DICTIONNAIRE FRANÇAIS~ANGLAIS ANGLAIS~FRANÇAIS

FRENCH~ENGLISH ENGLISH~FRENCH DICTIONARY

ROBERT·COLLINS JUNIOR DICTIONNAIRE FRANÇAIS-ANGLAIS ANGLAIS-FRANÇAIS

par

Beryl T. Atkins **Alain Duval**
Hélène M. A. Lewis **Rosemary C. Milne**

établi d'après le texte
abrégé et remanié du

DICTIONNAIRE
FRANÇAIS-ANGLAIS
ANGLAIS-FRANÇAIS
LE ROBERT & COLLINS

S.N.L. - Le Robert

Collins
London Glasgow Toronto

Webster's New World™ French Dictionary

Concise Edition

by

Beryl T. Atkins   Alain Duval
Hélène M. A. Lewis   Rosemary C. Milne

based on the

COLLINS-ROBERT
FRENCH-ENGLISH
ENGLISH-FRENCH
DICTIONARY

MACMILLAN • USA

FIRST PAPERBACK EDITION, 1992

EDITORS
Beryl T. Atkins
Alain Duval
Hélène M. A. Lewis
Rosemary C. Milne

Macmillan General Reference
A Simon & Schuster Macmillan Company
1633 Broadway
New York, NY 10019

A Webster's New World™ Book

Originally published in Great Britain
Published by arrangement with William Collins Sons & Co. Ltd.
and S.N.L.—Le Robert

Manufactured in the United States of America

6 7 8 9 10 11 97 98 99 00

TABLE DES MATIÈRES

TABLE OF CONTENTS

INTRODUCTION

Le Robert & Collins 'Junior' a été établi à partir du texte abrégé et remanié du dictionnaire français/anglais, anglais/français Le Robert & Collins. Il conserve de ce fait les principales caractéristiques de son aîné: refléter les deux langues, permettre au francophone et à l'anglophone de traduire à la fois dans sa propre langue et dans sa langue étrangère et de s'y exprimer avec assurance et précision.

'Il a été débordé par un diable qui a sauté le mou!'

Que penseriez-vous du malheureux anglophone vous annonçant cette nouvelle? Pourtant il voudrait seulement vous dire qu'un camion, en passant au feu rouge, a écrasé quelqu'un ('he was run over by a truck which jumped the lights').

Ne riez pas, vous pourriez affirmer des choses bien plus ridicules en essayant de parler anglais. Tout cela parce que vous utilisez des mots que vous ne connaissez pas. Des mots que vous avez trouvés dans un dictionnaire.

Justement, prenez le verbe **sauter**. Tout le monde vous dira que l'anglais est **to jump**. Mais est-ce toujours vrai? Ouvrez un dictionnaire et vous aurez le plus souvent une série de mots anglais inconnus, comme **to pop out; to blow up; to fuse; to be cancelled.** Comment choisir celui qui convient? S'il s'agit d'un bouchon de champagne qui saute, il faut utiliser **to pop out** (= partir), pour un pont, ce sera **to blow up** (= exploser), pour un circuit électrique **to fuse** (= fondre), enfin, si c'est un cours qui a sauté, vous devez prendre **to be cancelled** (= être supprimé).

Ce qu'il faut éviter, c'est de dire que le bouchon a fondu, que le cours a explosé ou que le pont est parti.

Vous comprenez donc que vous pouvez dire toutes sortes d'absurdités en anglais en choisissant la première traduction venue du mot français que vous cherchez. Pour trouver le mot juste, vous devez vous laisser guider par des 'panneaux de signalisation', et dans ce dictionnaire ils sont toujours en italiques.

En tournant la page, vous verrez comment cette signalisation fonctionne.

INTRODUCTION

The Collins–Robert Concise Dictionary is an abridged version of the Collins-Robert French Dictionary and has been written with the same main objectives: to reflect the two living languages and to enable the user of either nationality to translate both into and from the foreign language, and to express himself in it correctly and confidently.

'Attention not to make yourself squash, you've got to walk inside the nails.'

You'd probably back away from the poor Frenchman who said that, leaving him quite mystified, for he'd only been trying to warn you to cross at the pedestrian crossing if you didn't want to get run over. ('Attention de ne pas te faire écraser, tu dois marcher dans les clous.') Don't laugh – if you try to speak French you could find yourself saying even odder things. All because you're not using words that you know, but words that you've found in a dictionary.

Take the word **cut**: most people would say this is **couper** in French – but is it? If you look it up in the dictionary, you're often faced with a row of unknown French words, like **tondre**, **graver**, **réduire** or **sécher**. How are you going to decide which is the word you want? Of course it depends what you're going to cut. Cut the grass and you would use **tondre** (= to mow); cut a disc and it would be **graver** (= to engrave); if you're cutting expenses you'd need **réduire** (= to reduce), and if you're going to cut classes you'd be looking for **sécher** (= to miss).

What you don't want to say is that you're going to mow the disc, or engrave the lawn and so on.

You'll understand from this that if you look up an English word in the dictionary and take the first French word you come across, you could find yourself talking or writing nonsense. If you want to reach the right French word, you have to read the signposts, and in this dictionary these signposts are in italics.

If you turn this **page**, you'll see what kind of signposts we've given you …

COMMENT UTILISER LE DICTIONNAIRE

couche [kuʃ] *nf* **(a)** (*gén*) layer; *[peinture]* coat. ~ **sociale** social stratum; (*fig*) **en tenir une** ~* to be really thick*. **(b)** (*Horticulture*) hotbed. **(c)** *[bébé]* nappy, diaper (*US*). **(d)** (*Méd: accouchement*) ~s confinement; **mourir en** ~s to die in childbirth. **(e)** (*littér: lit*) bed.
coucher [kuʃe] (1) **1** *vt* **(a)** (*mettre au lit*) to put to bed; (*donner un lit*) to put up. **être/rester couché** to be/stay in bed. **(b)** *blessé* to lay out; *échelle etc* to lay down; *blés* to flatten. **être couché** to be lying. **(c)** (*inscrire*) to inscribe. **(d)** ~ **en joue** *fusil* to aim; *personne* to aim at. **2** *vi* (*dormir*) to sleep (*avec* with). **cela nous a fait** ~ **très tard** that meant we went to bed very late. **3 se** ~ *vpr* to go to bed; (*s'étendre*) to lie down; *[soleil, lune]* to set, go down; *[bateau]* to keel over. **4** *nm*: **le (moment du)** ~ bedtime; **le** ~ **des enfants** the children's bedtime; **(au)** ~ **du soleil** (at) sunset *ou* sundown (*US*). ♦ **couchette** *nf [voyageur]* berth, couchette; *[marin]* bunk.
coucou [kuku] *nm* (*oiseau*) cuckoo; (*pendule*) cuckoo clock; (*péj: avion*) (old) crate; (*fleur*) cowslip. ~ **(me voici)!** peek-a-boo!

Comment dire en anglais: 'le coucou pousse dans les bois'? L'article **coucou** vous donne plusieurs mots: cuckoo; cuckoo clock; (old) crate; cowslip. Sans autre indication, vous choisirez au hasard, vous prendrez sans doute la première solution en produisant un effet comique involontaire.

Aussi l'article contient-il autre chose, des mots français en *italique* placés entre parenthèses devant chaque traduction: (*oiseau*); (*pendule*); (*péj: avion*); (*fleur*). Voilà vos panneaux de signalisation. Ils correspondent chacun à un sens différent du mot 'coucou'. Vous pouvez choisir avec certitude ce que vous voulez, dans notre exemple, bien sûr (*fleur*) cowslip.

L'exemple est simple, mais prenez le mot 'coucher'. Il peut être verbe transitif (coucher quelqu'un ou quelque chose) ou verbe intransitif (coucher dans un lit) ou verbe pronominal (se coucher tard); il peut aussi être un nom (l'heure du coucher). Des chiffres vous indiquent ces différentes fonctions pour vous aider dans vos recherches: **1** *vt* (transitif) – **2** *vi* (intransitif) – **3 se** ~ *vpr* (pronominal) – **4** *nm* (nom masculin).

Vous savez aussi qu'on peut coucher des choses très différentes: un bébé dans son berceau, une échelle sur le sol, des mots sur le papier, on peut aussi coucher quelqu'un en joue. Pour vous mettre plus rapidement sur la voie, des lettres **(a)** – **(b)** – **(c)** – **(d)** séparent ces grandes zones d'emplois.

Si vous connaissez la traduction dans le premier cas: 'to put to bed', vous devinez qu'elle ne peut s'appliquer ni à l'échelle, ni au blé couché par le vent, c'est pourquoi ces deux mots en italique (ils sont compléments d'objet du verbe) vous renseignent: *échelle* to lay down; *blés* to flatten. Mais comment direz-vous, par exemple, 'coucher un meuble sur le côté'? Comme il n'est pas possible de citer tous les objets que l'on peut coucher c'est le mot *échelle* qui est chargé de les représenter, tout comme *blés* veut dire *herbe, avoine etc* ... donc, 'coucher un meuble' se dit 'to lay a piece of furniture down'.

Lorsqu'il s'agit de pourvoir quelqu'un d'un lit, vous pourriez logiquement croire que 'coucher un bébé' et 'coucher un ami pour la nuit' se disent de la même manière, mais de nouveaux panneaux (des synonymes entre parenthèses) vous avertissent que (*mettre au lit*) un bébé se dit 'to put to bed' et que (*donner un lit*) à un ami se dit 'to put up'.

Dans le verbe **se coucher**, de nouveaux panneaux vous aident à trouver votre chemin: [*soleil, lune*] to set, go down; [*bateau*] to keel over. Ce sont des sujets du verbe et ils sont placés entre crochets pour les distinguer des autres indications dont nous venons de parler.

Regardez maintenant l'article ♦ **couchette.** Comme il ne forme pas un article principal, il est précédé d'un losange pour le faire ressortir. Il y a d'autres mots entre crochets: [*voyageurs*] et [*marin*]. Ce sont des compléments du nom 'couchette'. Ils vous indiquent qu'une couchette de [*voyageur*] se dit 'berth' ou 'couchette' alors qu'une couchette de [*marin*] se dit 'bunk'.

Dans l'article **couche**, vous retrouvez un certain nombre d'indications du même type. Il y en a aussi de nouvelles. En voici quelques-unes:

... (*gén*) qui précède le mot anglais 'layer' signifie que cette traduction est la plus générale de couche, celle qui est valable dans le plus grand nombre de cas.

... (*US*) qui suit le mot 'diaper' indique que c'est la manière dont on dit 'couche de bébé' en américain.

Il y a aussi un astérisque: * à la fin de l'expression 'en tenir une ~*', ainsi qu'à la fin de la traduction 'to be really thick*'. Cet astérisque indique que l'une et l'autre sont familières. Si une expression est très familière, elle sera suivie de deux astérisques: **. Si par contre elle est démodée, elle sera suivie d'une croix: †.

Vous remarquerez enfin que le mot 'couche' n'est pas repris dans l'article. Il est remplacé par le signe ~ qui évite la répétition.

Dans la partie Anglais–Français du dictionnaire (cf. page ci-contre) vous remarquerez que les mots en *italique* sont en anglais, pour aider le lecteur anglophone. En tant que Français, vous-même n'avez pas besoin de précisions sur le sens des traductions françaises!

Les pages suivantes, à partir de deux colonnes prises dans le texte regroupent tous les éléments de cette signalisation.

USING THE DICTIONARY

aid [eɪd] **1** *n* **(a)** (*help*) aide *f*. **with the ~ of** *sb* avec l'aide de; *sth* à l'aide de; **in ~ of the blind** au profit des aveugles; (*fig*) **what is the meeting in ~ of?*** c'est dans quel but, cette réunion? **(b)** (*helper*) aide *mf*, assistant(e) *m(f)*; (*apparatus*) aide *f*, moyen *m*. **audio-visual ~s** support audio-visuel, moyens audio-visuels. **2** *vt* (*gen*) aider (*to do* à faire); *progress, recovery* contribuer à. (*Jur*) **to ~ and abet sb** être complice de qn.
aim [eɪm] **1** *n* **(a) to miss one's ~** manquer son coup; **to take ~** viser (*at sb/sth* qn/qch); **his ~ is bad** il vise mal. **(b)** (*purpose*) but *m*. **with the ~ of doing** dans le but de faire; **her ~ is to do** elle a pour but de faire. **2** *vt gun* braquer (*at* sur); *stone* lancer (*at* sur); *blow* décocher (*at* à); *remark* diriger (*at* contre). **3** *vi* viser. **to ~ at sth** viser qch; **to ~ at doing** *or* **to do** viser à faire, (*less formally*) avoir l'intention de faire. ♦ **aimless** *adj* sans but. ♦ **aimlessly** *adv wander* sans but; *stand around* sans trop savoir que faire; *chat, kick ball about* pour passer le temps.
alight[1] [əˈlaɪt] *vi [person]* descendre (*from* de); *[bird]* se poser (*on* sur).

Suppose you want to say in French 'with the aid of a dictionary': you look up **aid** in the dictionary. If you know that in your sentence the word 'aid' is a noun (*n*), and not a transitive verb (*vt*), then you will go straight to the section marked **1** *n*. This is in two parts, (**a**) and (**b**); the 'aid' that you're looking for is obviously the one marked (**a**) (*help*), and not (**b**) (*helper*) or (*apparatus*). You find the French word 'aide *f*'. Read on and you have the phrase you're looking for; 'a dictionary' is obviously a thing (*sth* means 'something') and not a person (*sb* means 'somebody'), so you can now translate your phrase 'with the aid of a dictionary' – 'à l'aide d'un dictionnaire' ('with the aid of his brother' would be 'avec l'aide de son frère'). You'll see in this particular dictionary the sign ~, which we use to avoid having to keep repeating the headword, in this case **aid**.

You will have noticed that the gender of a French noun is always given i.e. 'aide *f*'; normally this is done by using *f* for 'feminine' and *m* for 'masculine'. Sometimes the gender is already clear from the adjective which goes with the noun, and there is no need for *m* or *f*; thus, a few lines further on in the **aid** entry, **audio-visual ~s** is translated by 'support audio-visuel, moyens audio-visuels' – the masculine ending of 'audio-visuel' in both cases tells you that it is 'le support' and 'le moyen'.

Suppose however you'd been trying to put into French 'they aimed the searchlights at the plane'. From the entry **aim 2** *vt* (= verb transitive) you have to use the English in italics to help you choose the right French word to translate 'aim' in your sentence. Is 'aiming a *searchlight*' closer to 'aiming a *gun*' or to 'aiming a *stone*' at something? You obviously point a searchlight in the same way as you point a gun, you don't throw it, and so you would choose 'braquer': 'ils ont braqué les projecteurs sur l'avion'.

Further down the page you'll find **aimlessly** (the ♦ sign before it is just to help you find it more easily, since it's not a main headword like **aim**). If you want to talk about someone 'hanging about aimlessly on street corners' you'd pick *stand around* as nearest to 'hang about', and say 'il traînait au coin de la rue sans trop savoir que faire'.

Similarly under **alight**, for passengers who 'alight' from a coach, you would follow the signpost [*person*] and choose 'descendre', rather than 'se poser', which you'd use for a blackbird 'alighting' on a branch.

You may be puzzled by the word (*gen*) in **aid 2** *vt*: it means 'generally' or 'usually' and it tells you that usually the French for 'aid' is 'aider', but – look further on – if something is aiding *progress* or *recovery* (or *development* or anything else like that) then the translation of 'aid' would be 'contribuer à'; thus 'aider quelqu'un à faire quelque chose', but 'contribuer au progrès de quelque chose'.

Lastly, the asterisk (in **aid 1** *n*: **what is the meeting in ~ of?***) shows that this is something you'd happily *say* to someone, but not perhaps write in a formal piece of writing like an essay, or an application for a job. If an English or French phrase has two asterisks, this means that it is definitely slangy.

In the French-English side of the dictionary (see the opposite page) you'll notice that the words *in italics* are in French, to help the French user. As an English speaker, *you* don't need any help with your English!

If you want to know in more detail what all the signposts mean in this dictionary, turn over – they're all explained on the next page.

égide [eʒid] *nf*: **sous l'~ de** under the aegis of.
églantier [eglɑ̃tje] *nm* wild rose(-bush). ♦ **églantine** *nf* wild rose, eglantine.
église [egliz] *nf* (*gén*) church.
égoïsme [egɔism(ə)] *nm* selfishness, egoism. ♦ **égoïste 1** *adj* selfish, egoistic. **2** *nmf* egoist. ♦ **égoïstement** *adv* selfishly, egoistically.
égorger [egɔʀʒe] (3) *vt* (*lit*) to slit *ou* cut the throat of; (*) *client* to bleed white.
égout [egu] *nm* sewer. **les ~s** the sewerage system. ♦ **égoutier** *nm* sewer worker.
égoutter [egute] (1) **1** *vt* (*avec passoire*) to strain; (*en tordant*) to wring out. **2** *vi* [*vaisselle*] to drain; [*linge, eau*] to drip. **faire ~** *eau* to drain off; *linge* to hang up to drip; **'laisser ~'** 'drip dry'. **3 s'~** *vpr* to drip; to drain. ♦ **égouttoir** *nm* (*évier*) draining board; (*mobile*) draining rack; (*passoire*) strainer, colander.
égratigner [egʀatiɲe] (1) *vt* (*lit*) to scratch; (*fig*) to have a dig at. ♦ **égratignure** *nf* scratch; (*fig*) dig. **sans une ~** without a scratch, unscathed.
égrener [egʀəne] (5) *vt* *pois, blé, épi* to shell; *coton* to gin; *grappe* to pick grapes off. (*fig*) **~ son chapelet** to tell one's beads; **~ les heures** to mark the hours; **les maisons s'égrenaient le long de la route** the houses were dotted along the road.
égrillard, e [egʀijaʀ, aʀd(ə)] *adj* bawdy.
Égypte [eʒipt] *nf* Egypt. ♦ **égyptien, -ienne** *adj*, **É~(ne)** *nm(f)* Egyptian.
éhonté, e [eɔ̃te] *adj* shameless.
éjecter [eʒɛkte] (1) *vt* (*Tech*) to eject; (‡) to kick out*. **se faire ~**‡ to get o.s. kicked out*. ♦ **éjection** *nf* (*Tech*) ejection; (‡) kicking-out*.
élaborer [elabɔʀe] (1) *vt* (*gén*) to elaborate. ♦ **élaboration** *nf* elaboration.
élaguer [elage] (1) *vt* (*lit, fig*) to prune. ♦ **élagage** *nm* pruning. ♦ **élagueur** *nm* pruner.
élan¹ [elɑ̃] *nm* (*Zool*) elk, moose.
élan² [elɑ̃] *nm* **(a)** (*début de course*) run up. **saut avec/sans ~** running/standing jump. **(b)** (*vitesse acquise*) momentum. **prendre de l'~** to gather speed; **emporté par son ~** carried along by his own momentum. **(c)** [*enthousiasme, colère*] surge, burst. **~s (d'affection)** rushes of affection; **~s lyriques** lyrical outbursts. **(d)** [*troupes*] vigour, spirit. **~ patriotique** patriotic fervour.
élancer [elɑ̃se] (3) **1** *vi* [*blessure*] to give shooting pains. **2 s'~** *vpr* **(a)** (*se précipiter*) to rush, dash (*vers* towards). **s'~ d'un bond sur** to leap onto. **(b)** (*se dresser*) to soar (upwards). ♦ **élancé, e** *adj* *clocher etc* slender. ♦ **élancement** *nm* shooting pain.
élargir [elaʀʒiʀ] (2) **1** *vt* **(a)** (*gén*) to widen; *débat* to broaden. (*Pol*) **majorité élargie** increased majority; **ça lui élargit la taille** that makes his waist look fatter. **(b)** (*Jur: libérer*) to release, free. **2 s'~** *vpr* [*route*] to widen, get wider; [*idées*] to broaden. ♦ **élargissement** *nm* widening; broadening; release.
élastique [elastik] **1** *adj* *objet* elastic; *démarche* springy; *sens, esprit* flexible; (*péj*) *conscience* accommodating; (*Écon*) elastic. **2** *nm* (*de bureau*) elastic *ou* rubber band; (*Couture*) elastic. **en ~** elasticated. ♦ **élasticité** *nf* elasticity; spring; flexibility; accommodating nature.
électeur, -trice [elɛktœʀ, tʀis] *nm,f* **(a)** (*Pol*) voter. (*circonscription*) **~s** constituents. **(b)** (*Hist*) **É~** Elector; **É~trice** Electress. ♦ **élection** *nf* **(a)** (*Pol, gén*) election. **jour des ~s** polling *ou* election day; **~ partielle** ≃ by-election; **~s législatives** ≃ general election. **(b)** (*choix*) **patrie d'~** chosen country. ♦ **électoral, e, *mpl* -aux** *adj* election. ♦ **électorat** *nm* **(a)** electorate; (*d'un parti*) voters. **(b)** (*Hist*) electorate.

traductions interchangeables séparées par ,
signalisation par complément du verbe
chiffres isolant les fonctions grammaticales différentes du mot
signalisation par sujet du verbe
sens littéral et sens figuré
mot souche de l'article ou du sous-article repris par ~ (= 'égratignure')
différence minuscule/majuscule signalée
traductions non interchangeables séparées par ;
chiffres isolant les homographes
éléments non interchangeables à partir d'un tronc commun séparés par /
signalisation par complément de nom (= élan d'enthousiasme, de colère etc)
parenthèses isolant les mots que l'on peut omettre sans changer le sens
table de conjugaison V p.528
sens général, valable dans la plupart des cas
traductions non précisées du sous-article. Se reporter à la signalisation de l'article principal
signalisation par nom auquel se rapporte l'adjectif
indication du féminin
lettres isolant les sens différents du mot

alternative translations separated by ,
typical objects of headword to show shades of meaning which require different translations
numbers show different grammatical categories of the headword
typical subjects of verb shown in square brackets: [ ]
literal and figurative meanings
~ replaces main and secondary headword (= 'égratignure')
French adjectives and nouns of nationality shown
; separates shifts in meaning within a category
superior numbers separate homographs
/ shows alternatives in a phrase which are reflected exactly in the translation
noun complements shown in square brackets (= élan d'enthousiasme, de colère etc)
brackets round words which can be left out without altering meaning of phrase
French verb tables V p.528
indicates that the translation works generally or in most cases
translations separated by a ; with no explanations. Refer back to the main headword for indications as to shifts in meaning
noun complements of adjectives
feminine form of French nouns and adjectives
(a), (b) show distinct meanings of the headword

= Britannique; (US = Américain) — *= British; (US = American)*

admiral ['ædmərəl] *n* amiral *m* (d'escadre). **A~ of the Fleet** amiral (à cinq étoiles). ♦ **Admiralty Board** *n* (*Brit*) ≃ ministère *m* de la Marine.

équivalent culturel signalé par ≃ — *≃ 'is approximately equivalent of'*

admire [əd'maɪəʳ] *vt* admirer. ♦ **admirable** ['ædmərəbl] *adj* admirable. ♦ **admirably** *adv* admirablement. ♦ **admiration** *n* admiration *f* (*of, for* pour). **to be the admiration of** faire l'admiration de. ♦ **admirer** *n* admirateur *m*, -trice *f* (†: *suitor*) soupirant† *m*. ♦ **admiring** *adj* admiratif. ♦ **admiringly** *adv* avec admiration.

indication du genre: m = masculin; f = féminin — *gender: m = masculine; f = feminine*

emploi vieilli ou archaïque signalé par une croix † — *dagger means old-fashioned or obsolete*

admissible [əd'mɪsəbl] *adj plan* acceptable; *evidence* recevable.

admission [əd'mɪʃən] *n* **(a)** (*entry*) admission *f*, entrée *f* (*to* à). **~ free** entrée gratuite; **to gain ~ to** *person* trouver accès auprès de; *place* être admis dans. **(b)** (*confession*) aveu *m*. **by one's own ~** de son propre aveu.

genre indiqué une seule fois dans la catégorie — *gender shown once only per category*

admit [əd'mɪt] *vt* **(a)** (*let in*) laisser entrer. **children not ~ted** entrée interdite aux enfants; **this ticket ~s 2** ce billet est valable pour 2 personnes. **(b)** (*acknowledge*) reconnaître, admettre (*that* que); *crime* reconnaître avoir commis; *one's guilt* reconnaître. **I must ~ that ...** je dois avouer *or* admettre que ...; **I was wrong I ~** j'ai eu tort, j'en conviens.

prononciation (notation de l'Association Phonétique Internationale V p.xii) — *pronunciation in IPA, see p.xii*

mot souche de l'article repris par ~ ('admit') — *~ replaces main headword 'admit'*

admit of *vt fus* admettre, permettre.
admit to *vt fus crime* reconnaître avoir commis. **to ~ to having done** reconnaître avoir fait; **to ~ to a feeling of** avouer avoir un sentiment de.

traitement des verbes à particule séparé de l'article principal (ici: 'admit') V p.527 — *phrasal verbs dealt with separately from main entry ('admit') see p.527*

♦ **admittance** *n* droit *m* d'entrée, admission *f* (*to sth* à qch); accès *m* (*to sth* à qch; *to sb* auprès de qn); **I gained ~tance** on m'a laissé entrer; **no ~tance except on business** accès interdit à toute personne étrangère au service. ♦ **admittedly** *adv*: **~tedly this is true** je reconnais *or* il faut reconnaître que c'est vrai.

même dans les sous-articles ('admittance') le signe ~ remplace le mot souche ('admit') — *even in secondary entries ('admittance') ~ replaces main headword ('admit')*

éléments interchangeables de traduction à partir d'un tronc commun séparés par or — *separates alternative translations of part of a phrase*

admonish [əd'mɒnɪʃ] *vt* (*reprove*) réprimander (*for doing* pour avoir fait; *about, for* pour, à propos de); (*warn*) avertir (*against doing* de ne pas faire); (*exhort*) exhorter (*to do* à faire). ♦ **admonition** *n* réprimande *f*; avertissement *m*.

Précisions grammaticales à la suite de la traduction — *grammatical points given after French translations*

ad nauseam [ˌæd'nɔːsɪæm] *adv* à satiété.

ado [ə'duː] *n*: **much ~ about nothing** beaucoup de bruit pour rien; **without more ~** sans plus de cérémonies.

adolescent [ˌædəʊ'lesnt] *adj, n* adolescent(e) *m(f)*. ♦ **adolescence** *n* adolescence *f*.

adopt [ə'dɒpt] *vt child, method,* (*Pol*) *motion* adopter; *candidate, career* choisir. ♦ **adopted** *adj child* adopté; *country* d'adoption; *son, family* adoptif. ♦ **adoption** *n* adoption *f*; choix *m*. ♦ **adoptive** *adj parent, child* adoptif; *country* d'adoption.

sous-articles signalé par ♦ — *♦ highlights secondary headwords*

adore [ə'dɔːʳ] *vt* adorer. ♦ **adorable** *adj* adorable. ♦ **adoration** *n* adoration *f*. ♦ **adoringly** *adv* avec adoration.

classes grammaticales: verbe transitif, adjectif, nom, adverbe — *parts of speech: verb transitive, adjective, noun, adverb*

adorn [ə'dɔːn] *vt room* orner; *dress* parer (*with* de). **to ~ o.s.** se parer. ♦ **adornment** *n* ornement *m*; parure *f*.

adrenalin(e) [ə'drenəlɪn] *n* adrénaline *f*. (*fig*) **he felt the ~ rising** il a senti son pouls s'emballer.

genre non indiqué lorsque le nom est suivi d'un adjectif permettant de le déduire ('son') — *gender of nouns not specified when clear from accompanying adjective*

Adriatic (Sea) [ˌeɪdrɪ'ætɪk('siː)] *n* (mer *f*) Adriatique *f*.

parenthèses isolant les mots que l'on peut omettre — *brackets round words which may be left out*

adrift [ə'drɪft] *adv, adj* (*Naut*) à la dérive. **to turn ~** *boat* abandonner à la dérive; (*fig*) *person* laisser se débrouiller tout seul; **to come ~*** [*wire etc*] se détacher; [*plans*] tomber à l'eau.

*emploi familier indiqué par un astérisque * V p.vi* — *informal language; see note p.vii*

adroit [ə'drɔɪt] *adj* adroit. ♦ **adroitly** *adv* adroitement. ♦ **adroitness** *n* adresse *f*.

adulate ['ædjʊleɪt] *vt* aduler. ♦ **adulation** *n* adulation *f*.

adult ['ædʌlt] **1** *n* adulte *mf*. (*Cine etc*) **~s only** interdit aux moins de 18 ans. **2** *adj person, animal* adulte; *film, book, classes* pour adultes. **~ education** enseignement *m* post-scolaire.

= Cinéma; liste complète des abréviations V p.x — *= Cinema; for full list of such abbreviations see p.x*

ABRÉVIATIONS ABBREVIATIONS

abréviation	**abbr, abrév**	abbreviated, abbreviation
adjectif	**adj**	adjective
administration	**Admin**	administration
adverbe	**adv**	adverb
agriculture	**Agr**	agriculture
anatomie	**Anat**	anatomy
antiquité	**Antiq**	ancient history
approximativement	**approx**	approximately
archéologie	**Archeol, Archéol**	archaeology
architecture	**Archit**	architecture
argot	**arg**	slang
article	**art**	article
astrologie	**Astrol**	astrology
astronomie	**Astron**	astronomy
automobile	**Aut**	automobiles
auxiliaire	**aux**	auxiliary
aviation	**Aviat**	aviation
biologie	**Bio**	biology
botanique	**Bot**	botany
britannique, Grande-Bretagne	**Brit**	British, Great Britain
canadien, Canada	**Can**	Canadian, Canada
chimie	**Chem, Chim**	chemistry
cinéma	**Cine, Ciné**	cinema
commerce	**Comm**	commerce
comparatif	**comp**	comparative
conditionnel	**cond**	conditional
conjonction	**conj**	conjunction
construction	**Constr**	building trade
mots composés	**cpd**	compound, in compounds
cuisine	**Culin**	cookery
défini	**def, déf**	definite
démonstratif	**dem, dém**	demonstrative
dialectal, régional	**dial**	dialect
diminutif	**dim**	diminutive
direct	**dir**	direct
écologie	**Ecol**	ecology
économique	**Econ, Écon**	economics
par exemple	**eg**	for example
électricité, électronique	**Elec, Élec**	electricity, electronics
et cetera	**etc**	etcetera
euphémisme	**euph**	euphemism
par exemple	**ex**	for example
exclamation	**excl**	exclamation
féminin	**f**	feminine
figuré	**fig**	figuratively
finance	**Fin**	finance
football	**Ftbl**	football
fusionné	**fus**	fused
futur	**fut**	future
en général, généralement	**gen, gén**	in general, generally
géographie	**Geog, Géog**	geography
géologie	**Geol, Géol**	geology
géométrie	**Geom, Géom**	geometry
grammaire	**Gram**	grammar
gymnastique	**Gym**	gymnastics
héraldique	**Her, Hér**	heraldry
histoire	**Hist**	history
humoristique	**hum**	humorous
impératif	**imper, impér**	imperative
impersonnel	**impers**	impersonal
industrie	**Ind**	industry
indéfini	**indef, indéf**	indefinite
indicatif	**indic**	indicative
indirect	**indir**	indirect
infinitif	**infin**	infinitive
inséparable	**insep**	inseparable
interrogatif	**interrog**	interrogative
invariable	**inv**	invariable
irlandais, Irlande	**Ir**	Irish, Ireland
ironique	**iro**	ironic
irrégulier	**irrég**	irregular
droit, juridique	**Jur**	law, legal
linguistique	**Ling**	linguistics
littéral, au sens propre	**lit**	literally
littéraire	**liter**	literary
littérature	**Literat**	literature
littéraire	**littér**	literary
littérature	**Littérat**	literature
masculin	**m**	masculine
mathématique	**Math**	mathematics

médecine	**Med, Méd**	medicine
météorologie	**Met, Mét**	meteorology
métallurgie	**Metal, Métal**	metallurgy
militaire	**Mil**	military
mines	**Min**	mining
minéralogie	**Miner, Minér**	mineralogy
musique	**Mus**	music
mythologie	**Myth**	mythology
nom	**n**	noun
nautique	**Naut**	nautical, naval
négatif	**neg, nég**	negative
numéral	**num**	numerical
objet	**obj**	object
opposé	**opp**	opposite
optique	**Opt**	optics
ornithologie	**Orn**	ornithology
	o.s.	oneself
parlement	**Parl**	parliament
passif	**pass**	passive
péjoratif	**pej, péj**	pejorative
personnel	**pers**	personal
pharmacie	**Pharm**	pharmacy
philatélie	**Philat**	philately
philosophie	**Philos**	philosophy
photographie	**Phot**	photography
	phr vb elem	phrasal verb element
physique	**Phys**	physics
physiologie	**Physiol**	physiology
pluriel	**pl**	plural
politique	**Pol**	politics
possessif	**poss**	possessive
préfixe	**pref, préf**	prefix
préposition	**prep, prép**	preposition
prétérit	**pret, prét**	preterite
pronom	**pron**	pronoun
participe présent	**prp**	present participle
psychiatrie, psychologie	**Psych**	psychiatry, psychology
participe passé	**ptp**	past participle
quelque chose	**qch**	
quelqu'un	**qn**	
marque déposée	®	registered trademark
radio	**Rad**	radio
relatif	**rel**	relative
religion	**Rel**	religion
	sb	somebody, someone
sciences	**Sci**	science
école	**Scol**	school
écossais, Écosse	**Scot**	Scottish, Scotland
sculpture	**Sculp**	sculpture
séparable	**sep**	separable
singulier	**sg**	singular
argot	**sl**	slang
sociologie	**Soc, Sociol**	sociology, social work
Bourse	**St Ex**	Stock Exchange
	sth	something
subjonctif	**subj**	subjunctive
suffixe	**suf**	suffix
superlatif	**superl**	superlative
chirurgie	**Surg**	surgery
arpentage	**Surv**	surveying
technique	**Tech**	technical
télécommunication	**Telec, Téléc**	telecommunications
industrie textile	**Tex**	textiles
théâtre	**Theat, Théât**	theatre
télévision	**TV**	television
typographie	**Typ**	typography
université	**Univ**	university
américain, États-Unis	**US**	American, United States
voir	**V**	see
verbe	**vb**	verb
médecine vétérinaire	**Vet, Vét**	veterinary medicine
verbe intransitif	**vi**	intransitive verb
verbe pronominal	**vpr**	pronominal verb
verbe transitif	**vt**	transitive verb
verbe transitif et intransitif	**vti**	transitive and intransitive verb
verbe transitif indirect	**vt indir**	
zoologie	**Zool**	zoology
voir page vi	* ‡	see page vii
voir page vi	†	see page vii

Phonetic Transcription of French

Vowels

[i]	il, vie, lyre
[e]	blé, jouer
[ɛ]	lait, jouet, merci
[a]	plat, patte
[ɑ]	bas, pâte
[ɔ]	mort, donner
[o]	mot, dôme, eau, gauche
[u]	genou, roue
[y]	rue, vêtu
[ø]	peu, deux
[œ]	peur, meuble
[ə]	le, premier
[ɛ̃]	matin, plein
[ɑ̃]	sans, vent
[ɔ̃]	bon, ombre
[œ̃]	lundi, brun

Semi-consonants

[j]	yeux, paille, pied
[w]	oui, nouer
[ɥ]	huile, lui

Consonants

[p]	père, soupe
[t]	terre, vite
[k]	cou, qui, sac, képi
[b]	bon, robe
[d]	dans, aide
[g]	gare, bague
[f]	feu, neuf, photo
[s]	sale, celui, ça, dessous, tasse, nation
[ʃ]	chat, tache
[v]	vous, rêve
[z]	zéro, maison, rose
[ʒ]	je, gilet, geôle
[l]	lent, sol
[ʀ]	rue, venir
[m]	main, femme
[n]	nous, tonne, animal
[ɲ]	agneau, vigne
[h]	hop! (exclamative)
[']	haricot (no liaison)
[ŋ]	words borrowed from English: camping
[x]	words borrowed from Spanish or Arabic: jota

Transcription phonétique de l'anglais

Voyelles et diphtongues

[iː]	bead, see
[ɑː]	bard, calm
[ɔː]	born, cork
[uː]	boon, fool
[ɜː]	burn, fern, work
[ɪ]	sit, pity
[e]	set, less
[æ]	sat, apple
[ʌ]	fun, come
[ɒ]	fond, wash
[ʊ]	full, soot
[ə]	composer, above
[eɪ]	bay, fate
[aɪ]	buy, lie
[ɔɪ]	boy, voice
[əʊ]	no, ago
[aʊ]	now, plough
[ɪə]	tier, beer
[ɛə]	tare, fair
[ʊə]	tour

Consonnes

[p]	pat, pope
[b]	bat, baby
[t]	tab, strut
[d]	dab, mended
[k]	cot, kiss, chord
[g]	got, agog
[f]	fine, raffle
[v]	vine, river
[s]	pots, sit, rice
[z]	pods, buzz
[θ]	thin, maths
[ð]	this, other
[ʃ]	ship, sugar
[ʒ]	measure
[tʃ]	chance
[dʒ]	just, edge
[l]	little, place
[r]	ran, stirring
[m]	ram, mummy
[n]	ran, nut
[ŋ]	rang, bank
[h]	hat, reheat
[j]	yet, million
[w]	wet, bewail
[x]	loch

Divers

Un caractère en italique représente un son qui peut ne pas être prononcé.

[ʳ]	représente un [r] entendu s'il forme une liaison avec la voyelle du mot suivant
[ˈ]	accent tonique
[ˌ]	accent secondaire

DICTIONNAIRE FRANÇAIS–ANGLAIS
FRENCH–ENGLISH DICTIONARY

A

A, a [ɑ] *nm* (*lettre*) A, a. **de A à Z** from A to Z; **prouver par ~ plus b** to prove conclusively.

à [a] *prép* (*avec le, les:* **au, aux**) **(a)** (*déplacement*) to; (*dans*) into. **aller ~ Paris/au marché** to go to Paris/to (the) market; **aller ~ la pêche** to go fishing; **son voyage ~ Londres** his trip to London; **entrez au salon** go into the lounge.

(b) (*position*) at; (*dans*) in; (*sur*) on. **habiter ~ Paris/au 4e étage** to live in Paris/on the 4th floor; **être ~ l'école/~ domicile** to be at school/at home; **c'est ~ 3 km** it's 3 km away; **~ la télévision/radio** on television/the radio; **rester au chaud** to stay in the warm.

(c) (*temps*) at; (*date*) on; (*époque*) in; (*jusqu'à*) to, till, until. **~ 6 heures/Noël** at 6 o'clock/Christmas; **le 3 au soir** on the evening of the 3rd; **~ samedi!** see you on Saturday!; **au matin/19e siècle** in the morning/the 19th century; **de 2 ~ 4 heures** from 2 to *ou* till 4 (o'clock).

(d) (*rapport*) by, per; (*approximation*) to. **faire du 50 ~ l'heure** to do 50 km an *ou* per hour; **faire du 9 litres aux 100** to use 9 litres per 100 km; **être payé au poids/mois** to be paid by weight/the month; **entrer 2 ~ 2** to come in 2 by 2; **4 ~ 5 mètres** 4 to 5 metres; **gagner (par) 2 ~ 1** to win by 2 to 1.

(e) (*appartenance*) of, to. **ce sac est ~ moi/Peter** this bag is mine/Peter's, this bag belongs to me/Peter; **un ami ~ elle** a friend of hers, one of her friends; **ce n'est pas ~ moi de le faire** it's not for me *ou* up to me to do it.

(f) (*moyen*) on, by, with. **faire qch ~ la main** to do sth by hand; **aller ~ vélo/~ pied** to go by bike/on foot; **écrire qch au crayon** to write sth with a pencil *ou* in pencil; **jouer qch au piano** to play sth on the piano; **cuisiné au beurre** cooked in butter; **ils l'ont fait ~ 3** they did it between the 3 of them.

(g) (*caractérisation*) with. **robe ~ manches** dress with sleeves; **pompe ~ eau** water pump; **tasse ~ thé** tea cup; **elle est femme ~ le faire** she's the sort of woman to do it.

(h) (*destination*) for, to. **maison ~ vendre** house for sale; (*dédicace*) **~ ma sœur** to *ou* for my sister.

(i) (*conséquence*) to; (*hypothèse*) from. **~ leur grande surprise** much to their surprise; **~ ce que j'ai compris** from what I understood; **~ le voir si maigre** when I saw he was so thin; **~ bien réfléchir** if you think about it.

abaisser [abese] (1) **1** *vt* **(a)** (*gén*) *niveau* to lower; *store* to pull down; *température, taux* to bring down; *perpendiculaire* to drop. **(b)** to humiliate; (*Rel*) to humble. **2 s'~** *vpr* **(a)** *[température, taux]* to fall, drop; *[terrain]* to slope down; (*Théât*) *[rideau]* to fall (*sur* on). **(b)** (*s'humilier*) to humble o.s. **s'~ à faire** to stoop to doing. ♦ **abaissant, e** *adj* degrading. ♦ **abaissement** *nm* **(a)** (*action*) lowering; pulling down; dropping; humiliation; humbling. **(b)** (*chute*) fall, drop (*de* in); *[terrain]* downward slope; *[moralité]* decline. **(c)** (*abjection*) degradation.

abandon [abɑ̃dɔ̃] *nm* **(a)** (*délaissement*) desertion, abandonment; (*manque de soin*) neglected state, neglect. **laisser à l'~** to neglect. **(b)** *[idée, technique etc]* giving up; *[droit]* relinquishment; *[course]* withdrawal (*de* from). **faire ~ de ses biens à qn** to make over one's property to sb; (*fig*) **~ de soi-même** self-abnegation. **(c)** (*relâchement*) lack of constraint. **parler avec ~** to talk freely *ou* without constraint; **moments d'~** moments of abandon; **l'~ de son attitude** his relaxed attitude.

abandonner [abɑ̃dɔne] (1) **1** *vt* **(a)** (*délaisser*) *lieu, personne* to desert, abandon; *technique* to abandon, give up. **son courage l'abandonna** his courage deserted him. **(b)** (*se retirer de*) (*gén*) to give up; *études, projet* to abandon; *droit* to relinquish; *course* to withdraw from. (*lit, fig*) **~ la lutte** to give up the fight. **(c)** (*donner*) **~ à** (*gén*) to leave to; **~ ses biens à une bonne œuvre** to leave *ou* donate one's wealth to a good cause; **elle lui abandonna sa main** she let him take her hand; **~ à qn le soin de faire qch** to leave it to sb to do sth; **~ au pillage** to leave to be pillaged. **2 s'~** *vpr* to let o.s. go. **s'~ à** (*gén*) to give o.s. up to; *désespoir* to give way to; **il s'abandonna au sommeil** he let sleep overcome him. ♦ **abandonné, e** *adj attitude* relaxed; (*avec volupté*) abandoned; *usine* disused.

abasourdir [abazuʀdiʀ] (2) *vt* (*gén*) to stun.

abat-jour [abaʒuʀ] *nm inv* lampshade.

abats [aba] *nmpl [volaille]* giblets; *[bœuf]* offal.

abattage [abataʒ] *nm [animal]* slaughter; *[arbre]* felling; (*Min*) extracting.

abattant [abatɑ̃] *nm* flap (*of table, desk*).

abattement [abatmɑ̃] *nm* **(a)** (*dépression*) despondency; (*fatigue*) exhaustion. **(b)** (*rabais*) reduction; (*fiscal*) (tax) allowance.

abattis [abati] *nmpl [volaille]* giblets; (*: *membres*) limbs.

abattoir [abatwaʀ] *nm* slaughterhouse.

abattre [abatʀ(ə)] (41) **1** *vt* **(a)** *arbre* to cut down, fell; *adversaire, quilles, mur* to knock down; *roche* to hew; *avion* to shoot down. **la pluie abat la poussière** the rain settles the dust; **il abattit son bâton sur ma tête** he brought his stick down on my head. **(b)** (*tuer*) *personne, fauve* to shoot; *chien* to destroy, put down; *bœuf* to slaughter. **(c)** (*physiquement*) to weaken, exhaust; (*moralement*) to demoralize. **abattu par la chaleur** overcome by the heat; **ne te laisse pas ~** don't let things get you down; (*lit, fig*) **~ ses cartes** to lay *ou* put one's cards on the table; **~ du travail** to get through a lot of work. **2 s'~** *vpr* **(a)** *[personne]* to fall (down); *[cheminée]* to fall *ou* crash down. **(b) s'~ sur** *[pluie]* to beat down on; *[ennemi]* to swoop down on; *[coups, injures]* to rain on. ♦ **abattu, e** *adj* (*fatigué*) exhausted; (*déprimé*) demoralized, despondent.

abbaye [abei] *nf* abbey. ♦ **abbé** *nm [abbaye]* abbot; (*prêtre*) priest. ♦ **abbesse** *nf* abbess.

abc [abese] *nm*: **l'~ du métier** the first requirement of the job.

abcès [apsɛ] *nm* abscess. (*fig*) **vider l'~** to root out the evil.

abdication [abdikɑsjɔ̃] *nf* (*lit, fig*) abdication. ♦ **abdiquer** *vti [roi]* to abdicate; (*fig*) to give up.

abdomen [abdɔmɛn] *nm* abdomen. ♦ **abdominal, e,** *mpl* **-aux 1** *adj* abdominal. **2** *nmpl*: **~aux** stomach muscles.

abeille [abɛj] *nf* bee.

aberrant, e [abɛʀɑ̃, ɑ̃t] *adj conduite, (Bio)* aberrant; *histoire* absurd. ♦ **aberration** *nf (gén)* aberration.

abêtir *vt*, **s'~** *vpr* [abetiʀ] (2) to turn into a half-wit. ♦ **abêtissant, e** *adj travail* which reduces one to a half-wit. ♦ **abêtissement** *nm (état)* stupidity; *(action)* stupefying.

abhorrer [abɔʀe] (1) *vt (littér)* to abhor, loathe.

abîme [abim] *nm (lit, fig)* gulf, chasm. **au bord de l'~** *pays* on the brink of ruin; **au fond de l'~** *personne* in the depths of despair; **les ~s de l'enfer** the depths of hell; **dans un ~ de perplexité** utterly perplexed.

abîmer [abime] (1) **1** *vt* to damage, spoil. **2 s'~** *vpr* **(a)** *[objet]* to get spoilt *ou* damaged; *[fruits]* to go bad. **(b)** *(littér) [navire]* to founder. **s'~ dans la réflexion** to be plunged in thought.

abject, e [abʒɛkt] *adj* despicable, abject. ♦ **abjection** *nf* abjectness.

abjuration [abʒyʀɑsjɔ̃] *nf* abjuration, renunciation. ♦ **abjurer** (1) *vt* to abjure, renounce.

ablation [ablɑsjɔ̃] *nf (Méd)* removal.

ablutions [ablysjɔ̃] *nfpl (gén)* ablutions.

abnégation [abnegɑsjɔ̃] *nf* (self-)abnegation, self-denial. **avec ~** selflessly.

aboiement [abwamɑ̃] *nm [chien]* bark; *(péj: cri)* shout. **~s** barking.

abois [abwa] *nmpl*: **aux ~** at bay.

abolir [abɔliʀ] (2) *vt* to abolish. ♦ **abolition** *nf* abolition. ♦ **abolitionnisme** *nm* abolitionism. ♦ **abolitionniste** *adj, nmf* abolitionist.

abominable [abɔminabl(ə)] *adj* abominable; *(sens affaibli)* frightful, terrible. ♦ **abominablement** *adv* abominably; frightfully, terribly. ♦ **abomination** *nf (crime)* abomination; *(parole etc)* abominable remark *etc*. **avoir en ~** to loathe, abominate; **c'est une ~!** it's abominable! ♦ **abominer** (1) *vt* to abominate.

abondant, e [abɔ̃dɑ̃, ɑ̃t] *adj récolte, réserves* plentiful; *végétation* lush; *chevelure* thick; *larmes, conseils, repas* copious. **avec d'~es photographies** with numerous photographs; **les pêches sont ~es sur le marché** peaches are in plentiful *ou* good supply; **il lui faut une nourriture ~e** he must have plenty of food. ♦ **abondamment** *adv* abundantly; plentifully; *couler* profusely; *boire* copiously. ♦ **abondance** *nf (profusion)* abundance; *(opulence)* affluence. **des fruits en ~** fruit in plenty; **il y a (une) ~ de** there is an abundance of; **~ d'idées** wealth of ideas. ♦ **abonder** (1) *vi* **(a)** to abound, be plentiful. **~ en** to be full of, abound in. **(b) il abonda dans notre sens** he was in complete agreement with us.

abonné, e [abɔne] **1** *adj*: **être ~ à** *journal* to subscribe to; *téléphone, gaz* to have; *(fig)* **il y est ~!** he's making (quite) a habit of it! **2** *nm,f (Presse, Téléc)* subscriber; *(Élec, Gaz)* consumer; *(Rail, Théât)* season-ticket holder. ♦ **abonnement** *nm (Presse)* subscription; *(Téléc)* rental; *(Rail, Théât)* season ticket. ♦ **abonner** (1) **1** *vt*: **~ qn (à qch)** to take out a subscription (to sth) for sb; to buy sb a season ticket (for sth). **2 s'~** *vpr* to subscribe (*à* to); to buy a season ticket (*à* for).

abord [abɔʀ] *nm* **(a)** *(environs)* **~s** surroundings; **aux ~s de** around. **(b)** *(accès)* access, approach; *(accueil)* manner. **d'un ~ difficile** *livre* which is difficult to get into; *personne* unapproachable. **(c) allons d'~ chez le boucher** let's go to the butcher's first; **il fut (tout) d'~ poli, puis** he was polite at first *ou* initially, and then; **d'~, il n'a même pas 18 ans** for a start *ou* in the first place, he's not even 18; **dès l'~** from the outset; **au premier ~** at first sight. ♦ **abordable** *adj prix* reasonable; *personne* approachable; *lieu* accessible.

aborder [abɔʀde] (1) **1** *vt* **(a)** *lieu* to reach; *personne* to approach, come up to; *sujet* to tackle. **(b)** *(Naut) (attaquer)* to board; *(heurter)* to collide with. **2** *vi (Naut)* to land (*dans, sur* on). ♦ **abordage** *nm (assaut)* boarding; *(accident)* collision. **à l'~!** away boarders!

aborigène [abɔʀiʒɛn] **1** *adj* aboriginal. **2** *nmf* aborigine, native.

aboucher (s') [abuʃe] (1) *vpr*: **s'~ avec qn** to get in touch with sb.

aboutir [abutiʀ] (2) *vi* **(a)** *(réussir)* to succeed. **faire ~** to bring to a successful conclusion. **(b) ~ à** *ou* **dans** *lieu* to end (up) in; *désordre* to result in, lead to; **j'aboutis à 12 F** I get (it to come to) 12 francs; **il n'aboutira jamais à rien** he'll never get anywhere; **ça n'a abouti à rien** it has come to nothing. ♦ **aboutissement** *nm (résultat)* outcome; *(succès)* success.

aboyer [abwaje] (8) *vi* to bark; *(péj: crier)* to shout *(après* at).

abracadabrant, e [abʀakadabʀɑ̃, ɑ̃t] *adj* incredible, preposterous.

abrasif, -ive [abʀazif, iv] *adj, nm* abrasive.

abréger [abʀeʒe] (3 *et* 6) *vt (gén)* to shorten; *souffrances, visite* to cut short; *texte* to abridge; *mot* to abbreviate. **abrège!*** get to the point! ♦ **abrégé** *nm* summary. **faire un ~ de** to summarize; **en ~** *(en miniature)* in miniature; *(en bref)* in brief.

abreuver [abʀœve] (1) **1** *vt animal* to water. *(fig)* **~ qn de** to shower sb with; **terre abreuvée d'eau** waterlogged ground. **2 s'~** *vpr* to drink. ♦ **abreuvoir** *nm (mare)* watering place; *(récipient)* drinking trough.

abréviation [abʀevjɑsjɔ̃] *nf* abbreviation.

abri [abʀi] *nm (cabane)* shelter; *(fig)* refuge *(contre* from). **~ à vélos** bicycle shed; *(hum)* **tous aux ~s!** take cover!; **mettre à l'~** *(de la pluie, des regards)* to shelter (*de* from); **se mettre à l'~** to (take) shelter (*de* from); *(de soupçons)* to safeguard o.s. (*de* against); **c'est à l'~** *(de la pluie)* it's under shelter; *(du vol)* it's in a safe place; **à l'~ du mur** sheltered by the wall; **à l'~ du besoin** sheltered from want.

abricot [abʀiko] *nm, adj inv* apricot. ♦ **abricotier** *nm* apricot tree.

abriter [abʀite] (1) **1** *vt (pluie, vent)* to shelter; *(radiations)* to screen (*de* from). **le bâtiment peut ~ 20 personnes** the building can accommodate 20 people. **2 s'~** *vpr* to (take) shelter (*de* from). **s'~ derrière le règlement** to hide *ou* take cover behind the rules.

abrogation [abʀɔgɑsjɔ̃] *nf* abrogation. ♦ **abroger** (3) *vt* to abrogate.

abrupt, e [abʀypt, pt(ə)] **1** *adj pente* abrupt, steep; *personne* abrupt. **2** *nm* steep slope. ♦ **abruptement** *adv* steeply; abruptly.

abrutir [abʀytiʀ] (2) *vt*: **~ qn** to make sb stupid; **~ qn de** to drive sb stupid with; **abruti par l'alcool** stupefied with drink; **abruti de travail** dazed with work. ♦ **abruti, e*** *nm,f* idiot*, moron. ♦ **abrutissant, e** *adj bruit* stunning; *travail* mind-destroying. ♦ **abrutissement** *nm (fatigue)* exhaustion; *(abêtissement)* moronic state. **l'~ des masses par la télévision** the stupefying effect of television on the masses.

absence [apsɑ̃s] *nf [personne, objet]* absence; *[sentiment]* lack (*de* of). **il constata l'~ de sa valise** he noticed that his case was missing; **~ (de mémoire)** mental blank; **en l'~ de** in the absence of.

absent, e [apsɑ̃, ɑ̃t] **1** *adj* **(a)** *(gén)* away (*de* from); *(malade)* absent (*de* from). **conférence dont la France était ~e** conference from which France was absent. **(b)** *sentiment* lacking; *objet* missing. **toute émotion était ~e** there was no trace of emotion. **(c)** *(distrait) air* vacant. **2** *nm,f (gén)* absent person; *(Scol, Admin)* absentee; *(disparu)* missing person. **le grand ~ de la réunion** the most notable absentee at the meeting. ♦ **absentéisme** *nm* absenteeism. ♦ **absentéiste**

nmf absentee. (*gén*) **c'est un ~** he is always absent. ♦ **absenter (s')** (1) *vpr* (*gén*) to go out. **s'~ de** *pièce* to go out of; *ville* to leave; **elle s'absente souvent de son travail** she is frequently absent from work.
abside [apsid] *nf* apse.
absinthe [apsɛ̃t] *nf* absinth(e).
absolu, e [apsɔly] **1** *adj* **(a)** (*gén, Ling, Pol*) absolute. **en cas d'~e nécessité** if absolutely essential; **règle ~e** hard-and-fast rule. **(b)** *ton* peremptory; *jugement* rigid. **2** *nm*: **l'~** the absolute. ♦ **absolument** *adv* (*gén*) absolutely. **avoir ~ tort** to be quite *ou* absolutely wrong; **~ pas!** certainly not!
absolution [apsɔlysjɔ̃] *nf* (*Rel*) absolution (*de* from). **donner l'~ à qn** to give sb absolution.
absolutisme [apsɔlytism(ə)] *nm* absolutism.
absorber [apsɔʀbe] (1) *vt* **(a)** *aliment* to take; *parti, bruit, dette* to absorb; *firme* to take over; *liquide* to absorb, soak up; *tache* to remove. **(b)** *attention, temps* to occupy, take up. **s'~/être absorbé dans une lecture** to become/be absorbed in reading. ♦ **absorbant, e 1** *adj matière* absorbent; *tâche* absorbing; (*Bio*) absorptive. **2** *nm* absorbent. ♦ **absorption** *nf* **(a)** taking; absorption; takeover; removal. **(b)** (*méditation*) absorption.
absoudre [apsudʀ(ə)] (51) *vt* to absolve (*de* from).
abstenir (s') [apstəniʀ] (22) *vpr* **(a) s'~ de qch/de faire** to refrain *ou* abstain from sth/from doing; **je préfère m'~** I'd rather not. **(b)** (*Pol*) to abstain (*de voter* from voting). ♦ **abstention** *nf* abstention. ♦ **abstentionnisme** *nm* abstentionism. ♦ **abstentionniste** *adj, nmf* abstentionist.
abstinence [apstinɑ̃s] *nf* abstinence. **faire ~** to abstain (*from meat*). ♦ **abstinent, e** *adj* abstinent.
abstraction [apstʀaksjɔ̃] *nf* abstraction. **faire ~ de** to leave aside, disregard.
abstraire [apstʀɛʀ] (50) **1** *vt* to abstract (*de* from). **2 s'~** *vpr* to cut o.s. off (*de* from). ♦ **abstrait, e** *adj* abstract. **dans l'~** in the abstract; **l'(art) ~** abstract art. ♦ **abstraitement** *adv* abstractly.
absurde [apsyʀd(ə)] *adj* absurd. ♦ **absurdité** *nf* absurdity.
abus [aby] *nm* (*gén*) abuse. **faire ~ de** *force* to abuse; **l'~ qu'il fait d'aspirine** his excessive use *ou* overuse of aspirin; **nous avons fait des** *ou* **quelques ~ hier soir** we overdid it last night; **il y a de l'~!*** that's going a bit too far!; **~ de pouvoir** abuse *ou* misuse of power.
abuser [abyze] (1) **1 ~ de** *vt indir* **(a)** *situation, victime* to take advantage of; *autorité, hospitalité* to abuse. **je ne veux pas ~ de votre temps/gentillesse** I don't want to waste your time/to impose on your kindness; **tu abuses!** you're going too far! **(b)** (*user avec excès*) *médicaments* to overuse; *ses forces* to overtax; *plaisirs* to overindulge in. **~ de l'alcool** to drink to excess. **2** *vt [escroc]* to deceive; *[ressemblance]* to mislead. **3 s'~** *vpr* (*erreur*) to be mistaken; (*illusions*) to delude o.s.
abusif, -ive [abyzif, iv] *adj pratique* improper; *mère* over-possessive; *prix, punition* excessive. **usage ~ de** improper use *ou* misuse of; **c'est ~ de dire** it's putting it a bit strongly to say. ♦ **abusivement** *adv* improperly; excessively.
acabit [akabi] *nm* (*péj*) sort, type.
acacia [akasja] *nm* acacia.
académie [akademi] *nf* **(a)** (*société savante*) learned society; (*Antiq*) academy. (*officielle*) **A~** Academy; (*école*) **~ de dessin** art school, academy of art. **(b)** (*Univ*) ≃ regional education authority. ♦ **académicien, -ienne** *nm,f* (*gén*) academician; (*Antiq*) academic. ♦ **académique** *adj* (*gén, péj*) academic; *[Académie française]* of the French Academy; (*Univ*) ≃ of the regional education authority. (*Belgique, Can, Suisse*) **année ~** academic year.
acajou [akaʒu] *nm, adj inv* mahogany.
acariâtre [akaʀjɑtʀ(ə)] *adj* sour, cantankerous.
accabler [akɑble] (1) *vt* **(a)** (*gén*) to overwhelm. **accablé sous le nombre** overwhelmed *ou* overpowered by numbers; **sa déposition m'accable** his evidence is overwhelmingly against me. **(b) ~ qn de** *critiques* to heap on sb; *impôts, travail* to overburden sb with; *questions, conseils* to overwhelm sb with. ♦ **accablant, e** *adj chaleur, travail* exhausting; *témoignage, responsabilité* overwhelming; *douleur* excruciating. ♦ **accablement** *nm* (*abattement*) despondency; (*fatigue*) exhaustion.
accalmie [akalmi] *nf* (*gén*) lull (*de* in); *[fièvre]* respite (*dans* in); *[affaires]* slack period.
accaparer [akapaʀe] (1) *vt pouvoir, conversation, hôte* to monopolize; *temps, attention* to take up. **les enfants l'accaparent** the children take up all her time and energy. ♦ **accaparant, e** *adj* all-absorbing. ♦ **accaparement** *nm [pouvoir, production]* monopolizing; *[médecin etc]* involvement (*par* in). ♦ **accapareur, -euse 1** *adj* monopolistic. **2** *nm,f* monopolizer.
accéder [aksede] (6) **~ à** *vt indir* **(a)** *lieu* to reach, get to; *honneur, indépendance, pouvoir* to attain; *grade* to rise to. **(b)** *prière* to grant.
accélérer [akseleʀe] (6) **1** *vt* to speed up. **2** *vi* (*Aut, fig*) to accelerate, speed up. **accélère!*** get a move on!* **3 s'~** *vpr [pouls]* to quicken. ♦ **accélérateur** *nm* accelerator. ♦ **accélération** *nf* acceleration, speeding up; quickening.
accent [aksɑ̃] *nm* **(a)** (*prononciation*) accent. **(b)** (*Orthographe*) accent. **e ~ grave/aigu** e grave/acute; **~ circonflexe** circumflex (accent). **(c)** (*Phonétique*) accent, stress; (*fig*) stress, emphasis. **mettre l'~ sur** to stress. **(d)** (*inflexion*) tone (of voice). **~ plaintif** plaintive tone; **~ de sincérité** note of sincerity; **~s de rage/d'amour** accents of rage/of love; **les ~s de cette musique** the strains of this music.
accentuer [aksɑ̃tɥe] (1) **1** *vt* **(a)** *lettre* to accent; *syllabe* to stress. **(b)** *contraste* to emphasize, accentuate; *goût* to bring out; *effort* to intensify. **2 s'~** *vpr [tendance, traits]* to become more marked *ou* pronounced; *[inflation]* to increase. ♦ **accentuation** *nf* accentuation; stressing; emphasizing; intensification. (*Phonétique*) **les règles de l'~** the rules of stress.
accepter [aksɛpte] (1) *vt* (*gén, Comm*) to accept; *condition* to agree to, accept. **~ de faire** to agree to do; **elle accepte tout de sa fille** she puts up with anything from her daughter. ♦ **acceptable** *adj travail* satisfactory, fair; *repas* reasonable; *condition* acceptable. ♦ **acceptation** *nf* (*gén*) acceptance.
acception [aksɛpsjɔ̃] *nf* meaning, sense.
accès [aksɛ] *nm* **(a)** (*action d'entrer*) access; (*porte*) entrance. **interdire l'~ de qch** to bar entry *ou* prevent access to sth; **~ interdit** no entry, no admittance; **d'~ facile** *lieu* (easily) accessible; *personne* approachable; *manuel* easily understood; **tous les ~ de la ville** all approaches to the town; **donner/avoir ~ à** to give/have access to. **(b)** *[colère, toux, folie]* fit; *[fièvre]* attack, bout; *[enthousiasme]* burst.
accessible [aksesibl(ə)] *adj lieu* accessible (*à* to); *personne* approachable; *but* attainable. **~ à tous** (*financièrement*) within everyone's pocket; (*intellectuellement*) within the reach of everyone.
accession [aksɛsjɔ̃] *nf*: **~ à** *pouvoir, indépendance* attainment of; *rang* rise to.
accessit [aksesit] *nm* (*Scol*) ≃ certificate of merit.
accessoire [akseswaʀ] **1** *adj* (*gén*) secondary, incidental. **2** *nm* **(a)** (*Théât*) prop; (*Aut*) accessory. **~s de toilette** toilet requisites. **(b)** (*Philos*) **l'~** the unessential. ♦ **accessoirement** *adv*

secondarily, incidentally; (*si besoin est*) if necessary. ♦ **accessoiriste** *nmf* property man (*ou* girl).
accident [aksidɑ̃] *nm* **(a)** (*gén, Philos*) accident; (*Aut, Aviat*) crash; (*Méd*) illness, trouble; (*fig: revers*) setback. (*Admin*) **il n'y a pas eu d'~ de personnes** there were no casualties, no one was injured; (*hasard*) **par ~** by chance, by accident. **(b) ~ de terrain** undulation. ♦ **accidenté, e 1** *adj* **(a)** *région* undulating. **(b)** *véhicule* damaged. **2** *nm,f* casualty, injured person. ♦ **accidentel, -elle** *adj* (*gén*) accidental. ♦ **accidentellement** *adv* **(a)** (*par hasard*) accidentally, by accident *ou* chance. **(b)** *mourir* in an accident. ♦ **accidenter** (1) *vt personne* to injure, hurt; *véhicule* to damage.
acclamer [aklame] (1) *vt* to cheer, acclaim. ♦ **acclamation** *nf*: **~s** cheers; **par ~** by acclamation.
acclimater [aklimate] (1) **1** *vt* (*Bot, Zool*) to acclimatize. **2 s'~** *vpr* to become acclimatized (*à* to). ♦ **acclimatation** *nf* acclimatization.
accointances [akwɛ̃tɑ̃s] *nfpl* contacts, links.
accolade [akɔlad] *nf* **(a)** (*protocolaire*) embrace; (*Hist*) accolade. **donner l'~** to embrace. **(b)** (*Typ*) brace. **mots (mis) en ~** words bracketed together. ♦ **accoler** (1) *vt* (*gén*) to place side by side; (*Typ*) to bracket together.
accommoder [akɔmɔde] (1) **1** *vt* **(a)** *plat* to prepare (*à* in, with). **(b)** (*combiner*) to combine; (*adapter*) to adapt; (†: *arranger*) to arrange. **2** *vi* (*Opt*) to focus (*sur* on). **3 s'~** *vpr*: **s'~ de** to put up with; **elle s'accommode de tout** she can make do with anything; (*littér*) **s'~à qch** to adapt to sth; **s'~ avec qn** to come to an arrangement with sb (*sur* about). ♦ **accommodant, e** *adj* accommodating. ♦ **accommodation** *nf* (*Opt*) accommodation; (*adaptation*) adaptation. ♦ **accommodement** *nm* arrangement.
accompagner [akɔ̃paɲe] (1) *vt* (*gén*) to accompany. **il s'était fait ~ de sa mère** he had got his mother to go with him *ou* to accompany him; **tous nos vœux vous accompagnent** all our good wishes go with you; **il s'accompagna à la guitare** he accompanied himself on the guitar; **du chou accompagnait le rôti** cabbage was served with the roast. ♦ **accompagnateur, -trice** *nm,f* (*Mus*) accompanist; (*guide*) guide; (*Scol*) accompanying adult; (*Tourisme*) courier. ♦ **accompagnement** *nm* **(a)** (*Mus*) accompaniment. **sans ~** unaccompanied. **(b)** (*Culin*) accompanying vegetables.
accomplir [akɔ̃pliʀ] (2) *vt promesse* to fulfil, carry out; *mission, exploit* to perform, carry out, accomplish; *apprentissage* (*faire*) to do; (*terminer*) to complete. **la volonté de Dieu s'est accomplie** God's will was done. ♦ **accompli, e** *adj* (*expérimenté*) accomplished. ♦ **accomplissement** *nm* fulfilment; accomplishment; completion.
accord [akɔʀ] *nm* **(a)** (*gén, Gram*) agreement; (*harmonie*) harmony. **le bon ~ règne** harmony reigns; **~ à l'amiable** mutual agreement; **en ~ avec le paysage** in harmony *ou* in keeping with the landscape. **(b)** (*Mus*) (*notes*) chord. **~ parfait** triad; **~ de tierce** third. **(c) être d'~** to agree, be in agreement; **se mettre d'~ avec qn** to agree *ou* come to an agreement with sb; **mettre 2 personnes d'~** to make 2 people come to an agreement with each other; **c'est d'~ (pour demain)** it's agreed *ou* all right *ou* O.K.* (for tomorrow).
accordéon [akɔʀdeɔ̃] *nm* accordion. **en ~*** *voiture* crumpled; *pantalon* wrinkled. ♦ **accordéoniste** *nmf* accordionist.
accorder [akɔʀde] (1) **1** *vt* **(a)** (*gén*) to give, grant; *pension* to award (*à* to). **~ à qn que** to admit (to sb) that; **je vous l'accorde** I'll grant you that; **~ de la valeur à qch** to attach value to sth, value sth. **(b)** (*harmoniser*) *couleurs* to match; (*Mus*) to tune. (*fig*) **ils ont accordé leurs violons** they agreed on the line to take; (*Gram*) **(faire) ~ un verbe/un adjectif** to make a verb/an adjective agree (*avec* with). **2 s'~** *vpr* **(a)** (*être d'accord*) to agree. **ils s'accordent pour dire que le film est mauvais** they agree that it's a poor film; **(bien/mal) s'~ avec qn** to get on (well/badly) with sb. **(b)** *[couleurs]* to match; *[opinions]* to agree; *[caractères]* to be in harmony. **ses actions s'accordent avec ses opinions** his actions are in keeping with his opinions. **(c)** (*Ling*) to agree (*avec* with). ♦ **accordeur** *nm* (*Mus*) tuner.
accorte [akɔʀt(ə)] *adj f* (*hum*) winsome.
accoster [akɔste] (1) *vt personne* to accost; (*Naut*) to come alongside; (*emploi absolu*) to berth.
accotement [akɔtmɑ̃] *nm* (*Aut*) shoulder, verge; (*Rail*) shoulder.
accoter [akɔte] (1) *vt* to lean, rest. **s'~ à** *ou* **contre** to lean against.
accoucher [akuʃe] (1) **1** *vt*: **~ qn** to deliver sb's baby. **2** *vi* **(a)** (*être en travail*) to be in labour; (*donner naissance*) to give birth. **~ d'un garçon** to give birth to a boy, have a (baby) boy. **(b)** (*fig hum*) **~ de** *roman* to bring forth; **accouche!**‡ spit it out!* ♦ **accouchée** *nf* (new) mother. ♦ **accouchement** *nm* delivery. **~ prématuré** premature birth. ♦ **accoucheur, -euse 1** *nm,f*: **(médecin) ~** obstetrician. **2** *nf* (*sage-femme*) midwife.
accouder (s') [akude] (1) *vpr* to lean (on one's elbows) (*sur* on). ♦ **accoudoir** *nm* armrest.
accoupler [akuple] (1) **1** *vt* **(a)** *bœufs* to yoke; (*Tech*) to couple, connect (up) (*à* to); (*fig*) *mots* to link. **(b)** (*faire copuler*) to mate (*à* with). **2 s'~** *vpr* to mate. ♦ **accouplement** *nm* yoking; coupling; connecting (up); linking; mating.
accourir [akuʀiʀ] (11) *vi* (*lit*) to rush up, hurry (*à, vers* to).
accoutrement [akutʀəmɑ̃] *nm* (*péj*) getup*. ♦ **accoutrer** (1) *vt* (*péj*) to get up* (*de* in).
accoutumer [akutyme] (1) *vt*: **~ qn à qch/à faire** to accustom sb *ou* get sb used to sth/to doing; **s'~ à faire** to get used *ou* accustomed to doing. ♦ **accoutumé, e** *adj* usual. **comme à l'~e** as usual. ♦ **accoutumance** *nf* (*habitude*) habituation (*à* to); (*besoin*) addiction (*à* to).
accréditer [akʀedite] (1) **1** *vt rumeur* to substantiate; *personne* to accredit (*auprès de* to). **2 s'~** *vpr [rumeur]* to gain ground.
accroc [akʀo] *nm* **(a)** *[tissu]* tear; *[réputation]* blot (*à* on); *[règle]* breach (*à* of). **faire un ~ à** *règle* to twist; *tissu* to tear. **(b)** (*anicroche*) hitch. **sans ~s** without a hitch.
accrochage [akʀɔʃaʒ] *nm* (*Aut*) collision; (*Mil*) engagement; (*Boxe*) clinch; (*dispute*) clash.
accrocher [akʀɔʃe] (1) **1** *vt* **(a)** *tableau* to hang (up) (*à* on); *wagons* to couple (*à* to). **~ un ver à l'hameçon** to put a worm on the hook. **(b)** (*accident*) *jupe* to catch (*à* on); *voiture* to bump into; *piéton* to hit; *assiette* to knock. **(c)** (*: *fig*) *occasion* to get; *personne* to get hold of; *mots* to catch; *client* to attract. **~ le regard** to catch the eye. **(d)** (*Mil*) to engage; (*Boxe*) to clinch. **2** *vi* **(a)** *[fermeture éclair]* to jam; *[pourparlers]* to come up against a hitch. **cette planche accroche** this board catches on the cloth. **(b)** (*plaire*) *[slogan]* to catch on. **3 s'~** *vpr* **(a)** (*se cramponner*) to hang on. **s'~ à** *branche, espoir* to cling to. **(b)** (*) *[malade]* to cling on; *[étudiant]* to stick at it*; *[importun]* to cling. **(c)** *[voitures]* to bump (each other); (*Boxe*) to get into a clinch; (*Mil*) to engage; (*se disputer*) to have a clash (*avec* with). ♦ **accrocheur, -euse** *adj concurrent* tenacious; *affiche* eye-catching; *slogan* catchy.
accroire [akʀwaʀ] *vt*: **faire ~ à qn qch/que** to delude sb into believing sth/that.
accroître *vt*, **s'~** *vpr* [akʀwatʀ(ə)] (55) to increase. ♦ **accroissement** *nm* (*gén*) increase (*de*

in); *[production]* growth (*de* in).
accroupir (s') [akʀupiʀ] (2) *vpr* to squat *ou* crouch (down). ♦ **accroupi, e** *adj* squatting *ou* crouching (down).
accu* [aky] *nm* (*Aut etc*) battery.
accueil [akœj] *nm* (*gén*) welcome, reception; *[sinistrés, idée]* reception; (*logement*) accommodation. **faire bon** ~ **à** to welcome; **faire mauvais** ~ **à** to receive badly. ♦ **accueillant, e** *adj* welcoming. ♦ **accueillir** (12) *vt* **(a)** (*aller chercher*) to collect; (*recevoir*) to welcome; (*pouvoir héberger*) to accommodate. **bien/mal** ~ **qn** to give sb a good/bad reception; ~ **par des huées** to greet with jeers. **(b)** *nouvelle* to receive.
acculer [akyle] (1) *vt*: ~ **qn à** *mur* to drive sb back against; *ruine* to drive sb to the brink of; *choix* to force sb into; ~ **qn dans** *pièce* to corner sb in; (*lit, fig*) **nous sommes acculés** we're cornered.
accumuler [akymyle] (1) **1** *vt* (*gén*) to accumulate; *marchandises* to stockpile; *énergie* to store. **2 s'**~ *vpr* to accumulate; (*Fin*) to accrue. ♦ **accumulateur** *nm* battery. ♦ **accumulation** *nf* accumulation; stockpiling; storage; (*tas*) accumulation.
accusateur, -trice [akyzatœʀ, tʀis] **1** *adj* *regard* accusing; *preuves* incriminating. **2** *nm,f* accuser.
accusatif [akyzatif] *nm* (*Ling*) accusative.
accusation [akyzɑsjɔ̃] *nf* (*gén*) accusation; (*Jur*) charge. (*le procureur etc*) **l'**~ the prosecution; **mettre en** ~ to indict; **mise en** ~ indictment.
accuser [akyze] (1) **1** *vt* **(a)** (*gén*) to accuse (*de* of); (*blâmer*) to blame (*de* for). (*Jur*) ~ **de** to accuse of, charge with; **tout l'accuse** everything points to his guilt; ~ **qn d'incompétence** to blame sb for his incompetence. **(b)** *forme, contraste* to emphasize; *âge, fatigue* to show. (*lit, fig*) ~ **le coup** to stagger under the blow; ~ **réception** to acknowledge receipt (*de* of). **2 s'**~ *vpr* **(a) s'**~ **de qch/d'avoir fait** *[coupable]* to admit to sth/to having done; *[responsable]* to blame o.s. for sth/for having done. **(b)** *[tendance]* to become more marked. ♦ **accusé, e 1** *adj* (*marqué*) marked. **2** *nm,f* accused; *[procès]* defendant. **3**: ~ **de réception** acknowledgement of receipt.
acerbe [asɛʀb(ə)] *adj* caustic, acid.
acéré, e [aseʀe] *adj* *pointe* sharp; *raillerie* scathing, cutting.
acétate [asetat] *nm* acetate.
acétique [asetik] *adj* acetic.
acétone [asetɔn] *nf* acetone.
acétylène [asetilɛn] *nm* acetylene.
achalandé, e [aʃalɑ̃de] *adj*: **bien** ~ *[denrées]* well-stocked; *[clients]* well-patronized.
acharné, e [aʃaʀne] *adj* *combat, adversaire* fierce; *efforts, poursuivant, travailleur* relentless. ~ **à qch/à faire** bent on sth/on doing; ~ **contre** set against. ♦ **acharnement** *nm [combattant]* fierceness; *[poursuivant]* relentlessness; *[travailleur]* determination. **avec** ~ *poursuivre, travailler* relentlessly; *combattre* fiercely. ♦ **acharner (s')** (1) *vpr*: **s'**~ **sur** *ou* **contre qn** *[malchance]* to dog sb; *[adversaire]* to pursue sb (relentlessly); **je m'acharne à le leur faire comprendre** I'm desperately trying to explain it to them; **il s'acharne inutilement** he's wasting his efforts.
achat [aʃa] *nm* **(a)** purchase. **faire l'**~ **de qch** to purchase *ou* buy sth; **faire des** ~**s** to shop, go shopping; **c'est cher à l'**~ it's expensive to buy; ~ **judicieux** wise buy. **(b)** (*Bourse, Comm*) buying. **la livre vaut 8 F à l'**~ the buying rate for sterling is 8 francs.
acheminer [aʃmine] (1) **1** *vt* *colis* to dispatch; *troupes* to convey, transport; *trains* to route (*vers* to). **2 s'**~ *vpr*: **s'**~ **vers** *lieu, ruine* to head for; *solution* to move towards. ♦ **acheminement** *nm* dispatch; conveying, transporting; routing.
acheter [aʃte] (5) *vt* **(a)** to buy, purchase (*au vendeur* from the seller; *pour qn* for sb). **je lui ai acheté une robe** I bought her a dress. **(b)** (*péj*) *vote* to buy; *juge* to bribe. ♦ **acheteur, -euse** *nm,f* buyer; (*Jur*) vendee; (*profession*) buyer. **il est** ~ he'll buy it; **la foule des** ~**s** the crowd of shoppers.
achever [aʃve] (5) **1** *vt* **(a)** *discours, repas* to finish, end; *tâche* to complete, finish. ~ **(de parler)** to finish (speaking); **cette remarque acheva de l'exaspérer** this remark really brought his irritation to a head. **(b)** *blessé* to finish off; *cheval* to destroy. **ça m'a achevé!** it was the end of me! **2 s'**~ *vpr* (*se terminer*) to end (*par, sur* with). ♦ **achevé, e** *adj* *canaille* downright, thorough; *artiste* accomplished; *art* perfect. **d'un ridicule** ~ perfectly ridiculous. ♦ **achèvement** *nm [travaux]* completion.
achopper [aʃɔpe] (1) *vi*: ~ **sur** to stumble over.
acide [asid] **1** *adj* (*lit, fig*) acid, sour, tart; (*Chim*) acid. **2** *nm* acid. ♦ **acidité** *nf* (*lit, fig*) acidity. ♦ **acidulé, e** *adj* *goût* slightly acid *ou* sour.
acier [asje] *nm* steel. **d'**~ *poutre* steel, of steel; *regard* steely. ♦ **aciérie** *nf* steelworks.
acné [akne] *nf* acne. ~ **juvénile** teenage acne.
acolyte [akɔlit] *nm* (*péj*) confederate, associate.
acompte [akɔ̃t] *nm* (*arrhes*) deposit, down payment; (*régulier*) instalment; (*sur salaire*) advance.
acoquiner (s') [akɔkine] (1) *vpr* (*péj*) to team up (*avec* with).
à-côté [akote] *nm [problème]* side aspect; (*argent*) extra.
à-coup [aku] *nm* jolt. **par** ~**s** in fits and starts; **sans** ~**s** smoothly.
acoustique [akustik] **1** *adj* acoustic. **2** *nf* (*science*) acoustics (*sg*); (*sonorité*) acoustics (*pl*).
acquérir [akeʀiʀ] (21) *vt* *objet* to acquire, purchase, buy; *célébrité* to win; *habileté, valeur, expérience* to acquire, gain. ~ **la certitude de** to become certain of; **ça s'acquiert facilement** it's easy to pick up; ~ **la preuve de** to gain proof of. ♦ **acquéreur** *nm* buyer, purchaser. **se rendre** ~ **de qch** to purchase *ou* buy sth.
acquiescer [akjese] (3) *vi* (*approuver*) to approve, agree; (*de la tête*) to nod (one's approval *ou* agreement); (*consentir*) to acquiesce, assent (*à* to). ♦ **acquiescement** *nm* approval, agreement; acquiescence, assent.
acquis, e [aki, iz] **1** *adj* *droit, caractères* acquired; *fait* established. **tenir pour** ~ (*normal*) to take for granted; (*décidé*) to take as settled; **être** ~ **à un projet** to be strongly in favour of a plan. **2** *nm* (*savoir*) experience. **la connaissance de l'anglais représente un** ~ **précieux** knowledge of English is a valuable asset. ♦ **acquisition** *nf* acquisition; (*par achat*) purchase.
acquit [aki] *nm* (*Comm*) receipt. **par** ~ **de conscience** to set one's mind at rest.
acquitter [akite] (1) **1** *vt* **(a)** *accusé* to acquit. **(b)** *impôt, facture* to pay; (*Comm*) to receipt. ~ **qn de** to release sb from. **2 s'**~ *vpr*: **s'**~ **de** *dette, obligation, devoir* to discharge; *promesse, fonction* to fulfil, carry out; **comment m'**~ **(envers vous)?** how can I ever repay you? (*de* for). ♦ **acquittement** *nm* acquittal; payment; discharge; fulfilment.
acre [akʀ(ə)] *nf* (*Hist*) ≃ acre.
âcre [ɑkʀ(ə)] *adj* acrid, pungent. ♦ **âcreté** *nf* acridity, pungency.
acrimonie [akʀimɔni] *nf* acrimony.
acrobate [akʀɔbat] *nmf* (*lit, fig*) acrobat. ♦ **acrobatie** *nf* (*tour*) acrobatic feat; (*art, fig*) acrobatics (*sg*). ~ **aérienne** aerobatics; (*lit, fig*) **faire des** ~**s** to perform acrobatics. ♦ **acrobatique** *adj* (*lit, fig*) acrobatic.
acte [akt(ə)] **1** *nm* **(a)** (*action*) act. ~ **réflexe** reflex action; **des** ~**s!** let's have some action!; **il faut passer aux** ~**s** we must act *ou* take action; ~ **de bravoure** act of bravery, brave act *ou*

action. **(b)** (*Jur*) *[notaire]* deed; *[état civil]* certificate; (*Théât, fig*) act. *[congrès etc]* ~s proceedings. **(c) donner ~ de qch** to acknowledge sth formally; **faire ~ de citoyen** to act *ou* behave as a citizen; **faire ~ de clémence** to show mercy; **faire ~ de candidature** to apply; **faire ~ de présence** to put in an appearance; **prendre ~ de** to note, take note of.

2: **~ d'accusation** bill of indictment; **les A~s des Apôtres** the Acts of the Apostles; **~ de foi** act of faith; **~ gratuit** gratuitous act; **~ médical** (medical) consultation; **~ de vente** bill of sale.

acteur [aktœʀ] *nm* (*Théât, fig*) actor; *V* **actrice**.

actif, -ive [aktif, iv] **1** *adj* (*gén, Ling*) active; *armée* regular. **prendre une part ~ive à qch** to take an active part in sth. **2** *nm* **(a)** (*Ling*) active. **(b)** (*Fin*) assets; *[succession]* credits. **c'est à mettre à son ~** it is a point in his favour; **plusieurs crimes à son ~** several crimes to his name. **3** *nf* regular army.

action [aksjɔ̃] *nf* **(a)** (*acte*) action, act. **bonne ~** good deed; **~ d'éclat** brilliant feat *ou* deed; **commettre une mauvaise ~** to behave badly. **(b)** (*activité*) action. **passer à l'~** to take action; (*Mil*) to go into action; **entrer en ~** *[troupes, canon]* to go into action; **mettre en ~** *plan* to put into action; *dispositif* to put into operation. **(c)** (*effet*) action. **sans ~** ineffective; **sous l'~ de** under the action of. **(d)** (*Théât*) (*mouvement*) action; (*intrigue*) plot. **roman d'~** novel of events. **(e)** (*Jur*) action (at law). **(f)** (*Fin*) share. **~s** shares, stocks; **société par ~s** (joint) stock company; **~ de chasse** hunting rights; (*fig*) **ses ~s sont en baisse** things are not looking so good for him. **(g)** (*Rel*) **~ de grâce(s)** thanksgiving.

actionnaire [aksjɔnɛʀ] *nmf* shareholder.

actionner [aksjɔne] (1) *vt* to activate. **actionné par la vapeur** steam-powered. ♦ **actionnement** *nm* activation.

activement [aktivmɑ̃] *adv* actively.

activer [aktive] (1) **1** *vt travaux* to speed up; *feu* to stoke; (*Chim*) to activate. **2 s'~** *vpr* (*s'affairer*) to bustle about; (*: *se hâter*) to get a move on. **s'~ à faire** to be busy doing.

activisme [aktivism(ə)] *nm* activism. ♦ **activiste** *adj, nmf* activist.

activité [aktivite] *nf* (*gén*) activity; *[rue]* bustle. **être en ~** *[usine]* to be in operation; *[volcan]* to be active; *[fonctionnaire]* to be in active life.

actrice [aktʀis] *nf* (*Théât, fig*) actress.

actualité [aktɥalite] *nf* *[sujet]* topicality. **d'~** topical; (*événements*) **l'~** current events; (*nouvelles*) **les ~s** the news (*sg*). ♦ **actuel, -elle** *adj* **(a)** (*présent*) present. **à l'époque ~le** nowadays. **(b)** (*d'actualité*) topical. ♦ **actuellement** *adv* at present.

acuité [akɥite] *nf* *[son]* shrillness; *[sens, crise]* acuteness.

acupuncteur [akypɔ̃ktœʀ] *nm* acupuncturist. ♦ **acupuncture** *nf* acupuncture.

adage [adaʒ] *nm* adage.

adapter [adapte] (1) **1** *vt* (*gén*) to adapt (*à* to). (*Tech*) **~ qch à** to fit sth to; **adapté à la situation** suited to the situation. **2 s'~** *vpr* (*gén*) to adapt (o.s.) (*à* to). (*Tech*) **s'~ à** to fit. ♦ **adaptable** *adj* adaptable. ♦ **adaptateur, -trice** *nm,f* adapter. ♦ **adaptation** *nf* adaptation.

additionner [adisjɔne] (1) **1** *vt* to add up. **~ qch à** to add sth to. **2 s'~** *vpr* to add up. ♦ **additif** *nm* (*clause*) rider; (*substance*) additive. ♦ **addition** *nf* (*gén*) addition; (*facture*) bill, check (*US*). **par ~ de** by adding, by the addition of.

adepte [adɛpt(ə)] *nmf* follower.

adéquat, e [adekwa, at] *adj* appropriate, suitable.

adhérence [adeʀɑ̃s] *nf* (*gén*) adhesion (*à* to); *[pneus]* grip (*à* on). ♦ **adhérent, e 1** *adj*: **~ à** which sticks *ou* adheres to. **2** *nm,f* adherent.

adhérer [adeʀe] (6) **~ à** *vt indir* **(a)** (*coller*) to stick to, adhere to. **~ à la route** to grip the road. **(b)** *idée* to support. **(c)** (*s'inscrire*) to join; (*être inscrit*) to be a member of.

adhésif, -ive [adezif, iv] *adj, nm* adhesive.

adhésion [adezjɔ̃] *nf* **(a)** (*accord*) adherence (*à* to). **(b)** (*inscription*) joining; (*fait d'être membre*) membership (*à* of).

adieu, *pl* **~x** [adjø] **1** *nm* farewell, goodbye. (*lit, fig*) **dire ~ à** to say goodbye to; **faire ses ~x (à qn)** to say one's farewells (to sb). **2** *excl* goodbye, farewell (†).

adipeux, -euse [adipø, øz] *adj* (*Anat*) adipose; *visage* fleshy.

adjacent, e [adʒasɑ̃, ɑ̃t] *adj* adjacent, adjoining. **~ à** adjacent to.

adjectif, -ive [adʒɛktif, iv] **1** *adj* adjectival. **2** *nm* adjective.

adjoindre [adʒwɛ̃dʀ(ə)] (49) *vt* (*gén*) to add; *mécanisme* to attach, affix; *personne* to appoint (as an assistant) (*à* to). ♦ **adjoint, e** *adj, nm,f* assistant. **~ au maire** deputy mayor. ♦ **adjonction** *nf* addition; attaching; affixing; appointment.

adjudant [adʒydɑ̃] *nm* warrant officer.

adjudication [adʒydikɑsjɔ̃] *nf* **(a)** (*vente aux enchères*) sale by auction; (*marché administratif*) invitation to tender. **par (voie d')~** by auction; by tender. **(b)** (*attribution*) *[contrat]* awarding; *[meuble]* auctioning (*à* to).

adjuger [adʒyʒe] (3) *vt* **(a)** (*enchères*) to auction (*à* to). **adjugé, (vendu)!** going, going, gone!; **ceci fut adjugé pour 30 F** this went for 30 francs. **(b)** *récompense* to award; (*: *donner*) to give. **s'~ qch*** to grab sth.

adjurer [adʒyʀe] (1) *vt*: **~ qn de faire** to implore *ou* entreat sb to do. ♦ **adjuration** *nf* entreaty.

admettre [admɛtʀ(ə)] (56) *vt* **(a)** *visiteur* (*faire entrer*) to admit, let in; (*autoriser*) to allow in; (*recevoir*) to receive. **il fut admis dans le salon** he was ushered *ou* shown into the drawing room. **(b)** (*accepter*) *excuses, attitude* to accept; *nouveau membre* to admit. **je n'admets pas cette conduite** I won't accept *ou* permit such behaviour; **c'est chose admise** it's an accepted fact; **règle qui n'admet pas d'exception** rule which admits of *ou* allows of no exception; **se faire ~ dans un club** to gain admittance to a club. **(c)** (*reconnaître*) *erreur* to admit, acknowledge. **j'admets que vous avez raison** I admit *ou* acknowledge that you are right. **(d)** (*supposer*) to suppose, assume. **en admettant que** supposing *ou* assuming that. **(e)** (*Scol, Univ*) (*à un examen*) to pass; (*dans une classe*) to admit, accept. **il a été admis au concours** he passed *ou* got through the exam.

administrateur, -trice [administʀatœʀ, tʀis] *nm,f* (*gén*) administrator; *[entreprise]* director; *[fondation]* trustee.

administratif, -ive [administʀatif, iv] *adj* administrative. ♦ **administrativement** *adv* administratively.

administré, e [administʀe] *nm,f* citizen.

administrer [administʀe] (1) *vt* **(a)** *entreprise* to manage, run; *fondation, fortune* to administer; *pays* to run, govern. **(b)** *justice, remède* to administer; *coup* to deal; *preuve* to produce. ♦ **administration** *nf* **(a)** management; running; administration; government. **(b)** (*service public*) (government) department *ou* organisation. **l'A ~** ≃ the Civil Service; **l'~ locale** local government; **l'~ des Impôts** the tax department *ou* office.

admirable [admiʀabl(ə)] *adj* admirable. **être ~ de courage** to show admirable courage. ♦ **admirablement** *adv* admirably. ♦ **admirateur, -trice** *nm,f* admirer. ♦ **admiratif, -ive** *adj* admiring. ♦ **admiration** *nf* admiration. **faire l'~ de qn** to fill sb with admiration; **en ~ devant qch** filled with admiration for sth. ♦ **admirativement** *adv* admiringly. ♦ **admirer** (1) *vt* to admire.

admis, e [admi, iz] *nm,f* (*Scol*) successful candidate. ♦ **admissible 1** *adj conduite* acceptable; *postulant* eligible (*à* for). **2** *nmf* eligible candidate. ♦ **admissibilité** *nf* eligibility (*à* for).
admission [admisjɔ̃] *nf* **(a)** *[club]* admission, entry; *[école]* acceptance, entrance (*à* to). **demande d'~** application (*à* to join); **le nombre des ~s au concours** the number of successful candidates in this exam. **(b)** (*Tech: introduction*) intake; (*Aut*) induction.
admonestation [admɔnɛstasjɔ̃] *nf* admonition. ♦ **admonester** (1) *vt* to admonish.
adolescence [adɔlesɑ̃s] *nf* adolescence. ♦ **adolescent, e** *nm,f* adolescent, teenager.
adonner (s') [adɔne] (1) *vpr*: s'~ **à** *études* to devote o.s. to; *vice* to take to.
adopter [adɔpte] (1) *vt* (*gén*) to adopt. ♦ **adoptif, -ive** *adj enfant* adopted; *parent* adoptive. ♦ **adoption** *nf* adoption.
adorable [adɔʀabl(ə)] *adj personne* adorable, delightful; *chose* delightful. ♦ **adorablement** *adv* delightfully, adorably. ♦ **adorer** (1) *vt* (*gén*) to adore; (*Rel*) to worship. ♦ **adorateur, -trice** *nm,f* (*Rel, fig*) worshipper. ♦ **adoration** *nf* adoration; worship. **être en ~ devant** to worship.
adosser [adose] (1) *vt*: ~ **à qch** *meuble* to stand against sth; *bâtiment* to build against sth; **s'~ à** *ou* **contre qch** *[personne]* to lean with one's back against sth.
adoucir [adusiʀ] (2) **1** *vt* (*gén, Tech*) to soften; *goût* to make milder; (*avec sucre*) to sweeten; *aspérités* to smooth out; *caractère* to mellow; *conditions pénibles* to ease. **pour ~ ses vieux jours** to comfort him in his old age; **pour ~ sa solitude** to ease his loneliness; **cette averse a adouci la température** this shower has brought the temperature down. **2 s'~** *vpr [voix, couleur, peau]* to soften; *[caractère]* to mellow; *[température]* to get milder; *[pente]* to become gentler. ♦ **adoucissement** *nm* sweetening; softening; smoothing-out; mellowing; easing. **un ~ de la température** a spell of milder weather. ♦ **adoucisseur** *nm*: ~ **(d'eau)** water softener.
adresse[1] [adʀɛs] *nf* **(a)** (*domicile*) address. **(b)** (*message*) address. **à l'~ de** for the benefit of. **(c)** (*Lexicographie*) headword; (*Ordinateur*) address.
adresse[2] [adʀɛs] *nf* (*habileté*) deftness, skill; (*finesse*) shrewdness, skill; (*tact*) adroitness. **jeu d'~** game of skill.
adresser [adʀese] (1) **1** *vt lettre* (*envoyer*) to send; (*écrire l'adresse*) to address (*à* to); *remarque, requête* to address; *reproche, coup* to level, aim (*à* at); *compliment* to pay (*à* to); *sourire* to give. **~ la parole à qn** to speak to *ou* address sb; **il m'adressa un signe de tête** he nodded at me; **~ qn à un spécialiste** to refer sb to a specialist. **2 s'~** *vpr*: **s'~ à** *interlocuteur* to speak to, address; *responsable* to go and see; *bureau* to apply to, enquire at; *générosité* to appeal to. **livre qui s'adresse aux femmes** book intended *ou* written for women.
adroit, e [adʀwa, wat] *adj* (*habile*) skilful, deft; (*subtil*) shrewd; (*plein de tact*) adroit. **~ de ses mains** clever with one's hands. ♦ **adroitement** *adv* skilfully; deftly; shrewdly; cleverly; adroitly.
aduler [adyle] (1) *vt* to adulate. ♦ **adulateur, -trice** *nm,f* adulator. ♦ **adulation** *nf* adulation.
adulte [adylt(ə)] **1** *adj personne* adult; *animal, plante* fully-grown. **2** *nmf* adult, grown-up.
adultère [adyltɛʀ] **1** *adj désir* adulterous. **femme/homme ~** adulteress/adulterer. **2** *nm* adultery.
advenir [advəniʀ] (22) *vb impers* **(a)** (*survenir*) **~ que** to happen that; **~ à** to happen to; **il m'advint de** I happened to; **advienne que pourra** come what may. **(b)** (*devenir*) **~ de** to become of; **qu'en adviendra-t-il?** what will come of it?
adverbe [advɛʀb(ə)] *nm* adverb. ♦ **adverbial, e,** *mpl* **-aux** *adj* adverbial.
adversaire [advɛʀsɛʀ] *nmf* (*gén*) opponent, adversary. ♦ **adverse** *adj forces* opposing; *sort* adverse. ♦ **adversité** *nf* adversity.
ad vitam æternam* [advitametɛʀnam] *loc adv* till kingdom come.
aérer [aeʀe] (6) **1** *vt pièce* to air; *terre* to aerate; *présentation* to lighten. **2 s'~** *vpr [personne]* to get some fresh air. ♦ **aéré, e** *adj pièce* airy; *page* well spaced out. ♦ **aérateur** *nm* ventilator. ♦ **aération** *nf* ventilation.
aérien, -ienne [aeʀjɛ̃, jɛn] *adj* **(a)** (*Aviat, gén*) air; *navigation, photographie* aerial. **(b)** *silhouette* sylphlike; *démarche* floating; *musique* ethereal. **(c)** *racine* aerial; *câble* overhead; (*Géog*) *courant* air.
aérium [aeʀjɔm] *nm* sanatorium.
aéro-club [aeʀɔklœb] *nm* flying club.
aérodrome [aeʀɔdʀom] *nm* airfield.
aérodynamique [aeʀɔdinamik] **1** *adj ligne* streamlined, aerodynamic. **2** *nf* aerodynamics (*sg*).
aérofrein [aeʀɔfʀɛ̃] *nm* air brake.
aérogare [aeʀɔgaʀ] *nf [aéroport]* airport (buildings); (*en ville*) air terminal.
aéroglisseur [aeʀɔglisœʀ] *nm* hovercraft.
aérogramme [aeʀɔgʀam] *nm* air letter.
aéronautique [aeʀɔnotik] **1** *adj* aeronautical. **2** *nf* aeronautics (*sg*).
aéronaval, e, *pl* **~s** [aeʀɔnaval] *adj forces* air and sea. **l'A~e** ≈ the Fleet Air Arm.
aéroplane† [aeʀɔplan] *nm* aeroplane, airplane (*US*).
aéroport [aeʀɔpɔʀ] *nm* airport.
aéroporté, e [aeʀɔpɔʀte] *adj troupes* airborne; *matériel* air-lifted.
aérosol [aeʀɔsɔl] *nm* aerosol.
aérospatial, e, *mpl* **-aux** [aeʀɔspasjal, o] **1** *adj* aerospace. **2** *nf* aerospace science.
affabilité [afabilite] *nf* affability. ♦ **affable** *adj* affable. ♦ **affablement** *adv* affably.
affabuler [afabyle] (1) *vi* to make up stories.
affaiblir [afebliʀ] (2) **1** *vt* (*gén*) to weaken. **2 s'~** *vpr* (*gén*) to grow weaker; *[son]* to fade, grow fainter; *[tempête]* to abate, die down. ♦ **affaiblissement** *nm* (*gén*) weakening.
affaire [afɛʀ] **1** *nf* **(a)** (*gén: histoire*) matter, business; (*Jur*) case. **ce n'est pas une mince ~** it's no small matter; **il m'a tiré d'~** he helped me out; **ce n'est pas ton ~** it's none of your business; **j'en fais mon ~** I'll deal with that; **ça fait mon ~** that's (just) what I want *ou* need; **une grave ~ de corruption** a serious corruption case. **(b)** (*transaction*) deal, bargain. **une (bonne) ~** a good deal, a (good) bargain; **faire ~ avec qn** to make a bargain *ou* deal with sb. **(c)** (*firme*) business, concern. **(d) ~s** (*gén, Pol*) affairs; (*commerce*) business; (*habits*) clothes; (*objets*) things, belongings; **les ~s culturelles** cultural affairs; **venir pour ~s** to come on business; **mettre de l'ordre dans ses ~s** (*finances*) to put one's affairs in order; (*objets*) to tidy up one's things. **(e) avoir ~ à** *cas* to be faced with, have to deal with; *personne* to be dealing with; **tu auras ~ à moi!** you'll be hearing from me!; **être à son ~** to be in one's element; **cela ne fait rien à l'~** that's got nothing to do with it; **ce n'est pas une ~!** it's nothing to get worked up about!; **c'est toute une ~** it's quite a business; **(se) faire une ~ de qch** to make a fuss about sth; **c'est (une) ~ de goût** it's a matter of taste; **c'est l'~ de quelques minutes** it's a matter of a few minutes.
2: **~ de cœur** love affair; (*Pol*) **~ d'État** affair of state; **il en a fait une ~ d'état*** he made a great issue of it.
affairer (s') [afeʀe] (1) *vpr* to bustle about (*à faire* doing). **s'~ autour de qn** to fuss around sb.

♦ **affairé, e** *adj* busy. ♦ **affairement** *nm* bustling activity.
affaisser (s') [afese] (1) *vpr* **(a)** *[sol]* to subside; *[corps, poutre]* to sag; *[plancher]* to cave in. **(b)** (*s'écrouler*) to collapse. **affaissé sur le sol** slumped on the ground. ♦ **affaissement** *nm* subsidence; sagging. ~**(s) de terrain** subsidence.
affaler (s') [afale] (1) *vpr (tomber)* to collapse; (*se laisser tomber*) to slump (down).
affamer [afame] (1) *vt* to starve. ♦ **affamé, e** *adj* starving, famished. ~ **de gloire** greedy for fame.
affectation [afɛktɑsjɔ̃] *nf* **(a)** *[immeuble, somme]* allocation, allotment (*à* to, for). **(b)** (*nomination*) appointment; (*à une région*) posting. **(c)** (*simulation*) affectation.
affecter [afɛkte] (1) *vt* **(a)** (*feindre*) to affect. ~ **de faire** to pretend to do; ~ **une forme** to take on *ou* assume a shape. **(b)** (*destiner*) to allocate, allot (*à* to, for). **(c)** (*nommer*) to appoint; (*à une région*) to post (*à* to). **(d)** (*émouvoir*) to affect, move; (*concerner*) to affect. **(e)** (*Math*) to modify. **affecté du signe** + bearing a plus sign. ♦ **affecté, e** *adj* affected.
affectif, -ive [afɛktif, iv] *adj* (*gén*) *vie* emotional; *terme* affective; (*Psych*) affective.
affection [afɛksjɔ̃] *nf* **(a)** (*tendresse*) affection. **avoir de l'**~ **pour** to be fond of. **(b)** (*Méd*) ailment; (*Psych*) affection.
affectionner [afɛksjɔne] (1) *vt* to be fond of. **votre fils affectionné** your loving son.
affectivité [afɛktivite] *nf* affectivity.
affectueux, -euse [afɛktɥø, øz] *adj* affectionate. ♦ **affectueusement** *adv* affectionately.
afférent, e [aferɑ̃, ɑ̃t] *adj* (*Admin*) ~ **à** pertaining to; **questions** ~**es** related questions.
affermir [afɛrmir] (2) *vt* *pouvoir, position* to strengthen; *chairs* to tone up; *prise* to make firm *ou* firmer. ~ **sa voix** to steady one's voice. ♦ **affermissement** *nm* strengthening.
affiche [afiʃ] *nf* (*gén*) poster; (*Théât*) (play)bill. (*officielle*) **par voie d'**~ by (means of) public notices; (*Théât*) **mettre à l'**~ to bill; **quitter l'**~ to come off; **tenir longtemps l'**~ to have a long run.
afficher [afiʃe] (1) *vt* **(a)** *affiche, résultat* to stick up; (*Théât*) to bill. **défense d'**~ (stick) no bills. **(b)** (*péj*) *émotion, vice* to display. **s'**~ **avec sa maîtresse** to show o.s. off with one's mistress. ♦ **affichage** *nm* sticking up; billing. **l'**~ bill-sticking.
affilée[1] [afile] *nf*: **d'**~ in a row.
affiler [afile] (1) *vt* to sharpen. ♦ **affilé, e**[2] *adj* sharp.
affiliation [afiljɑsjɔ̃] *nf* affiliation. ♦ **affilié, e** *nm,f* affiliated member. ♦ **affilier** (7) **1** *vt* to affiliate (*à* to). **2 s'**~ *vpr* to become affiliated (*à* to).
affiner [afine] (1) *vt* **(a)** *métal* to refine; *fromage* to complete the maturing of. **(b)** *esprit, style* to refine; *sens* to sharpen. **son goût s'est affiné** his taste has become more refined. ♦ **affinage** *nm* refining; maturing. ♦ **affinement** *nm* refinement.
affinité [afinite] *nf* (*gén*) affinity.
affirmatif, -ive [afirmatif, iv] **1** *adj réponse, ton* affirmative. **il a été** ~ he was quite positive. **2** *nf*: **répondre par l'**~**ive** to answer yes *ou* in the affirmative; **dans l'**~**ive** in the event of an affirmative (reply). ♦ **affirmation** *nf* (*gén, Gram*) assertion. ♦ **affirmativement** *adv* in the affirmative, affirmatively.
affirmer [afirme] (1) *vt* **(a)** (*soutenir*) to maintain, assert. **pouvez-vous l'**~? can you swear to it *ou* be positive about it?; ~ **qch sur l'honneur** to maintain sth on one's word of honour; ~ **sa volonté de** to affirm *ou* assert one's wish to. **(b)** *originalité, autorité* to assert. **talent qui s'affirme** talent which is becoming more assured.
affleurer [aflœre] (1) **1** *vi [récifs, filon]* to show on the surface; *[sentiment]* to come to the surface. **2** *vt* (*Tech*) to make flush. ♦ **affleurement** *nm* (*Géol*) outcrop.
affliction [afliksjɔ̃] *nf* affliction.
affliger [afliʒe] (3) *vt* to distress, grieve. **s'**~ **de qch** to be grieved *ou* distressed about sth; **être affligé de** (*gén*) to be afflicted with; (*hum*) to be cursed with. ♦ **affligeant, e** *adj* distressing; (*iro*) pathetic.
affluence [aflyɑ̃s] *nf* crowd. **heure d'**~ peak *ou* rush hour.
affluent [aflyɑ̃] *nm* tributary.
affluer [aflye] (1) *vi [sang]* to rush, flow; *[foule]* to flock (*à, vers* to); *[lettres, argent]* to flood *ou* pour in. ♦ **afflux** *nm [fluide]* rush, flow; *[argent, foule]* influx.
affoler [afɔle] (1) **1** *vt* (*effrayer*) to throw into a panic; (*troubler*) to drive wild. **2 s'**~ *vpr* to panic. ♦ **affolant, e** *adj* alarming. ♦ **affolé, e** *adj* panic-stricken; driven wild. **je suis** ~ **de voir ça*** I'm appalled at that. ♦ **affolement** *nm* panic, (wild) turmoil. **pas d'**~**!*** don't panic!
affranchir [afrɑ̃ʃir] (2) *vt* **(a)** *lettre* to stamp; (*à la machine*) to frank. **non affranchi** unstamped; unfranked. **(b)** *esclave, esprit* to emancipate, free (*de* from); (*Cartes*) to clear. **s'**~ **des convenances** to free o.s. from convention; (‡: *prévenir*) ~ **qn** to give sb the low-down‡. ♦ **affranchissement** *nm* stamping; franking; emancipation, freeing; (*Poste: prix payé*) postage.
affres [afr(ə)] *nfpl*: **les** ~ **de** the pangs *ou* torments of; **les** ~ **de la mort** the throes of death.
affréter [afrete] (6) *vt* to charter. ♦ **affrètement** *nm* chartering.
affreux, -euse [afrø, øz] *adj* (*laid*) hideous, horrible, ghastly; (*abominable*) dreadful, awful. ♦ **affreusement** *adv souffrir* horribly. ~ **laid** hideously ugly; ~ **mauvais** really horrible; ~ **en retard*** dreadfully *ou* awfully late.
affrioler [afrijɔle] (1) *vt* to tempt, excite.
affront [afrɔ̃] *nm* affront. **faire (un)** ~ **à** to affront.
affronter [afrɔ̃te] (1) **1** *vt adversaire, danger* to confront, face; *mort, froid* to brave. **2 s'**~ *vpr [adversaires]* to confront each other; *[théories]* to conflict. ♦ **affrontement** *nm* confrontation.
affubler [afyble] (1) *vt*: ~ **qn de** *vêtement* to rig* sb out in; *nom* to give sb.
affût [afy] *nm* **(a)** ~ **(de canon)** (gun) carriage. **(b)** (*Chasse*) hide. **chasser à l'**~ to lie in wait for game; **être à l'**~ **de qch** to be on the look-out for sth.
affûter [afyte] (1) *vt* to sharpen. ♦ **affûtage** *nm* sharpening.
afin [afɛ̃] *prép*: ~ **de** to, in order to, so as to; ~ **que** + *subj* so that, in order that.
Afrique [afrik] *nf* Africa. **l'**~ **australe/du Sud** southern/South Africa. ♦ **africain, e** *adj*, **A**~**(e)** *nm(f)* African.
agacer [agase] (3) *vt*: ~ **qn** (*énerver*) to get on sb's nerves, irritate sb; (*taquiner*) to pester sb; **agacé par/de** irritated by/at. ♦ **agaçant, e** *adj* irritating. ♦ **agacement** *nm* irritation.
âge [ɑʒ] **1** *nm* (*gén*) age. **quel** ~ **avez-vous?** how old *ou* what age are you?; **d'un** ~ **avancé** elderly; **d'**~ **moyen** middle-aged; **sans** ~ ageless; **vieillir avant l'**~ to get old before one's time; **il a pris de l'**~ he has aged; **j'ai passé l'**~ **de le faire** I'm too old to do it; **être en** ~ **de** to be old enough to; **l'**~ **du bronze** the Bronze Age. **2**: **l'**~ **adulte** (*gén*) adulthood; (*homme*) manhood; (*femme*) womanhood; **l'**~ **ingrat** the awkward age; **avoir l'**~ **(légal)** to be of age; **l'**~ **mûr** maturity, middle age; **l'**~ **d'or** the golden age; **l'**~ **de raison** the age of reason. ♦ **âgé, e** *adj*: **être** ~ to be old; **être** ~ **de 9 ans** to be 9 (years old); **enfant** ~ **de 4 ans** 4 year-old child; **dame** ~**e** elderly lady.

agence [aʒɑ̃s] *nf* (*succursale*) branch (office); (*bureaux*) offices; (*organisme*) agency. ~ **immobilière** estate agent's (office); ~ **de placement** employment agency; ~ **de presse** news *ou* press agency.

agencer [aʒɑ̃se] (3) *vt* (*disposer*) to arrange; (*équiper*) to equip. ♦ **agencement** *nm* arrangement; equipment.

agenda [aʒɛ̃da] *nm* diary.

agenouiller (s') [aʒnuje] (1) *vpr* to kneel (down); (*fig*) to bow. **être agenouillé** to be kneeling.

agent [aʒɑ̃] **1** *nm* **(a)** ~ **(de police)** policeman; **pardon monsieur l'**~ excuse me, officer. **(b)** (*Chim, Gram, Sci*) agent. **(c)** (*Comm, Pol*) agent. **les** ~**s du lycée** the ancillary staff of the school.
2: ~ **d'assurances** insurance agent; ~ **de change** stockbroker; ~ **double** double agent; ~ **du gouvernement** government official; ~ **immobilier** estate agent; (*Mil*) ~ **de liaison** liaison officer; ~ **de maîtrise** supervisor.

agglomération [aglɔmeʀɑsjɔ̃] *nf* **(a)** (*ville*) town; (*Aut*) built-up area. **l'**~ **parisienne** Paris and its suburbs. **(b)** (*Tech*) conglomeration; (*gén*) agglomeration. ♦ **aggloméré** *nm* (*charbon*) briquette; (*bois*) chipboard; (*pierre*) conglomerate. ♦ **agglomérer (6) 1** *vt* (*Tech*) to agglomerate. **2 s'**~ *vpr* (*Tech*) to agglomerate; (*se rassembler*) to conglomerate.

agglutiner [aglytine] (1) *vt* to stick together; (*Bio*) to agglutinate. (*fig*) **s'**~ **devant la vitrine** to congregate in front of the shop window. ♦ **agglutination** *nf* (*Bio, Ling*) agglutination.

aggraver [agʀave] (1) **1** *vt* (*faire empirer*) to make worse, aggravate; (*renforcer*) to increase. **2 s'**~ *vpr* to get worse; to increase. ♦ **aggravation** *nf* worsening, aggravation; *[impôt, chômage]* increase.

agile [aʒil] *adj* agile, nimble. ♦ **agilement** *adv* nimbly, agilely. ♦ **agilité** *nf* agility, nimbleness.

agir [aʒiʀ] (2) **1** *vi* (*gén*) to act; (*se comporter*) to behave. **il faut** ~ **tout de suite** we must act *ou* take action at once; **il a bien/mal agi envers moi** he behaved well/badly towards me; ~ **sur qch** to act on sth; ~ **auprès de qn** to use one's influence with sb; **il a fait** ~ **ses amis** he got his friends to act *ou* take action; **le remède agit lentement** the medicine is slow to take effect *ou* acts slowly.
2 s'~ *vb impers* **(a)** (*il est question de*) **dans ce film il s'agit de 3 bandits** this film is about 3 gangsters; **les livres dont il s'agit** the books in question; **il s'agit de ta santé** your health is at stake; **il s'agirait/il s'agit d'un temple grec** it would appear to be/it is a Greek temple; **de quoi s'agit-il?** what's it (all) about?, what's the matter?; **il ne s'agit pas d'argent** it's not a question of money; **il ne s'agit pas de ça!** that's not it! *ou* the point! **(b)** (*il est nécessaire de faire*) **il s'agit pour lui de réussir** what he has to do is succeed; **il ne s'agit pas de plaisanter** this is no joking matter; **il s'agit de savoir ce qu'il va faire** it's a question of knowing what he's going to do; **s'agissant de telles sommes** when such large amounts are involved.

agissant, e [aʒisɑ̃, ɑ̃t] *adj* (*actif*) active; (*efficace*) effective.

agissements [aʒismɑ̃] *nmpl* (*péj*) schemes.

agitateur, -trice [aʒitatœʀ, tʀis] *nm,f* agitator.

agitation [aʒitɑsjɔ̃] *nf* *[personne]* (*remuant*) restlessness, fidgetiness; (*affairé*) bustle; (*troublé*) agitation; *[rue]* bustle; (*Pol*) unrest.

agité, e [aʒite] *adj* **(a)** *personne* (*remuant*) restless, fidgety; (*troublé*) agitated. **(b)** *mer* rough, choppy; *vie* hectic; *époque* troubled; *nuit* restless. **avoir le sommeil** ~ to toss in one's sleep.

agiter [aʒite] (1) **1** *vt* **(a)** *bras* to wave; *ailes* to flap; *liquide* to shake; *branches* to sway; (*fig*) *menace* to brandish. **agité par les vagues** tossed by the waves. **(b)** (*inquiéter*) to trouble, agitate. **(c)** *problème* to discuss, debate. **2 s'**~ *vpr [serveur]* to bustle about; *[malade]* to toss restlessly; *[élève]* to fidget; *[foule, pensées, mer]* to stir.

agneau, *pl* ~**x** [aɲo] *nm* lamb; (*fourrure*) lambskin.

agonie [agɔni] *nf* (*Méd, fig*) death throes. **être à l'**~ to be at death's door; **longue** ~ slow death. ♦ **agonisant, e** *adj* dying. ♦ **agoniser** (1) *vi* to be dying.

agrafe [agʀaf] *nf [vêtement]* hook; *[papiers]* staple; (*Méd*) clip. ♦ **agrafer** (1) *vt* to hook (up); to staple. ♦ **agrafeuse** *nf* stapler.

agraire [agʀɛʀ] *adj lois* agrarian; *surface* land.

agrandir [agʀɑ̃diʀ] (2) **1** *vt écart, passage* to widen; *trou, domaine, photographie* to enlarge; *activités* to expand. **ce miroir agrandit la pièce** this mirror makes the room look bigger; **(faire)** ~ **sa maison** to extend one's house. **2 s'**~ *vpr [ville, famille, entreprise]* to grow, expand; *[écart]* to widen; *[passage]* to get wider; *[trou]* to get bigger. ♦ **agrandissement** *nm [local]* extension; *[puissance, ville]* expansion; (*Phot*) enlargement.

agréable [agʀeabl(ə)] *adj* pleasant, agreeable, nice. **pour lui être** ~ in order to please him; **il me serait** ~ **de** it would be a pleasure for me to. ♦ **agréablement** *adv* pleasantly, agreeably.

agréer [agʀee] (1) **1** *vt demande* to accept. **veuillez** ~ **mes sincères salutations** yours sincerely; **fournisseur agréé** registered dealer. **2** ~ **à** *vt indir* to please, suit.

agrégat [agʀega] *nm* (*gén*) aggregate; (*péj*) medley.

agrégation [agʀegɑsjɔ̃] *nf* agrégation (*highest competitive examination for teachers in France*). ♦ **agrégé, e** *nm,f* agrégé.

agréger [agʀeʒe] (3 *et* 6) *vt particules* to aggregate. (*fig*) ~ **qn à un groupe** to incorporate sb into a group.

agrément [agʀemɑ̃] *nm* **(a)** *[personne]* attractiveness, charm; *[conversation, lieu]* pleasantness. **plein d'**~ very enjoyable *ou* pleasant; **sans** ~ unattractive; **les** ~**s de la vie** the pleasant things in life; **voyage d'**~ pleasure trip. **(b)** (*accord*) assent.

agrémenter [agʀemɑ̃te] (1) *vt habit* to embellish; *récit* to accompany (*de* with). **agrémenté de** accompanied by.

agrès [agʀɛ] *nmpl* (*Naut*) tackle; (*Sport*) (gymnastics) apparatus.

agresser [agʀese] (1) *vt* to attack. ♦ **agresseur** *nm* attacker; (*Pol*) aggressor. ♦ **agressif, -ive** *adj* aggressive. ♦ **agression** *nf* attack; (*Pol*) aggression. ♦ **agressivement** *adv* aggressively. ♦ **agressivité** *nf* aggressiveness.

agricole [agʀikɔl] *adj* (*gén*) agricultural; *ouvrier, produits* farm; *population* farming. ♦ **agriculteur** *nm* farmer. ♦ **agriculture** *nf* agriculture, farming.

agripper [agʀipe] (1) *vt* to grab *ou* clutch hold of. **s'**~ **à qch** to clutch *ou* grip sth.

agronome [agʀɔnɔm] *nm* agronomist. ♦ **agronomie** *nf* agronomy. ♦ **agronomique** *adj* agronomical.

agrumes [agʀym] *nmpl* citrus fruits.

aguerrir [ageʀiʀ] (2) *vt* to harden (*contre* to *ou* against). **troupes aguerries** seasoned troops; **s'**~ to become hardened.

aguets [agɛ] *nmpl*: **aux** ~ on the look-out.

aguicher [agiʃe] (1) *vt* to entice, tantalize.

ah [ɑ] *excl* ah!, oh! ~ **bon?** (*question*) really?; (*résignation*) oh well.

ahuri, e [ayʀi] **1** *adj* (*stupéfait*) stunned, dumbfounded; (*stupide*) stupefied. **2** *nm,f* (*péj*) blockhead*. ♦ **ahurir** (2) *vt* to dumbfound, stun. ♦ **ahurissant, e** *adj* stupefying, staggering. ♦ **ahurissement** *nm* stupefaction.

aide [ɛd] **1** *nf* help, assistance, aid. **crier à l'**~ to shout for help; **venir en** ~ **à qn** to help sb, come to sb's assistance *ou* aid; **à l'~!** help!; **sans l'~ de personne** without (any) help, completely unaided; **à l'~ de** with the help *ou* aid of. **2** *nm,f* assistant. **~-chimiste** assistant chemist; **~ de camp** *nm* aide-de-camp; **~ familiale** home help; **~-maçon** builder's mate. ♦ **aide-mémoire** *nm inv* crib (*Scol*), memorandum.

aider [ede] (1) **1** *vt* to help. **~ qn (à faire qch)** to help sb (to do sth); **~ qn de ses conseils** to help *ou* assist sb with one's advice; **je me suis fait ~ par** *ou* **de mon frère** I got my brother to help *ou* assist me; **~ à la clarté de qch** to help *ou* contribute towards the understanding of sth; **aidée de sa canne** with the help *ou* aid of her walking stick; **l'alcool aidant** helped on by the alcohol, with the help of alcohol. **2 s'~** *vpr*: **s'~ de** to use, make use of; **en s'aidant d'un escabeau** with the aid of a stool; **aide-toi, le Ciel t'aidera** God helps those who help themselves.

aïe [aj] *excl* (*douleur*) ouch! **~ ~ ~!** dear oh dear!

aïeul [ajœl] *nm* grandfather. **les ~s** the grandparents. ♦ **aïeule** *nf* grandmother. ♦ **aïeux** *nmpl* forefathers.

aigle [ɛgl(ə)] *nm,f* eagle. **~ royal** golden eagle; **regard d'~** eagle look; **ce n'est pas un ~*** he's no genius.

aigre [ɛgʀ(ə)] **1** *adj goût, lait* sour; *son* sharp; *vent* bitter, keen; *critique* harsh. **2**: **~-doux, ~-douce,** *mpl* **~s-doux** *adj sauce* sweet and sour; *fruit, propos* bitter-sweet. ♦ **aigrement** *adv dire* sourly.

aigrefin [ɛgʀəfɛ̃] *nm* swindler, crook.

aigrelet, -ette [ɛgʀəlɛ, ɛt] *adj goût* sourish; *voix* shrillish.

aigrette [ɛgʀɛt] *nf* (*plume*) aigrette; (*oiseau*) egret.

aigreur [ɛgʀœʀ] *nf [goût]* sourness; *[ton]* harshness, sharpness. **~s d'estomac** heartburn.

aigrir [egʀiʀ] (2) **1** *vt personne* to embitter; *caractère* to sour. **2 s'~** *vpr [aliment]* to turn sour. **il s'est aigri** he has become embittered.

aigu, -uë [egy] **1** *adj* **(a)** *son* high-pitched, shrill; (*Mus*) high. **(b)** *douleur, intelligence* acute, sharp. **(c)** (*pointu*) sharp, pointed. **2** *nm* (*Mus*) **les ~s** the high notes; **l'~** high pitch.

aiguillage [egɥijaʒ] *nm* (*Rail*) (*instrument*) points, switch (*US*).

aiguille [egɥij] *nf* (*gén*) needle; *[horloge]* hand; *[balance, cadran solaire]* pointer; *[clocher]* spire. **travail à l'~** needlework; **~ de glace** icicle; **~ de pin** pine needle.

aiguiller [egɥije] (1) *vt* to direct, steer (*vers* towards); (*Rail*) to shunt, switch (*US*). ♦ **aiguilleur** *nm* pointsman, switchman (*US*).

aiguillon [egɥijɔ̃] *nm [insecte]* sting; *[bouvier]* goad; (*fig*) spur. ♦ **aiguillonner** (1) *vt bœuf* to goad; (*fig*) to spur on.

aiguiser [egize] (1) *vt outil, esprit* to sharpen; *appétit* to whet.

ail, *pl* **~s, aulx** [aj, o] *nm* garlic.

aile [ɛl] *nf* (*gén*) wing; *[moulin]* sail; *[hélice]* blade; *[nez]* wing. **l'oiseau disparut d'un coup d'~** the bird disappeared with a flap of its wings; **avoir/donner des ~s** to have/lend wings; **prendre sous son ~** to take under one's wing. ♦ **aileron** *nm [raie]* fin; *[oiseau]* pinion; (*Aviat*) aileron. ♦ **ailette** *nf* fin; blade. ♦ **ailier** *nm* winger.

ailleurs [ajœʀ] *adv* **(a)** somewhere else, elsewhere. **nulle part/partout ~** nowhere/everywhere else. **(b) par ~** (*autrement*) otherwise; (*en outre*) moreover, furthermore; **d'~** (*de plus*) besides, moreover; (*entre parenthèses*) by the way.

aimable [ɛmabl(ə)] *adj* kind, nice. **c'est très ~ à vous** it's most kind of you; **soyez assez ~ pour** be so kind as to. ♦ **aimablement** *adv* kindly, nicely.

aimant[1] [ɛmɑ̃] *nm* magnet.

aimant[2]**, e** [ɛmɑ̃, ɑ̃t] *adj* loving, affectionate.

aimanter [ɛmɑ̃te] (1) *vt* to magnetize. **champ aimanté** magnetic field.

aimer [eme] (1) **1** *vt* **(a)** (*amour*) to love, to be in love with; (*amitié, goût*) to like, be fond of. **j'aime une bonne tasse de café** I like *ou* enjoy *ou* love a good cup of coffee; **je n'aime pas beaucoup cet acteur** I don't like that actor very much, I'm not very keen on that actor; **j'aime assez ce livre** I rather *ou* quite like this book; **elle aimerait bien venir** she would like *ou* love to come; **elle n'aime pas qu'il sorte le soir** she doesn't like him going out *ou* him to go out at night; **~ faire, ~à faire** to like doing *ou* to do. **(b)** (*avec autant, mieux*) **j'aime autant vous dire que** I may as well tell you that; **il aimerait autant ne pas sortir aujourd'hui** he'd just as soon not go out today, he'd be just as happy not going out today; **j'aime autant ça!*** (*menace*) that sounds more like it!*; (*soulagement*) what a relief!; **elle aimerait mieux des livres** she would rather *ou* sooner have books.

2 s'~ *vpr* to be in love, love each other. **se faire ~ de qn** to get sb to fall in love with one, win the love of sb.

aine [ɛn] *nf* groin (*Anat*).

aîné, e [ene] **1** *adj* (*entre 2*) elder, older; (*plus de 2*) eldest, oldest. **2** *nm,f* eldest child (*ou* boy *ou* girl). **il est mon ~ de 2 ans** he's 2 years older than me, he's 2 years my senior; **respectez vos ~s** respect your elders.

ainsi [ɛ̃si] *adv* **(a)** (*de cette façon*) in this way, thus; (*donc, de même*) so. **c'est ~ que ça s'est passé** that's the way *ou* how it happened; **s'il en était ~** if this were the case; **~ tu vas partir!** so, you're going to leave!; **~ que je le disais** just as I said; **sa beauté ~ que sa candeur** her beauty as well as her innocence. **(b) pour ~ dire** so to speak, as it were; **et ~ de suite** and so on (and so forth).

air[1] [ɛʀ] **1** *nm* **(a)** (*gaz*) air; (*vent*) (light) breeze; (*courant d'air*) draught. **sans ~** stuffy; **sortir à l'~ libre** to come out into the open air; **mettre la literie à l'~** to air the bedclothes; **sortir prendre l'~** to go out for a breath of fresh air; **vivre de l'~ du temps** to live on air alone. **(b)** (*espace*) air. **regarde en l'~** look up; **jeter qch en l'~** to throw sth (up) into the air; **l'avion a pris l'~** the plane has taken off. **(c)** (*ambiance*) atmosphere. **(d) être dans l'~** *[idée]* to be in the air; *[grippe]* to be about; *[orage, dispute]* to be brewing; **flanquer en l'~*** (*jeter*) to chuck away*; (*abandonner*) to chuck up‡; (*gâcher*) to mess up*; **en l'~** *paroles* idle, empty; *parler* rashly; (*en désordre*) upside down.

2: **~ comprimé** compressed air. **~ conditionné** air conditioning; (*Mil*) **~-sol** *adj inv* air-to-ground.

air[2] [ɛʀ] *nm* **(a)** (*expression*) look, air; (*manière*) manner, air; (*apparence*) appearance, air. **ils ont un ~ de famille** there's a family likeness between them; **prendre un ~ entendu** to put on a knowing look. **(b) ça m'a l'~ d'un mensonge** it looks to me *ou* sounds to me like a lie; **elle a l'~ intelligente** she looks *ou* seems intelligent; **il a eu l'~ de ne pas comprendre** he looked as if he didn't understand, he didn't seem to understand; **il a l'~ de vouloir neiger** it looks like snow; **cette plante n'a l'~ de rien, pourtant ...** this plant doesn't look up to much but ... .

air[3] [ɛʀ] *nm [opéra]* aria; (*mélodie*) tune, air. (*lit, fig*) **~ connu** familiar tune.

airain [ɛʀɛ̃] *nm* (*littér*) bronze.

aire [ɛʀ] *nf* (*gén, Math*) area; *[aigle]* eyrie. **~ de battage** threshing floor; **~ de lancement** launching site.

airelle [ɛʀɛl] *nf* bilberry.

aisance [ɛzɑ̃s] *nf* (*facilité*) ease; *[style]* fluency; (*richesse*) affluence. **vivre dans l'~** to be comfortably off; (*Couture*) **redonner de l'~ à**

qch to give more fullness to sth.
aise [ɛz] **1** *nf* **(a)** joy, pleasure. **combler d'~** to overjoy. **(b) être à l'~** *ou* **à son ~** (*situation*) to feel at ease; (*confort*) to feel *ou* be comfortable; (*richesse*) to be comfortably off; **mal à l'~** ill at ease; uncomfortable; **mettez-vous à l'~** make yourself at home *ou* comfortable; **vous en prenez à votre ~!** you're taking things nice and easy!; **à votre ~!** please yourself!; **aimer ses ~s** to be fond of (one's) creature comforts. **2** *adj* (*littér*) **être bien ~ d'avoir fini** to be delighted to have finished.
aisé, e [eze] *adj* **(a)** (*facile*) easy. **(b)** *démarche* easy; *style* flowing. **(c)** (*riche*) well-to-do, well-off. ♦ **aisément** *adv* easily.
aisselle [ɛsɛl] *nf* (*Anat*) armpit.
ajonc [aʒɔ̃] *nm*: **~(s)** gorse.
ajouré, e [aʒuʀe] *adj* *mouchoir* hemstitched; *sculpture* which has an openwork design.
ajourner [aʒuʀne] (1) **1** *vt* *assemblée* to adjourn; *élection, décision* to defer, adjourn; *candidat* to refer. **ajourné d'une semaine/au lundi suivant** adjourned for a week/until the following Monday. **2 s'~** *vpr* (*Pol*) to adjourn. ♦ **ajournement** *nm* adjournment; deferment; referring.
ajouter [aʒute] (1) **1** *vt* to add. **ajoutez à cela qu'il pleuvait** on top of that *ou* in addition to that it was raining; **~ foi aux dires de qn** to believe sb's statements. **2 ~ à** *vt indir* to add to, increase. **3 s'~** *vpr*: **s'~ à** to add to; **ceci, venant s'~ à ses difficultés** this adding further to his difficulties. ♦ **ajout** *nm* addition.
ajuster [aʒyste] (1) **1** *vt* **(a)** (*gén, Tech*) to adjust; *vêtement* to alter; *points de vue* to reconcile. **robe ajustée** close-fitting dress; **~ qch à** to fit sth to. **(b)** *tir* to aim; *cible* to aim at. **(c)** (†) *tenue* to tidy. **2 s'~** *vpr* (*s'emboîter*) to fit (together). ♦ **ajustage** *nm* (*Tech*) fitting. ♦ **ajustement** *nm* *[prix]* adjustment. ♦ **ajusteur** *nm* metal worker.
alambic [alɑ̃bik] *nm* still (*Chim*).
alanguir [alɑ̃giʀ] (2) **1** *vt* to make languid *ou* listless. **2 s'~** *vpr* to grow languid *ou* listless. ♦ **alangui, e** *adj* languid, listless. ♦ **alanguissement** *nm* languor.
alarme [alaʀm(ə)] *nf* (*gén*) alarm. **donner l'~** to give *ou* sound the alarm. ♦ **alarmant** *adj* alarming. ♦ **alarmer** (1) **1** *vt* to alarm. **2 s'~** *vpr* to become alarmed (*de, pour* about, at). ♦ **alarmiste** *adj, nmf* alarmist.
Albanie [albani] *nf* Albania. ♦ **albanais, e** *adj*, **A~(e)** *nm(f)* Albanian.
albâtre [albɑtʀ(ə)] *nm* alabaster.
albatros [albatʀos] *nm* albatross.
albinos [albinos] *nmf, adj inv* albino.
album [albɔm] *nm* album. **~ à colorier** colouring book.
albumine [albymin] *nf* albumin.
alcali [alkali] *nm* alkali.
alcalin, e [alkalɛ̃, in] *adj* alkaline.
alchimie [alʃimi] *nf* alchemy. ♦ **alchimiste** *nm* alchemist.
alcool [alkɔl] *nm* (*gén, Chim*) alcohol; (*type particulier*) spirit. **~ à brûler/à 90°** methylated/surgical spirit; **boire de l'~** (*gén*) to drink alcohol; (*eau de vie*) to drink spirits; **~ de prune** plum brandy. ♦ **alcoolique** *adj, nmf* alcoholic. ♦ **alcoolisé, e** *adj* alcoholic. ♦ **alcoolisme** *nm* alcoholism. ♦ **alcoo(l)test** *nm* (*objet*) Breathalyser; (*épreuve*) breath test.
alcôve [alkov] *nf* alcove.
aléa [alea] *nm* hazard, risk. **après bien des ~s** after many ups and downs.
aléatoire [aleatwaʀ] *adj* (*incertain*) uncertain; (*risqué*) chancy, risky.
alentour [alɑ̃tuʀ] *adv*: **~ (de)** around, round about. ♦ **alentours** *nmpl* *[ville]* surroundings, neighbourhood. **aux ~ de Dijon** in the vicinity *ou* neighbourhood of Dijon; **aux ~ de 8 heures/10 F** round about 8 o'clock/10 francs.
alerte [alɛʀt(ə)] **1** *adj* *personne* agile; *esprit* alert, agile; *style* brisk. **2** *nf* **(a)** (*signal, durée*) alert, alarm. **donner l'~** to give the alert *ou* alarm; **donner l'~ à qn** to alert sb; **~ aérienne** air raid warning. **(b)** (*fig*) (*avertissement*) warning sign; (*inquiétude*) alarm. **3** *excl*: **~!** watch out! ♦ **alertement** *adv* agilely; alertly; briskly. ♦ **alerter** (1) *vt* (*donner l'alarme*) to alert; (*informer*) to inform, notify; (*prévenir*) to warn.
alexandrin [alɛksɑ̃dʀɛ̃] *nm* alexandrine.
alezan, e [alzɑ̃, an] *adj, nm,f* chestnut (*horse*).
algarade [algaʀad] *nf* (*gronderie*) angry outburst; (*dispute*) row.
algèbre [alʒɛbʀ(ə)] *nf* (*Math*) algebra. **par l'~** algebraically; **c'est de l'~*** it's (all) Greek to me*. ♦ **algébrique** *adj* algebraic.
Alger [alʒe] *n* Algiers.
Algérie [alʒeʀi] *nf* Algeria. ♦ **algérien, -ienne** *adj*, **A~(ne)** *nm(f)* Algerian.
algue [alg(ə)] *nf*: **~(s)** seaweed.
alias [aljɑs] *adv* alias.
alibi [alibi] *nm* alibi.
aliénation [aljenɑsjɔ̃] *nf* (*gén*) alienation. (*Méd*) **~ (mentale)** (mental) derangement.
aliéné, e [aljene] *nm,f* mental patient.
aliéner [aljene] (6) *vt* **(a)** (*céder*) (*gén*) to give up; (*Jur*) to alienate. **(b)** *partisans, opinion* to alienate (*à qn* from sb). **s'~ un ami** to alienate a friend.
alignement [aliɲmɑ̃] *nm* (*action*) aligning, lining up, bringing into alignment; (*rangée*) alignment, line; (*Fin, Pol*) alignment. (*Mil*) **être à l'~** to be in line.
aligner [aliɲe] (1) **1** *vt* *objets* to line up, make lines of; *chiffres* to string together; *arguments* to reel off; (*Mil*) to form into lines. **des peupliers étaient alignés le long de la route** poplars stood in a straight line along the roadside; **~ sur qch** *[objets, conduite, politique]* to bring into line with sth. **2 s'~** *vpr* *[soldats]* to fall into line, line up. (*Pol*) **s'~ sur** *politique* to conform to the line of; *pays* to align o.s. with.
aliment [alimɑ̃] *nm*: **~(s)** food; **comment conserver vos ~s** how to keep (your) food *ou* foodstuffs fresh; **ça a fourni un ~ à la conversation** it gave us something to talk about. ♦ **alimentaire** *adj* *besoins* food. **denrées ~s** foodstuffs.
alimentation [alimɑ̃tɑsjɔ̃] *nf* **(a)** (*gén*) feeding; *[moteur]* supplying. **l'~ en eau des villes** supplying water to *ou* the supply of water to towns. **(b)** (*régime*) diet. **(c)** (*métier*) food trade; (*enseigne*) *[magasin]* grocery (store), groceries; *[rayon]* groceries.
alimenter [alimɑ̃te] (1) *vt* (*gén*) to feed; *conversation* to sustain; *moteur* to supply. **~ une ville en gaz** to supply a town with gas; **le malade recommence à s'~** the patient is starting to eat again.
alinéa [alinea] *nm* paragraph.
aliter (s') [alite] (1) *vpr* to take to one's bed. **rester alité** to remain confined to bed.
alizé [alize] *adj m, nm*: **(vent) ~** trade wind.
allaiter [alete] (1) *vt* *[femme]* to (breast-)feed; *[animal]* to suckle. **~ au biberon** to bottle-feed. ♦ **allaitement** *nm* (breast-)feeding; suckling; bottle-feeding.
allant, e [alɑ̃, ɑ̃t] **1** *adj* (*alerte*) active; (*entraînant*) lively. **2** *nm* (*dynamisme*) drive.
allécher [aleʃe] (6) *vt* *[odeur]* to make one's mouth water, tempt; *[proposition]* to entice, tempt. ♦ **alléchant, e** *adj* mouth-watering; enticing; tempting.
allée [ale] *nf* **(a)** (*gén*) path; *[parc]* walk; (*large*) avenue; (*menant à une maison*) drive; *[cinéma, bus]* aisle. **(b) leurs ~s et venues** their comings and goings; **j'ai perdu mon temps en ~s et venues** I've wasted my time going back and forth.

allégation [alegɑsjɔ̃] *nf* allegation.
allégeance [aleʒɑ̃s] *nf* allegiance.
alléger [aleʒe] (6 *et* 3) *vt poids, impôts* to lighten; *bagages* to make lighter; *douleur* to alleviate, soothe; *châtiment* to mitigate. ♦ **allégement** *nm* lightening; alleviation; mitigation.
allégorie [alegɔʀi] *nf* allegory. ♦ **allégorique** *adj* allegorical.
allègre [alɛgʀ(ə)] *adj personne* cheerful, light-hearted; *démarche* lively, jaunty; *musique* lively, merry. ♦ **allégrement** *adv* cheerfully; light-heartedly; jauntily; merrily. ♦ **allégresse** *nf* elation, exhilaration.
alléguer [alege] (6) *vt prétexte* to put forward. **il allégua que ...** he argued that ... .
Allemagne [almaɲ] *nf* Germany. ~ **de l'Ouest/de l'Est** West/East Germany. ♦ **allemand, e** *adj, nm,* **A~(e)** *nm(f)* German.
aller [ale] (9) **1** *vi* **(a)** (*gén*) to go (*à, vers* to, towards). ~ **et venir** to come and go; ~ **à Paris/au lit/à la pêche** to go to Paris/to bed/fishing; ~ **à la ville à pied/à vélo/en voiture** to go to town on foot/by bike/by car, walk/cycle/drive to town; (*lit, fig*) ~ **loin** to go far; ~ **jusqu'au ministre** to take a matter to the minister; ~ **à la catastrophe** to be heading for disaster; ~ **sur ses 8 ans** to be getting on for 8. **(b)** (*santé, situation*) **comment allez-vous? – ça va*** how are you? – fine *ou* not so bad*; **ça va bien/mal/ mieux** I'm well/unwell/feeling better; **ça va (les affaires)?*** how are you getting on?, how's business?*; **ça va mal à la maison** things aren't going too well at home; **ça va mal ~!** there's going to be trouble!; **ta pendule va bien?** is your clock right?; ~ **en empirant** to get worse and worse, go from bad to worse. **(c)** (*convenir*) ~ **à qn** *[mesure]* to fit sb; *[plan, genre]* to suit sb; *[climat]* to agree with sb; ~ **(bien) avec** to go (well) with; **la clef ne va pas dans la serrure** the key won't go in *ou* doesn't fit the lock; **ces ciseaux ne vont pas** these scissors won't do *ou* are no good. **(d)** (*excl*) **allons!, allez!** (*stimulation*) go on!; (*incrédulité, consolation*) come on now!; (*résignation*) all right!, O.K.!*; **allez, au revoir!** 'bye then!; **comme tu y vas!** you're going a bit far! **(e)** ~ **de soi** to be self-evident *ou* obvious; **cela va sans dire** it goes without saying; **il en va de même pour les autres** the same applies to the others; **il y va de votre vie** your life is at stake; **il y est allé de sa chanson** he gave us a song.
2 *vb aux* (+ *infin*) **(a)** (*futur immédiat*) to be going to. **ils allaient commencer** they were going *ou* were about to start. **(b)** ~ **faire qch** to go and do sth; **il est allé me chercher mes lunettes** he went to fetch my glasses; **allez donc voir si c'est vrai!** you'll never know if it's true!; **n'allez pas vous imaginer que** don't you go imagining that.
3 s'en ~ *vpr* **(a)** (*partir*) to go (away); (*déménager*) to move, leave; (*mourir*) to die; (*prendre sa retraite*) to retire. **ils s'en vont à Paris** they are going *ou* off to Paris; **je m'en vais leur montrer** I'll show them. **(b)** *[tache]* to come off; *[temps]* to pass, go by. **tout son argent s'en va en disques** all his money goes on records.
4 *nm* (*trajet*) outward journey; (*billet*) single *ou* one-way (*US*) ticket. **j'irai vous voir à l'~** I'll come and see you on the way there; **je ne fais que l'~-retour** I'm just going there and back; **prendre un ~-retour** to buy a return *ou* round-trip (*US*) ticket.
allergie [alɛʀʒi] *nf* allergy. ♦ **allergique** *adj* allergic (*à* to).
alliage [aljaʒ] *nm* alloy.
alliance [aljɑ̃s] *nf* **(a)** (*Pol*) alliance; (*Bible*) covenant. **(b)** (*mariage*) union, marriage. **oncle par ~** uncle by marriage. **(c)** (*bague*) (wedding) ring. **(d)** (*fig: mélange*) combination.
allier [alje] (7) **1** *vt efforts* to combine, unite; *couleurs* to match (*à* with). **2 s'~** *vpr [efforts]* to combine, unite; *[couleurs]* to match; (*Pol*) to become allies *ou* allied. **s'~ à** to become allied to *ou* with, ally o.s. with. ♦ **allié, e 1** *adj pays* allied. **2** *nm,f* (*Pol, fig*) ally; (*parent*) relative by marriage.
alligator [aligatɔʀ] *nm* alligator.
allô [alo] *excl* (*Téléc*) hullo!
allocation [alɔkɑsjɔ̃] *nf* **(a)** **(V allouer)** allocation; granting; allotment. **(b)** (*somme*) allowance. ~ **de chômage** unemployment benefit; ~**s familiales** family allowance(s), child benefits.
allocution [alɔkysjɔ̃] *nf* short speech.
allonger [alɔ̃ʒe] (3) **1** *vt* **(a)** (*rendre plus long*) to lengthen; (*étendre*) to stretch out. ~ **le pas** to quicken one's step. **(b)** (‡) *somme* to hand out; *coup* to deal. ~ **qn** to knock sb flat. **(c)** (*Culin*) *sauce* to thin (down). **2** *vi*: **les jours allongent** the days are growing longer. **3 s'~** *vpr* **(a)** *[ombres, jours]* to lengthen; *[enfant]* to grow taller; *[discours]* to drag on. (*fig*) **son visage s'allongea** his face fell; **la route s'allongeait devant eux** the road stretched away before them. **(b)** (*s'étendre*) to lie down, stretch out. ♦ **allongé, e** *adj* **(a)** (*étendu*) **être ~** to be stretched out, be lying; ~ **sur son lit/sur le dos** lying on one's bed/on one's back. **(b)** (*long*) long; (*étiré*) elongated; (*oblong*) oblong. ♦ **allongement** *nm* (*gén*) lengthening; (*Anat, Métal*) elongation.
allouer [alwe] (1) *vt argent* to allocate; *indemnité* to grant; (*Fin*) *actions* to allot; *temps* to allot, allow, allocate.
allumage [alymaʒ] *nm [poêle]* lighting; *[électricité]* putting *ou* switching on; (*Aut*) ignition.
allume-cigare [alymsigaʀ] *nm inv* cigar lighter.
allume-gaz [alymgaz] *nm inv* gas lighter (*for cooker*).
allumer [alyme] (1) **1** *vt* **(a)** *feu* to light. **le feu était allumé** the fire was lit. **(b)** *électricité* to put *ou* switch *ou* turn on; *gaz* to light, turn on. **laisse la lumière allumée** leave the light on; **ça n'allume pas** the light doesn't come on *ou* work; ~ **une pièce** to put the light on in a room; **sa fenêtre était allumée** there was a light on at his window. **(c)** *sentiment* to arouse, stir up; *guerre* to stir up.
2 s'~ *vpr [incendie]* to blaze, flare up; *[sentiment]* to be aroused; *[guerre]* to break out. **son regard s'alluma** his face lit up; **sa fenêtre s'alluma** a light came *ou* went on at his window; **où est-ce que ça s'allume?** where do you switch it on?
allumette [alymɛt] *nf* **(a)** match. ~ **de sûreté** safety match. **(b)** (*Culin*) flaky pastry finger.
allumeur [alymœʀ] *nm* (*Aut*) distributor; (*Tech*) igniter. (*Hist*) ~ **de réverbères** lamplighter.
allure [alyʀ] *nf* **(a)** (*vitesse*) *[véhicule]* speed; *[piéton]* pace. **à toute ~** at top *ou* full speed. **(b)** (*démarche*) walk; (*attitude*) air, look, appearance. **avoir fière/piètre ~** to cut a fine/shabby figure; **d'~ bizarre** odd-looking; **liberté d'~s** free behaviour.
allusion [alyzjɔ̃] *nf* allusion (*à* to), hint (*à* at). ~ **malveillante** innuendo; **faire ~ à** to allude to, hint at; **par ~** allusively. ♦ **allusif, -ive** *adj* allusive.
alluvions [alyvjɔ̃] *nfpl* alluvial deposits.
almanach [almana] *nm* almanac.
aloès [alɔɛs] *nm* aloe.
aloi [alwa] *nm*: **de bon ~** *gaieté* wholesome; *individu* worthy; *produit* of genuine quality; **de mauvais ~** unwholesome; of little worth; of doubtful quality.
alors [alɔʀ] *adv* (*à cette époque*) then, in those days, at that time; (*en conséquence*) then, in that case, so. ~ **que** (*simultanéité*) while, when; (*opposition*) whereas; ~ **même que** (*même si*) even if, though; (*au moment où*) while, just when; **elle est sortie ~ que le docteur le lui avait interdit** she went out although *ou* even though the doctor had told her not to; ~ **tu viens?** well (then), are you coming?; ~ **là d'accord** well then all right;

il pleut – et ~? it's raining – so (what)?

alouette [alwɛt] *nf* skylark.

alourdir [aluʀdiʀ] (2) **1** *vt* (*gén*) to make heavy; *impôts* to increase; *véhicule* to weigh down. **le gaz alourdissait l'air** the smell of gas hung heavy on the air, the air was heavy with the smell of gas. **2 s'~** *vpr* to become *ou* grow heavy. ♦ **alourdissement** *nm [véhicule, objet]* increased weight, heaviness; *[impôts]* increase (*de* in).

aloyau [alwajo] *nm* sirloin.

alpaga [alpaga] *nm* (*Tex, Zool*) alpaca.

Alpes [alp(ə)] *nfpl*: **les ~** the Alps. ♦ **alpage** *nm* high mountain pasture. ♦ **alpestre** *adj* alpine.

alphabet [alfabɛ] *nm* (*système*) alphabet; (*livre*) alphabet book. **~ morse** Morse code. ♦ **alphabétique** *adj* alphabetical. ♦ **alphabétiquement** *adv* alphabetically. ♦ **alphabétiser** (1) *vt*: **~ qn** to teach sb to read and write.

alpin, e [alpɛ̃, in] *adj* alpine.

alpinisme [alpinism(ə)] *nm* mountaineering, climbing. ♦ **alpiniste** *nmf* mountaineer, climber.

altérant, e [alteʀɑ̃, ɑ̃t] *adj* thirst-making.

altercation [altɛʀkɑsjɔ̃] *nf* altercation.

altérer [alteʀe] (6) **1** *vt* **(a)** (*assoiffer*) to make thirsty. **(b)** *texte, vérité* to distort, falsify; *aliments* to adulterate. **(c)** *denrées* to spoil; *matière, sentiments* to alter; *visage, voix* to distort; *santé* to impair. **(d)** (*modifier*) to alter, change. **2 s'~** *vpr [nourriture]* to go off; *[santé, relations]* to deteriorate; *[voix]* to break; *[vin]* to spoil. ♦ **altération** *nf* **(a)** distortion, falsification; alteration; adulteration; impairment; change. **l'~ de sa santé** the deterioration in his health; **l'~ de son visage/de sa voix** his distorted features/ broken voice. **(b)** (*Mus*) accidental.

alternance [altɛʀnɑ̃s] *nf* (*gén*) alternation. **être en ~** *[émissions]* to alternate; **travailler en ~** to work alternately (*avec* with).

alternateur [altɛʀnatœʀ] *nm* alternator.

alternatif, -ive [altɛʀnatif, iv] **1** *adj* alternate; (*Élec*) alternating. **2** *nf* (*dilemme*) alternative. **être dans une ~ive** to have to choose between two alternatives. ♦ **alternativement** *adv* alternately, in turn.

alterner [altɛʀne] (1) *vt* to alternate (*avec* with). **ils alternèrent à la présidence** they took turns in the chair. ♦ **alterne, alterné, e** *adj* alternate.

altesse [altɛs] *nf* (*titre*) highness.

altier, -ière [altje, jɛʀ] *adj* haughty.

altitude [altityd] *nf* altitude, height (above sea level). **à 500 mètres d'~** at a height *ou* an altitude of 500 metres; **en ~** at high altitude, high up; **prendre de l'~** to gain altitude.

alto [alto] *nm* (*instrument*) viola.

altruisme [altʀɥism(ə)] *nm* altruism. ♦ **altruiste** **1** *adj* altruistic. **2** *nmf* altruist.

alumine [alymin] *nf* alumina.

aluminium [alyminjɔm] *nm* aluminium.

alun [alœ̃] *nm* alum.

alunir [alyniʀ] (2) *vi* to land on the moon. ♦ **alunissage** *nm* (moon) landing.

alvéole [alveɔl] *nf ou m [ruche, poumon]* cell. **~ dentaire** tooth socket; **~s dentaires** alveolar *ou* teeth ridge.

amabilité [amabilite] *nf* kindness. **ayez l'~ de** be so kind as to; **faire des ~s à qn** to be polite to sb.

amadou [amadu] *nm* touchwood, tinder.

amadouer [amadwe] (1) *vt* (*enjôler*) to coax, cajole; (*adoucir*) to mollify.

amaigrir [amegʀiʀ] (2) *vt* to make thin *ou* thinner. ♦ **amaigrissant, e** *adj* *régime* slimming. ♦ **amaigrissement** *nm* (*pathologique*) thinness; (*volontaire*) slimming. **un ~ de 3 kg** a loss in weight of 3 kg.

amalgame [amalgam] *nm* (*péj*) (strange) combination; (*Métal*) amalgam. ♦ **amalgamer** (1) **1** *vt* to combine; to amalgamate. **2 s'~** *vpr* to combine.

amande [amɑ̃d] *nf* **(a)** (*fruit*) almond. **en ~** almond-shaped. **(b)** *[noyau]* kernel. ♦ **amandier** *nm* almond (tree).

amant [amɑ̃] *nm* lover. ♦ **amante**† *nf* mistress†.

amarrer [amaʀe] (1) *vt navire* to moor; *paquet* to make fast. ♦ **amarrage** *nm* mooring. ♦ **amarre** *nf* (mooring) rope. **les ~s** moorings.

amas [amɑ] *nm* (*lit*) heap, pile; *[idées]* mass; (*Astron*) star cluster; (*Min*) mass.

amasser [amɑse] (1) **1** *vt choses* to pile up, amass; *fortune* to amass; *preuves* to amass, gather (together). **2 s'~** *vpr [choses, preuves]* to pile up, accumulate; *[foule]* to gather.

amateur [amatœʀ] *nm* (*non-professionnel*) amateur; (*péj*) dilettante, mere amateur. **équipe ~** amateur team; **~ d'art** art lover; **être ~ de films** to be a keen film-goer; **faire qch en ~** to do sth as a mere amateur; **y a-t-il des ~s?** (*volontaires*) are there any volunteers?; (*acheteurs*) are there any takers? ♦ **amateurisme** *nm* (*Sport*) amateurism; (*péj*) amateurishness.

Amazone [amazon] **1** *nm* (*Géog*) Amazon. **2** *nf* (*Myth*) Amazon; (*fig*) amazon. (*écuyère*) **a~** horsewoman; **monter en a~** to ride sidesaddle.

ambages [ɑ̃baʒ] *nfpl*: **sans ~** without beating about the bush, in plain language.

ambassade [ɑ̃basad] *nf* (*Pol*) embassy; (*mission*) mission. ♦ **ambassadeur** *nm* (*Pol, fig*) ambassador. **~ extraordinaire** ambassador extraordinary (*auprès de* to). ♦ **ambassadrice** *nf* ambassador; (*épouse*) ambassadress.

ambiance [ɑ̃bjɑ̃s] *nf* atmosphere (*de* in, of).

ambiant, e [ɑ̃bjɑ̃, ɑ̃t] *adj* surrounding; *température* ambient.

ambidextre [ɑ̃bidɛkstʀ(ə)] *adj* ambidextrous.

ambigu, -uë [ɑ̃bigy] *adj* ambiguous. ♦ **ambiguïté** *nf* ambiguity. **sans ~** (*adj*) unambiguous; (*adv*) unambiguously.

ambitieux, -euse [ɑ̃bisjø, øz] *adj* ambitious. **~ de plaire** anxious to please. ♦ **ambitieusement** *adv* ambitiously. ♦ **ambition** *nf* ambition. ♦ **ambitionner** (1) *vt*: **il ambitionne de faire** his ambition is to do.

ambivalence [ɑ̃bivalɑ̃s] *nf* ambivalence. ♦ **ambivalent, e** *adj* ambivalent.

amble [ɑ̃bl(ə)] *nm [cheval]* amble.

ambre [ɑ̃bʀ(ə)] *nm*: **~ (jaune)** amber; **~ gris** ambergris. ♦ **ambré, e** *adj couleur* amber.

ambulance [ɑ̃bylɑ̃s] *nf* ambulance. ♦ **ambulancier, -ière** *nm,f* (*conducteur*) ambulance driver; (*infirmier*) ambulance man (*ou* woman).

ambulant, e [ɑ̃bylɑ̃, ɑ̃t] *adj musicien* strolling, travelling. **c'est un dictionnaire ~*** he's a walking dictionary.

âme [ɑm] *nf* **(a)** (*gén*) soul. (*fig*) **avoir l'~ chevillée au corps** to have nine lives; **avoir une ~ généreuse** to have great generosity of spirit; **avoir une ~ basse** to have an evil heart; **grandeur d'~** noble-mindedness; **en mon ~ et conscience** in all conscience; **ému jusqu'au fond de l'~** profoundly moved; **il est musicien dans l'~** he's a musician to the core. **(b)** (*personne*) soul. **on ne voyait ~ qui vive** you couldn't see a (living) soul; **bonne ~*** kind soul; **il erre comme une ~ en peine** he is wandering about like a lost soul; **son ~ damnée** his henchman; **trouver l'~ sœur** to find a soul mate; **l'~ d'un complot** the moving spirit in a plot. **(c)** (*Tech*) *[canon]* bore; *[violon]* soundpost.

améliorer *vt*, **s'~** *vpr* [ameljɔʀe] (1) (*gén*) to improve. ♦ **amélioration** *nf* improvement.

amen [amɛn] *adv* (*Rel, fig*) amen.

aménager [amenaʒe] (3) *vt* **(a)** (*équiper*) *local* to fit out; *territoire, parc* to develop. **(b)** (*créer*) *route* to make, build; *gradins* to fix up; *horaire* to work out. **~ un bureau dans une chambre** to fit up a study in a bedroom; **~ une chambre en bureau** to convert a bedroom into a study.

♦ **aménagement** *nm* (*gén*) development. ~s *[local]* fittings; *[quartier]* developments; *[horaire]* adjustments.
amende [amɑ̃d] *nf* fine. **mettre à l'~** to penalize; **donner une ~ à** to fine; **faire ~ honorable** to make amends.
amender [amɑ̃de] (1) **1** *vt* (*Pol*) to amend; (*Agr*) to enrich; *conduite* to improve, amend. **2 s'~** *vpr* to mend one's ways. ♦ **amendement** *nm* (*Pol*) amendment; (*Agr*) (*opération*) enrichment; (*substance*) enriching agent.
amène [amɛn] *adj* affable. **peu ~** unkind.
amener [amne] (5) **1** *vt* **(a)** *personne, objet* to bring; *catastrophe* to cause, bring about. **qu'est-ce qui vous amène ici?** what brings you here? **(b)** (*inciter*) **~ qn à faire qch** *[circonstances]* to lead *ou* bring sb to do sth; *[personne]* to get sb to do sth; **je suis amené à croire que** I am led to think that; **~ qn à ses propres idées** to bring sb round to one's own ideas; **~ la conversation sur un sujet** to lead the conversation on to a subject; **amené à un haut degré de complexité** brought to a high degree of complexity. **(c)** *transition, conclusion* to present, introduce. **bien amené** well-introduced. **(d)** *poisson* to draw in; *voile, drapeau* to strike. **2 s'~*** *vpr* (*venir*) to come along.
aménité [amenite] *nf* affability. **sans ~** unkindly.
amenuiser (s') [amənɥize] (1) *vpr [valeur, espoir]* to dwindle; *[chances]* to lessen; *[provisions]* to run low, dwindle. ♦ **amenuisement** *nm* dwindling; lessening.
amer, -ère [amɛʀ] *adj* bitter. ♦ **amèrement** *adv* bitterly.
américain, e [ameʀikɛ̃, ɛn] **1** *adj* American. **2** *nm* (*Ling*) American (English). **3** *nm(f)*: **A~(e)** American. ♦ **américaniser** (1) *vt* to americanize. ♦ **américanisme** *nm* americanism. ♦ **américaniste** *nmf* Americanist. ♦ **Amérique** *nf* America.
amerrir [ameʀiʀ] (2) *vi* (*Aviat*) to make a sea-landing; (*Espace*) to splash down. ♦ **amerrissage** *nm* (sea) landing; splashdown.
amertume [amɛʀtym] *nf* (*lit, fig*) bitterness.
améthyste [ametist(ə)] *nf, adj inv* amethyst.
ameublement [amœbləmɑ̃] *nm* (*meubles*) furniture. **articles d'~** furnishings.
ameublir [amœbliʀ] (2) *vt* (*Agr*) to loosen.
ameuter [amøte] (1) *vt* (*attrouper*) *curieux* to draw a crowd of; *voisins* to bring out; (*soulever*) to rouse, stir up (*contre* against). **des passants s'ameutèrent** a crowd of passers-by gathered (angrily).
ami, e [ami] **1** *nm,f* **(a)** friend. **~ d'enfance** childhood friend; **elle est avec ses ~es** she's with her (girl)friends; **se faire un ~ de qn** to make friends with sb; **~s des bêtes** animal lovers; **club des ~s de Balzac** Balzac society; **un professeur de mes ~s** a teacher friend of mine; **sans ~s** friendless. **(b)** (*amant*) boyfriend; (*maîtresse*) girlfriend, lady-friend. **(c) mes chers ~s** (ladies and) gentlemen; **mon cher ~** my dear fellow. **2** *adj* friendly. **être très ~ avec qn** to be very friendly *ou* be good friends with sb; **être ~ de l'ordre** to be a lover of order.
amiable [amjabl(ə)] *adj* (*Jur*) **à l'~** *vente* private; *accord* amicable. **régler qch à l'~** to settle sth out of court.
amiante [amjɑ̃t] *nm* asbestos.
amibe [amib] *nf* amoeba.
amical, e, mpl -aux [amikal, o] **1** *adj* friendly. **peu ~** unfriendly. **2** *nf* association, club. ♦ **amicalement** *adv* in a friendly way. *[lettre]* **(bien) ~** best wishes, yours.
amidon [amidɔ̃] *nm* starch. ♦ **amidonner** (1) *vt* to starch.
amincir [amɛ̃siʀ] (2) **1** *vt couche* to thin (down). **cette robe l'amincit** this dress makes her look slim(mer) *ou* thin(ner). **2 s'~** *vpr* to get thinner.
♦ **amincissement** *nm* thinning (down). **cure d'~** slimming treatment.
amiral, e *mpl* **-aux** [amiʀal, o] **1** *adj*: **vaisseau ~** flagship. **2** *nm* admiral. **3** *nf* admiral's wife. ♦ **amirauté** *nf* admiralty.
amitié [amitje] *nf* **(a)** (*sentiment*) friendship. **prendre qn en ~** to take a liking to sb; **se lier d'~ avec qn** to make friends with sb; **avoir de l'~ pour qn** to be fond of sb; **faites-moi l'~ de venir** do me the favour of coming. **(b)** *[lettre]* **~s, Paul** yours, Paul; **elle vous fait toutes ses ~s** she sends her regards.
ammoniac [amɔnjak] *nm* ammonia. ♦ **ammoniaque** *nf* liquid ammonia.
amnésie [amnezi] *nf* amnesia. ♦ **amnésique 1** *adj* amnesic. **2** *nmf* amnesiac.
amnistie [amnisti] *nf* amnesty. ♦ **amnistier** (7) *vt* to amnesty.
amocher: [amɔʃe] (1) *vt* to mess up*, make a mess of. **se faire ~** to get messed up*.
amoindrir [amwɛ̃dʀiʀ] (2) **1** *vt forces* to weaken; *quantité* to diminish, reduce. (*humilier*) **~ qn** to belittle sb. **2 s'~** *vpr* to grow weaker, weaken; to diminish. ♦ **amoindrissement** *nm* weakening; diminishing; reduction.
amollir [amɔliʀ] (2) **1** *vt chose, esprit* to soften; *forces* to weaken. **2 s'~** *vpr [chose]* to go soft; (*fig*) to weaken. ♦ **amollissement** *nm* softening; weakening.
amonceler [amɔ̃sle] (4) **1** *vt choses* to pile *ou* heap up; *difficultés* to accumulate. **2 s'~** *vpr* to pile *ou* heap up; to accumulate; *[nuages, neige]* to bank up. ♦ **amoncellement** *nm* **(a)** piling *ou* heaping up; accumulation. **(b)** (*tas*) pile, heap.
amont [amɔ̃] *nm [cours d'eau]* upstream water; *[pente]* uphill slope. **en ~** upstream; uphill (*de* from); **l'écluse d'~** the upstream lock.
amoral, e, mpl -aux [amɔʀal, o] *adj* amoral.
amorce [amɔʀs(ə)] *nf* **(a)** (*Pêche*) bait; (*de fond*) ground bait. **(b)** (*explosif*) cap. **(c)** (*début*) start, beginning. **l'~d'une réforme** the beginnings of a reform.
amorcer [amɔʀse] (3) *vt* **(a)** *hameçon* to bait; (*fig*) *client* to entice. **(b)** *pompe, syphon* to prime. **(c)** *négociations, travaux* to start, begin. **la construction est amorcée depuis 2 mois** work has been in progress *ou* been under way for 2 months; **une descente s'amorce après le virage** after the bend the road starts to go down; **une détente s'amorce** there are signs of a détente. ♦ **amorçage** *nm* baiting; ground baiting; priming.
amorphe [amɔʀf(ə)] *adj* passive.
amortir [amɔʀtiʀ] (2) *vt* **(a)** *coup* to cushion, soften; *bruit* to deaden, muffle; *douleur* to dull. (*Tennis*) **un amorti** a drop shot. **(b)** (*Fin*) *dette* to pay off; *action* to redeem; *matériel* to write off. **pour ~ la dépense** to recoup the cost. ♦ **amortissable** *adj* (*Fin*) redeemable. ♦ **amortissement** *nm* cushioning; softening; deadening; muffling; dulling; paying off; redemption. **l'~ de ce matériel se fait en 3 ans** it takes 3 years to recoup *ou* write off the cost of this equipment. ♦ **amortisseur** *nm* shock absorber.
amour [amuʀ] **1** *nm* **(a)** (*sentiment*) love. **roman d'~** love story; **faire l'~** to make love (*avec* to, with). **(b)** (*personne*) love; (*aventure*) love affair. **mon ~** my love; **cet enfant est un ~** that child's a real darling; **tu seras un ~** there's a darling *ou* a dear; **un ~ de bébé/de petite robe** a lovely *ou* sweet little baby/dress. **(c) pour l'~ de Dieu/de votre mère** for God's/your mother's sake; **faire qch pour l'~ de l'art*** to do sth for the love of it; **faire qch avec ~** to do sth with loving care. **2** *nfpl* (*littér*) **~s** (*personnes*) loves; (*aventures*) love affairs. **3: ~-propre** *nm* self-esteem, pride.
amoureux, -euse [amuʀø, øz] **1** *adj* **(a)** (*épris*) in love (*de* with). **être ~ de la nature** to be a lover of nature *ou* a nature-lover. **(b)** *aventures* amorous,

love; *tempérament* amorous; *regard* loving. **2** *nm,f* (†: *soupirant*) love, sweetheart. ♦ **amoureusement** *adv* lovingly, amorously.

amovible [amɔvibl(ə)] *adj* removable, detachable; (*Jur*) removable.

ampère [ɑ̃pɛʀ] *nm* ampere, amp. ♦ **ampèremètre** *nm* ammeter.

amphibie [ɑ̃fibi] **1** *adj* amphibious. **2** *nm* amphibian.

amphithéâtre [ɑ̃fiteɑtʀ(ə)] *nm* (*Archit, Géol*) amphitheatre; (*Univ*) lecture hall *ou* theatre; (*Théât*) upper gallery.

amphore [ɑ̃fɔʀ] *nf* amphora.

ample [ɑ̃pl(ə)] *adj jupe* full, ample, roomy; *geste* sweeping, grand; *voix* full; *style* grand; *projet* vast; *sujet* wide-ranging. **faire ~(s) provision(s) de** to gather a good supply of; **donner d' ~s détails** to give a wealth of detail *ou* full details; **jusqu'à plus ~ informé** until further information is available. ♦ **amplement** *adv mériter* fully, amply. **il a fait ~ ce qu'on lui demandait** he has fully accomplished what was asked of him; **ça suffit ~** that's more than enough, that's ample.

ampleur [ɑ̃plœʀ] *nf [vêtement]* fullness; *[style, geste]* grandeur; *[sujet]* scope, range; *[crise]* scale, extent. **sans grande ~** of limited scope, small-scale; **prendre de l'~** to grow in scale *ou* extent.

amplifier [ɑ̃plifje] (7) **1** *vt* (*gén*) to expand, develop, increase; (*péj*) *incident* to magnify; *son* to amplify. **2 s'~** *vpr* to grow, increase. ♦ **amplificateur** *nm* amplifier. ♦ **amplification** *nf* development; expansion; increase; amplification; magnification.

amplitude [ɑ̃plityd] *nf* (*Astron, Phys*) amplitude; *[températures]* range; *[catastrophe]* magnitude.

ampoule [ɑ̃pul] *nf* (*Élec*) bulb; (*Pharm*) phial; *[main]* blister.

amputer [ɑ̃pyte] (1) *vt* **(a)** (*Anat*) to amputate. **il est amputé (d'une jambe)** he has had a leg amputated, he has lost a leg. **(b)** *texte, budget* to cut drastically (*de* by). ♦ **amputation** *nf* amputation; drastic cut (*de* in).

amulette [amylɛt] *nt* amulet.

amusant, e [amyzɑ̃, ɑ̃t] *adj* (*distrayant*) amusing, entertaining; (*drôle*) amusing, funny.

amuse-gueule [amyzgœl] *nm inv* appetizer.

amusement [amyzmɑ̃] *nm* (*jeu*) game; (*passe-temps*) diversion, pastime; (*fait de (se) divertir*) amusement.

amuser [amyze] (1) **1** *vt* **(a)** (*divertir*) to amuse, entertain; (*faire rire*) to amuse. **ces remarques ne m'amusent pas** I'm not amused by such remarks; **si vous croyez que ces réunions m'amusent** if you think I enjoy these meetings. **(b)** (*détourner l'attention de*) to distract (the attention of); (*tromper*) to delude.

2 s'~ *vpr* **(a)** (*jouer*) *[enfants]* to play. **s'~ avec** *jouet* to play with; *stylo, ficelle* to play *ou* fiddle with; **s'~ à un jeu** to play a game; **s'~ à faire** to amuse o.s. doing; (*fig*) **ne t'amuse pas à recommencer, sinon!** don't do *ou* start that again, or else! **(b)** (*se divertir*) to have fun *ou* a good time, enjoy o.s.; (*rire*) to have a good laugh. **s'~ à faire** to have fun doing; **nous nous sommes bien amusés** we had great fun *ou* a great time*; **c'était juste pour s'~** it was just for fun *ou* for a laugh; **il ne faut pas qu'on s'amuse** (*se dépêcher*) we mustn't dawdle; (*travailler*) we mustn't idle. **(c)** (*se jouer de*) **s'~ de qn** to make a fool of sb. ♦ **amuseur, -euse** *nm,f* entertainer; (*péj*) clown.

amygdale [amidal] *nf* tonsil.

an [ɑ̃] *nm* year. **dans 3 ~s** in 3 years, in 3 years' time; **enfant de six ~s** six-year-old (child); **il a 22 ~s** he is 22 (years old); **il reçoit tant par ~** he gets so much a year *ou* per annum; **en l'~ de grâce ...** in the year of grace ...; **je m'en moque comme de l'~ quarante** I couldn't care less; **courbé sous le poids des ~s** bowed with age.

anachronique [anakʀɔnik] *adj* anachronistic. ♦ **anachronisme** *nm* anachronism.

anagramme [anagʀam] *nm* anagram.

analogie [analɔʒi] *nf* analogy. **par ~ avec** by analogy with. ♦ **analogique** *adj* analogical. ♦ **analogue 1** *adj* analogous, similar (*à* to). **2** *nm* analogue.

analphabète [analfabɛt] *adj, nmf* illiterate. ♦ **analphabétisme** *nm* illiteracy.

analyse [analiz] *nf* (*gén*) analysis; *[sang, urine]* test. **ça ne résiste pas à l'~** it doesn't stand up to analysis; **avoir l'esprit d'~** to have an analytical mind; **se faire faire des ~s** to have some tests done; **~ grammaticale** parsing; **~ logique** sentence analysis. ♦ **analyser** (1) *vt* to analyse; to test; to parse. ♦ **analyste** *nmf* analyst. ♦ **analytique** *adj* analytical.

ananas [anana(s)] *nm* (*fruit, plante*) pineapple.

anarchie [anaʀʃi] *nf* (*Pol, fig*) anarchy. ♦ **anarchique** *adj* anarchic. ♦ **anarchiquement** *adv* anarchically. ♦ **anarchisme** *nm* anarchism. ♦ **anarchiste 1** *adj* anarchistic. **2** *nmf* anarchist.

anathème [anatɛm] *nm* anathema. (*fig*) **jeter l'~ sur** to anathematize.

anatomie [anatɔmi] *nf* (*gén*) anatomy; (*analyse*) analysis. ♦ **anatomique** *adj* anatomical.

ancestral, e, *mpl* **-aux** [ɑ̃sɛstʀal, o] *adj* ancestral.

ancêtre [ɑ̃sɛtʀ(ə)] *nmf* (*aïeul*) ancestor; (*: *vieillard*) old man (*ou* woman); (*fig: précurseur*) ancestor, forerunner.

anchois [ɑ̃ʃwa] *nm* anchovy.

ancien, -ienne [ɑ̃sjɛ̃, jɛn] **1** *adj* **(a)** (*gén*) old; (*ancestral, antique*) ancient; *objet d'art* antique. **dans l'~ temps** in (the) olden days. **(b)** (*précédent*) former, old. **son ~ne femme** his former *ou* previous wife; **mon ~ne école** my old school. **2** *nm* (*mobilier*) l'~ antiques. **3** *nm,f* (*par l'âge*) elder, old man (*ou* woman); (*par l'expérience*) senior person; (*Hist*) les **~s** the Ancients; **~ combattant** war veteran, ex-serviceman; **~ élève** former pupil.

anciennement [ɑ̃sjɛnmɑ̃] *adv* formerly.

ancienneté [ɑ̃sjɛnte] *nf* **(a)** (*durée de service*) (length of) service; (*privilèges obtenus*) seniority. **à l'~** by seniority. **(b)** *[maison, famille]* oldness, age; *[objet d'art]* age, antiquity; *[loi, tradition]* ancientness.

ancre [ɑ̃kʀ(ə)] *nf* (*Naut, Tech*) anchor. **être à l'~** to be *ou* lie at anchor; **jeter/lever l'~** to cast *ou* drop/weigh anchor. ♦ **ancrage** *nm [grand bateau]* anchorage; *[petit bateau]* moorage.

ancrer [ɑ̃kʀe] (1) **1** *vt* (*Naut, Tech*) to anchor. **idée bien ancrée** firmly rooted idea. **2 s'~** *vpr* (*Naut*) to anchor. **il s'est ancré dans la tête que ...** he got it rooted *ou* fixed in his head that ... .

andouille [ɑ̃duj] *nf* **(a)** (*Culin*) andouille. **(b)** (*: *imbécile*) clot*, fool. **faire l'~** to act the fool.

âne [ɑn] *nm* (*Zool*) donkey, ass; (*fig*) ass, fool.

anéantir [aneɑ̃tiʀ] (2) *vt* **(a)** (*détruire*) to destroy, wipe out. **(b)** *[chaleur, chagrin]* to overwhelm; *[fatigue]* to exhaust. ♦ **anéantissement** *nm* (*destruction*) destruction; wiping out; (*fatigue*) exhaustion; (*abattement*) dejection.

anecdote [anɛkdɔt] *nf* anecdote. ♦ **anecdotique** *adj* anecdotal.

anémier [anemje] (7) **1** *vt* to make anaemic. **2 s'~** *vpr* to become anaemic. ♦ **anémie** *nf* anaemia. ♦ **anémique** *adj* anaemic.

anémone [anemɔn] *nf* anemone. **~ de mer** sea anemone.

ânerie [ɑnʀi] *nf* (*caractère*) stupidity; (*parole*) stupid remark; (*gaffe*) blunder. **dire des ~s** to talk rubbish.

ânesse [ɑnɛs] *nf* she-ass.

anesthésie [anɛstezi] *nf* (*technique*) anaesthesia; (*opération*) anaesthetic. **sous ~** under the anaesthetic, under anaesthesia; **faire une ~** to give an anaesthetic. ♦ **anesthésier** (7) *vt* to anaesthetize. ♦ **anesthésique** *adj, nm* anaesthetic. ♦ **anesthésiste** *nmf* anaesthetist.

ange [ɑ̃ʒ] *nm* (*Rel, fig*) angel; (*Zool*) angel fish. **oui mon ~** yes, darling; **tu seras un ~** there's an angel *ou* a dear; **avoir une patience d'~** to have the patience of a saint; **c'est un ~ de bonté** he's the soul of goodness; **un ~ passa** there was an awkward pause; **être aux ~s** to be in (the) seventh heaven; **~ déchu** fallen angel; **~ gardien** (*Rel, fig*) guardian angel; (*garde du corps*) bodyguard.

angélique [ɑ̃ʒelik] **1** *adj* angelic. **2** *nf* angelica. ♦ **angéliquement** *adv* angelically.

angelot [ɑ̃ʒlo] *nm* (*Art*) cherub.

angélus [ɑ̃ʒelys] *nm* angelus.

angine [ɑ̃ʒin] *nf* tonsillitis. **avoir une ~** to have a sore throat; **~ de poitrine** angina (pectoris).

anglais, e [ɑ̃glɛ, ɛz] **1** *adj* English. **2** *nm* **(a)** **A~** Englishman; **les A~** (*en général*) English people, the English; (*hommes*) Englishmen. **(b)** (*Ling*) English. **~ canadien** Canadian English. **3** *nf* **(a)** **A~e** Englishwoman. **(b)** (*Coiffure*) **~es** ringlets. **(c)** (*Écriture*) ≃ modern English handwriting. **(d) à l'~e** *légumes* boiled. **4** *adv*: **parler ~** to speak English.

angle [ɑ̃gl(ə)] *nm* [*meuble, rue*] corner; (*Math*) angle; (*aspect*) angle, point of view; (*fig*) [*caractère*] rough edge. **le magasin qui fait l'~** the shop on the corner; **à ~ droit** at right angles; **vu sous cet ~** seen from that angle; **~ de braquage** lock.

Angleterre [ɑ̃glətɛʀ] *nf* England.

anglican, e [ɑ̃glikɑ̃, an] *adj, nm,f* Anglican. ♦ **anglicanisme** *nm* Anglicanism.

angliciste [ɑ̃glisist(ə)] *nmf* (*étudiant*) student of English; (*spécialiste*) anglicist. ♦ **angliciser** (1) *vt* to anglicize. ♦ **anglicisme** *nm* anglicism.

anglo- [ɑ̃glɔ] *préf* anglo-. ♦ **anglo-américain** *nm* (*Ling*) American English. ♦ **anglo-normand, e** *adj, nm* Anglo-Norman. **les îles ~-~es** the Channel Islands. ♦ **anglo-saxon, onne** *adj, nm,f* Anglo-Saxon.

anglophile [ɑ̃glɔfil] **1** *adj* anglophilic. **2** *nmf* anglophile. ♦ **anglophilie** *nf* anglophilia.

anglophobe [ɑ̃glɔfɔb] **1** *adj* anglophobic. **2** *nmf* anglophobe. ♦ **anglophobie** *nf* anglophobia.

anglophone [ɑ̃glɔfɔn] **1** *adj* English-speaking. **2** *nmf* English speaker.

angoisse [ɑ̃gwas] *nf* (*gén, Psych*) anguish; (*peur*) fear. **une étrange ~ le saisit** a strange feeling of anguish gripped him; **il vivait dans l'~ d'un accident** he lived in fear and dread of an accident. ♦ **angoissant, e** *adj* harrowing, agonizing. **vivre des jours ~s** to suffer days of anguish *ou* agony. ♦ **angoissé, e** *adj voix* anguished; *question* agonized. **cri ~** cry of anguish; **être ~** (*inquiet*) to be in anguish; (*oppressé*) to feel choked. ♦ **angoisser** (1) *vt* to cause anguish to.

anguille [ɑ̃gij] *nf* eel. **filer entre les doigts de qn comme une ~** to slip right through sb's fingers; **il y a ~ sous roche** there's something in the wind.

angulaire [ɑ̃gylɛʀ] *adj* angular.

anguleux, -euse [ɑ̃gylø, øz] *adj* angular, bony.

anicroche* [anikʀɔʃ] *nf* hitch, snag. **sans ~s** smoothly, without a hitch.

ânier, -ière [ɑnje, jɛʀ] *nm,f* donkey-driver.

animal, e, *mpl* **-aux** [animal, o] *adj, nm* (*Bio, fig*) animal. **quel ~!*** what a lout!

animateur, -trice [animatœʀ, tʀis] *nm,f* [*spectacle*] compère; [*centres culturels*] leader, organizer; (*Ciné: technicien*) animator. **l' ~ de cette entreprise** the driving force behind this undertaking.

animation [animɑsjɔ̃] *nf* **(a)** (*vie*) life, liveliness; (*affairement*) (hustle and) bustle; [*discussion*] animation, liveliness. **parler avec ~** to speak with great animation; **mettre de l'~ dans une réunion** to liven up a meeting. **(b)** (*Ciné*) animation.

animé, e [anime] *adj* **(a)** (*affairé*) busy; (*plein de vie*) lively; *discussion* animated, lively; (*Comm*) *enchères, marché* brisk. **(b)** (*Ling, Philos*) animate.

animer [anime] (1) **1** *vt* **(a)** *entreprise, groupe* to lead; *réunion* to conduct; *spectacle* to compère; *soirée, conversation* to liven up. **~ une course** to set the pace in a race. **(b)** [*sentiment*] to drive, impel; [*désir, motif*] to prompt. **la joie qui anime son visage** the joy that shines in his face. **(c)** (*mouvoir*) to drive. **animé d'un mouvement régulier** moving in a steady rhythm. **(d)** (*Philos*) to animate. **2 s'~** *vpr* [*personne, rue, objet*] to come to life; [*conversation*] to become animated, liven up; [*yeux*] to light up.

animosité [animozite] *nf* animosity (*contre* towards, against).

anis [ani(s)] *nm* (*plante*) anise; (*Culin*) aniseed.

ankyloser [ɑ̃kiloze] (1) **1** *vt* to stiffen. **être ankylosé** to be stiff. **2 s'~** *vpr* to get stiff.

annales [anal] *nfpl* annals. **ça restera dans les ~*** that'll go down in history.

anneau, *pl* **~x** [ano] *nm* (*gén*) ring; [*chaîne*] link; [*serpent*] coil. (*Sport*) **~x** rings.

année [ane] *nf* year. **tout au long de l'~** the whole year round; **payé à l'~** paid annually; **étudiant de deuxième ~** second-year student; **les ~s 20/30** the 20s/30s; **d'~ en ~** from year to year; **~ bissextile/ civile** leap/calendar year; **~-lumière** *nf, pl* **~s -~s** light year.

annexe [anɛks(ə)] **1** *adj document* appended; *travail, dépenses* subsidiary. **les bâtiments ~s** the annexes. **2** *nf* (*Constr*) annexe; [*document*] annex (*de* to). ♦ **annexer** (1) *vt territoire* to annex; *document* to append (*à* to). ♦ **annexion** *nf* (*Pol*) annexation.

annihiler [aniile] (1) *vt efforts* to ruin, destroy; *résistance* to wipe out; *personnalité* to crush. ♦ **annihilation** *nf* ruin; destruction; crushing.

anniversaire [anivɛʀsɛʀ] *nm* [*naissance*] birthday; [*événement*] anniversary.

annonce [anɔ̃s] *nf* announcement; (*publicité*) advertisement; (*fig: indice*) sign, indication; (*Bridge*) declaration. **petites ~s** small ads.

annoncer [anɔ̃se] (3) **1** *vt* **(a)** *fait* to announce (*à* to); (*Comm*) *réclame* to advertise. **je lui ai annoncé la nouvelle** I announced the news to her; (*mauvaise nouvelle*) I broke the news to her; **on annonce un grave incendie** a serious fire is reported to have broken out. **(b)** (*prédire*) *pluie, chômage* to forecast; [*présage*] to foretell; [*signe avant-coureur*] to herald. **ça n'annonce rien de bon** it bodes no good; **ce radoucissement annonce la pluie** this warmer weather is a sign that rain is on the way *ou* is a sign of rain. **(c)** (*dénoter*) to indicate, point to. **(d)** *personne* to announce. **sans se faire ~** without being announced. **(e)** (*Cartes*) to declare. (*fig*) **~ la couleur** to lay one's cards on the table.

2 s'~ *vpr* [*personne*] to announce o.s., say who one is; [*événement*] to approach. **s'~ bien/mal** to look good/bad; **ça s'annonce difficile** it looks like being difficult.

annonceur [anɔ̃sœʀ] *nm* (*publicité*) advertiser; (*speaker*) announcer.

annonciateur, -trice [anɔ̃sjatœʀ, tʀis] *adj*: **signe ~ de** portent of.

Annonciation [anɔ̃sjɑsjɔ̃] *nf*: **l'~** (*événement*) the Annunciation; (*jour*) Annunciation Day, Lady Day.

annoter [anɔte] (1) *vt* to annotate. ♦ **annotation** *nf* annotation.

annuaire [anɥɛʀ] *nm* yearbook, annual; [*téléphone*] (telephone) directory, phone book*.

annuel, -elle [anɥɛl] *adj* annual, yearly. ♦ **annuellement** *adv* annually, yearly. ♦ **annuité** annual payment.

annulaire [anylɛʀ] *nm* ring *ou* third finger.

annuler [anyle] (1) **1** *vt contrat, élection* to nullify; *mariage* to annul; *commande* to cancel. **2 s'~** *vpr [poussées]* to nullify each other, cancel each other out. ♦ **annulation** *nf* nullification; cancellation; annulment.
anoblir [anɔbliʀ] (2) *vt* to ennoble. ♦ **anoblissement** *nm* ennoblement.
anode [anɔd] *nf* anode.
anodin, e [anɔdɛ̃, in] *adj personne, détail* insignificant; *blessure* harmless.
anomalie [anɔmali] *nf* (*gén*) anomaly; (*Bio*) abnormality; (*Tech*) (technical) fault.
ânon [ɑnɔ̃] *nm* ass's foal.
ânonner [ɑnɔne] (1) *vti*: ~ **(sa leçon)** to mumble (one's way) through one's lesson.
anonymat [anɔnima] *nm* anonymity. **garder l'~** to remain anonymous. ♦ **anonyme** *adj* (*sans nom*) anonymous; (*impersonnel*) impersonal. ♦ **anonymement** *adv* anonymously.
anorak [anɔʀak] *nm* anorak.
anormal, e, *mpl* **-aux** [anɔʀmal, o] *adj* (*gén*) abnormal. **il est ~ qu'il n'ait pas les mêmes droits** it's abnormal for him not to have the same rights. ♦ **anormalement** *adv* abnormally.
anse [ɑ̃s] *nf [tasse]* handle; (*Géog*) cove.
antagonisme [ɑ̃tagɔnism(ə)] *nm* antagonism. ♦ **antagoniste** **1** *adj* antagonistic. **2** *nmf* antagonist.
antan [ɑ̃tɑ̃] *nm*: **d'~** of yesteryear, of long ago.
antarctique [ɑ̃taʀktik] **1** *adj* antarctic. **2** *nm*: **l'A~** the Antarctic, Antarctica.
antécédent, e [ɑ̃tesedɑ̃, ɑ̃t] **1** *adj* antecedent. **2** *nm* (*Gram, Philos*) antecedent. **~s** previous history.
antédiluvien, -ienne [ɑ̃tedilyvjɛ̃, jɛn] *adj* (*lit, fig*) antediluvian.
antenne [ɑ̃tɛn] *nf* **(a)** (*Zool*) antenna, feeler; (*Rad*) aerial; (*fig: contact*) contact. (*fig*) **avoir des ~s** to have a sixth sense. **(b)** (*Rad, TV: écoute*) **sur** *ou* **à l'~** on the air; **gardez l'~** stay tuned in; **je donne l'~ à Paris** over to Paris; **hors ~** off the air; **sur nos ~s** on our station. **(c)** (*succursale*) subbranch; (*Mil*) outpost; (*Méd*) (emergency) unit.
antérieur, e [ɑ̃teʀjœʀ] *adj* **(a)** *époque, situation* previous, earlier, former. **c'est ~ à la guerre** it was prior to the war. **(b)** *partie* front. **membre ~** forelimb. ♦ **antérieurement** *adv* earlier. **~ à** prior *ou* previous to. ♦ **antériorité** *nf [événement]* precedence; (*Gram*) anteriority.
anthologie [ɑ̃tɔlɔʒi] *nf* anthology.
anthracite [ɑ̃tʀasit] **1** *nm* anthracite. **2** *adj inv* charcoal grey.
anthropoïde [ɑ̃tʀɔpɔid] *adj, nm* anthropoid.
anthropologie [ɑ̃tʀɔpɔlɔʒi] *nf* anthropology. ♦ **anthropologique** *adj* anthropological. ♦ **anthropologiste** *nmf* anthropologist.
anthropophage [ɑ̃tʀɔpɔfaʒ] *adj, nm* cannibal. ♦ **anthropophagie** *nf* cannibalism.
anti [ɑ̃ti] *préf* (*gén*) anti-; (*contraire à*) un-. **anticonformisme** nonconformism; **antimatière** antimatter; **antimilitariste** antimilitarist; **antipoétique** unpoetic; **antisémitisme** antisemitism; **sérum antitétanique/ antidiphtérique** tetanus/diphtheria serum; **campagne antialcoolique** campaign against alcohol.
antiaérien, -ienne [ɑ̃tiaeʀjɛ̃, jɛn] *adj canon* anti-aircraft; *abri* air-raid.
antiatomique [ɑ̃tiatɔmik] *adj*: **abri ~** fallout shelter.
antibiotique [ɑ̃tibjɔtik] *adj, nm* antibiotic.
antibrouillard [ɑ̃tibʀujaʀ] *adj, nm* (*Aut*) **(phare) ~** fog lamp.
antibuée [ɑ̃tibɥe] *adj inv:* **dispositif ~** demister; **bombe ~** anti-mist spray.
antichambre [ɑ̃tiʃɑ̃bʀ(ə)] *nf* antechamber, anteroom. **faire ~**† to wait (for an audience with sb).
antichoc [ɑ̃tiʃɔk] *adj montre* shockproof.
anticipation [ɑ̃tisipɑsjɔ̃] *nf*: **paiement par ~** payment in advance; **roman d'~** science fiction novel.
anticiper [ɑ̃tisipe] (1) **1** *vi* (*gén*) to anticipate; (*en imaginant*) to look *ou* think ahead; (*en racontant*) to jump ahead. **~ sur qch** to anticipate sth; **sans vouloir ~ sur ce que je dirai** without wishing to go into what I shall say later. **2** *vt* (*gén, Fin*) to anticipate. ♦ **anticipé, e** *adj retour* early; *paiement* advance. **avec mes remerciements ~s** thanking you in advance.
anticorps [ɑ̃tikɔʀ] *nm* antibody.
anticyclone [ɑ̃tisiklon] *nm* anticyclone.
antidater [ɑ̃tidate] (1) *vt* to backdate.
antidérapant, e [ɑ̃tideʀapɑ̃, ɑ̃t] *adj* non-skid.
antidote [ɑ̃tidɔt] *nm* (*lit, fig*) antidote (*contre, de* for, against).
antiesclavagisme [ɑ̃tiɛsklavaʒism(ə)] *nm* abolitionism.
antigang [ɑ̃tigɑ̃g] *adj inv*: **brigade ~** police commando squad.
antigel [ɑ̃tiʒɛl] *nm* antifreeze.
Antilles [ɑ̃tij] *nfpl*: **les ~** the West Indies. ♦ **antillais, e** *adj,* **A~(e)** *nm(f)* West Indian.
antilope [ɑ̃tilɔp] *nf* antelope.
antimite [ɑ̃timit] *nm* mothballs.
antimoine [ɑ̃timwan] *nm* antimony.
antinomie [ɑ̃tinɔmi] *nf* antinomy. ♦ **antinomique** *adj* antinomic(al).
antiparasite [ɑ̃tipaʀazit] *adj*: **dispositif ~** suppressor.
antipathie [ɑ̃tipati] *nf* antipathy. ♦ **antipathique** *adj* unpleasant.
antipode [ɑ̃tipɔd] *nm* (*Géog*) **les ~s** the antipodes; (*Géog*) **être à l'~** *ou* **aux ~s** to be on the other side of the world (*de* from, to); (*fig*) **votre théorie est aux ~s de la mienne** our theories are poles apart.
antique [ɑ̃tik] *adj* (*de l'antiquité*) antique, ancient; (*très ancien*) ancient; (*péj*) antiquated. ♦ **antiquaire** *nmf* antique dealer. ♦ **antiquité** *nf* (*gén*) antiquity; (*meuble*) antique.
antisepsie [ɑ̃tisɛpsi] *nf* antisepsis. ♦ **antiseptique** *adj, nm* antiseptic.
antithèse [ɑ̃titɛz] *nf* (*lit, fig*) antithesis. ♦ **antithétique** *adj* antithetical.
antivénéneux, -euse [ɑ̃tivenenø, øz] *adj* antidotal.
antivenimeux, -euse [ɑ̃tivənimø, øz] *adj*: **sérum ~** antivenom.
antivol [ɑ̃tivɔl] *nm, adj inv*: **(dispositif) ~** anti-theft device.
antonyme [ɑ̃tɔnim] *nm* antonym.
antre [ɑ̃tʀ(ə)] *nm* (*caverne*) cave; *[animal]* (*fig*) den, lair.
anus [anys] *nm* anus.
anxieux, -euse [ɑ̃ksjø, øz] **1** *adj personne, regard* anxious, worried; *attente* anxious. **~ de** anxious to. **2** *nm,f* worrier. ♦ **anxiété** *nf* anxiety. ♦ **anxieusement** *adv* anxiously.
aorte [aɔʀt(ə)] *nf* aorta.
août [u] *nm* August; *pour loc V* **septembre** *et* **quinze.**
apache [apaʃ] *nm* **(a)** (*indien*) **A~** Apache. **(b)** (†: *voyou*) tough.
apaisant, e [apɛzɑ̃, ɑ̃t] *adj* soothing.
apaisement [apɛzmɑ̃] *nm* (*calme*) calm, quiet; (*soulagement*) relief; (*pour rassurer*) reassurance. **donner des ~s à qn** to reassure sb; **cela lui procura un certain ~** this brought him some relief.
apaiser [apeze] (1) **1** *vt personne* to calm down, pacify; *désir, faim* to appease, assuage; *douleur, excitation* to soothe; *conscience* to salve; *scrupules* to allay. **2 s'~** *vpr [personne]* to calm down; *[vacarme, vagues, douleur]* to die down.
apanage [apanaʒ] *nm* (*privilège*) privilege. **avoir l'~ de qch** to have the sole *ou* exclusive right to sth.

aparté [apaʀte] *nm* (*entretien*) private conversation; (*Théât*) aside. **en ~** in an aside.

apathie [apati] *nf* apathy. ♦ **apathique** *adj* apathetic.

apatride [apatʀid] *nmf* stateless person.

apercevoir [apɛʀsəvwaʀ] (28) **1** *vt* **(a)** (*voir*) to see; (*brièvement*) to catch a glimpse of; (*remarquer*) to notice. **(b)** *danger* to see, perceive; *difficultés* to see, foresee. **2 s'~** *vpr*: **s'~ de** *erreur* to notice; *présence* to become aware of; **s'~ que** to notice *ou* realize that.

aperçu [apɛʀsy] *nm* (*idée générale*) general idea *ou* picture; (*compte-rendu*) general survey. **avoir des ~s sur qch** to have some insight into sth.

apéritif [apeʀitif] *nm* aperitif.

apesanteur [apəzɑ̃tœʀ] *nf* weightlessness.

à-peu-près [apøpʀɛ] *nm inv* vague approximation.

apeuré, e [apœʀe] *adj* frightened, scared.

aphone [afɔn] *adj* voiceless.

aphorisme [afɔʀism(ə)] *nm* aphorism.

aphrodisiaque [afʀɔdizjak] *adj, nm* aphrodisiac.

aphte [aft(ə)] *nm* mouth ulcer.

apiculteur, -trice [apikyltœʀ, tʀis] *nm,f* beekeeper. ♦ **apiculture** *nf* beekeeping.

apitoyer [apitwaje] (8) **1** *vt* to move to pity. **n'essaie pas de m'~** don't try and make me feel sorry for you. **2 s'~** *vpr*: **s'~ sur** to feel pity for. ♦ **apitoiement** *nm* (*pitié*) pity.

aplanir [aplaniʀ] (2) *vt terrain* to level; *difficultés* to smooth away. **les difficultés se sont aplanies** the difficulties smoothed themselves out *ou* were ironed out. ♦ **aplanissement** *nm* levelling; smoothing away.

aplatir [aplatiʀ] (2) **1** *vt* (*gén*) to flatten; *couture* to press flat; *pli* to smooth (out). **2 s'~** *vpr* **(a)** *[personne]* to flatten o.s. (*contre* against); (*s'étendre*) to lie flat on the ground; (*: *tomber*) to fall flat on one's face; (*s'humilier*) to grovel (*devant* before, to). **(b)** *[choses]* (*devenir plus plat*) to become flatter; (*s'écraser*) to smash (*contre* against). ♦ **aplati, e** *adj* flat. ♦ **aplatissement** *nm* (*gén*) flattening; (*humiliation*) grovelling.

aplomb [aplɔ̃] *nm* **(a)** (*assurance*) self-assurance; (*péj*) nerve, cheek*. **(b)** (*équilibre*) balance; (*verticalité*) plumb. **d'~** *corps* steady, balanced; *mur* plumb; **se tenir d'~ (sur ses jambes)** to be steady on one's feet; **tu n'as pas l'air d'~*** you look out of sorts; (*lit, fig*) **se remettre d'~** to get back on one's feet again; **le soleil tombait d'~** the sun was beating straight down.

apocalypse [apɔkalips(ə)] *nf* (*Rel*) **l'A~** (the book of) Revelation, the Apocalypse; **vision d'~** vision of doom. ♦ **apocalyptique** *adj* (*Rel*) apocalyptic; *vision* apocalyptic, of doom.

apogée [apɔʒe] *nm* (*Astron, fig*) apogee.

apolitique [apɔlitik] *adj* (*indifférent*) apolitical; (*neutre*) non-political.

apologie [apɔlɔʒi] *nf* apology. **faire l'~ de** to praise.

apoplexie [apɔplɛksi] *nf* apoplexy.

a posteriori [apɔsteʀjɔʀi] *loc adv, adj* (*gén*) after the event.

apostolat [apɔstɔla] *nm* (*Bible*) apostolate; (*prosélytisme*) proselytism; (*fig*) vocation. ♦ **apostolique** *adj* apostolic.

apostrophe [apɔstʀɔf] *nf* (*Gram*) apostrophe; (*interpellation*) rude remark. ♦ **apostropher** (1) *vt* to shout at.

apothéose [apɔteoz] *nf* apotheosis; (*Théât, gén: bouquet*) grand finale. **finir dans une ~** to end in a blaze of glory.

apothicaire† [apɔtikɛʀ] *nm* apothecary†.

apôtre [apotʀ(ə)] *nm* apostle. **faire le bon ~** to play the saint.

apparaître [apaʀɛtʀ(ə)] (57) *vi* (*se montrer*) to appear (*à* to); (*sembler*) to seem, appear (*à* to); *[fièvre, boutons]* to break out. **la vérité lui apparut soudain** the truth suddenly dawned on him; **il apparaît que** it appears *ou* turns out that.

apparat [apaʀa] *nm* (*pompe*) pomp. **d'~** ceremonial.

appareil [apaʀɛj] *nm* (*instrument*) piece of apparatus, device; (*électrique, ménager*) appliance; (*poste*) set; (*Phot*) camera; (*téléphone*) (tele)phone; (*Aviat*) aircraft (*inv*); (*dentier*) brace; (*pour fracture*) splint. **~ digestif** digestive system; **l'~ policier/du parti** the police/party machinery; **qui est à l'~?** who's speaking?; **~-photo** *nm, pl* **~s -~s** camera; **~ à sous** (*distributeur*) slot machine; (*jeu*) fruit machine.

appareiller [apaʀeje] (1) **1** *vi* (*Naut*) to cast off. **2** *vt* (*assortir*) to match up. ♦ **appareillage** *nm* casting off.

apparemment [apaʀamɑ̃] *adv* apparently.

apparence [apaʀɑ̃s] *nf* **(a)** (*gén*) appearance. **~ négligée** slovenly look *ou* appearance; **~ souriante** smiling exterior; **fausse ~** mere façade; **il n'a plus une ~ de respect pour** he no longer has the least semblance of respect for. **(b) malgré les ~s** in spite of appearances; **contre toute ~** against all expectations; **selon toute ~** in all probability; **en ~** (*apparemment*) apparently; (*hypocritement*) outwardly.

apparent, e [apaʀɑ̃, ɑ̃t] *adj* **(a)** (*visible*) *poutre* visible; *gêne, raison* apparent, obvious. **de façon ~e** visibly. **(b)** (*superficiel*) *solidité, contradictions* apparent.

apparenter (s') [apaʀɑ̃te] (1) *vpr*: **s'~ à** (*Pol*) to ally o.s. with; (*par mariage*) to marry into; (*ressembler à*) to be similar to.

appariteur [apaʀitœʀ] *nm* (*Univ*) attendant.

apparition [apaʀisjɔ̃] *nf* **(a)** (*arrivée*) (*gén*) appearance; *[boutons, fièvre]* outbreak. **faire son ~** to appear; to break out. **(b)** (*vision, fantôme*) apparition.

appartement [apaʀtəmɑ̃] *nm* flat, apartment (*US*); *[hôtel]* suite.

appartenance [apaʀtənɑ̃s] *nf* belonging (*à* to); membership (*à* of).

appartenir [apaʀtəniʀ] (22) **1 ~ à** *vt indir* (*possession*) to belong to; (*participation*) to belong to, be a member of; **pour des raisons qui m'appartiennent** for reasons of my own; **un médecin ne s'appartient pas** a doctor's time is not his own. **2** *vb impers*: **il m'appartient de le faire** it is for me *ou* up to me to do it.

appât [apɑ] *nm* (*gén*) bait. **mordre à l'~** to rise to the bait, bite; **l'~ du gain** the lure of gain. ♦ **appâter** (1) *vt gibier, client* to lure, entice; *piège* to bait.

appauvrir [apovʀiʀ] (2) **1** *vt* (*gén*) to impoverish; *sang* to make thin. **2 s'~** *vpr* (*gén*) to grow poorer; *[race]* to degenerate. ♦ **appauvrissement** *nm* impoverishment; degeneration.

appel [apɛl] **1** *nm* **(a)** (*cri*) call; (*demande pressante*) appeal. **~ à l'aide/aux armes** call for help/to arms; **elle a entendu des ~s** she heard cries; **à son ~, elle se retourna** she turned round when he called; **l'~ du devoir** the call of duty. **(b) faire ~ à** *générosité* to appeal to; *pompiers* to call on; *souvenirs* to call up; *courage* to summon up; **ça fait ~ à des connaissances spéciales** it calls for *ou* requires specialist knowledge. **(c)** (*présence*) **faire l'~** (*Scol*) to call the register; (*Mil*) to call the roll; (*Mil*) **l'~ d'une classe** the call-up of a class. **(d)** (*Jur*) appeal (*contre* against). **faire ~ (d'un jugement)** to appeal (against a judgment); **sans ~** (*Jur*) without appeal; (*fig*) final. **(e)** (*Cartes*) signal (*à* for). **(f)** (*élan*) take-off.

2: **~ d'air** draught; **~ de fonds** call for capital; (*Comm*) **~ d'offres** invitation to tender; **~ téléphonique** phone call; **faire un ~ de phares** to flash one's headlights.

appelé [aple] *nm* (*Mil*) conscript, draftee (*US*).

(*Rel, fig*) **il y a beaucoup d'~s et peu d'élus** many are called but few are chosen.
appeler [aple] (4) **1** *vt* **(a)** *personne, chien* to call; *nom* to call out; (*téléphoner à*) to call, phone. **~ qn par son prénom** to call *ou* address sb by his first name; **~ un chat un chat** to call a spade a spade; **~ (qn) à l'aide** to call (to sb) for help; **~ qn (d'un geste) de la main** to beckon to sb. **(b)** (*faire venir*) (*gén*) to call; *pompiers* to call out; *conscrits* to call up; *médecin* to send for; (*Jur*) to summon. **(c)** (*désigner*) **~ qn à** *poste* to appoint *ou* assign sb to; **être appelé à un brillant avenir** to be destined for a brilliant future; **la méthode est appelée à se généraliser** the method is bound to become general. **(d)** (*réclamer*) *[situation, conduite]* to call for. **une lâcheté en appelle une autre** one act of cowardice leads to another; **en ~ à** to appeal to; **en ~ de** to appeal against.
2 s'~ *vpr*: **il s'appelle Paul** his name is Paul, he's called Paul; **voilà ce qui s'appelle une gaffe** that's what's called a blunder!
appellation [apelɑsjɔ̃] *nf* designation, appellation; (*mot*) term, name. **~ d'origine** mark of the place of origin.
appendice [apɛ̃dis] *nm* (*Anat, gén*) appendix; (*hum: nez*) **~ nasal** proboscis (*hum*). ♦ **appendicite** *nf* appendicitis.
appentis [apɑ̃ti] *nm* lean-to.
appesantir [apəzɑ̃tiʀ] (2) **1** *vt membre, objet* to make heavy; *esprit* to dull; *autorité* to strengthen (*sur* over). **2 s'~** *vpr [tête, pas]* to grow heavier; *[esprit]* to grow duller; *[autorité]* to grow stronger. **s'~ sur un sujet** to dwell on a subject. ♦ **appesantissement** *nm [démarche]* heaviness; *[esprit]* dullness; *[autorité]* strengthening.
appétit [apeti] *nm* (*gén, fig*) appetite (*de* for). **avoir de l'~** to have a good *ou* hearty appetite; (*lit, fig*) **mettre qn en ~** to give sb an appetite; **avoir un ~ d'oiseau** to eat like a bird; **manger avec ~** to eat heartily; **l'~ vient en mangeant** (*lit*) eating whets the appetite; (*fig*) the more you have the more you want. ♦ **appétissant, e** *adj* appetizing.
applaudir [aplodiʀ] (2) **1** *vt* (*lit*) to applaud, clap; (*fig*) to applaud. **2** *vi* to applaud, clap. **~ à tout rompre** to bring the house down. **3 ~ à** *vt indir initiative* to applaud. **4 s'~** *vpr* to congratulate o.s, pat o.s. on the back (*d'avoir fait* for having done). ♦ **applaudissement** *nm*: **~s** applause.
applicable [aplikabl(ə)] *adj* applicable (*à* to).
applicateur [aplikatœʀ] *adj m, nm* applicator.
application [aplikasjɔ̃] *nf* **(a)** **(V appliquer)** application; use; implementation. **mettre en ~** *décision, loi* to implement. **(b)** **~s** *[théorie, méthode]* applications. **(c)** (*attention*) application (*à qch* to sth). **avec ~** industriously.
applique [aplik] *nf* wall lamp.
appliqué, e [aplike] *adj personne* industrious, painstaking; *écriture* careful. **bien ~** *baiser* firm; *coup* well-aimed; **linguistique** *etc* **~e** applied linguistics *etc*.
appliquer [aplike] (1) **1** *vt* (*gén*) to apply; *décision* to implement; *recette* to use; *gifle* to give. **~ un traitement/son esprit à qch** to apply a treatment/one's mind to sth; **~ une échelle contre un mur** to put *ou* lean a ladder against a wall; **~ sa main sur qch** to put one's hand on sth; **faire ~ la loi** to enforce the law. **2 s'~** *vpr [élève]* to apply o.s. (*à qch* to sth, *à faire qch* to doing sth); **s'~ à qch** *[remarque]* to apply to sth; **s'~ sur qch** *[calque]* to fit over sth.
appoint [apwɛ̃] *nm* (extra) contribution; (*monnaie*) right change. **faire l'~** to give the right money *ou* change; **salaire d'~** extra income.
appointer [apwɛ̃te] (1) *vt salarié* to pay. ♦ **appointements** *nmpl* salary.
appontement [apɔ̃tmɑ̃] *nm* landing stage.
apport [apɔʀ] *nm [capitaux, culture]* contribution; *[chaleur, eau]* supply. **le tourisme grâce à son ~ de devises** tourism, thanks to the currency it brings in; **l'~ en vitamines d'un aliment** the vitamins provided by a food.
apporter [apɔʀte] (1) (*gén*) to bring (*à* to); *modification* to introduce; *solution* to supply, provide; *soin* to exercise (*à faire* in doing). **apporte-le-lui** take it to him; **apporte-le en montant/en venant/en entrant** bring it up/along/in; **elle y a apporté toute son énergie** she put all her energy into it; **son livre n'apporte rien de nouveau** his book contributes nothing new.
apposer [apoze] (1) *vt* (*gén*) to affix; *signature* to append.
apposition [apozisjɔ̃] *nf* (*Gram*) apposition.
apprécier [apʀesje] (7) *vt* **(a)** *distance, importance* to estimate, assess, appraise; (*expertiser*) *objet* to value. **(b)** *nuance, qualité, repas* to appreciate. **mets très apprécié** much appreciated dish. ♦ **appréciable** *adj* appreciable. ♦ **appréciatif, -ive** *adj* (*estimatif*) appraising, evaluative; (*admiratif*) appreciative. ♦ **appréciation** *nf* assessment; appraisal; estimation; valuation. **je le laisse à votre ~** I leave you to judge for yourself; **~s du professeur sur un élève** teacher's assessment of a pupil.
appréhender [apʀeɑ̃de] (1) *vt* **(a)** (*arrêter*) to apprehend. **(b)** (*redouter*) to dread (*de faire* doing). **~ que** to fear that. ♦ **appréhensif, -ive** *adj* apprehensive, fearful (*de* of). ♦ **appréhension** *nf* apprehension. **voir qch avec ~** to dread sth; **avoir de l'~** to be apprehensive.
apprendre [apʀɑ̃dʀ(ə)] (58) *vt* **(a)** *leçon, métier* to learn; *fait* to hear of, learn of. **~ à connaître** to get to know; **ça s'apprend facilement** it's easy to learn; **apprenez que je ne me laisserai pas faire!** be warned that I won't be trifled with! **(b) ~ qch à qn** *nouvelle* to tell sb (of) sth; *science* to teach sb sth; (*iro*) **ça lui apprendra!** that'll teach him!
apprenti, e [apʀɑ̃ti] *nm,f [métier]* apprentice; (*débutant*) novice, beginner. ♦ **apprentissage** *nm* apprenticeship; (*fig*) initiation (*de* into). **mettre qn en ~** to apprentice sb (*chez* to); **école d'~** training school; **faire l'~ de** *métier* to serve one's apprenticeship in; *douleur* to be initiated into.
apprêter [apʀete] (1) **1** *vt* **(a)** (*préparer*) to get ready. **(b)** *peau* to dress; (*Peinture*) to size. **2 s'~** *vpr* **(a) s'~ à qch/à faire qch** to get ready for sth/to do sth. **(b)** (*toilette*) to prepare o.s. ♦ **apprêt** *nm* (*opération*) dressing; sizing; (*substance*) dressing; size. ♦ **apprêté, e** *adj* (*affecté*) affected.
apprivoiser [apʀivwaze] (1) *vt* to tame. **s'~** to become tame. ♦ **apprivoisable** *adj* tameable. ♦ **apprivoisé, e** *adj* tame. ♦ **apprivoisement** *nm* (*action*) taming; (*état*) tameness.
approbation [apʀɔbɑsjɔ̃] *nf* approval, approbation. **digne d'~** commendable. ♦ **approbateur, -trice** *adj* approving.
approchable [apʀɔʃabl(ə)] *adj* (*gén*) accessible.
approchant, e [apʀɔʃɑ̃, ɑ̃t] *adj style, genre* similar (*de* to); *résultat* close (*de* to). **rien d'~** nothing like that.
approche [apʀɔʃ] *nf* (*gén*) approach. **à l'~ de l'hiver** at the approach of winter, as winter draws near *ou* approaches; **d'~ difficile** *lieu* inaccessible; *auteur* difficult to understand; **travaux d'~** (*Mil*) approaches; (*fig*) manœuvres; **les ~s de** *ville, côte* the surrounding area of.
approché, e [apʀɔʃe] *adj* approximate.
approcher [apʀɔʃe] (1) **1** *vt* **(a)** *objet* to move near (*de* to); (*l'un de l'autre*) to bring *ou* move closer together. **approche ta chaise** draw *ou* bring your chair nearer; **il approcha le verre de ses lèvres** he lifted *ou* raised the glass to his lips. **(b)** *personne* (*lit*) to go near, approach; (*fig*) to approach. **2** *vi [date]* to approach, draw near; *[personne, orage]* to approach, come nearer. **le jour approche où** the

day is near when; **approche!** come here!; ~ **de** to approach, near. **3 s'~** *vpr* (*venir*) to come near, approach; (*aller*) to go near, approach. **il s'approcha de moi** he came up to me; **s'~ du micro** (*venir*) to go up to the mike; (*se rapprocher*) to get close to the mike; **approche-toi!** come here!

approfondir [apʀɔfɔ̃diʀ] (2) **1** *vt puits* to deepen, make deeper; *étude* to go (deeper) into; *connaissances* to deepen, increase. **2 s'~** *vpr [rivière]* to become deeper. ♦ **approfondi, e** *adj* thorough, detailed. ♦ **approfondissement** *nm* deepening.

approprier [apʀɔpʀije] (7) **1** *vt* to suit, adapt (*à* to). **2 s'~** *vpr bien, droit* to appropriate. **s'~ à** to suit. ♦ **appropriation** *nf* (*usurpation*) appropriation; (*adaptation*) suitability, appropriateness. ♦ **approprié, e** *adj* appropriate, suitable.

approuver [apʀuve] (1) *vt personne* to agree with; *décision* (*trouver louable*) to approve of; (*ratifier*) to approve.

approvisionner [apʀɔvizjɔne] (1) **1** *vt magasin* to supply (*en, de* with); *compte* to pay money into; *fusil* to load. **bien approvisionné en fruits** well stocked with fruit. **2 s'~** *vpr* to stock up (*en* with). **s'~ au marché** to shop at the market. ♦ **approvisionnement** *nm* (*action*) supplying (*en, de* of). (*réserves*) ~s supplies, provisions.

approximation [apʀɔksimɑsjɔ̃] *nf* approximation, (rough) estimate. ♦ **approximatif, -ive** *adj calcul, évaluation* rough; *nombre* approximate; *termes* vague. ♦ **approximativement** *adv* roughly; approximately; vaguely.

appui [apɥi] **1** *nm* (*lit, fig*) support. **prendre ~ sur** *[personne]* to lean on; *[objet]* to rest on; **il a des ~s au ministère** he has connections in the ministry; **à l'~ de son témoignage** in support of his evidence, to back up his evidence. **2**: **appui(e)-bras** *nm inv* armrest; ~ **de fenêtre** window-sill; **appui(e)-tête** *nm inv* headrest.

appuyé, e [apɥije] *adj regard* fixed, intent; *geste* emphatic.

appuyer [apɥije] (8) **1** *vt* (*presser*) to press (*sur* on); (*soutenir*) *personne, thèse* to support, back (up); *attaque* to back up. (*poser*) **~ qch contre qch** to lean *ou* rest sth against sth. **2** *vi* **~ sur** *sonnette* to press; *frein* to press on, press down; *levier* to press (down *etc*); *mot, argument* to stress, emphasize; (*Mus*) *note* to accentuate. ~ **sur des colonnes** to rest on pillars; ~ **sur la droite** to bear to the right. **3 s'~** *vpr* **(a) s'~ sur** *mur* to lean on; *preuve* to rely on; *parti* to rely on the support of. **(b)** (*:*) *importun, corvée* to put up with.

âpre [ɑpʀ(ə)] *adj* **(a)** *goût, hiver, vent* bitter; *temps* raw; *son* harsh. **(b)** *vie* harsh; *combat, discussion, résolution* bitter, grim; *concurrence, critique* fierce. ~ **au gain** grasping, greedy. ♦ **âprement** *adv* bitterly, grimly; fiercely. ♦ **âpreté** *nf* bitterness; rawness; harshness, grimness; fierceness.

après [apʀɛ] **1** *prép* **(a)** (*gén*) after. ~ **coup** after the event, afterwards; ~ **quoi** after which, and afterwards; **page ~ page** page after page; ~ **tout** after all; **j'étais ~ elle dans la queue** I was behind *ou* after her in the queue; **sa maison est (juste) ~ la mairie** his house is (just) past *ou* beyond the town hall; **collé ~ le mur** stuck on the wall; **crier ~ qn** to shout at sb; **en colère ~ qn** angry with sb; ~ **manger** after meals *ou* food; ~ **s'être reposé** after resting, after he had rested; ~ **que vous lui aurez parlé** after you have spoken to him. **(b) d'~ lui** according to him, in his opinion; **d'~ ce qu'il a dit** from *ou* according to what he said; **ne jugez pas d'~ les apparences** don't go by appearances; **d'~ les journaux** according to the papers; **d'~ Balzac** adapted from Balzac.

2 *adv* (*ensuite*) afterwards, after; (*plus tard*) later. **longtemps ~** long after(wards); **2 jours ~** 2 days later; ~ **nous avons des articles moins chers** otherwise we have cheaper things; **et (puis) ~?** (*lit*) and then what?, (*fig*) what of it?; ~ **tu iras dire que ...** next you'll be saying that ...; **le mois d'~** the following month, the month after; **il courut ~** he ran after it.

3: **~-demain** *adv* the day after tomorrow; **~-guerre** *nm* post-war years; **~-midi** *nm ou nf inv* afternoon; **~-rasage** *nm inv* after-shave; **~-ski** *nm inv* snow boot.

a priori [apʀijɔʀi] *loc adv, adj* a priori.

à-propos [apʀɔpo] *nm [remarque]* aptness. **avoir beaucoup d'~** to show great presence of mind.

apte [apt(ə)] *adj*: ~ **à qch** capable of sth; ~ **à faire** capable of doing, able to do; (*Mil*) ~ **(au service)** fit for service; (*Jur*) ~ **à** fit to *ou* for.

aptitude [aptityd] *nf* aptitude (*à faire* for doing); ability (*à faire* to do).

aquaplane [akwaplan] *nm* aquaplane.

aquarelle [akwaʀɛl] *nf* (*technique*) watercolours; (*tableau*) watercolour.

aquarium [akwaʀjɔm] *nm* aquarium.

aquatique [akwatik] *adj* aquatic.

aqueduc [akdyk] *nm* aqueduct.

aqueux, -euse [akø, øz] *adj* aqueous.

aquilin, e [akilɛ̃, in] *adj* aquiline.

aquilon [akilɔ̃] *nm* (*Poésie*) north wind.

ara [aʀa] *nm* macaw.

arabe [aʀab] **1** *adj désert, cheval* Arabian; *nation* Arab; *art, langue* Arabic, Arab. **2** *nm* (*Ling*) Arabic. **l'~ littéral** written Arabic. **3** *nmf*: **A~** Arab.

arabesque [aʀabɛsk(ə)] *nf* arabesque.

Arabie [aʀabi] *nf* Arabia. ~ **Saoudite**, ~ **Séoudite** Saudi Arabia.

arable [aʀabl(ə)] *adj* arable.

arachide [aʀaʃid] *nf* peanut, groundnut.

araignée [aʀeɲe] *nf* **(a)** (*animal*) spider. ~ **de mer** spider crab. **(b)** (*crochet*) spider.

aratoire [aʀatwaʀ] *adj* ploughing.

arbalète [aʀbalɛt] *nf* crossbow.

arbitraire [aʀbitʀɛʀ] **1** *adj* arbitrary. **2** *nm*: **l'~** the arbitrary; **l'~ de qch** the arbitrary nature of sth. ♦ **arbitrairement** *adv* arbitrarily.

arbitre [aʀbitʀ(ə)] *nm* **(a)** (*Jur*) arbitrator; (*gén*) arbiter. **(b)** (*Sport*) referee; (*Cricket, Hockey, Tennis*) umpire. ♦ **arbitrage** *nm* arbitration; refereeing; umpiring. ♦ **arbitrer** (1) *vt* to arbitrate; to referee; to umpire.

arborer [aʀbɔʀe] (1) *vt* (*gén*) to display; *vêtement, médaille* to sport; *sourire* to wear; *drapeau* to bear; *gros titre* to carry.

arboriculture [aʀbɔʀikyltyʀ] *nf* arboriculture. ♦ **arboriculteur, -trice** *nm,f* arboriculturist.

arbre [aʀbʀ(ə)] *nm* (*Bot*) tree; (*Tech*) shaft. **les ~s vous cachent la forêt** you can't see the wood for the trees; ~ **à cames** camshaft; ~ **fruitier** fruit tree; ~ **généalogique** family tree; ~ **de Noël** Christmas tree. ♦ **arbrisseau,** *pl* **~x** *nm* shrub. ♦ **arbuste** *nm* small shrub, bush.

arc [aʀk] *nm* (*arme*) bow; (*Géom, Élec*) arc; (*Anat, Archit*) arch. **en ~ de cercle** in a semi-circle.

arcade [aʀkad] *nf* (*Archit, Anat*) arch. **~s** arcade, arches.

arcanes [aʀkan] *nmpl* mysteries.

arc-boutant, *pl* **~s-~s** [aʀkbutɑ̃] *nm* flying buttress.

arc-bouter [aʀkbute] (1) **1** *vt* to buttress. **2 s'~** *vpr* to lean (*contre* against, *sur* on). **arc-bouté contre le mur** braced against the wall.

arceau, *pl* **~x** [aʀso] *nm* (*Archit*) arch; (*Croquet*) hoop.

arc-en-ciel, *pl* **~s-~-~** [aʀkɑ̃sjɛl] *nm* rainbow.

archaïque [aʀkaik] *adj* archaic. ♦ **archaïsme** *nm* archaism.

archange [aʀkɑ̃ʒ] *nm* archangel.

arche [aʀʃ(ə)] *nf* (*Archit*) arch; (*Rel*) ark. **l'~ de Noé** Noah's Ark.

archéologie [aʀkeɔlɔʒi] *nf* archaeology.

♦ **archéologique** *adj* archaeological. ♦ **archéologue** *nmf* archaeologist.
archer [aʀʃe] *nm* archer.
archet [aʀʃɛ] *nm* (*Mus, gén*) bow.
archétype [aʀketip] *nm* archetype.
archevêque [aʀʃəvɛk] *nm* archbishop. ♦ **archevêché** *nm* (*territoire*) archbishopric; (*palais*) archbishop's palace.
archi... [aʀʃi] *préf* **(a)** (*: *extrêmement*) tremendously, enormously. **~plein** chock-a-block*; **~millionnaire** millionaire several times over. **(b)** (*titre*) arch... . **~diacre/duc** archdeacon/archduke.
archipel [aʀʃipɛl] *nm* archipelago.
architecte [aʀʃitɛkt(ə)] *nm* (*lit, fig*) architect. ♦ **architectural, e,** *mpl* **-aux** *adj* architectural. ♦ **architecture** *nf* architecture.
archives [aʀʃiv] *nfpl* records, archives. **ça restera dans les ~!*** that will go down in history! ♦ **archiviste** *nmf* archivist.
arçon [aʀsɔ̃] *nm* (*d'avant*) pommel; (*d'arrière*) cantle.
arctique [aʀktik] **1** *adj* (*Géog*) Arctic. **2** *nm*: **l'~** the Arctic.
ardent, e [aʀdɑ̃, ɑ̃t] *adj* **(a)** *flambeau, chaleur* burning; *feu, soleil* blazing; *yeux* burning (*de* with). **(b)** *foi, partisan* fervent; *lutte, haine, amant* ardent; *discours* impassioned; *caractère* fiery. ♦ **ardemment** *adv* ardently, fervently. ♦ **ardeur** *nf* fervour; passion; ardour; fieriness. **son ~ au travail** his enthusiasm for work; **l'~ du soleil** the heat of the sun.
ardoise [aʀdwaz] **1** *nf* (*roche*) slate; (†: *dette*) unpaid bill. **2** *adj inv* (*couleur*) slate-grey.
ardu, e [aʀdy] *adj* *travail* arduous; *problème* difficult; *pente* steep.
are [aʀ] *nm* are, one hundred square metres.
arène [aʀɛn] *nf* (*lit, fig*) (*piste*) arena; (*Géol*) sand.
arête [aʀɛt] *nf* **(a)** (*Zool*) fishbone. **~ centrale** backbone, spine. **(b)** *[cube]* edge; *[montagne]* ridge; *[nez]* bridge.
argent [aʀʒɑ̃] **1** *nm* **(a)** (*métal, couleur*) silver. **en ~** silver. **(b)** (*Fin*) money. **se faire de l'~** to make money; **~ liquide** ready money, cash; **~ de poche** pocket money; **payer ~ comptant** to pay cash; (*fig*) **prendre qch pour ~ comptant** to take sth at face value; **on en a pour son ~** we get good value for money. **2** *adj inv* silver. ♦ **argenté, e** *adj* *couleur* silver, silvery; *couverts* silver-plated; **ils ne sont pas très ~s*** they're not very well-off. ♦ **argenter** (1) *vt* *miroir* to silver; *couverts* to silver-plate. ♦ **argenterie** *nf* silverware; (*de métal argenté*) silver plate. ♦ **argentin, e**[1] *adj* *son* silvery.
Argentine [aʀʒɑ̃tin] *nf*: **l'~** Argentina, the Argentine. ♦ **argentin, e**[2] *adj*, **A~(e)** *nm(f)* Argentinian.
argile [aʀʒil] *nf* clay. ♦ **argileux, -euse** *adj* clayey.
argot [aʀgo] *nm* slang. ♦ **argotique** *adj* slangy.
arguer [aʀgɥe] (1) *vt* to deduce. **~ que** to claim that.
argument [aʀgymɑ̃] *nm* argument. **tirer ~ de qch** to use sth as an argument. ♦ **argumentation** *nf* argumentation. ♦ **argumenter** (1) *vi* to argue.
argus [aʀgys] *nm*: guide to secondhand car prices.
aride [aʀid] *adj* (*lit, fig*) arid; *vent* dry; *travail* thankless. **cœur ~** heart of stone. ♦ **aridité** *nf* aridity; dryness; thanklessness. **~ du cœur** stony-heartedness.
aristocrate [aʀistɔkʀat] *nmf* aristocrat. ♦ **aristocratie** *nf* aristocracy. ♦ **aristocratique** *adj* aristocratic.
arithmétique [aʀitmetik] **1** *nf* arithmetic. **2** *adj* arithmetical. ♦ **arithmétiquement** *adv* arithmetically.
arlequin [aʀləkɛ̃] *nm* (*Théât*) Harlequin.
armateur [aʀmatœʀ] *nm* shipowner.
armature [aʀmatyʀ] *nf* (*gén*) frame; (*Constr, fig*) framework.
arme [aʀm(ə)] *nf* **(a)** (*gén*) weapon, arm; (*à feu*) gun; (*fig*) weapon. **sans ~(s)** (*lit*) unarmed; (*fig*) defenceless; **se battre à l'~ blanche** to fight with knives; **~ atomique** atomic weapon; **~ à feu** firearm; **~ à double tranchant** double-edged weapon. **(b)** (*Mil*) (*section*) arm. (*littér*) **les ~s** the army. **(c)** (*emblème*) **~s** (coat of) arms; **aux ~s de** bearing the arms of. **(d) à ~s égales** on equal terms; **déposer les ~s** to lay down (one's) arms; **faire ses premières ~s** to make one's début (*dans* in); **passer qn par les ~s** to shoot sb (*by firing squad*); **partir avec ~s et bagages** to pack up and go; **passer l'~ à gauche‡** to kick the bucket‡; **prendre le pouvoir par les ~s** to take power by force; **prendre les ~s** to take up arms; (*Escrime*) **faire des ~s** to fence; **en ~s** *soldats* at arms; *peuple* in arms; **aux ~s!** to arms!
armé, e[1] [aʀme] *adj* armed (*de* with). **~ jusqu'aux dents** armed to the teeth; **bien ~ contre le froid** well-armed *ou* well-equipped against the cold.
armée[2] [aʀme] **1** *nf* army. **quelle ~ d'incapables*** what a useless bunch*. **2**: **~ active** regular army; **l'~ de l'air** the Air Force; **l'~ de mer** the Navy; **l'~ de réserve** the reserve; **l'~ du Salut** the Salvation Army; **l'~ de terre** the Army.
armement [aʀməmɑ̃] *nm* **(a)** (*action*) *[pays]* armament; *[personne]* arming; *[fusil]* cocking; *[appareil-photo]* winding-on; *[navire]* fitting-out, equipping. **(b)** (*armes*) *[soldat]* arms, weapons; *[pays, navire]* arms, armament.
armer [aʀme] (1) **1** *vt* **(a)** *personne* to arm (*de* with); (*fig*) to arm, equip (*contre* against). (*Hist*) **~ qn chevalier** to dub sb knight. **(b)** *navire* to fit out, equip; *fusil* to cock; *appareil-photo* to wind on. **(c)** *béton, poutre* to reinforce (*de* with). **2 s'~** *vpr* to arm o.s. (*de* with, *contre* against).
armistice [aʀmistis] *nm* armistice.
armoire [aʀmwaʀ] *nf* (*gén*) cupboard; (*penderie*) wardrobe. **~ à pharmacie** medicine cabinet; **~ à glace** (*lit*) wardrobe with a mirror; (**fig: costaud*) hulking great brute*.
armoiries [aʀmwaʀi] *nfpl* coat of arms.
armure [aʀmyʀ] *nf* (*Mil, Zool*) armour; (*fig*) defence.
armurier [aʀmyʀje] *nm* *[fusils]* gunsmith; *[couteaux]* armourer. ♦ **armurerie** *nf* gunsmith's; armourer's.
arnaquer‡ [aʀnake] (1) *vt* to swindle. ♦ **arnaqueur, -euse‡** *nm,f* swindler, hustler*.
arnica [aʀnika] *nf* arnica.
aromate [aʀɔmat] *nm* (*thym etc*) herb; (*poivre etc*) spice. **~s** seasoning. ♦ **aromatique** *adj* aromatic. ♦ **aromatiser** (1) *vt* to flavour.
arôme [aʀom] *nm* aroma.
arpège [aʀpɛʒ] *nm* arpeggio.
arpenter [aʀpɑ̃te] (1) *vt* to pace up and down; (*Tech*) *terrain* to survey. ♦ **arpentage** *nm* surveying. ♦ **arpenteur** *nm* (land) surveyor.
arqué, e [aʀke] *adj* *forme, sourcils* arched, curved. **avoir le dos ~** to be hunchbacked; **il a les jambes ~es** he's bow-legged.
arquebuse [aʀkəbyz] *nf* (h)arquebus. ♦ **arquebusier** *nm* (h)arquebusier.
arquer [aʀke] (1) **1** *vt* *tige* to curve; *dos* to arch. **2** *vi*: **il ne peut plus ~‡** he can't walk any more. **3 s'~** *vpr* to curve.
arrachage [aʀaʃaʒ] *nm* **(V arracher)** lifting; pulling up; extraction; pulling out.
arraché [aʀaʃe] *nm* (*Sport*) snatch. (*fig*) **obtenir qch à l'~** to snatch sth.
arrachement [aʀaʃmɑ̃] *nm* (*chagrin*) wrench.
arrache-pied (d') [daʀaʃpje] *adv* relentlessly.
arracher [aʀaʃe] (1) **1** *vt* **(a)** *légume* to lift; *plante* to pull up; *dent* to take out, extract; *poil, clou* to pull out; *chemise, affiche* to tear off. **se faire ~ une dent** to have a tooth out; (*fig*) **je vais lui ~ les yeux** I'll scratch his eyes out; **ça lui arracha le cœur** it broke his heart. **(b)** (*enlever*) **~ à qn** *arme*

to snatch *ou* grab from sb; *larmes, promesse* to wring from sb; *victoire* to wrest from sb. **(c)** (*soustraire*) ~ **qn à** *famille, mort, sort, pays* to snatch sb away from; *vice, soucis* to rescue sb from; *rêve* to snatch sb out of.

2 s'~ *vpr*: **s'~ (les vêtements)** to tear one's clothes; **s'~ les cheveux** to tear one's hair; **s'~ qn/qch** to fight over sb/sth; **s'~ de** *famille* to tear o.s. away from; *habitude, lit* to force o.s. out of.

arraisonner [aʀɛzɔne] (1) *vt* (*Naut*) to inspect. ♦ **arraisonnement** *nm* inspection.

arrangeant, e [aʀɑ̃ʒɑ̃, ɑ̃t] *adj* obliging.

arrangement [aʀɑ̃ʒmɑ̃] *nm* **(a)** (*gén, Mil*) arrangement; *[mobilier]* layout; *[mots]* order. **l'~ de sa toilette** the way she is dressed. **(b)** (*accord*) settlement, arrangement.

arranger [aʀɑ̃ʒe] (3) **1** *vt* **(a)** (*disposer*) (*gén*) to arrange; *coiffure* to tidy up; *tenue* to straighten (up). **(b)** *voyage, rencontre* to arrange, organize. **c'était arrangé à l'avance** it was fixed (in advance). **(c)** *différend* to settle, sort out. **ça n'arrange rien** it doesn't help matters. **(d)** (*contenter*) to suit. **si ça vous arrange** if that suits you, if that's convenient for you. **(e)** *voiture, montre* to fix, put right; *robe* (*recoudre*) to mend; (*modifier*) to alter; (*Mus*) to arrange. ~ **ses notes** to sort out one's notes. **(f)** (*: *malmener*) to sort out*.

2 s'~ *vpr* **(a)** (*se mettre d'accord*) to come to an arrangement. **arrangez-vous avec le patron** sort it out with the boss. **(b)** *[querelle]* to be settled; *[situation]* to sort itself out; *[santé, temps, rapports]* to get better. **ça ne s'arrange pas*** things are no better. **(c)** (*se débrouiller*) to manage. **arrangez-vous comme vous voudrez mais ...** I don't mind how you do it but ...; **je ne sais pas comment tu t'arranges, mais ...** I don't know how you manage (it), but ...; **arrangez-vous pour venir** arrange it so that you can come. **(d) s'~ de qch** to make do with sth. **(e)** (*se rajuster*) to tidy o.s. up. **tu t'es bien arrangé!*** you look a mess!

arrérages [aʀeʀaʒ] *nmpl* arrears.

arrestation [aʀɛstɑsjɔ̃] *nf* arrest. **mettre en état d'~** to place *ou* put under arrest.

arrêt [aʀɛ] **1** *nm* **(a)** (*action*) stopping, checking, arrest; (*lieu, pause*) stop. **attendez l'~ complet (du train)** wait until the train stops *ou* is at a standstill; **5 minutes d'~** 5 minutes' stop, a 5-minute stop; **véhicule à l'~** stationary vehicle; **faire un ~** *[train]* to make a stop; (*Ftbl*) to make a save; **tomber en ~** to stop short; **sans ~** (*sans interruption*) without stopping, non-stop; (*très fréquemment*) continually, constantly; **~ d'autobus** bus stop. **(b)** (*Mil*) **~s** arrest; **mettre qn aux ~s** to put sb under arrest. **(c)** (*Jur: décision*) ruling, decision. **(d)** (*Tech*) *[machine]* stop mechanism; *[bouton]* stop button.

2: **~ du cœur** cardiac arrest; **l'~ des hostilités** the cessation of hostilities; (*Sport*) **~ de jeu** stoppage; **~ de mort** death sentence; **~ de travail** (*grève*) stoppage (of work); (*congé*) sick leave; (*certificat*) doctor's certificate.

arrêté, e [aʀete] **1** *adj volonté* firm; *idée* fixed, firm. **c'est une chose ~e** the matter is settled. **2** *nm* (*loi*) order. **~ municipal** ≃ bye-law; **~ de compte** (*fermeture*) settlement of account; (*relevé*) statement of account.

arrêter [aʀete] (1) **1** *vt* **(a)** (*gén*) to stop; *moteur* to switch off; *ennemi, progression* to check, halt; *hémorragie, criminel* to arrest. **arrêtez-moi près de la poste** drop me by the post office; **ici, je vous arrête!** I must stop you there!; **on n'arrête pas le progrès** there's no stopping progress; **nous avons été arrêtés par un embouteillage** we were held up by a traffic jam; **seul le prix l'arrête** it's only the price that stops him; (*Police*) **se faire ~** to get o.s. arrested. **(b)** *études, compétition* to give up; *envois, trafic aérien, représentations* to cancel. **~ la fabrication d'un produit** to discontinue a product; **on a dû ~ les travaux** we had to stop work *ou* call a halt to the work. **(c)** *compte (fermer)* to settle; (*relever*) to make up; *jour, lieu, plan* to decide on; *choix, décision* to make. **~ ses regards sur** to fix one's gaze on; **~ un marché** to settle a deal; (*Admin*) **~ que** to rule that.

2 *vi* to stop. **arrête de parler!** stop talking!; **~ de fumer** to give up *ou* stop smoking.

3 s'~ *vpr* **(a)** (*gén*) to stop; *[train]* to stop, come to a stop *ou* a halt. **nous nous arrêtâmes sur le bas-côté** we pulled up *ou* stopped by the roadside; **s'~ net** *[personne, bruit]* to stop dead; **s'~ pour manger** to break off *ou* stop to eat; **sans s'~** without stopping, without a break. **(b) s'~ sur** *[choix, regard]* to fall on; **s'~ à** *détails* to pay too much attention to; *projet* to settle *ou* fix on.

arrhes [aʀ] *nfpl* deposit.

arrière [aʀjɛʀ] **1** *nm* **(a)** *[voiture]* back; *[bateau]* stern; *[train]* rear; (*Sport*) fullback. (*Naut*) **à l'~** aft, at the stern; **à l'~ de** at the stern of, abaft; **se balancer d'avant en ~** to rock backwards and forwards; (*Mil*) **les ~s** the rear; **l'~ (du pays)** the homefront. **(b) en ~** (*derrière*) behind; (*vers l'arrière*) backwards; **rester en ~** to drop behind; **faire un pas en ~** to step back(wards); (*Naut*) **en ~ toute!** full astern!; **100 ans en ~** 100 years ago; **revenir en ~** (*gén*) to go back; *[civilisation]* to regress; (*avec magnétophone*) to rewind; **le chapeau en ~** his hat tilted back(wards); **en ~! vous gênez** stand *ou* get back! you're in the way; (*lit, fig*) **en ~ de** behind.

2 *adj inv*: **roue/feu ~** rear wheel/light; **siège ~** back seat.

3 *préf inv* (*le second élément prend la marque du pluriel et donne le genre*) **(a)** (*famille*) **~-grand-mère** great-grandmother; **~-petit-fils** great-grandson. **(b) ~-bouche** back of the mouth; **~-boutique** back shop; **~-cour** backyard; **~-cuisine** scullery; **~-garde** rearguard; **~-gorge** back of the throat; (*lit, fig*) **~-goût** aftertaste; **~-pays** hinterland; **~-pensée** (*raison intéressée*) ulterior motive; (*réserves*) mental reservation; **~-plan** background; **~-saison** autumn; **~-salle** back room; **~-train** hindquarters.

arriéré, e [aʀjeʀe] **1** *adj* **(a)** (*Comm*) overdue. **(b)** (*Psych*) backward, retarded; *pays* backward; *méthodes, personne* out-of-date. **2** *nm* (*travail*) backlog; (*paiement*) arrears.

arrimer [aʀime] (1) *vt* (*Naut*) *cargaison* to stow; (*gén*) *colis* to secure. ♦ **arrimage** *nm* stowage.

arrivage [aʀivaʒ] *nm [marchandises]* arrival; *[touristes]* fresh load *ou* influx.

arrivant, e [aʀivɑ̃, ɑ̃t] *nm,f* (*personne*) newcomer. (*arrivée*) **compter les ~s** to count the new arrivals.

arrivée [aʀive] *nf* **(a)** *[personne, train]* arrival; *[neige]* arrival, coming; *[course]* finish. **à son ~** when he arrived *ou* came in, on his arrival. **(b)** (*Tech*) **~ d'air/de gaz** (*robinet*) air/gas inlet; (*processus*) inflow of air/gas.

arriver [aʀive] (1) **1** *vt* **(a)** (*être au bout*) to arrive; (*approcher*) to come. (*atteindre*) **~ à** *lieu, résultat* to arrive at, get to, reach; *sujet, pouvoir* to come to; **~ chez soi** to arrive *ou* get *ou* reach home; **c'est arrivé jusqu'à lui** *[bruit, nouvelle]* it reached him; **~ le premier** (*course*) to come in first; (*soirée*) to be the first to arrive; **j'arrive!** (I'm) coming!, just coming!; **arrive!** come on!; **pour faire ~ l'eau jusqu'à la maison ...** to bring water up to the house ...; **je n'ai pas pu ~ jusqu'au chef** I wasn't able to get right to the boss; **l'eau lui arrivait aux genoux** the water came up to his knees; (*fig*) **il ne t'arrive pas à la cheville** he can't hold a candle to you. **(b)** (*réussir*) to succeed *ou* get on in life. **~ à faire qch** to succeed in doing sth, manage to do sth; **je n'arrive pas à comprendre son attitude** I simply cannot understand his attitude; **il n'arrivera jamais à rien**

he'll never get anywhere, he'll never achieve anything. **(c)** (*se produire*) to happen. **c'est arrivé hier** it took place *ou* happened yesterday; **il croit que c'est arrivé*** he thinks he's made it*; **faire ~ un accident** to bring about an accident; **tu vas nous faire ~ des ennuis** you'll get us into trouble. **(d) on en arrive à se demander si ...** we're beginning to wonder whether ...; **il faudra bien en ~ là!** it'll have to come to that (eventually).

2 *vb impers* **(a) il (lui) est arrivé un malheur** something dreadful has happened (to him); **il est arrivé un télégramme** a telegram has come *ou* arrived; **il lui arrivera des ennuis** he'll get (himself) into trouble; **quoi qu'il arrive** whatever happens; **comme il arrive souvent (dans ces cas-là)** as often happens, as is often the case. **(b) il m'arrive d'oublier, il arrive que j'oublie** I sometimes forget; **il peut ~ qu'elle se trompe** she may (occasionally) make mistakes; **s'il lui arrivait de faire une erreur** if she should happen to make a mistake.

arrivisme [aʀivism(ə)] *nm* pushfulness. ♦ **arriviste** *nmf* go-getter*.

arrogance [aʀɔgɑ̃s] *nf* arrogance. ♦ **arrogant, e** *adj* arrogant.

arroger (s') [aʀɔʒe] (3) *vpr pouvoirs, titre* to assume (without right).

arrondir [aʀɔ̃diʀ] (2) **1** *vt* **(a)** *objet* to (make) round; *angle* to round off; *caractère* to smooth the rough edges off. **~ les angles** to smooth things over. **(b)** *fortune* to swell; *domaine* to increase; *salaire* to supplement. **(c)** (*simplifier*) *somme, nombre* to round off (*à* to). **2 s'~** *vpr [relief]* to become round(ed); *[taille]* to fill out; *[fortune]* to swell. ♦ **arrondi, e 1** *adj forme* round, rounded; *visage* round. **2** *nm* (*gén: contour*) roundness; (*Couture*) hemline.

arrondissement [aʀɔ̃dismɑ̃] *nm* ≈ district.

arroser [aʀoze] (1) *vt* **(a)** (*gén*) to water; *rôti* to baste. **~ qch d'essence** to pour petrol over sth; **~ qn de balles** to spray sb with bullets; **se faire ~** to get drenched *ou* soaked; **ville très arrosée** very wet city; **mouchoir arrosé de sang/larmes** blood/tear-soaked handkerchief. **(b)** (*) *succès* to drink to; *repas* to wash down (with wine)*. ♦ **arrosage** *nm* watering. ♦ **arroseuse** *nf* water cart. ♦ **arrosoir** *nm* watering can.

arsenal, *pl* **-aux** [aʀsənal, o] *nm* (*Mil*) arsenal; (*: *attirail*) gear; (*: *collection*) collection.

arsenic [aʀsənik] *nm* arsenic.

arsouille† [aʀsuj] *nm ou nf* (*voyou*) ruffian.

art [aʀ] *nm* (*gén*) art; (*adresse*) skill. **l'~ de vivre** the art of living; **avec un ~ consommé** with consummate skill; **les ~s et métiers** industrial arts and crafts; **homme de l'~** expert; **avoir l'~ de faire qch** to have the art *ou* knack of doing sth.

artère [aʀtɛʀ] *nf* (*Anat*) artery; (*Aut*) main road. ♦ **artériel, -ielle** *adj* arterial.

arthrite [aʀtʀit] *nf* arthritis. ♦ **arthritique** *adj, nmf* arthritic. ♦ **arthrose** *nf* osteoarthritis.

artichaut [aʀtiʃo] *nm* artichoke.

article [aʀtikl(ə)] **1** *nm* **(a)** (*Comm*) item, article. **~ d'importation** imported product; **faire l'~ à qn** to give sb the sales patter. **(b)** *[loi, journal]* article; *[dictionnaire]* entry. **sur cet ~** on this point. **(c)** (*Gram*) article. **(d) à l'~ de la mort** at the point of death. **2: ~s de bureau** office accessories; **~ de foi** article of faith; **~ réclame** special offer; **~s de voyage** travel goods.

articuler [aʀtikyle] (1) *vt* **(a)** (*prononcer clairement*) to articulate; (*dire*) to pronounce, utter. **articule!** speak clearly! **(b)** *mécanismes, os* to articulate, joint; *idées* to link. **ses phrases s'articulent bien** his sentences link *ou* hang* together well. ♦ **articulation** *nf* (*Anat*) joint; (*Tech, Ling*) articulation; *[doigts]* knuckles; *[discours, raisonnement]* link. ♦ **articulé, e** *adj langage* articulate; *membre, objet* jointed, articulated; *poupée* with moveable joints.

artifice [aʀtifis] *nm* ingenious device, trick; (*péj*) trick. (*Art*) **l'~** artifice.

artificiel, -ielle [aʀtifisjɛl] *adj* (*gén*) artificial; *gaieté* forced, unnatural. ♦ **artificiellement** *adv* artificially.

artificieux, -ieuse [aʀtifisjø, jøz] *adj* guileful.

artillerie [aʀtijʀi] *nf* artillery. **~ de marine** naval guns; **tir d'~** artillery fire. ♦ **artilleur** *nm* artilleryman, gunner.

artimon [aʀtimɔ̃] *nm* mizzen.

artisan [aʀtizɑ̃] *nm* (*lit*) craftsman, artisan; (*fig*) architect, author. ♦ **artisanal, e,** *mpl* **-aux** *adj*: **profession ~e** craft, craft industry; **retraite ~e** pension for self-employed craftsmen; **fabrication ~e** production by craftsmen. ♦ **artisanalement** *adv* by craftsmen. ♦ **artisanat** *nm* (*métier*) craft industry; (*classe sociale*) artisans.

artiste [aʀtist(ə)] **1** *nmf* **(a)** (*Art*) artist; (*Spectacle*) artiste; (*chanteur*) singer; (*fantaisiste*) entertainer. **~ peintre** artist, painter; **~ dramatique** actor (*ou* actress); **les ~s saluèrent** the performers took a bow. **(b)** (*péj: bohème*) bohemian. **2** *adj personne, style* artistic. ♦ **artistique** *adj* artistic. ♦ **artistiquement** *adv* artistically.

aryen, -yenne [aʀjɛ̃, jɛn] *adj*, **A~(ne)** *nm(f)* Aryan.

as [ɑs] *nm* **(a)** (*carte, dé*) ace. **(b)** (*champion*) ace*. **un ~ de la route** a crack driver; **l'~ de l'école** the school's star pupil. **(c) être ficelé comme l'~ de pique*** to be dressed all anyhow*; **être (plein) aux ~‡** to be loaded*; **c'est passé à l'~‡** (*perdu*) it's gone down the drain*; (*inaperçu*) it went unnoticed.

ascendance [asɑ̃dɑ̃s] *nf* (*généalogique*) ancestry.

ascendant, e [asɑ̃dɑ̃, ɑ̃t] **1** *adj astre, trait* rising; *mouvement* upward; *progression* ascending. **2** *nm* **(a)** (*influence*) ascendancy (*sur* over). **(b)** (*Admin*) **~s** ascendants. **(c)** (*Astron*) rising star; (*Astrol*) ascendant.

ascenseur [asɑ̃sœʀ] *nm* lift, elevator (*US*).

ascension [asɑ̃sjɔ̃] *nf* **(a)** *[ballon, fusée]* ascent; (*fig: sociale*) rise. (*Rel*) **l'A~** the Ascension; (*jour*) Ascension Day. **(b)** *[montagne]* ascent, climb. **faire l'~ d'une montagne** to climb a mountain. ♦ **ascensionnel, -elle** *adj force* upward. **vitesse ~elle** climbing speed.

ascète [asɛt] *nmf* ascetic. ♦ **ascétique** *adj* ascetic. ♦ **ascétisme** *nm* asceticism.

asepsie [asɛpsi] *nf* asepsis. ♦ **aseptique** *adj* aseptic. ♦ **aseptiser** (1) *vt pièce* to fumigate; *pansement* to sterilize; *plaie* to disinfect.

Asie [azi] *nf* Asia. **~ Mineure** Asia Minor. ♦ **asiatique** *adj*, **A~** *nmf* Asian.

asile [azil] *nm* (*lit, fig*) refuge; (*Pol*) asylum; (*Hist*) sanctuary. **~ de vieillards** old people's home; **~ de fous** lunatic asylum; **~ de paix** haven of peace.

asocial, e, *mpl* **-aux** [asɔsjal, o] *adj* antisocial.

aspect [aspɛ] *nm* (*allure*) look, appearance; (*angle*) aspect, side; (*Astrol, Ling*) aspect. **d'~ sinistre** sinister-looking; **avoir l'~ de** to look like.

asperge [aspɛʀʒ(ə)] *nf* asparagus. (*: *personne*) **(grande) ~** beanpole*.

asperger [aspɛʀʒe] (3) *vt surface* to spray; *personne* to splash (*de* with).

aspérité [aspeʀite] *nf* bump. **~s** *[surface]* bumps, rough patches; *[caractère]* harshness.

asphalte [asfalt(ə)] *nm* asphalt. ♦ **asphalter** (1) *vt* to asphalt.

asphyxier [asfiksje] (7) **1** *vt* (*lit*) to suffocate, asphyxiate; (*fig*) to stifle. **mourir asphyxié** to die of suffocation *ou* asphyxiation. **2 s'~** *vpr* (*accident*) to suffocate, asphyxiate; (*suicide*) to suffocate o.s.; (*au gaz*) to gas o.s. ♦ **asphyxie** *nf* suffocation, asphyxiation.

aspic [aspik] *nm* (*Zool*) asp; (*Culin*) meat (*ou* fish *etc*) in aspic.
aspirant, e [aspiʀɑ̃, ɑ̃t] **1** *adj* suction. **2** *nm,f* (*candidat*) candidate (*à* for). **3** *nm* (*Mil*) officer cadet; (*Naut*) midshipman.
aspirateur [aspiʀatœʀ] *nm* vacuum cleaner, hoover ®. **passer à l'~** to vacuum, hoover.
aspirer [aspiʀe] (1) **1** *vt air* to inhale, breathe in; *liquide* to suck up; (*Ling*) to aspirate. **2** **~ à** *vt indir* to aspire to. ♦ **aspiration** *nf* **(a)** *[air]* inhalation; (*Ling*) aspiration; *[liquide]* sucking up. **(b)** (*ambition*) aspiration, longing (*vers, à* for).
aspirine [aspiʀin] *nf* aspirin.
assagir *vt,* **s'~** *vpr* [asaʒiʀ] (2) to quieten down.
assaillir [asajiʀ] (13) *vt* (*lit*) to assail, attack; (*fig*) to assail (*de* with). ♦ **assaillant, e** *nm,f* assailant.
assainir [aseniʀ] (2) *vt quartier, logement* to clean up; *marécage* to drain; *air* (*lit*) to purify; (*fig*) to clear; *finances, monnaie* to stabilize. **la situation s'est assainie** the situation has become healthier. ♦ **assainissement** *nm* cleaning up; stabilization.
assaisonner [asɛzɔne] (1) *vt* (*gén*) to season; *salade* to dress. **~ qn*** (*physiquement*) to knock sb about; (*verbalement*) to tell sb off; (*financièrement*) to clobber sb*. ♦ **assaisonnement** *nm* dressing; seasoning.
assassin, e [asasɛ̃, in] **1** *adj* provocative. **2** *nm* (*gén*) murderer; (*Pol*) assassin; (*Presse etc*) killer. **à l'~!** murder! ♦ **assassinat** *nm* murder; assassination. ♦ **assassiner** (1) *vt* to murder; to assassinate.
assaut [aso] *nm* (*Mil*) assault, attack (*de* on); (*Sport*) bout. **donner l'~** to attack; **les ~s de l'ennemi** the enemy's attacks *ou* onslaughts; (*lit, fig*) **prendre d'~** to take by storm, storm; **faire ~ de politesse** to vie with each other in politeness.
assécher [aseʃe] (6) *vt* to drain; *[évaporation]* to dry. ♦ **assèchement** *nm* drainage; drying.
assembler [asɑ̃ble] (1) **1** *vt* (*gén*) to assemble; *meuble etc* to put together; *comité* to convene. **2** **s'~** *vpr* to assemble, gather. ♦ **assemblage** *nm* **(a)** (*action*) assembling, putting together. **(b)** (*jointure*) joint; (*structure*) assembly; (*collection*) collection. ♦ **assemblée** *nf* (*foule*) gathering; (*convoquée*) meeting; (*Pol*) assembly. (*Rel*) **l'~ des fidèles** the congregation; **à la grande joie de l'~** to the great joy of those present.
asséner [asene] (5) *vt coup* to strike; *argument* to thrust forward.
assentiment [asɑ̃timɑ̃] *nm* (*consentement*) assent, consent; (*approbation*) approval (*à* to).
asseoir [aswaʀ] (26) **1** *vt* **(a)** **~ qn** (*personne debout*) to sit sb down; (*personne couchée*) to sit sb up; **faire ~ qn** to ask sb to sit down. **(b)** **être assis** to be sitting *ou* seated; **rester assis** to remain seated; **assis en tailleur** sitting cross-legged; (*fig*) **assis entre deux chaises** in an awkward position. **(c)** *réputation, autorité* to establish. **~ sa réputation sur qch** to build one's reputation on sth; **~ une théorie sur des faits** to base a theory on facts. **(d)** (*: *stupéfier*) to stagger, stun. **2** **s'~** *vpr* to sit down; *[personne couchée]* to sit up. **asseyez-vous donc** do sit down *ou* take a seat; **le règlement, je m'assieds dessus!*** you know what you can do with the rules!*
assermenté, e [asɛʀmɑ̃te] *adj policier, expert* sworn.
assertion [asɛʀsjɔ̃] *nf* assertion.
asservir [asɛʀviʀ] (2) *vt personne* to enslave; *pays* to subjugate; *nature* to master. ♦ **asservissement** *nm* (*action*) enslavement; (*lit, fig: état*) slavery, subservience (*à* to).
assesseur [asesœʀ] *nm* assessor.
assez [ase] *adv* **(a)** enough. **bien ~ grand** quite big enough; **pas ~ souvent** not often enough; **est-ce que 5 F c'est ~? – c'est bien ~** is 5 francs enough? *ou* will 5 francs do? – that will be plenty *ou* quite enough; **avez-vous acheté ~ de pain?** have you bought enough *ou* sufficient bread?; **as-tu trouvé une boîte ~ grande?** have you found a big enough box?; **je n'ai pas ~ d'argent pour m'offrir cette voiture** I can't afford (to buy myself) this car, I haven't enough money to buy myself this car; **il n'est pas ~ sot pour le croire** he is not so stupid as to believe him. **(b)** (*intensif*) **ce serait ~ agréable** it would be rather *ou* quite nice; **il était ~ tard** it was quite *ou* fairly late; **est-ce ~ bête!** how stupid (of me)!; **j'en ai ~ (de toi)!** I've had enough (of you)!, I'm fed up (with you)!; **~ de discours!** enough talk!, enough said!
assidu, e [asidy] *adj* (*ponctuel*) regular; (*appliqué*) assiduous, painstaking; (*empressé*) assiduous in one's attention (*auprès de* to). ♦ **assiduité** *nf* regularity; assiduity (*à* to). **son ~ aux cours** his regular attendance at classes; (*hum*) **~s** assiduous attentions. ♦ **assidûment** *adv* assiduously.
assiéger [asjeʒe] (3 *et* 6) *vt* (*Mil*) to besiege; *[tentations]* to beset. **la garnison assiégée** the beleagered *ou* besieged garrison; **assiégé par l'eau** hemmed in by water. ♦ **assiégeant, e** *nm,f* besieger.
assiette [asjɛt] *nf* **(a)** (*vaisselle*) plate. **~ anglaise** assorted cold roast meats; **~ creuse/plate** soup/dinner plate. **(b)** (*équilibre*) *[cavalier]* seat; *[navire]* trim. (*fig*) **il n'est pas dans son ~** he's feeling out of sorts. **(c)** *[impôt]* basis of assessment. ♦ **assiettée** *nf* (*gén*) plateful.
assigner [asiɲe] (1) *vt* **(a)** *place, rôle* to assign, allocate; *valeur* to attach; *cause* to ascribe, attribute; *somme* to allot, allocate; *limite* to set, fix (*à* to). **~ un objectif à qn** to set sb a goal. **(b)** (*Jur*) **~ (à comparaître)** *prévenu* to summons; *témoin* to subpoena, cite; **~ qn à résidence** to put sb under house arrest. ♦ **assignable** *adj* ascribable (*à* to). ♦ **assignation** *nf* allocation; summons.
assimiler [asimile] (1) **1** *vt* **(a)** *immigrants, substance* to assimilate, absorb. **notions mal assimilées** ill-digested notions. **(b)** **~ qn/qch à** (*comparer à*) to liken *ou* compare sb/sth to; (*classer comme*) to class sb/sth as; (*faire ressembler à*) to make sb/sth similar to. **2** **s'~** *vpr* to be assimilated. **s'~ à qn** to liken o.s. to sb. ♦ **assimilable** *adj* easily assimilated. **~ à** comparable to. ♦ **assimilation** *nf* assimilation; comparison (*à* to); classification (*à* as). ♦ **assimilé, e** *adj* comparable.
assis, e[1] [asi, iz] *adj* **(a)** *personne* sitting (down), seated; **V asseoir.** **(b)** *situation* stable; *autorité* well-established.
assise[2] [asiz] *nf* (*Constr*) course; (*Bio, Géol*) stratum; (*fig*) basis.
assises [asiz] *nfpl* (*Jur*) assizes; (*fig*) meeting.
assistance [asistɑ̃s] *nf* **(a)** *[conférence]* audience. **(b)** (*aide*) assistance; (*légale, technique*) aid. **donner ~ à qn** to give sb assistance; **~ médicale** medical care; **l'A~ publique** ≃ the Health Service; **enfant de l'A~** child in care. **(c)** (*présence*) attendance. ♦ **assistant, e** *nm,f* (*gén, Scol*) assistant; (*Univ*) assistant lecturer. **~e sociale** social worker; (*spectateurs*) **les ~s** those present.
assister [asiste] (1) **1** **~ à** *vt indir cérémonie, cours* to be (present) at, attend; *spectacle* to be at; *événement* to witness. **2** *vt pauvres* to assist; *mourant* to comfort.
association [asɔsjasjɔ̃] *nf* **(a)** (*société*) association; (*Comm, Écon*) partnership. **(b)** *[idées, images]* association; *[couleurs]* combination. **(c)** (*collaboration*) partnership. **son ~ à nos travaux** his joining us in our undertaking. ♦ **associatif, -ive** *adj* associative. ♦ **associé, e** *nm,f* (*gén*) associate; (*Comm, Fin*) partner.
associer [asɔsje] (7) **1** *vt* **(a)** **~ qn à** *profits* to give sb a share of; *affaire* to make sb a partner in; *triomphe* to include sb in. **(b)** *idées, mots* to associate; *couleurs, intérêts*

to combine (*à* with). ~ **qch à** (*relier*) to associate *ou* link sth with; (*mêler*) to combine sth with.

2 s'~ *vpr* **(a)** (*s'unir*) to join together; (*Comm*) to form a partnership; *[couleurs, qualités]* to be combined (*à* with). **s'~ qn** to take sb on as a partner; **s'~ à** to join with; (*Comm*) to go into partnership with. **(b) s'~ à** *projet* to join in; *opinion* associate o.s. with; *douleur* to share in; **je m'associe aux compliments que l'on vous faits** I should like to join with those who have complimented you.

assoiffer [aswafe] (1) *vt* to make thirsty. **assoiffé de** thirsting for. ♦ **assoiffant, e** *adj* thirst-giving.

assoler [asɔle] (1) *vt champ* to rotate crops on. ♦ **assolement** *nm* rotation of crops.

assombrir [asɔ̃bʀiʀ] (2) **1** *vt* (*lit*) to darken; *personne* to fill with gloom; *assistance, voyage* to cast a gloom *ou* shadow over. **2 s'~** *vpr [ciel, pièce]* to darken; *[personne, situation]* to become gloomy; *[visage, regard]* to cloud. ♦ **assombri, e** *adj ciel* darkened; *couleur* sombre; *visage, regard* gloomy, sombre. ♦ **assombrissement** *nm* darkening; gloominess.

assommer [asɔme] (1) *vt* (*tuer*) to batter sb's skull in; (*étourdir*) to knock out, stun; (*: *ennuyer*) to bore stiff*. **assommé par** *bruit* stunned by; *chaleur* overwhelmed by. ♦ **assommant, e*** *adj* deadly dull*.

Assomption [asɔ̃psjɔ̃] *nf* Assumption; (*jour*) Assumption Day.

assonance [asɔnɑ̃s] *nf* assonance.

assorti, e [asɔʀti] *adj bonbons* assorted. **'fromages ~s'** 'assortment of cheeses'; **bien/mal ~** *magasin* well/poorly-stocked; *couple* well/badly matched; **avec écharpe ~e** with matching scarf; **être ~ de** *conseils* to be accompanied by *ou* with.

assortiment [asɔʀtimɑ̃] *nm* **(a)** *[bonbons]* assortment; (*Comm: lot*) stock. **(b)** (*harmonie*) arrangement, ensemble.

assortir [asɔʀtiʀ] (2) **1** *vt* **(a)** (*accorder*) to match (*à, avec* to, with). **(b)** (*accompagner de*) **~ qch de** to accompany sth by *ou* with. **(c)** *commerçant* to supply; *magasin* to stock (*de* with). **2 s'~** *vpr* to match (*à* with). **s'~ de** to be accompanied by.

assoupir [asupiʀ] (2) **1** *vt personne* to make drowsy; *sens, douleur, intérêt* to dull; *passion* to lull. **2 s'~** *vpr [personne]* to doze off; (*fig*) to be dulled *ou* lulled. **il est assoupi** he is dozing. ♦ **assoupissement** *nm* (*sommeil*) doze; (*fig*) dulling; lulling.

assouplir [asupliʀ] (2) **1** *vt cuir, membres* to make supple; *règlements* to relax. **~ le caractère de qn** to make sb more amenable. **2 s'~** *vpr* to become supple; to relax. ♦ **assouplissement** *nm* suppling up; relaxing. **exercices d'~** limbering up exercises.

assourdir [asuʀdiʀ] (2) *vt personne* to deafen; *bruit* to deaden, muffle. ♦ **assourdissant, e** *adj* deafening.

assouvir [asuviʀ] (2) *vt* to satisfy, appease. ♦ **assouvissement** *nm* satisfaction, appeasement.

assujettir [asyʒetiʀ] (2) **1** *vt peuple* to subjugate. **~ qn à une règle** to subject sb to a rule. **2 s'~** *vpr*: **s'~ à qch** to submit to sth. ♦ **assujetti, e** *adj peuple* subjugated. **~ à** *règle, taxe* subject to. ♦ **assujettissant, e** *adj* demanding, exacting. ♦ **assujettissement** *nm* (*contrainte*) constraint; (*dépendance*) subjection. **~ à l'impôt** tax liability.

assumer [asyme] (1) *vt* **(a)** (*prendre*) *responsabilité, commandement, fonction* to take on, assume; *poste* to take up. **(b)** (*remplir*) *poste* to hold; *rôle* to fulfil. **(c)** (*accepter*) *conséquence* to accept.

assurance [asyʀɑ̃s] *nf* **(a)** (*confiance*) self-confidence, (self-)assurance. **avoir de l'~** to be self-confident *ou* (self-)assured. **(b)** (*garantie*) assurance. **veuillez agréer l'~ de ma considération distinguée** ≃ yours faithfully. **(c)** (*contrat*) insurance (policy); (*firme*) insurance company. (*métier*) **les ~s** insurance; **~ au tiers/tous risques** third party/comprehensive insurance; **~ sur la vie** life insurance; **être aux ~s sociales** ≃ to be in the National Insurance scheme.

assuré, e [asyʀe] **1** *adj réussite, situation* certain, assured; *air, voix* assured, confident; *main, pas* steady. **mal ~** unsteady; **tenir pour ~ que** to be confident that; **~ du succès** sure of success. **2** *nm,f* policyholder. **~ social** ≃ member of the National Insurance scheme.

assurément [asyʀemɑ̃] *adv* assuredly, most certainly.

assurer [asyʀe] (1) **1** *vt* **(a) ~ à qn que** to assure sb that; **~ que** to affirm *ou* contend that; **je vous assure!** I assure you!; **~ qn de** *amitié etc* to assure sb of. **(b)** (*Fin*) *maison, personne* to insure (*contre* against). **~ qn sur la vie** to insure sb's life. **(c)** *surveillance* to maintain; *service, ravitaillement, soins* to provide; *travaux* to carry out. **~ la protection de** to protect; **~ la liaison entre** to link. **(d)** *bonheur, succès, paix* to ensure; *fortune, situation* to secure. **(e)** *pas, prise* to steady; (*Alpinisme*) to belay. **2 s'~** *vpr* **(a) s'~ que/de qch** to make sure that/of sth, check that/sth. **(b)** (*Fin, fig*) to insure o.s. (*contre* against). **s'~ sur la vie** to insure one's life. **(c)** *aide, victoire* to secure, ensure; *revenu* to ensure o.s. **(d)** (*s'affermir*) to steady o.s. (*sur* on); (*Alpinisme*) to belay o.s.

assureur [asyʀœʀ] *nm* (*agent*) insurance agent; (*société*) insurance company.

astérisque [asteʀisk(ə)] *nm* asterisk.

asthmatique [asmatik] *adj, nmf* asthmatic. ♦ **asthme** *nm* asthma.

asticot [astiko] *nm* (*gén*) maggot; (*: *type*) guy*.

asticoter* [astikɔte] (1) *vt* to needle*.

astiquer [astike] (1) *vt* to polish.

astre [astʀ(ə)] *nm* star. ♦ **astral, e,** *mpl* **-aux** *adj* astral.

astreindre [astʀɛ̃dʀ(ə)] (49) **1** *vt*: **~ qn à faire** to compel *ou* force sb to do; **~ qn à un travail** to force a task upon sb. **2 s'~** *vpr*: **s'~ à (faire) qch** to force *ou* compel o.s. to do sth. ♦ **astreignant, e** [astʀɛɲɑ̃, ɑ̃t] *adj* exacting, demanding. ♦ **astreinte** *nf* constraint.

astringent, e [astʀɛ̃ʒɑ̃, ɑ̃t] *adj, nm* astringent.

astrologie [astʀɔlɔʒi] *nf* astrology. ♦ **astrologique** *adj* astrological. ♦ **astrologue** *nm* astrologer.

astronaute [astʀɔnot] *nmf* astronaut. ♦ **astronautique** *nf* astronautics (*sg*).

astronome [astʀɔnɔm] *nm* astronomer. ♦ **astronomie** *nf* astronomy. ♦ **astronomique** *adj* (*lit, fig*) astronomical.

astuce [astys] *nf* (*adresse*) shrewdness, astuteness, cleverness; (*truc*) trick; (*) (*jeu de mot*) pun; (*plaisanterie*) wisecrack*. **il a beaucoup d'~** he is very shrewd *ou* astute. ♦ **astucieusement** *adv* cleverly, astutely. ♦ **astucieux, -ieuse** *adj* shrewd, astute, clever.

asymétrique [asimetʀik] *adj* asymmetrical.

atavique [atavik] *adj* atavistic. ♦ **atavisme** *nm* atavism.

atelier [atəlje] *nm [artisan]* workshop; *[artiste]* studio; *[couturières]* workroom; *[usine]* workshop.

atemporel, -elle [atɑ̃pɔʀɛl] *adj vérité* timeless.

atermoyer [atɛʀmwaje] (8) *vi* to procrastinate. ♦ **atermoiement** *nm*: **~(s)** procrastination.

athée [ate] **1** *adj* atheistic. **2** *nmf* atheist. ♦ **athéisme** *nm* atheism.

athlète [atlɛt] *nmf* athlete. ♦ **athlétique** *adj* athletic. ♦ **athlétisme** *nm* athletics (*sg*).

atlantique [atlɑ̃tik] **1** *adj* Atlantic. **2** *nm*: **l'A~** the Atlantic.

atlas [atlɑs] *nm* (*livre, Anat*) atlas.

atmosphère [atmɔsfɛʀ] *nf* (*lit, fig*) atmosphere. ♦ **atmosphérique** *adj* atmospheric.
atoll [atɔl] *nm* atoll.
atome [atom] *nm* atom. ♦ **atomique** *adj* atomic. ♦ **atomiste** *nmf* atomic scientist.
atomiseur [atɔmizœʀ] *nm* (*gén*) spray; *[parfum]* atomizer.
atone [atɔn] *adj être* lifeless; *regard* expressionless; (*Ling*) unstressed.
atours [atuʀ] *nmpl* (†, *hum*) attire, finery.
atout [atu] *nm* **(a)** (*Cartes*) trump. ~ **cœur** hearts are trumps. **(b)** (*fig*) (*avantage*) asset; (*carte maîtresse*) trump card.
âtre [ɑtʀ(ə)] *nm* hearth.
atroce [atʀɔs] *adj crime* atrocious, heinous; *douleur* excruciating; *mort, sort* dreadful, terrible; *spectacle, goût, temps* ghastly, atrocious, dreadful. ♦ **atrocement** *adv souffrir* atrociously, horribly; *chanter* dreadfully, terribly. ♦ **atrocité** *nf* (*caractère*) atrocity, atrociousness; (*acte*) atrocity. **dire des** ~**s sur qn** to say atrocious things about sb.
atrophie [atʀɔfi] *nf* atrophy. ♦ **atrophier** (7) *vt*, **s'**~ *vpr* to atrophy.
attabler (s') [atable] (1) *vpr* to sit down at (the) table. **les clients attablés** the seated customers.
attachant, e [ataʃɑ̃, ɑ̃t] *adj* engaging.
attache [ataʃ] *nf [ficelle]* (piece of) string; *[métal]* clip, fastener; *[cuir]* strap. (*Anat*) ~**s** wrists and ankles; (*connaissances*) ~**s** ties, connections; **à l'**~ *animal* tethered; (*fig*) *personne* tied; *bateau* moored.
attacher [ataʃe] (1) **1** *vt* **(a)** *animal, plante, paquet* to tie up; (*ensemble*) to tie together; *volets* to fasten; *papiers* to attach. ~ **qch/qn à** to tie sth/sb to; **attachés avec une épingle** pinned together; ~ **son nom à une découverte** to put one's name to a discovery; **la ficelle qui attachait le paquet** the string that was round the parcel. **(b)** *robe, ceinture* to do up, fasten; *lacets* to do up, tie; *bouton* to do up. (*Aviat*) **attachez votre ceinture** fasten your seatbelt. **(c)** (*fig*) *importance, valeur* to attach (*à* to). ~ **son regard sur** to fix one's eyes on; ~ **qn à son service** to take sb on, engage sb; **ce qui l'attache à elle** what makes him feel attached to her, what keeps him with her; **être attaché à qn/qch** to be attached to sb/sth.
2 s'~ *vpr [robe]* to do up, fasten (up) (*avec, par* with). **s'**~ **à son siège** to fasten o.s. in one's seat; **s'**~ **à qn** to become attached to sb. ♦ **attaché** *nm* (*Pol, Presse*) attaché; (*Admin*) assistant. ♦ **attachement** *nm* attachment (*à* to).
attaquant, e [atakɑ̃, ɑ̃t] *nm,f* (*Mil, Sport*) attacker; (*Ftbl*) striker, forward.
attaque [atak] *nf* **(a)** (*Mil, fig*) attack. **passer à l'**~ to move into the attack. **(b)** (*Méd*) (*gén*) attack; *[épilepsie]* fit (*de* of). **avoir une** ~ (*cardiaque*) to have a heart attack, have a stroke. **(c)** (*) **d'**~ on form; **il n'est pas d'**~ he's a bit off form; **être assez d'**~ **pour faire** to feel up to doing.
attaquer [atake] (1) **1** *vt* **(a)** *pays, abus, métal* to attack; *passant* to attack, assault. ~ **(qn) par surprise** to make a surprise attack (on sb); ~ **qn en justice** to bring an action against sb. **(b)** *difficulté, chapitre* to tackle; *discours* to launch upon; (*Mus*) *morceau* to strike up; *note* to attack. **il attaqua les hors-d'œuvre*** he tucked into* the hors d'œuvres. **2 s'**~ *vpr*: **s'**~ **à** *personne, mal* to attack; *problème* to tackle.
attarder [ataʀde] (1) **1** *vt* to make late. **2 s'**~ *vpr* (*gén*) to linger. **s'**~ **chez des amis** to stay on at friends'; **s'**~ **derrière les autres** to lag behind the others; **s'**~ **à des détails** to linger over *ou* dwell on details. ♦ **attardé, e** *adj* (*Psych*) backward; (*en retard*) late; (*démodé*) old-fashioned.
atteindre [atɛ̃dʀ(ə)] (49) **1** *vt* **(a)** *lieu, objectif, objet haut placé* to reach. **cette tour atteint 30 mètres** this tower is 30 metres high; ~ **son but** to reach one's goal, achieve one's aim. **(b)** (*contacter*) to get in touch with, contact. **(c)** *[pierre, tireur]* to hit (*à* in); *[maladie, reproches]* to affect; *[malheur]* to strike. **il a été atteint dans son orgueil** his pride has been hurt. **2** ~ **à** *vt indir perfection* to attain, achieve. ♦ **atteint, e**[1] *adj* **(a)** (*malade*) **être** ~ **de** to be suffering from; **gravement** ~ *poumon* badly affected; *malade* seriously ill. **(b)** (*: *fou*) touched*. ♦ **atteinte**[2] *nf* **(a)** (*préjudice*) attack (*à* on). **porter** ~ **à** to undermine. **(b)** (*Méd*) attack (*de* of). **les premières** ~**s du mal** the first effects of the illness.
atteler [atle] (4) *vt cheval, charrette* to hitch up (*à* to); *wagons* to couple. **s'**~ **à** *tâche* to get down to. ♦ **attelage** *nm [chevaux, bœufs]* team.
attenant, e [atnɑ̃, ɑ̃t] *adj*: ~ **(à)** adjoining.
attendre [atɑ̃dʀ(ə)] (41) **1** *vt* **(a)** *[personne]* to wait for. **nous attendons qu'il vienne** we are waiting for him to come; ~ **la fin/un autre moment** to wait until the end/until another time; ~ **qn au train** to meet sb off the train; ~ **qch/de faire qch avec impatience** to look forward eagerly to sth/to doing sth. **(b)** *[voiture]* to be waiting for; *[maison, dîner]* to be ready for; *[surprise, gloire]* to be in store for, await. **(c)** (*sans objet*) to wait. **attendez voir*** let's see *ou* think; **attendez un peu** wait a second; (*iro*) **tu peux toujours** ~**!** you've got a hope!; **ces fruits ne peuvent pas** ~ this fruit won't keep. **(d) faire** ~ **qn** to keep sb waiting; **se faire** ~ *[personne]* to keep people waiting; *[événement]* to be a long time coming. **(e)** (*escompter*) to expect. ~ **qch de qn** to expect sth from sb; **j'attendais mieux de lui** I expected him to do better *ou* better of him. **(f)** ~ **son tour** to wait one's turn; ~ **un enfant** to be expecting a baby; **il attend son heure!** he's biding his time; **il m'attendait au tournant*** he waited for the chance to catch me out; **en attendant** (*pendant ce temps*) in the meantime; (*en dépit de cela*) all the same; **il a pris froid en attendant** he caught cold while (he was) waiting.
2 ~ **après*** *vt indir* to be waiting for; (*avoir besoin*) to be in a hurry for. **je n'attends pas après lui!** I can get along without him!
3 s'~ *vpr*: **s'**~ **à qch** to expect sth (*de* from); **est-ce que tu t'attends à ce qu'il écrive?** do you expect him to write?
attendrir [atɑ̃dʀiʀ] (2) **1** *vt viande* to tenderize; *personne* to move (to pity); *cœur* to soften. **se laisser** ~ **par** to be moved by. **2 s'**~ *vpr* to be moved (*sur* by). **s'**~ **sur qn** to feel sorry for sb. ♦ **attendri, e** *adj* tender. ♦ **attendrissant, e** *adj* moving, touching. ♦ **attendrissement** *nm* (*tendre*) emotion; (*apitoyé*) pity.
attendu, e [atɑ̃dy] **1** *adj* (*espéré*) long-awaited; (*prévu*) expected. **2** *prép* given, considering (*que* that).
attentat [atɑ̃ta] *nm* murder attempt; (*Pol*) assassination attempt; (*contre un bâtiment*) attack (*contre* on). ~ **à la bombe** bomb attack; ~ **aux droits** violation of rights; ~ **aux mœurs** offence against public decency.
attente [atɑ̃t] *nf* **(a)** wait. **dans l'**~ **des résultats** while waiting for the results; **dans l'**~ **de vos nouvelles** looking forward to hearing from you. **(b)** (*espoir*) expectation.
attenter [atɑ̃te] (1) *vi*: ~ **à** *vie* to make an attempt on; *droits* to violate; *sûreté nationale* to conspire against.
attentif, -ive [atɑ̃tif, iv] *adj personne, air* attentive; *travail* careful; *examen* careful, close. **être** ~ **à tout ce qui se passe** to pay attention to all that goes on; ~ **à ses devoirs** heedful of one's duty. ♦ **attentivement** *adv lire* attentively, carefully; *examiner* carefully, closely.
attention [atɑ̃sjɔ̃] *nf* **(a)** (*gén*) attention; (*soin*) care. **avec** ~ *écouter* carefully, attentively; *examiner* carefully, closely; ~**!** watch!, mind!, careful!; ~ **à la marche** mind the step; ~ **à la pein-**

ture (caution) wet paint; **fais ~** (*prends garde*) be careful; (*écoute*) listen carefully; (*regarde*) watch carefully; **prêter ~ à qch/qn** to pay attention to sth/sb, take notice of sth/sb; **fais ~ (à ce) que la porte soit fermée** be sure *ou* make sure *ou* mind the door's shut. **(b)** (*prévenance*) attention. **~s** attentions, thoughtfulness. ♦ **attentionné, e** *adj* thoughtful, considerate (*pour* towards).

atténuer [atenɥe] (1) **1** *vt* ***douleur*** to ease; ***propos*** to tone down; ***faute, punition*** to mitigate; ***faits*** to water down; ***couleur, son, coup*** to soften. **2 s'~** *vpr* ***[douleur, bruit]*** to die down; ***[violence]*** to subside. ♦ **atténuation** *nf* easing; toning down; watering down; softening; (*Jur*) ***[peine]*** mitigation; dying down.

atterrer [ateʀe] (1) *vt* to dismay, appal. **son air atterré** his look of utter dismay.

atterrir [ateʀiʀ] (2) *vi* to land, touch down. **~ sur le ventre** to make a belly landing; **~ en prison*** to land up* in prison. ♦ **atterrissage** *nm* landing. **à l'~** at touchdown; **~ forcé** emergency *ou* forced landing.

attester [atɛste] (1) *vt* ***fait*** to testify to. **~ (de) l'innocence de qn** to testify to *ou* vouch for sb's innocence; (*littér*) **j'atteste les dieux que ...** I call the gods to witness that ... . ♦ **attestation** *nf* **(a)** ***[fait]*** attestation. **(b)** (*document*) certificate.

attiédir [atjediʀ] (2) **1** *vt* ***eau*** to make lukewarm; ***climat*** to make more temperate; ***désir*** to cool. **2 s'~** *vpr* to become lukewarm; to become more temperate; to cool down.

attifer* [atife] (1) **1** *vt* (*habiller*) to get up*. **2 s'~** *vpr* to get o.s. up* (*de* in).

attiger* [atiʒe] (3) *vi* to go a bit far*.

attirail* [atiʀaj] *nm* gear, paraphernalia.

attirer [atiʀe] (1) *vt* **(a)** (*gén, Phys*) to attract; (*en appâtant*) to lure, entice; ***foule*** to draw, attract. **il m'attira dans un coin** he drew me into a corner; **être attiré par** to be attracted *ou* drawn to; **~ l'attention de qn sur qch** to draw sb's attention to sth; **ça attire le regard** it catches the eye; **elle attire les hommes** she appeals to *ou* attracts men. **(b)** ***colère*** to bring down (*sur* on); ***sympathie*** to win, gain. **s'~ des ennemis** to make enemies for o.s.; **tu vas t'~ des ennuis** you're going to cause trouble for yourself *ou* bring trouble upon yourself. ♦ **attirance** *nf* attraction (*pour* for). ♦ **attirant, e** *adj* attractive, appealing.

attiser [atize] (1) *vt* ***feu*** to poke (up); (*fig*) to stir up.

attitré, e [atitʀe] *adj* (*habituel*) regular, usual; (*agréé*) accredited.

attitude [atityd] *nf* (*maintien*) bearing; (*comportement*) attitude; (*affectation*) attitude, façade.

attraction [atʀaksjɔ̃] *nf* (*gén*) attraction. (*cirque etc*) **~s** programme of attractions *ou* entertainments.

attrait [atʀɛ] *nm* appeal, attraction. **~s** attractions; **ses romans ont pour moi beaucoup d'~** his novels appeal to me very much; **éprouver de l'~ pour qch** to find sth attractive *ou* appealing.

attraper [atʀape] (1) *vt* **(a)** (*gén*) to catch; (** fig*) to get; (*fig: saisir*) ***crayon, mots, accent*** to pick up. **~ qn à faire qch** to catch sb doing sth; **tu vas ~ froid** you'll catch cold; **la grippe s'attrape facilement** flu is very catching. **(b)** (*gronder*) to tell off*. **se faire ~ (par qn)** to get a telling off (from sb)*. **(c)** (*tromper*) to take in. **tu as été bien attrapé** (*trompé*) you were had all right*; (*surpris*) that startled you! ♦ **attrapade*** *nf* telling off*. ♦ **attrape** *nf* (*farce*) trick. ♦ **attrape-nigaud***, *pl* **~-~(s)** *nm* con*.

attrayant, e [atʀɛjɑ̃, ɑ̃t] *adj* (*gén*) attractive; ***idée*** appealing; ***lecture*** pleasant. **peu ~** unattractive, unappealing.

attribuer [atʀibɥe] (1) *vt* **(a)** ***prix*** to award; ***avantages*** to grant; ***rôle, part*** to allocate (*à* to). **s'~ le meilleur rôle** to give o.s. the best role. **(b)** ***pensée, échec*** to attribute, ascribe (*à* to). **(c)** ***invention, mérite*** to attribute (*à* to); ***intérêt*** to find (*à* in); ***importance*** to attach (*à* to). **s'~ tout le mérite** to claim all the merit for o.s. ♦ **attribuable** *adj* attributable (*à* to). ♦ **attribut** *nm* attribute. **(nom/adjectif) ~** predicative noun/adjective. ♦ **attribution** *nf* awarding; allocation; attribution.

attrister [atʀiste] (1) **1** *vt* to sadden. **2 s'~** *vpr* to be saddened (*de* by) *ou* be grieved (*de* at, *de voir que* at seeing that).

attrouper (s') [atʀupe] (1) *vpr* to gather (together), form a crowd. ♦ **attroupement** *nm* crowd, mob (*péj*).

au [o] *V* **à.**

aubade [obad] *nf* dawn serenade.

aubaine [obɛn] *nf* godsend; (*financière*) windfall. **profiter de l'~** to make the most of the opportunity.

aube [ob] *nf* **(a)** (*lit*) dawn, daybreak; (*fig*) dawn. **(b)** (*Rel*) alb. **(c)** ***[bateau]*** paddle; ***[moulin, turbine]*** vane. **roue à ~s** paddle wheel.

aubépine [obepin] *nf* hawthorn.

auberge [obɛʀʒ(ə)] *nf* inn. **~ de (la) jeunesse** youth hostel. ♦ **aubergiste** *nmf* innkeeper, landlord (*ou* lady).

aubergine [obɛʀʒin] **1** *nf* (*légume*) aubergine, eggplant. **2** *adj inv* aubergine(-coloured).

aucun, e [okœ̃, yn] **1** *adj* (*nég*) no, not any; (*positif*) any. **il n'a ~e preuve** he has no proof, he hasn't any proof; **sans faire ~ bruit** without making a noise *ou* any noise; **il lit plus qu'~ autre enfant** he reads more than any other child. **2** *pron* (*nég*) none; (*positif*) any (one). **il n'aime ~ de ces films** he doesn't like any of these films; **~ de ses enfants** none of his children; **pensez-vous qu'~ ait compris?** do you think anyone *ou* anybody understood?; **d'~s** some. ♦ **aucunement** *adv* in no way, not in the least.

audace [odas] *nf* (*témérité*) boldness, audacity; (*originalité*) daring; (*effronterie*) audacity; (*geste osé*) daring gesture; (*innovation*) daring idea. **avoir l'~ de** to have the audacity to, dare to. ♦ **audacieusement** *adv* daringly; boldly; audaciously. ♦ **audacieux, -ieuse** *adj* daring; bold; audacious.

au-deçà, au-dedans *etc V* **deçà, dedans** *etc.*

audible [odibl(ə)] *adj* audible. ♦ **audibilité** *nf* audibility.

audience [odjɑ̃s] *nf* (*entretien*) audience; (*Jur*) hearing. (*fig*) **ce projet eut beaucoup d'~** this project aroused much interest.

audio-visuel, -elle [odjɔvizɥɛl] **1** *adj* audio-visual. **2** *nm* audio-visual methods.

auditeur, -trice [oditœʀ, tʀis] *nm,f* (*gén, Rad*) listener. **les ~s** the audience. ♦ **auditif, -ive** *adj* auditory.

audition [odisjɔ̃] *nf* **(a)** (*Mus*) (*essai*) audition; (*récital*) recital; ***[disque]*** hearing. **(b)** (*ouïe*) hearing. (*Jur*) **procéder à l'~ d'un témoin** to examine a witness. ♦ **auditionner** (1) *vti* to audition. ♦ **auditoire** *nm* audience. ♦ **auditorium** *nm* (*Rad*) public studio.

auge [oʒ] *nf* trough.

augmenter [ɔgmɑ̃te] (1) **1** *vt* (*gén*) to increase, raise; ***collection*** to enlarge, extend; ***revenus*** to supplement (*en faisant* by doing). **~ les prix de 10%** to increase *ou* raise *ou* put up prices by 10%; **~ qn (de 50 F)** to increase sb's salary (by 50 francs), give sb a (50-franc) rise. **2** *vi* (*gén*) to increase; ***[prix]*** to rise, go up; ***[production, inquiétude]*** to grow. **~ de poids** to increase in weight. ♦ **augmentation** *nf* (*action*) increasing, raising (*de* of); (*résultat*) increase, rise (*de* in).

augure [ɔgyʀ] *nm* **(a)** (*devin*) (*Hist*) augur; (*fig hum*) oracle. **(b)** (*présage*) omen; (*Hist*) augury. **de bon/mauvais ~** of good/ill omen. ♦ **augurer** (1) *vt* to foresee (*de* from). **cela augure bien/mal de la suite** that augurs well/ill for what is to follow.

auguste [ɔgyst(ə)] *adj personnage* august; *geste* noble, majestic.

aujourd'hui [oʒuʀdɥi] *adv* today; (*de nos jours*) nowadays, today. **je le ferai dès ~** I'll do it this very day.

au(l)ne [on] *nm* alder.

aumône [ɔmon] *nf* alms. **vivre d'~(s)** to live on charity; **faire l'~** to give alms (*à* to); (*fig*) **faire l'~ d'un sourire à qn** to favour sb with a smile. ♦ **aumônerie** *nf* chaplaincy. ♦ **aumônier** *nm* chaplain.

auparavant [opaʀavɑ̃] *adv* (*d'abord*) before, first. (*avant*) **2 mois ~** 2 months before *ou* previously.

auprès [opʀɛ] **1** *prép*: **~ de** (*près de*) next to, close to, by; (*avec*) *malade, ami* with; (*comparé à*) compared with, in comparison with; (*dans l'opinion de*) in the view *ou* opinion of. **avoir de l'influence ~ de qn** to have a lot of influence on sb; **faire une demande ~ de qn** to apply to sb; **ambassadeur ~ de** ambassador to. **2** *adv* nearby.

auquel [okɛl] *V* **lequel.**

auréole [ɔʀeɔl] *nf* (*Art, Astron*) halo; (*tache*) ring. **l'~ du martyre** the crown of martyrdom. ♦ **auréoler** (1) *vt* (*glorifier*) to glorify. **être auréolé de prestige** to have an aura of prestige.

auriculaire [ɔʀikylɛʀ] **1** *nm* little finger. **2** *adj* auricular.

aurore [ɔʀɔʀ] *nf* dawn, daybreak; (*fig*) dawn. **à l'~** at dawn; **~ boréale** northern lights.

ausculter [ɔskylte] (1) *vt* to auscultate. ♦ **auscultation** *nf* auscultation.

auspices [ɔspis] *nmpl* (*Antiq, fig*) auspices. **sous de mauvais ~** under unfavourable auspices.

aussi [osi] **1** *adv* **(a)** (*également*) too, also. **je suis fatigué et eux ~** I'm tired and so are they *ou* and they are too; **il parle l'italien et ~ l'anglais** he speaks Italian and English too *ou* as well; **faites bon voyage – vous ~** have a good journey – you too *ou* the same to you. **(b)** (*comparaison*) **~ grand** *etc* **que** as tall *etc* as; **pas ~ souvent** *etc* **que** not so *ou* as often *etc* as. **(c)** (*si*) so. **je ne te savais pas ~ bête** I didn't think you were so stupid; **comment peut-on laisser passer une ~ bonne occasion?** how can one let slip such a good opportunity?; **~ léger qu'il fût** light though he was. **(d)** (*tout autant*) **ça m'a fait ~ mal** it hurt me just as much; **tu peux ~ bien dire non** you can just as easily *ou* well say no; **~ sec*** on the spot*. **2** *conj* (*en conséquence*) therefore, consequently.

aussitôt [osito] **1** *adv* straight away, immediately. **~ arrivé** as soon as he arrived; **~ dit, ~ fait** no sooner said than done; **~ après** straight *ou* immediately after; **~ que je le vis** as soon as I saw him. **2** *prép*: **~ mon arrivée** immediately on my arrival, as soon as I arrived.

austère [ɔstɛʀ] *adj personne, vie* austere; *livre* dry; *manteau* severely cut. ♦ **austèrement** *adv* austerely. ♦ **austérité** *nf* austerity; dryness.

austral, e, *mpl* **~s** [ɔstʀal] *adj* southern.

Australie [ɔstʀali] *nf* Australia. ♦ **australien, -ienne** *adj*, **A~(ne)** *nm(f)* Australian.

autant [otɑ̃] *adv* **(a) ~ de** (*quantité*) as much (*que* as); (*nombre*) as many (*que* as); **nous sommes ~ qu'eux** there are as many of us as of them; **elle mange deux fois ~ que lui** she eats twice as much as him *ou* as he does. **(b)** (*intensité*) as much (*que* as). **il peut crier ~ qu'il veut** he can scream as much as he likes; **courageux ~ que compétent** as courageous as he is competent. **(c)** (*tant*) **~ de** *succès, eau* so much, such; *personnes, bijoux* so many, such a lot of; **pourquoi travaille-t-il ~?** why does he work so much *ou* so hard? **(d)** (*avec en*) **je ne peux pas en dire/faire ~** I can't say/do as much *ou* the same. **(e)** (*avec de*) **ce sera augmenté d'~** it will be increased accordingly *ou* in proportion; **c'est d'~ plus dangereux qu'il n'y a pas de parapet** it's all the more dangerous since *ou* because there is no parapet; **nous le voyons d'~ moins qu'il habite très loin** we see him even less since *ou* because he lives a long way away. **(f) ~ il est généreux, ~ elle est avare** he is as generous as she is miserly; **~ que possible** as much *ou* as far as possible; **(pour) ~ que je sache** as far as I know, to the best of my knowledge; **c'est ~ de gagné** at least that's something; **~ dire qu'il est fou** you might as well say that he's mad; **il ne vous remerciera pas pour ~** for all that you won't get any thanks from him; **tous ~ que vous êtes** the whole lot of you; **~ prévenir la police** it would be as well to inform the police.

autarcie [otaʀsi] *nf* autarky.

autel [ɔtɛl] *nm* (*Rel, lit, fig*) altar. **conduire sa fille à l'~** to give one's daughter away in marriage; **dresser un ~ à qn** to worship sb.

auteur [otœʀ] *nm* (*gén*) author; *[opéra]* composer; *[tableau]* painter. **l'~ de l'accident** the person who caused the accident; **qui est l'~ de cette affiche?** who designed this poster?; (*Mus*) **~-compositeur** composer-songwriter; (*femme de lettres*) **c'est un ~ connu** she is a well-known author *ou* authoress.

authenticité [otɑ̃tisite] *nf* authenticity. ♦ **authentifier** (7) *vt* to authenticate. ♦ **authentique** *adj* authentic. ♦ **authentiquement** *adv* authentically.

auto [ɔto] **1** *nf* (*voiture*) car, automobile (*US*). **~s tamponneuses** dodgems. **2** *adj inv* car. **3** *préf* **(a)** self-. **~discipline/défense/portrait** self-discipline/defence/portrait; **s'~gérer** to be self-managing; **~-intoxication/suggestion** auto-intoxication/suggestion; **~-allumage** pre-ignition. **(b)** (*automobile*) car. **~(-)radio** car radio.

autobiographie [ɔtɔbjɔgʀafi] *nf* autobiography. ♦ **autobiographique** *adj* autobiographic(al).

autobus [ɔtɔbys] *nm* bus.

autocar [ɔtɔkaʀ] *nm* coach, bus (*US*).

autochtone [ɔtɔktɔn] *adj, nmf* native.

autoclave [ɔtɔklav] *nm* autoclave.

autocollant, e [ɔtɔkɔlɑ̃, ɑ̃t] **1** *adj* self-adhesive. **2** *nm* sticker.

autocrate [ɔtɔkʀat] *nm* autocrat. ♦ **autocratie** *nf* autocracy. ♦ **autocratique** *adj* autocratic.

autocuiseur [ɔtɔkɥizœʀ] *nm* pressure cooker.

autodafé [ɔtɔdafe] *nm* auto-da-fé.

autodidacte [ɔtɔdidakt(ə)] *adj* self-taught.

autodrome [ɔtɔdʀom] *nm* motor-racing track.

auto-école [ɔtɔekɔl] *nf* driving school.

autographe [ɔtɔgʀaf] *adj, nm* autograph.

automate [ɔtɔmat] *nm* (*lit, fig*) automaton.

automation [ɔtɔmɑsjɔ̃] *nf* automation.

automatique [ɔtɔmatik] **1** *adj* automatic. **2** *nm* (*Téléc*) ≃ subscriber trunk dialling, direct dialing (*US*); (*revolver*) automatic. ♦ **automatiquement** *adv* automatically. ♦ **automatisation** *nf* automation. ♦ **automatiser** (1) *vt* to automate. ♦ **automatisme** *nm* automatism.

automitrailleuse [ɔtɔmitʀɑjøz] *nf* armoured car.

automne [ɔtɔn] *nm* autumn, fall (*US*). ♦ **automnal, e,** *mpl* **-aux** *adj* autumnal.

automobile [ɔtɔmɔbil] **1** *adj véhicule, sport* motor; *assurance, industrie* motor, car, automobile (*US*). **2** *nf* motor car, automobile (*US*). **l'~** the car industry; (*Sport*) **l'~** motoring; **termes d'~** motoring terms. ♦ **automobiliste** *nmf* motorist.

autonome [ɔtɔnɔm] *adj* autonomous; *territoire* self-governed. ♦ **autonomie** *nf* autonomy; self-government; (*Aut, Aviat*) range. ♦ **autonomiste** *nmf* (*Pol*) autonomist.

autopsie [ɔtɔpsi] *nf* autopsy, post-mortem (examination). ♦ **autopsier** (7) *vt* to carry out an autopsy on.

autorail [ɔtɔʀɑj] *nm* railcar.
autoriser [ɔtɔʀize] (1) **1** *vt manifestation* to give permission for, authorize; *craintes* to justify. ~ **qn** to give sb permission *ou* allow sb (*à faire* to do); **ça autorise à croire que ...** that leads one to think that ...; **se croire autorisé à dire que ...** to feel one is entitled to say that ...; **loi qui autorise les abus** law which admits of abuses. **2 s'~** *vpr*: **s'~ de qch pour faire** to use sth as an excuse to do. ♦ **autorisation** *nf* permission (*de qch* for sth, *de faire* to do); (*permis*) permit. ♦ **autorisé, e** *adj agent, version* authorized; *opinion* authoritative. **milieux ~s** official circles.
autorité [ɔtɔʀite] *nf* (*pouvoir*) authority (*sur* over); (*expert*) authority. **avoir ~ pour faire** to have authority to do; (*Admin*) **l'~, les ~s** the authorities; **agent de l'~** representative of authority; **d'~** *ton* authoritative; *prendre* unhesitatingly; **de sa propre ~** on one's own authority; **faire ~** to be authoritative. ♦ **autoritaire** *adj, nmf* authoritarian. ♦ **autoritairement** *adv* in an authoritarian way. ♦ **autoritarisme** *nm* authoritarianism.
autoroute [ɔtɔʀut] *nf* motorway, highway (*US*). ♦ **autoroutier, -ière** *adj* motorway.
autosatisfaction [ɔtɔsatisfaksjɔ̃] *nf* self-satisfaction.
auto-stop [ɔtɔstɔp] *nm* hitch-hiking. **faire de l'~** to hitch-hike; **prendre qn en ~** to pick up sb, give a lift to sb. ♦ **auto-stoppeur, -euse** *nm,f* hitch-hiker.
autour [otuʀ] **1** *adv* around, round. **maison avec un jardin ~** house with a garden round it.
2 *prép*: **~ de** around, (round) about; **regarde ~ de toi** look around *ou* about you.
autre [otʀ(ə)] **1** *adj indéf* **(a)** (*différent*) other, different. **c'est une ~ question** that's another *ou* a different question; **parlons d'~ chose** let's talk about something else *ou* different; **revenez une ~ fois** come back some other *ou* another time. **(b)** (*supplémentaire*) other. **elle a 2 ~s enfants** she has 2 other *ou* 2 more children; **donnez-moi un ~ kilo** give me another kilo. **(c)** (*opposé*) other. **de l'~ côté de la rue** on the other *ou* opposite side of the street. **(d) et vous ~s qu'en pensez-vous?** what do you people think?; **nous ~ Français** we Frenchmen; **j'ai d'~s chats à fouetter** I've other fish to fry; **~ chose, Madame?** anything *ou* something else, madam?; **ce n'est pas ~ chose que de la jalousie** that's nothing but jealousy; **~ part** somewhere else; **d'~ part** (*par contre*) on the other hand; (*de plus*) moreover; **c'est une ~ paire de manches*** that's another story; (*Rel*) **l'~ monde** the next world.
2 *pron indéf* **(a)** (*qui est différent*) **un ~** another (one); **d'~s** others; **personne d'~** no one else, nobody else; **prendre une chose pour une ~** to take sth for sth else; **je n'en veux pas d'~** I don't want any other; **à d'~s!*** tell that to the marines!*; **il n'en fait jamais d'~s!** that's just typical of him; **un ~ que moi** anyone else but me; **il en a vu d'~s!** he's seen worse!; **les deux ~s** the other two, the two others; **X,Y,Z, et ~s** X,Y,Z etc. **(b)** (*supplémentaire*) **donnez m'en un ~** give me another (one) *ou* one more; **qui/rien d'~** who/nothing else. **(c)** (*opposition*) **l'~** the other (one); **les ~s** the others; **d'une minute à l'~** any minute.
autrefois [otʀəfwa] *adv* in the past. **d'~** of the past, of old, past; **~ je préférais le vin** in the past I used to prefer wine.
autrement [otʀəmɑ̃] *adv* **(a)** (*différemment*) differently. **il ne peut en être ~** it can't be any other way; **agir ~ que d'habitude** to act differently from usual; **comment aller à Londres ~ que par le train?** how can we get to London other than by train?; **~ appelé** otherwise known as; **faire qch ~** to do sth another way *ou* differently; **on ne peut pas faire ~** it's impossible to do otherwise *ou* to do anything else; **il n'a pas pu faire ~ que de me voir** he couldn't help seeing me; **~ dit** in other words. **(b)** (*sinon*) otherwise, or else; (*à part cela*) otherwise, apart from that. **cela ne m'a pas ~ surpris** that didn't particularly surprise me. **(c)** (*comparatif*) **~ bon/intelligent** far better/more intelligent (*que* than).
Autriche [otʀiʃ] *nf* Austria. ♦ **autrichien, -ienne** *adj*, **A~(ne)** *nm(f)* Austrian.
autruche [otʀyʃ] *nf* ostrich. (*fig*) **faire l'~** to bury one's head in the sand.
autrui [otʀɥi] *pron* others.
auvent [ovɑ̃] *nm* canopy.
aux [o] *V* **à.**
auxiliaire [ɔksiljɛʀ] **1** *adj* (*Ling, Mil, gén*) auxiliary; *cause* secondary, subsidiary; (*Scol*) assistant. **bureau ~** sub-office. **2** *nmf* (*assistant*) assistant. **~ médical** medical auxiliary. **3** *nm* (*Gram, Mil*) auxiliary.
auxquels [okɛl] *V* **lequel.**
avachir (s') [avaʃiʀ] (2) *vpr [cuir]* to become limp; *[vêtement]* to become shapeless; *[personne]* (*physiquement*) to become limp; (*moralement*) to get slack. **avachi sur son pupitre** slumped on his desk. ♦ **avachissement** *nm* loss of shape; limpness; slackness.
aval[1] [aval] *nm [cours d'eau]* downstream water; *[pente]* downhill slope. **en ~** downstream; downhill (*de* from).
aval[2], *pl* **~s** [aval] *nm* (*fig: soutien*) backing, support; (*Comm, Jur*) guarantee.
avalanche [avalɑ̃ʃ] *nf [neige, documents]* avalanche; *[compliments]* flood.
avaler [avale] (1) *vt repas, mensonge, affront* to swallow; *roman* to devour. *[fumeur]* **~ la fumée** to inhale; **~ à petites gorgées** to sip; **il a avalé de travers** sth went down the wrong way; **il n'a rien avalé depuis 2 jours*** he hasn't eaten a thing for 2 days; **ambitieux qui veut tout ~** ambitious man who thinks he can take on anything; **~ ses mots** to mumble; **tu as avalé ta langue?** have you lost your tongue?; **on dirait qu'il a avalé son parapluie** he's so stiff and starchy.
avaliser [avalize] (1) *vt plan* to back, support; (*Comm, Jur*) to guarantee.
avance [avɑ̃s] *nf* **(a)** (*marche*) advance. **accélérer/ralentir son ~** to speed up/slow down one's advance. **(b)** (*sur concurrent etc*) lead. **avoir de l'~ sur qn** to have a lead over sb; **10 minutes d'~** a 10 minute lead. **(c) avoir de l'~ (sur l'horaire)/dans son travail** to be ahead of schedule/ahead in one's work; **avoir 10 minutes d'~** *[train]* to be 10 minutes early *ou* ahead of schedule; *[montre]* to be 10 minutes fast; **le train a perdu son ~** the train has lost the time it had gained; **ma montre prend de l'~** my watch is gaining *ou* gains; **en ~** (*sur l'heure fixée*) early; (*sur l'horaire etc*) ahead of schedule; (*dans les études*) ahead (*sur qn* of sb); **dépêche-toi, tu n'es pas en ~!** hurry up you're running out of time!; **en ~ pour son âge** advanced for his age; **en ~ sur son temps** ahead of *ou* in advance of one's time; **à l'~, d'~** in advance, beforehand. **(d) ~ (de fonds)** advance; **~ à l'allumage** ignition advance; **~s** (*ouvertures*) overtures; (*galantes*) advances.
avancé, e[1] [avɑ̃se] *adj* **(a)** *élève, technique, idée,* (*Mil*) *poste* advanced. **la saison était ~e** it was late in the season; **à une heure ~e de la nuit** late at night; **son roman est déjà assez ~** he's already quite far ahead with his novel; **d'un âge ~** well on in years; **dans un état ~ de ...** in an advanced state of ...; **il n'en est pas plus ~** he's no further on than he was; (*iro*) **nous voilà bien ~s!*** a long way that's got us! **(b)** *fruit, fromage* overripe. **ce poisson est ~** this fish is going off.
avancée[2] [avɑ̃se] *nf* overhang.
avancement [avɑ̃smɑ̃] *nm* (*promotion*) promo-

tion; (*progrès*) *[travaux]* progress; *[sciences]* advancement.
avancer [avɑ̃se] (3) **1** *vt* **(a)** *objet* to move *ou* bring forward; *tête* to move forward; *main* to hold out, put out (*vers* to); *pendule* to put forward; *hypothèse* to put forward, advance; *date, départ* to bring forward. **(b)** (*faire progresser*) *travail* to speed up. **si cela peut vous ~** if it speeds things up (for you) *ou* helps you; **ça n'avance pas nos affaires** that doesn't improve matters for us; **cela ne t'avancera à rien de crier*** you won't get anywhere by shouting. **(c)** *argent* to advance; (*: *prêter*) to lend.
2 *vi* **(a)** to move forward; *[armée, procession]* to advance (*sur* on). **~ d'un pas** to move *ou* take a step forward; **faire ~ qn** to make sb move on. **(b)** (*fig*), *[travail]* to make progress; *[nuit]* to be wearing on. **faire ~** *travail* to speed up; *élève* to bring on; *science* to further; **~ lentement dans son travail** to make slow progress in one's work; **~ en grade** to be promoted, get promotion; **tout cela n'avance à rien** that doesn't get us any further *ou* anywhere. **(c)** *[montre]* **~ de 10 minutes par jour** to gain 10 minutes a day; **j'avance de 10 minutes** I'm 10 minutes fast. **(d)** *[cap, promontoire]* to project, jut out (*dans* into); *[lèvre, menton]* to protrude.
3 s'~ *vpr* to move forward; *[procession]* to advance; (*fig: s'engager*) to commit o.s. **il s'avança vers nous** he came towards us.
avanie [avani] *nf* snub. **faire des ~s à qn** to snub sb.
avant [avɑ̃] **1** *prép* **(a)** (*temps, lieu*) before. **~ de partir** *ou* **que je (ne) parte** before leaving, before I leave; **pas ~ 10 heures/une demi-heure** not until *ou* before 10/for another half hour; **j'étais ~ lui dans la queue** I was in front of him *ou* before him in the queue; **il me le faut ~ demain/un mois** I must have it by *ou* before tomorrow/within a month; **~ peu** shortly; **X, ce féministe bien ~ la lettre X,** a feminist long before the term existed *ou* had been coined. **(b)** (*priorité*) before. **~ tout** above all; **le travail passe ~ tout** work comes before everything; **en classe, elle est ~ sa sœur** at school she is ahead of her sister.
2 *adv* **(a)** (*d'abord*) before, beforehand; (*autrefois*) before. **quelques mois ~** a few months before *ou* previously *ou* earlier; **la semaine d'~** the week before, the previous week; **fort ~ dans la nuit** far into the night; **réfléchis ~** think first; **le train d'~ était plein** the previous train was full. **(b)** (*espace*) **aller plus ~/trop ~** (*lit, fig*) to go further (forward)/too far; **être assez ~ dans ses recherches** to be quite far ahead in one's research; **en ~** (*mouvement*) forward; (*position*) in front, ahead (*de* of); **en ~, marche!** forward march!; (*Naut*) **en ~ toute!** full steam ahead!; (*fig*) **regarder en ~** to look ahead; (*fig*) **mettre qch en ~** to put sth forward; (*fig*) **mettre qn en ~** (*pour se couvrir*) to use sb as a front; (*fig*) **il aime se mettre en ~** he likes to push himself forward.
3 *nm [voiture, train]* front; *[navire]* bow, stem; (*Sport: joueur*) forward; (*Mil*) front. **à l'~ (du train)** in the front of the train; (*fig*) **aller de l'~** to forge ahead.
4 *adj inv roue* front; *marche* forward. **traction ~** front-wheel drive; **la partie ~** the front part.
5 *préf inv* (*le second élément prend la marque du pluriel et donne le genre*) **~-bras** forearm; **~-centre** centre-forward; **~-coureur** *adj* precursory, premonitory; **signe ~-coureur** forerunner; **~-dernier** *adj* last but one; **~-garde** (*Mil*) vanguard; (*Art, Pol*) avant-garde; **d'~-garde** avant-garde; **~-goût** foretaste; **~-guerre** prewar years; **d'~-guerre** pre-war; **~-hier** the day before yesterday; **~-port** outer harbour; **~-poste** outpost; **~-première** preview; **~-projet** pilot study; **~-propos** foreword; **~-scène** (*scène*) apron; (*loge*) box; **~-train** *[animal]* forequarters; **l'~-veille** two days before *ou* previously; **l'~-veille de** two days before.
avantage [avɑ̃taʒ] *nm* **(a)** (*gén*) advantage. **avoir l'~** to have the advantage; **j'ai ~ à l'acheter** it's worth my while to buy it; **tirer ~ de la situation** to take advantage of the situation, turn the situation to one's advantage; **tu aurais ~ à te tenir tranquille*** you'd do well to keep quiet; **ils ont l'~ du nombre** they have the advantage of numbers (*sur* over). **(b)** (*Fin: gain*) benefit. **~s en nature** benefits in kind. **(c)** (*plaisir*) pleasure. **que me vaut l'~ de votre visite?** to what do I owe the pleasure of your visit? **(d) être à son ~** (*photo*) to look one's best; (*conversation*) to be at one's best; **se montrer à son ~** to show o.s. off to advantage; **c'est (tout) à ton ~** it's (entirely) to your advantage; **changer à son ~** to change for the better. ♦ **avantager** (3) *vt* (*donner un avantage à*) to favour, give an advantage to; (*mettre en valeur*) to flatter. ♦ **avantageusement** *adv vendre* at a good price; *décrire* favourably, flatteringly. ♦ **avantageux, -euse** *adj* **(a)** *affaire* worthwhile, profitable; *prix* attractive. **(b)** (*présomptueux*) conceited. **(c)** *portrait* flattering.
avare [avaʀ] **1** *adj* miserly. **~ de** *paroles, compliments* sparing of. **2** *nmf* miser. ♦ **avarice** *nf* miserliness, avarice. ♦ **avaricieux, -ieuse** *adj* miserly.
avarie [avaʀi] *nf*: **~(s)** damage.
avarier (s') [avaʀje] (7) *vpr* to go bad, rot. **viande avariée** rotting meat.
avatar [avataʀ] *nm* (*Rel*) avatar; (*fig*) metamorphosis. (*péripéties*) **~s*** misadventures.
avec [avɛk] **1** *prép* **(a)** (*gén*) with. **couteau ~ (un) manche en bois** knife with a wooden handle, wooden-handled knife; **ragoût fait ~ des restes** stew made out of *ou* from (the) left-overs; **c'est fait ~ du plomb** it's made of lead. **(b)** (*relations*) *combattre* with; *se comporter* with, towards. **doux/gentil ~ qn** gentle with/kind to sb; **se marier ~ qn** to marry sb; **son mariage ~ X** her marriage to X; **ils ont les syndicats ~ eux** they've got the unions on their side *ou* behind them. **(c)** (*cause etc*) with. **~ le temps** in the course of time, with the passing of time; **~ l'inflation et le prix de l'essence** what with inflation and the price of petrol; **~ toute ma bonne volonté** with the best will in the world; **ils sont partis ~ la pluie** they left in the rain. **(d) d'~** from; **séparer qch d'~ qch d'autre** to separate sth from sth else. **(e)** (*dans un magasin*) **et ~ ça?** is there anything else?; **il conduit mal et ~ ça il conduit trop vite** he drives badly and what's more he drives too fast; **~ cela que tu ne le savais pas!** as if you didn't know!; **~ tout ça j'ai oublié le pain** in the midst of all this I forgot about the bread.
2 *adv* (*) **tiens mes gants, je ne peux pas conduire ~** hold my gloves, I can't drive with them on.
aven [avɛn] *nm* swallow hole.
avenant, e [avnɑ̃, ɑ̃t] **1** *adj* pleasant. **2** *nm* **(a) à l'~** in keeping (*de* with). **(b)** *[contrat]* endorsement.
avènement [avɛnmɑ̃] *nm [roi]* accession (*à* to); *[régime, idée]* advent; *[Messie]* Advent, Coming.
avenir [avniʀ] *nm* (*gén*) future; (*postérité*) future generations. **dans un proche ~** in the near future; **à l'~** from now on, in future; **il a de l'~, c'est un homme d'~** he's a man with a future *ou* with good prospects.
Avent [avɑ̃] *nm*: **l'~** Advent.
aventure [avɑ̃tyʀ] *nf* (*péripétie*) adventure; (*entreprise*) venture; (*amoureuse*) affair; (*malencontreuse*) experience. **film d'~s** adventure film; **l'~** adventure; **marcher à l'~** to walk aimlessly; **si, par ~ *ou* d'~** if by any chance. ♦ **aventuré, e** *adj* risky. ♦ **aventurer** (1) **1** *vt*

somme, vie to risk; *remarque* to venture. **2 s'~** *vpr* to venture (*dans* into, *sur* onto). **s'~ à faire qch** to venture to do sth, risk doing sth. ♦ **aventureusement** *adv* adventurously, riskily. ♦ **aventureux, -euse** *adj personne, vie* adventurous; *projet* risky. ♦ **aventurier, -ière** *nm,f* adventurer, adventuress.

avenue [avny] *nf* avenue.

avérer (s') [aveʀe] (6) *vpr*: **il s'avère que** it turns out that; **cela s'avéra efficace** it proved (to be) *ou* turned out to be effective; **il est avéré que** it is a known *ou* recognised fact that.

averse [avɛʀs(ə)] *nf* (*lit, fig*) shower. **forte ~** heavy shower, downpour.

aversion [avɛʀsjɔ̃] *nf* aversion (*pour* to), loathing (*pour* for). **avoir en ~** to loathe.

avertir [avɛʀtiʀ] (2) *vt* (*mettre en garde*) to warn; (*renseigner*) to inform (*de qch* of sth). ♦ **averti, e** *adj public* informed, mature; *expert* well-informed (*de* about). **~ de** *problèmes etc* aware of. ♦ **avertissement** *nm* (*gén*) warning; (*Scol*) admonition. (*préface*) **~ (au lecteur)** foreword. ♦ **avertisseur, -euse 1** *adj* warning. **2** *nm* (*Aut*) horn. **~ (d'incendie)** (fire) alarm.

aveu, *pl* **~x** [avø] *nm*: **~x** confession, admission. **passer aux ~x** to make a confession; **de l'~ de qn** according to sb; **sans ~** *homme* disreputable; **sans l'~ de qn** without sb's consent.

aveugle [avœgl(ə)] **1** *adj* (*gén*) blind. **devenir ~** to go blind; **~ d'un œil** blind in one eye; **son amour le rend ~** he is blinded by love; **une confiance ~** an implicit trust; **être ~ aux défauts de qn** to be blind to sb's faults. **2** *nmf* blind man (*ou* woman). **les ~s** the blind; **faire qch en ~** to do sth blindly. ♦ **aveuglant, e** *adj* blinding, dazzling. ♦ **aveuglement** *nm* blindness. ♦ **aveuglément** *adv* (*lit, fig*) blindly. ♦ **aveugler** (1) *vt* (*lit, fig*) to blind; (*éblouir*) to dazzle, blind. **s'~ sur qn** to be blind to sb's defects. ♦ **aveuglette** *nf*: **à l'~** *décider* in the dark, blindly; **avancer à l'~** to grope (one's way) along.

aviation [avjɑsjɔ̃] *nf* (*Mil*) air force. **l'~** (*sport, métier*) flying; (*secteur*) aviation; (*transport*) air travel; **d'~** *coupe* flying; *usine* aircraft; *base* air; **~ de chasse** fighter force. ♦ **aviateur, -trice** *nm,f* aviator, pilot.

aviculture [avikyltyʀ] *nf* (*volailles*) poultry farming. ♦ **avicole** *adj* poultry. ♦ **aviculteur, -trice** *nm,f* poultry farmer.

avide [avid] *adj* (*cupidité*) greedy; *lecteur* avid, eager (*de qch* for sth). ♦ **avidement** *adv* eagerly; greedily; avidly. ♦ **avidité** *nf* eagerness; greed; avidity (*de* for).

avilir [aviliʀ] (2) **1** *vt* to degrade. **2 s'~** *vpr* to degrade o.s. ♦ **avilissant, e** *adj* degrading. ♦ **avilissement** *nm* degradation.

aviné, e [avine] *adj* inebriated.

avion [avjɔ̃] *nm* aeroplane, plane, airplane (*US*), aircraft (*pl inv*). (*sport*) **l'~** flying; **aller à Paris en ~** to go to Paris by air *ou* by plane, fly to Paris; **par ~** by air(mail); **~-cargo** (air) freighter, cargo aircraft; **~ de chasse** fighter (plane); **~ de ligne** airliner; **~ à réaction** jet (plane); **~-taxi** taxi-plane.

aviron [aviʀɔ̃] *nm* (*rame*) oar; (*sport*) rowing. **faire de l'~** to row.

avis [avi] *nm* **(a)** (*gén, Admin*) opinion. **donner son ~** to give one's opinion *ou* view (*sur* on, about); **les ~ sont partagés** opinion is divided; **être de l'~ de qn** to be of the same opinion as sb; **à mon ~** in my opinion, to my mind; **il était d'~ de partir** he thought *ou* was of the opinion that we should leave. **(b)** (*conseil*) advice. **un ~ amical** a friendly piece of advice, some friendly advice. **(c)** (*notification*) notice; (*Fin*) advice. **~ de crédit** credit advice; **jusqu'à nouvel ~** until further notice; **sauf ~ contraire** unless otherwise informed; (*sur étiquette*) unless otherwise indicated; **~ au lecteur** foreword; **~ au public** notice to the public.

aviser [avize] (1) **1** *vt* **(a)** (*avertir*) to advise, inform (*de* of), notify (*de* of, about). **(b)** (*apercevoir*) to catch sight of, notice. **2** *vi* to decide what to do. **~ au nécessaire** to see to the necessary, do what is necessary. **3 s'~** *vpr*: **s'~ de qch** to realize sth suddenly; **s'~ de faire qch** to take it into one's head to do sth. ♦ **avisé, e** *adj* sensible, wise. **bien/mal ~** well-/ill-advised.

avitaminose [avitaminoz] *nf* vitamin deficiency.

aviver [avive] (1) **1** *vt douleur, appétit* to sharpen; *chagrin* to deepen; *désir* to arouse, excite; *colère* to stir up; *regard, couleur* to brighten; *feu, souvenirs* to revive, stir up. **2 s'~** *vpr* to sharpen; to deepen; to be aroused; to be stirred up; to be excited; to brighten; to revive.

avocat, e [avɔka, at] **1** *nm,f* (*Jur: fonction*) barrister, attorney(-at-law) (*US*); (*fig*) advocate. **consulter son ~** to consult one's lawyer; **l'accusé et son ~** the accused and his counsel; **l'~ de la défense/de la partie civile** the counsel for the defence/the plaintiff; (*Rel, fig*) **l'~ du diable** the devil's advocate; **~ général** counsel for the prosecution; **se faire l'~ de qch** to advocate sth; **fais toi mon ~ auprès de lui** plead with him on my behalf.

2 *nm* (*fruit*) avocado (pear).

avoine [avwan] *nf* oats.

avoir [avwaʀ] (34) **1** *vt* **(a)** (*gén*) to have; (*recevoir, atteindre*) to get; (*porter*) *vêtements* to have on, wear. **il n'a pas d'argent** he has no money, he hasn't got any money; **essayez de m'~ Paris (au téléphone)** could you put me through to Paris; **on les aura!** we'll get them!; **il a les mains qui tremblent** his hands are shaking. **(b)** *âge, formes, couleur* to be. **ils ont le même âge** they are the same age; **~ 3 mètres de haut** to be 3 metres high; **ça a une jolie forme** it is a nice shape. **(c)** (*éprouver*) *joie, chagrin* to feel; *intérêt* to show. **~ faim/honte** to be *ou* feel hungry/ashamed; **~ le sentiment que** to have the feeling that; **qu'est-ce qu'il a?** what's the matter with him?; **qu'est-ce qu'il a à pleurer?** what's he crying for? **(d)** *geste, remarque* to make; *rire* to give; *cri* to utter. **(e)** (*: *duper*) to take in, con*. **se faire ~** to be had*, be taken in. **(f) en ~ après*** *ou* **contre qn*** to be mad at* *ou* cross with sb; **en ~ pour son argent** to have *ou* get one's money's worth; **j'en ai pour 10 F** it costs me 10 francs; **tu en as pour combien de temps?** how long are you going to be *ou* will it take you?; **en ~ assez*** *ou* **plein le dos*** to be fed up* (*de qch* with sth); **on en a encore pour 2 km/2 heures** it goes on for another 2 km/2 hours.

2 *vb aux* **(a)** (*avec ptp*) **dis-moi si tu l'as/l'avais vu** tell me if you have/had seen him; **je l'ai vu hier** I saw him yesterday; **il a dû trop manger** he must have eaten too much; **nous aurons terminé demain** we shall have finished tomorrow. **(b)** (+ *infin: devoir*) **~ qch à faire** to have sth to do; **j'ai à travailler** I have to work, I must work; **il n'a pas à se plaindre** he can't complain; **vous n'avez pas à vous en soucier** you needn't worry about it; **vous n'avez qu'à lui écrire** just write to him, you need only write to him; **tu n'avais qu'à ne pas y aller** you shouldn't have gone in the first place; **s'il n'est pas content, il n'a qu'à partir** if he doesn't like it, he can just go. **(c) ils ont eu leurs carreaux cassés** they had their windows broken; **vous aurez votre robe nettoyée** your dress will be cleaned.

3 *vb impers* **(a) il y a** (*avec sg*) there is; (*avec pl*) there are; **il y avait beaucoup d'eau/de gens** there was a lot of water/were a lot of people; **il n'y avait que moi** I was the only one; **il y avait une fois** ... once upon a time, there was ...; **il y en a, je vous jure!*** some people, honestly!*; **il n'y a pas de quoi** don't mention it; **qu'y a-t-il?** what's the matter?; **il**

y a que nous sommes mécontents* we're annoyed, that's what*; **il n'y a que lui pour faire cela!** only he would do that!; **il n'y a pas à dire*, il est très intelligent** there's no denying he's very intelligent; **il doit y ~ une raison** there must be a reason; **il n'y a qu'à les laisser partir** just let them go; **il n'y en a que pour mon petit frère, à la maison** my little brother gets all the attention at home. **(b)** (*temps écoulé*) **il y a 10 ans que je le connais** I have known him (for) 10 years; **il y a 10 ans, nous étions à Paris** 10 years ago we were in Paris. **(c)** (*distance*) **il y a 10 km d'ici à Paris** it is 10 km from here to Paris; **combien y a-t-il d'ici à Paris?** how far is it from here to Paris?

4 *nm* (*bien*) resources; (*Comm*) (*actif*) credit (side); (*billet de crédit*) credit note. (*Fin*) **~ fiscal** tax credit; **~s** holdings, assets.

avoisiner [avwazine] (1) *vt* (*lit, fig*) to border on. ♦ **avoisinant, e** *adj pays* neighbouring; *rue* nearby, neighbouring.

avorter [avɔʀte] (1) *vi* **(a)** **(se faire)** ~ to have an abortion; **faire ~ qn** *[personne]* to abort sb; *[remède etc]* to make sb abort. **(b)** (*fig*) to fail, come to nothing. **faire ~** to frustrate, wreck; **projet avorté** abortive plan. ♦ **avortement** *nm* (*Méd*) abortion; (*fig*) failure. ♦ **avorteur, -euse** *nm,f* abortionist. ♦ **avorton** *nm* (*péj: personne*) little runt (*péj*); (*arbre, animal*) puny specimen.

avouer [avwe] (1) **1** *vt amour* to confess; *fait* to admit; *faiblesse, crime* to admit to, confess to. **~ que** to admit *ou* confess that; **elle est douée, je l'avoue** she is gifted, I must admit. **2** *vi [coupable]* to confess, own up. (*fig*) **tu avoueras!** you must admit *ou* confess! **3 s'~** *vpr*: **s'~ coupable** to admit *ou* confess one's guilt; **s'~ vaincu** to admit defeat; **s'~ déçu** to admit to being disappointed. ♦ **avouable** *adj* respectable. **peu ~** disreputable. ♦ **avoué, e 1** *adj* avowed. **2** *nm* ≃ solicitor, attorney-at-law (*US*).

avril [avʀil] *nm* April. **en ~ ne te découvre pas d'un fil** ≃ never cast a clout till May is out; *V* **septembre.**

axe [aks(ə)] *nm* (*Tech*) axle; (*Sci, Math*) axis; (*route*) trunk *ou* main road; (*fig*) *[politique]* main line. **être dans l'~** to be on the same line (*de* as); **mets-toi dans l'~ de la cible** get directly in line with the target. ♦ **axer** (1) *vt*: **~ qch sur/autour de** to centre sth on/round. ♦ **axial, e,** *mpl* **-iaux** *adj* axial.

axiome [aksjom] *nm* axiom. ♦ **axiomatique 1** *adj* axiomatic. **2** *nf* axiomatics (*sg*).

axis [aksis] *nm* axis (vertebra).

ayant droit, *pl* **ayants droit** [ɛjɑ̃dʀwa] *nm* (*Jur*) assignee; *[prestation]* eligible party.

azalée [azale] *nf* azalea.

azimut [azimyt] *nm* azimuth. **dans tous les ~s*** all over the place.

azote [azɔt] *nf* nitrogen. ♦ **azoté, e** *adj* nitrogenous.

aztèque [aztɛk] *adj*, **A~** *nmf* Aztec.

azur [azyʀ] *nm* (*couleur*) azure; (*ciel*) sky. ♦ **azuré, e** *adj* azure. ♦ **azurer** (1) *vt* to tinge with blue.

azyme [azim] *adj* unleavened.

B

B, b [be] *nm* (*lettre*) B, b.
baba [baba] 1 *nm*: ~ **au rhum** rum baba. 2 *adj inv*: **en être** ~ * to be flabbergasted* *ou* dumbfounded.
babiller [babije] (1) *vi [personne]* to prattle, chatter; *[bébé]* to babble; *[oiseau]* to twitter. ♦ **babillage** *nm* babble; prattle; twitter; chatter.
babines [babin] *nfpl* (*Zool, fig*) chops.
babiole [babjɔl] *nf* (*bibelot*) trinket; (*fig: vétille*) triviality; (*petit cadeau*) token gift.
bâbord [babɔʀ] *nm* port side.
babouche [babuʃ] *nf* Turkish slipper.
babouin [babwɛ̃] *nm* baboon.
bac [bak] *nm* **(a)** *abrév de* **baccalauréat. (b)** (*bateau*) ferry, ferryboat. ~ **à voitures** car-ferry. **(c)** (*récipient*) tub; (*Ind*) tank, vat; (*Peinture, Phot*) tray; *[évier]* sink. ~ **à glace** ice-tray; ~ **à légumes** vegetable compartment.
baccalauréat [bakalɔʀea] *nm* baccalaureat, ≃ G.C.E. A-levels. ~ **en droit** ≃ degree of Bachelor of Laws.
bacchantes* [bakɑ̃t] *nfpl* moustache, whiskers*.
bâche [bɑʃ] *nf* canvas cover. ~ **goudronnée** tarpaulin. ♦ **bâcher** (1) *vt* to cover (with a canvas sheet *ou* a tarpaulin).
bachelier, -ière [baʃəlje, jɛʀ] *nm,f person who has passed the baccalauréat.*
bachot* [baʃo] *nm* = **baccalauréat.**
bachoter [baʃɔte] (1) *vi* to cram (for an exam). ♦ **bachotage** *nm* cramming.
bacille [basil] *nm* germ.
bâcler [bɑkle] (1) *vt devoir, ouvrage* to scamp; *cérémonie* to skip through. **c'est du travail bâclé** it's slapdash work.
bactérie [bakteʀi] *nf* bacterium. ♦ **bactérien, -ienne** *adj* bacterial. ♦ **bactériologie** *nf* bacteriology. ♦ **bactériologique** *adj* bacteriological. ♦ **bactériologiste** *nmf* bacteriologist.
badaud, e [bado, od] *nm,f* (*curieux*) curious onlooker; (*promeneur*) stroller.
baderne* [badɛʀn(ə)] *nf*: **(vieille)** ~ old fogey*.
badigeonner [badiʒɔne] (1) *vt intérieur* to distemper; *extérieur* to whitewash; (*en couleur*) to colourwash; (*péj*) to daub (*de* with); *gorge, plaie* to paint (*à, avec* with). ♦ **badigeon** *nm* distemper; whitewash.
badine [badin] *nf* switch.
badiner [badine] (1) *vi* (†: *plaisanter*) to jest†. **c'est qn qui ne badine pas** he's not a man to be trifled with; **il ne badine pas sur la discipline** he's a stickler for discipline; **et je ne badine pas!** I'm not joking! ♦ **badinage** *nm*: ~**(s)** banter, jesting talk.
baffe* [baf] *nf* slap, clout.
bafouer [bafwe] (1) *vt* to hold up to ridicule.
bafouiller [bafuje] (1) 1 *vi* to splutter, stammer. 2 *vt* to splutter (out), stammer (out). **qu'est-ce qu'il bafouille?** what's he babbling on about? ♦ **bafouilleur, -euse** *nm,f* splutterer, stammerer.
bâfrer‡ [bɑfʀe] (1) *vi* to guzzle, gobble.
bagage [bagaʒ] *nm* **(a)** (*valise*) bag, piece of luggage; (*Mil*) kit. ~**s** luggage, baggage; **faire/défaire ses** ~**s** to pack/unpack (one's luggage); ~**s accompagnés** registered luggage; ~**s à main** hand luggage. **(b)** (*diplômes*) qualifications. **son** ~ **intellectuel** his stock *ou* store of general knowledge. ♦ **bagagiste** *nm* baggage handler.
bagarre [bagaʀ] *nf* (*rixe*) fight, scuffle, brawl; (*dispute*) set-to, argument. **aimer la** ~ to love fighting *ou* a fight. ♦ **bagarrer*** (1) 1 *vi* (*lutter*) to fight. 2 **se** ~ *vpr* (*se battre*) to fight; (*se disputer*) to have a set-to. **ça s'est bagarré (dur)** there was (violent) rioting. ♦ **bagarreur, -euse*** 1 *adj caractère* aggressive. 2 *nm,f* fighter.
bagatelle [bagatɛl] *nf* (*objet*) trinket; (*petite somme*) small *ou* paltry sum; (*fig: vétille*) trifle. **perdre son temps à des** ~**s** to fritter away one's time.
bagne [baɲ] *nm* (*Hist*) (*prison*) penal colony; (*peine*) hard labour. (*fig*) **quel** ~**!*** what a grind!* ♦ **bagnard** *nm* convict.
bagnole* [baɲɔl] *nf* car, buggy‡. **vieille** ~ jalopy*.
bagou(t)* [bagu] *nm* volubility. **avoir du** ~ to have the gift of the gab.
bague [bag] *nf* (*bijou*) ring; *[cigare]* band; *[oiseau]* ring; (*Tech*) collar.
baguenauder (se)* [bagnode] (1) *vpr* (*faire un tour*) to go gallivanting about; (*traîner*) to mooch about*, trail around.
baguette [bagɛt] 1 *nf* **(a)** switch, stick. (*pour manger*) ~**s** chopsticks; ~ **de chef d'orchestre** conductor's baton; **sous la** ~ **de X** conducted by X; (*fig*) **mener qn à la** ~ to rule sb with an iron hand. **(b)** (*pain*) stick of French bread. 2: ~ **magique** magic wand; ~ **de sourcier** divining rod; ~ **de tambour** drumstick.
bah [ba] *excl* (*indifférence*) pooh!; (*doute*) really!
bahut [bay] *nm* **(a)** (*coffre*) chest; (*buffet*) sideboard. **(b)** (*arg Scol*) school.
bai, e[1] [bɛ] *adj cheval* bay.
baie[2] [bɛ] *nf* **(a)** (*Géog*) bay. **(b)** ~ **(vitrée)** picture window. **(c)** (*Bot*) berry.
baignade [bɛɲad] *nf* (*action*) bathing; (*bain*) bathe; (*lieu*) bathing place.
baigner [beɲe] (1) 1 *vt* **(a)** *bébé* to bath; *pieds, visage* to bathe. **visage baigné de larmes** face bathed in tears; **chemise baignée de sueur** shirt soaked with sweat, sweat-soaked shirt. **(b)** *[mer, rivière]* to wash, bathe; *[lumière]* to bathe. 2 *vi [linge, fruits]* to soak (*dans* in). ~ **dans son sang/la graisse** to lie in a pool of blood/grease; ~ **dans la brume/le mystère** to be shrouded *ou* wrapped in mist/mystery; (*fig*) **tout baigne dans l'huile*** everything's looking great*; **il baigne dans la joie** he is bursting with joy. 3 **se** ~ *vpr* (*mer*) to go bathing *ou* swimming; (*piscine*) to go swimming; (*baignoire*) to have a bath. ♦ **baigneur, -euse** 1 *nm,f* bather, swimmer. 2 *nm* (*jouet*) baby doll.
baignoire [bɛɲwaʀ] *nf* **(a)** bath(tub). ~ **sabot** ≃ hip-bath. **(b)** (*Théât*) ground floor box.
bail [baj], *pl* **baux** [bo] *nm* (*Jur*) lease. **prendre à** ~ to lease; **donner à** ~ to lease (out); (*fig*) **ça fait un** ~**!*** it's ages (*que* since).
bâiller [bɑje] (1) *vi [personne]* to yawn (*de* with); *[col, couture, soulier]* to gape; *[porte]* to be half-open. ~ **à s'en décrocher la mâchoire** to yawn one's head off. ♦ **bâillement** *nm* yawn.
bailleur, bailleresse [bajœʀ, bajʀɛs] *nm,f* lessor. ~ **de fonds** backer.
bâillon [bɑjɔ̃] *nm* (*lit, fig*) gag. ♦ **bâillonner** (1) *vt* to gag.

bain [bɛ̃] **1** *nm* **(a)** *[baignoire]* bath; *[piscine]* swim; *[mer]* bathe. **~ de boue/sang** mud/blood bath; **prendre un ~** to have a bath; to have a swim. **(b)** (*liquide*) bathwater; (*Chim, Phot*) bath. **(c)** (*récipient*) (*baignoire*) bath(tub); *[teinturier]* vat. **(d)** (*piscine*) **petit/grand ~** shallow/deep end; (*lieu*) **~s publics** public baths. **(e)** (*) **en avouant, il nous a tous mis dans le ~** by owning up he has got us all involved; **nous sommes tous dans le même ~** we're all in the same boat; **tu seras vite dans le ~** you'll soon get the hang of it*.

2: **prendre un ~ de foule** to mingle with the crowd, go on a walkabout; **j'ai pris un ~ de jouvence** it made me feel years younger; **faire chauffer au ~-marie** *sauce* to heat in a double boiler; *boîte de conserve* to immerse in boiling water; **~s de mer** sea bathing; **~ de mousse** bubble bath; **~ de pieds** (*récipient*) foot-bath; (*baignade*) paddle; **~ de siège** hipbath; **prendre un ~ de soleil** to sunbathe; **~s de soleil** sunbathing; **~ turc** Turkish bath; **~ de vapeur** steam bath.

baïonnette [bajɔnɛt] *nf* (*Élec, Mil*) bayonet. **~ au canon** with fixed bayonets.

baisemain [bɛzmɛ̃] *nm*: **il lui fit le ~** he kissed her hand.

baiser [beze] **1** *nm* kiss. (*fin de lettre*) **bons ~s** much love. **2** (1) *vt* **(a)** *main, visage* to kiss. **(b)** (**: avoir, l'emporter sur*) to outdo.

baisse [bɛs] *nf* (*gén*) fall, drop (*de* in). **être en ~** to be falling *ou* dropping; **~ sur le beurre** butter down in price *ou* reduced.

baisser [bese] (1) **1** *vt* **(a)** *main, bras, objet* to lower; *tête* to lower, bend; (*de chagrin, honte*) to hang (*de* in). **baisse la branche pour que je puisse l'attraper** pull the branch down so that I can reach it; **~ les yeux** to look down, lower one's eyes; **~ le nez dans son assiette*** to bow one's head over one's plate; (*fig*) **~ les bras** to give up; **~ pavillon** (*Naut*) to lower the flag; (*fig*) to show the white flag. **(b)** *chauffage, lampe, radio* to turn down; *voix* to lower. (*Aut*) **~ ses phares** to dip one's headlights; **baisse un peu le ton!*** pipe down!* **(c)** *prix* to bring down, reduce.

2 *vi* **(a)** (*gén*) to fall, drop; *[marée]* to go out, ebb; *[eaux]* to subside, go down; *[réserves, provisions]* to run *ou* get low; *[soleil]* to go down, sink. **il a baissé dans mon estime** he has sunk *ou* gone down in my estimation. **(b)** *[forces]* to fail; *[talent]* to decline. **le jour baisse** the light is failing; **il a beaucoup baissé ces derniers temps** he has got a lot weaker recently.

3 se ~ *vpr* (*pour ramasser*) to bend down, stoop; (*pour éviter*) to duck. **il n'y a qu'à se ~ pour les ramasser*** they are lying thick on the ground.

bajoues [baʒu] *nfpl* (*Zool*) chops; (*fig: joues*) heavy jowls.

bal, *pl* **~s** [bal] *nm* (*réunion*) dance; (*habillé*) ball; (*lieu*) dance hall. **aller au ~** to go dancing; **~ costumé/masqué** fancy dress/masked ball; **~ musette** popular dance (*to the accordion*).

balader* [balade] (1) **1** *vt* (*traîner*) to trail round; (*promener*) to take for a walk *ou* stroll. **2 se ~** *vpr* (*à pied*) to go for a walk *ou* stroll; (*en auto*) to go for a run; (*traîner*) to traipse round. **aller se ~ en Afrique** to go touring round Africa. ♦ **balade*** *nf* walk, stroll; run. **être en ~** to be out for a stroll (*ou* a run).

baladin† [baladɛ̃] *nm* wandering entertainer.

balafre [balafʀ(ə)] *nf* (*blessure*) gash; (*cicatrice*) scar. ♦ **balafrer** (1) *vt* to gash; to scar.

balai [balɛ] *nm* (*gén*) broom, brush; (*Élec*) brush; (*Aut*) *[essuie-glace]* blade. **passer le ~** to give the floor a sweep; **~-brosse** long-handled scrubbing brush; **~ mécanique** carpet sweeper.

balance [balɑ̃s] *nf* **(a)** (*gén*) pair of scales, scales; (*à bascule*) weighing machine; (*Chim, Phys*) balance. **(b)** **tenir la ~ égale entre** to hold the scales even between; **être en ~** *[proposition]* to hang in the balance; *[candidat]* to be under consideration; **mettre dans la ~ le pour et le contre** to weigh up the pros and cons; **il a mis toute son autorité dans la ~** he used his authority to tip the scales; **si on met dans la ~ son ancienneté** if you take his seniority into account. **(c)** (*Écon, Pol*) balance. **~ commerciale/des comptes/des forces** balance of trade/of payments/of power. **(d)** (*Astron*) **la B~** Libra. **(e)** (*Pêche*) drop-net.

balancer [balɑ̃se] (3) **1** *vt* **(a)** *chose, jambe* to swing; *branches, bateau, bébé* to rock; (*sur balançoire*) to swing. **(b)** (**: lancer*) to fling, chuck*. **(c)** (**: se débarrasser de*) *objet, employé* to chuck out*; *métier* to chuck up*. **(d)** (*équilibrer*) *compte, phrases, paquets* to balance. **tout bien balancé** everything considered. **2** *vi* **(a)** (†: *hésiter*) to waver. **(b)** (*osciller*) to swing. **3 se ~** *vpr [bras, jambes]* to swing; *[bateau]]* to rock; *[branches]* to sway; (*sur balançoire*) to swing; (*sur bascule*) to seesaw. **se ~ sur ses jambes** to sway from side to side; **ne te balance pas sur ta chaise!** don't tip back on your chair!; **je m'en balance*** I couldn't give a darn* (about it), I couldn't care less (about it). ♦ **balancé, e** *adj*: **bien ~** *phrase* nicely-balanced; (*) *personne* well-built. ♦ **balancement** *nm [corps]* sway; *[bras]* swinging; *[bateau]* rocking; *[hanches, branches]* swaying; (*Littérat, Mus*) balance. ♦ **balancier** *nm [pendule]* pendulum; *[équilibriste]* (balancing) pole. ♦ **balançoire** *nf (suspendue)* swing; (*sur pivot*) seesaw. **faire de la ~** to have a go on a swing (*ou* a seesaw).

balayer [baleje] (8) *vt* **(a)** *poussière* to sweep up; *pièce, trottoir* to sweep. **le vent balaie la plaine** the wind sweeps across the plain. **(b)** (*chasser*) *feuilles* to sweep away; *soucis, ennemi, objection* to sweep aside. **le gouvernement a été balayé** the government was swept out of office. **(c)** *[phares, tir]* to sweep (across); *[radar]* to scan. ♦ **balayage** *nm* sweeping; scanning. ♦ **balayette** *nf* small (hand)brush. ♦ **balayeur, -euse** *nm,f* roadsweeper.

balbutiement [balbysimɑ̃] *nm*: **~(s)** stammering, mumbling; *[bébé]* babbling; (*fig: débuts*) **~s** beginnings. ♦ **balbutier** (7) **1** *vi* to stammer, mumble. **2** *vt* to stammer *ou* falter out.

balcon [balkɔ̃] *nm* balcony. (*Théât*) **premier/deuxième ~** dress/upper circle.

baldaquin [baldakɛ̃] *nm* canopy.

Baléares [baleaʀ] *nfpl*: **les ~** the Balearic Islands.

baleine [balɛn] *nf* **(a)** whale. **(b)** *[corset]* stay; *[parapluie]* rib. ♦ **baleinier, -ière 1** *adj* whaling. **2** *nm* (*pêcheur, bateau*) whaler. **3** *nf* whaling boat.

balèze* [balɛz] *adj* (*musclé*) hefty*; (*doué*) great*.

balise [baliz] *nf* (*Naut, Aviat*) beacon. ♦ **balisage** *nm* **(a)** (*action*) beaconing; marking-out. **(b)** (*signaux*) beacons. ♦ **baliser** (1) *vt* to mark out with beacons.

balivernes [balivɛʀn] *nfpl* nonsense. **dire des ~s** to talk nonsense; **s'amuser à des ~s** to fool around.

ballade [balad] *nf* ballade.

ballant, e [balɑ̃, ɑ̃t] **1** *adj bras, jambes* dangling. **2** *nm* (*mou*) *[câble]* slack; *[chargement]* sway, roll. **avoir du ~** to be slack.

ballast [balast] *nm* (*Rail*) ballast; (*Naut*) ballast tank.

balle[1] [bal] *nf* **(a)** (*projectile*) bullet. **criblé de ~s** riddled with bullets. **(b)** (*Sport*) ball. **jouer à la ~** to play (with a) ball; **c'est une belle ~** that's a good shot; **faire des ~s** to have a knock-up; (*Tennis*) **~ de set** set point; (*fig*) **saisir la ~ au bond** to jump at the opportunity. **(c)** **~s*** francs.

balle[2] [bal] *nf* (*Agr, Bot*) husk, chaff; *[coton, laine]* bale; (*visage*) chubby face.

baller [bale] (1) *vi [bras, jambes]* to dangle, hang loosely; *[tête]* to hang; *[chargement]* to be slack *ou* loose.
ballerine [balRin] *nf* (*danseuse*) ballerina, ballet dancer; (*soulier*) ballet shoe.
ballet [balɛ] *nm* (*danse, spectacle, compagnie*) ballet; (*musique*) ballet music.
ballon [balɔ̃] *nm* **(a)** (*Sport*) ball. ~ **de football** football; (*fig*) le ~ **rond** soccer; le ~ **ovale** rugger. **(b)** ~ **(en baudruche)** (child's toy) balloon. **(c)** (*Aviat*) balloon. ~ **dirigeable** airship. **(d)** (*verre*) wineglass; (*contenu*) glass (of wine). **(e)** *[eau chaude]* tank; *[oxygène]* bottle.
ballonner [balɔne] (1) *vt ventre* to distend. **je suis ballonné** I feel bloated. ♦ **ballonnement** *nm*: ~**(s)** flatulence.
ballot [balo] *nm* **(a)** (*paquet*) bundle. **(b)** (*: *nigaud*) nitwit*. **c'est** ~ it's a bit daft*.
ballottage [balɔtaʒ] *nm*: **il y a** ~ there will have to be a second ballot.
ballotter [balɔte] (1) **1** *vi [objet]* to roll around, bang about; *[tête, membres]* to loll; *[poitrine]* to bounce; *[bateau]* to toss. **2** *vt personne* to shake about, jolt; *bateau* to toss. **ballotté entre 2 sentiments** torn between 2 feelings; **cet enfant a été ballotté entre plusieurs écoles** this child has been shifted around from school to school. ♦ **ballottement** *nm* banging about; rolling; lolling; bouncing; tossing, shaking.
balluchon [balyʃɔ̃] *nm* (†) bundle (of clothes). **faire son** ~* to pack up one's traps.
balnéaire [balneɛR] *adj* bathing.
balourd, e* [baluR, uRd(ə)] *nm,f* dolt, oaf. ♦ **balourdise** *nf* **(a)** (*manuelle*) clumsiness; (*manque de finesse*) doltishness. **(b)** (*gaffe*) blunder.
balte [balt] *adj pays, peuple* Baltic.
balustrade [balystRad] *nf* (*Archit*) balustrade; (*garde-fou*) railing.
bambin [bɑ̃bɛ̃] *nm* small child, little lad.
bambocher* [bɑ̃bɔʃe] (1) *vi* to live it up*, have a wild time. ♦ **bambocheur, -euse*** **1** *adj* revelling. **2** *nm,f* reveller.
bambou [bɑ̃bu] *nm* bamboo.
bamboula* [bɑ̃bula] *nf*: **faire la** ~ to live it up*, have a wild time.
ban [bɑ̃] *nm* **(a)** *[mariage]* ~s banns. **(b)** *[applaudissements]* round of applause. **un** ~ **pour X!** three cheers for X! **(c)** (*Hist*) proclamation. **(d) être au** ~ **de la société** to be outlawed from society; **le** ~ **et l'arrière-**~ **de** every last one of.
banal, e, *mpl* ~**s** [banal] *adj* (*gén*) banal; *idée* trite; *vie* humdrum; *personne* ordinary; *incident* (*courant*) commonplace; (*insignifiant*) trivial. **grippe** ~**e** common or garden case of flu; **peu** ~ unusual. ♦ **banalement** *adv* tritely; in a humdrum way. **tout** ~ simply. ♦ **banalité** *nf* **(a)** (*caractère*) banality; triteness; ordinariness; triviality. **(b)** (*propos*) truism, trite remark.
banaliser [banalize] (1) *vt* **(a)** *expression* to make trite; *vie* to rob of its originality. **(b)** *campus* to open to the police. **voiture banalisée** unmarked police vehicle. ♦ **banalisation** *nf* (*Univ*) opening to the police.
banane [banan] *nf* banana. ♦ **bananeraie** *nf* banana plantation. ♦ **bananier** *nm* (*arbre*) banana tree; (*bateau*) banana boat.
banc [bɑ̃] **1** *nm* **(a)** (*siège*) seat, bench. ~ **(d'école)** (desk) seat. **(b)** (*Géol*) (*couche*) layer; *[coraux]* reef. ~ **de sable/vase** sand/mudbank. **(c)** *[poissons]* shoal. **(d)** (*Tech*) (work)bench. **(e)** (*Mét*) bank, patch. **2:** ~ **des accusés** dock; ~ **des avocats** bar; ~ **d'église** pew; ~ **d'essai** (*Tech*) test bed; (*fig*) testing ground; (*Parl*) ~ **des ministres** government front bench.
bancaire [bɑ̃kɛR] *adj* banking. **chèque** ~ (bank) cheque.
bancal, e, *mpl* ~**s** [bɑ̃kal] *adj* **(a)** (*boiteux*) limping; (*jambes arquées*) bandy-legged. **(b)** *chaise* wobbly, rickety. **(c)** *idée* shaky.
bandage [bɑ̃daʒ] *nm* **(a)** (*objet*) bandage. ~ **herniaire** truss. **(b)** (*action*) bandaging.
bande[1] [bɑ̃d] **1** *nf* **(a)** (*tissu, métal*) band, strip; (*terre, papier*) strip; (*Ciné*) film; *[magnétophone, ordinateur]* tape; (*Presse*) wrapper; (*Méd*) bandage; (*Phys, Rad*) band. (*Mil*) ~ **(de mitrailleuse)** (ammunition) belt. **(b)** (*dessin, motif*) stripe; *[chaussée]* line. **(c)** (*Billard*) cushion. (*fig*) **par la** ~ in a roundabout way. **(d)** (*Naut*) list. **donner de la** ~ to list. **2:** ~ **dessinée** comic strip, strip cartoon; ~ **molletière** puttee; ~ **sonore** sound track; ~ **Velpeau** crêpe bandage.
bande[2] [bɑ̃d] *nf [gens]* band, group; *[oiseaux]* flock; *[animaux]* pack. **ils sont partis en** ~ they set off in a group; **toute une** ~ **d'amis** a whole crowd *ou* group of friends; **faire** ~ **à part** (*lit*) to make a separate group; (*fig*) to keep o.s. to o.s; ~ **d'imbéciles!** bunch *ou* pack of idiots!*
bandeau, *pl* ~**x** [bɑ̃do] *nm* (*ruban*) headband; (*pansement*) head bandage; (*pour les yeux*) blindfold. **avoir un** ~ **sur l'œil** to wear an eye patch; (*fig*) **avoir un** ~ **sur les yeux** to be blind (*fig*).
bandelette [bɑ̃dlɛt] *nf [momie]* wrapping, bandage.
bander [bɑ̃de] (1) *vt* **(a)** *plaie* to bandage. ~ **les yeux à qn** to blindfold sb; **les yeux bandés** blindfold(ed). **(b)** (*tendre*) to tense; *arc* to bend.
banderole [bɑ̃dRɔl] *nf* (*drapeau*) banderole. ~ **publicitaire** advertising streamer.
bandit [bɑ̃di] *nm* (*voleur*) gangster; (*brigand*) bandit; (*fig: escroc*) crook, shark*; (*: *enfant*) rascal. ~ **armé** gunman; ~ **de grand chemin** highwayman. ♦ **banditisme** *nm* crime.
bandoulière [bɑ̃duljɛR] *nf* shoulder strap. **en** ~ slung across the shoulder.
bang [bɑ̃g] *nm inv, excl* bang.
banjo [bɑ̃ʒo] *nm* banjo.
banlieue [bɑ̃ljø] *nf* suburbs. **proche/grande** ~ inner/outer suburbs; **de** ~ *maison* suburban; *train* commuter. ♦ **banlieusard, e** *nm,f* suburbanite.
bannière [banjɛR] *nf* banner; *[chemise]* shirt-tail.
bannir [baniR] (2) *vt* to banish (*de* from); *usage* to prohibit. ♦ **banni, e** *nm,f* exile. ♦ **bannissement** *nm* banishment.
banque [bɑ̃k] *nf* **(a)** (*établissement*) bank. **en** ~ in the bank; **la grande** ~ the big banks; ~ **d'affaires/du sang** commercial/blood bank. **(b)** (*activité*) banking. **(c)** (*Jeux*) bank. **tenir la** ~ to be (the) banker. ♦ **banquier** *nm* (*Fin, Jeux*) banker.
banqueroute [bɑ̃kRut] *nf* (*Fin, Pol*) bankruptcy; (*fig*) failure. **faire** ~ to go bankrupt.
banquet [bɑ̃kɛ] *nm* dinner; (*d'apparat*) banquet. ♦ **banqueter** (4) *vi* to banquet.
banquette [bɑ̃kɛt] *nf [train]* seat; *[auto, café]* (bench) seat.
banquise [bɑ̃kiz] *nf* ice field; (*flottante*) ice floe.
baptême [batɛm] **1** *nm* **(a)** (*sacrement*) baptism; (*cérémonie*) christening, baptism. **recevoir le** ~ to be baptized *ou* christened. **(b)** *[cloche]* blessing; *[navire]* christening. **2:** ~ **de l'air** first flight; ~ **du feu** baptism of fire.
baptiser [batize] (1) *vt* **(a)** (*Rel*) to baptize, christen. **(b)** *cloche* to bless; *navire* to christen. **(c)** (*appeler*) to call, christen, name; (*: *surnommer*) to dub. ♦ **baptismal, e,** *mpl* **-aux** *adj* baptismal. ♦ **baptisme** *nm* baptism. ♦ **baptiste** *nmf, adj* Baptist.
baquet [bakɛ] *nm* tub.
bar [baR] *nm* (*lieu*) bar; (*poisson*) bass.
baragouiner* [baRagwine] (1) *vt paroles* to gabble. **il baragouine un peu l'espagnol** he can speak a bit of Spanish; (*péj*) **qu'est-ce qu'il baragouine?** what's he gabbling on about?* ♦ **baragouin*** *nm* gibberish, double Dutch.
baraque [baRak] *nf* (*abri*) shed; (*boutique*) stall;

(*: *maison*) place*; (*péj: entreprise*) dump*.
baraqué, e* [baʀake] *adj*: **bien ~** well-built.
baraquement [baʀakmɑ̃] *nm*: **~(s)** group of huts; (*Mil*) camp.
baratin* [baʀatɛ̃] *nm* (*boniment*) sweet talk; (*verbiage*) chatter, hot air; (*Comm*) patter. **assez de ~!** cut the chat!* ♦ **baratiner*** (1) **1** *vt* to sweet-talk. **~ le client** to give a customer the patter. **2** *vi* (*bavarder*) to natter*. ♦ **baratineur, -euse*** *nm,f* (*beau parleur*) smooth talker; (*bavard*) gasbag‡.
baratte [baʀat] *nf [beurre]* churn.
barbant, e* [baʀbɑ̃, ɑ̃t] *adj* boring, deadly dull.
barbare [baʀbaʀ] **1** *adj invasion* barbarian; *crime* barbarous. **2** *nm* (*Hist, fig*) barbarian. ♦ **barbarement** *adv* barbarously. ♦ **barbarie** *nf* barbarism; (*cruauté*) barbarity. ♦ **barbarisme** *nm* (*Gram*) barbarism.
barbe [baʀb(ə)] **1** *nf* **(a)** (*Anat*) beard. **il a une ~ de 3 jours** he has 3 days' growth of beard; **sans ~** beardless. **(b)** (*aspérités*) **~s** *[papier]* ragged edge; *[métal]* jagged edge. **(c) à la ~ de qn** under sb's nose; **rire dans sa ~** to laugh up one's sleeve; **la ~!*** damn (it)!‡; **quelle ~!*** what a drag!*; **oh toi, la ~!*** oh shut up, you!* **2: B~ bleue** *nm* Bluebeard; **~ à papa** candy-floss.
barbecue [baʀbəkju] *nm* barbecue.
barbelé, e [baʀbəle] *adj, nm*: **(fil de fer) ~** barbed wire; **les ~s** the barbed wire (fence).
barber* [baʀbe] (1) *vt* to bore stiff*. **se ~** to be bored stiff* (*à faire* doing).
barbichette* [baʀbiʃɛt] *nf* goatee beard.
barbier† [baʀbje] *nm* barber.
barbiturique [baʀbityʀik] **1** *adj* barbituric. **2** *nm* barbiturate.
barbon [baʀbɔ̃] *nm* († *ou péj*) **(vieux) ~** old fogey*.
barboter [baʀbɔte] (1) **1** *vt* (*: *voler*) to pinch*, steal (*à* from). **2** *vi [canard, enfant]* to dabble, splash about; *[gaz]* to bubble.
barbouiller [baʀbuje] (1) *vt* **(a)** (*salir*) to smear (*de* with); (*péj: peindre*) to daub *ou* slap paint on. **il barbouille des toiles en amateur** he does a bit of painting as a hobby; **~ une feuille de dessins** to scribble drawings on a piece of paper. **(b)** (*) **~ l'estomac** to upset the stomach; **être barbouillé** to feel queasy. ♦ **barbouillage** *nm* (*peint*) daub; (*écrit*) scribble, scrawl. ♦ **barbouilleur, -euse** *nm,f* (*péj*) dauber; (*en bâtiment*) slapdash painter.
barbouze* [baʀbuz] *nf* **(a)** beard. **(b)** (*policier*) secret police agent; (*garde du corps*) bodyguard.
barbu, e [baʀby] *adj* bearded. **un ~** a man with a beard.
barda* [baʀda] *nm* gear; (*Mil*) kit.
barde [baʀd(ə)] **1** *nm* (*poète*) bard. **2** *nf* (*Culin*) bard.
barder [baʀde] (1) **1** *vt* **(a)** (*Culin*) to bard. **(b) bardé de fer** *cheval* barded; *soldat* armour-clad; *porte* with iron bars; **poitrine bardée de décorations** chest covered with medals; **être bardé (contre)** to be immune (to). **2** *vb impers* (*) **ça va ~** sparks are going to fly!
barème [baʀɛm] *nm* (*table*) table, list; (*tarif*) price list; (*Rail*) fare schedule; *[échelle]* scale.
baril [baʀi(l)] *nm* (*gén*) barrel; *[poudre]* keg; *[lessive]* drum.
barillet [baʀijɛ] *nm [revolver]* cylinder.
bariolé, e [baʀjɔle] *adj* gaily-coloured. ♦ **bariolure** *nf* gay colours.
baromètre [baʀɔmɛtʀ(ə)] *nm* barometer. **le ~ est au beau fixe/à la pluie** the barometer is set at fair/is pointing to rain. ♦ **barométrique** *adj* barometrical.
baron, -onne [baʀɔ̃, ɔn] *nm,f* baron; baroness.
baroque [baʀɔk] *adj idée* weird, wild; (*Art*) baroque.
baroud [baʀud] *nm*: **~ d'honneur** gallant last stand.
barque [baʀk(ə)] *nf* small boat.
barrage [baʀaʒ] *nm* **(a)** *[rivière]* dam; (*petit*) weir. **(b)** (*barrière*) barrier; (*Mil*) barrage. **~ de police** (police) roadblock; **faire ~ à** to stand in the way of.
barre [baʀ] **1** *nf* **(a)** (*gén*) bar; (*de fer, bois*) rod, bar; (*de savon*) cake, bar; (*Ftbl, Rugby*) crossbar; (*Danse*) barre. **(b)** (*Naut*) helm; (*petit*) tiller. (*lit, fig*) **être à la ~** to be at the helm. **(c)** (*Jur*) **~ du tribunal** bar; **~ (des témoins)** witness box; **comparaître à la ~** to appear as a witness. **(d)** (*houle*) (*gén*) race; (*à l'estuaire*) bore; (*banc de sable*) (sand) bar. **(e)** (*trait*) line; (*du t, f*) stroke. **mets une ~ à ton t** cross your t; (*Math*) **~ de fraction** fraction line. **2: ~ d'appui** (window) rail; **~ fixe** horizontal bar; (*Mus*) **~ de mesure** bar line; (*Tech*) **~ à mine** crowbar.
barreau, *pl* **~x** [baʀo] *nm* **(a)** *[échelle]* rung; *[cage]* bar. **(b)** (*Jur*) bar. **entrer au ~** to be called to the bar.
barrer [baʀe] (1) **1** *vt* **(a)** *porte* to bar; *fenêtre* to bar up; *route* (*par accident*) to block; (*pour travaux, par la police*) to close (off), shut off. (*lit, fig*) **~ la route à qn** to bar sb's way. **(b)** *mot* to cross *ou* score out; *feuille* to cross. **chèque barré/non barré** crossed/open *ou* uncrossed cheque. **(c)** (*Naut*) to steer. **quatre barré** coxed four. **2 se ~‡** *vpr* to clear off*.
barrette [baʀɛt] *nf [cheveux]* (hair) slide; (*Rel*) biretta.
barreur [baʀœʀ] *nm* (*gén*) helmsman; (*Aviron*) cox. **avec/sans ~** coxed/coxless.
barricader [baʀikade] (1) **1** *vt* to barricade. **2 se ~** *vpr*: **se ~ dans/derrière** to barricade o.s. in/behind; (*fig*) **se ~ chez soi** to lock o.s. in. ♦ **barricade** *nf* barricade.
barrière [baʀjɛʀ] *nf* (*clôture*) fence; (*porte*) gate; (*obstacle*) barrier. **~ douanière** trade *ou* tariff barrier; **~ (de passage à niveau)** level crossing gate.
barrique [baʀik] *nf* barrel, cask.
barrir [baʀiʀ] (2) *vi* to trumpet. ♦ **barrissement** *nm*: **~(s)** trumpeting.
baryton [baʀitɔ̃] *adj, nm* baritone.
bas¹, basse [bɑ, bɑs] **1** *adj* **(a)** (*gén*) low; *maison* low-roofed. **pièce basse de plafond** room with a low ceiling; **les basses branches** the lower *ou* bottom branches; **~ sur pattes** short-legged; **la Basse Seine** the lower Seine; **je l'ai eu à ~ prix** I got it cheap; **c'est la basse mer** the tide is out, it's low tide. **(b)** (*humble*) low, lowly; (*subalterne*) menial; (*abject*) base, mean. **(c) être au plus ~** *[personne]* to be very low; *[prix]* to be at their lowest; **au ~ mot** at the very least; **en ce ~ monde** here below; **de ~ étage** (*humble*) lowborn; (*médiocre*) poor, second-rate; **en ~ âge** young.

2 *adv* **(a)** *parler* softly, in a low voice. **très/trop** *etc* **~** very/too *etc* low; **mettez vos livres plus ~** put your books lower down; **voir plus ~** see below; **mettez la radio plus ~** turn the radio down. **(b) traiter qn plus ~ que terre** to treat sb like dirt; **mettre ~** to give birth; **mettre ~ les armes** (*Mil*) to lay down one's arms; (*fig*) to throw in the sponge; **~ les pattes!** (‡) paws off!‡; (*à un chien*) down!; **à ~ le fascisme!** down with fascism!

3 *nm [page]* foot, bottom; *[visage]* lower part; *[pantalon]* bottom. **dans le ~** at the bottom; **le tiroir du ~** the bottom drawer; **les appartements du ~** the downstairs flats; **lire de ~ en haut** to read from the bottom up; **il habite en ~** he lives downstairs *ou* down below.

4 *nf* (*Mus*) bass.

5: ~-côté *nm, pl* **~-~s** *[route]* verge; *[église]* side aisle; **basse-cour** *nf, pl* **basses-cours** (*lieu*) farmyard; (*volaille*) poultry; (*Naut*) **~-fond** *nm, pl* **~-~s** shallow, shoal; **les ~-~s de la société** the dregs of society; **les ~-~s de la ville** the seediest parts of the town; (*Boucherie*) **les ~ morceaux**

the cheap cuts; ~**-relief** *nm, pl* ~-~s bas relief, low relief; ~**-ventre** *nm, pl* ~-~s stomach, guts.

bas[2] [bɑ] *nm* stocking. *(fig)* ~ **de laine** savings.

basalte [bazalt(ə)] *nm* basalt. ♦ **basaltique** *adj* basalt(ic).

basané, e [bazane] *adj* tanned; *indigène* swarthy.

basculer [baskyle] (1) *vi [personne, objet]* to fall *ou* topple over; *[benne]* to tip up. **il bascula dans le vide** he toppled over the edge; *(Pol)* ~ **dans l'opposition** to swing over to the opposition; **faire** ~ *benne* to tip up; *contenu* to tip out; *personne* to topple over. ♦ **bascule** *nf (balançoire)* seesaw; *(balance)* weighing machine. *[personne]* ~ **(automatique)** scales; **fauteuil à** ~ rocking chair.

base [bɑz] **1** *nf* **(a)** *(lit, Chim, Mil)* base. *(Pol)* **la** ~ the rank and file, the grass roots. **(b)** *(principe fondamental)* basis. **des** ~**s solides en anglais** a sound basic knowledge of English. **(c) produit à** ~ **de soude** soda-based product; **être à la** ~ **de** to be at the root of; **sur la** ~ **de ces renseignements** on the basis of this information; **règles de** ~ basic rules. **2:** *(fig)* ~ **de départ** starting point *(fig)*; ~ **de lancement** launching site; ~ **de maquillage** make-up base. ♦ **baser** (1) *vt opinion, théorie* to base (*sur* on). *(Mil)* **être basé à** to be based at; **sur quoi vous basez-vous?** what basis *ou* grounds have you? *(pour dire* for saying).

base-ball [bɛzbol] *nm* baseball.

basilique [bazilik] *nf* basilica.

basket-ball [baskɛtbol] *nm* basketball. ♦ **basket*** *nm* basketball. ~**s** sneakers, trainers. ♦ **basketteur, -euse** *nm,f* basketball player.

basque [bask(ə)] *nf [habit]* skirt(s); *[robe]* basque.

basse [bɑs] *V* **bas**[1].

bassesse [bɑsɛs] *nf* **(a)** *(servilité)* servility; *(mesquinerie)* baseness; *(vulgarité)* vileness. **(b)** *(acte)* servile *ou* base act. **faire des** ~**s à qn pour obtenir** to grovel in order to get. ♦ **bassement** *adv* basely, meanly.

basset [basɛ] *nm* basset hound.

bassin [basɛ̃] *nm (pièce d'eau)* pond; *[piscine]* pool; *[fontaine]* basin; *(cuvette)* bowl; *(Méd)* bedpan; *(Géol)* basin; *(Anat)* pelvis; *(Naut)* dock. ~ **de radoub** dry dock; ~ **houiller** coalfield. ♦ **bassine** *nf* bowl; *(contenu)* bowlful.

bassiner [basine] (1) *vt* **(a)** *plaie* to bathe; *(Agr)* to spray (water on). **(b)** *lit* to warm (with a warming pan). **(c)** (*: *ennuyer*) to bore.

bassiste [bɑsist(ə)] *nmf* double bass player.

basson [bɑsɔ̃] *nm (instrument)* bassoon; *(musicien)* bassoonist.

bastingage [bastɛ̃gaʒ] *nm (Naut)* (ship's) rail; *(Hist)* bulwark.

bastion [bastjɔ̃] *nm* bastion.

bât [bɑ] *nm* packsaddle. *(fig)* **c'est là où le** ~ **blesse** that's where the shoe pinches. ♦ **bâter** (1) *vt* to put a packsaddle on.

bataclan* [bataklɑ̃] *nm* junk*. **et tout le** ~ and what have you, the whole caboodle*.

bataille [bataj] *nf* **(a)** *(Mil)* battle; *(rixe, fig)* fight. ~ **de rue** street fighting; ~ **rangée** pitched battle. **(b)** *(Cartes)* beggar-my-neighbour. **(c) il a les cheveux en** ~ his hair's all tousled; **le chapeau en** ~ with one's hat on askew. ♦ **batailler** (1) *vi* to fight, battle. ♦ **batailleur, -euse** *adj* aggressive. ♦ **bataillon** *nm (Mil)* battalion; *(fig)* crowd.

bâtard, e [bɑtaʀ, aʀd(ə)] **1** *adj enfant* illegitimate, bastard† *(péj)*; *(fig) œuvre* hybrid. **2** *nm,f (personne)* illegitimate child, bastard† *(péj)*; *(chien)* mongrel. **3** *nm* ≃ Vienna roll. ♦ **bâtardise** *nf* bastardy† *(péj)*, illegitimacy.

bateau, *pl* ~**x** [bato] **1** *nm* **(a)** *(gén)* boat; *(grand)* ship. **faire du** ~ *(à voiles)* to go sailing; *(à rames etc)* to go boating. **(b)** *[trottoir]* driveway entrance *(depression in kerb)*. **2** *adj inv* (*: *banal*) hackneyed. **3:** ~ **amiral** flagship; ~**-citerne** *nm, pl* ~**x-**~**s** tanker; ~ **de commerce** merchant ship; ~ **de guerre** warship, battleship; ~**-lavoir** *nm, pl* ~**x-**~**s** wash-shed; ~ **de sauvetage** lifeboat; ~ **à vapeur** steamer, steamship.

bateleur, -euse† [batlœʀ, øz] *nm,f* tumbler.

batelier [batəlje] *nm* boatman; *[bac]* ferryman.

batellerie [batɛlʀi] *nf* canal transport.

bâti, e [bɑti] **1** *adj* **(a) bien/mal** ~ *personne* well-built/of clumsy build; *dissertation* well/badly constructed. **(b) terrain** ~**/non** ~ developed/undeveloped site. **2** *nm* **(a)** *(Couture)* tacking. **(b)** *[porte, machine]* frame.

batifoler [batifɔle] (1) *vi* (†, *hum*) **(a)** *(folâtrer)* to lark about. **(b)** *(flirter)* to dally†, flirt (*avec* with).

bâtiment [bɑtimɑ̃] *nm* **(a)** *(édifice)* building. **(b)** *(industrie)* **le** ~ the building industry *ou* trade. **(c)** *(Naut)* ship.

bâtir [bɑtiʀ] (2) *vt* **(a)** *(Constr)* to build. **(se) faire** ~ **une maison** to have a house built; **terrain à** ~ building land. **(b)** *fortune, réputation, hypothèse* to build; *phrase* to construct. **(c)** *(Couture)* to tack, baste. ♦ **bâtisse** *nf* building. ♦ **bâtisseur, -euse** *nm,f* builder.

bâton [bɑtɔ̃] *nm* **(a)** *(canne)* stick; *(Rel)* staff; *(trique)* cudgel; *(Mil, Police)* baton. **(b)** *[craie etc]* stick. ~ **de rouge (à lèvres)** lipstick. **(c)** *(trait)* vertical stroke. **(d) il m'a mis des** ~**s dans les roues** he put a spoke in my wheel; **parler à** ~**s rompus** to talk casually about this and that.

batracien [batʀasjɛ̃] *nm* batrachian.

battage [bataʒ] *nm* **(a)** *[tapis]* beating; *[céréales]* threshing. **(b)** (*: *publicité*) publicity campaign. **faire du** ~ **autour de qch** to plug sth*.

battant [batɑ̃] *nm* **(a)** *[cloche]* tongue; *[porte]* flap, door; *[fenêtre]* window. **porte à double** ~ double door. **(b)** *(personne)* fighter *(fig)*.

batte [bat] *nf* bat.

battement [batmɑ̃] *nm* **(a)** ~**(s)** *[porte]* banging; *[pluie]* beating; *[voile, ailes]* flapping; *[paupières]* blinking; *[cœur]* beating. ~**s de jambes** leg movements; **avoir des** ~**s de cœur** to have palpitations. **(b)** *(intervalle)* interval. **2 minutes de** ~ *(pause)* a 2-minute break; *(attente)* 2 minutes' wait; *(temps libre)* 2 minutes to spare.

batterie [batʀi] *nf* **(a)** *(Mil)* battery. **mettre en** ~ to unlimber; *(fig)* **dévoiler ses** ~**s** to unmask one's guns. **(b)** *(Tech: série)* battery; *(Aut, Élec)* battery. *(Jazz)* **la** ~ the drums; ~ **de cuisine** pots and pans.

batteur [batœʀ] *nm (Culin)* whisk; *(Mus)* drummer; *(Agr)* thresher; *(Sport)* batsman. ♦ **batteuse** *nf* threshing machine.

battoir [batwaʀ] *nm [linge]* beetle; *[tapis]* beater. ~**s*** great paws*.

battre [batʀ(ə)] (41) **1** *vt* **(a)** *personne* to beat, strike, hit. ~ **qn à mort** to batter *ou* beat sb to death.

(b) *adversaire* to beat, defeat; *record* to beat. **se faire** ~ to be beaten; ~ **qn à plate(s) couture(s)** to beat sb hollow.

(c) *tapis, fer* to beat; *blé* to thresh. ~ **le fer pendant qu'il est chaud** to strike while the iron is hot; **il battit l'air des bras** his arms thrashed the air; **son manteau lui bat les talons** his coat is flapping round his ankles.

(d) *blanc d'œuf* to beat (up), whisk; *crème* to whip; *cartes* to shuffle. **œufs battus en neige** stiff egg whites.

(e) *(parcourir) région* to scour, comb. *(Chasse)* ~ **les buissons** to beat the bushes; **hors des sentiers battus** off the beaten track; *(fig)* ~ **la campagne** to wander in one's mind.

(f) *(heurter) [pluie]* to beat against. **battu par les tempêtes** storm-lashed.

(g) ~ **la mesure/le tambour** to beat time/the drum; ~ **le rappel** to call to arms; ~ **le rappel de ses amis** to rally one's friends; ~ **la retraite** to sound the retreat.

(h) ~ **en brèche une théorie** to demolish a theory; ~ **froid à qn** to give sb the cold shoulder;

~ son plein *[saison, fête]* to be at its height; ~ **pavillon britannique** to fly the British flag; ~ **monnaie** to strike *ou* mint coins.

2 *vi* **(a)** *[cœur]* to beat; *[pluie]* to beat, lash (*contre* against); *[porte]* to bang; *[drapeau]* to flap; *[tambour]* to beat.

(b) ~ **en retraite** to beat a retreat, fall back.

3 ~ **de** *vt indir:* ~ **des mains** to clap one's hands; (*fig*) to dance for joy; ~ **de l'aile** (*lit*) to flap its wings; (*fig*) to be in a shaky state.

4 se ~ *vpr* (*combat*) to fight (*avec* with, *contre* against); (*fig*) to fight, battle (*contre* against). **se** ~ **comme des chiffonniers** to fight like cat and dog; **se** ~ **la poitrine** to beat one's breast; (*fig*) **se** ~ **les flancs** to strain every nerve, rack one's brains. ♦ **battue** *nf* (*Chasse*) beat.

baudet [bodɛ] *nm* (*Zool*) donkey, ass.

baudrier [bodʀije] *nm [épée]* baldric; *[drapeau]* shoulder-belt.

baume [bom] *nm* (*lit, fig*) balm.

baux [bo] *nmpl de* **bail.**

bauxite [boksit] *nf* bauxite.

bavarder [bavaʀde] (1) *vi* to chat, chatter; (*péj*) to gossip; (*divulguer*) to talk. ♦ **bavard, e 1** *adj* talkative. **2** *nm,f* chatterbox*; (*péj*) gossip. ♦ **bavardage** *nm* **(a)** (*action*) chattering; gossiping. **(b)** ~**(s)** (*propos*) (idle) chatter; (*indiscrétion*) gossip.

baver [bave] (1) *vi* **(a)** *[personne]* to dribble; *[animal]* to slaver; *[chien enragé]* to foam at the mouth; *[stylo]* to leak; *[pinceau]* to drip; *[liquide]* to run. **(b) en** ~ **d'admiration*** to gasp in admiration; **en** ~**:** to have a rough time of it. ♦ **bave** *nf* dribble; slaver; foam; *[escargot]* slime; *[crapaud]* spittle. ♦ **baveux, -euse** *adj personne* dribbling; *omelette* runny. ♦ **bavoir** *nm* bib. ♦ **bavure** *nf* (*tache*) smudge; (*Tech*) burr; (*euph*) mistake. **sans** ~ (*adj*) flawless; (*adv*) flawlessly.

bayer [baje] (1) *vi:* ~ **aux corneilles** to stand gaping.

bazar [bazaʀ] *nm* **(a)** (*magasin*) general store; (*oriental*) bazaar. **(b)** (*) (*affaires*) gear; (*désordre*) clutter, jumble. **quel** ~! what a shambles!*; **et tout le** ~ the whole caboodle*. ♦ **bazarder*** (1) *vt* (*jeter*) to chuck out*; (*vendre*) to flog**:**, sell off.

bazooka [bazuka] *nm* bazooka.

béant, e [beɑ̃, ɑ̃t] *adj* gaping.

béat, e [bea, at] *adj* (*hum*) *personne* blissfully happy; (*péj*) smug; *sourire* beatific; *admiration* blind, dumb. ♦ **béatement** *adv* smugly; beatifically. ♦ **béatification** *nf* beatification. ♦ **béatifier** (7) *vt* to beatify. ♦ **béatitude** *nf* (*Rel*) beatitude; (*bonheur*) bliss.

beau [bo], **bel** *devant voyelle ou h muet,* **belle** *f, mpl* **beaux 1** *adj* **(a)** *objet, paysage, femme* beautiful, lovely; *homme* handsome, good-looking. **les beaux quartiers** the smart districts; **mettre ses beaux habits** to put on one's best clothes.

(b) *discours, match, roman* fine. **belle mort** fine death; ~ **geste** noble gesture.

(c) (*agréable*) *temps* fine, beautiful; *voyage* lovely; *mer* calm. **aux beaux jours** in (the) summertime; **il fait (très)** ~ **(temps)** the weather's very good, it's very fine; **c'est le bel âge** those are the best years of life; **c'est la belle vie!** this is the (good) life!

(d) (*: *intensif) revenu, profit* handsome, tidy*; *résultat, occasion* excellent, fine. **il en reste un** ~ **morceau** there's still a good bit (of it) left; **95 ans, c'est un bel âge** it's a good age, 95; **un** ~ **jour** one (fine) day.

(e) (*iro: déplaisant*) *désordre* fine; *gifle* good; *brûlure, peur* nasty; *vacarme* terrible. **c'est un bel escroc** he's a thorough crook; **la belle affaire!** so what?*; **en faire de belles** to get up to mischief; **en dire de belles sur qn*** to say some nice things about sb (*iro*); **être dans un** ~ **pétrin** to be in a fine old mess.

(f) (*locutions*) **ce n'est pas** ~ **de mentir** it isn't nice to tell lies; **ça me fait une belle jambe!*** a fat lot of good it does me!*; (*iro*) **c'est du** ~ **travail!** well done! (*iro*); **de plus belle** more than ever, even more; **crier de plus belle** to shout louder than ever *ou* even louder; **à la belle étoile** out in the open; **il y a belle lurette que** it is ages since; **faire qch pour les beaux yeux de qn** to do sth just to please sb; **le plus** ~ **de l'histoire, c'est que ...** the best part about it is that ...; **c'est trop** ~ **pour être vrai** it's too good to be true; **se faire** ~ to get dressed up; **on a** ~ **faire/**~ **protester, personne n'écoute** whatever you do/however much you protest no one listens; **on a** ~ **dire, il n'est pas bête** say what you like, he is not stupid; **bel et bien** well and truly.

(g) (*famille*) ~**-père,** *pl* ~**x-**~**s** father-in-law; (*remariage*) step-father; **belle-fille,** *pl* ~**s-**~**s** daughter-in-law; (*remariage*) step-daughter; **mes beaux-parents** my husband's (*ou* wife's) parents, my in-laws*.

2 *nm* **(a) le** ~ the beautiful, beauty; **elle n'achète que le** ~ she only buys the best quality.

(b) faire le ~ *[chien]* to sit up and beg; **être au** ~ to be set fair; **c'est du** ~**!** that's a fine thing to do!

3 *nf* **(a)** beauty, belle; (*compagne*) lady friend. **ma belle!*** my girl!; **la Belle au bois dormant** Sleeping Beauty.

(b) (*Jeux*) deciding match.

4: les beaux-arts *nmpl* (*Art*) fine arts; (*école*) the Art School; ~ **parleur** smooth talker; **le** ~ **sexe** the fair sex.

beaucoup [boku] *adv* **(a)** a lot, (very) much, a great deal. **elle ne lit pas** ~ she doesn't read much *ou* a great deal; **il s'intéresse** ~ **à la peinture** he is very interested in painting.

(b) ~ **de** (*quantité*) a great deal of, a lot of, much; (*nombre*) a lot of, a good many; ~ **de monde** a lot of people, a great *ou* good many people; **avec** ~ **de soin** with great care; **il ne reste pas** ~ **de pain** there isn't a lot of *ou* isn't (very) much bread left; **j'ai** ~ **(de choses) à faire** I have a lot (of things) to do; **il a eu** ~ **de chance** he's been very lucky.

(c) (*employé seul: personnes*) many. ~ **croient que** many *ou* a lot of people think that.

(d) (*avec trop, plus etc*) ~ **plus rapide** much *ou* a good deal *ou* a lot quicker; ~ **trop lentement** much *ou* far too slowly; ~ **moins de gens** a lot *ou* far fewer people.

(e) de ~ by far; **il est de** ~ **ton aîné** he is very much *ou* is a great deal older than you; **de** ~ **supérieur** greatly *ou* far superior; **il préférerait de** ~ **s'en aller** he'd much *ou* far rather go.

(f) (*locutions*) **c'est déjà** ~ **de l'avoir fait** it was quite something to have done it at all; **à** ~ **près** far from it; **c'est** ~ **dire** that's saying a lot; **être pour** ~ **dans une décision** to be largely responsible for a decision.

beaupré [bopʀe] *nm* bowsprit.

beauté [bote] *nf* **(a)** (*gén*) beauty; *[femme]* beauty, loveliness; *[homme]* handsomeness. **de toute** ~ very beautiful; **se (re)faire une** ~ to powder one's nose; **finir qch en** ~ to finish sth with a flourish. **(b)** (*femme*) beauty. **(c) les** ~**s de Rome** the beauties *ou* sights of Rome.

bébé [bebe] **1** *nm* (*gén*) baby; (*poupée*) dolly. **2** *adj* babyish.

bébête* [bebɛt] *adj* silly.

bec [bɛk] **1** *nm* **(a)** (*Orn*) beak, bill. **(nez en)** ~ **d'aigle** hook nose. **(b)** *[plume]* nib; *[carafe]* lip; *[théière]* spout. **(c)** (*: *bouche*) mouth. **(d) tomber sur un** ~***** to come unstuck*; **rester le** ~ **dans l'eau*** to be left in the lurch. **2:** ~ **Bunsen** Bunsen burner; ~**-de-cane** *nm, pl* ~**s-**~**-**~ doorhandle; ~ **fin*** gourmet; ~ **de gaz**

lamp post, gaslamp; (*Méd*) ~**-de-lièvre** *nm, pl* ~s-~-~ harelip; ~ **verseur** pouring lip.
bécane* [bekan] *nf* (*vélo*) bike.
bécarre [bekaʀ] *nm* (*Mus*) natural.
bêche [bɛʃ] *nf* spade. ♦ **bêcher** (1) *vt* to dig.
bécoter* [bekɔte] (1) **1** *vt* to kiss. **2 se** ~* *vpr* to smooch*. ♦ **bécot*** *nm* kiss.
becquée [beke] *nf* beakful. **donner la** ~ **à** to feed. ♦ **becqueter** (4) *vt* (*Orn*) to peck (at); (‡) to eat.
bedaine* [bədɛn] *nf* paunch, potbelly*.
bedeau, *pl* ~**x** [bədo] *nm* beadle.
bedonnant, e* [bədɔnɑ̃, ɑ̃t] *adj* potbellied*, portly.
bédouin, e [bedwɛ̃, in] *adj*, **B**~ **(e)** *nm(f)* Bedouin.
bée [be] *adj*: **être bouche** ~ to stand open-mouthed *ou* gaping.
beffroi [befʀwa] *nm* belfry.
bégayer [begeje] (8) **1** *vi* to stammer, stutter. **2** *vt* to stammer (out), falter (out). ♦ **bégaiement** *nm* stammering, stuttering. ♦ **bègue** *nmf* stammerer, stutterer.
bégonia [begɔnja] *nm* begonia.
béguin* [begɛ̃] *nm*: **avoir le** ~ **pour qn/qch** to fancy sb/sth.
beige [bɛʒ] *adj, nm* beige.
beignet [bɛɲɛ] *nm [fruits]* fritter; (*pâte frite*) doughnut.
bel [bɛl] *adj V* **beau.**
bêler [bele] (1) *vi* (*Zool, fig*) to bleat. ♦ **bêlement** *nm* bleating.
belette [bəlɛt] *nf* weasel.
belge [bɛlʒ(ə)] *adj*, **B**~ *nmf* Belgian. ♦ **Belgique** *nf* Belgium.
bélier [belje] *nm* (*Zool, Tech*) ram. (*Astron*) **le B**~ Aries, the Ram.
belladone [beladɔn] *nf* (*Bot*) deadly nightshade; (*Méd*) belladonna.
belle [bɛl] *V* **beau.**
belligérance [beliʒeʀɑ̃s] *nf* belligerence. ♦ **belligérant, e** *adj, nm,f* belligerent.
belliqueux, -euse [belikø, øz] *adj humeur* quarrelsome; *politique, peuple* warlike.
belvédère [bɛlvedɛʀ] *nm* belvedere; (*vue*) (panoramic) viewpoint.
bémol [bemɔl] *nm* (*Mus*) flat.
bénédicité [benedisite] *nm* grace. **dire le** ~ to say grace.
bénédiction [benediksjɔ̃] *nf* (*gén*) blessing; (*: *aubaine*) blessing, godsend.
bénéfice [benefis] *nm* **(a)** (*Comm*) profit. **faire du** ~ to make a profit. **(b)** (*avantage*) advantage, benefit. **concert donné au** ~ **de** concert given to raise funds for *ou* in aid of; **le** ~ **du doute** the benefit of the doubt; **au** ~ **de l'âge** by prerogative of age. **(c)** (*Rel*) benefice, living. ♦ **bénéficiaire** *nmf* (*gén*) beneficiary. **être le** ~ **de** to benefit by. ♦ **bénéficier de** (7) *vt indir* (*jouir de*) to have, enjoy; (*obtenir*) to get, have; (*tirer profit de*) to benefit by *ou* from. ~ **de circonstances atténuantes** to be granted extenuating circumstances; **faire** ~ **qn d'une remise** to give *ou* allow sb a discount. ♦ **bénéfique** *adj* beneficial.
Bénélux [benelyks] *nm*: **le** ~ the Benelux countries.
benêt [bənɛ] **1** *nm* simpleton. **2** *adj m* silly.
bénévole [benevɔl] *adj* voluntary, unpaid. ♦ **bénévolement** *adv* voluntarily.
bénin, -igne [benɛ̃, iɲ] *adj accident* slight, minor; *maladie, remède* mild; *tumeur* benign.
bénir [beniʀ] (2) *vt* **(a)** (*Rel*) to bless. **(b)** *occasion* to thank God for. *personne* **soyez béni!** bless you!; (*iro*) **ah, toi, je te bénis!** oh curse you! ♦ **bénit, e** *adj* consecrated; *eau* holy. ♦ **bénitier** *nm* (*Rel*) stoup.
benjamin, ine [bɛ̃ʒamɛ̃, in] *nm,f* youngest child (*ou* son *ou* daughter).
benjoin [bɛ̃ʒwɛ̃] *nm* benzoin.
benne [bɛn] *nf* **(a)** (*Min*) skip, truck. **(b)** *[camion]* (*basculante*) tipper; (*amovible*) skip; *[grue]* scoop; *[téléphérique]* (cable-)car.
benzène [bɛ̃zɛn] *nm* benzene.
béquille [bekij] *nf [infirme]* crutch; *[moto]* stand.
berbère [bɛʀbɛʀ] *adj*, **B**~ *nmf* Berber.
berceau, *pl* ~**x** [bɛʀso] *nm* (*lit*) cradle, crib; (*lieu d'origine*) birthplace; (*charmille*) arbour.
bercer [bɛʀse] (3) *vt* (*gén*) to rock; *douleur* to lull, soothe. (*tromper*) ~ **de** to delude with; **se** ~ **d'illusions** to delude o.s. ♦ **bercement** *nm* rocking movement. ♦ **berceur, -euse 1** *adj rythme* soothing. **2** *nf* (*chanson*) lullaby.
béret [beʀɛ] *nm* beret.
berge [bɛʀʒ(ə)] *nf [rivière]* bank. **il a 50** ~**s‡** he's 50 (years old).
berger [bɛʀʒe] *nm* (*lit, Rel*) shepherd. **(chien de)** ~ sheepdog; ~ **allemand** alsatian. ♦ **bergère** *nf* **(a)** shepherdess. **(b)** (*fauteuil*) wing chair. ♦ **bergerie** *nf* sheepfold.
bergeronnette [bɛʀʒəʀɔnɛt] *nf* wagtail.
berline [bɛʀlin] *nf* (*Aut*) saloon (car), sedan (*US*); (†: *à chevaux*) berlin; (*Min*) truck.
berlingot [bɛʀlɛ̃go] *nm* (*bonbon*) boiled sweet; (*emballage*) (pyramid-shaped) carton.
berlue [bɛʀly] *nf*: **avoir la** ~ to be seeing things.
bermuda(s) [bɛʀmyda] *nm* bermuda shorts.
Bermudes [bɛʀmyd] *nfpl* Bermuda.
bernard-l'(h)ermite [bɛʀnaʀlɛʀmit] *nm inv* hermit crab.
berne [bɛʀn(ə)] *nf*: **en** ~ ≃ at half-mast; **mettre en** ~ ≃ to half-mast.
berner [bɛʀne] (1) *vt* (*tromper*) to fool, hoax.
bernique [bɛʀnik] **1** *nf* limpet. **2** *excl* (*) nothing doing!*
besace [bəzas] *nf* beggar's bag.
besicles [bezikl(ə)] *nfpl* (*Hist*) spectacles.
besogne [bəzɔɲ] *nf* (*travail*) work, job.
besoin [bəzwɛ̃] *nm* **(a)** (*exigence*) need (*de* for, *de faire* to do). **il a de grands/petits** ~**s** his needs are great/small. **(b)** (*pauvreté*) **le** ~ need, want; **famille dans le** ~ needy family; **ceux qui sont dans le** ~ the needy. **(c)** (*euph*) ~**s naturels** nature's needs; **faire ses** ~**s** *[personne]* to relieve o.s.; *[animal domestique]* to do its business. **(d) avoir** ~ **de qch/de faire qch** to need sth/to do sth; **il n'a pas** ~ **de venir** he doesn't need *ou* have to come, there's no need for him to come; **il a** ~ **que vous l'aidiez** he needs your help *ou* you to help him; **pas** ~ **de dire que** it goes without saying that; (*iro*) **il avait bien** ~ **de ça!** that's just what he needed! (*iro*); **est-ce que tu avais** ~ **d'y aller?*** did you really have to go? **(e) au** ~, **si** ~ **est** if necessary, if need be; **pour les** ~**s de la cause** for the purpose in hand.
bestial, e, *mpl* **-aux** [bɛstjal, o] *adj* bestial, brutish. ♦ **bestialement** *adv* bestially, brutishly. ♦ **bestialité** *nf* bestiality, brutishness.
bestiaux [bɛstjo] *nmpl* (*gén*) livestock; (*bovins*) cattle.
bestiole [bɛstjɔl] *nf* (tiny) creature.
bêta, -asse* [bɛta, ɑs] *adj, nm,f* silly.
bétail [betaj] *nm* (*gén*) livestock; (*bovins, fig*) cattle. ♦ **bétaillère** *nf* cattle truck.
bête [bɛt] **1** *nf* **(a)** (*animal*) animal; (*insecte*) bug, creature. ~ **sauvage** wild beast *ou* creature; **pauvre petite** ~ poor little thing *ou* creature; **ces sales** ~**s** those wretched creatures. **(b)** (*personne*) (*bestial*) beast; (†: *stupide*) fool. (*hum*) **c'est une bonne** ~**!** he is a good-natured sort; (*terme d'affection*) **grosse** ~**!*** you big silly!*

2 *adj* **(a)** (*stupide*) stupid, silly, foolish. **ce qu'il peut être** ~**!** what a fool he is!; **être** ~ **comme ses pieds‡** to be as thick as a brick; **je ne suis pas si** ~ I'm not that silly; **c'est** ~ **j'ai oublié** it's silly *ou* stupid, I forgot; **ce n'est pas** ~ that's not a bad idea. **(b)** (*: *très simple*) **c'est tout** ~ it's quite *ou* dead* simple.

3: ~ **à bon dieu** ladybird; ~ **à cornes** horned animal; (*iro*) ~ **curieuse** strange animal; ~ **fauve**

big cat; **c'est ma ~ noire** *[chose]* that's my pet hate; *[personne]* I just can't stand him; **~ de somme** beast of burden.
♦ **bêtement** *adv* stupidly, foolishly. **tout ~** quite simply.

bêtise [betiz] *nf* **(a)** (*stupidité*) stupidity, folly. **j'ai eu la ~ de** I was foolish enough to. **(b)** (*action stupide*) silly *ou* stupid action; (*erreur*) blunder. **dire des ~s** to talk nonsense; **ne faites pas de ~s** don't do anything silly *ou* stupid. **(c)** (*bagatelle*) trifle. **dépenser son argent en ~s** to spend one's money on rubbish. **(d) ~ de Cambrai** ≃ mint humbug.

béton [betɔ̃] *nm* concrete. **~ armé** reinforced concrete.

betterave [bɛtʀav] *nf*: **~ fourragère** mangelwurzel, beet; **~ (rouge)** beetroot; **~ sucrière** sugar beet.

beugler [bøgle] (1) **1** *vi* **(a)** *[vache]* to moo; *[taureau]* to bellow. **(b)** (*) *[personne]* to bellow; *[radio]* to blare. **faire ~ sa télé** to have one's TV on full blast*. **2** *vt* (*) to bellow out. ♦ **beuglement** *nm* mooing; bellowing; blaring.

beurre [bœʀ] **1** *nm* **(a)** butter. **~ noir** brown (butter) sauce; **~ d'anchois** anchovy paste; **~ de cacahuètes** peanut butter. **(b)** (*) **entrer comme dans du ~** to go *ou* get in with the greatest (of) ease; **ça va mettre du ~ dans les épinards** that will add a little to the kitty; **faire son ~** to make a packet*. **2: ~-frais** *adj inv* buttercup yellow.
♦ **beurrer** (1) *vt* to butter. ♦ **beurrier** *nm* butter dish.

beuverie [bœvʀi] *nf* drinking bout.

bévue [bevy] *nf* blunder.

bi... [bi] *préf* bi.... **bilatéral/bivalent** bilateral/bivalent; **bicolore** two-coloured; **biréacteur** twin-engined jet; **biquotidien** twice-daily.

biais [bjɛ] *nm* **(a)** (*artifice*) device, means. **par le ~ de** by means of; (*aspect*) **abordons le problème par ce ~** let's tackle the problem from this angle. **(b)** (*Tex*) bias; (*ligne oblique*) slant. **en ~** *poser* slantwise; *couper* diagonally; **regarder qn de ~** to give sb a sidelong glance; **prendre une question de ~** to tackle a question in a roundabout way.
♦ **biaiser** (1) *vi* (*louvoyer*) to sidestep the issue, prevaricate; (*obliquer*) to change direction.

bibelot [biblo] *nm* (*sans valeur*) trinket; (*de valeur*) curio.

biberon [bibʀɔ̃] *nm* baby's bottle. **l'heure du ~** (baby's) feeding time; **nourrir au ~** to bottle-feed.

bibine* [bibin] *nf* weak beer.

bible [bibl(ə)] *nf* (*livre, fig*) bible. ♦ **biblique** *adj* biblical.

bibliographie [biblijɔgʀafi] *nf* bibliography.
♦ **bibliographique** *adj* bibliographic(al).

bibliophile [biblijɔfil] *nmf* booklover.

bibliothèque [biblijɔtɛk] *nf* (*édifice, collection*) library; (*meuble*) bookcase. **~ de gare** station bookstall. ♦ **bibliothécaire** *nmf* librarian.

bicarbonate [bikaʀbɔnat] *nm* bicarbonate. **~ de soude** sodium bicarbonate.

bicéphale [bisefal] *adj* two headed.

biceps [bisɛps] *nm* biceps. **avoir des ~*** to have a strong pair of arms.

biche [biʃ] *nf* doe. (*fig*) **ma ~** darling.

bicher* [biʃe] (1) *vi* to be pleased with o.s. **ça biche?** how's things?*

bichonner [biʃɔne] (1) **1** *vt* (*pomponner*) to titivate; (*prendre soin de*) to fuss over. **2 se ~** *vpr* to titivate.

bicoque [bikɔk] *nf* (*péj*) shack*.

bicorne [bikɔʀn(ə)] *nm* cocked hat.

bicyclette [bisiklɛt] *nf* bicycle, bike; (*sport*) cycling. **faire de la ~** (*promenade*) to go for a cycle ride; (*transport*) to go by bike.

bide [bid] *nm* (‡: *ventre*) belly*; (*arg Théât*) flop.

bidet [bidɛ] *nm* **(a)** bidet. **(b)** (*cheval*) nag.

bidon [bidɔ̃] **1** *nm* **(a)** (*gén*) can, tin; *[lait]* churn; *[campeur, soldat]* flask. **(b)** (‡) (*ventre*) belly*; (*bluff*) rubbish. **2** *adj inv* (‡) *attentat* mock. **société ~** ghost company. ♦ **bidonville** *nm* shanty town.

bidule* [bidyl] *nm* thingumabob*.

bielle [bjɛl] *nf* connecting rod.

bien [bjɛ̃] **1** *adv* **(a)** (*gén*) well; *fonctionner* properly, well. **être ~ portant** to be well, be in good health; **il parle ~ l'anglais** he speaks good English, he speaks English well; **il a ~ pris ce que je lui ai dit** he took what I had to say in good part; **il s'y est ~ pris (pour le faire)** he went about it the right way; **si je me rappelle ~** if I remember right *ou* correctly; **vous avez ~ fait** you did the right thing; **faire ~ les choses** to do things properly *ou* in style; **vous feriez ~ de** you'd do well *ou* you'd be well advised to; **on comprend ~ pourquoi** you can quite easily see why; **il peut très ~ le faire** he can quite easily do it.

(b) (*très*) very; (*beaucoup*) very much; (*trop*) rather. **~ mieux** much better; **~ souvent** quite often; **~ content** very glad; **~ plus heureux/cher** far *ou* much happier/more expensive; **nous avons ~ ri** we had a good laugh; **tout cela est ~ joli mais** that's all very well but; **c'est ~ long** it's rather long *ou* a bit on the long side.

(c) (*effectivement*) indeed, definitely. **j'avais ~ dit que** I DID say *ou* I certainly did say that; **c'est ~ une erreur** it's definitely *ou* certainly a mistake; **c'est ~ à ton frère que je pensais** it was indeed your brother I was thinking of; **est-ce ~ mon manteau?** is it really my coat?; **il s'agit ~ de cela!** as if that's the point!; **voilà ~ les femmes!** that's just like women!, that's women all over!; **c'est ~ ma veine!*** it's just my luck!; **c'était ~ la peine!** after all that trouble!; **où peut-il ~ être?** where on earth can he be?

(d) (*complètement*) **ferme ~ la porte** shut the door properly; **écoute-moi ~** listen to me carefully; **mets-toi ~ en face** stand right *ou* straight opposite; **ça m'est ~ égal** it's all the same to me; **c'est ~ compris?** is that clearly *ou* quite understood?

(e) (*hypothèse, fatalité*) **j'espère ~!** I should hope so!; **on verra ~** we'll see, time will tell; **il se pourrait ~ qu'il pleuve** it could well rain; **il fallait ~ que ça arrive** it was bound to happen; **il faut ~ le supporter** one just has to put up with it; **j'irais ~ mais ...** I'd willingly *ou* gladly go but ...; **je voudrais ~ t'y voir!** I'd like to see you try!

(f) (*au moins*) at least. **il y a ~ 3 jours que je ne l'ai vu** I haven't seen him for at least 3 days.

(g) ~ de: ~ des gens a good many *ou* quite a few (people); **ils ont eu ~ de la chance** they were really very lucky; **elle a eu ~ du mal à faire** she had a great deal of difficulty in doing.

(h) ~ que although, though.

(i) ah ~ (ça) alors! well really!; **~ sûr** of course; **ni ~ ni mal** so-so*; **c'est ~ fait (pour lui)** it serves him right.

2 *adj inv* **(a)** (*de qualité*) good; (*en bonne santé*) well; (*beau*) *personne* good-looking; *chose* nice. **donnez-lui quelque chose de ~** give him something really good; (*approbation*) **~!** good!, fine!; (*exaspération*) **c'est ~!** all right!, all right!

(b) (*à l'aise*) **il est ~ partout** he feels at home anywhere; **on est ~ à l'ombre** it's pleasant *ou* nice in the shade; **je suis ~ dans ce fauteuil** I'm very comfortable in this chair; **elle se trouve ~ dans son nouveau poste** she's very happy in her new job; **il est ~ où il est!** he's quite all right where he is; (*iro*) **vous voilà ~!** now you've done it!; **être/se mettre ~ avec qn** to be/get on good terms with sb.

(c) (*moralement*) nice. **ce n'est pas ~ de** it's not nice to; **c'est ~ à vous de les aider** it's good *ou* nice of you to help them.

3 *nm* **(a)** good. **faire le ~** to do good; **ça m'a fait**

du ~ it did me good; **c'est pour ton** ~! it's for your own good!; **ça a été un** ~ it was a good thing; **changer en** ~ to change for the better; **dire du** ~ **de** to speak highly of; **vouloir du** ~ **à qn** to wish sb well; **grand** ~ **vous fasse!** much good may it do you!

(b) (*gén: possession*) possession; (*argent*) fortune; (*terres*) estate. ~ **mal acquis ne profite jamais** ill-gotten gains seldom prosper.

4: ~**-aimé(e)** *adj, nm(f)* beloved; ~**s de consommation** consumer goods; ~**-être** *nm* (*physique*) well-being; (*matériel*) comfort; ~**-fondé** *nm [opinion]* validity; *[plainte]* cogency; ~ **pensant** *adj* (*Rel*) God-fearing; (*Pol, gén*) right-thinking.

bienfaisance [bjɛ̃fəzɑ̃s] *nf* charity. **œuvres de** ~ charities, charitable organisations. ♦ **bienfaisant, e** *adj* (*remède*) beneficial; *personne* beneficent, kind.

bienfait [bjɛ̃fɛ] *nm* kindness. **c'est un** ~ **du ciel!** it's a godsend! *ou* blessing!; **les** ~**s de** *science* the benefits of; *cure* the beneficial effects of. ♦ **bienfaiteur, -trice** *nm,f* benefactor, benefactress.

bienheureux, -euse [bjɛ̃nœʀø, øz] *adj* (*Rel*) blessed.

biennale [bjenal] *nf* biennial event.

bienséance [bjɛ̃seɑ̃s] *nf* propriety. ♦ **bienséant, e** *adj* proper, becoming.

bientôt [bjɛ̃to] *adv* soon. **à** ~! see you soon!; **on est** ~ **arrivé** we'll soon be there, we'll be there shortly; **c'est pour** ~? is it due soon?; **il est** ~ **minuit** it's nearly midnight; **il eut** ~ **fait de finir son travail**† he lost no time in finishing his work.

bienveillance [bjɛ̃vɛjɑ̃s] *nf* benevolence, kindness (*envers* to). **examiner avec** ~ to give favourable consideration to. ♦ **bienveillant, e** *adj* benevolent, kindly.

bienvenu, e [bjɛ̃vny] **1** *adj remarque* apposite, well-chosen. **2** *nm,f*: **être le** ~ (*ou* **la** ~**e**) to be most welcome. **3** *nf* welcome. **souhaiter la** ~**e à qn** to welcome sb.

bière¹ [bjɛʀ] *nf* beer. ~ **blonde** lager; ~ **brune** brown ale; ~ **pression** draught beer.

bière² [bjɛʀ] *nf* coffin.

biffer [bife] (1) *vt* to cross out.

bifteck [biftɛk] *nm* (piece of) steak.

bifurquer [bifyʀke] (1) *vi [route]* to fork, branch off; *[véhicule]* to turn off (*vers, sur* for). ~ **sur la droite** to bear right. ♦ **bifurcation** *nf* fork.

bigame [bigam] **1** *adj* bigamous. **2** *nmf* bigamist. ♦ **bigamie** *nf* bigamy.

bigarré, e [bigaʀe] *adj vêtement, groupe* gaily-coloured; (*fig*) *foule* motley; *peuple* mixed. ♦ **bigarrure** *nf* coloured pattern.

bigorneau, *pl* ~**x** [bigɔʀno] *nm* winkle.

bigot, e [bigo, ɔt] (*péj*) **1** *adj* over-devout. **2** *nm,f* (religious) bigot. ♦ **bigoterie** *nf* (religious) bigotry.

bigoudi [bigudi] *nm* (hair-)curler *ou* roller.

bigre [bigʀ(ə)] *excl* (*hum*) gosh!* ♦ **bigrement** *adv bon* darn*, dead*; *changer* a heck of a lot*.

bijou, *pl* ~**x** [biʒu] *nm* jewel; (*fig*) gem, marvel. **mon** ~ my love. ♦ **bijouterie** *nf* (*boutique*) jeweller's (shop); (*commerce*) jewellery business. ♦ **bijoutier, -ière** *nm,f* jeweller.

bikini [bikini] *nm* bikini.

bilan [bilɑ̃] *nm* **(a)** (*évaluation*) assessment; (*résultats*) results; (*conséquences*) consequences. **faire le** ~ **de** to take stock of, assess; ~ **de santé** (medical) checkup. **(b)** (*Fin*) balance sheet.

bilboquet [bilbɔkɛ] *nm* cup-and-ball game.

bile [bil] *nf* bile. **se faire de la** ~ **(pour)*** to get worried (about). ♦ **bileux, -euse*** **1** *adj* easily worried. **2** *nm,f* worrier, fretter*.

bilingue [bilɛ̃g] *adj* bilingual. ♦ **bilinguisme** *nm* bilingualism.

billard [bijaʀ] *nm* **(a)** (*jeu*) billiards (*sg*); (*table*) billiard table. **boule de** ~ billiard ball; **faire un** ~ to play a game of billiards; ~ **électrique** pinball machine. **(b)** (*) **passer sur le** ~ to have an operation; **c'est du** ~ it's dead easy*.

bille [bij] *nf* **(a)** *[enfant]* marble; *[billard]* (billiard) ball. **(b)** ~ **de bois** block of wood. **(c)** (*: *visage*) face, mug*.

billet [bijɛ] **1** *nm* **(a)** ticket. ~ **aller/aller-retour** single *ou* one-way (*US*)/return *ou* round-trip (*US*) ticket. **(b)** (*Fin*) note, bill (*US*). **(c)** (†: *lettre*) note, short letter. **je te fiche** *ou* **flanque mon** ~ **que*** I bet you my bottom dollar that*. **2:** ~ **de banque** banknote; ~ **de commerce** promissory note; ~ **doux** love letter; ~ **de faveur** complimentary ticket; (*Mil*) ~ **de logement** billet.

billion [biljɔ̃] *nm* billion, trillion (*US*).

billot [bijo] *nm* block.

binaire [binɛʀ] *adj* binary.

biner [bine] (1) *vt* to hoe, harrow. ♦ **binette** *nf* **(a)** (*Agr*) hoe. **(b)** (*: *visage*) face.

bing [biŋ] *excl* smack!, thwack!

biniou [binju] *nm* (*Mus*) Breton bagpipes.

binôme [binom] *nm* binomial.

biochimie [bjɔʃimi] *nf* biochemistry.

biographe [bjɔgʀaf] *nmf* biographer. ♦ **biographie** *nf* biography. ♦ **biographique** *adj* biographical.

biologie [bjɔlɔʒi] *nf* biology. ♦ **biologique** *adj* biological. ♦ **biologiste** *nmf* biologist.

bipartite [bipaʀtit] *adj* bipartite.

bipède [bipɛd] *adj, nm* biped.

biplan [biplɑ̃] *nm* biplane.

bique [bik] *nf* nanny-goat. (*péj*) **vieille** ~ old hag*. ♦ **biquet, -ette** *nm,f* (*Zool*) kid.

Birmanie [biʀmani] *nf* Burma. ♦ **birman, e** *adj*, **B**~**(e)** *nm(f)* Burmese.

bis¹ [bis] *adv* (*sur partition*) repeat. ~**!** encore!; (*numéro*) 12 ~ 12a.

bis², e [bi, biz] *adj* greyish-brown.

bisaïeul [bizajœl] *nm* great-grandfather.

bisaïeule [bizajœl] *nf* great-grandmother.

biscornu, e [biskɔʀny] *adj forme* crooked; *idée, esprit* tortuous, cranky. **chapeau** ~ shapeless hat.

biscoteaux* [biskɔto] *nmpl* biceps.

biscotte [biskɔt] *nf* rusk.

biscuit [biskɥi] *nm* (*mou*) sponge cake; (*sec*) biscuit, cracker (*US*). ~ **à la cuiller** sponge finger. ♦ **biscuiterie** *nf* (*usine*) biscuit factory.

bise [biz] *nf* **(a)** North wind. **(b)** kiss.

biseau, *pl* ~**x** [bizo] *nm [glace]* bevel; (*Menuiserie*) chamfer; (*outil*) bevel. **en** ~ bevelled; chamfered. ♦ **biseauter** (1) *vt* to bevel; to chamfer; *cartes* to mark.

bismuth [bismyt] *nm* bismuth.

bison [bizɔ̃] *nm* bison, American buffalo.

bisquer* [biske] (1) *vi* to be riled*. **faire** ~ to rile*.

bissecteur, -trice [bisɛktœʀ, tʀis] **1** *adj* bisecting. **2** *nf* bisector.

bisser [bise] (1) *vt acteur* to encore.

bistouri [bistuʀi] *nm* lancet.

bistre [bistʀ(ə)] *adj, nm* bistre. ♦ **bistré, e** *adj teint* swarthy.

bistro(t) [bistʀo] *nm* café, bar.

bitume [bitym] *nm* (*Chim, Min*) bitumen; (*revêtement*) asphalt, Tarmac ®. ♦ **bitum(in)er** (1) *vt* to asphalt, tarmac. ♦ **bitum(in)eux, -euse** *adj* bituminous.

bivouac [bivwak] *nm* bivouac. ♦ **bivouaquer** (1) *vi* to bivouac.

bizarre [bizaʀ] *adj* strange, odd, peculiar. **le** ~ **dans tout cela ...** the strange *ou* odd part about it all .... ♦ **bizarrement** *adv* strangely, oddly, peculiarly. ♦ **bizarrerie** *nf* strangeness, oddness. ~**s** peculiarities, oddities.

bizut(h) [bizy] *nm* (*arg Scol*) fresher (*arg*), first-year student. ♦ **bizuter** (1) *vt* (*arg Scol*) to rag.

blablabla* [blablabla] *nm* claptrap*.

blackbouler [blakbule] (1) *vt* (*élection*) to blackball; (*examen*) to fail.
blafard, e [blafaʀ, aʀd(ə)] *adj* wan, pale.
blague [blag] *nf* **(a)** (*) (*histoire*) joke; (*farce*) hoax. **faire une ~ à qn** to play a trick on sb; **sans ~?** you're kidding!‡; **~ à part** seriously, joking apart; **pas de ~s!** no messing about!* **(b)** (*: *erreur*) blunder. **(c) ~ (à tabac)** tobacco pouch. ♦ **blaguer*** (1) **1** *vi* to be joking *ou* kidding‡. **2** *vt* to tease, kid‡. ♦ **blagueur, -euse 1** *adj* teasing. **2** *nm,f* joker.
blaireau, *pl* **~x** [blɛʀo] *nm* (*Zool*) badger; (*pour barbe*) shaving brush.
blairer‡ [bleʀe] (1) *vt*: **je ne peux pas le ~** I can't stand him, he gives me the creeps‡.
blâme [blɑm] *nm* (*désapprobation*) blame; (*réprimande*) reprimand, rebuke; (*punition*) reprimand. **donner un ~** to reprimand. ♦ **blâmable** *adj* blameful. ♦ **blâmer** (1) *vt* to blame; to reprimand; to rebuke.
blanc, blanche [blɑ̃, blɑ̃ʃ] **1** *adj* **(a)** (*gén*) white (*de* with); (*pas bronzé*) pale. **il était ~ à 30 ans** he had white hair at 30; **~ comme un linge** as white as a sheet; (*fig*) **~ comme neige** as pure as the driven snow. **(b)** *page, copie* blank.
2 *nm* **(a)** (*couleur*) white; (*poudre*) white powder; (*vin*) white wine. (*lavage*) **le ~ et la couleur** white and coloureds; (*tissu*) **vente de ~** white sale, sale of household linen. **(b)** (*espace*) blank. **'laisser en ~'** 'leave (this space) blank'. **(c)** (*Culin*) **~ (d'œuf)** (egg) white; **~ (de poulet)** breast (of chicken). **(d)** (*homme*) **B~** White, white man. **(e) à ~** *charger* with blanks; **tirer à ~** to fire blanks; **cartouche à ~** blank (cartridge).
3 *nf* **(a)** (*femme*) **Blanche** white woman. **(b)** (*Mus*) minim.
4: ~ bec* greenhorn; **~ cassé** off-white; **~ d'Espagne** whitening; **Blanche-Neige** Snow White.
♦ **blanchâtre** *adj* whitish, off-white. ♦ **blancheur** *nf* whiteness.
blanchir [blɑ̃ʃiʀ] (2) **1** *vt* **(a)** (*gén*) to whiten, lighten; *cheveux* to turn grey *ou* white; *toile* to bleach. **~ à la chaux** to whitewash. **(b)** *linge* to launder. **il est blanchi** his laundry is done for him. **(c)** (*disculper*) to clear. **(d) (faire) ~** (*Culin, Agr*) to blanch. **2** *vi* *[cheveux]* to go grey *ou* white; *[couleur]* to become lighter. **3 se ~** *vpr* to clear one's name. ♦ **blanchissage** *nm* laundering. **note de ~** laundry bill. ♦ **blanchissement** *nm* whitening. ♦ **blanchisserie** *nf* laundry. ♦ **blanchisseur, euse** *nm,f* launderer, launderess.
blanquette [blɑ̃kɛt] *nf*: **~ de veau** blanquette of veal.
blaser [blaze] (1) *vt* to make blasé. **être blasé de** to be bored with. ♦ **blasé, e** *adj* blasé.
blason [blazɔ̃] *nm* coat of arms.
blasphémateur, -trice [blasfematœʀ, tʀis] *nm,f* blasphemer. ♦ **blasphématoire** *adj* blasphemous. ♦ **blasphème** *nm* blasphemy. ♦ **blasphémer** (6) *vti* to blaspheme.
blatte [blat] *nf* cockroach.
blé [ble] *nm* wheat. **~ dur** hard wheat; **~ noir** buckwheat.
bled* [blɛd] *nm* village. **~ perdu** hole*, dump‡.
blême [blɛm] *adj* pale, wan. **~ de rage** livid with rage. ♦ **blêmir** (2) *vi* to turn pale (*de* with).
blesser [blese] (1) *vt* **(a)** (*gén*) to hurt, injure; (*Mil*) to wound. **être blessé au bras** to have an arm injury *ou* wound; **il s'est blessé en tombant** he fell and injured himself; **ses souliers lui blessent le talon** his shoes hurt his heel; **couleurs qui blessent la vue** colours which offend *ou* shock the eye. **(b)** (*offenser*) *personne* to hurt (the feelings of), wound; *convenances* to offend against. **paroles qui blessent** wounding *ou* cutting remarks; **il se blesse pour un rien** he's easily hurt *ou* offended. ♦ **blessant, e** *adj* cutting. ♦ **blessé, e** *nm,f* wounded *ou* injured man (*ou* woman). **l'accident a fait 10 ~s** 10 people were injured *ou* hurt in the accident; **~ grave** seriously injured person; **les ~s de guerre** the war wounded; **~s de la route** road casualties. ♦ **blessure** *nf* injury; wound. **c'est une ~ d'amour-propre** his pride is hurt.
blet, blette [blɛ, blɛt] *adj* overripe.
bleu, e [blø] **1** *adj couleur* blue; *steak* very rare.
2 *nm* **(a)** (*couleur*) blue. (*fig*) **il n'y a vu que du ~*** he didn't smell a rat; **le ~ de ce ciel** the blueness of that sky; **~ marine/nuit/roi** navy/midnight/royal blue; **~-noir** blue-black. **(b) ~ (de lessive)** (dolly) blue. **(c)** (*sur la peau*) bruise. **(d)** (*vêtement*) **~(s) (de travail)** dungarees, overalls. **(e)** (*arg Mil: recrue*) rookie (*arg*), raw recruit; (*gén: débutant*) beginner, greenhorn. **(f)** (*fromage*) blue(-veined) cheese. **(g)** (*Culin*) **truite au ~** trout au bleu.
♦ **bleuâtre** *adj* bluish. ♦ **bleuet** *nm* cornflower. ♦ **bleuir** (2) *vti* to turn blue. ♦ **bleuté, e** *adj reflet* bluish; *verre* blue-tinted.
blinder [blɛ̃de] (1) *vt* **(a)** (*Mil*) to armour; *porte* to reinforce. **(b)** (*: *endurcir*) to harden, make immune (*contre* to). ♦ **blindage** *nm* armour plating; reinforcing. ♦ **blindé** *nm* (*Mil*) armoured car, tank. **les ~s** the armour.
blizzard [blizaʀ] *nm* blizzard.
bloc [blɔk] **1** *nm* **(a)** *[marbre, bois]* block. **fait d'un seul ~** made from a single piece. **(b)** (*papeterie*) pad. **(c)** (*système d'éléments*) unit; (*groupe*) group; (*Pol*) bloc. **(d)** (‡: *prison*) **mettre qn au ~** to clap sb in clink‡; **faire ~ avec/contre qn** to unite with/against sb; **visser qch à ~** to screw sth up tight; **vendre qch en ~** to sell sth as a whole; **il refuse en ~ tous mes arguments** he rejects all my arguments wholesale; **se retourner tout d'un ~** to swivel round. **2: ~-calendrier** *nm, pl* **~s-~s** tear-off calendar; **~-cuisine** *nm, pl* **~s-~s** kitchen unit; **~-évier** *nm, pl* **~s-~s** sink unit; (*Aut*) **~-moteur** *nm, pl* **~s-~s** engine block; **~-notes** *nm, pl* **~ s-~** desk-pad; (*Méd*) **~ opératoire** operating theatre suite.
blocage [blɔkaʒ] *nm* **(a)** *[prix]* freeze; *[compte]* freezing. **(b)** (*Psych*) block. **(c)** *[frein, roues]* locking; *[écrou]* overtightening.
blockhaus [blɔkos] *nm* (*Mil*) blockhouse.
blocus [blɔkys] *nm* blockade.
blond, e [blɔ̃, ɔ̃d] **1** *adj cheveux* fair, blond; *personne* fair, fair-haired; *blé, sable* golden. **~ cendré** ash-blond. **2** *nm* (*couleur*) blond, light gold; (*homme*) fair-haired man. **3** *nf* (*bière*) lager; (*cigarette*) Virginia cigarette; (*femme*) blonde. ♦ **blondinet, -ette** *nm,f* fair-haired child. ♦ **blondir** (2) *vi [cheveux]* to go fairer.
bloquer [blɔke] (1) **1** *vt* **(a)** (*grouper*) to lump *ou* group together. **(b)** *porte, machine* to jam; *écrou* to overtighten; *roue* (*accidentellement*) to lock; (*exprès*) to chock; *ballon* to block. **~ les freins** to jam on the brakes; **~ qn contre un mur** to pin sb against a wall; **bloqué par un accident** held up by an accident. **(c)** (*obstruer*) to block (up). **port bloqué par la glace** icebound port. **(d)** *marchandises* to stop, hold up; *salaires, compte* to freeze; *négociations* to block, hold up. **être bloqué** *[situation]* to be at a standstill. **2 se ~** *vpr [porte, frein, machine]* to jam; *[roue]* to lock.
blottir (se) [blɔtiʀ] (2) *vpr* to curl up, snuggle up. **blotti parmi les arbres** nestling among the trees.
blouse [bluz] *nf* (*tablier*) overall; *[médecin]* white coat; *[paysan]* smock.
blouson [bluzɔ̃] *nm* lumber jacket, windjammer. **~ noir** ≃ teddy-boy.
blue-jean, *pl* **~-~s** [bludʒin] *nm* jeans, denims.
blues [bluz] *nm inv* (*Mus*) blues.
bluff* [blœf] *nm* bluff. **c'est du ~!** he's just bluffing! ♦ **bluffer*** (1) **1** *vi* to bluff. **2** *vt* to fool; (*Cartes*) to bluff. ♦ **bluffeur, -euse*** *nm,f* bluffer.
boa [bɔa] *nm* (*Habillement, Zool*) boa.

bobard* [bɔbaʀ] *nm* lie, fib*.
bobine [bɔbin] *nf* **(a)** *[fil]* reel, bobbin; (*sur machine*) spool; (*Ciné*) reel; (*Aut, Élec*) coil. (*Phot*) ~ **de pellicule** roll of film. **(b)** (*: *visage*) face.
bobo* [bobo] *nm* (*plaie*) sore; (*coupure*) cut. **avoir ~** to have a pain; **ça (te) fait ~?** does it hurt?
bocage [bɔkaʒ] *nm* (*Géog*) bocage; (*bois*) grove. ♦ **bocager, -ère** *adj* (*boisé*) wooded; (*Géog*) bocage.
bocal, *pl* **-aux** [bɔkal, o] *nm* jar. **mettre en ~aux** to preserve, bottle.
bock [bɔk] *nm* glass of beer; (*verre*) beer glass.
bœuf [bœf], *pl* **~s** [bø] **1** *nm* (*bête*) *[labour]* ox; *[boucherie]* bullock; (*viande*) beef. **~s de boucherie** beef cattle. **2** *adj inv*: **effet ~*** fantastic effect*.
bohème [bɔɛm] **1** *adj* bohemian, happy-go-lucky. **2** *nmf* bohemian.
bohémien, -ienne [bɔemjɛ̃, jɛn] *nm,f* (*gitan*) gipsy.
boire [bwaʀ] (53) **1** *vt* **(a)** to drink. **~ un verre** to have a drink; **~ qch à longs traits** to take great gulps of sth; **donner à ~ à qn** to give sb sth to drink *ou* a drink; **~ à la santé/au succès de qn** to drink sb's health/to sb's success; **ça se boit bien** it is very drinkable; **faire ~** *personne* to give sth to drink to; *cheval* to water; **~ comme un trou*** to drink like a fish; **il boit (sec)** he's a (heavy) drinker. **(b)** *[plante, buvard]* to soak up. **(c) ~ les paroles de qn** to drink in sb's words; **~ le calice jusqu'à la lie** to drain one's cup to the last bitter drop; **~ un bouillon*** (*fortune*) to make a big loss; (*bain*) to swallow a mouthful; **~ du (petit) lait** to lap it up*; **il y a à ~ et à manger** you have to pick and choose what to believe.
2 *nm*: **le ~ et le manger** food and drink.
bois [bwa] **1** *nm* **(a)** (*gén*) wood. **en ~** made of wood, wooden; **chaise de** *ou* **en ~** wooden chair; **rester de ~** to remain impassive *ou* unmoved; **il va voir de quel ~ je me chauffe!** I'll show him (what I'm made of)! **(b)** (*Zool*) antler. (*Mus*) **les ~** the woodwind instruments. **2: ~ blanc** whitewood, deal; **~ de charpente** timber; **~ de chauffage** firewood; **~ de lit** bedstead. ♦ **boisé, e** *adj* wooded. ♦ **boiserie** *nf*: **~(s)** panelling.
boisson [bwasɔ̃] *nf* drink. **usé par la ~** ravaged by drink; **pris de ~** under the influence of drink.
boîte [bwat] **1** *nf* **(a)** (*gén*) box; (*en métal*) tin; *[conserves]* can. **mettre en ~** to can; (*fig*) **mettre qn en ~*** to pull sb's leg*. **(b)** (*) (*cabaret*) night club; (*firme*) firm; (*bureau*) office; (*école*) school. **quelle (sale) ~!** what a dump!‡
2: ~ d'allumettes box of matches; **~ crânienne** cranium; **~ à gants** glove compartment; **~ à** *ou* **aux lettres** letterbox; **~ à musique** musical box; **~ à ordures** dustbin, trash can (*US*); **~ à outils** toolbox; **~ à ouvrage** workbox; **~ postale 150** P.O. Box 150; **~ de vitesses** gearbox.
boiter [bwate] (1) *vi* to limp. **~ bas** to limp badly. ♦ **boitement** *nm* limping. ♦ **boiteux, -euse** *adj* *personne, explication* lame; *meuble* wobbly; *paix, raisonnement* shaky; *vers, phrase* faulty, clumsy.
boîtier [bwatje] *nm* case. **~ électrique** electric torch.
boitiller [bwatije] (1) *vi* to limp slightly, hobble.
bol [bɔl] *nm* bowl. **~ d'air** breath of fresh air; **avoir du ~‡** to be lucky.
boléro [bɔleʀo] *nm* (*gén*) bolero.
bolide [bɔlid] *nm* (*Astron*) meteor; (*voiture*) racing car. **comme un ~** at top speed, like a rocket.
bombance*† [bɔ̃bɑ̃s] *nf* revel. **faire ~** to revel.
bombarder [bɔ̃baʀde] (1) *vt* (*gén, Phys*) to bombard; (*bombes*) to bomb; (*obus*) to shell. (*fig*) **~ de** *cailloux* to pelt with; *questions, lettres* to bombard with; **on l'a bombardé directeur*** he was suddenly pitchforked into the position of manager. ♦ **bombardement** *nm* bombardment; bombing; shelling; pelting. **~ aérien** air raid; **~ atomique** atom-bomb attack. ♦ **bombardier** *nm* (*avion*) bomber.
bombe [bɔ̃b] **1** *nf* **(a)** (*Mil*) bomb. **éclater comme une ~** to come as a bombshell, be like a bolt out of the blue. **(b)** (*atomiseur*) **~ (insecticide)** *etc* (fly) *etc* spray. **(c)** (*Équitation*) riding hat. **(d) faire la ~*** to go on a binge*. **2: ~ au cobalt** telecobalt machine; **~ glacée** ice pudding.
bombé, e [bɔ̃be] *adj* (*gén*) rounded; *front* domed; *mur* bulging; *dos* humped; *route* steeply cambered.
bomber [bɔ̃be] (1) *vt*: **~ le torse** (*lit*) to throw out one's chest; (*fig*) to swagger about.
bon[1], bonne[1] [bɔ̃, bɔn] **1** *adj* **(a)** (*gén*) good; *outil, produit* good (quality); *odeur, ambiance* good, nice, pleasant; *placement, entreprise* sound. **être ~ en anglais** to be good at English; **une personne de ~ conseil** a man of sound judg(e)ment; **tout lui est ~ pour me discréditer** he'll stop at nothing to discredit me; **il a la bonne vie** he's got it easy*; **c'était le ~ temps!** those were the days!; **dans la bonne société** in polite society.
(b) (*charitable*) *personne, action* good, kind, kindly. **~ mouvement** nice gesture; **elle est bonne fille** she's a good-hearted girl; **mon ~ monsieur** my good man.
(c) (*utilisable*) *billet, passeport* valid. **médicament ~ jusqu'au 5 mai** medicine to be used before 5th May; **est-ce que ce vernis est encore ~?** is this varnish still usable?; **est-ce que cette eau est bonne?** is this water safe to drink?
(d) (*recommandé*) **est-ce bien ~ de fumer tant?** is it very wise to smoke so much?; **il est ~ de louer de bonne heure** it's as well *ou* it's advisable to book early; **croire ~ de faire** to think *ou* see fit to do; **comme ~ vous semble** as you think best.
(e) (*apte*) **~ pour le service** fit for service; **le voilà ~ pour recommencer** now he'll have to start all over again; **c'est ~ pour ceux qui n'ont rien à faire** it's all right *ou* fine for people who have nothing to do; **cet enfant n'est ~ à rien** this child is no good *ou* use at anything; **c'est ~ à jeter** it's fit for the dustbin; **c'est ~ à nous créer des ennuis** it will only create problems for us; **c'est ~ à savoir** it's useful to know that, that's worth knowing.
(f) (*correct*) *méthode, calcul* right; *fonctionnement* efficient, proper. **au ~ moment** at the right *ou* proper time; **le ~ usage** correct usage (of language); **il est de ~ ton de** it is good manners to; **si ma mémoire est bonne** if my memory serves me well, if I remember correctly.
(g) (*intensif*) good. **une bonne heure** a good hour; **bonne raclée*** thorough *ou* sound hiding; **une bonne averse** a heavy shower; **après un ~ moment** after quite some time; **faire ~ poids** to give good weight; **je te le dis une bonne fois** I'm telling you once and for all; **(un) ~ nombre de** a good many; **arriver ~ dernier** to come in a long way *ou* well behind the others.
(h) (*souhaits*) **~ anniversaire!** happy birthday!; **~ appétit!** enjoy your meal!; **~ courage!** good luck!; **~ retour!** safe journey back!, safe return!; **bonne santé!** I hope you keep well!; **bonnes vacances!** have a good holiday!
(i) (*locutions*) **c'est ~!** (all) right!, OK!*; **~ sang!** damn it!*; **~s baisers** much love; **~ débarras!** good riddance!; **~ gré mal gré** willy-nilly; **(à) ~ marché** cheap; **de ~ cœur** *manger, rire* heartily; *accepter* willingly, readily; **à ~ compte** *s'en sortir* lightly; *acheter* cheap; **de bonne heure** early; **à la bonne heure!** that's fine!; **être ~ enfant** to be good-natured; **cette fois-ci, on est ~!*** this time we've had it!*; **c'est de bonne guerre** that's fair enough; (*iro*) **elle est bien bonne**

celle-là!* that's a good one!; **tenir le ~ bout*** to be past the worst; **garder qch pour la bonne bouche** to save sth till the end; **voilà une bonne chose de faite** that's one good job done.

2 *adv*: **il fait ~ ici** it's nice *ou* pleasant here; **il ne ferait pas ~ le contredire** it would be unwise to contradict him.

3 *nm* (*personne*) good *ou* upright person. (*morceau*) **mange le ~ et laisse le mauvais** eat what's good and leave what's bad; **cette solution a du ~** this solution has its good points; *V aussi* **bon²**.

4 *nf*: **en voilà une bonne!** that's a good one!; (*iro*) **tu en as de bonnes, toi!*** you must be joking!*; **avoir qn à la bonne*** to like sb; *V aussi* **bonne²**.

5: bonne amie† sweetheart; **le B~ Dieu** the good Lord; **bonne étoile** lucky star; (*péj*) **bonne femme** woman; **~ mot** witty remark; **bonnes œuvres** charity; (*Rel*) **la bonne parole** the word of God; (*Scol*) **~ point** star; (*fig*) **un ~ point pour vous!** that's a point in your favour!; **~ à rien, bonne à rien** (*nm,f*) good-for-nothing; **~ sens** common sense; **bonne sœur*** nun; **~ vivant** (*adj*) jovial; (*nm*) jovial fellow.

bon² [bɔ̃] *nm* (*formulaire*) slip, form; (*coupon d'échange*) coupon, voucher; (*Fin*) bond. **~ d'épargne** savings bond; **~ de garantie** guarantee slip; **~ du Trésor** (Government) Treasury bond.

bonbon [bɔ̃bɔ̃] *nm* sweet, candy (*US*). **~ acidulé** acid drop; **~ à la menthe** mint, humbug.

bonbonne [bɔ̃bɔn] *nf* demijohn; (*Ind*) carboy.

bonbonnière [bɔ̃bɔnjɛʀ] *nf* (*boîte*) sweet box; (*fig: appartement*) bijou residence.

bond [bɔ̃] *nm* leap, bound; *[balle]* bounce. **faire des ~s** to leap about; **faire un ~ d'indignation** to leap up indignantly; **faire un ~ de surprise** to start with surprise; **se lever d'un ~** to leap *ou* spring up; **l'économie a fait un ~** there has been a boom in the economy; **les prix ont fait un ~** prices have shot up *ou* soared.

bonde [bɔ̃d] *nf* *[tonneau]* bung; *[évier]* plug; *[étang]* sluice gate; (*trou*) bung-hole; plughole.

bondé, e [bɔ̃de] *adj* packed, cram-full.

bondir [bɔ̃diʀ] (2) *vi* (*gén*) to leap *ou* spring up; *[balle]* to bounce; (*gambader*) to leap about; (*sursauter*) to start (*de* with). **~ de joie** to jump for joy; (*fig*) **cela me fait ~*** it makes me hopping mad*; **~ vers** to rush to; **~ sur sa proie** to pounce on one's prey. ♦ **bondissement** *nm* bound, leap.

bonheur [bɔnœʀ] *nm* **(a)** (*félicité*) **le ~** happiness; **avoir le ~ de voir son fils réussir** to have the joy of seeing one's son succeed; **faire le ~ de qn** to make sb happy; **quel ~!** what bliss!, what a delight! **(b)** (*chance*) (good) luck, good fortune. **il ne connaît pas son ~!** he doesn't know how lucky he is!; **par ~** fortunately, luckily; **au petit ~ (la chance)*** haphazardly.

bonhomme [bɔnɔm], *pl* **bonshommes** [bɔ̃zɔm] **1** *nm* (*) (*homme*) man, chap*, fellow; (*mari*) old man‡; (*enfant*) lad. **aller son petit ~ de chemin** to carry on in one's own sweet way; **~ de neige** snowman. **2** *adj inv* good-natured. ♦ **bonhomie** *nf* good-naturedness.

bonification [bɔnifikɑsjɔ̃] *nf* *[terre, vins]* improvement; (*Fin, Sport*) bonus. ♦ **bonifier** *vt*, **se ~** *vpr* (7) to improve.

boniment [bɔnimɑ̃] *nm* (*baratin*) patter; (*mensonge*) fib*.

bonjour [bɔ̃ʒuʀ] *nm* (*gén*) hello; (*matin*) good morning; (*après-midi*) good afternoon. **donnez-lui le ~ de ma part** give him my regards.

bonne² [bɔn] *nf* maid. **~ d'enfants** nanny; **~ à tout faire** general help; (*hum*) maid of all work; *V aussi* **bon¹**.

bonnement [bɔnmɑ̃] *adv*: **tout ~** quite simply.

bonnet [bɔnɛ] *nm* bonnet. **prendre qch sous son ~** to make sth one's concern; **c'est ~ blanc et blanc ~** it's six of one and half a dozen of the other; **~ d'âne/de bain** dunce's/bathing cap; **~ de nuit** nightcap; (**fig*) wet blanket; **~ à poils** bearskin. ♦ **bonneterie** *nf* (*objets*) hosiery; (*magasin*) hosier's shop; (*commerce*) hosiery trade. ♦ **bonnetier, -ière** *nm,f* hosier.

bonsoir [bɔ̃swaʀ] *nm* good evening; (*en se couchant*) good night. **~!*** (*rien à faire*) nothing doing!*

bonté [bɔ̃te] *nf* (*vertu*) kindness, goodness; (*acte*) (act of) kindness. **ayez la ~ de faire** would you be so kind *ou* good as to do?; **~ divine!** good heavens!

bonze [bɔ̃z] *nm* (*Rel*) bonze; (*: *chef*) bigwig*. **vieux ~ *** old fossil*.

boomerang [bumʀɑ̃g] *nm* (*lit, fig*) boomerang.

boqueteau, *pl* **~x** [bɔkto] *nm* copse.

bord [bɔʀ] *nm* **(a)** (*gén*) edge; *[route, lac]* side; *[précipice]* brink; *[verre]* brim, rim. **le ~ de la mer** the seashore; **~ du trottoir** kerb, curb (*US*); **au ~ de la rivière** *marcher* along the river bank; *s'asseoir* by the river; **passer ses vacances au ~ de la mer** to spend one's holidays at the seaside *ou* by the sea; **rempli à ras ~** full to the brim *ou* to overflowing; **chapeau à large(s) ~(s)** broad-brimmed hat.

(b) (*Naut*) side. **les hommes du ~** the crew; (*Aviat, Naut*) **à ~** on board, aboard; **jeter par-dessus ~** to throw overboard; **M X, à ~ d'une voiture bleue** Mr X, driving *ou* in a blue car.

(c) (*bordée*) tack. **tirer des ~s** to tack.

(d) au ~ de la ruine on the verge *ou* brink of ruin; **au ~ des larmes** on the verge of tears; **nous sommes du même ~** we are on the same side; **un peu fantaisiste sur les ~s*** a bit of an eccentric.

bordeaux [bɔʀdo] **1** *nm* Bordeaux (wine). **~ rouge** claret. **2** *adj inv* maroon, burgundy.

bordée [bɔʀde] *nf* (*salve*) broadside; (*quart*) watch; (*parcours*) tack. **tirer des ~s** to tack; (*fig*) **~ d'injures** torrent *ou* volley of abuse.

bordel‡ [bɔʀdɛl] *nm* brothel. (*fig*) **quel ~!** what a shambles!*

border [bɔʀde] (1) *vt* **(a)** (*Couture*) to edge (*de* with); (*ourler*) to hem. **(b)** *[arbres, maisons]* to line; *[sentier]* to run alongside. **bordé de fleurs** bordered with flowers. **(c)** *personne, couverture* to tuck in.

bordereau, *pl* **~x** [bɔʀdəʀo] *nm* note, slip; (*facture*) invoice.

bordure [bɔʀdyʀ] *nf* (*gén*) edge; (*cadre*) frame; (*de fleurs*) border; (*d'arbres*) line; (*Couture*) border. **en ~ de** (*le long de*) alongside, along the edge of; (*à côté de*) next to, by.

boréal, e, *mpl* **-aux** [bɔʀeal, o] *adj* boreal.

borgne [bɔʀɲ(ə)] *adj personne* one-eyed, blind in one eye; (*fig*) *hôtel* shady.

borne [bɔʀn(ə)] *nf* **(a)** *[route]* kilometre-marker, ≃ milestone; *[terrain]* boundary marker; *[monument]* post (of stone); (*Élec*) terminal. **3 ~s*** 3 kilometres. **(b)** (*fig*) **~s** limit(s), bounds; **dépasser les ~s** to go too far; **sans ~s** limitless, boundless; **mettre des ~s à** to limit. ♦ **borné, e** *adj personne* narrow-minded; *esprit, vie* narrow; *intelligence* limited. ♦ **borner** (1) *vt besoins, enquête, vue* to limit, restrict (*à faire* to doing, *à qch* to sth); *terrain* to mark out *ou* off. **arbres qui bornent un champ** trees which border a field; **se ~ à faire/à qch** *[personne]* to restrict *ou* limit o.s. to doing/to sth; **je me borne à vous faire remarquer que** I would just *ou* merely like to point out to you that.

bosquet [bɔskɛ] *nm* copse, grove.

bosse [bɔs] *nf* *[chameau, bossu]* hump; (*coup, monticule*) bump. **route pleine de ~s** bumpy road; **avoir la ~ du théâtre** to be a born actor.

bosseler [bɔsle] (4) *vt* (*déformer*) to dent; (*marteler*) to emboss.

bosser* [bɔse] (1) **1** *vi* to work; (*travailler dur*) to slog away*. **2** *vt examen* to swot for. ♦ **bosseur, -euse*** *nm,f* slogger*.

bossu, e [bɔsy] **1** *adj personne* hunchbacked. **dos**

~ hunched back. **2** *nm,f* hunchback.
bot [bo] *adj*: **pied** ~ club-foot.
botanique [bɔtanik] **1** *adj* botanical. **2** *nf* botany. ♦ **botaniste** *nmf* botanist.
botte [bɔt] *nf* **(a)** (high) boot; *[cavalier]* riding boot; *[égoutier]* wader. ~ **de caoutchouc** wellington (boot), gumboot; **sous la** ~ **de l'ennemi** under the enemy's heel. **(b)** *[légumes]* bunch; *[foin]* sheaf; (*au carré*) bale. **(c)** (*Escrime*) thrust.
botter [bɔte] (1) *vt* **(a)** to put boots on. **se** ~ to put one's boots on; **botté de cuir** with leather boots on, wearing leather boots; **ça me botte**‡ I like *ou* dig* that. **(b)** (*Ftbl*) to kick. ~ **les fesses de qn**‡ to give sb a kick in the pants‡. ♦ **bottier** *nm* bootmaker. ♦ **bottillon** *nm* ankle boot. ♦ **bottine** *nf* (ankle) boot.
Bottin [bɔtɛ̃] *nm* ® directory, phonebook.
bouc [buk] *nm* (*Zool*) (billy) goat; (*barbe*) goatee (beard). ~ **émissaire** scapegoat.
boucan* [bukɑ̃] *nm* din, racket. **faire du** ~ (*bruit*) to kick up* a din *ou* a racket; (*protestation*) to kick up* a fuss.
bouche [buʃ] **1** *nf* **(a)** (*gén*) mouth. **j'ai la** ~ **pâteuse** my tongue feels coated. **(b)** (*fig*) **fermer la** ~ **à qn** to shut sb up; **dans sa** ~**, ce mot choque** when he says *ou* uses it, that word sounds offensive; **il a toujours l'injure à la** ~ he's always ready with an insult; **il n'a que ce mot-là à la** ~ that word is never off his lips; **de** ~ **à oreille** by word of mouth; ~ **consue!*** mum's the word!*; **passer de** ~ **en** ~ to be rumoured about; **il en a plein la** ~ he can talk of nothing else; **faire la fine** ~ to turn one's nose up; **avoir la** ~ **en cœur** to simper.
2: ~ **d'aération** air vent; ~ **à** ~ (*nm inv*) kiss of life; ~ **d'égout** manhole; ~ **d'incendie** fire hydrant; ~ **de métro** metro entrance.
bouchée[1] [buʃe] *nf* **(a)** mouthful. **pour une** ~ **de pain** for a song; **mettre les** ~**s doubles** to put on a spurt; **ne faire qu'une** ~ **de** to make short work of. **(b) une** ~ **(au chocolat)** a chocolate; ~ **à la reine** savoury vol-au-vent.
boucher[1] [buʃe] (1) **1** *vt* **(a)** *bouteille* to cork, put the *ou* a cork in; *trou* to fill up; *fuite* to plug, stop; *fenêtre, nez, lavabo* to block (up); *vue* to block. ~ **le passage** to be in the way. **(b) ça lui en a bouché un coin**‡ it floored* *ou* threw* him. **2 se** ~ *vpr* *[évier]* to get blocked up; *[temps]* to become overcast. **se** ~ **le nez** to hold one's nose; **se** ~ **les oreilles** to put one's fingers in one's ears. ♦ **bouché, e**[2] *adj* *temps* overcast; (‡) *personne* thick‡. **les maths sont** ~**es** there's no future in maths. ♦ **bouche-trou,** *pl* ~**-**~**s** *nm* stopgap.
boucher[2] [buʃe] *nm* (*lit, fig*) butcher. ♦ **bouchère** *nf* (woman) butcher; (*épouse*) butcher's wife. ♦ **boucherie** *nf* (*magasin*) butcher's (shop); (*métier*) butchery (trade); (*fig*) slaughter.
bouchon [buʃɔ̃] *nm* **(a)** (*en liège*) cork; (*en verre, plastique*) stopper; (*en chiffon*) plug; *[bidon]* cap; *[tube]* top; *[évier]* plug. **(b)** (*Pêche*) float. **(c)** (*Aut*) holdup, traffic jam.
boucle [bukl(ə)] *nf [ceinture]* buckle; *[cheveux]* curl, lock; *[lacet]* bow; *[rivière]* loop; (*Sport*) lap; (*Aviat, Écriture, Ordinateurs*) loop. ~ **d'oreille** earring.
boucler [bukle] (1) **1** *vt* **(a)** *ceinture* to buckle, fasten (up); (*) *porte* to shut. (*lit, fig*) ~ **sa valise** to pack one's bags; **tu vas la** ~**!**‡ will you belt up!‡ **(b)** (*fig*) *affaire* to finish off; *circuit* to complete; *budget* to balance. **(c)** (*: *enfermer*) to lock up. **être bouclé chez soi** to be cooped up *ou* stuck at home. **(d)** (*Mil: encercler*) to seal off. **2** *vi* to curl, be curly. ♦ **bouclage** *nm* locking up; sealing off. ♦ **bouclé, e** *adj* curly.
bouclier [buklije] *nm* (*gén*) shield.
Bouddha [buda] *nm* Buddha. ♦ **bouddhique** *nm* Buddhistic. ♦ **bouddhisme** *adj* Buddhism. ♦ **bouddhiste** *adj, nmf* Buddhist.
bouder [bude] (1) **1** *vi* to sulk. **2** *vt* to refuse to have anything to do with. **il se boudent** they're not on speaking terms. ♦ **bouderie** *nf* (*état*) sulkiness; (*action*) sulk. ♦ **boudeur, -euse** *adj* sulky.
boudin [budɛ̃] *nm* **(a)** ~ **noir/blanc** ≃ black/white pudding. **(b)** (*bourrelet*) roll.
boudiné, e [budine] *adj* **(a)** *doigt* podgy. **(b)** (*serré*) ~ **dans** squeezed into, bulging out of.
boudoir [budwaʀ] *nm* (*salon*) boudoir; (*biscuit*) sponge finger.
boue [bu] *nf* (*gén, fig*) mud; *[canal]* sludge.
bouée [bwe] *nf* buoy; *[baigneur]* rubber ring. ~ **de sauvetage** lifebuoy.
boueux, -euse [bwø, øz] **1** *adj* muddy. **2** *nm* dustman, garbage collector (*US*).
bouffée [bufe] *nf [parfum]* whiff; *[pipe]* puff; *[colère]* outburst; *[orgueil]* fit; *[vent]* puff, gust. (*Méd*) ~ **de chaleur** hot flush.
bouffer[1] [bufe] (1) *vi [manche]* to puff out; *[cheveux]* to be bouffant. ♦ **bouffant, e** *adj* puffed-out; bouffant. **pantalon** ~ baggy breeches.
bouffer[2]* [bufe] (1) **1** *vt* to eat, gobble up*. **se** ~ **le nez** to scratch each other's eyes out; ~ **du curé** to be violently anti-church. **2** *vi* to eat, nosh‡. **on a bien bouffé** the grub was great‡. ♦ **bouffe**‡ *nf* grub‡.
bouffir [bufiʀ] (2) *vt* to puff up. ♦ **bouffi, e** *adj* *visage,* (*fig*) puffed up; *yeux* swollen. ♦ **bouffissure** *nf* puffiness.
bouffon, -onne [bufɔ̃, ɔn] **1** *adj* farcical, comical. **2** *nm* (*pitre*) buffoon, clown; (*Hist*) jester. ♦ **bouffonnerie** *nf* **(a)** (*caractère*) drollery. **(b)** ~**s** (*comportement*) antics; (*paroles*) jesting; **faire des** ~**s** to clown about.
bougeoir [buʒwaʀ] *nm* (*bas*) candle-holder; (*haut*) candlestick.
bouger [buʒe] (3) **1** *vi* to move, stir; (*protester*) to stir. **ne bouge pas** keep still, don't move; **il n'a pas bougé (de chez lui)** he stayed in *ou* at home; **ne pas** ~ *[idées, prix]* to stay the same; **ce tissu ne bouge pas** this cloth wears well; (*dimension*) this cloth is shrink-resistant; (*couleur*) this cloth will not fade. **2** *vt* (*) *objet* to move, shift. **il n'a pas bougé le petit doigt** he didn't lift a finger (to help). **3 se** ~ ‡ *vpr* to move. **bouge-toi de là!** shift over!*, shift out of the way!*; **il faut se** ~ **pour obtenir satisfaction** you have to put yourself out to get satisfaction. ♦ **bougeotte*** *nf*: **avoir la** ~ (*remuer*) to have the fidgets; (*voyager*) to be always on the move.
bougie [buʒi] *nf* **(a)** candle; (*Aut*) spark plug; (*Élec*) watt. **(b)** (*: *visage*) face.
bougon, -onne [bugɔ̃, ɔn] **1** *adj* grumpy, grouchy. **2** *nm,f* grumbler. ♦ **bougonnement** *nm* grumbling, grouching. ♦ **bougonner** (1) *vi* to grouch, grumble.
bougre* [bugʀ(ə)] *nm* fellow*. **pauvre** ~ poor devil*; ~ **d'idiot!** stupid idiot!* ♦ **bougrement*** *adv* damned*.
bouillant, e [bujɑ̃, ɑ̃t] *adj* (*brûlant*) boiling (hot); (*qui bout*) boiling; *tempérament* fiery.
bouille* [buj] *nf* (*visage*) face.
bouillie [buji] *nf [bébé]* baby cereal; *[vieillard]* porridge. **mettre en** ~ to reduce to a pulp.
bouillir [bujiʀ] (15) *vi* **(a)** (*lit*) to boil, be boiling. **faire** ~ *eau* to boil, bring to the boil; *linge* to boil; *biberon* to sterilize. **(b)** (*fig*) to boil. **faire** ~ **qn** to make sb's blood boil; ~ **d'impatience** to seethe with impatience. ♦ **bouilloire** *nf* kettle.
bouillon [bujɔ̃] **1** *nm* **(a)** (*soupe*) stock. **prendre un** ~* (*en nageant*) to swallow a mouthful; (*Fin*) to make a big loss. **(b)** (*bouillonnement*) bubble (in boiling liquid). **couler à gros** ~**s** to gush out. **2:** ~ **cube** stock cube; (*Bio*) ~ **de culture** (culture) medium.
bouillonner [bujɔne] (1) *vi [liquide chaud]* to bubble; *[torrent]* to foam; *[idées]* to bubble up;

[esprit] to seethe. **il bouillonne d'idées** his mind is teeming with ideas. ♦ **bouillonnement** *nm* bubbling; seething; foaming.
bouillotte [bujɔt] *nf* hot-water bottle.
boulanger [bulɑ̃ʒe] *nm* baker. ♦ **boulangère** *nf* (woman) baker; (*épouse*) baker's wife. ♦ **boulangerie** *nf* (*magasin*) baker's (shop), bakery; (*commerce*) bakery trade.
boule [bul] **1** *nf* **(a)** (*Billard*) ball; (*Boules*) bowl; (*Casino*) boule. **roulé en ~** rolled up in a ball. **(b) avoir une ~ dans la gorge** to have a lump in one's throat; **perdre la ~*** to go nuts*; **être/se mettre en ~*** to be/get mad*. **2: ~ de cristal** crystal ball; **~ de gomme** fruit pastille; **~ de neige** snowball; (*fig*) **faire ~ de neige** to snowball; ® **~ Quiès** earplug.
bouleau, *pl* **~x** [bulo] *nm* silver birch.
bouledogue [buldɔg] *nm* bulldog.
boulet [bulɛ] *nm* **(a)** *[forçat]* ball and chain. **~ (de canon)** cannonball; (*fig*) **traîner un ~** to have a millstone round one's neck. **(b)** *[charbon]* (coal) nut.
boulette [bulɛt] *nf* **(a)** *[papier]* pellet; (*Culin*) meatball; (*empoisonnée*) poison ball. **(b)** (**fig*) blunder, bloomer*.
boulevard [bulvaʀ] *nm* boulevard. **pièce de ~** light comedy.
bouleverser [bulvɛʀse] (1) *vt* **(a)** *objets* to turn upside down; *plans* to disrupt. **(b)** (*émouvoir*) to distress deeply, overwhelm, shatter. **bouleversé par la peur** distraught with fear. ♦ **bouleversant, e** *adj récit* deeply moving; *nouvelle* shattering. ♦ **bouleversement** *nm* upheaval, disruption. **le ~ de son visage** the utter distress on his face.
boulier [bulje] *nm* (*calcul*) abacus.
boulon [bulɔ̃] *nm* bolt. ♦ **boulonner** (1) **1** *vt* to bolt (down *ou* on *etc*). **2** *vi* (*) to work. **~ dur** to slog *ou* slave away*.
boulot[1], -otte [bulo, ɔt] *adj* plump, tubby*.
boulot[2]* [bulo] *nm* (*gén*) work; (*emploi*) job. **quel ~!** what a job!; **allons, au ~!** let's get cracking!*
boulotter* [bulɔte] (1) **1** *vi* to eat, nosh‡. **on a bien boulotté** we had a good meal *ou* nosh‡. **2** *vt* to eat.
boum [bum] *nm* bang. **~ par terre!** whoops a daisy!; **être en plein ~‡** to be in full swing.
bouquet [bukɛ] *nm* **(a)** *[fleurs]* bunch of flowers; (*soigneusement composé*) bouquet; *[thym etc]* bunch. **~ d'arbres** clump of trees. **(b)** *[feu d'artifice]* crowning piece. (*fig*) **c'est le ~!*** that takes the cake!* **(c)** *[vin]* bouquet. **(d)** (*crevette*) prawn.
bouquin* [bukɛ̃] *nm* book. ♦ **bouquiner*** (1) *vti* to read.
bourbier [buʀbje] *nm* quagmire; (*fig*) mess.
bourde* [buʀd(ə)] *nf* blunder, bloomer*.
bourdon [buʀdɔ̃] *nm* (*Zool*) bumblebee; (*cloche*) great bell. **avoir le ~*** to have the blues*.
bourdonnement [buʀdɔnmɑ̃] *nm [voix, insecte]* buzz; *[moteur]* drone. **avoir des ~s d'oreilles** to have a buzzing noise in one's ears. ♦ **bourdonner** (1) *vi* to buzz; to drone.
bourg [buʀ] *nm* market town; (*petit*) village. ♦ **bourgade** *nf* village, (small) town.
bourgeois, e [buʀʒwa, waz] **1** *adj* (*gén*) middle-class; (*Pol, péj*) bourgeois. **2** *nm,f* **(a)** bourgeois, middle-class person. **grand ~** upper middle-class person. **(b)** (*Hist*) (*citoyen*) burgess; (*riche roturier*) bourgeois. **3** *nf* (**hum: épouse*) **ma ~e** the wife*. ♦ **bourgeoisement** *adv penser* conventionally; *vivre* comfortably. ♦ **bourgeoisie** *nf* middle classes, bourgeoisie. **petite ~** lower middle class.
bourgeon [buʀʒɔ̃] *nm* bud. ♦ **bourgeonner** (1) *vi* to (come into) bud.
bourgmestre [buʀgmɛstʀ(ə)] *nm* burgomaster.
bourgogne [buʀgɔɲ] *nm* (*vin*) burgundy.
bourlinguer [buʀlɛ̃ge] (1) *vi* (*naviguer*) to sail; (*: *voyager*) to knock about a lot*.
bourrade [buʀad] *nf* (*du poing*) thump; (*du coude*) poke.
bourrage [buʀaʒ] *nm*: **~ de crâne*** brainwashing; (*Scol*) cramming.
bourrasque [buʀask(ə)] *nf* gust of wind, squall. **~ de neige** flurry of snow.
bourratif, -ive [buʀatif, iv] *adj* filling, stodgy.
bourre [buʀ] *nf [coussin]* stuffing; *[fusil]* wad. **à la ~‡** late.
bourré, e [buʀe] *adj* **(a)** (*plein*) packed, crammed (*de* with). **(b)** (‡: *ivre*) tight*, plastered‡.
bourreau, *pl* **~x** [buʀo] **1** *nm* (*tortionnaire*) torturer; (*Hist*) executioner; *[pendaison]* hangman. **2: ~ des cœurs** ladykiller; **~ d'enfants** child *ou* baby batterer; **~ de travail** glutton for work*.
bourrelet [buʀlɛ] *nm* (*gén*) roll; *[porte]* draught excluder. **~ (de chair)** roll of flesh, spare tyre*.
bourrer [buʀe] (1) *vt* **(a)** *coussin* to stuff; *pipe* to fill; *valise* to cram full. **~ un sac de papiers** to cram papers into a bag; **~ qn de nourriture** to stuff sb with food; **les frites, ça bourre!** chips are very filling! **(b) ~ le crâne à qn*** (*endoctriner*) to brainwash sb; (*tromper*) to feed sb a lot of eyewash*; (*Scol*) to cram sb; **~ qn de coups** to pummel sb.
bourrique [buʀik] *nf* **(a)** (*âne*) donkey, ass; (*ânesse*) she-ass. **(b)** (**fig*) (*imbécile*) ass; (*têtu*) mule. **faire tourner qn en ~** to drive sb mad*.
bourru, e [buʀy] *adj* surly.
bourse [buʀs(ə)] **1** *nf* **(a)** (*porte-monnaie*) purse. **la ~ ou la vie!** your money or your life!; **sans ~ délier** without spending a penny; **ils font ~ commune** they pool their resources; **ils font ~ à part** they keep their finances separate. **(b) la B~** ≃ the Stock Exchange *ou* Market (*US*); **la B~ monte/descend** the market is going up/down. **(c)** (*Univ*) **~ (d'études)** (student's) grant. **2: B~ du commerce** commodity market; **B~ du travail** ≃ trade union centre. ♦ **boursier, -ière 1** *adj* Stock Market. **2** *nm,f* (*Univ*) grant-holder.
boursoufler [buʀsufle] (1) **1** *vt* to puff up, bloat. **2 se ~** *vpr [peinture]* to blister. ♦ **boursouflé, e** *adj* puffy, bloated; blistered; *style* bombastic. ♦ **boursouflure** *nf* puffiness; pomposity; (*cloque*) blister.
bousculer [buskyle] (1) **1** *vt* (*pousser*) to jostle; (*heurter*) to bump into; (*presser*) to rush. (*fig*) **être très bousculé** to be rushed off one's feet. **2 se ~** *vpr* to jostle each other. ♦ **bousculade** *nf* (*remous*) jostle, crush; (*hâte*) rush, scramble.
bouse [buz] *nf* cow pat. **de la ~** (cattle) dung.
bousiller* [buzije] (1) *vt travail* to botch; *appareil, voiture* to smash up; *personne* to bump off‡.
boussole [busɔl] *nf* compass. (*fig*) **perdre la ~*** to go off one's head.
bout [bu] *nm* **(a)** (*extrémité*) (*gén*) end; *[nez, canne, oreille etc]* tip. **du ~ du pied** with one's toe; **à ~ de bras** at arm's length; (*fig*) **du ~ des lèvres** reluctantly, half-heartedly; **sur le ~ de la langue** on the tip of one's tongue; **jusqu'au ~ des ongles** to one's fingertips; **savoir qch sur le ~ du doigt** to have sth at one's fingertips.
(b) *[espace, durée]* end. **à l'autre ~ de la pièce** at the far *ou* other end of the room; **au ~ d'un mois** at the end of a month; **on n'en voit pas le ~** there doesn't seem to be any end to it; **d'un ~ à l'autre de ses œuvres/du voyage** throughout his works/the journey; (*fig*) **ce n'est pas le ~ du monde!** it's not the end of the world!
(c) (*morceau*) *[ficelle, pain]* piece, bit. **il m'a fait un ~ de conduite** he went part of the way with me; **cela fait un ~ (de chemin)** it's some distance *ou* quite a long way away; **il est resté un (bon) ~ de temps** he stayed a while *ou* quite some time; **un ~ de terrain/ciel** a patch of land/sky; **un petit ~ de chou*** a little kid*.
(d) être à ~ (*fatigué*) to be all in*; (*en colère*) to

have had enough; **à ~ de souffle** out of breath; **être à ~ de ressources** to have no money left; **être à ~ de nerfs** to be at the end of one's tether; **pousser qn à ~** to push sb to the limit (of his patience).

(e) (*locutions*) **au ~ du compte** in the end; **être au ~ de son rouleau*** (*idées*) to have run out of ideas; (*ressources*) to be running short of money; (*forces*) to be at the end of one's tether; **il n'est pas au ~ de ses peines** he's not out of the wood yet; **jusqu'au ~** right to the end; **~ à ~** end to end; **de ~ en ~** right through, from start to finish; **à ~ portant** at point-blank range.

boutade [butad] *nf* sally.

boute-en-train [butɑ̃tʀɛ̃] *nm inv* live wire*. **le ~ de la soirée** the life and soul of the party.

bouteille [butɛj] *nf* (*gén*) bottle; *[gaz]* cylinder. **® ~ Thermos** Thermos ® flask; **~ de vin** (*récipient*) wine bottle; (*contenu*) bottle of wine; **mettre en ~s** to bottle; **prendre de la ~*** to be getting on in years; **c'est la ~ à l'encre** the whole business is about as clear as mud.

boutique [butik] *nf* shop, store. **quelle sale ~!** what a dump!* ♦ **boutiquier, -ière** *nm,f* shopkeeper.

bouton [butɔ̃] **1** *nm* (*Couture*) button; (*Élec*) switch; *[porte, radio]* knob; *[sonnette]* (push-) button; (*Méd*) spot, pimple; (*Bot*) bud. **en ~** in bud; **~ de rose** rosebud. **2**: **~ de col** collar stud; **~ de manchette** cufflink; **~-d'or** *nm, pl* **~s-~** buttercup; **~-pression** *nm, pl* **~s-~** press-stud. ♦ **boutonner** (1) **1** *vt* to button (up). **2 se ~** *vpr* *[vêtement]* to button (up); *[personne]* to button (up) one's coat *etc.* ♦ **boutonneux, -euse** *adj* pimply, spotty. ♦ **boutonnière** *nf* buttonhole.

bouture [butyʀ] *nf* cutting. ♦ **bouturer** (1) *vt* to take a cutting from.

bouvier [buvje] *nm* herdsman.

bouvreuil [buvʀœj] *nm* bullfinch.

bovin, e [bɔvɛ̃, in] **1** *adj* (*lit, fig*) bovine. **2** *nmpl*: **~s** cattle.

bowling [buliŋ] *nm* (*jeu*) (tenpin) bowling; (*salle*) bowling alley.

box, *pl* **boxes** [bɔks] *nm [dortoir]* cubicle; *[écurie]* loose-box; (*garage*) lock-up (garage). **~ des accusés** dock.

boxe [bɔks(ə)] *nf* boxing. ♦ **boxer**[1] [bɔkse] (1) **1** *vi* to box, be a boxer. **2** *vt* to box against, fight; (**‡**: *frapper*) to thump. ♦ **boxeur** *nm* boxer.

boxer[2] [bɔksɛʀ] *nm* boxer (dog).

boyau, *pl* **~x** [bwajo] *nm* **(a)** (*intestins*) **~x** guts; **~ (de chat)** (cat)gut. **(b)** (*passage*) (narrow) passageway. **(c)** *[bicyclette]* racing tyre.

boycotter [bɔjkɔte] (1) *vt* to boycott. ♦ **boycott(age)** *nm* boycott.

bracelet [bʀaslɛ] *nm [poignet]* bracelet; *[bras, cheville]* bangle; *[montre]* strap. **~-montre** *nm, pl* **~s-~s** wrist watch.

braconnage [bʀakɔnaʒ] *nm* poaching. ♦ **braconner** (1) *vi* to poach. ♦ **braconnier** *nm* poacher.

brader [bʀade] (1) *vt* (*Comm, fig*) to sell off. ♦ **braderie** *nf* cut-price market.

braguette [bʀagɛt] *nf* fly, flies (*of trousers*).

brailler [bʀɑje] (1) **1** *vi* to bawl. **2** *vt chanson* to bawl out. ♦ **braillard, e 1** *adj* bawling. **2** *nm,f* bawler. ♦ **braillement** *nm* bawling.

braire [bʀɛʀ] (50) *vi* (*lit, fig*) to bray. **faire ~ qn‡** to get on sb's wick‡.

braise [bʀɛz] *nf*: **~(s)** embers; **de ~** *yeux* fiery.

braiser [bʀeze] (1) *vt* to braise.

bramer [bʀɑme] (1) *vi [cerf]* to bell; (**fig*) to wail.

brancard [bʀɑ̃kaʀ] *nm* (*bras*) shaft; (*civière*) stretcher. ♦ **brancardier, -ière** *nm,f* stretcher-bearer.

branche [bʀɑ̃ʃ] *nf* **(a)** (*Bot*) branch, bough. **asperges en ~s** asparagus spears; **céleri en ~s** sticks of celery. **(b)** *[nerfs, famille, rivière]* branch; *[lunettes]* side-piece; *[compas]* leg; *[ciseaux]* blade. **la ~ maternelle** the maternal branch *ou* the mother's side of the family. **(c)** (*secteur*) branch. **s'orienter vers une ~ technique** to go in for the technical side. ♦ **branchage** *nm* branches, boughs. **~s** fallen branches.

brancher [bʀɑ̃ʃe] (1) *vt prise* to plug in; *tuyau, téléphone* to connect up. **~ qch sur** to plug sth into; to connect sth up with; (*fig*) **~ qn sur un sujet** to start sb off *ou* launch sb on a subject. ♦ **branchement** *nm* (*action*) plugging-in; connecting-up; (*conduite*) connection.

branchies [bʀɑ̃ʃi] *nfpl* gills.

brandir [bʀɑ̃diʀ] (2) *vt* to brandish, flourish.

branlant, e [bʀɑ̃lɑ̃, ɑ̃t] *adj* (*gén*) shaky; *dent* loose.

branle [bʀɑ̃l] *nm [cloche]* swing. **mettre en ~** *cloche* to swing, set swinging; (*fig*) *forces* to set in motion, set off; **se mettre en ~** to get going *ou* moving.

branle-bas [bʀɑ̃lbɑ] *nm inv* bustle, commotion. **être en ~** to be in a state of commotion; **~ de combat!** 'action stations!'

branler [bʀɑ̃le] (1) **1** *vt*: **~ la tête** to shake one's head. **2** *vi* (*gén, fig*) to be shaky; *[dent]* to be loose. (*fig*) **ça branle dans le manche** the situation is very unsettled.

braquage [bʀakaʒ] *nm* (*Aut*) (steering) lock.

braquer [bʀake] (1) **1** *vt* **(a) ~ une arme** *etc* **sur** to point *ou* aim a weapon *etc* at; **~ les yeux sur qch** to fix one's eyes on sth. **(b)** (*Aut*) to turn. **(c)** (*fig: buter*) **~ qn** to antagonize sb; **~ qn contre qch** to turn sb against sth. **2** *vi* (*Aut*) to turn the steering wheel. *[voiture]* **~ bien/mal** to have a good/bad lock. **3 se ~** *vpr* to dig one's heels in. **se ~ contre** to set one's face against.

braquet [bʀakɛ] *nm* gear ratio.

bras [bʀa] *nm* **(a)** (*lit, fig*) arm. **donner le ~ à qn** to give sb one's arm; **être au ~ de qn** to be on sb's arm; **se donner le ~** to link arms; **~ dessus, ~ dessous** arm in arm; (*lit*) **les ~ croisés** with one's arms folded; (*fig*) **rester les ~ croisés** to sit idly by; (*fig*) **~ droit** right-hand man. **(b)** (*travailleur*) hand, worker. **manquer de ~** to be short-handed. **(c)** *[outil]* handle; *[fauteuil, électrophone]* arm; *[grue]* jib; *[croix]* limb; *[brancard]* shaft. **(d)** *[fleuve]* branch. **(e) en ~ de chemise** in one's shirt sleeves; **saisir qn à ~ le corps** to seize sb bodily; **avoir le ~ long** to have a long arm; (*lit, fig*) **à ~ ouverts** with open arms; **tomber sur qn à ~ raccourcis*** to set on sb; **lever les ~ au ciel** to throw up one's arms; **les ~ m'en tombent** I'm stunned; **avoir qch/qn sur les ~*** to have sth/sb on one's hands, be stuck* with sth/sb; **dans les ~ de Morphée** in the arms of Morpheus.

brasier [bʀɑzje] *nm* inferno.

brassage [bʀasaʒ] *nm* **(a)** *[bière]* brewing. **(b)** (*mélange*) mixing. **~ de races** intermixing of races.

brassard [bʀasaʀ] *nm* armband.

brasse [bʀas] *nf* **(a)** (*Sport*) breast-stroke. **~ papillon** butterfly(-stroke). **(b)** (*Naut*) fathom.

brassée [bʀase] *nf* armful.

brasser [bʀase] (1) *vt* **(a)** (*remuer*) to stir (up); (*mélanger*) to mix; *salade* to toss; *cartes* to shuffle; *argent* to handle a lot of. **~ des affaires** to be in big business. **(b)** *bière* to brew. ♦ **brasserie** *nf* (*café*) ≃ pub, bar, brasserie; (*usine*) brewery. ♦ **brasseur, -euse** *nm,f [bière]* brewer. **~ d'affaires** big businessman.

brassière [bʀasjɛʀ] *nf [bébé]* vest.

bravade [bʀavad] *nf* act of bravado. **par ~** out of bravado.

brave [bʀav] *adj* **(a)** (*courageux*) brave. **faire le ~** to put on a bold front. **(b)** (*bon*) nice; (*honnête*) decent, honest. **de ~s gens** good *ou* decent people; **mon ~ (homme)** my good man. ♦ **bravement** *adv* bravely.

braver [bʀave] (1) *vt autorité* to defy; *danger*

to brave. ~ **l'opinion** to fly in the face of (public) opinion.

bravo [bʀavo] **1** *excl* (*félicitation*) well done!, bravo!; (*approbation*) hear! hear! **2** *nm* cheer.

bravoure [bʀavuʀ] *nf* bravery.

break [bʀɛk] *nm* (*Aut*) estate (car), station wagon (*US*).

brebis [bʀəbi] *nf* (*Zool*) ewe; (*Rel: pl*) flock. ~ **égarée/galeuse** stray/black sheep.

brèche [bʀɛʃ] *nf* (*gén*) breach. **faire une ~ à sa fortune** to make a hole in one's fortune; (*fig*) **être toujours sur la ~** to be always hard at it*.

bredouille [bʀəduj] *adj* (*gén*) empty-handed.

bredouiller [bʀəduje] (1) **1** *vi* to stammer, mumble. **2** *vt* to mumble, stammer (out). ♦ **bredouillement** *nm* mumbling, stammering.

bref, brève [bʀɛf, ɛv] **1** *adj* (*gén*) brief, short; *voyelle, syllabe* short. **soyez ~** be brief; **à ~ délai** shortly. **2** *adv* (*pour résumer*) in short, in brief; (*passons*) anyway. **en ~** in short, in brief.

brelan [bʀəlɑ̃] *nm* (*Cartes*) three of a kind. ~ **d'as** three aces.

breloque [bʀəlɔk] *nf* bracelet charm.

Brésil [bʀezil] *nm* Brazil. ♦ **brésilien, -ienne** *adj*, **B~(ne)** *nm(f)* Brazilian.

Bretagne [bʀətaɲ] *nf* Brittany.

bretelle [bʀətɛl] *nf* **(a)** (*gén*) strap; *[fusil]* sling. *[pantalon]* ~**s** braces, suspenders (*US*). **(b)** (*Rail*) crossover; (*Aut*) link road. ~ **de raccordement** access road; ~ **de contournement** bypass.

breton, -onne [bʀətɔ̃, ɔn] *adj*, **B~(ne)** *nm(f)* Breton.

breuvage [bʀœvaʒ] *nm* drink, beverage.

brève [bʀɛv] *V* **bref.**

brevet [bʀəvɛ] *nm* (*diplôme*) diploma, certificate; (*Scol*) ≃ (G.C.E.) 'O' level; *[pilote]* licence; (*fig: garantie*) guarantee. (*Naut*) ~ **de capitaine** master's ticket; ~ **(d'invention)** patent. ♦ **brevetable** *adj* patentable. ♦ **breveté, e** *adj invention* patented; *technicien* qualified. ♦ **breveter** (4) *vt* to patent. **faire ~ qch** to take out a patent for sth.

bréviaire [bʀevjɛʀ] *nm* (*Rel*) breviary; (*fig*) bible.

bribe [bʀib] *nf* bit. ~**s de** *conversation* snatches of; *nourriture* scraps of; *fortune* remnants of; **par ~s** in snatches.

bric-à-brac [bʀikabʀak] *nm inv* (*objets, fig*) bric-a-brac; (*magasin*) junk shop.

bric et de broc [bʀikedbʀɔk] *loc adv*: **de ~** any old how*; *meublé* with bits and pieces.

brick [bʀik] *nm* (*Naut*) brig.

bricole* [bʀikɔl] *nf* (*babiole*) trifle; (*cadeau*) token; (*travail*) easy job. **il ne reste que des ~s** there are only a few bits and pieces left; **10 F et des ~s** 10 francs odd*.

bricoler [bʀikɔle] (1) **1** *vi* to do odd jobs; (*passe-temps*) to tinker about. **2** *vt* (*réparer*) to fix up, mend; (*fabriquer*) to knock up. ♦ **bricolage** *nm* odd jobs; tinkering about; (*réparation*) makeshift repair. **rayon ~** do-it-yourself department. ♦ **bricoleur, -euse** *nm,f* handyman (*ou* woman).

bride [bʀid] *nf* **(a)** (*Équitation*) bridle. **tenir en ~** *cheval, passions* to curb; **laisser la ~ sur le cou** *ou* **col à un cheval** to give a horse his head; **laisser la ~ sur le cou à qn** to leave sb a free hand; **à ~ abattue** hell for leather. **(b)** *[bonnet]* string; (*en cuir*) strap. ♦ **brider** (1) *vt* (*lit*) to bridle; (*fig*) to keep in check. **il est bridé dans son costume** his suit is too tight for him; **avoir les yeux bridés** to have slit eyes.

bridge [bʀidʒ(ə)] *nm* (*jeu, dents*) bridge; (*partie*) game of bridge. ♦ **bridger** (3) *vi* to play bridge. ♦ **bridgeur, -euse** *nm,f* bridge player.

brièvement [bʀijɛvmɑ̃] *adv* briefly. ♦ **brièveté** *nf* brevity.

brigade [bʀigad] *nf* (*Mil*) brigade; (*Police*) squad; (*équipe*) team. ♦ **brigadier** *nm* (*Police*) sergeant; (*Mil*) corporal.

brigand [bʀigɑ̃] *nm* (†) brigand; (*filou*) crook; (*hum: enfant*) rascal. ♦ **brigandage** *nm* brigandage. **(actes de) ~** robbery; (*fig*) **c'est du ~!** it's daylight robbery!

briguer [bʀige] (1) *vt* *emploi, faveur* to covet; *amitié, suffrages* to solicit.

brillant, e [bʀijɑ̃, ɑ̃t] **1** *adj* **(a)** (*luisant*) shiny; (*étincelant*) sparkling; *couleur* bright. **yeux ~s de fièvre/colère** eyes bright with fever/glittering with anger. **(b)** *personne, idées etc* brilliant. **ce n'est pas ~** it's not outstanding *ou* up to much. **2** *nm* **(a)** (*étincelant*) sparkle; (*luisant*) shine; *[couleur]* brightness; *[étoffe]* sheen; (*par usure*) shine; (*fig*) *[esprit]* brilliance. **donner du ~ à** to polish up. **(b)** (*diamant*) brilliant. ♦ **brillamment** *adv* brilliantly.

briller [bʀije] (1) *vi* **(a)** (*gén*) to shine; *[diamant]* to sparkle; *[étoile]* to twinkle; *[éclair]* to flash; *[surface humide]* to glisten. **faire ~** *meuble etc* to polish; (*fig*) *avantages* to paint a glowing picture of; **ses yeux brillaient de joie** his eyes shone *ou* sparkled with joy. **(b)** *[personne]* to shine. ~ **par son talent** to be outstandingly talented; **il ne brille pas par le courage** courage is not his strong point; ~ **par son absence** to be conspicuous by one's absence.

brimer [bʀime] (1) *vt* to bully; (*Mil, Scol*) to rag. **je suis brimé*** I'm being got at*. ♦ **brimade** *nf* vexation. ~**(s)** ragging.

brin [bʀɛ̃] *nm* **(a)** *[herbe]* blade; *[muguet]* sprig; *[osier]* twig; *[paille]* wisp. (*fig*) **un beau ~ de fille** a fine-looking girl. **(b)** *[corde]* strand. **(c) un ~ de** a touch *ou* grain of; **faire un ~ de causette** to have a bit of a chat*; **faire un ~ de toilette** to have a quick wash; **il n'y a pas un ~ de vent** there isn't a breath of wind; **un ~ embêté*/plus grand** a shade worried/bigger. ♦ **brindille** *nf* twig.

bringue* [bʀɛ̃g] *nf* **(a)** binge*. **faire la ~** to go on a binge*. **(b)** (*femme*) **grande ~** beanpole*.

bringuebaler* [bʀɛ̃gbale] (1) **1** *vi* *[tête, voiture]* to shake about, joggle; (*avec bruit*) to rattle. **2** *vt* to cart about. ♦ **bringuebalant, e*** *adj auto* ramshackle. ♦ **bringuebalement*** *nm* shaking (about); rattle.

brio [bʀijo] *nm* brilliance; (*Mus*) brio. **avec ~** brilliantly.

brioche [bʀijɔʃ] *nf* brioche, bun; (*: *ventre*) paunch.

brique [bʀik] **1** *nf* (*Constr*) brick; (*) a million (old) francs. **2** *adj inv* brick red.

briquer* [bʀike] (1) *vt* to polish up.

briquet [bʀikɛ] *nm* (cigarette) lighter.

bris [bʀi] *nm* breaking. ~ **de clôture** breaking-in; ~ **de glaces** broken windows.

brisant [bʀizɑ̃] *nm* (*vague*) breaker; (*écueil*) reef.

brise [bʀiz] *nf* breeze.

briser [bʀize] (1) **1** *vt* **(a)** (*gén*) to break. ~ **en mille morceaux** to smash to smithereens; (*lit, fig*) ~ **la glace** to break the ice. **(b)** (*fig*) *cœur, traité etc* to break; *carrière* to ruin, wreck; *volonté, espoir, rebelle* to crush. **d'une voix brisée par l'émotion** in a voice choked with emotion; **ça l'a brisé** it has left him a broken man; **brisé (de fatigue)** worn out, exhausted; **brisé (de chagrin)** broken-hearted.

2 *vi* to break (*avec* with, *contre* against).

3 se ~ *vpr* *[verre]* to break, smash; *[vagues]* to break (*contre* against); *[résistance]* to break down; *[assaut]* to break up; *[espoir]* to be dashed; *[cœur, voix]* to break.

♦ **brise-** *préf*: ~**fer** *nm inv* (*enfant*) wrecker; ~**glace** *nm inv* icebreaker; ~**lames** *nm inv* breakwater; ~**mottes** *nm inv* harrow. ♦ **briseur, -euse** *nm,f*: ~ **de grève** blackleg, strikebreaker. ♦ **brisure** *nf* break.

britannique [bʀitanik] **1** *adj* British. **2** *nmf*: **B~** British citizen *ou* person; **les B~s** the British.

broc [bʀo] *nm* pitcher.

brocante [bʀɔkɑ̃t] *nf* secondhand goods (trade).

♦ **brocanteur, -euse** *nm,f* secondhand (furniture) dealer.
broche [bRɔʃ] *nf* (*bijou*) brooch; (*Culin*) spit; (*Tech, Méd*) pin.
brocher [bRɔʃe] (1) *vt* to bind (*with paper*). **livre broché** paperback (book).
brochet [bRɔʃɛ] *nm* (*Zool*) pike.
brochette [bRɔʃɛt] *nf* (*ustensile*) skewer; (*plat*) kebab. (*fig*) ~ **de** *décorations etc* row *ou* string of.
brochure [bRɔʃyR] *nf* **(a)** (*magazine*) brochure, pamphlet. **(b)** (*reliure*) (paper) binding.
brodequin [bRɔdkɛ̃] *nm* (laced) boot.
broder [bRɔde] (1) *vti* (*lit, fig*) to embroider (*de* with). ~ **sur un sujet** to elaborate on a subject. ♦ **broderie** *nf* (*art*) embroidery; (*objet*) piece of embroidery. ♦ **brodeur, -euse** *nm,f* embroiderer, embroideress.
brome [bRom] *nm* bromine. ♦ **bromure** *nm* bromide.
bronche [bRɔ̃ʃ] *nf*: ~**s** bronchial tubes; **il est faible des ~s** he has a weak chest.
broncher [bRɔ̃ʃe] (1) *vi [cheval]* to stumble. **personne n'osait ~*** no one dared move a muscle *ou* make a move; **sans** ~ (*sans peur*) without flinching; (*sans protester*) uncomplainingly; (*sans se tromper*) without faltering.
bronchite [bRɔ̃ʃit] *nf*: **la** ~ bronchitis; **une** ~ a bout of bronchitis. ♦ **broncho-pneumonie,** *pl* ~-~**s** *nf* broncho-pneumonia.
bronze [bRɔ̃z] *nm* (*métal, objet*) bronze.
bronzer [bRɔ̃ze] (1) **1** *vt* to tan. **2** *vi* to get a tan. **3 se** ~ *vpr* to sunbathe. ♦ **bronzage** *nm* suntan. ♦ **bronzé, e** *adj* (sun)tanned, sunburnt.
brosse [bRɔs] *nf* **(a)** (*gén*) brush; (*en chiendent*) scrubbing-brush. ~ **à dents/à habits** *etc* tooth/clothesbrush *etc*; ~ **métallique** wire brush; **donne un coup de ~ à ta veste** give your jacket a brush. **(b)** (*Coiffure*) **avoir les cheveux en** ~ to have a crew-cut. ♦ **brossage** *nm* brushing. ♦ **brosser** (1) **1** *vt* **(a)** to brush; to scrub. ~ **qn** to brush sb's clothes. **(b)** (*Art, fig*) to paint. **2 se** ~ *vpr* to brush one's clothes. **se ~ les dents** to brush one's teeth; **tu peux te ~!*** you can whistle for it!*
brouette [bRuɛt] *nf* wheelbarrow.
brouhaha [bRuaa] *nm* hubbub.
brouillage [bRujaʒ] *nm* (*Rad*) (*intentionnel*) jamming; (*accidentel*) interference.
brouillard [bRujaR] *nm* fog; (*léger*) mist; (*avec fumée*) smog; (*très dense*) peasouper*. ~ **de chaleur** heat haze; **il fait du** ~ it's foggy; (*fig*) **être dans le** ~ to be lost.
brouillasser [bRujase] (1) *vi* to drizzle.
brouiller [bRuje] (1) **1** *vt* **(a)** *contour, vue* to blur; *papiers, idées* to muddle up; *message* to scramble. (*fig*) ~ **les pistes** *ou* **cartes** to cloud the issue. **(b)** (*fâcher*) to set at odds, put on bad terms (*avec* with). **être brouillé avec qn** to have fallen out with sb; **être brouillé avec les dates** to be hopeless at dates. **(c)** (*Rad*) (*exprès*) to jam; (*par accident*) to cause interference to. **2 se** ~ *vpr* **(a)** to become blurred; to get muddled up. **tout se brouilla dans sa tête** everything became confused in his mind. **(b)** (*se fâcher*) **se ~ avec qn** to fall out with sb. **(c)** *[ciel]* to cloud over. **le temps se brouille** the weather is breaking. ♦ **brouille** *nf* quarrel; (*légère*) tiff.
brouillon, -onne [bRujɔ̃, ɔn] **1** *adj* (*soin*) untidy; (*organisation*) muddle-headed. **élève** ~ careless pupil. **2** *nm,f* muddler. **3** *nm [devoir]* rough copy; (*ébauche*) (rough) draft; (*notes etc*) rough work. **(papier)** ~ rough paper; **prendre qch au** ~ to make a rough copy of sth.
broussaille [bRusaj] *nf*: ~**s** undergrowth, scrub; **en** ~ *cheveux* unkempt, tousled. ♦ **broussailleux, -euse** *adj* bushy, scrubby; *barbe* bushy.
brousse [bRus] *nf*: **la** ~ the bush; (*fig*) **en pleine ~*** in the middle of nowhere.
brouter [bRute] (1) **1** *vti [ruminant]* to graze; *[lapin]* to nibble. **2** *vi [embrayage]* to judder.
broutille [bRutij] *nf* trifle. **c'est de la ~*** (*mauvaise qualité*) it's cheap rubbish; (*sans importance*) it's not worth mentioning, it's nothing of any consequence.
broyer [bRwaje] (8) *vt* to grind; *main* to crush. (*fig*) ~ **du noir** to be down in the dumps*. ♦ **broyage** *nm* grinding. ♦ **broyeur, -euse 1** *adj* grinding. **2** *nm* grinder.
bru [bRy] *nf* daughter-in-law.
brugnon [bRyɲɔ̃] *nm* nectarine.
bruine [bRɥin] *nf* drizzle. ♦ **bruiner** (1) *vi* to drizzle.
bruire [bRɥiR] (2) *vi [tissu, vent]* to rustle; *[ruisseau]* to murmur; *[insectes]* to hum. ♦ **bruissement** *nm* rustle; murmur; humming.
bruit [bRɥi] *nm* **(a)** (*gén*) noise; (*sourd*) thud; (*strident*) screech; *[train]* rumble; *[coup de feu]* crack, bang; *[voix, moteur]* sound; *[vaisselle]* clatter. **des ~s de pas** footsteps; ~ **de fond** background noise; **on n'entend aucun** ~ you can't hear a sound; **faire du** ~ to make a noise; **travailler dans le** ~ to work against noise; **sans** ~ noiselessly. **(b)** (*fig*) **beaucoup de ~ pour rien** much ado about nothing; **faire grand ~ autour de** to make a great to-do about; **il fait plus de ~ que de mal** his bark is worse than his bite. **(c)** (*nouvelle*) rumour. **le ~ court que** rumour has it that; **faux ~s** false rumours. ♦ **bruitage** *nm* sound effects. ♦ **bruiteur** *nm* sound-effects engineer.
brûler [bRyle] (1) **1** *vt* **(a)** (*gén*) *[acide, flamme]* to burn; *[eau bouillante]* to scald; *[fer à repasser]* to scorch; *[gel]* to nip. **brûlé par le soleil** (*bronzage*) sunburnt, tanned; (*lésion*) burnt by the sun; *herbe* sun-scorched; ~ **ses dernières cartouches** to shoot one's bolt; ~ **ses vaisseaux** to burn one's boats; **brûlé vif** (*accident*) burnt alive *ou* to death; (*supplice*) burnt at the stake; **grand brûlé** badly burnt person. **(b)** *café* to roast. **(c)** *électricité* to burn, use. **ils ont brûlé tout leur bois** they've burnt up all their wood; ~ **la chandelle par les deux bouts** to burn the candle at both ends. **(d)** (*Aut*) ~ **un stop** to ignore a stop sign; ~ **un feu rouge** to go through a red light; ~ **une étape** to cut out a stop; (*fig*) ~ **les étapes** (*réussite*) to shoot ahead; (*précipitation*) to take short cuts. **(e)** (*sensation*) to burn. **les yeux me brûlent** my eyes are smarting; **j'ai la figure qui (me) brûle** my face is burning; **l'argent lui brûle les doigts** money burns a hole in his pocket; **le désir de l'aventure le brûlait** he was burning for adventure.
2 *vi* **(a)** *[lumière, feu]* to burn; *[maison]* to be on fire; (*Culin*) to burn. **ça sent le brûlé** (*lit*) there's a smell of burning; (*fig*) trouble's brewing; **goût de brûlé** burnt taste. **(b)** *[front, objet]* to be burning (hot); *[liquide]* to be scalding. **ça brûle** you'll burn yourself, you'll get burnt; (*jeu*) **tu brûles!** you're getting hot! **(c)** ~ **(d'envie) de faire qch** to be burning to do sth; ~ **d'impatience** to seethe with impatience; ~ **(d'amour) pour qn** to be madly in love with sb.
3 se ~ *vpr* to burn o.s.; (*s'ébouillanter*) to scald o.s. **se ~ la cervelle** to blow one's brains out. ♦ **brûlant, e** *adj objet* burning (hot); *plat, liquide* piping hot; *soleil* scorching; *regard, pages* fiery; *sujet* ticklish. ~ **(de fièvre)** burning (with fever); **c'est d'une actualité ~e** it's the burning question of the hour. ♦ **brûle-parfum** *nm inv* perfume burner. ♦ **brûle-pourpoint** *adv*: **à** ~ point-blank. ♦ **brûleur** *nm* burner. ♦ **brûlure** *nf* (*lésion*) burn; (*sensation*) burning sensation. ~ **(d'eau bouillante)** scald; ~**s d'estomac** heartburn.
brume [bRym] *nf* (*gén*) mist; (*dense*) fog; (*légère*) haze. ♦ **brumeux, -euse** *adj* misty; foggy; (*fig*) obscure, hazy.
brun, e [bRœ̃, yn] **1** *adj* (*gén*) brown; *cheveux, tabac* dark; *peau* swarthy; (*bronzé*) tanned, brown. **il est** ~ he's dark-haired; ~ **roux** (dark)

auburn. **2** *nm* (*couleur*) brown; (*homme*) dark-haired man. **3** *nf* (*bière*) brown ale; (*femme*) brunette. ♦ **brunâtre** *adj* brownish. ♦ **brunette** *nf* brunette. ♦ **brunir** (2) **1** *vi [personne]* to get sunburnt; *[cheveux]* to go darker. **2** *vt peau* to tan; *cheveux* to darken.
brushing [brœʃiŋ] *nm* blow-dry.
brusque [bʀysk(ə)] *adj* (*sec*) abrupt, blunt; (*soudain*) abrupt, sudden; *virage* sharp. ♦ **brusquement** *adv* abruptly; bluntly; suddenly; sharply. ♦ **brusquer** (1) *vt* (*gén*) to rush. **attaque brusquée** sudden attack. ♦ **brusquerie** *nf* abruptness, bluntness.
brut, e[1] [bʀyt] **1** *adj* **(a)** *diamant* rough; *pétrole* crude; *sucre* unrefined; *soie, métal* raw; *champagne* brut; *fait, idée* crude, raw. **à l'état ~** in the rough. **(b)** (*Comm*) gross. **ça fait 100 F/kg ~** that makes 100 francs/kg gross. **2** *nm* crude oil.
brutal, e, *mpl* -aux [bʀytal, o] *adj* **(a)** *caractère* rough, brutal; *instinct* savage; *jeu* rough. **force ~e** brute force. **(b)** *réponse, franchise* blunt; *vérité* plain; *réalité* stark. **(c)** *mort* sudden; *coup* brutal. ♦ **brutalement** *adv* roughly; brutally; bluntly; plainly; suddenly. ♦ **brutaliser** (1) *vt personne* to bully, manhandle; *machine* to ill-treat. ♦ **brutalité** *nf* brutality; roughness; suddenness; (*acte*) brutality. **~s** (*Sport*) rough play; **~s policières** police brutality. ♦ **brute**[2] *nf* (*brutal*) brute, animal; (*grossier*) boor, lout. **taper sur qch comme une ~*** to bash away at sth*; **~ épaisse*** brutish lout; **grosse ~!*** big bully!
Bruxelles [bʀysɛl] *n* Brussels.
bruyant, e [bʀɥijɑ̃, ɑ̃t] *adj* noisy. ♦ **bruyamment** *adv* noisily.
bruyère [bʀyjɛʀ] *nf* (*plante*) heather; (*terrain*) heath(land). **pipe en (racine de) ~** briar pipe.
bu, e [by] *ptp de* **boire.**
buanderie [bɥɑ̃dʀi] *nf* wash house, laundry.
bûche [byʃ] *nf* **(a)** log. **~ de Noël** Yule log. **(b)** (*) (*lourdaud*) blockhead*; (*chute*) fall. **ramasser une ~** to come a cropper*.
bûcher[1] [byʃe] *nm* **(a)** (*remise*) woodshed. **(b)** (*funéraire*) (funeral) pyre; (*supplice*) stake.
bûcher[2]* [byʃe] (1) **1** *vt* to swot up*. **2** *vi* to swot*.
bûcheron [byʃʀɔ̃] *nm* woodcutter, lumberjack.
bûcheur, -euse* [byʃœʀ, øz] **1** *adj* hard-working. **2** *nm,f* slogger*.
bucolique [bykɔlik] *adj, nf* bucolic.
budget [bydʒɛ] *nm* budget. ♦ **budgétaire** *adj* (*gén*) budgetary. **année ~** financial year.
buée [bɥe] *nf* mist, steam, condensation. **couvert de ~** misted up, steamed up; **faire de la ~** to make steam.
buffet [byfɛ] *nm* **(a)** (*meuble*) sideboard. **~ de cuisine** kitchen dresser. **(b)** *[réception]* buffet. **~ (de gare)** station buffet. **(c)** (*: *ventre*) belly*.
buffle [byfl(ə)] *nm* buffalo.
buis [bɥi] *nm* (*arbre*) box tree; (*bois*) box(wood).
buisson [bɥisɔ̃] *nm* bush.
bulbe [bylb(ə)] *nm* (*Bot, Anat*) bulb; (*Archit*) onion-shaped dome. ♦ **bulbeux, -euse** *adj* bulbous.
Bulgarie [bylgaʀi] *nf* Bulgaria. ♦ **bulgare** *adj, nm,* **B~** *nmf* Bulgarian.
bulldozer [buldozœʀ] *nm* bulldozer.
bulle [byl] *nf* **(a)** bubble; *[bande dessinée]* balloon. **faire des ~s** to blow bubbles. **(b)** (*Rel*) bull.
bulletin [byltɛ̃] **1** *nm* (*communiqué, magazine*) bulletin; (*formulaire*) form; (*certificat*) certificate; (*billet*) ticket; (*Scol*) report; (*Pol*) ballot paper. **2**: **~ météorologique** weather forecast; **~-réponse** *nm, pl* **~s -~s** reply form *ou* coupon; **~ de salaire** pay-slip.
bungalow [bœ̃galo] *nm* (*Inde*) bungalow; *[motel]* (holiday) chalet.
buraliste [byʀalist(ə)] *nmf [tabac]* tobacconist; *[poste]* clerk.
bureau, *pl* ~x [byʀo] **1** *nm* **(a)** (*meuble*) desk; (*chambre*) study; *[firme]* office. **heures de ~** office hours; **nos ~x seront fermés** the office will be closed. **(b)** (*section*) department; (*comité*) committee; (*exécutif*) board. **2**: **~ de change** bureau de change; **~ d'études** research unit; (*indépendant*) research consultancy; **~ de location** booking *ou* box office; **~ de placement** employment agency; **~ de poste** post office; **~ de tabac** tobacconist's (shop); **~ de vote** polling station.
bureaucrate [byʀokʀat] *nmf* bureaucrat. ♦ **bureaucratie** *nf* (*péj*) (*système*) bureaucracy, red tape; (*employés*) officialdom. ♦ **bureaucratique** *adj* bureaucratic.
burette [byʀɛt] *nf* (*Culin, Rel*) cruet; *[mécanicien]* oilcan.
burin [byʀɛ̃] *nm* (*Art*) burin; (*Tech*) (cold) chisel. ♦ **buriné, e** *adj visage* seamed, craggy.
burlesque [byʀlɛsk(ə)] *adj* (*Théât*) burlesque; (*comique*) comical; (*ridicule*) ludicrous.
bus* [bys] *nm* bus.
busqué, e [byske] *adj*: **nez ~** hooked nose.
buste [byst(ə)] *nm* (*torse*) chest; (*seins, sculpture*) bust.
but [by] *nm* **(a)** (*destination, objectif*) goal. **errer sans ~** to wander aimlessly about; **il a pour ~ de faire** he is aiming to do; **aller droit au ~** to go straight to the point; **nous touchons au ~** the end *ou* our goal is in sight; **nous sommes encore loin du ~** we still have a long way to go. **(b)** (*intention*) aim, purpose, object. **dans le ~ de faire** with the aim of doing; **le ~ de l'opération** the object *ou* point of the operation. **(c)** (*Ftbl*) goal; (*Tir*) target, mark. **(d) de ~ en blanc** *demander* point-blank; *répondre* off the cuff.
butane [bytan] *nm* (*Chim*) butane; (*en bouteille*) calor gas.
buter [byte] (1) **1** *vi* **(a) ~ contre** (*trébucher*) to stumble over; (*cogner*) to bump into; (*s'appuyer*) to rest against; (*fig*) *difficulté* to come up against; **nous butons sur ce problème** we are stuck over this problem. **(b)** (*Ftbl*) to score a goal. **2** *vt* (*irriter*) to antagonize; (*: *tuer*) to bump off*. **3 se ~** *vpr* to dig one's heels in. ♦ **buté, e**[1] *adj* stubborn, obstinate. ♦ **butée**[2] *nf* (*Tech*) stop. ♦ **buteur** *nm* (*Ftbl*) striker.
butin [bytɛ̃] *nm [armée]* spoils; *[voleur]* loot; (*fig*) booty.
butiner [bytine] (1) *vi* to gather nectar.
butoir [bytwaʀ] *nm* (*Tech*) stop.
butor [bytɔʀ] *nm* (*péj*) boor, lout.
butte [byt] *nf* mound, hillock. **~ de tir** butts; **~-témoin** outlier; (*fig*) **être en ~ à** to be exposed to.
buvable [byvabl(ə)] *adj* drinkable; (*Méd*) to be taken orally.
buvard [byvaʀ] *nm* (*papier*) blotting paper; (*sous-main*) blotter.
buvette [byvɛt] *nf* refreshment stall.
buveur, -euse [byvœʀ, øz] *nm,f* (*ivrogne*) drinker; *[café]* customer. **~ de bière** beer drinker.

C

C, c [se] *nm* (*lettre*) C, c.
c' [s] *abrév de* **ce.**
ça [sa] *pron dém* = **cela** (*dans la langue courante*).
çà [sa] *adv*: ~ **et là** here and there.
cabale [kabal] *nf* cabal. ♦ **cabalistique** *adj* cabalistic.
caban [kabɑ̃] *nm* reefer (jacket).
cabane [kaban] *nf* (*hutte*) cabin; (*remise*) shed; (*péj*) shack. (*: *prison*) **en** ~ in (the) clink*; ~ **à lapins** (*lit*) rabbit hutch; (*fig*) box. ♦ **cabanon** *nm* (*maison*) cottage, cabin; (*remise*) shed.
cabaret [kabaʀɛ] *nm* night club, cabaret; (*Hist: café*) inn. ♦ **cabaretier, -ière** *nm,f* innkeeper.
cabas [kabɑ] *nm* shopping bag.
cabestan [kabɛstɑ̃] *nm* capstan.
cabillaud [kabijo] *nm* (fresh) cod.
cabine [kabin] *nf* (*Espace, Naut*) cabin; *[avion]* cockpit; *[grue]* cab; *[piscine]* cubicle; (*Audio-visuel*) booth. ~ **d'ascenseur** lift (cage); ~ **de bain** bathing hut; ~ **d'essayage/de projection** fitting/projection room; ~ **téléphonique** phone box *ou* booth.
cabinet [kabinɛ] **1** *nm* **(a)** (*toilettes*) ~s toilet. **(b)** *[médecin]* surgery, consulting-room; *[notaire]* office; *[immobilier]* agency; (*clientèle*) practice. **(c)** (*gouvernement*) cabinet; *[ministre]* advisers. **(d)** *[exposition]* exhibition room. **(e)** (*meuble*) cabinet. **2:** ~ **d'affaires** business consultancy; ~ **d'aisances**† water closet†, lavatory; ~ **particulier** private dining room; ~ **de toilette** bathroom; ~ **de travail** study.
câble [kɑbl(ə)] *nm* (*gén*) cable. ~ **d'amarrage** mooring line. ♦ **câblage** *nm* cabling. ♦ **câbler** (1) *vt* to cable.
caboche* [kabɔʃ] *nf* head, nut*. ♦ **cabochard, e*** *adj* pigheaded*.
cabosser [kabɔse] (1) *vt* to dent.
cabot [kabo] *nm* (*péj: chien*) tyke (*péj*), cur (*péj*).
cabotage [kabɔtaʒ] *nm* coastal navigation. **faire du** ~ to ply along the coast. ♦ **caboteur** *nm* tramp, coaster.
cabotin, e [kabɔtɛ̃, in] **1** *adj* (*péj*) theatrical. **2** *nm,f* (*péj*) show-off; (*acteur*) ham (actor). ♦ **cabotinage** *nm* showing off; ham acting. ♦ **cabotiner** (1) *vi* to show off.
cabrer [kɑbʀe] (1) **1** *vt* *cheval* to make rear up; *avion* to nose up. ~ **qn** to put sb's back up; ~ **qn contre** to turn sb against. **2 se** ~ *vpr* to rear up; to nose up; *[personne]* to rebel (*contre* against).
cabri [kabʀi] *nm* (*Zool*) kid.
cabriole [kabʀijɔl] *nf [enfant, chevreau]* caper; *[gymnaste]* somersault. ♦ **cabrioler** (1) *vi* to caper about.
cabriolet [kabʀijɔlɛ] *nm* (*Hist*) cabriolet; (*décapotable*) convertible.
caca* [kaka] *nm*: **faire** ~ to do a job*; **marcher dans du** ~ to step on some muck; (*couleur*) ~ **d'oie** greenish-yellow.
cacah(o)uète [kakawɛt] *nf* peanut.
cacao [kakao] *nm* cocoa.
cacatoès [kakatɔɛs] *nm* cockatoo.
cachalot [kaʃalo] *nm* sperm whale.
cache [kaʃ] **1** *nm* (*gén*) card; (*Phot*) mask. **2** *nf* hiding place; (*pour butin*) cache.
cachemire [kaʃmiʀ] *nm* (*laine*) cashmere; (*dessin*) paisley pattern.
cacher [kaʃe] (1) **1** *vt* (*gén*) to hide, conceal. ~ **son jeu** (*lit*) to keep one's cards up; (*fig*) to hide one's game; **tu me caches la lumière** you're in my light; ~ **son âge** to keep one's age a secret; **il n'a pas caché que** he made no secret (of the fact) that. **2 se** ~ *vpr* (*gén*) to hide; *[évadé]* to be in hiding; *[maison, défaut]* to be concealed. **va te** ~**!** get out of my sight!; **faire qch sans se** ~ to do sth openly, do sth without hiding *ou* concealing the fact. ♦ **caché, e** *adj* (*gén*) hidden; (*à l'écart*) secluded; (*secret*) secret. ♦ **cache-cache** *nm inv* (*lit, fig*) hide-and-seek. ♦ **cache-col** *nm inv ou* ♦ **cache-nez** *nm inv* scarf, muffler. ♦ **cache-pot** *nm inv* flowerpot holder. ♦ **cache-radiateur** *nm inv* radiator cover. ♦ **cache-tampon** *nm inv* hunt-the-thimble.
cachet [kaʃɛ] *nm* **(a)** (*Pharm*) tablet. **(b)** (*timbre*) stamp; (*sceau*) seal. ~ **(de la poste)** postmark. **(c)** (*fig: caractère*) style, character. **robe qui a du** ~ stylish dress; **un** ~ **d'originalité** the stamp *ou* mark of originality. **(d)** (*rétribution*) fee. ♦ **cacheter** (4) *vt* to seal.
cachette [kaʃɛt] *nf* hiding-place. **en** ~ secretly; **en** ~ **de qn** unknown to sb.
cachot [kaʃo] *nm* (*cellule*) dungeon; (*punition*) solitary confinement.
cachotterie [kaʃɔtʀi] *nf* mystery. **faire des** ~**s** to be secretive, make mysteries about things. ♦ **cachottier, -ière** *adj* secretive.
cacophonie [kakɔfɔni] *nf* cacophony.
cactus [kaktys] *nm inv* cactus.
cadastre [kadastʀ(ə)] *nm* (*registre*) cadastre; (*service*) cadastral survey. ♦ **cadastral, e,** *mpl* **-aux** *adj* cadastral.
cadavre [kadɑvʀ(ə)] *nm* corpse, (dead) body; (*: *bouteille*) empty (bottle). ♦ **cadavérique** *adj* deathly pale.
cadeau, *pl* ~**x** [kado] *nm* present, gift (*de qn* from sb). ~ **de Noël** Christmas present; **faire** ~ **de qch à qn** (*offrir*) to give sb sth as a present; (*laisser*) to let sb keep sth, give sth away (to sb); (*fig*) **ils ne font pas de** ~**x** they don't let you off lightly.
cadenas [kadnɑ] *nm* padlock. ♦ **cadenasser** (1) *vt* to padlock.
cadence [kadɑ̃s] *nf [vers, chant]* rhythm; *[tir, production]* rate; *[marche]* pace. **en** ~ (*régulièrement*) rhythmically; (*en mesure*) in time. ♦ **cadencé, e** *adj* rhythmic(al). ♦ **cadencer** (3) *vt* to give rhythm to.
cadet, -ette [kadɛ, ɛt] **1** *adj* (*entre 2*) younger; (*plus de 2*) youngest. **2** *nm,f* **(a)** youngest child (*ou* boy *ou* girl). **mon (frère/fils)** ~ my younger brother/son; **il est mon** ~ **de 2 ans** he's 2 years younger than me, he's 2 years my junior; **c'est le** ~ **de mes soucis** it's the least of my worries. **(b)** (*Sport*) minor (*15-17 years*). **3** *nm* (*Hist Mil*) cadet.
cadrage [kɑdʀaʒ] *nm* (*Phot*) centring (of image).
cadran [kadʀɑ̃] *nm* (*gén*) dial; *[baromètre]* face. ~ **solaire** sundial.
cadre [kɑdʀ(ə)] *nm* **(a)** (*chassis*) frame; (*caisse*) crate; *[radio]* frame antenna; (*sur formulaire*) space, box. **(b)** (*décor*) setting; (*entourage*) surroundings. **le** ~ **étroit de** the strait jacket *ou* the narrow confines of. **(c)** (*limites*) scope; (*contexte*) framework. **dans le** ~ **de** *fonctions*

within the scope *ou* limits of; *festival* within the context *ou* framework of; **respecter le ~ de la légalité** to remain within (the bounds of) the law. **(d)** (*chef*) executive, manager; (*Mil*) officer. **les ~s** the managerial staff; **~ supérieur/moyen** senior/middle manager *ou* executive. **(e)** (*personnel*) **figurer sur les ~s** to be (placed) on the books; **rayé des ~s** (*licencié*) dismissed; (*libéré*) discharged.

cadrer [kɑdʀe] (1) **1** *vi* to tally (*avec* with), conform (*avec* to, with). **2** *vt* (*Phot*) to centre.

caduc, caduque [kadyk] *adj* (*Bot*) deciduous; (*Jur*) null and void; (*périmé*) outmoded, obsolete.

cafard[1] [kafaʀ] *nm* **(a)** (*insecte*) cockroach. **(b)** (*) **accès de ~** fit of the blues*; **avoir le ~** to have the blues*, be feeling blue*; **ça lui donne le ~** that gets him down*. ♦ **cafardeux, -euse** *adj personne* feeling blue*; *tempérament* gloomy.

cafard[2], **e** [kafaʀ, aʀd(ə)] *nm,f* (*péj*) sneak. ♦ **cafardage** *nm* sneaking. ♦ **cafarder** (1) *vi* to sneak.

café [kafe] *nm* (*produit, moment*) coffee; (*lieu*) café. **~ au lait** (*nm*) white coffee, coffee with milk; (*adj inv*) coffee-coloured; **~ liégeois** coffee ice cream (*with whipped cream topping*); **~ soluble** instant coffee. ♦ **caféier** *nm* coffee tree. ♦ **cafetier, -ière 1** *nm,f* café-owner. **2** *nf* (*pot*) coffeepot; (*percolateur*) coffee-maker; (ː: *tête*) nutː.

cafouiller* [kafuje] (1) *vi [organisation, discussion]* to be in a shambles; *[équipe]* to go to pieces; *[candidat]* to flounder; *[moteur]* to work in fits and starts. **~ (avec) le ballon** to fumble the ball. ♦ **cafouillage*** *nm* muddle, shambles (*sg*). ♦ **cafouilleur, -euse* 1** *adj* shambolic*. **2** *nm,f* muddler.

cage [kaʒ] *nf* (*gén, Anat, Min*) cage; (*Tech*) casing; (*Sport: buts*) goal. **~ d'ascenseur** lift shaft; **~ d'escalier** stairwell; **~ à lapins** (*lit*) (rabbit) hutch; (*péj*) box.

cageot [kaʒo] *nm [légumes, fruits]* crate.

cagibi [kaʒibi] *nm* box room.

cagneux, -euse [kaɲø, øz] *adj* knock-kneed. **genoux ~** knock knees.

cagnotte [kaɲɔt] *nf* (*caisse commune*) kitty; (*: *économies*) nest egg.

cagoule [kagul] *nf [moine]* cowl; *[pénitent, bandit]* hood; *[enfant]* balaclava.

cahier [kaje] *nm* (*Scol*) notebook, exercise book; (*revue*) journal. **~ de brouillon** roughbook; **~ de textes** homework notebook.

cahin-caha* [kaɛ̃kaa] *adv*: **aller ~** *[vie, marcheur]* to jog along; *[santé]* to be so-so*.

cahot [kao] *nm* jolt, bump. ♦ **cahotant, e** *adj route* bumpy, rough; *véhicule* bumpy, jolting. ♦ **cahoter** (1) **1** *vt* to jolt. **cahoté par la guerre** buffeted about by the war. **2** *vi* to jog *ou* trundle along.

cahute [kayt] *nf* shack.

caïd [kaid] *nm* (*meneur*) big chief*; (*: *as*) ace (*en* at). **le ~ de l'équipe*** the star of the team.

caillasse [kajas] *nf* loose stones.

caille [kɑj] *nf* quail.

caillebotis [kɑjbɔti] *nm* duckboard.

cailler [kɑje] (1) **1** *vt*: **(faire) ~** to curdle. **2** *vi*, **se ~** *vpr* **(a)** *[lait]* to curdle; *[sang]* to clot. **(b)** (ː: *avoir froid*) to be cold. **ça caille** it's freezing. ♦ **caillot** *nm* (blood) clot.

caillou, *pl* **~x** [kaju] *nm* (*gén*) stone; (*petit galet*) pebble; (*grosse pierre*) boulder; (*: *tête*) head, nutː; (*: *diamant*) stone. **il a un ~ à la place du cœur** he has a heart of stone; **il n'a pas un poil sur le ~*** he's as bald as a coot *ou* an egg. ♦ **caillouteux, -euse** *adj* stony; pebbly. ♦ **cailloutis** *nm* (*gén*) gravel; *[route]* (road) metal.

caïman [kaimɑ̃] *nm* cayman, caiman.

Caire [kɛʀ] *n*: **le ~** Cairo.

caisse [kɛs] **1** *nf* **(a)** (*boîte*) box; (*cageot*) crate; *[horloge]* casing; *[véhicule]* bodywork. **(b)** (*machine*) cash register, till; (*portable*) cashbox. **avoir de l'argent en ~** to have ready cash; **faire la ~** to do the till; **les ~s de l'état** the coffers of the state; **voler la ~** to steal the contents of the till, steal the takings. **(c)** *[boutique]* cashdesk; *[banque]* cashier's desk; *[supermarché]* check-out. **passer à la ~** (*lit*) to go to the cashdesk; (*payé*) to collect one's money; (*licencié*) to get paid off. **(d)** (*bureau*) office; (*organisme*) fund. **(e)** (*Mus*) drum. **2: ~ d'emballage** packing case; **~ enregistreuse** cash register; **~ d'épargne** savings bank; **~ noire** secret funds; **~ à outils** toolbox; **~ de résonance** resonance chamber. ♦ **caissette** *nf* (small) box. ♦ **caissier, -ière** *nm,f* (*gén*) cashier; *[banque]* teller; *[supermarché]* check-out assistant; *[cinéma]* box-office assistant.

caisson [kɛsɔ̃] *nm* (*Archit, Mil, Tech*) caisson. **le mal des ~s** caisson disease, the bends*.

cajoler [kaʒɔle] (1) *vt* to cuddle, make a fuss of. ♦ **cajolerie** *nf* cuddle. **faire des ~s à qn** to cuddle sb, make a fuss of sb.

cake [kɛk] *nm* fruit cake.

calage [kalaʒ] *nm [meuble]* wedging; *[roue]* chocking.

calamité [kalamite] *nf* (*malheur*) calamity. **quelle ~!*** what a calamity *ou* disaster! ♦ **calamiteux, -euse** *adj* calamitous.

calandre [kalɑ̃dʀ(ə)] *nf [automobile]* radiator grill; (*machine*) calender.

calcaire [kalkɛʀ] **1** *adj* (*gén*) chalky; *eau* hard; (*Géol*) limestone. **2** *nm* (*Géol*) limestone; *[bouilloire]* fur.

calciner [kalsine] (1) *vt* (*Tech*) to calcine; *rôti* to burn to a cinder. ♦ **calciné, e** *adj débris* charred, burned to ashes. **~ par le soleil** scorched by the sun.

calcium [kalsjɔm] *nm* calcium.

calcul [kalkyl] *nm* **(a)** (*gén, fig*) calculation; (*exercice scolaire*) sum. **erreur de ~** miscalculation; **d'après mes ~s** by my reckoning, according to my calculations; **par ~** with an ulterior motive, out of (calculated) self-interest. **(b)** (*discipline*) **le ~** arithmetic; **~ des probabilités** probability theory; **le ~ intégral** integral calculus. **(c)** (*Méd*) stone, calculus. ♦ **calculateur, -trice 1** *adj* (*intéressé*) calculating. **2** *nm* computer. **3** *nf* calculator. **4** *nm,f* (*personne*) calculator. ♦ **calculer** (1) **1** *vt prix, quantité, conséquences* to calculate, work out; *geste, effets* to plan, calculate. **~ son élan** to judge one's run-up; **~ son coup** to plan one's move (carefully); **avec une gentillesse calculée** with calculated kindness; **tout bien calculé** everything considered. **2** *vi* (*Math*) to calculate; (*économiser*) to count the pennies.

cale [kal] *nf* **(a)** (*soute*) hold; (*plan incliné*) slipway. **~ de radoub/sèche** graving/dry dock. **(b)** *[meuble]* wedge; *[roue]* chock, wedge.

calé, e* [kale] *adj personne* bright; *problème* tough.

calebasse [kalbɑs] *nf* calabash.

calèche [kalɛʃ] *nf* barouche.

caleçon [kalsɔ̃] *nm* (pair of) underpants. **~(s) de bain** bathing trunks.

calembour [kalɑ̃buʀ] *nm* pun.

calendes [kalɑ̃d] *nfpl* (*Antiq*) calends.

calendrier [kalɑ̃dʀije] *nm* (*jours et mois*) calendar; (*programme*) timetable.

cale-pied [kalpje] *nm inv [vélo]* toe clip.

calepin [kalpɛ̃] *nm* notebook.

caler [kale] (1) **1** *vt* **(a)** *meuble* to wedge; *roue* to chock, wedge; *malade, pile de livres* to prop up. **ça vous cale l'estomac*** it fills you up; **se ~ dans un fauteuil** to settle o.s. comfortably in an armchair. **(b)** *moteur* to stall. **2** *vi* **(a)** *[véhicule]* to stall. **(b)** (*: *abandonner*) to give up.

calfeutrer [kalføtʀe] (1) **1** *vt* to (make) draughtproof. **2 se ~** *vpr* to make o.s. snug. ♦ **calfeutrage** *nm* draughtproofing.
calibre [kalibʀ(ə)] *nm* **(a)** *[fusil]* calibre, bore; *[tuyau]* bore; *[obus]* calibre; *[câble]* diameter; *[œufs, fruits]* grade; *[boule]* size. **(b)** (*instrument*) gauge; (*fig: envergure*) calibre. ♦ **calibrer** (1) *vt œufs* to grade; (*Tech*) to gauge.
calice [kalis] *nm* (*Rel*) chalice; (*Bot*) calyx.
calicot [kaliko] *nm* (*tissu*) calico; (*banderole*) banner.
calife [kalif] *nm* caliph.
califourchon [kalifuʀʃɔ̃] *nm*: **à ~** astride.
câlin, e [kɑlɛ̃, in] **1** *adj enfant, chat* cuddly; *mère, ton* tender, loving. **2** *nm* cuddle. ♦ **câliner** (1) *vt* to fondle, cuddle. ♦ **câlinerie** *nf* tenderness. **~s** caresses.
calleux, -euse [kalø, øz] *adj peau* horny, callous.
calligraphier [kaligʀafje] (7) *vt* to write artistically.
callosité [kalozite] *nf* callosity.
calmant, e [kalmɑ̃, ɑ̃t] **1** *adj* (*pour les nerfs*) tranquillizing; (*contre la douleur*) painkilling; *paroles* soothing. **2** *nm* tranquillizer; painkiller.
calmar [kalmaʀ] *nm* squid.
calme [kalm(ə)] **1** *adj vie, atmosphère* quiet, peaceful; *air, ciel* still; *personne, mer* calm, quiet; *Bourse* quiet. **rester ~** to remain calm *ou* cool. **2** *nm* quietness, peacefulness; stillness; calm, calmness; (*sang-froid*) sangfroid. (*tranquillité*) **le ~** quietness, peace (and quiet); **du ~!** (*restez tranquille*) quieten down!; (*pas de panique*) keep cool! *ou* calm!; (*Pol*) **ramener le ~** to restore order; (*Naut*) **~ plat** dead calm; (*fig*) **c'est le ~ plat** things are at a standstill. ♦ **calmement** *adv agir* calmly; *se dérouler* quietly.
calmer [kalme] (1) **1** *vt personne* to calm (down); *querelle* to quieten down; *révolte, flots* to calm; *douleur, nerfs, crainte, fièvre* to soothe; *impatience, désir* to curb; *faim* to appease; *soif* to quench. **2 se ~** *vpr [personne, mer]* to calm down; *[discussion]* to quieten down; *[douleur, faim, inquiétude]* to ease; *[fièvre, colère, ardeur]* to subside.
calomnier [kalɔmnje] (7) *vt* to slander; (*par écrit*) to libel. ♦ **calomniateur, -trice** *nm,f* slanderer; libeller. ♦ **calomnie** *nf* slander; libel. **dire des ~s** to make slanderous remarks. ♦ **calomnieux, -euse** *adj* slanderous; libellous.
calorie [kalɔʀi] *nf* calorie. ♦ **calorifique** *adj* calorific.
calorifuger [kalɔʀifyʒe] (3) *vt* to lag, insulate. ♦ **calorifuge** *adj* (heat-)insulating. ♦ **calorifugeage** *nm* lagging, insulation.
calot [kalo] *nm* forage cap.
calotte [kalɔt] *nf* (*bonnet*) skullcap; (*partie supérieure*) crown; (*: *gifle*) slap. **la ~ des cieux** the vault of heaven; **~ glaciaire** icecap.
calque [kalk(ə)] *nm* (*dessin*) tracing; (*papier*) tracing paper; (*fig*) exact copy; (*Ling*) calque. ♦ **calquer** (1) *vt* to trace; to copy exactly.
calumet [kalymɛ] *nm* calumet. **le ~ de la paix** the pipe of peace.
calvaire [kalvɛʀ] *nm* (*croix, peinture*) Calvary; (*épreuve*) suffering, martyrdom. (*Rel*) **Le C~** Calvary.
calvinisme [kalvinism(ə)] *nm* Calvinism. ♦ **calviniste** *adj, nmf* Calvinist.
calvitie [kalvisi] *nf* baldness.
camaïeu [kamajø] *nm* monochrome.
camarade [kamaʀad] *nmf* companion, friend, mate*; (*Pol*) comrade. **~ d'atelier/d'école** workmate/schoolmate. ♦ **camaraderie** *nf* good-companionship.
Cambodge [kɑ̃bɔdʒ] *nm* Kampuchea, Cambodia†. ♦ **cambodgien, -ienne** *adj*, **C~(ne)** *nm(f)* Kampuchean, Cambodian†.
cambouis [kɑ̃bwi] *nm* dirty oil *ou* grease.
cambrer [kɑ̃bʀe] (1) **1** *vt pied, dos* to arch; *bois* to bend; *métal* to curve. **2 se ~** *vpr* to arch one's back. ♦ **cambré, e** *adj reins* arched; *pied, chaussures* with a high instep.
cambrioler [kɑ̃bʀijɔle] (1) *vt* to burgle, burglarize (*US*). ♦ **cambriolage** *nm* burglary. ♦ **cambrioleur** *nm* burglar.
cambrousse‡ [kɑ̃bʀus] *nf* country. **en pleine ~** in the middle of nowhere, out in the sticks*.
cambrure [kɑ̃bʀyʀ] *nf* **(a)** *[poutre, reins]* curve; *[pied]* arch; *[route]* camber. **(b)** (*partie*) **~ du pied** instep; **~ des reins** small of the back.
cambuse [kɑ̃byz] *nf* (‡: *chambre*) place*, pad‡; (*Naut*) storeroom.
came [kam] *nf* (*Tech*) cam; (*arg Drogue*) snow (*arg*), junk (*arg*); (‡: *marchandise*) stuff*; (* : *pacotille*) junk*. ♦ **camé, e**[1] *nm,f* (*arg*) junkie (*arg*).
camée[2] [kame] *nm* cameo.
caméléon [kameleɔ̃] *nm* chameleon.
camélia [kamelja] *nm* camellia.
camelot [kamlo] *nm* street pedlar.
camelote* [kamlɔt] *nf* (*pacotille*) junk*; (*marchandise*) stuff*.
caméra [kameʀa] *nf* (*Ciné, TV*) camera; *[amateur]* cine-camera, movie camera (*US*).
Cameroun [kamʀun] *nm* Cameroon. ♦ **camerounais, e** *adj*, **C~(e)** *nm(f)* Cameroonian.
camion [kamjɔ̃] *nm* (*ouvert*) lorry, truck (*US*); (*fermé*) van, truck (*US*). **~-citerne** *nm, pl* **~s-~s** tanker (lorry), tank truck (*US*); **~ de déménagement** removal van. ♦ **camionnage** *nm* haulage. ♦ **camionnette** *nf* (small) van. ♦ **camionneur** *nm* lorry *ou* truck (*US*) driver; (*entrepreneur*) road haulier.
camisole [kamizɔl] *nf*: **~ de force** strait jacket.
camomille [kamɔmij] *nf* camomile.
camoufler [kamufle] (1) *vt* (*Mil*) to camouflage; (*cacher*) to conceal; (*déguiser*) to disguise. ♦ **camouflage** *nm* (*Mil*) (*action*) camouflaging; (*résultat*) camouflage.
camp [kɑ̃] *nm* (*gén, Mil: emplacement*) camp; (*parti, Sport*) side; (*Pol*) camp. **~ d'extermination** death camp; **~ de toile** campsite.
campagne [kɑ̃paɲ] *nf* **(a)** (*gén*) country; (*paysage*) countryside. **en pleine ~** right in the middle of the country(side); **auberge de ~** country inn. **(b)** (*Mil, Pol, Presse*) campaign. **faire ~** to fight a campaign; **en ~** on campaign; **canon de ~** field gun; **mener une ~ pour/contre** to campaign for/against; **tout le monde se mit en ~** everybody set to work *ou* got busy (*pour faire* to do). ♦ **campagnard, e 1** *adj* country. **2** *nm* countryman. **~s** countryfolk. **3** *nf* countrywoman.
campanile [kɑ̃panil] *nm* campanile.
campanule [kɑ̃panyl] *nf* bellflower, campanula.
camper [kɑ̃pe] (1) **1** *vi* to camp. **2** *vt* **(a)** *troupes* to camp out. **(b)** *personnage* to portray; *portrait* to fashion, shape. **(c)** *lunettes etc* to plant (*sur* on). **se ~ devant** to plant o.s. in front of. ♦ **campement** *nm* camp, encampment. ♦ **campeur, -euse** *nm,f* camper. ♦ **camping** *nm* **(a)** (*activité*) **le ~** camping; **faire du ~** to go camping. **(b)** (*lieu*) campsite.
camphre [kɑ̃fʀ(ə)] *nm* camphor.
campus [kɑ̃pys] *nm* campus.
camus, e [kamy, yz] *adj personne* pug-nosed.
Canada [kanada] *nm* Canada. ♦ **canadianisme** *nm* Canadianism. ♦ **canadien, -ienne 1** *adj* Canadian. **2** *nm(f)*: **C~(ne)** Canadian. **3** *nf* (*veste*) fur-lined jacket.
canaille [kanɑj] **1** *adj* low, coarse. **2** *nf* (*salaud*) bastard‡; (*escroc*) crook; (*hum: enfant*) rascal. (*populace*) **la ~** the rabble (*péj*). ♦ **canaillerie** *nf* *[manières]* lowness, coarseness; *[procédés]* crookedness; (*action malhonnête*) dirty *ou* low trick.

canal, *pl* **-aux** [kanal, o] *nm* (*artificiel*) canal; (*détroit*) channel; (*tuyau, fossé*) conduit, duct; (*Anat*) canal, duct; (*TV*) channel. **par le ~ d'un collègue** through a colleague. ♦ **canalisation** *nf* (*tuyau*) (main) pipe; (*Élec*) cable. ♦ **canaliser** (1) *vt foule, demandes* to channel; *fleuve* to canalize; *plaine* to provide with a network of canals.
canapé [kanape] *nm* (*meuble*) settee, couch; (*Culin*) canapé.
canard [kanaʀ] *nm* (*gén*) duck; (*mâle*) drake; (*: *journal*) rag*. (*Mus*) **faire un ~** to hit a false note; **mon (petit) ~*** pet*; **~ de Barbarie** Muscovy *ou* musk duck.
canarder* [kanaʀde] (1) *vt* (*fusil*) to snipe at; (*pierres*) to pelt (*avec* with).
canari [kanaʀi] *nm* canary.
Canaries [kanaʀi] *nfpl*: **les (îles) ~** the Canary Islands.
cancans [kɑ̃kɑ̃] *nmpl* gossip. ♦ **cancaner** (1) *vi* to gossip, tittle-tattle. ♦ **cancanier, -ière** *adj* gossipy, tittle-tattling.
cancer [kɑ̃sɛʀ] *nm* cancer. ♦ **cancéreux, -euse** *adj tumeur* cancerous; *personne* with cancer. ♦ **cancérigène** *adj* carcinogenic. ♦ **cancérologie** *nf* cancerology. ♦ **cancérologue** *nmf* cancerologist.
cancre [kɑ̃kʀ(ə)] *nm* (*péj: élève*) dunce.
cancrelat [kɑ̃kʀəla] *nm* cockroach.
candélabre [kɑ̃delɑbʀ(ə)] *nm* candelabra.
candeur [kɑ̃dœʀ] *nf* naïvety.
candidat, e [kɑ̃dida, at] *nm,f* (*gén*) candidate (*à* at); *[poste]* applicant (*à* for). ♦ **candidature** *nf* candidature, candidacy (*US*); application (*à* for). **poser sa ~ à** *poste* to apply for.
candide [kɑ̃did] *adj* naïve. ♦ **candidement** *adv* naïvely.
cane [kan] *nf* (female) duck. ♦ **caneton** *nm,* **canette**[1] *nf* duckling.
canette[2] [kanɛt] *nf* (*bouteille*) bottle (of beer).
canevas [kanva] *nm* **(a)** *[livre]* framework. **(b)** (*toile*) canvas; (*ouvrage*) tapestry (work).
caniche [kaniʃ] *nm* poodle.
canicule [kanikyl] *nf* (*chaleur*) scorching heat; (*période*) heatwave. (*juillet-août*) **la ~** the dog days. ♦ **caniculaire** *adj* scorching.
canif [kanif] *nm* penknife, pocket knife.
canin, e [kanɛ̃, in] **1** *adj espèce* canine; *exposition* dog. **2** *nf* (*dent*) canine (tooth).
caniveau, *pl* **~x** [kanivo] *nm* (roadside) gutter.
cannage [kanaʒ] *nm* (*partie cannée*) canework; (*opération*) caning.
canne [kan] *nf* walking stick. **~ à pêche** fishing rod; **~ à sucre** sugar cane.
canneler [kanle] (4) *vt* to flute. ♦ **cannelure** *nf [colonne]* flute.
cannelle [kanɛl] *nf* cinnamon.
canner [kane] (1) *vt* to cane. **chaise cannée** cane chair. ♦ **canneur, -euse** *nm,f* cane worker.
cannibale [kanibal] **1** *adj* cannibal. **2** *nmf* cannibal, man-eater. ♦ **cannibalisme** *nm* cannibalism.
canoë [kanɔe] *nm* canoe. **faire du ~** to canoe. ♦ **canoéiste** *nmf* canoeist.
canon [kanɔ̃] *nm* **(a)** (*arme*) gun; (*Hist*) cannon; *[fusil, clé]* barrel. **(b)** (*Rel, Mus*) canon. (*code*) **~s** canons.
cañon [kaɲɔ̃] *nm* canyon.
canonique [kanɔnik] *adj* (*Rel*) canonical; *âge* venerable. ♦ **canonisation** *nf* canonization. ♦ **canoniser** (1) *vt* to canonize.
canonner [kanɔne] (1) *vt* to bombard, shell. ♦ **canonnade** *nf* cannonade. ♦ **canonnier** *nm* gunner. ♦ **canonnière** *nf* gunboat.
canot [kano] *nm* boat, ding(h)y. **~ automobile** motorboat; **~ pneumatique** rubber *ou* inflatable ding(h)y; **~ de sauvetage** lifeboat. ♦ **canotage** *nm* boating, rowing. **faire du ~** to go boating *ou* rowing. ♦ **canotier** *nm* (*chapeau*) boater.
cantate [kɑ̃tat] *nf* cantata.
cantatrice [kɑ̃tatʀis] *nf* (opera) singer.
cantine [kɑ̃tin] *nf* **(a)** *[usine]* canteen; *[école]* dining hall; (*service*) school meals. **(b)** (*malle*) tin trunk. ♦ **cantinière** *nf* (*Hist Mil*) canteen woman.
cantique [kɑ̃tik] *nm* hymn.
canton [kɑ̃tɔ̃] *nm* (*gén*) district; (*Admin*) canton. ♦ **cantonal, e,** *mpl* **-aux** *adj* district; cantonal.
cantonade [kɑ̃tɔnad] *nf*: **dire qch à la ~** to say sth to everyone in general.
cantonner [kɑ̃tɔne] (1) *vt* (*Mil*) to station; (*chez l'habitant etc*) to quarter, billet (*chez, dans* on). (*fig*) **~ qn dans un travail** to confine sb to a job; **se ~ dans** to confine o.s. to. ♦ **cantonnement** *nm* (*action*) stationing; billeting, quartering; (*lieu*) quarters, billet; (*camp*) camp.
cantonnier [kɑ̃tɔnje] *nm* roadman.
canular [kanylaʀ] *nm* hoax.
caoutchouc [kautʃu] *nm* (*matière*) rubber; (*élastique*) rubber *ou* elastic band. ® **~ mousse** foam *ou* sponge rubber. ♦ **caoutchouter** (1) *vt* to rubberize. ♦ **caoutchouteux, -euse** *adj* rubbery.
cap [kap] *nm* **(a)** (*Géog*) cape; (*promontoire*) point, headland. **le ~ Horn** Cape Horn; **le ~ de Bonne Espérance** the Cape of Good Hope; **doubler un ~** to round a cape; **passer le ~ de l'examen** to get over the hurdle of the exam; **franchir le ~ des 40 ans** to turn 40; **franchir le ~ des 50 millions** to pass the 50-million mark. **(b)** (*lit, fig*) **changer de ~** to change course; (*Aut, Naut*) **mettre le ~ sur** to head for.
capable [kapabl(ə)] *adj* able, capable. **~ de faire/de qch** capable of doing/of sth; **te sens-tu ~ de tout manger?** do you feel you can eat it all?, do you feel up to eating it all?; **il est ~ de l'avoir perdu** he's quite likely to have lost it, he may well have lost it.
capacité [kapasite] *nf* (*contenance*) capacity; (*aptitude*) ability (*à faire* to do); (*civile, légale*) capacity. **~s intellectuelles** intellectual abilities *ou* capacities; **avoir ~ pour** to be (legally) entitled to.
caparaçonner [kapaʀasɔne] (1) *vt cheval* to caparison. (*fig*) **caparaçonné de cuir** all clad in leather.
cape [kap] *nf* (*courte*) cape; (*longue*) cloak.
capharnaüm* [kafaʀnaɔm] *nm* clutter, muddle.
capillaire [kapilɛʀ] **1** *adj* (*Sci*) capillary; *lotion* hair. **2** *nm* (*Anat*) capillary.
capilotade [kapilɔtad] *nf*: **mettre en ~** *fruits* to squash to a pulp; *adversaire* to beat to a pulp; **il avait les reins en ~** his back was aching like hell‡.
capitaine [kapitɛn] *nm* (*Mil, Naut, Sport*) captain; (*armée de l'air*) flight lieutenant; (*littér: chef*) (military) leader. **~ d'industrie** captain of industry; **~ au long cours** master mariner; **~ des pompiers** fire chief.
capital, e, *mpl* **-aux** [kapital, o] **1** *adj* (*gén*) major, main; *erreur* chief, major; *importance* cardinal, capital; *peine* capital. **il est ~ d'y aller** it is vital *ou* absolutely essential that we go. **2** *nm* (*Fin, Pol*) capital. **~aux** money, capital; (*fig*) **~ de connaissances** stock *ou* fund of knowledge; **cela constitue un ~ appréciable** it is a major asset; **le ~ artistique du pays** the artistic wealth *ou* resources of the country. **3** *nf* **(a)** **(lettre) ~e** capital (letter); **en ~es d'imprimerie** in block capitals. **(b)** (*métropole*) capital (city).
capitaliser [kapitalize] (1) **1** *vt* **(a)** *somme* to amass; (*fig*) *expériences* to build up, accumulate. **l'intérêt capitalisé pendant un an** interest accrued *ou* accumulated in a year. **(b)** (*Fin: ajouter au capital*) *intérêts* to capitalize. **2** *vi* to save. ♦ **capitalisation** *nf* capitalization. ♦ **capitalisme** *nm* capitalism. ♦ **capitaliste** *adj, nmf* capitalist.

capiteux, -euse [kapitø, øz] *adj vin* heady; *beauté* intoxicating.
capitonner [kapitɔne] (1) *vt* to pad (*de* with). ♦ **capitonnage** *nm* padding.
capituler [kapityle] (1) *vi* to capitulate, surrender. ♦ **capitulation** *nf* capitulation, surrender.
caporal, *pl* **-aux** [kapɔʀal, o] *nm* corporal.
capot [kapo] *nm* bonnet, hood (*US*).
capote [kapɔt] *nf [voiture]* hood, top (*US*); (*manteau*) greatcoat.
capoter [kapɔte] (1) *vi* to overturn.
câpre [kɑpʀ(ə)] *nf* (*Culin*) caper.
caprice [kapʀis] *nm* whim, caprice. **faire un ~** to throw a tantrum; **cet enfant fait des ~s** this child is being awkward; **~ de la nature** freak of nature; ~s *[chemin]* windings; *[mode]* vagaries, whims; *[sort]* quirks. ♦ **capricieusement** *adv* capriciously, whimsically. ♦ **capricieux, -ieuse** *adj* capricious, whimsical; (*péj*) temperamental; awkward.
Capricorne [kapʀikɔʀn(ə)] *nm*: **le ~** Capricorn; **être du ~** to be (a) Capricorn.
capsule [kapsyl] *nf* (*Espace, Sci*) capsule; *[bouteille]* capsule, cap; *[arme]* cap. ♦ **capsuler** (1) *vt* to put a capsule *ou* cap on.
capter [kapte] (1) *vt suffrages, confiance* to win; *émission* to pick up; *source* to harness; *courant* to tap.
captif, -ive [kaptif, iv] *adj, nm,f* captive. ♦ **captiver** (1) *vt* to captivate. ♦ **captivité** *nf* captivity.
capturer [kaptyʀe] (1) *vt* to catch, capture. ♦ **capture** *nf* (*action*) capture, catching; (*animal*) catch; (*personne*) capture.
capuche [kapyʃ] *nf* hood. ♦ **capuchon** *nm* hood; (*Rel*) cowl; (*pèlerine*) hooded raincoat; *[stylo]* top, cap.
capucine [kapysin] *nf* (*Bot*) nasturtium.
caquet [kakɛ] *nm* (*) *[personne]* prattle; *[poule]* cackle. **rabattre le ~ à qn*** to bring sb down a peg or two. ♦ **caqueter** (4) *vi* to prattle; to cackle.
car[1] [kaʀ] *nm* coach, bus (*US*). **~ de police** police van.
car[2] [kaʀ] *conj* because, for.
carabine [kaʀabin] *nf* rifle.
carabiné, e* [kaʀabine] *adj fièvre* raging, violent; *facture* stiff.
carabinier [kaʀabinje] *nm* (*Espagne*) carabinero; (*Italie*) carabiniere.
caracoler [kaʀakɔle] (1) *vi* to caracole.
caractère [kaʀaktɛʀ] *nm* **(a)** (*gén*) character, nature. **avoir bon/mauvais ~** to be good-/ill-natured, be good-/bad-tempered; *[personne, maison]* **avoir du ~** to have character; **la situation n'a aucun ~ de gravité** the situation shows no sign *ou* evidence of seriousness. **(b)** (*gén pl: caractéristique*) characteristic, feature. **(c)** (*Typ*) character, letter. **~s gras** bold type; **~s d'imprimerie** block capitals.
♦ **caractériel, -elle** *adj traits* character; *troubles* emotional. **(enfant) ~** emotionally disturbed child, problem child. ♦ **caractériser** (1) *vt* (*être typique de*) to characterize, be characteristic of; (*décrire*) to characterize. **se ~ par** to be characterized by; **erreur caractérisée** blatant mistake. ♦ **caractéristique 1** *adj* characteristic (*de* of). **2** *nf* characteristic, (typical) feature.
carafe [kaʀaf] *nf* (*gén*) carafe; (*en cristal*) decanter.
caraïbe [kaʀaib] *adj* Caribbean. **les C~s** the Caribbean.
carambolage [kaʀɑ̃bɔlaʒ] *nm* pileup. ♦ **se caramboler** (1) *vpr* to collide.
caramel [kaʀamɛl] *nm* (*Culin*) caramel; (*mou*) fudge; (*dur*) toffee, butterscotch. ♦ **caraméliser** (1) *vt sucre* to caramelize; *moule* to coat with caramel; *boisson* to flavour with caramel.
carapace [kaʀapas] *nf* (*lit, fig*) shell.
carat [kaʀa] *nm* carat.
caravane [kaʀavan] *nf* (*convoi*) caravan; (*fig*) stream; (*véhicule*) caravan, trailer (*US*). ♦ **caravanier, -ière 1** *adj* caravan. **2** *nm* caravanner. ♦ **caravaning** *nm* caravanning. ♦ **caravansérail** *nm* (*lit, fig*) caravanserai.
caravelle [kaʀavɛl] *nf* caravel.
carbone [kaʀbɔn] *nm* carbon. ♦ **carbonate** *nm* carbonate. ♦ **carbonique** *adj* carbonic.
carboniser [kaʀbɔnize] (1) *vt bois* to carbonize; *maison* to burn to the ground; *rôti* to burn to a cinder. ♦ **carbonisé, e** *adj restes* charred. **mort ~** burned to death.
carburant [kaʀbyʀɑ̃] *nm* fuel. ♦ **carburateur** *nm* carburettor. ♦ **carburation** *nf [essence]* carburation. ♦ **carbure** *nm* carbide. ♦ **carburer** (1) *vi*: **~ bien/mal** *[moteur]* to be well/badly tuned; (*: *fig*) to be going well/badly.
carcan [kaʀkɑ̃] *nm* (*Hist*) iron collar; (*contrainte*) yoke; (*fig:col*) vice (*fig*).
carcasse [kaʀkas] *nf [corps]* carcass; *[abat-jour]* frame; *[bateau, immeuble]* skeleton.
cardan [kaʀdɑ̃] *nm* universal joint.
carder [kaʀde] (1) *vt* to card.
cardiaque [kaʀdjak] **1** *adj* cardiac. **être ~** to have a heart condition. **2** *nmf* heart patient.
cardinal, e, *mpl* **-aux** [kaʀdinal, o] **1** *adj* cardinal. **2** *nm* (*Rel*) cardinal; (*nombre*) cardinal number.
cardiologie [kaʀdjɔlɔʒi] *nf* cardiology. ♦ **cardiologue** *nmf* cardiologist, heart specialist. ♦ **cardio-vasculaire** *adj* cardiovascular.
carême [kaʀɛm] *nm* (*jeûne*) fast. (*Rel: période*) **le C~** Lent.
carence [kaʀɑ̃s] *nf* (*incompétence*) incompetence; (*manque*) shortage (*en* of); (*Méd*) deficiency. **les ~s de** the shortcomings of.
carène [kaʀɛn] *nf* (*Naut*) hull. ♦ **caréner** (6) *vt* (*Naut*) to careen; *véhicule* to streamline.
caresser [kaʀese] (1) *vt* **(a)** to caress, stroke. **~ qn du regard** to give sb a caressing look. **(b)** *projet* to entertain, toy with. ♦ **caressant, e** *adj enfant* affectionate; *voix, brise* caressing.
cargaison [kaʀgɛzɔ̃] *nf* cargo, freight; (*fig*) load, stock. ♦ **cargo** *nm* cargo boat, freighter.
carguer [kaʀge] (1) *vt voiles* to furl.
caricature [kaʀikatyʀ] *nf* **(a)** caricature; (*politique*) cartoon. **une ~ de procès** a mockery of a trial; **une ~ de la vérité** a caricature *ou* gross distortion of the truth. **(b)** (*: *personne*) fright*. ♦ **caricatural, e,** *mpl* **-aux** *adj* (*ridicule*) ridiculous, grotesque; (*exagéré*) caricatured. ♦ **caricaturer** (1) *vt* to caricature. ♦ **caricaturiste** *nmf* caricaturist; (satirical) cartoonist.
carie [kaʀi] *nf*: **la ~ dentaire** tooth decay, (dental) caries; **j'ai une ~** I've got a bad tooth *ou* a hole in my tooth. ♦ **carier** (7) *vt*, **se ~** *vpr* to decay. **dent cariée** bad *ou* decayed tooth.
carillon [kaʀijɔ̃] *nm* (*cloches*) peal of bells; (*horloge*) chiming clock; (*sonnette*) (door) chime; (*air*) chimes. ♦ **carillonner** (1) **1** *vi [cloches]* to ring, chime; (*à la porte*) to ring very loudly. **2** *vt heure* to chime, ring; (*fig*) *nouvelle* to broadcast.
carlingue [kaʀlɛ̃g] *nf* (*Aviat*) cabin.
carmin [kaʀmɛ̃] *nm, adj inv* carmine.
carnage [kaʀnaʒ] *nm* (*lit, fig*) carnage, slaughter.
carnassier, -ière [kaʀnasje, jɛʀ] **1** *adj animal* carnivorous, flesh-eating. **2** *nm* carnivore.
carnaval, *pl* **~s** [kaʀnaval] *nm* carnival. ♦ **carnavalesque** *adj* carnivalesque.
carne [kaʀn(ə)] *nf* (*péj*) tough *ou* leathery meat.
carnet [kaʀnɛ] *nm* (*calepin*) notebook; *[timbres etc]* book. **~ de chèques** cheque book; **~ de notes** school report.
carnivore [kaʀnivɔʀ] **1** *adj animal* carnivorous, flesh-eating. **2** *nm* carnivore.
carotide [kaʀɔtid] *adj, nf* carotid.
carotte [kaʀɔt] **1** *nf* carrot; (*Tech*) core; *[tabac]*

plug. **les ~s sont cuites!*** they've (*ou* we've *etc*) had it!*. **2** *adj inv* carroty.

carotter‡ [kaʀɔte] (1) *vt objet* to swipe‡, pinch* (*à* from); *client* to do* (*de* out of).

carpe [kaʀp(ə)] **1** *nf* carp. **2** *nm* (*Anat*) carpus.

carpette [kaʀpɛt] *nf* (*tapis*) rug; (*fig, péj*) doormat (*fig*).

carquois [kaʀkwa] *nm* quiver.

carre [kaʀ] *nf [ski]* edge.

carré, e [kaʀe] **1** *adj* **(a)** (*Math, forme*) square. **mètre ~** square metre. **(b)** (*franc*) *personne* forthright, straightforward; *réponse* straight(forward). **2** *nm* (*gén, Math, écharpe*) square; (*Naut: mess*) wardroom. **~ de terre** patch *ou* plot (of land); **3 au ~** 3 squared; **mettre un nombre au ~** to square a number; (*Cartes*) **un ~ d'as** four aces. **3** *nf* (‡: *chambre*) pad‡.

carreau, *pl* **~x** [kaʀo] *nm* **(a)** (*par terre*) (floor) tile; (*au mur*) (wall) tile; (*sol*) (tiled) floor; *[mine]* bank. **(b)** (*vitre*) (window) pane. (*: *lunettes*) **~x** specs*. **(c)** (*sur un tissu*) check; (*sur du papier*) square. **à ~x** checked; **à petits ~x** with a small check. **(d)** (*Cartes*) diamond. **(e)** (*flèche*) bolt. **(f)** (‡) **il est resté sur le ~** (*bagarre*) he was laid out cold*; (*examen*) he didn't make the grade; **se tenir à ~** to keep one's nose clean*.

carrefour [kaʀfuʀ] *nm* (*gén*) crossroads. **au ~ de plusieurs sciences** at the junction *ou* meeting point of many different sciences; **~ d'idées** forum for ideas.

carreler [kaʀle] (4) *vt* to tile. ♦ **carrelage** *nm* (*action*) tiling; (*sol*) tiled floor. ♦ **carreleur** *nm* tiler.

carrelet [kaʀlɛ] *nm* (*poisson*) plaice; (*filet*) *square fishing net.*

carrément [kaʀemɑ̃] *adv* (*crûment*) bluntly, straight out; (*directement*) straight. **vas-y ~** go right ahead; **il est ~ timbré*** he's definitely cracked*.

carrer (se) [kaʀe] (1) *vpr* to settle (o.s.) firmly (*dans* in).

carrière [kaʀjɛʀ] *nf* **(a)** *[sable]* (sand)pit; *[roches etc]* quarry. **(b)** (*profession*) career. **faire ~ dans la banque** (*gén*) to make banking one's career; (*réussir*) to make a good career for o.s. in banking. **(c)** (*littér*) **le jour achève sa ~** the day has run its course; **donner (libre) ~ à** to give free rein to. ♦ **carriériste** *nmf* (*péj*) careerist.

carriole [kaʀjɔl] *nf* (*péj*) (ramshackle) cart.

carrossable [kaʀɔsabl(ə)] *adj* suitable for (motor) vehicles.

carrosse [kaʀɔs] *nm* (horse-drawn) coach.

carrosserie [kaʀɔsʀi] *nf* body, coachwork; (*métier*) coachbuilding. ♦ **carrossier** *nm* coachbuilder.

carrousel [kaʀuzɛl] *nm* (*Équitation*) carrousel; (*fig*) whirligig.

carrure [kaʀyʀ] *nf [personne]* build; *[vêtement]* breadth across the shoulders; (*fig*) calibre, stature. **de forte ~** well-built, burly.

cartable [kaʀtabl(ə)] *nm* (school)bag; (*à bretelles*) satchel.

carte [kaʀt(ə)] *nf* **(a)** (*gén*) card; (*Rail*) season ticket. **~ de crédit/de vœux** credit/New Year card; **~ grise** logbook; **~ de lecteur** library ticket; **~ postale** postcard; **~ de visite** visiting card; **avoir ~ blanche** to have carte blanche *ou* a free hand. **(b)** (*Jeux*) **~ (à jouer)** (playing) card; **faire les ~s à qn** to read sb's cards; **~ maîtresse** (*lit*) master (card); (*fig*) trump card; (*lit, fig*) **~s sur table** cards on the table. **(c)** (*Géog*) map; (*Astron, Mét, Naut*) chart. **~ routière** roadmap; **~ d'état-major** ≃ Ordnance Survey map. **(d)** (*au restaurant*) menu. **repas à la ~** à la carte meal; **~ des vins** wine list; (*fig*) **programme à la ~** free-choice curriculum.

cartel [kaʀtɛl] *nm* (*Pol, Écon*) cartel; (*pendule*) wall clock.

carter [kaʀtɛʀ] *nm [bicyclette]* chain guard; *[moteur]* crankcase.

cartilage [kaʀtilaʒ] *nm* (*Anat*) cartilage; *[viande]* gristle. ♦ **cartilagineux, -euse** *adj* cartilaginous; gristly.

cartographe [kaʀtɔgʀaf] *nmf* cartographer. ♦ **cartographie** *nf* cartography. ♦ **cartographique** *adj* cartographic(al).

cartomancie [kaʀtɔmɑ̃si] *nf* fortunetelling (*with cards*). ♦ **cartomancien, -ienne** *nm,f* fortuneteller.

carton [kaʀtɔ̃] **1** *nm* **(a)** (*matière*) cardboard; (*morceau*) piece of cardboard; (*boîte*) (cardboard) box, carton; (*cartable*) (school)bag; (*dossier*) file. **(b)** (*cible*) target. **faire un ~** (*à la fête*) to have a go at the rifle range; (*: *sur l'ennemi*) to take a potshot* (*sur* at); **faire un bon ~** to make a good score. **(c)** (*Peinture*) sketch. **2: ~ à chapeau** hatbox; **~ à dessin** portfolio; **~ pâte** pasteboard; **de ~ pâte** cardboard. ♦ **cartonnage** *nm* (*emballage*) cardboard (packing); (*couverture*) binding.

cartouche [kaʀtuʃ] **1** *nf* (*gén*) cartridge; *[cigarettes]* carton. **2** *nm* (*Archéol, Archit*) cartouche. ♦ **cartoucherie** *nf* (*fabrique*) cartridge factory; (*dépôt*) cartridge depot. ♦ **cartouchière** *nf* (*ceinture*) cartridge belt; (*sac*) cartridge pouch.

cas [kɑ] *nm* (*gén*) case; (*situation*) case, situation; (*événement*) occurrence; (*exemple*) case, instance. **comme c'est son ~** as is the case with him; **il s'est mis dans un mauvais ~** he's got himself into a tricky situation *ou* position; (*hum*) **c'est un ~ pendable** he deserves to be shot (*hum*); **faire (grand) ~ de/peu de ~ de** to set great/little store by; **il ne fait jamais aucun ~ de nos observations** he never pays any attention to *ou* takes any notice of our comments; **c'est bien le ~ de le dire!** you've said it!; **au ~ où il pleuvrait** in case it rains; **en ce ~** in that case; **le ~ échéant** if such is the case; **en ~ de** in case of, in the event of; **en ~ de besoin** if need be; **en ~ d'urgence** in an emergency; **en aucun ~** on no account, under no circumstances; **en tout ~** in any case, at any rate; **selon les ~** as the case may be; **il a un ~ de conscience** he's in a moral dilemma.

casanier, -ière [kazanje, jɛʀ] *adj, nm,f* stay-at-home.

casaque [kazak] *nf [jockey]* blouse; *[mousquetaire]* tabard.

cascade [kaskad] *nf* waterfall, cascade; *[mots etc]* stream, torrent; *[rires]* peal. (*fig*) **des démissions en ~** a spate of resignations. ♦ **cascader** (1) *vi* to cascade. ♦ **cascadeur, -euse** *nm,f* stuntman; stuntgirl.

case [kɑz] *nf* **(a)** (*carré*) square. **(b)** *[courrier]* pigeonhole; *[tiroir]* compartment. **il a une ~ vide*** he has a screw loose*. **(c)** (*hutte*) hut, cabin.

casemate [kazmat] *nf* blockhouse.

caser* [kaze] (1) **1** *vt* (*placer*) *objets* to put, tuck; (*loger*) to put up; (*marier*) to find a husband (*ou* wife) for; (*dans un métier*) to find a job for. **il est casé** (*mariage*) he's married; (*emploi*) he's fixed up. **2 se ~** *vpr* (*mariage*) to settle down; (*emploi*) to find a (steady) job; (*logement*) to find a place (to live).

caserne [kazɛʀn(ə)] *nf* (*Mil, fig*) barracks (*gén sg*). **~ de pompiers** fire station. ♦ **casernement** *nm* (*action*) quartering in barracks; (*bâtiments*) barrack buildings. ♦ **caserner** (1) *vt* to barrack.

cash* [kaʃ] *adv*: **payer ~** to pay cash down.

casier [kɑzje] *nm* (*gén*) compartment; (*tiroir*) drawer; (*fermant à clef*) locker; *[courrier]* pigeonhole; (*meuble*) cabinet; (*Pêche*) (lobster *etc*) pot. **~ à bouteilles** bottle rack; **~ judiciaire** police record.

casino [kazino] *nm* casino.

casque [kask(ə)] *nm* (*gén*) helmet; *[motocycliste etc]* crash helmet; (*sèche-cheveux*) (hair-)drier.

~ **(à écouteurs)** headphones, headset (*US*); **les C~s bleus** the U.N. peace-keeping troops. ♦ **casqué, e** *adj* wearing a helmet. ♦ **casquette** *nf* cap.

casquer* [kaske] (1) *vi* (*payer*) to fork out*.

cassable [kɑsabl(ə)] *adj* breakable.

cassant, e [kɑsɑ̃, ɑ̃t] *adj substance* brittle; *bois* easily broken; *ton, manières* brusque, abrupt. **ce n'est pas ~*** it's not exactly tiring work.

cassation [kɑsɑsjɔ̃] *nf* (*Jur*) cassation; (*Mil*) reduction to the ranks.

casse [kɑs] **1** *nf* (*action*) breaking, breakage; (*objets cassés*) damage, breakages. **il va y avoir de la ~*** there's going to be (some) rough stuff*; **mettre à la ~** to scrap; **bon pour la ~** ready for the scrap heap. **2** *nm* (*arg Crime*) break-in. **3** *préf V* **casser.**

cassé, e [kɑse] *adj voix* broken; *vieillard* bent.

cassement [kɑsmɑ̃] *nm*: **~ de tête** headache (*fig*), worry.

casser [kɑse] (1) **1** *vt* **(a)** (*gén*) to break; *noix* to crack; *branche* to snap; (*) *appareil* to bust*. **~ un bras à qn** to break sb's arm; **~ les prix** to slash prices. **(b)** (*dégrader*) (*Mil*) to reduce to the ranks, break; (*Admin*) to demote. **(c)** *jugement* to quash; *mariage, arrêt* to annul. **(d) ~ la croûte*** to have a bite to eat; **~ la figure à qn*** to smash sb's face in‡; **~ les pieds à qn*** (*fatiguer*) to bore sb stiff; (*irriter*) to get on sb's nerves; **~ sa pipe*** to snuff it‡, kick the bucket‡; **ça ne casse rien*** it's nothing special, it's no great shakes*; **~ du sucre sur le dos de qn** to talk about sb behind his back; **il nous casse la tête avec sa trompette** he deafens us with his trumpet; **à tout ~*** (*extraordinaire*) fantastic*; (*tout au plus*) at the outside, at the most.

2 *vi* to break; to snap. *[pantalon]* **~ sur la chaussure** to rest on the instep.

3 se ~ *vpr [objet]* to break. *[personne]* **se ~ une jambe** to break a leg; **se ~ la figure*** (*faire faillite, tomber*) to come a cropper*; (*d'une certaine hauteur*) to crash down; (*se tuer*) to smash o.s. up*; **se ~ le nez** to find no one in; **il ne s'est pas cassé (la tête)*** he didn't overtax himself; **se ~ la tête sur un problème*** to rack one's brains over a problem.

4: casse-cou* *nmf inv* daredevil, reckless person; **casse-croûte** *nm inv* snack, lunch (*US*); **casse-noisettes** *nm inv*, **casse-noix** *nm inv* (pair of) nutcrackers; **casse-pieds*** *nmf inv* (*importun*) nuisance, pain in the neck*; (*ennuyeux*) bore; (*Mil*) **aller au casse-pipes** to go to the front; **casse-tête** *nm inv* (*problème*) headache; (*jeu*) puzzle, brain teaser; (*massue*) club.

casserole [kasʀɔl] *nf* (*Culin*) saucepan; (*péj: piano*) tinny piano. **passer à la ~‡** (*tuer*) to bump off‡.

cassette [kasɛt] *nf* (*coffret*) casket; *[roi]* privy purse; *[magnétophone]* cassette.

casseur [kɑsœʀ] *nm* (*: *bravache*) tough guy‡; (*ferrailleur*) scrap dealer; (*manifestant*) rioter, demonstrator; (*arg Crime: cambrioleur*) burglar.

cassis [kasis] *nm* (*fruit*) blackcurrant; (‡: *tête*) nut‡; *[route]* bump, ridge.

cassure [kɑsyʀ] *nf* **(a)** (*lit, fig*) break; *[col]* fold. **(b)** (*Géol*) (*gén*) break; (*fissure*) crack; (*faille*) fault.

castagnettes [kastaɲɛt] *nfpl* castanets. **avoir les dents qui jouent des ~*** to feel one's teeth chattering.

caste [kast(ə)] *nf* (*lit, péj*) caste.

castor [kastɔʀ] *nm* beaver.

castrer [kastʀe] (1) *vt* (*gén*) to castrate; *cheval* to geld; *chat, chien* to neuter. ♦ **castration** *nf* castration; gelding; neutering.

cataclysme [kataklism(ə)] *nm* cataclysm.

catacombes [katakɔ̃b(ə)] *nfpl* catacombs.

catafalque [katafalk(ə)] *nm* catafalque.

catalepsie [katalɛpsi] *nf* catalepsy. **tomber en ~** to have a cataleptic fit. ♦ **cataleptique** *adj, nmf* cataleptic.

catalogue [katalɔg] *nm* catalogue. **prix de ~** list price. ♦ **cataloguer** (1) *vt objets* to catalogue, list; (*) *personne* to label.

catalyse [kataliz] *nf* catalysis. ♦ **catalyseur** *nm* (*Chim, fig*) catalyst. ♦ **catalytique** *adj* catalytic.

cataplasme [kataplasm(ə)] *nm* (*Méd*) poultice; (*fig*) lead weight.

catapulte [katapylt(ə)] *nf* catapult. ♦ **catapulter** (1) *vt* to catapult.

cataracte [kataʀakt(ə)] *nf* (*gén, Méd*) cataract. (*fig*) **des ~s de pluie** torrents of rain.

catarrhe [kataʀ] *nm* catarrh.

catastrophe [katastʀɔf] *nf* disaster, catastrophe. **en ~** *partir* in a mad rush; **atterrir en ~** to make an emergency landing. ♦ **catastropher*** (1) *vt* to shatter, stun. ♦ **catastrophique** *adj* disastrous, catastrophic.

catch [katʃ] *nm* (all-in) wrestling. ♦ **catcheur, -euse** *nm,f* (all-in) wrestler.

catéchisme [kateʃism(ə)] *nm* (*gén*) catechism. ♦ **catéchiser** (1) *vt* to catechize. ♦ **catéchiste** *nmf* catechist.

catégorie [kategɔʀi] *nf* (*gén, Philos*) category; (*Boxe, Hôtellerie*) class; *[personnel]* grade. ♦ **catégorique** *adj* (*gén*) categorical; *refus* flat. ♦ **catégoriquement** *adv* categorically; flatly. ♦ **catégorisation** *nf* (*gén*) categorization; (*Admin*) grading. ♦ **catégoriser** (1) *vt* to categorize.

caténaire [katenɛʀ] *adj, nf* (*Rail*) catenary.

cathédrale [katedʀal] *nf* cathedral.

cathode [katɔd] *nf* cathode. ♦ **cathodique** *adj* cathodic.

catholique [katɔlik] **1** *adj* (*Rel*) (Roman) Catholic. **pas (très) ~*** fishy*, shady. **2** *nmf* (Roman) Catholic. ♦ **catholicisme** *nm* (Roman) Catholicism.

catimini [katimini] *adv*: **en ~** on the sly; **sortir en ~** to steal *ou* sneak out; **il me l'a dit en ~** he whispered it in my ear.

catin [katɛ̃] *nf* (*prostituée*) trollop.

cation [katjɔ̃] *nm* cation.

Caucase [kokɑz] *nm*: **le ~** the Caucasus.

cauchemar [koʃmaʀ] *nm* (*lit, fig*) nightmare. ♦ **cauchemardesque** *adj* nightmarish.

causalité [kozalite] *nf* causality.

causant, e [kozɑ̃, ɑ̃t] *adj* talkative, chatty.

cause [koz] *nf* **(a)** (*raison*) cause (*de* of). **la chaleur en est la ~** it is caused by the heat; **les ~s qui l'ont poussé à agir** the reasons that caused him to act. **(b)** (*Jur*) case; (*à plaider*) brief. (*fig*) **la ~ est entendue** there's no doubt in our minds; **plaider sa ~** to plead one's case; **avocat sans ~** briefless barrister. **(c)** (*parti*) cause. **faire ~ commune avec qn** to make common cause with sb, take sides with sb. **(d) à ~ de** (*en raison de*) because of, owing to, on account of; (*par égard pour*) because of, for the sake of; **être en ~** *[personne, intérêts etc]* to be involved; **son honnêteté n'est pas en ~** his honesty is not in question; **mettre en ~** *projet* to call into question; *personne* to implicate; **ça remet tout en ~** it re-opens the whole question, we're back to square one*; **mettre qn hors de ~** to clear *ou* exonerate sb; **c'est hors de ~** it is out of the question; **pour ~ de** on account of; **et pour ~!** and for (a very) good reason!; **non sans ~!** not without (good) reason!

causer¹ [koze] (1) *vt* (*provoquer*) to cause; (*entraîner*) to bring about. **~ des ennuis à qn** to get sb into trouble, bring trouble to sb; **~ de la peine à qn** to hurt sb.

causer² [koze] (1) *vti* (*s'entretenir*) to chat, talk (*de* about); (*: *discourir*) to speak, talk; (*jaser*) to talk, gossip (*sur qn* about sb); (‡: *avouer*) to talk. **~ politique** to talk politics; **~ à qn*** to talk *ou* speak to sb. ♦ **causerie** *nf* (*conférence*) talk; (*conversation*) chat. ♦ **causette** *nf*: **faire la** ~ to have a chat *ou* natter* (*avec* with). ♦ **causeur, -euse 1** *adj* talkative, chatty. **2** *nm,f* talker.

causticité [kostisite] *nf* (*lit, fig*) causticity. ♦ **caustique** *adj, nmf* caustic.

cautère [kɔtɛʀ] *nm* cautery. ♦ **cautérisation** *nf* cauterization. ♦ **cautériser** (1) *vt* to cauterize.

caution [kosjɔ̃] *nf* (*Fin*) guarantee, security; (*Jur*) bail (bond); (*morale*) guarantee; (*appui*) backing, support. **libéré sous** ~ released on bail; **payer la** ~ **de qn** to stand bail for sb, bail sb out. ♦ **cautionnement** *nm* (*somme*) guaranty, guarantee, security; *[politique]* backing. ♦ **cautionner** (1) *vt* (*Fin, fig*) to guarantee; *politique* to support, back.

cavalcade [kavalkad] *nf* (*désordonnée*) stampede; (*défilé*) cavalcade.

cavaler‡ [kavale] (1) **1** *vi* (*courir*) to run. **2** *vt* (*ennuyer*) to bore, annoy. **3 se** ~ *vpr* (*se sauver*) to clear off‡.

cavalerie [kavalʀi] *nf* (*Mil*) cavalry; *[cirque]* stable (of circus horses). (*Mil*) ~ **légère** light cavalry *ou* horse; (*: *Comm*) **c'est de la grosse** ~ it's the heavy stuff.

cavalier, -ière [kavalje, jɛʀ] **1** *adj* **(a)** (*impertinent*) cavalier, offhand. **(b) allée/piste** ~**ière** riding path/track. **2** *nm,f* (*Équitation*) rider; (*partenaire*) partner. (*fig*) **faire** ~ **seul** to go it alone. **3** *nm* **(a)** (*Mil*) trooper, cavalryman. **troupe de 20** ~**s** troop of 20 horses. **(b)** (*accompagnateur*) escort. **(c)** (*Échecs*) knight. ♦ **cavalièrement** *adv* in cavalier fashion, offhandedly.

cave [kav] **1** *nf* (*gén*) cellar. **2** *adj joues* hollow, sunken. ♦ **caveau,** *pl* ~**x** *nm* (*sépulture*) vault, tomb; (*cave*) (small) cellar.

caverne [kavɛʀn(ə)] *nf* cave, cavern. ♦ **caverneux, -euse** *adj* (*gén*) cavernous.

caviar [kavjaʀ] *nm* (*Culin*) caviar. ~ **rouge** salmon roe.

caviste [kavist(ə)] *nm* cellarman.

cavité [kavite] *nf* cavity.

ce [sə], **cet** [sɛt] *devant voyelle ou h muet au masculin,* **cette** [sɛt] *f,* **ces** [se] *pl* **1** *adj dém* **(a)** (*proximité*) this; (*pl*) these; (*non-proximité*) that; (*pl*) those. **ce chapeau(-ci)/(-là)** this/that hat; **et ce rhume?*** and how's the cold (doing)?*; **cette nuit** (*qui vient*) tonight; (*passée*) last night; **en ces temps troublés** (*de nos jours*) in these troubled days; (*dans le passé*) in those troubled days; **un de ces jours** one of these days; **ces messieurs sont en réunion** the gentlemen are in a meeting; **cette ami chez qui elle habite** the friend she's living with; **c'est un de ces livres que l'on lit en vacances** it's one of those books *ou* the sort of book you read on holiday.

(b) (*intensif*) **aurait-il vraiment ce courage?** would he really have that sort of *ou* that much courage?; **cette idée!** what an idea!; **cette générosité me semble suspecte** such *ou* this generosity strikes me as suspicious.

2 *pron dém* **(a) qui est-ce? – c'est un médecin** (*en désignant*) who's he? *ou* who's that? – he is a doctor; (*au téléphone*) who is it? – it's a doctor; **c'était le bon temps!** those were the days!; **qui est-ce qui a crié? – c'est lui** who shouted? – HE did *ou* it was him; **c'est eux*** *ou* **ce sont eux qui mentaient** they (are the ones who) *ou* it's they who were lying; **c'est toi qui le dis!** that's what YOU say!; **c'est à se demander si** you really wonder *ou* it makes you wonder if.

(b) ce qui, ce que what; (*reprenant une proposition*) which; **elle fait ce qu'on/tout ce qu'on lui dit** she does what *ou* as she is told/all that she is told; **il ne comprenait pas ce à quoi on faisait allusion/ce dont on l'accusait** he didn't understand what they were hinting at/what he was being accused of; **il faut être diplômé, ce qu'il n'est pas** you have to have qualifications, which *ou* and he hasn't; **ce que ce film est lent!** how slow this film is!, what a slow film this is!; **voilà ce que c'est que de conduire trop vite** that's what comes of driving too fast.

(c) c'est (vous) dire s'il a eu peur that shows (you) how frightened he was; **à ce qu'on dit** from *ou* according to what they say; **ce faisant** in so doing; **ce disant** so saying; **pour ce faire** to this end, with this end in view; **il a refusé, et ce, après toutes nos prières** he refused, (and this) after all our entreaties.

ceci [səsi] *pron dém* this. **ce cas a** ~ **de surprenant que** ... this case is surprising in that ...; **à** ~ **près que** except that; ~ **compense cela** one thing makes up for another.

cécité [sesite] *nf* blindness.

céder [sede] (6) **1** *vt* **(a)** *part, tour* to give up. ~ **qch à qn** to let sb have sth; **je cède l'antenne à Paris** over to Paris; (*Jur*) ~ **ses biens** to make over one's property. **(b)** ~ **le pas à qn/qch** to give precedence to sb/sth; ~ **du terrain** (*Mil*) to yield ground; (*fig*) to make concessions; *[épidémie]* to recede; **son courage ne le cède en rien à son intelligence** he's as brave as he is intelligent. **2** *vi* *[personne]* to give in; *[branche]* to give way; *[colère]* to subside. ~ **à** (*succomber*) to give way to, yield to; (*consentir*) to give in to.

cédille [sedij] *nf* cedilla.

cèdre [sɛdʀ(ə)] *nm* cedar.

ceindre [sɛ̃dʀ(ə)] (52) *vt* (*littér*) *écharpe* to put on; *épée* to gird. **la tête ceinte d'un diadème** wearing a diadem; **ville ceinte de murs** town surrounded *ou* encircled by walls.

ceinture [sɛ̃tyʀ] *nf* **(a)** *[pantalon]* belt; *[pyjamas]* cord; (*écharpe*) sash; (*gaine*) girdle. **se mettre la** ~* to tighten one's belt (*fig*); (*Judo*) ~ **noire** black belt; ~ **de flanelle** flannel binder; ~ **de natation** swimming ring; ~ **de sauvetage** life belt; ~ **de sécurité** seat *ou* safety belt; (*Boxe, fig*) **au-dessous de la** ~ below the belt. **(b)** (*taille*) (*Couture*) waistband; (*Anat*) waist. **l'eau lui arrivait à la** ~ he was waist-deep in *ou* up to his waist in water. **(c)** *[murailles]* ring; *[arbres]* belt; (*métro, bus*) circle line. ♦ **ceinturer** (1) *vt personne* to seize round the waist; *ville* to surround, encircle. ♦ **ceinturon** *nm* belt.

cela [s(ə)la] *pron dém* **(a)** that; (*sujet apparent*) it. **qu'est-ce que** ~ **veut dire?** what does that *ou* this mean?; ~ **vaut la peine qu'il essaie** it's worth his trying; **faire des études,** ~ **ne le tentait guère** studying did not really appeal to him. **(b)** (*pour renforcer*) ~ **fait 10 jours qu'il est parti** it is 10 days since he left, he left 10 days ago; **j'ai vu X – qui** ~**?/quand** ~**?/où** ~**?** I've seen X – who do you mean? *ou* who is that?/when was that?/where was that?; **voyez-vous** ~**!** did you ever hear of such a thing!; **à** ~ **près que** except that; **il y a** ~ **de bien que** the (one) good thing is that.

célébrer [selebʀe] (6) *vt mariage, messe, fête* to celebrate; *cérémonie* to hold. ~ **les louanges de qn** to sing sb's praises. ♦ **célébrant** *nm* celebrant. ♦ **célébration** *nf* celebration. ♦ **célèbre** *adj* famous, celebrated (*par* for). ♦ **célébrité** *nf* (*renommée*) fame, celebrity; (*personne*) celebrity.

céleri [sɛlʀi] *nm*: ~ **en branche(s)** celery; ~**(-rave)** celeriac.

célérité [seleʀite] *nf* promptness, swiftness.

céleste [selɛst(ə)] *adj* (*Rel*) celestial, heavenly; (*fig*) heavenly.

célibat [seliba] *nm* *[homme]* bachelorhood; *[femme]* spinsterhood; *[prêtre]* celibacy. ♦ **célibataire 1** *adj* single, unmarried; *prêtre* celibate. **2** *nm* bachelor; (*Admin*) single man. **la vie de** ~ (the) single life. **3** *nf* single *ou* unmarried woman; (*moins jeune*) spinster.

celle [sɛl] *pron dém* **V celui.**

cellier [selje] *nm* storeroom (*for wine and food*).
cellophane [selɔfan] *nf* ® cellophane ®.
cellule [selyl] *nf* (*gén*) cell; *[électrophone]* cartridge. ♦ **cellulaire** *adj* (*Bio*) cellular. **fourgon ~** prison van.
cellulite [selylit] *nf* cellulitis.
celluloïd [selylɔid] *nm* celluloid.
cellulose [selyloz] *nf* cellulose. ♦ **cellulosique** *adj* cellulose.
celte [sɛlt(ə)] **1** *adj* Celtic. **2** *nmf*: **C~** Celt. ♦ **celtique** *adj, nm* Celtic.
celui [səlɥi], **celle** [sɛl], *mpl* **ceux** [sø], *fpl* **celles** [sɛl] *pron dém* **(a) celui-ci, celle-ci** this one; **ceux-ci, celles-ci** these (ones); **celui-là, celle-là** that one; **ceux-la, celles-là** those (ones).
(b) (*avec antécédent*) **j'ai vu mon frère et mon oncle: celui-ci était malade** I saw my brother and my uncle - the latter was ill; **elle écrivit à son frère; celui-ci ne répondit pas** she wrote to her brother, but he did not answer; **ceux-là, ils auront de mes nouvelles** as for them, I'll give them a piece of my mind; **il a vraiment de la chance, celui-là!** that fellow certainly has a lot of luck!; **elle est bien bonne, celle-là!** that's a bit much!
(c) (+ *de, que*) **je n'aime pas cette pièce, celle de X est meilleure** I don't like this play, X's is better; **il n'a qu'un désir, celui de devenir ministre** he only wants one thing and that's to become a minister; **s'il cherche un appartement, celui d'en-dessous est libre** if he's looking for a flat, the one below is free; **ses romans sont ceux qui se vendent le mieux** his novels are the ones that sell best; **celui dont je t'ai parlé** the one I told you about; **cette marque est celle recommandée par X** this is the brand recommended by X.
cénacle [senakl(ə)] *nm* (literary) coterie; (*Rel*) cenacle.
cendre [sɑ̃dʀ(ə)] *nf* (*gén*) ash. **~(s)** *[charbon]* ash, ashes, cinders; (*braises*) embers; *[mort]* **~s** ashes; **couleur de ~** ashen, ash-coloured; (*Rel*) **les C~s** Ash Wednesday; (*Géol*) **~s volcaniques** volcanic ash. ♦ **cendré, e 1** *adj* ash. **2** *nf* (*piste*) cinder track. ♦ **cendreux, -euse** *adj* ashy; *teint* ashen. ♦ **cendrier** *nm [fumeur]* ashtray; *[poêle]* ash pan.
Cendrillon [sɑ̃dʀijɔ̃] *nf* (*lit, fig*) Cinderella.
Cène [sɛn] *nf*: **la ~** the Last Supper.
cénotaphe [senɔtaf] *nm* cenotaph.
cens [sɑ̃s] *nm*: **~ électoral** (electoral) property qualification.
censé, e [sɑ̃se] *adj*: **être ~ faire qch** to be supposed to do sth. ♦ **censément** *adv* (*en principe*) supposedly; (*pratiquement*) virtually.
censeur [sɑ̃sœʀ] *nm* (*Hist, Presse*) censor; (*fig*) critic; (*Scol*) ≃ deputy *ou* assistant head.
censurer [sɑ̃syʀe] (1) *vt* (*Ciné, Presse*) to censor; (*fig, Pol, Rel*) to censure. ♦ **censure** *nf* (*Ciné, Presse*) (*examen*) censorship; (*censeurs*) (board of) censors; (*Psych*) censor. **les ~s de** the censure of.
cent [sɑ̃] **1** *adj* **(a)** one hundred, a hundred. **quatre ~ treize** four hundred and thirteen; **deux ~s chaises** two hundred chairs; (*ordinal: inv*) **page quatre ~** page four hundred. **(b) il a ~ fois raison** he's absolutely right; **~ fois mieux** a hundred times better; **je préférerais ~ fois faire votre travail** I'd far rather do your job; **il est aux ~ coups** he is frantic; **faire les ~ pas** to pace up and down; **quatre ~s mètres haies** 400 metres hurdles; **tu ne vas pas attendre ~ sept ans*** you can't wait for ever; **je vous le donne en ~** you'll never guess.
2 *nm* **(a)** a hundred. **il y a ~ contre un à parier que** it's a hundred to one that; **~ pour ~** a hundred per cent; *pour autres locutions V* **six. (b)** (*US, Can: monnaie*) cent.
centaine [sɑ̃tɛn] *nf* hundred. (*environ cent*) **une ~ de** about a hundred, a hundred or so; **plusieurs ~s (de)** several hundred; **des ~s de** hundreds of; **10 F la ~** 10 francs a hundred; *V* **soixantaine.**
centaure [sɑ̃tɔʀ] *nm* centaur.
centenaire [sɑ̃tnɛʀ] **1** *adj*: **cet arbre est ~** this tree is a hundred years old, this is a hundred-year-old tree. **2** *nmf* (*personne*) centenarian. **3** *nm* (*anniversaire*) centenary.
centième [sɑ̃tjɛm] **1** *adj, nmf* hundredth; *pour loc V* **sixième. 2** *nf* (*Théât*) hundredth performance.
centigrade [sɑ̃tigʀad] *adj* centigrade. ♦ **centigramme** *nm* centigramme. ♦ **centilitre** *nm* centilitre. ♦ **centime** *nm* centime. (*fig*) **je n'ai pas un ~** I haven't got a penny *ou* a cent (*US*). ♦ **centimètre** *nm* centimetre; (*ruban*) tape measure.
centrage [sɑ̃tʀaʒ] *nm* centring.
central, e, *mpl* **-aux** [sɑ̃tʀal, o] **1** *adj* (*gén*) central; *partie* centre; *bureau* main. **2** *nm* (*Téléc*) **~ (téléphonique)** (telephone) exchange. **3** *nf* (*prison*) (central) prison. **~e (électrique)** power station; **~e syndicale** trade union.
centraliser [sɑ̃tʀalize] (1) *vt* to centralize. ♦ **centralisateur, -trice** *adj* centralizing. ♦ **centralisation** *nf* centralization.
centre [sɑ̃tʀ(ə)] **1** *nm* (*gén*) centre. **le C~ (de la France)** central France; **~-ville** town *ou* city centre; **il se croit le ~ du monde** he thinks the universe revolves around him; **les grands ~s universitaires** the great academic centres; (*Pol*) **~ gauche** centre left. **2: ~ commercial** shopping centre; **~ hospitalier** hospital complex; (*Poste*) **~ de tri** sorting office; (*lit, fig*) **~s vitaux** vital organs.
centrer [sɑ̃tʀe] (1) *vt* (*Sport, Tech*) to centre. **~ une discussion sur** to centre *ou* focus a discussion on.
centrifuge [sɑ̃tʀifyʒ] *adj* centrifugal. ♦ **centrifuger** (3) *vt* to centrifuge. ♦ **centrifugeuse** *nf* centrifuge.
centripète [sɑ̃tʀipɛt] *adj* centripetal.
centuple [sɑ̃typl(ə)] **1** *adj* a hundred times as large (*de* as). **2** *nm*: **le ~ de 10** a hundred times 10; **au ~** a hundredfold. ♦ **centupler** (1) *vti* to increase a hundred times *ou* a hundredfold.
centurion [sɑ̃tyʀjɔ̃] *nm* centurion.
cep [sɛp] *nm*: **~ (de vigne)** vine stock. ♦ **cépage** *nm* (type of) vine.
cèpe [sɛp] *nm* (*Culin*) cepe; (*Bot*) boletus.
cependant [s(ə)pɑ̃dɑ̃] *conj* **(a)** (*pourtant*) nevertheless, however. **et ~ c'est vrai** yet *ou* but nevertheless it is true. **(b)** (*pendant ce temps*) meanwhile. **~ que** while.
céramique [seʀamik] *nf* ceramic. (*art*) **la ~** ceramics; **vase en ~** ceramic vase.
cerceau, *pl* **~x** [sɛʀso] *nm* hoop.
cercle [sɛʀkl(ə)] *nm* **(a)** (*lit*) circle, ring; (*Géom*) circle. **faire ~ (autour de qn/qch)** to make a circle *ou* ring (round sb/sth); **~ vicieux** vicious circle. **(b)** *[famille, amis]* circle; *[connaissances]* scope, range; (*club*) club. **~ littéraire** literary circle *ou* society. **(c)** *[tonneau]* hoop, band; *[roue]* metal rim. ♦ **cercler** (1) *vt* to ring; to hoop; to rim (*de* with). **lunettes cerclées d'écaille** horn-rimmed spectacles.
cercueil [sɛʀkœj] *nm* coffin, casket (*US*).
céréale [seʀeal] *nf* cereal.
cérébral, e, *mpl* **-aux** [seʀebʀal, o] *adj* (*Méd*) cerebral; *travail* mental.
cérémonie [seʀemɔni] *nf* ceremony. **sans ~** *manger* informally; *réception* informal; **faire des ~s** to stand on ceremony; **habit(s) de ~** formal dress. ♦ **cérémonial,** *pl* **~s** *nm* ceremonial. ♦ **cérémonieusement** *adv* ceremoniously, formally. ♦ **cérémonieux, -euse** *adj* ceremonious, formal.
cerf [sɛʀ] *nm* stag. ♦ **cerf-volant,** *pl* **~s-~s** *nm* kite. **jouer au ~** to fly a kite.
cerfeuil [sɛʀfœj] *nm* chervil.

cerise [s(ə)ʀiz] **1** *nf* cherry. **2** *adj inv* cherry (-red). ♦ **cerisier** *nm* cherry tree.

cerner [sɛʀne] (1) *vt ennemi* to encircle, surround; *problème* to delimit, define. **avoir les yeux cernés** to have dark rings under one's eyes. ♦ **cerne** *nm* (*gén*) ring.

certain, e [sɛʀtɛ̃, ɛn] **1** *adj* **(a)** (*après n: incontestable*) (*gén*) certain; *preuve* positive, sure, definite; *cause* undoubted, sure. **c'est la raison ~e de son départ** it's undoubtedly the reason for his going; **c'est ~** there's no doubt about it, that's quite certain. **(b)** (*convaincu*) sure, certain (*de qch* of sth, *de faire* of doing).

2 *adj indéf* (*avant n*) **(a)** (*mal défini*) certain. **elle a un ~ charme** she's got a certain charm; **dans un ~ village où** in a certain *ou* some village where; **un ~ M. X** a (certain) *ou* one Mr. X; **dans un ~ sens** in a way, in a certain sense, in some senses; **dans ~s cas** in some *ou* certain cases. **(b)** (*intensif*) some. **c'est à une ~e distance d'ici** it's quite a *ou* some distance from here; **d'un ~ âge** elderly.

3 *pron indéf pl:* **~s** (*personnes*) some (people); (*choses*) some.

♦ **certainement** *adv* certainly. ♦ **certes** *adv* (*concession*) certainly, admittedly; (*affirmation*) indeed, most certainly; (*bien sûr*) of course.

certificat [sɛʀtifika] *nm* (*attestation*) certificate, attestation; (*diplôme*) certificate, diploma; (*recommandation*) *[domestique]* testimonial; (*fig*) guarantee. **~ médical** doctor's certificate.

certifier [sɛʀtifje] (7) *vt document* to certify; *signature* to attest, witness. **~ qch à qn** to assure sb of sth, guarantee sth to sb; **copie certifiée conforme à l'original** certified copy of the original.

♦ **certification** *nf* attestation, witnessing.

certitude [sɛʀtityd] *nf* certainty. **j'ai la ~ d'être le plus fort** I am certain *ou* (quite) sure of being the strongest.

cerveau, *pl* **~x** [sɛʀvo] *nm* brain; (*personne, intelligence*) brain, mind; (*fig: centre de direction*) brain(s). **avoir le ~ dérangé** to be deranged *ou* (a bit) cracked*; **le ~ de la bande** the brain(s) *ou* the mastermind of the gang.

cervelas [sɛʀvəla] *nm* saveloy.

cervelet [sɛʀvəlɛ] *nm* cerebellum.

cervelle [sɛʀvɛl] *nf* (*Anat*) brain; (*Culin*) brains; (*tête*) head. **se brûler la ~** to blow one's brains out; **avoir une ~ d'oiseau** to be feather-brained.

cervical, e, *mpl* **-aux** [sɛʀvikal, o] *adj* cervical.

ces [se] *adj dém V* **ce.**

césarienne [sezaʀjɛn] *nf* Caesarean (section).

cessation [sɛsasjɔ̃] *nf* cessation; *[paiements]* suspension.

cesse [sɛs] *nf* **(a) sans ~** (*tout le temps*) continually, incessantly; (*sans interruption*) continuously, without ceasing. **(b) il n'a de ~ que** he will not rest until.

cesser [sese] (1) **1** *vt* (*gén*) to stop; *relations* to (bring to an) end, break off; *fabrication* to discontinue; (*Admin*) *fonctions* to relinquish, give up. **~ le combat** to stop (the) fighting. **2 ~ de** *vt indir:* **~ de faire qch** (*gén*) to stop doing sth; (*renoncer*) to give up doing sth; **ça a cessé d'exister** it has ceased to exist; **son effet n'a pas cessé de se faire sentir** its effect is still making itself felt; **il ne cesse de dire que** he is constantly *ou* he keeps on saying that. **3** *vi* (*gén*) to stop; *[bruit, activités]* to stop, cease; *[fonctions]* to come to an end; *[fièvre]* to pass, die down. **faire ~** *bruit* to put a stop to, stop; *scandale* to put an end *ou* a stop to. ♦ **cessez-le-feu** *nm inv* ceasefire.

cession [sɛsjɔ̃] *nf* transfer. **faire ~ de** to transfer.

c'est-à-dire [setadiʀ] *conj* that is (to say). **~ que** (*conséquence*) which means that; (*excuse*) the thing is that.

cet [sɛt] *adj dém V* **ce.**

ceux [sø] *adj dém V* **celui.**

Ceylan [selɑ̃] *nm* Ceylon.

chacal, *pl* **~s** [ʃakal] *nm* jackal.

chacun, e [ʃakœ̃, yn] *pron indéf* **(a)** (*isolément*) each (one). **~ de** each (one) *ou* every one of; **~ à notre/leur tour** each (of us/of them) in turn. **(b)** (*tous*) everyone, everybody. **~ son tour!** everyone in turn!, each in turn!; **~ son goût/pour soi** every man to his (own) taste/for himself.

chagrin, e [ʃagʀɛ̃, in] **1** *adj* (*triste*) woeful, dejected; (*bougon*) ill-humoured, morose. **2** *nm* grief, sorrow. **~ d'amour** unhappy love affair; **faire du ~ à qn** to grieve *ou* distress sb; **avoir du ~** to be sorry *ou* upset. ♦ **chagrinant, e** *adj* distressing. ♦ **chagriner** (1) *vt* (*désoler*) to grieve, distress, upset; (*tracasser*) to worry, bother.

chah [ʃa] *nm* = **shah.**

chahut [ʃay] *nm* uproar. ♦ **chahuter** (1) **1** *vi* (*faire du bruit*) to make an uproar; (*faire les fous*) to scrap, romp. **2** *vt professeur* to rag, play up; (*: *cahoter*) *objet* to knock about. ♦ **chahuteur, -euse 1** *adj* rowdy, unruly. **2** *nm,f* rowdy.

chai [ʃɛ] *nm* wine and spirits store(house).

chaîne [ʃɛn] *nf* (*gén*) chain; *[montagnes]* range, chain; *[magasins]* string, chain; (*Tex*) warp; (*TV, Rad*) channel. (*fig: esclavage*) **~s** chains, bonds; **~ d'arpenteur** chain measure; **~ hi-fi** hi-fi system; **~ de fabrication/de montage** production/assembly line; **produire à la ~** to mass-produce. ♦ **chaînette** *nf* (small) chain. ♦ **chaînon** *nm* (*lit, fig*) link; (*Géog*) secondary range.

chair [ʃɛʀ] *nf* flesh. **les ~s** the flesh; **en ~ et en os** in the flesh; **(couleur) ~** flesh-coloured; **donner la ~ de poule** to give gooseflesh *ou* goosebumps (*US*); **~ à saucisse** sausage meat; (*fig*) **je vais en faire de la ~ à pâté** I'm going to make mincemeat of him; **bien en ~** well-padded (*hum*), plump; **sa propre ~** his own flesh and blood.

chaire [ʃɛʀ] *nf [prédicateur]* pulpit; *[pape]* throne; *[professeur]* (*estrade*) rostrum; (*poste*) chair.

chaise [ʃɛz] *nf* chair. **~ de bébé** highchair; **~ électrique** electric chair; **~ longue** deckchair; **~ (à porteurs)** sedan(-chair). ♦ **chaisière** *nf* (female) chair attendant.

chaland [ʃalɑ̃] *nm* (*Naut*) barge.

châle [ʃɑl] *nm* shawl.

chalet [ʃalɛ] *nm* chalet.

chaleur [ʃalœʀ] *nf* **(a)** (*gén, Phys*) heat; (*agréable*) warmth. **les grandes ~s (de l'été)** the hot (summer) days *ou* weather; **'craint la ~'** 'to be kept in a cool place'. **(b)** *[discussion]* heat; *[accueil]* warmth; *[convictions]* fervour. **défendre avec ~** to defend hotly *ou* heatedly. **(c)** (*Zool*) **être en ~** to be on *ou* in heat; (*Méd*) **avoir des ~s** to have hot flushes. ♦ **chaleureusement** *adv* warmly. ♦ **chaleureux, -euse** *adj* warm.

challenge [ʃalɑ̃ʒ] *nm* (*épreuve*) contest, tournament; (*trophée*) trophy.

chaloupe [ʃalup] *nf* launch. **~ de sauvetage** lifeboat.

chaloupé, e [ʃalupe] *adj danse* swaying; *démarche* rolling.

chalumeau, *pl* **~x** [ʃalymo] *nm* (*Tech*) blowlamp, blowtorch (*US*).

chalut [ʃaly] *nm* trawl (net). **pêcher au ~** to trawl. ♦ **chalutier** *nm* (*bateau*) trawler; (*pêcheur*) trawlerman.

chamailler (se)* [ʃamɑje] (1) *vpr* to squabble, bicker. ♦ **chamaillerie*** *nf* squabble. ♦ **chamailleur, -euse* 1** *adj* quarrelsome. **2** *nm,f* squabbler.

chamarré, e [ʃamaʀe] *adj* richly coloured. **~ d'or** bedecked with gold.

chambard* [ʃɑ̃baʀ] *nm* (*vacarme*) row, rumpus*; (*bagarre*) scuffle, brawl; (*désordre*) shambles* (*sg*), mess; (*bouleversement*) upheaval. ♦ **chambardement*** *nm* upheaval. ♦ **chambarder*** (1) *vt* (*bouleverser*) to turn upside down; (*se débarrasser de*) to chuck out*.

chambellan [ʃɑ̃belɑ̃] *nm* chamberlain.

chamboulement* [ʃɑ̃bulmɑ̃] *nm* (*désordre*) chaos; (*bouleversement*) upheaval. ♦ **chambouler*** (1) *vt objets* to turn upside down; *projets* to mess up*, make a mess of.

chambranle [ʃɑ̃bʀɑ̃l] *nm* *[porte]* frame; *[cheminée]* mantelpiece.

chambre [ʃɑ̃bʀ(ə)] **1** *nf* **(a)** bedroom; (*littér: pièce*) chamber (*littér*). **faire ~ à part** to sleep in separate rooms; **travailler en ~** to work at home. **(b)** (*Pol*) House, Chamber; (*Jur: section*) division; (*tribunal*) court; (*Admin, groupement*) chamber. **(c)** (*Anat, Tech*) chamber.

2: ~ à air inner tube; **~ d'amis** spare *ou* guest room; **~ de bonne** maid's room; **~ de commerce** Chamber of Commerce; **la C~ des communes** the House of Commons; **~ à coucher** (*pièce*) bedroom; (*mobilier*) bedroom suite; **la C~ des députés** the Chamber of Deputies; **~ forte** strongroom; **~ froide** cold room; **~ à gaz** gas chamber; **la C~ des lords** the House of Lords; (*Phot*) **~ noire** dark room.

♦ **chambrée** *nf* room; *[soldats]* barrack-room.

♦ **chambrer** (1) *vt vin* to bring to room temperature.

chameau, *pl* **~x** [ʃamo] *nm* (*Zool*) camel; (**péj*) beast*. ♦ **chamelier** *nm* camel driver. ♦ **chamelle** *nf* she-camel.

chamois [ʃamwa] *nm* chamois.

champ [ʃɑ̃] **1** *nm* **(a)** (*Agr, Sci*) field; (*fig: domaine*) field, area. (*campagne*) **les ~s** the country(side); **fleurs des ~s** wild flowers; (*Phot*) **être dans le/sortir du ~** to be in/go out of shot; **pas assez de ~** not enough depth of focus. **(b) avoir du ~** to have elbowroom, have room to move; **laisser le ~ libre à qn** to leave sb a clear field; **prendre du ~** (*lit, fig*) to draw back. **2: ~ d'action** sphere of activity; **~ d'aviation** airfield; **~ de bataille** battlefield; **~ de courses** racecourse; **~ de foire** fairground; **mort au ~ d'honneur** killed in action; **~ de tir** (*terrain*) rifle range; (*visée*) field of fire. ♦ **champêtre** *adj* (*gén*) rural; *vie* country.

champignon [ʃɑ̃piɲɔ̃] *nm* (*gén*) mushroom; (*vénéneux*) toadstool; (*Méd, terme de botanique*) fungus; (*Aut**) accelerator.

champion, -onne [ʃɑ̃pjɔ̃, ɔn] **1** *adj* (*) first-rate. **2** *nm,f* (*gén*) champion. **se faire le ~ d'une cause** to champion a cause. ♦ **championnat** *nm* championship.

chance [ʃɑ̃s] *nf* **(a)** (*bonne fortune*) (good) luck. **il a la ~ d'y aller** he's lucky *ou* fortunate enough to be going, he has the good luck *ou* good fortune to be going; **par ~** luckily, fortunately; **pas de ~!** hard *ou* bad luck!; (*iro*) **c'est bien ma ~** (that's) just my luck! **(b)** (*hasard*) luck, chance. **tenter sa ~** to try one's luck; **mettre toutes les ~s de son côté** to take no chances; **mauvaise ~** ill-luck. **(c)** (*possibilité*) chance. **quelles sont ses ~s?** what are his chances *ou* what chance has he got?; **il y a toutes les ~s que** the chances are that.

chanceler [ʃɑ̃sle] (4) *vi* *[personne]* to totter; *[objet]* to wobble, totter; *[autorité]* to totter, falter; *[résolution]* to waver, falter. ♦ **chancelant, e** *adj pas* unsteady, faltering; *objet* wobbly; *mémoire, santé, autorité* shaky.

chancelier [ʃɑ̃səlje] *nm* (*Pol*) chancellor; *[ambassade]* secretary. **le C~ de l'Échiquier** the Chancellor of the Exchequer. ♦ **chancellerie** *nf* chancellery.

chanceux, -euse [ʃɑ̃sø, øz] *adj* lucky, fortunate.

chancre [ʃɑ̃kʀ(ə)] *nm* canker.

chandail [ʃɑ̃daj] *nm* (thick) jersey *ou* sweater.

Chandeleur [ʃɑ̃dlœʀ] *nf*: **la ~** Candlemas.

chandelier [ʃɑ̃dəlje] *nm* candlestick; (*à plusieurs branches*) candelabra.

chandelle [ʃɑ̃dɛl] *nf* (*bougie*) (tallow) candle; (*Aviat*) chandelle; (*Rugby*) up-and-under; (*Tennis*) lob; (*Gym*) shoulder stand. **dîner aux ~s** dinner by candlelight; **~ romaine** roman candle.

change [ʃɑ̃ʒ] *nm* (*Fin*) *[devises]* exchange; (*taux*) exchange rate. (*Banque*) **faire le ~** to exchange money; (*fig*) **gagner/perdre au ~** to gain/lose on the exchange *ou* deal; **donner le ~ à qn** to throw sb off the scent.

changeant, e [ʃɑ̃ʒɑ̃, ɑ̃t] *adj personne, fortune* changeable, fickle, changing; *paysage* changing; *temps* changeable, unsettled.

changement [ʃɑ̃ʒmɑ̃] *nm* (*gén*) change (*de* in, of); (*transformation*) alteration; (*Admin: mutation*) transfer. **le ~ de la roue** changing the wheel, the wheel change; **la situation reste sans ~** the situation remains unchanged *ou* unaltered; **~ en bien** change for the better; **~ de programme** (*projet*) change of plan; (*spectacle etc*) change in the programme; **~ de direction** (*sens*) change of direction; (*dirigeants*) change of management; **~ de vitesse** (*dispositif*) gears, gear lever; (*action*) change of gears; *[bicyclette]* gear(s).

changer [ʃɑ̃ʒe] (3) **1** *vt* **(a)** (*modifier*) to change, alter. **ce chapeau la change** this hat makes her look different; **cela change tout!** that makes all the difference!, that changes everything!; **une promenade lui changera les idées** a walk will take his mind off things; **cela ne change rien au fait que** it doesn't change *ou* alter the fact that; **~ qch/qn en** to change *ou* turn sth/sb into; **cela les changera de leur routine** it will be *ou* make a change for them from their routine. **(b)** (*remplacer*) (*gén*) to change; *décor* to change, shift; *marchandise, argent* to exchange (*contre* for). **j'ai changé ma place contre la sienne** I changed *ou* swapped* places with him, I exchanged my place for his; **~ un malade** to change a patient. **(c)** (*déplacer*) to move. **~ qn/qch de place** to move sb/sth to a different place, shift sb/sth; (*fig*) **~ son fusil d'épaule** to change *ou* alter one's stand.

2 ~ de *vt indir* (*gén*) to change; (*modifier*) to alter; (*échanger*) to exchange. **~ de nom** to change one's name; **~ de domicile** to move house; **~ d'avis** to change one's mind; **elle a changé de visage** (*d'émotion*) her expression changed *ou* altered; **change de disque!*** put another record on!*; **~ de train** to change trains; **~ de camp** to change sides; **~ de position** to alter *ou* change one's position; **~ de côté** (*dans la rue*) to cross over (to the other side); **~ de propriétaire** *ou* **de mains** to change hands; **changeons de sujet** let's change the subject; (*Naut*) **~ de cap** to change *ou* alter course; **~ de place avec qn** to change *ou* swap* places with sb.

3 *vi* (*se transformer*) to change, alter; (*Rail*) to change. **~ en bien/en mal** to change for the better/the worse; **pour (ne pas) ~!** (just) for *ou* by way of a change!; **ça change (de la routine)** it makes a change (from the routine).

4 se ~ *vpr* to change (one's clothes). **se ~ en** to change *ou* turn into.

changeur [ʃɑ̃ʒœʀ] *nm* moneychanger. **~ (de disques)** record changer; **~ de monnaie** change machine.

chanoine [ʃanwan] *nm* (*personne*) canon.

chanson [ʃɑ̃sɔ̃] *nf* song. **c'est toujours la même ~** it's always the same old story; **~ folklorique** folksong; **~ de geste** chanson de geste. ♦ **chansonnette** *nf* ditty.

chant [ʃɑ̃] *nm* (*action, art*) singing; (*chanson*) song; (*Poésie: chapitre*) canto. **le ~ de l'oiseau** (*musique*) the warbling *ou* singing of the bird; (*mélodie*) the song of the bird; **au ~ du coq** at cockcrow; (*lit, fig*) **~ du cygne** swan song; **~ de Noël** (Christmas) carol; **~ religieux** hymn; **cours de ~** singing lessons; **~ grégorien** Gregorian chant.

chantage [ʃɑ̃taʒ] *nm* blackmail. **faire du ~ à qn** to blackmail sb.

chanter [ʃɑ̃te] (1) **1** *vt* (*gén*) to sing; *exploits* to sing (of). **qu'est-ce qu'il nous chante là?*** what's this he's telling us?; **~ qch sur tous les tons** to harp on *ou* go on about sth. **2** *vi* (*gén*) to sing; *[oiseau]* to sing, warble; *[coq]* to crow; *[poule]* to cackle; *[ruisseau]* to babble. **c'est comme si on chantait*** it's like talking to a deaf man, it's a waste of breath; (*par chantage*) **faire ~ qn** to blackmail sb; **vas-y si le programme te chante*** go if the programme appeals to you *ou* if you fancy the programme. ♦ **chantant, e** *adj voix* singsong, lilting; *musique* tuneful. ♦ **chanteur, -euse** *nm,f* singer.

chantier [ʃɑ̃tje] *nm* (*Constr*) (building) site; *[route]* roadworks; (*entrepôt*) depot, yard. **quel ~ dans ta chambre!*** what a shambles* *ou* mess in your room!; **avoir/mettre un ouvrage en ~** to have/put a piece of work in hand; **nous sommes en ~ depuis 2 mois** we've had workmen in *ou* alterations going on for 2 months; **~ de démolition** demolition site; **~ naval** shipyard.

chantonner [ʃɑ̃tɔne] (1) *vti* to sing softly, hum, croon.

chantre [ʃɑ̃tʀ(ə)] *nm* (*Rel*) cantor; (*poète*) bard; (*laudateur*) exalter.

chanvre [ʃɑ̃vʀ(ə)] *nm* (*Bot, Tex*) hemp.

chaos [kao] *nm* (*lit, fig*) chaos. ♦ **chaotique** *adj* chaotic.

chaparder* [ʃapaʀde] (1) *vti* to pinch*, pilfer (*à* from). ♦ **chapardage*** *nm* petty theft. ♦ **chapardeur, -euse*** **1** *adj* light-fingered. **2** *nm,f* pilferer.

chapeau, *pl* **~x** [ʃapo] *nm* (*gén*) hat; (*Bot, Tech*) cap. **tirer son ~ à qn*** to take off one's hat to sb; **~!*** well done, jolly good*; (*Aut*) **~ de roue** hub cap; **sur les ~x de roues*** at top speed; **~ haut-de-forme** top hat; **~ melon** bowler (hat); **~ mou** trilby, fedora (*US*). ♦ **chapeauter** (1) *vt* (*Admin etc*) to head, oversee.

chapelain [ʃaplɛ̃] *nm* chaplain.

chapelet [ʃaplɛ] *nm* (*Rel*) rosary. **dévider son ~*** to recite one's grievances; **~ de** *oignons, injures* string of; *bombes* stick of.

chapelier, -ière [ʃapəlje, jɛʀ] **1** *adj* hat. **2** *nm,f* hatter.

chapelle [ʃapɛl] *nf* chapel; (*coterie*) coterie, clique. **~ ardente** chapel of rest.

chapelure [ʃaplyʀ] *nf* (dried) bread-crumbs.

chaperon [ʃapʀɔ̃] *nm* (*personne*) chaperon. **le petit ~ rouge** Little Red Riding Hood. ♦ **chaperonner** (1) *vt* to chaperon.

chapiteau, *pl* **~x** [ʃapito] *nm [colonne]* capital; *[cirque]* big top.

chapitre [ʃapitʀ(ə)] *nm [livre]* chapter; *[budget]* section, item; (*Rel*) chapter. **sur ce ~** on that subject *ou* score. ♦ **chapitrer** (1) *vt* (*réprimander*) to admonish, reprimand; (*sermonner*) to lecture.

chaque [ʃak] *adj* (*défini*) every, each; (*indéfini*) every. **~ élève** every *ou* each pupil; **10 F ~** 10 francs each *ou* apiece; **~ homme naît libre** every man is born free; **à ~ instant** every other second.

char [ʃaʀ] *nm* (*Mil*) tank; *[carnaval]* (carnival) float; (*charrette*) waggon, cart; (*Antiq*) chariot. (*fig*) **le ~ de l'État** the ship of state.

charabia* [ʃaʀabja] *nm* gibberish, gobbledygook*.

charade [ʃaʀad] *nf* (*parlée*) riddle; (*mimée*) charade.

charbon [ʃaʀbɔ̃] *nm* coal; (*Méd*) anthrax; (*crayon*) piece of charcoal; *[arc électrique]* carbon. **~ actif** active carbon; **~ de bois** charcoal; **être sur des ~s ardents** to be like a cat on hot bricks. ♦ **charbonnages** *nmpl* (*houillères*) collieries, coalmines; (*ministère*) Coal Board. ♦ **charbonnier** *nm* (*personne*) coalman; (*navire*) collier.

charcutier, -ière [ʃaʀkytje, jɛʀ] *nm,f* pork butcher; (*traiteur*) delicatessen dealer; (**fig*) butcher* (*fig*). ♦ **charcuter*** (1) *vt* to butcher*. ♦ **charcuterie** *nf* (*magasin*) pork butcher's shop and delicatessen; (*produits*) cooked pork meats; (*commerce*) pork meat trade; delicatessen trade.

chardon [ʃaʀdɔ̃] *nm* thistle.

chardonneret [ʃaʀdɔnʀɛ] *nm* goldfinch.

charge [ʃaʀʒ(ə)] *nf* **(a)** (*lit, fig: fardeau*) burden; *[véhicule, voûte]* load; *[navire]* freight, cargo. **(b)** (*responsabilité*) responsibility; (*poste*) office. **(c)** (*dépenses*) **~s** expenses, costs, outgoings; *[locataire]* maintenance charges; **~s sociales** social security contributions; **les ~s de l'État** government expenditure. **(d)** (*Mil, Jur*) charge; (*caricature*) caricature. **(e)** *[fusil]* (*action*) loading, charging; (*explosifs*) charge; (*Élec*) (*action*) charging; (*quantité*) charge. **mettre une batterie en ~** to put a battery on charge. **(f) être à la ~ de qn** *[frais]* to be chargeable to sb, be payable by sb; *[personne]* to be dependent upon sb, be supported by sb; **~s de famille** dependents; **enfants à ~** dependent children; **les enfants confiés à sa ~** the children in his care; **avoir la ~ de qn/de faire qch** to be responsible for sb/for doing sth; **à ~ pour lui de payer** on condition that he meets the costs; **prendre en ~** *personne* to take charge of; *frais* to take care of; *[taxi]* to pick up, take on; **prise en ~** *[taxi]* minimum (standard) charge; *[Sécurité sociale]* acceptance (of financial liability).

chargé, e [ʃaʀʒe] **1** *adj* (*gén*) loaded; *estomac* overloaded; *programme* full, busy; *conscience* troubled. **~ de** *honneurs* laden with; *sens, menaces* full of; *nuages, parfums* heavy with; *tâche, enfant* in charge of; **homme au passé ~** man with a past; **avoir la langue ~e** to have a coated *ou* furred tongue. **2**: **~ d'affaires** *nm* chargé d'affaires; **~ de famille** *adj* with family responsibilities; **~ de mission** *nm* official representative.

chargement [ʃaʀʒəmɑ̃] *nm* (*action*) loading; (*marchandises*) load; *[navire]* freight, cargo.

charger [ʃaʀʒe] (3) **1** *vt* **(a)** (*gén*) to load; (*à l'excès*) to overload. **table chargée de mets** table laden with dishes; **~ qn de** *paquets* to load sb up *ou* weigh sb down with; *impôts* to burden sb with, weigh sb down with; *[taxi]* **~ un client** to pick up a passenger. **(b)** *fusil, caméra* to load; (*Élec*) to charge; *chaudière* to stoke. **(c)** (*responsabilité*) **~ qn de qch** to put sb in charge of sth; **~ qn de faire** to give sb the responsibility *ou* job of doing, ask sb to do; **on l'a chargé d'une mission importante** he was given *ou* assigned an important mission; **on m'a chargé d'appliquer le règlement** I've been instructed to apply the rule; **il m'a chargé de ses amitiés pour vous** he asked me to give you his regards. **(d)** (*accuser*) to bring all possible evidence against. **~ qn de** *crime* to charge sb with. **(e)** (*Mil: attaquer*) *ennemi* to charge (at). **(f)** (*caricaturer*) *portrait* to make a caricature of; *description* to overdo, exaggerate; *rôle* to overact.

2 se ~ *vpr*: **se ~ de** to see to, take care of, attend to; **se ~ de faire** to undertake to do; **je me charge de lui** leave it to me to look after him; **je me charge de le faire venir** I'll make sure he comes.

chargeur [ʃaʀʒœʀ] *nm* **(a)** (*personne*) (*gén, Mil*) loader; (*Naut: négociant*) shipper. **(b)** (*Phot*) cartridge; *[arme]* magazine; (*balles*) clip. **~ de batterie** (battery) charger.

chariot [ʃaʀjo] *nm* (*charrette*) waggon; (*petit*) cart; (*à roulettes*) trolley; (*de manutention*) truck; *[machine à écrire]* carriage.

charitable [ʃaʀitabl(ə)] *adj* (*gén*) charitable; (*gentil*) kind (*envers* towards); (*iro*) *conseil* friendly, kindly. ♦ **charitablement** *adv* charitably; kindly.

charité [ʃaʀite] *nf* **(a)** (*gén, Rel*) charity; (*gentillesse*) kindness. **ayez la ~ de** have the kind-

ness to, be kind enough to. **(b)** (*aumône*) charity. **demander la ~** (*lit*) to beg for charity; (*fig*) to come begging; **faire la ~ à** to give (something) to; **la ~ publique** (public) charity; **~ bien ordonnée commence par soi-même** charity begins at home; **vente de ~** sale of work.
charivari* [ʃaʀivaʀi] *nm* hullabaloo*.
charlatan [ʃaʀlatɑ̃] *nm* (*péj*) (*gén*) charlatan; (*médecin*) quack; (*vendeur*) mountebank. ♦ **charlatanesque** *adj* (*de guérisseur*) quack; (*d'escroc*) phoney, bogus. ♦ **charlatanisme** *nm* charlatanism.
charme [ʃaʀm(ə)] *nm* **(a)** (*attrait*) charm, appeal; (*envoûtement*) spell. **le ~ de la nouveauté** the attraction(s) of novelty; **ça offre peu de ~ pour moi** it does not really appeal to me, it holds few attractions for me; (*hum*) **~s** charms (*hum*); **exercer un ~ sur qn** to have sb under one's spell; **tenir qn sous le ~ (de)** to captivate sb (with), hold sb spellbound (with); **faire du ~ à qn** to make eyes at sb; **se porter comme un ~** to be *ou* feel as fit as a fiddle. **(b)** (*Bot*) hornbeam. ♦ **charmant, e** *adj* (*gén*) charming, delightful; *soirée* delightful, lovely. (*iro*) **c'est ~!** charming! (*iro*). ♦ **charmer** (1) *vt* to charm, delight; *serpents* to charm. **être charmé de faire** to be delighted to do. ♦ **charmeur, -euse 1** *adj* winning, engaging. **2** *nm,f* charmer. **~ de serpent** snake charmer.
charnel, -elle [ʃaʀnɛl] *adj instincts* carnal; *créature* earthly. ♦ **charnellement** *adv désirer* sexually.
charnier [ʃaʀnje] *nm* mass grave.
charnière [ʃaʀnjɛʀ] *nf* (*lit*) hinge; (*fig*) turning point; (*Mil, Sport*) linchpin. **discipline-~** interlinking field of study; **époque-~** transition period.
charnu, e [ʃaʀny] *adj* fleshy.
charogne [ʃaʀɔɲ] *nf* (*cadavre*) carrion; (*: *salaud*) swine* (*inv*). ♦ **charognard** *nm* (*lit, fig*) vulture.
charpente [ʃaʀpɑ̃t] *nf* (*gén*) framework; (*carrure*) build, frame. ♦ **charpenté, e** *adj*: **bien ~** well built. ♦ **charpentier** *nm* carpenter; (*Naut*) shipwright.
charpie [ʃaʀpi] *nf* (*pansement*) shredded linen. (*lit, fig*) **être/mettre en ~** to be/tear in shreds.
charrette [ʃaʀɛt] *nf* cart. **~ à bras** handcart, barrow. ♦ **charretée** *nf* cartload (*de* of). (**fig*) **des ~s de** loads* *ou* stacks* of. ♦ **charretier** *nm* carter. **de ~** *langage* coarse.
charrier [ʃaʀje] (7) **1** *vt* **(a)** (*avec brouette*) to cart (along), wheel (along); (*sur le dos*) to heave (along); *[camion]* to carry, cart; *[fleuve]* to carry (along), sweep (along). **(b)** (*: *se moquer de*) **~ qn** to take sb for a ride*, kid sb on*. **2** *vi* (*) (*abuser*) to go too far. (*plaisanter*) **tu charries** you must be kidding* *ou* joking.
charron [ʃaʀɔ̃] *nm* cartwright, wheelwright.
charrue [ʃaʀy] *nf* plough, plow (*US*). **mettre la ~ avant les bœufs** to put the cart before the horse.
charte [ʃaʀt(ə)] *nf* charter; (*Hist: titre*) title, deed.
charter [ʃaʀtɛʀ] **1** *nm* (*vol*) charter flight; (*avion*) chartered plane. **2** *adj inv billet* charter; *avion* chartered.
chas [ʃa] *nm* eye (*of needle*).
chasse [ʃas] **1** *nf* **(a)** (*gén*) hunting; (*au fusil*) shooting. **aller à la ~ aux papillons** to go butterfly-hunting; **habits de ~** hunting clothes. **(b)** (*période*) hunting *ou* shooting season; (*gibier*) game; (*terrain*) hunting ground. **faire (une) bonne ~** to get a good bag; **~ gardée** (*lit*) private hunting (ground); (*fig*) private ground. **(c) la ~** (*chasseurs*) the hunt; (*Aviat*) the fighters. **(d)** (*poursuite*) chase. **faire la ~ à** *moustiques, abus* to hunt down; **faire la ~ aux appartements** to be *ou* go flat-hunting; **donner la ~** to give chase (*à* to); **se mettre en ~ pour trouver qch** to go hunting for sth. **2: ~ à l'affût** hunting (from a hide); **~ à courre** hunting; **~ d'eau** toilet flush; **tirer la ~ (d'eau)** to flush the toilet; **~ à l'homme** manhunt; **~ sous-marine** harpoon fishing.
♦ **chasse-clou**, *pl* **~-~s** *nm* nail punch. ♦ **chassé-croisé** *nm* (*Danse*) chassé-croisé; (*erreur*) mix-up. **avec tous ces ~s-~s** with all these to-ings and fro-ings *ou* mix-ups. ♦ **chasse-neige** *nm inv* snowplough.
châsse [ʃɑs] *nf* (*reliquaire*) reliquary, shrine.
chasser [ʃase] (1) **1** *vt* **(a)** (*gén*) to hunt; (*au fusil*) to shoot, hunt. **~ à l'affût** to hunt from a hide; **~ le faisan** to go pheasant-shooting. **(b)** *importun, ennemi* to drive *ou* chase away; *domestique, manifestant* to turn out; *immigrant* to drive out, expel. **chassant de la main les insectes** brushing away the insects with his hand; **chassez le naturel, il revient au galop** what's bred in the bone comes out in the flesh. **(c)** *odeur, doute* to dispel, drive away; *idée* to dismiss, chase away. **le vent a chassé le brouillard** the wind dispelled *ou* blew away the fog. **(d)** *clou* to drive in. **2** *vi* **(a)** (*gén*) to go hunting; (*au fusil*) to go shooting. **(b)** *[véhicule]* to skid; *[ancre]* to drag.
chasseur [ʃasœʀ] **1** *nm* **(a)** hunter, huntsman. **c'est un grand ~ de perdrix** he's a great one for partridge-shooting. **(b)** (*Mil*) (*soldat*) chasseur; (*avion*) fighter. (*régiment*) **le 3e ~** the 3rd chasseurs. **(c)** *[hôtel]* page (boy), messenger (boy). **2: ~ alpin** mountain infantryman; **~-bombardier** *nm, pl* **~s-~s** fighter-bomber; **~ d'images** roving photographic enthusiast; **~ de têtes** headhunter.
chassis [ʃɑsi] *nm [véhicule]* chassis, subframe; (*Agr*) cold frame.
chaste [ʃast(ə)] *adj* chaste; *oreilles* innocent. ♦ **chastement** *adv* chastely. ♦ **chasteté** *nf* chastity.
chasuble [ʃazybl(ə)] *nf* chasuble.
chat [ʃa] **1** *nm* (*gén*) cat; (*mâle*) tomcat. **petit ~** kitten; **mon petit ~*** pet*, love; **jouer à ~** to play tig *ou* tag; **(c'est toi le) ~!** you're it! *ou* he!; **il n'y avait pas un ~ dehors** there wasn't a soul outside; **avoir un ~ dans la gorge** to have a frog in one's throat; **~ échaudé craint l'eau froide** once bitten, twice shy. **2: le C~ Botté** Puss in Boots; **~ de gouttière** alley cat; **~ sauvage** wild cat.
châtaigne [ʃatɛɲ] *nf* (*fruit*) chestnut; (*: *coup*) clout, biff*. ♦ **châtaignier** *nm* chestnut (tree).
châtain [ʃatɛ̃] *adj inv cheveux* chestnut (brown); *personne* brown-haired.
château, *pl* **~x** [ʃato] *nm* (*forteresse*) castle; (*palais*) palace, castle; (*manoir*) mansion; (*en France*) château. **bâtir des ~x en Espagne** to build castles in the air *ou* in Spain; **~ de cartes** house of cards; **~ d'eau** water tower; **~ fort** stronghold, fortified castle.
châtelain [ʃatlɛ̃] *nm* (*Hist*) (feudal) lord; (*propriétaire*) squire; (*nouveau riche*) manor-owner. ♦ **châtelaine** *nf* manor-owner; (*épouse*) lady of the manor.
châtier [ʃatje] (7) *vt coupable, faute* to punish; *style, langage* to refine. ♦ **châtiment** *nm* punishment.
chatoiement [ʃatwamɑ̃] *nm* glistening, shimmer(ing), sparkle.
chaton [ʃatɔ̃] *nm* **(a)** (*Zool*) kitten; (*Bot*) catkin. **~s** *[saule]* pussy willows; *[poussière]* balls of fluff. **(b)** (*monture*) setting; (*pierre*) stone.
chatouiller [ʃatuje] (1) *vt* (*lit*) to tickle; (*fig*) to titillate. ♦ **chatouille*** *nf* tickle. **craindre les ~s** to be ticklish. ♦ **chatouillement** *nm*: **~(s)** (*gén*) tickling; *[nez, gorge]* tickle. ♦ **chatouilleux, -euse** *adj* (*lit*) ticklish; (*susceptible*) touchy, (over-) sensitive (*sur* on, about).
chatoyer [ʃatwaje] (8) *vi* to glisten, shimmer, sparkle.
châtrer [ʃatʀe] (1) *vt* (*gén*) to castrate; *cheval* to geld; *chat* to neuter.

chatte [ʃat] *nf* (she-)cat. **ma (petite) ~*** (my) pet*, love.

chatterie [ʃatʀi] *nf* **(a)** **~s** (*caresses*) playful caresses; (*minauderies*) kittenish ways. **(b)** (*friandise*) titbit.

chatterton [ʃatɛʀtɔn] *nm* insulating tape.

chaud, e [ʃo, od] **1** *adj* **(a)** (*agréable*) warm; (*brûlant*) hot. **cela sort tout ~ du four** it's (piping) hot from the oven. **(b)** *félicitations* warm, hearty; *partisan* keen, ardent; *discussion* heated; *nouvelle, tempérament* hot; *voix, couleur* warm; *bataille* fierce. **il n'est pas très ~ pour le faire*** he is not very keen on doing it; **l'alerte a été ~e** it was a near *ou* close thing; **points ~s** hot spots.

2 *nm*: **le ~** (the) heat, the warmth; (*Méd*) **~ et froid** chill; **elle souffre du ~** she suffers from the heat; **restez au ~** stay in the warmth; **garder qch au ~** to keep sth warm *ou* hot; **il a été opéré à ~** he had an emergency operation.

3 *adv*: **avoir ~** to be *ou* feel warm; (*trop*) to be *ou* feel hot; **j'ai eu ~!** I got a real fright; **ça ne me fait ni ~ ni froid** I couldn't care less; **servir ~** serve hot; **tenir ~ à qn** to keep sb warm. ♦ **chaudement** *adv s'habiller* warmly; *féliciter* warmly, heartily; *défendre* heatedly, hotly.

chaudière [ʃodjɛʀ] *nf* boiler.

chaudron [ʃodʀɔ̃] *nm* cauldron. ♦ **chaudronnerie** *nf* (*métier*) boilermaking; (*boutique*) coppersmith's workshop; (*usine*) boilerworks. ♦ **chaudronnier** *nm* (*artisan*) coppersmith; (*ouvrier*) boilermaker.

chauffage [ʃofaʒ] *nm* (*action*) heating; (*appareils*) heating (system). **~ central** central heating.

chauffard [ʃofaʀ] *nm* (*péj*) reckless driver. **~!*** roadhog!

chauffer [ʃofe] (1) **1** *vt* **(a)** **(faire) ~** *soupe* to warm up, heat up; *assiette* to warm, heat. **(b)** (*gén, Tech*) to heat; *[soleil]* to warm; *[soleil brûlant]* to heat. **~ qch à blanc** to make sth white-hot; (*fig*) **~ qn à blanc** to fire sb into action. **(c)** (*) *candidat* to cram; *commando* to train up. **2** *vi [aliment, eau, assiette]* to be heating (up), be warming (up); *[moteur]* to warm up; *[four]* to heat up; (*trop chaud*) to overheat. **ça va ~!*** sparks will fly!; **le but chauffe** they're on the brink of a goal; (*cache-tampon*) **tu chauffes!** you're getting warm(er)! **3 se ~** *vpr* to warm o.s. **se ~ au bois/gaz** to use wood/gas for heating. ♦ **chauffe-eau** *nm inv* immersion heater. ♦ **chauffe-plats** *nm inv* plate-warmer, hotplate.

chaufferie [ʃofʀi] *nf [usine]* boiler room; *[navire]* stokehold.

chauffeur [ʃofœʀ] *nm* **(a)** driver; (*privé*) chauffeur. **voiture sans ~** self-drive car. **(b)** *[chaudière]* fireman, stoker.

chaume [ʃom] *nm [champ]* stubble; *[toit]* thatch. ♦ **chaumière** *nf* (little) cottage; (*de chaume*) thatched cottage.

chaussée [ʃose] *nf* (*route*) road, roadway; (*surélevée*) causeway. **~ bombée** cambered road; '**~ déformée**' 'uneven road surface'.

chausser [ʃose] (1) *vt souliers, lunettes* to put on. **~ du 40** to take size 40 in shoes; **chausse les enfants** put the children's shoes on (for them); **se ~** to put one's shoes on; **chaussé de bottes** wearing boots; **se (faire) ~ chez** to buy *ou* get one's shoes at; **ces chaussures chaussent large/bien** these are wide-fitting/well-fitting shoes. ♦ **chausse-pied,** *pl* **~-~s** *nm* shoehorn. ♦ **chaussetrappe,** *pl* **~-~s** *nf* trap. ♦ **chaussette** *nf* sock. ♦ **chausseur** *nm* shoemaker.

chausson [ʃosɔ̃] *nm* slipper; *[bébé]* bootee; *[danseur]* ballet shoe; (*Culin*) turnover.

chaussure [ʃosyʀ] *nf* (*basse*) shoe; (*montante*) boot. **la ~** (*industrie*) the shoe industry; (*commerce*) the shoe trade; **rayon ~s** shoe *ou* footwear department.

chauve [ʃov] *adj personne* bald(-headed); *crâne* bald; *colline* bare. **~ comme un œuf*** as bald as a coot. ♦ **chauve-souris,** *pl* **~s-~** *nf* bat.

chauvin, e [ʃovɛ̃, in] **1** *adj* chauvinistic. **2** *nm,f* chauvinist. ♦ **chauvinisme** *nm* chauvinism.

chaux [ʃo] *nf* lime. **blanchi à la ~** whitewashed.

chavirer [ʃaviʀe] (1) **1** *vi* (*lit*) to capsize, keel over, overturn; *[paysage, esprit]* to ree[illegible] **(a)** **(faire) ~** *bateau* to capsize, overturn **(b)** (*bouleverser*) to bowl over.

chef [ʃɛf] **1** *nm [usine]* head, boss*; *[tribu]* chief(tain), headman; *[mouvement]* leader; (*Culin*) chef; (*littér: tête*) head. **tu es un ~*** you're the greatest*; **commandant en ~** commander-in-chief; **rédacteur en ~** chief editor; **de son propre ~** on his own initiative; **au premier ~** greatly; **de ce ~** accordingly.

2 *adj inv*: **gardien ~** chief warden.

3: **~ d'accusation** charge; **~ d'atelier** (shop) foreman; **~ de bataillon** major; **~ de bureau** head clerk; **~ comptable** chief accountant; **~ d'entreprise** company manager; **~ d'État** head *ou* chief of state; **~ d'état-major** chief of staff; **~ de famille** head of the family; **~ de file** leader; **~ de gare** station master; **~-lieu** *nm, pl* **~-~x** ≈ county town; **~ d'œuvre** *nm, pl* **~s-~** masterpiece, chef d'œuvre; **~ d'orchestre** conductor; **~ de service** section *ou* departmental head; **~ de train** guard.

cheftaine [ʃɛftɛn] *nf [louveteaux]* cubmistress; *[éclaireuses]* (guide) captain.

cheik [ʃɛk] *nm* sheik.

chelem [ʃlɛm] *nm*: **petit/grand ~** small/grand slam.

chemin [ʃ(ə)mɛ̃] **1** *nm* **(a)** (*gén*) path; *[campagne]* lane; *[piste]* track. **le ~ de la ruine** the road *ou* path to ruin. **(b)** (*trajet, direction*) way (*de, pour* to). **il y a une heure de ~** it's an hour's walk (*ou* drive); **quel ~ a-t-elle pris?** which way did she go?; **ils ont fait tout le ~ à pied** they walked all the way; **se mettre en ~** to set out *ou* off; **poursuivre son ~** to carry on one's way; **nous avons pris le ~ des écoliers** we came the long way round. **(c)** (*fig*) **il a encore du ~ à faire** he's still got a long way to go; **se mettre en travers du ~** to stand in the way *ou* path; **faire du ~** *[véhicule, chercheur]* to come a long way; *[idée]* to gain ground; *[ambitieux]* to make one's way; (*concession*) **faire la moitié du ~** to go half-way (to meet sb); **cela n'en prend pas le ~** it doesn't look likely; **il ne doit pas s'arrêter en si beau ~** he mustn't stop (now) when he's doing so well; **être sur le bon ~** to be on the right track *ou* lines.

2: **~ creux** sunken lane; **le ~ de croix** the Way of the Cross; **~ de fer** railway, railroad (*US*); **par ~ de fer** by rail; **~ de halage** tow-path.

cheminée [ʃ(ə)mine] *nf* (*extérieure*) chimney (stack); (*Naut, Rail*) funnel; (*intérieure*) fireplace; (*encadrement*) mantelpiece; *[volcan, lampe]* chimney. **~ d'aération** ventilation shaft.

cheminement [ʃ(ə)minmɑ̃] *nm [marcheurs]* progress, advance; *[sentier]* course, way; *[pensée]* development, progression. ♦ **cheminer** (1) *vi [personne]* to walk (along); *[ruisseau etc]* to follow its course (*dans* along).

cheminot [ʃ(ə)mino] *nm* railwayman, railroad man (*US*).

chemise [ʃ(ə)miz] *nf [homme]* shirt; *[femme, bébé]* vest; *[dossier]* folder. **être en bras de ~** to be in one's shirt sleeves; **il s'en moque comme de sa première ~** he doesn't care a fig*; **~ de nuit** *[femme]* nightdress; *[homme]* nightshirt. ♦ **chemiserie** *nf* (*magasin*) man's shop; (*commerce*) shirt(-making) trade. ♦ **chemisette** *nf* short-sleeved shirt. ♦ **chemisier** *nm* (*marchand*) shirt-maker; (*vêtement*) blouse.

chenal, *pl* **-aux** [ʃənal, o] *nm* (*canal*) channel, fairway; (*rigole*) channel; *[moulin]* millrace; *[usine]* flume.

chenapan [ʃ(ə)napɑ̃] *nm* rascal.
chêne [ʃɛn] *nm* oak. **~-liège** *nm, pl* **~s-~s** cork-oak; **~ vert** holm oak.
chenet [ʃ(ə)nɛ] *nm* fire-dog, andiron.
chènevis [ʃɛnvi] *nm* hempseed.
chenil [ʃ(ə)ni(l)] *nm* kennels.
chenille [ʃ(ə)nij] *nf* (*Aut, Zool*) caterpillar. ♦ **chenillette** *nf* tracked vehicle.
cheptel [ʃɛptɛl] *nm* livestock.
chèque [ʃɛk] *nm* cheque, check (*US*); (*bon*) voucher. **~ de 100 F** cheque for 100 francs; **~-repas** luncheon voucher; **~-cadeau** gift token; (*lit, fig*) **~ en blanc** blank cheque; **~ postal** ≈ (Post Office) Girocheque; **~ sans provision** bad *ou* dud* cheque; **~ de voyage** traveller's cheque. ♦ **chéquier** *nm* cheque book.
cher, chère[1] [ʃɛʀ] **1** *adj* **(a)** (*aimé*) dear (*à* to). **les êtres ~s** the loved ones; **c'est mon vœu le plus ~** it's my fondest *ou* dearest wish; **son bien le plus ~** his most precious possession; **ce ~ (vieux) Louis!*** dear old Louis!; **ses ~s parents** his beloved parents. **(b)** (*coûteux*) expensive, dear. **pas ~** cheap, inexpensive; **la vie est chère** the cost of living is high. **2** *nm,f*: **mon ~, ma chère** my dear. **3** *adv coûter, payer* a lot *ou* a great deal (of money). **vendre ~** to charge high prices; **je ne l'ai pas acheté ~** I bought it very cheaply, I didn't pay much for it; **ça vaut ~** it's expensive, it costs a lot; (*fig*) **il ne vaut pas ~** he's a bad lot; (*fig*) **ça lui a coûté ~** it cost him dear, he paid dearly for it.
chercher [ʃɛʀʃe] (1) *vt* **(a)** (*gén*) to look for, search for, try to find; *ombre, moyen* to look for, seek; *gloire, alliance* to seek; *danger* to court; (*sur un livre*) to look up; (*dans sa mémoire*) to try to think of. **~ qn des yeux** to look (around) for sb; **il n'a pas bien cherché** he didn't look *ou* search very hard; **~ ses mots** to search for words; (*à un chien*) **cherche! cherche!** find it, boy!; **il ne cherche que son intérêt** he is concerned only with his own interest; **~ la difficulté** to look for difficulties; **~ la bagarre** to be looking for a fight; **tu l'auras cherché!** you've been asking for it!; **~ à faire** to try *ou* attempt to do.
(b) aller ~ qch/qn to go for sth/sb, go and fetch *ou* get sth/sb; **va me ~ mon sac** go and fetch *ou* get me my bag; **il est venu le ~ à la gare** he came to meet *ou* collect him at the station; **envoyer (qn) ~ le médecin** to send (sb) for the doctor; **où va-t-il ~ tout cela!** where does he get all that from!; **ça va ~ dans les 30 F** it'll add up to something like 30 francs.
(c) (*fig*) **~ fortune** to seek one's fortune; **~ des histoires à qn** to try to make trouble for sb; **~ midi à quatorze heures** to look for complications; **~ noise à qn** to seek a quarrel with sb; **~ la petite bête** to split hairs; **~ une aiguille dans une meule de foin** to look for a needle in a haystack; **~ son salut dans la fuite** to seek *ou* take refuge in flight; **artiste qui se cherche** artist who is searching for an identity.
chercheur, -euse [ʃɛʀʃœʀ, øz] **1** *adj esprit* inquiring. **2** *nm,f* researcher, research worker. **~ de** (*gén*) seeker of; **~ d'or** gold digger; **~ de trésors** treasure hunter.
chère[2] [ʃɛʀ] *nf* (*littér*) food, fare. **faire bonne ~** to eat well.
chèrement [ʃɛʀmɑ̃] *adv aimer* dearly, fondly; *conserver* lovingly; *vendre* at a high price. **~ payé** *victoire* dearly bought *ou* won; **vendre ~ sa vie** to sell one's life dearly.
chérir [ʃeʀiʀ] (2) *vt* to cherish. ♦ **chéri, e 1** *adj* beloved. **maman ~e** mother dear *ou* darling. **2** *nm,f* darling.
cherté [ʃɛʀte] *nf* high price, dearness. **la ~ de la vie** the high cost of living.
chérubin [ʃeʀybɛ̃] *nm* (*lit, fig*) cherub.
chétif, -ive [ʃetif, iv] *adj enfant* puny; *plante* puny, stunted; *récolte* meagre; *repas* meagre, scanty; *raisonnement* paltry. ♦ **chétivement** *adv* punily.
cheval, pl -aux [ʃ(ə)val, o] **1** *nm* (*animal*) horse. (*Aut*) **~ ou ~aux (vapeur)** horsepower; **ce n'est pas le mauvais ~*** he's not a bad sort; **au travail, c'est un vrai ~** he works like a Trojan; **à ~** on horseback; **à ~ sur une chaise** (sitting) astride a chair; **à ~ sur deux mois** overlapping two (different) months; **être (très) à ~ sur le règlement** to be a (real) stickler for the rules; **de ~*** *remède* drastic; *fièvre* raging. **2: ~ d'arçons** (vaulting) horse; **~ à bascule** rocking horse; (*fig*) **~ de bataille** hobby horse; **~aux de bois** roundabout, merry-go-round, carousel (*US*); **~ de course** racehorse; **~aux de frise** chevaux-de-frise; **~ de labour** cart-horse, plough horse; **(vieux) ~ de retour** old lag; **~ de trait** draught horse; (*lit, fig*) **~ de Troie** Trojan horse.
chevalet [ʃ(ə)valɛ] *nm* *[peintre]* easel; (*Menuiserie*) trestle; *[violon etc]* bridge.
chevalier [ʃ(ə)valje] *nm* (*Hist*) knight; *[légion d'honneur]* chevalier. **faire qn ~** to knight sb, dub sb knight; **~ errant** knight-errant; **~ servant** (attentive) escort. ♦ **chevaleresque** *adj* chivalrous, gentlemanly; *honneur* knightly. ♦ **chevalerie** *nf* (*institution*) chivalry; (*chevaliers*) knighthood.
chevalière [ʃ(ə)valjɛʀ] *nf* signet ring.
chevalin, e [ʃ(ə)valɛ̃, in] *adj race* equine; *visage* horsy.
chevaucher [ʃ(ə)voʃe] (1) **1** *vt* to be *ou* sit astride; *[pont]* to span; *[tuiles]* to overlap. **2 se ~** *vpr* to overlap. **3** *vi* to ride (on horseback). ♦ **chevauchée** *nf* (*course*) ride; (*cavaliers*) cavalcade. ♦ **chevauchement** *nm* (*gén*) overlapping.
chevet [ʃ(ə)vɛ] *nm* **(a)** *[lit]* bed(head). **au ~ de qn** at sb's bedside. **(b)** (*Archit*) chevet.
cheveu, pl ~x [ʃ(ə)vø] *nm* **(a)** (*poil*) hair. (*chevelure*) **~x** hair; **aux ~x blonds** fair-haired; **2 ~x blancs** 2 white hairs; **épingle à ~x** hairpin. **(b) leur vie n'a tenu qu'à un ~** their life hung by a thread; **il s'en est fallu d'un ~ qu'ils ne se tuent** they escaped death by a hair's breadth, they were within an ace of being killed; **avoir un ~* (sur la langue)** to have a lisp; **se faire des ~x* (blancs)** to worry o.s. grey *ou* stiff*; **arriver comme un ~ sur la soupe*** *[visiteur]* to come at the most awkward moment; *[remarque]* to be completely irrelevant; **tiré par les ~x** far-fetched; **il y a un ~*** there's a hitch *ou* snag. ♦ **chevelu, e** *adj* long-haired. ♦ **chevelure** *nf* (*cheveux*) hair; *[comète]* tail. **elle avait une ~ abondante** she had thick hair *ou* a thick head of hair.
cheville [ʃ(ə)vij] *nf* (*Anat*) ankle; (*pour joindre*) peg, pin; (*pour clou*) rawlplug; *[poème]* cheville. (*Aut, fig*) **~ ouvrière** kingpin; **il n'arrive pas à la ~ de son frère** he can't hold a candle to his brother; **être en ~ avec qn** to be in contact *ou* touch with sb. ♦ **cheviller** (1) *vt* (*Menuiserie*) to peg.
chèvre [ʃɛvʀ(ə)] **1** *nf* (she-)goat, (nanny-)goat. **rendre qn ~*** to drive sb up the wall*. **2** *nm* goat('s milk) cheese. ♦ **chevreau, pl ~x** *nm* kid.
chèvrefeuille [ʃɛvʀəfœj] *nm* honeysuckle.
chevreuil [ʃəvʀœj] *nm* (*Zool*) roe deer; (*mâle*) roebuck; (*Culin*) venison.
chevron [ʃəvʀɔ̃] *nm* (*poutre*) rafter; (*galon*) stripe, chevron. (*motif*) **~s** herring bone (pattern); (*grands*) chevron pattern.
chevronné, e [ʃəvʀɔne] *adj* practised, seasoned.
chevroter [ʃəvʀɔte] (1) *vi* to quaver. ♦ **chevrotement** *nm* quavering.
chevrotine [ʃəvʀɔtin] *nf*: **~(s)** buckshot.
chez [ʃe] *prép*: **rentrer ~ soi** to go (back) home; **faites comme ~ vous** make yourself at home; **~ nous** (*gén*) at home; (*maison*) at our place *ou* house; (*famille*) in our family; (*pays*) in our country; **il est ~ sa tante** he's at his aunt's (place

ou house); **c'est petit ~ lui** his place *ou* house is small; **être/aller ~ le boucher** to be at/go to the butcher's; (*adresse*) **~ M X** c/o Mr. X; **c'est une coutume bien de ~ nous** it's one of our typical local customs; **~ les Romains** among the Romans; **on trouve cela ~ les animaux/Balzac** you find this in animals/Balzac; **c'est une habitude ~ lui** it's a habit with him.

chiader‡ [ʃjade] (1) **1** *vt examen* to swot for*. **2** *vi* to swot*. ♦ **chiadé, e‡** *adj* (*difficile*) tough*, stiff*; (*approfondi*) brainy*; (*perfectionné*) clever.

chialer‡ [ʃjale] (1) *vi* to blubber*.

chiasse‡ [ʃjas] *nf*: **avoir la ~** (*colique*) to have the runs*; (*peur*) to be in a funk‡.

chic [ʃik] **1** *nm [toilette]* stylishness; *[personne]* style. **avoir du ~** to have style; **habillé avec ~** stylishly dressed; **avoir le ~ pour faire qch** to have the knack of doing sth; **de ~** *peindre* without a model, from memory; *écrire* off the cuff. **2** *adj inv* (*élégant*) stylish, smart; (*riche*) smart, posh*; (*: *gentil*) decent, nice (*avec* to). **3** *excl*: **~** terrific!*, great!*

chicane [ʃikan] *nf* **(a)** *[route]* in and out. **(b)** (*querelle*) squabble. ♦ **chicaner** (1) **1** *vt*: **~ qn** to quibble *ou* squabble with sb (*sur qch* over sth). **2** *vi* to quibble (*sur* about). ♦ **chicanier, -ière 1** *adj* quibbling. **2** *nm,f* quibbler.

chiche[1] [ʃiʃ] *adj*: **pois ~** chick pea.

chiche[2] [ʃiʃ] *adj* **(a)** *personne, rétribution* niggardly, mean; *repas* scanty, meagre. **être ~ de paroles** to be sparing with one's words. **(b)** (*) **es-tu ~ de le faire?** are you game to do it?; **~ que je le fais!** I bet you I do it!* ♦ **chichement** *adv* meanly, meagrely.

chichis* [ʃiʃi] *nmpl* fuss. **faire des ~** to make a fuss; **sans ~** informally.

chicorée [ʃikɔʀe] *nf* (*salade*) endive; (*à café*) chicory. **~ frisée** curly endive (lettuce).

chicot [ʃiko] *nm* (*dent*) stump.

chien [ʃjɛ̃] **1** *nm* (*animal*) dog; *[fusil]* hammer. **petit ~** (*jeune*) puppy; **en ~ de fusil** curled up; **vie de ~** dog's life; **de ~** *temps, métier* rotten*; **comme un ~** like a dog; **elle a du ~*** she has a certain something*; **entre ~ et loup** in the twilight *ou* dusk; **être comme ~ et chat** to fight like cat and dog; **recevoir qn comme un ~ dans un jeu de quilles** to give sb a cold reception. **2** *adj inv* (*avare*) mean, stingy*; (*méchant*) rotten*. **3: ~ d'arrêt** pointer; **~ d'aveugle** guide dog; **~ de berger** sheepdog; **~ de chasse** retriever; **~ couchant** setter; **faire le ~ couchant** to toady; **~ courant** hound; **~ de garde** watch dog; **~-loup** *nm, pl* **~s-~s** wolfhound; **~ policier** police dog.

chiendent [ʃjɛ̃dɑ̃] *nm* couch grass.

chienne [ʃjɛn] *nf* bitch.

chier‡ [ʃje] (7) *vi* to shit‡. **faire ~ qn** (*ennuyer*) to bore the pants off sb‡; (*tracasser*) to bug sb‡.

chiffe [ʃif] *nf* (*péj*) spineless individual, wet*. **je suis comme une ~** (*fatigué*) I feel like a wet rag.

chiffon [ʃifɔ̃] *nm* (piece of) rag. **mettre en ~** to crumple; **parler ~s*** to talk (about) clothes; **~ à chaussures** shoe cloth; **~ de papier** scrap of paper; **~ à poussière** duster. ♦ **chiffonner** (1) **1** *vt* **(a)** *papier* to crumple; *habits* to crease, crumple. **(b)** (*: *contrarier*) **ça me chiffonne** it bothers me. **2 se ~** *vpr* to crease *ou* crumple easily. ♦ **chiffonnier** *nm* (*personne*) ragman; (*meuble*) chiffonier. **se battre comme des ~s** to fight like cat and dog.

chiffre [ʃifʀ(ə)] *nm* **(a)** (*caractère*) figure, numeral. **~ arabe** Arab numeral; **nombre de 7 ~s** 7-figure number; **science des ~s** science of numbers. **(b)** (*somme*) sum; (*total*) total. **ça atteint des ~s astronomiques** it reaches an astronomical figure *ou* sum; le **~ des chômeurs** the unemployment figures *ou* total; **~ (d'affaires)** turnover. **(c)** *[message]* code; *[coffre-fort]* combination. **écrire une lettre en ~s** to write a letter in code. **(d)** (*initiales*) initials, monogram; (*Mus: indice*) figure.

chiffrer [ʃifʀe] (1) **1** *vt* (*coder*) to encode; (*évaluer*) to put a figure on, assess (the amount of); (*numéroter*) to number; *linge* to mark (with one's initials); (*Mus*) to figure. **2** *vi*, **se ~** *vpr*: **(se) ~ à** to add up to, amount to; **ça finit par ~*** it adds up to *ou* amounts to quite a lot in the end. ♦ **chiffrage** *nm* encoding; assessing; numbering; marking; figuring.

chignole [ʃiɲɔl] *nf* drill.

chignon [ʃiɲɔ̃] *nm* bun, chignon.

Chili [ʃili] *nm* Chile. ♦ **chilien, -ienne** *adj*, **C~(ne)** *nm(f)* Chilean.

chimère [ʃimɛʀ] *nf* (*utopie*) chimera; (*irréalisable*) pipe dream, (idle) fancy; (*Myth*) Chim(a)era. ♦ **chimérique** *adj* **(a)** *esprit, projet* fanciful; *rêve* idle. **(b)** (*imaginaire*) imaginary, chimerical.

chimie [ʃimi] *nf* chemistry. ♦ **chimique** *adj* chemical. ♦ **chimiquement** *adv* chemically. ♦ **chimiste** *nmf* chemist (*scientist*).

chimpanzé [ʃɛ̃pɑ̃ze] *nm* chimpanzee.

Chine [ʃin] *nf* China. **~ populaire** communist China.

chiné, e [ʃine] *adj* (*Tex*) chiné.

chiner* [ʃine] (1) *vt* to tease, rag.

chinois, e [ʃinwa, waz] **1** *adj* **(a)** (*de Chine*) Chinese. **(b)** (*péj*) *personne* fussy; *règlement* hair-splitting. **2** *nm* **(a)** (*Ling*) Chinese. (*péj*) **c'est du ~*** it's all Greek to me*. **(b) C~** Chinese(man); **les C~** the Chinese. **(c)** (**péj*: *maniaque*) hair-splitter. **3** *nf*: **C~e** Chinese woman. ♦ **chinoiseries** *nfpl* unnecessary fuss. **les ~ de l'administration** red tape.

chiot [ʃjo] *nm* pup(py).

chiper* [ʃipe] (1) *vt objet* to pinch*, filch*; *rhume* to catch.

chipie [ʃipi] *nf* minx.

chipoter* [ʃipɔte] (1) *vi* (*manger*) to pick at one's food; (*ergoter*) to quibble (*sur* over); (*marchander*) to haggle (*sur* over). ♦ **chipoteur, -euse* 1** *adj* haggling; quibbling; (*en mangeant*) fussy. **2** *nm,f* haggler; quibbler; fussy eater.

chips [ʃip(s)] *nfpl* (*Culin*) crisps.

chique [ʃik] *nf* (*tabac*) quid; (*: *enflure*) lump (on the cheek).

chiqué* [ʃike] *nm*: **le ~** (*pour impressionner*) bluffing; (*factice*) sham; (*maniéré*) airs and graces; **il a fait ça au ~** he bluffed it out; **c'est du ~** it's all put on*; **c'est pas du ~** that's for real*; **faire du ~** to put on airs (and graces).

chiquement* [ʃikmɑ̃] *adv s'habiller* smartly, stylishly; *traiter*, kindly, decently.

chiquenaude [ʃiknod] *nf* flick.

chiquer [ʃike] (1) **1** *vt* to chew. **2** *vi* to chew tobacco.

chiromancie [kiʀɔmɑ̃si] *nf* palmistry. ♦ **chiromancien, -ienne** *nm,f* palmist.

chiropracteur [kiʀɔpʀaktœʀ] *nm* chiropractor. ♦ **chiropraxie** *nf* chiropractic.

chirurgie [ʃiʀyʀʒi] *nf* surgery (*science*). ♦ **chirurgical, e,** *mpl* **-aux** *adj* surgical. ♦ **chirurgien** *nm* surgeon. **~-dentiste** dental surgeon.

chlore [klɔʀ] *nm* chlorine. ♦ **chlorer** (1) *vt* to chlorinate. ♦ **chlorhydrique** *adj* hydrochloric. ♦ **chlorure** *nm* chloride.

chloroforme [klɔʀɔfɔʀm(ə)] *nm* chloroform. ♦ **chloroformer** (1) *vt* to chloroform.

chlorophylle [klɔʀɔfil] *nf* chlorophyll. ♦ **chlorophyllien, -ienne** *adj* chlorophyllous.

choc [ʃɔk] *nm* **(a)** (*heurt*) *[objets]* impact, shock; *[vagues, véhicules]* crash; *[troupes, intérêts]* clash; (*sur la tête etc*) blow, bump. **cela se brise au moindre ~** it breaks at the slightest bump; **ça s'est déformé sous le ~** it twisted under the impact; **résister au ~** *[instrument]* to be shock-resistant; *[armée]* to stand up to the onslaught; ~ **opératoire** post-operative shock. **(b)** (*bruit*) (*violent*) crash; (*sourd*) thud; (*métallique*) clang; (*cristallin*) clink. **(c)** (*émotion*) shock. **ça m'a fait un drôle de** ~ it gave me a nasty shock. **(d) de** ~ *troupe, traitement* shock; *patron* dynamic, high-powered; **argument/photo(-)**~ shock argument/photo; **prix-**~ special price.

chocolat [ʃɔkɔla] **1** *nm* (*gén*) chocolate. **mousse au** ~ chocolate mousse; ~ **en poudre/à croquer** drinking/plain chocolate. **2** *adj inv* chocolate (-coloured). ♦ **chocolaté, e** *adj* chocolate-flavoured. ♦ **chocolaterie** *nf* chocolate factory. ♦ **chocolatier, -ière 1** *adj* chocolate. **2** *nm,f* chocolate maker.

chocottes‡ [ʃɔkɔt] *nfpl*: **avoir les** ~ to have the jitters*.

chœur [kœʀ] *nm* (*gén, fig*) chorus; (*Rel: chanteurs*) choir; (*nef*) choir, chancel. **en** ~ in chorus; **tous en** ~! all together now!

choir [ʃwaʀ] *vi* (*littér*) to fall. **faire** ~ to cause to fall; **laisser** ~ *objet* to drop; *amis* to let down; **se laisser** ~ **dans un fauteuil** to sink into an armchair.

choisir [ʃwaziʀ] (2) *vt* (*gén*) to choose; *candidat, produit* to select. **il faut savoir** ~ **ses amis** you must know how to pick *ou* choose your friends; **se** ~ **un mari** to choose a husband; ~ **de faire qch** to choose to do sth. ♦ **choisi, e** *adj passages* selected; *langage* carefully chosen; *clientèle* select.

choix [ʃwa] *nm* **(a)** (*décision*) choice; (*échantillonnage*) choice, selection. **un aménagement de son** ~ alterations of one's (own) choosing; **le** ~ **d'un cadeau** choosing a gift, the choice of a gift; **il y a du** ~ there is a choice *ou* a wide selection; **vous avez, au** ~, **fruits ou fromages** you have a choice between *ou* of fruit or cheese; **faire son** ~ to make one's choice; **je n'avais pas le** ~ I had no option *ou* choice; **laisser le** ~ **à qn (de faire)** to leave sb (free) to choose (to do), give sb the choice (of doing); **porter son** ~ **sur qch** to settle on sth. **(b)** (*qualité*) **de** ~ choice, selected; **de premier** ~ *fruits, viande* top grade; **de** ~ **courant** standard quality; **de second** ~ grade two; **articles de second** ~ seconds.

choléra [kɔleʀa] *nm* cholera. ♦ **cholérique 1** *adj* choleraic. **2** *nmf* cholera patient.

cholestérol [kɔlɛsteʀɔl] *nm* cholesterol.

chômage [ʃomaʒ] *nm* unemployment. **(être) au** ~ (to be) unemployed *ou* out of work; **s'inscrire au** ~ to apply for unemployment benefit; **mettre qn au** ~ to make sb redundant, put sb out of work; ~ **partiel** short-time working; ~ **technique** lay-offs; **mettre en** ~ **technique** to lay off. ♦ **chômer** (1) *vi* **(a)** (*gén*) to be idle; *[travailleur]* to be unemployed; *[usine]* to be at a standstill. **(b)** (*en congé*) to have a holiday. **jour chômé** public holiday. ♦ **chômeur, -euse** *nm,f* (*gén*) unemployed person; (*mis au chômage*) redundant worker. **les** ~**s** the unemployed, people out of work.

chope [ʃɔp] *nf* tankard; (*contenu*) pint.

choper‡ [ʃɔpe] (1) *vt objet* to pinch*; *rhume* to catch; *voleur* to nab*.

chopine* [ʃɔpin] *nf* bottle (of wine).

choquer [ʃɔke] (1) **1** *vt* **(a)** (*scandaliser*) to shock, appal. **ce roman risque de** ~ people may find this novel offensive *ou* shocking; **j'ai été choqué par son indifférence** I was shocked *ou* appalled by his indifference. **(b)** *délicatesse, raison* to offend against; *vue, oreilles* to offend. **(c)** *[chute]* to shake (up); *[accident]* to shake (up), shock; *[deuil]* to shake. **(d)** *objet* to knock (against); *verres* to clink. **2 se** ~ *vpr* (*s'offusquer*) to be shocked. ♦ **choquant, e** *adj* shocking; appalling; offensive.

choral, e, *mpl* ~**s** [kɔʀal] **1** *adj* choral. **2** *nm* choral(e). **3** *nf* choral society, choir.

chorégraphe [kɔʀegʀaf] *nmf* choreographer. ♦ **chorégraphie** *nf* choreography. ♦ **chorégraphique** *adj* choreographic.

choriste [kɔʀist(ə)] *nmf* (*Rel*) choir member, chorister; (*Théât*) member of the chorus. **les** ~**s** the choir; the chorus.

chorus [kɔʀys] *nm*: **faire** ~ **(avec qn)** to voice one's agreement (with sb).

chose [ʃoz] **1** *nf* **(a)** (*gén*) thing. ~ **étrange, il a accepté** the strange thing is that he accepted, strangely enough he accepted; **c'est une** ~ **admise que** it's an accepted fact that; **c'est** ~ **faite** it's done; **peu de** ~ nothing much; **avant toute** ~ above all else; **de 2** ~**s l'une** it's got to be one thing or the other; **faire bien les** ~**s** to do things in style; **dites-lui bien des** ~**s de ma part** give him my regards; **nous avons parlé de** ~**s et d'autres** we talked about this and that *ou* about one thing and another.

(b) (*question*) matter. **la** ~ **en question** the matter in hand; **c'est tout autre** ~ it's another matter; **dans l'état actuel des** ~**s** as things *ou* matters stand at present.

(c) (*situation*) it, things. **il va vous expliquer la** ~ he'll tell you about it; **il a bien pris la** ~ he took it very well; **les** ~**s se sont passées ainsi** it *ou* things happened like this; **en mettant les** ~**s au mieux/pire** at best/worst.

2 *nm* (*) (*truc*) thing, contraption; (*personne*) what's-his-name*, thingumajig*. **eh! C**~ hey you.

3 *adj inv*: **être tout** ~ (*bizarre*) to feel a bit peculiar; (*malade*) to be out of sorts; **ça l'a rendu tout** ~ it made him go all funny*.

chou[1], *pl* ~**x** [ʃu] *nm* (*Bot*) cabbage; (*ruban*) rosette; (*gâteau*) puff. **notre projet est/il est dans les** ~**x*** our plan has/he has had it*; **faire** ~ **blanc*** to draw a blank; ~ **de Bruxelles** Brussels sprout; ~**-fleur** *nm, pl* ~**x-**~**s** cauliflower; ~ **rouge** red cabbage. ♦ **chou**[2], **-te***, *mpl* ~**x 1** *nm,f* (*amour*) darling. **2** *adj inv* (*ravissant*) delightful. ♦ **chouchou, -te*** *nm,f* pet. ♦ **chouchouter*** (1) *vt* to pamper, pet. ♦ **choucroute** *nf* sauerkraut.

choucas [ʃukɑ] *nm* jackdaw.

chouette[1]* [ʃwɛt] *adj* (*beau*) smashing*, great*; (*gentil*) nice. **sois** ~ be a dear *ou* sport*; ~ **(alors)!** smashing!*, great!*

chouette[2] [ʃwɛt] *nf* owl. (*péj*) **vieille** ~ old harpy.

choyer [ʃwaje] (8) *vt* to pamper, spoil.

chrétien, -ienne [kʀetjɛ̃, jɛn] *adj*, **C**~**(ne)** *nm(f)* Christian. ♦ **chrétiennement** *adv* as a Christian. ♦ **chrétienté** *nf* Christendom.

christ [kʀist] *nm* **(a) le C**~ Christ. **(b)** (*objet*) figure of Christ. ♦ **christianisation** *nf* conversion to Christianity. ♦ **christianiser** (1) *vt* to convert to Christianity. ♦ **christianisme** *nm* Christianity.

chromatique [kʀɔmatik] *adj* (*Mus, Peinture*) chromatic; (*Bio*) chromosomal.

chrome [kʀom] *nm* (*Chim*) chromium. (*Aut*) **faire les** ~**s*** to polish the chrome. ♦ **chromer** (1) *vt* to chromium-plate.

chromo [kʀɔmo] *nm* chromo.

chromosome [kʀɔmozom] *nm* chromosome. ♦ **chromosomique** *adj* chromosomal.

chronique [kʀɔnik] **1** *adj* chronic. **2** *nf* (*Littérat*) chronicle; (*Presse*) column, page. ♦ **chroniquement** *adv* chronically. ♦ **chroniqueur** *nm* (*Littérat*) chronicler; (*Presse, gén*) columnist. ~ **sportif** sports editor; ~ **dramatique** drama critic.

chrono* [kʀɔno] *nm* stopwatch. (*Aut*) **faire du 80 (km/h) (au)** ~ to be timed at 80; **faire un bon** ~ to do a good time.

chronologie [kʀɔnɔlɔʒi] *nf* chronology. ♦ **chronologique** *adj* chronological. ♦ **chronologiquement** *adv* chronologically.

chronomètre [kʀɔnɔmɛtʀ(ə)] *nm* chronometer; (*Sport*) stopwatch. ♦ **chronométrage** *nm* timing. ♦ **chronométrer** (6) *vt* to time. ♦ **chronométreur** *nm* timekeeper. ♦ **chronométrique** *adj* chronometric.

chrysalide [kʀizalid] *nf* chrysalis.
chrysanthème [kʀisɑ̃tɛm] *nm* chrysanthemum.
chuchoter [ʃyʃɔte] (1) *vti* (*gén, fig*) to whisper; *[ruisseau]* to murmur. ♦ **chuchotement** *nm* whisper; murmur.
chuinter [ʃɥɛ̃te] (1) *vi* to hiss softly. ♦ **chuintement** *nm* soft hiss.
chut [ʃyt] *excl* sh!
chute [ʃyt] *nf* **(a)** (*gén*) fall; *[cheveux]* loss; *[empire, commerce]* collapse; *[régime]* downfall (*de* of); *[monnaie, température]* drop (*de* in); (*Théât*) *[pièce]* failure (*de* of). **faire une ~ de 3 mètres** to fall 3 metres; **faire une ~ de cheval** to fall off a horse; **loi de la ~ des corps** law of gravity; **~ libre** free fall; **économie en ~ libre** plummeting economy; **attention, ~ de pierres** danger, falling rocks. **(b)** (*Géog*) **~ d'eau** waterfall; **les ~s du Niagara/Zambèze** the Niagara/Victoria Falls; **fortes ~s de pluie/neige** heavy rainfalls/snowfalls. **(c)** (*déchet*) *[tissu]* clipping, scrap; *[bois]* off-cut. **(d) la ~ des reins** the small of the back; **~ du jour** nightfall.
chuter [ʃyte] (1) *vi* to fall; (*échouer*) to come a cropper*; (*Théât*) to flop. (*lit, fig*) **faire ~ qn** to bring sb down.
Chypre [ʃipʀ(ə)] *n* Cyprus. ♦ **chypriote** *adj*, **C~** *nmf* = **cypriote.**
ci [si] **1** *adv*: **celui-~, celle-~** this one; **ceux-~** these (ones); **ce livre-~** this book; **à cette heure-~** (*indue*) at this hour of the day; (*actuelle*) by now; **ces jours-~** (*avenir*) in the next few days; (*passé*) these past few days; (*présent*) these days; **de ~ de là** here and there. **2: ~-après** below; **~-contre** opposite; **~-dessous** below; **~-dessus** above; **~-gît** here lies; **~-inclus une enveloppe** envelope enclosed; **les papiers ~-joints** the enclosed papers.
cible [sibl(ə)] *nf* (*lit, fig*) target.
ciboire [sibwaʀ] *nm* (*Rel*) ciborium (*vessel*).
ciboule [sibul] *nf*, **ciboulette** [sibulɛt] *nf* chives.
cicatrice [sikatʀis] *nf* (*lit, fig*) scar. ♦ **cicatrisation** *nf* healing. ♦ **cicatriser** *vt*, **se ~** *vpr* (1) to heal (over).
cidre [sidʀ(ə)] *nm* cider.
ciel [sjɛl] **1** *nm* **(a)** (*espace: pl littér* **cieux**) sky, heavens (*littér*). **sous des cieux plus cléments** (*climat*) beneath more clement skies; (*hum: moins dangereux*) in healthier climes. **(b)** (*Peinture: pl* **ciels**) sky. **(c)** (*Rel*) **le ~, les cieux** heaven; **juste ~!** good heavens!; **c'est le ~ qui vous envoie!** you're heaven-sent! **(d) à ~ ouvert** *égout* open; *piscine* open-air; *mine* opencast. **2: ~ de lit** canopy.
cierge [sjɛʀʒ(ə)] *nm* (*Rel*) candle.
cigale [sigal] *nf* cicada.
cigare [sigaʀ] *nm* cigar; (*: *tête*) head, nut‡. ♦ **cigarette** *nf* cigarette. **~ (à) bout filtre** filter-tip(ped) cigarette.
cigogne [sigɔɲ] *nf* (*Orn*) stork.
ciguë [sigy] *nf* hemlock.
cil [sil] *nm* (*Anat*) eyelash. **~s vibratiles** cilia. ♦ **ciller** [sije] (1) *vi*: **~ (des yeux)** to blink (one's eyes).
cime [sim] *nf [montagne]* summit; *[arbre]* top; *[gloire]* peak, height.
ciment [simɑ̃] *nm* cement. **~ armé** reinforced concrete. ♦ **cimenter** (1) *vt* to cement. ♦ **cimenterie** *nf* cement works.
cimetière [simtjɛʀ] *nm [ville]* cemetery; *[église]* graveyard, churchyard. **~ de voitures** scrapyard.
cinéma [sinema] *nm* (*gén*) cinema; (*salle*) cinema, movie theater (*US*). **~ muet/parlant** silent/talking films; **faire du ~** to be a film actor (*ou* actress); **de ~** *producteur, studio* film; *écran* cinema; **être dans le ~** to be in the film business; **aller au ~** to go to the pictures *ou* movies (*US*); **quel ~!** (*frime*) what a performance, what an act; (*complication*) what a to-do *ou* fuss. ♦ **ciné*** *nm abrév de* **cinéma.** ♦ **cinéaste** *nmf* filmmaker. ♦ **ciné-club,** *pl* **~-~s** *nm* film society. ♦ **cinémascope** *nm* ® Cinemascope ®. ♦ **cinémathèque** *nf* film library; (*salle*) film theatre. ♦ **cinématographique** *adj* film, cinema. ♦ **cinéphile** *nmf* film enthusiast.
cingler [sɛ̃gle] (1) **1** *vt* (*gén, fig*) to lash. **le visage cinglé par le vent** with his face stung *ou* whipped by the wind. **2** *vi* (*Naut*) **~ vers** to make for. ♦ **cinglant, e** *adj vent* biting, bitter; *pluie* lashing; *propos* scathing, cutting. ♦ **cinglé, e*** **1** *adj* nutty‡, cracked*. **2** *nm,f* crackpot*, nut‡.
cinq [sɛ̃k] *adj, nm* five. **en ~ sec‡** in a flash, in two ticks*; *V* **six.**
cinquante [sɛ̃kɑ̃t] *adj, nm* fifty. ♦ **cinquantaine** *nf* about fifty. ♦ **cinquantenaire** *nm* fiftieth anniversary, golden jubilee. ♦ **cinquantième** *adj, nmf* fiftieth; *V* **six, soixantaine, sixième.**
cinquième [sɛ̃kjɛm] **1** *adj, nmf* fifth. **être la ~ roue du carrosse*** to count for nothing; *V* **sixième. 2** *nf* (*Scol*) second year. ♦ **cinquièmement** *adv* in the fifth place.
cintre [sɛ̃tʀ(ə)] *nm* (*Archit*) arch; *[manteau]* coat hanger. (*Théât*) **les ~s** the flies. ♦ **cintré, e** *adj porte* arched; *veste* waisted; *chemise* slim-fitting.
cirage [siʀaʒ] *nm* (*produit*) (shoe) polish; (*action*) polishing. **être dans le ~*** (*malaise*) to be dazed; (*ignorance*) to be all at sea*.
circoncire [siʀkɔ̃siʀ] (37) *vt* to circumcize. ♦ **circoncision** *nf* circumcision.
circonférence [siʀkɔ̃feʀɑ̃s] *nf* circumference.
circonflexe [siʀkɔ̃flɛks(ə)] *adj*: **accent ~** circumflex.
circonlocution [siʀkɔ̃lɔkysjɔ̃] *nf* circumlocution.
circonscription [siʀkɔ̃skʀipsjɔ̃] *nf* district, area. **~ (électorale)** constituency.
circonscrire [siʀkɔ̃skʀiʀ] (39) *vt feu, épidémie* to contain, confine; *territoire* to mark out; *sujet* to define. **se ~** *ou* **être circonscrit à qch** to be limited *ou* confined *ou* restricted to sth.
circonspection [siʀkɔ̃spɛksjɔ̃] *nf* caution, wariness, circumspection. ♦ **circonspect, e** *adj* circumspect, cautious, wary.
circonstance [siʀkɔ̃stɑ̃s] *nf* (*occasion*) occasion; *[accident]* circumstance. (*situation*) **~s** circumstances; **en la ~** on this occasion; **dans ces ~s** in these circumstances; **~s atténuantes** mitigating circumstances; **de ~** *mine* appropriate; *poésie* occasional. ♦ **circonstancié, e** *adj* detailed. ♦ **circonstanciel, -ielle** *adj* adverbial.
circonvenir [siʀkɔ̃vniʀ] (22) *vt* to circumvent.
circonvolution [siʀkɔ̃vɔlysjɔ̃] *nf* (*Anat*) convolution; *[itinéraire]* twist.
circuit [siʀkɥi] *nm* (*touristique*) tour, (round) trip; (*compliqué*) roundabout *ou* circuitous route; (*Sport, Élec*) circuit; (*Écon*) circulation. **mettre qch en ~** to connect sth up; **être dans le ~*** to be around; **~ de distribution** distribution network; **~ fermé** (*Élec, fig*) closed circuit; **~ intégré/imprimé** integrated/printed circuit.
circulaire [siʀkylɛʀ] *adj, nf* (*gén*) circular.
circulation [siʀkylɑsjɔ̃] *nf [air, sang, argent]* circulation; *[marchandises, travailleurs]* movement; *[trains]* running; (*Aut, Aviat*) traffic. **mettre en ~** *argent* to put into circulation; *livre, voiture* to put on the market, bring out; **mise en ~** circulation; marketing. ♦ **circulatoire** *adj* circulatory.
circuler [siʀkyle] (1) *vi* **(a)** (*Anat, Écon*) to circulate; *[rumeur]* to circulate, go round. **faire ~** (*lit*) to circulate; *bruits* to spread, circulate (*sur* about). **(b)** *[voiture]* to go; *[passant]* to walk; *[foule]* to move (along); *[plat]* to be handed round. **circulez!** move along!; **faire ~** *voitures* to move on; *plat* to hand round.
cire [siʀ] *nf* (*gén*) wax; *[meubles]* polish; *[oreille]*

(ear)wax. ~ **d'abeille** beeswax; ~ **à cacheter** sealing wax. ♦ **ciré** *nm* oilskin. ♦ **cirer** (1) *vt* to polish. ♦ **cireur, -euse 1** *nm,f [souliers]* bootblack. **2** *nf* floor polisher. ♦ **cireux, -euse** *adj matière* waxy; *teint* waxen.
cirque [siʀk(ə)] *nm* (*spectacle*) circus; (*Antiq: arène*) amphitheatre; (*Géog*) cirque. **quel** ~!* (*tracas*) what a carry-on*!; (*désordre*) what absolute chaos!
cirrhose [siʀoz] *nf* cirrhosis.
cisailles [sizaj] *nfpl [métal, arbre]* shears; *[fil de fer]* wire cutters. ♦ **cisailler** (1) *vt métal* to cut; *arbuste* to clip; (*par l'usure*) to shear off; (*: *maladroitement*) to hack; (*) *personne* to cripple the career of.
ciseau, *pl* ~**x** [sizo] *nm* **(a)** **(paire de)** ~**x** (*gén*) (pair of) scissors; *[métal, laine]* shears. **(b)** (*Sculp, Tech*) chisel. ~ **à froid** cold chisel. **(c)** (*Sport: prise*) scissors (hold).
ciseler [sizle] (5) *vt pierre* to chisel, engrave; *métal* to chase, engrave. ♦ **ciselure** *nf* chased pattern, engraving.
citadelle [sitadɛl] *nf* (*lit, fig*) citadel.
citadin, e [sitadɛ̃, in] **1** *adj* urban, town, city. **2** *nm,f* city dweller.
citation [sitɑsjɔ̃] *nf [auteur]* quotation. ~ **à comparaître** (*à accusé*) summons to appear; (*à témoin*) subpoena; ~ **à l'ordre de l'armée** mention in dispatches.
cité [site] *nf* city; (*petite*) town. ~**-dortoir** *nf, pl* ~**s**-~**s** dormitory town; ~**-jardin** *nf, pl* ~**s**-~**s** garden city; ~ **ouvrière** ≈ (workers') housing estate; ~ **universitaire** (student) halls of residence.
citer [site] (1) *vt* to quote, cite. ~ **qn (en exemple)** to cite sb *ou* hold sb up as an example; ~ **un soldat à l'ordre du jour** to mention a soldier in dispatches; ~ **(à comparaître)** *accusé* to summon to appear; *témoin* to subpoena.
citerne [sitɛʀn(ə)] *nf* tank.
citoyen, -enne [sitwajɛ̃, ɛn] **1** *nm,f* citizen. **2** *nm* (*: *type*) fellow, guy*. ♦ **citoyenneté** *nf* citizenship.
citron [sitʀɔ̃] **1** *nm* (*fruit*) lemon; (‡: *tête*) head, nut‡. **2** *adj inv* lemon(-coloured). ♦ **citronnade** *nf* lemon squash. ♦ **citronnier** *nm* lemon tree.
citrouille [sitʀuj] *nf* pumpkin; (‡: *tête*) head, nut‡.
civet [sivɛ] *nm* stew.
civière [sivjɛʀ] *nf* stretcher.
civil, e [sivil] **1** *adj guerre, mariage* civil; (*non militaire*) civilian; (*poli*) civil, courteous. **2** *nm* civilian. **en** ~ *soldat* in civilian clothes; *policier* in plain clothes; **dans le** ~ in civilian life. ♦ **civilement** *adv* **(a)** **être** ~ **responsable** to be legally responsible; **se marier** ~ to have a civil wedding. **(b)** (*poliment*) civilly.
civilisation [sivilizɑsjɔ̃] *nf* civilization. ♦ **civiliser** (1) **1** *vt* to civilize. **2 se** ~ *vpr* to become civilized.
civilité [sivilite] *nf* civility. ~**s** civilities, compliments.
civique [sivik] *adj* civic. ♦ **civisme** *nm* public-spiritedness.
clac [klak] *excl [porte]* slam!; *[élastique]* snap!; *[fouet]* crack!
clair, e [klɛʀ] **1** *adj* **(a)** *pièce* bright, light; *couleur* (*vive*) bright; (*pâle*) light; *robe* light-coloured. **bleu** ~ light blue. **(b)** *soupe, cheveux, tissu usé* thin. **(c)** (*lit, fig: limpide*) clear. **par temps** ~ on a clear day; **avoir un esprit** ~ to be a clear thinker; **il est** ~ **qu'il se trompe** it is clear *ou* plain that he's mistaken; ~ **comme le jour** as clear as daylight, crystal-clear. **2** *adv parler, voir* clearly. **il fait** ~ it is daylight; **il ne fait guère** ~ it's not very light. **3** *nm*: **tirer qch au** ~ to clear sth up; **en** ~ (*c'est-à-dire*) to put it plainly; (*non codé*) in clear; **gaspiller le plus** ~ **de son temps/argent** to waste most of one's time/the better part of one's money; **au** ~ **de lune** in the moonlight. ♦ **clairement** *adv* clearly. ♦ **claire-voies,** *pl* ~**s**-~**s** *nf* openwork fence. **à** ~-~ openwork.
clairière [klɛʀjɛʀ] *nf* clearing, glade.
clairon [klɛʀɔ̃] *nm* bugle; (*joueur*) bugler. ♦ **claironnant, e** *adj voix* resonant. ♦ **claironner** (1) *vt nouvelle* to trumpet.
clairsemé, e [klɛʀsəme] *adj maisons, auditoire* scattered; *gazon* sparse.
clairvoyance [klɛʀvwajɑ̃s] *nf* clear-sightedness, perceptiveness. ♦ **clairvoyant, e** *adj* clear-sighted, perceptive.
clamecer‡ [klamse] (3) *vi* to kick the bucket‡.
clamer [klame] (1) *vt* (*gén*) to shout out; *innocence* to proclaim. ♦ **clameur** *nf* (*cris*) clamour. ~**s** protests.
clan [klɑ̃] *nm* (*lit, fig*) clan.
clandestin, e [klɑ̃dɛstɛ̃, in] *adj réunion* secret, clandestine; *mouvement* underground; *commerce* clandestine, illicit. **(passager)** ~ stowaway. ♦ **clandestinement** *adv* secretly; clandestinely; illicitly. ♦ **clandestinité** *nf [activité]* secret nature. **dans la** ~ *travailler* in secret, clandestinely; *vivre* underground.
clapet [klapɛ] *nm* (*Tech*) valve. **ferme ton** ~* hold your tongue*.
clapier [klapje] *nm* (*lit*) hutch; (*péj*) dump‡, hole*.
clapoter [klapɔte] (1) *vi* to lap. ♦ **clapotement** *nm ou* ♦ **clapotis** *nm* lap(ping).
clapper [klape] (1) *vi*: ~ **de la langue** to click one's tongue.
claquage [klakaʒ] *nm* (*blessure*) strained muscle.
claque [klak] **1** *nf* (*gifle*) slap; (*Théât*) claque. **2** *adj, nm*: **(chapeau)** ~ opera hat.
claquer [klake] (1) **1** *vi* **(a)** *[volet]* to bang; *[drapeau]* to flap; *[fouet]* to crack; *[coup de feu]* to ring out. **faire** ~ *porte* to bang, slam; *fouet* to crack; *doigts* to snap; *langue* to click; ~ **dans ses mains** to clap (one's hands); ~ **des talons** to click one's heels; **il claquait des dents** his teeth were chattering. **(b)** (‡: *mourir*) *[personne]* to kick the bucket‡; *[lampe]* to conk out‡, pack in‡; *[élastique]* to snap. ~ **dans les mains de qn** *[malade]* to die on sb*; *[affaire]* to go bust on sb‡. **2** *vt* (*gifler*) to slap; (*fermer*) to snap shut; (*: *fatiguer*) to exhaust, tire out; (*: *casser*) to bust; (‡: *dépenser*) to blow‡, blue‡. ~ **la porte** (*lit*) to slam the door; (*fig*) to leave in a huff; **se** ~ **un muscle** to strain a muscle. ♦ **claquement** *nm* bang; slam; crack; click; snap. (*répété*) **le** ~ *ou* **les** ~**s de** the banging (*ou* flapping *ou* cracking *etc*) of.
claquette [klakɛt] *nf* (*danse*) ~**s** tap-dancing.
clarifier *vt,* **se** ~ *vpr* [klaʀifje] (7) (*lit, fig*) to clarify. ♦ **clarification** *nf* clarification.
clarinette [klaʀinɛt] *nf* clarinet. ♦ **clarinettiste** *nmf* clarinettist.
clarté [klaʀte] *nf* (*gén: lumière*) light; *[flamme, pièce, ciel]* brightness; *[eau, son]* clearness; *[explication, pensée]* clarity. (*fig: précisions*) ~**s** knowledge (*sur* about); **à la** ~ **de la lampe/lune** in the lamplight/moonlight; ~ **d'esprit** clear thinking.
classe [klɑs] *nf* **(a)** (*catégorie*) (*gén*) class; (*grade*) grade; *[utilisateurs]* category. **les** ~**s moyennes** the middle classes; **société sans** ~ classless society; **de première** ~ *employé* top *ou* first grade; *hôtel, billet* 1st class; (*Aviat*) ~ **touriste** economy class; ~ **d'âge** age group. **(b)** (*gén, Sport: valeur*) class. **de (grande)** ~ of great distinction; **de** ~ **internationale** of international status; **elle a de la** ~ she's got class. **(c)** (*Scol*) (*élèves, cours*) class; (*année*) year, grade (*US*); (*salle*) classroom. **la** ~ (*l'école*) school; **il est (le) premier/(le) dernier de la** ~ he is top/bottom of the class; **aller en** ~ to go to school; **après la** ~ after school (hours); **c'est M X qui leur fait la** ~ Mr X is their teacher; **turbulent en** ~ disruptive in class *ou* in the classroom. **(d)** (*Mil*) **soldat de**

1ère (*ou* **2ème**) ~ ≃ private; **la ~ 1972** the class of '72; **faire ses ~s** to do one's training.

classer [klɑse] (1) **1** *vt* **(a)** *papiers* to file; *livres, plantes* to classify. **(b)** (*hiérarchiser*) to grade. **X, que l'on classe parmi** X, who ranks among. **(c)** (*clore*) *affaire* to close. **(d)** (*péj: cataloguer*) *personne* to size up, categorize. **2 se ~** *vpr*: **se ~ parmi les premiers** to be *ou* come among the first; **se ~ parmi les meilleurs** to rank among the best; **être bien classé** to be well placed. ♦ **classé, e** *adj monument* listed; *vins* classified; *joueur* graded. ♦ **classement** *nm* **(a)** (*action*) filing; classification; grading; closing. **j'ai fait du ~ toute la journée** I've spent all day filing. **(b)** (*rang*) *[élève]* place; *[coureur]* placing; (*liste*) *[élèves]* class list; *[coureurs]* finishing list. **je vais vous lire le ~** I'm going to read you your placings; **~ général** overall placing(s). ♦ **classeur** *nm* (*meuble*) filing cabinet; (*dossier*) (loose-leaf) file.

classifier [klasifje] (7) *vt* to classify. ♦ **classification** *nf* classification.

classique [klasik] **1** *adj auteur, musique, études* classical; *vêtement, ameublement* classic(al); *argument* standard, classic; *conséquence* usual. **c'est ~!** it's the usual *ou* classic situation!; **grâce à une opération maintenant ~** thanks to an operation which is now quite usual *ou* standard; (*Scol*) **il est en section ~** he's in the classics stream. **2** *nm* (*auteur*) (*Antiq*) classical author; (*XVIIème siècle*) classic, classicist; (*écrivain, œuvre célèbre*) classic. **le ~** (*musique*) classical music; (*mobilier*) the classic(al) style. ♦ **classicisme** *nm* (*Art*) classicism; (*conformisme*) conventionality. ♦ **classiquement** *adv* classically.

clause [kloz] *nf* (*gén*) clause.

claustrophobie [klostrɔfɔbi] *nf* claustrophobia.

clavecin [klavsɛ̃] *nm* harpsichord.

clavicule [klavikyl] *nf* collarbone.

clavier [klavje] *nm* (*lit*) keyboard; *[orgue]* manual; (*fig*) range.

clé *ou* **clef** [kle] **1** *nf* (*gén, fig*) key (*de* to); (*Tech*) spanner; *[violon]* peg; *[gamme]* clef. **altération à la ~** change in the key signature; **avec un récompense à la ~** with a reward into the bargain; **prix ~s en main** *[voiture]* price on the road; *[appartement]* price with immediate entry *ou* possession; **mettre sous ~** to put under lock and key; **mettre la ~ sous la porte** to clear out; **prendre la ~ des champs** to run away. **2** *adj inv*: **position- etc ~** key position *etc*. **3**: **~ anglaise** (monkey) wrench; **~ à molette** adjustable wrench *ou* spanner; (*lit, fig*) **~ de voûte** keystone.

clématite [klematit] *nf* clematis.

clémence [klemɑ̃s] *nf [temps]* mildness; *[juge]* clemency, leniency. ♦ **clément, e** *adj* mild; lenient.

clémentine [klemɑ̃tin] *nf* clementine.

clenche [klɑ̃ʃ] *nf* latch.

cleptomane [klɛptɔman] *nmf* = **kleptomane.**

clerc [klɛʀ] *nm [notaire etc]* clerk; (*Rel*) cleric; (*Hist*) (learned) scholar. **être (grand) ~ en la matière** to be an expert on the subject.

clergé [klɛʀʒe] *nm* clergy. ♦ **clérical, e, *mpl* -aux** *adj, nmf* (*Rel*) clerical.

clic [klik] *nm* click. **le ~-clac de** the clickety-clack of.

cliché [kliʃe] *nm* (*banal*) cliché; (*Phot*) negative; (*Typ*) plate.

client, e [klijɑ̃, ɑ̃t] *nm,f* (*gén*) customer; *[avocat]* client; *[hôtel]* guest, patron; *[médecin]* patient; *[taxi]* fare; (* *péj: individu*) fellow, guy*; (*Antiq: protégé*) client. **être ~ d'un magasin** to patronize a shop, be a regular customer at a shop. ♦ **clientèle** *nf [magasin]* customers, clientèle; *[avocat, médecin]* practice; *[parti]* supporters. **accorder sa ~ à qn** to give sb one's custom, patronize sb.

cligner [kliɲe] (1) *vt, vt indir*: **~ les** *ou* **des yeux** to blink; (*à moitié*) to screw up one's eyes; **~ de l'œil** to wink (*en direction de* at). ♦ **clignement** *nm*: **~(s)** blinking; **un ~ d'œil** a wink.

clignoter [kliɲɔte] (1) *vi [yeux]* to blink; *[étoile]* to twinkle; *[lampe]* to flicker; (*pour signal*) to flash, wink. ♦ **clignotant** *nm* (*Aut*) indicator. ♦ **clignotement** *nm*: **~(s)** blinking; twinkling; flickering; flashing, winking.

climat [klima] *nm* (*lit, fig*) climate; (*littér: contrée*) clime (*littér*). ♦ **climatique** *adj* climatic. ♦ **climatisation** *nf* air conditioning. ♦ **climatiser** (1) *vt* to air-condition. ♦ **climatiseur** *nm* air conditioner.

clin [klɛ̃] *nm*: **~ d'œil** wink; **faire un ~ d'œil** to wink (*à* at); **en un ~ d'œil** in the twinkling of an eye.

clinique [klinik] **1** *adj* clinical. **2** *nf* (*établissement*) nursing home; (*section*) clinic. **~ d'accouchement** maternity home.

clinquant, e [klɛ̃kɑ̃, ɑ̃t] **1** *adj* flashy. **2** *nm* (*lit*) tinsel; (*bijoux*) tawdry jewellery; *[style]* flashiness.

clip [klip] *nm* brooch.

clique [klik] *nf* (*Mus*) band; (*péj*) clique, set. **prendre ses ~s et ses claques*** to pack up (and go).

cliqueter [klikte] (4) *vi* (*gén*) to clink; *[vaisselle]* to clatter; *[chaînes, ferraille]* to jangle; *[armes]* to clash. ♦ **cliquetis** *nm* clink; clatter; jangle; clash.

clivage [klivaʒ] *nm* (*action*) cleaving; (*résultat*) cleavage; (*fig*) split (*de* in).

cloaque [klɔak] *nm* cesspool, cesspit.

clochard, e* [klɔʃaʀ, aʀd(ə)] *nm,f* down-and-out, tramp.

cloche [klɔʃ] **1** *nf* (*gén*) bell; *[plat]* lid; *[plantes]* cloche; (*: *imbécile*) idiot*. **~ à fromage** cheese cover; **~ à plongeur** diving bell. **2** *adj* **(a)** *jupe* bell-shaped. **chapeau ~** cloche hat. **(b)** (*: *idiot*) idiotic. ♦ **cloche-pied** *adv*: **a ~** *sauter* to hop. ♦ **clochette** *nf* small bell; (*fleur*) bellflower.

clocher[1] [klɔʃe] *nm* (*en pointe*) steeple; (*quadrangulaire*) church tower; (*fig: village*) village. **de ~** *mentalité* parochial. ♦ **clocheton** *nm* (*Archit*) pinnacle.

clocher*[2] [klɔʃe] (1) *vi*: **il y a qch qui cloche** there's sth up* *ou* wrong (*dans* with).

cloison [klwazɔ̃] *nf* (*gén*) partition; (*Naut*) bulkhead; (*fig*) barrier. ♦ **cloisonnement** *nm* compartmentalization. ♦ **cloisonner** (1) *vt activités etc* to compartmentalize.

cloître [klwatʀ(ə)] *nm* cloister. ♦ **cloîtrer** (1) **1** *vt* to shut away (*dans* in); (*Rel*) to cloister. **religieux cloîtré** enclosed monk. **2 se ~** *vpr* to shut o.s. up *ou* away (*dans* in). **vivre cloîtré** to live a cloistered life.

clopiner [klɔpine] (1) *vi* to hobble *ou* limp along. ♦ **clopin-clopant** *adv*: **aller ~** *[marcheur]* to hobble along; *[affaires]* to be so-so*.

cloque [klɔk] *nf* blister. ♦ **cloquer** (1) *vi* to blister.

clore [klɔʀ] (45) *vt* (*terminer*) to close, end, conclude; (*entourer*) to enclose (*de* with); (*fermer*) *porte* to close, shut; *lettre* to seal. **~ le bec à qn*** to shut sb up*. ♦ **clos, e 1** *adj système, yeux* closed; *espace* enclosed. **2** *nm* (*pré*) (enclosed) field; (*vignoble*) vineyard.

clôture [klotyʀ] *nf* **(a)** (*planches*) fence; (*fil de fer*) (wire) fence; (*haies*) hedge; (*ciment*) wall. **mur de ~** outer wall. **(b)** *[débat, liste, compte]* closing, closure; *[bureaux]* closing. (*Théât*) **~ annuelle** annual closure; **avant la ~** before it closes; **date etc de ~** closing date *etc*. ♦ **clôturer** (1) *vt champ* to enclose; *liste* to close.

clou [klu] *nm* **(a)** (*gén*) nail; (*décoratif, pour chaussée*) stud; *[tapissier]* tack. **traverser dans les ~s** to cross at the pedestrian crossing. **(b)** (*Méd*) boil. **(c)** (*fig*) *[spectacle]* star attraction *ou* turn. **mettre sa montre au ~*** to pawn one's watch, put one's watch in hock*; **(vieux) ~*** (*gén*) ancient machine; (*voiture*) old banger; **des ~s!**‡ nothing doing!*; **~ de girofle** clove. ♦ **clouer** (1) *vt* (*lit*) to nail down; *ennemi* to pin down. **~ qn sur place** to nail *ou* root sb to the spot; **~ qn au lit** to keep sb confined to bed; **~ le bec à qn*** to shut sb up*. ♦ **clouté, e** *adj ceinture* studded; *souliers* hob-nailed.

clown [klun] *nm* clown. **faire le ~** to clown (about), play the fool. ♦ **clownerie** *nf* silly trick. **~s** clowning.

club [klœb] *nm* (*gén*) club.

co [kɔ] *préf* co-, joint. **coaccusé** codefendant; **coacquéreur** joint purchaser; **codétenu** fellow prisoner; **coéquipier** team mate.

coaguler *vti,* **se ~** *vpr* [kɔagyle] (1) to coagulate; *[sang]* to clot, congeal; *[lait]* to curdle. ♦ **coagulant, e 1** *adj* coagulative. **2** *nm* coagulant. ♦ **coagulation** *nf* coagulation.

coaliser *vt,* **se ~** *vpr* [kɔalize] (1) to unite (in a coalition). ♦ **coalition** *nf* coalition.

coasser [kɔase] (1) *vi* to croak. ♦ **coassement** *nm*: **~(s)** croaking.

cobalt [kɔbalt] *nm* cobalt.

cobaye [kɔbaj] *nm* (*lit, fig*) guinea-pig.

cobra [kɔbʀa] *nm* cobra.

cocaïne [kɔkain] *nf* cocaine.

cocarde [kɔkaʀd(ə)] *nf* rosette; (*Hist*) cockade; *[avion]* roundel; (*sur voiture*) sticker.

cocasse [kɔkas] *adj* comical, funny. ♦ **cocasserie** *nf* comicalness, funniness.

coccinelle [kɔksinɛl] *nf* ladybird.

coccyx [kɔksis] *nm* coccyx.

cocher[1] [kɔʃe] (1) *vt* (*crayon*) to tick (off); (*entaille*) to notch.

cocher[2] [kɔʃe] *nm* coachman; *[fiacre]* cabman.

cochon[1] [kɔʃɔ̃] *nm* (*animal*) pig; (*: *viande*) pork. **~ d'Inde** guinea-pig; **~ de lait** sucking-pig; **un ~ n'y retrouverait pas ses petits** it's like a pigsty in there. ♦ **cochon**[2]**, -onne 1** *adj* (‡: *obscène*) dirty, smutty. **2** *nm,f* (‡*péj: personne*) (*sale, vicieux*) dirty pig‡ *ou* beast‡; (*méchant*) swine‡. **quel temps de ~!** what lousy weather!* ♦ **cochonner*** (1) *vt* to mess up*. ♦ **cochonnerie*** *nf* (*histoire*) dirty joke; (*tour*) dirty trick. **de la ~** (*nourriture*) disgusting food; (*marchandise*) rubbish; (*saleté*) filth; **faire des ~s** to make a mess. ♦ **cochonnet** *nm* (*Zool*) piglet; (*Boules*) jack.

cocktail [kɔktɛl] *nm* (*réunion*) cocktail party; (*boisson*) cocktail; (*fig*) mixture.

coco [koko] *nm* (*: *œuf*) eggie*; (*réglisse*) liquorice powder. **oui mon ~** yes, darling; (*: *péj*) **drôle de ~** odd guy*.

cocon [kɔkɔ̃] *nm* cocoon; (*fig*) shell.

cocorico [kɔkɔʀiko] *nm, excl* cock-a-doodle-do.

cocotier [kɔkɔtje] *nm* coconut palm.

cocotte [kɔkɔt] *nf* (*: *poule*) hen; (*marmite*) casserole; (**péj: femme*) tart*. **hue ~!** gee up!; **oui ma ~** yes darling; **~ minute** ® pressure cooker.

cocu, e‡ [kɔky] *adj, nm,f* cuckold. **faire qn ~** to be unfaithful to sb.

code [kɔd] *nm* (*gén*) code. **C~ de la route** highway code; **écrire qch en ~** to write sth in code, (en)code sth; **(phares) ~** dipped headlights, low beams (*US*); **se mettre en ~** to dip one's headlights. ♦ **codage** *nm* (en)coding. ♦ **coder** (1) *vt* to code.

codifier [kɔdifje] (7) *vt* to codify. ♦ **codification** *nf* codification.

coefficient [kɔefisjɑ̃] *nm* (*Math, Phys*) coefficient. **~ d'erreur** margin of error.

coercition [kɔɛʀsisjɔ̃] *nf* coercion.

cœur [kœʀ] *nm* **(a)** (*Anat, Cartes, forme*) heart. **en (forme de) ~** heart-shaped; **on l'a opéré à ~ ouvert** he had an open-heart operation.

(b) (*fig: estomac*) **avoir mal au ~** to feel sick; **il faut avoir le ~ bien accroché** you need guts* *ou* a strong stomach; **odeur qui soulève le ~** nauseating *ou* sickening smell.

(c) (*âme*) heart. **c'est un ~ pur** he is a candid soul; **avoir le ~ sensible** to be tender-hearted; **elle lui a donné son ~** she has lost her heart to him; **spectacle à vous fendre le ~** heartrending *ou* heartbreaking sight; **avoir le ~ gros** to have a heavy heart; **il avait la rage au ~** he was inwardly seething with anger; **ce geste lui est allé (droit) au ~** this gesture went straight to his heart; **connaître le fond du ~ de qn** to know sb's innermost feelings; **des paroles venues (du fond) du ~** heartfelt words; **au fond de son ~** in his heart of hearts; **il m'a parlé à ~ ouvert** he had a heart-to-heart talk with me.

(d) (*bonté, générosité*) **avoir bon ~** to be kind-hearted; **avoir le ~ sur la main** to be open-handed; **sans ~** heartless; **c'est un ~ de pierre/d'or** he has a heart of stone/gold; **femme de ~** noble-hearted woman.

(e) (*humeur*) **avoir le ~ gai** to feel happy; **je n'ai pas le ~ à rire** I do not feel like laughing, I am not in the mood for laughing; **si le ~ vous en dit** if you feel like it.

(f) (*courage*) heart, courage. **le ~ lui manqua** his heart *ou* courage failed him; **mettre tout son ~ dans qch/à faire qch** to put all one's heart into sth/into doing sth; **comment peut-on avoir le ~ de refuser?** how can one have the heart to refuse?; **donner du ~ au ventre à qn*** to buck sb up*; **avoir du ~ au ventre*** to have guts*.

(g) *[chou]* heart; *[arbre]* heart, core; *[fruit]* core; *[problème, ville]* heart. **au ~ de** in the heart of; **~ de palmier** heart of palm; **~ d'artichaut** artichoke heart.

(h) par ~ by heart; **ça m'est resté sur le ~** I still feel sore about it; **je vais lui dire ce que j'ai sur le ~** I'm going to tell him what's on my mind; **à ~ joie** to one's heart's content; **je suis de tout ~ avec vous** I DO sympathize with you; **ne pas porter qn dans son ~** to have no great liking for sb; **je veux en avoir le ~ net** I want to be clear in my own mind (about it); **avoir à ~ de faire** to make a point of doing; **prendre les choses à ~** to take things to heart; **ce voyage me tient à ~** I have set my heart on this journey; **ce sujet me tient à ~** this subject is close to my heart.

coexister [kɔɛgziste] (1) *vi* to coexist. ♦ **coexistence** *nf* coexistence.

coffre [kɔfʀ(ə)] *nm* (*meuble*) chest; (*Aut*) boot, trunk (*US*); (*coffrage*) case; (*Hist, fig: cassette*) coffer; (*: *poitrine*) chest. **~-fort** *nm, pl* **~s-~s** safe; **~ à jouets** toybox. ♦ **coffrage** *nm [bois]* case; *[béton]* form. ♦ **coffrer*** (1) *vt* to throw *ou* put inside*. ♦ **coffret** *nm* casket. **~ à bijoux** jewel box.

cognac [kɔɲak] *nm* cognac, French brandy.

cogner [kɔɲe] (1) **1** *vt objet* to knock; (‡: *battre*) to beat up. **2 ~ sur** *vt indir clou* to hammer; *mur* to knock on; (*fort*) to bang on; **~ du poing sur la table** to thump one's fist on the table; **~ à** *porte* to knock at; (*fort*) to bang at; **~ contre** to hit, strike. **3** *vi [volet]* to bang (*contre* against); (*) *[boxeur]* to hit out (hard); *[soleil]* to beat down; *[moteur]* to knock. **ça va ~*** there's going to be some rough stuff*. **4 se ~** *vpr*: **se ~/se ~ le genou contre** to bang o.s/one's knee against; (*fig*) **c'est à se ~ la tête contre les murs** it's enough to drive you up the wall. ♦ **cognée** *nf* felling axe. ♦ **cognement** *nm*: **~(s)** banging; knocking. ♦ **cogneur*** *nm* bruiser*.

cohabiter [kɔabite] (1) *vi* to live together, cohabit. **~ avec** to live with. ♦ **cohabitation** *nf* living together, cohabitation.

cohérent, e [kɔeʀɑ̃, ɑ̃t] *adj* coherent, consistent. ♦ **cohérence** *nf* coherence, consistency.

cohésion [kɔezjɔ̃] *nf* cohesion.

cohorte [kɔɔʀt(ə)] *nf* (*groupe*) troop; (*Hist Mil*) cohort.

cohue [kɔy] *nf* (*foule*) crowd; (*bousculade*) crush

coi, coite [kwa, kwat] *adj* silent.
coiffe [kwaf] *nf* headdress.
coiffer [kwafe] (1) *vt* **(a)** ~ **qn** to do sb's hair; **se faire** ~ to have one's hair done; **se** ~ to do one's hair. **(b)** (*mettre*) *chapeau* to put on. **se** ~ **d'une casquette** to put on a cap; ~ **qn** to put a hat on sb's head; **ça te coiffe bien** it suits you; **coiffé d'un chapeau** wearing a hat; **pic coiffé de neige** snow-capped peak. **(c)** (*fig*) *organismes* to have overall responsibility for; (*) *concurrent* to get the better of, beat. ♦ **coiffé, e** *adj*: **il est toujours mal/bien** ~ his hair always looks untidy/nice; **être** ~ **en brosse** to have a crew cut; **il était** ~ **en arrière** he had his hair brushed back. ♦ **coiffeur, euse 1** *nm,f* hairdresser. **2** *nf* (*meuble*) dressing table. ♦ **coiffure** *nf* hair style, hairdo*; (*chapeau*) hat. (*métier*) **la** ~ hairdressing.
coin [kwɛ̃] *nm* **(a)** (*angle*) corner. **au** ~ **du feu** by the fireside; **le magasin qui fait le** ~ the corner shop, the shop at the corner; **à tous les** ~**s de rue** on every street corner; **sourire en** ~ half smile; **regard en** ~ side glance; **surveiller qn du** ~ **de l'œil** to watch sb out of the corner of one's eye. **(b)** (*région*) area; (*village*) place; (*endroit*) *[plage, mémoire]* corner. **le** ~ **du bricoleur** the handyman's corner; **un** ~ **de terre/ciel** a patch of land/sky; **je l'ai mis dans un** ~ I put it somewhere; **dans tous les** ~**s (et recoins)** in every nook and cranny; ~**-repas** dining area; **l'épicier du** ~ the local grocer; **un** ~ **perdu** a place miles from anywhere; **un petit** ~ **pas cher** somewhere nice and cheap, a nice inexpensive spot. **(c)** (*cale*) wedge; (*poinçon*) hallmark; (*pour graver*) die; (*pour sous-main*) corner-piece.
coincer [kwɛ̃se] (3) **1** *vt* **(a)** (*intentionnellement*) to wedge; (*accidentellement*) to jam. **le tiroir est coincé** the drawer is stuck *ou* jammed; **il se trouva coincé contre un mur** he was pinned against a wall; **il m'a coincé pour me dire** he cornered me to tell me. **(b)** (*) *voleur* to nab*; *fraudeur* to catch up with; *candidat* to catch out. **coincé entre son désir et la peur** caught between his desire and fear; **nous sommes coincés** we are stuck *ou* cornered. **2 se** ~ *vpr* to jam, stick, get jammed *ou* stuck.
coïncidence [kɔɛ̃sidɑ̃s] *nf* (*gén*) coincidence. ♦ **coïncident, e** *adj* coincident. ♦ **coïncider** (1) *vi* to coincide (*avec* with). **faire** ~ **les dates** to get the dates to coincide.
coing [kwɛ̃] *nm* quince.
coke [kɔk] *nm* coke.
col [kɔl] *nm* **(a)** *[chemise]* collar. ~ **roulé** polo-neck sweater; ~ **bleu** (*ouvrier*) blue-collar worker; (*marin*) blue jacket. **(b)** (*Géog*) pass; (*Anat, fig*) neck.
colchique [kɔlʃik] *nm* autumn crocus.
coléoptère [kɔleɔptɛʀ] *nm* beetle.
colère [kɔlɛʀ] **1** *nf* (*gén*) anger; (*littér*) wrath; (*accès*) (fit of) rage. **être/se mettre/mettre qn en** ~ to be/get/make sb angry (*contre* with); **faire une** ~ to throw a tantrum. **2** *adj inv*: **être** ~* to be cross *ou* angry. ♦ **coléreux, -euse** *ou* ♦ **colérique** *adj* quick-tempered.
colibacille [kɔlibasil] *nm* colon bacillus.
colibri [kɔlibʀi] *nm* hummingbird.
colifichet [kɔlifiʃɛ] *nm* trinket.
colimaçon [kɔlimasɔ̃] *nm* snail. **escalier en** ~ spiral staircase.
colin [kɔlɛ̃] *nm* hake.
colin-maillard [kɔlɛ̃majaʀ] *nm* blind man's buff.
colique [kɔlik] *nf* (*diarrhée*) diarrhoea. (*douleurs*) ~**s** stomach pains, colic; ~**s néphrétiques** renal colic.
colis [kɔli] *nm* parcel. **par** ~ **postal** by parcel post.
collaborateur, -trice [kɔlabɔʀatœʀ, tʀis] *nm,f* (*gén*) colleague; *[journal]* contributor; *[livre]* collaborator; (*Pol*) collaborationist. ♦ **collaboration** *nf* collaboration (*à* on); contribution (*à* to). **en** ~ **avec** in collaboration with. ♦ **collaborer** (1) *vi* to collaborate (*à* on); to contribute (*à* to).
collage [kɔlaʒ] *nm* **(a)** sticking, gluing; pasting. ~ **de papiers peints** paperhanging; ~ **d'affiches** billposting. **(b)** (*Art*) collage.
collant, e [kɔlɑ̃, ɑ̃t] **1** *adj* (*ajusté*) tight-fitting, clinging; (*poisseux*) sticky. (*importun*) **être** ~* to cling. **2** *nm* (*maillot*) *[femme]* body stocking; *[danseur]* leotard; (*bas*) tights.
collation [kɔlasjɔ̃] *nf* snack.
colle [kɔl] *nf* **(a)** (*gén*) glue; (*à papier*) paste. **(b)** (*: *question*) poser*. **(c)** (*examen blanc*) mock oral exam; (*retenue*) detention.
collecteur, -trice [kɔlɛktœʀ, tʀis] **1** *nm,f* collector. **2** *nm*: **(égout)** ~ main sewer. ♦ **collecte** *nf* collection. ♦ **collecter** (1) *vt* to collect.
collectif, -ive [kɔlɛktif, iv] **1** *adj* (*gén*) collective; *billet* group; *hystérie, licenciements* mass; *installations* public. **immeuble** ~ block of flats. **2** *nm* (*Gram*) collective noun. (*Fin*) ~ **budgétaire** ≃ Finance Bill. ♦ **collectivement** *adv* (*gén*) collectively. ♦ **collectiviser** (1) *vt* to collectivize.
collection [kɔlɛksjɔ̃] *nf* (*gén*) collection; (*Comm*) *[échantillons]* line. ♦ **collectionner** (1) *vt* to collect. ♦ **collectionneur, -euse** *nm,f* collector.
collectivité [kɔlɛktivite] *nf* **(a)** (*groupe*) group; (*organisation*) body, organisation. **la** ~ the community; **vivre en** ~ to lead a communal life. **(b)** (*possession commune*) collective ownership.
collège [kɔlɛʒ] *nm* **(a)** (*Scol*) secondary school, high school (*US*); (†: *privé*) private school. ~ **technique** technical school. **(b)** (*Pol, Rel*) college. ~ **électoral** electoral college. ♦ **collégial, e,** *mpl* **-iaux** *adj* collegiate. ♦ **collégien, -ienne** *nm,f* schoolboy; schoolgirl; (*fig*) novice.
collègue [kɔlɛg] *nmf* colleague.
coller [kɔle] (1) **1** *vt* **(a)** *timbre* to stick; *affiche* to stick up (*à, sur* on); *enveloppe* to stick down; *papier peint* to hang. ~ **2 morceaux (ensemble)** to stick *ou* glue 2 pieces together; ~ **son oreille à la porte** to press one's ear to the door; **il colla l'armoire contre le mur** he stood the wardrobe right against the wall; **il m'a collé (après) toute la journée*** he clung to me all day. **(b)** (*) (*mettre*) to stick*, shove*; (*donner*) to give; (*écrire*) to write. **colle tes valises dans un coin** stick* *ou* shove* *ou* dump* your bags in a corner; **ils l'ont collé ministre** they've gone and made him a minister*; **on lui a collé la responsabilité** he's got stuck* *ou* landed* with the responsibility. **(c)** (*arg Scol*) (*consigner*) to give a detention to, keep in; (*poser une question*) to catch out; (*recaler*) to fail. **se faire** ~ to be given a detention; to be failed.
2 *vi* **(a)** (*être poisseux*) to be sticky; (*adhérer*) to stick (*à* to). ~ **au peloton** to stick to the pack; **robe qui colle au corps** tight-fitting *ou* clinging dress; ~ **au sujet** to stick to the subject. **(b)** (*: *bien marcher*) **ça colle?** O.K.?*; **ça ne colle pas** it doesn't work, there's sth wrong.
3 se ~ *vpr* **(a)** (*) *tâche, personne* to get stuck *ou* landed with*. **se** ~ **à (faire) qch** to get down to (doing) sth. **(b) se** ~ **à qn** *[danseur, importun]* to cling to sb; **se** ~ **devant la télé*** to be glued to the telly*; **ils sont toujours collés ensemble*** they are always together.
collet [kɔlɛ] *nm* (*piège*) noose; *[dent]* neck; (*Tech*) collar, flange. **prendre qn au** ~ to seize sb by the collar; **elle est très** ~ **monté** she's very strait-laced. ♦ **colleter** (4) *vt* to collar. (*lit, fig*) **se** ~ **avec*** to wrestle *ou* grapple with.
colleur, -euse [kɔlœʀ, øz] *nm,f*: ~ **d'affiches** billsticker; ~ **de papiers peints** wallpaperer.
collier [kɔlje] *nm* *[femme]* necklace; *[maire]* chain; *[animal]* collar; (*Tech*) collar. ~ **de fleurs** garland of flowers; **reprendre le** ~* to get back into harness; ~ **(de barbe)** *narrow beard along the line of the jaw.*
collimateur [kɔlimatœʀ] *nm* collimator. (*lit, fig*)

avoir qn dans son ~ to have sb in one's sights.
colline [kɔlin] *nf* hill.
collision [kɔlizjɔ̃] *nf [véhicules]* collision; (*fig*) clash. **entrer en ~** to collide (*avec* with).
colloque [kɔlɔk] *nm* colloquium.
collusion [kɔlyzjɔ̃] *nf* collusion.
collyre [kɔliʀ] *nm* eye lotion.
colmater [kɔlmate] (1) *vt fuite* to seal (off); *fissure* to fill in, plug. (*fig, Mil*) **~ une brèche** to seal a gap.
colombe [kɔlɔ̃b] *nf* dove. ♦ **colombier** *nm* dovecote.
Colombie [kɔlɔ̃bi] *nf* Colombia. ♦ **colombien, -ienne** *adj*, **C~(ne)** *nm(f)* Colombian.
colon [kɔlɔ̃] *nm* (*pionnier*) settler, colonist; (*enfant*) child, boarder; (*arg Mil*) colonel.
côlon [kolɔ̃] *nm* (*Anat*) colon.
colonel [kɔlɔnɛl] *nm* colonel; (*armée de l'air*) group captain.
colonie [kɔlɔni] *nf* (*gén*) colony. **~ de vacances** holiday camp. ♦ **colonial, e,** *mpl* **-aux 1** *adj* colonial. **2** *nm* (*habitant*) colonial. ♦ **colonialisme** *nm* colonialism. ♦ **colonialiste** *adj, nmf* colonialist.
coloniser [kɔlɔnize] (1) *vt* to colonize. **les colonisés** the colonized peoples. ♦ **colonisateur, -trice 1** *adj* colonizing. **2** *nm,f* colonizer. ♦ **colonisation** *nf* colonization.
colonne [kɔlɔn] *nf* (*gén*) column. **~ blindée** armoured column; **~ montante** rising main; **~ de secours** rescue party; **~ vertébrale** spine, spinal column. ♦ **colonnade** *nf* colonnade. ♦ **colonnette** *nf* small column.
colorer [kɔlɔʀe] (1) **1** *vt substance* to colour; *tissu* to dye; *bois* to stain; *récit* to colour (*de* with). **~ qch en bleu** to colour sth blue. **2 se ~** *vpr [tomate, visage]* to turn red. **le ciel se colore de rose** the sky takes on a rosy tinge; (*fig*) **se ~ de** to be coloured *ou* tinged with. ♦ **colorant, e** *adj, nm* colouring. ♦ **coloration** *nf* **(a)** (*action*) colouring; dyeing; staining. **(b)** (*couleur*) colouring, colour; *[peau]* colouring; *[voix]* coloration. ♦ **coloré, e** *adj teint* ruddy; *objet* coloured; *foule, récit* colourful.
colorier [kɔlɔʀje] (7) *vt* to colour (in). ♦ **coloriage** *nm* (*action*) colouring; (*dessin*) coloured drawing. ♦ **coloris** *nm* (*gén*) colour, shade; *[peau]* colouring.
colosse [kɔlɔs] *nm* (*personne*) giant; (*institution*) colossus, giant. ♦ **colossal, e,** *mpl* **-aux** *adj* colossal, huge.
colporter [kɔlpɔʀte] (1) *vt* to hawk, peddle. ♦ **colportage** *nm* hawking, peddling. ♦ **colporteur, -euse** *nm,f* hawker, pedlar. **~ de fausses nouvelles** newsmonger.
coltiner [kɔltine] (1) **1** *vt colis* to carry *ou* lug* around. **2 se ~*** *vpr colis* to lug around*, carry; (‡) *travail, personne* to get stuck *ou* landed with*.
colza [kɔlza] *nm* rape(seed).
coma [kɔma] *nm* (*Méd*) coma. **dans le ~** in a coma. ♦ **comateux, -euse** *adj*: **état ~** comatose state.
combat [kɔ̃ba] *nm* (*gén*) fight; (*Mil*) battle; (*fig*) fight, struggle; (*Sport*) match. **tué au ~** killed in action; **aller au ~** to go into battle; **les ~s continuent** the fighting goes on; **~ de rues** street fighting; **~ singulier** single combat. ♦ **combatif, -ive** *adj troupes* ready to fight; *personne* of a fighting spirit; *humeur* fighting. ♦ **combativité** *nf [troupe]* readiness to fight; *[personne]* fighting spirit. ♦ **combattant, e 1** *adj* fighting, combatant. **2** *nm,f [guerre]* combatant; *[bagarre]* brawler. ♦ **combattre** (41) **1** *vt* to fight; (*fig*) *théorie, vice* to combat, fight (against). **2** *vi* to fight.
combien [kɔ̃bjɛ̃] **1** *adv*: **~ de** (*quantité*) how much; (*nombre*) how many; **~ y en a-t-il (en moins)?** (*quantité*) how much (less) is there (of it)?; (*nombre*) how many (fewer) are there (of them)?; **(depuis) ~ de temps?** how long?; **~ vous avez raison!** how right you are!; **~ d'ennui je vous cause** what a lot of trouble I'm causing you; **~ mesure-t-il?** how big is it?; **ça va faire une différence de ~?** what will the difference be?; **~ y a-t-il d'ici à la ville?** how far is it from here to the town? **2** *nm* (*) (*rang*) **le ~ êtes-vous?** where were you placed?; (*date*) **le ~ sommes-nous?** what date is it?; (*fréquence*) **il y en a tous les ~?** how often do they come?
combinaison [kɔ̃binɛzɔ̃] *nf* **(a)** (*gén, Math*) combination. **~ (ministérielle)** government. **(b)** (*vêtement*) *[femme]* slip; *[aviateur]* flying suit; *[mécanicien]* boiler suit. **(c)** (*astuce*) device; (*manigance*) scheme. ♦ **combinard, e** *adj, nm,f* (*péj*) **il est ~** he's a schemer. ♦ **combine** *nf* (*astuce*) trick; (*péj*) scheme. **il est dans la ~** he's in on it*. ♦ **combiné** *nm* (*Chim*) compound; *[téléphone]* receiver; (*Sport*) combination. ♦ **combiner** (1) **1** *vt* (*grouper*) to combine (*avec* with); (*élaborer*) to devise, work out. **2 se ~** *vpr* to combine (*avec* with).
comble [kɔ̃bl(ə)] **1** *adj* packed. **2** *nm* **(a) le ~ de** the height of; **au ~ du désespoir** in the depths of despair; **pour ~ (de malheur) il ...** to cap *ou* crown it all he ...; **c'est le** *ou* **un ~!** that's the last straw! **(b)** (*charpente*) roof timbers. (*pièce*) **les ~s** the attic.
comblement [kɔ̃bləmɑ̃] *nm [cavité]* filling(-in).
combler [kɔ̃ble] (1) *vt* **(a)** *trou* to fill in; *déficit* to make good; *lacune* to fill. **~ son retard** to make up lost time. **(b)** *désir, besoin* to fulfil; *personne* to gratify. **c'est une femme comblée** she has all that she could wish for; **~ qn de** *cadeaux* to shower sb with; *joie* to fill sb with; **comblé d'honneurs** laden with honours; **vraiment, vous nous comblez!** really, you're too good to us!
combustible [kɔ̃bystibl(ə)] **1** *adj* combustible. **2** *nm* fuel. ♦ **combustion** *nf* combustion.
comédie [kɔmedi] *nf* (*Théât*) comedy. **~ musicale** musical; **de ~** (*Théât*) comedy; (*fig*) comic; (*fig*) **jouer la ~** to put on an act; **faire la ~** to make a fuss *ou* a scene. ♦ **comédien, -ienne** *nm,f* (comedy) actor *ou* actress; (*hypocrite*) sham; (*pitre*) show-off.
comestible [kɔmɛstibl(ə)] **1** *adj* edible. **2** *nmpl*: **~s** (fine) foods, delicatessen.
comète [kɔmɛt] *nf* comet.
comique [kɔmik] **1** *adj* (*Théât*) comic; (*fig*) comical. **2** *nm* **(a)** comic aspect *ou* character. **d'un ~ irrésistible** hilariously funny; **le ~ de la chose, c'est que ...** the funny thing about it is that ... . **(b)** (*Littérat*) **le ~** comedy; **~ de caractère** character comedy; **avoir le sens du ~** to have a sense of the comic. **(c)** (*artiste*) comic, comedian; (*dramaturge*) comedy writer. ♦ **comiquement** *adv* comically.
comité [kɔmite] *nm* (*gén*) committee. (*fig*) **se réunir en petit ~** to have a small get-together; **~ directeur** board of management.
commandant [kɔmɑ̃dɑ̃] *nm* **(a)** (*gén*) commander, commandant; (*armée de terre*) major; (*armée de l'air*) squadron leader. **(b)** (*Aviat, Naut*) captain. **~ en second** second in command.
commande [kɔmɑ̃d] *nf* **(a)** (*Comm*) order. **passer une ~** to put in an order (*de* for); **en ~** on order; **fait sur ~** made to order. **(b)** (*Tech*) (*action*) control, controlling. (*dispositif*) **~(s)** controls; **être/se mettre aux ~s** to be in/take control. **(c) de ~** *sourire* forced, artificial; (*Art*) *œuvre* commissioned; **agir sur ~** to act on orders; **s'amuser sur ~** to enjoy o.s. to order; **ouvrage écrit/composé sur ~** commissioned work/composition.
commandement [kɔmɑ̃dmɑ̃] *nm* (*direction, ordre, état-major*) command; (*Rel*) commandment. **prendre le ~ de** to take command of; **ton de ~** commanding tone; **à mon ~** on my command.
commander [kɔmɑ̃de] (1) **1** *vt* **(a)** *obéissance* to order, command. **il me commanda le silence** he

ordered *ou* commanded me to keep quiet; ~ **l'admiration** to compel admiration; **la prudence commande que ...** prudence demands that ... . **(b)** *marchandise, repas* to order; (*Art*) *œuvre* to commission. **(c)** *armée* to command; (*emploi absolu*) to be in command *ou* in charge. **je n'aime pas qu'on me commande** I don't like to be ordered about; **ce bouton commande la sirène** this switch controls the siren. **2** ~ **à** *vt indir passions, muscles* to have command *ou* control over. **3 se** ~ *vpr [pièces]* to lead into one another; *[personne]* to control o.s. **ces choses-là ne se commandent pas** you can't help these things. ♦ **commandeur** *nm* commander (*of an Order*). ♦ **commanditaire** *nm* sleeping partner. ♦ **commanditer** (1) *vt* (*Comm: financer*) to finance.

commando [kɔmɑ̃do] *nm* (*groupe, homme*) commando.

comme [kɔm] **1** *conj* **(a)** (*temps*) as; (*cause*) as, since. **(juste)** ~ **le rideau se levait** (just) as the curtain was rising; ~ **il pleut** seeing that it's raining, since it's raining. **(b)** (*comparaison*) as, like (*devant n et pron*). **il pense** ~ **nous** he thinks as we do *ou* like us; **c'est un homme** ~ **lui qu'il nous faut** we need a man like him *ou* such as him; **en ville** ~ **à la campagne** in town and *ou* as well as in the country; **il écrit** ~ **il parle** he writes as *ou* the way he speaks; **dur** ~ **du fer** (as) hard as iron; **il y eut** ~ **une lueur** there was a sort *ou* kind of light. **(c)** (*en tant que*) as. ~ **étudiant** as a student. **(d)** ~ **si** as if, as though; ~ **pour faire** as if to do; ~ **si nous ne savions pas!** as if we didn't know!; ~ **quoi il ne fallait pas l'écouter** which goes to show that you shouldn't have listened to him; **il était** ~ **fasciné** it was as though *ou* as if he were fascinated. **(e)** ~ **cela** like that; ~ **ci** ~ **ça** so-so, (fair to) middling; **alors,** ~ **ça, vous nous quittez?** so you're leaving us?; ~ **il vous plaira** as you wish; ~ **de juste** naturally; ~ **par hasard, il était absent** he just HAPPENED to be away; ~ **il faut** *manger* properly; *personne* decent; **c'était amusant** ~ **tout** it was terribly funny.

2 *adv*: ~ **ces enfants sont bruyants!** how noisy these children are!; ~ **il fait beau!** what a lovely day!, what lovely weather!

commémorer [kɔmemɔʀe] (1) *vt* to commemorate. ♦ **commémoratif, -ive** *adj* commemorative, memorial. ♦ **commémoration** *nf* commemoration. **en** ~ **de** in commemoration of.

commencer [kɔmɑ̃se] (3) **1** *vt* to begin, start, commence. ~ **un élève (en maths)** to start a pupil (off) (in maths). **2** *vi* to begin, start, commence. **le concert va** ~ the concert is about to begin *ou* start; **ça commence bien!** that's a good start!; **pour** ~ to begin *ou* start with; ~ **à** (*ou* **de**) **faire** to begin *ou* start to do *ou* doing; **ça commence à bien faire*** it's getting a bit much*; ~ **par qch/par faire qch** to start *ou* begin with sth/by doing sth. ♦ **commençant, e 1** *adj* beginning. **2** *nm,f* beginner. ♦ **commencement** *nm* (*début*) beginning; (*départ*) start. **au/dès le** ~ in/from the beginning, at/from the outset *ou* start; **du** ~ **à la fin** from beginning to end, from start to finish; ~**s** *[science, métier]* beginnings.

comment [kɔmɑ̃] **1** *adv* **(a)** how. ~ **appelles-tu cela?** what do you call that?; ~ **allez-vous?** how are you?; ~ **faire?** how shall we do it?; ~ **se fait-il que ...?** how is it that ...? **(b)** (*excl*) ~? pardon?, sorry?, what?*; ~ **cela?** what do you mean?; ~, **il est mort?** what! is he dead?; **et** ~**!*** not half!*, and how!*; ~ **donc!** by all means!, of course! **2** *nm*: **le** ~ the how.

commentaire [kɔmɑ̃tɛʀ] *nm* (*remarque*) comment; (*gén, Littérat: exposé*) commentary (*sur, de* on). ~**s de presse** press comments; **et pas de** ~**s!** and that's final!; **ça se passe de** ~**s** it speaks for itself. ♦ **commentateur, -trice** *nm,f* (*gén*) commentator. ♦ **commenter** (1) *vt poème, match* to give a commentary on; *conduite, événement* to comment on.

commérage [kɔmeʀaʒ] *nm*: ~**(s)** gossip.

commerçant, e [kɔmɛʀsɑ̃, ɑ̃t] **1** *adj nation* trading; *ville* commercial; *rue* shopping. **il est très** ~ he's got good business sense. **2** *nm* shopkeeper, tradesman. **3** *nf* shopkeeper.

commerce [kɔmɛʀs(ə)] *nm* **(a) le** ~ trade, commerce; (*affaires*) business. (*commerçants*) **le petit** ~ small shopkeepers; **opération de** ~ commercial operation; ~ **de gros/demi-gros/détail** wholesale/retail-wholesale/retail trade; **faire du** ~ **avec** to trade with; **dans le** ~ *objet* in the shops; **vendu hors-**~ sold direct to the public. **(b)** (*boutique*) business. **(c)** (*littér*) (*compagnie*) company; (*rapport*) dealings. ♦ **commercer** (3) *vi* to trade (*avec* with). ♦ **commercial, e,** *mpl* **-iaux 1** *adj* commercial. **2** *nf* (*véhicule*) (light) van. ♦ **commercialisation** *nf* marketing. ♦ **commercialiser** (1) *vt* to market.

commère [kɔmɛʀ] *nf* (*péj: bavarde*) gossip.

commettre [kɔmɛtʀ(ə)] (56) **1** *vt* **(a)** *crime* to commit; *erreur* to make. **(b)** (*confier*) ~ **qch à qn** to commit *ou* entrust sth to sb. **(c)** (*nommer*) to appoint, nominate (*à* to). **2 se** ~ *vpr* (*péj*) to lower o.s. **se** ~ **avec** to associate with.

commis [kɔmi] *nm* (shop) assistant. ~ **de bureau** office clerk; ~ **voyageur** commercial traveller.

commisération [kɔmizeʀɑsjɔ̃] *nf* commiseration.

commissaire [kɔmisɛʀ] *nm (police)* (police) superintendent; (*Sport etc*) steward; (*envoyé*) representative; *[commission]* commissioner. (*Naut*) ~ **du bord** purser; ~**-priseur** *nm, pl* ~**s-**~**s** auctioneer. ♦ **commissariat** *nm* **(a)** (*poste*) ~ **(de police)** police station. **(b)** (*ministère*) board.

commission [kɔmisjɔ̃] *nf* **(a)** (*nommée*) commission; (*comité*) committee. **travail en** ~ work in committee. **(b)** (*message*) message. **(c)** (*course*) errand; (*Comm, Jur: mandat*) commission. (*emplettes*) ~**s** shopping; **faire les** ~**s** to do the *ou* go shopping. **(d)** (*pourcentage*) commission (*sur* on). ♦ **commissionnaire** *nm* (*livreur*) delivery man; (*messager*) messenger; (*Comm: intermédiaire*) agent, broker. ♦ **commissionner** (1) *vt* to commission.

commissure [kɔmisyʀ] *nf [bouche]* corner.

commode [kɔmɔd] **1** *adj* **(a)** (*gén*) convenient; *outil* handy (*pour faire* for doing). **(b)** (*facile*) easy. ~ **à vivre** easy to get on with; **il n'est pas** ~ he's an awkward customer. **2** *nf* (*meuble*) chest of drawers. ♦ **commodément** *adv s'asseoir* comfortably; *transporter* easily. ♦ **commodité** *nf* convenience.

commotion [kɔmosjɔ̃] *nf* (*secousse*) shock; (*révolution*) upheaval. ~ **cérébrale** concussion. ♦ **commotionner** (1) *vt*: ~ **qn** to give sb a shock, shake sb.

commuer [kɔmɥe] (1) *vt peine* to commute (*en* to).

commun, e[1] [kɔmœ̃, yn] **1** *adj* **(a)** (*gén, Math*) common; *effort, démarche* joint; *ami* mutual; *pièce* shared. **d'un** ~ **accord** of one accord; **il y a une cuisine** ~**e** there is a communal *ou* shared kitchen; **être** ~ **à** to be shared by; **la vie** ~**e** *[couple]* conjugal life; *[communauté]* communal life; **ils n'ont rien de** ~ they have nothing in common (*avec* with); **il n'y a pas de** ~**e mesure entre eux** there's no possible comparison between them. **(b) avoir qch en** ~ to have sth in common; **faire la cuisine en** ~ to share (in) the cooking; **vivre en** ~ to live communally; **mettre ses ressources en** ~ to share *ou* pool one's resources. **(c)** *accident, métal, (péj) manières* common; *opinion* commonly held, widespread. **peu** ~ uncommon, unusual. **2** *nm* **(a) le** ~ **des mortels** the common run of people. **(b)** (*bâtiments*) **les** ~**s** the outbuildings. ♦ **communément** *adv* commonly.

communauté [kɔmynote] *nf* **(a)** *[idées]* identity;

[culture] community. **(b)** (*Pol, Rel etc*) community. ~ **urbaine** urban community; **vivre en** ~ to live communally; **mettre qch en** ~ to pool sth; **la C~ Économique Européenne** the European Economic Community. **(c)** (*entre époux*) shared estate. ♦ **communautaire** *adj* community; (*Pol*) Community.

commune² [kɔmyn] *nf* **(a)** (*ville*) town; (*territoire*) district; (*autorités*) town (*ou* district) council. **(b)** (*Brit Pol*) **les C~s** the (House of) Commons. ♦ **communal, e,** *mpl* **-aux** *adj* (*Admin*) district; (*local*) local.

communicatif, -ive [kɔmynikatif, iv] *adj rire* infectious; *personne* communicative.

communication [kɔmynikɑsjɔ̃] *nf* **(a)** (*gén, fig: liaison*) communication. **les ~s sont coupées** communications are cut (off); **porte de** ~ communicating door; **être en** ~ **avec** to be in communication *ou* contact with; **mettre qn en** ~ **avec qn** to put sb in touch *ou* contact with sb. **(b)** *[fait]* communication; *[dossier]* transmission. **avoir** ~ **d'un fait** to be informed of a fact; **demander** ~ **d'un dossier** to ask for a file. **(c)** (*message*) message, communication; (*Univ: exposé*) paper. **(d)** ~ **(téléphonique)** (phone) call; **mettre qn en** ~ **(avec)** to put sb through (to), connect sb (with); ~ **en PCV** reverse charge call, collect call (*US*); **je n'ai pas pu avoir la** ~ I couldn't get through.

communier [kɔmynje] (7) *vi* (*Rel*) to receive communion. ~ **dans** *sentiment* to be united in. ♦ **communiant, e** *nm,f* communicant. **premier** ~ child making his first communion. ♦ **communion** *nf* (*Rel, fig*) communion. **faire sa (première)** ~ to make one's first communion; (*fig*) **être en** ~ **avec** *personne* to be in communion with; *sentiments* to be in sympathy with.

communiquer [kɔmynike] (1) **1** *vt nouvelle, mouvement, peur* to communicate; *dossier* (*donner*) to give; (*envoyer*) to send; *maladie* to pass on, give; *lumière, chaleur* to transmit (*à* to). **2** *vi [personnes, pièces]* to communicate (*avec* with). **3 se** ~ *vpr [feu etc]* **se** ~ **à** to spread to. ♦ **communiqué** *nm* communiqué. ~ **de presse** press release.

communisme [kɔmynism(ə)] *nm* communism. ♦ **communisant, e 1** *adj* communistic. **2** *nm,f* communist sympathizer, fellow traveller. ♦ **communiste** *adj, nmf* communist.

commuter [kɔmyte] (1) *vt* to commute. ♦ **commutateur** *nm* (*Élec*) switch. ♦ **commutation** *nf* commutation.

compact, e [kɔ̃pakt, akt(ə)] *adj* dense; *véhicule, appareil* compact; *majorité* solid.

compagnie [kɔ̃paɲi] *nf* **(a)** (*présence*) company. **en** ~ **de** in company with; **en bonne/mauvaise** ~ in good/bad company; **tenir** ~ **à qn** to keep sb company; **bonsoir la** ~! goodnight all! **(b)** (*Comm, Mil, Théât*) company; *[perdreaux]* covey. **la banque X et** ~ the bank of X and company; **tout ça, c'est voleurs et** ~* they're all the same thieving lot*. ♦ **compagne** *nf* companion; (*maîtresse*) ladyfriend; *[animal]* mate. ~ **de classe** classmate. ♦ **compagnon** *nm* **(a)** (*gén*) companion. ~ **de travail** fellow worker, workmate; ~ **d'armes** companion- *ou* comrade-in-arms; ~ **de bord** shipmate; ~ **de voyage** travelling companion; ~ **de misère** companion in suffering. **(b)** (*ouvrier*) craftsman, journeyman†.

comparaison [kɔ̃paʀɛzɔ̃] *nf* **(a)** (*gén*) comparison (*à* to, *avec* with). **mettre qch en** ~ **avec** to compare sth with; **il n'y a pas de** ~ **(entre)** there is no comparison (between); **en** ~ **(de)** in comparison (with); **il est sans** ~ **le meilleur** he is far and away the best. **(b)** (*Gram*) comparison; (*Littérat*) simile, comparison. ♦ **comparable** *adj* comparable (*à* to, *avec* with).

comparaître [kɔ̃paʀɛtʀ(ə)] (57) *vi* (*Jur*) to appear.

comparer [kɔ̃paʀe] (1) *vt* (*confronter*) to compare (*à, avec* with); (*identifier*) to compare, liken (*à* to). **ça ne se compare pas** there's no comparison. ♦ **comparatif, -ive** *adj, nm* comparative. ♦ **comparativement** *adv* comparatively. ~ **à** by comparison with. ♦ **comparé, e** *adj* comparative.

comparse [kɔ̃paʀs(ə)] *nmf* (*Théât*) walker-on; (*péj*) stooge. (*péj, fig*) **rôle de** ~ minor part.

compartiment [kɔ̃paʀtimɑ̃] *nm* compartment. ♦ **compartimentage** *nm [armoire]* partitioning; *[administration]* compartmentalization. ♦ **compartimenter** (1) *vt* to partition; to compartmentalize.

comparution [kɔ̃paʀysjɔ̃] *nf* (*Jur*) appearance.

compas [kɔ̃pa] *nm* (*Géom*) (pair of) compasses; (*Naut*) compass. (*fig*) **avoir le** ~ **dans l'œil** to have an accurate eye.

compassion [kɔ̃pɑsjɔ̃] *nf* compassion.

compatible [kɔ̃patibl(ə)] *adj* compatible. ♦ **compatibilité** *nf* compatibility.

compatir [kɔ̃patiʀ] (2) *vi* to sympathize. ~ **à la douleur de qn** to sympathize *ou* commiserate with sb in his grief. ♦ **compatissant, e** *adj* compassionate, sympathetic.

compatriote [kɔ̃patʀijɔt] *nmf* compatriot, fellow countryman (*ou* woman).

compenser [kɔ̃pɑ̃se] (1) **1** *vt perte* to make good, compensate for, offset; *infirmité* to compensate (for). ~ **qch par** to make up for sth with; **pour** ~ to compensate, to make up for it. **2 se** ~ *vpr [forces]* to compensate each other; *[gains et pertes]* to cancel each other out. ♦ **compensation** *nf* (*gén, Phys, Psych*) compensation; (*équilibrage*) balancing. **en** ~ **(des dégâts)** in compensation (for the damage). ♦ **compensatoire** *adj* compensatory. ♦ **compensé, e** *adj semelles* platform.

compère [kɔ̃pɛʀ] *nm* **(a)** (*complice*) accomplice; (*aux enchères*) puffer. **(b)** (†: *ami*) comrade.

compétence [kɔ̃petɑ̃s] *nf* (*gén, Jur*) competence. ~s abilities; **ce n'est pas de ma** ~ that's not (in) my sphere. ♦ **compétent, e** *adj* competent, capable; (*Jur*) competent. ~ **en** competent in; **l'autorité ~e** the authority concerned.

compétition [kɔ̃petisjɔ̃] *nf* **(a)** (*épreuve*) event. (*activité*) **faire de la** ~ to go in for competitive sport; **la** ~ **automobile** motor racing. **(b)** (*concurrence*) competition. **être en** ~ to be competing *ou* in competition (*avec* with). ♦ **compétitif, -ive** *adj* competitive. ♦ **compétitivité** *nf* competitiveness.

compiler [kɔ̃pile] (1) *vt* to compile. ♦ **compilateur, -trice** *nm,f* compiler. ♦ **compilation** *nf* compilation.

complainte [kɔ̃plɛ̃t] *nf* lament.

complaire [kɔ̃plɛʀ] (54) **1** ~ **à** *vt indir* to (try to) please. **2 se** ~ *vpr*: **se** ~ **dans qch/à faire qch** to delight *ou* revel in sth/in doing sth.

complaisance [kɔ̃plɛzɑ̃s] *nf* (*obligeance*) kindness (*envers* to, towards); (*indulgence*) indulgence; (*connivence*) connivance; (*fatuité*) smugness, complacency. ♦ **complaisamment** *adv* obligingly, kindly; smugly, complacently. ♦ **complaisant, e** *adj* kind; indulgent; conniving; smug; complacent. **prêter une oreille ~e à qn/qch** to lend a willing ear to sb/sth.

complément [kɔ̃plemɑ̃] *nm* **(a)** (*gén, Bio, Math*) complement; (*reste*) rest, remainder. ~ **d'information** further *ou* additional information. **(b)** (*Gram*) (*gén*) complement. ~ **circonstanciel de lieu** adverbial phrase of place; ~ **(d'objet) direct/indirect** direct/indirect object; ~ **d'agent** agent; ~ **de nom** possessive phrase. ♦ **complémentaire** *adj* (*gén, Math*) complementary; (*additionnel*) supplementary; *renseignement* further, additional.

complet, -ète [kɔ̃plɛ, ɛt] **1** *adj* **(a)** (*exhaustif*) (*gén*) complete, full; *rapport* comprehensive; *examen* thorough. **le dossier est-il ~?** is the file complete? **(b)** *échec, obscurité* complete, utter.

(c) (*après n*) *acteur* complete. **athlète** ~ all-round *ou* complete athlete. **(d)** *train* full. (*écriteau*) '~' *[hôtel]* 'no vacancies'; *[parking]* 'full (up)'; **eh bien! c'est** ~!* well, that's the limit! **2** *nm* **(a) nous sommes au** ~ we are all here; **la famille au grand** ~ the whole *ou* entire family. **(b)** ~**(-veston)** suit. ♦ **complètement** *adv* *démonter* completely; *lire* right through; *étudier* fully, thoroughly; *citer* in full; *faux* completely, utterly. ~ **nu** stark naked.

compléter [kɔ̃plete] (6) **1** *vt* **(a)** (*terminer*) *somme, effectifs* to make up; *collection, dossier* to complete; *études, repas* to round off. **et pour** ~ **le tableau** and to crown it all *ou* as a finishing touch. **(b)** (*augmenter*) *formation* to complement, supplement; *garde-robe* to add to. **2 se** ~ *vpr [caractères, fonctions]* to complement one another.

complexe [kɔ̃plɛks(ə)] *adj, nm* complex. ~ **d'Œdipe** Oedipus complex; **être bourré de** ~**s*** to have loads of hang-ups*. ♦ **complexer** (1) *vt*: **ça le complexe** it gives him a complex; **être très complexé** to be full of complexes *ou* hang-ups*. ♦ **complexité** *nf* complexity.

complication [kɔ̃plikɑsjɔ̃] *nf* (*complexité*) complexity; (*ennui*) complication. (*Méd*) ~s complications; **faire des** ~s to make life difficult *ou* complicated.

complice [kɔ̃plis] **1** *adj regard* knowing; *attitude* conniving. **être** ~ **de qch** to be (a) party to sth. **2** *nmf* (*criminel*) accomplice; (*amant*) lover; (*maîtresse*) mistress. ♦ **complicité** *nf* (*Jur, fig*) complicity.

compliment [kɔ̃plimɑ̃] *nm* (*louange*) compliment. ~s (*félicitations*) congratulations; (*hommages*) compliments; **faire des** ~**s à qn (pour)** to compliment *ou* congratulate sb (on); **avec les** ~**s de la direction** with the compliments of the management. ♦ **complimenter** (1) *vt* to congratulate, compliment (*pour, sur, de* on).

compliquer [kɔ̃plike] (1) **1** *vt* to complicate. **2 se** ~ *vpr* to become *ou* get complicated. **se** ~ **l'existence** to make life difficult *ou* complicated for o.s. ♦ **compliqué, e** *adj* (*gén*) complicated; *esprit* tortuous; (*Méd*) *fracture* compound. **ce n'est pas** ~, **moi je pars** that simplifies the problem - I'm leaving.

complot [kɔ̃plo] *nm* plot. ♦ **comploter** (1) *vti* to plot (*de faire* to do, *contre* against). ♦ **comploteur** *nm* plotter.

comporter [kɔ̃pɔrte] (1) **1** *vt* (*consister en*) to be composed of, consist of, comprise; (*être muni de*) *dispositif, exceptions* to have, include; (*impliquer*) *risques* to entail, involve. **2 se** ~ *vpr [personne]* to behave (*en* like); *[voiture]* to perform. **notre équipe s'est très bien comportée** our team played very well *ou* put up a good performance. ♦ **comportement** *nm* (*gén*) behaviour (*envers* towards); *[pneus]* performance.

composer [kɔ̃poze] (1) **1** *vt* **(a)** (*confectionner*) *plat* to concoct, make (up); *équipe* to select; *assemblée* to form, set up; *lettre* to write, compose; *symphonie* to compose; *tableau* to paint; *numéro de téléphone* to dial; *programme* to work out, draw up; *bouquet* to arrange, make up; *étalage* to lay out, set up; (*Typ*) to set. **(b)** (*constituer*) *ensemble, produit* to make up, form. **(c)** (*littér*) ~ **son visage** to assume an affected expression. **2** *vi* **(a)** (*Scol*) to do a test. ~ **en anglais** to take an English test. **(b)** (*traiter*) to compromise (*avec* with). **3 se** ~ *vpr*: **se** ~ **de** *ou* **être composé de** to be composed of, consist of, comprise. ♦ **composant, e** *adj, nm,f* component. ♦ **composé, e 1** *adj* compound; (*guindé*) studied. **2** *nm* (*Chim, Gram*) compound; (*fig*) combination, mixture.

composite [kɔ̃pozit] *adj éléments* heterogeneous; *foule* motley; (*Archit*) composite.

compositeur, -trice [kɔ̃pozitœʀ, tʀis] *nm,f* (*Mus*) composer; (*Typ*) typesetter.

composition [kɔ̃pozisjɔ̃] *nf* **(a)** (*action: V composer*) concocting, making(-up); formation, setting-up; selection; writing; composition; painting; drawing up; laying out; (type)setting. **une œuvre de ma** ~ a work of my own composition. **(b)** (*résultat, œuvre*) composition; (*structure*) structure. **quelle est la** ~ **du gâteau?** what is the cake made of? **(c)** (*Scol: examen*) test, exam. ~ **de français** (*en classe*) French test *ou* exam; (*à l'examen*) French paper; (*rédaction*) ~ **française** French essay. **(d) venir à** ~ to come to terms; **amener qn à** ~ to get sb to come to terms.

compost [kɔ̃pɔst] *nm* compost.

composter [kɔ̃pɔste] (1) *vt* (*dater*) to (date) stamp; (*poinçonner*) to punch.

compote [kɔ̃pɔt] *nf* (*Culin*) stewed fruit, compote. ~ **de pommes** stewed apples, compote of apples; **en** ~* *jambes* like jelly* *ou* cotton wool; *visage* black and blue. ♦ **compotier** *nm* fruit dish.

comprendre [kɔ̃pʀɑ̃dʀ(ə)] (58) *vt* **(a)** (*être composé de*) to be composed of, consist of, comprise. **le loyer ne comprend pas le chauffage** the rent doesn't include *ou* cover (the) heating.

(b) *problème, langue, personne* to understand. **vous m'avez mal compris** you've misunderstood me; **il ne comprend pas la plaisanterie** he can't take a joke; **c'est à n'y rien** ~ it's beyond me, I can't understand it; **se faire** ~ to make o.s. understood; **j'espère que je me suis bien fait** ~ I hope I've made myself quite clear; **tu comprends, ce que je veux c'est ...** you see, what I want is ...; **dois-je** ~ **que ...?** am I to take it *ou* understand that ...?

(c) (*concevoir*) (*gén*) to understand; *point de vue* to see; *difficultés* to appreciate; *gravité* to realize. **c'est comme ça que je le comprends** that's how I see *ou* understand it; **ça se comprend** it's quite understandable; **il m'a fait** ~ **que je devais faire attention** he made me realize that I should be careful.

♦ **compréhensible** *adj* (*clair*) comprehensible; (*concevable*) understandable. ♦ **compréhensif, -ive** *adj* (*tolérant*) understanding; (*Logique*) comprehensive. ♦ **compréhension** *nf* understanding; (*Logique*) comprehension.

compression [kɔ̃pʀesjɔ̃] *nf* (*gén, Aut, Phys*) compression; (*Écon*) reduction, cutback (*de* in). ~**s budgétaires** cutbacks in spending, budget restrictions. ♦ **compresse** *nf* compress. ♦ **compresseur** *nm* compressor. ♦ **compressible** *adj* (*Phys*) compressible; *dépenses* reducible.

comprimer [kɔ̃pʀime] (1) *vt* **(a)** *air, artère* to compress; (*pour emballer*) to press *ou* pack tightly together. **ça lui comprimait l'estomac** it was pressing into his stomach; **comprimés dans l'ascenseur** packed tightly together in the lift. **(b)** *dépenses, personnel* to cut down, reduce; *larmes, colère* to hold back. ♦ **comprimé** *nm* (*Pharm*) tablet.

compris, e [kɔ̃pʀi, iz] *adj* **(a)** (*inclus*) **emballage (y)/non** ~ including/excluding packaging, packaging included/not included. **(b)** (*situé*) **être** ~ **entre** to be contained between *ou* by; **les chapitres** ~ **entre les pages 12 et 145** the chapters contained *ou* included in pages 12 to 145. **(c)** (*d'accord*) **(c'est)** ~! (it's) agreed!; **pars tout de suite,** ~! go immediately, understand? *ou* is that understood?

compromettre [kɔ̃pʀɔmɛtʀ(ə)] (56) **1** *vt réputation, chances* to compromise, jeopardize. **2 se** ~ *vpr* to compromise o.s. ♦ **compromettant, e** *adj lettres* compromising. **ce n'est pas très** ~ you won't commit yourself to much, there's no great commitment involved. ♦ **compromis** *nm* compromise. ♦ **compromission** *nf* shady deal.

comptabiliser [kɔ̃tabilize] (1) *vt* (*Fin*) to post. ♦ **comptabilité** *nf* (*science*) accountancy, book-keeping; (*comptes*) accounts, books; (*service*) accounts department; (*profession*) accountancy. **s'occuper de la ~** to keep the books. ♦ **comptable 1** *adj* (*Fin*) accounts. **2** *nmf* accountant.

comptant [kɔ̃tɑ̃] **1** *adv payer* (in) cash; *acheter* for cash. **verser 10 F ~** to pay 10 francs down. **2** *nm* (*argent*) cash. **vente au ~** cash sale.

compte [kɔ̃t] **1** *nm* **(a)** (*calcul*) count. **faire le ~ de** *prisonniers* to count (up), make a count of; *dépenses* to calculate, work out.

(b) (*nombre*) number. le **~** y est (*paiement*) that's the right amount; (*inventaire*) that's the right number; **~ rond** round number *ou* figure; **nous sommes loin du ~** we are a long way short of the target.

(c) (*Banque, comptabilité*) account; (*facture*) account, bill. **faire/tenir ses ~s** to do/keep one's accounts *ou* books; **être en ~ avec qn** to have an *ou* be in account with sb; **donner son ~ à un employé** (*payer*) to settle up with an employee; (*renvoyer*) to give an employee his cards*; **il avait son ~*** (*mort*) he'd had it*; (*soûl*) he'd had more than he could hold; **son ~ est bon** he's had it*; **devoir/rendre des ~s à qn** to owe/give sb an explanation; **cela fait mon ~** that suits me.

(d) (*responsabilité*) **prendre qch à son ~** *dépense* to pay for sth; *maxime* to make sth one's own; **s'installer à son ~** to set up one's own business; **mettre qch sur le ~ de** to put sth down to, attribute sth to; **dire qch sur le ~ de qn** to say sth about sb; **pour le ~ de** on behalf of; **pour mon ~** (*opinion*) personally; (*usage*) for my own use.

(e) (*locutions*) (*Boxe*) **aller au tapis pour le ~** to go down for the count; **tenir ~ de qch** to take sth into account; **ne pas tenir ~ de qch** to disregard *ou* ignore sth; **~ tenu de** considering, in view of; **à ce ~-là** (*dans ce cas*) in this case; (*à ce train-là*) at this rate; **tout ~ fait** all things considered, when all is said and done.

2: ~ en banque bank account; **~ chèque postal** ≃ Giro account; **~ à rebours** countdown; **~ rendu** (*gén*) account, report. *[film]* review.

compte- [kɔ̃t] *préf*: **~-gouttes** *nm inv* (*pipette*) dropper; **au ~-gouttes** (*fig*) sparingly; **~-tours** *nm inv* revolution counter.

compter [kɔ̃te] (1) **1** *vt* **(a)** (*calculer*) to count. **combien en avez-vous compté?** how many did you count?, how many did you make it?; **il a 50 ans bien comptés** he's a good 50 (years old); **ses gaffes ne se comptent plus** we can't keep count of his blunders. **(b)** (*prévoir*) to allow, reckon. **j'ai compté qu'il nous en fallait 10** I reckoned we'd need 10; **il faut (bien) ~ 10 jours** you must allow (a good) 10 days, you must reckon on it taking (a good) 10 days. **(c)** (*tenir compte de*) to take into account; (*inclure*) to include. **t'es-tu compté?** did you count *ou* include yourself?; **sans ~** (*sans inclure*) not counting; (*sans parler de*) not to mention, to say nothing of. **(d)** (*facturer*) to charge for; (*payer*) to pay. **combien vous ont-ils compté le café?** how much did they charge you for the coffee? **(e)** (*avoir*) to have. **il ne compte pas d'ennemis** he has no enemies. **(f)** (*classer, ranger*) to consider. **il le compte au nombre de ses amis** he considers him one of his friends, he numbers him among his friends. **(g)** (*parcimonie*) *argent* to count; *permissions* to ration. **il ne compte pas sa peine** he spares no trouble; **ses jours sont comptés** his days are numbered. **(h)** (*avoir l'intention de*) to intend, plan, mean (*faire* to do); (*s'attendre à*) to expect. **je ne compte pas qu'il vienne aujourd'hui** I am not expecting him to come today.

2 *vi* **(a)** (*calculer*) to count. **tu as mal compté** you counted wrong, you miscounted; **à ~ de** (starting *ou* as) from. **(b)** (*être économe*) to economize. **sans ~** (*lit*) regardless of expense; **se dépenser sans ~** to spare no effort. **(c)** (*avoir de l'importance*) to count, matter. **35 ans de mariage, ça compte!** 35 years of marriage, that's quite something!; **~ double** to count double; **ça compte pour beaucoup dans sa décision** it has a lot to do with his decision. **(d)** (*tenir compte de*) **~ avec qch** to reckon with sth, take account of sth, allow for sth. **(e)** (*figurer*) **~ parmi** to be *ou* rank among. **(f)** (*se fier à*) **~ sur** to count on, rely on; **nous comptons sur vous (pour) demain** we're relying on you for tomorrow; **j'y compte bien!** I should hope so!; **vous pouvez ~ là-dessus** you can depend upon it; **ne comptez pas sur moi** (you can) count me out.

compteur [kɔ̃tœʀ] *nm* meter. **~ Geiger** Geiger counter; **~ (kilométrique)** milometer; **~ (de vitesse)** speedometer.

comptoir [kɔ̃twaʀ] *nm* **(a)** *[magasin]* counter; *[bar]* bar. **(b)** (*colonial*) trading post. **(c)** (*agence*) branch.

compulser [kɔ̃pylse] (1) *vt* to consult, examine.

comte [kɔ̃t] *nm* count; (*Brit*) earl. ♦ **comté** *nm* (*Hist*) earldom; (*Admin*) county. ♦ **comtesse** *nf* countess.

concasser [kɔ̃kɑse] (1) *vt* to crush; *poivre* to grind. ♦ **concassage** *nm* crushing; grinding. ♦ **concasseur** *nm* crusher.

concave [kɔ̃kav] *adj* concave. ♦ **concavité** *nf* (*Opt*) concavity; (*cavité*) cavity.

concéder [kɔ̃sede] (6) *vt droit, point* to grant, concede; *but* to concede, give away. **je vous concède que** I'll grant you that.

concentrer *vt*, **se ~** *vpr* [kɔ̃sɑ̃tʀe] (1) (*gén*) to concentrate; *attention, regards* to fix, focus (*sur* on). ♦ **concentration** *nf* (*gén*) concentration. **~ urbaine** conurbation; (*Écon*) **~ horizontale** horizontal integration; **~ d'esprit** concentration. ♦ **concentré, e 1** *adj acide* concentrated; *lait* condensed; *candidat* in a state of concentration. **2** *nm* (*chimique*) concentrated solution; (*bouillon*) concentrate, extract. **~ de tomates** tomato purée.

concentrique [kɔ̃sɑ̃tʀik] *adj cercle* concentric.

conception [kɔ̃sɛpsjɔ̃] *nf* **(a)** (*Bio*) conception. **(b)** (*action*) *[idée]* conception. **d'une ~ géniale** brilliantly conceived; **voilà quelle est ma ~ de la chose** this is how I see it. **(c)** (*idée*) notion, idea; (*réalisation*) creation. ♦ **concept** *nm* concept. ♦ **conceptualiser** (1) *vt* to conceptualize.

concerner [kɔ̃sɛʀne] (1) *vt* to concern. **des mesures concernant ce problème** steps concerning *ou* regarding this matter; **en ce qui concerne cette question** with regard to this question, as far as this question is concerned; **en ce qui me concerne** as far as I'm concerned.

concert [kɔ̃sɛʀ] *nm* (*Mus*) concert; (*accord*) entente, agreement. (*fig*) **~ de louanges/d'avertisseurs** chorus of praise/horns; **de ~** (*ensemble*) together, in unison; (*d'accord*) in concert; **de ~ avec** (*accord*) in conjunction with; (*ensemble*) together with. ♦ **concertiste** *nmf* concert artiste. ♦ **concerto** *nm* concerto.

concertation [kɔ̃sɛʀtɑsjɔ̃] *nf* (*dialogue*) dialogue; (*rencontre*) meeting. **sans ~ préalable** without preliminary consultations. ♦ **concerté, e** *adj* concerted. ♦ **concerter** (1) **1** *vt* to devise. **2 se ~** *vpr* to consult (each other).

concession [kɔ̃sesjɔ̃] *nf* (*gén*) concession (*à* to); *[cimetière]* plot. ♦ **concessionnaire** *nmf* (*Comm*) agent, dealer.

concevoir [kɔ̃s(ə)vwaʀ] (28) *vt* **(a)** *idée* to conceive of; *solution, projet* to conceive, devise, think up; *déception* to understand. **~ que** to conceive *ou* imagine that; **leur maison est bien/mal conçue** their house is well/badly designed; **voilà comment je conçois la chose** that's how I see it *ou* view it; **cela se conçoit facilement** it's quite understandable; **lettre ainsi conçue** letter expressed *ou* couched in these terms. **(b)** (*littér:*

éprouver) *doutes* have, feel; *jalousie* to feel. **(c)** (*engendrer*) to conceive. ♦ **concevable** *adj* conceivable.

concierge [kɔ̃sjɛʀʒ(ə)] *nmf* caretaker.

concile [kɔ̃sil] *nm* (*Rel*) council.

conciliabule [kɔ̃siljabyl] *nm* confabulation.

concilier [kɔ̃silje] (7) *vt* **(a)** *exigences* to reconcile (*avec* with). **(b)** *partisans, amitié* to win, gain. **se ~ (les bonnes grâces de) qn** to win *ou* gain sb's favour. ♦ **conciliable** *adj* reconcilable. ♦ **conciliant, e** *adj* conciliatory. ♦ **conciliateur, -trice** *nm,f* conciliator. ♦ **conciliation** *nf* (*apaisement*) conciliation; (*compatibilité*) reconciliation.

concis, e [kɔ̃si, iz] *adj* concise. ♦ **concision** *nf* concision, conciseness.

concitoyen, -yenne [kɔ̃sitwajɛ̃, jɛn] *nm,f* fellow citizen.

conclave [kɔ̃klav] *nm* (*Rel*) conclave.

conclure [kɔ̃klyʀ] (35) **1** *vt* **(a)** *accord* to conclude; *marché* to conclude, clinch. **marché conclu!** it's a deal! **(b)** (*gén*), *texte* to conclude, end (*par* with); *discours* to wind up, bring to a close. **et pour ~** and to conclude. **(c)** (*déduire*) to conclude (*qch de qch* sth from sth). **2 ~ à** *vt indir*: **ils ont conclu au suicide** they concluded that it was suicide. ♦ **concluant, e** *adj* conclusive. ♦ **conclusion** *nf* (*gén*) conclusion; *[discours]* close. **~s** (*Jur*) *[demandeur]* submissions; *[avocat]* summing-up; *[jury]* findings; **en ~** in conclusion.

concocter* [kɔ̃kɔkte] (1) *vt breuvage* to concoct; *discours* to elaborate.

concombre [kɔ̃kɔ̃bʀ(ə)] *nm* cucumber.

concorder [kɔ̃kɔʀde] (1) *vi [faits, dates, résultats]* to agree, tally; *[idées, caractères]* to match. **ses actes concordent-ils avec ses idées?** is his behaviour in accordance with his ideas? ♦ **concordance** *nf [témoignages]* agreement (*de* of); *[résultats]* similarity (*de* of *ou* between). (*Gram*) **~ des temps** sequence of tenses. ♦ **concordant, e** *adj résultats* similar; **témoignages ~s** testimonies which agree *ou* tally. ♦ **concordat** *nm* (*Rel*) concordat. ♦ **concorde** *nf* concord.

concourir [kɔ̃kuʀiʀ] (11) **1** *vi* **(a)** *[concurrent]* to compete (*pour* for). **(b)** (*converger*) to converge (*vers* towards, on). **2 ~ à** *vt indir*: **~ à qch/à faire qch** to work towards sth/towards doing sth. ♦ **concours** *nm* **(a)** (*gén: jeu*) competition; (*examen*) competitive examination. **~ hippique/agricole** horse/agricultural show; **~ de beauté** beauty contest. **(b)** (*participation*) aid, help. **prêter son ~ à qch** to lend one's support to sth; **~ de circonstances** combination of circumstances.

concret, -ète [kɔ̃kʀɛ, ɛt] *adj* (*gén*) concrete; *avantages* positive. ♦ **concrètement** *adv* in concrete terms. ♦ **concrétiser** (1) **1** *vt* to put in concrete form. **2 se ~** *vpr* to materialize.

concubinage [kɔ̃kybinaʒ] *nm* cohabitation.

concupiscence [kɔ̃kypisɑ̃s] *nf* concupiscence. ♦ **concupiscent, e** *adj* concupiscent.

concurremment [kɔ̃kyʀamɑ̃] *adv* (*conjointement*) jointly.

concurrence [kɔ̃kyʀɑ̃s] *nf* (*gén, Comm*) competition. **prix défiant toute ~** absolutely unbeatable price; **faire ~ à qn** to compete with sb; **jusqu'à ~ de ...** up to ..., to a limit of .... ♦ **concurrencer** (3) *vt* to compete with. ♦ **concurrent, e** *nm,f* (*Comm, Sport*) competitor; *[concours]* candidate. ♦ **concurrentiel, -elle** *adj* (*Écon*) competitive.

condamner [kɔ̃dɑne] (1) *vt* **(a)** *coupable* to sentence (*à* to, *pour* for); *livre, délit, expression* to condemn. **~ à mort** to sentence to death; **~ qn à une amende** to fine sb; **X, plusieurs fois condamné pour vol ...** X, several times convicted of theft ...; **il ne faut pas le ~ d'avoir fait cela** you mustn't condemn *ou* blame him for doing that; **sa rougeur le condamne** his blushes condemn him; **je suis condamné à me lever tôt** I'm doomed to get up early. **(b)** (*Méd*) *malade* to give up hope for. **il était condamné** *[malade, projet]* he (*ou* it) was doomed *ou* done for; **c'est condamné à sombrer dans l'oubli** it's doomed to sink into oblivion. **(c)** *porte* to fill in, block up; *pièce* to lock up. (*fig*) **~ sa porte à qn** to bar one's door to sb. ♦ **condamnable** *adj* reprehensible, blameworthy. ♦ **condamnation** *nf* **(a)** *[coupable]* (*action*) sentencing (*à* to, *pour* for); (*peine*) sentence. **il a 3 ~s à son actif** he (already) has 3 convictions; **~ à mort** death sentence; **~ à une amende** imposition of a fine. **(b)** *[livre, délit, conduite]* condemnation. **(c)** (*fig: échec*) end. ♦ **condamné, e** *nm,f* sentenced person, convict. **~ (à mort)** condemned man.

condenser *vt*, **se ~** *vpr* [kɔ̃dɑ̃se] (1) to condense. ♦ **condensateur** *nm* condenser. ♦ **condensation** *nf* condensation. ♦ **condensé** *nm* (*Presse*) digest.

condescendance [kɔ̃desɑ̃dɑ̃s] *nf* condescension. ♦ **condescendant, e** *adj* condescending. ♦ **condescendre** (41) *vi*: **~ à (faire)** to condescend to (do).

condiment [kɔ̃dimɑ̃] *nm* condiment.

condisciple [kɔ̃disipl(ə)] *nm* (*Scol*) schoolfellow; (*Univ*) fellow student.

condition [kɔ̃disjɔ̃] *nf* **(a)** (*circonstances*) **~s** conditions; **dans ces ~s** under these conditions. **(b)** (*stipulation*) condition; (*exigence*) condition, requirement. **~ préalable** prerequisite; **poser ses ~s** to lay down one's conditions; **remplir les ~s requises** to fulfil the requirements; **sans ~(s)** (*adj*) unconditional; (*adv*) unconditionally; **à une ~** on one condition; **à ~ d'être *ou* que tu sois sage** provided *ou* on condition that you're good; **sous ~** *libérer* conditionally. **(c)** (*Comm*) **~s** terms; **faire ses ~s** to make one's terms. **(d)** (*état*) **en bonne ~** *envoi* in good condition; *athlète* in condition, fit; **(se) mettre en ~** to get into condition, get fit; **la mise en ~ des téléspectateurs** the conditioning of viewers. **(e)** (*socialement*) (*métier*) profession, trade; (*rang*) station, condition. **étudiant de ~ modeste** student from a modest home *ou* background; **améliorer la ~ des ouvriers** to improve the conditions of the workers. ♦ **conditionnel, -elle** *adj, nm* conditional. ♦ **conditionnellement** *adv* conditionally. ♦ **conditionner** (1) *vt* (*emballer*) to package, prepack; (*influencer*) to condition. ♦ **conditionnement** *nm* packaging; conditioning.

condoléances [kɔ̃dɔleɑ̃s] *nfpl* condolences. **faire ses ~ à qn** to offer sb one's sympathy *ou* condolences.

conducteur, -trice [kɔ̃dyktœʀ, tʀis] **1** *adj* (*Élec*) conductive, conducting. **2** *nm,f* (*Aut, Rail*) driver; *[machine]* operator. **~ d'hommes** leader. **3** *nm* (*Élec*) conductor. ♦ **conductibilité** *nf* conductivity. ♦ **conductible** *adj* conductive. ♦ **conduction** *nf* (*Méd, Phys*) conduction.

conduire [kɔ̃dɥiʀ] (38) **1** *vt* **(a) ~ qn quelque part** *[personne, véhicule]* to take sb somewhere; *[guide, route, études]* to lead sb somewhere; **~ qn à la gare** (*en voiture*) to take *ou* drive sb to the station; (*à pied*) to walk sb to the station; **~ les hommes à l'assaut** to lead the men into the attack; **cela nous conduit à penser que** that leads us to think that; **ça l'a conduit en prison** it landed him in prison. **(b)** *véhicule* to drive; *embarcation* to steer; *avion* to pilot; *cheval [cavalier]* to ride; *[cocher]* to drive. **il conduit bien** he is a good driver, he drives well. **(c)** *affaires, pays* to run; *travaux* to supervise; *négociations, enquête* to conduct; *orchestre [chef]* to conduct; *[violon]* to lead. **(d)** *électricité* to conduct; *eau* to carry. **2 se ~** *vpr* to behave (*comme* as). **il s'est mal conduit** he behaved badly. ♦ **conduit** *nm* (*Tech*) conduit, pipe; (*Anat*) duct, canal; *[fumée]* flue. **~ de**

ventilation ventilation shaft; ~ **d'aération** air duct.
♦ **conduite** *nf* **(a)** (*V* **conduire (b)**) driving; steering; piloting. **voiture avec** ~ **à gauche** left-hand drive car; **faire un brin de** ~ **à qn*** to walk along with sb for a bit. **(b)** (*V* **conduire (c)**) running; supervision; conducting. **sous la** ~ **de** *guide* under the leadership of. **(c)** (*comportement*) behaviour; (*Scol*) conduct. **(d)** (*tuyau*) pipe; *[eau, gaz]* main.
cone [kon] *nm* (*gén*) cone.
confectionner [kɔ̃fɛksjɔne] (1) *vt mets* to prepare, make; *vêtement* to make. ♦ **confection** *nf* making; preparation. **être dans la** ~ to be in the ready-made clothes business.
confédéral, e, *mpl* **-aux** [kɔ̃fedeʀal, o] *adj* confederal. ♦ **confédération** *nf* confederation, confederacy. ♦ **confédéré, e** *adj, nm,f* confederate.
conférence [kɔ̃feʀɑ̃s] *nf* (*exposé*) lecture; (*réunion*) conference, meeting. **être en** ~ to be in *ou* at a meeting; ~ **de presse** press conference. ♦ **conférencier, -ière** *nm,f* speaker, lecturer.
conférer [kɔ̃feʀe] (6) **1** *vt* (*gén*) to give (*à* to); *prestige, dignité* to confer (*à* on). **2** *vi* to confer (*sur* on, about).
confesser [kɔ̃fese] (1) **1** *vt péchés* to confess. ~ **qn** to hear sb's confession, confess sb. **2 se** ~ *vpr* (*Rel*) to go to confession. **se** ~ **à** to confess to; **se** ~ **de** (*littér*) to confess. ♦ **confesse** *nf*: **aller à** ~ to go to confession. ♦ **confesseur** *nm* confessor. ♦ **confession** *nf* (*aveu*) confession; (*religion*) denomination. ♦ **confessional,** *pl* **-aux** *nm* confessional. ♦ **confessionnel, -elle** *adj* denominational.
confetti [kɔ̃feti] *nm*: ~**(s)** confetti.
confiance [kɔ̃fjɑ̃s] *nf* (*en l'honnêteté*) confidence, trust; (*en la valeur*) confidence, faith (*en* in). **avoir** ~ **en, faire** ~ **à** to have confidence in; (*Pol*) **voter la** ~ to pass a vote of confidence; **mettre qn en** ~ to win sb's trust; **avec** ~ *se confier* trustingly; *espérer* confidently; **de** ~ *acheter* with confidence; *homme, maison* trustworthy, reliable; **un poste de** ~ a position of trust; ~ **en soi** self-confidence. ♦ **confiant, e** *adj* (*assuré*) confident; (*sans défiance*) confiding.
confidence [kɔ̃fidɑ̃s] *nf* confidence. **faire une** ~ **à qn** to confide sth to sb; **en** ~ in confidence; **mettre qn dans la** ~ to let sb into the secret. ♦ **confident, e** *nm,f* confidant; confidante. ♦ **confidentiel, -ielle** *adj* confidential; (*sur enveloppe*) private. ♦ **confidentiellement** *adv* confidentially.
confier [kɔ̃fje] (7) **1** *vt secret, projet, espoir* to confide (*à* to). **je vous confie le soin de le faire** I entrust you with the task of doing it. **2 se** ~ *vpr*: **se** ~ **à qn** (*secret*) to confide in sb; (*protection*) to place o.s. in sb's hands.
configuration [kɔ̃figyʀɑsjɔ̃] *nf* (general) shape, configuration; *[lieux]* layout.
confiner [kɔ̃fine] (1) **1** *vt*: ~ **qn dans** to confine sb in. **2** ~ **à** *vt indir* to border on. **3 se** ~ *vpr* to confine o.s. (*à* to). **se** ~ **chez soi** to shut o.s. up at home. ♦ **confiné, e** *adj* close, stuffy. ♦ **confinement** *nm* confining.
confins [kɔ̃fɛ̃] *nmpl* borders; (*limite extrême*) furthermost bounds.
confire [kɔ̃fiʀ] (37) *vt* to preserve; (*vinaigre*) to pickle. ♦ **confit, e 1** *adj fruit* crystallized, candied; *cornichon etc* pickled. **2** *nm*: ~ **d'oie** conserve of goose. ♦ **confiture** *nf* jam. ~ **d'oranges/de citrons** (orange)/lemon marmalade; (*fig*) **donner de la** ~ **aux cochons** to cast pearls before swine.
confirmer [kɔ̃fiʀme] (1) *vt* (*gén, Rel*) to confirm. **la nouvelle se confirme** there is some confirmation of the news. ♦ **confirmation** *nf* confirmation. **en** ~ **de** in confirmation of; **c'est la** ~ **de** it is confirmation of.
confiserie [kɔ̃fizʀi] *nf* (*magasin*) confectioner's (shop); (*métier, marchandise*) confectionery. **manger une** ~ to eat a sweet. ♦ **confiseur, -euse** *nm,f* confectioner.
confisquer [kɔ̃fiske] (1) *vt* (*gén, Jur*) to confiscate. ♦ **confiscation** *nf* confiscation.
conflit [kɔ̃fli] *nm* (*gén, Mil*) conflict, clash. **entrer en** ~ **avec qn** to clash with sb.
confluent [kɔ̃flyɑ̃] *nm* (*endroit*) confluence.
confondre [kɔ̃fɔ̃dʀ(ə)] (41) **1** *vt* **(a)** *choses, dates* to mix up, confuse. ~ **qch avec qch d'autre** to mistake sth for sth else; **j'ai dû** ~ I must have made a mistake. **(b)** (*déconcerter*) to astound (*par* with). **confondu de reconnaissance** overcome with gratitude. **(c)** *menteur* to confound. **(d)** (*fusionner*) to join. **2 se** ~ *vpr* **(a)** *[couleurs, silhouettes]* to merge; *[souvenirs]* to become confused; *[fleuves]* to join. **nos intérêts se confondent** our interests are one and the same. **(b) se** ~ **en excuses/remerciements** to apologize (to sb)/thank sb profusely.
conforme [kɔ̃fɔʀm(ə)] *adj* true. ~ **à** *modèle* true to; *plan, règle* in accordance *ou* conformity with; *moyens, opinions* in keeping with; **c'est peu** ~ **à ce que j'ai dit** it bears little resemblance to what I said.
conformer [kɔ̃fɔʀme] (1) **1** *vt*: ~ **qch à** to model sth on. **2 se** ~ *vpr*: **se** ~ **à** to conform to. ♦ **conformation** *nf* conformation. ♦ **conformé, e** *adj*: **bien/mal** ~ well/ill-formed. ♦ **conformément** *adv*: ~ **à** in accordance with.
conformisme [kɔ̃fɔʀmism(ə)] *nm* (*gén*) conformity. ♦ **conformiste** *adj, nmf* (*gén*) conformist.
conformité [kɔ̃fɔʀmite] *nf* (*identité*) similarity; (*fidélité*) faithfulness (*à* to). **en** ~ **avec** *plan, ordres* in accordance with; *idées* in keeping *ou* in conformity with.
confort [kɔ̃fɔʀ] *nm* comfort. **appartement tout** ~ flat with all mod cons. ♦ **confortable** *adj* (*gén, fig*) comfortable. **peu** ~ rather uncomfortable. ♦ **confortablement** *adv* comfortably. **vivre** ~ (*confort*) to live in comfort; (*richesse*) to live very comfortably.
confrère [kɔ̃fʀɛʀ] *nm [profession]* colleague; *[association]* fellow member; (*journal*) (fellow) newspaper. ♦ **confrérie** *nf* brotherhood.
confronter [kɔ̃fʀɔ̃te] (1) *vt opinions* to confront; *textes* to compare. ♦ **confrontation** *nf* confrontation; comparison.
confus, e [kɔ̃fy, yz] *adj* **(a)** (*gén*) confused; *esprit, style* muddled; *idée* hazy. **(b)** (*honteux*) ashamed, embarrassed (*de qch* of sth, *d'avoir fait* at having done). ♦ **confusément** *adv distinguer, ressentir* vaguely; *parler* confusedly. ♦ **confusion** *nf* (*honte*) embarrassment; (*trouble, désordre*) confusion; (*erreur*) confusion (*de* in). **vous avez fait une** ~ you've made a mistake; **mettre la** ~ **dans les esprits** to throw people into disarray *ou* confusion.
congé [kɔ̃ʒe] *nm* **(a)** (*vacances*) holiday, vacation (*US*); (*Mil*) leave. **3 jours de** ~ **pour** *ou* **à Noël** 3 days' holiday *ou* 3 days off at Christmas; **en** ~ on holiday; **quand avez-vous** ~**?** when are you off?, when do you get a holiday?; **avoir** ~ **le mercredi** to have Wednesdays off; ~**s payés/scolaires** paid/school holidays. **(b)** (*arrêt*) **prendre/donner du** ~ to take/give time off *ou* some leave; ~ **sans solde/de maladie** unpaid/sick leave. **(c)** (*départ*) notice. **donner son** ~ *[employé]* to give in one's notice; *[employeur, locataire]* to give notice (*à* to); **il a demandé son** ~ he's asked to leave. **(d)** (*adieu*) **prendre** ~ **(de qn)** to take one's leave (of sb). **(e)** (*Admin: autorisation*) clearance certificate; *[alcool]* release. ♦ **congédier** (7) *vt* to dismiss.
congeler [kɔ̃ʒle] (5) **1** *vt* to freeze. **produits congelés** (deep-)frozen *ou* deep-freeze foods. **2 se** ~ *vpr* to freeze. ♦ **congélateur** *nm* (*meuble*) deep-

freeze; (*compartiment*) freezer compartment. ♦ **congélation** *nf* freezing.

congénère [kɔ̃ʒenɛʀ] *nmf* fellow creature. ♦ **congénital, e,** *mpl* **-aux** *adj* congenital.

congère [kɔ̃ʒɛʀ] *nf* snowdrift.

congestionner [kɔ̃ʒɛstjɔne] (1) *vt rue* to congest; *personne* to flush, make flushed. **être congestionné** to be flushed. ♦ **congestion** *nf* congestion. ~ **(cérébrale)** stroke.

Congo [kɔ̃gɔ] *nm*: **le** ~ the Congo. ♦ **congolais, e** *adj*, **C~(e)** *nm(f)* Congolese.

congratuler [kɔ̃gʀatyle] (1) *vt* to congratulate. ♦ **congratulations** *nfpl* congratulations.

congre [kɔ̃gʀ(ə)] *nm* conger eel.

congrégation [kɔ̃gʀegɑsjɔ̃] *nf* (*Rel*) congregation.

congrès [kɔ̃gʀɛ] *nm* congress. ♦ **congressiste** *nmf* participant at a congress.

conifère [kɔnifɛʀ] *nm* conifer.

conique [kɔnik] *adj* cone-shaped.

conjecture [kɔ̃ʒɛktyʀ] *nf* conjecture. ♦ **conjecturer** (1) *vt* to conjecture.

conjoint, e [kɔ̃ʒwɛ̃, wɛ̃t] **1** *adj action* joint. **2** *nm,f* (*époux*) spouse. **les** ~**s** the couple, the husband and wife. ♦ **conjointement** *adv* jointly. ~ **avec** together with.

conjonction [kɔ̃ʒɔ̃ksjɔ̃] *nf* conjunction. ♦ **conjonctif, -ive** *adj* (*Gram*) conjunctive.

conjoncture [kɔ̃ʒɔ̃ktyʀ] *nf* circumstances. **crise de** ~ economic crisis.

conjugaison [kɔ̃ʒygɛzɔ̃] *nf* (*Bio, Gram*) conjugation; (*union*) union.

conjugal, e, *mpl* **-aux** [kɔ̃ʒygal, o] *adj amour* conjugal; *vie* married, conjugal. ♦ **conjugalement** *adv vivre* as a married couple.

conjuguer [kɔ̃ʒyge] (1) **1** *vt* (*Gram*) to conjugate; (*combiner*) to combine. **action conjuguée** joint *ou* combined action. **2 se** ~ *vpr [efforts]* to combine. *[verbe]* **se** ~ **(avec)** to be conjugated (with).

conjurer [kɔ̃ʒyʀe] (1) **1** *vt* **(a)** *échec* to avert; *diable, sort* to ward off. **(b)** ~ **qn de faire qch** to beseech *ou* entreat sb to do sth. **2 se** ~ *vpr* to conspire (*contre* against). ♦ **conjuration** *nf* conspiracy. ♦ **conjuré, e** *nm,f* conspirator.

connaissance [kɔnɛsɑ̃s] *nf* **(a)** (*savoir*) knowledge. **une profonde** ~ **du cœur humain** a deep understanding of the human heart; **faire étalage de ses** ~**s** to display one's knowledge *ou* learning; **c'est un garçon qui a des** ~**s** he's a knowledgeable fellow. **(b)** (*personne*) acquaintance. **(c)** (*conscience*) consciousness. **sans** ~ unconscious; **reprendre** ~ to regain consciousness, come round. **(d) (pas) à ma** ~ (not) to my knowledge, (not) as far as I know; **venir à la** ~ **de qn** to come to sb's knowledge; **donner** ~ **de qch à qn** to inform sb of sth; **en** ~ **de cause** with full knowledge of the facts; **en pays de** ~ (*gens*) among familiar faces; (*sujet*) on familiar ground; **qn de sa** ~ someone he knew; **faire** ~ **avec qn** to meet sb; **prendre** ~ **de qch** to read sth; **je leur ai fait faire** ~ I introduced them (to each other). ♦ **connaisseur, -euse 1** *adj* expert. **2** *nm,f* connoisseur.

connaître [kɔnɛtʀ(ə)] (57) **1** *vt* **(a)** (*gén*) to know; *fait, personne* to be acquainted with; *texte, coutume* to be familiar with; *restaurant* to know of. **connaît-il la nouvelle?** has he heard the news?; ~ **qn de vue** to know sb by sight; **apprendre à** ~ **qn** to get to know sb; **il l'a connu à l'université** he met *ou* knew him at university; **tu connais les oiseaux/la mécanique?** do you know anything about birds/engineering?; ~ **la vie** to know about life; **il connaît son affaire** he knows what he's talking about; **elle n'y connaît rien** she doesn't know a thing about it, she hasn't a clue about it*; (*fig*) **je connais la chanson** I've heard it all before. **(b)** *succès* to enjoy, have; *privations* to know, experience. **nous connaissons de tristes heures** we are going through sad times. **(c) faire** ~ **(qn/qch)** to make (sb/sth) known; **il m'a fait** ~ **son frère/la pêche** he introduced me to his brother/fishing; **se faire** ~ (*gén*) to make o.s. known; *[artiste]* to make a name for o.s.

2 se ~ *vpr* **(a) se** ~ **(soi-même)** to know o.s.; (*rage*) **il ne se connaît plus** he's beside himself with anger. **(b)** (*se rencontrer*) to meet. **(c) s'y** ~ **en qch** to know a lot about sth, be an expert on sth. ♦ **connu, e** *adj terre, animal* known; *idée, auteur* well-known. **mal** ~ little known; **il est** ~ **comme le loup blanc** everybody knows him.

connecter [kɔnɛkte] (1) *vt* to connect. ♦ **connexion** *nf* connection.

connétable [kɔnetabl(ə)] *nm* (*Hist*) constable.

connivence [kɔnivɑ̃s] *nf* connivance. **de** ~ **avec** in connivance with; **sourire de** ~ smile of complicity.

conquérir [kɔ̃keʀiʀ] (21) *vt* (*gén*) to conquer; *galons* to win; *estime* to win, gain; *personnage influent* to win over. **conquis à une doctrine** won over to a doctrine. ♦ **conquérant, e 1** *adj peuple* conquering; *ardeur* masterful; *regard* swaggering. **2** *nm,f* conqueror. ♦ **conquête** *nf* conquest. **faire la** ~ **de** to conquer; to win over.

consacrer [kɔ̃sakʀe] (1) *vt* **(a)** ~ **à** (*dédier à*) to devote to, dedicate to, consecrate to; (*affecter à*) to devote to, give to; **pouvez-vous me** ~ **un instant?** can you spare me a moment?; **se** ~ **à Dieu** to dedicate *ou* give o.s. to God. **(b)** (*Rel*) to consecrate; *coutume, droit* to establish; *abus* to sanction. ♦ **consacré, e** *adj expression* accepted; *itinéraire* traditional; *écrivain* established, recognized.

conscience [kɔ̃sjɑ̃s] *nf* **(a)** (*psychologique*) **la** ~ **de qch** the awareness *ou* consciousness of sth; (*Philos, Psych*) **la** ~ consciousness; **avoir** ~ **que** to be aware *ou* conscious that; **prendre** ~ **de qch** to become aware of sth, realize sth; **perdre/reprendre** ~ to lose/regain consciousness. **(b)** (*morale*) conscience. **avoir qch sur la** ~ to have sth on one's conscience; **avoir bonne/mauvaise** ~ to have a good *ou* clear/bad *ou* guilty conscience; **en (toute)** ~ in all conscience *ou* honesty. **(c)** ~ **(professionnelle)** conscientiousness. ♦ **consciemment** *adv* consciously. ♦ **consciencieusement** *adv* conscientiously. ♦ **consciencieux, -ieuse** *adj* conscientious. ♦ **conscient, e** *adj* (*non évanoui*) conscious; (*lucide*) lucid; *décision* conscious. ~ **de** conscious *ou* aware of.

conscrit [kɔ̃skʀi] *nm* conscript, draftee (*US*). ♦ **conscription** *nf* conscription, draft (*US*).

consécration [kɔ̃sekʀɑsjɔ̃] *nf* (*Rel*) consecration; *[coutume, droit]* establishment; *[abus]* sanctioning; *[artiste]* consecration.

consécutif, -ive [kɔ̃sekytif, iv] *adj* consecutive. ~ **à** following upon. ♦ **consécutivement** *adv* consecutively. ~ **à** following upon.

conseil [kɔ̃sɛj] **1** *nm* **(a)** ~**(s)** advice; **un** ~ some advice, a piece of advice; **prendre** ~ **de qn** to take advice from sb; **un petit** ~ a word of advice; ~ **d'ami** friendly piece of advice; ~**s à la ménagère** hints *ou* tips for the housewife. **(b)** (*personne*) **ingénieur-**~ consulting engineer; **avocat-**~ legal consultant. **(c)** (*groupe*) *[entreprise]* board; *[organisme]* council, committee; (*séance*) meeting. **tenir** ~ (*se réunir*) to hold a meeting; (*délibérer*) to deliberate.

2: ~ **d'administration** *[société]* board of directors; *[hôpital]* board of governors; ~ **de classe** staff meeting; ~ **de discipline** disciplinary committee; ~ **de guerre** (*réunion*) council of war; (*tribunal*) court-martial; **le C~ des ministres** the Cabinet; ~ **municipal** town council; ~ **de révision** recruiting board; **C~ de Sécurité** Security Council.

conseiller[1] [kɔ̃seje] (1) *vt* **(a)** *prudence, méthode* to recommend (*à qn* to sb). ~ **à qn de faire qch** to advise sb to do sth; **la peur lui conseilla de ...** fear

prompted him to ...; **il est conseillé de** it is advisable to; **il est conseillé aux parents de ...** parents are advised to ... . **(b)** (*guider*) to advise, give advice to. **bien/mal conseillé** well/badly advised.
conseiller[2], **-ère** [kɔ̃seje, kɔ̃sɛjɛʀ] *nm,f* (*expert*) adviser; (*Admin, Pol*) council member, councillor. ~ **municipal** town councillor.
consentir [kɔ̃sɑ̃tiʀ] (16) **1** *vi* to agree, consent (*à* to). ~ **(à ce) que qn fasse qch** to consent *ou* agree to sb's doing sth. **2** *vt délai, prêt* to grant (*à* to). ♦ **consentant, e** *adj* willing; (*Jur*) consenting. **êtes-vous** ~? do you consent to it?, does it have your consent? ♦ **consentement** *nm* consent.
conséquence [kɔ̃sekɑ̃s] *nf* **(a)** (*gén*) consequence; (*conclusion*) conclusion. **cela a eu pour** ~ **de** the result *ou* consequence of this was that; **avoir d'heureuses** ~**s** to have a happy outcome *ou* happy results; **tirer les** ~**s** to draw conclusions *ou* inferences (*de* from). **(b) de** ~ of (some) consequence; **en** ~ (*donc*) consequently; *agir* accordingly; **en** ~ **de** (*par suite de*) in consequence of; **sans** ~ (*fâcheuse*) without repercussions; (*sans importance*) of no consequence; **cela ne tire pas à** ~ it's of no consequence. ♦ **conséquent, e** *adj* (*logique*) consistent; (*: *important*) sizeable; (*Géol*) consequent. **par** ~ consequently.
conservateur, -trice [kɔ̃sɛʀvatœʀ, tʀis] **1** *adj* (*gén*) conservative. **2** *nm,f [musée]* curator; *[bibliothèque]* librarian; (*Pol*) conservative. ♦ **conservatisme** *nm* conservatism.
conservatoire [kɔ̃sɛʀvatwaʀ] *nm* school, academy (*of music, drama*). **le C**~ the (Paris) Conservatoire.
conserver [kɔ̃sɛʀve] (1) **1** *vt* **(a)** (*gén*) to keep; *denrée* to store; *vitesse* to maintain; *habitude* to keep up; *espoir, sens* to retain; *qualité, droits, vie* to conserve. **il a conservé sa tête** (*calme*) he kept his head; (*lucidité*) he still has his wits about him. **(b)** (*en bon état*) to preserve. **bien conservé** *personne* well-preserved. **(c)** (*Culin*) to preserve; (*au vinaigre*) to pickle; (*en bocal*) to bottle. **2 se** ~ *vpr [aliments]* to keep. ♦ **conservation** *nf [archives]* keeping; *[aliments, monuments]* preservation. **en bon état de** ~ well-preserved. ♦ **conserve 1** *nf*: **les** ~**s** tinned (*ou* canned *ou* bottled) food(s); **l'industrie de la** ~ the canning industry; **mettre en** ~ (*boîte*) to can; (*bocal*) to bottle. **2** *adv*: **de** ~ *naviguer* in convoy; *agir* in concert. ♦ **conserverie** *nf* (*usine*) canning factory.
considérable [kɔ̃sideʀabl(ə)] *adj* (*gén*) considerable; *rôle* significant; *dégâts* extensive; (*littér*) *personnage* eminent. ♦ **considérablement** *adv* considerably; significantly; extensively.
considération [kɔ̃sideʀɑsjɔ̃] *nf* **(a)** (*examen*) consideration. **ceci mérite** ~ this is worth considering *ou* consideration; **prendre qch en** ~ to take sth into consideration *ou* account; **en** ~ **de** (*en raison de*) because of; (*par rapport à*) considering; **sans** ~ **de** *dangers* regardless of; *personne* without taking into consideration. **(b)** (*motif*) consideration. **(c)** (*remarques*) ~**s** reflections. **(d)** (*respect*) esteem, respect. **'veuillez agréer l'assurance de ma** ~ **distinguée'** 'yours faithfully *ou* truly'. ♦ **considérer** (6) *vt* **(a)** (*gén*) to consider. ~ **qch avec inquiétude** to view sth with anxiety; **tout bien considéré** all things considered; **je le considère comme mon fils** I look upon him as my son; **il se considère comme un génie** he considers himself a genius; **considérant que** considering that. **(b)** (*respecter*) to respect, have a high regard for.
consigner [kɔ̃siɲe] (1) *vt* **(a)** *fait* to record. **(b)** *soldat* to confine to barracks; *élève* to keep in (after school); *salle* to bar entrance to. **(c)** *bagages* to put in the left-luggage office. **(d)** *bouteille* to put a deposit on. ♦ **consigne** *nf* (*instructions*) orders; (*punition*) (*Mil*) confinement to barracks; (*Scol*) detention; *[bagages]* left-luggage (office); *[bouteille]* deposit. ~ **automatique** left-luggage lockers. ♦ **consigné, e** *adj emballage* returnable. **non** ~ non-returnable.
consistance [kɔ̃sistɑ̃s] *nf* consistency. **prendre** ~ *[liquide]* to thicken; **sans** ~ *substance* lacking in consistency; *caractère* spineless; *rumeur* ill-founded, groundless. ♦ **consistant, e** *adj repas* substantial; *nourriture, argument* solid; *sirop* thick.
consister [kɔ̃siste] (1) *vi* (*se composer de*) ~ **en** to consist of, be made up of; (*résider dans*) ~ **dans** to consist in; ~ **à faire** to consist in doing.
consoler [kɔ̃sɔle] (1) **1** *vt personne* to console; *chagrin* to soothe. **si ça peut te** ~ **...** if it is of any consolation *ou* comfort to you ... . **2 se** ~ *vpr* to console o.s., find consolation. **se** ~ **d'une perte** to be consoled for *ou* get over a loss. ♦ **consolant, e** *adj* consoling, comforting. ♦ **consolation** *nf* (*action*) consolation. (*réconfort*) ~**(s)** consolation, comfort; **c'est une** ~ that's one consolation.
consolider [kɔ̃sɔlide] (1) **1** *vt* (*gén*) to strengthen; *accord, fortune* to consolidate. **2 se** ~ *vpr [régime]* to strengthen *ou* consolidate its position. ♦ **consolidation** *nf* strengthening; consolidation.
consommer [kɔ̃sɔme] (1) *vt* **(a)** (*gén*) to consume; *nourriture* to eat; *boissons* to drink; *carburant* to use. **il se consomme beaucoup de vin** a lot of wine is consumed *ou* drunk; **je désirerais** ~ I would like a drink; (*Aut*) **elle consomme beaucoup d'essence** it's heavy on petrol, it uses a lot of petrol. **(b)** *acte sexuel* to consummate; *crime* to perpetrate, commit; *ruine* to confirm. ♦ **consommateur, -trice** *nm,f* (*acheteur*) consumer; *[café]* customer. ♦ **consommation** *nf* **(a)** consumption; consummation; perpetration; confirmation. **il fait une grande** ~ **de papier** he goes through* *ou* uses a lot of paper; **de** ~ *biens, société* consumer. **(b)** (*boisson*) drink. **prendre les** ~**s** to take the orders. ♦ **consommé, e 1** *adj habileté* consummate; *écrivain* accomplished. **2** *nm* consommé.
consonne [kɔ̃sɔn] *nf* consonant.
consortium [kɔ̃sɔʀsjɔm] *nm* consortium.
conspirer [kɔ̃spiʀe] (1) *vi* to conspire, plot (*contre* against). ~ **à faire** to conspire to do. ♦ **conspirateur, -trice 1** *adj* conspiratorial. **2** *nm,f* conspirer, plotter. ♦ **conspiration** *nf* conspiracy.
conspuer [kɔ̃spɥe] (1) *vt* to boo.
constant, e [kɔ̃stɑ̃, ɑ̃t] **1** *adj* (*gén*) constant; *effort* steadfast. **2** *nf* (*Math*) constant; (*fig*) permanent feature. ♦ **constamment** *adv* constantly. ♦ **constance** *nf* constancy, steadfastness.
constater [kɔ̃state] (1) *vt* **(a)** (*remarquer*) to note, notice, see. **je constatai sa disparition** I noticed *ou* saw that it had disappeared; **je ne fais que** ~ I'm merely stating a fact, I'm merely making an observation; **constatez par vous-même** see for yourself. **(b)** (*consigner*) *effraction* to record; *décès* to certify. ♦ **constat** *nm*: ~ **(d'huissier)** certified report; ~ **(d'accident)** (accident) report. ♦ **constatation** *nf* **(a)** (*action*) noting; noticing; seeing; recording; certifying. **(b)** (*remarque*) observation. ~**s** *[enquête]* findings.
constellation [kɔ̃stelɑsjɔ̃] *nf* (*gén*) constellation. ♦ **constellé, e** *adj*: ~ **de** *astres, lumières* spangled *ou* studded with; *taches* spotted *ou* dotted with.
consternation [kɔ̃stɛʀnɑsjɔ̃] *nf* consternation, dismay. ♦ **consterner** (1) *vt* to dismay, fill with consternation. **air consterné** air of consternation *ou* dismay.
constiper [kɔ̃stipe] (1) *vt* to constipate. ♦ **constipation** *nf* constipation. ♦ **constipé, e** *adj* (*péj: guindé*) stiff; (*Méd*) constipated.
constituer [kɔ̃stitɥe] (1) **1** *vt* **(a)** (*fonder*) *comité, gouvernement* to set up, form; *bibliothèque* to

build up; *dossier* to make up, put together. **(b)** (*composer*) *[éléments]* to make up, constitute. **constitué de plusieurs morceaux** made up *ou* composed of several pieces. **(c)** *délit, motif* to constitute. **(d)** (*Jur*) *rente* to settle (*à* on); *avocat* to retain. ~ **qn son héritier** to appoint sb one's heir. **2 se** ~ *vpr*: **se** ~ **prisonnier** to give o.s. up. ♦ **constituant, e** *adj* (*gén, Pol*) constituent. ♦ **constitué, e** *adj*: **bien/mal** ~ of sound/unsound constitution. ♦ **constitutif, -ive** *adj* constituent, component. ♦ **constitution** *nf* **(a)** setting-up, formation; building-up; putting together; making-up; settlement; retaining. **(b)** (*composition*) composition, make-up. **(c)** (*Méd, Pol*) constitution. ♦ **constitutionnel, -elle** *adj* constitutional.

construire [kɔ̃stʀɥiʀ] (38) *vt* (*gén*) to build, construct; (*Géom*) to construct; *théorie, phrase* to construct, put together, build up. **ça s'est beaucoup construit ici** there's a lot of building here; **ça se construit avec le subjonctif** it takes the subjunctive. ♦ **constructeur, -trice** *nmf* (*fabricant*) maker, manufacturer; (*bâtisseur*) builder, constructor. ~ **de navires** shipbuilder. ♦ **constructif, -ive** *adj* constructive. ♦ **construction** *nf* **(a)** (*action*) building; construction. **de** ~ **française/robuste** French/ solidly built; **matériaux de** ~ building materials; **en** ~ under construction. **(b)** (*industrie*) **la** ~ the building trade; **les** ~**s navales** shipbuilding; **les** ~**s aéronautiques** the aircraft industry. **(c)** (*édifice*) building.

consul [kɔ̃syl] *nm* consul. ~ **général** consul general. ♦ **consulaire** *adj* consular. ♦ **consulat** *nm* **(a)** (*bureaux, charge*) consulate. **(b)** (*Hist française*) **le C**~ the Consulate.

consulter [kɔ̃sylte] (1) **1** *vt* (*gén*) to consult. **ne** ~ **que sa raison** to be guided only by one's reason. **2** *vi [médecin]* to hold surgery. **3 se** ~ *vpr* to confer, consult each other. **se** ~ **du regard** to look questioningly at one another. ♦ **consultatif, -ive** *adj* consultative, advisory. ♦ **consultation** *nf* **(a)** (*action*) consultation. **après** ~ **de son agenda** (after) having consulted his diary; **d'une** ~ **difficile** difficult to consult. **(b)** *[médecin, expert]* consultation. **aller à la** ~ to go to the surgery, pay a visit to the doctor; **les heures de** ~ surgery *ou* consulting hours. **(c)** (*échange de vues*) consultation. **en** ~ **avec** in consultation with.

consumer [kɔ̃syme] (1) **1** *vt [incendie]* to consume, burn; *[fièvre, ambition]* to consume, devour; *forces* to expend; *fortune* to squander, fritter away. **débris consumés** charred debris. **2 se** ~ *vpr [bois]* to burn; (*littér: dépérir*) to waste away.

contact [kɔ̃takt] *nm* (*gén*) contact; (*toucher*) touch. (*Aut*) **mettre le** ~ to switch on the ignition; **prendre** ~ (*Rad*) to make contact; (*affaires*) to get in touch *ou* contact (*avec* with); **mettre en** ~ *objets* to bring into contact; (*affaires*) to put in touch; (*Rad*) to put in contact; **prise de** ~ (*entrevue*) first meeting; **au** ~ **de l'air** in contact with (the) air. ♦ **contacter** (1) *vt* to contact, get in touch with.

contagion [kɔ̃taʒjɔ̃] *nf* (*Méd*) contagion; (*fig: épidémie*) epidemic. **la** ~ **de la violence** the infectiousness of violence. ♦ **contagieux, -euse** *adj maladie* (*gén*) infectious; (*par le contact*) contagious; *peur, rire* infectious, contagious.

contaminer [kɔ̃tamine] (1) *vt* to contaminate. ♦ **contamination** *nf* contamination.

conte [kɔ̃t] *nm* tale, story. (*lit, fig*) ~ **de fée** fairy tale *ou* story.

contempler [kɔ̃tɑ̃ple] (1) *vt* to contemplate, gaze at. ♦ **contemplatif, -ive** *adj* (*gén*) contemplative. ♦ **contemplation** *nf* contemplation.

contemporain, e [kɔ̃tɑ̃pɔʀɛ̃, ɛn] **1** *adj* contemporary (*de* with). **2** *nm* contemporary.

contenir [kɔ̃tniʀ] (22) **1** *vt* **(a)** (*en capacité*) *[récipient]* to hold, take; *[cinéma, avion]* to seat, hold. **(b)** (*en contenu*) *[récipient, livre, minerai]* to contain. **(c)** (*maîtriser*) (*gén*) to contain; *larmes* to hold back; *foule, ennemi* to hold in check. **2 se** ~ *vpr* to contain o.s. ♦ **contenance** *nf* **(a)** (*capacité*) capacity. **(b)** (*attitude*) attitude. **pour se donner une** ~ to give an impression of composure; **faire bonne** ~ **(devant)** to put on a bold front (in the face of); **perdre** ~ to lose one's composure. ♦ **contenant** *nm*: **le** ~ the container.

content, e [kɔ̃tɑ̃, ɑ̃t] **1** *adj* pleased, glad, happy. ~ **de** *élève, voiture* pleased *ou* happy with; *changement* pleased *ou* glad at *ou* about; **être** ~ **de soi** to be pleased with o.s.; **non** ~ **d'être/d'avoir fait ...** not content with being/with having done .... **2** *nm*: **avoir (tout) son** ~ **de qch** to have had one's fill of sth. ♦ **contentement** *nm* contentment, satisfaction. ~ **de soi** self-satisfaction. ♦ **contenter** (1) **1** *vt besoin, curiosité* to satisfy; *personne* to satisfy, please. **cette explication l'a contenté** he was satisfied *ou* happy with this explanation. **2 se** ~ *vpr*: **se** ~ **de qch/de faire qch** to content o.s. *ou* make do with sth/with doing sth.

contentieux, -euse [kɔ̃tɑ̃sjø, øz] **1** *adj* (*Jur*) contentious. **2** *nm* (*Comm*) litigation; (*Pol*) disputes; (*service*) legal department.

contenu, e [kɔ̃tny] **1** *adj colère* restrained, suppressed. **2** *nm [récipient]* contents; *[texte]* content.

conter [kɔ̃te] (1) *vt* (*littér*) *histoire* to recount, relate. ~ **qch à qn** to tell sth to sb; **il lui en a conté de belles!** he told him some incredible stories!; **elle ne s'en laisse pas** ~ she's not easily taken in; ~ **fleurette à qn** to murmur sweet nothings to sb.

contester [kɔ̃tɛste] (1) **1** *vt* to question, dispute, contest. **roman/écrivain très contesté** very controversial novel/author. **2** *vi* to protest. **il ne conteste jamais** he never takes issue over anything. ♦ **contestable** *adj* questionable, disputable. ♦ **contestataire 1** *adj* anti-establishment. **2** *nmf* protester. ♦ **contestation** *nf* **(a)** (*action*) contesting; questioning; disputing. **(b)** (*discussion*) dispute; (*objection*) objection. **(c)** (*Pol*) **la** ~ anti-establishment activity; **faire de la** ~ to protest (against the establishment). ♦ **conteste** *nf*: **sans** ~ unquestionably, indisputably.

conteur, -euse [kɔ̃tœʀ, øz] *nm,f* (*écrivain*) storywriter; (*narrateur*) storyteller.

contexte [kɔ̃tɛkst(ə)] *nm* context.

contigu, -uë [kɔ̃tigy] *adj choses* adjoining, adjacent; *sujets* closely related. **être** ~ **à qch** to be adjacent *ou* next to sth. ♦ **contiguïté** *nf [choses]* proximity; *[sujets]* relatedness.

continence [kɔ̃tinɑ̃s] *nf* continence. ♦ **continent**[1], **e** *adj* continent.

continent[2] [kɔ̃tinɑ̃] *nm* continent. (*terre ferme*) **le** ~ the mainland. ♦ **continental, e,** *mpl* **-aux** *adj* continental.

contingence [kɔ̃tɛ̃ʒɑ̃s] *nf* (*gén*) contingency. ♦ **contingent, e 1** *adj* contingent. **2** *nm* **(a)** (*Mil: groupe*) contingent. (*en France*) **le** ~ *soldiers on national service*, the draft (*US*). **(b)** (*quota*) quota; (*part*) share. ♦ **contingenter** (1) *vt* (*Comm*) to place *ou* fix a quota on.

continu, e [kɔ̃tiny] *adj* (*gén*) continuous; *ligne, silence* unbroken. ♦ **continuateur, -trice** *nm,f* continuator. ♦ **continuation** *nf* continuation. ♦ **continuel, -elle** *adj* (*continu*) continuous; (*qui se répète*) continual. ♦ **continuellement** *adv* continuously; continually.

continuer [kɔ̃tinɥe] (1) **1** *vt effort* to continue (with), carry on with; *droite, route* to continue. ~ **son chemin** to go on, continue on one's way. **2** *vi [bruit, spectacle]* to continue, go on. ~ **de** *ou* **à manger** *etc* to go on *ou* keep on *ou* continue eating *etc*; **s'il continue ...** if he goes on *ou* keeps on *ou* continues ... . **3 se** ~ *vpr* to go on, continue

(*jusqu'à* as far as). ♦ **continuité** *nf [politique]* continuation; *[action]* continuity. ♦ **continûment** *adv* continuously. ♦ **continuum** *nm* continuum.
contondant, e [kɔ̃tɔ̃dɑ̃, ɑ̃t] *adj* blunt.
contorsion [kɔ̃tɔʀsjɔ̃] *nf* contortion. ♦ **contorsionner (se)** (1) *vpr* to contort o.s. ♦ **contorsionniste** *nmf* contortionist.
contour [kɔ̃tuʀ] *nm* outline, contour. ♦ **contourner** (1) *vt* (*gén*) to go (*ou* walk *ou* drive *etc*) round; *ville* to bypass; *difficulté* to get round.
contraception [kɔ̃tʀasɛpsjɔ̃] *nf* contraception. ♦ **contraceptif, -ive** *adj, nm* contraceptive.
contracter [kɔ̃tʀakte] (1) **1** *vt* **(a)** (*raidir*) *muscle, visage* to tense; (*fig*) *personne* to make tense. **la peur lui contracta la gorge** fear gripped his throat. **(b)** (*Phys: réduire*) ~ **un corps** to make a body contract. **(c)** *dette, alliance, maladie* to contract; *assurance* to take out. **2 se** ~ *vpr [muscle, visage]* to tense; *[gorge]* to tighten; (*fig*) *[personne]* to become tense; (*Phys*) *[corps]* to contract. ♦ **contracté, e** *adj* (*Ling*) contracted; *personne* tense. ♦ **contraction** *nf* (*action*) tensing, contraction; (*état*) tenseness; (*spasme*) contraction.
contractuel, -elle [kɔ̃tʀaktɥɛl] **1** *adj* contractual. **2** *nm,f* (*Police*) ≃ traffic warden; (*Admin*) contract employee.
contradiction [kɔ̃tʀadiksjɔ̃] *nf* contradiction. **être en** ~ **avec** to contradict. ♦ **contradictoire** *adj* contradictory, conflicting. **débat** ~ debate; ~ **à** in contradiction to, in conflict with.
contraindre [kɔ̃tʀɛ̃dʀ(ə)] (52) *vt*: ~ **qn à faire qch** to force *ou* compel *ou* constrain sb to do sth; **se** ~ **avec peine** to restrain o.s. with difficulty. ♦ **contraignant, e** *adj* restricting, constraining. ♦ **contraint, e**[1] *adj air* constrained, forced. **être** ~ **et forcé de faire** to be forced to do. ♦ **contrainte**[2] *nf* **(a)** (*violence*) constraint. **sous la** ~ under constraint *ou* duress. **(b)** (*gêne*) constraint, restraint. **sans** ~ unrestrainedly, unconstrainedly.
contraire [kɔ̃tʀɛʀ] **1** *adj* (*gén*) opposite; *vent, action* contrary; *intérêts* conflicting; *destin* adverse. **l'alcool m'est** ~ alcohol doesn't agree with me; **le sort lui fut** ~ fate was against him; ~ **à la santé** bad for the health. **2** *nm [mot, concept]* opposite. **c'est tout le** ~ it's just the reverse *ou* opposite; **je ne vous dis pas le** ~ I'm not saying anything to the contrary, I'm not disputing it; **tout au** ~ on the contrary; **au** ~ **des autres** unlike the others. ♦ **contrairement** *adv*: ~ **à** contrary to; ~ **aux autres ...** unlike the others ...
contrarier [kɔ̃tʀaʀje] (7) *vt* (*irriter*) to annoy; (*gêner*) *projets* to frustrate, thwart; *mouvement* to impede. ♦ **contrariant, e** *adj* annoying. ♦ **contrariété** *nf* annoyance.
contraste [kɔ̃tʀast(ə)] *nm* (*gén*) contrast. **par** ~ by contrast; **en** ~ **avec** in contrast to; **mettre en** ~ to contrast. ♦ **contrasté, e** *adj couleurs* contrasting. (*Phot*) **trop** ~ with too much contrast. ♦ **contraster** (1) **1** *vt éléments* to contrast; *photo* to give contrast to. **2** *vi* to contrast (*avec* with).
contrat [kɔ̃tʀa] *nm* (*gén*) contract; (*fig: accord*) agreement. *[équipe]* **remplir son** ~ to fulfil one's pledges.
contravention [kɔ̃tʀavɑ̃sjɔ̃] *nf* **(a)** (*Aut*) (*gén*) fine; (*papillon*) parking ticket. **dresser** ~ **(à qn)** to book* *ou* fine sb. **(b)** (*Jur: infraction*) ~ **à** contravention of.
contre [kɔ̃tʀ(ə)] **1** *prép et adv* **(a)** (*contact*) against. **appuyez-vous** ~ lean against *ou* on it; **serrer qn** ~ **son cœur** to clasp sb to one's breast; **son garage est juste** ~ **notre maison** his garage is built onto our house; **joue** ~ **joue** cheek to cheek. **(b)** (*hostilité*) against. (*Sport*) **Poitiers** ~ **Lyon** Poitiers versus *ou* against Lyons; **en colère** ~ **qn** angry with sb; **je n'ai rien** ~ **(cela)** I have nothing against it. **(c)** (*protection*) **s'abriter** ~ **le vent** to shelter from the wind; **des comprimés** ~ **la grippe** flu tablets, tablets for flu; **s'assurer** ~ **les accidents** to insure (o.s.) against *ou* for accidents. **(d)** (*échange*) *argent* (in exchange) for; *promesse* in return for. **envoi** ~ **remboursement** cash on delivery. **(e)** (*rapport*) **1 bon** ~ **3 mauvais** 1 good one for 3 bad ones; **9 voix** ~ **4** 9 votes to 4. **(f)** (*locutions*) ~ **toute attente** contrary to (all) expectations; ~ **toute apparence** despite (all) appearances to the contrary; **par** ~ on the other hand.
2 *nm* (*riposte*) retort; (*Cartes*) double.
3 *préf* (*le second élément donne le genre et prend seul la marque du pl*) ~**-attaque/-révolution/-espionnage** counter-attack/revolution/espionage; ~**-expertise/-visite** *etc* second assessment/(medical) opinion *etc*; ~**-allée** (*ville*) service road; (*parc*) side path; ~**-amiral** rear admiral; ~**-braquer** to steer into the skid; ~**-courant** counter-current; **à** ~**-courant** against the current; **en** ~**-haut (de)** above; ~**-indication** contraindication; ~**-indiqué, e** (*Méd*) contraindicated; (*déconseillé*) unadvisable; ~**-interrogatoire** cross-examination; **faire subir un** ~**-interrogatoire à qn** to cross-examine sb; ~**-jour** (*éclairage*) backlighting; (*photographie*) backlit shot; **à** ~**-jour** *se profiler* against the sunlight; *photographier* into the light; *lire* with one's back to the light; ~ **la montre** against the clock; **épreuve** ~ **la montre** time-trial; ~**-performance** substandard performance; **prendre le** ~**-pied de ce que dit qn** to say exactly the opposite of sb else; (*Sport*) **à** ~**-pied** on the wrong foot; ~**-plaqué** plywood; ~**-ut** top *ou* high C; ~**-valeur** exchange value; ~**-vérité** untruth, falsehood.
contrebalancer [kɔ̃tʀəbalɑ̃se] (3) *vt [poids]* to counterbalance; *[influence]* to offset.
contrebande [kɔ̃tʀəbɑ̃d] *nf* (*activité*) contraband, smuggling. **faire de la** ~ to do some smuggling; **produits de** ~ contraband, smuggled goods. ♦ **contrebandier, -ière** *nm,f* smuggler.
contrebas [kɔ̃tʀəbɑ] *nm*: **en** ~ (down) below; **en** ~ **de** below.
contrebasse [kɔ̃tʀəbɑs] *nf* (*instrument*) (double) bass; (*musicien*) (double) bass player.
contrebasson [kɔ̃tʀəbasɔ̃] *nm* contrabassoon.
contrecarrer [kɔ̃tʀəkaʀe] (1) *vt* to thwart.
contrecœur [kɔ̃tʀəkœʀ] *adv*: **à** ~ reluctantly.
contrecoup [kɔ̃tʀəku] *nm* repercussions.
contredire [kɔ̃tʀədiʀ] (37) *vt [personne]* to contradict; *[faits]* to be at variance with. ♦ **contredit** *nm*: **sans** ~ unquestionably.
contrée [kɔ̃tʀe] *nf* (*littér*) (*pays*) land; (*région*) region.
contrefaire [kɔ̃tʀəfɛʀ] (60) *vt* (*imiter*) to imitate; (*déguiser*) to disguise; (*falsifier*) to counterfeit, forge; (†: *feindre*) to feign. ♦ **contrefaçon** *nf* (*action*) counterfeiting; forgery, forging; (*produit*) imitation; (*billets, signature*) forgery, counterfeit.
contrefort [kɔ̃tʀəfɔʀ] *nm* **(a)** (*Archit*) buttress. **(b)** *[soulier]* stiffener. **(c)** (*Géog*) *[arête]* spur. *[chaîne]* ~**s** foothills.
contremaître, -maîtresse [kɔ̃tʀəmɛtʀ(ə), mɛtʀɛs] *nm,f* foreman; forewoman.
contrepartie [kɔ̃tʀəparti] *nf* compensation. **en** ~ (*en échange*) in return; (*en revanche*) in compensation (*de* for).
contrepoids [kɔ̃tʀəpwa] *nm* (*lit*) counterweight, counterbalance; *[acrobate]* balancing-pole. **faire** ~ to act as a counterbalance.
contrepoint [kɔ̃tʀəpwɛ̃] *nm* counterpoint.
contrepoison [kɔ̃tʀəpwazɔ̃] *nm* antidote.
contrer [kɔ̃tʀe] (1) **1** *vt* (*gén*) to counter; (*Cartes*) to double. **2** *vi* (*Cartes*) to double.
contresens [kɔ̃tʀəsɑ̃s] *nm* misinterpretation; (*traduction*) mistranslation. **à** ~ (*Aut*) the wrong way; (*Couture*) against the grain; **à** ~ **de** against.

contresigner [kɔ̃tʀəsiɲe] (1) *vt* to countersign.

contretemps [kɔ̃tʀətɑ̃] *nm* (*retard*) hitch. **à ~** (*Mus*) off the beat; (*fig*) at an inopportune moment.

contrevenir [kɔ̃tʀəvniʀ] (22) **~ à** *vt indir* to contravene. ♦ **contrevenant, e** *nm,f* offender.

contrevent [kɔ̃tʀəvɑ̃] *nm* (*volet*) shutter.

contribuer [kɔ̃tʀibɥe] (1) **~ à** *vt indir* to contribute to(wards). ♦ **contribuable** *nmf* taxpayer. ♦ **contribution** *nf* **(a)** (*participation*) contribution. **mettre qn à ~** to make use of sb. **(b)** (*impôts*) **~s** *[commune]* rates; *[état]* taxes; (*administration*) tax office; **~s directes** direct taxation.

contrit, e [kɔ̃tʀi, it] *adj* contrite. ♦ **contrition** *nf* contrition.

contrôler [kɔ̃tʀole] (1) **1** *vt* **(a)** (*vérifier*) (*gén*) to check; *billets* to inspect; *qualité* to control. **(b)** (*surveiller*) *opérations, employés* to supervise; *prix* to control. **(c)** (*maîtriser*) *colère*, (*Écon, Sport*) to control; (*Mil*) to be in control of. **2 se ~** *vpr* to control o.s. ♦ **contrôle** *nm* **(a)** (*action*) checking; inspecting; controlling; supervising. **(b)** (*opération*) check; inspection; control; supervision. **exercer un ~ sur** to maintain control over; **~ d'identité** identity check; **~ de soi-même** self-control; **garder le ~ de sa voiture** to remain in control of one's vehicle. **(c)** (*Théât: bureau*) (advance) booking office. (*Mil: registres*) **~s** lists. ♦ **contrôleur** *nm* (*gén*) inspector.

contrordre [kɔ̃tʀɔʀdʀ(ə)] *nm* counter-order.

controverse [kɔ̃tʀɔvɛʀs(ə)] *nf* controversy. ♦ **controversé, e** *adj* much debated.

contumace [kɔ̃tymas] *nf* (*Jur*) **par ~** in his (*ou* her *etc*) absence.

contusion [kɔ̃tyzjɔ̃] *nf* bruise. ♦ **contusionner** (1) *vt* to bruise.

conurbation [kɔnyʀbɑsjɔ̃] *nf* conurbation.

convaincre [kɔ̃vɛ̃kʀ(ə)] (42) *vt* to convince (*de qch* of sth). **~ qn de faire qch** to persuade sb to do sth, talk sb into doing sth; **~ qn de meurtre** to prove sb guilty of *ou* convict sb of murder. ♦ **convaincant, e** *adj* convincing. ♦ **convaincu, e** *adj* convinced. **d'un ton ~** with conviction.

convalescence [kɔ̃valesɑ̃s] *nf* convalescence. **être en ~** to be convalescing; **maison de ~** convalescent home. ♦ **convalescent, e** *adj, nm,f* convalescent.

convection [kɔ̃vɛksjɔ̃] *nf* convection.

convenable [kɔ̃vnabl(ə)] *adj* **(a)** (*approprié*) fitting, suitable. **(b)** (*décent*) decent, respectable. **peu ~** improper. **(c)** (*acceptable*) *devoir, salaire* acceptable, adequate. **à peine ~** scarcely acceptable *ou* adequate. ♦ **convenablement** *adv placé* suitably; *s'habiller* acceptably, decently; *payé, logé* adequately; *manger, se tenir* properly.

convenance [kɔ̃vnɑ̃s] *nf* (*préférence*) convenience; *[caractères]* affinity; *[équipement]* suitability. **est-ce à votre ~?** is it to your liking?; **les ~s** (*préférences*) preferences; (*sociales*) the proprieties.

convenir [kɔ̃vniʀ] (22) **1 ~ à** *vt indir*: **~ à qn** *[offre]* to suit sb; *[lecture]* to be suitable for sb; *[climat]* to agree with sb; *[date]* to be convenient for sb. **2 ~ de** *vt indir* **(a)** *erreur* to admit, recognize. **~ d'avoir fait** to admit (to) having done. **(b)** *date, lieu* to agree upon. **comme convenu** as agreed. **3** *vt*: **~ que** (*avouer*) to admit that; (*s'accorder sur*) to agree that. **4** *vb impers*: **il convient de faire** (*il vaut mieux*) it's advisable to do; (*il est bienséant de*) it is polite *ou* proper to do; **il convient de faire remarquer** we should point out.

convention [kɔ̃vɑ̃sjɔ̃] *nf* (*gén*) agreement; (*tacite*) understanding; (*Art, Pol, bienséance*) convention. ♦ **conventionnel, -elle** *adj* (*gén*) conventional.

converger [kɔ̃vɛʀʒe] (3) *vi* (*gén*) to converge; *[regards]* to focus (*sur* on). ♦ **convergence** *nf* convergence. ♦ **convergent, e** *adj* convergent.

conversation [kɔ̃vɛʀsɑsjɔ̃] *nf* (*gén*) conversation; (*Pol*) talk. **en (grande) ~ avec** (deep) in conversation with; **faire la ~ à** to make conversation with, speak to; **avoir de la ~** to be a good conversationalist; **dans la ~ courante** in informal *ou* conversational speech. ♦ **converser** (1) *vi* to converse (*avec* with).

convertir [kɔ̃vɛʀtiʀ] (2) **1** *vt* to convert (*à* to, *en* into). **2 se ~** *vpr* to be converted (*à* to). ♦ **conversion** *nf* conversion (*à* to, *en* into). ♦ **converti, e 1** *adj* converted. **2** *nm,f* convert. ♦ **convertible 1** *adj* convertible (*en* into). **2** *nm* (*canapé*) bed-settee. ♦ **convertisseur** *nm* converter.

convexe [kɔ̃vɛks(ə)] *adj* convex. ♦ **convexité** *nf* convexity.

conviction [kɔ̃viksjɔ̃] *nf* (*gén*) conviction.

convier [kɔ̃vje] (7) *vt*: **~ à** *soirée etc* to invite to. ♦ **convive** *nmf* guest.

convoiter [kɔ̃vwate] (1) *vt* to covet. ♦ **convoitise** *nf*: **la ~** covetousness; **la ~ de qch** the lust for sth; **l'objet de sa ~** *ou* **de ses ~s** the object of his desire; **regard de ~** covetous look.

convoler [kɔ̃vɔle] (1) *vi* († *ou hum*) **~ (en justes noces)** to be wed.

convoquer [kɔ̃vɔke] (1) *vt assemblée* to convene; *membre de club etc* to invite (*à* to); *candidat* to ask to attend; *prévenu, subordonné* to summon. **le chef m'a convoqué** I was summoned by *ou* called before the boss. ♦ **convocation** *nf* **(a)** (*action*) convening; inviting; summoning. **(b)** (*gén, Jur: avis*) summons; (*lettre*) (letter of) notification to appear *ou* attend.

convoyer [kɔ̃vwaje] (8) *vt* (*gén*) to escort; (*Mil, Naut*) to escort, convoy. ♦ **convoi** *nm* (*funèbre*) funeral procession; (*train*) train; (*véhicules*) convoy. ♦ **convoyeur** *nm* (*navire*) convoy, escort ship; (*personne*) escort. **~ de fonds** security guard.

convulser [kɔ̃vylse] (1) *vt* to convulse, distort. ♦ **convulsif, -ive** *adj* convulsive. ♦ **convulsion** *nf* (*gén*) convulsion. ♦ **convulsionner** (1) *vt* to convulse. ♦ **convulsivement** *adv* convulsively.

coopérer [kɔɔpeʀe] (6) *vi* to cooperate (*à* in). ♦ **coopérant** *nm person serving in the coopération.* ♦ **coopératif, -ive** *adj, nf* cooperative. ♦ **coopération** *nf* (*gén*) cooperation; (*Pol*) *scheme of aid to developing countries,* ≈ Voluntary Service Overseas (*Brit*), Peace Corps (*US*).

coopter [kɔɔpte] (1) *vt* to coopt. ♦ **cooptation** *nf* coopting.

coordonner [kɔɔʀdɔne] (1) *vt* to coordinate. ♦ **coordination** *nf* coordination. ♦ **coordonnateur, -trice 1** *adj* coordinating. **2** *nm,f* coordinator. ♦ **coordonné, e 1** *adj* (*gén*) coordinated; *proposition* coordinate. **2 ~es** *nfpl* (*Math*) coordinates; (*adresse*) whereabouts.

copain*, copine* [kɔpɛ̃, in] **1** *nm,f* pal*, chum*, buddy* (*US*). **2** *adj*: **très ~ avec** (very) pally* with.

copeau, *pl* **~x** [kɔpo] *nm [bois]* shaving; *[métal]* turning.

copier [kɔpje] (7) **1** *vt* (*gén*) to copy; (*Scol*) to crib (*sur* from). **~ qch au propre** to make a fair copy of sth; **vous me la copierez*** that's one to remember! **2** *vi* (*Scol*) to crib (*sur* from). ♦ **copie** *nf* **(a)** (*action*) copying; (*exemplaire, Presse, Typ*) copy. (*Admin*) **~ certifiée conforme** certified copy; **prendre ~ de** to make a copy of; **pâle ~** pale imitation; **c'est la ~ de sa mère** she's the (spitting) image of her mother. **(b)** (*Scol*) (*feuille*) sheet (of paper); (*devoir*) exercise; (*examen*) paper. ♦ **copieur, -euse** *nm,f* (*Scol*) cribber.

copieux, -euse [kɔpjø, øz] *adj* (*gén*) copious; *repas* hearty; *portion* generous. ♦ **copieusement** *adv* copiously, heartily; generously. **on s'est fait ~ arroser** we got thoroughly soaked.

copilote [kɔpilɔt] *nmf* co-pilot; (*Aut*) navigator.

copiner* [kɔpine] (1) *vi* to be pally꞉ (*avec* with). ♦ **copine** *nf V* **copain.**

copiste [kɔpist(ə)] *nmf* copyist.

copuler [kɔpyle] (1) *vi* to copulate. ♦ **copulation** *nf* copulation.

coq[1] [kɔk] *nm* cock. (*Boxe*) **poids** ~ bantamweight; **être comme un** ~ **en pâte** to be in clover; **mollets de** ~ wiry legs; **sauter du** ~ **à l'âne** to jump from one subject to another; **le** ~ **gaulois** the French cockerel; (*fig*) ~ **du village** cock of the walk; (*Culin*) ~ **au vin** coq au vin. ♦ **coquelet** *nm* (*Culin*) cockerel.

coq[2] [kɔk] *nm* (*Naut*) (ship's) cook.

coque [kɔk] *nf* **(a)** *[bateau]* hull; *[avion]* fuselage; *[auto]* body; *[œuf]* shell. (*Culin*) **à la** ~ boiled. **(b)** (*mollusque*) cockle. ♦ **coquetier** *nm* egg cup.

coquelicot [kɔkliko] *nm* poppy.

coqueluche [kɔklyʃ] *nf* (*Méd*) whooping cough. (*fig*) **être la** ~ **de** to be the idol of.

coquerie [kɔkʀi] *nf* (*Naut*) (ship's) galley.

coquet, -ette [kɔkɛ, ɛt] **1** *adj* **(a)** *ville* pretty, charming; *logement, vêtement* smart, stylish; *personne* (*dans sa tenue*) smart; (*par tempérament*) clothes-conscious. **(b)** (*) *revenu* tidy*. **(c)** (†) flirtatious, coquettish. **2** *nf* (†) coquette, flirt. ♦ **coquettement** *adv* smartly, stylishly; prettily; coquettishly. ♦ **coquetterie** *nf* **(a)** (*élégance*) smartness, stylishness; (*caractère*) consciousness of one's appearance. **(b)** (*amoureuse*) coquetry, flirtatiousness. ~**s** coquetries; (*amour propre*) **il mettait sa** ~ **à marcher sans canne** he prided himself on walking without a stick.

coquillage [kɔkijaʒ] *nm* (*coquille*) shell. (*mollusque*) ~**(s)** shellfish.

coquille [kɔkij] **1** *nf* (*gén*) shell; (*récipient*) scallop; (*Typ*) misprint; (*Méd: plâtre*) spinal bed. **2:** ~ **de beurre** whorl of butter; (*Naut*) ~ **de noix*** cockleshell; ~ **Saint-Jacques** (*animal*) scallop; (*carapace*) scallop shell. ♦ **coquillettes** *nfpl* pasta shells.

coquin, e [kɔkɛ̃, in] **1** *adj* (*malicieux*) mischievous; (*grivois*) naughty. ~ **de sort!*** the devil!* **2** *nm,f* (*enfant*) rascal, mischief. **3** *nm* (†: *gredin*) rogue. **4** *nf* (†) strumpet †. ♦ **coquinerie** *nf* **(a)** (*caractère*) mischievousness, roguishness. **(b)** (*acte*) mischievous trick; rascally trick.

cor [kɔʀ] *nm* **(a)** (*Mus*) horn. ~ **anglais** cor anglais; ~ **de chasse** hunting horn; ~ **d'harmonie** French horn; **demander qch à** ~ **et à cri** to clamour for sth. **(b)** ~ **(au pied)** corn.

corail, *pl* **-aux** [kɔʀaj, o] *nm, adj inv* coral.

coran [kɔʀɑ̃] *nm* Koran.

corbeau, *pl* ~**x** [kɔʀbo] *nm* (*gén*) crow. **(grand)** ~ raven.

corbeille [kɔʀbɛj] *nf* **(a)** (*panier*) basket. ~ **de mariage** wedding presents; ~ **à papiers** waste paper basket. **(b)** (*Théât*) (dress) circle.

corbillard [kɔʀbijaʀ] *nm* hearse.

corde [kɔʀd(ə)] **1** *nf* **(a)** (*câble*) rope. (*Boxe*) ~**s** ropes; (*fig*) **mériter la** ~ to deserve to be hanged; **de** ~ *semelle* rope; *tapis* whipcord; **monter à la** ~ to climb a rope. **(b)** *[violon, arc, raquette]* string. **les (instruments à)** ~**s** the stringed instruments, the strings; **quatuor à** ~**s** string quartet. **(c)** *[tissu]* thread; (*Math*) chord. **(d) se mettre la** ~ **au cou** to put one's head in the noose; **avoir plusieurs** ~**s à son arc** to have more than one string to one's bow; **c'est dans ses** ~**s** it's in his line; (*Courses*) **tenir la** ~ to be on the inside (lane); **prendre un virage à la** ~ to hug the bend; **tirer sur la** ~ to go too far; **il pleut des** ~**s*** it's bucketing (down)*.
2: ~ **à linge** clothes line; ~ **à nœuds** knotted climbing rope; ~ **à piano** pianowire; ~ **raide** tightrope; ~ **à sauter** skipping rope; ~**s vocales** vocal cords.
♦ **cordage** *nm* rope. *[voilure]* ~**s** rigging. ♦ **cordeau,** *pl* ~**x** *nm* **(a)** *[jardinier]* line. (*fig*) **tiré au** ~ as straight as a die. **(b)** (*mèche*) fuse. ♦ **cordée** *nf* roped party. ♦ **cordelette** *nf* cord.

cordial, e, *mpl* **-iaux** [kɔʀdjal, jo] **1** *adj* warm, cordial. **2** *nm* cordial. ♦ **cordialement** *adv* warmly, cordially. ~ **(vôtre)** ever yours. ♦ **cordialité** *nf* warmth, cordiality.

cordillère [kɔʀdijɛʀ] *nf*: **la** ~ **des Andes** the Andes cordillera.

cordon [kɔʀdɔ̃] **1** *nm [rideau]* cord; *[tablier]* tie; *[sac]* string; *[souliers]* lace; *[soldats]* cordon; (*décoration*) ribbon. ~ **de sonnette** bell-pull; (*fig*) **tenir les** ~**s de la bourse** to hold the purse strings. **2:** ~**-bleu*** *nm, pl* ~**s-**~**s** cordon-bleu cook; ~ **littoral** offshore bar; ~ **ombilical** umbilical cord; (*Méd, Pol*) ~ **sanitaire** quarantine line.

cordonnerie [kɔʀdɔnʀi] *nf* (*boutique*) shoemender's (shop); (*métier*) shoemending. ♦ **cordonnier, -ière** *nm,f* (*réparateur*) shoemender, cobbler.

coriace [kɔʀjas] *adj* (*lit, fig*) tough.

cormoran [kɔʀmɔʀɑ̃] *nm* cormorant.

corne [kɔʀn(ə)] **1** *nf* (*gén, instrument*) horn; *[cerf]* antler; *[page]* dog-ear. **à** ~**s** horned; **donner un coup de** ~ **à qn** to butt sb; **blesser qn d'un coup de** ~ to gore sb; (*fig*) **faire les** ~**s à qn** to make a face at sb; (*peau*) **de la** ~ hard skin. **2:** ~ **d'abondance** horn of plenty; ~ **de brume** foghorn; ~ **à chaussures** shoehorn.

cornée [kɔʀne] *nf* cornea.

corneille [kɔʀnɛj] *nf* crow.

cornemuse [kɔʀnəmyz] *nf* bagpipes. **joueur de** ~ bagpiper.

corner[1] [kɔʀne] (1) **1** *vt* **(a)** *livre* to make dog-eared; *page* to turn down the corner of. **(b)** *nouvelle* to shout out. **2** *vi* (*Aut*) to sound one's horn.

corner[2] [kɔʀnɛʀ] *nm* (*Ftbl*) corner (kick).

cornet [kɔʀnɛ] *nm* (*récipient*) cornet; *[orgue]* cornet stop. ~ **acoustique** ear trumpet; ~ **à dés** dice cup; (*Mus*) ~ **(à pistons)** cornet.

corniaud [kɔʀnjo] *nm* (*chien*) mongrel; (꞉: *imbécile*) nitwit*.

corniche [kɔʀniʃ] *nf* (*Archit*) cornice; (*Géog*) ledge. **(route en)** ~ cliff road.

cornichon [kɔʀniʃɔ̃] *nm* (*lit*) gherkin; (*: *fig*) nitwit*.

Cornouailles [kɔʀnwaj] *nf* Cornwall.

cornue [kɔʀny] *nf* (*Tech*) retort.

corollaire [kɔʀɔlɛʀ] *nm* corollary.

corolle [kɔʀɔl] *nf* corolla.

coronaire [kɔʀɔnɛʀ] *adj* coronary.

corporatif, -ive [kɔʀpɔʀatif, iv] *adj système* corporative; *esprit* corporate. ♦ **corporation** *nf* professional body; (*Hist*) guild.

corporel, -elle [kɔʀpɔʀɛl] *adj châtiment* corporal; *besoin* bodily.

corps [kɔʀ] **1** *nm* (*gén, Chim, fig*) body; (*cadavre*) corpse, (dead) body. **trembler de tout son** ~ to tremble all over; **n'avoir rien dans le** ~ to feel empty; **se donner** ~ **et âme à qch** to give o.s. heart and soul to sth; **perdu** ~ **et biens** lost with all hands; (*fig*) **à** ~ **perdu** headlong; **donner** ~ **à qch** to give substance to sth; **faire** ~ *[idées]* to form one body (*avec* with); *[choses concrètes]* to be joined (*avec* to); **prendre** ~ to take shape; **à son** ~ **défendant** against one's will; **mais qu'est-ce qu'il a dans le** ~? what HAS got into him?
2: ~ **d'armée** army corps; ~ **de ballet** corps de ballet; ~ **de bâtiment** building; ~ **à** ~ (*adv*) hand-to-hand; (*nm*) hand-to-hand fight; ~ **diplomatique** diplomatic corps; ~ **électoral** electorate; **le** ~ **enseignant** the teaching profession; ~ **expéditionnaire** task force; ~ **franc** irregular force; ~ **de garde** (*local*) guardroom; ~ **gras** greasy substance; **le** ~ **médical** the medical profession; ~ **de métier** trade association; ~ **de sapeurs-pompiers** fire-brigade; ~ **de troupe** unit (of troops).

corpulence [kɔʀpylɑ̃s] *nf* stoutness, corpulence. **de moyenne** ~ of medium build. ♦ **corpulent, e** *adj* stout, corpulent.

corpus [kɔʀpys] *nm* corpus. ♦ **corpuscule** *nm* (*Anat, Phys*) corpuscle.

correct, e [kɔʀɛkt, ɛkt(ə)] *adj* (*gén*) correct; *réponse* right; *fonctionnement, tenue* proper; (*: *acceptable*) adequate. ~ **en affaires** correct in business matters. ♦ **correctement** *adv* correctly; properly; adequately. ♦ **correcteur, -trice 1** *adj* corrective. **2** *nm,f [examen]* marker; (*Typ*) proof-reader. **3** *nm* (*Tech*) corrector. ♦ **correctif, -ive 1** *adj* corrective. **2** *nm* (*mise au point*) qualifying statement.

correction [kɔʀɛksjɔ̃] *nf* **(a)** (*action*) (*gén*) correction; (*Typ*) proofreading; *[examen]* marking. **(b)** (*résultat*) correction; (*châtiment*) thrashing. **(c)** (*exactitude*) correctness; propriety. ♦ **correctionnel, -elle** *adj, nf*: **le tribunal** ~, **la** ~**le*** the criminal court.

corrélation [kɔʀelɑsjɔ̃] *nf* correlation.

correspondance [kɔʀɛspɔ̃dɑ̃s] *nf* **(a)** (*conformité*) correspondence. **(b)** (*Math*) relation; (*fig: rapport*) relation, connection. **(c)** (*échange de lettres*) correspondence; (*courrier*) mail. **être en** ~ to be in correspondence; **apprendre qch par** ~ to learn sth by a correspondence course. **(d)** (*transports*) connection. **assurer la** ~ **avec** to connect with. ♦ **correspondant, e 1** *adj* corresponding. **2** *nm,f* (*gén, Presse*) correspondent; (*Scol*) penfriend.

correspondre [kɔʀɛspɔ̃dʀ(ə)] (41) **1** ~ **à** *vt indir goûts* to suit; *capacités, description* to fit; *dimension, système* to correspond to. **ça ne correspond pas à la réalité** it doesn't tally with *ou* fit the facts. **2** *vi* (*écrire*) to correspond; *[chambres]* to communicate (*avec* with). (*Transport*) ~ **avec** to connect with. **3 se** ~ *vpr* to communicate.

corrida [kɔʀida] *nf* bullfight; (**fig*) to-do*.

corridor [kɔʀidɔʀ] *nm* corridor.

corriger [kɔʀiʒe] (3) **1** *vt* **(a)** (*gén*) to correct; (*Typ*) to proofread; *examen* to mark; *abus* to remedy. **(b)** ~ **qn de** *défaut* to cure sb of. **(c)** (*punir*) to thrash. **2 se** ~ *vpr* (*devenir raisonnable*) to mend one's ways. **se** ~ **de** *défaut* to cure *ou* rid o.s. of. ♦ **corrigé** *nm [exercice]* correct version; *[traduction]* fair copy. **recueil de** ~**s** key to exercises.

corroborer [kɔʀɔbɔʀe] (1) *vt* to corroborate.

corroder [kɔʀɔde] (1) *vt* to corrode.

corrompre [kɔʀɔ̃pʀ(ə)] (4) *vt témoin* to bribe, corrupt; *mœurs, texte* to corrupt; *langage* to debase; *aliments* to taint. ♦ **corrompu, e** *adj* corrupt.

corrosion [kɔʀozjɔ̃] *nf* corrosion. ♦ **corrosif, -ive** *adj* corrosive; (*fig*) caustic, scathing.

corruption [kɔʀypsjɔ̃] *nf* corruption. ♦ **corrupteur, -trice 1** *adj* corrupting. **2** *nm,f* briber; (*littér: dépravateur*) corrupter. ♦ **corruptible** *adj* corruptible.

corsage [kɔʀsaʒ] *nm* (*chemisier*) blouse; *[robe]* bodice.

corsaire [kɔʀsɛʀ] *nm* (*Hist*) privateer.

Corse [kɔʀs(ə)] *nf* Corsica. ♦ **corse** *adj*, **C**~ *nmf* Corsican.

corser [kɔʀse] (1) *vt repas* to make spicier; *difficulté* to intensify, aggravate; *récit* to liven up. **ça se corse** things are hotting up. ♦ **corsé, e** *adj vin* full-bodied; *café* strong (and flavourful); *mets, histoire* spicy; *problème* stiff.

corset [kɔʀsɛ] *nm* corset.

corso [kɔʀso] *nm*: ~ **(fleuri)** procession of floral floats.

cortège [kɔʀtɛʒ] *nm [prince]* retinue. (*littér*) ~ **de** *malheurs* trail of; *souvenirs* succession of.

corvée [kɔʀve] *nf* (*Mil*) fatigue duty; (*gén*) chore. **être de** ~ to be on fatigue duty; ~ **de ravitaillement** supply duty; **quelle** ~! what a chore!

corvette [kɔʀvɛt] *nf* corvette.

cosaque [kɔzak] *nm* cossack.

cosmétique [kɔsmetik] *nm* hair oil.

cosmos [kɔsmos] *nm* (*univers*) cosmos; (*Espace*) outer space. ♦ **cosmique** *adj* cosmic. ♦ **cosmonaute** *nmf* cosmonaut. ♦ **cosmopolite** *adj* cosmopolitan.

cosse [kɔs] *nf [pois]* pod; (*Élec*) terminal spade tag. **avoir la** ~* to be in a lazy mood.

cossu, e [kɔsy] *adj personne* well-off; *maison* grand.

costaud, e* [kɔsto, od] *adj* strong, sturdy.

costume [kɔstym] *nm* (*régional*) costume, dress; (*Théât*) costume; (*complet*) suit. ~ **de bain** bathing costume. ♦ **costumer** (1) **1** *vt*: ~ **qn en** to dress sb up as. **2 se** ~ *vpr [acteur]* to get into costume; **se** ~ **en** to dress up as; **être costumé** to wear fancy dress.

cotation [kɔtɑsjɔ̃] *nf* (*Bourse*) quotation; *[voiture]* valuation; *[devoir]* marking.

cote [kɔt] *nf* **(a)** (*Bourse*) (*cours*) quotation; (*liste*) share index; *[timbre]* quoted value; *[devoir]* mark; *[cheval]* odds (*de* on); *[film]* rating; (*Impôts*) assessment. **(b)** (*popularité*) rating. **avoir la** ~* to be very popular (*auprès de* with) *ou* highly rated (*auprès de* by); **sa** ~ **est en baisse** his popularity is on the decline. **(c)** *[carte]* spot height; *[croquis]* dimensions; *[bibliothèque]* classification mark. (*Mil*) **la** ~ **215** hill 215; ~ **d'alerte** *[rivière, prix]* danger mark; *[situation]* crisis point; ~ **mal taillée** rough-and-ready settlement.

côte [kot] *nf* **(a)** (*Anat, Bot*) rib. **se tenir les** ~**s (de rire)** to split one's sides (with laughter); ~ **à** ~ side by side. **(b)** *[bœuf]* rib; *[veau, agneau]* cutlet; *[mouton, porc]* chop. ~ **première** loin chop. **(c)** *[colline]* slope; (*Aut*) *[route]* hill. **(d)** (*littoral*) coast. **les** ~**s de France** the coasts of France; **la** ~ **d'Azur** the Riviera; **la C**~**-d'Ivoire** the Ivory Coast.

côté [kote] **1** *nm* **(a)** side. **l'épée au** ~ (with) his sword by his side; **à son** ~ at *ou* by his side, beside him; **appartement** ~ **rue** flat overlooking the street; **se mettre du** ~ **du plus fort** to side *ou* take sides with the strongest. **(b)** (*aspect*) side. **les bons** ~**s de qch** the good sides *ou* points of sth; **prendre qch du bon/mauvais** ~ to take sth well/badly; **prendre qn par son** ~ **faible** to attack sb's weak spot; **par certains** ~**s** in some respects *ou* ways; **d'un** ~ ... **d'un autre** ~ ... (*alternative*) on (the) one hand ... on the other hand ...; (*hésitation*) in one respect ... in another respect ...; **(du)** ~ **santé*** healthwise*, as far as his *etc* health is concerned. **(c)** (*précédé de 'de': direction*) way, direction. **de ce** ~**-ci** this way; **de l'autre** ~ the other way, in the other direction; **aller/venir du** ~ **de la mer** to go towards/come from the sea; **de tous** ~**s** everywhere; (*fig*) **je l'ai entendu dire de divers** ~**s** I've heard it from several quarters *ou* sources; (*fig*) **de mon** ~ for my part.

2 à ~ *adv* **(a)** (*proximité*) nearby. **les gens (d')à** ~ the people next door, our next-door neighbours; **à** ~ **de** next to, beside; **(tout) à** ~ close by. **(b) viser à** ~ **(du but)** to miss (the goal); **à** ~ **de la cible** wide of the target; **à** ~ **de la question** off the point; (*fig*) **passer à** ~ **de qch*** to miss sth (narrowly). **(c)** (*comparaison*) by comparison. **à** ~ **de** compared to; (*par contre*) **à** ~ **de ça** but on the other hand.

3 de ~ *adv se tourner* sideways; *sauter, laisser* aside, to one side. **mettre qch de** ~ to put sth aside; **regard de** ~ sidelong look.

coteau, *pl* ~**x** [kɔto] *nm* (*colline*) hill; (*versant*) hillside.

côtelette [kotlɛt] *nf [mouton, porc]* chop; *[veau, agneau]* cutlet.

coter [kɔte] (1) *vt* **(a)** to quote; *timbre* to quote the market price of; *devoir* to mark; *film* to rate. **bien/mal coté** highly/not highly thought of; **coté à**

l'Argus listed in the secondhand car book. **(b)** *carte* to put spot heights on; *croquis* to mark in the dimensions on; (*en bibliothèque*) to put a classification mark on.

coterie [kɔtRi] *nf* (*gén péj*) set.

côtier, -ière [kotje, jɛR] *adj pêche* inshore; *navigation, région* coastal.

cotisation [kɔtizɑsjɔ̃] *nf [club]* subscription; *[sécurité sociale, syndicat]* contributions. ♦ **cotisant, e** *nm,f* subscriber; contributor. ♦ **cotiser** (1) **1** *vi* to subscribe, pay one's subscription; to pay one's contributions (*à* to). **2 se ~** *vpr* to club together.

côtoiement [kotwamɑ̃] *nm* (*fréquentation*) association; (*coudoiement*) mixing (*de* with).

coton [kɔtɔ̃] **1** *nm* (*gén*) cotton; (*tampon*) (cotton-wool) swab. **~ à repriser** darning thread; **~ hydrophile** cotton wool; **avoir du ~ dans les oreilles*** to have cloth ears*; **j'ai les jambes en ~** my legs feel like cotton wool. **2** *adj* (*: *ardu*) stiff*. ♦ **cotonnade** *nf* cotton fabric. ♦ **cotonneux, -euse** *adj brouillard* wispy; *nuage* fluffy. ♦ **cotonnier, -ière 1** *adj* cotton. **2** *nm* (*Bot*) cotton plant.

côtoyer [kotwaje] (8) **1** *vt* **(a)** (*longer*) to drive (*ou* walk *etc*) alongside; *[rivière, route]* to run alongside. **(b)** (*coudoyer*) to rub shoulders with. **~ la malhonnêteté** to be bordering *ou* verging on dishonesty. **2 se ~** *vpr [individus]* to rub shoulders; *[genres]* to meet.

cotte [kɔt] *nf* **(a)** (*Hist*) **~ de mailles** coat of mail; **~ d'armes** coat of arms (*surcoat*). **(b)** (*salopette*) dungarees, overalls.

cou [ku] **1** *nm* neck. **jusqu'au ~** *enlisé, endetté* up to one's neck; **sauter au ~ de qn** to throw one's arms around sb's neck. **2: ~-de-pied** *nm, pl* **~s-~-~** instep.

couac [kwak] *nm* false note.

couchage *nm* (*installation*) sleeping arrangements. **matériel de ~** sleeping equipment.

couchant [kuʃɑ̃] **1** *adj*: **soleil ~** setting sun. **2** *nm* (*ouest*) west; (*ciel du soir*) sunset.

couche [kuʃ] *nf* **(a)** (*gén*) layer; *[peinture]* coat. **~ sociale** social stratum; (*fig*) **en tenir une ~*** to be really thick*. **(b)** (*Horticulture*) hotbed. **(c)** *[bébé]* nappy, diaper (*US*). **(d)** (*Méd: accouchement*) **~s** confinement; **mourir en ~s** to die in childbirth. **(e)** (*littér: lit*) bed.

coucher [kuʃe] (1) **1** *vt* **(a)** (*mettre au lit*) to put to bed; (*donner un lit*) to put up. **être/rester couché** to be/stay in bed. **(b)** *blessé* to lay out; *échelle etc* to lay down; *blés* to flatten. **être couché** to be lying. **(c)** (*inscrire*) to inscribe. **(d) ~ en joue** *fusil* to aim; *personne* to aim at. **2** *vi* (*dormir*) to sleep (*avec* with). **cela nous a fait ~ très tard** that meant we went to bed very late. **3 se ~** *vpr* to go to bed; (*s'étendre*) to lie down; *[soleil, lune]* to set, go down; *[bateau]* to keel over. **4** *nm*: **le (moment du) ~** bedtime; **le ~ des enfants** the children's bedtime; **(au) ~ du soleil** (at) sunset *ou* sundown (*US*). ♦ **couchette** *nf [voyageur]* berth, couchette; *[marin]* bunk.

coucou [kuku] *nm* (*oiseau*) cuckoo; (*pendule*) cuckoo clock; (*péj: avion*) (old) crate; (*fleur*) cowslip. **~ (me voici)!** peek-a-boo!

coude [kud] *nm* (*Anat*) elbow; *[route, tuyau]* bend. (*fig*) **se serrer les ~s** to stick together; **~ à ~** shoulder to shoulder. ♦ **coudée** *nf*: **avoir les ~s franches** to have elbow room; (*fig*) **dépasser qn de cent ~s**† to stand head and shoulders above sb.

coudoyer [kudwaje] (8) *vt* (*fréquenter*) to rub shoulders with; (*être à côté de*) to be next to. ♦ **coudoiement** *nm* mixing.

coudre [kudR(ə)] (48) *vt* to sew; *bouton* to sew on; *vêtement, plaie* to sew up; (*Reliure*) to stitch.

coudrier [kudRije] *nm* hazel tree.

couenne [kwan] *nf [lard]* rind; (*: *peau*) hide*.

couiner [kwine] (1) *vi* to squeal.

couler [kule] (1) **1** *vi* **(a)** *[liquide, paroles]* to flow; *[larmes, sueur]* to run down; *[fromage, bougie]* to run. *[vin]* **~ à flots** to flow freely; **le sang a coulé** blood has been shed; **faire ~** *eau, bain* to run; **faire ~ le sang** to shed blood; (*fig*) **ça a fait ~ beaucoup d'encre** it caused much ink to flow; **~ de source** (*être clair*) to be obvious; (*s'enchaîner*) to follow naturally. **(b)** *[robinet, nez]* to run; (*fuir*) to leak. **(c)** *[vie, temps]* to slip by. **(d)** *[bateau, personne]* to sink. **~ à pic** to sink straight to the bottom. **2** *vt* **(a)** *ciment* to pour; *métal, statue* to cast. **(b)** *bateau* to sink; (*) *personne* to discredit; *candidat* to bring down. **(c)** *regard* to steal. **~ des jours heureux** to enjoy happy days. **3 se ~** *vpr*: **se ~ dans/à travers** to slip into/through; **se la ~ douce*** to have an easy time of it. ♦ **coulant, e 1** *adj pâte* runny; *style* flowing; (*: *indulgent*) easy-going. **2** *nm [ceinture]* sliding loop. ♦ **coulée** *nf [métal]* casting. **~ de lave** lava flow; **~ de boue** mud slide.

couleur [kulœR] *nf* **(a)** (*gén, fig*) colour; (*nuance*) shade, tint; (*peinture*) paint; (*Cartes*) suit. **de ~ claire** light-coloured; **(de) ~ chair/paille** flesh/straw-coloured; **film en ~s** colour film; **de ~** *personne* coloured; *vêtements* colourful; **les ~s** (*linge*) coloureds; (*emblème*) the colours; **boîte de ~s** paintbox; **reprendre des ~s** to get back one's colour; **sans ~** colourless; **~ locale** local colour. **(b)** (*locutions*) **sous ~ de qch** under the guise of sth; **sous ~ de faire** while pretending to do; **sous de fausses ~s** in a false light; **peindre qch sous les plus sombres ~s** to paint sth in the darkest colours; **elle n'a jamais vu la ~ de son argent*** she's never seen the colour of his money*.

couleuvre [kulœvR(ə)] *nf* grass snake.

coulisse [kulis] *nf* **(a)** (*Théât: gén pl*) wings; **en ~** (*Théât*) in the wings; (*fig*) behind the scenes. **(b)** *[porte]* runner. **porte à ~** sliding door; (*fig*) **regard en ~** sidelong look. ♦ **coulisser** (1) *vi [porte]* to slide.

couloir [kulwaR] *nm* corridor, passage; *[wagon]* corridor; (*bande de circulation*) lane; (*ravin*) gully. **~ d'avalanches** avalanche corridor.

coup [ku] **1** *nm* **(a)** (*choc*) knock; (*affectif*) blow. **se donner un ~ à la tête** to hit *ou* bang one's head; **donner des ~s dans la porte** to bang at the door.

(b) (*hostile*) blow. **~ de pied** kick; **~ de poing** punch; **donner un ~** to hit; **recevoir un ~ de bâton** to be struck with a stick; **il a reçu un ~ de griffe/de couteau** he was clawed/knifed; **tuer qn à ~s de pierres** to stone sb to death; **donner un ~ de dents/de bec** to bite/peck (*dans* at); **~ de feu** shot; **tuer qn d'un ~ de fusil** to shoot sb dead (with a rifle).

(c) (*avec le corps*) **~ d'œil** (*regard*) glance; (*spectacle*) view; **jeter un ~ d'œil à** to glance at; **~ de coude** nudge; **~ d'ongle** scratch; **l'oiseau donna un ~ d'aile** the bird flapped its wings *ou* gave a flap of its wings; **d'un ~ de tête/de genou** with a nudge *ou* thrust of his head/knee.

(d) (*habileté*) **avoir le ~*** to have the knack; **avoir le ~ d'œil** to have a good eye.

(e) (*avec instrument*) **~ de crayon** stroke of a pencil; **~ de marteau** blow of a hammer; **passer un ~ de chiffon/balai à qch** to give sth a wipe/sweep sth; **donner un ~ de peinture à un mur** to give a wall a coat of paint; **~ de téléphone** phone call; **donner un ~ de frein** to brake.

(f) (*Golf, Tennis*) stroke; (*Boxe*) punch; (*Échecs*) move. (*Boxe, fig*) **~ bas** punch below the belt; (*Ftbl, Rugby*) **~ d'envoi** kick-off; (*Ftbl*) **~ franc** free kick.

(g) (*bruit*) **~ de tonnerre** (*lit*) thunderclap; (*fig*) bombshell; **~ de sonnette** ring; **arrêtez au ~ de sifflet** stop when the whistle blows; **les douze ~s de midi** the twelve strokes of noon.

(h) (*produit par les éléments*) **~ de vent** gust of

wind; **passer en ~ de vent** to rush past like a whirlwind; (*visite*) to pay a flying visit; **~(s) de soleil** sunburn; **prendre un ~ de soleil** to get sunburnt; **prendre un ~ de froid** to catch a chill.

(i) (*événement fortuit*) **~ du sort** blow dealt by fate; **~ de chance** stroke of luck; **~ dur** hard blow; **c'est un sale ~*** it's a dreadful blow.

(j) (*entreprise*) *[cambrioleurs]* job*. **tenter le ~*** to have a go*; **réussir un beau ~** to pull it off; **être dans le ~/hors du ~** to be/not to be in on it.

(k) (*:*contre qn*) trick. **faire un sale ~ à qn** to play a dirty trick on sb; **il nous fait le ~ chaque fois** he never fails to do that.

(l) (*: *verre*) **boire un ~** to have a drink; **il a bu un ~ de trop** he's had one too many*.

(m) (*: *fois*) time. **à tous (les) ~s** every time; **du premier ~** first time; **pour un ~** for once; **rire un bon ~** to have a good laugh.

(n) (*effet*) **sous le ~ de** *surprise* in the grip of, affected by; (*Admin*) **tomber sous le ~ de la loi** to be a statutory offence.

(o) (*locutions*) **à ~ sûr** definitely; **après ~** after the event; **~ sur ~** in quick succession; **c'est pour le ~ qu'il se fâcherait** then he'd really get angry; **sur le ~** (*gén*) outright; *tué* instantly; **sur le ~ je n'ai pas compris** at the time I didn't understand; **d'un seul ~** at one go; **tout à ~** all of a sudden; **tenir le ~** to hold out.

2: (*fig*) **~ d'arrêt** sharp check; (*Jur*) **~s et blessures** assault and grievous bodily harm; **~ de boutoir** thrust; (*lit, fig*) **~ de dés** toss of the dice; **~ d'éclat** glorious feat; **~ d'essai** first attempt; **~ d'État** coup (d'état); (*fig*) **~ de filet** haul; **~ de force** armed takeover; (*fig*) **~ de foudre** love at first sight; (*lit, fig*) **~ de grâce** finishing blow; **~ de grisou** firedamp explosion; **~ de main** (*aide*) helping hand; (*raid*) raid; **donne-moi un ~ de main** give me a hand; **~ de maître** master stroke; **~ de pouce** (*pour aider qn*) push in the right direction; **~ de sang** stroke; **~ de tête** sudden impulse; **~ de théâtre** (*Théât*) coup de théâtre; (*gén*) dramatic turn of events.

coupable [kupabl(ə)] **1** *adj personne* guilty (*de* of); *désirs* guilty; *négligence* culpable. **2** *nmf* culprit.

coupage [kupaʒ] *nm* (*action*) blending; (*avec de l'eau*) dilution; (*résultat*) blend. **~s** blended wines.

coupant, e [kupɑ̃, ɑ̃t] *adj lame, ton* sharp.

coupe¹ [kup] *nf* **(a)** (*à fruits*) dish; (*contenu*) dishful; (*à boire*) goblet. **(b)** (*Sport*) cup.

coupe² [kup] *nf* **(a)** (*action*) (*gén*) cutting; *[tissu]* cutting-out; *[arbre]* cutting-down. **(b)** (*résultat*) cut. **~ de cheveux** haircut. **(c)** (*section*) section. **(d) être sous la ~ de qn** to be under sb's control; **faire des ~s sombres dans** to make drastic cuts in; **mettre en ~ réglée** to bleed systematically (*fig*); *V aussi* **couper 5.**

coupé [kupe] *nm* (*Aut, Danse*) coupé.

couper [kupe] (1) **1** *vt* **(a)** (*gén*) to cut; *bois* to chop; *arbre* to cut down; *rôti* to carve; (*Couture*) *vêtement* to cut out; *gâteau* to slice; (*fig*) *[vent]* to sting. **~ la gorge à qn** to slit sb's throat; **~ la tête à qn** to chop sb's head off; **se faire ~ les cheveux** to get one's hair cut. **(b)** (*raccourcir, retrancher*) to cut; (*séparer*) to cut off; (*entailler*) to slit. **(c)** *route, relations, vivres* to cut off; *fièvre* to bring down; *appétit* to take away; *eau, gaz* to cut off; (*au compteur*) to turn off. (*Aut*) **~ le contact** to switch off the ignition; **~ le vent** to cut out the wind; **~ la route à qn** to cut in front of sb; **~ qn de** to cut sb off from; **~ les ponts avec qn** to break off communications with sb. **(d)** *voyage* to break; *journée* to break up. **(e)** *[ligne]* to cut; *[route]* to cut across. **(f)** (*Cartes*) *jeu* to cut; (*avec l'atout*) to trump. **(g)** *[vin]* to blend; (*avec de l'eau*) to dilute. **(h)** (*locutions*) **~ les bras à qn** to dishearten sb; **~ la poire en deux** to meet halfway; **~ les cheveux en quatre** to split hairs; **~ ses effets à qn** to steal sb's thunder; **~ l'herbe sous le pied à qn** to cut the ground from under sb's feet; **~ la parole à qn** *[personne]* to cut sb short; *[émotion]* to render sb speechless; **~ le sifflet* à qn** to shut sb up*; **~ le souffle à qn** (*lit*) to wind sb; (*fig*) to take sb's breath away; **brouillard/accent à ~ au couteau** fog/accent you could cut with a knife.

2 ~ à *vt indir* **(a)** *corvée* to get out of. **tu n'y couperas pas** you won't get out of it. **(b) ~ court à** to cut short.

3 *vi* (*gén*) to cut; (*jouer atout*) to trump. **~ à travers champs** to cut across country; **~ au plus court** to take the quickest way.

4 se ~ *vpr* **(a)** to cut o.s. **se ~ à la jambe/les ongles** to cut one's leg/one's nails. **(b)** (*) to give o.s. away.

5: coupe-circuit *nm inv* cutout; **coupe-coupe** *nm inv* machete; **coupe-feu** *nm inv* firebreak; **coupe-gorge** *nm inv* death-trap; **coupe-papier** *nm inv* paper knife.

couperet [kupʀɛ] *nm [boucher]* cleaver, chopper; *[guillotine]* blade.

couple [kupl(ə)] *nm* (*gén*) couple; (*patineurs, animaux*) pair; (*moteur, de torsion*) torque. ◆ **coupler** (1) *vt* to couple together.

couplet [kuplɛ] *nm [chanson]* verse.

coupole [kupɔl] *nf* dome; (*petite*) cupola.

coupon [kupɔ̃] *nm* **(a)** (*Couture*) (*reste*) remnant; (*rouleau*) roll. **(b)** (*Fin: ticket*) coupon. **~-réponse** reply coupon.

coupure [kupyʀ] *nf* (*gén*) cut; (*fig: fossé*) break; (*billet de banque*) note. **~ (de presse)** (newspaper) cutting; **~ (de courant)** power cut.

cour [kuʀ] *nf* **(a)** (*gén*) (court)yard; *[gare]* forecourt; *[caserne]* square. **être sur (la) ~** to look onto the (court)yard; **~ d'école** schoolyard, playground; **~ de ferme** farmyard; **~ de récréation** playground. **(b)** (*Jur*) court. **~ d'appel/de cassation** Court of Appeal/of Cassation; (*Mil*) **~ martiale** court martial. **(c)** *[roi]* court; *[écrivain, femme]* following. **faire sa ~ à** *roi* to pay court to; *supérieur* to pay one's respects to; **être bien/mal en ~** to be in/out of favour (*auprès de qn* with sb); **faire la ~ à une femme** to court a woman.

courage [kuʀaʒ] *nm* (*bravoure*) courage, bravery; (*ardeur*) will, spirit. **vous n'aurez pas le ~ de** you won't have the heart to; **entreprendre qch avec ~** to undertake sth with a will; **je ne m'en sens pas le ~** I don't feel up to it; **ça vous donnera du ~** it'll buck you up*; **~!** cheer up!, take heart!; **perdre ~** to lose heart; **reprendre ~** to take fresh heart. ◆ **courageusement** *adv* bravely, courageously; *entreprendre* with a will. ◆ **courageux, -euse** *adj* brave, courageous. **il n'est pas très ~ pour l'étude** he hasn't got much will for studying.

couramment [kuʀamɑ̃] *adv* **(a)** (*aisément*) fluently. **(b)** (*souvent*) commonly. **ce mot s'emploie ~** this word is in current usage; **cela se fait ~** it's quite common practice.

courant, e [kuʀɑ̃, ɑ̃t] **1** *adj* **(a)** *dépenses, usage* everyday, standard; (*Comm*) *modèle* standard; *incident* common. **il n'est pas ~ de voir** it is quite uncommon to see. **(b)** (*en cours*) *année* current. (*Comm*) **votre lettre du 5 ~** your letter of the 5th inst. **2** *nm* **(a)** *[cours d'eau]* current; *[populations, commerce]* movement; *[opinions]* trend. **~ (atmosphérique)** airstream, current; **un ~ de sympathie** a wave of sympathy; (*Littérat*) **le ~ surréaliste** the surrealist movement. **(b)** (*Élec*) current. **couper le ~** to cut off the power. **(c) dans le ~ du mois** in the course of the month; **être au ~ de** *nouvelle* to know about; *science* to be well-informed about; *méthodes* to be up to date on; **mettre qn au ~ de** *faits* to tell sb (about); *théories* to bring sb up to date on; **tenez-moi au ~** keep me informed; **il se tient au ~** he keeps himself up to date *ou* informed.

courbature [kurbatyr] *nf* ache. ♦ **courbaturé, e** *adj* aching (all over).
courber [kurbe] (1) **1** *vt* to bend. **l'âge l'avait courbé** he was bowed *ou* bent with age; ~ **la tête** (*lit*) to bow *ou* bend one's head; (*fig*) to submit. **2** *vi* to bend. **3 se** ~ *vpr [branche]* to bend; (*lit, fig*) *[personne]* to bend down. ♦ **courbe 1** *adj* curved. **2** *nf* curve. ~ **de niveau** contour line; ~ **de température** temperature curve. ♦ **courbette** *nf* low bow. (*fig*) **faire des** ~**s à** *ou* **devant qn** to bow and scrape to sb. ♦ **courbure** *nf* curve.
courette [kurɛt] *nf* small courtyard.
coureur, -euse [kurœr, øz] **1** *nm,f* (*Athlétisme*) runner. ~ **de fond** long-distance runner; ~ **automobile** racing(-car) driver; ~ **cycliste** racing cyclist; ~ **de dot** fortune hunter. **2** *nm*: **c'est un** ~ **de cafés** he hangs round cafés; ~ **(de filles)** womanizer. **3** *nf* (*péj*) manhunter.
courge [kurʒ(ə)] *nf* (*plante*) gourd; (*Culin*) marrow, squash (*US*). ♦ **courgette** *nf* courgette.
courir [kurir] (11) **1** *vi* **(a)** (*gén*) to run; (*Aut, Cyclisme*) to race. **entrer/sortir en courant** to run in/out; ~ **à toutes jambes** to run like the wind; ~ **ventre à terre** to run flat out; **faire** ~ **un cheval** to race a horse. **(b)** (*se précipiter*) to rush. ~ **chercher le docteur** to rush *ou* run for the doctor; **je cours l'appeler** I'll run and call him; **faire qch en courant** to do sth in a rush; **tu peux toujours** ~**!*** you can whistle for it!* **(c)** (*avec à, après, sur*) ~ **à l'échec** to be heading for failure; ~ **après qch** to chase after sth; (*lit, fig*) ~ **après qn** to run after sb; ~ **sur ses 20 ans** to be approaching 20. **(d)** *[nuages, ombres, reflets]* to speed, race; *[eau]* to rush; *[chemin]* to run. **un frisson lui courut par tout le corps** a shiver ran through his body. **(e)** **faire** ~ **un bruit** to spread a rumour; **le bruit court que** ... there is a rumour going round that .... **(f)** (*se passer*) **le mois qui court** the current month; **par les temps qui courent** nowadays; **laisser** ~* to let things alone. **(g)** (*Fin*) *[intérêt]* to accrue.
2 *vt* **(a)** (*Sport*) *épreuve* to compete in. ~ **un 100 mètres** to run (in) *ou* compete in a 100 metres race; ~ **le Grand Prix** to race in the Grand Prix. **(b)** (*Chasse*) ~ **le cerf** to go staghunting; (*fig*) ~ **deux lièvres à la fois** to have one's finger in more than one pie. **(c)** (*rechercher*) *honneurs, aventure* to seek; *risque* to run. **il court de graves dangers** he's running a great risk; ~ **sa chance** to try one's luck. **(d)** *le monde, les bois* to roam; *les magasins* to go round. ~ **les rues** (*lit*) to roam the streets; (*fig*) to be run-of-the-mill; **ça ne court pas les rues** it is hard to find; ~ **les théâtres** to do the rounds of the theatres; ~ **les filles** to chase the girls.
couronne [kurɔn] *nf* **(a)** *[fleurs]* wreath. ~ **mortuaire/de lauriers** funeral/laurel wreath; ~ **d'épines** crown of thorns. **(b)** *[roi, pape]* crown; *[noble]* coronet. **(c)** (*objet*) *[dent]* crown; (*Astron*) corona. ♦ **couronnement** *nm [roi]* coronation, crowning; *[édifice]* top, crown; *[carrière]* crowning achievement. ♦ **couronner** (1) **1** *vt* (*gén, Méd, fig*) to crown; *ouvrage, auteur* to award a prize to. **front couronné de fleurs** head crowned with flowers; (*iro*) **et pour** ~ **le tout** and to crown it all; **couronné de succès** crowned with success. **2 se** ~ *vpr*: **se** ~ **le genou** to graze its (*ou* one's) knee.
courrier [kurje] *nm* **(a)** (*reçu*) mail, letters; (*à écrire*) letters. **(b)** (†) (*avion, bateau*) mail; (*Mil: estafette*) courier. **(c)** (*Presse*) (*rubrique*) column, page. ~ **du cœur** broken hearts' column, problem page; ~ **des lecteurs** letters to the Editor.
courroie [kurwa] *nf* strap; (*Tech*) belt.
courroucer [kuruse] (3) (*littér*) *vt* to incense. ♦ **courroux** *nm* wrath.
cours [kur] *nm* **(a)** (*déroulement, Astron, gén*) course; *[guerre, maladie]* progress; *[rivière]* (*cheminement*) course; (*écoulement*) flow. **descendre le** ~ **de la Seine** to go down the Seine; ~ **d'eau** river, stream. **(b)** (*Fin*) *[monnaie]* currency; *[titre, objet]* price; *[devises]* rate. ~ **légal** legal tender. **(c)** (*leçon*) (*Scol*) class; (*Univ*) lecture; (*série de leçons*) course; (*manuel*) coursebook. **faire un** ~ **sur** to give a class on; ~ **du soir** (*pl*) evening classes; ~ **par correspondance** correspondence course. **(d)** (*Scol*) (*établissement*) school. (*année*) ~ **élémentaire** *etc* primary *etc* class *ou* year; ~ **privé** private school. **(e)** (*avenue*) walk. **(f)** (*locutions*) **avoir** ~ *[monnaie]* to be legal tender; (*fig*) to be current; **en** ~ *année* current; *affaires* in hand; *essais* in progress; **en** ~ **de réparation** in the process of being repaired; **en** ~ **de route** on the way; **au** ~ **de** in the course of; **donner libre** ~ **à** to give free expression to.
course [kurs(ə)] *nf* **(a)** (*action*) running. **prendre sa** ~ to start running. **(b)** (*épreuve*) race; (*discipline*) (*Athlétisme*) running; (*Aut, Courses, Cyclisme*) racing. **faire de la** ~ to go running; ~ **de fond** (*specialité*) long-distance running; (*épreuve*) long-distance race; (*fig*) **la** ~ **aux armements** the arms race; **faire la** ~ **avec qn** to race with sb; (*Courses*) **parier aux** ~**s** to bet on the races; ~ **de taureaux** bullfight; ~ **de trot** trotting race; ~ **de vitesse** sprint. **(c)** (*fig*) *[projectile]* flight; *[navire]* course; *[nuages, temps]* swift passage. **(d)** (*excursion*) (*à pied*) hike; (*ascension*) climb; (*voyage*) journey. (*taxi*) **payer la** ~ to pay the fare. **(e)** (*commission*) errand. **faire une** *or* **des** ~**s** *[ménagère]* to do some shopping; *[coursier]* to run an errand *ou* errands. **(f)** (*Tech*) movement; *[piston]* stroke. **(g)** **être à bout de** ~ to be worn out; **il n'est plus dans la** ~* he's out of things now.
coursier, -ière [kursje, jɛr] **1** *nm,f* messenger. **2** *nm* (*littér, cheval*) steed, horse.
court[1]**, e** [kur, kurt(ə)] **1** *adj* **(a)** (*gén*) short. **il a été très** ~ he was very brief; **de** ~**e durée** *joie* short-lived; **c'est plus** ~ **par le bois** it's quicker *ou* shorter through the wood; **avoir le souffle** ~ to be short-winded. **(b)** (*insuffisant*) **c'est** ~ **un peu** it's a bit on the short side. **(c)** **tirer à la** ~**e paille** to draw straws; **à sa** ~**e honte** to his great shame; **être à** ~ **d'argent** to be short of money; **prendre au plus** ~ to go the shortest way; **prendre qn de** ~ to catch sb unprepared. **2** *adv* short. **s'arrêter** ~ to stop short. **3:** ~**-bouillon** *nm, pl* ~**s-**~**s** court-bouillon; (*Élec*) ~**-circuit** *nm, pl* ~**s-**~**s** short (-circuit); ~**-circuiter** (1) *vt* (*lit, fig*) to short-circuit; **faire la** ~**e échelle à qn** to give sb a leg up; ~ **métrage** short film.
court[2] [kur] *nm* tennis court.
courtaud, e [kurto, od] *adj* dumpy, squat.
courtier, -ière [kurtje, jɛr] *nm,f* broker.
courtiser [kurtize] (1) *vt* to pay court to. ♦ **courtisan** *nm* (*Hist*) courtier; (*fig*) sycophant. ♦ **courtisane** *nf* (*Hist*) courtesan.
courtoisie [kurtwazi] *nf* courtesy. ♦ **courtois, e** *adj* courteous; (*Littérat*) courtly. ♦ **courtoisement** *adv* courteously.
couru, e [kury] *adj restaurant* popular. **c'est** ~* it's a sure thing.
cousin, e [kuzɛ̃, in] **1** *nm,f* cousin. ~ **germain** first cousin. **2** *nm* mosquito.
coussin [kusɛ̃] *nm* cushion.
cousu, e [kuzy] *adj* sewn, stitched. (*fig*) **c'est** ~ **de fil blanc** it doesn't hold *ou* hang together; ~ **main** (*lit*) handsewn; (**fig*) **c'est du** ~ **main** it's top quality stuff.
coût [ku] *nm* (*lit, fig*) cost. **le** ~ **de la vie** the cost of living. ♦ **coûtant** *adj m*: **prix** ~ cost price.
couteau, *pl* ~**x** [kuto] *nm* **(a)** (*pour couper*) knife; *[balance]* knife edge; (*coquillage*) razor-shell. ~ **à poisson** fish knife; ~ **à cran d'arrêt** flick-knife; ~ **à découper** carving knife. **(b)** **vous me mettez le** ~ **sous la gorge** you're holding a pistol at my head; **être à** ~**x tirés** to be at daggers drawn (*avec*

with); **remuer le ~ dans la plaie** to twist the knife in the wound.

coutellerie [kutɛlʀi] *nf* (*industrie*) cutlery industry; (*magasin*) cutler's (shop); (*produits*) cutlery.

coûter [kute] (1) **1** *vi* to cost. **les vacances, ça coûte!** holidays are expensive *ou* cost a lot!; **ça coûte une fortune** it costs a fortune; (*fig*) **ça va lui ~ cher** it will cost him dear; **ça ne coûte rien d'essayer** it costs nothing to try; **cet aveu m'a coûté** this confession cost me; **cette démarche me coûte** it costs me a great effort to take this step; **coûte que coûte** at all costs. **2** *vt fatigue, larmes* to cost. **ça lui a coûté la vie** it cost him his life. ♦ **coûteusement** *adv* expensively. ♦ **coûteux, -euse** *adj* costly, expensive.

coutume [kutym] *nf* (*gén, Jur*) custom. **avoir ~ de** to be in the habit of; **plus que de ~** more than usual; **comme de ~** as usual; **selon sa ~** following his usual custom. ♦ **coutumier, -ière** *adj* customary, usual. (*gén péj*) **il est ~ du fait** that is what he usually does.

couture [kutyʀ] *nf* **(a)** (*activité, ouvrage*) sewing. **la ~** (*métier*) dressmaking; (*industrie*) the fashion industry; **faire de la ~** to sew. **(b)** (*suite de points*) seam; (*cicatrice*) scar; (*suture*) stitches. **sans ~(s)** seamless; **sous toutes les ~s** from every angle. ♦ **couturier** *nm* couturier, fashion designer. ♦ **couturière** *nf* dressmaker.

couvent [kuvɑ̃] *nm* [*sœurs*] convent; [*moines*] monastery; (*internat*) convent school.

couver [kuve] (1) **1** *vi* **(a)** [*feu, incendie, haine*] to smoulder; [*émeute*] to be brewing; [*complot*] to be hatching. **(b)** [*poule*] to sit on its eggs. **2** *vt* **(a)** *œufs* [*poule*] to sit on; [*appareil*] to hatch. **(b)** (*fig*) *enfant* to be overcareful with; *maladie* to be sickening for; *vengeance* to brew, plot. **~ qch des yeux** (*tendresse*) to look lovingly at sth; (*convoitise*) to look longingly at sth. ♦ **couvée** *nf* [*poussins, enfants*] brood, clutch; [*œufs*] clutch.

couvercle [kuvɛʀkl(ə)] *nm* (*gén*) lid; [*aérosol*] cap, top.

couvert, e [kuvɛʀ, ɛʀt(ə)] **1** *adj* **(a)** (*habillé*) covered (up). **trop ~** too wrapped up; (*chapeau*) **il est resté ~** he kept his hat on. **(b) ~ de** covered in *ou* with; **~ de chaume** thatched. **(c)** *ciel* overcast. **(d)** *rue* covered. **(e)** (*fig: protégé*) covered. **2** *nm* **(a)** (*ustensiles*) place setting. **les ~s en argent** the silver cutlery; **mettre 4 ~s** to lay *ou* set 4 places, lay *ou* set the table for 4; **le gîte et le ~** board and lodging. **(b)** (*au restaurant*) cover charge. **(c)** (*abri*) shelter. **à ~ de** sheltered from; (*Mil*) **être/se mettre à ~** to be/get under *ou* take cover; **se mettre à ~ (contre des réclamations)** to cover o.s. (against claims); **sous (le) ~ de** *prétexte* under cover of; **sous (le) ~ de la plaisanterie** while trying to appear to be joking.

couverture [kuvɛʀtyʀ] *nf* **(a)** (*literie*) blanket. **~ de voyage** travelling rug; (*fig*) **tirer la ~ à soi** to take all the credit. **(b)** (*toiture*) roofing; [*cahier*] cover; (*jaquette*) dust cover; (*Mil, Fin, fig*) cover.

couveuse [kuvøz] *nf* (*poule*) broody hen. **~ (artificielle)** incubator.

couvre- [kuvʀ(ə)] *préf V* **couvrir.**

couvreur [kuvʀœʀ] *nm* roofer.

couvrir [kuvʀiʀ] (18) **1** *vt* **(a)** (*gén*) to cover (*de, avec* with). **~ un toit de chaume/de tuiles** to thatch/tile a roof; **couvre bien les enfants** wrap the children up well; **un châle lui couvrait les épaules** her shoulders were covered with *ou* by a shawl; **couvert de bleus** bruised all over, covered in bruises; **~ qn d'injures/de cadeaux** to shower insults/gifts on sb; **ça l'a couvert de ridicule** it covered him with ridicule. **(b)** *voix* to drown; *énigme, sentiments* to conceal; (*lit, fig*) *personne* to cover, shield. **~ qch du nom de charité** to pass sth off as charity. **(c)** *distance, frais* to cover.

2 se ~ *vpr* [*personne*] to wrap (o.s.) up; (*chapeau*) to put one's hat on; [*ciel*] to become overcast; (*Boxe, Escrime*) to cover. **se ~ de** *taches* to get o.s. covered in; *boutons* to become covered in *ou* with; *gloire, honte* to cover o.s. with.

3: (*hum*) **couvre-chef** *nm, pl* **~-~s** hat; **couvre-feu** *nm, pl* **~-~x** curfew; **couvre-lit** *nm, pl* **~-~s** bedspread; **couvre-pied(s)** *nm, pl* **~-~s** quilt.

coyote [kɔjɔt] *nm* coyote, prairie wolf.

crabe [kʀɑb] *nm* (*Zool*) crab. **marcher en ~** to walk crab-wise.

crac [kʀak] *excl* [*bois, glace etc*] crack; [*étoffe*] rip; (*fig*) bang.

cracher [kʀaʃe] (1) **1** *vi* **(a)** to spit (*sur* at). **il ne crache pas sur le caviar*** he doesn't turn his nose up at caviar; **c'est comme si je crachais en l'air*** it's like banging my head against a brick wall. **(b)** [*stylo, plume*] to sputter; [*micro*] to crackle. **2** *vt* **(a)** *sang etc* to spit; *bouchée, injures* to spit out; (‡) *argent* to cough up*, stump up*. **(b)** [*canon*] to spit out; [*cheminée*] to belch out. ♦ **crachat** *nm*: **~(s)** spit, spittle. ♦ **craché, e*** *adj*: **c'est son père tout ~** he's the spitting image of his father. ♦ **crachement** *nm* [*vapeur*] burst; [*étincelles*] shower. **~(s)** [*salive etc*] spitting; [*radio*] crackle.

crachin [kʀaʃɛ̃] *nm* drizzle.

crack [kʀak] *nm* (*poulain*) star horse; (*: *as*) wizard*; (*en sport*) ace.

craie [kʀɛ] *nf* chalk.

craindre [kʀɛ̃dʀ(ə)] (52) *vt* **(a)** [*personne*] to fear, be afraid *ou* scared of. **craignant de manquer le train** afraid of missing *ou* afraid he might miss the train; **elle craignait qu'il ne se blesse** she was afraid that he would *ou* might hurt himself. **(b) ~ pour** *vie, réputation, personne* to fear for. **(c)** [*aliment*] **~ le froid** to be easily damaged by the cold; **'craint l'humidité'** 'keep *ou* store in a dry place'; **c'est un vêtement qui ne craint pas** it's a hard-wearing garment; **il craint la chaleur** he can't stand the heat.

crainte [kʀɛ̃t] *nf* fear. **avoir la ~ de qch** to fear *ou* be afraid of sth; **soyez sans ~** have no fear; **j'ai des ~s à son sujet** I'm worried about him; **sans ~** (*adj*) fearless; (*adv*) fearlessly; **avec ~** fearfully; **par ~ de** for fear of; **de ~ que** for fear that, fearing that. ♦ **craintif, -ive** *adj personne* timorous, timid; *ton* timid. ♦ **craintivement** *adv* timorously, timidly.

cramoisi, e [kʀamwazi] *adj* crimson.

crampe [kʀɑ̃p] *nf*: **~(s)** cramp.

crampon [kʀɑ̃pɔ̃] *nm* (*Tech*) cramp, clamp; [*chaussure*] stud; (*: *personne*) clinging bore. **~ (à glace)** crampon. ♦ **cramponner** (1) **1** *vt* (**fig*) to cling to. **2 se ~** *vpr* to hold on. **se ~ à** *branche* to cling to.

cran [kʀɑ̃] *nm* **(a)** [*crémaillère*] notch; [*arme*] catch; [*ceinture*] hole; (*Couture, Typ*) nick; [*cheveux*] wave. **(b) avoir du ~*** to have guts*; **monter/descendre d'un ~** to go up/down a notch *ou* peg (*dans* in); **être à ~** to be very edgy. ♦ **cranté, e** *adj* notched.

crâne [kʀɑn] **1** *nm* (*Anat*) skull; (*fig*) head. **2** *adj* (†) gallant. ♦ **crânien, -ienne** *adj* cranial.

crâner* [kʀɑne] (1) *vi* to show off. ♦ **crâneur, -euse*** *nm,f* show-off.

crapaud [kʀapo] *nm* (*Zool*) toad.

crapule [kʀapyl] *nf* scoundrel. ♦ **crapulerie** *nf* villainy. ♦ **crapuleux, -euse** *adj action* villainous.

craqueler *vt*, **se ~** *vpr* [kʀakle] (4) to crack. ♦ **craquelure** *nf* crack.

craquer [kʀake] (1) **1** *vi* **(a)** (*bruit*) [*parquet*] to creak; [*feuilles*] to crackle; [*neige, biscuit*] to crunch; [*chaussures*] to squeak. **(b)** (*céder*) [*bas*] to rip; [*glace etc*] to crack; [*branche*] to snap; [*entreprise*] to collapse. **2** *vt pantalon, bas* to rip; *allumette* to strike. ♦ **craquement** *nm*: **~(s)** creak; squeak; crackle; crunch; **casser avec un ~** to break with a crack *ou* a snap.

crasse [kʀas] **1** *nf* (*saleté*) grime, filth; (*: *sale*

tour) dirty trick*. 2 *adj bêtise* crass. ♦ **crasseux, -euse** *adj* grimy, filthy.
cratère [kratɛr] *nm* crater.
cravache [kravaʃ] *nf* riding crop. (*fig*) **mener qn à la ~** to drive sb ruthlessly. ♦ **cravacher** (1) **1** *vt cheval* to use the crop on. **2** *vi* (*) (*foncer*) to belt along*; (*travailler*) to work like mad*.
cravate [kravat] *nf* tie; (*décoration*) ribbon; (*Lutte*) headlock. ♦ **cravater** (1) *vt* to put a tie on. **cravaté** wearing a tie; **se ~** to put one's tie on.
crayeux, -euse [krɛjø, øz] *adj* chalky.
crayon [krɛjɔ̃] *nm* (*gén*) pencil; (*dessin*) pencil drawing. **notes au ~** pencilled notes; **~ à bille** ball-point pen; **~ de couleur** crayon, coloured pencil; **~ noir** lead pencil; **~ pour les yeux** eyeliner pencil. ♦ **crayonner** (1) *vt notes* to scribble; *dessin* to sketch.
créance [kreɑ̃s] *nf* **(a)** *[créancier]* financial claim; (*titre*) letter of credit. **(b)** (†: *foi*) credence. **donner ~ à qch** (*rendre croyable*) to lend credibility to sth; (*ajouter foi à*) to give credence to sth. ♦ **créancier, -ière** *nm,f* creditor.
créateur, -trice [kreatœr, tris] **1** *adj* creative. **2** *nm,f* (*gén, Rel*) creator. ♦ **création** *nf* (*gén*) creation; (*Théât: représentation*) first production; (*Comm: produit*) product. ♦ **créativité** *nf* creativity.
créature [kreatyr] *nf* (*gén*) creature.
crécelle [kresɛl] *nf* rattle.
crèche [krɛʃ] *nf* **(a)** (*Rel: de Noël*) crib. **(b)** (*établissement*) crèche, day nursery.
crédibilité [kredibilite] *nf* credibility.
crédit [kredi] *nm* **(a)** (*Fin*) credit. **faire ~ à qn** to give sb credit; **acheter/vendre qch à ~** to buy/sell sth on credit *ou* easy terms; **porter une somme au ~ de qn** to credit a sum to sb; **~ hypothécaire** mortgage; **~ bail** leasing; **~s budgétaires** budget allocation; **~s extraordinaires** extraordinary funds. **(b)** (*prestige, confiance*) credit. **donner du ~ à qch** to give credit to sth; **avoir du ~** *[firme]* to be creditworthy; *[théorie]* to be widely accepted; **faire ~ à** to trust *ou* have faith in; **trouver/perdre ~ auprès de qn** to win/lose sb's confidence. ♦ **créditer** (1) *vt* (*Fin, Sport*) **~ qn de** to credit sb with. ♦ **créditeur, -trice 1** *adj* in credit. **solde ~** credit balance. **2** *nm,f* customer in credit.
credo [kredo] *nm* (*Rel, fig*) creed.
crédule [kredyl] *adj* credulous, gullible. ♦ **crédulité** *nf* credulity, gullibility.
créer [kree] (1) *vt* **(a)** (*gén*) to create. **la joie de ~** the joy of creation; **se ~ une clientèle** to build up a clientèle; **~ des ennuis à qn** to create problems for sb. **(b)** (*Théât*) *rôle* to create; *pièce* to produce for the first time.
crémaillère [kremajɛr] *nf* **(a)** *[cheminée]* trammel. (*fig*) **pendre la ~** to have a house-warming party. **(b)** (*Rail, Tech*) rack.
crémation [kremɑsjɔ̃] *nf* cremation. ♦ **crématoire 1** *adj* crematory. **2** *nm* crematorium.
crème [krɛm] **1** *nf* (*gén*) cream; (*peau du lait*) skin; (*entremets*) cream dessert. (*liqueur*) **~ de bananes** crème de bananes; **gâteau à la ~** cream cake; (*fig: les meilleurs*) **la ~** the cream; **la ~ des pères** the best of fathers. **2** *adj inv* cream-coloured. **3** *nm* (*café*) white coffee. **4**: **~ anglaise** egg custard; **~ de beauté** beauty cream; **~ Chantilly** *ou* **fouettée** whipped cream; **~ glacée** ice cream; **~ pâtissière** confectioner's custard; **~ à raser** shaving cream. ♦ **crémerie** *nf* (*magasin*) dairy. ♦ **crémeux, -euse** *adj* creamy. ♦ **crémier, -ière** *nm,f* dairyman (*ou* woman).
crémone [kremɔn] *nf* espagnolette bolt.
créneau, *pl* **~x** [kreno] *nm* **(a)** *[rempart]* crenel. **les ~x** the battlements. **(b)** (*Aut*) **faire un ~** to park (*between two cars*). **(c)** *[horaire etc]* gap; (*Rad*) slot. ♦ **crénelé, e** *adj mur* crenellated.
créole [kreɔl] **1** *adj* creole. **2** *nmf* Creole.
crêpe [krɛp] **1** *nf* (*Culin*) pancake. **2** *nm* (*matière*) crepe; (*ruban de deuil*) black ribbon; (*au bras*) black armband.
crêper [krepe] (1) *vt cheveux* to backcomb. **se ~ le chignon*** to have a set-to.
crêperie [krɛpri] *nf* pancake shop.
crépir [krepir] (2) *vt* to roughcast. ♦ **crépi, e** *adj, nm* roughcast. ♦ **crépissage** *nm* roughcasting.
crépiter [krepite] (1) *vi [feu]* to crackle; *[friture]* to splutter; *[mitrailleuse]* to rattle out; *[grésil]* to rattle, patter; *[applaudissements]* to break out. ♦ **crépitement** *nm*: **~(s)** crackling; spluttering; rattle, patter.
crépu, e [krepy] *adj cheveux* frizzy.
crépuscule [krepyskyl] *nm* (*lit, fig*) twilight. ♦ **crépusculaire** *adj*: **lumière ~** twilight glow.
crescendo [kreʃɛndo] *adv, nm* (*Mus*) crescendo. (*fig*) **aller ~** to rise in a crescendo, grow louder and louder.
cresson [kresɔ̃] *nm*: **~ (de fontaine)** watercress.
crête [krɛt] *nf* **(a)** *[oiseau]* crest. **~ de coq** cockscomb. **(b)** *[mur]* top; *[toit, montagne]* ridge; *[vague]* crest; *[graphique]* peak.
crétin, e [kretɛ̃, in] **1** *adj* (*péj*) cretinous*. **2** *nm,f* (*péj*) cretin*; (*Méd*) cretin. ♦ **crétinerie** *nf* idiocy.
creuser [krøze] (1) **1** *vt* **(a)** (*gén*) to dig; *puits* to sink, bore; *sillon* to plough; (*fig*) *abîme* to create; *problème, idée* to go into deeply, look into closely. **(b)** (*évider*) *bois* to hollow out; *sol* to dig out, dig a hole in. **(c)** (*locutions*) **la fatigue lui creusait les joues** his face looked gaunt with tiredness; **visage creusé de rides** face furrowed with wrinkles; **~ les reins** to draw o.s. up; **ça creuse (l'estomac)*** it gives you a real appetite; **se ~ (la cervelle)*** to rack one's brains; **il ne s'est pas beaucoup creusé!*** he didn't overtax himself! **2** *vi* to dig (*dans* into). ♦ **creusement** *nm* digging.
creuset [krøzɛ] *nm* crucible; (*fig: lieu de brassage*) melting pot.
creux, -euse [krø, øz] **1** *adj objet, son* hollow; *estomac* empty; *paroles* empty, hollow; *idées* barren, futile; *raisonnement* weak, flimsy. **les heures ~euses** (*gén*) slack periods; (*pour électricité etc*) off-peak periods. **2** *nm* **(a)** (*gén*) hollow; (*trou*) hole. **le ~ des reins** the small of the back; **le ~ de la main** the hollow of one's hand; **manger dans le ~ de la main** to eat out of one's hand; **le ~ de l'estomac** the pit of the stomach; **avoir un ~ (dans l'estomac)** to feel empty. **(b)** (*Écon: période*) slack period. **(c)** (*Naut*) *[voile]* belly; *[vague]* trough. **des ~ de 2 mètres** 2-metre high waves; (*fig*) **il est dans le ~ de la vague** his fortunes are at their lowest ebb.
crevaison [krəvɛzɔ̃] *nf* (*Aut*) puncture, flat.
crevant, e: [krəvɑ̃, ɑ̃t] *adj* (*gén*) killing*.
crevasse [krəvas] *nf* (*gén*) crack; *[mur]* crevice; *[glacier]* crevasse. ♦ **crevasser** *vt*, **se ~** *vpr* (1) to crack.
crever [krəve] (5) **1** *vt* **(a)** (*gén*) to burst; *pneu* to puncture. **~ les yeux à qn** to blind sb; **j'ai un pneu (de) crevé** I've got a flat *ou* a puncture; (*fig*) **~ le cœur à qn** to break sb's heart; (*fig*) **cela crève les yeux** it stares you in the face! **(b)** (*: *exténuer*) **~ qn** *[personne]* to work sb to death; *[tâche]* to kill sb*; **se ~ (au travail)** to work o.s. to death. **(c)** (:) **~ la faim** to be starving* *ou* famished*.

2 *vi* **(a)** *[pneu]* to puncture. **~ de jalousie** to be bursting with jealousy. **(b)** (*mourir*) *[animal, plante]* to die (off); (:) *[personne]* to die, snuff it:. **chien crevé** dead dog; **~ de faim/froid:** to starve/freeze to death; **~ de soif:** to die of thirst; **on crève de chaud ici*** it's boiling in here*; **faire ~ qn:** to kill sb. **(c)** (*Aut*) to have a puncture, have a flat tyre.
♦ **crevé, e:** *adj* (*mort*) dead; (*las*) dead-beat*. ♦ **crève-cœur** *nm inv* heartbreak. ♦ **crève-la-faim** *nmf inv* down-and-out.

crevette [kʀəvɛt] *nf*: ~ **(rose)** prawn; ~ **grise** shrimp.

cri [kʀi] *nm* **(a)** (*gén*) shout, cry; (*hurlement*) yell, howl; (*aigu*) squeal; *[peur]* scream, shriek; (*appel*) call; (*exclamation*) cry. ~ **du cœur** cry from the heart; ~ **de guerre** war cry; **elle jeta un ~ de douleur** she cried out in pain, she gave a cry of pain. **(b)** *[animal]* (*appel*) call; (*douleur*) squeal. (*générique*) **quel est le ~ du chien?** what noise does a dog make? **(c)** (*littér: crissement*) screech.

criailler [kʀiɑje] (1) *vi* (*rouspéter*) to grouse*, grumble. ~ **après qn** to nag at sb. ♦ **criailleries** *nfpl* grousing*, grumbling; nagging.

criant, e [kʀijɑ̃, ɑ̃t] *adj* (*gén*) glaring; *vérité* striking. **portrait ~ de vérité** portrait strikingly true to life.

criard, e [kʀijaʀ, aʀd(ə)] *adj* (*péj*) *enfant* squalling; *femme* scolding; *oiseau* squawking; *son* piercing; *couleurs, vêtement* loud, garish.

cribler [kʀible] (1) *vt graines* to sift; *charbon* to riddle, screen. ~ **qn de** *balles* to riddle sb with; *questions* to bombard sb with. ♦ **criblage** *nm* sifting; riddling; screening. ♦ **crible** *nm* (*à main*) riddle; (*Ind*) screen. **passer au ~** (*lit*) to riddle; (*fig*) to examine closely. ♦ **criblé, e** *adj*: ~ **de** *taches* covered in; *dettes* crippled with.

cric [kʀik] *nm* (car) jack.

criée [kʀije] *nf* (*salle*) auction room. **(vente à la) ~** (sale by) auction.

crier [kʀije] (7) **1** *vi* **(a)** (*gén*) to shout, cry out; (*hurler*) to yell, howl; (*aigu*) to squeal; *[peur]* to scream, shriek; *[appel]* to call out. ~ **de douleur** to cry *ou* scream out in pain; ~ **contre qn** to nag at *ou* go on at sb; **tes parents vont ~** your parents are going to make a fuss; ~ **contre qch** to shout about sth; ~ **au scandale** to call it a scandal; ~ **au loup** to cry wolf. **(b)** *[animal]* (*appel*) to call; (*douleur*) to squeal; *[plancher]* to creak; *[frein]* to screech.

2 *vt ordre, injures* to shout out, yell out; *mépris, innocence* to proclaim; *marchandise* to shout, cry. ~ **à qn de se taire** to shout at sb to be quiet; ~ **qch sur les toits** to cry sth from the rooftops; ~ **casse-cou** to warn of a danger; **sans ~ gare** without a warning; ~ **grâce** to beg for mercy; ~ **famine** to cry famine; ~ **vengeance** to cry out for vengeance.

♦ **crieur, -euse** *nm,f*: ~ **de journaux** newspaper seller; (*Hist*) ~ **public** town crier.

crime [kʀim] *nm* (*gén*) crime; (*meurtre*) murder. ~**s de guerre** war crimes; **le ~ ne paie pas** crime doesn't pay; **ce n'est pas un ~**! it's not a crime! ♦ **criminalité** *nf* criminality. ♦ **criminel, -elle** **1** *adj* (*gén, Jur*) criminal. **2** *nm,f* murderer (*ou* murderess); criminal. (*hum*) **voilà le ~** there's the culprit *ou* the guilty party. ♦ **criminellement** *adv agir* criminally. ♦ **criminologie** *nf* criminology.

crin [kʀɛ̃] *nm* horsehair. (*fig*) **à tout ~** diehard. ♦ **crinière** *nf [animal]* mane; *[personne]* mop of hair.

crique [kʀik] *nf* creek, inlet.

criquet [kʀikɛ] *nm* locust.

crise [kʀiz] *nf* **(a)** (*Méd*) attack; *[épilepsie]* fit; (*fig: accès*) outburst, fit; (*lubie*) mood. ~ **cardiaque/de foie** heart/liverish attack; ~ **de nerfs** fit of hysterics; **piquer une ~*** to throw a tantrum. **(b)** (*moral, Pol, Écon*) crisis. **en état de ~** in a state of crisis. **(c)** (*pénurie*) shortage. ~ **du logement** housing shortage.

crisper [kʀispe] (1) **1** *vt* **(a)** (*contracter*) *visage* to contort; *muscles* to tense; *poings* to clench. **(b)** (*: *agacer*) ~ **qn** to get on sb's nerves*. **2 se ~** *vpr [visage]* to tense; *[sourire]* to become strained; *[poing]* to clench; *[personne]* to get tense. **ses mains se crispèrent sur le volant** his hands tightened *ou* tensed on the wheel. ♦ **crispant, e** *adj* (*énervant*) irritating. ♦ **crispation** *nf* **(a)** *[traits, visage]* contortion; *[muscles]* contraction. **(b)** (*spasme*) twitch. **des ~s nerveuses** nervous twitches. **(c)** (*nervosité*) state of tension. ♦ **crispé, e** *adj* tense.

crisser [kʀise] (1) *vi [gravier]* to crunch; *[pneus]* to screech; *[soie]* to rustle. ♦ **crissement** *nm*: ~**(s)** crunch; screech; rustle.

cristal, *pl* **-aux** [kʀistal, o] *nm* crystal; (*objet*) piece of crystal. ~ **de roche** rock crystal; ~**aux de soude** washing soda; ~**aux de givre** ice crystals. ♦ **cristallerie** *nf* crystal glassworks. ♦ **cristallin, e** **1** *adj* (*Min*) crystalline; *son* crystal-clear. **2** *nm* (*Anat*) crystalline lens. ♦ **cristallisation** *nf* (*gén*) crystallization. ♦ **cristalliser** *vti,* **se ~** *vpr* (1) to crystallize.

critère [kʀitɛʀ] *nm* criterion.

critérium [kʀiteʀjɔm] *nm* (*Cyclisme*) rally; (*Natation*) gala.

critique [kʀitik] **1** *adj* (*gén, Sci*) critical. **avoir l'esprit ~** to have a critical mind; **il s'est montré très ~ (au sujet de ...)** he was very critical (of ...). **2** *nf* **(a)** (*blâme*) criticism. **la ~ est aisée** it's easy to criticize. **(b)** *[œuvre]* appreciation, critique; *[livre, spectacle]* review. **la ~** (*métier*) criticism; (*personnes*) the critics; **faire la ~ de** *film* to review; *poème* to write an appreciation *ou* a critique of. **3** *nmf* critic. ~ **d'art** art critic. ♦ **critiquable** *adj* open to criticism. ♦ **critiquer** (1) *vt* (*blâmer*) to criticize, find fault with; (*juger*) *œuvre* to write a critique of.

croasser [kʀɔase] (1) *vi* to caw. ♦ **croassement** *nm* caw.

croc [kʀo] *nm* (*dent*) fang; (*crochet*) hook. (*lit, fig*) **montrer les ~s** to bare its (*ou* one's) teeth. ♦ **croc-en-jambe,** *pl* **~s-~-~** *nm* (*lit, fig*) **faire un ~ à qn** to trip sb up.

croche [kʀɔʃ] *nf* (*Mus*) quaver.

croche-pied, *pl* **~-~s** [kʀɔʃpje] *nm* = **croc-en-jambe.**

crochet [kʀɔʃɛ] **1** *nm* **(a)** (*gén, Boxe*) hook; *[vêtement]* fastener; *[serpent]* fang; *[cambrioleur]* picklock. (*Typ*) **entre ~s** in square brackets; **vivre aux ~s de qn** to live off sb. **(b)** (*aiguille*) crochet hook; (*technique*) crochet. **faire qch au ~** to crochet sth. **(c)** *[véhicule]* sudden swerve; *[route]* sudden turn; *[voyage]* detour. **faire ~** (*pour éviter*) to swerve; (*par une ville*) to make a detour (*par* through). **2**: ~ **radiophonique** talent show. ♦ **crocheter** (5) *vt serrure* to pick; *porte* to pick the lock on. ♦ **crochu, e** *adj nez* hooked; *doigts* claw-like.

crocodile [kʀɔkɔdil] *nm* crocodile.

crocus [kʀɔkys] *nm* crocus.

croire [kʀwaʀ] (44) **1** *vt* **(a)** to believe. **auriez-vous cru cela de lui?** would you have believed it of him?; **je te crois sur parole** I'll take your word for it; **le croira qui voudra, mais ...** believe it or not (but) ... . **(b)** (*penser*) to believe, think. **elle croyait avoir perdu son sac** she thought she had lost her bag; **il a cru bien faire** he meant well; **je crois que oui** I think so; **on les croyait morts/en France** they were believed dead/to be in France; **il n'a pas cru utile de me prévenir** he didn't think it necessary to warn me. **(c) en ~ : à l'en ~** if you were to listen to what he says; **s'il faut en ~ les journaux** if we are to believe the papers; **vous pouvez m'en ~** you can take it from me; **si vous m'en croyez** if you want my opinion; **il n'en croyait pas ses yeux** he couldn't believe his eyes. **(d)** (*locutions*) **c'est à ~ qu'il est sourd** you'd think he was deaf; **c'est à n'y pas ~**! it's unbelievable!; **il est à ~ que, il faut ~ que** it would seem that; **il ne croyait pas si bien dire!** he didn't know how right he was!; **on croirait une hirondelle** it looks like a swallow; **on croirait une clarinette** it sounds like a clarinet; **on croirait qu'elle ne comprend pas** she doesn't seem to understand; **tu ne peux pas ~ combien il nous manque** you cannot imagine how much we miss him; **je vous crois!*** you bet!*, rather!; **on croit rêver!*** the mind boggles!* **2** *vi* (*Rel*) to be a believer. **3 ~ à, ~ en** *vt indir* to believe in; (*avec confiance*) to have faith *ou* confidence in. **on a cru d'abord à un accident** at first they took it for an accident; **veuillez ~ à mes sentiments dévoués** yours sincerely; **il croit trop en lui-même** he is too self-confident. **4 se ~** *vpr* to have an inflated opinion of o.s. **il se croit malin** he thinks he's clever.

croisade [kʀwazad] *nf* (*Hist, fig*) crusade.

croisé, e [kʀwaze] **1** *adj veste* double-breasted; *rimes* alternate. **2** *nm* (*Hist*) crusader. **3** *nf* (*littér: fenêtre*) casement (*littér*). (*lit, fig*) **à la ~ des chemins** at the crossroads, at the parting of the ways.

croisement [kʀwazmɑ̃] *nm* **(a)** *[fils]* crossing; *[véhicules]* passing. **(b)** (*Bio, Zool*) (*action*) crossing (*avec* with); (*résultat*) cross. **(c)** (*carrefour*) crossroads, junction. **au ~ des deux routes** where the two roads cross.

croiser [kʀwaze] (1) **1** *vt* **(a)** (*gén*) to cross; *bras* to fold; *[route, ligne]* to cut across. **elle croisa son châle sur sa poitrine** she folded her shawl across her chest; **les jambes croisées** cross-legged; (*lit, fig*) **~ le fer** to cross swords (*avec* with). **(b)** *véhicule, passant* to pass. **son regard croisa le mien** his eyes met mine. **(c)** *animaux, plantes* to cross (*avec* with). **2** *vi* (*Habillement*) to overlap; (*Naut*) to cruise. **3 se ~** *vpr [chemins, lignes, lettres]* to cross; *[regards]* to meet; *[personnes, véhicules]* to pass each other. (*fig*) **se ~ les bras** to sit around idly.

croiseur [kʀwazœʀ] *nm* cruiser (*warship*).

croisière [kʀwazjɛʀ] *nf* cruise. **faire une ~** to go on a cruise.

croissance [kʀwasɑ̃s] *nf* growth, development.

croissant [kʀwasɑ̃] *nm* (*forme*) crescent; (*Culin*) croissant. **en ~** crescent-shaped.

croître [kʀwatʀ(ə)] (55) *vi [enfant, plante]* to grow; *[sentiment, bruit, quantité]* to grow, increase; *[jours]* to get longer; *[chaleur]* to get more and more intense, keep on rising; *[lune]* to wax.

croix [kʀwa] *nf* (*gén*) cross. **C~-Rouge/de guerre** *etc* Red/Military *etc* Cross; **~ gammée** swastika; **disposé en ~** arranged crosswise; **mettre en ~** to crucify; **mise en ~** crucifixion; **les bras en ~** with one's arms out-spread; **pour le faire sortir, c'est la ~ et la bannière*** it's the devil's own job to get him to go out; **les noms marqués d'une ~** the names with a cross against them; **tu peux faire une ~ dessus*** you might as well forget it!*, you can kiss that goodbye*.

croquant, e [kʀɔkɑ̃, ɑ̃t] *adj* crisp, crunchy.

croquer [kʀɔke] (1) **1** *vt* **(a)** *bonbons* to crunch; *fruits* to munch. **~ de l'argent** to squander money. **(b)** (*dessiner*) to sketch. **joli à ~** as pretty as a picture. **2** *vi [fruit]* to be crunchy, be crisp; *[salade]* to be crisp. **~ dans une pomme** to bite into an apple. ♦ **croque-mitaine,** *pl* **~-~s** *nm* bog(e)y man, ogre. ♦ **croque-monsieur** *nm inv toasted cheese sandwich with ham.* ♦ **croque-mort,** *pl* **~-~s** *nm* undertaker's assistant.

croquet [kʀɔkɛ] *nm* croquet.

croquette [kʀɔkɛt] *nf* croquette.

croquis [kʀɔki] *nm* sketch.

crosse [kʀɔs] *nf* **(a)** *[fusil]* butt; *[revolver]* grip; *[violon]* head. **(b)** (*bâton*) (*Rel*) crook, crosier. (*Sport*) **~ de golf** golf club; **~ de hockey** hockey stick. **(c) chercher des ~s à qn*** to pick a quarrel with sb.

crotale [kʀɔtal] *nm* rattlesnake.

crotte [kʀɔt] *nf*: **de la ~** (*excrément*) manure, dung; (*boue*) mud; **~s** *[lapin]* droppings; **des ~s** *ou* **une ~ de chien** some dog's dirt; **~ de chocolat** chocolate. ♦ **crotter** (1) *vt* to muddy. **souliers tout crottés** muddy shoes. ♦ **crottin** *nm* dung, manure.

crouler [kʀule] (1) *vi* (*lit, fig: s'écrouler*) to collapse; *[toit]* to cave in; *[civilisation]* to totter; *[empire, mur]* to crumble. **la salle croulait sous les applaudissements** the room shook with the applause. ♦ **croulant, e** *adj mur* crumbling, tumbledown; *autorité, empire* crumbling.

croup [kʀup] *nm* (*Méd*) croup.

croupe [kʀup] *nf [cheval]* rump, hindquarters; (*) *[personne]* rump; *[colline]* top. **monter en ~** to ride pillion.

croupier [kʀupje] *nm* croupier.

croupir [kʀupiʀ] (2) *vi [eau]* to stagnate. (*fig*) **~ dans le vice** to wallow in vice. ♦ **croupi, e** *adj eau* stagnant.

croustiller [kʀustije] (1) *vi [pâte]* to be crusty; *[chips]* to be crisp.

croûte [kʀut] *nf* **(a)** *[pain]* crust; *[fromage]* rind; *[vol-au-vent]* case; *[terre, glace]* layer; *[plaie]* scab. **la ~ terrestre** the earth's crust; **à la ~!*** (*allons manger*) let's go and eat! **(b)** (*cuir*) hide. **(c)** (*péj: tableau*) daub.

croûton [kʀutɔ̃] *nm* (*bout du pain*) crust; (*Culin*) crouton; (*péj: personne*) old fossil*.

croyance [kʀwajɑ̃s] *nf* belief (*à, en* in). ♦ **croyable** *adj* credible. **pas ~** unbelievable, incredible. ♦ **croyant, e** *nm,f* believer.

cru[1], e[1] [kʀy] *adj* **(a)** (*Culin, Tech*) raw; *fruits* uncooked, raw. **(b)** *lumière, couleur* harsh; *description* (*réaliste*) forthright, blunt; (*grossière*) crude, coarse.

cru[2] [kʀy] *nm* (*vignoble*) vineyard; (*vin*) wine. (*lit, fig*) **du ~** local; **grand ~** great wine *ou* vintage; **de son (propre) ~** of his own invention.

cruauté [kʀyote] *nf* cruelty (*envers* to); *[animal]* ferocity.

cruche [kʀyʃ] *nf* **(a)** (*récipient*) pitcher, jug. **(b)** (*: *imbécile*) ass*, twit*.

crucial, e, *mpl* **-aux** [kʀysjal, o] *adj* crucial.

crucifier [kʀysifje] (7) *vt* (*lit, fig*) to crucify. ♦ **crucifix** *nm* crucifix. ♦ **crucifixion** *nf* crucifixion.

crudité [kʀydite] *nf* **(a)** *[langage]* crudeness, coarseness; *[description]* bluntness; *[couleur]* harshness. **(b)** (*Culin*) **~s** ≈ mixed salad.

crue[2] [kʀy] *nf* (*montée des eaux*) rise in the water level; (*inondation*) flood. **en ~** in spate.

cruel, -elle [kʀyɛl] *adj* (*gén*) cruel; *animal* ferocious; *sort* harsh; *froid, nécessité* bitter. ♦ **cruellement** *adv* cruelly; ferociously; harshly; bitterly. **~ éprouvé** sorely distressed.

crûment [kʀymɑ̃] *adv* (*nettement*) bluntly, forthrightly; (*grossièrement*) crudely, coarsely. **éclairer ~** to cast a harsh light over.

crustacé [kʀystase] *nm* (*Zool*) shellfish. (*Culin*) **~s** seafood, shellfish.

crypte [kʀipt(ə)] *nf* crypt.

Cuba [kyba] *nf* Cuba. ♦ **cubain, e** *adj*, **C~(e)** *nm(f)* Cuban.

cube [kyb] **1** *nm* (*gén*) cube; *[jeu]* wooden brick. **élever au ~** to cube. **2** *adj*: **mètre ~** cubic metre. ♦ **cubage** *nm* cubage. **~ d'air** air space. ♦ **cuber** (1) **1** *vt* to cube. **2** *vi* (*: *augmenter*) to mount up. ♦ **cubique** *adj* cubic. ♦ **cubisme** *nm* cubism. ♦ **cubiste** *adj, nmf* cubist.

cubitus [kybitys] *nm* ulna.

cueillir [kœjiʀ] (12) *vt fleurs, fruits* to pick, gather; (*isolément*) to pick, pluck; *ballon* to catch; *baiser* to snatch; (*) *voleur* to catch, nab*. (*fig*) **il m'a cueilli à froid** he caught me off guard. ♦ **cueillette** *nf* (*action*) picking; gathering; (*récolte*) harvest *ou* crop of fruit.

cuiller, cuillère [kɥijɛʀ] *nf* spoon; (*contenu*) spoonful; (*Pêche*) spoon-bait. **serrer la ~ à qn*** to shake sb's paw*; **~ à café** coffee spoon, ≈ teaspoon; **~ à soupe** soupspoon, ≈ tablespoon. ♦ **cuillerée** *nf* spoonful.

cuir [kɥiʀ] *nm* leather; (*avant tannage*) hide. ~ **brut** rawhide; ~ **chevelu** scalp.

cuirasse [kɥiʀas] *nf* cuirass; (*fig*) armour. ♦ **cuirassé** *nm* battleship. ♦ **cuirasser** (1) *vt chevalier* to cuirass; *navire* to armour-plate; (*fig: endurcir*) to harden (*contre* against). **se** ~ **contre** to harden o.s. against. ♦ **cuirassier** *nm* (*Hist*) cuirassier. (*régiment*) **le 3e** ~ the 3rd armoured cavalry.

cuire [kɥiʀ] (38) **1** *vt* **(a)** (*aussi* **faire** ~) to cook. ~ **à petit feu** to simmer *ou* cook gently; ~ **au bain-marie** ≃ to heat in a double saucepan; ~ **à la broche** to roast on the spit; ~ **au four** *gâteau* to bake; *viande* to roast; ~ **à la vapeur/au gril/à la poêle/à l'eau** to steam/grill/fry/boil; **faire trop** ~ **qch** to overcook sth; **ne pas faire assez** ~ **qch** to undercook sth. **(b)** *pain* to bake; *briques* to fire. **(c) à** ~ *chocolat, pommes* cooking; *poires* stewing. **2** *vi* **(a)** *[aliment]* to cook. ~ **à gros bouillon(s)** to boil hard. **(b)** *[personne]* ~ **au soleil** to roast in the sun; **on cuit ici!*** it's boiling in here!* **(c) les mains/yeux me cuisaient** my hands/eyes were smarting; **mon dos me cuit** my back is burning. **(d) il vous en cuira** you'll rue the day you did it.

cuisant, e [kɥizɑ̃, ɑ̃t] *adj douleur* smarting, burning; *froid, échec, regret* bitter; *remarque* stinging.

cuisine [kɥizin] *nf* **(a)** (*pièce*) kitchen; (*art*) cookery, cooking; (*nourriture*) cooking, food. **elle fait la** ~ (*en général*) she does the cooking *ou* is the cook; (*en ce moment*) she's cooking the meal. **(b)** (*péj*) shady manoeuvres. ♦ **cuisiner** (1) *vt plat* to cook; (*‡ fig*) *personne* to grill*. ♦ **cuisinier, -ière 1** *nm,f* (*personne*) cook. **2** *nf* cooker; (*vieux modèle*) kitchen range.

cuissardes [kɥisaʀd(ə)] *nfpl [pêcheur]* waders; (*mode féminine*) thigh boots.

cuisse [kɥis] *nf* (*Anat*) thigh. ~ **de poulet** chicken leg; (*fig*) **se croire sorti de la** ~ **de Jupiter*** to think a lot of o.s.

cuisson [kɥisɔ̃] *nf [aliments]* cooking; *[pain]* baking; *[gigot]* roasting; *[briques]* firing.

cuistance‡ [kɥistɑ̃s] *nf* (*nourriture*) grub‡.

cuistot* [kɥisto] *nm* cook.

cuit, e [kɥi, kɥit] **1** *adj* **(a)** *plat* cooked; *pain, viande* ready, done. **bien** ~ well cooked *ou* done; **trop** ~ overdone; **pas assez** ~ underdone; ~ **à point** (*parfaitement*) done to a turn; (*peu saignant*) medium-cooked. **(b) c'est du tout** ~* it's a cinch* *ou* a walkover*; **il est** ~* he's had it*. **2** *nf*: **prendre une** ~‡ to get plastered‡.

cuivre [kɥivʀ(ə)] *nm*: ~ **(rouge)** copper; ~ **jaune** brass; **faire les** ~**s** to do the brass (*ou* the copper); (*Mus*) **les** ~**s** the brass. ♦ **cuivré, e** *adj reflets* coppery; *teint* bronzed; *voix* resonant.

cul [ky] **1** *nm* (*Anat*:‡) backside*; *[bouteille]* bottom. **faire** ~ **sec** to down one's drink in one go*. **2:** ~**-de-jatte** *nm, pl* ~**s**-~-~ legless cripple; ~**-de-sac** *nm, pl* ~**s**-~-~ (*rue*) cul-de-sac, dead end; (*fig*) blind alley. **3** *adj inv* (‡: *stupide*) silly, clottish*.

culasse [kylas] *nf [moteur]* cylinder head; *[fusil]* breech.

culbute [kylbyt] *nf* (*cabriole*) somersault; (*chute*) tumble, fall; (*: *ruine*) collapse. **faire la** ~ (*ruine*) to collapse; (*profit*) to double one's money.

culbuter [kylbyte] (1) **1** *vi [personne]* to tumble; *[chose]* to topple over; *[voiture]* to overturn. **2** *vt chaise etc* to knock over; *ennemi* to overwhelm; *ministère etc* to bring down, topple.

culinaire [kylinɛʀ] *adj* culinary.

culminer [kylmine] (1) *vi* **(a)** *[sommet]* to tower (*au-dessus de* above). ~ **à** to reach its highest point at. **(b)** (*fig*) *[colère]* to reach a peak.

culot [kylo] *nm* **(a)** (*: *effronterie*) cheek*. **(b)** *[ampoule]* cap; *[obus]* base.

culotte [kylɔt] *nf* **(a)** (*pantalon*) trousers; (*Hist*) breeches; (*sous-vêtement*) pants. ~**(s) courte(s)/longue(s)** short/long trousers; ~ **de cheval** riding breeches; ~ **de golf** plus-fours; (*fig*) **c'est elle qui porte la** ~ she wears the trousers. **(b)** (*Boucherie*) rump.

culotté, e [kylɔte] *adj* **(a)** (*) cheeky*. **(b)** *pipe* seasoned.

culpabilité [kylpabilite] *nf* guilt.

culte [kylt(ə)] *nm* (*vénération*) cult, worship; (*pratiques*) cult; (*religion*) religion; (*office*) church service. **le** ~ **de Dieu** the worship of God; **avoir le** ~ **de** to worship; **les objets du** ~ liturgical objects.

cultiver [kyltive] (1) **1** *vt champ, art, personne, don* to cultivate; *légumes* to grow, cultivate. ~ **la terre** to cultivate the soil, farm the land. **2 se** ~ *vpr* to cultivate one's mind. ♦ **cultivable** *adj terrain* cultivable. ♦ **cultivateur, -trice** *nm,f* farmer. ♦ **cultivé, e** *adj* (*instruit*) cultured.

culture [kyltyʀ] *nf* **(a)** *[champ]* cultivation; *[légumes]* growing, cultivation. **méthodes de** ~ farming methods; ~ **intensive/fruitière** intensive/fruit farming; (*terres*) ~**s** land under cultivation. **(b)** *[esprit]* cultivation. **la** ~ culture; ~ **générale** general knowledge *ou* education; **faire de la** ~ **physique** to do physical training. **(c)** (*Bio*) culture. ♦ **culturel, -elle** *adj* cultural. ♦ **culturisme** *nm* body-building.

cumin [kymɛ̃] *nm* (*Culin*) caraway seeds, cumin.

cumuler [kymyle] (1) *vt fonctions* to hold concurrently *ou* simultaneously. ~ **2 traitements** to draw 2 separate salaries. ♦ **cumul** *nm [fonctions]* plurality; *[avantages]* amassing; *[traitements]* concurrent drawing.

cupide [kypid] *adj* greedy. ♦ **cupidement** *adv* greedily. ♦ **cupidité** *nf* greed.

cure [kyʀ] *nf* **(a)** (*traitement*) course of treatment. ~ **d'amaigrissement** slimming course; ~ **de fruits/de repos** fruit/rest cure. **(b)** (*Rel*) (*fonction, paroisse*) cure; (*maison*) presbytery. **(c)** (*littér*) **je n'en ai** ~! I care not a whit! ♦ **curable** *adj* curable. ♦ **curatif, -ive** *adj* curative.

curé [kyʀe] *nm* parish priest. (*péj*) **les** ~**s** clerics.

curée [kyʀe] *nf* (*Chasse*) quarry; (*fig: ruée*) scramble.

curer [kyʀe] (1) **1** *vt* to clean out. **se** ~ **les dents** to pick one's teeth; **se** ~ **les ongles** to clean one's nails. **2: cure-dent** *nm, pl* ~**-**~**s** toothpick; **cure-pipe** *nm, pl* ~**-**~**s** pipe cleaner. ♦ **curage** *nm* cleaning-out.

curieux, -euse [kyʀjø, øz] **1** *adj* **(a)** (*intéressé*) *esprit* inquiring. ~ **de qch** interested in *ou* keen on sth; ~ **de savoir** interested *ou* curious to know. **(b)** (*indiscret*) curious, inquisitive. **(c)** (*bizarre*) curious, funny. **2** *nm*: **le** ~**, dans cette affaire** the funny *ou* curious thing about this business. **3** *nm,f* (*indiscret*) busybody, nosey-parker*; (*badaud*) onlooker, bystander. **venir en** ~ to come just for a look. ♦ **curieusement** *adv* strangely, curiously. ♦ **curiosité** *nf* **(a)** (*intérêt*) curiosity; (*indiscrétion*) curiosity, inquisitiveness. ~**s malsaines** unhealthy curiosity. **(b)** (*site*) curious *ou* unusual sight *ou* feature; (*bibelot*) curio.

curiste [kyʀist(ə)] *nmf* person taking the waters at a spa.

cutané, e [kytane] *adj* skin.

cuti(-réaction) [kyti(ʀeaksjɔ̃)] *nf* skin test.

cuve [kyv] *nf [vin, teinture]* vat; *[mazout, eau, photo]* tank. ♦ **cuvée** *nf* (*contenu*) vatful; (*produit, année*) vintage. ♦ **cuver** (1) **1** *vt*: ~ **son vin** to sleep it off*. **2** *vi [vin]* to ferment.

cuvette [kyvɛt] *nf* (*gén*) bowl; *[évier]* basin; *[W.-C.]* pan; (*Géog*) basin.

cyanure [sjanyʀ] *nm* cyanide.

cyclamen [siklamɛn] *nm* cyclamen.

cycle [sikl(ə)] *nm* (*gén*) cycle; (*vélo*) bicycle, cycle. **premier/deuxième** ~ (*Scol*) lower/upper school; (*Univ*) first and second/final year. ♦ **cyclique** *adj* cyclical. ♦ **cyclisme** *nm* cycling. ♦ **cycliste 1** *adj course* cycle; *coureur* racing. **2** *nmf* cyclist. ♦ **cyclomoteur** *nm* moped. ♦ **cyclomotoriste** *nmf* moped rider.

cyclone [siklon] *nm* (*Mét*) cyclone; (*fig*) whirlwind.

Cyclope [siklɔp] *nm* (*Myth*) Cyclops.

cygne [siɲ] *nm* swan; (*jeune*) cygnet; (*mâle*) cob.

cylindre [silɛ̃dʀ(ə)] *nm* (*Aut, Typ, Géom*) cylinder; (*rouleau*) roller. ♦ **cylindrée** *nf* capacity. **les petites** ~**s** small-engined cars. ♦ **cylindrique** *adj* cylindrical.

cymbale [sɛ̃bal] *nf* cymbal.

cynique [sinik] **1** *adj* cynical. **2** *nm* cynic. ♦ **cyniquement** *adv* cynically. ♦ **cynisme** *nm* cynicism.

cyprès [sipʀɛ] *nm* cypress.

cypriote [sipʀijɔt] *adj*, **C**~ *nmf* Cypriot.

cytise [sitiz] *nm* laburnum.

D

D, d [de] *nm* (*lettre*) D, d. ◆ **d'** *V* **de.**
dactylo [daktilo] *nf* typist. ◆ **dactylo(graphie)** *nf* typing, typewriting. ◆ **dactylographier** (7) *vt* to type (out).
dada [dada] *nm* (*: *cheval*) horsy*; (*fig: marotte*) hobby-horse, pet subject.
dadais [dadɛ] *nm*: **grand ~** awkward lump.
dague [dag] *nf* dagger.
dahlia [dalja] *nm* dahlia.
daigner [deɲe] (1) *vt* to deign, condescend. **daignez nous excuser** be so good as to excuse us.
daim [dɛ̃] *nm* fallow deer; (*mâle*) buck; (*peau*) buckskin, doeskin; (*cuir*) suede. ◆ **daine** *nf* doe.
dais [dɛ] *nm* canopy.
dalle [dal] *nf* paving stone, flag(stone). **~ funéraire** gravestone; **je n'y vois que ~**‡ I can't see a damn‡ thing. ◆ **dallage** *nm* (*gén*) paving. ◆ **daller** (1) *vt* to pave.
daltonien, -ienne [daltɔnjɛ̃, jɛn] *adj* colour-blind.
dam [dɑ̃] *nm*: **au ~ de** (*détriment*) to the detriment of; (*déplaisir*) to the displeasure of.
dame [dam] **1** *nf* **(a)** (*gén*) lady; (*: *épouse*) wife. **pour ~s** *coiffeur* ladies'; **de ~** *sac* lady's. **(b)** (*Cartes, Échecs*) queen; (*Dames*) crown. **le jeu de ~s** draughts, checkers (*US*); **aller à ~** (*Dames*) to make a crown; (*Échecs*) to queen. **2** *excl* (†) **~ oui/non!** why yes/no! **3: ~ de charité** benefactress; **~ de compagnie** lady's companion; **~ d'honneur** lady-in-waiting; **~ patronnesse** patroness.
damer [dame] (1) *vt terre* to pack down. (*fig*) **~ le pion à qn** to get the better of sb.
damier [damje] *nm* (*Dames*) draughtboard, checkerboard (*US*). (*dessin*) **à ~** chequered.
damnation [dɑnɑsjɔ̃] *nf* damnation. ◆ **damné, e 1** *adj* (*: *maudit*) cursed*. **2** *nm,f* damned person. **les ~s** the damned. ◆ **damner** (1) *vt* to damn. **faire ~ qn*** to drive sb mad*.
dancing [dɑ̃siŋ] *nm* dance hall.
dandiner (se) [dɑ̃dine] (1) *vpr* to waddle. ◆ **dandinement** *nm* waddle.
Danemark [danmaʀk] *nm* Denmark.
danger [dɑ̃ʒe] *nm* danger. **hors de/en ~** out of/in danger; **mettre en ~** to endanger; **il est en ~ de mort** he is in danger *ou* peril of his life; **courir un ~** to run a risk; **en cas de ~** in case of emergency; **~ public** public menace; **les ~s de la route** road hazards; **sans ~** (*adj*) safe; (*adv*) safely; **pas de ~ qu'il vienne!*** there's no fear *ou* danger that he'll come. ◆ **dangereusement** *adv* dangerously. ◆ **dangereux, -euse** *adj* (*gén*) dangerous (*pour* to); *entreprise* hazardous, risky. **zone ~euse** danger zone.
danois, e [danwa, waz] **1** *adj* Danish. **2** *nm* (*Ling*) Danish; (*chien*) Great Dane. **3 D~(e)** *nm(f)* Dane.
dans [dɑ̃] *prép* **(a)** (*lieu*) in; (*mouvement*) into; (*but*) to; (*parcours*) through; (*intérieur*) inside; (*limites*) within. **être/pénétrer ~ la forêt** to be in/go into the forest; **ils sont partis ~ la montagne** they have gone off to the mountains; **elle erra ~ la ville** she wandered round *ou* about *ou* through the town; **~ un rayon restreint** within a restricted radius; **ils ont voyagé ~ le même train** they travelled on the same train; **cherche ~ la boîte** look inside *ou* in the box; **jeter l'eau sale ~ l'évier** to pour the dirty water down the sink; **~ le fond de l'armoire** at the back of the wardrobe; **boire ~ une tasse** to drink out of *ou* from a cup. **(b)** (*temps*) in; (*limites*) within, inside. **il est ~ sa 6e année** he's in his 6th year; **~ le temps** in the past, at one time; **cela pourrait se faire ~ le mois** it could be done within the month; **je l'attends ~ la nuit** I'm expecting him some time tonight. **(c)** (*état etc*) in. **être ~ les affaires** to be in business; **~ la plus grande confusion** in a state of great confusion; **il est ~ le secret** he's in on the secret; **il l'a fait ~ ce but** he did it with this aim in view. **(d)** (*approximation*) about. **cela coûte ~ les 50 F** it costs in the region of 50 francs *ou* about 50 francs; **il vous faut ~ les 3 mètres de tissu** you'll need about *ou* something like 3 metres of fabric; **la pièce fait ~ les 8 m²** the room is about 8 m².
dansant, e [dɑ̃sɑ̃, ɑ̃t] *adj mouvement* dancing; *musique* lively. **soirée ~e** dance.
danse [dɑ̃s] *nf* (*valse etc*) dance. **la ~** (*art*) dancing; **~ de guerre** war dance; **la ~ classique** ballet dancing; **avoir la ~ de Saint Guy** (*Méd*) to have St Vitus's dance; (*fig*) to have the fidgets; **de ~** *professeur* dancing; *musique* dance. ◆ **danser** (1) *vti* (*gén*) to dance. **faire ~ qn** to dance with sb; **~ de joie** to dance for joy. ◆ **danseur, -euse** *nm,f* (*gén*) dancer; (*partenaire*) partner; *[ballet]* ballet dancer.
dard [daʀ] *nm [animal]* sting.
darder [daʀde] (1) *vt* **(a)** (*lancer*) *flèche, regard* to shoot (*sur* at). **le soleil dardait ses rayons** the sun's rays beat down (*sur* on). **(b)** (*dresser*) *piquants* to point.
dare-dare* [daʀdaʀ] *loc adv* double-quick.
datation [datɑsjɔ̃] *nf* dating.
date [dat] *nf* date. **~ de naissance** date of birth; **à quelle ~?** on what date?; **à cette ~-là** by that time, by then; **lettre en ~ du 23 mai** letter dated May 23rd; **~ limite** deadline; **prendre ~ avec qn** to set *ou* fix a date with sb; **faire ~** *[événement]* to stand out (*dans* in); **le premier/dernier en ~** the first/latest *ou* most recent; **sans ~** undated; **de longue ~** (*adj*) long-standing; **de fraîche ~** (*adj*) recent; **connaître qn de longue/fraîche ~** to have known sb for a long/short time.
dater [date] (1) **1** *vt* to date. **daté du 6/de Paris** dated from the 6th/from Paris; **non daté** undated. **2** *vi* **(a) ~ de** to date back to, date from; **à ~ de demain** as from tomorrow, from tomorrow onwards; **de quand date votre dernière rencontre?** when did you last meet? **(b)** (*faire date*) *[événement]* to stand out (*dans* in); (*être démodé*) to be dated.
datif, -ive [datif, iv] *adj, nm* dative.
datte [dat] *nf* date. ◆ **dattier** *nm* date palm.
daube [dob] *nf* stew, casserole. **bœuf en ~** casserole of beef, beef stew.
dauphin [dofɛ̃] *nm* **(a)** (*Zool*) dolphin. **(b)** (*Hist*) **le D~** the Dauphin. **(c)** (*fig: successeur*) heir apparent.
Dauphine [dofin] *nf* Dauphine.
daurade [dɔʀad] *nf* sea bream.
davantage [davɑ̃taʒ] *adv* **(a)** (*plus*) more; (*négatif*) any more; (*interrogatif*) (any) more (*que* than). **bien/encore ~** much/still more. **(b)**

(*plus longtemps*) longer; (*négatif, interrogatif*) any longer (*que* than). **(c)** (*de plus en plus*) more and more. **chaque jour** ~ more and more every day. **(d)** ~ **de** (some) more; (*négatif*) any more.

de [d(ə)] (*devant voyelle et h muet:* **d'**; *contraction avec* **le, les: du, des**) **1** *prép* **(a)** (*provenance*) out of, from; (*localisation*) in, on. **sortir** ~ **la maison** to come out of the house; **arriver du Japon** to arrive from Japan; **l'avion** ~ **Londres** (*provenance*) the plane from London; (*destination*) the plane for London, the London plane; **les magasins** ~ **Paris** the Paris shops, the shops in Paris; **les voisins du 2e** the neighbours on the 2nd floor; **le meilleur** ~ **la classe/du monde** the best in the class/in the world; **né** ~ **parents pauvres** born of poor parents; ~ **6 qu'ils étaient au départ** (out) of the original 6.

(b) (*appartenance*) of. **la maison** ~ **mon ami** the house of my friend, my friend's house; **un roman** ~ **Wells** a novel by Wells, a novel of Wells'; **le pied** ~ **la table** the leg of the table, the table leg.

(c) (*caractérisation*) of. **regard** ~ **haine** look of hatred; **le professeur d'anglais** the English teacher, the teacher of English; **objet** ~ **cristal/métal** crystal/metal object; **il est d'une bêtise!** he's so stupid!; **c'est bien** ~ **lui!** it's just like him *ou* typical of him!; **2 verres** ~ **cassés** 2 broken glasses, 2 glasses broken.

(d) (*contenu*) of. **une tasse** ~ **thé** a cup of tea.

(e) (*temps*) ~ **jour** by day, during the day; ~ **6 à 8** from 6 to 8; **3 heures du matin** 3 (o'clock) in the morning; **il n'a rien fait** ~ **l'année** he hasn't done a thing all year; **d'une minute à l'autre** (*incessamment*) any minute now; (*progressivement*) from one minute to the next; **3 jours** ~ **libre** 3 days free.

(f) (*mesure*) **pièce** ~ **6 m²** room measuring 6 m²; **enfant** ~ **5 ans** 5-year-old child; **promenade** ~ **3 heures/km** 3-hour/3-km walk; **ce poteau a 5 mètres** ~ **haut** this post is 5 metres high; **plus grand** ~ **5 cm** 5 cm taller; **il gagne 9 F** ~ **l'heure** he earns 9 francs an hour *ou* per hour.

(g) (*moyen, manière, cause*) **frapper** ~ **la main** to strike with one's hand; **se nourrir** ~ **racines** to live on roots; **il vit** ~ **sa peinture** he lives by his painting; **faire qch** ~ **rien** to make sth out of nothing; **parler d'une voix ferme** to speak in a firm voice; **mourir** ~ **vieillesse** to die of old age; **rougir** ~ **honte** to blush with shame; ~ **colère, il la gifla** he slapped her in anger; **étonné** ~ **voir** astonished at seeing *ou* to see.

(h) (*copule*) **décider** ~ **faire** to decide to do; **empêcher qn** ~ **faire** to prevent sb from doing; **content** ~ **qch** pleased with sth; **le mois** ~ **juin** the month of June; **le prénom** ~ **Paul** the name Paul; **ton idiot** ~ **fils** that stupid son of yours; **ce cochon** ~ **temps** this rotten weather; **et elle** ~ **se moquer** ~ **nous!** and she poked fun at us!

2 *art partitif* (*affirmation*) some (*souvent omis*); (*interrogation*) any, some; (*négation*) any, no. **boire** ~ **l'eau au robinet** to drink (some) water from the tap; **voulez-vous du pain?** do you want any bread?; **il n'y a plus d'espoir** there is no hope left; **c'est du vol!** that's robbery!; **faire du bruit** to make a noise; **avoir** ~ **l'humour** to have a sense of humour; **il y a** ~ **la lumière** there's a light on.

3 des, de *art indéf pl* some (*souvent omis*); (*négation*) any, no. **des enfants ont cassé les carreaux** some children have broken the window panes; **je n'ai pas de voisins** I haven't any neighbours, I have no neighbours; **j'ai attendu des heures (et des heures)** I waited for hours (and hours).

dé [de] *nm* **(a)** ~ **(à coudre)** thimble; (*petit verre*) tiny glass. **(b)** (*Jeux*) die, dice. ~**s** dice; **les** ~**s sont jetés** the die is cast; (*Culin*) **couper en** ~**s** to dice.

déambuler [deɑ̃byle] (1) *vi* to stroll (about).

débâcle [debɑkl(ə)] *nf [armée]* rout; *[régime]* collapse; *[glaces]* breaking up.

déballer [debale] (1) *vt affaires* to unpack; *marchandises* to display; (*) *sentiments* to pour out. ♦ **déballage** *nm* (*action*) unpacking; (*marchandises*) display (*of loose goods*).

débandade [debɑ̃dad] *nf* (*déroute*) headlong flight; (*dispersion*) scattering. **en** ~ in disorder.

débander [debɑ̃de] (1) **1** *vt* (*Méd*) to unbandage. ~ **les yeux de qn** to remove the blindfold from sb's eyes. **2 se** ~ *vpr [armée]* to scatter.

débaptiser [debatize] (1) *vt* to rename.

débarbouiller *vt*, **se** ~ *vpr* [debaʀbuje] (1) to wash.

débarcadère [debaʀkadɛʀ] *nm* landing stage.

débardeur [debaʀdœʀ] *nm* (*ouvrier*) docker; (*vêtement*) slipover.

débarquer [debaʀke] (1) **1** *vt* (*gén, Mil*) to land; *marchandises* to unload. **2** *vi* to disembark, land. **il a débarqué chez moi*** he turned up at my place; **tu débarques!*** where have you been? ♦ **débarquement** *nm* landing; unloading.

débarras [debaʀa] *nm* (*pièce*) lumber room; (*placard*) cupboard. **bon** ~! good riddance!

débarrasser [debaʀase] (1) **1** *vt* **(a)** *local* to clear (*de* of). ~ **(la table)** to clear the table; **débarrasse le plancher!*** clear off!*, make yourself scarce!*. **(b)** ~ **qn de** *fardeau* to relieve sb of; *ennemi, mal* to rid sb of; *liens* to release sb from. **2 se** ~ *vpr*: **se** ~ **de** (*gén*) to get rid of, rid o.s. of; *vêtement* to take off, remove.

débat [deba] *nm* discussion, debate. (*Jur, Pol*) ~**s** debates.

débattre [debatʀ(ə)] (41) **1** *vt* to discuss, debate. **2 se** ~ *vpr* to struggle, wrestle (*contre* with).

débauchage [deboʃaʒ] *nm* (*Écon*) laying off.

débauche [deboʃ] *nf* **(a)** (*vice*) debauchery. **partie de** ~ orgy. **(b)** (*abondance*) ~ **de** profusion of; ~ **de couleurs** riot of colour.

débaucher [deboʃe] (1) **1** *vt* (†: *corrompre*) to debauch; (*licencier*) to lay off. **2 se** ~ *vpr* to become debauched. ♦ **débauché, e 1** *adj* debauched. **2** *nm,f* debauchee.

débile [debil] *adj corps, esprit* feeble; (*péj*) moronic. **c'est un** ~ **mental** (*lit*) he is mentally deficient; (*péj*) he's a moron. ♦ **débilité** *nf*: ~ **(mentale)** mental deficiency.

débiliter [debilite] (1) *vt [climat]* to debilitate, enervate; *[propos]* to demoralize.

débiner* [debine] (1) **1** *vt* to run down. **2 se** ~ *vpr* to clear off*.

débit [debi] **1** *nm* **(a)** (*Fin*) debit. **mettre 10 F au** ~ **de qn** to debit sb with 10 francs. **(b)** (*Comm: vente*) turnover. **cette boutique a du** ~ this shop has a quick turnover. **(c)** *[fleuve, pompe]* flow; *[tuyau]* discharge; *[machine, gaz]* output. **(d)** (*élocution*) delivery. **2:** ~ **de boissons** (*Admin*) drinking establishment; ~ **de tabac** tobacconist's (shop).

débitant, e [debitɑ̃, ɑ̃t] *nm,f*: ~ **(de boissons)** ≃ licensed grocer; ~ **(de tabac)** tobacconist.

débiter [debite] (1) *vt compte* to debit; *marchandises* to retail, sell; *[usine]* to produce; (*péj: dire*) to pour out; (*tailler*) to cut up.

débiteur, -trice [debitœʀ, tʀis] **1** *adj solde* debit. **mon compte est** ~ **de 50 F** my account has a debit balance of 50 francs. **2** *nm,f* (*Fin, fig*) debtor.

déblayer [debleje] (8) *vt décombres* to clear away; *chemin* to clear; *pièce* to clear up; *travail* to prepare. ♦ **déblaiement** *nm* clearing. ♦ **déblais** *nmpl* (*gravats*) rubble; (*terre*) earth.

débloquer [deblɔke] (1) **1** *vt* **(a)** *compte, prix* to free; *stocks, crédits* to release. **(b)** *machine* to unjam; *écrou, freins* to release; *route* to unblock. **2** *vi* (‡) (*dire des bêtises*) to talk twaddle*; (*être fou*) to be off one's rocker‡. ♦ **déblocage** *nm* freeing; releasing; unjamming; unblocking.

déboires [debwaʀ] *nmpl* (*déceptions*) disappointments; (*échecs*) setbacks; (*ennuis*) difficulties.

déboiser [debwaze] (1) *vt montagne* to deforest; *forêt* to clear of trees. ♦ **déboisement** *nm* deforestation; clearing.

déboîter [debwate] (1) **1** *vt membre* to dislocate; *tuyaux* to disconnect; *objet* to dislodge. **se ~ l'épaule** to dislocate one's shoulder. **2** *vi* (*Aut*) to pull out. ♦ **déboîtement** *nm* dislocation; pulling out.

débonnaire [debɔnɛʀ] *adj personne* good-natured; *air* kindly.

débordant, e [debɔʀdɑ̃, ɑ̃t] *adj activité* exuberant; *joie* overflowing. (*Mil*) **mouvement ~** outflanking manoeuvre.

débordement [debɔʀdəmɑ̃] *nm* **(a)** **~(s)** *[liquide]* overflowing; (*par ébullition*) boiling over; (*Mil, Sport*) outflanking. **(b)** *[joie]* outburst; *[paroles]* torrent; *[activité]* explosion. (*débauches*) **~s** excesses.

déborder [debɔʀde] (1) **1** *vi* **(a)** *[liquide]* (*gén*) to overflow; (*en bouillant*) to boil over. **plein à ~** full to the brim *ou* to overflowing (*de* with); **~ de la casserole** to overflow (*ou* boil over) the saucepan; (*fig*) **cela a fait ~ le vase, c'est la goutte qui a fait ~ le vase** that was the last straw; **~ de santé** *etc* to be bursting with health *etc*. **(b)** (*d'un alignement*) to stick out; (*en dessinant*) to go over the edge. **2** *vt* **(a)** (*dépasser*) (*gén*) to extend beyond; (*Mil, Sport*) to outflank; (*d'un alignement*) to stick *ou* jut out beyond. **être débordé de travail** to be snowed under with work*. **(b)** *lit* to untuck.

déboucher [debuʃe] (1) **1** *vt tuyau* to unblock; *bouteille* to uncork; *tube* to uncap. **2** *vi*: **~ de** to emerge from, come out of; **~ sur qch** *[rue]* to run *ou* open into sth; *[voiture]* to come out *ou* emerge into sth; *[discussion]* to lead up to sth. **3 se ~** *vpr [tuyau]* to come unblocked. ♦ **débouchage** *nm* unblocking; uncorking. ♦ **débouché** *nm [pays, économie]* outlet; *[vallée, carrière]* opening.

déboucler [debukle] (1) *vt ceinture* to unbuckle, undo.

débouler [debule] (1) **1** *vi [lapin]* to bolt; (*dégringoler*) to tumble down. **2** *vt* (*: *dévaler*) to belt down*.

débourser [debuʀse] (1) *vt* to pay out, lay out. ♦ **débours** *nm* outlay.

debout [dəbu] *adv, adj inv* **(a)** *personne* standing; (*levé*) up. **être ~** to stand; (*levé*) to be up; (*guéri*) to be up and about; **se mettre ~** to stand up, get up; **rester ~** to remain standing; (*veiller*) to stay up; **il l'aida à se remettre ~** he helped him back up *ou* back to his feet; **~!** get up!, on your feet! **(b)** *objet* standing upright. **mettre qch ~** to stand sth upright; **tenir ~** *[objet]* to stand up; *[édifice]* to be standing; *[théorie]* to stand, hold; **ça ne tient pas ~ ce que tu dis** what you say doesn't stand up *ou* doesn't hold water.

déboutonner [debutɔne] (1) **1** *vt* to unbutton, undo. **2 se ~** *vpr [personne]* to unbutton *ou* undo o.s.; *[habit]* to come unbuttoned *ou* undone.

débraillé, e [debʀaje] **1** *adj tenue* untidy; *manières* slovenly; *style* sloppy. **2** *nm* slovenliness; sloppiness.

débrancher [debʀɑ̃ʃe] (1) *vt* (*gén*) to disconnect.

débrayer [debʀeje] (8) *vi* (*Aut*) to disengage the clutch; (*faire grève*) to stop work. ♦ **débrayage** *nm* clutch; stoppage.

débridé, e [debʀide] *adj* unbridled.

débris [debʀi] *nm* (*gén*) fragment. **les ~** (*décombres*) the debris (*sg*); (*détritus*) the rubbish; *[repas]* the leftovers *ou* scraps; *[armée, fortune]* the remains.

débrouiller [debʀuje] (1) **1** *vt fils* to disentangle; *papiers, problème* to sort out; *mystère* to unravel. **~ qn*** to teach sb the basics. **2 se ~** *vpr* to manage. **il m'a laissé me ~ tout seul** he left me to cope alone *ou* sort things out myself. ♦ **débrouillard, e*** *adj* smart*, resourceful. ♦ **débrouillardise*** *nf* smartness*, resourcefulness.

débroussailler [debʀusɑje] (1) *vt terrain* to clear; *problème* to do the spadework on.

débusquer [debyske] (1) *vt* to drive out.

début [deby] *nm* **(a)** (*gén*) beginning, start. **du ~ à la fin** from beginning to end; **salaire de ~** starting salary; **dès le ~** from the outset *ou* start *ou* beginning; **au ~** at first, in the beginning; **au ~ du mois prochain** early next month. **(b) ~s** start; **à ses ~s** *projet* in its early stages; **faire ses ~s** (*gén*) to start; (*Théât*) to make one's début.

débutant, e [debytɑ̃, ɑ̃t] **1** *adj* novice. **2** *nm,f* (*gén*) beginner, novice; (*Théât*) debutant actor (*ou* actress).

débuter [debyte] (1) **1** *vi* to start, begin (*par, sur* with); *[acteur]* to make one's début (*dans* in). **2** *vt* (*) to start, begin.

déca [deka] *préf* deca.

deçà [dəsa] *adv* **(a) en ~ de** *fleuve* on this side of; **en ~ de ses moyens** within his means; **c'est très en ~ de la vérité** it is far short of the truth. **(b)** (*littér*) **~, delà** here and there.

décacheter [dekaʃte] (4) *vt lettre* to unseal, open. ♦ **décachetage** *nm* unsealing, opening.

décade [dekad] *nf* (*décennie*) decade; (*dix jours*) period of ten days.

décadence [dekadɑ̃s] *nf* (*processus*) decline; (*état*) decadence. **tomber en ~** to fall into decline. ♦ **décadent, e 1** *adj* decadent, declining. **2** *nm,f* decadent.

décaféiner [dekafeine] (1) *vt* to decaffeinate.

décalage [dekalaʒ] *nm* (*entre concepts*) gap; (*entre cause et effet*) interval, time-lag (*entre* between). **~ horaire** time difference.

décalaminer [dekalamine] (1) *vt* to decarbonize.

décalcifier [dekalsifje] (7) *vt* to decalcify. ♦ **décalcification** *nf* decalcification.

décalcomanie [dekalkɔmani] *nf* (*image*) transfer. **faire de la ~** to do transfers.

décaler [dekale] (1) *vt* **(a)** (*avancer*) to move forward; (*reculer*) to move back. **se ~ d'un rang** to move forward (*ou* back) a row; **décalé par rapport aux autres** out of line with *ou* sticking out beyond the others; **décalé d'une heure** (*avancé*) brought forward an hour; (*retardé*) put back an hour. **(b)** (*déséquilibrer*) to unwedge.

décalquer [dekalke] (1) *vt* to trace; (*par pression*) to transfer. ♦ **décalque** *nm* tracing; transfer.

décamper* [dekɑ̃pe] (1) *vi* to clear off*.

décanter [dekɑ̃te] (1) **1** *vt* to allow to settle. **2 se ~** *vpr [vin]* to settle; *[idées]* to become clear. **laisser les choses se ~** to let things clarify themselves, allow the dust to settle. ♦ **décantation** *nf* settling; clarification.

décaper [dekape] (1) *vt* (*gén*) to clean; (*à l'abrasif*) to scour; (*à l'acide*) to pickle; (*à la brosse*) to scrub; (*au papier de verre*) to sand.

décapiter [dekapite] (1) *vt personne* to behead; (*accidentellement*) to decapitate; (*fig*) *parti* to remove the top men from. ♦ **décapitation** *nf* beheading.

décapotable [dekapɔtabl(ə)] *adj* (*Aut*) convertible.

décapsuler [dekapsyle] (1) *vt* to take the cap *ou* top off. ♦ **décapsuleur** *nm* bottle-opener.

décarcasser (se)* [dekaʀkase] (1) *vpr* to go to a lot of trouble (*pour* to).

décati, e [dekati] *adj* (*péj*) *vieillard* decrepit; *visage* aged; *beauté* faded.

décéder [desede] (6) *vi* to die. ♦ **décédé, e** *adj* deceased.

déceler [desle] (5) *vt* (*trouver*) to detect; (*montrer*) to indicate. ♦ **décelable** *adj* detectable.

décélération [deseleʀasjɔ̃] *nf* deceleration.

décembre [desɑ̃bʀ(ə)] *nm* December; *V* **septembre.**

décence [desɑ̃s] *nf* (*bienséance*) decency.

♦ **décemment** *adv* decently. ♦ **décent, e** *adj* decent.
décennie [deseni] *nf* decade.
décentraliser [desɑ̃tʀalize] (1) *vt* to decentralize. ♦ **décentralisation** *nf* decentralization.
déception [desɛpsjɔ̃] *nf* disappointment.
décerner [desɛʀne] (1) *vt* to award.
décès [desɛ] *nm* death.
décevoir [desvwaʀ] (28) *vt* to disappoint. ♦ **décevant, e** *adj* disappointing.
déchaîner [deʃene] (1) **1** *vt violence* to unleash; *enthousiasme* to arouse; *opinion publique* to rouse; *campagne* (*organiser*) to set up; (*avoir comme résultat*) to trigger off. ~ **les huées/les rires** to raise a storm of booing/laughter. **2 se** ~ *vpr [fureur]* to burst out; *[rires, tempête]* to break out; *[personne]* to loose one's anger (*contre* upon). ♦ **déchaîné, e** *adj passions, flots* raging; *enthousiasme, personne* wild; *opinion publique* furious. **il est** ~ **contre moi** he is furious with me. ♦ **déchaînement** *nm* bursting out; breaking out; *[passions etc]* fury. **un** ~ **d'injures** a torrent of abuse.
déchanter [deʃɑ̃te] (1) *vi* to become disillusioned.
décharge [deʃaʀʒ(ə)] *nf* **(a)** (*salve*) volley of shots. ~ **(électrique)** electrical discharge. **(b)** (*Jur*) discharge; (*Comm: reçu*) receipt. (*fig*) **il faut dire à sa** ~ **que ...** it must be said in his defence that ... . **(c)** (*dépôt*) ~ **(publique)** rubbish *ou* garbage (*US*) dump.
décharger [deʃaʀʒe] (3) *vt véhicule, bagages* to unload (*de* from); *conscience* to unburden (*auprès de* to); *accusé, arme* to discharge. ~ **sa colère** to vent one's anger (*sur qn* on sb); ~ **qn de** *tâche* to relieve sb of; **se** ~ **de ses responsabilités** to pass off *ou* off-load one's responsibilities (*sur qn* onto sb); (*Élec*) **se** ~ to go flat, lose its charge. ♦ **déchargement** *nm* unloading.
décharné, e [deʃaʀne] *adj corps* emaciated; *doigts* bony; *visage* gaunt; *paysage* bare.
déchausser [deʃose] (1) **1** *vt*: ~ **un enfant** to take a child's shoes off. **2 se** ~ *vpr [personne]* to take one's shoes off; *[dents]* to come loose. ♦ **déchaussé, e** *adj personne* barefooted.
déchéance [deʃeɑ̃s] *nf* (*morale*) decay; (*physique*) degeneration; (*Rel*) fall; (*Pol*) *[souverain]* deposition.
déchet [deʃɛ] *nm [viande, tissu]* scrap; (*perte*) waste. ~**s radio-actifs** radioactive waste; **jeter les** ~**s à la poubelle** to throw the rubbish out; **il y a du** ~ there is some wastage; (*péj*) ~ **(humain)** human wreck.
déchiffrer [deʃifʀe] (1) *vt message* to decipher; *code* to decode; (*Mus*) to sight-read; *énigme* to unravel. ♦ **déchiffrable** *adj* decipherable; decodable. ♦ **déchiffrage** *nm* deciphering; decoding; sight-reading; unravelling.
déchiqueter [deʃikte] (4) *vt* (*lit, fig*) to tear to pieces. **déchiqueté par l'explosion** blown to pieces by the explosion. ♦ **déchiqueté, e** *adj relief* jagged; *corps* mutilated.
déchirer [deʃiʀe] (1) **1** *vt* **(a)** (*lacérer*) to tear up; (*faire un accroc*) to tear, rip; (*arracher*) to tear out (*de* from); (*ouvrir*) to tear open. ~ **en deux** to tear in two. **(b)** *[querelle, remords]* to tear apart. **cris qui déchirent l'air/les oreilles** cries which rend the air/split one's ears; **spectacle qui déchire le cœur** heartrending *ou* harrowing sight. **2 se** ~ *vpr [vêtement]* to tear, rip; *[sac]* to burst; *[cœur]* to break; *[couple]* to tear each other apart. **se** ~ **un muscle** to tear a muscle; **se** ~ **les mains** to graze one's hands. ♦ **déchirant, e** *adj* heartbreaking. ♦ **déchirement** *nm* (*douleur*) wrench, heartbreak. (*Pol: divisions*) ~**s** rifts. ♦ **déchirure** *nf [tissu]* tear, rip; *[ciel]* break in the clouds. **se faire une** ~ **musculaire** to tear a muscle.
déchoir [deʃwaʀ] (25) *vi [personne]* to demean o.s.; *[réputation, influence]* to wane. ♦ **déchu, e** *adj roi* deposed; (*Rel*) fallen. (*Jur*) **être** ~ **de ses droits** to be deprived of one's rights.
déci [desi] *préf* deci.
décidé, e [deside] *adj air, ton* determined, decided; *personne* determined (*à faire* to do); *question* settled, decided. **bon, c'est** ~ right, that's settled then.
décidément [desidemɑ̃] *adv* (*certainement*) certainly, undoubtedly, indeed; (*vraiment*) really. ~, **il est fou** he's really mad.
décider [deside] (1) **1** *vt* **(a)** (*établir*) ~ **qch** to decide on sth; ~ **que** to decide that; ~ **de faire qch/de ne pas faire qch** to decide to do sth/against doing sth; **c'est à lui de** ~ it's up to him to decide. **(b)** (*persuader*) *[personne]* to persuade; *[conseil, événement]* to decide. ~ **qn à faire** to persuade sb to do. **(c)** *[chose]* (*provoquer*) to cause, bring about. **2** ~ **de** *vt indir*: ~ **de qch** *[personne]* to decide on sth; *[événements]* to decide *ou* determine sth; **le sort en a décidé autrement** fate has decided *ou* ordained otherwise. **3 se** ~ *vpr* **(a)** *[personne]* to come to *ou* make a decision, make up one's mind. **se** ~ **à** *ou* **pour qch** to decide on sth; **je ne peux pas me** ~ **à lui mentir** I cannot bring myself *ou* I cannot make up my mind to lie to him. **(b)** *[problème]* to be decided *ou* settled. **est-ce qu'il va se** ~ **à faire beau?*** do you think it'll turn out fine after all?
décimal, e, *mpl* **-aux** [desimal, o] *adj, nf* decimal.
décimer [desime] (1) *vt* to decimate. ♦ **décimation** *nf* decimation.
décisif, -ive [desizif, iv] *adj* (*gén*) decisive; *argument* conclusive; *coup, facteur* deciding.
décision [desizjɔ̃] *nf* (*choix, verdict*) decision; (*fermeté*) decisiveness. **soumettre qch à la** ~ **de qn** to submit sth to sb for his decision.
déclamer [deklame] (1) **1** *vt* to declaim; (*péj*) to spout. **2** *vi* (*péj*) to rant. (*littér*) ~ **contre** to inveigh against. ♦ **déclamation** *nf* (*art*) declamation. (*péj*) ~**(s)** ranting. ♦ **déclamatoire** *adj* (*gén*) declamatory; (*péj*) *ton* ranting.
déclarable [deklaʀabl(ə)] *adj* declarable.
déclaration [deklaʀɑsjɔ̃] **1** *nf* (*proclamation*) declaration; (*discours, commentaire*) statement; (*aveu*) admission; (*révélation*) revelation; *[décès]* registration; *[vol]* notification. **2:** ~ **(d'amour)** declaration of love; ~ **de guerre** declaration of war; ~ **d'impôts** statement of income; (*formulaire*) tax return; ~ **sous serment** statement under oath.
déclaré, e [deklaʀe] *adj opinion* professed; *athée, ennemi* avowed; *intention* avowed, declared.
déclarer [deklaʀe] (1) **1** *vt* (*gén*) to declare; (*annoncer*) to announce; (*avouer*) to admit; *décès* to register; *vol* to notify. ~ **la guerre** to declare war (*à* on); ~ **qn coupable** to find sb guilty; ~ **que** ... to declare that ...; **je vous déclare que** I tell you that. **2 se** ~ *vpr* **(a) se** ~ **en faveur de** to declare o.s. *ou* come out in favour of; **se** ~ **satisfait** to declare o.s. satisfied; **se** ~ **offensé** to say one is offended. **(b)** *[incendie, épidémie]* to break out. **(c)** *[amoureux]* to declare one's love.
déclasser [deklɑse] (1) *vt coureur* to relegate; *fiches* to get out of order. ♦ **déclassement** *nm* relegation.
déclencher [deklɑ̃ʃe] (1) **1** *vt mécanisme* to release; *sonnerie* to set off; *ouverture* to activate; *attaque, grève* to launch; *catastrophe, commentaires* to trigger off; (*Mil*) *tir* to open. **2 se** ~ *vpr [mécanisme]* to release itself; *[sonnerie]* to go off; *[attaque, grève]* to start; *[crise]* to be triggered off. ♦ **déclenchement** *nm* release; setting off; triggering off; activating; launching; starting; opening. ♦ **déclencheur** *nm* (*Tech*) release mechanism.
déclic [deklik] *nm* (*bruit*) click; (*mécanisme*) trigger mechanism.

décliner [dekline] (1) **1** *vt* **(a)** *nom, identité* to state, give; *offre* to decline, refuse. ~ **toute responsabilité** to decline *ou* refuse to accept any responsibility. **(b)** (*Ling*) to decline. **2** *vi* **(a)** (*s'affaiblir*) (*gén*) to decline; *[santé]* to deteriorate; *[ardeur, beauté]* to wane, fade. **(b)** (*baisser*) *[jour]* to draw to a close; *[soleil]* to go down; *[lune]* to wane; *[astre]* to set. ♦ **déclin** *nm* decline; deterioration; waning; fading (*de* in). **le ~ du jour/de la vie** the close of day/of life; **être à son ~** *[soleil]* to be setting; *[lune]* to be waning; **être en ~** to be on the decline. ♦ **déclinable** *adj* declinable. ♦ **déclinaison** *nf* (*Ling*) declension; (*Astron, Phys*) declination.
déclivité [deklivite] *nf* incline.
décocher [dekɔʃe] (1) *vt flèche, regard* to shoot; *coup* to throw; *ruade, remarque* to let fly.
décoder [dekɔde] (1) *vt code* to decode; *message* to decipher. ♦ **décodage** *nm* decoding; deciphering.
décoiffer [dekwafe] (1) *vt*: ~ **qn** (*cheveux*) to disarrange sb's hair; (*chapeau*) to take sb's hat off; **je suis toute décoiffée** my hair is in a mess; **se ~** to take one's hat off.
décoincer [dekwɛ̃se] (3) *vt* (*gén*) to unjam.
décolérer [dekɔleʀe] (6) *vi*: **il ne décolère pas depuis hier** he hasn't calmed down *ou* cooled off* since yesterday.
décoller [dekɔle] (1) **1** *vt* (*gén*) to unstick; (*) *poursuivants* to shake off. **2** *vi* (*Aviat, fig*) to take off; (*) *[gêneur]* to budge. **3 se ~** *vpr [timbre]* to come unstuck. ♦ **décollage** *nm* (*Aviat*) takeoff.
décolleté, e [dekɔlte] **1** *adj robe* low-cut. ~ **dans le dos** cut low at the back. **2** *nm* low neckline.
décoloniser [dekɔlɔnize] (1) *vt* to decolonize. ♦ **décolonisateur, -trice 1** *adj* decolonizing. **2** *nm,f* decolonizer. ♦ **décolonisation** *nf* decolonization.
décolorer [dekɔlɔʀe] (1) **1** *vt liquide* to decolour; *cheveux* to bleach; *tissu* to fade. **lèvres décolorées** colourless lips. **2 se ~** *vpr* (*gén*) to lose its colour; *[tissu]* to fade. ♦ **décoloration** *nf* (*gén*) decoloration. **se faire faire une ~** to have one's hair bleached.
décombres [dekɔ̃bʀ(ə)] *nmpl* rubble, debris (*sg*).
décommander [dekɔmɑ̃de] (1) **1** *vt marchandise, invitation* to cancel; *invités* to put off. **2 se ~** *vpr* to cancel an appointment.
décomposer [dekɔ̃poze] (1) **1** *vt* **(a)** *mouvement, lumière* to break up; *problème, phrase* to break down; (*Chim*) to decompose. **(b)** (*altérer*) *visage* to contort; *viande* to cause to decompose. **2 se ~** *vpr [viande]* to decompose; *[visage]* to change dramatically. ♦ **décomposition** *nf* decomposition; breaking up; breaking down; contortion. **en ~** *cadavre* in a state of decomposition; *société* in decay.
décompte [dekɔ̃t] *nm* (*compte*) detailed account; (*déduction*) deduction. **faire le ~ des points** to count up the points. ♦ **décompter** (1) *vt* to deduct.
déconcentrer [dekɔ̃sɑ̃tʀe] (1) **1** *vt* (*Admin*) to devolve, decentralize; (*Ind*) to disperse. **2 se ~** *vpr* (*Sport*) to lose concentration.
déconcerter [dekɔ̃sɛʀte] (1) *vt* to disconcert.
déconfit, e [dekɔ̃fi, it] *adj* crestfallen, downcast.
déconfiture* [dekɔ̃fityʀ] *nf* defeat; (*financière*) (financial) collapse.
décongeler [dekɔ̃ʒle] (5) *vt* to thaw (out).
décongestionner [dekɔ̃ʒɛstjɔne] (1) *vt* (*Méd*), *rue* to relieve congestion in; *administration* to relieve the pressure on.
déconnecter [dekɔnɛkte] (1) *vt* to disconnect.
déconseiller [dekɔ̃seje] (1) *vt*: ~ **qch à qn** to advise sb against sth; **c'est déconseillé** it's inadvisable.
déconsidérer [dekɔ̃sideʀe] (6) *vt* to discredit.
décontenancer [dekɔ̃tnɑ̃se] (3) *vt* to disconcert.
décontracter *vt*, **se ~** *vpr* [dekɔ̃tʀakte] (1) to relax. ♦ **décontraction** *nf* relaxation.
déconvenue [dekɔ̃vny] *nf* disappointment.
décor [dekɔʀ] *nm* **(a)** (*Théât*) **le ~, les ~s** the scenery, the décor; ~ **de cinéma/théâtre** film/stage set; **quel beau ~!** what a lovely set!; *[véhicule]* **entrer dans le ~*** to run off the road; **envoyer qn dans le ~*** to force sb off the road. **(b)** (*paysage*) scenery; (*milieu*) setting. ♦ **décorateur, -trice** *nm,f* **(a)** (*d'intérieurs*) (interior) decorator. **(b)** (*Théât*) set designer. ♦ **décoratif, -ive** *adj* decorative. ♦ **décoration** *nf* decoration. ♦ **décorer** (1) *vt* (*gén*) to decorate; *robe* to trim.
décortiquer [dekɔʀtike] (1) *vt crevettes* to shell; *riz* to hull; *texte* to dissect.
décorum [dekɔʀɔm] *nm*: **le ~** decorum.
découcher [dekuʃe] (1) *vi* to stay out all night.
découdre [dekudʀ(ə)] (48) **1** *vt* **(a)** *vêtement* to unpick; *bouton* to take off. **(b)** (*littér*) **en ~** to fight. **2 se ~** *vpr [robe]* to come unstitched; *[bouton]* to come off.
découler [dekule] (1) *vi* to ensue, follow (*de* from).
découpage [dekupaʒ] *nm* **(a)** *[papier, gâteau]* cutting up; *[viande]* carving; *[image, métal]* cutting out; (*Ciné*) cutting. ~ **électoral** division into constituencies. **(b)** (*image*) cut-out (figure).
découpé, e [dekupe] *adj relief, côte* jagged, indented; *feuille* jagged.
découper [dekupe] (1) **1** *vt viande* to carve; *gâteau, papier, tissu* to cut up; *images, métal* to cut out. **indentations qui découpent la côte** indentations which cut into the coastline. **2 se ~** *vpr [silhouette]* to stand out (*sur* against).
découpure [dekupyʀ] *nf* **(a)** (*contour*) jagged *ou* indented outline. **~s** *[côte]* indentations. **(b)** (*morceau*) piece cut out.
décourager [dekuʀaʒe] (3) **1** *vt* (*démoraliser*) to discourage, dishearten; (*dissuader*) to discourage, put off. ~ **qn d'une entreprise** to discourage sb from an undertaking, put sb off an undertaking. **2 se ~** *vpr* to lose heart, become discouraged. ♦ **décourageant, e** *adj* disheartening, discouraging. ♦ **découragement** *nm* discouragement, despondency.
décousu, e [dekuzy] *adj* (*Couture*) unstitched; (*fig*) disjointed.
découvert, e [dekuvɛʀ, ɛʀt(ə)] **1** *adj tête* bare, uncovered; *lieu* open, exposed. **être à ~** to be exposed; **agir à ~** to act openly. **2** *nm [compte]* overdraft; *[caisse]* deficit. **tirer de l'argent à ~** to overdraw one's account. **3** *nf* discovery. **aller à la ~e de** to go in search of.
découvrir [dekuvʀiʀ] (18) **1** *vt* **(a)** (*trouver*) to discover; *cause, vérité* to discover, find out, unearth. ~ **que/comment** to find out *ou* discover that/how; **elle s'est découvert un cousin en Amérique** she found out *ou* discovered she had a cousin in America; ~ **le pot aux roses*** to find out about the fiddle*. **(b)** *casserole* to take the lid off; *statue* to unveil; *corps, ruines* to uncover; *membres* to bare, uncover. **il resta découvert devant elle** he kept his hat off in her presence; **robe qui découvre le dos** dress which reveals the back. **(c)** *panorama* to see, have a view of. **(d)** ~ **ses projets** to reveal *ou* disclose one's plans (*à qn* to sb); **se ~ à qn** to confide in sb.
2 se ~ *vpr* **(a)** *[personne]* (*chapeau*) to take off one's hat; (*habits*) to take off one's clothes; (*couvertures*) to uncover o.s. **il ne faut pas se ~** you must keep covered up. **(b)** (*Boxe, Escrime*) to leave o.s. open to attack. **(c)** *[ciel, temps]* to clear.
décrasser [dekʀase] (1) *vt* (*gén*) to clean; *chaudière* to clean out. **se ~** to give o.s. a good clean-up. ♦ **décrassage** *nm* cleaning; cleaning-out; clean-up.
décrépitude [dekʀepityd] *nf [personne]* decrepitude; *[nation]* decay. **tomber en ~** to

become decrepit; to decay. ♦ **décrépit, e** *adj* decrepit.

décréter [dekʀete] (6) *vt mobilisation, nomination* to order; *état d'urgence* to declare; *mesure* (*hum: décider*) to decree. ♦ **décret** *nm* (*gén*) decree.

décrier [dekʀije] (7) *vt* (*gén*) to disparage.

décrire [dekʀiʀ] (39) *vt* (*dépeindre*) to describe; (*parcourir*) to follow, describe. **l'avion décrivait des cercles** the plane flew in circles.

décrocher [dekʀɔʃe] (1) **1** *vt* **(a)** *rideau* to take down, unhook; *fermoir* to undo; *wagon* to uncouple; *téléphone* (*pour répondre*) to pick up, lift; (*pour l'empêcher de sonner*) to take off the hook; *objet coincé* to free. **le rideau s'est décroché** the curtain came unhooked. **(b)** (*: *obtenir*) to get, land*. **2** *vi* **(a)** (*Téléc*) to pick up *ou* lift the receiver. **(b)** (*Mil*) to break off the action. **(c)** (*) (*ne pas comprendre*) to fail to keep up; (*se désintéresser*) to drop out; (*cesser d'écouter*) to switch off*. ♦ **décroché** *nm* (*Constr*) recess.

décroiser [dekʀwaze] (1) *vt* to uncross.

décroître [dekʀwatʀ(ə)] (55) *vi* (*gén*) to decrease; *[fièvre, crue]* to go down; *[lune]* to wane; *[jour]* to get shorter; *[lumière]* to fade. ♦ **décroissance** *nf* (*gén*) decrease, decline (*de* in). ♦ **décrue** *nf [rivière]* fall in the level (*de* of).

décrotter [dekʀɔte] (1) *vt chaussures* to get the mud off.

déçu, e [desy] *adj* disappointed.

décupler [dekyple] (1) *vti* to increase tenfold; (*fig*) to double.

dédaigner [dedeɲe] (1) *vt* (*mépriser*) to scorn, disdain; (*négliger*) *offre, adversaire* to spurn; *menaces* to disregard. **ce n'est pas à ~** (*offre*) it's not to be sniffed at *ou* despised; (*danger*) it can't just be shrugged off; (*littér*) **il dédaigna d'y aller** he did not deign to go; **il ne dédaigne pas la plaisanterie** *ou* **de plaisanter** he's not averse to a good joke. ♦ **dédaigneusement** *adv* disdainfully. ♦ **dédaigneux, -euse** *adj* disdainful (*de* of). ♦ **dédain** *nm* disdain (*de* for).

dédale [dedal] *nm [rues, idées]* maze.

dedans [d(ə)dɑ̃] **1** *adv* inside. **nous sommes restés (au-)~ toute la journée** we stayed indoors all day; **elle cherche son sac, tout son argent est ~** she is looking for her bag - all her money is in it; **du ~** from inside; **en** *ou* **au ~ (de lui)** deep down; **au ~ (de)** inside; **il est rentré ~*** (*accident*) he ran *ou* crashed straight into it; (*bagarre*) he laid into him*; **il s'est fichu ~*** he got it all wrong. **2** *nm* inside.

dédicacer [dedikase] (3) *vt* to autograph (*à qn* for sb), inscribe (*à qn* to sb). ♦ **dédicace** *nf* dedication; (*manuscrite*) inscription.

dédier [dedje] (7) *vt*: **~ à** (*gén, Rel*) to dedicate to; *efforts* to devote to.

dédire (se) [dediʀ] (37) *vpr* (*engagements*) to go back on one's word; (*affirmation*) to withdraw. ♦ **dédit** *nm* (*caution*) forfeit, penalty. **en cas de ~** if you fail to keep your word.

dédommager [dedɔmaʒe] (3) *vt*: **~ qn** to compensate sb (*de* for); **comment vous ~ du dérangement?** how can I ever make up for the trouble? ♦ **dédommagement** *nm* compensation. **en ~** in compensation (*de* for).

dédouaner [dedwane] (1) *vt* (*Comm*) to clear through customs; (*) *personne* to clear. ♦ **dédouanement** *nm* customs clearance.

dédoubler [deduble] (1) *vt classe* to divide in two. **~ un train** to put on a relief train; **je ne peux pas me ~*** I can't be in two places at once. ♦ **dédoublement** *nm* (*Psych*) **~ de la personnalité** dual personality.

déduction [dedyksjɔ̃] *nf* **(a)** (*Comm*) deduction. **~ faite de** after deduction of. **(b)** (*raisonnement*) deduction, inference; (*conclusion*) conclusion. ♦ **déductible** *adj* deductible. ♦ **déductif, -ive** *adj* deductive.

déduire [dedɥiʀ] (38) *vt* (*Comm*) to deduct (*de* from); (*conclure*) to deduce, infer (*de* from).

déesse [deɛs] *nf* goddess.

défaillance [defajɑ̃s] *nf* (*évanouissement*) blackout; (*lit, fig: faiblesse*) weakness; (*panne*) fault, failure, breakdown (*de* in). **avoir une ~** (*évanouissement*) to faint, have a blackout; (*faiblesse*) to feel faint; **élève qui a des ~s** pupil who has certain shortcomings *ou* weak points (*en* in); **mémoire sans ~** faultless memory; **~ cardiaque** heart failure; **~ de mémoire** lapse of memory. ♦ **défaillant, e** *adj forces, mémoire* failing; *courage* weakening; *voix, pas* unsteady; *personne* weak, faint (*de* with). **candidat ~** candidate who fails to appear. ♦ **défaillir** (13) *vi [personne]* to faint; *[forces, courage]* to weaken. **sans ~** without flinching.

défaire [defɛʀ] (60) **1** *vt* **(a)** *installation* to take down, dismantle; *nœud, fermeture, robe* to undo; *valise* to unpack. **~ le lit** (*changer les draps*) to strip the bed; (*se coucher*) to pull back the sheets; (*désordre*) to unmake the bed. **(b)** *contrat* to break. **elle se plaît à ~ tout ce que je fais** she takes pleasure in undoing everything I do. **(c)** (*littér*) *ennemi, armée* to defeat. **(d) ~ qn de** *liens, gêneur* to rid sb of; *habitude* to break sb of. **2 se ~** *vpr* **(a)** *[ficelle]* to come undone. **(b) se ~ de** *gêneur* to get rid of; *idée* to put out of one's mind; *habitude* to break o.s. of; *collaborateur* to part with. ♦ **défait, e**[1] *adj visage* haggard; *cheveux* tousled; *lit* rumpled; *armée* defeated. ♦ **défaite**[2] *nf* (*Mil, fig*) defeat. ♦ **défaitisme** *nm* defeatism. ♦ **défaitiste** *adj, nmf* defeatist.

défalquer [defalke] (1) *vt* to deduct. ♦ **défalcation** *nf* deduction.

défaut [defo] *nm* **(a)** *[diamant, verre]* flaw; *[étoffe, machine]* fault; *[roman, système]* flaw, defect; *[personne]* fault, failing. **~ de prononciation** speech defect; **c'est un vilain ~** it's a bad fault; **sans ~** flawless, faultless. **(b)** (*désavantage*) drawback. **le ~ avec cette voiture, c'est que ...** the snag *ou* drawback with this car is that.... **(c)** (*manque*) **~ de** *raisonnement* lack of; *main-d'œuvre* shortage of. **(d) faire ~** *[argent]* to be lacking; **le temps lui fait ~** he lacks time; **mes amis m'ont fait ~** my friends let me down; **à ~ de** for lack *ou* want of; **à ~ prenez du vinaigre** failing that use some vinegar; **être en ~** to be at fault; **prendre qn en ~** to catch sb out; **juger qn par ~** to judge sb in his absence; **calculer qch par ~** to calculate sth to the nearest decimal point; (*lit, fig*) **le ~ de la cuirasse** the chink in the armour.

défaveur [defavœʀ] *nf* disfavour (*auprès de* with). ♦ **défavorable** *adj* unfavourable (*à* to). ♦ **défavorablement** *adv* unfavourably.

défavoriser [defavɔʀize] (1) *vt [décision]* to penalize; *[timidité]* to put at a disadvantage. **j'ai été défavorisé par rapport aux autres** I was put at an unfair disadvantage compared with the others; **les couches défavorisées de la population** the underprivileged *ou* disadvantaged sections of the population.

défectif, -ive [defɛktif, iv] *adj verbe* defective.

défection [defɛksjɔ̃] *nf [amis]* desertion; *[troupes]* failure to assist; *[candidats, invités]* failure to appear. **faire ~** *[partisans]* to fail to lend support.

défectueux, -euse [defɛktɥø, øz] *adj* defective. ♦ **défectuosité** *nf* (*état*) defectiveness; (*défaut*) defect, fault (*de* in).

défendable [defɑ̃dabl(ə)] *adj* defensible.

défendeur, -deresse [defɑ̃dœʀ, dʀɛs] *nm,f* (*Jur*) defendant.

défendre [defɑ̃dʀ(ə)] (41) **1** *vt* **(a)** (*protéger*) (*gén*) to defend; *opinion* to stand up for; *cause* to champion (*contre* against); (*du froid*) to protect (*de* from). **(b)** (*interdire*) ~ **qch à qn** to forbid sb sth; ~ **à qn de faire** to forbid sb to do; **il est défendu de fumer** smoking is prohibited *ou* not allowed. **2 se** ~ *vpr* **(a)** (*se protéger*) to defend o.s. (*contre* against). **se** ~ **de la pluie** to protect o.s. from the rain; **il se défend bien/mal en affaires** he does quite well/he doesn't do very well in business. **(b)** (*se justifier*) **se** ~ **d'avoir fait qch** to deny doing sth; **sa position se défend** his position is quite defensible. **(c)** (*s'empêcher de*) **se** ~ **de faire** to refrain from doing.

défense [defɑ̃s] *nf* **(a)** (*gén, Jur, Mil*) defence. (*fortifications etc*) ~**s** defences; **prendre la** ~ **de qn** to stand up for sb, defend sb; **sans** ~ defenceless; **la parole est à la** ~ the defence may speak. **(b)** (*interdiction*) ~ **d'entrer** no admittance; **danger:** ~ **d'entrer** danger - keep out; ~ **de fumer** no smoking, smoking prohibited; **j'ai oublié la** ~ **qu'il m'a faite** I forgot that he forbade me to do that. **(c)** *[éléphant]* tusk.

défenseur [defɑ̃sœʀ] *nm* (*gén, Mil*) defender; *[cause]* champion; *[doctrine]* advocate; (*Jur*) counsel for the defence.

défensif, -ive [defɑ̃sif, iv] **1** *adj* defensive. **2** *nf*: **sur la** ~**ive** on the defensive.

déférence [defeʀɑ̃s] *nf* deference. **par** ~ **pour** in deference to. ♦ **déférent, e** *adj* deferential.

déférer [defeʀe] (6) *vt* **(a)** (*Jur*) *affaire* to refer to the court. ~ **qn à la justice** to hand sb over to the law. **(b)** (*céder*) to defer (*à* to).

déferler [defɛʀle] (1) *vi [vagues]* to break. ~ **sur le pays** *[violence]* to sweep through the country; *[touristes]* to pour into the country. ♦ **déferlement** *nm [vagues]* breaking; *[violence]* spread; *[véhicules, touristes]* flood; *[enthousiasme]* wave.

défi [defi] *nm* challenge. **lancer un** ~ **à qn** to challenge sb; **mettre qn au** ~ to defy sb (*de faire* to do); **c'est un** ~ **au bon sens** it defies common sense; **d'un air de** ~ defiantly.

défiance [defjɑ̃s] *nf* mistrust. **sans** ~ (*adj*) unsuspecting; (*adv*) unsuspectingly. ♦ **défiant, e** *adj* mistrustful.

déficience [defisjɑ̃s] *nf* (*Méd, fig*) deficiency. ~ **de mémoire** lapse of memory. ♦ **déficient, e** *adj* (*gén*) deficient; *raisonnement* weak.

déficit [defisit] *nm* deficit. ♦ **déficitaire** *adj* (*Fin*) in deficit; *année* poor (*en* in), bad (*en* for).

défier [defje] (7) **1** *vt adversaire* to challenge (*à* to); *adversité* to defy. **à des prix qui défient toute concurrence** at absolutely unbeatable prices; ~ **qn de faire qch** to defy sb to do sth. **2 se** ~ *vpr*: **se** ~ **de** to mistrust; (†) **défie-toi de lui!** beware of him!

défigurer [defigyʀe] (1) *vt visage [blessure]* to disfigure; *[bouton]* to spoil; *pensée, réalité* to distort; *texte, tableau* to mutilate, deface; *paysage* to disfigure, mar.

défilé [defile] *nm* **(a)** (*cortège*) procession; (*manifestation*) march; (*Mil*) march-past, parade. ~ **de mode** fashion parade. **(b)** *[voitures, impressions]* stream. **(c)** (*Géog*) narrow pass.

défiler [defile] (1) **1** *vi* (*Mil*) to march past, parade; *[manifestants]* to march (*devant* past); *[paysage, souvenirs]* to pass (*dans* through, *devant* before). **2 se** ~ *vpr* (*s'éclipser*) to slip away. (*refuser*) **il s'est défilé** he wriggled out of it.

définir [definiʀ] (2) *vt* to define. **notre politique se définit comme ...** our policies can be defined as ... . ♦ **défini, e** *adj* (*gén, Gram*) definite. ♦ **définissable** *adj* definable.

définitif, -ive [definitif, iv] **1** *adj* (*gén*) final; *victoire, fermeture, édition* definitive; *refus* definite. **2** *nf*: **en** ~**ive** (*à la fin*) eventually; (*somme toute*) when all is said and done. ♦ **définitivement** *adv partir* for good; *résoudre* conclusively, definitively; *refuser* definitely; *nommer* permanently.

définition [definisjɔ̃] *nf* definition; *[mots croisés]* clue.

déflagration [deflagʀɑsjɔ̃] *nf* (*gén*) explosion.

déflation [deflɑsjɔ̃] *nf* deflation.

défoncer [defɔ̃se] (3) *vt caisse, porte* to stave in; *sommier* to break the springs of; *route* to break up. **fauteuil défoncé** sunken armchair.

déformer [defɔʀme] (1) **1** *vt objet* to put out of shape; *corps* to deform; *visage, image, vision, vérité* to distort; *esprit, goût* to warp. **déformé par son métier** conditioned by one's job; **chaussée déformée** uneven road surface. **2 se** ~ *vpr* to lose its shape. ♦ **déformant, e** *adj miroir* distorting. ♦ **déformation** *nf* (*action*) putting out of shape; deformation; distortion; warping; (*résultat*) loss of shape; (*Méd*) deformation. **c'est de la** ~ **professionnelle** it's force of habit (because of his job).

défouler (se) [defule] (1) *vpr* to release one's pent-up feelings, unwind. ♦ **défoulement** *nm* release.

défraîchir (se) [defʀeʃiʀ] (2) *vpr* (*passer*) to fade; (*s'user*) to become worn.

défrayer [defʀeje] (8) *vt*: ~ **qn** to pay sb's expenses; ~ **la chronique** to be widely talked about.

défricher [defʀiʃe] (1) *vt terrain* to clear (*for cultivation*); *sujet* to do the spadework on. (*fig*) ~ **le terrain** to clear the way. ♦ **défrichage** *nm* clearing (*for cultivation*). (*fig*) ~ **d'un sujet** spadework done on a subject.

défroisser [defʀwase] (1) *vt* to smooth out.

défunt, e [defœ̃, œ̃t] **1** *adj personne* late; *espoir, année* which is dead and gone; *projet* defunct. **son** ~ **père** his late father. **2** *nm,f* deceased.

dégagé, e [degaʒe] *adj route, ciel* clear; *vue* wide, open; *front* bare; *ton, manières* casual.

dégagement [degaʒmɑ̃] *nm* **(a)** (*action: V* **dégager**) freeing; relief; clearing; release; redemption. (*Aut*) **voie de** ~ slip road; (*Aut*) **itinéraire de** ~ alternative route. **(b)** (*émanation*) emission. **(c)** (*Ftbl*) clearance. **(d)** (*espace libre*) *[forêt]* clearing; *[appartement]* passage.

dégager [degaʒe] (3) **1** *vt* **(a)** *personne, objet* to free; (*Mil*) to relieve; *ballon* to clear; *crédits* to release; *objet en gage* to redeem. **cela devrait se** ~ **facilement** it should come free easily; ~ **qn de sa promesse** to free sb from his promise; ~ **sa responsabilité d'une affaire** to disclaim responsibility in a matter; **robe qui dégage le cou** dress which leaves the neck bare. **(b)** *passage, nez* to clear (*de* of). **allons, dégagez!*** move along! **(c)** *odeur, chaleur* to give off, emit. **(d)** *conclusion* to draw; *sens* to bring out; *impressions* to single out. ~ **la vérité de l'erreur** to separate truth from untruth.

2 se ~ *vpr* **(a)** *[personne]* to free *ou* extricate o.s.; (*Mil*) to extricate itself (*de* from). **se** ~ **de** *obligation* to free o.s. from; *affaire* to back out of; *promesse* to go back on. **(b)** *[ciel, rue, nez]* to clear. **(c)** *[odeur, chaleur]* to be given off; *[enthousiasme]* to radiate; *[rumeur]* to rise (*de* from). **(d)** *[conclusion]* to be drawn; *[impression]* to emerge (*de* from).

dégainer [degene] (1) *vt épée, pistolet* to draw.

dégarnir [degaʀniʀ] (2) **1** *vt maison* to empty, clear; *compte* to drain; (*Mil*) to withdraw troops from. **2 se** ~ *vpr [salle]* to empty; *[tête]* to go bald; *[arbre]* to lose its leaves; *[rayons, stock]* to be cleaned out. ♦ **dégarni, e** *adj front, salle, rayon* bare; *compte* low; *tête* balding.

dégât [degɑ] *nm*: **du** ~, **des** ~**s** damage.

dégeler [deʒle] (5) **1** *vt lac, invité, réunion* to thaw; *atmosphère, crédits* to unfreeze. **2** *vi* to thaw. (*Culin*) **faire** ~ to thaw, leave to thaw. **3** *vb impers:* **ça dégèle** it's thawing. **4 se** ~ *vpr [personne]* (*lit*) to warm up; (*fig*) to thaw. ♦ **dégel** *nm* (*lit, fig*) thaw.

dégénérer [deʒeneʀe] (6) *vi* (*gén*) to degenerate

(*en* into). ♦ **dégénéré, e** *adj, nm,f* degenerate. ♦ **dégénérescence** *nf* degeneracy.
dégingandé, e* [deʒɛ̃gɑ̃de] *adj* gangling.
dégivrer [deʒivʀe] (1) *vt* to defrost; (*Aviat*) to de-ice. ♦ **dégivrage** *nm* defrosting; de-icing.
déglinguer* [deglɛ̃ge] (1) **1** *vt objet, appareil* to knock to pieces. **2 se ~** *vpr* to fall apart. **fauteuil déglingué** armchair which is falling apart.
dégonfler [degɔ̃fle] (1) **1** *vt pneu, ballon* to deflate; *enflure* to reduce. **2 se ~** *vpr* (*lit*) to go down; (*: *avoir peur*) to chicken out*, back out. ♦ **dégonflé, e** *adj* **(a)** *pneu* flat. **(b)** (‡: *lâche*) yellow‡, cowardly. **c'est un ~** he's a yellow-belly‡. ♦ **dégonflement** *nm* deflation; reduction.
dégorger [degɔʀʒe] (3) **1** *vt* (*déboucher*) to clear out; (*lit, fig: déverser*) to pour out. **2** *vi [étoffe, viande]* to soak; *[concombres]* to sweat. **faire ~** to soak; to sweat.
dégot(t)er* [degɔte] (1) *vt* to dig up*, unearth.
dégouliner [deguline] (1) *vi [filet]* to trickle; *[goutte]* to drip. ♦ **dégoulinade** *nf* trickle.
dégourdir [deguʀdiʀ] (2) **1** *vt membres* to bring the circulation back to. **le service militaire le dégourdira** military service will teach him a thing or two. **2 se ~** *vpr [provincial]* to get a bit livelier. **se ~ (les jambes)** to stretch one's legs a bit. ♦ **dégourdi, e*** *adj* (*malin*) smart, bright.
dégoût [degu] *nm*: **le ~** disgust, distaste (*pour, de* for); **~ de la vie** world-weariness. ♦ **dégoûtant, e** *adj* disgusting. ♦ **dégoûté, e** *adj*: **je suis ~!** I am fed up!*; **être ~ de** to be sick of. ♦ **dégoûter** (1) *vt* to disgust. **ce plat me dégoûte** I find this dish disgusting; **~ qn de qch** to put sb off sth; **se ~ de qn/qch** to get sick of sb/sth.
dégoutter [degute] (1) *vi* to drip.
dégrader [degʀade] (1) **1** *vt* **(a)** *personne* to degrade; *qualité* to debase. **(b)** *[pluie]* to erode; *[vandales]* to deface, damage. **(c)** (*Art*) *couleurs* to shade off. **2 se ~** *vpr* (*moralement*) to degrade o.s.; *[situation, santé, bâtiment]* to deteriorate; *[temps]* to break. ♦ **dégradant, e** *adj* degrading. ♦ **dégradation** *nf* degradation; debasement; erosion; damaging, defacing; deterioration. ♦ **dégradé** *nm [couleurs]* gradation.
dégrafer [degʀafe] (1) **1** *vt* to unfasten, undo. **2 se ~** *vpr* (*par accident*) to come undone *ou* unfastened.
dégraisser [degʀese] (1) *vt vêtement* to take the grease marks out of; *bouillon* to skim; *viande* to remove the fat from.
degré [dəgʀe] *nm* **(a)** (*gén: niveau*) degree. **à un ~ avancé de** at an advanced stage of; **au plus haut ~** in the extreme, to a degree; **jusqu'à un certain ~** to some extent *ou* degree; **par ~(s)** by degrees. **(b)** (*Gram, Mus, Sci*) degree. **équation du 1er/2e ~** equation of the 1st/2nd degree; **~ en alcool d'un liquide** percentage of alcohol in a liquid; **alcool à 90 ~s** 90% proof alcohol; **vin de 11 ~s** 11° wine; **~ centigrade/Fahrenheit** degree centigrade/Fahrenheit. **(c)** (*Méd*) **brûlure du premier/deuxième ~** first/second degree burn; (*Scol*) **enseignement du premier/second ~** primary/secondary education; **~ de parenté** degree of family relationship; **cousins au premier/au second ~** first/second cousins; **parents au premier/deuxième ~** relatives of the first/second degree. **(d)** (*littér: marche*) step.
dégressif, -ive [degʀesif, iv] *adj* degressive.
dégrever [degʀəve] (5) *vt produit* to reduce the tax(es) on; *contribuable* to grant tax relief to. ♦ **dégrèvement** *nm* reduction of tax (*de* on).
dégringoler [degʀɛ̃gɔle] (1) **1** *vi* to tumble down. **elle a fait ~ toute la pile** she toppled the whole pile over. **2** *vt pente* to rush *ou* leap down. ♦ **dégringolade** *nf* tumble.
dégriser *vt*, **se ~** *vpr* [degʀize] (1) (*lit, fig*) to sober up.
dégrossir [degʀosiʀ] (2) *vt bois* to trim; *marbre* to rough-hew; *travail* to rough out; (*) *personne* to knock the rough edges off. **il est mal dégrossi** he is unrefined.
dégrouiller (se)* [degʀuje] (1) *vpr* to hurry up, get a move on*.
déguenillé, e [degnije] *adj* ragged, tattered.
déguerpir* [degɛʀpiʀ] (2) *vi* to clear off*. **faire ~** to drive off.
déguiser [degize] (1) **1** *vt voix, pensée* to disguise; *étonnement* to conceal; *enfant* to dress up (*en* as). **non déguisé** undisguised. **2 se ~** *vpr* (*pour tromper*) to disguise o.s.; (*pour s'amuser*) to dress up. ♦ **déguisement** *nm* (*pour tromper*) disguise; (*pour s'amuser*) fancy dress.
déguster [degyste] (1) **1** *vt vins* to taste; *fromages* to sample; *repas, spectacle* to enjoy, savour. **2** *vi* (*: *souffrir*) to have a rough time of it*. ♦ **dégustateur** *nm* wine taster. ♦ **dégustation** *nf* sampling. **~ de vin(s)** wine-tasting session.
dehors [dəɔʀ] **1** *adv* **(a)** outside. **passer la journée (au) ~** to spend the day out of doors *ou* outside; **de ~** from (the) outside; **passez par ~** go round the outside; **dîner ~** to eat *ou* dine out; **mettre qn ~*** to throw *ou* kick* sb out. **(b)** (*locutions*) **en ~ de** *maison, fenêtre* outside; *sujet* outside, irrelevant to; **en ~ de cela** apart from that; **il a voulu rester en ~** he wanted to stay uninvolved; **au ~, elle paraît calme** outwardly she looks relaxed. **2** *nm* **(a)** (*extérieur*) outside. **les bruits du ~** the noise from outside. **(b)** (*apparences: pl*) appearances. **sous des ~ aimables** under a friendly exterior.
déifier [deifje] (7) *vt* to deify. ♦ **déification** *nf* deification.
déisme [deism(ə)] *nm* deism. ♦ **déiste** *adj, nmf* deist.
déjà [deʒa] *adv* **(a)** already. **est-il ~ rentré?** has he come home yet?; **j'aurais ~ fini si** I would have finished by now *ou* already if; **je suis sûr de l'avoir ~ rencontré** I'm sure I've met him before *ou* I've already met him. **(b)** (*intensif*) **c'est ~ pas mal*** that's not bad at all; **c'est ~ un gros camion** that's quite a big truck, that's a fair-sized truck; **il est ~ assez paresseux** he's lazy enough as it is; **c'est ~ quelque chose!** it's better than nothing! **(c)** (*: *interrogatif*) **c'est combien, ~?** how much is it again?
déjeuner [deʒœne] (1) **1** *vi* to have lunch; (*le matin*) to have breakfast. **inviter qn à ~** to invite sb to lunch; **nous avons déjeuné sur l'herbe** we had a picnic lunch. **2** *nm* lunch, luncheon; (*du matin*) breakfast; (*tasse et soucoupe*) breakfast cup and saucer. **prendre son ~** to have lunch; **à ~** for lunch; **ça a été un vrai ~ de soleil** it didn't last long.
déjouer [deʒwe] (1) *vt complot* to foil; *ruse* to outsmart; *surveillance* to elude.
déjuger (se) [deʒyʒe] (3) *vpr* to go back on one's decision.
delà [dəla] **1** *adv*: **au-~, par-~** beyond (that); **ça coûte bien au-~** it costs much more (than that). **2** *prép*: **au ~ de** beyond; *somme* over, above; (*littér*) **au ~ des mers, par ~ les mers** overseas, beyond *ou* over the seas; **par ~ les apparences** beneath appearances; **par ~ les siècles** across the centuries. **3** *nm*: **l'au-~** the beyond.
délabrer [delɑbʀe] (1) **1** *vt* to ruin. **2 se ~** *vpr [mur]* to become dilapidated, fall into decay; *[santé]* to break down. ♦ **délabré, e** *adj maison* dilapidated; *santé* broken; *affaires* in a poor state; *fortune* depleted. ♦ **délabrement** *nm [maison]* dilapidation; *[santé, affaires]* poor state; *[fortune]* depletion. **état de ~** dilapidated state.
délacer [delase] (3) **1** *vt chaussures* to undo; *corset* to unlace. **2 se ~** *vpr* (*par accident*) to come unlaced *ou* undone.
délai [delɛ] **1** *nm* **(a)** (*limite*) time limit. **c'est un ~ trop court pour ...** it's too short a time for ...; **~ impératif** *ou* **de rigueur, dernier ~** absolute

deadline; **dans un ~ de 6 jours** within a period of 6 days. **(b)** (*période d'attente*) waiting period. **il faut compter un ~ de huit jours** you'll have to allow a week. **(c)** (*sursis*) extension (of time). **il va demander un ~** he's going to ask for more time. **(d) dans le(s) plus bref(s) ~(s)** as soon *ou* as quickly as possible; **dans les ~s** within the time limit; **à bref ~** (*vite*) at short notice; (*bientôt*) shortly, very soon; **sans ~** without delay. **2: ~ de livraison** delivery time; **~ de paiement** term of payment, time for payment.

délaisser [delese] (1) *vt travail, enfant* (*abandonner*) to abandon; (*négliger*) to neglect. **épouse délaissée** deserted wife. ♦ **délaissement** *nm* (*action*) abandonment, desertion; (*état*) state of neglect.

délasser [delɑse] (1) **1** *vt* (*reposer*) to refresh, relax; (*divertir*) to entertain. **2 se ~** *vpr* to relax. ♦ **délassement** *nm* relaxation.

délation [delɑsjɔ̃] *nf* informing. ♦ **délateur, -trice** *nm,f* informer.

délavé, e [delave] *adj tissu* faded; *inscription* washed-out; *terre* waterlogged.

délayer [deleje] (8) *vt farine, poudre* to mix (*dans* with); (*péj*) *idée* to spin out; *texte* to pad out. ♦ **délayage** *nm* (*Culin*) mixing. (*péj*) **du ~** padding.

delco [dɛlko] *nm* ® distributor.

délecter (se) [delɛkte] (1) *vpr*: **se ~ de qch/à faire** to delight *ou* revel in sth/in doing. ♦ **délectable** *adj* delectable. ♦ **délectation** *nf* delight.

délégation [delegɑsjɔ̃] *nf* (*groupe, mandat*) delegation. **venir en ~** to come as a delegation; **agir par ~** to act on sb's authority; **~ de pouvoirs** delegation of powers. ♦ **délégué, e 1** *adj*: **membre ~** delegate. **2** *nm,f* delegate. ♦ **déléguer** (6) *vt* to delegate (*à* to).

délester [delɛste] (1) **1** *vt ballon* to unballast; (*Élec*) to cut off power from. **~ qn de qch** to relieve sb of sth. **2 se ~** *vpr*: **se ~ de** *lest* to jettison; *colis* to unload. ♦ **délestage** *nm* (*Élec*) power cut.

délétère [deletɛʀ] *adj* deleterious.

délibération [delibeʀɑsjɔ̃] *nf* deliberation. **~s** (*discussion*) deliberations; (*décision*) resolutions; **après ~ du jury** after the jury's deliberation.

délibéré, e [delibeʀe] *adj* (*intentionnel*) deliberate; (*assuré*) resolute. ♦ **délibérément** *adv* deliberately; resolutely.

délibérer [delibeʀe] (6) *vi* (*gén*) to deliberate. **après avoir mûrement délibéré** after duly considering the matter; **~ sur qch** to deliberate upon sth; **~ de qch** to deliberate sth; **~ de faire qch** to resolve to do sth.

délicat, e [delika, at] *adj* **(a)** (*gén*) delicate; *voile, travail* fine; *mets* dainty; *nuance* subtle; *oreille* sensitive; *toucher, mouvement* gentle; *prévenance* thoughtful. **(b)** (*difficile*) delicate, tricky. **(c)** (*scrupuleux*) scrupulous; (*plein de tact*) tactful. **peu ~** unscrupulous, dishonest. **(d)** (*exigeant*) particular. **faire le ~** (*nourriture*) to be particular; (*spectacle*) to be squeamish; (*propos*) to be easily shocked. ♦ **délicatement** *adv* delicately; finely; daintily; subtly; gently; thoughtfully; tactfully. ♦ **délicatesse** *nf* delicacy; daintiness; fineness; subtlety; sensitivity; gentleness; thoughtfulness; scrupulousness; tact.

délice [delis] *nm* delight. **c'est un vrai ~** it is quite delightful *ou* delicious; **les ~s de l'étude** the delights of study; **faire ses ~s de qch** to take delight in sth; **ça ferait les ~s de mon père** it would delight my father. ♦ **délicieusement** *adv* (*gén*) delightfully; *beau* exquisitely; *parfumé* deliciously; (*avec délice*) with delight. ♦ **délicieux, -ieuse** *adj fruit* delicious; *lieu, sensation* delightful.

délié, e [delje] **1** *adj* **(a)** *doigts* nimble; *esprit* astute. **avoir la langue ~e** to have a long tongue. **(b)** *taille* slender; *fil, écriture* fine. **2** *nm* [*lettre*] upstroke.

délier [delje] (7) *vt* to untie. **~ la langue de qn** to loosen sb's tongue; **~ qn de** to free sb from.

délimiter [delimite] (1) *vt* (*gén*) to delimit. ♦ **délimitation** *nf* delimitation.

délinquance [delɛ̃kɑ̃s] *nf* delinquency. **~ juvénile** juvenile delinquency. ♦ **délinquant, e 1** *adj* delinquent. **2** *nm,f* delinquent, offender.

déliquescence [delikesɑ̃s] *nf* (*Chim*) deliquescence; (*fig*) decay. ♦ **déliquescent, e** *adj* deliquescent; decaying.

délire [deliʀ] *nm* (*Méd*) delirium; (*frénésie*) frenzy. **avoir le ~** to be delirious; **c'est du ~!*** it's sheer madness!; **foule en ~** frenzied crowd; **quand l'acteur parut, ce fut le ~*** when the actor appeared there was frenzied excitement; **~ de persécution** persecution mania. ♦ **délirer** (1) *vi* to be delirious (*de* with). **il délire!*** he's raving!*

délit [deli] *nm* offence.

délivrer [delivʀe] (1) **1** *vt* **(a)** *prisonnier* to set free. **~ qn de** to relieve sb of. **(b)** *reçu* to issue, give. **2 se ~** *vpr* to free o.s. (*de* from); (*fig*) to get relief (*de* from). ♦ **délivrance** *nf* **(a)** [*prisonniers*] release; [*pays*] deliverance. **(b)** (*fig: soulagement*) relief. **(c)** [*reçu*] issue.

déloger [delɔʒe] (3) **1** *vt locataire* to turn out; *fugitif* to flush out; *ennemi* to dislodge (*de* from). **2** *vi* to move out.

déloyal, e, *mpl* **-aux** [delwajal, o] *adj personne* disloyal (*envers* towards); *procédé* unfair. ♦ **déloyalement** *adv* disloyally. ♦ **déloyauté** *nf* disloyalty; unfairness; (*acte*) disloyal act.

delta [dɛlta] *nm* (*Géog, Ling*) delta.

déluge [delyʒ] *nm* (*pluie*) downpour; [*larmes, paroles*] flood; [*coups*] shower. (*Bible*) **le ~** the Flood; **ça remonte au ~** it's as old as the hills.

déluré, e [delyʀe] *adj* (*éveillé*) smart; (*péj*) forward, pert.

démagogie [demagɔʒi] *nf* demagogy. ♦ **démagogique** *adj* demagogic. ♦ **démagogue** *nm* demagogue.

démailler (se) [demaje] (1) *vpr* [*bas*] to ladder, run.

demain [d(ə)mɛ̃] *adv* tomorrow. **~ matin** tomorrow morning; **~ il fera jour** tomorrow is another day; **ce n'est pas ~ la veille*** it's not just around the corner; **le monde de ~** tomorrow's world.

demande [d(ə)mɑ̃d] *nf* (*requête*) request (*de* for); (*revendication*) demand (*de* for); (*question*) question; [*emploi, naturalisation*] application (*de* for); [*remboursement*] claim (*de* for); (*Écon: opposé à offre*) demand. **adressez votre ~ au ministère** apply to the ministry; **~ (en mariage)** proposal (of marriage); **faire sa ~ (en mariage)** to propose; **~ de divorce** divorce petition; **à** *ou* **sur la ~ de qn** at sb's request; **sur ~** on request; (*Admin*) on application.

demandé, e [d(ə)mɑ̃de] *adj* (*Comm etc*) in demand.

demander [d(ə)mɑ̃de] (1) **1** *vt* **(a)** *conseil, entrevue* to ask for, request; *emploi, divorce* to apply for; *indemnité* to claim; *réunion, volontaire* to call for. **~ qch à qn** to ask sb for sth; **~ un service à qn** to ask sb a favour; **~ la permission de** to ask permission to; **~ à voir qn** to ask to see sb; **~ à qn de faire** *ou* **qu'il fasse qch** to ask sb to do sth; **~ des nouvelles de qn** to inquire *ou* ask after sb; **vous n'avez qu'à ~** you only have to ask.

(b) *médecin, plombier* to send for; *personne, numéro* to ask for. (*au téléphone*) **demandez-moi M X** get me Mr X; **le patron vous demande** the boss wants to see you.

(c) (*désirer*) to be asking for, want. **il demande qu'on le laisse partir** he wants us *ou* is asking us to let him go; **il ne demandera pas mieux que de**

vous aider he'll be only too pleased to help you; **'on demande une vendeuse'** 'shop assistant wanted'.

(d) *heure, nom, chemin* to ask. **~ qch à qn** to ask sb sth; **je ne te demande rien** I'm not asking you.

(e) (*nécessiter*) *[travail, décision etc]* to require, need. **ce travail va (lui) ~ 6 heures** this job will require 6 hours, he'll need 6 hours to do this job; **ça demande toute votre attention** it calls for *ou* requires your full attention.

(f) (*exiger*) **~ qch de qn** to ask sth of sb; **il ne faut pas trop lui en ~!** you mustn't ask too much of him!

(g) (*locutions*) **~ la paix** to sue for peace; **~ l'impossible** to ask the impossible; **~ la lune** to ask for the moon; **~ la parole** to ask to be allowed to speak; **~ qn en mariage, ~ la main de qn** to ask for sb's hand in marriage; **sans ~ son reste** without further ado.

2 se ~ *vpr* to wonder. **il se demanda: suis-je vraiment aussi bête?** he asked himself *ou* wondered: am I really so stupid?

demandeur[1], -deresse [d(ə)mɑ̃dœʀ, dʀɛs] *nm,f* (*Jur*) plaintiff.

demandeur[2], -euse [d(ə)mɑ̃dœʀ, øz] *nm,f*: **~ d'emploi** person looking for work, job-seeker.

démanger [demɑ̃ʒe] (3) *vt*: **ça (me *etc*) démange** it itches, it's itching; (*fig*) **ça me démange de faire ...** I'm dying *ou* itching to do ... . ♦ **démangeaison** *nf* itching sensation. **avoir des ~s** to be itching; **j'ai une ~** I've got an itch; (*fig*) **~ de faire** itch *ou* urge to do.

démanteler [demɑ̃tle] (5) *vt* (*Mil*) to demolish; *gang* to break up; *empire* to bring down. ♦ **démantèlement** *nm* demolition; breaking up; bringing down.

démantibuler* [demɑ̃tibyle] (1) **1** *vt* to demolish. **2 se ~*** *vpr* to fall apart.

démaquiller [demakije] (1) **1** *vt* to remove the make-up from. **2 se ~** *vpr* to remove one's make-up. ♦ **démaquillage** *nm* removal of make-up. ♦ **démaquillant, e 1** *adj* make-up removing. **2** *nm* make-up remover.

démarcation [demaʀkasjɔ̃] *nf* demarcation (*de, entre* between).

démarche [demaʀʃ(ə)] *nf* **(a)** *[personne]* gait, walk; *[pensée]* processes. **(b)** (*intervention*) step. **faire des ~s** to take steps; **faire une ~ auprès de qn (pour obtenir qch)** to approach sb (to obtain sth).

démarcheur, -euse [demaʀʃœʀ, øz] *nm,f* door-to-door salesman (*ou* woman).

démarquer [demaʀke] (1) **1** *vt* (*Comm*) *article* to mark down; *œuvre, auteur* to plagiarize. **2 se ~** *vpr*: **se ~ de** to dissociate o.s. from. ♦ **démarqué, e** *adj joueur* unmarked.

démarrage [demaʀaʒ] *nm* **(a)** *[véhicule]* (*départ*) moving off; (*mise en marche*) starting. **à chaque ~ du bus** every time the bus moved off; **~ en côte** hill start. **(b)** *[affaire, élève]* (*action*) starting; (*résultat*) start. **le ~ d'une campagne** getting a campaign going. **(c)** (*Sport*) **placer plusieurs ~s** to pull ahead several times.

démarrer [demaʀe] (1) **1** *vi [moteur, conducteur]* to start up; *[véhicule]* to move off; *[coureur]* to pull away; *[campagne]* to get moving; *[débutant]* to start off. **l'affaire a bien démarré** the affair got off to a good start *ou* started off well; **~ en trombe** to shoot off; **il ne veut pas ~ de son idée** he just won't let go of his idea. **2** *vt* (*plus courant:* **faire ~**) *véhicule* to start, get started; *affaire, travail* to get going on. ♦ **démarreur** *nm* (*Aut*) starter.

démasquer [demaske] (1) **1** *vt* (*gén*) to unmask; *plan* to unveil. **2 se ~** *vpr [imposteur]* to drop one's mask.

démêlé [demele] *nm* dispute, quarrel. **~s** problems.

démêler [demele] (1) **1** *vt ficelle* to disentangle; *cheveux* to untangle; *problème, situation* to sort out. **~ qch d'avec** *ou* **de** to distinguish *ou* tell sth from. **2 se ~** *vpr*: **se ~ de** *embarras* to extricate o.s. from.

démembrer [demɑ̃bʀe] (1) *vt domaine* to carve up.

déménager [demenaʒe] (3) **1** *vt affaires* to move, remove; *maison* to move the furniture out of. **2** *vi* **(a)** to move (house). **~ à la cloche de bois** to shoot the moon. **(b)** (‡) (*partir*) to clear off‡; (*être fou*) to be off one's rocker‡. ♦ **déménagement** *nm [meubles]* removal; (*changement de domicile*) move. **le ~ du bureau** moving the furniture out of the office. ♦ **déménageur** *nm* (*entrepreneur*) furniture remover; (*ouvrier*) removal man.

démence [demɑ̃s] *nf* madness, insanity. ♦ **dément, e 1** *adj* mad, insane. **c'est ~!** it's incredible! **2** *nm,f* (*Méd*) lunatic. ♦ **démentiel, -ielle** *adj* insane.

démener (se) [dɛmne] (5) *vpr* (*se débattre*) to thrash about, struggle; (*se dépenser*) to exert o.s.

démentir [demɑ̃tiʀ] (16) **1** *vt* **(a)** *[personne] nouvelle* to deny; *personne* to contradict. **(b)** *[faits] témoignage* to refute; *apparences* to belie; *espoirs* to disappoint. **ses actes démentent ses paroles** his actions belie his words. **2 se ~** *vpr*: **ça ne s'est jamais démenti** it has never failed. ♦ **démenti** *nm* denial; refutation.

démériter [demeʀite] (1) **1 ~ de** *vt indir* to show o.s. unworthy of. **2** *vi* to do badly. ♦ **démérite** *nm* (*littér*) demerit.

démesure [deməzyʀ] *nf [personnage]* immoderation; *[propos]* outrageousness. ♦ **démesuré, e** *adj orgueil, taille* immoderate; *territoire, membres* enormous. ♦ **démesurément** *adv* immoderately; enormously.

démettre [demɛtʀ(ə)] (56) *vt* **(a)** *articulation* to dislocate. **se ~ le poignet** to dislocate one's wrist. **(b)** *fonctionnaire* to dismiss (*de* from). **se ~ de ses fonctions** to resign (from) one's duties, hand in one's resignation.

demeure [dəmœʀ] *nf* residence. **à ~** *installations* permanent; *s'installer* permanently; **mettre qn en ~ de faire qch** to order sb to do sth; (*Jur*) **mettre qn en ~ de payer** to give sb notice to pay.

demeurer [dəmœʀe] (1) *vi* **(a)** (*avec avoir*) (*habiter*) to live. **il demeure rue d'Ulm** he lives in the rue d'Ulm. **(b)** (*avec être*) (*rester*) to remain, stay. **~ fidèle** to remain faithful; **la conversation en est demeurée là** the conversation was taken no further *ou* was left at that; **la maison leur est demeurée** the house was left to them; **au demeurant** for all that. ♦ **demeuré, e 1** *adj* half-witted. **2** *nm,f* half-wit.

demi, e [d(ə)mi] **1** *adv*: **(à) ~ plein** *etc* half-full *etc*; **il ne te croit qu'à ~** he only half believes you; **il a fait le travail à ~** he has only done half the work; **je ne fais pas les choses à ~** I don't do things by halves. **2** *adj* (*après n*) **une livre et ~e** one and a half pounds, a pound and a half; **à six heures et ~e** at half past six; **2 fois et ~e plus grand** 2 and a half times greater. **3** *nm,f* (a) half. **une bouteille? – non une ~e** one bottle? – no, a half *ou* half a bottle *ou* a half-bottle; **deux ~s** two halves. **4** *nf* (*à l'horloge*) **la ~e a sonné** the half-hour has struck; **c'est déjà la ~e** it's already half past. **5** *nm* **(a)** (*bière*) ≈ half-pint, half*. **(b)** (*Sport*) half-back. **~ de mêlée/d'ouverture** scrum/stand-off half. **6** *préf inv* (*le 2ème élément donne le genre et porte la marque du pluriel*) half. **une ~-douzaine d'œufs** half a dozen *ou* a half-dozen eggs; **dans une ~-heure** in half an hour; **la première ~-heure** the first half-hour; **~-litre/-journée/-sommeil/-teinte** *etc* half-litre/-day/-sleep/-tone *etc*; **~-cercle** semicircle; **en ~-cercle** semicircular; **~-dieu** demigod; **~-finale** semifinal; **~-fond** (*discipline*) medium-distance running; **~-frère** half-brother; (*Comm*)

~-**gros** wholesale trade; ~-**mal: ce n'est que** ~-**mal** it could have been worse; ~-**mot: se faire comprendre à** ~-**mot** to make o.s. understood without having to spell it out; ~-**pension** half-board; ~-**pensionnaire** half-boarder; ~-**saison: manteau de** ~-**saison** light coat; ~-**sel** (*adj inv*) *beurre* slightly salted; ~-**sœur** half-sister; ~-**tarif: billet** *etc* **(à)** ~-**tarif** half-price ticket *etc*; **voyager à** ~-**tarif** to travel at half-fare; ~-**tour** (*sur soi-même*) about-turn; (*Aut*) U-turn; (*de clé*) half-turn; (*repartir*) **faire** ~-**tour** to go back.

démilitarisation [demilitaʀizɑsjɔ̃] *nf* demilitarization. ♦ **démilitariser** (1) *vt* to demilitarize.

démission [demisjɔ̃] *nf* (*lit*) resignation; (*fig*) abdication. **donner sa** ~ to hand in *ou* tender one's resignation. ♦ **démissionner** (1) *vi* to resign; (*fig*) *[parents]* to give up.

démobilisation [demɔbilizɑsjɔ̃] *nf* demobilization. ♦ **démobiliser** (1) *vt* to demobilize.

démocrate [demɔkʀat] **1** *adj* democratic. **2** *nmf* democrat. ♦ **démocratie** *nf* democracy. ~ **populaire** people's democracy. ♦ **démocratique** *adj* democratic. ♦ **démocratiquement** *adv* democratically. ♦ **démocratisation** *nf* democratization. ♦ **démocratiser** *vt*, **se** ~ *vpr* (1) to democratize.

démodé, e [demɔde] *adj* old-fashioned, out-of-date. ♦ **démoder (se)** (1) *vpr* to become old-fashioned, go out of fashion.

démographie [demɔgʀafi] *nf* demography. ♦ **démographique** *adj* demographic. **poussée** ~ population increase.

demoiselle [d(ə)mwazɛl] *nf* (*jeune*) young lady; (*âgée*) single lady. **la** ~ **du téléphone** the telephone lady; ~ **d'honneur** *[mariage]* bridesmaid; *[reine]* maid of honour.

démolir [demɔliʀ] (2) *vt maison, objet, doctrine* to demolish; *santé* to ruin; *autorité* to overthrow, shatter; *personne* (*: *épuiser*) to do for*; (‡: *battre*) to beat up; (*: *critiquer*) to tear to pieces. ♦ **démolisseur** *nm* demolition worker; (*entrepreneur*) demolition contractor. ♦ **démolition** *nf* demolition. **en** ~ in the course of being demolished.

démon [demɔ̃] *nm* (*Rel*) demon, fiend; (*Myth*) genius; (*fig*) (*harpie*) harpy; (*enfant*) demon. **le** ~ the Devil; **le** ~ **du jeu** a passion for gambling; **le** ~ **de la curiosité** the demon curiosity; **mauvais** ~ evil spirit. ♦ **démoniaque** *adj* demoniacal, fiendish.

démonstration [demɔ̃stʀɑsjɔ̃] *nf* *[vérité]* demonstration; *[théorème]* proof; (*Comm*) demonstration. **faire une** ~ to give a demonstration; **appareil de** ~ demonstration model; ~**s de** *joie, force* show of. ♦ **démonstrateur, -trice** *nm,f* (*gén*) demonstrator (*of commercial products*). ♦ **démonstratif, -ive** *adj* demonstrative. **peu** ~ undemonstrative.

démonter [demɔ̃te] (1) **1** *vt* **(a)** (*gén*) to dismantle; *étagères* to take down; *appareil* to take to pieces, take apart; *pneu, porte* to take off. **(b)** (*déconcerter*) to disconcert. **il ne se laisse jamais** ~ he never gets flustered. **(c)** *cavalier* to throw. **2 se** ~ *vpr [assemblage]* to come apart; *[personne]* to become flustered. ♦ **démontable** *adj* (*gén*) that can be dismantled. ♦ **démontage** *nm* dismantling; taking down; taking to pieces; taking apart; taking off. ~ **difficile** difficult dismantling operation. ♦ **démonté, e** *adj mer* raging. ♦ **démonte-pneu**, *pl* ~-~**s** *nm* tyre lever.

démontrer [demɔ̃tʀe] (1) *vt vérité, fonctionnement* to demonstrate; *théorème* to prove; *nécessité* to show, demonstrate. ~ **qch (à qn) par A plus B** to prove sth conclusively (to sb); **ça démontrait son inquiétude** that clearly indicated his anxiety. ♦ **démontrable** *adj* demonstrable.

démoraliser [demɔʀalize] (1) **1** *vt* to demoralize. **2 se** ~ *vpr* to become demoralized. ♦ **démoralisant, e** *adj* demoralizing. ♦ **démoralisation** *nf* demoralization.

démordre [demɔʀdʀ(ə)] (41) *vi*: **il ne démord pas de sa décision** he is sticking to his decision; **il ne veut pas en** ~ he won't budge an inch, he is sticking to his guns.

démouler [demule] (1) *vt statue* to remove from the mould; *gâteau* to turn out. ♦ **démoulage** *nm* removal from the mould; turning out.

démultiplier [demyltiplije] (7) *vt* to reduce, gear down. ♦ **démultiplication** *nf* (*procédé*) reduction; (*rapport*) reduction ratio.

démunir [demyniʀ] (2) **1** *vt*: ~ **qn de** to deprive sb of; ~ **qch de** to divest sth of. **2 se** ~ *vpr*: **se** ~ **de** to part with. ♦ **démuni, e** *adj* (*sans ressources*) impoverished. ~ **de** without; ~ **de protection** unprotected; ~ **d'intérêt** lacking in *ou* without interest; ~ **de tout** destitute.

démystifier [demistifje] (7) *vt* to enlighten. ♦ **démystification** *nf* enlightenment.

dénatalité [denatalite] *nf* fall in the birth rate.

dénaturer [denatyʀe] (1) *vt faits* to distort, misrepresent; (*Tech*) to denature; *goût* to alter completely. ♦ **dénaturé, e** *adj mœurs, parents* unnatural.

dénégation [denegɑsjɔ̃] *nf* (*gén, Jur*) denial.

déni [deni] *nm* (*Jur*) ~ **de justice** denial of justice.

déniaiser [denjeze] (1) *vt*: ~ **qn** to teach sb a thing or two.

dénicher [deniʃe] (1) *vt* **(a)** (*) *objet* to unearth; *bistro* to discover; *personne* to track down. **(b)** (*débusquer*) *fugitif, animal* to drive out of hiding.

denier [dənje] *nm* (*à Rome*) denarius; (*en France, Tex*) denier. **pas un** ~† not a farthing; **de mes** ~**s**† out of my own pocket; **le** ~ **du culte** the (church) collection; **les** ~**s publics** public monies.

dénier [denje] (7) *vt responsabilité* to deny, disclaim; *faute* to deny. ~ **qch à qn** to deny sb sth.

dénigrer [denigʀe] (1) *vt* to denigrate. ♦ **dénigrement** *nm* denigration.

dénivellation [denivɛlɑsjɔ̃] *nf* (*pente*) slope. ~ **entre deux points** difference in level between two points.

dénombrer [denɔ̃bʀe] (1) *vt* (*compter*) to count; (*énumérer*) to enumerate. ♦ **dénombrable** *adj* countable. ♦ **dénombrement** *nm* counting.

dénominateur [denɔminatœʀ] *nm* denominator.

dénommer [denɔme] (1) *vt* to name. **le dénommé X** the man called X. ♦ **dénomination** *nf* designation.

dénoncer [denɔ̃se] (3) **1** *vt* **(a)** (*révéler*) *coupable, injustice, traité* to denounce; *forfait* to expose. **sa hâte le dénonça** his haste betrayed him; ~ **qn à la police** to inform against sb. **(b)** (*littér: dénoter*) to indicate. **2 se** ~ *vpr* to give o.s. up. **se** ~ **à la police** to give o.s. up to the police. ♦ **dénonciateur, -trice** **1** *adj* denunciatory. **2** *nm,f* denouncer, informer; exposer. ♦ **dénonciation** *nf* denunciation; exposure.

dénoter [denɔte] (1) *vt* to denote.

dénouement [denumɑ̃] *nm* (*Théât*) dénouement; *[aventure]* outcome.

dénouer [denwe] (1) **1** *vt lien* to untie, undo; *situation* to untangle, resolve. **2 se** ~ *vpr* to come untied *ou* undone; to be resolved.

dénoyauter [denwajote] (1) *vt fruit* to stone, pit. ♦ **dénoyauteur** *nm* stoner, pitter.

denrée [dɑ̃ʀe] *nf* (*aliment*) food, foodstuff; (*fig: hum*) commodity. ~**s coloniales** colonial produce.

densité [dɑ̃site] *nf* (*Phys*) density; *[brouillard]* denseness, thickness; *[foule]* denseness. **à forte/faible** ~ **de population** densely/sparsely populated. ♦ **dense** *adj* dense, thick; *style* condensed.

dent [dɑ̃] *nf* **(a)** *[homme, scie, peigne]* tooth; *[fourche]* prong; *[engrenage]* cog. ~ **de lait/de sagesse** milk/wisdom tooth; **en** ~**s de scie**

couteau serrated; *montagne* jagged. **(b)** (*locutions*) **avoir la ~*** to be hungry; **avoir la ~ dure** to be scathing in one's comments; **avoir/garder une ~ contre qn** to have/hold a grudge against sb; **avoir les ~s longues** (*ambitieux*) to have one's sights fixed high; **être sur les ~s** (*épuisé*) to be worn out; (*très occupé*) to be working flat out*; **faire** *ou* **percer ses ~s** to teethe; **croquer qch à belles ~s** to bite into sth with gusto; **manger du bout des ~s** to eat half-heartedly; **n'avoir rien à se mettre sous la ~** not to have a bite to eat. ♦ **dentaire** *adj* dental. ♦ **denté, e** *adj* (*Tech*) toothed; (*Bot*) dentate.

dentelé, e [dɑ̃tle] *adj arête, côte* jagged; *timbre* perforated; *bord* serrated.

dentelle [dɑ̃tɛl] *nf* lace. ♦ **dentellière** *nf* lacemaker; (*machine*) lacemaking machine.

dentelure [dɑ̃tlyʀ] *nf [timbre]* perforations; *[feuille]* serration; *[côte, arête]* jagged outline.

dentiste [dɑ̃tist(ə)] *nmf* dentist. ♦ **dentier** *nm* denture. ♦ **dentifrice** *nm* toothpaste, dentifrice. ♦ **dentition** *nf* dentition. ♦ **denture** *nf* teeth (*pl*).

dénuder [denyde] (1) **1** *vt* to bare, strip. **2 se ~** *vpr [personne]* to strip; *[colline]* to become bare. ♦ **dénudé, e** *adj* (*gén*) bare; *crâne* bald.

dénué, e [denɥe] *adj*: **~ de** *bon sens* devoid of; *talent* lacking in, without; **~ de tout** destitute; **~ de tout fondement** completely unfounded *ou* groundless. ♦ **dénuement** *nm* destitution.

déodorant [deɔdɔʀɑ̃] *adj m, nm*: **(produit) ~** deodorant.

dépanner [depane] (1) *vt véhicule* to fix, repair; *automobiliste* to fix the car of; (*: *tirer d'embarras*) to help out. ♦ **dépannage** *nm* fixing; repairing; helping out. **service de ~** breakdown service; **ils ont fait 3 ~s** they've fixed 3 breakdowns; **partir pour un ~** to go out on a repair *ou* breakdown job. ♦ **dépanneur** *nm* (*Aut*) breakdown mechanic; (*TV*) television repairman. ♦ **dépanneuse** *nf* breakdown truck.

dépareillé, e [depaʀeje] *adj collection* incomplete; *objet* odd. (*Comm*) **articles ~s** oddments.

déparer [depaʀe] (1) *vt* to spoil, mar.

départ [depaʀ] *nm* **(a)** *[voyageur, train]* departure. **observer le ~ du train** to watch the train leave *ou* depart; **mon ~ de l'hôtel** my departure from *ou* my leaving the hotel; **le ~ du courrier se fait à 9 heures** the mail leaves town at 9 o'clock. **(b)** (*Sport*) start. (*lit, fig*) **faux ~** false start; **donner le ~ aux coureurs** to give the runners the starting signal. **(c)** *[employé]* departure. **le ~ du ministre a fait l'effet d'une bombe** the minister's leaving *ou* departure was something of a bombshell. **(d)** *[processus]* start. **la substance de ~** the original substance. **(e) être sur le ~** to be about to leave *ou* go; **excursions au ~ de Chamonix** excursions (leaving *ou* departing) from Chamonix; (*fig*) **au ~** at the start *ou* outset. **(f)** (*littér: distinction*) distinction.

départager [depaʀtaʒe] (3) *vt* to decide between. **~ l'assemblée** to settle the voting in the assembly.

département [depaʀtəmɑ̃] *nm* (*gén*) department. ♦ **départemental, e,** *mpl* **-aux** *adj* departmental. **route ~e** secondary road.

départir (se) [depaʀtiʀ] (16) *vpr* (*gén nég*) **se ~ de** to abandon.

dépassé, e [depɑse] *adj* (*périmé*) out-moded.

dépassement [depɑsmɑ̃] *nm* **(a)** (*Aut*) overtaking, passing. **après plusieurs ~s ...** after overtaking several vehicles ... . **(b) ~ (de soi-même)** surpassing of oneself.

dépasser [depɑse] (1) **1** *vt* **(a)** *endroit* to pass, go past; *véhicule, piéton* to overtake, pass. **(b)** *alignement* (*horizontalement*) to jut *ou* stick out beyond; (*verticalement*) to jut out above. **(c)** *limite, quantité* to exceed. **~ qch en hauteur/largeur** to be higher/wider than sth, exceed sth in height/width; **~ en nombre** to outnumber; **tout colis qui dépasse 20 kg** all parcels exceeding *ou* over 20 kg; **~ le nombre prévu** to be more than expected; **la réunion ne devrait pas ~ 3 heures** the meeting shouldn't last longer than 3 hours; **il ne veut pas ~ 100 F** he won't go above 100 francs; **elle a dépassé la quarantaine** she is over forty. **(d)** *valeur, prévisions* to exceed; *rival* to outstrip. **~ qn (en intelligence *etc*)** to surpass sb (in intelligence *etc*); **pour la paresse il dépasse tout le monde** he beats everybody for laziness; **il dépasse tous ses camarades** he surpasses all his friends; **sa bêtise dépasse tout ce qu'on peut imaginer** his stupidity goes beyond all imagining; **l'homme doit se ~** man must try to surpass himself. **(e)** *instructions, attributions* to go beyond, overstep; *crédits* to exceed. **cela dépasse les bornes** that's going too far; **cela a dépassé le stade de la plaisanterie** it has gone beyond a joke; **cela dépasse mes forces/ma compétence** it's beyond my strength/capabilities; **il a dépassé ses forces** he has overtaxed himself. **(f)** (*: *dérouter*) **cela me dépasse!** it is beyond me!; **être dépassé par les événements** to be overtaken by events; **il est complètement dépassé!** he is completely out of his depth!

2 *vi* **(a)** (*Aut*) to overtake, pass. **(b)** *[tour, balcon, clou]* to stick out (*de* of); *[jupon]* to show (*de* below).

dépassionner [depasjɔne] (1) *vt débat* to take the heat out of.

dépaysement [depeizmɑ̃] *nm* (*désorientation*) disorientation; (*agréable*) change of surroundings. ♦ **dépaysé, e** *adj*: **être ~** to be completely disoriented. ♦ **dépayser** (1) *vt* to disorientate; to give a change of surroundings to.

dépecer [depəse] (5) *vt [boucher]* to joint, cut up; *[lion]* to dismember; *territoire* to carve up. ♦ **dépeçage** *nm* jointing, cutting up; dismembering; carving up.

dépêche [depɛʃ] *nf* dispatch. **~ télégraphique** telegram, wire.

dépêcher [depeʃe] (1) **1** *vt* to dispatch, send (*auprès de* to). **2 se ~** *vpr* to hurry. **dépêche-toi!** hurry up!; **se ~ de faire qch** to hurry to do sth.

dépeigner [depeɲe] (1) *vt*: **~ qn** to make sb's hair untidy; **dépeigné** with dishevelled hair.

dépeindre [depɛ̃dʀ(ə)] (52) *vt* to depict.

dépenaillé, e [depənaje] *adj* (*en haillons*) tattered.

dépendance [depɑ̃dɑ̃s] *nf* **(a)** (*interdépendance*) dependence, dependency. **~s** dependencies. **(b)** (*asservissement*) subordination. **sous la ~ de qn** subordinate to sb. **(c)** (*bâtiment*) outbuilding; (*territoire*) dependency. **(d)** (*Drogue*) dependence, dependency.

dépendre [depɑ̃dʀ(ə)] (41) **1 ~ de** *vt indir* (*gén*) to depend on, be dependent on; *[employé]* to be answerable to. **ce terrain dépend de leur domaine** this piece of land is part of their property; **ne ~ que de soi-même** to be answerable only to oneself; **– ça dépend –** it (all) depends; **il ne dépend que de vous que ...** it depends entirely on you whether ..., it's entirely up to you whether ... . **2** *vt lustre* to take down.

dépens [depɑ̃] *nmpl* **(a)** (*Jur*) costs. **condamné aux ~** ordered to pay costs. **(b) aux ~ de** at the expense of; **je l'ai appris à mes ~** I learnt this to my cost.

dépense [depɑ̃s] *nf* **(a)** (*argent dépensé*) expense; (*sortie*) outlay, expenditure. **contrôler les ~s de qn** to control sb's expenditure *ou* spending; **c'est une grosse ~** it's a large outlay, it's a lot to lay out; **~s publiques** public expenditure *ou* spending; **pousser qn à la ~** to make sb spend money; **faire la ~ de qch** to spend money on sth; **regarder à la ~** to watch one's spending. **(b)** *[électricité, essence]* consumption; *[imagination]* expenditure. ~ **physique** (physical) exercise; ~ **de temps** spending of time.

dépenser [depɑ̃se] (1) **1** *vt argent, temps* to spend; *électricité* to use; *énergie, jeunesse* to use up. ~ **inutilement qch** to waste sth. **2 se** ~ *vpr* to exert o.s. ♦ **dépensier, -ière 1** *adj* extravagant. **2** *nm,f* spendthrift.

déperdition [depɛʀdisjɔ̃] *nf* (*Sci, gén*) loss.

dépérir [depeʀiʀ] (2) *vi [personne]* to waste away; *[forces]* to fail; *[plante]* to wither; *[affaire]* to go downhill. ♦ **dépérissement** *nm* wasting away; failing; withering.

dépêtrer [depetʀe] (1) **1** *vt*: ~ **qn de** to extricate sb from. **2 se** ~ *vpr* to extricate o.s. (*de* from).

dépeupler [depœple] (1) **1** *vt ville* to depopulate; *rivière* to empty of fish; *région* to empty of wildlife; *forêt* to clear (of trees *etc*). **2 se** ~ *vpr* to be depopulated; to be emptied of fish (*ou* wildlife); to be cleared (of trees *etc*). ♦ **dépeuplement** *nm* depopulation; emptying of fish (*ou* wildlife); clearing (of trees *etc*); (*résultat*) disappearance of fish (*ou* wildlife *ou* trees *etc*).

dépilatoire [depilatwaʀ] *adj* depilatory.

dépister [depiste] (1) *vt gibier, criminel* to track down; *maladie* to detect; *cause* to unearth, detect. ♦ **dépistage** *nm* tracking down; detection; unearthing.

dépit [depi] *nm* vexation. **causer du** ~ **à qn** to vex sb greatly; **en** ~ **de** in spite of; **en** ~ **du bon sens** contrary to good sense. ♦ **dépiter** (1) *vt* (*littér*) to vex greatly.

déplacer [deplase] (3) **1** *vt meuble, élève* to move, shift; *usine, fonctionnaire* to transfer, move; (*fig*) *problème* to shift the emphasis of; (*Naut*) to displace. **se** ~ **une articulation** to displace a joint. **2 se** ~ *vpr* (*gén*) to move; *[air]* to move, be displaced. ♦ **déplacé, e** *adj propos* uncalled-for, out of place. ♦ **déplacement** *nm* (*action*) moving; shifting; transfer; displacement; (*mouvement*) movement; displacement; (*voyage*) trip; (*Naut*) displacement. **ça vaut le** ~ it's worth the journey; **frais de** ~ travelling expenses.

déplaire [deplɛʀ] (54) *vt*: ~ **à qn** (*être antipathique*) to be disliked by sb; (*irriter*) to displease sb; **ça me déplaît** I dislike *ou* don't like it; **il cherche à** ~ he is trying to be disagreeable; **n'en déplaise à son mari** with all due respect to her husband; **elle se déplaît ici** she dislikes it *ou* doesn't like it here. ♦ **déplaisant, e** *adj* disagreeable, unpleasant. ♦ **déplaisir** *nm* displeasure.

déplâtrer [deplɑtʀe] (1) *vt* (*Méd*) to take out of plaster.

déplier [deplije] (7) *vt serviette, carte* to unfold; *jambes* to stretch out. ♦ **dépliant, e 1** *adj* extendible. **2** *nm* leaflet, folder.

déplorer [deplɔʀe] (1) *vt incident* to deplore; (*littér*) *mort* to lament. ♦ **déplorable** *adj* deplorable. ♦ **déplorablement** *adv* deplorably.

déployer [deplwaje] (8) **1** *vt carte* to spread out; *voile* to unfurl; *ailes* to spread; *troupes* to deploy; *échantillons* to spread out, lay out; *richesses, talents, forces* to display. ~ **en éventail** *troupes* to fan out. **2 se** ~ *vpr [drapeau]* to unfurl; *[ailes]* to spread; *[troupes]* to deploy; *[cortège]* to spread out. ♦ **déploiement** *nm* unfurling; spreading; deployment; *[forces]* display.

déplumer (se) [deplyme] (1) *vpr [oiseau]* to moult; (*) *[personne]* to go bald.

dépoétiser [depɔetize] (1) *vt* to make prosaic.

dépolitiser [depɔlitize] (1) *vt* to depoliticize.

dépopulation [depɔpylɑsjɔ̃] *nf* depopulation.

déporter [depɔʀte] (1) *vt* **(a)** (*exiler*) to deport; (*interner*) to send to a concentration camp. **(b)** *[vent]* to carry off course. **se** ~ **vers la gauche** to swerve to the left. ♦ **déportation** *nf* deportation; imprisonment (in a concentration camp). ♦ **déporté, e** *nm,f* deportee; prisoner (in a concentration camp).

déposer [depoze] (1) **1** *vt* **(a)** *gerbe, armes* to lay down; *ordures* to dump; *colis* to leave; *passager* to drop; (*Fin*) to deposit. **est-ce que je peux vous** ~ **quelque part?** can I give you a lift anywhere?, can I drop you anywhere?; **ce vin dépose de la lie** this wine has some sediment. **(b)** *plainte* to lodge; *réclamation* to file; *marque de fabrique* to register; *projet de loi* to bring in; *rapport* to send in. ~ **son bilan** to go into voluntary liquidation. **(c)** (*destituer*) *souverain* to depose. **(d)** *tenture* to take down; *tapis* to take up; *moteur* to take out. **2** *vi* **(a)** *[liquide]* to leave some sediment. **laisser** ~ to leave to settle. **(b)** (*Jur*) to testify. **3 se** ~ *vpr [poussière, lie]* to settle. ♦ **dépositaire** *nmf [objet confié]* depository; *[secret, vérité]* possessor; (*Comm*) agent (*de* for). ♦ **déposition** *nf* (*gén*) deposition.

déposséder [depɔsede] (6) *vt*: ~ **qn de** *terres* to dispossess sb of; *place, charge* to deprive sb of. ♦ **dépossession** *nf* dispossession; deprivation.

dépôt [depo] *nm* **(a)** (*action*) **procéder au** ~ **d'une gerbe** to lay a wreath; **le** ~ **des manteaux au vestiaire est obligatoire** coats must be left *ou* deposited in the cloakroom. **(b)** (*garde*) **avoir qch en** ~ to hold sth in trust; **confier qch en** ~ **à qn** to entrust sth to sb; ~ **sacré** sacred trust. **(c)** (*Comm*) *[marque]* registration. **(d)** (*garantie*) deposit. (*Fin*) ~ **de bilan** statement of affairs. **(e) du** ~, **un** ~ *[liquide]* sediment, deposit; *[tartre]* fur. **(f)** (*entrepôt*) warehouse; *[autobus, trains]*, (*Mil*) depot. **il y a un** ~ **de pain à l'épicerie** the grocer supplies *ou* sells bread; ~ **de munitions** ammunition dump; ~ **d'ordures** rubbish dump. **(g)** (*prison*) jail, prison.

dépotoir [depɔtwaʀ] *nm* (*lit, fig*) dumping ground.

dépouille [depuj] *nf* (*peau*) skin, hide. (*cadavre*) ~ **(mortelle)** (mortal) remains; (*butin*) ~**s** plunder, spoils.

dépouillé, e [depuje] *adj style, décor* bare, bald. ~ **de** lacking in, stripped of.

dépouiller [depuje] (1) **1** *vt* **(a)** *comptes, courrier* to go through, peruse; *scrutin* to count. **(b)** *animal* to skin; *arbre* to strip; *voyageur* to strip of his possessions; *héritier* to deprive of his inheritance. ~ **de qch** (*gén*) to strip of sth; *droits* to divest *ou* deprive of sth; ~ **le pays** to plunder the country, lay the country bare. **(c)** (*se défaire de*) to shed.

2 se ~ *vpr*: **se** ~ **de** *vêtements* to shed; *possessions* to divest o.s. of; *arrogance* to cast aside; **les arbres se dépouillent** the trees are shedding their leaves; **la campagne se dépouille** the countryside is beginning to look bare. ♦ **dépouillement** *nm* **(a)** perusal; *[scrutin]* counting. **(b)** (*sobriété*) lack of ornamentation. **(c)** (*de biens, droits*) deprivation.

dépourvu, e [depuʀvy] **1** *adj*: ~ **de** (*gén*) lacking in, without; *bons sens* devoid of; ~ **d'ornements** unornamented, bare of ornaments; ~ **d'argent** penniless; **des gens** ~**s (de tout)** destitute people. **2** *nm*: **prendre qn au** ~ to catch sb unprepared *ou* unawares.

dépravation [depʀavɑsjɔ̃] *nf* (*état*) depravity. ♦ **dépravé, e 1** *adj* depraved. **2** *nm, f* degenerate. ♦ **dépraver** (1) *vt* to deprave.

déprécier *vt*, **se** ~ *vpr* [depʀesje] (7) to depreciate. ♦ **dépréciatif, -ive** *adj* disparaging, derogatory. ♦ **dépréciation** *nf* depreciation (*de* in).

déprédations [depʀedɑsjɔ̃] *nfpl* (*dégâts*) damage.

dépression [depʀɛsjɔ̃] *nf*: ~ **(de terrain)** depression; ~ **atmosphérique** atmospheric depression, trough of low pressure; **une** ~ **(nerveuse)** a (nervous) breakdown; **elle fait de la** ~ she is having a bad fit of depression; ~ **(économique)** (economic) depression *ou* slump. ♦ **dépressif, -ive** *adj* depressive.

déprimer [depʀime] (1) *vt* (*moralement*) to

depress; (*physiquement*) to debilitate. ♦ **déprimant, e** *adj* (*moralement*) depressing; (*physiquement*) debilitating. ♦ **déprimé, e** *adj* (*moralement*) depressed; (*physiquement*) low; *terrain* low-lying.

depuis [dəpɥi] **1** *prép* **(a)** (*temps: point de départ*) since, ever since (*intensif*). **il attend/attendait ~ hier** he has/had been waiting since yesterday; **~ son plus jeune âge** since *ou* from early childhood; **~ cette affaire il est très méfiant** (ever) since that affair he has been very suspicious; **~ quand le connaissez-vous?** how long have you known him?; **~ quelle date êtes-vous ici?** since when have you been here?; **~ cela, ~ lors** since then *ou* that time, ever since; **~ le matin jusqu'au soir** from morning till night.

(b) (*durée*) for. **il est malade ~ une semaine** he has been ill for a week (now); **~ ces derniers mois il a bien changé** he has changed a great deal in *ou* over the last few months; **tu le connais ~ longtemps? – ~ toujours** have you known him long? *ou* for a long time? – I've known him all my life; **je la connaissais ~ peu quand elle est partie** I had known her only a short time when she left; **~ peu elle a recommencé à sortir** lately *ou* recently she has started going out again.

(c) (*lieu*) since, from. **~ Nice il a fait le plein 3 fois** he's filled up 3 times since Nice; **le concert est retransmis ~ Paris** the concert is broadcast from Paris.

(d) (*rang, quantité*) from. **~ le premier jusqu'au dernier** from the first to the last; **toutes les tailles ~ le 36** all sizes from 36 upwards.

(e) ~ que, ~ le temps que: ~ qu'il est ministre since he became a minister; **~ le temps qu'il apprend le français** considering how long he's been learning French; **~ le temps que je voulais voir ce film!** I had been waiting to see that film for ages!

2 *adv* ever since, since (then). **je ne l'ai pas revu ~** I haven't seen him since (then).

député [depyte] *nm* deputy, ≃ member of Parliament, ≃ representative (*US*). ♦ **députation** *nf* (*groupe*) deputation, delegation. **candidat à la ~** parliamentary candidate. ♦ **députer** (1) *vt*: **~ qn pour faire** to delegate sb to do; **~ qn auprès de** to send sb as representative to.

déraciner [deʀasine] (1) *vt arbre, personne* to uproot; *erreur* to eradicate. ♦ **déracinement** *nm* uprooting; eradication.

dérailler [deʀɑje] (1) *vi [train]* to be derailed; (*: *divaguer*) to rave; (*: *mal fonctionner*) to be on the blink*. **faire ~ un train** to derail a train. ♦ **déraillement** *nm* derailment. ♦ **dérailleur** *nm [bicyclette]* dérailleur gears.

déraisonner [deʀɛzɔne] (1) *vi* to rave. ♦ **déraisonnable** *adj* unreasonable.

déranger [deʀɑ̃ʒe] (3) **1** *vt papiers, personne* to disturb; *coiffure* to ruffle; *projets, routine* to disrupt, upset; *machine* to put out of order; *temps* to unsettle. **~ qn inutilement** to bother *ou* trouble sb unnecessarily; **ça vous dérange si je fume?** do you mind if I smoke?; **il a le cerveau dérangé** his mind is deranged *ou* unhinged; **il a l'estomac dérangé** his stomach is upset. **2 se ~** *vpr* **(a)** *[médecin]* to come out; (*pour une démarche*) to go along, come along. **sans vous ~** without leaving your home; **surtout, ne vous dérangez pas pour moi** please don't put yourself out on my account. **(b)** (*changer de place*) to move. ♦ **dérangement** *nm* (*gêne*) trouble, inconvenience; (*déplacement*) trip; (*bouleversement*) disorder (*de* in). **en ~** *machine* out of order.

déraper [deʀape] (1) *vi [véhicule]* to skid; *[personne, échelle]* to slip. ♦ **dérapage** *nm* skid.

dérégler [deʀegle] (6) **1** *vt* (*gén*) to upset; *temps* to unsettle. **2 se ~** *vpr [appareil]* to go wrong; *[pouls, estomac, temps]* to be upset. ♦ **déréglé, e** *adj* out of order; upset; unsettled; *mœurs* dissolute. ♦ **dérèglement** *nm* upset. *[mœurs]* **~(s)** dissoluteness.

dérider *vt*, **se ~** *vpr* [deʀide] (1) *personne* to brighten up; *front* to uncrease.

dérision [deʀizjɔ̃] *nf* derision, mockery. **par ~** derisively, mockingly; **tourner en ~** to mock, ridicule. ♦ **dérisoire** *adj* derisory. ♦ **dérisoirement** *adv* pathetically.

dérivatif, -ive [deʀivatif, iv] **1** *adj* derivative. **2** *nm* distraction.

dérivation [deʀivɑsjɔ̃] *nf [rivière]* diversion; (*Ling, Math*) derivation; (*Élec*) shunt; (*Aviat, Naut*) deviation.

dérive [deʀiv] *nf* **(a)** (*déviation*) drift. (*lit*) **à la ~** adrift; (*fig*) **aller à la ~** to drift. **(b)** (*dispositif*) (*Aviat*) fin; (*Naut*) centre-board.

dériver [deʀive] (1) **1** *vt rivière* to divert; (*Chim, Ling, Math*) to derive; (*Élec*) to shunt. **2 ~ de** *vt indir* to derive from. **3** *vi* (*Aviat, Naut*) to drift; *[orateur]* to drift off the subject. ♦ **dérivé, e 1** *adj* derived. **2** *nm* (*Chim, Ling, Math*) derivative; (*produit*) by-product. **3** *nf* (*Math*) derivative.

dermatologie [dɛʀmatɔlɔʒi] *nf* dermatology. ♦ **dermatologue** *nmf* dermatologist.

dernier, -ière [dɛʀnje, jɛʀ] **1** *adj* **(a)** (*espace*) (*gén*) last; *étage* top; *rang* back; *branche* highest. **arriver ~** to come in last; **la ~ière marche** (*en bas*) the bottom step; (*en haut*) the top step; (*Presse*) **en ~ière page** on the back page; **les 100 ~ières pages** the last 100 pages.

(b) (*temps*) (*gén*) last; (*plus récent*) latest; (*final*) final; (*précédent*) previous. **durant les ~s jours du mois** in the last few days of the month; **voici les ~ières nouvelles** here is the latest news; **l'artiste dans ses ~ières œuvres** the artist in his final *ou* last works; **les ~s propriétaires étaient belges** the previous *ou* last owners were Belgians; **il faut payer avant le 15, ~ délai** it must be paid by the 15th at the latest, the 15th is the final date for payment; **le mois ~** last month; **ces ~s temps** lately, of late; **c'est le ~ cri** it's the very latest thing *ou* fashion.

(c) (*en mérite*) *élève* bottom, last; *qualité* lowest, poorest. **de ~ ordre** very inferior; **il est toujours ~ (en classe)** he's always bottom (of the class), he's always last (in the class).

(d) (*extrême*) **grossier au ~ point** *ou* **degré** extremely rude, rude in the extreme; **il a protesté avec la ~ière énergie** he protested most vigorously *ou* with the utmost vigour; **c'est du ~ chic** it's the last word in elegance; **c'est de la ~ière importance** it is of the utmost importance.

(e) (*ultime*) *grade* top, highest; *regard, effort* last, final. **quel est votre ~ prix?** (*pour vendre*) what's the lowest you'll go?; (*pour acheter*) what's your final offer?; **en ~ière analyse** in the final *ou* last analysis; **en ~ lieu** finally; **mettre la ~ière main à qch** to put the finishing touches to sth; **avoir le ~ mot** to have the last word; **en ~ ressort** in the last instance; **en ~ recours** as a last resort; **rendre le ~ soupir** to breathe one's last; **accompagner qn à sa ~ière demeure** to accompany sb to his final resting place.

2 *nm,f* last (one); (*enfant*) youngest (child). **sortir le ~** to leave last; **les ~s arrivés** the last ones to arrive; **il est le ~ de sa classe** he's at the bottom of the class; **il est le ~ à pouvoir faire cela** he's the last person to be able to do that; **c'est le ~ de mes soucis** it's the least of my worries; (*péj*) **le ~ des imbéciles** a complete and utter fool; (*péj*) **c'est le ~ des ~s!** he's the lowest of the low; **ce ~, cette ~ière** (*de deux*) the latter; (*de plusieurs*) this last, the last-mentioned; **~-né** youngest (child).

3 *nm* (*étage*) top floor. **acheter qch en ~** to buy sth last.

4 *nf* (*Théât*) last performance. **vous con-**

naissez la ~ière?* have you heard the latest?
dernièrement [dɛʀnjɛʀmɑ̃] *adv* recently.
dérober [deʀɔbe] (1) **1** *vt* **(a)** (*voler*) to steal (*à qn* from sb). **(b)** (*cacher*) to hide, conceal (*à qn* from sb). **~ qn à la justice** to shield sb from justice. **2 se ~** *vpr* **(a)** (*refuser d'assumer*) to shy away. **je lui ai posé la question mais il s'est dérobé** I put the question to him but he evaded it. **(b)** (*se cacher de*) to hide, conceal o.s. (*à* from). **(c)** (*se libérer*) to slip away. **se ~ à l'étreinte de qn** to slip out of sb's arms. **(d)** *[sol, genoux]* to give way. **(e)** (*Équitation*) to refuse. ♦ **dérobade** *nf* evasion; (*Équitation*) refusal. ♦ **dérobé, e 1** *adj porte* secret, hidden. **2** *nf*: **à la ~e** secretly, surreptitiously.
dérogation [deʀɔgasjɔ̃] *nf* (special) dispensation. ♦ **dérogatoire** *adj* dispensatory.
déroger [deʀɔʒe] (3) *vi* **(a)** (*déchoir*) (*gén*) to lower o.s.; (*Hist*) to lose rank and title. **(b)** (*enfreindre*) **~ à qch** to go against sth.
dérouler [deʀule] (1) **1** *vt fil* to unwind; *cordage* to uncoil; *nappe* to unroll. **~ qch dans son esprit** to go over sth in one's mind. **2 se ~** *vpr* **(a)** *[fil]* to unwind; *[cordage]* to uncoil; *[carte]* to unroll; *[paysage]* to unfold. **(b)** (*se produire, se situer*) to take place. **c'est là que toute ma vie s'est déroulée** it was there that my whole life was spent. **(c)** (*se développer*) *[histoire]* to develop, unfold. **la manifestation s'est déroulée dans le calme** the demonstration went off peacefully; **à mesure que l'histoire se déroulait** as the story unfolded *ou* developed. ♦ **déroulement** *nm* **(a)** *[cérémonie]* progress; *[action]* development. **pendant le ~ des opérations** during the course of the operations, while the operations were in progress. **(b)** unwinding; uncoiling; unrolling.
déroute [deʀut] *nf* rout. **en ~** routed; **mettre en ~** to rout.
dérouter [deʀute] (1) *vt avion* to reroute; *candidat* to disconcert; *poursuivants* to throw off the scent. ♦ **déroutant, e** *adj* disconcerting.
derrick [dɛʀik] *nm* derrick.
derrière [dɛʀjɛʀ] **1** *prép* **(a)** (*gén, fig*) behind. **passe (par) ~ la maison** go round the back of *ou* round behind the house; **faire qch ~ (le dos de) qn** to do sth behind sb's back; (*fig*) **je suis ~ vous** I'll back you up, I'm on your side; **il faut toujours être ~ son dos** you've always got to keep an eye on him; **vin de ~ les fagots** extra-special wine. **(b)** (*Naut*) (*dans le bateau*) abaft; (*sur la mer*) astern of.
2 *adv* **(a)** behind. **assis 3 rangs ~** sitting 3 rows back *ou* behind; (*Aut*) **monter ~** to sit in the back; **regarde ~** (*tourne-toi*) look behind *ou* back; (*au fond de la voiture*) look in the back; (*derrière un objet*) look behind it; **par-~** *entrer* by the back; *attaquer* from behind, from the rear; *s'attacher* at the back; *médire* behind sb's back. **(b)** (*Naut*) (*dans le bateau*) abaft; (*sur la mer*) astern.
3 *nm [personne]* bottom, behind*; *[animal]* hindquarters, rump; *[objet]* back; *[maison]* back, rear. **habiter sur le ~** to live at the back (of the house); **porte de ~** back *ou* rear door.
derviche [dɛʀviʃ] *nm* dervish. **~ tourneur** dancing dervish.
des [de] *V* **de.**
dès [dɛ] *prép* **(a)** (*temps*) from. **il a commencé à pleuvoir ~ le matin** it rained from the morning onwards; **~ le début** from the start; **~ qu'il aura fini il viendra** as soon as he's finished he'll come; **~ son retour il fera le nécessaire** as soon as he's back he'll do what's necessary; **~ l'époque romaine** as early as *ou* as far back as Roman times; **~ son enfance** since (his) childhood, ever since he was a child; **~ maintenant** right now. **(b)** (*espace etc*) **~ Lyon il a plu sans arrêt** it never stopped raining from Lyons onwards *ou* after Lyons; **~ l'entrée je sentis qu'il se passait qch** as soon as I walked in at the door I sensed that sth was going on; **~ le premier verre il roula sous la table** after the first glass he collapsed under the table. **(c) ~ lors** from that moment; **~ lors que** (*puisque*) since, as.
désabusé, e [dezabyze] *adj* disenchanted, disillusioned.
désaccord [dezakɔʀ] *nm* **(a)** (*mésentente*) discord. **être en ~ avec sa famille** to be at odds with one's family. **(b)** (*divergence*) (*entre points de vue*) disagreement; (*entre intérêts*) conflict. **leurs intérêts sont en ~ avec les nôtres** their interests conflict with ours. **(c)** (*contradiction*) discrepancy. **ce qu'il dit est en ~ avec ce qu'il fait** there is a discrepancy between what he says and what he does.
désaccordé, e [dezakɔʀde] *adj piano* out of tune.
désaccoutumer [dezakutyme] (1) *vt*: **~ qn de qch/de faire** to get sb out of the habit of sth/of doing; **se ~ de qch/de faire** to lose the habit of sth/of doing.
désaffecter [dezafɛkte] (1) *vt* to close down. ♦ **désaffectation** *nf* closing down. ♦ **désaffecté, e** *adj* disused.
désaffection [dezafɛksjɔ̃] *nf* loss of affection (*pour* for).
désagréable [dezagʀeabl(ə)] *adj* disagreeable. ♦ **désagréablement** *adv* disagreeably.
désagréger *vt*, **se ~** *vpr* [dezagʀeʒe] (3 *et* 6) to disintegrate, break up. ♦ **désagrégation** *nf* disintegration, breaking up.
désagrément [dezagʀemɑ̃] *nm* (*déboire*) annoyance; (*déplaisir*) displeasure. **malgré tous les ~s que cela entraîne** despite all the annoyances *ou* trouble it involves.
désaltérer [dezalteʀe] (6) **1** *vt* to quench the thirst of. **2 se ~** *vpr* to quench one's thirst. ♦ **désaltérant, e** *adj* thirst-quenching.
désamorcer [dezamɔʀse] (3) *vt fusée* to remove the primer from; *pompe* to drain; (*fig*) *situation* to defuse.
désappointer [dezapwɛ̃te] (1) *vt* to disappoint. ♦ **désappointement** *nm* disappointment.
désapprouver [dezapʀuve] (1) *vt* to disapprove of. **elle désapprouve qu'il vienne** she disapproves of his coming. ♦ **désapprobateur, -trice** *adj* disapproving. ♦ **désapprobation** *nf* disapproval.
désarçonner [dezaʀsɔne] (1) *vt* (*lit*) to unseat; (*fig*) *[réponse]* to nonplus.
désargenté, e* [dezaʀʒɑ̃te] *adj* (*sans un sou*) broke*.
désarmer [dezaʀme] (1) **1** *vt* (*Mil, fig*) to disarm; (*Naut*) to lay up. **2** *vi [pays]* to disarm; (*fig*) *[haine]* to abate. **il ne désarme pas contre son fils** he is unrelenting in his attitude towards his son. ♦ **désarmant, e** *adj* disarming. ♦ **désarmé, e** *adj* (*lit*) unarmed; (*fig*) helpless. ♦ **désarmement** *nm [forteresse]* disarming; *[pays]* disarmament; *[navire]* laying up.
désarroi [dezaʀwa] *nm [personne]* helplessness; *[armée, équipe]* confusion.
désarticuler (se) [dezaʀtikyle] (1) *vpr [acrobate]* to contort o.s. **se ~ l'épaule** to dislocate one's shoulder.
désastre [dezastʀ(ə)] *nm* (*lit, fig*) disaster. **les ~s causés par la tempête** the damage caused by the storm. ♦ **désastreux, -euse** *adj* (*gén*) disastrous; *conditions, temps* terrible, appalling.
désavantage [dezavɑ̃taʒ] *nm* (*gén*) disadvantage; (*handicap*) handicap; (*inconvénient*) drawback. **avoir un ~ sur qn** to be at a disadvantage *ou* be handicapped in comparison with sb; **se montrer à son ~** to show o.s. to one's disadvantage *ou* in an unfavourable light.
désavantager [dezavɑ̃taʒe] (3) *vt* to put at a disadvantage (*par rapport à* by comparison with). **cela désavantage surtout les plus pauvres** this puts the very poor at the greatest disadvan-

tage, this penalizes the very poor in particular. ♦ **désavantageusement** *adv* unfavourably, disadvantageously. ♦ **désavantageux, -euse** *adj* unfavourable, disadvantageous.

désavouer [dezavwe] (1) **1** *vt* to disclaim, disavow; (*blâmer*) to repudiate. **2 se ~** *vpr* to retract. ♦ **désaveu** *nm* (*rétractation*) retraction; (*reniement*) disavowal; (*blâme*) repudiation.

désaxer [dezakse] (1) *vt esprit* to unhinge.

desceller [desele] (1) *vt pierre* to pull free.

descendance [desɑ̃dɑ̃s] *nf* (*enfants*) descendants; (*origine*) descent.

descendant, e [desɑ̃dɑ̃, ɑ̃t] **1** *adj direction* downward, descending; *gamme* falling, descending; (*Rail*) *voie, train* down. **2** *nm,f* descendant.

descendre [desɑ̃dʀ(ə)] (41) **1** *vi* **(a)** (*aller*) to go down; (*venir*) to come down (*à, vers* to, *dans* into); *[avion]* to come down, descend. **descends me voir** come down and see me; **~ à pied/en parachute** to walk/parachute down; **~ en train** to go down by train; **nous sommes descendus en 10 minutes** we got down in 10 minutes; **~ à Marseille** to go down to Marseilles; **~ en ville** to go into town; **la rue descend en pente douce** the street slopes gently down; **cheveux qui descendent sur les épaules** shoulder-length hair.

(b) ~ de *arbre* to climb *ou* come down from; *voiture* to get out of; **fais ~ le chien du fauteuil** get the dog down off the armchair; **~ à terre** to go ashore; **~ de cheval** to dismount; **~ de bicyclette** to get off one's bicycle.

(c) *[obscurité, neige]* to fall; *[soleil]* to go down (*sur* on); *[brouillard]* to come down (*sur* over); *[prix, température]* to fall, drop; *[marée]* to go out.

(d) (*s'abaisser*) **~ dans l'estime de qn** to go down in sb's estimation; **il est descendu jusqu'à mendier** he has stooped to begging.

(e) (*lieu*) **~ à l'hôtel** to put up *ou* stay at a hotel; **la police est descendue dans cette boîte de nuit** the police have raided the night club.

2 ~ de *vt indir ancêtre* to be descended from.

3 *vt* **(a)** *escalier, rivière, gamme* to go down. **~ la rue en courant** to run down the street.

(b) (*apporter*) *valise* to take *ou* bring down. **faire ~ ses bagages** to have one's luggage brought *ou* taken down; **descends-moi mes lunettes** bring *ou* fetch me my glasses down; **je te descends en ville** I'll take you into town, I'll give you a lift into town.

(c) (*baisser*) *store, étagère, rayon* to lower.

(d) (*: *abattre*) *avion* to shoot down; *personne* to bump off*; *bouteille* to down. **se faire ~** to get o.s. bumped off*; **~ qn en flammes** to shoot sb down in flames.

descente [desɑ̃t] **1** *nf* **(a)** (*gén, Aviat*) descent. **la ~ dans le puits est dangereuse** going down the well is dangerous; **la ~ des bagages prend du temps** it takes time to bring down the luggage; **le téléphérique est tombé en panne dans la ~** the cable-car broke down on the way down; **~ en parachute** parachute drop; (*Ski*) **(épreuve de) ~** downhill race *ou* run; **accueillir qn à la ~ du train** to meet sb off the train; **à ma ~ de voiture** as I got out of the car. **(b)** (*raid*) raid. **faire une ~ sur** *ou* **dans** to raid, make a raid on. **(c)** (*partie descendante*) downward slope, incline. **freiner dans les ~s** to brake going downhill; **la ~ de la cave/du garage** the entrance into the cellar/garage. **2: ~ de croix** Deposition; **~ aux enfers** descent into Hell; **~ de lit** bedside rug.

description [dɛskʀipsjɔ̃] *nf* description. **faire la ~ de** to describe. ♦ **descriptif, -ive** *adj* descriptive.

désembuer [dezɑ̃bye] (1) *vt vitre* to demist.

désemparé, e [dezɑ̃paʀe] *adj* bewildered, distraught; *navire* crippled.

désemparer [dezɑ̃paʀe] (1) *vi*: **sans ~** without stopping.

désemplir [dezɑ̃pliʀ] (2) *vi*: **le magasin ne désemplit jamais** the shop is never empty *ou* is always full.

désenchantement [dezɑ̃ʃɑ̃tmɑ̃] *nm* disenchantment, disillusion. ♦ **désenchanté, e** *adj* disenchanted, disillusioned.

désenfler [dezɑ̃fle] (1) *vi* to go down, become less swollen.

désennuyer [dezɑ̃nɥije] (8) *vt*: **~ qn** to relieve sb's boredom.

désépaissir [dezepesiʀ] (2) *vt cheveux* to thin (out).

déséquilibre [dezekilibʀ(ə)] *nm* (*entre quantités*) imbalance; (*mental*) unbalance; *[objet]* unsteadiness. **en ~** *armoire* unsteady; *budget* unbalanced. ♦ **déséquilibré, e 1** *adj* unbalanced. **2** *nm,f* unbalanced person. ♦ **déséquilibrer** (1) *vt* (*lit*) to throw off balance; *esprit* to unbalance.

désert, e [dezɛʀ, ɛʀt(ə)] **1** *adj* deserted. **2** *nm* desert. ♦ **désertique** *adj* desert.

déserter [dezɛʀte] (1) *vti* to desert. ♦ **déserteur** *nm* deserter. ♦ **désertion** *nf* desertion.

désespérer [dezɛspeʀe] (6) **1** *vt* to drive to despair. **2** *vi* to despair. **3 ~ de** *vt indir*: **~ de qn/de faire** to despair of sb/of doing; **je ne désespère pas de réussir** I haven't lost hope *ou* given up hope of succeeding. **4 se ~** *vpr* to despair. ♦ **désespérant, e** *adj lenteur, nouvelle* appalling; *enfant* hopeless; *temps* maddening, sickening. ♦ **désespéré, e 1** *adj* (*gén*) *cas* hopeless. **appel ~** cry of despair. **2** *nm,f* (*suicidé*) suicide (*person*). ♦ **désespérément** *adv tenter* desperately. **~ vide** hopelessly empty.

désespoir [dezɛspwaʀ] *nm* despair. **faire le ~ de qn** to be the despair of sb, drive sb to despair; **être au ~** to be in despair; **je suis au ~ de ne pouvoir venir** I'm desperately sorry not to be able to come; **en ~ de cause** in desperation.

déshabiller [dezabije] (1) **1** *vt* to undress. **2 se ~** *vpr* to undress; (*manteau etc*) to take off one's coat *ou* things. ♦ **déshabillé** *nm* négligée.

déshabituer [dezabitɥe] (1) **1** *vt*: **~ qn de (faire) qch** to break sb of the habit of (doing) sth. **2 se ~** *vpr*: **se ~ de qch/de faire qch** to get out of the habit of sth/of doing sth.

désherber [dezɛʀbe] (1) *vt* to weed. ♦ **désherbage** *nm* weeding. ♦ **désherbant** *nm* weed-killer.

déshériter [dezeʀite] (1) *vt héritier* to disinherit; (*désavantager*) to deprive. **déshérité par la nature** ill-favoured by nature; **les déshérités** the deprived.

déshonorer [dezɔnɔʀe] (1) **1** *vt profession* to disgrace, dishonour; *personne* to dishonour, bring disgrace *ou* dishonour upon. **2 se ~** *vpr* to bring disgrace *ou* dishonour on o.s. ♦ **déshonneur** *nm* disgrace, dishonour. ♦ **déshonorant, e** *adj* dishonourable, degrading.

déshydrater *vt*, **se ~** *vpr* [dezidʀate] (1) to dehydrate. ♦ **déshydratation** *nf* dehydration.

désigner [deziɲe] (1) *vt* **(a)** (*du doigt*) to point out; (*d'un mot*) to refer to. **tout le désigne comme coupable** everything points to his guilt. **(b)** (*nommer*) to appoint, designate (*à un poste* to a post). **que des volontaires se désignent!** volunteers step forward!; **successeur désigné** successor elect *ou* designate. **(c)** (*qualifier*) to mark out. **sa hardiesse le désigne pour cette tentative** his boldness marks him out for this attempt; **c'était la victime désignée** he was the classic victim; **être tout désigné pour faire qch** to be cut out to do sth. ♦ **désignation** *nf* designation.

désillusionner [dezilyzjɔne] (1) *vt* to disillusion. ♦ **désillusion** *nf* disillusion.

désinence [dezinɑ̃s] *nf* (*Ling*) ending, inflexion.

désinfecter [dezɛ̃fɛkte] (1) *vt* to disinfect. ♦ **désinfectant, e** *adj, nm* disinfectant. ♦ **désinfection** *nf* disinfection.

désintégrer [dezɛ̃tegʀe] (6) **1** *vt* (*Phys*) to split; (*fig*) to split up, break up. **2 se ~** *vpr* (*gén*) to disintegrate; (*Phys*) to split. ♦ **désintégration** *nf* splitting; splitting-up; breaking-up; disintegration.

désintéresser [dezɛ̃teʀese] (1) **1** *vt créancier* to pay off. **2 se ~** *vpr*: **se ~ de** to lose interest in. ♦ **désintéressé, e** *adj* disinterested. ♦ **désintéressement** *nm* (*gén*) disinterestedness; *[créancier]* paying off. ♦ **désintérêt** *nm* disinterest.

désintoxiquer [dezɛ̃tɔksike] (1) *vt* to treat for alcoholism (*ou* drug addiction). ♦ **désintoxication** *nf* treatment for alcoholism (*ou* drug addiction).

désinvolte [dezɛ̃vɔlt(ə)] *adj* casual, offhand, airy. ♦ **désinvolture** *nf* casualness.

désir [deziʀ] *nm* (*souhait*) wish, desire; (*convoitise*) desire (*de qch* for sth, *de faire* to do). **vos ~s sont des ordres** your wish is my command; **prendre ses ~s pour des réalités** to indulge in wishful thinking. ♦ **désirable** *adj* desirable. **peu ~** undesirable.

désirer [deziʀe] (1) *vt* (*vouloir*) to want; (*convoiter*) to desire. **~ faire qch** to want *ou* wish to do sth; **que désirez-vous?** (*au café*) what would you like?; (*dans un bureau*) what can I do for you?; **il désire que tu viennes tout de suite** he wants you to come at once; **ça laisse beaucoup à ~** it leaves a lot to be desired. ♦ **désireux, -euse** *adj*: **~ de** anxious to.

désister (se) [deziste] (1) *vpr* to withdraw. ♦ **désistement** *nm* withdrawal.

désobéir [dezɔbeiʀ] (2) *vi* to be disobedient. **~ à qn/à un ordre** to disobey sb/an order. ♦ **désobéissance** *nf* disobedience (*à* to). ♦ **désobéissant, e** *adj* disobedient.

désobliger [dezɔbliʒe] (3) *vt* to offend. ♦ **désobligeant, e** *adj* disagreeable, offensive.

désodoriser [dezɔdɔʀize] (1) *vt* to deodorize. ♦ **désodorisant, e** *adj, nm* deodorant.

désœuvré, e [dezœvʀe] *adj* idle. **rester ~ pendant des heures** to be at a loose end *ou* have nothing to do for hours on end. ♦ **désœuvrement** *nm* idleness. **par ~** for want of anything better to do.

désoler [dezɔle] (1) **1** *vt* to distress, upset; (*dévaster*) to desolate. **2 se ~** *vpr* to be upset. ♦ **désolant, e** *adj nouvelle, situation* distressing; *enfant, temps* disappointing. **il est ~ que** it's a terrible shame *ou* such a pity that. ♦ **désolation** *nf* (*consternation*) distress, grief; (*dévastation*) desolation. ♦ **désolé, e** *adj* **(a)** *endroit* desolate. **(b)** (*affligé*) distressed; (*contrit*) sorry. **(je suis) ~ de vous avoir dérangé** (I'm) sorry to have disturbed you.

désolidariser (se) [desɔlidaʀize] (1) *vpr*: **se ~ de** to dissociate o.s. from.

désopilant, e [dezɔpilɑ̃, ɑ̃t] *adj* hilarious.

désordre [dezɔʀdʀ(ə)] *nm* **(a)** *[pièce, vêtements]* untidiness, disorderliness; *[service public]* disorder; *[esprits]* confusion; (*Méd*) disorder; *[vie]* dissoluteness. **mettre/être en ~** to make/be untidy; **quel ~!** what a muddle! *ou* mess! **(b)** (*agitation*) disorder. **faire du ~** *[élève]* to cause a commotion *ou* a disturbance; *[agitateur]* to spread unrest; (*émeute*) **de graves ~s** serious disturbances, serious outbreaks of disorder. ♦ **désordonné, e** *adj personne* untidy, disorderly; *mouvements* uncoordinated; *fuite, vie* disorderly; *esprit* muddled. **~ dans son travail** disorganized in one's work.

désorganiser [dezɔʀganize] (1) *vt* (*gén*) to disorganize. ♦ **désorganisation** *nf* disorganization.

désorienter [dezɔʀjɑ̃te] (1) *vt* to disorientate.

désormais [dezɔʀmɛ] *adv* in future, henceforth.

désosser [dezɔse] (1) *vt viande* to bone.

despote [dɛspɔt] **1** *adj* despotic. **2** *nm* despot; (*fig*) tyrant. ♦ **despotique** *adj* despotic; (*fig*) tyrannical. ♦ **despotisme** *nm* despotism; (*fig*) tyranny.

desquels, desquelles [dekɛl] *V* **lequel.**

dessaisir [deseziʀ] (2) **1** *vt*: **~ un tribunal d'une affaire** to remove a case from a court. **2 se ~** *vpr*: **se ~ de** to part with.

dessaler [desale] (1) *vt* **(a)** (*aussi*: **faire ~** *ou* **mettre à ~**) *viande* to soak. **(b)** (*: *délurer*) **~ qn** to teach sb a thing or two*.

dessécher [deseʃe] (6) **1** *vt terre* to dry out; *plante* to wither; (*fig*) *cœur* to harden. **2 se ~** *vpr* (*gén*) to dry out; *[terre, bouche]* to become parched; *[plante]* to wither; *[aliments]* to go dry.

dessein [desɛ̃] *nm* (*gén*) design; (*intention*) intention; (*projet*) plan. **il a le ~ de faire** he intends *ou* means to do; **avoir des ~s sur qn** to have designs on sb; **dans le ~ de faire** with the intention of doing; **faire qch à ~** to do sth intentionally.

desseller [desele] (1) *vt* to unsaddle.

desserrer [deseʀe] (1) **1** *vt* (*gén*) to loosen; *nœud* to slacken; *étreinte* to relax; *poing, dents* to unclench; *écrou* to unscrew; *frein, étau* to release; *mots* to space out. **~ sa ceinture de 2 crans** to loosen *ou* slacken one's belt 2 notches; (*fig*) **il n'a pas desserré les dents** he hasn't opened his mouth *ou* lips. **2 se ~** *vpr [nœud, écrou]* to come loose *ou* undone; *[frein]* to release itself; *[étreinte]* to relax, loosen. ♦ **desserré, e** *adj* loose; *nœud* slack.

dessert [desɛʀ] *nm* dessert.

desserte [desɛʀt(ə)] *nf* **(a)** (*meuble*) sideboard table. **(b)** (*transport*) service. **la ~ de la ville est assurée par un car** there is a bus service to the town.

desservir[1] [desɛʀviʀ] (14) *vt* **(a)** *plat, table* to clear away. **(b)** (*nuire à*) *personne* to go against; *intérêts* to harm. **il m'a desservi auprès de mes amis** he did me a disservice with my friends.

desservir[2] [desɛʀviʀ] (14) *vt* **(a)** (*Transport*) to serve. **le village est desservi par 3 lignes d'autobus** the village is served by *ou* has 3 bus services. **(b)** *[couloir]* to lead into.

dessin [desɛ̃] *nm* **(a)** (*gén*) drawing. **~ animé** cartoon film; **~ humoristique** cartoon; **il faut lui faire un ~!*** you'll have to spell it out for him. **(b)** (*art*) **le ~** drawing; **école de ~** drawing school; **~ de mode** fashion design; **planche à ~** drawing board. **(c)** (*motif*) pattern, design. **tissu avec des ~s jaunes** material with a yellow pattern on it. **(d)** (*contour*) outline, line. ♦ **dessinateur, -trice** *nm,f* (*artiste*) drawer. **~ industriel** draughtsman; **~ humoristique** cartoonist; **~ de mode** fashion designer.

dessiner [desine] (1) **1** *vt* **(a)** (*gén*) to draw; *véhicule* to design; *jardin* to lay out, landscape. **~ au crayon** to draw in pencil; **bouche bien dessinée** finely delineated mouth. **(b)** *[chose]* **les champs dessinent un damier** the fields are laid out like a checkerboard; **vêtement qui dessine bien la taille** garment that shows off the waist well. **2 se ~** *vpr [contour]* to stand out; *[tendance]* to become apparent; *[projet]* to take shape. **un sourire se dessina sur ses lèvres** a smile formed on his lips.

dessoûler* [desule] (1) *vti* to sober up.

dessous [d(ə)su] **1** *adv* **(a)** (*sous*) under, underneath, beneath; (*plus bas*) below. **mettez votre valise ~** put your suitcase underneath (it) *ou* under it; **retirer qch de ~ le lit** to get sth from under the bed. **(b) en ~, au-~** (*sous*) under, underneath; (*plus bas*) below; **en ~ de, au-~ de** below; **les enfants au-~ de 7 ans** children under 7; **20° au-~ de zéro** 20° below zero; **être au-~ de tout** to be quite hopeless; **les locataires d'en ~** the people who rent the flat below, the tenants downstairs *ou* underneath; **regarder qn en ~** to give sb a shifty look; **faire qch en ~** to do sth in an underhand manner.

2 *nm* **(a)** *[objet]* bottom, underside; *[pied]* sole; *[voiture, animal]* underside. **drap du ~** bottom sheet; **les gens du ~** the people downstairs; **le ~ de la table est poussiéreux** the table is dusty underneath; **les fruits du ~** the fruit at the bottom, the fruit underneath; **avoir le ~** to get the worst of it. **(b)** (*côté secret*) **les ~ de la politique** the hidden side of politics; **connaître le ~ des cartes** to have inside information. **(c)** (*Habillement*) les ~ underwear.

3: ~ **de bouteille** bottle mat; ~ **de plat** table mat; ~ **de robe** slip, petticoat; ~ **de table** under the counter payment; ~ **de verre** coaster.

dessus [d(ə)sy] **1** *adv* **(a)** *placé* on top (of it); *collé, écrit* on it; *lancer* over (it); (*plus haut*) above. **montez ~** (*échelle*) get up on it; **passez (par) ~** go over it; **ôter qch de ~ la table** to take sth off the table; **il lui a tapé/tiré ~** he hit him/shot at him. **(b) au-~** above; (*étage*) upstairs; (*posé sur*) on top; (*plus cher etc*) over, above; **au-~ de** (*plus haut que*) above; (*sur*) on top of; *prix, limite* over, above; *possibilités* beyond; **les enfants au-~ de 7 ans** children over 7; **20° au-~ de zéro** 20° above zero; **être au-~ de tout soupçon/reproche** to be above all suspicion/beyond all reproach.

2 *nm* top. **drap du ~** top sheet; **les gens du ~** the people upstairs; (*fig*) **le ~ du panier** the pick of the bunch; (*élite sociale*) the upper crust; **avoir/prendre le ~** to have/get the upper hand; **reprendre le ~** to get over it.

3: ~ **de cheminée** mantelpiece; ~ **de lit** bedspread; ~ **de table** table runner.

destin [dɛstɛ̃] *nm* (*sort*) fate; (*avenir, vocation*) destiny.

destinataire [dɛstinatɛʀ] *nmf [lettre]* addressee; *[marchandise]* consignee; *[mandat]* payee.

destination [dɛstinɑsjɔ̃] *nf* (*direction*) destination; (*usage*) purpose. **à ~ de** *avion, train* to; *bateau* bound for; *voyageur* travelling to; **arriver à ~** to reach one's destination.

destiner [dɛstine] (1) *vt* **(a)** (*attribuer*) **~ qch à qn** (*gén*) to intend *ou* mean sth for sb; *ballon* to aim sth at sb; **livre destiné aux enfants** book (intended *ou* meant) for children; **il vous destine ce poste** he intends *ou* means you to have this post; **le sort qui lui était destiné** the fate that was in store for him. **(b)** (*affecter*) **~ une somme à l'achat de qch** to intend to use a sum *ou* earmark a sum to buy sth; **les fonds seront destinés à la recherche** the money will be devoted to *ou* used for research. **(c)** (*vouer*) **~ qn à une fonction/à être médecin** to destine sb for a post/to be a doctor; **destiné à mourir jeune** destined *ou* fated to die young; **il se destine à l'enseignement** he intends to go into teaching. ♦ **destinée** *nf* (*sort*) fate; (*avenir, vocation*) destiny.

destituer [dɛstitɥe] (1) *vt ministre* to dismiss; *roi* to depose; *fonctionnaire* to dismiss from office. ♦ **destitution** *nf* dismissal; deposition.

destruction [dɛstʀyksjɔ̃] *nf*: **~(s)** (*gén*) destruction; *[rats]* extermination. ♦ **destructeur, -trice 1** *adj* destructive. **2** *nm,f* destroyer. ♦ **destructible** *adj* destructible. ♦ **destructif, -ive** *adj* destructive.

désuet, -ète [desɥɛ, ɛt] *adj* (*gén*) outdated; *mot* obsolete; *charme* old-fashioned. ♦ **désuétude** *nf* disuse. **tomber en ~** *[loi]* to fall into abeyance; *[coutume]* to become obsolete, fall into disuse.

désunir [dezyniʀ] (2) *vt famille* to divide, disunite. ♦ **désunion** *nf* disunity.

détacher [detaʃe] (1) **1** *vt* **(a)** *prisonnier, paquet* to untie; *wagon* to take off, detach (*de* from). **(b)** (*dénouer*) (*gén*) to undo; *nœud* to untie; *soulier, ceinture* to unfasten. **(c)** (*ôter*) (*gén*) to remove, take off; *papier collé* to unstick; *rideau* to take down (*de* from); *reçu* to tear out (*de* of), detach (*de* from). **il ne pouvait ~ son regard du spectacle** he could not take his eyes off the sight; **'~ suivant le pointillé'** 'tear off along the dotted line'. **(d)** (*envoyer*) *personne* to send, dispatch; (*Admin: affecter*) to second. **être détaché** to be on secondment. **(e)** (*mettre en relief*) *mots* to separate; *contour* to bring out; (*Mus*) *notes* to detach. **(f)** (*éloigner*) **~ qn de qch/qn** to turn sb away from sth/sb. **(g)** (*nettoyer*) to clean.

2 se ~ *vpr* **(a)** *[prisonnier]* to free o.s., get loose (*de* from); *[paquet, nœud]* to come undone *ou* untied. **(b)** *[écorce, papier collé]* to come off; *[page, épingle]* to come out; *[rideau]* to come down. **(c)** *[coureur etc]* to pull *ou* break away (*de* from). **(d)** (*ressortir*) to stand out (*sur* against). **(e) se ~ de** (*renoncer à*) to renounce; (*se désintéresser de*) to grow away from.

♦ **détachable** *adj* detachable. ♦ **détachage** *nm* (*nettoyage*) stain removal. ♦ **détachant** *nm* stain remover. ♦ **détaché, e** *adj air* detached. ♦ **détachement** *nm* (*indifférence*) detachment; (*Mil*) detachment; *[fonctionnaire]* secondment.

détail [detaj] *nm* **(a)** (*particularité*) detail. **entrer dans les ~s** to go into details *ou* particulars. **(b)** *[facture, compte]* breakdown. **faire le ~ de qch** to give a breakdown of sth; **il nous a fait le ~ de ses aventures** he gave us a detailed account of his adventures; **en *ou* dans le ~** in detail. **(c)** (*Comm*) retail. **vendre au ~** *vin* to (sell) retail; *articles* to sell separately; **marchand de ~** retailer, retail dealer. ♦ **détaillant, e** *nm,f* retailer, retail dealer. ♦ **détaillé, e** *adj* detailed. ♦ **détailler** (1) *vt* **(a)** (*Comm*) *articles* to sell separately; *marchandise* to sell retail. **(b)** *plan, raison* to detail, explain in detail. **il m'a détaillé de la tête aux pieds** he examined me from head to foot.

détaler [detale] (1) *vi [lapin]* to bolt; (*) *[personne]* to scarper*.

détartrer [detaʀtʀe] (1) *vt dents* to scale; *chaudière etc* to descale.

détaxer [detakse] (1) *vt* (*réduire*) to reduce the tax on; (*supprimer*) to remove the tax on. ♦ **détaxe** *nf* reduction in tax; removal of tax (*de* from); (*remboursement*) tax refund.

détecter [detɛkte] (1) *vt* to detect. ♦ **détecteur, -trice 1** *adj* detecting, detector. **2** *nm* detector. ♦ **détection** *nf* detection.

détective [detɛktiv] *nm*: **~ (privé)** private detective.

déteindre [detɛ̃dʀ(ə)] (52) **1** *vt* to take the colour out of. **2** *vi* (*gén*) to lose its colour; (*au lavage*) to run; (*au soleil*) to fade. **~ sur** *[couleur]* to run into; *[caractère]* to rub off on.

dételer [detle] (4) **1** *vt chevaux etc* to unharness; *voiture* to unhitch. **2** *vi* (*) to leave off working*. **sans ~** without a break.

détendre [detɑ̃dʀ(ə)] (41) **1** *vt ressort* to release; *corde* to slacken, loosen; *corps, esprit* to relax; *atmosphère* to relieve, ease; *nerfs* to calm, soothe. **2 se ~** *vpr [ressort]* to lose its tension; *[corde]* to become slack, slacken; *[atmosphère, esprit, corps]* to relax; *[nerfs]* to calm down. **détendez-vous!** relax!, let yourself unwind!*; **se ~ les jambes** to unbend one's legs. ♦ **détendu, e** *adj personne, atmosphère* relaxed; *câble* slack; *ressort* unextended.

détenir [detniʀ] (22) *vt titre* to hold; *secret, objets volés* to be in possession of; *moyen* to have (in one's possession); *prisonnier* to detain. **~ le pouvoir** to be in power.

détente [detɑ̃t] *nf* **(a)** (*délassement*) relaxation; (*dans les relations*) easing (*dans* of). (*Pol*) **la ~** détente. **(b)** (*élan*) *[sauteur]* spring; *[lanceur]* thrust. **d'une ~ rapide** with a swift bound. **(c)** (*lit, fig: gâchette*) trigger.

détention [detɑ̃sjɔ̃] *nf* **(a)** *[armes]* possession; *[titres]* holding. **(b)** (*captivité*) detention. **~ préventive** custody. ♦ **détenteur, -trice** *nm,f* possessor; holder. ♦ **détenu, e** *nm,f* prisoner.

détergent, e [detɛʀʒɑ̃, ɑ̃t] *adj, nm* detergent.

détériorer [deteʀjɔʀe] (1) **1** *vt* to damage, spoil. **2 se ~** *vpr* to deteriorate. ♦ **détérioration** *nf* damaging (*de* of), damage (*de* to); deterioration (*de* in). **~s** damage.

déterminer [detɛʀmine] (1) *vt* (*gén*) to determine; (*par calcul*) to calculate, work out; (*motiver*) *retard* to cause, bring about. ♦ **déterminant, e** *adj* determining. ♦ **détermination** *nf* (*précision*) determining; (*résolution*) decision, resolution; (*fermeté*) determination. ♦ **déterminé, e** *adj air* determined; *but* definite, well-defined. **quantité ~e** given quantity.

déterrer [deteʀe] (1) *vt* (*gén*) to dig up; (*lit, fig*) *objet* to unearth; *mort* to disinter. **avoir une tête de déterré** to look deathly pale.

détersif, -ive [detɛʀsif, iv] *adj, nm* detergent.

détester [detɛste] (1) *vt* to hate, detest. **elle déteste attendre** she hates *ou* can't bear having to wait; **il ne déteste pas le chocolat** he is rather fond of *ou* is not averse to chocolate. ♦ **détestable** *adj temps, repas* foul, dreadful, appalling; *habitude, caractère* odious, detestable. ♦ **détestablement** *adv* appallingly, dreadfully.

détoner [detɔne] (1) *vi* to detonate, explode. ♦ **détonateur** *nm* detonator. ♦ **détonation** *nf [obus]* detonation, explosion; *[fusil]* bang.

détonner [detɔne] (1) *vi [couleurs]* to clash; *[conduite]* to be out of place.

détour [detuʀ] *nm* **(a)** (*sinuosité*) bend, curve. **faire des ~s** to wind about; **au ~ du chemin** at the bend of the path. **(b)** (*déviation*) detour. **(c)** (*subterfuge*) roundabout means; (*circonlocution*) circumlocution. **sans ~s** plainly, without beating about the bush.

détourner [detuʀne] (1) **1** *vt* **(a)** *route, convoi* to divert; *avion [pirate de l'air]* to hijack; *soupçon, conversation* to divert (*sur* on to); *coup, colère* to ward off. **~ les yeux** to look away; **~ la tête** to turn one's head away; **~ qn de** *chemin, devoir, soucis* to divert sb from; *projet* to dissuade sb from; *sa famille* to turn sb away from; **~ qn du droit chemin** to lead sb astray. **(b)** (*voler*) to misappropriate. **2 se ~** *vpr* to turn away. **se ~ de sa route** (*pour aller ailleurs*) to make a detour; (*par erreur*) to go off the right road. ♦ **détourné, e** *adj chemin, moyen* roundabout. **de façon ~e** in a roundabout way. ♦ **détournement** *nm [rivière]* diversion. **~ d'avion** hijacking; **~ de fonds** misappropriation of funds; **~ de mineur** (*perversion*) corruption of a minor.

détraquer [detʀake] (1) **1** *vt machine* to put out of order; *personne* (*physiquement*) to put out of sorts; (*nerveusement*) to upset; (*mentalement*) to unhinge. **ces orages ont détraqué le temps** these storms have unsettled the weather; **c'est un détraqué*** he's a headcase‡, he's cracked*. **2 se ~** *vpr [machine]* to go wrong; *[estomac]* to be upset; *[temps]* to break. ♦ **détraquement** *nm [machine]* breakdown; *[santé, nerfs]* upset, breakdown.

détremper [detʀɑ̃pe] (1) *vt* to soak. **chemins détrempés** sodden paths; **chemise détrempée** soaking (wet) shirt.

détresse [detʀɛs] *nf* distress. **en ~** *personne, bateau* in distress; *entreprise* in difficulties; *cœur* anguished; **appel de ~** distress call.

détriment [detʀimɑ̃] *nm*: **au ~ de** to the detriment of.

détritus [detʀitys] *nmpl* rubbish, refuse.

détroit [detʀwa] *nm* (*Géog*) strait. **le ~ de Gibraltar** the straits of Gibraltar.

détromper [detʀɔ̃pe] (1) **1** *vt personne* to disabuse (*de* of). **2 se ~** *vpr* to be disillusioned.

détrôner [detʀone] (1) *vt* (*lit, fig*) to dethrone.

détrousser [detʀuse] (1) *vt* († *ou hum*) to rob.

détruire [detʀɥiʀ] (38) *vt* (*gén*) to destroy; *population* to wipe out; *insectes* to exterminate; *santé, espoir, projet* to ruin, wreck. **les effets se détruisent** the effects cancel each other out.

dette [dɛt] *nf* (*Fin, fig*) debt. **faire des ~s** to get into debt; **avoir 1000 F de ~s** to be 1,000 francs in debt; **la ~ publique** the national debt; (*fig*) **je suis en ~ envers vous** I am indebted to you.

deuil [dœj] *nm* **(a)** (*perte*) bereavement. **plusieurs ~s dans sa famille** several deaths in his family. **(b)** (*affliction*) grief. **plonger qn dans le ~** to plunge sb into mourning *ou* grief. **(c)** (*vêtements*) mourning (clothes). **en grand ~** in deep mourning; **être/se mettre en ~** to be in/go into mourning. **(d)** (*durée*) mourning. **jour de ~** day of mourning; **~ national** national mourning. **(e)** **faire son ~ de qch*** to say goodbye to sth*.

deux [dø] **1** *adj* **(a)** two. **~ fois** twice; **je les ai vus tous (les) ~** I saw them both, I saw both of them, I saw the two of them; (*lit, fig*) **à ~ tranchants** double-edged; **des ~ côtés de la rue** on both sides *ou* on either side of the street; **tous les ~ jours** every other day, every two days; (*en épelant*) **~ t/l** double t/l. **(b)** (*quelques*) a couple, a few. **c'est à ~ minutes d'ici** it's just a few minutes *ou* only a couple of minutes from here; **vous y serez en ~ secondes** you'll be there in no time (at all); **j'ai ~ mots à vous dire** I want to have a word with you. **(c)** (*deuxième*) second. **(d)** (*locutions*) **essayer et réussir, cela fait ~** to try and to succeed are two entirely different things; **pris entre ~ feux** caught in the crossfire; **il ne faut plus qu'il y ait ~ poids (et) ~ mesures** we must no longer have two sets of standards; (*fig*) **être assis entre ~ chaises** to be in an awkward position; **~ précautions valent mieux qu'une** better safe than sorry; **en ~ temps, trois mouvements** in two ticks*.

2 *nm* two. **couper en ~** to cut in two *ou* in half; **marcher ~ par ~** to walk two by two *ou* in pairs; **à nous ~** (*à un ennemi*) now let's fight it out!; *V* **six.**

3: ~-pièces *nm inv* (*ensemble*) two-piece suit; (*maillot*) two-piece (costume); (*appartement*) two-room flat; **~-points** *nm inv* colon; **~-roues** *nm inv* two-wheeled vehicle.

♦ **deuxième** *adj, nmf* second. (*Mil*) **~ classe** private; *V* **sixième.** ♦ **deuxièmement** *adv* second(ly).

dévaler [devale] (1) **1** *vt* to tear down, hurtle down. **2** *vi [rochers]* to hurtle down; *[lave]* to rush down; *[terrain]* to fall away sharply. *[personne]* **~ dans les escaliers** to tumble down the stairs.

dévaliser [devalize] (1) *vt maison* to burgle; *banque, personne* to rob. (*fig*) *[clients]* **~ un magasin** to buy up a shop.

dévaloriser *vt,* **se ~** *vpr* [devalɔʀize] (1) to depreciate. ♦ **dévalorisation** *nf* depreciation.

dévaluer *vt,* **se ~** *vpr* [devalɥe] (1) to devalue. ♦ **dévaluation** *nf* devaluation.

devancer [dəvɑ̃se] (3) *vt* (*distancer*) to get ahead of; (*précéder*) to arrive ahead of; *objection, désir* to anticipate. (*Mil*) **~ l'appel** to enlist before call-up. ♦ **devancier, -ière** *nm,f* precursor.

devant [d(ə)vɑ̃] **1** *prép* **(a)** (*position*) in front of; (*distance*) ahead of; (*dépassement*) past. **il est passé ~ moi sans me voir** he walked past me without seeing me; **assis ~ la fenêtre** sitting at *ou* by the window; **va-t-en de ~ la vitrine** move away from (in front of) the window; **il marchait ~ moi** he was walking in front of *ou* ahead of me; **il est ~ moi en classe** (*lit*) he sits in front of me at school; (*fig*) he is ahead of me at school; **fuir ~ qn** to flee before *ou* from sb; **avoir du temps/de l'argent ~ soi** to have time/money to spare; (*lit, fig*) **aller droit ~ soi** to go straight on. **(b)** (*en présence de*) before. **s'incliner ~ qn** to bow before sb; **imperturbable ~ le malheur d'autrui** unmoved by other people's misfortune; (*fig*) **reculer ~ ses responsabilités** to shrink from one's responsibilities; **par-~ notaire** in the presence of a notary; **~ la situation** (*étant donné*) in view of *ou* considering the situation; (*face à*) faced *ou* confronted with the situation; **rester ferme ~ le danger** to stand fast in the face of danger.

2 *adv*: **vous êtes juste ~** you are right in front of it; **corsage qui se boutonne (par-)~** blouse which buttons up at the front; **il est loin ~** he's a long way ahead; **je suis passé ~** *boutique* I went past *ou* by it; *coureur* I went ahead of *ou* in front of him; **fais passer le plateau ~** pass the tray forward; **il a pris des places ~** he has got seats at the front; (*Aut*) **monter ~** to sit in the front; **marchez ~, les enfants** walk in front, children.

3 *nm* **(a)** (*gén*) front; *[bateau]* fore, bows. **habiter sur le ~** to live at the front; **roue de ~** front wheel. **(b) prendre les ~s** to make the first move, take the initiative; **je suis allé au-~ (de lui)** I went to meet him; **aller au-~ des désirs de qn** to anticipate sb's wishes; **courir au-~ du danger** to court danger; **aller au-~ des ennuis** to be looking for trouble.

devanture [d(ə)vɑ̃tyʀ] *nf* (*étalage*) display; (*vitrine*) (shop) window; (*façade*) (shop) front.

dévaster [devaste] (1) *vt* to devastate. ♦ **dévastateur, -trice** *adj orage* devastating; *passion* destructive. ♦ **dévastation** *nf*: **~(s)** devastation.

déveine* [devɛn] *nf* rotten luck*.

développer [devlɔpe] (1) **1** *vt* (*gén, Phot*) to develop; *commerce* to expand; *argument* to enlarge (up)on; *paquet* to unwrap; *parchemin* to unroll; *coupon de tissu* to unfold; *troupes* to deploy. **poitrine bien/peu développée** well-developed/underdeveloped bust. **2 se ~** *vpr [personne, plante]* to develop; *[affaire]* to expand, develop; *[armée]* to spread out; *[habitude]* to spread. ♦ **développement** *nm* development; expansion. **en plein ~** fast-expanding, fast-developing.

devenir [dəvniʀ] (22) **1** *vi* **(a)** to become. **~ médecin** to become a doctor; **que veux-tu ~ dans la vie?** what do you want to do *ou* be in life?; **cet enfant est devenu un homme solide** that child has turned into *ou* has become a strong man; **il est devenu tout rouge** he turned *ou* went quite red; **~ vieux** to grow *ou* get old; **c'est à ~ fou!** it's enough to drive you mad! **(b)** (*advenir de*) **bonjour, que devenez-vous?*** hullo, how are you getting on? *ou* doing?*; **que sont devenues mes lunettes?** where have my glasses got to?; **qu'allons-nous ~?** what will become of us? **2** *nm* evolution.

dévergonder (se) [devɛʀgɔ̃de] (1) *vpr* to run wild. ♦ **dévergondé, e** *adj* shameless.

déverser [devɛʀse] (1) **1** *vt ordures* to tip (out), dump; *bombes* to unload; *voyageurs* to disgorge; *colère* to pour out. **2 se ~** *vpr* to pour out (*dans* into).

dévêtir *vt*, **se ~** *vpr* [devetiʀ] (20) to undress.

déviation [devjɑsjɔ̃] *nf* (*lit, fig: écart*) deviation; (*Aut*) diversion; *[colonne vertébrale]* curvature.

dévider [devide] (1) *vt bobine* to unwind; *reproches* to reel off. ♦ **dévidoir** *nm* reel.

dévier [devje] (7) **1** *vi* **(a)** *[aiguille]* to deviate; *[bateau, projectile]* to veer off course. **le poteau a fait ~ le ballon** the post deflected the ball. **(b)** *[doctrine]* to alter. **la conversation déviait dangereusement** the conversation was taking a dangerous turn; **~ par rapport au projet initial** to move away *ou* diverge from the original plan; **~ de sa ligne politique** to deviate *ou* depart from one's political line; **il fit ~ la conversation** he turned *ou* diverted the conversation (*sur* onto). **2** *vt circulation* to divert; *coup* to deflect.

deviner [d(ə)vine] (1) *vt* (*gén*) to guess; *énigme* to solve. **~ l'avenir** to foretell the future; **devine pourquoi** guess why. ♦ **devin, devineresse** *nm,f* soothsayer. **je ne suis pas ~*** I haven't got second sight. ♦ **devinette** *nf* riddle.

devis [d(ə)vi] *nm* estimate, quotation.

dévisager [devizaʒe] (3) *vt* to stare at, look hard at.

devise [d(ə)viz] *nf* motto; (*Comm*) slogan. (*Fin*) **~s** (foreign) currency.

dévisser [devise] (1) *vt* to unscrew.

dévoiler [devwale] (1) *vt statue, secret* to unveil; *nom, date* to reveal, disclose.

devoir [d(ə)vwaʀ] (28) **1** *vt argent, respect etc* to owe. **il réclame ce qui lui est dû** he is asking for what is owing *ou* due to him; **il ne veut rien ~ à personne** he doesn't want to be indebted to anyone *ou* to owe anyone anything; **je dois à mes parents d'avoir réussi** I have my parents to thank for my success, I owe my success to my parents; **il lui doit bien cela!** it's the least he can do for him!; **avec les honneurs dûs à son rang** with honours befitting his rank.

2 *vb aux* **(a)** (*obligation*) to have to. **il aurait dû la prévenir** he should have *ou* ought to have warned her; **dois-je lui écrire tout de suite?** must I *ou* do I have to *ou* have I got to write to him straight away?; **vous ne devez pas entrer sans frapper** you are not to *ou* you must not come in without knocking; **non, tu ne dois pas le rembourser** no, you need not *ou* don't have to pay it back. **(b)** (*fatalité*) **cela devait arriver** it was bound to happen; **elle ne devait pas apprendre la nouvelle avant le lendemain** she was not to hear the news until the next day; **même s'il devait être condamné, il refuserait** even if he were (to be) found guilty he would refuse; **les choses semblent ~ s'arranger** things seem to be sorting themselves out. **(c)** (*prévision*) **il doit arriver ce soir** he is due to arrive tonight, he is to arrive tonight; **vous deviez le lui cacher** you were (supposed) to hide it from him. **(d)** (*probabilité*) **vous devez vous tromper** you must be mistaken; **elle ne doit pas être bête** she can't be stupid; **cela devrait pouvoir s'arranger** it should be possible to put that right.

3 se ~ *vpr*: **se ~ à qn/qch** to have to devote o.s. to sb/sth; **nous nous devons de le lui dire** it is our duty to tell him; **comme il se doit** (*comme il faut*) as is proper *ou* right; (*comme prévu*) as expected.

4 *nm* **(a)** (*obligation*) duty. **agir par ~** to act from a sense of duty; **se faire un ~ de faire** to make it one's duty to do; **~s religieux** religious duties; **se mettre en ~ de faire** to set about doing; **présenter ses ~s à qn** to pay one's respects to sb. **(b)** (*Scol*) (*à la maison*) homework; (*en classe*) exercise. **faire ses ~s** to do one's homework.

dévolu, e [devɔly] *adj*: **être ~ à qn** *[droits]* to be devolved upon sb; *[charge]* to be handed down to sb; **budget ~ à la recherche** funds allotted to research.

dévorer [devɔʀe] (1) *vt* **(a)** *aliment, livre* to devour; *fortune* to consume; *larmes* to choke back. **cet enfant dévore!** this child has a huge appetite!; **dévoré par les moustiques** eaten alive by mosquitoes; **~ qn du regard** to eye sb greedily. **(b)** *[jalousie, feu]* to consume, devour. **la soif le dévore** he has a burning thirst; **voiture qui dévore les kilomètres** car which eats up the miles; **c'est une tâche qui dévore tous mes loisirs** it's a task which swallows up all my free time. ♦ **dévorant, e** *adj faim* raging; *curiosité, soif* burning; *passion* devouring, consuming.

dévot, e [devo, ɔt] *adj* (*gén*) devout, pious; (*péj*) over-pious. ♦ **dévotement** *adv* devoutly, piously. ♦ **dévotion** *nf* (*piété*) devoutness; (*culte*) devotion. **avoir une ~ pour qn** to worship sb.

dévouer (se) [devwe] (1) *vpr* (*se sacrifier*) to sacrifice o.s. (*pour* for). (*se consacrer à*) **se ~ à** to devote *ou* dedicate o.s. to. ♦ **dévoué, e** *adj* devoted, dedicated (*à* to). ♦ **dévouement** *nm* devotion, dedication. **avec ~** devotedly.

dévoyer [devwaje] (8) **1** *vt* to lead astray. **2 se ~** *vpr* to go astray. ♦ **dévoyé, e** *adj, nm,f* delinquent.

dextérité [dɛksteʀite] *nf* skill, dexterity.

diabète [djabɛt] *nm* diabetes (*sg*). ♦ **diabétique** *adj, nmf* diabetic.
diable [djɑbl(ə)] *nm* **(a)** devil. **il a le ~ au corps** he is the very devil; **il est très ~** he is a real little devil; **tirer le ~ par la queue** to live from hand to mouth; **habiter au ~ vauvert** to live miles from anywhere; **il faisait un vent du ~** there was the devil of a wind; **il est menteur en ~** he is the devil of a liar; **ce ~ de temps** this wretched weather. **(b)** (*excl*) **D~!** well!; **qu'il aille au ~!** the devil take him!; **du courage que ~!** cheer up, dash it!; **pourquoi/quand ~ l'as-tu jeté?** why/when the devil did you throw it out?; **c'est bien le ~ si** it would be most unusual if; **ce n'est pas le ~!** it's not the end of the world! **(c)** (*enfant*) devil, rogue. (*personne*) **pauvre ~** poor devil; **grand ~** tall fellow; **ce n'est pas un mauvais ~** he's not a bad fellow. **(d)** (*chariot*) hand truck. (*jouet*) **~ (à ressort)** jack-in-the-box. ♦ **diablement*** *adv* dashed*. ♦ **diabolique** *adj* diabolical, devilish. ♦ **diaboliquement** *adv* diabolically.
diabolo [djabɔlo] *nm* (*jouet*) diabolo. (*boisson*) **~ menthe** mint and lemonade.
diacre [djakʀ(ə)] *nm* deacon.
diadème [djadɛm] *nm* (*lit, fig*) diadem; (*bijou*) tiara.
diagnostiquer [djagnɔstike] (1) *vt* (*lit, fig*) to diagnose. ♦ **diagnostic** *nm* diagnosis.
diagonal, e, *mpl* **-aux** [djagɔnal, o] *adj, nf* diagonal. **en ~e** diagonally; **lire en ~e** to skim through.
diagramme [djagʀam] *nm* (*schéma*) diagram; (*graphique*) chart, graph.
dialecte [djalɛkt(ə)] *nm* dialect. ♦ **dialectal, e,** *mpl* **-aux** *adj* dialectal.
dialectique [djalɛktik] *adj, nf* dialectic.
dialogue [djalɔg] *nm* (*gén*) dialogue; (*conversation*) conversation. **c'est un ~ de sourds** it's a dialogue of the deaf. ♦ **dialoguer** (1) *vi [amis]* to have a conversation; *[syndicats]* to have a dialogue.
diamant [djamɑ̃] *nm* (*gén*) diamond. ♦ **diamantaire** *nm* (*tailleur*) diamond-cutter; (*vendeur*) diamond merchant.
diamètre [djamɛtʀ(ə)] *nm* diameter. ♦ **diamétralement** *adv* diametrically.
diantre [djɑ̃tʀ(ə)] *excl* (†, *hum*) by Jove! (†, *hum*). **qui ~ ...?** who the devil ...?†. ♦ **diantrement** *adv* (†, *hum*) devilish†.
diapason [djapazɔ̃] *nm* (*gén*) diapason. **se mettre au ~ de qn** to get in tune with sb.
diaphane [djafan] *adj* diaphanous.
diaphragme [djafʀagm(ə)] *nm* (*gén*) diaphragm.
diapositive [djapozitiv] *nf* (*Phot*) slide.
diarrhée [djaʀe] *nf* diarrhœa.
diatribe [djatʀib] *nf* diatribe.
dichotomie [dikɔtɔmi] *nf* dichotomy.
dictateur [diktatœʀ] *nm* dictator. ♦ **dictatorial, e,** *mpl* **-aux** *adj* dictatorial. ♦ **dictature** *nf* dictatorship. (*fig*) **c'est de la ~!** this is tyranny!
dicter [dikte] (1) *vt lettre, condition* to dictate (*à* to); *volonté* to impose (*à* upon). **je n'aime pas qu'on me dicte ce que je dois faire!** I won't be dictated to! ♦ **dictée** *nf* dictation. **écrire sous la ~ de qn** to take down sb's dictation.
diction [diksjɔ̃] *nf* (*débit*) diction, delivery; (*art*) speech production.
dictionnaire [diksjɔnɛʀ] *nm* dictionary. **c'est un vrai ~** he's a walking encyclopaedia.
dicton [diktɔ̃] *nm* saying, dictum.
dièse [djɛz] *adj, nm* (*Mus*) sharp. **fa ~** F sharp.
diesel [djezɛl] *nm* diesel.
diète [djɛt] *nf* **(a)** (*Méd*) (*jeûne*) starvation diet; (*régime*) diet. **mettre qn à la ~** to put sb on a starvation diet. **(b)** (*Hist*) diet. ♦ **diététicien, -ienne** *nm,f* dietician. ♦ **diététique 1** *adj* dietary. **2** *nf* dietetics (*sg*).
dieu, *pl* **~x** [djø] *nm* **(a)** (*Myth, fig*) god. **(b) D~** God; **D~ le père** God the Father; **société sans D~** godless society; **le bon D~** the good Lord; **on lui donnerait le bon D~ sans confession** he looks as if butter wouldn't melt in his mouth. **(c)** (*locutions*) **mon D~!** my goodness!, goodness me!; **mon D~ oui** well yes; **D~ vous bénisse!** God bless you!; **à D~ ne plaise!, D~ m'en garde!** God forbid!; **D~ vous entende!** may God hear you!; **D~ seul le sait** God only *ou* alone knows; **D~ sait s'il est généreux!** God knows he is generous!; **D~ soit loué!** praise God! *ou* the Lord!; **D~ merci, il n'a pas plu** it didn't rain, thank goodness; **à-D~-vat!** (*entreprise risquée*) well, it's in God's hands; (*départ*) God be with you; **tu vas te taire bon D~!‡** for Christ's sake‡ will you be quiet!
diffamer [difame] (1) *vt* (*en paroles*) to slander; (*par écrit*) to libel. ♦ **diffamateur, -trice** *nm,f* slanderer. ♦ **diffamation** *nf*: **~(s)** slander; libel. ♦ **diffamatoire** *adj* slanderous; libellous.
différé, e [difeʀe] *adj* (*TV*) (pre-)recorded.
différemment [difeʀamɑ̃] *adv* differently.
différence [difeʀɑ̃s] *nf* (*gén*) difference. **~ d'âge** difference in age, age difference; **quelle ~ avec les autres!** what a difference from the others!; **ne pas faire de ~** to make no distinction (*entre* between); **à la ~ de** unlike; **à cette ~ que** with this difference that.
différencier [difeʀɑ̃sje] (7) **1** *vt* to differentiate. **2 se ~** *vpr* (*être différent de*) to differ (*de* from); (*devenir différent*) to become differentiated (*de* from); (*se rendre différent*) to differentiate o.s. (*de* from). ♦ **différenciation** *nf* differentiation.
différend [difeʀɑ̃] *nm* difference of opinion, disagreement.
différent, e [difeʀɑ̃, ɑ̃t] *adj* **(a)** (*dissemblable*) different (*de* from). **(b)** (*pl: divers*) different, various. **à ~es heures de la journée** at different times of day; **pour ~es raisons** for various reasons.
différentiel, -elle [difeʀɑ̃sjɛl] *adj, nm, nf* (*gén*) differential.
différer [difeʀe] (6) **1** *vi* **(a)** (*être dissemblable*) to differ, be different (*de* from, *en, par* in). **(b)** (*diverger*) to differ. **2** *vt* (*gén*) to postpone, put off; *jugement* to defer.
difficile [difisil] *adj* **(a)** *travail, problème* difficult; *situation* difficult, awkward, tricky*. **il a eu un moment ~** he went through a difficult *ou* hard *ou* trying time; **il a trouvé l'expédition ~** he found the expedition hard going *ou* heavy going; **~ à faire** difficult *ou* hard to do; **ils ont des fins de mois ~s** they find things difficult at the end of the month. **(b)** *personne* (*contrariant*) difficult, trying; (*exigeant*) fussy. **être ~ sur la nourriture** to be difficult *ou* fussy about one's food; **faire le ~** to be hard to please.
♦ **difficilement** *adv marcher, s'exprimer* with difficulty. **c'est ~ visible** it's difficult *ou* hard to see; **il gagne ~ sa vie** he finds it difficult *ou* hard to earn a living. ♦ **difficulté** *nf* (*gén*) difficulty. **avoir de la ~ à faire qch** to have difficulty (in) doing sth, find it difficult *ou* hard to do sth; **avoir des ~s financières** to be in financial difficulties; **faire des ~s pour accepter** to make *ou* raise difficulties about accepting; **être en ~** to be in difficulties *ou* in trouble; **mettre qn en ~** to put sb in a difficult position.
difforme [difɔʀm(ə)] *adj corps* deformed, misshapen; *visage, arbre* twisted. ♦ **difformité** *nf* deformity, misshapenness; twistedness. (*Méd*) **~s** deformities.
diffus, e [dify, yz] *adj* (*gén*) diffuse.
diffuser [difyze] (1) *vt lumière, chaleur* to diffuse; *livres* to distribute; *émission* to broadcast. **programme diffusé en direct** live broadcast *ou* programme. ♦ **diffuseur** *nm* (*Presse: distributeur*) distributor. ♦ **diffusion** *nf* diffusion; distribution; broadcasting.

digérer [diʒeʀe] (6) *vt aliment, connaissance* to digest; *insulte* to stomach*, put up with. ~ **bien/mal** to have a good/bad digestion. ♦ **digeste** *adj aliment* easily digested, digestible. ♦ **digestif, -ive 1** *adj* digestive. **2** *nm* (*liqueur*) liqueur. ♦ **digestion** *nf* digestion.

digital, e, *mpl* **-aux** [diʒital, o] **1** *adj* (*Anat*) digital. **2** *nf* digitalis.

digne [diɲ] *adj* (*auguste*) dignified; (*à la hauteur*) worthy. **son ~ fils** his worthy son; **~ de** worthy of; **~ d'éloges** praiseworthy; **~ de foi** trustworthy; **~ de pitié** pitiable; **~ d'envie** enviable; **il n'est pas ~ de vivre** he's not fit to live; (*lit, péj*) **tu es le ~ fils de ton père!** you're fit to be your father's son!; **avec une attitude peu ~ d'un juge** with an attitude ill-befitting a judge. ♦ **dignement** *adv se conduire* with dignity; *récompenser* fittingly, justly. ♦ **dignitaire** *nm* dignitary. ♦ **dignité** *nf* (*gén*) dignity. **la ~ de la personne humaine** human dignity.

digression [digʀesjɔ̃] *nf* digression.

digue [dig] *nf* (*gén*) dyke; (*pour protéger la côte*) sea wall; (*fig*) barrier.

dilapider [dilapide] (1) *vt* to squander, waste. ♦ **dilapidation** *nf* squandering, wasting.

dilater [dilate] (1) **1** *vt* (*gén*) to dilate; *métal, gaz* to cause to expand. **2 se ~** *vpr* to dilate; to expand. **se ~ la rate*** to split one's sides (laughing)*. ♦ **dilatation** *nf* dilation; expansion.

dilemme [dilɛm] *nm* dilemma.

dilettante [dilɛtɑ̃t] *nmf* (*en art*) dilettante; (*péj: amateur*) amateur. ♦ **dilettantisme** *nm* amateurishness.

diligence [diliʒɑ̃s] *nf* **(a)** (*empressement*) haste. **faire ~** to make haste. **(b)** (*soin*) diligence. **(c)** (*Hist: voiture*) stagecoach. ♦ **diligent, e** *adj* (*rapide*) speedy, prompt; (*assidu*) diligent.

diluer [dilɥe] (1) *vt liquide,* (*fig*) to dilute; *peinture* to thin down. ♦ **dilution** *nf* dilution; thinning down.

diluvienne [dilyvjɛn] *adj f pluie* torrential.

dimanche [dimɑ̃ʃ] *nm* Sunday. **le ~ de Pâques** Easter Sunday; **ses habits du ~** one's Sunday clothes, one's Sunday best; **peintre du ~** spare-time painter; **chauffeur du ~** Sunday driver; *V* **samedi.**

dime [dim] *nf* (*Hist*) tithe.

dimension [dimɑ̃sjɔ̃] *nf* **(a)** (*taille*) size. **avoir la même ~** to be the same size; **de grande/petite ~** large/small-sized; **une tâche à la ~ de son talent** a task equal to *ou* commensurate with one's talent. **(b)** (*mesures*) **~s** dimensions; **quelles sont les ~s de la pièce?** what are the dimensions *ou* measurements of the room?; **dans la plus grande ~** at the widest (*ou* longest) point; **à 2/3 ~s** 2/3 dimensional. **(c)** (*Philos*) dimension.

diminuer [diminɥe] (1) **1** *vt* **(a)** (*gén*) to reduce, decrease; *frais* to cut down; *prix* to bring down; *son* to lower, turn down; *plaisir, intérêt* to lessen, diminish. **ça l'a beaucoup diminué** this has greatly undermined his health; **c'est un homme très diminué** he has really gone downhill, he is not at all the man he was; **~ un employé** to cut *ou* reduce the salary of an employee. **(b)** (*dénigrer*) to belittle.

2 *vi* **(a)** *[violence, intensité]* to diminish; *[circulation]* to decrease; *[pluie]* to let up; *[orage, bruit]* to die down *ou* away. **~ d'intensité** to decrease in intensity, subside. **(b)** *[nombre]* to decrease, diminish; *[prix, valeur, pression]* to go down, fall, decrease; *[jours]* to grow shorter. **ça a diminué de volume** it has been reduced in volume.

♦ **diminutif, -ive** *adj, nm* diminutive. ♦ **diminution** *nf* **(a)** (*réduction*) reduction. **consentir une ~ à** to allow a reduction to. **(b)** (*décroissance*) diminishing; decrease. **une ~ du nombre des accidents** a decrease in the number of accidents.

dinde [dɛ̃d] *nf* turkey(hen). ♦ **dindon** *nm* turkey(cock). **être le ~ (de la farce)** to be made a fool of. ♦ **dindonneau,** *pl* **~x** *nm* turkey poult.

dîner [dine] (1) **1** *vi* to have dinner. **~ d'une tranche de pain** to have a slice of bread for dinner; **avoir qn à ~** to have sb for *ou* to dinner. **2** *nm* dinner; (*réception*) dinner party. ♦ **dînette** *nf* (*jeu*) doll's tea party. (*repas*) **on fera la ~*** we'll have a snack. ♦ **dîneur, -euse** *nm,f* diner.

dingue* [dɛ̃g] **1** *adj* nuts*, crazy* (*de* about). **2** *nmf* nutcase*, loony‡. **c'est un ~ de la voiture** he's crazy* *ou* nuts* about cars.

dinosaure [dinozɔʀ] *nm* dinosaur.

diocèse [djɔsɛz] *nm* diocese.

diphtérie [difteʀi] *nf* diphtheria. ♦ **diphtérique** *adj* diphtherial.

diphtongue [diftɔ̃g] *nf* diphthong.

diplomate [diplɔmat] **1** *adj* diplomatic. **2** *nmf* (*Pol*) diplomat; (*fig*) diplomatist. **3** *nm* (*Culin*) ≃ trifle. ♦ **diplomatie** *nf* (*Pol, fig*) diplomacy. ♦ **diplomatique** *adj* diplomatic.

diplôme [diplom] *nm* (*titre*) diploma; (*examen*) examination. **avoir des ~s** to have qualifications. ♦ **diplômé, e 1** *adj* qualified. **2** *nm,f* holder of a diploma.

dire [diʀ] (37) **1** *vt* **(a)** *paroles* to say. **'j'ai froid' dit-il** 'I'm cold' he said; **~ bonjour à qn** to say hullo to sb; **comme disent les Anglais** as the English put it *ou* say; **~ ce qu'on pense** to speak one's mind; **il n'a pas dit un mot** he hasn't said *ou* spoken *ou* uttered a single word; **qu'est-ce que les gens vont ~!** whatever will people say!; **il ne croyait pas si bien ~** he didn't know how right he was, he never spoke a truer word; **ce n'est pas une chose à ~** it is better left unsaid; **que dis-je!** what am I saying?

(b) ~ que to say that; **doit-il venir? – elle dit que oui** is he coming? – she says he is *ou* she says so; **la loi dit clairement que** the law says clearly that *ou* clearly states that; **l'espoir fait vivre, dit-on** you can live on hope, as the saying goes; **on le dit malade** he's rumoured to be ill; **il sait ce qu'il dit** he knows what he's talking about.

(c) ~ à qn que to tell sb that, say to sb that; **~ qch à qn** to tell sb sth; **j'ai qch à vous ~** there's sth I want to tell you; **~ la bonne aventure à qn** to tell sb's fortune; **il nous a dit sa joie** he told us of his joy, he told us how happy he was; **ce nom me dit qch** this name rings a bell; **dites-lui de partir/qu'il parte ce soir** tell him to go/that he must leave tonight; **fais ce qu'on te dit!** do as you are told!; **'méfie-toi' me dit-il** he told me *ou* he said to me, 'be cautious'.

(d) (*objecter*) to say (*à, contre* against). **tu n'as rien à ~, tu es bien servi** you can't complain, you've done all right.

(e) *poèmes, messe, prière* to say; *rôle* to speak; *mensonge, renseignement* to tell. **~ des bêtises** to talk nonsense.

(f) (*plaire*) **cela vous dit de sortir?** do you feel like going out?; **rien ne me dit en ce moment** I am not in the mood for anything just now; **cela ne me dit rien qui vaille** I don't like the look of that.

(g) *[chose]* (*indiquer*) to say, show. **son silence en dit long** his silence speaks for itself.

(h) (*penser*) to think. **qu'est-ce que tu dis de ma robe?** what do you think of *ou* how do you like my dress?; **qu'est-ce que vous dites de la question?** what do you think about the matter?; **qu'est-ce que vous diriez d'une promenade?** what would you say to a walk?, how about a walk?; **on dirait qu'il n'aime pas cette ville** he doesn't seem to like this town; **on dirait qu'il va pleuvoir** it looks like rain; **on dirait du poulet** it tastes like chicken; **on dirait du Brahms** it sounds like Brahms; **qui l'eût dit!** who would have thought it!

(i) (*décider*) **venez bientôt, disons demain** come soon, let's make it tomorrow *ou* let's say tomorrow; **il est dit que je ne gagnerai jamais** I'm destined never to win; **bon, voilà qui est dit** right, it's settled; **à l'heure dite** at the appointed time.

(j) (*admettre*) to say, admit. **il faut bien ~ que** I must say *ou* admit that; **disons-le, il nous ennuie** let's be frank, he bores us.

(k) (*locutions*) **X, dit le Chacal** X, known as the Jackal; **qui dit argent dit problèmes** money means problems; **tu l'as dit!** you've said it!; **ceci dit** having said this; **pour ainsi ~** so to speak; **comme qui dirait*** as you might say; **ou pour mieux ~** ... or, to put it another way ...; **dis donc!** (*à propos*) by the way; (*holà*) hey!; **comme dit l'autre*** as they say, so to speak; **pour tout ~** in fact; **je vous l'avais bien dit!** I told you so!; **que tu dis!‡** sez you!‡; **à qui le dites-vous!** you're telling ME!*; **cela va sans ~** it goes without saying; **à vrai ~** to tell (you) the truth; **il n'y a pas à ~** there's no doubt about it; **je ne vous dis que cela!** just let me tell you!; **on a beau ~** say what you like; **comment dirais-je** ... how shall I put it?; **c'est ~ s'il est content** that just shows you how pleased he is; **c'est beaucoup ~** that's saying a lot; **c'est peu ~** that's an understatement; **c'est (tout) ~** that (just) shows you; **c'est moi qui vous le dis** you take my word for it; **ce n'est pas pour ~, mais ...** (*se vanter*) I don't wish to boast but ...; (*se plaindre*) I don't wish to complain but ...; **c'est-à-~** that is to say; **c'est-à-~ que je ne le savais pas** well actually I didn't know; **entre nous soit dit** between the two of us *ou* you and me; **soit dit en passant** incidentally.

(l) (*avec faire, laisser, vouloir*) **faire ~ qch à qn** to send word of sth to sb; **faire ~ à qn de venir** to send for sb; **il ne se l'est pas fait ~ deux fois** he did not need to be told twice; **je ne lui ai pas fait ~** I didn't make him say it; **laisser ~** to let people talk; **je me suis laissé ~ que** I heard that, I was told that; **vouloir ~** to mean; **cette phrase ne veut rien ~** this sentence does not mean a thing.

2 se ~ *vpr* **(a) il se dit qu'il était tard** he said to himself that it was late; **il se dit malade** he claims to be ill; **elles se dirent au revoir** they said goodbye (to each other). **(b)** (*sens passif*) **cela ne se dit pas** it's not the sort of thing one says; **cela ne se dit plus** this expression is no longer used; **comment se dit ... en français?** what is the French for ...?

3 *nm* (*déclaration*) statement. **d'après ses ~s** according to him *ou* what he says.

direct, e [diʀɛkt, ɛkt(ə)] **1** *adj* (*gén*) direct. **il m'a parlé de manière très ~e** he spoke to me in a very direct *ou* straightforward way; **ses chefs ~s** his immediate superiors; **être en rapport ~ avec** to deal directly *ou* be in direct contact with; **il a pris une part très ~e à cette affaire** he was directly involved in this business; **ce train est ~ jusqu'à Lyon** this is a fast *ou* non-stop train to Lyons. **2** *nm* (*Rail*) express (train), fast train; (*Boxe*) jab. **~ du gauche** straight left; (*Rad, TV*) **c'est du ~** it's live; **en ~ de New York** live from New York.

directement [diʀɛktəmɑ̃] *adv* (*immédiatement*) straight, directly; (*personnellement*) directly; (*sans intermédiaire*) direct, straight; (*tout à fait*) completely. **il est ~ allé se coucher** he went straight *ou* directly to bed, he went to bed straight away; **tout ceci ne me concerne pas ~ mais ...** none of this concerns me directly but ...; **adressez-vous ~ au patron** apply to the boss direct *ou* in person; **~ contraire** completely contrary.

directeur, -trice [diʀɛktœʀ, tʀis] **1** *adj* (*dirigeant*) directing; *idée* leading, main; *principe* guiding. **2** *nm [banque, usine]* (*responsable*) manager; (*administrateur*) director; (*Admin*) head; (*Ciné, TV*) director. **~ (d'école)** headmaster, principal (*US*); (*Pol*) **~ de cabinet (d'un ministre)** principal private secretary; **~ de journal** newspaper editor. **3** *nf [entreprise]* manageress; (*propriétaire*) director; (*Admin*) head. **~trice d'école** headmistress, principal (*US*).

direction [diʀɛksjɔ̃] *nf* **(a)** (*lit, fig: sens*) direction. **dans quelle ~ est-il parti?** which way did he go?; **prendre la ~ de Paris** to go towards *ou* in the direction of Paris; **train en ~ de ...** train for *ou* going to ... . **(b)** (*gén*) running; *[firme]* management; *[journal]* editorship; *[parti]* leadership; *[opérations]* directing; *[recherches]* supervision. **on lui a confié la ~ des travaux** he has been put in charge of the work; **prendre la ~ de** *entreprise* to take over the running of; *opérations* to take charge *ou* control of. **(c)** (*fonction*) *[entreprise]* post of manager; *[école]* headship; *[journal]* editorship; (*Admin*) post of chief executive. (*personnel dirigeant*) **la ~** the management. **(d)** (*bureau*) director's *ou* manager's *ou* headmaster's *ou* editor's office. **(e)** (*service*) department. **la ~ du personnel** the personnel department. **(f)** (*Aut: mécanisme*) steering. **~ assistée** power assisted steering. ♦ **directorial, e,** *mpl* **-iaux** *adj* (*Comm, Ind*) managerial. **bureau ~** manager's *ou* director's *ou* headmaster's *ou* principal's (*US*) *etc* office.

directive [diʀɛktiv] *nf* directive.

directrice [diʀɛktʀis] *V* **directeur.**

dirigeable [diʀiʒabl(ə)] *adj, nm* airship.

dirigeant, e [diʀiʒɑ̃, ɑ̃t] **1** *adj classe* ruling. **2** *nm,f [entreprise]* manager; *[parti, pays]* leader.

diriger [diʀiʒe] (3) **1** *vt* **(a)** (*gén*) to run; *entreprise* to manage; *journal* to edit; *pays, parti* to lead; *opération* to direct; *recherches* to supervise, oversee; *enquête, débat* to lead; *orchestre* to conduct. (*Mil*) **~ le tir** to direct the firing; **cette idée dirige toute notre politique** this idea guides *ou* determines our whole policy. **(b)** *voiture, bateau* to steer; *avion* to pilot, fly. (*fig*) **bien ~ sa barque** to run one's affairs well. **(c)** (*acheminer*) *marchandises* to send; *personnes* to direct, send (*sur, vers* to). **(d)** *arme* to point, aim (*sur* at); *critique* to aim, direct (*contre* at); *lampe* to shine (*sur* on). **~ son attention sur qch** to turn one's attention to sth; **~ son regard sur qch** to look towards sth; **la flèche est dirigée vers la gauche** the arrow is pointing left *ou* to the left; **~ ses pas vers un lieu** to make one's way towards a place; **on devrait ~ ce garçon vers les sciences** we should steer this boy towards the sciences.

2 se ~ *vpr* **(a) se ~ vers** *lieu* to make one's way towards; *carrière* to turn towards; **l'avion se dirigea vers le nord** the plane flew *ou* headed northwards; **se ~ droit sur qch** to make a beeline *ou* make straight for sth. **(b)** (*se guider*) to find one's way. **se ~ au radar** to navigate by radar.

discerner [disɛʀne] (1) *vt* **(a)** (*distinguer*) *forme* to discern, make out; *bruit* to detect. **(b)** (*différencier*) to distinguish, discriminate (*entre* between). **~ le vrai du faux** to distinguish *ou* tell truth from falsehood. ♦ **discernable** *adj* discernible. ♦ **discernement** *nm* (*sagesse*) discernment; (*action*) distinguishing, discriminating. **sans ~** (*réflexion*) without proper judgment; (*distinction*) without distinction.

disciple [disipl(ə)] *nm* disciple.

discipliner [disipline] (1) *vt élèves* to discipline; *cheveux* to control. **se ~** to discipline oneself. ♦ **disciplinable** *adj* disciplinable. ♦ **disciplinaire** *adj* disciplinary. ♦ **disciplinairement** *adv* in a disciplinary way. ♦ **discipline** *nf* (*règle*) discipline; (*matière*) discipline, subject. ♦ **discipliné, e** *adj* well-disciplined.

discontinu, e [diskɔ̃tiny] *adj* (*gén*) discontinuous; *bruit* intermittent. (*Aut*) **bande jaune ~e** dotted yellow line. ♦ **discontinuer** (1) *vi*: **sans ~** without stopping, without a break. ♦ **discontinuité** *nf* discontinuity.

disconvenir [diskɔ̃vniʀ] (22) *vi*: **je n'en disconviens pas** I don't deny it.

discorder [diskɔʀde] (1) *vi [sons]* to be discordant; *[couleurs]* to clash; *[témoignages]* to conflict. ♦ **discordance** *nf [caractères]* conflict; *[sons]* discordance; *[couleurs]* clash. *[témoignages]* **présenter des ~s** to show discrepancies, conflict. ♦ **discordant, e** *adj* (*gén*) discordant; *caractères, opinions* conflicting; *bruits* harsh; *couleurs* clashing. ♦ **discorde** *nf* discord, dissension. **mettre la ~** to cause dissension.

discothèque [diskɔtɛk] *nf* (*collection*) record collection; (*meuble*) record cabinet; (*bâtiment*) record library; (*club*) disco.

discours [diskuʀ] *nm* **(a)** (*allocution*) speech. (*péj*) **tous ces beaux ~** all this fine talk; **suis-moi sans faire de ~!** follow me and no arguing; **perdre son temps en ~** to waste one's time talking. **(b)** (*Ling*) **(au) ~ direct/indirect** (in) direct/indirect speech. **(c)** (*Philos:traité*) discourse. ♦ **discourir** (11) *vi* (*faire un discours*) to discourse; (*péj*) to hold forth (*sur, de* upon); (*bavarder*) to chat.

discourtois, e [diskuʀtwa, waz] *adj* discourteous.

discréditer [diskʀedite] (1) **1** *vt* (*gén*) to discredit. **2 se ~** *vpr [personne]* to discredit o.s. ♦ **discrédit** *nm* discredit, disrepute. **tomber dans le ~** to fall into disrepute.

discret, -ète [diskʀɛ, ɛt] *adj* **(a)** (*réservé, silencieux*) discreet. **(b)** (*timide, neutre*) *personne* unassuming; *maquillage, regard* discreet; *vêtement* sober, plain; *couleur, endroit* quiet; *lumière* subdued. **'envoi ~'** 'sent under plain cover'. ♦ **discrètement** *adv* discreetly; soberly; quietly. **il a ~ fait allusion à** he made a discreet allusion to. ♦ **discrétion** *nf* discretion; sobriety; plainness; (*discernement*) discretion. **vin** *etc* **à ~** unlimited wine *etc*.

discrimination [diskʀiminɑsjɔ̃] *nf* discrimination. ♦ **discriminatoire** *adj mesures* discriminatory. ♦ **discriminer** (1) *vt* to discriminate.

disculper [diskylpe] (1) **1** *vt* to exonerate (*de* from). **2 se ~** *vpr* to exonerate o.s. (*auprès de qn* in sb's eyes). ♦ **disculpation** *nf* exoneration.

discuter [diskyte] (1) **1** *vt* **(a)** (*gén*) to discuss; *projet de loi* to debate; *prix* to argue about. **(b)** (*contester*) *ordre* to question, dispute. **théorie très discutée** very controversial theory; **ça se discute** that's debatable. **(c) ~ le coup*** (*parler*) to have a chat; (*parlementer*) to argue away. **2** *vi* (*conférer*) to confer; (*parler*) to talk; (*parlementer, protester*) to argue (*avec* with). **~ de qch** to discuss sth; **j'en ai discuté avec lui** I have discussed the matter *ou* talked the matter over with him. ♦ **discussion** *nf* (*gén*) discussion; (*débat*) debate; (*pourparlers*) discussion, talks; (*conversation*) talk; (*querelle*) argument. **suis-moi et pas de ~s** follow me and no argument. ♦ **discutable** *adj* debatable, questionable.

disette [dizɛt] *nf* (*manque*) scarcity, shortage; (*famine*) food shortage.

diseuse [dizøz] *nf*: **~ de bonne aventure** fortune-teller.

disgrâce [disgʀɑs] *nf* disgrace. **tomber en ~** to fall into disgrace. ♦ **disgracier** (7) *vt* to disgrace.

disgracieux, -ieuse [disgʀasjø, jøz] *adj démarche* awkward, ungainly; *visage* ill-favoured; *forme* unsightly.

disjoindre [disʒwɛ̃dʀ(ə)] (49) **1** *vt planches* to take apart; *problèmes* to separate. **2 se ~** *vpr* to come apart *ou* loose.

disjoncteur [disʒɔ̃ktœʀ] *nm* (*Élec*) circuit breaker.

disloquer [dislɔke] (1) **1** *vt* **(a)** *bras* to dislocate. **(b)** *machine, cortège, empire* to break up. **2 se ~** *vpr* **(a) se ~ le bras** to dislocate one's arm. **(b)** *[meuble]* to come apart; *[cortège]* to disperse, break up. ♦ **dislocation** *nf* dislocation; breaking up; dispersal.

disparaître [dispaʀɛtʀ(ə)] (57) *vi* **(a)** (*gén*) to disappear, vanish. **le fuyard disparut dans la foule** the fugitive disappeared *ou* vanished into the crowd; **~ discrètement** to slip away quietly; **~ furtivement** to sneak away *ou* out; **il a disparu de son domicile** he has gone missing *ou* has disappeared from home. **(b)** (*mourir*) *[race, coutume]* to die out; *[personne]* to die; *[navire]* to sink, be lost. **~ en mer** to be lost at sea; (*Naut*) **~ corps et biens** to go down with all hands. **(c) faire ~** *tache, obstacle* to remove; *personne* to get rid of; *crainte* to dispel; **cela a fait ~ la douleur/la rougeur** it made the pain/red mark go away, it got rid of the pain/all trace of the red mark; **faire ~ un objet** *[prestidigitateur]* to make an object vanish; *[voleur]* to conceal an object; (*enlever*) to remove an object; (*jeter*) to dispose of *ou* get rid of an object.

disparate [dispaʀat] *adj éléments* disparate; *couple* ill-assorted. ♦ **disparité** *nf* disparity (*de* in); ill-assortedness.

disparition [dispaʀisjɔ̃] *nf* (*gén*) disappearance; *[soleil]* setting; *[tache, obstacle]* removal; *[objet, bateau]* loss; (*mort*) death.

disparu, e [dispaʀy] **1** *adj époque* bygone, vanished; *bonheur* lost, departed; (*mort*) *personne* dead; *coutume* vanished. **il a été porté ~** he has been reported missing; **marin ~ en mer** sailor lost at sea. **2** *nm,f* (*mort*) dead person; (*manquant*) missing person. **le cher ~** the dear departed.

dispendieux, -ieuse [dispɑ̃djø, jøz] *adj* extravagant.

dispensaire [dispɑ̃sɛʀ] *nm* community clinic.

dispenser [dispɑ̃se] (1) **1** *vt* **(a)** (*exempter*) to exempt (*de faire* from doing, *de qch* from sth). **dispensez-moi de sa vue** spare me the sight of him; **se faire ~** to get exempted. **(b)** *bienfaits, lumière* to dispense. **~ à qn son dévouement** to lavish one's devotion on sb; (*Méd*) **~ des soins à un malade** to give medical care to a patient. **2 se ~** *vpr*: **se ~ de** *corvée* to avoid, get out of; *remarque* to refrain from making; **se ~ de faire qch** to get out of doing sth; **il peut se ~ de travailler** he doesn't need to work. ♦ **dispense** *nf* (*exemption*) exemption (*de* from); (*permission*) special permission; (*Rel*) dispensation (*de* from).

disperser [dispɛʀse] (1) **1** *vt papiers* to scatter, spread about; *brouillard* to disperse; *collection* to break up; *foule, ennemi* to scatter, disperse; *ses efforts* to dissipate. **tous nos amis sont maintenant dispersés** all our friends are scattered now. **2 se ~** *vpr [foule]* to scatter, disperse; *[élève]* to dissipate one's efforts. ♦ **dispersé, e** *adj habitat* scattered; *esprit* unselective; *travail* disorganized. ♦ **dispersion** *nf* scattering; dispersal; breaking up; dissipation; (*Chim, Phys*) dispersion. **évitez la ~ dans votre travail** don't attempt to do too many things at once.

disponible [dispɔnibl(ə)] *adj* **(a)** *livre, place* available. **je ne suis pas ~ ce soir** I'm not free tonight. **(b)** *auditoire* receptive. ♦ **disponibilité** *nf* availability; receptiveness. (*Fin*) **~s** liquid assets; (*Admin*) **mettre en ~** *fonctionnaire* to grant leave of absence to.

dispos, e [dispo, oz] *adj personne* refreshed. **avoir l'esprit ~** to have a fresh mind.

disposer [dispoze] (1) **1** *vt* **(a)** (*mettre*) to place, set, lay; (*arranger*) to arrange. **(b) ~ qn à faire/à qch** (*engager à*) to dispose *ou* incline sb to do/towards sth; (*préparer à*) to prepare sb to do/for sth. **2** *vi* (*partir*) to leave. **vous pouvez ~** you may leave. **3 ~ de** *vt indir argent, moyens* to have (available *ou* at one's disposal). **il disposait de quelques heures** he had a few hours to spare;

vous pouvez en ~ you can use it; **il dispose de ses amis de manière abusive** he takes advantage of his friends; **droit des peuples à ~ d'eux-mêmes** right of nations to self-determination. **4 se ~** *vpr*: **se ~ à faire** (*se préparer à*) to prepare to do, be about to do. ♦ **disposé, e** *adj* **(a) être ~ à faire** to be disposed *ou* prepared to do; **bien/mal ~** in a good/bad mood; **bien/mal ~ à l'égard de** *ou* **pour** *ou* **envers qn** well-/ill-disposed towards sb. **(b)** *terrain* situated. **bien/mal ~** *pièces, vitrine* well-/badly-laid-out.

dispositif [dispozitif] *nm* **(a)** (*mécanisme*) device. **(b)** (*moyens*) plan of action. **~ de défense** defence system; **un important ~ (policier) a été mis en place** a large police operation was set up. **(c)** (*Jur*) *[jugement]* pronouncement; *[loi]* purview.

disposition [dispozisjɔ̃] *nf* **(a)** *[meubles]* arrangement; *[invités]* placing; *[terrain]* situation; *[pièces]* layout. **(b)** (*usage*) disposal. **mettre qch/être à la ~ de qn** to put sth/be at sb's disposal; **mis à la ~ de la justice** handed over to the law. **(c)** (*mesures*) **~s** (*préparatifs*) arrangements; (*précautions*) measures, steps; **prendre des** *ou* **ses ~s** to make arrangements. **(d)** (*humeur*) mood, frame of mind. **être dans de bonnes ~s pour faire qch** to be in the right mood to do sth; **être dans de bonnes ~s à l'égard de qn** to feel well-disposed towards sb; **est-il toujours dans les mêmes ~s à l'égard de ce projet?** does he still feel the same way about this plan? **(e)** (*aptitude*) **~s** aptitude, natural ability; **avoir des ~s pour les langues** to have a special aptitude for *ou* a gift for languages. **(f)** (*tendance*) tendency (*à* to). **(g)** (*Jur*) clause. **~s testamentaires** provisions of a will.

disproportion [disprɔpɔrsjɔ̃] *nf* disproportion (*de* in). ♦ **disproportionné, e** *adj* *objet* disproportionately large. **~ à** disproportionate to, out of all proportion with.

disputer [dispyte] (1) **1** *vt* **(a) ~ qch/qn à qn** to fight with sb for *ou* over sth/sb; **elle essaya de lui ~ la gloire de son invention** she tried to rob him of the glory of his invention; **le ~ en beauté à qn** to rival sb in beauty. **(b)** *combat* to fight; *match* to play. **(c)** (*: *gronder*) to tell off*. **se faire ~** to get a telling-off* (*par* from). **2 se ~** *vpr* **(a)** (*se quereller*) to quarrel, have an argument (*avec* with). **(b)** *objet* to fight over; *poste* to contest. ♦ **dispute** *nf* argument, quarrel. ♦ **disputé, e** *adj* *match* close, closely fought.

disquaire [diskɛʀ] *nm* record-dealer.

disqualifier [diskalifje] (7) *vt* (*Sport*) to disqualify; (*fig: discréditer*) to bring discredit on. ♦ **disqualification** *nf* disqualification.

disque [disk(ə)] *nm* (*gén, Méd*) disc; (*Sport*) discus; (*Mus*) record.

dissection [disɛksjɔ̃] *nf* dissection.

dissemblable [disɑ̃blabl(ə)] *adj* dissimilar (*de* to). ♦ **dissemblance** *nf* dissimilarity (*de* in).

disséminer *vt*, **se ~** *vpr* [disemine] (1) to scatter, spread (out). ♦ **dissémination** *nf* (*action*) scattering, spreading; (*état*) dispersal.

dissension [disɑ̃sjɔ̃] *nf* dissension.

dissentiment [disɑ̃timɑ̃] *nm* disagreement.

disséquer [diseke] (6) *vt* (*lit, fig*) to dissect.

disserter [disɛʀte] (1) *vi*: **~ sur** (*parler*) to speak on; (*écrire*) to write an essay on; (*péj*) to hold forth about. ♦ **dissertation** *nf* (*Scol, hum*) essay.

dissidence [disidɑ̃s] *nf* (*Pol*) dissidence; (*Rel*) dissent; (*divergence*) disagreement, dissidence. ♦ **dissident, e 1** *adj* (*Pol*) dissident; (*Rel*) dissenting. **2** *nm,f* (*Pol*) dissident; (*Rel*) dissenter.

dissimilitude [disimilityd] *nf* dissimilarity.

dissimuler [disimyle] (1) **1** *vt* to conceal, hide (*à qn* from sb). **je ne vous dissimulerai pas que** I won't disguise *ou* conceal the fact that; **savoir ~** to be good at pretending. **2 se ~** *vpr* to conceal *ou* hide o.s. ♦ **dissimulateur, -trice 1** *adj* dissembling. **2** *nm,f* dissembler. ♦ **dissimulation** *nf* (*duplicité*) dissimulation; (*action de cacher*) concealment. ♦ **dissimulé, e** *adj* *caractère, enfant* secretive.

dissiper [disipe] (1) **1** *vt* **(a)** *fumée* to dispel; *nuage* to disperse; *soupçon, crainte* to dispel; *malentendu* to clear up. **(b)** *fortune* to dissipate, squander; *jeunesse* to waste. **(c) ~ qn** (*corrompre*) to lead sb astray; (*distraire*) to distract sb. **2 se ~** *vpr* **(a)** *[fumée]* to drift away; *[nuages]* to disperse; *[brouillard]* to clear, lift; *[inquiétude]* to vanish; *[malaise]* to disappear, wear off. **(b)** *[élève]* to misbehave; *[personne]* to lead a dissolute *ou* dissipated life. ♦ **dissipation** *nf* **(a)** (*indiscipline*) misbehaviour; (*débauche*) dissipation. **(b)** *[fortune]* squandering, dissipation. **(c)** *[fumée, nuage]* dispersal; *[brouillard]* clearing, lifting; *[craintes]* dispelling.

dissocier [disɔsje] (7) **1** *vt* to dissociate. **2 se ~** *vpr [éléments]* to break up, split up. (*fig*) **se ~ de qn** to dissociate o.s. from sb. ♦ **dissociable** *adj* *molécules* dissociable; *problèmes* separable. ♦ **dissociation** *nf* dissociation.

dissolu, e [disɔly] *adj* dissolute.

dissolution [disɔlysjɔ̃] *nf* (*Jur*) dissolution; *[groupe]* breaking-up; *[empire, unité]* crumbling. **prononcer la ~ de** to dissolve; *[sucre etc]* **tourner jusqu'à ~ complète** stir until it has completely dissolved.

dissolvant, e [disɔlvɑ̃, ɑ̃t] **1** *adj* solvent. **2** *nm* solvent; (*pour ongles*) nail varnish remover.

dissonance [disɔnɑ̃s] *nf*: **~(s)** dissonance. ♦ **dissonant, e** *adj* *sons* dissonant; *couleurs* clashing.

dissoudre [disudʀ(ə)] (51) **1** *vt* **(a)** (*aussi:* **faire ~**) *sel* to dissolve. **(b)** (*Jur, Pol*) to dissolve; *parti* to break up. **2 se ~** *vpr* **(a)** *[sel]* to dissolve. **(b)** *[association]* to break up.

dissuader [disɥade] (1) *vt* to dissuade (*de qch* from sth, *de faire* from doing). ♦ **dissuasion** *nf* dissuasion.

dissymétrie [disimetʀi] *nf* dissymmetry. ♦ **dissymétrique** *adj* dissymmetrical.

distance [distɑ̃s] *nf* **(a)** (*lit*) distance. **à quelle ~ est la gare?** how far away is the station?, what's the distance to the station?; **habiter à une grande ~/à quelques kilomètres de ~** to live a long way away/a few kilometres away (*de* from); **à 2 ans de ~ je m'en souviens encore** 2 years later I can still remember it; **nés à quelques années de ~** born within a few years of one another. **(b)** (*fig: écart*) gap. **(c)** (*locutions*) **garder ses ~s** to keep one's distance (*vis à vis de* from); **tenir qn à ~** to keep sb at a distance *ou* at arm's length; **se tenir à ~** to keep one's distance; **faire qch à ~** to do sth at *ou* from a distance; **mettre en marche à ~** *appareil* to start up by remote control; **~ focale** focal length. ♦ **distancer** (3) *vt* *voiture* to outdistance, leave behind; *concurrent* to outstrip, leave behind. **se laisser ~** to be left behind. ♦ **distant, e** *adj* *lieu, événement* distant, far-off; *attitude* distant, aloof. **une ville ~e de 10 km** a town 10 km away.

distendre [distɑ̃dʀ(ə)] (41) **1** *vt* *peau* to distend; *muscle*, (*fig*) *lien* to strain. **2 se ~** *vpr [lien]* to slacken; *[peau]* to distend. ♦ **distension** *nf* distension; slackening.

distiller [distile] (1) *vt* (*lit*) to distil; (*fig*) to exude. ♦ **distillateur** *nm* distiller. ♦ **distillation** *nf* distillation, distilling. ♦ **distillerie** *nf* (*usine*) distillery; (*industrie*) distilling.

distinct, e [distɛ̃(kt), distɛ̃kt(ə)] *adj* (*gén*) distinct (*de* from). ♦ **distinctement** *adv* distinctly. ♦ **distinctif, -ive** *adj* distinctive. ♦ **distinction** *nf* (*gén*) distinction. **faire la ~ entre** to make a distinction between.

distinguer [distɛ̃ge] (1) **1** *vt* **(a)** *objet, bruit* to make out, distinguish. ~ **qn dans la foule** to pick out *ou* spot sb in the crowd; **il distingue mal sans lunettes** he can't see very well without his glasses. **(b)** (*différencier*) to distinguish. ~ **une chose d'avec une autre** to distinguish *ou* tell one thing from another. **(c)** (*rendre différent*) to distinguish, set apart (*de* from). **(d)** (*choisir*) to single out; (*honorer*) to honour. **2 se** ~ *vpr* **(a)** (*différer*) to be distinguished (*de* from). **ces objets se distinguent par leur couleur** these objects can be distinguished by their colour; **il se distingue par son accent** his accent makes him stand out. **(b)** (*réussir*) to distinguish o.s. **il se distingue par son absence** he is conspicuous by his absence. ♦ **distinguable** *adj* distinguishable. ♦ **distingué, e** *adj* distinguished. **veuillez agréer l'expression de ma considération** ~**e** yours faithfully. ♦ **distinguo** *nm* (*nuance*) distinction.

distordre *vt*, **se** ~ *vpr* [distɔʀdʀ(ə)] (41) to twist.

distorsion [distɔʀsjɔ̃] *nf* (*gén*) distortion; (*Écon*) imbalance.

distraction [distʀaksjɔ̃] *nf* **(a)** (*inattention*) absent-mindedness. **j'ai eu une** ~ my concentration lapsed. **(b)** (*passe-temps*) distraction, amusement. **la** ~ recreation. **(c)** (*Jur: vol*) abstraction.

distraire [distʀɛʀ] (50) **1** *vt* (*divertir*) to entertain, amuse; (*déranger*) to distract, divert; (*voler*) to abstract (*de* from). ~ **qn de son chagrin** to take sb's mind off his grief. **2 se** ~ *vpr* to amuse o.s., enjoy o.s. ♦ **distrait, e** *adj* *personne* absent-minded; *attitude* inattentive, abstracted. ♦ **distraitement** *adv* absent-mindedly, abstractedly. ♦ **distrayant, e** *adj* entertaining.

distribuer [distʀibɥe] (1) *vt* **(a)** (*donner*) (*gén*) to distribute; *gâteau* to share out; *courrier* to deliver; *travail, rôle* to allocate, assign; *cartes* to deal (out); *ordres* to hand out; *saluts, enseignement* to dispense (*à* to). **(b)** (*disposer*) (*gén*) to distribute; *emploi du temps* to arrange; *plan de maison* to lay out. **savoir** ~ **son temps** to know how to divide up one's time. **(c)** (*gén, Comm: acheminer*) to distribute; *eau* to supply. ♦ **distributeur, -trice 1** *nm,f* distributor. **2** *nm* (*appareil*) machine; (*Aut*) distributor. ~ **automatique** slot machine. ♦ **distribution** *nf* **(a)** distribution; sharing out; delivery; allocation; deal; arrangement; layout; supply. ~ **gratuite** free gifts; ~ **des prix** prize giving. **(b)** (*Ciné, Théât: acteurs*) cast. **(c)** (*Comm, Aut, Tech*) distribution.

district [distʀik(t)] *nm* district.

dithyrambique [ditiʀɑ̃bik] *adj* *éloges* extravagant.

diurétique [djyʀetik] *adj, nm* diuretic.

diurne [djyʀn(ə)] *adj* diurnal.

divaguer [divage] (1) *vi* (*délirer*) to ramble; (*) to rave. ♦ **divagation** *nf* rambling; (*) raving.

divan [divɑ̃] *nm* divan.

diverger [divɛʀʒe] (3) *vi* to diverge. ♦ **divergence** *nf* divergence. ♦ **divergent, e** *adj* divergent.

divers, e [divɛʀ, ɛʀs(ə)] *adj* **(a)** (*pl*) (*varié*) diverse, varied; (*différent*) different, various; (*plusieurs*) various, several. **frais** ~ miscellaneous expenses. **(b)** (*changeant*) varied. ♦ **diversement** *adv* in various ways.

diversifier [divɛʀsifje] (7) **1** *vt* *exercices* to vary; *production* to diversify. **2 se** ~ *vpr* to diversify.

diversion [divɛʀsjɔ̃] *nf* diversion. **faire** ~ to create a diversion.

diversité [divɛʀsite] *nf* (*variété*) variety, diversity; (*divergence*) diversity.

divertir [divɛʀtiʀ] (2) **1** *vt* (*amuser*) to amuse, entertain, divert; (*voler*) to divert; (†: *détourner*) to distract (*de* from). **2 se** ~ *vpr* to amuse o.s., enjoy o.s. **se** ~ **l'esprit** to occupy one's mind; **se** ~ **de qn** to laugh at sb. ♦ **divertissant, e** *adj* amusing, entertaining. ♦ **divertissement** *nm* (*passe-temps*) distraction, entertainment, amusement; (*Mus*) divertissement; (*Jur: vol*) misappropriation; (*Philos*) distraction. **le** ~ recreation.

dividende [dividɑ̃d] *nm* (*Fin, Math*) dividend.

divin, e [divɛ̃, in] *adj* (*gén*) divine; (*: *excellent*) divine, heavenly. **notre** ~ **Sauveur** our Holy Saviour. ♦ **divinement** *adv* divinely. ♦ **divinité** *nf* divinity.

diviniser [divinize] (1) *vt* to deify. ♦ **divinisation** *nf* deification.

diviser [divize] (1) **1** *vt* (*gén, Math*) to divide; *tâche, ressources* to share out; *gâteau* to divide up. ~ **en 3/en 3 parties** to divide *ou* split in 3/into 3 parts; ~ **pour régner** divide and rule; **les historiens sont divisés à ce sujet** historians are divided on this subject. **2 se** ~ *vpr* (*se scinder*) to split up, divide (*en* into); (*se ramifier*) to fork, divide. **se** ~ **en 3 chapitres** to be divided into 3 chapters. ♦ **diviseur** *nm* (*Math*) divisor; (*personne*) divisive influence. ♦ **divisibilité** *nf* divisibility. ♦ **divisible** *adj* divisible. ♦ **division** *nf* (*gén*) division; (*dans un parti*) split, rift. ~ **du travail** division of labour; **semer la** ~ to sow discord (*entre* among); (*Math*) **faire une** ~ to do a division (sum).

divorcer [divɔʀse] (3) *vi* **(a)** (*Jur*) to get divorced. ~ **d'avec sa femme** to divorce one's wife. **(b)** (*fig*) to break (*d'avec* with). ♦ **divorce** *nm* (*lit, fig*) divorce (*d'avec* from). **obtenir le** ~ to get a divorce. ♦ **divorcé, e 1** *adj* (*lit, fig*) divorced (*de* from). **2** *nm,f* divorcee.

divulguer [divylge] (1) *vt* to divulge, disclose. ♦ **divulgation** *nf* disclosure.

dix [dis] **1** *adj inv, nm* ten. **2:** ~**-huit** *adj inv, nm* eighteen; ~**-huitième** *adj, nmf* eighteenth; ~**-neuf** *adj inv, nm* nineteen; ~**-neuvième** *adj, nmf* nineteenth; ~**-sept** *adj inv, nm* seventeen; ~**-septième** *adj, nmf* seventeenth. ♦ **dixième** *adj, nmf* tenth; (*de la Loterie*) *tenth share in a ticket.* ♦ **dixièmement** *adv* tenthly. ♦ **dizaine** *nf* (*dix*) ten; (*environ dix*) about ten; *V* **soixantaine.**

do [do] *nm inv* (*note*) C; (*chanté*) doh.

docile [dɔsil] *adj* docile; *cheveux* manageable. ♦ **docilement** *adv* docilely. ♦ **docilité** *nf* docility.

dock [dɔk] *nm* (*bassin*) dock; (*bâtiment*) warehouse. ♦ **docker** [dɔkɛʀ] *nm* docker.

docteur [dɔktœʀ] *nm* (*gén, Univ*) doctor (*ès, en* of). **le** ~ **Lebrun** Dr Lebrun. ♦ **doctorat** *nm* doctorate (*ès, en* in). ~ **de 3e cycle** ≃ Ph.D. ♦ **doctoresse** *nf* lady doctor.

doctrine [dɔktʀin] *nf* doctrine. ♦ **doctrinaire 1** *adj* (*dogmatique*) doctrinaire; (*sentencieux*) sententious. **2** *nmf* doctrinarian. ♦ **doctrinal, e,** *mpl* **-aux** *adj* doctrinal.

document [dɔkymɑ̃] *nm* document. ♦ **documentaire 1** *adj* *intérêt* documentary. **2** *nm* (*film*) documentary (film). ♦ **documentaliste** *nmf* archivist. ♦ **documentation** *nf* documentation, literature. ♦ **documenté, e** *adj* *personne* well-informed; *livre* well-documented. ♦ **se documenter** (1) *vpr* to gather information *ou* material (*sur* on, about).

dodeliner [dɔdline] (1) *vi*: **il dodelinait de la tête** his head kept nodding (gently) forward.

dodo* [dodo] *nm* bye-byes*, sleep. **aller au** ~ to go to bye-byes*.

dodu, e [dɔdy] *adj* (*gén*) plump; *enfant, joue* chubby.

doge [dɔʒ] *nm* doge.

dogme [dɔgm(ə)] *nm* (*lit, fig*) dogma. ♦ **dogmatique** *adj* dogmatic.

dogue [dɔg] *nm* (*Zool*) mastiff.

doigt [dwa] *nm* **(a)** *[main, gant]* finger; *[animal]* digit. ~ **de pied** toe; **se mettre les** ~**s dans le nez** to pick one's nose. **(b)** (*mesure*) inch. **un** ~ **de vin** a drop of wine; **il a été à deux** ~**s de se tuer** he was within an ace *ou* an inch *ou* a hairsbreadth of being killed. **(c)** (*locutions*) **avoir des ~s de fée** *[ménagère]* to have nimble fingers; *[infirmière]* to have gentle hands; **il ne sait rien faire de ses dix ~s** he's a good-for-nothing; **faire marcher qn au ~ et à l'œil** to have sb at one's beck and call; **se mettre le ~ dans l'œil*** to be kidding o.s.*; **il n'a pas levé le petit ~ pour nous aider** he didn't lift a finger to help us; **son petit ~ le lui a dit** a little bird told him; **mettre le ~ sur le problème** to put one's finger on the problem; **mettre le ~ dans l'engrenage** to get involved in something; **je le ferais les ~s dans le nez*** I could do it standing on my head. ♦ **doigté** *nm [chirurgien]* touch; (*fig: tact*) tact. ♦ **doigtier** *nm* fingerstall.

doléances [dɔleɑ̃s] *nfpl* (*plaintes*) complaints; (*réclamations*) grievances.

dolent, e [dɔlɑ̃, ɑ̃t] *adj* doleful.

dollar [dɔlaʀ] *nm* dollar.

domaine [dɔmɛn] *nm* (*propriété*) estate, domain, property; (*sphère*) domain, sphere.

dôme [dom] *nm* dome. (*fig*) **~ de verdure** canopy of foliage.

domestique [dɔmɛstik] **1** *nmf* servant. **2** *adj travaux* domestic, household; *soucis* domestic, family; (*Zool*) domestic, domesticated. ♦ **domesticité** *nf* (*personnel*) domestic staff, household. ♦ **domestiquer** (1) *vt animal* to domesticate; *marée* to harness.

domicile [dɔmisil] *nm* home, domicile (*Admin*); (*adresse*) address. **le ~ conjugal** the marital home; **dernier ~ connu** last known address; **travailler à ~** to work at home; **'livraisons à ~'** 'deliveries'. ♦ **domiciliation** *nf* domiciliation. ♦ **domicilier** (7) *vt chèque* to domicile. **être domicilié** to be domiciled (*Admin*), have one's home (*à* in).

dominant, e [dɔminɑ̃, ɑ̃t] **1** *adj* (*gén*) dominant; *opinion, vent* prevailing; *idée, préoccupation* main, chief; *position* dominating. **2** *nf* (*caractéristique*) dominant characteristic; (*couleur*) dominant colour; (*Mus*) dominant.

dominateur, -trice [dɔminatœʀ, tʀis] *adj caractère* domineering; *geste* imperious; *pays* dominating; *passion* ruling.

domination [dɔminɑsjɔ̃] *nf* domination. **les pays sous la ~ britannique** countries under British rule *ou* dominion; **exercer sa ~ sur qn** to exert one's influence on sb; **~ de soi-même** self-control, self-domination.

dominer [dɔmine] (1) **1** *vt* (*gén*) to dominate; *concurrent* to outclass, surpass; *sentiment, situation* to master; (*par la taille*) to tower above. **~ le monde** to rule the world; **~ ses élèves** to keep control over one's pupils; **parler fort pour ~ le bruit de la rue** to speak loudly to overcome the noise from the street; **ce problème domine tous les autres** this problem overshadows all others; **se ~** to control o.s., keep o.s. under control; **la préoccupation que domine toute son œuvre** the preoccupation which dominates his whole work; **rocher qui domine la mer** rock which overlooks the sea. **2** *vi* **(a)** *[orateur, concurrent]* to be in the dominant position; *[équipe]* to be on top. (*fig*) **~ de la tête et des épaules** to be head and shoulders above the others. **(b)** (*prédominer*) (*gén*) to dominate; *[idée, théorie]* to prevail. **c'est le jaune qui domine** it is yellow which stands out *ou* which is the dominant colour.

dominion [dɔminjɔn] *nm* (*Brit: état*) dominion.

domino [dɔmino] *nm* (*gén*) domino. (*jeu*) **les ~s** dominoes (*sg*).

dommage [dɔmaʒ] **1** *nm* (*préjudice*) harm, injury. (*dégât*) **~(s)** damage; **causer un ~ à qn** to do sb harm; **c'est ~!, quel ~!** what a pity! *ou* shame! **2: ~(s) corporel(s)** physical injury; **~s de guerre** war damages; **~s et intérêts** damages. ♦ **dommageable** *adj* harmful, injurious (*à* to).

dompter [dɔ̃te] (1) *vt animal, nature* to tame; *cheval* to break in; *fauve* to train; *rebelles* to subdue; *passions* to master, control. ♦ **domptage** *nm* taming. ♦ **dompteur, -euse** *nm,f* (*gén*) trainer. **~ de lions** liontamer; **~ de chevaux** horsebreaker.

don [dɔ̃] *nm* **(a)** (*aptitude*) gift, talent (*pour* for). **elle a le ~ de m'énerver** she has a knack of getting on my nerves; **ça n'a pas eu le ~ de lui plaire** it didn't happen to please him. **(b)** (*cadeau*) gift; (*offrande*) donation. **faire ~ de** *fortune* to donate; *livre* to give (as a present); **le ~ de soi** self-sacrifice. ♦ **donataire** *nmf* donee. ♦ **donateur, -trice** *nm,f* donor. ♦ **donation** *nf* donation.

donc [dɔ̃k] *conj* **(a)** (*par conséquent*) therefore, thus; (*après digression, marquant la surprise*) so, then. **c'était ~ un espion?** he was a spy then?, so he was a spy? **(b)** (*de renforcement*) **allons ~!** come on!; **tais-toi ~!** do be quiet!; **regardez ~ ça** just look at that; **dis ~** (*question*) tell me, I say; (*menace*) look here.

donjon [dɔ̃ʒɔ̃] *nm* keep.

don Juan [dɔ̃ʒɥɑ̃] *nm* Don Juan.

donnant, e [dɔnɑ̃, ɑ̃t] *adj* (†) generous. **c'est ~, ~** it's fifty-fifty.

donne [dɔn] *nf* (*Cartes*) deal. **mauvaise ~** misdeal.

donné, e [dɔne] **1** *adj lieu, date* given, fixed. **étant ~ la situation** in view of *ou* given *ou* considering the situation. **2** *nf* (*Math, Sci*) datum; (*gén*) fact. **~es** data; facts.

donner [dɔne] (1) **1** *vt* **(a)** (*gén*) to give (*à* to); *lettre* to hand; *copie d'examen* to hand *ou* give in; *parts de gâteau* to hand *ou* give out; *vieux habits* to give away; *cartes* to deal (out); *sa vie, sa place* to give up; *permission* to grant; *décoration* to award. **~ à manger à qn** to give sb sth to eat; **pouvez-vous me ~ l'heure?** could you tell me the time?; **ça lui donne un air triste** it makes him look sad; **donne-toi un coup de peigne** give your hair a quick comb; **~ une gifle à qn** to slap sb's face; **~ un ordre à qn** to give sb an order, order sb to do sth; **il n'est pas donné à tout le monde d'être riche** it is not given to everybody to be rich; **c'est donné*** it's dirt cheap; (*fig*) **~ le ton** to set the tone; **je vous le donne en mille** you'll never guess; **on lui donnerait le bon Dieu sans confession** he looks as if butter wouldn't melt in his mouth. **(b)** (*causer*) *plaisir, courage* to give (*à* to); *mal* to cause, give (*à* to). **~ de l'appétit à qn** to give sb an appetite; **cela donne soif** this makes you (feel) thirsty. **(c)** (*avec à + infin: faire*) **il m'a donné à penser que** he made me think that; **ça nous a donné à réfléchir** it has given us food for thought; **~ à rire** to give cause for laughter; **~ ses chaussures à ressemeler** to take one's shoes (in) to be mended *ou* to the cobbler's. **(d)** (*organiser*) *réception* to give, hold (*à* for); *film* to show; *pièce* to perform, put on. **ça se donne encore?** *[film]* is it still on *ou* showing? **(e)** (*attribuer*) **quel âge lui donnez-vous?** how old do you take him to be *ou* would you say he was?; **~ un fait pour certain** to present a fact as a certainty; **on le donne pour un homme habile** he is said to be a clever man. **(f)** (*produire*) *récolte* to yield; *résultat* to produce. **les pommiers ont bien donné** the apple trees have produced a good crop *ou* given a good yield; **elle lui a donné un fils** she bore him a son. **(g)** (*‡: dénoncer*) *complice* to shop‡, give away.

2 *vi* **(a)** (*frapper*) **aller ~ sur** to strike; **~ de la tête contre** to knock one's head against; **le soleil donne en plein sur la voiture** the sun is beating down on the car; **ne savoir où ~ de la tête*** not to know which way to turn. **(b) ~ dans** *piège* to fall into; *défaut* to lapse into; **~ dans le snobisme** to be rather snobbish. **(c) ~ sur** *[pièce, porte]* to give onto, open onto; **la maison donne sur la mer** the house faces *ou* looks onto the sea front.

3 se ~ *vpr* **(a) se ~ à** *cause* to devote o.s. to; **se**

~ **à fond** to give one's all. **(b) se ~ à un maître** to choose o.s. a master; **se ~ de la peine** to take (great) trouble; **se ~ du bon temps** to have a good time; **se ~ un air sévère** to put on a strict air; **se ~ pour généreux** to profess *ou* make o.s. out to be generous.

donneur, -euse [dɔnœʀ, øz] *nm,f* (*gén*) giver; (*Cartes*) dealer; (*: *dénonciateur*) squealer*, informer; (*Méd*) donor.

dont [dɔ̃] *pron rel* **(a)** (*reprenant complément de nom*) (*chose*) whose, of which; (*personne*) whose. **la maison ~ on voit le toit** the house the roof of which *ou* whose roof you can see. **(b)** (*partie d'un tout*) **ils ont 3 filles ~ 2 sont mariées** they have 3 daughters, 2 of whom are married; **l'histoire, ~ l'essentiel est ...** the story, the main point of which is ... . **(c)** (*reprenant* **de**) **la façon ~ elle s'habille** the way (in which) she dresses, her way of dressing; **la maladie ~ elle souffre** the illness she suffers from *ou* from which she suffers.

doper [dɔpe] (1) **1** *vt* to dope. **2 se ~** *vpr* to dope o.s. ♦ **doping** *nm* (*action*) doping. (*excitant*) **~(s)** dope.

dorénavant [dɔʀenavɑ̃] *adv* from now on.

dorer [dɔʀe] (1) **1** *vt objet* to gild; *rôti* to brown; *peau* to bronze, tan. **faire ~ un cadre** to have a frame gilded; **~ la pilule à qn*** to sugar the pill for sb; **se ~ au soleil** to lie and get brown in the sun. **2** *vi [rôti]* to brown. **faire ~ au four** to put in the oven to brown. ♦ **doré, e 1** *adj objet* gilt, gilded; *peau* bronzed, tanned; *blé, cheveux, rêves* golden. **2** *nm* (*matière*) gilt.

dorique [dɔʀik] *adj, nm* Doric.

dorloter [dɔʀlɔte] (1) *vt* to pamper, cosset. **trop dorloté** mollycoddled.

dormir [dɔʀmiʀ] (16) *vi* **(a)** to sleep; (*être endormi*) to be asleep, be sleeping. **avoir envie de ~** to feel sleepy; **ça m'empêche de ~** *[café]* it keeps me awake; *[soucis]* I'm losing sleep over it; **parler en dormant** to talk in one's sleep. **(b)** *[eau, nature]* to be still; *[argent]* to lie idle. **tout dormait dans la ville** everything was quiet *ou* still in the town; **ce n'est pas le moment de ~!** this is no time for slacking *ou* idling! **(c)** (*locutions*) **je dors debout** I'm asleep on my feet; **histoire à ~ debout** cock-and-bull story; **~ comme un loir** to sleep like a log; **ne ~ que d'un œil** to sleep with one eye open; **il dort à poings fermés** he is sound *ou* fast asleep, he's dead to the world; (*fig*) **~ tranquille** (*sans soucis*) to rest easy. ♦ **dormant, e 1** *adj eau* still; *châssis* fixed. **2** *nm [porte]* frame. ♦ **dormeur, -euse** *nm,f* sleeper.

dorsal, e, *mpl* **-aux** [dɔʀsal, o] *adj* (*gén*) dorsal.

dortoir [dɔʀtwaʀ] *nm* dormitory. **cité-~** dormitory town.

dorure [dɔʀyʀ] *nf* (*couche d'or*) gilt, gilding; (*action*) gilding.

dos [do] *nm* **(a)** (*gén*) back; *[livre]* spine; *[langue]* back; *[lame]* blunt edge. **avoir le ~ rond** to be round-shouldered; **au ~ de la lettre** on the back of the letter; **robe décolletée dans le ~** low-backed dress; **'voir au ~'** 'see over'; **aller à ~ d'âne** to ride on a donkey; **(vu) de ~** (seen) from behind *ou* from the back. **(b) ~ à ~** back to back; **le train a bon ~*** (that's right) blame the train; **se mettre qn à ~** to turn sb against one; (*fig*) **avoir qn sur le ~** to have sb breathing down one's neck; **on l'a dans le ~**‡ that's really messed us up‡; **mettre qch sur le ~ de qn** (*responsabilité*) to saddle sb with sth; (*accusation*) to pin sth on sb; **il s'est mis une sale affaire sur le ~** he has got himself mixed up in a nasty bit of business; **faire des affaires sur le ~ de qn** to do a bit of business at sb's expense; **il n'a rien à se mettre sur le ~** he hasn't got a thing to wear; **tomber sur le ~ de qn** (*arriver*) to drop in on sb; (*attaquer*) to go for sb; **faire qch derrière le ~ de qn** to do sth behind sb's back; **il n'y va pas avec le ~ de la cuiller*** he certainly doesn't go in for half-measures; **(pont en) ~ d'âne** humpback bridge.

dose [doz] *nf* (*Pharm*) dose; (*gén: proportion*) amount, quantity. **en avoir sa ~*** to have one's share of it; **forcer la ~** to overstep the mark; **~ d'ironie** touch of irony; **à petites ~s** in small doses. ♦ **dosage** *nm* (*action*) measuring out; correct proportioning; (*mélange*) mixture; (*équilibre*) balance. ♦ **doser** (1) *vt* (*Chim, gén*) to measure out; *mélange* to proportion correctly; (*fig: équilibrer*) to strike a balance between. **savoir ~ ses efforts** to know how much effort to expend. ♦ **doseur** *nm* measure.

dossier [dosje] *nm [siège]* back; (*documents*) file, dossier; (*classeur*) file.

doter [dɔte] (1) *vt épouse* to provide with a dowry; *institution* to endow. **~ de** *matériels* to equip with; *qualités* to endow with. ♦ **dot** *nf* dowry. **apporter qch en ~** to bring a dowry of sth. ♦ **dotation** *nf* endowment.

douairière [dwɛʀjɛʀ] *nf* dowager.

douane [dwan] *nf* (*service*) **les ~s** the Customs; (*poste*) **la ~** the customs; **marchandises en ~** goods in bond; **passer à la ~** to go through customs. ♦ **douanier, -ière 1** *adj* customs. **2** *nm,f* customs officer.

doublage [dublaʒ] *nm* (*gén*) doubling; *[film]* dubbing. **le ~ d'un acteur** standing in for an actor.

double [dubl(ə)] **1** *adj* double; *avantage* double, twofold. **le prix est ~ de ce qu'il était** the price is double *ou* twice what it was; **faire qch en ~ exemplaire** to make two copies of sth; **ustensile à ~ usage** dual-purpose utensil; **faire ~ emploi** to be redundant; **fermer à ~ tour** to double-lock; (*lit, fig*) **à ~ tranchant** double-edged; **valise à ~ fond** case with a false bottom; **jouer un ~ jeu** to play a double game; **phrase à ~ sens** sentence with a double meaning. **2** *nm* **(a) manger le ~ (de qn)** to eat twice as much (as sb) *ou* double the amount (that sb does); **4 est le ~ de 2** 4 is two times *ou* twice 2; **c'est le ~ du prix normal** it is twice *ou* double the normal price. **(b)** (*copie*) copy; (*sosie*) double. **avoir qch en ~** (*document*) to have a copy of sth; (*timbre*) to have two *ou* a duplicate of sth; **plier qch en ~** to fold sth in half *ou* two. **(c)** (*Tennis*) doubles. **faire un ~** to play a doubles match. **3** *adv* double. **4: ~ commande** *nf* dual controls; **~ croche** *nf* semiquaver, sixteenth note (*US*); **~-décimètre** *nm* (20-cm) ruler; **~s rideaux** *nmpl* double curtains; **~ vue** *nf* second sight.

doubler [duble] (1) **1** *vt* (*augmenter*) to double; *ficelle* to use double; (*Scol*) *classe* to repeat; *acteur* to stand in for; *film* to dub; (*Couture*) to line (*de* with); (*dépasser*) *véhicule* to overtake, pass; (*Naut*) *cap* to round. **~ le cap des 50 ans** to turn 50; **~ le pas** to quicken one's pace, speed up; **veste non doublée** unlined jacket. **2** *vi* (*augmenter*) to double, increase twofold; (*Aut*) to overtake, pass. **~ de poids** to double in weight. **3 se ~** *vpr*: **se ~ de** to be coupled with; **c'est un savant doublé d'un pédagogue** he is a teacher as well as a scholar. ♦ **doublé** *nm* (*victoire*) double. ♦ **doublement 1** *adv* (*pour deux raisons*) for a double reason; (*à un degré double*) doubly. **2** *nm* doubling; (*Aut*) overtaking, passing. ♦ **doublure** *nf* **(a)** (*étoffe*) lining. **(b)** (*Théât*) understudy; (*Ciné*) stand-in; (*cascadeur*) stuntman (*ou* stuntwoman).

douce [dus] *V* **doux.**

douceur [dusœʀ] *nf* **(a)** *[peau]* softness; *[temps]* mildness; *[personne]* gentleness. **prendre qn par la ~** to deal gently with sb; **les ~s de l'amitié** the pleasures of friendship. **(b)** (*sucrerie*) sweet. **(c) en ~** *démarrer* smoothly; *commencer* gently. ♦ **douceâtre** *adj saveur* sickly sweet, cloying; *air* mawkish.

♦ **doucement** *adv* (*sans violence*) gently, softly; (*gentiment*) gently; (*sans bruit*) quietly; (*prudemment*) carefully; *rouler* slowly; *démarrer* smoothly. **comment allez-vous? – (tout) ~** how are you? – so-so*; **allez-y ~!*** easy *or* gently does it! ♦ **doucereux, -euse** *adj goût* sickly sweet; *ton* sugary; *manières* smooth.

douche [duʃ] *nf* (*jet, système*) shower; (*: *averse*) soaking, drenching. (*salle*) **~s** shower room; **~ (froide)** (*déception*) let-down; **c'est vraiment la ~ écossaise** it's all up one minute and down the next. ♦ **doucher** (1) **1** *vt*: **~ qn** to give sb a shower; *[orage]* to soak *ou* drench sb. **2 se ~** *vpr* to have *ou* take a shower.

doué, e [dwe] *adj* (*talentueux*) gifted, talented (*en* in). **être ~ pour** to have a gift for; (*pourvu de*) **~ de** *vie, raison* endowed with.

douille [duj] *nf [cartouche]* (cartridge) case; (*Élec*) socket.

douillet, -ette [dujɛ, ɛt] *adj* **(a)** (*péj*) *personne* soft. **(b)** *atmosphère, lit* cosy. ♦ **douillettement** *adv* cosily. (*péj*) **élever ~** to mollycoddle.

douleur [dulœʀ] *nf* (*physique*) pain; (*morale*) distress. **'nous avons la ~ d'apprendre que...'** 'it is with great sorrow that we learn that ...'. ♦ **douloureusement** *adv* painfully; distressingly. ♦ **douloureux, -euse** *adj* painful; distressing; *regard* distressed, pained.

doute [dut] *nm* doubt. **être dans le ~** to be doubtful *ou* uncertain (*sur* about); **laisser qn dans le ~** to leave sb in (a state of) uncertainty; **le ~ n'est plus permis** there is no more room for doubt; **il a émis des ~s à propos de ...** he expressed (his) doubts *ou* misgivings about ...; **dans le ~, abstiens-toi** when in doubt, don't!; **sans ~** doubtless, no doubt; **sans aucun ~** without a doubt; **ceci ne fait aucun ~** there is no doubt about it; **mettre en ~** to question, challenge.

douter [dute] (1) **1 ~ de** *vt indir* (*gén*) to doubt, have (one's) doubts as to; *réussite* to be doubtful of; *authenticité* to question. **j'en doute** I have my doubts, I doubt it; **n'en doutez pas** there's no doubt about that; **je doute d'avoir jamais fait cela** I doubt that I ever did that; **je doute qu'il vienne** I doubt if *ou* whether he'll come; **à n'en pas ~** undoubtedly; **il ne doute de rien!*** he's got some nerve! **2 se ~** *vpr*: **se ~ de qch** to suspect sth; **se ~ que** to suspect that, have an idea that; **je m'en doute** I can well imagine that.

douteux, -euse [dutø, øz] *adj* **(a)** (*incertain*) (*gén*) doubtful; *fait* questionable; *résultat* uncertain. **il est ~ que** it is doubtful *ou* questionable that *ou* whether; **il n'est pas ~ que** there is no doubt that. **(b)** (*péj*) *qualité, goût* dubious, questionable; *aliment* dubious-looking; *individu* dubious, doubtful.

douve [duv] *nf [château]* moat.

Douvres [duvʀ(ə)] *n* Dover.

doux, douce [du, dus] **1** *adj* (*au toucher*) soft; *temps* mild; *brise, chaleur* gentle; (*sucré, agréable*) sweet; *moutarde* mild; *son* sweet, gentle; *lumière, couleur* soft; *pente* gentle; *démarrage* smooth; *caractère, manières* mild, gentle. **~ comme un agneau** as meek *ou* gentle as a lamb; **cuire à feu ~** to simmer gently (over a low flame); **se faire une douce violence** to inflict a pleasant burden upon o.s.; **cette pensée lui était douce** this thought gave him great pleasure; **en douce*** on the quiet; **préférer le ~ à l'amer** to prefer sweet tastes *ou* things to sour. **2** *adv*: **ça va tout ~*** things are going so-so*; († *ou hum*) **tout ~!** gently (now)!

douze [duz] *adj, nm inv* twelve; *V* **six.** ♦ **douzaine** *nf* (*douze*) dozen. (*environ douze*) **une ~** about twelve, a dozen or so. ♦ **douzième** *adj, nmf* twelfth; *V* **sixième.** ♦ **douzièmement** *adv* in twelfth place, twelfthly.

doyen, -enne [dwajɛ̃, ɛn] *nm,f* (*Rel, Univ*) dean; *[groupe]* most senior member; *[assemblée]* doyen.

draconien, -ienne [dʀakɔnjɛ̃, jɛn] *adj* draconian.

dragée [dʀaʒe] *nf* sugared almond. **tenir la ~ haute à qn** to be a fair *ou* good match for sb. ♦ **dragéifié** *adj* sugared.

dragon [dʀagɔ̃] *nm* (*Myth, fig*) dragon; (*Hist Mil*) dragoon.

draguer [dʀage] (1) *vt* **(a)** (*Pêche*) to fish with a dragnet; (*pour nettoyer, trouver*) to dredge; *mines* to sweep. *[ancre]* **~ (le fond)** to drag. **(b)** (**fig*) to chat up*. ♦ **drague** *nf* (*Pêche*) dragnet; (*machine*) dredge; (*navire*) dredger. ♦ **dragueur** *nm* (*bateau*) dredger. **~ de mines** minesweeper.

drainer [dʀene] (1) *vt* (*gén*) to drain. ♦ **drain** *nm* drain. ♦ **drainage** *nm* drainage.

drame [dʀam] *nm* **(a)** (*Théât*) drama. **(b)** (*événement tragique*) drama, tragedy. **n'en faites pas un ~** don't make such a drama out of it. ♦ **dramatique 1** *adj* (*Théât*) dramatic; (*tragique*) tragic; (*spectaculaire*) dramatic. **2** *nf* (*TV*) (television) play *ou* drama. ♦ **dramatiquement** *adv* tragically. ♦ **dramatisation** *nf* dramatization. ♦ **dramatiser** (1) *vt* to dramatize. ♦ **dramaturge** *nmf* dramatist, playwright.

drap [dʀa] *nm* **(a)** (*tissu*) woollen cloth. **(b) ~ (de lit)** sheet; (*fig*) **mettre qn dans de beaux ~s** to land sb in a fine mess.

drapeau, *pl* **~x** [dʀapo] *nm* (*gén*) flag. **le ~ tricolore** the tricolour; **être sous les ~x** to do one's national service.

draper [dʀape] (1) **1** *vt* to drape. **2 se ~** *vpr*: **se ~ dans** to drape o.s. in; (*fig péj*) **se ~ dans sa dignité** to stand on one's dignity. ♦ **draperie** *nf* drapery. ♦ **drapier** *nm* draper.

dresser [dʀese] (1) **1** *vt* **(a)** *liste, acte* to draw up. **~ (une) contravention à qn** to report sb, book sb*; **~ le bilan de qch** to give a review of sth. **(b)** (*ériger*) (*gén*) to put up, erect; *échelle* to set up; *tente* to pitch; *mât* to raise. **~ un buffet** to set *ou* lay out a buffet; **~ la table** to lay *ou* set the table. **(c)** (*inciter*) **~ qn contre** to set sb against. **(d)** *tête* to raise, lift. (*fig*) **~ l'oreille** to prick up one's ears; **faire ~ les cheveux sur la tête à qn** to make sb's hair stand on end. **(e)** *lion* to tame; *cheval* to break in; *chien* to train. (*Cirque*) **animaux dressés** performing animals; **ça le dressera!*** that'll teach him a lesson; **~ un enfant*** to teach a child his place. **2 se ~** *vpr* (*gén*) to stand; *[tour, sommet]* to tower; *[personne]* to stand up; *[cheveux]* to stand on end. **se ~ de toute sa taille** to draw o.s. up to one's full height; **se ~ contre qn** to rise up against sb; **se ~ en justicier** to set o.s. up as a dispenser of justice. ♦ **dressage** *nm* (*domptage*) taming; breaking in; training. ♦ **dresseur, -euse** *nm,f* trainer. **~ de lions** liontamer.

dressoir [dʀeswaʀ] *nm* dresser.

drille [dʀij] *nm* (†) **joyeux ~** cheerful character.

drogue [dʀɔg] *nf* drug. **la ~** drugs. ♦ **drogué, e** *nm,f* drug addict. ♦ **droguer** (1) *vt malade* (*péj*) to dose up; *victime* to drug. **il se drogue** he's on drugs, he's taking drugs.

droguiste [dʀɔgist(ə)] *nmf* hardware merchant. ♦ **droguerie** *nf* (*commerce*) hardware trade; (*magasin*) hardware shop.

droit[1], e[1] [dʀwa, dʀwat] **1** *adj bras* right; *poche* right(-hand). **du côté ~** on the right-hand side. **2** *nm* (*Boxe*) right. **3** *nf* **(a) la ~e** (*gén, Aut, Pol*) the right; (*côté*) the right-hand side; **à ~e** *rue, rouler* on the right; *tourner* to the right; **chemin de ~e** right-hand path; **à ~e de la fenêtre** to the right of the window; **de ~e à gauche** from right to left; (*fig*) **de ~e et de gauche** everywhere; **garder sa ~e** to keep to the right; **idées de ~e** right-wing ideas. **(b)** (*Boxe*) right. ♦ **droitier, -ière** *adj* right-handed.

droit[2], e[2] [dʀwa, dʀwat] **1** *adj* **(a)** *ligne, route* straight. **4 km en ligne ~e** 4 km as the crow flies;

(*fig*) **cela vient en ~e ligne de ...** that comes straight *ou* direct from ...; (*Rel*) **le ~ chemin** the straight and narrow way. **(b)** *arbre, mur* upright, straight. **tiens ta tasse ~e** hold your cup straight *ou* level; **tiens-toi ~** (*debout*) stand up straight; (*assis*) sit up straight. **(c)** (*loyal*) *personne* upright, straight. **(d)** (*judicieux*) *jugement* sound, sane. **2** *nf*: **(ligne) ~e** straight line. **3** *adv couper* straight. **c'est ~ devant vous** it's straight ahead of you *ou* right in front of you; (*fig*) **aller ~ au but** to go straight to the point. ♦ **droiture** *nf* uprightness.

droit[3] [dRwa] **1** *nm* **(a)** (*prérogative*) right. **c'est bien votre ~** you've every right to do so, you're perfectly within your rights; **de quel ~ est-il entré?** what right had he to come in?; **avoir ~ de regard sur** to have the right to examine; **avoir le ~ de faire** (*permission*) to be allowed to do; (*Admin, Jur*) to have the right to do; **avoir ~ à qch** to be entitled to sth; (*hum*) **il a eu ~ à une bonne raclée*** he earned himself a good hiding; **être dans son (bon) ~** to be quite within one's rights; **c'est à lui de (plein) ~** it's his by right; **le ~ du plus fort** the law of the jungle; **faire ~ à** *requête* to grant; **monarque de ~ divin** monarch by divine right. **(b)** (*Jur*) **le ~** law; (*Univ*) **faire son ~** to study law; **délit de ~ commun** common law crime. **(c)** (*gén pl*) (*taxe*) duty, tax; (*d'inscription etc*) fee, fees. **~ d'entrée** entrance fee; **~s de douane/de succession** customs/death duties. **2: ~ d'aînesse** birthright; **~ d'asile** right of asylum; **~s d'auteur** royalties; **avoir ~ de cité dans** to be established in; **~ de grâce** right of reprieve; **le ~ de vote** the right to vote, the vote.

drôle [dRol] *adj* (*amusant*) funny, comical, amusing; (*bizarre*) funny, peculiar, strange; (*: *intensif*) fantastic. **ça me fait (tout) ~ (de le voir)*** it gives me a funny *ou* an odd feeling (to see him); **faire une ~ de tête** to pull a wry face, look disgruntled; **de ~s de progrès** fantastic *ou* terrific progress*. ♦ **drôlement** *adv* funnily; comically; amusingly; peculiarly; strangely. **il fait ~ froid*** it's terribly *ou* awfully cold; **il a ~ changé*** he really has changed, he's changed an awful lot. ♦ **drôlerie** *nf* funny remark *etc.* **la ~** funniness.

dromadaire [dRɔmadɛR] *nm* dromedary.

dru, e [dRy] **1** *adj herbe* thick; *barbe* bushy; *pluie* heavy. **2** *adv* thickly; heavily; *[coups]* thick and fast.

druide [dRɥid] *nm* druid.

du [dy] *V* **de.**

dû, due [dy] **1** *adj* (*à restituer*) owing, owed; (*à échéance*) due. **la somme qui lui est due** the sum owing to him; **troubles ~s à ...** troubles due to ...; **en (bonne et) due forme** in due form. **2** *nm* due; (*argent*) dues. ♦ **dûment** *adv* duly.

dualité [dɥalite] *nf* duality.

duc [dyk] *nm* duke. ♦ **ducal, e,** *mpl* **-aux** *adj* ducal. ♦ **duché** *nm* dukedom. ♦ **duchesse** *nf* duchess.

duel [dɥɛl] *nm* duel. **se battre en ~** to fight a duel (*avec* with); **~ d'artillerie** artillery battle. ♦ **duelliste** *nm* duellist.

dulcinée [dylsine] *nf* († *ou hum*) lady-love.

dune [dyn] *nf* dune.

Dunkerque [dœ̃kɛRk] *n* Dunkirk.

duo [dɥo] *nm* (*Mus*) duet; (*Théât, fig*) duo.

duodénum [dyɔdenɔm] *nm* duodenum.

dupe [dyp] *nf* dupe. **être (la) ~ de qn** to be taken in *ou* fooled by sb; **je ne suis pas ~** I'm not taken in by it. ♦ **duper** (1) *vt* to dupe, deceive. **se ~ (soi-même)** to deceive o.s. ♦ **duperie** *nf* deception. **la ~** dupery.

duplex [dyplɛks] *nm* (*appartement*) maisonette, duplex; (*Télec*) link-up.

duplicata [dyplikata] *nm inv* duplicate. ♦ **duplicateur** *nm* duplicator.

duplicité [dyplisite] *nf* duplicity.

dur, e [dyR] **1** *adj* **(a)** (*résistant*) (*gén*) hard; *carton, serrure, brosse* stiff; *viande* tough. **être ~ d'oreille** to be hard of hearing. **(b)** (*difficile*) (*gén*) hard, stiff, tough; *enfant* difficult. **~ à croire** hard to believe. **(c)** (*pénible, sévère*) (*gén*) harsh, hard; *combat* fierce; *vin* bitter. **les temps sont ~s** times are hard; **être ~ avec qn** to be tough with sb, be hard on sb; **il a le cœur ~** he's a hard-hearted man. **(d)** (*endurant*) **être ~ à la douleur** to be inured to suffering; **être ~ à l'ouvrage** to be a tireless worker. **2** *adv* (*) (*gén*) hard. **le soleil tape ~** the sun is beating down; **croire à qch ~ comme fer** to believe firmly in sth. **3** *nm,f* (*: *gén*) tough one *ou* guy*; (*Pol: intransigeant*) hard-liner. **un ~ à cuire*** a hard nut to crack; **construction en ~** permanent structure; **élevé à la ~e** brought up the hard way; **coucher sur la ~e** to sleep rough; **en voir de ~es*** to have a hard *ou* tough time of it. ♦ **durement** *adv* harshly; fiercely; hard-heartedly. **~ éprouvé** sorely tried; **élever qn ~** to bring sb up the hard way.

durable [dyRabl(ə)] *adj* (*gén*) lasting; *étoffe* durable, long-lasting. ♦ **durablement** *adv s'installer* on a long-term basis. **bâti ~** built to last.

durant [dyRɑ̃] *prép* (*au cours de*) during, in the course of; (*mesure de temps*) for. **il a plu ~ la nuit** it rained in (the course of) *ou* during the night; **2 heures ~** for (a whole) 2 hours; **sa vie ~** throughout his life.

durcir *vt*, **se ~** *vpr* [dyRsiR] (2) (*lit, fig*) to harden. ♦ **durcissement** *nm* hardening.

durée [dyRe] *nf* (*gén*) duration, length; *[bail]* term; *[matériau, ampoule]* life. **pendant une ~ d'un mois** for a period of one month; **pendant la ~ des réparations** for the duration of repairs; **de courte ~** *séjour* short; *bonheur* short-lived; **de longue ~** long-lasting; **croire en la ~ de qch** to believe in the continuance of sth, believe that sth will last.

durer [dyRe] (1) *vi* (*gén*) to last. **la fête a duré toute la nuit** the party went on *ou* lasted all night; **sa maladie dure depuis 2 mois** he has been ill for 2 months (now); **ça ne peut plus ~!** this can't go on any longer!; (*iro*) **faire ~ le plaisir** to prolong the agony; **le temps me dure** time hangs heavy on my hands; **cette somme doit te ~ un mois** the sum will have to last you a month.

dureté [dyRte] *nf* (*gén*) hardness; *[brosse]* stiffness; *[viande]* toughness; *[traitement]* harshness. **~ de cœur** hard-heartedness.

durillon [dyRijɔ̃] *nm* callus.

duvet [dyvɛ] *nm* (*gén*) down; (*sac de couchage*) sleeping bag. ♦ **duveteux, -euse** *adj* downy.

dynamique [dinamik] **1** *adj* (*gén*) dynamic. **2** *nf* (*Phys*) dynamics (*sg*). ♦ **dynamiquement** *adv* dynamically. ♦ **dynamisme** *nm* dynamism.

dynamite [dinamit] *nf* (*lit, fig*) dynamite. ♦ **dynamiter** (1) *vt* to dynamite.

dynamo [dinamo] *nf* dynamo.

dynastie [dinasti] *nf* dynasty. ♦ **dynastique** *adj* dynastic.

dysenterie [disɑ̃tRi] *nf* dysentery. ♦ **dysentérique** *adj* dysenteric.

E

E, e [ə] *nm* (*lettre*) E, e.
eau, *pl* **~x** [o] **1** *nf* **(a)** (*gén, Bijouterie*) water; (*pluie*) rain. **sans ~** *vin* neat; **cuire à l'~** to boil. **(b)** (*locutions*) **apporter de l'~ au moulin de qn** to strengthen *ou* back sb's case *ou* argument; (*Méd*) **aller aux ~x** to take the waters; **j'en avais l'~ à la bouche** it made my mouth water; **être en ~** to be bathed in perspiration *ou* sweat; **faire ~ (de toutes parts)** to leak (like a sieve); (*Naut*) **mettre à l'~** to launch; **mettre de l'~ dans son vin** (*lit*) to water down one's wine; (*fig*) to climb down; *[chaussures]* **prendre l'~** to leak, let in water; **il passera beaucoup d'~ sous les ponts** much water will have flowed under the bridge; **il y a de l'~ dans le gaz*** things aren't running too smoothly. **2: ~ bénite** holy water; **~ de Cologne** eau de Cologne; **~ courante** running water; **~ douce** fresh water; **~ forte** (*Art*) etching; (*Chim*) aqua fortis; **~ gazeuse** soda water; **~ de javel** bleach; **~ oxygénée** hydrogen peroxide; **roman à l'~ de rose** sentimental novel; **~ salée** salt water; **~ de toilette** toilet water; **~x usées** liquid waste; **~ de vie (de prune** *etc***)** (plum *etc*) brandy.
ébahir [ebaiʀ] (2) *vt* to astound. ♦ **ébahissement** *nm* astonishment.
ébattre (s') [ebatʀ(ə)] (41) *vpr* to frolic, gambol about. ♦ **ébats** *nmpl* frolics.
ébaucher [eboʃe] (1) **1** *vt livre, tableau* to sketch out; *plan* to outline; *amitié, conversation* to start up. **~ un sourire** to give a faint smile; **~ un geste** to give a hint of a movement. **2 s'~** *vpr [plan, solution, livre]* to take shape; *[amitié]* to form; *[conversation]* to start up. ♦ **ébauche** *nf* **(a)** (*action*) sketching out; outlining; starting up. **(b)** (*résultat*) *[livre, projet]* rough outline; *[amitié]* beginnings. **une ~ de sourire** the ghost of a smile; **l'~ d'un geste** the hint of a gesture; **première ~** rough draft; **à l'état d'~** in the early stages.
ébène [ebɛn] *nf* ebony. **cheveux d'~** ebony hair. ♦ **ébéniste** *nm* cabinetmaker. ♦ **ébénisterie** *nf* (*métier*) cabinetmaking; (*façon*) cabinetwork.
éberluer [ebɛʀlɥe] (1) *vt* to astound.
éblouir [ebluiʀ] (2) *vt* (*lit, fig*) to dazzle. ♦ **éblouissement** *nm* **(a)** *[lampe]* dazzle. **(b)** (*émerveillement*) bedazzlement; (*spectacle*) dazzling sight. **(c)** (*Méd*) **avoir un ~** to have a dizzy turn.
ébonite [ebɔnit] *nf* ebonite.
éborgner [ebɔʀɲe] (1) *vt*: **~ qn** to blind sb in one eye, poke sb's eye out.
éboueur [ebwœʀ] *nm* dustman, garbage collector (*US*).
ébouillanter [ebujɑ̃te] (1) *vt* (*gén*) to scald.
ébouler [ebule] (1) **1** *vt* to cause to collapse *ou* crumble. **2 s'~** *vpr* (*progressivement*) to crumble; (*soudainement*) to collapse; *[sable]* to fall. ♦ **éboulement** *nm* **(a)** (*action*) crumbling; collapse; fall. **(b)** (*amas*) heap of rocks, earth *etc.* ♦ **éboulis** *nm* heap of fallen rocks, earth *etc.* **pente couverte d'~** scree-covered slope.
ébouriffer [ebuʀife] (1) *vt* **(a)** (*gén*) to ruffle. **~ qn** to tousle *ou* ruffle sb's hair. **(b)** (*: *surprendre*) to astound. ♦ **ébouriffant, e*** *adj vitesse, prix* hair-raising.
ébranler [ebʀɑ̃le] (1) **1** *vt* (*gén*) to shake; (*affaiblir*) to weaken; *esprit* to disturb. **ébranlé par cette nouvelle** shaken *ou* shattered by the news; **se laisser ~ par des prières** to allow o.s. to be swayed by pleas. **2 s'~** *vpr [cortège]* to move off. ♦ **ébranlement** *nm* (*action*) shaking; weakening; disturbance; (*résultat*) shock.
ébrécher [ebʀeʃe] (6) *vt assiette* to chip; *lame* to nick; *fortune* to break into. ♦ **ébréchure** *nf* chip; nick.
ébriété [ebʀijete] *nf* intoxication.
ébrouer (s') [ebʀue] (1) *vpr [cheval]* to snort; *[personne, chien]* to shake o.s.
ébruiter [ebʀɥite] (1) **1** *vt* to spread about. **2 s'~** *vpr* to leak out. ♦ **ébruitement** *nm* spreading.
ébullition [ebylisjɔ̃] *nf [eau]* boiling point; (*fig: agitation*) turmoil. **porter à (l')~** to bring to the boil; **avant l'~** before boiling point is reached; **être en ~** *[liquide]* to be boiling; *[maison]* to be in an uproar; *[pays]* to be seething with unrest.
écaille [ekɑj] *nf [poisson, reptile]* scale; *[huître]* shell; *[peinture]* flake. **lunettes d'~** horn-rimmed spectacles; **peigne en ~** tortoiseshell comb. ♦ **écailler** (1) **1** *vt poisson* to scale; *peinture etc* to chip. **2 s'~** *vpr [peinture]* to flake off.
écarlate [ekaʀlat] *adj, nf* scarlet.
écarquiller [ekaʀkije] (1) *vt*: **~ les yeux** to stare wide-eyed (*devant* at).
écart [ekaʀ] **1** *nm* **(a)** *[objets, dates]* gap; *[chiffres, températures, opinions]* difference (*entre* between). **~ par rapport à la règle** departure from the rule; **~ important de prix** big difference in price; (*lit, fig*) **réduire l'~ entre** to narrow the gap between. **(b) faire un ~** *[cheval]* to shy; *[voiture]* to swerve; *[piéton]* to leap aside; (*Danse*) **faire le grand ~** to do the splits. **(c) être à l'~** *[hameau]* to be isolated; **tirer qn à l'~** to take sb aside; **tenir qn à l'~** (*fig*) to keep sb in the background; (*lit*) to hold sb back; **rester à l'~** (*s'isoler*) to hold o.s. aloof; (*ne pas approcher*) to stay in the background; (*ne pas participer*) to keep out of things; **à l'~ de la route** (well) off the road, off the beaten track; **tenir qn à l'~ d'un lieu** to keep sb well away from a place; **tenir qn à l'~ d'une affaire** to keep sb out of an affair. **2: ~ de conduite** misdemeanour; **~ de langage** bad language; **~ de régime** lapse in one's diet.
écarteler [ekaʀtəle] (5) *vt* (*Hist*) to quarter. (*fig*) **écartelé entre 2 choses** torn between 2 things. ♦ **écartèlement** *nm* quartering.
écartement [ekaʀtəmɑ̃] *nm* space, gap (*de, entre* between). (*Rail*) **~ (des rails)** gauge.
écarter [ekaʀte] (1) **1** *vt* **(a)** *objets* to move apart; *doigts* to spread; *rideaux* to draw (back). **il écarta la foule pour passer** he pushed his way through the crowd; **les jambes écartées** with his legs wide apart; **les bras écartés** with his arms outspread. **(b)** *objection, idée* to dismiss; *candidature* to turn down; *personne* to remove (*de* from). **(c)** (*éloigner*) *meuble* to move away; *personne* to push back; (*fig: de l'étude*) to distract (*de* from). **tout danger est maintenant écarté** there is no further risk of danger; **ça nous écarte de notre propos** this is leading us off the subject. **2 s'~** *vpr* (*se séparer*) to draw aside, part; (*s'éloigner*) to withdraw, move away; (*reculer*) to step back (*de* from). **s'~ de** *route, sujet* to stray *ou* wander off; *norme* to deviate *ou* depart from. ♦ **écarté, e** *adj*

lieu remote, isolated. **chemin** ~ lonely road.
ecchymose [ekimoz] *nf* bruise.
ecclésiastique [eklezjastik] **1** *adj* ecclesiastical. **2** *nm* ecclesiastic.
écervelé, e [esɛʀvəle] **1** *adj* scatterbrained. **2** *nm,f* scatterbrain.
échafaud [eʃafo] *nm* scaffold. **il risque l'~** he's risking his neck.
échafauder [eʃafode] (1) *vt* **(a)** *fortune* to build up; *théorie* to construct. **(b)** (*empiler*) to pile up. ♦ **échafaudage** *nm* **(a)** (*Constr*) ~**(s)** scaffolding. **(b)** *[objets]* heap, pile. **(c)** building up, construction.
échalote [eʃalɔt] *nf* shallot.
échancré, e [eʃɑ̃kʀe] *adj robe* with a scooped neckline; *côte* indented; *feuille* serrated. ♦ **échancrure** *nf* scooped neckline; indentation; serration.
échange [eʃɑ̃ʒ] *nm* (*gén*) exchange; (*troc*) swap. ~**s commerciaux** trade; **en** ~ (*par contre*) on the other hand; (*troc*) in exchange (*de* for); (*pour compenser*) to make up for it; **faire (l')~ de qch** to swap *ou* exchange sth. ♦ **échanger** (3) *vt* (*gén*) to exchange, swap (*contre* for); *injures* to bandy. ♦ **échangeur** *nm* (*Aut*) interchange.
échantillon [eʃɑ̃tijɔ̃] *nm* sample. ♦ **échantillonnage** *nm* (*action*) sampling; (*collection*) range.
échapper [eʃape] (1) **1** *vi* **(a)** ~ **à** (*gén*) to escape; (*en fuyant*) to escape (from), get away from; (*par ruse*) to evade; ~ **à la règle** to be an exception to the rule; **il échappe à tout contrôle** he is beyond control; **tu ne m'échapperas pas!** I'll get you yet!; **son nom m'échappe** his name escapes me *ou* has slipped my mind; **ce qu'il a dit m'a échappé** (*entendre*) I did not catch what he said; (*comprendre*) I did not grasp what he said; **l'opportunité d'une telle mesure m'échappe** I fail to see the point of such a measure; **rien ne lui échappe** he doesn't miss a thing. **(b)** ~ **des mains de qn** to slip out of sb's hands. **(c) laisser** ~ *parole, occasion, objet* to let slip; *détail* to overlook; **laisser** ~ **un prisonnier** to let a prisoner escape; **il l'a échappé belle** he had a narrow escape.
2 s'~ *vpr* **(a)** *[prisonnier]* to escape (*de* from), break out (*de* of); *[oiseau]* to fly away; *[coureur]* to pull away; *[cri]* to escape, burst (*de* from). **la voiture réussit à s'**~ the car got away; (*fig*) **je m'échappe un instant** I'll slip away for a moment. **(b)** *[gaz]* to escape, leak; *[odeur, lumière]* to come (*de* from). **des flammes s'échappaient du toit** flames were coming out of the roof.
♦ **échappatoire** *nf* way out. ♦ **échappé, e 1** *nm,f* (*Sport*) **les** ~**s** the breakaway group. **2** *nf* **(a)** (*Sport*) breakaway. **(b)** (*vue*) vista; (*soleil*) gleam. ♦ **échappement** *nm* (*Aut*) exhaust; (*Tech*) escapement. ~ **libre** cutout.
écharde [eʃaʀd(ə)] *nf* splinter (of wood).
écharpe [eʃaʀp(ə)] *nf [femme]* scarf; *[maire]* sash; (*bandage*) sling. **bras en** ~ arm in a sling.
écharper [eʃaʀpe] (1) *vt* (*lit, fig*) to tear to pieces.
échasse [eʃɑs] *nf* (*gén*) stilt. ♦ **échassier** *nm* wader (*bird*).
échauder [eʃode] (1) *vt* (*ébouillanter*) to scald. (*faire réfléchir*) ~ **qn** to teach sb a lesson.
échauffer [eʃofe] (1) **1** *vt moteur* to overheat; *imagination* to fire. **échauffé par la course** hot after the race; **les esprits étaient très échauffés** people were getting very heated *ou* worked up. **2 s'**~ *vpr* (*Sport*) to warm up; *[débat]* to become heated. ♦ **échauffement** *nm* (*Sport*) warm-up; *[moteur]* overheating.
échauffourée [eʃofuʀe] *nf* (*Police*) clash; (*Mil*) skirmish.
échéance [eʃeɑ̃s] *nf* **(a)** *[délai]* expiry date; *[bon]* maturity date; *[traite]* redemption date; *[loyer]* date of payment; *[facture, dette]* settlement date. **(b)** (*règlements*) **l'~ de fin de mois** the end-of-month payments; **faire face à ses** ~**s** to meet one's financial obligations *ou* commitments. **(c)** (*laps de temps*) term. (*Fin*) **à longue/courte** ~ long-/short-term; (*fig*) **à longue** ~ in the long run; (*fig*) **à courte** ~ before long.
échec [eʃɛk] *nm* **(a)** (*insuccès*) failure; (*revers*) setback. **voué à l'~** bound to fail, doomed to failure; **tenir qn en** ~ to hold sb in check; **faire** ~ **à qn** to foil sb *ou* sb's plans. **(b)** (*Jeux*) **les** ~**s** chess; **jeu d'**~**s** (*échiquier*) chessboard; (*pièces*) chessmen; **être en** ~ to be in check; **faire** ~ **au roi** to check the king; **faire** ~ **et mat** to checkmate.
échelle [eʃɛl] *nf* **(a)** (*objet*) ladder. (*fig*) **il n'y a plus qu'à tirer l'~** we may as well give it up. **(b)** *[croquis, salaires etc]* scale. **à grande** ~ large-scale; **à l'~ mondiale** on a world scale; ~ **sociale** social scale. **(c)** *[bas]* ladder, run. ♦ **échelon** *nm [échelle]* rung; *[hiérarchie]* grade; (*Admin: niveau*) level. **grimper rapidement les** ~**s** to get quick promotion; **à l'~ national** at the national level.
échelonner [eʃlɔne] (1) *vt objets, paiements* to space out; *congés* to stagger; *difficultés* (*en complexité*) to grade; (*dans le temps*) to introduce gradually (*sur* over). **service d'ordre échelonné sur le parcours** police guard stationed at intervals along the route; **s'~ sur 3 km** to stretch over *ou* be spaced out over a distance of 3 km. ♦ **échelonnement** *nm* spacing out; staggering; grading; gradual introduction.
écheveau, *pl* ~**x** [eʃvo] *nm* skein, hank; (*fig*) tangle.
échevelé, e [eʃəvle] *adj personne* tousled; *rythme* frenzied.
échevin [ɛʃvɛ̃] *nm* (*Hist*) alderman; (*Belgique*) deputy burgomaster.
échine [eʃin] *nf* backbone, spine; (*Culin*) loin. **courber l'~** to submit. ♦ **s'échiner** (1) *vpr* (*fig*) to work o.s. to death (*à faire qch* doing sth).
échiquier [eʃikje] *nm* chessboard. **l'~ mondial** the scene of world affairs.
écho [eko] *nm* **(a)** (*lit*) echo; (*rumeur*) rumour, echo; (*témoignage*) account, report; (*réponse*) response. **se faire l'~ de** to echo, repeat; **sa proposition est restée sans** ~ his suggestion wasn't taken up. **(b)** (*Presse*) item of gossip. (*rubrique*) ~**s** gossip column.
échoir [eʃwaʀ] *vi* **(a) il vous échoit de faire** it falls to you to do. **(b)** *[loyer]* to fall due; *[délai]* to expire.
échoppe† [eʃɔp] *nf* workshop.
échouer [eʃwe] (1) **1** *vi* **(a)** *[personne]* to fail; *[plan]* to fail, fall through. ~ **à un examen/dans une tentative** to fail an exam/in an attempt; **faire** ~ *complot* to foil; *projet* to wreck; **faire** ~ **les plans de qn** to foil sb's plans. **(b)** (*aboutir*) to end up (*dans* in). **(c)** (*Naut: aussi* **s'**~) *[bateau]* to run aground; *[débris]* to be washed up. **le bateau s'est échoué** *ou* **a échoué sur un écueil** the boat ran onto a reef. **2** *vt* (*Naut*) (*accidentellement*) to ground; (*volontairement*) to beach.
éclabousser [eklabuse] (1) *vt* to splash, spatter (*de* with). **ils ont été éclaboussés par le scandale** their good name has been smeared by the scandal; ~ **qn de son luxe** (*éblouir*) to show off one's wealth to sb. ♦ **éclaboussure** *nf [boue]* splash; *[sang]* spatter; *[eau]* spot; (*fig*) smear, blot.
éclair [eklɛʀ] **1** *nm* **(a)** (*Mét*) flash of lightning; (*Phot*) flash. ~**s de chaleur** summer lightning; ~ **de** *génie etc* flash *ou* spark of; **passer comme un** ~ to flash past *ou* by; **en un** ~ in a flash; **un** ~ **dans sa vie** a ray of sunshine in his life. **(b)** (*Culin*) éclair. **2** *adj inv visite* lightning. **raid** ~ hit-and-run raid.
éclairage [eklɛʀaʒ] *nm* (*intérieur*) lighting; (*luminosité*) light (level). (*lit, fig*) **sous cet** ~ in this light. ♦ **éclairagiste** *nm* (*Théât*) electrician; (*Ciné*) lighting engineer.

éclairant, e [eklɛʀɑ̃, ɑ̃t] *adj* (*fig*) illuminating, enlightening; (*lit*) *propriétés* lighting.
éclaircir [eklɛʀsiʀ] (2) **1** *vt* **(a)** *teinte* to lighten. **(b)** *soupe* to make thinner; *plantes, cheveux* to thin. **(c)** *mystère* to clear up; *pensée, situation* to clarify. **pouvez-vous nous ~ sur ce point?** can you enlighten us on this point? **2 s'~** *vpr* **(a)** *[ciel]* to clear; *[temps]* to clear up. **s'~ la voix** to clear one's throat. **(b)** *[arbres, foule]* to thin out; *[cheveux]* to get thin *ou* thinner. **(c)** *[idées, situation]* to become clearer; *[mystère]* to be cleared up. ♦ **éclaircie** *nf* (*de soleil*) bright interval, sunny spell; (*dans nuages*) break; (*fig: dans la vie*) ray of sunshine. ♦ **éclaircissement** *nm [mystère]* clearing up; *[texte obscur]* clarification. **j'exige des ~s** I demand an explanation.
éclairer [ekleʀe] (1) **1** *vt* **(a)** *[lampe]* to light (up); *[soleil]* to shine (down) on; *[fenêtre]* to give light to. **une seule fenêtre était éclairée** only one window was lit up; **un sourire éclaira son visage** his face lit up in a smile; **bien/mal éclairé** well-/badly-lit. **(b)** *situation, texte* to throw light on. **(c) ~ qn** (*lit*) to light the way for sb; (*fig: renseigner*) to enlighten sb (*sur* about). **(d)** (*Mil*) **~ le terrain** to scout out the ground. **2** *vi*: **~ bien/mal** to give a good/poor light. **3 s'~** *vpr [rue]* to be lit; *[visage]* to light up, brighten; *[situation]* to get clearer. **tout s'éclaire!** everything's becoming clear!; **s'~ à la bougie** to use candlelight. ♦ **éclairé, e** *adj minorité* enlightened.
éclaireur [eklɛʀœʀ] *nm* **(a)** (*Mil*) scout. (*lit, fig*) **partir en ~** to go off to have a scout around. **(b)** (*Scoutisme*) (boy) scout. ♦ **éclaireuse** *nf* (girl) guide.
éclat [ekla] *nm* **(a)** *[os, bois]* splinter; *[grenade, pierre]* fragment. **~ d'obus** piece of shrapnel. **(b)** *[lumière, diamant, couleur]* brilliance; *[braise]* glow; *[vernis]* shine; *[satin, perle]* sheen; *[phares]* glare; *[yeux]* sparkle; *[teint, jeunesse]* radiance. **(c)** *[nom]* fame; *[cérémonie, époque]* brilliance; *[personnage]* glamour. **réception donnée avec ~** dazzling reception. **(d)** (*scandale*) fuss. **faire un ~** to make a fuss. **(e) ~s de voix** shouts; **~ de colère** angry outburst; **~ de rire** roar *ou* burst of laughter. ♦ **éclatant, e** *adj* **(a)** *lumière, couleur* bright; *soleil* blazing; *blancheur* dazzling; *teint* radiant. **(b)** *succès* dazzling; *revanche* shattering; *gloire* shining; *vérité* manifest; *exemple* striking; *mensonge* blatant. **il a des dons ~s** he is brilliantly gifted; **~ de santé** radiant with health. **(c)** *rire, bruit* loud; *voix* ringing.
éclater [eklate] (1) *vi* **(a)** *[bombe]* to explode, blow up; *[bourgeon]* to burst open; *[pneu, chaudière]* to burst; *[verre]* to shatter; *[parti]* to break up. **(b)** *[fléau, applaudissement]* to break out; *[scandale, orage]* to break. **des cris ont éclaté** shouts were raised; **un coup de tonnerre éclata** there was a peal of thunder. **(c)** *[vérité]* to shine out. **la joie éclate dans ses yeux** joy shines in his eyes. **(d) ~ de rire** to burst out laughing; **~ (de rage)** to explode (with rage); **~ en sanglots** to burst into tears; **~ en applaudissements** to burst into applause. **(e) faire ~** *mine* to detonate, blow up; *bombe* to explode; *pétard* to let off; *ballon, tuyau* to burst; *verre* to shatter; **faire *ou* laisser ~ sa joie/colère** to give free rein to one's joy/anger. ♦ **éclatement** *nm* explosion; bursting (*de* of); break-up (*de* in).
éclectique [eklɛktik] *adj* eclectic.
éclipse [eklips(ə)] *nf* (*Astron, fig*) eclipse. ♦ **éclipser** (1) **1** *vt* (*Astron*) to eclipse; *[gloire]* to eclipse, overshadow. **2 s'~*** *vpr* to slip away.
éclopé, e [eklɔpe] **1** *adj* lame. **2** *nm,f* (*hum*) (slightly) injured person.
éclore [eklɔʀ] (45) *vi [œuf]* to hatch; *[poussin]* to hatch (out); *[fleur]* to open out; *[amour, jour]* to dawn. **faire ~** *œuf* to hatch; *sentiment* to kindle. ♦ **éclosion** *nf* hatching; opening; dawn.
écluse [eklyz] *nf* (*Naut*) lock. ♦ **éclusier, -ière** *nm,f* lock keeper.
écœurer [ekœʀe] (1) *vt*: **~ qn** *[gâteau]* to make sb feel sick; *[conduite]* to disgust sb, make sb sick; *[échec]* to sicken sb. ♦ **écœurant, e** *adj conduite* disgusting, sickening; *gâteau* sickly; *chance, avantage* disgusting. ♦ **écœurement** *nm* (*lit*) nausea; (*fig*) disgust; (*lassitude*) discouragement.
école [ekɔl] *nf* school. (*éducation*) **l'~** education; **navire-~** training ship; **être à bonne ~** to be in good hands; **il a été à dure ~** he learned about life the hard way; **faire l'~** to teach; **faire l'~ buissonnière** to play truant *ou* hooky; **faire ~** *[personne]* to collect a following; *[théorie]* to gain widespread acceptance; **~ hôtelière** catering school; **~ maternelle** nursery school; **~ normale** ≃ teachers' training college; **~ de secrétariat** secretarial college. ♦ **écolier** *nm* schoolboy; (*fig: novice*) novice. ♦ **écolière** *nf* schoolgirl.
écologie [ekɔlɔʒi] *nf* ecology. ♦ **écologique** *adj* ecological. ♦ **écologiste** *nmf* ecologist.
éconduire [ekɔ̃dɥiʀ] (38) *vt visiteur* to dismiss; *soupirant* to reject; *solliciteur* to put off.
économat [ekɔnɔma] *nm* (*fonction*) bursarship; (*bureau*) bursar's office; (*magasin*) staff cooperative.
économe [ekɔnɔm] **1** *adj* thrifty. **être ~ de son temps** *etc* to be sparing of one's time *etc.* **2** *nmf* (*Admin*) bursar.
économie [ekɔnɔmi] *nf* **(a)** (*science*) economics (*sg*); (*Pol: système*) economy. **(b)** (*épargne*) economy, thrift. **(c)** (*gain*) saving. **faire une ~ de temps** to save time; **~s** savings; **faire des ~s** to save up, save money; **faire des ~s de chauffage** to economize on heating; **il n'y a pas de petites ~s** every little helps; (*fig péj*) **faire des ~s de bouts de chandelle** to make footling economies. ♦ **économique** *adj* (*Écon*) economic; (*bon marché*) economical. ♦ **économiquement** *adv* economically. **les ~ faibles** the lower-income groups. ♦ **économiser** (1) *vt électricité* to economize on, save on; *temps, forces* to save; *argent* to save up. **~ sur** to economize on, cut down on. ♦ **économiste** *nmf* economist.
écoper [ekɔpe] (1) *vti* (*Naut*) to bale (out). **~ (d')une punition*** to catch it*. ♦ **écope** *nf* (*Naut*) baler.
écorce [ekɔʀs(ə)] *nf [arbre]* bark; *[orange]* peel, skin. **l'~ terrestre** the earth's crust.
écorcher [ekɔʀʃe] (1) *vt* **(a)** (*dépecer*) *animal* to skin; *criminel* to flay. **(b)** (*égratigner*) to graze; (*par frottement*) to chafe, rub. **(c)** (*fig*) *mot* to mispronounce. **il écorche l'allemand** he speaks broken German. **(d)** (*) **~ le client** to fleece one's customers; **~ les oreilles de qn** to grate on sb's ears. ♦ **écorchure** *nf* graze.
écorner [ekɔʀne] (1) *vt meuble* to chip the corner of; *fortune* to make a hole in. **livre écorné** dog-eared book.
écossais, e [ekɔsɛ, ɛz] **1** *adj temps, caractère* Scottish; *whisky* Scotch; *tissu* tartan. **2** *nm*: **É~** Scot, Scotsman; **les É~** the Scots. **3** *nf*: **É~e** Scot, Scotswoman. ♦ **Écosse** *nf* Scotland.
écosser [ekɔse] (1) *vt* to shell, pod.
écot [eko] *nm* share (of a bill).
écouler [ekule] (1) **1** *vt* (*Comm*) to sell; *faux billets* to get rid of. **2 s'~** *vpr* **(a)** (*suinter*) to seep out; (*fuir*) to leak out; (*couler*) to flow out. **(b)** (*fig*) *[temps]* to pass, go by; *[argent]* to melt away; *[foule]* to drift away; (*Comm*) to sell. **sa vie écoulée** his past life. ♦ **écoulement** *nm [eau, voitures]* flow; *[pus]* discharge; *[foule]* dispersal; *[temps]* passage, passing; (*Comm*) selling.
écourter [ekuʀte] (1) *vt* (*gén*) to shorten; *visite* to cut short; *texte* to cut down.
écouter [ekute] (1) **1** *vt disque, confidence, conseil* to listen to; *discours,* (*Jur*) *témoin* to hear. ~

qn jusqu'au bout to hear sb out; ~ **qn parler** to hear sb speak; ~ **aux portes** to eavesdrop; **faire ~ un disque à qn** to play a record to sb; **ses conseils sont très écoutés** his advice is greatly valued; ~ **ses parents** to listen to one's parents; **faire ~ qn** to get sb to listen *ou* obey; **n'écoutant que son courage** letting courage be his only guide. **2 s'~** *vpr*: **elle s'écoute trop** she coddles herself; **si je m'écoutais je n'irais pas** I've a good mind not to go; **s'~ parler** to savour one's words.
♦ **écoute** *nf* (*Rad*) listening (*de* to). (*Police*) **~(s) téléphonique(s)** (phone) tapping; **nous restons à l'~** we are staying tuned in; (*TV*) **heures de grande ~** peak viewing hours; **avoir une grande ~** to have a large audience; **être aux ~s** to be listening (*de* to). ♦ **écouteur, -euse 1** *nm,f* (*attentif*) listener; (*indiscret*) eavesdropper. **2** *nm [téléphone]* receiver. (*Rad*) **~s** earphones, headphones.

écrabouiller* [ekʀabuje] (1) *vt* to crush. **se faire ~ par une voiture** to get crushed by a car.

écran [ekʀɑ̃] *nm* (*gén*) screen. **porter un roman à l'~** to film a novel; **faire ~ à qn** (*abriter*) to screen *ou* shelter sb; (*gêner*) to get in the way of sb; (*éclipser*) to put sb in the shade.

écraser [ekʀɑze] (1) **1** *vt* **(a)** (*gén*) to crush; *mouche* to swat; *mégot* to stub out; (*en purée*) to mash; (*en poudre*) to grind (*en* to); (*pour le jus*) to squeeze; (*en aplatissant*) to flatten out; (*en piétinant*) to trample down. ~ **sous la dent** *biscuit* to crunch; **vous m'écrasez les pieds** you're treading on my feet. **(b)** (*tuer*) *[voiture]* ~ **qn** to run sb over; **il s'est fait ~** he was run over. **(c)** (*fig: accabler*) to crush. **être écrasé de** *impôts* to be crushed by; *chaleur, sommeil* to be overcome by; *travail* to be snowed under with. **(d)** (*vaincre*) *ennemi* to crush. **notre équipe s'est fait ~** our team was beaten hollow; **il écrase tout le monde** he outdoes everyone (*en* at). **2** *vi*: **en ~‡** to sleep like a log*. **3 s'~** *vpr* **(a)** *[avion]* to crash; *[objet, corps]* to be dashed (*contre* on, against); (*dans le métro*) to get crushed (*dans* in). **(b)** (‡: *se taire*) to pipe down*. ♦ **écrasant, e** *adj* (*gén*) crushing; *travail* back-breaking; *victoire, chaleur, responsabilité, nombre* overwhelming. ♦ **écrasé, e** *adj nez* flat; *relief* dwarfed. ♦ **écrasement** *nm* crushing.

écrémer [ekʀeme] (6) *vt lait* to skim.

écrevisse [ekʀəvis] *nf* (freshwater) crayfish.

écrier (s') [ekʀije] (7) *vpr* to exclaim, cry out.

écrin [ekʀɛ̃] *nm* (jewellery) case.

écrire [ekʀiʀ] (39) *vt* (*gén*) to write; (*orthographier*) to spell; (*inscrire*) to write down. ~ **gros** to have large handwriting; ~ **à la machine** to type; **c'était écrit** it was bound to happen; **il est écrit que je ne pourrai jamais y arriver!** I'm doomed never to succeed! ♦ **écrit** *nm* (*ouvrage*) piece of writing; (*examen*) written paper; (*Jur*) document. **par ~** in writing. ♦ **écriteau,** *pl* **~x** *nm* notice, sign. ♦ **écriture** *nf* **(a)** (*à la main*) (hand)-writing; (*alphabet*) writing, script; (*style*) style. **(b)** (*Fin, Comm*) **~s** accounts, books; **tenir les ~s** to do the book-keeping. **(c)** (*Rel*) **l'É~ (Sainte)** the Scriptures. ♦ **écrivain** *nm* (*homme*) writer. **(femme-)~** woman writer.

écrou [ekʀu] *nm* (*Tech*) nut.

écrouer [ekʀue] (1) *vt* to imprison.

écrouler (s') [ekʀule] (1) *vpr* (*gén*) to collapse; *[empire, espoir]* to crumble; *[personne]* (*tomber*) to collapse; (*: *s'endormir*) to fall fast asleep; *[accusé]* to break down. **s'~ de fatigue** to be overcome with weariness. ♦ **écroulé, e** *adj*: **à moitié ~** *maison* half-ruined, tumbledown; **être ~** (*par le malheur*) to be prostrate with grief; (*de rire*) to be doubled up with laughter. ♦ **écroulement** *nm* collapse.

écru, e [ekʀy] *adj tissu* raw; *couleur* natural-coloured. **toile ~e** unbleached linen.

écu [eky] *nm* (*Hist Fin*) crown; (*arme*) shield.

écueil [ekœj] *nm* (*lit*) reef; (*problème*) stumbling block; (*piège*) pitfall.

écuelle [ekɥɛl] *nf* bowl.

éculé, e [ekyle] *adj soulier* down-at-heel; *plaisanterie* hackneyed, worn.

écumer [ekyme] (1) **1** *vt* **(a)** *bouillon* to skim. **(b)** (*piller*) to plunder; (*chercher*) to scour. ~ **les mers** to scour the seas. **2** *vi* (*gén*) to foam; *[cheval]* to lather. (*fig*) ~ **(de rage)** to foam with rage. ♦ **écume** *nf* (*gén*) foam; *[cheval]* lather. **pipe en ~ de mer** meerschaum pipe; (*fig*) **l'~ de la société** the dregs of society. ♦ **écumeux, -euse** *adj* foamy. ♦ **écumoire** *nf* skimmer.

écureuil [ekyʀœj] *nm* squirrel.

écurie [ekyʀi] *nf* stable; (*fig: sale*) pigsty. **mettre à l'~** to stable; ~ **de course** racing stable.

écusson [ekysɔ̃] *nm* badge.

écuyer [ekɥije] *nm* (*cavalier*) rider, horseman; (*d'un chevalier*) squire; (*à la cour*) equerry. ♦ **écuyère** *nf* rider, horsewoman.

eczéma [ɛgzema] *nm* eczema.

Éden [edɛn] *nm*: **l'~** Eden.

édicter [edikte] (1) *vt* to decree.

édifier [edifje] (7) *vt maison* to build, erect; *fortune, empire* to build (up); (*moralement*) to edify. ♦ **édification** *nf* erection; *[esprit]* edification. ♦ **édifice** *nm* edifice, building; (*social*) structure, fabric.

Édimbourg [edɛ̃buʀ] *n* Edinburgh.

édit [edi] *nm* (*Hist*) edict.

éditer [edite] (1) *vt* (*publier*) to publish; (*annoter*) to edit. ♦ **éditeur, -trice** *nm,f* publisher; editor. ♦ **édition** *nf* (*action*) publishing; editing; (*livre*) edition. **l'~** the publishing business.

éditorial, *pl* **-iaux** [editɔʀjal, jo] *nm* leader, editorial. ♦ **éditorialiste** *nmf* leader writer.

édredon [edʀədɔ̃] *nm* eiderdown.

éducation [edykɑsjɔ̃] *nf* (*Scol, gén*) education; (*familiale*) upbringing; *[goût]* training. **j'ai fait mon ~ à Paris** I was educated *ou* went to school in Paris; ~ **physique** physical training *ou* education; **sans ~** (*instruction*) ill-educated; (*bonnes manières*) ill-mannered, ill-bred. ♦ **éducateur, -trice 1** *adj* educational. **2** *nm,f* educator. ♦ **éducatif, -ive** *adj* educational.

édulcorer [edylkɔʀe] (1) *vt* (*Pharm*) to sweeten; (*fig*) to tone down.

éduquer [edyke] (1) *vt* (*à l'école*) to educate; (*à la maison*) to bring up; *peuple* to educate; *goût* to train. **bien éduqué** well-mannered, well-bred.

effacer [efase] (3) **1** *vt* (*gén*) to efface, erase; *[gomme]* to rub out; *[chiffon]* to wipe off; *[grattoir]* to scratch out; *souvenir* to efface; *faute* to erase; *craintes* to dispel; *concurrent* to outshine. ~ **son passé** to blot out one's past; **le temps efface tout** everything fades with time; ~ **le corps** to draw o.s. in. **2 s'~** *vpr* **(a)** (*gén*) to fade; *[inscription]* to wear off. **ça s'efface bien** *[crayon]* it rubs out easily; *[tableau]* it's easy to clean. **(b)** (*lit: s'écarter*) to move *ou* step aside; (*fig: se tenir en arrière*) to keep in the background; (*se retirer*) to withdraw. ♦ **effacé, e** *adj teinte* (*passé*) faded; (*sans éclat*) subdued; *personne, vie* retiring; *rôle* unobtrusive. ♦ **effacement** *nm* **(a)** erasing; effacing; dispelling; fading. ~ **des épaules** drawing one's shoulders back. **(b)** (*modestie*) retiring *ou* self-effacing manner; (*retrait*) withdrawal; (*éclipse*) eclipse.

effarer [efaʀe] (1) *vt* to alarm. **cette bêtise m'effare** I am aghast at *ou* appalled by such stupidity. ♦ **effarant, e** *adj* (*gén*) alarming. ♦ **effarement** *nm* alarm.

effaroucher [efaʀuʃe] (1) **1** *vt* (*gén*) to frighten *ou* scare away; (*choquer*) to shock. **2 s'~** *vpr* (*timidité*) to take fright (*de* at); (*pudeur*) to be shocked (*de* by).

effectif, -ive [efɛktif, iv] **1** *adj aide, travail*

effective, actual. **être ~ à partir de** to take effect *ou* become effective as from. **2** *nm [lycée]* size; *[parti]* size, strength. (*Mil, Pol*) **~s** numbers; (*Mil*) **l'~ est au complet** we are at full strength. ♦ **effectivement** *adv aider* effectively; *se produire* actually, really. **c'est ~ plus rapide** it's actually faster; **oui, ~!** yes, indeed!

effectuer [efɛktɥe] (1) **1** *vt* (*gén*) to make; *opération, expérience* to carry out, perform; *geste* to execute; *paiement* to effect; *trajet* to complete. **2 s'~** *vpr* to be made. **le voyage s'est effectué sans incident** the journey went off without a hitch.

efféminé, e [efemine] *adj* effeminate.

effervescence [efɛʀvesɑ̃s] *nf* (*lit*) effervescence; (*fig*) agitation. **être en ~** to be in a turmoil. ♦ **effervescent, e** *adj* effervescent.

effet [efɛ] *nm* **(a)** (*résultat*) effect. **c'est l'~ du hasard** it is quite by chance; **être sans ~** to be ineffective, have no effect; **~ de surprise** effect of surprise; **avoir pour ~ de** to result in; **ce médicament (me) fait de l'~/a fait son ~** this medicine is effective *ou* works (on me)/has taken effect *ou* has worked. **(b)** (*impression*) impression (*sur* on). **il a fait son petit ~** he managed to cause a bit of a stir; **c'est tout l'~ que ça te fait?** is that all it means to you?; **faire bon/mauvais ~ sur qn** to make a good/bad impression on sb; **il me fait l'~ d'(être) une belle crapule** he seems like a real crook to me; **cette déclaration a fait l'~ d'une bombe** this statement came as a bombshell. **(c)** (*procédé*) effect. **~ de style/de perspective** stylistic/visual effect; **elle lui a coupé ses ~s** she stole his thunder; **manquer son ~** *[personne]* to spoil one's effect; *[plaisanterie]* to fall flat. **(d)** (*Sport*) *[balle]* spin. **donner de l'~ à** to spin. **(e)** (*Jur*) **avec ~ rétroactif** backdated; **prendre ~ à la date de** to take effect as from. **(f)** (*Comm: valeur*) **~ (de commerce)** bill (of exchange). **(g)** (*vêtements*) **~s** things, clothes. **(h) en ~** (*parce que*) because; **oui, en ~** yes indeed; **c'est en ~ plus rapide** it's actually faster. **(i)** (*locutions*) **mettre à ~** to put into effect; **à cet ~** to that effect *ou* end; **sous l'~ de** *alcool* under the effect *ou* influence of; **il était encore sous l'~ de la colère** he was still angry.

efficace [efikas] *adj mesure* effective; *remède* efficacious; *personne, machine* efficient. ♦ **efficacement** *adv* effectively; efficaciously; efficiently. ♦ **efficacité** *nf* effectiveness; efficacy; efficiency.

effigie [efiʒi] *nf* effigy. **à l'~ de** bearing the effigy of.

effiler [efile] (1) **1** *vt étoffe* to fray. **2 s'~** *vpr [objet]* to taper; *[étoffe]* to fray. ♦ **effilé, e** *adj* slender, tapering.

effilocher *vt*, **s'~** *vpr* [efilɔʃe] (1) to fray.

efflanqué, e [eflɑ̃ke] *adj animal* raw-boned; *personne* emaciated.

effleurer [eflœʀe] (1) *vt* (*frôler*) to touch lightly, brush (against); (*érafler*) to graze; (*fig*) *sujet* to touch (lightly) upon. **~ l'esprit de qn** to cross sb's mind. ♦ **effleurement** *nm* light touch.

effluve [eflyv] *nm*: **~s** exhalations.

effondrer (s') [efɔ̃dʀe] (1) *vpr* (*gén*) to collapse; *[empire, espoir]* to crumble; *[accusé]* to break down. ♦ **effondré, e** *adj* (*abattu*) crushed (*de* by). ♦ **effondrement** *nm* **(a)** collapse; break-down. **(b)** (*abattement*) utter dejection.

efforcer (s') [efɔʀse] (3) *vpr*: **s'~ de faire** to try hard to do, do one's best to do.

effort [efɔʀ] *nm* **(a)** effort. **après bien des ~s** after much effort; **~ financier** financial outlay; **~ de volonté** effort of will; **faire un ~ de mémoire** to make an effort to remember; **faire de gros ~s pour réussir** to make a great effort to succeed, try very hard to succeed; **faire tous ses ~s** to do one's utmost, make every effort; **faire l'~ de** to make the effort to; **sans ~** effortlessly. **(b)** (*Tech*) stress, strain.

effraction [efʀaksjɔ̃] *nf* (*action*) breaking-in. **plusieurs ~s** several break-ins; **entrer par ~** to break in.

effranger *vt*, **s'~** *vpr* [efʀɑ̃ʒe] (3) to fray.

effrayer [efʀeje] (8) **1** *vt* to frighten. **2 s'~** *vpr* to be frightened (*de* by), take fright (*de* at). ♦ **effrayant, e** *adj* frightening, fearsome; (*sens affaibli*) frightful.

effréné, e [efʀene] *adj course* frantic; *passion, luxe* unbridled.

effriter [efʀite] (1) **1** *vt biscuit* to crumble; *roche* to cause to crumble. **2 s'~** *vpr* (*lit, fig*) to crumble (away). ♦ **effritement** *nm* crumbling(-away).

effroi [efʀwa] *nm* terror, dread.

effronté, e [efʀɔ̃te] *adj* insolent; *mensonge, menteur* brazen, shameless. ♦ **effrontément** *adv* insolently; brazenly, shamelessly. ♦ **effronterie** *nf* insolence; shamelessness.

effroyable [efʀwajabl(ə)] *adj* horrifying, appalling. ♦ **effroyablement** *adv* appallingly, horrifyingly.

effusion [efyzjɔ̃] *nf* effusion. **avec ~** effusively; **~ de sang** bloodshed.

égal, e, *mpl* **-aux** [egal, o] **1** *adj* **(a)** (*valeur*) equal (*en* in, *à* to). **de poids ~** of equal weight; **à poids ~** weight for weight; **à ~e distance de** equidistant from. **(b)** *justice, pas* even, unvarying; *climat, caractère* equable; *terrain* even, level; *bruit, vent* steady. **(c) ça m'est ~** I don't mind; (*je m'en fiche*) I don't care; **c'est ~, il aurait pu écrire** all the same he might have written; **la partie n'est pas ~e (entre eux)** they are not evenly matched; **ça n'a d'~ que** it is matched *ou* equalled only by; **rester ~ à soi-même** to remain true to form. **2** *nm,f* (*personne*) equal. **d'~ à ~** as equals; **être à l'~ de** (*égal à*) to be equalled *ou* matched by; (*comme*) to be just like; **sans ~** matchless, unequalled. ♦ **égalable** *adj*: **difficilement ~** difficult to equal *ou* match. ♦ **également** *adv* (*gén*) equally. (*aussi*) **elle lui a ~ parlé** she spoke to him too *ou* as well. ♦ **égaler** (1) **1** *vt* to equal (*en* in). **2 plus 2 égalent 4** 2 plus 2 equals 4; **~ qn à** to rank sb with; **~ qn en qch** to equal sb in sth, match sb for sth. **2 s'~** *vpr*: **s'~ à** to equal, be equal to; (*comparaison*) to liken o.s. to.

égaliser [egalize] (1) **1** *vt chances* to equalize; *sol, revenus* to level (out). **2** *vi* (*Sport*) to equalize. ♦ **égalisateur, -trice** *adj* equalizing. ♦ **égalisation** *nf* equalization; levelling.

égalité [egalite] *nf [chances, hommes]* equality; (*Math*) identity; *[climat]* equableness; *[pouls]* regularity; *[surface]* evenness, levelness. **~ d'humeur** equanimity; **être à ~** (*gén*) to be equal; (*match nul*) to draw. ♦ **égalitariste** *adj, nmf* egalitarian.

égard [egaʀ] *nm* **(a)** (*respect*) **~s** consideration; **montrer beaucoup d'~s pour** to show great consideration for, be very considerate towards. **(b) à l'~ de** (*envers*) towards; (*contre*) concerning, with regard to; **par ~ pour** out of consideration for; **sans ~ pour** without regard for; **à tous ~s** in all respects; **à cet ~** in this respect.

égarer [egaʀe] (1) **1** *vt voyageur* to lead out of his way; *enquêteurs* to mislead; *objet* to mislay; (*moralement*) to lead astray. **égaré par la douleur** distraught with grief. **2 s'~** *vpr [voyageur, lettre]* to get lost; *[discussion]* to wander from the point. (*fig, Rel*) **s'~ hors du droit chemin** to wander from the straight and narrow; **mon esprit s'égare** I feel distraught. ♦ **égaré, e** *adj voyageur* lost; *animal, obus* stray; *village* remote; *air* distraught. ♦ **égarement** *nm* (*trouble*) distraction. (*dérèglements*) **~s** aberrations.

égayer [egeje] (8) **1** *vt* (*gén*) to brighten up; (*divertir*) to amuse, cheer up. **2 s'~** *vpr* to amuse

o.s. **s'~ aux dépens de qn** to amuse o.s. at sb's expense.
égide [eʒid] *nf*: **sous l'~ de** under the aegis of.
églantier [eglɑ̃tje] *nm* wild rose(-bush). ♦ **églantine** *nf* wild rose, eglantine.
église [egliz] *nf* (*gén*) church.
égoïsme [egɔism(ə)] *nm* selfishness, egoism. ♦ **égoïste 1** *adj* selfish, egoistic. **2** *nmf* egoist. ♦ **égoïstement** *adv* selfishly, egoistically.
égorger [egɔʀʒe] (3) *vt* (*lit*) to slit *ou* cut the throat of; (*) *client* to bleed white.
égout [egu] *nm* sewer. **les ~s** the sewerage system. ♦ **égoutier** *nm* sewer worker.
égoutter [egute] (1) **1** *vt* (*avec passoire*) to strain; (*en tordant*) to wring out. **2** *vi [vaisselle]* to drain; *[linge, eau]* to drip. **faire ~** *eau* to drain off; *linge* to hang up to drip; **'laisser ~'** 'drip dry'. **3 s'~** *vpr* to drip; to drain. ♦ **égouttoir** *nm* (*évier*) draining board; (*mobile*) draining rack; (*passoire*) strainer, colander.
égratigner [egʀatiɲe] (1) *vt* (*lit*) to scratch; (*fig*) to have a dig at. ♦ **égratignure** *nf* scratch; (*fig*) dig. **sans une ~** without a scratch, unscathed.
égrener [egʀəne] (5) *vt pois, blé, épi* to shell; *coton* to gin; *grappe* to pick grapes off. (*fig*) **~ son chapelet** to tell one's beads; **~ les heures** to mark the hours; **les maisons s'égrenaient le long de la route** the houses were dotted along the road.
égrillard, e [egʀijaʀ, aʀd(ə)] *adj* bawdy.
Égypte [eʒipt] *nf* Egypt. ♦ **égyptien, -ienne** *adj*, **É~(ne)** *nm(f)* Egyptian.
éhonté, e [eɔ̃te] *adj* shameless.
éjecter [eʒɛkte] (1) *vt* (*Tech*) to eject; (‡) to kick out*. **se faire ~‡** to get o.s. kicked out*. ♦ **éjection** *nf* (*Tech*) ejection; (‡) kicking-out*.
élaborer [elabɔʀe] (1) *vt* (*gén*) to elaborate. ♦ **élaboration** *nf* elaboration.
élaguer [elage] (1) *vt* (*lit, fig*) to prune. ♦ **élagage** *nm* pruning. ♦ **élagueur** *nm* pruner.
élan[1] [elɑ̃] *nm* (*Zool*) elk, moose.
élan[2] [elɑ̃] *nm* **(a)** (*début de course*) run up. **saut avec/sans ~** running/standing jump. **(b)** (*vitesse acquise*) momentum. **prendre de l'~** to gather speed; **emporté par son ~** carried along by his own momentum. **(c)** *[enthousiasme, colère]* surge, burst. **~s (d'affection)** rushes of affection; **~s lyriques** lyrical outbursts. **(d)** *[troupes]* vigour, spirit. **~ patriotique** patriotic fervour.
élancer [elɑ̃se] (3) **1** *vi [blessure]* to give shooting pains. **2 s'~** *vpr* **(a)** (*se précipiter*) to rush, dash (*vers* towards). **s'~ d'un bond sur** to leap onto. **(b)** (*se dresser*) to soar (upwards). ♦ **élancé, e** *adj clocher etc* slender. ♦ **élancement** *nm* shooting pain.
élargir [elaʀʒiʀ] (2) **1** *vt* **(a)** (*gén*) to widen; *débat* to broaden. (*Pol*) **majorité élargie** increased majority; **ça lui élargit la taille** that makes his waist look fatter. **(b)** (*Jur: libérer*) to release, free. **2 s'~** *vpr [route]* to widen, get wider; *[idées]* to broaden. ♦ **élargissement** *nm* widening; broadening; release.
élastique [elastik] **1** *adj objet* elastic; *démarche* springy; *sens, esprit* flexible; (*péj*) *conscience* accommodating; (*Écon*) elastic. **2** *nm* (*de bureau*) elastic *ou* rubber band; (*Couture*) elastic. **en ~** elasticated. ♦ **élasticité** *nf* elasticity; spring; flexibility; accommodating nature.
électeur, -trice [elɛktœʀ, tʀis] *nm,f* **(a)** (*Pol*) voter. (*circonscription*) **~s** constituents. **(b)** (*Hist*) **É~** Elector; **É~trice** Electress. ♦ **élection** *nf* **(a)** (*Pol, gén*) election. **jour des ~s** polling *ou* election day; **~ partielle** = by-election; **~s législatives** = general election. **(b)** (*choix*) **patrie d'~** chosen country. ♦ **électoral, e,** *mpl* **-aux** *adj* election. ♦ **électorat** *nm* **(a)** electorate; (*d'un parti*) voters. **(b)** (*Hist*) electorate.
électricité [elɛktʀisite] *nf* electricity. (*fig*) **il y a de l'~ dans l'air*** the atmosphere is electric. ♦ **électricien** *nm* electrician. ♦ **électrification** *nf* electrification. ♦ **électrifier** (7) *vt* to electrify. ♦ **électrique** *adj* electrical. ♦ **électriquement** *adv* electrically. ♦ **électriser** (1) *vt* (*lit, fig*) to electrify.
électro [elɛktʀɔ] *préf* electro. **~-aimant** electromagnet; **~cardiogramme** electrocardiogram; **~choc(s)** electric shock treatment.
électrocuter [elɛktʀɔkyte] (1) *vt* to electrocute. ♦ **électrocution** *nf* electrocution.
électrode [elɛktʀɔd] *nf* electrode.
électroménager [elɛktʀɔmenaʒe] *adj appareil* (domestic) electrical.
électron [elɛktʀɔ̃] *nm* electron.
électronique [elɛktʀɔnik] **1** *adj* (*gén*) electronic; *optique* electron. **2** *nf* electronics (*sg*). ♦ **électronicien, -ienne** *nm,f* electronics engineer.
électrophone [elɛktʀɔfɔn] *nm* record player.
élégant, e [elegɑ̃, ɑ̃t] *adj* (*gén*) elegant; *conduite* generous. ♦ **élégamment** *adv* elegantly. ♦ **élégance** *nf* elegance; generosity.
élégie [eleʒi] *nf* elegy.
élément [elemɑ̃] *nm* (*gén, Chim*) element; *[machine]* part, component; *[pile]* cell; (*Mil*) unit; (*fait*) fact. (*rudiments*) **~s** rudiments, elements; **~s préfabriqués de cuisine** ready-made kitchen units; **aucun ~ nouveau n'est survenu** there have been no new developments, no new facts have come to light; **c'est le meilleur ~ de ma classe** he's the best pupil in my class; **les ~s (naturels)** the elements; **être dans son ~*** to be in one's element. ♦ **élémentaire** *adj* elementary; rudimentary; (*Chim*) elemental.
éléphant [elefɑ̃] *nm* elephant. **comme un ~ dans un magasin de porcelaine** like a bull in a china shop.
élevage [ɛlvaʒ] *nm* **(a)** (*gén*) breeding. **l'~ (du bétail)** cattle breeding *ou* rearing; **l'~ des abeilles** beekeeping; **faire l'~ de** to breed; **pays d'~** cattle-breeding area. **(b)** (*ferme*) cattle farm. **~ de poulets** poultry farm.
élévation [elevɑsjɔ̃] *nf* (*action d'élever*) raising; (*action de s'élever*) rise (*de* in); (*tertre*) elevation, rise (in the ground); (*coupe, plan*) elevation; *[pensée, style]* loftiness; *[âme]* elevation. (*Rel*) **l'~** the Elevation.
élève [elɛv] *nmf* pupil, student. **~ infirmière** student nurse.
élevé, e [ɛlve] *adj* (*gén*) high; *pertes* heavy; *cime* lofty. **peu ~** low; *pertes* slight; **bien ~** well-mannered; **mal ~** (*rustre*) ill-mannered; (*impoli*) rude; **c'est mal ~ de** it's bad manners *ou* it's rude to.
élever [ɛlve] (5) **1** *vt* **(a)** *enfant* to bring up, raise; *bétail* to rear, breed; *abeilles* to keep; *plantes* to grow. **(b)** *mur* (*dresser*) to put up. (*hausser*) **~ (d'un étage)** to raise (by one storey), make (one storey) higher. **(c)** *objection* to raise, *critique* to make. **(d)** *poids, regard* to lift, raise; *niveau, prix, voix* to raise. **(e)** (*promouvoir*) to raise, elevate (*au rang de* to the rank of). **(f)** (*gén, Math*) to raise. **~ un nombre au carré** to square a number.
2 s'~ *vpr* **(a)** *[niveau, prix]* to rise, go up. *[somme]* **s'~ à** to add up to, amount to. **(b)** *[immeuble]* (*se dresser*) to rise; (*se bâtir*) to go up. **un mur s'élevait entre** a wall stood between. **(c)** *[avion]* to go up; *[oiseau]* to fly up; (*dans la société*) to rise. **s'~ jusqu'au sommet de l'échelle** to climb to the top of the ladder. **(d)** *[discussions]* to arise; *[objections, doutes]* to be raised, arise; *[voix]* to rise. **s'~ contre** to rise up against.
éleveur, -euse [ɛlvœʀ, øz] *nm,f* stockbreeder.
elfe [ɛlf(ə)] *nm* elf.
éligible [eliʒibl(ə)] *adj* (*Pol*) eligible. ♦ **éligibilité** *nf* eligibility.
élimer *vt*, **s'~** *vpr* [elime] (1) to fray.
éliminer [elimine] (1) *vt* to eliminate; *données*

secondaires to discard; (*euph*) *témoin* to dispose of. ♦ **élimination** *nf* elimination. ♦ **éliminatoire 1** *adj épreuve* eliminatory; *note* disqualifying. **2** *nf* (*Sport*) heat.
élire [eliʀ] (43) *vt* to elect.
élite [elit] *nf* élite. **d'~** *élève* first-class; *âme* noble; (*Mil*) **corps d'~** crack corps. ♦ **élitisme** *nm* élitism.
élixir [eliksiʀ] *nm* elixir.
elle [ɛl] *pron pers f* **(a)** (*sujet*) (*personne, nation*) she; (*chose*) it; (*animal, bébé*) she, it. **~s** they; **~**, **~ n'aurait jamais fait ça** SHE would never have done that; **~ renoncer?** HER give up? **(b)** (*objet*) (*personne, nation*) her; (*animal*) her, it; (*chose*) it. **c'est ~ qui me l'a dit** she told me herself, it's she who told me; (*iro*) **c'est ~s qui le disent** that's what THEY say!; **c'est ~ que j'avais invitée** it's her I had invited. **(c)** (*avec prép*) (*personne*) her; (*animal*) her, it; (*chose*) it. **ce livre est à ~** this book belongs to her *ou* is hers; **elle ne pense qu'à ~** she only thinks of herself; **elle a un appartement à ~** she has a flat of her own; **ses enfants à ~** HER children. **(d)** (*comparaison*) (*sujet*) she; (*objet*) her. **il est plus grand qu'~s** he is taller than they are *ou* than them. **(e)** (*interrog, emphatique*) **sa lettre est-~ arrivée?** has his (*ou* her) letter come?; **ta tante, ~ n'est pas très aimable!** your aunt isn't very nice!
ellipse [elips(ə)] *nf* (*Géom*) ellipse; (*Ling*) ellipsis.
élocution [elɔkysjɔ̃] *nf* (*débit*) delivery; (*clarté*) diction. **défaut d'~** speech impediment.
éloge [elɔʒ] *nm* **(a)** (*louange*) **~(s)** praise; **faire des ~s à qn** to praise sb; **faire l'~ de** to praise; **faire son propre ~** to sing one's own praises. **(b)** (*panégyrique*) eulogy. **~ funèbre** funeral oration. ♦ **élogieusement** *adv parler* very highly. ♦ **élogieux, -ieuse** *adj* laudatory.
éloigné, e [elwaɲe] *adj lieu, son* distant, far-off; *événement* distant, remote (*de* from); *parent* distant; *ancêtre* remote. **est-ce très ~ de la gare? – oui, c'est très ~** is it very far *ou* a long way from the station? – yes, it's a long way; **~ de 3 km** 3 km away; **dans un avenir peu ~** in the not-too-distant future; **sentiment pas très ~ de la haine** emotion not far removed from hatred; **rien n'est plus ~ de mes pensées** nothing is farther from my thoughts; **tenir ~ de** to keep away from; **se tenir ~ des querelles** to steer clear of quarrels.
éloignement [elwaɲmɑ̃] *nm* (*gén*) removal; (*report*) postponement; (*désaffection*) estrangement; (*banissement*) banishment; (*distance*) distance. **avec l'~** (*temps, espace*) from a distance.
éloigner [elwaɲe] (1) **1** *vt* **(a)** *objet* to move *ou* take away; *personne* to take away; (*fig: exiler*) to send away (*de* from). (*fig*) **~ qn de** *être aimé* to estrange sb from; *tentations* to remove sb from. **(b)** (*fig: dissiper*) (*gén*) to remove; *idée, crainte* to dismiss; *danger* to ward off; *soupçons* to avert (*de* from). **(c)** *visite* (*reporter*) to put off, postpone; (*espacer*) to space out. **2 s'~** *vpr* (*gén*) to go away (*de* from); *[souvenir]* to grow more distant *ou* remote. **s'~ en courant** to run away *ou* off; **éloignez-vous, les enfants** move *ou* stand back, children; **s'~ de** *être aimé* to grow away from; *sujet* to wander from; *position prise* to move away from; *devoir, vérité* to stray from; **s'~ du droit chemin** to stray from the straight and narrow.
élongation [elɔ̃gɑsjɔ̃] *nf*: **se faire une ~** to strain a muscle.
éloquent, e [elɔkɑ̃, ɑ̃t] *adj* eloquent. **ces chiffres sont ~s** these figures speak for themselves. ♦ **éloquemment** *adv* eloquently. ♦ **éloquence** *nf* eloquence.
élu, e [ely] **1** *adj* (*Rel*) chosen; (*Pol*) elected. **2** *nm,f* (*député*) elected member; (*conseiller*) councillor. (*hum*) **l'heureux ~** the lucky man; (*Rel*) **les É~s** the Chosen ones, the Elect.
élucider [elyside] (1) *vt* to elucidate. ♦ **élucidation** *nf* elucidation.
élucubrations [elykybʀɑsjɔ̃] *nfpl* (*péj*) wild imaginings.
éluder [elyde] (1) *vt* to evade, elude.
émacié, e [emasje] *adj* emaciated.
émailler [emaje] (1) *vt* (*lit*) to enamel; *[étoiles]* to spangle; *[fautes]* to pepper. ♦ **émail,** *pl* **-aux** *nm* enamel. **en ~** enamel; (*Art*) **~aux** pieces of enamel work. ♦ **émaillage** *nm* enamelling.
émanation [emanɑsjɔ̃] *nf* **(a)** (*odeurs*) **~s** exhalations. **(b)** (*fig*) product.
émanciper [emɑ̃sipe] (1) **1** *vt* (*Jur*) to emancipate; *esprit* to liberate. **2 s'~** *vpr* to become liberated. ♦ **émancipation** *nf* emancipation; liberation.
émaner [emane] (1) **~ de** *vt indir [pouvoir, ordres]* to come from; *[chaleur, odeur]* to emanate *ou* come from; *[charme]* to emanate from.
émarger [emaʀʒe] (3) **1** *vt* to sign. **2** *vi* to be paid. ♦ **émargement** *nm* signing. **feuille d'~** (*paye*) paysheet; (*présence*) attendance sheet.
emballer [ɑ̃bale] (1) **1** *vt* **(a)** (*empaqueter*) to pack (up); (*dans du papier*) to wrap up. **(b)** (‡: *emprisonner*) to run in‡. **(c)** *moteur* to race. **(d)** (*: *enthousiasmer*) to thrill. **2 s'~** *vpr* **(a)** (*) (*enthousiasme*) to get carried away; (*colère*) to fly off the handle*. **(b)** *[moteur]* to race; *[cheval]* to bolt. **cheval emballé** bolting horse. ♦ **emballage** *nm* packing; wrapping-up; (*boîte etc*) packet, package. ♦ **emballement** *nm* **(a)** (*) (*enthousiasme*) craze; (*colère*) angry outburst. **(b)** *[moteur]* racing; *[cheval]* bolting.
embarcadère [ɑ̃baʀkadɛʀ] *nm* landing stage.
embarcation [ɑ̃baʀkɑsjɔ̃] *nf* (small) boat *ou* craft (*inv*).
embardée [ɑ̃baʀde] *nf* (*Aut*) swerve. **faire une ~** to swerve.
embargo [ɑ̃baʀgo] *nm* embargo. **mettre l'~ sur** to put an embargo on.
embarquer [ɑ̃baʀke] (1) **1** *vt passagers* to embark; *cargaison* to load; (‡) (*emporter, emprisonner*) to cart off*; (*voler*) to pinch*. **~ qn dans une histoire** to get sb mixed up in* *ou* involved in an affair. **2** *vi* (*aussi* **s'~**) (*en bateau*) to embark, board; (*en train, avion*) to board. **~ pour la France** to sail for France. **3 s'~** *vpr* **(a)** = **2. (b) s'~ dans** *aventure* to embark on. ♦ **embarquement** *nm* loading; embarkation; boarding.
embarras [ɑ̃baʀa] *nm* (*ennui*) hindrance, obstacle; (*gêne*) confusion, embarrassment; (*situation délicate*) predicament, awkward position. **être dans l'~** to be in a predicament *ou* an awkward position; (*dans un dilemme*) to be in a quandary *ou* in a dilemma; (*sans argent*) to be in financial difficulties; **~ gastrique** stomach upset; **~ de circulation** (road) congestion; **faire des ~** (*chichis*) to make a fuss; (*ennuis*) to make trouble (*à qn* for sb); **je ne veux pas être un ~ pour vous** I don't want to hinder you *ou* to be in your way; **ne vous mettez pas dans l'~ pour moi** don't put yourself out for me; **elle a l'~ du choix** her only problem is that she has too great a choice.
embarrasser [ɑ̃baʀase] (1) **1** *vt* **(a)** *[paquets]* to clutter; *[vêtements]* to hinder, hamper. **ça m'embarrasse** it's in my way; **~ l'estomac** to lie heavy on the stomach. **(b)** (*désorienter*) **~ qn** to put sb in a predicament *ou* an awkward position; **ça m'embarrasse de te le dire mais ...** I don't like to tell you this but ...; **il y a qch qui m'embarrasse là-dedans** there's sth about it that bothers me. **2 s'~** *vpr*: **s'~ de** *paquets, scrupules* to burden o.s. with; *détails* to trouble o.s. *ou* worry about; **s'~ dans** *vêtements* to get tangled up in; *explications* to get in a muddle with, get mixed up in. ♦ **embarrassant, e** *adj* **(a)** *situation* embarrass-

ing; *problème* awkward. **(b)** *paquets* cumbersome. **cet enfant est ~!** this child is always in the way! ♦ **embarrassé, e** *adj* (*gêné*) embarrassed; (*peu clair*) muddled, confused; (*encombré*) cluttered. **avoir l'estomac ~** to have an upset stomach; **j'ai les mains ~es** my hands are full.
embaucher [ɑ̃boʃe] (1) *vt* to take on, hire. ♦ **embauche** *nf* hiring. **est-ce qu'il y a de l'~?** are there any vacancies?; **bureau d'~** labour office.
embaumer [ɑ̃bome] (1) **1** *vt cadavre* to embalm. **l'air embaumait le lilas** the air was fragrant with the scent of lilac. **2** *vi* to be fragrant. ♦ **embaumé, e** *adj air* balmy, fragrant. ♦ **embaumement** *nm* embalming.
embellir [ɑ̃beliʀ] (2) **1** *vt* (*gén*) to make (more) attractive; *récit* to embellish. **2** *vi* to grow more attractive. ♦ **embellissement** *nm* improvement; *[récit]* embellishment.
embêter* [ɑ̃bete] (1) **1** *vt* (*gén*) to bother, worry; (*importuner*) to pester; (*irriter*) to annoy; (*lasser*) to bore. **2 s'~** *vpr* to be bored. ♦ **embêtant, e*** *adj* worrying, annoying; *situation* awkward, tricky. ♦ **embêtement*** *nm* annoyance. **~(s)** trouble.
emblée [ɑ̃ble] *adv*: **d'~** straightaway, right away.
emblème [ɑ̃blɛm] *nm* emblem.
emboîter [ɑ̃bwate] (1) **1** *vt* to fit together. **~ qch dans** to fit sth into; **~ le pas à qn** (*lit*) to follow close on sb's heels; (*fig*) to follow suit. **2 s'~** *vpr* to fit together.
embonpoint [ɑ̃bɔ̃pwɛ̃] *nm* stoutness. **prendre de l'~** to grow stout.
embouchure [ɑ̃buʃyʀ] *nf [fleuve]* mouth; (*Mus*) mouthpiece.
embourber *vt*, **s'~** *vpr* [ɑ̃buʀbe] (1) *voiture* to get stuck in the mud.
embourgeoiser (s') [ɑ̃buʀʒwaze] (1) *vpr* to become middle-class.
embout [ɑ̃bu] *nm [canne]* tip; *[tuyau]* nozzle.
embouteiller [ɑ̃buteje] (1) *vt* (*Aut*) to jam, block; (*Téléc*) *lignes* to block. ♦ **embouteillage** *nm* (*Aut*) traffic jam, holdup.
emboutir [ɑ̃butiʀ] (2) *vt métal* to stamp; (*Aut: percuter*) to crash *ou* run into.
embranchement [ɑ̃bʀɑ̃ʃmɑ̃] *nm* (*jonction*) junction; (*route*) side road; (*voie*) branch line; (*rivière*) embranchment; (*Bot, Zool: catégorie*) branch.
embraser [ɑ̃bʀɑze] (1) **1** *vt forêt etc* to set ablaze; *cœur* to fire. **2 s'~** *vpr* to blaze up; to be fired (*de* with). ♦ **embrasement** *nm* (*action*) blazing-up; (*résultat*) blaze.
embrasser [ɑ̃bʀase] (1) **1** *vt* to kiss; (*étreindre*) to embrace; *cause, aspects* to embrace; *carrière* to take up. **~ qch du regard** to take sth in at a glance. **2 s'~** *vpr* to kiss (each other). ♦ **embrassade** *nf* embrace.
embrasure [ɑ̃bʀɑzyʀ] *nf* embrasure. **dans l'~ de la porte** in the doorway.
embrayer [ɑ̃bʀeje] (8) **1** *vt* (*Aut, Tech*) to put into gear. **2** *vi* (*Aut*) to let in *ou* engage the clutch. ♦ **embrayage** *nm* (*mécanisme*) clutch; (*action*) engaging the clutch.
embrigader [ɑ̃bʀigade] (1) *vt* to dragoon (*dans* into).
embrocher [ɑ̃bʀɔʃe] (1) *vt* (*Culin*) (*broche*) to spit; (*brochette*) to skewer. (*fig*) **~ qn** to run sb through.
embrouiller [ɑ̃bʀuje] (1) **1** *vt* (*gén*) to muddle up; *ficelle* to tangle (up). **2 s'~** *vpr [idées, situation]* to become muddled *ou* confused; *[personne]* to get in a muddle, become confused. **s'~ dans** to get in a muddle with. ♦ **embrouillement** *nm* (*action*) tangling; muddling up; confusion; (*état*) tangle; muddle; confusion.
embroussaillé, e [ɑ̃bʀusɑje] *adj chemin* overgrown; *barbe* bushy, shaggy.
embrumer [ɑ̃bʀyme] (1) *vt* to mist over, cloud over (*de* with).
embruns [ɑ̃bʀœ̃] *nmpl* spindrift, sea spray.
embryon [ɑ̃bʀijɔ̃] *nm* embryo. ♦ **embryonnaire** *adj* embryonic.
embûche [ɑ̃byʃ] *nf* pitfall, trap.
embuer [ɑ̃bɥe] (1) *vt* to mist up *ou* over.
embuscade [ɑ̃byskad] *nf* ambush. **être en ~** to lie in ambush. ♦ **s'embusquer** (1) *vpr* to lie in ambush.
éméché, e [emeʃe] *adj* tipsy, merry.
émeraude [ɛmʀod] *nf, adj inv* emerald.
émerger [emeʀʒe] (3) *vi* to emerge; (*faire saillie*) to stand out. **~ du brouillard** to rise out of the fog. ♦ **émergence** *nf* emergence.
émeri [ɛmʀi] *nm* emery. **toile ~** emery paper.
émerveiller [emɛʀveje] (1) **1** *vt* to fill with wonder. **2 s'~** *vpr* to be filled with wonder. **s'~ de** to marvel at. ♦ **émerveillement** *nm* (*sentiment*) wonder; (*vision*) marvel.
émettre [emɛtʀ(ə)] (56) *vt* (*gén*) to emit; *lumière* to give out; *son* to send out; *odeur* to give off; (*Rad, TV*) to transmit; *monnaie, emprunt* to issue; *chèque* to draw; *hypothèse* to put forward; *vœux* to express. **~ sur ondes courtes** to broadcast on short wave. ♦ **émetteur, -trice 1** *adj* (*Rad*) transmitting; (*Fin*) issuing. **2** *nm* transmitter. **~-récepteur** transmitter-receiver.
émeute [emøt] *nf* riot. **~s** riots, rioting. ♦ **émeutier, -ière** *nm,f* rioter.
émietter *vt*, **s'~** *vpr* [emjete] (1) *pain, terre* to crumble; *pouvoir* to disperse; *énergie* to dissipate. ♦ **émiettement** *nm* crumbling; dispersion; dissipation.
émigrer [emigʀe] (1) *vi* to emigrate. ♦ **émigrant, e** *nm,f* emigrant. ♦ **émigration** *nf* emigration. ♦ **émigré, e** *nm,f* (*Hist*) émigré; (*Pol*) expatriate.
émincer [emɛ̃se] (3) *vt* to slice thinly.
éminence [eminɑ̃s] *nf [terrain]* hill, rise; *[qualité]* distinction, eminence; (*cardinal*) Eminence. (*fig*) **~ grise** éminence grise. ♦ **éminemment** *adv* eminently. ♦ **éminent, e** *adj* distinguished, eminent.
émir [emiʀ] *nm* emir. ♦ **émirat** *nm* emirate.
émissaire [emisɛʀ] *nm* (*gén*) emissary.
émission [emisjɔ̃] *nf* **(a)** (*V* **émettre**) emission; transmission; broadcast; issue; drawing. **(b)** (*Rad, TV: spectacle*) programme, broadcast.
emmagasiner [ɑ̃magazine] (1) *vt* (*lit, fig: amasser*) to accumulate; (*Comm*) to store. ♦ **emmagasinage** *nm* accumulation; storage.
emmailloter [ɑ̃majɔte] (1) *vt* to wrap up.
emmêler [ɑ̃mele] (1) **1** *vt fil* to tangle (up); (*fig*) *affaire* to confuse, muddle. (*fig*) **tu emmêles tout** you're getting everything muddled (up) *ou* confused. **2 s'~** *vpr* (*lit*) to get in a tangle; (*fig*) to get in a muddle (*dans* with). ♦ **emmêlement** *nm* (*action*) tangling; (*état*) tangle; muddle.
emménager [ɑ̃menaʒe] (3) *vi* to move in. **~ dans** to move into. ♦ **emménagement** *nm* moving in.
emmener [ɑ̃mne] (5) *vt* (*gén*) to take; *otage* to take away. **~ qn au cinéma** to take sb to the cinema; **~ promener qn** to take sb for a walk.
emmitoufler [ɑ̃mitufle] (1) *vt* to wrap *ou* muffle up. **s'~** to wrap *ou* muffle o.s. up.
emmurer [ɑ̃myʀe] (1) *vt* to wall up, immure.
émoi [emwa] *nm* (*trouble*) agitation, emotion; (*de joie*) excitement; (*tumulte*) commotion. **en ~** *cœur* in a flutter; *sens* agitated, excited; *rue* in a commotion.
émoluments [emɔlymɑ̃] *nmpl* (*Admin*) emolument, fee.
émotion [emosjɔ̃] *nf* emotion; (*peur*) fright. **donner des ~s à qn*** to give sb a nasty turn* *ou* fright. ♦ **émotif, -ive** *adj* emotional. ♦ **émotionnel, -elle** *adj* emotional. ♦ **émotionner*** (1) **1** *vt* to upset. **2 s'~** *vpr* to get upset (*de* about). ♦ **émotivité** *nf* emotionalism.
émoulu, e [emuly] *adj*: **frais ~ (de l'école)** fresh from school, just out of school.

émoussé, e [emuse] *adj couteau* blunt; *goût* blunted, dulled.
émoustiller* [emustije] (1) *vt* to tantalize.
émouvoir [emuvwaʀ] (27) **1** *vt [beauté]* to rouse, stir; *[misère]* to affect, touch, move; *[menace]* to disturb, worry, upset. **~ qn jusqu'aux larmes** to move sb to tears; **se laisser ~ par des prières** to be moved by entreaties; **~ la pitié de qn** to move sb to pity, rouse sb's pity. **2 s'~** *vpr* to be roused *ou* stirred *ou* affected *ou* touched *ou* moved *ou* disturbed *ou* worried *ou* upset (*de* by). **il ne s'émeut de rien** nothing upsets *ou* disturbs him. ♦ **émouvant, e** *adj* moving, touching.
empailler [ɑ̃pɑje] (1) *vt animal* to stuff. ♦ **empailleur, -euse** *nm,f* taxidermist.
empaqueter [ɑ̃pakte] (4) *vt marchandises* to pack; *colis* to wrap up.
emparer (s') [ɑ̃paʀe] (1) *vpr* **(a)** *[personne]* **s'~ de** (*gén*) to seize; *objet* to grab (hold of), snatch up; *conversation* to take over; *prétexte* to seize on. **(b)** *[sentiment]* **s'~ de** to take *ou* seize hold of; **le remords s'empara d'elle** she was seized with remorse.
empâter [ɑ̃pɑte] (1) **1** *vt bouche* to coat, fur (up); *traits* to thicken, coarsen. **2 s'~** *vpr [silhouette]* to thicken out.
empêcher [ɑ̃peʃe] (1) **1** *vt* to prevent, stop. **~ que qch (ne) se produise** to prevent sth from happening, stop sth happening; **~ qn de faire** to prevent sb from doing, stop sb (from) doing; (*fig*) **ça ne m'empêche pas de dormir** I don't lose any sleep over it; **ça n'empêche rien*** it makes no odds* *ou* no difference; **(il) n'empêche qu'il a tort** nevertheless *ou* all the same he's wrong. **2 s'~** *vpr*: **s'~ de faire** to stop o.s. (from) doing; **il n'a pas pu s'~ de rire** he couldn't help laughing, he couldn't stop himself (from) laughing. ♦ **empêché, e** *adj* (*retenu*) detained, held up. **il a été ~ par ses obligations** his commitments prevented him from coming; **tu es bien ~ de le dire** you seem at a loss to know what to say. ♦ **empêchement** *nm* (unexpected) difficulty, hitch. **il a eu un ~** sth prevented him from coming.
empereur [ɑ̃pʀœʀ] *nm* emperor.
empeser [ɑ̃pəze] (5) *vt* to starch. ♦ **empesé, e** *adj col* starched; (*fig*) stiff, starchy.
empester [ɑ̃pɛste] (1) *vt odeur* to stink of, reek of; *pièce* to stink out (*de* with). **ça empeste ici** it stinks in here.
empêtrer (s') [ɑ̃petʀe] (1) *vpr*: **s'~ dans** *habits, explications* to get tangled up in; *affaire* to get (o.s.) mixed up in.
emphase [ɑ̃fɑz] *nf* pomposity. **sans ~** simply. ♦ **emphatique** *adj* pompous; (*Ling*) emphatic.
empiéter [ɑ̃pjete] (6) *vi*: **~ sur** (*lit, fig*) to encroach (up)on; *[terrain]* to overlap into; *attributions* to trespass on. ♦ **empiètement** *nm* encroachment (*sur* upon).
empiffrer (s')‡ [ɑ̃pifʀe] (1) *vpr* to stuff o.s.* (*de* with), gorge o.s. (*de* on).
empiler [ɑ̃pile] (1) **1** *vt* to pile, stack. **2 s'~** *vpr* to be piled up (*sur* on). **s'~ dans** *véhicule* to squeeze into. ♦ **empilement** *nm* (*action*) piling, stacking; (*pile*) pile, stack.
empire [ɑ̃piʀ] *nm* **(a)** (*Pol*) empire. **pas pour un ~!** not for all the world! **(b)** (*emprise*) influence, authority. **sous l'~ de** *colère* in the grip of; *boisson* under the influence of; **~ sur soi-même** self-control, self-command.
empirer [ɑ̃piʀe] (1) **1** *vi* to get worse, deteriorate. **2** *vt* to make worse.
empirique [ɑ̃piʀik] *adj* empirical. ♦ **empirisme** *nm* empiricism.
emplacement [ɑ̃plasmɑ̃] *nm* site, location. **sur l'~ de** on the site of.
emplâtre [ɑ̃plɑtʀ(ə)] *nm* (*Méd*) plaster; (*Aut*) patch.
emplette† [ɑ̃plɛt] *nf* purchase. **faire l'~ de** to purchase; **faire des ~s** to do some shopping.
emplir [ɑ̃pliʀ] (2) **1** *vt verre, pièce* to fill (*de* with). **2 s'~** *vpr*: **s'~ de** to fill with.
employer [ɑ̃plwaje] (8) *vt* (*gén*) to use; *moyen, ouvrier* to employ; *temps* to spend (*à qch* on sth, *à faire qch* doing sth). **~ toute son énergie à faire qch** to apply *ou* devote all one's energies to doing sth; **mal ~** to misuse; **s'~ à faire qch/à qch** to apply *ou* devote o.s. to doing sth/to sth. ♦ **emploi** *nm* **(a)** (*gén*) use; *[mot]* usage. **je n'en ai pas l'~** I have no use for it; **~ du temps** timetable, schedule. **(b)** (*poste*) job. **l'~** employment; **sans ~** unemployed, jobless. ♦ **employé, e** *nm,f* employee. **~ de bureau** office worker, clerk; **~ des postes** postal worker; **l'~ du gaz** the gas man; **~ de maison** domestic employee; **les ~s de cette firme** the staff *ou* employees of this firm. ♦ **employeur, -euse** *nm,f* employer.
empocher* [ɑ̃pɔʃe] (1) *vt* to pocket.
empoigner [ɑ̃pwaɲe] (1) **1** *vt* to grasp, grab hold of. **2 s'~*** *vpr* to have a row. ♦ **empoignade** *nf* row.
empoisonner [ɑ̃pwazɔne] (1) **1** *vt* **(a)** **~ qn** *[assassin]* to poison sb; *[aliments]* to give sb food poisoning; (*fig*:*) *[contretemps]* to annoy sb; *[gêneur, travail]* to drive sb mad*. **(b)** *air* to make foul; *relations* to poison. **2 s'~** *vpr* (*lit*) to poison o.s.; (*intoxication*) to get food poisoning. (*fig*:*) to get bored. ♦ **empoisonnant, e*** *adj* annoying. **empoisonné, e** *adj flèche* poisoned; *paroles* poisonous. ♦ **empoisonnement** *nm* poisoning. (*: *ennui*) **~(s)** bother. ♦ **empoisonneur, -euse** *nm,f* (*lit*) poisoner; (*fig*:*) bore.
emporté, e [ɑ̃pɔʀte] *adj* quick-tempered.
emportement [ɑ̃pɔʀtəmɑ̃] *nm* fit of anger, rage. **avec ~** angrily.
emporte-pièce [ɑ̃pɔʀtəpjɛs] *nm inv* (*Tech*) punch. (*fig*) **à l'~** incisive.
emporter [ɑ̃pɔʀte] (1) **1** *vt* **(a)** (*comme bagage*) to take; (*enlever*) to take away. **si vous gagnez, vous pouvez l'~ (avec vous)** if you win, you can take it away (with you); **plats chauds à ~** take-away hot meals; **il ne l'emportera pas en Paradis!** he'll soon be smiling on the other side of his face! **(b)** *[vent, train]* to carry along; *[colère, imagination]* to carry away. **emporté par son élan** carried along by his own momentum. **(c)** (*arracher*) *bras* to take off; *cheminée* to blow off; *pont* to wash away; (*euph: tuer*) *[maladie]* to carry off. **la vague a emporté 3 passagers** the wave swept 3 passengers overboard; (*fig*) **plat qui emporte la bouche** dish that takes the roof off your mouth*. **(d)** *prix* to carry off; (*Mil*) *position* to take, win. **~ la décision** to carry *ou* win the day; **l'~ (sur)** *[personne]* to get the upper hand (of); *[méthode]* to prevail (over); **l'~ sur son adversaire** to get the better of one's opponent; **l'~ sur qn en adresse** to outmatch sb in skill. **2 s'~** *vpr* **(a)** (*de colère*) to lose one's temper (*contre* with). **(b)** *[cheval]* to bolt.
empoté, e* [ɑ̃pɔte] **1** *adj* awkward. **2** *nm,f* (*péj*) awkward lump*.
empourprer *vt*, **s'~** *vpr* [ɑ̃puʀpʀe] (1) to turn crimson.
empreindre [ɑ̃pʀɛ̃dʀ(ə)] (52) *vt* (*littér*) to imprint. **empreint de** *regret* tinged with; *bonté* stamped with; *menaces* fraught with.
empreinte [ɑ̃pʀɛ̃t] *nf* **(a)** (*gén*) imprint, impression; *[animal]* track. **~ de pas** footprint; **~s digitales** fingerprints. **(b)** (*fig*) stamp.
empresser (s') [ɑ̃pʀese] (1) *vpr* **(a)** (*s'affairer*) to bustle about; (*péj*) to fuss about. **s'~ auprès *ou* autour de qn** to surround sb with attentions, fuss around sb. **(b)** (*se hâter*) **s'~ de faire** to hasten to do. ♦ **empressé, e** *adj serveur* attentive; *aide* willing; *admirateur* assiduous; *subordonné* overzealous. **faire l'~ (auprès d'une femme)** to fuss

around (a woman). ♦ **empressement** *nm* **(a)** (*zèle*) attentiveness; willingness; assiduity; overzealousness. **(b)** (*hâte*) eagerness. **il montrait peu d'~ à ...** he showed little desire to ... .

emprise [ɑ̃pʀiz] *nf* hold, ascendancy (*sur* over). **sous l'~ de** under the influence of.

emprisonner [ɑ̃pʀizɔne] (1) *vt* (*prison*) to imprison; (*chambre*) to shut up; *[vêtement]* to confine; *[doctrine, routine]* to trap. ♦ **emprisonnement** *nm* imprisonment. **10 ans d'~** 10 years in prison.

emprunter [ɑ̃pʀœ̃te] (1) *vt argent, idée* to borrow (*à* from); *chaleur* to derive (*à* from); *nom, autorité* to assume, take on; *style* to use, adopt; *route* to take; *itinéraire* to follow. ♦ **emprunt** *nm* (*action*) borrowing; (*somme*) loan; (*Ling: mot*) borrowing. (*Fin*) **faire un ~ (d'un million)** to raise a loan (of a million); **d'~** *nom, autorité* assumed; *matériel* borrowed. ♦ **emprunté, e** *adj air, personne* ill-at-ease, awkward; *gloire, éclat* sham, feigned. ♦ **emprunteur, -euse** *nm,f* borrower.

empuantir [ɑ̃pɥɑ̃tiʀ] (2) *vt* to stink out (*de* with).

ému, e [emy] *adj* (*compassion, gratitude*) moved, touched; (*joie*) excited; (*timidité, peur*) nervous, agitated; *air* filled with emotion; *voix* emotional; *souvenirs* tender. **encore tout ~, il la remercia** still quite overcome he thanked her.

émulation [emylɑsjɔ̃] *nf* emulation. ♦ **émule** *nmf* (*littér*) imitator; (*égal*) equal.

émulsion [emylsjɔ̃] *nf* emulsion.

en[1] [ɑ̃] *prép* **(a)** (*lieu*) in; (*direction*) to. **vivre ~ France** to live in France; **aller ~ Angleterre** to go to England; **de ville ~ ville** from town to town; **il voyage ~ Grèce** he's travelling around Greece; **aller ~ ville** to go (in)to town. **(b)** (*date*) in. **~ semaine** in *ou* during the week; **de jour ~ jour** from day to day, daily. **(c)** (*moyen de transport*) by. **~ taxi** by taxi; **aller à Londres ~ avion** to fly to London; **ils y sont allés ~ voiture** they went by car *ou* in a car, they drove there. **(d)** (*état, manière*) in, on. **~ sang** covered in *ou* with blood; **partir ~ vacances** to go on holiday; **~ flammes** on fire, in flames; **être ~ noir** to be dressed in black, be wearing black; **elle était ~ bigoudis** she was in her rollers; **~ guerre** at war; **carte ~ couleur** coloured postcard; **~ groupe/cercle** in a group/circle. **(e)** (*transformation*) *traduire, changer etc* into. **se déguiser ~** to dress up as; **casser ~ deux/en deux morceaux** to cut in two/into two pieces. **(f)** (*variante*) in. **la même valise ~ plus grand** the same suitcase in a bigger size. **(g)** (*conformité*) as. **~ tant qu'ami** as a friend; **agir ~ tyran** to act like a tyrant; **~ bon commerçant (qu'il est)** good tradesman that he is; **donné ~ cadeau** given as a present. **(h)** (*composition*) made of; (*présentation*) in. **c'est ~ or** it is made of gold; **une bague ~ or** a gold ring; **c'est ~ quoi?*** what's it made of?; **~ 6 volumes** in 6 volumes; **écrit ~ prose** written in prose. **(i)** (*matière*) in, at, of. **~ musique** in music; **bon ~ géographie** good at geography; **docteur ~ droit** doctor of law. **(j)** (*mesure*) in. **compter ~ francs** to count in francs; **~ long** lengthwise; **~ hauteur** in height. **(k)** (*avec gérondif*) **monter/entrer ~ courant** to run up/in; **endormir un enfant ~ le berçant** to rock a child to sleep; **faire obéir qn ~ le punissant** to make sb obey by punishing him; **se couper ~ ouvrant qch** to cut o.s. opening sth; **il a fait une folie ~ achetant cette bague** it was very extravagant of him to buy this ring; **aller jusqu'à la poste ~ se promenant** to go for a walk as far as the post office; **~ apprenant la nouvelle** when he heard the news, on hearing the news; **il a buté ~ montant dans l'autobus** he tripped getting into *ou* as he got into the bus; **il s'est endormi ~ lisant le journal** he fell asleep while reading the newspaper; **fermez la porte ~ sortant** shut the door as you go out; **il est sorti ~ haussant les épaules** he left with a shrug of his shoulders.

en[2] [ɑ̃] *pron* **(a)** (*lieu*) **il ~ revient** he's just come back (from there); **le bénéfice qu'il ~ a tiré** the profit he got out of it *ou* from it; **où ~ sommes-nous?** where are we now? **(b)** (*agent etc*) **il saisit sa canne et l'~ frappa** he seized his stick and struck him with it; **~ mourir** (*maladie*) to die of it; (*blessure*) to die because of it *ou* as a result of it; **elle ~ est aimée** she is loved by him. **(c)** (*complément de vb, d'adj, de n*) **qu'est-ce que tu ~ feras?** what will you do with it (*ou* them)?; **je t'~ donne/offre 10 F** I'll give/offer you 10 francs for it. **(d)** (*quantitatif, indéf*) of it, of them (*souvent omis*). **si vous aimez les pommes, prenez-~ plusieurs** if you like apples, take several; **il n'y ~ a pas beaucoup** there isn't much (of it); **si j'~ avais** if I had any; **il n'y ~ a plus** there isn't (*ou* aren't) any left, there's (*ou* there are) none left; **j'~ ai assez** I've had enough (of it); **il ~ aime une autre** he loves somebody else. **(e)** (*renforcement*) *non traduit*. **il s'~ souviendra de cette réception** he'll certainly remember that party. **(f)** (*locutions verbales*) *non traduit*. **il ~ est à penser que** he has come to think that; **ne vous ~ faites pas** don't worry, never mind; **il ~ va de même pour** the same goes for.

encadrer [ɑ̃kɑdʀe] (1) *vt tableau* to frame; *visage, plaine* to frame, surround; *étudiants, recrues* to train; *prisonnier* to surround; (*par 2 personnes*) to flank. **je ne peux pas l'~‡** I can't stand him*. ♦ **encadrement** *nm* **(a)** framing; training. **personnel d'~** (*Admin*) executive staff. **(b)** (*embrasure, cadre*) frame. **dans l'~ de la porte** in the doorway.

encaisser [ɑ̃kese] (1) *vt* **(a)** *argent* to collect, receive; *chèque* to cash. **(b)** (*) *coups, défaite* to take. **qu'est-ce qu'il a encaissé!** what a hammering he got!* **(c)** (‡) **je ne peux pas l'~** *personne* I can't stand him*; *décision* I can't take it*. ♦ **encaissé, e** *adj vallée* deep; *route* hemmed in by steep hills. ♦ **encaissement** *nm* (*Fin*) collection; receipt; cashing; *[vallée]* depth. ♦ **encaisseur** *nm* collector (*of debts etc*).

en-cas [ɑ̃kɑ] *nm* (*nourriture*) snack.

encastrer [ɑ̃kastʀe] (1) **1** *vt* (*dans mur*) to embed (*dans* in); (*dans boîtier*) to fit (*dans* into). **2 s'~** *vpr [pièces]* to fit (*dans* into).

encaustique [ɑ̃kɔstik] *nf* polish. ♦ **encaustiquer** (1) *vt* to polish.

enceindre [ɑ̃sɛ̃dʀ(ə)] (52) *vt* to encircle, surround.

enceinte[1] [ɑ̃sɛ̃t] *adj f* pregnant (*de qn* by sb). **~ de 5 mois** 5 months pregnant.

enceinte[2] [ɑ̃sɛ̃t] *nf* **(a)** (*mur*) wall; (*palissade*) enclosure, fence. **mur d'~** surrounding wall. **(b)** (*espace clos*) enclosure; *[couvent]* precinct. **dans l'~ de la ville** inside the town. **(c) ~ (acoustique)** loudspeaker.

encens [ɑ̃sɑ̃] *nm* incense. ♦ **encenser** (1) *vt* to incense; (*fig*) to heap praise upon. ♦ **encensoir** *nm* censer.

encercler [ɑ̃sɛʀkle] (1) *vt* to surround. ♦ **encerclement** *nm* surrounding.

enchaîner [ɑ̃ʃene] (1) **1** *vt* **(a)** *prisonnier* to chain up (*à* to); (*fig*) *peuple* to enslave; *presse* to muzzle; *[secret, sentiment]* to bind. **(b)** *faits, épisodes* to link together. **2** *vi* to go on, continue; (*Ciné, Théât*) to move on. **3 s'~** *vpr* to be linked (together). ♦ **enchaînement** *nm* (*liaison*) linking; (*Danse*) enchaînement. (*série*) **~ de circonstances** series *ou* string of.

enchanter [ɑ̃ʃɑ̃te] (1) *vt* (*ensorceler*) to enchant, bewitch; (*ravir*) to enchant, delight. ♦ **enchanté, e** *adj* **(a)** (*ravi*) enchanted (*de* by), delighted (*de* with). **~ (de vous connaître)** pleased to meet you. **(b)** (*magique*) enchanted. ♦ **enchantement** *nm* (*magie*) enchantment; (*ravissement*) delight, enchantment. **comme par ~** as if by magic.

♦ **enchanteur, -teresse** 1 *adj* enchanting. 2 *nm* (*sorcier*) enchanter; (*fig*) charmer. 3 *nf* enchantress.
enchère [ɑ̃ʃɛʀ] *nf* **(a)** (*Comm, Cartes: offre*) bid. **les ~s** the bidding. **(b)** (*vente*) **mettre aux ~s** to put up for auction; **vendu aux ~s** sold by auction.
enchérir [ɑ̃ʃeʀiʀ] (2) *vi* (*Comm*) to make a higher bid. (*fig*) **~ sur** to go further than.
enchevêtrer [ɑ̃ʃ(ə)vetʀe] (1) **1** *vt ficelle* to tangle (up); *idées, intrigue* to confuse, muddle. **2 s'~** *vpr [ficelles]* to become entangled; *[situations]* to become confused *ou* muddled. **s'~ dans** *explications* to get tangled up in. ♦ **enchevêtrement** *nm [ficelles]* (*action*) entanglement; (*résultat*) tangle; *[idées, situation]* confusion, muddle.
enclave [ɑ̃klav] *nf* (*lit, fig*) enclave. ♦ **enclavement** *nm* (*action*) enclosing; (*résultat*) enclosed situation. ♦ **enclaver** (1) *vt* to enclose.
enclencher [ɑ̃klɑ̃ʃe] (1) *vt mécanisme* to engage; *affaire* to set in motion, get under way.
enclin, e [ɑ̃klɛ̃, in] *adj*: **~ à qch/à faire qch** inclined *ou* prone to sth/to do sth.
enclore [ɑ̃klɔʀ] (45) *vt* to enclose, shut in. ♦ **enclos** *nm* (*gén*) enclosure; *[chevaux]* paddock; *[moutons]* fold.
enclume [ɑ̃klym] *nf* anvil.
encoche [ɑ̃kɔʃ] *nf* notch (*à* in).
encoignure [ɑ̃kɔɲyʀ] *nf* corner.
encoller [ɑ̃kɔle] (1) *vt papier* to paste; (*colle forte*) to glue.
encolure [ɑ̃kɔlyʀ] *nf* (*cou*) neck; (*mesure*) collar size.
encombrer [ɑ̃kɔ̃bʀe] (1) **1** *vt pièce, mémoire* to clutter (up); *couloir* to obstruct; *profession* to saturate; (*Téléc*) *lignes* to block; (*Comm*) *marché* to glut. **ces boîtes m'encombrent** (*je les porte*) I'm loaded down with these boxes; (*elles gênent*) these boxes are in my way. **2 s'~** *vpr*: **s'~ de** *paquets* to load o.s. with; *enfants* to burden o.s. with; **il ne s'encombre pas de scrupules** he's not overburdened with scruples. ♦ **encombrant, e** *adj paquet* cumbersome, bulky; *présence* burdensome. ♦ **encombre** *nm*: **sans ~** without mishap *ou* incident. ♦ **encombrement** *nm* **(a)** (*gén*) congestion; (*Aut*) traffic jam. **à cause de l'~ des lignes téléphoniques** because of the telephone lines being blocked. **(b)** (*volume*) bulk.
encontre [ɑ̃kɔ̃tʀ(ə)] *prép*: **à l'~ de** (*contre*) against; (*au contraire de*) contrary to; **aller à l'~ de** *[décision]* to go against.
encore [ɑ̃kɔʀ] *adv* **(a)** (*toujours*) still. **il n'est ~ que caporal** he's only a corporal as yet, he's still only a corporal; **le malfaiteur court ~** the criminal is still at large. **(b) pas ~** not yet; **il n'est pas ~ prêt** he's not ready yet; **ça ne s'était ~ jamais vu** that had never been seen before. **(c)** (*pas plus tard que*) only. **ce matin ~** only this morning. **(d)** (*de nouveau*) again. **ça s'est ~ défait** it has come undone (yet) again *ou* once more; **~ vous!** (not) you again! **(e)** (*de plus*) more. **~ un rhume** (yet) another cold; **~ un peu de thé?** a little more tea?, more tea?; **j'en veux ~** I want some more; **que te faut-il ~?** what else *or* more do you want?; **pendant ~ 2 jours** for another 2 days, for 2 more days; **mais ~?** is that all?, what else? **(f)** (*avec comp*) even, still. **il fait ~ plus froid qu'hier** it's even *ou* still colder than yesterday; **~ pire** even *ou* still worse; **~ autant** as much again. **(g)** (*aussi*) too, also, as well. **(h)** (*restriction*) **~ ne sait-il pas tout** even then he doesn't know everything; **~ faut-il le faire** you still have to do it; **~ heureux qu'il ne se soit pas plaint** (still) at least he didn't complain; **c'est passable, et ~!** it'll do, but only just!; **si ~** if only. **(i)** (*littér*) **~ que** even though.
encourager [ɑ̃kuʀaʒe] (3) *vt* (*gén*) to encourage. **~ qn à l'effort** to encourage sb to make an effort. ♦ **encourageant, e** *adj* encouraging. ♦ **encouragement** *nm* encouragement.
encourir [ɑ̃kuʀiʀ] (11) *vt frais* to incur; *punition* to bring upon o.s.
encrasser (s') [ɑ̃kʀase] (1) *vpr [arme]* to foul up; *[cheminée, bougie]* to soot up; *[poêle, piston]* to clog up. ♦ **encrassement** *nm* fouling up; sooting up; clogging up.
encre [ɑ̃kʀ(ə)] *nf* ink. **écrire à l'~** to write in ink; **~ de Chine** Indian ink. ♦ **encrier** *nm* inkwell.
encroûter (s')* [ɑ̃kʀute] (1) *vpr [personne]* to stagnate, get into a rut. **s'~ dans** *préjugés* to become entrenched in.
encyclique [ɑ̃siklik] *adj, nf*: **(lettre) ~** encyclical.
encyclopédie [ɑ̃siklɔpedi] *nf* encyclopaedia. ♦ **encyclopédique** *adj* encyclopaedic.
endémique [ɑ̃demik] *adj* (*Méd, fig*) endemic.
endetter *vt*, **s'~** *vpr* [ɑ̃dete] (1) to get into debt. ♦ **endetté, e** *adj* (*lit*) in debt. (*fig*) **~ envers qn** indebted to sb. ♦ **endettement** *nm* (*action*) getting into debt; (*dettes*) debts.
endeuiller [ɑ̃dœje] (1) *vt* to plunge into mourning; *épreuve sportive* to cast a tragic shadow over.
endiablé, e [ɑ̃djɑble] *adj* furious, wild.
endiguer [ɑ̃dige] (1) *vt fleuve* to dyke up; *révolte, invasion* to hold back, contain; *progrès* to check, hold back.
endimanché, e [ɑ̃dimɑ̃ʃe] *adj* in one's Sunday best.
endive [ɑ̃div] *nf*: **~(s)** chicory.
endoctriner [ɑ̃dɔktʀine] (1) *vt* to indoctrinate. ♦ **endoctrinement** *nm* indoctrination.
endolori, e [ɑ̃dɔlɔʀi] *adj* painful, aching.
endommager [ɑ̃dɔmaʒe] (3) *vt* to damage. ♦ **endommagement** *nm* damaging.
endormir [ɑ̃dɔʀmiʀ] (16) **1** *vt* **(a)** (*lit, fig*) *personne* to send to sleep. **(b)** *douleur* to deaden; *soupçons* to allay, lull. **(c)** (*tromper*) to beguile. **se laisser ~ par des promesses** to let o.s. be beguiled by promises. **2 s'~** *vpr* **(a)** to go to sleep, fall asleep; (*euph: mourir*) to pass away. (*fig*) **ce n'est pas le moment de nous ~** we can't afford to slow down now; **s'~ sur ses lauriers** to rest on one's laurels. **(b)** *[ville]* to fall asleep; *[douleur]* to die down; *[facultés]* to go to sleep. ♦ **endormant, e** *adj* deadly boring. ♦ **endormi, e** *adj* (*lit*) sleeping, asleep; (*: *apathique*) sluggish; (*engourdi*) numb; *passion, facultés* dormant; *ville, rue* sleepy, drowsy. **à moitié ~** half asleep; **quel ~*** what a sleepyhead.
endosser [ɑ̃dose] (1) *vt vêtement* to put on; *responsabilité* to take, shoulder (*de* for); (*Comm, Fin*) to endorse. ♦ **endossement** *nm* endorsement.
endroit [ɑ̃dʀwa] *nm* **(a)** (*gén*) place; *[récit]* passage, part. **un ~ idéal pour le pique-nique** an ideal spot *ou* place for a picnic; **les gens de l'~** the local people; **il arrêta sa lecture à cet ~** he stopped reading at that point; **à quel ~?** whereabouts?, where exactly?; **par ~s** in places; **à l'~ de** (*à l'égard de*) regarding, with regard to. **(b)** (*bon côté*) right side. **à l'~** *vêtement* the right way out; *objet posé* the right way round; **remets tes chaussettes à l'~** turn your socks right side out; **une maille à l'~, une maille à l'envers** knit one, purl one.
enduire [ɑ̃dɥiʀ] (38) *vt* to coat (*de* with). ♦ **enduit** *nm* coating.
endurance [ɑ̃dyʀɑ̃s] *nf* endurance. ♦ **endurant, e** *adj* (*fort*) tough, hardy; (*patient*) patient.
endurcir [ɑ̃dyʀsiʀ] (2) **1** *vt corps* to toughen; *âme* to harden. **2 s'~** *vpr* to become tough; to become hardened. ♦ **endurci, e** *adj criminel* hardened; *célibataire* confirmed. ♦ **endurcissement** *nm* (*action*) becoming tough; becoming hardened; (*état*) toughness; hardness. **~ à la douleur** being hardened to pain.
endurer [ɑ̃dyʀe] (1) *vt* to endure, bear.

énergétique [enɛʀʒetik] *adj ressources* energy; *aliment* energy-giving.

énergie [enɛʀʒi] *nf* **(a)** (*physique*) energy; (*morale*) spirit. **avec toute son ~** with all one's energy; **être sans ~** to feel unenergetic, be lacking in energy. **(b)** (*Phys*) energy; (*Tech*) power. **réaction qui libère de l'~** reaction that releases energy; **consommation d'~** power consumption. ♦ **énergique** *adj* (*physiquement*) energetic; (*moralement*) spirited; *résistance, ton, refus* forceful, vigorous; *remède* powerful; *mesures* drastic; *punition* severe. ♦ **énergiquement** *adv* energetically; spiritedly; forcefully; vigorously; powerfully; drastically; severely.

énergumène [enɛʀgymɛn] *nmf* rowdy character.

énerver [enɛʀve] (1) **1** *vt*: **~ qn** (*agiter*) to set sb's nerves on edge; (*agacer*) to irritate sb, annoy sb, get on sb's nerves. **2 s'~** *vpr* to get worked up. ♦ **énervant, e** *adj* irritating, annoying. ♦ **énervé, e** *adj* (*agacé*) irritated, annoyed; (*agité*) nervous. ♦ **énervement** *nm* irritation, annoyance; nervousness.

enfant [ɑ̃fɑ̃] **1** *nmf* (*gén*) child; (*garçon*) (little) boy; (*fille*) (little) girl. **quand il était ~** when he was a child; **c'est un grand ~** he's such a child; **il est resté très ~** he has stayed very childlike; **faire l'~** to behave childishly; **sans ~** childless; (*fig*) **ce livre est son ~** this book is his baby; **c'est un ~ du pays** he's a native of these parts; (*: *personnes*) **les ~s! folks!*** **2: ~ de chœur** altar boy; (*ingénu*) innocent; **ce n'est pas un ~ de chœur!*** he's no angel; **~ prodige** child prodigy; **~ prodigue** prodigal son; **~ trouvé** foundling; **~ unique** only child. ♦ **enfance** *nf* (*jeunesse*) childhood; *[garçon]* boyhood; *[fille]* girlhood; (*petite enfance*) infancy; (*fig: début*) infancy. **c'est l'~ de l'art** it's child's play; (*enfants*) **~ déshéritée** deprived children.

enfanter [ɑ̃fɑ̃te] (1) **1** *vt* (†, *Bible*) to bring forth†. **2** *vi* to give birth. ♦ **enfantement** *nm* (†, *Bible*) childbirth; *[œuvre]* giving birth (*de* to).

enfantillage [ɑ̃fɑ̃tijaʒ] *nm* (*conduite*) childishness. **se livrer à des ~s** to behave childishly.

enfantin, e [ɑ̃fɑ̃tɛ̃, in] *adj* childlike; (*puéril*) childish. (*facile*) **c'est ~** it's simple, it's child's play; **rire/jeu ~** child's laugh/game.

enfer [ɑ̃fɛʀ] *nm* (*lit, fig*) hell. (*Myth*) **les ~s** Hell; **l'~ est pavé de bonnes intentions** the road to hell is paved with good intentions; **l'~ de la guerre** the purgatory of war; **bruit/vision d'~** hellish *ou* infernal noise/vision; **feu d'~** raging fire; **rouler à un train d'~** to go hell for leather *ou* flat out.

enfermer [ɑ̃fɛʀme] (1) **1** *vt* (*gén*) to shut up; (*à clef*) to lock up (*dans* in); (*dans conventions*) to imprison, confine (*dans* within); (*dans un dilemme*) to trap (*dans* in). **il est bon à ~ (à l'asile)*** he ought to be locked up; (*littér*) **les collines qui enfermaient le vallon** the hills that enclosed the valley. **2 s'~** *vpr* (*lit*) to shut o.s. up *ou* in. **s'~ à clef** to lock o.s. away *ou* in; **s'~ dans** *mutisme* to retreat into; *rôle* to stick to.

enferrer (s') [ɑ̃feʀe] (1) *vpr* to tie o.s. in knots. **s'~ dans** *contradictions* to get embroiled in, get tangled up in.

enfiévrer [ɑ̃fjevʀe] (6) *vt imagination* to fire; *esprits* to rouse. ♦ **enfiévré, e** *adj* feverish.

enfilade [ɑ̃filad] *nf*: **une ~ de** *maisons* a row *ou* string of; **prendre en ~** (*Mil*) to rake, enfilade.

enfiler [ɑ̃file] (1) **1** *vt aiguille, perles* to thread; *rue* to take; (*) *vêtement* to slip on. **~ qch sur une tringle** to slip sth onto a rod; (*: *fourrer*) **~ un objet dans** to stick* an object into. **2 s'~** *vpr* **(a) s'~ dans** *couloir* to disappear into. **(b)** (*: *nourriture*) to down; *corvée* to get landed with*.

enfin [ɑ̃fɛ̃] *adv* **(a)** (*à la fin*) at last, finally. **il y est ~ arrivé** he has at last *ou* finally succeeded; **~ seuls!** alone at last! **(b)** (*en dernier lieu*) lastly, finally. **~ et surtout** and last but not least. **(c)** (*en conclusion*) **~ (bref)** in short, in a word. **(d)** (*restrictif*) well. **~, dans un sens, oui** well – in a way, yes; **mais ~** but; **car ~** because. **(e)** (*somme toute*) after all. **c'est un élève qui, ~, n'est pas bête** this pupil is not stupid, after all. **(f)** (*toutefois*) still. **~, si ça vous plaît prenez-le** still, if you like it take it. **(g)** (*exclamatif*) **~! que veux-tu y faire!** still, what can you do!; **~, tu aurais pu le faire!** all the same *ou* even so, you could have done it!; **(mais) ~! je viens de te le dire!** but I've just TOLD you!; **~! un grand garçon comme toi!** come now, a big boy like you!

enflammer [ɑ̃flame] (1) **1** *vt bois* to set on fire, set fire to; *allumette* to strike; *ciel* to set ablaze; *colère, désir* to inflame; *imagination* to fire. **2 s'~** *vpr [bois]* to catch fire; *[visage]* to blaze; *[désir]* to flare up; *[imagination]* to be fired; *[orateur]* to become impassioned. **s'~ (de colère)** to flare up (in anger). ♦ **enflammé, e** *adj allumette* burning; *torche, ciel* blazing; *caractère, paroles* fiery, passionate; *déclaration* impassioned; *plaie* inflamed.

enfler [ɑ̃fle] (1) **1** *vt membre, fleuve* to cause to swell; (*littér*) *voiles* to swell. **se faire ~ de 10 F*** to be done out of 10 francs*. **2** *vi [membre]* to become swollen, swell (up); (*grossir*) to fill out. **3 s'~** *vpr [voix]* to rise; *[son, fleuve, voiles]* to swell. ♦ **enflé, e** *nm,f* (*: *imbécile*) twit*, clot*. ♦ **enflure** *nf* (*Méd*) swelling; (*: *imbécile*) twit*, clot*.

enfoncer [ɑ̃fɔ̃se] (3) **1** *vt* **(a)** *pieu* to drive in; *punaise* to stick in, push in. **~ un couteau dans** to plunge a knife into; **~ qch à coups de marteau** to hammer sth in. **(b)** (*mettre*) **~ les mains dans ses poches** to thrust one's hands into one's pockets; **~ son chapeau jusqu'aux yeux** to pull one's hat down over one's eyes; **qui a bien pu lui ~ ça dans la crâne?** who on earth put that into his head?; **~ qn dans la misère** to plunge sb into poverty. **(c)** *porte* to break down; *véhicule* to smash in; (*fig*) *ennemi* to break through. (*fig*) **~ une porte ouverte** to labour an obvious point. **(d)** (*) (*battre*) to beat hollow*; (*surpasser*) to lick*. **2** *vi* (*pénétrer*) to sink in; (*céder*) to give way, cave in. **3 s'~** *vpr* **(a)** (*gén*) to sink (*dans* in, into). **s'~ dans** *forêt* to disappear into; *vice* to plunge into; **s'~ sous les édredons*** to snuggle down under the eiderdown; **il s'est enfoncé jusqu'au cou dans une sale histoire** he's up to his neck in a nasty bit of business; **à mentir, tu ne fais que t'~ davantage** by lying, you're just getting yourself into deeper and deeper water. **(b)** (*céder*) to give way. **(c) s'~ une arête dans la gorge** to get a bone stuck in one's throat; **s'~ une aiguille dans la main** to stick a needle into one's hand; **enfoncez-vous bien ça dans le crâne*** now get this into your head*. ♦ **enfoncé, e** *adj yeux* deep-set; *côtes* broken; *recoin* deep. **la tête ~e dans les épaules** with his head sunk between his shoulders. ♦ **enfoncement** *nm* **(a)** (*action*) driving in; breaking down; breaking through; giving way; sinking. **avoir un ~ de la cage thoracique** to have broken ribs. **(b)** (*recoin*) recess, nook.

enfouir [ɑ̃fwiʀ] (2) **1** *vt* to bury (*dans* in). **2 s'~** *vpr*: **s'~ dans/sous** to bury o.s. in/under. ♦ **enfouissement** *nm* burying.

enfourcher [ɑ̃fuʀʃe] (1) *vt* to mount. (*fig*) **~ son dada** to get on one's hobby-horse.

enfourner [ɑ̃fuʀne] (1) *vt* to put in the oven; (*: *avaler*) to down. (*: *enfoncer*) **~ qch dans** to stuff* sth into.

enfreindre [ɑ̃fʀɛ̃dʀ(ə)] (52) *vt* to infringe.

enfuir (s') [ɑ̃fɥiʀ] (17) *vpr* to run away (*chez, dans* to); (*s'échapper*) to run away, escape (*de* from); (*littér*) *[temps]* to fly.

enfumer [ɑ̃fyme] (1) *vt pièce* to fill with smoke; *ruche* to smoke out. **pièce enfumée** smoky room.

engagé, e [ɑ̃gaʒe] **1** *adj écrivain* committed. (*Pol*) **non ~** uncommitted. **2** *nm* (*soldat*) enlisted man; (*coureur*) competitor; (*cheval*) runner. **~ volontaire** volunteer.

engageant, e [ɑ̃gaʒɑ̃, ɑ̃t] *adj mine, proposition* attractive; *air, sourire* engaging, winning; *gâteau* inviting.

engagement [ɑ̃gaʒmɑ̃] *nm* **(a)** (*promesse*) agreement, promise. **sans ~ de votre part** without obligation on your part; **prendre l'~ de** to undertake to. **(b)** (*Théât: contrat*) engagement. **(c)** (*embauche*) taking on, engaging. **(d)** *[capitaux]* investing; *[dépenses]* incurring. **~s financiers** financial commitments *ou* liabilities. **(e)** *[débat, négociations]* start. **(f)** (*Sport*) (*inscription*) entry; (*coup d'envoi*) kick-off; (*Boxe*) attack; (*Escrime*) engagement. **(g)** (*Mil*) *[recrues]* enlistment; *[combat, troupes fraîches]* engaging. **tué dans un ~** killed in an engagement. **(h)** (*Littérat, Pol*) commitment. **politique de non ~** policy of non-commitment. **(i)** (*mise en gage*) pawning. **(j)** (*encouragement*) encouragement. **(k)** (*introduction*) *[clef]* insertion; *[voiture]* entry.

engager [ɑ̃gaʒe] (3) **1** *vt* **(a)** *[promesse]* to bind. **ça n'engage à rien** it doesn't commit you to anything; **~ sa parole** to give one's word. **(b)** *ouvrier* to take on, engage; *artiste* to engage. **(c)** (*entraîner*) to involve (*dans* in). **(d)** (*encourager*) **~ qn à faire qch** to urge sb to do sth. **(e)** (*introduire*) to insert (*dans* in(to)). **~ sa voiture dans une ruelle** to drive (one's car) into a lane. **(f)** *discussion* to start (up); *négociations* to enter into; (*Jur*) *poursuites* to institute (*contre* against). **(g)** (*mettre en gage*) to pawn; (*investir*) to invest. **(h)** (*Sport*) *concurrents* to enter. **la partie est bien engagée** the match is well under way. **(i)** (*Mil*) *recrues* to enlist; *troupes fraîches* to throw in, engage. **~ le combat contre l'ennemi** to engage the enemy.

2 s'~ *vpr* **(a)** (*promettre*) to commit o.s. **s'~ à faire** to undertake to do. **(b)** (*s'embaucher*) to take a job (*chez* with). **(c) s'~ dans** *frais* to incur; *discussion* to enter into; *affaire* to become involved in; **le pays s'engage dans une politique dangereuse** the country is embarking on a dangerous policy. **(d) s'~ dans** *[mécanisme]* to fit into; *[véhicule]* to turn into; **s'~ sur la chaussée** to step onto the road. **(e)** *[pourparlers]* to start, get under way. **(f)** (*Sport*) to enter (*dans* for). **(g)** (*Mil*) *[recrues]* to enlist. **s'~ dans l'armée de l'air** to join the air force; **le combat s'engagea** the fight began.

engelure [ɑ̃ʒlyʀ] *nf* chilblain.

engendrer [ɑ̃ʒɑ̃dʀe] (1) *vt* (*littér*) *enfant* to father; (*Ling, Math, Phys*) to generate; *malheurs* to breed.

engin [ɑ̃ʒɛ̃] *nm* (*machine*) machine; (*outil*) instrument; (*Aut*) large vehicle; (*Aviat*) aircraft; (*: *truc*) contraption, gadget. **~ balistique** ballistic missile; **~ explosif** explosive device.

englober [ɑ̃glɔbe] (1) *vt* to include (*dans* in).

engloutir [ɑ̃glutiʀ] (2) **1** *vt nourriture* to gobble up, gulp down; *navire* to engulf; *fortune* to devour. **2 s'~** *vpr [navire]* to be engulfed. ♦ **engloutissement** *nm* gobbling up; engulfing; devouring.

engoncer [ɑ̃gɔ̃se] (3) *vt* (*gén ptp*) to cramp.

engorger [ɑ̃gɔʀʒe] (3) *vt tuyau* to block; (*Comm*) to glut. ♦ **engorgement** *nm* blocking; glut.

engouer (s') [ɑ̃gwe] (1) *vpr*: **s'~ de qch** to develop a passion for sth; **s'~ de qn** to become infatuated with sb. ♦ **engouement** *nm* infatuation; passion (*pour* for).

engouffrer [ɑ̃gufʀe] (1) **1** *vt charbon* to shoot (*dans* into); (*) *fortune* to devour; (*) *nourriture* to gobble up; *navire* to swallow up, engulf. **2 s'~** *vpr* (*gén*) to rush.

engourdir [ɑ̃guʀdiʀ] (2) **1** *vt membres* to numb; *esprit, douleur* to dull; *[chaleur]* to make sleepy *ou* drowsy. **2 s'~** *vpr* to go numb; to grow dull. ♦ **engourdissement** *nm* **(a)** (*état*) numbness; sleepiness, drowsiness; dullness. **(b)** (*action*) numbing; dulling.

engrais [ɑ̃gʀɛ] *nm* (*chimique*) fertilizer; (*animal*) manure. **mettre à l'~** to fatten up.

engraisser [ɑ̃gʀese] (1) **1** *vt volailles* to cram; *bétail* to fatten (up); *terre* to manure, fertilize; (*) *personne* to fatten up. **2** *vi* (*) to put on weight. ♦ **engraissement** *nm* fattening up; cramming.

engrenage [ɑ̃gʀənaʒ] *nm* gearing; (*fig*) chain. **être pris dans l'~** to get caught up in the system.

engueuler* [ɑ̃gœle] (1) **1** *vt*: **~ qn** to bawl sb out*; **se faire ~** to get bawled out*. **2 s'~** *vpr* to have a row (*avec* with). ♦ **engueulade*** *nf* (*dispute*) row; (*réprimande*) bawling out*.

enguirlander* [ɑ̃giʀlɑ̃de] (1) *vt*: **~ qn** to give sb a telling-off.

enhardir [ɑ̃aʀdiʀ] (2) **1** *vt* to make bolder. **2 s'~** *vpr* to get bolder.

énigme [enigm(ə)] *nf* (*mystère*) enigma, riddle; (*jeu*) riddle, puzzle. ♦ **énigmatique** *adj* enigmatic. ♦ **énigmatiquement** *adv* enigmatically.

enivrer [ɑ̃nivʀe] (1) **1** *vt* to intoxicate. **2 s'~** *vpr* to get drunk (*de* on), become intoxicated (*de* with). ♦ **enivrant, e** *adj* intoxicating. ♦ **enivrement** *nm* intoxication.

enjamber [ɑ̃ʒɑ̃be] (1) *vt obstacle* to stride *ou* step over; *fossé* to step *ou* stride across; *[pont]* to span, stretch across. (*s'asseoir*) **~ qch** to sit down astride sth. ♦ **enjambée** *nf* stride.

enjeu, *pl* ~x [ɑ̃ʒø] *nm [pari, guerre]* stake, stakes (*de* in). **quel est l'~?** what is at stake?

enjoindre [ɑ̃ʒwɛ̃dʀ(ə)] (49) *vt*: **~ à qn de faire** to enjoin sb to do.

enjôler [ɑ̃ʒole] (1) *vt*: **~ qn** to get round sb; **~ qn pour obtenir qch** to coax *ou* wheedle sb into giving sth. ♦ **enjôleur, -euse** **1** *adj* coaxing, wheedling. **2** *nm,f* (*charmeur*) coaxer, wheedler.

enjoliver [ɑ̃ʒɔlive] (1) *vt objet* to embellish; *récit* to embroider. ♦ **enjoliveur** *nm* (*Aut*) hub cap.

enjoué, e [ɑ̃ʒwe] *adj* cheerful. ♦ **enjouement** *nm* cheerfulness.

enlacer [ɑ̃lɑse] (3) **1** *vt* (*étreindre*) to clasp, hug; (*enchevêtrer*) to intertwine; (*s'enrouler autour*) to wind round, entwine. **2 s'~** *vpr* to hug *ou* clasp each other; to intertwine. **s'~ autour de** to twine *ou* wind round. ♦ **enlacement** *nm* (*étreinte*) embrace; (*enchevêtrement*) intertwining.

enlaidir [ɑ̃lediʀ] (2) **1** *vt* to make ugly. **2** *vi* to become ugly.

enlever [ɑ̃lve] (5) **1** *vt* **(a)** (*gén*) to remove; *étiquette, vêtement* to take off; *tache* to take out; (*en brossant ou lavant etc*) to brush *ou* wash *etc* off; *lustre* to take down. **~ le couvert** to clear the table; **enlève tes coudes de la table** take your elbows off the table. **(b)** *craintes, scrupules* to allay; *doutes* to dispel. **~ à qn** *courage* to rob sb of; *espoir* to deprive sb of; *commandement* to relieve sb of; **on lui a enlevé la garde de l'enfant** the child was taken from his care; **ça lui enlèvera le goût de recommencer** that'll cure him of trying that again; **ça n'enlève rien à son mérite** that doesn't detract from his worth. **(c)** (*emporter*) *objet* to take away, remove; *ordures* to collect. **faire ~ qch** to have sth taken away; **enlevé par un mal foudroyant** borne off by a sudden illness; **la mort nous l'a enlevé** death has taken him from us. **(d)** (*kidnapper*) to kidnap, abduct. **se faire ~ par son amant** to elope with one's lover. **(e)** *victoire* to win; (*Mil*) *position* to capture, take. **~ la décision** to carry the day; **~ une affaire** (*tractation*) to pull off a deal; (*commande*) to get *ou* secure an order; (*marchandise*) to carry off a bargain; **ça a été vite enlevé** (*marchandise*) it sold quickly; (*: *travail*) it was done in no time.

2 s'~ *vpr [tache]* to come off; *[peinture, écorce]* to peel off, come off. **enlève-toi de là*** mind out of

the way!; **ça s'enlève comme des petits pains*** it's selling like hot cakes*.
♦ **enlevé, e** *adj récit* spirited; *musique* executed with spirit. ♦ **enlèvement** *nm [personne]* kidnapping, abduction; *[objet]* taking away; *[ordures, bagages]* collection; (*Mil*) *[position]* capture; *[organe]* removal.

enliser [ɑ̃lize] (1) **1** *vt*: ~ **sa voiture** to get one's car stuck in the mud (*ou* sand *etc*). **2 s'~** *vpr* to sink (*dans* into); (*dans les détails*) to get bogged down (*dans* in). ♦ **enlisement** *nm* sinking.

enneigé, e [ɑ̃neʒe] *adj montagne* snow-covered; *route* blocked by snow, snowed up. ♦ **enneigement** *nm* depth of snow. **bulletin d'~** snow report.

ennemi, e [ɛnmi] **1** *adj* (*Mil*) enemy; (*hostile*) hostile. **2** *nm,f* enemy. **se faire un ~ de qn** to make an enemy of sb; **être ~ de qch** to be opposed to sth.

ennui [ɑ̃nɥi] *nm* (*désœuvrement*) boredom; (*monotonie*) tedium, tediousness; (*tracas*) trouble, worry. **avoir des ~s** to have troubles; **avoir des ~s d'argent** to have money worries; **avoir des ~s avec la police** to be in trouble with the police; **faire des ~s à qn** to make trouble for sb; **j'ai eu un ~ avec ma montre** I had some trouble *ou* bother with my watch; **si ça vous cause le moindre ~** if it's any bother to you; **l'~, c'est que ...** the trouble is that ....

ennuyer [ɑ̃nɥije] (8) **1** *vt* (*lasser*) to bore; (*préoccuper*) to worry; (*importuner*) to bother. (*irriter*) **~ qn** to annoy sb, get on sb's nerves; **il y a qch qui m'ennuie** there's sth that worries *ou* bothers me; **ça m'ennuierait beaucoup de te voir fâché** I'd really hate to see you cross; **ça m'ennuierait beaucoup d'y aller** it would really annoy me to go; **si cela ne vous ennuie pas trop** if you wouldn't mind, if it isn't too much bother; **je ne voudrais pas vous ~** I don't want to put you to any trouble, I don't want to bother you. **2 s'~** *vpr* to be bored (*de, à* with). **s'~ à mourir** to be bored to tears, be bored stiff*; **s'~ de qn** to miss sb. ♦ **ennuyé, e** *adj* (*préoccupé*) worried, bothered (*de* about); (*contrarié*) annoyed (*de* at, about). ♦ **ennuyeux, -euse** *adj* (*lassant*) boring, tedious; (*qui importune*) annoying, tiresome; (*préoccupant*) worrying.

énoncer [enɔ̃se] (3) *vt* (*gén*) to say; *idée* to express; *conditions* to state. ♦ **énoncé** *nm* (*Scol*) *[sujet]* exposition; *[problème]* terms; (*Jur*) *[loi]* wording; (*Ling*) utterance; *[faits, décision]* statement. (*Scol*) **pendant l'~ du sujet** while the subject is being read out.

enorgueillir (s') [ɑ̃nɔʀgœjiʀ] (2) *vpr*: **s'~ de** (*être fier de*) to pride o.s. on, boast about; (*avoir*) to boast.

énorme [enɔʀm(ə)] *adj* enormous, tremendous, huge. **ça lui a fait un bien ~** it's done him a great deal of good; **il a accepté, c'est déjà ~** he has accepted and that's quite something. ♦ **énormément** *adv* **(a)** enormously, tremendously, hugely. **ça m'a ~ déçu** it greatly disappointed me. **(b) ~ d'argent** a tremendous *ou* an enormous amount of money; **~ de gens** a tremendous *ou* an enormous number of people, a great many people. ♦ **énormité** *nf [poids, somme]* hugeness; *[demande]* enormity; (*propos*) outrageous remark; (*erreur*) howler*.

enquérir (s') [ɑ̃keʀiʀ] (21) *vpr* to inquire, ask (*de* about).

enquête [ɑ̃kɛt] *nf* (*gén, Jur*) inquiry; (*après décès*) inquest; (*Police*) investigation; (*sondage*) survey. ♦ **enquêter** (1) *vi* to hold an inquiry; to investigate; to conduct a survey. **~ sur qch** to investigate sth, carry out an investigation into sth. ♦ **enquêteur, -euse** *nm,f* (*Police*) officer; *[sondage]* pollster. **les ~s poursuivent leurs recherches** the police are continuing their investigations.

enquiquiner* [ɑ̃kikine] (1) **1** *vt* (*importuner*) to bother; (*préoccuper*) to worry; (*lasser*) to bore. **2 s'~** *vpr* to be bored. ♦ **enquiquinement*** *nm*: **quel ~!** what a flipping nuisance!*; **avoir des ~s** to have trouble (*avec* with). ♦ **enquiquineur, -euse*** *nm,f* pest*.

enraciner [ɑ̃ʀasine] (1) **1** *vt* to root. **solidement enraciné** *préjugé* deep-rooted; *famille* firmly rooted. **2 s'~** *vpr [arbre, préjugé]* to take root.

enrager [ɑ̃ʀaʒe] (3) *vi* **(a) faire ~ qn*** (*taquiner*) to tease sb; (*importuner*) to pester sb. **(b)** to be furious (*de faire* at doing). ♦ **enragé, e** *adj* **(a)** *chasseur, joueur* keen (*de* on). **c'est un ~ de la voiture** he's mad about cars*, he's a car fanatic. **(b)** (*en colère*) furious; (*Vét*) rabid.

enrayer [ɑ̃ʀeje] (8) **1** *vt maladie* to check, stop; *arme* to jam. **2 s'~** *vpr* to jam.

enrégimenter [ɑ̃ʀeʒimɑ̃te] (1) *vt* (*péj*) to enrol.

enregistrer [ɑ̃ʀʒistʀe] (1) *vt voix* to record; (*sur bande*) to tape(-record); (*Jur*) *acte* to register; (*Comm*) *commande* to enter; *constatation* to note; (*mentalement*) to retain, register. **d'accord, j'enregistre*** all right, I'll bear it in mind; **(faire) ~ ses bagages** to register one's luggage; (*Aviat*) to check in one's luggage. ♦ **enregistrement** *nm* registration; check-in. **~ magnétique** tape recording. ♦ **enregistreur, -euse 1** *adj* recording. **2** *nm* recorder, recording machine.

enrhumer [ɑ̃ʀyme] (1) **1** *vt* to give a cold to. **être enrhumé** to have a cold. **2 s'~** *vpr* to catch (a) cold.

enrichir [ɑ̃ʀiʃiʀ] (2) **1** *vt esprit, collection* to enrich; *[argent]* to make rich. **2 s'~** *vpr [commerçant]* to grow rich; *[esprit]* to grow richer (*de* in); *[collection]* to be enriched (*de* with). ♦ **enrichi, e** *adj* (*Tech*) enriched. ♦ **enrichissant, e** *adj* enriching. ♦ **enrichissement** *nm* enrichment.

enrober [ɑ̃ʀɔbe] (1) *vt bonbon* to coat (*de* with); *paroles* to wrap up (*de* in). ♦ **enrobage** *nm* coating.

enrôler *vt*, **s'~** *vpr* [ɑ̃ʀole] (1) to enlist. ♦ **enrôlé** *nm* recruit. ♦ **enrôlement** *nm* enlistment.

enrouer [ɑ̃ʀwe] (1) **1** *vt* to make hoarse. **2 s'~** *vpr* (*froid*) to go hoarse; (*cri*) to make o.s. hoarse. ♦ **enroué, e** *adj* hoarse. ♦ **enrouement** *nm* hoarseness.

enrouler [ɑ̃ʀule] (1) **1** *vt* (*gén*) to roll up; *cheveux* to coil up; *fil* to wind (*autour de* round). **2 s'~** *vpr [serpent]* to coil up; *[fil]* to wind. **s'~ dans une couverture** to wrap *ou* roll o.s. up in a blanket.

ensabler *vt*, **s'~** *vpr* [ɑ̃sɑble] (1) *port* to silt up; *voiture* to get stuck in the sand.

ensanglanter [ɑ̃sɑ̃glɑ̃te] (1) *vt visage* to cover with blood; *vêtement* to soak with blood.

enseignant, e [ɑ̃sɛɲɑ̃, ɑ̃t] **1** *adj* teaching. **2** *nm,f* teacher.

enseigne [ɑ̃sɛɲ] **1** *nf* (*Comm*) (shop) sign; (*drapeau*) ensign. **~ lumineuse** neon sign; (*littér*) **à telle(s) ~(s) que** so much so that. **2** *nm* (*Hist*) ensign. **~ de vaisseau** lieutenant.

enseignement [ɑ̃sɛɲmɑ̃] *nm* **(a)** (*Admin*) education. **~ ménager** home economics; **~ par correspondance** postal tuition; **~ secondaire/technique** secondary/technical education; **~ professionnel** vocational training; **~ programmé** programmed learning. **(b)** (*art d'enseigner*) teaching. **~ moderne** modern teaching methods. **(c)** (*carrière*) teaching profession. **être dans l'~** to be a teacher. **(d)** (*leçon*) lesson. ♦ **enseigner** (1) *vt* to teach. **~ qch à qn** to teach sb sth; **~ à qn à faire qch** to teach sb (how) to do sth.

ensemble [ɑ̃sɑ̃bl(ə)] **1** *adv* together. **tous ~** all together; **ils ont répondu ~** (*deux*) they both answered together; (*plusieurs*) they all answered together; **ils vont bien ~** they go together well; **l'armoire et la table vont mal ~** the wardrobe and the table don't go (very well) together; **être bien/mal ~** to be on good/bad terms. **2** *nm* **(a)** (*unité*) unity. **avec un parfait ~** simultaneously, with one accord. **(b)** (*totalité*) whole. **l'~ du personnel** the entire *ou* whole staff, all the members of staff; **dans l'~** on the whole, by and large; **les spectateurs dans leur ~** the audience as a whole; **d'~** *vue etc* overall, general. **(c)** *[personnes]* group; *[objets]* set; *[lois]* body; (*Mus*) ensemble; (*zone résidentielle*) housing scheme; (*Math*) set; (*Couture*) outfit, suit.

ensemencer [ɑ̃smɑ̃se] (3) *vt* (*Agr*) to sow. ♦ **ensemencement** *nm* sowing.

ensevelir [ɑ̃səvliʀ] (2) *vt* (*gén*) to bury; (*d'un linceul*) to shroud (*de* in). ♦ **ensevelissement** *nm* burying; shrouding.

ensoleiller [ɑ̃sɔleje] (1) *vt* (*lit*) to fill with sunshine; (*fig*) to brighten, light up. ♦ **ensoleillé, e** *adj* sunny. ♦ **ensoleillement** *nm* hours of sunshine.

ensommeillé, e [ɑ̃sɔmeje] *adj* sleepy, drowsy.

ensorceler [ɑ̃sɔʀsəle] (4) *vt* (*lit, fig*) to bewitch.

ensuite [ɑ̃sɥit] *adv* (*puis*) then, next; (*par la suite*) afterwards, later; (*en fin de compte*) in the end. **~ de quoi** after which.

ensuivre (s') [ɑ̃sɥivʀ(ə)] (40) *vpr* to follow. **et tout ce qui s'ensuit** and all the rest; **torturé jusqu'à ce que mort s'ensuive** tortured to death.

entaille [ɑ̃taj] *nf* (*gén*) cut; (*profonde*) gash; (*sur objet*) notch; (*allongée*) groove. ♦ **entailler** (1) *vt* to cut; to gash; to notch.

entamer [ɑ̃tame] (1) *vt* **(a)** *pain* to start (upon); *bouteille* to start, open; *patrimoine* to dip into; *journée, livre* to start; *travail* to start on; *discussion* to open; *poursuites* to institute. **la journée est déjà bien entamée** we are already well into the day; (*Cartes*) **~ la partie** to open the game. **(b)** *résistance* to wear down, break down; *conviction* to shake, weaken; *réputation* to damage, harm. **(c)** (*inciser*) to cut (into). ♦ **entame** *nf* first slice.

entartrer *vt*, **s'~** *vpr* [ɑ̃taʀtʀe] (1) to scale. ♦ **entartrage** *nm* scaling.

entasser *vt*, **s'~** *vpr* [ɑ̃tɑse] (1) to pile up (*sur* onto). **s'~ dans** to cram *ou* pack into. ♦ **entassement** *nm* **(a)** (*action*) piling up; cramming in, packing together. **(b)** (*tas*) pile, heap.

entendre [ɑ̃tɑ̃dʀ(ə)] (41) **1** *vt* **(a)** *voix, témoin, messe* to hear; *conseil, discours* to listen to. **j'entendais qn parler** I heard *ou* could hear sb speaking; (*fig*) **il ne l'entend pas de cette oreille** he doesn't see it like that; **à l'~** to hear him talk, to listen to him; **~ raison** to listen to *ou* see reason. **(b)** (*comprendre*) to understand; (*vouloir*) to intend, mean; (*vouloir dire*) to mean. **laisser ~ à qn que** (*faire comprendre*) to give sb to understand that; (*donner l'impression*) to give sb the impression that; **faites comme vous l'entendez** do as you see fit *ou* think best; **j'entends être obéi** I intend *ou* mean to be obeyed, I WILL be obeyed. **(c)** (*locutions*) **~ parler de** to hear of *ou* about; (*fig*) **il ne veut pas en ~ parler** he won't hear of it; **d'après ce que j'ai entendu dire** from what I have heard; **on entend dire que** it is said *ou* rumoured that; **sa voix se fit ~** his voice was heard.

2 s'~ *vpr* **(a)** (*être d'accord*) to agree (*sur* on). **ils s'entendent bien/ne s'entendent pas** they get on well (together)/don't get on (together). **(b)** (*s'y connaître*) **il s'y entend pour le faire** he's very good at it, he knows how to do it. **(c)** (*se comprendre*) **quand je dis énorme je m'entends, disons grand** when I say huge what I really mean is big; (*bien sûr*) **(cela) s'entend** of course; **entendons-nous bien!** let's be quite clear about this; **ça s'entend de 2 manières** that can be taken 2 ways *ou* to mean 2 different things. **(d)** (*être entendu*) **on ne s'entend plus ici** you can't hear yourself think in here.

♦ **entendement** *nm* (*Philos*) understanding. ♦ **entendeur** *nm*: **à bon ~, salut** a word to the wise is enough. ♦ **entendu, e** *adj* **(a)** (*convenu*) agreed. (*évidemment*) **bien ~!** of course!; (*concessif*) **c'est ~** all right. **(b)** *sourire, air* knowing. ♦ **entente** *nf* (*amitié, compréhension*) understanding; (*accord*) agreement. **vivre en bonne ~** to live in harmony.

entériner [ɑ̃teʀine] (1) *vt* to ratify, confirm.

entérite [ɑ̃teʀit] *nf* enteritis.

enterrer [ɑ̃teʀe] (1) *vt* (*gén*) to bury; *projet* to drop. **tu nous enterreras tous!** you'll outlive us all! ♦ **enterrement** *nm [mort]* burial; *[espoir]* end, death; (*cérémonie*) funeral; (*convoi*) funeral procession. **faire une tête d'~*** to look gloomy.

en-tête, *pl* **en-têtes** [ɑ̃tɛt] *nm* heading.

entêter [ɑ̃tete] (1) **1** *vt [parfum]* to go to the head of. **2 s'~** *vpr* to persist (*dans qch* in sth, *à faire qch* in doing sth). ♦ **entêtant, e** *adj vin* heady. ♦ **entêté, e** *adj* stubborn. ♦ **entêtement** *nm* stubbornness.

enthousiasme [ɑ̃tuzjasm(ə)] *nm* enthusiasm. ♦ **enthousiasmant, e** *adj* exciting, exhilarating. ♦ **enthousiasmer** (1) **1** *vt* to fill with enthusiasm. **2 s'~** *vpr* to be enthusiastic (*pour* about, over). ♦ **enthousiaste** *adj* enthusiastic (*de* about, over).

enticher (s') [ɑ̃tiʃe] (1) *vpr* (*péj*) **s'~ de** *femme* to become infatuated with; *choses* to have a passion for.

entier, -ière [ɑ̃tje, jɛʀ] **1** *adj* **(a)** *quantité* whole, full; *surface* whole, entire. **payer place ~ière** to pay the full price; **une heure ~ière** a whole *ou* full hour; **dans la France ~ière** throughout France, in the whole of France; **tout ~** entirely, completely. **(b)** (*intact*) intact; (*absolu*) absolute, complete. **la question reste ~ière** the matter still remains unresolved. **(c)** *personne, caractère* unyielding, unbending. **(d) pain ~** wholemeal bread; **lait ~** full-cream milk. **2** *nm* **(a)** (*Math*) whole. **(b) en ~** entirely; **boire une bouteille en ~** to drink a whole bottle; **lire qch en ~** to read the whole of sth, read sth right through; **la nation dans son ~** the nation as a whole. ♦ **entièrement** *adv* entirely, completely, wholly, fully.

entité [ɑ̃tite] *nf* entity.

entonner [ɑ̃tɔne] (1) *vt chanson* to strike up.

entonnoir [ɑ̃tɔnwaʀ] *nm* (*Culin*) funnel.

entorse [ɑ̃tɔʀs(ə)] *nf* (*Méd*) sprain; *[loi]* infringement (*à* of). **se faire une ~ au poignet** to sprain one's wrist; **faire une ~ à** *vérité* to twist; *habitudes* to break; *règlement* to bend.

entortiller [ɑ̃tɔʀtije] (1) *vt* **(a)** *ficelle* to twist, wind; *objet* to wrap (up). **(b)** (*duper*) to hoodwink.

entourer [ɑ̃tuʀe] (1) **1** *vt* **(a)** (*mettre autour*) **~ qch de** (*gén*) to surround sth with; *couverture* to wrap sth in; **~ qn de ses bras** to put one's arms round sb. **(b)** (*être autour*) (*gén*) to surround; *[écharpe]* to be round; (*fig*) *personne souffrante* to rally round. **le monde qui nous entoure** the world about us. **2 s'~** *vpr*: **s'~ de** to surround o.s. with; **s'~ de précautions** to take elaborate precautions. ♦ **entourage** *nm* (*famille*) family circle; (*compagnie*) set, circle; *[président]* entourage; *[fenêtre etc]* surround. ♦ **entouré, e** *adj* (*admiré*) popular.

entracte [ɑ̃tʀakt(ə)] *nm [spectacle],* (*Ciné*) interval; (*fig*) interlude.

entraide [ɑ̃tʀɛd] *nf* mutual aid. ♦ **entraider (s')** (1) *vpr* to help one another.

entrailles [ɑ̃tʀɑj] *nfpl* (*gén*), (*littér*) entrails; *[mère]* womb; (*fig*) *[terre]* bowels. **sans ~** heartless; **spectacle qui vous prend aux ~** sight that grips your very soul.

entrain [ɑ̃tʀɛ̃] *nm* spirit, drive, liveliness. **avec ~** *répondre, manger* with gusto; *travailler* spiritedly; **faire qch sans ~** to do sth half-heartedly. ♦ **entraînant, e** *adj paroles* stirring, rousing.

entraîner [ɑ̃tʀene] (1) **1** *vt* **(a)** *objets arrachés* to carry *ou* drag along; (*Tech*) *machine* to drive; (*tirer*) *wagons* to pull. **il entraîna son camarade dans sa chute** he pulled *ou* dragged his friend down in his fall; **il m'entraîna vers la sortie** he took me off towards the exit. **(b)** (*fig: influencer*) to lead. ~ **qn à voler qch** to get sb to steal sth; ~ **ses camarades à boire** to encourage one's friends to drink. **(c)** *dépenses, chutes* (*impliquer*) to entail, mean; (*causer*) to bring about, lead to. ~ **qn à une dépense** to lead sb to incur some expense. **(d)** *[rythme]* to carry along; *[enthousiasme]* to carry away. **se laisser** ~ **par ses passions** to (let o.s.) get *ou* be carried away by one's passions. **(e)** (*préparer*) *athlète* to train, coach; *cheval* to train (*à* for). **2 s'**~ *vpr* (*gén*) to train o.s.; (*Sport*) to train (*à, pour* for). **s'**~ **à faire un mouvement** to practise a movement; **il s'entraîne à parler en public** he is training himself to speak in public. ♦ **entraînement** *nm [roue]* driving; *[athlète]* training. **manquer d'**~ to be out of training. ♦ **entraîneur** *nm [cheval]* trainer; *[coureur]* coach, trainer.

entraver [ɑ̃tʀave] (1) *vt circulation* to hold up; *action* to hinder, hamper; *animal* to fetter; *prisonnier* to chain up. ♦ **entrave** *nf* hindrance (*à* to). *[prisonnier]* ~**s** chains; (*fig*) **les** ~**s de** the fetters of.

entre [ɑ̃tʀ(ə)] *prép* **(a)** (*gén*) between. **la vérité est** ~ **les deux** the truth is somewhere in between.

(b) (*parmi*) (*gén*) among, amongst; *choisir* between. **lui,** ~ **autres, n'est pas d'accord** he, for one, doesn't agree; ~ **autres (choses)** among other things; **l'un d'**~ **eux** one of them; **cette heure** ~ **toutes** this (hour) of all hours; **difficile** ~ **tous** exceptionally difficult.

(c) (*dans*) in, into. **prendre** ~ **ses bras** to take in one's arms; ~ **parenthèses** in brackets.

(d) (*à travers*) through. (*lit, fig*) **passer** ~ **les mailles du filet** to slip through the net.

(e) (*relation*) (*deux choses*) between; (*plus de deux*) among. ~ **nous** between you and me, between ourselves; ~ **eux 4** among the 4 of them; **il n'y a rien de commun** ~ **eux** they have nothing in common; **ils préfèrent rester** ~ **eux** they prefer to be on their own; **ils se sont disputés** ~ **eux** they have quarrelled with each other *ou* with one another; **on ne va pas se battre** ~ **nous** we're not going to fight among ourselves.

(f) (*locutions*) ~ **chien et loup** when the shadows are falling; ~ **deux âges** middle-aged; (*fig*) ~ **deux portes** briefly; ~ **deux eaux** just below the surface; **pris** ~ **deux feux** caught in the crossfire; **parler** ~ **ses dents** to mumble.

entrebâiller [ɑ̃tʀəbɑje] (1) *vt* to half-open. ♦ **entrebâillé, e** *adj*: **être** ~ to be ajar *ou* half-open. ♦ **entrebâillement** *nm*: **dans l'**~ **de la porte** in the half-open door.

entrechoquer [ɑ̃tʀəʃɔke] (1) **1** *vt* (*gén*) to knock together; *verres* to clink. **2 s'**~ *vpr* (*gén*) to knock together; *[verres]* to clink; *[dents]* to chatter; *[épées]* to clash together; *[idées, mots]* to jostle together.

entrecôte [ɑ̃tʀəkot] *nf* entrecôte *ou* rib steak.

entrecouper [ɑ̃tʀəkupe] (1) **1** *vt*: ~ **de** (*gén*) to interrupt with; *citations* to intersperse with; **voix entrecoupée** broken voice. **2 s'**~ *vpr [lignes]* to intersect, cut across each other.

entrecroiser *vt,* **s'**~ *vpr* [ɑ̃tʀəkʀwaze] (1) *fils* to intertwine; *lignes* to intersect.

entrée [ɑ̃tʀe] *nf* **(a)** (*arrivée*) *[personnne]* entry, entrance; *[véhicule, marchandise]* entry. (*Théât*) ~ **(en scène)** entrance; **à son** ~ as he entered; **faire une** ~ **discrète** to enter discreetly; **faire son** ~ **dans le monde** to make one's début (in society). **(b)** (*accès*) admission (*de, dans* to); (*sur pancarte*) 'way in'. '~ **libre**' 'admission free'; '~ **interdite**' 'no admittance'; **on lui a refusé l'**~ **de la salle** he was refused admission *ou* entrance to the hall; **billet d'**~ (entrance) ticket; **depuis son** ~ **à l'université/dans le club** since he went to university/joined the club; **avoir ses** ~**s auprès de qn** to have easy access to sb. **(c)** (*Tech*) *[pièce]* insertion. ~ **d'air** air inlet. **(d)** (*billet*) ticket. **les** ~**s couvriront tous les frais** the takings will cover all expenses. **(e)** (*porte*) entrance; *[trou]* mouth. (*Théât*) ~ **des artistes** stage door; ~ **de service** service entrance. **(f)** (*vestibule*) entrance (hall). **(g)** (*début*) **à l'**~ **de l'hiver** at the beginning of winter; **à l'**~ **de la vie** at life's outset; **d'**~ **(de jeu)** from the outset; ~ **en matière** introduction. **(h)** (*Culin*) first *ou* main course. **(i)** (*Comm, Statistique*) entry; (*Lexicographie*) headword.

entrefaites [ɑ̃tʀəfɛt] *nfpl*: **sur ces** ~ at that moment.

entre-jambes [ɑ̃tʀəʒɑ̃b] *nm inv* (*Couture*) crotch.

entrelacer *vt,* **s'**~ *vpr* [ɑ̃tʀəlase] (3) to intertwine, interlace. ♦ **entrelacement** *nm*: **un** ~ **de ...** a network of ....

entremêler [ɑ̃tʀəmele] (1) **1** *vt choses* to intermingle, intermix. ~ **un récit de** to intersperse a tale with. **2 s'**~ *vpr* to intermingle.

entremets [ɑ̃tʀəmɛ] *nm* (cream) sweet *ou* dessert.

entremettre (s') [ɑ̃tʀəmɛtʀ(ə)] (56) *vpr* to intervene (*dans* in). ♦ **entremetteur, -euse** *nm,f* (*péj*) go-between. ♦ **entremise** *nf* intervention. **par l'**~ **de** through.

entreposer [ɑ̃tʀəpoze] (1) *vt* to store, put into storage. ♦ **entrepôt** *nm* (*gén*) warehouse; (*port*) entrepot.

entreprendre [ɑ̃tʀəpʀɑ̃dʀ(ə)] (58) *vt* (*gén*) to begin *ou* start on, embark upon. ~ **qn** (*pour bavarder*) to buttonhole sb; (*sur un problème*) to tackle sb; ~ **de faire qch** to undertake to do sth. ♦ **entreprenant, e** *adj* (*gén*) enterprising; (*avec les femmes*) forward.

entrepreneur, -euse [ɑ̃tʀəpʀənœʀ, øz] *nm,f* contractor. ~ **(en bâtiment)** building contractor; ~ **de pompes funèbres** undertaker.

entreprise [ɑ̃tʀəpʀiz] *nf* (*firme*) firm; (*dessein*) undertaking, venture.

entrer [ɑ̃tʀe] (1) **1** *vi* **(a)** (*aller*) to go in, enter; (*venir*) to come in; (*à pied*) to walk in; (*en voiture*) to drive in. ~ **dans** to go *ou* come into, enter; ~ **en coup de vent** to burst in, come bursting in; **entrez!** come in!; **les gens entraient et sortaient** people were going in and out; ~ **par la fenêtre** to get in by the window; **je suis entré chez eux** I called in at their house.

(b) *[marchandises, devises]* to enter; *[objet]* to go in; (*s'adapter*) to fit in. **ça n'entre pas** it won't go *ou* fit in; **son coude m'entrait dans les côtes** his elbow was digging into my ribs; **l'eau entre par le toit** water comes in through the roof; **l'air entre dans la pièce** air comes into *ou* enters the room; **la rage est entrée dans son cœur** his heart was filled with rage; **à force d'explications ça finira par** ~* explain it for long enough and it'll sink in*; **alors ces maths, ça entre?*** are you getting the hang of maths then?*; **c'est entré comme dans du beurre*** it went (in) like a hot knife through butter.

(c) laisser ~ to let in; **laisser** ~ **qn dans** to let sb into.

(d) faire ~ *visiteur* to show in; *objet* to fit in; *marchandises* to take *ou* bring in; (*en fraude*) to smuggle in; **il m'a fait** ~ **dans leur club** (*persuadé*) he got me to join their club; (*aidé*) he got me into their club; (*contraint*) he made me join their club; (*comme employé*) he got me a job in their club; **il me fit** ~ **dans la cellule** he showed me into the cell.

(e) (*commencer*) ~ **en convalescence** to begin convalescence; ~ **en ébullition** to reach boiling point, begin to boil.

(f) ~ **dans** *club, parti* to join; *groupe, métier* to go into; *profession libérale* to enter; ~ **dans les affaires** to go into business; ~ **en religion** to enter the religious life; ~ **dans les ordres** to take orders; ~ **au service de qn** to enter sb's service; ~

dans l'histoire to go down in history; ~ **dans la légende** to become a legend.

(g) ~ **dans** *arbre* to hit, go into; (*Aut*) **on lui est entré dedans*** sb banged into him.

(h) ~ **dans** *vues, peines de qn* to share.

(i) ~ **dans** *catégorie* to fall into, come into; *mélange* to go into; **c'est entré pour beaucoup dans sa décision** it counted for a good deal in his decision; **il n'entre pas dans mes intentions de le faire** I don't have any intention of doing so; **faire ~ qch dans une catégorie** to put sth into a category.

(j) ~ **dans** *période, discussion* to enter into; *rêverie, considérations, colère* to go into; ~ **dans la vie active** to enter active life; ~ **dans la cinquantaine** to turn fifty; ~ **dans le vif du sujet** to get to the heart of the matter.

2 *vt*: ~ **les bras dans les manches** to put one's arms into the sleeves; **ne m'entre pas ta canne dans les côtes** don't dig your stick into my ribs.

entresol [ɑ̃tʀəsɔl] *nm* mezzanine.

entre-temps [ɑ̃tʀətɑ̃] *adv* meanwhile, (in the) meantime.

entretenir [ɑ̃tʀətniʀ] (22) **1** *vt* **(a)** *propriété* to maintain, look after; *route, machine* to maintain; *famille* to support, keep; *souvenir, espoir* to keep alive; *craintes* to have; *correspondance* to keep up. **ça entretient de l'humidité** (*qualité*) it keeps up *ou* maintains the humidity; (*défaut*) it holds the damp; ~ **le feu** to keep the fire going *ou* burning; ~ **qn dans l'erreur** to keep sb in ignorance; ~ **sa forme, s'~ (en bonne forme)** to keep (o.s.) fit. **(b)** (*converser*) ~ **qn** to speak to sb (*de* about). **2 s'~** *vpr* **(a)** (*converser*) **s'~ avec qn** to speak to sb (*de* about). **(b)** (*pourvoir à ses besoins*) to be self-supporting. ♦ **entretenu, e** *adj femme* kept. **jardin bien/mal** ~ well-/badly-kept garden. ♦ **entretien** *nm* **(a)** *[maison]* upkeep; *[route, machine]* maintenance; *[famille]* keep. **(b)** (*conversation*) conversation; (*entrevue*) interview; (*débat*) discussion. (*Pol*) **~(s)** talks, discussions.

entre-tuer (s') [ɑ̃tʀətɥe] (1) *vpr* to kill one another.

entrevoir [ɑ̃tʀəvwaʀ] (30) *vt* (*indistinctement*) to make out; (*brièvement*) to catch sight of; (*fig: pressentir*) to glimpse.

entrevue [ɑ̃tʀəvy] *nf* (*discussion*) meeting; (*audience*) interview; (*Pol*) talks, discussions.

entrouvrir *vt*, **s'~** *vpr* [ɑ̃tʀuvʀiʀ] (18) to half-open. ♦ **entrouvert, e** *adj* (*gén*) half-open; *porte* ajar.

envahir [ɑ̃vaiʀ] (2) *vt [ennemi, herbes]* to invade, overrun; *[douleur, sommeil]* to overcome. **la foule envahit la place** the crowd swarmed into the square; (*déranger*) ~ **qn** to invade sb's privacy. ♦ **envahissant, e** *adj personne* intrusive; *passion* invading. ♦ **envahisseur, -euse 1** *adj* invading. **2** *nm,f* invader.

envaser [ɑ̃vɑze] (1) **1** *vt port* to silt up. **2 s'~** *vpr [port]* to silt up; *[bateau]* to stick in the mud. ♦ **envasement** *nm* silting up.

enveloppe [ɑ̃vlɔp] *nf* **(a)** (*pli postal*) envelope. **sous ~** *envoyer* under cover; **mettre sous ~** to put in an envelope. **(b)** (*emballage*) (*gén*) covering; (*en papier, toile*) wrapping; (*en métal*) casing; *[graine]* husk; *[pneu]* cover. **(c)** (*apparence*) exterior.

envelopper [ɑ̃vlɔpe] (1) *vt* **(a)** *objet, enfant* to wrap up. **il s'enveloppa dans une cape** he wrapped himself in a cape; (*fig*) ~ **qn de son affection** to surround sb with one's affection; ~ **sa pensée** to veil one's thoughts. **(b)** *[brume]* to envelop, shroud. **le silence enveloppe la ville** the town is wrapped *ou* shrouded in silence; **enveloppé de mystère** shrouded *ou* veiled in mystery; ~ **qn du regard** to envelop sb with one's gaze; ~ **dans sa réprobation**† to include in one's disapproval.

envenimer [ɑ̃vnime] (1) **1** *vt plaie* to make septic; *querelle, situation* to inflame. **2 s'~** *vpr [plaie]* to go septic; *[querelle, situation]* to grow more bitter.

envergure [ɑ̃vɛʀgyʀ] *nf [oiseau, avion]* wingspan; *[voile]* breadth; *[personne]* calibre; *[entreprise]* scale, scope; *[intelligence]* scope, range. **de grande ~** large-scale.

envers[1] [ɑ̃vɛʀ] *prép* towards, to. ~ **et contre tous** despite all opposition.

envers[2] [ɑ̃vɛʀ] *nm* **(a)** *[étoffe]* wrong side; *[papier]* back; *[médaille]* reverse (side). **l'~ et l'endroit** the wrong (side) and the right side; (*fig*) **l'~ du décor** the other side of the picture. **(b) à l'~** *vêtement* inside out; *objet* (*vertical*) upside down; (*horizontal*) the wrong way round, back to front; **tout va à l'~** everything is upside down; **faire qch à l'~** (*à rebours*) to do sth the wrong way round; (*mal*) to do sth all wrong; **elle avait la tête à l'~** her mind was in a whirl.

envie [ɑ̃vi] *nf* **(a)** ~ **de qch/de faire** (*désir*) desire for sth/to do; (*grand désir*) longing for sth/to do; (*besoin*) need for sth/to do; **avoir ~ de** to want; **j'ai ~ d'y aller** I feel like going, I would like to go; **avoir bien/presque ~ de faire qch** to have a good mind/half a mind to do sth; **j'ai ~ qu'il s'en aille** I would like him to go away, I wish he would go away; **avoir ~ de rire** to feel like laughing; **cela lui a donné (l')~ de rire** it made him want to laugh; **avoir ~*** (*d'aller aux toilettes*) to need to go to the toilet. **(b)** (*convoitise*) envy. **mon bonheur lui fait ~** he envies my happiness. **(c)** (*Anat*) *[peau]* birthmark; *[ongles]* hangnail. ♦ **enviable** *adj* enviable. ♦ **envier** (7) *vt* to envy, be envious of. **je vous envie votre maison** I wish I had your house, I envy you your house; **il n'a rien à m'~** (*comme avantage*) he has no cause to be jealous of me; (*comme désavantage*) he's just as badly off as I am. ♦ **envieusement** *adv* enviously. ♦ **envieux, -euse** *adj* envious. **faire des ~** to arouse envy.

environ [ɑ̃viʀɔ̃] **1** *adv* about. **c'est à 100 km ~ d'ici** it's about 100 km from here, it's 100 km or so from here. **2** *nmpl*: **les ~s** the surroundings; **aux ~s de 10 F** round about 10 francs, 10 francs or thereabouts; **dans les ~s du château** in the vicinity of the castle. ♦ **environnant, e** *adj* surrounding. ♦ **environnement** *nm* environment. ♦ **environner** (1) *vt* to surround, encircle. **s'~ de** to surround o.s. with.

envisager [ɑ̃vizaʒe] (3) *vt* to envisage, contemplate (*de faire* doing).

envoi [ɑ̃vwa] *nm* **(a)** (*V* **envoyer**) sending; sending off; dispatching; shipment. ~ **contre remboursement** cash on delivery. **(b)** (*colis*) parcel. ~ **en nombre** mass mailing.

envoler (s') [ɑ̃vɔle] (1) *vpr [oiseau]* to fly away; *[avion]* to take off; *[chapeau]* to blow off; *[temps]* to fly (past); *[espoirs, objet volé]* to vanish. ♦ **envol** *nm [oiseau]* taking flight; *[avion]* takeoff; *[pensée]* flight. **prendre son ~** *[oiseau]* to take flight. ♦ **envolée** *nf*: ~ **(poétique)** flight of poetry.

envoûter [ɑ̃vute] (1) *vt* to bewitch, cast a spell on. **être envoûté par qn** to be under sb's spell. ♦ **envoûtement** *nm* bewitchment.

envoyer [ɑ̃vwaje] (8) **1** *vt* **(a)** (*gén*) to send; *marchandises* to dispatch, send off; (*par bateau*) to ship; (*en vacances*) to send off; (*en mission*) to send out (*chez* to); *candidature* to send in. **envoie-moi un mot** drop me a line. **(b)** *pierre* to throw; (*avec force*) to hurl; *obus* to fire; *signaux* to send out; *ballon* to send. ~ **des baisers à qn** to blow sb kisses; ~ **des sourires à qn** to smile at sb; ~ **des coups de poing à qn** to punch sb; **ne m'envoie pas ta fumée dans les yeux** don't blow smoke in my eyes; ~ **qn à terre** to knock sb down; (*Naut*) ~ **par le fond** to send down *ou* to the bottom; (*Mil*) ~ **les**

couleurs to run up the colours. **(c)** ~ **chercher qn/qch** to send for sb/sth; ~ **promener qn*** to send sb packing*; ~ **valser qch*** to send sth flying; **il a tout envoyé promener*** he has chucked (up) everything‡; **il ne le lui a pas envoyé dire*** he told him straight to his face. **2 s'**~‡ *vpr corvée* to get stuck with; *nourriture* to down. **je m'enverrais des gifles*** I could kick myself*. ♦ **envoyé, e 1** *adj réponse* well-aimed, sharp. **2** *nm,f* (*gén*) messenger; (*Pol*) envoy; (*Presse*) correspondent. ♦ **envoyeur, -euse** *nm,f* sender.

épagneul, e [epaɲœl] *nm,f* spaniel.

épais, -aisse [epɛ, ɛs] **1** *adj* **(a)** (*gén*) thick; *neige, silence* deep; *barbe* bushy; *corps* thickset; *nuit* pitch-black. ~ **de 5 cm** 5 cm thick. **(b)** (*péj*) *esprit* dull; *personne* dense, thickheaded; *plaisanterie* clumsy. **2** *adv semer* thick, thickly. **il n'y en a pas** ~**!*** there's not much of it! ♦ **épaisseur** *nf* thickness; depth; dullness. **la neige a un mètre d'**~ the snow is a metre deep. ♦ **épaissir** (2) **1** *vt* (*lit*) to thicken. **l'air était épaissi par les fumées** the air was thick with smoke. **2** *vi* (*gén*) to get thicker, thicken; *[personne]* to thicken out. **3 s'**~ *vpr* (*lit*) to thicken, get thicker; *[ténèbres, mystère]* to deepen. ♦ **épaississement** *nm* thickening.

épancher [epɑ̃ʃe] (1) **1** *vt sentiments* to pour forth. **2 s'**~ *vpr [personne]* to pour out one's feelings; *[sang]* to pour out. ♦ **épanchement** *nm [sang]* effusion; *[sentiments]* outpouring.

épanouir (s') [epanwiʀ] (2) *vpr [fleur]* to bloom, open out; *[visage]* to light up; *[personne]* to blossom. ♦ **épanoui, e** *adj fleur* in full bloom; *visage, sourire* radiant. ♦ **épanouissement** *nm* opening out; blossoming.

épargner [epaʀɲe] (1) *vt* **(a)** (*économiser*) to save. **je n'épargnerai rien pour le faire** I'll spare nothing to get it done. **(b)** (*éviter*) ~ **qch à qn** to spare sb sth; **pour t'**~ **des explications** to save giving you *ou* to spare you explanations; **pour m'**~ **la peine de venir** to save *ou* spare myself the bother of coming. **(c)** (*ménager*) *ennemi etc* to spare. ♦ **épargnant, e** *nm,f* saver. ♦ **épargne** *nf* (*somme*) savings. (*vertu*) **l'**~ saving.

éparpiller [epaʀpije] (1) **1** *vt* (*gén*) to scatter; *efforts* to dissipate. **2 s'**~ *vpr* to scatter; to dissipate one's efforts. ♦ **éparpillement** *nm* scattering; dissipation. ♦ **épars, e** *adj* scattered.

épatant, e* [epatɑ̃, ɑ̃t] *adj* splendid, great*.

épaté, e [epate] *adj nez* flat.

épater* [epate] (1) *vt* (*étonner*) to amaze, stagger; (*impressionner*) to impress.

épaule [epol] *nf* (*Anat, Culin*) shoulder.

épauler [epole] (1) *vt* **(a)** *personne* to back up, support. **(b)** *fusil* to raise. **il épaula** he took aim.

épaulette [epolɛt] *nf* (*Mil*) epaulette.

épave [epav] *nf* (*lit, fig*) wreck; (*débris*) piece of wreckage.

épée [epe] *nf* sword.

épeler [eple] (4 *ou* 5) *vt mot* to spell; *texte* to spell out.

éperdu, e [epeʀdy] *adj* **(a)** *personne* distraught, overcome (*de* with). **(b)** *gratitude* boundless; *regard* wild, distraught; *amour* passionate; *fuite* headlong; *désir* frantic. ♦ **éperdument** *adv* frantically; *aimer* passionately. **je m'en moque** ~ I couldn't care less.

éperonner [epʀɔne] (1) *vt cheval* to spur on; *navire* to ram. ♦ **éperon** *nm* (*gén*) spur.

épervier [epeʀvje] *nm* (*Orn*) sparrowhawk; (*filet*) casting net.

éphémère [efemeʀ] *adj* fleeting, short-lived.

épi [epi] *nm [blé]* ear; *[fleur]* spike; *[cheveux]* tuft.

épice [epis] *nf* spice. ♦ **épicé, e** *adj* (*gén*) spicy. ♦ **épicer** (3) *vt* to spice.

épicerie [episʀi] *nf* (*magasin*) grocer's (shop); (*nourriture*) groceries; (*métier*) grocery trade. **aller à l'**~ to go to the grocer's; ~ **fine** ≃ delicatessen. ♦ **épicier, -ière** *nm,f* (*gén*) grocer; (*fruits et légumes*) greengrocer.

épidémie [epidemi] *nf* epidemic. ♦ **épidémique** *adj* (*lit*) epidemic; (*fig*) contagious.

épiderme [epidɛʀm(ə)] *nm* skin. ♦ **épidermique** *adj* (*Anat*) skin. (*fig*) **réaction** ~ automatic reaction.

épier [epje] (7) *vt personne* to spy on; *geste* to watch closely; *bruit* to listen out for; *occasion* to watch out for.

épilepsie [epilɛpsi] *nf* epilepsy. ♦ **épileptique** *adj, nmf* epileptic.

épiler [epile] (1) *vt jambes* to remove the hair from; *sourcils* to pluck.

épilogue [epilɔg] *nm* (*littér*) epilogue; (*fig*) conclusion.

épinard [epinaʀ] *nm*: ~**(s)** spinach.

épine [epin] *nf* **(a)** *[buisson]* thorn; *[hérisson, oursin]* spine, prickle; *[porc-épic]* quill. ~ **dorsale** backbone; **vous m'enlevez une belle** ~ **du pied** you have got me out of a spot*. **(b)** (*arbre*) thorn bush. ~ **blanche** hawthorn. ♦ **épineux, -euse** *adj plante* thorny, prickly; *problème* thorny, tricky.

épingle [epɛ̃gl(ə)] *nf* pin. **virage en** ~ **à cheveux** hairpin bend; ~ **à linge** clothes peg *ou* pin (*US*); ~ **de nourrice** safety pin; **tirer son** ~ **du jeu** to manage to extricate o.s. ♦ **épingler** (1) *vt* (*attacher*) to pin (on) (*à , sur* to); (‡: *arrêter*) to nick‡, nab*.

Épiphanie [epifani] *nf*: **l'**~ Epiphany, Twelfth Night.

épique [epik] *adj* (*lit, fig*) epic.

épiscopat [episkɔpa] *nm* (*siège*) bishopric; (*corps*) episcopacy. ♦ **épiscopal, e,** *mpl* **-aux** *adj* episcopal.

épisode [epizɔd] *nm* episode. **film à** ~**s** serial. ♦ **épisodique** *adj* (*occasionnel*) occasional; (*secondaire*) minor, secondary. ♦ **épisodiquement** *adv* occasionally.

épitaphe [epitaf] *nf* epitaph.

épithète [epitɛt] *nf* **(a)** (*Gram*) attribute. **adjectif** ~ attributive adjective. **(b)** (*qualificatif*) epithet.

épître [epitʀ(ə)] *nf* epistle.

éploré, e [eplɔʀe] *adj* (*littér*) *visage* bathed in tears; *personne, voix* tearful.

éplucher [eplyʃe] (1) *vt* (*gén*) to peel; *salade* to clean; *bonbon* to unwrap; *comptes* to dissect. ♦ **épluchage** *nm* cleaning; peeling; unwrapping; dissection. ♦ **épluchure** *nf* (piece of) peeling.

éponge [epɔ̃ʒ] *nf* sponge. **passons l'**~**!** let's forget all about it!; ~ **métallique** scouring pad. ♦ **éponger** (3) *vt liquide* to mop *ou* sponge up; *front* to mop; *dette* to absorb.

épopée [epɔpe] *nf* (*lit, fig*) epic.

époque [epɔk] *nf* (*gén*) time; (*Hist*) age, era, epoch; (*Géol*) period. **à l'**~ at the time; **meuble d'**~ genuine antique.

époumoner (s') [epumɔne] (1) *vpr* to shout *etc* o.s. hoarse.

épouser [epuze] (1) *vt* **(a)** *personne* to marry; *idée* to embrace, take up. **(b)** *[robe]* to fit; *[route, tracé]* to follow. ♦ **épouse** *nf* wife.

épousseter [epuste] (4) *vt* to dust.

époustoufler* [epustufle] (1) *vt* to stagger, flabbergast.

épouvanter [epuvɑ̃te] (1) *vt* (*gén*) to appal. ♦ **épouvantable** *adj* appalling, dreadful. ♦ **épouvantablement** *adv* appallingly, dreadfully. ♦ **épouvantail** *nm* (*à oiseaux*) scarecrow; (*menace*) (*personne*) bogey; (*chose*) bugbear. ♦ **épouvante** *nf* terror. **saisi d'**~ terror-stricken; **avec** ~ with dread; **film d'**~ horror film.

époux [epu] *nm* husband. **les** ~ the husband and wife.

éprendre (s') [epʀɑ̃dʀ(ə)] (58) *vpr* (*littér*) **s'**~ **de** to fall in love with.

épreuve [epʀœv] *nf* **(a)** (*essai*) test. (*fig*) ~ **de force** test of strength; **mettre à l'**~ to put to the

test; **à l'~ des balles/du feu** bulletproof/fireproof; **courage à toute ~** unfailing courage. **(b)** (*initiatique*) ordeal; (*malheur*) ordeal, trial. **(c)** (*Scol*) test; (*Sport*) event. **~ de sélection** heat; **~ contre la montre** time-trial. **(d)** (*Typ*) proof; (*Phot*) print.
épris, e [epʀi, iz] *adj* (*littér*) in love (*de* with).
éprouver [epʀuve] (1) *vt* **(a)** *sensation* to feel, experience; *perte* to suffer; *difficultés* to experience. **(b)** (*tester*) to test. **(c)** *[maladie]* to afflict; *[nouvelle]* to distress. ♦ **éprouvant, e** *adj* testing. ♦ **éprouvé, e** *adj remède* well-tried, proven; *spécialiste* well-proven.
éprouvette [epʀuvɛt] *nf* test-tube.
épuiser [epɥize] (1) **1** *vt* (*gén*) to exhaust; *personne* to tire out, wear out. **2 s'~** *vpr [réserves]* to run out; *[source]* to dry up; *[forces]* to fail; *[personne]* to exhaust o.s., wear *ou* tire o.s. out (*à faire qch* doing sth). ♦ **épuisant, e** *adj* exhausting. ♦ **épuisé, e** *adj* (*gén*) exhausted; (*Comm*) *article* sold out; *livre* out of print. **~ de fatigue** tired out, worn out. ♦ **épuisement** *nm* (*gén*) exhaustion. **devant l'~ de ses finances** seeing that his money was exhausted *ou* had run out.
épuisette [epɥizɛt] *nf* landing net; (*à crevettes*) shrimping net.
épurer [epyʀe] (1) *vt* (*lit*) to purify; (*Pol*) to purge. ♦ **épuration** *nf* purification; purge.
équateur [ekwatœʀ] *nm* equator. ♦ **équatorial, e,** *mpl* **-aux** *adj* equatorial.
équation [ekwɑsjɔ̃] *nf* equation.
équerre [ekɛʀ] *nf* (*pour tracer*) set square; (*de soutien*) brace. **en ~** at right angles; **être d'~** to be straight *ou* level.
équestre [ekɛstʀ(ə)] *adj* equestrian.
équidistant, e [ekɥidistɑ̃, ɑ̃t] *adj* equidistant (*de* from).
équilatéral, e, *mpl* **-aux** [ekɥilateʀal, o] *adj* equilateral.
équilibre [ekilibʀ(ə)] *nm* (*gén*) balance, equilibrium; (*harmonie*) harmony. **perdre l'~** to lose one's balance; **être en ~ sur** *[personne]* to balance on; *[objet]* to be balanced on; **mettre qch en ~** to balance sth (*sur* on); **~ (mental)** (mental) equilibrium *ou* stability; **~ budgétaire** balance in the budget; **budget en ~** balanced budget; **l'~ du monde** the world balance of power. ♦ **équilibrage** *nm* (*Aut*) balancing. ♦ **équilibré, e** *adj personne* stable, well-balanced; *vie* well-regulated. **mal ~** unbalanced. ♦ **équilibrer** (1) **1** *vt* (*gén*) to balance; (*contrebalancer*) to counterbalance. **2 s'~** *vpr [forces etc]* to counterbalance each other, cancel each other out. ♦ **équilibriste** *nmf* tightrope walker; (*fig*) juggler.
équinoxe [ekinɔks(ə)] *nm* equinox.
équipage [ekipaʒ] *nm* (*Aviat*) (air)crew; (*Naut*) crew; (†) *[seigneur, chevaux]* equipage†.
équipe [ekip] *nf* (*Sport, gén*) team; *[rameurs]* crew; *[ouvriers]* gang; (*par roulement*) shift; (*: *péj, fig*) bunch*, crew*. **~ de secours** rescue party; **~ de nuit** night shift; **faire ~ avec** to team up with. ♦ **équipier, -ière** *nm,f* (*Sport*) team member.
équipée [ekipe] *nf [prisonnier]* escape; *[aventurier]* undertaking, venture; *[promeneur]* jaunt.
équiper [ekipe] (1) *vt* (*gén*) to equip; *local* to fit out; *sportif* to kit out (*de* with). **~ une machine de** to fit a machine out with; **s'~** *[sportif]* to equip o.s., kit o.s. out. ♦ **équipement** *nm* (*action*) equipping; fitting out; kitting out (*de* with); (*matériel*) equipment, kit. **l'~ hôtelier d'une région** the hotel resources of a region.
équitable [ekitabl(ə)] *adj jugement* equitable, fair; *personne* fair. ♦ **équitablement** *adv* equitably, fairly.
équitation [ekitɑsjɔ̃] *nf* (horse-)riding.
équité [ekite] *nf* equity.
équivalence [ekivalɑ̃s] *nf* equivalence. ♦ **équivalent, e 1** *adj* equivalent (*à* to). **à prix ~** for the same *ou* equivalent price. **2** *nm* equivalent (*de* of). ♦ **équivaloir** (29) *vi* to be equivalent (*à* to).
équivoque [ekivɔk] **1** *adj* (*ambigu*) equivocal, ambiguous; (*louche*) dubious. **2** *nf* (*ambiguïté*) ambiguity; (*incertitude*) doubt; (*malentendu*) misunderstanding. **sans ~** *conduite* unequivocal.
érable [eʀabl(ə)] *nm* maple.
érafler [eʀɑfle] (1) *vt* to scratch, graze. ♦ **éraflure** *nf* scratch, graze.
éraillé, e [eʀɑje] *adj voix* rasping, hoarse.
ère [ɛʀ] *nf* era. **avant notre ~** B.C.; **de notre ~** A.D.
érection [eʀɛksjɔ̃] *nf* (*lit*) erection; *[société etc]* setting-up.
éreinter [eʀɛ̃te] (1) *vt* (*épuiser*) to exhaust, wear out; (*critiquer*) to pull to pieces. ♦ **éreintant, e*** *adj* exhausting, back-breaking. ♦ **éreinté, e*** *adj* worn out, shattered*.
ergot [ɛʀgo] *nm [coq]* spur.
ergoter [ɛʀgɔte] (1) *vi* to quibble (*sur* about). ♦ **ergotage** *nm*: **~(s)** quibbling. ♦ **ergoteur, -euse** *nm,f* quibbler.
ériger [eʀiʒe] (3) *vt bâtiment* to erect; *société etc* to set up. **~ ses habitudes en doctrine** to give one's habits the status of a doctrine; **il s'érige en maître** he sets himself up as a master.
ermite [ɛʀmit] *nm* hermit. ♦ **ermitage** *nm* hermitage; (*fig*) retreat.
éroder [eʀɔde] (1) *vt* to erode. ♦ **érosion** *nf* erosion.
érotisme [eʀɔtism(ə)] *nm* eroticism. ♦ **érotique** *adj* erotic.
errer [ɛʀe] (1) *vi* (*littér*) **(a)** *[voyageur, regard]* to wander, roam (*sur* over); *[sourire]* to hover. **(b)** (*se tromper*) to err. ♦ **errant, e** *adj* (*gén*) wandering. **chien ~** stray dog.
erreur [ɛʀœʀ] *nf* **(a)** (*gén*) mistake, error. **~ de calcul** miscalculation; **~ typographique** misprint, typographical error; **~ de sens** wrong meaning; **~ de traduction** mistranslation; **~ judiciaire** miscarriage of justice; **sauf ~** unless I'm (very much) mistaken; **par ~** by mistake; **faire ~** to be wrong *ou* mistaken; **l'~ est humaine** to err is human. **(b)** (*dérèglements*) **~s** errors; **~s de jeunesse** errors of youth. ♦ **erroné, e** *adj* erroneous.
ersatz [ɛʀzats] *nm* (*lit, fig*) ersatz.
érudit, e [eʀydi, it] **1** *adj* erudite, scholarly. **2** *nm,f* scholar. ♦ **érudition** *nf* erudition, scholarship.
éruption [eʀypsjɔ̃] *nf* eruption. **entrer en ~** to erupt.
ès [ɛs] *prép*: **licencié ~ lettres** ≈ Bachelor of Arts.
escabeau, *pl* **~x** [ɛskabo] *nm* (*tabouret*) stool; (*échelle*) stepladder.
escadre [ɛskadʀ(ə)] *nf* (*Naut*) squadron; (*Aviat*) wing. ♦ **escadrille** *nf* (*Aviat*) flight. ♦ **escadron** *nm* (*Mil*) squadron; (*fig: bande*) crowd.
escalader [ɛskalade] (1) *vt* to climb; *forteresse* to scale. ♦ **escalade** *nf* (*action*) climbing; scaling; (*Pol etc*) escalation. (*sport*) **l'~** (rock) climbing; **une belle ~** a beautiful climb.
escale [ɛskal] *nf* **(a)** (*endroit*) (*Naut*) port of call; (*Aviat*) stop. **faire ~ à** (*Naut*) to call at; (*Aviat*) to stop over at. **(b)** (*temps d'arrêt*) (*Naut*) call; (*Aviat*) stop. **vol sans ~** non-stop flight; (*Aviat*) **~ technique** refuelling stop.
escalier [ɛskalje] *nm* (*marches*) stairs; (*cage*) staircase. **dans l'~** on the stairs; **~ de service** backstairs; **~ roulant** escalator; **~ de secours** fire escape.
escalope [ɛskalɔp] *nf* escalope.
escamoter [ɛskamɔte] (1) *vt cartes etc* to conjure away; *difficulté, question* to evade; *mot* to skip; (*: *voler*) to pinch*; (*Aviat*) to retract. ♦ **escamotable** *adj* (*gén*) retractable; *lit* collapsible, fold-away. ♦ **escamotage** *nm [train d'atterrissage]* retraction. ♦ **escamoteur, -euse** *nm,f* conjurer.

escapade [ɛskapad] *nf* (*promenade*) jaunt. *[écolier]* **faire une ~** to run away.
escargot [ɛskaʀgo] *nm* snail.
escarmouche [ɛskaʀmuʃ] *nf* (*lit, fig*) skirmish.
escarpé, e [ɛskaʀpe] *adj* steep. ♦ **escarpement** *nm* (*côte*) steep slope.
escarpin [ɛskaʀpɛ̃] *nm* flat shoe.
escient [esjɑ̃] *nm*: **à bon ~** advisedly; **à mauvais ~** ill-advisedly.
esclaffer (s') [ɛsklafe] (1) *vpr* to burst out laughing.
esclandre [ɛsklɑ̃dʀ(ə)] *nm* scene.
esclave [ɛsklav] *nm* slave (*de qn/qch* to sb/sth). ♦ **esclavage** *nm* slavery. **réduire en ~** to enslave. ♦ **esclavagisme** *nm* proslavery.
escompte [ɛskɔ̃t] *nm* discount. ♦ **escompter** (1) *vt* to discount; (*fig*) to expect.
escorte [ɛskɔʀt(ə)] *nf* (*gén*) escort. **sous bonne ~** under escort. ♦ **escorter** (1) *vt* to escort.
escouade [ɛskwad] *nf* (*gén, Mil*) squad.
escrime [ɛskʀim] *nf* fencing. **faire de l'~** to fence. ♦ **escrimer (s')*** (1) *vpr*: **s'~ à faire qch** to wear o.s. out doing sth. ♦ **escrimeur, -euse** *nm,f* fencer.
escroc [ɛskʀo] *nm* swindler. ♦ **escroquer** (1) *vt* to swindle. **~ qch à qn** to swindle sb out of sth. ♦ **escroquerie** *nf* (*gén*) swindle; (*Jur*) fraud.
ésotérique [ezɔteʀik] *adj* esoteric.
espace [ɛspas] *nm* (*gén*) space. (*Phys*) **~-temps** space time; **~ de temps** space of time, interval; **manquer d'~** to be short of space *ou* room; **laisser un ~ entre** to leave a space *ou* gap between; **en l'~ de 3 minutes** within the space of 3 minutes; **~ parcouru** distance covered; **~s verts** green spaces; **~ vital** living space. ♦ **espacement** *nm* (*action*) spacing out; (*résultat*) spacing. ♦ **espacer** (3) **1** *vt* to space out. **2 s'~** *vpr* to become less frequent.
espadon [ɛspadɔ̃] *nm* swordfish.
espadrille [ɛspadʀij] *nf* rope-soled sandal.
Espagne [ɛspaɲ] *nf* Spain. ♦ **espagnol, e 1** *adj* Spanish. **2** *nm* (*Ling*) Spanish. **3** *nm(f)*: **E~(e)** Spaniard.
espèce [ɛspɛs] *nf* **(a)** (*Bio, Philos, Rel*) species. **~ humaine** human race. **(b)** (*sorte*) sort, kind, type. **ça n'a aucune ~ d'importance** that is of absolutely no importance; **de la pire ~** of the worst kind *ou* sort; **une** *ou* **un ~ d'excentrique** an eccentric sort of person; **~ de maladroit!** you clumsy clot!* **(c)** (*Fin*) **~s** cash; **en ~s** in cash.
espérance [ɛspeʀɑ̃s] *nf* hope. **dans l'~ de faire** hoping to do, in the hope of doing; **contre toute ~** against all expectations *ou* hope; **donner de grandes ~s** to show great promise; **avoir de grandes ~s (d'avenir)** to have great prospects; **garder l'~ de pouvoir ...** to remain hopeful of being able to ...; **~ de vie** life expectancy, expectation of life.
espérer [ɛspeʀe] (6) **1** *vt succès etc* to hope for. **~ réussir** to hope to succeed; **– je l'espère (bien)** – I hope so; **ceci nous laisse ~ un succès rapide** this gives us hope of quick success; **j'espère bien n'avoir rien oublié** I hope I haven't forgotten anything. **2** *vi* (*avoir confiance*) to have faith. **il faut ~** you must have faith; **~ en** *Dieu etc* to trust in.
espiègle [ɛspjɛgl(ə)] **1** *adj enfant* mischievous; *air* roguish. **2** *nmf* imp. ♦ **espièglerie** *nf* mischievousness; roguishness; (*tour*) prank.
espion, -onne [ɛspjɔ̃, ɔn] *nm,f* spy. ♦ **espionnage** *nm* espionage, spying. **film d'~** spy film. ♦ **espionner** (1) *vt* to spy on.
esplanade [ɛsplanad] *nf* esplanade.
espoir [ɛspwaʀ] *nm* (*gén*) hope. **dans l'~ de vous voir** hoping to see *ou* in the hope of seeing you; **avoir l'~ que** to be hopeful that; **avoir bon ~ de faire/que** to be confident of doing/that; **sans ~** *situation* hopeless; *aimer* without hope.
esprit [ɛspʀi] **1** *nm* **(a)** (*gén: pensée*) mind. **avoir l'~ large/étroit** to be broad-/narrow-minded; **à l'~ lent** slow-witted; **avoir l'~ clair** to have a clear head *ou* mind; **où ai-je l'~?** what am I thinking of?; **il m'est venu à l'~ que** it crossed my mind that, it occurred to me that. **(b)** (*humour*) wit. **faire de l'~** to try to be witty *ou* funny. **(c)** (*être humain*) person; (*savant*) mind; (*fantôme*) spirit. **c'est un ~ subtil** he is a shrewd man, he has a shrewd mind. **(d)** *[loi, époque, texte]* spirit. **(e)** (*aptitude*) **avoir l'~ d'analyse** to have an analytical mind; **avoir l'~ des affaires** to have a good head for business; **avoir l'~ critique** to have a critical eye; **avoir l'~ de critique** to be a fault-finder. **(f)** (*attitude*) spirit. **l'~ de cette classe** the attitude of this class; **~ de clan** clannishness; **~ de compétition/d'équipe** competitive/team spirit; **faire preuve de mauvais ~** to be a disruptive influence. **2: ~ de contradiction** argumentativeness; **~ de famille** family feeling; (*péj*) clannishness; **~ frappeur** spirit-rapper; **l'~ malin** the Evil spirit; (*Rel*) **l'E~ Saint** the Holy Ghost; **~ de suite** consistency of thought.
esquimau, -aude, *mpl* **~x** [ɛskimo, od] **1** *adj* Eskimo. **2** *nm* (*Ling*) Eskimo; (*glace*) choc-ice; (*chien*) husky. **3** *nm(f)*: **E~(de)** Eskimo.
esquinter* [ɛskɛ̃te] (1) **1** *vt objet* to mess up; *santé* to ruin; *adversaire* to bash up*; *voiture* to smash up; (*critiquer*) to pull to pieces. **2 s'~** *vpr* to tire o.s. out (*à faire* doing).
esquisse [ɛskis] *nf* (*Peinture*) sketch; *[projet]* outline; *[geste]* suggestion. ♦ **esquisser** (1) *vt* to sketch (out); to outline. **~ un geste** to half-make a gesture; **un progrès commence à s'~** one can begin to detect some progress.
esquiver [ɛskive] (1) **1** *vt coup* to dodge; *question* to evade. **2 s'~** *vpr* to slip *ou* sneak away. ♦ **esquive** *nf* dodge; evasion.
essai [esɛ] *nm* **(a)** (*test*) (*action*) trying out; testing; (*épreuve*) test. (*Aut*) **~s** trials; **prendre qn à l'~** to take sb on for a trial period; **mettre à l'~** to test (out), put to the test; (*première utilisation*) **faire l'~ d'un produit** to try out a product. **(b)** (*tentative*) attempt, try; (*Sport*) attempt. **premier ~** first try *ou* attempt *ou* go. **(c)** (*Rugby*) try. **(d)** (*Littérat*) essay.
essaim [esɛ̃] *nm* (*lit, fig*) swarm. ♦ **essaimer** [eseme] (1) *vi* (*lit*) to swarm; *[famille]* to scatter; *[firme]* to spread.
essayer [eseje] (8) **1** *vt* **(a)** (*tester*) to test (out), try (out); (*pour la première fois*) to try (out); *vêtement* to try on. **(b)** (*tenter*) to try. **~ de faire** to try *ou* attempt to do; **essaie de le faire** try to do it, try and do it; **je vais ~** I'll try, I'll have a go *ou* a try. **2 s'~** *vpr*: **s'~ à qch/à faire** to try one's hand at sth/at doing. ♦ **essayage** *nm* (*Couture*) fitting.
essence [esɑ̃s] *nf* **(a)** (*carburant*) petrol, gas(oline) (*US*); (*solvant*) spirit. **~ minérale** mineral oil. **(b)** (*extrait*) *[plantes etc]* oil, essence. **~ de rose** rose oil. **(c)** *[question, doctrine]* gist, essence; (*Philos*) essence. **par ~** in essence, essentially. **(d)** (*espèce*) species.
essentiel, -elle [esɑ̃sjɛl] **1** *adj* (*indispensable*) essential (*à, pour* for); (*de base*) essential, basic. **2** *nm*: **l'~** (*objets nécessaires*) the basic essentials; (*points principaux*) the essentials, the essential *ou* basic points; (*l'important*) the main thing; **l'~ de** the main part of; **l'~ de ce qu'il dit** most of what he says. ♦ **essentiellement** *adv* essentially; basically.
essieu, *pl* **~x** [esjø] *nm* axle(-tree).
essor [esɔʀ] *nm* *[oiseau, imagination]* flight; *[pays]* expansion; *[art]* blossoming. **prendre son ~** *[oiseau]* to fly off; *[société]* to expand rapidly.
essorer [esɔʀe] (1) *vt* (*manuellement*) to wring (out); (*force centrifuge*) to spin-dry. ♦ **essorage** *nm* wringing; spin-drying. ♦ **essoreuse** *nf* wringer; spin-dryer.
essouffler [esufle] (1) **1** *vt* to make breathless.

être essoufflé to be out of breath. 2 s'~ *vpr [coureur]* to get out of breath; *[travail]* to fall off; *[romancier]* to exhaust o.s. ♦ **essoufflement** *nm* breathlessness.
essuyer [esɥije] (8) **1** *vt* **(a)** *(gén)* to wipe; *tableau noir* to clean, wipe; *poussière* to dust; *eau* to wipe up, mop up. **s'~ les mains** to wipe one's hands (dry), dry one's hands; **~ la vaisselle** to wipe *ou* dry up; **nous avons essuyé les plâtres*** we had a lot of teething troubles. **(b)** *pertes, reproches* to suffer; *refus* to meet with; *tempête* to weather. **~ le feu de l'ennemi** to come under enemy fire; **~ un coup de feu** to be shot at. **2 s'~** *vpr [baigneur]* to dry o.s. **3: essuie-glace** *nm inv* windscreen *ou* windshield (*US*) wiper; **essuie-mains** *nm inv* hand towel.
est[1] [ɛ] *V* **être.**
est[2] [ɛst] **1** *nm* east. **vent d'~** east wind; **à l'~** (*situation*) in the east; (*direction*) to the east, east(wards); **à l'~ de** east of, to the east of; (*Pol*) **les pays de l'E~** the eastern countries. **2** *adj inv région* eastern; *côté* east; *direction* eastward, easterly.
estafilade [ɛstafilad] *nf* slash.
estaminet† [ɛstaminɛ] *nm* tavern†.
estampe [ɛstɑ̃p] *nf* (*image*) engraving, print; (*outil*) stamp.
estamper [ɛstɑ̃pe] (1) *vt* (‡: *voler*) to swindle, diddle* (*de qch* out of sth); (*Tech*) to stamp.
estampille [ɛstɑ̃pij] *nf* stamp.
esthétique [ɛstetik] **1** *adj jugement* aesthetic; *carrosserie* attractive. **2** *nf* attractiveness. (*discipline*) **l'~** aesthetics (*sg*); **l'~ industrielle** industrial design. ♦ **esthète** *nmf* aesthete. ♦ **esthéticien, -ienne** *nm,f* (*Méd*) beautician. ♦ **esthétiquement** *adv* aesthetically. ♦ **esthétisme** *nm* aestheticism.
estimer [ɛstime] (1) *vt* **(a)** *objet* to appraise, value; *distance, dégâts, prix* to assess, estimate. **(b)** (*respecter*) *personne* to esteem. **estimé de tous** respected *ou* esteemed by everyone. **(c)** *qualité* to value greatly, prize. **savoir ~ un service rendu** to know how to appreciate a favour; **c'est un plat très estimé** this dish is considered a great delicacy. **(d)** (*considérer*) **~ que ...** to consider that ...; **nous estimons nécessaire de dire** we consider it necessary to say; **~ inutile de faire** to see no point in doing, consider it pointless to do; **s'~ heureux d'un résultat** to consider o.s. fortunate with a result. ♦ **estimable** *adj* (*respectable*) estimable; (*assez bon*) honest, sound; (*déterminable*) assessable. ♦ **estimation** *nf* appraisal, valuation; assessment, estimation; (*chiffre*) estimate. ♦ **estime** *nf* **(a)** (*considération*) esteem, respect. **(b)** (*Naut*) **à l'~** by dead reckoning.
estival, e, *mpl* **-aux** [ɛstival, o] *adj* summer. ♦ **estivant, e** *nm,f* holiday-maker.
estomac [ɛstɔma] *nm* **(a)** stomach. **partir l'~ creux** to set off on an empty stomach; **avoir l'~ creux/bien rempli** to feel empty/full (up). **(b)** (‡) **avoir de l'~** (*du culot*) to have a nerve; (*du courage*) to have guts*; **il lui a fait ça à l'~** he hoodwinked him.
estomaquer* [ɛstɔmake] (1) *vt* to stagger*.
estomper [ɛstɔ̃pe] (1) **1** *vt dessin* to shade off; *contours, souvenir* to blur. **2 s'~** *vpr* to become blurred.
estourbir‡ [ɛsturbir] (2) *vt* (*assommer*) to stun; (*tuer*) to do in‡.
estrade [ɛstrad] *nf* platform, rostrum.
estragon [ɛstragɔ̃] *nm* tarragon.
estropier [ɛstrɔpje] (7) *vt personne* to cripple, disable; *citation* to twist, distort; *langue étrangère, musique* to murder. ♦ **estropié, e** *nm,f* cripple.
estuaire [ɛstɥɛr] *nm* estuary.
estudiantin, e [ɛstydjɑ̃tɛ̃, in] *adj* student.
esturgeon [ɛstyrʒɔ̃] *nm* sturgeon.
et [e] *conj* and. **~ lui ~ vous** both he and you; **j'aime beaucoup ça, ~ vous?** I'm very fond of that, aren't you? *ou* what about you?; **~ moi alors?** what about me then?; **~ puis** and then; (*qu'importe*) so what?*; **~ moi, je peux venir?** can I come too?; **vingt/trente** *etc* **~ un** twenty-/thirty-*etc* one; **à midi ~ quart** at a quarter past twelve; **le vingt ~ unième** the twenty-first.
étable [etabl(ə)] *nf* cowshed.
établi [etabli] *nm* workbench.
établir [etablir] (2) **1** *vt* **(a)** (*gén*) to establish; *usine, record, communications* to set up; *règlement* to lay down, institute. **~ son camp/Q.G. dans** to pitch one's camp/set up one's H.Q. in; **~ son fils médecin** to set one's son up *ou* establish one's son in medical practice; **~ son pouvoir sur le pays** to establish control over the country; **il est établi que** it's an established fact that. **(b)** *empire, fortune* to build up; *démonstration* to base (*sur* on). **(c)** *liste* to draw up, make out; *programme* to arrange; *chèque* to make out; *plans* to draw up; *prix* to fix.
2 s'~ *vpr [commerçant, colon]* to establish o.s; *[usage]* to become customary; *[pouvoir]* to become established; *[amitié, contacts]* to develop. **une nouvelle usine s'est établie** a new factory has been set up; **l'ennemi s'est établi sur la colline** the enemy has taken up position on the hill; **s'~ boulanger** to set o.s. up as a baker; **un grand silence s'établit** a great silence fell.
♦ **établissement** *nm* **(a)** (*action*) establishing; setting-up; institution; laying-down; building up; basing; drawing-up; making-out; arranging; fixing; development. **(b)** (*bâtiment*) establishment; (*colonie*) settlement. **~ hospitalier** hospital; **~ religieux** religious institution; **~ industriel** factory; **avec les compliments des ~s X** with the compliments of X and Co.
étage [etaʒ] *nm [bâtiment]* floor, storey; *[fusée]* stage; *[mine, jardin]* level; *[gâteau]* tier. **au premier ~** on the first floor; **maison à deux ~s** three-storeyed house; **il grimpa 3 ~s** he went up *ou* walked up 3 floors *ou* flights. ♦ **étagement** *nm* terracing. ♦ **étager** (3) **1** *vt* to lay out in tiers. **2 s'~** *vpr* to rise in tiers *ou* terraces. ♦ **étagère** *nf* (*tablette*) shelf; (*meuble*) shelves.
étai [etɛ] *nm* (*gén, Naut*) stay.
étain [etɛ̃] *nm* (*Min*) tin; (*Orfèvrerie*) (*matière*) pewter; (*objet*) piece of pewterware.
étal [etal] *nm* stall.
étalage [etalaʒ] *nm* **(a)** (*Comm*) (*action*) displaying; (*devanture*) shop window; (*tréteaux*) stand; (*articles*) display. **disposer l'~** to dress the window; **chemise qui a fait l'~** shop-soiled shirt. **(b)** *[luxe, connaissances]* display, show. **faire ~ de** to show off. ♦ **étalagiste** *nmf* window dresser.
étale [etal] *adj mer, situation* slack.
étaler [etale] (1) **1** *vt* **(a)** *objets* to spread (*sur* over); *journal* to spread out (*sur* on); *marchandise* to display, lay out (*sur* on). **~ ses cartes** to display one's cards. **(b)** *beurre, peinture* to spread (*sur* on); *crème solaire* to apply. **(c)** *paiements* to spread; *vacances* to stagger (*sur* over). **étalez vos envois** space out your consignments. **(d)** *luxe, savoir* to flaunt; *malheurs* to make a show of. **2 s'~** *vpr [plaine, cultures]* to stretch out; *[vacances]* to be staggered (*sur* over); *[vaniteux]* to flaunt o.s. **son ignominie s'étale au grand jour** his ignominy is plain for all to see; **s'~ sur un divan** to sprawl on a divan; **étalé sur le tapis** sprawling on *ou* stretched out on the carpet; **s'~ (par terre)*** to fall flat on one's face*. ♦ **étalement** *nm* spreading; spreading-out; displaying; laying-out; application; staggering.
étalon [etalɔ̃] *nm* (*mesure*) standard; (*fig*) yardstick; (*cheval*) stallion. **~-or** gold standard.
étamine [etamin] *nf* (*Bot*) stamen.
étanche [etɑ̃ʃ] *adj vêtements, montre* waterproof;

compartiment, (*fig*) watertight. ~ **à l'air** airtight. ♦ **étanchéité** *nf* waterproofness; watertightness; airtightness.

étancher [etɑ̃ʃe] (1) *vt sang* to stem; *soif* to quench, slake.

étang [etɑ̃] *nm* pond.

étape [etap] *nf* (*gén*) stage; (*but*) (*gén*) stop; (*Sport*) stopover point. **faire** ~ **à** to stop off at; **par petites** ~**s** in easy stages.

état [eta] *nm* **(a)** *[personne]* state. ~ **(de santé)** health; ~ **de veille** waking state; ~ **d'âme** mood; ~ **d'esprit** frame *ou* state of mind; **il n'est pas en** ~ **de le faire** he's in no condition *ou* (fit) state to do it; **il était dans tous ses** ~**s** he was all worked up* *ou* in a terrible state; **il n'était pas dans son** ~ **normal** he wasn't his normal self. **(b)** *[connaissances, corps chimique]* state. (*situation*) ~ **d'alerte/de siège/d'urgence** state of alert/of siege/of emergency; ~ **de choses** situation; **quel est l'**~ **de la question?** where *ou* how do things stand in the matter?, what stage have things reached? **(c)** *[objet]* condition, state. **en bon/mauvais** ~ in good/poor *ou* bad condition; (*Naut*) **en** ~ **de naviguer** sea-worthy; **en** ~ **de marche** in working order; **remettre en** ~ to repair, do up; **sucre à l'**~ **brut** sugar in its raw *ou* unrefined state; **à l'**~ **(de) neuf** as good as new. **(d)** (*nation*) state. **(e)** (†: *métier*) profession, trade; (*statut social*) station. **tailleur de son** ~ tailor by trade; ~ **civil** civil status. **(f)** (*comptes*) statement, account; (*inventaire*) inventory. ~**s de service** service record. **(g) faire** ~ **de** *ses services etc* to instance, put forward; **mettre en** ~ **d'arrestation** to put under arrest; **en tout** ~ **de cause** in any case; **c'est un** ~ **de fait** it is an established fact; **en** ~ **d'ivresse** in a drunken state, under the influence (of drink); **mettre qn hors d'**~ **de nuire** to make sb harmless.

♦ **étatisé, e** *adj* state-controlled. ♦ **étatiser** (1) *vt* to establish state control over. ♦ **état-major,** *pl* ~**s-**~**s** *nm* (*officiers*) staff; (*bureaux*) staff headquarters; *[parti politique]* administrative staff; *[entreprise]* top management. ♦ **États-Unis** *nmpl*: **les** ~ **(d'Amérique)** the United States (of America).

étau, *pl* ~**x** [eto] *nm* (*Tech*) vice. (*fig*) **l'**~ **se resserre** the noose is tightening; **se trouver pris comme dans un** ~ to find o.s. caught in a stranglehold.

étayer [eteje] (8) *vt mur* to prop up; (*fig*) *théorie* to support. ♦ **étayage** *nm* propping-up.

et cetera [ɛtsetera] *locution* et cetera, and so on (and so forth).

été [ete] *nm* summer. ~ **de la Saint-Martin** Indian summer; **en** ~ in (the) summer *ou* summertime.

éteindre [etɛ̃dʀ(ə)] (52) **1** *vt* **(a)** *flamme* to put out, extinguish; *bougie* to blow out; *gaz, lampe, radio* to turn off, switch off; *pièce* to put out the lights in. **laisse** ~ **le feu** let the fire go out; **tous feux éteints** without lights. **(b)** *colère* to subdue; *envie* to kill; *soif* to quench. **2 s'**~ *vpr [agonisant]* to pass away, die; *[colère]* to abate; *[amour]* to die; *[feu, gaz etc]* to go out; *[dette]* to be nullified; *[famille]* to die out. ♦ **éteint, e** *adj couleur* faded; *race, volcan* extinct; *regard* dull; *voix* faint. **c'est un homme** ~ he's a broken man.

étendard [etɑ̃daʀ] *nm* (*lit, fig*) standard.

étendre [etɑ̃dʀ(ə)] (41) **1** *vt* **(a)** *journal* to spread out; *beurre, ailes* to spread; *bras, blessé* to stretch out. ~ **du linge** (*sur un fil*) to hang out *ou* hang up the washing; **étendu sur le sol** stretched (out) *ou* lying on the ground. **(b)** (*) *adversaire* to floor*; *candidat* to fail. **se faire** ~ to be flattened*. **(c)** (*agrandir*) (*gén*) to extend (*sur* over); *domaine* to expand; *fortune* to increase; *vocabulaire* to widen. **cette mesure s'étend à tous** this measure applies to everyone. **(d)** *vin, sauce* to let down (*de* with).

2 s'~ *vpr* **(a)** (*s'allonger*) to stretch out; (*se reposer*) to lie down; (*fig: en expliquant*) to elaborate (*sur* on). **(b)** *[forêt, travaux]* to stretch, extend (*sur* over). **la plaine s'étendait à perte de vue** the plain stretched away as far as the eye could see. **(c)** *[brouillard, épidémie]* to spread; *[pouvoirs, parti, fortune]* to expand; *[connaissances, vocabulaire]* to widen.

♦ **étendu, e**[1] *adj* (*gén*) wide; *vocabulaire, pouvoirs* extensive, wide. ♦ **étendue**[2] *nf* **(a)** (*surface*) area; (*durée*) duration, length. **sur une** ~ **de** over an area of; over a period of; **grande** ~ **de sable** large stretch *ou* expanse of sand; **l'**~ **du territoire** the size *ou* extent of the territory. **(b)** (*importance*) extent; *[connaissances]* range, scope. **(c)** (*Mus*) range; (*Philos*) extent.

éternel, -elle [etɛʀnɛl] **1** *adj* (*Philos, Rel*) eternal; (*sans fin*) eternal, everlasting; (*perpétuel*) perpetual. **soucis** ~**s** never-ending worries; **son** ~ **chapeau sur la tête*** the inevitable hat on his head. **2** *nm* (*Rel*) **l'É**~ the Eternal, the Everlasting; (*hum*) **grand joueur devant l'É**~ inveterate gambler. ♦ **éternellement** *adv* eternally; everlastingly; perpetually.

éterniser [etɛʀnize] (1) **1** *vt débats* to drag *ou* draw out. **2 s'**~ *vpr [attente]* to drag on; *[visiteur]* to linger too long. **on ne peut pas s'**~ **ici** we can't stay here for ever.

éternité [etɛʀnite] *nf* eternity. **il y a des** ~**s que tu m'as promis cela** you promised me that ages ago; **ça a duré une** ~ it lasted for ages; **de toute** ~ from time immemorial; **pour l'**~ to all eternity.

éternuer [etɛʀnɥe] (1) *vi* to sneeze. ♦ **éternuement** *nm* sneeze.

éther [etɛʀ] *nm* (*Chim, Poésie*) ether.

Éthiopie [etjɔpi] *nf* Ethiopia. ♦ **éthiopien, -ienne** *adj*, **É**~**(ne)** *nm(f)* Ethiopian.

éthique [etik] **1** *adj* ethical. **2** *nf* (*Philos*) ethics (*sg*); (*code moral*) moral code.

ethnie [ɛtni] *nf* ethnic group. ♦ **ethnique** *adj* ethnic.

ethnologie [ɛtnɔlɔʒi] *nf* ethnology. ♦ **ethnologique** *adj* ethnological. ♦ **ethnologue** *nmf* ethnologist.

étinceler [etɛ̃sle] (4) *vi [diamant, lame]* to sparkle, glitter; *[étoile]* to twinkle; *[esprit, beauté]* to sparkle. *[yeux]* ~ **de colère** to glitter *ou* flash with anger; ~ **de joie** to sparkle *ou* shine with joy. ♦ **étincelle** *nf* **(a)** (*incandescente*) spark. **jeter des** ~**s** to throw out sparks; (*fig*) **faire des** ~**s*** *[élève]* to shine; *[dispute]* to make the sparks fly. **(b)** *[lame, regard]* flash, glitter; *[raison]* glimmer. ~ **de génie** spark *ou* flash of genius. ♦ **étincellement** *nm* sparkle; glitter; twinkling; flash; shining.

étioler [etjɔle] (1) **1** *vt plante* to blanch; *personne* to weaken. **2 s'**~ *vpr [plante]* to wilt; *[personne]* to wither away. ♦ **étiolement** *nm* blanching; weakening; wilting; withering away.

étiquette [etikɛt] *nf* label. (*protocole*) **l'**~ etiquette. ♦ **étiquetage** [etiktaʒ] *nm* labelling. ♦ **étiqueter** [etikte] (4) *vt* to label.

étirer [etiʀe] (1) **1** *vt* to stretch; *métal* to draw out. **2 s'**~ *vpr [personne]* to stretch; *[convoi, route]* to stretch out.

étoffe [etɔf] *nf* material, fabric. (*fig*) **avoir l'**~ **de** to have the makings of; **avoir de l'**~ to have a strong personality.

étoffer [etɔfe] (1) **1** *vt style* to enrich; *discours* to fill out. **2 s'**~ *vpr [personne]* to fill out.

étoile [etwal] *nf* star. ~ **filante** shooting star; ~ **polaire** pole *ou* north star; ~ **du berger** evening star; ~ **de mer** starfish; **sans** ~ starless; **à la clarté des** ~**s** by starlight; **dormir à la belle** ~ to sleep out in the open; **(hôtel) trois** ~**s** three-star hotel; ~ **de la danse** dancing star; **avoir foi en son** ~ to trust one's lucky star; **né sous une bonne/mauvaise** ~ born under a lucky/an unlucky

star; **son ~ a pâli** his star has set. ♦ **étoilé, e** *adj nuit* starry, starlit; *ciel* starry.
étole [etɔl] *nf (Rel, gén)* stole.
étonner [etɔne] (1) **1** *vt* to surprise, amaze, astonish. **2 s'~** *vpr* to be amazed, wonder, marvel (*de qch* at sth, *de voir* at seeing, *que* + *subj* that). ♦ **étonnamment** *adv* surprisingly, amazingly, astonishingly. ♦ **étonnant, e** *adj* (*surprenant*) surprising, amazing, astonishing; (*remarquable*) *personne* amazing, incredible. **l'~ est que** the astonishing *ou* amazing thing is that; **vous êtes ~** you're incredible *ou* amazing. ♦ **étonnement** *nm* surprise, amazement, astonishment.
étouffer [etufe] (1) **1** *vt* **(a)** *[assassin]* to smother; *[chaleur]* to suffocate; *[sanglots, aliment]* to choke. **les scrupules ne l'étouffent pas** he isn't hampered by scruples. **(b)** *bruit* to muffle; *bâillement, cris* to smother, suppress, stifle. **(c)** *scandale* to hush up; *rumeurs, sentiments* to stifle; *révolte* to put down, quell. **(d)** *flammes* to extinguish; *feu* to put out, smother. **2** *vi* (*mourir*) to die of suffocation; (*fig*) to suffocate. **~ de colère** to choke with anger; **~ de chaleur** to be overcome with the heat. **3 s'~** *vpr* (*mourir*) to suffocate; (*en mangeant*) to choke. ♦ **étouffant, e** *adj* stifling. ♦ **étouffé, e**[1] *adj rire* suppressed; *voix* subdued; *rumeur* muffled. ♦ **étouffée**[2] *nf*: **cuire à l'~** *poisson, légumes* to steam; *viande* to braise. ♦ **étouffement** *nm* **(a)** (*mort*) suffocation. (*Méd*) **sensation d'~** feeling of suffocation. **(b)** (*action*) hushing-up; stifling; suppression.
étoupe [etup] *nf [lin]* tow; *[cordes]* oakum.
étourdir [eturdir] (2) *vt [coup]* to stun, daze; *[bruit]* to deafen. **~ qn** *[altitude, vin]* to make sb dizzy; *[succès]* to go to sb's head; **s'~ de paroles** to get drunk on words. ♦ **étourderie** *nf* (*caractère*) thoughtlessness, heedlessness; (*faute*) thoughtless blunder. ♦ **étourdi, e 1** *adj* thoughtless, heedless. **2** *nm,f* scatterbrain. ♦ **étourdiment** *adv* thoughtlessly. ♦ **étourdissant, e** *adj bruit* deafening; *succès, beauté* stunning; *rythme* intoxicating. ♦ **étourdissement** *nm* (*syncope*) blackout; (*vertige*) dizzy spell; (*littér: griserie*) intoxication. **ça me donne des ~s** it makes me feel dizzy.
étourneau, *pl* **~x** [eturno] *nm* (*Orn*) starling; (*: *distrait*) scatterbrain.
étrange [etrɑ̃ʒ] *adj* strange; (*bizarre*) odd, queer. **et chose ~** strangely enough. ♦ **étrangement** *adv* strangely, oddly; (*étonnamment*) surprisingly, amazingly.
étranger, -ère [etrɑ̃ʒe, ɛr] **1** *adj* **(a)** (*autre pays*) foreign. **être ~** to be a foreigner, come from abroad. **(b)** (*autre groupe*) strange (*à* to). **être ~ à un groupe** not to belong to a group, be an outsider; **entrée interdite à toute personne ~ère** no entry for unauthorized persons. **(c)** (*inconnu*) strange, unfamiliar (*à* to). **son nom ne m'est pas ~** his name is not unknown *ou* not unfamiliar to me. **(d)** *donnée, fait* extraneous (*à* to). **~ au sujet** irrelevant to the subject; **être ~ à un complot** to have nothing to do with a plot. **(e)** (*Méd, fig*) **corps ~** foreign body. **2** *nm,f* (*autre pays*) foreigner; (*péj, Admin*) alien; (*inconnu*) stranger. **3** *nm* (*pays*) **l'~** foreign parts; **vivre à l'~** to live abroad *ou* in a foreign country.
étrangeté [etrɑ̃ʒte] *nf* strangeness, oddness, queerness; (*événement*) odd *ou* strange event.
étrangler [etrɑ̃gle] (1) **1** *vt* **(a)** (*tuer*) to strangle, throttle. **(b)** *[rage etc]* to choke. **voix étranglée par l'émotion** voice choking with emotion. **(c)** *presse* to strangle, stifle. (*financièrement*) **~ qn** to bleed sb white. **(d)** (*resserrer*) to squeeze. **taille étranglée** tightly constricted waist. **2 s'~** *vpr* **(a) s'~ de rire/en mangeant** to choke with laughter/whilst eating. **(b)** *[voix]* to catch in one's throat. **(c)** *[rue]* to narrow. ♦ **étranglement** *nm [victime]* strangulation; *[presse]* stifling; *[vallée]* neck; *[rue]* bottleneck; *[taille]* constriction; *[voix]* strain. ♦ **étrangleur, -euse** *nm,f* strangler.
être [ɛtr(ə)] (61) **1** *vb copule* **(a)** (*gén*) to be. **elle veut ~ médecin** she wants to be a doctor; **soyez sages!** be good!; **si j'étais vous** if I were you; **nous sommes 10 à vouloir partir** there are 10 of us wanting *ou* who want to go. **(b)** (*date*) **nous sommes le 12 janvier** it is January 12th. **(c)** (*appartenance*) **à qui est ce livre? – il est à moi** whose book is this? – it's mine *ou* it belongs to me; **je suis à vous** I'll be with you; **c'était à elle de protester** it was up to her to protest; **~ de l'expédition** to take part in the expedition; **je ne pourrai pas ~ des vôtres jeudi** I shan't be able to join you on Thursday. **(d)** (*état, fait etc*) to be. **il n'est pas à son travail** his mind is not on his work; **il est au travail** he is working; **elle n'y est pour rien** it has nothing to do with her; **je suis pour dormir ici** I am for sleeping here*, I am in favour of sleeping here.

2 *vb aux* **(a)** (*temps composés actifs*) **est-il venu?** has he come?; **il est passé hier** he came yesterday. **(b)** (*passif*) **~ fabriqué par ...** to be made by ...; **il a été blessé** he was injured. **(c)** (*avec à* + *infin*) **le poisson est à manger tout de suite** the fish is to be eaten *ou* must be eaten at once; **il est à travailler** he is busy working; **elle est toujours à le taquiner** she's forever teasing him.

3 *vi* **(a)** (*exister*) to be. **que la lumière soit** let there be light; **un menteur s'il en est** a liar if ever there was one. **(b)** (*habiter*) **il est maintenant à Lille** he now lives *ou* he is now in Lille; **elle n'y est pour personne** she is not at home *ou* available to anyone. **(c)** (*: *être allé*) **il n'avait jamais été à Londres** he'd never been to London; **j'ai été en Italie l'an dernier** I went to Italy last year.

4 *vb impers* **(a)** (*avoir atteint*) **en ~ à la page 9** to be at page 9, have reached page 9; **où en est-il dans ses études?** how far has he got with his studies?; **l'affaire en est là** that's how the matter stands. **(b)** (*se voir réduit à*) **j'en suis à me demander si** I've come to wonder if; **il en est à mendier** he has been reduced to begging. **(c)** (*locutions*) **il était une fois** once upon a time; **il n'en est rien** it's nothing of the sort; **tu y es?*** (*tu es prêt*) are you ready?; (*comprends-tu*) do you get it?* **(d)** (*pour mettre en relief*) **c'est lui qui me l'a dit** he (is the one who) told me; **c'est à qui dira son mot** they all want to have their say; **est-ce que vous saviez?** did you know?; **il fait beau, n'est-ce pas?** it's a lovely day, isn't it?; **vous viendrez, n'est-ce pas?** you will come, won't you? **(e)** (*supposition*) **si ce n'était** were it not for; **ne serait-ce que pour nous ennuyer** if only to annoy us; **comme si de rien n'était** as if nothing had happened; (*Math*) **soit une droite XY** let XY be a straight line.

5 *nm* (*gén, Sci*) being. **~ humain** human being; **un ~ cher** a loved one; **un ~ merveilleux** a wonderful person; **de tout son ~** with all his heart; **au plus profond de notre ~** deep down in our souls.
étreindre [etrɛ̃dr(ə)] (52) *vt ami* to embrace, clasp in one's arms; *ennemi* to seize, grasp; (*avec les mains*) to clutch, grip; *[douleur]* to grip. ♦ **étreinte** *nf* embrace; grip; clutch; grasp.
étrenner [etrene] (1) **1** *vt* to use for the first time. **2** *vi* (‡: *écoper*) to catch it*, get it*.
étrennes [etrɛn] *nfpl [enfant]* New Year's gift; *[facteur etc]* ≃ Christmas box.
étrier [etrije] *nm* stirrup.
étriqué, e [etrike] *adj habit* skimpy, tight; *esprit, vie* narrow. **il fait tout ~ dans son manteau** he looks cramped in his coat.
étroit, e [etrwa, wat] *adj* **(a)** (*lit*) (*gén*) narrow; *espace* cramped, confined; *vêtement, étreinte* tight. **être à l'~** (*logé*) to live in cramped conditions; (*habillé*) to be cramped in one's clothes. **(b)** (*borné*) narrow, limited. **à l'esprit ~** narrow-

minded. **(c)** *amitié, surveillance, liens* close; *subordination* strict. **en collaboration ~e avec** in close collaboration with. **(d)** (*Ling*) *acception* narrow, strict. ♦ **étroitement** *adv lier* closely; *obéir* strictly; *tenir* tightly. **être ~ logé** to live in cramped conditions. ♦ **étroitesse** *nf* narrowness; crampedness; tightness; closeness. **~ (d'esprit)** narrow-mindedness.

étude [etyd] *nf* **(a)** (*action*) (*gén*) study. **mettre un projet à l'~** to investigate *ou* study a project; **avoir le goût de l'~** to like study *ou* studying; **~(s) de marché** market research. **(b)** (*Scol, Univ*) **~s** studies; **payer ses ~s** to pay for one's education; **faire des ~s (de droit)** to study (law). **(c)** (*ouvrage*) study. **~s de fleurs** studies of flowers. **(d)** (*Scol*) **(salle d')~** study *ou* prep room; **l'~ (du soir)** preparation. **(e)** (*Jur*) (*bureau*) office; (*clientèle*) practice.

étudiant, e [etydjɑ̃, ɑ̃t] *adj, nm,f* student.

étudier [etydje] (7) *vt* **(a)** (*gén*) to study; *leçon* to learn. **les deux adversaires s'étudiaient de près** the two opponents observed each other closely. **(b)** (*concevoir*) *procédé* to devise; *machine* to design. **(c)** *gestes, ton* to study. ♦ **étudié, e** *adj geste* studied; *conception* carefully designed; *prix* keen.

étui [etɥi] *nm* (*gén*) case; *[revolver]* holster.

étuve [etyv] *nf* (*bains*) steamroom; (*de désinfection*) sterilizer; (*fig*) oven.

étymologie [etimɔlɔʒi] *nf* etymology. ♦ **étymologique** *adj* etymological.

eucalyptus [økaliptys] *nm* eucalyptus.

Eucharistie [økaʀisti] *nf*: **l'~** the Eucharist.

euh [ø] *excl* er! ... .

eunuque [ønyk] *nm* eunuch.

euphémisme [øfemism(ə)] *nm* euphemism. ♦ **euphémique** *adj* euphemistic.

euphorie [øfɔʀi] *nf* euphoria. ♦ **euphorique** *adj* euphoric.

Europe [øʀɔp] *nf* Europe. **~ Centrale** Central Europe; **l'~ verte** European *ou* Community agriculture. ♦ **eurodollar** *nm* Eurodollar. ♦ **européaniser** (1) *vt* to europeanize. ♦ **européen, -éenne** *adj,* **E~(ne)** *nm(f)* European. ♦ **Eurovision** *nf* Eurovision.

euthanasie [øtanazi] *nf* euthanasia.

eux [ø] *pron pers* (*sujet*) they; (*objet*) them. **nous y allons, ~ non** we are going but they aren't *ou* but not them; **~ mentir?** them tell a lie?; **ce sont ~ qui répondront** they are the ones who will reply, they'll reply; **cette maison est-elle à ~?** does this house belong to them?, is this house theirs?; **ils ne pensent qu'à ~** they only think of themselves.

évacuer [evakɥe] (1) *vt* (*gén*) to evacuate. ♦ **évacuation** *nf* evacuation. ♦ **évacué, e** *nm,f* evacuee.

évader (s') [evade] (1) *vpr* (*lit, fig*) to escape (*de* from). **faire s'~ qn** to help sb escape. ♦ **évadé, e** *nm,f* escaped prisoner.

évaluer [evalɥe] (1) *vt bijou* to appraise, value; *dégâts, prix* to assess, evaluate; (*approximativement*) to estimate (*à* at). **faire ~ qch par un expert** to have sth valued by an expert. ♦ **évaluable** *adj* assessable. ♦ **évaluation** *nf* appraisal; valuation; assessment; estimation.

évangile [evɑ̃ʒil] *nm* (*Rel, fig*) gospel. **ce n'est pas parole d'~** it's not gospel. ♦ **évangélique** *adj* evangelical. ♦ **évangéliser** (1) *vt* to evangelize. ♦ **évangéliste** *nm* evangelist.

évanouir (s') [evanwiʀ] (2) *vpr* to faint (*de* from); *[rêves, craintes]* to vanish, disappear. ♦ **évanoui, e** *adj* unconscious. **tomber ~** to faint. ♦ **évanouissement** *nm* (*syncope*) fainting fit; (*accident etc*) loss of consciousness; (*fig*) disappearance.

évaporer [evapɔʀe] (1) **1** *vt* (*gén* **faire ~**) to evaporate. **2 s'~** *vpr* (*lit*) to evaporate; (*: *disparaître*) to vanish into thin air. ♦ **évaporation** *nf* evaporation. ♦ **évaporé, e 1** *adj* (*péj*) *personne* scatterbrained. **2** *nm,f* scatterbrain.

évaser *vt,* **s'~** *vpr* [evɑze] (1) *tuyau* to open out; *jupe* to flare. **à bords évasés** with a curving rim. ♦ **évasement** *nm* opening-out; flare.

évasion [evazjɔ̃] *nf* (*lit, fig: fuite*) escape. **besoin d'~** need to escape; **~ des capitaux** flight of capital; **~ fiscale** tax evasion. ♦ **évasif, -ive** *adj* evasive. ♦ **évasivement** *adv* evasively.

évêché [eveʃe] *nm* (*région*) bishopric; (*palais*) bishop's palace; (*ville*) cathedral town.

éveiller [eveje] (1) **1** *vt* **(a)** (*littér: réveiller*) to awaken. **tenir éveillé** to keep awake. **(b)** *curiosité, sentiment* to arouse, awaken; *passion* to kindle; *intelligence* to stimulate. **2 s'~** *vpr* (*lit*) to awaken; *[ville, nature]* to wake (up); *[sentiment, curiosité]* to be aroused; *[intelligence]* to develop. **s'~ à** *amour* to awaken to. ♦ **éveil** *nm* awakening; arousing. **être en ~** *[personne]* to be on the alert; *[sens]* to be alert *ou* aroused; **donner l'~** to raise the alarm *ou* alert. ♦ **éveillé, e** *adj* (*alerte*) alert, sharp, bright; (*réveillé*) (wide-) awake.

événement [evɛnmɑ̃] *nm* event. **semaine chargée en ~s** eventful week.

éventail [evɑ̃taj] *nm* (*instrument*) fan; (*fig: gamme*) range. **en ~** fan-shaped.

éventaire [evɑ̃tɛʀ] *nm* (*corbeille*) tray; (*étalage*) stand.

éventer [evɑ̃te] (1) **1** *vt* **(a)** (*avec éventail*) to fan. **(b)** *secret* to discover. **2 s'~** *vpr [bière]* to go flat; *[parfum]* to go stale.

éventrer [evɑ̃tʀe] (1) *vt* **(a)** (*couteau*) to disembowel; (*corne*) to gore. **(b)** *sac* to tear open; *coffre* to smash open; *matelas* to rip open. ♦ **éventration** *nf* (*Méd*) rupture.

éventualité [evɑ̃tɥalite] *nf* possibility. **dans cette ~** in that case. ♦ **éventuel, -elle** *adj* possible. **les profits ~s seraient réinvestis** any profits which might be made would be reinvested. ♦ **éventuellement** *adv* possibly.

évêque [evɛk] *nm* bishop.

évertuer (s') [evɛʀtɥe] (1) *vpr*: **s'~ à faire** to struggle hard to do.

éviction [eviksjɔ̃] *nf* (*Jur*) eviction; *[rival]* ousting.

évidence [evidɑ̃s] *nf* (*caractère*) obviousness, evidence; (*fait*) obvious fact. **se rendre à l'~** to yield to the facts *ou* the evidence; **nier l'~** to deny the obvious *ou* the facts; **c'est une ~ que de dire** it's a statement of the obvious to say; **(être) en ~** (to be) conspicuous *ou* in evidence; **mettre en ~** *personne, fait* to bring to the fore; *objet* to put in a conspicuous position; **se mettre en ~** to make o.s. conspicuous; **de toute ~** quite obviously *ou* evidently. ♦ **évidemment** *adv* (*gén*) obviously; (*bien sûr*) of course. ♦ **évident, e** *adj* obvious, evident.

évider [evide] (1) *vt* to hollow out.

évier [evje] *nm* sink.

évincer [evɛ̃se] (3) *vt* to oust, supplant. ♦ **évincement** *nm* ousting, supplanting.

éviter [evite] (1) *vt* (*gén*) to avoid; *coup* to dodge; *regard* to evade. **~ qu'une situation n'empire** to avoid *ou* prevent the worsening of a situation; **~ de faire qch** to avoid doing sth; **~ le sel** to avoid *ou* keep off salt; **ça lui a évité d'avoir à se déplacer** that saved him the bother of going. ♦ **évitable** *adj* avoidable.

évocation [evɔkasjɔ̃] *nf* evocation. ♦ **évocateur, -trice** *adj* evocative (*de* of).

évoluer [evɔlɥe] (1) *vi* **(a)** (*changer*) (*gén*) to evolve; *[maladie]* to develop. **ses parents ont évolué** his parents have moved with the times. **(b)** *[danseur]* to move about; *[avion]* to circle; *[troupes]* to manoeuvre. ♦ **évolué, e** *adj peuple* (highly) developed, advanced; *personne* (*compréhensif*) broad-minded; (*indépendant*) independent. ♦ **évolution** *nf* evolution; development; advancement; movement.

évoquer [evɔke] (1) *vt* (*gén*) to evoke; *souvenir* to recall; *scène* to conjure up; *problème* to touch on.

exacerber [ɛgzasɛʀbe] (1) *vt* to exacerbate.

exact, e [ɛgza, akt(ə)] *adj* **(a)** *reproduction, compte rendu* exact, accurate; *réponse, calcul* correct, right; (*précis*) *dimension* exact, precise. **est-il ~ que?** is it right *ou* correct that?; **c'est l'~e vérité** that's the exact truth; **l'heure ~e** the exact time. **(b)** (*ponctuel*) punctual; (*littér: strict*) strict. ♦ **exactement** *adv* exactly; accurately; correctly; precisely; strictly. ♦ **exactitude** *nf* exactness; accuracy; correctness; precision; punctuality; (*littér: minutie*) exactitude.

exaction [ɛgzaksjɔ̃] *nf* exaction.

ex æquo [ɛgzeko] **1** *adj inv* equally placed. **2** *adv classer* equal.

exagérer [ɛgzaʒeʀe] (6) **1** *vt* (*gén*) to exaggerate. **sans ~** without any exaggeration; **il exagère** he goes too far. **2 s'~** *vpr difficultés* to exaggerate; *avantages* to overrate. ♦ **exagération** *nf* (*gén*) exaggeration. ♦ **exagéré, e** *adj* (*amplifié*) exaggerated; (*excessif*) excessive. **c'est un peu ~** it's a bit much*; **il n'est pas ~ de dire** it is not an exaggeration to say. ♦ **exagérément** *adv* excessively, exaggeratedly.

exalter [ɛgzalte] (1) *vt* **(a)** *esprit, courage* to fire, excite. **exalté par** (*excité*) excited by; (*euphorique*) elated by; **il s'exalte facilement** he is easily carried away. **(b)** (*glorifier*) to exalt, praise. ♦ **exaltant, e** *adj* exalting, elating. ♦ **exaltation** *nf* **(a)** (*nerveuse*) intense excitement; (*joyeuse*) elation; (*mystique*) exaltation. **(b)** (*glorification*) praising, exalting. ♦ **exalté, e 1** *adj sentiments* elated; *imagination* wild; *esprit* excited. **2** *nm,f* (*péj*) fanatic.

examiner [ɛgzamine] (1) *vt* **(a)** (*analyser*) (*gén*) to examine; *demande* to consider; *comptes* to go through. **~ en détail** to scrutinize. **(b)** *objet, visage* to examine, study; *ciel* to scan; *appartement* to have a look round. **s'~ devant la glace** to examine o.s. in the mirror. **(c)** (*Méd, Scol*) to examine. **se faire ~** to be examined. ♦ **examen** *nm* **(a)** (*action*) examination; consideration. **~ détaillé** scrutiny; **la question est à l'~** the matter is under consideration. **(b)** (*Méd*) medical examination. **se faire faire des ~s** to have some tests done. **(c)** (*Scol*) exam, examination. **~ blanc/de passage** mock/end-of-the-year exam. ♦ **examinateur, -trice** *nm,f* examiner.

exaspérer [ɛgzaspeʀe] (6) *vt* (*irriter*) to exasperate; (*littér: aviver*) to exacerbate, aggravate. ♦ **exaspération** *nf* exasperation.

exaucer [ɛgzose] (3) *vt vœu, prière* to grant. **~ qn** to grant sb's wish. ♦ **exaucement** *nm* fulfilment.

excavation [ɛkskavasjɔ̃] *nf* excavation.

excédent [ɛksedɑ̃] *nm* surplus (*sur* over). **un ~ de poids** some excess weight; **budget en ~** surplus budget. ♦ **excédentaire** *adj production* excess, surplus.

excéder [ɛksede] (6) *vt* **(a)** *longueur, prix* to exceed. **les avantages excèdent les inconvénients** the advantages outweigh the disadvantages. **(b)** *pouvoir* to overstep, exceed; *forces* to overtax. **(c)** (*accabler: gén pass*) to exhaust. **excédé de fatigue** exhausted, tired out; **excédé de travail** overworked. **(d)** (*agacer: gén pass*) to exasperate.

excellence [ɛksɛlɑ̃s] *nf* **(a)** excellence. **par ~** *héros* par excellence; *aimer* above all else. **(b) Son E~** his Excellency. ♦ **excellemment** *adv* excellently. ♦ **excellent, e** *adj* excellent. ♦ **exceller** (1) *vi* to excel (*dans* in, *à faire* in doing).

excentrique [ɛksɑ̃tʀik] **1** *adj personne,* (*Math*) eccentric; *quartier* outlying. **2** *nmf* eccentric. ♦ **excentricité** *nf* eccentricity.

excepter [ɛksɛpte] (1) *vt* to except (*de* from). **sans ~ personne** without excluding anyone. ♦ **excepté, e 1** *adj*: **sa mère ~e** apart from *ou* except his mother. **2** *prép* except, apart from. **~ quand/que** except when/that. ♦ **exception** *nf* exception. **d'~** *mesure* special, exceptional; **faire une ~ à** *règle* to make an exception to; **faire ~ (à la règle)** to be an exception (to the rule); **faire ~ de** to make an exception of; **à l'~ de** except for. ♦ **exceptionnel, -elle** *adj* exceptional. ♦ **exceptionnellement** *adv* (*à titre d'exception*) in this particular instance; (*très*) exceptionally.

excès [ɛksɛ] *nm* **(a)** (*surplus*) *[argent]* excess, surplus; *[marchandises]* glut, surplus. **il y a un ~ d'acide** there is too much acid; **~ de précautions** excessive care; **~ de zèle** overzealousness. **(b)** (*abus*) excess. **des ~ de langage** immoderate language; **tomber dans l'~ inverse** to go to the opposite extreme; **faire un ~ de vitesse** to exceed the speed limit; **faire des ~ de table** to overindulge; **jusqu'à l'~, avec ~** to excess, excessively. ♦ **excessif, -ive** *adj* excessive. **elle est ~ive en tout** she takes everything to extremes; **c'est ~!** that's far too much!, that's excessive! ♦ **excessivement** *adv* excessively.

exciter [ɛksite] (1) **1** *vt* **(a)** *désir* to arouse, excite; *rire* to cause; *pitié* to rouse; *imagination* to fire, stir; *appétit* to whet; *ardeur* to increase. **cela ne fit qu'~ sa colère** that only made him even more angry. **(b)** (*enthousiasmer*) to thrill, excite. **excitant pour l'esprit** mentally stimulating. **(c)** (*rendre nerveux*) *personne* to arouse; *chien* to excite. **le café excite** coffee acts as a stimulant. **(d)** (*: *irriter*) to irritate. **il commence à m'~** he's getting on my nerves. **(e)** (*encourager*) to urge on. **~ qn contre qn** to set sb against sb; **~ qn à faire qch** to urge sb to do sth. **(f)** (*Méd, Élec*) to excite. **2 s'~** *vpr* (*enthousiaste*) to get excited (*sur* about, over); (*nerveux*) to get worked up*; (*: *fâché*) to get angry, fly off the handle*. ♦ **excitable** *adj* excitable. ♦ **excitant, e 1** *adj* (*gén*) exciting. **2** *nm* stimulant. ♦ **excitation** *nf* (*gén*) excitement; (*Méd, Élec*) excitation. (*incitation*) **~ à** incitement to. ♦ **excité, e** *nm,f* hothead.

exclamer (s') [ɛksklame] (1) *vpr* to exclaim. **s'~ de colère** to cry out in anger. ♦ **exclamation** *nf* exclamation.

exclure [ɛksklyʀ] (35) *vt* **(a)** (*d'une salle*) to turn out; (*d'un parti, d'une école*) to expel. **se faire ~ de** to get o.s. expelled from. **(b)** *solution, hypothèse* to exclude. **~ qch de son régime** to cut sth out of one's diet; **je tiens à être exclu de cette affaire** count me out of this business; **c'est tout à fait exclu** it's quite out of the question. ♦ **exclusif, -ive** *adj* exclusive. (*Comm*) **droits ~s** sole *ou* exclusive rights. ♦ **exclusion** *nf* exclusion; expulsion (*de* from). **à l'~ de** (*sauf*) with the exclusion of; (*en écartant*) to the exclusion of. ♦ **exclusivement** *adv* (*seulement*) exclusively, solely. **~ réservé au personnel** reserved for staff only; (*non inclus*) **du 10 au 15 ~** from the 10th to the 15th exclusive. ♦ **exclusivité** *nf* (*Comm*) exclusive rights; *[sentiments]* exclusiveness. **ce film passe en ~ à** this film is showing exclusively at.

excommunier [ɛkskɔmynje] (7) *vt* to excommunicate. ♦ **excommunication** *nf* excommunication.

excrément [ɛkskʀemɑ̃] *nm*: **~(s)** excrement.

excrétion [ɛkskʀesjɔ̃] *nf* excretion.

excroissance [ɛkskʀwasɑ̃s] *nf* outgrowth.

excursion [ɛkskyʀsjɔ̃] *nf* (*en car etc*) excursion, trip; (*à pied*) walk, hike. ♦ **excursionniste** *nmf* (day) tripper; hiker, walker.

excuser [ɛkskyze] (1) **1** *vt* **(a)** (*pardonner*) to excuse, forgive. **excusez-moi** excuse me, I'm sorry; **excusez-moi de ne pas venir** excuse my not coming, I'm sorry I can't come. **(b)** (*justifier, dispenser*) to excuse. **se faire ~** to ask to be excused; **'M Dupont: (absent) excusé'** 'Mr Dupont has sent an apology'. **2 s'~** *vpr*: **s'~ de qch** to apologize for sth (*auprès de* to). ♦ **excusable** *adj* excusable, forgivable. ♦ **excuse** *nf* **(a)** (*prétexte*) excuse. **mauvaise ~** poor excuse; **sans ~** inexcusable; **prendre qch pour ~** to use sth as an excuse. **(b)** (*regret*) **~s** apology; **faire des ~s** to apologize; **je vous dois des ~s** I owe you an apology.

exécrer [ɛgzekʀe] (6) *vt* to loathe, execrate. ♦ **exécrable** *adj* atrocious, execrable. ♦ **exécrablement** *adv* atrociously, execrably. ♦ **exécration** *nf* execration, loathing.

exécuter [ɛgzekyte] (1) **1** *vt* **(a)** (*accomplir*) (*gén*) to carry out; *travail, mouvements* to execute; *promesse* to fulfil; *tâche* to perform. **il a fait ~ des travaux** he had some work done. **(b)** *objet* to produce, make; *tableau* to paint; *commande* to make up; (*Mus*) *morceau* to perform, execute. **(c)** (*tuer*) to execute, put to death. **(d)** *décret* to enforce. **2 s'~** *vpr* (*obéir*) to comply; (*payer*) to pay up. ♦ **exécutant, e** *nm,f* (*Mus*) performer; (*fig péj: agent*) underling. ♦ **exécuteur** *nm* (*Jur*) **~ (testamentaire)** executor. ♦ **exécutif, -ive** *adj, nm* executive. ♦ **exécution** *nf* execution; carrying out; fulfilment; performance; production; making; painting; making up; enforcement. **mettre à ~** *projet, idées* to carry out; **en ~ de la loi** in compliance with the law; **~ capitale** capital execution.

exemplaire [ɛgzɑ̃plɛʀ] **1** *adj* exemplary. **2** *nm* *[livre]* copy; (*échantillon*) example.

exemple [ɛgzɑ̃pl(ə)] *nm* (*modèle*) example; (*spécimen*) example, instance. **citer qn en ~** to quote sb as an example; **donner l'~** to set an example (*de* of); **prendre ~ sur qn** to take sb as an example; **à l'~ de son père** just like his father; **faire un ~ de qn** to make an example of sb; **le seul ~ que je connaisse** the only example *ou* instance I know of; **par ~** (*explicatif*) for example *ou* instance; (*: *par contre*) on the other hand; **(ça) par ~!** (*surprise*) my word!; (*indignation*) oh really!

exempt, e [ɛgzɑ̃, ɑ̃t] *adj*: **~ de** *corvée* exempt from; *dangers* free from; **~ de taxes** duty-free. ♦ **exempter** (1) *vt* to exempt (*de* from). ♦ **exemption** *nf* exemption.

exercer [ɛgzɛʀse] (3) **1** *vt* **(a)** *profession* to practise; *fonction* to fulfil; *talents, droit, charité* to exercise; *contrôle, influence* to exert (*sur* over); *représailles* to take (*sur* on); *poussée* to exert (*sur* on). **quel métier exercez-vous?** what job do you do?; (*Jur*) **~ des poursuites contre qn** to bring an action against sb. **(b)** (*aguerrir*) *corps, esprit* to train, exercise (*à* to, for); *facultés* to exercise. **(c)** (*éprouver*) *patience* to tax. **2 s'~** *vpr [pianiste, sportif]* to practise. **s'~ à** *technique* to practise; **s'~ à faire qch** to train o.s. to do sth. ♦ **exercé, e** *adj oreille* keen, trained.

exercice [ɛgzɛʀsis] *nm* **(a)** *[métier]* practice; *[droit]* exercising; *[facultés, culte]* exercise. **dans l'~ de ses fonctions** in the execution of his duties; **être en ~** *[médecin]* to be in practice; *[fonctionnaire]* to hold office. **(b)** (*entraînement, devoir*) exercise. **faire de l'~** to take some exercise; (*Mil*) **l'~** drill; (*Ling*) **~s structuraux** structure drills.

exhaler [ɛgzale] (1) *vt* (*littér*) *odeur* to exhale; *soupir* to breathe; *plainte* to utter. **s'~ de** to rise from. ♦ **exhalaison** *nf* exhalation.

exhaustif, -ive [ɛgzostif, iv] *adj* exhaustive. ♦ **exhaustivement** *adv* exhaustively.

exhiber [ɛgzibe] (1) **1** *vt* (*péj*) *savoir, richesse* to flaunt; *chiens savants, passeport* to show. **2 s'~** *vpr* (*péj*) to show o.s. off; (*indécemment*) to expose o.s. ♦ **exhibition** *nf* flaunting; showing. (*péj*) **~(s)** showing off. ♦ **exhibitionnisme** *nm* exhibitionism. ♦ **exhibitionniste** *nmf* exhibitionist.

exhorter [ɛgzɔʀte] (1) *vt* to exhort (*à faire* to do, *à qch* to sth). ♦ **exhortation** *nf* exhortation.

exhumer [ɛgzyme] (1) *vt corps* to exhume; *ruines* to excavate; *faits, vieux livres* to unearth; *souvenirs* to recollect. ♦ **exhumation** *nf* exhumation; excavation; unearthing; recollection.

exiger [ɛgziʒe] (3) *vt* to demand, require (*qch de qn* sth of *ou* from sb). **j'exige que vous le fassiez** I insist on your doing it, I demand that you do it; **des titres universitaires sont exigés** university degrees are required; **trop ~ de ses forces** to overtask o.s.; **cette plante exige beaucoup d'eau** this plant needs *ou* requires a lot of water. ♦ **exigeant, e** *adj client* demanding, hard to please; *travail* demanding, exacting. ♦ **exigence** *nf* **(a)** *[client]* particularity; *[maître]* strictness. **(b)** (*revendication, besoin*) demand, requirement.

exigible [ɛgziʒibl(ə)] *adj* (*Comm, Jur*) payable. ♦ **exigibilité** *nf* payability.

exigu, -uë [ɛgzigy] *adj lieu* cramped; *ressources* scanty; *délais* short. ♦ **exiguïté** *nf* crampedness; scantiness; shortness.

exil [ɛgzil] *nm* exile. ♦ **exilé, e** *nm,f* exile. ♦ **exiler** (1) **1** *vt* (*Pol*) to exile; (*fig*) to banish. **2 s'~** *vpr* (*Pol*) to go into exile. (*fig*) **s'~ loin du monde** to cut o.s. off from the world.

exister [ɛgziste] (1) *vi* to exist. **la vie existe-t-elle sur Mars?** is there life on Mars?; (*il y a*) **il existe** there is, there are; **il en existe en plusieurs couleurs** they come *ou* are found in several colours. ♦ **existant, e** *adj* existing. ♦ **existence** *nf* (*gén*) existence. **dans l'~** in life.

exode [ɛgzɔd] *nm* (*lit, fig*) exodus. **~ rural** drift from the land.

exonérer [ɛgzɔneʀe] (6) *vt* (*Fin*) to exempt (*de* from). ♦ **exonération** *nf* exemption.

exorbitant, e [ɛgzɔʀbitɑ̃, ɑ̃t] *adj* exorbitant.

exorciser [ɛgzɔʀsize] (1) *vt* to exorcize. ♦ **exorcisme** *nm* exorcism. ♦ **exorciste** *nm* exorcist.

exotique [ɛgzɔtik] *adj* exotic. ♦ **exotisme** *nm* exoticism.

expansion [ɛkspɑ̃sjɔ̃] *nf* **(a)** (*extension*) expansion. **en ~** *économie* booming, fast-expanding; *univers* expanding. **(b)** (*effusion*) expansiveness. **avec de grandes ~s** expansively. ♦ **expansif, -ive** *adj* expansive. **peu ~** not very forthcoming. ♦ **expansivité** *nf* expansiveness.

expatrier [ɛkspatʀije] (7) **1** *vt* to expatriate. **2 s'~** *vpr* to expatriate o.s. ♦ **expatriation** *nf* expatriation. ♦ **expatrié, e** *nm,f* expatriate.

expectative [ɛkspɛktativ] *nf* (*incertitude*) state of uncertainty. **être dans l'~** to be still waiting (to see *etc*).

expectorer [ɛkspɛktɔʀe] (1) *vti* to expectorate. ♦ **expectoration** *nf* expectoration.

expédient, e [ɛkspedjɑ̃, ɑ̃t] *adj, nm* expedient.

expédier [ɛkspedje] (7) *vt* **(a)** *lettre* to send, dispatch. **~ par la poste** to send through the post; **~ par le train** to send by rail; **~ par bateau** *lettres* to send surface mail; *produits* to ship. **(b)** (*) *client, affaire* to dispose of, deal with; *déjeuner* to polish off. ♦ **expéditeur, -trice 1** *adj* dispatching. **2** *nm,f* sender. ♦ **expéditif, -ive** *adj* expeditious. ♦ **expédition** *nf* (*action*) dispatch; shipping; (*paquet*) consignment; (*par bateau*) shipment; (*Mil, Sci*) expedition. ♦ **expéditionnaire 1** *adj* (*Mil*) expeditionary. **2** *nmf* (*Comm*) forwarding clerk. ♦ **expéditivement** *adv* expeditiously.

expérience [ɛkspeʀjɑ̃s] *nf* **(a)** (*gén*) experience. **sans ~** inexperienced; **savoir par ~** to know by *ou* from experience; **il a une longue ~ de l'enseignement** he has a lot of teaching experience; **tente l'~** try it; **faire l'~ de qch** to experience sth. **(b)** (*scientifique*) experiment. **vérité d'~** experimental truth; **faire une ~ sur** to do an experiment on.

expérimenter [ɛkspeʀimɑ̃te] (1) *vt appareil* to test; *remède* to experiment with; *méthode* to test out. ♦ **expérimental, e,** *mpl* **-aux** *adj* experimental. ♦ **expérimentalement** *adv* experimentally. ♦ **expérimentateur, -trice** *nm,f* experimenter. ♦ **expérimentation** *nf* experimentation. ♦ **expérimenté, e** *adj* experienced.

expert, e [ɛkspɛʀ, ɛʀt(ə)] **1** *adj* expert, skilled (*en* in, *à* at). **2** *nm* expert (*en* in, at); (*d'assurances*) valuer. **~-comptable** ≈ chartered accountant. ♦ **expertement** *adv* expertly.

expertiser [ɛkspɛʀtize] (1) *vt bijou* to value, appraise; *dégâts* to assess, evaluate. **faire ~ qch** to have sth valued. ♦ **expertise** *nf* (*évaluation*) valuation; (*rapport*) expert's report.

expier [ɛkspje] (7) *vt* to expiate, atone for. ♦ **expiation** *nf* expiation (*de* of), atonement (*de* for).

expirer [ɛkspiʀe] (1) **1** *vt air* to breathe out. **2** *vi* (*mourir, prendre fin*) to expire. ♦ **expiration** *nf* (*gén*) expiration. **venir à ~** to expire; **à l'~ de** at the expiry of.

explication [ɛksplikɑsjɔ̃] *nf* explanation (*de* for); (*discussion*) discussion; (*dispute*) argument; (*Scol*) analysis (*de* of). **j'exige des ~s** I demand an explanation. ♦ **explicable** *adj* explicable.

expliciter [ɛksplisite] (1) *vt* to make explicit. ♦ **explicite** *adj* explicit. ♦ **explicitement** *adv* explicitly.

expliquer [ɛksplike] (1) **1** *vt* (*faire comprendre*) to explain (*à qn* to sb); (*rendre compte de*) to account for, explain; (*Scol*) *texte* to analyse. **2 s'~** *vpr* **(a)** (*préciser*) to explain o.s., make o.s. clear. **s'~ sur ses projets** to explain one's plans. **(b)** (*comprendre*) to understand. **(c)** (*être compréhensible*) **ça s'explique par le mauvais temps** it is explained by the bad weather; **tout s'explique!** it's all clear now! **(d)** (*discuter*) **s'~ avec qn** to explain o.s. to sb; **après s'être longuement expliqués** after having discussed the matter for a long time; **ils sont allés s'~ dehors*** they went off to sort it out outside.

exploit [ɛksplwa] *nm* exploit, feat.

exploiter [ɛksplwate] (1) *vt mine* to work; *entreprise* to run; *ressources, idée, personne* to exploit. ♦ **exploitable** *adj* (*gén*) exploitable. ♦ **exploitant, e** *nm,f* farmer. ♦ **exploitation** *nf* **(a)** (*action*) working; exploitation; running. **mettre en ~** to exploit; **frais d'~** running costs. **(b)** (*entreprise*) concern. **~ agricole** farming concern; **~ minière** mining development. ♦ **exploiteur, -euse** *nm,f* exploiter.

explorer [ɛksplɔʀe] (1) *vt* to explore. ♦ **explorateur, -trice** *nm,f* explorer. ♦ **exploration** *nf* exploration.

exploser [ɛksploze] (1) *vi* (*lit, fig*) to explode; *[joie]* to burst out; *[bombe]* to blow up. **~ (de colère)** to explode with anger; **faire ~** *bombe* to explode; *bâtiment* to blow up; **cette remarque le fit ~** he blew up at that remark. ♦ **explosif, -ive** *adj, nm* explosive. ♦ **explosion** *nf* explosion; outburst. **faire ~** to explode; to blow up.

exporter [ɛkspɔʀte] (1) *vt* to export. ♦ **exportable** *adj* exportable. ♦ **exportateur, -trice 1** *adj* exporting. **2** *nm,f* exporter. ♦ **exportation** *nf* (*gén*) export.

exposer [ɛkspoze] (1) **1** *vt* **(a)** *marchandises* to display; *tableaux* to show. **c'est resté exposé pendant 3 mois** it has been on display for 3 months. **(b)** (*expliquer*) (*gén*) to explain; *faits, théorie* to expound, set out. **(c)** (*mettre en danger*) *personne, objet* to expose (*à* to); *vie, réputation* to risk. **sa conduite l'expose à des reproches** his behaviour lays him open to blame; **c'est exposé à être découvert** it is liable to be discovered. **(d)** (*gén, Phot: orienter*) to expose. **exposé au sud** facing (due) south; **maison bien exposée** well-situated house; **endroit très exposé** very exposed place. **2 s'~** *vpr* to expose o.s. **s'~ à** to expose o.s. to, lay o.s. open to. ♦ **exposant, e 1** *nm,f [foire]* exhibitor. **2** *nm* (*Math*) exponent. ♦ **exposé** *nm* (*action*) account, statement; (*conférence: gén, Scol*) talk (*sur* on). ♦ **exposition** *nf* **(a)** *[marchandises]* display; *[raisons]* exposition; (*au danger*) exposure (*à* to). **(b)** (*foire*) exhibition. **l'E~ Universelle** the World Fair. **(c)** (*Phot*) exposure. **(d)** (*Littérat, Mus*) exposition. **scène d'~** introductory scene. **(e)** (*orientation*) *[maison]* aspect.

exprès[1] [ɛkspʀɛ] *adv* (*spécialement*) specially; (*intentionnellement*) on purpose.

exprès[2]**, -esse** [ɛkspʀɛs] *adj* **(a)** *interdiction* formal. **(b)** (*inv*) **(lettre) ~** express letter; **envoyer qch en ~** to send sth express.

express [ɛkspʀɛs] *adj, nm inv*: **(train) ~** fast train; **(café) ~** espresso coffee.

expressément [ɛkspʀɛsemɑ̃] *adv* (*formellement*) expressly; (*spécialement*) specially.

expression [ɛkspʀɛsjɔ̃] *nf* (*gén*) expression. **au-delà de toute ~** inexpressible; **visage sans ~** expressionless face; (*locution*) **~ figée** set expression *ou* phrase. ♦ **expressif, -ive** *adj* expressive. ♦ **expressivement** *adv* expressively. ♦ **expressivité** *nf* expressiveness.

exprimer [ɛkspʀime] (1) **1** *vt* **(a)** (*gén*) to express. **le signe + exprime l'addition** the sign + stands for addition. **(b)** *jus* to press out. **2 s'~** *vpr [personne]* to express o.s.; *[sentiment]* to be expressed. **si je peux m'~ ainsi** if I may put it like that. ♦ **exprimable** *adj* expressible.

exproprier [ɛkspʀɔpʀije] (7) *vt* to place a compulsory purchase order on.

expulser [ɛkspylse] (1) *vt* (*gén*) *élève* to expel; *étranger* to deport, expel; *locataire* to evict; *manifestant* to eject (*de* from); *joueur* to send off; (*Anat*) to evacuate. ♦ **expulsion** *nf* expulsion; deportation; eviction; ejection; sending off; evacuation.

expurger [ɛkspyʀʒe] (3) *vt* to expurgate.

exquis, -ise [ɛkski, iz] *adj* (*lit*) exquisite; *personne, temps* delightful.

extase [ɛkstɑz] *nf* (*Rel, fig*) ecstasy. **être en ~ devant** to be in ecstasies over. ♦ **extasier (s')** (7) *vpr* to go into ecstasies (*sur* over). ♦ **extatique** *adj* ecstatic.

extension [ɛkstɑ̃sjɔ̃] *nf [membre, ressort]* stretching; *[épidémie]* extension, spreading; *[commerce, domaine]* expansion; *[loi, sens]* extension (*à* to). **par ~ (de sens)** by extension; **prendre de l'~** to spread. ♦ **extensible** *adj matière* extensible; *définition* extendable. ♦ **extensif, -ive** *adj* extensive.

exténuer [ɛkstenɥe] (1) **1** *vt* to exhaust. **2 s'~** *vpr* to exhaust o.s. (*à faire* doing).

extérieur, e [ɛksteʀjœʀ] **1** *adj* **(a)** (*gén*) outside; *cour* outer; *bruit, réalité* external; *décoration* exterior; *[personne] apparence* outward; *amabilité* superficial. **signes ~s de richesse** outward signs of wealth; **être ~ à un sujet** to be external to *ou* outside a subject; **interdit à toute personne ~e au chantier** site workers only. **(b)** *commerce, politique* foreign. **2** *nm [objet, maison]* outside, exterior; *[personne]* exterior, outward appearance. **c'est à l'~ (de la ville)** it's outside (the town); (*Ciné*) **~s** location shots; (*pays*) **l'~** foreign countries; **vendre à l'~** to sell abroad. ♦ **extérieurement** *adv* (*du dehors*) on the outside, externally; (*en apparence*) outwardly. ♦ **extérioriser** (1) *vt joie etc* to show.

exterminer [ɛkstɛʀmine] (1) *vt* (*lit, fig*) to exterminate. ♦ **extermination** *nf* extermination.

externe [ɛkstɛʀn(ə)] **1** *adj surface etc* external, outer; *angle* exterior. **à usage ~** for external use only. **2** *nmf* (*Scol*) day pupil; (*Méd*) non-resident student. ♦ **externat** *nm* (*Scol*) day school.

extincteur [ɛkstɛ̃ktœʀ] *nm* fire extinguisher.
extinction [ɛkstɛ̃ksjɔ̃] *nf [incendie]* extinguishing; *[peuple]* extinction; *[droit]* extinguishment. **~ de voix** loss of voice.
extirper [ɛkstiʀpe] (1) *vt* to eradicate. **impossible de lui ~ une parole!*** it's impossible to drag a word out of him!; **s'~ de son manteau** to extricate o.s. from one's coat. ♦ **extirpation** *nf* eradication.
extorquer [ɛkstɔʀke] (1) *vt* to extort (*à qn* from sb). ♦ **extorqueur, -euse** *nm,f* extortioner. ♦ **extorsion** *nf* extortion.
extra [ɛkstʀa] **1** *nm inv* (*domestique*) extra servant *ou* help; (*gâterie*) special treat. **2** *adj inv fromage, vin* first-rate; *tissu* top-quality; (*) *film, personne* terrific*, great*. **de qualité ~** of the finest quality. **3** *préf* extra. **~-fin** superfine, extra fine.
extraction [ɛkstʀaksjɔ̃] *nf* (*V* **extraire**) extraction; mining; quarrying; (†: *origine*) extraction.
extrader [ɛkstʀade] (1) *vt* to extradite. ♦ **extradition** *nf* extradition.
extraire [ɛkstʀɛʀ] (50) *vt* (*gén, Méd, Math*) to extract; *charbon* to mine; *marbre* to quarry. **~ de** *poche* to take *ou* bring out of; *prison* to get out of; **passage extrait d'un livre** extract from a book, passage taken from a book; **s'~ de son manteau*** to extricate o.s. from one's coat. ♦ **extrait** *nm* (*gén*) extract; *[livre]* extract, excerpt. **~ de naissance** *etc* birth *etc* certificate.
extraordinaire [ɛkstʀaɔʀdinɛʀ] *adj* (*étrange*) extraordinary; (*exceptionnel*) exceptional, extraordinary; (*Pol*) special. **acteur ~** extraordinary *ou* remarkable actor; **ce n'est pas ~** it isn't up to much*; **si par ~** if by some unlikely chance; **quand par ~** on those rare occasions when. ♦ **extraordinairement** *adv* extraordinarily; exceptionally.
extravagance [ɛkstʀavagɑ̃s] *nf* (*caractère*) eccentricity, extravagance. (*acte*) **~(s)** eccentric *ou* extravagant behaviour. ♦ **extravagant, e** *adj idée, prix* extravagant; *conduite* eccentric.
extrême [ɛkstʀɛm] **1** *adj* (*gén*) extreme; *point* furthest; *mesures* drastic. **à l'~ opposé (de)** at the opposite extreme (of). **2** *nm* (*gén*) extreme. **jusqu'à l'~** in the extreme, to a degree. **3: ~ droite/gauche** extreme right/left (wing); **~-onction** Extreme Unction; **E~-Orient** Far East. ♦ **extrêmement** *adv* extremely. ♦ **extrémisme** *nm* extremism. ♦ **extrémiste** *adj, nmf* extremist.
extrémité [ɛkstʀemite] *nf* **(a)** (*bout*) (*gén*) end; *[aiguille]* point; *[objet mince]* tip; *[village, île]* extremity, limit. (*Anat*) **~s** extremities. **(b) à la dernière ~** (*misère*) in the most dire plight; (*mort*) on the point of death; **se porter à des ~s** to go to extremes.
exubérance [ɛgzybeʀɑ̃s] *nf* (*caractère*) exuberance. (*action*) **~(s)** exuberant behaviour. ♦ **exubérant, e** *adj* (*gén*) exuberant.
exulter [ɛgzylte] (1) *vi* to exult. ♦ **exultation** *nf* exultation.
exutoire [ɛgzytwaʀ] *nm* outlet, release.
ex-voto [ɛksvɔto] *nm inv* monumental tablet.

F

F, f [ɛf] ***nm ou nf*** *(lettre)* F, f.
fa [fɑ] ***nm inv*** *(Mus)* F; *(en chantant)* fa.
fable [fɑbl(ə)] ***nf*** *(gén)* fable; *(mensonge)* tale. **être la ~ de toute la ville** to be the laughing stock of the whole town.
fabriquer [fabʀike] (1) ***vt*** *(gén)* to make; *(industriellement)* to manufacture; *histoire* to fabricate, make up; *fausse monnaie* to forge. **~ en série** to mass-produce; **il s'est fabriqué une cabane** he built *ou* made himself a shed; **qu'est-ce qu'il fabrique?*** what on earth is he up to?* ♦ **fabricant** ***nm*** manufacturer. ♦ **fabrication** ***nf*** making; manufacturing; forging; fabricating. **~ en série** mass production; **de ~ française** made in France, of French make; **de bonne ~** well-made; **une robe de sa ~** a dress of her own making. ♦ **fabrique** ***nf*** *(établissement)* factory. **~ de papier** paper mill.
fabuleux, -euse [fabylø, øz] ***adj*** *(gén)* fabulous. ♦ **fabuleusement** ***adv*** fabulously.
fac [fak] ***nf*** *(arg Univ)* *abrév de* **faculté.**
façade [fasad] ***nf*** **(a)** *[maison]* façade, front; *(latérale)* side; *[magasin]* front. **la ~ arrière de la maison** the back of the house. **(b)** *(fig: apparence)* façade. **de ~** *luxe* sham.
face [fas] ***nf*** **(a)** *(visage)* face. **les blessés de la ~** people with facial injuries; **sauver/perdre la ~** to save/lose face. **(b)** *[objet]* side; *[médaille]* front; *(lit, fig)* *[monde]* face. **question à double ~** two-sided question; **sous *ou* sur toutes ses ~s** from all sides; **la pièce est tombée sur ~** the coin fell face up; *(jeu de pile ou face)* **~!** heads!; **la ~ des choses** the face of things. **(c) faire ~** to face up to things; **faire ~ à** *lieu, difficulté* to face; *épreuve* to face up to, face; *engagement* to meet; **se faire ~** to be facing each other. **(d) en ~** opposite; **la dame d'en ~** the lady from across the street, the lady opposite; **regarder qn en ~** to look sb in the face; **il lui a dit en ~ que** he told him to his face that; **il faut voir les choses en ~** one must face facts. **(e) ~ à, en ~ de** *maison* opposite, facing; *examinateur* in front of; *danger* confronted *ou* faced with; **être ~ à ~** to be facing each other, be face to face; *(TV)* **un ~ à ~** a face to face discussion; **les deux ennemis étaient maintenant l'un en ~ de l'autre** the two enemies now stood facing each other *ou* face to face. **(f) de ~** *portrait* full-face; *attaque* frontal; *(Théât)* *place* facing the stage; **voir qn de ~** to see sb face on; **avoir une vue de ~ sur qch** to have a front view of sth.
facétie [fasesi] ***nf*** *(drôlerie)* joke; *(farce)* prank. ♦ **facétieux, -euse** ***adj*** facetious.
facette [fasɛt] ***nf*** *(lit, fig)* facet.
fâcher [fɑʃe] (1) **1** ***vt*** *(mettre en colère)* to anger, make angry; *(contrarier)* to distress. **2 se ~** ***vpr*** *(se mettre en colère)* to get angry (*contre* with); *(se brouiller)* to fall out (*avec* with). ♦ **fâché, e** ***adj*** *(en colère)* angry, cross (*contre* with); *(contrarié)* sorry (*de qch* about sth). **je suis ~ de ne pas venir** I am sorry that I cannot come; *(hum)* **je ne serais pas ~ de m'asseoir** I wouldn't mind a seat. ♦ **fâcherie** ***nf*** *(brouille)* quarrel.
fâcheux, -euse [fɑʃø, øz] ***adj*** *exemple* unfortunate; *situation* unfortunate, awkward. **il est ~ que** it's unfortunate *ou* a pity that. ♦ **fâcheusement** ***adv*** unfortunately, awkwardly. **~ surpris** unpleasantly surprised.
facile [fasil] **1** ***adj*** **(a)** *(aisé)* easy (*à faire* to do). **plus ~ à dire qu'à faire** easier said than done; **avoir la larme ~** to be easily moved to tears; **il a le couteau ~** he's very ready with his knife. **(b)** *(péj)* **effet/ironie ~** facile effect/irony. **(c)** *caractère* easy-going. **il est ~ à vivre** he's easy to get on with; *(péj)* **fille ~** woman of easy virtue. **2** ***adv*** (‡) **elle a 50 ans ~** she's easily 50. ♦ **facilement** ***adv*** *(gén)* easily. **~ toléré par l'organisme** easily *ou* readily tolerated by the body.
facilité [fasilite] ***nf*** **(a)** *[problème]* easiness; *[succès]* ease; *[style]* fluency. **il travaille avec ~** he works with ease. **(b)** *(aptitude)* ability, aptitude; *(tendance)* tendency. **il a beaucoup de ~ pour les langues** he has a great aptitude for languages. **(c)** *(gén pl: possibilité)* facility. **avoir toutes ~s de faire qch** to have every opportunity to do sth; **~s de transport** transport facilities; *(Comm)* **~s de paiement** easy terms. ♦ **faciliter** (1) ***vt*** to make easier, facilitate. **ça ne va pas ~ les choses** that's not going to make matters any easier.
façon [fasɔ̃] ***nf*** **(a)** *(manière)* way. **de quelle ~ est-ce arrivé?** how did it happen?; **je le ferai à ma ~** I shall do it my own way; **à la ~ d'un enfant** like a child, as a child would do; **(c'est une) ~ de parler** it's a way of putting it; **d'une certaine ~** in a way, in some ways; **d'une ~ générale** generally speaking; **de toute(s) ~(s)** in any case, at any rate; **de cette ~** (in) this way; **d'une ~ ou d'une autre** one way or another; **en aucune ~** in no way; **un plat de ma ~** a dish of my own making; **de ~ à ne pas le déranger** so as not to disturb him; **de ~ à ce qu'il puisse regarder** so that he can see. **(b) sans ~** *accepter* without fuss; *repas* unpretentious; *personne* unaffected; **merci, sans ~** no thanks honestly; **et sans plus de ~s** and without further ado. **(c) ~s** manners, behaviour; **en voilà des ~s!** that's no way to behave!; **faire des ~s** *(minauderies)* to be affected; *(chichis)* to make a fuss. **(d)** *(Couture)* *[robe]* cut, making-up. **payer la ~** to pay for the tailoring *ou* making-up. **(e)** *(imitation)* **veste ~ daim** jacket in imitation suede. **(f)** (†: *genre*) **une ~ de roman** a novel of sorts.
façonner [fasɔne] (1) ***vt*** *(gén)* to make; *(industriellement)* to manufacture; *argile* to shape, fashion; *personne* to mould, form.
fac-similé, *pl* **~-~s** [faksimile] ***nm*** facsimile.
facteur [faktœʀ] ***nm*** *(Poste)* postman; *(élément, Math)* factor. *(fabricant)* **~ de pianos** piano maker.
factice [faktis] ***adj*** *marbre, beauté* artificial; *bijou* imitation; *barbe* false; *bouteille en vitrine* dummy; *enthousiasme* feigned.
factieux, -euse [faksjø, øz] **1** ***adj*** factious. **2** ***nm,f*** seditionary.
faction [faksjɔ̃] ***nf*** **(a)** *(groupe)* faction. **(b)** *[soldat]* guard; *(fig)* long watch. **être de *ou* en ~** to be on *ou* stand guard; *(fig)* to keep watch. ♦ **factionnaire** ***nm*** guard.
factrice [faktʀis] ***nf*** postwoman.
facture [faktyʀ] ***nf*** *(gén)* bill; *(Comm)* invoice. ♦ **facturer** (1) ***vt*** *(établir une facture)* to invoice.

(*compter*) ~ **qch 20 F (à qn)** to charge (sb) 20 francs for sth.
facultatif, -ive [fakyltatif, iv] *adj* optional. **arrêt** ~ request stop.
faculté [fakylte] *nf* **(a)** (*Univ*) faculty. **quand j'étais en** ~ when I was at university. **(b)** (*don*) faculty; (*pouvoir*) power; (*propriété*) property. **avoir une grande** ~ **de mémoire** to have great powers of memory; **avoir la** ~ **de marcher** to have the power of walking; (*aptitudes*) ~s faculties. **(c)** (*droit*) right; (*possibilité*) freedom. **je te laisse la** ~ **de choisir** I'll give you the freedom to choose.
fadaise [fadɛz] *nf* (*littér*) ~**(s)** nonsense.
fade [fad] *adj plat* tasteless, insipid, bland; *teinte* dull; *plaisanterie* tame; *décor, individu, conversation* dull, insipid. ♦ **fadeur** *nf* tastelessness; insipidness; blandness; dullness. (*platitudes*) ~s sweet nothings.
fagot [fago] *nm* bundle of sticks.
fagoter* [fagɔte] (1) **1** *vt* (*péj*) to rig out*. **2 se** ~ *vpr* to rig o.s. out*.
faible [fɛbl(ə)] **1** *adj* (*gén*) weak; *somme, intensité* low; *quantité, différence* small, slight; *espoir, bruit, odeur* slight, faint; *lumière* dim; *voix, pouls* faint, feeble; *vent* light; *rendement, devoir, raisonnement* poor. **avoir la vue** ~ to have weak *ou* poor eyesight; **il est trop** ~ **avec elle** he is too soft with her; **à une** ~ **profondeur** at a slight depth below the surface; (*Pol*) **une** ~ **majorité** a narrow *ou* slight majority; ~ **en alcool** low in alcohol; ~ **en français** poor at French. **2** *nm* **(a)** (*sans volonté*) weakling. (*sans défense*) **les** ~s the weak; **un** ~ **d'esprit** a feeble-minded person. **(b)** (*déficience*) weak point; (*penchant*) weakness. **il a un** ~ **pour sa fille** he has a soft spot for his daughter.
♦ **faiblement** *adv* weakly; slightly; faintly; dimly; lightly. ♦ **faiblesse** *nf* **(a)** weakness; softness; smallness; slightness; faintness; feebleness; dimness; lightness. **la** ~ **de la demande** the low *ou* poor demand; ~ **d'esprit** feeble-mindedness; **avoir la** ~ **d'accepter** to be weak enough to accept. **(b)** (*syncope*) sudden weakness. **(c)** (*défaut*) weakness. **chacun a ses petites** ~s we all have our little foibles *ou* weaknesses. ♦ **faiblir** (2) *vi* to get weaker (*ou* slighter *ou* smaller *etc*); *[résolution, résistance]* to weaken; *[forces, courage, vue]* to fail; *[vent]* to slacken; *[rendement]* to slacken off. **l'écart faiblit entre eux** the gap is narrowing between them.
faïence [fajɑ̃s] *nf* **(a) la** ~ (*substance*) earthenware; (*objets*) crockery, earthenware. **(b)** (*objet*) piece of earthenware.
faille [faj] *nf* (*Géol*) fault; *[raisonnement]* flaw; *[amitié]* rift.
faillir [fajiʀ] *vi* **(a)** (*manquer*) **j'ai failli tomber** I almost *ou* very nearly fell. **(b)** ~ **à** *devoir* to fail in; *promesse* to fail to keep; **sans** ~ unfailingly. **(c)** (†: *fauter*) to lapse.
faillite [fajit] *nf* (*Comm*) bankruptcy; *[espoir, méthode, gouvernement]* collapse. **faire** ~ (*Comm*) to go bankrupt; (*fig*) to collapse; **mettre qn en** ~ to make sb bankrupt.
faim [fɛ̃] *nf* hunger. **donner/avoir** ~ to make sb/be hungry; **manger à sa** ~ to eat one's fill; **avoir** ~ **de** *honneur etc* to hunger for; **sa** ~ **de richesses** his yearning for wealth; **j'ai une** ~ **de loup** I'm ravenous *ou* famished.
fainéant, e [feneɑ̃, ɑ̃t] **1** *adj* lazy, idle. **2** *nm,f* idler. ♦ **fainéanter** (1) *vi* to idle about. ♦ **fainéantise** *nf* laziness, idleness.
faire [fɛʀ] (60) **1** *vt* **(a)** (*fabrication*) (*gén*) to make; *maison* to build; *pain* to bake; *repas* to cook; *liste* to draw up; *chèque* to make out; *cours* to give; *livre* to write; *tableau* to paint; *dessin* to draw; *farce* to play; *faute, promesse* to make. ~ **du thé** to make (some) tea; **qu'avez-vous fait de votre sac?** what have you done with your bag?, where have you left *ou* put your bag? **(b)** (*activité*) (*gén*) to do; *piano, tennis, match* to play; *rêve, chute* to have; *geste, projet* to make. **que faites-vous?** (*dans la vie*) what do you do?, what is your job?; (*en ce moment*) what are you doing?; ~ **du français** to do *ou* study French; **elle fait du tricot/un peu de tricot** she knits/does a bit of knitting. **(c)** (*fonction*) (*Théât*) *rôle* to play, be. ~ **le malade** to pretend to be ill; ~ **l'innocent** to play *ou* act the innocent; **il fait le jardinier pendant les vacances** he is acting as gardener during the holidays; **quel idiot je fais!** what a fool I am! *ou* I look!; **il en a fait un avocat/son héritier** he's made a lawyer of him/made him his heir; **on le fait plus riche qu'il n'est** people make him out to be richer than he is; **ils ont fait de cette pièce une cuisine** they made *ou* turned the room into a kitchen; **la cuisine fait salle à manger** the kitchen serves as *ou* is used as a dining room; **cet hôtel fait aussi restaurant** this hotel is also run as a restaurant. **(d)** (*parcours*) to do. ~ **un voyage/une promenade** to go on a journey/go for *ou* take a walk; ~ **du 100 km/h** to do 100 km/h; ~ **les magasins** to go round the shops. **(e)** (*Comm*) *l'épicerie* to sell, deal in; *blé* to grow, produce. **nous ne faisons pas cette marque** we don't stock *ou* keep that make. **(f)** (*nettoyage*) *ménage* to do; *lit* to make; *chaussures* to clean. ~ **la vaisselle** to do the washing-up *ou* the dishes. **(g)** (*Méd*) *diabète etc* to have, suffer from. ~ **de la fièvre** to have *ou* run a temperature; ~ **ses besoins** to go to the toilet. **(h)** (*mesure*) to be. **2 et 2 font 4** 2 and 2 are *ou* make 4; **ça fait 3 mètres de long** it is 3 metres long; **ça fait 3 kg** it weighs 3 kg; **combien fait cette chaise?** how much is this chair? *ou* does this chair cost?; **je vous la fais 100 F** I'll let you have it *ou* I'll give it to you for 100 F. **(i)** (*effet*) *piqûres etc* to give. ~ **du bien/du mal à ...** to do good/harm to ...; ~ **du chagrin à qn** to cause unhappiness to sb, make sb unhappy; ~ **le bonheur de qn** to make sb happy; **qu'est-ce que cela peut bien te** ~**?** what does it matter to you?; **la mort de son père ne lui a rien fait** his father's death didn't affect him; **cela ne vous ferait rien de sortir?** would you mind going out?; **qu'est-ce qu'on t'a donc fait!** whatever have they done to you!; **ça ne fait rien** it doesn't matter. **(j)** (*locutions*) **pour ce qu'on en fait!** for all that we do with it!; **n'en faites rien** do nothing of the sort; **n'avoir que** ~ **de** to have no need of; **ne** ~ **que de protester** to keep on and on protesting, be constantly protesting; **je ne fais que d'arriver** I've only just arrived.
2 *vi* **(a)** (*agir*) to do. ~ **vite** to act quickly, be quick; **il a bien fait** he did the right thing; ~ **de son mieux** to do one's best; **on ferait bien de le prévenir** it would be a good idea to warn him; **je ferais mieux de partir** I'd better go; **faites comme vous voulez** do as you please; **faites comme chez vous** make yourself at home; **il n'y a rien à** ~ it's no use. **(b)** (*dire*) to say. **vraiment? fit-il** really? he said; **il fit un 'ah' de surprise** he gave a surprised 'ah'. **(c)** (*durer*) **ce chapeau (me) fera encore un hiver** this hat will last *ou* do me another winter. **(d)** (*paraître*) to look. **ce vase fait bien sur la table** the vase looks nice on the table; ~ **vieux/jeune** to look old/young (for one's age). **(e)** (*devenir*) to make, be. **cet enfant fera un bon musicien** this child will make a good musician; **il veut** ~ **médecin** he wants to be a doctor.
3 *vb impers*: **il fait jour** it is daylight; **il fait du soleil** the sun is shining, it is sunny; **il fait lourd** it *ou* the weather is close; **cela fait 2 ans que je ne l'ai pas vu** it is 2 years since I last saw him, I haven't seen him for 2 years; **ça fait 2 ans qu'il est parti** he left 2 years ago, it's 2 years since he left; **il fait bon se promener** it is nice to go for a walk; **il ne fait pas bon le contredire** it is better not to

contradict him; **cela fait que nous devons partir** the result is that we must leave.

4 *vb substitut* to do. **il travaille mieux que je ne fais** he works better than I do; **- faites, je vous en prie -** (yes) please do, (yes) by all means.

5 se ~ *vpr* **(a)** *robe, amis* to make o.s. **il se fait sa cuisine** he does his own cooking; **il se fait 4000 F par mois** he earns *ou* makes 4,000 francs a month; **s'en ~** to worry. **(b)** *[fromage, vin]* to mature. (*fig*) **il s'est fait tout seul** he is a self-made man. **(c)** (*devenir*) *prêtre etc* to become. **se ~ vieux** to be getting old; **il se faisait tard** it was getting late; **se ~ beau** to make o.s. beautiful. **(d) se ~ à** to get used to; **il ne peut pas se ~ au climat** he can't get used to the climate. **(e) cela ne se fait pas** it's not done; **une chose qui se fait** a done thing; **ça ne se fera pas** it won't take place. **(f)** (*impers*) **il peut/il pourrait se ~ qu'il pleuve** it may/it might rain; **comment se fait-il qu'il soit absent?** how is it that he is absent? **(g) se ~ +** *infin*: **se ~ vomir** to make o.s. vomit; **il s'est fait remettre le document** he had the document handed over to him; **il s'est fait ouvrir par le voisin** he got the neighbour to let him in.

6 *vb aux + infin*: **j'ai fait démarrer la voiture** I made the car start, I got the car started; **~ traverser la rue à un aveugle** to help a blind man across the road; **~ entrer** *visiteur* to show *ou* ask in; *livreur* to let in; **(se) ~ faire une robe** to have a dress made; **~ faire la vaisselle à qn** to get sb to do the dishes; **il lui a fait ouvrir le coffre-fort** he made him open *ou* forced him to open the safe.

7: ~-part *nm inv* announcement (of a birth *ou* death *etc*); **~-part de mariage** ≃ wedding invitation.

faisable [fəzabl(ə)] *adj* feasible. **est-ce ~ en 2 jours?** can it be done in 2 days?

faisan [fəzɑ̃] *nm* pheasant. ♦ **faisandé, e** *adj goût* high; (*péj*) corrupt.

faisceau, *pl* **~x** [fɛso] *nm* (*fagot*) bundle; (*Élec, Phys*) beam. **~ de preuves** body of proof.

fait[1] [fɛ] *nm* **(a)** (*événement*) event, occurrence; (*donnée, acte*) fact. **~ nouveau** new development; **le ~ de bouger** the fact of moving; **~ d'armes** feat of arms; **~ divers** (short) news item; (*rubrique*) **~s divers** news in brief; **~s et gestes** actions. **(b) au ~** (*à propos*) by the way; **en venir au ~** to get to the point; **être au ~ (de)** to be informed (of); **mettre qn au ~ (d'une affaire)** to inform sb of *ou* acquaint sb with a matter; **de ~** (*de facto*) de facto; (*en fait*) in fact; **il est de ~ que** it is a fact that; **de ce ~** therefore; **du ~ de qch** on account of sth; **en ~** in fact; **en ~ de** (*en guise de*) by way of a; (*en matière de*) as regards, in the way of; **le ~ est là** it's a fact; **être le ~ de** (*être typique de*) to be typical of; (*être causé par*) to be the work of; **par ce ~** by this very fact; **dire son ~ à qn** to talk straight to sb; **prendre ~ et cause pour qn** to side with sb; **comme par un ~ exprès** almost as if on purpose; **mettre qn devant le ~ accompli** to present sb with a fait accompli.

fait[2], **e** [fɛ, fɛt] *adj* **(a) être ~ pour** to be made *ou* meant for; **ceci n'est pas ~ pour lui plaire** this is not likely to please him; **il est ~ pour être médecin** he's cut out to be a doctor. **(b)** (*fini*) **c'en est ~ de notre vie calme** that's the end of our quiet life; **c'est toujours ça de ~** that's one job done. **(c)** (*mûr*) *personne* mature; *fromage* ripe. **(d)** (*locutions*) **comment est-il ~?** what is he like?, what does he look like?; **avoir la jambe bien ~e** to have nice legs; **il est ~ (comme un rat)*** he's cornered!; **c'est bien ~!** it serves them right!

faîte [fɛt] *nm [montagne]* summit; *[arbre]* top. **~ du toit** rooftop; **~ de la gloire** height of glory.

faitout *nm* [fɛtu] stewpot.

fakir [fakiʀ] *nm* (*Rel*) fakir; (*Music-Hall*) wizard.

falaise [falɛz] *nf* cliff.

fallacieux, -euse [falasjø, øz] *adj* fallacious. ♦ **fallacieusement** *adv* fallaciously.

falloir [falwaʀ] (29) **1** *vb impers* **(a)** (*besoin*) **il me le faut à tout prix** I must have it at all costs; **il lui faut qn pour l'aider** he needs sb to help him; **il vous faut tourner à gauche** you have to *ou* need to turn left; (*au magasin*) **qu'est-ce qu'il vous faut?** what are you looking for?; **il n'en faut pas beaucoup pour qu'il se mette à pleurer** it doesn't take much to make him cry; **s'il le faut** if need be. **(b)** (*obligation*) **il va ~ y aller** we'll have to go; **il faut que tu y ailles** you must go; **il faudrait qu'il parte** he ought to *ou* should go; **que faut-il leur dire?** what shall I tell them?; **il ne faut pas être en retard** we mustn't be *ou* we can't afford to be late; **il va ~ qu'il parte** he'll have to go. **(c)** (*intensif*) **il fallait me le dire** you should have told me; **il faut voir ce spectacle** this show is a must, you must see this show; **il ne faudrait pas qu'il essaie!** he'd better not try!; **(il) faut dire qu'il est culotté*** you've got to admit he's got a cheek; **il a fallu qu'elle le perde!** she HAD to go and lose it! **(d)** (*probabilité*) **il faut que tu te sois trompé** you must have made a mistake; **faut-il donc être bête!** some people are so stupid; **faut-il qu'il soit bête!** he must be so *ou* really stupid; **il ne faut pas être intelligent pour dire ça** it's not very clever to say sth like that. **(e)** (*locutions*) **(il) faut le faire!** (*admiratif*) that takes some doing!; **il faut de tout pour faire un monde** it takes all sorts to make a world; **il ne faut jamais remettre au lendemain ce qu'on peut faire le jour même** procrastination is the thief of time; **ce qu'il faut entendre!** the things you hear!

2 s'en ~ *vpr*: **il ne s'en fallait que de 100 F pour qu'il ait la somme** he was only *ou* just 100 francs short of the full amount; **il s'en faut de beaucoup qu'il soit heureux** he is far from happy; **il s'en est fallu d'un cheveu qu'il ne soit pris** he was within a hair's breadth *ou* an ace of being caught; **peu s'en est fallu qu'il pleure** he almost *ou* very nearly wept.

falot[1] [falo] *nm* lantern.

falot[2], **e** [falo, ɔt] *adj personne* colourless; *lumière* wan, pale.

falsifier [falsifje] (7) *vt* to falsify, alter, tamper with.

famélique [famelik] *adj* half-starved.

fameux, -euse [famø, øz] *adj* **(a)** (*: *bon*) *mets, voiture* first-rate; *idée* bright, great*. **pas ~** *mets, roman* not too good, not up to much*; **il n'est pas ~ en maths** he's not too hot at maths*. **(b)** (*: *avant n: intensif*) **c'est un ~ problème** it's a real *ou* it's quite a problem; **c'est une ~euse vaisselle** that's an awful lot of washing-up; **c'est un ~ gaillard** (*bien bâti*) he's a strapping fellow. **(c)** (*: *référence*) **quel est le nom de cette ~euse rue?** what's the name of that (famous) street? **(d)** (*célèbre*) famous (*pour* for). ♦ **fameusement** *adv* remarkably, really.

familial, e, *mpl* **-aux** [familjal, o] **1** *adj* family. **2** *nf* family estate car, station wagon (*US*).

familiariser [familjaʀize] (1) **1** *vt*: **~ qn avec** to familiarize sb with. **2 se ~** *vpr*: **se ~ avec** *lieu, méthode* to familiarize o.s. with; *personne* to get to know, become acquainted with; *bruit, danger* to get used *ou* accustomed to; **être (peu) familiarisé avec** to be (un)familiar with.

familier, -ière [familje, jɛʀ] **1** *adj* **(a)** (*bien connu*) familiar. **ça m'est ~** I'm familiar with it; **cette attitude lui est ~ière** this is a familiar *ou* customary attitude of his; **le mensonge lui était devenu ~** he had become quite used to lying. **(b)** (*amical*) informal, friendly; (*désinvolte*) *personne, surnom* (over)familiar; *attitude* offhand, casual; (*non recherché*) *expression, style* familiar, colloquial. **expression ~ière** colloquialism. **2** *nm [club, théâtre]* regular visitor (*de* to); *[famille]* friend (*de* of). ♦ **familiarité** *nf*

familiarity. (*privautés*) ~s familiarities; ~ **avec** *langue, méthode* familiarity with. ♦ **familièrement** *adv* informally; familiarly; colloquially.
famille [famij] *nf* (*gén*) family. **on a prévenu la** ~ the relatives *ou* the next of kin have been informed; **dîner de** ~ family dinner; **ça tient de** ~ it runs in the family; **passer ses vacances en** ~ to spend one's holidays with the family.
famine [famin] *nf* (*épidémie*) famine. **nous allons à la** ~ we are heading for starvation.
fan* [fan] *nm* (*admirateur*) fan.
fanal, *pl* -aux [fanal, o] *nm* (*gén*) lantern; *[train]* headlight; (*phare*) beacon.
fanatique [fanatik] **1** *adj* fanatical (*de* about). **2** *nmf* (*gén, Sport*) fanatic. ♦ **fanatiquement** *adv* fanatically. ♦ **fanatiser** (1) *vt* to rouse to fanaticism. ♦ **fanatisme** *nm* fanaticism.
fane [fan] *nf [radis etc]* top.
faner [fane] (1) **1** *vi* to make hay. **2** *vt* **(a)** *herbe* to toss. **(b)** *fleur, beauté* to fade. **3 se** ~ *vpr [plante, teint]* to fade; *[peau]* to wither.
fanfare [fɑ̃faʀ] *nf* (*orchestre*) brass band; (*musique*) fanfare. **en** ~ *réveil* clamorous, tumultuous; *partir* noisily, with great commotion; **annoncer en** ~ *réforme etc* to blazon *ou* trumpet forth.
fanfaron, -onne [fɑ̃faʀɔ̃, ɔn] **1** *adj* boastful. **2** *nm,f* braggart. **faire le** ~ to brag. ♦ **fanfaronnade** *nf*: ~**(s)** bragging. ♦ **fanfaronner** (1) *vi* to brag.
fanfreluche [fɑ̃fʀəlyʃ] *nf* trimming.
fange [fɑ̃ʒ] *nf* (*littér*) mire.
fanion [fanjɔ̃] *nm* pennant.
fantaisie [fɑ̃tezi] *nf* **(a)** (*caprice*) whim; (*extravagance*) extravagance. **je me suis payé une petite** ~ I bought myself a little present; **il veut vivre à sa** ~ he wants to live as he pleases; **il lui a pris la** ~ **de faire** he took it into his head to do; **à votre** ~ as it may please you. **(b)** (*imagination*) fancy, imagination. **manquer de** ~ *[vie]* to be monotonous; *[personne]* to be lacking in imagination. **(c) rideaux/boutons** *etc* ~ fancy curtains/buttons *etc.* **(d)** (*œuvre*) (*Littérat*) fantasy; (*Mus*) fantasia. ♦ **fantaisiste 1** *adj* (*faux*) fanciful; (*bizarre*) eccentric; (*farceur*) whimsical. **2** *nmf* (*Théât*) variety artist; (*original*) eccentric; (*péj: fumiste*) phoney*.
fantasme [fɑ̃tasm(ə)] *nm* fantasy.
fantasque [fɑ̃task(ə)] *adj humeur* whimsical; *chose* weird, fantastic.
fantassin [fɑ̃tasɛ̃] *nm* foot soldier, infantryman.
fantastique [fɑ̃tastik] *adj* **(a)** (*étrange*) uncanny, weird, fantastic. **le cinéma** ~ the cinema of the fantastic. **(b)** (*: *excellent, énorme, incroyable*) fantastic*. ♦ **fantastiquement** *adv* fantastically.
fantoche [fɑ̃tɔʃ] *nm, adj* puppet.
fantôme [fɑ̃tom] **1** *nm* (*spectre*) ghost. **2** *adj firme* bogus. **bateau** ~ ghost *ou* phantom ship. ♦ **fantomatique** *adj* ghostly.
faon [fɑ̃] *nm* (*Zool*) fawn.
faramineux, -euse* [faʀaminø, øz] *adj bêtise etc* staggering; *prix* astronomical; *idée* brilliant.
farce [faʀs(ə)] *nf* **(a)** (*tour*) practical joke, hoax. **faire une** ~ **à qn** to play a joke on sb; **magasin de** ~**s-attrapes** joke shop. **(b)** (*Théât*) farce. **grosse** ~ slapstick comedy. **(c)** (*Culin*) stuffing. ♦ **farceur, -euse** *nm,f* (*blagueur*) joker; (*péj: fumiste*) phoney*.
farcir [faʀsiʀ] (2) **1** *vt* (*Culin*) to stuff. **farci de fautes** crammed *ou* packed with mistakes. **2 se** ~ *vpr* (‡) *travail, personne* to get landed with*; *mets* to knock back*. **il faut se le** ~! (*bavard*) he's a bit of a pain in the neck*.
fard [faʀ] *nm* make-up; (†: *poudre*) rouge; *[acteur]* greasepaint. **sans** ~ *parler* openly.
fardeau, *pl* ~**x** [faʀdo] *nm* (*lit*) load; (*fig*) burden. **sous le** ~ **de** under the weight *ou* burden of.
farder [faʀde] (1) **1** *vt acteur* to make up; *visage* to rouge; *vérité* to disguise. **2 se** ~ *vpr* to make o.s. up; to rouge one's face.
farfelu, e* [faʀfəly] **1** *adj* cranky, scatty*. **2** *nm,f* eccentric.
farfouiller* [faʀfuje] (1) *vi* to rummage about (*dans* in).
farine [faʀin] *nf [blé]* flour. ~ **d'avoine** oatmeal. ♦ **fariner** (1) *vt* to flour. ♦ **farineux, -euse 1** *adj aspect, goût* floury, chalky. **2** *nm*: **(aliment)** ~ starchy food.
farouche [faʀuʃ] *adj* **(a)** (*timide*) shy, timid; (*peu sociable*) unsociable. **(b)** (*hostile*) fierce. **ennemi** ~ bitter enemy. **(c)** (*opiniâtre*) *volonté, résistance* unshakeable; *énergie* irrepressible. **(d)** (*indompté*) savage, wild. ♦ **farouchement** *adv* fiercely.
fart [faʀ(t)] *nm* (ski) wax. ♦ **farter** (1) *vt* to wax.
fascicule [fasikyl] *nm [livre]* instalment.
fasciner [fasine] (1) *vt* (*gén*) to fascinate; *[charme]* to bewitch. ♦ **fascination** *nf* fascination (*sur* on, over).
fascisme [faʃism(ə)] *nm* fascism. ♦ **fasciste** *adj, nmf* fascist.
faste[1] [fast(ə)] *nm* splendour.
faste[2] [fast(ə)] *adj* (*littér*) lucky.
fastidieux, -euse [fastidjø, øz] *adj* tedious, boring. ♦ **fastidieusement** *adv* tediously, boringly.
fastueux, -euse [fastɥø, øz] *adj décor* sumptuous; *repas, réception* lavish. ♦ **fastueusement** *adv* sumptuously; lavishly.
fatal, e, *mpl* ~**s** [fatal] *adj accident* fatal; *coup* fatal, deadly; *ton, instant* fateful. **erreur** ~**e!** grievous *ou* fatal error!; **être** ~ **à qn** to be *ou* prove fatal to *ou* for sb; **c'était** ~! it was inevitable, it was bound to happen. ♦ **fatalement** *adv* inevitably. ♦ **fatalisme** *nm* fatalism. ♦ **fataliste 1** *adj* fatalistic. **2** *nmf* fatalist. ♦ **fatalité** *nf* (*destin*) fate; (*coïncidence*) fateful coincidence; (*inévitabilité*) inevitability.
fatidique [fatidik] *adj* fateful.
fatigant, e [fatigɑ̃, ɑ̃t] *adj* (*épuisant*) tiring; (*agaçant*) tiresome, tedious. **c'est** ~ **pour le cœur** it's a strain on the heart; **tu es vraiment** ~ you really are tiresome *ou* a nuisance.
fatigue [fatig] *nf* (*gén*) tiredness; (*Méd, Tech*) fatigue. **tomber de** ~ to be dead tired; **il a voulu nous épargner cette** ~ he wanted to spare us the strain; **les** ~**s du voyage** the strain *ou* the tiring effects of the journey.
fatiguer [fatige] (1) **1** *vt* **(a)** *personne* to tire; *moteur* to strain; *poutre* to put a strain on; *terre* to exhaust, impoverish. *[patron]* ~ **qn/qch** to overwork sb/sth; **ça vous fatigue** it tires *ou* wears you out; **ça fatigue le cœur** it puts a strain on the heart. **(b)** (*fig: agacer*) to annoy; (*lasser*) to wear out. **2** *vi [moteur]* to labour, strain; *[poutre]* to become strained; *[personne]* to tire. **3 se** ~ *vpr* to get tired; (*se surmener*) to overwork o.s. **se** ~ **à faire qch** to tire o.s. out doing sth; **se** ~ **les yeux** to strain one's eyes; (*se lasser de*) **se** ~ **de qch/de faire** to get tired of sth/of doing; **pas la peine de te** ~* there's no need to wear yourself out *ou* no point wearing yourself out. ♦ **fatigué, e** *adj personne, voix, traits* tired, weary; *yeux, cœur* strained; *estomac* upset; *poutre, joint, habit* worn. ~ **de** tired of.
fatras [fatʀa] *nm* jumble.
fatuité [fatɥite] *nf* self-complacency.
faubourg [fobuʀ] *nm* (inner) suburb. ♦ **faubourien, -ienne** *adj accent* working-class.
fauchaison [foʃɛzɔ̃] *nf* (*époque, action*) mowing, reaping.
faucher [foʃe] (1) *vt* **(a)** *blé* to reap; *champs* to mow; *herbe* to mow, cut; (*avec une faux*) to scythe. **(b)** (*fig*) *[véhicule, tir]* to mow down. **la mort l'a fauché** death cut him down; **avoir une jambe fauchée par le train** to have a leg cut off by

the train. **(c)** (*: *voler*) to pinch*, swipe*. ♦ **fauche*** *nf* (*vol*) pinching*, swiping*. ♦ **fauché, e*** *adj* (*sans argent*) stony-broke*. ♦ **faucheur, -euse** *nm,f* mower, reaper.

faucille [fosij] *nf* sickle.

faucon [fokɔ̃] *nm* falcon, hawk.

faufiler (se) [fofile] (1) *vpr*: **se ~ parmi la foule** to worm *ou* inch one's way through the crowd; **se ~ entre les voitures** to thread one's way through the traffic; **se ~ à l'intérieur/au dehors** to slip *ou* sneak in/out.

faune[1] [fon] *nm* (*Myth*) faun.

faune[2] [fon] *nf* (*Zool*) wildlife; (*péj*) set.

faussaire [fosɛʀ] *nmf* forger.

faussement [fosmɑ̃] *adv accuser* wrongly; *croire* falsely. **~ modeste** falsely modest; **d'un ton ~ indifférent** in a tone of feigned indifference.

fausser [fose] (1) *vt calcul, réalité, sens* to distort; *esprit* to disturb; *clef* to bend; *serrure* to break; *charnière* to buckle; *hélice* to warp. **~ compagnie à qn** to give sb the slip.

fausseté [foste] *nf* **(a)** *[accusation, dogme]* falseness, falsity; *[caractère, personne]* duplicity. **(b)** (†: *mensonge*) falsehood.

faute [fot] *nf* (*erreur*) mistake, error; (*mauvaise action*) misdeed; (*Jur*) offence; (*péché*) sin; (*Ftbl etc*) offence; (*Tennis*) fault; (*responsabilité*) fault. **~ de frappe** typing error; **~ d'impression** misprint; **~ d'inattention** careless mistake; **~ d'orthographe** spelling mistake; **faire une ~** to make a mistake (*de* in); **c'est de la ~ de Richard** it's Richard's fault, it's because of Richard; **à qui la ~?** whose fault is it?, who's to blame?; **être/se sentir en ~** to be/feel at fault *ou* in the wrong; **prendre qn en ~** to catch sb out; **il ne se fait pas ~ de faire** he doesn't fail to do; **~ d'argent** for want of money; **~ de quoi** failing which.

fauteuil [fotœj] *nm* (*gén*) armchair, easy chair; *[président]* chair; *[théâtre, académicien]* seat. (*fig*) **il est arrivé dans un ~*** he romped home; **~ à bascule** rocking chair; **~ roulant** wheelchair.

fauteur [fotœʀ] *nm*: **~ de troubles** troublemaker; **~ de guerre** warmonger.

fautif, -ive [fotif, iv] **1** *adj* **(a)** *élève* naughty, guilty. **être ~** to be at fault *ou* in the wrong. **(b)** *liste, calcul* faulty. **2** *nm,f*: **c'est moi le ~** I'm the one to blame *ou* the culprit. ♦ **fautivement** *adv* by mistake.

fauve [fov] **1** *adj couleur* tawny, fawn. **2** *nm* big cat.

faux[1] [fo] *nf* scythe.

faux[2], **fausse** [fo, fos] **1** *adj* **(a)** *argent, documents* forged, fake; *marbre* imitation; *tableau* fake; (*fig*) *savant* bogus; *dent, nez* false. **~ papiers** forged identity papers. **(b)** *bonhomie, colère* feigned; *attitude, promesse* false; *situation* awkward. **fausse dévotion** false piety. **(c)** (*inexact*) (*gén*) wrong; *affirmation* untrue; *balance, raisonnement* inaccurate, faulty; *piano, voix* out of tune; *rumeur, soupçons* false. **c'est ~** that's wrong; **faire fausse route** (*lit*) to go the wrong way; (*fig*) to be on the wrong track; **faire un ~ pas** (*lit*) to stumble; (*fig*) to make a foolish mistake; **avoir de fausses craintes** to have groundless fears.

2 *nm* **(a)** (*mensonge, Philos*) **le ~** falsehood. **(b)** (*contrefaçon*) forgery; (*tableau, document*) fake, forgery. **faire un ~** to commit a forgery.

3 *adv chanter* out of tune. **sonner ~** *[rire]* to have a false ring.

4: **fausse alerte** false alarm; **~ ami** (*traître*) false friend; (*Ling*) faux ami, deceptive cognate; **faire ~ bond à qn** to let sb down; **fausse clef** skeleton key; **~ col** detachable collar; **fausses côtes** floating ribs; **fausse couche** miscarriage; (*lit, fig*) **~ départ** false start; **fausse fenêtre** blind window; **~-filet** sirloin; **~ frais** (*pl*) incidental expenses; **~-fuyant** evasion, equivocation; **user de ~-fuyants** to equivocate; **~ jeton*** devious character; **fausse joie** vain joy; **~ jour** (*lit*) deceptive light; (*fig*) **sous un ~ jour** in a false light; **fausse manœuvre** wrong move; **~-monnayeur** forger; **~ mouvement** awkward movement; **~ nom** false name; **fausse note** (*Mus*) wrong note; (*fig*) sour note; (*lit, fig*) **fausse piste** wrong track; **~ pli** crease; **fausse porte** false door; **~ problème** non-problem; **~ semblant** sham, pretence; **~ sens** mistranslation; **~ témoignage** false evidence; (*délit*) perjury; **~ témoin** lying witness.

faveur [favœʀ] *nf* **(a)** favour. **faites-moi la ~ de ...** would you be so kind as to ...; **gagner/perdre la ~ du public** to win/lose public favour; **être en ~** to be in favour (*auprès de qn* with sb); **de ~** *billet* complimentary; *régime* preferential; **en ~ de** (*à cause de*) on account of; (*au profit de*) in favour of; (*but charitable*) in aid of; **être en ~ de qch** to be in favour of sth; **à la ~ de** thanks to; **à la ~ de la nuit** under cover of darkness. **(b)** (*ruban*) favour. ♦ **favorable** *adj* favourable. **sous un jour ~** in a favourable light; **prêter une oreille ~ à** to lend a sympathetic ear to; **d'un œil ~** with a favourable eye; **être ~ à** to be favourable to. ♦ **favorablement** *adv* favourably. ♦ **favori, -ite** *adj, nm,f* favourite. ♦ **favoris** *nmpl* side whiskers. ♦ **favoriser** (1) *vt* (*gén*) to favour. ♦ **favoritisme** *nm* favouritism.

fébrile [febʀil] *adj* (*lit, fig*) feverish. ♦ **fébrilement** *adv* feverishly. ♦ **fébrilité** *nf* feverishness.

fécond, e [fekɔ̃, ɔ̃d] *adj femelle* (*non stérile*) fertile; (*prolifique*) prolific; *sujet, idée, terre* fruitful; *esprit* fertile. **~ en** abounding in. ♦ **féconder** (1) *vt femme* to make pregnant; *animal, fleur* to fertilize. ♦ **fécondation** *nf* impregnation; fertilization. ♦ **fécondité** *nf* fertility, fruitfulness.

fécule [fekyl] *nf* starch. ♦ **féculent, e** *adj* starchy. **~s** starchy foods.

fédéral, e, *mpl* **-aux** [federal, o] *adj* federal. ♦ **fédéraliser** (1) *vt* to federalize. ♦ **fédéralisme** *nm* federalism. ♦ **fédéraliste** *adj, nmf* federalist.

fédération [fedeʀasjɔ̃] *nf* federation.

fée [fe] *nf* fairy.

féerie [fe(e)ʀi] *nf* (*Ciné, Théât*) extravaganza; (*vision*) enchantment. ♦ **féerique** *adj* magical.

feindre [fɛ̃dʀ(ə)] (52) **1** *vt enthousiasme, ignorance* to feign. **~ d'être/de faire** to pretend to be/do. **2** *vi* to dissemble. ♦ **feint, e**[1] *adj* feigned.

feinter [fɛ̃te] (1) **1** *vt* (*Ftbl*) to dummy; (*Boxe*) to feint at; (*: *rouler*) to trick, take in. **2** *vi* (*Escrime*) to feint. ♦ **feinte**[2] *nf* (*manœuvre*) dummy move; (*Boxe*) feint; (*ruse*) ruse. **parler sans ~** to speak without dissimulation.

fêler *vt*, **se ~** *vpr* [fele] (1) to crack.

félicité [felisite] *nf* (*Rel*) bliss.

féliciter [felisite] (1) **1** *vt* to congratulate (*qn de ou sur qch* sb on sth). **2 se ~** *vpr* to congratulate o.s. (*de* on). **je n'y suis pas allé et je m'en félicite** I didn't go and I'm glad *ou* very pleased I didn't. ♦ **félicitations** *nfpl* congratulations (*pour* on).

félin, e [felɛ̃, in] **1** *adj race* feline; *allure* feline, catlike. **2** *nm* feline.

félon, -onne [felɔ̃, ɔn] **1** *adj* perfidious. **2** *nm* traitor. **3** *nf* traitress. ♦ **félonie** *nf* perfidy.

fêlure [felyʀ] *nf* (*lit, fig*) crack.

femelle [fəmɛl] **1** *adj* (*gén*) female; *souris etc* she-; *oiseau* hen-; *baleine, éléphant* cow-. **2** *nf* (*Zool, péj*) female.

féminin, e [feminɛ̃, in] **1** *adj* (*gén, Ling*) feminine; *sexe* female; *mode, équipe* women's. **2** *nm* (*Ling*) feminine. **au ~** in the feminine. ♦ **féminisme** *nm* feminism. ♦ **féministe** *adj, nmf* feminist. ♦ **féminité** *nf* femininity.

femme [fam] **1** *nf* (*individu*) woman; (*épouse*) wife. **la ~** woman; **~ médecin/professeur** (lady *ou* woman) doctor/teacher. **2** *adj inv*: **être ~** (*nubile*) to have reached womanhood; **être très ~** to be very womanly. **3: ~ d'affaires** business-woman; **~ auteur** authoress; **~ de chambre** chambermaid; **~ d'intérieur** (conscientious) housewife; **~ de lettres** woman of letters; **~ de ménage** domestic help, cleaning lady; **~ du monde** society woman.

fémur [femyʀ] *nm* thighbone, femur.

fenaison [fənɛzɔ̃] *nf* haymaking.

fendiller *vt*, **se ~** *vpr* [fɑ̃dije] (1) *vernis* to craze; *bois* to spring; *peau* to chap.

fendre [fɑ̃dʀ(ə)] (41) **1** *vt* (*gén*) to split; *rochers* to cleave; *plâtre* to crack. **~ du bois** to chop wood; **il lui fendit le crâne** he split his skull open; **~ la foule** to cut *ou* push one's way through the crowd; **récit qui fend le cœur** story which breaks one's heart, heartbreaking story. **2 se ~** *vpr* **(a)** (*se fissurer*) to crack. **se ~ la lèvre** to cut one's lip; **se ~ la pipe**‡ to laugh one's head off. **(b)** (*Escrime*) to lunge. **(c)** (‡) **se ~ de** *somme* to shell out*; *cadeau* to lash out on*. ♦ **fendu, e** *adj manche* slashed; *veste* with a vent; *jupe* slit. **la bouche ~e jusqu'aux oreilles** with a grin stretching from ear to ear.

fenêtre [f(ə)nɛtʀ(ə)] *nf* (*gén*) window. (*train*) **coin ~** window seat; **~ à guillotine** sash window; **~ à battants** casement window.

fente [fɑ̃t] *nf* **(a)** (*fissure*) crack; *[rocher]* cleft. **(b)** *[volet]* slit; *[boîte à lettres]* slot; *[veston]* vent.

féodal, e, *mpl* **-aux** [feɔdal, o] **1** *adj* feudal. **2** *nm* feudal lord. ♦ **féodalité** *nf* feudalism.

fer [fɛʀ] **1** *nm* **(a)** (*métal*) iron. **volonté de ~** iron will. **(b)** (*poutre*) (iron) girder; (*épée*) sword; *[cheval]* shoe; *[soulier]* steel tip; *[flèche, lance]* head, point; *[rabot]* blade. **(c) ~s** (†: *chaînes*) chains, irons; (*Méd* †) forceps. **2: ~-blanc** tin-plate; **~ forgé** wrought iron; **~ à friser** curling tongs; (*fig*) **~ de lance** spearhead; **~ à repasser** iron; **~ à souder** soldering iron.

férié, e [feʀje] *adj*: **jour ~** public holiday; **le lundi est ~** the Monday is a holiday.

ferme[1] [fɛʀm(ə)] **1** *adj* (*gén*) firm; *viande* tough; *écriture* steady; *trait* confident; *résolution, acheteur* definite. **~ sur ses jambes** steady on one's legs; **d'un pas ~** with a firm step; **rester ~ dans l'adversité** to remain steadfast in adversity; **prix ~s et définitifs** firm prices. **2** *adv travailler* hard; *discuter* vigorously; (*Comm*) *acheter* definitely.

ferme[2] [fɛʀm(ə)] *nf* (*domaine*) farm; (*habitation*) farmhouse.

fermé, e [fɛʀme] *adj* **(a)** *porte etc* shut, closed; (*à clef*) locked; *espace* closed-in; *angle* narrow; *ensemble* closed; *robinet* off. **(b)** *milieu, club* exclusive. **cette carrière lui est ~e** this career is closed to him. **(c)** *visage* impassive; *personne* uncommunicative. **(d) être ~ à** *sentiment* to be impervious to; *art* to have no feeling for.

fermement [fɛʀməmɑ̃] *adv* (*lit, fig*) firmly.

ferment [fɛʀmɑ̃] *nm* (*lit, fig*) ferment. ♦ **fermentation** *nf* fermentation. **en ~** (*lit*) fermenting; (*fig*) in a ferment. ♦ **fermenter** (1) *vi* to ferment.

fermer [fɛʀme] (1) **1** *vt* **(a)** (*lit*) to close, shut; *lettre, poing,* (*fig*) *compte, liste* to close; *manteau* to do up, fasten; *gaz* to turn *ou* switch off; *robinet* to turn off. **~ à clef** to lock; **~ au verrou** to bolt; **~ la porte au nez de qn** to shut *ou* slam the door in sb's face; (*fig*) **toutes les portes lui sont fermées** all doors are closed to him; **ferme-la!**‡ shut *ou* belt up!‡; **je n'ai pas fermé l'œil de la nuit** I didn't sleep a wink all night; **~ les yeux sur** *misère* to close one's eyes to; *abus* to turn a blind eye to. **(b)** *chemin* to block, bar; *accès* to shut off; *frontière, col* to close; *aéroport* to close *ou* shut down. **champ fermé par une haie** field enclosed by a hedge; **~ la marche** to bring up the rear. **(c)** (*cesser d'exploiter*) *magasin, école* to close *ou* shut down. **~ boutique** to close down. **2** *vi* (*gén*) to close, shut; *[vêtement]* to do up, fasten. **ça ferme mal** it doesn't close *ou* shut properly; **ça ferme à 7 heures** closing time is 7 o'clock. **3 se ~** *vpr* to close, shut; *[fleur, blessure]* to close up; *[vêtement]* to do up, fasten. **se ~ à la pitié** to close one's heart to pity.

fermeté [fɛʀməte] *nf* (*V* **ferme**[1]) firmness; steadiness; confidence; steadfastness.

fermette [fɛʀmɛt] *nf* country cottage.

fermeture [fɛʀmətyʀ] *nf* **(a)** (*action*) (*gén*) closing; shutting; (*à clef*) locking; (*au verrou*) bolting; (*Comm: définitive*) closing down. **~ annuelle** annual closure; **à (l'heure de) la ~** at closing time. **(b)** (*mécanisme*) *[coffre-fort]* catch; *[vêtement]* fastener. **~ éclair** ® zip (fastener), zipper.

fermier, -ière [fɛʀmje, jɛʀ] **1** *adj* farm. **2** *nm* (*cultivateur*) farmer. **3** *nf* farmer's wife; (*indépendante*) (woman) farmer.

fermoir [fɛʀmwaʀ] *nm [collier]* clasp.

féroce [feʀɔs] *adj* (*lit*) ferocious; *envie, joie* savage; *appétit* ravenous. ♦ **férocement** *adv* ferociously; savagely. ♦ **férocité** *nf* ferocity; savagery.

ferraille [fɛʀɑj] *nf* (*déchets*) scrap iron; (*: *monnaie*) small change. **bruit de ~** clanking noise; **mettre à la ~** to scrap. ♦ **ferrailleur** *nm* scrap merchant.

ferrer [fɛʀe] (1) *vt* **(a)** *cheval* to shoe; *soulier* to nail. **(b)** *poisson* to strike. ♦ **ferré, e** *adj* **(a)** *canne* steel-tipped; *soulier* hobnailed; *cheval* shod; *roue* steel-rimmed. **(b)** (*: *calé*) **être ~ sur un sujet** to be well up* in a subject.

ferreux [fɛʀø] *adj m* ferrous.

ferronnerie [fɛʀɔnʀi] *nf* (*atelier*) ironworks; (*métier*) ironwork; (*objets*) ironware. **grille en ~** wrought iron gate. ♦ **ferronnier** *nm* (*artisan*) craftsman in wrought iron; (*commerçant*) ironware merchant.

ferroviaire [fɛʀɔvjɛʀ] *adj* railway, railroad (*US*), rail.

ferry-boat, *pl* **~-~s** [fɛʀibot] *nm [voitures]* (car) ferry; *[trains]* (train) ferry.

fertile [fɛʀtil] *adj* (*gén*) fertile, fruitful. **journée ~ en événements** eventful day. ♦ **fertilisation** *nf* fertilization. ♦ **fertiliser** (1) *vt* to fertilize. ♦ **fertilité** *nf* (*lit, fig*) fertility.

fervent, e [fɛʀvɑ̃, ɑ̃t] **1** *adj* fervent. **2** *nm,f* devotee. **~ de musique** music lover. ♦ **ferveur** *nf* fervour.

fesse [fɛs] *nf* (*Anat*) buttock. **les ~s** the buttocks, the bottom, the backside*. ♦ **fessée** *nf* spanking. ♦ **fesser** (1) *vt* to spank.

festin [fɛstɛ̃] *nm* feast.

festival, *pl* **~s** [fɛstival] *nm* festival.

festivités [fɛstivite] *nfpl* (*gén*) festivities.

festoyer [fɛstwaje] (8) *vi* to feast.

fêtard, e* [fɛtaʀ, aʀd(ə)] *nm,f* (*péj*) roisterer.

fête [fɛt] **1** *nf* **(a)** (*religieuse*) feast; (*civile*) holiday. **Noël est la ~ des enfants** Christmas is the children's festival. **(b)** (*prénom*) feast *ou* name day. **la ~ de la Saint-Jean** Saint John's day; **souhaiter sa ~ à qn** to wish sb a happy feast day. **(c)** (*congé*) holiday. **3 jours de ~** 3 days off, 3 days' holiday; **les ~s (de fin d'année)** the (Christmas and New Year) holidays. **(d)** (*foire*) fair; (*kermesse*) fête, fair; (*exposition*) festival, show. **~ de la bière/de la moisson** beer/harvest festival; **la ~ de la ville** the town festival; **la foule en ~** the festive crowd; **air de ~** festive air. **(e)** (*réception*) party. **les ~s** the celebrations (*en l'honneur de* in honour of). **(f)** (*locutions*) **être à la ~** to have a great time; **je n'étais pas à la ~** it was no picnic for me*; **être de la ~** to be one of the party; **faire sa ~ à qn**‡ to bash sb up‡; **faire la ~*** to live it up*; **faire ~ à qn** to give sb a warm reception; [chien] to fawn on sb; **elle se faisait une ~ d'y aller** she was really looking forward to going.

2: ~ **de charité** charity fair; ~ **de famille** family celebration; ~ **foraine** fun fair; ~ **légale** public holiday; **la** ~ **des Mères** Mother's Day; ~ **nationale** national holiday; ~ **de village** village fête. ♦ **fêter** (1) *vt anniversaire* to celebrate; *personne* to have a celebration for.

fétiche [fetiʃ] *nm* (*lit*) fetish; (*mascotte*) mascot. ♦ **fétichisme** *nm* fetishism. ♦ **fétichiste** *adj, nmf* fetishist.

fétide [fetid] *adj* fetid.

fétu [fety] *nm*: ~ **(de paille)** wisp of straw.

feu[1], *pl* ~**x** [fø] **1** *nm* **(a)** (*source de chaleur*) fire. **faire du** ~ to make a fire; (*cigarette*) **avez-vous du** ~**?** do you have a light?; **prendre** ~ to catch fire; **mettre le** ~ **à qch** to set fire to sth; **en** ~ on fire; **il y a le** ~ there's a fire; (*fig*) **il n'y a pas le** ~**!*** there's no panic!*; (*fig*) **j'ai la gorge en** ~ my throat is burning. **(b)** (*lumineux*) light. **le** ~ **était (au) rouge** the lights were at red; **être sous le** ~ **des projecteurs** (*lit*) to be in the glare of the spotlights; (*fig*) to be in the limelight; **mettre pleins** ~**x sur** to put the spotlight on; **les** ~**x de la rampe** the footlights. **(c)** (*Culin*) (*brûleur*) ring. **mettre qch/être sur le** ~ to put sth/be on the stove; **plat qui va au** ~ ovenproof *ou* fireproof dish; **faire cuire à** ~ **vif** to cook over a brisk heat; **faire cuire à petit** ~ to cook gently. **(d)** (*Mil*) (*combat*) action; (*tir*) fire. **faire** ~ to fire; (*lit, fig*) ~ **roulant** running fire; **des** ~**x croisés** crossfire. **(e)** (*ardeur*) fire. **dans le** ~ **de la discussion** in the heat of the discussion; **tempérament de** ~ fiery temperament. **(f)** [*diamant*] ~**x** fire; **jeter mille** ~**x** to flash *ou* sparkle brilliantly. **(g) avoir le** ~ **sacré** to be dedicated; **mettre le** ~ **aux poudres** to touch off a crisis; **mettre une ville à** ~ **et à sang** to put a town to fire and the sword; **mettre à** ~ **une fusée** to fire off a rocket; **au moment de la mise à** ~ at the moment of blast-off.

2 *adj inv*: **rouge** ~ flame red.

3: ~ **d'artifice** firework; ~ **de Bengale** Bengal light; ~ **follet** will-o'-the-wisp; ~ **de joie** bonfire; (*fig*) ~ **de paille** flash in the pan; ~ **de position** sidelight; ~ **rouge** set of traffic lights; (*lit, fig*) ~ **vert** green light.

feu[2] [fø] *adj*: ~ **ma tante, ma** ~**e tante** my late aunt.

feuille [fœj] **1** *nf* [*plante*] leaf; [*papier, acier*] sheet; (*bulletin*) slip; (*formulaire*) form; (*journal*) paper. **2:** ~ **de chou** (*péj: journal*) rag; ~ **d'impôt** tax form; ~ **de paye** pay slip; ~ **de présence** attendance sheet; ~ **de route** travel warrant; ~ **de température** temperature chart; ~ **volante** loose sheet. ♦ **feuillage** *nm*: ~**(s)** foliage. ♦ **feuillet** *nm* leaf, page.

feuilleter [fœjte] (4) *vt* **(a)** *livre* to leaf through. **(b)** (*Culin*) **pâte feuilletée** puff pastry. ♦ **feuilleté** *nm* pastry.

feuilleton [fœjtɔ̃] *nm* (*à suivre*) serial; (*histoire complète*) series (*sg*).

feuillu, e [fœjy] **1** *adj* leafy. **2** *nm* broad-leaved tree.

feutre [føtʀ(ə)] *nm* (*Tex*) felt; (*chapeau*) felt hat; (*stylo*) felt(-tip) pen. ♦ **feutré, e** *adj étoffe* felt-like; *atmosphère, bruit* muffled.

fève [fɛv] *nf* (*Bot*) broad bean; [*gâteau*] charm.

février [fevʀije] *nm* February; *V* **septembre.**

fi [fi] *excl* (*hum*) pooh! **faire** ~ **de** to snap one's fingers at.

fiable [fjabl(ə)] *adj* reliable. ♦ **fiabilité** *nf* reliability.

fiacre [fjakʀ(ə)] *nm* hackney cab.

fiancer [fjɑ̃se] (3) **1** *vt* to betroth (*avec, à* to). **2 se** ~ *vpr* to become engaged (*avec, à* to). ♦ **fiançailles** *nfpl* engagement. ♦ **fiancé, e 1** *adj* engaged. **2** *nm* fiancé. (*couple*) **les** ~**s** the engaged couple. **3** *nf* fiancée.

fiasco [fjasko] *nm* fiasco. **faire** ~ to be a fiasco.

fibre [fibʀ(ə)] *nf* **(a)** (*lit: gén*) fibre. ~ **de verre** glass fibre; **dans le sens des** ~**s** with the grain. **(b)** (*fig: âme*) **elle a la** ~ **maternelle** she has a strong maternal streak in her. ♦ **fibreux, -euse** *adj texture* fibrous; *viande* stringy.

ficelle [fisɛl] *nf* (*matière*) string; (*morceau*) piece of string; (*pain*) stick of French bread. **tirer les** ~**s** to pull the strings; **connaître les** ~**s du métier** to know the tricks of the trade. ♦ **ficeler** (4) *vt* (*: *habiller*) to rig out*.

fiche [fiʃ] *nf* **(a)** (*carte*) index card; (*feuille*) sheet, slip; (*formulaire*) form. ~ **perforée** perforated card; ~ **de paye** pay slip; **mettre en** ~ to index. **(b)** (*cheville*) pin; (*Élec*) (*broche*) pin; (*prise*) plug.

ficher[1] [fiʃe] (1) *vt* **(a)** *renseignements* to file; *suspects* to put on file. **(b)** ~ **qch en terre** to drive sth into the ground; **se** ~ **une épine dans le doigt** to get a thorn stuck in one's finger.

ficher[2]* [fiʃe] (1) **1** *vt* **(a)** (*faire*) to do. **qu'est-ce qu'il fiche?** what on earth is he doing?; **je n'en ai rien à fiche** I couldn't care less (*de* about). **(b)** (*donner*) to give. **ce truc me fiche la migraine** this thing gives me a headache; **fiche-moi la paix!** leave me in peace!; **ça va nous** ~ **la poisse** that'll bring us bad luck; **je vous fiche mon billet que ...** I bet you my bottom dollar that* ... . **(c)** (*mettre*) to put. **fiche-le dans le tiroir** stick it in the drawer*; ~ **qn à la porte** to chuck sb out*; ~ **qch en l'air** (*gâcher*) to mess sth up*; (*jeter*) to chuck sth up*; ~ **le camp** to clear off*. **2 se** ~ *vpr* **(a)** (*se mettre*) **tu vas te** ~ **ce truc dans l'œil** you're going to stick that thing in your eye; **se** ~ **qch dans le crâne** to get sth into one's head; **se** ~ **par terre** to fall flat on one's face. **(b)** (*se gausser*) **se** ~ **de qn** to pull sb's leg; **se** ~ **de qch** to make fun of sth; (*être indifférent*) **il s'en fiche** he couldn't care less about it; **ce garagiste se fiche du monde!** that garage man has got a darned nerve!*; **là, ils ne se sont vraiment pas fichus de nous** they really did us proud!; **va te faire fiche!**‡ get lost!*, take a running jump!‡

fichier [fiʃje] *nm* file.

fichu[1] [fiʃy] *nm* (head)scarf.

fichu[2], e* [fiʃy] *adj* **(a)** (*avant n*) *temps, métier* wretched, rotten*, lousy*. **il y a une** ~**e différence** there's one heck of a *ou* a heck of a difference*. **(b)** (*après n: perdu*) *malade, vêtement* done for. **le pique-nique est** ~ the picnic has had it*. **(c)** (*habillé*) rigged out*. **(d)** (*conçu*) **ce livre est bien/mal** ~ this is a clever/hopeless book; **comment c'est** ~ **ce truc?** how does this thing work? **(e)** [*malade*] **être mal** ~ to feel rotten* *ou* out of sorts. **(f)** (*capable*) **il est** ~ **d'y aller** he's quite likely *ou* liable to go; **il n'est (même) pas** ~ **de réparer ça** he can't even mend the darned thing*.

fictif, -ive [fiktif, iv] *adj* (*imaginaire*) imaginary; (*faux*) fictitious. ♦ **fiction** *nf* (*imagination*) fiction; (*fait*) invention. ♦ **fictivement** *adv* in fiction.

fidèle [fidɛl] **1** *adj* (*gén*) faithful (à to); *lecteur, client* regular; *récit, appareil* accurate. **rester** ~ **à une promesse** to remain faithful *ou* true to a promise; ~ **serviteur** trusty *ou* loyal servant; ~ **à lui-même** *ou* **à son habitude** true to form, true to character. **2** *nmf* (*Rel*) believer; (*client*) regular customer; (*lecteur*) regular reader; [*doctrine*] follower. **les** ~**s** (*croyants*) the faithful; (*assemblée*) the congregation. ♦ **fidèlement** *adv* faithfully, loyally; regularly; accurately. ♦ **fidélité** *nf* faithfulness; loyalty; accuracy; (*à un produit, sa femme*) fidelity.

fief [fjɛf] *nm* (*Hist*) fief; [*firme*] preserve; [*parti*] stronghold; (*hum: domaine*) kingdom.

fiel [fjɛl] *nm* (*lit, fig*) gall.

fier[1]**, fière** [fjɛʀ] *adj* **(a)** proud. ~ **comme Artaban** as proud as a peacock; **faire le** ~ (*méprisant*) to be aloof; (*brave*) to be full of o.s.; **c'est qn de pas** ~* he's not stuck-up*; **avoir fière allure** to cut a fine figure; **il n'y a pas de quoi être** ~ there's nothing to be proud of *ou* to boast about. **(b)** (*avant n*) *imbécile* first-class, prize; *canaille* downright; *toupet* incredible. **je te dois une fière chandelle** I'm terribly indebted to you. ♦ **fièrement** *adv* proudly. ♦ **fierté** *nf* (*gén*) pride. **tirer** ~ **de** to get a sense of pride from.

fier[2] **(se)** [fje] (7) *vpr*: **se** ~ **à** (*gén*) to trust; *appareil, mémoire* to rely on; **ne vous fiez pas aux apparences** don't go by *ou* trust appearances.

fièvre [fjɛvʀ(ə)] *nf* **(a)** (*température*) fever, temperature. **avoir beaucoup de** ~ to have *ou* run a high temperature; **avoir 39 de** ~ to have a temperature of 104(°F) *ou* 39(°C); **une** ~ **de cheval** a raging fever. **(b)** (*maladie*) fever. ~ **jaune** yellow fever; ~ **aphteuse** foot-and-mouth disease. **(c)** (*fig: agitation*) fever, excitement. **avec** ~ excitedly; **la** ~ **des élections** election fever; **pris d'une** ~ **d'écrire** seized with a feverish urge to write. ♦ **fiévreusement** *adv* feverishly, excitedly. ♦ **fiévreux, -euse** *adj* feverish.

fifre [fifʀ(ə)] *nm* fife; (*joueur*) fife player.

figer *vti*, **se** ~ *vpr* [fiʒe] (3) *huile* to congeal; *sang* to clot, coagulate; *attitude* to freeze. **histoire à vous** ~ **le sang** bloodcurdling story. ♦ **figé, e** *adj style, manières* stiff; *mœurs* rigid; *sourire* fixed. **expression** ~**e** set expression; ~ **par la peur** terror-stricken; ~ **par la mort** rigid in death.

fignoler* [fiɲɔle] (1) *vt* to put the finishing touches to. **du travail fignolé** a really neat job*.

figue [fig] *nf* (*Bot*) fig. ~ **de Barbarie** prickly pear. ♦ **figuier** *nm* fig tree. ~ **de Barbarie** prickly pear.

figurant, e [figyʀɑ̃, ɑ̃t] *nm,f* (*Ciné*) extra; (*Théât*) walker-on; (*fig*) (*pantin*) puppet; (*complice*) stooge.

figuratif, -ive [figyʀatif, iv] *adj* (*Art*) representational.

figuration [figyʀɑsjɔ̃] *nf*: **faire de la** ~ (*Théât*) to do walk-on parts; (*Ciné*) to work as an extra.

figure [figyʀ] *nf* (*visage*) face; (*personnage*) figure; (*Cartes*) face card; (*image*) illustration; (*Danse, Math*) figure. **faire** ~ **de favori** to be looked on as the favourite; **faire bonne** ~ to put up a good show; **faire triste** ~ to look a sorry sight; ~ **de style** stylistic device.

figurer [figyʀe] (1) **1** *vt* to represent. **2** *vi* to appear. **3 se** ~ *vpr* to imagine. **figurez-vous que** would you believe that. ♦ **figuré, e** *adj* figurative. **mot employé au** ~ word used figuratively *ou* in the figurative sense.

figurine [figyʀin] *nf* figurine.

fil [fil] **1** *nm* **(a)** (*brin*) *[coton, araignée]* thread; *[laine]* yarn; *[cuivre]* wire; *[haricots, marionnette]* string. (*téléphone*) **j'ai ta mère au bout du** ~ I have your mother on the line *ou* phone; **haricots pleins de** ~**s/sans** ~**s** stringy/stringless beans. **(b)** (*Tex: matière*) linen. **(c)** *[bois, viande]* grain. **dans le sens du** ~ with the grain. **(d)** (*tranchant*) edge. **passer au** ~ **de l'épée** to put to the sword. **(e)** *[discours, pensée]* thread. **au** ~ **des jours** with the passing days; **le** ~ **de l'eau** the current. **(f)** (*locutions*) **donner du** ~ **à retordre à qn** to make life difficult for sb; **ne tenir qu'à un** ~ to hang by a thread; **de** ~ **en aiguille** one thing leading to another. **2:** ~ **conducteur** *[enquête]* vital lead; *[récit]* main theme; ~ **de fer** wire; ~ **(à linge)** washing *ou* clothes line; ~ **(à pêche)** fishing line; ~ **à plomb** plumbline.

filament [filamɑ̃] *nm* (*Bio, Élec*) filament; *[bave]* thread.

filandreux, -euse [filɑ̃dʀø, øz] *adj viande* stringy; *discours* long-winded.

filasse [filas] **1** *nf* tow. **2** *adj inv* tow-coloured.

filature [filatyʀ] *nf* **(a)** (*Tex*) (*action*) spinning; (*usine*) mill. **(b)** (*surveillance*) shadowing.

file [fil] *nf* line; (*Aut: couloir*) lane. ~ **(d'attente)** queue; **se garer en double** ~ to double-park; **se mettre en** ~ to line up; **prendre la** ~ to join the queue; **marcher en** ~ to walk in line; **entrer à la** ~ to file in; **en** ~ **indienne** in single file; **à la** ~ (*à la suite*) in succession, one after the other.

filer [file] (1) **1** *vt* **(a)** (*gén*) to spin; *comparaison, note* to draw out. ~ **un mauvais coton*** to be in a bad way. **(b)** (*Police etc: suivre*) to shadw. **(c)** (*: *donner*) *argent, objet* to slip; *coup* to land. **(d)** *bas* to ladder. **(e) navire qui file 20 nœuds** ship which does 20 knots. **2** *vi* **(a)** *[liquide]* to run; *[lampe]* to smoke. ~ **qch entre ses doigts** to run sth through one's fingers. **(b)** (*) (*courir*) to fly by; (*s'en aller*) to slip off *ou* away. **il fila comme une flèche** he darted away; ~ **voir qn** to dash to see sb; **il faut que je file** I must dash *ou* fly*; **allez, file!** off with you!; ~ **à l'anglaise** to take French leave; ~ **entre les doigts de qn** to slip between sb's fingers; ~ **doux** to behave o.s. **(c)** *[maille]* to run; *[collant]* to ladder.

filet [filɛ] *nm* **(a)** *[eau]* trickle; *[fumée]* wisp; *[lumière]* streak; *[vinaigre]* drop, dash; (*trait*) thread. **(b)** *[poisson, viande]* fillet. **(c)** (*Pêche, Sport*) net; (*piège*) snare. ~ **(à provisions)** string bag; ~ **(à bagages)** luggage rack; ~ **à cheveux/de pêche** hair/fishing net; **travailler sans** ~ to work without a safety net.

filial, e, *mpl* **-aux** [filjal, o] **1** *adj* filial. **2** *nf* (*Comm*) subsidiary company.

filière [filjɛʀ] *nf [carrière]* path; *[administration]* channels; *[drogue]* network.

filiforme [filifɔʀm(ə)] *adj antenne* threadlike; (*) *corps* spindly.

filigrane [filigʀan] *nm [billet]* watermark; *[objet]* filigree. **mais on devinait, en** ~**, sa colère** but his anger was showing through.

filin [filɛ̃] *nm* rope.

fille [fij] *nf* (*opp de* **fils**) daughter; (*opp de* **garçon**) girl; (†*péj: prostituée*) whore. **brave** ~ nice girl, good sort; **rester** ~† to remain unmarried; **vieille** ~ old maid; ~ **de ferme** farm girl; ~ **d'auberge** serving maid; ~ **d'honneur** maid of honour; (*péj*) ~**-mère** unmarried mother. ♦ **fillette** *nf* (little) girl. **rayon** ~**s** girls' department.

filleul, -eule [fijœl] *nm,f* godchild, godson (*ou* goddaughter).

film [film] *nm* **(a)** (*pellicule*) film; (*œuvre*) film, picture, movie (*US*). (*fig*) **le** ~ **des événements** the pattern of events. **(b)** (*couche*) film. ♦ **filmer** (1) *vt personne* to film; *scène* to film, shoot.

filon [filɔ̃] *nm* (*Minér*) vein; (*sujet*) theme, line; (*: *combine*) cushy number*. (*fig*) **trouver le** ~ to strike it lucky *ou* rich.

filou* [filu] *nm* rogue. ♦ **filouter*** (1) *vti* to cheat (*de* out of).

fils [fis] *nm* son. **M Martin** ~ young Mr Martin; (*Comm*) Mr Martin junior; **le** ~ **Martin** the Martin boy; ~ **de famille** young man of means; (*péj*) ~ **à papa** daddy's boy.

filtre [filtʀ(ə)] *nm* (*gén*) filter; *[cigarette]* filter tip. **(café-)**~ (filter) coffee. ♦ **filtrer** (1) **1** *vt* (*lit*) to filter; *nouvelles, spectateurs* to screen. **2** *vi* to filter (*à travers* through). ♦ **filtrage** *nm* filtering; screening. ♦ **filtrant, e** *adj substance* filtering; *pouvoir* of filtration; *verre* filter.

fin[1]**, fine**[1] [fɛ̃, fin] **1** *adj* **(a)** (*en épaisseur*) thin; (*en grosseur*) fine; *lame* sharp; *taille, jambe* slender, slim. **(b)** (*de qualité*) fine. **perles fines** real pearls; **fines herbes** (sweet) herbs; **petits pois** ~**s** (graded) garden peas; **la fine fleur de** the flower of; **le** ~ **du** ~ the last word (*de* in). **(c)** *vue, ouïe* sharp; *goût, odorat* fine. **(d)** *personne, esprit* shrewd; *remarque* subtle. **fine mouche** sharp customer; ~ **limier** (keen) sleuth; **il n'est pas très** ~ he's not very bright; (*iro*) **c'est** ~ **ce que tu as**

fait! that was clever of you! (*iro*); **tu as l'air ~!** you look a fool!; **jouer au plus ~ avec qn** to try to outsmart sb. **(e)** (*avant n: connaisseur*) expert. **~ connaisseur** connoisseur; **~ tireur** crack shot. **(f)** (*avant n: intensif*) **au ~ fond de la campagne** in the depths of the country; **au ~ fond du tiroir** right at the back of the drawer; **savoir le ~ mot de l'histoire** to know the real story behind it all. **2** *adv* **moudre** finely. **écrire ~** to write small; **~ prêt** quite *ou* all ready.

fin[2] [fɛ̃] *nf* **(a)** (*gén*) end. **~ juin** at the end of June; **jusqu'à la ~ des temps** until the end of time; **à la ~** eventually, in the end, finally; **ça suffit à la ~!*** that's enough now!; **en ~ de compte** in the end; **sans ~** (*adj*) endless; (*adv*) endlessly; **prendre ~** to come to an end; **tirer à sa ~** to be coming to an end, be drawing to a close; **mettre ~ à** to put an end to, end; **mener qch à bonne ~** to bring sth to a successful conclusion; **faire une ~** to settle down; **c'est la ~ des haricots*** it's all up!*; **avoir une ~ tragique** to die a tragic death; (*Comm*) **~ de série** oddment. **(b)** (*but*) end, aim, purpose; (*Philos*) end. **la ~ justifie les moyens** the end justifies the means; **à seule ~ de faire** for the sole purpose of doing; **à toutes ~s utiles** for your information.

final, e, *mpl* **~s** [final] **1** *adj* final. **2** *nm* (*Mus*) finale. **3** *nf* (*Sport*) final. **quart de ~e** quarter final. ♦ **finalement** *adv* in the end, finally. ♦ **finaliste** *adj, nmf* finalist. ♦ **finalité** *nf* finality.

finance [finɑ̃s] *nf*: **~s** finances; (*administration*) **les F~s** ≃ the Treasury; **la haute ~** (*activité*) high finance; (*personne*) top financiers. ♦ **financement** *nm* financing. ♦ **financer** (3) *vt* to finance. ♦ **financier, -ière 1** *adj* financial. **2** *nm* financier. ♦ **financièrement** *adv* financially.

fine[2] [fin] *nf* **(a)** (*alcool*) liqueur brandy. **(b)** (*huître*) **~ de claire** oyster.

finement [finmɑ̃] *adv* **ciselé** finely, delicately; **faire remarquer** subtly; **agir** cleverly, shrewdly.

finesse [finɛs] *nf* **(a)** (*V* **fin**[1]) thinness; fineness; sharpness; slimness; shrewdness; subtlety. **(b)** **~s** *[langue]* niceties; *[affaire]* ins and outs; **il connaît toutes les ~s** he knows all the tricks.

fini, e [fini] **1** *adj* **(a)** (*gén, Ind*) finished. **tout est ~** it's all over. **(b)** (*péj*) **menteur, escroc** utter, out-and-out. **(c)** (*Math, Philos*) finite. **2** *nm* *[ouvrage]* finish.

finir [finiʀ] (2) **1** *vt* **(a)** **travail, parcours** to finish, complete; **discours, affaire** to end. **il a fini ses jours à Paris** he ended his days in Paris; **finis ton pain!** eat up *ou* finish your bread! **(b)** (*arrêter*) to stop (**de faire** doing). **(c)** (*parachever*) to put the finishing touches to. **2** *vi* **(a)** (*gén*) to finish, end; *[réunion]* to draw to a close. **les vacances finissent demain** the holidays are over tomorrow; **il finira en prison** he will end up in prison; **il a fini dans un accident de voiture** he died in a car accident; **ça finit en pointe** it ends in a point; **il a fini par se décider** he finally *ou* eventually made up his mind, he made up his mind in the end; **tu finis par m'ennuyer** you're beginning to annoy me. **(b)** **en ~ avec une situation** to put an end to a situation; **nous en aurons bientôt fini** we'll soon be finished with it; **quand en auras-tu fini avec tes jérémiades?** when will you ever stop moaning?; **pour vous en ~** to cut the story short; **qui n'en finit pas** never-ending, endless; **elle n'en finit pas de se préparer** she takes an age to get ready; **on n'en aurait jamais fini de raconter ses bêtises** you could go on for ever recounting the stupid things he has done.

finish [finiʃ] *nm* (*Sport*) finish.

finition [finisjɔ̃] *nf* (*action*) finishing; (*résultat*) finish.

Finlande [fɛ̃lɑ̃d] *nf* Finland. ♦ **finlandais, e** *ou* ♦ **finnois, e 1** *adj, nm* Finnish. **2** *nm(f)*: **F~(e)** Finn.

fiole [fjɔl] *nf* phial; (*: *tête*) face.

fioriture [fjɔʀityʀ] *nf* flourish.

firmament [fiʀmamɑ̃] *nm* firmament. (*fig*) **au ~ de** at the height of.

firme [fiʀm(ə)] *nf* firm.

fisc [fisk] *nm* ≃ Inland Revenue (*Brit*), ≃ Internal Revenue (*US*). ♦ **fiscal, e,** *mpl* **-aux** *adj* fiscal, tax. ♦ **fiscalité** *nf* (*système*) tax system; (*impôts*) taxation.

fission [fisjɔ̃] *nf* fission. **~ de l'atome** atomic fission.

fissurer *vt*, **se ~** *vpr* [fisyʀe] (1) to crack, fissure. ♦ **fissure** *nf* crack, fissure.

fiston* [fistɔ̃] *nm* son, lad.

fixateur [fiksatœʀ] *nm* (*Art*) fixative spray; (*Phot*) fixer.

fixation [fiksɑsjɔ̃] *nf* **(a)** (*Chim, Psych, Zool*) fixation; (*Phot*) fixing. **(b)** (*attache*) fastening. (*Ski*) **~ (de sécurité)** (safety) binding.

fixe [fiks(ə)] **1** *adj* (*gén*) fixed; **emploi** permanent, steady. **à heure ~** at a set time. **2** *nm* (*paye*) fixed salary.

fixer [fikse] (1) **1** *vt* **(a)** (*attacher*) to fix, fasten (*à, sur* to); **regard** to fix, fasten (*sur* on). **il le fixa longuement** he stared at him; **~ qch dans sa mémoire** to fix sth firmly in one's memory. **(b)** **prix, date** to fix, set; **règle** to lay down. (*fig*) **~ son choix sur qch** to decide *ou* settle on sth; (*fig*) **je ne suis pas encore fixé** I haven't made up my mind yet; **à l'heure fixée** at the agreed time; **~ ses idées sur le papier** to set one's ideas down on paper; **mot fixé par l'usage** word fixed by usage. **(c)** (*renseigner*) **~ qn sur qch*** to put sb in the picture about sth*; **être fixé sur le compte de qn** to have sb sized up*; **alors, es-tu fixé maintenant?*** have you got the picture now?* **(d)** (*Phot*) to fix. **2 se ~** *vpr* (*s'installer*) to settle; *[usage]* to become fixed.

fixité [fiksite] *nf [opinions]* fixedness; *[regard]* steadiness.

fjord [fjɔʀ(d)] *nm* fiord, fjord.

flac [flak] *excl* splash!

flacon [flakɔ̃] *nm* bottle; (*Chim*) flask.

flageller [flaʒele] (1) *vt* to flog, scourge.

flageoler [flaʒɔle] (1) *vi*: **~ sur ses jambes** (*de faiblesse*) to be sagging at the knees; (*de peur*) to quake at the knees.

flagrant, e [flagʀɑ̃, ɑ̃t] *adj* **erreur** blatant, glaring. **prendre qn en ~ délit** to catch sb red-handed.

flair [flɛʀ] *nm [chien]* nose; (*fig*) sixth sense, intuition. ♦ **flairer** (1) *vt* to sniff (at); (*Chasse*) to scent; (*fig*) to scent, sense.

flamand, e [flamɑ̃, ɑ̃d] **1** *adj, nm* Flemish. **2** *nm(f)*: **F~(e)** Flemish man (*ou* woman).

flamant [flamɑ̃] *nm*: **~ (rose)** (pink) flamingo.

flambant [flɑ̃bɑ̃] *adv*: **~ neuf** brand new.

flambeau, *pl* **~x** [flɑ̃bo] *nm* (*lit, fig*) torch; (*chandelier*) candlestick.

flamber [flɑ̃be] (1) **1** *vi [bois]* to burn; *[feu]* to blaze. **2** *vt* **crêpe** to flambé; **volaille, cheveux** to singe; (*Méd*) **aiguille** to sterilize. ♦ **flambé, e**[1]* *adj* finished. ♦ **flambée**[2] *nf* **(a)** (*feu*) quick blaze. **(b)** *[violence]* outburst; *[prix]* explosion.

flamboyer [flɑ̃bwaje] (8) *vi [flamme]* to blaze; *[yeux]* to flash; *[ciel]* to blaze; *[épée]* to gleam, flash. ♦ **flamboiement** *nm* blaze; flash; gleam. ♦ **flamboyant, e** *adj* (*Archit*) flamboyant.

flamme [flam] *nf* **(a)** (*lit*) flame. **en ~s** on fire; (*Aviat, fig*) **descendre en ~s** to shoot down in flames. **(b)** (*fig: ardeur, éclat*) fire; (*littér: amour*) ardour, love. **plein de ~** passionate, fiery. **(c)** (*drapeau*) pennant, pennon.

flan [flɑ̃] *nm* (*Culin*) custard tart.

flanc [flɑ̃] *nm* side; *[animal, armée]* flank; *[montagne]* slope. **tirer au ~*** to swing the lead*; **être sur le ~** to be laid up; (*:*fig*) to be all in*; *[maladie]* **mettre qn sur le ~*** to knock sb out; **à ~ de coteau** on the hillside; **prendre de ~** (*Naut, fig*)

to catch broadside on; (*Mil*) to attack on the flank.
flancher* [flɑ̃ʃe] (1) *vi [cœur]* to pack up*; *[troupes]* to quit; *[accusé]* to lose one's nerve. **sa mémoire a flanché** his memory failed him; ~ **en math** to come down in maths.
Flandre [flɑ̃dʀ(ə)] *nf*: **la** ~, **les** ~**s** Flanders.
flanelle [flanɛl] *nf* (*Tex*) flannel.
flâner [flɑne] (1) *vi* to stroll, saunter; (*péj*) to hang about. ♦ **flânerie** *nf* stroll, saunter. (*péj*) ~**(s)** idling about. ♦ **flâneur, -euse 1** *adj* idle. **2** *nm,f* stroller; (*péj*) idler.
flanquer [flɑ̃ke] (1) *vt* **(a)** to flank. **flanqué de** flanked by. **(b)** (*: *jeter*) ~ **qch par terre** (*lit*) to fling sth to the ground; (*fig*) to put paid to sth; ~ **qn à la porte** to chuck sb out‡; (*licencier*) to sack *ou* fire sb; ~ **tout en l'air** to chuck it all up‡; **se** ~ **par terre** to fall flat on one's face. **(c)** (*: *donner*) to give. ~ **2 ans de prison à qn** to put sb behind bars for 2 years.
flaque [flak] *nf*: ~ **de sang** *etc* pool of blood *etc*; ~ **d'eau** puddle.
flash [flaʃ] *nm* **(a)** (*Phot*) flash. **au** ~ by flash. **(b)** (*Rad, TV*) newsflash.
flasque [flask(ə)] *adj peau* flabby; (*fig*) limp.
flatter [flate] (1) **1** *vt* **(a)** *personne, goût* to flatter; *vice* to pander to, encourage; *regard* to delight, charm. ~ **servilement qn** to fawn upon sb. **(b)** (*caresser*) to stroke, pat. **2 se** ~ *vpr* (*se leurrer*) to delude o.s. **il se flatte de le faire** he flatters himself he can do it; **se** ~ **de qch** to pride o.s. on sth; **et je m'en flatte!** and I'm proud of it! ♦ **flatterie** *nf* flattery. ♦ **flatteur, -euse 1** *adj* flattering. **2** *nm,f* flatterer.
fléau, *pl* ~**x** [fleo] *nm* **(a)** (*calamité*) scourge, curse. **(b)** *[balance]* beam; (*Agr*) flail.
flèche [flɛʃ] *nf* **(a)** (*arme*) arrow; (*de direction*) arrow, pointer; (*critique*) shaft. ~ **en caoutchouc** rubber-tipped dart; **monter en** ~ (*lit*) to rise like an arrow; (*fig*) to soar, rocket; **partir comme une** ~ to set off like a shot; **la** ~ **du Parthe** the Parthian shot; **il fait** ~ **de tout bois** he'll use any means he can. **(b)** *[église]* spire; *[grue]* jib; *[attelage, mât]* pole. ♦ **flécher** (1) *vt* to arrow, mark with arrows. ♦ **fléchette** *nf* dart.
fléchir [fleʃiʀ] (2) **1** *vt* **(a)** (*plier*) to bend; *articulation* to flex. ~ **le genou devant qn** to bend the knee to sb. **(b)** (*apaiser*) *personne* to sway; *colère* to soothe. **2** *vi* **(a)** (*gén*) to bend; *[planches, genoux]* to sag; *[armée]* to yield; *[volonté]* to weaken; *[attention]* to flag; *[nombre]* to fall off; *[prix]* to drop. **(b)** (*s'apaiser*) to yield. **se laisser** ~ to allow o.s. to be swayed. ♦ **fléchissement** *nm* (*gén*) bending; *[prix]* drop.
flegme [flɛgm(ə)] *nm* composure, phlegm. ♦ **flegmatique** *adj* phlegmatic. ♦ **flegmatiquement** *adv* phlegmatically.
flemme* [flɛm] *nf* laziness. **j'ai la** ~ **de le faire** I can't be bothered doing it. ♦ **flemmard, e* 1** *adj* bone-idle*. **2** *nm,f* lazybones*, slacker.
flétrir [fletʀiʀ] (2) **1** *vt* (*faner*) to wither, fade; (*stigmatiser*) to condemn. **2 se** ~ *vpr* to wither.
fleur [flœʀ] *nf* **(a)** (*lit, fig*) flower; *[arbre]* blossom. **en** ~**(s)** in blossom; in flower; ~ **d'oranger** orange blossom; **assiette à** ~**s** flower-patterned *ou* flowery plate; (*fig*) **couvrir qn de** ~**s** to shower praise on sb. **(b) dans la** ~ **de l'âge** in the prime of life; **arriver premier comme une** ~ to win hands down*; **à** ~ **de terre/d'eau** just above the ground/the water; **j'ai les nerfs à** ~ **de peau** my nerves are all on edge; **faire une** ~ **à qn*** to do sb a good turn; **ils s'envoient des** ~**s** they pat each other on the back.
fleurer [flœʀe] (1) *vt*: **ça fleure bon la lavande** *etc* there's a lovely smell of lavender *etc*.
fleuret [flœʀɛ] *nm* (*épée*) foil.
fleurir [flœʀiʀ] (2) **1** *vi* **(a)** *[arbre]* to blossom, flower; *[fleur]* to flower, bloom; *[sentiment]* to blossom. **(b)** (*imparfait* **florissait**, *ptp* **florissant**) *[commerce, arts]* to flourish. **2** *vt salon* to decorate with flowers. ~ **une tombe** to put flowers on a grave. ♦ **fleuri, e** *adj fleur* in bloom; *branche* in blossom; *jardin* in flower *ou* bloom; *tissu* flowery; *style* flowery, florid. ♦ **fleuriste** *nmf* (*personne*) florist; (*boutique*) florist's (shop).
fleuron [flœʀɔ̃] *nm [couronne]* floweret; *[bâtiment]* finial; (*fig*) jewel.
fleuve [flœv] **1** *nm* river. **2** *adj inv discours* interminable.
flexible [flɛksibl(ə)] **1** *adj* (*lit*) flexible, pliable; *caractère* (*compréhensif*) flexible, adaptable; (*faible*) pliable. **2** *nm* (*tuyau*) flexible tubing. ♦ **flexibilité** *nf* flexibility.
flexion [flɛksjɔ̃] *nf* (*courbure*) flexion, bending; (*Ling*) inflection.
flibustier [flibystje] *nm* freebooter.
flic* [flik] *nm* cop*.
flic flac [flikflak] *excl* splash! **faire** ~ to go splish splash.
flingue‡ [flɛ̃g] *nm* gun, rod‡. ♦ **flinguer‡** (1) *vt* to gun down.
flipper [flipœʀ] *nm* (*électrique*) pin-ball machine.
flirt [flœʀt] *nm* (*amourette*) brief romance; (*amoureux*) boyfriend (*ou* girlfriend). (*action*) **le** ~ flirting. ♦ **flirter** (1) *vi* to flirt. (*fig*) ~ **avec** *idée* to flirt with; *personne* to go about with.
floc [flɔk] *nm, excl* plop.
flocon [flɔkɔ̃] *nm [neige, purée]* flake; *[écume]* fleck; *[laine]* flock.
floraison [flɔʀɛzɔ̃] *nf [fleurs, talents]* flowering, blossoming; *[affiches]* rash; (*époque*) flowering time.
floral, e, *mpl* **-aux** [flɔʀal, o] *adj* floral; *exposition* flower.
floralies [flɔʀali] *nfpl* flower show.
flore [flɔʀ] *nf* flora.
florilège [flɔʀilɛʒ] *nm* anthology.
florin [flɔʀɛ̃] *nm* florin.
florissant, e [flɔʀisɑ̃, ɑ̃t] *adj pays* flourishing; *santé, teint* blooming.
flot [flo] *nm [véhicules, insultes]* flood, stream. (*marée*) **le** ~ the floodtide; **les** ~**s** the waves; **à (grands)** ~**s** in streams; **la lumière entre à** ~**s** light is streaming in *ou* flooding in; **être à** ~ *[bateau]* to be afloat; *[personne, entreprise]* to be on an even keel; **remettre à** ~ *bateau* to refloat; *entreprise* to bring back onto an even keel; (*lit, fig*) **mettre à** ~ to launch.
flottaison [flɔtɛzɔ̃] *nf*: **ligne de** ~ waterline.
flottant [flɔtɑ̃] *nm* (*short*) shorts.
flotte [flɔt] *nf* **(a)** (*Aviat, Naut*) fleet. **(b)** (*) (*pluie*) rain; (*eau*) water. **(c)** (*flotteur*) float.
flottement [flɔtmɑ̃] *nm [foule]* wavering, hesitation; *[électeurs]* indecision; *[soldats]* sway; *[copie]* vagueness; *[travail]* unevenness (*dans* in).
flotter [flɔte] (1) **1** *vi [bateau, monnaie]* to float; *[brume, parfum]* to hang; *[pensée]* to wander; (*en hésitant*) to waver; *[cheveux]* to stream out; *[drapeau]* to flap, flutter (*au vent* in the wind). **il flotte dans ses vêtements** his clothes are too big for him; **faire** ~ to float. **2** *vb impers* (*: *pleuvoir*) to rain. **3** *vt bois* to float.
flotteur [flɔtœʀ] *nm* (*gén*) float; *[chasse d'eau]* ballcock.
flottille [flɔtij] *nf [bateaux]* flotilla; *[avions]* squadron.
flou, e [flu] **1** *adj contour, photo* blurred; *image* hazy; *robe* loose(-fitting); *coiffure* soft; *théorie* woolly, vague. **2** *nm* blurredness; looseness; vagueness, woolliness.
fluctuer [flyktɥe] (1) *vi* to fluctuate. ♦ **fluctuation** *nf* fluctuation (*de* in).
fluet, -ette [flyɛ, ɛt] *adj corps* slight, slender; *taille* slender, slim; *voix* thin.
fluide [flyid] **1** *adj* (*lit, fig*) fluid; *main d'œuvre* flexible. **la circulation est** ~ traffic flows freely. **2** *nm* fluid; (*fig: pouvoir*) mysterious power.

♦ **fluidité** *nf* fluidity; flexibility; free flow.
fluor [flyɔʀ] *nm* fluorine.
fluorescent, e [flyɔʀesɑ̃, ɑ̃t] *adj* fluorescent.
flûte [flyt] **1** *nf* flute; (*verre*) flute glass; (*pain*) long French loaf. **petite** ~ piccolo; ~ **à bec** recorder; ~ **de Pan** Pan's pipes. **2** *excl* (*) drat it!*, dash it!* ♦ **flûtiste** *nmf* flautist, flutist.
fluvial, e, *mpl* **-aux** [flyvjal, o] *adj eaux* river; *érosion* fluvial.
flux [fly] *nm [argent etc]* flood; (*Phys*) flux. (*marée*) **le** ~ the floodtide; **le** ~ **et le reflux** the ebb and flow.
fluxion [flyksjɔ̃] *nf* swelling; (*dentaire*) gumboil. ~ **de poitrine** pneumonia.
foc [fɔk] *nm* jib.
focal, e, *mpl* **-aux** [fɔkal, o] **1** *adj* focal. **2** *nf* focal distance.
fœtus [fetys] *nm* foetus.
foi [fwa] *nf* **(a)** (*croyance*) faith. **avoir la** ~ to have faith; **il faut avoir la** ~**!*** you've got to be really dedicated!; **sans** ~ **ni loi** fearing neither God nor man. **(b)** (*confiance*) faith, trust. **avoir** ~ **en** to have faith *ou* trust in; **digne de** ~ reliable, trustworthy. **(c)** (*assurance*) word. ~ **d'honnête homme!** on my word as a gentleman!; **cette lettre en fait** ~ this letter proves it; **sous la** ~ **du serment** under *ou* on oath; **sur la** ~ **de** on the strength of; **de bonne/mauvaise** ~ in good/bad faith; **ma** ~ ... well ... .
foie [fwa] *nm* liver. ~ **gras** foie gras.
foin [fwɛ̃] *nm* hay. **faire les** ~**s** to make hay; (*saison*) **les** ~**s** the haymaking season; **faire du** ~* to kick up a fuss*.
foire [fwaʀ] *nf* (*marché*) fair; (*fête*) fun fair. **faire la** ~* to go on a spree; **c'est la** ~ **ici!*** it's bedlam in here!; **c'est une** ~ **d'empoigne** it's a free-for-all.
foirer [fwaʀe] (1) *vi* (*) *[vis]* to slip; *[obus]* to hang fire; (‡) *[projet]* to fall through.
fois [fwa] *nf* **(a)** time. **une** ~ once; **deux** ~ twice; **trois** ~ three times; (*aux enchères*) **une** ~**, deux** ~**, trois** ~ **adjugé** going, going, gone!; **quand je l'ai vu pour la première/dernière** ~ when I first/last saw him; **c'est bon pour cette** ~ I'll let you off this time; **peu de** ~ on few occasions; **y regarder à deux** ~ **avant d'acheter qch** to think twice before buying sth; **s'y prendre à plusieurs** ~ **pour faire qch** to take several attempts to do sth; **payer en plusieurs** ~ to pay in several instalments. **(b)** (*calcul*) **une** ~ **tous les deux jours** once every two days, once every other day; **3** ~ **par an** 3 times a year; **9** ~ **sur 10** 9 times out of 10; **4** ~ **plus d'eau/de voitures** 4 times as much water/as many cars; **6** ~ **moins d'argent/de gens** 6 times less money/fewer people; **il avait deux** ~ **rien** (*argent*) he had absolutely nothing; (*blessure*) he had the merest scratch. **(c) une** ~ once; **il était une** ~ once upon a time there was; **une** ~ **n'est pas coutume** once in a while does no harm; **pour une** ~! for once!; **une (bonne)** ~ **pour toutes** once and for all; **une** ~ **(qu'il sera) parti** once he has left. **(d)** (*) **des** ~ (*parfois*) sometimes; **si des** ~ **vous le rencontrez** if you should happen to meet him; **non mais, des** ~! (*scandalisé*) do you MIND!; **attendons, des** ~ **qu'il viendrait** let's wait in case he comes. **(e) à la** ~ *répondre* at once, at the same time; **il était à la** ~ **grand et gros** he was both tall and fat.
foison [fwazɔ̃] *nf*: **il y a des légumes à** ~ there is an abundance of vegetables. ♦ **foisonnement** *nm* profusion, abundance. ♦ **foisonner** (1) *vi* to abound. **foisonnant d'idées** teeming with ideas.
folâtrer [fɔlɑtʀe] (1) *vi* to frolic. **au lieu de** ~ instead of playing about. ♦ **folâtre** *adj* playful.
folichon, -onne* [fɔliʃɔ̃, ɔn] *adj*: **ce n'est pas très** ~ it's not much fun.
folie [fɔli] *nf* **(a) la** ~ madness, lunacy; ~ **furieuse** (*Méd*) raving madness; (*fig*) sheer lunacy; **avoir la** ~ **des grandeurs** to have delusions of grandeur; **il a la** ~ **des timbres-poste** he is mad about stamps; **aimer qn à la** ~ to be madly in love with sb; **il a eu la** ~ **de refuser** he was mad enough to refuse. **(b)** (*erreur*) extravagance. ~**s de jeunesse** youthful follies; **vous avez fait des** ~**s en achetant ce cadeau** you have been far too extravagant in buying this present; **il ferait des** ~**s pour elle/pour la revoir** he would do anything for her/to see her again.
folklore [fɔlklɔʀ] *nm* folklore. ♦ **folklorique** *adj costume* folk; (*: *excentrique*) outlandish. ♦ **folk song** *nm* folk music.
folle [fɔl] *V* **fou.**
follement [fɔlmɑ̃] *adv* madly, wildly. **on s'est** ~ **amusé** we had a fantastic time; **il désire** ~ **lui parler** he is longing to speak to her.
fomenter [fɔmɑ̃te] (1) *vt* (*lit, fig*) to foment, stir up.
foncer[1]* [fɔ̃se] (3) *vi* to tear along*. ~ **sur** to charge at, make a rush at; ~ **dans la foule** to charge into the crowd; ~ **(tête baissée) dans le piège** to walk straight into the trap; (*fig*) ~ **dans le brouillard** to forge ahead in the dark. ♦ **fonceur, -euse*** *nm,f* fighter (*fig*).
foncer[2] [fɔ̃se] (3) **1** *vt couleur* to make darker. **2** *vi* to turn *ou* go darker. ♦ **foncé, e** *adj* dark.
foncier, -ière [fɔ̃sje, jɛʀ] *adj* **(a)** *impôt* land; *propriété* landed. **(b)** (*fondamental*) fundamental, basic. ♦ **foncièrement** *adv* fundamentally, basically.
fonction [fɔ̃ksjɔ̃] *nf* **(a)** (*métier*) post, office. (*tâches*) ~**s** duties; **entrer en** ~**s** to take up one's post; **être en** ~ to be in office; **la** ~ **publique** the public service. **(b)** (*gén, Gram: rôle*) function. **faire** ~ **de directeur** to act as a manager; **il n'y a pas de porte, ce rideau en fait** ~ there is no door but this curtain does instead *ou* does duty for it. **(c)** (*Math*) function. (*fig*) **sa réussite est** ~ **de son travail** his success depends on how well he works; **en** ~ **de** according to.
fonctionnaire [fɔ̃ksjɔnɛʀ] *nmf* (*gén*) state employee; *[ministère]* ≃ civil servant; *[municipalité]* local authority employee.
fonctionnel, -elle [fɔ̃ksjɔnɛl] *adj* functional.
fonctionner [fɔ̃ksjɔne] (1) *vi* (*gén*) to work, operate; *[entreprise]* to function. **faire** ~ *machine* to operate. ♦ **fonctionnement** *nm* working, operating; functioning. **en état de bon** ~ in good working order; **mauvais** ~ **du carburateur** fault in the carburettor; **pendant le** ~ **de l'appareil** while the machine is in operation.
fond [fɔ̃] **1** *nm* **(a)** *[récipient, vallée etc]* bottom; *[gorge]* back; *[pièce]* far end, back; *[chapeau]* crown; *[chaise]* seat. (*Min*) **le** ~ the coal face; **être/tomber au** ~ **de l'eau** to be at/fall to the bottom of the water; (*Naut*) **envoyer par le** ~ to send to the bottom; **y a-t-il beaucoup de** ~? is it very deep?; **l'épave repose par 10 mètres de** ~ the wreck is lying 10 metres down; **au** ~ **du couloir** at the far end of the corridor; **au** ~ **de la province** in the depths *ou* heart of the country; (*lit, fig*) **sans** ~ bottomless. **(b)** (*fig: tréfonds*) **merci du** ~ **du cœur** I thank you from the bottom of my heart; **au** ~ **de son cœur** deep down, in his heart of hearts; **je vais vous dire le** ~ **de ma pensée** I shall tell you what I really think; **regarder qn au** ~ **des yeux** to look deep into sb's eyes; **il a un bon** ~ he's a good person at heart; **il y a chez lui un** ~ **d'honnêteté** he's fundamentally honest; ~ **de vérité** element of truth; **toucher le** ~ **de la douleur** to plumb the depths of sorrow. **(c)** (*Littérat, gén: contenu*) content; (*Jur*) substance; (*arrière-plan*) background; *[question]* heart; *[discours]* basis. **il faut aller jusqu'au** ~ **de cette histoire** we must get to the root of this business; **ouvrage de** ~ basic work; **article de** ~ leading article, leader; **avec** ~ **musical** with background

music. **(d)** (*lie*) sediment. (*petite quantité*) **juste un ~ (de verre)** just a drop; **ils ont vidé les ~s de bouteilles** they emptied what was left in the bottles; **~ de magasin** old stock; **racler les ~s de tiroirs** to scrape around for pennies. **(e)** (*Sport*) **de ~** long-distance. **(f)** (*locutions*) **le ~ de l'air est frais*** it's a bit chilly; **au ~, dans le ~** in fact; **à ~** *étudier* thoroughly, in depth; *soutenir* to the hilt; *visser* right home; **à ~ de train** hell for leather*, full tilt; **de ~ en comble** *fouiller, détruire* from top to bottom; *modifier* completely. **2: ~ d'artichaut** artichoke heart; **les ~s marins** the sea-bed; **~ de robe** (full-length) slip *ou* petticoat; **~ de teint** (make-up) foundation.

fondamental, e, *mpl* **-aux** [fɔ̃damɑ̃tal, o] *adj* fundamental, basic. ♦ **fondamentalement** *adv* fundamentally, basically.

fonder [fɔ̃de] (1) **1** *vt* **(a)** (*créer*) to found; *famille* to start. **(b)** (*baser*) (*gén*) to base, found; *richesse* to build; *espoirs* to place (*sur* on). **2 se ~** *vpr*: **se ~ sur** *[personne]* to go on; *[théorie]* to be based on; **sur quoi vous fondez-vous pour l'affirmer?** what grounds do you have for saying this? ♦ **fondateur, -trice** *nm,f* founder. ♦ **fondation** *nf* (*action*) foundation. (*Constr*) **~s** foundations. ♦ **fondé, e 1** *adj* well-founded, justified. **mal ~** ill-founded; **~ sur des ouï-dire** based on hearsay; **être ~ à dire** to have good reason to say. **2** *nm*: **~ (de pouvoir)** (*Jur*) authorized representative; (*Banque*) senior executive. ♦ **fondement** *nm* foundation. **sans ~** without foundation, unfounded.

fondre [fɔ̃dʀ(ə)] (41) **1** *vt* **(a)** (*aussi* **faire ~**) (*lit, fig*) to melt; *minerai* to smelt. **(b)** *statue* to cast, found; *couleurs* to blend; *idées* to fuse together (*en* into). **2** *vi* **(a)** (*à la chaleur*) to melt; (*dans l'eau*) to dissolve. **(b)** (*fig*) *[colère]* to melt away; *[réserves]* to vanish. **j'ai fondu de 5 kg** I've lost 5 kg; **~ en larmes** to dissolve into tears. **(c) ~ sur qn** *[ennemi]* to swoop down on sb; *[malheurs]* to sweep down on sb. **3 se ~** *vpr* to merge (*dans* into). ♦ **fonderie** *nf* (*usine*) smelting works; (*de moulage*) foundry.

fondrière [fɔ̃dʀijɛʀ] *nf* pothole, rut.

fonds [fɔ̃] *nm* **(a) ~ de commerce** business. **(b)** *[musée]* collection; *[œuvre d'entraide]* fund. **le F~ Monétaire International** the International Monetary Fund; (*fig*) **~ folklorique** folk heritage. **(c)** (*Fin: pl*) (*argent*) money; (*capital*) capital; (*pour un achat*) funds. **~ publics/secrets** public/secret funds; **mise de ~ initiale** initial (capital) outlay; **ne pas être/être en ~** to be out of/be in funds; **prêter de l'argent à ~ perdus** to lend money for an indefinite period; **~ de roulement** working capital.

fondu, e [fɔ̃dy] **1** *adj* *beurre* melted; *métal* molten; *contours* blurred, hazy; *couleurs* blending. **neige ~e** slush. **2** *nf* (*Culin*) (cheese) fondue. **~e bourguignonne** meat fondue.

fontaine [fɔ̃tɛn] *nf* (*ornementale*) fountain; (*naturelle*) spring. (*fig*) **~ de** fountain of.

fonte [fɔ̃t] *nf* **(a)** (*action*) (*gén*) melting; *[minerai]* smelting; *[cloche]* casting, founding. **à la ~ des neiges** when the snow melts. **(b)** (*métal*) cast iron. **~ brute** pig-iron; **en ~** *tuyau* cast-iron.

fonts [fɔ̃] *nmpl*: **~ baptismaux** font.

football [futbol] *nm* football, soccer. **jouer au ~** to play football. ♦ **foot*** *nm abrév de* **football.** ♦ **footballeur** *nm* footballer.

footing [futiŋ] *nm*: **faire du ~** to go jogging; **faire un ~** to go for a jog.

forage [fɔʀaʒ] *nm [roche]* drilling, boring; *[puits]* sinking, boring.

forain, e [fɔʀɛ̃, ɛn] **1** *adj* fairground. **2** *nm* (*acteur*) fairground entertainer. **(marchand) ~** stallholder.

forban [fɔʀbɑ̃] *nm* (*Hist*) pirate; (*fig*) shark, crook.

forçat [fɔʀsa] *nm* (*bagnard*) convict; (*galérien, fig*) galley slave.

force [fɔʀs(ə)] **1** *nf* **(a)** *[personne]* **la ~, les ~s** strength; **avoir de la ~ dans les bras** to be strong in the arm; **à la ~ du poignet** (*lit*) by the strength of one's arms; (*fig*) by the sweat of one's brow; **c'est une ~ de la nature** he's a mighty figure; **dans la ~ de l'âge** in the prime of life; **de toutes ses ~s** *frapper* with all one's might; *désirer* with all one's heart. **(b)** (*violence*) force. **la ~ brutale** brute force. **(c)** (*de la nature*) force; *[argument, alcool etc]* strength. **vent de ~ 4** force 4 wind; **dans toute la ~ du terme** in the strongest sense of the word; **par la ~ des choses** by force of circumstances; **avoir ~ de loi** to have force of law. **(d)** (*Mil*) strength. **~s** forces; **d'importantes ~s de police** large contingents of police; **dans une position de ~** in a position of strength. **(e)** (*valeur*) **de la même ~** *joueurs* evenly matched; *cartes* of the same value; **il est de première ~ au bridge** he's a first-class bridge player; **il est de ~ à le faire** he's equal to it; **tu n'es pas de ~ à lutter avec lui** you're no match for him; **à ~s égales** on equal terms. **(f)** (*Phys*) force. (*Élec*) **la ~** 30-amp circuit; **~ de gravité** force of gravity. **(g) en ~** *attaquer* in force; *venir* in strength; **de ~, par ~** by force; **faire entrer qn de ~** *ou* **par la ~** to force sb to enter; **entrer de ~ chez qn** to force one's way into sb's house; **avec ~** firmly; **vouloir à toute ~** to want at all costs; **à ~ d'essayer/de gentillesse** by dint of trying/kindness; **à ~, tu vas le casser*** you'll end up breaking it; **~ lui est d'accepter** he has no choice but to accept, he is forced to accept. **2** *adv* (*hum*) many. **3: ~ d'âme** fortitude; **la ~ armée** the army; **les ~s armées** the armed forces; **~ de caractère** strength of character; **~ de dissuasion** deterrent power; **~ de frappe** strike force; **les ~s de l'ordre** the police.

forcé, e [fɔʀse] *adj* (*gén*) forced; *bain* unintended; *conséquence* inevitable; *amabilité* affected. **atterrissage ~** forced *ou* emergency landing; **c'est ~!** it's inevitable!

forcément [fɔʀsemɑ̃] *adv* (*inévitablement*) inevitably; (*évidemment*) of course. **ça devait ~ arriver** it was bound to happen; **pas ~** not necessarily.

forcené, e [fɔʀsəne] **1** *adj* (*fou*) deranged; *ardeur, travailleur* frenzied; *partisan* fanatical. **2** *nm,f* (*fou*) maniac; (*fanatique*) fanatic.

forceps [fɔʀsɛps] *nm* forceps.

forcer [fɔʀse] (3) **1** *vt* **(a)** (*contraindre*) to force, compel (*à faire* to do). **ils m'ont forcé la main** they forced my hand; **~ qn au silence** to force sb to keep silent. **(b)** *serrure, porte* to force open; *blocus* to run; *barrage* to force; *ville* to take by force. **~ le passage** to force one's way through; **sa conduite force le respect** his behaviour commands respect; (*Sport*) **~ la décision** to settle the outcome. **(c)** *cerf* to hunt down; *ennemi* to track down. **(d)** (*pousser*) *cheval* to override; *plantes* to force; *talent, voix* to strain; *allure* to increase; *destin* to tempt. **~ le sens d'un texte** to stretch the meaning of a text; (*fig*) **~ la dose*** *ou* **la note*** to overdo it. **2** *vi* (*exagérer*) to overdo it; (*en tirant*) to force it; (*être coincé*) to jam. **sans ~*** easily; **il force sur l'alcool*** he overdoes the drink a bit*. **3 se ~** *vpr* to force o.s. (*pour faire* to do).

forcing [fɔʀsiŋ] *nm* pressure. **faire du ~** to pile on the pressure.

forcir [fɔʀsiʀ] (2) *vi* to fill out.

forer [fɔʀe] (1) *vt* *roche* to drill, bore; *puits* to sink, bore. ♦ **foret** *nm* drill.

forêt [fɔʀɛ] *nf* (*lit, fig*) forest. **~ vierge** virgin forest. ♦ **forestier, -ière 1** *adj* *région* forest. **exploitation ~ière** (*activité*) forestry; (*lieu*) forestry site. **2** *nm* forester.

forfait [fɔʀfɛ] *nm* **(a)** (*à payer*) fixed *ou* set price; (*à percevoir*) lump sum. **~-vacances** package holiday. **(b)** (*abandon*) withdrawal. **gagner par ~** to win by default; **déclarer ~** to withdraw. **(c)** (*crime*) infamy. ♦ **forfaitaire** *adj* standard, uniform. ♦ **forfaitairement** *adv* uniformly.

forger [fɔʀʒe] (3) *vt métal* to forge; (*fig*) *caractère* to form, mould; *mot* to coin; *prétexte* to make up. **c'est forgé de toutes pièces** it's a complete fabrication; **se ~** *illusions* to build up; *réputation* to earn o.s.; *idéal* to create for o.s. ♦ **forge** *nf* (*atelier*) forge, smithy; (*fourneau*) forge. (*fonderie*) **~s** ironworks. ♦ **forgeron** *nm* blacksmith.

formaliser [fɔʀmalize] (1) **1** *vt* to formalize. **2 se ~** *vpr* to take offence (*de* at). ♦ **formalisation** *nf* formalization.

formalisme [fɔʀmalism(ə)] *nm* (*péj*) formality; (*Art, Philos*) formalism. ♦ **formaliste 1** *adj* (*péj*) formalistic; (*Art, Philos*) formalist. **2** *nmf* formalist.

formalité [fɔʀmalite] *nf* formality. (*fig*) **sans autre ~** without any further ado.

format [fɔʀma] *nm* format.

formation [fɔʀmɑsjɔ̃] *nf* **(a)** (*développement*) formation, forming. **en cours de ~** in the process of formation. **(b)** (*apprentissage*) training; (*éducation*) education. **(c)** (*groupement*) (*gén*) formation. **~ musicale** music group. ♦ **formateur, -trice** *adj* formative.

forme [fɔʀm(ə)] *nf* **(a)** (*contour*) form, shape; (*silhouette*) figure. **en ~ de cloche** bell-shaped; **sans ~** *chapeau* shapeless; *pensée* formless; **prendre la ~ d'un entretien** to take the form of a talk; **prendre ~** *[statue, projet]* to take shape; **sous ~ de comprimés** in tablet form; **sous toutes ses ~s** in all its forms. **(b)** (*genre*) **~ de vie** form of life; (*coutumes*) way of life; **~ de pensée** way of thinking. **(c)** (*Art, Jur*) form. **de pure ~** purely formal; **pour la ~** as a matter of form, for form's sake; **en bonne (et due) ~** in due form; (*fig*) **sans autre ~ de procès** without further ado. **(d)** (*convenances*) **~s** proprieties; **refuser en y mettant des ~s** to decline as tactfully as possible. **(e)** (*Ling*) form. **mettre à la ~ passive** to put in the passive. **(f)** (*Tech, Typ*) form; *[cordonnier]* last; *[modiste]* (dress) form. **(g)** (*physique*) form. **être en ~** to be on form; **hors de ~** off form.

formel, -elle [fɔʀmɛl] *adj* (*catégorique*) definite, positive; (*Art, Philos*) formal; *politesse* formal. ♦ **formellement** *adv* positively; formally.

former [fɔʀme] (1) **1** *vt* **(a)** (*gén*) to form; *train, phrase* to make up. **formé de 3 éléments** made up of 3 elements; **~ l'idée de faire** to form *ou* have the idea of doing; **ça forme un rond** it makes *ou* forms a circle. **(b)** *ingénieurs* to train; *intelligence, caractère* to form, develop. **2 se ~** *vpr* (*gén*) to form; *[autodidacte]* to teach *ou* train o.s.

formidable [fɔʀmidabl(ə)] *adj* (*très important*) tremendous; (*: *très bien*) fantastic*, great*, tremendous*; (*: *incroyable*) incredible; (*effrayant*) fearsome. ♦ **formidablement** *adv* tremendously*; fantastically*.

formol [fɔʀmɔl] *nm* formalin.

formulaire [fɔʀmylɛʀ] *nm* form.

formule [fɔʀmyl] *nf* **(a)** (*Chim, Math*) formula. **(b)** (*expression*) phrase, expression; (*magique, consacrée*) formula. **~ de politesse** (*en fin de lettre*) letter ending; **~ publicitaire** advertising slogan. **(c)** (*méthode*) system, way. **~ de paiement** method of payment; **~ de vacances** holiday schedule. **(d)** (*formulaire*) form.

formuler [fɔʀmyle] (1) *vt plainte* to formulate, set out; *sentiment* to formulate, express. ♦ **formulation** *nf* formulation; expression.

fornication [fɔʀnikɑsjɔ̃] *nf* fornication.

fort, e [fɔʀ, fɔʀt(ə)] **1** *adj* **(a)** (*gén*) strong; (*euph: gros*) large; *bruit* loud; *pluie, rhume* heavy; *fièvre, augmentation* high; *chaleur, sentiment* great; *différence, somme* great, large, big; *secousse* hard; *pente* steep. **~ comme un bœuf** as strong as an ox; **armée ~e de 20.000 hommes** army 20,000 strong; **la dame est plus ~e que le valet** the queen is higher than the jack; **avoir affaire à ~e partie** to have a strong *ou* tough opponent; **user de la manière ~e** to use strong-arm methods; **rayon (pour) femmes ~es** outsize department; **il avait une ~e envie de rire** he very much wanted to laugh; **il y a de ~es chances pour qu'il vienne** there's a good chance he'll come, he's very likely to come; **faire payer le prix ~** to charge the full price; **être ~ dans l'adversité** to be strong in adversity; **âme ~e** steadfast soul; **~e tête** rebel. **(b)** (*doué*) good (*en, à* at). **il a trouvé plus ~ que lui** he has met (more than) his match; **ce n'est pas très ~ de sa part*** that's not very bright of him. **(c) ~ de cette garantie** fortified by this guarantee; **être ~ de son bon droit** to be confident of one's rights; **il se fait ~ de le faire** he's quite sure *ou* confident he can do it; **au sens ~ du terme** in the strongest sense of the term; **à plus ~e raison, tu aurais dû venir** all the more reason for you to have come; **c'est plus ~ que moi** I can't help it; **c'est plus ~ que de jouer au bouchon!** it's a real puzzle!; **c'est trop ~!** that's too much!; **c'est trop ~ pour moi** it's above *ou* beyond me; **elle est ~e celle-là!*** that takes the biscuit!*; **et le plus ~ c'est que ...** and the best part of it is that ... .

2 *adv* **(a)** *crier* loudly, loud; *lancer, frapper* hard. **parlez plus ~** speak up *ou* louder; **respirez bien ~** take a deep breath; **tu y vas un peu ~*** you're going a bit far. **(b)** *détester* greatly; *mécontent* most, highly. **j'en doute ~** I very much doubt it; **j'ai ~ à faire avec lui** I have a hard job with him; **il y avait ~ peu de monde** there were very few people; **tu le sais ~ bien** you know very well.

3 *nm* **(a)** (*forteresse*) fort. **(b)** (*personne*) **le ~ et le faible** the strong and the weak; **~ des Halles** market porter. **(c)** (*spécialité*) strong point. **(d)** (*milieu*) **au ~ de** *été* at the height of; *hiver* in the depths of; *combat* in the thick of.

fortement [fɔʀtəmɑ̃] *adv conseiller* strongly; *tenir* fast; *frapper* hard; *serrer* hard, tight. **~ marqué** strongly marked; **il en est ~ question** it is being seriously considered; **j'espère ~ que** I very much hope that; **~ intéressé par** most interested in.

forteresse [fɔʀtəʀɛs] *nf* fortress, stronghold.

fortifier [fɔʀtifje] (7) *vt* to strengthen, fortify. ♦ **fortifiant, e 1** *adj médicament* fortifying; *air* invigorating, bracing. **2** *nm* tonic. ♦ **fortification** *nf* fortification.

fortuit, e [fɔʀtɥi, ɥit] *adj* fortuitous, chance. ♦ **fortuitement** *adv* fortuitously, by chance.

fortune [fɔʀtyn] *nf* **(a)** (*richesse*) fortune. **situation de ~** financial situation; **avoir de la ~** to have private means; **faire ~** to make one's fortune; **le mot a fait ~** the word has become really popular. **(b)** (*chance*) luck, fortune; (*destinée*) fortune. **chercher ~** to seek one's fortune; **connaître des ~s diverses** to have varying luck; **il a eu la (bonne) ~ de le rencontrer** he was fortunate enough to meet him, he had the good fortune to meet him; **mauvaise ~** misfortune; **venez dîner à la ~ du pot** come to dinner and take pot luck with us. **(c) de ~** *installation* makeshift, rough-and-ready. ♦ **fortuné, e** *adj* (*riche*) wealthy; (*heureux*) fortunate.

forum [fɔʀɔm] *nm* forum.

fosse [fos] *nf* (*trou*) pit; (*tombe*) grave; (*pour le saut*) sandpit. **~ d'aisances** cesspool; **~ commune** communal grave; (*lit, fig*) **~ aux lions** lions' den; **~ d'orchestre** orchestra pit; **~ septique** septic tank.

fossé [fose] *nm* (*gén*) ditch; (*fig*) gulf, gap.

fossette [fosɛt] *nf* dimple.

fossile [fosil] *nm, adj* (*lit, fig*) fossil. ♦ **fossiliser** *vt*, **se** ~ *vpr* (1) to fossilize.
fossoyeur [foswajœʀ] *nm* gravedigger.
fou [fu], **fol** *devant n commençant par une voyelle ou h muet*, **folle** [fɔl] *f* **1** *adj* **(a)** *personne, idée etc* mad, crazy, insane; *imagination, gestes, course* wild. **devenir/rendre** ~ to go/drive mad *ou* crazy; ~ **à lier** raving mad; ~ **de colère** beside o.s. with anger; ~ **d'amour** madly *ou* wildly in love (*pour* with); **elle est folle de lui** she's mad* *ou* crazy* about him; **pas folle, la guêpe*** he's (*ou* she's) not stupid *ou* daft* you know!; **avoir le** ~ **rire** to have the giggles. **(b)** (*) *courage, vitesse, succès* fantastic*, terrific, tremendous; *prix* enormous, huge. **j'ai eu un mal** ~ **pour venir** I had a terrific *ou* terrible job to get here; **tu as mis un temps** ~ you've taken absolutely ages*; **dépenser un argent** ~ to spend loads *ou* pots of money*; **il y a un monde** ~ there are masses of people; **c'est** ~ **ce qu'il a changé** it's incredible *ou* unbelievable how he has changed. **(c)** *boussole* erratic; *camion, cheval* runaway; *cheveux* unruly. **2** *nm,f* (*insensé*) madman (*ou* madwoman), lunatic; (*bête*) fool. **faire le** ~ to play *ou* act the fool. **3** *nm* (*Échecs*) bishop; (*Hist: bouffon*) jester, fool.
foudre [fudʀ(ə)] *nf* lightning; (*Myth*) thunderbolt. **frappé par la** ~ struck by lightning; **s'attirer les** ~**s de qn** to bring down sb's wrath upon o.s.
foudroyer [fudʀwaje] (8) *vt [foudre]* to strike; *[maladie etc]* to strike down. ~ **qn du regard** to look daggers at sb. ♦ **foudroyant, e** *adj vitesse* lightning; *poison, maladie* violent; *succès* stunning. **nouvelle** ~**e** devastating piece of news.
fouetter [fwete] (1) *vt* (*gén, fig*) to whip; (*punition*) to flog; (*Culin*) to whisk; *imagination* to fire; *désir* to whip up. **la pluie fouette les vitres** the rain lashes *ou* whips the window panes; **il n'y a pas de quoi** ~ **un chat** it's nothing to make a fuss about. ♦ **fouet** *nm* whip; whisk.
fougère [fuʒɛʀ] *nf* fern. **couvert de** ~**(s)** overgrown with bracken.
fougue [fug] *nf* ardour, spirit. **plein de** ~ fiery. ♦ **fougueusement** *adv* with spirit, ardently. ♦ **fougueux, -euse** *adj* fiery, ardent; *jeunesse* hotheaded; *cheval* mettlesome; *attaque* spirited.
fouiller [fuje] (1) **1** *vt* (*gén*) to search; *personne* to frisk; *région* to scour; *ciel* to scan; *question* to go (deeply) into; *sol* to dig. **il fouilla l'obscurité des yeux** he peered into the darkness; **très fouillé** very detailed. **2** *vi*: ~ **dans** *armoire* to rummage in; *bagages* to go through; *mémoire* to search. **3 se** ~ *vpr* to search one's pockets. ♦ **fouille** *nf* search. (*Archéol*) ~s excavation(s); **faire des** ~**s** to carry out excavations.
fouillis [fuji] *nm [objets]* jumble; *[branchages]* tangle. **faire du** ~ to make a mess; **être en** ~ to be in a mess.
fouine [fwin] *nf* (*Zool*) stone marten; (*péj*) snooper*. **visage de** ~ weasel face. ♦ **fouiner** (1) *vi* (*péj*) to nose around *ou* about. ♦ **fouineur, -euse** (*péj*) **1** *adj* prying, nosey*. **2** *nm,f* snooper*.
fouir [fwiʀ] (2) *vi* to dig.
foulant, e* [fulɑ̃, ɑ̃t] *adj* killing, back-breaking.
foulard [fulaʀ] *nm* (*écharpe*) scarf; (*tissu*) foulard.
foule [ful] *nf* (*gén*) crowd; (*péj*) mob. (*le peuple*) **la** ~ the masses; **il n'y avait pas** ~! there was hardly anyone there!; **une** ~ **de** *gens* a crowd of; *objets, questions* masses *ou* heaps* of; **ils vinrent en** ~ **à l'exposition** they came in crowds *ou* they flocked to the exhibition.
fouler [fule] (1) **1** *vt raisins* to press; *sol* to walk *ou* tread upon. (*fig*) ~ **aux pieds** to trample underfoot. **2 se** ~ *vpr* **(a) se** ~ **la cheville** to sprain one's ankle. **(b)** (*: *travailler*) to flog o.s. to death*. ♦ **foulée** *nf [cheval, coureur]* stride. **être dans la** ~ **de qn** to follow (close) on sb's heels; (*fig*) **il l'a fait dans la** ~ he did it while he was at it *ou* while he was in his stride. ♦ **foulure** *nf* sprain.
four [fuʀ] *nm* **(a)** (*Culin*) oven; *[potier]* kiln; (*Ind*) furnace. **cuire au** ~ *gâteau* to bake; *viande* to roast; **plat allant au** ~ ovenproof dish; ~ **crématoire** crematorium furnace. **(b)** (*arg Théât*) flop, fiasco. **faire un** ~ to be a flop. **(c) (petit)** ~ fancy cake.
fourbe [fuʀb(ə)] *adj* deceitful, treacherous. ♦ **fourberie** *nf* (*acte*) deceit. **la** ~ deceitfulness, treachery.
fourbi* [fuʀbi] *nm* (*attirail*) gear*; (*fouillis*) mess. **et tout le** ~ and the whole caboodle*.
fourbu, e [fuʀby] *adj* exhausted.
fourche [fuʀʃ(ə)] *nf* (*gén*) fork; (*à foin*) pitchfork. *[route]* **faire une** ~ to fork. ♦ **fourcher** (1) *vi*: **ma langue a fourché** it was a slip of the tongue. ♦ **fourchette** *nf* (*lit*) fork; (*Statistique*) margin. **il a une bonne** ~ he has a hearty appetite. ♦ **fourchu, e** *adj arbre* forked. **pied** ~ cloven hoof.
fourgon [fuʀgɔ̃] *nm* (*wagon*) waggon; (*camion*) (large) van; (*diligence*) coach. ~ **mortuaire** hearse. ♦ **fourgonnette** *nf* small van.
fourgonner [fuʀgɔne] (1) *vi* to poke about, rake about (*dans* in).
fourguer* [fuʀge] (1) *vt* to unload* (*à* onto).
fourmi [fuʀmi] *nf* ant. **avoir des** ~**s dans les jambes** to have pins and needles in one's legs. ♦ **fourmilière** *nf* (*monticule*) ant-hill; (*intérieur*) ants' nest; (*fig*) hive of activity.
fourmiller [fuʀmije] (1) *vi* to swarm. ~ **de** to be swarming *ou* teeming with. ♦ **fourmillement** *nm* swarming. **un** ~ **d'idées** a welter of ideas; (*picotement*) ~s pins and needles (*dans* in).
fournaise [fuʀnɛz] *nf* blaze; (*fig*) furnace, oven.
fourneau, *pl* ~**x** [fuʀno] *nm* **(a)** (*poêle*) stove. **(b)** *[forge]* furnace; *[pipe]* bowl.
fournée [fuʀne] *nf* (*lit, fig*) batch.
fourni, e [fuʀni] *adj herbe, barbe* thick. **peu** ~ sparse, thin; **bien** ~ (*en marchandises*) well-stocked.
fourniment* [fuʀnimɑ̃] *nm* gear*.
fournir [fuʀniʀ] (2) **1** *vt* **(a)** (*approvisionner*) to supply. ~ **qn en** to supply sb with. **(b)** (*procurer*) (*gén*) to supply, provide; *pièce d'identité* to produce; *prestation, exemple* to give; *effort* to put in. ~ **qch à qn** to supply *ou* provide sb with sth; (*Cartes*) ~ **à cœur** to follow suit in hearts. **2** ~ **à** *vt indir besoins* to provide for. **3 se** ~ *vpr* to provide o.s. (*de* with). **je me fournis chez cet épicier** I shop at this grocer's. ♦ **fournisseur** *nm* (*commerçant*) tradesman; (*détaillant*) stockist, retailer; (*Comm, Ind*) supplier. ♦ **fourniture** *nf* supply. ~**s de bureau** office supplies.
fourrage [fuʀaʒ] *nm* fodder. ~ **vert** silage.
fourrager [fuʀaʒe] (3) *vi*: ~ **dans** to rummage through.
fourré[1] [fuʀe] *nm* thicket. **les** ~**s** the bushes.
fourreau, *pl* ~**x** [fuʀo] *nm [épée]* sheath; *[parapluie]* cover. **robe** ~ sheath dress.
fourrer [fuʀe] (1) **1** *vt* **(a)** (*: *mettre*) to stick*. ~ **qch dans un sac** to stick* *ou* shove* sth into a bag; ~ **son nez partout** to poke *ou* stick* one's nose into everything; ~ **qn dans le pétrin** to land sb in the soup*. **(b)** *volaille* to stuff; *manteau* to line (with fur). **2 se** ~* *vpr*: **il s'est fourré dans la tête que ...** he has got it into his head that ...; **se** ~ **dans un coin** to get in a corner; **où a-t-il encore été se** ~? where has he got to now?; **il ne savait plus où se** ~ he didn't know where to put himself. ♦ **fourré**[2], **e** *adj bonbon* filled; *gants* fur-lined. **chocolats** ~**s** chocolate creams; ~ **à la crème** cream(-filled). ♦ **fourre-tout** *nm inv* (*placard*) junk cupboard, glory-hole; (*sac*) holdall.
fourreur [fuʀœʀ] *nm* furrier.
fourrière [fuʀjɛʀ] *nf* pound. **emmener une voiture à la** ~ to tow away a car.

fourrure [fuʀyʀ] *nf* (*pelage*) coat; (*manteau etc*) fur.

fourvoyer [fuʀvwaje] (8) **1** *vt*: ~ **qn** *[guide]* to mislead sb; *[mauvais exemple]* to lead sb astray. **2 se** ~ *vpr* (*lit, fig*) to go astray. **se** ~ **dans** *lieu* to stray into; *aventure* to get involved in.

foutaise‡ [futɛz] *nf*: **de la** ~, **des** ~**s** rubbish*.

foutre‡ [futʀ(ə)] **1** *vt* (*faire*) to do; (*donner*) to give; (*mettre*) to stick*, shove*. **qu'est-ce qu'il fout** what the hell‡ is he doing *ou* up to; ~ **qn à la porte** to give sb the boot*, kick sb out*; **tout** ~ **en l'air** (*métier*) to chuck it all up‡; (*objet*) to chuck it all away‡; **fous-moi le camp!** clear off! **2 se** ~ *vpr*: **se** ~ **dedans** to boob*; **se** ~ **par terre** to go sprawling; **se** ~ **de qn** to take the mickey out of sb‡; **je m'en fous** I couldn't give a damn‡. ♦ **foutu, e‡** *adj*: **être** ~ *[malade]* to be done for; *[appareil]* to be bust*; **être bien/mal** ~ *[appareil]* to be damned clever/hopeless‡; (*habillé*) to be well/badly got up*; **se sentir mal** ~ to feel lousy‡; **il n'est pas** ~ **de le faire** he's damn well incapable of doing it‡; **ce** ~ **temps** this damned weather‡.

fox(-terrier), *pl* **fox(-terriers)** [fɔks(tɛʀje)] *nm* fox terrier.

foyer [fwaje] *nm* **(a)** (*maison*) home; (*famille*) family. **(b)** *[chaudière]* firebox; (*âtre*) hearth, fireplace. **(c)** *[vieillards, soldats]* home; *[étudiants]* hostel; (*club*) club; (*Théât*) foyer. ~ **des artistes** greenroom. **(d)** (*Opt, Phys*) focus. **(e)** ~ **de** *incendie, infection* seat of; *lumière* source of; *agitation, extrémistes* centre of.

fracas [fʀaka] *nm* (*gén*) crash; *[train, tonnerre]* roar; *[bataille]* din. ♦ **fracassant, e** *adj bruit* deafening; *déclaration* shattering, sensational. ♦ **fracasser** (1) **1** *vt* to smash, shatter. **2 se** ~ *vpr*: **se** ~ **contre** *ou* **sur** to crash against.

fraction [fʀaksjɔ̃] *nf* (*Math*) fraction; (*gén: partie*) part. **une** ~ **de seconde** a split second; **par** ~ **de** in fractions of. ♦ **fractionnement** *nm* splitting up, division. ♦ **fractionner** *vt*, **se** ~ *vpr* (1) to divide (up), split up.

fracture [fʀaktyʀ] *nf* (*Géol, Méd*) fracture. ♦ **fracturer** (1) *vt* (*Géol, Méd*) to fracture; *serrure* to break.

fragile [fʀaʒil] *adj* (*lit, fig: gén*) fragile; *peau* delicate; *verre* brittle; *équilibre* shaky; *bonheur, argument* frail, flimsy. (*sur étiquette*) **'attention** ~**'** 'fragile, with care'. ♦ **fragilité** *nf* fragility; delicacy; brittleness; shakiness; flimsiness, frailty.

fragment [fʀagmɑ̃] *nm* fragment, bit; *[conversation, chanson]* snatch; *[lettre]* part; (*extrait*) passage, extract. ♦ **fragmentaire** *adj* sketchy, fragmentary.

fragmenter [fʀagmɑ̃te] (1) **1** *vt état, terrain* to fragment, split up; *travail, somme* to split up (*en* into). **2 se** ~ *vpr [roches]* to fragment. ♦ **fragmentation** *nf* fragmentation; splitting up.

frais¹, fraîche [fʀɛ, fʀɛʃ] **1** *adj* **(a)** *vent, accueil* cool. **il fait** ~ it's rather cool. **(b)** *couleur, joues, parfum* fresh; *voix* clear; *joie, âme* pure. **(c)** *plaie, traces, nouvelles* fresh; *peinture* wet; *aliment, vêtement, troupes* fresh. **un peu d'air** ~ a breath of fresh air; ~ **et dispos,** ~ **comme une rose** as fresh as a daisy; ~ **comme un gardon** bright as a button; (*Comm*) **argent** ~ ready cash; **nous voilà** ~**!*** we're in a fix!* **2** *adv* **(a) il fait** ~ it's cool; **en été, il faut boire** ~ in summer you need cool drinks. **(b)** (*récemment*) newly. ~ **débarqué de sa province** fresh *ou* newly up from the country; **habillé de** ~ freshly changed. **3** *nm*: **prendre le** ~ to take a breath of cool air; **mettre (qch) au** ~ to put (sth) in a cool place. ♦ **fraîchement** *adv* (*récemment*) freshly, newly; *accueillir* coolly. **comment ça va? –** ~**!*** how are you? – a bit chilly! ♦ **fraîcheur** *nf* coolness; freshness; chilliness; purity. **la** ~ **du soir** the cool of the evening.

frais² [fʀɛ] *nmpl* **(a)** (*gén*) expenses; (*charges*) costs; (*Admin: droits*) charges, fees. ~ **de déplacement** travelling expenses; ~ **d'entretien** *[machine]* maintenance costs; ~ **de timbre** stamp charges; ~ **d'enregistrement** registration fees; ~ **généraux** overheads; ~ **divers** miscellaneous expenses; ~ **de scolarité** school fees; **séjour tous** ~ **compris** all-in holiday. **(b)** (*lit*) **se mettre en** ~ to go to great expense; **se mettre en** ~ **pour qn** to put o.s. out for sb; **faire les** ~ **de la conversation** (*parler*) to keep the conversation going; (*en être le sujet*) to be the main topic of conversation; **faire les** ~ **d'une erreur** to bear the brunt of a mistake; **j'en ai été pour mes** ~ I was wasting my time; **à ses** ~ at one's own expense; **aux** ~ **de la princesse*** at the firm's (*ou* the taxpayer's *etc*) expense; **à peu de** ~ *acheter* cheaply; *s'en tirer* lightly.

fraise [fʀɛz] *nf* **(a)** (*fruit*) strawberry. ~ **des bois** wild strawberry. **(b)** *[métallurgiste]* milling-cutter; *[dentiste]* drill. ♦ **fraiser** (1) *vt trou* to countersink; *pièce* to mill. ♦ **fraisier** *nm* strawberry plant.

framboise [fʀɑ̃bwaz] *nf* (*fruit*) raspberry. ♦ **framboisier** *nm* raspberry bush.

franc¹, franche [fʀɑ̃, fʀɑ̃ʃ] **1** *adj* **(a)** *personne, regard* frank, candid; *gaieté* open. ~ **comme l'or** perfectly frank. **(b)** *situation, différence* clear-cut; *cassure* clean; *répugnance* clear, definite; *couleur* clear, pure. **5 jours** ~**s** 5 clear days. **(c)** (*péj: total*) *imbécile, ingratitude* downright. **(d)** *zone, ville* free. (*Comm*) ~ **de port** postage paid. **2** *adv*: **à vous parler** ~ to be frank with you. **3**: ~**-maçon** *nm, pl* ~**s-**~**s** freemason; ~**-maçonnerie** *nf* freemasonry; ~**-parler** *nm* outspokenness; ~**-tireur** *nm, pl* ~**s-**~**s** (*Mil*) irregular; (*fig*) freelance; **agir en** ~**-tireur** to act independently.

franc² [fʀɑ̃] *nm* (*monnaie*) franc.

français, e [fʀɑ̃sɛ, ɛz] **1** *adj* French. **2** *nm* **(a) F**~ Frenchman; **les F**~ (*gens*) the French, French people; (*hommes*) Frenchmen. **(b)** (*Ling*) **le** ~ French. **3** *nf*: **F**~**e** Frenchwoman. ♦ **France** *nf* France.

Francfort [fʀɑ̃kfɔʀ] *n* Frankfurt.

franchement [fʀɑ̃ʃmɑ̃] *adv* **(a)** (*honnêtement*) *parler* frankly, candidly; *agir* openly. ~, **qu'en penses-tu?** what do you honestly think?; **il y a des gens,** ~! really! *ou* honestly! some people!; ~ **non** frankly no. **(b)** (*sans hésiter*) *frapper* boldly; *demander* clearly, straight out. **allez-y** ~ (*explication*) go straight to the point; (*manœuvre etc*) go right ahead; **c'est** ~ **plus lourd** it's distinctly heavier. **(c)** (*tout à fait*) *mauvais, laid* downright, really; *bon* really. **on s'est** ~ **bien amusé** we really *ou* thoroughly enjoyed ourselves; **c'est** ~ **trop cher** it's much *ou* far too dear.

franchir [fʀɑ̃ʃiʀ] (2) *vt obstacle* to clear, jump over; *rue, seuil* to cross; *porte* to go through; *distance* to cover; *mur du son* to break (through); *difficulté* to surmount; *limite* to overstep. **il lui reste 10 mètres à** ~ he still has 10 metres to go; ~ **le cap de la soixantaine** to turn sixty. ♦ **franchissement** *nm* clearing; crossing; overstepping.

franchise [fʀɑ̃ʃiz] *nf* **(a)** *[personne, réponse]* frankness; *[regard]* candour. **(b)** (*exemption*) exemption; (*Hist*) *[ville]* franchise. **'**~ **postale'** ≃ 'official paid'; ~ **de bagages** baggage allowance. **(c)** (*Assurance*) excess.

franco [fʀɑ̃ko] *adv* (*Comm*) ~ **(de port)** postage-paid; **y aller** ~***** (*explication*) to go straight to the point; (*manœuvre*) to go right ahead.

franco- [fʀɑ̃ko] *préf* franco-. ♦ **franco-canadien** *nm* French Canadian. ♦ **francophile** *adj, nmf* francophile. ♦ **francophilie** *nf* francomania. ♦ **francophobe** *adj, nmf* francophobe. ♦ **francophobie** *nf* francophobia. ♦ **francophone** **1** *adj* French-speaking. **2** *nmf* (native) French speaker. ♦ **francophonie** *nf* French-speaking communities.

frange [fʀɑ̃ʒ] *nf* (*lit*) fringe; *[conscience]* threshold. ♦ **franger** (3) *vt* to fringe (*de* with).

frangin* [fʀɑ̃ʒɛ̃] *nm* brother. ♦ **frangine*** *nf* sister.

franquette* [fʀɑ̃kɛt] *nf*: **à la bonne ~** simply, without any fuss.

frappant, e [fʀapɑ̃, ɑ̃t] *adj* striking.

frappe [fʀap] *nf* **(a)** *[médaille]* (*action*) striking; (*empreinte*) stamp. **(b)** *[dactylo]* (*souplesse*) touch; (*impression*) typeface. **la lettre est à la ~** the letter is being typed; **la première ~** the top copy.

frapper [fʀape] (1) **1** *vt* **(a)** (*lit, fig*) to strike; *[projectile, mesure]* to hit; *[couteau]* to stab. **~ le sol du pied** to stamp one's foot on the ground; **~ le regard/l'imagination** to catch the eye/the imagination; **la pluie/la lumière frappait le mur** the rain lashed against/the light fell on the wall; **frappé à mort** fatally wounded; **frappé de paralysie/par le malheur** stricken with paralysis/by misfortune; **frappé de stupeur** thunderstruck; **frappé de panique** panic-stricken; **~ qn d'une amende/d'un impôt** to impose a fine/a tax upon sb; **la loi doit ~ les coupables** the law must punish the guilty. **(b)** *monnaie, médaille* to strike. **(c)** (*glacer*) *vin* to put on ice; *café* to ice. **à boire frappé** serve chilled. **2** *vi* to strike (*sur* on, *contre* against). **~ sur la table** to bang on the table (*avec* with); **~ dans ses mains** to clap one's hands; **entrez sans ~** come in without knocking, come straight in; (*fig*) **~ à toutes les portes** to try every door; (*fig*) **~ à la bonne/mauvaise porte** to go to the right/wrong person *ou* place. **3 se ~** *vpr* **(a) se ~ la poitrine** to beat one's breast; **se ~ le front** to tap one's forehead. **(b)** (*: *se tracasser*) to get (o.s.) worked up*.

frasque [fʀask(ə)] *nf* escapade.

fraternel, -elle [fʀatɛʀnɛl] *adj* brotherly, fraternal. ♦ **fraternisation** *nf* fraternization. ♦ **fraterniser** (1) *vi* to fraternize (*avec* with). ♦ **fraternité** *nf* fraternity.

fraude [fʀod] *nf*: **la ~** fraud; (*à un examen*) cheating; **en ~** *vendre* fraudulently; *lire* secretly; **passer qch en ~** to smuggle sth in; **~ électorale** electoral fraud; **~ fiscale** tax evasion. ♦ **frauder** (1) **1** *vt* to cheat. **~ le fisc** to evade taxation. **2** *vi* (*gén*) to cheat (*sur* over). ♦ **fraudeur, -euse** *nm,f* (*gén*) person guilty of fraud; (*à la douane*) smuggler; (*envers le fisc*) tax evader. ♦ **frauduleusement** *adv* fraudulently. ♦ **frauduleux, -euse** *adj* fraudulent.

frayer [fʀeje] (8) **1** *vt* *chemin* to open up, clear. (*fig*) **~ la voie** to pave the way. **2 se ~** *vpr*: **se ~ un passage (dans la foule)** to force one's way through (the crowd).

frayeur [fʀɛjœʀ] *nf* fright. **cri de ~** cry of fear.

fredaine [fʀədɛn] *nf* escapade.

fredonner [fʀədɔne] (1) *vt* to hum.

freezer [fʀizœʀ] *nm* ice-box, freezer (*of refrigerator*).

frégate [fʀegat] *nf* frigate.

frein [fʀɛ̃] *nm* (*lit, fig*) brake; *[cheval]* bit. **mets le ~** put the brake on; **mettre un ~ à** to curb, check; **sans ~** unbridled, unchecked; **~ à main** hand-brake; **~ moteur** engine braking. ♦ **freinage** *nm* braking. ♦ **freiner** (1) **1** *vt* *véhicule* to pull up, slow down; *progression* to hold up; *joie, évolution* to check. **2** *vi* (*Aut*) to brake; (*à ski etc*) to slow down.

frelaté, e [fʀəlate] *adj* *aliment* adulterated; *milieu* tainted.

frêle [fʀɛl] *adj* (*lit, fig*) frail.

frelon [fʀəlɔ̃] *nm* hornet.

frémir [fʀemiʀ] (2) *vi* **(a)** (*de peur*) to shiver, shudder; (*de fièvre, froid*) to shiver, tremble; (*de colère*) to shake; (*d'espoir*) to tremble (*de* with). **toute la salle frémissait** the whole audience trembled. **(b)** *[lèvres, feuillage]* to tremble, quiver; *[eau chaude]* to simmer. ♦ **frémissement** *nm* shudder; shiver; quiver. **un ~ de plaisir** a thrill *ou* quiver of pleasure; **le ~** *ou* **les ~s de** *lèvres* the trembling *ou* quivering of; *eau* the simmering of.

frêne [fʀɛn] *nm* ash (tree).

frénésie [fʀenezi] *nf* frenzy. ♦ **frénétique** *adj* frenzied, frenetic. ♦ **frénétiquement** *adv* frenetically, furiously.

fréquent, e [fʀekɑ̃, ɑ̃t] *adj* frequent. ♦ **fréquemment** *adv* frequently. ♦ **fréquence** *nf* frequency.

fréquenter [fʀekɑ̃te] (1) *vt* *lieu* to frequent; *voisins* to see frequently; *jeune fille* to go around with. **~ la bonne société** to move in fashionable circles. ♦ **fréquentable** *adj*: **sont-ils ~s?** are they the sort of people one can associate with? ♦ **fréquentation** *nf* **(a)** *[établissement]* frequenting. **la ~ de ces gens** frequent contact with these people. **(b)** (*relations*) **~s** company. ♦ **fréquenté, e** *adj* *lieu* busy. (*fig*) **bien/mal ~** of good/ill repute.

frère [fʀɛʀ] *nm* (*gén*) brother. **partager en ~s** to share like brothers; **~s d'armes** brothers in arms; **peuples ~s** sister countries; (*Rel*) **mes ~s** brethren; **~ lai** lay brother; **~ Antoine** Brother Antoine, Friar Antoine; **mettre qn chez les ~s** to send sb to a Catholic boarding school.

fresque [fʀɛsk(ə)] *nf* (*Art*) fresco; (*Littérat*) portrait.

fret [fʀɛ] *nm* (*prix*) (*Aviat, Naut*) freightage; (*Aut*) carriage; (*cargaison*) (*Aviat, Naut*) freight, cargo; (*Aut*) load. ♦ **fréter** (6) *vt* (*prendre à fret*) to charter; (*donner à fret*) to freight.

frétiller [fʀetije] (1) *vi* *[poisson, personne]* to wriggle; *[chien]* to wag its tail. **~ de joie** to quiver with joy. ♦ **frétillement** *nm* *[poisson]* **~(s)** wriggling; **~ d'impatience** quiver of impatience.

friable [fʀijabl(ə)] *adj* crumbly, flaky.

friand, e [fʀijɑ̃, ɑ̃d] **1** *adj*: **~ de** fond of. **2** *nm* (*pâté*) (minced) meat pie. ♦ **friandise** *nf* titbit, delicacy.

fric: [fʀik] *nm* (*argent*) dough:, cash*, lolly:.

fric-frac*, *pl* **~-~(s)** [fʀikfʀak] *nm* break-in.

friche [fʀiʃ] *nf* fallow land. (*lit, fig*) **être/laisser en ~** to lie/let lie fallow.

friction [fʀiksjɔ̃] *nf* (*Phys, Tech, fig*) friction; (*massage*) rub-down; (*chez le coiffeur*) scalp massage. ♦ **frictionner** (1) *vt* to rub.

frigidaire [fʀiʒidɛʀ] *nm* ®, **frigo*** [fʀigo] *nm* refrigerator, fridge. ♦ **frigorifier** (7) *vt* (*lit*) to refrigerate. **être frigorifié*** to be frozen stiff. ♦ **frigorifique** *adj* *camion* refrigerator.

frileux, -euse [fʀilø, øz] *adj* *personne* sensitive to the cold; *geste* shivery. ♦ **frileusement** *adv* shiveringly.

frime* [fʀim] *nf*: **c'est de la ~** that's a lot of eyewash*; **c'est pour la ~** it's all *ou* just for show.

frimousse [fʀimus] *nf* (sweet) little face.

fringale* [fʀɛ̃gal] *nf* raging hunger.

fringant, e [fʀɛ̃gɑ̃, ɑ̃t] *adj* *cheval* frisky; *personne* dashing.

fringuer (se): [fʀɛ̃ge] (1) *vpr* to get dressed. ♦ **fringues**: *nfpl* togs*.

friper *vt*, **se ~** *vpr* [fʀipe] (1) to crumple.

fripier, -ière [fʀipje, jɛʀ] *nm,f* secondhand clothes dealer.

fripon, -onne [fʀipɔ̃, ɔn] **1** *adj* roguish. **2** *nm,f* rogue. ♦ **friponnerie** *nf* (*acte*) piece of mischief, prank.

fripouille [fʀipuj] *nf* (*péj*) rogue.

frire [fʀiʀ] *vti*: **~, faire ~** to fry.

frise [fʀiz] *nf* (*Archit, Art*) frieze.

friser [fʀize] (1) **1** *vt* **(a)** *cheveux* to curl; *moustache* to twirl. **~ qn** to curl sb's hair. **(b)** *surface* to graze, skim; *mort* to come within a hair's breadth of; *insolence* to border on. ~ **la soixantaine** to be nearly sixty. 2 *vi [cheveux]* to curl; *[personne]* to have curly hair. **se faire** ~ to have one's hair curled. ♦ **frisé, e** 1 *adj cheveux* curly; *personne* curly-haired. 2 *nf* (*chicorée*) curly endive. ♦ **frisette** *nf* little curl.

frisquet* [fʀiskɛ] *adj m* chilly.

frissonner [fʀisɔne] (1) *vi* **(a)** (*de peur*) to shiver, shudder; (*de fièvre, froid*) to shiver, tremble; (*de désir*) to quiver, tremble; (*de colère*) to shake (*de* with). **(b)** *[feuillage]* to quiver, tremble; *[lac]* to ripple. ♦ **frisson** *nm* shiver; shudder; quiver. ~ **de désir** quiver of desire; **ça me donne le** ~ it gives me the shivers*. ♦ **frissonnement** *nm* shiver, shudder. **le** ~ **du feuillage** the quivering of the leaves.

frit, e [fʀi, fʀit] 1 *adj* fried. 2 *nf* chip. ~**s** chips, French fries (*US*). ♦ **friteuse** *nf* chip pan, deep fryer. ♦ **friture** *nf* **(a)** (*Culin*) (*méthode*) frying; (*graisse*) deep fat; (*mets*) fried fish. **(b)** (*Rad**) crackle.

frivole [fʀivɔl] *adj* frivolous. ♦ **frivolement** *adv* frivolously. ♦ **frivolité** *nf* frivolity.

froc [fʀɔk] *nm* (*Rel*) frock, habit; (‡: *pantalon*) trousers, bags*.

froid, e [fʀwa, fʀwad] 1 *adj* (*gén*) cold; *accueil* cold, cool; *calcul* cool. **ça me laisse** ~ it leaves me cold; **garder la tête** ~**e** to keep cool, keep a cool head; **souder à** ~ to cold-weld; **démarrer à** ~ to start (from) cold; **cueillir qn à** ~* to catch sb unawares *ou* off guard. 2 *nm* **(a) le** ~ (*gén*) the cold; (*industrie*) refrigeration; **j'ai** ~ I am cold; **j'ai** ~ **aux pieds** my feet are cold; **il fait un** ~ **de canard*** it's freezing cold *ou* perishing*; **ça me fait** ~ **dans le dos** (*lit*) it makes my back cold; (*fig*) it sends shivers down my spine; **prendre (un coup de)** ~ to catch cold *ou* a chill; **vague de** ~ cold spell; **n'avoir pas** ~ **aux yeux** to be adventurous. **(b)** (*brouille*) coolness. **être en** ~ **avec qn** to be on bad terms with sb. ♦ **froidement** *adv accueillir* coldly; *calculer* coolly; *tuer* in cold blood. ♦ **froideur** *nf* coldness. **recevoir qn avec** ~ to greet sb coldly.

froisser [fʀwase] (1) 1 *vt habit* to crumple, crease; *personne* to hurt, offend. 2 **se** ~ *vpr [tissu]* to crease, crumple; *[personne]* to take offence (*de* at). **se** ~ **un muscle** to strain a muscle. ♦ **froissement** *nm [tissu]* crumpling, creasing; (*bruit*) rustle.

frôler [fʀole] (1) *vt* (*lit*) (*toucher*) to brush against; (*passer près de*) to skim. ~ **la mort** to come within a hair's breadth of death. ♦ **frôlement** *nm* (*contact*) light touch *ou* contact; (*bruit*) rustle.

fromage [fʀɔmaʒ] *nm* cheese. **plat au** ~ cheese dish; **trouver un (bon)** ~* to find a cushy job*; ~ **blanc** soft white cheese; ~ **de chèvre** goat's milk cheese; ~ **de tête** pork brawn. ♦ **fromager, -ère** 1 *adj* cheese. 2 *nm* (*marchand*) cheesemonger. ♦ **fromagerie** *nf* cheese dairy.

froment [fʀɔmɑ̃] *nm* wheat.

froncer [fʀɔ̃se] (3) *vt* (*Couture*) to gather. ~ **les sourcils** to frown, knit one's brows. ♦ **fronce** *nf* gather. **à** ~**s** gathered. ♦ **froncement** *nm*: ~ **de sourcils** frown.

fronde [fʀɔ̃d] *nf* (*arme*) sling; (*jouet*) catapult; (*fig*) revolt. ♦ **frondeur, -euse** *adj* rebellious.

front [fʀɔ̃] *nm* (*Anat*) forehead, brow; *[bâtiment]* façade, front; (*Mét, Mil, Pol*) front. **marcher le** ~ **haut** to hold one's head up high; **la honte sur son** ~ the shame on his face; ~ **de mer** sea front; **tué au** ~ killed in action; **de** ~ *attaque* frontal; *choc, heurter* head-on; **marcher à trois de** ~ to walk three abreast; **mener plusieurs tâches de** ~ to have several tasks on the go at one time; **aborder de** ~ **un problème** to tackle a problem head-on; **faire** ~ to face up to things; **faire** ~ **à l'ennemi** to face up *ou* stand up to the enemy; **faire** ~ **commun contre** to join forces against; **avoir le** ~ **de faire** to have the effrontery *ou* front to do. ♦ **frontal, e,** *mpl* **-aux** *adj collision* head-on; *attaque,* (*Anat, Géom*) frontal.

frontière [fʀɔ̃tjɛʀ] *nf* (*Géog, Pol*) frontier, border. **à l'intérieur et au-delà de nos** ~**s** at home and abroad; ~ **naturelle** natural boundary; **les** ~**s du savoir** the frontiers of knowledge; (*fig*) **à la** ~ **du rêve et de la réalité** on the borderline between dream and reality; **ville** ~ frontier *ou* border town. ♦ **frontalier, -ière** 1 *adj* border, frontier. 2 *nm,f* inhabitant of the frontier zone.

fronton [fʀɔ̃tɔ̃] *nm* pediment.

frotter [fʀɔte] (1) 1 *vt* (*gén*) to rub; *allumette* to strike; *meubles, chaussures* to rub up, shine; *plancher* to scrub; (*pour enlever la terre*) to scrape. ~ **les oreilles à qn** to box sb's ears. 2 *vi* to rub, scrape. 3 **se** ~ *vpr* to rub o.s. (*lit, fig*) **se** ~ **les mains** to rub one's hands; **se** ~ **à qn** to cross swords with sb. ♦ **frottement** *nm* (*action*) rubbing; (*lit, fig: friction*) friction.

frousse* [fʀus] *nf* fright. **avoir la** ~ to be scared stiff*. ♦ **froussard, e*** *nm,f* (*péj*) coward.

fructifier [fʀyktifje] (7) *vi [investissement]* to yield a profit. **faire** ~ to increase.

fructueux, -euse [fʀyktɥø, øz] *adj* fruitful, profitable. ♦ **fructueusement** *adv* fruitfully, profitably.

frugal, e, *mpl* **-aux** [fʀygal, o] *adj* frugal. ♦ **frugalement** *adv* frugally. ♦ **frugalité** *nf* frugality.

fruit [fʀɥi] *nm* fruit. **il y a des** ~**s** there is some fruit; **3** ~**s** 3 pieces of fruit; (*espèce*) 3 fruits; **les** ~**s de son travail** the fruits of one's work; **porter ses** ~**s** to bear fruit; **avec** ~ fruitfully; **sans** ~ fruitlessly; ~**s confits** candied fruits; ~**s de mer** seafood. ♦ **fruité, e** *adj* fruity. ♦ **fruitier, -ière** 1 *adj* fruit. 2 *nm,f* fruiterer, greengrocer.

frusques [fʀysk(ə)] *nfpl* (*péj*) togs*. **vieilles** ~ rags.

fruste [fʀyst(ə)] *adj* coarse, unrefined.

frustrer [fʀystʀe] (1) *vt* to frustrate. ~ **qn de** *satisfaction* to deprive sb of; *biens* to defraud sb of. ♦ **frustration** *nf* frustration.

fuel(-oil) [fjul(ɔjl)] *nm* fuel oil.

fugitif, -ive [fyʒitif, iv] 1 *adj personne* runaway; *impression etc* fleeting. 2 *nm,f* fugitive.

fugue [fyg] *nf* **(a) faire une** ~ to run away, abscond. **(b)** (*Mus*) fugue.

fuir [fɥiʀ] (17) 1 *vt personne, danger* to shun, avoid; *obligation* to evade, shirk; *patrie, bourreaux* to flee from, run away from. 2 *vi* **(a)** *[prisonnier]* to run away, escape; *[troupes]* to take flight, flee. **faire** ~ (*Mil*) to put to flight; (*fig*) to chase off *ou* away; ~ **devant** to run away from. **(b)** *[bateau]* to glide swiftly along; *[temps]* to fly by, slip by; *[paysage]* to recede. **(c)** *[liquide, récipient]* to leak. ♦ **fuite** *nf* **(a)** *[fugitif]* flight, escape. **la** ~ **des capitaux** the flight of capital; **prendre la** ~ to take (to) flight; **mettre qn en** ~ to put sb to flight; **les prisonniers sont en** ~ the prisoners are on the run; **les voleurs en** ~ the runaway thieves. **(b)** *[temps, bateau]* swift passage. **(c)** *[liquide, nouvelle, récipient]* leak. **avaries dues à des** ~**s** damage caused by leakage.

fulgurant, e [fylgyʀɑ̃, ɑ̃t] *adj vitesse, réplique* lightning; *regard* blazing; *douleur* searing.

fulminer [fylmine] (1) *vi* to be enraged. ~ **contre** to fulminate against.

fumer [fyme] (1) 1 *vi [feu]* to smoke; *[liquide]* to steam; *[produit chimique]* to fume; (*: *être en colère*) to be fuming* (*de* with). ~ **comme un sapeur** to smoke like a chimney. 2 *vt tabac* to smoke; (*Culin*) to smoke; (*Agr*) to manure. ♦ **fumé, e**[1] *adj* smoked. ♦ **fume-cigarette** *nm inv* cigarette holder. ♦ **fumée**[2] *nf* smoke; steam. (*Chim*) ~**s** fumes; **la** ~ **ne vous gêne pas?** do you mind my smoking?; **sans** ~ smokeless;

partir en ~ to go up in smoke; **il n'y a pas de** ~ **sans feu** there's no smoke without fire.
fumet [fymɛ] *nm* aroma.
fumeur, -euse[1] [fymœʀ, øz] *nm,f* smoker. **non-**~ non-smoker.
fumeux, -euse[2] [fymø, øz] *adj* **(a)** (*confus*) woolly. **(b)** *flamme* smoky; *horizon* misty.
fumier [fymje] *nm* (*engrais*) dung, manure; (‡: *salaud*) bastard‡.
fumiste [fymist(ə)] **1** *nm* (*réparateur*) heating mechanic; (*ramoneur*) chimney sweep. **2** *nmf* (*péj*) (*employé*) shirker; (*philosophe*) phoney*. ♦ **fumisterie** *nf* (*péj*) **c'est une** ~ it's a fraud *ou* a con‡.
fumure [fymyʀ] *nf* (*engrais*) manure.
funambule [fynɑ̃byl] *nmf* tightrope walker.
funèbre [fynɛbʀ(ə)] *adj* (*gén*) funeral; *ton* mournful, funereal; *atmosphère* gloomy, dismal. **veillée** ~ deathbed vigil.
funérailles [fyneʀɑj] *nfpl* funeral.
funéraire [fyneʀɛʀ] *adj* funeral. **pierre** ~ gravestone.
funeste [fynɛst(ə)] *adj* **(a)** (*désastreux*) (*gén*) disastrous; *erreur* grievous; *conseil, influence* harmful. **jour** ~ fateful *ou* ill-fated day. **(b)** (*de mort*) *vision* of death. **(c)** *accident* fatal; *coup* fatal, lethal, deadly; *projet* lethal, deadly.
funiculaire [fynikylɛʀ] *nm* funicular railway.
fur [fyʀ] *nm*: **au** ~ **et à mesure** (*gén*) little by little; **dépenser au** ~ **et à mesure** to spend as fast *ou* as soon as one earns; **passe-moi les assiettes au** ~ **et à mesure** pass the plates to me as you go along; **au** ~ **et à mesure que vous les recevez** as (soon as) you receive them; **au** ~ **et à mesure de vos besoins** as and when you need it.
furax‡ [fyʀaks] *adj inv* hopping mad*.
furet [fyʀɛ] *nm* (*animal*) ferret.
fureter [fyʀte] (5) *vi* to nose *ou* ferret *ou* pry about. ♦ **fureteur, -euse** *adj* prying, inquisitive.
fureur [fyʀœʀ] *nf* (*gén*) fury. **crise de** ~ fit of rage; **être en** ~ to be infuriated *ou* enraged; **mettre en** ~ to infuriate, enrage; **la** ~ **du jeu** a passion for gambling; **avec** ~ *dire* with rage, furiously; *aimer* madly, passionately; **faire** ~ to be all the rage. ♦ **furibond, e** *adj* furious. ♦ **furie** *nf* (*péj: mégère*) shrew; (*Myth*) Fury; (*colère, violence*) fury. **la** ~ **du jeu** a passion for gambling; **en** ~ *personne* infuriated, enraged; *mer* raging. ♦ **furieux, -euse** *adj* (*gén*) furious (*contre* with, at); (*hum: fort*) *envie, coup* tremendous. ♦ **furieusement** *adv* furiously; tremendously.
furoncle [fyʀɔ̃kl(ə)] *nm* boil.
furtif, -ive [fyʀtif, iv] *adj* furtive, stealthy. ♦ **furtivement** *adv* furtively, stealthily.
fusain [fyzɛ̃] *nm* (*crayon*) charcoal crayon; (*croquis*) charcoal drawing; (*arbre*) spindle-tree.
fuseau, *pl* ~**x** [fyzo] *nm [fileuse]* spindle; *[dentelière]* bobbin. **(pantalon)** ~, ~**x** stretch ski pants; **en (forme de)** ~ *colonne* swelled; *jambes* slender; ~ **horaire** time zone.
fusée [fyze] *nf* (*gén*) rocket; *[obus, mine]* fuse. ~ **éclairante** flare; ~ **spatiale** space rocket.
fuselage [fyzlaʒ] *nm* fuselage.
fuselé, e [fyzle] *adj colonne* swelled; *jambes* slender.
fuser [fyze] (1) *vi [cris]* to burst forth; *[liquide]* to gush *ou* spurt out; *[étincelles]* to fly; *[lumière]* to stream out.
fusible [fyzibl(ə)] *nm* fuse.
fusil [fyzi] *nm* **(a)** (*arme*) rifle, gun; (*de chasse*) shotgun. (*fig*) **c'est un bon** ~ he's a good shot; **changer son** ~ **d'épaule** to change one's plans; ~ **mitrailleur** machine gun; ~ **sous-marin** (underwater) speargun. **(b)** (*allume-gaz*) gas lighter; (*à aiguiser*) steel. ♦ **fusilier** *nm* (*Hist*) fusilier. ~ **marin** marine. ♦ **fusillade** *nf* (*bruit*) gunfire, shooting; (*combat*) shooting battle. ♦ **fusiller** (1) *vt* (*lit*) to shoot; (*: *casser*) to mess up*. ~ **qn du regard** to look daggers at sb.
fusion [fyzjɔ̃] *nf* **(a)** (*gén, Phys*) fusion; *[métal, glace]* melting; *[idées]* merging, blending. **(b)** (*Comm*) merger, amalgamation. ♦ **fusionner** (1) *vti* (*Comm*) to merge, amalgamate; (*Pol*) to merge.
fustiger [fystiʒe] (3) *vt adversaire* to flay; *pratiques* to censure, denounce.
fût [fy] *nm* **(a)** *[arbre]* trunk; *[colonne]* shaft. **(b)** (*tonneau*) barrel.
futaie [fytɛ] *nf* forest.
futé, e [fyte] *adj* crafty, sly.
futile [fytil] *adj* (*gén*) futile; *personne* frivolous. ♦ **futilité** *nf* futility; frivolousness. ~**s** trivialities.
futur, e [fytyʀ] **1** *adj* future. ~**e maman** mother-to-be; ~ **champion** budding *ou* future champion. **2** *nm* (*Ling, avenir*) **le** ~ the future; **le** ~ **proche** the immediate future; **le** ~ **antérieur** the future perfect. **3** *nm,f* fiancé(e), husband-(*ou* wife-) to-be.
fuyant, e [fɥijɑ̃, ɑ̃t] *adj regard, personne* evasive; *front* receding; *lignes, vision* fleeting.
fuyard, e [fɥijaʀ, aʀd(ə)] *nm,f* runaway.

G

G, g [ʒe] *nm* (*lettre*) G, g.
gabardine [gabaʀdin] *nf* (*tissu*) gabardine; (*manteau*) gabardine (raincoat).
gabarit [gabaʀi] *nm* (*dimension*) size; (*fig: valeur*) calibre; (*maquette*) template.
Gabon [gabɔ̃] *nm*: **le ~** the Gabon.
gâcher [gɑʃe] (1) *vt* **(a)** *plâtre* to temper; *mortier* to mix. **(b)** (*gaspiller*) to waste; (*bâcler*) to botch; (*gâter*) to spoil. **il nous a gâché notre plaisir** he spoiled our pleasure. ♦ **gâcheur, -euse 1** *adj* wasteful. **2** *nm,f* wasteful person; (*d'argent*) spendthrift. ♦ **gâchis** *nm* (*désordre*) mess; (*gaspillage*) waste.
gâchette [gɑʃɛt] *nf [arme]* trigger. **il a la ~ facile** he's trigger-happy.
gadget [gadʒɛt] *nm* (*gén: machin*) thingummy*; (*ustensile*) gadget; (*trouvaille*) gimmick.
gadoue [gadu] *nf* (*boue*) mud, sludge; (*neige*) slush.
gaffe [gaf] *nf* **(a)** (*bévue*) blunder, boob*. **(b)** (*Naut*) boat hook; (*Pêche*) gaff. **(c)** (*) **faire ~** to be careful (*à* of). ♦ **gaffer** (1) **1** *vi* to blunder, boob*. **2** *vt* to hook; to gaff. ♦ **gaffeur, -euse** *nm,f* blunderer.
gag [gag] *nm* (*Ciné, Théât*) gag.
gaga* [gaga] *adj* gaga*, senile.
gage [gaʒ] *nm* **(a)** (*à créancier*) security; (*à prêteur*) pledge. **mettre qch en ~** to pawn sth; **laisser qch en ~** to leave sth as (a) security; **~ de sincérité** proof *ou* evidence of one's sincerity; **~ d'amour** token of one's love; **en ~ de notre amitié** as a token *ou* in token of our friendship. **(b)** (*Jeux*) forfeit. **(c)** (*salaire*) **~s** wages; **tueur à ~s** hired killer; **être aux ~s de qn** (*gén*) to be employed by sb; (*péj*) to be in the pay of sb.
gager [gaʒe] (3) *vt* **(a)** (*parier*) **~ que** to wager that, bet that. **(b)** *emprunt* to guarantee.
gageure [gaʒyʀ] *nf* (*pari*) wager. **c'est une véritable ~ que de vouloir le faire** it's attempting the impossible to try to do it.
gagner [gɑɲe] (1) **1** *vt* **(a)** (*par le travail, l'effort*) to earn. **~ sa vie/sa croûte*** to earn one's living/one's bread and butter; **~ de l'argent** (*dans une affaire*) to make money. **(b)** (*par le hasard, la lutte*) to win. (*lit, fig*) **~ le gros lot** to hit *ou* win the jackpot; **~ qn de vitesse** to beat sb to it*. **(c)** (*obtenir*) to gain. **vous n'y gagnerez rien** you'll gain nothing by it; **~ du temps** (*temporiser*) to gain time; (*économiser*) to save time; (*lit, fig*) **~ du terrain** to gain ground; **vous y gagnerez un bon rhume** you'll get nothing but a bad cold. **(d)** *gardiens, témoins* to win over; *confiance* to win, gain. **se laisser ~ par les prières de qn** to be won over by sb's prayers. **(e)** *lieu, refuge* to reach. **~ qn** *[sommeil, peur]* to overcome sb, creep over sb; **le feu gagna le toit** the fire spread to the roof.

2 *vi* **(a)** (*être vainqueur*) to win. **~ aux courses** to win on the horses *ou* at the races; **il gagne sur tous les tableaux** he's winning all the way; **tu as gagné!*** you got what you asked for! **(b)** (*trouver un avantage*) **vous y gagnez** it's in your interest, it's to your advantage; **qu'est-ce que j'y gagne?** what do I get out of it? *ou* gain from it?; **vous gagneriez à partir en groupe** you'd be better off going in a group; **~ au change** to make on the deal. **(c)** (*s'améliorer*) **~ en hauteur** to increase in height; **il gagne à être connu** he improves on acquaintance; **ce roman gagne à être relu** this novel gains by a second reading. **(d)** *[incendie, épidémie]* to spread, gain ground.
♦ **gagnant, e 1** *adj* winning. **on le donne ~** he is the favourite to win. **2** *nm,f* winner. ♦ **gagne-pain*** *nm inv* job.
gai, e [ge] *adj* **(a)** *personne, voix* cheerful, happy; *caractère* cheerful, merry. **~ luron** cheery fellow; **~ comme un pinson** happy as a lark. **(b)** (*euph: ivre*) merry, tipsy. **(c)** *couleur, robe* bright, gay; *pièce* bright, cheerful. **(d)** (*iro: amusant*) **c'est ~!** that's great*; **ça va être ~, les vacances avec lui!** the holidays are going to be great fun with him around! ♦ **gaiement** *adv* cheerfully; happily; cheerily; merrily. (*iro*) **allons-y ~!** let's get on with it! ♦ **gaieté** *nf [personne, roman]* cheerfulness, gaiety; *[couleur]* brightness, gaiety. **de ~ de cœur** lightheartedly; (*joies*) **les ~s de** the delights *ou* joys of.
gaillard, e [gajaʀ, aʀd(ə)] **1** *adj* **(a)** *personne* strong; *allure* lively, sprightly. **(b)** (*grivois*) bawdy. **2** *nm* (*costaud*) strapping *ou* robust fellow; (*: *type*) fellow, guy*. **toi, mon ~, je t'ai à l'œil!** I've got my eye on you, mate!* **3** *nf* (*) strapping woman*. **4: ~ (d'avant)** forecastle, fo'c'sle; (*Hist*) **~ d'arrière** quarter-deck.
♦ **gaillardement** *adv* stoutly, vigorously.
gain [gɛ̃] *nm* **(a)** (*salaire*) earnings, wages. **(b)** (*lucre*) **le ~** gain. **(c)** (*bénéfices*) **~s** *[société]* profits; (*au jeu*) winnings. **(d)** (*avantage*) gains; (*spirituel*) benefit. **tirer un ~ de qch** to draw benefit from sth. **(e)** (*économie*) saving. **ça nous permet un ~ de temps** it saves us time. **(f)** (*obtention*) *[bataille]* winning; *[voix d'électeurs]* gaining. **obtenir ~ de cause** (*lit*) to win the case; (*fig*) to win the day; **donner ~ de cause à qn** (*Jur*) to decide the case in favour of sb; (*fig*) to pronounce sb right.
gaine [gɛn] *nf* (*Habillement*) girdle; (*Bot, fourreau*) sheath. **~ d'aération** ventilation shaft.
galant, e [galɑ̃, ɑ̃t] **1** *adj* **(a)** (*courtois*) gallant, courteous, gentlemanly. **(b)** *propos* flirtatious, gallant; *rendez-vous* romantic. **en ~e compagnie** with a lady (*ou* gentleman) friend. **2** *nm* suitor.
♦ **galamment** *adv* courteously, gallantly.
♦ **galanterie** *nf* gallantry; (*propos*) gallant remark.
galaxie [galaksi] *nf* galaxy.
galbe [galb(ə)] *nm* curve. ♦ **galbé, e** *adj* curved.
gale [gal] *nf* (*Méd*) scabies, itch; (*Vét*) *[chien, chat]* mange; *[mouton]* scab. **je n'ai pas la ~!** I'm not infectious!; **il est méchant comme la ~** he's a nasty piece of work*.
galère [galɛʀ] *nf* (*Hist*) galley. **qu'est-il allé faire dans cette ~?** why did he have to get involved in this business?
galerie [galʀi] *nf* **(a)** (*couloir*) gallery. **~ marchande** shopping arcade. **(b)** (*Art*) (*magasin*) gallery; (*salle de musée*) room, gallery. **(c)** (*Théât*) circle. **premières/deuxièmes ~s** dress/upper circle. **(d)** (*public*) gallery, audience. **pour amuser la ~** to amuse the audience. **(e)** (*Aut*) roof rack.
galérien [galeʀjɛ̃] *nm* galley slave.
galet [galɛ] *nm* pebble. **~s** shingle.

galette [galɛt] *nf* (*gâteau*) *round, flat cake*; (*crêpe*) pancake; (*: *argent*) dough*, lolly*.
galeux, -euse [galø, øz] *adj personne* affected with scabies; *chien* mangy; *mouton* scabby. **traiter comme un chien** ~ to treat like dirt.
galimatias [galimatja] *nm* gibberish.
galipette* [galipɛt] *nf* somersault. **faire la** ~ to somersault.
Galles [gal] *nfpl*: **le pays de** ~ Wales. ♦ **gallois, e** **1** *adj* Welsh. **2** *nm* **(a)** G~ Welshman; **les G~** the Welsh. **(b)** (*Ling*) Welsh. **3** *nf*: G~e Welshwoman.
gallicisme [galisism(ə)] *nm* gallicism.
gallon [galɔ̃] *nm* gallon.
galoche [galɔʃ] *nf* clog.
galon [galɔ̃] *nm* (*Couture*) (piece of) braid; (*Mil*) stripe. (*fig*) **prendre du** ~ to get promotion.
galop [galo] *nm* gallop. **petit** ~ canter; ~ **d'essai** (*lit*) trial gallop; (*fig*) trial run; **cheval au** ~ galloping horse; **se mettre au** ~ to break into a gallop; **partir au** ~ *[cheval]* to set off at a gallop; *[personne]* to rush off *ou* away; **va chercher tes affaires au** ~! go and get your things, at the double! ♦ **galopade** *nf* stampede. ♦ **galopant, e** *adj inflation* galloping. ♦ **galoper** (1) *vi [cheval]* to gallop; *[imagination]* to run wild, run riot; *[enfant]* to run.
galopin* [galɔpɛ̃] *nm* rascal.
galvaniser [galvanize] (1) *vt* (*Tech*) to galvanize; (*fig*) to galvanize into action. ♦ **galvanisation** *nf* galvanization.
galvauder [galvode] (1) **1** *vt réputation* to tarnish; *talent* to prostitute; *expression* to debase. **2** *vi* (*vagabonder*) to idle around.
gambade [gɑ̃bad] *nf* leap, caper. ♦ **gambader** (1) *vi* to gambol, leap (about), caper (about). ~ **de joie** to jump for joy.
gamelle [gamɛl] *nf [soldat]* mess tin; *[ouvrier]* billy-can. **prendre une** ~* to come a cropper*.
gamin, e [gamɛ̃, in] **1** *adj* (*espiègle*) mischievous, playful; (*puéril*) childish. **2** *nm,f* (*) kid*. ♦ **gaminerie** *nf* playfulness; childishness. **faire des** ~**s** to get up to mischief; to be childish.
gamme [gam] *nf* (*Mus*) scale; (*fig*) range. **faire des** ~**s** to practise scales.
gang [gɑ̃g] *nm* gang (of crooks).
ganglion [gɑ̃glijɔ̃] *nm* ganglion.
gangrène [gɑ̃gʀɛn] *nf* (*Méd*) gangrene; (*fig*) corruption.
gangster [gɑ̃gstɛʀ] *nm* gangster; (*fig*) shark, crook. ♦ **gangstérisme** *nm* gangsterism.
gant [gɑ̃] *nm* glove. ~**s de boxe** boxing gloves; ~ **de crin** massage glove; ~ **de toilette** face flannel, wash glove; **ça me va comme un** ~ *[robe]* it fits me like a glove; *[idée]* it suits me down to the ground; **tu ferais mieux de prendre des** ~**s avec lui** you'd better handle him with kid gloves; **il va falloir prendre des** ~**s pour lui annoncer la nouvelle** we'll have to break the news to him gently; (*lit, fig*) **jeter/relever le** ~ to throw down/take up the gauntlet. ♦ **se ganter** (1) *vpr* to put on one's gloves. **ganté de cuir** wearing leather gloves.
garage [gaʀaʒ] *nm* (*Aut*) garage. ~ **d'autobus** bus depot; ~ **d'avions** hangar; ~ **de bicyclettes** bicycle shed; ~ **de canots** boathouse. ♦ **garagiste** *nm* (*propriétaire*) garage owner; (*mécanicien*) garage mechanic.
garantir [gaʀɑ̃tiʀ] (2) *vt* **(a)** (*gén, Comm: assurer*) to guarantee. ~ **que** to assure *ou* guarantee that; **je te garantis que ça ne se passera pas comme ça!*** I can assure you things won't turn out like that! **(b)** (*protéger*) ~ **qch de** to protect sth from; **se** ~ **du soleil** to protect o.s. from the sun. ♦ **garant, e** *nm,f* (*personne, état*) guarantor (*de* for); (*chose*) guarantee (*de* of). **servir de** ~ **à qn** to stand surety for sb; **se porter** ~ **de qch** to vouch for sth, guarantee sth. ♦ **garanti, e**[1] *adj*: ~ **étanche/3 ans** guaranteed waterproof/for 3 years; **c'est** ~ **sur facture*** it's as sure as anything, it's a cert*. ♦ **garantie**[2] *nf* (*gén, Comm*) guarantee; (*gage*) security, surety; (*protection*) safeguard. *[police d'assurance]* ~**s** cover; **si on a la** ~ **qu'ils se conduiront bien ...** if we have a firm undertaking *ou* a guarantee that they'll behave ...; **servir de** ~ to be used as a security; **sous** ~ under guarantee; **c'est une** ~ **de succès** it's a guarantee of success; **c'est une** ~ **contre le chômage** it's a safeguard against unemployment; (*caution*) **donner sa** ~ **à** to guarantee, stand security *ou* surety for; **je vous dis ça, mais c'est sans** ~ I can't guarantee that what I'm telling you is right.
garçon [gaʀsɔ̃] **1** *nm* **(a)** boy. **traiter qn comme un petit** ~ to treat sb like a child *ou* a little boy; ~ **manqué** tomboy; **c'est un brave** ~ he's a good sort *ou* a nice fellow *ou* a nice young man. **(b)** (*commis*) shop assistant; (*serveur*) waiter. ~ **boucher** butcher's assistant. **(c)** (*célibataire*) bachelor. **rester** ~ to remain a bachelor. **2**: ~ **de bureau** office assistant; ~ **de café** waiter; ~ **de courses** messenger; ~ **d'écurie** stable lad; ~ **d'étage** bellboy; ~ **de ferme** farm hand; ~ **d'honneur** best man. ♦ **garçonnet** *nm* small boy. **taille** ~ boy's size. ♦ **garçonnière** *nf* bachelor flat.
garde[1] [gaʀd(ə)] *nf* **(a)** (*surveillance*) **se charger de la** ~ **de qch** to undertake to look after *ou* to guard *ou* to keep an eye on sth; **prendre en** ~ to take into one's care; **laisser qch en** ~ **à qn** to leave sth in sb's care; **sous la** ~ **de la police** under police guard; **être/mettre qn sous bonne** ~ to be/put sb under guard; ~ **à vue** police custody; **l'enfant a été laissé à la** ~ **de la mère** the child was left in the custody of the mother. **(b)** (*service*) *[soldat]* guard duty; *[infirmière etc]* ward duty. **être de** ~ *[infirmière, sentinelle]* to be on duty; **pharmacie de** ~ duty chemist's. **(c)** (*escorte*) guard. **(d)** (*infirmière*) nurse. ~ **d'enfant** childminder. **(e)** (*Boxe, Escrime*) guard. **en** ~! on guard!; **se mettre en** ~ to take one's guard. **(f)** *[épée]* hilt. (*lit, fig*) **jusqu'à la** ~ (up) to the hilt. **(g) mettre qn en** ~ to put sb on his guard (*contre* against); **mise en** ~ warning; **faire bonne** ~ to keep a close watch; **prenez** ~ **de ne pas tomber** mind you don't fall, be careful not to fall; **prends** ~! (*exhortation*) watch out!; (*menace*) watch it!*; **prends** ~ **aux voitures** watch out for *ou* mind the cars; **sans prendre** ~ **au danger** without considering the danger; **sans y prendre** ~ without realizing it; **être sur ses** ~**s** to be on one's guard.
garde[2] [gaʀd(ə)] *nm [prisonnier]* guard; *[château]* warden; *[jardin public]* keeper; (*soldat*) guardsman; (*sentinelle*) guard. ~ **champêtre** rural policeman; ~ **du corps** body-guard; ~ **forestier** forest warden; ~ **des Sceaux** ≈ Lord Chancellor.
garde- [gaʀd(ə)] *préf*: **garde-barrière** *nmf, pl* ~**s-**~**(s)** level-crossing keeper; **garde-boue** *nm inv* mudguard; **garde-chasse** *nm, pl* ~**s-**~**(s)** gamekeeper; **garde-chiourme** *nm, pl* ~**(s)-**~**(s)** martinet; **garde-côte** *nm, pl* ~**-**~**(s)** coastguard ship; **garde-fou** *nm, pl* ~**-**~**s** (*en fer*) railing; (*en pierre*) parapet; **garde-malade** *nmf, pl* ~**s-**~**s** home nurse; **garde-manger** *nm inv* (*armoire*) meat safe; (*pièce*) pantry, larder; **garde-meuble** *nm, pl* ~**-**~**(s)** furniture store; **garde-pêche** *nm inv* (*personne*) water bailiff; (*frégate*) fisheries protection ship; **garde-robe** *nf, pl* ~**-**~**s** (*habits*) wardrobe; (*Mil*) **garde-à-vous (fixe)!** attention!; **se mettre au garde-à-vous** to stand to attention.
garder [gaʀde] (1) **1** *vt* **(a)** (*surveiller*) to look after, guard; (*défendre*) to guard. ~ **qn à vue** ≈ to keep sb in custody; ~ **des enfants (à domicile)** to baby-sit; **garde ma valise** look after *ou* keep an eye on my suitcase; **on n'a pas gardé les cochons ensemble!*** you've a nerve to take liberties like that!*; **ça vous gardera du froid** it'll protect you from the cold; **Dieu vous garde** God be with you;

le musée qui garde ces trésors the museum which houses these treasures; **passage à niveau gardé/non gardé** manned/unmanned level-crossing. **(b)** (*conserver*) (*gén*) to keep; *jeunesse* to retain; *habitude* to keep up; *vêtement* to keep on; *[police]* to detain. ~ **la chambre/le lit** to stay in one's room/in bed; ~ **qn à déjeuner** to have sb stay for lunch; ~ **en retenue** to keep in detention; **je lui ai gardé une côtelette pour ce soir** I've kept *ou* saved a chop for him for tonight; **je lui garde un chien de ma chienne*** he's got it coming to him from me*; ~ **une poire pour la soif** to keep sth by for a rainy day; **gardez cela pour vous** keep this to yourself; **il a gardé toutes ses facultés** he still has all his faculties; ~ **son calme/le silence** to keep calm/silent; ~ **l'anonymat** to remain anonymous; ~ **la ligne** to keep one's figure; ~ **rancune à qn** to bear sb a grudge. **2 se** ~ *vpr* **(a)** *[denrées]* to keep. **(b) se** ~ **de qch** (*se défier de*) to be wary of sth; (*se protéger de*) to protect o.s. from sth, guard against sth; **gardez-vous de vos amis** be wary of your own friends; **se** ~ **de faire qch** to be careful not to do sth; **je m'en garderai bien!** that's the last thing I'd do!

garderie [gaRdəRi] *nf*: ~ **(d'enfants)** day nursery, crèche.

gardien, -ienne [gaRdjɛ̃, jɛn] *nm,f* (*gén*) guard; *[prison]* officer; *[château]* warden; *[musée, hôtel]* attendant; *[jardin public, phare, zoo]* keeper; (*fig: défenseur*) guardian. ~ **de but** goalkeeper; ~ **d'immeuble** caretaker; ~ **de nuit** night watchman; ~ **de la paix** policeman.

gare[1] [gaR] *nf* station. ~ **de marchandises** goods station; ~ **maritime** harbour station; ~ **routière** (*camions*) haulage depot; (*autocars*) coach *ou* bus station; ~ **de triage** marshalling yard.

gare[2]* [gaR] *excl*: ~ **à toi!** just watch it!*; ~ **au premier qui bouge!** the first one to move will be for it!*; **sinon** ~! or else!*; ~ **à ta tête** mind your head; ~ **aux conséquences** beware of the consequences.

garer [gaRe] (1) **1** *vt véhicule* to park; *embarcation* to dock. **2 se** ~ *vpr* to park; *[véhicule]* to draw into the side; *[piéton]* to get out of the way.

gargariser (se) [gaRgaRize] (1) *vpr* to gargle. (*fig péj*) **se** ~ **de grands mots** to revel in big words. ♦ **gargarisme** *nm* gargle.

gargote [gaRgɔt] *nf* (*péj*) cheap restaurant.

gargouille [gaRguj] *nf* (*Archit*) gargoyle. ♦ **gargouiller** (1) *vi [eau]* to gurgle; *[intestin]* to rumble. ♦ **gargouillement** *nm ou* ♦ **gargouillis** *nm* gurgling; rumbling.

garnement [gaRnəmɑ̃] *nm* (*gamin*) rascal; (*adolescent*) tearaway.

garnir [gaRniR] (2) **1** *vt* **(a)** (*équiper*) *bibliothèque, caisse* to fill; *réfrigérateur* to stock; *chaudière* to stoke; *hameçon* to bait (*de* with). ~ **qch de pneus** *etc* to put tyres *etc* on sth, fit sth out with tyres *etc*; ~ **une muraille de canons** to range guns along a wall; ~ **une boîte de tissu** to line a box with material. **(b)** (*remplir*) to fill; (*couvrir*) to cover. **la foule garnissait les rues** the crowd packed the streets; **boîte garnie de chocolats** box full of *ou* filled with chocolates; **les canons qui garnissent la muraille** the guns which line the wall *ou* which are ranged along the wall. **(c)** (*décorer*) *robe* to trim; *aliment* to garnish (*de* with). ~ **de fleurs** to decorate with flowers. **2 se** ~ *vpr [salle]* to fill up (*de* with). ♦ **garni, e 1** *adj plat* (*décoré*) garnished; (*accompagné*) served with vegetables. **bien** ~ *portefeuille* well-lined; *réfrigérateur* well-stocked; *estomac, boîte* full. **2** *nm* furnished rooms *ou* accommodation.

garnison [gaRnizɔ̃] *nf* garrison. **(ville de)** ~ garrison town; **être en** ~ **à** to be stationed *ou* garrisoned at.

garniture [gaRnityR] *nf [chaudière]* lagging; *[coffret, freins]* lining; *[aliment]* (*décoration*) garnish; (*légumes*) vegetables. *[robe]* ~**(s)** trimming; (*Aut*) ~ **intérieure** upholstery, interior trim; ~ **de cheminée** mantelpiece ornaments; ~ **de toilette** toilet set; ~ **périodique** sanitary towel *ou* napkin (*US*); **avec** ~ **en cuir** with leather fittings.

garrot [gaRo] *nm [cheval]* withers; (*Méd*) tourniquet; (*supplice*) garrotte. ♦ **garrotter** (1) *vt* to tie up.

gars* [gɑ] *nm* (*enfant*) lad; (*type*) fellow, guy*. **au revoir les** ~! cheerio boys!* *ou* fellows!*

gas-oil [gɑzɔjl] *nm* diesel oil.

gaspiller [gaspije] (1) *vt* (*gén*) to waste; *fortune* to squander. ♦ **gaspillage** *nm* wasting; squandering. ♦ **gaspilleur, -euse 1** *adj* wasteful. **2** *nm,f* waster; squanderer.

gastrique [gastRik] *adj* gastric. ♦ **gastrite** *nf* gastritis.

gastronome [gastRɔnɔm] *nmf* gourmet, gastronome. ♦ **gastronomie** *nf* gastronomy. ♦ **gastronomique** *adj* gastronomic.

gâteau, *pl* ~**x** [gɑto] *nm* cake; (*au restaurant*) gateau. ~ **de riz** rice pudding; ~ **sec** biscuit; ~ **de miel** honeycomb; **se partager le** ~* to share the loot*; **c'est du** ~* it's a piece of cake*, it's a walk-over*.

gâter [gɑte] (1) **1** *vt* (*gén*) to ruin, spoil; *enfant* to spoil; *jugement* to have a harmful effect on. ~ **des fruits** to make fruit go bad; **avoir les dents gâtées** to have bad teeth; **et, ce qui ne gâte rien** and, which is all to the good; **nous avons été gâtés cette année** we've been really lucky this year. **2 se** ~ *vpr [viande]* to go bad, go off; *[relations]* to go sour. **le temps va se** ~ the weather's going to break; **ça commence à se** ~ **(entre eux)** things are beginning to go wrong (between them); **ça va se** ~! there's going to be trouble!, things are going to turn nasty! ♦ **gâterie** *nf* little treat. **se payer une** ~ to treat o.s. to sth.

gâteux, -euse* [gɑtø, øz] **1** *adj* senile, gaga*. **2** *nm,f*: **(vieux)** ~ doddering old man. ♦ **gâtisme** *nm* senility.

gauche [goʃ] **1** *adj* **(a)** *bras* left; *poche* left-hand. **du côté** ~ on the left-hand side. **(b)** (*maladroit*) clumsy, awkward; (*tordu*) warped. **2** *nm* (*Boxe*) left. **3** *nf* **(a) la** ~ (*gén, Aut, Pol*) the left; (*côté*) the left-hand side; **à** ~ *rue, rouler* on the left; *tourner* to the left; **tiroir de** ~ left-hand drawer; **à** ~ **de la porte** to the left of the door; **garder sa** ~ to keep to the left; **idées de** ~ left-wing ideas; **mettre de l'argent à** ~* to put money aside. **(b)** (*coup*) left. ♦ **gauchement** *adv* clumsily, awkwardly. ♦ **gaucher, -ère** *adj* left-handed. ♦ **gaucherie** *nf* awkwardness, clumsiness. ♦ **gauchir** (2) **1** *vt* (*lit*) to warp; *fait* to distort. **2 se** ~ *vpr* to warp. ♦ **gauchisme** *nm* leftism. ♦ **gauchissement** *nm* warping; distortion. ♦ **gauchiste** *adj, nmf* leftist.

gaudriole* [godRijɔl] *nf* (*propos*) broad joke.

gaufre [gofR(ə)] *nf* waffle. ♦ **gaufré, e** *adj papier* embossed; *tissu* goffered. ♦ **gaufrette** *nf* wafer. ♦ **gaufrier** *nm* waffle iron.

Gaule [gol] *nf* Gaul.

gaule [gol] *nf* pole; (*Pêche*) fishing rod. ♦ **gauler** (1) *vt arbre* to beat; *fruits* to bring down, shake down.

gaullisme [golism(ə)] *nm* Gaullism. ♦ **gaulliste** *adj, nmf* Gaullist.

gaulois, e [golwa, waz] **1** *adj* **(a)** (*de Gaule*) Gallic. **(b)** (*grivois*) bawdy. **2** *nm(f)*: **G**~**(e)** Gaul. **3** *nf* (®: *cigarette*) Gauloise. ♦ **gauloiserie** *nf* (*propos*) bawdy story. **la** ~ bawdiness.

gausser (se) [gose] (1) *vpr* (*littér*) (*rire*) to laugh; (*se moquer*) to be joking. **se** ~ **de** to poke fun at.

gaver [gave] (1) **1** *vt animal* to force-feed; *personne* to fill up (*de* with). **je suis gavé!** I'm full (up)! **2 se** ~ *vpr*: **se** ~ **de** *nourriture* to stuff o.s. with; *romans* to devour.

gaz [gɑz] **1** *nm inv* (*Chim*) gas. (*Mil*) **les ~** gas; **l'employé du ~** the gasman; **vous avez le ~?** are you on gas?; **il s'est suicidé au ~** he gassed himself; (*Aut*) **mettre les ~*** to step on the gas*; (*euph*) **avoir des ~** to have wind. **2: ~ asphyxiant** poison gas; **~ carbonique** carbon dioxide; **~ d'échappement** exhaust gas; **~ lacrymogène** teargas; **~ de ville** town gas. ♦ **gazoduc** *nm* gas pipeline. ♦ **gazogène** *nm* gas producer (*plant*). ♦ **gazole** *nm* diesel oil. ♦ **gazomètre** *nm* gasometer.

gaze [gɑz] *nf* gauze.

gazelle [gazɛl] *nf* gazelle.

gazer [gɑze] (1) **1** *vi* (*) **ça gaze?** how's things?*, how goes it?*; **ça a gazé?** did it go O.K.?*; **ça ne gaze pas fort** things aren't too good *ou* too hot*; **il y a qch qui ne gaze pas** there's sth wrong somewhere. **2** *vt* (*Mil*) to gas.

gazette [gazɛt] *nf* (*hum*) newspaper.

gazeux, -euse [gɑzø, øz] *adj* (*Chim*) gaseous; *boisson* fizzy.

gazon [gɑzɔ̃] *nm* (*pelouse*) lawn. (*herbe*) **le ~** turf, grass; **une motte de ~** a turf, a sod.

gazouiller [gazuje] (1) *vi [oiseau]* to chirp, warble; *[ruisseau, bébé]* to babble. ♦ **gazouillement** *nm ou* ♦ **gazouillis** *nm* chirping, warbling; babbling.

geai [ʒɛ] *nm* jay.

géant, e [ʒeɑ̃, ɑ̃t] **1** *adj* gigantic; *paquet* giant-sized, giant. **2** *nm* (*lit, fig*) giant; (*Écon, Pol*) giant power. **3** *nf* giantess.

geindre [ʒɛ̃dʀ(ə)] (52) *vi* (*gémir*) to groan, moan (*de* with); (*péj*) to moan. ♦ **geignard, e*** *nm,f* moaner. ♦ **geignement** *nm*: **~(s)** moaning.

gel [ʒɛl] *nm* **(a)** (*froid*) frost. **'craint le ~'** 'keep away from extreme cold'. **(b)** *[crédits]* freezing. **(c)** (*pâte*) gel.

gélatine [ʒelatin] *nf* gelatine. ♦ **gélatineux, -euse** *adj* gelatinous.

geler [ʒ(ə)le] (5) **1** *vt* **(a)** *eau, sol* to freeze; *membre* to cause frostbite to. **mourir gelé** to freeze to death; **j'ai les mains gelées** (*froides*) my hands are frozen (stiff); (*blessées*) my hands are frost-bitten; **tu nous gèles*** you're making us freeze. **(b)** (*Fin*) to freeze. **2 se ~*** *vpr* to freeze. **3** *vi* **(a)** *[eau]* to freeze (over), ice over; *[sol, plante]* to freeze; *[récoltes]* to be blighted by frost; *[membre]* to be frostbitten. **(b)** (*avoir froid*) to freeze. **4** *vb impers:* **il gèle** it's freezing; **il a gelé à pierre fendre** it froze hard. ♦ **gelé, e**[1] *adj public* cold, unresponsive; (*: *soûl*) tight*. ♦ **gelée**[2] *nf* **(a)** (*gel*) frost. **~ blanche** hoarfrost. **(b)** (*Culin*) jelly.

gélule [ʒelyl] *nf* (*Méd*) capsule.

gelure [ʒ(ə)lyʀ] *nf* (*Méd*) **~(s)** frostbite.

Gémeaux [ʒemo] *nmpl* (*Astron*) Gemini.

gémir [ʒemiʀ] (2) *vi [blessé]* to groan, moan (*de* with); *[plancher]* to creak; *[vent]* to moan, whine. ♦ **gémissement** *nm*: **~(s)** groaning; moaning; creaking; whining.

gênant, e [ʒɛnɑ̃, ɑ̃t] *adj situation, témoin* awkward, embarrassing; *révélations* embarrassing. (*irritant*) **c'est ~** it's a nuisance.

gencive [ʒɑ̃siv] *nf* gum.

gendarme [ʒɑ̃daʀm(ə)] *nm* gendarme, policeman. ♦ **gendarmer (se)** (1) *vpr*: **se ~ pour obtenir qch** to have to take a strong line to get sth. ♦ **gendarmerie** *nf* (*corps*) gendarmerie, police force; (*bureaux*) police station; (*caserne*) police barracks.

gendre [ʒɑ̃dʀ(ə)] *nm* son-in-law.

gène [ʒɛn] *nm* gene.

gêne [ʒɛn] *nf* (*physique*) discomfort; (*dérangement*) trouble, bother; (*manque d'argent*) financial difficulties; (*embarras*) embarrassment. **il ressentait une certaine ~ à respirer** he experienced some difficulty in breathing; **je ne voudrais vous causer aucune ~** I wouldn't like to put you to any trouble *ou* bother, I wouldn't want to be a nuisance.

généalogie [ʒenealɔʒi] *nf* genealogy. ♦ **généalogique** *adj* genealogical.

gêner [ʒene] (1) **1** *vt* **(a)** *[fumée]* to bother; *[bruit]* to bother, disturb; *[vêtement étroit, obstacle]* to hamper. **~ le passage** to be in the way; **ça me gêne pour respirer** it hampers my breathing. **(b)** (*déranger*) *personne* to bother; *projet* to hamper, hinder. **j'espère que ça ne vous gêne pas d'y aller** I hope it won't inconvenience you to go; **cela vous gênerait de ne pas fumer?** would you mind not smoking?; **et alors, ça te gêne?*** so what?* **(c)** (*financièrement*) to put in financial difficulties. **(d)** (*embarrasser*) **~ qn** to make sb feel ill-at-ease *ou* uncomfortable; **ça me gêne de vous dire ça mais ...** I hate to tell you but .... **2 se ~** *vpr* **(a)** (*se contraindre*) **ne vous gênez pas pour moi** don't mind me, don't put yourself out for me; **il ne faut pas vous ~ avec moi** don't stand on ceremony with me; **il ne s'est pas gêné pour le lui dire** he didn't mind telling him. **(b)** (*économiser*) to tighten one's belt. ♦ **gêné, e** *adj personne, air* embarrassed, self-conscious; *silence* uncomfortable, embarrassed, awkward. (*financièrement*) **être ~ (aux entournures)** to be short of money *ou* hard up*.

général, e, *mpl* **-aux** [ʒeneʀal, o] **1** *adj* general. **un tableau ~ de la situation** a general *ou* an overall picture of the situation; **dans l'intérêt ~** in the general interest; **à la surprise ~e** to the surprise of most *ou* many people; **en ~, de façon ~e** generally, in general; **secrétaire ~** (*gén*) general secretary; *[organisation internationale]* secretary-general. **2** *nm* general. **~ de brigade** brigadier; **~ en chef** general-in-chief. **3** *nf* **(a)** (*épouse*) general's wife. **(b)** (*Théât*) **(répétition) ~e** (final) dress rehearsal. ♦ **généralement** *adv* generally, usually. **~ parlant** generally speaking; **coutume assez ~ répandue** fairly widespread custom.

généraliser [ʒeneʀalize] (1) **1** *vt* (*gén*) to generalize; *méthode* to put *ou* bring into general use. **cancer généralisé** general cancer. **2 se ~** *vpr* to become widespread. ♦ **généralisable** *adj* which can be applied generally. ♦ **généralisation** *nf* generalization.

généraliste [ʒeneʀalist(ə)] *nm* (*Méd*) G.P., general practitioner.

généralité [ʒeneʀalite] *nf* **(a)** (*majorité*) majority. **(b) ~s** (*introduction*) general points; (*péj: banalités*) generalities.

générateur, -trice [ʒeneʀatœʀ, tʀis] **1** *adj* generative, generating. **~ de désordres** which causes trouble. **2** *nf* (*Élec*) generator.

générer [ʒeneʀe] (6) *vt* to generate. ♦ **génération** *nf* generation.

généreux, -euse [ʒeneʀø, øz] *adj* generous. ♦ **généreusement** *adv* generously. ♦ **générosité** *nf* generosity. (*largesses*) **~s** kindnesses.

générique [ʒeneʀik] **1** *adj* generic. **2** *nm* (*Ciné*) credit titles, credits.

genêt [ʒ(ə)nɛ] *nm* (*Bot*) broom.

génétique [ʒenetik] **1** *adj* genetic. **2** *nf* genetics (*sg*).

gêneur, -euse [ʒɛnœʀ, øz] *nm,f* (*importun*) intruder. **supprimer un ~** to do away with a person who stands in one's way.

Genève [ʒ(ə)nɛv] *n* Geneva.

génial, e, *mpl* **-aux** [ʒenjal, o] *adj écrivain, invention* of genius; *idée* inspired; (*: *formidable*) fantastic*, tremendous*. ♦ **génialement** *adv* with genius, brilliantly.

génie [ʒeni] *nm* **(a)** (*savant, talent*) genius. **avoir du ~** to have genius; **avoir le ~ des affaires** to have a genius for business; **avoir le ~ du mal** to have an evil bent. **(b)** (*Myth*) (*gén*) spirit; (*arabe*) genie. **le bon/mauvais ~ de qn** sb's good/evil genius. **(c)** (*Mil*) **le** ~ ≃ the Engineers; **soldat du** ~ engineer; ~ **civil** (*branche*) civil engineering; (*corps*) civil engineers.

genièvre [ʒənjɛvʀ(ə)] *nm* (*boisson*) Hollands gin; (*arbre*) juniper; (*fruit*) juniper berry.

génisse [ʒenis] *nf* heifer.

génital, e, *mpl* **-aux** [ʒenital, o] *adj* genital.

génitif [ʒenitif] *nm* genitive (case).

génocide [ʒenɔsid] *nm* genocide.

genou, *pl* ~**x** [ʒ(ə)nu] *nm* knee. **il était à** ~**x** he was kneeling, he was on his knees; **se mettre à** ~**x** to kneel down; (*fig*) **se mettre à** ~**x devant qn** to go down on one's knees to sb; **c'est à se mettre à** ~**x!*** it's out of this world!*; **j'en suis tombé à** ~**x!*** I just about dropped!*; **demander qch à (deux)** ~**x** to ask for sth on bended knee; **prendre qn sur ses** ~**x** to take sb on one's knee; **faire du** ~ **à qn*** to play footsie with sb*; **plier le** ~ **devant qn** to bend the knee to sb; **être sur les** ~**x*** to be on one's knees*, be tired out.

genre [ʒɑ̃ʀ] *nm* **(a)** (*espèce*) kind, type, sort. ~ **de vie** lifestyle, way of life; **cette maison n'est pas mauvaise en son** ~ that house isn't bad of its type; **ce qui se fait le mieux dans le** ~ the best of its kind; **chaussures en tout** ~ all kinds of shoes; **qch du même** ~ sth of the kind; **il a écrit un** ~ **de roman** he wrote a novel of sorts. **(b)** (*allure*) manner. **avoir bon** ~ to look a nice sort; **avoir mauvais** ~ to be coarse-looking; **il a un drôle de** ~ he's a bit weird; **avoir le** ~ **artiste** to be an arty type; **faire du** ~ to stand on ceremony; **ce n'est pas son** ~ **de ne pas répondre** it's not like him not to answer. **(c)** (*Art*) genre; (*Gram*) gender; (*Philos, Sci*) genus. **le** ~ **humain** mankind, the human race.

gens [ʒɑ̃] *nmpl* (*accord féminin de l'adjectif antéposé*) people, folk; (*serviteurs*) servants. **les** ~ **de la ville** townspeople, townsfolk; **les** ~ **du pays** *ou* **du coin*** the local people, the locals; **de braves** ~ good people *ou* folk; **les** ~ **d'Église** the clergy; ~ **de lettres** men of letters; **les** ~ **de loi**† the legal profession; ~ **de maison** people in service.

gentil, -ille [ʒɑ̃ti, ij] *adj* **(a)** (*aimable*) kind, nice (*avec, pour* to). **c'est** ~ **à toi de ...** it's very kind *ou* nice *ou* good of you to ...; **tout ça, c'est bien** ~ **mais** ... that's all very nice but ...; **sois** ~**, va me le chercher** be a dear and go and get it for me, would you mind going to get it for me. **(b)** (*sage*) good. **il n'a pas été** ~ he hasn't been a good boy. **(c)** *visage, endroit* nice, pleasant; *somme* tidy, fair. ♦ **gentillesse** *nf* (*gén*) kindness. **une** ~ **en vaut une autre** one good turn deserves another. ♦ **gentiment** *adv* kindly, nicely.

gentilhomme [ʒɑ̃tijɔm], *pl* **gentilshommes** [ʒɑ̃tizɔm] *nm* gentleman. ~ **campagnard** country squire. ♦ **gentilhommière** *nf* manor house.

génuflexion [ʒenyflɛksjɔ̃] *nf* genuflexion.

géodésie [ʒeɔdezi] *nf* geodesy. ♦ **géodésique** *adj* geodesic.

géographie [ʒeɔgʀafi] *nf* geography. ♦ **géographe** *nmf* geographer. ♦ **géographique** *adj* geographical.

geôle [ʒol] *nf* gaol, jail. ♦ **geôlier, -ière** *nm,f* gaoler, jailer.

géologie [ʒeɔlɔʒi] *nf* geology. ♦ **géologique** *adj* geological. ♦ **géologue** *nmf* geologist.

géométrie [ʒeɔmetʀi] *nf* geometry. ~ **dans l'espace** solid geometry; **à** ~ **variable** swing-wing. ♦ **géomètre** *nm* (*arpenteur*) surveyor; (*mathématicien*) geometer. ♦ **géométrique** *adj* geometrical. ♦ **géométriquement** *adv* geometrically.

géothermique [ʒeɔtɛʀmik] *adj* geothermal.

gérance [ʒeʀɑ̃s] *nf* management. **prendre qch en** ~ to take over the management of sth; **mettre qch en** ~ to appoint a manager for sth. ♦ **gérant** *nm* manager; *[immeuble]* managing agent. ♦ **gérante** *nf* manageress.

géranium [ʒeʀanjɔm] *nm* geranium.

gerbe [ʒɛʀb(ə)] *nf [blé]* sheaf; *[osier]* bundle; *[preuves]* collection. ~ **de fleurs** spray of flowers; ~ **d'eau** spray *ou* shower of water; (*fusée*) **retomber en** ~ to fall in a shower *ou* burst of sparks.

gercer *vt*, **se** ~ *vpr* [ʒɛʀse] (3) *peau* to chap; *sol* to crack. ♦ **gerçure** *nf* crack.

gérer [ʒeʀe] (6) *vt* to manage. **mal** ~ to mismanage.

gériatrie [ʒeʀjatʀi] *nf* geriatrics (*sg*). ♦ **gériatrique** *adj* geriatric.

germain, e [ʒɛʀmɛ̃, ɛn] *adj*: **cousin** ~ first cousin.

germe [ʒɛʀm(ə)] *nm [embryon, idée]* germ; *[pomme de terre]* eye; *[erreur, vie]* seed; (*microbe*) germ. **avoir en** ~ to contain in embryo, contain the seeds of. ♦ **germer** (1) *vi* to germinate. **pomme de terre germée** sprouting potato. ♦ **germination** *nf* germination.

gérondif [ʒeʀɔ̃dif] *nm* gerund.

gérontologie [ʒeʀɔ̃tɔlɔʒi] *nf* gerontology. ♦ **gérontologique** *adj* gerontological.

gésier [ʒezje] *nm* gizzard.

gésir [ʒeziʀ] *vi*: **il gît/gisait sur le sol** he is lying/was lying *ou* lay on the ground.

gestation [ʒɛstɑsjɔ̃] *nf* gestation. **en** ~ in gestation.

geste [ʒɛst(ə)] *nm* **(a)** (*mouvement*) gesture. **pas un** ~ **ou je tire!** one move and I'll shoot!; **faire un** ~ **de la tête** (*affirmatif*) to nod (one's head); (*négatif*) to shake one's head; **il le fit entrer d'un** ~ he motioned *ou* gestured *ou* waved to him to come in; **il ne fit pas un** ~ **pour l'aider** he didn't lift a finger *ou* make a move to help him. **(b)** (*action*) act, deed; (*généreux*) gesture. **faites un** ~ make a gesture.

gesticuler [ʒɛstikyle] (1) *vi* to gesticulate. ♦ **gesticulation** *nf* gesticulation.

gestion [ʒɛstjɔ̃] *nf* management. **mauvaise** ~ mismanagement, bad management. ♦ **gestionnaire 1** *adj* administrative, management. **2** *nmf* administrator.

geyser [ʒɛzɛʀ] *nm* geyser.

ghetto [gɛto] *nm* ghetto.

gibecière [ʒibsjɛʀ] *nf* (*gén*) shoulder bag; *[chasseur]* gamebag; *[écolier]* satchel.

gibet [ʒibɛ] *nm* gallows.

gibier [ʒibje] *nm* (*lit*) game; (*fig*) prey. ~ **d'eau** waterfowl; ~ **à poil** game animals; ~ **à plume** game birds; ~ **de potence** gallows bird; (*lit, fig*) **le gros** ~ big game.

giboulée [ʒibule] *nf* (sudden) shower. ~ **de mars** April shower.

giboyeux, -euse [ʒibwajø, øz] *adj* well-stocked with game.

gicler [ʒikle] (1) *vi* to spurt. **faire** ~ **de l'eau** (*d'un robinet*) to squirt water; *[véhicule]* to send up a spray of water. ♦ **giclée** *nf* spurt. ♦ **gicleur** *nm* (*Aut*) jet.

gifler [ʒifle] (1) *vt*: ~ **qn** to smack sb's face, slap sb in the face. ♦ **gifle** *nf* slap in the face.

gigantesque [ʒigɑ̃tɛsk(ə)] *adj* gigantic, immense.

gigolo [ʒigɔlo] *nm* gigolo.

gigot [ʒigo] *nm* joint. ~ **de mouton** leg of mutton; ~ **de chevreuil** haunch of venison.

gigoter* [ʒigɔte] (1) *vi* to wriggle (about).

gilet [ʒilɛ] *nm* (*de complet*) waistcoat, vest (*US*); (*cardigan*) cardigan. ~ **(de corps)** vest, undershirt (*US*); ~ **pare-balles** bulletproof jacket; ~ **de sauvetage** life jacket.

gin [dʒin] *nm* gin.

gingembre [ʒɛ̃ʒɑ̃bʀ(ə)] *nm* ginger.

girafe [ʒiʀaf] *nf* (*Zool*) giraffe; (*péj: personne*) beanpole*.

giration [ʒiʀɑsjɔ̃] *nf* gyration. ♦ **giratoire** *adj* gyrating.

girofle [ʒiʀɔfl(ə)] *nm*: **clou de** ~ clove.

giroflée [ʒiʀɔfle] *nf* wallflower.
girolle [ʒiʀɔl] *nf* chanterelle.
giron [ʒiʀɔ̃] *nm* (*genoux*) lap; (*fig: sein*) bosom.
girouette [ʒiʀwɛt] *nf* weather cock. (*fig*) **c'est une vraie ~** he changes (his mind) with the weather.
gisement [ʒizmɑ̃] *nm* (*Minér*) deposit.
gisent [ʒiz], **gît** [ʒi] *V* **gésir.**
gitan, e [ʒitɑ̃, an] **1** *adj*, **G~(e)** *nm(f)* gipsy. **2** *nf* (®: *cigarette*) Gitane.
gîte [ʒit] *nm* (*abri*) shelter; (*maison*) home; *[lièvre]* form; *[minerai]* deposit. **le ~ et le couvert** board and lodging; **~ (à la noix)** topside.
givre [ʒivʀ(ə)] *nm* hoarfrost. ♦ **givré, e** *adj* **(a)** *arbre* covered in frost; *fenêtre, hélice* frosted-up, iced-up. **(b)** (*) (*ivre*) tight*; (*fou*) cracked*, nuts*. ♦ **givrer** *vt*, **se ~** *vpr* (1) to frost up, ice up.
glaçage [glasaʒ] *nm [papier, aliment]* glazing; (*au sucre*) icing.
glace [glas] *nf* **(a)** (*eau*) ice. (*lit, fig*) **briser la ~** to break the ice; (*Géog*) **~s** ice sheets *ou* fields; **~s flottantes** ice floes; **bloqué par les ~s** *canal* blocked with ice; *bateau* icebound. **(b)** (*Culin*) ice cream. **~ à l'eau/à la crème** water/dairy ice. **(c)** (*miroir*) mirror. **(d)** (*plaque de verre*) sheet of plate glass; *[vitrine]* glass; *[véhicule]* window.
glacer [glase] (3) **1** *vt* **(a)** *liquide* (*geler*) to freeze; (*rafraîchir*) to chill, ice. **mettre à ~** to put to chill; **ce vent glace les oreilles** this wind is freezing to the ears *ou* freezes your ears. **(b) ~ qn** (*lit, fig: réfrigérer*) to turn sb cold; (*paralyser*) to make sb's blood run cold; **glacé d'horreur** frozen with horror. **(c)** *papier, aliment* to glaze; (*au sucre*) to ice. **2 se ~** *vpr* (*lit, fig*) to freeze. ♦ **glacé, e** *adj* *lac* frozen; *vent, chambre* icy, freezing; *boisson* iced, ice-cold; *papier* glazed; *fruit* glacé; *accueil* icy, frosty. **je suis ~** I'm frozen (stiff); **j'ai les mains ~es** my hands are frozen; **à servir ~** serve iced *ou* ice-cold; **café ~** iced coffee.
glaciaire [glasjɛʀ] *adj période, calotte* ice; *relief* glacial.
glacial, e, mpl ~s ou -aux [glasjal, o] *adj* icy, freezing; (*fig*) icy, frosty.
glaciation [glasjɑsjɔ̃] *nf* glaciation.
glacier [glasje] *nm* **(a)** (*Géog*) glacier. **(b)** (*fabricant*) ice-cream maker; (*vendeur*) ice-cream man.
glacière [glasjɛʀ] *nf* (*lit, fig*) icebox.
glaçon [glasɔ̃] *nm [rivière]* block of ice; *[toit]* icicle; *[boisson]* ice cube; (*péj: personne*) iceberg. **un whisky avec des ~s** a whisky on the rocks.
gladiateur [gladjatœʀ] *nm* gladiator.
glaïeul [glajœl] *nm* gladiolus.
glaire [glɛʀ] *nf [œuf]* white; (*Méd*) phlegm.
glaise [glɛz] *nf* clay. ♦ **glaiseux, -euse** *adj* clayey.
gland [glɑ̃] *nm* (*Bot*) acorn; (*ornement*) tassel.
glande [glɑ̃d] *nf* gland. ♦ **glandulaire** *adj* glandular.
glaner [glane] (1) *vt* (*lit, fig*) to glean. ♦ **glaneur, -euse** *nm,f* gleaner.
glapir [glapiʀ] (2) *vi* (*lit, fig*) to yelp. ♦ **glapissement** *nm*: **~(s)** yelping.
glas [glɑ] *nm* knell. **on sonne le ~** they are tolling the knell.
glissade [glisad] *nf* (*par jeu*) slide; (*chute*) slip; (*dérapage*) skid; (*Danse*) glissade.
glissant, e [glisɑ̃, ɑ̃t] *adj* slippery.
glissement [glismɑ̃] *nm*: **~ électoral** electoral swing; **~ de sens** shift in meaning; **~ de terrain** landslide.
glisser [glise] (1) **1** *vi* **(a)** (*gén*) to slide; *[voilier, nuages]* to glide along. **il fit ~ le fauteuil sur le sol** he slid the armchair along the floor; **il se laissa ~ le long du mur** he slid down the wall; **une larme glissa le long de sa joue** a tear trickled *ou* slid down his cheek; **le pays glisse vers l'anarchie/la droite** the country is slipping *ou* sliding towards anarchy/is swinging towards the right. **(b)** (*déraper*) *[personne]* to slip; *[véhicule]* to skid; *[parquet]* to be slippery. **il m'a fait ~** he made me slip. **(c)** (*échapper de*) **~ de la table/des mains** to slip *ou* slide off the table/out of one's hands; **le voleur leur a glissé entre les mains** the thief slipped (right) through their fingers. **(d)** (*effleurer*) **ses doigts glissaient sur les touches** his fingers slipped over the keys; **les reproches glissent sur lui** reproaches roll off him; **~ sur un sujet** to skate over a subject; **la balle glissa sur le blindage** the bullet glanced off the armour plating. **2** *vt* (*introduire*) **~ qch sous/dans qch** to slip sth under/into sth; **il me glissa un regard en coulisse** he gave me a sidelong glance; **il me glissa que ...** he whispered to me that ... . **3 se ~** *vpr*: **se ~ dans** *[personne]* to slip into; *[soupçon, erreur]* to creep into; **se ~ dans les draps** to slip *ou* slide between the sheets; **le voleur se glissa dans la maison** the thief slipped into the house; **se ~ jusqu'au premier rang** to edge *ou* worm one's way to the front.
glissière [glisjɛʀ] *nf* groove. **porte à ~** sliding door; **~ de sécurité** crash barrier.
global, e, mpl -aux [glɔbal, o] *adj* (*gén*) overall; *somme* total, aggregate; *vue* global. ♦ **globalement** *adv* (*en bloc*) globally; (*dans son ensemble*) taken as a whole.
globe [glɔb] *nm* globe. **~ oculaire** eyeball; **le ~ terrestre** the globe; (*fig*) **mettre qch sous ~** to keep sth under glass.
globule [glɔbyl] *nm* (*gén, Chim*) globule. **~s rouges/blancs** red/white corpuscles. ♦ **globulaire** *adj* global; corpuscular. ♦ **globuleux, -euse** *adj* *forme* globular; *œil* protruding.
gloire [glwaʀ] *nf* **(a)** (*renommée*) glory, fame; (*Rel: éclat*) glory. **en pleine ~** at the height of one's fame; **couvert de ~** covered in glory; **elle a eu son heure de ~** she has had her hour of glory; **pour la ~** for the glory of it. **(b)** (*distinction*) **sa plus grande ~ a été de faire** his greatest distinction *ou* his greatest claim to fame was to do; **s'attribuer toute la ~ de qch** to give o.s. all the credit for sth; **tirer ~ de qch** to vaunt sth; **il s'en fait ~!** he's proud of it! **(c)** (*louange*) glory, praise. **~ à Dieu** glory to God, praise be to God; **à la ~ de** in praise of; **célébrer la ~ de** to sing the praises of. **(d)** (*personne: célébrité*) celebrity. ♦ **glorieusement** *adv* gloriously. ♦ **glorieux, -euse** *adj* glorious; (*fier*) proud.
glorifier [glɔʀifje] (7) **1** *vt* to glorify. **2 se ~** *vpr*: **se ~ de** to glory in, take great pride in. ♦ **glorification** *nf* glorification.
gloriole [glɔʀjɔl] *nf* vainglory.
glossaire [glɔsɛʀ] *nm* glossary.
glotte [glɔt] *nf* glottis. **coup de ~** glottal stop.
glouglou [gluglu] *nm [eau]* gurgling; *[dindon]* gobble-gobble. **faire ~** to gurgle; to gobble.
glousser [gluse] (1) *vi [personne]* to chuckle; *[poule]* to cluck. ♦ **gloussement** *nm* chuckle; cluck.
glouton, -onne [glutɔ̃, ɔn] **1** *adj* *personne* gluttonous; *appétit* voracious. **2** *nm,f* glutton. ♦ **gloutonnement** *adv* gluttonously; voraciously. ♦ **gloutonnerie** *nf* gluttony.
glu [gly] *nf* (*pour oiseaux*) birdlime. **on dirait de la ~** it's like glue. ♦ **gluant, e** *adj* sticky, gummy.
glucose [glykoz] *nm* glucose.
glycérine [gliseʀin] *nf* glycerine.
glycine [glisin] *nf* wisteria.
gnangnan* [ɲɑ̃ɲɑ̃] *nmf* moan*, drip*.
gnognote* [ɲɔɲɔt] *nf*: **c'est de la ~!** it's rubbish!
gnôle* [ɲol] *nf* firewater*, hooch*.
gnome [gnom] *nm* gnome.
gnon* [ɲɔ̃] *nm* bash*. **prendre un ~** to get bashed*.
go [go] *loc adv*: **tout de ~** *dire* straight out; *aller* straightaway.
goal [gol] *nm* goalkeeper, goalie*.
gobelet [gɔblɛ] *nm [enfant]* beaker; *[étain]* tum-

bler; *[dés]* cup. ~ **en papier** paper cup.
gober [gɔbe] (1) *vt œuf, mensonge* to swallow.
godasse* [gɔdas] *nf* shoe.
godet [gɔdɛ] *nm* (*gén*) pot; (*: *verre*) glass.
godiche [gɔdiʃ] *adj* (*péj*) lumpish, oafish.
godille [gɔdij] *nf* (*Sport*) scull. (*: *péj*) **à la** ~ *système* ropey*, crappy* (*US*).
godillot* [gɔdijo] *nm* boot.
goéland [gɔelɑ̃] *nm* seagull, gull.
goélette [gɔelɛt] *nf* schooner.
goémon [gɔemɔ̃] *nm* wrack.
gogo* [gogo] **1** *nm* sucker*, mug‡. **c'est bon pour les** ~**s** it's a mug's game‡. **2** *adv*: **du vin** *etc* **à** ~ wine *etc* galore.
goguenard, e [gɔgnaʀ, aʀd(ə)] *adj* mocking.
goguette* [gɔgɛt] *nf*: **être en** ~ to be on the binge*.
goinfre* [gwɛ̃fʀ(ə)] (*glouton*) **1** *adj* piggish*. **2** *nm* pig*. ♦ **se goinfrer*** (1) *vpr* to make a pig of o.s.*. **se** ~ **de** to guzzle. ♦ **goinfrerie*** *nf* piggishness*.
goitre [gwatʀ(ə)] *nm* goitre.
golden [gɔldɛn] *nf inv* Golden Delicious.
golf [gɔlf] *nm* (*Sport*) golf; (*terrain*) golf course *ou* links. ~ **miniature** miniature golf.
golfe [gɔlf(ə)] *nm* gulf; (*petit*) bay. **le** ~ **de Gascogne** the Bay of Biscay; **le** ~ **du Lion** the Gulf of Lions; **le** ~ **Persique** the Persian Gulf.
gomme [gɔm] *nf* (*substance*) gum; (*pour effacer*) rubber, eraser (*US*). **mettre toute la** ~* to put one's foot right down*; **à la** ~* useless, hopeless. ♦ **gommer** (1) *vt mot* to rub out, erase; (*fig*) to erase. **papier gommé** gummed paper. ♦ **gommage** *nm* rubbing-out; erasing.
gond [gɔ̃] *nm* hinge.
gondole [gɔ̃dɔl] *nf* gondola. ♦ **gondolier, -ière** *nm,f* gondolier.
gondoler [gɔ̃dɔle] (1) **1** *vi [papier]* to crinkle; *[planche]* to warp; *[tôle]* to buckle. **2 se** ~ *vpr* to crinkle; to warp; to buckle; (*: *rire*) to split one's sides laughing*. ♦ **gondolant, e*** *adj* side-splitting*.
gonfler [gɔ̃fle] (1) **1** *vt* **(a)** *ballon etc* (*gén*) to inflate; (*avec pompe*) to pump up; (*en soufflant*) to blow up; *poitrine* to puff out. **(b)** *rivière, voiles* to swell. **un paquet gonflait sa poche** his pocket was bulging with a package; **gonflé d'eau** swollen with water; **ça me gonfle l'estomac** it makes me feel bloated; **gonflé d'orgueil** *personne* puffed up (with pride); *cœur* swollen with pride; **cœur gonflé de joie** heart bursting with joy. **(c)** *prix, résultat* to inflate; *effectif* (*augmenter*) to swell; (*exagérer*) to exaggerate. **2** *vi [cheville, bois]* to swell; *[pâte]* to rise. **faire** ~ **le riz** to leave the rice to swell. **3 se** ~ *vpr* to swell. **son cœur se gonfle (de tristesse)** his heart is heavy (with sorrow). ♦ **gonflage** *nm* inflation. ♦ **gonflé, e** *adj* **(a)** *yeux, visage* puffy, swollen. **joues bien** ~**es** chubby cheeks; **je me sens** ~ I feel bloated. **(b)** (**fig*) **il est** ~! (*courageux*) he's got some nerve!*; (*impertinent*) he's got a nerve!* *ou* some cheek!*; **être** ~ **à bloc** to be raring to go*. ♦ **gonflement** *nm* inflation; swelling; exaggeration. ♦ **gonfleur** *nm* air pump.
gong [gɔ̃(g)] *nm* (*Mus*) gong; (*Boxe*) bell.
gorge [gɔʀʒ(ə)] *nf* **(a)** (*gosier*) throat; (*poitrine*) breast. **avoir la** ~ **sèche** to have a dry throat; **avoir la** ~ **serrée** to have a lump in one's throat; **à** ~ **déployée** *rire* heartily; *chanter* at the top of one's voice; **prendre qn à la** ~ *[créancier]* to put a gun to sb's head (*fig*); *[agresseur]* to grab sb by the throat; *[fumée]* to get in sb's throat; *[peur]* to grip sb by the throat; (*fig*) **ça lui est resté en travers de la** ~ he found it hard to take, he couldn't swallow it. **(b)** (*vallée, défilé*) gorge. **(c)** (*rainure*) *[poulie]* groove; *[serrure]* tumbler.
gorgée [gɔʀʒe] *nf* mouthful. **boire à petites** ~**s** to sip; **boire à grandes** ~**s** to gulp; **d'une seule** ~ in one gulp.
gorger [gɔʀʒe] (3) **1** *vt* to fill, stuff (*de* with). **gorgé d'eau** saturated with *ou* full of water; **gorgé de soleil** bursting with sunshine. **2 se** ~ *vpr* to gorge o.s., stuff o.s.* (*de* with).
gorille [gɔʀij] *nm* gorilla; (*: *garde*) bodyguard.
gosier [gozje] *nm* throat.
gosse* [gɔs] *nmf* kid*. **sale** ~ little brat*.
gothique [gɔtik] *adj* Gothic.
gouache [gwaʃ] *nf* gouache.
goudron [gudʀɔ̃] *nm* tar. ♦ **goudronner** (1) *vt route* to tar.
gouffre [gufʀ(ə)] *nm* (*Géog*) abyss, gulf. **le** ~ **de l'oubli** the depths of oblivion; **c'est un** ~ **d'ignorance** he's abysmally ignorant; **au bord du** ~ on the brink of the abyss.
goujat [guʒa] *nm* boor. ♦ **goujaterie** *nm* boorishness.
goulée [gule] *nf* gulp. ~ **d'air frais** gulp *ou* lungful of fresh air.
goulet [gulɛ] *nm* (*Naut*) narrows; (*Géog*) gully.
goulot [gulo] *nm [bouteille]* neck. **boire au** ~ to drink straight from the bottle; (*fig*) ~ **d'étranglement** bottleneck.
goulu, e [guly] **1** *adj* greedy, gluttonous. **2** *nm,f* glutton. ♦ **goulûment** *adv* greedily, gluttonously.
goupille [gupij] *nf* (*Tech*) pin.
goupiller [gupije] (1) **1** *vt* **(a)** (*: *combiner*) to fix*. **bien/mal goupillé** *machine* well/badly thought out. **(b)** (*Tech*) to pin. **2 se** ~ * *vpr* to work. **comment est-ce que ça se goupille pour demain?** what's the set up* for tomorrow?
goupillon [gupijɔ̃] *nm* (*Rel*) sprinkler; (*à bouteille*) bottle brush.
gourde [guʀd(ə)] **1** *nf* (*Bot*) gourd; (*à eau*) flask; (*: *empoté*) clot*. **2** *adj* (*) thick*.
gourdin [guʀdɛ̃] *nm* club, bludgeon.
gourer (se)‡ [guʀe] (1) *vpr* to boob‡, slip up. **se** ~ **de numéro** to boob‡ over the number; **se** ~ **dans** to boob in‡.
gourmand, e [guʀmɑ̃, ɑ̃d] **1** *adj* (*lit, fig*) greedy (*de* for). **2** *nm,f* gourmand. **3** *nm* (*Agr*) sucker. ♦ **gourmandise** *nf* **(a)** greed, greediness. **(b)** (*gâterie*) delicacy, titbit.
gourmet [guʀmɛ] *nm* gourmet.
gourmette [guʀmɛt] *nf [poignet]* chain bracelet.
gousse [gus] *nf [vanille etc]* pod. ~ **d'ail** clove of garlic.
gousset [gusɛ] *nm [gilet]* fob; *[slip]* gusset.
goût [gu] *nm* **(a)** (*sens*) taste. **ça a mauvais** ~ it has a bad taste, it tastes nasty; **ça a un** ~ **de fraise** it tastes like strawberry, it has a strawberry taste *ou* flavour; **la soupe a un** ~ the soup has a funny taste; **sans** ~ tasteless, flavourless. **(b)** (*jugement*) taste. **sans/avec** ~ tastelessly/tastefully; **elle s'habille avec beaucoup de** ~ she has very good taste in dress, she has very good dress sense; **à mon/son** ~ for my/his liking *ou* my/his taste; **de bon** ~ tasteful, in good taste; **de mauvais** ~ tasteless, in bad *ou* poor taste; (*iro*) **il serait de bon** ~ **d'y aller** it would be as well to go. **(c)** (*penchant*) taste, liking (*de, pour* for). **il n'a aucun** ~ **pour les sciences** the sciences don't appeal to him, he has no taste for *ou* he is not keen on the sciences; **prendre** ~ **à qch** to get a taste for sth, get to like sth; **il n'avait** ~ **à rien** he didn't feel like (doing) anything; **il la trouve à son** ~ she suits his taste; **avoir des** ~**s modestes** to have simple tastes; **tous les** ~**s sont dans la nature** it takes all sorts to make a world. **(d)** (*style*) style. **dans le** ~ **classique** in the classical style; **ou qch dans ce** ~**-là*** or sth of that sort; **se mettre au** ~ **du jour** to bring o.s. into line with current tastes.
goûter [gute] (1) **1** *vt aliment* to taste; *repos, spectacle* to enjoy; *plaisanterie* to appreciate. **2** ~ **à** *vt indir aliment, plaisir* to taste, sample. **il y a à peine goûté** he's hardly touched it. **3** ~ **de** *vt indir* to have a taste of. **4** *vi* (*manger*) to have tea. **5** *nm* tea. **donner un** ~ to give a tea party.

goutte [gut] *nf* **(a)** (*lit, fig*) drop. ~ **de rosée** dewdrop; ~ **de sueur** bead of sweat; **pleuvoir à grosses** ~s to rain heavily; **il est tombé quelques** ~s a few spots *ou* drops of rain have fallen; **tomber** ~ **à** ~ to drip. **(b)** (*: *eau-de-vie*) **prendre la** ~ to have a nip*. **(c)** (*Méd*) gout. **(d) avoir la** ~ **au nez** to have a running nose; **c'est une** ~ **d'eau dans la mer** it's a drop in the ocean; **c'est la** ~ **(d'eau) qui fait déborder le vase** it's the last straw (that breaks the camel's back). ♦ **goutte-à-goutte** *nm inv* drip. **faire du** ~**-à-**~ **à qn** to put sb on the drip. ♦ **gouttelette** *nf* droplet. ♦ **goutter** (1) *vi* to drip (*de* from).

gouttière [gutjɛʀ] *nf* (*horizontale*) gutter; (*verticale*) drainpipe; (*Méd*) (plaster) cast.

gouvernail [guvɛʀnaj] *nm* (*pale*) rudder; (*barre*) helm, tiller. (*fig*) **tenir le** ~ to be at the helm.

gouvernante [guvɛʀnɑ̃t] *nf* (*institutrice*) governess; (*intendante*) housekeeper.

gouvernants [guvɛʀnɑ̃] *nmpl* (*Pol*) **les** ~ the government.

gouverne [guvɛʀn(ə)] *nf*: **pour ta** ~ for your guidance.

gouvernement [guvɛʀnəmɑ̃] *nm* (*régime*) government; (*cabinet*) Cabinet, Government. **sous un** ~ **socialiste** under socialist rule *ou* government. ♦ **gouvernemental, e,** *mpl* **-aux** *adj député* of the governing party; *politique* government, governmental; *journal* pro-government. **le parti** ~ the party in office.

gouverner [guvɛʀne] (1) **1** *vt* **(a)** (*Pol*) to govern, rule; (*fig: contrôler*) to control. **le parti qui gouverne** the party in power *ou* in office. **(b)** (*Naut*) to steer. **(c)** (*Gram*) to govern, take. **2 se** ~ *vpr [peuple]* to govern it's own affairs; *[personne]* to control o.s.

gouverneur [guvɛʀnœʀ] *nm* governor.

grabat [gʀaba] *nm* pallet. ♦ **grabataire** *adj* bedridden.

grabuge* [gʀabyʒ] *nm*: **il va y avoir du** ~ there'll be a rumpus*.

grâce [gʀɑs] *nf* **(a)** (*charme*) *[personne]* grace; *[paysage]* charm. **plein de** ~ graceful; **faire des** ~s to put on airs and graces. **(b)** (*faveur*) favour. **il nous a fait la** ~ **d'accepter** he did us the honour of accepting; **être dans les bonnes** ~**s de qn** to be in sb's good books; **rentrer en** ~ to come back into favour; **gagner les bonnes** ~**s de qn** to gain sb's favour; **donner à qn une semaine de** ~ to give sb a week's grace; ~ **à qn/qch** thanks to sb/sth; ~ **à Dieu!** thank God, thank goodness! **(c) de** *ou* **avec bonne/mauvaise** ~ with (a) good/bad grace; **il a eu la bonne** ~ **de** he had the grace to; **il aurait mauvaise** ~ **à refuser** it would be in bad taste for him to refuse. **(d)** (*miséricorde*) mercy; (*Jur*) pardon. **crier** ~ to beg *ou* cry for mercy; ~! (have) mercy!; **de** ~ for pity's sake, for goodness' sake; **je vous fais** ~ **des détails** I'll spare you the details. **(e)** (*Rel*) grace; (*fig: don*) gift. (*fig*) **c'est la** ~ **que nous lui souhaitons** that is what we wish for him; **à la** ~ **de Dieu!** it's in God's hands! **(f)** (*déesse*) **les trois G**~**s** the three Graces. **(g)** (*titre*) **Sa G**~ ... His *ou* Her Grace ....

gracier [gʀasje] (7) *vt* to pardon.

gracieux, -ieuse [gʀasjø, jøz] *adj* (*élégant*) graceful; (*aimable*) kindly; (*gratuit*) gratuitous. **notre** ~**euse souveraine** our gracious sovereign. ♦ **gracieusement** *adv* gracefully; kindly; (*gratuitement*) free of charge. ♦ **gracieuseté** *nf* (*amabilité*) kindliness; (*geste élégant*) graceful gesture; (*cadeau*) free gift.

gracile [gʀasil] *adj* slender.

gradation [gʀadɑsjɔ̃] *nf* gradation.

grade [gʀad] *nm* (*Admin, Mil*) rank; (*diplôme*) degree; (*Mil, Tech*) grade. **monter en** ~ to be promoted; **en prendre pour son** ~* to get a proper dressing-down*. ♦ **gradé** *nm* (*gén*) officer.

gradin [gʀadɛ̃] *nm* (*Théât*) tier; *[stade]* step (of the terracing); (*Agr*) terrace. **en** ~s terraced.

graduer [gʀadɥe] (1) *vt difficultés* to increase gradually; *thermomètre* to graduate. ♦ **graduation** *nf* graduation. ♦ **gradué, e** *adj exercices* graded; *règle* graduated. ♦ **graduel, -elle** *adj progression* gradual; *difficultés* progressive. ♦ **graduellement** *adv* gradually.

graffiti [gʀafiti] *nmpl* graffiti.

grain [gʀɛ̃] *nm* **(a)** *[blé, sable]* grain; *[café]* bean; *[poussière]* speck; *[chapelet]* bead. (*fig*) ~ **de vérité** *etc* grain of truth *etc*; **alcool de** ~**(s)** grain alcohol; (*Rel*) **le bon** ~ the good seed; ~ **de raisin** grape; ~ **de poivre** peppercorn; ~ **de groseille/cassis** red currant/blackcurrant (berry); ~ **de beauté** mole, beauty spot; **mettre son** ~ **de sel*** to put one's oar in*; **un** ~ **de fantaisie** a touch of fantasy; **un** ~ **de bon sens** a grain *ou* an ounce of common sense; **il n'y a pas un** ~ **de vérité dans ce qu'il dit** there's not a grain *ou* scrap of truth in what he says; **il a un (petit)** ~ he's a bit touched*. **(b)** (*texture*) grain. **à gros** ~s coarse-grained. **(c)** (*averse*) heavy shower; (*bourrasque*) squall.

graine [gʀɛn] *nf* (*Agr*) seed. **prends-en de la** ~* take a leaf out of his (*ou* her) book*. ♦ **graineterie** *nf* (*commerce*) seed trade; (*magasin*) seed shop. ♦ **grainetier, -ière** *nm,f* seed merchant.

graisse [gʀɛs] *nf* (*gén*) fat; (*lubrifiant*) grease. ♦ **graissage** *nm* greasing. (*Aut*) **faire faire un** ~ to have a lubricating job done. ♦ **graisser** (1) *vt* (*gén*) to grease; (*salir*) to get grease on. (*fig*) ~ **la patte à qn*** to grease sb's palm. ♦ **graisseux, -euse** *adj objet* greasy; *tumeur* fatty.

grammaire [gʀamɛʀ] *nf* grammar. **règle de** ~ grammatical rule; **livre de** ~ grammar book. ♦ **grammairien, -ienne** *nm,f* grammarian. ♦ **grammatical, e,** *mpl* **-aux** *adj* grammatical. ♦ **grammaticalement** *adv* grammatically.

gramme [gʀam] *nm* gramme.

grand, e [gʀɑ̃, gʀɑ̃d] **1** *adj* **(a)** (*gén*) big; (*haut*) tall; (*important, remarquable*) great; *distance* long; *quantité* large; (*lit, fig*) *marge* wide; *bruit* loud; *vent* strong, high; *chaleur* intense; *soupir* deep; *dégâts* extensive. **plus** ~ **que nature** larger than life; **ouvrir la fenêtre toute** ~**e** to open the window wide; **la** ~**e majorité des gens** the great *ou* vast majority of people; **le** ~ **capital** big money; **les** ~**s esprits se rencontrent** great minds think alike. **(b)** (*plus âgé*) **son** ~ **frère** his big *ou* older brother; **ils ont 2** ~**s enfants** they have 2 grown-up children; **il est assez** ~ **pour savoir** he's big *ou* old enough to know; **les** ~**es classes** the senior forms. **(c)** (*principal*) main. **c'est la** ~**e question** (*problème*) it's the main *ou* major issue; (*interrogation*) it's the big question. **(d)** (*intensif*) *travailleur* hard; *collectionneur, ami, menteur* great; *buveur* heavy; *mangeur* big. ~**e jeunesse** extreme youth; ~ **âge** great age, old age; **un** ~ **mois** a good month; **un** ~ **panier de champignons** a full basket of mushrooms; **les** ~**s malades** the seriously ill; **un** ~ **invalide** a seriously disabled person; **de** ~**s mots** high-sounding words; **prendre de** ~**s airs** to put on airs, give o.s. airs. **(e)** (*de gala*) *dîner* grand. **en** ~**e pompe** with great pomp; **en** ~**e tenue** in full dress. **(f)** (*noble*) *âme* noble, great. **se montrer** ~ **(et généreux)** to be big-hearted *ou* magnanimous. **(g)** (*locutions*) ~**-chose**: **cela ne vaut pas** ~**-chose** it's not worth much, it's not up to much*; **il n'y a pas** ~**-chose à dire** there's nothing much to say; **à ma** ~**e surprise** much to my surprise, to my great surprise; **de** ~**e classe** *produit* high-class; *œuvre* admirable; **de** ~ **cœur** wholeheartedly; **le groupe au** ~ **complet** the whole group; **à** ~**s cris** vociferously; **de** ~**e envergure** *opération* large-scale; *auteur* of great stature; *réforme* far-reaching; **à** ~**s frais** at great expense; **au** ~ **jour** (*lit*) in broad daylight; (*fig*) in the open; **de** ~ **matin** very early in the morning; **en** ~**e partie** largely; **à** ~**-peine** with great difficulty; **à ~ renfort de** *publicité* with the help of much; *arguments* with the help of many; **à ~ spectacle** *revue* spectacular; **boire qch à ~s traits** to take big gulps of sth. **(h)** (*beaucoup de*) **avoir ~e allure** to look very impressive; **cela te fera (le plus) ~ bien** that'll do you the world of good; **faire ~ bruit** to cause quite a stir; **faire ~ cas de** to attach great importance to, set great store by; **il n'y a pas ~ monde** there aren't very many (people) here; **avoir ~-peine à faire qch** to have great difficulty in doing sth. **(i)** (*bien, très*) **avoir ~ avantage à** to be well advised to; **il a ~ besoin d'un bain** he is in great need of a bath, he badly needs a bath; **elle avait ~e envie de faire** she very much wanted to do, she was longing to do; **avoir ~ faim** to be very hungry; **il fait ~ jour** it's broad daylight; **avoir ~ peur** to be very much afraid; **il est ~ temps de faire ceci** it's high time this was done.

2 *adv*: **voir ~** to think big*; **ces souliers chaussent ~** these shoes are big-fitting; **faire qch en ~** to do sth on a large scale *ou* in a big way; **ouvrir ~ la fenêtre** to open the window wide.

3 *nm* **(a)** (*Scol*) older *ou* bigger *ou* senior boy. **pour petits et ~s** for old and young alike, for the young and the not-so-young. **(b)** (*terme d'affection*) **mon ~** son, my lad. **(c) les ~s de ce monde** those in high places; (*Pol*) **les quatre G~s** the Big Four. **(d) Pierre** *etc* **le G~** Peter *etc* the Great.

4 *nf* older *ou* bigger *ou* senior girl. (*terme d'affection*) **ma ~e** (my) dear.

5: **le ~ air** the open air; (*Phot*) **~ angle** wide-angle lens; (*Aut*) **~s axes** (main) trunk roads; **la ~e banlieue** the outer suburbs; **la G~e-Bretagne** Great Britain; **~ chef** big boss; **~-duc** *nm, pl* **~s-~s** (*prince*) grand duke; (*Orn*) eagle owl; **les ~es eaux de Versailles** the fountains of Versailles; **le ~ écart** the splits; **la ~e échelle (des pompiers)** the (firemen's) big (turntable) ladder; (*Univ*) **~e école** grande école, *school of university level with competitive entrance examination;* (*Scol*) **être à la ~e école*** to be at the big school; **~ ensemble** housing scheme; **le ~ film** the main film; **les G~s Lacs** the Great Lakes; **le ~ large** the high seas; **~ magasin** department store; **~ manitou*** big boss*; **~ mât** mainmast; **~-mère** *nf, pl* **~s-~s** grandmother; (*: *vieille dame*) granny*; **~-messe** *nf, pl* **~-~s** high mass; **le ~ monde** high society; **le G~ Nord** the far North; **~-oncle** *nm, pl* **~s-~s** great-uncle; **~s-parents** *nmpl* grandparents; **~-père** *nm, pl* **~s-~s** grandfather; (*: *vieux monsieur*) old man; **~e personne** grown-up; **~ prêtre** high priest; **le ~ public** the general public; (*Pol*) **~e puissance** major power; **la ~-rue** the high *ou* main street; **~e surface** hypermarket; **~-tante** *nf, pl* **~s-~s** great-aunt; **~ teint** *adj inv* colourfast; **les ~es vacances** the summer holidays *ou* vacation (*US*); (*Univ*) the long vacation; **~-voile** *nf, pl* **~s-~s** mainsail.

grandement [grɑ̃dmɑ̃] *adv*: **se tromper ~** to be greatly mistaken; **avoir ~ tort** to be absolutely wrong; **il a ~ le temps** he has plenty of time; **nous ne sommes pas ~ logés** we haven't (very) much room; **il est ~ temps de partir** it's high time we went.

grandeur [grɑ̃dœr] *nf* **(a)** *[objet]* size; *[sacrifice]* greatness. **~ nature** life-size; (*fig*) **de première ~** of the first order. **(b)** (*gloire, dignité*) greatness; (*magnanimité*) magnanimity. **~ d'âme** nobility of soul; **~ et décadence de** rise and fall of; **politique de ~** politics of grandeur.

grandiloquent, e [grɑ̃dilɔkɑ̃, ɑ̃t] *adj* grandiloquent.

grandiose [grɑ̃djoz] *adj* grandiose.

grandir [grɑ̃dir] (2) **1** *vi* (*en taille*) to grow; (*en importance*) to grow, increase; *[bruit]* to grow louder; *[ombre]* to grow bigger. **~ de 10 cm** to grow 10 cm; **~ dans l'estime de qn** to grow *ou* go up in sb's estimation; **en grandissant tu verras que** as you grow up you'll see that. **2** *vt [microscope]* to magnify. **~ les dangers** to exaggerate the dangers; **ça le grandit** (*en taille*) it makes him look taller; (*en prestige*) it increases his stature.

grange [grɑ̃ʒ] *nf* barn.

granit(e) [granit] *nm* granite.

granulé, e [granyle] *nm* granule.

granuleux, -euse [granylø, øz] *adj* granular.

graphique [grafik] **1** *adj* graphic. **2** *nm* (*courbe*) graph.

graphite [grafit] *nm* graphite.

graphologie [grafɔlɔʒi] *nf* graphology.

grappe [grap] *nf* cluster. **~ de raisin** bunch of grapes; **en ~s** in clusters.

grappin [grapɛ̃] *nm* grapnel. **mettre le ~ sur** to grab.

gras, grasse [grɑ, grɑs] **1** *adj* **(a)** *bouillon* fatty. **fromage ~** full fat cheese. **(b)** (*gros*) *personne* fat; *volaille* plump. **(c)** (*graisseux*) *mains, cheveux* greasy; *sol* slimy. **(d)** (*épais*) *trait* thick. **(e)** *toux* loose, phlegmy; *voix, rire* throaty. **(f)** (*vulgaire*) coarse, crude. **(g)** (*abondant*) *pâturage* rich; *récompense* fat*. **la paye n'est pas grasse** it's not much of a salary. **(h) faire la grasse matinée** to have a long lie. **2** *nm* (*Culin*) fat; (*sale*) grease. **~-double** tripe; **le ~ de la jambe** the fleshy part of the leg. ♦ **grassement** *adv rétribuer* generously; *rire* coarsely. **~ payé** highly paid, well paid. ♦ **grassouillet, -ette*** *adj* podgy, plump.

gratification [gratifikɑsjɔ̃] *nf* (*Admin*) bonus.

gratifier [gratifje] (7) *vt*: **~ qn de** *récompense, amende* to present sb with; *sourire* to favour sb with; *punition* to reward sb with.

gratin [gratɛ̃] *nm* (*Culin*) (*plat*) cheese(-topped) dish; (*croûte*) cheese topping. (*: *haute société*) **le ~** the upper crust; **au ~** au gratin. ♦ **gratiné, e 1** *adj* **(a)** (*Culin*) au gratin. **(b)** (*) *épreuve* stiff*; *plaisanterie* wild*. **c'est un type ~** he's absolutely incredible. **2** *nf* onion soup au gratin. ♦ **gratiner** (1) *vi [sauce]* to stick.

gratis [gratis] **1** *adj* free. **2** *adv* free, for nothing.

gratitude [gratityd] *nf* gratitude.

gratter [grate] (1) **1** *vt* **(a)** *surface* to scratch; (*avec un outil*) to scrape; *tache* to scratch off; *inscription* to scratch out; *boue* to scrape off. **(b)** (*irriter*) **ce drap me gratte** this sheet is making me itch; **ça (me) gratte** I've got an itch; **vin qui gratte la gorge** wine which catches in one's throat. **(c)** (*) **~ quelques francs** to make a few francs*; **~ les fonds de tiroir** to raid the piggy bank. **2** *vi* **(a)** *[plume]* to scratch. **(b)** *[drap]* (*irriter*) to be scratchy; (*démanger*) to be itchy. **(c)** (*) (*économiser*) to save; (*travailler*) to slog (away)*; (*écrire*) to scribble. **3 se ~** *vpr* to scratch (o.s.). ♦ **gratte-ciel** *nm inv* skyscraper. ♦ **gratte-papier** *nm inv* (*péj*) penpusher. ♦ **gratte-pieds** *nm inv* shoe-scraper. ♦ **grattoir** *nm* scraper.

gratuit, e [gratɥi, ɥit] *adj* **(a)** (*sans payer*) free. **(b)** *affirmation* unwarranted; *cruauté, geste* gratuitous. ♦ **gratuité** *nf* **(a) la ~ de l'éducation** *etc* free education *etc.* **(b)** unwarranted nature; gratuitousness. ♦ **gratuitement** *adv* **(a)** free of charge. **(b)** gratuitously.

gravats [gravɑ] *nmpl* (*Constr*) rubble.

grave [grav] **1** *adj* (*solennel*) grave, solemn; (*important, alarmant*) serious, grave; (*Ling*) *accent* grave; *note* low; *son, voix* deep. **blessé ~** seriously injured man; **ce n'est pas ~** there's no harm done, it's not serious. **2** *nm* (*Rad*) **'~-aigu'** 'bass-treble'; **les ~s** (*Rad*) the bass tones; (*Mus*) the low notes. ♦ **gravement** *adv* gravely, solemnly; seriously.

graver [grave] (1) *vt* (*gén*) to engrave; (*sur bois*) to carve (*dans* on); *disque* to cut. **~ à l'eau-forte** to etch; **faire ~ des cartes de visite** to get some visiting cards printed; **c'est gravé sur son front** it's written all over his face. ♦ **graveur** *nm* engraver; (*sur bois*) woodcutter. ~ **à l'eau-forte** etcher.

gravier [gʀavje] *nm* (*caillou*) bit of gravel. **le ~** gravel; **allée de ~** gravel path.

gravillon [gʀavijɔ̃] *nm* (*caillou*) bit of grit *ou* gravel. **du ~, des ~s** loose chippings.

gravir [gʀaviʀ] (2) *vt* (*lit, fig*) to climb. ~ **péniblement une côte** to struggle up a slope.

gravité [gʀavite] *nf* **(a)** *[ton, assemblée]* gravity, solemnity; *[situation, faute]* seriousness. **c'est un accident sans ~** it wasn't a serious accident. **(b)** (*Phys*) gravity.

graviter [gʀavite] (1) *vi* (*lit, fig*) to revolve (*autour de* round). **il gravite dans les milieux diplomatiques** he moves in diplomatic circles.

gravure [gʀavyʀ] *nf* **(a)** (*gén*) engraving; (*sur bois*) carving; *[disque]* cutting. **(b)** (*dans une revue*) plate; (*au mur*) print. ~ **sur bois** (*technique*) woodcutting; (*dessin*) woodcut; ~ **sur cuivre** copperplate engraving; ~ **à l'eau-forte** etching; ~ **de mode** fashion plate.

gré [gʀe] *nm* **(a)** *[personnes]* **à mon/votre ~** (*goût*) to my/your liking *ou* taste; (*désir, choix*) as I/you like *ou* please; **contre le ~ de qn** against sb's will; **de ~ à ~** by mutual agreement; **il le fera de ~ ou de force** he'll do it whether he likes it or not; **de son plein ~** of one's own free will, of one's own accord; **de bon ~** willingly; **de mauvais ~** grudgingly. **(b)** *[choses]* **flottant au ~ de l'eau** drifting on *ou* with the current; **volant au ~ du vent** flying in the wind; **agir au ~ des événements** to act according to events; **au ~ de sa fantaisie** as the fancy took him (*ou* her).

Grèce [gʀɛs] *nf* Greece. ♦ **grec, grecque 1** *adj* (*gén*) Greek; *vase, beauté* Grecian. **2** *nm* (*Ling*) Greek. **3** *nm(f)*: **G~(que)** Greek.

gredin [gʀədɛ̃] *nm* rascal.

gréer [gʀee] (1) *vt* (*Naut*) to rig. ♦ **gréement** *nm* rigging.

greffe[1] [gʀɛf] *nf* *[organe]* transplant; *[tissu, branche]* graft. **une ~ du cœur** a heart transplant; (*action*) **la ~ de qch** the transplanting (*ou* grafting) of sth. ♦ **greffer** (1) *vt* to transplant; to graft. *[problème]* **se ~ sur qch** to come on top of *ou* in addition to sth. ♦ **greffon** *nm* transplant; graft.

greffe[2] [gʀɛf] *nm* Clerk's Office (*of courts*). ♦ **greffier** *nm* clerk of the court.

grégaire [gʀegɛʀ] *adj* gregarious.

grêle[1] [gʀɛl] *adj* *jambes* spindly; *personne* lanky; *son* shrill.

grêle[2] [gʀɛl] *nf* hail. **averse de ~** hail storm; ~ **de** *coups etc* hail *ou* shower of. ♦ **grêlé, e** *adj* *peau* pockmarked. ♦ **grêler** (1) *vb impers*: **il grèle** it is hailing. ♦ **grêlon** *nm* hailstone.

grelot [gʀəlo] *nm* bell.

grelotter [gʀəlɔte] (1) *vi* (*trembler*) to shiver (*de* with).

grenade [gʀənad] *nf* (*Bot*) pomegranate; (*explosif*) grenade. ~ **lacrymogène** teargas grenade; ~ **sous-marine** depth charge. ♦ **grenadine** *nf* grenadine.

grenat [gʀəna] **1** *nm* garnet. **2** *adj inv* dark red.

grenier [gʀənje] *nm* attic, garret; (*pour grain etc*) loft. ~ **à blé** granary; ~ **à foin** hayloft.

grenouille [gʀənuj] *nf* frog. (*péj*) ~ **de bénitier** Holy Joe*.

grès [gʀɛ] *nm* (*Géol*) sandstone; (*Poterie*) stoneware. **pot de ~** stoneware pot.

grésil [gʀezi(l)] *nm* (*Mét*) (fine) hail.

grésiller [gʀezije] (1) *vi* *[huile]* to sizzle; *[radio]* to crackle. ♦ **grésillement** *nm*: **~(s)** sizzling; crackling.

grève [gʀɛv] *nf* **(a)** (*arrêt de travail*) strike. **se mettre en ~** to go on strike, strike; **être en ~, faire ~** to be on strike; ~ **de la faim** hunger strike; ~ **sauvage** wildcat strike; ~ **de solidarité** sympathy strike; ~ **sur le tas** sit-down strike; ~ **tournante** strike by rota; ~ **du zèle** ≃ work-to-rule. **(b)** *[mer]* shore; *[rivière]* bank.

grever [gʀəve] (5) *vt* *budget* to put a strain on; *pays* to burden. **grevé d'impôts** weighed down with *ou* crippled by taxes.

gréviste [gʀevist(ə)] *nmf* striker.

gribouiller [gʀibuje] (1) **1** *vt* (*écrire*) to scribble, scrawl; (*dessiner*) to scrawl. **2** *vi* (*dessiner*) to doodle. ♦ **gribouillage** *nm ou* ♦ **gribouillis** *nm* scribble; doodle. ♦ **gribouilleur, -euse** *nm,f* scribbler.

grief [gʀijɛf] *nm* grievance. **faire ~ à qn de qch** to hold sth against sb.

grièvement [gʀijɛvmɑ̃] *adv*: ~ **blessé** (very) seriously injured.

griffe [gʀif] *nf* **(a)** (*Zool*) claw. **le chat fait ses ~s** the cat is sharpening its claws; (*lit, fig*) **sortir** *ou* **montrer/rentrer ses ~s** to show/draw in one's claws; **arracher qn des ~s d'un ennemi** to snatch sb from the clutches of an enemy. **(b)** *[couturier]* maker's label; *[fonctionnaire]* signature stamp; (*fig: empreinte*) stamp. ♦ **griffer** (1) *vt* to scratch; (*avec force*) to claw.

griffonner [gʀifɔne] (1) **1** *vt* (*écrire*) to scribble, scrawl; (*dessiner*) to scrawl. **2** *vi* (*dessiner*) to doodle. ♦ **griffonnage** *nm* scribble; doodle.

grignoter [gʀiɲɔte] (1) **1** *vt* **(a)** *[personne, souris]* to nibble (at). **(b)** *libertés* to eat away at; *avantage* to win gradually. ~ **du terrain** to gain ground gradually. **2** *vi* to nibble (at one's food). ♦ **grignotement** *nm*: **~(s)** nibbling.

gril [gʀi(l)] *nm* (*Culin*) steak pan, grill pan. **être sur le ~*** to be on tenterhooks. ♦ **grillade** *nf* (*viande*) grill.

grillage [gʀijaʒ] *nm* wire netting; *[clôture]* wire fencing. ♦ **grillager** (3) *vt* to put wire netting (*ou* wire fencing) on.

grille [gʀij] *nf* **(a)** (*clôture*) railings; (*portail*) (metal) gate. **(b)** *[cellule]* bars; *[parloir]* grille; *[égout]* (metal) grate *ou* grating; *[poêle à charbon]* grate. **(c)** *[salaires, tarifs]* scale; *[horaires]* schedule; (*codage*) (code) grid. ~ **de mots croisés** crossword puzzle (grid).

griller [gʀije] (1) **1** *vt* **(a)** (*Culin: aussi* **faire ~**) *pain, amandes* to toast; *viande* to grill; *café, châtaignes* to roast. **(b)** *corps* to burn; *végétation* to scorch. **se ~ au soleil** to roast in the sun. **(c)** *lampe* to blow; *moteur* to burn out. **(d)** (*) ~ **une cigarette** to have a smoke; ~ **un feu rouge** to jump the lights; ~ **une étape** to cut out a stop; ~ **qn à l'arrivée** to pip sb at the post*. **2** *vi*: ~ **(d'envie) de faire** to be itching to do; **on grille ici!*** we're *ou* it's roasting in here!* ♦ **grille-pain** *nm inv* toaster.

grillon [gʀijɔ̃] *nm* cricket.

grimace [gʀimas] *nf* (*gén*) grimace; (*sourire*) grin. **s'amuser à faire des ~s** to play at making *ou* pulling (funny) faces; **il fit une ~** he pulled a wry face, he grimaced; **il fit la ~ quand il connut la décision** he pulled a face when he learned of the decision. ♦ **grimacer** (3) *vi* (*sourire*) to grin. ~ **(de douleur)** to grimace with pain; ~ **(sous l'effort)** to grimace *ou* screw one's face up (with the effort); **il grimaça de dégoût** he grimaced *ou* his face twisted with disgust.

grimer *vt*, **se ~** *vpr* [gʀime] (1) (*Théât*) to make up.

grimoire [gʀimwaʀ] *nm* (*littér*) book.

grimper [gʀɛ̃pe] (1) **1** *vi* to climb; (*avec difficulté*) to clamber up; *[fièvre, prix]* to soar. ~ **aux arbres** to climb trees; ~ **à l'échelle** to climb (up) the ladder; **ça grimpe dur!** it's a stiff *ou* steep climb! **2** *vt* to climb, go up. **3** *nm* (*Athlétisme*) **le ~** (rope)-climbing. ♦ **grimpant, e** *adj* climbing. ♦ **grimpette*** *nf* (steep little) climb.

grincer [gʀɛ̃se] (3) *vi* *[métal]* to grate; *[plancher]* to creak; *[plume]* to scratch. ~ **des dents (de**

colère) to grind one's teeth (in anger); **ce bruit vous fait ~ des dents** this noise sets your teeth on edge. ♦ **grinçant, e** *adj* (*lit, fig*) grating. ♦ **grincement** *nm*: **~(s)** grating; creaking; scratching.
grincheux, -euse [gʀɛ̃ʃø, øz] *adj* grumpy.
grippe [gʀip] *nf*: **la ~** (the) flu; **une petite ~** a slight touch of flu; **~ intestinale** gastric flu; **prendre qn/qch en ~** to take a sudden dislike to sb/sth. ♦ **grippé, e** *adj*: **il est ~** he's got (the) flu.
gripper [gʀipe] (1) *vti* (*Tech*) to jam. **le moteur a grippé** the engine has seized up.
gris, e [gʀi, gʀiz] **1** *adj* (*lit*) grey, gray (*US*); (*morne*) dull; (*soûl*) tipsy. **~ perle/-bleu** pearl/blue-grey; **il fait ~** it's a grey *ou* dull day; **faire ~e mine à qn** to give sb a cool reception; **faire ~e mine** to look put out. **2** *nm* grey. ♦ **grisaille** *nf* greyness; dullness. ♦ **grisâtre** *adj* greyish.
griser [gʀize] (1) **1** *vt*: **~ qn** to intoxicate sb, go to sb's head; **se laisser ~ par l'ambition** to be carried away by ambition. **2 se ~** *vpr*: **se ~ de** *vitesse* to get drunk on; *paroles* to be intoxicated by *ou* carried away by. ♦ **griserie** *nf* intoxication.
grisonner [gʀizɔne] (1) *vi* to be going grey.
grisou [gʀizu] *nm* firedamp.
grive [gʀiv] *nf* (*Orn*) thrush.
grivois, e [gʀivwa, waz] *adj* saucy. ♦ **grivoiserie** *nf* (*attitude*) sauciness; (*histoire*) saucy story.
Groënland [gʀɔenlɑ̃d] *nm* Greenland.
grog [gʀɔg] *nm* grog.
grogner [gʀɔɲe] (1) *vi [personne]* to grumble, growl; *[cochon]* to grunt; *[sanglier]* to snort; *[ours, chien]* to growl. ♦ **grognement** *nm* growl; grunt; snort. ♦ **grognon 1** *adj* grumpy, surly. **2** *nmf* grumbler.
groin [gʀwɛ̃] *nm [animal]* snout.
grommeler [gʀɔmle] (4) **1** *vi* to mutter, grumble to o.s. **2** *vt insultes* to mutter. ♦ **grommellement** *nm*: **~(s)** muttering, grumbling.
gronder [gʀɔ̃de] (1) **1** *vt enfant* to scold, tell off*. **2** *vi [canon, orage]* to rumble; *[chien]* to growl; *[foule]* to mutter (angrily); *[colère, émeute]* to be brewing. ♦ **grondement** *nm*: **~(s)** rumbling; growling; (angry) muttering. ♦ **gronderie** *nf* scolding. ♦ **grondeur, -euse** *adj* grumbling.
groom [gʀum] *nm* bellboy.
gros, grosse [gʀo, gʀos] **1** *adj* **(a)** (*gén*) big, large; (*épais*) thick; (*gras*) fat; (*lourd*) heavy. **c'est ~ comme une tête d'épingle** it's the size of *ou* it's no bigger than a pinhead. **(b)** (*fig*) *travail* big; *somme, firme* large; *progrès* great; *dégâts* extensive, serious; *mer, rhume, averse* heavy; *fièvre* high; *soupir* deep. **les grosses chaleurs** the height of summer, the hot season; (*fig*) **c'est un ~ morceau*** (*travail*) it's a big job; (*obstacle*) it's a big hurdle; **la grosse industrie** heavy industry; **~ rire** guffaw; **un ~ banquier/mangeur** a big banker/eater; **un ~ buveur** a heavy drinker; **~ nigaud*** big *ou* great silly*. **(c)** *drap* coarse; *traits du visage* thick, heavy. **le ~ travail** the heavy work; **grosse plaisanterie** obvious *ou* unsubtle joke; **c'est vraiment un peu ~** it's a bit thick*. **(d) avoir les yeux ~ de larmes** to have eyes filled with tears; **cœur ~ de chagrin** heart heavy with sorrow; **femme grosse de 6 mois** woman 6 months pregnant; **jouer ~ jeu** to play for high stakes; **avoir le cœur ~** to have a heavy heart; **le chat fait le ~ dos** the cat is arching its back; **faire les ~ yeux (à un enfant)** to glower (at a child).
2 *nm* **(a)** (*personne*) (*corpulent*) fat man; (*riche*) rich man. **mon ~*** old man*. **(b)** (*principal*) **le ~ du travail** the bulk of *ou* the main part of the work; **le ~ de l'armée** the main body of the army; **le ~ de l'orage** the worst of the storm; **dites-moi, en ~, ce qui s'est passé** tell me roughly what happened. **(c)** (*milieu*) **au ~ de l'hiver** in the depth of winter; **au ~ de l'été** at the height of summer. **(d)** (*Comm*) **le (commerce de) ~** the wholesale business; **prix de ~** wholesale price; **papetier en ~** wholesale stationer; **vendre en ~** to sell wholesale.
3 *nf* (*personne*) fat woman.
4 *adv*: **écrire ~** to write big, write in large letters; **il risque ~** he's risking a great deal; **il y a ~ à parier que ...** it's a safe bet that ...; **en avoir ~ sur le cœur** to be upset.
5: **~ bétail** cattle; **~ bonnet*** bigwig*, big shot*; (*Mus*) **grosse caisse** (bass) drum; **grosse cavalerie*** heavy stuff*; **~ gibier** big game; **~ intestin** large intestine; **grosse légume*** = **~ bonnet***; (*lit, fig*) **~ lot** jackpot; **~ mot** coarse word; **~ orteil** big toe; **~ plan** close-up; **~ sel** cooking salt; **par ~ temps** in rough weather; **~ titre** headline.
groseille [gʀozɛj] **1** *nf*: **~ (rouge)** red currant; **~ (blanche)** white currant; **~ à maquereau** gooseberry. **2** *adj inv* (cherry-)red. ♦ **groseillier** *nm* currant bush. **~ à manquereau** gooseberry bush.
grossesse [gʀosɛs] *nf* pregnancy.
grosseur [gʀosœʀ] *nf* **(a)** *[objet]* size; *[fil, bâton]* thickness; *[personne]* weight, fatness. **(b)** (*tumeur*) lump.
grossier, -ière [gʀosje, jɛʀ] *adj* **(a)** (*sans finesse*) *matière, traits* coarse; *esprit* unrefined; *imitation, instrument, ruse* crude; *plaisanterie* unsubtle; *plaisirs* base; *travail* roughly done; *dessin, réparation, estimation* rough. **(b)** *erreur* stupid, gross; *ignorance* crass. **(c)** (*insolent*) rude (*envers* to); (*vulgaire*) coarse. ♦ **grossièrement** *adv* roughly; crudely; coarsely; rudely. **se tromper ~** to make a gross error. ♦ **grossièreté** *nf* rudeness; crudeness; coarseness. **dire des ~s** to use coarse language; **la ~ de ses manières** his crude manners.
grossir [gʀosiʀ] (2) **1** *vi* **(a)** *[personne]* to put on weight. **(b)** (*en quantité etc*) to grow; (*en taille*) to get bigger; *[bruit]* to get louder. **2** *vt* **(a)** *[lunettes]* to enlarge, magnify; (*exagérer*) to exaggerate. *[vêtement]* **~ qn** to make sb look fatter. **(b)** *foule, cours d'eau* to swell; *voix* to raise; *somme* to increase, add to. **~ les rangs de** to swell the ranks of. ♦ **grossissement** *nm [tumeur]* swelling; *[objet, dangers etc]* magnification.
grossiste [gʀosist(ə)] *nmf* wholesaler.
grosso modo [gʀosomɔdo] *adv* (*en gros*) roughly; (*tant bien que mal*) after a fashion.
grotesque [gʀɔtɛsk(ə)] *adj* (*risible*) ludicrous; (*difforme*) grotesque.
grotte [gʀɔt] *nf* (*naturelle*) cave; (*artificielle*) grotto.
grouiller [gʀuje] (1) **1** *vi [foule]* to mill about; *[rue]* to be swarming with people. **2 se ~** *vpr* (*) to get a move on*. ♦ **grouillement** *nm* milling; swarming.
groupe [gʀup] *nm* group. **le ~ de la majorité** the M.P.s of the majority party; **des ~s de gens** groups *ou* knots of people; **un ~ de touristes** a group *ou* party of tourists; **par ~s de 3** in groups of 3, in threes; **marcher en ~** to walk in a group; **~ d'arbres** clump of trees; **~ électrogène** generating set; **~ hospitalier/scolaire** hospital/school complex; **~ de pression** pressure group; **~ sanguin** blood group. ♦ **groupement** *nm* (*action*) grouping; (*groupe*) group. ♦ **grouper** (1) **1** *vt* to group; (*Comm*) *colis* to bulk; *efforts, ressources* to pool; *idées* to put together, order. **2 se ~** *vpr [foule]* to gather; (*en association*) to band together. **se ~ autour d'un chef** to rally round a leader. ♦ **groupuscule** *nm* (*Pol péj*) small group.
gruau [gʀyo] *nm*: **farine de ~** fine wheat flour.
grue [gʀy] *nf* (*Tech, Orn*) crane; (*‡péj: prostituée*) tart‡ (*péj*).
grumeau, *pl* **~x** [gʀymo] *nm [sauce]* lump.
gruyère [gʀyjɛʀ] *nm* gruyère (cheese).

gué [ge] *nm* ford. **passer qch à ~** to ford sth.
guenille [gənij] *nf* rag. **~s** (old) rags.
guenon [gənɔ̃] *nf* (*Zool*) female monkey.
guépard [gepaʀ] *nm* cheetah.
guêpe [gɛp] *nf* wasp. ♦ **guêpier** *nm* (*piège*) trap; (*nid*) wasp's nest.
guère [gɛʀ] *adv* hardly, scarcely. **il n'y a ~ de monde** there's hardly *ou* scarcely anybody there; **il n'y a ~ que lui qui ...** he's about the only one who ...; **ça ne fera ~ moins de 100F** that won't be (very) much less than 100 francs; **je n'aime ~ qu'on me questionne** I don't much like being questioned; **cela ne durera ~** that won't last (for) very long.
guéridon [geʀidɔ̃] *nm* pedestal table.
guérilla [geʀija] *nf* guerrilla warfare. ♦ **guérillero** *nm* guerrilla.
guérir [geʀiʀ] (2) **1** *vt malade, maladie* to cure; *membre, blessure* to heal. **2** *vi [malade]* to recover (*de* from), be cured (*de* of); *[blessure, chagrin]* to heal. **3 se ~** *vpr* to recover, be cured. **se ~ d'une habitude** to cure o.s. of a habit. ♦ **guérison** *nf [malade]* recovery; *[maladie]* curing; *[membre, plaie]* healing. ♦ **guérissable** *adj* curable. ♦ **guérisseur, -euse** *nm,f* healer; (*péj*) quack (doctor).
guérite [geʀit] *nf* (*Mil*) sentry box; (*sur chantier*) site hut.
Guernesey [gɛʀn(ə)zɛ] *nf* Guernsey.
guerre [gɛʀ] *nf* **(a)** (*conflit*) war; (*technique*) warfare. **correspondant** *etc* **de ~** war correspondent *etc*; **~ froide/mondiale** cold/world war; **la ~ de Sécession** the American Civil War; **la ~ d'embuscade** guerrilla warfare. **(b) entre eux c'est la ~ ouverte** there's open war(fare) between them; (*lit, fig*) **en ~** at war (*avec, contre* with, against); **faire la ~ à** *pays, abus* to wage war on; **soldat qui a fait la ~** soldier who was in the war; **ton chapeau a fait la ~*** your hat has been in the wars*; **faire la ~ à qn pour obtenir qch** to battle with sb to get sth; **de ~ lasse elle accepta** she gave up the struggle and accepted; **à la ~ comme à la ~** we'll just have to make the best of things. ♦ **guerrier, -ière 1** *adj nation, air* warlike; *danse, exploits* war. **2** *nm,f* warrior.
guet [gɛ] *nm* **(a) faire le ~** to be on the watch *ou* look-out; **avoir l'œil au ~** to keep one's eyes open. **(b)** (*Hist*) watch. ♦ **guet-apens,** *pl* **~s-~** *nm* (*lit, fig*) ambush.
guêtre [gɛtʀ(ə)] *nf* gaiter.
guetter [gete] (1) *vt* (*épier*) to watch (intently); (*attendre*) to watch out for, be on the look-out for; (*hostilement*) to lie in wait for. **~ le passage de qn** to watch out for sb (to pass by); (*fig*) **la crise cardiaque le guette** there's a heart attack lying in wait for him. ♦ **guetteur** *nm* (*Mil*) look-out; (*Hist*) watch.
gueule [gœl] *nf* **(a)** (:) (*bouche*) mouth; (*figure*) face; (*aspect*) look. **ferme ta ~!** shut your trap!: *ou* face!:; **faire la ~** to look sulky; **il a fait une sale ~** he pulled a face; **ça a une drôle de ~** it looks really weird. **(b)** *[animal, four]* mouth; *[canon]* muzzle. (*fig*) **se jeter dans la ~ du loup** to throw o.s. into the lion's jaws. ♦ **gueule-de-loup,** *pl* **~s-~-~** *nf* snapdragon. ♦ **gueulement:** *nm* (*cri*) bawl; (*de douleur*) yell. ♦ **gueuler:** (1) **1** *vi* **(a)** to bawl; (*de douleur*) to yell (*de* with); (*protester*) to get stroppy*, bellyache: (*contre* about). **ça va ~** there'll be one hell of a row:. **(b)** *[poste]* to blare out. **faire ~ sa télé** to turn one's telly up full blast*. **2** *vt ordres* to bawl out.
gueuleton* [gœltɔ̃] *nm* blow-out*.
gueux [gø] *nm* (*mendiant*) beggar; (*coquin*) rogue.
gui [gi] **(a)** (*Bot*) mistletoe. **(b)** (*Naut*) boom.
guibol(l)e* [gibɔl] *nf* (*jambe*) leg.
guichet [giʃɛ] *nm* **(a)** *[banque]* counter; *[théâtre]* box office; *[gare]* ticket office. **adressez-vous au ~ d'à côté** inquire at the next window; (*à la poste*) '**~ fermé**' 'position closed'. **(b)** *[mur]* hatch; (*grillage*) grille. ♦ **guichetier, -ière** *nm,f* counter clerk.
guide [gid] **1** *nm* (*gén*) guide; (*livre*) guide(book). **2** *nfpl* (*rênes*) **~s** reins. ♦ **guidage** *nm* (*Aviat*) guidance. ♦ **guider** (1) *vt* (*gén*) to guide. **organisme qui guide les étudiants** organization that provides guidance for students; **se laissant ~ par son instinct** letting himself be guided by his instinct; **se guidant sur les étoiles** using the stars as a guide.
guidon [gidɔ̃] *nm [vélo]* handlebars.
guigne* [giɲ(ə)] *nf* rotten luck*. **avoir la ~** to be jinxed*.
guigner [giɲe] (1) *vt* to eye.
guignol [giɲɔl] *nm* (*marionnette*) guignol (*name of French puppet*); (*péj*) clown; (*spectacle*) puppet show (= *Punch and Judy show*). **c'est du ~!** it's a real farce!
guillemet [gijmɛ] *nm* inverted comma, quotation mark. **ouvrez les ~s** open the inverted commas; **mettre un mot entre ~s** to put a word in quotation marks *ou* inverted commas.
guilleret, -ette [gijʀɛ, ɛt] *adj* **(a)** (*enjoué*) perky. **être tout ~** to be full of beans*. **(b)** (*grivois*) saucy.
guillotine [gijɔtin] *nf* guillotine. ♦ **guillotiner** (1) *vt* to guillotine.
guimauve [gimov] *nf* marshmallow.
guimbarde* [gɛ̃baʀd(ə)] *nf*: **(vieille) ~** old banger*, old rattletrap* (*US*).
guindé, e [gɛ̃de] *adj personne* stiff, starchy; *style* stilted. **il est ~ dans ses vêtements** his clothes make him look stiff.
Guinée [gine] *nf* Guinea.
guingois* [gɛ̃gwa] *adv*: **de ~** skew-whiff*.
guinguette [gɛ̃gɛt] *nf open-air café or dance hall.*
guirlande [giʀlɑ̃d] *nf* garland. **~ de papier** paper chain.
guise [giz] *nf*: **n'en faire qu'à sa ~** to do as one pleases *ou* likes; **en ~ de** by way of.
guitare [gitaʀ] *nf* guitar. ♦ **guitariste** *nmf* guitarist.
guitoune [gitun] *nf* tent.
gus* [gys] *nm* (*type*) guy*.
guttural, e, *mpl* **-aux** [gytyʀal, o] *adj* guttural.
Guyane [gɥijan] *nf* Guiana.
gym [ʒim] *nf* gym, P.E.
gymkhana [ʒimkana] *nm* rally. **~ motocycliste** motorcycle scramble.
gymnastique [ʒimnastik] *nf* gymnastics (*sg*). **professeur de ~** physical education *ou* P.E. teacher; **~ corrective** remedial gymnastics; **faire de la ~** (*Sport*) to do gymnastics; (*au réveil*) to do exercises; **~ intellectuelle** mental gymnastics; **quelle ~ pour aller d'une banlieue à une autre*** what a palaver* to get from one suburb to another. ♦ **gymnase** *nm* gymnasium, gym. ♦ **gymnaste** *nmf* gymnast.
gynécologie [ʒinekɔlɔʒi] *nf* gynaecology. ♦ **gynécologique** *adj* gynaecological. ♦ **gynécologue** *nmf* gynaecologist.
gyroscope [ʒiʀɔskɔp] *nm* gyroscope.

H

H, h [aʃ] *nm ou nf* (*lettre*) H, h. **H aspiré/muet** aspirate/silent *ou* mute h.
habile [abil] *adj mains, ouvrier* skilful, skilled; *diplomate, tactique* skilful, clever. **être ~ à (faire) qch** to be clever *ou* skilful at (doing) sth. ♦ **habilement** *adv* skilfully; cleverly. ♦ **habileté** *nf* skill, skilfulness; cleverness.
habiller [abije] (1) **1** *vt* **(a)** (*vêtir*) to dress (*de* in); (*déguiser*) to dress up (*en* as). **cette robe vous habille bien** that dress really suits you. **(b)** *miséreux* to clothe; *recrues* to provide with uniforms. (*Couture*) **c'est X qui l'habille** X makes all her clothes. **(c)** *mur, fauteuil* to cover (*de* with). **2 s'~** *vpr* to dress, get dressed; (*se déguiser*) to dress up (*en* as). **elle s'habille long** she wears long skirts; **elle ne sait pas s'~** she has no dress sense; (*Couture*) **s'~ chez un tailleur** to buy *ou* get one's clothes from a tailor. ♦ **habillé, e** *adj* **(a)** *robe, soirée* dressy. **(b)** *personne* **bien/mal ~** well/badly dressed; **être ~ de noir** to be dressed in *ou* wearing black; **tout ~** fully dressed, with all one's clothes on. ♦ **habillement** *nm* (*action*) clothing; (*costume*) clothes; (*profession*) clothing trade.
habit [abi] *nm* **(a) ~s** clothes; **~s de travail/du dimanche** working/Sunday clothes. **(b)** (*costume*) suit; (*Théât*) costume; (*de cérémonie*) tails. (*tenue*) **son ~** his dress; **l'~ ne fait pas le moine** do not judge by appearances; **en ~** wearing tails; **l'~ ecclésiastique** clerical dress; **~ de gala** formal dress; **~ religieux** (monk's) habit.
habitable [abitabl(ə)] *adj* (in)habitable.
habitacle [abitakl(ə)] *nm* (*Naut*) binnacle; (*Aviat*) cockpit.
habitant, e [abitɑ̃, ɑ̃t] *nm,f [maison]* occupant; *[ville, pays]* inhabitant. **loger chez l'~** *[touristes]* to stay with the locals; *[soldats]* to be billeted on the locals.
habitat [abita] *nm* (*Bot, Zool*) habitat. (*Géog*) **~ rural** rural settlement.
habitation [abitɑsjɔ̃] *nf* (*maison*) house; (*domicile*) place of residence. **conditions d'~** housing *ou* living conditions; **~ à loyer modéré** (*appartement*) ≃ council flat, public housing unit (*US*); (*immeuble*) ≃ (block of) council flats, public housing (*US*).
habiter [abite] (1) **1** *vt maison* to live in; *région* to inhabit; *[idée]* to dwell in. **la maison n'a pas l'air habitée** the house doesn't look lived-in *ou* occupied. **2** *vi* to live (*en, dans* in).
habitude [abityd] *nf* **(a)** (*accoutumance*) habit. **avoir l'~ de faire** to be used to doing, be in the habit of doing; **mauvaises ~s** bad habits; **faire perdre une ~ à qn** to break sb of a habit; **avoir une longue ~ de** to have long experience of; **j'ai l'~!** I'm used to it; **il a ses petites ~s** he has his (pet) ways *ou* habits; **d'~** usually; **par ~** out of habit; **comme d'~** as usual; **comme à son ~** as he usually does. **(b)** (*coutume*) **~s** customs.
habituer [abitɥe] (1) **1** *vt*: **~ qn à qch/à faire** (*endurcir*) to accustom sb to sth/to doing, get sb used to sth/to doing; (*apprendre*) to teach sb sth/to do. **2 s'~** *vpr*: **s'~ à qch/à faire** to get used *ou* accustomed to sth/to doing. ♦ **habitué, e** *nm,f [maison]* regular visitor; *[café]* regular customer. ♦ **habituel, -elle** *adj* usual, customary, habitual. ♦ **habituellement** *adv* usually.
hacher ['aʃe] (1) *vt* (*au couteau*) to chop; (*avec un appareil*) to mince; (*fig*) *discours* to break up; *récolte* to slash to pieces. **~ menu** to mince, chop finely; **il se ferait ~ pour vous** he'd go through fire for you. ♦ **hache** *nf* axe. **~ de guerre** hatchet; (*fig*) **déterrer la ~ de guerre** to take up the hatchet. ♦ **haché, e 1** *adj viande* minced; *style* jerky. **2** *nm* mince, ground beef (*US*). ♦ **hache-légumes** *nm inv* vegetable-chopper. ♦ **hachette** *nf* hatchet. ♦ **hache-viande** *nm inv* (meat-) mincer. ♦ **hachis** *nm [légumes]* chopped vegetables; *[viande]* mince. **~ Parmentier** ≃ shepherd's pie. ♦ **hachoir** *nm* (*couteau*) chopper; (*appareil*) (meat-)mincer.
hachisch ['aʃiʃ] *nm* hashish.
haddock ['adɔk] *nm* haddock.
hagard, e ['agaʀ, aʀd(ə)] *adj* distraught, wild.
haie ['ɛ] *nf* **(a)** (*clôture*) hedge. **~ vive** quickset hedge. **(b)** *[coureur]* hurdle; *[chevaux]* fence. **course de ~s** *[coureur]* hurdles (race); *[chevaux]* steeplechase; **110 mètres ~s** 110 metres hurdles. **(c)** *[spectateurs]* line, row.
haillon ['ɑjɔ̃] *nm* rag. **en ~s** in rags.
haine ['ɛn] *nf* hatred, hate (*de, pour* of). **prendre qn en ~** to take a violent dislike to sb; **avoir de la ~ pour** to be filled with hate *ou* hatred for. ♦ **haineusement** *adv* with hatred. ♦ **haineux, -euse** *adj parole* full of hatred *ou* hate; *joie* malevolent.
haïr ['aiʀ] (10) *vt* to detest, hate. ♦ **haïssable** *adj* detestable, hateful.
halage ['alaʒ] *nm* towing. **chemin de ~** towpath.
hâle ['ɑl] *nm* tan, sunburn. ♦ **hâlé, e** *adj* tanned, sunburnt.
haleine [alɛn] *nf* (*souffle*) breath; (*respiration*) breathing. **hors d'~** out of breath, breathless; **d'une seule ~** *dire* in one breath; **avoir mauvaise ~** to have bad breath; **tenir qn en ~** (*attention*) to hold sb spellbound; (*incertitude*) to keep sb in suspense; **travail de longue ~** long-term job; **à perdre ~** until one is out of breath.
haler ['ale] (1) *vt ancre* to haul in; *bateau* to tow.
haleter ['alte] (5) *vi* **(a)** (*manquer d'air*) to pant, gasp for breath; (*de soif, d'émotion*) to pant (*de* with). **(b)** *[poitrine]* to heave; *[moteur]* to puff. ♦ **haletant, e** *adj* panting; puffing; heaving; *voix* breathless. **être ~** to be out of breath. ♦ **halètement** *nm*: **~(s)** panting; puffing; heaving.
hall ['ol] *nm [hôtel, immeuble]* hall, foyer; *[gare]* arrival (*ou* departure) hall.
halle ['al] *nf* (*marché*) (covered) market. **les H~s (de Paris)** *the central food market of Paris.*
hallucination [alysinɑsjɔ̃] *nf* hallucination. **tu as des ~s!*** you must be seeing things! ♦ **hallucinant, e** *adj* staggering, incredible.
halo ['alo] *nm* (*Astron, Tech*) halo. **~ de gloire** cloud of glory.
halte ['alt(ə)] *nf* (*pause*) stop, break; (*fig*) pause; (*endroit*) stopping place; (*Rail*) halt. **faire ~** to (make a) stop; **~(-là)!** (*gén*) stop!; (*Mil*) halt!; (*fig*) hold on!; **~ aux essais nucléaires!** no more nuclear tests!
haltère [altɛʀ] *nm* (*à boules*) dumbbell; (*à dis-*

ques) barbell. **faire des ~s** to do weight lifting.
hamac ['amak] *nm* hammock.
hameau, *pl* **~x** ['amo] *nm* hamlet.
hameçon [amsɔ̃] *nm* fish hook.
hampe ['ɑ̃p] *nf [drapeau]* pole; *[lance]* shaft; *[cerf]* breast; *[bœuf]* flank.
hanche ['ɑ̃ʃ] *nf [personne]* hip; *[cheval]* haunch.
hand-ball ['ɑ̃dbal] *nm* handball.
handicap ['ɑ̃dikap] *nm* (*lit, fig*) handicap. ♦ **handicapé, e 1** *adj* handicapped. **2** *nm,f* handicapped person. ♦ **handicaper** (1) *vt* to handicap.
hangar ['ɑ̃gaʀ] *nm* (*gén*) shed; *[marchandises]* warehouse; *[avions]* hangar.
hanneton ['antɔ̃] *nm* maybug.
hanter ['ɑ̃te] (1) *vt* to haunt.
hantise ['ɑ̃tiz] *nf* obsessive fear.
happer ['ape] (1) *vt* (*avec la gueule*) to snap up; (*avec la main*) to snatch up. **se faire ~ par une voiture** to be hit by a car.
harangue ['aʀɑ̃g] *nf* harangue. ♦ **haranguer** (1) *vt* to harangue.
haras ['aʀɑ] *nm* stud farm.
harassement ['aʀasmɑ̃] *nm* exhaustion. ♦ **harasser** (1) *vt* to exhaust. **harassé de travail** overwhelmed with work.
harceler ['aʀsəle] (5) *vt* to harass (*de* with); *gibier* to hunt down. ♦ **harcèlement** *nm* harassing.
hardi, e ['aʀdi] *adj* (*gén*) bold, daring. **~ les gars!** come on lads! ♦ **hardiesse** *nf* boldness, daring. **~s** *[livre]* bold statements; *[domestique]* liberties; **~s de langage** bold language. ♦ **hardiment** *adv* boldly, daringly.
harem ['aʀɛm] *nm* harem.
hareng ['aʀɑ̃] *nm* herring. **~ saur** smoked herring, kipper.
hargne ['aʀɲ(ə)] *nf* aggressiveness. ♦ **hargneusement** *adv* aggressively. ♦ **hargneux, -euse** *adj* aggressive.
haricot ['aʀiko] *nm* bean. **des ~s!‡** nothing doing!*; **~ blanc** haricot bean; **~ à rame** runner bean; **~ vert** French bean; **~ de mouton** mutton stew.
harmonica [aʀmɔnika] *nm* harmonica, mouth organ.
harmonie [aʀmɔni] *nf* (*gén*) harmony; (*fanfare*) wind band. **être en ~ avec** to be in harmony with; **vivre en bonne ~** to get on well together (*avec* with). ♦ **harmonieusement** *adv* harmoniously. ♦ **harmonieux, -euse** *adj* (*gén*) harmonious; *couleurs* well-matched.
harmoniser *vt*, **s'~** *vpr* [aʀmɔnize] (1) to harmonize. ♦ **harmonisation** *nf* harmonization.
harmonium [aʀmɔnjɔm] *nm* harmonium.
harnacher ['aʀnaʃe] (1) *vt cheval* to harness; (*péj: habiller*) to rig out*. ♦ **harnachement** *nm [cheval]* (*action*) harnessing; (*objet*) harness; *[personne]* rig-out*.
harnais ['aʀnɛ] *nm* harness.
harpe ['aʀp(ə)] *nf* (*Mus*) harp. ♦ **harpiste** *nmf* harpist.
harpie ['aʀpi] *nf* (*Myth, péj*) harpy.
harpon ['aʀpɔ̃] *nm* harpoon. ♦ **harponner** (1) *vt baleine* to harpoon; (‡) *malfaiteur* to collar*; (‡) *passant* to waylay.
hasard ['azaʀ] *nm* **(a)** (*coïncidence*) coincidence. **un ~ heureux/malheureux** a stroke *ou* piece of luck/bad luck; **par le plus grand des ~s** quite by chance *ou* coincidence; **les ~s de la vie** the fortunes of life. **(b)** (*destin*) chance, fate, luck; (*Statistique*) chance. **les caprices du ~** the whims of fate; **il ne laisse jamais rien au ~** he never leaves anything to chance; **le ~ a voulu qu'il soit absent** as luck would have it he was not there. **(c)** (*risques*) **~s** hazards. **(d) au ~** *aller* aimlessly; *agir* haphazardly; *tirer, citer* at random; **il a acheté ces livres au ~ de ses voyages** he bought these books haphazardly in the course of his journeys; **à tout ~** (*en cas de besoin*) just in case; **je suis entré à tout ~** I looked in on the off chance; **par ~** by chance, by accident; **tu n'aurais pas par ~ 100 F?** you wouldn't by any chance have *ou* you wouldn't happen to have 100 francs on you? ♦ **hasarder** (1) **1** *vt vie* to risk; *hypothèse* to hazard, venture. **2 se ~** *vpr*: **se ~ dans** to venture into; **se ~ à faire** to risk doing, venture to do. ♦ **hasardeux, -euse** *adj entreprise* hazardous, risky; *hypothèse* dangerous, rash.
hâte ['ɑt] *nf* (*empressement*) haste; (*impatience*) impatience. **à la ~** hurriedly, hastily, in a hurry; **en toute ~** posthaste; **avoir ~ de faire** to be eager *ou* anxious to do; **sans ~** unhurriedly. ♦ **hâter** (1) **1** *vt* (*gén*) to hasten. **~ le pas** to quicken one's pace. **2 se ~** *vpr* to hurry, hasten (*de faire* to do). **hâtez-vous** hurry up; **je me hâte de dire que** I hasten to say that. ♦ **hâtif, -ive** *adj développement* precocious; *fruit* early; *travail* hurried; *décision* hasty. ♦ **hâtivement** *adv* hurriedly, hastily.
hausse ['os] *nf* rise, increase (*de* in). **~ de salaire** (pay) rise; **être en ~** to be going up (in price); (*fig*) **ses actions sont en ~** things are looking up for him.
hausser ['ose] (1) **1** *vt* (*gén*) to raise; (*surélever*) to heighten. **~ les épaules** to shrug one's shoulders. **2 se ~** *vpr*: **se ~ sur la pointe des pieds** to stand up on tiptoe; **se ~ au niveau de qn** to raise o.s. up to sb's level. ♦ **haussement** *nm*: **~ d'épaules** shrug.
haut, e ['o, 'ot] **1** *adj* **(a)** (*gén*) high; (*en taille*) tall. **un mur ~ de 3 mètres** a wall 3 metres high; **les plus ~es branches de l'arbre** the topmost branches of the tree; (*lit, fig*) **marcher la tête ~e** to walk with one's head held high; **la mer est ~e** it is high tide, the tide is in; **en ~e mer** on the open sea; **pousser les ~s cris** to exclaim in horror; **à voix ~e** aloud, out loud; **le prix de l'or est au plus ~** the price of gold has reached a peak. **(b)** (*supérieur*) *qualité, rang* high; *âme, pensée* lofty, noble. **du plus ~ comique** highly amusing; **~ en couleur** (*pittoresque*) colourful; **avoir la ~e main sur qch** to have supreme control of sth; **de ~e naissance** of noble *ou* high birth; **~e cuisine** *etc* haute cuisine *etc*; **~ fonctionnaire** high-ranking civil servant; **la ~e bourgeoisie** the upper middle classes. **(c)** (*ancien*) **dans la plus ~e antiquité** in earliest antiquity; **le ~ moyen âge** the Early Middle Ages. **(d)** (*Géog*) **la H~e Normandie** Upper Normandy.

2 *nm* **(a)** top. **le mur a 3 mètres de ~** the wall is 3 metres high; **en ~ de l'arbre** at the top of the tree; **le ~ du visage** the top part of the face; **les pièces du ~** the upstairs rooms; **l'étagère du ~** the top shelf; **des ~s et des bas** ups and downs; **du ~ d'un arbre** from the top of a tree; **parler du ~ d'une tribune** to speak from a platform. **(b) voir les choses de ~** to take a detached view of things; **tomber de ~** (*lit*) to fall from a height; (*fig*) to have one's hopes dashed; **prendre qch de ~** to take sth in a high and mighty way; **traiter qn de ~** to look down on sb; **regarder qn de ~ en bas** to look sb up and down; **frapper de ~ en bas** to strike downwards; **d'en ~** from above.

3 *nf*: **(les gens de) la ~e‡** the upper crust*, the swells‡.

4 *adv* high; (*sur colis*) 'this side up'. **mettez vos livres plus ~** put your books higher up; **lire tout ~** to read aloud *ou* out loud; **des gens ~ placés** people in high places; **aussi ~ qu'on peut remonter** as far back as we can go; **'voir plus ~'** 'see above'; **~ les mains!** hands up!, stick 'em up!‡; **gagner ~ la main** to win hands down.

5: **~-le-cœur** *nm inv* retch; **avoir un ~-le-cœur** to retch; **~ commissaire** high commissioner; **~-le-corps** *nm inv* sudden start, jump; **avoir un ~-le-corps** to start, jump; **~e fidélité** hi-fi, high fidelity; **~-fond** *nm, pl* **~s-~s** shallow, shoal; **~-**

de-forme *nm, pl* ~s-~-~ top hat; ~-**fourneau** *nm, pl* ~s-~x blast furnace; **le ~ lieu de la culture** the Mecca of culture; **en ~ lieu** in high places; ~-**parleur** *nm, pl* ~-~s loudspeaker; ~**e trahison** high treason.
hautain, e ['otɛ̃, ɛn] *adj* haughty.
hautbois ['obwɑ] *nm* oboe.
hautement ['otmɑ̃] *adv* (*extrêmement*) highly; (*ouvertement*) openly.
hauteur ['otœʀ] *nf* **(a)** *[tour, personne]* height; *[son]* pitch. (*Aut*) ~ **maximum 3 mètres** headroom 3 metres; **tomber de toute sa** ~ to come *ou* go crashing down; **prendre de la** ~ to climb, gain height; **à ~ des yeux** at eye level; **arriver à la ~ de qn** to draw level with sb; (*fig*) **être à la ~ de la situation** to be equal to the situation; **il n'est pas à la ~*** he's not up to it. **(b)** (*Géom*) perpendicular height; (*ligne*) perpendicular; (*Astron*) altitude. **(c)** (*colline*) hill. **(d)** (*noblesse*) loftiness, nobility; (*arrogance*) haughtiness.
hâve ['ɑv] *adj* gaunt, haggard.
havre ['ɑvʀ(ə)] *nm* (*lit, fig*) haven.
Haye ['ɛ] *nf*: **La** ~ the Hague.
hé ['e, he] *excl* (*pour appeler*) hey!; (*pour renforcer*) well.
hebdomadaire [ɛbdɔmadɛʀ] *adj, nm* weekly.
héberger [ebɛʀʒe] (3) *vt* (*gén*) to accommodate; (*provisoirement*) to put up; *réfugiés* to take in. ♦ **hébergement** *nm* accommodation; putting up; taking in.
hébéter [ebete] (6) *vt [alcool]* to stupefy; *[fatigue, télévision]* to daze. ♦ **hébétement** *nm* stupor.
hébraïque [ebʀaik] *adj* Hebrew, Hebraic.
hébreu, *pl* ~**x** [ebʀø] *adj m, nm* Hebrew. **pour moi, c'est de l'~*** it's all Greek to me!
hécatombe [ekatɔ̃b] *nf* slaughter.
hectare [ɛktaʀ] *nm* hectare.
hecto ... [ɛkto] *préf* hecto ... . ~**litre/mètre** hectolitre/metre.
hégémonie [eʒemɔni] *nf* hegemony.
hein* ['ɛ̃, hɛ̃] *excl* eh.
hélas ['elɑs] *excl* alas! ~ **non!** I'm afraid not!, unfortunately not.
héler ['ele] (6) *vt* to hail.
hélice [elis] *nf* propeller, screw.
hélicoptère [elikɔptɛʀ] *nm* helicopter. ♦ **héligare** *nf* heliport. ♦ **héliport** *nm* heliport. ♦ **héliporté, e** *adj* transported by helicopter.
hélium [eljɔm] *nm* helium.
hellénique [elenik] *adj* Hellenic.
helvétique [ɛlvetik] *adj* Swiss.
hématie [emati] *nf* red (blood) corpuscle.
hématome [ematom] *nm* bruise.
hémicycle [emisikl(ə)] *nm* semicircle, hemicycle. (*Pol*) **l'~** the benches (*of the Assemblée Nationale*).
hémisphère [emisfɛʀ] *nm* (*gén*) hemisphere. ~ **sud/nord** southern/northern hemisphere. ♦ **hémisphérique** *adj* hemispherical.
hémistiche [emistiʃ] *nm* hemistich.
hémoglobine [emɔglɔbin] *nf* haemoglobin.
hémophile [emɔfil] **1** *adj* haemophilic. **2** *nmf* haemophiliac. ♦ **hémophilie** *nf* haemophilia.
hémorragie [emɔʀaʒi] *nf* bleeding, haemorrhage.
hémorroïde [emɔʀɔid] *nf* (*gén pl*) haemorrhoid, pile.
hémostatique [emɔstatik] *adj, nm* haemostatic.
hennir ['eniʀ] (2) *vi* to neigh, whinny. ♦ **hennissement** *nm* neigh, whinny.
hep ['ɛp, hɛp] *excl* hey!
hépatique [epatik] **1** *adj* hepatic. **2** *nmf* person who suffers from a liver complaint. ♦ **hépatite** *nf* hepatitis.
héraldique [eʀaldik] **1** *adj* heraldic. **2** *nf* heraldry.
héraut ['eʀo] *nm* (*Hist, fig*) herald.
herbage [ɛʀbaʒ] *nm* pasture.
herbe [ɛʀb(ə)] *nf*: **l'~** grass; **une ~** (*espèce*) a grass; (*brin*) a blade of grass; (*Culin, Méd*) a herb; **mauvaise ~** weed; ~**s folles** wild grasses; ~**s potagères** pot herbs; **en ~** *blé* green, unripe; *avocat* budding; **couper l'~ sous les pieds de qn** to cut the ground from under sb's feet. ♦ **herbeux, -euse** *adj* grassy. ♦ **herbicide 1** *adj* herbicidal. **2** *nm* weed-killer. ♦ **herbier** *nm* herbarium. ♦ **herbivore 1** *adj* herbivorous. **2** *nm* herbivore.
herboriste [ɛʀbɔʀist(ə)] *nmf* herbalist. ♦ **herboristerie** *nf* (*commerce*) herb trade; (*magasin*) herbalist's shop.
Hercule [ɛʀkyl] *nm* (*Myth*) Hercules. (*fig*) **c'est un h~** he's a real Hercules. ♦ **herculéen, -éenne** *adj* Herculean.
héréditaire [eʀeditɛʀ] *adj* hereditary. ♦ **hérédité** *nf* (*Bio*) heredity; (*droit*) right of inheritance; (*caractère*) hereditary nature.
hérésie [eʀezi] *nf* (*Rel*) heresy. (*fig*) **c'est une ~!** it's sacrilege! ♦ **hérétique 1** *adj* heretical. **2** *nmf* heretic.
hérisser ['eʀise] (1) **1** *vt* **(a) le chat hérisse ses poils** the cat makes its coat bristle; **l'oiseau hérisse ses plumes** the bird ruffles its feathers; **le vent hérisse mes cheveux** the wind makes my hair stand on end. **(b)** (*armer*) ~ **une planche de clous** to spike a plank with nails; **de nombreuses difficultés hérissent le texte** numerous difficulties are scattered throughout the text. **(c)** (*mettre en colère*) ~ **qn** to put sb's back up*. **2 se ~** *vpr* **(a)** *[poils]* to stand on end, bristle; *[animal]* to bristle. **(b)** (*se fâcher*) to bristle, get one's back up*. ♦ **hérissé, e** *adj cheveux* standing on end, bristling. ~ **de** *poils, obstacles* bristling with; *épines* spiked with.
hérisson ['eʀisɔ̃] *nm* hedgehog.
héritage [eʀitaʒ] *nm* inheritance; (*culturel*) heritage, legacy. **faire un ~** to come into an inheritance; **laisser qch en ~ à qn** to leave sth to sb, bequeath sth to sb; **tante à ~** wealthy *ou* rich aunt. ♦ **hériter** (1) *vti* to inherit. ~ **(de) qch de qn** to inherit sth from sb; ~ **de son oncle** to inherit one's uncle's property; **il a hérité d'un rhume*** he's picked up a cold. ♦ **héritier, -ière** *nm,f* heir; heiress.
hermétique [ɛʀmetik] *adj joint* airtight, watertight, hermetic; *barrage, secret, visage* impenetrable; *écrivain, livre* (*obscur*) abstruse, obscure; (*Littérat*) hermetic. ♦ **hermétiquement** *adv* tightly, hermetically; abstrusely, obscurely. **secret ~ gardé** closely guarded secret. ♦ **hermétisme** *nm* (*obscurité*) abstruseness, obscurity; (*Alchimie, Littérat*) hermetism.
hermine [ɛʀmin] *nf* ermine; (*avec pelage d'été*) stoat.
hernie ['ɛʀni] *nf* (*Méd*) hernia, rupture; *[pneu]* bulge. ~ **discale** slipped disc. ♦ **herniaire** *adj* hernial.
héroïne [eʀɔin] *nf* (*femme*) heroine; (*drogue*) heroin.
héroïque [eʀɔik] *adj* heroic. **l'époque ~** the pioneering days. ♦ **héroïquement** *adv* heroically. ♦ **héroïsme** *nm* heroism.
héron ['eʀɔ̃] *nm* heron.
héros ['eʀo] *nm* hero.
herse ['ɛʀs(ə)] *nf* (*Agr*) harrow; *[château]* portcullis.
hertz [ɛʀts] *nm* hertz. ♦ **hertzien, -ienne** *adj* Hertzian.
hésiter [ezite] (1) *vi* (*gén*) to hesitate. **il n'y a pas à ~** there are no two ways about it; **il hésitait sur la route à suivre** he hesitated over which road to take; ~ **entre plusieurs possibilités** to waver between several possibilities; ~ **en récitant sa leçon** to falter in reciting one's lesson. ♦ **hésitant, e** *adj* (*gén*) hesitant; *caractère* wavering; *voix, pas* faltering. ♦ **hésitation** *nf* hesitation. **sans ~** without hesitation, unhesitatingly; **après bien des ~s** after much hesitation.

hétéroclite [eteʀɔklit] *adj ensemble* heterogeneous; *objets* assorted.

hétérogène [eteʀɔʒɛn] *adj* heterogeneous. ♦ **hétérogénéité** *nf* heterogeneousness.

hêtre ['ɛtʀ(ə)] *nm* (*arbre*) beech (tree); (*bois*) beech (wood).

heure [œʀ] *nf* **(a)** (*mesure*) hour; (*Scol*) period, class. **pendant les ~s de bureau** during office hours; **gagner 20 F de l'~** to earn 20 francs an hour *ou* per hour; **1 ~/3 ~s de travail** 1 hour's/3 hours' work; **il y a 2 ~s de route** it's a 2-hour drive, it's 2 hours away by road; **faire des/10 ~s supplémentaires** to work *ou* do overtime/10 hours' overtime.
(b) (*de la journée*) **avez-vous l'~?** have you got the time?; **quelle ~ est-il?** what time is it?; **il est 6 ~s/6 ~s 10/6 ~s moins 10/6 ~s et demie** it is 6 (o'clock)/10 past 6/10 to 6/half past 6; **10 ~s du matin/du soir** 10 (o'clock) in the morning/at night, 10 a.m./p.m.; **il est 8 ~s passées** it's after 8 o'clock; **à 4 ~s juste(s)** at 4 sharp; **à une ~ avancée (de la nuit)** at a late hour (of the night).
(c) (*fixée*) time. **c'est l'~** it's time; **avant l'~** before time, ahead of time, early; **à l'~** on time; **après l'~** late; **~ d'été** summer time; **mettre sa montre à l'~** to set *ou* put one's watch right; **l'~ c'est l'~** on time is on time.
(d) (*moment*) time. **l'~ du déjeuner** lunchtime; **aux ~s des repas** at mealtimes; **~ de pointe** (*trains*) rush hour; (*magasin*) peak (shopping) period; (*téléphone*) peak period; **les ~s creuses** (*gén*) the slack periods; (*pour électricité*) off-peak periods; **les problèmes de l'~** the problems of the moment; **à l'~ H** at zero hour; **l'~ de vérité** the hour of truth.
(e) (*avec adj poss*) **il est poète à ses ~s** he writes poetry when the fancy takes him; **elle a eu son ~ de gloire** she has had her hour of glory; **il attend son ~** he is biding his time; **son ~ viendra** his time will come.
(f) (*locutions*) **à l'~ qu'il est il doit être arrivé** he must have arrived by now; **repas chaud à toute ~** hot meals all day; **24 ~s sur 24** round the clock, 24 hours a day; **d'~ en ~** hourly, hour by hour; **d'une ~ à l'autre** *varier* from one hour to the next; *attendre* any time now; **'Paris à l'~ écossaise'** 'Paris goes Scottish'; **la France à l'~ de l'ordinateur** France in the computer age; **tout à l'~** (*passé*) a short while ago; (*futur*) in a little while, shortly.

heureusement [œʀøzmɑ̃] *adv* (*par bonheur*) fortunately, luckily; (*judicieusement*) happily. **il est parti, ~!** he has gone, thank goodness!; **mot ~ choisi** well *ou* happily chosen word.

heureux, -euse [œʀø, øz] *adj* **(a)** (*content, comblé*) happy. **vivre ~** to live happily; **~ comme un poisson dans l'eau** happy as a sandboy; **ces jouets vont faire des ~** these toys will make some children happy; **c'est une ~euse nature** he has a happy *ou* cheerful nature; **je suis très ~ d'apprendre la nouvelle** I am very glad *ou* happy *ou* pleased to hear the news; **je suis ~ du résultat** I am pleased *ou* happy with the result. **(b)** (*chanceux*) *effet, résultat* happy; *choix* fortunate, happy; *personne* fortunate, lucky. **~ en amour** lucky in love; (*iro*) **c'est encore ~!** it's just as well!; **par un ~ hasard** by a fortunate coincidence; **attendre un ~ événement** to be expecting a happy event.

heurt ['œʀ] *nm* (*lit: choc*) collision; (*fig: conflit*) clash. **sans ~s** (*adj*) smooth; (*adv*) smoothly.

heurter ['œʀte] (1) **1** *vt* **(a)** *objet* to strike, hit; *personne* to collide with; (*bousculer*) to jostle. **~ des verres** *etc* to knock glasses *etc* against each other. **(b)** (*fig: choquer*) *personne* to offend; *bon sens, tradition* to go against; *opinions* to conflict *ou* clash with. **~ qn de front** to clash head-on with sb. **2** *vt indir*: **~ à la porte** to knock at the door; **~ contre qch** to strike against sth. **3 se ~** *vpr* to collide (with each other); (*fig*) to clash (with each other). **se ~ à un problème/refus** to come up against a problem/refusal. ♦ **heurté, e** *adj couleurs* clashing; *style, rythme* jerky.

hexagone [ɛgzagɔn] *nm* (*Géom*) hexagon. (*fig*) **l'~ (national)** France. ♦ **hexagonal, e,** *mpl* **-aux** *adj* hexagonal.

hiberner [ibɛʀne] (1) *vi* to hibernate. ♦ **hibernation** *nf* hibernation.

hibou, *pl* **~x** ['ibu] *nm* owl.

hic* ['ik] *nm*: **c'est là le ~** that's the snag.

hideux, -euse ['idø, øz] *adj* hideous. ♦ **hideusement** *adv* hideously.

hier [jɛʀ] *adv* yesterday. **~ (au) soir** yesterday evening, last night; **toute la journée d'~** all day yesterday; **je ne suis pas né d'~** I wasn't born yesterday.

hiérarchie ['jeʀaʀʃi] *nf* hierarchy. ♦ **hiérarchique** *adj* hierarchical. **chef ~** senior in rank. ♦ **hiérarchiquement** *adv* hierarchically.

hiéroglyphe ['jeʀɔglif] *nm* hieroglyphic.

hi-fi ['ifi] *adj, nf* hi-fi.

hilarité [ilaʀite] *nf* hilarity, mirth. ♦ **hilare** *adj* mirthful.

hindou, e [ɛ̃du] *adj*, **H~(e)** *nm(f)* (*citoyen*) Indian; (*croyant*) Hindu. ♦ **hindouisme** *nm* Hinduism.

hippie ['ipi] *adj, nmf* hippy.

hippique [ipik] *adj*: **concours ~** horse show; **le sport ~** equestrian sport.

hippocampe [ipɔkɑ̃p] *nm* sea horse.

hippodrome [ipɔdʀom] *nm* racecourse.

hippopotame [ipɔpɔtam] *nm* hippopotamus, hippo.

hirondelle [iʀɔ̃dɛl] *nf* swallow.

hirsute [iʀsyt] *adj tête* tousled; *personne* shaggy-haired; *barbe* shaggy.

hispanique [ispanik] *adj* Hispanic.

hisser ['ise] (1) *vt* (*Naut, fig*) to hoist; *objet* to hoist, haul up. **se ~ sur un toit** to haul o.s. up onto a roof.

histoire [istwaʀ] *nf* **(a)** (*science*) **l'~** history; **l'~ jugera** posterity will be the judge; **l'H~ sainte** Biblical history; **la petite ~** the footnotes of history; **pour la petite ~** for the record; **c'est de l'~ ancienne*** all that's ancient history*. **(b)** (*récit*) story; (*historique*) history; (*: *mensonge*) story*, fib*. **~ drôle** funny story, joke; **~ de fous** shaggy-dog story; **c'est une ~ à dormir debout** it's a cock-and-bull story; **qu'est-ce que c'est que cette ~?** what on earth is all this about?; **~ de prendre l'air*** just for a breath of fresh air; **tu me racontes des ~s** you're pulling my leg. **(c)** (*: *affaire*) business. **c'est une drôle d'~** it's a funny business; **il vient de lui arriver une drôle d'~** sth funny has just happened to him; **c'est toujours la même ~!** it's always the same old story. **(d)** (*) **~s** (*ennuis*) trouble; (*complications*) fuss; **faire des ~s à qn** to make trouble for sb; **quelle ~ pour si peu!** what a to-do *ou* fuss over so little. ♦ **historien, -ienne** *nm,f* historian. ♦ **historique 1** *adj étude* historical; *événement* historic. **2** *nm*: **faire l'~ de** *problème* to review; *institution* to examine the history of. ♦ **historiquement** *adv* historically.

hiver [ivɛʀ] *nm* winter. **il fait un temps d'~** it's like winter, it's wintry weather; **sports d'~** winter sports. ♦ **hivernal, e,** *mpl* **-aux** *adj* (*lit*) winter; (*fig: glacial*) *temps* wintry.

hocher ['ɔʃe] (1) *vt*: **~ la tête** (*affirmativement*) to nod (one's head); (*négativement*) to shake one's head. ♦ **hochement** *nm*: **~ de tête** nod (of the head); shake of the head. ♦ **hochet** *nm* [*bébé*] rattle.

hockey ['ɔkɛ] *nm* hockey. **~ sur glace** ice hockey; **~ sur gazon** field hockey.

holà ['ɔla, hɔla] **1** *excl* hold! **2** *nm*: **mettre le ~ à qch** to put a stop *ou* an end to sth.

hold-up ['ɔldœp] *nm inv* hold-up.

Hollande ['ɔlɑ̃d] **1** *nf* Holland. **2** *nm*: **h~** (*fromage*) Dutch cheese. ♦ **hollandais, e 1** *adj* Dutch. **2** *nm* **(a) H~** Dutchman. **(b)** (*Ling*) Dutch. **3** *nf*: **H~e** Dutchwoman.

holocauste [ɔlɔkost(ə)] *nm* (*Rel, fig*) sacrifice; (*Rel juive*) holocaust.

homard ['ɔmaʀ] *nm* lobster.

homélie [ɔmeli] *nf* homily.

homéopathe [ɔmeɔpat] *nmf* homoeopath. ♦ **homéopathie** *nf* homoeopathy. ♦ **homéopathique** *adj* homoeopathic.

homérique [ɔmeʀik] *adj* Homeric.

homicide [ɔmisid] *nm* murder, homicide (*US*). **~ involontaire, ~ par imprudence** manslaughter.

hommage [ɔmaʒ] *nm* **(a)** (*marque d'estime*) tribute. **rendre ~ à qn** to pay homage *ou* tribute to sb. **(b)** (*civilités*) **~s** respects; **présenter ses ~s à une dame** to pay one's respects to a lady. **(c)** (*don*) **en ~ de ma gratitude** as a mark *ou* token of my gratitude; **faire ~ d'un livre** to give a presentation copy of a book; **~ de l'éditeur** with the publisher's compliments. **(d)** (*Hist*) homage.

homme [ɔm] **1** *nm* man. (*espèce*) **l'~** man, mankind; **des vêtements d'~** men's clothes; **parler d'~ à ~** to have a man-to-man talk; **il n'est pas ~ à mentir** he's not one to lie *ou* a man to lie; **comme un seul ~** as one man; **un ~ averti en vaut deux** forewarned is forearmed. **2**: **~ d'action** man of action; **~ d'affaires** businessman; **~ des cavernes** cave man; **~ de confiance** right-hand man; **~ d'équipage** member of a ship's crew; **navire avec 30 ~s d'équipage** ship with a crew of 30 (men); **~ d'État** statesman; **~ fort du régime** muscleman of the regime; **~-grenouille** *nm, pl* **~s-~s** frogman; **l'~ de la rue** the man in the street; **~ de lettres** man of letters; **~ de loi** man of law; **~ de main** hired man; **~ du monde** society man; **~-orchestre** *nm, pl* **~s-~s** one-man band; **~ de paille** stooge; **~ de peine** workhand; **~ de science** man of science; **~ à tout faire** odd-job man; **~ de troupe** private.

homogène [ɔmɔʒɛn] *adj* homogeneous. ♦ **homogénéisation** *nf* homogenization. ♦ **homogénéiser** (1) *vt* to homogenize. ♦ **homogénéité** *nf* homogeneity.

homologue [ɔmɔlɔg] **1** *adj* homologous (*de* to). **2** *nm* (*personne*) counterpart, opposite number.

homologuer [ɔmɔlɔge] (1) *vt* to ratify. ♦ **homologation** *nf* ratification.

homonyme [ɔmɔnim] **1** *adj* homonymous. **2** *nm* (*Ling*) homonym; (*personne*) namesake. ♦ **homonymie** *nf* homonymy.

homosexualité [ɔmɔsɛksɥalite] *nf* homosexuality. ♦ **homosexuel, -elle** *adj, nm,f* homosexual.

Hongrie ['ɔ̃gʀi] *nf* Hungary. ♦ **hongrois, e** *adj, nm,* **H~(e)** *nm(f)* Hungarian.

honnête [ɔnɛt] *adj* (*intègre*) honest; (*satisfaisant*) reasonable, fair; (*hum: poli*) courteous. **d'~s gens** decent people; **~ homme** gentleman. ♦ **honnêtement** *adv* honestly; decently; fairly; reasonably; courteously. **~, vous le saviez bien!** come now, you knew! ♦ **honnêteté** *nf* honesty; decency; fairness; courtesy.

honneur [ɔnœʀ] *nm* **(a)** (*réputation*) honour. **mettre son (point d')~ à faire qch** to make it a point of honour to do sth; **jurer sur l'~** to swear on one's honour. **(b)** (*mérite*) credit. **avec ~** creditably; **c'est tout à son ~** it is much to his credit; **faire ~ à sa famille** to be a credit *ou* an honour to one's family. **(c)** (*faveur*) honour. **avoir l'~ de** to have the honour of; (*Admin*) **j'ai l'~ de solliciter ...** I am writing to ask ...; **invité d'~** guest of honour; **membre d'~** honorary member; **couvert d'~s** covered in honours; **avoir les ~s de la première page** to get a mention on the first page. **(d)** (*Cartes*) honour. **(e)** (*titre*) **votre H~** Your Honour. **(f) ~ aux dames** ladies first; **à vous l'~** after you; *[mode]* **être en ~** to be in favour; **en l'~ de nos hôtes** in honour of our guests; **en l'~ de cet événement** in honour of this event; **à qui ai-je l'~?** to whom do I have the honour of speaking?; **faire les ~s de la maison** to do the honours of one's house; **faire ~ à un repas** to do justice to a meal.

honorable [ɔnɔʀabl(ə)] *adj* **personne, buts** honourable; ***sentiments*** creditable; ***résultats*** decent. ♦ **honorabilité** *nf* worthiness. ♦ **honorablement** *adv* honourably; creditably; decently.

honoraire [ɔnɔʀɛʀ] **1** *adj* honorary. **professeur ~** professor emeritus. **2** *nmpl*: **~s** fee, fees.

honorer [ɔnɔʀe] (1) **1** *vt* (*vénérer*) to honour; (*estimer*) to hold in high regard *ou* esteem; (*faire honneur à*) ***pays*** to be a credit to; ***signature*** to honour. **~ qn de qch** to honour sb with sth; **je suis très honoré** I am highly *ou* greatly honoured; **cette franchise l'honore** this frankness does him credit. **2 s'~** *vpr*: **s'~ de** to pride o.s. upon.

honorifique [ɔnɔʀifik] *adj* honorary.

honte ['ɔ̃t] *nf* **(a)** (*déshonneur*) disgrace, shame. **couvrir qn de ~** to bring disgrace *ou* shame on sb, disgrace sb; **c'est une ~!** that's disgraceful! *ou* a disgrace! **(b)** (*gêne*) shame. **à ma grande ~** to my great shame; **sans ~** shamelessly; **avoir ~ (de qch/de faire)** to be *ou* feel ashamed (of sth/of doing); **faire ~ à qn** to make sb feel ashamed. ♦ **honteusement** *adv* shamefully; disgracefully. ♦ **honteux, -euse** *adj* (*déshonorant*) shameful; (*confus*) ashamed (*de* of). **c'est ~!** it's a disgrace!, it's disgraceful!

hôpital, *pl* **-aux** [ɔpital, o] *nm* hospital. **c'est l'~ qui se moque de la charité!** ≈ it's the pot calling the kettle black.

hoquet ['ɔkɛ] *nm* hiccough. **avoir le ~** to have (the) hiccoughs. ♦ **hoqueter** (4) *vi* to hiccough.

horaire [ɔʀɛʀ] **1** *adj* hourly. **débit ~** rate per hour. **2** *nm* timetable, schedule.

horde ['ɔʀd(ə)] *nf* horde.

horizon [ɔʀizɔ̃] *nm* **(a)** horizon. **la ligne d'~** the horizon; **à l'~** ***voir*** on the horizon; ***disparaître*** below the horizon. **(b)** (*paysage*) landscape, view; (*fig: perspective*) horizon. **changer d'~** to have a change of scene; **l'~ politique** the political scene. ♦ **horizontal, e,** *mpl* **-aux 1** *adj* horizontal. **2** *nf* horizontal. **à l'~e** in a horizontal position. ♦ **horizontalement** *adv* horizontally. ♦ **horizontalité** *nf* horizontality.

horloge [ɔʀlɔʒ] *nf* clock. **il a la régularité d'une ~** he's as regular as clockwork; **il est 2 heures à l'~** it's 2 o'clock by *ou* according to the clock; **l'~ parlante** the speaking clock; **~ normande** grandfather clock. ♦ **horloger, -ère 1** *adj* watch-making. **2** *nm,f* watchmaker. **~ bijoutier** watchmaker and jeweller. ♦ **horlogerie** *nf* (*métier*) watch-making; (*magasin*) watchmaker's (shop). **~ bijouterie** watchmaker's and jeweller's shop.

hormis ['ɔʀmi] *prép* save.

hormone [ɔʀmɔn] *nf* hormone. ♦ **hormonal, e,** *mpl* **-aux** *adj* hormonal, hormone.

horoscope [ɔʀɔskɔp] *nm* horoscope.

horreur [ɔʀœʀ] *nf* (*gén*) horror; (*répugnance*) loathing. **frappé d'~** horror-stricken; **vision d'~** horrific *ou* horrifying sight; **l'esclavage dans toute son ~** slavery in all its horror; **les ~s de la guerre** the horrors of war; **c'est une ~*** *[film]* it is terrible *ou* dreadful; *[chapeau]* it is a fright, it is hideous; **quelle ~!** how dreadful! *ou* awful!; **débiter des ~s sur qn** to say dreadful *ou* terrible things about sb; **avoir ~ de qch** to loathe *ou* detest sth; **le mensonge me fait ~** I loathe *ou* detest lying, I have a horror of lying.

horrible [ɔʀibl(ə)] *adj* (*effrayant*) horrible; (*laid*) hideous; (*mauvais*) terrible, dreadful. ♦ **horriblement** *adv* horribly; hideously; terribly, dreadfully. ♦ **horrifier** (7) *vt* to horrify.

horripiler [ɔʀipile] (1) *vt* to exasperate.

hors ['ɔʀ] **1** *prép* **(a)** (*excepté*) except (for), apart from. **(b)** (*espace, temps*) ~ **de** out of; **vivre ~ de la ville** to live out of town *ou* outside the town; **habiter ~ du centre** to live away from *ou* outside the centre; ~ **d'ici!** get out of here! **(c)** (*fig*) **il est ~ d'affaire** he's over the worst; ~ **d'atteinte** (*lit*) out of reach (*de* of); (*fig*) beyond reach; **mettre ~ de combat** to put out of the fight; **être ~ de danger** to be out of danger; **il est ~ de doute que** it is beyond doubt that; **mettre ~ d'état de nuire** to render harmless; ~ **d'haleine** out of breath; ~ **de prix** exorbitant, prohibitive; ~ **de propos** untimely; **c'est ~ de question** it is out of the question; **être ~ de soi** to be beside o.s. (with anger); **mettre ~ d'usage** to put out of action. **2**: ~**-bord** *nm inv* speedboat; ~**-concours** *adj inv* hors concours; ~**-d'œuvre** *nm inv* hors d'œuvre; ~**-jeu** *adj inv, nm inv* offside; ~**-la-loi** *nm inv* outlaw; ~ **ligne,** ~ **pair** *adj inv* outstanding, matchless; ~**-taxe** *adj inv, adv* duty-free; ~**-texte** *nm inv* plate; ~ **tout** *adj longueur* overall.

hortensia [ɔʀtɑ̃sja] *nm* hydrangea.

horticole [ɔʀtikɔl] *adj* horticultural. ♦ **horticulteur, -trice** *nm,f* horticulturist. ♦ **horticulture** *nf* horticulture.

hospice [ɔspis] *nm* **(a)** (*hôpital*) home. ~ **de vieillards** old people's home. **(b)** *[monastère]* hospice.

hospitalier, -ière [ɔspitalje, jɛʀ] *adj* (*Méd*) hospital; (*accueillant*) hospitable.

hospitaliser [ɔspitalize] (1) *vt* to hospitalize. ♦ **hospitalisation** *nf* hospitalization.

hospitalité [ɔspitalite] *nf* hospitality.

hostie [ɔsti] *nf* (*Rel*) host.

hostile [ɔstil] *adj* hostile (*à* to). ♦ **hostilité** *nf* hostility. (*Mil*) **les ~s** hostilities.

hôte [ot] **1** *nm* (*maître de maison*) host; (*aubergiste*) landlord. **2** *nmf* (*invité*) guest. ~ **payant** paying guest.

hôtel [otɛl] *nm* hotel. ~**-meublé** *nm, pl* ~**s**-~**s** lodging house; ~ **particulier** (private) mansion; ~ **des ventes** salerooms; ~ **de ville** town hall. ♦ **hôtelier, -ière** **1** *adj* hotel. **2** *nm,f* hotelier. ♦ **hôtellerie** *nf* (*auberge*) inn; (*profession*) hotel business.

hôtesse [otɛs] *nf* hostess; (*aubergiste*) landlady. ~ **de l'air** air hostess; ~ **d'accueil** receptionist, hostess.

hotte ['ɔt] *nf* (*panier*) basket; *[cheminée]* hood. ~ **aspirante** cooker hood; **la ~ du Père Noël** Father Christmas's sack.

hou ['u, hu] *excl [peur]* boo!; *[honte]* tut-tut!

houblon ['ublɔ̃] *nm* (*plante*) hop; (*dans la bière*) hops.

houe ['u] *nf* hoe.

houille ['uj] *nf* coal. ~ **blanche** hydroelectric power. ♦ **houiller, -ère** **1** *adj* coal. **2** *nf* coalmine.

houle ['ul] *nf* swell. ♦ **houleux, -euse** *adj mer* heavy; *séance* stormy; *foule* turbulent.

houppe ['up] *nf [cheveux]* tuft; *[fils]* tassel. ♦ **houppette** *nf* powder puff.

hourra ['uʀa] *excl* hurrah!

houspiller ['uspije] (1) *vt* to scold, tell off.

housse ['us] *nf* dust cover; (*pour recouvrir à neuf*) loose cover; (*élastique*) stretch cover.

houx ['u] *nm* holly.

hublot ['yblo] *nm* porthole.

huche ['yʃ] *nf* (*coffre*) chest. ~ **à pain** bread bin.

hue ['y, hy] *excl* gee up! (*fig*) **ils tirent tous à ~ et à dia** they are all pulling in opposite directions.

huer ['ɥe] (1) *vt* to boo. ♦ **huées** *nfpl* boos.

huile [ɥil] *nf* **(a)** (*liquide*) oil. ~ **de table** salad oil; ~ **de foie de morue** cod-liver oil; ~ **de lin** linseed oil; **jeter de l'~ sur le feu** to add fuel to the flames; **une mer d'~** a glassy sea. **(b)** (*: *notabilité*) bigwig*, big shot*. **(c)** (*Peinture*) oil painting. **fait à l'~** done in oils. ♦ **huiler** (1) *vt machine* to oil, lubricate. ♦ **huileux, -euse** *adj* oily.

huis [ɥi] *nm* (*littér*) door. (*Jur*) **à ~ clos** in camera.

huissier [ɥisje] *nm* (*appariteur*) usher; (*Jur*) ≃ bailiff.

huit ['ɥi(t)] *adj, nm inv* eight. **lundi en ~** a week on Monday; **dans ~ jours** in a week; **donner à qn ses ~ jours** to give sb notice; *V* **six.** ♦ **huitaine** *nf* eight or so, about eight. **dans une ~ (de jours)** in a week or so. ♦ **huitante** *adj inv* (*Suisse*) eighty. ♦ **huitième** *adj, nmf* eighth. **la ~ merveille du monde** the eighth wonder of the world; *V* **sixième.** ♦ **huitièmement** *adv* eighthly.

huître [ɥitʀ(ə)] *nf* oyster.

hululer [ylyle] (1) *vi* to hoot. ♦ **hululement** *nm*: ~**(s)** hooting.

hum ['œm, hœm] *excl* hem!, h'm!

humain, e [ymɛ̃, ɛn] **1** *adj* (*gén*) human; (*compatissant*) humane. **se montrer ~** to show humanity, act humanely (*envers* towards); **c'est ~!** it's only human! **2** *nm* human (being). ♦ **humainement** *adv* (*avec bonté*) humanely; (*par l'homme*) humanly. ♦ **humaniser** (1) *vt* to humanize. ♦ **humanisme** *nm* humanism. ♦ **humaniste** **1** *adj* humanistic. **2** *nmf* humanist. ♦ **humanitaire** *adj* humanitarian.

humanité [ymanite] *nf* (*gén*) humanity. (*humaine*) **l'~** humanity, mankind.

humble [œ̃bl(ə)] *adj* humble. ♦ **humblement** *adv* humbly.

humecter [ymɛkte] (1) *vt linge* to dampen; *front* to moisten.

humer ['yme] (1) *vt plat* to smell; *air* to breathe in.

humérus [ymeʀys] *nm* humerus.

humeur [ymœʀ] *nf* **(a)** (*momentanée*) mood, humour. **de bonne ~** in a good mood *ou* humour, in good spirits; **de mauvaise ~** in a bad mood; **se sentir d'~ à travailler** to feel in the mood for work; **plein de bonne ~** good-humoured, full of good humour. **(b)** (*tempérament*) temper, temperament. **il est d'~ inégale/égale** he has an uneven/even temper. **(c)** (*irritation*) bad temper, ill humour. **geste d'~** bad-tempered gesture; **dire qch avec ~** to say sth ill-humouredly. **(d)** (*Méd*) secretion.

humide [ymid] *adj* (*gén*) damp; *mains* moist; *climat* (*chaud*) humid; (*froid*) damp; *cave* dank, damp; *saison* wet. ♦ **humidificateur** *nm* humidifier. ♦ **humidification** *nf* humidification. ♦ **humidifier** (7) *vt* to humidify. ♦ **humidité** *nf* dampness; humidity; dankness. **traces d'~** traces of moisture *ou* of damp; **'craint l'~', 'à protéger de l'~'** 'keep in a dry place'.

humilier [ymilje] (7) *vt* to humiliate. **s'~ devant** to humiliate *ou* humble o.s. before. ♦ **humiliation** *nf* humiliation.

humilité [ymilite] *nf* humility.

humoriste [ymɔʀist(ə)] *nmf* humorist. ♦ **humoristique** *adj* humorous.

humour [ymuʀ] *nm* humour. ~ **noir** sick humour; **avoir beaucoup d'~** to have a good sense of humour.

humus [ymys] *nm* humus.

hune ['yn] *nf* (*Naut*) top.

huppé, e* ['ype] *adj* (*riche*) posh*, classy*.

hurler ['yʀle] (1) **1** *vi* (*gén*) to howl; *[foule]* to roar (*de* with); *[sirène]* to wail; *[couleurs]* to clash. **2** *vt* to roar, bellow out. ♦ **hurlement** *nm* howl; roar; wail.

hurluberlu [yʀlybɛʀly] *nm* crank.

hutte ['yt] *nf* hut.

hybride [ibrid] *adj, nm* hybrid. ♦ **hybridation** *nf* hybridization. ♦ **hybrider** (1) *vt* to hybridize. ♦ **hybridité** *nf* hybridism.

hydrate [idʀat] *nm* hydrate. ~ **de carbone** carbohydrate. ♦ **hydratant, e** *adj* moisturizing. ♦ **hydratation** *nf* moisturizing, hydration. ♦ **hydrater** (1) *vt* to moisturize.

hydraulique [idʀolik] **1** *adj* hydraulic. **2** *nf* hydraulics (*sg*).
hydravion [idʀavjɔ̃] *nm* seaplane, hydroplane.
hydrocarbure [idʀɔkaʀbyʀ] *nm* hydrocarbon.
hydrocution [idʀɔkysjɔ̃] *nf* immersion syncope.
hydroélectricité [idʀɔelɛktʀisite] *nf* hydroelectricity. ♦ **hydro-électrique** *adj* hydroelectric.
hydrofoil [idʀɔfɔjl] *nm* hydrofoil (*boat*).
hydrogène [idʀɔʒɛn] *nm* hydrogen.
hydroglisseur [idʀɔglisœʀ] *nm* hydroplane (*boat*).
hydrolyse [idʀɔliz] *nf* hydrolysis.
hydromel [idʀɔmɛl] *nm* mead.
hydropisie [idʀɔpizi] *nf* dropsy.
hydroxyde [idʀɔksid] *nm* hydroxide.
hyène [jɛn] *nf* hyena.
hygiène [iʒjɛn] *nf* hygiene. ♦ **hygiénique** *adj* hygienic.
hymne [imn(ə)] *nm* (*Littérat, Rel*) hymn. ~ **national** national anthem.
hyper ... [ipɛʀ] *préf* hyper ... .
hyperbole [ipɛʀbɔl] *nf* (*Math*) hyperbola; (*Littérat*) hyperbole.
hyperémotivité [ipɛʀemɔtivite] *nf* excess emotionality.
hypermarché [ipɛʀmaʀʃe] *nf* hypermarket.
hypermétrope [ipɛʀmetʀɔp] *adj* long-sighted. ♦ **hypermétropie** *nf* long-sightedness.
hypernerveux, -euse [ipɛʀnɛʀvø, øz] *adj* over-excitable. ♦ **hypernervosité** *nf* over-excitability.
hypersensibilité [ipɛʀsɑ̃sibilite] *nf* hypersensitivity. ♦ **hypersensible** *adj* hypersensitive.
hypertension [ipɛʀtɑ̃sjɔ̃] *nf* high blood pressure, hypertension. ♦ **hypertendu, e** *adj* suffering from high blood pressure.
hypertrophie [ipɛʀtʀɔfi] *nf* hypertrophy. ♦ **hypertrophier** (7) *vt* to hypertrophy.
hypnose [ipnoz] *nf* hypnosis. ♦ **hypnotique** *adj* hypnotic. ♦ **hypnotiser** (1) *vt* to hypnotize. **s'~ sur un problème** to be hypnotized by a problem. ♦ **hypnotiseur** *nm* hypnotist. ♦ **hypnotisme** *nm* hypnotism.
hypo ... [ipɔ] *préf* hypo ... .
hypocrisie [ipɔkʀizi] *nf* hypocrisy. ♦ **hypocrite** **1** *adj* hypocritical. **2** *nmf* hypocrite. ♦ **hypocritement** *adv* hypocritically.
hypodermique [ipɔdɛʀmik] *adj* hypodermic.
hypotension [ipɔtɑ̃sjɔ̃] *nf* low blood pressure.
hypoténuse [ipɔtenyz] *nf* hypotenuse.
hypothèque [ipɔtɛk] *nf* mortgage. ♦ **hypothécaire** *adj* hypothecary. **garantie ~** mortgage security. ♦ **hypothéquer** (6) *vt maison* to mortgage; *créance* to secure (by mortgage).
hypothèse [ipɔtɛz] *nf* hypothesis. ♦ **hypothétique** *adj* hypothetical.
hystérie [isteʀi] *nf* hysteria. ~ **collective** mass hysteria. ♦ **hystérique** **1** *adj* hysterical. **2** *nmf* (*Méd*) hysteric; (*péj*) hysterical sort.

I

I, i [i] *nm* (*lettre*) I, i.
ibérique [ibeʀik] *adj* Iberian.
ibis [ibis] *nm* ibis.
iceberg [isbɛʀg] *nm* iceberg.
ici [isi] *adv* **(a)** here. **d'~ à Paris** from here to Paris; **passez par ~** come this way; **c'est ~ que** this is the place where, it is (*ou* was *etc*) here that; **le bus vient jusqu'~** the bus comes as far as this. **(b)** (*temporel*) **d'~ demain** by tomorrow; **d'~ peu** before long, shortly; **d'~ là** in the meantime; **jusqu'~** (up) until now; **d'~ à ce qu'il accepte, ça risque de faire long** it might be (quite) some time before he says yes. **(c) les gens d'~** the local people; **je vois ça d'~!*** I can just see that!; **vous êtes ~ chez vous** please make yourself (quite) at home; **~ présent** here present; '**~ X**' (*au téléphone*) 'X speaking'; (*à la radio*) 'this is X'; **~ et là** here and there; (*Rel, hum*) **~-bas** here below; **par ~** (*dans le coin*) around here.
icône [ikon] *nf* icon.
idéal, e, *mpl* **-aux** [ideal, o] *adj, nm* ideal. **l'~ serait d'y aller** the ideal thing would be for us to go. ♦ **idéalement** *adv* ideally. ♦ **idéalisation** *nf* idealization. ♦ **idéaliser** (1) *vt* to idealize. ♦ **idéalisme** *nm* idealism. ♦ **idéaliste 1** *adj* idealistic. **2** *nmf* idealist.
idée [ide] **1** *nf* **(a)** (*gén*) idea. **il a eu l'~ de faire** he had the idea *ou* hit upon the idea of doing; **ça m'a donné l'~ qu'il ne viendrait pas** that made me think that he wouldn't come; **à l'~ de faire qch** at the idea *ou* thought of doing sth; **avoir une ~ derrière la tête** to have something at the back of one's mind; **tu te fais des ~s** you're imagining things; **je n'en ai pas la moindre ~** I haven't the faintest *ou* slightest idea; **vous n'avez pas ~ de sa bêtise** you have no idea how stupid he is; **j'ai ~ que** I have an idea *ou* a feeling that; **on n'a pas ~!*** it's incredible!; **de nouvelles ~s-vacances** some new holiday tips *ou* hints. **(b)** (*opinion*) **~s** ideas, views; **ce n'est pas dans ses ~s** he doesn't hold with that; **avoir les ~s larges/étroites** to be broad-minded/narrow-minded. **(c)** (*goût*) **agir selon son ~** to act as one sees fit; **il n'en fait qu'à son ~** he does just as he likes; **il faut un peu d'~** you have to have some imagination *ou* a few ideas; **il y a de l'~*** there's sth in it, it's an idea. **(d)** (*esprit*) **avoir dans l'~ que** to have it in one's mind that; **il a dans l'~ de partir au Mexique** he's thinking of going to Mexico; **il s'est mis dans l'~ de faire** he took it into his head to do. **2: ~ fixe** idée fixe, obsession; **~ de génie** brainwave; **~ noire** black thought; **~ reçue** generally accepted idea.
identique [idɑ̃tik] *adj* identical (*à* to). ♦ **identifiable** *adj* identifiable. ♦ **identification** *nf* identification. ♦ **identifier** *vt,* **s'~** *vpr* (7) to identify (*à* with). ♦ **identiquement** *adv* identically. ♦ **identité** *nf* (*gén*) identity. **une ~ de goûts** *etc* similar *ou* shared tastes *etc*.
idéologie [ideɔlɔʒi] *nf* ideology. ♦ **idéologique** *adj* ideological.
idiome [idjom] *nm* idiom (*language*). ♦ **idiomatique** *adj* idiomatic. **expression ~** idiom.
idiot, e [idjo, idjɔt] **1** *adj* idiotic, stupid; (*Méd*) idiotic. **2** *nm,f* idiot. **ne fais pas l'~*** (*n'agis pas bêtement*) don't be an idiot; (*ne simule pas la bêtise*) stop acting stupid*. ♦ **idiotement** *adv* idiotically, stupidly. ♦ **idiotie** *nf* idiocy, stupidity. **c'est une ~** (*gén*) it's an idiotic thing to do (*ou* say); (*film*) it's rubbish; **ne fais pas d'~s** don't do anything stupid.
idiotisme [idjɔtism(ə)] *nm* idiom, idiomatic phrase.
idole [idɔl] *nf* (*Rel, fig*) idol. ♦ **idolâtre** *adj* idolatrous (*de* of). ♦ **idolâtrer** (1) *vt* to idolize. ♦ **idolâtrie** *nf* idolatry.
idylle [idil] *nf* (*gén*) idyll. ♦ **idyllique** *adj* idyllic.
if [if] *nm* yew (tree).
igloo, iglou [iglu] *nm* igloo.
ignare [iɲaʀ] (*péj*) **1** *adj* ignorant. **2** *nmf* ignoramus.
ignifuger [ignifyʒe] (3) *vt* to fireproof. ♦ **ignifuge 1** *adj produit* fireproofing. **2** *nm* fireproofing material.
ignoble [iɲɔbl(ə)] *adj* vile, base; (*sens affaibli*) revolting.
ignominie [iɲɔmini] *nf* (*caractère*) ignominy; (*acte*) ignominious *ou* disgraceful act. ♦ **ignominieux, -euse** *adj* ignominious.
ignorance [iɲɔʀɑ̃s] *nf* ignorance. **être dans l'~ de qch** to be in ignorance of *ou* in the dark about sth; **dans l'~ des résultats** ignorant of the results; **il a de graves ~s en maths** there are serious gaps in his knowledge of maths. ♦ **ignorant, e 1** *adj* ignorant (*en* about). **~ des usages** ignorant *ou* unaware of the customs. **2** *nm,f* ignoramus. **ne fais pas l'~** stop pretending you don't know what I mean.
ignorer [iɲɔʀe] (1) *vt* **(a)** (*ne pas connaître*) not to know. **vous n'ignorez pas que** you know *ou* are aware that; **j'ignore tout de cette affaire** I don't know anything about this business; **j'ignore avoir dit cela** I am not aware of having said that; **~ la misère** to have had no experience of poverty; **c'est un poète qui s'ignore** he's an unconscious poet. **(b)** (*bouder*) *personne* to ignore. ♦ **ignoré, e** *adj* unknown. **~ de tous** (*inconnu*) unknown to anybody; (*boudé*) ignored by all.
iguane [igwan] *nm* iguana.
il [il] *pron pers m* **(a)** (*personne*) he; (*bébé, animal*) it, he; (*chose*) it; (*bateau, nation*) she, it. **~s** they; **~ était journaliste** he was a journalist. **(b)** (*impers*) it. **~ fait beau** it's a fine day; **~ y a 3 enfants** there are 3 children; **~ est vrai que** it is true that. **(c)** (*non traduit*) **Paul est-~ rentré?** is Paul back?; **~ est si beau cet arbre** this tree is so beautiful.
île [il] *nf* island. **les ~s anglo-normandes** the Channel Islands; **les ~s Britanniques** the British Isles; **~ flottante** floating island.
illégal, e, *mpl* **-aux** [ilegal, o] *adj* illegal, unlawful. ♦ **illégalement** *adv* illegally, unlawfully. ♦ **illégalité** *nf* illegality.
illégitime [ileʒitim] *adj* illegitimate. ♦ **illégitimité** *nf* illegitimacy.
illettré, e [iletʀe] *adj, nm,f* illiterate.
illicite [ilisit] *adj* illicit. ♦ **illicitement** *adv* illicitly.
illico* [iliko] *adv* at once, pronto*.
illimité, e [ilimite] *adj* (*gén*) unlimited; *confiance* boundless.

illisibilité [ilizibilite] *nf* illegibility. ♦ **illisible** *adj* (*indéchiffrable*) illegible; (*mauvais*) unreadable.

illogique [ilɔʒik] *adj* illogical. ♦ **illogiquement** *adv* illogically. ♦ **illogisme** *nm* illogicality.

illuminer [ilymine] (1) **1** *vt* (*lit, fig*) to light up, illuminate; *[projecteurs]* to floodlight. **2 s'~** *vpr [visage, ciel]* to light up (*de* with); *[rue]* to be lit up. ♦ **illumination** *nf* **(a)** lighting; illumination; floodlighting. (*lumières*) ~s illuminations, lights. **(b)** (*inspiration*) flash of inspiration. ♦ **illuminé, e** *nm,f* (*péj: visionnaire*) crank (*péj*).

illusion [ilyzjɔ̃] *nf* illusion. ~ **d'optique** optical illusion; **tu te fais des ~s** you're deluding yourself; **ça ne fera pas ~ longtemps** it won't delude *ou* fool people for long. ♦ **s'illusionner** (1) *vpr* to delude o.s. (*sur* about). ♦ **illusionniste** *nmf* conjurer. ♦ **illusoire** *adj* illusory.

illustrer [ilystʀe] (1) **1** *vt* to illustrate (*de* with). **2 s'~** *vpr* to win fame, become famous (*par, dans* through). ♦ **illustrateur, -trice** *nm,f* illustrator. ♦ **illustration** *nf* (*gén*) illustration. ♦ **illustre** *adj* illustrious, renowned. ♦ **illustré, e 1** *adj* illustrated. **2** *nm* (*journal*) comic.

îlot [ilo] *nm* (*île*) small island; (*maisons*) block; (*fig: zone*) island. ~ **de résistance** pocket of resistance.

image [imaʒ] *nf* (*dessin, représentation*) picture; (*métaphore, ressemblance, Phys*) image; (*reflet*) reflexion. **les ~s d'un film** the frames of a film; **popularisé par l'~** popularized by the camera; **Dieu créa l'homme à son ~** God created man in his own image; ~ **de marque** *[produit]* brand image; *[parti, firme]* public image. ♦ **imagé, e** *adj* full of imagery.

imaginer [imaʒine] (1) **1** *vt* **(a)** (*supposer*) to imagine. **je l'imaginais plus vieux** I imagined him to be older; **qu'allez-vous ~ là?** what on earth are you thinking of? **(b)** (*inventer*) to devise, dream up. **qu'est-il encore allé ~?*** now what has he dreamed up? **2 s'~** *vpr* **(a)** (*se figurer*) to imagine. **s'~ que** to imagine *ou* think that. **(b)** (*se voir*) to imagine o.s., picture o.s. ♦ **imaginable** *adj* conceivable, imaginable. ♦ **imaginaire** *adj* imaginary; *monde* make-believe. ♦ **imaginatif, -ive** *adj* imaginative. ♦ **imagination** *nf* (*faculté*) imagination. **ce sont de pures ~s** that's sheer imagination, those are pure fancies.

imbattable [ɛ̃batabl(ə)] *adj* unbeatable.

imbécile [ɛ̃besil] **1** *adj* stupid, idiotic; (*Méd*) imbecilic. **2** *nmf* idiot, imbecile. **ne fais pas l'~*** (*n'agis pas bêtement*) don't be an idiot*; (*ne simule pas la bêtise*) stop acting stupid*; **c'est un ~ heureux** he's living in a fool's paradise. ♦ **imbécillité** *nf* idiocy, imbecility. **c'est une ~** (*gén*) it's an idiotic thing to do (*ou* say); (*film*) it's rubbish.

imberbe [ɛ̃bɛʀb(ə)] *adj* beardless.

imbiber [ɛ̃bibe] (1) **1** *vt*: ~ **un tampon de** to moisten a pad with; **imbibé d'eau** *étoffe* saturated (with water); *terre* waterlogged. **2 s'~** *vpr*: **s'~ de** to become saturated with.

imbriquer (s') [ɛ̃bʀike] (1) *vpr [problèmes]* to be linked *ou* interwoven; *[plaques]* to overlap; *[cubes]* to fit into each other. ♦ **imbrication** *nf* interweaving; overlapping.

imbroglio [ɛ̃bʀɔljo] *nm* imbroglio.

imbu, e [ɛ̃by] *adj*: ~ **de** full of.

imbuvable [ɛ̃byvabl(ə)] *adj* (*lit*) undrinkable; (*) *personne* unbearable, insufferable.

imiter [imite] (1) *vt* **(a)** (*gén*) to imitate; *personnage* to impersonate; *geste* to mimic; *signature* to forge. **il se leva et tout le monde l'imita** he got up and everybody did likewise *ou* followed suit. **(b)** *[matière]* to look like. ♦ **imitateur, -trice 1** *adj* imitative. **2** *nm,f* (*gén*) imitator; (*Théât*) *[personnage]* impersonator. ♦ **imitatif, -ive** *adj* imitative. ♦ **imitation** *nf* imitation; impersonation; mimicry; forgery. **à l'~ de** in imitation of; **c'est en ~ cuir** it's imitation leather.

immaculé, e [imakyle] *adj* spotless, immaculate. **d'un blanc ~** spotlessly white.

immangeable [ɛ̃mɑ̃ʒabl(ə)] *adj* uneatable, inedible.

immanquable [ɛ̃mɑ̃kabl(ə)] *adj cible* impossible to miss. **c'était ~!** it was inevitable! ♦ **immanquablement** *adv* inevitably.

immatriculer [imatʀikyle] (1) *vt* to register. **faire ~, se faire ~** to register. ♦ **immatriculation** *nf* registration. **numéro d'~** registration *ou* license (*US*) number.

immédiat, e [imedja, at] **1** *adj* (*gén*) immediate. **2** *nm*: **dans l'~** for the time being. ♦ **immédiatement** *adv* immediately.

immémorial, e, *mpl* -aux [imemɔʀjal, o] *adj* age-old. **de temps ~** from time immemorial.

immense [imɑ̃s] *adj* (*gén*) immense; *espace* boundless; *foule* huge; *avantage* tremendous. ♦ **immensément** *adv* immensely, tremendously. ♦ **immensité** *nf* immensity, hugeness.

immerger [imɛʀʒe] (3) *vt objet* to immerse, submerge; *déchets* to dump at sea; *câble* to lay under water; *corps* to bury at sea. ♦ **immergé, e** *adj terres* submerged. ~ **par 100 mètres de fond** lying 100 metres down. ♦ **immersion** *nf* immersion; submersion; dumping at sea; underwater laying; burying at sea.

immérité, e [imeʀite] *adj* undeserved, unmerited.

immettable [ɛ̃mɛtabl(ə)] *adj vêtement* unwearable.

immeuble [imœbl(ə)] *nm* (*bâtiment*) building; (*d'habitation*) block of flats, apartment building (*US*). ~ **de bureaux** office block.

immigrer [imigʀe] (1) *vi* to immigrate (*à, dans* into). ♦ **immigrant, e** *adj, nm,f* immigrant. ♦ **immigration** *nf* immigration.

imminence [iminɑ̃s] *nf* imminence. ♦ **imminent, e** *adj* imminent, impending.

immiscer (s') [imise] (3) *vpr*: **s'~ dans** to interfere in. ♦ **immixtion** *nf*: ~ **dans** interference in.

immobile [imɔbil] *adj* motionless. **rester ~** to keep still.

immobilier, -ière [imɔbilje, jɛʀ] **1** *adj vente* property; *biens* in real estate. **2** *nm*: **l'~** the property *ou* real-estate business.

immobiliser [imɔbilize] (1) **1** *vt* (*gén*) to immobilize; *véhicule* to stop, bring to a standstill. **ça l'immobilise à son domicile** it keeps him housebound; **immobilisé par la peur** paralyzed with fear. **2 s'~** *vpr [personne]* to stop, stand still; *[véhicule]* to come to a standstill. ♦ **immobilisation** *nf* immobilization. **attendez l'~ totale de l'avion** wait until the aircraft has come to a complete standstill. ♦ **immobilité** *nf* stillness, motionlessness. **le médecin lui a ordonné l'~ complète** the doctor ordered him not to move (at all); ~ **forcée** forced immobility; ~ **politique** political inertia.

immodéré, e [imɔdeʀe] *adj* immoderate, inordinate.

immoler [imɔle] (1) *vt* (*gén*) to sacrifice (*à* to). ♦ **immolation** *nf* sacrifice.

immonde [imɔ̃d] *adj taudis* squalid, foul; *personne* base, vile. ♦ **immondices** *nfpl* (*ordures*) refuse.

immoral, e, *mpl* -aux [imɔʀal, o] *adj* immoral. ♦ **immoralité** *nf* immorality.

immortaliser [imɔʀtalize] (1) **1** *vt* to immortalize. **2 s'~** *vpr* to win immortality. ♦ **immortalité** *nf* immortality. ♦ **immortel, -elle 1** *adj* immortal. **2** *nf* (*fleur*) everlasting flower.

immotivé, e [imɔtive] *adj action* unmotivated; *crainte* groundless.

immuable [imɥabl(ə)] *adj* (*gén*) unchanging; *loi* immutable. **son chapeau ~** his eternal hat. ♦ **immuablement** *adv* immutably.

immuniser [imynize] (1) *vt* (*Méd*) to immunize. (*fig*) **être immunisé contre les tentations** to be immune to temptation. ♦ **immunisation** *nf* immunization. ♦ **immunité** *nf* (*Bio, Jur*) immunity. ~ **parlementaire** ≃ parliamentary privilege.

impact [ɛ̃pakt] *nm* (*lit, fig*) impact.

impair, e [ɛ̃pɛʀ] **1** *adj* odd. **2** *nm* (*gaffe*) blunder. (*Casino*) **l'**~ the odd numbers.

impalpable [ɛ̃palpabl(ə)] *adj* impalpable.

imparable [ɛ̃paʀabl(ə)] *adj* unstoppable.

impardonnable [ɛ̃paʀdɔnabl(ə)] *adj* unforgivable, unpardonable.

imparfait, e [ɛ̃paʀfɛ, ɛt] **1** *adj* (*gén*) imperfect. **2** *nm* (*Ling*) **l'**~ the imperfect (tense). ♦ **imparfaitement** *adv* imperfectly.

impartial, e, *mpl* **-aux** [ɛ̃paʀsjal, o] *adj* impartial, unbiased. ♦ **impartialement** *adv* impartially. ♦ **impartialité** *nf* impartiality.

impasse [ɛ̃pas] *nf* **(a)** (*cul-de-sac*) dead end; (*sur panneau*) 'no through road'. **(b)** (*fig*) impasse. **être dans l'**~ *[négociations]* to be at deadlock; ~ **budgétaire** budget deficit. **(c)** (*Cartes*) finesse. (*Scol*) **j'ai fait 3** ~**s** I missed out 3 topics.

impassibilité [ɛ̃pasibilite] *nf* impassiveness. ♦ **impassible** *adj* impassive. ♦ **impassiblement** *adv* impassively.

impatience [ɛ̃pasjɑ̃s] *nf* impatience. **il était dans l'**~ **de la revoir** he was impatient to see her again. ♦ **impatiemment** *adv* impatiently. ♦ **impatient, e** *adj* impatient. ~ **de faire** eager to do. ♦ **impatienter** (1) **1** *vt* to irritate, annoy. **2 s'**~ *vpr* to get impatient (*contre* with, at).

impayable* [ɛ̃pɛjabl(ə)] *adj* (*drôle*) priceless*.

impayé, e [ɛ̃peje] *adj* unpaid.

impeccable [ɛ̃pekabl(ə)] *adj* (*gén*) impeccable. ♦ **impeccablement** *adv* impeccably.

impénétrable [ɛ̃penetʀabl(ə)] *adj* (*gén*) impenetrable (*à* to, by); *visage* inscrutable.

impénitent, e [ɛ̃penitɑ̃, ɑ̃t] *adj* unrepentant.

impensable [ɛ̃pɑ̃sabl(ə)] *adj* *événement hypothétique* unthinkable; *événement arrivé* unbelievable.

imper* [ɛ̃pɛʀ] *nm* (*abrév de* **imperméable**) mac.

impératif, -ive [ɛ̃peʀatif, iv] **1** *adj* (*obligatoire*) imperative; (*impérieux*) *ton* commanding. **2** *nm* **(a)** (*Ling*) **l'**~ the imperative (mood). **(b)** *[fonction]* requirement; *[mode, horaire]* demand; *[situation]* necessity; (*Mil*) imperative. ♦ **impérativement** *adv* imperatively.

impératrice [ɛ̃peʀatʀis] *nf* empress.

imperceptible [ɛ̃pɛʀsɛptibl(ə)] *adj* imperceptible (*à* to). ♦ **imperceptiblement** *adv* imperceptibly.

imperfection [ɛ̃pɛʀfɛksjɔ̃] *nf* (*gén*) imperfection.

impérial, e, *mpl* **-aux** [ɛ̃peʀjal, o] **1** *adj* imperial. **2** *nf [autobus]* top deck. **autobus à** ~**e** ≃ double-decker (bus). ♦ **impérialisme** *nm* imperialism. ♦ **impérialiste** *adj, nmf* imperialist.

impérieux, -euse [ɛ̃peʀjø, øz] *adj* (*autoritaire*) imperious; (*pressant*) urgent, pressing. ♦ **impérieusement** *adv* imperiously; urgently.

impérissable [ɛ̃peʀisabl(ə)] *adj œuvre* imperishable; *souvenir* undying.

imperméable [ɛ̃pɛʀmeabl(ə)] **1** *adj roches* impermeable; *tissu* waterproof. ~ **à l'eau** waterproof; ~ **à l'air** airtight; (*fig: insensible*) ~ **à** impervious to. **2** *nm* (*manteau*) raincoat. ♦ **imperméabiliser** (1) *vt* to waterproof. ♦ **imperméabilité** *nf* impermeability.

impersonnel, -elle [ɛ̃pɛʀsɔnɛl] *adj* impersonal.

impertinence [ɛ̃pɛʀtinɑ̃s] *nf* impertinence. ♦ **impertinent, e** *adj* impertinent.

imperturbable [ɛ̃pɛʀtyʀbabl(ə)] *adj* imperturbable. **rester** ~ to remain unruffled. ♦ **imperturbablement** *adv* imperturbably.

impétueux, -euse [ɛ̃petɥø, øz] *adj* (*gén*) impetuous; *torrent* raging. ♦ **impétueusement** *adv* impetuously. ♦ **impétuosité** *nf* impetuosity.

impie [ɛ̃pi] *adj* impious, ungodly. ♦ **impiété** *nf* impiety, ungodliness.

impitoyable [ɛ̃pitwajabl(ə)] *adj* merciless, pitiless. ♦ **impitoyablement** *adv* mercilessly, pitilessly.

implacable [ɛ̃plakabl(ə)] *adj* implacable. ♦ **implacablement** *adv* implacably.

implanter [ɛ̃plɑ̃te] (1) **1** *vt usage* to introduce; *race* to settle; *usine* to set up, establish; *idée,* (*Méd*) to implant. **2 s'**~ *vpr [usines]* to be set up *ou* established; *[race]* to settle. **des traditions solidement implantées** deeply-rooted *ou* deeply-entrenched traditions. ♦ **implantation** *nf* introduction; settlement; establishment; implantation.

implication [ɛ̃plikɑsjɔ̃] *nf* (*gén*) implication.

implicite [ɛ̃plisit] *adj* implicit. ♦ **implicitement** *adv* implicitly.

impliquer [ɛ̃plike] (1) *vt* **(a)** (*supposer*) to imply (*que* that). **(b)** ~ **qn dans** to implicate sb in.

implorer [ɛ̃plɔʀe] (1) *vt* to implore. ~ **qn de faire** to implore *ou* beseech sb to do. ♦ **imploration** *nf* entreaty.

impoli, e [ɛ̃pɔli] *adj* impolite, rude (*envers* to). ♦ **impoliment** *adv* impolitely, rudely. ♦ **impolitesse** *nf* (*attitude*) impoliteness, rudeness; (*remarque*) impolite *ou* rude remark; (*acte*) impolite action. **c'est une** ~ **que de faire** it is impolite *ou* rude to do.

impondérable [ɛ̃pɔ̃deʀabl(ə)] *adj, nm* imponderable.

impopulaire [ɛ̃pɔpylɛʀ] *adj* unpopular. ♦ **impopularité** *nf* unpopularity.

importance [ɛ̃pɔʀtɑ̃s] *nf* (*gén*) importance; *[fait]* significance; *[somme]* size; *[dégâts]* extent. **avoir de l'**~ to be important; **sans** ~ unimportant, insignificant; **ça n'a pas d'**~ it doesn't matter; **d'une certaine** ~ *firme* sizeable; *dégâts* considerable; **prendre de l'**~ (*gén*) to become more important; *[firme]* to increase in size; (*péj*) **se donner de l'**~ to put on self-important airs. ♦ **important, e** *adj* important; significant; sizeable; extensive; (*péj*) *airs* self-important. **peu** ~ of little importance *ou* significance; **l'**~ **est de** the important thing is to.

importer¹ [ɛ̃pɔʀte] (1) *vt* to import (*de* from). ♦ **importateur, -trice** **1** *adj* importing. **2** *nm,f* importer. ♦ **importation** *nf* (*action*) importation; (*produit*) import. **articles d'**~ imported articles.

importer² [ɛ̃pɔʀte] (1) *vi* (*être important*) to matter. **que lui importe!** what does he care about it!, what does it matter to him!; **il importe de faire/que** it is important to do/that; **peu m'importe** (*pas de préférence*) I don't mind; (*je m'en moque*) I don't care; **n'importe** it doesn't matter, I don't mind; **n'importe qui** anybody, anyone; **n'importe quoi** anything; **n'importe comment** anyhow; **n'importe où** anywhere; **n'importe quand** anytime; **venez à n'importe quelle heure** come any time.

importun, e [ɛ̃pɔʀtœ̃, yn] **1** *adj présence* troublesome; *visite* inopportune; *personne* importunate. **2** *nm,f* (*gêneur*) irksome individual; (*visiteur*) intruder. ♦ **importunément** *adv* importunately, inopportunely. ♦ **importuner** (1) *vt* to importune, bother. **je ne veux pas vous** ~ I don't wish to bother you *ou* to disturb you *ou* to intrude. ♦ **importunité** *nf* importunity.

imposer [ɛ̃poze] (1) **1** *vt* (*gén*) to impose; *tâche* to set; *conditions* to lay down; (*Fin: taxer*) to tax. ~ **sa présence à qn** to impose *ou* force one's company on sb; ~ **un régime à qn** to put sb on a diet; ~ **son nom** *[artiste]* to make o.s. known; *[firme]* to establish itself; **sa conduite impose le respect** his behaviour compels respect; (*Rel*) ~ **les mains** to lay on hands; **en** ~ **à qn** to impress sb. **2 s'**~ *vpr* **(a)** (*être nécessaire*) to be essential *ou* vital *ou* imperative. **une visite au Louvre s'impose** a visit to the Louvre is a must. **(b) s'~ une tâche** to set o.s. a task; **s'~ de faire** to make it a rule to do. **(c)** *[artiste]* to make o.s. known; *[firme]* to become firmly established; *[sportif]* to emerge as the best. **(d)** (*importuner*) **s'~ à qn** to impose (o.s.) upon sb; **je ne voudrais pas m'~** I do not want to impose. ♦ **imposable** *adj* taxable. ♦ **imposant, e** *adj stature* imposing; *allure* stately; (*considérable*) imposing. ♦ **imposition** *nf* (*Fin*) taxation. (*Rel*) **l'~ des mains** the laying on of hands.

impossibilité [ɛ̃pɔsibilite] *nf* impossibility. **être dans l'~ de faire qch** to find it impossible to do sth; **se heurter à des ~s** to come up against insuperable obstacles. ♦ **impossible 1** *adj* (*gén*) impossible. **il m'est ~ de le faire** it's impossible for me to do it, I can't possibly do it. **2** *nm*: **je ferai l'~ (pour venir)** I'll do my utmost (to come); **par ~** by some miracle.

imposteur [ɛ̃pɔstœʀ] *nm* impostor. ♦ **imposture** *nf* imposture.

impôt [ɛ̃po] *nm* (*taxe*) tax; (*taxation*) taxation. **payer des ~s** to pay tax; **~s locaux** rates; **~ sur les plus-values** ≃ capital gains tax; **~ sur le revenu** income tax.

impotent, e [ɛ̃pɔtɑ̃, ɑ̃t] **1** *adj* disabled, crippled. **2** *nm,f* cripple. ♦ **impotence** *nf* disability.

impraticable [ɛ̃pʀatikabl(ə)] *adj idée* impracticable, unworkable; (*Sport*) *terrain* unfit for play; *route* impassable.

imprécation [ɛ̃pʀekɑsjɔ̃] *nf* imprecation, curse.

imprécis, e [ɛ̃pʀesi, iz] *adj* (*gén*) imprecise; *tir* inaccurate. ♦ **imprécision** *nf* imprecision; inaccuracy.

imprégner [ɛ̃pʀeɲe] (6) *vt tissu* to impregnate; *air* to permeate, fill; *esprit* to imbue (*de* with). **imprégné de lumière** flooded with light; **s'~ d'eau** to become soaked with water; **s'~ d'une langue** to immerse o.s. in a language. ♦ **imprégnation** *nf* (*gén*) impregnation; permeation; immersion.

imprenable [ɛ̃pʀənabl(ə)] *adj forteresse* impregnable. **vue ~** open *ou* unrestricted outlook.

imprésario [ɛ̃pʀesaʀjo] *nm* (*Théât*) manager.

impression [ɛ̃pʀesjɔ̃] *nf* **(a)** (*sensation*) impression. **faire bonne/mauvaise ~** to create a good/bad impression; **avoir l'~ que** to have a feeling *ou* the impression that; **faire ~** to make an impression. **(b)** *[livre]* (*action*) printing; (*tirage*) impression. **(c)** (*motif*) pattern. **(d)** (*Phot*) exposure. **(e)** (*Peinture*) undercoat.

impressionner [ɛ̃pʀesjɔne] (1) *vt* **(a)** (*frapper*) to impress; (*bouleverser*) to upset. **(b)** (*Opt, Phot*) *[image]* to show up on; *[photographe]* to expose. ♦ **impressionnable** *adj* impressionable. ♦ **impressionnant, e** *adj* impressive; upsetting.

imprévisibilité [ɛ̃pʀevizibilite] *nf* unpredictability. ♦ **imprévisible** *adj* unpredictable.

imprévoyance [ɛ̃pʀevwajɑ̃s] *nf* lack of foresight; (*d'argent*) improvidence. ♦ **imprévoyant, e** *adj* lacking (in) foresight; improvident.

imprévu, e [ɛ̃pʀevy] **1** *adj événement* unforeseen, unexpected; *geste* unexpected; *dépense* unforeseen. **2** *nm*: **l'~** the unexpected, the unforeseen; **plein d'~** full of surprises; **en cas d'~** if anything unexpected *ou* unforeseen crops up; **tous ces ~s** all these unexpected *ou* unforeseen events.

imprimer [ɛ̃pʀime] (1) *vt livre* to print; *cachet* to stamp; *rides, marque* to imprint (*dans* in, on); (*publier*) to publish. **~ un mouvement à** to transmit a movement to. ♦ **imprimé, e 1** *adj* printed. **2** *nm* (*formulaire*) printed form. (*Poste*) **~(s)** printed matter; (*tissu*) **l'~** printed material. ♦ **imprimerie** *nf* (*firme*) printing works; (*atelier*) printing house; (*section*) printery. (*technique*) **l'~** printing. ♦ **imprimeur** *nm* printer.

improbabilité [ɛ̃pʀɔbabilite] *nf* unlikelihood, improbability. ♦ **improbable** *adj* unlikely, improbable.

improductif, -ive [ɛ̃pʀɔdyktif, iv] *adj* unproductive.

impromptu, e [ɛ̃pʀɔ̃pty] **1** *adj départ* sudden; *visite* surprise; *repas, exposé* impromptu. **2** *nm* (*Littérat, Mus*) impromptu. **3** *adv* impromptu.

imprononçable [ɛ̃pʀɔnɔ̃sabl(ə)] *adj* unpronounceable.

impropre [ɛ̃pʀɔpʀ(ə)] *adj terme* inappropriate. **~ à** unsuitable for; **~ à la consommation** unfit for (human) consumption. ♦ **improprement** *adv* improperly. ♦ **impropriété** *nf [forme]* incorrectness. **~ (de langage)** (language) error, mistake.

improviser [ɛ̃pʀɔvize] (1) **1** *vt* to improvise. **2 s'~** *vpr*: **s'~ cuisinier** to act as cook; **on ne s'improvise pas menuisier** you don't become a joiner just like that. ♦ **improvisation** *nf* improvisation. ♦ **improvisé, e** *adj* (*de fortune*) improvised, makeshift; (*impromptu*) improvised.

improviste [ɛ̃pʀɔvist(ə)] *nm*: **à l'~** unexpectedly, without warning; **prendre qn à l'~** to catch sb unawares.

imprudent, e [ɛ̃pʀydɑ̃, ɑ̃t] **1** *adj* (*gén*) careless, imprudent, foolish; *remarque* unwise. **il est ~ de** it's unwise to. **2** *nm,f* imprudent *ou* careless person. ♦ **imprudemment** *adv* carelessly, imprudently, foolishly; unwisely. ♦ **imprudence** *nf* (*caractère*) carelessness, imprudence, foolishness. (*action*) **commettre une ~** to do something foolish *ou* imprudent.

impudence [ɛ̃pydɑ̃s] *nf* impudence; (*acte*) impudent action. ♦ **impudent, e** *adj* impudent.

impudeur [ɛ̃pydœʀ] *nf* immodesty. ♦ **impudique** *adj* immodest.

impuissance [ɛ̃pɥisɑ̃s] *nf [personne]* powerlessness, helplessness; (*sexuelle*) impotence; *[efforts]* ineffectiveness. ♦ **impuissant, e** *adj* powerless, helpless; impotent; ineffectual.

impulsion [ɛ̃pylsjɔ̃] *nf* (*Phys, Psych*) impulse; (*fig: élan*) impetus. **l'~ donnée à l'économie** the boost *ou* impetus given to the economy. ♦ **impulsif, -ive** *adj* impulsive.

impunément [ɛ̃pynemɑ̃] *adv* with impunity. ♦ **impuni, e** *adj* unpunished. ♦ **impunité** *nf* impunity.

impur, e [ɛ̃pyʀ] *adj* impure. ♦ **impureté** *nf* (*gén*) impurity.

imputer [ɛ̃pyte] (1) *vt*: **~ à** to impute to, attribute to, ascribe to; (*Fin*) to charge to. ♦ **imputable** *adj*: **~ à** ascribable to, attributable to; chargeable to. ♦ **imputation** *nf* (*accusation*) imputation. (*Fin*) **~ à** charging to.

inabordable [inabɔʀdabl(ə)] *adj personne* unapproachable; *lieu* inaccessible; *prix* prohibitive.

inaccentué, e [inaksɑ̃tɥe] *adj* unstressed.

inacceptable [inaksɛptabl(ə)] *adj offre* unacceptable; *propos* inadmissible.

inaccessible [inaksesibl(ə)] *adj* inaccessible. **~ à** (*insensible à*) impervious to.

inaccoutumé, e [inakutyme] *adj* unusual. **~ à** unaccustomed to, unused to.

inachevé, e [inaʃve] *adj* unfinished, uncompleted. ♦ **inachèvement** *nm* incompletion.

inactif, -ive [inaktif, iv] *adj* **(a)** (*oisif*) idle, inactive; *population* non-working. **(b)** (*inefficace*) ineffective. ♦ **inaction** *nf* inactivity, idleness. ♦ **inactivité** *nf* inactivity.

inadapté, e [inadapte] *adj personne* maladjusted. **~ à** not adapted *ou* adjusted to. ♦ **inadaptation** *nf* maladjustment.

inadéquat, e [inadekwa, at] *adj* inadequate.

inadmissible [inadmisibl(ə)] *adj* (*gén*) inadmissible.

inadvertance [inadvɛʀtɑ̃s] *nf*: **par ~** inadvertently.

inaliénable [inaljenabl(ə)] *adj* inalienable.
inaltérable [inalteʀabl(ə)] *adj substance* stable; *encre* permanent; *principes etc* steadfast, unshakeable. ~ **à l'air** unaffected by air.
inamical, e, *mpl* **-aux** [inamikal, o] *adj* unfriendly.
inamovible [inamɔvibl(ə)] *adj fonctionnaire* irremovable; *panneau* fixed; (*hum*) *casquette etc* eternal.
inanimé, e [inanime] *adj matière* inanimate; (*évanoui*) unconscious; (*mort*) lifeless.
inanité [inanite] *nf [conversation]* inanity; *[efforts]* futility.
inanition [inanisjɔ̃] *nf*: **tomber d'**~ to faint with hunger.
inaperçu, e [inapɛʀsy] *adj* unnoticed. **passer** ~ to pass unnoticed.
inapplicable [inaplikabl(ə)] *adj* inapplicable (*à* to).
inapplication [inaplikɑsjɔ̃] *nf [élève]* lack of application. ♦ **inappliqué, e** *adj* lacking in application.
inappréciable [inapʀesjabl(ə)] *adj aide* invaluable; *bonheur* inestimable; *nuance* imperceptible.
inapte [inapt(ə)] *adj* incapable (*à faire* of doing). ~ **aux affaires** unsuited to business; (*Mil*) ~ **(au service)** unfit (for military service). ♦ **inaptitude** *nf* (*mentale*) inaptitude, incapacity; (*physique*) unfitness (*à* for).
inarticulé, e [inaʀtikyle] *adj* inarticulate.
inassouvi, e [inasuvi] *adj* unappeased.
inattaquable [inatakabl(ə)] *adj position* unassailable; *preuve* irrefutable; *conduite* irreproachable.
inattendu, e [inatɑ̃dy] **1** *adj* unexpected, unforeseen. **2** *nm*: **l'**~ **d'une remarque** the unexpectedness of a remark.
inattention [inatɑ̃sjɔ̃] *nf* **(a)** inattention. **(faute d')**~ careless mistake. **(b)** ~ **à** *détails* lack of concern for. ♦ **inattentif, -ive** *adj* inattentive (*à* to); unconcerned (*à* by).
inaudible [inodibl(ə)] *adj* inaudible.
inaugurer [inɔgyʀe] (1) *vt* (*gén, fig*) to inaugurate; *monument* to unveil; *exposition* to open; (*hum*) *chapeau* to christen. ♦ **inaugural, e,** *mpl* **-aux** *adj* (*gén*) inaugural. **voyage** ~ maiden voyage. ♦ **inauguration** *nf* inauguration; unveiling; opening. **(cérémonie d')**~ inaugural ceremony.
inavouable [inavwabl(ə)] *adj* shameful. ♦ **inavoué, e** *adj* unconfessed.
incalculable [ɛ̃kalkylabl(ə)] *adj* (*gén*) incalculable.
incandescence [ɛ̃kɑ̃desɑ̃s] *nf* incandescence. **en** ~ white-hot, incandescent. ♦ **incandescent, e** *adj* incandescent, white-hot.
incantation [ɛ̃kɑ̃tɑsjɔ̃] *nf* incantation. ♦ **incantatoire** *adj* incantatory.
incapable [ɛ̃kapabl(ə)] **1** *adj* (*gén*) incapable (*de faire* of doing). ~ **de bouger** unable to move, incapable of movement *ou* of moving. **2** *nmf*: **c'est un** ~ he's useless*, he's an incompetent. ♦ **incapacité** *nf* (*incompétence*) incapability; (*invalidité*) disablement; (*Jur*) incapacity. (*impossibilité*) ~ **de faire** incapability *ou* inability to do; **être dans l'**~ **de faire** to be unable to do, be incapable of doing.
incarcérer [ɛ̃kaʀseʀe] (6) *vt* to incarcerate. ♦ **incarcération** *nf* incarceration.
incarner [ɛ̃kaʀne] (1) **1** *vt* to embody; (*Théât*) to play; (*Rel*) to incarnate. **2 s'**~ *vpr*: **s'**~ **dans** to be embodied in; (*Rel*) to be incarnate in. ♦ **incarnation** *nf* incarnation; embodiment. ♦ **incarné, e** *adj* **(a)** incarnate. **c'est la méchanceté** ~**e** he is wickedness incarnate. **(b)** *ongle* ingrown.
incartade [ɛ̃kaʀtad] *nf* prank.
incassable [ɛ̃kɑsabl(ə)] *adj* unbreakable.
incendier [ɛ̃sɑ̃dje] (7) *vt* **(a)** (*mettre le feu à*) to set fire to; (*brûler complètement*) to burn down. **(b)** *désir, imagination* to fire; *gorge* to burn. **(c)** (*: *réprimander*) ~ **qn** to give sb a telling-off*. ♦ **incendiaire 1** *nmf* arsonist. **2** *adj balle, discours* incendiary; *œillade* passionate. ♦ **incendie** *nm* fire. ~ **criminel** case of arson; ~ **de forêt** forest fire.
incertain, e [ɛ̃sɛʀtɛ̃, ɛn] *adj* **(a)** *personne* uncertain, unsure (*de, sur* about). **(b)** *démarche, temps* uncertain; *contour* indistinct, blurred; *lumière* dim. **(c)** *succès, fait* uncertain, doubtful. ♦ **incertitude** *nf* (*gén*) uncertainty. **être dans l'**~ to be in a state of uncertainty.
incessamment [ɛ̃sesamɑ̃] *adv* (very) shortly.
incessant, e [ɛ̃sɛsɑ̃, ɑ̃t] *adj* (*gén*) incessant, unceasing; *efforts* ceaseless, unremitting.
inceste [ɛ̃sɛst(ə)] *nm* incest. ♦ **incestueux, -euse** *adj* incestuous.
inchangé, e [ɛ̃ʃɑ̃ʒe] *adj* unchanged, unaltered. ♦ **inchangeable** *adj* unchangeable.
incidemment [ɛ̃sidamɑ̃] *adv* incidentally, in passing.
incidence [ɛ̃sidɑ̃s] *nf* (*conséquence*) effect; (*Écon, Phys*) incidence.
incident [ɛ̃sidɑ̃] *nm* (*gén*) incident. ~ **imprévu** unexpected incident; ~ **de parcours** (*gén*) (slight) setback; (*lit, fig*) ~ **technique** technical hitch; **l'**~ **est clos** that's an end of the matter.
incinérer [ɛ̃sineʀe] (6) *vt* to incinerate; (*au crématorium*) to cremate. ♦ **incinérateur** *nm* incinerator. ♦ **incinération** *nf* incineration; cremation.
inciser [ɛ̃size] (1) *vt* to incise. ♦ **incisif, -ive 1** *adj ton* cutting, incisive; *regard* piercing. **2** *nf* (*dent*) incisor. ♦ **incision** *nf* incision.
inciter [ɛ̃site] (1) *vt*: ~ **qn à faire** to incite *ou* urge sb to do; **ça n'incite pas au travail** it's no incentive to work. ♦ **incitation** *nf* incitement (*à* to).
incivilité [ɛ̃sivilite] *nf* incivility, rudeness; (*propos*) uncivil *ou* rude remark.
inclassable [ɛ̃klɑsabl(ə)] *adj* unclassifiable.
incliner [ɛ̃kline] (1) **1** *vt* **(a)** (*pencher*) to tilt; (*courber*) to bend. ~ **la tête** to bow *ou* incline one's head; ~ **le buste** (*saluer*) to bow; (*pencher*) to lean *ou* bend forward. **(b)** ~ **qn à** to encourage sb to; **ceci m'incline à penser que** that leads me to believe that. **2** *vi* **(a)** ~ **à** to be inclined to. **(b)** (*bifurquer*) ~ **vers** to veer towards *ou* to. **3 s'**~ *vpr* **(a)** (*se courber*) to bow; (*s'avouer battu*) to admit defeat. (*lit, fig*) **s'**~ **devant qn** to bow before *ou* to sb; **s'**~ **devant un ordre** to accept an order; **Marseille s'est incliné devant Saint-Étienne** Marseilles went down to *ou* lost to Saint-Étienne. **(b)** *[arbre]* to bend over; *[mur]* to lean; *[chemin]* to slope.
♦ **inclinaison** *nf [route]* gradient; *[toit]* slope, pitch; *[mur]* lean; *[chapeau, tête]* tilt; *[navire]* list; (*Géom*) *[droite]* angle. ♦ **inclination** *nf* **(a)** (*penchant*) inclination. **avoir de l'**~ **pour** to have a strong liking *ou* a penchant for. **(b)** ~ **de (la) tête** (*acquiescement*) nod; (*salut*) inclination of the head; ~ **(du buste)** bow. ♦ **incliné, e** *adj* **(a)** *pente* steep; *mur* leaning; *récipient* tilted. **(b) être** ~ **à penser que** ... to be inclined to think that ...; **être** ~ **au mal** to have a tendency towards what is bad.
inclure [ɛ̃klyʀ] (35) *vt* to include; (*dans une enveloppe*) to enclose (*dans* in). **jusqu'au 10 mars inclus** until March 10th inclusive, up to and including March 10th. ♦ **inclusion** *nf* inclusion. ♦ **inclusivement** *adv* inclusively. **jusqu'au 1er janvier** ~ until January 1st inclusive, up to and including January 1st.
incognito [ɛ̃kɔɲito] **1** *adv* incognito. **2** *nm*: **garder l'**~ to remain incognito.
incohérent, e [ɛ̃kɔeʀɑ̃, ɑ̃t] *adj* (*confus*) incoherent; (*illogique*) inconsistent. ♦ **incohérence** *nf* incoherence; inconsistency. ~**s dans un texte**

inconsistencies *ou* discrepancies in a text.
incolore [ɛ̃kɔlɔʀ] *adj* colourless; *vernis* clear.
incomber [ɛ̃kɔ̃be] (1) ~ **à** *vt indir [responsabilité]* to be incumbent (up)on; *[frais]* to be sb's responsibility. **il nous incombe de** it falls to us to.
incombustible [ɛ̃kɔ̃bystibl(ə)] *adj* incombustible.
incommode [ɛ̃kɔmɔd] *adj heure* awkward, inconvenient; *outil* impractical; *siège* uncomfortable; *position* awkward, uncomfortable. ♦ **incommodément** *adv* inconveniently; awkwardly, uncomfortably. ♦ **incommodité** *nf* inconvenience; awkwardness; impracticality; lack of comfort.
incommoder [ɛ̃kɔmɔde] (1) *vt*: ~ **qn** to disturb *ou* bother sb. ♦ **incommodant, e** *adj odeur* unpleasant, offensive; *bruit* annoying; *chaleur* uncomfortable. ♦ **incommodé, e** *adj* indisposed, unwell.
incomparable [ɛ̃kɔ̃paʀabl(ə)] *adj* (*sans pareil*) incomparable, matchless; (*dissemblable*) not comparable. ♦ **incomparablement** *adv* incomparably.
incompatibilité [ɛ̃kɔ̃patibilite] *nf* incompatibility. ~ **d'humeur** (mutual) incompatibility. ♦ **incompatible** *adj* incompatible (*avec* with).
incompétence [ɛ̃kɔ̃petɑ̃s] *nf* incompetence. ♦ **incompétent, e** *adj* incompetent.
incomplet, -ète [ɛ̃kɔ̃plɛ, ɛt] *adj* incomplete. ♦ **incomplètement** *adv renseigné* incompletely; *guéri* not completely.
incompréhension [ɛ̃kɔ̃pʀeɑ̃sjɔ̃] *nf* (*par ignorance*) lack of understanding; (*par hostilité*) lack of sympathy. ♦ **incompréhensible** *adj* (*gén*) incomprehensible. ♦ **incompréhensif, -ive** *adj* unsympathetic. ♦ **incompris, e** *adj* misunderstood.
inconcevable [ɛ̃kɔ̃svabl(ə)] *adj* (*gén*) inconceivable.
inconciliable [ɛ̃kɔ̃siljabl(ə)] *adj* irreconcilable.
inconditionnel, -elle [ɛ̃kɔ̃disjɔnɛl] **1** *adj* unconditional; *partisan* unquestioning. **2** *nm,f* (*hum: fanatique*) enthusiast, fanatic.
inconduite [ɛ̃kɔ̃dɥit] *nf* wild *ou* loose behaviour.
inconfort [ɛ̃kɔ̃fɔʀ] *nm [logement]* lack of comfort, discomfort. ♦ **inconfortable** *adj maison* uncomfortable; (*lit, fig*) *position* uncomfortable, awkward.
incongru, e [ɛ̃kɔ̃gʀy] *adj attitude* unseemly; *remarque* incongruous, ill-placed. ♦ **incongruité** *nf* incongruity, unseemliness. **une** ~ an unseemly remark (*ou* action).
inconnu, e [ɛ̃kɔny] **1** *adj* unknown. **son visage m'était** ~ his face was new *ou* unknown to me; **une joie** ~**e** a strange joy; ~ **à cette adresse** not known at this address. **2** *nm,f* stranger, unknown person. **3** *nm*: **l'**~ the unknown. **4** *nf* (*Math, fig*) unknown quantity.
inconscient, e [ɛ̃kɔ̃sjɑ̃, ɑ̃t] **1** *adj* (*évanoui, machinal*) unconscious; (*irréfléchi*) thoughtless, reckless; (*: *fou*) mad*. ~ **de** unaware of. **2** *nm* (*Psych*) **l'**~ the unconscious. **3** *nm,f* (*) nutcase*. ♦ **inconsciemment** *adv* unconsciously; thoughtlessly; recklessly. ♦ **inconscience** *nf* unconsciousness; thoughtlessness; recklessness. **c'est de l'**~ that's sheer madness.
inconséquent, e [ɛ̃kɔ̃sekɑ̃, ɑ̃t] *adj* (*illogique*) inconsistent, inconsequent; (*irréfléchi*) thoughtless. ♦ **inconséquence** *nf* inconsistency; thoughtlessness.
inconsidéré, e [ɛ̃kɔ̃sideʀe] *adj* thoughtless, rash. ♦ **inconsidérément** *adv* thoughtlessly, rashly.
inconsistant, e [ɛ̃kɔ̃sistɑ̃, ɑ̃t] *adj preuve* flimsy; *caractère* weak; *crème* runny. ♦ **inconsistance** *nf* flimsiness; weakness; runniness.
inconsolable [ɛ̃kɔ̃sɔlabl(ə)] *adj* inconsolable.
inconstance [ɛ̃kɔ̃stɑ̃s] *nf [temps, sort]* fickleness; *[amour]* inconstancy; *[comportement]* inconsistency. ♦ **inconstant, e** *adj* fickle; inconstant; inconsistent.
incontestable [ɛ̃kɔ̃tɛstabl(ə)] *adj* incontestable, indisputable. ♦ **incontestablement** *adv* incontestably, indisputably. ♦ **incontesté, e** *adj* uncontested, undisputed.
incontinence [ɛ̃kɔ̃tinɑ̃s] *nf* incontinence. ♦ **incontinent, e** *adj* incontinent.
incontrôlable [ɛ̃kɔ̃tʀolabl(ə)] *adj* (*non vérifiable*) unverifiable; (*irrépressible*) uncontrollable. ♦ **incontrôlé, e** *adj* unverified; uncontrolled.
inconvenant, e [ɛ̃kɔ̃vnɑ̃, ɑ̃t] *adj comportement* improper, unseemly; *question* improper; *personne* ill-mannered. ♦ **inconvenance** *nf* **(a)** impropriety, unseemliness. **(b)** (*acte, remarque*) impropriety.
inconvénient [ɛ̃kɔ̃venjɑ̃] *nm* (*désavantage*) disadvantage, drawback, inconvenience; (*risque*) risk. **nous ne voulons pas en supporter les** ~**s** we don't want to have to suffer the consequences; **peut-on en boire sans** ~? can one safely drink it?, is there any risk in drinking it?; **l'**~ **c'est que** the annoying thing is that, the one drawback is that; **si vous n'y voyez pas d'**~ ... if you have no objections ... .
incorporer [ɛ̃kɔʀpɔʀe] (1) *vt* (*gén*) to incorporate; (*Mil*) to enlist (*dans* into); *substance* to mix (*à, avec* with). **se faire** ~ **dans l'infanterie** to enlist in the infantry. ♦ **incorporation** *nf* incorporation; mixing; enlistment.
incorrect, e [ɛ̃kɔʀɛkt, ɛkt(ə)] *adj* **(a)** *réglage* faulty; *solution* incorrect, wrong. **(b)** *langage* improper; *tenue* indecent; *personne* discourteous, impolite. **(c)** (*déloyal*) *personne, procédé* underhand. ♦ **incorrectement** *adv* faultily; incorrectly; wrongly; improperly; indecently; discourteously, impolitely; in an underhand way. ♦ **incorrection** *nf* **(a)** **l'**~ impropriety, incorrectness. **(b)** (*terme*) impropriety; (*action*) impolite action.
incorrigible [ɛ̃kɔʀiʒibl(ə)] *adj* incorrigible.
incorruptible [ɛ̃kɔʀyptibl(ə)] *adj* incorruptible.
incrédule [ɛ̃kʀedyl] **1** *adj* (*sceptique*) incredulous; (*Rel*) unbelieving. **2** *nmf* (*Rel*) nonbeliever. ♦ **incrédulité** *nf* incredulity; unbelief.
increvable [ɛ̃kʀəvabl(ə)] *adj pneu* puncture-proof; (*: *infatigable*) tireless.
incriminer [ɛ̃kʀimine] (1) *vt personne* to incriminate, accuse; *conduite* to bring under attack; *honnêteté* to call into question.
incrochetable [ɛ̃kʀɔʃtabl(ə)] *adj serrure* burglar-proof.
incroyable [ɛ̃kʀwajabl(ə)] *adj* incredible, unbelievable. ♦ **incroyablement** *adv* incredibly, unbelievably.
incroyance [ɛ̃kʀwajɑ̃s] *nf* (*Rel*) unbelief. ♦ **incroyant, e** **1** *adj* unbelieving. **2** *nm,f* nonbeliever.
incruster [ɛ̃kʀyste] (1) **1** *vt* (*Art*) to inlay. **2 s'**~ *vpr* **(a)** *[caillou]* **s'**~ **dans** to become embedded in. **(b)** (*fig*) *[invité]* to take root. **(c)** *[radiateur]* to become incrusted (*de* with). ♦ **incrustation** *nf* (*Art*) (*technique*) inlaying; (*ornement*) inlay; (*sur roche*) incrustation.
incuber [ɛ̃kybe] (1) *vt* to incubate. ♦ **incubateur** *nm* incubator. ♦ **incubation** *nf* incubation.
inculper [ɛ̃kylpe] (1) *vt* to charge (*de* with). ♦ **inculpation** *nf* charging. **sous l'**~ **de** on a charge of. ♦ **inculpé, e** *nm,f* accused.
inculquer [ɛ̃kylke] (1) *vt*: ~ **à qn** to inculcate in sb.
inculte [ɛ̃kylt(ə)] *adj terre* uncultivated; *barbe* unkempt; *personne* uneducated. ♦ **inculture** *nf* lack of education.
incurable [ɛ̃kyʀabl(ə)] *adj, nmf* incurable.
incursion [ɛ̃kyʀsjɔ̃] *nf* (*lit, fig*) incursion, foray (*en, dans* into).
incurver *vt*, **s'**~ *vpr* [ɛ̃kyʀve] (1) to curve.
Inde [ɛ̃d] *nf* India. **les** ~**s** the Indies.

indécent, e [ɛ̃desɑ̃, ɑ̃t] *adj* indecent; (*fig*) *chance* disgusting. ♦ **indécemment** *adv* indecently. ♦ **indécence** *nf* indecency.
indéchiffrable [ɛ̃deʃifRabl(ə)] *adj* (*illisible*) indecipherable; (*incompréhensible*) incomprehensible; *regard* inscrutable.
indéchirable [ɛ̃deʃiRabl(ə)] *adj* tear-proof.
indécis, e [ɛ̃desi, iz] *adj personne* (*par nature*) indecisive; (*temporairement*) undecided (*sur* about); *résultat* undecided; *temps, paix* unsettled; *réponse* vague; *forme* indistinct. ♦ **indécision** *nf* indecisiveness; (*temporaire*) indecision (*sur* about).
indéfendable [ɛ̃defɑ̃dabl(ə)] *adj* (*lit, fig*) indefensible.
indéfini, e [ɛ̃defini] *adj* (*vague*) undefined; (*indéterminé*) indefinite. ♦ **indéfiniment** *adv* indefinitely. ♦ **indéfinissable** *adj* indefinable.
indélébile [ɛ̃delebil] *adj* (*lit, fig*) indelible.
indélicat, e [ɛ̃delika, at] *adj* (*mufle*) indelicate; (*malhonnête*) dishonest. ♦ **indélicatement** *adv* indelicately; dishonestly. ♦ **indélicatesse** *nf* indelicacy; dishonesty.
indémaillable [ɛ̃demɑjabl(ə)] *adj* run-resist.
indemne [ɛ̃dɛmn(ə)] *adj* unharmed, unhurt, unscathed.
indemniser [ɛ̃dɛmnize] (1) *vt* (*gén*) to indemnify (*de* for); (*d'une perte*) to compensate (*de* for). **se faire** ~ to get indemnification *ou* compensation. ♦ **indemnisation** *nf* (*action*) indemnification; (*somme*) indemnity, compensation. **10 F d'**~ 10 francs compensation. ♦ **indemnité** *nf [perte]* indemnity; *[frais]* allowance. ~ **de transport** travel allowance; ~ **parlementaire** M.P.'s salary.
indéniable [ɛ̃denjabl(ə)] *adj* undeniable. ♦ **indéniablement** *adj* undeniably.
indentation [ɛ̃dɑ̃tɑsjɔ̃] *nf* indentation.
indépendance [ɛ̃depɑ̃dɑ̃s] *nf* (*gén*) independence. ♦ **indépendamment** *adv* (*seul*) independently. ~ **de cela** apart from that. ♦ **indépendant, e** *adj* (*gén*) independent (*de* of). **pour des causes** ~**es de notre volonté** for reasons beyond our control; **'à louer: chambre** ~**e'** to let: self-contained bedsitter.
indescriptible [ɛ̃dɛskRiptibl(ə)] *adj* indescribable.
indésirable [ɛ̃deziRabl(ə)] *adj, nmf* undesirable.
indestructible [ɛ̃dɛstRyktibl(ə)] *adj* indestructible.
indéterminé, e [ɛ̃detɛRmine] *adj date, cause* unspecified; *quantité* indeterminate; *impression, contours* vague. **pour des raisons** ~**es** for reasons which were not determined; **je suis encore** ~ **sur** I'm still undecided *ou* uncertain about. ♦ **indétermination** *nf* (*imprécision*) vagueness; (*irrésolution*) indecision.
index [ɛ̃dɛks] *nm* (*doigt*) forefinger; (*repère*) pointer; (*liste, indice*) index. ♦ **indexation** *nf* indexing. ♦ **indexer** (1) *vt* to index (*sur* to).
indication [ɛ̃dikɑsjɔ̃] *nf* (*gén*) indication (*de* of); (*directive*) instruction, direction; (*renseignement*) piece of information. **quelle** ~ **porte la pancarte?** what does the notice say?; **sauf** ~ **contraire** unless otherwise stated. ♦ **indicateur, -trice 1** *nm,f:* ~ **(de police)** (police) informer. **2** *nm* (*guide*) guide; (*horaire*) timetable; (*Tech*) gauge, indicator. ~ **des rues** street directory; ~ **de vitesse** (*Aut*) speedometer; (*Aviat*) airspeed indicator. ♦ **indicatif, -ive 1** *adj* indicative (*de* of). **2** *nm* **(a)** (*Rad*) (*mélodie*) signature tune. *[poste émetteur]* ~ **(d'appel)** call sign; ~ **téléphonique** (dialling) code. **(b)** (*Ling*) **l'**~ the indicative.
indice [ɛ̃dis] *nm* **(a)** (*signe*) indication, sign; (*élément d'enquête*) clue; (*Jur: preuve*) piece of evidence. **(b)** (*Math*) suffix; (*Admin: grade*) grading. ~ **des prix** price index.
indicible [ɛ̃disibl(ə)] *adj* inexpressible.
indien, -ienne [ɛ̃djɛ̃, jɛn] **1** *adj* Indian. **2** *nm(f)*: **I**~**(ne)** *[Inde]* Indian; *[Amérique]* (Red *ou* American) Indian.
indifférence [ɛ̃difeRɑ̃s] *nf* (*gén*) indifference (*envers* to, towards). ♦ **indifféremment** *adv*: **supporter** ~ **le froid et le chaud** to stand cold and heat equally well, stand either cold or heat; **manger de tout** ~ to eat anything. ♦ **indifférent, e** *adj* indifferent (*à* to). **cela m'est** ~ it is immaterial to me, it doesn't matter to me; **parler de choses** ~**es** to talk of this and that. ♦ **indifférer** (6) *vt*: **ceci l'indiffère** he's indifferent to this, he couldn't care less about this.
indigence [ɛ̃diʒɑ̃s] *nf* (*misère*) poverty, destitution; (*fig*) poverty. ♦ **indigent, e 1** *adj* destitute, poor. **2** *nm,f* pauper.
indigène [ɛ̃diʒɛn] **1** *adj* (*du pays*) local; (*aux colonies*) native; (*Bot, Zool*) indigenous. **2** *nmf* local; native.
indigestion [ɛ̃diʒɛstjɔ̃] *nf* indigestion. **avoir une** ~ to get indigestion *ou* an attack of indigestion; (*fig*) **avoir une** ~ **de qch** to be sick of sth. ♦ **indigeste** *adj* (*lit, fig*) indigestible.
indigne [ɛ̃diɲ] *adj acte* shameful; *personne* unworthy. ~ **de** *amitié* unworthy of; **il est** ~ **de vivre** he doesn't deserve to live, he's not fit to live. ♦ **indignement** *adv* shamefully. ♦ **indignité** *nf* **(a)** *[personne]* unworthiness; *[conduite]* shamefulness. **(b)** (*acte*) shameful act.
indigner [ɛ̃diɲe] (1) **1** *vt*: ~ **qn** to make sb indignant. **2 s'**~ *vpr* to get indignant (*de* about, at, *contre* with). ♦ **indignation** *nf* indignation. **avec** ~ indignantly. ♦ **indigné, e** *adj* indignant (*par* at).
indigo [ɛ̃digo] *nm, adj inv* indigo.
indiqué, e [ɛ̃dike] *adj* (*conseillé*) advisable; (*adéquat*) appropriate, suitable. **c'est tout** ~ it's just what we need, it's just the thing.
indiquer [ɛ̃dike] (1) *vt* **(a)** (*montrer*) to show, indicate. ~ **qch du doigt** to point sth out (*à qn* to sb), point to sth; *[montre]* ~ **l'heure** to show *ou* tell the time; ~ **la réception à qn** to direct sb to *ou* show sb the way to reception; **qu'indique la pancarte?** what does the sign say?; **cela indique de la négligence** it points to *ou* indicates negligence. **(4)** (*dire*) *solution* to tell; *dangers* to point out. ~ **un hôtel à qn** to tell sb of a hotel, suggest a hotel to sb. **(c)** (*fixer*) *date* to give, name. **à l'heure indiquée** at the agreed *ou* appointed time. **(d)** *[étiquette]* to show; *[facture]* to give, mention. ~ **qch sur un plan** to mark *ou* draw sth on a plan.
indirect, e [ɛ̃diRɛkt, ɛkt(ə)] *adj* (*gén*) indirect. ♦ **indirectement** *adv* indirectly; *apprendre qch* in a roundabout way.
indiscipline [ɛ̃disiplin] *nf* lack of discipline. ♦ **indiscipliné, e** *adj* undisciplined, unruly.
indiscret, -ète [ɛ̃diskRɛ, ɛt] *adj* (*gén*) indiscreet; (*curieux*) inquisitive. **à l'abri des regards** ~**s** away from prying *ou* inquisitive eyes. ♦ **indiscrétion** *nf* **(a)** indiscretion; inquisitiveness. **sans** ~ without being indiscreet. **(b)** (*parole*) indiscreet word, indiscretion.
indiscutable [ɛ̃diskytabl(ə)] *adj* indisputable, unquestionable. ♦ **indiscutablement** *adv* indisputably, unquestionably. ♦ **indiscuté, e** *adj* undisputed.
indispensable [ɛ̃dispɑ̃sabl(ə)] **1** *adj* (*vital*) essential, vital; (*nécessaire*) necessary. **se rendre** ~ to make o.s. indispensable; **ça m'est** ~ it's indispensable to me, I can't do without it. **2** *nm*: **faire l'**~ to do what is essential *ou* absolutely necessary.
indisponible [ɛ̃dispɔnibl(ə)] *adj* unavailable.
indisposer [ɛ̃dispoze] (1) *vt* (*rendre malade*) to upset; (*mécontenter*) to antagonize, alienate. ♦ **indisposé, e** *adj* (*malade*) indisposed, unwell. ♦ **indisposition** *nf* (slight) indisposition, upset.
indissociable [ɛ̃disɔsjabl(ə)] *adj problèmes* indissociable.

indissoluble [ɛ̃disɔlybl(ə)] *adj* indissoluble.
indistinct, e [ɛ̃distɛ̃(kt), ɛ̃kt(ə)] *adj* (*gén*) indistinct; *murmure* confused; *couleurs* vague. ♦ **indistinctement** *adv* **(a)** indistinctly; vaguely; confusedly. **(b)** (*indifféremment*) **ça marche ~ au gaz ou à l'électricité** it runs equally well *ou* just as well on gas or on electricity; **tuant ~ femmes et enfants** killing women and children indiscriminately.
individu [ɛ̃dividy] *nm* (*gén*) individual; (*corps*) body; (*péj: homme*) fellow. **un drôle d'~** an odd-looking character *ou* individual.
individualiser [ɛ̃dividɥalize] (1) **1** *vt* (*caractériser*) to individualize; (*personnaliser*) to personalize; *horaire* to tailor to individual requirements. **2 s'~** *vpr* to acquire an identity of one's own. ♦ **individualisé, e** *adj caractères, groupe* distinctive. ♦ **individualisme** *nm* individualism. ♦ **individualiste 1** *adj* individualistic. **2** *nmf* individualist. ♦ **individualité** *nf* (*gén*) individuality; (*personnalité*) personality. ♦ **individuel, -elle** *adj* (*gén*) individual; *liberté* personal; *caractères* distinctive. ♦ **individuellement** *adv* individually.
indivisibilité [ɛ̃divizibilite] *nf* indivisibility. ♦ **indivisible** *adj* indivisible.
Indochine [ɛ̃dɔʃin] *nf* Indochina. ♦ **indochinois, e** *adj*, **I~(e)** *nm(f)* Indochinese.
indolence [ɛ̃dɔlɑ̃s] *nf* (*gén*) indolence; *[pouvoirs publics]* apathy, lethargy. ♦ **indolent, e** *adj* indolent; apathetic, lethargic.
indolore [ɛ̃dɔlɔʀ] *adj* painless.
indomptable [ɛ̃dɔ̃tabl(ə)] *adj* (*gén*) untameable; *enfant* unmanageable; *volonté* indomitable. ♦ **indompté, e** *adj* untamed, wild.
Indonésie [ɛ̃dɔnezi] *nf* Indonesia. ♦ **indonésien, -enne** *adj*, **I~(ne)** *nm(f)* Indonesian.
indu, e [ɛ̃dy] *adj joie* unseemly; *dépenses* unwarranted. **sans optimisme ~** without undue optimism.
indubitable [ɛ̃dybitabl(ə)] *adj* indubitable. ♦ **indubitablement** *adv* indubitably.
induction [ɛ̃dyksjɔ̃] *nf* (*gén*) induction.
induire [ɛ̃dɥiʀ] (38) *vt* **(a) ~ qn en erreur** to mislead sb, lead sb astray. **(b)** (*inférer*) to infer, induce (*de* from).
indulgent, e [ɛ̃dylʒɑ̃, ɑ̃t] *adj* (*gén*) indulgent (*avec* with); *juge, examinateur* lenient (*envers* towards). ♦ **indulgence** *nf* indulgence; leniency. **critique sans ~** harsh criticism.
indûment [ɛ̃dymɑ̃] *adv protester* unduly; *détenir* wrongfully.
industrie [ɛ̃dystʀi] *nf* **(a)** (*activité*) industry. **doter un pays d'une ~** to provide a country with an industrial infrastructure; **l'~ du spectacle** show business. **(b)** (*entreprise*) industry, industrial concern. **(c)** (*ingéniosité*) ingenuity. ♦ **industrialisation** *nf* industrialization. ♦ **industrialiser** (1) **1** *vt* to industrialize. **2 s'~** *vpr* to become industrialized. ♦ **industriel, -elle 1** *adj* industrial. **2** *nm* industrialist, manufacturer. ♦ **industriellement** *adv* industrially.
industrieux, -euse [ɛ̃dystʀijø, øz] *adj* industrious.
inébranlable [inebʀɑ̃labl(ə)] *adj* (*résolu*) unshakeable, steadfast, unwavering; (*inamovible*) immovable.
inédit, e [inedi, it] *adj texte* unpublished; *trouvaille* new, original.
ineffable [inefabl(ə)] *adj* ineffable.
inefficace [inefikas] *adj mesure* ineffective; *machine* inefficient. ♦ **inefficacité** *nf* ineffectiveness; inefficiency.
inégal, e, *mpl* **-aux** [inegal, o] *adj* (*irrégulier*) uneven; (*disproportionné*) unequal. ♦ **inégalable** *adj* incomparable, matchless. ♦ **inégalé, e** *adj* unequalled, unmatched. ♦ **inégalement** *adv* unequally; unevenly. ♦ **inégalité** *nf* (*différence*) difference (*de* between); (*injustice*) inequality; (*irrégularité*) unevenness. **~s de terrain** unevenness of the ground, bumps in the ground.
inélégant, e [inelegɑ̃, ɑ̃t] *adj toilette* inelegant; *procédés* discourteous.
inéligibilité [ineliʒibilite] *nf* (*Pol*) ineligibility. ♦ **inéligible** *adj* ineligible.
inéluctable [inelyktabl(ə)] *adj, nm* inescapable. ♦ **inéluctabilité** *nf* inescapability. ♦ **inéluctablement** *adv* inescapably.
inénarrable [inenaʀabl(ə)] *adj* (*désopilant*) priceless*; (*incroyable*) incredible.
inepte [inɛpt(ə)] *adj* inept. ♦ **ineptie** *nf* (*gén*) ineptitude. **dire des ~s** to talk nonsense.
inépuisable [inepɥizabl(ə)] *adj* inexhaustible.
inerte [inɛʀt(ə)] *adj* (*gén*) inert; *corps* lifeless; *personne* passive, apathetic. ♦ **inertie** *nf* inertia; passivity, apathy.
inescompté, e [inɛskɔ̃te] *adj*, **inespéré, e** [inɛspeʀe] *adj* unexpected, unhoped-for.
inestimable [inɛstimabl(ə)] *adj aide* inestimable, invaluable; *valeur* incalculable.
inévitable [inevitabl(ə)] *adj obstacle, accident* unavoidable; *résultat* inevitable, inescapable. **c'était ~!** it was inevitable!, it was bound to happen!; **l'~** the inevitable. ♦ **inévitablement** *adv* inevitably.
inexact, e [inɛgza(kt), akt(ə)] *adj* (*faux*) inaccurate, inexact; (*sans ponctualité*) unpunctual. ♦ **inexactitude** *nf* inaccuracy; unpunctuality.
inexcusable [inɛkskyzabl(ə)] *adj* inexcusable, unforgivable.
inexistant, e [inɛgzistɑ̃, ɑ̃t] *adj* non-existent.
inexorable [inɛgzɔʀabl(ə)] *adj destin* inexorable; *juge* inflexible. ♦ **inexorabilité** *nf* inexorability; inflexibility. ♦ **inexorablement** *adv* inexorably.
inexpérience [inɛkspeʀjɑ̃s] *nf* inexperience. ♦ **inexpérimenté, e** *adj personne* inexperienced; *gestes* inexpert.
inexplicable [inɛksplikabl(ə)] *adj* inexplicable. ♦ **inexplicablement** *adv* inexplicably. ♦ **inexpliqué, e** *adj* unexplained.
inexploitable [inɛksplwatabl(ə)] *adj* unexploitable. ♦ **inexploité, e** *adj* unexploited.
inexploré, e [inɛksplɔʀe] *adj* unexplored.
inexpressif, -ive [inɛkspʀesif, iv] *adj visage* expressionless, inexpressive.
inexprimable [inɛkspʀimabl(ə)] *adj, nm* inexpressible.
inextinguible [inɛkstɛ̃gibl(ə)] *adj* (*littér*) *passion* inextinguishable; *soif* unquenchable.
in extremis [inɛkstʀemis] **1** *loc adv arriver* at the last minute. **2** *loc adj sauvetage* last-minute.
inextricable [inɛkstʀikabl(ə)] *adj* inextricable. ♦ **inextricablement** *adv* inextricably.
infaillible [ɛ̃fajibl(ə)] *adj* infallible. ♦ **infaillibilité** *nf* infallibility. ♦ **infailliblement** *adv* (*à coup sûr*) inevitably; (*sans erreur*) infallibly.
infaisable [ɛ̃fəzabl(ə)] *adj* impossible, impracticable.
infâme [ɛ̃fɑm] *adj* (*gén*) vile; *action* unspeakable; *traître* infamous; *taudis* revolting, disgusting. ♦ **infamant, e** *adj acte* infamous; *propos* defamatory. ♦ **infamie** *nf* **(a)** infamy. **(b)** (*insulte*) scandalous remark; (*action*) infamous *ou* vile action.
infanterie [ɛ̃fɑ̃tʀi] *nf* infantry.
infantile [ɛ̃fɑ̃til] *adj maladie* infantile; *médecine* child; (*puéril*) infantile, childish. ♦ **infantilisme** *nm* (*Méd, Psych*) infantilism. **c'est de l'~!** how childish!
infarctus [ɛ̃faʀktys] *nm*: **~ (du myocarde)** coronary thrombosis; **il a fait trois ~** he has had three coronaries.
infatigable [ɛ̃fatigabl(ə)] *adj* indefatigable, tireless. ♦ **infatigablement** *adv* indefatigably, tirelessly.
infatuer (s') [ɛ̃fatɥe] (1) *vpr*: **s'~ de** to become

infatuated with. ♦ **infatuation** *nf* self-conceit. ♦ **infatué, e** *adj air* conceited. ~ **de lui-même** full of self-conceit.

infect, e [ɛ̃fɛkt, ɛkt(ə)] *adj* (*gén*) vile, revolting; *temps* filthy, foul.

infecter [ɛ̃fɛkte] (1) **1** *vt atmosphère* to contaminate; (*Méd, fig*) to poison, infect. **2 s'~** *vpr [plaie]* to become infected, turn septic. ♦ **infectieux, -euse** *adj* infectious. ♦ **infection** *nf* (*Méd*) infection; (*puanteur*) stench.

inférer [ɛ̃feʀe] (6) *vt* to infer, gather (*de* from).

inférieur, e [ɛ̃feʀjœʀ] **1** *adj partie, rang, vitesse* lower; *quantité, nombre* smaller; *qualité, intelligence* inferior. **descendez à l'étage ~** go to the next floor down; ~ **à** *nombre* less *ou* smaller than, below; ~ **à la moyenne** below average; **roman ~ à un autre** novel inferior to another. **2** *nm,f* inferior. ♦ **infériorité** *nf* inferiority. ~ **en nombre** inferiority in numbers; **en état d'~** in an inferior position.

infernal, e, *mpl* **-aux** [ɛ̃fɛʀnal, o] *adj* (*gén*) infernal; *douleur, enfant* diabolical.

infertile [ɛ̃fɛʀtil] *adj* (*lit, fig*) infertile.

infester [ɛ̃fɛste] (1) *vt* (*gén*) to infest. **infesté de souris** infested with *ou* overrun with mice.

infidèle [ɛ̃fidɛl] **1** *adj ami, récit* unfaithful (*à* to); *mémoire* unreliable; (*Rel*) infidel. **2** *nmf* (*Rel*) infidel. ♦ **infidélité** *nf* **(a)** unfaithfulness; unreliability. **(b)** (*acte déloyal*) infidelity. **faire une ~ à qn** to be unfaithful to sb.

infiltrer (s') [ɛ̃filtʀe] (1) *vpr* (*gén*) to infiltrate; *[liquide]* to percolate (through); *[lumière]* to filter through. **s'~ dans** to infiltrate; to percolate (through); to filter into. ♦ **infiltration** *nf* infiltration; percolation. (*Méd*) **se faire faire des ~s** to have injections.

infime [ɛ̃fim] *adj* tiny, minute.

infini, e [ɛ̃fini] **1** *adj* (*gén*) infinite; *patience* unlimited; *douleur* immense; *propos* interminable, never-ending. **2** *nm*: **l'~** (*Philos*) the infinite; (*Math, Phot*) infinity; **à l'~** endlessly. ♦ **infiniment** *adv* (*gén*) infinitely. **avec ~ de soin** with infinite care; **je regrette ~** I'm extremely sorry; **l'~ grand** the infinitely great; **l'~ petit** the infinitesimal. ♦ **infinité** *nf* infinity. **une ~ de** an infinite number of. ♦ **infinitésimal, e,** *mpl* **-aux** *adj* infinitesimal.

infinitif, -ive [ɛ̃finitif, iv] *adj, nm* infinitive.

infirme [ɛ̃fiʀm(ə)] **1** *adj* crippled, disabled; (*avec l'âge*) infirm. **2** *nmf* cripple. ~ **du travail** industrially disabled person; ~ **de guerre** war cripple. ♦ **infirmerie** *nf* (*gén*) infirmary; *[école, navire]* sick bay. ♦ **infirmier** *nm* male nurse. ♦ **infirmière** *nf* nurse. ♦ **infirmité** *nf* disability. **les ~s de la vieillesse** the infirmities of old age.

infirmer [ɛ̃fiʀme] (1) *vt* to invalidate.

inflammable [ɛ̃flamabl(ə)] *adj* inflammable, flammable.

inflammation [ɛ̃flamɑsjɔ̃] *nf* inflammation. ♦ **inflammatoire** *adj* inflammatory.

inflation [ɛ̃flɑsjɔ̃] *nf* inflation. ♦ **inflationniste** *adj danger* inflationary; *politique* inflationist.

infléchir [ɛ̃fleʃiʀ] (2) **1** *vt* (*lit, fig*) to bend; *rayons* to inflect. **2 s'~** *vpr [route]* to bend; *[poutre]* to sag; *[politique]* to shift.

inflexible [ɛ̃flɛksibl(ə)] *adj* (*gén*) inflexible; *caractère* unyielding; *règle* rigid. ♦ **inflexibilité** *nf* inflexibility; rigidity.

inflexion [ɛ̃flɛksjɔ̃] *nf [direction]* bend; *[voix]* inflexion; *[politique]* shift (*de* in). **d'une ~ de la tête/du corps** with a nod/bow.

infliger [ɛ̃fliʒe] (3) *vt* (*gén*) to inflict; *amende* to impose (*à* on).

influence [ɛ̃flyɑ̃s] *nf* influence (*sur* on). **il a de l'~** he's an influential person; **avoir une ~ néfaste sur** to have a harmful effect on; **sous l'~ de** under the influence of. ♦ **influençable** *adj* easily influenced. ♦ **influencer** (3) *vt* (*gén*) to influence; (*agir sur*) to act upon. ♦ **influent, e** *adj* influential. ♦ **influer** (1) *vi*: ~ **sur** to influence, have an influence on.

influx [ɛ̃fly] *nm*: ~ **nerveux** (nerve) impulse.

informateur, -trice [ɛ̃fɔʀmatœʀ, tʀis] *nm,f* informer.

informaticien, -ienne [ɛ̃fɔʀmatisjɛ̃, jɛn] *nm,f* computer scientist.

information [ɛ̃fɔʀmɑsjɔ̃] *nf* **(a)** (*renseignement*) piece of information; (*nouvelle*) piece of news. **voici nos ~s** here is the news; **une ~ de dernière minute** some last-minute news. **(b)** (*diffusion*) information. **pour l'~ des voyageurs** for the information of travellers; **mettre la main sur l'~** to get hold of the information network. **(c)** (*connaissances*) information. **(d)** (*Ordinateurs, Sci*) **l'~** information; **traitement de l'~** data processing. **(e)** (*Jur*) ~ **officielle** (judicial) inquiry.

informatique [ɛ̃fɔʀmatik] **1** *nf* (*science*) computer science; (*techniques*) data processing. **l'ère de l'~** the age of the computer. **2** *adj* computer.

informe [ɛ̃fɔʀm(ə)] *adj masse* shapeless, formless; *visage* misshapen.

informer [ɛ̃fɔʀme] (1) **1** *vt* to inform, tell (*de* of, about). **on vous a mal informé** you've been misinformed; **milieux bien informés** well-informed circles. **2 s'~** *vpr* (*d'un fait*) to inquire, find out, ask (*de* about); (*dans une matière*) to inform o.s. (*sur* about).

infortune [ɛ̃fɔʀtyn] *nf* misfortune. ♦ **infortuné, e** **1** *adj* ill-fated, wretched. **2** *nm,f* (poor) wretch.

infraction [ɛ̃fʀaksjɔ̃] *nf* (*délit*) offence. (*Aut*) **être en ~** to be committing an offence, be in breach of the law.

infranchissable [ɛ̃fʀɑ̃ʃisabl(ə)] *adj* (*lit*) impassable; (*fig*) insurmountable, insuperable.

infrarouge [ɛ̃fʀaʀuʒ] *adj, nm* infrared.

infrastructure [ɛ̃fʀastʀyktyʀ] *nf* (*Constr*) substructure; (*Écon, fig*) infrastructure.

infroissable [ɛ̃fʀwasabl(ə)] *adj* uncrushable, crease-resistant.

infructueux, -euse [ɛ̃fʀyktɥø, øz] *adj* fruitless, unfruitful.

infuser [ɛ̃fyze] (1) *vt* **(a)** (*plus gén faire ~*) *tisane* to infuse. **laisser ~ le thé** to leave the tea to brew *ou* infuse. **(b)** (*fig*) to infuse (*à* into). ♦ **infusion** *nf* (*action*) infusion; (*tisane*) infusion, herb tea. ~ **de tilleul** lime tea.

ingénier (s') [ɛ̃ʒenje] (7) *vpr*: **s'~ à faire** to try hard to do.

ingénieur [ɛ̃ʒenjœʀ] *nm* engineer. ~ **chimiste** chemical engineer; ~ **du son** sound engineer.

ingénieux, -euse [ɛ̃ʒenjø, øz] *adj* ingenious. ♦ **ingénieusement** *adv* ingeniously. ♦ **ingéniosité** *nf* ingenuity.

ingénu, e [ɛ̃ʒeny] *adj* naïve, artless. ♦ **ingénuité** *nf* naïvety, artlessness. ♦ **ingénument** *adv* naïvely, artlessly.

ingérer [ɛ̃ʒeʀe] (6) **1** *vt* to ingest. **2 s'~** *vpr*: **s'~ dans** to interfere in. ♦ **ingérence** *nf* interference (*dans* in). ♦ **ingestion** *nf* ingestion.

ingouvernable [ɛ̃guvɛʀnabl(ə)] *adj* (*Pol*) ungovernable.

ingrat, e [ɛ̃gʀa, at] *adj personne* ungrateful (*envers* to); *métier, sujet* thankless; *sol* sterile; *visage* unattractive. ♦ **ingratitude** *nf* ingratitude, ungratefulness (*envers* towards). **avec ~** ungratefully.

ingrédient [ɛ̃gʀedjɑ̃] *nm* ingredient.

inguérissable [ɛ̃geʀisabl(ə)] *adj* (*gén*) incurable; *chagrin* inconsolable.

ingurgiter [ɛ̃gyʀʒite] (1) *vt nourriture* to swallow, ingurgitate; (*fig*) to ingest, ingurgitate.

inhabile [inabil] *adj* (*manuellement*) clumsy; (*tactiquement*) inept. ♦ **inhabilité** *nf* clumsiness; ineptitude.

inhabitable [inabitabl(ə)] *adj* uninhabitable. ♦ **inhabité, e** *adj* uninhabited.
inhabituel, -elle [inabitɥɛl] *adj* unusual.
inhaler [inale] (1) *vt* to inhale, breathe in. ♦ **inhalation** *nf* inhalation. **prendre une ~** to use an inhalation bath.
inhérent, e [ineʀɑ̃, ɑ̃t] *adj* inherent (*à* in).
inhiber [inibe] (1) *vt* to inhibit. ♦ **inhibition** *nf* inhibition.
inhospitalier, -ière [inɔspitalje, jɛʀ] *adj* inhospitable.
inhumain, e [inymɛ̃, ɛn] *adj* inhuman.
inhumer [inyme] (1) *vt* to inter. ♦ **inhumation** *nf* interment.
inimaginable [inimaʒinabl(ə)] *adj* unimaginable.
inimitable [inimitabl(ə)] *adj* inimitable.
inimitié [inimitje] *nf* enmity.
ininflammable [inɛ̃flamabl(ə)] *adj* non-flammable.
inintelligent, e [inɛ̃teliʒɑ̃, ɑ̃t] *adj* unintelligent.
inintelligible [inɛ̃teliʒibl(ə)] *adj* unintelligible. ♦ **inintelligibilité** *nf* unintelligibility.
inintéressant, e [inɛ̃teʀɛsɑ̃, ɑ̃t] *adj* uninteresting.
ininterrompu, e [inɛ̃tɛʀɔ̃py] *adj ligne* unbroken; *flot* steady, uninterrupted.
inique [inik] *adj* iniquitous. ♦ **iniquité** *nf* iniquity.
initial, e, *mpl* **-aux** [inisjal, o] *adj, nf* initial. ♦ **initialement** *adv* initially.
initiative [inisjativ] *nf* (*gén*) initiative. **prendre l'~ d'une action/de faire** to take the initiative for an action/in doing; **avoir de l'~** to have *ou* show initiative.
initier [inisje] (7) **1** *vt* (*gén*) to initiate (*à* into); (*à un sport*) to introduce (*à* to). **2 s'~** *vpr* to become initiated. ♦ **initiateur, -trice** *nm,f* (*gén*) initiator; *[mode]* innovator. ♦ **initiation** *nf* initiation (*à* into). (*titre*) **~ à la philosophie** introduction to philosophy. ♦ **initié, e 1** *adj* initiated. **2** *nm,f* initiated person. **les non ~s** the uninitiated.
injecter [ɛ̃ʒɛkte] (1) *vt* (*Méd, Tech*) to inject. **yeux injectés de sang** bloodshot eyes. ♦ **injectable** *adj* injectable. ♦ **injection** *nf* injection.
injonction [ɛ̃ʒɔ̃ksjɔ̃] *nf* injunction, command.
injure [ɛ̃ʒyʀ] *nf* insult. **bordée d'~s** string of abuse *ou* insults; **il m'a fait l'~ de ne pas venir** he insulted *ou* affronted me by not coming. ♦ **injurier** (7) *vt* to abuse, insult. ♦ **injurieusement** *adv* abusively, insultingly. ♦ **injurieux, -euse** *adj* abusive, insulting (*pour* to).
injuste [ɛ̃ʒyst(ə)] *adj* (*gén*) unjust; (*partial*) unfair (*avec* to). ♦ **injustement** *adv* unjustly; unfairly. ♦ **injustice** *nf* **(a)** injustice; unfairness. **(b)** (*acte*) injustice.
injustifiable [ɛ̃ʒystifjabl(ə)] *adj* unjustifiable. ♦ **injustifié,** e *adj* unjustified, unwarranted.
inlassable [ɛ̃lɑsabl(ə)] *adj* tireless, unflagging. ♦ **inlassablement** *adv* tirelessly, unflaggingly.
inné, e [ine] *adj* innate, inborn.
innocent, e [inɔsɑ̃, ɑ̃t] **1** *adj* (*gén*) innocent (*de* of); *farce* harmless. **2** *nm,f* innocent. **l'~ du village** the village simpleton *ou* idiot. ♦ **innocemment** *adv* innocently. ♦ **innocence** *nf* innocence; harmlessness. ♦ **innocenter** (1) *vt* to clear, prove innocent (*de* of).
innombrable [inɔ̃bʀabl(ə)] *adj détails* innumerable, countless; *foule* vast.
innommable [inɔmabl(ə)] *adj conduite* unspeakable; *ordures* unspeakably foul.
innover [inɔve] (1) **1** *vi* to innovate. **ce peintre innove** this painter is breaking new ground. **2** *vt* to create, invent. ♦ **innovateur, -trice 1** *adj* innovatory. **2** *nm,f* innovator. ♦ **innovation** *nf* innovation.
inoccupé, e [inɔkype] *adj* (*gén*) unoccupied.
inoculer [inɔkyle] (1) *vt*: **~ un virus à qn** (*volontairement*) to inoculate sb with a virus; (*accidentellement*) to infect sb with a virus; **~ une passion** *etc* **à qn** to infect sb with a passion *etc.* ♦ **inoculation** *nf* inoculation; infection.
inodore [inɔdɔʀ] *adj gaz* odourless; *fleur* scentless.
inoffensif, -ive [inɔfɑ̃sif, iv] *adj* harmless, innocuous.
inonder [inɔ̃de] (1) *vt* to flood; (*fig: de produits*) to flood, swamp, inundate (*de* with). **inondé de soleil/de sueur** bathed in sunlight/in sweat; **inondé de larmes** *joues* streaming with tears; *yeux* full of tears; **se faire ~ (par la pluie)** to get soaked *ou* drenched (by the rain). ♦ **inondation** *nf* (*action*) flooding; swamping; inundation; (*résultat*) flood.
inopérable [inɔpeʀabl(ə)] *adj* inoperable.
inopiné, e [inɔpine] *adj* (*gén*) unexpected; *mort* sudden. ♦ **inopinément** *adv* unexpectedly.
inopportun, e [inɔpɔʀtœ̃, yn] *adj* ill-timed, inopportune, untimely. ♦ **inopportunément** *adv* inopportunely.
inorganisé, e [inɔʀganize] *adj* unorganized.
inoubliable [inublijabl(ə)] *adj* unforgettable.
inouï, e [inwi] *adj événement* unprecedented, unheard-of; *nouvelle, vitesse* incredible. **il est ~!*** he's incredible!
inox [inɔks] *ou* **inoxydable** [inɔksidabl(ə)] **1** *adj acier* stainless; *couteau* stainless steel. **2** *nm* stainless steel.
inqualifiable [ɛ̃kalifjabl(ə)] *adj* unspeakable.
inquiet, -ète [ɛ̃kjɛ, ɛt] **1** *adj* (*momentanément*) worried; (*par nature*) anxious; *gestes, attente* uneasy. **je suis ~ de ne pas le voir** I'm worried *ou* anxious at not seeing him. **2** *nm,f* worrier. ♦ **inquiétant, e** *adj* disturbing, worrying. ♦ **inquiéter** (6) **1** *vt* (*gén*) to worry, disturb; (*Mil*) to harass. **être inquiété (par la police)** to be troubled *ou* bothered by the police. **2 s'~** *vpr* to worry. **s'~ de** (*s'enquérir*) to inquire about; (*se soucier*) to worry about, trouble (o.s.) about, bother about. ♦ **inquiétude** *nf* anxiety. **donner des ~s à qn** to give sb cause for worry *ou* anxiety; **soyez sans ~** have no fear.
inquisiteur, -trice [ɛ̃kizitœʀ, tʀis] **1** *adj* inquisitive. **2** *nm* inquisitor. ♦ **inquisition** *nf* inquisition.
insaisissable [ɛ̃sezisabl(ə)] *adj fugitif* elusive; *nuance* imperceptible.
insalubre [ɛ̃salybʀ(ə)] *adj climat* insalubrious. ♦ **insalubrité** *nf* insalubrity.
insanité [ɛ̃sanite] *nf* (*folie*) insanity, madness; (*acte*) insane act. (*propos*) **~(s)** insane talk.
insatiable [ɛ̃sasjabl(ə)] *adj* insatiable. ♦ **insatiablement** *adv* insatiably.
insatisfait, e [ɛ̃satisfɛ, ɛt] *adj* (*non comblé*) unsatisfied; (*mécontent*) dissatisfied. ♦ **insatisfaction** *nf* dissatisfaction.
inscription [ɛ̃skʀipsjɔ̃] *nf* **(a)** (*écrite*) inscription. **l'~ d'une question à l'ordre du jour** putting a question on the agenda. **(b)** (*immatriculation*) enrolment, registration; (*à l'université*) matriculation (*à* at); (*à un concours*) enrolment (*à* in). **l'~ à un club** joining a club; **il y a déjà 20 ~s pour jeudi** 20 people have already signed on *ou* enrolled for Thursday; **votre ~ sur la liste dépend de ...** the inclusion of your name on the list depends on ... .
inscrire [ɛ̃skʀiʀ] (39) **1** *vt* **(a)** *nom, date* to note down, write down; (*dans la pierre*) to inscribe, engrave. **~ une question à l'ordre du jour** to put a question on the agenda; **il est inscrit sur la liste** his name is (written) on the list. **(b)** *étudiant* to register, enrol; (*pour rendez-vous*) to put down. **(faire) ~ un enfant à l'école** to put a child's name down for school, enrol *ou* register a child for school. **2 s'~** *vpr* **(a)** (*à un club*) to join (*à* non traduit); (*sur une liste*) to put one's name down (*sur* on); (*à l'université*) to register, enrol (*à* at). **(b)** (*s'insérer*) (*Math*) to be inscribed. (*fig*) **s'~ dans le cadre de qch** to lie *ou* come within the framework of sth, fit into sth. **(c) s'~ en faux**

contre qch to deny sth strongly. ♦ **inscrit, e** *nm,f* registered member (*ou* student *ou* candidate).

insecte [ɛ̃sɛkt(ə)] *nm* insect. ♦ **insecticide** *adj, nm* insecticide.

insécurité [ɛ̃sekyʀite] *nf* insecurity.

inséminer [ɛ̃semine] (1) *vt* to inseminate. ♦ **insémination** *nf* insemination.

insensé, e [ɛ̃sɑ̃se] *adj* insane. **c'est un ~!** he's demented! *ou* insane!

insensible [ɛ̃sɑ̃sibl(ə)] *adj* **(a)** insensible, insensitive (*à* to). **(b)** (*imperceptible*) imperceptible. ♦ **insensibiliser** (1) *vt* to anaesthetize. ♦ **insensibilité** *nf* insensitivity, insensibility. ♦ **insensiblement** *adv* imperceptibly.

inséparable [ɛ̃sepaʀabl(ə)] *adj* inseparable (*de* from).

insérer [ɛ̃seʀe] (6) **1** *vt* to insert (*dans* into). **2 s'~** *vpr*: **s'~ dans** *ensemble etc* to fit into. ♦ **insertion** *nf* insertion.

insidieux, -euse [ɛ̃sidjø, øz] *adj* insidious. ♦ **insidieusement** *adv* insidiously.

insigne[1] [ɛ̃siɲ] *adj honneur* distinguished; *faveur* notable; *maladresse* remarkable.

insigne[2] [ɛ̃siɲ] *nm* (*cocarde*) badge. (*emblème*) **l'~ de, les ~s de** the insignia of.

insignifiant, e [ɛ̃siɲifjɑ̃, ɑ̃t] *adj* (*gén*) insignificant; *somme* trifling. ♦ **insignifiance** *nf* insignificance.

insinuer [ɛ̃sinɥe] (1) **1** *vt* to insinuate, imply. **2 s'~** *vpr*: **s'~ dans** *[personne]* to worm one's way into, insinuate o.s. into; *[eau]* to seep *ou* creep into. ♦ **insinuation** *nf* insinuation, innuendo.

insipide [ɛ̃sipid] *adj* (*gén*) insipid.

insister [ɛ̃siste] (1) *vi* **(a)** ~ **sur** *sujet* to stress; *syllabe* to emphasize, stress; **n'insistons pas!** let us not dwell on it. **(b)** (*s'obstiner*) to be insistent (*auprès de* with), insist. **sonnez encore, insistez, elle est un peu sourde** ring again and keep (on) trying because she's a little deaf; **je n'insiste pas, je m'en vais*** I won't insist - I'll go. ♦ **insistance** *nf* insistence (*à faire* on doing). **avec ~** insistently. ♦ **insistant, e** *adj* insistent.

insolation [ɛ̃sɔlɑsjɔ̃] *nf* **(a)** (*malaise*) sunstroke. **une ~** a touch of sunstroke. **(b)** (*ensoleillement*) (period of) sunshine. **(c)** (*exposition au soleil*) exposure.

insolent, e [ɛ̃sɔlɑ̃, ɑ̃t] *adj personne, attitude* insolent; *luxe, joie* unashamed. **il a une chance ~e!** he has the luck of the devil! ♦ **insolemment** *adv* insolently; unashamedly. ♦ **insolence** *nf* insolence; (*remarque*) insolent remark.

insolite [ɛ̃sɔlit] *adj* unusual, strange.

insoluble [ɛ̃sɔlybl(ə)] *adj problème* insoluble, insolvable. ~ **(dans l'eau)** insoluble (in water).

insolvable [ɛ̃sɔlvabl(ə)] *adj* insolvent. ♦ **insolvabilité** *nf* insolvency.

insomnie [ɛ̃sɔmni] *nf* insomnia. **nuits d'~** sleepless nights; **ses ~s** his (periods of) insomnia. ♦ **insomniaque** *nmf* insomniac.

insondable [ɛ̃sɔ̃dabl(ə)] *adj* unfathomable.

insonore [ɛ̃sɔnɔʀ] *adj* soundproof. ♦ **insonorisation** *nf* soundproofing. ♦ **insonoriser** (1) *vt* to soundproof.

insouciant, e [ɛ̃susjɑ̃, ɑ̃t] *adj personne* carefree, happy-go-lucky; *paroles* carefree. ~ **de** careless *ou* heedless of. ♦ **insouciance** *nf* heedless *ou* happy-go-lucky attitude. **vivre dans l'~** to live a carefree life. ♦ **insoucieux, -euse** *adj* carefree.

insoumis, e [ɛ̃sumi, iz] **1** *adj enfant* rebellious; *tribu* unsubdued; *soldat* absent without leave. **2** *nm* (*Mil*) absentee. ♦ **insoumission** *nf* rebelliousness; (*Mil*) absence without leave.

insoupçonnable [ɛ̃supsɔnabl(ə)] *adj* above suspicion. ♦ **insoupçonné, e** *adj* unsuspected (*de* by).

insoutenable [ɛ̃sutnabl(ə)] *adj douleur* unbearable; *théorie* untenable.

inspecter [ɛ̃spɛkte] (1) *vt* to inspect. ♦ **inspecteur, -trice** *nm,f* (*gén*) inspector. ~ **de police** police inspector. ♦ **inspection** *nf* **(a)** (*examen*) inspection. **faire l'~ de** to inspect. **(b)** (*inspecteurs*) inspectorate.

inspirer [ɛ̃spiʀe] (1) **1** *vt* (*gén*) to inspire. **cette idée ne m'inspire pas beaucoup*** I'm not all that keen on this idea; **il ne m'inspire pas confiance** he doesn't inspire me with confidence; ~ **de l'horreur à qn** to fill sb with horror; **être bien/mal inspiré de faire qch** to be truly inspired/ill-inspired to do sth. **2** *vi* (*respirer*) to breathe in. **3 s'~** *vpr*: **s'~ d'un modèle** to be inspired by a model. ♦ **inspirateur, -trice** *nm,f* (*animateur*) inspirer; (*instigateur*) instigator. ♦ **inspiration** *nf* **(a)** (*poétique etc*) inspiration. **avoir de l'~** to have inspiration; **selon l'~ du moment** according to the mood of the moment; **j'eus la bonne ~ de refuser** I had the bright idea of refusing. **(b)** (*instigation*) instigation. **sous l'~ de qn** at sb's instigation, prompted by sb. **(c)** (*respiration*) inspiration.

instable [ɛ̃stabl(ə)] *adj* (*gén*) unstable; *temps* unsettled; *échafaudage* unsteady. ♦ **instabilité** *nf* instability; unsteadiness. **l'~ du temps** the unsettled weather.

installateur [ɛ̃stalatœʀ] *nm* fitter.

installation [ɛ̃stalɑsjɔ̃] *nf* **(a)** *[téléphone]* installation, putting in; *[rideaux]* putting up; *[local]* fitting out. **(b)** *[locataire]* settling in; *[artisan]* setting up. **il voulait fêter son ~** he wanted to celebrate moving in. **(c)** (*appareils etc: gén pl*) fittings, installations. **l'~ électrique est défectueuse** the wiring is faulty; **les ~s industrielles d'une région** the industrial plant of a region. **(d)** (*ameublement etc*) **ils ont une ~ provisoire** they have temporary living arrangements.

installer [ɛ̃stale] (1) **1** *vt* **(a)** *électricité, meuble* to install, put in; *étagère, tente* to put up; *appartement* to fit out. **cuisine bien installée** well equipped *ou* fitted kitchen; **ils ont installé leur bureau dans le grenier** they've turned the attic into a study. **(b)** *malade, jeune couple* to get settled, settle; *invité, fonctionnaire* to install. **il a installé son fils dentiste** he set his son up as a dentist. **2 s'~** *vpr* **(a)** *[commerçant]* to set o.s. up (*comme* as), set up shop (*comme* as). **s'~ à son compte** to set up on one's own. **(b)** (*se loger*) to settle, set up house; (*emménager*) to settle in. **il s'est installé chez des amis** he has moved in *ou* he is living with friends; **ils sont bien installés** they have made themselves a very comfortable home. **(c)** (*à un emplacement*) to settle down. **installe-toi comme il faut** (*confortablement*) make yourself comfortable; (*tiens-toi bien*) sit properly. **(d)** *[grève, maladie]* to take a firm hold, become firmly established. **s'~ dans la guerre** to settle into war.

instamment [ɛ̃stamɑ̃] *adv* insistently, earnestly.

instance [ɛ̃stɑ̃s] *nf* **(a)** (*autorité*) authority. **les ~s internationales** the international authorities. **(b)** (*Jur*) **introduire une ~** to institute (legal) proceedings; **en seconde ~** on appeal; **tribunal de première ~** court of first instance; **tribunal d'~** ≃ magistrates' court; **tribunal de grande ~** ≃ County court. **(c)** (*prière*) **demander qch avec ~** to ask earnestly for sth; **~s** entreaties. **(d)** (*en cours*) **l'affaire est en ~** the matter is pending; **être en ~ de divorce** to be waiting for a divorce; **en ~ de départ** on the point of departure.

instant[1] [ɛ̃stɑ̃] *nm* moment, instant. **vivre dans l'~** to live in the present (moment); **il faut le faire à l'~** we must do it this instant *ou* minute; **à l'~ où je vous parle** as I'm speaking to you now; **à chaque ~, à tout ~** (*d'un moment à l'autre*) at any moment *ou* minute; (*tout le temps*) all the time, every minute; **dans un ~** in a moment *ou* minute; **en un ~** in an instant; **de tous les ~s** constant; **par ~s** at times; **pour l'~** for the moment, for the time being.

instant[2]**, e** [ɛ̃stɑ̃, ɑ̃t] *adj* (*pressant*) insistent.
instantané, e [ɛ̃stɑ̃tane] **1** *adj* instantaneous; *café* instant. **2** *nm* (*Phot*) snapshot. ♦ **instantanément** *adv* instantaneously; *dissoudre* instantly.
instaurer [ɛ̃stɔʀe] (1) *vt* to institute. ♦ **instauration** *nf* institution.
instigation [ɛ̃stigɑsjɔ̃] *nf* instigation. ♦ **instigateur, -trice** *nm,f* instigator.
instinct [ɛ̃stɛ̃] *nm* (*gén*) instinct. **d'~** instinctively. ♦ **instinctif, -ive** *adj* instinctive. ♦ **instinctivement** *adv* instinctively.
instituer [ɛ̃stitɥe] (1) *vt* (*gén*) to institute.
institut [ɛ̃stity] *nm* institute. **~ de beauté** beauty salon; **I~ Universitaire de Technologie** ≃ Polytechnic; **~ médico-légal** mortuary.
instituteur, -trice [ɛ̃stitytœʀ, tʀis] *nm,f* (primary school) teacher.
institution [ɛ̃stitysjɔ̃] *nf* (*gén*) institution; (*école*) private school.
institutionnel, -elle [ɛ̃stitysjɔnɛl] *adj* institutional.
instructeur [ɛ̃stʀyktœʀ] *nm* instructor.
instructif, -ive [ɛ̃stʀyktif, iv] *adj* instructive.
instruction [ɛ̃stʀyksjɔ̃] *nf* **(a)** education. **~ civique** civics (*sg*); **~ militaire** army training; **~ religieuse** religious instruction; **avoir de l'~** to be well educated. **(b)** (*Jur*) investigation (*by juge d'instruction*). **(c)** (*Admin: circulaire*) directive. **(d) ~s** (*ordres*) instructions; (*mode d'emploi*) instructions, directions.
instruire [ɛ̃stʀɥiʀ] (38) **1** *vt* **(a)** (*gén*) to teach, educate; *recrue* to train. **instruit par son exemple** having learnt from his example. **(b) ~ qn de qch** to inform *ou* advise sb of sth. **(c)** (*Jur*) *affaire* to conduct the investigation for. **2 s'~** *vpr* to educate o.s. **s'~ de qch** to obtain information about sth, find out about sth. ♦ **instruit, e** *adj* educated.
instrument [ɛ̃stʀymɑ̃] *nm* (*lit, fig*) instrument. **~ de musique** musical instrument; **~s de travail** tools; (*fig*) **être l'~ de qn** to be sb's tool. ♦ **instrumental, e,** *mpl* **-aux** *adj* (*Ling, Mus*) instrumental. ♦ **instrumentation** *nf* instrumentation, orchestration. ♦ **instrumenter** (1) *vt* (*Mus*) to orchestrate. ♦ **instrumentiste** *nmf* instrumentalist.
insu [ɛ̃sy] *nm* **(a)** (*en cachette de*) **à l'~ de qn** without sb's knowledge, without sb's knowing. **(b)** (*inconsciemment*) **à mon ~** without my *ou* me knowing it.
insubmersible [ɛ̃sybmɛʀsibl(ə)] *adj* unsinkable.
insubordination [ɛ̃sybɔʀdinɑsjɔ̃] *nf* insubordination. ♦ **insubordonné, e** *adj* (*gén*) insubordinate.
insuccès [ɛ̃syksɛ] *nm* failure.
insuffisant, e [ɛ̃syfizɑ̃, ɑ̃t] *adj* (*en quantité*) insufficient; (*en qualité*) inadequate. **c'est ~** it's not enough; **il est ~ en math** he's not up to standard in maths; **en nombre ~** insufficient in number. ♦ **insuffisamment** *adv* insufficiently; inadequately. ♦ **insuffisance** *nf* insufficiency; inadequacy. **une ~ de personnel** a shortage of staff; **~s** (*faiblesses*) inadequacies; (*Méd*) insufficiency.
insuffler [ɛ̃syfle] (1) *vt* (*lit, fig*) to blow (*à, dans* into).
insulaire [ɛ̃sylɛʀ] **1** *adj population* island; *attitude* insular. **2** *nmf* islander.
insuline [ɛ̃sylin] *nf* insulin.
insulte [ɛ̃sylt(ə)] *nf* insult. **hurler des ~s** to shout insults *ou* abuse. ♦ **insultant, e** *adj* insulting (*pour* to). ♦ **insulter** (1) *vt* to insult.
insupportable [ɛ̃sypɔʀtabl(ə)] *adj* unbearable, insufferable.
insurger (s') [ɛ̃syʀʒe] (3) *vpr* (*lit, fig*) to rebel, revolt (*contre* against). ♦ **insurgé, e** *adj, nm,f* rebel, insurgent.
insurmontable [ɛ̃syʀmɔ̃tabl(ə)] *adj obstacle* insurmountable, insuperable; *dégoût* unconquerable.
insurrection [ɛ̃syʀɛksjɔ̃] *nf* insurrection, revolt. ♦ **insurrectionnel, -elle** *adj* insurrectionary.
intact, e [ɛ̃takt, akt(ə)] *adj* intact.
intangible [ɛ̃tɑ̃ʒibl(ə)] *adj* inviolable. ♦ **intangibilité** *nf* inviolability.
intarissable [ɛ̃taʀisabl(ə)] *adj* (*lit, fig*) inexhaustible. ♦ **intarissablement** *adv* inexhaustibly.
intégral, e, *mpl* **-aux** [ɛ̃tegʀal, o] **1** *adj* complete. **le remboursement ~ de qch** the repayment in full of sth; (*Ciné*) **version ~e** uncut version; (*Presse*) **texte ~** unabridged version. **2** *nf* (*Math*) integral; (*œuvre*) complete works. ♦ **intégralement** *adv* in full, fully. ♦ **intégralité** *nf* whole. **l'~ de la somme** the whole of the sum, the whole *ou* full sum; **dans son ~** in its entirety, in full.
intégrer [ɛ̃tegʀe] (6) **1** *vt* to integrate (*à, dans* into). **2** *vi* (*arg Univ*) **~ à** to get into. **3 s'~** *vpr* to become integrated (*à, dans* into). ♦ **intégration** *nf* integration (*à, dans* into). (*arg Univ*) **après son ~** after getting into the college.
intégrité [ɛ̃tegʀite] *nf* (*totalité*) integrity; (*honnêteté*) integrity, honesty, uprightness. ♦ **intègre** *adj* upright, honest.
intellect [ɛ̃telɛkt] *nm* intellect. ♦ **intellectuel, -elle 1** *adj* (*gén*) intellectual; *fatigue* mental; (*péj*) highbrow. **2** *nm,f* intellectual; (*péj*) highbrow. ♦ **intellectuellement** *adv* mentally; intellectually.
intelligence [ɛ̃teliʒɑ̃s] *nf* **(a)** (*aptitude*) intelligence. **avoir l'~ vive** to have a sharp *ou* quick mind; **les grandes ~s** great minds *ou* intellects. **(b)** (*compréhension*) **~ de** understanding of; **avoir l'~ des affaires** to have a good grasp *ou* understanding of business matters, have a good head for business. **(c)** (*complicité*) secret agreement. **agir d'~ avec qn** to act in (secret) agreement with sb; **signe d'~** sign of complicity; **vivre en bonne/mauvaise ~ avec qn** to be on good/bad terms with sb; **avoir des ~s dans la place** to have secret contacts in the place. ♦ **intelligent, e** *adj* (*gén*) intelligent; (*à l'esprit vif*) clever, bright. ♦ **intelligemment** *adv* intelligently; cleverly.
intelligible [ɛ̃teliʒibl(ə)] *adj* intelligible. **à haute et ~ voix** loudly and clearly. ♦ **intelligibilité** *nf* intelligibility. ♦ **intelligiblement** *adv* intelligibly.
intempérant, e [ɛ̃tɑ̃peʀɑ̃, ɑ̃t] *adj* intemperate. ♦ **intempérance** *nf* intemperance. **~s** excesses; **une telle ~ de langage** such excessive language.
intempéries [ɛ̃tɑ̃peʀi] *nfpl* bad weather.
intempestif, -ive [ɛ̃tɑ̃pɛstif, iv] *adj* (*gén*) untimely; *zèle* excessive. ♦ **intempestivement** *adv* at an untimely moment.
intemporel, -elle [ɛ̃tɑ̃pɔʀɛl] *adj* (*sans durée*) timeless; (*immatériel*) immaterial.
intenable [ɛ̃tnabl(ə)] *adj situation* intolerable, unbearable; *personne* unruly; *théorie* untenable.
intendance [ɛ̃tɑ̃dɑ̃s] *nf* (*Mil*) (*service*) Supply Corps; (*bureau*) Supplies office; (*Scol*) (*métier*) school management; (*bureau*) bursar's office. ♦ **intendant** *nm* (*Mil*) quartermaster; (*Scol*) bursar; (*régisseur*) steward. ♦ **intendante** *nf* (*Scol*) bursar; (*régisseur*) steward.
intense [ɛ̃tɑ̃s] *adj* (*gén*) intense; *circulation* dense, heavy. ♦ **intensément** *adv* intensely. ♦ **intensif, -ive** *adj* intensive. ♦ **intensification** *nf* intensification. ♦ **intensifier** *vt,* **s'~** *vpr* (7) to intensify. ♦ **intensité** *nf* intensity; density, heaviness. (*Ling*) **accent d'~** stress accent. ♦ **intensivement** *adv* intensively.
intenter [ɛ̃tɑ̃te] (1) *vt*: **~ un procès contre** *ou* **à qn** to start *ou* institute proceedings against sb.
intention [ɛ̃tɑ̃sjɔ̃] *nf* **(a)** intention. **agir dans une bonne ~** to act with good intentions; **c'est l'~ qui compte** it's the thought that counts; **à cette ~** with this intention, to this end; **avoir l'~ de faire** to intend *ou* mean to do, have the intention of doing. **(b) à l'~ de qn** *collecte* in aid of sb; *cadeau,*

messe for sb; **livre à l'~ des enfants** book aimed at children. ♦ **intentionné, e** *adj*: **bien ~** well-meaning, well-intentioned; **mal ~** ill-intentioned. ♦ **intentionnel, -elle** *adj* intentional. ♦ **intentionnellement** *adv* intentionally.

inter [ɛ̃tɛʀ] **1** *nm* (*Téléc*) = **interurbain**; (*Sport*) ~ **gauche/droit** inside-left/-right. **2** *préf* inter... . ~ **continental/ministériel/syndical** *etc* intercontinental/departmental/union *etc*; ~**allié** inter-Allied; **opération ~armes** combined arms operation; **tournoi ~scolaire** inter-schools tournament.

interaction [ɛ̃tɛʀaksjɔ̃] *nf* interaction.

intercaler [ɛ̃tɛʀkale] (1) **1** *vt mot* to insert; *feuillet* to inset, insert. ~ **quelques jours de repos dans un mois de stage** to fit a few days' break into a training month. **2 s'~** *vpr*: **s'~ entre** to come in between. ♦ **intercalaire** *adj*: **feuillet ~** inset, insert.

intercéder [ɛ̃tɛʀsede] (6) *vi* to intercede (*auprès de* with).

intercepter [ɛ̃tɛʀsɛpte] (1) *vt* to intercept. ♦ **interception** *nf* interception.

interchangeable [ɛ̃tɛʀʃɑ̃ʒabl(ə)] *adj* interchangeable.

interclasse [ɛ̃tɛʀklɑs] *nm* (*Scol*) break (*between classes*).

interdépendance [ɛ̃tɛʀdepɑ̃dɑ̃s] *nf* interdependence. ♦ **interdépendant, e** *adj* interdependent.

interdire [ɛ̃tɛʀdiʀ] (37) **1** *vt* **(a)** (*prohiber*) to forbid; (*Admin*) *stationnement etc* to prohibit, ban; *journal* to ban. **on a interdit les camions dans la ville** lorries have been banned from *ou* prohibited in the town. **(b)** *[difficulté]* to preclude, prevent; *[obstacle]* to block. **son état de santé lui interdit tout travail** his state of health does not allow *ou* permit him to do any work; **la gravité de la crise interdit tout espoir** the gravity of the crisis precludes all hope; **une porte interdisait le passage** a door blocked *ou* barred the way. **2 s'~** *vpr*: **s'~ toute remarque** to refrain *ou* abstain from making any remark; **s'~ la boisson** to abstain from drink *ou* drinking; **il s'interdit d'y penser** he doesn't allow himself to think about it. ♦ **interdiction** *nf* (*gén*) ban (*de* on). '**~ absolue de fumer**' 'smoking strictly prohibited'; '**~ de tourner à droite**' 'no right turn'; **~ de parler à quiconque** it is (strictly) forbidden to talk to anyone; **écriteau portant une ~** notice prohibiting *ou* forbidding sth. ♦ **interdit, e 1** *adj* **(a)** *livre* banned. **film ~ aux moins de 18/13 ans** ≈ X/A film; **stationnement ~** no parking; **il est strictement ~ de faire** it is strictly forbidden *ou* prohibited to do. **(b)** (*surpris*) dumbfounded, taken aback. **2** *nm* (*interdiction*) (*Rel*) interdict; (*social*) prohibition.

intéresser [ɛ̃teʀese] (1) **1** *vt* (*captiver*) to interest; (*concerner*) to affect, concern. ~ **qn à** *problème* to interest sb in; *bénéfices* to give sb a share *ou* an interest in; **ça pourrait vous ~** this might interest you *ou* be of interest to you; (*Fin*) **être intéressé dans une affaire** to have an interest *ou* a stake in a business. **2 s'~** *vpr*: **s'~ à qch/qn** to be interested in sth/sb, take an interest in sth/sb. ♦ **intéressant, e** *adj* (*captivant*) interesting; (*avantageux*) attractive, worthwhile. (*péj*) **un personnage peu ~** a worthless individual; **faire son ~** to show off. ♦ **intéressé, e** *adj* **(a)** (*en cause*) concerned, involved. **c'est lui le principal ~** he is the person *ou* party principally involved *ou* concerned. **(b)** (*égoïste*) *personne* self-interested; *motif* interested. **une visite ~e** a visit motivated by self-interest. ♦ **intéressement** *nm*: **l'~ des travailleurs aux bénéfices** the workers' sharing of the profits.

intérêt [ɛ̃teʀɛ] *nm* **(a)** (*attention*) interest. **porter de l'~ à qn** to take an interest in sb. **(b)** (*valeur*) *[livre]* interest; *[recherches, découverte]* significance, relevance. **dénué d'~** devoid of interest; **considérations sans ~** unimportant *ou* minor considerations; **c'est sans ~ pour la suite de l'histoire** it's of no relevance *ou* importance for the rest of the story. **(c)** (*avantage*) interest. **dans l'~ général** in the general interest; **il y trouve son ~** he finds it worth his while; **il sait où est son ~** he knows which side his bread is buttered; **il a ~ à accepter** it's in his interest to accept, he'd be well advised to accept; **y a-t-il un ~ quelconque à se réunir?** is there any point at all in getting together? **(d)** (*Fin, Écon*) interest. 7% **d'~** 7% interest; **prêter à ~** to lend at *ou* with interest; (*péj*) **agir par ~** to act out of self-interest; **il a des ~s dans l'affaire** he has a stake *ou* a financial interest in the business.

interférence [ɛ̃tɛʀfeʀɑ̃s] *nf* (*gén*) interference (*dans* in). **l'~ de ces problèmes** (*fusion*) the conjunction of these problems; (*immixtion*) the intrusion of these problems (*dans* into). ♦ **interférer** (6) *vi* to interfere (*avec* with, *dans* in).

intérieur, e [ɛ̃teʀjœʀ] **1** *adj* (*gén*) inner; *poche* inside; *paroi, angle* interior; *navigation, mer* inland; *marché* home; *politique*, (*Aviat*) *vol* domestic, internal. **2** *nm* **(a)** *[tiroir]* inside; *[maison]* inside, interior. **à l'~ (de la ville)** inside (the town); **à l'~ de lui-même** inwardly, within himself; **rester à l'~** (*gén*) to stay inside; (*de la maison*) to stay indoors; **veste d'~** indoor jacket; **chaussures d'~** house shoes. **(b)** *[pays]* interior. **les villes de l'~** the inland cities, the cities of the interior; **l'~ est sauvage** the hinterland is wild; **à l'~ de nos frontières** within *ou* inside our frontiers. **(c)** (*mobilier*) interior. **(d)** (*Ftbl*) ~ **gauche/droit** inside-left/-right. ♦ **intérieurement** *adv* inwardly. **rire ~** to laugh inwardly *ou* to o.s. ♦ **intérioriser** (1) *vt* to internalize, interiorize.

intérim [ɛ̃teʀim] *nm* (*période*) interim period. **il assure l'~ en l'absence du directeur** he deputizes for the manager in his absence *ou* in the interim; **ministre par ~** acting *ou* interim minister. ♦ **intérimaire 1** *adj directeur* acting, interim; *secrétaire* temporary; *mesure* interim; *gouvernement* caretaker. **2** *nmf* (*secrétaire*) temporary secretary, temp*; (*fonctionnaire*) deputy; (*médecin, prêtre*) locum (tenens).

interjection [ɛ̃tɛʀʒɛksjɔ̃] *nf* interjection.

interligne [ɛ̃tɛʀliɲ] *nm* space between the lines. **double ~** double spacing.

interlocuteur, -trice [ɛ̃tɛʀlɔkytœʀ, tʀis] *nm,f* speaker. **mon ~** the person I was speaking to; (*Pol*) **~ valable** authorized negotiator.

interlope [ɛ̃tɛʀlɔp] *adj* (*équivoque*) shady; (*illégal*) illicit, unlawful.

interloquer [ɛ̃tɛʀlɔke] (1) *vt* to take aback.

interlude [ɛ̃tɛʀlyd] *nm* (*Mus, TV*) interlude.

intermède [ɛ̃tɛʀmɛd] *nm* (*Théât, gén*) interlude.

intermédiaire [ɛ̃tɛʀmedjɛʀ] **1** *adj* intermediate, middle, intermediary. **une couleur ~ entre** a colour halfway between. **2** *nm*: **sans ~** *vendre* directly; **par l'~ de** *personne* through (the intermediary of); *presse* through the medium of. **3** *nmf* intermediary, go-between; (*Comm, Écon*) middleman.

interminable [ɛ̃tɛʀminabl(ə)] *adj* endless, interminable, never-ending. ♦ **interminablement** *adv* endlessly, interminably.

intermittent, e [ɛ̃tɛʀmitɑ̃, ɑ̃t] *adj* sporadic, intermittent. ♦ **intermittence** *nf*: **par ~** sporadically, intermittently.

international, e, *mpl* **-aux** [ɛ̃tɛʀnasjɔnal, o] **1** *adj* international. **2** *nm,f* (*Ftbl, Tennis etc*) international player.

interne [ɛ̃tɛʀn(ə)] **1** *adj* (*gén*) internal; *oreille* inner; *angle* interior. **2** *nmf* (*Scol*) boarder. (*Univ, Méd*) ~ **(des hôpitaux)** houseman, intern (*US*).

♦ **internat** *nm* (*Scol*) boarding school; (*Univ Méd*) (*stage*) ≈ period as a houseman *ou* an intern (*US*); (*concours*) entrance examination (for hospital work).

interner [ɛ̃tɛʀne] (1) *vt* (*Pol*) to intern; (*Méd*) to confine to a mental hospital. **on devrait l'~*** he ought to be certified*. ♦ **interné, e** *nm,f* internee; inmate (of a mental hospital). ♦ **internement** *nm* internment; confinement (to a mental hospital).

interpeller [ɛ̃tɛʀpele] (1) *vt* (*appeler*) to call out to, shout out to; (*apostropher*) to shout at; *orateur, malfaiteur* to question. ♦ **interpellation** *nf*: **il y a eu une dizaine d'~s** about ten people were taken in for questioning.

interphone [ɛ̃tɛʀfɔn] *nm* intercom.

interpoler [ɛ̃tɛʀpɔle] (1) *vt* to interpolate.

interposer [ɛ̃tɛʀpoze] (1) **1** *vt* (*lit, fig*) to interpose (*entre* between). **2 s'~** *vpr* to intervene.

interpréter [ɛ̃tɛʀpʀete] (6) *vt* **(a)** (*Mus, Théât, gén*) to perform, interpret; *personnage, sonate* to play; *chanson* to sing. **(b)** (*expliquer*) to interpret. **mal ~** to misinterpret. ♦ **interprétariat** *nm* interpreting. **école d'~** interpreting school. ♦ **interprétation** *nf* interpretation. ♦ **interprète** *nmf* **(a)** (*Mus, Théât*) performer, interpreter; singer. **(b)** (*traducteur*) interpreter. (*porte-parole*) **servir d'~ à qn/aux idées de qn** to act *ou* serve as a spokesman for sb/for sb's ideas.

interroger [ɛ̃teʀɔʒe] (3) **1** *vt* (*gén*) to question, ask (*sur* about); (*minutieusement*) to interrogate; *données, ciel* to examine; *mémoire* to search; *élève* to test, examine (orally). **~ qn du regard** to give sb a questioning *ou* an inquiring look. **2 s'~** *vpr* to question o.s. (*sur* about). **s'~ sur la conduite à tenir** to wonder what course to follow. ♦ **interrogateur, -trice 1** *adj air* questioning, inquiring. **2** *nm,f* (oral) examiner. ♦ **interrogatif, -ive** *adj, nm air,* (*Ling*) interrogative. ♦ **interrogation** *nf* **(a)** (*V* **interroger**) questioning; interrogation; examination; testing. **(b)** (*question*) question. (*Scol*) **~ (écrite)** (written) test; **~ (orale)** oral (test); (*Gram*) **~ directe/indirecte** direct/indirect question; (*réflexions*) **ses ~s** his questioning. ♦ **interrogatoire** *nm* (*Police*) questioning; (*au tribunal*) cross-examination; (*fig*) interrogation.

interrompre [ɛ̃tɛʀɔ̃pʀ(ə)] (41) **1** *vt voyage, études* to break off, interrupt; *grossesse* to terminate. **il a interrompu la conversation pour dire** he broke *ou* cut into the conversation to say; **~ qn** to interrupt sb; **je ne veux pas ~ mais ...** I don't want to cut in *ou* interrupt but ... . **2 s'~** *vpr [personne, conversation]* to break off. ♦ **interrupteur** *nm* (*Élec*) switch. ♦ **interruption** *nf* (*action*) interruption; (*état*) break, interruption. **~ de grossesse** termination of pregnancy; **sans ~** without a break; **un moment d'~** a moment's break.

intersection [ɛ̃tɛʀsɛksjɔ̃] *nf* intersection.

interstice [ɛ̃tɛʀstis] *nm* crack, chink, interstice.

interurbain, e [ɛ̃tɛʀyʀbɛ̃, ɛn] **1** *adj communication* long-distance. **2** *nm*: **l'~** the long-distance telephone service.

intervalle [ɛ̃tɛʀval] *nm* (*espace*) space; (*temps*) interval; (*Mus*) interval. **c'est arrivé à 2 jours d'~** it happened after an interval of 2 days; **dans l'~** (*temporel*) in the meantime, meanwhile; (*spatial*) in between.

intervenir [ɛ̃tɛʀvəniʀ] (22) *vi* **(a)** (*entrer en action*) to intervene. **on a dû faire ~ l'armée** the army had to be brought in. **(b)** (*Méd*) to operate. **(c)** *[événement]* to take place, occur; *[accord]* to be reached; *[décision]* to be taken; *[élément nouveau]* to arise, come up. ♦ **intervention** *nf* (*gén, Jur*) intervention; (*Méd*) operation. **prix d'~** intervention price.

intervertir [ɛ̃tɛʀvɛʀtiʀ] (2) *vt* to invert (the order of).

interview [ɛ̃tɛʀvju] *nf* (*Presse, TV*) interview. ♦ **interviewé, e** [ɛ̃tɛʀvjuve] *nm,f* interviewee. ♦ **interviewer**[1] [ɛ̃tɛʀvjuve] (1) *vt* to interview. ♦ **interviewer**[2] [ɛ̃tɛʀvjuvœʀ] *nm* interviewer.

intestin [ɛ̃tɛstɛ̃] *nm* intestine. **~s** intestines, bowels. ♦ **intestinal, e,** *mpl* **-aux** *adj* intestinal.

intime [ɛ̃tim] **1** *adj* **(a)** *vie* private; *confidences, hygiène* intimate; *cérémonie* quiet; *atmosphère* intimate, cosy. **journal ~** private diary; **être ~ avec qn** to be close to sb. **(b)** *mélange, conviction* intimate. **2** *nmf* close friend. ♦ **intimement** *adj* intimately. **~ persuadé** deeply *ou* firmly convinced.

intimer [ɛ̃time] (1) *vt* **(a) ~ à qn l'ordre de faire** to order sb to do. **(b)** (*Jur*) (*assigner*) to summon; (*signifier*) to notify.

intimider [ɛ̃timide] (1) *vt* to intimidate. ♦ **intimidable** *adj* easily intimidated. ♦ **intimidant, e** *adj* intimidating. ♦ **intimidateur, -trice** *adj* intimidating. ♦ **intimidation** *nf* intimidation.

intimité [ɛ̃timite] *nf* **(a)** (*vie privée*) privacy. **nous serons dans l'~** there will only be a few of us; **se marier dans l'~** to have a quiet wedding; **dans la plus stricte ~** in the strictest privacy; **pénétrer dans l'~ de qn** to be admitted into sb's private life; **vivre dans l'~ de qn** to be in close contact with sb. **(b)** (*familiarité*) intimacy. **dans l'~ conjugale** in the intimacy of one's married life. **(c)** (*confort*) cosiness, intimacy.

intituler [ɛ̃tityle] (1) **1** *vt* to entitle, call. **2 s'~** *vpr [livre]* to be entitled *ou* called; *[personne]* to call o.s. ♦ **intitulé** *nm* title.

intolérable [ɛ̃tɔleʀabl(ə)] *adj* intolerable. ♦ **intolérablement** *adv* intolerably.

intolérance [ɛ̃tɔleʀɑ̃s] *nf* intolerance. ♦ **intolérant, e** *adj* intolerant.

intonation [ɛ̃tɔnɑsjɔ̃] *nf* (*Ling, Mus*) intonation. **voix aux ~s douces** soft-toned voice.

intouchable [ɛ̃tuʃabl(ə)] *adj, nmf* untouchable.

intoxiquer [ɛ̃tɔksike] (1) **1** *vt* (*lit*) to poison; (*Pol*) to brainwash. **2 s'~** *vpr* to poison o.s. ♦ **intoxication** *nf* poisoning; brainwashing. **~ alimentaire** food poisoning. ♦ **intoxiqué, e** *nm,f* (*drogue*) drug addict; (*tabac*) smoking addict; (*alcool*) alcoholic.

intraduisible [ɛ̃tʀadɥizibl(ə)] *adj texte* untranslatable; *idée* inexpressible.

intraitable [ɛ̃tʀɛtabl(ə)] *adj* uncompromising, inflexible.

intramusculaire [ɛ̃tʀamyskylɛʀ] *adj* intramuscular.

intransigeant, e [ɛ̃tʀɑ̃ziʒɑ̃, ɑ̃t] *adj personne* uncompromising, intransigent; *morale* uncompromising. **les ~s** the intransigents. ♦ **intransigeance** *nf* intransigence.

intransitif, -ive [ɛ̃tʀɑ̃zitif, iv] *adj, nm* intransitive.

intransportable [ɛ̃tʀɑ̃spɔʀtabl(ə)] *adj objet* untransportable; *malade* unfit to travel.

intraveineux, -euse [ɛ̃tʀavenø, øz] **1** *adj* intravenous. **2** *nf* intravenous injection.

intrépide [ɛ̃tʀepid] *adj* (*courageux*) intrepid, dauntless; *menteur* barefaced, unashamed. ♦ **intrépidité** *nf* intrepidity, dauntlessness.

intriguer [ɛ̃tʀige] (1) **1** *vt* to intrigue, puzzle. **2** *vi* to scheme, intrigue. ♦ **intrigant, e 1** *adj* scheming. **2** *nm,f* schemer, intriguer. ♦ **intrigue** *nf* (*manœuvre*) intrigue, scheme; (*liaison*) (love) affair, intrigue; (*Théât*) plot.

intrinsèque [ɛ̃tʀɛ̃sɛk] *adj* intrinsic. ♦ **intrinsèquement** *adv* intrinsically.

introduire [ɛ̃tʀɔdɥiʀ] (38) **1** *vt* (*gén*) to introduce (*dans* into, *auprès de* to); *visiteur* to show in; *idées nouvelles* to bring in. **il introduisit sa clef dans la serrure** he placed his key in the lock, he inserted his key into the lock; **on m'introduisit dans le salon** I was shown into *ou* ushered into the lounge;

~ **des marchandises en contrebande** to smuggle in goods. **2 s'~** *vpr* **(a)** (*pénétrer*) to get in. **s'~ dans un groupe** to work one's way into a group; **s'~ chez qn par effraction** to break into sb's home; **s'~ dans une pièce** to get into *ou* enter a room. **(b)** *[usage]* to be introduced (*dans* into). ♦ **introduction** *nf* introduction. **chapitre d'~** introductory chapter; **lettre d'~** letter of introduction.

introuvable [ɛ̃tʀuvabl(ə)] *adj* which (*ou* who) cannot be found.

intrus, e [ɛ̃tʀy, yz] *nm,f* intruder. ♦ **intrusion** *nf* (*gén*) intrusion (*dans* in).

intuition [ɛ̃tɥisjɔ̃] *nf* intuition. ♦ **intuitif, -ive** *adj* intuitive. ♦ **intuitivement** *adv* intuitively.

inusable [inyzabl(ə)] *adj* *vêtement* hard-wearing.

inusité, e [inyzite] *adj* uncommon.

inutile [inytil] *adj* (*qui ne sert pas*) useless; (*superflu*) needless, unnecessary. **c'est ~ d'insister!** it's no use *ou* no good insisting!, there's no point insisting!; ~ **de vous dire que** I hardly need say that. ♦ **inutilement** *adv* needlessly, unnecessarily. ♦ **inutilité** *nf* uselessness; needlessness.

inutilisable [inytilizabl(ə)] *adj* unusable.

inutilisé, e [inytilize] *adj* unused.

invaincu, e [ɛ̃vɛ̃ky] *adj* unconquered; (*Sport*) unbeaten.

invalide [ɛ̃valid] **1** *nmf* disabled person. ~ **de guerre** disabled ex-serviceman; ~ **du travail** industrially disabled person. **2** *adj* (*Méd*) disabled. ♦ **invalidité** *nf* disablement.

invalider [ɛ̃valide] (1) *vt* (*Jur*) to invalidate; *député* to remove from office. ♦ **invalidation** *nf* invalidation; removal (from office).

invariable [ɛ̃vaʀjabl(ə)] *adj* invariable. ♦ **invariablement** *adv* invariably. ♦ **invariant, e** *adj, nm* invariant.

invasion [ɛ̃vɑzjɔ̃] *nf* invasion.

invective [ɛ̃vɛktiv] *nf* invective. **~s** abuse, invectives. ♦ **invectiver** (1) **1** *vt* to hurl *ou* shout abuse at. **s'~** to hurl *ou* shout abuse at each other. **2** *vi* to inveigh, rail (*contre* against).

invendable [ɛ̃vɑ̃dabl(ə)] *adj* (*gén*) unsaleable; (*Comm*) unmarketable.

invendu, e [ɛ̃vɑ̃dy] **1** *adj* unsold. **2** *nm* unsold article.

inventaire [ɛ̃vɑ̃tɛʀ] *nm* (*gén, Jur*) inventory; (*Comm*) (*liste*) stocklist; (*opération*) stocktaking; (*fig: recensement*) survey. (*fig*) **faire l'~ de** to assess, take stock of.

inventer [ɛ̃vɑ̃te] (1) *vt* (*gén*) to invent; *moyen* to devise; *mot* to coin; *jeu* to make *ou* think up. **il n'a pas inventé la poudre** he'll never set the Thames on fire; **je n'invente rien** I'm not making anything up, I'm not inventing a thing. ♦ **inventeur, -trice** *nm,f* inventor. ♦ **inventif, -ive** *adj* resourceful, inventive. ♦ **invention** *nf* (*gén*) invention. **esprit d'~** inventiveness; **c'est une pure ~** it is a pure invention *ou* fabrication; **un cocktail de mon ~** a cocktail of my own creation.

invérifiable [ɛ̃veʀifjabl(ə)] *adj* unverifiable.

inverse [ɛ̃vɛʀs(ə)] **1** *adj* (*gén*) opposite. **arriver en sens ~** to arrive from the opposite direction; **dans l'ordre ~** in the reverse order. **2** *nm*: **l'~** (*gén*) the opposite, the reverse; **t'a-t-il attaqué ou l'~?** did he attack you or was it the other way round?; **à l'~** conversely. ♦ **inversé, e** *adj* *image* reversed; *relief* inverted. ♦ **inversement** *adv* (*gén*) conversely; (*Math*) inversely. **... et ~** ... and vice versa. ♦ **inverser** (1) *vt* *ordre* to reverse, invert; (*Élec*) to reverse. ♦ **inversion** *nf* (*gén*) inversion; (*Élec*) reversal.

invertébré, e [ɛ̃vɛʀtebʀe] *adj, nm* invertebrate.

investigation [ɛ̃vɛstigɑsjɔ̃] *nf* investigation. **après de minutieuses ~s** after a detailed investigation *ou* inspection.

investir [ɛ̃vɛstiʀ] (2) *vt* (*Fin, Mil*) to invest; *fonctionnaire* to induct; *évêque* to invest. **~ qn de pouvoirs** to invest *ou* vest sb with powers; **~ qn de sa confiance** to place one's trust in sb. ♦ **investissement** *nm* (*Écon*) investment; (*Mil*) investing. ♦ **investiture** *nf* *[candidat]* nomination, appointment; *[évêché]* investiture.

invétéré, e [ɛ̃veteʀe] *adj* inveterate.

invincible [ɛ̃vɛ̃sibl(ə)] *adj* (*gén*) invincible; *timidité* insurmountable. ♦ **invincibilité** *nf* invincibility.

inviolable [ɛ̃vjɔlabl(ə)] *adj* *droit* inviolable; *serrure* impregnable; *diplomate* immune.

invisible [ɛ̃vizibl(ə)] **1** *adj* (*impossible à voir*) invisible; (*minuscule*) barely visible (*à* to); (*Écon*) invisible. **danger ~** unseen *ou* hidden danger; **M. X est ~** (*occupé*) Mr X cannot be seen; (*disparu*) Mr X isn't to be found. **2** *nm*: **l'~** the invisible. ♦ **invisibilité** *nf* invisibility.

inviter [ɛ̃vite] (1) *vt* (*gén*) to invite (*à* to). **~ qn à dîner** to invite *ou* ask sb to *ou* for dinner; **il s'est invité** he invited himself; **il m'invita à avancer** he motioned (to) me to come forward; **ceci invite à croire que ...** this leads us to believe that ...; **la chaleur invitait au repos** the heat tempted one to rest. ♦ **invitation** *nf* invitation (*à* to). **à *ou* sur son ~** at his invitation. ♦ **invité, e** *nm,f* guest.

invivable [ɛ̃vivabl(ə)] *adj* unbearable.

invocation [ɛ̃vɔkɑsjɔ̃] *nf* invocation (*à* to).

involontaire [ɛ̃vɔlɔ̃tɛʀ] *adj* *mouvement* involuntary; *peine* unintentional; *complice* unwitting. ♦ **involontairement** *adv* involuntarily; unintentionally; unwittingly.

invoquer [ɛ̃vɔke] (1) *vt* **(a)** *excuse* to put forward; *témoignage* to call upon; *ignorance* to plead; *loi* to cite, refer to. **(b)** *Dieu* to invoke, call upon.

invraisemblable [ɛ̃vʀɛsɑ̃blabl(ə)] *adj* *nouvelle* unlikely, improbable; *argument* implausible; *insolence, habit* incredible. ♦ **invraisemblance** *nf* unlikelihood, improbability; implausibility. **plein d'~s** full of improbabilities *ou* implausibilities.

invulnérable [ɛ̃vylneʀabl(ə)] *adj* invulnerable (*à* to). ♦ **invulnérabilité** *nf* invulnerability.

iode [jɔd] *nm* iodine.

ion [jɔ̃] *nm* ion. ♦ **ionisation** *nf* ionization. ♦ **ioniser** (1) *vt* to ionize.

Irak [iʀak] *nm* Iraq. ♦ **irakien, -ienne** *adj, nm,* **I~(ne)** *nm(f)* Iraqi.

Iran [iʀɑ̃] *nm* Iran. ♦ **iranien, -ienne** *adj, nm,* **I~(ne)** *nm(f)* Iranian.

irascible [iʀasibl(ə)] *adj* irascible. ♦ **irascibilité** *nf* irascibility.

iris [iʀis] *nm* (*gén*) iris.

Irlande [iʀlɑ̃d] *nf*: **l'~** (*pays*) Ireland; (*État*) the Irish Republic; **l'~ du Nord** Northern Ireland, Ulster. ♦ **irlandais, e** **1** *adj* Irish. **2** *nm* **(a)** (*Ling*) Irish. **(b)** **I~** Irishman; **les I~** the Irish. **3** *nf*: **I~e** Irishwoman.

ironie [iʀɔni] *nf* irony. ♦ **ironique** *adj* ironic(al). ♦ **ironiquement** *adv* ironically. ♦ **ironiser** (1) *vi* to be ironic(al) (*sur* about).

irradier [iʀadje] (7) **1** *vt* to irradiate. **2** *vi* to radiate.

irraisonné, e [iʀɛzɔne] *adj* irrational.

irrationnel, -elle [iʀasjɔnɛl] *adj* (*gén, Math*) irrational. ♦ **irrationalité** *nf* irrationality.

irréalisable [iʀealizabl(ə)] *adj* *but* unrealizable, unachievable; *projet* unworkable.

irrecevable [iʀəsvabl(ə)] *adj* *témoignage* inadmissible; *demande* unacceptable.

irréconciliable [iʀekɔ̃siljabl(ə)] *adj* irreconcilable.

irrécupérable [iʀekypeʀabl(ə)] *adj* *argent* irretrievable; *ferraille* unreclaimable; *voiture* beyond repair; *personne* irredeemable.

irrécusable [iʀekyzabl(ə)] *adj* *témoin* unimpeachable; *preuve* indisputable.

irréductible [iʀedyktibl(ə)] *adj* (*gén, Sci*) irreducible; *obstacle* insurmountable; *ennemi*

implacable. ♦ **irréductiblement** *adv* implacably.
irréel, -elle [iʀeɛl] *adj* unreal.
irréfléchi, e [iʀefleʃi] *adj action* thoughtless, unconsidered; *personne* unthinking. ♦ **irréflexion** *nf* thoughtlessness.
irréfutable [iʀefytabl(ə)] *adj* irrefutable. ♦ **irréfutabilité** *nf* irrefutability.
irrégulier, -ière [iʀegylje, jɛʀ] *adj* (*gén*) irregular; *terrain, travail* uneven; *vent* fitful; *élève, athlète* erratic; *homme d'affaires* dubious. ♦ **irrégularité** *nf* irregularity. ♦ **irrégulièrement** *adv* irregularly; unevenly; fitfully; erratically; dubiously.
irrémédiable [iʀemedjabl(ə)] *adj perte* irreparable; *mal* incurable, irremediable. **essayer d'éviter l'~** to try to avoid reaching the point of no return. ♦ **irrémédiablement** *adv* irreparably; incurably, irremediably.
irremplaçable [iʀɑ̃plasabl(ə)] *adj* irreplaceable.
irréparable [iʀepaʀabl(ə)] *adj* (*lit, fig*) irreparable. **la voiture est ~** the car is beyond repair *ou* is a write-off.
irrépressible [iʀepʀesibl(ə)] *adj* irrepressible.
irréprochable [iʀepʀɔʃabl(ə)] *adj conduite* irreproachable; *tenue* impeccable.
irrésistible [iʀezistibl(ə)] *adj* (*gén*) irresistible. **il est ~!** (*amusant*) he's hilarious! ♦ **irrésistiblement** *adv* irresistibly.
irrésolu, e [iʀezɔly] *adj personne* irresolute, indecisive. ♦ **irrésolution** *nf* irresoluteness, indecisiveness.
irrespectueux, -euse [iʀɛspɛktɥø, øz] *adj* disrespectful (*envers* to, towards).
irrespirable [iʀɛspiʀabl(ə)] *adj* (*lit*) unbreathable; (*étouffant*) oppressive, stifling; (*dangereux*) unsafe, unhealthy.
irresponsable [iʀɛspɔ̃sabl(ə)] *adj* irresponsible. ♦ **irresponsabilité** *nf* irresponsibility.
irrévérencieux, -euse [iʀeveʀɑ̃sjø, øz] *adj* irreverent. ♦ **irrévérence** *nf* (*caractère*) irreverence; (*propos*) irreverent word.
irréversible [iʀevɛʀsibl(ə)] *adj* irreversible.
irrévocable [iʀevɔkabl(ə)] *adj* (*gén*) irrevocable. ♦ **irrévocablement** *adv* irrevocably.
irriguer [iʀige] (1) *vt* (*Agr, Méd*) to irrigate. ♦ **irrigation** *nf* irrigation.
irriter [iʀite] (1) **1** *vt* **(a)** (*agacer*) to irritate, annoy. **(b)** *peau* to irritate. **2 s'~** *vpr*: **s'~ de qch/contre qn** to feel irritated *ou* annoyed at sth/with sb. ♦ **irritabilité** *nf* irritability. ♦ **irritable** *adj* irritable. ♦ **irritant, e 1** *adj* irritating, annoying; (*Méd*) irritant. **2** *nm* irritant. ♦ **irritation** *nf* (*colère*) irritation, annoyance; (*Méd*) irritation.
irruption [iʀypsjɔ̃] *nf* irruption. **faire ~ (chez qn)** to burst in (on sb).
Islam [islam] *nm*: **l'~** Islam. ♦ **islamique** *adj* Islamic.
Islande [islɑ̃d] *nf* Iceland. ♦ **islandais, e 1** *adj, nm* Icelandic. **2** *nm(f)*: **I~(e)** Icelander.
isocèle [izɔsɛl] *adj* isoceles.
isoler [izɔle] (1) **1** *vt* (*gén*) to isolate; (*Élec*) to insulate; (*contre le bruit*) to soundproof. **ville isolée du reste du monde** town cut off from the rest of the world. **2 s'~** *vpr* (*gén*) to isolate o.s. **ils s'isolèrent quelques instants** they stood aside for a few seconds. ♦ **isolant, e 1** *adj* (*gén*) insulating; (*insonorisant*) soundproofing. **2** *nm* insulator. ♦ **isolation** *nf* insulation. **~ phonique** soundproofing. ♦ **isolationnisme** *nm* isolationism. ♦ **isolationniste** *adj, nmf* isolationist. ♦ **isolé, e 1** *adj* (*gén*) isolated; *lieu* lonely, remote. **tireur ~** lone sniper. **2** *nm,f* (*théoricien*) loner; (*personne délaissée*) lonely person. ♦ **isolement** *nm* (*gén*) isolation; *[personne délaissée, maison]* loneliness; (*Élec*) insulation. ♦ **isolément** *adv* in isolation, individually, separately. ♦ **isoloir** *nm* polling booth.
isorel [izɔʀɛl] *nm* ® hardboard.
isotherme [izɔtɛʀm(ə)] *adj* isothermal. **camion ~** refrigerated lorry.
isotope [izɔtɔp] **1** *adj* isotopic. **2** *nm* isotope.
Israël [isʀaɛl] *nm* Israel. ♦ **israélien, -ienne** *adj*, **I~(ne)** *nm(f)* Israeli. ♦ **israélite 1** *adj* Jewish. **2** *nm*: **I~** (*gén*) Jew; (*Hist*) Israelite. **3** *nf*: **I~** Jewess; Israelite.
issu, e¹ [isy] *adj*: **être ~ de** (*résulter de*) to stem from; (*être né de*) to be descended from.
issue² [isy] *nf* **(a)** (*sortie*) exit; *[vapeur]* outlet. **voie sans ~** (*lit, fig*) dead end; (*panneau*) 'no through road'; **~ de secours** emergency exit; (*fig*) **se ménager une ~** to leave o.s. a way out. **(b)** (*solution*) way out. **la situation est sans ~** there is no way out of *ou* no solution to the situation; **un avenir sans ~** a future without prospects. **(c)** (*fin*) outcome. **~ fatale** fatal outcome; **à l'~ de** at the conclusion *ou* close of.
isthme [ism(ə)] *nm* (*Anat, Géog*) isthmus.
Italie [itali] *nf* Italy. ♦ **italien, -ienne** *adj, nm*, **I~(ne)** *nm(f)* Italian.
italique [italik] *nm* (*Typ*) italics. **mettre un mot en ~(s)** to put a word in italics, italicize a word.
itinéraire [itineʀɛʀ] *nm* (*chemin*) route, itinerary; (*intellectuel*) itinerary.
itinérant, e [itineʀɑ̃, ɑ̃t] *adj* itinerant. **ambassadeur ~** roving ambassador.
ivoire [ivwaʀ] *nm* ivory.
ivre [ivʀ(ə)] *adj* (*lit*) drunk. **~ de colère/de joie** wild *ou* beside o.s. with anger/joy; **~ mort** dead *ou* blind drunk. ♦ **ivresse** *nf* drunkenness. **l'~ de la victoire** the exhilaration of victory; **l'~ du plaisir** the (wild) ecstasy of pleasure; **avec ~** rapturously, ecstatically. ♦ **ivrogne** *nmf* drunkard. ♦ **ivrognerie** *nf* drunkenness.

J

J, j [ʒi] *nm* (*lettre*) J, j.

j' [ʒ(ə)] *V* **je.**

jabot [ʒabo] *nm* (*Zool*) crop; (*Habillement*) jabot.

jacasser [ʒakase] (1) *vi* (*gén*) to chatter. ♦ **jacassement** *nm*: **~(s)** chatter.

jachère [ʒaʃɛʀ] *nf*: **mettre une terre en ~** to leave a piece of land fallow; **rester en ~** to lie fallow.

jacinthe [ʒasɛ̃t] *nf* hyacinth. **~ des bois** bluebell.

Jacques [ʒak] *nm*: **faire le ~*** to play *ou* act the fool.

jade [ʒad] *nm* (*pierre*) jade; (*objet*) jade object.

jadis [ʒadis] **1** *adv* formerly, long ago. **mes amis de ~** my friends of long ago. **2** *adj*: **dans le temps ~** in days of old.

jaguar [ʒagwaʀ] *nm* (*Zool*) jaguar.

jaillir [ʒajiʀ] (2) *vi [liquide]* to spurt out, gush forth; *[larmes]* to flow; *[flammes]* to shoot up; *[étincelles]* to fly out; *[lumière]* to flash; *[cris]* to burst out; *[idée, vérité]* to spring (*de* from). **il jaillit dans la pièce** he burst into the room. ♦ **jaillissement** *nm [liquide]* spurt, gush.

jais [ʒɛ] *nm* (*Minér*) jet; (*couleur*) jet black.

jalon [ʒalɔ̃] *nm* (*lit*) ranging-pole; (*fig*) step. (*fig*) **poser les premiers ~s de qch** to prepare the ground for sth. ♦ **jalonner** (1) *vt* (*pour construire*) to mark out *ou* off; (*border, s'espacer sur*) to line. **carrière jalonnée de succès** career punctuated with successes.

jaloux, -ouse [ʒalu, uz] *adj* (*gén*) jealous. **faire des ~** to make people jealous. ♦ **jalousement** *adv* jealously. ♦ **jalouser** (1) *vt* to be jealous of. ♦ **jalousie** *nf* **(a)** (*sentiment*) jealousy. **être malade de ~** to be green with envy. **(b)** (*persienne*) venetian blind, jalousie.

Jamaïque [ʒamaik] *nf* Jamaica. ♦ **jamaïquain, e** *adj*, **J~(e)** *nm(f)* Jamaican.

jamais [ʒamɛ] *adv* **(a)** (*négatif*) never. **il ne lui a ~ plus écrit** he never wrote to her again, he has never written to her since; **il partit pour ne ~ plus revenir** he departed never to return; **nous sommes restés 2 ans sans ~ recevoir de nouvelles** we went for 2 years without ever hearing any news; **ça ne fait ~ que 2 heures qu'il est parti** it's no more than 2 hours since he left; ce **n'est ~ qu'un enfant** he is only *ou* but a child (after all); **~, au grand ~!, ~ de la vie!** never!; **~ plus!** never again!; **presque ~** hardly ever, practically never; **c'est le moment ou ~** it's now or never; **~ deux sans trois!** there's always a third time! **(b)** (*temps indéfini*) ever. **si ~ j'avais un poste pour vous je vous préviendrais** if I ever had a job for you I'd let you know; **si ~ tu rates le train, reviens** if by any chance you miss *ou* if you should happen to miss the train come back; les **œufs sont plus chers que ~** eggs are dearer than ever; **à tout ~** for ever (and ever).

jambe [ʒɑ̃b] *nf* leg. **~ de pantalon** trouser leg; **~ de bois** wooden leg; (*Constr*) **~ de force** strut; **avoir les ~s comme du coton** to have legs like jelly *ou* cotton wool; (*fig*) **n'avoir plus de ~s** to be worn out; **traîner la ~** to limp along; **elle ne peut plus se tenir sur ses ~s** she can hardly stand; **prendre ses ~s à son cou** to take to one's heels; **faire qch par dessous *ou* par dessus la ~*** to do sth in a slipshod way; **tenir la ~ à qn*** to detain sb; **elle est toujours dans mes ~s*** she's always getting in my way.

jambon [ʒɑ̃bɔ̃] *nm* ham. **~ fumé** smoked ham, gammon; **~ blanc *ou* de Paris** boiled ham. ♦ **jambonneau,** *pl* **~x** *nm* knuckle of ham.

jante [ʒɑ̃t] *nf [charrette]* felly; *[voiture, vélo]* rim.

janvier [ʒɑ̃vje] *nm* January; *V* **septembre.**

Japon [ʒapɔ̃] *nm* Japan. ♦ **japonais, e** *adj, nm*, **J~(e)** *nm(f)* Japanese.

japper [ʒape] (1) *vi* to yap, yelp. ♦ **jappement** *nm* yap, yelp.

jaquette [ʒakɛt] *nf [homme]* morning coat; *[livre]* (dust) jacket.

jardin [ʒaʀdɛ̃] *nm* garden. **siège de ~** garden seat; **~ d'agrément** pleasure garden; **~ botanique** botanical garden(s); **~ d'enfants** nursery school, kindergarten; **~ potager** vegetable garden; **~ public** (public) park, public gardens. ♦ **jardinage** *nm* gardening. ♦ **jardiner** (1) *vi* to garden, do some gardening. ♦ **jardinier, -ière 1** *adj* garden. **2** *nm,f* gardener. **3** *nf* **(a)** (*caisse à fleurs*) window box. **(b)** **~ière (de légumes)** mixed vegetables, jardiniere. **(c)** **~ière d'enfants** nursery school *ou* kindergarten teacher.

jargon [ʒaʀgɔ̃] *nm* (*baragouin*) gibberish, double Dutch*; (*professionnel*) jargon. **~ administratif** officialese, official jargon; **~ de métier** trade jargon *ou* slang.

jarret [ʒaʀɛ] *nm [homme]* back of the knee, ham; *[animal]* hock. (*Culin*) **~ de veau** knuckle of veal.

jarretelle [ʒaʀtɛl] *nf* suspender, garter (*US*).

jarretière [ʒaʀtjɛʀ] *nf* garter.

jars [ʒaʀ] *nm* gander.

jaser [ʒaze] (1) *vi [enfant]* to chatter, prattle; *[oiseau]* to twitter; *[ruisseau]* to babble; (*arg Police*) to talk; *[personne]* (*parler*) to chat; (*médire*) to gossip. **cela va faire ~ les gens** that'll set tongues wagging.

jasmin [ʒasmɛ̃] *nm* jasmine.

jauge [ʒoʒ] *nf* **(a)** (*compteur*) gauge; (*règle graduée*) dipstick. **(b)** (*capacité*) *[réservoir]* capacity; *[navire]* tonnage, burden. ♦ **jauger** (3) **1** *vt réservoir* to gauge the capacity of; *navire* to measure the tonnage of; *personne* to size up. **il le jaugea du regard** he gave him an appraising look. **2** *vi* to have a capacity of. **navire qui jauge 500 tonneaux** ship of 500 tonnes *ou* tons burden.

jaune [ʒon] **1** *adj* yellow. **~ d'or** golden yellow; **~ paille** straw-coloured. **2** *nm* **(a)** **J~** Asiatic, Asian; **les J~s** the yellow races. **(b)** (*couleur*) yellow. **(c)** **~ (d'œuf)** (egg) yolk. **(d)** (*péj: non gréviste*) blackleg, scab‡. **3** *nf* **(a)** **J~** Asiatic *ou* Asian woman. **(b)** (*péj*) blackleg, scab‡. ♦ **jaunâtre** *adj* yellowish. ♦ **jaunir** (2) *vti* to turn yellow. ♦ **jaunisse** *nf* (*Méd*) jaundice. **en faire une ~*** (*de dépit*) to be pretty miffed*; (*de jalousie*) to be *ou* turn green with envy.

java [ʒava] *nf* (*danse*) popular waltz. (*fig*) **faire la ~‡** to live it up*, have a rave-up‡.

javelliser [ʒavelize] (1) *vt* to chlorinate.

javelot [ʒavlo] *nm* (*Mil, Sport*) javelin.

jazz [dʒaz] *nm* jazz.

je, j' [ʒ(ə)] *pron pers* I. **elle a un je ne sais quoi qui attire** there's (a certain) something about her that is very attractive; **son je-m'en-fichisme*** his (I-)couldn't-care-less attitude*.

jean [dʒin] *nm* (pair of) jeans.
jeep [ʒip] *nf* jeep.
jérémiades* [ʒeʀemjad] *nfpl* moaning, whining.
jerrycan [ʒeʀikan] *nm* jerry can.
jersey [ʒɛʀzɛ] **1** *nm* (*tissu*) jersey (cloth). **point de ~** stocking stitch. **2: J~** *nf* Jersey.
jésuite [ʒezɥit] *nm, adj* Jesuit.
jésus [ʒezy] *nm* **(a) J~** Jesus; **J~ Christ** Jesus Christ; **en 300 avant/après J~ Christ** in 300 B.C./A.D. **(b)** (*statue*) statue of the infant Jesus. (*terme d'affection*) **mon ~** (my) darling.
jet¹ [ʒɛ] *nm* **(a)** *[eau etc]* jet; *[sang]* spurt; *[salive]* stream; *[lumière]* beam. **(b)** *[pierre]* (*action*) throwing; (*résultat*) throw. **à un ~ de pierre** at a stone's throw. **(c) premier ~** first sketch; **écrire d'un (seul) ~** to write in one go*; **à ~ continu** in a continuous *ou* an endless stream; **~ d'eau** (*fontaine*) fountain; (*gerbe*) spray.
jet² [dʒɛt] *nm* (*Aviat*) jet.
jetée [ʒ(ə)te] *nf* jetty; (*grande*) pier.
jeter [ʒ(ə)te] (4) **1** *vt* **(a)** (*lancer*) to throw; (*avec force*) to fling, hurl; (*au rebut*) to throw away *ou* out. (*: *mettre rapidement*) **~ une veste sur ses épaules** to slip a jacket over one's shoulders; **~ une idée sur le papier** to jot down an idea; **~ qch à qn** (*pour qu'il l'attrape*) to throw sth to sb; (*agressivement*) to throw sth at sb; **~ qch par terre/par la fenêtre** to throw sth on the ground/out of the window; **~ qch à la poubelle** to throw sth in the dustbin; **jette l'eau sale dans l'évier** pour the dirty water down the sink; **~ dehors** *visiteur* to throw out; *employé* to sack. **(b)** (*construire*) *pont* to throw (*sur* over); *fondations* to lay. **(c)** *lueur* to give, give out, cast, shed; *cri* to give, utter, let out; *regard* to cast. **~ un coup d'œil sur qch** (*rapidement*) to glance at sth; (*pour surveiller*) to take a look at sth; **le diamant jette mille feux** the diamond sparkles brilliantly. **(d)** (*dans le désespoir*) to plunge; (*dans l'embarras*) to throw (*dans* into). **ça me jette hors de moi** it drives me frantic *ou* wild. **(e)** *discrédit, sort* to cast. **~ le trouble chez qn** to disturb *ou* trouble sb; **sa remarque a jeté un froid** his remark cast a chill. **(f)** (*dire*) to say (*à* to); *insultes* to hurl (*à* at). **il me jeta en passant que c'était commencé** he mentioned to me as he went by that it had begun. **(g)** (*locutions*) **~ son dévolu sur qch/qn** to set one's heart on sth/sb; **~ du lest** (*lit*) to dump ballast; (*fig*) to sacrifice sth, make concessions; **on va s'en ~ un derrière la cravate‡** we'll have a quick one*; **~ l'argent par les fenêtres** to spend money like water; **~ sa gourme** to sow one's wild oats; **~ le manche après la cognée** to throw in one's hand; **~ de la poudre aux yeux de qn** to impress sb.
2 se ~ *vpr* **(a) se ~ par la fenêtre/à genoux** to throw o.s. out of the window/down on one's knees; **se ~ sur qn** to launch o.s. at sb, rush at sb; **se ~ sur sa proie** to pounce on one's prey; **sa voiture s'est jetée contre un arbre** his car crashed into a tree; **se ~ à l'eau** (*lit*) to plunge into the water; (*fig*) to take the plunge; **se ~ à corps perdu dans une entreprise** to throw o.s. wholeheartedly into an enterprise. **(b)** *[rivière]* to flow (*dans* into).
jeton [ʒ(ə)tɔ̃] *nm* **(a)** (*pièce*) (*gén*) token; (*Jeu*) counter; (*Roulette*) chip. **~ de téléphone** telephone token; **~ (de présence)** (*argent*) director's fees. **(b)** (‡) (*coup*) biff*. **avoir les ~s** to have the jitters*.
jeu, *pl* ~x [ʒø] **1** *nm* **(a)** (*gén avec règles*) game. **~ d'adresse/de hasard** game of skill/chance; **~ de société** parlour game; **~-concours** competition; **~ télévisé** (*avec questions*) television quiz; **~ de patience** jigsaw puzzle. **(b)** (*Sport*) (*partie*) game. (*Tennis*) **mener par 5 ~x à 2** to lead by 5 games to 2; **hors ~** (*Tennis*) out (of play); (*Ftbl*) off-side; **remettre en ~** to throw in; **remise en ~** throw-in. **(c)** (*série*) *[pions, clefs]* set. **~ de construction** building set; **~ de cartes** pack of cards. **(d)** (*lieu*) **~ de boules** bowling ground; **~ de quilles** skittle alley. **(e)** (*Cartes: main*) hand. **avoir du ~** to have a good hand; (*fig*) **cacher son ~** to conceal one's hand. **(f)** (*façon de jouer*) (*Sport*) game; (*Théât*) acting. **il a un ~ rapide** (*Sport*) he plays a swift game; (*Mus*) he plays quickly; **j'observais son petit ~** I watched his little game. **(g) le ~** (*amusement*) play; (*Casino*) gambling; **le ~ est nécessaire à l'homme** play is necessary to man, man needs to play. **(h)** (*fonctionnement*) *[institutions]* working, interplay; (*Tech*) play. **donner du ~ à qch** to give a bit of play to sth, loosen sth up a bit; **il y a du ~** it's a bit loose, there's a bit of play. **(i)** (*locutions*) **le ~ n'en vaut pas la chandelle** the game is not worth the candle; **il a beau ~ de protester maintenant** it's easy for him to complain now; **les forces en ~** the forces at work; **ce qui est en ~** what is at stake; **mettre/entrer en ~** to bring/come into play; **faire le ~ de qn** to play into sb's hands; **faire ~ égal avec qn** to be evenly matched (against sb); **c'est un ~ d'enfant** it's child's play; **par ~** for fun; **être pris à son propre ~** to be caught out at one's own game.
2: (*Comm*) **~ d'écritures** dummy entry; **~ de massacre** (*à la foire*) Aunt Sally; (*fig*) wholesale slaughter; **~ de mots** play on words, pun; **~ de l'oie** ≃ snakes and ladders; **J~x Olympiques** Olympic games; **J~x Olympiques d'hiver** Winter Olympics.
jeudi [ʒødi] *nm* Thursday. **le ~ de l'Ascension** Ascension Day; **le ~ saint** Maundy Thursday; *V* **samedi.**
jeun [ʒœ̃] *adv*: **être à ~** to have eaten (*ou* drunk) nothing; (*pas ivre*) to be sober; (*Méd*) **à prendre à ~** to be taken on an empty stomach.
jeune [ʒœn] **1** *adj* **(a)** (*gén*) young; *apparence* youthful; *industrie* new. **dans mon ~ âge** in my younger days, in my youth; **il n'est plus tout ~** he's not as young as he was; **il est plus ~ que moi de 5 ans** he's 5 years younger than me, he's 5 years my junior; **s'habiller ~** to dress young for one's age; **être ~ d'allure** to be young-looking, be youthful in appearance; **être ~ de caractère** (*puéril*) to be childish; (*dynamique*) to have a youthful outlook. **(b)** (*inexpérimenté*) inexperienced, green*. **être ~ dans le métier** to be new *ou* a newcomer to the trade. **(c)** (*cadet*) junior. **mon ~ frère** my younger brother; **mon plus ~ frère** my youngest brother; **Durand ~** Durand junior. **(d)** (*: *insuffisant*) short, skimpy. **c'est un peu ~** *[temps]* it's cutting it a bit short *ou* fine; *[argent]* it's a bit on the short side, it's pretty tight*.
2 *nm* youth, young man. **les ~s** young people; **club de ~s** youth club.
3 *nf* girl.
4: ~ chien puppy; **~ femme** young woman; **~ fille** girl; **la ~ génération** the younger generation; **~s gens** young people; **~ homme** young man; **~ marié** bridegroom; **~ mariée** bride; **les ~s mariés** the newly-weds; (*Théât*) **~ premier** leading man; **~ première** leading lady.
jeûne [ʒøn] *nm* fast. ♦ **jeûner** (1) *vi* (*gén*) to go without food; (*Rel*) to fast.
jeunesse [ʒœnɛs] *nf* **(a)** (*gén*) youth; *[apparence, esprit]* youthfulness; *[vin]* youngness. **dans ma ~** in my youth, in my younger days; **erreur de ~** youthful mistake; **il faut que ~ se passe** youth must have its fling; **la ~ de son visage** his youthful face. **(b)** (*personnes*) **la ~** young people; **la ~ des écoles** young people at school; **les ~s communistes** the Communist Youth Movement.
joaillerie [ʒɔɑjʀi] *nf* (*commerce*) jeweller's trade; (*marchandise*) jewellery; (*magasin*) jeweller's (shop). ♦ **joaillier, -ière** *nm,f* jeweller.
jobard, e‡ [ʒɔbaʀ, aʀd(ə)] **1** *adj* gullible. **2** *nm,f* (*dupe*) sucker*, mug*.
jockey [ʒɔkɛ] *nm* jockey.

joie [ʒwa] *nf* joy. **à ma grande ~** to my great joy *ou* delight; **être au comble de la ~** to be overjoyed; **quand aurons-nous la ~ de vous revoir?** when shall we have the pleasure of seeing you again?; **les ~s du mariage** the joys of marriage; **être plein de ~ de vivre** to be full of the joys of life; **faire la ~ de qn** to delight sb, give great pleasure to sb; **il se faisait une telle ~ d'y aller** he was so looking forward to going; **je me ferai une ~ de le faire** I shall be delighted *ou* only too pleased to do it.

joindre [ʒwɛ̃dʀ(ə)] (49) **1** *vt* **(a)** (*gén*) to join (*à* to); *objets* to put together; *villes* to link (*à* with); *efforts* to combine. **les talons joints** with one's heels together; **~ l'utile à l'agréable** to combine work with pleasure; **~ le geste à la parole** to suit the action to the word; (*fig*) **~ les deux bouts*** to make (both) ends meet. **(b)** (*inclure*) *timbre, chèque etc* to enclose (*à* with). **les avantages joints à ce poste** the advantages attached to this post; **carte jointe à un cadeau** card attached to a gift. **(c)** (*communiquer avec*) *personne* to get in touch with, contact. **2** *vi [fenêtre, porte]* to shut, close; *[planches etc]* to join. **3 se ~** *vpr* **(a)** (*s'unir à*) **se ~ à** *groupe* to join; **se ~ à la foule** to mingle *ou* mix with the crowd; **se ~ à la discussion** to join in the discussion. **(b)** *[mains]* to join.

♦ **joint** *nm* **(a)** (*articulation*) joint; (*ligne de jonction*) join; (*en ciment, mastic*) pointing. **~ de robinet** washer; **~ de cardan** cardan joint; **~ de culasse** cylinder head gasket. **(b)** (*arg Drogue*) joint (*arg*). **(c) faire le ~*** *[personne]* to last *ou* hold out; *[argent]* to bridge the gap; **trouver le ~*** to come up with the answer. ♦ **jointure** *nf* joint; join. **faire craquer ses ~s** to crack one's knuckles.

joker [ʒɔkɛʀ] *nm* (*Cartes*) joker.

joli, e [ʒɔli] *adj* **(a)** (*gén*) nice; *femme* pretty; *vue* attractive. **~ comme un cœur** pretty as a picture; **il est ~ garçon** he is (quite) good-looking. **(b)** (*) *profit, résultat* nice, good. **ça fait une ~e somme** it's a tidy *ou* handsome sum of money. **(c)** (*iro: déplaisant*) fine (*iro*), nice (*iro*). **un ~ gâchis** a fine mess; **un ~ monsieur** a nasty character. **(d)** (*locutions*) **tout ça c'est bien ~ mais** that's all very well but; **le plus ~ (de l'histoire) c'est que** the best bit of it all is that; **vous avez fait du ~!** you've made a fine mess of things!; **faire le ~ cœur** to play the ladykiller; **ce n'est pas ~ de mentir** it's not nice to tell lies; **elle est ~e, votre idée!** that's a nice *ou* great* idea! ♦ **joliment** *adv* nicely; attractively; prettily. **il était ~ en retard*** he was pretty* late.

jonc [ʒɔ̃] *nm* (*plante*) bulrush; (*canne*) cane, rattan.

joncher [ʒɔ̃ʃe] (1) *vt*: **~ qch de** to strew sth with.

jonction [ʒɔ̃ksjɔ̃] *nf* junction. **point de ~** junction, meeting point.

jongler [ʒɔ̃gle] (1) *vi* (*lit, fig*) to juggle (*avec* with). ♦ **jonglerie** *nf* jugglery, juggling. ♦ **jongleur, -euse** *nm,f* juggler; (*Hist*) jongleur.

jonque [ʒɔ̃k] *nf* (*Naut*) junk.

jonquille [ʒɔ̃kij] *nf* daffodil, jonquil.

Jordanie [ʒɔʀdani] *nf* Jordan. ♦ **jordanien, -ienne** *adj*, **J~(ne)** *nm(f)* Jordanian.

joue [ʒu] *nf* **(a)** (*Anat*) cheek. **~ contre ~** cheek to cheek. **(b)** (*Mil*) **en ~!** take aim!; **mettre en ~** *cible* to aim at; *fusil* to aim.

jouer [ʒwe] (1) **1** *vi* **(a)** to play (*avec* with). **~ à la poupée/aux soldats/aux cartes/à courir** to play with one's dolls/(at) soldiers/cards/at running; (*fig*) **~ avec** *son crayon, une idée* to toy with; *sa santé* to gamble with; (*fig*) **on ne joue pas avec ces choses-là** matters like these are not to be treated lightly; **~ au chat et à la souris avec qn** to play cat and mouse with sb; **~ avec** *ou* **contre X aux échecs** to play X at chess; **~ au héros** to play the hero. **(b)** (*Mus*) to play. **~ du piano** to play the piano. **(c)** (*Casino*) to gamble. **~ à la Bourse** to speculate *ou* gamble on the Stock Exchange; **~ à la roulette** to play roulette; **~ aux courses** to bet on the horses; **ils ont joué sur la surprise** they were banking *ou* relying on the element of surprise. **(d)** (*Théât*) to act. **elle joue bien** she is a good actress, she acts well; **on joue à guichets fermés** the performance is fully booked *ou* is booked out. **(e)** (*fonctionner*) to work. **faire ~ un ressort** to activate *ou* trigger a spring. **(f)** (*joindre mal*) to fit loosely, be loose; *[bois]* (*travailler*) to warp. **(g)** (*intervenir*) *[facteur]* to matter, count. **cette mesure joue pour tout le monde** this measure applies to everybody; **ça a joué en ma faveur** it worked in my favour; **il a fait ~ ses appuis politiques** he made use of his political connections. **(h)** (*locutions*) **~ sur les mots** to play with words; **faire qch pour ~** to do sth for fun; **~ serré** to play a close game; **~ perdant/gagnant** to play a losing/winning game; **~ au plus fin** to try to outsmart sb; **~ de malheur** to be dogged by ill luck; (*lit, fig*) **à vous de ~!** your go! *ou* turn!; (*Échecs*) your move!; **bien joué!** well done!; **~ avec le feu** to play with fire.

2 *vt* **(a)** (*Théât*) *rôle* to play, act; (*représenter*) *film* to put on, show. **on joue 'Macbeth' ce soir** 'Macbeth' is on this evening; (*fig*) **~ un rôle** to play a part; (*fig*) **~ la comédie** to put on an act; (*fig*) **le drame s'est joué très rapidement** the tragedy happened very quickly. **(b)** (*simuler*) **~ les victimes** to play the victim; **~ la surprise** to affect *ou* feign surprise. **(c)** (*Mus, Sport*) to play; *pion* to play, move. **~ atout** to play trumps. **(d)** *argent* (*Casino*) to stake, wager; (*Courses*) to bet, stake (*sur* on); *cheval* to back, bet on; *réputation* to wager. **~ les consommations** to play for drinks. **(e)** (*littér: tromper*) *personne* to deceive. **(f)** (*locutions*) **il faut ~ le jeu** you've got to play the game; **~ franc jeu** to play fair; **~ un double jeu** to play a double game; **~ son va-tout** to stake one's all; **~ un tour à qn** to play a trick on sb; **~ sa dernière carte** to play one's last card.

3 ~ de *vt indir couteau, influence* to use, make use of. **~ des jambes*** to run away, take to one's heels; **~ des coudes pour entrer** to elbow one's way in; **il joue de sa maladie pour ne rien faire** he plays on his illness to get out of doing anything.

4 se ~ *vpr* (*littér*) **se ~ de qn** to deceive sb; **se ~ des difficultés** to make light of the difficulties; **il a réussi cet examen comme en se jouant** that exam was a walkover for him*.

♦ **jouet** *nm* toy, plaything. **être le ~ d'une illusion** to be the victim of an illusion. ♦ **joueur, -euse** *nm,f* player; (*Casino*) gambler. **~ de golf** golfer; **être beau/mauvais ~** to be a good/bad loser; *[enfant]* **il est très ~** he's very playful.

joufflu, e [ʒufly] *adj enfant* chubby-cheeked; *visage* chubby.

joug [ʒu] *nm* **(a)** (*Agr, fig*) yoke. **sous le ~** under the yoke. **(b)** *[balance]* beam.

jouir [ʒwiʀ] (2) **1 ~ de** *vt indir* (*gén, Jur*) to enjoy. **~ de toutes ses facultés** to be in full possession of one's faculties. **2** *vi* (‡) (*plaisir*) to have a great time*. ♦ **jouissance** *nf* **(a)** (*volupté*) pleasure. **(b)** (*Jur: usage*) use, enjoyment.

joujou*, *pl* **~x** [ʒuʒu] *nm* toy. **faire ~** to play (*avec* with).

jour [ʒuʀ] **1** *nm* **(a)** (*lumière*) day(light); (*période*) day(-time). **il fait ~** it is daylight; **je fais ça le ~** I do it during the day *ou* in the daytime; **voyager de ~** to travel by day; **se lever avant le ~** to get up before dawn *ou* daybreak; **avoir le ~ dans les yeux** to have the light in one's eyes; **c'est le ~ et la nuit!** there's absolutely no comparison! **(b)** (*espace de temps*) day. **d'un ~** *célébrité, joie* short-lived, fleeting; **c'est à 2 ~s de marche de ...** it is a 2 days' walk from ...; **dans 2 ~s** in 2 days' time, in 2 days; **un de ces ~s** one of these days; **à**

un de ces ~s! see you again sometime!, be seeing you!*; **le ~ d'avant** the day before, the previous day; **le ~ d'après** the day after, the next day, the following day; **le ~ de Pâques** Easter Day; (*iro*) **c'est mon ~!** it's just not my day today!; **ce n'est vraiment pas le ~!** you (*ou* we *etc*) have picked the wrong day!; **le goût du ~** the style of the day; **un œuf du ~** an egg laid today. **(c)** (*indéterminé*) **la fuite des ~s** the swift passage of time; **mettre fin à ses ~s** to put an end to one's life; **nous gardons cela pour nos vieux ~s/pour les mauvais ~s** we're keeping that for our old age/for a rainy day *ou* for hard times. **(d)** (*éclairage: lit, fig*) light. **jeter un ~ nouveau sur** to throw (a) new light on; **se présenter sous un ~ favorable** *[projet]* to look promising; *[personne]* to show o.s. in a favourable light; **nous le voyons sous son véritable ~** we see him in his true colours. **(e)** (*ouverture*) *[mur, haie]* gap. (*Couture*) **~s** hemstitching. **(f)** (*locutions*) **donner le ~ à** to give birth to; **voir le ~** to be born; **mettre au ~** (*révéler*) to bring to light; **se faire ~** to become clear; **vivre au ~ le ~** to live from day to day; **être/mettre à ~** to be/bring up to date; **mise à ~** updating; **un ~ ou l'autre** sooner or later; **du ~ au lendemain** overnight; **chose de tous les ~s** everyday *ou* ordinary thing; **de nos ~s** these days, nowadays; **il y a 2 ans ~ pour ~** 2 years ago to the day.

2: le ~ de l'An New Year's day; **~ de congé** day off, holiday; **~ férié** public holiday; **~ de fête** feastday, holiday; **le ~ J** D-day; **le ~ des Morts** All Souls' Day; **~ ouvrable** weekday; **le ~ des Rois** Epiphany, Twelfth Night; **le ~ du Seigneur** Sunday; **~ de sortie** day off; **~ de travail** working day.

journal, *pl* **-aux** [ʒuʀnal, o] *nm* **(a)** (*Presse*) (news)paper; (*magazine*) magazine; (*bulletin*) journal. **(b)** (*intime*) diary, journal; (*Rad*) news. **~ de bord** ship's log; **~ pour enfants** children's comic *ou* paper; (*TV*) **~ télévisé** television news.

journalier, -ière [ʒuʀnalje, jɛʀ] *adj* (*de chaque jour*) daily; (*banal*) everyday, humdrum. **c'est ~** it happens every day.

journalisme [ʒuʀnalism(ə)] *nm* journalism. ♦ **journaliste** *nmf* journalist. ♦ **journalistique** *adj* journalistic.

journée [ʒuʀne] *nf* **(a)** day. **pendant la ~** during the day; **dans la ~ d'hier** yesterday, in the course of yesterday. **(b)** *[ouvrier]* **~ (de travail)** day's work; **~ (de salaire)** day's wages *ou* pay; **faire de dures ~s** to put in a heavy day's work; **être payé à la ~** to be paid by the day; **faire la ~ continue** to work over lunch; **la ~ de 8 heures** the 8-hour day; **~ de repos** day off.

journellement [ʒuʀnɛlmɑ̃] *adv* (*quotidiennement*) daily; (*souvent*) every day.

joute [ʒut] *nf* (*Hist, fig*) joust. **~s nautiques** water tournament. ♦ **jouter** (1) *vi* (*Hist, fig*) to joust (*contre* against).

jouvenceau, *pl* **~x** [ʒuvɑ̃so] *nm* (†, *hum*) stripling†. ♦ **jouvencelle** *nf* (†, *hum*) damsel (†).

jouxter [ʒukste] (1) *vt* to adjoin, be next to.

jovial, e, *mpl* **-aux** *ou* **~s** [ʒɔvjal, o] *adj* jovial, jolly. ♦ **jovialement** *adv* jovially. ♦ **jovialité** *nf* joviality, jollity.

joyau, *pl* **~x** [ʒwajo] *nm* (*lit, fig*) gem, jewel.

joyeux, -euse [ʒwajø, øz] *adj* (*gén*) joyful; *groupe* merry; *repas* cheerful. **un ~ luron** a jolly fellow; **il était tout ~ à l'idée de partir** he was overjoyed at the idea of going; **~ Noël!** merry *ou* happy Christmas!; **~euse fête!** many happy returns! ♦ **joyeusement** *adv* joyfully; merrily; cheerfully.

jubilé [ʒybile] *nm* jubilee.

jubiler* [ʒybile] (1) *vi* to be jubilant. ♦ **jubilation** *nf* jubilation.

jucher *vt*, **se ~** *vpr* [ʒyʃe] (1) to perch (*sur* on).

judaïque [ʒydaik] *adj loi* Judaic; *religion* Jewish. ♦ **judaïsme** *nm* Judaism. ♦ **judéo-** *préf* Judeo-.

judiciaire [ʒydisjɛʀ] *adj* judicial. **poursuites ~s** judicial *ou* legal proceedings.

judicieux, -euse [ʒydisjø, øz] *adj* judicious. ♦ **judicieusement** *adv* judiciously.

judo [ʒydo] *nm* judo. ♦ **judoka** *nmf* judoka.

juge [ʒyʒ] **1** *nm* (*gén*) judge. **oui, Monsieur le J~** yes, your Honour; **le ~ X** Mr Justice X; **être à la fois ~ et partie** to be both judge and judged; **je vous fais ~** I'll let you be the judge; **il est seul ~ en la matière** he is the only one who can judge. **2: ~-arbitre** referee; **~ d'instruction** examining judge *ou* magistrate; **~ de paix** justice of the peace, magistrate; **~ de touche** linesman.

jugé [ʒyʒe] *nm*: **au ~** by guesswork; **tirer au ~** to fire blind.

jugement [ʒyʒmɑ̃] *nm* **(a)** (*Jur*) *[criminel]* sentence; *[civil]* decision, award. **rendre un ~** to pass sentence; **passer en ~** to stand trial; **poursuivre qn en ~** to sue sb, take legal proceedings against sb; **~ par défaut** judgment by default. **(b)** (*opinion*) judgment, opinion. **porter un ~ sur** to pass judgment on; **~ préconçu** prejudgment. **(c)** (*discernement*) judgment. **manquer de ~** to lack judgment. **(d)** (*Rel*) judgment.

jugeote* [ʒyʒɔt] *nf* gumption*.

juger [ʒyʒe] (3) **1** *vt* **(a)** *affaire* to judge, try; *accusé* to try (*pour* for); *différend* to arbitrate in. **le jury a jugé qu'il n'était pas coupable** the jury found him not guilty; **l'affaire doit se ~ à l'automne** the case is to be heard in the autumn. **(b)** (*décider*) to judge. **à vous de ~** it's up to you to decide *ou* to judge. **(c)** (*apprécier*) to judge. **il ne faut pas ~ d'après les apparences** you must not judge *ou* go by appearances; **jugez combien j'étais surpris** imagine how surprised I was. **(d)** (*estimer*) **~ qch/qn ridicule** to consider *ou* find sth/sb ridiculous; **~ que** to think *ou* consider that; **~ mal qn** to think badly of sb; **~ bon de faire** to consider it a good thing *ou* advisable to do; **il se juge capable de le faire** he thinks *ou* reckons he can do it. **2 ~ de** *vt indir* to appreciate, judge. **si j'en juge par mon expérience** judging by my experience; **autant que je puisse en ~** as far as I can judge. **3** *nm* = **jugé.**

juguler [ʒygyle] (1) *vt maladie* to arrest; *envie* to suppress; *inflation* to curb; *révolte* to put down.

juif, juive [ʒɥif, ʒɥiv] **1** *adj* Jewish. **2** *nm*: **J~** Jew. **3** *nf*: **Juive** Jewess.

juillet [ʒɥijɛ] *nm* July; *V* **septembre.**

juin [ʒɥɛ̃] *nm* June; *V* **septembre.**

jumeau, -elle, *mpl* **~x** [ʒymo, ɛl] **1** *adj* (*gén*) twin. **mon frère ~** my twin brother; **maisons ~elles** semidetached houses. **2** *nm,f* (*personne*) twin; (*sosie*) double. **3** *nf*: **~elle(s)** binoculars; **~elles de théâtre** opera glasses. ♦ **jumelage** *nm* twinning. ♦ **jumelé, e** *adj colonnes* twin; *roues, billets* double. ♦ **jumeler** (4) *vt villes* to twin; *efforts* to join.

jument [ʒymɑ̃] *nf* mare.

jungle [ʒɔ̃gl(ə)] *nf* (*lit, fig*) jungle.

junior [ʒynjɔʀ] *adj, nmf* junior.

junte [ʒœ̃t] *nf* junta.

jupe [ʒyp] *nf* skirt. (*fig*) **être toujours dans les ~s de sa mère** to cling to one's mother's apron strings. ♦ **jupon** *nm* waist petticoat *ou* slip. **courir le ~** to chase anything in a skirt.

jurer [ʒyʀe] (1) **1** *vt* to swear. **~ fidélité à qn** to swear *ou* pledge loyalty to sb; **~ la perte de qn** to swear to ruin sb; **faire ~ à qn de garder le secret** to swear *ou* pledge sb to secrecy; **il jurait ses grands dieux qu'il n'avait rien fait** he swore blind* *ou* to heaven that he hadn't done anything; **ah! je vous jure!** honestly!; **on ne jure plus que par lui** everyone swears by him. **2 ~ de** *vt indir* to swear to. **j'en jurerais** I'd swear to it; **il ne faut ~ de rien** you never can tell. **3** *vi* **(a)** (*pester*) to swear, curse. **(b)** *[couleurs]* to clash, jar; *[propos]*

to jar. **4 se** ~ *vpr*: **se** ~ **qch** (*à soi-même*) to vow sth (to o.s.); (*l'un à l'autre*) to pledge *ou* swear *ou* vow sth to each other. ♦ **juré, e 1** *adj* sworn. **2** *nm,f* juror, juryman (*ou* woman). **les** ~**s** the members of the jury.

juridiction [ʒyridiksjɔ̃] *nf* (*compétence*) jurisdiction; (*tribunal*) court(s) of law.

juridique [ʒyridik] *adj* legal. ♦ **juridiquement** *adv* legally.

juriste [ʒyrist(ə)] *nm [compagnie]* lawyer; (*auteur*) jurist.

juron [ʒyrɔ̃] *nm* oath, swearword. **dire des** ~**s** to swear, curse.

jury [ʒyri] *nm* (*Jur*) jury; (*Art, Sport*) panel of judges; (*Scol*) board of examiners.

jus [ʒy] *nm* **(a)** (*liquide*) juice. ~ **de fruit** fruit juice; ~ **de viande** gravy. **(b)** (*) (*café*) coffee; (*courant*) juice*; (*eau*) water. **au** ~! coffee's ready!; **tomber dans le** ~ to fall into the water.

jusant [ʒyzɑ̃] *nm* ebb tide.

jusque [ʒysk(ə)] **1** *prép* **(a)** (*lieu*) **jusqu'à là, jusqu'au** to; **j'ai couru jusqu'à la maison** I ran all the *ou* right the way home; **j'ai marché jusqu'au village** I walked to *ou* as far as the village; **jusqu'où?** how far?; **il avait de la neige jusqu'aux genoux** he was knee-deep in snow; **la nouvelle est venue jusqu'à moi** the news has reached me; **en avoir** ~**-là*** to be fed up*; **s'en mettre** ~**-là*** to stuff o.s.* **(b)** (*temps*) **jusqu'à, jusqu'en** until, till, up to; **jusqu'à quand?** until when?, how long?; **jusqu'à présent** until now, so far; **jusqu'au bout** to the end; **du matin jusqu'au soir** from morning till night; **jusqu'à 5 ans** until *ou* up to the age of 5. **(c)** (*limite*) up to. **jusqu'à 20 kg** up to 20 kg, not exceeding 20 kg; **pousser l'indulgence jusqu'à la faiblesse** to carry indulgence to the point of weakness; **aller jusqu'à dire/faire** to go so far as to say/do; **tu vois jusqu'à quel point tu t'es trompé** you see how wrong you were. **(d)** (*y compris*) even. **ils ont regardé** ~ **sous le lit** they even looked under the bed; **tous jusqu'au dernier** every single one of them. **2** *adv*: ~ **et y compris** up to and including; **jusqu'à** (*même*) even; **tout jusqu'au paysage avait changé** even the landscape had changed. **3** *conj*: **jusqu'à ce que** until.

juste [ʒyst(ə)] **1** *adj* **(a)** (*légitime*) just; (*équitable*) just, fair; *colère* righteous, justifiable. **pour être** ~ **envers lui** in fairness to him, to be fair to him; **les** ~**s** (*gén*) the just; (*Rel*) the righteous; **à** ~ **titre** with just cause *ou* reason; ~ **ciel!**† heavens above! **(b)** *calcul, réponse* right; *raisonnement* sound; *remarque* apt; *appareil* accurate; *oreille* good; *note de musique, voix* true; *piano* well-tuned. **à l'heure** ~ right on time; **à 6 heures** ~**s** on the stroke of 6; **apprécier qch à son** ~ **prix** to appreciate the true worth of sth; **le** ~ **milieu** the happy medium; **très** ~**!** quite right! **(c)** (*trop court*) *vêtement* tight; (*longueur*) on the short side. (*quantité*) **1 kg pour 6, c'est un peu** ~ 1 kg for 6 people - it's barely enough *ou* it's a bit on the short side; **elle n'a pas raté son train mais c'était** ~ she didn't miss her train but it was a close thing.

2 *adv* **(a)** *compter, viser* accurately; *raisonner* soundly; *deviner* rightly; *chanter* in tune. **tomber** ~ (*deviner*) to hit the nail on the head; **la pendule va** ~ the clock is keeping good time. **(b)** (*exactement*) just, exactly. ~ **au-dessus** just above; **3 kg** ~ 3 kg exactly. **(c)** (*seulement*) only, just. **il est parti il y a** ~ **un moment** he left just *ou* only a moment ago. **(d) (un peu)** ~ *prévoir* not quite enough, too little; **il a mesuré trop** ~ he cut it a bit too fine. **(e)** (*locutions*) **que veut-il au** ~**?** what exactly does he want?; **au plus** ~ **prix** at the minimum price; **comme de** ~ of course; **tout** ~ (*seulement*) only just; (*à peine*) hardly, barely; (*exactement*) exactly.

justement [ʒystəmɑ̃] *adv* **(a)** (*précisément*) just, precisely. **on parlait** ~ **de vous** we were just talking about you. **(b)** *remarquer* rightly, justly, soundly. ~ **puni** justly punished; ~ **fier** justifiably proud.

justesse [ʒystɛs] *nf* (*gén*) accuracy; *[raisonnement]* soundness; *[remarque]* aptness. **de** ~ *gagner* by a narrow margin, narrowly; *s'en tirer* by the skin of one's teeth, narrowly.

justice [ʒystis] *nf* **(a)** (*gén*) justice. **rendre la** ~ to dispense justice; **rendre** ~ **à qn** to do sb justice; **rendre** ~ **au talent de qn** to give fair recognition to sb's talent; **on doit lui rendre cette** ~ **que** it must be said in fairness to him that; **ce n'est que** ~ it's only fair; **se faire** ~ (*se venger*) to take the law into one's own hands; (*se suicider*) to take one's life. **(b)** (*tribunal*) court; (*autorités*) law. **la** ~ **le recherche** he is wanted by the law; ~ **administrative** administrative law; **passer en** ~ to stand trial; **aller en** ~ to take the case to court. ♦ **justiciable** *adj*: ~ **de** subject to. ♦ **justicier, -ière** *nm,f* (*gén*) upholder of the law.

justifier [ʒystifje] (7) **1** *vt* (*gén*) to justify. **ça justifie mon point de vue** it bears out *ou* vindicates my opinion. **2** ~ **de** *vt indir* to prove. **3 se** ~ *vpr* to justify o.s. **se** ~ **d'une accusation** to clear o.s. of an accusation. ♦ **justifiable** *adj* justifiable. ♦ **justificatif, -ive** *adj* justificatory. **pièce** ~**ive** written proof *ou* evidence. ♦ **justification** *nf* (*explication*) justification; (*preuve*) proof.

jute [ʒyt] *nm* jute.

juteux, -euse [ʒytø, øz] *adj fruit* juicy.

juvénile [ʒyvenil] *adj allure* youthful.

juxtaposer [ʒykstapoze] (1) *vt* to juxtapose. ♦ **juxtaposition** *nf* juxtaposition.

K

K, k [ka] *nm* (*lettre*) K, k.
kaki [kaki] **1** *adj* khaki. **2** *nm* **(a)** (*couleur*) khaki. **(b)** (*Agr*) persimmon.
kaléidoscope [kaleidɔskɔp] *nm* kaleidoscope.
kamikaze [kamikaze] *nm* kamikaze.
kangourou [kɑ̃guʀu] *nm* kangaroo.
kaolin [kaɔlɛ̃] *nm* kaolin.
kapok [kapɔk] *nm* kapok.
karaté [kaʀate] *nm* karate.
kayak [kajak] *nm* (*eskimo*) kayak; (*Sport*) canoe, kayak. **faire du ~** to go canoeing.
képi [kepi] *nm* kepi.
kermesse [kɛʀmɛs] *nf* fair; (*de charité*) bazaar, fête. (*fig*) **c'est une vraie ~ là-dedans*** it's absolute bedlam in there.
kérosène [keʀozɛn] *nm* kerosene, (aviation) fuel.
kidnapper [kidnape] (1) *vt* to kidnap. ♦ **kidnappeur, -euse** *nm,f* kidnapper.
kif [kif] *nm* **(a)** (*Drogue*) kef, kif. **(b)** (*) **c'est du ~, c'est ~-~** it's all the same, it makes no odds*.
kilo [kilo] **1** *nm* kilo. **2** *préf* kilo.... ♦ **kilogramme** *nm* kilogramme. ♦ **kilométrage** *nm* ≈ *[voiture]* mileage. ♦ **kilomètre** *nm* kilometre. ♦ **kilowatt** *nm* kilowatt. **~-heure** *nm* kilowatt-hour.
kimono [kimɔno] *nm* kimono.
kinésithérapeute [kineziteʀapøt] *nmf* physiotherapist. ♦ **kinésithérapie** *nf* physiotherapy.
kiosque [kjɔsk(ə)] *nm [journaux etc]* kiosk, stall; *[jardin]* pavilion. **~ à musique** bandstand.
kirsch [kiʀʃ] *nm* kirsch.
kiwi [kiwi] *nm* kiwi.
klaxon [klaksɔn] *nm* ® (*Aut*) horn. ♦ **klaxonner** (1) *vi* to hoot (one's horn), sound one's horn.
kleptomane [klɛptɔman] *adj, nmf* kleptomaniac. ♦ **kleptomanie** *nf* kleptomania.
knock-out [nɔkawt] (*Boxe*, ‡) **1** *adj* knocked out. **mettre qn ~** to knock sb out. **2** *nm* knock-out.
koala [kɔala] *nm* koala (bear).
krach [kʀak] *nm* (*Bourse*) crash.
kyrielle [kiʀjɛl] *nf [réclamations, personnes]* stream; *[objets]* pile.
kyste [kist(ə)] *nm* cyst.

L

L, l [ɛl] *nm ou nf* (*lettre*) L, l.
l' [l(ə)] *V* **le¹, le².**
la¹ [la] *V* **le¹, le².**
la² [la] *nm inv* (*note*) A; (*chanté*) la. **donner le ~** (*lit*) to give an A; (*fig*) to set the tone.
là [la] **1** *adv* **(a)** (*espace*) there. **c'est ~ où** *ou* **que je suis né** that's where I was born; **c'est à 3 km de ~** it's 3 km away (from there); **quelque part par ~** somewhere around there; **passez par ~** go that way; **M X n'est pas ~** Mr X isn't there *ou* in; **qu'est-ce que tu fais ~?** (*lit*) what are you doing here?; (*fig: manigancer*) what are you up to? **(b)** (*temps*) then. **c'est ~ qu'il comprit** that was when he realized, it was then that he realized; **à partir de ~** from then on, after that; **à quelques jours de ~** a few days later. **(c)** (*situation*) that. **il faut en rester ~** we'll have to leave it at that; **la situation en est ~** that's how the situation stands at the moment; **ils en sont ~** that's the stage they've reached; **~ est la difficulté** that's where the difficulty lies. **(d)** (*intensif*) that. **ce jour-~** that day; **en ce temps-~** in those days; **ce qu'il dit ~ n'est pas bête** what he has just said isn't a bad idea; **de ~ son désespoir** hence his despair; **de ~ vient que nous ne le voyons plus** that's why we don't see him any more; **de ~ à prétendre qu'il a tout fait seul, il y a loin** there's a big difference between saying that and claiming that he did it all himself; **loin de ~** far from it; **tout est ~** that's the whole question; **comme menteur, il est** *ou* **se pose ~** he isn't half a liar*; **alors ~, ça ne me surprend pas** (oh) now, that doesn't surprise me; **hé ~!** (*appel*) hey!; (*surprise*) good grief!; **~, ~ du calme** now, now *ou* there, there, calm down; **oh ~ ~ (~ ~)** dear! dear!
2: **~-bas** (over) there; **~-bas dans le nord** up (there) in the north; **~-dedans** (*lit*) inside; (*fig*) in that; **~-dessous** underneath; (*fig*) **il y a qch ~-dessous** there's sth odd about it *ou* that; **~-dessus** on that; (*sur ces mots*) at that point; (*à ce sujet*) about that; **~-haut** up there; (*dessus*) up on top; (*à l'étage*) upstairs; (*fig: au ciel*) in heaven above.
label [labɛl] *nm* (*Comm*) stamp, seal.
labeur [labœʀ] *nm* (*littér*) labour.
laboratoire [labɔʀatwaʀ] *nm* laboratory. ♦ **labo*** *nm* lab*. ♦ **laborantin, e** *nm,f* laboratory *ou* lab* assistant.
laborieux, -euse [labɔʀjø, øz] *adj* **(a)** (*pénible*) (*gén*) laborious; *récit* laboured; *digestion* heavy. **ça a été ~!*** it has been heavy going. **(b)** (*travailleur*) hard-working, industrious. **les classes ~euses** the working classes; **une vie ~euse** a life of hard work. ♦ **laborieusement** *adv* laboriously, with much effort.
labourer [labuʀe] (1) *vt* **(a)** (*avec charrue*) to plough, plow (*US*); (*avec bêche*) to dig (over). **terre qui se laboure bien** land which ploughs well. **(b)** *visage, corps* to gash. **labouré de rides** lined *ou* furrowed with wrinkles; **ça me laboure les côtes** it is digging into my sides. ♦ **labour** *nm* (*action*) ploughing, plowing (*US*); digging; (*champ*) ploughed field. ♦ **labourage** *nm* ploughing, plowing (*US*); digging. ♦ **laboureur** *nm* ploughman, plowman (*US*).
Labrador [labʀadɔʀ] *nm* (*Géog, chien*) Labrador.
labyrinthe [labiʀɛ̃t] *nm* (*lit, fig*) maze, labyrinth.
lac [lak] *nm* lake. **le ~ Léman** Lake Geneva; **c'est dans le ~*** it has fallen through.
lacer [lɑse] (3) *vt chaussure* to tie (up); *corset* to lace up. **ça se lace (par) devant** it laces up at the front.
lacérer [laseʀe] (6) *vt vêtement* to tear *ou* rip up; *corps* to lacerate. ♦ **lacération** *nf* ripping up, tearing up; laceration.
lacet [lɑsɛ] *nm* **(a)** *[chaussure]* (shoe) lace; *[corset]* lace. **chaussures à ~s** lace-up shoes. **(b)** *[route]* sharp bend, twist. **en ~** winding, twisty. **(c)** (*piège*) snare.
lâche [lɑʃ] **1** *adj* **(a)** *corde* slack; *nœud, style, règlement* loose; *discipline* lax. **(b)** (*couard*) cowardly. **se montrer ~** to show o.s. a coward. **2** *nmf* coward. ♦ **lâchement** *adv* loosely; in a cowardly way.
lâcher [lɑʃe] (1) **1** *vt* **(a)** *ceinture* to loosen, let out, slacken. **(b)** *main, proie* to let go of; *bombes* to drop; *pigeon, frein* to release. **lâche-moi!** let *ou* leave go (of me)!; **attention! tu vas ~ le verre** careful, you're going to drop the glass; **~ un chien sur qn** to set a dog on sb; **il va falloir qu'il les lâche*** *ou* **qu'il lâche ses sous*** he'll have to part with the cash*. **(c)** *bêtise, juron* to come out with. **(d)** (*: *abandonner*) *personne* to throw over*; *métier* to give up, throw up*. (*Sport*) **~ le peloton** to leave the rest of the field behind; **il ne m'a pas lâché** *[poursuivant]* he stuck to me; *[mal de tête]* it didn't leave me; **une bonne occasion, ça ne se lâche pas** you don't pass up an opportunity like that*. **(e)** (*locutions*) **~ prise** (*lit*) to let go; (*fig*) to loosen one's grip; **~ pied** to fall back; **~ du lest** (*Naut*) to throw out ballast; (** fig*) to climb down; **~ la bride à un cheval/à qn** to give a horse/sb his head. **2** *vi* *[corde]* to break, give way; *[frein]* to fail. **ses nerfs ont lâché** he broke down. **3** *nm*: **~ de ballons/de pigeons** release of balloons/of pigeons.
lâcheté [lɑʃte] *nf* cowardice, cowardliness; (*acte*) cowardly act, act of cowardice.
lâcheur, -euse* [lɑʃœʀ, øz] *nm,f* unreliable so-and-so*.
laconique [lakɔnik] *adj* laconic, terse. ♦ **laconiquement** *adv* laconically, tersely. ♦ **laconisme** *nm* terseness.
lacté, e [lakte] *adj sécrétion* milky; *régime, farine* milk.
lacune [lakyn] *nf [manuscrit]*, (*Anat, Bot*) lacuna; *[connaissances, texte]* gap, deficiency.
ladite [ladit] *adj V* **ledit.**
lagon [lagɔ̃] *nm* lagoon. ♦ **lagune** *nf* lagoon.
lai, e [lɛ] *adj* (*Rel*) lay. **frère ~** lay brother.
laïciser [laisize] (1) *vt* to secularize. ♦ **laïcité** *nf* (*caractère*) secularity.
laid, e [lɛ, lɛd] *adj* **(a)** (*gén*) ugly; *région* unattractive; *bâtiment* unsightly. **~ comme un pou** ugly as sin; **il est ~ de visage** he's got an ugly face. **(b)** *action* low, mean. **c'est ~ de montrer du doigt** it's rude *ou* not nice to point. ♦ **laideron** *nm* ugly girl *ou* woman. ♦ **laideur** *nf* ugliness; unattractiveness; unsightliness; lowness, meanness. **la guerre dans toute sa ~** the full horror of war; **les ~s de la vie** the ugly things in life.
laine [lɛn] *nf* wool. **de ~** *vêtement* wool, woollen; **~ peignée** *[veston]* worsted wool; *[pull]* combed

wool; ~ **de verre** glass wool; ~ **vierge** new wool. ♦ **lainage** *nm* (*vêtement*) woollen (garment); (*étoffe*) woollen material. ♦ **laineux, -euse** *adj* woolly. ♦ **lainier, -ière** *adj industrie* woollen; *région* wool-producing.

laïque [laik] **1** *adj tribunal* lay, civil; *vie* secular; *habit* ordinary; *collège* non-religious. **l'enseignement** ~ state education (*in France*). **2** *nm* layman. **les** ~**s** laymen, the laity. **3** *nf* laywoman.

laisse [lɛs] *nf* leash, lead. **tenir en** ~ to keep on a leash *ou* lead.

laisser [lese] (1) **1** *vt* **(a)** (*abandonner*) (*gén*) to leave. **laisse-moi ta clé** leave me your key, leave your key with me; **laisse-lui du gâteau** leave *ou* save him some cake; **il m'a laissé ce vase pour 10 F** he let me have this vase for 10 francs; **laisse-moi le soin de le lui dire** leave it to me to tell him; **laisse-moi le temps d'y réfléchir** give me time to think about it; **il a laissé un bras dans l'accident** he lost an arm in the accident; **il y a laissé sa vie** it cost him his life; ~ **qn indifférent** to leave sb unmoved; ~ **qn debout** to keep sb standing (up); **on lui a laissé ses illusions** we didn't disillusion him; **vous laissez le village sur votre droite** you go past the village on your right; ~ **la vie à qn** to spare sb's life; ~ **qn en liberté** to allow sb to stay free. **(b)** (*locutions*) (*lit, fig*) ~ **la porte ouverte** to leave the door open; **il ne laisse jamais rien au hasard** he never leaves anything to chance; **c'était à prendre ou à** ~ it was a case of take it or leave it; **avec lui il faut en prendre et en** ~ you must take what he tells you with a pinch of salt; **on l'a laissé pour mort** he was left for dead; **il laisse tout le monde derrière en math** he is head and shoulders above *ou* streets* ahead of the others in maths; (*littér*) **cela n'a pas laissé de me surprendre** I couldn't fail to be surprised by *ou* at that; (*littér*) **ça ne laisse pas d'être vrai** it is true nonetheless.

2 *vb aux*: ~ **(qn) faire qch** to let sb do sth; **le gouvernement laisse faire!** the government does nothing!; **laissez-moi rire** don't make me laugh; ~ **voir ses sentiments** to let one's feelings show; **il faut** ~ **faire le temps** we must let things take their course.

3 se ~ *vpr*: **se** ~ **exploiter** to let o.s. be exploited; **se** ~ **attendrir** to be moved; **je me suis laissé surprendre par la pluie** I got caught in the rain; **se** ~ **aller** to let o.s. go; **je me suis laissé faire*** I let myself be persuaded; **je n'ai pas l'intention de me** ~ **faire** I'm not going to let myself be pushed around; **laisse-toi faire!** (*à qn qu'on soigne*) let me do it!

♦ **laisser-aller** *nm inv* (*gén*) casualness, carelessness. ♦ **laisser-faire** *nm* (*Écon*) laissez-faire. ♦ **laissez-passer** *nm inv* pass. ♦ **laissé-pour-compte,** *pl* ~**s**-~-~ **1** *adj* (*lit, fig*) rejected. **2** *nm* (*Comm*) (*refusé*) reject; (*invendu*) unsold article. (*fig*) **les** ~**s**-~-~ **de la société** society's rejects; **ce sont les** ~**s**-~-~ **du progrès** these people are the casualties of progress.

lait [lɛ] **1** *nm* milk. ~ **de vache** cow's milk; **petit** ~ whey; (*fig*) **boire du (petit)** ~ to lap it up; **cela se boit comme du petit** ~ you don't notice you're drinking it; **frère de** ~ foster brother; **chocolat au** ~ milk chocolate. **2:** ~ **de beauté** beauty lotion; ~ **caillé** curds; ~ **de chaux** lime water; ~ **de coco** coconut milk; ~ **démaquillant** cleansing milk; ~ **entier** unskimmed milk; ~ **maternel** mother's milk, breast milk; ~ **en poudre** dried *ou* powdered milk. ♦ **laitage** *nm* milk product. ♦ **laitance** *nf* soft roe. ♦ **laiterie** *nf* (*magasin*) dairy; (*industrie*) dairy industry. ♦ **laiteux, -euse** *adj* milky. ♦ **laitier, -ière 1** *adj* dairy. **2** *nm* **(a)** (*livreur*) milkman; (*vendeur*) dairyman. **(b)** (*Ind*) slag. **3** *nf* (*vendeuse*) dairywoman. (*vache*) **une (bonne)** ~**ière** a (good) milker.

laiton [lɛtɔ̃] *nm* brass.

laitue [lety] *nf* lettuce.

lama [lama] *nm* (*Zool*) llama; (*Rel*) lama.

lambeau, *pl* ~**x** [lɑ̃bo] *nm* scrap. **en** ~**x** *vêtements* in tatters *ou* rags; *affiche* in tatters; **mettre en** ~**x** to tear to shreds; **tomber en** ~**x** to fall to pieces.

lambin, e* [lɑ̃bɛ̃, in] **1** *adj* slow. **2** *nm,f* slowcoach*, slowpoke* (*US*). ♦ **lambiner*** (1) *vi* to dawdle.

lambris [lɑ̃bʀi] *nm* panelling.

lame [lam] **1** *nf* **(a)** *[métal, verre]* strip; *[ressort]* leaf; (*pour microscope*) slide. **(b)** *[poignard, tondeuse]* blade. **visage en** ~ **de couteau** hatchet face. **(c)** (*épée*) sword; (*escrimeur*) swordsman. **(d)** (*vague*) wave. **2:** ~**s de fond** ground swell; ~ **de parquet** floorboard; ~ **de rasoir** razor blade. ♦ **lamé, e** *adj, nm* lamé. ♦ **lamelle** *nf* (*gén*) (small) strip; *[persiennes]* slat; *[champignon]* gill; (*pour microscope*) coverglass. **couper en** ~**s** to cut into thin strips.

lamentable [lamɑ̃tabl(ə)] *adj* (*gén*) appalling, awful; *état* lamentable; *spectacle* pitiful. ♦ **lamentablement** *adv échouer* lamentably.

lamenter (se) [lamɑ̃te] (1) *vpr* to moan, lament. **se** ~ **sur qch** to moan over sth, bemoan sth; **arrête de te** ~ **sur ton propre sort** stop feeling sorry for yourself. ♦ **lamentation** *nf* lamentation. (*péj*) ~**(s)** moaning.

laminer [lamine] (1) *vt métal* to laminate. ♦ **laminage** *nm* lamination. ♦ **laminoir** *nm* rolling mill.

lampadaire [lɑ̃padɛʀ] *nm [intérieur]* standard lamp; *[rue]* street lamp. **(pied de)** ~ *[intérieur]* lamp standard; *[rue]* lamp-post.

lampe [lɑ̃p(ə)] *nf* lamp; (*ampoule*) bulb; (*Rad*) valve. ~ **de bureau** desk light; ~ **de chevet** bedside light; ~ **à pétrole** oil lamp; ~ **de poche** torch, flashlight (*US*); ~ **à souder** blowlamp. ♦ **lampion** *nm* Chinese lantern.

lance [lɑ̃s] *nf* **(a)** (*arme*) spear; *[tournoi]* lance. **(b)** (*tuyau*) hose. ~ **d'incendie** fire hose.

lancer [lɑ̃se] (3) **1** *vt* **(a)** (*gén*) to throw; (*violemment*) to hurl, fling; *bombes* to drop; (*Sport*) *poids* to put. ~ **qch à qn** to throw sth to sb; (*hostilement*) to throw *ou* hurl sth at sb; ~ **une balle en l'air** to throw *ou* toss a ball up in the air; ~ **les jambes en avant** to fling one's legs forward; ~ **un coup de poing** to lash out with one's fist; ~ **son poing dans la figure de qn** to punch sb in the face. **(b)** *fumée* to send up *ou* out; *flammes, lave* to throw out. *[yeux, bijoux]* ~ **des éclairs** to flash (fire). **(c)** *menaces* to hurl, fling; *proclamation* to issue; *S.O.S.* to send out; *fausse nouvelle* to put out; *hurlement* to give out. ~ **un cri** to cry out; **elle lui lança un coup d'œil furieux** she flashed *ou* darted a furious glance at him; **'je refuse' lança-t-il** 'I refuse' he said. **(d)** *navire, idée, produit* to launch; *entreprise* to start up; *emprunt* to issue, float. **ne le lancez pas sur son sujet favori** don't set him off on *ou* don't let him get launched on his pet subject; ~ **ses hommes à l'assaut** to launch one's men into the attack; ~ **qn dans la politique** to launch sb into politics; **ce chanteur est lancé** this singer has made a name for himself. **(e)** *moteur* to open up; *voiture* to get up to full speed; *balançoire* to set going. ~ **un cheval** to give a horse its head.

2 se ~ *vpr* (*prendre de l'élan*) to build up *ou* get up momentum *ou* speed; (*sauter*) to leap, jump; (*se précipiter*) to dash, rush (*contre* at). **se** ~ **à l'assaut** to leap to the attack; **se** ~ **dans la bagarre** to pitch into the fight; **n'hésite pas, lance-toi** don't hesitate, off you go *ou* let yourself go; **se** ~ **dans** *discussion etc* to launch into, embark on; **acteur qui cherche à se** ~ actor who's trying to make a name for himself.

3 *nm* **(a)** (*Sport*) **un** ~ a throw; **le** ~ **du poids** *etc* *V* **lancement. (b)** (*Pêche*) (*attirail*) rod and reel;

(*genre de pêche*) rod and reel fishing. ♦ **lance-flammes** *nm inv* flamethrower. ♦ **lance-grenades** *nm inv* grenade launcher. ♦ **lance-missiles** *nm inv* missile launcher. ♦ **lance-pierre(s)** *nm inv* catapult. ♦ **lance-torpilles** *nm inv* torpedo tube. ♦ **lancée** *nf*: **être sur sa** ~ to be *ou* have got under way; **continuer sur sa** ~ to keep going; **je peux encore courir 2 km sur ma** ~ now I'm in my stride I can run another 2 km. ♦ **lancement** *nm [navire, campagne etc]* launching; *[emprunt]* issuing, floating. **le** ~ **du disque** throwing the discus; **le** ~ **du poids** putting the shot. ♦ **lanceur, -euse 1** *nm,f* (*Sport*) thrower; *[entreprise]* promoter. **2** *nm* (*Espace*) launcher.

lanciner [lɑ̃sine] (1) **1** *vi* to throb. **2** *vt [pensée]* to haunt; (*) *[enfant]* to torment. ♦ **lancinant, e** *adj douleur* shooting, throbbing; *souvenir* haunting; *musique* insistent. **ce que tu peux être** ~* you get on my nerves.

landau [lɑ̃do] *nm* (*d'enfant*) pram, baby carriage (*US*); (*carrosse*) landau.

lande [lɑ̃d] *nf* moor.

langage [lɑ̃gaʒ] *nm* language. **changer de** ~ to change one's tune; ~ **argotique** slang speech; ~ **chiffré** cipher, code (language).

lange [lɑ̃ʒ] *nm* baby's flannel blanket. (*Hist*) ~**s** swaddling clothes. ♦ **langer** (3) *vt bébé* to change (the nappy of). **table à** ~ changing table.

langoureux, -euse [lɑ̃guʀø, øz] *adj* languorous. ♦ **langoureusement** *adv* languorously.

langouste [lɑ̃gust(ə)] *nf* crawfish, spiny lobster (*US*). ♦ **langoustine** *nf* Dublin bay prawn. (*Culin*) ~**s** scampi.

langue [lɑ̃g] *nf* **(a)** (*Anat*) tongue. **tirer la** ~ to stick out *ou* put out one's tongue; (*: *être dans le besoin*) to have a rough time of it*; (*: *avoir soif*) **il tirait la** ~ his tongue was hanging out. **(b)** (*organe de la parole*) tongue. **avoir la** ~ **bien pendue** to have a ready tongue in one's head; **il a la** ~ **trop longue** he talks too much; **il n'a pas la** ~ **dans sa poche** he's never at a loss for words; **perdre/retrouver sa** ~ to lose/find one's tongue; **donner sa** ~ **au chat** to give in *ou* up; **j'ai le mot sur (le bout de) la** ~ the word is on the tip of my tongue. **(c)** (*personne*) **mauvaise** ~, ~ **de vipère** spiteful gossip. **(d)** (*Ling*) language. **la** ~ **française** the French language; **les gens de** ~ **anglaise** English-speaking people; ~ **maternelle** mother tongue; ~ **populaire** (*idiome*) popular language; (*usage*) popular speech; (*lit, fig*) **nous ne parlons pas la même** ~ we don't speak the same language. **(e)** ~ **de terre** spit of land. ♦ **languette** *nf [bois, cuir]* tongue.

langueur [lɑ̃gœʀ] *nf* languidness, languor. ♦ **languir** (2) *vi* **(a)** *[personne]* to languish; *[conversation etc]* to flag. ~ **après qn/qch** to languish for *ou* pine for sb/sth. **(b)** (*: *attendre*) to wait, hang around*. **faire** ~ **qn** to keep sb waiting. ♦ **languissant, e** *adj personne* languid; *regard* languishing; *récit* dull; *affaires* slack.

lanière [lanjɛʀ] *nf [cuir]* strap; *[étoffe]* strip; *[fouet]* lash.

lanterne [lɑ̃tɛʀn(ə)] *nf* lantern; (*électrique*) lamp, light. (*Aut*) **se mettre en** ~**s** to switch on one's (side)lights; ~ **magique** magic lantern; ~ **rouge** (*fig: dernier*) tail-ender; ~ **vénitienne** Chinese lantern.

laper [lape] (1) **1** *vt* to lap up. **2** *vi* to lap.

lapider [lapide] (1) *vt* to stone.

lapin [lapɛ̃] *nm* (buck) rabbit; (*fourrure*) rabbit-skin. ~ **de garenne** wild rabbit; **mon petit** ~ my lamb; **poser un** ~ **à qn*** to stand sb up*. ♦ **lapine** *nf* (doe) rabbit.

laps [laps] *nm*: ~ **de temps** lapse of time.

lapsus [lapsys] *nm* slip (of the tongue).

laquais [lakɛ] *nm* lackey, footman; (*péj*) flunkey.

laque [lak] *nf* (*produit brut*) shellac; (*peinture*) lacquer; (*pour cheveux*) hair lacquer *ou* spray.

laquelle [lakɛl] *V* **lequel**.

laquer [lake] (1) *vt* to lacquer. **meuble (en) laqué blanc** piece of furniture with a white lacquer finish.

larbin‡ [laʀbɛ̃] *nm* (*péj*) flunkey.

larcin [laʀsɛ̃] *nm* (*vol*) theft; (*butin*) spoils.

lard [laʀ] *nm* (*gras*) fat (of pig); (*viande*) bacon. ~ **(maigre)** ≃ streaky bacon; (*péj*) **un gros** ~**‡** a fat lump‡. ♦ **larder** (1) *vt* (*Culin*) to lard. ~ **qn de coups de couteau** to hack at sb with a knife. ♦ **lardon** *nm* lardon.

large [laʀʒ(ə)] **1** *adj* **(a)** *surface* wide, broad; *concessions, pouvoirs* wide. **trop** ~ **de 3 mètres** 3 metres too wide; **chapeau à** ~**s bords** broad-brimmed *ou* wide-brimmed hat; **ouvrir une** ~ **bouche** to open one's mouth wide; **d'un geste** ~ with a broad *ou* sweeping gesture; **être** ~ **d'épaules** *[personne]* to be broad-shouldered; *[vêtements]* to be wide *ou* broad at the shoulders; **faire une** ~ **part à qch** to give great weight to sth; **dans une** ~ **mesure** to a great *ou* large extent. **(b)** (*généreux*) *personne* generous. **1 kg de viande pour 4, c'est** ~ 1 kg of meat for 4 is ample *ou* plenty; **une vie** ~ a life of ease. **(c)** *sens, esprit* broad; *conscience* accommodating. ~ **d'idées** broad-minded. **2** *adv*: **prévoir** ~ to allow a bit extra; **cette marque taille** ~ the sizes in this brand tend to be on the large side. **3** *nm* **(a)** (*largeur*) width. **avenue de 8 mètres de** ~ avenue 8 metres wide *ou* 8 metres in width; **être au** ~ (*place*) to have plenty of room; (*argent*) to have plenty of money; **cela se fait en 2 mètres de** ~ that comes in 2-metre widths. **(b)** (*Naut*) **le** ~ the open sea; **au** ~ **de Calais** off Calais; (*fig*) **prendre le** ~* to clear off*, hop it*.

largement [laʀʒəmɑ̃] *adv* **(a)** (*gén*) widely. **fenêtre** ~ **ouverte** wide open window; **idée** ~ **répandue** widely held *ou* widespread view. **(b)** (*de loin*) considerably, greatly. **déborder** ~ **le sujet** to go well beyond the limits of the subject; **elle vaut** ~ **son frère** she's every bit as good as *ou* at least as good as her brother. **(c)** (*amplement*) **vous avez** ~ **le temps** you have ample time *ou* plenty of time; **c'est** ~ **suffisant** that's plenty, that's more than enough; **il est** ~ **temps de commencer** it's high time we started; **j'ai été** ~ **récompensé** I have been amply rewarded; **ça vaut** ~ **la peine** it's well worth the trouble. **(d)** (*généreusement*) generously. **vivre** ~ to live handsomely. **(e)** (*au moins*) easily, at least. **il est** ~ **2 heures** it's well past 2 o'clock.

largesse [laʀʒɛs] *nf* generosity; (*cadeau*) generous gift.

largeur [laʀʒœʀ] *nf* (*lit*) width, breadth; *[idées]* broadness. **sur toute la** ~ all the way across; **dans le sens de la** ~ widthways, widthwise; ~ **d'esprit** broad-mindedness.

larguer [laʀge] (1) *vt amarres* to cast off, slip; *parachutiste* to drop; (*) *objet, personne, emploi* to chuck‡. **être largué*** to be all at sea*.

larme [laʀm(ə)] *nf* (*lit*) tear; (*: *goutte*) drop. **en** ~**s** in tears; **verser toutes les** ~**s de son corps** to cry one's eyes out; ~**s de crocodile** crocodile tears. ♦ **larmoyant, e** *adj voix* tearful; *récit* maudlin. ♦ **larmoyer** (8) *vi* **(a)** *[yeux]* to water, run. **(b)** (*pleurnicher*) to whimper, snivel.

larron [laʀɔ̃] *nm* (†, *Bible*) thief. **s'entendre comme** ~**s en foire** to be as thick as thieves.

larve [laʀv(ə)] *nf* (*Zool*) larva; (*asticot*) grub; (*péj*) worm. ♦ **larvé, e** *adj guerre* latent.

larynx [laʀɛ̃ks] *nm* larynx. ♦ **laryngite** *nf* laryngitis. ♦ **laryngologiste** *nmf* throat specialist, laryngologist.

las, lasse [lɑ, lɑs] *adj* weary, tired (*de* of).

lascar* [laskaʀ] *nm* (*louche*) character; (*malin*) rogue.

lascif, -ive [lasif, iv] *adj* lascivious, lustful. ♦ **lascivité** *nf* lasciviousness, lustfulness.

laser [lazɛʀ] *nm* laser.
lasser [lɑse] (1) **1** *vt* to weary, tire. **2 se ~** *vpr*: **se ~ de qch/de faire qch** to grow weary of sth/of doing sth; **sans se ~** without tiring. ♦ **lassant, e** *adj* wearisome, tiresome. ♦ **lassitude** *nf* weariness, lassitude.
lasso [laso] *nm* lasso. **prendre au ~** to lasso.
latent, e [latɑ̃, ɑ̃t] *adj* (*gén*) latent. ♦ **latence** *nf* latency.
latéral, e, *mpl* **-aux** [lateʀal, o] *adj* side, lateral. ♦ **latéralement** *adv* (*gén*) laterally; *être situé* on the side.
latex [latɛks] *nm inv* latex.
latin, e [latɛ̃, in] *adj, nm,* **L~(e)** *nm(f)* Latin. **~ de cuisine** dog Latin; **j'y perds mon ~** I can't make head nor tail of it. ♦ **latino-américain, e** *adj* Latin-American.
latitude [latityd] *nf* (*gén, fig*) latitude. **Paris est à 48° de ~ Nord** Paris is situated at latitude 48° north; **avoir toute ~ de faire qch** to be quite free *ou* have full scope to do sth.
latte [lat] *nf* (*gén*) lath; *[plancher]* board.
lauréat, e [lɔʀea, at] **1** *adj* prize-winning. **2** *nm,f* prize winner.
laurier [lɔʀje] *nm* (*Bot*) laurel; (*Culin*) bay leaves. **feuille de ~** bay leaf. ♦ **laurier-rose,** *pl* **~s-~s** *nm* oleander.
lavande [lavɑ̃d] *nf* lavender.
lavandière [lavɑ̃djɛʀ] *nf* washerwoman.
lave [lav] *nf*: **~(s)** lava.
laver [lave] (1) **1** *vt* **(a)** (*gén*) to wash; *plaie* to bathe; *tache* to wash out *ou* off; (*Méd*) *intestin* to wash out; (*à la brosse*) to scrub (down); (*à l'éponge*) to (wash with a) sponge. **~ à grande eau** to swill down; **~ la vaisselle** to wash the dishes, do the washing up. **(b)** (*emploi absolu*) *[savon]* to wash; *[personne]* to do the washing. **(c)** *affront* to avenge; *honte* to wash away. **~ qn de qch** to clear sb of sth.
2 se ~ *vpr* to have a wash. **se ~ la figure** to wash one's face; **se ~ les dents** to clean *ou* brush one's teeth; **ce tissu se lave bien** this material washes well; **ça ne se lave pas** it isn't washable *ou* won't wash; **se ~ de** *accusation* to clear o.s. of; **je m'en lave les mains** I wash my hands of the matter.
♦ **lave-glace,** *pl* **~-~s** *nm* windscreen *ou* windshield (*US*) washer. ♦ **lave-mains** *nm inv* wash-stand. ♦ **lave-vaisselle** *nm inv* dishwasher. ♦ **lavable** *adj* washable. ♦ **lavabo** *nm* washbasin. (*euph*) **~s** toilets. ♦ **lavage** *nm* (*gén*) washing; (*lessive*) wash; *[plaie]* bathing. **pour un meilleur ~, utilisez ...** for a better wash, use ...; **on a dû faire 3 ~s** it had to be washed 3 times; **~ d'estomac** stomach wash; **~ de cerveau** brainwashing; **on lui a fait subir un ~ de cerveau** he was brainwashed. ♦ **lavasse*** *nf* dishwater*. ♦ **lavement** *nm* enema. ♦ **laverie** *nf*: **~ automatique** launderette. ♦ **lavette** *nf* (*chiffon*) dish cloth; (*péj*) drip*. ♦ **laveur** *nm* washer. **~ de carreaux** window cleaner. ♦ **laveuse** *nf* washerwoman. ♦ **lavoir** *nm* (*dehors*) washing-place; (*édifice*) wash house; (*bac*) washtub.
laxatif, -ive [laksatif, iv] *adj, nm* laxative.
laxisme [laksism(ə)] *nm* laxity. ♦ **laxiste** **1** *adj* lax. **2** *nmf* latitudinarian.
layette [lɛjɛt] *nf* baby clothes, layette. **rayon ~** babywear department.
le[1] [l(ə)], **la** [la], **les** [le] *art déf* (*avec à, de* **au, aux, du, des**) **(a)** (*détermination*) the. **les enfants sont en retard** the children are late; **il n'a pas ~ droit de le faire** he has no right to do it; **la femme de l'épicier** the grocer's wife; **l'Italie de Mussolini** Mussolini's Italy. **(b)** (*temps*) the (*souvent omis*). **venez ~ dimanche de Pâques** come on Easter Sunday; **l'hiver dernier** last winter; **il ne travaille pas ~ samedi** he doesn't work on Saturdays *ou* on a Saturday; **~ matin** in the morning; **vers les 5 heures** at about 5 o'clock; **il est parti ~ 5 mai** he left on the 5th of May *ou* on May the 5th (*style parlé*); he left on May 5th (*style écrit*). **(c)** (*distribution*) a, an. **5 F ~ mètre/la pièce** 5 francs a metre/each *ou* apiece; **60 km à l'heure** 60 km an *ou* per hour; **j'en ai fait la moitié/~ dixième** I have done half/a tenth of it. **(d)** (*généralisation, abstraction*) *gén non traduit*. **~ hibou vole surtout la nuit** owls fly *ou* the owl flies mainly at night; **l'homme est un roseau pensant** man is a thinking reed; **l'enfant n'aime pas** *ou* **les enfants n'aiment pas l'obscurité** children don't like the dark; **la tuberculose** tuberculosis; **la jeunesse** youth; **~ café est cher** coffee is dear; **j'aime la musique** I like music; **~ beau** the beautiful; **les riches** the rich. **(e)** (*possession*) **elle ouvrit les yeux** she opened her eyes; **j'ai mal au pied** I've a pain in my foot; **il a la jambe cassée** he has got a broken leg; **avoir mal à la tête** to have a headache; **il a les cheveux noirs** he has black hair. **(f)** (*valeur démonstrative*) **faites attention, les enfants!** be careful children!; **oh ~ beau chien!** what a lovely dog!, (just) look at that lovely dog!
le[2] [l(ə)], **la** [la], **les** [le] *pron m,f,pl* **(a)** (*homme*) him; (*femme, nation, bateau*) her; (*animal, bébé*) it, him, her; (*chose*) it. **les** them; **regarde-~/-la/-les** look at him *ou* it/her *ou* it/them. **(b)** (*emphatique*) **cette femme-là, je la déteste** I can't bear that woman; **vous l'êtes, beau** you really DO look smart. **(c)** (*neutre: souvent non traduit*) **je l'ai entendu dire** I have heard it said, so I have heard; **demande-~-lui** ask him; **je ~ savais bien** I thought so.
lécher [leʃe] (6) *vt* **(a)** (*gén*) to lick; *assiette* to lick clean; *[vagues]* to wash *ou* lap against. **se ~ les doigts** to lick one's fingers; (*fig*) **s'en ~ les doigts** to lick one's lips over it; **~ les bottes de qn*** to suck up to sb*, lick sb's boots*. **(b)** (*: *fignoler*) to polish up. ♦ **lèche*** *nf* bootlicking*. **faire de la ~** to be a bootlicker*. ♦ **lèche-bottes*** *nmf inv* bootlicker*. ♦ **lèche-vitrines*** *nm*: **faire du ~** to go window-shopping. ♦ **lécheur, -euse*** *nm,f* bootlicker*.
leçon [l(ə)sɔ̃] *nf* (*gén*) lesson. **~s particulières** private lessons *ou* tuition; (*fig*) **il peut vous donner des ~s** he could teach you a thing or two; **faire la ~ à qn** (*endoctriner*) to give sb instructions; (*réprimander*) to give sb a lecture; **que cela te serve de ~** let that be a lesson to you.
lecteur, -trice [lɛktœʀ, tʀis] *nm,f* **(a)** (*gén*) reader. **le nombre de ~s de ce journal** the readership of this paper. **(b)** (*Univ*) (foreign language) assistant. **(c) ~ de cassettes** cassette player.
lecture [lɛktyʀ] *nf* (*gén*) reading. **d'une ~ facile** easy to read, very readable; **~ à haute voix** reading aloud; **faire la ~ à qn** to read to sb; **donner ~ de qch** to read sth out (*à qn* to sb); **apportez-moi de la ~** bring me something to read; **~s pour la jeunesse** books for children.
ledit [lədi], **ladite** [ladit], *m(f)pl* **lesdit(e)s** [ledi(t)] *adj* the aforementioned, the aforesaid.
légal, e, *mpl* **-aux** [legal, o] *adj* (*gén*) legal; *adresse* official. ♦ **légalement** *adv* legally. ♦ **légalisation** *nf* legalization. ♦ **légaliser** (1) *vt* to legalize. ♦ **légalité** *nf* *[acte]* legality. **rester dans la ~** to keep within the law.
légat [lega] *nm*: **~ (du Pape)** (papal) legate.
légataire [legatɛʀ] *nmf* legatee. **~ universel** sole legatee.
légation [legɑsjɔ̃] *nf* (*Diplomatie*) legation.
légende [leʒɑ̃d] *nf* **(a)** (*mythe*) legend. **entrer dans la ~** to go down in legend. **(b)** *[médaille]* legend; *[dessin]* caption; *[carte]* key. **(c)** (*péj: mensonge*) fairy tale. ♦ **légendaire** *adj* (*gén*) legendary.
léger, -ère [leʒe, ɛʀ] *adj* **(a)** *poids, parfum* light. **construction ~ère** light *ou* flimsy (*péj*) building; **faire qch d'un cœur ~** to do sth with a light heart. **(b)** *allure* light, nimble; *taille* light, slender. **d'un**

pas ~ with a light *ou* springy step. **(c)** *bruit, surprise* slight, faint; *thé* weak; *vin, coup* light; *maladie, châtiment* mild, slight. **une ~ère pointe d'ironie** a light touch of irony; **un blessé ~** a slightly injured person. **(d)** (*superficiel*) *personne, propos* thoughtless; *argument* lightweight, flimsy. **agir à la ~ère** to act thoughtlessly; **il prend toujours tout à la ~ère** he never takes anything seriously. **(e)** (*frivole*) *personne* fickle; *plaisanterie* ribald, broad. **femme ~ère** woman of easy virtue. ♦ **légèrement** *adv* lightly; nimbly; slightly; faintly; thoughtlessly. **~ plus grand** slightly bigger. ♦ **légèreté** *nf* lightness; flimsiness; nimbleness; mildness; thoughtlessness; fickleness; ribaldry.

légion [leʒjɔ̃] *nf* legion. **ils sont ~** they are legion. ♦ **légionnaire** *nm* (*Hist*) legionary; *[Légion étrangère]* legionnaire.

législation [leʒislasjɔ̃] *nf* legislation. ♦ **législateur, -trice** *nm,f* legislator. ♦ **législatif, -ive 1** *adj* legislative. **élections ~ives** ≃ general election. **2** *nm*: **le ~** the legislature. ♦ **législature** *nf* (*Parl*) (*durée*) term (of office); (*corps*) legislature. ♦ **légiste** *nm* legist, jurist.

légitime [leʒitim] *adj* (*gén*) legitimate; *femme* lawful; *colère* justifiable, justified; *revendication* rightful. **j'étais en état de ~ défense** I was acting in self-defence. ♦ **légitimement** *adv* (*gén*) rightfully; (*Jur*) legitimately. ♦ **légitimer** (1) *vt* to legitimate. ♦ **légitimité** *nf* (*gén*) legitimacy.

legs [lɛg] *nm* (*Jur, fig*) legacy. **faire un ~ à qn** to leave sb a legacy. ♦ **léguer** (6) *vt* (*Jur*) to bequeath; *tradition, tare* to hand down, pass on.

légume [legym] **1** *nm* vegetable. **~s secs/verts** dry/green vegetables. **2** *nf*: **une grosse ~*** a bigwig*. ♦ **légumier** *nm* vegetable dish. ♦ **légumineuse** *nf* leguminous plant.

lendemain [lɑ̃dmɛ̃] *nm* **(a)** (*jour suivant*) **le ~** the next *ou* following day, the day after; **le ~ de son arrivée** the day after he arrived, the day following his arrival; **le ~ soir** the next *ou* following evening; **il ne faut jamais remettre au ~ ce qu'on peut faire le jour même** never put off till tomorrow what you can do today; **au ~ de la défaite** soon after *ou* in the days following the defeat. **(b)** (*avenir*) **le ~** tomorrow, the future; **succès sans ~** short-lived success. **(c) ~s** (*conséquences*) consequences; (*perspectives*) prospects.

lent, e¹ [lɑ̃, lɑ̃t] *adj* (*gén*) slow; *poison* slow-acting. **à l'esprit ~** slow-witted. ♦ **lentement** *adv* slowly. ♦ **lenteur** *nf* slowness. **~ d'esprit** slow-wittedness; **la ~ de la construction** the slow progress of the building.

lente² [lɑ̃t] *nf* (*Zool*) nit.

lentille [lɑ̃tij] *nf* (*Bot, Culin*) lentil; (*Opt*) lens. **~s cornéennes** contact lenses.

léopard [leɔpaʀ] *nm* leopard; (*fourrure*) leopard-skin.

lèpre [lɛpʀ(ə)] *nf* (*Méd*) leprosy; (*fig: mal*) plague. ♦ **lépreux, -euse 1** *adj* (*lit*) leprous; *mur* flaking, peeling. **2** *nm,f* (*lit, fig*) leper. ♦ **léproserie** *nf* leper-house.

lequel [ləkɛl], **laquelle** [lakɛl], *m(f)pl* **lesquel(le)s** [lekɛl] (*avec à, de* **auquel, auxquels, auxquelles, duquel, desquels, desquelles**) **1** *pron* **(a)** (*relatif*) (*personne: sujet*) who; (*personne: objet*) whom; (*chose*) which. **j'ai écrit au directeur, ~ n'a jamais répondu** I wrote to the manager, who has never answered; **le règlement d'après ~** the ruling whereby ...; **la femme à laquelle j'ai acheté mon chien** the woman from whom I bought my dog; **le pont sur ~ vous êtes passé** the bridge you came over *ou* over which you came. **(b)** (*interrogatif*) which. **~ des 2 acteurs préférez-vous?** which of the 2 actors do you prefer?; **va voir ma sœur – laquelle?** go and see my sister – which one? **2** *adj*: **son état pourrait empirer, auquel cas je reviendrais** his condition could worsen, in which case I would come back.

les [le] *V* **le¹, le²**.

lesbienne [lɛsbjɛn] *nf* lesbian.

lèse-majesté [lɛzmaʒɛste] *nf* lese-majesty.

léser [leze] (6) *vt* **(a)** *personne* to wrong; *droits* to infringe on; *intérêts* to damage. **(b)** (*Méd*) to injure.

lésiner [lezine] (1) *vi* to skimp (*sur qch* on sth). ♦ **lésinerie** *nf* stinginess.

lésion [lezjɔ̃] *nf* (*Jur, Méd*) lesion.

lessiver [lesive] (1) *vt* **(a)** (*lit*) to wash. **(b)** (*: *battre*) (*au jeu*) to clean out*; *adversaire* to lick*. ♦ **lessivage** *nm* washing. ♦ **lessive** *nf* (*produit*) washing powder; (*linge*) washing; (*lavage*) washing, wash. **faire la ~** to do the washing; **faire 4 ~s par semaine** to do 4 washes a week. ♦ **lessivé, e*** *adj* (*fatigué*) **être ~** to be dead beat* *ou* all in*. ♦ **lessiveuse** *nf* (laundry) boiler.

lest [lɛst] *nm* ballast. ♦ **lester** (1) *vt* (*lit*) to ballast; (*: *remplir*) *poches* to fill.

leste [lɛst(ə)] *adj* **(a)** (*agile*) nimble, agile, sprightly. **(b)** *plaisanterie* risqué. ♦ **lestement** *adv* nimbly, agilely. **mener ~ une affaire** to conduct a piece of business briskly.

léthargie [letaʀʒi] *nf* lethargy. **tomber en ~** to fall into a state of lethargy. ♦ **léthargique** *adj* lethargic.

lettre [lɛtʀ(ə)] **1** *nf* **(a)** (*caractère*) letter. **c'est écrit en toutes ~s** it's there *ou* it's written in black and white; **écrire en (toutes) ~s** *nom, somme* to write in full. **(b)** (*missive*) letter. **~s** (*courrier*) letters, mail; **mettre une ~ à la boîte** to post a letter; **écris-lui une petite ~** write him a note. **(c) les (belles) ~s** literature; **homme de ~s** man of letters; **avoir des ~s** to be well-read. **(d)** (*Scol*) **fort en ~s** good at arts subjects; **professeur de ~s** teacher of French (*in France*); **~s modernes** French language and literature; **~s classiques** classics (*sg*). **(e)** (*locutions*) **rester ~ morte** *[protestation]* to go unheeded; **devenir ~ morte** *[loi]* to become a dead letter; **c'est passé comme une ~ à la poste*** it went off smoothly *ou* without a hitch; **prendre qch au pied de la ~** to take sth literally; **exécuter qch à la ~** to carry out sth to the letter.

2: ~ de change bill of exchange; **~s de créance** credentials; **~s de noblesse** letters patent of nobility; **~ recommandée** (*attestant sa remise*) recorded delivery letter; (*assurant sa valeur*) registered letter. ♦ **lettré, e** *adj* well-read.

leucémie [løsemi] *nf* leukaemia. ♦ **leucémique 1** *adj* leukaemic. **2** *nmf* person suffering from leukaemia.

leur [lœʀ] **1** *pron pers mf* them. **il ~ est facile de le faire** it is easy for them to do it. **2** *adj poss* **(a)** their. **ils ont ~s petites manies** they have their little fads. **(b)** (*littér*) theirs, their own. **ils ont fait ~s ces idées** they made these ideas their own. **3** *pron poss*: **le ~, la ~, les ~s** theirs; **ces sacs sont les ~s** these bags are theirs. **4** *nm* **(a) ils ont mis du ~** they pulled their weight. **(b) les ~s** (*famille*) their family; (*partisans*) their own people; **ils ont encore fait des ~s*** they've (gone and) done it again*; **nous étions des ~s** we were with them.

leurre [lœʀ] *nm* (*illusion*) delusion; (*duperie*) deception; (*piège*) trap, snare; (*Pêche, Chasse*) lure. ♦ **leurrer** (1) **1** *vt* to delude. **2 se ~** *vpr* to delude o.s.

levage [ləvaʒ] *nm* (*Tech*) lifting.

levain [ləvɛ̃] *nm* *[pain]* leaven. **sans ~** unleavened.

levant [ləvɑ̃] **1** *adj*: **soleil ~** rising sun; **au soleil ~** at sunrise. **2** *nm*: **le ~** the East; (*pays*) **le L~** the Levant.

lever [l(ə)ve] (5) **1** *vt* **(a)** (*lit*) (*gén*) to raise; *objet* to lift; *yeux, tête* to lift up; *main* (*en classe*) to put up. ~ **le visage vers qn** to look up at sb. **(b)** *blocus* to raise; *séance* to close; *difficulté, scrupules* to remove; *interdiction* to lift. **(c)** *impôts, armée* to levy. **(d)** *plan, carte* to draw. **(e)** *enfant, malade* to get up. **faire ~ qn** (*d'une chaise*) to make sb stand up; (*du lit*) to get sb up; (*lit, fig*) ~ **un lièvre** to start a hare. **(f)** (*locutions*) ~ **l'ancre** (*Naut*) to weigh anchor; (*fig*) to make tracks*; ~ **le camp** (*lit*) to break camp; (*fig*) to break up; ~ **le siège** (*lit*) to raise the siege; (*fig*) to take o.s. off; **il n'a pas levé le petit doigt pour m'aider** he didn't lift a finger to help me; *[chien]* ~ **la patte** to cock its leg; ~ **le pied** (*disparaître*) to vanish; (*Aut: ralentir*) to slow down; ~ **la main sur qn** to raise one's hand to sb; ~ **le voile** to reveal the truth (*sur* about); ~ **son verre à la santé de qn** to drink to sb's health.

2 *vi* **(a)** *[plante]* to come up. **(b)** (*Culin*) to rise. **faire ~ la pâte** to make the dough rise.

3 se ~ *vpr* **(a)** *[rideau, main]* to go up. **(b)** *[personne]* to get up. **se ~ de table** to get up from the table; **faire se ~ qn** (*du lit*) to get sb up; (*d'une chaise*) to make sb stand up; (*fig*) **il s'est levé du pied gauche** he got out of bed on the wrong side; **se ~ sur son séant** to sit up. **(c)** *[soleil, lune]* to rise; *[jour]* to break. **(d)** *[vent, orage]* to get up, rise; *[brume]* to lift, clear. **le temps se lève** the weather is clearing.

4 *nm* **(a)** ~ **de soleil** sunrise; ~ **du jour** daybreak, dawn. **(b)** (*au réveil*) **prenez 3 comprimés au ~** take 3 tablets when you get up *ou* on rising; **le ~ du roi** the levee of the king. **(c)** (*Théât*) **le ~ du rideau** (*commencement*) the curtain; (*action*) the raising of the curtain; (*pièce*) **un ~ de rideau** a curtain raiser.

♦ **levé**[1] *nm* (*plan*) survey. ♦ **levé**[2], **e**[1] *adj*: **être ~** to be up. ♦ **levée**[2] **1** *nf* **(a)** *[siège]* raising; *[séance]* closing; *[interdiction]* lifting. **(b)** (*Poste*) collection. **(c)** (*Cartes*) trick. **faire une ~** to take a trick. **(d)** *[impôts, armée]* levying. **(e)** (*remblai*) levee. **2:** ~ **de boucliers** general outcry; **la ~ du corps aura lieu à 10 heures** the funeral will start from the house at 10 o'clock; ~ **d'écrou** release (from prison). ♦ **lève-tard** *nm inv* late riser. ♦ **lève-tôt** *nm inv* early riser.

levier [ləvje] *nm* lever. **faire ~ sur qch** to lever sth up; (*fig*) **être aux ~s de commande** to be in control *ou* command.

lèvre [lɛvʀ(ə)] *nf* (*gén*) lip; (*Géog*) *[faille]* side.

lévrier [levʀije] *nm* greyhound.

levure [l(ə)vyʀ] *nf* (*ferment*) yeast.

lexique [lɛksik] *nm* vocabulary; (*glossaire*) lexicon. ♦ **lexicographie** *nf* lexicography.

lézard [lezaʀ] *nm* (*animal*) lizard; (*peau*) lizardskin. **faire le ~ (au soleil)*** to bask in the sun.

lézarde [lezaʀd(ə)] *nf* (*fissure*) crack. ♦ **se lézarder** (1) *vpr* to crack.

liaison [ljɛzɔ̃] *nf* **(a)** (*fréquentation*) ~ **(amoureuse)** (love) affair; ~ **(d'affaires)** business relationship *ou* connection. **(b)** (*contact*) **entrer en ~ avec qn** to get in contact with sb; **travailler en ~ étroite avec qn** to work in close collaboration with sb; ~ **radio** radio contact; **officier de ~** liaison officer. **(c)** (*entre événements, idées*) connection. **(d)** (*Phonétique*) liaison. (*Gram*) **mot de ~** linkword. **(e)** (*Transport*) link.

liane [ljan] *nf* creeper, liana.

liant, e [ljɑ̃, ɑ̃t] *adj* sociable.

liasse [ljas] *nf* bundle, wad.

Liban [libɑ̃] *nm*: **le ~** (the) Lebanon. ♦ **libanais, e** *adj*, **L~(e)** *nm(f)* Lebanese.

libations [libɑsjɔ̃] *nfpl* libations.

libeller [libele] (1) *vt acte* to draw up; *chèque* to make out (*au nom de* to); *lettre* to word. ♦ **libellé** *nm* wording.

libellule [libelyl] *nf* dragonfly.

libéral, e, *mpl* **-aux** [libeʀal, o] *adj, nm,f* (*gén*) liberal. ♦ **libéralement** *adv* liberally. ♦ **libéralisation** *nf* liberalization. ♦ **libéraliser** (1) *vt* to liberalize. ♦ **libéralisme** *nm* liberalism. ♦ **libéralité** *nf* liberality; (*don*) generous *ou* liberal gift.

libérer [libeʀe] (6) **1** *vt* **(a)** *prisonnier* to release; *soldat* to discharge (*de* from). **libéré sous caution/sur parole** released on bail/on parole. **(b)** *pays, peuple* to free, liberate; (*d'une promesse*) to release (*de* from). **(c)** *énergie, gaz, cran d'arrêt* to release; *échanges commerciaux* to ease restrictions on. ~ **le passage** to free *ou* unblock the way. **(d)** *conscience* to unburden; *instincts* to give free rein to. **2 se ~** *vpr* (*de ses liens*) to free o.s. (*de* from); (*d'une promesse*) to release o.s. (*de* from); (*d'une dette*) to clear o.s. (*de* of). **jeudi je ne peux pas me ~** I can't be free on Thursday. ♦ **libérateur, -trice 1** *adj* (*Psych*) liberating. **guerre ~trice** war of liberation. **2** *nm,f* liberator. ♦ **libération** *nf* release; discharge; freeing; liberation.

liberté [libɛʀte] *nf* **(a)** (*gén, Jur*) freedom, liberty. **mettre en ~** to free, release; **être mis en ~ surveillée** to be put on probation; **mise en ~** *[prisonnier]* release; **être en ~** *[animal]* to be free; **animaux en ~** animals in freedom; **le voleur est encore en ~** the thief is still at large; *[épouse]* **elle a repris sa ~** she has regained her independence; **avoir toute ~ pour agir** to have full freedom to act; ~, **égalité, fraternité** liberty, equality, fraternity. **(b)** (*loisir*) **moments de ~** free moments, spare *ou* free time; **jour de ~** free day, day off. **(c)** (*absence de contrainte*) liberty. ~ **de mœurs** freedom of morals; **prendre la ~ de faire** to take the liberty of doing; **prendre des ~s avec** *texte* to take liberties with. **(d)** (*droit*) right. **les ~s syndicales** the rights of the unions.

libertin, e [libɛʀtɛ̃, in] *adj, nm,f* libertine.

libraire [libʀɛʀ] *nmf* bookseller. ♦ **librairie** *nf* (*magasin*) bookshop. **~-papeterie** bookseller's and stationer's; **la ~** (*activité*) bookselling.

libre [libʀ(ə)] *adj* **(a)** (*sans contrainte*) free. **en vente ~** on open sale; **garder l'esprit ~** to keep one's mind free, keep a clear mind; **être ~ comme l'air** to be as free as a bird; **rester ~** (*non marié*) to remain unattached; ~ **de tout préjugé** free from all prejudice; **vous êtes ~ de refuser** you're free *ou* at liberty to refuse; **le sujet de la dissertation est ~** the subject of this essay is left open. **(b)** (*non occupé*) (*gén*) free; *passage* clear; *taxi* empty. (*Téléc*) **la ligne n'est pas ~** the line is engaged; **est-ce que cette place est ~?** is this seat free? *ou* vacant?; **avoir du temps ~** to have some spare *ou* free time; (*non payant*) **'entrée ~'** entrance free. **(c)** (*Scol*) *enseignement* private and Roman Catholic. **(d)** (*sans retenue*) *personne* free *ou* open in one's behaviour; *plaisanteries* broad; *propos* blunt. **être très ~ avec qn** to be very free with sb; **donner ~ cours à sa colère** to give free rein *ou* give vent to one's anger. ♦ **libre arbitre** *nm* free will. ♦ **libre-échange** *nm* free trade. ♦ **libre penseur** *nm* freethinker. ♦ **libre-service,** *pl* **~s-~s** *nm* (*restaurant*) self-service restaurant; (*magasin*) self-service store. ♦ **librement** *adv* freely.

Libye [libi] *nf* Libya. ♦ **libyen, -enne** *adj*, **L~(ne)** *nm(f)* Libyan.

licence [lisɑ̃s] *nf* **(a)** (*Univ*) degree. ~ **ès lettres** Arts degree, ≃ B.A.; ~ **ès sciences** Science degree, ≃ B.Sc. **(b)** (*autorisation, Sport*) permit; (*Comm, Jur*) licence. **(c)** ~ **(des mœurs)** licentiousness; ~ **poétique** poetic licence. ♦ **licencié, e** *nm,f* **(a)** ~ **ès lettres/ès sciences/en droit** Bachelor of Arts/of Science/of Law, arts/science/law graduate. **(b)** (*Sport*) permit-holder.

licencier [lisɑ̃sje] (7) *vt* (*débaucher*) to

make redundant; (*renvoyer*) to dismiss. ♦ **licenciement** *nm* (*action*) dismissal. (*résultat*) **plusieurs ~s** several redundancies.
licencieux, -euse [lisɑ̃sjø, øz] *adj* licentious.
lichen [likɛn] *nm* lichen.
lichette* [liʃɛt] *nf*: **~ de pain** *etc* nibble of bread *etc.*
licite [lisit] *adj* lawful, licit.
licorne [likɔʀn(ə)] *nf* unicorn.
lie [li] **1** *nf [vin]* dregs, sediment. **la ~ de la société** the dregs of society. **2:** **~ de vin** *adj* wine (-coloured).
liège [ljɛʒ] *nm* cork.
lien [ljɛ̃] *nm* **(a)** (*lit, fig: attache*) bond, tie. **~s de parenté** family ties; **~s d'amitié** bonds of friendship. **(b)** (*corrélation*) link, connection.
lier [lje] (7) **1** *vt* **(a)** (*attacher*) to bind, tie up. **~ qn à un arbre** to tie sb to a tree. **(b)** (*relier*) to link up. **tous ces événements sont étroitement liés** all these events are closely linked *ou* connected. **(c)** (*unir*) *personnes* to bind, unite. **(d)** (*Culin*) *sauce* to thicken. **(e)** **~ amitié/conversation** to strike up a friendship/conversation. **2 se ~** *vpr* to make friends (*avec qn* with sb); (*par un serment*) to bind o.s. **ils sont très liés** they are very close friends.
lierre [ljɛʀ] *nm* ivy.
liesse [ljɛs] *nf* (*littér: joie*) jubilation. **en ~** jubilant.
lieu, *pl* **~x** [ljø] **1** *nm* **(a)** (*gén: endroit*) place; *[événement]* scene. **en quelque ~ qu'il soit** wherever he is; **en tous ~x** everywhere; **en ~ sûr** in a safe place; **être sur les ~x de l'accident** to be on the scene of the accident. **(b)** (*locaux*) **les ~x** the premises; **quitter les ~x** (*Admin*) to vacate the premises; (*) to get out. **(c)** (*temps*) **en premier ~** in the first place; **en dernier ~** lastly; **en son ~** in due course. **(d)** **au ~ de qch** instead of sth; **en ~ et place de qn** on behalf of sb; **avoir ~** (*se produire*) to take place; **avoir ~ d'être inquiet** to have (good) grounds for being worried, have (good) reason to be worried; **s'il y a ~** if necessary; **donner ~ à des critiques** to give rise to criticism; **tenir ~ de qch** to take the place of sth, serve as sth.
2: **~x d'aisances**† lavatory; **~ commun** commonplace; **~-dit,** *pl* **~x-~s** locality; **~ de naissance** (*gén*) birthplace; (*Admin*) place of birth; **~ de passage** passing through place; **~ de vacances** (*ville*) holiday resort.
lieue [ljø] *nf* league. **j'étais à cent ~s de supposer cela** that never occurred to me.
lieuse [ljøz] *nf* (*Agr*) binder.
lieutenant [ljøtnɑ̃] *nm* (*Mil, fig*) lieutenant; (*marine marchande*) mate. **~-colonel** lieutenant colonel.
lièvre [ljɛvʀ(ə)] *nm* hare.
ligament [ligamɑ̃] *nm* ligament.
ligature [ligatyʀ] *nf* ligature. ♦ **ligaturer** (1) *vt* to ligature.
ligne [liɲ] **1** *nf* **(a)** (*trait, limite*) line. **~ brisée** broken *ou* dotted line; **~ de départ/d'arrivée** starting/finishing line; **la ~ des x/des y** the X/Y axis; **courir en ~ droite** to run in a straight line; (*Aut*) **~ droite** stretch of straight road. **(b)** *[meuble, voiture]* line(s); *[femme]* figure. **garder la ~** to keep one's figure; **la ~ lancée par la mode** the look launched by the collections. **(c)** (*règle*) line. **~ de conduite** line of conduct; **les grandes ~s d'un programme** the broad lines of a programme. **(d)** (*rangée*) line, row. **mettre des personnes en ~** to line people up; **se mettre en ~** to line up, get into line. **(e)** (*Rail*) line. **~ d'autobus** (*service*) bus service; (*parcours*) bus route; **~ d'aviation** (*compagnie*) air line; (*trajet*) (air) route; **~ de métro** underground line. **(f)** (*Élec*) (*gén*) line; (*câbles*) wires. **être en ~** to be connected. **(g)** *[texte]* line. (*dictée*) **'à la ~'** 'new paragraph'. **(h)** (*Pêche*) fishing line. **(i)** (*locutions*) **mettre sur la même ~** to put on the same level; **faire entrer en ~ de compte** to take into account *ou* consideration; **sur toute la ~** all along the line.
2: **~ de but** goal line; **~ de flottaison** water line; (*Pêche*) **~ de fond** ledger line; **~ d'horizon** skyline; (*Sport*) **~ médiane** halfway line; **~ de mire** line of sight; **~ de partage des eaux** watershed; **~ de touche** touchline.
♦ **lignée** *nf* (*postérité*) descendants; (*race*) line; (*tradition*) tradition.
ligoter [ligɔte] (1) *vt personne* to bind hand and foot. **~ à un arbre** to tie to a tree.
ligue [lig] *nf* league. ♦ **liguer** (1) **1** *vt* to unite (*contre* against). **être ligué avec** to be in league with. **2 se ~** *vpr* to form a league, be in league (*contre* against).
lilas [lilɑ] *nm, adj inv* lilac.
limace [limas] *nf* (*Zool*) slug; (*: *chemise*) shirt; (*: *personne*) slowcoach, slowpoke (*US*).
limande [limɑ̃d] *nf* (*poisson*) dab. **~-sole** lemon sole.
lime [lim] *nf* file. **~ à ongles** nail file. ♦ **limer** (1) *vt* to file; *aspérité* to file off.
limier [limje] *nm* (*Zool*) bloodhound; (*fig*) sleuth.
limite [limit] **1** *nf* (*gén*) limit; *[jardin]* boundary. **~ de rupture** breaking point; **~ d'âge** age limit; **sans ~** boundless, limitless; **la bêtise a des ~s!** foolishness has its limits!; **il dépasse les ~s!** he's going a bit too far!; **à la ~ on croirait qu'il le fait exprès** you'd almost think he is doing it on purpose; **à la ~ tout roman est réaliste** at a pinch any novel could be said to be realistic; **dans une certaine ~** up to a point, to a certain extent; **dans les ~s de mes moyens** (*aptitude*) within (the limits of) my capabilities; (*argent*) within my means; **jusqu'à la dernière ~** to the end; **jusqu'à la ~ de ses forces** to the point of exhaustion; (*Boxe*) **tenir jusqu'à la ~** to go the distance. **2** *adj*: **cas ~** borderline case; **vitesse/âge ~** maximum speed/age; **date ~** deadline.
♦ **limitatif, -ive** *adj* restrictive. ♦ **limitation** *nf* (*gén*) limitation. **~ des prix/des naissances** price/birth control; **sans ~ de temps** with no time limit; **~ de vitesse** speed limit. ♦ **limiter** (1) **1** *vt* **(a)** (*restreindre*) to limit, restrict. **~ les dégâts*** to stop things getting any worse; (*financièrement*) to cut one's losses. **(b)** *[frontière, montagnes]* to border. **2 se ~** *vpr [personne]* **se ~ (à qch/à faire)** to limit *ou* confine o.s. (to sth/to doing); *[chose]* **se ~ à** to be limited to.
limitrophe [limitʀɔf] *adj département* border.
limoger [limɔʒe] (3) *vt* to dismiss, fire.
limon [limɔ̃] *nm* (*Géog*) silt; *[attelage]* shaft.
limonade [limɔnad] *nf* lemonade.
limpide [lɛ̃pid] *adj* (*gén*) limpid; *explication* lucid. ♦ **limpidité** *nf [eau, ciel]* clearness; *[regard]* limpidity; *[explication]* clarity, lucidity.
lin [lɛ̃] *nm* (*plante*) flax; (*tissu*) linen.
linceul [lɛ̃sœl] *nm* (*lit, fig*) shroud.
linéaire [lineɛʀ] *adj* linear.
linge [lɛ̃ʒ] *nm* **(a)** **le ~, du ~** linen; **le gros/petit ~** the main/small items of linen; **~ de corps/de table** body/table linen; **~ de toilette** bathroom linen. **(b)** (*lessive*) **le ~** the washing. **(c)** (*morceau*) cloth. **blanc comme un ~** as white as a sheet. ♦ **lingerie** *nf* (*local*) linen room; (*sous-vêtements*) lingerie, underwear.
lingot [lɛ̃go] *nm* ingot.
linguiste [lɛ̃gɥist(ə)] *nmf* linguist. ♦ **linguistique** **1** *nf* linguistics (*sg*). **2** *adj* linguistic.
linoléum [linɔleɔm] *nm* linoleum.
lion [ljɔ̃] *nm* lion. ♦ **lionceau,** *pl* **~x** *nm* lion cub. ♦ **lionne** *nf* lioness.
lippu, e [lipy] *adj* thick-lipped.
liquéfier *vt,* **se ~** *vpr* [likefje] (7) to liquefy. ♦ **liquéfaction** *nf* liquefaction.

liqueur [likœʀ] *nf* (*boisson*) liqueur; (*Chim*) solution.
liquide [likid] **1** *adj* liquid. **sauce trop** ~ sauce which is too runny *ou* too thin. **2** *nm* **(a)** (*substance*) liquid. **(b)** (*argent*) **du** ~ ready money, ready cash.
liquider [likide] (1) *vt* **(a)** *société, biens* to liquidate; (*lit, fig*) *compte* to settle; *retraite* to pay. **(b)** (*vendre*) to sell (off). **(c)** (‡) (*tuer*) to liquidate; (*se débarrasser de*) to get rid of; (*finir*) to finish off. **c'est liquidé maintenant** it is all finished *ou* over now. ♦ **liquidation** *nf* liquidation; settlement; payment; sale. **mettre en** ~ *compagnie* to liquidate.
liquidité [likidite] *nf* (*Chim, Jur*) liquidity. ~**s** liquid assets.
liquoreux, -euse [likɔʀø, øz] *adj vin* syrupy.
lire[1] [liʀ] (43) *vt* (*gén*) to read; *discours* to read out. **il l'a lu dans le journal** he read (about) it in the paper; **ça se lit très vite** it makes quick reading; ~ **entre les lignes** to read between the lines; **lu et approuvé** read and approved; ~ **dans le cœur de qn** to see into sb's heart; **elle m'a lu les lignes de la main** she read my hand; ~ **dans le jeu de qn** to see sb's game; **nous espérons vous** ~ **bientôt** we hope to hear from you soon.
lire[2] [liʀ] *nf* lira.
lis [lis] *nm* lily.
liseron [lizʀɔ̃] *nm* bindweed, convolvulus.
liseur, -euse [lizœʀ, øz] **1** *nm,f* reader. **2** *nf* (*vêtement*) bed jacket.
lisible [lizibl(ə)] *adj écriture* legible; *livre* readable. ♦ **lisibilité** *nf* legibility. ♦ **lisiblement** *adv* legibly.
lisière [lizjɛʀ] *nf [bois, village]* edge.
lisse [lis] *adj* (*gén*) smooth; *cheveux* sleek. ♦ **lisser** (1) *vt cheveux* to smooth (down); *papier froissé* to smooth out. **l'oiseau se lisse les plumes** the bird is preening its feathers.
liste [list(ə)] *nf* list. **faire la** ~ **de** to make out a list of, list; ~ **électorale** electoral roll; ~ **noire** blacklist.
lit [li] **1** *nm* bed. ~ **d'une personne/de deux personnes** single/double bed; ~ **de fer** iron bedstead; **se mettre au** ~ to go to bed; **faire le** ~ to make the bed; **faire** ~ **à part** to sleep in separate beds; **au** ~ **les enfants!** bedtime *ou* off to bed children!; **enfants du premier** ~ children of the first marriage. **2:** ~ **de camp** campbed; ~ **d'enfant** cot; ~ **gigogne** bunk bed; ~ **de mort** deathbed; ~ **en portefeuille** apple pie bed; (*Naut*) **le** ~ **du vent** the set of the wind.
litanie [litani] *nf* (*Rel, péj*) litany.
literie [litʀi] *nf* bedding.
lithographie [litɔgʀafi] *nf* (*technique*) lithography; (*image*) lithograph.
litière [litjɛʀ] *nf* litter.
litige [litiʒ] *nm* (*gén*) dispute; (*Jur*) lawsuit. **objet de** ~ object of contention. ♦ **litigieux, -ieuse** *adj* litigious, contentious.
litre [litʀ(ə)] *nm* (*mesure*) litre; (*récipient*) litre bottle.
littéral, e, *mpl* **-aux** [liteʀal, o] *adj* literal. ♦ **littéralement** *adv* (*lit, fig*) literally.
littérature [liteʀatyʀ] *nf* literature; (*profession*) writing. ♦ **littéraire** *adj* (*gén*) literary.
littoral, e, *mpl* **-aux** [litɔʀal, o] **1** *adj* coastal. **2** *nm* coast.
liturgie [lityʀʒi] *nf* liturgy. ♦ **liturgique** *adj* liturgical.
livide [livid] *adj* (*pâle*) pallid; (*bleuâtre*) livid.
livraison [livʀɛzɔ̃] *nf* delivery. (*avis*) '~ **à domicile**' 'we deliver'.
livre[1] [livʀ(ə)] *nm* book. (*commerce*) **le** ~ the book trade *ou* industry; ~ **blanc** report (*on disasters, atrocities etc published by independent organization*); ~ **de bord** logbook; ~ **de caisse** cashbook; ~ **de classe** schoolbook; ~ **d'or** visitors' book; ~ **de poche** paperback.
livre[2] [livʀ(ə)] *nf* **(a)** (*poids*) ≈ pound, half a kilo. **(b)** (*monnaie*) pound; (*Hist française*) livre. ~ **sterling** pound sterling.
livrée [livʀe] *nf* (*uniforme*) livery.
livrer [livʀe] (1) **1** *vt* **(a)** (*Comm*) to deliver. **(b)** (*à l'ennemi*) to hand over (*à* to). ~ **qn à la mort** to send sb to his death; **être livré au pillage** to be given over to pillage; ~ **son âme au diable** to give one's soul to the devil; **être livré à soi-même** to be left to o.s. *ou* to one's own devices. **(c)** *confidence* to give away, reveal. **(d)** ~ **bataille** to join *ou* do battle (*à* with); ~ **passage à qn** to let sb pass. **2 se** ~ *vpr* **(a) se** ~ **à** *destin* to abandon o.s. to; *excès, douleur* to give o.s. over to; *boisson* to indulge in; *sport* to practise; *occupation* to be engaged in; *recherches* to do, carry out; *enquête* to hold; **se** ~ **à l'étude** to devote o.s. to study. **(b)** (*à la police*) to give o.s. up; (*à un confident*) to open up (*à* to). ♦ **livreur, -euse** *nm,f* delivery boy (*ou* girl).
livret [livʀɛ] *nm* **(a)** (*Mus*) libretto. **(b)** ~ **de caisse d'épargne** (savings) bank-book; ~ **de famille** (official) family record book; ~ **scolaire** (school) report book.
lobe [lɔb] *nm* (*Anat, Bot*) lobe.
local, e, *mpl* **-aux** [lɔkal, o] **1** *adj* local. **2** *nm* (*salle*) room. (*bureaux*) ~**aux** offices, premises; **dans les** ~**aux de la police** in the police station. ♦ **localement** *adv* (*ici*) locally; (*par endroits*) in places. ♦ **localisation** *nf* localization. ♦ **localiser** (1) *vt* (*gén*) to localize; *épidémie* to confine. ♦ **localité** *nf* locality.
location [lɔkɑsjɔ̃] *nf* **(a)** (*par locataire*) *[maison]* renting; *[voiture]* hiring. **prendre en** ~ *maison* to rent; *bateau* to hire. **(b)** (*par propriétaire*) *[maison]* renting (out), letting; *[voiture]* hiring (out). **donner en** ~ *maison* to rent out, let; *véhicule* to hire out; ~ **de voitures** (*écriteau*) 'cars for hire'. **(c)** (*bail*) **(contrat de)** ~ lease; ~**-vente** hire purchase. **(d)** (*maison*) **il a une** ~ *[locataire]* he is renting a house; *[propriétaire]* he has property for letting. **(e)** (*réservation*) booking. **bureau de** ~ (advance) booking office. ♦ **locataire** *nmf [appartement]* tenant; *[chambre]* lodger.
locomotion [lɔkɔmosjɔ̃] *nf* locomotion.
locomotive [lɔkɔmɔtiv] *nf* locomotive, engine.
locution [lɔkysjɔ̃] *nf* phrase, locution. ~ **figée** set phrase.
logarithme [lɔgaʀitm(ə)] *nm* logarithm.
loge [lɔʒ] *nf [concierge, francs-maçons]* lodge; *[bûcheron]* hut; *[artiste]* dressing room; (*spectateur*) box. (*fig*) **être aux premières** ~**s** to have a ringside seat.
loger [lɔʒe] (3) **1** *vi* to live (*dans* in, *chez* with, at). ~ **rue X** to live in X street; (*Mil*) ~ **chez l'habitant** to be billeted on the local inhabitants. **2** *vt* **(a)** *amis* to put up; *clients* to accommodate; *objet* to put; *soldats* (*chez l'habitant*) to billet. **(b)** (*contenir*) to accommodate. **salle qui loge beaucoup de monde** room which can hold *ou* accommodate a lot of people. **(c)** (*envoyer*) ~ **une balle dans** to lodge a bullet in. **3 se** ~ *vpr* **(a)** *[jeunes mariés]* to find somewhere to live; *[touristes]* to find accommodation; *[étudiant]* to find lodgings *ou* accommodation. **(b)** (*tenir*) **se** ~ **dans qch** to fit into sth. **(c)** (*se coincer dans*) **se** ~ **dans/entre** to lodge itself in/between.
♦ **logé, e** *adj*: **être** ~ **et nourri** to have board and lodging; **être bien/mal** ~ to have good/poor lodgings *ou* accommodation; **être** ~ **à la même enseigne** to be in the same boat. ♦ **logeable** *adj* (*habitable*) habitable; (*spacieux*) roomy. ♦ **logement** *nm* **(a)** (*hébergement*) housing. **(b)** (*appartement*) flat, apartment (*US*). **trouver un** ~ to find lodgings *ou* accommodation *ou* a flat. **(c)** (*Mil*) (*à la caserne*) quartering; (*chez*

l'habitant) billeting. **~s** quarters; billet. ♦ **logeur, -euse** *nm,f* landlord (*ou* landlady). ♦ **logis** *nm* (*littér*) dwelling. **le ~ paternel** the paternal home.

loggia [lɔdʒja] *nf* loggia.

logique [lɔʒik] **1** *nf* logic. **cela est dans la ~ des choses** it's in the nature of things. **2** *adj* logical. ♦ **logiquement** *adv* logically.

logistique [lɔʒistik] **1** *adj* logistic. **2** *nf* logistics (*sg*).

loi [lwa] *nf* law. **se faire une ~ de faire** to make it a rule to do; **il n'a pas la ~ chez lui!*** he's not the boss in his own house!*; **ce qu'il dit fait ~** his word is law; **les ~s de la mode** the dictates of fashion; **les ~s de l'honneur** the code of honour; **les ~s de l'étiquette** the rules of etiquette; **~-cadre** *nf, pl* **~s-~s** outline *ou* blueprint law; **~ martiale** martial law.

loin [lwɛ̃] *adv* **(a)** (*distance*) far. **plus ~** further, farther; **moins ~** not so far (*de* from); **il est ~ derrière** he's far *ou* a long way behind; **au ~** in the distance, far off; **de ~** from a distance; **de ~ en ~** at distant intervals, here and there; **ça ne doit pas faire ~ de 5 km** it can't be far off 5 km. **(b)** (*temps*) **il n'est pas ~ de minuit** it isn't far off midnight; **de ~ en ~** every now and then; **il n'y a pas ~ de 5 ans qu'il est parti** it's not far off 5 years since he left; **c'est ~ tout cela!** (*passé*) that was a long time ago!; (*futur*) that's a long way off!; **~ dans le passé** in the remote past, in far-off times; **voir ~** to see a long way *ou* far ahead. **(c)** (*fig*) **~ de là** far from it; **être très ~ du sujet** to be way off the subject; **~ de moi la pensée de vous blâmer!** far be it from me to blame you!

lointain, e [lwɛ̃tɛ̃, ɛn] **1** *adj* (*lit, fig*) distant, remote; *regard* faraway. **2** *nm*: **dans le ~** in the distance.

loir [lwaʀ] *nm* dormouse.

loisir [lwaziʀ] *nm* **(a) ~s** (*temps libre*) leisure (time), spare time; (*activités*) leisure *ou* spare-time activities. **(b)** (*littér*) **avoir le ~ de faire** to have leisure *ou* time to do; **donner à qn le ~ de faire** to allow sb (the opportunity) to do. ♦ **loisible** *adj* (*littér*) **il vous est ~ de faire** you are at liberty to do.

Londres [lɔ̃dʀ(ə)] *n* London. ♦ **londonien, -ienne** **1** *adj* London. **2** *nm(f)*: **L~(ne)** Londoner.

long, longue [lɔ̃, lɔ̃g] **1** *adj* **(a)** (*gén*) long; *voyage* lengthy; *amitié* long-standing. **un pont ~ de 30 mètres** a bridge 30 metres long; **ce travail est ~ à faire** this work takes a long time; **il a été ~ à s'habiller** he took a long time to get dressed; **il était ~ à venir** he was a long time coming. **(b)** (*locutions*) **ils se connaissent de longue date** they have known each other for a very long time; **à ~ terme** *prévoir* in the long term *ou* run; *projet* long-term; **à plus ou moins longue échéance** sooner or later; **ça n'a pas fait ~ feu** it didn't last long; **de longue haleine** *travail* long-term; **préparé de longue main** prepared well beforehand; **à longue portée** *canon* long-range. **2** *adv*: **s'habiller ~** to wear long clothes; **en savoir ~/trop ~/plus ~** to know a lot/too much/more (*sur* about); **en dire ~** *[attitude etc]* to speak volumes. **3** *nm* **(a) un bateau de 7 mètres de ~** a boat 7 metres long; **en ~** lengthways, lengthwise. **(b) tomber de tout son ~** to measure one's length; **étendu de tout son ~** spread out at full length; **(tout) le ~ du fleuve** (all) along the river; **tout au ~ de son récit** throughout his story; **l'eau coule le ~ de la gouttière** the water flows down *ou* along the gutter; **grimper le ~ d'un mât** to climb up a mast; **tout au** *ou* **du ~** from beginning to end; **de ~ en large** back and forth, to and fro, up and down; **en ~ et en large** at great length. **4** *nf*: **à la longue** in the end. ♦ **long-courrier,** *pl* **~-~s** *nm* (*Naut*) ocean liner; (*Aviat*) long-haul *ou* long-distance aircraft. ♦ **long métrage** *nm* full-length film. ♦ **longue-vue,** *pl* **~s-~s** *nf* telescope. ♦ **longuement** *adv* (*longtemps*) for a long time; (*en détail*) at length. ♦ **longuet, -ette*** *adj* a bit long.

longer [lɔ̃ʒe] (3) *vt [mur, sentier]* to border; *[personne, train]* to go along *ou* alongside. **~ la côte** *[bateau, route]* to hug the coast; *[voiture]* to drive along *ou* keep to the coast.

longévité [lɔ̃ʒevite] *nf* longevity.

longitude [lɔ̃ʒityd] *nf* longitude. **à** *ou* **par 50° de ~ est** at 50° longitude east. ♦ **longitudinal, e,** *mpl* **-aux** *adj* longitudinal.

longtemps [lɔ̃tɑ̃] *adv* (for) a long time; (*dans phrase nég ou interrog*) (for) long. **pendant ~** (for) a long time; (for) long; **pas avant ~** not for a long time; **~ avant/après** long before/after; **il n'en a plus pour ~** (*finir*) he hasn't much longer to go; (*mourir*) he can't last much longer now; **je n'en ai pas pour ~** I shan't be long, it won't take me long; **il habite ici depuis ~, il y a ~ qu'il habite ici** he has been living here (for) a long time; **c'était il y a ~/il n'y a pas ~** that was a long time ago/not long ago.

longue [lɔ̃g] *V* **long.**

longueur [lɔ̃gœʀ] *nf* (*gén*) length. **la plage s'étend sur une ~ de 7 km** the beach stretches for 7 km; **dans le sens de la ~** lengthways, lengthwise; (*lit, fig*) **~ d'onde** wavelength; **à ~ de journée** all day long; **à ~ de temps** all the time; **traîner en ~** to drag on; **prendre 2 ~s d'avance** to go into a 2-length lead; (*dans un film*) **~s** monotonous moments.

lopin [lɔpɛ̃] *nm*: **~ (de terre)** patch of land, plot (of land).

loquace [lɔkas] *adj* talkative.

loque [lɔk] *nf*: **~s** rags; **tomber en ~s** to be in tatters; (*fig péj*) **une ~ (humaine)** a (human) wreck.

loquet [lɔkɛ] *nm* latch.

lorgner* [lɔʀɲe] (1) *vt objet* to eye; *héritage* to have one's eye on. ♦ **lorgnette** *nf* spyglass. ♦ **lorgnon** *nm* pince-nez.

lors [lɔʀ] *adv*: **~ de** at the time of; **~ même que** even though *ou* if.

lorsque [lɔʀsk(ə)] *conj* when.

losange [lɔzɑ̃ʒ] *nm* diamond, lozenge.

lot [lo] *nm* **(a)** (*Loterie*) prize. **le gros ~** the first prize, the jackpot. **(b)** (*portion*) share. **~ (de terre)** plot (of land). **(c)** (*assortiment*) batch; *[draps, vaisselle]* set; (*aux enchères*) lot. **(d)** (*littér: destin*) lot, fate.

loterie [lɔtʀi] *nf* (*lit, fig*) lottery. **gagner à la ~** to win on the lottery.

lotion [losjɔ̃] *nf* lotion.

lotir [lɔtiʀ] (2) *vt* (*diviser*) to divide up. **~ qn de qch** to allot sth to sb, provide sb with sth; **être bien/mal loti** to be well-/badly off. ♦ **lotissement** *nm* **(a)** (*ensemble*) housing estate; (*parcelle*) plot, lot. **(b)** (*action*) division.

loto [lɔto] *nm* (*jeu*) lotto; (*matériel*) lotto set. **~ (national)** ≃ national lottery.

lotus [lɔtys] *nm* lotus.

louable [lwabl(ə)] *adj* praiseworthy, laudable. ♦ **louange** *nf* praise. **à la ~ de qn** in praise of sb. ♦ **louangeur, -euse** *adj* laudatory.

loubar(d) [lubaʀ] *nm* (young) thug.

louche¹ [luʃ] *adj* shady, fishy*, suspicious. **c'est ~** that's funny *ou* odd.

louche² [luʃ] *nf* ladle.

loucher [luʃe] (1) *vi* to squint, have a squint.

louer¹ [lwe] (1) **1** *vt* to praise. **~ qn de qch** to praise sb for sth; (*fig*) **Dieu soit loué!** thank God! **2 se ~** *vpr*: **se ~ de** *employé, appareil* to be very pleased with; **se ~ d'avoir fait qch** to congratulate o.s. on having done sth.

louer² [lwe] (1) *vt* **(a)** *[propriétaire] maison* to let, rent out; *voiture* to hire out, rent (out). **(b)** *[locataire] maison* to rent; *voiture* to hire, rent; *place* to book. **à ~** *chambre etc* to let; *voiture etc* for hire. ♦ **loueur, -euse** *nm,f* (*propriétaire*) hirer.

loufoque* [lufɔk] **1** *adj* crazy, barmy*. **2** *nmf* crackpot*.

loup [lu] **1** *nm* (*carnassier*) wolf; (*poisson*) bass; (*masque*) (eye) mask. **mon petit ~*** (my) pet* *ou* love; **mettre le ~ dans la bergerie** to set the fox to mind the geese. **2: ~-garou** *nm, pl* **~s-~s** werewolf; (*hum*) **le ~-garou** Mr Bogeyman; **~ de mer** (*: *marin*) old salt*; (*vêtement*) (short-sleeved) jersey.

loupe [lup] *nf* magnifying glass.

louper* [lupe] (1) *vt train* to miss; *travail* to mess up*, spoil; *examen* to flunk*. **il a loupé son coup** he bungled *ou* botched* it; **ça va tout faire ~** that'll muck everything up*.

lourd, e [luʀ, luʀd(ə)] *adj* (*lit, fig*) heavy; *temps, chaleur* sultry, close; *faute* serious; *plaisanterie* heavy-handed. **yeux ~s de sommeil** eyes heavy with sleep; **avoir l'estomac ~** to feel bloated; **j'ai la tête ~e** my head feels fuzzy, I feel a bit headachy; **avoir l'esprit ~** to be slow-witted; **~ de menaces** heavy with threat; **~ de conséquences** fraught with consequences; **il n'y a pas ~ de pain*** there isn't much bread; **il n'en sait pas ~** he doesn't know much.
♦ **lourdaud, e** **1** *adj* oafish. **2** *nm,f* oaf.
♦ **lourdement** *adv* (*gén*) heavily. **se tromper ~** to make a big mistake; **insister ~ sur qch** to insist strenuously on sth. ♦ **lourdeur** *nf* (*gén*) heaviness. **~ d'esprit** slow-wittedness; **avoir des ~s d'estomac** to feel bloated.

loustic* [lustik] *nm* (*enfant*) kid*; (*taquin*) villain* (*hum*); (*type*) (funny) guy*.

loutre [lutʀ(ə)] *nf* (*animal*) otter; (*fourrure*) otter-skin.

louve [luv] *nf* she-wolf. ♦ **louveteau,** *pl* **~x** *nm* (*Zool*) (wolf) cub; (*scout*) cub scout.

louvoyer [luvwaje] (8) *vi* (*Naut*) to tack; (*fig*) to hedge, evade the issue.

loyal, e, *mpl* **-aux** [lwajal, o] *adj* (*fidèle*) loyal, faithful, trusty; (*honnête*) fair, honest.
♦ **loyalement** *adv* loyally, faithfully; fairly, honestly. ♦ **loyauté** *nf* loyalty, faithfulness; fairness, honesty.

loyer [lwaje] *nm* rent.

lubie [lybi] *nf* whim, craze, fad. **il lui a pris la ~ de faire** he has taken it into his head to do.

lubrifier [lybʀifje] (7) *vt* to lubricate.
♦ **lubrifiant, e** **1** *adj* lubricating. **2** *nm* lubricant.
♦ **lubrification** *nf* lubrication.

lubrique [lybʀik] *adj* lewd.

lucarne [lykaʀn(ə)] *nf* [*toit*] skylight; (*en saillie*) dormer window.

lucide [lysid] *adj vieillard* lucid; *accidenté* conscious; *observateur* clear-headed; *raisonnement* lucid, clear. ♦ **lucidement** *adv* lucidly, clearly.
♦ **lucidité** *nf* lucidity; consciousness; clear-headedness; clearness.

lucratif, -ive [lykʀatif, iv] *adj* lucrative. **association à but non ~** non-profit-making organization.
♦ **lucrativement** *adv* lucratively.

lueur [lɥœʀ] *nf*: **~(s)** (*lit*) (faint) light; [*braises, soleil couchant*] glow; [*flamme, raison, espoir*] glimmer; [*désir, colère*] gleam; **à la ~ d'une bougie** by candlelight; **les premières ~s de l'aube** the first light of dawn.

luge [lyʒ] *nf* sledge, sled (*US*). **faire de la ~** to sledge, sled (*US*).

lugubre [lygybʀ(ə)] *adj* gloomy, dismal.

lui [lɥi] **1** *pron pers mf* (*objet indirect*) (*homme*) him; (*femme, bateau, nation*) her; (*animal, bébé*) it, him, her; (*chose*) it. **je ne le ~ ai jamais caché** I have never kept it from him *ou* her; **il ~ est facile de le faire** it's easy for him *ou* her to do it. **2** *pron m* **(a)** (*fonction objet*) (*personne*) him; (*pays, bateau*) her; (*animal*) him, her, it; (*chose*) it. **c'est ~, je le reconnais** it's him, I recognize him. **(b)** (*sujet, gén emphatique*) (*personne*) he, him; (*chose*) it; (*animal*) it, she, he; (*nation*) she, her. **elle est venue mais pas ~** she came but not him *ou* but he didn't; **c'est ~ qui me l'a dit** he told me himself, it's he who told me; **chasse ce chien, c'est ~ qui m'a mordu** chase that dog away – it's the one that bit me. **(c)** (*avec prép*) (*personne*) him; (*chose*) it. **ce livre est à ~** this book belongs to him *ou* is his; **il a un appartement à ~** he has a flat of his own; **un ami à ~** a friend of his, one of his friends; **il ne pense qu'à ~** he only thinks of himself; **elle veut une photo de ~** she wants a photo of him. **(d)** (*dans comparaisons*) (*sujet*) he, him*; (*objet*) him. **j'ai mangé plus que ~** I ate more than he did *ou* than him*; **ne fais pas comme ~** don't do as he did.

luire [lɥiʀ] (38) *vi* (*gén*) to shine; (*reflet humide*) to glisten; (*reflet moiré*) to shimmer, glimmer; (*éclat bref*) to glint; (*rougeoiement*) to glow. **rendu luisant par l'usure** shiny with wear; **yeux luisants de fièvre** eyes bright with fever.
♦ **luisant** *nm* [*étoffe*] sheen; [*pelage*] gloss.

lumbago [lɔ̃bago] *nm* lumbago.

lumière [lymjɛʀ] *nf* (*gén*) light. **la ~ du jour** daylight; **la ~ du soleil l'éblouit** he was dazzled by the sunlight; **donne-nous de la ~** switch *ou* put the light on, will you?; **il y a de la ~ dans sa chambre** there's a light on in his room; **à la ~ des récents événements** in the light of recent events; **faire (toute) la ~ sur qch** to make sth (wholly) clear; **le pauvre garçon n'est pas une ~** the poor boy doesn't really shine; **avoir des ~s sur une question** to have some knowledge of a question.
♦ **luminaire** *nm* light, lamp. ♦ **lumineux, -euse** *adj* (*gén*) luminous; *fontaine, enseigne* illuminated; *rayon* of light; (*iro*) *exposé* limpid, brilliant. **source ~euse** light source; **c'est ~!** it's as clear as daylight! ♦ **luminosité** *nf* luminosity. **il y a beaucoup de ~** the light is very bright.

lunch [lœntʃ] *nm* buffet lunch.

lundi [lœ̃di] *nm* Monday; *V* **samedi.**

lune [lyn] *nf* moon. **pleine/nouvelle ~** full/new moon; **nuit sans ~** moonless night; **~ de miel** honeymoon; **être dans la ~** to be in a dream; **demander la ~** to ask for the moon. ♦ **lunaire** *adj paysage* lunar. ♦ **lunatique** *adj* quirky, temperamental. ♦ **luné, e*** *adj*: **être bien/mal ~** to be in a good/bad mood.

lunette [lynɛt] *nf* **(a)** **~s** glasses, specs*; (*de protection*) goggles; **~s de soleil** sunglasses. **(b)** (*télescope*) telescope; [*fusil*] sight(s). **~ d'approche** telescope; (*Aut*) **~ arrière** rear window.

luron* [lyʀɔ̃] *nm* lad*. **gai ~** gay dog.

lustre [lystʀ(ə)] *nm* **(a)** [*peau, vernis*] lustre, shine; [*cérémonie*] lustre. **(b)** (*luminaire*) chandelier. **(c)** **depuis des ~s** for ages.

lustrer [lystʀe] (1) *vt* (*Tech*) *étoffe* to lustre; (*gén: faire briller*) to shine; (*par l'usure*) to make shiny. ♦ **lustré, e** *adj poil* glossy; *manche usée* shiny.

luth [lyt] *nm* lute.

lutin [lytɛ̃] *nm* (*lit, fig*) imp.

lutte [lyt] *nf* **(a)** (*bataille*) struggle, fight. (*action*) **la ~** fighting; **~ armée** armed struggle; **~ des classes** class-struggle *ou* war; **~ d'intérêts** clash of interests; **être en ~ contre qn** to be in conflict with sb; **le pays en ~** the country at war. **(b)** (*Sport*) wrestling. **~ libre** all-in wrestling.
♦ **lutter** (1) *vi* to struggle, fight. **~ contre** *adversaire* to struggle *ou* fight against; *incendie* to fight; *sommeil, mort* to battle against; **ils luttaient de vitesse** they were racing each other.
♦ **lutteur, -euse** *nm,f* (*Sport*) wrestler; (*fig*) fighter.

luxe [lyks(ə)] *nm* (*richesse*) luxury; [*maison, objet*] luxuriousness. **de ~** *voiture* luxury; (*Comm*) *produits* de luxe; **je ne peux pas me payer le ~ d'être malade** I can't afford the luxury

of being ill; **un ~ de détails** a host *ou* wealth of details. ♦ **luxueusement** *adv* luxuriously. ♦ **luxueux, -euse** *adj* luxurious.
Luxembourg [lyksɑ̃buʀ] *nm* Luxembourg. ♦ **luxembourgeois, e 1** *adj* of Luxembourg. **2** *nm(f)*: **L~(e)** native of Luxembourg.
luxer [lykse] (1) *vt* to dislocate. **se ~ un membre** to dislocate a limb. ♦ **luxation** *nf* dislocation.
luxure [lyksyʀ] *nf* lust.
luxuriance [lyksyʀjɑ̃s] *nf* luxuriance. ♦ **luxuriant, e** *adj* luxuriant.
luzerne [lyzɛʀn(ə)] *nf* lucerne, alfalfa.
lycée [lise] *nm* lycée, ≈ secondary school, high school (*US*). **~ technique** technical school. ♦ **lycéen, -enne** *nm,f* secondary school *ou* high-school (*US*) pupil (*ou* boy *ou* girl).
lymphe [lɛ̃f] *nf* lymph. ♦ **lymphatique** *adj* (*Bio*) lymphatic; (*fig*) sluggish.
lyncher [lɛ̃ʃe] (1) *vt* to lynch.
lynx [lɛ̃ks] *nm* lynx.
lyre [liʀ] *nf* lyre. ♦ **lyrique** *adj* **(a)** (*Mus, Poésie*) lyric. **artiste ~** opera singer. **(b)** (*enthousiaste*) lyrical. ♦ **lyrisme** *nm* lyricism.
lys [lis] *nm* = **lis.**

M

M, m [ɛm] *nm ou nf* (*lettre*) M, m.
m' [m(ə)] *V* **me.**
ma [ma] *adj poss V* **mon.**
macabre [makɑbʀ(ə)] *adj* macabre, gruesome.
macadam [makadam] *nm [pierres]* macadam; *[goudron]* Tarmac(adam) ®; (*fig: rue*) road. ♦ **macadamiser** (1) *vt* to macadamize; to tarmac.
macaron [makaʀɔ̃] *nm* (*Culin*) macaroon; (*insigne*) (round) badge; (*autocollant*) (round) sticker.
macaroni [makaʀɔni] *nm* piece of macaroni. **manger des** ~**s** to eat macaroni.
macchabée* [makabe] *nm* stiff* (*corpse*).
macédoine [masedwan] *nf*: ~ **de légumes** mixed vegetables; ~ **de fruits** fruit salad.
macérer [maseʀe] (6) *vti*: **(faire)** ~ to macerate. ♦ **macération** *nf* maceration.
Mach [mak] *nm* mach. **voler à** ~ **2** to fly at mach 2.
mâche [mɑʃ] *nf* corn salad, lambs' lettuce.
mâchefer [mɑʃfɛʀ] *nm* clinker, cinders.
mâcher [mɑʃe] (1) *vt [personne]* to chew; (*avec bruit*) to munch; *[animal]* to chomp. **il faut lui** ~ **tout le travail** you have to do half his work for him; **il ne mâche pas ses mots** he doesn't mince his words.
machiavélique [makjavelik] *adj* Machiavellian.
machin, e[1]* [maʃɛ̃, in] **1** *nm,f* thing; (*dont le nom échappe*) thingummyjig*, what-d'you-call-it*. **2** *nm* (*personne*) **M**~ **(chouette)** what's-his-name*, what d'you-call-him*; **hé! M**~! hey there you!; **le père M**~ Mr what's-his-name*. **3 M**~**e** *nf* (*personne*) what's-her-name*.
machine[2] [maʃin] **1** *nf* (*gén, fig*) machine; (*locomotive*) engine, locomotive; (*Naut: moteur*) engine; (*avion*) plane; (*: *moto*) bike. **la** ~ **administrative** the bureaucratic machinery; **à la** ~ by machine, with a machine; **fait à la** ~ machine-made; **faire** ~ **arrière** (*Naut*) to go astern; (*fig*) to back-pedal, draw back. **2:** ~ **à affranchir/à calculer** franking/calculating machine; ~ **à coudre** sewing machine; ~ **à écrire** typewriter; ~ **à laver** washing machine; ~ **à laver la vaisselle** dishwasher; ~**-outil** *nf, pl* ~**s-**~**s** machine tool; ~ **à sous** (*Casino*) one-armed bandit, fruit machine; (*distributeur*) slot machine; ~ **à vapeur** steam engine. ♦ **machinal, e,** *mpl* **-aux** *adj* mechanical. ♦ **machinalement** *adv* mechanically. ♦ **machinisme** *nm* mechanization. ♦ **machiniste** *nm* (*Théât*) stagehand; (*Transport*) driver.
machiner [maʃine] (1) *vt trahison etc* to plot, engineer. **il a tout machiné** he engineered the whole thing. ♦ **machination** *nf* (*complot*) plot, machination. **odieuses** ~**s** foul machinations *ou* schemings.
mâchoire [mɑʃwaʀ] *nf* jaw.
mâchonner* [mɑʃɔne] (1) *vt*, **mâchouiller*** [mɑʃuje] (1) *vt* to chew at *ou* on.
maçon [masɔ̃] *nm* (*gén*) builder; *[pierre]* (stone)mason; *[briques]* bricklayer. ♦ **maçonnerie** *nf* **(a)** *[pierres]* masonry, stonework; *[briques]* brickwork. **(b)** (*travail*) building; bricklaying. **entreprise de** ~ building firm.
macro ... [makʀɔ] *préf* macro ... .
maculer [makyle] (1) *vt* to stain (*de* with).
Madame [madam], *pl* **Mesdames** [medam] *nf* **(a)** (*s'adressant à qn*) **bonjour** ~ (*courant*) good morning; (*nom connu*) good morning, Mrs X; (*avec déférence*) good morning, Madam; (*devant un auditoire*) **Mesdames (, Messieurs)** ladies (and gentlemen); ~ **la Présidente** Madam Chairman; **oui** ~ **la Marquise** yes Madam; (*Scol*) ~! please Mrs X!, please Miss! **(b)** (*parlant de qn*) ~ **X est malade** Mrs X is ill; **je vais le dire à** ~ I will inform Mrs X; ~ **dit que c'est à elle** the lady says it belongs to her; ~ **la Présidente** the chairman. **(c)** (*sur une enveloppe*) ~ **X** Mrs X; **Mesdames X** the Mrs X; **Mesdames X et Y** Mrs X and Mrs Y; **Monsieur X et** ~ Mr and Mrs X; ~ **la Maréchale X** Mrs X; ~ **la Marquise de X** the Marchioness of X. **(d)** (*en-tête de lettre*) Dear Madam. **Chère** ~ Dear Mrs X; ~**, Mademoiselle, Monsieur** Dear Sir or Madam; ~ **la Maréchale** Dear Madam. **(e)** (*sans majuscule, pl* ~s: * *ou péj*) lady.
Mademoiselle [madmwazɛl], *pl* **Mesdemoiselles** [medmwazɛl] *nf* **(a)** (*s'adressant à qn*) **bonjour** ~ (*courant*) good morning; (*nom connu*) good morning, Miss X; **bonjour Mesdemoiselles** good morning ladies; (*au restaurant*) **et pour vous** ~? and for the young lady?, and for you, miss? **(b)** (*parlant de qn*) ~ **X est malade** Miss X is ill; ~ **est sortie** Miss X is out; **je vais le dire à** ~ I shall tell Miss X. **(c)** (*sur une enveloppe*) ~ **X** Miss X; **Mesdemoiselles X** the Misses X; **Mesdemoiselles X et Y** Miss X and Miss Y. **(d)** (*en-tête de lettre*) Dear Madam. **Chère** ~ Dear Miss X.
Madère [madɛʀ] **1** *nf* Madeira. **2** *nm*: **m**~ Madeira (wine).
madone [madɔn] *nf* madonna.
maf(f)ia [mafja] *nf* **(a) la M**~ the Maf(f)ia. **(b)** *[trafiquants]* gang, ring. ~ **d'anciens élèves** old boys' network.
magasin [magazɛ̃] *nm* **(a)** (*boutique*) shop, store; (*entrepôt*) warehouse. ~ **à grande surface** hypermarket; ~ **à succursales multiples** chain *ou* multiple store; **faire les** ~**s** to go shopping; **nous ne l'avons pas en** ~ we haven't got it in stock. **(b)** (*Tech*) *[fusil, appareil-photo]* magazine. ♦ **magasinier** *nm [usine]* storeman; *[entrepôt]* warehouseman.
magazine [magazin] *nm* (*Presse*) magazine. (*Rad, TV*) ~ **féminin** woman's hour.
mage [maʒ] *nm* magus.
Maghreb [magʀɛb] *nm*: **le** ~ the Maghreb, NW Africa.
magie [maʒi] *nf* magic. **comme par** ~ like magic, as if by magic. ♦ **magicien, -ienne** *nm,f* magician. ♦ **magique** *adj* (*lit*) magic; (*fig: enchanteur*) magical. ♦ **magiquement** *adv* magically.
magistral, e, *mpl* **-aux** [maʒistʀal, o] *adj* (*éminent*) masterly; (*hum: gigantesque*) thorough, colossal; (*doctoral*) *ton* authoritative, masterful. (*Univ*) **cours** ~ lecture. ♦ **magistralement** *adv* in a masterly manner.
magistrat [maʒistʀa] *nm* magistrate. ♦ **magistrature** *nf* (*Jur*) magistracy; (*Admin, Pol*) public office. **la** ~ **suprême** the supreme *ou* highest office.
magma [magma] *nm* (*Sci*) magma; (*fig*) jumble.
magnanime [maɲanim] *adj* magnanimous. ♦ **magnanimité** *nf* magnanimity.

magnat [magna] *nm* tycoon, magnate. ~ **de la presse** press baron *ou* lord.

magner (se)‡ [maɲe] (1) *vpr* to get a move on*, hurry up.

magnésium [maɲezjɔm] *nm* magnesium.

magnétiser [maɲetize] (1) *vt* (*Phys, fig*) to magnetize; (*hypnotiser*) to hypnotize. ♦ **magnétique** *adj* (*Phys, fig*) magnetic. ♦ **magnétisation** *nf* magnetization; hypnotization. ♦ **magnétiseur, -euse** *nm,f* hypnotizer. ♦ **magnétisme** *nm* magnetism; hypnotism.

magnéto [maɲeto] **1** *nf* (*Élec*) magneto. **2** *préf* magneto. **3** *nm* (*) tape recorder. ♦ **magnétophone** *nm* tape recorder. ~ **à cassettes** cassette recorder. ♦ **magnétoscope** *nm* (*appareil*) video (-tape) recorder; (*bande*) video-tape.

magnificence [maɲifisɑ̃s] *nf* (*faste*) magnificence.

magnifique [maɲifik] *adj* (*gén*) magnificent; *fleur, temps* gorgeous, superb; *projet* marvellous. ~!* fantastic!*, great!* ♦ **magnifiquement** *adv* magnificently; gorgeously, superbly; marvellously.

magot [mago] *nm* **(a)** (*Zool*) Barbary ape. **(b)** (*Sculp*) magot. **(c)** (*) (*somme d'argent*) pile (of money)*, packet*; (*économies*) savings, nest egg.

magouiller* [maguje] (1) *vi* (*péj*) to graft*.

mahara(d)jah [maaʀa(d)ʒa] *nm* Maharajah.

mai [mɛ] *nm* May; *V* **septembre.**

maigre [mɛgʀ(ə)] **1** *adj* **(a)** *personne* thin, skinny (*péj*); *visage* thin, lean. ~ **comme un clou*** as thin as a rake. **(b)** *bouillon* clear; *viande* lean; *fromage* low-fat. **(c)** (*Rel*) **jour** ~ day of abstinence; **faire** ~ to eat no meat. **(d)** *profit* small, slim, scanty; *ration, résultat, salaire* meagre, poor; *exposé* sketchy, skimpy; *espoir* slim, slight. **c'est un peu** ~ it's a bit skimpy, it's a bit on the short side. **(e)** *végétation* thin, sparse; *récolte, terre* poor. **un** ~ **filet d'eau** a thin trickle of water. **2** *nmf* thin person. **3** *nm* (*viande*) lean meat; (*jus*) thin gravy.

♦ **maigrement** *adv* poorly, meagrely. ♦ **maigreur** *nf* thinness; leanness; smallness, scantiness; meagreness; sketchiness; sparseness; poverty. **il est d'une** ~! he's so thin! ♦ **maigrir** (2) **1** *vi* to get thinner, lose weight. **il a maigri de 5 kg** he has lost 5 kg; **se faire** ~ to slim, diet (to lose weight). **2** *vt*: ~ **qn** *[vêtement]* to make sb look slim (*ou* slimmer); *[maladie]* to make sb lose weight.

maille [maj] *nf* **(a)** (*Couture*) stitch. *[bas]* ~ **filée** ladder, run; **une** ~ **à l'endroit, une** ~ **à l'envers** knit one, purl one; **tissu à fines** ~s fine-knit material. **(b)** *[filet]* mesh. (*lit, fig*) **passer à travers les** ~**s (du filet)** to slip through the net; **filet à larges/fines** ~s wide/fine mesh net. **(c)** *[armure, grillage]* link. **(d) avoir** ~ **à partir avec qn** to get into trouble with sb.

maillet [majɛ] *nm* mallet.

mailloche [majɔʃ] *nf* (*Tech*) beetle.

maillon [mɑjɔ̃] *nm* (*lit, fig*) link.

maillot [majo] *nm* (*gén*) vest; (*Danse*) leotard; (*Sport*) jersey; *[bébé]* baby's wrap. ~ **de bain** *[homme]* swimming trunks; *[femme]* swimming costume, swimsuit; ~ **de corps** vest, undershirt (*US*).

main [mɛ̃] **1** *nf* **(a)** hand. **donner la** ~ **à qn** to hold sb's hand; **il me salua de la** ~ he waved to me; **être adroit de ses** ~s to be clever with one's hands; **des deux** ~s with both hands; **la** ~ **dans la** ~ *[promeneurs]* hand in hand; *[escrocs]* hand in glove; **les** ~**s en l'air!** hands up!, stick 'em up!*; **trouver une** ~ **secourable** to find a helping hand; **tomber aux** ~**s de l'ennemi** to fall into the hands of the enemy; **accorder la** ~ **de sa fille à qn** to give sb one's daughter's hand in marriage.

(b) (*locutions*) **à** ~ **droite/gauche** on the right-hand/left-hand side; **de** ~ **de maître** with a master's hand; **en** ~**s sûres** in(to) safe hands; **avoir une voiture bien en** ~ to have the feel of a car; **de la** ~ **à la** ~ directly (*without receipt*); **préparé de longue** ~ prepared long beforehand; **de première/seconde** ~ firsthand/secondhand; **à la** ~ by hand; **fait (à la)** ~ handmade; **cousu (à la)** ~ hand-sewn; **vol à** ~ **armée** armed robbery; **(pris) la** ~ **dans le sac** caught red-handed, caught in the act; **en sous** ~ *agir* secretly; **les** ~**s vides** empty-handed; **avoir tout sous la** ~ to have everything at hand; **à** ~ **levée** *vote* by a show of hands; *dessin* freehand.

(c) (*locutions verbales*) **avoir la** ~ **heureuse** to be lucky; **avoir la** ~ **lourde** to be heavy-handed; (*gifler*) **avoir la** ~ **leste** to be free with one's hands; **je ne suis pas à ma** ~ I can't get a proper hold *ou* grip; **perdre la** ~ to lose one's touch; **se faire la** ~ to get one's hand in; **faire** ~ **basse sur qch** to run off with sth; **laisser les** ~**s libres à qn** to give sb a free hand *ou* rein; **mettre la** ~ **au collet de qn** to arrest sb; **en venir aux** ~s to come to blows; **mettre la** ~ **sur** to lay hands on; **mettre la** ~ **à la pâte** to lend a hand; **mettre la dernière** ~ **à** to put the finishing touches to; **avoir la situation (bien) en** ~ to have the situation well in hand; **prendre qch/qn en** ~ to take sth/sb in hand; **remettre qch en** ~**s propres à qn** to hand sth to sb personally; **il n'y va pas de** ~ **morte** (*exagérer*) he doesn't do things by halves; (*frapper*) he doesn't pull his punches; **j'en mettrais ma** ~ **au feu** *ou* **à couper** I'd stake my life on it; **prêter** ~**-forte à qn** to come to sb's assistance.

2: ~ **courante** handrail; ~**-d'œuvre** *nf* labour, manpower.

mainmise [mɛ̃miz] *nf* (*Jur, Pol*) seizure (*sur* of).

maint, e [mɛ̃, ɛ̃t] *adj* (*littér*) many. ~ **étranger** many a foreigner; ~**s étrangers** many foreigners.

maintenant [mɛ̃tnɑ̃] *adv* now. **il doit être arrivé** ~ he must have arrived by now; **les jeunes de** ~ young people nowadays *ou* today.

maintenir [mɛ̃tniʀ] (22) **1** *vt* (*gén*) to keep; *édifice* to hold *ou* keep up, support; *tradition* to maintain, uphold; *décision* to stand by; *affirmation* to maintain. ~ **qch en équilibre** to keep *ou* hold sth balanced; ~ **la tête hors de l'eau** to keep one's head above water; ~ **l'ordre** to keep *ou* maintain law and order. **2 se** ~ *vpr [temps]* to stay fair; *[amélioration, préjugé]* to persist; *[malade]* to hold one's own; *[prix]* to hold steady. (*Scol*) **se** ~ **dans la moyenne** to keep up with the middle of the class. ♦ **maintien** *nm* **(a)** (*sauvegarde*) (*gén*) maintenance; *[tradition]* upholding. **(b)** (*posture*) bearing, deportment. **professeur de** ~ teacher of deportment.

maire [mɛʀ] *nm* mayor. ♦ **mairie** *nf* (*bâtiment*) town hall; (*administration*) town council.

mais [mɛ] **1** *conj* but. **tu me crois? –** ~ **oui** do you believe me? – (but) of course *ou* of course I do; ~ **ne te fais pas de soucis!** don't you worry!; ~ **dites-moi, c'est intéressant!** well now that's interesting!; ~ **j'y pense, ...** by the way I've just thought, ...; **ah** ~**!, non** ~ **(des fois)!** look here! **2** *nm*: **je ne veux pas de** ~ I don't want any buts; **il y a un** ~ there's one snag.

maïs [mais] *nm* maize, corn (*US*).

maison [mɛzɔ̃] **1** *nf* **(a)** (*bâtiment*) house; (*immeuble*) building; (*locatif*) block of flats. ~ **individuelle** (detached) house. **(b)** (*foyer*) home. **être/rester à la** ~ to be/stay at home; **rentrer à la** ~ to go (back) home; **les dépenses de la** ~ household expenses; **fait à la** ~ home-made. **(c)** (*famille*) family. **il n'est pas heureux à la** ~ he doesn't have a happy home *ou* family life. **(d)** (*entreprise*) firm, company; (*magasin*) (*grand*) store; (*petit*) shop. **(e)** (*famille royale*) House. **(f)** (*domesticité*) household. **la** ~ **du Roi** the Royal Household; **employés de** ~ domestic staff.

2 *adj inv* **(a)** *gâteau* home-made; *ingénieur* trained by the firm. **pâté ~** pâté maison, chef's own pâté. **(b)** (*: *très réussi*) first-rate. **une bagarre ~** an almighty* *ou* a stand-up row.

3: **~ d'arrêt** prison; **la M~ Blanche** the White House; **~ de campagne** (*grande*) house in the country; (*petite*) (country) cottage; **~ close** *ou* **de passe** brothel; **~ de jeu** gambling club; **~ des jeunes et de la culture** ≃ youth club and arts centre; (*Comm*) **~ mère** parent company; **~ de poupée** doll's house; **~ de repos** convalescent home; **~ de retraite** old people's home; **~ de santé** (*clinique*) nursing home; (*asile*) mental home. ♦ **maisonnée** *nf* household, family. ♦ **maisonnette** *nf* small house.

maître, maîtresse [mɛtʀ(ə), mɛtʀɛs] **1** *adj* **(a)** (*gén*) main; *œuvre* major; *qualité* chief, major; (*Cartes*) *atout* master. **position maîtresse** major *ou* key position; **idée maîtresse** principal *ou* governing idea. **(b)** (*intensif*) **un ~ filou** an arrant *ou* out-and-out rascal; **une maîtresse femme** a managing woman.

2 *nm* **(a)** (*gén*) master; (*Pol: dirigeant*) ruler. **agir en ~** to act authoritatively; **d'un ton de ~** in an authoritative *ou* a masterful tone; **le ~ de céans** the master of the house; **~ (d'école)** teacher, (school)master; **~ charpentier** master carpenter. **(b)** (*titre*) (*pour artistes etc*) **M~** Sir; **mon cher M~** Dear Mr X; (*Jur*) **M~ X** Mr X. **(c)** (*locutions*) **être ~ chez soi** to be master in one's own home; **être son propre ~** to be one's own master; **être ~ de faire** to be free to do; **rester ~ de soi** to keep one's self-control; **être ~ de soi** to have control of o.s.; **être ~ de la situation** to be in control of the situation; **se rendre ~ de** *pays* to gain control of; *incendie* to bring under control; **il est passé ~ dans l'art de mentir** he's a past master in the art of lying.

3 *nf* **(a)** (*gén*) mistress. **(b)** (*Scol*) **maîtresse (d'école)** teacher, (school)mistress; **maîtresse!** Miss!

4: **~ d'armes** fencing master; **~ de cérémonie** master of ceremonies; (*Crime*) **~ chanteur** blackmailer; **~ de conférences** ≃ senior lecturer; **~ d'équipage** boatswain; **~ d'hôtel** *[maison]* butler; *[restaurant]* head waiter; **~ de maison** host; **maîtresse de maison** (*ménagère*) housewife; (*hôtesse*) hostess; **~ nageur** swimming teacher *ou* instructor.

maîtrise [metʀiz] *nf* **(a)** (*sang-froid*) **~ (de soi)** self-control, self-possession. **(b)** (*contrôle*) mastery, control. (*Mil*) **avoir la ~ de** to have control of, control. **(c)** (*habileté*) skill, expertise. **(d)** (*Ind*) supervisory staff. **(e)** (*Rel*) (*école*) choir school; (*groupe*) choir. **(f)** (*Univ*) *research degree* ≃ master's degree. **~ de conférence** ≃ senior lectureship. ♦ **maîtriser** (1) **1** *vt forcené* to control; *adversaire* to overcome, overpower; *émeute*, *révolte* to suppress, bring under control; *difficulté, langue* to master; *inflation* to curb; *larmes, rire* to force back, restrain. **2 se ~** *vpr* to control o.s. ♦ **maîtrisable** *adj* controllable.

majesté [maʒɛste] *nf* (*gén*) majesty. **Votre M~** Your Majesty; **Sa M~** (*roi*) His Majesty; (*reine*) Her Majesty. ♦ **majestueusement** *adv* majestically. ♦ **majestueux, -euse** *adj* (*gén*) majestic; *taille* imposing.

majeur, e [maʒœʀ] **1** *adj* **(a)** (*principal*) major. **sa préoccupation ~e** his major *ou* main concern; **en ~e partie** for the most part; **la ~e partie des gens** most people, the majority (of people). **(b)** (*Jur*) **être ~** to be of age; **il sera ~ en 1995** he will come of age in 1995. **(c)** (*Mus*) major. **2** *nm,f* (*Jur*) major. **3** *nm* middle finger.

major [maʒɔʀ] *nm* (*Mil*) **(médecin) ~** medical officer; (*Univ etc*) **être ~ de promotion** ≃ to be first in one's year.

majorer [maʒɔʀe] (1) *vt impôt, prix* to increase, raise (*de* by). ♦ **majoration** *nf* (*hausse*) rise, increase (*de* in); (*supplément*) surcharge.

majorité [maʒɔʀite] *nf* (*gén*) majority; (*parti majoritaire*) government, party in power. **élu à une ~ de** elected by a majority of; **être en ~** to be in the majority; **groupe composé en ~ de** group mainly composed of; (*Jur*) **atteindre sa ~** to come of age, reach one's majority. ♦ **majoritaire** *adj* majority. **être ~** to be in the majority.

majuscule [maʒyskyl] **1** *adj* capital. **2** *nf* capital letter; (*Typ*) upper case letter.

mal [mal] **1** *adv* **(a)** (*de façon défectueuse*) badly, not properly. **cette porte ferme ~** this door shuts badly *ou* doesn't shut properly; **nous sommes ~ nourris** the food we're given is poor *ou* bad; **il a ~ pris ce que je lui ai dit** he took exception to what I said to him; **il s'y est ~ pris** he set about it the wrong way; **de ~ en pis** from bad to worse. **(b) ~ choisi** *etc* ill-chosen *etc*; **~ à l'aise** (*gêné*) ill-at-ease; (*malade*) unwell; **~ famé** of ill fame, disreputable; **~ en point** in a bad state; **~ à propos** at the wrong moment; **avoir l'esprit ~ tourné** to have a low mind; **il est ~ venu de se plaindre** he is scarcely in a position to complain. **(c) ~ comprendre** to misunderstand; **~ interpréter** to misinterpret; **~ renseigner** to misinform. **(d)** (*avec difficulté*) with difficulty. **on comprend ~ pourquoi** it is not easy *ou* it is difficult to understand why. **(e)** (*de façon répréhensible*) badly, wrongly. **trouves-tu ~ qu'il y soit allé?** do you think it was wrong of him to go? **(f)** (*malade*) **se sentir ~** to feel ill; **être ~ portant** to be in poor health; **se trouver ~** to faint. **(g) il n'a pas ~ travaillé ce trimestre** he's worked quite well this term; **vous (ne) feriez pas ~ de le surveiller** it wouldn't be a bad thing if you kept an eye on him. **(h)** (*beaucoup*) **pas ~ (de)*** quite a lot (of); **on a pas ~ travaillé aujourd'hui** we've worked pretty hard today*; **je m'en fiche pas ~!** I couldn't care less!, I don't give a damn!‡

2 *adj inv* **(a)** (*contraire à la morale*) wrong, bad. **c'est ~ à lui de dire cela** it's bad *ou* wrong of him to say this. **(b)** (*malade*) ill. **il est au plus ~** he is very ill. **(c)** (*mal à l'aise*) uncomfortable. **il est ~ dans sa peau** he's at odds with himself; **on n'est pas ~ (assis) dans ces fauteuils** these armchairs are quite comfortable. **(d) être ~ avec qn** to be on bad terms with sb; **se mettre ~ avec qn** to get on the wrong side of sb. **(e) pas ~*** (*bien*) not bad*, quite *ou* rather good; (*beau*) quite attractive; (*compétent*) quite competent.

3 *nm, pl* **maux** [mo] **(a)** (*ce qui est mauvais*) evil, ill. **le ~** evil; **~ nécessaire** necessary evil; **penser/dire du ~ de qn** to think/speak ill of sb. **(b)** (*qui cause un dommage*) harm. **faire du ~ à** to harm, hurt; **il n'y a pas de ~ à cela** there's no harm in that; **~ m'en a pris de sortir** going out was a grave mistake (on my part). **(c)** (*douleur*) pain; (*maladie*) illness, disease; (*tristesse*) sorrow, pain. **avoir ~ partout** to be aching all over; **se faire (du) ~** to hurt o.s.; **ça fait ~, j'ai ~** it hurts; **j'ai ~ dans le dos** I've got a pain in my back, my back hurts; **avoir un ~ de tête** to have a headache; **avoir ~ aux dents** to have toothache; **avoir ~ au pied** to have a sore foot; **des maux d'estomac** stomach pains, an upset stomach; **un ~ blanc** a whitlow; **avoir le ~ de mer** to be seasick; **contre le ~ de mer** against seasickness; **~ du pays** homesickness. **(d)** (*effort*) difficulty, trouble. **se donner du ~ à faire qch** to take trouble *ou* pains over sth; **avoir du ~ à faire qch** to have trouble *ou* difficulty doing sth; **on n'a rien sans ~** you get nothing without (some) effort.

malabar* [malabaʀ] *nm* muscle man*.

malade [malad] **1** *adj homme* ill, sick, unwell; *organe, plante* diseased; *dent, jambe* bad. **être ~ du cœur** to have heart trouble *ou* a bad heart; **tomber ~** to fall ill *ou* sick; **ça me rend ~** it makes me sick (*de* with); (*fou*) **tu n'es pas ~?*** are you mad *ou* out of your mind?; **l'entreprise est bien ~** the business is in a shaky state. **2** *nmf* invalid, sick person; (*d'un médecin*) patient. **~ mental** mentally sick person; **les ~s** the sick. ♦ **maladie** *nf* **(a)** (*Méd*) illness, disease; *[plante, vin]* disease. **~ de cœur/foie** heart/liver complaint *ou* disease; **il en a fait une ~*** he was in a terrible state about it. **(b)** (*: *obsession*) mania. **avoir la ~ de la vitesse** to be a speed maniac. ♦ **maladif, -ive** *adj* (*lit*) sickly; *obsession* pathological.

maladroit, e [maladʀwa, wat] **1** *adj* (*gén*) clumsy, awkward. **~ de ses mains** useless with one's hands; **ce serait ~ de lui en parler** it would be a mistake to mention it to him. **2** *nm,f* clumsy clot. ♦ **maladresse** *nf* **(a)** clumsiness, awkwardness. **(b)** (*gaffe*) blunder, gaffe. ♦ **maladroitement** *adv* clumsily, awkwardly.

malaise [malɛz] *nm* **(a)** (*Méd*) dizzy turn. **avoir un ~** to feel faint *ou* dizzy. **(b)** (*fig: trouble*) uneasiness, disquiet. **le ~ étudiant** student discontent *ou* unrest.

malaisé, e [maleze] *adj* difficult. ♦ **malaisément** *adv* with difficulty.

malappris, e [malapʀi, iz] **1** *adj* boorish. **2** *nm,f* lout, boor.

malavisé, e [malavize] *adj* ill-advised, unwise.

malaxer [malakse] (1) *vt* (*triturer*) to knead; *muscle* to massage; (*mélanger*) to mix.

malchance [malʃɑ̃s] *nf* (*déveine*) bad luck, misfortune; (*mésaventure*) misfortune. **par ~** unfortunately. ♦ **malchanceux, -euse** *adj* unlucky.

malcommode [malkɔmɔd] *adj* inconvenient.

mâle [mɑl] **1** *adj* (*Bio, Tech*) male; (*viril*) manly. **2** *nm* male. **(éléphant) ~** bull (elephant); **(lapin) ~** buck (rabbit); **(moineau) ~** cock (sparrow); **(ours) ~** he-bear.

malédiction [malediksjɔ̃] *nf* curse.

maléfice [malefis] *nm* evil spell. ♦ **maléfique** *adj* evil.

malencontreux, -euse [malɑ̃kɔ̃tʀø, øz] *adj* unfortunate. ♦ **malencontreusement** *adv arriver* at the wrong moment; *faire tomber* inadvertently.

malentendu [malɑ̃tɑ̃dy] *nm* misunderstanding.

malfaçon [malfasɔ̃] *nf* fault, defect.

malfaisant, e [malfəzɑ̃, ɑ̃t] *adj* evil, harmful.

malfaiteur, -trice [malfɛtœʀ, tʀis] *nm,f* (*gén*) lawbreaker; (*voleur*) burglar, thief. **dangereux ~** dangerous criminal.

malformation [malfɔʀmɑsjɔ̃] *nf* malformation.

malgré [malgʀe] *prép* in spite of, despite. **~ son intelligence** in spite of *ou* for all his intelligence; **j'ai signé ~ moi** I signed reluctantly *ou* against my better judgment; **~ tout, c'est dangereux** all the same *ou* after all it's dangerous.

malhabile [malabil] *adj* clumsy, awkward. ♦ **malhabilement** *adv* clumsily, awkwardly.

malheur [malœʀ] *nm* **(a)** misfortune; (*accident*) accident. **un ~ ne vient jamais seul** it never rains but it pours; **grand ~** great tragedy. **(b) le ~** (*adversité*) adversity; (*malchance*) bad luck, misfortune; **famille dans le ~** family in misfortune *ou* faced with adversity; **le ~ a voulu qu'un agent le voie** as bad luck would have it a policeman saw him. **(c)** (*maudit*) **de ~*** wretched. **(d) par ~** unfortunately; **le ~ c'est que** ... the trouble *ou* snag is that ...; **faire le ~ de ses parents** to bring sorrow to one's parents; **faire un ~*** *[artiste]* to make a great hit; (*par colère*) to do sth violent, go wild; **quel ~ qu'il ne soit pas venu** what a shame *ou* pity he didn't come. ♦ **malheureusement** *adv* unfortunately. ♦ **malheureux, -euse** **1** *adj* **(a)** *victime, geste, parole* unfortunate; *enfant, vie* unhappy, miserable; *air* distressed; *candidat* unsuccessful, unlucky. **c'est bien ~** it's a great pity *ou* shame; **il est ~ de ne pas venir** he's distressed *ou* upset at not coming; **rendre qn ~** to make sb unhappy. **(b)** (*: *insignifiant*) wretched, miserable. **il y avait 2 ou 3 ~ spectateurs** there was a miserable handful of spectators. **2** *nm,f* (*infortuné*) poor wretch; (*indigent*) needy person. **le ~!** the poor man!; **ne fais pas cela, petit ~!** don't do that, you so-and-so!*

malhonnête [malɔnɛt] *adj* (*déloyal*) dishonest, crooked; (*impoli*) rude. ♦ **malhonnêtement** *adv* dishonestly, crookedly; rudely. ♦ **malhonnêteté** *nf* dishonesty, crookedness; rudeness. **une ~** (*action*) a crooked deal; (*parole*) a rude remark.

malice [malis] *nf* (*espièglerie*) mischief, mischievousness; (*méchanceté*) malice, spite. **il n'y entend pas ~** he means no harm by it; **boîte à ~** box of tricks. ♦ **malicieusement** *adv* mischievously. ♦ **malicieux, -euse** *adj* mischievous.

malin, -igne [malɛ̃, iɲ] *ou* **-ine*** [in] **1** *adj* **(a)** (*intelligent*) smart, clever. **il est ~ comme un singe** he is as artful as a cartload of monkeys; (*iro*) **c'est ~!** that's clever *ou* bright, isn't it? **(b)** (*: *difficile*) **ce n'est pourtant pas bien ~** but it isn't difficult *ou* tricky. **(c)** (*mauvais*) *influence* malignant, malicious; (*Méd*) malignant. **2** *nm,f*: **c'est un (petit) ~** he's a crafty one, he knows a thing or two; **le M~** the Devil.

malingre [malɛ̃gʀ(ə)] *adj* puny.

malintentionné, e [malɛ̃tɑ̃sjɔne] *adj* ill-intentioned (*envers* towards).

malle [mal] *nf* (*valise*) trunk; (*Aut*) boot, trunk (*US*). **ils ont fait la ~**‡ they've scarpered‡. ♦ **mallette** *nf* (small) suitcase.

malléable [maleabl(ə)] *adj* malleable. ♦ **malléabilité** *nf* malleability.

malmener [malməne] (5) *vt* to manhandle, handle roughly.

malnutrition [malnytʀisjɔ̃] *nf* malnutrition.

malodorant, e [malɔdɔʀɑ̃, ɑ̃t] *adj* foul- *ou* ill-smelling.

malotru, e [malɔtʀy] *nm,f* lout, boor.

malpoli, e [malpɔli] *adj* impolite, discourteous.

malpropre [malpʀɔpʀ(ə)] *adj objet* dirty; *travail* shoddy; *histoire* smutty; *action* dishonest. ♦ **malproprement** *adv* in a dirty way. ♦ **malpropreté** *nf* dirtiness.

malsain, e [malsɛ̃, ɛn] *adj* unhealthy.

malséant, e [malseɑ̃, ɑ̃t] *adj* unseemly, unbecoming.

malt [malt] *nm* malt.

Malte [malt] *nf* Malta. ♦ **maltais, e** *adj, nm,* **M~(e)** *nm(f)* Maltese.

malthusien, -ienne [maltyzjɛ̃, jɛn] *adj* Malthusian. ♦ **malthusianisme** *nm* Malthusianism.

maltraiter [maltʀete] (1) *vt personne* to manhandle, handle roughly, ill-treat; *grammaire* to misuse.

malveillance [malvɛjɑ̃s] *nf* malevolence. **avec ~** malevolently. ♦ **malveillant, e** *adj* malevolent.

maman [mamɑ̃] *nf* mummy, mother.

mamelle [mamɛl] *nf* (*Zool*) teat; (*pis*) udder, dug; *[femme]* breast. ♦ **mamelon** *nm* (*Anat*) nipple; (*Géog*) knoll, hillock.

mamie [mami] *nf* (*grand-mère*) granny*, gran*.

mammifère [mamifɛʀ] *nm* mammal.

mammouth [mamut] *nm* mammoth.

manche[1] [mɑ̃ʃ] *nf* **(a)** (*Habillement*) sleeve. **à ~s longues** long-sleeved; **sans ~s** sleeveless; (*fig*) **avoir qn dans sa ~** to have sb in one's pocket. **(b)** (*partie*) (*gén, Pol, Sport*) round; (*Cartes*) game. **(c)** (*Géog*) **la M~** the English Channel. **(d) ~ à air** (*Aviat*) wind sock; (*Naut*) ventilator.

manche[2] [mɑ̃ʃ] *nm* **(a)** (*gén*) handle; (*long*) shaft. **~ à balai** (*gén*) broomstick; (*Aviat*) joystick. **(b)** (*: *incapable*) clumsy fool.

manchette [mɑ̃ʃɛt] *nf* **(a)** *[chemise]* cuff; (*protectrice*) over-sleeve. **(b)** (*Presse*) headline. **(c)** (*Lutte*) forearm blow.

manchon [mɑ̃ʃɔ̃] *nm* muff.
manchot, -ote [mɑ̃ʃo, ɔt] **1** *adj* (*d'un bras*) one-armed; (*des deux bras*) armless; (*d'une main*) one-handed; (*des deux mains*) with no hands, handless. (*adroit*) **il n'est pas ~!*** he's clever with his hands! **2** *nm* (*Orn*) penguin.
mandarin [mɑ̃daʀɛ̃] *nm* (*Hist, péj*) mandarin.
mandarine [mɑ̃daʀin] *nf* mandarin (orange), tangerine.
mandat [mɑ̃da] *nm* **(a)** (*gén, Pol*) mandate. **donner à qn ~ de faire** to give sb a mandate to do. **(b)** (*Poste*) postal order, money order. **(c)** (*Jur: procuration*) power of attorney, proxy; (*Police etc*) warrant. **~ d'amener** ≃ summons; **~ d'arrêt** ≃ warrant for arrest; **placer qn sous ~ de dépôt** ≃ to place sb under a committal order; **~ de perquisition** search warrant. ♦ **mandataire** *nmf* (*Jur*) proxy, attorney; (*représentant*) representative; (*aux Halles*) (sales) agent. ♦ **mandater** (1) *vt* **(a)** *personne* to commission. **(b)** *somme* to make over.
mandoline [mɑ̃dɔlin] *nf* mandolin(e).
manège [manɛʒ] *nm* **(a) ~ (de chevaux de bois)** roundabout, merry-go-round. **(b)** (*Équitation*) (*école*) riding school; (*piste*) ring, school. **(c)** (*fig: agissements*) game, ploy.
manette [manɛt] *nf* lever, tap.
manger [mɑ̃ʒe] (3) **1** *vt* **(a)** to eat. **il ne mange pas en ce moment** he's off his food at present; **vous mangerez bien un morceau avec nous?*** won't you have a bite to eat with us?; **cela se mange?** can you eat it?; **ça se mange chaud** it should be eaten hot; **donner à ~ à qn, faire ~ qn** to feed sb; **faire ~ qch à qn** to give sb sth to eat; **mange!** eat up!; **on mange bien/mal à cet hôtel** the food is good/bad at this hotel. **(b)** (*faire un repas*) **~ au restaurant** to eat out, have a meal out; **c'est l'heure de ~** (*midi*) it's lunchtime; (*soir*) it's dinnertime; **inviter qn à ~** to invite sb for a meal; **boire en mangeant** to drink with a meal; **~ sur le pouce** to have a (quick) snack. **(c)** *[soleil]* to fade; *[rouille]* to eat away. **mangé aux mites** moth-eaten. **(d)** *électricité, économies* to go through; *temps* to take up; *mots* to swallow. **les grosses entreprises mangent les petites** the big firms swallow up the smaller ones; **l'entreprise mange de l'argent** the business is wasting money. **(e)** (*locutions*) **~ la consigne** to forget one's errand; **~ comme quatre** to eat like a horse; **~ à sa faim** to have enough to eat; **~ du bout des dents** to pick at one's food; (*fig*) **~ le morceau‡** to spill the beans‡; **je ne mange pas de ce pain-là!** I'm having nothing to do with that!; **~ à tous les rateliers*** to cash in* on all sides; **~ qn des yeux** to devour sb with one's eyes.
2 *nm* (*nourriture*) food; (*repas*) meal.
♦ **mangeable** *adj* edible, eatable. ♦ **mangeaille** *nf* (*péj*) food. ♦ **mangeoire** *nf* trough, manger. ♦ **mangeur, -euse** *nm,f* eater.
mangue [mɑ̃g] *nf* mango (*fruit*).
maniaque [manjak] **1** *adj* finicky, fussy. **2** *nmf* (*fou*) maniac, lunatic; (*fanatique*) fanatic; (*méticuleux*) fusspot*.
manichéen, -enne [manikeɛ̃, ɛn] *adj, nm,f* Manich(a)ean. ♦ **manichéisme** *nm* (*Philos*) Maniche(an)ism. **faire du ~** to see things in black and white.
manie [mani] *nf* (*habitude*) odd *ou* queer habit; (*obsession*) mania. **une de ses ~s** one of his funny habits.
manier [manje] (7) *vt* to handle. ♦ **maniabilité** *nf* handiness, manageability. ♦ **maniable** *adj* handy, manageable, easy to handle. ♦ **maniement** *nm* handling. **d'un ~ difficile** difficult to handle; **~ d'armes** arms drill, manual of arms (*US*).
manière [manjɛʀ] *nf* **(a)** (*façon*) way; (*Art: style*) style. **sa ~ de parler** his way of speaking, the way he speaks; **il le fera à sa ~** he'll do it his own way; **~ de vivre** way of life; **de quelle ~ as-tu fait cela?** how did you do that?; **à la ~ d'un singe** like a monkey; **c'est une ~ de pastiche** it's a kind of pastiche. **(b)** (*locutions*) **employer la ~ forte** to use strong-arm measures; **en ~ d'excuse** by way of (an) excuse; **d'une certaine ~** in a way, in some ways; **d'une ~ générale** generally speaking; **de toute(s) ~(s)** in any case, anyway; **d'une ~ ou d'une autre** somehow or other; **en aucune ~** in no way; **de ~ à faire** so as to do; **de ~ (à ce) que nous arrivions à l'heure** so that we get there on time. **(c) ~s: avoir de bonnes/mauvaises ~s** to have good/bad manners; **ce ne sont pas des ~s!** that's no way to behave!; **faire des ~s** (*minauderies*) to put on airs; (*chichis*) to make a fuss. ♦ **maniéré, e** *adj* (*péj: affecté*) affected; (*Art*) *genre* mannered.
manifester [manifɛste] (1) **1** *vt* (*gén*) to show; *sentiment* to express; *courage* to demonstrate. **~ le désir de faire** to indicate one's wish to do. **2** *vi* (*Pol*) to demonstrate. **3 se ~** *vpr* **(a)** *[émotion]* to show itself, express itself; *[difficultés]* to emerge, arise. **une certaine détente se manifesta** there was evidence of a certain thaw in the atmosphere. **(b)** *[candidat, témoin]* to come forward; *[personne]* (*se présenter*) to appear, turn up; (*se faire remarquer*) to make o.s. known, attract attention; (*dans un débat*) to make o.s. heard. **Dieu s'est manifesté aux hommes** God revealed himself to mankind. ♦ **manifestant, e** *nm,f* demonstrator. ♦ **manifestation** *nf* **(a)** (*Pol*) demonstration. **(b)** *[opinion, sentiment]* expression; *[maladie]* (*apparition*) appearance; (*symptômes*) outward sign. **~ de mauvaise humeur** show of bad temper. **(c)** *[Dieu, vérité]* revelation. **(d)** (*réunion, fête*) event. ♦ **manifeste 1** *adj* obvious, evident, manifest. **erreur ~** glaring error. **2** *nm* (*Littérat, Pol*) manifesto. ♦ **manifestement** *adv* obviously, evidently, manifestly.
manigancer [manigɑ̃se] (3) *vt* to plot, devise. **qu'est-ce qu'il manigance maintenant?** what's he up to now? ♦ **manigance** *nf* trick.
manipuler [manipyle] (1) *vt* *objet* to handle; (*péj*) *électeurs* to manipulate; *comptes* to rig, fiddle*. ♦ **manipulateur, -trice** *nm,f* (*technicien*) technician. ♦ **manipulation** *nf* (*maniement*) handling; (*Scol: Chim, Phys*) experiment. (*Méd, péj*) **~s** manipulation.
manitou [manitu] *nm* **(a) grand ~*** big shot*. **(b)** (*Rel*) manitou.
manivelle [manivɛl] *nf* crank.
manne [man] *nf* (*aubaine*) godsend. (*Rel*) **la ~** manna.
mannequin [mankɛ̃] *nm* (*personne*) model; (*objet*) dummy; (*fig: pantin*) stuffed dummy.
manœuvrer [manœvʀe] (1) **1** *vt* *véhicule* to manœuvre; *machine* to operate, work. **2** *vi* (*gén*) to manœuvre. ♦ **manœuvre 1** *nf* (*gén*) manœuvre. **la ~ d'un bateau est difficile** manœuvring a boat is difficult; (*Rail*) **faire la ~** to shunt; **~ d'encerclement** encircling movement; **~ d'obstruction** obstructive move; **~s frauduleuses** fraudulent schemes *ou* devices; **terrain de ~** drill *ou* parade ground; **grandes ~s** army manœuvres *ou* exercises. **2** *nm* labourer, unskilled worker. **~ agricole** farm labourer.
manoir [manwaʀ] *nm* manor house.
manomètre [manɔmɛtʀ(ə)] *nm* gauge, manometer.
manquer [mɑ̃ke] (1) **1** *vt* **(a)** *photo, gâteau* to spoil, make a mess of; *examen* to fail; *but, train, personne* to miss. **je l'ai manqué de peu/de 5 minutes** I missed him by a fraction/by 5 minutes; **c'est à ne pas ~** it's a must*; (*iro*) **il n'en manque jamais une!*** he puts his foot in it every time!*; **~ sa vie** to waste one's life; **ils ont manqué leur coup** their attempt failed. **(b)** (*être absent de*) to be absent from, miss.

2 *vi* **(a)** (*faire défaut*) (*gén*) to be lacking. **l'argent vint à ~** money ran out *ou* ran short; **ce qui me manque c'est le temps** what I need *ou* lack is time; **les mots me manquent pour exprimer** I can't find (the) words to express; **le temps me manque pour dire** there's no time for me to say; **le pied lui manqua** his foot slipped, he missed his footing. **(b)** (*être absent*) to be absent; (*avoir disparu*) to be missing. **(c)** (*échouer*) to fail.

3 ~ à *vt indir*: **~ à son honneur** to fail in one's honour; **~ à tous ses devoirs** to neglect all one's duties; **~ à l'appel** (*lit*) to be absent from roll call; (*fig*) to be missing; **il nous manque, sa présence nous manque** we miss him.

4 ~ de *vt indir* **(a)** *intelligence* to lack; *argent, main d'œuvre* to be short of, lack. **le pays ne manque pas d'un certain charme** the country is not without a certain charm; **on manque d'air ici** there's no air in here; **il ne manque pas d'audace!** he's got a nerve! **(b)** (*faillir*) **il a manqué mourir** he nearly *ou* almost died. **(c)** (*formules nég*) **ne manquez pas de le remercier** don't forget to thank him; **il n'a pas manqué de le lui dire** he made sure he told him; **on ne peut ~ d'être frappé par** one cannot fail to marvel at, one cannot help but be struck by; **ça ne va pas ~ (d'arriver)*** it's bound to happen.

5 *vb impers*: **il (nous) manque 2 chaises** (*elles ont disparu*) there are 2 chairs missing; (*on en a besoin*) we are 2 chairs short, we are short of 2 chairs; **il ne manquera pas de gens pour dire** there'll be no shortage of people to say; **il ne manquait plus que ça** that's all we needed, that's the last straw.

6 se ~ *vpr* (*suicide*) to fail.

♦ **manquant, e** *adj* missing. ♦ **manque** *nm* **(a) ~ de** (*faiblesse*) lack of, want of; (*pénurie*) shortage of; **quel ~ de chance!** what bad *ou* hard luck!; **~ à gagner** loss of profit. **(b) ~s** *[roman]* faults; *[personne]* failings, shortcomings; *[connaissances]* gaps. **(c)** (*vide*) gap, emptiness; (*Drogue*) withdrawal. **(d) à la ~**: *chanteur, idée* crummy:. ♦ **manqué, e** *adj essai* failed, abortive; *rendez-vous* missed; *photo* spoilt; (*Tech*) *pièce* faulty; *occasion* lost, wasted. **c'est un écrivain ~** (*mauvais écrivain*) he is a failure as a writer; (*il aurait dû être écrivain*) he should have been a writer. ♦ **manquement** *nm*: **~ à** *règle* breach of; **au moindre ~** at the slightest lapse.

mansarde [mɑ̃saʀd(ə)] *nf* attic. ♦ **mansardé, e** *adj*: **chambre ~e** attic room.

mansuétude [mɑ̃sɥetyd] *nf* leniency, indulgence.

manteau, *pl* **~x** [mɑ̃to] *nm* coat. **sous le ~** clandestinely, on the sly; **~ de cheminée** mantelpiece.

mantille [mɑ̃tij] *nf* mantilla.

manucure [manykyʀ] *nmf* manicurist.

manuel, -elle [manɥɛl] **1** *adj* manual. **2** *nm* (*livre*) manual, handbook. **~ de lecture** reader. ♦ **manuellement** *adv* manually.

manufacture [manyfaktyʀ] *nf* (*usine*) factory; (*fabrication*) manufacture. ♦ **manufacturer** (1) *vt* to manufacture.

manuscrit, e [manyskʀi, it] **1** *adj* handwritten. **pages ~es** manuscript pages. **2** *nm* manuscript; (*dactylographié*) typescript.

manutention [manytɑ̃sjɔ̃] *nf* (*opération*) handling; (*local*) storehouse. ♦ **manutentionnaire** *nmf* packer.

mappemonde [mapmɔ̃d] *nf* (*carte*) map of the world; (*sphère*) globe.

maquereau, *pl* **~x** [makʀo] *nm* mackerel; (:) pimp, ponce:.

maquette [makɛt] *nf* (scale) model.

maquiller [makije] (1) **1** *vt visage* to make up; *vérité, faits* to fake, doctor; *chiffres* to fiddle*; *voiture* to do over*, disguise. **meurtre maquillé en accident** murder faked up to look like an accident. **2 se ~** *vpr* to make up. ♦ **maquillage** *nm* make-up. **le ~ des faits** faking the facts.

maquis [maki] *nm* (*Géog*) scrub, bush; (*labyrinthe*) maze; (*Hist*) maquis. **prendre le ~** to go underground. ♦ **maquisard, e** *nm,f* maquis.

maraîcher, -ère [maʀeʃe, maʀɛʃɛʀ] **1** *nm,f* market gardener, truck farmer (*US*). **2** *adj*: **produits ~s** market garden produce, truck (*US*).

marais [maʀɛ] *nm* marsh, swamp. **~ salant** salt marsh.

marasme [maʀasm(ə)] *nm* **(a)** (*Écon, Pol*) stagnation, slump. **(b)** (*accablement*) dejection, depression.

marathon [maʀatɔ̃] *nm* (*Sport, fig*) marathon.

marâtre [maʀɑtʀ(ə)] *nf* cruel mother.

marauder [maʀode] (1) *vi* to thieve, pilfer. ♦ **maraude** *nf* thieving, pilfering. **taxi en ~** cruising *ou* prowling taxi. ♦ **maraudeur, -euse** *nm,f* (*voleur*) prowler; (*soldat*) marauder.

marbre [maʀbʀ(ə)] *nm* (*Géol*) marble; (*surface*) marble top; (*Typ*) stone, bed. **rester de ~** to be stony-faced. ♦ **marbrer** (1) *vt papier, cuir* to marble; *peau, bois* to mottle. ♦ **marbrier** *nm* (*funéraire*) monumental mason. ♦ **marbrure** *nf*: **~(s)** marbling; mottling.

marc [maʀ] *nm* (*raisin*) marc; (*alcool*) brandy. **~ (de café)** (coffee) grounds *ou* dregs.

marcassin [maʀkasɛ̃] *nm* young wild boar.

marchand, e [maʀʃɑ̃, ɑ̃d] **1** *adj valeur* market. **2** *nm,f* shopkeeper; (*sur un marché*) stallholder; *[vins, fruits, charbon, grains]* merchant; *[meubles, bestiaux]* dealer. **~ au détail** retailer; **~ en gros** wholesaler; **la ~e de chaussures** the woman in the shoeshop. **3: ~ ambulant** hawker, pedlar; **~ de biens** ≃ estate agent; **~ de couleurs** ironmonger, hardware dealer; **~ de journaux** newsagent; **~ de légumes** greengrocer; **~ de quatre saisons** costermonger; **~ de sable** sandman.

marchander [maʀʃɑ̃de] (1) *vt objet* to haggle over, bargain over; (*emploi absolu*) to haggle, bargain. **il n'a pas marchandé ses compliments** he wasn't sparing with his compliments. ♦ **marchandage** *nm* bargaining, haggling. ♦ **marchandise** *nf* (*article*) commodity. **~s** goods, merchandise; (*stock*) **la ~** the goods *ou* merchandise; **gare de ~** goods station; **il a de la bonne ~** he sells good stuff; **vanter la ~*** to show o.s. off to advantage.

marche[1] [maʀʃ(ə)] *nf* **(a)** (*action, Sport*) walking. **poursuivre sa ~** to walk on; **chaussures de ~** walking shoes. **(b)** (*démarche*) walk, step; (*rythme*) pace, step. **(c)** (*trajet*) walk. **c'est à 2 heures de ~** it's a 2-hour walk from here. **(d)** (*Mus, Mil, Pol*) march. **chanson de ~** marching song; **fermer la ~** to bring up the rear; **ouvrir la ~** to lead the way; **faire ~ sur** to march upon; **en avant, ~!** forward march! **(e)** *[véhicule]* running; *[machine, usine]* running, working; *[navire]* sailing; *[étoile]* course; *[horloge]* working. **dans le sens de la ~** facing the engine; **véhicule en ~** moving vehicle; **en état de ~** in working order; (*Tech*) **~ - arrêt** on - off; **~ arrière** reverse; **faire ~ arrière** (*Aut*) to reverse; (*fig*) to back-pedal, backtrack; **~ à suivre** (correct) procedure. **(f)** *[maladie]* progress; *[événements]* course; *[temps, progrès]* march. **(g) être en ~** *[personnes]* to be on the move; *[moteur etc]* to be running; **se mettre en ~** *[personne]* to get moving; *[machine]* to start; **mettre en ~** *voiture* to start (up); *machine* to set going.

marche[2] [maʀʃ(ə)] *nf [escalier]* step. **sur les ~s** on the stairs; (*escalier extérieur, escabeau*) on the steps.

marché [maʀʃe] **1** *nm* **(a)** (*lieu*) market; (*ville*) trading centre. **faire son ~** to go to the market; (*plus gén*) to go shopping. **(b)** (*Écon, Fin*) market. **lancer qch sur le ~** to launch sth on the market; **le ~ du travail** the labour market; **le ~ des valeurs**

the stockmarket. **(c)** (*transaction*) bargain, deal. **passer un ~ avec qn** to make a deal with sb; **~ conclu!** it's a deal!; **mettre le ~ en main à qn** to force sb to accept or refuse. **2: le M~ commun** the Common Market, the E.E.C; **~ noir** black market; **~ aux puces** flea market.

marchepied [maʀʃəpje] *nm* (*Rail*) step; (*Aut*) running board; (*fig*) stepping stone.

marcher [maʀʃe] (1) *vi* **(a)** to walk; *[soldats]* to march. **~ à grands pas** to stride (along); **on va ~ un peu** let's have a walk, let's go for a walk; **faire ~ un bébé** to help a baby walk; **son père saura le faire ~ droit** his father will soon have him toeing the line; **~ dans une flaque d'eau** to step in a puddle; **défense de ~ sur les pelouses** keep off the grass; (*lit, fig*) **~ sur les pieds de qn** to tread on sb's toes; **~ sur une ville** to advance on a town. **(b)** (*) (*consentir*) to agree; (*être dupé*) to be taken in. **il n'a pas voulu ~ dans la combine** he did not want to get mixed up in the business; **faire ~ qn** (*taquiner*) to pull sb's leg; (*tromper*) to take sb for a ride*. **(c)** (*avec véhicule*) **le train a bien marché jusqu'à Lyon** the train made good time as far as Lyons; **nous marchions à 100 à l'heure** we were doing a hundred. **(d)** *[appareil, usine]* to work; *[ruse]* to come off; *[affaires, études]* to go (well). **faire ~** *appareil* to work, operate; *entreprise* to run; **ça fait ~ les affaires** it's good for business; **est-ce que le métro marche?** is the underground running?; **ces deux opérations marchent ensemble** these two procedures go *ou* work together; **les études, ça marche?*** how's the work going? ♦ **marcheur, -euse** *nm,f* (*gén*) walker; (*Pol etc*) marcher.

mardi [maʀdi] *nm* Tuesday. **M~ gras** Shrove Tuesday; *V* **samedi.**

mare [maʀ] *nf* (*étang*) pond; (*flaque*) pool. **~ de sang** pool of blood.

marécage [maʀekaʒ] *nm* marsh, swamp, bog. ♦ **marécageux, -euse** *adj* marshy, swampy, boggy.

maréchal, *pl* **-aux** [maʀeʃal, o] *nm* (*Mil*) marshal. **~-ferrant** blacksmith; **~ des logis** sergeant.

marée [maʀe] *nf* **(a)** tide. **~ montante/descendante** flood *ou* rising/ebb tide; **à ~ basse/haute** at low/high tide *ou* water; **~ noire** oil slick. **(b)** (*fig*) flood. **(c)** (*poissons*) **la ~** fresh (sea) fish.

marelle [maʀɛl] *nf* hopscotch.

margarine [maʀgaʀin] *nf* margarine, marge*.

marge [maʀʒ(ə)] **1** *nf* (*gén*) margin. **j'ai encore de la ~** I still have time (*ou* money *etc*) to spare; **en ~ de la société** on the fringe of society; **vivre en ~ du monde** to live cut off from the world. **2: ~ bénéficiaire** profit margin; **~ d'erreur** margin of error; **~ de manœuvre** room to manœuvre; **~ de sécurité** safety margin. ♦ **marginal, e,** *mpl* **-aux** *adj* (*gén, Écon*) marginal. (*fig*) **les ~aux** (*contestataires*) dropouts; (*déshérités*) second-class citizens.

marguerite [maʀgəʀit] *nf* (*Bot*) marguerite, (oxeye) daisy.

mari [maʀi] *nm* husband.

mariage [maʀjaʒ] *nm* **(a)** (*union*) marriage. **50 ans de ~** 50 years of married life *ou* of marriage; **on parle de ~ entre eux** there is talk of their getting married; **donner qn en ~ à** to give sb in marriage to; **~ d'amour** love match; **faire un ~ d'argent** to marry for money. **(b)** (*cérémonie*) wedding. **cadeau de ~** wedding present. **(c)** *[couleurs, parfums]* marriage, blend. ♦ **marié, e 1** *adj* married. **non ~** unmarried, single. **2** *nm* (bride)groom. **les ~s** (*jour du mariage*) the bride and (bride)groom; (*après le mariage*) the newlyweds. **3** *nf* bride. **trouver que la ~e est trop belle** to object that everything's too good to be true; **robe de ~e** wedding dress. ♦ **marier** (7) **1** *vt personne* to marry; *couleurs, goûts* to blend, harmonize. **il a encore 2 filles à ~** he still has 2 daughters to marry off. **2 se ~** *vpr [personne]* to get married; *[couleurs, goûts]* to blend, harmonize. **se ~ à** *ou* **avec qn** to marry sb, get married to sb.

marijuana [maʀiʒɥana] *nf* marijuana, pot (*arg*).

marin, e[1] [maʀɛ̃, in] **1** *adj air* sea; *faune* marine, sea. **costume ~** sailor suit. **2** *nm* sailor; (*grade*) ordinary seaman. **~ d'eau douce** landlubber.

marine[2] [maʀin] **1** *nf* **(a)** navy. **terme de ~** nautical term; **~ (de guerre)** navy; **~ marchande** merchant navy. **(b)** (*tableau*) seascape. **2** *nm* (*soldat*) marine.

mariner [maʀine] (1) *vti* to marinade. **harengs marinés** soused herrings.

marionnette [maʀjɔnɛt] *nf* (*lit, fig*) puppet. (*spectacle*) **~s** puppet show; **~ à fils** marionette; **~ à gaine** glove puppet. ♦ **marionnettiste** *nmf* puppeteer.

marital, e, *mpl* **-aux** [maʀital, o] *adj* marital, husband's. ♦ **maritalement** *adv*: **vivre ~** to live as husband and wife.

maritime [maʀitim] *adj* (*gén*) maritime; *province* seaboard, coastal; *commerce, droit* shipping.

marmaille* [maʀmɑj] *nf* gang of kids* *ou* brats* (*péj*).

marmelade [maʀməlad] *nf* stewed fruit, compote. (*lit, fig*) **réduire en ~** to reduce to a pulp.

marmite [maʀmit] *nf* (cooking-)pot.

marmonner [maʀmɔne] (1) *vt* to mumble, mutter. ♦ **marmonnement** *nm*: **~(s)** mumbling, muttering.

marmot* [maʀmo] *nm* kid*, brat* (*péj*).

marmotte [maʀmɔt] *nf* (*Zool*) marmot; (*fig*) dormouse.

marmotter [maʀmɔte] (1) *vt* to mumble, mutter.

Maroc [maʀɔk] *nm* Morocco. ♦ **marocain, e** *adj,* **M~(e)** *nm(f)* Moroccan.

maroquin [maʀɔkɛ̃] *nm* (*cuir*) morocco (leather); (*fig: portefeuille*) (minister's) portfolio. ♦ **maroquinerie** *nf* (*boutique*) shop selling fine leather goods; (*métier*) fine leather trade. **(articles de) ~** fine leather goods. ♦ **maroquinier** *nm* dealer in fine leather goods.

marotte [maʀɔt] *nf* hobby, craze.

marquer [maʀke] (1) **1** *vt* **(a)** (*par une trace*) (*gén, fig*) to mark; *animal, criminel* to brand; *arbre* to blaze; *marchandise* to label, stamp. **j'ai marqué nos places avec nos valises** I've reserved our seats with our cases; **pour ~ cette journée** to mark this day; **la souffrance l'a marqué** suffering has left its mark on him. **(b)** (*indiquer, montrer*) (*gén*) to show; *[balance]* to register. **la pendule marque 6 heures** the clock points to *ou* shows 6 o'clock; **robe qui marque la taille** dress which shows off *ou* emphasizes the waistline; **cela marque bien que le pays veut la paix** that definitely indicates that the country wants peace; **la déception se marquait sur son visage** disappointment showed in his face *ou* was written all over his face. **(c)** (*écrire*) to note down, make a note of. **on l'a marqué absent** he was marked absent; **qu'y a-t-il de marqué?** what does it say?, what's written on it? **(d)** (*Sport*) *joueur* to mark; *but* to score. **(e)** (*locutions*) **~ le coup*** to mark the occasion; **~ un point sur qn** to be one up on sb; **~ la mesure** to keep the beat; (*lit, fig*) **~ le pas** to mark time; **~ un temps d'arrêt** to mark a pause.

2 *vi* **(a)** *[événement, personnalité]* to stand out; *[coup]* to reach home, tell. **(b)** *[crayon]* to write; *[tampon]* to stamp. **ne pose pas le verre là, ça marque** don't put the glass down there, it will leave a mark.

♦ **marquant, e** *adj personnage, événement* outstanding; *souvenir* vivid. ♦ **marque** *nf* **(a)** (*repère, trace*) (*lit, fig*) mark; *[linge personnel]* name tab; *[viande, œufs]* stamp. **~s de doigts** fingermarks; **~s de pas** footmarks, footprints; (*Sport*) **à vos ~s! prêts! partez!** on your marks!, get set!, go!; **~ de confiance** sign *ou* mark of confidence; **la ~ du génie** the hallmark of genius. **(b)** (*Comm*) *[nourriture]* brand; *[produits manufacturés]* make. **~ de fabrique** trademark, trade name; **~ déposée** registered trademark; **produits de ~** high-class products; **visiteur de ~** important *ou* distinguished visitor, V.I.P. **(c)** (*Sport, Cartes: décompte*) **la ~** the score. ♦ **marqué, e** *adj* (*accentué*) pronounced; (*Ling*) marked. **le prix ~** the marked price, the price on the label; (*fig*) **c'est un homme ~** he's a marked man. ♦ **marqueur** *nm* (*stylo*) felt-tip (marker) pen.

marquis [maʀki] *nm* marquess.

marquise [maʀkiz] *nf* **(a)** (*noble*) marchioness. **(b)** (*auvent*) glass canopy.

marraine [maʀɛn] *nf [enfant]* godmother; *[navire]* christener, namer.

marre‡ [maʀ] *adv*: **en avoir ~** to be fed up* (*de* with), be sick* (*de* of).

marrer (se)‡ [maʀe] (1) *vpr* to laugh. ♦ **marrant, e*** *adj* (*amusant*) funny, killing*; (*étrange*) funny, odd.

marron [maʀɔ̃] **1** *nm* **(a)** chestnut. **~ d'Inde** horse chestnut; **~ glacé** marron glacé; **tirer les ~s du feu** (*profiter*) to steal a march; (*être victime*) to be a cat's paw. **(b)** (*couleur*) brown. **(c)** (‡: *coup*) thump, clout*. **2** *adj inv* **(a)** (*couleur*) brown. **(b)** (‡: *être trompé*) **être ~** to be had*. ♦ **marronnier** *nm* chestnut tree. **~ (d'Inde)** horse chestnut tree.

Mars [maʀs] *nm* (*Astron, Myth*) Mars.

mars [maʀs] *nm* (*mois*) March; *V* **septembre.**

marsouin [maʀswɛ̃] *nm* (*Zool*) porpoise.

marteau, *pl* **~x** [maʀto] **1** *nm* hammer; *[horloge]* striker; *[porte]* knocker. **entre le ~ et l'enclume** between the devil and the deep blue sea; **être ~*** to be nuts* *ou* cracked*. **2: ~-pilon** *nm, pl* **~x-~s** power hammer; **~-piqueur** *nm, pl* **~x-~s** pneumatic drill. ♦ **martèlement** *nm*: **~(s)** hammering, pounding. ♦ **marteler** (5) *vt* to hammer, pound; *mots* to hammer out.

martial, e, *mpl* **-aux** [maʀsjal, o] *adj* martial.

martien, -ienne [maʀsjɛ̃, jɛn] *adj, nm,f* Martian.

martinet [maʀtinɛ] *nm* **(a)** small whip. **(b)** (*Orn*) swift.

martin-pêcheur, *pl* **~s-~s** [maʀtɛ̃pɛʃœʀ] *nm* kingfisher.

martre [maʀtʀ(ə)] *nf* marten. **~ zibeline** sable.

martyr, e[1] [maʀtiʀ] **1** *adj peuple* martyred. **mère ~e** stricken mother; **enfant ~** battered child. **2** *nm,f* martyr. ♦ **martyre**[2] *nm* (*Rel, fig*) martyrdom. **mettre au ~** to martyrize; **souffrir le ~** to suffer agonies. ♦ **martyriser** (1) *vt personne, animal* to martyrize; *élève* to bully; *enfant* to batter; (*Rel*) to martyr.

marxisme [maʀksism(ə)] *nm* Marxism. ♦ **marxiste** *adj, nmf* Marxist.

mascarade [maskaʀad] *nf* masquerade.

mascotte [maskɔt] *nf* mascot.

masculin, e [maskylɛ̃, in] **1** *adj* (*gén*) male; (*viril*) manly; (*péj: hommasse*) mannish; (*Gram*) masculine. **2** *nm* (*Gram*) masculine.

masochisme [mazɔʃism(ə)] *nm* masochism. ♦ **masochiste** **1** *adj* masochistic. **2** *nmf* masochist.

masque [mask(ə)] *nm* (*gén, fig*) mask. **jeter le ~** to unmask o.s.; **~ antirides** face pack; **~ à gaz/de plongée** gas/diving mask. ♦ **masqué, e** *adj bandit* masked; *enfant* wearing a mask. (*Aut*) **sortie ~e** concealed exit. ♦ **masquer** (1) **1** *vt* (*gén*) to mask, conceal (*à qn* from sb); *lumière* to screen, shade. **~ la vue** to block (out) the view; **~ l'essentiel** to mask *ou* obscure the essential point. **2 se ~** *vpr* (*lit, fig*) to hide, conceal (*derrière* behind).

massacre [masakʀ(ə)] *nm* slaughter, massacre. *[gibier]* **c'est du ~** it is sheer butchery; (*sabotage*) **c'est un vrai ~!*** it's a real mess! ♦ **massacrer** (1) *vt* **(a)** (*tuer*) to slaughter, massacre; *animaux* to slaughter. **(b)** (*) *opéra* to murder; *travail* to make a mess *ou* hash* of; *adversaire* to make mincemeat* of. ♦ **massacreur, -euse*** *nm,f* (*saboteur*) bungler.

masse [mas] *nf* **(a)** (*volume, Phys*) mass; (*forme*) massive shape. **~ de nuages** bank of clouds; **~ monétaire** amount of money in circulation; **taillé dans la ~** carved from the block; **tomber comme une ~** to fall in a heap. **(b)** (*foule*) **la ~, les ~s** the masses; **la ~ des lecteurs** the majority of readers; **manifestation de ~** mass demonstration; **une ~ de*, des ~s de*** *objets* masses of, loads of*; *touristes* crowds of; **il n'y en a pas des ~s*** *[objets]* there aren't very many; *[argent]* there isn't very much. **(c)** (*Élec*) earth, ground (*US*). **faire ~** to act as an earth. **(d)** (*maillet*) sledgehammer; *[huissier]* mace. **~ d'armes** mace. **(e) exécutions en ~** mass executions; **fabriquer en ~** to mass-produce; **venir en ~** to come in a body *ou* en masse.

massepain [maspɛ̃] *nm* marzipan.

masser[1] *vt*, **se ~** *vpr* [mase] (1) to mass.

masser[2] [mase] (1) *vt personne* to massage. **se faire ~** to have a massage. ♦ **massage** *nm* massage. ♦ **masseur, -euse** *nm,f* masseur, masseuse. **~ kinésithérapeute** physiotherapist.

massif, -ive [masif, iv] **1** *adj* **(a)** *meuble, bâtiment* massive, solid; *personne* sturdily built. **(b)** (*pur*) **or/chêne ~** solid gold/oak. **(c)** *dose* massive, heavy. **départs ~s** mass exodus (*sg*). **2** *nm* (*Géog*) massif; *[fleurs, arbres]* clump. ♦ **massivement** *adv répondre* en masse; *injecter* in massive doses.

mass(-)media [masmedja] *nmpl* mass media.

massue [masy] *nf* club, bludgeon.

mastiquer [mastike] (1) *vt* **(a)** (*Bio*) to chew, masticate. **(b)** *vitre* to putty; *fissure* to fill. ♦ **mastic** **1** *nm [vitrier]* putty; *[menuisier]* filler, mastic. **2** *adj* putty-coloured, off-white.

mastodonte [mastɔdɔ̃t] *nm* (*Zool*) mastodon; (*fig hum*) great hulk.

masure [mazyʀ] *nf* hovel.

mat[1] [mat] (*Échecs*) **1** *adj inv*: **être ~** to be checkmate; **faire ~** to checkmate. **2** *nm* checkmate.

mat[2]**, e** [mat] *adj métal, couleur* mat(t), dull; *peinture, teint* mat(t). **bruit ~** dull noise, thud.

mât [mɑ] *nm* (*Naut*) mast; (*pylône*) pole, post; (*hampe*) flagpole; (*Sport*) climbing pole. **~ d'artimon** mizzenmast; **~ de charge** derrick; **~ de cocagne** greasy pole; **~ de misaine** foremast.

match [matʃ] *nm* (*Sport*) match, game (*US*). **~ aller/retour** first/second leg; **~ nul** draw; **faire ~ nul** to draw.

matelas [matla] *nm* mattress. **~ pneumatique** air mattress *ou* bed, Lilo ®. ♦ **matelasser** (1) *vt meuble* to pad; *tissu* to quilt. ♦ **matelassier, -ière** *nm,f* mattress maker.

matelot [matlo] *nm* sailor, seaman.

mater [mate] (1) *vt* **(a)** *rebelles, enfant* to subdue; *révolution* to put down, quell; *incendie* to bring under control. **(b)** (*Échecs*) to checkmate, mate. **(c)** (*marteler*) to burr.

matérialiser [mateʀjalize] (1) **1** *vt* (*concrétiser*) to make materialize; (*symboliser*) to embody. **2 se ~** *vpr* to materialize. ♦ **matérialisation** *nf* materialization.

matérialisme [mateʀjalism(ə)] *nm* materialism. ♦ **matérialiste** **1** *adj* materialistic. **2** *nmf* materialist.

matériau [mateʀjo] *nm inv* (*Constr*) material. ♦ **matériaux** *nmpl* (*Constr*) materials; (*documents*) material.

matériel, -elle [mateʀjɛl] **1** *adj* (*gén*) material; (*financier*) financial; (*pratique*) *organisation* practical. **je n'ai pas le temps ~ de le faire** I simply have not the time to do it. **2** *nm* (*équipement*) equipment, materials; (*attirail*) gear; (*fig: corpus*) material. **~ de bureau** (*meubles*) office equipment; (*fournitures*) office materials; **~**

d'exploitation plant; ~ **roulant** rolling stock. ♦ **matériellement** *adv* materially; financially; practically.

maternel, -elle [matɛʀnɛl] *adj* **(a)** (*gén*) maternal; *geste, amour* motherly. **il avait gardé les habitudes ~les** he had retained his mother's habits. **(b)** **(école) ~le** (state) nursery school. ♦ **maternellement** *adv* maternally, like a mother. ♦ **maternité** *nf* **(a)** (*bâtiment*) maternity hospital. **(b)** (*accouchement*) pregnancy. **(c)** (*état de mère*) motherhood, maternity.

mathématique [matematik] **1** *adj* mathematical. **2** *nfpl*: **les ~s** mathematics. ♦ **math(s)*** *nfpl* maths*, math* (*US*). ♦ **mathématicien, -ienne** *nm,f* mathematician. ♦ **mathématiquement** *adv* mathematically. ♦ **matheux, -euse*** *nm,f* (*Scol*) maths specialist; (*hum*) maths expert.

matière [matjɛʀ] **1** *nf* (*produit*) material, substance; (*sujet, Scol*) subject. **la ~** matter; **fournir la ~ d'un discours** to provide the material *ou* subject matter for a speech; **ignorant en la ~** ignorant on the matter *ou* subject; **en ~ poétique** as far as poetry is concerned, as regards poetry; **donner ~ à plaisanter** to give cause for laughter; **il n'y a pas là ~ à se réjouir** this is no matter for rejoicing. **2: ~(s) grasse(s)** fat content, fat; **~s fécales** faeces; (*lit, fig*) **~ grise** grey matter; **~ plastique** plastic; **~ première** raw material.

matin [matɛ̃] *nm* morning. **le 10 au ~** on the morning of the 10th; **2h du ~** 2 a.m., 2 in the morning; **du ~ au soir** from morning till night; **de bon ~** early in the morning. ♦ **matinal, e,** *mpl* **-aux** *adj tâches* morning; *heure* early. **être ~** to be an early riser, get up early. ♦ **matinée** *nf* **(a)** (*matin*) morning. **en fin de ~** at the end of the morning. **(b)** (*Ciné, Théât*) matinée, afternoon performance. **~ dansante** afternoon dance.

matois, e [matwa, waz] *adj* wily, sly, crafty.

matou [matu] *nm* tomcat.

matraque [matʀak] *nf [police]* truncheon, billy (*US*); *[malfaiteur]* cosh. ♦ **matraquer** (1) *vt* **(a)** *[police]* to beat up; *[malfaiteur]* to cosh. (**fig*) **~ le client** to soak‡ *ou* overcharge customers. **(b)** (*Rad*) *publicité* to plug; *public* to bombard (*de* with). ♦ **matraquage** *nm* beating up; plugging; bombarding.

matrice [matʀis] *nf* (*utérus*) womb; (*Tech*) mould, die; (*Typ, Ling, Math*) matrix.

matricule [matʀikyl] *nm* (*Mil*) regimental number; (*Admin*) reference number.

matrimonial, e, *mpl* **-aux** [matʀimɔnjal, o] *adj* matrimonial.

matrone [matʀɔn] *nf* matronly woman.

mâture [mɑtyʀ] *nf* masts. **dans la ~** aloft.

maturité [matyʀite] *nf* maturity. **venir à ~** to come to maturity; **manquer de ~** to be immature.

maudire [modiʀ] (2) *vt* to curse. ♦ **maudit, e** **1** *adj* **(a)** (*: *sacré*) blasted*, confounded*. **(b)** (*littér*) **poète ~** accursed poet; **~e soit la guerre!** cursed be the war! **2** *nm,f* damned soul. **les ~s** the damned. **3** *nm*: **le M~** the Devil.

maugréer [mogʀee] (1) *vi* to grouse, grumble (*contre* about, at).

mausolée [mozɔle] *nm* mausoleum.

maussade [mosad] *adj* (*gén*) gloomy, sullen.

mauvais, e [mɔvɛ, ɛz] **1** *adj* **(a)** (*en qualité*) (*gén*) bad; *appareil* faulty; *santé, film, élève* poor. **~e excuse** poor *ou* lame excuse; (*Élec*) **~ contact** faulty contact; **~ en géographie** bad *ou* weak at geography. **(b)** (*erroné*) wrong; (*qui ne convient pas*) awkward. **le ~ numéro** the wrong number; **il a choisi un ~ moment** he picked an awkward *ou* a bad time; **c'est un ~ calcul de sa part** he's badly misjudged it; **il ne serait pas ~ de se renseigner** it wouldn't be a bad idea if we found out more about this. **(c)** (*nuisible*) (*gén*) bad; *blessure* nasty; *temps, goût, odeur* unpleasant; *sourire, joie, personne* malicious, spiteful. (*Scol*) **~e note** bad mark; **la mer est ~e** the sea is rough; **être en ~e posture** to be in a tricky *ou* nasty position; **la soupe a un ~ goût** the soup tastes nasty; **il a passé un ~ quart d'heure** he had a nasty time of it; **ce n'est pas un ~ garçon** he's not a bad boy; **aujourd'hui il fait ~** today the weather is bad; **prendre qch en ~e part** to take sth in bad part, take sth amiss; **se faire du ~ sang** to worry, get in a state.

2 *nm*: **enlève le ~ et mange le reste** cut out the bad part and eat the rest; (*personnes*) **les ~** the wicked.

3: ~ coucheur awkward customer; **recevoir un ~ coup** to get a nasty blow; **faire un ~ coup** to commit a crime; **~ esprit** troublemaker; **~ garçon** tough; **c'est de la ~e graine** he's (*ou* she's) a bad lot; **~e herbe** weed; **~e langue** gossip, scandalmonger; **~ lieu** place of ill repute; **le ~ œil** the evil eye; **~ pas** tight spot; **~e passe** difficult situation; **~ plaisant** hoaxer; **faire la ~e tête** to sulk; **~ traitement** ill treatment; **faire subir de ~ traitements à** to ill-treat.

mauve [mov] **1** *adj, nm* (*couleur*) mauve. **2** *nf* (*Bot*) mallow.

mauviette [movjɛt] *nf* (*péj*) weakling.

maxi ... [maksi] *préf*: maxi ... .

maxillaire [maksilɛʀ] **1** *adj* maxillary. **2** *nm* jawbone.

maxime [maksim] *nf* maxim.

maximum [maksimɔm], *f* **~** *ou* **maxima** [maksima], *pl* **~s** *ou* **maxima** *adj, nm* maximum. **la température ~** the maximum *ou* highest temperature; **au (grand) ~** at the (very) maximum, at the (very) most; **il faut rester au** *ou* **le ~ à l'ombre** one must stay as much as possible in the shade. ♦ **maximal, e,** *mpl* **-aux** *adj* maximal.

mayonnaise [majɔnɛz] *nf* mayonnaise.

mazout [mazut] *nm* (fuel) oil. **poêle à ~** oil-fired stove.

me, m' [m(ə)] *pron pers* me; (*réfléchi*) myself. **il m'en a parlé** he spoke to me about it; **je ne ~ vois pas dans ce rôle-là** I can't see myself in that part.

méandre [meɑ̃dʀ(ə)] *nm* (*Art, Géog*) meander; (*fig*) twists and turns.

mec‡ [mɛk] *nm* guy.

mécanique [mekanik] **1** *adj* (*gén*) mechanical; *jouet* clockwork. **les industries ~s** mechanical engineering industries; (*Aut, Aviat*) **avoir des ennuis ~s** to have engine trouble. **2** *nf* (*gén*) mechanics (*sg*); (*science*) (mechanical) engineering; (*mécanisme*) mechanism. ♦ **mécanicien, -ienne** *nm,f* (*Aut*) (garage *ou* motor) mechanic; (*Naut*) engineer; (*Rail*) engine driver, engineer (*US*). ♦ **mécaniquement** *adv* mechanically. ♦ **mécanisation** *nf* mechanization. ♦ **mécaniser** (1) *vt* to mechanize. ♦ **mécanisme** *nm* mechanism. ♦ **mécanographie** *nf* (*procédé*) (mechanical) data processing; (*service*) comptometer department.

méchant, e [meʃɑ̃, ɑ̃t] **1** *adj* **(a)** nasty, wicked; (*sens affaibli*) *enfant* naughty. **ce n'est pas un ~ homme** he's not such a bad fellow; **ce n'est pas bien ~*** *[blessure]* it's not too serious; *[examen]* it's not too difficult *ou* stiff*. **(b)** (*insignifiant*) **un ~ morceau de fromage** one miserable bit of cheese; **que de bruit pour une ~e clef perdue** what a fuss over one wretched lost key. **(c)** (‡: *sensationnel*) **il a une ~e moto** he's got a fantastic* *ou* terrific* bike; **une ~e cicatrice** a hell of a scar‡. **2** *nm,f* (*enfant*) naughty child; (*personne*) wicked person. **les ~s** (*dans un western*) the baddies*, the bad guys* (*US*); **faire le ~*** to be difficult, be nasty. ♦ **méchamment** *adv* (*cruellement*) nastily, wickedly; (*: *très*) *bon* fantastically*, terrifically*; *abîmé* badly. ♦ **méchanceté** *nf* **(a)** nastiness, wickedness; naughtiness. **par ~** out of spite. **(b)** (*action, parole*) nasty *ou* wicked action *ou* remark. **dire des ~s à qn** to say spiteful things to sb.

mèche [mɛʃ] *nf [lampe]* wick; *[bombe]* fuse; *[cheveux]* lock of hair; *[chignole]* bit. ~ **postiche** hairpiece; **être de ~ avec qn*** to be hand in glove with sb*, be in league with sb.

mécompte [mekɔ̃t] *nm* disappointment.

méconnaître [mekɔnɛtʀ(ə)] (57) *vt faits* to be unaware of, not to know; *gravité d'un problème* to misjudge; *mérites, personne* to underrate, underestimate; *devoirs* to ignore. ♦ **méconnaissable** *adj* unrecognizable; (*presque*) hardly recognizable. ♦ **méconnaissance** *nf* (*ignorance*) lack of knowledge (*de* about), ignorance (*de* of). ♦ **méconnu, e** *adj* (*gén*) unrecognized; *inventeur* misunderstood.

mécontentement [mekɔ̃tɑ̃tmɑ̃] *nm* (*Pol*) discontent; (*déplaisir*) dissatisfaction, displeasure; (*irritation*) annoyance. ♦ **mécontent, e 1** *adj* displeased, dissatisfied; annoyed (*de* with). **2** *nm,f* grumbler; (*Pol*) malcontent. ♦ **mécontenter** (1) *vt* to dissatisfy, displease; to annoy.

médaille [medaj] *nf* **(a)** (*décoration*) medal. **(b)** (*insigne*) *[employé]* badge; *[chien]* name tag; *[volaille]* guarantee tag. ♦ **médaillé, e** *nm,f* medalholder. ♦ **médailler** (1) *vt* to award a medal to. ♦ **médaillon** *nm* (*Art, Culin*) medallion; (*bijou*) locket.

médecin [mɛdsɛ̃] *nm* doctor. ~ **d'hôpital** ≃ consultant; ~ **légiste** forensic surgeon; ~ **généraliste** general practitioner, G.P.; ~ **militaire** army medical officer. ♦ **médecine** *nf* medicine. ~ **générale** general medicine; ~ **du travail** occupational *ou* industrial medicine.

médiation [medjɑsjɔ̃] *nf* (*gén, Pol*) mediation; (*Ind*) arbitration. ♦ **médiateur, -trice 1** *nm,f* mediator; arbitrator. **2** *nf* (*Géom*) median.

médical, e, *mpl* **-aux** [medikal, o] *adj* medical. ♦ **médicalement** *adv* medically. ♦ **médicament** *nm* medicine, drug. ♦ **médicinal, e,** *mpl* **-aux** *adj* medicinal.

médiéval, e, *mpl* **-aux** [medjeval, o] *adj* medieval.

médiocre [medjɔkʀ(ə)] *adj* (*gén*) mediocre; *qualité, salaire* poor; *personne, emploi* second-rate. **il a montré un intérêt ~ pour ce projet** he showed little interest in the project. ♦ **médiocrement** *adv intelligent* not particularly; *satisfait* barely; *travailler* indifferently. **gagner ~ sa vie** to earn a poor living. ♦ **médiocrité** *nf* mediocrity; poorness. **cet homme est une ~** this man is a complete mediocrity *ou* second-rater.

médire [mediʀ] (37) *vi*: **~ de qn** to speak ill of sb; (*à tort*) to malign *ou* slander sb. ♦ **médisance** *nf* (*propos*) piece of scandal. **la ~** scandalmongering; **dire des ~s** to spread scandal *ou* malicious gossip. ♦ **médisant, e 1** *adj paroles* slanderous. **être ~** to spread scandal. **2** *nm,f* scandalmonger, slanderer.

méditer [medite] (1) **1** *vt pensée* to meditate on, ponder (over); *projet* to meditate. **~ de faire qch** to contemplate doing sth, plan to do sth. **2** *vi* to meditate. **~ sur qch** to ponder over sth. ♦ **méditatif, -ive** *adj* meditative, thoughtful. ♦ **méditation** *nf* meditation. **après de longues ~s** after much *ou* deep thought, after lengthy meditation.

Méditerranée [mediteʀane] *nf*: **la (mer) ~** the Mediterranean (Sea). ♦ **méditerranéen, -enne** *adj* Mediterranean.

méduse [medyz] *nf* jellyfish. (*Myth*) **M~** Medusa.

méduser [medyze] (1) *vt* (*gén pass*) to dumbfound.

meeting [mitiŋ] *nm* (*Pol, Sport*) meeting. **~ d'aviation** air show.

méfait [mefɛ] *nm* misdemeanour; (*hum*) misdeed. **les ~s de** *temps, épidémie, alcoolisme* the ravages of.

méfiance [mefjɑ̃s] *nf* distrust, mistrust, suspicion. **éveiller la ~ de qn** to arouse sb's suspicion(s); **venir sans ~** to come unsuspectingly. ♦ **méfiant, e** *adj* distrustful, mistrustful, suspicious. ♦ **méfier (se)** (7) *vpr*: **se ~ de** *personne, conseil* to distrust, mistrust; *ses impulsions* to be wary of; **méfiez-vous de lui** don't trust him; **il faut vous ~** you must be careful; **méfie-toi de cette marche** mind *ou* watch the step.

méga [mega] **1** *préf* mega ... . **~tonne** megaton. **2** *adj inv* (*ǃ*) enormous. **~ dissertation** hell of a long essayǃ.

mégalomanie [megalɔmani] *nf* megalomania. ♦ **mégalomane** *adj, nmf* megalomaniac.

mégarde [megaʀd(ə)] *nf*: **par ~** (*accidentellement*) accidentally, by accident; (*par erreur*) by mistake, inadvertently.

mégère [meʒɛʀ] *nf* (*péj: femme*) shrew.

mégot* [mego] *nm* cigarette butt *ou* end.

meilleur, e [mɛjœʀ] **1** *adj* better (*que* than). **le ~ des deux** the better of the two; **le ~ de tous** the best of the lot; **ce gâteau est ~ avec du rhum** this cake tastes *ou* is better with rum; **~ marché** cheaper; **le ~ marché** the cheapest; **~s vœux** best wishes; **il n'y a rien de ~** there's nothing better, there's nothing to beat it. **2** *adv sentir* better, nicer. **3** *nm,f*: **le ~, la ~e** the best one; **les ~s** the best (people). **4** *nm*: **le ~** the best; **pour le ~ et pour le pire** for better or for worse; **donner le ~ de soi-même** to give of one's best; **le ~ de son temps** the best part of one's time; **prendre le ~ sur qn** to get the better of sb.

mélancolie [melɑ̃kɔli] *nf* melancholy. ♦ **mélancolique** *adj* melancholy. ♦ **mélancoliquement** *adv* melancholically.

mélanger [melɑ̃ʒe] (3) **1** *vt* (*gén*) to mix; *couleurs, vins, tabacs* to blend; *dates, documents* to mix up, muddle up. **public très mélangé** very varied *ou* mixed public. **2 se ~** *vpr* to mix; to blend. **tout se mélange dans ma tête** I'm getting all mixed up. ♦ **mélange** *nm* **(a)** (*opération*) mixing; blending. **(b)** (*résultat*) mixture; blend. **~ détonant** explosive mixture; **joie sans ~** unalloyed joy; (*Littérat*) **~s** miscellanies.

mélasse [melas] *nf* (*Culin*) treacle, molasses (*US*); (*boue*) muck. **être dans la ~*** (*ennuis*) to be in the soup*; (*misère*) to be on one's beam ends*.

mêler [mele] (1) **1** *vt* **(a)** (*unir*) to mingle; *races* to mix; (*Vét*) to cross; (*Culin*) to mix, blend; *traits de caractère* to combine. **~ la douceur à la fermeté** to combine gentleness with firmness. **(b)** *papiers* to muddle up, mix up; (*battre*) *cartes* to shuffle. **~ la réalité et le rêve** to confuse reality and dream. **(c) ~ qn à** *affaire* to involve sb in, get sb mixed up in; *conversation* to bring *ou* draw sb into. **2 se ~** *vpr* **(a)** to mix; to mingle; to combine. **(b) se ~ à** *querelle* to get involved in; *conversation* to join in; *groupe* to join, mix with; *[cris, sentiments]* to mingle with. **(c) se ~ de qch** to meddle with sth; **mêle-toi de tes affaires!** mind your own business!; **se ~ de faire qch** to take it upon o.s. to do sth. ♦ **mêlé, e 1** *adj sentiments* mixed, mingled; *monde* mixed. **2** *nf* (*bataille*) mêlée; (*Rugby*) scrum. **~e générale** free-for-all; **rester au-dessus de la ~e** to keep clear of the fray.

mélèze [melɛz] *nm* larch.

méli-mélo* [melimelo] *nm [situation]* muddle; *[objets]* jumble.

mélodie [melɔdi] *nf* (*gén*) tune. (*genre*) **les ~s de Debussy** Debussy's melodies. ♦ **mélodieusement** *adv* melodiously, tunefully. ♦ **mélodieux, -euse** *adj* melodious, tuneful. ♦ **mélodique** *adj* melodic.

mélodrame [melɔdʀam] *nm* (*Littérat, péj*) melodrama. ♦ **mélodramatique** *adj* melodramatic.

mélomane [melɔman] *adj, nmf*: **être ~** to be a music lover.

melon [m(ə)lɔ̃] *nm* (*Bot*) melon. **(chapeau) ~** bowler hat.

membrane [mɑ̃bʀan] *nf* membrane.

membre [mɑ̃bʀ(ə)] *nm* **(a)** (*Anat*) limb. **(b)** (*personne*) member. **être ~ de** to be a member of; **ce club a 300 ~s** this club has a membership of 300; **pays ~** member country. **(c)** (*Math, Ling*) member.

même [mɛm] **1** *adj* **(a)** (*identique*) same. **ils ont la ~ taille, ils sont de ~ taille** they are the same size; **ils ont la ~ voiture que nous** they have the same car as we have *ou* as us; **c'est toujours la ~ chose!** it's always the same (old story)!; **arriver en ~ temps (que)** to arrive at the same time (as). **(b)** (*réel*) very. **ce sont ses paroles ~s** those are his very *ou* actual words; **il est la générosité ~** he is generosity itself *ou* the soul of generosity. **(c) moi-~** myself; **toi-~** yourself; **lui-~** himself; **elle-~** herself; **nous-~s** ourselves; **vous-~** yourself; **vous-~s** yourselves; **eux-** *ou* **elles-~s** themselves; **on est soi-~ conscient de ses propres erreurs** one is aware (oneself) of one's own mistakes; **au plus profond d'eux-~s** in their heart of hearts; **elle fait ses robes elle-~** she makes her own dresses, she makes her dresses herself; **elle se disait en elle-~ que ...** she thought to herself that ...; **faire qch de soi-~** to do sth on one's own initiative; **faire qch (par) soi-~** to do sth (by) oneself.

2 *pron indéf*: **le** *ou* **la ~** the same one; (*fig*) **ce sont toujours les ~s** it's always the same ones.

3 *adv* **(a)** even. **il n'a ~ pas de quoi écrire** he hasn't even got anything to write with; **personne ne sait, ~ pas lui** nobody knows, not even him; **~ si** even if, even though. **(b)** (*précisément*) **ici ~** in this very place; **c'est celui-là ~ qui** he's the very one who; **c'est cela ~** that's just *ou* exactly it. **(c) boire à ~ la bouteille** to drink straight from the bottle; **coucher à ~ le sol** to lie on the bare ground; **à ~ la peau** next to the skin; **être à ~ de faire** to be able *ou* in a position to do; **il fera de ~** he'll do the same *ou* likewise; **vous le détestez? moi de ~** you hate him? so do I *ou* I do too; **de ~ qu'il nous a dit que ...** just as he told us that ...; **il en est de ~ pour moi** it's the same for me, same here*; **quand ~, tout de ~** all the same, even so.

mémé* [meme] *nf*, **mémère*** [memɛʀ] *nf* granny*.

mémoire¹ [memwaʀ] *nf* (*gén*) memory. **de ~** from memory; **pour ~** as a matter of interest; **avoir la ~ des noms** to have a good memory for names; **si j'ai bonne ~** if I remember rightly, if my memory serves me right; **avoir la ~ courte** to have a short memory; **j'ai gardé la ~ de cette conversation** I remember this conversation; **ça me revient en ~** it comes back to me; **il me l'a remis en ~** he reminded me of it; **de glorieuse ~** of blessed memory; **à la ~ de** in memory of, to the memory of.

mémoire² [memwaʀ] *nm* (*requête*) memorandum; (*rapport*) report; (*exposé*) paper; (*facture*) bill. (*souvenirs*) **~s** memoirs.

mémorable [memɔʀabl(ə)] *adj* memorable.

mémorandum [memɔʀɑ̃dɔm] *nm* memorandum.

mémorial, *pl* **-aux** [memɔʀjal, o] *nm* (*Archit*) memorial.

mémoriser [memɔʀize] (1) *vt* to memorize.

menace [mənas] *nf* threat. **paroles de ~** threatening words; **sous la ~** under threat; **~ d'épidémie** impending epidemic, threat of an epidemic. ♦ **menaçant, e** *adj* threatening, menacing. ♦ **menacer** (3) *vt* to threaten. **~ qn de mort/d'un revolver** to threaten sb with death/with a gun; **la pluie menace** it looks like rain; **chaise qui menace de se casser** chair which is about to break *ou* which looks like breaking; **ça menace de durer** it threatens *ou* looks set to last some time.

ménage [menaʒ] *nm* **(a)** (*entretien*) housework. **tenir son ~** to look after one's house; **faire le ~** to do the housework; **faire des ~s** to go out charring. **(b)** (*couple*) couple. **être heureux en ~** to have a happy married life; **se mettre en ~ avec qn** to set up house with sb; **scènes de ~** domestic rows; **faire bon/mauvais ~ avec qn** to get on well/badly with sb.

ménager¹, -ère [menaʒe, ɛʀ] **1** *adj* **(a)** *ustensiles* household, domestic. **travaux ~s** housework. **(b)** (*économe*) **~ de** sparing of. **2** *nf* (*femme*) housewife; (*couverts*) canteen of cutlery.

ménager² [menaʒe] (3) *vt* **(a)** *adversaire* to handle carefully; *susceptibilité* to spare; *temps, argent* to use carefully *ou* sparingly; *forces* to conserve; *santé* to take care of; *paroles* to moderate, tone down. **il faut vous ~** you should take things easy; **il n'a pas ménagé ses efforts** he spared no effort; **elle est très sensible, il faut la ~** she is very sensitive, you must treat her gently; **~ les deux partis** to humour both parties; **~ la chèvre et le chou** to keep both parties sweet*. **(b)** *rencontre* to arrange, organize; *transition* to bring about. **~ l'avenir** to prepare for the future; **il nous ménage une surprise** he has a surprise in store for us. **(c)** *porte* to put in; *chemin* to cut. **~ une place pour** to make room for; **se ~ une porte de sortie** to leave o.s. a way out. ♦ **ménagement** *nm* care. **traiter avec ~** *interlocuteur* to treat considerately; *malade* to treat gently; **traiter sans ~** to handle roughly; **elle a besoin de ~** she needs care and attention; (*égards*) **~s** (respectful) consideration *ou* attention.

ménagerie [menaʒʀi] *nf* (*lit, fig*) menagerie.

mendier [mɑ̃dje] (7) **1** *vt* to beg (for). **~ qch à qn** to beg sb for sth, beg sth from sb. **2** *vi* to beg (for alms). ♦ **mendiant, e** *nm,f* beggar. ♦ **mendicité** *nf* begging.

mener [məne] (5) *vt* **(a)** (*conduire*) (*gén*) to lead; (*vers un lieu*) to take; (*en voiture*) to drive (*à* to, *dans* into). **~ un enfant à l'école** to take a child to school; **mène ton ami à sa chambre** show *ou* take your friend to his room; **chemin qui mène à la mer** path (leading) to the sea; **où tout cela va-t-il nous ~?** where's all this going to get *ou* lead us?; **ces études mènent au journalisme** this training prepares one for journalism; **de telles infractions pourraient le ~ loin** offences such as these could get him into trouble; **~ qn à faire** to lead sb to do.

(b) (*diriger*) (*gén*) to lead; *pays, entreprise* to run; *enquête* to carry out, conduct. **~ les choses rondement** to manage things efficiently; **~ qch à bien** to carry sth through to a successful conclusion; **~ qn par le bout du nez** to lead sb by the nose; **~ qn à la baguette** to rule sb with an iron hand; **l'argent mène le monde** money rules the world; **~ les débats** to chair the discussion.

(c) (*Sport*) to lead. **la France mène (l'Écosse par 2 buts à 1)** France is in the lead (by 2 goals to 1 against Scotland), France is leading (Scotland by 2 goals to 1).

(d) ~ la vie dure à qn to rule sb with an iron hand; **~ qn en bateau*** to take sb for a ride*; **il n'en menait pas large** his heart was in his boots; **~ grand bruit autour d'une affaire** to give an affair a lot of publicity.

♦ **menées** *nfpl* intrigues, machinations. **~ subversives** subversive activities. ♦ **meneur, -euse** *nm,f* (*chef*) ringleader; (*agitateur*) agitator. **~ d'hommes** born leader; **~ de jeu** (*spectacle*) compère; (*jeu*) quiz-master.

ménestrel [menɛstʀɛl] *nm* minstrel.

menhir [meniʀ] *nm* menhir, standing stone.

méninge [menɛ̃ʒ] *nf* (*Méd*) meninx. **~s** meninges; **se creuser les ~s** to rack one's brains. ♦ **méningite** *nf* meningitis.

ménopause [menɔpoz] *nf* menopause.

menotte [mənɔt] *nf* **(a) ~s** handcuffs; **mettre les ~s à qn** to handcuff sb. **(b)** (*: *main*) hand, handy*.

mensonge [mɑ̃sɔ̃ʒ] *nm* lie, fib*, untruth. (*acte*) **le**

~ lying, untruthfulness. ♦ **mensonger, -ère** *adj* untrue, false.
menstruation [mɑ̃stʀyasjɔ̃] *nf* menstruation.
mensuel, -elle [mɑ̃sɥɛl] **1** *adj* monthly. **2** *nm,f* employee paid by the month. **3** *nm* (*Presse*) monthly (magazine). ♦ **mensualiser** (1) *vt* to pay on a monthly basis. ♦ **mensualité** *nf* (*traite*) monthly payment; (*salaire*) monthly salary. ♦ **mensuellement** *adv* monthly, every month.
mensuration [mɑ̃syʀasjɔ̃] *nf* (*calcul*) mensuration. (*mesures*) ~s measurements.
mental, e, *mpl* **-aux** [mɑ̃tal, o] *adj* mental. ♦ **mentalement** *adv* mentally. ♦ **mentalité** *nf* mentality.
menteur, -euse [mɑ̃tœʀ, øz] **1** *adj proverbe* false; *enfant* untruthful, lying. **il est très** ~ he is a great liar. **2** *nm,f* liar, fibber*.
menthe [mɑ̃t] *nf* (*Bot*) mint; (*boisson*) peppermint cordial. ~ **poivrée** peppermint; ~ **verte** spearmint; **de** ~, **à la** ~ mint.
mention [mɑ̃sjɔ̃] *nf* **(a)** (*action*) mention. **faire** ~ **de** to mention, make mention of. **(b)** (*annotation*) note, comment. (*Admin*) **'rayer la** ~ **inutile'** 'delete as appropriate'. **(c)** (*Scol*) ~ **passable/assez bien/bien/très bien** (*examen*) ≃ grade D/C/B/A pass; (*Univ: licence*) IIIrd class/lower IInd class/upper IInd class/Ist class Honours; **être reçu avec** ~ to pass with distinction. ♦ **mentionner** (1) *vt* to mention.
mentir [mɑ̃tiʀ] (16) *vi* to lie (*à qn* to sb, *sur* about). **sans** ~ quite honestly; **il ment comme il respire** he's a compulsive liar; **faire** ~ **le proverbe** to give the lie to the proverb; ~ **à sa réputation** to belie one's reputation; **se** ~ **à soi-même** to fool o.s.
menton [mɑ̃tɔ̃] *nm* chin.
menu[1] [məny] *nm* (*repas*) meal; (*carte*) menu; (*régime*) diet. ~ **(à prix fixe)** set menu; ~ **du jour** today's menu; ~ **touristique** standard menu; ~ **gastronomique** gourmet's menu.
menu[2]**, e** [məny] **1** *adj tige* slender; *taille, personne* slim, slight; *herbe* fine; *écriture, pas* small, tiny; *voix* thin; *incidents* minor, trifling. **en** ~**s morceaux** in tiny pieces; **dans les** ~**s détails, par le** ~ in minute detail; (*lit, fig*) ~ **fretin** small fry; ~**e monnaie** small *ou* loose change. **2** *adv hacher* fine. **écrire** ~ to write small.
menuisier [mənɥizje] *nm [meubles]* joiner; *[bâtiment]* carpenter. ~ **d'art** cabinetmaker. ♦ **menuiserie** *nf* **(a)** (*métier*) joinery; carpentry. ~ **d'art** cabinet work. **(b)** (*atelier*) joiner's workshop. **(c)** (*ouvrage*) piece of woodwork *ou* joinery.
méprendre (se) [mepʀɑ̃dʀ(ə)] (58) *vpr* (*littér*) to make a mistake, be mistaken (*sur* about).
mépris [mepʀi] *nm* contempt, scorn. **avec** ~ contemptuously, scornfully; **avoir le** ~ **des convenances** to have no regard for conventions; **au** ~ **du danger** regardless *ou* in defiance of danger. ♦ **mépriser** (1) *vt* (*gén*) to scorn, despise; *personne* to look down on; *conseil* to spurn. ♦ **méprisable** *adj* contemptible, despicable. ♦ **méprisant, e** *adj* contemptuous, scornful.
méprise [mepʀiz] *nf* (*erreur*) mistake, error; (*malentendu*) misunderstanding.
mer [mɛʀ] *nf* **(a)** sea. ~ **fermée** inland sea; ~ **de sable** sea of sand; ~ **d'huile** glassy sea; **vent de** ~ sea breeze; **gens de** ~ sailors. **(b)** (*marée*) tide. **la** ~ **est haute/basse** the tide is high *ou* in/low *ou* out; **c'est la haute/basse** ~ it is high/low tide. **(c) en** ~ at sea; **en haute** *ou* **pleine** ~ on the open sea; **prendre la** ~ to put out to sea; **mettre (une embarcation) à la** ~ to bring *ou* get out a boat; (*fig*) **ce n'est pas la** ~ **à boire!** it's not asking the impossible!
mercenaire [mɛʀsənɛʀ] *adj, nm* mercenary.
mercerie [mɛʀsəʀi] *nf* (*boutique*) haberdasher's shop, notions store (*US*); (*articles*) haberdashery, notions (*US*). ♦ **mercier, -ière** *nm,f* haberdasher.
merci [mɛʀsi] **1** *excl* thank you (*de, pour* for); (*pour refuser*) no, thank you. ~ **bien** *ou* **beaucoup** thank you very much, many thanks; ~ **d'avoir répondu** thank you for replying; **dire** ~ **à qn** to thank sb, say thank you to sb. **2** *nm* thank-you. **je n'ai pas eu un** ~ I didn't get a word of thanks; **mille** ~s (very) many thanks. **3** *nf* mercy. **crier** ~ to cry for mercy; **sans** ~ *combat etc* merciless, ruthless; **à la** ~ **de** at the mercy of.
mercredi [mɛʀkʀədi] *nm* Wednesday. ~ **des Cendres** Ash Wednesday; *V* **samedi.**
mercure [mɛʀkyʀ] *nm* mercury. ♦ **mercurochrome** *nm* mercurochrome.
merde* [mɛʀd(ə)] **1** *nf* shit*; (*fig: ennuis*) mess. **2** *excl* hell!*
mère [mɛʀ] *nf* **(a)** mother. ~ **de famille** mother, housewife; **M**~ **Supérieure** Mother Superior; (*péj*) **la** ~ **X*** old Mrs X. **(b) cellule/maison** ~ parent cell/company.
méridien, -enne [meʀidjɛ̃, ɛn] *adj, nm* meridian.
méridional, e, *mpl* **-aux** [meʀidjɔnal, o] **1** *adj* southern. **2** *nm(f)*: **M**~**(e)** Southerner.
meringue [məʀɛ̃g] *nf* meringue.
mériter [meʀite] (1) *vt louange, châtiment* to deserve, merit. **il mérite la prison** he deserves to go to gaol; **repos bien mérité** well-deserved rest; **ça mérite d'être noté** it is worth noting; **ceci mérite réflexion** (*exiger*) this calls for *ou* requires careful thought; (*valoir*) this deserves careful thought; **ça lui a mérité le respect de tous** this earned him everyone's respect. ♦ **méritant, e** *adj* deserving. ♦ **mérite** *nm* (*gén*) merit. **il n'y a aucun** ~ **à cela** there's no merit in that, one deserves no credit for that; **de grand** ~ of great worth *ou* merit; **si nombreux que soient ses** ~**s** however many qualities he may have; **ça a le** ~ **d'être simple** it has the merit of being simple. ♦ **méritoire** *adj* meritorious, commendable.
merlan [mɛʀlɑ̃] *nm* whiting.
merle [mɛʀl(ə)] *nm* blackbird.
merlu [mɛʀly] *nm* hake.
merveille [mɛʀvɛj] *nf* marvel, wonder. **à** ~ *fonctionner* perfectly; **se porter à** ~ to be in excellent health; **ça tombe à** ~ this comes just at the right time; **faire** ~ to work wonders; **c'est** ~ **que** it's a wonder *ou* a marvel that; **on en dit** ~ it's praised to the skies. ♦ **merveilleusement** *adv* marvellously, wonderfully. ♦ **merveilleux, -euse 1** *adj* (*magnifique*) marvellous, wonderful; (*après n: surnaturel*) magic. **2** *nm*: **le** ~ the supernatural.
mes [me] *adj poss V* **mon.**
mésalliance [mezaljɑ̃s] *nf* misalliance.
mésange [mezɑ̃ʒ] *nf* tit(mouse).
mésaventure [mezavɑ̃tyʀ] *nf* misadventure, misfortune.
Mesdames [medam] *nfpl V* **Madame.**
Mesdemoiselles [medmwazɛl] *nfpl V* **Mademoiselle.**
mésentente [mezɑ̃tɑ̃t] *nf* dissension, disagreement.
mésestimer [mezɛstime] (1) *vt difficulté* to underestimate, underrate; *personne* to have little regard for.
mesquin, e [mɛskɛ̃, in] *adj* (*avare*) mean, stingy; (*vil*) mean, petty. ♦ **mesquinement** *adv agir* meanly, stingily; pettily. ♦ **mesquinerie** *nf* meanness, stinginess; pettiness. **une** ~ a mean *ou* petty trick.
mess [mɛs] *nm* (*Mil*) mess.
message [mesaʒ] *nm* message. ~ **publicitaire** advertisement. ♦ **messager, -ère** *nm,f* messenger. ♦ **messageries** *nfpl* freight company.
messe [mɛs] *nf* mass. **aller à la** ~ to go to mass; ~ **basse** low mass; **finissez vos** ~**s basses** stop muttering together.
messie [mesi] *nm* messiah. **le M**~ the Messiah.
Messieurs [mesjø] *nmpl V* **Monsieur.**
mesure [m(ə)zyʀ] *nf* **(a)** (*évaluation, dimension*)

measurement. **prendre les ~s de qch** to take the measurements of sth. **(b)** (*étalon, quantité*) measure. **~ de longueur** measure of length; **faire bonne ~** to give good measure; **la bonne ~** the happy medium; **la ~ est comble** that's the limit; **dépasser la ~** to overstep the mark; **boire outre ~** to drink to excess. **(c)** (*fig*) *[forces, sentiments]* measure. **monde à la ~ de l'homme** world on a human scale; **il est à ma ~** *[travail]* it is within my capabilities; *[adversaire]* he's a good match for me; **donner toute sa ~** to show one's worth. **(d)** (*modération*) moderation. **avec ~** in moderation; **il a beaucoup de ~** he's very moderate; **sans ~** *orgueil* immoderate, measureless; **se dépenser sans ~** (*se dévouer*) to give one's all. **(e)** (*moyen*) measure, step. **prendre des ~s d'urgence** to take emergency action *ou* measures; **des ~s de rétorsion** reprisals; **j'ai pris mes ~s pour qu'il vienne** I have made arrangements for him to come. **(f)** (*Mus*) (*cadence*) time, tempo; (*division*) bar. **être/ne pas être en ~** to be in/out of time; **jouer quelques ~s** to play a few bars. **(g)** (*Habillement*) **prendre les ~s de qn** to take sb's measurements; **est-ce que ce costume est bien à ma ~?** is this suit my size?, will this suit fit me?; **s'habiller sur ~** to have one's clothes made to measure; **j'ai un patron sur ~** my boss suits me down to the ground. **(h)** (*locutions*) **dans la ~ du possible/de mes moyens** as far as possible/as I am able; **dans la ~ où** inasmuch as, insofar as; **dans une certaine/large ~** to some/to a large extent; **être en ~ de faire qch** to be in a position to do sth; **(au fur et) à ~ que** as; **donne-les moi (au fur et) à ~** hand them to me one by one *ou* as you go along. ♦ **mesurable** *adj* measurable.

mesurer [məzyʀe] (1) **1** *vt* **(a)** *chose* to measure; *personne* to take the measurements of, measure (up); (*par calcul*) to calculate. **il me mesura 3 mètres de tissu** he measured me off *ou* out 3 metres of fabric. **(b)** *dégâts, valeur* to assess; *conséquences* to consider, weigh up. **(c)** (*hostilement*) **~ ses forces avec qn** to pit o.s. against sb; **~ qn du regard** to look sb up and down; **se ~ des yeux** to weigh *ou* size each other up. **(d)** (*avoir pour mesure*) to measure. **cette pièce mesure 3 mètres sur 10** this room measures 3 metres by 10; **il mesure 1 mètre 80** it (*ou* he) measures 1 metre 80. **(e)** (*avec parcimonie*) to limit. **le temps nous est mesuré** our time is limited. **(f)** (*avec modération*) **~ ses paroles** to moderate one's language. **(g)** (*proportionner*) to match (*à, sur* to). **2 se ~** *vpr*: **se ~ avec** *personne* to pit o.s. against; *difficulté* to confront, tackle. ♦ **mesuré, e** *adj ton, pas* measured; *personne* moderate (*dans* in).

métabolisme [metabɔlism(ə)] *nm* metabolism.

métal, *pl* **-aux** [metal, o] *nm* metal. ♦ **métallique** *adj* (*gén, fig*) metallic; *objet* (*en métal*) metal; (*qui ressemble au métal*) metallic. **bruit ~** jangle, clank. ♦ **métallisé, e** *adj peinture* metallic. ♦ **métallurgie** *nf* (*industrie*) metallurgical industry; (*technique*) metallurgy. ♦ **métallurgique** *adj* metallurgic. ♦ **métallurgiste** *nm* (*ouvrier*) steel *ou* metal-worker; (*industriel*) metallurgist.

métamorphose [metamɔʀfoz] *nf* metamorphosis. ♦ **métamorphoser** (1) **1** *vt* to transform, metamorphose (*en* into). **2 se ~** *vpr* to be metamorphosed *ou* transformed (*en* into).

métaphore [metafɔʀ] *nf* metaphor. ♦ **métaphorique** *adj* metaphorical. ♦ **métaphoriquement** *adv* metaphorically.

météore [meteɔʀ] *nm* meteor. ♦ **météorique** *adj* meteoric. ♦ **météorite** *nm ou f* meteorite.

météorologie [meteɔʀɔlɔʒi] *nf* (*Sci*) meteorology; (*services*) Meteorological Office, Met Office*. ♦ **météo** *nf* (*bulletin*) weather forecast. ♦ **météorologique** *adj phénomène, observation* meteorological; *carte, station* weather. ♦ **météorologiste** *nmf ou* ♦ **météorologue** *nmf* meteorologist.

métèque [metɛk] *nmf* (*péj*) wog‡ (*péj*), wop‡ (*péj*).

méthane [metan] *nm* methane.

méthode [metɔd] *nf* **(a)** method. **avoir sa ~ pour faire qch** to have one's own way *ou* method for *ou* of doing sth; **il a beaucoup de ~** he's very methodical; **faire qch avec/sans ~** to do sth methodically/unmethodically. **(b)** (*livre*) manual, tutor. **~ de latin** latin primer. ♦ **méthodique** *adj* methodical. ♦ **méthodiquement** *adv* methodically.

méticuleux, -euse [metikylø, øz] *adj* meticulous. ♦ **méticuleusement** *adv* meticulously.

métier [metje] *nm* **(a)** (*gén: travail*) job; (*Admin*) occupation; (*manuel*) trade; (*artisanal*) craft; (*intellectuel*) profession. **les ~s manuels** (the) manual occupations; **il est plombier de son ~** he is a plumber by *ou* to trade; **il est du ~** he is in the trade *ou* profession *ou* business; **il connaît son ~** he knows his job. **(b)** (*expérience*) (acquired) skill *ou* technique, experience. **avoir du ~** to have practical experience; **avoir 2 ans de ~** to have been 2 years in the trade *ou* profession; **homme de ~** expert, professional, specialist. **(c) ~ à tisser** (weaving) loom.

métis, -isse [metis] **1** *adj personne* half-caste, half-breed; *animal* crossbreed, mongrel; *plante* hybrid. **2** *nm,f* (*personne*) half-caste, half-breed; (*animal, plante*) mongrel. **3** *nm* (*Tex*) fabric made of cotton and linen mixture. ♦ **métisser** (1) *vt* to crossbreed, cross.

métonymie [metɔnimi] *nf* metonymy.

mètre [mɛtʀ(ə)] *nm* (*gén*) metre; (*instrument*) (metre) rule. **~ carré/cube** square/cubic metre; **~ pliant** folding rule; **~ à ruban** tape measure, measuring tape; (*Sport*) **un 100 ~s** a 100-metre race. ♦ **métrage** *nm* (*Couture*) length, yardage; (*mesure*) measurement. ♦ **métrer** (6) *vt* to measure (in metres); *[vérificateur]* to survey. ♦ **métreur, -euse** *nm,f*: **~ (vérificateur)** quantity surveyor. ♦ **métrique** *adj* metric.

métro [metʀo] *nm* underground, subway (*US*). **le ~ de Londres** the tube.

métronome [metʀɔnɔm] *nm* metronome.

métropole [metʀɔpɔl] *nf* (*ville*) metropolis; (*état*) home country. ♦ **métropolitain, e** *adj* metropolitan.

mets [mɛ] *nm* (*Culin*) dish.

mettable [mɛtabl(ə)] *adj* wearable, decent.

metteur [mɛtœʀ] *nm*: **~ en ondes** producer; **~ en scène** (*Théât*) producer; (*Ciné*) director.

mettre [mɛtʀ(ə)] (56) **1** *vt* **(a)** (*placer*) to put (*dans* in, into, *sur* on). **elle lui mit la main sur l'épaule** she put *ou* laid her hand on his shoulder; **elle met son travail avant sa famille** she puts her work before her family; **je mets Molière parmi les plus grands écrivains** I rank *ou* rate Molière among the greatest writers; **~ qch à plat** to lay sth down flat; **~ qch droit** to put *ou* set sth straight; **ne mets pas d'encre sur la nappe** don't get ink on the tablecloth; **~ un enfant à l'école** to send a child to school; (*combat*) **qu'est-ce qu'ils nous ont mis!*** what a hiding they gave us!*; **~ qch à cuire** to put sth on to cook. **(b)** *vêtements, lunettes* to put on. **je ne mets plus mon gilet** I've stopped wearing my cardigan; **mets-lui son chapeau** put his hat on (for him). **(c)** (*consacrer*) **j'ai mis 2 heures à le faire** I took 2 hours to do it, I spent 2 hours on *ou* over it; **~ beaucoup de soin à faire** to take great care in doing; **il y a mis le temps!** he's taken his time (about it)! **(d)** *radio, chauffage* to put *ou* switch *ou* turn on. **~ le réveil (à 7 heures)** to set the alarm (for 7 o'clock); **~ le verrou** to bolt the door. **(e)** (*installer*) *placards* to put in; *eau* to lay on. **(f)** (*écrire*) **~ en anglais/au pluriel** to put into English/the plural; **~ un mot à qn*** to drop a line to sb*; **mettez bien clairement que** put (down) quite clearly that; **il met qu'il est bien arrivé** he says in his letter *ou* writes that he arrived safely. **(g)** *argent (gén)* to put. ~ **de l'argent sur un cheval** to put money on a horse; **je suis prêt à ~ 500 F** I'm willing to give 500 francs; **il faut y ~ le prix** you have to pay for it. **(h)** (*supposer*) **mettons que je me sois trompé** let's say *ou* (just) suppose I've got it wrong.

2 se ~ *vpr* **(a)** *[personne]* to put o.s.; *[objet]* to go. **mets-toi là** (*debout*) (go and) stand there; (*assis*) (go and) sit there; **se ~ dans un fauteuil** to sit down in an armchair; (*fig*) **elle ne savait plus où se ~** she didn't know where to hide herself; **se ~ autour (de)** to gather round; **ces verres se mettent dans le placard** these glasses go in the cupboard; **se ~ une idée dans la tête/de l'encre sur les doigts** to get an idea into one's head/ink on one's fingers. **(b)** *[temps]* **se ~ au froid** to turn cold; **ça se met à la pluie** it looks like rain. **(c)** (*s'habiller*) **se ~ en robe** to put on a dress; **se ~ en bras de chemise** to take off one's jacket; **je n'ai rien à me ~** I've got nothing to wear. **(d) se ~ à rire** to start laughing, start *ou* begin to laugh; **se ~ au travail** to set to work, get down to work; **se ~ à boire** to take to drink; **il s'est bien mis à l'anglais** he's really taken to English. **(e)** (*se grouper*) **ils se sont mis à plusieurs/2 pour pousser la voiture** several of them/the 2 of them joined forces to push the car; **se ~ avec qn** (*faire équipe*) to team up with sb; (*prendre parti*) to side with sb; **se ~ d'un parti** to join a party. **(f) qu'est-ce qu'ils se sont mis!*** (*manger*) they had a real blowout!‡; (*combat*) they didn't half lay into each other!‡

meuble [mœbl(ə)] **1** *nm* (*objet*) piece of furniture. **les ~s** the furniture; (*ameublement*) **le ~** furniture; **~ de rangement** cupboard, storage unit; **être dans ses ~s** to be settled in one's own home. **2** *adj* **(a)** *terre* loose; *roche* soft. **(b)** (*Jur*) **biens ~s** movables. ♦ **meublé, e 1** *adj* furnished. **non ~** unfurnished. **2** *nm* (*appartement*) furnished flat *ou* rooms. ♦ **meubler** (1) **1** *vt pièce* to furnish; *loisirs* to fill (*de* with). **~ la conversation** to keep the conversation going. **2 se ~** *vpr* to buy *ou* get (some) furniture.

meugler [møgle] (1) *vi* to moo. ♦ **meuglement** *nm*: **~(s)** mooing.

meule [møl] *nf* (*à moudre*) millstone; (*à polir*) buff wheel; (*de paille*) stack. **~ (à aiguiser)** grindstone; **~ (de gruyère)** round of gruyère; **~ de foin** haystack.

meunier, -ière [mønje, jɛʀ] **1** *adj* (*Tech*) milling. **sole ~ière** sole meunière. **2** *nm* miller. **3** *nf* miller's wife.

meurtre [mœʀtʀ(ə)] *nm* murder. **au ~!** murder! ♦ **meurtrier, -ière 1** *adj intention* murderous; *arme, combat* deadly; *épidémie* fatal. **cette route est ~ière** this road is lethal *ou* a deathtrap. **2** *nm* murderer. **3** *nf* **(a)** murderess. **(b)** (*Archit*) loophole.

meurtrir [mœʀtʀiʀ] (2) *vt* to bruise. **être tout meurtri** to be covered in bruises, be black and blue all over. ♦ **meurtrissure** *nf* bruise.

meute [møt] *nf* (*Chasse, fig*) pack.

mévente [mevɑ̃t] *nf* slump in sales.

Mexique [mɛksik] *nm* Mexico. ♦ **mexicain, e** *adj*, **M~(e)** *nm(f)* Mexican. ♦ **Mexico** *n* Mexico City.

mi [mi] *nm* (*Mus*) E; (*en chantant*) mi.

mi- [mi] *préf* half, mid-. **la mi-janvier** the middle of January, mid-January; **la mi-carême** the third Thursday in Lent; **les yeux mi-clos** with half-closed eyes; **mi-long** *bas* knee-length; *manteau* calf-length; **manche mi-longue** elbow-length sleeve; **mi-pleurant** half-crying; **mi-figue mi-raisin** *sourire, remarque* wry; *accueil* mixed; **à mi-chemin** halfway, midway; **à mi-côte** halfway up *ou* down the hill; **il a de l'eau à mi-cuisses** he is thigh-deep in water, water comes up to his thighs; **à mi-corps/mi-jambes** up (*ou* down) to the waist/knees; **à mi-vitesse** at half-speed; **à mi-voix** in a low voice; *V* **mi-temps.**

miaou [mjau] *nm* miaow. **faire ~** to miaow.

miauler [mjole] (1) *vi* to mew; (*fortement*) to caterwaul. ♦ **miaulement** *nm*: **~(s)** mewing; caterwauling.

mica [mika] *nm* (*roche*) mica.

miche [miʃ] *nf* round loaf, cob loaf.

micheline [miʃlin] *nf* railcar.

micmac* [mikmak] *nm* (*péj*) (*intrigue*) (little) game*; (*complications*) fuss, carry-on*.

micro [mikʀo] *nm* microphone, mike*.

micro ... [mikʀo] *préf* micro ... . **~film** *etc* microfilm *etc.*

microbe [mikʀɔb] *nm* germ, microbe; (*: *enfant*) tich*; (*péj: nabot*) little runt*. ♦ **microbien, -ienne** *adj culture* microbial. **maladie ~ienne** bacterial disease.

microcosme [mikʀɔkɔsm(ə)] *nm* microcosm.

micron [mikʀɔ̃] *nm* micron.

microphone [mikʀɔfɔn] *nm* microphone.

microscope [mikʀɔskɔp] *nm* microscope. **au ~** under a microscope. ♦ **microscopique** *adj* microscopic.

microsillon [mikʀɔsijɔ̃] *nm* (*sillon*) microgroove. **(disque) ~** long-playing record, L.P.

midi [midi] *nm* **(a)** (*heure*) 12 (o'clock). **~ 10** 10 past 12; **de ~ à 2 heures** from 12 *ou* (12) noon to 2; **à ~** at 12 o'clock, at noon, at midday. **(b)** (*déjeuner*) lunchtime. **à ~** at lunchtime; **qu'est-ce que tu as eu à ~?** what did you have for lunch? **(c)** (*période*) **ça s'est passé en plein ~** it happened right in the middle of the day. **(d)** (*Géog: sud*) south. **le M~ (de la France)** the South of France, the Midi.

mie [mi] *nf* crumb (of the loaf).

miel [mjɛl] *nm* honey. **bonbon au ~** honey sweet; *[personne]* **être tout ~** to be unctuous *ou* syrupy. ♦ **mielleusement** *adv* (*péj*) unctuously. ♦ **mielleux, -euse** *adj* (*péj*) *personne* unctuous; *paroles* honeyed; *sourire* sugary; *saveur* sickly sweet.

mien, mienne [mjɛ̃, mjɛn] **1** *pron poss*: **le ~, la mienne, les ~s, les miennes** mine, my own. **2** *nm*: **les ~s** my family; *V* **sien. 3** *adj poss*: **un ~ cousin** a cousin of mine.

miette [mjɛt] *nf [pain]* crumb; *[conversation]* scrap. **en ~s** *verre* in bits *ou* pieces; *gâteau* in crumbs; *casser* to bits, to smithereens; **les ~s de sa fortune** the remnants of his fortune; **je n'en prendrai qu'une ~** I'll just have a tiny bit; **il n'en a pas laissé une ~** he didn't leave a scrap.

mieux [mjø] (*comp, superl de* **bien**) **1** *adv* **(a)** better. **aller ~** to be better; **elle joue ~ que lui** she plays better than he does; **espérer ~** to hope for better (things). **(b) le ~, la ~, les ~** (the) best; (*de deux*) (the) better; **c'est ici qu'il dort le ~** this is where he sleeps best; **tout va le ~ du monde** everything's going beautifully; **un dîner des ~ réussis** a most *ou* highly successful dinner; **j'ai fait le ~ ou du ~ que j'ai pu** I did my best *ou* the best I could; **elle est la ~ habillée** (*de deux*) she is the better dressed; (*de toutes*) she is the best dressed. **(c) ~ que jamais** better than ever; **~ vaut tard que jamais** better late than never; **~ vaut prévenir que guérir** prevention is better than cure; **il va de ~ en ~** he's getting better and better; **il nous a écrit, ~ il est venu nous voir** he wrote to us, and better still he came to see us; **ils criaient à qui ~ ~** each tried to outdo the other in shouting; **c'est on ne peut ~** it's (just) perfect.

2 *adj inv* **(a)** (*gén*) better; (*plus beau*) better-looking, more attractive. **le ~ serait de** the best thing would be to; **être le ~ du monde** to be in perfect health *ou* excellent form; **c'est à l'ombre qu'elle sera le ~** she'll be best *ou* most comfortable in the shade; **son aînée est la ~** (*de 2*) his elder daughter is the better-looking; (*de toutes*) his eldest daughter is the best-looking. **(b) au ~** (*gén*) at best; **faites pour le ~** do what you think best; **être le ~ du monde avec qn** to be on the best of terms with sb; **tu n'as rien de ~ à faire?** haven't you got anything better to do?; **qui ~ est** even better, better still.

3 *nm* **(a)** best. **aider qn de son ~** to do one's best to help sb, help sb the best one can. **(b)** (*progrès*) improvement.

mièvre [mjɛvʀ(ə)] *adj* (*gén*) vapid; (*sentimental*) mawkish. ♦ **mièvrerie** *nf* vapidity; mawkishness. **~(s)** (*comportement*) childish *ou* silly behaviour; (*propos*) vapid *ou* silly talk.

mignard, e [miɲaʀ, aʀd(ə)] *adj style* mannered.

mignon, -onne [miɲɔ̃, ɔn] **1** *adj* pretty, nice, sweet. **donne-le-moi, tu seras ~ne*** give it to me there's a dear*. **2** *nm,f* (little) darling.

migraine [migʀɛn] *nf* headache; (*Méd*) migraine.

migration [migʀɑsjɔ̃] *nf* (*gén*) migration. ♦ **migrateur** *nm* migrant, migratory bird. ♦ **migratoire** *adj* migratory.

mijaurée [miʒɔʀe] *nf* affected woman *ou* girl.

mijoter [miʒɔte] (1) **1** *vt* **(a)** (*Culin*) **(faire) ~** (*lentement*) to simmer; (*avec soin*) to cook lovingly. **(b)** (*) *tour* to plot, cook up*; *complot* to hatch. **qu'est-ce qu'il peut bien ~?** what's he up to?*; **laisser qn ~ dans son jus** to leave sb to stew*. **2** *vi [plat]* to simmer.

mil [mil] *nm* (*dans une date*) a *ou* one thousand.

milice [milis] *nf* militia. ♦ **milicien** *nm* militiaman. ♦ **milicienne** *nf* woman serving in the militia.

milieu, *pl* **~x** [miljø] *nm* **(a)** (*centre*) middle. **la porte du ~** the middle *ou* centre door; **celui du ~** the one in the middle, the middle one; **vers le ~ de l'après-midi** towards the middle of the afternoon, about mid-afternoon; **au ~ de** (*au centre de*) in the middle of; (*parmi*) among, in the midst of; **au beau ~ (de)** right in the middle (of), in the very middle (of); **au ~ de son affolement** in the middle *ou* midst of his panic; **au ~ de la nuit** in the middle of the night, at dead of night; **comment travailler au ~ de ce vacarme?** how can anyone work in *ou* surrounded by this din?; **au ~ de la descente** halfway down (the hill); **au ~ de l'hiver** in mid-winter.

(b) (*état intermédiaire*) middle course *ou* way. **il n'y a pas de ~ (entre)** there is no middle course *ou* way (between); **le juste ~** the happy medium, the golden mean; **il est innocent ou coupable, il n'y a pas de ~** he is either innocent or guilty, he can't be both.

(c) (*Bio, Géog*) environment. (*Phys*) **~ réfringent** refractive medium.

(d) (*entourage*) milieu, environment; (*groupe*) set, circle; (*provenance*) background. **le ~ familial** the family circle; (*Sociol*) the family background, the home environment; **elle est dans son ~ chez nous** she feels (quite) at home with us; **de quel ~ sort-il?** what is his (social) background?; **~x bien informés** well-informed circles; **~ très fermé** exclusive set; (*Crime*) **le ~, les gens du ~** (people of) the underworld.

militaire [militɛʀ] **1** *adj* military, army. **2** *nm* serviceman. **~ de carrière** regular (soldier). ♦ **militairement** *adv saluer* in military fashion. **occupé ~** occupied by the army. ♦ **militarisation** *nf* militarization. ♦ **militariser** (1) *vt* to militarize.

militer [milite] (1) *vi [personne]* to be a militant. *[arguments]* **~ pour/contre** to militate in favour of/against, argue for/against. ♦ **militant, e** *adj, nm,f* militant. ♦ **militantisme** *nm* militancy.

mille[1] [mil] **1** *adj inv* a *ou* one thousand. **~ un** a *ou* one thousand and one; **trois ~** three thousand; **deux ~ neuf cents** two thousand nine hundred; **~ regrets** I'm terribly *ou* extremely sorry; **c'est ~ fois trop grand** it's far too big. **2** *nm inv* **(a)** (*Comm, Math*) a *ou* one thousand. **2 ~ de boulons** 2 thousand bolts. **(b)** *[cible]* bull's-eye. (*lit, fig*) **mettre dans le ~** to hit the bull's-eye. ♦ **mille-pattes** *nm inv* centipede.

mille[2] [mil] *nm* **(a) ~ (marin)** nautical mile. **(b)** (*Can*) mile (*1,609 km*).

millénaire [milenɛʀ] **1** *nm* millennium. **2** *adj* (*lit*) millennial; (*fig: très vieux*) ancient.

millésime [milezim] *nm* (*date*) year, date; *[vin]* year, vintage. ♦ **millésimé, e** *adj*: **bordeaux ~** vintage Bordeaux.

millet [mijɛ] *nm* (*Agr*) millet.

milli ... [mili] *préf* milli ... . **~gramme** *etc* milligram(me) *etc.*

milliard [miljaʀ] *nm* thousand million, milliard, billion (*US*). **10 ~s de francs** 10 thousand million francs, 10 billion francs (*US*). ♦ **milliardaire** *nmf* millionaire, billionaire (*US*). ♦ **milliardième** *adj, nmf* thousand millionth, billionth (*US*).

millième [miljɛm] *adj, nmf* thousandth.

millier [milje] *nm* thousand. **un ~ de gens** a thousand (or so) people, (about) a thousand people; **il y en a des ~s** there are thousands (of them).

million [miljɔ̃] *nm* million. **2 ~s de francs** 2 million francs; **être riche à ~s** to be a millionaire. ♦ **millionième** *adj, nmf* millionth. ♦ **millionnaire** *nmf* millionaire.

mime [mim] *nm* **(a)** (*personne*) mimic; (*professionnel*) mime. **(b)** (*art, pièce*) mime. ♦ **mimer** (1) *vt* (*Théât*) to mime; (*singer*) to mimic, take off*. ♦ **mimique** *nf* (*expression*) comical expression, funny face; (*geste*) expressive gesture.

mimosa [mimoza] *nm* mimosa.

minable [minabl(ə)] *adj* (*décrépit*) shabby-looking, seedy-looking; (*médiocre*) hopeless*, pathetic*; *salaire, vie* miserable, wretched. **c'est un ~** he's a washout*, he's (just) hopeless* *ou* pathetic*.

minauder [minode] (1) *vi* to mince about. ♦ **minauderies** *nfpl* mincing ways.

mince [mɛ̃s] **1** *adj* **(a)** (*peu épais*) thin; (*svelte*) slim, slender. **(b)** *profit, preuve, chances* slender; *salaire* meagre, small; *prétexte, connaissances, rôle* slight. **l'intérêt du film est bien ~** the film is decidedly lacking in interest; **ce n'est pas une ~ affaire** it's no easy task; **c'est un peu ~ comme réponse** that's not much of an answer. **2** *adv couper* thinly, in thin slices. **3** *excl* (*) **~ (alors)!** drat (it)!* ♦ **minceur** *nf* slenderness. ♦ **mincir** (2) *vi* to get slimmer *ou* thinner.

mine[1] [min] *nf* **(a)** (*physionomie*) expression, look; (*allure*) appearance. **ne fais pas cette ~-là** stop pulling that face; (*péj*) **faire des ~s** to put on simpering airs; **tu as la ~ de qn qui n'a rien compris** you look as if you haven't understood a single thing; **faire triste ~** to look a sorry sight. **(b)** (*teint*) **avoir bonne ~** to look well; **il a mauvaise ~** he doesn't look well; **il a meilleure ~** he looks better; **votre poulet a bonne ~** your chicken looks good *ou* inviting; (*iro*) **tu as bonne ~ maintenant!** now you look an utter idiot! **(c) faire ~ de faire** to make a show *ou* pretence of doing; **j'ai fait ~ de lui donner une gifle** I made as if to slap him; **il est venu pour voir ~ de rien*** he came all casual like* to have a look.

mine[2] [min] *nf* (*gén, Mil, fig*) mine. (*lit, fig*) **~ d'or** gold mine; **la nationalisation des ~s** the nationalization of the mining industry; **~ de charbon** (*gén*) coalmine; (*puits*) pit, mine; (*entreprise*) colliery; **ingénieur des M~s** (state qualified) mining engineer; **~ de renseignements** mine of information; **~ (de crayon)** lead (of pencil).

miner [mine] (1) *vt falaise, société, énergie* to undermine; (*avec explosifs*) to mine. **miné par le chagrin** worn down by grief; **miné par la jalousie** consumed by jealousy.

minerai [minʀɛ] *nm* ore.

minéral, e, *mpl* **-aux** [mineʀal, o] **1** *adj huile, sel* mineral; (*Chim*) inorganic. **2** *nm* mineral. ♦ **minéralogie** *nf* mineralogy. ♦ **minéralogiste** *nmf* mineralogist.

minéralogique [mineʀalɔʒik] *adj* (*Géol*) mineralogical. (*Aut*) **numéro** ~ registration *ou* licence (*US*) number; **plaque** ~ number plate.

minet, -ette* [minɛ, ɛt] *nm,f* (*chat*) puss*, pussy (-cat).

mineur, e [minœʀ] **1** *adj* (*gén, Jur*) minor. **en do** ~ in C minor; **être** ~ to be under age. **2** *nm,f* (*Jur*) minor. **3** *nm* **(a)** (*Mus*) minor. **en** ~ in a minor key. **(b)** (*Ind*) miner; *[houille]* (coal)miner. ~ **de fond** pitface worker; **village de** ~**s** mining village.

mini ... [mini] *préf* mini ... . ~**-budget** mini-budget; ~**-cassette** cassette recorder; **elle s'habille (en)** ~ she wears minis.

miniature [minjatyʀ] **1** *nf* (*gén*) miniature; (*: *nabot*) (little) shrimp*. **en** ~ in miniature. **2** *adj* miniature. ♦ **miniaturisation** *nf* miniaturization. ♦ **miniaturiser** (1) *vt* to miniaturize.

minier, -ière [minje, jɛʀ] *adj* mining.

minimum [minimɔm], *f* ~ *ou* **minima** [minima], *pl* ~**s** *ou* **minima 1** *adj* minimum. **2** *nm* (*gén, Math*) minimum; (*Jur*) minimum sentence. **dans le** ~ **de temps** in the shortest time possible; **un** ~ **de temps** a minimum amount of time; **travailler un** ~ to do a minimum of work; **la production a atteint son** ~ production has sunk to its lowest level (yet) *ou* an all-time low; **il faut rester le** ~ **au soleil** you must stay in the sun as little as possible. ♦ **minimal, e,** *mpl* **-aux** *adj* minimum. ♦ **minime** *adj dégât, rôle* minor; *différence* minimal; *fait* trivial; *salaire* paltry. ♦ **minimiser** (1) *vt* to minimize.

ministère [ministɛʀ] *nm* **(a)** (*département*) ministry, department (*surtout US*). ~ **de l'Intérieur** Ministry of the Interior, ≃ Home Office (*Brit*), Department of the Interior (*US*). **(b)** (*cabinet*) government. ~ **de coalition** coalition government. **(c)** (*Jur*) **le** ~ **public** the Prosecution, the State Prosecutor. **(d)** (*Rel*) ministry. **exercer son** ~ **à la campagne** to have a country parish. **(e)** (*littér: entremise*) agency. ♦ **ministériel, -elle** *adj* (*gén*) ministerial; *remaniement* cabinet. ♦ **ministre** *nm* **(a)** *[gouvernement]* minister, secretary (*surtout US*). ~ **de l'Intérieur** Minister of the Interior, ≃ Home Secretary (*Brit*), Secretary of the Interior (*US*); ~ **sans portefeuille** minister without portfolio. **(b)** *[ambassade]* envoy. ~ **plénipotentiaire** minister plenipotentiary. **(c)** (*Rel*) ~ **(du culte)** minister (of religion). **(d)** (*littér: représentant*) agent.

minium [minjɔm] *nm* red lead paint.

minois [minwa] *nm* (pretty) little face.

minorer [minɔʀe] (1) *vt* to cut, reduce. ♦ **minoration** *nf* cut, reduction (*de* in).

minorité [minɔʀite] *nf* (*gén*) minority; (*groupe*) minority (group). (*Jur*) **pendant sa** ~ while he is under age, during his minority; **être en** ~ to be in the minority; **le gouvernement a été mis en** ~ the government was defeated (*sur* on). ♦ **minoritaire** *adj groupe* minority. **être** ~ to be a minority *ou* in the minority.

minoterie [minɔtʀi] *nf* (*industrie*) flour-milling (industry); (*usine*) (flour-)mill. ♦ **minotier** *nm* miller.

minou* [minu] *nm* pussy(-cat)*, puss*.

minuit [minɥi] *nm* midnight, twelve (o'clock) (at night).

minuscule [minyskyl] **1** *adj* minute, tiny, minuscule. **2** *nf*: **(lettre)** ~ small letter; (*Typ*) lower case letter. ♦ **minus** *nmf* (*péj*) dimwit*, moron*.

minute [minyt] *nf* **(a)** minute; (*moment*) minute, moment. **une** ~ **d'inattention a suffi** a moment's inattention was enough; ~ **papillon!*** hey, just a minute!; **la** ~ **de vérité** the moment of truth; **steak** ~ minute steak; **talons** ~ heels repaired while you wait, heel-bar; **on me l'a apporté à la** ~ it has just this instant *ou* moment been brought to me; **il faut toujours tout faire à la** ~ you always have to do things there and then. **(b)** (*Jur*) minute, draft. ♦ **minutage** *nm* timing. ♦ **minuter** (1) *vt* (*organiser*) to time (carefully); (*limiter*) to time. **emploi du temps minuté** strict schedule.

minuterie [minytʀi] *nf [lumière]* time switch.

minutie [minysi] *nf* **(a)** *[personne, travail]* meticulousness; *[inspection]* detail. **ça demande beaucoup de** ~ it requires a great deal of precision. **(b)** (*détails: péj*) ~**s** trifling details, minutiae. ♦ **minutieusement** *adv* (*avec soin*) meticulously; (*dans le détail*) in minute detail. ♦ **minutieux, -euse** *adj personne, soin* meticulous; *inspection* minute. **il s'agit d'un travail** ~ it's a job that demands great care.

mioche [mjɔʃ] *nmf* (*: *gosse*) kid*, nipper*; (*péj*) brat*.

mirabelle [miʀabɛl] *nf* cherry plum.

miracle [miʀɑkl(ə)] *nm* miracle. **cela tient du** ~ it's a miracle; (*lit, fig*) **faire des** ~**s** to work miracles; **par** ~ miraculously; **le remède** ~ the miracle cure. ♦ **miraculé, e** *adj, nm,f* **(malade)** ~ (person) who has been miraculously cured. ♦ **miraculeusement** *adv* miraculously. ♦ **miraculeux, -euse** *adj* miraculous. **ça n'a rien de** ~ there's nothing so extraordinary about that.

mirador [miʀadɔʀ] *nm* (*Mil*) watchtower.

mirage [miʀaʒ] *nm* (*lit, fig*) mirage.

mire [miʀ] *nf* (*TV*) test card.

mirobolant, e* [miʀɔbɔlɑ̃, ɑ̃t] *adj* fabulous*, fantastic.

miroir [miʀwaʀ] *nm* mirror. **est-ce le** ~ **de la réalité?** is it a reflexion of reality?, does it mirror *ou* reflect reality?; (*lit, fig*) ~ **aux alouettes** lure. ♦ **se mirer** (1) *vpr* to gaze at o.s.; *[chose]* to be mirrored *ou* reflected (*in the water etc*).

miroiter [miʀwate] (1) *vi* (*étinceler*) to sparkle, gleam; (*chatoyer*) to shimmer. (*fig*) **il lui fit** ~ **les avantages** he painted in glowing colours the advantages. ♦ **miroitement** *nm*: ~**(s)** sparkling, gleaming; shimmering.

miroiterie [miʀwatʀi] *nf* **(a)** (*Comm*) mirror trade; (*Ind*) mirror industry. **(b)** (*usine*) mirror factory. ♦ **miroitier, -ière** *nm,f* (*vendeur*) mirror dealer; (*fabricant*) mirror manufacturer.

mis, e[1] [mi, miz] *adj*: **bien** ~ well-dressed.

misaine [mizɛn] *nf*: **(voile de)** ~ foresail.

misanthrope [mizɑ̃tʀɔp] **1** *nmf* misanthropist. **2** *adj* misanthropic. ♦ **misanthropie** *nf* misanthropy.

mise[2] [miz] **1** *nf* **(a)** (*action de mettre*) putting, setting. ~ **en service** putting into service; ~ **en bouteilles** bottling; ~ **en marche** starting; ~ **à jour** updating. **(b)** (*enjeu*) stake; (*Comm*) outlay. **(c)** (*habillement*) clothing. **(d) être de** ~ *[remarque]* to be in place; **ces propos ne sont pas de** ~ those remarks are out of place.

2: ~ **en accusation** impeachment; *[fusée]* ~ **à feu** blast-off; (*Fin*) ~ **de fonds** capital outlay; ~ **en garde** warning; ~ **en liberté** release; ~ **à mort** kill; (*Coiffure*) ~ **en plis** set; ~ **au point** (*Aut*) tuning; (*Phot*) focusing; (*Tech*) adjustment; (*explication*) clarification; ~ **à prix** (*enchères*) reserve price, upset price (*US*); ~ **en scène** production; (*fig*) performance; ~ **en valeur** *[terre]* development; *[maison]* improvement; *[tableau]* setting-off.

miser [mize] (1) *vt argent* to stake, bet (*sur* on). (*: *compter sur*) ~ **sur** to bank on, count on.

misère [mizɛʀ] *nf* **(a)** (*pauvreté*) poverty, destitution. **être dans la** ~ to be destitute *ou* poverty-stricken; **vivre dans la** ~ to live in poverty; **salaire de** ~ starvation wage. **(b)** (*malheur*) ~**s**

woes, miseries; (*: *ennuis*) **petites ~s** little troubles; **faire des ~s à qn*** to be nasty to sb; **quelle ~!** what a wretched shame! **(c)** (*somme*) **il l'a eu pour une ~** he got it for a song *ou* for next to nothing. ♦ **misérable 1** *adj* **(a)** (*pauvre*) *personne* destitute; *région* impoverished, poverty-stricken; *logement* seedy, mean. **(b)** (*pitoyable*) *existence, conditions* miserable, wretched, pitiful; *personne* pitiful, wretched. **(c)** (*sans valeur*) *somme d'argent* paltry, miserable. **tout ça pour un ~ billet de 10 F** all this because of a paltry *ou* measly* 10-franc note. **2** *nmf* (*méchant*) wretch; (*pauvre*) poor wretch. **petit ~!** you (little) wretch! ♦ **misérablement** *adv* (*pitoyablement*) miserably, wretchedly; (*pauvrement*) in wretched poverty. ♦ **miséreux, -euse 1** *adj* poverty-stricken. **2** *nm,f* down-and-out.

miséricorde [mizeʀikɔʀd(ə)] *nf* mercy. ♦ **miséricordieux, -ieuse** *adj* merciful.

misogyne [mizɔʒin] **1** *adj* misogynous. **2** *nmf* misogynist. ♦ **misogynie** *nf* misogyny.

miss [mis] *nf* **(a)** beauty queen. **M~ France** Miss France. **(b)** (*gouvernante*) governess.

missel [misɛl] *nm* missal.

missile [misil] *nm* missile.

mission [misjɔ̃] *nf* (*gén*) mission; (*Pol*) assignment. **~ lui fut donnée de** he was commissioned to; **il s'est donné pour ~ de faire** he set himself the task of doing. ♦ **missionnaire** *adj, nmf* missionary.

missive [misiv] *nf* (*littér*) missive.

mite [mit] *nf* clothes moth. ♦ **se miter** (1) *vpr* to be *ou* become moth-eaten. ♦ **miteux, -euse** *adj lieu* seedy, dingy; *vêtement, personne* shabby.

mi-temps [mitɑ̃] *nf inv* **(a)** (*Sport*) (*période*) half; (*repos*) half-time. **à la ~** at half-time. **(b) travailler à ~** to work part-time.

mitigé, e [mitiʒe] *adj ardeur* mitigated; *convictions* lukewarm; *sentiments* mixed.

mitonner [mitɔne] (1) **1** *vt* (*à feu doux*) to simmer; (*avec soin*) to cook with loving care. **2** *vi* to simmer.

mitoyen, -enne [mitwajɛ̃, ɛn] *adj*: **mur ~** party wall.

mitrailler [mitʀɑje] (1) *vt* (*Mil*) to machine gun. **~ qn avec des élastiques*** to pelt sb with rubber bands; **~ qn de questions** to bombard sb with questions; (*Phot*) **~ un monument** to snap away at a monument. ♦ **mitraille** *nf* (*projectiles*) grapeshot; (*décharge*) hail of bullets; (*monnaie*) loose *ou* small change. ♦ **mitraillette** *nf* submachine gun. ♦ **mitrailleuse** *nf* machine gun.

mitre [mitʀ(ə)] *nf* (*Rel*) mitre.

mitron [mitʀɔ̃] *nm* baker's boy.

mixage [miksaʒ] *nm* (*Ciné, Rad*) (sound) mixing.

mixer, mixeur [miksœʀ] *nm* liquidizer.

mixte [mikst(ə)] *adj* **(a)** (*deux sexes*) (*gén*) mixed; *école* coeducational. **(b)** (*hétérogène*) (*gén*) mixed; *équipe* combined; *commission* joint; *rôle* dual. **lycée ~** comprehensive school; **outil à usage ~** dual-purpose tool; **cargo ~** cargo-passenger ship; **cuisinière ~** gas and electric cooker. ♦ **mixité** *nf* coeducation.

mixture [mikstyʀ] *nf* (*lit*) mixture; (*péj, fig*) concoction.

mobile [mɔbil] **1** *adj pièce de moteur* moving; *casier, panneau* movable; *feuillets* loose; *main d'œuvre, population, troupes* mobile; *reflet* changing; *traits, regard* mobile. **avec la voiture on est très ~** having a car makes you very mobile. **2** *nm* **(a)** (*impulsion*) motive (*de* for). **(b)** (*Art*) mobile. **(c)** (*Phys*) moving object *ou* body.

mobilier, -ière [mɔbilje, jɛʀ] **1** *adj bien* personal; *valeurs* transferable. **2** *nm* (*ameublement*) furniture; (*Jur*) personal *ou* movable property.

mobiliser [mɔbilize] (1) *vt* (*gén*) to mobilize. **~ les esprits** to rouse people's interest. ♦ **mobilisation** *nf* mobilization.

mobilité [mɔbilite] *nf* (*gén*) mobility.

mobylette [mɔbilɛt] *nf* ® moped.

mocassin [mɔkasɛ̃] *nm* mocassin.

moche* [mɔʃ] *adj* (*laid*) ugly, awful, ghastly*; (*mauvais*) rotten*. ♦ **mocheté*** *nf* **(a)** (*laideur*) ugliness. **(b)** (*femme*) fright; (*objet*) eyesore.

mode[1] [mɔd] *nf* (*gén*) fashion; (*péj: engouement*) craze. **suivre la ~** to keep in fashion; **à la ~** *personne, vêtement* fashionable; (*dans le vent*) trendy*; **c'est la ~ des boucles d'oreilles** earrings are in fashion *ou* are in*; **habillé à la ~** fashionably *ou* trendily* dressed; **travailler dans la ~** to work in the fashion industry *ou* business; **journal de ~** fashion magazine; **coloris ~** fashion colours; **selon la ~ de l'époque** according to the custom of the day; **à la ~ du 18e siècle** in the style of the 18th century.

mode[2] [mɔd] *nm* **(a)** (*méthode*) method; (*genre*) way. **~ de vie** way of life; **~ de paiement** method *ou* mode of payment; **~ d'emploi** directions for use. **(b)** (*Gram*) mood; (*Mus, Philos*) mode. ♦ **modal, e,** *mpl* **-aux** *adj* modal. ♦ **modalité** *nf* **(a)** (*forme*) mode. **~ d'application de la loi** mode of enforcement of the law; **~s de paiement** methods *ou* modes of payment. **(b)** (*Ling, Mus, Philos*) modality. **(c)** (*Jur: condition*) clause.

modèle [mɔdɛl] **1** *nm* (*gén, Écon*) model; (*Tech*) pattern; (*type*) type; (*exemple*) example, model; (*Scol: corrigé*) fair copy **~ réduit/de série** small-scale/production model; **~ déposé** registered design; **petit/grand ~** small/large; (*Mode*) **X présente ses ~s d'automne** X presents his autumn models *ou* styles; **X est le ~ du bon élève** X is a model pupil; **prendre qn pour ~** to model o.s. upon sb. **2** *adj conduite, ouvrier, ferme* model.

modeler [mɔdle] (5) *vt statue* to model, mould; *caractère* to shape, mould. **corps bien modelé** shapely body; **~ ses attitudes sur** to model one's attitudes on; **se ~ sur qn/qch** to model o.s. on sb/sth. ♦ **modelage** *nm* (*activité*) modelling; (*statue*) piece of sculpture. ♦ **modelé** *nm [corps]* contours; (*Géog*) relief.

modérer [mɔdeʀe] (6) **1** *vt* (*gén*) to curb, moderate; *vitesse* to reduce. **modérez vos expressions!** moderate *ou* mind your language! **2 se ~** *vpr* (*s'apaiser*) to calm down, control o.s.; (*montrer de la mesure*) to restrain o.s. ♦ **modérateur, -trice 1** *adj* moderating, restraining. **2** *nm* (*Tech*) regulator; (*atomique*) moderator. ♦ **modération** *nf* (*retenue*) moderation, restraint; (*diminution*) reduction. ♦ **modéré, e** *adj* (*gén*) moderate. ♦ **modérément** *adv manger* in moderation. **être ~ satisfait** to be moderately satisfied.

moderne [mɔdɛʀn(ə)] **1** *adj* (*gén*) modern; *équipement* up-to-date. **la jeune fille ~** the young woman of today. **2** *nm* (*style*) modern style; (*meubles*) modern furniture. ♦ **modernisation** *nf* modernization. ♦ **moderniser** (1) *vt* to modernize, bring up to date. ♦ **modernisme** *nm* modernism. ♦ **moderniste 1** *nmf* modernist. **2** *adj* modernistic.

modeste [mɔdɛst(ə)] *adj* (*gén*) modest. **c'est un cadeau bien ~** it's a very modest gift; **je ne suis qu'un ~ ouvrier** I'm only a simple working man; **d'origine ~** from a modest *ou* humble background; **faire le ~** to make a show of modesty; **avoir le triomphe ~** to be modest about one's successes. ♦ **modestement** *adv* modestly. ♦ **modestie** *nf* modesty. **fausse ~** false modesty.

modifier [mɔdifje] (7) **1** *vt* to modify, alter. **2 se ~** *vpr* to alter, be modified. ♦ **modification** *nf* modification, alteration.

modique [mɔdik] *adj* (*gén*) modest, low; *salaire* meagre. ♦ **modicité** *nf* lowness.

modiste [mɔdist(ə)] *nf* milliner.

module [mɔdyl] *nm* (*Espace*) module; (*Math, Phys*) modulus.

moduler [mɔdyle] (1) *vti* to modulate.

♦ **modulation** *nf* modulation. **poste à ~ de fréquence** VHF *ou* FM radio.
moelle [mwal] *nf* (*Anat*) marrow; (*Bot*) pith. **~ épinière** spinal cord; (*lit, fig*) **pourri jusqu'à la ~** rotten to the core.
moelleux, -euse [mwalø, øz] **1** *adj tapis, couleur* soft; *aliment* creamy, smooth; *son, vin* mellow. **2** *nm* softness; creaminess, smoothness; mellowness. ♦ **moelleusement** *adv s'étendre* luxuriously.
mœurs [mœʀ(s)] *nfpl* **(a)** (*morale*) morals. **avoir des ~ sévères** to have strict moral standards; **contraire aux bonnes ~** contrary to accepted standards of behaviour; **femme de ~ légères** woman of easy virtue; (*Jur, Presse*) **affaire de ~** sex case; **la police des ~** ≃ the vice squad. **(b)** (*coutumes*) customs, habits. **c'est entré dans les ~** it's become normal practice; **les ~ politiques** the political practices *ou* usages; **avoir des ~ simples** to have simple tastes. **(c)** (*manières*) manners, ways. **quelles ~!** what a way to behave!, what manners!; **comédie de ~** comedy of manners.
moi [mwa] **1** *pron pers* **(a)** (*objet*) me. **il nous a regardés ma femme et ~** he looked at my wife and me; **écoute-~ ça!*** just listen to that!; **il n'obéit qu'à ~** he only obeys me, I'm the only one he obeys; **~ elle me déteste** she hates me *ou* ME. **(b)** (*sujet*) I, me*. **qui a fait cela? - (ce n'est) pas ~** who did this? - I didn't *ou* not me*; **~, le saluer?, jamais!** me, greet him?, never!; **mon mari et ~ refusons** my husband and I refuse; **~ parti que ferez-vous?** when I'm gone what will you do?, what will you do with me away?; **et ~ de rire de plus belle!** and so I (just) laughed all the more!; **je ne l'ai pas vu, ~** I (myself) didn't see him. **(c)** (*avec qui, que*) **~ qui vous parle, je l'ai vu** I myself *ou* personally saw him; **c'est ~ qu'elle veut voir** it's me she wants to see; **et ~ qui avais espéré gagner!** and to think that I had hoped to win! **(d)** (*avec prép*) **venez chez ~** come to my place; **le poème n'est pas de ~** the poem isn't one I wrote *ou* isn't one of mine; **un élève à ~** a pupil of mine; **j'ai un appartement à ~** I have a flat of my own; **ce livre est à ~** this book belongs to me *ou* is mine; **il veut une photo de ~** he wants a photo of me. **(e)** (*dans comparaisons*) I, me. **il mange plus que ~** he eats more than I (do) *ou* than me; **fais comme ~** do as I do, do like me*; *V* **même**. **2** *nm*: **le ~** the self, the ego; **notre vrai ~** our true self.
moignon [mwaɲɔ̃] *nm* stump.
moindre [mwɛ̃dʀ(ə)] *adj* **(a)** (*moins grand*) less, lesser; (*inférieur*) lower, poorer. **les dégâts sont bien ~s** the damage is much less; **à un ~ degré** to a lesser degree; **à ~ prix** at a lower price. **(b) le ~, la ~, les ~s** the least, the slightest; (*de deux*) the lesser; **la ~ idée** the slightest *ou* remotest idea; **le ~ de deux maux** the lesser of two evils; **c'est la ~ de mes difficultés** that's the least of my difficulties; **c'est la ~ des choses!** it's a pleasure!, it's the least I could do!; **certains spécialistes et non des ~s disent que** some specialists and important ones at that say that. ♦ **moindrement** *adv*: **il n'était pas le ~ surpris** he was not in the least *ou* slightest surprised.
moine [mwan] *nm* monk, friar.
moineau, *pl* **~x** [mwano] *nm* sparrow.
moins [mwɛ̃] **1** *adv* **(a)** less. **3 fois ~** 3 times less; **il est ~ grand que son frère/que je ne pensais** he is not as tall as his brother/as I thought, he is less tall than his brother/than I thought; **il a fait encore ~ beau qu'en juillet** the weather was even worse than in July; **rien n'est ~ sûr** nothing is less certain; **c'est tellement ~ cher** it's so much cheaper *ou* so much less expensive; **~ je fume, plus je mange** the less I smoke the more I eat; **c'est le même genre, en ~ bien** it's the same kind, only (it's) not so good. **(b)** (*superl*) least. **c'est la ~ douée de mes élèves** she is the least gifted of my pupils; **la température la ~ haute de l'été** the lowest temperature of the summer; **celui que je lis le ~ souvent** the one I read (the) least often.

2 *nm* **(a)** (*quantité*) less. **donner ~** to give less; **vous ne l'obtiendrez pas à ~** you won't get it for less. **(b) ~ de** (*quantité*) less, not so much; (*nombre*) fewer, not so many; (*heure*) before, not yet; (*durée, âge, distance*) less than, under; **mange ~ de bonbons et de chocolat** eat fewer sweets and less chocolate; **les enfants de ~ de 4 ans** children under 4 *ou* of less than 4 years of age; **il est ~ de minuit** it is not yet midnight; **vous ne pouvez pas lui donner ~ de 100 F** you can't give him less than 100 francs; **il a eu ~ de mal que nous** he had less trouble than we had; **nous l'avons fait en ~ de 5 minutes** we did it in less than *ou* in under 5 minutes; **en ~ de deux*** in a flash; **il y aura ~ de monde demain** there will be fewer people tomorrow. **(c) le ~** the least; **c'est (bien) le ~ qu'on puisse faire** it's the least one can do; **si vous êtes le ~ du monde soucieux** if you are the slightest (bit) *ou* the least (bit) worried. **(d)** (*quantité qui se soustrait*) **il gagne 500 F de ~ qu'elle** he earns 500 francs less than she does; **vous avez 5 ans de ~ qu'elle** you are 5 years younger than she is; **il y a 3 verres en ~** (*qui manquent*) there are 3 glasses missing; (*trop peu*) we are 3 glasses short; **c'est le même climat, le brouillard en ~** it's the same climate except for the fog *ou* minus the fog. **(e)** (*signe algébrique*) minus (sign). **(f)** (*locutions*) **à ~ qu'il ne vienne** unless he comes; **au ~** at least; **pour le ~** to say the least, at the very least; **de ~ en ~** less and less; **du ~ je le pense** I think so at least; **laissez-le sortir, si du ~ il ne fait pas froid** let him go out, that is (only) if it is not cold.

3 *prép* **(a)** (*soustraction*) **6 ~ 2 font 4** 6 minus 2 equals 4, 2 from 6 makes 4; **j'ai retrouvé mon sac, ~ le portefeuille** I found my bag, minus the wallet. **(b)** (*heure*) to. **il est 4 heures ~ 5 (minutes)** it is 5 (minutes) to 4; **il n'est que ~ 10*** it's only 10 to*. **(c)** (*température*) below. **il fait ~ 5°** it is 5° below freezing *ou* minus 5°.
moire [mwaʀ] *nf* moiré. ♦ **moiré, e** *adj, nm* moiré.
mois [mwa] *nm* **(a)** (*période*) month. **dans un ~** in a month('s time); **être payé au ~** to be paid monthly; **louer au ~** to rent by the month; **30 F par ~** 30 francs a *ou* per month; **un bébé de 6 ~** a 6-month(-old) baby; **devoir 3 ~ de loyer** to owe 3 months' rent. **(b)** (*salaire*) monthly pay *ou* salary. **~ double** extra month's pay (*as end-of-year bonus*).
moisir [mwaziʀ] (2) **1** *vt* to make mouldy. **2** *vi* **(a)** to go mouldy. **(b)** (*en province*) to stagnate; (*dans un cachot*) to rot. **on ne va pas ~ ici jusqu'à la nuit!*** we're not going to hang around here till night-time!* ♦ **moisi, e 1** *adj* mouldy, mildewed. **2** *nm* mould, mildew. **odeur de ~** musty smell; **ça sent le ~** it smells musty. ♦ **moisissure** *nf* (*gén*) mould; (*aspect*) mouldiness; (*par l'humidité*) mildew. **enlever les ~s sur un fromage** to scrape the mould *ou* mildew off a piece of cheese.
moisson [mwasɔ̃] *nf* harvest. **faire la ~** to harvest; **~ de renseignements** wealth of information. ♦ **moissonner** (1) *vt céréale* to harvest, gather in; *champ* to reap; *renseignements, souvenirs* to gather, collect. ♦ **moissonneur, -euse 1** *nm,f* harvester. **2** *nf* (*machine*) harvester. **3: ~euse-batteuse** *nf, pl* **~s-~s** combine harvester.
moite [mwat] *adj* (*gén*) sticky; *mains* sweaty; *atmosphère* muggy. ♦ **moiteur** *nf* stickiness; sweatiness; mugginess.
moitié [mwatje] *nf* **(a)** (*partie*) half. **partager qch en deux ~s** to halve sth, divide sth in half *ou* into two halves; **donne-m'en la ~** give me half (of it); **faire la ~ du chemin** to go halfway *ou* half of the

way; **la ~ du temps** half the time; **il en faut ~ plus/moins** you need half as much again/half (of) that. **(b)** (*milieu*) halfway mark, half. **à la ~ du chemin** having reached halfway *ou* the half-way mark; **arrivé à la ~ du travail** having done half the work *ou* got halfway through the work. **(c)** (*hum: épouse*) **ma ~** my better half*, my wife. **(d)** **il a fait le travail à ~** he has (only) half done the work; **il ne fait jamais rien à ~** he never does things by halves; **à ~ plein** half-full; **à ~ chemin** (at) halfway, at the halfway mark; **à ~ prix** (at) half-price; **réduire de ~** to cut by half, halve; **plus grand de ~** half as big again, bigger by half; **diviser qch par ~** to divide sth in two *ou* in half; **on a partagé le pain ~ ~** we shared the bread half-and-half *ou* fifty-fifty*.

moka [mɔka] *nm* (*gâteau*) coffee cream cake, mocha cake; (*café*) mocha coffee.

molaire [mɔlɛʀ] *nf* (*dent*) molar.

môle [mol] *nm* (*digue*) breakwater, jetty; (*quai*) pier, jetty.

molécule [mɔlekyl] *nf* molecule. ♦ **moléculaire** *adj* molecular.

molester [mɔlɛste] (1) *vt* to manhandle, maul.

molette [mɔlɛt] *nf* toothed wheel; *[briquet]* knurl. ♦ **moleté, e** *adj* knurled.

mollesse [mɔlɛs] *nf [substance, contours]* softness; *[relief]* gentleness; *[traits du visage]* flabbiness; *[geste]* lifelessness; *[protestations]* weakness, feebleness; *[personne]* (*indolence*) sluggishness; (*manque d'autorité*) spinelessness; (*grande indulgence*) laxness. ♦ **mollasse*** *adj* (*péj*) (*apathique*) sluggish; (*flasque*) flabby, flaccid. ♦ **molle** *adj f V* **mou.** ♦ **mollement** *adv tomber* softly; *couler* gently; *travailler* half-heartedly; *protester* feebly, weakly.

mollet [mɔlɛ] *nm* (*Anat*) calf.

molletonner [mɔltɔne] (1) *vt* to line warmly.

mollir [mɔliʀ] (2) *vi* **(a)** *[sol, ennemi]* to yield, give way; *[père]* to come round, relent; *[courage]* to flag. **(b)** *[substance]* to soften, go soft. **(c)** *[vent]* to die down.

mollusque [mɔlysk(ə)] *nm* (*Zool*) mollusc; (* *péj*) lazy lump*.

molosse [mɔlɔs] *nm* big dog *ou* hound.

môme [mom] *nmf* (*: *enfant*) kid*; (*péj*) brat*; (‡: *fille*) bird‡.

moment [mɔmɑ̃] *nm* **(a)** (*instant*) while, moment. **je ne l'ai pas vu depuis un (bon) ~** I haven't seen him for a (good) while *ou* for quite a time *ou* while; **ça va prendre un ~** it will take some time *ou* a good while; **il réfléchit (pendant) un ~** he thought for a moment; **c'est l'affaire d'un ~** it won't take a minute *ou* moment; **dans un ~** in a little while, in a moment; **un ~!** just a moment *ou* a minute! **(b)** (*période*) time. **à quel ~ est-ce arrivé?** at what point *ou* when exactly did this occur?; **ce n'est pas le ~** this is not the time *ou* the moment (*de* to); **passer de bons ~s** to spend (some) happy times; **arriver au bon ~** to come at the right time; **passer un mauvais ~** to have a rough *ou* difficult time; **il est dans un de ses mauvais ~s** it's one of his off* *ou* bad spells; **à ses ~s perdus** in his spare time; **les grands ~s de l'histoire** the great moments of history; **le succès du ~** the success of the moment *ou* day; **profiter du ~** to take advantage of the opportunity (*de* to). **(c)** (*Tech*) moment; (*Phys*) momentum. **(d)** (*locutions*) **en ce ~** at the moment, at present, just now; **au ~ de l'accident** at the time of the accident, when the accident took place; **au ~ de partir** just as I (*ou* he *etc*) was about to leave; **au ~ où elle entrait** when *ou* as she was going in; **à un ~ donné** at a certain point; **le ~ venu** when the time comes (*ou* came); **il peut arriver à tout ~ *ou* d'un ~ à l'autre** he may arrive (at) any time (now) *ou* any moment (now); **à ce ~-là** (*temps*) at that time; (*circonstance*) in that case; **le bruit grandissait de ~ en ~** the noise grew louder every moment; **du ~ où *ou* que** since, seeing that; **dès le ~ que *ou* où** as soon as; **par ~s** now and then, at times; **pour le ~** for the time being; **sur le ~** at the time. ♦ **momentané, e** *adj* momentary. ♦ **momentanément** *adv* (*en ce moment*) at the moment, at present; (*un court instant*) momentarily.

momie [mɔmi] *nf* mummy.

mon [mɔ̃], **ma** [ma], **mes** [me] *adj poss* my. **j'ai ~ samedi cette année*** I've got Saturday(s) off this year; **~ vieux*** my dear fellow, old chap* *ou* fellow*; (*Rel*) **oui ~ Père** yes Father; **~ Dieu** (*Rel*) dear Lord; (*excl*) good heavens!; **oui ~ général** yes sir *ou* general; *V* **son.**

monarchie [mɔnaʀʃi] *nf* monarchy. ♦ **monarchique** *adj* monarchistic. ♦ **monarchiste** *adj, nmf* monarchist. ♦ **monarque** *nm* monarch.

monastère [mɔnastɛʀ] *nm* monastery. ♦ **monastique** *adj* monastic.

monceau, *pl* **~x** [mɔ̃so] *nm* heap.

mondain, e [mɔ̃dɛ̃, ɛn] **1** *adj* **(a)** *réunion, chronique* society; *obligations* social; *public* fashionable. **plaisirs ~s** pleasures of society; **vie ~e** social *ou* society life. **(b)** *politesse, ton* refined. **(c)** (*Philos*) mundane; (*Rel*) worldly, earthly. **(d) la (police) ~e** ≃ the vice squad. **2** *nm,f* society man (*ou* woman), socialite. ♦ **mondanités** *nfpl* (*divertissements*) society life; (*propos*) society small talk.

monde [mɔ̃d] *nm* **(a)** world. **dans le ~ entier** all over the world, the world over, throughout the world; **le ~ entier s'indigna** the whole world was outraged; **il se moque *ou* se fiche* du ~** he's got a nerve *ou* cheek*; **mettre/venir au ~** to bring/come into the world; **si je suis encore de ce ~** if I'm still here *ou* in the land of the living *ou* of this world; **dans ce bas ~** here below; **l'Ancien/le Nouveau M~** the Old/New World; **le ~ de la folie** the world *ou* realm of madness.

(b) (*intensif*) **le meilleur du ~** the best in the world; **c'est le meilleur homme du ~** he's the finest man alive; **tout s'est passé le mieux du ~** everything went (off) perfectly *ou* like a dream*; **il n'était pas le moins du ~ anxieux** he was not the least bit worried; **pour rien au ~** not for all the world; **nul au ~ ne peut ...** nobody in the world can ...; **j'en pense tout le bien du ~** I have the highest opinion of him (*ou* her *ou* it).

(c) (*locutions*) **c'est le ~ à l'envers** it's a topsy-turvy *ou* crazy world; **comme le ~ est petit!** it's a small world!; **se faire tout un ~ de qch** to make a fuss about sth; **c'est un ~!*** if that doesn't beat all!*; **il y a un ~ entre ces deux concepts** there is a world of difference between these two concepts.

(d) (*gens*) **j'entends du ~ à côté** I can hear people in the next room; **est-ce qu'il y a du ~?** (*qn est-il présent*) is there anybody there?; (*y a-t-il foule*) are there a lot of people there?; **il y a du ~** (*ce n'est pas vide*) there are some people there; (*il y a foule*) there's quite a crowd; **il y a beaucoup de ~** there's a real crowd; **ils reçoivent beaucoup de ~** they entertain a lot; **ce week-end nous avons du ~** we have people coming *ou* visitors this weekend; **tout ce petit ~ s'est bien amusé?** and have all these children had a nice time?; **il connaît son ~** he knows the people he deals with.

(e) (*milieu social*) set, circle. **le (grand) ~** (high) society; **il n'est pas de notre ~** he's not one of our set *ou* crowd*; **homme/femme/gens du ~** society man/woman/people.

♦ **mondial, e,** *mpl* **-aux** *adj guerre, population* world; *crise* world-wide. **à l'échelle ~e** on a world-wide scale. ♦ **mondialement** *adv* throughout the world. **~ connu** world-famous. ♦ **mond(i)ovision** *nf* television broadcast by satellite.

mongolien, -ienne [mɔ̃gɔljɛ̃, jɛn] *adj, nm,f* (*Méd*) mongol. ♦ **mongolisme** *nm* mongolism.

moniteur, -trice [mɔnitœʀ, tʀis] *nm,f* (*Sport*) instructor, instructress; *[colonie de vacances]* supervisor, (camp) counsellor (*US*).
monnaie [mɔnɛ] *nf* **(a)** (*devises*) currency. **(b)** (*pièce, médaille*) coin. **(c)** (*appoint*) change. **petite** *ou* **menue** ~ small change; **auriez-vous de la** ~? could you give me some change?; **faire la** ~ **de 100 F** to get change for 100 francs. **(d) c'est** ~ **courante** *[faits]* it's a common occurrence; *[pratiques]* it's common practice; (*fig*) **rendre à qn la** ~ **de sa pièce** to pay sb back in his own coin; **servir de** ~ **d'échange** to be used as money *ou* as a currency; (*fig*) to be used as bargaining counters; **payer qn en** ~ **de singe** to fob sb off with empty promises. ♦ **monétaire** *adj* (*gén*) monetary. **la circulation** ~ the circulation of currency. ♦ **monnayer** (8) *vt terres, titres* to convert into cash; *talent* to capitalize on.
mono... [mɔnɔ] *préf* mono... .
monochrome [mɔnɔkʀom] *adj* monochrome, monochromatic.
monocle [mɔnɔkl(ə)] *nm* monocle, eyeglass.
monocoque [mɔnɔkɔk] *adj, nm* monocoque.
monocorde [mɔnɔkɔʀd(ə)] *adj voix, discours* monotonous.
monoculture [mɔnɔkyltyʀ] *nf* single-crop farming, monoculture.
monogramme [mɔnɔgʀam] *nm* monogram.
monographie [mɔnɔgʀafi] *nf* monograph.
monokini [mɔnɔkini] *nm* topless swimsuit.
monolingue [mɔnɔlɛ̃g] *adj* monolingual.
monolithique [mɔnɔlitik] *adj* (*lit, fig*) monolithic.
monologue [mɔnɔlɔg] *nm* monologue, soliloquy. ♦ **monologuer** (1) *vi* to soliloquize.
monôme [mɔnom] *nm* (*Math*) monomial; (*arg Scol*) ≃ students' rag.
monomoteur, -trice [mɔnɔmɔtœʀ, tʀis] **1** *adj* single-engined. **2** *nm* single-engined aircraft.
monophonie [mɔnɔfɔni] *nf* monophony. ♦ **monophonique** *adj* monophonic.
monoplace [mɔnɔplas] *nmf* single-seater.
monopole [mɔnɔpɔl] *nm* (*Écon, fig*) monopoly. ♦ **monopolisateur, -trice** *nm,f* monopolizer. ♦ **monopolisation** *nf* monopolization. ♦ **monopoliser** (1) *vt* (*lit, fig*) to monopolize.
monosyllabe [mɔnɔsilab] *nm* (*lit, fig*) monosyllable. ♦ **monosyllabique** *adj* monosyllabic.
monothéisme [mɔnɔteism(ə)] *nm* monotheism. ♦ **monothéiste 1** *adj* monotheistic. **2** *nmf* monotheist.
monotone [mɔnɔtɔn] *adj* (*gén*) monotonous; *spectacle* dull, dreary; *vie* humdrum. ♦ **monotonie** *nf* monotony; dullness, dreariness.
monseigneur [mɔ̃sɛɲœʀ], *pl* **messeigneurs** [mesɛɲœʀ] *nm* **(a)** (*formule d'adresse*) (*à archevêque, duc*) Your Grace; (*à cardinal*) Your Eminence; (*à prince*) Your Highness. **(b)** (*à la troisième personne*) His Grace; His Eminence; His Highness.
Monsieur [məsjø], *pl* **Messieurs** [mesjø] *nm* **(a)** (*s'adressant à qn*) **bonjour** ~ (*courant*) good morning; (*nom connu*) good morning Mr X; (*avec déférence*) good morning sir; (*au restaurant*) **et pour (vous)** ~/**Messieurs?** and for you, sir/gentlemen?; ~ **le Président** Mr President; **oui,** ~ **le Juge** ≃ yes, Your Honour *ou* Your Worship; ~ **le curé** Father; ~ **le ministre** Minister; ~ **le duc** Your Grace, your Lordship; **mon bon** *ou* **pauvre** ~* my dear sir. **(b)** (*parlant de qn*) ~ **est sorti** Mr X is not at home; ~ **dit que c'est à lui** the gentleman says it's his; ~ **le Président** the President; ~ **le juge X** ≃ (His Honour) Judge X; ~ **le duc de X** (His Grace) the Duke of X; ~ **l'abbé (X)** Father X; ~ **tout le monde** the average man. **(c)** (*sur une enveloppe*) ~ **X** Mr X; (*à un enfant*) Master John *etc* X; **Messieurs X et Y** Messrs X and Y. **(d)** (*en-tête de lettre*) (*gén*) Dear Sir; (*personne connue*) Dear Mr X; ~ **le Président** Dear Mr President.

(e) (*sans majuscule*) gentleman. **c'est un grand m**~ he is a great man.
monstre [mɔ̃stʀ(ə)] **1** *nm* (*gén*) monster. **c'est un** ~ **de laideur** he is monstrously ugly; (*Ciné, Théât*) ~ **sacré** superstar, public idol. **2** *adj* (*) *rabais etc* monstrous, colossal. **j'ai un travail** ~ I've got loads* of work to do. ♦ **monstrueusement** *adv laid* monstrously; *intelligent* stupendously. ♦ **monstrueux, -euse** *adj* monstrous. ♦ **monstruosité** *nf* (*gén*) monstrosity; (*Méd*) deformity. **dire des** ~**s** to say monstrous things.
mont [mɔ̃] *nm* mountain. (*avec nom propre*) **le** ~ **Everest** *etc* Mount Everest *etc*; **être toujours par** ~**s et par vaux*** to be always on the move. ♦ **mont-de-piété**, *pl* ~**s-**~**-**~ *nm* (state-owned) pawnshop. **mettre qch au** ~ to pawn sth.
montage [mɔ̃taʒ] *nm [appareil]* assembly; *[bijou]* setting; (*Ciné*) editing. (*Élec*) ~ **en parallèle** connection in parallel; ~ **de photographies** photomontage.
montagne [mɔ̃taɲ] **1** *nf* (*sommet*) mountain. (*région*) **la** ~ the mountains; **moyenne** ~ medium mountains; **plantes des** ~**s** mountain plants; (*fig*) **une** ~ **de** mountains of; **il se fait une** ~ **de cet examen** he's making far too much of this exam. **2: les** ~**s Rocheuses** the Rocky Mountains, the Rockies; ~**s russes** big dipper, roller coaster. ♦ **montagnard, e 1** *adj* mountain. **2** *nm,f* mountain dweller. ♦ **montagneux, -euse** *adj* (*gén, Géog*) mountainous; (*accidenté*) hilly.
montant, e [mɔ̃tɑ̃, ɑ̃t] **1** *adj mouvement* upward, rising; *col* high; *robe* high-necked; *chemin* uphill. **chaussures** ~**es** boots; **train** ~ up train. **2** *nm* **(a)** *[échelle, fenêtre]* upright; *[lit]* post. **(b)** (*somme*) sum total, total amount.
montée [mɔ̃te] *nf* **(a)** (*escalade*) climb, climbing. **c'est une** ~ **difficile** it's a difficult climb; **on a fait la** ~ **à pied** we walked up, we went up on foot. **(b)** *[ballon, avion]* ascent. **pendant la** ~ **de l'ascenseur** while the lift is going up. **(c)** *[eaux, sève, prix]* rise. **(d)** (*côte*) hill, uphill slope.
monter¹ [mɔ̃te] (1) **1** *vi* **(a)** (*gén*) to go up (*à* to, *dans* into); *[oiseau]* to fly up; *[avion]* to climb. ~ **à pied/à vélo** to walk/cycle up; ~ **par l'ascenseur** to go up in the lift; ~ **en courant dans sa chambre** to run up(stairs) to one's room; **monte me voir** come up and see me. **(b)** ~ **sur** *table, toit* to climb (up) on; *colline, échelle* to climb up; **il était monté sur une chaise** he was standing on a chair; **monté sur un cheval** riding *ou* on a horse. **(c)** (*moyen de transport*) ~ **dans un train** to get on *ou* into a train, board a train; ~ **à bord d'un navire** to go on board *ou* aboard a ship; ~ **à cheval** (*se mettre en selle*) to get on *ou* mount a horse; (*faire du cheval*) to ride, go riding. **(d)** *[vedette]* to be on the way up; *[réputation]* to rise, go up. ~ **en grade** to be promoted; **les générations montantes** the rising generations. **(e)** *[eau, vêtements]* ~ **à** to come up to; **robe qui monte jusqu'au cou** high-necked dress. **(f)** *[colline, route]* to go up, rise; *[soleil, flamme]* to rise. ~ **en pente douce** to slope gently upwards, rise gently; **un bruit montait de la cave** a noise was coming from down in the cellar. **(g)** *[mer]* to come in; *[fleuve, colère]* to rise; *[prix, température]* to rise, go up; (*Mus*) *[voix, note]* to go up. **les prix montent en flèche** prices are rocketing *ou* soaring; **ça a fait** ~ **les prix** it put prices up; (*Culin*) **(faire)** ~ **des blancs en neige** to whisk up egg whites. **(h)** (*émotions*) **le sang lui monta au visage** the blood rushed to his face; **les larmes lui montent aux yeux** tears come into his eyes; **le vin lui monte à la tête** wine goes to his head; **un cri lui monta à la gorge** a cry rose in his throat. **(i)** *[plante]* ~ **(en graine)** to bolt, go to seed. **(j)** (*locutions*) ~ **à l'assaut** to go into the attack; ~ **à l'assaut de** to launch an attack on; ~ **sur ses ergots** to get one's hackles up; ~ **sur ses grands chevaux** to get on one's high horse;

~ **sur le trône** to come to *ou* ascend the throne.
2 *vt* **(a)** to go up. ~ **l'escalier** to go upstairs; ~ **la gamme** to go up the scale. **(b)** *valise* to take *ou* carry up. **faire ~ ses valises** to have one's luggage brought up. **(c) ~ un cheval** to ride a horse. **(d) ~ qn contre qn** to set sb against sb; **on lui a monté la tête** sb has got him all worked up. **(e)** (*Mil*) ~ **la garde** to mount guard.
3 **se ~** *vpr [prix, frais]* **se ~ à** to come to, add up to; **se ~ la tête** to get worked up.
♦ **monte-charge** *nm inv* service elevator. ♦ **monte-plats** *nm inv* dumbwaiter.

monter² [mɔ̃te] (1) *vt* **(a)** *machine, robe* to assemble; *tente* to pitch; *film* to edit; *diamant* to set; *pneu* to put on. (*Élec*) ~ **en série** to connect in series. **(b)** *pièce de théâtre* to put on, produce; *affaire* to set up; *farce* to play; *complot* to hatch. ~ **un coup** to plan a job; ~ **le coup à qn‡** to take sb for a ride‡; **coup monté** put-up job*, frame-up*. **(c)** (*équiper*) to equip. **être bien/mal monté en qch** to be well-/ill-equipped with sth; **tu es bien montée, avec deux garnements pareils!*** you're well set up with that pair of rascals!* ♦ **monteur, -euse** *nm,f* (*Tech*) fitter; (*Ciné*) (film) editor.

monticule [mɔ̃tikyl] *nm* (*colline*) hillock; (*tas*) mound.

montre¹ [mɔ̃tʀ(ə)] *nf* watch. ~**-bracelet** wrist watch; ~ **de plongée** diver's watch; **il est 2 heures à ma ~** it is 2 o'clock by my watch; **j'ai mis 2 heures ~ en main** it took me exactly *ou* precisely 2 hours.

montre² [mɔ̃tʀ(ə)] *nf*: **faire ~ de** *courage* to show.

montrer [mɔ̃tʀe] (1) **1** *vt* **(a)** (*gén*) to show; (*par un geste*) to point to; *détail* to point out; *surprise, courage* to display; (*ostensiblement*) *richesse* to show off, display (*à* to). **je vais vous ~ le jardin** I'll show you (round) the garden; **l'avenir montrera qui avait raison** the future will show *ou* prove who was right; ~ **à qn à faire qch** to show sb how *ou* the way to do sth. **(b)** (*locutions*) **c'est l'avocat qui montre le bout de l'oreille** it's the lawyer in him showing through; **je lui montrerai de quel bois je me chauffe** I'll show him what I'm made of; (*lit, fig*) ~ **les dents** to bare one's teeth; ~ **le bon exemple** to set a good example; (*lit, fig*) ~ **le chemin** to show the way; ~ **le bout du nez** to show one's face; ~ **patte blanche** to show one's pass. **2 se ~** *vpr* to appear, show o.s.; (*se faire respecter*) to assert o.s. **se ~ ferme** to appear firm, show firmness; **se ~ désagréable** to be unpleasant, behave unpleasantly; **se ~ lâche** to show cowardice; **se ~ efficace** to prove effective.

monture [mɔ̃tyʀ] *nf* **(a)** (*cheval*) mount. **(b)** (*Tech*) mounting; *[lunettes]* frame; *[bijou]* setting.

monument [mɔnymɑ̃] *nm* (*gén, fig*) monument; (*commémoratif*) memorial. ~ **(funéraire)** monument; ~ **aux morts** war memorial; ~ **historique** ancient monument; **c'est un ~ de bêtise!*** what monumental stupidity! ♦ **monumental, e,** *mpl* **-aux** *adj* monumental.

moquer (se) [mɔke] (1) *vpr*: **se ~ de** to make fun of, laugh at, poke fun at; **on va se ~ de toi** people will laugh at you, you'll make yourself a laughing stock; **vous vous moquez du monde!** you've got an absolute nerve!; **je m'en moque (pas mal)*** I couldn't care less; **elle se moque du qu'en-dira-t-on** she doesn't care what people say (about her). ♦ **moquerie** *nf*: ~**(s)** mockery. ♦ **moqueur, -euse** *adj* mocking. ♦ **moqueusement** *adv* mockingly.

moquette [mɔkɛt] *nf* fitted carpet.

moral, e, *mpl* **-aux** [mɔʀal, o] **1** *adj* (*gén*) moral. **2** *nm* **(a) au ~ comme au physique** mentally as well as physically. **(b)** (*état d'esprit*) morale. **avoir bon/mauvais ~** to be in good/low spirits; **les troupes ont bon/mauvais ~** the morale of the troops is high/low. **3** *nf* **(a)** (*doctrine*) moral code; (*mœurs*) morals; (*valeurs traditionnelles*) moral standards. (*Philos*) **la ~e** moral philosophy; **action conforme à la ~e** act in keeping with morality *ou* moral standards; **faire la ~e à qn** to lecture sb. **(b)** *[fable]* moral.
♦ **moralement** *adv* morally. ♦ **moralisateur, -trice 1** *adj ton* moralizing; *histoire* edifying. **2** *nm,f* moralizer. ♦ **moraliser** (1) **1** *vi* to moralize. **2** *vt*: ~ **qn** to lecture sb. ♦ **moraliste 1** *adj* moralistic. **2** *nmf* moralist. ♦ **moralité** *nf* **(a)** (*mœurs*) morals, morality, moral standards. **d'une haute ~** of high moral standards; **la ~ publique** public morality. **(b)** (*valeur*) *[attitude, action]* morality. **(c)** *[fable]* moral. ~**, j'ai eu une indigestion*** the result was (that) I had indigestion.

morbide [mɔʀbid] *adj* morbid. ♦ **morbidité** *nf* morbidity.

morceau, *pl* ~**x** [mɔʀso] *nm* (*gén*) piece; (*bout*) bit; (*Littérat, Mus: passage*) passage; *[sucre]* lump; *[terre]* patch, plot; (*chez le boucher*) cut. ~ **de choix** choice cut; **manger un ~** to have a bite to eat *ou* a snack; **lâcher le ~‡** to spill the beans*, talk*; **couper en ~x** to cut into pieces; **mettre qch en ~x** to pull sth to pieces; ~**x choisis** selected extracts *ou* passages; ~ **de bravoure** purple passage; **sacré ~*** (*personne, objet*) great *ou* solid lump*. ♦ **morceler** (4) *vt* (*gén*) to divide up, split up. ♦ **morcellement** *nm* division.

mordoré, e [mɔʀdɔʀe] *adj, nm* lustrous bronze.

mordre [mɔʀdʀ(ə)] (41) **1** *vt* **(a)** to bite. ~ **qn à la jambe** to bite sb's leg, bite sb on the leg; ~ **une pomme** to bite into an apple; ~ **la poussière** to bite the dust. **(b)** *[lime, vis]* to bite into; *[acide]* to eat into; *[froid]* to bite, nip. **la jalousie lui mordait le cœur** jealousy was gnawing at his heart. **(c)** (*empiéter sur*) **la balle a mordu la ligne** the ball (just) touched the line. **2 ~ sur** *vt indir* (*empiéter sur*) to go over into, overlap into; (*corroder*) to bite into. **3** *vi* **(a) ~ dans une pomme** to bite into an apple. **(b)** (*Pêche, fig*) to bite; (*lit, fig*) ~ **à l'hameçon** to bite, rise to the bait; **il a mordu aux maths*** he's taken to maths; **l'engrenage ne mord plus** the gear won't mesh any more. **4 se ~** *vpr*: **se ~ la langue** (*lit, se repentir*) to bite one's tongue; (*se retenir*) to hold one's tongue; **maintenant il s'en mord les doigts** he could kick himself now.
♦ **mordant, e 1** *adj ton* cutting, scathing; *polémiste* scathing; *froid* biting. **2** *nm [personne]* spirit, drive; *[style]* bite, punch; *[scie]* bite.
♦ **mordiller** (1) *vt* to nibble at. ♦ **mordu, e*** *adj*: **être ~ de** to be mad* *ou* crazy* about; **c'est un ~ du football** he is a great football fan *ou* buff (*US*).

morfondre (se) [mɔʀfɔ̃dʀ(ə)] (42) *vpr* to languish.

morgue [mɔʀg(ə)] *nf* **(a)** pride, haughtiness. **(b)** (*Police*) morgue; *[hôpital]* mortuary.

moribond, e [mɔʀibɔ̃, ɔ̃d] *adj* (*lit, fig*) dying, moribund. **un ~** a dying man.

morille [mɔʀij] *nf* morel.

morne [mɔʀn(ə)] *adj visage* doleful, glum; *ton, temps* gloomy, dismal; *vie, paysage* dreary.

morose [mɔʀoz] *adj* sullen, morose. ♦ **morosité** *nf* sullenness, moroseness.

morphine [mɔʀfin] *nf* morphine.

morphologie [mɔʀfɔlɔʒi] *nf* morphology. ♦ **morphologique** *adj* morphological.

mors [mɔʀ] *nm* (*Équitation*) bit; (*Tech*) jaw. (*lit, fig*) **prendre le ~ aux dents** to take the bit between its (*ou* one's) teeth.

morse [mɔʀs(ə)] *nm* **(a)** (*Zool*) walrus. **(b)** (*code*) Morse (code).

morsure [mɔʀsyʀ] *nf* bite.

mort¹ [mɔʀ] *nf* **(a)** death. **donner la ~ à qn** to kill sb; **en danger de ~** in danger of dying *ou* of one's life; **mourir dans son sommeil, c'est une belle ~** dying in one's sleep is a good way to go; **à la ~ de sa mère** on the death of his mother, when his mother died; **il n'y a pas eu ~ d'homme** no one was killed, there was no loss of life; **le super-**

marché sera la ~ du petit commerce supermarkets will mean the end of *ou* the death of small businesses; **~ au tyran!, à ~ le tyran!** death to the tyrant! **(b) silence de ~** deathly hush; **engin de ~** deadly weapon; **peine de ~** death penalty; **menaces de ~** threats of death. **(c) lutte à ~** fight to the death; **blessé à ~** (*combat*) mortally wounded; (*accident*) fatally injured; **condamnation à ~** death sentence; **frapper qn à ~** to strike sb dead; **mettre qn à ~** to put sb to death; **nous sommes fâchés à ~** we're at daggers drawn; **en vouloir à qn à ~** to be bitterly resentful of sb; **freiner à ~*** to jam on the brakes. **(d)** (*douleur*) **souffrir mille ~s** to suffer agonies; **il avait la ~ dans l'âme** his heart ached.

mort², e [mɔʀ, mɔʀt(ə)] **1** *adj* (*lit, fig*) dead. **il est ~ depuis 2 ans** he's been dead (for) 2 years, he died 2 years ago; **laissé pour ~** left for dead; **~ et enterré** dead and buried; **~ ou vif** dead or alive; **~ au champ d'honneur** killed in action; **~ (de fatigue)** dead tired, dead beat*; **~ de peur** frightened to death, scared stiff*. **2** *nm* **(a)** dead man. **les ~s** the dead; **il y a eu un ~** one man was killed; **prière des ~s** prayer for the dead; **cet homme est un ~ vivant** this man is more dead than alive; **faire le ~** (*lit*) to pretend to be dead; (*fig*) to lie low. **(b)** (*Cartes*) dummy. **être le ~** to be dummy. **3** *nf* dead woman. ♦ **mort-né,e,** *pl* **~-~(e)s** *adj* stillborn. ♦ **mort-aux-rats** *nf* rat poison. ♦ **morte-saison** *nf* slack *ou* off season.

mortadelle [mɔʀtadɛl] *nf* mortadella.

mortalité [mɔʀtalite] *nf* mortality, death rate. **~ infantile** infant mortality.

mortel, -elle [mɔʀtɛl] **1** *adj* (*gén*) mortal; *blessure* fatal; *poison* deadly, lethal; *froid, attente* deadly; *pâleur, silence* deathly; *livre, soirée* deadly boring *ou* dull. **cette révélation lui serait ~elle** such a discovery would kill him; **il est ~*** he's a deadly* bore. **2** *nm,f* (*littér, hum*) mortal. **heureux ~!*** lucky chap!* ♦ **mortellement** *adv blesser* fatally; *vexer* mortally. **~ pâle** deathly pale; **~ ennuyeux** deadly boring *ou* dull.

mortier [mɔʀtje] *nm* (*gén*) mortar.

mortifier [mɔʀtifje] (7) *vt* to mortify. ♦ **mortification** *nf* mortification.

mortuaire [mɔʀtɥɛʀ] *adj chapelle, rites* mortuary. **chambre ~** death chamber; **la maison ~** the house of the deceased.

morue [mɔʀy] *nf* (*Zool*) cod.

mosaïque [mɔzaik] *nf* mosaic.

Moscou [mɔsku] *n* Moscow.

mosquée [mɔske] *nf* mosque.

mot [mo] **1** *nm* **(a)** (*gén*) word. **c'est bien le ~!** that's the right word for it!; **à/sur ces ~s** at/with these words; **à ~s couverts** in veiled terms; **en un ~** in brief, in a word; **~ à ~** word for word; **~ pour ~** word for word, verbatim. **(b)** (*message*) word; (*courte lettre*) note. **~ d'excuse** excuse note; **en toucher un ~ à qn** to have a word with sb about it; **se donner le ~** to pass the word round *ou* on. **(c)** (*locutions*) **avoir des ~s avec qn** to have words with sb; **avoir toujours le ~ pour rire** to be a born joker; **tenir le ~ de l'énigme** to hold the key to the mystery; **avoir le ~ de la fin** to get the last word; **j'estime avoir mon ~ à dire dans cette affaire** I think I'm entitled to have my say in this matter; **je vais lui dire deux ~s** I'll give him a piece of my mind; **prendre qn au ~** to take sb at his word. **2: ~-clé** *nm, pl* **~s-~s** keyword; **~s croisés** crossword (puzzle); **~ d'enfant** child's (funny) remark *ou* saying; **~ d'esprit, bon ~** witticism, witty remark; **~ d'ordre** watchword; **~ de passe** password.

motard [mɔtaʀ] *nm* motorcyclist; (*Police*) motorcycle policeman.

motel [mɔtɛl] *nm* motel.

moteur¹ [mɔtœʀ] *nm* motor, engine. **~ électrique** electric motor; **~ à 2/4 temps** 2-/4-stroke engine; **à ~** power-driven, motor; (*fig*) **être le ~ de qch** to be the driving force behind sth.

moteur², -trice¹ [mɔtœʀ, tʀis] *adj muscle, nerf* motor; *troubles* motory; (*Tech*), (*lit, fig*) *force* driving.

motif [mɔtif] *nm* **(a)** (*gén*) reason, grounds; (*Jur*) motive (*de* for). **(b)** *[tissu, papier]* pattern; (*Peinture, Mus*) motif.

motion [mosjɔ̃] *nf* (*Pol*) motion. **~ de censure** censure motion.

motiver [mɔtive] (1) *vt* (*justifier*) *action, attitude* to justify, account for; (*fournir un motif à*) *refus, jugement* to motivate. ♦ **motivation** *nf* motivation. ♦ **motivé, e** *adj* justified, well-founded, motivated; *personne* motivated.

moto* [mɔto] *nf* (motor)bike*. ♦ **moto-cross** *nm inv* motocross. ♦ **motoculteur** *nm* (motorized) cultivator. ♦ **motocyclette** *nf* motorcycle. ♦ **motocycliste** *nmf* motorcyclist. ♦ **motonautisme** *nm* speedboat racing. ♦ **motopompe** *nf* motor-pump.

motoriser [mɔtɔʀize] (1) *vt* (*Mil, Tech*) to motorize. **être motorisé*** to have a car. ♦ **motorisation** *nf* motorization.

motrice² [mɔtʀis] *nf* motor unit; *V* **moteur²**.

motte [mɔt] *nf*: **~ (de terre)** lump of earth, clod (of earth); **~ de gazon** turf, sod; **~ de beurre** lump *ou* block of butter.

motus* [mɔtys] *excl* not a word!

mou, molle [mu, mɔl] (*masc.* **mol** [mɔl] *devant voyelle ou h muet*) **1** *adj substance* soft; *tige, geste* limp; *chair* flabby; *relief* soft, gentle; *traits du visage* weak; *protestations, opposition* weak, feeble; *style,* (*Mus*) *exécution* dull. **personne molle** (*sans énergie*) lethargic *ou* sluggish person; (*sans autorité*) spineless character; (*trop indulgent*) lax *ou* soft person; **bruit ~** muffled noise. **2** *nm* **(a)** *[corde]* **avoir du ~** to be slack; **donner du ~ (à qch)** to slacken (sth). **(b)** (*Boucherie*) lights.

mouchard [muʃaʀ] *nm* **(a)** (*) (*Scol*) sneak*; (*arg Police*) grass (*arg*). **(b)** *[veilleur de nuit]* control clock; (*Mil*) spy plane. ♦ **moucharder*** (1) *vt* (*Scol*) to sneak on*; (*arg Police*) to grass on (*arg*).

mouche [muʃ] *nf* fly; (*en taffetas*) patch. **~ bleue, ~ à vers** bluebottle, blowfly; **quelle ~ t'a piqué?** what has bitten you?*; **tomber comme des ~s** to fall like flies; **prendre la ~** to take the huff*; **faire ~** (*Tir*) to score a bull's-eye; (*fig*) to hit home.

moucher [muʃe] (1) **1** *vt* **(a) ~ (le nez de) qn** to blow sb's nose. **(b)** (* *fig*) **~ qn** to snub sb, put sb in his place. **2 se ~** *vpr* to blow one's nose.

moucheron [muʃʀɔ̃] *nm* midge; (*: *enfant*) kid*.

moucheté, e [muʃte] *adj œuf* speckled; *laine* flecked; *fleuret* buttoned.

mouchoir [muʃwaʀ] *nm* handkerchief. **~ en papier** tissue, paper hanky; **grand comme un ~ de poche** as big as *ou* no bigger than a pocket handkerchief; **ils sont arrivés dans un ~** it was a close finish.

moudre [mudʀ(ə)] (47) *vt* (*gén*) to grind.

moue [mu] *nf* pout. **faire la ~** (*tiquer*) to pull a face; *[enfant gâté]* to pout.

mouette [mwɛt] *nf* seagull.

moufle [mufl(ə)] *nf* mitten.

mouiller [muje] (1) **1** *vt* **(a)** (*gén*) to wet. **se faire ~** to get wet *ou* drenched *ou* soaked. **(b)** *vin, lait* to water (down). **(c)** (*Naut*) *mine* to lay; *sonde* to heave. **~ l'ancre** to cast *ou* drop anchor. **(d)** (*Ling*) to palatalize. **2** *vi* (*Naut*) to lie at anchor. **3 se ~** *vpr* **(a)** to get o.s. wet. **se ~ les pieds** to get one's feet wet. **(b)** *[yeux]* to fill with tears. **(c)** (‡: *risquer*) to get one's feet wet, commit o.s. ♦ **mouillage** *nm* (*rade*) anchorage, moorage. ♦ **mouillé, e** *adj* wet. **tout ~** soaked through; **ne marche pas dans le ~** don't walk in the wet.

moulage [mulaʒ] *nm [briques]* moulding; *[statue]* casting; (*objet*) cast.

moule[1] [mul] *nm* (*lit, fig*) mould; (*Typ*) matrix. ~ **à gâteaux** cake tin; ~ **à gaufre** waffle-iron; ~ **à tarte** pie plate, flan case.

moule[2] [mul] *nf* **(a)** (*Zool*) mussel. ~**s marinières** mussels (cooked) in white wine. **(b)** (*: *idiot*) idiot, twit*.

mouler [mule] (1) *vt* **(a)** *briques* to mould; *caractères d'imprimerie, statue* to cast; *lettre* to form with care. ~ **son style sur** to model one's style on. **(b)** *[robe]* to hug, fit closely round. **robe qui moule** close- *ou* tight-fitting dress.

moulin [mulɛ̃] *nm* mill; (*: *moteur*) engine. ~ **à eau** water mill; ~ **à vent** windmill. ♦ **mouliner** (1) *vt* (*Culin*) to put through a vegetable mill; (*Pêche*) to reel in. ♦ **moulinet** *nm* (*Pêche*) reel; (*Escrime*) flourish. **faire des** ~**s avec une canne** to twirl *ou* whirl a stick. ♦ **moulinette** *nf* ® vegetable mill.

moulu, e [muly] *adj*: ~ **(de coups)** thrashed; ~ **(de fatigue)*** dead-beat*, worn-out.

moulure [mulyʀ] *nf* moulding.

mourir [muʀiʀ] (19) *vi* **(a)** to die. ~ **de sa belle mort** to die a natural death; ~ **avant l'âge** to die before one's time; ~ **assassiné** to be murdered; ~ **en héros** to die a hero's death; **faire** ~ **qn** to kill sb; (*hum*) **tu n'en mourras pas!*** it won't kill you! **(b)** *[feu, coutume]* to die out; *[bruit, vague]* to die away; *[jour]* to fade, die; *[flamme]* to die down. **(c)** ~ **d'inquiétude** to be worried to death; **il meurt d'envie de le faire** he's dying to do it; **s'ennuyer à** ~ to be bored to death *ou* to tears; ~ **de faim** (*lit*) to starve to death; (*fig*) to be famished *ou* starving; **je meurs de soif** I am parched; **faire** ~ **qn à petit feu** (*lit*) to kill sb slowly; (*fig*) to torment the life out of sb; **c'est à** ~ **de rire** it would make you die laughing*. ♦ **mourant, e** *adj* dying; *voix* faint; (*) *rythme* deadly (dull). **un** ~ a dying man; **les** ~**s** the dying.

mousquetaire [muskətɛʀ] *nm* musketeer.

mousse[1] [mus] *nf* (*Bot*) moss; *[bière, eau]* froth, foam; *[savon]* lather; *[champagne]* bubbles; (*Culin*) mousse. ~ **au chocolat** chocolate mousse; **balle (en)** ~ rubber ball; **collant** ~ stretch tights; ~ **de caoutchouc** foam rubber; **se faire de la** ~* to worry o.s. sick*.

mousse[2] [mus] *nm* ship's boy.

mousseline [muslin] *nf* (*coton*) muslin; (*soie, tergal*) chiffon.

mousser [muse] (1) *vi [bière, eau]* to froth, foam; *[champagne]* to bubble, sparkle; *[savon]* to lather. **se faire** ~* to give o.s. a boost* (*auprès de* with). ♦ **mousseux, -euse 1** *adj* sparkling; frothy. **2** *nm* sparkling wine.

mousson [musɔ̃] *nf* monsoon.

moustache [mustaʃ] *nf [homme]* moustache. *[animal]* ~s whiskers.

moustique [mustik] *nm* (*Zool*) mosquito; (*: *enfant*) tich*, (little) kid*. ♦ **moustiquaire** *nf* (*rideau*) mosquito net; *[fenêtre]* screen.

moutarde [mutaʀd(ə)] *nf* mustard. ~ **forte** English mustard; ~ **à l'estragon** French mustard; (*fig*) **la** ~ **me monta au nez** I flared up, I lost my temper.

mouton [mutɔ̃] *nm* **(a)** (*Zool, fig*) sheep; (*Culin*) mutton. **doublé de** ~ lined with sheepskin; **se conduire en** ~**s de Panurge** to behave like a lot of sheep. **(b)** ~s (*sur la mer*) white horses; (*sur le plancher*) (bits of) fluff; (*dans le ciel*) fluffy *ou* fleecy clouds. ♦ **moutonneux, -euse** *adj mer* flecked with white horses; *ciel* flecked with fleecy *ou* fluffy clouds.

mouvement [muvmɑ̃] *nm* **(a)** (*geste*) movement. ~**s de gymnastique** (physical) exercises; **il approuva d'un** ~ **de tête** he gave a nod of approval; **elle eut un** ~ **de recul** she started back. **(b)** (*impulsion*) impulse, reaction. **avoir un bon** ~ to make a kind gesture; ~ **de colère** burst *ou* upsurge of anger; ~**s dans l'auditoire** a stir in the audience; **discours accueilli avec des** ~**s divers** speech which got a mixed reception; **agir de son propre** ~ to act of one's own accord. **(c)** (*activité*) activity, bustle. **rue pleine de** ~ busy *ou* lively street. **(d)** (*déplacement*) movement; (*Mil: manœuvre*) move. **être sans cesse en** ~ to be constantly on the move *ou* on the go*; **mettre qch en** ~ to set sth in motion, set sth going; **se mettre en** ~ to start *ou* set off; **suivre le** ~ to follow the general movement; **le** ~ **perpétuel** perpetual motion; ~ **de foule** sway in the crowd; ~**s de population** shifts in population; ~**s de troupes** troop movements; ~ **de fonds** movement of capital; ~ **de personnel** changes in staff. **(e)** (*évolution*) **le** ~ **des idées** the evolution of ideas; **être dans le** ~ to keep up-to-date; ~ **d'opinion** trend of opinion; **le** ~ **des prix** the trend of prices; ~ **de baisse** downward trend. **(f)** *[phrase]* rhythm; *[tragédie]* action; *[draperie]* drape; *[collines]* undulations. **(g)** (*groupe*) movement. ~ **politique** political movement. **(h)** *[symphonie]* movement. **(i)** (*Tech: mécanisme*) movement. **par un** ~ **d'horlogerie** by clockwork.

♦ **mouvant, e** *adj situation* unsettled, fluid; *ombre, flamme* moving, changing; *terrain* shifting. ♦ **mouvementé, e** *adj vie, poursuite, récit* eventful; *séance* turbulent, stormy. ♦ **mouvoir** (27) **1** *vt* **(a)** *machine* to drive; *bras, levier* to move. **comme mû par un ressort** as if propelled by a spring. **(b)** *[sentiment]* to drive, prompt. **2 se** ~ *vpr* to move.

moyen, -enne [mwajɛ̃, ɛn] **1** *adj* (*gén*) average. **être** ~ **en maths** to be average at maths; **résultats très** ~s mediocre *ou* poor results; **de taille** ~**enne** *personne* of medium *ou* average height; *entreprise, bâtiment* medium-sized; **avoir un temps** ~ to have mixed weather; **une solution** ~**enne** a middle-of-the-road solution.

2 *nm* **(a)** means, way. ~**s de défense/production** *etc* means of defence/production *etc*; **trouver un** ~ **terme** to find a middle course; **c'est l'unique** ~ **de s'en sortir** it's the only way out; **employer les grands** ~s to have to resort to drastic means *ou* measures; **se débrouiller avec les** ~**s du bord** *ou* **avec des** ~**s de fortune** to make do with what's available, use makeshift devices; **au** ~ **de** by means of. **(b) est-ce qu'il y a** ~ **de lui parler?** is it possible to speak to him?; **il n'y a pas** ~ **de sortir par ce temps** you can't go out in this weather; **le** ~ **de dire autre chose!** what else could I say! **(c)** (*physiques*) ~s abilities; **être en possession de tous ses** ~s to be at one's peak; **par ses propres** ~s all by himself. **(d)** (*financiers*) ~s means; **c'est au-dessus de ses** ~s he can't afford it, it's beyond his means; **avoir de gros/petits** ~s to have a large/small income.

3 *nf* **(a)** (*gén*) average. **la** ~**enne d'âge** the average age; **la** ~**enne des gens** most people; **faire du 100 de** ~**enne** to average 100 km/h; ~**enne arithmétique** arithmetic mean; **en** ~**enne** on average. **(b)** (*Scol*) **avoir la** ~**enne** (*devoir*) to get half marks; (*examen*) to get a pass; ~**enne générale (de l'année)** average (for the year); **cet élève est dans la** ~**enne/la bonne** ~**enne** this pupil is about/above average.

♦ **moyen âge** *nm*: **le** ~ the Middle Ages. ♦ **moyenâgeux, -euse** *adj ville* medieval; (*péj*) antiquated. ♦ **moyen-courrier**, *pl* ~**s-**~**s** *nm* medium-haul (aeroplane). ♦ **Moyen-Orient** *nm*: **le** ~ the Middle East. ♦ **moyennant** *prép argent* for; *service* in return for; *travail, effort* with. ~ **finance** for a fee *ou* a consideration; ~ **quoi** in return for which. ♦ **moyennement** *adv content* fairly, moderately; *travailler* fairly *ou* moderately well.

moyeu, *pl* ~**x** [mwajø] *nm [roue]* hub.

muer [mɥe] (1) **1** *vi* (*gén*) to moult; *[serpent]* to slough. **sa voix mue** his voice is breaking. **2** *vt*, **se** ~ *vpr* to change *ou* turn (*en* into). ♦ **mue** *nf* moulting; sloughing; (*époque*) moulting *ou* sloughing season; (*peau, plumes*) slough; moulted hair, feathers *etc.* *[voix]* **au moment de la ~** when the voice breaks.

muet, -ette [mɥɛ, ɛt] **1** *adj* (*infirme*) dumb; (*lit, fig: silencieux*) silent; (*Ling*) mute, silent; (*Géog*) *carte* blank. **en rester ~** to stand speechless (*de* with); **il est resté ~ comme une carpe** he never opened his mouth. **2** *nm,f* dumb man (*ou* woman). **3** *nm*: **le ~** the silent cinema.

mufle [myfl(ə)] *nm* **(a)** *[chien etc]* muzzle. **(b)** (*: *goujat*) boor, lout. ♦ **muflerie** *nf* boorishness. **une ~** a boorish remark (*ou* thing to do).

mugir [myʒiʀ] (2) *vi [vache]* to moo; *[bœuf]* to bellow; *[vent, sirène]* to howl. ♦ **mugissement** *nm*: **~(s)** mooing; bellowing; howling.

muguet [mygɛ] *nm* (*Bot*) lily of the valley.

mulâtre, -esse [mylɑtʀ(ə), ɛs] *nm,f* mulatto.

mule [myl] *nf* (*Zool*) (she-)mule; (*pantoufle*) mule. ♦ **mulet** *nm* (*âne*) (he-)mule; (*poisson*) mullet. ♦ **muletier, -ière 1** *adj*: **sentier ~** mule track. **2** *nm,f* mule-driver.

mulot [mylo] *nm* field mouse.

multicolore [myltikɔlɔʀ] *adj* multicoloured.

multiforme [myltifɔʀm(ə)] *adj apparence* multiform; *problème* many-sided.

multimillionnaire [myltimiljɔnɛʀ] *nmf* multimillionaire.

multinational, e, *mpl* **-aux** [myltinasjɔnal, o] *adj* multinational.

multiple [myltipl(ə)] **1** *adj occasions, raisons* numerous, multiple; *fracture* multiple; *aspects* multifarious, manifold; *problème* many-sided. **à usages ~s** multi-purpose; **100 est ~ de 10** 100 is a multiple of 10. **2** *nm* multiple. ♦ **multiplication** *nf* (*prolifération*) increase in the number of; (*Bot, Math*) multiplication. ♦ **multiplicité** *nf* multiplicity. ♦ **multiplier** (7) **1** *vt* (*gén*) to multiply (*par* by). **2 se ~** *vpr* (*gén*) to multiply; *[infirmier]* to do one's utmost.

multirisque [myltiʀisk(ə)] *adj* multiple-risk.

multitude [myltityd] *nf* **(a) une ~ de** a multitude of, a vast number of; **la ~ de** the mass of; **la ~ des gens** the (vast) majority of people. **(b)** (*littér: foule*) multitude, throng.

municipal, e, *mpl* **-aux** [mynisipal, o] *adj élection, stade* municipal; *conseil* local, town. **arrêté ~** local by-law; **piscine ~e** public swimming pool. ♦ **municipalité** *nf* (*ville*) town; (*conseil*) town council.

munir [myniʀ] (2) **1** *vt personne, objet* to provide, equip (*de* with). **muni de ces conseils** armed with this advice. **2 se ~** *vpr*: **se ~ de** to provide o.s. with; **se ~ de patience** to arm o.s. with patience.

munitions [mynisjɔ̃] *nfpl* ammunition.

muqueuse [mykøz] *nf* mucous membrane.

mur [myʀ] *nm* (*gén*) wall. **~ d'enceinte** outer wall *ou* walls; **une maison aux ~s de brique** a brick house; **faire le ~*** to jump the wall; **l'ennemi est dans nos ~s** the enemy is within our gates; **M X est dans nos ~s aujourd'hui** we have Mr X with us today; **avoir le dos au ~** to have one's back to the wall; **on parle à un ~** it's like talking to a brick wall; **franchir le ~ du son** to break the sound barrier. ♦ **muraille** *nf* (high) wall. **couleur (de) ~** stone grey. ♦ **mural, e,** *mpl* **-aux** *adj* wall; (*Art*) mural. ♦ **murer** (1) **1** *vt ouverture* to wall up, brick up. **2 se ~** *vpr* (*chez soi*) to shut o.s. up. **se ~ dans son silence** to immure o.s. in silence.

mûr, e[1] [myʀ] *adj fruit, projet* ripe; *tissu* worn; *personne, esprit* mature. **pas ~** unripe; **trop ~** overripe; **il est ~ pour le mariage** he is ready for marriage; **après ~e réflexion** after mature reflection. ♦ **mûrement** *adv*: **ayant ~ réfléchi** after much thought, after lengthy deliberation. ♦ **mûrir** (2) **1** *vi [fruit]* to ripen; *[idée, personne]* to mature; *[abcès]* to come to a head. **2** *vt fruit* to ripen; *projet* to nurture; *personne* to make mature.

mûre[2] [myʀ] *nf [ronce]* blackberry, bramble; *[mûrier]* mulberry. ♦ **mûrier** *nm* mulberry bush.

murmurer [myʀmyʀe] (1) **1** *vt* to murmur. **on murmure que ...** it's whispered that ..., rumour has it that ... . **2** *vi* (*chuchoter*) to murmur; (*protester*) to mutter, grumble (*contre* about). ♦ **murmure** *nm* murmur. **obéir sans ~** to obey without a murmur; **~s** (*protestations*) murmurings, grumblings; (*objections*) objections.

muscade [myskad] *nf* nutmeg.

muscat [myska] *nm* (*raisin*) muscat grape; (*vin*) muscatel (wine).

muscle [myskl(ə)] *nm* muscle. ♦ **musclé, e** *adj corps* muscular; *homme* brawny; *régime* strong-arm. ♦ **musculaire** *adj force* muscular. **fibre ~** muscle fibre. ♦ **musculature** *nf* muscle structure.

muse [myz] *nf* (*Littérat, Myth*) Muse.

museau, *pl* **~x** [myzo] *nm [chien, bovin]* muzzle; *[porc]* snout; (*Culin*) brawn; (*: *visage*) face. ♦ **museler** (4) *vt* (*lit, fig*) to muzzle. ♦ **muselière** *nf* muzzle.

musée [myze] *nm* (*art*) art gallery; (*technique*) museum. (*lit, fig*) **pièce de ~** museum piece. ♦ **muséum** *nm* museum.

musique [myzik] *nf* (*art*) music; (*orchestre*) band. **~ sacrée/d'ambiance/de chambre** sacred/background/chamber music; **elle fait de la ~** she plays an instrument; **mettre un poème en ~** to set a poem to music; **c'est toujours la même ~*** it's always the same old refrain. ♦ **musical, e,** *mpl* **-aux** *adj* musical. ♦ **musicalement** *adv* musically. ♦ **musicalité** *nf* musicality, musical quality. ♦ **music-hall,** *pl* **~-~s** *nm* (*salle*) variety theatre, music hall. **faire du ~** to be in variety; **numéro de ~** variety turn. ♦ **musicien, -ienne 1** *adj* musical. **2** *nm,f* musician.

musulman, e [myzylmɑ̃, an] *adj, nm,f* Moslem, Muslim.

muter [myte] (1) *vt* (*Admin*) to transfer. ♦ **mutation** *nf* (*gén*) transformation; (*Bio*) mutation; (*Admin, Jur*) transfer.

mutiler [mytile] (1) *vt* (*gén*) to mutilate; *personne* to maim; *statue, arbre* to deface. **se ~** to maim *ou* injure o.s. ♦ **mutilation** *nf* mutilation. ♦ **mutilé, e 1** *adj*: **être ~** to be disabled. **2** *nm,f* cripple, disabled person. **~ de la face** disfigured person; **~ de guerre** disabled ex-serviceman.

mutiner (se) [mytine] (1) *vpr* (*Mil, Naut*) to mutiny; (*gén*) to rebel, revolt. ♦ **mutin, e 1** *adj* (*espiègle*) mischievous. **2** *nm* mutineer; rebel. ♦ **mutiné, e 1** *adj* mutinous. **2** *nm* mutineer. ♦ **mutinerie** *nf* mutiny; rebellion, revolt.

mutisme [mytism(ə)] *nm* (*gén*) silence; (*Méd*) muteness.

mutuel, -elle [mytɥɛl] **1** *adj* mutual. **2** *nf* mutual benefit society. ♦ **mutuellement** *adv s'aider* one another, each other. **~ ressenti** mutually felt.

myope [mjɔp] *adj* short- *ou* near-sighted, myopic. **~ comme une taupe*** (as) blind as a bat. ♦ **myopie** *nf* short- *ou* near-sightedness, myopia.

myosotis [mjɔzɔtis] *nm* forget-me-not.

myriade [miʀjad] *nf* myriad.

myrtille [miʀtij] *nf* bilberry.

mystère [mistɛʀ] *nm* mystery. ♦ **mystérieusement** *adv* mysteriously. ♦ **mystérieux, -euse** *adj* mysterious.

mystifier [mistifje] (7) *vt* to fool, take in. ♦ **mystification** *nf* (*farce*) hoax; (*péj: mythe*) myth. ♦ **mystificateur, -trice** *nm,f* hoaxer.

mystique [mistik] **1** *adj* mystical. **2** *nmf* (*personne*) mystic. **3** *nf* (*science*) mysticism; (*péj: vénération*) blind belief (*de* in). ♦ **mysticisme** *nm* mysticism. ♦ **mystiquement** *adv* mystically.

mythe [mit] *nm* (*gén*) myth. ♦ **mythique** *adj* mythical. ♦ **mythologie** *nf* mythology. ♦ **mythologique** *adj* mythological. ♦ **mythomane** *adj, nmf* mythomaniac.

myxomatose [miksɔmatoz] *nf* myxomatosis.

N

N, n [ɛn] *nm* (*lettre*) N, n.
n' [n] *V* **ne.**
nacre [nakʀ(ə)] *nf* mother-of-pearl. ♦ **nacré, e** *adj* pearly.
nager [naʒe] (3) **1** *vi [personne]* to swim; *[objet]* to float. **ça nage dans la graisse** it is swimming in fat; ~ **dans l'opulence** to be rolling in money*; **il nage dans ses vêtements** he is lost in his clothes; **en allemand, je nage complètement*** I'm completely at sea* in German. **2** *vt* to swim. ~ **la brasse** to swim breast-stroke. ♦ **nage** *nf* **(a)** swimming; (*manière*) stroke, style of swimming. ~ **sur le dos** backstroke; ~ **libre** freestyle; **gagner la rive à la** ~ to swim to the bank. **(b) être en** ~ to be bathed in sweat; **cela m'a mis en** ~ that made me sweat. ♦ **nageoire** *nf [poisson]* fin; *[phoque etc]* flipper. ♦ **nageur, -euse** *nm,f* swimmer.
naguère [nagɛʀ] *adv* (*récemment*) not long ago; (*autrefois*) formerly.
naïf, naïve [naif, naiv] **1** *adj* naïve. **2** *nm,f* gullible fool, innocent. ♦ **naïvement** *adv* naïvely. ♦ **naïveté** *nf* naïvety.
nain, e [nɛ̃, nɛn] **1** *adj* dwarfish. **chêne** ~ dwarf oak. **2** *nm,f* dwarf.
naissance [nɛsɑ̃s] *nf* (*gén*) birth; *[rivière]* source; *[cheveux, ongles]* root; *[cou]* base. **à la** ~ at birth; **de** ~ *aveugle* from birth; *français* by birth; **prendre** ~ to take form; **donner** ~ **à** *enfant* to give birth to; *rumeurs* to give rise to.
naître [nɛtʀ(ə)] (59) *vi* **(a)** to be born. **il vient de** ~ he has just been born; **X est né le 4 mars** X was born on March 4; **l'homme naît libre** man is born free; **il est né poète** he is a born poet; **en naissant** at birth; **il naît plus de filles que de garçons** there are more girls born than boys; **Mme Durand, née Dupont** Mme Durand, née Dupont; **être né de parents français** to be born of French parents; **être né coiffé** to be born lucky; **il n'est pas né d'hier** he wasn't born yesterday. **(b)** *[idée]* to be born; *[ville]* to spring up; *[jour]* to break; *[sentiment, difficultés]* to arise; *[plante]* to burst forth; *[rivière]* to rise. **un sourire naquit sur son visage** a smile crept over his face; **faire** ~ *industrie* to create; *soupçons, désir* to arouse; **la haine née de ces querelles** the hatred which sprang from these quarrels; ~ **à l'amour** to awaken to love.
nana* [nana] *nf* (*femme*) bird‡, chick‡.
nantir [nɑ̃tiʀ] (2) *vt* to provide (*de* with). **se** ~ **de** to provide o.s. with. ♦ **nanti, e** *adj* affluent, well-to-do.
napalm [napalm] *nm* napalm.
naphtaline [naftalin] *nf* mothballs.
nappe [nap] *nf* tablecloth; *[gaz, pétrole]* layer; *[brouillard]* blanket; *[eau, feu]* sheet. ~ **de mazout** oil slick. ♦ **napper** (1) *vt* (*Culin*) to coat (*de* with). ♦ **napperon** *nm* doily.
narcisse [naʀsis] *nm* (*Bot*) narcissus; (*péj: égocentrique*) narcissistic individual.
narcotique [naʀkɔtik] *adj, nm* narcotic.
narguer [naʀge] (1) *vt danger* to flout; *personne* to scoff at.
narine [naʀin] *nf* nostril.
narquois, e [naʀkwa, waz] *adj* mocking, derisive. ♦ **narquoisement** *adv* mockingly, derisively.
narrer [naʀe] (1) *vt* to narrate. ♦ **narrateur, -trice** *nm,f* narrator. ♦ **narratif, -ive** *adj* narrative. ♦ **narration** *nf* (*action*) narration; (*récit*) narrative, account; (*Scol: rédaction*) essay.
nasal, e, mpl -aux [nazal, o] *adj* nasal.
naseau, pl ~**x** [nazo] *nm [cheval]* nostril.
nasiller [nazije] (1) *vi [personne]* to have a (nasal) twang; *[micro]* to whine. ♦ **nasillard, e** *adj* nasal; whiny. ♦ **nasillement** *nm* (nasal) twang; whine.
nasse [nas] *nf* hoop net.
natal, e, mpl ~**s** [natal] *adj* native. ♦ **natalité** *nf* birth rate.
natation [natɑsjɔ̃] *nf* swimming.
natif, -ive [natif, iv] *adj, nm,f* (*gén*) native.
nation [nɑsjɔ̃] *nf* nation. **les N**~**s Unies** the United Nations. ♦ **national, e, mpl -aux** *adj* (*gén*) national; *obsèques, éducation* state. **(route)** ~**e** ≈ 'A' *ou* trunk road, state highway (*US*). ♦ **nationalisation** *nf* nationalization. ♦ **nationaliser** (1) *vt* to nationalize. ♦ **nationalisme** *nm* nationalism. ♦ **nationaliste** *adj, nmf* nationalist. ♦ **nationalité** *nf* nationality.
natte [nat] *nf* (*tresse*) pigtail, plait; (*paillasse*) mat.
naturaliser [natyʀalize] (1) *vt* to naturalize. **se faire** ~ **français** to become a naturalized Frenchman. ♦ **naturalisation** *nf* naturalization.
nature [natyʀ] **1** *nf* **(a)** (*caractère*) nature. **la** ~ **humaine** human nature; **c'est/ce n'est pas de** ~ **à** it's liable to/not likely to; **il n'est pas de** ~ **à** he's not the sort of person who would. **(b)** (*monde*) **la** ~ nature; **vivre (perdu) dans la** ~ to live (out) in the country *ou* at the back of beyond; **disparaître dans la** ~* to vanish into thin air. **(c)** (*sorte*) nature, kind. **de toute(s)** ~**(s)** of all kinds, of every kind. **(d)** (*Art*) **peindre d'après** ~ to paint from life; **plus grand que** ~ more than life-size, larger than life; ~ **morte** still life. **(e)** (*Fin*) **en** ~ in kind. **2** *adj inv eau, thé etc* plain. **café** ~ black coffee; **boire le whisky** ~ to drink whisky neat.
naturel, -elle [natyʀɛl] **1** *adj* (*gén*) natural; *besoins* bodily. **avec sa voix** ~**elle** in his normal voice; **c'est** ~ **chez lui** it's natural for him, it comes naturally to him; **ne me remerciez pas, c'est tout** ~ please don't mention it. **2** *nm* **(a)** (*caractère*) nature, disposition. **(b)** (*absence d'affectation*) naturalness. **(c)** (*indigène*) native. **(d) au** ~ (*Culin*) served plain, au naturel; **elle est mieux en photo qu'au** ~ she's better in photos than in real life. ♦ **naturellement** *adv* (*gén*) naturally; (*bien sûr*) naturally, of course.
naufrage [nofʀaʒ] *nm [bateau]* wreck; (*fig*) ruin. **un** ~ a shipwreck; **faire** ~ *[bateau]* to be wrecked; *[marin]* to be shipwrecked. ♦ **naufragé, e 1** *adj* shipwrecked. **2** *nm,f* shipwrecked person; (*sur une île*) castaway.
nausée [noze] *nf* (feeling of) nausea *ou* sickness. **avoir la** ~ to feel sick; **avoir des** ~**s** to have bouts of nausea; (*lit, fig*) **ça me donne la** ~ it makes me (feel) sick. ♦ **nauséabond, e** *adj* (*lit, fig*) nauseating, sickening.
nautique [notik] *adj* nautical. **sports** ~**s** water sports; **fête** ~ water festival.
naval, e, mpl ~**s** [naval] *adj* (*gén*) naval; *industrie* ship-building.
navet [navɛ] *nm* **(a)** turnip. **(b)** (*péj*) third-rate film (*ou* novel).

navette [navɛt] *nf* **(a)** (*Tex*) shuttle. **(b)** (*transport*) shuttle (service). **faire la ~ entre** *[banlieusard]* to commute between; *[véhicule]* to operate a shuttle service between; *[bateau]* to ply between.

naviguer [navige] (1) *vi* **(a)** (*voyager*) *[bateau, marin]* to sail; *[avion, pilote]* to fly. **ce type a beaucoup navigué*** this guy has been around a lot*; **bateau en état de ~** seaworthy ship. **(b)** (*piloter*) *[marin]* to navigate, sail; *[aviateur]* to navigate, fly. (*fig*) **il sait ~*** he knows the ropes. ♦ **navigabilité** *nf [rivière]* navigability; *[bateau]* seaworthiness; *[avion]* airworthiness. ♦ **navigable** *adj rivière* navigable. ♦ **navigant, e** *adj* (*Aviat*) **personnel ~** flying personnel. ♦ **navigateur** *nm* (*gén*) navigator. **~ solitaire** single-handed sailor. ♦ **navigation** *nf* **(a)** (*Naut*) sailing, navigation; (*trafic*) (sea) traffic. **ouvert à la ~** open to shipping *ou* ships; **terme de ~** nautical term. **(b)** (*Aviat*) (*trafic*) air traffic; (*pilotage*) navigation, flying.

navire [naviʀ] *nm* ship; (*Jur*) vessel. **~ amiral** flagship; **~ de guerre** warship.

navrer [navʀe] (1) *vt [conduite, nouvelle]* to distress, upset; *[contretemps]* to annoy. ♦ **navré, e** *adj* sorry (*de* to). **ton ~** (*excuse*) apologetic tone; (*compassion*) sympathetic tone; (*émotion*) distressed *ou* upset voice.

nazi, e [nazi] *adj, nm,f* Nazi. ♦ **nazisme** *nm* Nazism.

ne [n(ə)] *adv nég, n' devant voyelles et h muet* **(a)** not. **il n'a rien dit** he did not *ou* didn't say anything, he said nothing; **nul n'a compris** nobody *ou* no one understood; **je n'ai pas d'argent** I have no money, I haven't any money; **~ me dérangez pas** don't *ou* do not disturb me; **il ~ sait pas parler** he can't *ou* cannot speak; **pas un seul ~ savait** not a single one knew; **il n'a que faire de vos conseils** he has no use for your advice; **que n'a-t-il songé à me prévenir** if only he had thought to warn me; **n'était la situation internationale, il serait parti** had it not been for *ou* were it not for the international situation he would have left; **cela fait des années que je n'ai été au cinéma** it's years since I (last) went to the cinema. **(b) ~ ... que** only; **elle n'a confiance qu'en nous** she trusts only us; **il n'a que trop d'assurance** he is only too self-assured; **il n'y a pas que vous** you're not the only one; **et il n'y a pas que ça!** and that's not all! **(c)** (*sans valeur nég*) **j'ai peur qu'il ~ vienne** I am afraid (that) he will come; **mangez avant que le rôti ~ refroidisse** do eat before the roast gets cold; **il est plus malin qu'on ~ pense** he is more cunning than you think.

né, e [ne] *adj, nm,f* born. **son premier/dernier ~** her first-/last-born.

néanmoins [neɑ̃mwɛ̃] *adv* nevertheless, yet.

néant [neɑ̃] *nm*: **le ~** nothingness; **le ~ de la vie** the worthlessness of life; **signes particuliers: ~** special peculiarities: none.

nébuleux, -euse [nebylø, øz] **1** *adj ciel* cloudy; *discours* nebulous. **2** *nf* (*Astron*) nebula.

nécessaire [nesesɛʀ] **1** *adj* (*gén*) necessary; *personne* indispensable (*à* to). **il est ~ qu'on le fasse** we need to do it, we have (got) to do it, we must do it, it's necessary for us to do it; **~ à la vie/aux hommes** necessary for life/to man; **un bon repos vous est ~** you need a good rest; **avoir le temps ~ (pour qch/pour faire)** to have the necessary time *ou* the time required (for sth/to do). **2** *nm*: **je n'ai pas le ~ pour le faire** I haven't got what's needed *ou* necessary to do it; **le strict ~** the bare necessities *ou* essentials; **je vais faire le ~** I'll see to it, I'll make the necessary arrangements. **3: ~ à couture** sewing box; **~ à ongles** manicure set; **~ de toilette** toilet bag; **~ de voyage** grip. ♦ **nécessairement** *adv faux etc* necessarily. **dois-je ~ m'en aller?** is it necessary for me to go?, must I go?, do I have to go?; **il va ~ échouer** he's bound to fail, he'll inevitably fail. ♦ **nécessité** *nf* **(a)** necessity. **je ne vois pas la ~ de le faire** I don't see the necessity of doing that *ou* the need for doing that; **être dans la ~ de faire qch** to have no choice *ou* alternative but to do sth. **(b) les ~s de la vie** the necessities *ou* essentials of life; **les ~s du service** the demands *ou* requirements of the job. **(c)** (†: *pauvreté*) destitution. ♦ **nécessiter** (1) *vt* to necessitate, require. ♦ **nécessiteux, -euse** *adj* needy.

nécrologie [nekʀɔlɔʒi] *nf* (*liste*) obituary column; (*biographie*) obituary. ♦ **nécrologique** *adj* obituary.

nécropole [nekʀɔpɔl] *nf* necropolis.

nectar [nɛktaʀ] *nm* (*Bot, Myth, fig*) nectar.

néerlandais, e [neɛʀlɑ̃dɛ, ɛz] **1** *adj* Dutch. **2** *nm* **(a) N~** Dutchman; **les N~** the Dutch. **(b)** (*Ling*) Dutch. **3** *nf*: **N~e** Dutchwoman.

nef [nɛf] *nf* nave. **~ latérale** side aisle.

néfaste [nefast(ə)] *adj* (*nuisible*) harmful (*à* to); (*funeste*) ill-fated, unlucky.

négatif, -ive [negatif, iv] **1** *adj* negative. **2** *nm* (*Phot*) negative. **3** *nf*: **dans la ~ive** in the negative. ♦ **négation** *nf* negation. ♦ **négativement** *adv* negatively.

négliger [negliʒe] (3) **1** *vt* (*gén*) to neglect; *tenue* to be careless about; *conseil* to disregard; *occasion* to miss. **ce n'est pas à ~** (*offre*) it's not to be sneezed at; (*difficulté*) it mustn't be overlooked; **ne rien ~ pour réussir** to leave no stone unturned in an effort to succeed; **il a négligé de le faire** he did not bother *ou* he neglected to do it. **2 se ~** *vpr* (*santé*) to neglect o.s.; (*tenue*) to neglect one's appearance. ♦ **négligé, e** **1** *adj épouse* neglected; *tenue* slovenly; *travail, style* slipshod. **2** *nm* (*laisser-aller*) slovenliness; (*vêtement*) négligée. ♦ **négligeable** *adj* (*gén*) negligible; *détail* trivial; *adversaire* insignificant. **non ~** not inconsiderable. ♦ **négligemment** *adv* (*sans soin*) carelessly, negligently; (*nonchalamment*) casually. ♦ **négligence** *nf* negligence, slovenliness; (*erreur*) omission. ♦ **négligent, e** *adj* (*sans soin*) negligent, careless; (*nonchalant*) casual.

négocier [negɔsje] (7) *vti* (*gén*) to negotiate. ♦ **négoce** *nm* (†: *commerce*) business. ♦ **négociable** *adj* negotiable. ♦ **négociant, e** *nm,f* merchant. **~ en gros** wholesaler. ♦ **négociateur, -trice** *nm,f* negotiator. ♦ **négociation** *nf* negotiation.

nègre [nɛgʀ(ə)] **1** *nm* (*péj*) (*indigène*) Negro, nigger (*péj*); (*écrivain*) ghost writer. **2** *adj* Negro. ♦ **négresse** *nf* Negress.

neige [nɛʒ] *nf* (*gén, arg*) snow. **aller à la ~*** to go to the ski resorts; **~ carbonique** dry ice; **~ fondue** (*pluie*) sleet. ♦ **neiger** (3) *vb impers* to snow, be snowing. ♦ **neigeux, -euse** *adj sommet* snow-covered, snow-clad; *aspect* snowy.

nénuphar [nenyfaʀ] *nm* water lily.

néo- [neɔ] *préf* neo-.

néolithique [neɔlitik] *adj, nm* neolithic.

néologisme [neɔlɔʒism(ə)] *nm* neologism.

néon [neɔ̃] *nm* (*gaz*) neon; (*éclairage*) neon lighting.

néophyte [neɔfit] *nmf* (*gén*) beginner; (*Rel*) neophyte.

néo-zélandais, e [neɔzelɑ̃dɛ, ɛz] **1** *adj* New Zealand. **2** *nm(f)*: **N~(e)** New Zealander.

nerf [nɛʀ] *nm* nerve. **avoir les ~s malades** to suffer from nerves; **avoir les ~s à vif** to be very nervy *ou* edgy, be on edge; **avoir ses ~s** to have a fit of nerves; **être sur les ~s** to be all keyed up; **taper* sur les ~s de qn** to get on sb's nerves; **ses ~s ont lâché*** his nerves have gone to pieces, he has cracked up*; **allons du ~!** come on, buck up!*; **ça manque de ~** it has got no go about it; **l'argent est le ~ de la guerre** money is the sinews of war. ♦ **nerveusement** *adv* (*excité*) nervously, tensely;

(*agacé*) touchily, nervily. **ébranlé** ~ shaken. ♦ **nerveux, -euse** *adj* **(a)** *tension, système* nervous; *cellule* nerve. **(b)** (*agité*) nervous, tense; (*irritable*) touchy, nervy. **c'est un grand** ~ he's very highly strung. **(c)** (*vigoureux*) *corps, style* energetic, vigorous; *moteur* responsive. **(d)** (*sec*) *personne* wiry; *main* sinewy; *viande* stringy. ♦ **nervosité** *nf* **(a)** (*agitation*) (*permanente*) nervousness; (*passagère*) agitation, tension. **(b)** (*irritabilité*) irritability, nerviness.

nervure [nɛʀvyʀ] *nf* (*Bot*) nervure; (*Archit*) rib.

n'est-ce pas [nɛspɑ] *adv*: **il est fort,** ~? he is strong, isn't he?; **il l'ignore,** ~? he doesn't know, does he?

net, nette [nɛt] **1** *adj* **(a)** *surface* clean; *intérieur, travail* neat, tidy; *conscience* clear. **mettre qch au** ~ to make a fair copy of sth. **(b)** *prix, poids* net. ~ **de** free of. **(c)** *idée, explication, voix* clear; *réponse* straight, plain; *refus* flat; *situation* clear-cut. **(d)** *différence, amélioration etc* marked, distinct. **il est très** ~ **qu'il le savait** it is quite clear *ou* obvious that he knew. **(e)** *dessin, écriture, souvenir* clear; *contour,* (*Phot*) *image* sharp; *cassure* clean. **2** *adv* **(a)** *s'arrêter* dead; *tué* outright. **se casser** ~ to break clean through. **(b)** *parler* frankly, bluntly; *refuser* flatly. **pour vous parler** ~ to be blunt *ou* frank with you. **(c)** (*Comm*) net. **2 kg** ~ 2 kg net. ♦ **nettement** *adv* (*gén*) clearly; *refuser* flatly; *dire* bluntly, frankly; *apparaître* distinctly, sharply; *s'améliorer* markedly. ♦ **netteté** *nf [tenue, travail]* neatness; *[explication, souvenir, voix]* clearness, clarity; *[contour, image]* sharpness; *[cassure]* cleanness.

nettoyer [nɛtwaje] (8) *vt* **(a)** (*gén*) *objet* to clean; *jardin* to clear. ~ **au chiffon** to dust; ~ **avec du savon** to wash with soap; ~ **à la brosse** to brush; ~ **à sec** to dry-clean. **(b)** (*) (*tuer*) to finish off*; (*ruiner*) to clean out; (*vider*) to clean out, empty. **(c)** (*Mil, Police*) to clean up. ♦ **nettoiement** *nm* cleaning. ♦ **nettoyage** *nm* (*gén*) cleaning; (*Mil, Police*) cleaning up. ~ **de printemps** spring-cleaning; ~ **à sec** dry cleaning.

neuf[1] [nœf] *adj inv, nm inv* nine; *V* **six.**

neuf[2], **neuve** [nœf, nœv] **1** *adj* (*gén*) new; *pensée* fresh; *pays* young. **à l'état** ~ as good as new. **2** *nm*: **il y a du** ~ there has been a new development; **vêtu de** ~ dressed in new clothes; **remettre à** ~ to do up like new.

neurasthénie [nøʀasteni] *nf* (*gén*) depression. **faire de la** ~ to be depressed. ♦ **neurasthénique** *adj* depressed.

neurologie [nøʀɔlɔʒi] *nf* neurology. ♦ **neurologue** *nmf* neurologist.

neutre [nøtʀ(ə)] **1** *adj* (*gén*) neutral; (*Ling, Zool*) neuter. **2** *nm* (*Ling*) neuter; (*Élec*) neutral; (*Pol*) neutral country. ♦ **neutralisation** *nf* neutralization. ♦ **neutraliser** (1) *vt* to neutralize. ♦ **neutralité** *nf* neutrality. ♦ **neutron** *nm* neutron.

neuvième [nœvjɛm] *adj, nmf* ninth; *V* **sixième.** ♦ **neuvièmement** *adv* ninthly; *V* **sixièmement.**

neveu, *pl* ~**x** [n(ə)vø] *nm* nephew.

névralgie [nevʀalʒi] *nf* neuralgia. ♦ **névralgique** *adj* neuralgic. (*Méd, fig*) **point** ~ nerve centre.

névrose [nevʀoz] *nf* neurosis. ♦ **névrosé, e** *adj, nm,f* neurotic. ♦ **névropathe** *adj, nmf* neurotic. ♦ **névrotique** *adj* neurotic.

nez [ne] *nm* **(a)** (*gén*) nose. **parler du** ~ to talk through one's nose; **comme le** ~ **au milieu du visage** as plain as the nose on your face *ou* as a pikestaff; **cela sent le brûlé à plein** ~ there's a strong smell of burning; **tu as le** ~ **dessus!** it's right under your nose! **(b)** (*visage*) **baisser/lever le** ~ to bow/raise one's head, look down/up; **mettre le** ~ **à la fenêtre** to show one's face at the window; **fermer la porte au** ~ **de qn** to shut the door in sb's face; ~ **à** ~ face to face (*avec* with); **faire un drôle de** ~ to pull a funny face. **(c)** (*flair*) **avoir du** ~ to have flair; **j'ai eu le** ~ **creux de m'en aller*** I was quite right to leave. **(d) au** ~ **et à la barbe de qn** under sb's very nose; **il m'a dans le** ~* he can't stand me*, he has got sth against me; **se bouffer le** ~‡ to be at each others' throats; **mettre son** ~ **dans qch** to poke one's nose into sth; **l'affaire lui est passée sous le** ~* the bargain slipped through his fingers.

ni [ni] *conj* nor, or. **ni ... ni ...** neither ... nor ...; **il ne pouvait (**~**) parler** ~ **entendre** he could neither speak nor hear, he couldn't speak or hear; **je ne veux** ~ **ne peux accepter** I neither wish to nor can accept; ~ **plus** ~ **moins** no more no less; ~ **l'un** ~ **l'autre** neither one nor the other, neither of them; ~ **vu** ~ **connu*** no one'll know; **cela ne me fait** ~ **chaud** ~ **froid** it makes no odds to me.

niais, e [njɛ, ɛz] **1** *adj* (*gén*) silly, simple; *rire* inane. **2** *nm,f* simpleton. ♦ **niaisement** *adv* inanely. ♦ **niaiserie** *nf* silliness, simpleness; inaneness. ~**s** foolish remarks *etc.*

niche [niʃ] *nf* **(a)** (*alcôve*) niche, recess; *[chien]* kennel. **(b)** (*farce*) trick.

nichée [niʃe] *nf [oiseaux, enfants]* brood; *[chiens]* litter.

nicher [niʃe] (1) **1** *vi [oiseau]* to nest; (*) *[personne]* to hang out‡. **2 se** ~ *vpr [oiseau]* to nest; *[village etc]* to nestle; (*) *[personne]* to stick* *ou* put o.s.; *[objet]* to lodge itself.

nickel [nikɛl] **1** *nm* nickel. **2** *adj* (*: *impeccable*) spick and span. ♦ **nickeler** (4) *vt* to nickel-plate.

nicotine [nikɔtin] *nf* nicotine.

nid [ni] *nm* (*Zool*) nest; (*foyer*) cosy little nest; (*repaire*) den. **surprendre qn au** ~ to find sb at home *ou* in; ~ **de mitrailleuses** nest of machine guns; ~ **de poule** pothole; ~ **à poussière** dust trap; ~ **de résistance** centre of resistance.

nièce [njɛs] *nf* niece.

nier [nje] (7) *vt* to deny (*avoir fait* having done). **l'accusé nia** the accused denied the charges.

nigaud, e [nigo, od] **1** *adj* silly, simple. **2** *nm,f* simpleton. **gros** ~! big silly *ou* ninny!*

nipper* [nipe] (1) **1** *vt* to tog out*. **2 se** ~ *vpr* to get togged up*. ♦ **nippes**†* *nfpl* togs*.

nippon, e *ou* **-onne** [nipɔ̃, ɔn] *adj,* **N**~**(e)** *nm(f)* Japanese, Nipponese.

nitrate [nitʀat] *nm* nitrate. ♦ **nitrique** *adj* nitric. ♦ **nitroglycérine** *nf* nitroglycerine.

niveau, *pl* ~**x** [nivo] *nm* **(a)** *[huile, eau]* level. **au** ~ **du sol** at ground level; **la neige m'arrivait au** ~ **des genoux** the snow came up to my knees *ou* was knee-deep; **serré au** ~ **de la taille** tight at the waist; **au** ~ **du village, il s'arrêta** once level with the village he stopped; **de** ~ **avec, au même** ~ **que** level with; **mettre/être de** *ou* **à** ~ to make/be level. **(b)** *[études]* standard; *[intelligence, qualité]* level. ~ **de langue** register; ~ **social** social standing; ~ **de vie** standard of living; **atteindre son** ~ **le plus bas** to reach its lowest ebb *ou* level; (*Scol*) **au** ~ up to standard; **au** ~ **européen** at a European level. **(c)** (*objet*) (*Constr*) level; (*Aut: jauge*) gauge. ♦ **niveler** (4) *vt* (*gén*) to level; *[érosion]* to wear down *ou* away. ~ **par le bas** to level down. ♦ **nivelage** *nm ou* ♦ **nivellement** *nm* levelling.

noble [nɔbl(ə)] **1** *adj* noble. **2** *nmf* nobleman; noblewoman. **les** ~**s** the nobility. ♦ **noblement** *adv* nobly. ♦ **noblesse** *nf* (*gén*) nobility. **la petite** ~ the gentry.

noce [nɔs] *nf* (*cérémonie*) wedding; (*cortège*) wedding party. ~**s** wedding; **être de** ~ to be invited to a wedding; **repas de** ~**(s)** wedding banquet; ~**s d'or** golden wedding; **il l'avait épousée en premières** ~**s** she was his first wife; **faire la** ~* to live it up*, have a wild time; **je n'étais pas à la** ~ I was having a pretty uncomfortable time. ♦ **noceur, -euse*** *nm,f* reveller.

nocif, -ive [nɔsif, iv] *adj* noxious, harmful. ♦ **nocivité** *nf* noxiousness, harmfulness.

noctambule [nɔktɑ̃byl] *nmf* night-owl.
nocturne [nɔktyʀn(ə)] **1** *adj* nocturnal, night. **2** *nm* (*Zool*) night hunter; (*Mus*) nocturne; (*Sport*) evening fixture.
Noël [nɔɛl] *nm* (*fête*) Christmas; (*chant*) (Christmas) carol; (*cadeau*) Christmas present.
nœud [nø] **1** *nm* (*gén*) knot; (*ruban*) bow; (*Phys*) node. **faire son ~ de cravate** to knot *ou* tie one's tie; **avoir un ~ dans la gorge** to have a lump in one's throat; **il y a un ~!*** there's a hitch *ou* snag!; **le ~ de** *problème,* (*Théât*) *intrigue* the knot of; (*littér: lien*) **les ~s de l'amitié** the bonds *ou* ties of friendship. **2: ~ coulant** slipknot; **~ ferroviaire** rail junction; **~ gordien** Gordian knot; **~ papillon** bow tie; **~ de vipères** nest of vipers.
noir, e [nwaʀ] **1** *adj* **(a)** (*couleur*) black; *peau* (*par le soleil*) tanned; (*par les coups etc*) black and blue; *yeux, cheveux* dark. **je l'ai vu ~ sur blanc** I saw it in black and white; **~ de saleté** black with dirt. **(b)** *race* black, coloured. **l'Afrique ~e** black Africa; **le problème ~** the colour problem. **(c)** (*obscur*) dark. **il faisait ~ comme dans un four*** it was as black as pitch; **il faisait nuit ~e** it was pitch-dark; **rue ~e de monde** street teeming with people. **(d)** *désespoir, humeur, avenir, colère* black; *misère* utter; *idée* gloomy; (*macabre*) *film* macabre. **(e)** (*hostile*) black. **regarder qn d'un œil ~** to give sb a black look. **(f)** (*: *ivre*) drunk, tight.
2 *nm* **(a)** (*couleur*) black; (*pour les yeux*) mascara. **elle avait du ~ sur le menton** she had a black mark on her chin; **elle est en ~** she is in black; (*en deuil*) she is in mourning; **voir les choses en ~** to look on the black side. **(b)** (*obscurité*) dark, darkness. **(c) vendre au ~** to sell on the black market; **travailler au ~** to work on the side, moonlight*. **(d)** (*personne*) **N~** black.
3 *nf* **(a)** (*personne*) **N~e** black, black woman. **(b)** (*Mus*) crotchet.
♦ **noirâtre** *adj* blackish. ♦ **noirceur** *nf* blackness; darkness; (*acte perfide*) black deed. ♦ **noircir** (2) **1** *vt* (*gén, fig*) to blacken; *[charbon]* to dirty; (*à la cire*) to darken. (*fig*) **~ du papier** to cover paper with writing; **le soleil l'a noirci** the sun has tanned him; **~ la situation** to paint a black picture of the situation. **2** *vi [peau]* to tan; *[ciel, couleur]* to darken. **3 se ~** *vpr [ciel, couleur]* to darken; *[temps]* to turn stormy. ♦ **noircissement** *nm* blackening; dirtying; darkening. ♦ **noircissure** *nf* black mark.
noise [nwaz] *nf*: **chercher ~ à qn** to try to pick a quarrel with sb.
noisette [nwazɛt] **1** *adj inv* hazel. **2** *nf* (*fruit*) hazelnut. **~ de beurre** knob of butter. ♦ **noisetier** *nm* hazel tree.
noix [nwa] *nf* (*fruit*) walnut; *[côtelette]* eye. **à la ~*** rubbishy; **~ de beurre** knob of butter; **~ de coco** coconut; **~ de muscade** nutmeg; **~ de veau** cushion of veal.
nom [nɔ̃] **1** *nm* (*gén*) name. **petit ~** Christian *ou* first name; **le beau ~ de liberté** the great name of liberty; **il n'est spécialiste que de ~** he is a specialist in name only; **un crime sans ~** *ou* **qui n'a pas de ~** an unspeakable crime; **se faire un ~** to make a name for o.s.; **parler au ~ de qn** to speak for *ou* on behalf of sb; **au ~ de la loi, ouvrez** open up in the name of the law; **au ~ de quoi vous permettez-vous ...?** whatever gives you the right to ...?; **au ~ du ciel!** in heaven's name!; **au ~ de ce que vous avez de plus cher** in the name of everything you hold most dear; **~ de ~ *** *ou* **d'un chien!*** damn‡ *ou* dash* it!; **traiter qn de tous les ~s** to call sb names, call sb everything under the sun. **2: ~ de baptême** Christian name, given name (*US*); **~ commun** common noun; **~ déposé** (registered) trademark; **~ d'emprunt** alias, assumed name; **~ de famille** surname; **~ de femme mariée** married name; **~ de guerre** nom de guerre; **~ de jeune fille** maiden name; **~ propre** proper noun; **~ de théâtre** stage name.
nomade [nɔmad] **1** *adj* nomadic. **2** *nmf* nomad.
nombre [nɔ̃bʀ(ə)] *nm* **(a)** (*gén*) number. **depuis ~ d'années** for several years, for a number of years; **les gagnants sont au ~ de 3** there are 3 winners; **supérieur en ~** superior in numbers; **à ~ égal** with equal numbers; **des ennemis sans ~** innumerable enemies. **(b)** (*masse*) numbers. **être en ~** to be in large numbers; **faire ~** to make up the numbers; **submergé par le ~** overcome by sheer weight of numbers; **le plus grand ~** the great majority of people. **(c)** (*parmi*) **je le compte au ~ de mes amis** I number him among my friends; **est-il du ~ des reçus?** is he among those who passed?; **il y en avait dans le ~ qui riaient** some among them were laughing.
nombreux, -euse [nɔ̃bʀø, øz] *adj* **(a)** numerous, many. **les ~euses personnalités** the numerous *ou* many personalities; **de ~ accidents** many *ou* numerous accidents; **être ~** to be numerous; **les gens étaient venus ~** people had come in great numbers; **peu ~** few; **le public était moins/plus ~ hier** there were fewer/more spectators yesterday. **(b)** *foule, collection* large.
nombril [nɔ̃bʀi] *nm* navel, belly button*. **il se prend pour le ~ du monde*** he thinks he is the cat's whiskers*.
nomenclature [nɔmɑ̃klatyʀ] *nf* (*gén: liste*) list; (*Ling, Sci*) nomenclature.
nominal, e, *mpl* **-aux** [nɔminal, o] *adj* (*gén*) nominal; (*Ling*) noun. **liste ~e** list of names. ♦ **nominalement** *adv* (*gén, Ling*) nominally. ♦ **nominatif, -ive 1** *adj* (*Fin*) registered. **liste ~ive** list of names. **2** *nm* (*Ling*) nominative. ♦ **nominativement** *adv* by name.
nommer [nɔme] (1) **1** *vt* **(a)** *fonctionnaire* to appoint; *candidat* to nominate (*à* to). **(b)** (*citer*) to name; (*appeler*) *personne* to call, name. **ce que nous nommons le bonheur** what we name *ou* call happiness; **qn que je ne nommerai pas** sb who shall remain nameless. **2 se ~** *vpr* (*s'appeler*) to be called; (*se présenter*) to introduce o.s. ♦ **nomination** *nf* (*promotion*) appointment, nomination (*à* to); (*document*) appointment *ou* nomination papers. ♦ **nommément** *adv* **(a)** (*par son nom*) by name. **(b)** (*spécialement*) particularly.
non [nɔ̃] **1** *adv* **(a)** no. **le connaissez-vous? – ~** do you know him? – no (I don't); **est-elle chez elle? – ~** is she at home? – no (she isn't); **je ne dis pas ~** (*ce n'est pas de refus*) I wouldn't say no; (*je n'en disconviens pas*) I don't disagree; **certes ~!** most certainly *ou* definitely not!; **bien sûr que ~!** of course not!, I should think not!; **répondre (par) ~** to answer no; **faire ~ de la tête** to shake one's head. **(b)** (*remplaçant une proposition*) not. **je pense que ~** I don't think so; **je crains que ~** I am afraid not; **elle veut mais lui ~** she wants to but he doesn't; **ah ~?** really?, no?; **partez-vous ou ~?** are you going or not?; **erreur ou ~** mistake or no mistake. **(c)** (*littér: pas*) not. **c'est mon avis ~ (pas) le vôtre** it's my opinion not yours; **~ (pas) que ...** not that .... **(d)** (*impatience, indignation*) **tu vas cesser de pleurer ~?** WILL you stop crying?; **~ par exemple!** good gracious! **(e)** (*doute*) no? **il me l'a dit lui-même – ~?** he told me so himself – no?; **c'est bon ~?** it's good isn't it? **(f) nous ne l'avons pas vu – nous ~ plus** we didn't see him – neither did we *ou* we didn't either; **il parle ~ plus en médecin mais en ami** he is talking now not as a doctor but as a friend. **(g)** (*modifiant adv*) not. **~ loin de là il y a ...** not far from there there's ...; **c'est ~ moins intéressant** it's no less interesting; **~ sans raison/ ~ sans peine** not without reason/difficulty; **~ seulement il est impoli mais** ... not only is he impolite but .... **(h)** (*modifiant adj, participe*) **toutes les places ~ réservées** all

the unreserved seats, all seats not reserved.

2 *nm inv* no. **il y a eu 30 ~** there were 30 votes against *ou* 30 noes.

3 *préf* non-, un-. **~-ferreux** non-ferrous; **~-vérifié** unverified.

4: non-agression non-aggression; **non-alignement** non-alignment; **non-assistance à personne en danger** failure to render assistance to a person in danger; **non-combattant** non-combatant; **non-conformisme** nonconformism; **non-croyant** non-believer; **non-existant** non-existent; **non-intervention** non-intervention; **non-lieu** not proven verdict; **non-paiement** non-payment; **non-parution** failure to appear *ou* be published; **non-retour** no return; **non-sens** (*absurdité*) (piece of) nonsense; (*en traduction*) meaningless word; **non-stop** non-stop.

nonante [nɔnɑ̃t] *adj* (*Belgique, Suisse*) ninety.

nonchalance [nɔ̃ʃalɑ̃s] *nf* nonchalance. ♦ **nonchalant, e** *adj* nonchalant. ♦ **nonchalamment** *adv* nonchalantly.

nord [nɔʀ] **1** *nm* north. **le vent du ~** the north wind; **un vent du ~** a northerly *ou* north wind; **le vent est au ~** the wind is blowing from the north; **au ~** (*situation*) in the north; (*direction*) to the north, northwards; **au ~ de** north of; **l'Europe du ~** Northern Europe; **l'Amérique du N~** North America. **2** *adj inv région* northern; *entrée, pôle* north; *direction* northward; (*Mét*) northerly. **3: ~-africain** *etc* North African *etc*; **~-est/-ouest** north-east/-west. ♦ **nordique 1** *adj* Nordic. **2** *nmf*: **N~** Scandinavian. ♦ **nordiste 1** *adj* Northern, Yankee. **2** *nmf*: **N~** Northerner, Yankee.

normal, e, *mpl* **-aux** [nɔʀmal, o] **1** *adj* (*gén*) normal; (*courant*) normal, usual. **de dimension ~e** normal-sized, standard-sized; **il n'est pas ~** there's sth wrong with him; **c'est ~!** it's (quite) natural! **2** *nf*: **s'écarter de la ~e** to diverge from the norm; **revenir à la ~e** to return to normality, get back to normal; **au-dessus de la ~e** above average. ♦ **normalement** *adv* normally, usually. ♦ **normaliser** (1) *vt situation* to normalize; *produit* to standardize. ♦ **normalisation** *nf* normalization; standardization.

Normandie [nɔʀmɑ̃di] *nf* Normandy. ♦ **normand, e** *adj*, **N~(e)** *nm(f)* Norman.

norme [nɔʀm(ə)] *nf* (*gén*) norm; (*Tech*) standard. **rester dans la ~** to keep within limits.

Norvège [nɔʀvɛʒ] *nf* Norway. ♦ **norvégien, -ienne** *adj, nm*, **N~(ne)** *nm(f)* Norwegian.

nos [no] *adj poss V* **notre.**

nostalgie [nɔstalʒi] *nf* nostalgia. ♦ **nostalgique** *adj* nostalgic.

notable [nɔtabl(ə)] *adj, nm* notable. ♦ **notabilité** *nf* notability. ♦ **notablement** *adv* notably.

notaire [nɔtɛʀ] *nm* ≃ solicitor, notary (public).

notamment [nɔtamɑ̃] *adv* notably.

note [nɔt] *nf* **(a)** (*écrite*) note. **prendre des ~s** to take notes; **prendre bonne ~ de qch** to take good note of sth; **prendre qch en ~** to make a note of sth, write sth down; **~ en bas de page** footnote; **~ de service** memorandum. **(b)** (*chiffrée*) mark. **bonne/mauvaise ~** good/bad mark. **(c)** (*facture*) bill, check (*US*). **(d)** (*Mus, fig*) note. **ses paroles étaient dans la ~** his words struck the right note; **~ de tristesse** note *ou* touch of sadness. ♦ **notation** *nf [signes]* notation; *[devoir, employé]* marking. (*remarque*) **une ~ intéressante** an interesting touch. ♦ **noter** (1) *vt* **(a)** *adresse etc* to write down, note down. **notez-le** make a note of it; **notez que nous serons absents** note that we'll be away. **(b)** (*remarquer*) *faute, progrès* to notice. **notez (bien) que je n'ai rien dit** I didn't say anything, mark you; **il faut ~ qu'il a des excuses** he has an excuse mind *ou* mark you. **(c)** (*cocher*) to mark. **~ d'une croix** to mark with a cross, put a cross against. **(d)** *devoir* to mark; *élève, employé* to give a mark to. ♦ **notice** *nf* (*gén*) note; (*mode d'emploi*) directions, instructions.

notifier [nɔtifje] (7) *vt* to notify. ♦ **notification** *nf* notification.

notion [nosjɔ̃] *nf* notion. **perdre la ~ du temps** to lose all notion of time; **avoir quelques ~s de grammaire** to have some notion of grammar.

notoire [nɔtwaʀ] *adj criminel* notorious; *fait* well-known. **il est ~ que** it is common knowledge that. ♦ **notoirement** *adv* notoriously. **~ reconnu** well known. ♦ **notoriété** *nf [fait]* notoriety; (*renommée*) fame. **c'est de ~ publique** that's common knowledge.

notre [nɔtʀ(ə)], *pl* **nos** [no] *adj poss* our; (*emphatique*) our own. **~ homme a filé** the chap *ou* fellow has run off; **~ esprit** our minds; **N~ Seigneur** Our Lord.

nôtre [notʀ(ə)] **1** *pron poss*: **le ~, la ~, les ~s** ours, our own. **2** *nm* **(a) nous y mettrons du ~** we'll do our bit. **(b) les ~s** (*famille*) our family; (*partisans*) our own people; **il sera des ~s** he will join us. **3** *adj poss* (*littér*) ours, our own. **ces principes, nous les avons faits ~s** we have made these principles our own; *V* **sien.**

nouba* [nuba] *nf*: **faire la ~** to live it up*.

nouer [nwe] (1) **1** *vt ficelle* to tie, knot, fasten; *paquet* to tie up, do up; *alliance, amitié* to form; (*Littérat*) *action* to build up. **avoir la gorge nouée** to have a lump in one's throat; **~ conversation avec qn** to start *ou* strike up a conversation with sb. **2 se ~** *vpr [mains]* to join together; *[amitié]* to be formed; *[conversation]* to start; *[intrigue]* to build up. ♦ **noueux, -euse** *adj* gnarled.

nougat [nuga] *nm* (*Culin*) nougat. (*pieds*) **~s*** feet; **c'est du ~*** it's dead easy*.

nouille [nuj] *nf* **(a)** (*Culin*) **~s** pasta, noodles. **(b)** (*) (*imbécile*) noodle*, idiot; (*mollasson*) big lump*.

nounou* [nunu] *nf* nanny.

nounours [nunuʀs] *nm* teddy (bear).

nourrice [nuʀis] *nf* **(a)** (*gardienne*) child-minder; (*qui allaite*) wet nurse. **~ sèche** dry nurse; **mettre un enfant en ~** to foster a child. **(b)** (*bidon*) jerrycan.

nourrir [nuʀiʀ] (2) **1** *vt* (*lit*) to feed; *feu* to stoke; *projet* to nurse; *espoir, haine* to nourish. **~ au sein** to breast-feed; **bien/mal nourri** well-/poorly-fed; **cette entreprise nourrit 10 000 ouvriers** this firm provides work for 10,000 workers; **ça ne nourrit pas son homme** it doesn't earn a man his bread *ou* doesn't give a man a living wage. **2** *vi* to be nourishing. **3 se ~** *vpr* to eat. **se ~ de** *viande* to feed (o.s.) on, eat; *illusions* to feed on, live on. ♦ **nourri, e** *adj fusillade* heavy; *conversation* lively. ♦ **nourrissant, e** *adj* nourishing, nutritious. ♦ **nourrisson** *nm* infant. ♦ **nourriture** *nf* (*aliments, fig*) food. (*alimentation*) **une ~ saine** a healthy diet.

nous [nu] *pron pers* **(a)** (*sujet*) we. **~ vous écrirons** we'll write to you; **~ accepter?, jamais!** us accept that?, never!; **c'est ~ qui sommes fautifs** we are the ones to blame. **(b)** (*objet*) us. **écoutez-~** listen to us; **~, elle ~ déteste** she hates us; **c'est ~ qu'elle veut voir** it's us she wants to see. **(c)** (*avec prép*) us. **à ~ cinq** between the 5 of us; **cette maison est à ~** this house belongs to us *ou* is ours; **un élève à ~** one of our pupils. **(d)** (*comparaison*) we, us. **il est aussi fort que ~** he is as strong as we are *ou* as us*; **faites comme ~** do as we do, do the same as us*. **(e)** (*avec vpr*) **~ ~ sommes bien amusés** we thoroughly enjoyed ourselves; **~ ~ détestons** we hate each other; **asseyons-~ donc** let's sit down.

nouveau, nouvelle[1] [nuvo, nuvɛl] (**nouvel** [nuvɛl] *devant nm commençant par voyelle ou h muet*), *mpl* **nouveaux** [nuvo] **1** *adj* **(a)** (*gén*) new. **carottes nouvelles** spring carrots; **c'est tout ~** this is brand-new; **ce travail est ~ pour lui** he's new to this job; **le ~ président** the new *ou* newly-elected president. **(b)** (*original*) *idée* novel, new; *méthode* new, up-to-date. **(c)** (*qui s'ajoute*) new, fresh. **avez-vous lu son ~ livre?** have you read his new *ou* latest book?; **un ~ Napoléon** a second Napoleon; **il y a eu un ~ tremblement de terre** there has been a further *ou* a fresh earthquake.

2 *nm,f* new man (*ou* woman); (*Scol*) new boy (*ou* girl).

3 *nm*: **y a-t-il du ~ à ce sujet?** is there anything new on this?; **il y a du ~ dans cette affaire** there has been a fresh *ou* a new development in this business; **faire qch de** *ou* **à ~** to do sth again; **nous examinerons la question à ~** we'll examine the question anew.

4: Nouvel An New Year; **Nouvelle-Angleterre** New England; **Nouvelle-Calédonie** New Caledonia; **nouvelle lune** new moon; **nouveaux mariés** newly-weds; **N~ Monde** New World; **~-né, *mpl* ~-nés** (*adj*) newborn; (*nm*) newborn child; **~ venu, nouvelle venue** newcomer; **Nouvelle-Zélande** New Zealand.

nouveauté [nuvote] *nf* (*actualité, originalité*) novelty; (*chose*) new thing; (*livre*) new publication. **il n'aime pas la ~** he hates anything new; **c'est une ~!** that's new!; (*Habillement*) **~s de printemps** new spring fashions.

nouvelle[2] [nuvɛl] *nf* **(a)** (*écho*) **une ~** a piece of news; **vous connaissez la ~?** have you heard the news?; **aller aux ~s** to go and find out what is happening; **avez-vous de ses ~s?** have you heard from him?, have you had any news from him?; **j'irai prendre de ses ~s** I'll go and see how he's getting on; **pas de ~s, bonnes ~s** no news is good news; **il aura de mes ~s!*** I'll give him what for!*; **(goûtez mon vin) vous m'en direz des ~s** (taste my wine,) I'm sure you'll like it; (*Presse*) **voici les ~s** here is the news. **(b)** (*court récit*) short story.

nouvellement [nuvɛlmɑ̃] *adv* recently, newly.

novembre [nɔvɑ̃bʀ(ə)] *nm* November; *V* **septembre.**

novice [nɔvis] **1** *adj* inexperienced (*dans* in), green* (*dans* at). **2** *nmf* novice, beginner; (*Rel*) novice.

noyau, *pl* ~x [nwajo] *nm [fruit]* stone, pit (*US*); (*Astron, Bio, Ling, Phys*) nucleus; (*Géol*) core; (*groupe de fidèles*) circle; (*manifestants*) small group. **~ de résistance** centre of resistance.

noyer[1] [nwaje] *nm* (*arbre*) walnut (tree); (*bois*) walnut.

noyer[2] [nwaje] (8) **1** *vt* **(a)** (*gén*) to drown; *moteur, rives* to flood. **les yeux noyés de larmes** with his eyes full of *ou* brimming with tears; **~ le poisson*** to draw a red herring across the trail; **~ qn sous un déluge d'explications** to swamp sb with explanations; **noyé dans l'obscurité** shrouded in darkness; **noyé dans la foule** lost in the crowd; **noyé dans la masse** put together with the rest. **(b)** (*Tech*) *pilier* to embed. **2 se ~** *vpr* (*accidentellement*) to drown; (*volontairement*) to drown o.s. **se ~ dans les détails** to get bogged down in details; **se ~ dans un verre d'eau** to make a mountain out of a molehill. ♦ **noyade** *nf* drowning. **de nombreuses ~s** many drowning accidents, many deaths by drowning. ♦ **noyé, e 1** *adj* (*fig: perdu*) **être ~** to be out of one's depth, be all at sea (*en* in). **2** *nm,f* drowned person.

nu, e [ny] **1** *adj* **(a)** *personne* naked, bare. **~-pieds** barefoot, with bare feet; **(la) tête ~e** bareheaded; **~ jusqu'à la ceinture** stripped to the waist; **à moitié ~** half-naked; **tout ~** stark naked; **se mettre ~** to strip (off), take one's clothes off. **(b)** *mur, arbre, plaine* bare; *vérité* plain, naked. **(c) en ~e-propriété** without usufruct; **mettre à ~** *fil électrique* to strip; **mettre son cœur à ~** to lay bare one's heart. **2** *nm* nude. ♦ **nu-pieds** *nmpl* (*sandales*) flip-flops.

nuage [nɥaʒ] *nm* cloud. **le ciel se couvre de ~s** the sky is clouding over; **juste un ~ de lait** just a drop of milk; (*fig*) **il est dans les ~s** his head is in the clouds; **sans ~s** *ciel* cloudless; *bonheur* unmarred, unclouded. ♦ **nuageux, -euse** *adj temps* cloudy; *ciel* cloudy, overcast.

nuance [nɥɑ̃s] *nf [couleur]* shade; (*Littérat*) shade of meaning, nuance; (*différence*) slight difference; (*touche*) touch, note. **~ politique** shade of political opinion; **tout en ~s** *discours* subtle; **sans ~** unsubtle. ♦ **nuancer** (3) *vt opinion* to qualify.

nucléaire [nykleɛʀ] *adj* nuclear.

nudité [nydite] *nf [personne]* nakedness, nudity; *[mur]* bareness. ♦ **nudisme** *nm* nudism. ♦ **nudiste** *adj, nmf* nudist.

nuée [nɥe] *nf* (*littér: nuage*) cloud; *[insectes, flèches]* cloud; *[ennemis]* horde, host.

nues [ny] *nfpl*: **porter qn aux ~s** to praise sb to the skies; **tomber des ~s** to be completely taken aback.

nuire [nɥiʀ] (38) **1 ~ à** *vt indir* to harm, injure. **sa laideur lui nuit beaucoup** his ugliness is very much against him *ou* is a great disadvantage to him. **2 se ~** *vpr* (*à soi-même*) to do o.s. a lot of harm; (*l'un l'autre*) to harm each other's interests. ♦ **nuisible** *adj* harmful, injurious (*à* to). **animaux ~s** pests.

nuit [nɥi] *nf* **(a)** (*obscurité*) darkness, night. **il fait ~ noire** it's pitch dark; **la ~ tombe** night is falling; **à la ~ tombante** at nightfall, at dusk; **rentrer avant la ~** to come home before dark; **la ~ polaire** the polar night *ou* darkness. **(b)** (*temps*) night. **cette ~** (*passée*) last night; (*qui vient*) tonight; **dans la ~ de jeudi** during Thursday night; **~ blanche** sleepless night; **ouvert la ~** open at night; **rouler la ~** *ou* **de ~** to drive at night; **de ~** *service etc* night; **dans la ~ des temps** in the mists of time; **la ~ de Noël** Christmas Eve.

nul, nulle [nyl] **1** *adj indéf* **(a)** (*aucun*) no. **il n'avait ~ besoin de sortir** he had no need to go out; **~ autre** no one else; **il ne l'a trouvé nulle part** he couldn't find it anywhere, he could find it nowhere; **sans ~ doute** without any doubt. **(b)** *résultat, risque* nil; *testament, élection* null and void; *récolte etc* non-existent. **le score est ~** (*zéro à zéro*) the result is a nil draw; (*2 à 2 etc*) the result is a draw; **~ et non avenu** invalid, null and void; **rendre ~** to annul, nullify. **(c)** *personne, travail* worthless, useless. **~ en géographie** hopeless *ou* useless at geography. **2** *pron indéf* no one. **~ d'entre vous** none of you. ♦ **nullement** *adv* not at all, not in the least. ♦ **nullité** *nf* **(a)** (*Jur*) nullity; *[personne]* uselessness; *[objection]* invalidity. **(b)** (*personne*) nonentity, wash-out*.

numéraire [nymeʀɛʀ] *nm* cash.

numéro [nymeʀo] *nm* **(a)** (*gén, Aut, Phys*) number. **j'habite au ~ 6** I live at number 6; **~ minéralogique** registration *ou* license (*US*) number, car number; **composer un ~** to dial a number. **(b)** (*Presse*) issue, number. **vieux ~** back number, back issue. **(c)** *[chant, danse]* number; *[cirque, music-hall]* act, turn. **il nous a fait son petit ~** he put on his usual act for us. **(d)** (*personne*) **c'est un drôle de ~!*** what a character! ♦ **numéral, e, *mpl* -aux** *adj, nm* numeral. ♦ **numérique** *adj* numerical. ♦ **numériquement** *adv* numerically. ♦ **numéroter** (1) *vt* to number.

nuptial, e, *mpl* -aux [nypsjal, o] *adj bénédiction* nuptial; *cérémonie* wedding.

nuque [nyk] *nf* nape (of the neck).

nurse [nœʀs(ə)] *nf* nanny, (children's) nurse.

nutrition [nytʀisjɔ̃] *nf* nutrition. ♦ **nutritif, -ive** *adj* (*nourrissant*) nourishing, nutritious; (*Méd*) nutritive. **valeur ~ive** food *ou* nutritional value.

nylon [nilɔ̃] *nm* ® nylon.

nymphe [nɛ̃f] *nf* (*Myth, fig*) nymph.

O

O, o [o] *nm* (*lettre*) O, o.
oasis [ɔazis] *nf* (*lit, fig*) oasis.
obéir [ɔbeiʀ] (2) ~ **à** *vt indir* **(a)** (*gén*) to obey. **il sait se faire** ~ he knows how to make people obey him *ou* how to enforce obedience; ~ **à une impulsion** to act on an impulse. **(b)** *[voilier, moteur, monture]* to respond to. ♦ **obéissance** *nf* obedience (*à* to). ♦ **obéissant, e** *adj* obedient (*à* to).
obélisque [ɔbelisk(ə)] *nm* obelisk (*monument*).
obèse [ɔbɛz] *adj* obese. ♦ **obésité** *nf* obesity.
objecter [ɔbʒɛkte] (1) *vt* **(a)** (*à une suggestion*) ~ **une raison à un argument** to put forward a reason against an argument; **il m'objecta que ...** he objected to me that ...; **je n'ai rien à** ~ I have no objection (to make). **(b)** (*à une demande*) **il objecta la fatigue** he pleaded tiredness; **il m'objecta mon manque d'expérience** he objected that I lacked experience. ♦ **objecteur** *nm*: ~ **de conscience** conscientious objector. ♦ **objection** *nf* objection. **faire une** ~ to raise *ou* make an objection, object.
objectif, -ive [ɔbʒɛktif, iv] **1** *adj* (*gén*) objective. **2** *nm* (*gén*) objective; *[caméra]* lens, objective. **braquer son** ~ **sur** to train one's camera on. ♦ **objectivement** *adv* objectively. ♦ **objectivité** *nf* objectivity.
objet [ɔbʒɛ] *nm* **(a)** (*article*) object, thing. ~**s de première nécessité** basic essentials, essential items *ou* things; ~**s de toilette** toilet requisites *ou* articles; **les** ~**s trouvés** the lost property office. **(b)** *[rêve, désir]* object; *[discussion, litige, science]* subject. **il était l'**~ **de la curiosité des autres** he was an object of curiosity to the others; **faire** *ou* **être l'**~ **de** *discussion, recherches* to be the subject of; *enquête* to be subjected to; *soins* to be given *ou* shown. **(c)** *[visite, démarche]* object, purpose. **votre plainte est sans** ~ your complaint is not applicable. **(d)** (*Ling, Philos*) object.
obligation [ɔbligɑsjɔ̃] *nf* **(a)** (*gén*) obligation. **avoir l'**~ **de faire** to be under an obligation to do; **sans** ~ **d'achat** with no obligation to buy; ~**s** *militaires, scolaires etc* obligations, duties. **(b)** (*Fin*) bond, debenture. ♦ **obligatoire** *adj* compulsory, obligatory. **c'était** ~**!*** it was inevitable!, it was bound to happen! ♦ **obligatoirement** *adv* **(a)** **devoir** ~ **faire** to be strictly obliged to do. **(b)** (*: *sans doute*) inevitably.
obliger [ɔbliʒe] (3) *vt* **(a)** (*forcer*) ~ **qn à faire** *[règlement]* to require sb to do; *[circonstances]* to force *ou* oblige *ou* compel sb to do; **mes principes m'y obligent** I'm bound by my principles (to do it); **je suis obligé de vous laisser** I have to *ou* I must leave you, I'm obliged to leave you; **il est bien obligé** he has no choice *ou* alternative. **(b)** (*rendre service à*) to oblige. **je vous serais très obligé de bien vouloir** I should be greatly obliged if you would kindly; **entre voisins, il faut bien s'**~ we neighbours have to help each other. ♦ **obligé, e** **1** *adj* **(a)** (*redevable*) **être** ~ **à qn** to be obliged *ou* indebted to sb (*de qch* for sth). **(b)** (*: *inévitable*) **c'était** ~**!** it had to happen!, it was bound to happen! **2** *nm,f* **(a)** (*Jur*) debtor. **(b)** **être l'**~ **de qn** to be under an obligation to sb. ♦ **obligeamment** *adv* obligingly. ♦ **obligeance** *nf*: **il a eu l'**~ **de me reconduire** he was obliging *ou* kind enough to take me back. ♦ **obligeant, e** *adj personne* obliging; *offre* kind.
oblique [ɔblik] **1** *adj* (*gén*) oblique. **regard** ~ sidelong glance. **2** *nf* (*Math*) oblique line. ♦ **obliquement** *adv* obliquely. ♦ **obliquer** (1) *vi*: **obliquez avant l'église** turn off before the church.
oblitérer [ɔbliteʀe] (6) *vt timbre* to cancel. ♦ **oblitération** *nf* cancelling, cancellation.
oblong, -ongue [ɔblɔ̃, ɔ̃g] *adj* oblong.
obnubiler [ɔbnybile] (1) *vt* to obsess.
obole [ɔbɔl] *nf* (*contribution*) offering.
obscène [ɔpsɛn] *adj* obscene. ♦ **obscénité** *nf* obscenity.
obscur, e [ɔpskyʀ] *adj* (*lit*) dark; (*fig*) obscure; *pressentiment* vague, dim. **de naissance** ~**e** of obscure *ou* humble birth. ♦ **obscurcir** (2) **1** *vt* to darken; (*fig*) to obscure. **2 s'**~ *vpr [ciel]* to darken, grow dark; *[jour]* to grow dark; *[style]* to become obscure; *[vue]* to grow dim; *[mystère]* to deepen. ♦ **obscurcissement** *nm* darkening; obscuring; dimming. ♦ **obscurément** *adv* obscurely. ♦ **obscurité** *nf* (*lit*) darkness; (*fig*) obscurity. **dans l'**~ in the dark, in darkness; (*fig*) **laisser qch dans l'**~ to throw no light on sth.
obséder [ɔpsede] (6) *vt* to haunt, obsess. **être obsédé par** to be haunted *ou* obsessed by. ♦ **obsédant, e** *adj* haunting, obsessive. ♦ **obsédé, e** *nm,f*: ~ **(sexuel)** sex maniac; (*hum*) **un** ~ **du tennis** a tennis fanatic.
obsèques [ɔpsɛk] *nfpl* funeral.
obséquieux, -euse [ɔpsekjø, øz] *adj* obsequious. ♦ **obséquiosité** *nf* obsequiousness.
observer [ɔpsɛʀve] (1) **1** *vt* **(a)** (*regarder*) to observe; *adversaire* to watch; (*au microscope*) to examine. **(b)** (*contrôler*) ~ **ses gestes** to watch one's gestures. **(c)** (*remarquer*) to notice, observe. **faire** ~ **que** to point out *ou* remark *ou* observe that; **faire** ~ **un détail à qn** to point out a detail to sb. **(d)** (*respecter*) (*gén*) to observe; *jeûne* to keep; *attitude, maintien* to keep (up), maintain. **2 s'**~ *vpr* (*surveiller sa tenue*) to keep a check on o.s., be careful of one's behaviour. ♦ **observance** *nf* observance. ♦ **observateur, -trice** **1** *adj* observant. **2** *nm,f* observer. ♦ **observation** *nf* **(a)** (*obéissance*) observance. **(b)** (*expérience, surveillance*) observation. (*Méd*) **être en** ~ to be under observation. **(c)** (*remarque*) observation, remark; (*objection*) objection; (*reproche*) reproof. **je lui en fis l'**~ I pointed it out to him; **ce film appelle quelques** ~**s** this film calls for some comment; **faire une** ~ **à qn** to reprove sb. ♦ **observatoire** *nm* (*Astron*) observatory; (*gén: lieu*) observation *ou* look-out post.
obsession [ɔpsesjɔ̃] *nf* obsession. **il avait l'**~ **de la mort** he had an obsession with death. ♦ **obsessionnel, -elle** *adj* obsessional.
obstacle [ɔpstakl(ə)] *nm* (*lit, fig*) obstacle; (*Équitation*) jump, fence. **faire** ~ **à** *la lumière* to block, obstruct; *un projet* to hinder.
obstétrique [ɔpstetʀik] *nf* obstetrics (*sg*).
obstination [ɔpstinɑsjɔ̃] *nf* obstinacy, stubbornness. ~ **à faire** obstinate *ou* stubborn determination to do. ♦ **obstiné, e** *adj personne* obstinate, stubborn; *efforts, demandes* persistent, obstinate. ♦ **obstinément** *adv* obstinately, stubbornly; persistently. ♦ **s'obstiner** (1) *vpr* to insist, dig

one's heels in. **s'~ à faire** to persist obstinately *ou* stubbornly in doing; **s'~ au silence** to remain obstinately silent.
obstruer [ɔpstʀye] (1) *vt* to obstruct, block. ♦ **obstruction** *nf* obstruction, blockage; (*tactique*) obstruction. **faire de l'~** to be obstructive.
obtempérer [ɔptɑ̃peʀe] (6) **~ à** *vt indir* to obey.
obtenir [ɔptəniʀ] (22) *vt* **(a)** *permission, diplôme* to obtain, get. **il m'a fait ~ de l'avancement** he got me promoted; **il obtint de lui parler** he was (finally) allowed to speak to him; **elle a obtenu qu'il paie** she got him to pay, she managed to make him pay. **(b)** *résultat* to achieve, obtain; *total* to reach, arrive at. **cette couleur s'obtient par un mélange** this colour is obtained by blending. ♦ **obtention** *nf* obtaining, achievement. **pour l'~ du visa** to obtain the visa.
obturer [ɔptyʀe] (1) *vt* (*gén*) to seal; *dent* to fill. ♦ **obturateur** *nm* (*Phot*) shutter; (*Tech*) obturator. ♦ **obturation** *nf* sealing; filling. (*Phot*) **vitesse d'~** shutter speed.
obtus, e [ɔpty, yz] *adj* (*lit, fig*) obtuse.
obus [ɔby] *nm* shell.
occasion [ɔkɑzjɔ̃] *nf* **(a)** (*circonstance*) occasion; (*conjoncture favorable*) opportunity, chance. **avoir l'~ de faire** to have the chance *ou* opportunity of doing; **à l'~ de** on the occasion of; **la robe des grandes ~s** the dress kept for special *ou* great occasions; **à l'~ venez dîner** come and have dinner some time; **à la première ~** at the first opportunity. **(b)** (*Comm*) secondhand buy; (*: *avantageuse*) bargain. **d'~** (*adj, adv*) secondhand. ♦ **occasionnel, -elle** *adj* (*gén*) occasional; *client* casual; (*fortuit*) chance. ♦ **occasionnellement** *adv* occasionally. ♦ **occasionner** (1) *vt* to cause, bring about. **~ du dérangement à qn** to put sb to *ou* cause sb a lot of trouble.
occident [ɔksidɑ̃] *nm* west. ♦ **occidental, e,** *mpl* **-aux 1** *adj* western. **2** *nm(f)*: **O~(e)** Westerner.
occulte [ɔkylt(ə)] *adj* occult.
occuper [ɔkype] (1) **1** *vt* (*gén*) to occupy; *logement* to live in; *surface, temps* to take up; *poste* to hold; *main d'œuvre* to employ. **leurs bureaux occupent tout l'étage** their offices take up *ou* occupy the whole floor; **ça occupe une trop petite part de mon temps** it takes up *ou* fills *ou* occupies far too little of my time; **comment ~ ses loisirs?** how should one occupy *ou* employ one's free time?; **mon travail m'occupe beaucoup** my work keeps me very busy; **ils ont occupé tout le pays** they took over *ou* occupied the whole country. **2 s'~** *vpr* **(a) s'~ de** (*s'attaquer à*) to deal with, take care of; (*être chargé de*) to be in charge of; (*s'intéresser à*) to take an interest in; *enfant, malade* to look after; *client* to attend to. **je m'occupe de tout** I'll see to everything, I'll take care of everything; **occupe-toi de tes affaires*** mind your own business; **est-ce qu'on s'occupe de vous Madame?** are you being attended to? *ou* served? **(b) s'~ à faire qch/à qch** to busy o.s. doing sth/with sth; **il y a de quoi s'~** there is plenty to do *ou* to keep one busy *ou* occupied. ♦ **occupant, e 1** *adj* (*Mil*) occupying. **2** *nm,f [maison]* occupant, occupier; *[place, voiture]* occupant. **3** *nm*: **l'~** the occupying forces. ♦ **occupation** *nf* (*Mil*) occupation; (*logement*) occupancy, occupation; (*passe-temps*) occupation; (*emploi*) occupation, job. **vaquer à ses ~s** to go about one's business. ♦ **occupé, e** *adj personne* busy; *toilettes, téléphone* engaged; *places* taken, occupied; *zone, usine* occupied.
occurrence [ɔkyʀɑ̃s] *nf* **(a)** instance, case. **en l'~** in this case. **(b)** (*Ling*) occurrence.
océan [ɔseɑ̃] *nm* (*lit*) ocean. **~ de verdure** sea of greenery. ♦ **Océanie** *nf* Oceania. ♦ **océanique** *adj* oceanic.
ocre [ɔkʀ(ə)] *nf, adj inv* ochre.
octane [ɔktan] *nm* octane.
octante [ɔktɑ̃t] *adj inv* (*dialectal*) eighty.
octave [ɔktav] *nf* (*Mus*) octave.
octobre [ɔktɔbʀ(ə)] *nm* October; *V* **septembre.**
octogénaire [ɔktɔʒenɛʀ] *adj, nmf* octogenarian.
octogone [ɔktɔgɔn] *nm* octagon. ♦ **octogonal, e,** *mpl* **-aux** *adj* octagonal, eight-sided.
octroyer [ɔktʀwaje] (8) **1** *vt* to grant (*à* to). **2 s'~** *vpr* to accord *ou* grant o.s. ♦ **octroi** *nm* **(a)** granting. **(b)** (*Hist*) city toll.
oculaire [ɔkylɛʀ] *adj* (*Anat*) ocular. ♦ **oculiste** *nmf* eye specialist, oculist.
ode [ɔd] *nf* ode.
odeur [ɔdœʀ] *nf* (*gén*) smell, odour; (*de fleurs etc*) fragrance, scent. **sans ~** odourless; **mauvaise ~** bad *ou* unpleasant smell *ou* odour; **~ de brûlé** smell of burning; **avoir une bonne/une mauvaise ~** to smell nice/bad; **être/ne pas être en ~ de sainteté** to be in favour/out of favour (*auprès de* with). ♦ **odorant, e** *adj* sweet-smelling. ♦ **odorat** *nm* sense of smell.
odieux, -euse [ɔdjø, øz] *adj* (*gén*) odious; *élève* unbearable; *tâche, conduite* obnoxious; *crime* heinous. **ça m'est ~** I can't bear it. ♦ **odieusement** *adv* odiously; obnoxiously.
odyssée [ɔdise] *nf* odyssey.
œdème [edɛm] *nm* oedema.
œil [œj], *pl* **yeux** [jø] *nm* **(a)** (*Anat*) eye. **aux yeux bleus** blue-eyed; **avoir de bons/mauvais yeux** to have good/bad eyes *ou* eyesight; **à l'~ nu** with the naked eye; **avoir un ~ au beurre noir** to have a black eye. **(b)** (*expression*) look. **il a un ~ malin** there's a mischievous look in his eye; **d'un ~ d'envie** with an envious look. **(c)** (*jugement*) **voir qch d'un bon/mauvais ~** to view sth favourably/unfavourably; **d'un ~ critique** with a critical eye; **il ne voit pas cela du même ~ qu'elle** he doesn't see *ou* view that in the same light as she does. **(d)** (*coup d'œil*) **avoir l'~ du spécialiste** to have a trained eye; **il a l'~** he has sharp eyes; **risquer un ~ au dehors** to take a quick look outside. **(e)** (*regard*) **sous l'~ de** under the eye *ou* gaze of; **faire qch aux yeux de tous** to do sth in full view of everyone; **chercher qn des yeux** to glance *ou* look (a)round for sb; **n'avoir d'yeux que pour qch/qn** to have eyes only for sth/sb. **(f)** *[aiguille, pomme de terre, cyclone]* eye; (*bourgeon*) bud. **les yeux du bouillon** the globules of fat in the stock. **(g)** (*locutions avec* **œil**) **à l'~*** (*gratuitement*) for nothing, for free*; **mon ~!*** (*je n'y crois pas*) my eye!*, my foot!*; (*je ne le donnerai pas*) nothing doing!*, no way!*; **avoir qn à l'~** to keep a watch *ou* an eye on sb; **faire de l'~ à qn** to make eyes at sb, give sb the eye*. **(h)** (*locutions avec* **yeux**) à ses yeux in his eyes; **ouvrir de grands yeux** to look surprised; **coûter les yeux de la tête** to cost the earth; (*lit, fig*) **les yeux fermés** with one's eyes shut; **faire les yeux doux à qn** to make sheep's eyes at sb; **faire des yeux ronds** to stare round-eyed; **avoir les yeux battus** to have rings under one's eyes. ♦ **œillade** *nf* wink. **faire des ~s à qn** to make eyes at sb. ♦ **œillères** *nfpl* (*lit, fig*) blinkers.
œillet [œjɛ] *nm* carnation. **~ d'Inde** French marigold; **~ (mignardise)** pink.
œsophage [ezɔfaʒ] *nm* œsophagus.
œuf [œf], *pl* **~s** [ø] *nm* **(a)** egg. **~ frais** new-laid *ou* fresh egg; **~s brouillés** scrambled eggs; **~ à la coque** (soft-)boiled egg; **~ dur** hard-boiled egg; **~ sur le plat** fried egg; **détruire qch dans l'~** to nip sth in the bud; **mettre tous ses ~s dans le même panier** to put all one's eggs in one basket. **(b)** (*idiot*) blockhead*.
œuvre [œvʀ(ə)] **1** *nf* **(a)** (*livre etc*) work; (*production globale*) works. **~s complètes/choisies** complete/selected works. **(b)** (*travail*) (*à faire*) undertaking, task; (*achevé*) work. **ce beau gâchis est l'~ des enfants** this fine mess is the children's doing *ou* work; **être/se mettre à l'~** to be at/get down to work; **voir qn à l'~** to see sb at work;

mettre en ~ *moyens* to implement; **mise en ~** implementation; **il avait tout mis en ~ pour les aider** he had done everything possible to help them. **(c)** (*acte*) deed, work. **(bonnes) ~s** good *ou* charitable works; **ce sera une bonne ~** that will be a kind act; **faire ~ utile** to do valuable work; **faire ~ de pionnier** to act as a pioneer; **le feu avait fait son ~** the fire had wrought its havoc. **(d)** (*organisation*) **~ (de bienfaisance)** charitable organization, charity. **2** *nm* (*littér*) **l'~ gravé de Picasso** the etchings of Picasso.

offenser [ɔfɑ̃se] (1) **1** *vt personne, souvenir, bon goût* to offend; *règles* to offend against. **2 s'~** *vpr* to take offence (*de qch* at sth). ♦ **offensant, e** *adj* offensive, insulting. ♦ **offense** *nf* (*affront*) insult; (*Rel: péché*) trespass, offence. **~ envers** *chef d'État* libel against; *Dieu* offence against.

offensif, -ive [ɔfɑ̃sif, iv] **1** *adj* (*Mil, Pol*) offensive. **2** *nf* offensive. **passer à l'~ive** to go into the offensive; (*fig*) **l'~ive de l'hiver** the onslaught of winter.

office [ɔfis] **1** *nm* **(a)** (*métier*) office; (*fonction*) function. **l'~ de directeur** the office of manager; **faire ~ de** to act *ou* serve as; **remplir son ~** *[objet]* to fulfil its function; *[fonctionnaire]* to perform one's duties. **(b)** (*bureau*) bureau, agency. **~ de publicité** advertising agency; **~ du tourisme** tourist bureau. **(c)** (*messe*) (church) service. (*prières*) **l'~ (divin)** the divine office. **(d) être nommé d'~** to be appointed automatically. **(e)** (*littér: service*) office. (*Pol*) **bons ~s** good offices. **2** *nm ou f* (*cuisine*) pantry.

officiel, -elle [ɔfisjɛl] **1** *adj* (*gén*) official. **2** *nm,f* official. ♦ **officialiser** (1) *vt* to make official. ♦ **officiellement** *adv* officially.

officier[1] [ɔfisje] *nm* officer. **~ de marine** naval officer; **~ de police** ≃ police officer; **~ ministériel** member of the legal profession; **~ de l'état civil** ≃ registrar.

officier[2] [ɔfisje] (7) *vi* (*Rel, hum*) to officiate.

officieux, -euse [ɔfisjø, øz] *adj* unofficial. ♦ **officieusement** *adv* unofficially.

offrir [ɔfʀiʀ] (18) **1** *vt* **(a)** *cadeau* (*donner*) to give (*à* to); (*acheter*) to buy (*à* for). **c'est pour ~?** is it for a present?; **la joie d'~** the joy of giving. **(b)** *aide, marchandise, choix* to offer; *démission* to tender. **puis-je vous ~ à boire?** can I offer you a drink?; **~ de faire** to offer to do; **~ sa vie à la patrie** to offer up one's life to the homeland. **(c)** *spectacle, avantage* to present, offer; *exemple, explication* to provide; *analogie* to offer, have. **cela n'offre rien de particulier** there is nothing special about that; **~ de la résistance** to offer resistance. **2 s'~** *vpr* **(a)** *[femme]* to offer o.s. (*à* to). **s'~ aux regards** *[personne]* to expose o.s. to the public gaze; *[spectacle]* to present itself to the gaze. **(b)** *repas, vacances* to treat o.s. to; *disque* to buy o.s. **(c) s'~ à faire qch** to offer to do sth. ♦ **offrande** *nf* offering. ♦ **offrant** *nm*: **au plus ~** to the highest bidder. ♦ **offre** *nf* (*gén*) offer; (*aux enchères*) bid. (*Écon*) **l'~ et la demande** supply and demand; (*Presse*) **~s d'emploi** situations vacant column, job ads*; **il y avait plusieurs ~s d'emploi** there were several jobs advertised; **~ publique d'achat** takeover bid; **~s de service** offers of service; **~s de paix** peace overtures.

offusquer [ɔfyske] (1) **1** *vt* to offend. **2 s'~** *vpr* to take offence (*de* at).

ogive [ɔʒiv] *nf* **(a)** (*Archit*) rib. **voûte en ~** rib vault. **(b)** *[fusée etc]* nose cone. **~ nucléaire** nuclear warhead.

ogre, ogresse [ɔgʀ(ə), ɔgʀɛs] *nm,f* ogre, ogress. **manger comme un ~** to eat like a horse.

oie [wa] *nf* (*Zool*) goose; (*péj*) silly goose.

oignon [ɔɲɔ̃] *nm* (*légume*) onion; *[tulipe etc]* bulb; (*Méd*) bunion. **petits ~s** pickling onions; **ce n'est pas mes ~s!** it's no business of mine.

oiseau, *pl* **~x** [wazo] *nm* bird. **~ de mauvais augure** bird of ill omen; **~-mouche** *nm, pl* **~x-~s** hummingbird; **~ de paradis** bird of paradise; **~ de proie** bird of prey; **trouver l'~ rare** to find the man (*ou* woman) in a million; **drôle d'~*** queer fish* *ou* customer*. ♦ **oiseleur** *nm* bird-catcher. ♦ **oiselier, -ière** *nm,f* bird-seller. ♦ **oisellerie** *nf* (*magasin*) birdshop; (*commerce*) bird-selling.

oiseux, -euse [wazø, øz] *adj propos* pointless; *question* trivial, trifling.

oisif, -ive [wazif, iv] **1** *adj* idle. **2** *nm,f* man (*ou* woman) of leisure. ♦ **oisiveté** *nf* idleness. **~ forcée** forced inactivity.

oléagineux, -euse [ɔleaʒinø, øz] **1** *adj* oleaginous. **2** *nm* oleaginous plant.

oléoduc [ɔleɔdyk] *nm* oil pipeline.

olive [ɔliv] **1** *nf* olive. **2** *adj inv* olive(-green). ♦ **olivâtre** *adj* (*gén*) olive-greenish; *teint* sallow. ♦ **oliveraie** *nf* olive grove. ♦ **olivier** *nm* (*arbre*) olive tree; (*bois*) olive(-wood).

olympique [ɔlɛ̃pik] *adj* Olympic. ♦ **olympiade** *nf* Olympiad.

ombrage [ɔ̃bʀaʒ] *nm* **(a)** (*ombre*) shade. **(b) prendre ~ de qch** to take umbrage *ou* offence at sth. ♦ **ombragé, e** *adj* shaded, shady. ♦ **ombrager** (3) *vt* to shade. ♦ **ombrageux, -euse** *adj personne* touchy, easily offended; *cheval* skittish, nervous.

ombre [ɔ̃bʀ(ə)] *nf* **(a)** shade; (*ombre portée*) shadow; (*obscurité*) darkness. **25° à l'~** 25° in the shade; **tu me fais de l'~** you're in my light; **places sans ~/pleines d'~** shadeless/shady squares. **(b)** (*forme vague*) shadow, shadowy figure; (*fantôme*) shade. **(c)** (*fig*) (*anonymat*) obscurity; (*secret, incertitude*) dark. **laisser dans l'~** to leave in the dark; **rester dans l'~** *[artiste]* to remain in obscurity; *[meneur]* to keep in the background; *[détail]* to be still obscure. **(d)** (*soupçon*) **une ~ de moustache** a hint *ou* suspicion of a moustache; **il n'y a pas l'~ d'un doute** there's not the shadow of a doubt; **pas l'~ d'une chance** not the ghost of a chance. **(e)** (*locutions*) **jeter une ~ sur qch** to cast a gloom over sth; **mettre qn à l'~*** to put sb behind bars, lock sb up; **il y a une ~ au tableau** there's a fly in the ointment; **n'être plus que l'~ de soi-même** to be the mere shadow of one's former self; **~s chinoises** (*improvisées*) shadowgraph; (*spectacle*) shadow show. ♦ **ombrelle** *nf* parasol, sunshade. ♦ **ombreux, -euse** *adj* shady.

omelette [ɔmlɛt] *nf* omelette.

omettre [ɔmɛtʀ(ə)] (56) *vt* to leave out, miss out, omit. **~ de faire qch** to fail *ou* omit to do sth. ♦ **omission** *nf* (*action*) omission; (*chose oubliée*) omission, oversight.

omnibus [ɔmnibys] *nm* slow *ou* stopping train; (*Hist: bus*) omnibus.

omnipotence [ɔmnipɔtɑ̃s] *nf* omnipotence. ♦ **omnipotent, e** *adj* omnipotent.

omniprésent,e [ɔmnipʀezɑ̃, ɑ̃t] *adj* omnipresent.

omniscient, e [ɔmnisjɑ̃, ɑ̃t] *adj* omniscient.

omnivore [ɔmnivɔʀ] *adj* omnivorous.

omoplate [ɔmɔplat] *nf* shoulder blade.

on [ɔ̃] *pron* **(a)** (*indétermination*) **~ l'interrogea** he was questioned; **~ va encore augmenter l'essence** petrol is going up again; **~ prétend que** they say that, it is said that; **~ se précipita sur les places vides** there was a rush for the empty seats. **(b)** (*quelqu'un*) someone. **~ frappa à la porte** there was a knock at the door; **est-ce qu'~ est venu réparer la porte?** has anyone *ou* someone been to repair the door?; **~ peut très bien aimer la pluie** some people may well like the rain. **(c)** (*celui qui parle*) you, one, we. **~ aimerait être sûr que ...** one *ou* we would like to be sure that ...; **~ a trop chaud ici** it's too hot here; **~ ne pense jamais à tout** one *ou* you can't think of everything. **(d)** (*éloignement*) they, people. **en Chine ~ mange avec des baguettes** in China they eat with chopsticks. **(e)** (*: *nous*) we. **~ a décidé tous les trois**

de partir the three of us decided to leave; ~ **a amené notre chien** we've brought along the dog; (*hum*) ~ **ne dit plus bonjour?** don't we say hullo any more? **(f)** (*intensif*) **c'est** ~ **ne peut plus beau** it couldn't be lovelier.

once [ɔ̃s] *nf* ounce.

oncle [ɔ̃kl(ə)] *nm* uncle.

onctueux, -euse [ɔ̃ktɥø, øz] *adj* (*lit*) creamy; (*fig*) unctuous, smooth. ♦ **onctueusement** *adv* unctuously. ♦ **onctuosité** *nf* unctuousness, smoothness; creaminess.

onde [ɔ̃d] *nf* **(a)** (*gén, Phys*) wave. **petites** ~**s**, ~**s moyennes** medium waves; ~**s courtes** short waves; **sur les** ~**s et dans la presse** on the radio and in the press; **il passe sur les** ~**s demain** he's on the air tomorrow; **mettre en** ~s to produce for the radio. **(b)** (*littér: lac, mer*) **l'**~ the waters.

ondée [ɔ̃de] *nf* shower (*of rain*).

on-dit [ɔ̃di] *nm inv* rumour. **ce ne sont que des** ~ it's only hearsay.

onduler [ɔ̃dyle] (1) *vi* (*gén*) to undulate; *[drapeau]* to ripple, wave; *[route]* to snake up and down; *[cheveux]* to be wavy. ♦ **ondulation** *nf* undulation. *[cheveux]* ~s waves. ♦ **onduleux, -euse** *adj ligne* wavy; *plaine* undulating; *démarche* swaying, supple.

onéreux, -euse [ɔneʀø, øz] *adj* costly.

ongle [ɔ̃gl(ə)] *nm [personne]* (finger)nail; *[animal]* claw. ~ **de pied** toenail; **se faire les** ~s to cut (*ou* file) one's nails.

onomatopée [ɔnɔmatɔpe] *nf* onomatopoeia.

onyx [ɔniks] *nm* onyx.

onze [ɔ̃z] *adj, nm inv* eleven. **le** ~ **novembre** Armistice Day; **le** ~ **de France** the French eleven *ou* team; *V* **six**. ♦ **onzième** *adj, nmf* eleventh. ♦ **onzièmement** *adv* in the eleventh place.

opale [ɔpal] *nf* opal.

opaque [ɔpak] *adj verre, corps* opaque (*à* to); *brouillard, nuit* impenetrable. ♦ **opacité** *nf* opaqueness; impenetrableness.

opéra [ɔpeʀa] *nm* (*œuvre*) opera; (*édifice*) opera house. ~ **bouffe** opera bouffe, comic opera; ~**-comique** light opera, opéra comique. ♦ **opérette** *nf* operetta, light opera.

opercule [ɔpɛʀkyl] *nm* protective cap.

opérer [ɔpeʀe] (6) **1** *vt* **(a)** *malade, organe* to operate on (*de* for); *tumeur* to remove. **se faire** ~ **des amygdales** to have one's tonsils removed *ou* out*. **(b)** *transformation, réforme* to carry out, implement; *choix, redressement* to make. ~ **des miracles** to work wonders; **ça a opéré un changement** it brought about a change; **un changement s'était opéré** a change had taken place *ou* had occurred. **2** *vi [remède]* to work, take effect; *[technicien etc]* to proceed. **comment faut-il** ~? what's the procedure? (*pour* for). ♦ **opérable** *adj* operable. ♦ **opérateur, -trice** *nm,f* (*sur machine*) operator; (*Ciné*) cameraman. ♦ **opération** *nf* **(a)** (*gén, Math, Méd, Mil*) operation. **salle d'**~ operating theatre. **(b)** (*Comm*) deal. ~ **financière** financial deal; ~**s de bourse** stock exchange dealings. **(c)** (*Tech, gén*) process, operation. (*iro*) **par l'**~ **du Saint-Esprit** by magic. ♦ **opérationnel, -elle** *adj* operational. ♦ **opératoire** *adj* (*Méd*) operating. ♦ **opéré, e** *nm,f* (*Méd*) patient.

ophtalmologie [ɔftalmɔlɔʒi] *nf* ophthalmology. ♦ **ophtalmologique** *adj* ophthalmological. ♦ **ophtalmologiste** *nmf* ophthalmologist.

opiner [ɔpine] (1) *vi*: ~ **de la tête** to nod one's agreement, nod assent.

opiniâtre [ɔpinjɑtʀ(ə)] *adj personne* stubborn, obstinate; *efforts, haine* unrelenting. ♦ **opiniâtrement** *adv* stubbornly, obstinately; unrelentingly. ♦ **opiniâtreté** *nf* stubbornness, obstinacy; unrelentingness.

opinion [ɔpinjɔ̃] *nf* (*gén*) opinion (*sur* on, about). **j'ai la même** ~ I am of *ou* I hold the same opinion *ou* view; **l'**~ **française** French public opinion.

opium [ɔpjɔm] *nm* opium.

opportun, e [ɔpɔʀtœ̃, yn] *adj* timely, opportune. **il serait** ~ **de faire** it would be appropriate *ou* advisable to do; **en temps** ~ at the appropriate *ou* right time. ♦ **opportunément** *adv* opportunely. ♦ **opportunisme** *nm* opportunism. ♦ **opportuniste** *adj, nmf* opportunist. ♦ **opportunité** *nf* timeliness, opportuneness; appropriateness.

opposer [ɔpoze] (1) **1** *vt* **(a)** *équipes* to bring together; *rivaux* to bring into conflict (*à* with); *idées, couleurs* to contrast (*à* with). **ce qui nous oppose** what divides us. **(b)** *arguments* to put forward; *résistance* to put up. ~ **son refus/des protestations** to refuse/protest; ~ **une armée à qn** to set an army against sb; **il nous opposa que cela coûtait cher** he objected that it was expensive. **2 s'**~ *vpr* **(a)** *[équipes]* to confront each other, meet; *[rivaux]* to clash; *[théories]* to conflict; *[styles]* to contrast (*à* with). **haut s'oppose à bas** high is the opposite of low. **(b) s'**~ **à** *parents* to rebel against; *mesure, progrès* to oppose; **rien ne s'oppose à leur bonheur** nothing stands in the way of their happiness; **je m'oppose à ce que vous y alliez** I am opposed to *ou* I am against your going there; **ma conscience s'y oppose** it goes against my conscience. ♦ **opposant, e** *nm,f* opponent (*à* of). ♦ **opposé, e 1** *adj* **(a)** *rive, direction* opposite; *équipe* opposing. **la maison** ~**e à la nôtre** the house opposite *ou* facing ours; **l'équipe** ~**e à la nôtre** the team playing against ours. **(b)** *intérêts, opinions* conflicting; *caractères* opposite; *forces* opposing; *couleurs, styles* contrasting. **ils sont d'un avis** ~ (*au nôtre*) they are of the opposite opinion; (*l'un à l'autre*) they are of conflicting opinions; ~ **à** opposed to, against. **2** *nm* **(a)** (*contraire*) **l'**~ the opposite, the reverse (*de* of); **à l'**~ **de Paul, je pense que ...** contrary to *ou* unlike Paul, I think that ... . **(b) à l'**~ (*dans l'autre direction*) the other *ou* opposite way (*de* from); (*de l'autre côté*) on the other *ou* opposite side (*de* from). ♦ **opposition** *nf* **(a)** (*résistance*) opposition (*à* to). (*Pol*) **l'O**~ the Opposition. **(b)** (*conflit*) (*gén*) opposition; *[idées, intérêts]* conflict; *[styles, caractères]* contrast. **mettre en** ~ to oppose, contrast; **ceci est en** ~ **avec les faits** this conflicts with the facts; **mettre** ~ **à** *décision* to oppose; *chèque* to stop; **par** ~ **à** as opposed to, in contrast with.

oppresser [ɔpʀese] (1) *vt* (*gén*) to oppress; *[vêtement serré]* to suffocate; *[remords]* to weigh down. **avoir une respiration oppressée** to have difficulty with one's breathing. ♦ **oppressant, e** *adj* oppressive. ♦ **oppresseur** *nm* oppressor. ♦ **oppressif, -ive** *adj* oppressive. ♦ **oppression** *nf* (*asservissement*) oppression; (*gêne*) feeling of suffocation *ou* oppression.

opprimer [ɔpʀime] (1) *vt* **(a)** *peuple* to oppress; *opinion* to suppress, stifle. **(b)** *[chaleur etc]* to suffocate, oppress.

opprobre [ɔpʀɔbʀ(ə)] *nm* (*littér*) opprobrium, shame.

opter [ɔpte] (1) *vi*: ~ **pour** to opt for, decide upon; ~ **entre** to choose *ou* decide between.

opticien, -ienne [ɔptisjɛ̃, jɛn] *nm,f* optician.

optimisme [ɔptimism(ə)] *nm* optimism. ♦ **optimiste 1** *adj* optimistic. **2** *nmf* optimist.

optimum, *pl* ~**s** *ou* **optima** [ɔptimɔm, a] **1** *nm* optimum. **2** *adj* optimum, optimal. ♦ **optimal, e,** *mpl* **-aux** *adj* optimal, optimum.

option [ɔpsjɔ̃] *nf* (*gén*) option. **matière à** ~ optional subject.

optique [ɔptik] **1** *adj verre* optical; *nerf* optic. **2** *nf* **(a)** (*science, appareils*) optics (*sg*). **instrument d'** ~ optical instrument. **(b)** (*perspective*) perspective. **voir qch avec une certaine** ~ to look at sth from a certain angle *ou* viewpoint.

opulent, e [ɔpylɑ̃, ɑ̃t] *adj pays, prairie* rich; *personne* wealthy, rich; *luxe, vie* opulent.

♦ **opulence** *nf* richness; wealthiness; opulence.
opuscule [ɔpyskyl] *nm* opuscule.
or[1] [ɔʀ] *nm* **(a)** (*métal*) gold. **~ noir** black gold; **blés/cheveux d'~** golden cornfields/hair; **en lettres d'~** in gilt *ou* gold lettering; **étalon ~** gold standard. **(b) en ~** *objet* gold; *occasion* golden; *mari, sujet* marvellous, wonderful; **c'est une affaire en ~** (*achat*) it's a real bargain; (*commerce, magasin*) it's a gold mine; **pour tout l'~ du monde** for all the money in the world; **faire des affaires d'~** to run a gold mine.
or[2] [ɔʀ] *conj* (*transition*) now; (*pourtant*) but, yet.
oracle [ɔʀɑkl(ə)] *nm* (*gén*) oracle.
orage [ɔʀaʒ] *nm* (*tempête*) (thunder)storm; (*dispute*) row, upset. **pluie d'~** thundery *ou* stormy shower; **les ~s de la vie** the turmoils of life; (*lit, fig*) **il y a de l'~ dans l'air** there is a storm brewing. ♦ **orageux, -euse** *adj ciel, vie, séance* stormy; *pluie, temps* thundery.
oraison [ɔʀɛzɔ̃] *nf* orison, prayer. **~ funèbre** funeral oration.
oral, e, mpl -aux [ɔʀal, o] *adj, nm* (*gén, Scol*) oral. ♦ **oralement** *adv* orally.
orange [ɔʀɑ̃ʒ] **1** *adj inv, nm* (*couleur*) orange. **2** *nf* (*fruit*) orange. **~ sanguine** blood orange. ♦ **orangé, e** *adj* orangey. ♦ **orangeade** *nf* orangeade. ♦ **oranger** *nm* orange tree. ♦ **orangeraie** *nf* orange grove. ♦ **orangerie** *nf* (*serre*) orangery.
orang-outan(g), *pl* **~s-~s** [ɔʀɑ̃utɑ̃] *nm* orang-outang.
orateur, -trice [ɔʀatœʀ, tʀis] *nm,f* (*gén*) speaker. **être bon ~** to be a good speaker *ou* orator. ♦ **oratoire 1** *adj* oratorical. **2** *nm* (*chapelle*) oratory.
oratorio [ɔʀatɔʀjo] *nm* oratorio.
orbite [ɔʀbit] *nf* (*Anat*) (eye-)socket; (*Astron, Phys*) orbit; (*zone d'influence*) sphere of influence. **mettre sur ~** *satellite* to put into orbit; *projet* to launch; **être sur ~** to be in orbit. ♦ **orbital, e, mpl -aux** *adj* orbital.
orchestre [ɔʀkɛstʀ(ə)] *nm* **(a)** (*musiciens*) orchestra; *[jazz, danse]* band. **(b)** (*Ciné, Théât: emplacement*) stalls, orchestra (*US*). ♦ **orchestral, e, mpl -aux** *adj* orchestral. ♦ **orchestration** *nf* orchestration; organization. ♦ **orchestrer** (1) *vt* (*Mus*) to orchestrate; *propagande* to organize.
orchidée [ɔʀkide] *nf* orchid.
ordinaire [ɔʀdinɛʀ] **1** *adj* **(a)** (*habituel*) ordinary, usual; *session* ordinary. **peu ~** *fait* unusual; (*) *audace* incredible. **(b)** *vin* ordinary; *service de table* everyday; *qualité* standard; (*péj: commun*) common. **2** *nm*: **l'~** (*banalité*) the ordinary; (*nourriture*) the food; **qui sort de l'~** which is out of the ordinary; **comme à l'~** as usual; **d'~** usually, as a rule; **plus que d'~** more than usual. ♦ **ordinairement** *adv* usually, as a rule.
ordinal, e, mpl -aux [ɔʀdinal, o] **1** *adj* ordinal. **2** *nm* ordinal number.
ordinateur [ɔʀdinatœʀ] *nm* computer. **mettre sur ~** to computerize; **mise sur ~** computerization.
ordonnance [ɔʀdɔnɑ̃s] *nf* **(a)** (*Méd*) prescription. **(b)** (*Jur: arrêté*) order. **(c)** *[phrase, tableau]* organization, layout; *[bâtiment]* plan, layout; *[cérémonie]* organization. **(d)** (*Mil: domestique*) batman.
ordonner [ɔʀdɔne] (1) **1** *vt* **(a)** *idées, éléments, discours* to organize. **(b)** *traitement* to prescribe; *huis-clos* to order. **~ que** to order that; **il nous ordonna le silence** he ordered us to be quiet. **(c)** (*Rel*) *prêtre* to ordain. **2 s'~** *vpr [idées, faits]* to organize themselves. ♦ **ordonné, e 1** *adj maison, enfant* tidy, orderly; *employé* methodical; *vie* well-ordered. **2** *nf* (*Math*) ordinate.
ordre [ɔʀdʀ(ə)] *nm* **(a)** (*succession*) order. **par ~ alphabétique** in alphabetical order; (*Mil*) **en ~ de marche** in marching order. **(b)** (*Archit, Bio: catégorie*) order. **(c)** (*nature*) **dans le même ~ d'idées** similarly; **dans un autre ~ d'idées** in a different connection; **motifs d'~ personnel** reasons of a personal nature; **c'est dans l'~ des choses** it's in the nature of things; **du même ~** of the same nature *ou* order; **un chiffre de l'~ de 2 millions** a figure of the order of 2 million; **donnez-nous un ~ de grandeur** give us a rough estimate *ou* a rough idea; **de premier ~** first-rate; **de dernier ~** third-rate. **(d)** (*organisation*) **l'~** order; **l'~ public** law and order; **rentrer dans l'~** to be back in order. **(e)** *[personne, chambre]* tidiness, orderliness. **sans ~** untidy, disorderly; **avoir de l'~** (*rangements*) to be tidy *ou* orderly; (*travail*) to be methodical; **en ~** *maison* tidy, orderly; *comptes* in order; **mettre en ~** to tidy up; **mettre bon ~ à qch** to put sth to rights, sort out sth. **(f)** (*état*) **en ~ de marche** in working order. **(g)** (*association*) order. (*Rel*) **entrer dans les ~s** to take (holy) orders; **l'~ des médecins** ≈ the Medical Association; **l'~ des avocats** = the Bar. **(h)** (*commandement*) (*gén, Fin*) order; (*Mil*) order, command. **~ de mission** orders (*for a mission*); (*Mil*) **~ de route** marching orders; **par ~ du ministre** by order of the minister; **j'ai reçu des ~s formels** I have formal instructions; **être aux ~s de qn** to be at sb's disposal; (*formule de politesse*) **je suis à vos ~s** I am at your service; (*Mil*) **à vos ~s!** yes sir!; **combattre sous les ~s de qn** to fight under sb's command; **payable à l'~ de** payable to the order of. **(i) l'~ du jour** (*Mil*) the order of the day; (*programme*) the agenda; **cité à l'~ du jour** mentioned in dispatches; **être à l'~ du jour** (*lit*) to be on the agenda; (*d'actualité*) to be topical.
ordure [ɔʀdyʀ] *nf* (*saleté*) (*lit*) dirt, filth; (*fig*) filth; (*péj: personne*) swine‡. **~s** (*saleté*) dirt; (*grossièretés*) obscenities, filth; (*détritus*) rubbish, refuse, garbage (*US*); **jeter qch aux ~s** to throw sth into the dustbin *ou* garbage can (*US*); **écrire des ~s** to write filth. ♦ **ordurier, -ière** *adj* lewd, filthy.
orée [ɔʀe] *nf [bois]* edge.
oreille [ɔʀɛj] *nf* **(a)** (*Anat*) ear. **les ~s ont dû lui tinter** his ears must have been burning; **écouter de toutes ses ~s** to be all ears; **venir aux ~s de qn** to come to sb's attention; **dire qch à qn dans le creux de l'~** to have a word in sb's ear about sth; **n'écouter que d'une ~** to listen with only one ear; **avoir les ~s rebattues de qch** to have heard enough of sth, be sick of hearing sth; **tirer les ~s à qn** (*lit*) to tweak sb's ears; (*fig*) to tell sb off*; **se faire tirer l'~** to need a lot of persuading; **ouvre tes ~s** listen to what you are told; **l'~ basse** crestfallen. **(b)** (*ouïe*) hearing, ear. **avoir l'~ fine** to be sharp of hearing, have a sharp ear; **avoir de l'~** to have a good ear (for music). ♦ **oreiller** *nm* pillow. ♦ **oreillons** *nmpl*: **les ~** (the) mumps.
orfèvre [ɔʀfɛvʀ(ə)] *nm* silversmith, goldsmith. **être ~ en la matière** to be an expert on the subject. ♦ **orfèvrerie** *nf* (*commerce*) silversmith's *ou* goldsmith's trade; (*magasin*) silversmith's *ou* goldsmith's shop; (*ouvrage*) (silver) plate, (gold) plate.
organe [ɔʀgan] *nm* (*gén, Anat*) organ; (*porte-parole*) spokesman; (*littér: voix*) voice. **~s de commande** controls; **~s de transmission** transmission system.
organigramme [ɔʀganigʀam] *nm* (*hiérarchie*) organization chart; (*procédure*) flow chart.
organique [ɔʀganik] *adj* (*Chim, Jur, Méd*) organic.
organiser [ɔʀganize] (1) **1** *vt* (*gén*) to organize, arrange. **2 s'~** *vpr* to organize o.s. (*ou* itself), get (o.s. *ou* itself) organized. ♦ **organisateur, -trice 1** *adj* organizing. **2** *nm,f* organizer. ♦ **organisation** *nf* **(a)** (*action*) organization, arranging; (*résultat*) organization, arrangement. **(b)** (*parti, syndicat*) organization.

organisme [ɔʀganism(ə)] *nm* (*organes, bureaux*) body, organism; (*Zool: individu*) organism.

organiste [ɔʀganist(ə)] *nmf* organist.

orgasme [ɔʀgasm(ə)] *nm* orgasm, climax.

orge [ɔʀʒ(ə)] *nf* barley.

orgie [ɔʀʒi] *nf* orgy. **une ~ de** a profusion of.

orgue [ɔʀg(ə)] *nm* organ. **~ de Barbarie** barrel organ, hurdy-gurdy.

orgueil [ɔʀgœj] *nm* pride. **tirer ~ de qch** to take pride in sth, pride o.s. on sth; **mettre son ~ à faire qch** to take a pride in doing sth. ♦ **orgueilleusement** *adv* proudly. ♦ **orgueilleux, -euse** *adj* proud.

orgues [ɔʀg(ə)] *nfpl* organ. **les grandes ~** the great organs.

orient [ɔʀjɑ̃] *nm* (*littér: est*) orient. **l'O~** the East, the Orient (*littér*). ♦ **oriental, e** *mpl* **-aux 1** *adj* *région* eastern; *langue, produits* oriental. **2** *nm*: **O~** Oriental. **3** *nf*: **O~e** Oriental woman.

orienter [ɔʀjɑ̃te] (1) **1** *vt* **(a)** *objet* to position, adjust. **~ une maison vers le sud** to build a house facing south; **~ une antenne vers le nord** to turn *ou* direct an aerial towards the north; **maison bien orientée** well-positioned house, house with a good aspect. **(b)** *élèves* to orientate; *voyageurs, recherches* to direct (*vers* towards). **~ la conversation vers un sujet** to turn the conversation onto a subject. **(c)** (*marquer*) *carte* to orientate; (*Math*) *droite* to orient. **2 s'~** *vpr [voyageur]* to find one's bearings. **s'~ vers** (*lit, fig*) to turn towards; *[société]* to move towards. ♦ **orientable** *adj* *antenne* adjustable. ♦ **orientation** *nf* **(a)** (*action*) positioning, adjustment; directing; orientation. **l'~ professionnelle** careers advising; **conseiller d'~** careers adviser. **(b)** (*position*) *[maison]* aspect; *[antenne]* direction. **l'~ du jardin au sud** the garden's southern aspect. **(c)** (*tendance*) *[recherches]* direction, orientation; *[science]* trends; *[magazine]* leanings, (political) tendencies. **quelle ~ va-t-il choisir?** *[parti]* which line will they move towards?; *[élève]* which direction will he take? ♦ **orienté, e** *adj* (*partial*) *article* slanted.

orifice [ɔʀifis] *nm* (*gén*) opening; *[tuyau]* mouth; *[organe]* orifice.

originaire [ɔʀiʒinɛʀ] *adj* **(a) ~ de** *plante, mets* native to; **il est ~ de** he is a native of, he was born in. **(b)** *propriétaire* original; *vice* innate. ♦ **originairement** *adv* originally, at first.

original, e, *mpl* **-aux** [ɔʀiʒinal, o] **1** *adj* original; (*péj: bizarre*) eccentric, odd. **2** *nm,f* eccentric. **3** *nm* (*tableau*) original; (*document*) original (copy); (*texte dactylographié*) top copy. ♦ **originalement** *adv* originally. ♦ **originalité** *nf* **(a)** originality; eccentricity, oddness. **(b)** (*caractéristique*) original aspect *ou* feature. (*conduite*) **~(s)** eccentric behaviour.

origine [ɔʀiʒin] *nf* (*gén*) origin. **avoir son ~ dans** to have one's origins in, originate in; **d'~** *pays* of origin; *pneus* original; **d'~ française** of French origin *ou* extraction; **coutume d'~ ancienne** long-standing custom, custom of long standing; **à l'~** originally, to begin with; **dès l'~** at *ou* from the outset *ou* the very beginning; **à l'~ de** at the origin of. ♦ **originel, -elle** *adj* original. ♦ **originellement** *adv* (*primitivement*) originally; (*dès le début*) from the outset.

oripeaux [ɔʀipo] *nmpl* rags.

orme [ɔʀm(ə)] *nm* elm.

orner [ɔʀne] (1) *vt* **(a)** *chambre, vêtement* to decorate; *discours* to embellish (*de* with). **robe ornée d'un galon** dress trimmed with braid. **(b)** *[statue, bibelot]* to adorn, decorate. ♦ **orné, e** *adj* *style* ornate, florid. ♦ **ornement** *nm* (*gén*) ornament; (*Archit, Art*) embellishment, adornment. **sans ~(s)** *toilette, style* plain, unadorned; **d'~** *arbre, jardin* ornamental. ♦ **ornemental, e,** *mpl* **-aux** *adj* *plante* ornamental; *motif* decorative. ♦ **ornementation** *nf* ornamentation.

ornière [ɔʀnjɛʀ] *nf* (*lit*) rut. (*fig*) **il est sorti de l'~ maintenant** he's out of the wood now.

ornithologie [ɔʀnitɔlɔʒi] *nf* ornithology. ♦ **ornithologique** *adj* ornithological. ♦ **ornithologiste** *nmf ou* ♦ **ornithologue** *nmf* ornithologist.

orphelin, e [ɔʀfəlɛ̃, in] **1** *adj* orphan(ed). **2** *nm,f* orphan. **être ~ de père** to be fatherless, have lost one's father. ♦ **orphelinat** *nm* (*lieu*) orphanage; (*orphelins*) children of the orphanage.

orteil [ɔʀtɛj] *nm* toe. **gros ~** big toe.

orthodoxe [ɔʀtɔdɔks(ə)] **1** *adj* (*Rel, gén*) orthodox. **2** *nmf* orthodox. ♦ **orthodoxie** *nf* orthodoxy.

orthographe [ɔʀtɔgʀaf] *nf* (*gén*) spelling; (*système*) spelling (system). ♦ **orthographier** (7) *vt* to spell (*in writing*). ♦ **orthographique** *adj* spelling, orthographical.

orthopédie [ɔʀtɔpedi] *nf* orthopaedics (*sg*). ♦ **orthopédique** *adj* orthopaedic. ♦ **orthopédiste** *nmf* orthopaedist.

ortie [ɔʀti] *nf* (stinging) nettle. **~ blanche** white dead-nettle.

os [ɔs] *nm* bone. **~ de seiche** cuttle-bone; **viande sans ~** boned meat; **à manche en ~** bone-handled; **trempé jusqu'aux ~** soaked to the skin, wet through; **il y a un ~*** there's a snag *ou* hitch; **tomber sur un ~*** to come across *ou* hit* a snag.

oscar [ɔskaʀ] *nm* (*Ciné*) Oscar; (*gén*) prize (*de* for).

osciller [ɔsile] (1) *vi* (*Sci*) to oscillate; *[pendule]* to swing; *[tête, navire]* to rock. **le vent fit ~ la flamme** the wind made the flame flicker; (*fig*) **~ entre** *[personne]* to waver between; *[prix]* to fluctuate between. ♦ **oscillation** *nf* oscillation; fluctuation. ♦ **oscillatoire** *adj* oscillatory.

oseille [ozɛj] *nf* (*Bot*) sorrel; (*‡: argent*) dough‡.

oser [oze] (1) *vt* to dare. **il faut ~** one must take risks; **il n'osait (pas) bouger** he did not dare (to) move; **je n'ose pas** I dare not; **si j'ose dire** if I may say so; **j'ose l'espérer** I like to hope so. ♦ **osé, e** *adj* *tentative, toilette* bold, daring; *sujet* risqué, daring.

osier [ozje] *nm* (*Bot*) willow; (*fibres*) wicker. **corbeille en ~** wicker(work) basket.

ossature [ɔsatyʀ] *nf [corps]* frame, bone structure; *[machine, discours]* framework. ♦ **osselets** *nmpl* knucklebones. ♦ **ossements** *nmpl* (*squelettes*) bones. ♦ **osseux, -euse** *adj* (*Anat, Méd*) bone; (*maigre*) bony.

ostensible [ɔstɑ̃sibl(ə)] *adj* conspicuous. ♦ **ostensiblement** *adv* conspicuously.

ostentation [ɔstɑ̃tɑsjɔ̃] *nf* ostentation. **avec ~** ostentatiously; **faire qch sans ~** to do sth unostentatiously. ♦ **ostentatoire** *adj* ostentatious.

ostraciser [ɔstʀasize] (1) *vt* to ostracize. ♦ **ostracisme** *nm* ostracism.

otage [ɔtaʒ] *nm* hostage.

otarie [ɔtaʀi] *nf* sea-lion.

ôter [ote] (1) **1** *vt* **(a)** (*gén*) to remove (*de* from); *ornement, scrupules, somme* to take away; *vêtement* to take off; *arêtes, tache* to take out (*de* of). **ôte les assiettes** clear the dishes; **ôte tes mains de la porte!** take your hands off the door! **(b)** (*prendre*) **~ qch à qn** (*lit*) to take sth (away) from sb; **~ à qn ses forces** to deprive sb of his strength; **~ à qn toute envie de faire** to rid sb of any desire to do; **on ne m'ôtera pas de l'idée que ...** I can't get it out of my mind *ou* head that ... . **2 s'~** *vpr*: **ôtez-vous de là!** move yourself!, get out of there!

otite [ɔtit] *nf* ear infection.

oto-rhino(-laryngologie) [ɔtɔʀinɔlaʀɛ̃gɔlɔʒi] *nf* otorhinolaryngology. ♦ **oto-rhino(-laryngologiste)** *nmf* ear, nose and throat specialist.

ou [u] *conj* or. **aujourd'hui ~ demain** (either) today or tomorrow; **avec ~ sans sucre?** with or without sugar?; **que vous le vouliez ~ non** whether you like it or not; ~ **pour mieux dire** or rather; ~ **il est malade** ~ **(bien) il est fou** he's either sick or mad, either he's sick or (else) he's mad.

où [u] **1** *pron* **(a)** (*lit*) where. **la ville** ~ **j'habite** the town I live in *ou* where I live; **le mur** ~ **il est appuyé** the wall he's leaning against; **le livre** ~ **il a copié ceci** the book from which he copied this; **le village par** ~ **il est passé** the village he went through. **(b)** (*abstrait*) **la famille d'**~ **il sort** the family he comes from; **dans l'état** ~ **il est** in the state he is in; **la mélancolie** ~ **il se complaît** the melancholy in which he wallows; **au prix** ~ **c'est** at the price it is. **(c)** (*temporel*) when. **le jour** ~ **je l'ai rencontré** the day (when *ou* on which) I met him; **à l'instant** ~ **il est arrivé** the moment he arrived. **2** *adv rel* where. **s'établir** ~ **l'on veut** to settle where one likes; ~ **que l'on aille** wherever one goes; **savoir** ~ **s'arrêter** to know where *ou* when to stop; **d'**~ **l'on peut conclure que ...** from which one may conclude that ... ; **d'**~ **son silence** hence his silence. **3** *adv interrog* where. ~ **es-tu?** where are you?; **par** ~ **y aller?** which way should we go?; **d'**~ **vient cette attitude?** what's the reason for this attitude?; ~ **voulez-vous en venir?** what are you getting at?

ouailles [waj] *nfpl* (*Rel, hum*) flock.

ouate [wat] *nf* (*pour pansement*) cotton wool; (*pour rembourrage*) padding. ♦ **ouaté, e** *adj vêtement* quilted; *bruit* muffled; *ambiance* cocoon-like.

oublier [ublije] (7) **1** *vt* (*gén*) to forget; *soucis, client* to forget (about); *fautes d'orthographe* to miss; *phrase* to leave out. ~ **de faire/pourquoi** to forget to do/why; **il essaie de se faire** ~ he's trying to keep out of the limelight; **on l'a oublié sur la liste** he's been left off the list. **2 s'**~ *vpr [personne]* to forget o.s. **ça s'oublie facilement** it's easily forgotten. ♦ **oubli** *nm* **(a)** forgetting. **l'**~ **de cet objet** forgetting this thing; **l'**~ **de soi (-même)** self-effacement. **(b)** (*trou de mémoire*) lapse of memory; (*omission*) omission; (*négligence*) oversight. **cet** ~ **lui coûta la vie** this omission *ou* oversight cost him his life. **(c) l'**~ oblivion, forgetfulness.

ouest [wɛst] **1** *nm* west. **le vent d'**~ the west wind; **un vent d'**~ a west(erly) wind; **à l'**~ (*situation*) in the west; (*direction*) to the west, westwards; **à l'**~ **de** west of; **l'Europe de l'**~ Western Europe; **Allemagne de l'**~ West Germany; (*Pol*) **l'O**~ the West. **2** *adj inv région* western; *entrée* west; *direction* westward, westerly. ~**-allemand** West German.

ouf [uf] *excl* phew! **sans avoir le temps de dire** ~* before they had time to catch their breath.

oui [wi] **1** *adv* **(a)** yes. **le connaissez-vous?** — ~ do you know him? — yes (I do); **est-elle chez elle?** — ~ is she at home? — yes (she is); **ah, ça** ~! I should say so!, yes indeed!; **vous en voulez?** — ~**, bien sûr** do you want some? — of course (I do) *ou* I most certainly do; **répondre (par)** ~ to answer yes; **faire** ~ **de la tête** to nod (one's head). **(b)** (*remplaçant une proposition*) **je pense que** ~ (yes) I think so; **j'espère que** ~ I hope so; **j'ai demandé si elle était venue, lui dit que** ~ I asked if she had been and he says she has. **(c)** (*intensif*) **il va accepter,** ~ **ou non?** is he or isn't he going to accept?; **tu te presses,** ~ **ou non?** will you PLEASE hurry up. **2** *nm inv* yes. **il y a eu 30** ~ there were 30 votes for, there were 30 ayes; **pleurer pour un** ~ **ou pour un non** to cry at the drop of a hat.

ouïe [wi] *nf* hearing. ♦ **ouï-dire** *nm inv*: **par** ~ by hearsay. ♦ **ouïr** (10) *vt* (*littér, Jur*) to hear. **j'ai ouï dire que** I've heard it said that.

ouïes [wi] *nfpl* (*Zool*) gills; (*Mus*) sound-hole.

ouille [uj] *excl* ouch!

ouragan [uʀagɑ̃] *nm* (*lit*) hurricane. (*fig*) **déchaîner un** ~ to create a storm; **arriver comme un** ~ to arrive like a whirlwind *ou* tornado.

ourler [uʀle] (1) *vt* to hem. ♦ **ourlet** *nm* hem.

ours [uʀs] *nm* (*Zool*) bear; (*péj: misanthrope*) (old) bear. (*jouet*) ~ **(en peluche)** teddy bear; ~ **blanc** polar bear; ~ **brun** brown bear; ~ **mal léché*** lout. ♦ **ourse** *nf* she-bear. ♦ **ourson** *nm* bear cub.

oursin [uʀsɛ̃] *nm* sea urchin.

oust(e)* [ust(ə)] *excl* beat it!*, off with you!

outil [uti] *nm* (*lit, fig*) tool; (*agricole*) implement. ♦ **outillage** *nm [bricoleur]* set of tools; *[jardinier]* implements; *[usine]* equipment. ♦ **outiller** (1) *vt* (*gén*) to equip; *ouvrier* to supply with tools, kit out; *atelier* to fit out. **bien/mal outillé** well-/badly-equipped.

outrage [utʀaʒ] *nm* insult (*à* to). **faire** ~ **à** *mémoire* to insult, offend; *pudeur* to outrage; ~ **à agent** insulting a police officer; ~ **à magistrat** contempt of court; ~ **à la pudeur** indecent behaviour. ♦ **outragé, e** *adj* gravely offended. ♦ **outrageant, e** *adj* offensive. ♦ **outrager** (3) *vt* (*littér*) *personne* to offend gravely; *mœurs* to outrage; *raison* to insult.

outrageux, -euse [utʀaʒø, øz] *adj* outrageous, excessive. ♦ **outrageusement** *adv* outrageously, excessively.

outrance [utʀɑ̃s] *nf* (*excès*) excess. **l'**~ excessiveness; **méticuleux à** ~ meticulous in the extreme. ♦ **outrancier, -ière** *adj* extreme.

outre [utʀ(ə)] **1** *prép* besides. ~ **son salaire** on top of *ou* in addition to his salary; ~ **le fait que** as well as *ou* besides the fact that; **en** ~ moreover, besides; **en** ~ **de** on top of; ~ **mesure** to excess; **passer** ~ to carry on regardless; **passer** ~ **à** to disregard; ~ **qu'il a le temps, il sait le faire** apart from having the time he knows how to do it.

2: ~**-Atlantique** across the Atlantic; ~**-Manche** across the Channel; ~**-mer** overseas; **les territoires d'**~**-mer** overseas territories; **voix d'**~**-tombe** lugubrious voice.

outrepasser [utʀəpɑse] (1) *vt droits, pouvoir, ordres* to exceed; *limites* to go beyond, overstep.

outrer [utʀe] (1) *vt* (*exagérer*) to exaggerate; (*indigner*) to outrage. ♦ **outré, e** *adj* **(a)** *éloges* excessive, exaggerated; *description* exaggerated, extravagant. **(b)** (*indigné*) outraged (*de, par* at, by).

outsider [awtsajdœʀ] *nm* (*Sport, fig*) possible winner.

ouvert, e [uvɛʀ, ɛʀt] *etc V* **ouvrir.**

ouvrage [uvʀaʒ] *nm* **(a)** (*travail*) work. **se mettre à l'**~ to set to *ou* start work. **(b)** (*objet*) piece of work; (*Couture, Constr*) work; (*livre*) (*œuvre*) work; (*volume*) book. ~ **d'art** structure (*bridge or tunnel etc*). ♦ **ouvragé, e** *adj meuble* finely carved; *napperon* finely embroidered; *bijou* finely worked.

ouvrier, -ière [uvʀije, ijɛʀ] **1** *adj quartier* working-class; *conflit, agitation, législation* industrial, labour. **2** *nm* worker, workman. ~ **d'usine** factory worker *ou* hand; ~ **agricole** farm labourer, farm hand; ~ **qualifié/spécialisé** skilled/unskilled worker. **3** *nf* female worker. ~**ière (d'usine)** female factory worker *ou* factory hand.

ouvrir [uvʀiʀ] (18) **1** *vt* **(a)** (*gén*) to open; *porte fermée à clef* to unlock; *ailes* to spread; *manteau* to undo, unfasten. ~ **par effraction** to break open; **il a ouvert brusquement la porte** he threw *ou* flung the door open; ~ **la porte aux abus** to throw the door open to abuses; **on a frappé: va** ~! there was a knock: go and open *ou* answer the door!; **fais-toi** ~ **par la concierge** ask *ou* get the caretaker to let you in; ~ **l'œil** to keep one's eyes open (*fig*); **ça m'a ouvert les yeux** it opened my eyes, it was an eye-opener (to me); ~ **les oreilles** to pin back one's ears*; **ça m'a ouvert l'appétit** that whetted my appetite; ~ **sa bourse (à qn)** to put one's hand in one's pocket (to help sb). **(b)** (*percer*) *mur* to open up; *membre, ventre* to open up, cut open; *autoroute* to build; *perspectives* to open up. **ils lui ont ouvert un passage dans la foule** they made a passage for him through the crowd; (*fig*) ~ **la voie (à qn)** to lead the way (for sb). **(c)** (*commencer*) *théâtre, magasin* to open (up); *compte, enquête, bal* to open. ~ **les hostilités** to start up *ou* begin hostilities; ~ **le feu** to open fire; ~ **le jeu** (*Sport*) to open up the game; (*Cartes*) to open play. **(d)** (*être au début de*) *liste* to head; *procession* to lead. ~ **la marche** to take the lead. **(e)** *gaz, radio* to turn on, switch on, put on; *eau, robinet* to turn on; *vanne* to open.

2 *vi* to open (*sur* on, *par* with).

3 s'~ *vpr* **(a)** (*gén*) to open; *[fleur]* to open out. **robe qui s'ouvre par devant** dress that undoes *ou* unfastens at the front; **la foule s'ouvrit pour le laisser passer** the crowd parted to let him through; **s'**~ **un passage dans la foule** to cut one's way through the crowd; **la porte a dû s'**~ the door must have come open; **la vie qui s'ouvre devant elle** the life which is opening in front of *ou* before her. **(b) s'**~ **à** *amour, problèmes* to become aware of; *confident* to open one's heart to (*de qch* about sth). **(c) s'**~ **les veines** to cut *ou* slash one's wrists; **s'**~ **la jambe** to cut open *ou* gash one's leg. ♦ **ouvre-boîte(s)** *nm inv* tin opener. ♦ **ouvre-bouteille(s)** *nm inv* bottle-opener. ♦ **ouvert, e** *adj* (*gén, fig*) open; *angle* wide; *ensemble* open-ended; *robinet* on, running; *col* undone. **la bouche** ~**e** open-mouthed, with open mouth; **entrez, c'est** ~**!** come in, the door isn't locked!; ~ **au public** open to the public; **à l'esprit** ~ open-minded. ♦ **ouvertement** *adv dire* openly; *agir* openly, overtly. ♦ **ouverture** *nf* **(a)** (*action: V* **ouvrir**) opening; unlocking; opening up; opening-out. **heures d'**~ opening hours; **à l'**~ at opening time; **l'**~ **de la porte est automatique** the door opens automatically. **(b)** (*trou*) opening; (*Phot*) aperture; (*Mus*) overture; (*Cartes*) opening. ~ **d'esprit** open-mindedness. **(c)** (*avances*) ~**s** overtures; **faire des** ~**s de paix** to make peace overtures (*à qn* to sb). ♦ **ouvrable** *adj*: **jour** ~ weekday, working day; **heures** ~**s** business hours. ♦ **ouvreuse** *nf* usherette.

ovaire [ɔvɛʀ] *nm* ovary.

ovale [ɔval] *adj, nm* oval.

ovation [ɔvɑsjɔ̃] *nf* ovation. **faire une** ~ **à qn** to give sb an ovation.

ovin, e [ɔvɛ̃, in] **1** *adj* ovine. **2** *nm*: **les** ~**s** the ovine race.

ovule [ɔvyl] *nm* (*Physiol*) ovum. ♦ **ovulation** *nf* ovulation.

oxyder [ɔkside] (1) **1** *vt* to oxidize. **2 s'**~ *vpr* to become oxidized. ♦ **oxydant, e 1** *adj* oxidizing. **2** *nm* oxidizer. ♦ **oxydation** *nf* oxidization, oxidation. ♦ **oxyde** *nm* oxide. ~ **de carbone** carbon monoxide.

oxygène [ɔksiʒɛn] *nm* oxygen. ♦ **oxygénation** *nf* oxygenation. ♦ **oxygéner** (6) **1** *vt* (*Chim*) to oxygenate. **2 s'**~ *vpr* (*) to get some fresh air.

ozone [ozon] *nm* ozone.

P

P, p [pe] *nm* (*lettre*) P, p.
pacage [pakaʒ] *nm* pasture (land).
pacha [paʃa] *nm* pasha. **mener une vie de** ~ to live like a lord.
pachyderme [paʃidɛʀm(ə)] *nm* (*éléphant*) elephant.
pacifique [pasifik] **1** *adj* **(a)** *coexistence* peaceful; *humeur* peaceable; *intention* pacific. **utilisé à des fins** ~s used for peaceful purposes. **(b)** (*Géog*) Pacific. **2** *nm* (*Géog*) **le P**~ the Pacific. ♦ **pacificateur, -trice 1** *adj* pacificatory. **2** *nm,f* (*personne*) peacemaker; (*chose*) pacifier. ♦ **pacification** *nf* pacification. ♦ **pacifier** (7) *vt* to pacify. ♦ **pacifiquement** *adv* peacefully; peaceably; pacifically. ♦ **pacifisme** *nm* pacifism. ♦ **pacifiste** *nmf, adj* pacifist.
pacotille [pakɔtij] *nf* poor-quality stuff, cheap and nasty goods; (*clinquant*) showy stuff. **c'est de la** ~ it's cheap rubbish; **meubles de** ~ cheap furniture.
pacte [pakt(ə)] *nm* pact. ♦ **pactiser** (1) *vt* (*péj*) (*se liguer*) to take sides (*avec* with); (*transiger*) to come to terms (*avec* with).
pactole [paktɔl] *nm* gold mine.
pagaie [pagɛ] *nf* paddle.
pagaïe, pagaille [pagaj] *nf* (*objets*) mess, shambles; (*désorganisation*) chaos. **mettre la** ~ **dans qch** to mess sth up; **il y en a en** ~* there are loads* *ou* masses of them.
paganisme [paganism(ə)] *nm* paganism, heathenism.
pagayer [pageje] (8) *vi* to paddle. ♦ **pagayeur, -euse** *nm,f* paddler.
page[1] [paʒ] *nf* **(a)** page. ~ **de garde** flyleaf; **une** ~ **d'écriture** a page of writing; **les plus belles** ~**s de Corneille** the finest passages of Corneille; **une** ~ **glorieuse de notre histoire** a glorious page *ou* chapter in our history; **mettre en** ~ to make up (into pages). **(b) être à la** ~ (*mode*) to be up-to-date *ou* with it*; (*actualité*) to keep in touch *ou* up-to-date; **ne plus être à la** ~ to be out of touch *ou* behind the times.
page[2] [paʒ] *nm* (*Hist*) page (boy).
pagne [paɲ] *nm* loincloth.
pagode [pagɔd] *nf* pagoda.
paie [pɛ] *nf* (*gén*) pay; *[ouvrier]* wages. **feuille de** ~ paysheet; **ça fait une** ~ **que nous ne nous sommes pas vus*** it's ages since we last saw each other. ♦ **paiement** *nm* payment. ~ **comptant** cash payment.
païen, -ïenne [pajɛ̃, jɛn] *adj, nm,f* pagan, heathen.
paille [pɑj] **1** *nf* straw; (*pour boire*) (drinking) straw; (*Tech: défaut*) flaw. ~ **de fer** steel wool; ~ **de riz** straw; **chapeau de** ~ straw hat; **être sur la** ~ to be penniless; **mettre sur la** ~ to reduce to poverty; **2 millions de francs? une** ~**!*** 2 million francs? peanuts!* **2** *adj inv* straw-coloured. ♦ **paillasse** *nf* **(a)** (*matelas*) straw mattress. **(b)** *[évier]* draining board. ♦ **paillasson** *nm* (*lit, péj*) doormat. ♦ **paillé, e** *adj* straw-bottomed.
paillette [pajɛt] *nf* **(a)** (*Habillement*) sequin, spangle. **(b)** *[or]* speck; *[mica, lessive]* flake. ♦ **pailleté, e** *adj robe* sequined. ♦ **pailleter** (4) *vt* to spangle.
pain [pɛ̃] **1** *nm* (*gén*) bread; (*miche*) loaf; *[cire]* bar; *[savon]* bar, cake. (*Culin*) ~ **de poisson** *etc* fish *etc* loaf; **avoir du** ~ **sur la planche*** to have a lot on one's plate; **le** ~ **quotidien** one's daily bread. **2:** ~ **brioché** brioche loaf; ~ **de campagne** farmhouse bread; ~ **complet** wholemeal bread; ~ **d'épice(s)** ≈ gingerbread; ~ **de Gênes** Genoa cake; ~ **grillé** toast; ~ **de gruau** *ou* **viennois** Vienna loaf; ~ **de mie** sandwich loaf; ~ **aux raisins** currant bun; **petit** ~ **(au lait)** ≈ plain bun; **se vendre comme des petits** ~**s** to sell like hot cakes.
pair[1] [pɛʀ] *nm* (*personne*) peer; (*Fin*) par. **remboursé au** ~ repayable at par; **travailler au** ~ to work in exchange for board and lodging; **jeune fille au** ~ au pair girl; **ça va de** ~ it goes hand in hand (*avec* with). ♦ **pairesse** *nf* peeress. ♦ **pairie** *nf* peerage.
pair[2]**, e**[1] [pɛʀ] *adj nombre* even. **le côté** ~ **de la rue** the even-numbers side of the street; **jours** ~**s** even dates.
paire[2] [pɛʀ] *nf* (*gén*) pair; *[bœufs]* yoke; *[pigeons]* brace. **donner une** ~ **de gifles à qn** to box sb's ears; (*hum*) **les deux font la** ~ they're two of a kind; **c'est une autre** ~ **de manches*** that's another story.
paisible [pezibl(ə)] *adj* peaceful, quiet; (*sans agressivité*) peaceable. ♦ **paisiblement** *adv* peacefully, quietly; peaceably.
paître [pɛtʀ(ə)] (57) **1** *vi* to graze. **faire** ~ to take to pasture; **envoyer** ~ **qn**ᵻ to send sb packing*. **2** *vt*: ~ **l'herbe d'un pré** to graze.
paix [pɛ] *nf* **(a)** (*gén, Mil*) peace. **signer la** ~ to sign a peace treaty; **en temps de** ~ in peacetime; **faire la** ~ **avec qn** to make one's peace with sb, make it up with sb; **ramener la** ~ **entre** to make peace between. **(b)** (*tranquillité*) peace, quiet; (*silence*) stillness, peacefulness. **avoir la** ~ to have a bit of peace and quiet; ~ **à sa mémoire** God rest his soul; **avoir la conscience en** ~ to have a clear conscience; **fiche-moi* la** ~! leave me alone!; **la** ~**!*** shut up!*
Pakistan [pakistɑ̃] *nm* Pakistan. ♦ **pakistanais, e** *adj*, **P**~**(e)** *nm(f)* Pakistani.
palace [palas] *nm* luxury hotel.
palais [palɛ] *nm* (*édifice*) palace; (*Anat*) palate. ~ **des expositions** exhibition hall; **le P**~ **de Justice** the Law Courts; ~ **des sports** sports stadium.
palan [palɑ̃] *nm* hoist.
pale [pal] *nf [hélice]* blade; *[roue]* paddle.
pâle [pɑl] *adj* pale; (*maladif*) pallid; *style* weak; *imitation* poor; *sourire* faint, wan. ~ **comme un linge** as white as a sheet; ~ **de peur** white with fear.
palefrenier [palfʀənje] *nm [auberge]* ostler; *[château]* groom.
Palestine [palɛstin] *nf* Palestine. ♦ **palestinien, -ienne** *adj*, **P**~**(ne)** *nm(f)* Palestinian.
paletot [palto] *nm* knitted jacket. **il m'est tombé sur le** ~ᵻ he jumped on me.
palette [palɛt] *nf* (*Peinture*) palette; (*Boucherie*) shoulder; *[roue]* paddle.
pâleur [pɑlœʀ] *nf* paleness; (*maladive*) pallor.
palier [palje] *nm [escalier]* landing; *[route]* level; (*Tech*) bearing; (*fig: étape*) stage. **habiter sur le même** ~ to live on the same floor; **les prix ont**

atteint un nouveau ~ prices have risen to a new level.
pâlir [pɑliʀ] (2) **1** *vi [personne]* to turn *ou* go pale (*de* with); *[étoiles]* to grow dim; *[ciel]* to grow pale; *[couleur]* to fade; *[souvenir]* to fade (away), dim. **faire** ~ **qn d'envie** to make sb green with envy. **2** *vt* to turn pale. ♦ **pâlissant, e** *adj teinte, lumière* wan, fading.
palissade [palisad] *nf [pieux]* fence; *[planches]* boarding.
pallier [palje] (7) *vt difficulté* to get round; *manque* to offset, compensate for, make up for. ♦ **palliatif** *nm* (*mesure*) palliative, stopgap measure; (*réparation*) makeshift.
palmarès [palmaʀɛs] *nm* (*Scol*) prize list; (*Sport*) (list of) medal winners; *[athlète etc]* record (of achievements).
palme [palm(ə)] *nf* (*Bot*) palm leaf; (*symbole*) palm; *[nageur]* flipper. **vin de** ~ palm wine. ♦ **palmé, e** *adj patte* webbed; *oiseau* webfooted. ♦ **palmeraie** *nf* palm grove. ♦ **palmier** *nm* (*Bot*) palm tree; (*gâteau*) palmier.
palombe [palɔ̃b] *nf* woodpigeon.
pâlot, -otte* [pɑlo, ɔt] *adj* pale, peaky*.
palourde [paluʀd(ə)] *nf* clam.
palper [palpe] (1) *vt objet* to feel, finger; (*Méd*) to palpate; (‡) *argent* to get, make. ♦ **palpable** *adj* (*lit, fig*) palpable.
palpiter [palpite] (1) *vi [cœur]* to beat; (*violemment*) to pound; *[narines, flamme]* to quiver. ♦ **palpitant, e** *adj livre* thrilling, exciting. **être** ~ **d'émotion** to be quivering with emotion. ♦ **palpitation** *nf*: ~**(s)** *[cœur]* pounding; *[flamme]* quivering; (*Méd*) **avoir des** ~**s** to have palpitations.
paluche‡ [palyʃ] *nf* (*main*) hand, paw*.
paludisme [palydism(ə)] *nm* malaria.
pamphlet [pɑ̃flɛ] *nm* satirical tract, lampoon.
pamplemousse [pɑ̃pləmus] *nm* grapefruit.
pan¹ [pɑ̃] *nm* (*morceau*) piece; (*basque*) tail; (*côté*) side, face. ~ **de ciel** patch of sky; ~ **de mur** (section of) wall; **il est en** ~ **de chemise** he has just his shirt on.
pan² [pɑ̃] *excl [coup de feu]* bang!; *[gifle]* slap!, whack!
pan³ [pɑ̃], *devant voyelle* [pan] *préf* Pan-. **panaméricain** *etc* Pan-American *etc*.
panacée [panase] *nf* panacea.
panache [panaʃ] *nm* (*plumet*) plume; (*héroïsme*) gallantry. ~ **de fumée** plume of smoke.
panaché, e [panaʃe] **1** *adj fleur* many-coloured; *foule, assortiment* motley; *glace* mixed-flavour. **2** *nm* (*boisson*) shandy.
panard‡ [panaʀ] *nm* foot, hoof‡.
panaris [panaʀi] *nm* whitlow.
pancarte [pɑ̃kaʀt(ə)] *nf* (*gén*) sign, notice; (*Aut*) (road)sign; *[manifestant]* placard.
pancréas [pɑ̃kʀeɑs] *nm* pancreas.
paner [pane] (1) *vt* to coat with breadcrumbs.
panier [panje] **1** *nm* (*gén, Sport*) basket; (*contenu*) basket(ful). (*fig*) **ils sont tous à mettre dans le même** ~ they are all much of a muchness; **jeter au** ~ to throw out. **2:** ~ **à bouteilles** bottle-carrier; **c'est un** ~ **de crabes** they fight to get ahead of each other; ~ **percé** spendthrift; ~ **à salade** (*Culin*) salad shaker *ou* basket; (**fig*) police van, Black Maria*.
panique [panik] *nf* panic. **pris de** ~ panic-stricken; **peur** ~ pathological fear. ♦ **paniquer** *vi*, **se** ~* *vpr* (1) to panic.
panne [pan] *nf* breakdown. **je suis tombé en** ~ my car has broken down; **je suis tombé en** ~ **sèche** I have run out of petrol *ou* gasoline (*US*); ~ **de courant** power failure; ~ **de moteur** engine failure; **rester en** ~ **devant une difficulté** to be stuck over a difficulty; **laisser qn en** ~ to let sb down.
panneau, *pl* ~**x** [pano] *nm [porte etc]* panel; (*écriteau*) sign, notice. ~ **d'affichage** (*pour résultats*) notice board; (*pour publicité*) hoarding, billboard (*US*); ~ **indicateur** signpost; ~ **de signalisation** road-sign; ~ **vitré** glass panel; **tomber dans le** ~* to fall *ou* walk (right) into the trap, fall for it*. ♦ **panonceau,** *pl* ~**x** *nm* (*plaque*) plaque; (*publicitaire*) sign.
panoplie [panɔpli] *nf* (*jouet*) outfit; *[moyens etc]* range. ~ **d'armes** (*collection*) display of weapons; (*équipement*) armoury.
panorama [panɔʀama] *nm* (*lit, fig*) panorama. ♦ **panoramique** *adj* panoramic.
panse [pɑ̃s] *nf* paunch; (*: *ventre*) belly‡. **se remplir la** ~* to eat one's fill.
panser [pɑ̃se] (1) *vt* **(a)** *plaie* to dress; *bras* to put a dressing on; *blessé* to dress the wounds of. **(b)** *cheval* to groom. ♦ **pansage** *nm* grooming. ♦ **pansement** *nm* dressing; (*bandage*) bandage. **faire un** ~ to dress a wound; **couvert de** ~**s** all bandaged up; ~ **(adhésif)** (sticking) plaster, bandaid ® (*US*).
pantalon [pɑ̃talɔ̃] *nm* (pair of) trousers *ou* pants (*US*). **10** ~**s** 10 pairs of trousers.
pantelant, e [pɑ̃tlɑ̃, ɑ̃t] *adj personne* panting (*de* with); *gorge, chair* heaving.
panthéon [pɑ̃teɔ̃] *nm* pantheon.
panthère [pɑ̃tɛʀ] *nf* panther; (*fig: mégère*) hellcat*.
pantin [pɑ̃tɛ̃] *nm* (*jouet*) jumping jack; (*péj: personne*) puppet.
pantomime [pɑ̃tɔmim] *nf* (*art*) mime; (*spectacle*) mime show; (*fig*) scene, fuss.
pantoufle [pɑ̃tufl(ə)] *nf* slipper. ♦ **pantouflard, e*** *adj caractère* stay-at-home; *vie* quiet.
paon [pɑ̃] *nm* peacock.
papa [papa] *nm* dad, daddy. **la musique de** ~* old-fashioned music; **conduire à la** ~* to potter along in one's car; **c'est un** ~ **gâteau** he spoils his (grand)children.
pape [pap] *nm* pope. ♦ **papal, e,** *mpl* **-aux** *adj* papal. ♦ **papauté** *nf* papacy.
papelard* [paplaʀ] *nm* paper.
paperasse [papʀas] *nf* (*péj*) ~**(s)** papers; (*à remplir*) forms. ♦ **paperasserie** *nf* (*péj*) papers; (*à remplir*) forms; (*routine*) red tape. **il y a trop de** ~ **à faire dans ce travail** there's too much paperwork in this job.
papeterie [papetʀi] *nf* (*magasin*) stationer's (shop); (*fourniture*) stationery; (*fabrique*) paper mill; (*fabrication*) papermaking industry; (*commerce*) stationery trade. ♦ **papetier, -ière** *nm,f* (*vendeur*) stationer; (*fabricant*) paper-maker.
papier [papje] **1** *nm* **(a)** (*matière*) paper. **sac en** ~ paper bag; **mettre qch sur** ~ to write sth down; **sur** ~ **libre** on plain paper; **sur le** ~ (*théoriquement*) on paper. **(b)** (*feuille écrite*) paper; (*feuille blanche*) sheet *ou* piece of paper; (*Presse: article*) article. **un** ~ **à signer** a form to be signed; ~**s (d'identité)/militaires** *etc* (identity)/army *etc* papers; (*Aut*) **vos** ~**s, s'il vous plaît!** may I see your (driving) licence, please?; **rayez cela de vos** ~**s!** you can forget about that!; **être dans les petits** ~**s de qn** to be in sb's good books.
2: ~ **aluminium** aluminium foil, tinfoil; ~ **d'argent** silver foil *ou* paper, tinfoil; ~ **brouillon** scrap paper; ~ **buvard** blotting paper; ~ **calque** tracing paper; ~ **carbone** carbon paper; ~ **à cigarettes** cigarette paper; ~ **collant** gummed paper; ~ **à dessin** drawing paper; ~ **d'emballage** wrapping paper; ~ **filtre** filter paper; ~ **hygiénique** toilet paper; ~ **journal** newspaper; ~ **à lettres** writing paper, notepaper; ~ **mâché** papier-mâché; (*fig*) **mine de** ~ **mâché** pasty complexion; ~ **machine** typing paper; ~ **monnaie** paper money; ~ **peint** wallpaper; ~ **de soie** tissue paper; ~ **timbré** stamped paper; ~ **de verre** glass-paper, sandpaper.
papillon [papijɔ̃] *nm* (*insecte*) butterfly; (*écrou*) wing *ou* butterfly nut; (*contravention*) (parking)

ticket; (*autocollant*) sticker. ~ **de nuit** moth.
papillote [papijɔt] *nf [cheveux]* curlpaper; *[bonbon]* (sweet) paper; *[gigot]* frill.
papilloter [papijɔte] (1) *vi [lumière]* to twinkle; *[paupières]* to flicker; *[yeux]* to blink. ♦ **papillotement** *nm*: ~**(s)** twinkling; flickering; blinking.
papoter [papɔte] (1) *vi* to chatter. ♦ **papotage** *nm* (*action*) chattering. (*propos*) ~**(s)** (idle) chatter.
paquebot [pakbo] *nm* liner, (steam)ship.
pâquerette [pɑkʀɛt] *nf* daisy.
Pâques [pɑk] **1** *nm* Easter. (*fig*) **à** ~ **ou à la Trinité** never in a month of Sundays. **2** *nfpl*: **joyeuses** ~ Happy Easter; **faire ses** ~ to carry out one's Easter duties.
paquet [pakɛ] *nm* **(a)** *[café]* bag; *[cigarettes]* packet, pack (*US*); *[cartes]* pack; *[linge]* bundle. **(b)** (*colis*) parcel. **faire un** ~ to make up a parcel. **(c)** ~ **de** *neige* pile *ou* mass of; *boue* lump of; *billets* wad of; **il a touché un bon** ~* he got a fat sum*. **(d)** (*Rugby*) ~ **(d'avants)** pack. **(e)** (*Naut*) ~ **de mer** heavy sea, big wave. **(f) faire ses** ~**s** to pack one's bags; **il y a mis le** ~* (*argent*) he spared no expense; (*efforts*) he put everything into it. ♦ **paquetage** *nm* (*Mil*) pack, kit.
par [paʀ] *prép* **(a)** (*agent, cause*) by. **cassé** ~ **l'orage** broken by the storm; **accablé** ~ **le désespoir** overwhelmed with despair; **il a appris la nouvelle** ~ **un ami** he learned the news from *ou* through a friend; **elle veut tout faire** ~ **elle-même** she wants to do everything (for) herself; **la décision** ~ **le patron de ...** the boss's decision to ... .
(b) (*manière, moyen*) by. **obtenir qch** ~ **la force/la persuasion/la ruse** to obtain sth by force/with persuasion/by *ou* through cunning; **la porte ferme** ~ **un verrou** the gate is locked with a bolt *ou* by means of a bolt; **payer** ~ **chèque** to pay by cheque; ~ **le train** by rail *ou* train; ~ **bien des côtés** in many ways; **honnête** ~ **nature** honest by nature.
(c) (*motif etc*) out of, from, for. **étonnant** ~ **son érudition** amazing for his learning; ~ **manque de temps** owing to lack of time; ~ **habitude** out of *ou* from habit; ~ **plaisir/pitié** for pleasure/out of pity; ~ **hasard/erreur** by chance/mistake.
(d) (*lieu, état*) through. **il est sorti** ~ **la fenêtre** he went out by (way of) *ou* through the window; **nous sommes venus** ~ **l'Espagne** we came via *ou* through Spain; **se promener** ~ **les champs** to walk through *ou* across the fields; ~ **tout le pays** throughout *ou* all over the (entire) country; **il habite** ~ **ici** he lives round here; **sortez** ~ **ici** go out this way; ~ **où est-il venu?** which way did he come (by)?; **passer** ~ **de dures épreuves** to go through some very trying times; ~ **5 mètres de fond** at a depth of 5 metres; ~ **10° de latitude sud** at a latitude of 10° south; **arriver** ~ **le nord** to arrive from the north.
(e) (*distribution, mesure*) a, per, by. **marcher 2** ~ **2** to walk 2 by 2 *ou* in 2's; **50 F** ~ **personne** 50 francs per person *ou* a head *ou* apiece; **3 fois** ~ **jour** 3 times daily *ou* a day; **6 étudiants** ~ **appartement** 6 students to a flat *ou* per flat; ~ **an** a *ou* per year, per annum; ~ **moments** at times; **ils sont venus** ~ **milliers** they came in their thousands; ~ **poignées** in handfuls, by the handful; ~ **3 fois, on lui a demandé** 3 times he has been asked.
(f) (*atmosphère*) in; (*moment*) on. ~ **une belle nuit** one *ou* on a beautiful night; ~ **ce froid/cette chaleur** in this cold/heat; ~ **temps de pluie** in wet weather; **sortir** ~ **moins 10°** to go out when it's minus 10°.
(g) commencer ~ **qch**/~ **faire** to begin with sth/by doing; **il a fini** ~ **ennuyer tout le monde** he ended up *ou* finished up boring everyone; ~ **où allons-nous commencer?** where shall we begin?
(h) (*exclamations*) by. ~ **tout ce que j'ai de plus cher** by all that I hold most dear.
(i) ~ **trop** far too, excessively; **de** ~ ... in the name of ..., by order of ... .
parabole [paʀabɔl] *nf* (*Math*) parabola; (*Rel*) parable. ♦ **parabolique 1** *adj* parabolic. **2** *nm* (*radiateur*) electric fire.
parachever [paʀaʃve] (5) *vt* to perfect, put the finishing touches to. ♦ **parachèvement** *nm* perfection.
parachute [paʀaʃyt] *nm* parachute. ♦ **para*** *nm* para*. ♦ **parachutage** *nm* parachuting. ♦ **parachuter** (1) *vt* to parachute. **ils m'ont parachuté à ce poste*** I was pitchforked into this job. ♦ **parachutisme** *nm* parachuting. **faire du** ~ to go parachuting. ♦ **parachutiste** *nmf* parachutist; (*Mil*) paratrooper.
parade [paʀad] *nf* **(a)** (*ostentation*) show. **faire** ~ **de** to parade, show off; **de** ~ *uniforme* ceremonial. **(b)** (*spectacle*) parade. ~ **militaire/foraine** military/circus parade. **(c)** (*Escrime, Boxe*) parry; (*fig*) answer, reply. ♦ **parader** (1) *vi* to show off.
paradis [paʀadi] *nm* (*lit, fig*) paradise, heaven. **le P**~ **terrestre** (*Bible*) the Garden of Eden; (*fig*) heaven on earth. ♦ **paradisiaque** *adj* heavenly.
paradoxe [paʀadɔks(ə)] *nm* paradox. ♦ **paradoxal, e,** *mpl* **-aux** *adj* paradoxical. ♦ **paradoxalement** *adv* paradoxically.
paraffine [paʀafin] *nf* paraffin wax.
parages [paʀaʒ] *nmpl* **(a) dans les** ~ in the area, in the vicinity; **dans les** ~ **de** round about, in the vicinity of. **(b)** (*Naut*) waters, region.
paragraphe [paʀagʀaf] *nm* paragraph.
paraître [paʀɛtʀ(ə)] (57) *vi* **(a)** (*se montrer*) to appear (*sur* on). **il n'a pas paru à la réunion** he didn't appear *ou* turn up at the meeting; ~ **en public** to appear in public, make a public appearance. **(b)** (*Presse*) to appear, come out. **faire** ~ **qch** *[éditeur]* to bring sth out; *[auteur]* to have sth published. **(c)** (*être visible*) to show (through). **il en paraît toujours qch** one can always see some sign of it *ou* traces of it; **laisser** ~ **son irritation** to let one's annoyance show; (*péj*) **chercher à** ~ to show off. **(d)** (*sembler*) to look, seem, appear. **cela me paraît une erreur** it looks *ou* seems like a mistake to me; **cette robe la fait** ~ **plus grande** that dress makes her look taller; **il lui paraissait impossible de refuser** he didn't see how he could refuse; **il paraît que oui** so it seems *ou* appears, apparently so.
parallèle [paʀalɛl] **1** *adj* **(a)** (*Math*) parallel (*à* to). **(b)** (*comparable*) similar; (*indépendant*) separate; (*non officiel*) unofficial. **2** *nf* (*Math*) parallel line. (*Élec*) **en** ~ in parallel. **3** *nm* (*Géog, fig*) parallel. **mettre en** ~ *choses opposées* to compare; *choses semblables* to parallel. ♦ **parallèlement** *adv* (*lit*) parallel (*à* to); (*ensemble*) at the same time; (*similairement*) in the same way. ♦ **parallélisme** *nm* (*lit, fig*) parallelism; (*Aut*) wheel alignment. ♦ **parallélogramme** *nm* parallelogram.
paralyser [paʀalize] (1) *vt* (*Méd, fig*) to paralyse. ♦ **paralysie** *nf* paralysis. ♦ **paralytique** *adj, nmf* paralytic.
paramètre [paʀamɛtʀ(ə)] *nm* parameter.
paranoïaque [paʀanɔjak] *adj, nmf* paranoiac.
parapet [paʀapɛ] *nm* parapet.
paraphe [paʀaf] *nm* (*trait*) flourish; (*initiales*) initial; (*signature*) signature. ♦ **parapher** (1) *vt* (*Admin*) to initial; to sign.
paraphrase [paʀafʀɑz] *nf* paraphrase. ♦ **paraphraser** (1) *vt* to paraphrase.
parapluie [paʀaplɥi] *nm* umbrella.
parasite [paʀazit] **1** *nm* (*lit, fig*) parasite. (*Rad, TV*) ~**s** interference, atmospherics, static. **2** *adj* parasitic(al). ♦ **parasiter** (1) *vt* (*Bot, Vét*) to live as a parasite on; (*Rad, TV*) to cause interference on.
parasol [paʀasɔl] *nm [plage]* beach umbrella,

parasol; *[café]* sunshade, parasol.
paratonnerre [paʀatɔnɛʀ] *nm* lightning conductor.
paravent [paʀavɑ̃] *nm* folding screen *ou* partition.
parc [paʀk] **1** *nm (jardin public)* park; *[château]* grounds; (*Mil: entrepôt*) depot; (*fig, Écon: ensemble*) stock. **2:** ~ **d'attractions** amusement park; ~ **automobile** *[pays]* number of vehicles on the road; *[entreprise]* car fleet; ~ **à bébé** playpen; ~ **à huîtres** oyster bed; ~ **à moutons** sheep pen, sheepfold; ~ **naturel** nature reserve; ~ **de stationnement** car park, parking lot (*US*); ~ **zoologique** zoological gardens.
parcelle [paʀsɛl] *nf* (*lit*) fragment; (*vérité]* grain, scrap; *[bonheur]* bit; (*sur cadastre*) parcel (*of land*). ~ **de terre** plot of land.
parce que [paʀsk(ə)] *conj* because.
parchemin [paʀʃəmɛ̃] *nm* (piece of) parchment.
parcimonie [paʀsimɔni] *nf* parsimony. ♦ **parcimonieusement** *adv* parsimoniously. ♦ **parcimonieux, -euse** *adj* parsimonious.
par-ci par-là [paʀsipaʀla] *adv* (*espace*) here and there; (*temps*) now and then.
parcmètre [paʀkmɛtʀ(ə)] *nm* (parking) meter.
parcourir [paʀkuʀiʀ] (11) *vt* **(a)** *distance* to cover, travel; (*en tous sens*) *lieu* to go all over; *pays* to travel up and down. ~ **les mers** to sail all over the seas; **un frisson parcourut tout son corps** a shiver ran through his body. **(b)** *livre* to glance *ou* skim through. **il parcourut la foule des yeux** he ran his eye over the crowd. ♦ **parcours** *nm* (*distance*) distance; (*trajet*) journey; (*itinéraire*) route; *[fleuve]* course; *[golf]* round. (*Sport*) **sur un** ~ **difficile** over a difficult course; **le prix du** ~ the fare.
par-delà [paʀdəla] *prép* beyond.
par-derrière [paʀdɛʀjɛʀ] **1** *prép* (round) behind. **2** *adv passer* round the back; *attaquer* from behind; *se boutonner* at the back. **dire du mal de qn** ~ to speak ill of sb behind his back.
par-dessous [paʀd(ə)su] *prép, adv* under(neath).
pardessus [paʀdəsy] *nm* overcoat.
par-dessus [paʀd(ə)sy] **1** *prép* over. ~ **tout** above all; **j'en ai** ~ **la tête** I'm sick and tired of it; ~ **le marché** into the bargain, on top of all that; ~ **bord** overboard. **2** *adv* over (the top).
par-devant [paʀd(ə)vɑ̃] **1** *prép*: ~ **notaire** in the presence of *ou* before a lawyer. **2** *adv passer* round the front; *attaquer* from the front; *se boutonner* at the front.
pardon [paʀdɔ̃] *nm* **(a)** (*grâce*) forgiveness, pardon (*Jur*). **(b)** (*en Bretagne*) pardon (*religious festival*). **(c) demander** ~ **à qn d'avoir fait qch** to apologize to sb for doing *ou* having done sth; **demande** ~! say you're sorry!; **(je vous demande)** ~ (I'm) sorry, I beg your pardon; ~ **Monsieur, avez-vous l'heure?** excuse me, could you tell me the time?; **et puis** ~!* **il travaille dur** he works hard I can tell you. ♦ **pardonnable** *adj* pardonable, forgivable. ♦ **pardonner** (1) **1** *vt* to forgive, pardon. ~ **qch à qn/à qn d'avoir fait qch** to forgive sb for sth/for doing *ou* having done sth; **pour se faire** ~ so as to be forgiven; **pardonnez-moi de vous avoir dérangé** I'm sorry to have disturbed you; **je ne me le pardonnerai jamais** I'll never forgive myself. **2** *vi* to forgive. **erreur qui ne pardonne pas** fatal mistake.
pare- [paʀ] *préf V* **parer**[2].
pareil, -eille [paʀɛj] **1** *adj* **(a)** (*identique*) similar. **il n'y en a pas deux** ~**s** there aren't two the same *ou* alike; ~ **que,** ~ **à** the same as, similar to, just like; **c'est toujours** ~ it's always the same; **il est** ~ **à lui-même** he's the same as ever; **j'en ai un** ~ I have one the same *ou* just like it; **l'an dernier à** ~**eille époque** this time last year. **(b)** (*tel*) such (a). **je n'ai jamais entendu un discours** ~ I've never heard such a speech *ou* a speech like it. **2** *nm,f*: **nos** ~**s** (*semblables*) our fellow men; (*égaux*) our equals *ou* peers; **ne pas avoir son** ~ to be second to none; **vous et vos** ~**s** people like you; **sans** ~ unparalleled, unequalled; **c'est du** ~ **au même*** it comes to the same thing. **3** *adv* (*) *s'habiller* the same, in the same way, alike. **faire** ~ to do the same thing (*que* as). ♦ **pareillement** *adv* (*de la même manière*) in the same way (*à* as); (*également*) likewise, also, equally. **à vous** ~! the same to you!
parent, e [paʀɑ̃, ɑ̃t] **1** *adj* related (*de* to). **2** *nm,f* **(a)** relative, relation. **être** ~ **de qn** to be related to sb; (*fig*) ~ **pauvre** poor relation. **(b)** (*Bio*) parent. **3** *nmpl*: ~**s** (*père et mère*) parents; (*ancêtres*) ancestors, forefathers. ♦ **parenté** *nf* (*rapport*) relationship, kinship; (*famille*) relations, relatives.
parenthèse [paʀɑ̃tɛz] *nf* (*digression*) digression; (*signe*) bracket, parenthesis. **entre** ~**s** (*lit*) in brackets; (*fig*) incidentally, in parenthesis; (*fig*) **ouvrir une** ~ to digress.
parer[1] [paʀe] (1) **1** *vt* **(a)** (*orner*) to adorn. **robe richement parée** richly trimmed dress. **(b)** *viande* to dress, trim; *cuir* to dress. **2 se**~ *vpr* (*se faire beau*) to put on all one's finery. **se** ~ **de** *bijoux* to adorn o.s. with; *faux titre* to assume.
parer[2] [paʀe] (1) **1** *vt coup* to ward off, stave off, fend off; (*Boxe, Escrime, fig*) to parry. **2** ~ **à** *vt indir inconvénient* to deal with, remedy; *danger* to ward off; *éventualité* to be prepared for. ~ **au plus pressé** to attend to the most urgent things first. ♦ **paré, e** *adj* (*prêt*) ready, all set; (*préparé*) prepared (*contre* against). ♦ **pare-balles** *adj inv* bulletproof. ♦ **pare-brise** *nm inv* windscreen, windshield (*US*). ♦ **pare-chocs** *nm inv* (*Aut*) bumper, fender (*US*). ♦ **pare-soleil** *nm inv* sun visor.
paresseux, -euse [paʀesø, øz] **1** *adj personne* lazy, idle; *esprit* slow; *allure* lazy; *estomac* sluggish. ~ **comme une couleuvre** bone-idle*. **2** *nm,f* lazy *ou* idle person, lazybones*. ♦ **paresse** *nf* laziness; idleness; slowness; sluggishness; (*péché*) sloth. ♦ **paresser** (1) *vi* to laze about *ou* around. ♦ **paresseusement** *adv* lazily.
parfait, e [paʀfɛ, ɛt] **1** *adj* (*gén*) perfect; *raisonnement, manières* flawless, faultless; *tranquillité* complete, total; *crétin* utter, downright. **(c'est)** ~! (that's) perfect! *ou* great!* **2** *nm* **(a)** (*Culin*) ~ **au café** coffee parfait. **(b)** (*Ling*) perfect. ♦ **parfaire** (60) *vt* to perfect. ♦ **parfaitement** *adv* perfectly; completely, totally; utterly. **tu as fait ça tout seul?** — ~! you did it all on your own? — I certainly did! *ou* I did indeed!
parfois [paʀfwa] *adv* sometimes.
parfum [paʀfœ̃] *nm* (*substance*) perfume, scent; (*odeur*) scent, fragrance; *[café]* aroma; *[glace]* flavour. **être au** ~‡ to be in the know*; **mettre qn au** ~‡ to put sb in the picture*. ♦ **parfumé, e** *adj savon* scented; *air, fleur* fragrant. ~ **au café** coffee-flavoured. ♦ **parfumer** (1) **1** *vt [fleurs]* to perfume, scent; *[café, tabac]* to fill with its aroma; *mouchoir* to put scent *ou* perfume on; (*Culin*) to flavour (*à* with). **2 se** ~ *vpr* to use perfume *ou* scent. ♦ **parfumerie** *nf* (*gén*) perfumery; (*boutique*) perfume shop. ♦ **parfumeur, -euse** *nm,f* perfumer.
pari [paʀi] *nm* bet, wager; (*Sport*) bet. (*fig*) **les** ~**s sont ouverts** it's anyone's bet*. ♦ **parier** (7) *vt* **(a)** (*gager*) to bet, wager. **je (te) parie que c'est lui** I bet you it's him; **il y a gros à** ~ **que ...** the odds are that ...; **je l'aurais parié** I might have known. **(b)** (*Courses*) *argent* to bet, lay, stake. ~ **sur un cheval** to bet on a horse. ♦ **parieur, -euse** *nm,f* punter.
parisien, -ienne [paʀizjɛ̃, jɛn] **1** *adj* (*gén*) Paris; *ambiance* Parisian. **la vie** ~**ienne** Paris *ou* Parisian life. **2** *nm(f)*: **P**~**(ne)** Parisian.
parité [paʀite] *nf* parity. ♦ **paritaire** *adj*

commission joint; *représentation* equal.
parjure [paʀʒyʀ] **1** *adj personne* faithless; *serment* false. **2** *nm* (*violation de serment*) betrayal; (*faux serment*) perjury. **3** *nmf* traitor; perjurer. ♦ **parjurer (se)** (1) *vpr* to be faithless to one's promise; to perjure o.s.
parking [paʀkiŋ] *nm* (*lieu*) car park, parking lot (*US*); (*action*) parking.
parlement [paʀləmɑ̃] *nm* parliament. ♦ **parlementaire 1** *adj* parliamentary. **2** *nmf* (*Pol*) member of Parliament; (*négociateur*) negociator, mediator. ♦ **parlementer** (1) *vi* (*négocier*) to parley.
parler [paʀle] (1) **1** *vi* **(a)** (*faculté physique*) to talk. **votre perroquet parle?** can your parrot talk?; **parlez plus fort!** talk *ou* speak louder!, speak up! **(b)** (*exprimer sa pensée*) to speak; (*bavarder*) to talk. **~ franc** to speak frankly; **faire ~ un suspect** to make a suspect talk; **~ à tort et à travers** to talk through one's hat*; **voilà qui est bien parlé!** well said! **(c) ~ à qn** to talk *ou* speak to sb; **nous ne nous parlons pas** we're not on speaking terms; **moi qui vous parle** I myself; (*fig*) **trouver à qui ~** to meet one's match. **(d) ~ de qch/qn** to talk about sth/sb; **~ de faire qch** to talk of doing sth; **faire ~ de soi** to get o.s. talked about; **~ mal de qn** to speak ill of sb; **toute la ville en parle** it's the talk of the town; **il n'en parle jamais** he never mentions it *ou* refers to it *ou* talks about it; **quand on parle du loup (on en voit la queue)** speak of the devil (and he will appear). **(e) ~ de qch à qn** to tell sb about sth; **je lui parlerai de cette affaire** I'll speak to him *ou* I'll have a word with him about this business; **on m'a beaucoup parlé de vous** I've heard a lot about you. **(f) ~ par gestes** to use sign language; **~ à l'imagination** to appeal to the imagination; **les faits parlent d'eux-mêmes** the facts speak for themselves; **de quoi ça parle, ton livre? — ça parle de bateaux*** what is your book about? — it's about ships. **(g)** (*locutions*) **vous parlez!*** (*bien sûr*) you're telling me!*, you bet!*; (*iro*) no chance!*, you must be joking!*; **tu parles d'une brute!** talk about a brute!; **n'en parlons plus!** let's forget (about) it, let's not mention it again; **sans ~ de ...** not to mention ..., to say nothing of ...; **vous n'avez qu'à ~** just say the word.
2 *vt langue* to speak. **~ (l')anglais** to speak English; **~ politique** to talk politics.
3 *nm* speech; (*régional*) dialect.
♦ **parlant, e 1** *adj être* speaking, talking; (*fig*) *portrait* lifelike; *comparaison* graphic, vivid; *regard* eloquent, meaningful. **2** *adv*: **économiquement** *etc* **~** economically *etc* speaking. ♦ **parlé, e** *adj langue* spoken. ♦ **parleur, -euse** *nm,f* talker. **beau ~** fine talker. ♦ **parloir** *nm [école, prison]* visiting room; *[couvent]* parlour.
parmi [paʀmi] *prép* (*gén*) among. **~ nous** among us, in our midst; **aller ~ les rues désertes** to go through the deserted streets.
parodie [paʀɔdi] *nf* parody. (*fig*) **une ~ de procès** a mockery of a trial. ♦ **parodier** (7) *vt* to parody.
paroi [paʀwa] *nf* (*gén*) wall; *[véhicule]* side; (*cloison*) partition. **~ rocheuse** rock face.
paroisse [paʀwas] *nf* parish. ♦ **paroissial, e**, *mpl* **-aux** *adj* parish. **salle ~e** church hall. ♦ **paroissien, -ienne** *nm,f* parishioner. **drôle de ~*** funny customer*.
parole [paʀɔl] *nf* **(a)** (*mot*) word; (*remarque*) remark. **comprenez-vous le sens de ses ~s?** can you understand (the meaning of) what he says?; **c'est ~ d'évangile** it's the gospel truth; (*iro*) **de belles ~s** fair *ou* fine words! (*iro*); **assez de ~s, des actes!** enough talk *ou* enough said, let's have some action!; **tout cela est bien joli en ~s mais ...** this sounds all very well but ... . **(b)** *[chanson]* **~s** words, lyrics; **histoire sans ~s** wordless cartoon. **(c)** (*promesse*) word. **tenir ~** to keep one's word; **c'est un homme de ~** he's a man of his word; **je l'ai cru sur ~** I took his word for it; **~ d'honneur!** you have my word (of honour); **ma ~!*** (upon) my word! **(d)** (*faculté*) speech. **avoir la ~ facile** to be a fluent speaker; **la ~ est d'argent, le silence est d'or** speech is silver, silence is golden. **(e)** (*Ling*) speech, parole. **(f)** (*dans un débat*) **droit de ~** right to speak; **passer la ~ à qn** to hand over to sb; **prendre la ~** to speak.
paroxysme [paʀɔksism(ə)] *nm [maladie]* crisis (point); *[sentiment]* height. **au ~ de la joie** beside o.s. with joy; **atteindre son ~** to be at its height.
parpaing [paʀpɛ̃] *nm* (*aggloméré*) breeze-block.
parquer [paʀke] (1) **1** *vt voiture* to park; *bétail* to pen (in *ou* up). **2 se ~** *vpr* (*Aut*) to park.
parquet [paʀkɛ] *nm* **(a)** (*plancher*) (wooden *ou* parquet) floor. **(b)** (*Jur*) public prosecutor's department.
parrain [paʀɛ̃] *nm* (*Rel*) godfather; (*fig*) sponsor. ♦ **parrainage** *nm* sponsorship. ♦ **parrainer** (1) *vt* to sponsor.
parricide [paʀisid] **1** *adj* parricidal. **2** *nmf* parricide. **3** *nm* (*crime*) parricide.
parsemer [paʀsəme] (5) *vt* **(a)** (*répandre*) **~ de** to sprinkle with, strew with; **~ un texte de citations** to scatter quotations through a text. **(b)** (*être répandu sur*) to be scattered *ou* sprinkled over. **ciel parsemé d'étoiles** sky sprinkled *ou* studded with stars; **parsemé de difficultés** riddled with difficulties.
part [paʀ] *nf* **(a)** (*portion*) (*gén, Fin*) share; *[légumes]* portion. **la ~ du lion** the lion's share.
(b) (*participation*) part. **cela prend une grande ~ dans sa vie** it plays a great part in his life; **prendre ~ à** *débat* to participate in, take part in; *douleur* to share in; **faire la ~ de la fatigue** to take tiredness into account, make allowances for tiredness.
(c) (*partie*) part, portion, fraction. **pour une large ~** to a great extent; **pour une petite ~** in a small way.
(d) à ~ (*de côté*) aside, on one side; (*séparément*) separately, on its (*ou* their) own; (*excepté*) except for, apart from; **prendre qn à ~** to take sb aside; **plaisanterie à ~** joking apart; **c'est un homme à ~** he's an exceptional man, he's in a class of his own; **un cas à ~** a special case.
(e) faire ~ de qch à qn to inform sb of sth, tell sb about sth; **de la ~ de** (*provenance*) from; (*au nom de*) on behalf of; **cela m'étonne de sa ~** I'm surprised at that (coming) from him; **pour ma ~** as for me, as far as I'm concerned; **c'est gentil de sa ~** that's nice of him; (*Téléc*) **c'est de la ~ de qui?** who's calling? *ou* speaking?; **prendre qch en bonne ~** to take sth in good part; **prendre qch en mauvaise ~** to take offence at sth; **de toute(s) ~(s)** from all sides; **d'autre ~** (*de plus*) moreover; **d'une ~ ... d'autre ~** on the one hand ... on the other hand; **de ~ et d'autre** on both sides; **de ~ en ~** right through; **membre à ~ entière** full member.
partage [paʀtaʒ] *nm* **(a)** (*division*) division; *[gâteau]* cutting. **faire le ~ de qch** to divide sth up. **(b)** (*distribution*) sharing out. **le ~ n'est pas juste** it isn't fairly shared out. **(c)** (*participation*) sharing. **il y a ~ des responsabilités** the responsibility is shared; **fidélité sans ~** undivided loyalty. **(d)** (*part*) share; (*fig: sort*) portion, lot. (*Jur*) **recevoir qch en ~** to receive sth in a will.
partager [paʀtaʒe] (3) **1** *vt* **(a)** (*fractionner*) to divide up; (*distribuer*) to share out. **~ en 2/en 2 bouts** to divide in 2/into 2 bits; **~ son temps entre** to divide one's time between. **(b)** *héritage, sort* to share (*avec* with). **les torts sont partagés** all (*ou* both) parties are at fault. **(c)** *bonheur, goûts* to share (in); *idée* to share, agree with. **amour partagé** mutual love. **(d)** *[conflit]* to divide.

partagé entre l'amour et la haine torn between love and hatred. **2 se**~ *vpr*: **ça peut facilement se ~ en 3** it can easily be divided in 3; **le pouvoir ne se partage pas** power is not sth which can be shared; **ils se sont partagé le butin** they shared the booty between them. ♦ **partagé, e** *adj* **(a)** *opinions* divided. **(b)** (*littér: doté*) endowed. **il est bien ~ par le sort** fate has been kind to him.
partance [paʀtɑ̃s] *nf*: **en ~** *train* due to leave; *avion* outbound; *bateau* sailing; **en ~ pour Londres** for London.
partant [paʀtɑ̃] *nm* **(a)** (*coureur*) starter; (*cheval*) runner. **tous ~s** all horses running; **non ~** non-runner. **(b)** (*personne*) person leaving.
partenaire [paʀtənɛʀ] *nmf* partner.
parterre [paʀtɛʀ] *nm* **(a)** (*plate-bande*) border, (flower)bed. **(b)** (*Théât*) stalls, orchestra (*US*); (*public*) audience.
parti [paʀti] *nm* **(a)** (*groupe*) party. **prendre le ~ de qn, prendre ~ pour qn** to stand up for sb, take sb's side; **il ne veut pas prendre ~** he does not want to take a stand *ou* take sides. **(b)** (*solution*) option, course of action. **prendre le ~ de faire** to make up one's mind to do, decide to do; **prendre son ~ de qch** to come to terms with sth. **(c)** (*personne à marier*) match. **(d) tirer ~ de** *situation* to take advantage of, turn to (good) account; *ressources* to put to good use; **faire un mauvais ~ à qn** to deal roughly with sb. **(e) ~ pris** prejudice, bias; **juger sans ~ pris** to take an unbiased *ou* objective view.
partial, e, *mpl* **-aux** [paʀsjal, o] *adj jugement* biased. **être ~** to be biased *ou* partial. ♦ **partialement** *adv* in a biased way. ♦ **partialité** *nf*: **~ (en faveur de qn)** partiality (for sb); **~ (contre qn)** bias (against sb).
participer [paʀtisipe] (1) **1 ~ à** *vt indir* (*gén*) to take part in; *discussion, jeu* to participate in; *concours* to enter; *complot* to be involved in; *frais* to contribute to; *profits* to share in. *[artiste]* **~ à un spectacle** to appear in a show; **~ à la joie de qn** to share sb's joy; **~ (financièrement) à** *projet* to cooperate in. **2 ~ de** *vt indir* (*littér*) to partake of (*littér*). ♦ **participant, e 1** *adj* participant, participating. **2** *nm,f [concours, course]* entrant (*à* in); *[débat]* participant; *[association]* member (*à* of). **les ~s à la cérémonie** those taking part in the ceremony. ♦ **participation** *nf* **(a)** *[débat]* participation; *[spectacle]* appearance; *[complot]* involvement (*à* in). **c'est la ~ qui compte** what counts is taking part; **'~ aux frais: 50 F'** 'cost: 50 francs'. **(b)** (*Écon*) (*détention d'actions*) interest. **la ~ (ouvrière)** worker participation; **~ aux bénéfices** profit-sharing. ♦ **participe** *nm* participle.
particulariser [paʀtikylaʀize] (1) **1** *vt* to particularize. **2 se ~** *vpr* to be distinguished *ou* characterized (*par* by). ♦ **particularité** *nf* particularity, distinctive characteristic *ou* feature.
particule [paʀtikyl] *nf* (*Ling, Phys*) particle. **nom à ~** title.
particulier, -ière [paʀtikylje, jɛʀ] **1** *adj* **(a)** (*spécifique*) particular; *style* distinctive. **dans ce cas ~** in this particular case; **cette habitude lui est ~ière** this habit is peculiar to him. **(b)** (*inhabituel*) unusual. **rien de ~ à signaler** nothing in particular *ou* unusual to report; **avec un soin tout ~** with very special care, with particular care. **(c)** (*étrange*) peculiar, odd. **(d)** (*privé*) private. **leçons ~ières** private lessons *ou* tuition. **(e) en ~** (*en privé*) *parler* in private; (*séparément*) *examiner* separately; (*surtout, entre autres choses*) in particular. **2** *nm* **(a)** (*personne*) person; (*Admin*) private individual. **comme un simple ~** like any ordinary person; **vente de ~ à ~** private sale; **drôle de ~*** odd character *ou* individual. **(b)** (*chose*) **du général au ~** from the general to the particular. ♦ **particulièrement** *adv* particularly. **tout ~** especially.
partie [paʀti] *nf* **(a)** (*fraction*) part. **une petite ~ de l'argent** a small part *ou* amount of the money; **la majeure ~ du temps** most of *ou* the greater part of the time; **en ~** partly, in part; **en majeure ~** largely, for the most part; **faire ~ de** *ensemble, risques* to be part of; *club* to belong to; *gagnants* to be among; **faire ~ intégrante de** to be an integral part of, be part and parcel of. **(b)** (*spécialité*) field, subject. **il n'est pas de la ~** it's not his line *ou* field. **(c)** (*Cartes, Sport*) game. (*fig*) **abandonner la ~** to give up the fight; **la ~ n'est pas égale** it's not an even match. **(d)** (*Jur*) *[contrat]* party; *[procès]* litigant; (*Mil: adversaire*) opponent. **se porter ~ civile** to associate in an action with the public prosecutor; **avoir affaire à forte ~** to have a tough opponent to contend with; **être ~ prenante dans une négociation** to be a party to a negotiation. **(e)** (*Mus*) part. (*Ling*) **les ~s du discours** the parts of speech; (*Anat*) **~s sexuelles** private parts. **(f)** (*sortie, réunion*) party. **~ de pêche** fishing party *ou* expedition; **~ de campagne** outing in the country; **ce n'est pas une ~ de plaisir!** it's not my idea of fun! **(g)** (*locutions*) **ils ont la ~ belle** it's easy for them; **se mettre de la ~** to join in; **je veux être de la ~** I want to be in on this*; **ce n'est que ~ remise** it will be for another time; **prendre qn à ~** to attack sb; **comptabilité en ~ simple/double** single-/double-entry book-keeping.
partiel, -elle [paʀsjɛl] **1** *adj* (*gén*) partial. **paiement ~** part payment. **2** *nm* (*Univ*) class exam. ♦ **partiellement** *adv* partially, partly.
partir [paʀtiʀ] (16) *vi* **(a)** (*gén*) to go (*dans, pour* to); (*quitter un lieu*) to leave (*pour* for); (*se mettre en route*) to set off, set out (*pour* for); (*s'éloigner*) to go away *ou* off. **il est parti chercher du pain/faire des courses/en vacances** he has gone to buy some bread/gone (out) shopping/gone (off) on holiday; **allez, je pars** I'm off now; **sa femme est partie de la maison** his wife has left home; **faire ~ qn** to drive sb *ou* chase sb away; (*fig*) **~ en fumée** to go up in smoke; **fais ~ le chat de ma chaise** get the cat off my chair.
(b) *[moteur]* to start; *[avion]* to take off; *[train]* to leave; *[coureur]* to be off; *[plante]* to take. **~ en courant** to dash off; **la voiture partit** the car drove off; **attention, prêts? partez!** ready, steady, go!; **c'est parti mon kiki!‡** here we go!*; **faire ~ une voiture** to start (up) a car.
(c) *[fusée, coup de feu]* to go off; *[bouchon]* to pop *ou* shoot out. **ces cris partaient de la foule** these cries came from the crowd; **faire ~** *fusée* to launch; *pétard* to set off.
(d) (*être engagé*) **~ sur une idée fausse** to start off with the wrong idea; *[affaire]* **~ bien/mal** to get off to a good/bad start, start (off) well/badly; **le pays est mal parti** the country is in a bad way *ou* in a mess; **il est bien parti pour gagner** he's all set to win; **~ dans des digressions** to launch into digressions; **~ d'un éclat de rire** to burst out laughing; **la pluie est partie pour toute la journée** the rain has set in for the day; **on est parti pour ne pas déjeuner** at this rate *ou* the way things are going, we won't get any lunch.
(e) ~ de *[contrat, vacances]* to begin on, run from; *[course]* to start *ou* leave from; *[analyse]* to be based on; **un chemin qui part de l'église** a path going from the church; **si tu pars du principe que tu as toujours raison** if you start from the notion that you're always right; **cela part d'un bon sentiment** that comes from his (*ou* her *etc*) kindness.
(f) (*disparaître*) (*gén*) to go; *[tache]* to come out; *[bouton, crochet]* to come off; *[odeur]* to clear. **toute la couleur est partie** all the colour has gone *ou* faded; **faire ~** *tache* to remove; *odeur* to clear, get rid of.

(g) à ~ de from; **à ~ d'aujourd'hui** from today onwards; **à ~ de maintenant** from now on; **à ~ de** *ou* **en partant de la gauche, c'est le troisième** it is (the) third along from the left; **pantalons à ~ de 50 F** trousers from 50 francs (upwards).
partisan, e [paʀtizɑ̃, an] **1** *adj* **(a)** (*partial*) partisan. **(b) être ~ de qch/de faire qch** to be in favour of sth/of doing sth. **2** *nm,f* (*gén*) supporter; (*Mil*) partisan.
partitif, -ive [paʀtitif, iv] *adj* partitive.
partition [paʀtisjɔ̃] *nf* **(a)** (*Mus*) score. **(b)** (*division*) partition.
partout [paʀtu] *adv* everywhere. **~ où** wherever; **avoir mal ~** to ache all over; **tu as mis des papiers ~** you've put papers all over the place; (*Sport*) **2/15 ~** 2/15 all; (*Tennis*) **40 ~** deuce.
partouze‡ [paʀtuz] *nf* orgy.
parure [paʀyʀ] *nf* (*toilette*) costume; (*bijoux*) jewels; (*fig littér*) finery. **~ de lit** set of bed linen.
parution [paʀysjɔ̃] *nf* appearance, publication.
parvenir [paʀvəniʀ] (22) **1 ~ à** *vt indir* **(a)** (*arriver*) (*gén*) to reach; *sommet* to get to; *honneurs* to achieve. **~ à maturité** to become ripe; **faire ~ qch à qn** to send sth to sb; **~ à ses fins** to achieve one's ends. **(b)** (*réussir*) **~ à faire qch** to manage to do sth, succeed in doing sth; **il y est parvenu** he managed it. **2** *vi* (*faire fortune*) to succeed *ou* get on in life. ♦ **parvenu, e** *adj, nm,f* (*péj*) parvenu, upstart.
parvis [paʀvi] *nm* square (*in front of church*).
pas[1] [pɑ] *nm* **(a)** (*gén*) step; (*bruit*) footstep; (*trace*) footprint; (*démarche*) tread. **faire un ~ en arrière** to step *ou* take a step back; **marcher à grands ~** to stride along; (*lit, fig*) **~ à ~** step by step; **ne le quittez pas d'un ~** follow him wherever he goes; **arriver sur les ~ de qn** to follow close on sb's heels. **(b)** (*distance*) pace. **c'est à deux ~ d'ici** it's just a stone's throw from here. **(c)** (*vitesse*) pace; (*Mil, Danse*) step; *[cheval]* walk. **d'un bon ~** at a good *ou* brisk pace; **marcher d'un ~ lent** to walk slowly; **marcher au ~** to march; **mettre son cheval au ~** to walk one's horse; (*Aut*) **rouler au ~** to drive dead slow*; **au ~ cadencé** in quick time; **au ~ de charge** at the charge; **au ~ de course** at a run; **au ~ de gymnastique** at a jog trot; **faire le ~ de l'oie** to goose-step. **(d)** *[montagne]* pass; *[mer]* strait. **le ~ de Calais** the Straits of Dover. **(e) ~ (de vis)** thread. **(f) le ~ de la porte** the doorstep; (*Jur*) **~ de porte** key money (*for shop etc*). **(g) avancer à ~ de géant** to take gigantic steps forward; **à ~ de loup, à ~ feutrés** stealthily; **j'y vais de ce ~** I'll go straightaway *ou* at once; **mettre qn au ~** to bring sb to heel, make sb toe the line; **avoir le ~ sur qn** to rank before sb; **prendre le ~ sur** *considérations* to override; *méthode* to supplant; *personne* to steal a lead over; **sauter le ~** to take the plunge.
pas[2] [pɑ] *adv nég* **(a)** (*avec ne*) not. **ce n'est ~ vrai, c'est ~ vrai*** it isn't *ou* it's not *ou* it is not true; **je ne trouve ~ mon sac** I can't *ou* cannot find my bag; **ils n'ont ~ de voiture** they don't have *ou* haven't got a car, they have no car; **il m'a dit de ne ~ le faire** he told me not to do it; **je n'en sais ~ plus que vous** I know no more *ou* I don't know any more about it than you (do); **il n'est ~ moins intelligent que vous** he is no less intelligent than you. **(b)** (*opposition*) **elle travaille, mais lui ~** she works, but he doesn't; **ils sont 4 et non ~ 3** there are 4 of them, not 3. **(c)** (*réponses négatives*) **~ de sucre, merci!** no sugar, thanks!; **~ du tout** not at all; **~ encore** not yet; **~ des masses‡** not a lot; **qui l'a prévenu? — ~ moi** who told him? — not me *ou* I didn't. **(d)** (*excl*) **~ un n'est venu** not one *ou* none (of them) came; **~ possible!*** no!, you don't say!*; **~ de chance!*** hard *ou* bad luck!, too bad!*; **tu es content, ~ vrai?*** you're pleased, aren't you?; **~ d'histoires** no nonsense; **(c'est) ~ bête!** that's not a bad idea!; **~ de ça!** none of that!; **ce n'est ~ trop tôt!** it's not before time! **(e)** (*locutions*) **~ plus tard qu'hier** only *ou* just yesterday; **ils ont ~ mal d'argent** they have quite a lot of money.
passable [pɑsabl(ə)] *adj* passable, reasonable, tolerable. (*Univ*) **mention ~** pass(mark). ♦ **passablement** *adv travailler* reasonably well; *irritant, long* rather, fairly; (*beaucoup*) quite a lot *ou* a bit* (*de* of).
passade [pɑsad] *nf* passing fancy.
passage [pɑsaʒ] **1** *nm* **(a)** (*venue*) **attendre le ~ de l'autobus** to wait for the bus to come (by *ou* past); **observer le ~ des oiseaux** to watch the birds fly by; **lors de votre ~ à la douane** when you go through customs; **l'autobus fait 4 ~s par jour** the bus goes past 4 times a day; **'~ de troupeaux'** 'cattle crossing'; **commerçant qui travaille avec le ~** shopkeeper catering for the casual *ou* passing trade; **il est de ~ à Paris** he is in *ou* visiting Paris at the moment; **je l'ai saisi au ~** I grabbed him as I went by *ou* past. **(b)** (*transfert*) **le ~ de l'enfance à l'adolescence** the transition from childhood to adolescence; **le ~ du jour à la nuit** the change from day to night; **le ~ de l'alcool dans le sang** the entry of alcohol into the bloodstream. **(c)** (*lieu*) passage; (*chemin*) way, passage; (*itinéraire*) route; (*rue*) passage(way), alley(way). **on se retourne sur son ~** people turn round and look when he goes past; **barrer le ~ à qn** to block sb's way; **laisser le ~ à qn** to let sb pass *ou* past, make way for sb. **(d)** (*Naut*) **payer son ~** to pay for one's passage, pay one's fare. **(e)** *[livre, symphonie]* passage. **(f)** (*traversée*) *[rivière, limite]* crossing. **2: ~ clouté** pedestrian crossing; **'~ interdit'** 'no entry'; **~ à niveau** level crossing; **~ souterrain** subway, underground passage (*US*); **~ à tabac** beating up; **~ à vide** blank spell.
passager, -ère [pɑsaʒe, ɛʀ] **1** *adj* **(a)** *hôte* temporary, making a short stay. **(b)** *malaise etc* passing; *inconvénient* temporary; *bonheur, beauté* transient. **pluies ~ères** intermittent *ou* occasional showers *ou* rain. **(c)** *rue* busy. **2** *nm,f* passenger. **~ clandestin** stowaway. ♦ **passagèrement** *adv* temporarily.
passant, e [pɑsɑ̃, ɑ̃t] **1** *adj rue* busy. **2** *nm,f* passer-by. **3** *nm [ceinture]* loop.
passation [pɑsasjɔ̃] *nf [contrat]* signing. **~ de pouvoirs** transfer of power.
passe [pɑs] **1** *nf* (*gén*) pass; (*Roulette*) passe; (*chenal*) pass, channel. **être en ~ de faire** to be on the way to doing; **être dans une mauvaise ~** to be in a bad way; **traverser une mauvaise ~** to go through a bad patch; (*fig*) **~ d'armes** heated exchange. **2** *nm* (*) skeleton *ou* master key. ♦ **passe-droit,** *pl* **~-~s** *nm* undeserved privilege. ♦ **passe-montagne,** *pl* **~-~s** *nm* balaclava. ♦ **passe-partout 1** *nm inv* skeleton *ou* master key. **2** *adj inv*: **formule** *etc* **~** all-purpose phrase *etc*. ♦ **passe-plat,** *pl* **~-~s** *nm* serving hatch. ♦ **passe-temps** *nm inv* pastime.
passé, e [pɑse] **1** *adj* **(a)** (*dernier*) last. **le mois ~** last month; **au cours des années ~es** over the past years. **(b)** (*révolu*) past. **~ de mode** out of fashion, out of date; **sa gloire ~e** his past *ou* former glory; **cette époque est ~e maintenant** that era is now over; **il se rappelait le temps ~** he was thinking back to days *ou* time gone by. **(c)** (*fané*) faded. **(d)** (*plus de*) **il est 8 heures ~es** it's past *ou* gone 8 o'clock; **ça fait une heure ~e que je t'attends** I've been waiting for you for more than *ou* over an hour. **2** *nm* **(a)** (*gén*) past. **c'est du ~** it's (all) in the past now. **(b)** (*Gram*) past tense. **~ antérieur** past anterior; **~ composé** perfect; **~ simple** past historic. **3** *prép* after. **~ 6 heures/cette maison** after 6 o'clock/this house.
passementerie [pɑsmɑ̃tʀi] *nf* braid, trimming.
passeport [pɑspɔʀ] *nm* passport.
passer [pɑse] (1) **1** *vi* **(a)** (*gén*) to pass; *[train]* to come *ou* go past; *[démarcheur]* to call. **~ devant la**

maison de qn to pass *ou* go past sb's house; ~ **en courant** to run past; **il passait dans la rue** he was walking down the street; **l'air passe sous la porte** a draught comes in under the door; **où passe la route?** where does the road go?; **la Seine passe à Paris** the Seine flows through Paris; **faire ~ qn d'abord** to let sb go first; **une lueur passa dans son regard** a gleam came into his eyes; ~ **au bureau** to call (in) *ou* drop in at the office; ~ **prendre qn** to call for sb; **le facteur est passé** the postman has been; **j'irai le voir en passant** I'll call to see him on my way past; (*fig*) **soit dit en passant** let me say in passing *ou* by the way. **(b)** (*changer*) to go. ~ **d'une pièce dans une autre** to go from one room to another; ~ **d'un état à l'autre** to change *ou* pass from one state to another; ~ **à l'ennemi** to go over to the enemy; **la photo passa de main en main** the photo was passed *ou* handed round; ~ **dans la langue** to pass *ou* come into the language; **son argent de poche passe en bonbons** his pocket money (all) goes on sweets. **(c)** *[temps]* to go by, pass. **comme le temps passe!** how time flies!; **cela fait ~ le temps** it passes the time. **(d)** *[liquide]* to go through; *[courant électrique]* to get through. **(e)** (*être accepté*) *[proposition, candidat]* to pass, get through; *[plaisanterie, erreur]* to be acceptable; *[aliment]* to go down. **mon déjeuner ne passe pas** my lunch hasn't settled; **il est passé dans la classe supérieure** he's moved up to the next class; ~ **directeur** to become *ou* be appointed director; **qu'il soit menteur, passe encore, mais voleur, c'est plus grave** it's one thing if he's a liar, but it's more serious if he's a thief; **passe pour cette fois** I'll let you off this time. **(f)** *[film]* to be showing, be on; (*TV*) *[émission]* to be on; *[personne]* to be on, appear. ~ **à la télé*** to be on TV*. **(g)** (*dépasser*) *[oreilles, queue]* to stick out. **son manteau est trop court, la robe passe** her coat is too short — her dress shows underneath (it); **ne laisse pas ~ ton bras par la portière** don't put your arm out of the window. **(h)** *[couleur, beauté]* to fade; *[mode]* to die out; *[douleur]* to pass (off), wear off; *[colère, orage]* to die down; *[jeunesse]* to pass; (*mourir*) to pass on *ou* away. **faire ~ à qn l'envie de faire** to cure sb of doing; **cela fera ~ votre rhume** that will get you over your cold *ou* get rid of your cold for you; **le plus dur est passé** the worst is over now; **ça lui passera!*** he'll grow out of it! **(i)** (*Cartes*) to pass. **(j)** (*Aut*) ~ **en première** to go into first (gear); ~ **en seconde** to change into second; **les vitesses passent mal** the gears are stiff. **(k)** ~ **par** (*lit, fig*) to go through; **par où êtes-vous passé?** which way did you go?; ~ **par des difficultés** to have difficulties *ou* a difficult time; **nous sommes tous passés par là** we've all been through that; **il faudra bien en ~ par là** there's no way round it, we'll have to put up with it. **(l)** ~ **pour un imbécile/pour un Allemand** to be taken for a fool/for a German; ~ **pour un séducteur** to be regarded as a lady's man; **il passe pour intelligent** he is supposed to be intelligent; **cela passe pour vrai** it's thought to be true; **se faire ~ pour** to pass o.s. off as; **faire ~ qn pour** to make sb out to be. **(m)** ~ **sous/sur/derrière** *etc* to go under/over/behind *etc*; **passez donc devant** you go first; ~ **devant une juridiction** to come before a court; **il est passé sous l'autobus** he was run over by the bus; **le travail passe avant les loisirs** work comes before leisure; **les poissons sont passés au travers du filet** the fish slipped through the net; ~ **sur** *faute, détail* to pass over. **(n)** **y** ~*: **tout le monde y a** *ou* **y est passé** everybody got it, nobody escaped it; **toute sa fortune y a passé** *ou* **y est passée** his whole fortune went on it. **(o)** **laisser** ~ *air* to let in; *personne* to let through (*ou* past, in, out *etc*); *erreur* to overlook, miss; *occasion* to let slip, miss; **nous ne pouvons pas laisser ~ cette affaire sans protester** we cannot let this matter pass without a protest.

2 *vt* **(a)** *frontière* to cross; *porte* to go through; *obstacle* to get through; *haie* to jump *ou* get over. ~ **une rivière à la nage** to swim across a river. **(b)** *examen* to sit, take; *douane* to go through, clear. *visite médicale* to have. **(c)** *temps* to spend (*à faire* doing). **pour ~ le temps** to while away *ou* pass the time. **(d)** (*assouvir*) ~ **sa colère sur qn** to work off *ou* vent one's anger on sb. **(e)** (*omettre*) *mot* to miss *ou* leave out. ~ **son tour** to miss one's turn; **et j'en passe!** and that's not all! **(f)** (*permettre*) ~ **une faute à qn** to overlook sb's mistake; ~ **un caprice à qn** to indulge sb's whim; **on lui passe tout** he gets away with anything; **passez-moi l'expression** (if you'll) pardon the expression. **(g)** *consigne, maladie* to pass on; *objet* to pass, give, hand; *faux billets* to pass; (*Sport*) *ballon* to pass (*à* to). ~ **(en fraude) de l'alcool** to smuggle spirits; **tu (le) fais ~** pass *ou* hand it round; **passe-moi du feu** give me a light; (*au téléphone*) **je vous passe M X** (*gén*) here's Mr X; (*standard*) I'm putting you through to Mr X; **passe-lui un coup de fil** give him a ring *ou* call. **(h)** *pull* to slip on; *robe* to slip into. ~ **une bague au doigt de qn** to slip a ring on sb's finger; ~ **un lacet dans qch** to thread a lace through sth. **(i)** ~ **la tête à la porte** to poke one's head round the door; ~ **la main à la fenêtre** to stick one's hand out of the window. **(j)** (*dépasser*) *maison* to pass, go past. ~ **les bornes** to go too far; **tu as passé l'âge (de ces jeux)** you are too old (for these games); **il ne passera pas la nuit** he won't last the night. **(k)** *soupe, thé* to strain; *café* to pour the water on. **(l)** (*Aut*) ~ **la seconde** to go *ou* change (up *ou* down) into second (gear). **(m)** *film* to show; *disque* to put on, play. **que passent-ils au cinéma?** what's on *ou* showing at the cinema? **(n)** (*Comm*) *écriture* to enter; *commande* to place; *accord* to reach, come to; *contrat* to sign. **(o)** ~ **le balai** to sweep up; **passe le chiffon dans le salon** dust the sitting room, give the sitting room a dust; ~ **une couche de peinture sur qch** to give sth a coat of paint; **elle lui passa la main dans les cheveux** she ran her hand through his hair; **se ~ les mains à l'eau** to rinse one's hands.

3 se ~ *vpr* **(a)** (*avoir lieu*) to take place; (*arriver*) to happen. **qu'est-ce qu'il se passe?** what's going on?; **tout s'est bien passé** everything went off smoothly; **cela ne se passera pas ainsi!** I shan't let it rest at that!; **il ne se passe pas un seul jour sans qu'il ne pleuve** not a day goes by without rain. **(b)** (*finir*) *[douleur, orage]* to pass off, be over. **(c)** **se ~ de qch/de faire** to do without sth/doing; **se ~ de qn** to manage without sb; **la citation se passe de commentaires** the quotation needs no comment *ou* speaks for itself.

passerelle [pasʀɛl] *nf* (*pont*) footbridge; (*Aviat, Naut*) gangway; (*du commandant*) bridge; (*fig: passage*) (inter)link.

passeur [pasœʀ] *nm [rivière]* ferryman; *[frontière]* smuggler.

passible [pasibl(ə)] *adj*: ~ **d'une amende** *personne* liable to a fine; *délit* punishable by a fine; ~ **d'un impôt** liable for (a) tax.

passif, -ive [pasif, iv] **1** *adj* (*gén*) passive. **2** *nm* (*Ling*) passive; (*Fin*) liabilities. ♦ **passivement** *adv* passively. ♦ **passivité** *nf* passivity, passiveness.

passion [pɑsjɔ̃] *nf* passion. **avoir la ~ du jeu** to have a passion for gambling; **aimer/discuter avec ~** to love/argue passionately; **sans ~** dispassionately; (*Rel*) **la P~** the Passion. ♦ **passionnant, e** *adj personne* fascinating; *film* fascinating, gripping, exciting. ♦ **passionné, e 1** *adj personne, haine* passionate; *orateur, jugement* impassioned. **être ~ de** to have a passion for. **2** *nm,f*: **un ~ de voitures** a car fanatic. ♦ **passionnel, -elle** *adj sentiment* passionate; *crime* of passion. ♦ **passionnément** *adv* passionately. ♦ **passionner** (1) **1** *vt personne* to fascinate, grip; *débat* to inflame. **la musique le passionne** music is his passion, he has a passion for music. **2 se ~** *vpr*: **se ~ pour** *livre* to be fascinated by; *sport, science* to have a passion for.

passoire [pɑswaʀ] *nf* (*gén, fig*) sieve; *[thé]* strainer; *[légumes]* colander.

pastel [pastɛl] *nm, adj inv* pastel.

pastèque [pastɛk] *nf* watermelon.

pasteur [pastœʀ] *nm* (*prêtre*) minister, pastor; (*littér, Rel: berger*) shepherd.

pasteuriser [pastœʀize] (1) *vt* to pasteurize. ♦ **pasteurisation** *nf* pasteurization.

pastiche [pastiʃ] *nm* pastiche. ♦ **pasticher** (1) *vt* to write a pastiche of.

pastille [pastij] *nf* (*bonbon*) pastille, lozenge; *[couleur]* block; *[papier]* disc. **~s de menthe** mints; **~s pour la toux** cough pastilles *ou* drops.

pastoral, e, *mpl* -aux [pastɔʀal, o] **1** *adj* (*gén*) pastoral. **2** *nf* (*gén*) pastoral; (*Mus*) pastorale.

patate [patat] *nf* (*: *pomme de terre*) spud‡; (‡: *imbécile*) fathead‡, chump*. **~ (douce)** sweet potato.

patati* [patati] *excl*: **et ~ et patata** and so on and so forth.

patatras [patatʀa] *excl* crash!

pataud, e [pato, od] *adj* lumpish, clumsy.

patauger [patoʒe] (3) *vi* (*avec effort*) to wade about; (*avec plaisir*) to splash about; (*fig: être perdu*) to flounder.

pâte [pɑt] **1** *nf* **(a)** (*à tarte*) pastry; (*à gâteaux*) mixture; (*à pain*) dough; (*à frire*) batter. **(b)** *[fromage]* cheese. **(c) ~s (alimentaires)** pasta; (*dans la soupe*) noodles. **(d)** (*gén: substance*) paste; (*crème*) cream. **2: ~ d'amandes** almond paste; **~ brisée** shortcrust pastry; **~ dentifrice** toothpaste; **~ feuilletée** puff *ou* flaky pastry; **~ de fruits** fruit jelly; **~ à modeler** modelling clay, Plasticine ®; **~ à papier** paper pulp; **~ sablée** sablé pastry. ♦ **pâté** *nm* (*Culin*) pâté; (*d'encre*) inkblot. **~ en croûte** ≃ meat pie; **~ de maisons** block (of houses); **~ (de sable)** sandpie, sandcastle. ♦ **pâtée** *nf* **(a)** *[chien, volaille]* mash, feed; *[porcs]* swill. **(b)** (*: *correction*) hiding*.

patelin* [patlɛ̃] *nm* village.

patent, e[1] [patɑ̃, ɑ̃t] *adj* obvious, patent.

patente[2] [patɑ̃t] *nf* (trading) licence. ♦ **patenté, e** *adj* licensed.

patère [patɛʀ] *nf* (hat- *ou* coat-)peg.

paternel, -elle [patɛʀnɛl] **1** *adj* paternal; (*bienveillant*) fatherly. **quitter le domicile ~** to leave one's father's house; **ma tante ~elle** my aunt on my father's side, my paternal aunt. **2** *nm* (‡) old man‡. ♦ **paternalisme** *nm* paternalism. ♦ **paternaliste** *adj* paternalistic. ♦ **paternellement** *adv* paternally; in a fatherly way. ♦ **paternité** *nf* paternity.

pâteux, -euse [pɑtø, øz] *adj* (*gén*) pasty; *langue* coated; *voix* thick, husky.

pathétique [patetik] **1** *adj* moving, pathetic; (*Anat*) pathetic. **2** *nm* pathos.

pathogène [patɔʒɛn] *adj* pathogenic.

pathologique [patɔlɔʒik] *adj* pathological. ♦ **pathologiquement** *adv* pathologically.

patibulaire [patibylɛʀ] *adj* sinister.

patience [pasjɑ̃s] *nf* (*gén*) patience. **prendre ~** to be patient, have patience; **il faut avoir une ~ d'ange** it takes the patience of a saint *ou* of Job; (*Cartes*) **faires des ~s** to play patience; **~, j'arrive!** wait a minute! *ou* hang on!*, I'm coming. ♦ **patiemment** *adv* patiently. ♦ **patient, e 1** *adj* patient. **2** *nm,f* (*Méd*) patient. ♦ **patienter** (1) *vi* to wait. **faites-le ~** ask him to wait; **~ un instant** to wait *ou* hang on* a moment; **pour ~ il regardait les tableaux** to fill in *ou* pass the time he looked at the paintings.

patin [patɛ̃] *nm [patineur]* skate; *[luge]* runner; (*pour le parquet*) cloth pad. **~ (de frein)** brake block; **~s à glace** iceskates; **~s à roulettes** roller skates; **faire du ~ à glace** to go ice-skating. ♦ **patinage** *nm* skating. **~ artistique** figure skating. ♦ **patiner**[1] (1) *vi* (*Sport*) to skate; (*Aut*) *[roue]* to spin; *[embrayage]* to slip. ♦ **patinette** *nf* scooter. ♦ **patineur, -euse** *nm,f* skater. ♦ **patinoire** *nf* skating rink, ice rink.

patine [patin] *nf* patina, sheen. ♦ **patiner**[2] (1) *vt* (*naturellement*) to give a sheen to; (*artificiellement*) to give a patina to.

pâtir [pɑtiʀ] (2) *vi* (*littér*) to suffer (*de* because of).

pâtisserie [pɑtisʀi] *nf* (*magasin*) cake shop, confectioner's; (*gâteau*) cake, pastry; (*art ménager*) cake- *ou* pastry-making, baking; (*commerce*) confectionery. ♦ **pâtissier, -ière** *nm,f* confectioner, pastrycook.

patois [patwa] *nm* patois.

patraque* [patʀak] *adj* peaky*, out of sorts.

pâtre [pɑtʀ(ə)] *nm* (*littér*) shepherd.

patriarche [patʀijaʀʃ(ə)] *nm* patriarch.

patricien, -ienne [patʀisjɛ̃, jɛn] *adj, nm,f* patrician.

patrie [patʀi] *nf* (*gén*) homeland, fatherland. **Limoges, ~ de la porcelaine** Limoges, the home of porcelain.

patrimoine [patʀimwan] *nm* (*gén*) inheritance; (*Jur*) patrimony; (*fig*) heritage.

patriote [patʀiɔt] **1** *adj* patriotic. **2** *nmf* patriot. ♦ **patriotique** *adj* patriotic. ♦ **patriotisme** *nm* patriotism.

patron [patʀɔ̃] *nm* **(a)** (*propriétaire*) owner, boss*; (*gérant*) manager, boss*; (*employeur*) employer, boss*; (*Hist, Rel: protecteur*) patron. **saint ~** patron saint; **~ (pêcheur)** skipper. **(b)** (*Couture*) pattern. **taille demi-~/~/grand ~** small/medium/large size. ♦ **patronne** *nf* boss*, lady owner (*ou* manager *ou* employer); (*sainte*) patron saint. ♦ **patronage** *nm* **(a)** (*protection*) patronage. **(b)** (*organisation*) youth club. ♦ **patronal, e, *mpl* -aux** *adj* employer's. ♦ **patronat** *nm*: **le ~** the employers. ♦ **patronner** (1) *vt* to sponsor, support.

patrouille [patʀuj] *nf* patrol. ♦ **patrouiller** (1) *vi* to patrol, be on patrol. **~ dans les rues** to patrol the streets. ♦ **patrouilleur** *nm* (*soldat*) patroller; (*Naut*) patrol boat.

patte [pat] **1** *nf* **(a)** (*jambe*) leg; (*pied*) *[chat]* paw; *[oiseau]* foot; (*: *main*) hand, paw*. **~s de devant** forelegs; forefeet; **~s de derrière** hindlegs; hind feet; **le chat retomba sur ses ~s** the cat fell on its feet; *[chat]* **faire ~ de velours** to draw in *ou* sheathe its claws; **court sur ~s** *personne* short-legged; *table* low; **il est toujours dans mes ~s*** he's always under my feet; **s'il me tombe sous la ~*** if I get my hands *ou* paws* on him; **tomber dans les ~s de qn*** to fall into sb's clutches. **(b)** *[ancre]* fluke; (*languette*) tongue; *[vêtement]* strap; (*sur l'épaule*) epaulette. **(c)** (*favoris*) **~s (de lapin)** sideburns. **2: pantalon à ~s d'éléphant** bell-bottom trousers; **~s de mouche** spidery scrawl; **~-d'oie** *nf, pl* **~s-~** (*à l'œil*) crow's-foot; (*carrefour*) branching crossroads.

pâturer [pɑtyʀe] (1) *vti* to graze. ♦ **pâturage** *nm* (*lieu*) pasture; (*action*) grazing. ♦ **pâture** *nf* (*nourriture*) food; (*pâturage*) pasture.

paume [pom] *nf [main]* palm.

paumer‡ [pome] (1) **1** *vt* (*perdre*) to lose. **2 se ~** *vpr* to get lost. ♦ **paumé, e‡ 1** *adj* lost. **habiter un bled ~** to live in a godforsaken hole‡. **2** *nmf* drop-out*.

paupière [popjɛʀ] *nf* eyelid.

paupiette [popjɛt] *nf*: **~ de veau** veal olive.

pause [poz] *nf* (*arrêt*) break; (*en parlant, Mus*) pause; (*Sport*) half-time.

pauvre [povʀ(ə)] **1** *adj* (*gén*) poor; *végétation* sparse; *mobilier* shabby; *excuse, orateur, sourire* weak. **minerai ~ en cuivre** ore with a low copper content, ore poor in copper; **air ~ en oxygène** air low in oxygen; **pays ~ en ressources** country short of *ou* lacking resources; **de ~s chances de succès** only a slim *ou* slender chance of success; **elle avait un ~ petit air** she looked miserable *ou* wretched. **(b) ~ crétin‡** stupid ass‡; **~ hère** poor wretch; **~ d'esprit** half-wit; **mon ~ mari** my poor husband; **~ de moi!** poor (little) me!; **mon ~ ami** my dear friend. **2** *nmf* poor man *ou* woman. **les ~s** the poor, poor people; **mon ~!** my dear fellow; **le ~!** the poor guy!* ♦ **pauvrement** *adv* poorly; *vêtu* shabbily. ♦ **pauvreté** *nf* (*gén*) poverty; *[mobilier]* shabbiness.

pavaner (se) [pavane] (1) *vpr* to strut about.

pavé [pave] *nm [chaussée]* cobblestone; *[cour]* paving stone; (*viande*) thick piece of steak; (*péj: livre*) hefty tome*. **être sur le ~** (*sans domicile*) to be on the streets; (*sans emploi*) to be out of a job; **mettre qn sur le ~** to throw sb out; **jeter un ~ dans la mare** to set the cat among the pigeons. ♦ **paver** (1) *vt cour* to pave; *chaussée* to cobble. ♦ **pavage** *nm* (*revêtement*) paving; cobbles.

pavillon [pavijɔ̃] *nm* **(a)** (*villa*) house; (*de gardien*) lodge; (*d'hôpital*) ward, pavilion. **~ de banlieue** house in the suburbs; **~ de chasse** hunting lodge. **(b)** (*Naut*) flag. **(c)** *[instrument]* bell; *[phonographe]* horn; *[oreille]* pavilion, pinna.

pavoiser [pavwaze] (1) **1** *vt navire* to dress; *monument* to deck with flags. **2** *vi* to put out flags; (*fig*) to exult.

pavot [pavo] *nm* poppy.

payer [peje] (8) **1** *vt* **(a)** *somme, employé* to pay; *dette* to pay, settle; *entrepreneur* to pay, settle up with. **~ comptant** to pay cash; **~ qn de promesses** to fob sb off with promises; (*fig*) **il est payé pour le savoir** he has learnt that to his cost. **(b)** *travail, marchandise* to pay for. **je l'ai payé de ma poche** I paid for it out of my own pocket; **il m'a fait ~ 10F** he charged me 10 francs (*pour* for); **travail bien/mal payé** well-/badly-paid work. **(c)** (*: *offrir*) **~ qch à qn** (*gén*) to buy sth for sb; *restaurant, apéritif* to treat sb to sth, stand sb sth; **~ un voyage à qn** to pay for sb to go on a trip. **(d)** (*récompenser*) to reward (*de* for). **(e)** *faute, crime* to pay for. **il l'a payé de sa vie** it cost him his life; **il me le paiera!** he'll pay for this!

2 *vi* **(a)** *[effort]* to pay off; *[métier]* to be well-paid. **le crime ne paie pas** crime doesn't pay; **~ pour qn** (*lit*) to pay for sb; (*fig*) to carry the can for sb*. **(b) ~ de sa personne** to give of o.s., sacrifice o.s.; **ça ne paie pas de mine, mais** it isn't much to look at but; **~ d'audace** to act with great daring.

3 se ~ *vpr* **(a) tout se paie** everything must be paid for. **(b)** (*: *s'offrir*) *objet* to buy o.s., treat o.s. to; *maladie* to get. **se ~ une pinte de bon sang** to have a good laugh*; **se ~ la tête de qn** to make a fool of sb.

♦ **payable** *adj*: **~ en 3 fois** payable in 3 instalments; **l'impôt est ~ par tous** taxes must be paid by everyone. ♦ **payant, e** *adj* **(a)** *spectateur* who pays (for his seat). **spectacle ~** show for which there is an admission charge. **(b)** (*rentable*) *affaire* profitable; *politique, conduite* which pays off. ♦ **paye** *nf* = **paie.** ♦ **payement** *nm* = **paiement.** ♦ **payeur, -euse 1** *adj*: **service ~** payments office. **2** *nm,f* payer; (*Mil, Naut*) paymaster. **mauvais ~** bad debtor.

pays [pei] **1** *nm* **(a)** (*contrée*) country. **des ~ lointains** far-off countries *ou* lands. **(b)** (*région*) region. **gens/vin du ~** local people/wine; **~ de légumes/d'élevage** vegetable-growing/cattle-breeding region; **le ~ du vin** the wine country. **(c)** (*village*) village. **(d) voir du ~** to travel around (a lot); **être en ~ de connaissance** (*dans une réunion*) to be among familiar faces; (*sur un sujet*) to be on home ground. **2: les P~-Bas** *nmpl* the Netherlands; **~ de Cocagne** land of plenty; **le ~de Galles** Wales.

paysage [peizaʒ] *nm* (*point de vue*) landscape; (*décor*) scenery. ♦ **paysagiste** *nmf* (*Peinture*) landscape painter. (*Agr*) **(jardinier) ~** landscape gardener.

paysan, -anne [peizɑ̃, an] **1** *adj problème* farming; *revendications* farmers'; *coutumes* country; (*péj*) *manières* peasant. **2** *nm* countryman, farmer; (*péj*) peasant. **3** *nf* peasant woman, countrywoman; (*péj*) peasant. ♦ **paysannerie** *nf* peasantry, farmers.

péage [peaʒ] *nm* (*droit*) toll; (*barrière*) tollgate. **pont à ~** toll bridge.

peau, *pl* **~x** [po] **1** *nf* **(a)** (*gén*) skin. **n'avoir que la ~ et les os** to be all skin and bones; **attraper qn par la ~ du cou** to grab sb by the scruff of his *ou* her neck; **faire ~ neuve** *[administration]* to find a new image; (*en changeant d'habit*) to change (one's clothes). **(b)** (*: *corps, vie*) **risquer sa ~** to risk one's neck* *ou* hide*; **sauver sa ~** to save one's skin; **j'aurai sa ~!** I'll have his hide for this!*; **être bien/mal dans sa ~** (*physiquement*) to feel great*/awful; (*mentalement*) to feel quite at ease/ill-at-ease; **avoir qn dans la ~** to be crazy about sb*; **avoir le jeu** *etc* **dans la ~** to have gambling *etc* in one's blood; **se mettre dans la ~ de qn** to put o.s in sb's place *ou* shoes. **(c)** (*cuir*) hide; (*fourrure*) pelt. **gants de ~** leather gloves. **(d)** *[fromage]* rind; (*épluchure*) peel. **2: ~ de chamois** chamois leather, shammy; **~ de mouton** sheepskin; **~ de porc** pigskin; **P~-Rouge** *nmf, pl* **P~x-R~s** Red Indian, redskin; **~ de vache‡** (*homme*) bastard‡; (*femme*) bitch‡.

pébroque* [pebrɔk] *nm* brolly*, umbrella.

peccadille [pekadij] *nf* (*vétille*) trifle; (*délit*) peccadillo.

pêche[1] [pɛʃ] *nf* (*fruit*) peach; (‡: *coup*) slap, clout. **~-abricot/blanche** yellow/white peach. ♦ **pêcher**[1] *nm* peach tree.

pêche[2] [pɛʃ] *nf* **(a)** (*activité*) fishing; (*saison*) fishing season. **la ~ à la ligne** (*mer*) line fishing; (*rivière*) angling; **la ~ aux moules** the gathering of mussels; **aller à la ~** to go fishing; **barque de ~** fishing boat. **(b)** (*poissons*) catch. ♦ **pêcher**[2] (1) **1** *vt* (*être pêcheur de*) to fish for; (*attraper*) to catch, land; *coquillages* to gather. **~ la baleine/la crevette** to go whaling/shrimping; **où as-tu été ~ cette idée?*** where did you dig that idea up from?* **2** *vi* to go fishing; to go angling. **~ à l'asticot** to fish with maggots. ♦ **pêcherie** *nf* fishery, fishing ground. ♦ **pêcheur 1** *nm* fisherman; angler. **~ de crevettes** shrimper; **~ de perles** pearl diver. **2** *adj bateau* fishing. ♦ **pêcheuse** *nf* fisherwoman; (*à la ligne*) (woman) angler.

péché [peʃe] *nm* sin. **~ capital** *ou* **mortel** deadly sin; **~ de jeunesse** youthful indiscretion; **c'est son ~ mignon** he has a weakness for it. ♦ **pécher** (6) *vi* (*Rel*) to sin. **~ par imprudence** to be too reckless; **~ par ignorance** to err through ignorance; **~ par excès de prudence** to be over-careful; **ça pèche par bien des points** it has a lot of weaknesses *ou* shortcomings. ♦ **pécheur, pécheresse** *nm,f* sinner.

pécule [pekyl] *nm* (*économies*) savings; *[détenu, soldat]* earnings, wages.

pécuniaire [pekynjɛʀ] *adj* financial.

pédagogie [pedagɔʒi] *nf* (*science, méthode*) education. ♦ **pédagogique** *adj méthodes* educational; (*clair*) *exposé* clear. **stage (de formation) ~** teacher-training course. ♦ **pédagogue** *nmf* teacher.

pédale [pedal] *nf* (*gén*) pedal; *[machine à coudre, tour]* treadle. ♦ **pédaler** (1) *vi* to pedal. ♦ **pédalier** *nm* pedal and gear mechanism. ♦ **pédalo** *nm* pedal-boat.

pédant, e [pedɑ̃, ɑ̃t] **1** *adj* pedantic. **2** *nm,f* pedant. ♦ **pédantisme** *nm* pedantry.

pédéraste [pedeʀast(ə)] *nm* homosexual.

pédiatre [pedjatʀ(ə)] *nmf* paediatrician. ♦ **pédiatrie** *nf* paediatrics (*sg*).
pédicure [pedikyʀ] *nmf* chiropodist.
pedigree [pedigʀe] *nm* pedigree.
pègre [pɛgʀ(ə)] *nf*: **la ~** the underworld.
peigne [pɛɲ] *nm [cheveux]* comb; (*Tex*) card. **passer qch au ~ fin** to go through sth with a fine-tooth comb. ♦ **peignée*** *nf* (*raclée*) thrashing, hiding. ♦ **peigner** (1) **1** *vt cheveux* to comb; *enfant* to comb the hair of; (*Tex*) to card. **mal peigné** dishevelled, tousled. **2 se ~** *vpr* to comb one's hair.
peignoir [pɛɲwaʀ] *nm* dressing gown. **~ (de bain)** bathrobe.
peinard, e* [pɛnaʀ, aʀd(ə)] *adj travail, vie* cushy‡. **être ~** to take it easy.
peindre [pɛ̃dʀ(ə)] (52) *vt* (*gén*) to paint; (*fig: décrire*) to portray, depict. **~ qch en jaune** to paint sth yellow; **se faire ~ par X** to have one's portrait painted by X; **le désespoir se peignait sur leur visage** despair was written on their faces.
peine [pɛn] *nf* **(a)** (*chagrin*) sorrow, sadness. **avoir de la ~** to be sad *ou* (*moins fort*) upset; **elle m'a fait de la ~** (*pitié*) I felt sorry for her; (*chagrin*) she upset me *ou* made me sad; **~s de cœur** emotional troubles; **il faisait ~ à voir** he looked a pitiful sight. **(b)** (*effort*) effort, trouble. **cela demande de la ~** that requires an effort; **se donner de la ~ pour faire** to go to a lot of trouble to do; **si tu te donnais seulement la ~ d'essayer** if you would only bother to try; **donnez-vous donc la ~ d'entrer** do come in; **est-ce que c'est la ~ d'y aller?** is it worth going?; **ce n'est pas la ~ de me le répéter** there's no point in repeating that, you've no need to repeat that; **ce n'est pas la ~** don't bother; **c'était bien la ~ de sortir!** it was a waste of time going out; **tu as été sage, pour la ~, tu auras un bonbon** here's a sweet for being good; **ne vous mettez pas en ~ pour moi** don't go to *ou* put yourself to any trouble for me. **(c)** (*difficulté*) difficulty. **avoir de la ~ à faire** to have difficulty in doing, find it difficult *ou* hard to do; **sans ~** without difficulty, easily; **il n'est pas en ~ pour trouver des secrétaires** he has no difficulty finding secretaries; **je serais bien en ~ de vous le dire** I'd be hard pushed to tell you. **(d)** (*punition*) punishment, penalty; (*Jur*) sentence. **~ capitale *ou* de mort** capital punishment, death sentence; **sous ~ de mort** on pain of death; **défense d'afficher sous ~ d'amende** billposters will be fined; **pour la ~ tu mettras la table** for that you can lay the table. **(e) à ~** hardly; **il est à ~ 2 heures** it's only just 2 o'clock; **à ~ rentré, il a dû ressortir** he had hardly *ou* scarcely got in when he had to go out again, no sooner had he got in than he had to go out again; **il était à ~ aimable** he was barely *ou* scarcely civil.
♦ **peiner** (1) **1** *vi [personne]* to work hard; *[moteur]* to labour. **~ sur un problème** to struggle with a problem. **2** *vt* to sadden, distress. **ton peiné** aggrieved tone; **il avait l'air peiné** he looked upset.
peintre [pɛ̃tʀ(ə)] *nmf* (*lit*) painter; (*fig: écrivain*) portrayer. **~ en bâtiment** house painter. ♦ **peinture** *nf* (*action, art*) painting; (*ouvrage*) painting, picture; (*surface peinte*) paintwork; (*matière*) paint; (*fig*) portrayal. **faire de la ~ (à l'huile/à l'eau)** to paint (in oils/watercolours); **attention à la ~!** wet paint!; **~ à l'huile** (*tableau*) oil painting; (*matière*) oil paint; (*pour le bâtiment*) oil-based paint; **~ au pistolet** spray painting. ♦ **peinturlurer** (1) *vt* to daub (with paint). **visage peinturluré** painted face.
péjoratif, -ive [peʒɔʀatif, iv] *adj* derogatory, pejorative.
Pékin [pekɛ̃] *n* Peking. ♦ **pékinois, e** *adj, nm,* **P~(e)** *nm(f)* Pekinese.
pelage [pəlaʒ] *nm* coat, fur.
pêle-mêle [pɛlmɛl] *adv* higgledy-piggledy.
peler [pəle] (5) *vti* (*gén*) to peel. ♦ **pelé, e 1** *adj personne* bald(-headed); *animal* hairless; *vêtement* threadbare; *terrain* bare. **2** *nm*: **il n'y avait que quatre ~s et un tondu*** there was hardly anyone there.
pèlerin [pɛlʀɛ̃] *nm* pilgrim. ♦ **pèlerinage** *nm* pilgrimage. **faire un ~ à** to go on a pilgrimage to.
pèlerine [pɛlʀin] *nf* cape.
pélican [pelikɑ̃] *nm* pelican.
pelle [pɛl] *nf* (*gén*) shovel; *[enfant]* spade. **~ à ordures** dustpan; **~ à tarte** cake *ou* pie server; **il y en a à la ~*** there are loads of them*; **prendre une ~‡** to come a cropper. ♦ **pelletée** *nf* shovelful; spadeful. ♦ **pelleteuse** *nf* mechanical shovel *ou* digger.
pellicule [pelikyl] *nf* (*gén, Phot*) film. (*Méd*) **~s** dandruff.
pelote [p(ə)lɔt] *nf [laine]* ball; *[épingles]* pin cushion. (*fig*) **faire sa ~** to feather one's nest; **~ (basque)** pelota.
peloter* [p(ə)lɔte] (1) *vt* to pet*, paw*.
peloton [p(ə)lɔtɔ̃] *nm* (*Mil*) platoon; (*Sport*) pack. **~ d'exécution** firing squad; **être dans le ~ de tête** (*Sport*) to be up with the leaders; (*en classe*) to be among the top few.
pelouse [p(ə)luz] *nf* lawn; (*Ftbl, Rugby*) field, ground.
peluche [p(ə)lyʃ] *nf* (*Tex*) plush; (*poil*) bit of fluff. **jouets en ~** soft toys; **chien en ~** fluffy dog.
pelure [p(ə)lyʀ] *nf* (*épluchure*) peeling, piece of peel; (‡: *manteau*) (over)coat. (*Bot*) **~ d'oignon** onion skin.
pénal, e, *mpl* **-aux** [penal, o] *adj* penal. ♦ **pénaliser** (1) *vt* to penalize. ♦ **pénalité** *nf* (*Fin, Sport*) penalty. ♦ **penalty,** *pl* **~ies** *nm* (*Ftbl*) penalty (kick).
pénates [penat] *nmpl* (*Myth*) Penates; (*fig hum*) home.
penaud, e [pəno, od] *adj* sheepish.
penchant [pɑ̃ʃɑ̃] *nm* (*tendance*) tendency, propensity (*à faire* to do); (*faible*) liking, fondness (*pour qch* for sth). **avoir un ~ pour la boisson** to be partial to drink.
pencher [pɑ̃ʃe] (1) **1** *vt objet* to tip up, tilt. **~ la tête** (*en avant*) to bend one's head forward; (*sur le côté*) to lean *ou* tilt one's head to one side. **2** *vi* **(a)** *[mur, arbre]* to lean over; *[navire]* to list; *[objet]* to tilt, tip (to one side). (*fig*) **faire ~ la balance** to tip the scales. **(b) ~ pour qch** to favour sth; **~ à croire que** to be inclined to believe that. **3 se ~** *vpr* **(a)** to lean over; (*se baisser*) to bend down. **défense de se ~ au dehors** do not lean out of the window. **(b) se ~ sur un cas** to look into *ou* study a case; **se ~ sur les malheurs de qn** to turn one's attention to sb's misfortunes. ♦ **penché, e** *adj tableau, poteau* slanting; *objet* tilting, tipping; *écriture* sloping. **être ~ sur ses livres** to be bent over one's books.
pendaison [pɑ̃dɛzɔ̃] *nf* hanging. **~ de crémaillère** house-warming party.
pendant¹, e [pɑ̃dɑ̃, ɑ̃t] **1** *adj* **(a)** *jambes* hanging, dangling; *oreilles* drooping; *branches* hanging, drooping. **la langue ~e** with his (*ou* its) tongue hanging out. **(b)** (*Admin*) *question* outstanding; *affaire, procès* pending. **2** *nm* **(a) ~ (d'oreille)** drop earring. **(b)** (*contrepartie*) **le ~ de** *meuble* the matching piece to; *personne* the counterpart of; **faire ~ à, se faire ~** to match.
pendant² [pɑ̃dɑ̃] **1** *prép* (*au cours de*) during; (*durée*) for. **~ la journée/la guerre** during the day/the war; **~ ce temps** meanwhile, in the meantime; **marcher ~ des kilomètres/des heures** to walk for miles/for hours. **2: ~ que** *conj* while; **~ que vous serez à Paris, pourriez-vous aller le voir?** while you're in Paris could you go and see him?; (*iro*) **finissez le plat ~ que vous y êtes** why don't you eat it all (up) while you're at it (*iro*).

pendentif [pãdãtif] *nm* (*bijou*) pendant.
penderie [pãdʀi] *nf* (*meuble*) wardrobe; (*débarras*) walk-in cupboard *ou* closet (*US*).
pendre [pãdʀ(ə)] (41) **1** *vt objet* to hang up; *criminel* to hang. ~ **le linge au dehors** to hang the washing out to dry; ~ **la crémaillère** to have a house-warming party; **qu'il aille se faire ~ ailleurs!*** he can go hang!* **2** *vi [objet]* to hang (down) (*de* from); *[bras, jambes]* to dangle; *[joue]* to sag. **laisser ~ ses jambes** to dangle one's legs; **cela lui pend au nez*** he's got it coming to him*. **3 se ~** *vpr* (*se tuer*) to hang o.s. **se ~ à** *branche* to hang from; **se ~ au cou de qn** to throw one's arms round sb's neck. ♦ **pendu, e 1** *adj* **(a)** *chose* hung up, hanging up. ~ **à** hanging from. **(b) être ~ au téléphone*** to spend all one's time on the telephone; **être ~ aux lèvres de qn** to hang on sb's every word. **2** *nm,f* hanged man (*ou* woman).
pendule [pãdyl] **1** *nf* clock. **2** *nm* pendulum. ♦ **pendulette** *nf* small clock.
pénétrer [penetʀe] (6) **1** *vi* **(a)** *[personne, véhicule]* ~ **dans** *bâtiment* to enter; *groupe* to penetrate; **faire ~ qn dans le salon** to show *ou* let sb into the lounge; **des voleurs ont pénétré dans la maison** thieves broke into the house. **(b)** *[air, liquide]* to come *ou* get in. **le soleil pénètre dans la pièce** the sun is shining into the room; ~ **dans le bois** *[balle]* to penetrate the wood; *[vernis]* to soak into the wood; **faire ~ de l'air (dans)** to let fresh air in(to); **faire ~ une crème (dans la peau)** to rub a cream in(to the skin). **2** *vt* (*gén, fig*) to penetrate; *[odeur, sentiment]* to fill. **le froid les pénétrait jusqu'aux os** the cold cut *ou* went right through them; ~ **les intentions de qn** to fathom sb's intentions; **pénétré de pitié** filled with pity. **3 se ~** *vpr*: **se ~ d'une idée** to get an idea firmly set in one's mind, become convinced of a idea. ♦ **pénétrable** *adj* penetrable (*à* by). ♦ **pénétrant, e** *adj pluie* drenching; *froid* piercing, biting; *odeur, regard, esprit* penetrating. ♦ **pénétration** *nf* (*gén*) penetration. ♦ **pénétré, e** *adj air, ton* earnest. **être ~ de** *sa propre importance* to be full of; *ses obligations* to be highly conscious of.
pénible [penibl(ə)] *adj travail* tiresome, tedious; *personne* tiresome; *nouvelle, maladie* painful (*à* to). ~ **à lire** hard *ou* difficult to read; **l'hiver a été ~** the winter has been unpleasant; **il est vraiment ~*** he's a thorough nuisance; **la lumière violente lui est ~** bright light hurts his eyes; **il m'est ~ de constater que** I am sorry to find that. ♦ **péniblement** *adv* (*difficilement*) with difficulty; (*tristement*) painfully.
péniche [peniʃ] *nf* barge.
pénicilline [penisilin] *nf* penicillin.
péninsule [penɛ̃syl] *nf* peninsula.
pénitence [penitãs] *nf* (*gén*) punishment; (*Rel*) (*repentir*) penitence; (*peine, sacrement*) penance. **faire ~** to repent (*de* of); **mettre qn en ~** to make sb stand in the corner. ♦ **pénitencier** *nm* penitentiary. ♦ **pénitent, e** *adj, nm,f* penitent. ♦ **pénitentiaire** *adj* prison.
pénombre [penɔ̃bʀ(ə)] *nf* (*faible clarté*) half-light; (*obscurité*) darkness.
pensée[1] [pãse] *nf* (*gén*) thought. **si vous voulez connaître le fond de ma ~** if you want to know what I really think (about it) *ou* how I really feel about it; **venir à la ~ de qn** to occur to sb; **les soucis qui hantent sa ~** the worries that haunt his thoughts *ou* his mind; **la ~ marxiste** Marxist thinking.
pensée[2] [pãse] *nf* (*Bot*) pansy.
penser [pãse] (1) **1** *vi* to think. ~ **à qch/à faire** (*réfléchir*) to think about sth/about doing; (*prévoir*) to think of sth/of doing; (*se souvenir*) to remember sth/to do; **pensez-y avant d'accepter** think it over *ou* give it some thought before you accept; **il me fait ~ à mon père** he makes me think of *ou* he reminds me of my father; **fais m'y ~** don't let me forget, remind me about that; **faire qch sans y ~** to do sth without thinking (about it); **il vient? — pensez-vous!** is he coming? — you must be joking!*; **il va accepter? — je pense bien!** will he accept? — of course he will!
2 *vt* **(a)** (*avoir une opinion*) to think. **il en pense du bien/du mal** he has a high/poor opinion of it; **que pensez-vous de ce projet?** what do you think *ou* how do you feel about this plan?; **que penseriez-vous d'un voyage à Rome?** what would you say to *ou* how would you fancy a trip to Rome? **(b)** (*supposer*) to think. **je pense que oui/non** I think so/don't think so; **ce n'est pas si bête qu'on le pense** it's not such a silly idea as you might think; **ils pensent avoir trouvé une maison** they think they've found a house; **vous pensez bien qu'elle a refusé** you can well imagine that she refused; **j'ai pensé mourir** I thought I was going to die. **(c) ~ faire** (*avoir l'intention de*) to be thinking of doing, consider doing, intend to do; (*espérer*) to hope *ou* expect to do. **(d)** (*concevoir*) *projet, machine* to think out.
♦ **penseur** *nm* thinker. ♦ **pensif, -ive** *adj* pensive, thoughtful. ♦ **pensivement** *adv* pensively, thoughtfully.
pension [pãsjɔ̃] *nf* **(a)** (*allocation*) pension. ~ **de retraite** retirement *ou* old age pension; ~ **alimentaire** *[étudiant]* living allowance; *[divorcée]* alimony. **(b)** (*hôtel*) boarding house; (*Scol*) boarding school; (*hébergement*) board and lodging. ~ **de famille** ≃ boarding house, guesthouse. **être en ~ chez qn** to board with sb; **chambre sans/avec demi-~** room (*with no meals provided*)/with half-board; ~ **complète** full board. ♦ **pensionnaire** *nmf* (*Scol*) boarder; *[famille]* lodger; *[hôtel]* resident. ♦ **pensionnat** *nm* boarding school. ♦ **pensionné, e** *nm,f* pensioner. ♦ **pensionner** (1) *vt* to give a pension to.
pentagone [pɛ̃tagɔn] *nm* pentagon.
pente [pãt] *nf* slope; **être en ~ douce/raide** to slope (down) gently/steeply; **en ~** *toit* sloping; *allée* on a slope. **rue en ~** steep street; **suivre sa ~ naturelle** to follow one's natural tendency; **être sur une mauvaise ~** to be going downhill; (*fig*) **remonter la ~** to get on one's feet again; (*fig*) ~ **glissante** slippery slope.
Pentecôte [pãtkot] *nf* (*dimanche*) Whit Sunday; (*période*) Whitsun.
pénurie [penyʀi] *nf* shortage. ~ **de** shortage *ou* lack of.
pépé* [pepe] *nm* grandad*, grandpa*.
pépée‡ [pepe] *nf* (*fille*) bird‡, chick*.
pépère* [pepɛʀ] **1** *nm* (*pépé*) grandad*, grandpa*; (*homme*) (old) man. **2** *adj vie, endroit* quiet; *travail* cushy*.
pépie [pepi] *nf*: **avoir la ~*** to be parched*.
pépier [pepje] (7) *vi* to chirp, chirrup, tweet.
pépin [pepɛ̃] *nm* **(a)** (*Bot*) pip. **sans ~s** seedless. **(b)** (*: *ennui*) snag, hitch. **avoir un ~** to hit a snag*. **(c)** (*: *parapluie*) brolly*.
pépinière [pepinjɛʀ] *nf* (*lit*) tree nursery; (*fig*) nest. ♦ **pépiniériste** *nm* nurseryman.
perception [pɛʀsɛpsjɔ̃] *nf* **(a)** (*sensation*) perception. **(b)** *[impôt]* collection; (*bureau*) tax (collector's) office.
♦ **percepteur** *nm* tax collector, tax man*. ♦ **perceptible** *adj* **(a)** *son, ironie* perceptible (*à* to). **(b)** *impôt* collectable.
percer [pɛʀse] (3) **1** *vt* **(a)** (*trouer*) to pierce; (*avec perceuse*) to drill *ou* bore through; *chaussette* to wear a hole in; *coffre-fort* to break open; *abcès* to lance; *tympan* to burst; *nuages, lignes ennemies* to pierce, break through. **avoir une poche percée** to have a hole in one's pocket; **percé de trous** full of holes. **(b)** *trou, ouverture* to pierce, make; *canal* to build; *tunnel* to bore, drive (*dans* through). **mur percé de petites fenêtres** wall with small windows set in it. **(c)** *mystère* to

penetrate. ~ **qch à jour** to see (right) through sth. **(d)** ~ **une dent** to cut a tooth.

2 *vi [abcès]* to burst; *[plante]* to come up; *[soleil, armée]* to break through; *[émotion]* to show; *[vedette]* to become famous. **il a une dent qui perce** he's cutting a tooth; **rien n'a percé des négociations** no news of the negotiations has filtered through.

♦ **perçant, e** *adj* (*gén*) piercing; *vue* sharp, keen. ♦ **perce** *nf*: **mettre en** ~ *tonneau* to broach, tap. ♦ **percée** *nf [forêt]* opening, clearing; *[mur]* breach, gap; (*Mil, Sci*) breakthrough; (*Rugby*) break. ♦ **percement** *nm [trou]* piercing; drilling, boring; *[rue]* building, driving; *[fenêtre]* making. ♦ **perce-neige** *nm inv* snowdrop. ♦ **perceur** *nm* driller. ~ **de coffre-fort*** safe-breaker. ♦ **perceuse** *nf* drill.

percevoir [pɛʀsəvwaʀ] (28) *vt* **(a)** (*ressentir*) to perceive, detect, make out. **(b)** *taxe* to collect; *indemnité* to receive, get. ♦ **percevable** *adj impôt* collectable, payable.

perche [pɛʀʃ(ə)] *nf* **(a)** (*poisson*) perch. **(b)** (*bâton*) pole; (*: *personne*) beanpole*.

percher [pɛʀʃe] (1) **1** *vi [oiseau]* to perch; *[volailles]* to roost; (*: *habiter*) to live; (*pour la nuit*) to stay, kip*. **2** *vt* (*: *mettre*) to stick*. **3 se** ~ *vpr* (*lit, fig*) to perch. **être perché sur** to be perched upon. ♦ **perchoir** *nm* (*lit, fig*) perch.

percolateur [pɛʀkɔlatœʀ] *nm* (commercial) percolator.

percuter [pɛʀkyte] (1) **1** *vt* (*gén*) to strike. **2** *vi*: ~ **contre** *[avion, voiture]* to crash into. ♦ **percussion** *nf* (*gén*) percussion. ♦ **percussionniste** *nmf* percussionist. ♦ **percutant, e** *adj discours* forceful, explosive. ♦ **percuteur** *nm* firing pin.

perdre [pɛʀdʀ(ə)] (41) **1** *vt* **(a)** (*gén*) to lose; *nom, date* to forget; *habitude* to get out of. (*lit, fig*) ~ **qn de vue** to lose sight of sb; **j'ai perdu le goût de rire** I don't feel like laughing any longer; ~ **espoir/l'appétit/la vie** to lose hope/one's appetite/one's life; **l'arbre perd ses feuilles** the tree is shedding *ou* losing its leaves. **(b)** *temps, argent* to waste (*à qch* on sth, *à faire* doing); *occasion* to lose, miss; *aliment* to spoil. **tu ne l'as jamais vu? tu n'y perds rien!** you've never seen him? you haven't missed anything!; **il ne perd rien pour attendre!** I'll be quits with him yet! **(c)** (*causer préjudice à*) to ruin. **son ambition l'a perdu** ambition was his downfall *ou* the ruin of him. **2** *vi* **(a)** (*gén*) to lose (*sur* on). **tu as perdu en ne venant pas** you missed something by not coming. **(b)** *[réservoir]* to leak. **3 se** ~ *vpr* **(a)** (*s'égarer*) to get lost, lose one's way. **se** ~ **dans les détails** to get bogged down *ou* get lost in the details; **il y a trop de chiffres, je m'y perds** there are too many figures, I'm all confused. **(b)** (*disparaître*) to disappear, vanish; *[coutume]* to die out; (*Naut*) to sink. **se** ~ **dans la foule** to disappear *ou* vanish into the crowd; **son cri s'est perdu dans le vacarme** his shout was lost in the din. **(c)** (*devenir inutilisable*) to be wasted; *[denrées]* to go bad. **il y a des gifles qui se perdent** he (*ou* she *etc*) deserves a good slap.

♦ **perdant, e 1** *adj numéro, cheval* losing. **je suis** ~ I lose out*. **2** *nm,f* loser. ♦ **perdition** *nf* **(a)** (*Rel*) perdition. **lieu de** ~ den of vice *ou* iniquity. **(b)** (*Naut*) **en** ~ in distress. ♦ **perdu, e** *adj* **(a)** (*gén*) lost; *malade* done for; *balle* stray. **je suis** ~ (*égaré*) I'm lost; (*désespéré*) I'm done for; (*embrouillé*) I'm lost *ou* all at sea; **c'est de l'argent** ~ it's money down the drain, it's a waste of money; **pendant ses moments** ~**s** in his spare time; **ma récolte est** ~**e** my harvest is ruined. **(b)** *endroit* out-of-the-way, isolated. **(c)** *emballage* non-returnable.

perdrix [pɛʀdʀi] *nf* partridge. ♦ **perdreau,** *pl* ~**x** *nm* (young) partridge.

père [pɛʀ] *nm* **(a)** father. ~ **de famille** father; **Martin (le)** ~ Martin senior; **de** ~ **en fils** from father to son. **(b)** (*ancêtres*) ~s forefathers, ancestors. **(c)** (*Zool*) *[animal]* sire. **(d)** (*Rel*) father. **le P~ X** Father X; **mon P~** Father; **le P~ éternel** the Heavenly Father. **(e)** (*: *monsieur*) **le** ~ **Benoit** old (man) Benoit*; **un** ~ **tranquille** a quiet fellow; **le** ~ **Noël** Father Christmas, Santa Claus.

péremptoire [peʀɑ̃ptwaʀ] *adj* peremptory.

perfection [pɛʀfɛksjɔ̃] *nf* perfection. **à la** ~ to perfection. ♦ **perfectionné, e** *adj* sophisticated. ♦ **perfectionnement** *nm* perfection (*de* of), improvement (*de* in). **cours de** ~ proficiency course. ♦ **perfectionner** (1) **1** *vt* to improve, perfect. **2 se** ~ *vpr [chose]* to improve; *[personne]* to improve o.s. **se** ~ **en anglais** to improve one's English.

perfide [pɛʀfid] *adj* (*littér*) perfidious. ♦ **perfidie** *nf* (*vice*) perfidy; (*acte*) perfidious act.

perforer [pɛʀfɔʀe] (1) *vt* (*trouer*) to pierce; (*poinçonner*) to punch; (*Méd*) to perforate. **carte perforée** punch card; **bande perforée** punched tape. ♦ **perforateur, -trice 1** *nm,f* (*ouvrier*) punch-card operator. **2** *nf* (*Ordinateurs*) card punch. ♦ **perforation** *nf* (*Méd*) perforation; (*Ordinateurs*) punch.

performance [pɛʀfɔʀmɑ̃s] *nf* performance.

perfusion [pɛʀfyzjɔ̃] *nf* perfusion.

péricliter [peʀiklite] (1) *vi [affaire]* to collapse.

péril [peʀil] *nm* (*littér*) peril, danger. **mettre en** ~ to imperil, endanger; **au** ~ **de sa vie** at the risk of one's life; **le** ~ **jaune** the yellow peril. ♦ **périlleux, -euse** *adj* perilous.

périmé, e [peʀime] *adj*: **être** ~ *[billet]* to be out-of-date *ou* no longer valid; *[idée]* to be outdated.

périmètre [peʀimɛtʀ(ə)] *nm* (*Math*) perimeter; (*zone*) area.

période [peʀjɔd] *nf* (*gén*) period. **une** ~ **de chaleur** a hot period *ou* spell; **pendant la** ~ **électorale** at election time. ♦ **périodicité** *nf* periodicity. ♦ **périodique 1** *adj* periodic. **2** *nm* (*Presse*) periodical. ♦ **périodiquement** *adv* periodically.

péripétie [peʀipesi] *nf* event, episode. **les** ~**s d'une révolution** the turns taken by a revolution; **après bien des** ~**s** after many ups and downs.

périphérie [peʀifeʀi] *nf* (*limite*) periphery; (*banlieue*) outskirts. ♦ **périphérique 1** *adj* (*Anat, Math*) peripheral; *quartier* outlying. **2** *nm*: **(boulevard)** ~ ring road, circular route (*US*).

périphrase [peʀifʀɑz] *nf* circumlocution.

périple [peʀipl(ə)] *nm* (*par mer*) voyage; (*par terre*) journey.

périr [peʀiʀ] (2) *vi* (*littér*) to perish (*littér*), die; *[navire]* to go down, sink. ~ **noyé** to drown; **faire** ~ to kill. ♦ **périssable** *adj* perishable.

périscope [peʀiskɔp] *nm* periscope.

péritonite [peʀitɔnit] *nf* peritonitis.

perle [pɛʀl(ə)] *nf* (*bijou*) pearl; (*boule*) bead; *[eau, sang]* drop; *[sueur]* bead; (*fig: trésor, hum: erreur*) gem. ~ **fine/de culture** natural/cultured pearl.

permanence [pɛʀmanɑ̃s] *nf* **(a)** (*durée*) permanence. **en** ~ *siéger* permanently; *crier* continuously. **(b)** (*service*) **être de** ~ to be on duty *ou* on call; **une** ~ **est assurée le dimanche** there is someone on duty *ou* on call on Sundays. **(c)** (*bureau*) (duty) office; (*Pol*) committee room; (*Scol*) study room. ♦ **permanent, e 1** *adj* (*gén*) permanent; *armée, comité* standing; *spectacle* continuous. (*Ciné*) ~ **de 2 heures à minuit** continuous showings from 2 o'clock to midnight. **2** *nm* (*Pol*) (party) official. **3** *nf* (*Coiffure*) perm.

perméable [pɛʀmeabl(ə)] *adj* permeable.

permettre [pɛʀmɛtʀ(ə)] (56) **1** *vt* **(a)** (*gén*) to allow, permit. ~ **à qn de faire** (*autoriser*) to allow *ou* permit sb to do, let sb do; (*donner la possibilité*) to enable sb to do; (*donner le droit*) to entitle sb to do; **il se croit tout permis** he thinks he can do what he likes *ou* as he pleases; **est-il**

permis d'être aussi bête! how can anyone be so stupid!; **mes moyens ne me le permettent pas** I cannot afford it; **mes occupations ne me le permettent pas** I'm too busy to be able to do it. **(b)** (*sollicitation*) **vous permettez?** may I?; **permettez-moi de vous dire que** may I say that, let me tell you that; **vous permettez que je fume?** do you mind if I smoke?; **permettez! je ne suis pas d'accord** if you don't mind! *ou* pardon me! I disagree.

2 se ~ *vpr* (*gén*) to allow o.s.; *fantaisie* to indulge o.s. in. **je ne peux pas me ~ d'acheter ce manteau** I can't afford to buy this coat; **il s'est permis de partir sans permission** he took the liberty of going without permission; **je me permettrai de vous dire que** let me tell you that; **je me permets de vous écrire au sujet de ...** I am writing to you in connection with ... .

♦ **permis, e 1** *adj limites* permitted. **il est ~ d'en douter** one might *ou* may well doubt this. **2** *nm* permit, licence. **~ de conduire** (*carte*) driving licence; (*épreuve*) driving test; **~ de construire** planning permission; **~ d'inhumer** burial certificate; **~ de séjour** residence permit; **~ de travail** work permit. ♦ **permission** *nf* **(a)** permission. **demander/donner la ~** to ask/give permission (*de* to). **(b)** (*Mil*) (*congé*) leave; (*certificat*) pass. **en ~** on leave; **~ de minuit** late pass. ♦ **permissionnaire** *nm* soldier on leave.

permuter [pɛʀmyte] (1) **1** *vt* (*gén*) to change round, permutate; (*Math*) to permutate. **2** *vi* to change, swap (seats *ou* jobs *etc*). ♦ **permutation** *nf* permutation.

pernicieux, -euse [pɛʀnisjø, øz] *adj* pernicious.

pérorer [peʀɔʀe] (1) *vi* to hold forth (*péj*), declaim (*péj*).

Pérou [peʀu] *nm* Peru. **ce n'est pas le ~*** it's no great fortune.

perpendiculaire [pɛʀpɑ̃dikylɛʀ] *adj, nf* perpendicular (*à* to). ♦ **perpendiculairement** *adv* perpendicularly. **~ à** at right angles to, perpendicular to.

perpétrer [pɛʀpetʀe] (6) *vt* to perpetrate.

perpétuel, -elle [pɛʀpetɥɛl] *adj* (*gén*) perpetual; *secrétaire* permanent; *rente* life. ♦ **perpétuellement** *adv* perpetually. ♦ **perpétuer** (1) **1** *vt* to perpetuate. **2 se ~** *vpr [usage]* to be perpetuated; *[espèce]* to survive. ♦ **perpétuité** *nf* perpetuity. **à ~** *condamnation* for life; *concession* in perpetuity.

perplexe [pɛʀplɛks(ə)] *adj* perplexed, puzzled. **laisser ~** to perplex, puzzle. ♦ **perplexité** *nf* perplexity.

perquisition [pɛʀkizisjɔ̃] *nf* (*Police*) search. ♦ **perquisitionner** (1) *vi* to carry out a search. **~ au domicile de qn** to search sb's house.

perron [pɛʀɔ̃] *nm* steps (*leading to entrance*).

perroquet [pɛʀɔkɛ] *nm* (*Orn, fig*) parrot.

perruche [peʀyʃ] *nf* (*Orn*) budgerigar, budgie*; (*bavard*) chatterbox*.

perruque [peʀyk] *nf* wig.

persécuter [pɛʀsekyte] (1) *vt* to persecute. ♦ **persécuteur, -trice** *nm,f* persecutor. ♦ **persécution** *nf* persecution.

persévérer [pɛʀseveʀe] (6) *vi* to persevere. ♦ **persévérance** *nf* perseverance.

persienne [pɛʀsjɛn] *nf* (metal) shutter.

persiflage [pɛʀsiflaʒ] *nm* mockery.

persil [pɛʀsi] *nm* parsley.

persister [pɛʀsiste] (1) *vi* to persist. **~ dans qch/à faire** to persist in sth/in doing; **~ dans son opinion** to stick to one's opinion; **je persiste à croire que ...** I still believe that ... . ♦ **persistance** *nf* persistence (*à faire* in doing). **avec ~** (*tout le temps*) persistently; (*avec obstination*) persistently, doggedly, stubbornly. ♦ **persistant, e** *adj* persistent.

personne [pɛʀsɔn] **1** *nf* **(a)** (*être humain*) person. **deux ~s** two people, two persons (*US*); **les ~s qui ...** those who ..., the people who ...; **100 F par ~** 100 francs per head *ou* per person; **par ~ interposée** through an intermediary, through a third party. **(b)** (*corps*) **être bien (fait) de sa ~** to be good-looking; **toute sa ~ inspire confiance** his whole being inspires confidence; **il prend soin de sa petite ~** he looks after himself; **je l'ai vu en ~** I saw him in person; **je m'en occupe en ~** I'll see to it personally; **c'est la bonté en ~** he's *ou* she's kindness itself *ou* personified. **(c)** (*Gram*) person. **à la première ~** in the first person. **2** *pron* (*quelqu'un*) anyone, anybody; (*aucun*) no one, nobody. **elle le sait mieux que ~** she knows that better than anyone *ou* anybody (else); **presque ~** hardly anyone *ou* anybody, practically no one *ou* nobody; **il n'y a ~** there's no one *ou* nobody there, there isn't anyone *ou* anybody there; **ce n'est la faute de ~** it's no one's *ou* nobody's fault. **3: ~ âgée** elderly person; **~ à charge** dependent; (*Jur*) **~ civile** *ou* **morale** artificial person; **la ~ humaine** the individual; (*Jur*) **~ physique** individual. ♦ **personnage** *nm* (*individu*) character, individual; (*célébrité*) personage, (very) important person; *[roman]* character; *[tableau]* figure. **~ influent** influential person; (*lit, fig*) **jouer un ~** to play a part. ♦ **personnalité** *nf* (*gén*) personality.

personnel, -elle [pɛʀsɔnɛl] **1** *adj* (*gén, Gram*) personal; (*égoïste*) selfish, self-centred. **fortune ~elle** personal *ou* private fortune; **mon opinion ~elle** my own *ou* personal opinion. **2** *nm [école, château]* staff; *[usine, service public]* personnel, employees. **faire partie du ~** to be on the staff; **chef du ~** personnel officer *ou* manager. ♦ **personnellement** *adv* personally.

personnifier [pɛʀsɔnifje] (7) *vt* to personify, embody. **être la bêtise personnifiée** to be stupidity itself *ou* personified. ♦ **personnification** *nf* personification, embodiment.

perspective [pɛʀspɛktiv] *nf* **(a)** (*Art*) perspective. **(b)** (*point de vue*) (*lit*) view; (*fig*) angle, viewpoint. **(c)** (*idée, possibilité*) prospect. **en ~** in prospect; **à la ~ de** at the prospect of.

perspicace [pɛʀspikas] *adj* perspicacious. ♦ **perspicacité** *nf* insight, perspicacity.

persuader [pɛʀsɥade] (1) *vt* to persuade, convince (*qn de qch* sb of sth). **j'en suis persuadé** I'm quite sure *ou* convinced (of it); **se ~ de qch** to convince o.s. of sth, be convinced of sth. ♦ **persuasif, -ive** *adj* persuasive, convincing. ♦ **persuasion** *nf* (*action, art*) persuasion; (*croyance*) conviction, belief.

perte [pɛʀt(ə)] *nf* (*gén*) loss; (*ruine*) ruin. **~ de** *chaleur* loss of; *temps* waste of; **vendre à ~** to sell at a loss; (*Mil*) **de lourdes ~s** heavy losses; **il court à sa ~** he is on the road to ruin; **à ~ de vue** as far as the eye can see; (*Fin*) **~ sèche** dead loss; (*lit, fig*) **être en ~ de vitesse** to lose momentum.

pertinent, e [pɛʀtinɑ̃, ɑ̃t] *adj remarque* pertinent, relevant; *analyse, esprit* judicious, discerning; (*Ling*) significant. ♦ **pertinemment** *adv parler* pertinently, to the point. **savoir ~ que** to know full well that. ♦ **pertinence** *nf* pertinence, relevance.

perturber [pɛʀtyʀbe] (1) *vt services publics, réunion* to disrupt, disturb; *personne* to perturb, disturb. ♦ **perturbateur, -trice 1** *adj* disruptive. **2** *nm,f* troublemaker. ♦ **perturbation** *nf* disruption; disturbance; perturbation. **~ (atmosphérique)** (atmospheric) disturbance.

pervenche [pɛʀvɑ̃ʃ] *nf* (*Bot*) periwinkle.

pervers, e [pɛʀvɛʀ, ɛʀs(ə)] **1** *adj joie* perverse; *personne* perverted. **2** *nm,f* pervert. ♦ **perversion** *nf* perversion. ♦ **perversité** *nf* perversity. ♦ **pervertir** (2) **1** *vt* to pervert. **2 se ~** *vpr* to become perverted.

peser [pəze] (5) **1** *vt* (*lit*) to weigh; (*fig: évaluer*) to weigh up. **tout bien pesé** everything considered. **2** *vi* to weigh. ~ **lourd** *[objet]* to be heavy; *[argument, homme politique]* to carry weight; (*fig*) **il n'a pas pesé lourd devant son adversaire** he was no match for his opponent; ~ **sur** *objet* to press on; *estomac, conscience* to lie heavy on; *décision* to influence; **le soupçon/la menace qui pèse sur lui** the suspicion/the threat which hangs over him; **toute la responsabilité pèse sur ses épaules** all the responsibility rests on his shoulders, he has to shoulder all the responsibility; **le temps lui pèse** time hangs heavy on his hands; **ses responsabilités lui pèsent** he feels weighed down by his responsibilities, his responsibilities weigh heavy on him.

♦ **pesamment** *adv* heavily. ♦ **pesant, e 1** *adj* (*gén: lit, fig*) heavy; *sommeil* deep; *architecture* massive; *style* ponderous; *présence* burdensome. **2** *nm*: **valoir son** ~ **d'or** to be worth one's weight in gold. ♦ **pesanteur** *nf* (*Phys*) gravity; (*lourdeur*) heaviness; weightiness; massiveness; ponderousness. ♦ **pesée** *nf [objet]* weighing; (*poussée*) push, thrust. ♦ **pèse-bébé,** *pl* ~**-**~**s** *nm* baby scales. ♦ **pèse-lettre,** *pl* ~**-**~**s** *nm* letter scales. ♦ **pèse-personne,** *pl* ~**-**~**s** *nm* scales.

pessimisme [pesimism(ə)] *nm* pessimism. ♦ **pessimiste 1** *adj* pessimistic (*sur* about). **2** *nmf* pessimist.

peste [pɛst(ə)] *nf* (*Méd*) plague; (*fig: personne*) pest, nuisance. (*fig*) **fuir qch comme la** ~ to avoid sth like the plague.

pester [pɛste] (1) *vi* to curse. ~ **contre qn/qch** to curse sb/sth.

pestilence [pɛstilɑ̃s] *nf* stench. ♦ **pestilentiel, -elle** *adj* stinking.

pet [pɛ] *nm* **(a)** (‡) fart‡. **(b) faire le** ~* to be on (the) watch *ou* on (the) look-out.

pétale [petal] *nm* petal.

pétarader [petaʀade] (1) *vi [moteur]* to backfire.

pétard [petaʀ] *nm* **(a)** banger, firecracker; (*Rail*) detonator, torpedo (*US*). **(b)** (‡: *tapage*) din, racket. **faire du** ~ to kick up a stink‡; **être en** ~ to be raging mad*. **(c)** (‡: *revolver*) gun, gat‡. **(d)** (‡: *derrière*) bottom*.

péter [pete] (6) **1** *vi* **(a)** (‡) to fart‡. **(b)** (*) *[détonation]* to go off; *[tuyau, ballon]* to burst; *[ficelle]* to bust*, snap. **2** *vt* (*) *ficelle* to bust*, snap; *objet* to bust*. ~ **la santé** to be bursting with health.

pétiller [petije] (1) *vi [feu]* to crackle; *[liquide]* to bubble; *[yeux, joie]* to sparkle. ♦ **pétillant, e** *adj eau* bubbly, fizzy; *vin* sparkling. ♦ **pétillement** *nm*: ~**(s)** crackling; bubbling; sparkling.

petit, e [p(ə)ti, it] **1** *adj* **(a)** *objet, pointure etc* small; (*nuance affective*) little. (*fig*) **se faire tout** ~ to make o.s. inconspicuous; **être de** ~**e taille** to be short *ou* small. **(b)** (*mince*) *taille* slim, slender; *membre* thin, slender. **une** ~**e pluie fine** a fine drizzle. **(c)** (*jeune*) small, young; (*nuance affective*) little. **son** ~ **frère** his younger *ou* little brother; (*bébé*) his baby brother; ~ **chat/chien** (little) kitten/puppy; **un** ~ **Anglais** an English boy; **les** ~**s Anglais** English children; **dans sa** ~**e enfance** when he was very small; **le** ~ **Jésus** baby Jesus. **(d)** *voyage, distance, lettre* short, little. **par** ~**es étapes** in short *ou* easy stages; **il en a pour une** ~**e heure** it won't take him more than an hour; **j'en ai pour un** ~ **moment** (*longtemps*) it'll take me quite a while; (*peu de temps*) it won't take me long. **(e)** *bruit, espoir* faint, slight; *coup* light, gentle; *opération, détail, fonctionnaire* minor; *rhume* slight; *cadeau* little. ~**e robe d'été** light summer dress; **il a un** ~ **appétit** he hasn't much of an appetite; **avoir une** ~**e santé** to be in poor health; **ce n'est pas une** ~**e affaire que de le faire obéir** getting him to obey is no easy matter; **la** ~**e industrie** light industry; **le** ~ **commerce** small businesses; **les** ~**es gens** ordinary people; **la** ~**e histoire** the footnotes of history. **(f)** (*péj: mesquin*) mean, petty, low. **(g)** (*affectif, intensif*) little. **ma** ~**e maman** my (dear) mummy; **mon** ~ **chou** *etc* (my little) pet*, darling; **un** ~ **coin tranquille** a nice quiet spot; **un bon** ~ **souper** a nice little supper; (*euph*) **le** ~ **coin** *ou* **endroit** the bathroom (*euph*); **être/ne pas être dans les** ~**s papiers de qn** to be in sb's good/bad books; **mettre les** ~**s plats dans les grands** to lay on a first rate meal; **être aux** ~**s soins pour qn** to dance attendance on sb; **être dans ses** ~**s souliers** to be shaking in one's shoes.

2 *adv*: ~ **à** ~ little by little.

3 *nm* (*enfant*) (little) boy; (*Scol*) junior (boy); (*homme petit*) small man; (*personne inférieure*) little man. **les** ~**s** children; **viens ici,** ~ come here, son; **pauvre** ~ poor little thing; **le** ~ **Durand** young Durand, the Durand boy; **les tout** ~**s** the very young, the tiny tots; **la chatte et ses** ~**s** the cat and her kittens; **la lionne et ses** ~**s** the lioness and her young *or* cubs; **faire des** ~**s** to have kittens (*ou* puppies *ou* lambs *etc*); (*fig*) **son argent a fait des** ~**s** his money has made more money; **c'est le monde en** ~ it is the world in miniature.

4 *nf* (*enfant*) (little) girl; (*femme*) small woman. **la** ~**e Durand** the Durand's daughter.

5: ~ **ami** boyfriend; ~**e amie** girlfriend; ~**-beurre** *nm, pl* ~**s-**~ petit beurre biscuit; ~ **cousin** (*enfant*) little *ou* young cousin; (*parent éloigné*) distant cousin; ~ **déjeuner** breakfast; **le** ~ **doigt** the little finger; **le** ~ **écran** television, TV; ~**-enfant** *nm, pl* ~**s-**~**s** grandchild; ~**e-fille** *nf, pl* ~**es-**~**s** granddaughter; ~**-fils** *nm, pl* ~**s-**~**s** grandson; ~**-neveu** *nm, pl* ~**s-**~**s** great-nephew; ~**e-nièce** *nf, pl* ~**es-**~**s** great-niece; ~ **nom*** Christian name, first name; ~**-pois** *nm, pl* ~**s-**~ (garden) pea; (*Culin*) ~ **salé** salt pork; ~**-suisse** *nm, pl* ~**s-**~**s** petit-suisse.

♦ **petitement** *adv* (*chichement*) poorly; (*mesquinement*) meanly, pettily. **nous sommes** ~ **logés** our accommodation is cramped. ♦ **petitesse** *nf [taille, endroit]* smallness, small size; *[somme]* smallness; *[acte]* meanness, pettiness.

pétition [petisjɔ̃] *nf* petition. **faire une** ~ **auprès de qn** to petition sb. ♦ **pétitionnaire** *nmf* petitioner.

pétrifier [petʀifje] (7) *vt* (*Géol*) to petrify; *personne* to paralyze, transfix (*de* with). ♦ **pétrification** *nf* petrification.

pétrin [petʀɛ̃] *nm* **(a)** (*: *ennui*) mess*. **être dans le** ~ to be in a mess* *ou* jam* *ou* fix*. **(b)** (*Boulangerie*) kneading-trough. ♦ **pétrir** (2) *vt* to knead.

pétrole [petʀɔl] *nm* (*brut*) oil, petroleum. ~ **(lampant)** paraffin (oil); **lampe à** ~ paraffin *ou* oil lamp. ♦ **pétrochimie** *nf* petrochemistry. ♦ **pétrolier, -ière 1** *adj* petroleum, oil; *pays* oil-producing. **2** *nm* (*navire*) (oil) tanker; (*financier*) oil magnate. ♦ **pétrolifère** *adj* oil-bearing.

peu [pø] **1** *adv* **(a)** (*petite quantité*) little, not much; (*petit nombre*) few, not many. **il gagne très** ~ he doesn't earn very much, he earns very little; **il se contente de** ~ he is satisfied with little; **il mange trop** ~ he doesn't eat (nearly) enough. **(b)** (*modifiant adj etc*) (a) little, not very. **il est** ~ **sociable** he is not very sociable; **il conduit** ~ **prudemment** he doesn't drive very carefully; **ils sont trop** ~ **nombreux** there are too few of them; **c'est un** ~ **grand** it's a little *ou* a bit (too) big. **(c)** ~ **de** (*quantité*) little, not much; (*nombre*) few, not (very) many; **nous avons eu (très)** ~ **de soleil/d'orages** we had (very) little sunshine/(very) few storms, we didn't have (very) much sunshine/(very) many storms (at all); **il est ici pour** ~ **de temps** he is here for (only) a short time *ou* while. **(d)** (*locutions*) **il l'a battu de** ~ he just beat him; **à** ~ **près terminé** almost *ou* nearly *ou* more or less finished; **à** ~ **près 10 kilos**

roughly *ou* approximately 10 kilos; **rester dans l'à ~ près** to remain vague; **à ~ de chose près** more or less, just about; **(c'est) ~ de chose** it's nothing; **~ à ~** gradually, little by little, bit by bit.

2 *nm* **(a)** little. **le ~ (d'argent) qu'elle a** what little (money) *ou* the little (money) she has; **son ~ de patience lui a nui** his lack of patience has done him harm; **le ~ d'amis qu'elle avait** the few friends she had. **(b) un ~** a little; **un petit ~** a little bit; **il boite un ~** he limps slightly *ou* a little *ou* a bit, he is slightly *ou* a bit lame; **il est un ~ artiste** he's a bit of an artist*, he's something of an artist; **nous avons un ~ moins de clients** we have slightly fewer customers; **pour un ~** *ou* **un ~ plus il écrasait le chien** he all but *ou* he very nearly ran over the dog. **(c) un ~ d'eau** a little water; **un ~ de patience** a little patience, a bit of patience; **un ~ de silence!** let's have some quiet *ou* a bit of quiet!; **il a un ~ de sinusite** he has a touch of sinusitis. **(d)** (*: *intensif*) **un ~!, un ~ mon neveu!‡** you bet!*, and how!*; **montre-moi un ~ comment tu fais** just show me how you do it; **comme menteur il est un ~ là!** as liars go, he'd be hard to beat!; **un ~ partout** just about everywhere; **c'est un ~ beaucoup*** that's a bit much*.

peuple [pœpl(ə)] *nm* (*gén*) people; (*foule*) crowd (of people). **les gens du ~** the common people, ordinary people. ♦ **peuplade** *nf* (small) tribe, people. ♦ **peuplé, e** *adj* populated. ♦ **peupler** (1) **1** *vt* **(a)** (*pourvoir*) *colonie* to populate; *étang* to stock; *forêt* to plant out; (*fig*) *esprit* to fill (*de* with). **(b)** (*habiter*) *terre, maison* to inhabit. **2 se ~** *vpr [région]* to become populated; (*fig: s'animer*) to fill (up), be filled (*de* with). ♦ **peuplement** *nm* **(a)** (*action*) populating; stocking; planting (with trees). **(b)** (*population*) population.

peuplier [pøplije] *nm* poplar (tree).

peur [pœʀ] *nf* fear. **être vert** *ou* **mort de ~** to be frightened *ou* scared out of one's wits; **prendre ~** to take fright; **sans ~** (*adj*) fearless (*de* of); (*adv*) fearlessly; **avoir une ~ bleue de qch** to be scared stiff* of sth; **il m'a fait une de ces ~s!** he gave me a dreadful fright *ou* scare; **avoir ~** to be frightened *ou* afraid *ou* scared (*de* of); (*fig*) **j'ai bien ~/très ~ qu'il ne pleuve** I'm afraid/very much afraid it's going to rain; **il y a eu plus de ~ que de mal** it caused more fright than real harm, it was more frightening than anything else; **faire ~ à qn** to frighten *ou* scare sb; **cette pensée fait ~** it's a frightening thought; **laid à faire ~** frightfully ugly; **il a couru de ~ de manquer le train** he ran for fear of missing the train. ♦ **peureusement** *adv* fearfully, timorously. ♦ **peureux, -euse** *adj* fearful, timorous.

peut-être [pøtɛtʀ(ə)] *adv* perhaps, maybe. **~ bien qu'il pleuvra** it may *ou* might well rain; **~ que oui** perhaps so; **tu le sais mieux que moi ~?** so (you think) you know more about it than I do, do you?

pèze‡ [pɛz] *nm* (*argent*) dough‡, bread‡.

phalange [falɑ̃ʒ] *nf* phalanx.

pharaon [faʀaɔ̃] *nm* Pharaoh.

phare [faʀ] *nm* **(a)** (*tour*) lighthouse; (*Aviat, fig*) beacon. **(b)** (*Aut*) headlight, headlamp. **rouler pleins ~s** to drive on full beam *ou* high beams (*US*); **~s code** dipped headlights *ou* beams; **~ antibrouillard** fog lamp; **~ de recul** reversing light.

pharmacie [faʀmasi] *nf* **(a)** (*magasin*) chemist's (shop), pharmacy, drugstore (*Can, US*). **(b)** (*science*) pharmacology; (*profession*) pharmacy. **(c)** (*produits*) pharmaceuticals, medicines. **(armoire à) ~** medicine cabinet; **~ portative** first-aid kit. ♦ **pharmaceutique** *adj* pharmaceutical. ♦ **pharmacien, -ienne** *nm,f* (dispensing) chemist, pharmacist, druggist (*US*).

pharynx [faʀɛ̃ks] *nm* pharynx.

phase [fɑz] *nf* phase.

phénol [fenɔl] *nm* phenol.

phénomène [fenɔmɛn] *nm* (*gén*) phenomenon; (*excentrique*) character; (*anormal*) freak. ♦ **phénoménal, e, *mpl* -aux** *adj* (*gén*) phenomenal. ♦ **phénoménalement** *adv* phenomenally.

philanthrope [filɑ̃tʀɔp] *nmf* philanthropist. ♦ **philanthropie** *nf* philanthropy. ♦ **philanthropique** *adj* philanthropic(al).

philatélie [filateli] *nf* philately, stamp collecting. ♦ **philatélique** *adj* philatelic. ♦ **philatéliste** *nmf* philatelist, stamp collector.

philharmonique [filaʀmɔnik] *adj* philharmonic.

philosophie [filɔzɔfi] *nf* philosophy. ♦ **philosophe 1** *nmf* philosopher. **2** *adj* philosophical. ♦ **philosopher** (1) *vi* to philosophize. ♦ **philosophique** *adj* philosophical. ♦ **philosophiquement** *adv* philosophically.

phlébite [flebit] *nf* phlebitis.

phobie [fɔbi] *nf* phobia.

phonétique [fɔnetik] **1** *nf* phonetics (*sg*). **2** *adj* phonetic. ♦ **phonétiquement** *adv* phonetically.

phonique [fɔnik] *adj* phonic.

phonographe [fɔnɔgʀaf] *nm* (wind-up) gramophone, phonograph (*US*).

phoque [fɔk] *nm* (*animal*) seal; (*fourrure*) sealskin.

phosphate [fɔsfat] *nm* phosphate.

phosphore [fɔsfɔʀ] *nm* phosphorus. ♦ **phosphorescence** *nf* luminosity, phosphorescence. ♦ **phosphorescent, e** *adj* luminous, phosphorescent.

photo [fɔto] *nf* photo, snap(shot). **prendre qn en ~** to take a photo *ou* snap(shot) of sb. ♦ **photo-électrique** *adj* photo-electric.

photocopie [fɔtɔkɔpi] *nf* (*action*) photocopying, photostatting; (*copie*) photocopy, photostat (copy). ♦ **photocopier** (7) *vt* to photocopy, photostat. ♦ **photocopieur** *nm* photocopier, photostat.

photographie [fɔtɔgʀafi] *nf* (*art*) photography; (*image*) photograph. **faire de la ~** to take photographs, do photography; **~ d'identité** passport photograph. ♦ **photographe** *nmf* (*artiste*) photographer; (*commerçant*) camera dealer. (*boutique*) **chez un ~** at a camera shop *ou* store (*US*). ♦ **photographier** (7) *vt* to photograph. **se faire ~** to have one's photo(graph) taken. ♦ **photographique** *adj* photographic.

photogravure [fɔtɔgʀavyʀ] *nf* photoengraving.

phrase [fʀɑz] *nf* (*Ling*) sentence; (*Mus, fig: expression*) phrase. **faire des ~s** to talk in flowery language; **~ toute faite** stock phrase.

phtisie [ftizi] *nf* consumption.

physicien, -ienne [fizisjɛ̃, jɛn] *nm,f* physicist.

physiologie [fizjɔlɔʒi] *nf* physiology. ♦ **physiologique** *adj* physiological. ♦ **physiologiste** *nmf* physiologist.

physionomie [fizjɔnɔmi] *nf* (*lit, fig*) face. ♦ **physionomiste** *adj, nmf*: **il est ~** he has a good memory for faces.

physique [fizik] **1** *adj* (*gén*) physical. **2** *nm* physique. **au ~** physically; **avoir un ~ agréable** to be quite good-looking; **avoir le ~ de l'emploi** to look the part. **3** *nf* physics (*sg*). ♦ **physiquement** *adv* physically.

piaffer [pjafe] (1) *vi [cheval]* to stamp, paw the ground. **~ d'impatience** to fidget with impatience.

piailler [pjɑje] (1) *vi* (*lit, péj*) to squawk. ♦ **piaillement** *nm*: **~(s)** squawking.

piano [pjano] **1** *nm* piano. **~ droit/à queue** upright/grand piano. **2** *adv* (*Mus*) piano; (**fig*) gently. ♦ **pianiste** *nmf* pianist.

pic [pik] *nm* **(a)** (*cime*) peak. **(b)** (*pioche*) pick(axe). **~ à glace** ice pick. **(c)** (*oiseau*) **~ (vert)** (green) woodpecker. **(d) à ~** *falaise* sheer; **couler à ~** to go straight down; **arriver à ~*** to come just at the right time *ou* in the nick of time.

pichet [piʃɛ] *nm* pitcher, jug.
picoler* [pikɔle] (1) *vi* to booze‡, tipple*.
picorer [pikɔʀe] (1) *vti* to peck.
picoter [pikɔte] (1) **1** *vt* **(a)** *gorge* to tickle; *peau* to make smart; *yeux* to sting; (*avec une épingle*) to prick. **(b)** (*picorer*) to peck at. **2** *vi [gorge]* to tickle; *[peau]* to smart, prickle; *[yeux]* to smart, sting. ♦ **picotement** *nm*: ~**(s)** tickling; smarting; prickling; stinging.
picrate‡ [pikʀat] *nm* plonk*, (cheap) wine.
pie [pi] **1** *nf* (*oiseau*) magpie; (*bavard*) chatterbox*. **2** *adj inv cheval* piebald; *vache* black and white.
pièce [pjɛs] **1** *nf* **(a)** (*fragment*) piece. **en ~s** in pieces; (*lit, fig*) **mettre en ~s** to pull *ou* tear to pieces; **c'est inventé de toutes ~s** it's a complete fabrication. **(b)** (*objet, pion*) piece; (*Mil*) gun; (*Chasse, Pêche: prise*) specimen. **se vendre à la ~** to be sold separately *ou* individually; **2 F ~** 2 francs each *ou* apiece; **travail à la ~** *ou* **aux ~s** piecework; (*costume*) **un deux ~s** a two-piece (suit). **(c)** (*Tech*) ~ **(détachée)** part, component; **~s (de rechange)** spares, spare parts; **livré en ~s détachées** delivered in kit form. **(d)** (*document*) paper, document. ~ **d'identité** identity paper; ~ **à conviction** exhibit; **juger sur ~s** to judge on actual evidence. **(e)** (*Couture: reprise*) patch. **(f)** *[maison]* room. **un deux-~s** a 2-room(ed) flat *ou* apartment (*US*). **(g)** (*Littérat, Mus*) piece. ~ **(de théâtre)** play. **(h)** ~ **(de monnaie)** coin; **une ~ de 5 francs** a 5-franc piece *ou* coin; **donner la ~ à qn*** to give *ou* slip sb a tip.
2: ~ **de bétail** head of cattle; ~ **de blé** wheat field; ~ **d'eau** ornamental lake *ou* pond; (*Culin*) ~ **montée** tiered cake; (*noce*) wedding cake; ~ **de musée** museum piece; ~ **de terre** piece *ou* patch of land; ~ **de vin** cask of wine.
pied [pje] *nm* **(a)** (*gén*) foot. **aller ~s nus** *ou* **nu-pieds** to go barefoot(ed); **avoir les ~s plats** to have flat feet, be flatfooted; **à ~s joints** with one's feet together; **le ~ lui a manqué** he lost his footing, his foot slipped; **aller à ~** to go on foot, walk; (*lit, fig*) **~s et poings liés** bound hand and foot. **(b)** *[arbre, mur etc]* foot, bottom; *[table]* leg; *[appareil-photo, lampadaire]* stand, tripod; *[lampe]* base; *[verre]* stem; *[colonne]* base, foot. **(c)** *[salade, tomate]* plant. ~ **de céleri** head of celery; ~ **de vigne** vine; **blé sur ~** standing corn *ou* wheat. **(d)** (*Culin*) *[porc, veau]* trotter. **(e)** (*mesure*) foot. **un poteau de 6 ~s** a 6-foot pole. **(f)** (*Poésie*) foot. **(g)** (*niveau*) **vivre sur un grand ~** to live in (great *ou* grand) style; **sur un ~ d'amitié/d'égalité** on a friendly/equal footing. **(h)** (‡: *idiot*) twit*, idiot. **il chante comme un ~** he's a useless* *ou* lousy‡ singer. **(i)** (*avec prép*) ~ **à ~** *lutter* every inch of the way; **au ~ de la lettre** literally; **au ~ levé** at a moment's notice; **à ~ d'œuvre** ready to to get down to the job; **à ~ sec** without getting one's feet wet; **de ~ ferme** resolutely; **des ~s à la tête** from head to foot; **sur le ~ de guerre** ready for action. **(j)** (*avec verbes*) **avoir ~** to be able to touch the bottom (*in swimming*); **perdre ~** to be *ou* get out of one's depth; **avoir bon ~ bon œil** to be as fit as a fiddle; **avoir le ~ marin** to be a good sailor; **avoir les ~s sur terre** to have one's feet firmly on the ground; **avoir un ~ dans la tombe** to have one foot in the grave; **être sur ~** *[projet]* to be under way; *[malade]* to be up and about; **faire du ~ à qn** (*prévenir*) to give sb a kick (*to warn him*); (*galamment*) to play footsy with sb*; **faire le ~ de grue*** to kick one's heels; **faire des ~s et des mains pour faire qch*** to move heaven and earth to do sth; **faire un ~ de nez à qn** to thumb one's nose at sb; **cela lui fera les ~s*** that'll teach him (a thing or two)*; **mettre qn à ~** to dismiss sb; **mettre ~ à terre** to dismount; **mettre les ~s chez qn** to set foot in sb's house; **mettre qn au ~ du mur** to put sb to the test; **mettre les ~s dans le plat*** (*gaffer*) to put one's foot in it; (*intervenir*) to put one's foot down; **mettre qch sur ~** to set sth up; **remettre qn sur ~** to set sb back on his feet again; **prendre ~ dans/sur** to get a foothold in/on; **c'est le ~!‡** it's a real turn-on!‡; it's great!*
♦ **pied-noir,** *pl* **~s-~s** *nm* pied-noir (*Algerian-born Frenchman*). ♦ **pied-de-poule 1** *nm, pl* **~s-~-~** hound's-tooth cloth. **2** *adj inv* hound's tooth. ♦ **pied-à-terre** *nm inv* pied-à-terre.
piédestal, *pl* **-aux** [pjedɛstal, o] *nm* (*lit, fig*) pedestal.
piège [pjɛʒ] *nm* (*lit, fig*) trap; (*fosse*) pit; (*collet*) snare. **les ~s d'une dictée** the pitfalls of a dictation; **pris à son propre ~** caught in one's own trap; **tendre un ~ à qn** to set a trap for sb; ~ **à loups** mantrap. ♦ **piégé, e** *adj*: **engin ~** booby trap; **voiture/lettre ~e** car-/letter-bomb. ♦ **piéger** (3) *vt* **(a)** *animal, personne* to trap. **se faire ~** to be trapped. **(b)** *objet* to set a trap in; (*avec explosifs*) to booby-trap.
pierre [pjɛʀ] **1** *nf* (*gén, Méd*) stone. **cœur de ~** heart of stone; **faire d'une ~ deux coups** to kill two birds with one stone; ~ **qui roule n'amasse pas mousse** a rolling stone gathers no moss; **c'est une ~ dans son jardin** it's a dig at him; **jour à marquer d'une ~ blanche/noire** red-letter/black day.
2: ~ **d'achoppement** stumbling block; ~ **à aiguiser** whetstone; ~ **à briquet** flint; ~ **ponce** pumice stone; ~ **précieuse** precious stone, gem; **mur en ~s sèches** drystone wall *ou* dyke; ~ **de taille** freestone; ~ **tombale** tombstone; (*lit, fig*) ~ **de touche** touchstone. ♦ **pierraille** *nf* loose stones, chippings. ♦ **pierreries** *nfpl* gems, precious stones. ♦ **pierreux, -euse** *adj* stony.
pierrot [pjɛʀo] *nm* **(a)** (*Théât*) pierrot. **(b)** (*Orn*) sparrow.
piété [pjete] *nf* piety. **articles de ~** devotional articles.
piétiner [pjetine] (1) **1** *vi* (*trépigner*) to stamp (one's foot *ou* feet); (*ne pas avancer*) *[personne]* to stand about; *[discussion, enquête]* to be at a standstill, hang fire; *[science]* to be at a standstill. ~ **dans la boue** to trudge through the mud. **2** *vt sol* to trample *ou* tread on; (*fig*) *adversaire* to trample underfoot. ♦ **piétinement** *nm* (*marche sur place*) standing about; (*bruit*) stamping. **le ~ de la discussion** the fact that the discussion is not making progress.
piéton[1] [pjetɔ̃] *nm* pedestrian. ♦ **piéton**[2], **-onne** *ou* ♦ **piétonnier, -ière** *adj* pedestrian. **rue ~onne** *ou* **~ière** pedestrian precinct.
piètre [pjɛtʀ(ə)] *adj* very poor, mediocre. **c'est une ~ consolation** it's small *ou* little comfort; **avoir ~ allure** to be a sorry sight.
pieu, *pl* **~x**[1] [pjø] *nm* **(a)** post; (*pointu*) stake; (*Constr*) pile. **(b)** (‡: *lit*) bed. **se mettre au ~** to turn in*.
pieuvre [pjœvʀ(ə)] *nf* octopus.
pieux[2], **-euse** [pjø, øz] *adj* pious, devout. ~ **mensonge** white lie. ♦ **pieusement** *adv* piously.
pif‡ [pif] *nm* (*nez*) beak‡, nose. **au ~** at a rough guess.
pigeon [piʒɔ̃] *nm* (*oiseau*) pigeon; (*: *dupe*) mug‡. ~ **ramier** woodpigeon; ~ **voyageur** carrier *ou* homing pigeon. ♦ **pigeonnier** *nm* dovecote.
piger‡ [piʒe] (3) *vi* to twig‡, understand. **je ne pige pas** I don't get it*, I don't twig‡.
pigment [pigmɑ̃] *nm* pigment. ♦ **pigmentation** *nf* pigmentation. ♦ **pigmenter** (1) *vt* to pigment.
pignon [piɲɔ̃] *nm* (*Archit*) gable; (*Tech*) gear-wheel; (*petite roue*) pinion.
pile [pil] **1** *nf* **(a)** (*tas*) pile, stack. **(b)** *[pont]* pile, pier. **(c)** (*Élec*) battery. **à ~(s)** battery-operated; ~ **atomique** nuclear reactor. **(d)** *[pièce]* ~ **ou face?** heads or tails?; **tirer à ~ ou face pour savoir si ...** to toss up to find out if ... . **2** *adv* (*) (*net*) dead*; (*juste*) just, right. **s'arrêter ~** to stop

dead*; **ça tombe** ~! that's just *ou* exactly what I (*ou* we *etc*) need(ed)!; **arriver** ~ to come just at the right time; **à 2 heures** ~ (at) dead on 2*, at 2 on the dot*.

piler [pile] (1) *vt* (*lit*) to crush, pound. ~ **qn*** (*rosser*) to give sb a hammering‡; (*vaincre*) to beat sb hollow*.

pilier [pilje] *nm* pillar; (*Rugby*) prop (forward).

piller [pije] (1) *vt* ***ville, maison*** to loot, ransack, pillage; *personne* to fleece; (*fig: plagier*) to plagiarize. ♦ ***pillage*** *nm* looting, ransacking, pillaging; fleecing; plagiarizing. ♦ **pillard, e 1** *adj* pillaging, looting. **2** *nm,f* looter.

pilon [pilɔ̃] *nm* (*instrument*) pestle; (*jambe*) wooden leg; *[poulet]* drumstick. ♦ **pilonner** (1) *vt* (*Culin*) to pound; (*Mil*) to pound, shell, bombard. ♦ **pilonnage** *nm* pounding; shelling, bombardment.

pilori [pilɔʀi] *nm* pillory. **mettre au** ~ (*lit*) to put in the stocks; (*fig*) to pillory.

pilote [pilɔt] **1** *adj ferme* experimental; *magasin* cut-price. **2** *nm* (*Aviat, Naut*) pilot; (*Aut*) driver; (*fig: guide*) guide. ~ **automatique/d'essai/de ligne** automatic/test/airline pilot; ~ **de course** racing driver. ♦ **pilotage** *nm* piloting, flying. ♦ **piloter** (1) *vt avion* to pilot, fly; *navire* to pilot; *voiture* to drive. ~ **qn** to show *ou* guide sb round.

pilotis [pilɔti] *nm* pile.

pilule [pilyl] *nf* pill. **prendre la** ~ (*contraceptive*) to be on *ou* take the pill; (‡*fig*) to take a hammering‡.

piment [pimɑ̃] *nm* chilli (pepper); (*fig*) spice. ~ **doux** pepper, capsicum; **avoir du** ~ to be spicy. ♦ **pimenté, e** *adj plat* hot; *récit* spicy.

pimpant, e [pɛ̃pɑ̃, ɑ̃t] *adj* spruce.

pin [pɛ̃] *nm* (*arbre*) pine (tree); (*bois*) pine(wood). ~ **maritime/parasol** maritime/umbrella pine.

pinard‡ [pinaʀ] *nm* plonk*, (cheap) wine.

pince [pɛ̃s] *nf* **(a)** (*outil*) ~**(s)** (*gén*) pliers; (*à sucre, charbon, de forgeron*) tongs; ~ **à épiler** tweezers; ~ **à linge** clothes peg. **(b)** (*levier*) crowbar. **(c)** *[crabe]* pincer, claw. **(d)** (*Couture*) dart. **faire des** ~**s à** to put darts in. **(e)** (‡: *main*) mitt‡, paw‡. **(f)** (‡: *jambe*) leg. **aller à** ~**s** to foot it*. ♦ **pince-monseigneur**, *pl* ~**s-**~ *nf* jemmy.

pinceau, *pl* ~**x** [pɛ̃so] *nm* (*Peinture*) (paint)brush; (‡: *pied*) foot, hoof‡. ~ **lumineux** pencil of light.

pincer [pɛ̃se] (3) **1** *vt* **(a)** (*pour faire mal*) to pinch, nip; *[froid, chien]* to nip; (*Agr*) to pinch out; (*Mus*) to pluck. **se** ~ **le doigt dans la porte** to trap *ou* catch one's finger in the door; **il s'est fait** ~ **par un crabe** he was nipped by a crab. **(b)** (*serrer*) to grip. ~ **les lèvres** to purse (up) one's lips; **se** ~ **le nez** to hold one's nose; **robe qui pince la taille** dress which is tight at the waist. **(c)** (*Couture*) *veste* to put darts in. **(d)** (**fig: arrêter*) to catch, cop‡. **(e) en** ~ **pour qn‡** to be stuck on sb‡, be mad about sb*. **2** *vi* (‡) **ça pince (dur)** it's freezing (cold). ♦ **pincé, e**[1] *adj air, ton* stiff. ♦ **pincée**[2] *nf [sel, poivre]* pinch. ♦ **pincement** *nm*: ~ **au cœur** lump in one's throat. ♦ **pince-sans-rire** *nm inv*: **c'est un** ~ he's the deadpan type.

pincettes [pɛ̃sɛt] *nfpl* (fire) tongs; *[horloger]* tweezers. **il n'est pas à toucher avec des** ~**s** (*sale*) he's filthy dirty; (*mécontent*) he's like a bear with a sore head.

pinède [pinɛd] *nf* pinewood, pine forest.

pingouin [pɛ̃gwɛ̃] *nm [arctique]* auk; (*gén*) penguin.

ping-pong [piŋpɔ̃g] *nm* table tennis.

pingre [pɛ̃gʀ(ə)] (*péj*) **1** *adj* stingy, niggardly. **2** *nmf* skinflint, niggard. ♦ **pingrerie** *nf* (*péj*) stinginess.

pinson [pɛ̃sɔ̃] *nm* chaffinch.

pintade [pɛ̃tad] *nf* guinea-fowl.

pioche [pjɔʃ] *nf* mattock, pickaxe. ♦ **piocher** (1) *vt terre* to dig up; (*) *sujet* to cram for; (*Jeu*) *carte* to pick up (from the pile).

piolet [pjɔlɛ] *nm* ice axe.

pion [pjɔ̃] *nm* **(a)** (*Échecs*) pawn; (*Jeu*) piece. **(b)** (*Scol: péj*) ≃ supervisor.

pioncer‡ [pjɔ̃se] (3) *vi* to have a kip‡, sleep.

pionnier [pjɔnje] *nm* (*lit, fig*) pioneer.

pipe [pip] *nf* pipe. ~ **de bruyère** briar pipe.

pipeau [pipo] *nm* (*Mus*) (reed-)pipe.

pipelet, -ette* [piplɛ, ɛt] *nm,f* (*péj*) concierge.

pipe-line, *pl* ~**-**~**s** [pajplajn, piplin] *nm* pipeline.

pipi* [pipi] *nm* wee(wee)*. **faire** ~ to go to the toilet.

piquant, e [pikɑ̃, ɑ̃t] **1** *adj barbe* prickly; (*Bot*) *tige* thorny; *froid* biting; *critique* biting, cutting; *détail* titillating, spicy; *moutarde* hot; *goût, fromage* pungent; *vin* sour, tart. (*Culin*) **sauce** ~**e** piquant sauce. **2** *nm [hérisson, oursin]* spine; *[rosier]* thorn; *[chardon]* prickle; *[barbelé]* barb; *[conversation]* piquancy; *[aventure]* spice. **et, détail qui ne manque pas de** ~, ... and here's a diverting detail ....

pique [pik] **1** *nf* (*arme*) pike; (*critique*) cutting remark. **2** *nm* (*carte*) spade; (*couleur*) spades.

piqué, e [pike] **1** *adj* **(a)** (*Couture*) (*cousu*) (machine-)stitched; *couvre-lit* quilted. **(b)** *glace, linge* mildewed; *meuble* worm-eaten; *vin* sour. ~ **par la rouille** *métal* pitted with rust; *linge* covered in rust spots. **(c)** (*: *fou*) nuts*, barmy*. **2** *nm* **(a)** (*Aviat*) dive. **(b)** (*tissu*) piqué.

piquer [pike] (1) **1** *vt* **(a)** *[guêpe]* to sting; *[moustique, serpent]* to bite; (*avec une pointe*) to prick; (*Méd*) to give an injection to. **se faire** ~ to have an injection; (*euph*) **faire** ~ **un chat** to have a cat put to sleep (*euph*); ~ **la viande avec une fourchette** to prick the meat with a fork; ~ **qch au mur** to put *ou* stick *ou* pin sth up on the wall. **(b)** *aiguille* to stick, stab, jab (*dans* into). **(c)** (*Couture*) ~ **qch (à la machine)** to (machine) stitch sth, sew sth up. **(d)** *[barbe]* to prick, prickle; *[ortie]* to sting; *[froid]* to bite, sting. **ça (me) pique** *[démangeaison]* it itches; *[barbe, tissu]* it's prickly; *[liqueur]* it burns; *[ronces]* it prickles; *[alcool sur une plaie]* it stings *ou* burns; **les yeux me piquent** my eyes are smarting *ou* stinging. **(e)** (*exciter*) *curiosité* to arouse, excite; (*vexer*) to pique, nettle. ~ **qn au vif** to cut sb to the quick. **(f)** (*: *faire*) ~ **un cent mètres** to put on a burst of speed; ~ **une crise de larmes** to have a fit of tears; ~ **une colère** to fly into a rage; ~ **une suée** to break out in a sweat; ~ **un plongeon** to dive. **(g)** (*: *prendre*) *accent* to pick up; *manie, maladie* to pick up, catch, get; *portefeuille* to pinch*, whip‡; *idée* to pinch* (*à* from); *voleur* to nab‡, nick‡. ~ **dans le tas** to choose *ou* pick at random.

2 *vi* **(a)** *[avion]* to go into a dive. **il faudrait** ~ **vers le village** we'll have to head towards the village; ~ **du nez** *[avion]* to go into a nose-dive; *[bateau]* to dip her head; *[fleurs]* to droop; *[personne]* to fall headfirst. **(b)** *[moutarde, radis]* to be hot; *[vin]* to be sour; *[fromage]* to be pungent.

3 se ~ *vpr* **(a)** (*avec une aiguille*) to prick o.s.; (*dans les orties*) to get stung; (*Méd*) to give o.s. an injection, inject o.s. **(b)** *[miroir, linge]* to go mildewed; *[métal]* to be pitted; *[vin, cidre]* to go *ou* turn sour. **(c) se** ~ **de littérature** to pride o.s. on one's knowledge of literature; **se** ~ **de faire qch** to pride o.s. on one's ability to do sth. **(d)** (*se vexer*) to take offence. **(e) il s'est piqué au jeu** it grew on him; **se** ~ **le nez‡** to booze‡.

♦ **pique-assiette*** *nmf inv* scrounger*, sponger*. ♦ **pique-nique**, *pl* ~**-**~**s** *nm* picnic. ♦ **pique-niquer** (1) *vi* to have a picnic, picnic.

piquet [pikɛ] *nm* (*pieu*) post, stake; *[tente]* peg. ~ **(de grève)** (strike-)picket; (*Scol*) **mettre qn au** ~ to put sb in the corner.

piqueter [pikte] (4) *vt* (*moucheter*) to dot (*de* with).

piquette [pikɛt] *nf* (*vin*) (cheap) wine; (‡: *défaite*)

hammering:, thrashing*. **prendre une ~** to be hammered: *ou* thrashed*.
piqûre [pikyʀ] *nf* **(a)** *[épingle]* prick; *[guêpe, ortie]* sting; *[moustique]* bite; (*trace, trou*) hole. **~ d'amour-propre** injury to one's pride. **(b)** (*Méd*) injection, shot*. **faire/se faire faire une ~** to give/have an injection. **(c)** (*Couture*) (*point*) (straight) stitch; (*rang*) (straight) stitching.
pirate [piʀat] **1** *adj* pirate. **2** *nm* pirate; (*fig: escroc*) swindler, shark*. **~ de l'air** hijacker, skyjacker*. ♦ **pirater** (1) *vt* to pirate. ♦ **piraterie** *nf* piracy; (*acte*) act of piracy. **~ aérienne** hijacking, skyjacking*; **c'est de la ~!** it's daylight robbery!
pire [piʀ] **1** *adj* **(a)** (*comp*) worse. **c'est ~ que jamais** it's worse than ever. **(b)** (*superl*) **le ~, la ~** the worst. **2** *nm*: **le ~** the worst; **le ~ c'est que ...** the worst thing *ou* the worst of it is that ...; **au ~** at (the very) worst.
pirogue [piʀɔg] *nf* dugout canoe.
pirouette [piʀwɛt] *nf* (*lit*) pirouette; (*fig: volte-face*) about-turn (*fig*); (*faux-fuyant*) evasive reply.
pis[1] [pi] *nm [vache]* udder.
pis[2] [pi] (*littér*) **1** *adj* worse. **qui ~ est** what is worse. **2** *adv* worse. **de ~ en ~** worse and worse; **dire ~ que pendre de qn** to malign sb. **3** *nm*: **le ~** the worst (thing); **au ~ aller** if the worst comes to the worst. ♦ **pis-aller** *nm inv* (*personne, solution*) stopgap; (*chose*) makeshift.
pisciculture [pisikyltyʀ] *nf* fish breeding.
piscine [pisin] *nf* swimming pool.
pissenlit [pisɑ̃li] *nm* dandelion.
pisser: [pise] (1) **1** *vi [personne]* to pee:; *[récipient]* to gush out. **2** *vt*: **ça pisse le sang/l'eau** it's gushing blood/water, there's blood/water gushing from it. ♦ **pisse**: *nf* pee:.
pistache [pistaʃ] *nf* pistachio (nut).
piste [pist(ə)] *nf* **(a)** *[animal, suspect]* track, trail; (*Police: indice*) lead. **être sur la bonne ~** to be on the right track; **perdre la ~ du meurtrier** to lose the murderer's trail. **(b)** *[hippodrome]* course; *[stade]* track; *[patinage]* rink; *[danse]* (dance)-floor; *[skieurs]* (ski)run; *[cirque]* ring; (*Aviat*) runway. **~ cavalière** bridle path; **~ cyclable** cycle track; (*Athlétisme*) **~ 3** lane 3. **(c)** (*sentier*) track; *[désert]* trail. **(d)** *[magnétophone]* track. (*Ciné*) **~ sonore** sound track. ♦ **pister** (1) *vt* to track, trail.
pistolet [pistɔlɛ] *nm* (*arme*) pistol, gun; *[peintre]* spray gun. **peindre au ~** to spray-paint; **~ mitrailleur** submachine gun.
piston [pistɔ̃] *nm* (*Tech*) piston; (*Mus*) valve; (*: *aide*) string-pulling*. ♦ **pistonner*** (1) *vt* to pull strings for* (*auprès de* with). **se faire ~** to get sb to pull strings (for one)*.
piteux, -euse [pitø, øz] *adj* (*minable*) pitiful, pathetic; (*honteux*) shamefaced. **en ~ état** in a sorry *ou* pitiful state. ♦ **piteusement** *adv* pathetically.
pitié [pitje] *nf* **(a)** (*compassion*) pity. **avoir ~ de qn** to pity sb, feel pity for sb; **prendre qn en ~** to take pity on sb; **il me fait ~** I feel sorry for him, I pity him; **quelle ~ de voir ça** it's pitiful to see (that). **(b)** (*miséricorde*) pity, mercy. **avoir ~ d'un ennemi** to have pity *ou* mercy on an enemy; **~!** (*lit: grâce*) (have) mercy!; (*: *assez*) for goodness' *ou* pity's sake!; **sans ~** *agir* pitilessly, mercilessly, ruthlessly; *personne* pitiless, merciless, ruthless.
piton [pitɔ̃] *nm* **(a)** (*à anneau*) eye; (*à crochet*) hook; *[alpiniste]* piton, peg. **(b)** (*Géog*) peak.
pitoyable [pitwajabl(ə)] *adj* (*gén*) pitiful, pitiable.
pitre [pitʀ(ə)] *nm* (*lit, fig*) clown. **faire le ~** to clown *ou* fool about. ♦ **pitrerie** *nf*: **~(s)** clowning.
pittoresque [pitɔʀɛsk(ə)] **1** *adj* picturesque; *récit* colourful, vivid. **2** *nm*: **le ~ de qch** the picturesque quality of sth.
pivert [pivɛʀ] *nm* green woodpecker.
pivoine [pivwan] *nf* peony.
pivot [pivo] *nm* (*gén*) pivot; *[dent]* post. ♦ **pivotant, e** *adj panneau* pivoting, revolving; *fauteuil* swivel. ♦ **pivoter** (1) *vi [porte]* to revolve, pivot. *[personne]* **~ (sur ses talons)** to turn *ou* swivel round; **faire ~ qch** to swing *ou* swivel sth round.
placage [plakaʒ] *nm* (*en bois*) veneer; (*en pierre*) facing.
placard [plakaʀ] *nm* **(a)** (*armoire*) cupboard. **(b)** (*affiche*) poster, notice. **~ publicitaire** display advertisement. **(c)** (*: *couche*) thick layer. ♦ **placarder** (1) *vt affiche* to stick up, put up; *mur* to stick posters on, placard.
place [plas] *nf* **(a)** (*esplanade*) square. (*fig*) **sur la ~ publique** in public. **(b)** *[objet]* place. **remettre qch en ~** to put sth back where it belongs *ou* in its proper place; **changer qch de ~** to move *ou* shift sth. **(c)** *[personne]* (*lit, fig*) place; (*assise*) seat. **~ d'honneur** place *ou* seat of honour; **prenez ~** take your place *ou* seat; (*lit, fig*) **prendre la ~ de qn** to take sb's place; **il ne tient pas en ~** he can't keep still; (*fig*) **remettre qn à sa ~** to put sb in his place; **laisser la ~ à qn** (*lit*) to give (up) one's seat to sb; (*fig*) to hand over to sb; **il n'est pas à sa ~ dans ce milieu** he is out of place in this setting; **être en bonne ~ pour gagner** to be well-placed *ou* in a good position to win; **se mettre à la ~ de qn** to put o.s. in sb's place *ou* in sb's shoes; **à votre ~** if I were you, in your place. **(d)** (*espace libre*) room, space. **prendre/faire de la ~** to take up/make room *ou* space. **(e)** (*siège, billet*) seat; (*prix d'un trajet*) fare; (*emplacement réservé*) space. **payer ~ entière** (*au cinéma etc*) to pay full price; (*dans le bus etc*) to pay full fare; **~ de parking** parking space; **cinéma de 400 ~s** cinema seating 400 (people) *ou* with a seating capacity of 400; **~ assise** seat; **une voiture de 4 ~s** a 4-seater car; **j'ai 3 ~s dans ma voiture** I've room for 3 in my car. **(f)** (*rang*) (*Scol*) place; (*Sport*) place, placing. **il a eu une ~ de 2e en histoire** he came *ou* was (placed) 2nd in history. **(g)** (*emploi*) job; *[domestique]* position, situation. **une ~ d'employé** a job as a clerk; (*Pol*) **les gens en ~** influential people. **(h)** (*Mil*) **~ (forte)** fortified town; (*lit, fig*) **s'introduire dans la ~** to get on the inside; **~ d'armes** parade ground. **(i)** (*Comm, Fin*) market. **~ financière** money market. **(j) de ~ en ~** here and there, in places; **rester sur/se rendre sur ~** to stay on/go to the spot; **à la ~ (de)** (*en échange*) instead (of), in place (of); **répondre à la ~ de qn** to reply in sb's place *ou* on sb's behalf; **être en ~** to be ready; **mettre qch en ~** to set sth up, get sth ready; **faire ~ à qn** (*lit*) to let sb pass; (*fig*) to give way to sb; **faire ~ nette** to make a clean sweep.
placement [plasmɑ̃] *nm* (*Fin*) investment.
placer [plase] (3) **1** *vt* **(a)** (*mettre*) (*gén*) to place, put; *invité, spectateur* to seat; *sentinelle* to post, station; (*Boxe*) *coup* to land, place; *parole* to put in, get in; (*Tech: installer*) to put in, fit in. **vous me placez dans une situation délicate** you're placing *ou* putting me in a tricky position; **il a placé l'action de son roman en Provence** he has set *ou* situated the action of his novel in Provence. **(b)** *malade, écolier* to place (*dans* in). **~ qn comme vendeur** to get *ou* find sb a job as a salesman; **~ qn comme apprenti (chez X)** to apprentice sb (to X); **l'orchestre est placé sous la direction de ...** the orchestra is conducted by ... . **(c)** (*Comm: vendre*) to place, sell; *argent* (*Bourse*) to invest; (*Caisse d'Épargne*) to deposit; (*sur son compte*) to put, pay (*sur* into).
2 se ~ *vpr* **(a)** *[personne]* to take up a position; (*debout*) to stand; (*assis*) to sit (down); *[événement]* to take place, occur, happen. **si nous nous plaçons dans cette perspective** if we look at things from this point of view *ou* angle; **plaçons-**

nous dans cette hypothèse let us suppose that this happens. **(b)** (*Scol, Sport*) **se ~ 2e** to be *ou* come 2nd, be in 2nd place; **il s'est bien placé** he was well placed. **(c)** *[ouvrier]* to get *ou* find a job; *[retraité]* to find a place in a home.

♦ **placé, e** *adj*: **la fenêtre est ~e à gauche** the window is (situated) on the left; **être bien/mal ~** *[terrain]* to be well/badly situated; *[objet, concurrent]* to be well/badly placed; *[spectateur]* to have a good/a poor seat; **sa fierté est mal ~e** his pride is misplaced *ou* out of place; **je suis bien/mal ~ pour vous répondre** I'm in a/in no position to answer.

placide [plasid] *adj* placid. ♦ **placidité** *nf* placidity.

plafond [plafɔ̃] *nm* (*gén, fig*) ceiling; *[voiture, caverne]* roof. **prix ~** ceiling *ou* maximum price. ♦ **plafonner** (1) *vi* to reach a ceiling *ou* maximum. ♦ **plafonnier** *nm* *[voiture]* courtesy light; *[chambre]* ceiling light.

plage [plaʒ] *nf* *[mer, lac]* beach; *[disque]* track; (*ville*) (seaside) resort; (*fig: zone*) area. **~ de prix** price range *ou* bracket; **~ arrière** (*Naut*) quarter-deck; (*Aut*) parcel *ou* back shelf.

plagiat [plaʒja] *nm* plagiarism. ♦ **plagier** (7) *vt* to plagiarize.

plaider [plede] (1) **1** *vt* to plead. **~ la légitime défense** to plead self-defence; **~ la cause de qn** (*fig*) to plead sb's cause; (*Jur*) to plead sb's case; **l'affaire s'est plaidée à Paris** the case was heard in Paris. **2** *vi* *[avocat]* to plead; (*intenter un procès*) to go to court. (*fig*) **~ pour qn** *[personne]* to speak for sb; *[qualités]* to be a point in sb's favour. ♦ **plaideur, -euse** *nm,f* litigant. ♦ **plaidoirie** *nf* (defence *ou* prosecution) speech. ♦ **plaidoyer** *nm* (*Jur*) speech for the defence; (*fig*) defence, plea.

plaie [plɛ] *nf* (*gén*) wound; (*coupure*) cut; (*fig: fléau*) scourge. **quelle ~!*** what a bind!* *ou* pest!* *ou* nuisance!; **remuer le fer dans la ~** to twist the knife in the wound.

plaignant, e [plɛɲɑ̃, ɑ̃t] **1** *adj* *partie* litigant. **2** *nm,f* plaintiff.

plaindre [plɛ̃dʀ(ə)] (52) **1** *vt* **(a)** *personne* to pity, feel sorry for. **elle n'est pas à ~** (*c'est bien fait*) she doesn't deserve to be pitied; (*elle a de la chance*) she's got nothing to complain about; **je vous plains** I pity you (*de faire* for doing). **(b)** (*: *donner chichement*) to begrudge. **2 se ~** *vpr* (*gémir*) to moan; (*protester*) to complain, grumble, moan* (*de* about); (*Jur: réclamer*) to make a complaint (*de* about, *auprès de* to). **se ~ de** *maux de tête etc* to complain of.

plaine [plɛn] *nf* plain.

plain-pied [plɛ̃pje] *adv*: **de ~** (*pièce*) on the same level (*avec* as); (*maison*) (built) at street-level; (*fig*) **entrer de ~ dans le sujet** to come straight to the point.

plainte [plɛ̃t] *nf* (*gémissement*) moan, groan; (*protestation*) complaint. **porter ~ contre qn** to lodge a complaint against *ou* about sb. ♦ **plaintif, -ive** *adj* plaintive, doleful. ♦ **plaintivement** *adv* plaintively, dolefully.

plaire [plɛʀ] (54) **1** *vi* *[personne]* **~ à qn** to be liked by sb; **ça me plaît** *[livre, spectacle, travail]* I like *ou* enjoy it; *[plan]* it suits me; *[sport, activité]* I'm keen on it, I enjoy it; **ce genre de musique ne me plaît pas beaucoup** I'm not keen on *ou* I don't care for that kind of music, that kind of music doesn't appeal to me very much; **c'est une chose qui me plairait beaucoup à faire** it's something I'd very much like to do *ou* I'd love to do; **il cherche à ~ à tout le monde** he tries to please everyone; **ça te plairait d'aller au cinéma?** would you like to go to the pictures?, do you fancy* going *ou* do you feel like going to the pictures?; **quand ça me plaît** when I feel like it, when it suits me, when the fancy takes me; **je fais ce qui me plaît** I do as I like *ou* please; *[idée, repas]* **cela plaît toujours** it always goes down well, it's always popular. **2** *vb impers*: **et s'il me plaît d'y aller?** and what if I want to go?; **comme il vous plaira** just as you like *ou* please; **s'il te plaît, s'il vous plaît** please; **plaît-il?** I beg your pardon? **3 se ~** *vpr*: **il se plaît à Londres** he likes *ou* enjoys being in London; **les fougères se plaisent dans les sous-bois** ferns do well *ou* thrive in the undergrowth; **tu te plais avec ton chapeau?** do you like *ou* fancy* yourself in your hat?; **ces deux-là se plaisent** those two get on well together; **se ~ à lire** to take pleasure in reading.

plaisance [plɛzɑ̃s] *nf*: **la navigation de ~** sailing, yachting; **bateau de ~** yacht; **maison de ~** country cottage. ♦ **plaisancier** *nm* yachtsman.

plaisant, e [plɛzɑ̃, ɑ̃t] *adj* (*agréable*) pleasant, agreeable; (*amusant*) amusing, funny; (*ridicule*) laughable, ridiculous. ♦ **plaisamment** *adv* pleasantly; agreeably; amusingly; laughably.

plaisanter [plɛzɑ̃te] (1) **1** *vi* to joke (*sur* about). **et je ne plaisante pas!** and I'm not joking!; **vous plaisantez** you must be joking; **pour ~** for fun *ou* a joke *ou* a laugh*; **il ne plaisante pas sur la discipline** there's no joking with him over matters of discipline. **2** *vt*: **~ qn sur qch** to tease sb about sth. ♦ **plaisanterie** *nf* **(a)** (*blague, raillerie*) joke (*sur* about); (*farce*) practical joke, prank. **aimer la ~** to be fond of a joke; **il est en butte aux ~s de ses amis** his friends are always making fun of him *ou* poking fun at him; **mauvaise ~** (nasty) practical joke. ♦ **plaisantin** *nm* (*blagueur*) joker; (*fumiste*) clown.

plaisir [pleziʀ] *nm* **(a)** (*joie*) pleasure. **prendre ~ à faire qch** to find *ou* take pleasure in doing sth, delight in doing sth; **j'ai le ~ de vous annoncer que ...** I have pleasure in announcing that ...; **ranger pour le ~ de ranger** to tidy up just for the sake of it; (*iro*) **je vous souhaite bien du ~!** good luck to you! (*iro*); **au ~ de vous revoir, au ~*** (I'll) see you again sometime. **(b)** (*distraction*) pleasure; (*dada*) hobby. **(c)** (*littér: volonté*) pleasure (*littér*), wish. **si c'est votre (bon) ~** if such is your will *ou* wish. **(d) faire ~ à qn** to please sb; **cela me fait ~ de vous voir** I'm pleased *ou* delighted to see you; **ça fait ~ à voir** it is a pleasure to see; **fais-moi ~: mange ta soupe** eat your soup, there's a dear; **voulez-vous me faire le ~ de venir dîner?** would you do me the pleasure of dining with me?; **fais-moi le ~ de te taire!** would you mind just being quiet!, do me a favour and be quiet!; **il se fera un ~ de vous reconduire** he'll be (only too) pleased *ou* glad to drive you back; **bon, c'est bien pour vous faire ~** all right, if it will make you happy.

plan¹ [plɑ̃] *nm* **(a)** *[maison, machine]* plan; *[ville, région]* map. **faire des ~s** to draw up plans. **(b)** (*Math etc: surface*) plane. (*dans cuisine*) **~ de travail** work-top; **~ incliné** inclined plane; **en ~ incliné** sloping; **~ d'eau** stretch of water. **(c)** (*Ciné*) shot. **premier ~** foreground; **dernier ~** background; (*Peinture*) **au deuxième ~** in the middle distance. **(d)** (*fig: niveau*) plane. **mettre qch au deuxième ~** to consider sth of secondary importance; **ce problème vient au premier ~ de nos préoccupations** this problem is uppermost in our minds; **personnalité de premier/second ~** key/minor *ou* secondary figure; **au premier ~ de l'actualité** in the forefront of the news. **(e)** (*projet*) plan. **~ de travail** work plan *ou* programme *ou* schedule; **~ d'action** plan of action. **(f)** *[livre]* plan; *[dissertation]* plan, framework. **(g) laisser en ~*** *personne* to leave in the lurch *ou* stranded; *affaires, voiture* to abandon, ditch*; **il a tout laissé en ~*** he dropped everything; **rester en ~*** *[projet]* to be left in mid air.

plan², plane [plɑ̃, plan] *adj* (*gén*) flat; (*Math*) plane.

planche [plɑ̃ʃ] *nf* **(a)** (*en bois*) plank; (*plus large*) board; (*rayon*) shelf; (*Naut: passerelle*) gangplank; (*plongeoir*) diving board. ~ **à dessin/à repasser** drawing/ironing board; ~ **à laver** washboard; (*fig*) ~ **de salut** last hope; (*Théât*) **monter sur les** ~**s** to go on the stage; (*Natation*) **faire la** ~ to float on one's back; **cabine en** ~**s** wooden hut. **(b)** (*Typ, illustration*) plate. **(c)** (*Horticulture*) bed. ♦ **plancher** *nm* (*Constr*) floor. **(prix)** ~ minimum *ou* floor *ou* bottom price.

plancton [plɑ̃ktɔ̃] *nm* plankton.

planer [plane] (1) *vi [oiseau]* to glide, hover; *[avion]* to glide; *[fumée]* to float, hover; (*fig*) *[rêveur]* to have one's head in the clouds. ~ **sur** *[regard]* to look down over; *[danger, soupçons]* to hang over.

planète [planɛt] *nf* planet. ♦ **planétaire** *adj* (*Astron, Tech*) planetary. ♦ **planétarium** *nm* planetarium.

planeur [planœʀ] *nm* (*Aviat*) glider.

planifier [planifje] (7) *vt* to plan. ♦ **planification** *nf* (economic) planning. ♦ **planning** *nm* (*Écon, Ind*) programme, schedule. ~ **familial** family planning.

planque‡ [plɑ̃k] *nf* (*cachette*) hideaway, hideout; (*travail*) cushy‡ *ou* soft* job. ♦ **planquer**‡ (1) **1** *vt* to hide *ou* stash* away. **2 se** ~ *vpr* to take cover.

plant [plɑ̃] *nm* (*plante*) seedling, young plant; (*plantation*) bed; *[arbres]* plantation. **un** ~ **de vigne** a young vine.

plantation [plɑ̃tɑsjɔ̃] *nf* (*action*) planting; (*culture*) plant; (*terrain*) bed; *[arbres]* plantation. **faire des** ~**s de fleurs** to plant flowers (out).

plante [plɑ̃t] *nf* **(a)** (*Bot*) plant. ~ **fourragère** fodder plant; ~ **grasse** succulent (plant); ~ **grimpante** creeper; ~ **verte** green (foliage) plant. **(b)** (*Anat*) ~ **(des pieds)** sole (of the foot).

planter [plɑ̃te] (1) *vt* **(a)** *plante* to plant, put in; *jardin* to put plants in; (*repiquer*) to plant out. **avenue plantée d'arbres** tree-lined avenue. **(b)** *clou* to hammer in, knock in; *pieu* to drive in; *aiguille* to stick in. ~ **un poignard dans le dos de qn** to knife *ou* stab sb in the back; **se** ~ **une épine dans le doigt** to get a thorn stuck in one's finger. **(c)** (*mettre*) *objet* to stick*, put. **il se planta devant moi** he planted himself in front of me; **rester planté devant une vitrine*** to stand looking at a shop window; ~ **là*** *personne, voiture* to dump*, ditch*; *outils* to dump*, drop; *métier* to chuck up‡, pack in*. **(d)** *tente* to put up, pitch; (*Théât*) *décors* to set up. ~ **une échelle contre un mur** to stand a ladder (up) against a wall. ♦ **planteur** *nm* (*colon*) planter. ♦ **plantoir** *nm* dibble.

planton [plɑ̃tɔ̃] *nm* (*Mil*) orderly. **faire le** ~* to hang about*.

plantureux, -euse [plɑ̃tyʀø, øz] *adj repas* copious; *région* fertile. **récolte** ~**euse** bumper *ou* heavy crop.

plaquage [plakaʒ] *nm* (*Rugby*) tackle.

plaque [plak] *nf [métal, verre]* sheet, plate; *[marbre, chocolat]* slab; (*de verglas, sur la peau*) patch; (*Élec, Phot, de revêtement*) plate; (*portant une inscription*) plaque; (*insigne*) badge. ~ **d'identité** identity disc; (*Aut*) ~ **minéralogique** number *ou* license (*US*) plate; ~ **tournante** (*Rail*) turntable; (*fig*) centre.

plaquer [plake] (1) *vt* **(a)** *bois* to veneer; *bijoux* to plate. **(b)** (‡: *abandonner*) *personne* to ditch*; *emploi* to chuck (in *ou* up)‡, pack in*. **(c)** (*aplatir*) *cheveux* to plaster down. ~ **qn au sol** to pin sb to the ground; **se** ~ **contre un mur** to flatten o.s. against a wall. **(d)** (*Rugby*) to tackle, bring down. **(e)** (*Mus*) *accord* to play. ♦ **plaqué, e 1** *adj*: ~ **(or** *etc***)** (gold *etc*) plated. **2** *nm* plate. **c'est du** ~ it's plated.

plasma [plasma] *nm* (*Anat, Phys*) plasma.

plastic [plastik] *nm* gelignite.

plastifier [plastifje] (7) *vt* to coat with plastic.

plastique [plastik] **1** *adj* plastic. **en matière** ~ plastic. **2** *nm* plastic. **3** *nf* plastic art.

plastiquer [plastike] (1) *vt* to plant a plastic bomb in.

plastron [plastʀɔ̃] *nm [chemise]* shirt front; *[escrimeur]* plastron.

plastronner [plastʀɔne] (1) *vi* to swagger.

plat[1], **plate** [pla, plat] **1** *adj* **(a)** (*gén*) flat; *angle, cheveux* straight; *style* flat, dull; (*obséquieux*) obsequious. **bateau à fond** ~ flat-bottomed boat; **chaussure à talon** ~ flat(-heeled) shoe. **(b) poser qch à** ~ to lay sth (down) flat; **être à** ~ *[pneu, batterie]* to be flat; *[automobiliste]* to have a flat tyre; (*) *[personne]* to be washed out*; **la grippe l'a mis à** ~* his flu laid him low; **tomber à** ~ *[plaisanterie]* to fall flat; **tomber à** ~ **ventre** to fall flat on one's face; **se mettre à** ~ **ventre** to lie face down; (*fig*) **se mettre à** ~ **ventre devant qn** to crawl to sb. **2** *nm* (*partie plate*) flat (part). **course de** ~ flat race; (*fig*) **faire du** ~ **à*** *supérieur* to crawl to; *femme* to sweet-talk*. ♦ **plate-bande,** *pl* ~**s-**~**s** *nf* (*Horticulture*) flower bed. **piétiner les** ~**s-**~**s de qn*** to tread on sb else's patch. ♦ **plate-forme,** *pl* ~**s-**~**s** *nf* (*gén, fig*) platform; (*Rail: wagon*) flat wagon *ou* car (*US*).

plat[2] [pla] *nm* (*récipient, mets*) dish; (*partie du repas*) course. **il en a fait tout un** ~* he made a great fuss about it; **mettre les petits** ~**s dans les grands** to lay on a first-rate meal; ~ **du jour** today's special; ~ **de résistance** *[repas]* main course; (*fig*) pièce de résistance.

platane [platan] *nm* plane tree.

plateau, *pl* ~**x** [plato] *nm* (*de serveur*) tray; *[balance]* pan; *[électrophone]* turntable, deck; *[table]* top; *[graphique]* plateau; (*Géog*) plateau; (*Théât*) stage; (*Ciné, TV*) set; (*Rail: wagon*) flat wagon *ou* car (*US*); (*plate-forme roulante*) trailer. ~ **de fromages** cheeseboard.

platine [platin] **1** *nm, adj inv* platinum. **2** *nf [électrophone]* deck, turntable.

platitude [platityd] *nf [livre]* dullness; (*propos*) platitude.

plâtre [plɑtʀ(ə)] *nm* (*matière*) plaster; (*objet*) plaster cast. (*Constr*) **les** ~**s** the plasterwork. ♦ **plâtras** *nm* (*débris*) rubble. ♦ **plâtrer** (1) *vt mur* to plaster; *jambe* to set *ou* put in plaster. ♦ **plâtrier** *nm* plasterer.

plausible [plozibl(ə)] *adj* plausible.

plébiscite [plebisit] *nm* plebiscite. ♦ **plébisciter** (1) *vt* (*Pol*) to elect by plebiscite. (*fig*) **se faire** ~ to be elected by an overwhelming majority.

pléiade [plejad] *nf* (*gén*) pleiad.

plein, pleine [plɛ̃, plɛn] **1** *adj* **(a)** (*rempli*) full; *vie, journée* full, busy. ~ **à déborder** full to overflowing; ~ **à craquer** full to bursting, crammed full; **un** ~ **panier de pommes** a whole basketful of apples; **avoir le ventre** ~* to be full, have eaten one's fill; **être** ~ **aux as**‡ to be rolling in money*; (*péj*) **un gros** ~ **de soupe**‡ a big fat slob‡ (*péj*); ~ **comme une barrique**‡ as drunk as a lord; ~ **de** (*gén*) full of; *taches* covered in *ou* with; *idées* bursting with; **salle pleine de monde** room full of people, crowded room; **remarque pleine de finesse** very shrewd remark. **(b)** *succès, confiance* complete, total. **accord** ~ **et entier** wholehearted consent; **absent un jour** ~ absent for a whole day; **à** ~ **temps** full-time; **avoir les** ~**s pouvoirs** to have full powers; **politique de** ~**-emploi** policy of full employment. **(c)** *lune* full. **la mer est pleine** the tide is in, it is high tide; **en pleine mer** on the open sea. **(d)** *paroi* solid; *trait* unbroken, continuous; *voix* rich, sonorous. **(e)** (*Vét*) pregnant, in calf (*ou* foal, lamb *etc*). **(f)** (*intensité*) **la pleine lumière** the bright light; **avoir pleine conscience de qch** to be fully aware of sth; **être en pleine forme*** to be in *ou* on top form; **de son** ~ **gré** of one's own free will; **de** ~

droit *membre* rightful; *réclamer* rightfully; **heurter qch de ~ fouet** to crash headlong into sth; *[usine]* **marcher à ~ rendement** to work at full capacity; **ça sent l'ammoniaque à ~ nez** there's a terrible smell *ou* stench of ammonia; **respirer à ~s poumons** to take deep breaths; **prendre qch à pleines mains** to grasp sth firmly. **(g) ~ air** open air; **les enfants ont ~ air le mercredi** the children have games *ou* sport on Wednesdays; **jeux de ~ air** outdoor games; **en ~ air** *spectacle, cirque* open-air; *s'asseoir* in the open (air). **(h) en ~ milieu** right *ou* bang* in the middle; **en pleine tête** right in the head; **oiseau en ~ vol** bird in full flight; **en pleine jeunesse** in the bloom of youth; **en ~ jour** in broad daylight; **le jardin est en ~ soleil** the garden is in full sun; **affaire en pleine croissance** rapidly expanding *ou* growing business; **en pleine saison** at the height of the season; **je suis en ~ travail** I'm in the middle of work *ou* working; **en pleine obscurité** in complete darkness.

2 *adv* **(a) avoir de l'encre ~ les mains** to have ink all over one's hands, have one's hands covered in ink; **il a des jouets ~ un placard** he's got a cupboardful *ou* a cupboard full of toys; **se diriger ~ ouest** to head due west; **en avoir ~ le dos de qch*** to be fed up with sth*; **en avoir ~ les jambes*** to be all-in*; **il a voulu nous en mettre ~ la vue*** he wanted to dazzle us. **(b) ~ de*** *argent, gens etc* lots of; **il a mis ~ de chocolat sur sa veste** he has got chocolate all over his jacket. **(c) en ~: la lumière frappait son visage en ~** the light was shining straight into his face; **en ~ devant toi** right *ou* straight in front of you. **(d) à ~** *fonctionner* at full capacity; *utiliser* to the full; **les légumes donnent à ~** it is the height of the vegetable season.

3 *nm* **(a) faire le ~** (*Aut*) to fill up; (*Théât*) to have a full house; **le ~, s'il vous plaît** fill it up please. **(b)** *[animation, fête]* height.

pleinement [plɛnmɑ̃] *adv* *vivre* to the full; *approuver* wholeheartedly, fully; *responsable* wholly, entirely, fully. **utiliser qch ~** to make full use of sth.

plénipotentiaire [plenipɔtɑ̃sjɛʀ] *adj, nm* plenipotentiary.

pléonasme [pleɔnasm(ə)] *nm* pleonasm.

pléthore [pletɔʀ] *nf* overabundance, plethora. ♦ **pléthorique** *adj* *nombre* excessive; *effectifs* overabundant.

pleurer [plœʀe] (1) **1** *vi* **(a)** *[personne]* to cry, weep (*sur* over); *[yeux]* to water, run. **~ de rire/de rage** to shed tears of laughter/rage; **faire ~ qn** *[peine]* to make sb cry; *[oignons]* to make sb's eyes water; **~ comme une madeleine** to cry one's eyes *ou* one's heart out; **sur le point de ~** almost in tears, on the verge of tears; **triste à ~** terribly sad; **bête à ~** pitifully stupid. **(b)** (*péj: réclamer*) to moan. **2** *vt* **(a)** *personne* to mourn (for); *chose* to bemoan. **~ des larmes de joie** to weep *ou* shed tears of joy; **~ toutes les larmes de son corps** to cry one's eyes out. **(b)** (*péj*) (*quémander*) to shout for; (*lésiner sur*) to begrudge, stint. **~ misère** to moan about one's lot. ♦ **pleur** *nm*: **en ~s** in tears.

pleurésie [plœʀezi] *nf* pleurisy.

pleurnicher [plœʀniʃe] (1) *vi* to snivel*. ♦ **pleurnicherie** *nf*: **~(s)** snivelling*. ♦ **pleurnicheur, -euse 1** *adj* snivelling*. **2** *nm,f* crybaby*.

pleuviner [pløvine] (1) *vi* to drizzle.

pleuvoir [pløvwaʀ] (23) **1** *vb impers* to rain. **il pleut** it's raining; **il pleut à torrents, il pleut des cordes** it's pouring (down). **2** *vi [coups, projectiles]* to rain down; *[critiques, invitations]* to shower down. **faire ~ des coups sur qn** to rain blows (up)on sb.

plexiglas [plɛksiglas] *nm* ® plexiglass ®.

pli [pli] *nm* **(a)** *[rideau etc]* fold; (*Couture*) pleat. **(faux) ~** crease; **~ de pantalon** trouser crease; **ton manteau fait un ~ dans le dos** your coat creases (up) at the back; **garder un bon ~** to keep its shape; *[vêtement]* **prendre un mauvais ~** to go out of shape; **les ~s et les replis de sa cape** the many folds of his cloak; (*fig*) **cela ne fait pas un ~*** there's no doubt about it. **(b)** *[genou, bras]* bend; *[menton, ventre]* (skin-)fold; *[bouche, yeux]* crease; *[front]* crease, furrow, line. **(c)** (*habitude*) habit. **prendre le ~ de faire** to get into the habit of doing; **mauvais ~** bad habit. **(d)** (*enveloppe*) envelope; (*lettre*) letter. **(e)** (*Cartes*) trick. **faire un ~** to win *ou* take a trick. **(f)** (*Géol*) fold. **~ de terrain** undulation.

pliant, e [plijɑ̃, ɑ̃t] **1** *adj table etc* collapsible, folding. **2** *nm* folding *ou* collapsible stool, camp-stool.

plie [pli] *nf* plaice.

plier [plije] (7) **1** *vt* **(a)** (*gén*) to fold; (*ranger*) to fold up; *volets* to fold back. (*fig*) **~ bagage** to pack up and go. **(b)** *branche, genou* to bend. (*fig*) **~ le genou devant qn** to bow before sb; **plié par l'âge** bent (double) with age; **plié (en deux) de rire/par la douleur** doubled up with laughter/pain; **~ qn à une discipline** to force a discipline upon sb. **2** *vi* **(a)** *[branche]* to bend (over); *[plancher]* to sag. **~ sous le poids des ans** to be weighed down by years. **(b)** *[personne]* to yield, give in; *[armée]* to give way, lose ground. **faire ~ qn** to make sb give in. **3 se ~** *vpr [chaise]* to fold (up). **se ~ à** *règle* to submit to; *circonstances* to bow to, yield to; *désirs* to give in to.

plinthe [plɛ̃t] *nf* skirting board.

plisser [plise] (1) **1** *vt jupe* to pleat; *papier* to fold (over); (*en chiffonnant*) to crease; *lèvres* to pucker (up); *yeux* to screw up; *front* to crease, wrinkle; (*Géol*) to fold. **2** *vi* to become creased. **3 se ~** *vpr [front]* to crease (up), furrow; *[lèvres]* to pucker (up). ♦ **plissé, e** *adj jupe* pleated; *peau* creased, wrinkled. ♦ **plissement** *nm*: **~ de terrain** fold. ♦ **plissure** *nf* pleats.

pliure [plijyʀ] *nf* (*gén*) fold; *[bras, genou]* bend.

plomb [plɔ̃] *nm* (*métal*) lead; (*Pêche*) sinker; (*Chasse*) piece of (lead) shot; (*Typ*) type; (*Élec: fusible*) fuse. **de ~** *tuyau* lead; *soldat* tin; *ciel* leaden; *soleil* blazing; *sommeil* deep, heavy; **avoir du ~ dans l'aile** to be in a bad way; **avoir du ~ dans la tête** to have common sense; **le soleil tombe à ~** the sun is blazing straight down; **les ~s ont sauté** the fuses have blown.

plomber [plɔ̃be] (1) *vt canne, ligne* to weight (with lead); *dent* to fill; *colis* to seal (with lead). ♦ **plombage** *nm [dent]* filling. ♦ **plombé, e** *adj couleur* leaden. ♦ **plomberie** *nf* (*métier, installations*) plumbing; (*atelier*) plumber's (work)shop. ♦ **plombier** *nm* plumber.

plonger [plɔ̃ʒe] (3) **1** *vi [personne, sous-marin, avion]* to dive (*dans* into, *sur* on, onto); *[route, terrain]* to plunge down; *[racines]* to go down. **il plongea dans sa poche pour prendre son mouchoir** he plunged his hand *ou* he dived into his pocket to get his handkerchief out. **2** *vt* (*lit, fig*) **~ qch/qn dans** to plunge *ou* thrust sth/sb into; **~ qn dans la surprise** to surprise sb greatly; **~ qn dans le désespoir** to throw *ou* plunge sb into despair; **~ son regard sur/vers** to cast one's eyes at/towards. **3 se ~** *vpr*: **se ~ dans** *lecture* to bury *ou* immerse o.s. in; *eau* to plunge into. ♦ **plongé, e**[1] *adj*: **~ dans** *obscurité, misère* plunged in; *vice* steeped in; *méditation* immersed in, deep in; *livre* buried *ou* immersed in; **~ dans le sommeil** sound asleep, in a deep sleep. ♦ **plongeant, e** *adj décolleté, tir* plunging. **vue ~e** view from above. ♦ **plongée**[2] *nf* (*action*) diving; (*exercice*) dive; *[sous-marin]* submersion. **~ sous-marine** (*gén*) diving; (*sans scaphandre*) skin diving. ♦ **plongeoir** *nm* diving board. ♦ **plongeon** *nm* dive. **faire un ~** to dive. ♦ **plongeur, -euse** *nm,f* **(a)** (*Sport*) diver; (*sans* *scaphandre*) skin diver. **(b)** *[restaurant]* dishwasher.

plouf [pluf] *nm, excl* splash.

ployer [plwaje] (8) (*littér*) **1** *vi* (*lit, fig*) to bend; *[poutre]* to sag; *[armée]* to yield, give in. **2** *vt* to bend.

pluie [plɥi] *nf* **(a)** rain; (*averse*) shower. **le temps est à la ~** it looks like rain; **temps de ~** wet *ou* rainy weather; **~ battante** driving *ou* lashing rain; **~ diluvienne** downpour; **~ fine** drizzle. **(b)** *[cadeaux]* shower; *[coups]* hail, shower. **verser qch en ~** to sprinkle sth in *ou* on. **(c) faire la ~ et le beau temps** to rule the roost; **il n'est pas né de la dernière ~** he wasn't born yesterday.

plumage [plymaʒ] *nm* plumage, feathers.

plumard‡ [plymaʀ] *nm* bed.

plume [plym] *nf* **(a)** *[oiseau]* feather. **chapeau à ~s** feathered hat; **oreiller de ~s** feather pillow; **soulever qch comme une ~** to lift sth up as if it were a featherweight; **il y a laissé des ~s*** he got his fingers burnt. **(b)** (*pour écrire*) pen; (*pour vacciner*) vaccine point. **il a la ~ facile** writing comes easily to him; **prendre la ~** to take up one's pen. ♦ **plumeau,** *pl* **~x** *nm* feather duster. ♦ **plumer** (1) *vt volaille* to pluck; (*‡fig*) *personne* to fleece*. ♦ **plumet** *nm* plume.

plumier [plymje] *nm* pencil box.

plupart [plypaʀ] *nf*: **la ~ des gens** most people, the majority of people; **la ~ des gens qui se trouvaient là** most of the people there; **dans la ~ des cas** in most cases, in the majority of cases; **pour la ~** for the most part; **la ~ du temps** most of the time.

pluriel, -elle [plyʀjɛl] **1** *adj* plural. **2** *nm* plural. **au ~** in the plural; **la première personne du ~** the first person plural.

plus 1 *adv nég* [ply] **(a)** (*temps*) no longer. **il n'en a ~ besoin** he doesn't need it any longer, he no longer needs it; **il n'a ~ dit un mot** he didn't say another word; (*euph*) **son père n'est ~** his father has passed away (*euph*); **elle n'est ~ très jeune** she's not as young as she was; **~ de doute** no doubt now; **il n'y a ~ d'enfants!** children aren't what they used to be. **(b)** (*quantité*) no more. **elle n'a ~ de pain** she hasn't (got) any more bread, she's got no (more) bread left; **des fruits? il n'y en a ~** fruit? there is none left; **il n'y a ~ personne** there's no one left; **il n'y a ~ rien** there's nothing left; **il n'y a ~ rien d'autre à faire** there's nothing else to do; **on n'y voit ~ guère *ou* presque ~ rien** you can hardly see anything now. **(c)** (*avec que: seulement*) **il n'y a ~ que des miettes** there are only crumbs left; **~ que huit jours avant les vacances** only a week to go before the holidays; **~ que 5 km à faire** only another 5 km to go.

2 *adv emploi comparatif* [ply(s)] **(a)** *travailler etc* more (*que* than). **il est ~ intelligent/âgé (que moi)** he is more intelligent/he is older (than me *ou* than I am); **trois fois ~ cher/souvent que ...** three times as expensive/often as ...; **il est ~ qu'intelligent** he's clever to say the least; **j'aime dix fois ~ le théâtre que le cinéma** I like the theatre ten times better than the cinema. **(b) ~ de pain** *etc* more bread *etc*; **il n'y aura pas ~ de monde demain** there won't be any more people tomorrow; **il y aura ~ de 100 personnes** there will be more than *ou* over 100 people; **les enfants de ~ de 4 ans** children over 4; **il n'y avait pas ~ de 10 personnes** there were no more than 10 people; **il est ~ de 9 heures** it's after *ou* past 9 o'clock; **~ d'un** more than one. **(c) ~ on est de fous, ~ on rit** the more the merrier; **~ on boit, ~ on a soif** the more you drink, the thirstier you get; **~ il gagne, moins il est content** the more he earns, the less happy he is. **(d) elle a 10 ans de ~ (que lui)** she's 10 years older (than him); **il y a 10 personnes de ~ qu'hier** there are 10 more people than yesterday; **les faux frais sont en ~** the incidental expenses are not included *ou* are extra; **deux verres de ~ *ou* en ~** two more *ou* extra glasses; (*de trop*) two glasses too many; **en ~ de son travail** on top of *ou* in addition to his work. **(e) de ~ en ~** more and more; **aller de ~ en ~ vite** to go faster and faster; **~ ou moins** more or less; **~ que jamais** more than ever; **qui ~ est** what is more, moreover.

3 *adv emploi superlatif* [ply(s)]: **le film le ~ long/beau que j'aie vu** the longest/most beautiful film I've ever seen; **la ~ grande partie de son temps** most of his time; **le livre que je lis le ~ souvent** the book I read most often; **il a couru le ~ vite** he ran the fastest; **ce que j'aime le ~** what I like (the) most *ou* (the) best; **c'est le samedi qu'il y a le ~ de monde** it's on Saturdays that there are (the) most people; **prends le ~ possible de livres/de beurre** take as many books/as much butter as possible *ou* as you can; **au ~** at the most, at the outside; **tout au ~** at the very most.

4 *conj* [plys] plus. **les voisins, ~ leurs enfants** the neighbours, plus *ou* and their children; (*degré*) **il fait ~ deux** it's plus two (degrees), it's two above freezing.

5 *nm* [plys] (*Math*) **(signe) ~** plus (sign).

♦ **plus-que-parfait** [plyskəpaʀfɛ] *nm* pluperfect (tense), past perfect. ♦ **plus-value,** *pl* **~-~s** [plyvaly] *nf* (*bénéfice*) profit; (*imposable*) capital gains.

plusieurs [plyzjœʀ] *adj et pron indéf pl* several. **nous nous sommes mis à ~ pour ...** several of us got together to... .

plutonium [plytɔnjɔm] *nm* plutonium.

plutôt [plyto] *adv* **(a)** (*de préférence*) rather; (*à la place*) instead. **prends ce livre ~ que celui-là** take this book rather than *ou* instead of that one; **cette maladie affecte ~ les enfants** this illness affects children for the most part *ou* tends to affect children; **~ souffrir que mourir** it is better to suffer than to die. **(b)** (*plus exactement*) rather. **il est ignorant ~ que sot** he's ignorant rather *ou* more than stupid. **(c)** (*assez*) *chaud, bon* rather, quite. **c'est ~ bon signe** that's quite *ou* rather a good sign; **il est ~ petit** he is rather *ou* somewhat on the small side, he is rather *ou* fairly small.

pluvieux, -euse [plyvjø, øz] *adj* rainy, wet.

pneu [pnø] *nm* (*abrév de* **pneumatique**) *[véhicule]* tyre, tire (*US*); (*message*) letter sent by pneumatic despatch *ou* tube.

pneumatique [pnømatik] **1** *adj* (*Sci*) pneumatic; (*gonflable*) inflatable. **2** *nm* = **pneu.**

pneumonie [pnømɔni] *nf*: **la ~** pneumonia; **une ~** an attack *ou* a bout of pneumonia.

poche [pɔʃ] *nf* (*gén*) pocket; *[kangourou]* pouch; (*sac*) bag. **~ revolver/intérieure** hip/inside pocket; **~ de pantalon/d'air** trouser/air pocket; **de ~** *mouchoir* pocket; *livre* paperback; **format de ~** pocket-size; **j'avais 10 F en ~** I had 10 francs on me; **en être de sa ~*** to be out of pocket; **il a payé de sa ~** he paid for it out of his (own) pocket; **mettre qn dans sa ~*** to twist sb round one's little finger; **c'est dans la ~!*** it's in the bag!*; **faire les ~s à qn*** to go through sb's pockets; **connaître un endroit comme sa ~** to know a place like the back of one's hand; *[veste]* **faire des ~s** to bag, go out of shape.

pocher [pɔʃe] (1) *vt* (*Culin*) to poach. **~ un œil à qn** to give sb a black eye.

pochette [pɔʃɛt] *nf* (*mouchoir*) pocket handkerchief; (*petite poche*) breast pocket; (*enveloppe*) envelope; (*étui*) case. **~ surprise** lucky bag; **~ d'allumettes** book of matches.

podium [pɔdjɔm] *nm* podium.

poêle¹ [pwal] *nf*: **~ (à frire)** frying pan; **passer à la ~** to fry.

poêle², poële [pwal] *nm* stove.

poème [pɔɛm] *nm* poem. **c'est tout un ~*** (*compliqué*) it's a real palaver*; (*indescriptible*) it defies description. ♦ **poésie** *nf* (*art*) poetry; (*poème*) poem. ♦ **poète** 1 *nm* poet. 2 *adj* *tempérament* poetic. **être** ~ to be a poet. ♦ **poétesse** *nf* poetess. ♦ **poétique** *adj* poetic(al). ♦ **poétiquement** *adv* poetically.

pognon‡ [pɔɲɔ̃] *nm* dough‡, lolly‡.

poids [pwa] 1 *nm* **(a)** (*lit, fig*) weight. **prendre du** ~ to gain *ou* put on weight; **vendu au** ~ sold by weight; **quel** ~ **pèse-t-il?** what weight is he?, what does he weigh?; **plier sous le** ~ **des sacs/des soucis** to be weighed down with bags/by worries; **il ne fait pas le** ~ *[acteur, homme politique]* he doesn't measure up; *[lutteur]* he's no match for his opponent; **enlever un** ~ **(de la conscience) à qn** to take a weight *ou* a load off sb's mind; **avoir un** ~ **sur l'estomac** to have something lying heavy on one's stomach; **argument de** ~ weighty argument. **(b)** (*Sport*) shot. **lancer le** ~ to put(t) the shot. **2:** ~ **lourd** (*Sport, *fig: personne grosse*) heavyweight; (*camion*) lorry, truck (*US*); (*Tech*) ~ **mort** dead load; ~ **plume** (*Sport, *fig*) featherweight; ~ **spécifique** specific gravity.

poignant, e [pwaɲɑ̃, ɑ̃t] *adj* poignant, heart-rending.

poignard [pwaɲaʀ] *nm* dagger. **coup de** ~ stab. ♦ **poignarder** (1) *vt* to stab, knife.

poigne [pwaɲ] *nf* (*étreinte*) grip; (*main*) hand. **avoir de la** ~ (*lit*) to have a strong grip; (*fig*) to be firm-handed.

poignée [pwaɲe] *nf* (*quantité*) handful; *[porte etc]* handle. ~ **de main** handshake; **donner une** ~ **de main à qn** to shake hands with sb.

poignet [pwaɲɛ] *nm* (*Anat*) wrist; (*Habillement*) cuff.

poil [pwal] 1 *nm* **(a)** (*Anat*) hair; *[brosse]* bristle; *[étoffe]* strand. **avoir du** ~ *ou* **des** ~**s sur la poitrine** to have hairs on one's chest; **manteau en** ~ **de lapin/de chameau** rabbit-skin/camel-hair coat; (*pelage*) **chat qui a un beau** ~ cat with a sleek coat *ou* with sleek fur; **les** ~**s d'un tapis/d'un tissu** the pile of a carpet/of a fabric. **(b)** (*: *un peu*) **ça mesure un mètre, à un** ~ **près** it measures roughly one metre; **il n'y a pas un** ~ **de différence entre les deux** there isn't the slightest difference between the two (of them); **il s'en est fallu d'un** ~ it was a near thing *ou* a close shave. **(c) être à** ~‡ to be in the altogether* *ou* in one's birthday suit*; **se mettre à** ~‡ to strip off; **c'est au** ~* it's great* *ou* fantastic*; **avoir un** ~ **dans la main*** to be bone-idle*; **être de bon/de mauvais** ~* to be in a good/bad mood; **tomber sur le** ~ **à qn*** to go for* *ou* lay into* sb; **reprendre du** ~ **de la bête*** to regain strength. **2:** ~ **de carotte** *personne* red-haired; *cheveux* red; ~ **à gratter** itching powder. ♦ **poilu, e** 1 *adj* hairy. 2 *nm* poilu (*French soldier in First World War*).

poinçon [pwɛ̃sɔ̃] *nm* **(a)** *[cordonnier]* awl; *[graveur]* style; (*pour estampiller*) die, stamp. **(b)** (*estampille*) hallmark. ♦ **poinçonner** (1) *vt* *marchandise* to stamp; *or etc* to hallmark; *billet* to punch. ♦ **poinçonneur, -euse** 1 *nm,f* (*personne*) ticket-puncher. 2 *nf* (*machine*) punching machine.

poindre [pwɛ̃dʀ(ə)] (49) *vi* (*littér*) *[jour]* to break; *[plante]* to come up, peep through.

poing [pwɛ̃] *nm* fist. **taper du** ~ **sur la table** to thump the table; **mettre son** ~ **dans la figure de qn** to punch sb in the face; **revolver au** ~ revolver in hand; **menacer qn du** ~ to shake one's fist at sb.

point[1] [pwɛ̃] 1 *nm* **(a)** (*endroit, degré*) point. **pour aller d'un** ~ **à un autre** to go from one point *ou* place *ou* spot to another; **avoir atteint le** ~ **où ...** to have reached the point *ou* stage where ...; **nous en sommes toujours au même** ~ we haven't got any further; **au** ~ **où on en est** considering the situation we're in; ~ **d'ébullition** boiling point; **jusqu'à un certain** ~ up to a point, to a certain extent; **au plus haut** ~ extremely; **au plus haut** ~ **de la gloire** at the height *ou* peak *ou* summit of glory; **est-il possible d'être bête à ce** ~**(-là)!** how stupid can you get?*; **sa colère avait atteint un** ~ **tel que ...** he was so angry that ..., his anger was such that ...; **il a mangé au** ~ **de se rendre malade** he ate so much (that) he was sick.

(b) (*détail, subdivision*) point. ~ **de droit** point of law; **passons au** ~ **suivant de l'ordre du jour** let us move on to the next item on the agenda; ~ **de détail** minor point, point of detail; **ils sont d'accord sur ce** ~ they agree on this point *ou* score; **se ressembler en tout** ~ to resemble each other in every respect.

(c) (*position*) (*Aviat, Naut*) position. (*Naut*) **faire le** ~ to plot one's position; **faire le** ~ **de la situation** (*analyse*) to take stock of the situation; (*résumé*) to sum up the situation.

(d) (*marque*) (*en morse, sur i etc*) dot; (*ponctuation*) full stop, period; (*tache*) spot, speck; *[dé]* pip. (*fig*) **mettre les** ~**s sur les i** to spell it out; **mettre un** ~ **final à qch** to put an end to sth; **tu n'iras pas, un** ~ **c'est tout** you're not going — period *ou* full stop.

(e) (*score*) (*Cartes, Sport*) point; (*Scol, Univ*) mark, point; *[retraite]* unit; *[salaire]* point. (*Boxe*) **aux** ~**s** on points; **bon/mauvais** ~ (*Scol*) good/bad mark (*for conduct etc*); (*fig*) plus/minus (mark).

(f) (*Couture*) stitch. **faire un** ~ **à qch** to put a stitch in sth.

(g) à ~ *viande* medium; **arriver à** ~ **(nommé)** to arrive just at the right moment; **au** ~ *photo* in focus; *procédé* perfected; *discours* up to scratch; **mettre au** ~ to (bring into) focus; to perfect; **mettre une affaire au** ~ **avec qn** to finalize *ou* settle all the details of a matter with sb; *[machine, spectacle]* **ce n'est pas encore au** ~ it isn't quite up to scratch yet; **j'étais sur le** ~ **de faire du café** I was just going to *ou* (just) about to make some coffee.

2: ~ **d'appui** *[levier]* fulcrum; *[personne]* **chercher un** ~ **d'appui** to look for sth to lean on; ~**s cardinaux** cardinal points; ~ **chaud** (*Mil*) trouble spot; (*de l'actualité*) major issue; ~ **de côté** stitch (*pain in the side*); ~ **culminant** *[gloire, épidémie]* height; *[scandale]* climax; *[montagne]* peak, summit; ~ **de départ** *[train]* point of departure; *[aventure]* starting point; (*Sport*) start; (*fig*) **nous voilà revenus au** ~ **de départ** (so) we're back to square one*, we're back where we started; ~ **d'eau** (*source*) watering place; *[camping]* water (supply) point; ~ **d'exclamation** exclamation mark *ou* point (*US*); ~ **faible** weak point; ~ **fort** strong point; ~ **d'honneur** point of honour; ~ **d'interrogation** question mark; **le** ~ **du jour** daybreak; ~ **de mire** (*lit*) target; (*fig*) focal point; (*Aut*) ~ **mort** neutral; (*fig*) **au** ~ **mort** at a standstill; ~ **névralgique** (*Méd*) nerve centre; (*fig*) sensitive spot; ~ **de non-retour** point of no return; ~ **de rencontre** meeting point; ~ **de repère** (*dans l'espace*) landmark; (*dans le temps*) point of reference; ~ **stratégique** key point; ~**s de suspension** suspension points; (*Méd*) ~ **de suture** stitch; ~ **de vente** shop, store; ~ **virgule** semicolon; ~ **de vue** (*lit*) view(point); (*fig*) point of view, standpoint; **du** *ou* **au** ~ **de vue argent** from the financial point of view.

point[2] [pwɛ̃] *adv* (*littér, hum*) = **pas**[2].

pointage [pwɛ̃taʒ] *nm* **(a)** (*sur une liste*) ticking *ou* checking *ou* marking off; *[employé]* checking in; (*à la sortie*) checking out; *[canon]* aiming. **(b)** (*contrôle*) check.

pointe [pwɛ̃t] 1 *nf* **(a)** (*pointue*) point; *[montagne]* peak, top; *[chaussure]* toe; *[grille]* spike. **à la** ~ **de l'île** at the tip of the island; **la côte s'avance en** ~ the coast forms a headland; **objet qui forme une** ~ object that tapers to a point; (*Danse*) **faire des** ~**s** to dance on points; **en** ~ *barbe* in a point, pointed. **(b)** (*clou*) tack; (*Sport*) *[chaussure]* spike; (*outil pointu*) point. **(c)** (*foulard*) triangular (neck)scarf. **(d)** ~ **de** *ail, ironie, jalousie* touch *ou* hint of; *accent* hint of. **(e)** (*maximum*) peak. ~ **de vitesse** burst of speed; **à la** ~ **de** *actualité etc* in the forefront of; **de** ~ *industrie* leading; *technique* latest; *vitesse* top, maximum; *[circulation]* **heure de** ~ rush *ou* peak hour; **faire une** ~ **jusqu'à Paris** to push *ou* press on as far as Paris. **2:** ~ **d'asperge** asparagus tip; **la** ~ **des pieds** the toes; **(se mettre) sur la** ~ **des pieds** (to stand) on tiptoe; ~ **de terre** spit of land.

pointer [pwɛ̃te] (1) **1** *vt* **(a)** (*cocher*) to tick off, check off, mark off. (*Naut*) ~ **(sa position)** to plot one's position. **(b)** (*Ind*) *employé* (*à l'arrivée*) to check in; (*au départ*) to check out. **(c)** *fusil* to aim (*vers, sur* at); *jumelles* to train (*vers, sur* on); *lampe* to direct (*vers, sur* towards); *doigt* to point (*sur* at). **(d)** *[chien]* ~ **les oreilles** to prick up its ears. **2** *vi* **(a)** *[employé]* (*arrivée*) to clock in, check in; (*départ*) to clock out, check out. **(b)** (*apparaître*) (*gén*) to appear; *[plante]* to peep out; (*fig*) *[ironie]* to pierce through; *[jour]* to break, dawn. **(c)** (*s'élever*) *[tour]* to soar up. **3 se** ~* *vpr* (*arriver*) to turn up*, show up*.

pointillé, e [pwɛ̃tije] **1** *adj* dotted. **2** *nm* dotted line.

pointilleux, -euse [pwɛ̃tijø, øz] *adj* particular, pernickety.

pointu, e [pwɛ̃ty] *adj* pointed; (*aiguisé*) sharp.

pointure [pwɛ̃tyʀ] *nf* size. **quelle est votre** ~? what size are you?

poire [pwaʀ] *nf* (*fruit*) pear; (*: *tête*) face, mug‡; (*: *dupe*) mug‡, sucker*. ~ **électrique** (*pear-shaped*) switch.

poireau, *pl* ~**x** [pwaʀo] *nm* leek. **faire le** ~* to hang about*. ♦ **poireauter*** (1) *vi* to hang about*.

poirier [pwaʀje] *nm* pear tree. (*fig*) **faire le** ~ to do a headstand.

pois [pwa] **1** *nm* (*légume*) pea; (*dessin*) (polka) dot, spot. **petits** ~ (garden) peas; **robe à** ~ dotted *ou* spotted dress. **2:** ~ **cassés** split peas; ~ **chiche** chickpea; ~ **de senteur** sweet pea.

poison [pwazɔ̃] *nm* (*lit, fig*) poison. **quel** ~**!*** what a pest* *ou* nuisance!

poisse‡ [pwas] *nf* bad *ou* rotten* luck. **avoir la** ~ to have bad *ou* rotten* luck.

poisser [pwase] (1) *vt* **(a)** (‡: *attraper*) to nab‡. **(b)** (*salir*) to make sticky. ♦ **poisseux, -euse** *adj* sticky.

poisson [pwasɔ̃] *nm* fish. **2/3** ~**s** 2/3 fish *ou* fishes; **comme un** ~ **dans l'eau** in one's element; (*Astron*) **P**~**s** Pisces; (*blague*) ~ **d'avril** April fool's trick; ~ **rouge** goldfish. ♦ **poissonnerie** *nf* (*boutique*) fishmonger's (shop); (*métier*) fish trade. ♦ **poissonneux, -euse** *adj* full of fish. ♦ **poissonnier, -ière** *nm,f* fishmonger.

poitrine [pwatʀin] *nf* (*gén*) chest, breast (*littér*); (*seins*) bust, bosom; (*Culin*) *[veau, mouton]* breast. *[porc]* ~ **(salée *ou* fumée)** streaky bacon. ♦ **poitrail** *nm* (*Zool*) breast; (*hum: poitrine*) chest.

poivre [pwavʀ(ə)] *nm* pepper. ~ **en grains** whole pepper, peppercorns; ~ **et sel** *cheveux* pepper-and-salt. ♦ **poivré, e** *adj* *plat* peppery; *histoire* spicy, juicy*. ♦ **poivrer** (1) *vt* to pepper. ♦ **poivrier** *nm* (*Bot*) pepper plant; (*objet*) pepperpot.

poivron [pwavʀɔ̃] *nm*: ~ **(vert)** green pepper, capsicum; ~ **rouge** red pepper, capsicum.

poivrot, e* [pwavʀo, ɔt] *nm,f* drunkard.

poix [pwa] *nf* pitch (*tar*).

poker [pɔkɛʀ] *nm* (*Cartes*) (*jeu*) poker; (*partie*) game of poker. (*fig*) **coup de** ~ gamble.

pôle [pol] *nm* pole. **P**~ **Nord/Sud** North/South Pole; (*fig*) ~ **d'attraction** centre of attraction, focus of attention. ♦ **polaire** *adj* polar. ♦ **polariser** (1) *vt* (*Élec, Phys*) to polarize; (*fig: attirer*) to attract. ~ **son attention** *ou* **se** ~ **sur qch** to focus *ou* centre one's attention on sth.

polémique [pɔlemik] **1** *adj* controversial. **2** *nf* controversy, argument, polemic.

poli, e [pɔli] **1** *adj* **(a)** polite (*avec* to). **soyez** ~**!** don't be so rude. **(b)** *bois, métal* polished; *caillou* smooth. **2** *nm* shine. ♦ **poliment** *adv* politely.

police [pɔlis] **1** *nf* **(a)** (*corps*) police, police force. **voiture de** ~ police car; **être dans *ou* de la** ~ to be in the police (force), be a policeman; **la** ~ **est à ses trousses** the police are after him *ou* are on his tail. **(b)** (*maintien de l'ordre*) enforcement of law and order. **faire la** ~ to keep law and order (*dans* in). **(c)** (*règlements*) regulations. **(d)** ~ **(d'assurance)** (insurance) policy; ~ **d'assurance vie** life insurance policy. **2:** ~ **judiciaire** ≃ Criminal Investigation Department, CID; ~ **des mœurs** ≃ vice squad; ~ **parallèle** *unofficial governmental police service*; ~ **de la route** traffic police; ~ **secours** police (*special service for emergencies*), ≃ emergency services. ♦ **policier, -ière 1** *adj* (*gén*) police; *roman* detective. **2** *nm* policeman.

Polichinelle [pɔliʃinɛl] *nm* (*marionnette*) Punch; (*péj*) buffoon.

polio(myélite) [pɔljɔ(mjelit)] *nf* polio(myelitis).

polir [pɔliʀ] (2) *vt* (*gén, fig*) to polish; *discours* to polish (up); *caractère* to refine.

polisson, -onne [pɔlisɔ̃, ɔn] **1** *adj* (*espiègle*) naughty; (*grivois*) naughty, saucy. **2** *nm,f* (*enfant*) (little) devil*. ♦ **polissonnerie** *nf* naughty trick.

politesse [pɔlitɛs] *nf* politeness; (*parole*) polite remark; (*action*) polite gesture.

politique [pɔlitik] **1** *adj* political; (*littér: habile*) diplomatic, politic. **homme** ~ politician. **2** *nf* **(a)** (*science, carrière*) politics (*sg*). **faire de la** ~ (*militantisme*) to be a political activist; (*métier*) to be in politics. **(b)** (*ligne de conduite*) policy; (*manière de gouverner*) policies. ~ **extérieure** foreign policy; **la** ~ **du gouvernement** the government's policies; **pratiquer la** ~ **de l'autruche** to bury one's head in the sand. ♦ **politicien, -ienne** (*péj*) **1** *adj* politicking (*péj*). **2** *nm,f* political schemer. ♦ **politiquement** *adv* (*lit*) politically; (*fig littér*) diplomatically. ♦ **politisation** *nf* politicization. ♦ **politiser** (1) *vt* to politicize.

polka [pɔlka] *nf* polka.

pollen [pɔlɛn] *nm* pollen.

polluer [pɔlɥe] (1) *vt* to pollute. ♦ **polluant, e** *adj* polluting. **produit** ~ pollutant. ♦ **pollution** *nf* pollution.

polo [pɔlo] *nm* **(a)** (*Sport*) polo. **(b)** (*chemise*) sweat shirt.

polochon* [pɔlɔʃɔ̃] *nm* bolster.

Pologne [pɔlɔɲ] *nf* Poland. ♦ **polonais, e 1** *adj* Polish. **2** *nm* **(a) P**~ Pole. **(b)** (*Ling*) Polish. **3** *nf* **(a) P**~**e** Pole. **(b)** (*Mus, Culin*) polonaise.

poltron, -onne [pɔltʀɔ̃, ɔn] **1** *adj* cowardly. **2** *nm,f* coward. ♦ **poltronnerie** *nf* cowardice.

polychrome [pɔlikʀom] *adj* polychrome, polychromatic.

polyclinique [pɔliklinik] *nf* polyclinic.

polycopier [pɔlikɔpje] (7) *vt* to duplicate, stencil. **machine à** ~ duplicator.

polyculture [pɔlikyltyʀ] *nf* mixed farming.

polyester [pɔliɛstɛʀ] *nm* polyester.

polygame [pɔligam] **1** *adj* polygamous. **2** *nm* polygamist. ♦ **polygamie** *nf* polygamy.

polyglotte [pɔliglɔt] *adj, nmf* polyglot.

polygone [pɔligɔn] *nm* (*Math*) polygon; (*fig: zone*) area, zone. (*Mil*) ~ **de tir** rifle range.

Polynésie [pɔlinezi] *nf* Polynesia. ♦ **polynésien, -ienne** *adj*, **P**~**(ne)** *nm(f)* Polynesian.

polysémie [pɔlisemi] *nf* polysemy.

polyvalent, e [pɔlivalɑ̃, ɑ̃t] *adj* (*Chim, Méd*) polyvalent; *rôle* varied; *usages* various, many; *personne* versatile.

pommade [pɔmad] *nf* *[peau]* ointment; *[cheveux]*

cream, pomade. (*fig*) **passer de la ~ à qn*** to butter sb up*, soft-soap sb*.
pomme [pɔm] **1** *nf* **(a)** (*fruit*) apple. **tomber dans les ~s*** to faint, pass out*. **(b)** *[laitue]* heart; *[canne]* knob; *[arrosoir]* rose. **(c)** (*) (*tête*) head, nut*; (*visage*) face. **c'est pour ma ~** it's for my own sweet self*.
2: ~ **d'Adam** Adam's apple; **(~s) chips** (potato) crisps *ou* chips (*US*); **~s frites** chips, French fries (*US*); ~ **de pin** pine *ou* fir cone; ~ **de terre** potato.
pommeau, *pl* **~x** [pɔmo] *nm [épée, selle]* pommel; *[canne]* knob.
pommelé, e [pɔmle] *adj cheval* dappled; *ciel* mackerel, flecked with clouds. **gris ~** dapple-grey.
pommette [pɔmɛt] *nf* cheekbone.
pommier [pɔmje] *nm* apple tree.
pompe [pɔ̃p] *nf* **(a)** (*machine*) pump; (‡: *chaussure*) shoe. ~ **à air** air pump; **à toute ~‡** at top speed, flat out*; ~ **à essence** (*distributeur*) petrol *ou* gasoline (*US*) pump; (*station*) petrol *ou* gas (*US*) station; ~ **à incendie** fire engine (*apparatus*). **(b)** (*littér: solennité*) pomp. **en grande ~** with great pomp. **(c) ~s funèbres** funeral director's, undertaker's; **entreprise de ~s funèbres** funeral parlour. ♦ **pomper** (1) *vt* to pump; (*évacuer*) to pump out; *[éponge, buvard]* to soak up; (*arg Scol: copier*) to crib* (*sur* from); (‡: *boire*) to drink, knock back‡; (‡: *épuiser*) to wear *ou* tire out. ♦ **pompeusement** *adv* pompously. ♦ **pompeux, -euse** *adj* (*ampoulé*) pompous; (*imposant*) solemn. ♦ **pompier 1** *adj* (*) *style* pompous, pretentious. **2** *nm* fireman. **appeler les ~s** to call the fire brigade. ♦ **pompiste** *nmf* petrol *ou* gasoline (*US*) pump attendant.
pompon [pɔ̃pɔ̃] *nm* pompon, bobble. **c'est le ~!*** it's the last straw!, that beats everything!*
pomponner [pɔ̃pɔne] (1) **1** *vt* to titivate, doll up*. **2 se ~** *vpr* to titivate (o.s.), get dolled up*.
poncer [pɔ̃se] (3) *vt* to sand, rub down. ♦ **ponçage** *nm* sanding, rubbing down. ♦ **ponce** *nf*: **pierre ~** pumice (stone). ♦ **ponceuse** *nf* sander.
ponction [pɔ̃ksjɔ̃] *nf* (*lombaire*) puncture; (*pulmonaire*) tapping; *[argent]* withdrawal. **faire une ~ dans ses économies** to dip into one's savings.
ponctuel, -elle [pɔ̃ktɥɛl] *adj* punctual. ♦ **ponctualité** *nf* punctuality. ♦ **ponctuellement** *adv* punctually.
ponctuer [pɔ̃ktɥe] (1) *vt* (*lit, fig*) to punctuate (*de* with). ♦ **ponctuation** *nf* punctuation.
pondérer [pɔ̃deʀe] (6) *vt* (*équilibrer*) to balance; (*Écon*) to weight. ♦ **pondéré, e** *adj personne* level-headed. ♦ **pondération** *nf* level-headedness; balancing; weighting.
pondéreux, -euse [pɔ̃deʀø, øz] *adj* heavy.
pondre [pɔ̃dʀ(ə)] (41) **1** *vt œuf* to lay; (*) *enfant, devoir* to produce. **œuf frais pondu** new-laid egg. **2** *vi* to lay.
poney [pɔnɛ] *nm* pony.
pont [pɔ̃] **1** *nm* (*Constr*) bridge; (*fig: lien*) bridge, link; (*Naut*) deck; (*Aut*) axle. **vivre sous les ~s** to be a tramp; **faire un ~ d'or à qn** to offer sb a fortune to take on a job; (*vacances*) **on a un ~ de 3 jours** we have 3 days (off); **faire le ~** to make a long weekend of it. **2:** ~ **basculant/suspendu/tournant/transbordeur** bascule/suspension/swing/transporter bridge; ~ **aérien** airlift; **les P~s et chaussées** the department of civil engineering; ~ **de graissage** ramp (*in a garage*); **~-levis** *nm, pl* **~s-~** drawbridge.
ponte¹ [pɔ̃t] *nf* (*action*) laying (of eggs); (*saison*) (egg-)laying season.
ponte²* [pɔ̃t] *nm* big shot*, big noise*.
pontife [pɔ̃tif] *nm* (*Rel*) pontiff. ♦ **pontifical, e,** *mpl* **-aux** *adj messe* pontifical; *gardes, états* papal. ♦ **pontificat** *nm* pontificate. ♦ **pontifier*** (7) *vi* to pontificate.
ponton [pɔ̃tɔ̃] *nm* pontoon, landing stage.
pop [pɔp] *adj inv* pop.
pope [pɔp] *nm* (Orthodox) priest.
popeline [pɔplin] *nf* poplin.
popote* [pɔpɔt] **1** *nf* (*cuisine*) cooking. **2** *adj inv* stay-at-home.
populace [pɔpylas] *nf* (*péj*) rabble.
populaire [pɔpylɛʀ] *adj* (*gén, fig*) popular; *quartier* working-class; (*Ling*) *expression* colloquial. **république ~** people's republic; **manifestation ~** mass demonstration.
♦ **populariser** (1) *vt* to popularize. ♦ **popularité** *nf* popularity.
population [pɔpylɑsjɔ̃] *nf* (*gén*) population. ♦ **populeux, -euse** *adj pays* densely populated; *rue* crowded.
porc [pɔʀ] *nm* (*animal*) pig, hog (*US*); (*viande*) pork; (*péj: personne*) pig; (*peau*) pigskin.
porcelaine [pɔʀsəlɛn] *nf* (*matière*) porcelain, china; (*objet*) piece of porcelain.
porcelet [pɔʀsəlɛ] *nm* piglet.
porc-épic, *pl* **~s-~s** [pɔʀkepik] *nm* porcupine.
porche [pɔʀʃ(ə)] *nm* porch.
porcherie [pɔʀʃəʀi] *nf* (*lit, fig*) pigsty.
pore [pɔʀ] *nm* pore. ♦ **poreux, -euse** *adj* porous.
pornographie [pɔʀnɔgʀafi] *nf* pornography. ♦ **pornographique** *adj* pornographic.
port¹ [pɔʀ] *nm* harbour, port. ~ **d'attache** (*Naut*) port of registry; (*fig*) home base; **arriver à bon ~** to arrive safe and sound.
port² [pɔʀ] *nm* **(a) le ~ de la barbe** *etc* wearing a beard *etc*; ~ **d'armes prohibées** illegal carrying of firearms. **(b)** (*prix*) (*poste*) postage; (*transport*) carriage. **franco de ~** carriage paid; **(en) ~ dû** postage due. **(c)** (*comportement*) bearing, carriage.
portail [pɔʀtaj] *nm* portal.
portant, e [pɔʀtɑ̃, ɑ̃t] *adj*: **être bien/mal ~** to be in good/poor health.
portatif, -ive [pɔʀtatif, iv] *adj* portable.
porte [pɔʀt(ə)] **1** *nf* **(a)** (*gén*) door; *[forteresse, jardin, écluse, ski]* gate; (*seuil*) doorstep; (*embrasure*) doorway. **sonner à la ~** to ring the (door)-bell; **c'est à ma ~** it's on the doorstep; **le bus me descend à ma ~** the bus takes me to my door; **faire du ~ à ~** to sell from door to door, be a door-to-door salesman; **Dijon, ~ de la Bourgogne** Dijon, the gateway to Burgundy. **(b) être à la ~** to be locked out; **mettre qn à la ~** (*licencier*) to sack sb; (*éjecter*) to throw sb out; **claquer la ~ au nez de qn** to slam the door in sb's face; **frapper à la bonne/mauvaise ~** to get hold of the right/wrong person; **laisser la ~ ouverte à** *compromis, abus* to leave the door open to; **parler à qn entre deux ~s** to have a quick word with sb, speak to sb very briefly; **prendre la ~** to go away, leave; **aimable comme une ~ de prison** like a bear with a sore head.
2: ~ **cochère** carriage entrance; ~ **à deux battants** double door; ~ **d'embarquement** departure gate; ~ **d'entrée** front door; **~-fenêtre** *nf, pl* **~s-~s** French window; ~ **de secours** emergency exit; ~ **de service** tradesman's entrance; (*lit, fig*) ~ **de sortie** way out.
porte- [pɔʀt(ə)] *préf formant nm*: **~-avions** *inv* aircraft carrier; **~-bagages** *inv* (luggage) rack; **~-bonheur** *inv* lucky charm; **~-clefs** *inv* (*anneau*) key ring; (*étui*) key case; **~-couteau,** *pl* **~-~(x)** knife rest; **~-documents** *inv* attaché case; (*lit, fig*) **~-drapeau,** *pl* **~-~(x)** standard bearer; **en ~-à-faux** *objet* precariously balanced; *situation* awkward; **~-mine,** *pl* **~-~(s)** propelling pencil; **~-monnaie** *inv* purse; **~-parapluies** *inv* umbrella stand; **~-parole** *inv* (*homme*) spokesman; (*femme*) spokeswoman; (*revue politique etc*) mouthpiece; **~-plume** *inv* penholder; **~-revues** *inv* magazine rack; **~-savon,** *pl* **~-~(s)** soapdish; **~-serviettes** *inv* towel

rail; **~-voix** *inv* megaphone; (*électrique*) loudhailer.

porté, e[1] [pɔʀte] *adj*: **être ~ à faire** to be inclined to do, tend to do; **être ~ à colère** to be prone to anger; **être ~ sur qch** to be partial to sth.

portée[2] [pɔʀte] *nf* **(a)** (*distance*) range, reach; *[fusil]* range. **canon à faible/longue ~** short-/long-range gun; **à ~ de voix** within earshot; **restez à ~ de vue** don't go out of sight; **c'est à la ~ de toutes les bourses** it's within everyone's means; **hors de ~** out of reach (*de* of). **(b)** *[intelligence]* reach, scope, capacity. **se mettre à la ~ des enfants** to come down to a child's level. **(c)** *[parole]* impact, import; *[acte]* significance. **(d)** (*Archit*) (*poussée*) loading; (*distance*) span. **(e)** (*Mus*) stave, staff. **(f)** (*Vét*) litter.

portefeuille [pɔʀtəfœj] *nm [argent]* wallet; (*Bourse, Pol*) portfolio.

portemanteau, *pl* **~x** [pɔʀtmɑ̃to] *nm* coat hanger; (*accroché au mur*) coat rack; (*sur pied*) hat stand.

porter [pɔʀte] (1) **1** *vt* **(a)** *paquet* to carry; *responsabilité* to bear, carry. **pouvez-vous me ~ ma valise?** can you carry my case for me?; **~ la tête droite** to hold one's head up; **cette poutre porte tout le poids** this beam bears *ou* carries *ou* takes the whole weight. **(b)** (*amener*) to take. **porte-lui ce livre** take this book to him, take him this book; **il s'est fait ~ à manger** he had food brought to him; **~ qch à sa bouche** to lift *ou* put sth to one's lips; **~ une œuvre à l'écran** to transfer a work to the screen; **~ bonheur/malheur (à qn)** to be lucky/unlucky (for sb), bring (sb) (good) luck/misfortune. **(c)** *vêtement* to wear; *barbe* to have, wear; *nom* to have, bear; *blessure, inscription* to bear; *trace* to show. **~ les cheveux longs** to wear one's hair long, have long hair; **~ le nom de Jérôme** to be called Jerome; **elle porte bien le pantalon** trousers suit her; **cela ne se porte plus** that's out of fashion, nobody wears that any more. **(d)** (*inscrire*) to write down, put down (*sur* on, in); (*Comm*) *somme* to enter (*sur* in). **~ de l'argent au crédit/débit d'un compte** to credit/debit an account with a sum; **se faire ~ absent** to go absent; **se faire ~ malade** to report sick; **porté disparu** reported missing. **(e)** *sentiment* to have, feel (*à* for); *coup* to deal (*à* to); *accusation, attaque* to make (*contre* against); *pas* to turn (*vers* towards). **faire ~** *regard, choix, effort* to direct (*sur* towards); *attention* to focus, turn (*sur* on). **(f)** (*faire arriver*) to bring. **~ au pouvoir/à la perfection** to bring to power/to perfection; **~ la température/le nombre à** to bring the temperature/the number up to. **(g)** (*inciter*) **~ qn à (faire) qch** to prompt *ou* lead sb to do sth; **tout (nous) porte à croire que ...** everything leads us to believe that ... . **(h)** (*Méd*) *enfant* to carry; *intérêts, récolte* to yield; *fruit* to bear. **je ne le porte pas dans mon cœur** I am not exactly fond of him. **(i)** (*conduire*) to carry; *[foi]* to carry along; *[vent, foule]* to carry away.

2 *vi* **(a)** *[bruit]* to carry. **le son a porté à 500 mètres** the sound carried 500 metres. **(b)** *[conseil]* to be effective. *[reproche, coup]* **~ (juste)** to hit *ou* strike home; **tous les coups portaient** every blow told. **(c)** (*Vét*) *[animal]* to carry its young. **(d) ~ sur** *[édifice, pilier]* to be supported by *ou* on; *[débat]* to turn on, be about; *[revendications]* to concern; *[étude, action]* to focus on; *[accent]* to fall on; **faire ~ son exposé sur qch** to focus on sth in one's talk; **sa tête a porté sur le trottoir** his head struck the pavement.

3 se ~ *vpr* **(a) se ~ bien/mal** to be well/unwell; **se ~ mieux/plus mal** to feel better/worse; **se ~ comme un charme** to be fighting fit, be as fit as a fiddle. **(b) se ~ candidat** to stand as a candidate; **se ~ acquéreur (de)** to put in a bid (for). **(c)** *[regard, soupçon, choix]* **se ~ sur** to fall on; **son attention se porta sur ce point** he focused *ou* concentrated his attention on this point. **(d) se ~ à** *violences* to commit; **se ~ à la rencontre de qn** to go to meet sb.

porteur, -euse [pɔʀtœʀ, øz] **1** *adj fusée* booster; *courant* carrier. **2** *nm,f [colis]* porter; *[message, chèque]* bearer; *[actions]* (share)holder. **~ d'eau/de germes** water/germ carrier; **il était ~ de faux papiers** he was carrying forged papers; **le ~ du ballon** the holder of the (foot)ball; (*Fin*) **payable au ~** payable to bearer.

portier [pɔʀtje] *nm* commissionnaire, janitor.

portière [pɔʀtjɛʀ] *nf* (*Aut, Rail*) door.

portillon [pɔʀtijɔ̃] *nm* gate.

portion [pɔʀsjɔ̃] *nf* (*gén*) portion; (*Culin*) helping. **~ congrue** smallest share; **~ de route** stretch of road.

portique [pɔʀtik] *nm* (*Archit*) portico; (*Sport*) crossbar.

porto [pɔʀto] **1** *nm* port (wine). **2**: **P~** *n* (*Géog*) Oporto.

portrait [pɔʀtʀɛ] *nm* (*peinture, description*) portrait; (*photo*) photograph. **~-robot** identikit picture, photo-fit picture; **c'est tout le ~ de son père** he's the spitting image of his father; **faire le ~ de qn** to paint sb's portrait.

portuaire [pɔʀtɥɛʀ] *adj* port, harbour.

Portugal [pɔʀtygal] *nm* Portugal. ♦ **portugais, e** *adj, nm,* **P~(e)** *nm(f)* Portuguese.

pose [poz] *nf* **(a)** (*installation*) installation. **la ~ d'une serrure** fitting a lock. **(b)** (*Art, attitude*) pose; (*affectation*) posing. **prendre une ~** to strike a pose. **(c)** (*Phot*) exposure; (*bouton*) time exposure. **prendre une photo en ~** to take a photo in time exposure.

posé, e [poze] *adj personne* calm, level-headed; *attitude* steady, sober. ♦ **posément** *adv parler* calmly, steadily.

poser [poze] (1) **1** *vt* **(a)** (*placer*) to put (down), lay (down), set down (*sur* on); (*debout*) to stand, put (*contre* against); (*Math*) *opération* to write, set down. **~ son manteau** to take off one's coat; **~ son regard sur qch** to look at sth; **réussir à ~ son avion** to manage to land one's plane; **~ un lapin à qn*** to stand sb up*. **(b)** *carrelage, fondations etc* to lay; *gaz* to install; *rideaux* to hang, put up; *tapis, vitre* to put in; *moquette, serrure* to fit (*sur* on). **~ des jalons** (*lit*) to put stakes up; (*fig*) to prepare the ground. **(c)** *principe, condition* to lay down, set out, state; *problème* to pose; *devinette* to set. **~ une question à qn** to ask sb a question, put a question to sb; (*à l'examen*) to set sb a question; **~ la question de confiance** to ask for a vote of confidence; **~ sa candidature** to apply (*à* for); (*Pol*) to put o.s. up *ou* stand *ou* run (*US*) for election; **posons que ...** let us suppose *ou* assume that ... . **(d)** (*donner de l'importance*) to give standing to; (*professionnellement*) to establish the reputation of.

2 *vi* **(a)** (*Art, Phot*) to pose, sit (*pour* for); (*se vanter*) to show off. **~ à l'artiste** to play *ou* act the artist. **(b)** *[poutre]* **~ sur** to bear *ou* rest on.

3 se ~ *vpr* **(a)** *[oiseau]* to alight (*sur* on); *[avion]* to land, touch down; *[regard]* to settle, fix (*sur* on). (*Aviat*) **se ~ sur le ventre** to make a belly-landing. **(b) se ~ comme victime** to pretend *ou* claim to be a victim; **comme menteur, il se pose là*** he's a terrible liar; (*poids*) **il se pose là!*** he's enormous. **(c)** *[question]* to come up, crop up, arise. **le problème qui se pose** the problem we are faced with; **il commence à se ~ des questions** he's beginning to wonder; **il y a une question que je me pose** there's one thing I'd like to know.

poseur, -euse [pozœʀ, øz] **1** *adj* affected. **2** *nm,f* **(a)** (*péj*) show-off, poseur. **(b)** (*ouvrier*) **~ de tuyaux** *etc* pipe *etc* layer.

positif, -ive [pozitif, iv] *adj, nm* (*gén*) positive. ♦ **positivement** *adv* (*gén*) positively.

position [pozisjɔ̃] *nf* (*gén*) position. (*lit, fig*) **rester sur ses ~s** to stand one's ground; **avoir une ~ de repli** (*Mil*) to have a position to fall back on; (*fig*) to have other proposals to fall back on; **prendre ~** (*gén, Mil*) to take up (one's) position; (*se déclarer*) to take a stand; **être en première/seconde/dernière ~** to be first/second/last; **dormir dans une mauvaise ~** to sleep in the wrong position; **être dans une ~ fausse** to be in a false position; **le gouvernement doit définir sa ~ sur cette question** the government must make its position *ou* stance on this question clear; (*Fin*) **demander sa ~** to ask for the balance of one's account.

posologie [pozɔlɔʒi] *nf* directions for use.

posséder [pɔsede] (6) **1** *vt* **(a)** (*gén*) to have; *fortune, qualité* to possess; *maison* to own; *diplôme* to hold. **bien ~ une langue** to have a thorough knowledge of a language. **(b)** *[démon]* to possess. **la jalousie le possède** he is consumed with jealousy. **(c)** (*: *duper*) **~ qn** to take sb in*; **se faire ~** to be had*. **2 se ~** *vpr* to control o.s. **elle ne se possédait plus de joie** she was beside herself *ou* was overcome with joy.

♦ **possédant, e 1** *adj* propertied. **2** *nmpl*: **les ~s** the wealthy. ♦ **possédé, e 1** *adj* possessed (*de* by). **2** *nm,f* person possessed. ♦ **possesseur** *nm* possessor, owner; holder. **être ~ de** *objet* to have. ♦ **possessif, -ive** *adj, nm* possessive. ♦ **possession** *nf* **(a)** (*gén*) possession; *[bien]* ownership. **la ~ d'une arme** possessing *ou* having a weapon; **avoir qch en sa ~** to have sth in one's possession; **prendre ~ de** *fonction* to take up; *appartement* to take possession of; **en ~ de toutes ses facultés** in possession of all one's faculties. **(b)** (*chose possédée*) possession; (*Rel: envoûtement*) possession. (*maîtrise*) **~ de soi** self-control.

possibilité [pɔsibilite] *nf* (*gén*) possibility; *[projet]* feasibility. **ai-je la ~ de faire cela?** is it possible for me to do that?, can I do that?; **quelles sont vos ~s de logement?** what is your position as regards accommodation?

possible [pɔsibl(ə)] **1** *adj* (*gén*) possible; *projet* feasible. **lui serait-il ~ d'arriver plus tôt?** could he possibly *ou* would it be possible for him to come earlier?; **arrivez tôt si (c'est) ~** arrive early if possible *ou* if you can; **ce n'est pas ~ autrement** there's no other way; **il est ~ qu'il vienne** he may *ou* might (possibly) come, it's possible (that) he'll come; **il a eu toutes les difficultés ~s et imaginables à obtenir un visa** he had all kinds of problems *ou* every imaginable problem getting a visa; **venez aussitôt que ~** come as soon as possible *ou* as soon as you (possibly) can; **il a acheté la valise la plus légère ~** he bought the lightest possible suitcase; **cette situation n'est plus ~** this situation has become impossible *ou* intolerable; **ce n'est pas ~** (*faux*) that can't be true; (*étonnant*) well I never!; (*irréalisable*) it's impossible; **c'est (bien) ~** (quite) possibly, maybe. **2** *nm*: **dans le ~, dans les limites du ~** within the realms of possibility; **faire tout son ~** to do one's utmost, do all one can (*pour* to); **énervant au ~** extremely annoying.

post- [pɔst] *préf* post-.

postal, e, *mpl* **-aux** [pɔstal, o] *adj* (*gén*) postal; *colis* sent by post *ou* mail.

postdater [pɔstdate] (1) *vt* to postdate.

poste[1] [pɔst(ə)] *nf* **(a)** (*administration, bureau*) post office. **la ~ principale** the main *ou* head post office. **(b)** (*service*) postal *ou* mail service. **envoyer qch par la ~** to send sth by post *ou* mail; **mettre une lettre à la ~** to post *ou* mail a letter; **~ aérienne** airmail; **~ restante** poste restante.

poste[2] [pɔst(ə)] **1** *nm* **(a)** (*emplacement*) post. **~ de douane** *etc* customs *etc* post; **à vos ~s!** to your stations! *ou* posts! **(b)** (*emploi*) (*gén*) job; *[fonctionnaire]* post; (*dans une hiérarchie*) position; (*nomination*) appointment. **toujours fidèle au ~?*** still at the same job? **(c)** (*Rad, TV*) set. **~ émetteur/récepteur** transmitting/receiving set, transmitter/receiver; **éteindre le ~** to turn the set off. **(d)** (*Téléc*) **~ 23** extension 23. **(e)** *[budget]* item. **(f)** (*Ind*) shift. **~ de 8 heures** 8-hour shift. **2: ~ d'aiguillage** signal box; **~ de commandement** headquarters; **~ de contrôle** checkpoint; **~ d'équipage** crew's quarters; **~ d'essence** petrol *ou* gas (*US*) station; **~ d'incendie** fire point; **~ de pilotage** cockpit; **~ de police** police station.

poster[1] [pɔste] (1) **1** *vt lettre* post, mail; *sentinelle* to post, station. **2 se ~** *vpr* to position *ou* station o.s.

poster[2] [pɔstɛʀ] *nm* poster.

postérieur, e [pɔsteʀjœʀ] **1** *adj* (*dans le temps*) later; (*dans l'espace*) back. **~ à 1800** after 1800. **2** *nm* (*) behind*. ♦ **postérieurement** *adv* later. **~ à** after.

postérité [pɔsteʀite] *nf* posterity.

posthume [pɔstym] *adj* posthumous.

postiche [pɔstiʃ] **1** *adj* (*gén*) false. **2** *nm* hairpiece, postiche.

postier, -ière [pɔstje, jɛʀ] *nm,f* post office worker.

postillon [pɔstijɔ̃] *nm* (*Hist*) postilion.

postopératoire [pɔstɔpeʀatwaʀ] *adj* post-operative.

postposition [pɔstpozisjɔ̃] *nf* postposition. **verbe à ~** phrasal verb.

postscolaire [pɔstskɔlɛʀ] *adj enseignement* further.

post-scriptum [pɔstskʀiptɔm] *nm inv* postscript.

postsynchroniser [pɔstsɛ̃kʀɔnize] (1) *vt* to dub (*a film*).

postuler [pɔstyle] (1) *vt* **(a)** *emploi* to apply for, put in for. **(b)** *principe* to postulate. ♦ **postulant, e** *nm,f* applicant. ♦ **postulat** *nm* postulate.

posture [pɔstyʀ] *nf* posture, position. **en bonne/mauvaise ~** in a good/bad position.

pot [po] **1** *nm* **(a)** (*en verre*) jar; (*en terre*) pot; (*en carton*) carton. **mettre en ~** *fleur* to pot; *confiture* to put in jars; **mettre un enfant sur le ~** to put a child on the potty; **tu viens boire un ~?*** are you coming for a drink? **(b)** (*: *chance*) luck. **avoir du/manquer de ~** to be lucky/unlucky; **coup de ~** stroke of luck. **(c)** (*Cartes*) (*enjeu*) kitty; (*restant*) pile.

2: ~ de chambre chamberpot; **~ de colle** (*lit*) pot of glue; (*péj: crampon*) leech; **~ à eau** water jug; **~ d'échappement** exhaust pipe; **~-au-feu** (*nm inv*) (*plat*) (beef) stew; (*viande*) stewing beef; **~ de fleurs** (*récipient*) flowerpot; (*fleurs*) pot of flowers; **~ à lait** (*pour transporter*) milk can; (*sur la table*) milk jug; (*Mus*) **~-pourri** *nm, pl* **~s-~s** potpourri, medley; **~-de-vin** *nm, pl* **~s-~-~** bribe, backhander*.

potable [pɔtabl(ə)] *adj* (*lit*) drinkable; (**fig*) decent. **eau ~** drinking water.

potage [pɔtaʒ] *nm* soup.

potager, -ère [pɔtaʒe, ɛʀ] **1** *adj* vegetable. **2** *nm* kitchen *ou* vegetable garden.

potasser* [pɔtase] (1) *vt* to cram for.

pote* [pɔt] *nm* pal*, mate*.

poteau, *pl* **~x** [pɔto] *nm* post. **au ~!*** down with him!; **~ (d'exécution)** execution post; **~ d'arrivée/de départ** finishing/starting post; **~ de but** goal-post; **~ indicateur** signpost; **~ télégraphique** telegraph post *ou* pole.

potelé, e [pɔtle] *adj enfant* plump, chubby; *bras* plump.

potence [pɔtɑ̃s] *nf* (*gibet*) gallows (*sg*); (*support*) bracket.

potentiel, -elle [pɔtɑ̃sjɛl] *adj, nm* (*gén*) potential. ♦ **potentiellement** *adv* potentially.

poterie [pɔtʀi] *nf* (*atelier, art*) pottery; (*objet*) piece of pottery. ♦ **potiche** *nf* oriental vase; (*fig*) figurehead. ♦ **potier** *nm* potter.

potin* [pɔtɛ̃] *nm* **(a)** (*vacarme*) din, racket. **faire du ~** (*lit*) to make a noise; (*fig*) to kick up a fuss*. **(b)** (*commérage*) ~s gossip.

potion [posjɔ̃] *nf* potion.

potiron [pɔtiʀɔ̃] *nm* pumpkin.

pou, *pl* **~x** [pu] *nm* louse. **couvert de ~x** covered in lice.

pouah [pwa] *excl* ugh!

poubelle [pubɛl] *nf [ordures]* (dust)bin, trash can (*US*). **mettre à la ~** to throw away.

pouce [pus] *nm* **(a)** *[main]* thumb; *[pied]* big toe. **se tourner les ~s** to twiddle one's thumbs; (*au jeu*) **~!** pax!, truce!; **manger sur le ~*** to have a quick snack. **(b)** (*mesure*) inch.

poudre [pudʀ(ə)] *nf* (*gén*) powder; (*poussière*) dust; (*fard*) (face) powder; (*explosif*) (gun)-powder. **réduire qch en ~** to grind sth to a powder; **en ~** *lait* dried, powdered; *chocolat* drinking; *sucre* granulated; **prendre la ~ d'escampette*** to take to one's heels; **~ à laver/à récurer** soap/scouring powder. ♦ **poudrer** (1) *vt* to powder. ♦ **poudrerie** *nf* gunpowder factory. ♦ **poudreux, -euse** *adj* (*poussiéreux*) dusty. **neige ~euse** powder snow. ♦ **poudrier** *nm* (powder) compact. ♦ **poudrière** *nf* powder magazine; (*fig*) powder keg (*fig*).

pouf [puf] **1** *nm* pouffe. **2** *excl* thud! **faire ~** to tumble (over).

pouffer [pufe] (1) *vi*: **~ (de rire)** to snigger.

pouilleux, -euse [pujø, øz] **1** *adj* (*lit*) lousy, verminous; *quartier* squalid, seedy; *personne* dirty, filthy. **2** *nm,f* (*pauvre*) down-and-out.

poulailler [pulɑje] *nm* henhouse. (*Théât*) **le ~*** the gods*.

poulain [pulɛ̃] *nm* foal; (*fig*) promising young athlete; (*protégé*) protégé.

poularde [pulaʀd(ə)] *nf* fatted chicken.

poule[1] [pul] **1** *nf* **(a)** (*Zool*) hen; (*Culin*) (boiling) fowl. **se lever/se coucher avec les ~s** to get up/go to bed early; **quand les ~s auront des dents** when pigs can fly. **(b)** (*) (*maîtresse*) mistress; (*prostituée*) whore. **ma ~** (my) pet. **2: ~ d'eau** moorhen; **~ faisane** hen pheasant; **~ mouillée*** coward, softy*; **la ~ aux œufs d'or** the goose that lays the golden eggs; **~ au pot** boiled chicken.

poule[2] [pul] *nf* **(a)** (*enjeu*) pool, kitty. **(b)** (*tournoi*) (*gén*) tournament; (*Escrime*) pool; (*Rugby*) group.

poulet [pulɛ] *nm* chicken; (*:*flic*) cop*.

pouliche [puliʃ] *nf* filly.

poulie [puli] *nf* pulley; (*avec sa caisse*) block.

poulpe [pulp(ə)] *nm* octopus.

pouls [pu] *nm* pulse. **prendre le ~ de qn** to take sb's pulse.

poumon [pumɔ̃] *nm* lung. **~ d'acier** iron lung.

poupe [pup] *nf* (*Naut*) stern.

poupée [pupe] *nf* (*jouet*) doll, dolly; (*:*femme jolie*) doll*; (*: *fille*) bird*; (*pansement*) finger bandage.

poupon [pupɔ̃] *nm* little baby. ♦ **pouponner** (1) *vi* to play mother. ♦ **pouponnière** *nf* day nursery, crèche.

pour [puʀ] **1** *prép* **(a)** (*direction*) for, to. **il part ~ l'Espagne demain** he leaves for Spain *ou* he is off to Spain tomorrow; **le train ~ Londres** the London train, the train for London.

(b) (*temps*) for. **il lui faut sa voiture ~ demain** he must have his car for *ou* by tomorrow; **~ l'instant** for the moment; **~ toujours** for ever; **gardez le meilleur ~ la fin** keep the best till the end.

(c) (*intention*) for. **il ferait tout ~ sa mère** he would do anything for his mother *ou* for his mother's sake; **faire qch ~ la gloire** to do sth for the glory of it; **son amour ~ les bêtes** his love of animals; **c'est mauvais/bon ~ vous** it's bad/good for you; **il a été très gentil ~ ma mère** he was very kind to my mother; **sirop ~ la toux** cough mixture; **le plombier est venu ~ la chaudière** the plumber came about the boiler; **~ le meilleur et ~ le pire** for better or for worse.

(d) (*approbation*) for, in favour of. **je suis ~!*** I'm all for it*, I'm all in favour (of it).

(e) (*point de vue*) **~ moi** (*à mon avis*) in my opinion, in my view; (*en ce qui me concerne*) personally, for my part; **sa fille est tout ~ lui** his daughter is everything to him.

(f) (*cause*) **condamné ~ vol** convicted for theft; **puni ~ avoir menti** punished for lying *ou* having lied; **félicité ~ son audace** congratulated on his boldness; **fermé ~ cause de maladie** closed because of *ou* on account of illness; **pourquoi se faire du souci ~ cela?** why worry about that?; **il y est ~ qch/~ beaucoup** he is partly/largely responsible for it.

(g) (*à la place de*) **payer ~ qn** to pay for sb; (*Comm etc*) **~ le directeur** p.p. Manager; **il a parlé ~ nous** he spoke on our behalf; **donnez-moi ~ 30 F d'essence** give me 30 francs' worth of petrol; **il l'a eu ~ 5 F** he got it for 5 francs.

(h) (*rapport*) for. **~ cent** per cent; **petit ~ son âge** small for his age; **jour ~ jour** to the (very) day; **mourir ~ mourir, je préfère que ce soit ici** if I have to die I should prefer it to be here.

(i) (*comme*) for, as. **prendre qn ~ un imbécile** to take sb for an idiot; **il a ~ adjoint son cousin** he has his cousin as his deputy; **il passe ~ filou** he's said to be a crook; **il a ~ principe de faire ...** his principle is to do ...; **~ de bon*** truly, really.

(j) (*emphatique*) **~ (ce qui est de) notre voyage** as for our journey, as far as our journey goes *ou* is concerned; **~ une malchance c'est une malchance!** this is a most unfortunate thing indeed!

(k) (*but*) to. **nous avons assez d'argent ~ l'aider** we have enough money to help him; **je n'ai rien dit ~ ne pas le blesser** I didn't say anything in order not to *ou* so as not to hurt him; **il étendit le bras ~ prendre la boîte** he reached (out) for the box; **le travail n'est pas ~ l'effrayer** he's not afraid of hard work; **il a dit ça ~ rire** he said it in fun *ou* as a joke; **il est parti ~ ne plus revenir** he left never to return; **j'étais ~ partir*** I was just going, I was just about to go.

(l) ~ que+*subj* so that, in order that; **écris ta lettre ~ qu'elle parte ce soir** write your letter so that it leaves this evening; **il est trop tard ~ qu'on le prévienne** it's too late to warn him.

(m) (*restriction*) **~ riche qu'il soit, il n'est pas généreux** rich though he is, he's not generous; **~ peu qu'il soit sorti ...** if on top of it all he has gone out ...; **~ autant que je sache** as far as I know.

2 *nm*: **le ~ et le contre** the arguments for and against, the pros and the cons.

pourboire [puʀbwaʀ] *nm* tip.

pourcentage [puʀsɑ̃taʒ] *nm* percentage. **travailler au ~** to work on commission.

pourchasser [puʀʃase] (1) *vt [ennemi]* to pursue, hunt down; *[créancier, importun]* to hound. **~ le crime** to hunt out crime.

pourparlers [puʀpaʀle] *nmpl* talks, negotiations, discussions. **être en ~ avec** to have talks with.

pourpre [puʀpʀ(ə)] **1** *adj, nm* (*couleur*) crimson. **2** *nf* (*matière, étoffe, symbole*) purple.

pourquoi [puʀkwa] **1** *conj* why. **~ est-il venu?** why did he come?, what did he come for? **2** *adv* why. **tu viens? — ~ pas?** are you coming? — why not? *ou* why shouldn't I?; **allez savoir ~*!** I don't know why! **3** *nm inv* (*raison*) reason (*de* for); (*question*) question.

pourrir [puʀiʀ] (2) **1** *vi [fruit]* to go rotten *ou* bad; *[bois, cadavre]* to rot away. **~ en prison** to rot in prison; **laisser ~ la situation** to let the situation deteriorate *ou* get worse. **2** *vt fruit* to make rotten, rot; (*fig*) *enfant etc* to spoil. ♦ **pourri, e**

1 *adj* **(a)** (*gén*) rotten; *feuille, cadavre* rotting; *viande* bad. **être ~** to have gone rotten *ou* bad. **(b)** *temps* wet, rainy; *société* rotten; *enfant* spoilt. **2** *nm* **(a)** (*morceau*) rotten *ou* bad part; *odeur* putrid smell. **(b)** (‡:*crapule*) swine‡, bastard‡. ♦ **pourrissement** *nm [situation]* deterioration, worsening (*de* in, of). ♦ **pourriture** *nf* **(a)** (*lit, Agr*) rot; *[société]* rottenness. **(b)** (*péj: personne*) swine‡.

poursuivre [puʀsɥivʀ(ə)] (40) **1** *vt* **(a)** (*courir après*) (*gén*) to pursue; *animal* to hunt down; *malfaiteur* to chase (after). **(b)** *[importun, souvenir]* to hound; *[idée]* to haunt. **~ qn de sa colère** to hound sb through anger. **(c)** *rêve etc* to pursue; *gloire* to seek (after); *idéal* to strive towards. **(d)** (*continuer*) (*gén*) to continue, go *ou* carry on with; *avantage* to follow up, pursue. **~ sa marche** to keep going, walk on. **(e)** (*Jur*) **~ qn (en justice)** (*au criminel*) to prosecute sb; (*au civil*) to sue sb. **2** *vi* (*continuer*) to carry on, go on, continue; (*persévérer*) to keep at it, keep it up. **3 se ~** *vpr* to go on, continue. ♦ **poursuite** *nf* **(a)** *[fugitif]* chase (*de* after), pursuit (*de* of); *[gloire]* pursuit (*de* of). **se mettre à la ~ de qn** to go in pursuit of sb. **(b) ~s (judiciaires)** legal proceedings; **engager des ~s contre** to take legal action against; **s'exposer à des ~s** to run the risk of prosecution. **(c)** (*continuation*) continuation. **(d)** (*Sport*) **(course) ~** track race. ♦ **poursuivant, e** *nm,f* pursuer.

pourtant [puʀtɑ̃] *adv* yet, nevertheless. **frêle mais ~ résistant** frail but nevertheless *ou* yet resilient; **il n'est ~ pas très intelligent** (and) yet he's not very clever, he's not very clever though.

pourtour [puʀtuʀ] *nm [cercle]* circumference; *[rectangle]* perimeter; (*bord*) surround. **sur le ~ de** around.

pourvoir [puʀvwaʀ] (25) **1** *vt*: **~ qn de qch** to provide *ou* equip *ou* supply sb with sth, provide sth for sb; **~ sa cave de vin** to stock one's cellar with wine. **2 ~ à** *vt indir éventualité, besoins* to provide for, cater for; *emploi* to fill. **j'y pourvoirai** I'll see to it *ou* deal with it. **3 se ~** *vpr*: **se ~ de** *argent* to provide o.s. with. ♦ **pourvoyeur, -euse** *nm,f* supplier. ♦ **pourvu**[1], **e** *adj emploi* filled. **~ de** *intelligence* gifted *ou* endowed with; *dispositif* equipped *ou* fitted with; **nous voilà ~s pour l'hiver** we're stocked up *ou* well provided for for the winter; **feuille de papier ~e d'une marge** sheet of paper with a margin.

pourvu[2] [puʀvy] *conj*: **~ que** (*souhait*) let's hope; (*condition*) provided (that), so long as.

pousse [pus] *nf* **(a)** (*bourgeon*) shoot. **(b)** (*action*) *[feuilles]* sprouting; *[cheveux]* growth.

poussé, e[1] [puse] *adj études* advanced; *enquête* exhaustive. **très ~** *technique, dessin* elaborate.

pousse-café* [puskafe] *nm inv* (after-dinner) liqueur.

poussée[2] [puse] *nf* **(a)** (*pression*) pressure; (*coup*) push, shove; (*Tech, Mil*) thrust. **sous la ~** under the pressure. **(b)** *[acné]* attack; *[prix]* rise, upsurge; (*électorale*) upsurge. **~ de fièvre** (sudden) high temperature.

pousser [puse] (1) **1** *vt* **(a)** (*gén*) to push; *verrou* to slide; *objet gênant* to move, push aside; (*du coude*) to nudge; (*en bousculant*) to jostle. **~ la porte** (*fermer*) to push the door to *ou* shut; (*ouvrir*) to push the door open; **~ un caillou du pied** to kick a stone (along); **le vent nous poussait vers la côte** the wind was blowing us towards the shore; (*balançoire*) **peux-tu me ~?** can you give me a push? **(b)** *cheval* to ride hard, push; *moteur* to drive hard; *feu* to stoke up; *chauffage* to turn up; *élève* (*stimuler*) to urge on, push; (*mettre en valeur*) to push. **c'est l'ambition qui le pousse** he is driven by ambition. **(c) ~ qn à faire qch** *[faim, curiosité]* to drive sb to do sth; *[personne]* (*inciter*) to urge *ou* press sb to do sth; (*persuader*) to persuade *ou* induce sb to do sth; **son échec nous pousse à croire que ...** his failure leads us to think that ...; **~ qn au crime** to drive sb to crime; **~ qn à la dépense** to encourage sb to spend money. **(d)** *études, marche* to continue; *avantage* to press (home), follow up. **~ la plaisanterie un peu loin** to carry *ou* take the joke a bit far; **~ qch à la perfection** to carry *ou* bring sth to perfection; **il a poussé la gentillesse jusqu'à faire** he was kind enough to do; **~ qn dans ses derniers retranchements** to drive sb into a corner; **~ qn à bout** to push sb to breaking point. **(e)** *cri* to let out, utter, give; *soupir* to heave. **~ des cris** to shout, scream; **~ des rugissements** to roar.

2 *vi* **(a)** (*grandir*) (*gén*) to grow; *[graine]* to sprout. **faire ~ des tomates** to grow tomatoes; **ça pousse comme du chiendent** they grow like weeds; **se laisser ~ la barbe/les cheveux** to grow a beard/one's hair; **il a une dent qui pousse** he's cutting a tooth, he's got a tooth coming through; **de nouvelles villes poussaient comme des champignons** new towns were springing up *ou* mushrooming. **(b)** (*faire un effort*) to push. (*fig*) **~ à la roue** to do a bit of pushing, push a bit; **faut pas ~!‡** this is going a bit far! **(c)** (*aller*) **~ jusqu'à Lyon** to go on *ou* push on as far as Lyons.

3 se ~ *vpr* (*se déplacer*) to move, shift*.

poussette [pusɛt] *nf* push chair.

poussière [pusjɛʀ] *nf* dust. **faire de la ~** to raise a dust; **avoir une ~ dans l'œil** to have a speck of dust in one's eye; **3 F et des ~s*** just over 3 francs; **tomber en ~** to crumble into dust. ♦ **poussiéreux, -euse** *adj* dusty.

poussif, -ive [pusif, iv] *adj personne* short-winded; *moteur* puffing, wheezing.

poussin [pusɛ̃] *nm* chick. **mon ~!*** pet!

poussoir [puswaʀ] *nm [sonnette]* button.

poutre [putʀ(ə)] *nf* (*en bois*) beam; (*en métal*) girder. ♦ **poutrelle** *nf* girder.

pouvoir[1] [puvwaʀ] (33) **1** *vb aux* **(a)** (*permission*) can, may, to be allowed to. **peut-il venir?** can he *ou* may he come?; **il peut ne pas venir** he doesn't have to come, he needn't come, he's not bound to come; **il pourrait venir s'il nous prévenait** he could come *ou* he would be able *ou* allowed to come if he notified us; **est-ce qu'on peut fermer la fenêtre?** may we *ou* do you mind if we shut the window? **(b)** (*possibilité*) can, to be able to. **il ne peut pas ne pas venir** he can't not come, he HAS to *ou* he MUST come; **il n'a (pas) pu venir** he couldn't *ou* wasn't able to *ou* was unable to come; **il ne peut pas s'empêcher de tousser** he can't help coughing; **comme il pouvait comprendre la fiche technique, il a pu réparer le poste** since he could understand the technical information he was able to *ou* he managed to repair the set; **pourriez-vous nous apporter du thé?** could you bring us some tea? **(c)** (*éventualité*) **il peut être français** he may *ou* might *ou* could be French; **il ne peut pas être français** he can't be French; **quel âge peut-il avoir?** how old might he be?; **qu'est-ce que cela peut bien lui faire?*** what's that (got) to do with him?*; **il peut être très méchant, parfois** he can be very nasty at times; **où ai-je bien pu mettre mon stylo?** where on earth can I have put my pen?; **cela pourrait se faire** that might *ou* could be arranged. **(d)** (*suggestion*) **elle pourrait arriver à l'heure!** she might *ou* could (at least) be punctual! **(e)** (*littér: souhait*) **puisse Dieu les aider!** may God help them!; **puissiez-vous dire vrai!** let us pray *ou* hope you're right!

2 *vb impers*: **il peut** *ou* **pourrait pleuvoir** it may *ou* might *ou* could rain, it is possible that it will rain.

3 *vt* can. **il partira dès qu'il le pourra** he will leave as soon as he can *ou* is able (to); **que puis-je pour vous?** what can I do for you?; **il a été on ne peut plus aimable** he couldn't have been kinder, he was as kind as could be; **il n'en peut plus** (*fatigué*) he's all-in* *ou* tired out; (*à bout*) he can't take any more; **on n'y peut rien** there's nothing we can do (about it), it can't be helped.

4 se ~ *vpr*: **il se peut/se pourrait qu'elle vienne** she may *ou* could/might *ou* could (well) come; **cela se pourrait bien** that's quite possible, that might *ou* could well be.

pouvoir[2] [puvwaʀ] *nm* **(a)** (*gén*) power. ~ **absorbant** absorption power; ~ **d'achat** purchasing power; **avoir le** ~ **de faire** (*capacité*) to have the power *ou* ability to do; (*autorisation*) to have authority *ou* power to do; **ce n'est pas en mon** ~ it is not within *ou* in my power, it is beyond my power; **avoir du** ~ **sur qn** to have influence *ou* power over sb; **avoir du** ~ **sur soi-même** to have will power; **dépasser ses** ~**s** to exceed one's powers. **(b)** (*Pol*) **le** ~ (*direction*) power; (*dirigeants*) the government; **le parti au** ~ the party in power *ou* in office; **avoir le** ~ to hold power, rule, govern; **prendre le** ~ (*légalement*) to come to power *ou* into office; (*illégalement*) to seize power; **le** ~ **exécutif** the executive power; **les** ~**s publics** the authorities. **(c)** (*Jur: procuration*) proxy. **donner** ~ **à qn de faire** to give sb proxy to do.

prairie [pʀeʀi] *nf* meadow.

praline [pʀalin] *nf* sugared almond. ♦ **praliné, e 1** *adj* praline-flavoured. **2** *nm* praline-flavoured ice cream.

pratique [pʀatik] **1** *adj* **(a)** (*non théorique, réaliste*) practical. **avoir le sens** ~ to be practical-minded. **(b)** (*commode*) (*gén*) practical; *instrument* handy; *emploi du temps* convenient. **2** *nf* **(a)** (*application, procédé*) practice; (*expérience*) practical experience. **en** ~ in practice; **mettre qch en** ~ to put sth into practice; **il a une longue** ~ **des élèves** he has a long practical experience of teaching; **il a perdu la** ~ he is out of practice; **des** ~**s malhonnêtes** dishonest practices. **(b)** *[règle]* observance; *[sport]* practising; *[vertu]* exercise, practice. **la** ~ **du golf** golfing, (playing) golf; ~ **(religieuse)** church attendance; **la** ~ **de la médecine** the practising of medicine. ♦ **pratiquement** *adv* (*en pratique*) in practice; (*presque*) practically. ♦ **praticable** *adj* (*gén*) practicable; *projet* feasible; *chemin* passable, negotiable. ♦ **praticien, -ienne** *nm,f* (*gén*) practitioner. ♦ **pratiquant, e 1** *adj* practising. **il est très** ~ he goes to church regularly. **2** *nm,f* (*d'une foi*) follower; (*assidu*) regular churchgoer.

pratiquer [pʀatike] (1) **1** *vt* **(a)** *art etc* to practise, practice (*US*); *règle* to observe; *vertu* to exercise; *football* to play. ~ **l'escrime** to go in for fencing. **(b)** *ouverture* to make; *trou* to pierce, bore; *route* to build, open up; (*Méd*) *intervention* to carry out (*sur* on). **(c)** *méthode* to use. **2** *vi* (*Rel*) to go to church; (*Méd*) to be in practice. **3 se** ~ *vpr* *[méthode]* to be the practice; *[religion]* to be practised. **les prix qui se pratiquent à Paris** prices which prevail *ou* are current in Paris.

pré [pʀe] *nm* meadow.

pré ... [pʀe] *préf* pre ... .

préalable [pʀealabl(ə)] **1** *adj* *entretien, condition* preliminary; *accord, avis* prior, previous. ~ **à** preceding, prior to. **2** *nm* precondition, prerequisite. **au** ~ first, beforehand. ♦ **préalablement** *adv* first, beforehand. ~ **à** prior to.

préambule [pʀeɑ̃byl] *nm [loi]* preamble; (*fig: prélude*) prelude (*à* to).

préau, *pl* ~**x** [pʀeo] *nm [école]* covered playground; *[prison, couvent]* inner courtyard.

préavis [pʀeavi] *nm* (advance) notice. **sans** ~ without advance *ou* previous notice.

précaire [pʀekɛʀ] *adj* (*gén*) precarious; *santé* shaky.

précaution [pʀekosjɔ̃] *nf* **(a)** (*disposition*) precaution. **prendre se** ~**s** to take precautions. **(b)** (*prudence*) caution, care. **par** ~ as a precaution; **pour plus de** ~ to be on the safe side; **avec** ~ cautiously.

♦ **précautionneux, -euse** *adj* (*prudent*) cautious; (*soigneux*) careful.

précéder [pʀesede] (6) **1** *vt* **(a)** (*venir avant*) to precede, come before; (*dans une file*) to be in front *ou* ahead of, precede. **faire** ~ **son discours d'une remarque** to precede one's speech by a remark. **(b)** (*devancer*) to precede, get ahead of. **il m'a précédé de 5 minutes** he got there 5 minutes before me *ou* ahead of me, he preceded me by 5 minutes.

2 *vi* to precede. **tout ce qui a précédé** all that has been said *etc* before *ou* so far; **dans le chapitre qui précède** in the preceding chapter.

♦ **précédemment** *adv* before, previously. ♦ **précédent, e 1** *adj* previous. **un discours** ~ a previous *ou* an earlier speech; **le film** ~ the preceding *ou* previous film. **2** *nm* precedent. **sans** ~ unprecedented.

précepte [pʀesɛpt(ə)] *nm* precept.

précepteur [pʀesɛptœʀ] *nm* private tutor.

prêcher [pʀeʃe] (1) **1** *vt* (*Rel, fig*) to preach; *personne* to preach to. (*hum*) ~ **la bonne parole** to spread the good word. **2** *vi* to preach. ~ **d'exemple** to preach by example.

précieux, -euse [pʀesjø, øz] *adj* (*lit, fig, péj*) precious; *conseil* invaluable; *ami* valued, precious. ♦ **précieusement** *adv* preciously.

précipice [pʀesipis] *nm* (*gouffre*) chasm; (*fig*) abyss. (*paroi*) **au bord du** ~ at the brink of the precipice.

précipiter [pʀesipite] (1) **1** *vt* **(a)** (*jeter*) to throw *ou* hurl down; (*dans le malheur*) to plunge (*dans* into). **(b)** (*hâter*) *pas, événement* to hasten. **il ne faut rien** ~ we mustn't rush things. **2** *vti* (*Chim*) to precipitate. **3 se** ~ *vpr* **(a)** (*se ruer*) to rush forward. **se** ~ **vers/sur** to rush towards/at; **se** ~ **contre** *[personne]* to throw o.s. against; *[voiture]* to smash into; **se** ~ **dans le vide** to hurl o.s. into space; **se** ~ **sur l'ennemi** to rush at *ou* hurl o.s. at the enemy; **il se précipita au-dehors** he raced *ou* dashed *ou* rushed outside. **(b)** (*s'accélérer*) to speed up; *[pouls]* to quicken. **les choses se précipitaient** events started to move faster. **(c)** (*se dépêcher*) to hurry, rush. ♦ **précipitamment** *adv* hastily. **sortir** ~ to rush out. ♦ **précipitation** *nf* (*hâte*) haste. (*Mét*) ~**s** precipitation. ♦ **précipité, e 1** *adj* *départ, pas, décision* hasty; *fuite* headlong; *rythme* swift. **2** *nm* (*Chim*) precipitate.

précis, e [pʀesi, iz] **1** *adj* (*juste*) precise, accurate; (*défini*) precise, definite; (*net*) *contours* distinct, precise. **je ne pense à rien de** ~ I'm not thinking of anything in particular; **à cet instant** ~ at that precise *ou* very moment; **à 4 heures** ~**es** at 4 o'clock sharp *ou* on the dot*. **2** *nm* (*résumé*) précis, summary; (*manuel*) handbook. ♦ **précisément** *adv* (*gén*) precisely; (*avec exactitude*) accurately; (*distinctement*) distinctly. **je venais** ~ **de sortir** in fact *ou* as a matter of fact I had just gone out, as it happened I'd just gone out; **il est arrivé** ~ **à ce moment-là** he arrived right *ou* just at that moment *ou* at that very moment; **ce n'est pas** ~ **beau** it's not exactly beautiful. ♦ **préciser** (1) **1** *vt* *intention* to specify, make clear, clarify; *fait* to be more specific about. **je vous préciserai la date plus tard** I'll let you know the exact date later; **je dois** ~ **que** ... I must point out *ou* add *ou* explain that ... . **2 se** ~ *vpr [idée]* to take shape; *[danger]* to become clear *ou* clearer. ♦ **précision** *nf* **(a)** precision; accuracy; distinctness. **outil de** ~ precision tool. **(b)** (*détail*) point, piece of information; (*explication*) explanation.

précoce [pʀekɔs] *adj* early; *sénilité* premature; *enfant* precocious, advanced for his *ou* her age.

♦ **précocement** *adv* precociously. ♦ **précocité** *nf* earliness; precocity, precociousness.
préconçu, e [prekɔ̃sy] *adj* preconceived.
préconiser [prekɔnize] (1) *vt remède* to recommend; *méthode* to advocate.
précurseur [prekyrsœr] **1** *adj m* precursory. ~ **de** preceding. **2** *nm* forerunner, precursor.
prédécesseur [predesesœr] *nm* predecessor.
prédestiner [predɛstine] (1) *vt* to predestine (*à qch* for sth, *à faire* to do). ♦ **prédestination** *nf* predestination.
prédicateur [predikatœr] *nm* preacher.
prédiction [prediksjɔ̃] *nf* prediction.
prédilection [predilɛksjɔ̃] *nf* predilection, partiality (*pour* for). **de** ~ favourite.
prédire [predir] (37) *vt [prophète]* to foretell; (*gén*) to predict. ~ **l'avenir** to tell *ou* predict the future; **il m'a prédit que je ...** he predicted (that) I ..., he told me (that) I ... .
prédisposer [predispoze] (1) *vt* to predispose (*à* to). ♦ **prédisposition** *nf* predisposition (*à* to).
prédominer [predɔmine] (1) *vi* (*gén*) to predominate. ♦ **prédominance** *nf* predominance. ♦ **prédominant, e** *adj* predominant.
prééminence [preeminɑ̃s] *nf* pre-eminence. ♦ **prééminent, e** *adj* pre-eminent.
préexister [preɛgziste] (1) *vi* to pre-exist. ♦ **préexistant, e** *adj* pre-existent. ♦ **préexistence** *nf* pre-existence.
préfabriqué, e [prefabrike] **1** *adj* prefabricated. **2** *nm* (*maison*) prefabricated house.
préface [prefas] *nf* preface.
préfecture [prefɛktyr] *nf* prefecture. ~ **de police** Paris police headquarters. ♦ **préfectoral, e, mpl -aux** *adj* prefectural.
préférer [prefere] (6) *vt* to prefer (*à* to). **je te préfère avec les cheveux courts** I like you better *ou* I prefer you with short hair; **je préfère aller au cinéma** I prefer to go *ou* I would rather go to the cinema; **nous avons préféré attendre (plutôt que)** we preferred to wait *ou* thought it better to wait (rather than); **si tu préfères** if you prefer, if you like. ♦ **préférable** *adj* preferable (*à qch* to sth), better (*à qch* than sth). **il serait ~ d'y aller** it would be better if you (*ou* we *etc*) went, it would be better for you (*ou* us *etc*) to go. ♦ **préféré, e** *adj, nm,f* favourite, pet*. ♦ **préférence** *nf* preference. **de** ~ preferably; **de** ~ **à** in preference to, rather than; **je n'ai pas de** ~ I don't mind. ♦ **préférentiel, -ielle** *adj* preferential.
préfet [prefɛ] *nm* prefect.
préfigurer [prefigyre] (1) *vt* to foreshadow.
préfixe [prefiks] *nm* prefix.
préhistoire [preistwar] *nf* prehistory. ♦ **préhistorique** *adj* prehistoric; (*péj*) antediluvian, ancient.
préjudice [preʒydis] *nm* (*matériel*) loss; (*moral*) harm, damage, wrong. **porter** ~ **à qn** (*gén*) to harm sb; *[décision]* to be detrimental to sb; **au** ~ **de sa santé** at the expense of his health. ♦ **préjudiciable** *adj* prejudicial, detrimental, harmful (*à* to).
préjugé [preʒyʒe] *nm* prejudice. **avoir un** ~ **contre** to be prejudiced *ou* biased against.
préjuger [preʒyʒe] (3) *vt*, ~ **de** *vt indir* to prejudge.
prélasser (se) [prelɑse] (1) *vpr* to lounge.
prélat [prela] *nm* prelate.
prélever [prelve] (5) *vt échantillon* to take (*sur* from); *impôt* to levy (*sur* on); *retenue* to deduct *sur* from); *argent sur un compte* to withdraw (*sur* from). ♦ **prélèvement** *nm* taking; levying; deduction; withdrawal. **faire un** ~ **de sang** to take a blood sample.
préliminaire [preliminer] **1** *adj* preliminary. **2** *nmpl*: ~s preliminaries.
prélude [prelyd] *nm* prelude (*à* to). ♦ **préluder à** (1) *vt indir* to be a prelude to.
prématuré, e [prematyre] **1** *adj* (*gén*) premature; *mort* untimely. **2** *nm,f* premature baby. ♦ **prématurément** *adv* prematurely.
préméditer [premedite] (1) *vt* to premeditate. ~ **de faire** to plan to do. ♦ **préméditation** *nf* premeditation. **avec** ~ *crime* premeditated; *tuer* with intent.
premier, -ière [prəmje, jɛr] **1** *adj* **(a)** (*gén*) first; *impression* initial; *enfance* early; *rang* front; *ébauche* rough; *branche* lower, bottom. **être** ~ to be first; (*Sport*) **être en ~ière position** to be in the lead; (*Presse*) **en ~ière page** on the front page; **les 100 ~ières pages** the first 100 pages; **la ~ière marche de l'escalier** the bottom step; **le ~ mouchoir de la pile** the first *ou* top handkerchief in the pile; **ses ~s poèmes** his first *ou* early poems; **lire qch de la ~ière à la dernière ligne** to read sth from beginning to end; (*lit, fig*) **poser la ~ière pierre** to lay the foundation stone *ou* first stone; **au ~ signe de résistance** at the first sign of resistance. **(b)** (*dans un ordre*) first; (*à un examen*) first, top; (*en importance*) leading, foremost. ~ **secrétaire** first secretary; ~ **commis** chief shop assistant; ~ **danseur/rôle** leading dancer/part; **de ~ière qualité** top-quality; **de ~ ordre** first-rate; **c'est de ~ière urgence** it's a matter of the utmost urgency, it's (a) top priority; ~ **en classe** top of the class, first in the class; **de ~ière importance** of paramount *ou* prime *ou* the first importance; **de ~ière nécessité** absolutely essential; **cela m'intéresse au ~ chef** it's of the greatest *ou* utmost interest to me; **c'est le ~ écrivain français vivant** he's the leading *ou* foremost French writer alive today. **(c)** (*du début*) *grade, prix* bottom. **c'était le ~ prix** it was the cheapest; **les ~s rudiments** the first *ou* basic rudiments. **(d)** (*après n: fondamental*) *cause* basic; *objectif, qualité* prime; *état* initial, original. **(e) au ~ abord** at first sight; **au** *ou* **du ~ coup** at the first go *ou* try; **il n'est plus de la ~ière jeunesse** he's not as young as he used to be; **en ~ lieu** in the first place; (*fig*) **être aux ~ières loges** to have a front seat; **il n'en sait pas le ~ mot** he doesn't know the first thing about it; **~ière nouvelle!** it's news to me!; **faire ses ~s pas** to take one's first steps; **faire les ~s pas** to make the first move; **dans un ~ temps** as a first step, at first; **dans les ~s temps** at first, at the outset; **à ~ière vue** at first sight.
2 *nm,f* first (one). **passer le ~** to go first; **il a été le ~ à le dire** he was the first to say so; **il a été reçu dans les ~s** he was in the first few.
3 *nm* (*gén*) first; (*étage*) first floor, second floor (*US*); (*enfant*) first child. **le ~ de l'an** New Year's Day; **en ~** *arriver* first; *dire* first(ly).
4 *nf* (*gén*) first; (*Rail etc*) first class; (*Théât*) first night; (*Ciné*) première; (*Alpinisme*) first ascent; (*Scol*) ≃ lower sixth, junior year (*US*). (*Aut*) **passer en ~ière** to go into first gear; **c'est de ~ière!*** it's first-class!
5: le ~ âge the first 3 months of life; **le ~ avril** the first of April, April Fool's Day; **~ière communion** first communion; ~ **jour** *[exposition]* first *ou* opening day; **le P~ Mai** the first of May, May Day; ~ **ministre** Prime Minister, Premier; ~ **né** first *ou* eldest child; ~ **plan** (*Phot*) foreground; (*fig*) forefront; **rôle de ~ plan** principal role; **les ~s secours** first aid; **le ~ venu** (*lit*) the first to come; (*fig*) anybody; ~ **violon** leader.
premièrement [prəmjɛrmɑ̃] *adv* (*d'abord*) first(ly); (*en premier lieu*) in the first place, to start with; (*objection*) firstly, for a start.
prémonition [premɔnisjɔ̃] *nf* premonition. ♦ **prémonitoire** *adj* premonitory.
prémunir [premynir] (2) **1** *vt* to protect (*contre* against). **2 se ~** *vpr* to protect o.s. (*contre* from).
prenant, e [prənɑ̃, ɑ̃t] *adj film, activité* absorbing, engrossing; *voix* fascinating, captivating.

prendre [pʀɑ̃dʀ(ə)] (58) **1** *vt* **(a)** (*saisir*) to take. **il l'a pris dans le tiroir** he took *ou* got it out of the drawer; **il prit un journal sur la table** he picked up *ou* took a newspaper from the table; **prends tes lunettes pour lire** put your glasses on to read; **il la prit par le cou** he put his arms round her neck.

(b) (*aller chercher*) *chose* to get, fetch; *personne* to pick up; (*emmener*) to take. **je ne veux plus de ce manteau, tu peux le ~** I don't want this coat any more so you can take *ou* have it; **prends ta chaise et viens ici** bring *ou* fetch your chair over here; **prends du beurre dans le frigo** get some butter out of the fridge.

(c) (*s'emparer de*) (*gén*) to take; *poisson, voleur* to catch. **le voleur s'est fait ~** the robber was caught.

(d) (*surprendre*) to catch; (*duper*) to take in. **~ qn à faire qch** to catch sb doing sth; **se laisser ~ à des paroles aimables** to let o.s. be taken in by soft talk.

(e) *repas* to have; *médicament* to take; *bain, repos* to take, have. **est-ce que vous prendrez du café?** will you have *ou* would you like (some) coffee?; **fais-lui ~ son médicament** give him his medicine; **il a pris son temps!** he took his time (over *ou* about it)!

(f) *métro, direction* to take. **il a pris le train** he took the train *ou* went by train; **je prends le train de 4 heures** I'm catching the 4 o'clock train; **il a pris sa voiture/l'avion pour aller à Lyon** he drove/flew to Lyons, he went by car/air to Lyons.

(g) *billet, essence* to get; *assurance-vie* to take out; *couchette* to book. **nous avons pris une maison** (*loué*) we have taken *ou* rented a house; (*acheté*) we have bought a house.

(h) *client, pensionnaire* to take; *passager* to pick up; *locataire* to take (in); *personnel* to take on.

(i) *renseignement, adresse* to write down, make a note of; *mesures, température* to take; (*sous la dictée*) to take (down). **~ des notes** to take notes; **~ qn en photo** to take a photo of sb.

(j) *risque etc* to take; *air, ton* to put on, assume; *décision* to take, make, come to.

(k) *autorité* to gain. **~ du ventre** to get fat; **~ du poids** to put on weight; **les feuilles prenaient une couleur dorée** the leaves were turning golden-brown.

(l) (*coûter, prélever*) *temps, place, argent* to take; (*faire payer*) to charge. **cela me prend tout mon temps** it takes up all my time; **ce spécialiste prend très cher** this specialist charges very high fees; **~ de l'argent à la banque** to draw (out) *ou* withdraw money from the bank; **la cotisation est prise sur le salaire** the contribution is taken off *ou* deducted from one's salary; **il a dû ~ sur ses économies** he had to dip into his savings.

(m) *coup* to get; *maladie* to catch; *nouvelle, plaisanterie* to take. **~ froid/un rhume** to catch cold/a cold; **qu'est-ce qu'on a pris!** (*reproches*) we didn't half catch it!*; (*défaite*) we took a beating*; (*averse*) we got drenched!

(n) (*manier*) *personne, problème* to handle, tackle.

(o) **~ qn/qch pour** (*considérer*) to take sb/sth for; (*se servir de*) to take *ou* use sb/sth as; **pour qui me prenez-vous?** what do you take me for?, who do you think I am?; **~ qn pour un autre** to mistake sb for sb else.

(p) *[fièvre, remords]* to strike; *[doute, colère]* to seize, sweep over. **être pris de panique** to be panic-stricken; **il me prend l'envie de faire** I feel like doing, I've got an urge to do; **qu'est-ce qui te prend?*** what's the matter with you?, what's come over you?; **quand le froid vous prend** when the cold hits you.

(q) (*coincer*) to catch, trap. **j'ai pris mon manteau *ou* mon manteau s'est pris dans la porte** I caught *ou* trapped my coat in the door, my coat got stuck *ou* caught in the door.

(r) (*locutions*) **à tout ~** on the whole, all in all; **c'est à ~ ou à laisser** take it or leave it; **il faut en ~ et en laisser** you have to take it with a pinch of salt; **c'est toujours ça de pris** that's something at least; **~ sur soi de faire qch** to take it upon o.s. to do sth.

2 *vi* **(a)** *[ciment, pâte]* to set.

(b) *[plante]* to take root; *[vaccin]* to take; *[mode]* to catch on; *[spectacle]* to be a success. **avec moi, ça ne prend pas*** it doesn't work with me*.

(c) *[feu de buches]* to go; *[incendie]* to start; *[bois]* to catch fire.

(d) (*se diriger*) to go. **~ à gauche** to go *ou* turn *ou* bear left.

3 se ~ *vpr* **(a) se ~ au sérieux** to take o.s. seriously; **il se prend pour un intellectuel** he thinks *ou* likes to think he's an intellectual.

(b) s'y ~ to set about (doing) it; **s'y ~ bien/mal pour faire qch** to set about doing sth the right/wrong way; **s'y ~ à deux fois pour faire qch** to try twice to do sth, take two attempts to do sth; **il faut s'y ~ à deux** it needs two of us (to do it); **je ne sais pas comment tu t'y prends, mais ...** I don't know how you manage it but ... .

(c) s'en ~ à (*agresser*) to lay into, set about; (*passer sa colère sur*) to take it out on; (*blâmer*) to lay *ou* put the blame on.

(d) (*se solidifier*) to set hard. **se ~ en glace** to freeze over.

preneur, -euse [pʀənœʀ, øz] *nm,f* (*acheteur*) buyer; (*locataire*) tenant. **je suis ~ à 100 F** I'll buy *ou* take it for 100 francs.

prénom [pʀenɔ̃] *nm* Christian name, first name; (*Admin*) forename, given name (*US*). ◆ **prénommer** (1) *vt* to call, name. **le prénommé Paul** the said Paul; **se ~** to be called *ou* named.

préoccuper [pʀeɔkype] (1) **1** *vt* (*inquiéter*) to worry, bother; (*absorber*) to preoccupy. **l'avenir le préoccupe** he is concerned *ou* anxious about the future; **tu as l'air préoccupé** you look worried, you look as though you've got sth on your mind; **il est uniquement préoccupé de sa petite personne** he only thinks about himself *ou* number one*. **2 se ~** *vpr* (*s'occuper*) to concern o.s. (*de* with); (*s'inquiéter*) to worry (*de* about). **il ne s'en préoccupe guère** he doesn't bother very much about it. ◆ **préoccupant, e** *adj* worrying. ◆ **préoccupation** *nf* (*inquiétude*) worry, anxiety; (*ennui*) worry; (*problème à résoudre*) preoccupation, concern.

préparer [pʀepaʀe] (1) **1** *vt* **(a)** (*gén*) to prepare; *repas* to make; *complot* to hatch; *plan* to draw up; *bagages* to get ready; *peaux, poisson* to dress; *voyage* to get ready for; *examen* to prepare for, study for. **~ l'avenir** to prepare for the future; **il a préparé la rencontre des 2 ministres** he organized the meeting of the 2 ministers; (*Mil, fig*) **~ le terrain** to prepare the ground. **(b) ~ qn à qch/à faire qch** to prepare sb for sth/to do sth; **~ qn à un examen** to prepare *ou* coach sb for an exam; **je n'y étais pas préparé** I wasn't prepared for it, I wasn't expecting it. **(c) ~ qch à qn** to have sth in store for sb; **il nous prépare une surprise** he has a surprise in store for us.

2 se ~ *vpr* **(a)** (*s'apprêter*) to prepare (o.s.), get ready; *[athlète]* to train (*à qch* for sth, *à faire* to do). **elle se prépare** she's getting ready; **préparez-vous à venir** be prepared to come. **(b)** (*lit, fig*) *[orage]* to be brewing. **il se prépare une bagarre** there's going to be a fight; **il se prépare qch de louche** there's sth fishy in the air.

◆ **préparateur, -trice** *nm,f* assistant. ◆ **préparatifs** *nmpl* preparations (*de* for). ◆ **préparation** *nf* (*gén*) preparation (*d'un repas etc* of a meal *etc*, *d'un voyage etc* for a trip *etc*);

[peaux, poisson] dressing (*de* of); (*à épreuve sportive*) training (*à* for). **annoncer qch sans ~** to announce sth abruptly *ou* without preparation; **avoir qch en ~** to have sth in hand *ou* preparation. ♦ **préparatoire** *adj* preparatory, preliminary.

prépondérance [prepɔ̃derɑ̃s] *nf [nation, théorie]* supremacy; *[trait de caractère]* domination. ♦ **prépondérant, e** *adj rôle* dominating.

préposer [prepoze] (1) *vt* to appoint (*à* to). **être préposé à** to be in charge of. ♦ **préposé** *nm* (*Postes*) postman (*ou* woman); (*gén*) employee; *[vestiaire]* attendant.

préposition [prepozisjɔ̃] *nf* preposition.

préretraite [prer(ə)trɛt] *nf* early retirement.

prérogative [prerɔgativ] *nf* prerogative.

près [prɛ] *adv* **(a)** (*espace*) near(by), close (by), near *ou* close at hand; (*temps*) near, close. **c'est plus/moins ~ que je ne croyais** it's nearer *ou* closer than I thought/not as near *ou* close as I thought. **(b) ~ de** (*dans le temps*) close to; (*dans l'espace*) close to, near (to); (*presque*) nearly, almost; **le moins ~ possible de Noël** as far away as possible from Christmas; **ils étaient très ~ l'un de l'autre** they were very close to each other; **elle est ~ de sa mère** she's with her mother; **il est ~ de la retraite** he is close to *ou* nearing retirement; **il en a dépensé ~ de la moitié** he has spent nearly *ou* almost half of it; **il a été ~ de refuser** he was on the point of refusing *ou* about to refuse; (*iro*) **je ne suis pas ~ de partir** at this rate, I'm not likely to be going (yet); (*fig*) **être ~ de son argent** to be close- *ou* tight-fisted. **(c) de ~** (*gén*), *examiner* closely; *surveiller* carefully; **le coup a été tiré de ~** the shot was fired at close range; **il voit mal de ~** he can't see very well close to; **il a vu la mort de ~** he has stared *ou* looked death in the face, he has come within an inch of death. **(d) à peu de chose ~** more or less; **ce n'est pas aussi bon, à beaucoup ~** it's nothing like as good, it's nowhere near as good; **ils sont identiques, à la couleur ~** they are identical apart from *ou* except for the colour; **à cela ~ que ...** apart from the fact that ...; **je vais vous donner le chiffre à un franc ~** I'll give you the figure to within about a franc; **il a raté le bus à une minute ~** he missed the bus by a minute or so; **il n'est pas à 10 minutes/à un kilo de sucre ~** he can spare 10 minutes/a kilo of sugar.

présage [prezaʒ] *nm* omen, sign. **mauvais ~** ill omen. ♦ **présager** (3) *vt* (*annoncer*) to be a sign *ou* an omen of; (*prévoir*) to predict, foresee. **rien ne laissait ~ que** there was nothing to indicate *ou* foretell that.

presbytère [prɛsbitɛr] *nm* presbytery.

prescience [presjɑ̃s] *nf* prescience, foresight.

prescrire [prɛskrir] (39) *vt* (*Méd, Jur*) to prescribe; (*stipuler*) to stipulate; (*ordonner*) to order, command. ♦ **prescription** *nf* prescription; stipulation; order.

préséance [preseɑ̃s] *nf* precedence.

présélectionner [preselɛksjɔne] (1) *vt* (*Rad*) to preset; *candidats* to short-list. ♦ **présélection** *nf* (*gén*) preselection; *[candidats]* short-listing.

présence [prezɑ̃s] *nf* (*gén*) presence; (*au bureau, à l'école*) attendance. **avoir de la ~** to have great presence; **en ~** *armées* opposing; **mettre deux personnes en ~** to bring two people together *ou* face to face; **en ~ de** in (the) presence of; **hors de ma ~** while I was not there, in my absence; **en ~ de tels incidents** faced with such incidents; **~ d'esprit** presence of mind.

présent[1], e [prezɑ̃, ɑ̃t] **1** *adj* (*gén*) present. **ici ~** here present; **être ~ à une cérémonie** to be present at *ou* attend a ceremony; **métal ~ dans un minerai** metal present *ou* found in an ore; **avoir qch ~ à l'esprit** to have sth fresh in one's mind, not to forget about sth. **2** *nm* (*Gram*) present tense. (*époque*) **le ~** the present; (*personnes*) **les ~s** those present; **il y avait 5 ~s** there were 5 people present *ou* there; **à ~** at present, presently (*US*), now; (*de nos jours*) nowadays; **les gens d'à ~** people of today.

présent[2] [prezɑ̃] *nm* (*littér*) gift, present.

présentation [prezɑ̃tasjɔ̃] *nf* (*gén*) presentation; *[nouveau venu]* introduction. **sur ~ du billet** on presentation of the ticket; **faire les ~s** to make the introductions; **~ de mode** fashion show; *[personne]* **avoir une bonne/mauvaise ~** to have a good/poor appearance. ♦ **présentable** *adj* presentable. ♦ **présentateur, -trice** *nm,f* (*Rad, TV*) introducer, presenter.

présentement [prezɑ̃tmɑ̃] *adv* at present, presently (*US*).

présenter [prezɑ̃te] (1) **1** *vt* **(a)** (*gén*), *tableau, pièce de théâtre* to present; *personne* to introduce (*à* to, *dans* into); *marchandises* to display (*à* to), set out (*à* before); (*TV*) *nouvelles* to present; *émission* to compere. **(b)** *facture etc* to present, submit; *passeport* to present, show; *requête, candidat* to put in; *plat* to hold out. **~ le flanc à l'ennemi** to turn one's flank towards the enemy; **~ sa candidature à un poste** to apply for *ou* put in for a job; **présentez armes!** present arms! **(c)** *excuses, félicitations* to present, offer; *respects* to present, pay; *objection* to raise. **(d)** (*exposer*) *problème, idée, théorie* to set out, expound. **travail bien/mal présenté** well-/badly presented *ou* laid-out piece of work; **~ qch sous un jour favorable** to present sth in a favourable light; **il nous a présenté son ami comme un héros** he spoke of his friend as a hero. **(e)** (*laisser paraître*) *avantage, symptôme, danger, obstacle* to show. **cette route présente beaucoup de détours** there are a lot of bends on this road. **(f)** (*Tech: placer*) to position, line up.

2 *vi [personne]* **~ bien/mal** to have a good/poor appearance.

3 se ~ *vpr* **(a)** (*se rendre*) to go, come, appear. **se ~ chez qn** to go to sb's house; **il ne s'est présenté personne** no one came *ou* appeared *ou* turned up. **(b)** *[candidat]* to come forward. **se ~ pour un emploi** to apply for *ou* put in for a job; **se ~ à** *élection* to stand *ou* put o.s. up *ou* run (*US*) for; *examen* to sit, take; *concours* to go in for, enter for. **(c)** (*donner son nom*) to introduce o.s. **(d)** *[solution etc]* to present itself; *[occasion]* to arise, present itself; *[difficulté]* to crop *ou* come up. **un problème se présente à nous** we are faced with a problem; **si une nouvelle occasion se présente** if another opportunity arises; **se ~ à l'esprit** to come *ou* spring to mind. **(e)** (*apparaître*) **se ~ sous forme de cachets** to come in the form of tablets; **l'affaire se présente bien/mal** things are looking good/aren't looking too good; **se ~ sous un nouveau jour** to appear in a new light; **comment cela se présente-t-il?** (*lit*) what does it look like?; (**fig*) how's it going?

préserver [prezerve] (1) *vt* to protect (*de* from, against). **se ~ du soleil** to protect o.s. from the sun; **Dieu m'en préserve!** Heaven preserve me! ♦ **préservation** *nf* preservation, protection.

président [prezidɑ̃] *nm [pays, club]* president; *[comité, firme]* chairman; *[université]* vice-chancellor, president (*US*); *[tribunal]* presiding judge *ou* magistrate. **~ du jury** (*Scol*) chief examiner; (*Jur*) foreman of the jury; **~ du conseil** prime minister; **~ directeur général** chairman and managing director; **Monsieur le ~** (*gén*) Mr President; (*Jur*) your Honour. ♦ **présidence** *nf* presidency; chairmanship; vice-chancellorship; (*résidence*) presidential residence *ou* palace. (*Pol*) **candidat à la ~** presidential candidate. ♦ **présidente** *nf* (*en titre*) (lady *ou* woman) president *etc*; (*épouse*) president's *etc* wife. ♦ **présidentiel, -elle** *adj* presidential.

présider [prezide] (1) **1** *vt* (*gén*) to preside over; *débat* to chair. **~ un dîner** to be the guest of honour at a dinner; **c'est X qui préside** (*séance*) X is in the chair. **2** ~ **à** *vt indir*: ~ **à qch** to govern sth.

présomption [pʀezɔ̃psjɔ̃] *nf* (*supposition*) presumption; (*prétention*) presumptuousness. ♦ **présomptueux, -euse** *adj* presumptuous.

presque [pʀɛsk(ə)] *adv* almost, nearly; (*négatif*) hardly, scarcely. **c'est** ~ **de la folie** it's little short of madness; ~ **rien** hardly *ou* scarcely anything, next to nothing; **la** ~ **totalité des lecteurs** almost *ou* nearly all the readers.

presqu'île [pʀɛskil] *nf* peninsula.

pressant, e [pʀɛsɑ̃, ɑ̃t] *adj besoin, danger* pressing; *travail, désir* urgent; *demande* insistent.

presse [pʀɛs] *nf* **(a)** (*institution*) press; (*journaux*) (news)papers. ~ **automobile** car magazines; (*lit, fig*) **avoir bonne/mauvaise** ~ to be well/badly thought of; **agence** *etc* **de** ~ press agency *etc*. **(b)** (*appareil*) (*gén*) press; (*Typ*) (printing) press. **mettre sous** ~ *livre* to send to press; *journal* to put to bed. **(c)** (*littér: foule*) throng (*littér*), press (*littér*). **(d)** (*urgence*) **il n'y a pas de** ~* there's no rush *ou* hurry. ♦ **presse-citron** *nm inv* lemon squeezer. ♦ **presse-papiers** *nm inv* paperweight. ♦ **presse-purée** *nm inv* potato-masher.

pressentir [pʀesɑ̃tiʀ] (16) *vt* **(a)** *danger* to sense. ~ **que ...** to have a feeling *ou* a premonition that ...; **rien ne laissait** ~ **sa mort** there was nothing to forewarn of *ou* to hint at his death. **(b)** *personne* to sound out, approach. ♦ **pressentiment** *nm* (*intuition*) presentiment, premonition; (*idée*) feeling.

presser [pʀese] (1) **1** *vt* **(a)** *éponge, fruit, objet* to squeeze; *bouton* to press, push; *raisin, disque* to press. **les gens étaient pressés les uns contre les autres** people were squashed up *ou* crushed up against one another. **(b)** ~ **qn de faire** to urge *ou* press sb to do. **(c)** *départ* to hasten, speed up. **(faire)** ~ **qn** to hurry sb (up); **(faire)** ~ **les choses** to speed things up; ~ **le pas** to speed up; **rien ne vous presse** there's no hurry, we're in no rush. **(d)** *débiteur, ennemi* to press. **pressé par le besoin** driven *ou* pressed by need; ~ **qn de questions** to bombard *ou* ply sb with questions. **2** *vi* [*affaire*] to be urgent. **le temps presse** time is short, time presses; **rien ne presse** there's no hurry *ou* rush. **3 se** ~ *vpr* **(a) se** ~ **contre qn** to squeeze up against sb; **se** ~ **autour de qn** to press *ou* crowd round sb; **les gens se pressaient pour entrer** people were pushing to get in. **(b)** (*se hâter*) to hurry (up). **sans se** ~ without hurrying. ♦ **pressé, e** *adj pas* hurried. **être** ~ **(de partir)** to be in a hurry (to leave); **il faut parer au plus** ~ we must do the most urgent thing(s) first, first things first.

pressing [pʀesiŋ] *nm* **(a)** (*repassage*) steam-pressing; (*établissement*) dry-cleaner's. **(b)** (*Sport*) pressure.

pression [pʀesjɔ̃] *nf* **(a)** (*gén, fig, Sci*) pressure. (*Tech*) **mettre sous** ~ to pressurize; **faire** ~ **sur** *objet* to press on; *personne* to put pressure on; **être soumis à des** ~**s** to be under pressure; **bière à la** ~ draught beer. **(b)** (*bouton*) press stud, snap fastener (*US*).

pressoir [pʀeswaʀ] *nm* (*appareil*) press; (*local*) press-house.

pressuriser [pʀesyʀize] (1) *vt* to pressurize. ♦ **pressurisation** *nf* pressurization.

prestance [pʀɛstɑ̃s] *nf* imposing bearing, presence.

prestation [pʀɛstasjɔ̃] *nf* **(a)** (*allocation*) benefit, allowance. ~**s sociales** social security benefits. **(b)** [*hôtel*] ~(s) service. **(c)** [*artiste, sportif*] performance.

preste [pʀɛst(ə)] *adj* (*littér*) nimble.

prestidigitation [pʀɛstidiʒitasjɔ̃] *nf* conjuring. ♦ **prestidigitateur, -trice** *nm,f* conjurer.

prestige [pʀɛstiʒ] *nm* prestige. **voiture** *etc* **de** ~ prestige car *etc*. ♦ **prestigieux, -euse** *adj* prestigious.

présumer [pʀezyme] (1) **1** *vt* to presume, assume. **2** ~ **de** *vt indir*: **trop** ~ **de** to overestimate, overrate.

présupposer [pʀesypoze] (1) *vt* to presuppose.

prêt[1]**, e** [pʀɛ, ɛt] *adj* **(a)** (*préparé*) ready (*à qch* for sth, *à faire* to do). **poulet** ~ **à cuire** oven-ready chicken; **tout est** ~ everything is ready, everything is in readiness; **il est** ~ **à tout** he will do anything, he will stop at nothing. **(b)** (*disposé*) ~ **à** ready *ou* prepared *ou* willing to. ♦ **prêt-à-porter** *nm* ready-to-wear (clothes).

prêt[2] [pʀɛ] *nm* (*action*) loan, lending; (*somme*) loan; (*sur salaire*) advance.

prétendant, e [pʀetɑ̃dɑ̃, ɑ̃t] **1** *nm* (*prince*) pretender; (*amoureux*) suitor. **2** *nm,f* (*candidat*) candidate (*à* for).

prétendre [pʀetɑ̃dʀ(ə)] (41) **1** *vt* **(a)** (*affirmer*) to claim, maintain, assert. **il se prétend médecin** he makes out *ou* claims he's a doctor; **on le prétend très riche** he is said *ou* alleged to be very rich; **à ce qu'il prétend** according to him *ou* to what he says. **(b)** (*avoir la prétention de*) to claim, pretend. **tu ne prétends pas le faire tout seul?** you don't pretend *ou* expect to do it on your own? **(c)** (*littér*) (*vouloir*) to want; (*avoir l'intention de*) to mean, intend. **2** ~ **à** *vt indir* to lay claim to, aspire to. ~ **à faire** to aspire to do. ♦ **prétendu, e** *adj chose* alleged; *personne* so-called, would-be. ♦ **prétendument** *adv* supposedly, allegedly.

prétention [pʀetɑ̃sjɔ̃] *nf* **(a)** (*exigence*) claim. **avoir des** ~**s sur** to lay claim to. **(b)** (*ambition*) pretension, claim (*à* to). **avoir la** ~ **de faire** to claim to be able to do; **sans** ~ *maison, repas* unpretentious; *robe* simple. **(c)** (*vanité*) pretentiousness, pretension. ♦ **prétentieusement** *adv* pretentiously. ♦ **prétentieux, -euse** *adj* pretentious.

prêter [pʀete] (1) **1** *vt* **(a)** *objet, argent* to lend. ~ **qch à qn** to lend sth to sb, lend sb sth; (*fig*) **c'est un prêté pour un rendu** it's tit for tat. **(b)** *sentiment, intention* to attribute, ascribe (*à* to). **on lui prête l'intention de démissionner** he is alleged *ou* claimed *ou* supposed to be going to resign. **(c)** *aide* to give, lend. ~ **main forte à qn** to lend sb a hand, go to sb's help; ~ **la main à un complot** to get involved in *ou* take part in a plot. **(d)** (*locutions*) ~ **attention à** to pay attention to, take notice of; ~ **le flanc à la critique** to lay o.s. open to criticism, invite criticism; ~ **l'oreille** to listen (*à* to); ~ **serment** to take an *ou* the oath; ~ **de l'importance à qch** to accord importance to sth, consider sth to be important. **2** ~ **à** *vt indir*: ~ **à la critique** to be open to *ou* give rise to criticism; ~ **à rire** to be ridiculous *ou* laughable. **3 se** ~ *vpr* **(a)** (*gén*) **se** ~ **à qch** to lend o.s. to sth. **(b)** [*chaussures, cuir*] to give, stretch. ♦ **prêteur, -euse 1** *adj* unselfish. **il n'est pas** ~ he doesn't like lending his things. **2** *nm,f* (money)lender. ~ **sur gages** pawnbroker. ♦ **prête-nom,** *pl* ~**-**~**s** *nm* figurehead.

prétérit [pʀeteʀit] *nm* preterite.

prétexte [pʀetɛkst(ə)] *nm* pretext, excuse. **mauvais** ~ poor *ou* lame excuse; **sous** ~ **de/que** on the pretext *ou* pretence of/that; **sous aucun** ~ on no account. ♦ **prétexter** (1) *vt*: ~ **qch** to give sth as a pretext *ou* an excuse.

prêtre [pʀɛtʀ(ə)] *nm* priest. ♦ **prêtresse** *nf* priestess. ♦ **prêtrise** *nf* priesthood.

preuve [pʀœv] *nf* **(a)** (*gén, Jur, Math*) proof. **pouvez-vous apporter la** ~ **de ce que vous dites?** can you prove what you're saying?, can you produce proof *ou* evidence of what you're saying?; **j'avais prévu cela, la** ~**, j'ai déjà mon billet*** I'd thought of that and to prove it I've already got my ticket; **je n'ai pas de** ~**s** I have no proof *ou* evidence; **il y a 3** ~**s irréfutables qu'il ment** there are

3 definite pieces of evidence to show that he's lying. **(b)** (*locutions*) **faire ~ de** to show; **faire ses ~s** *[personne]* to prove o.s.; *[technique]* to be well-tried; **professeur qui a fait ses ~s** experienced teacher.

prévaloir [prevalwar] (29) **1** *vi* to prevail (*sur* over, *contre* against). **faire ~ ses droits** to insist upon one's rights; **faire ~ son opinion** to win acceptance for one's opinion. **2 se ~** *vpr*: **se ~ de** (*se flatter*) to pride o.s. on; (*profiter*) to take advantage of.

prévenance [prevnɑ̃s] *nf*: **~(s)** thoughtfulness, consideration, kindness. ♦ **prévenant, e** *adj* considerate, kind (*envers* to), thoughtful.

prévenir [prevnir] (22) *vt* **(a)** (*menacer*) to warn (*de qch* about *ou* against sth); (*aviser*) to inform, tell, let know (*de qch* about sth). **~ le médecin** to call the doctor; **partir sans ~** to leave without telling anyone. **(b)** *accident, malheur* to prevent, avoid. **mieux vaut ~ que guérir** prevention is better than cure. **(c)** *besoin, désir* to anticipate; *objection* to forestall. **(d) ~ qn contre qn/en faveur de qn** to prejudice sb against sb/in sb's favour. ♦ **préventif, -ive** *adj* preventive. **à titre ~** as a preventive. ♦ **prévention** *nf* **(a)** *[accident, crime]* prevention. **~ routière** road safety. **(b)** (*Jur*) custody, detention. **(c)** (*préjugé*) prejudice (*contre* against). ♦ **préventivement** *adv* *agir* preventively. ♦ **préventorium** *nm* sanatorium. ♦ **prévenu, e** (*Jur*) **1** *adj* charged (*de* with). **2** *nm,f* defendant, accused (person).

prévoir [prevwar] (24) *vt* **(a)** *événement, conséquence* to foresee, anticipate; *temps* to forecast. **tout laisse ~ une issue rapide** everything points to a rapid solution; **rien ne faisait** *ou* **ne laissait ~ que ...** there was nothing to suggest *ou* to make one think that ...; **on ne peut pas tout ~** you can't think of everything; **plus tôt que prévu** earlier than expected *ou* anticipated. **(b)** *voyage, construction* to plan. **~ de faire qch** to plan to do sth; **au moment prévu** at the appointed *ou* scheduled time; **comme prévu** as planned; **prévu pour lundi** scheduled for Monday. **(c)** *temps, place, argent* to allow; *équipements, repas* to provide. **tout est prévu pour l'arrivée de nos hôtes** everything is organized for the arrival of our guests; **cette voiture est prévue pour 4 personnes** this car is designed to take 4 people; **déposez vos lettres dans la boîte prévue à cet effet** put your letters in the box provided. **(d)** *[loi]* to provide for, make provision for.
♦ **prévisible** *adj* foreseeable. ♦ **prévision** *nf* (*gén*) prediction; (*attente*) expectation. **~s budgétaires** budget estimates; **~s météorologiques** weather forecast; (*action*) **la ~ du temps** weather forecasting; **en ~ de son arrivée** in anticipation *ou* expectation of his arrival.

prévoyance [prevwajɑ̃s] *nf* foresight, forethought. **société de ~** provident society. ♦ **prévoyant, e** *adj* provident.

prier [prije] (7) **1** *vt* (*Rel*) to pray to; (*implorer*) to beg. **il m'a prié de venir** (*demande*) he begged me to come; (*invitation*) he asked *ou* invited me to come; (*ordre*) he requested me to come; **je vous prie de sortir** will you please leave the room; **je vous en prie** (*faites donc*) please do, of course; (*après vous*) after you; (*de rien*) don't mention it, not at all; **voulez-vous ouvrir la fenêtre je vous prie?** would you mind opening the window please?; **il s'est fait ~** he needed coaxing *ou* persuading; **sans se faire ~** without hesitation. **2** *vi* to pray (*pour* for). ♦ **prière** *nf* (*Rel*) prayer; (*demande*) request; (*supplication*) plea, entreaty. **être en ~** to be at prayer *ou* praying; **à la ~ de qn** at sb's request; **~ de ne pas fumer** no smoking (please).

primaire [primer] **1** *adj* (*gén*) primary; (*péj*) *personne* simple-minded; *raisonnement* simplistic. **2** *nm* (*Géol*) Primary, Palaeozoic. (*Scol*) **être en ~** to be in primary school.

primauté [primote] *nf* primacy.

prime[1] [prim] *nf* **(a)** (*cadeau*) free gift. **(b)** (*bonus*) bonus; (*subvention*) premium, subsidy; (*indemnité*) allowance. **~ de transport** transport allowance. **(c)** (*Assurance, Bourse*) premium.

prime[2] [prim] *adj*: **de ~ abord** at first glance; **~ jeunesse** earliest youth; (*Math*) **n ~** n prime.

primer [prime] (1) **1** *vt* (*surpasser*) to prevail over, take precedence over; (*récompenser*) to award a prize to. **2** *vi* to be of prime importance.

primeur [primœr] **1** *nfpl* (*Comm*) **~s** early fruit and vegetables; **marchand de ~s** greengrocer. **2** *nf*: **avoir la ~ d'une nouvelle** to be the first to hear a piece of news.

primevère [primvɛr] *nf* primrose, primula.

primitif, -ive [primitif, iv] **1** *adj* (*gén, Sociol*) primitive; (*originel*) original, first; *couleur* primary; (*sommaire*) *installation* primitive, crude. **2** *nm,f* primitive. ♦ **primitivement** *adv* originally.

primo [primo] *adv* first (of all), firstly.

primordial, e, *mpl* **-aux** [primɔrdjal, o] *adj* essential, primordial.

prince [prɛ̃s] *nm* prince. **être bon ~** to be generous; **habillé comme un ~** dressed like a prince; **~ charmant** Prince Charming; **~ consort** Prince Consort; **~ héritier** crown prince. ♦ **princesse** *nf* princess. ♦ **princier, -ière** *adj* (*lit, fig*) princely.

principal, e, *mpl* **-aux** [prɛ̃sipal, o] **1** *adj bâtiment* main; *employé* chief, head; *question, raison* principal, main. **il a eu l'un des rôles ~aux** he played a major role, he was one of the leading *ou* main figures. **2** *nm* (*Fin*) principal; (*Scol*) principal, head(master); (*Admin*) chief clerk. **c'est le ~** that's the main thing. **3** *nf* (*Gram*) main clause. ♦ **principalement** *adv* principally, mainly, chiefly.

principauté [prɛ̃sipote] *nf* principality.

principe [prɛ̃sip] *nm* principle. **partir du ~ que** to work on the principle *ou* assumption that; **avoir pour ~ de faire** to make it a principle to do, make a point of doing; **par ~** on principle; **en ~** (*d'habitude*) as a rule; (*théoriquement*) in principle; **de ~** *opposition etc* mechanical, automatic; **faire qch pour le ~** to do sth on principle.

printemps [prɛ̃tɑ̃] *nm* spring. **au ~** in (the) spring(time). ♦ **printanier, -ière** *adj soleil* spring; *temps, vêtement* spring-like.

priorité [prijɔrite] *nf* (*gén*) priority. **en ~** as a (matter of) priority; (*Aut*) **avoir la ~** to have right of way (*sur* over). ♦ **prioritaire** *adj* having priority; (*Aut*) having right of way.

pris, prise[1] [pri, priz] *adj* **(a)** *place* taken. **avoir les mains prises** to have one's hands full; **tous les billets sont ~** the tickets are sold out. **(b)** *personne* busy, engaged. **si vous n'êtes pas ~ ce soir ...** if you're free *ou* if you're not busy this evening ... . **(c)** (*Méd*) *nez* stuffed-up; *gorge* hoarse. **les poumons sont ~** the lungs are affected. **(d)** *crème* set; (*gelé*) *eau* frozen. **(e) ~ de peur/remords** stricken with *ou* by fear/remorse; **~ de boisson** under the influence of drink.

prise[2] [priz] **1** *nf* **(a)** (*pour empoigner*) hold, grip; (*pour soulever*) purchase; (*Judo, Alpinisme*) hold. **cette construction offre trop de ~ au vent** this building is too open to the wind. **(b)** (*Chasse, Pêche*) catch; (*Mil, Dames, Échecs*) capture. **(c)** (*Aut*) **être en ~** to be in gear; **en ~ (directe)** in direct drive; (*fig*) **en ~ directe avec** *ou* **sur** switched on to. **(d)** (*Méd*) dose. **(e)** (*locutions*) **avoir ~ sur** to have a hold over; **son attitude donne ~ aux soupçons** his attitude gives rise to *ou* lays him open to suspicion; **aux ~s avec qn/qch** battling *ou* grappling with sb/sth. **2: ~ d'air** air inlet *ou* intake; **~ de bec*** row*, set-to*; **~**

de conscience awareness, realization; ~ **de contact** initial contact *ou* meeting; ~ **de courant** (*mâle*) plug; (*femelle*) socket; ~ **d'eau** water (supply) point; (*robinet*) tap; ~ **d'otages** taking *ou* seizure of hostages; ~ **de position** stand; ~ **de sang** blood test; (*Ciné*) ~ **de son** sound recording; (*Élec, Rad*) ~ **de terre** earth, ground (*US*); ~ **de vue** (*opération*) filming, shooting; (*photo*) shot.

priser [pRize] (1) **1** *vt tabac* to take; (*fig: apprécier*) to prize, value. **2** *vi* to take snuff.

prisme [pRism(ə)] *nm* prism.

prison [pRizɔ̃] *nf* (*lieu*) prison, jail; (*peine*) imprisonment. **mettre/être en** ~ to send to/be in prison *ou* jail; **peine de** ~ prison sentence; **condamné à 3 mois de** ~ **ferme** sentenced to 3 months' imprisonment; **faire de la** ~ **préventive** to be remanded in custody. ♦ **prisonnier, -ière 1** *adj soldat* captive. **être** ~ to be a prisoner (*de* of); ~ **de ses vêtements** imprisoned in one's clothes. **2** *nm,f* prisoner. **faire/retenir qn** ~ to take/hold sb prisoner.

privation [pRivɑsjɔ̃] *nf* (*suppression*) deprivation; (*gén pl: sacrifice*) privation, hardship. **la** ~ **de la vue** the loss of one's sight.

privatiser [pRivatize] (1) *vt entreprise* to put into private hands.

privautés [pRivote] *nfpl* liberties.

privé, e [pRive] **1** *adj* (*gén*) private; (*Presse*) *source* unofficial; (*Jur*) *droit* civil. **2** *nm* (*vie*) private life; (*Comm: secteur*) private sector. **en** ~ in private.

priver [pRive] (1) **1** *vt*: ~ **qn de qch** to deprive sb of sth; ~ **qch d'un élément** to remove an element from sth, strip sth of one of its elements; **privé de connaissance** unconscious; **privé de voix** speechless, unable to speak; **il a été privé de sommeil** he didn't get any sleep; **cela ne me prive pas** (*de vous le donner*) I can spare it; (*de ne plus en manger*) I don't miss it; (*de ne pas y aller*) I don't mind. **2 se** ~ *vpr* to go *ou* do without. **se** ~ **de qch** to go *ou* do without sth, manage without sth; **se** ~ **de dessert** to do without sweet, forego the sweet; **se** ~ **inutilement de qch** to deprive o.s. of sth unnecessarily; **il ne s'est pas privé de le dire** he had no hesitation in saying so; **si tu veux y aller, ne t'en prive pas pour moi** if you want to go don't hold back for me.

privilège [pRivilɛʒ] *nm* (*gén*) privilege. **j'ai eu le** ~ **de faire** I had the privilege of doing, I was privileged to do. ♦ **privilégié, e** *adj* (*gén*) privileged; (*par le sort*) favoured. ♦ **privilégier** (7) *vt* to favour.

prix [pRi] *nm* **(a)** (*gén, fig*) price; *[location, transport]* cost. **quel est le** ~ **du billet de métro?** how much does a ticket on the underground cost?, what is the fare on the underground?; ~ **de revient** cost price; **menu à** ~ **fixe** set price menu; **votre** ~ **sera le mien** name *ou* state your price; **acheter qch à** ~ **d'or** to pay a (small) fortune for sth; **ça n'a pas de** ~ it is priceless; **je vous fais un** ~ **(d'ami)** I'll let you have it at a reduced price, I'll knock a bit off for you*; **y mettre le** ~ to pay a lot for sth; **c'est dans mes** ~ that's within my price-range; (*enchères*) **mettre qch à** ~ to set a reserve price *ou* an upset price (*US*) on sth; **mettre à** ~ **la tête de qn** to put a price on sb's head; **objet de** ~ expensive *ou* pricey object; **j'apprécie votre geste à son juste** ~ I appreciate your gesture for what it's worth; **donner du** ~ **à qch** to make sth more precious; **à tout** ~ at all costs; **à aucun** ~ on no account; **au** ~ **de grands efforts** at the expense of great effort. **(b)** (*récompense*) prize. **le** ~ **Nobel de la paix** the Nobel Peace Prize. **(c)** (*vainqueur*) (*personne*) prizewinner; (*livre*) prize winning book. **(d)** (*Courses*) race. (*Aut*) **Grand** ~ **(automobile)** Grand Prix.

pro [pRo] *nm, préf* pro-.

probable [pRɔbabl(ə)] *adj* probable, likely. **il est peu** ~ **qu'il vienne** he is unlikely to come, there is little chance of his coming. ♦ **probabilité** *nf* probability, likelihood; (*chance*) probability. ♦ **probablement** *adv* probably.

probant, e [pRɔbɑ̃, ɑ̃t] *adj* convincing.

probité [pRɔbite] *nf* probity, integrity.

problème [pRɔblɛm] *nm* problem; (*à débattre*) issue; (*Math*) problem, sum. **enfant à** ~**s** problem child. ♦ **problématique** *adj* problematic(al).

procéder [pRɔsede] (6) **1** *vi* (*agir*) to proceed; (*moralement*) to behave. **2** ~ **à** *vt indir enquête etc* to conduct, carry out. ~ **à l'ouverture de qch** to proceed to open sth. **3** ~ **de** *vt indir* (*littér*) to come from, proceed from. ♦ **procédé** *nm* (*méthode*) process. (*conduite*) ~**(s)** behaviour, conduct.

procédure [pRɔsedyR] *nf* (*gén, Jur*) procedure; (*procès*) proceedings.

procès [pRɔsɛ] *nm* (*civil*) (legal) proceedings, (court) action, lawsuit; (*criminel*) trial. **engager un** ~ **contre qn** to take (court) action against sb, take sb to court, sue sb; **gagner/perdre son** ~ to win/lose one's case; (*fig*) **faire le** ~ **de qn** to put sb on trial (*fig*). ♦ **procès-verbal,** *pl* ~**-**~**aux** *nm* (*compte-rendu*) minutes; (*constat*) report; (*de contravention*) statement. **dresser un** ~ **contre qn** to book sb.

procession [pRɔsesjɔ̃] *nf* (*gén*) procession.

processus [pRɔsesys] *nm* process.

prochain, e [pRɔʃɛ̃, ɛn] **1** *adj* **(a)** (*suivant*) next. **le mois** ~ next month; **la** ~**e fois** next time; **à la** ~**e occasion** at the next *ou* first opportunity; **au revoir, à une** ~**e fois!** goodbye, see you again!; **ce sera pour une** ~**e fois** it'll have to be some other time; **je descends à la** ~**e*** I'm getting off at the next stop. **(b)** (*proche*) *arrivée* imminent; *avenir* near, immediate. **un jour** ~ soon, in the near future. **2** *nm* fellow man. ♦ **prochainement** *adv* soon, shortly.

proche [pRɔʃ] **1** *adj* **(a)** *village* neighbouring, nearby. **être** ~ to be near, be close (by); ~ **de** near, close to; **le magasin le plus** ~ the nearest shop; **de** ~ **en** ~ gradually; **le P**~**-Orient** the Near-East. **(b)** *mort* close, at hand; *départ* imminent. **dans un** ~ **avenir** in the near future; **être** ~ to be drawing near, be at hand; **être** ~ **de** to be close to. **(c)** *événement* close, recent. **(d)** *parent* close, near. **2** *nmpl*: ~**s** close relations, next of kin.

proclamer [pRɔklame] (1) *vt* (*gén*) to proclaim; *décret* to publish; *résultats d'élection* to declare; *résultats d'examen* to announce. ♦ **proclamation** *nf* proclamation; declaration; announcement.

procréer [pRɔkRee] (1) *vt* to procreate. ♦ **procréation** *nf* procreation.

procuration [pRɔkyRɑsjɔ̃] *nf* proxy; (*Fin*) power of attorney.

procurer [pRɔkyRe] (1) **1** *vt* to bring, give. ~ **qch à qn** to get *ou* obtain sth for sb, provide sb with sth. **2 se** ~ *vpr* to get, find, obtain (for o.s.); (*acheter*) to buy (o.s.).

procureur [pRɔkyRœR] *nm* (*Jur*) ~ **(de la République)** public *ou* state prosecutor.

prodigalité [pRɔdigalite] *nf* (*gén*) prodigality, extravagance; (*fig: profusion*) profusion. ~**s** extravagance.

prodige [pRɔdiʒ] **1** *nm* (*événement*) marvel, wonder; (*personne*) prodigy. **tenir du** ~ to be extraordinary; **faire des** ~**s** to work wonders; **grâce à des** ~**s de courage** thanks to his (*ou* her *etc*) prodigious *ou* extraordinary courage. **2** *adj*: **enfant** ~ child prodigy. ♦ **prodigieusement** *adv* fantastically, incredibly, prodigiously. ♦ **prodigieux, -euse** *adj* (*gén*) fantastic, incredible; *effort, personne* prodigious.

prodigue [pRɔdig] **1** *adj* (*dépensier*) extravagant, wasteful, prodigal; (*généreux*) generous. **être** ~ **de** *compliments, argent* to be free with; *temps* to be unsparing of; (*Rel*) **le fils ~** the prodigal son. **2** *nmf* spendthrift.

prodiguer [prɔdige] (1) *vt énergie* to be unsparing of; *conseils* to give; *argent* to be lavish with. **~ qch à qn** to lavish sth on sb.

produire [prɔdɥiʀ] (38) **1** *vt* (*gén, Ciné, Jur*) to produce; *voitures etc* to produce, make; (*Agr*) to produce, grow; *intérêt* to yield, return. **2 se ~** *vpr* **(a)** (*survenir*) to happen, occur, take place. **(b)** *[acteur]* to give a performance, appear. ♦ **producteur, -trice 1** *adj* (*gén, Agr*) producing. **pays ~ de pétrole** oil-producing country, oil producer. **2** *nm,f* (*gén, Ciné, Agr*) producer. ♦ **productif, -ive** *adj* productive. (*Fin*) **~ d'intérêts** interest-bearing. ♦ **production** *nf* **(a)** (*action*) production. **(b)** (*rendement*) (*Ind*) production, output; (*Agr*) production, yield. **(c)** (*produit*) product. **~s** (*Agr*) produce; (*Comm, Ind*) goods. **(d)** (*Ciné*) production. ♦ **productivité** *nf* productivity.

produit [prɔdɥi] *nm* **(a)** (*article*) product; (*Chim*) chemical. **~s** (*Agr*) produce; (*Comm, Ind*) goods, products; **~s finis** finished goods *ou* products; **~s alimentaires** foodstuffs; **~s de beauté** cosmetics; **~ pharmaceutique** pharmaceutical (product). **(b)** (*rapport*) product, yield; (*bénéfice*) profit; (*revenu*) income. **le ~ de la collecte** the proceeds *ou* takings from the collection; **~ national brut** gross national product. **(c)** (*Math*) product.

proéminent, e [prɔeminɑ̃, ɑ̃t] *adj* prominent.

prof* [prɔf] *abrév de* **professeur.**

profane [prɔfan] **1** *adj fête etc* secular. **2** *nmf* **(a)** (*gén*) layman, lay person. **(b)** (*Rel*) non-believer. **3** *nm* (*Rel*) **le ~** the secular. ♦ **profaner** (1) *vt église* to desecrate, profane; *souvenir* to defile. ♦ **profanateur, -trice 1** *adj* profaning. **2** *nm,f* profaner. ♦ **profanation** *nf* desecration, profanation; defilement.

proférer [prɔfeʀe] (6) *vt parole* to utter.

professer [prɔfese] (1) *vt* **(a)** *opinion etc* to profess, declare. **(b)** (*Scol*) to teach.

professeur [prɔfɛsœʀ] *nm* (*gén*) teacher; (*Scol*) (school)teacher; (*Univ*) ≈ lecturer; (*avec chaire*) professor. **~ de piano** piano teacher *ou* master (*ou* mistress).

profession [prɔfɛsjɔ̃] *nf* (*gén*) occupation; (*manuelle*) trade; (*libérale*) profession. (*Admin*) **'sans ~'** 'occupation: none'; **faire ~ d'être artiste** to profess *ou* declare o.s. an artist; (*Rel, fig*) **~ de foi** profession of faith. ♦ **professionnel, -elle 1** *adj activité, maladie* occupational; *formation* vocational; *sportif, secret, faute* professional. **école ~elle** training college. **2** *nm,f* (*gén, Sport*) professional.

professoral, e, *mpl* **-aux** [prɔfɛsɔʀal, o] *adj ton* professorial. ♦ **professorat** *nm*: **le ~** teaching.

profil [prɔfil] *nm* (*gén, fig*) profile; *[voiture]* line. **de ~** in profile. ♦ **profiler** (1) **1** *vt* (*Tech*) (*dessiner*) to profile; (*fabriquer*) to shape. **2 se ~** *vpr [objet]* to stand out, be outlined (*sur, contre* against); *[ennuis, solution]* to emerge.

profit [prɔfi] *nm* (*Comm, Fin*) profit; (*avantage*) benefit, advantage, profit. **être d'un grand ~ à qn** to be of great benefit to sb; **faire du ~** (*gén*) to be economical; *[vêtement]* to wear well; *[rôti]* to go a long way; **vous avez ~ à faire cela** it's in your interest *ou* to your advantage to do that; **tirer ~ de, mettre à ~** *leçon* to profit *ou* benefit from; *malheur des autres* to take advantage of; *invention* to turn to good account; *jeunesse, temps libre* to make the most of; **collecte au ~ des aveugles** collection in aid of the blind. ♦ **profitable** *adj* (*utile*) beneficial, of benefit; (*lucratif*) profitable (*à* to). ♦ **profiter** (1) **1 ~ de** *vt indir* to take advantage of; *jeunesse, vacances* to make the most of. **2 ~ à** *vt indir*: **~ à qn** *[repas, conseil]* to benefit sb; **cette affaire lui a profité** he benefited by that business; **à qui cela profite-t-il?** who stands to gain by it? **3** *vi* (*) *[enfant]* to thrive, grow; (*être économique*) to be economical. ♦ **profiteur, -euse** *nm,f* profiteer.

profond, e [prɔfɔ̃, ɔ̃d] **1** *adj* **(a)** (*lit*) deep. **peu ~** shallow; **~ de 3 mètres** 3 metres deep. **(b)** *nuit, couleur, voix* deep; *soupir* deep, heavy; *sommeil* deep, sound; *silence, mystère, réflexion* deep, profound; *erreur, intérêt, sentiment* profound; *révérence* deep, low; *cause, signification* underlying, deeper; *tendance* deep-seated, underlying. **2** *nm*: **au plus ~ de** (*gén*) in the depths of; **au plus ~ de la nuit** at dead of night. **3** *adv creuser* deep; *planter* deep (down). ♦ **profondément** *adv* deeply; profoundly; *creuser* deep; *s'incliner* low. **~ différent** vastly *ou* profoundly different; **il dort ~** he is sound *ou* fast asleep; **idée ~ ancrée dans les esprits** idea deeply rooted in people's minds; **ça m'est ~ égal** I really couldn't care less. ♦ **profondeur** *nf* **(a)** (*lit*) depth. **à cause du peu de ~** because of the shallowness; **creuser en ~** to dig deep; **avoir 10 mètres de ~** to be 10 metres deep *ou* in depth; **les ~s** the depths (*de* of). **(b)** *[personne, remarque]* profundity; *[sentiment, regard]* depth. **en ~** *agir* in depth; *réforme* radical.

profusion [prɔfyzjɔ̃] *nf* (*gén*) profusion; *[idées]* wealth. **il y a des fruits à ~** there is fruit galore* *ou* in plenty, there is plenty of fruit.

progéniture [prɔʒenityʀ] *nf* offspring.

programme [prɔgʀam] *nm* **(a)** (*gén*) programme, program (*US*); (*emploi du temps*) timetable; (*Ordinateurs*) program. **au ~** in the programme. **(b)** (*Scol*) (*d'une matière*) syllabus; (*d'une classe, d'une école*) curriculum. **les œuvres du ~** the set books, the books on the syllabus. ♦ **programmation** *nf* programming. ♦ **programmer** (1) *vt émission* to bill; *ordinateur* to program; (*: *prévoir*) to plan. ♦ **programmeur, -euse** *nm,f* (computer) programmer.

progrès [prɔgʀɛ] *nm* (*gén*) progress. **faire des ~** to make progress; **élève en ~** pupil who is making progress *ou* who is getting on (well); **il y a du ~** there is some progress *ou* improvement; **suivre les ~ de** to follow the progress of. ♦ **progresser** (1) *vi* **(a)** (*s'améliorer*) to progress, get *ou* come on well. **(b)** (*avancer*) to advance, progress; *[théorie]* to gain ground, make headway. ♦ **progressif, -ive** *adj* progressive. ♦ **progression** *nf* **(a)** (*gén*) progress; *[ennemi]* advance; *[maladie]* progression. **(b)** (*Math, Mus*) progression. ♦ **progressiste** *adj, nmf* progressive. ♦ **progressivement** *adv* progressively.

prohiber [prɔibe] (1) *vt* to prohibit, ban, forbid. ♦ **prohibitif, -ive** *adj* prohibitive. ♦ **prohibition** *nf* prohibition.

proie [pʀwa] *nf* (*lit, fig*) prey. **être la ~ de** to fall prey to, be the prey of; **être en ~ à** *maladie* to be a victim of; *douleur* to be tortured by; *émotion* to be prey to.

projecteur [prɔʒɛktœʀ] *nm* **(a)** *[film]* projector. **(b)** (*lampe*) *[théâtre]* spotlight; *[bateau]* searchlight; *[monument]* floodlight.

projectile [prɔʒɛktil] *nm* missile, projectile.

projection [prɔʒɛksjɔ̃] *nf* **(a)** *[film]* (*action*) projection; (*séance*) showing. **appareil de ~** projector; **salle de ~** film theatre; **cabine de ~** projection room. **(b)** *[pierres etc]* throwing; *[vapeur]* discharge. ♦ **projectionniste** *nmf* projectionist.

projet [prɔʒɛ] *nm* **(a)** (*dessein*) plan. **faire le ~ de faire** to make plans to do; **ce ~ de livre** this plan for a book; **c'est encore en ~** it's still only at the planning stage. **(b)** (*ébauche*) *[roman]* (preliminary) draft; *[maison]* plan. **~ de loi** bill; **établir un ~ de contrat** to draft a contract.

projeter [prɔʒte] (4) **1** *vt* **(a)** (*envisager*) to plan (*de faire* to do). **(b)** (*jeter*) (*gén*) to throw, fling; *gravillons* to throw up; *étincelles* to throw off; *fumée* to send out, discharge. **(c)** *ombre, reflet* to cast, project, throw; *diapositive* to project, show. **2 se** ~ *vpr [ombre]* to be cast, fall (*sur* on).

prolétaire [pʀɔletɛʀ] *nm* proletarian. ♦ **prolétariat** *nm* proletariat. ♦ **prolétarien, -ienne** *adj* proletarian.

prolifération [pʀɔlifeʀɑsjɔ̃] *nf* proliferation. ♦ **proliférer** (6) *vi* to proliferate. ♦ **prolifique** *adj* prolific.

prologue [pʀɔlɔg] *nm* prologue (*à* to).

prolonger [pʀɔlɔ̃ʒe] (3) **1** *vt* (*gén*) to prolong; *billet* to extend; *rue, mur* to extend, continue. **2 se** ~ *vpr* (*gén*) to go on, carry on, continue; *[effet]* to last, persist.
♦ **prolongation** *nf* prolongation; extension. (*Ftbl*) ~s extra time. ♦ **prolongé, e** *adj* prolonged. ♦ **prolongement** *nm [route]* continuation; *[bâtiment, affaire]* extension. **être dans le** ~ **de qch** to run *ou* lead straight on from sth; (*suites*) ~s repercussions, effects.

promenade [pʀɔmnad] *nf* **(a)** (*à pied*) walk, stroll; (*en voiture*) drive, ride; (*en bateau*) sail; (*en vélo, à cheval*) ride. **faire une** ~/**être en** ~ to go out/be out for a walk (*ou* a drive *etc*). **(b)** (*avenue*) walk, esplanade. ♦ **promener** (5) **1** *vt*: **(emmener)** ~ **qn** to take sb (out) for a walk *ou* stroll; **cela te promènera** that will get you out for a while; (*péj*) ~ **qch/qn partout*** to trail sb/sth everywhere; ~ **ses regards/ses doigts sur qch** to run one's eyes/one's fingers over sth. **2 se** ~ *vpr* to go for a walk (*ou* drive *etc*); *[regards, doigts]* to wander. **ses affaires se promènent toujours partout*** his things are always lying around all over the place. ♦ **promeneur, -euse** *nm,f* walker, stroller.

promesse [pʀɔmɛs] *nf* promise; (*Comm*) commitment, undertaking. ~ **en l'air** empty *ou* vain promise; ~ **d'achat** commitment to buy; **faire une** ~ to make a promise, give one's word; **j'ai sa** ~ I have his word for it; (*fig*) **plein de** ~s very promising.

prometteur, -euse [pʀɔmɛtœʀ, øz] *adj début, signe* promising.

promettre [pʀɔmɛtʀ(ə)] (56) **1** *vt* (*gén, fig*) to promise. **je te le promets** I promise (you); **il a promis de venir** he promised to come; **il m'a promis de venir** *ou* **qu'il viendrait** he promised me that he would come; ~ **la lune** to promise the moon *ou* the earth; ~ **son cœur** to pledge one's heart; **on nous promet du beau temps** we are promised *ou* we are in for* some fine weather; **le dîner promet d'être réussi** the dinner promises to be a success; **cet enfant promet** this child shows promise *ou* is promising; (*iro*) **ça promet!** that's a good start! (*iro*), that's promising! (*iro*).
2 se ~ *vpr*: **se** ~ **de faire** to mean *ou* resolve to do; **se** ~ **du bon temps** to promise o.s. a good time.
♦ **promis, e** *adj*: **être** ~ **à qch** to be destined for sth.

promiscuité [pʀɔmiskɥite] *nf* lack of privacy (*de* in).

promontoire [pʀɔmɔ̃twaʀ] *nm* headland, promontory.

promotion [pʀɔmosjɔ̃] *nf [employé, produit]* promotion; (*Scol: année*) year. ~ **sociale** social advancement; **(article en)** ~ (item on) special offer. ♦ **promoteur, -trice** *nm,f* (*Constr*) property developer; (*instigateur*) promoter. ♦ **promotionnel, -elle** *adj article* on (special) offer; *vente* promotional. ♦ **promouvoir** (27) *vt* to promote (*à* to).

prompt, prompte [pʀɔ̃, pʀɔ̃t] *adj* (*gén*) swift, rapid, quick; *réaction* prompt, swift; *départ, changement* sudden. ~ **rétablissement!** get well soon!; ~ **à agir** swift *ou* quick to act. ♦ **promptement** *adv* swiftly; rapidly; quickly; promptly; suddenly. ♦ **promptitude** *nf* swiftness; rapidity; quickness; promptness; suddenness.

promulguer [pʀɔmylge] (1) *vt* to promulgate.

prôner [pʀone] (1) *vt* (*vanter*) to extol; (*préconiser*) to advocate.

pronom [pʀɔnɔ̃] *nm* pronoun. ♦ **pronominal, e,** *mpl* **-aux** *adj* pronominal. **verbe** ~ reflexive verb.

prononcer [pʀɔnɔ̃se] (3) **1** *vt* **(a)** (*articuler*) to pronounce. **mal** ~ **un mot** to mispronounce a word; ~ **distinctement** to speak clearly. **(b)** (*dire*) *parole, nom* to utter; *discours* to make, deliver. **(c)** *sentence, dissolution* to pronounce. **2 se** ~ *vpr* **(a)** to reach *ou* come to a decision, give a verdict (*sur* on). **se** ~ **en faveur de** to pronounce o.s. in favour of. **(b)** *[mot]* to be pronounced.
♦ **prononcé, e** *adj accent, goût, trait* marked, pronounced. ♦ **prononciation** *nf* pronunciation. **il a une bonne** ~ he speaks clearly; (*langue étrangère*) he has a good pronunciation; **défaut de** ~ speech impediment *ou* defect.

pronostic [pʀɔnɔstik] *nm* forecast. ♦ **pronostiquer** (1) *vt* (*prédire*) to forecast; (*être le signe de*) to foretell, be a sign of. ♦ **pronostiqueur, -euse** *nm,f* (*gén*) forecaster; (*Courses*) tipster.

propagande [pʀɔpagɑ̃d] *nf* propaganda. **faire de la** ~ **pour qch/qn** to push *ou* plug* sth/sb.

propager [pʀɔpaʒe] (3) **1** *vt foi, idée* to propagate; *nouvelle, maladie* to spread. **2 se** ~ *vpr* (*gén*) to spread; (*Phys*) *[onde]* to be propagated; (*Bio*) *[espèce]* to propagate. ♦ **propagateur, -trice** *nm,f* propagator; spreader. ♦ **propagation** *nf* propagation; spreading.

propane [pʀɔpan] *nm* propane.

propension [pʀɔpɑ̃sjɔ̃] *nf* propensity (*à qch* for sth, *à faire* to do).

prophète [pʀɔfɛt] *nm* prophet. ♦ **prophétesse** *nf* prophetess. ♦ **prophétie** *nf* prophecy. ♦ **prophétique** *adj* prophetic. ♦ **prophétiser** (1) *vt* to prophesy.

propice [pʀɔpis] *adj* (*gén*) favourable (*à* to); *circonstance* auspicious, propitious. **moment** ~ opportune moment.

proportion [pʀɔpɔʀsjɔ̃] *nf* (*gén*) proportion. (*rapport*) **la** ~ **entre hauteur et largeur** the proportion *ou* relation of height to width, the ratio between height and width; **en** ~ in proportion (*de* to); **hors de** ~ out of proportion (*avec* to); **toutes** ~**s gardées** relatively speaking, making due allowance(s). ♦ **proportionné, e** *adj*: ~ **à** proportional *ou* proportionate to; **bien** ~ well-proportioned. ♦ **proportionnel, -elle** *adj* proportional. ~ **à** proportional *ou* proportionate to. ♦ **proportionnellement** *adv* proportionally, proportionately (*à* to). ♦ **proportionner** (1) *vt* to proportion.

propos [pʀɔpo] *nm* **(a)** (*paroles*) talk, remarks, words. **(b)** (*littér: intention*) intention. **de** ~ **délibéré** deliberately, on purpose. **(c)** (*sujet*) subject. **à quel** ~ **voulait-il me voir?** what did he want to see me about?; **à** ~ **de ta voiture** about your car, on the subject of your car; **je vous écris à** ~ **de l'annonce** I am writing regarding *ou* concerning the advertisement *ou* in connection with the advertisement; **à ce** ~ in this connection. **(d)** (*lit, fig*) **arriver à** ~ to come at the right moment *ou* time; *[fait]* **arriver mal à** ~ to happen (just) at the wrong moment *ou* time; **juger à** ~ **de faire qch** to see fit to do sth; **à** ~**, dis-moi ...** incidentally *ou* by the way, tell me ... .

proposer [pʀɔpoze] (1) **1** *vt* **(a)** (*suggérer*) (*gén*) to suggest, propose (*de faire* doing); *solution, candidat* to put forward. ~ **qch à qn** to suggest sth to sb; **je vous propose de passer me voir** I would suggest that you come round and see me. **(b)** (*offrir*) *aide, prix, situation* to offer. ~ **de faire** to offer to do; ~ **qch à qn** to offer sth to sb, offer sb sth.
2 se ~ *vpr* **(a)** (*offrir ses services*) to offer one's services. **se** ~ **pour faire qch** to offer to do sth. **(b)** *but, tâche* to set o.s. **se** ~ **de faire qch** to intend *ou* mean *ou* propose to do sth.
♦ **proposition** *nf* **(a)** (*suggestion, offre*) proposal,

proposition. (*Pol*) ~ **de loi** private bill; **sur** ~ **de** at the proposal of. **(b)** (*Math, Philos, déclaration*) proposition. **(c)** (*Gram*) clause. ~ **principale** main clause.

propre[1] [pʀɔpʀ(ə)] **1** *adj* **(a)** (*pas sali*) clean; (*net*) *personne, vêtement* neat, tidy; *travail, cahier* neat. ~ **comme un sou neuf** as neat *ou* clean as a new pin; **ce n'est pas** ~ **de manger avec les doigts** it's messy to eat with your fingers; **nous voilà** ~**s!*** now we're in a fine *ou* proper mess!* **(b)** (*qui ne salit pas*) *chien* house-trained; *enfant* toilet-trained. **(c)** (*honnête*) honest, decent. **2** *nm*: **sentir le** ~ to smell clean; **recopier qch au** ~ to make a fair copy of sth; **c'est du** ~**!*** (*gâchis*) what a mess!; (*comportement*) it's an absolute disgrace!

propre[2] [pʀɔpʀ(ə)] **1** *adj* **(a)** (*possessif*) own. **par ses** ~**s moyens** *réussir* on one's own; *rentrer* under one's own steam; **ce sont ses** ~**s mots** those are his own *ou* his very *ou* his actual words; **de son** ~ **chef** on his own initiative. **(b)** (*spécifique*) ~ **à** peculiar to, characteristic of; **c'est un trait qui lui est** ~ it's a distinctive *ou* specific characteristic of his. **(c)** (*qui convient*) suitable, appropriate (*à* for). **le mot** ~ the right *ou* proper word. **(d)** (*de nature à*) **un poste** ~ **à lui apporter des satisfactions** a job likely to bring him satisfaction. **(e)** (*Ling*) *sens d'un mot* literal. **2** *nm* **(a)** (*qualité*) **c'est le** ~ **de qch** it's a peculiarity *ou* (distinctive) feature of sth; **avoir qch en** ~ to have exclusive possession of sth; **cette caractéristique que la France possède en** ~ this feature which is peculiar *ou* exclusive to France. **(b)** (*Ling*) **au** ~ in the literal sense, literally.

propre-à-rien, *pl* ~**s-**~**-**~ [pʀɔpʀaʀjɛ̃] *nmf* good-for-nothing.

proprement [pʀɔpʀəmɑ̃] *adv* **(a)** (*avec propreté*) cleanly; (*avec netteté*) neatly, tidily; (*comme il faut*) properly; (*fig: décemment*) decently. **mange** ~! eat properly! **(b)** (*exactement*) exactly, literally; (*exclusivement*) specifically, strictly. **à** ~ **parler** strictly speaking; **le village** ~ **dit** the actual village, the village itself; **c'est** ~ **scandaleux** it's absolutely disgraceful.

propreté [pʀɔpʀəte] *nf* (*V* **propre**[1]) cleanliness, cleanness; neatness; tidiness; (*hygiène*) hygiene.

propriété [pʀɔpʀijete] *nf* **(a)** (*droit*) ownership, property. ~ **artistique** artistic copyright; **posséder en toute** ~ to have sole ownership of. **(b)** (*maison*) property; (*terres*) property, land. ~ **bâtie/non bâtie** developed/undeveloped property; ~ **privée** private property. **(c)** (*qualité*) property. **(d)** (*correction*) *[mot]* appropriateness, suitability. ♦ **propriétaire 1** *nm* (*gén*) owner; *[entreprise]* proprietor; *[appartement loué]* landlord. **il est** ~ he owns his house; ~ **récoltant** grower; ~ **terrien** landowner; ~ **foncier** property owner. **2** *nf* owner; proprietress; landlady.

propulser [pʀɔpylse] (1) *vt* **(a)** *[moteur]* to propel, drive. **(b)** (*projeter*) to hurl, fling. ♦ **propulseur 1** *adj* propulsive, driving. **2** *nm* propeller. ♦ **propulsion** *nf* propulsion. **à** ~ **atomique** atomic-powered.

prorata [pʀɔʀata] *nm inv*: **au** ~ **de** in proportion to.

proroger [pʀɔʀɔʒe] (3) *vt durée* to extend; *échéance* to put back, defer; *séance* to adjourn; (*Parl*) to prorogue. ♦ **prorogation** *nf* extension; deferment; adjournment; prorogation.

prosaïque [prozaik] *adj* mundane, prosaic. ♦ **prosaïquement** *adv* mundanely, prosaically.

proscrire [pʀɔskʀiʀ] (39) *vt chose* to ban, prohibit, proscribe; *personne* (*mettre hors la loi*) to outlaw, proscribe; (*exiler*) to banish, exile. ~ **une expression de son style** to banish an expression from one's style. ♦ **proscription** *nf* banning; prohibition; proscription; banishment. ♦ **proscrit, e** *nm,f* (*hors-la-loi*) outlaw; (*exilé*) exile.

prose [pʀoz] *nf* (*gén*) prose; (*hum: lettre*) letter. **poème en** ~ prose poem.

prospecter [pʀɔspɛkte] (1) *vt* (*Min*) to prospect; (*Comm*) to canvass. ♦ **prospecteur, -trice** *nm,f* prospector. ♦ **prospection** *nf* prospecting; canvassing.

prospectus [pʀɔspɛktys] *nm* (*tract*) leaflet, handout; (*dépliant*) brochure, leaflet.

prospère [pʀɔspɛʀ] *adj commerce, santé* flourishing; *finances* thriving; *pays, commerçant* prosperous, affluent. ♦ **prospérer** (6) *vi* to flourish; to thrive; to prosper. ♦ **prospérité** *nf* (*matérielle, économique*) prosperity; *[finances]* thriving state.

prostate [pʀɔstat] *nf* prostate (gland).

prosterner [pʀɔstɛʀne] (1) **1** *vt* (*littér*) to bow low. **2 se** ~ *vpr* (*s'incliner*) to bow down, prostrate o.s. (*devant* before); (*fig: s'humilier*) to grovel (*devant* before). ♦ **prosterné, e** *adj* prostrate.

prostituer [pʀɔstitɥe] (1) **1** *vt* to prostitute. **2 se** ~ *vpr* (*lit, fig*) to prostitute o.s. ♦ **prostituée** *nf* prostitute. ♦ **prostitution** *nf* (*lit, fig*) prostitution.

prostration [pʀɔstʀɑsjɔ̃] *nf* prostration. ♦ **prostré, e** *adj* prostrate.

protagoniste [pʀɔtagɔnist(ə)] *nm* protagonist.

protection [pʀɔtɛksjɔ̃] *nf* (*défense*) protection; (*patronage*) patronage; (*blindage*) armour-plating. **mesures de** ~ protective measures; **prendre qn sous sa** ~ to give sb one's protection (*ou* patronage); ~ **de la nature** preservation *ou* protection of the countryside. ♦ **protecteur, -trice 1** *adj* (*gén*) protective (*de* of); *ton, air* patronizing. **2** *nm,f* (*défenseur*) protector, guardian; *[arts]* patron. **3** *nm* (*souteneur*) pimp (*péj*). ♦ **protectionnisme** *nm* protectionism. ♦ **protectionniste** *adj, nmf* protectionist. ♦ **protectorat** *nm* protectorate.

protéger [pʀɔteʒe] (6 *et* 3) **1** *vt* (*gén*) to protect; (*moralement*) to guard, shield; (*des éléments*) to protect, shelter (*de* from); (*fig: patronner*) to patronize. **2 se** ~ *vpr* to protect o.s. ♦ **protégé, e** *nm,f* protégé; protégée; (*:*favori*) favourite, pet*. ♦ **protège-cahier,** *pl* ~**-**~**s** *nm* exercise-book cover.

protéine [pʀɔtein] *nf* protein.

protestant, e [pʀɔtɛstɑ̃, ɑ̃t] *adj, nm,f* Protestant. ♦ **protestantisme** *nm* Protestantism.

protester [pʀɔtɛste] (1) *vti* to protest (*contre* against, about). ~ **de son innocence** to protest one's innocence. ♦ **protestataire 1** *adj personne* protesting; *marche* protest. **2** *nmf* protester. ♦ **protestation** *nf* (*plainte*) protest; (*déclaration*) protestation, profession.

prothèse [pʀɔtɛz] *nf* prosthesis. ~ **(dentaire)** dentures.

protocole [pʀɔtɔkɔl] *nm* **(a)** (*étiquette*) etiquette; (*Pol*) protocol. **(b)** (*procès-verbal*) protocol. ~ **d'accord** draft treaty. ♦ **protocolaire** *adj cérémonie* formal.

prototype [pʀɔtɔtip] *nm* prototype.

protubérance [pʀɔtybeʀɑ̃s] *nf* bulge, protuberance. ♦ **protubérant, e** *adj* bulging, protuberant, protruding.

proue [pʀu] *nf* bow, bows, prow.

prouesse [pʀuɛs] *nf* (*littér*) feat. (*fig*) **faire des** ~**s** to work miracles.

prouver [pʀuve] (1) *vt* (*gén*) to prove. **cela prouve que ...** it proves *ou* shows that ...; **cela n'est pas prouvé** there's no proof of it, that hasn't been proved; **il a voulu se** ~ **qu'il en était capable** he wanted to prove to himself that he was capable of it.

provenir [pʀɔvniʀ] (22) ~ **de** *vt indir pays* to come from; *cause* to be due to, be the result of. ♦ **provenance** *nf [objet]* origin; *[coutume]* source. **j'ignore la** ~ **de cette lettre** I don't know where this letter comes from; **en** ~ **de l'Angleterre** from England.

proverbe [pRɔvɛRb(ə)] *nm* proverb. ♦ **proverbial, e,** *mpl* **-aux** *adj* proverbial.
providence [pRɔvidɑ̃s] *nf* (*Rel*) providence; (*fig: sauveur*) guardian angel. (*fig*) **ça a été notre** ~ it was our salvation. ♦ **providentiel, -elle** *adj* providential. ♦ **providentiellement** *adv* providentially.
province [pRɔvɛ̃s] *nf* province. **vivre en** ~ to live in the provinces; **ville de** ~ provincial town. ♦ **provincial, e,** *mpl* **-aux** *adj, nm,f* provincial.
proviseur [pRɔvizœR] *nm* head(master) (*of a lycée*).
provision [pRɔvizjɔ̃] *nf* **(a)** (*réserve*) stock, supply. **faire** ~ **de** to stock up with, get in a stock *ou* supply of. **(b)** ~s (*vivres*) provisions, food; (*courses*) groceries; **faire ses** ~**s** to go shopping; **filet à** ~**s** shopping bag. **(c)** (*arrhes*) deposit. (*Banque*) **y a-t-il** ~ **au compte?** are there sufficient funds in the account?
provisoire [pRɔvizwaR] *adj mesure, gouvernement* provisional, temporary; *bonheur, installation* temporary. **à titre** ~ temporarily, provisionally; **c'est du** ~ it's a temporary arrangement. ♦ **provisoirement** *adv* for the time being.
provoquer [pRɔvɔke] (1) *vt* **(a)** (*inciter*) ~ **qn à** to incite sb to. **(b)** (*défier*) to provoke. ~ **qn en duel** to challenge sb to a duel. **(c)** *accident, révolte etc* to cause; *réaction* to provoke, produce; *gaieté, commentaires* to give rise to; *colère, curiosité* to arouse. **le malade est sous sommeil provoqué** the patient is in an induced sleep. ♦ **provocant, e** *adj* provocative. ♦ **provocateur, -trice 1** *adj* provocative. **2** *nm* agitator. ♦ **provocation** *nf* provocation.
proxénète [pRɔksenɛt] *nm* procurer.
proximité [pRɔksimite] *nf* proximity. **à** ~ close by, near at hand; **à** ~ **de** near (to), in proximity to.
prude [pRyd] **1** *adj* prudish. **2** *nf* prude.
prudent, e [pRydɑ̃, ɑ̃t] *adj* (*circonspect*) cautious, prudent; (*sage*) wise, sensible; (*réservé*) cautious. **il serait** ~ **de faire** you would be well-advised to do, it is advisable to do; **ce n'est pas** ~ it's not advisable; **c'est plus** ~ it's wiser *ou* safer; **soyez** ~! be careful!, take care! ♦ **prudemment** *adv* cautiously, prudently; wisely, sensibly. ♦ **prudence** *nf* caution, cautiousness, prudence; wisdom. **par** ~ as a precaution, to be on the safe side; **il a eu la** ~ **de partir** he had the good sense *ou* he was wise enough to leave.
prune [pRyn] **1** *nf* (*fruit*) plum; (*alcool*) plum brandy. **pour des** ~**s*** for nothing; **des** ~**s!*** not likely!* **2** *adj inv* plum-coloured. ♦ **pruneau,** *pl* ~**x** *nm* prune; (*: *balle*) slug*. ♦ **prunier** *nm* plum tree.
prunelle [pRynɛl] *nf* **(a)** (*Bot*) sloe; (*eau-de-vie*) sloe gin. **(b)** (*pupille*) pupil. **il y tient comme à la** ~ **de ses yeux** it's the apple of his eye.
psalmodier [psalmɔdje] (7) *vt* to chant.
psaume [psom] *nm* psalm.
pseudo- [psødɔ] *préf* (*gén*) pseudo-; (*péj*) bogus (*péj*).
pseudonyme [psødɔnim] *nm* (*gén*) assumed name; *[écrivain]* pen name; *[comédien]* stage name.
psychanalyse [psikanaliz] *nf* psychoanalysis. ♦ **psychanalyser** (1) *vt* to psychoanalyze. ♦ **psychanalyste** *nmf* psychoanalyst. ♦ **psychanalytique** *adj* psychoanalytic(al).
psychiatre [psikjatR(ə)] *nmf* psychiatrist. ♦ **psychiatrie** *nf* psychiatry. ♦ **psychiatrique** *adj troubles* psychiatric; *hôpital* psychiatric, mental.
psychique [psiʃik] *adj* psychological, psychic(al). ♦ **psychisme** *nm* psyche.
psychologie [psikɔlɔʒi] *nf* psychology. ♦ **psychologique** *adj* psychological. ♦ **psychologiquement** *adv* psychologically. ♦ **psychologue** *nmf* psychologist. (*fig*) **être** ~ to be a good psychologist. ♦ **psychose** *nf* (*Psych*) psychosis; (*fig: obsession*) obsessive fear (*de* of).
puant, e [pɥɑ̃, ɑ̃t] *adj* (*lit*) stinking, foul-smelling; (*fig*) *personne* obnoxious. ♦ **puanteur** *nf* stink, stench.
puberté [pybɛRte] *nf* puberty.
public, -ique [pyblik] **1** *adj* (*gén*) public. **danger** ~ public danger; **rendre** ~ *nouvelle* to make public.
2 *nm* (*population*) (general) public; (*assistance*) audience. **des huées s'élevèrent du** ~ boos rose from the audience *ou* public; **un** ~ **clairsemé assistait au match** the match was attended by very few spectators; **le** ~ **est informé que ...** the public is advised that ...; **en** ~ in public; **roman destiné au grand** ~ novel written for the general reader *ou* public.
publication [pyblikɑsjɔ̃] *nf* (*gén*) publication.
publicité [pyblisite] *nf* **(a)** (*méthode, profession*) advertising. (*Comm, fig*) **faire de la** ~ **pour qch** to advertise sth. **(b)** (*annonce*) advertisement, ad(vert)*. **(c)** (*révélations*) publicity. **faire de la** ~ **autour de qch** to give sth a lot of publicity. ♦ **publicitaire** *adj* (*gén*) advertising; *film, voiture* publicity. **vente** ~ promotional sale.
publier [pyblije] (7) *vt* to publish. **ça vient d'être publié** it has just come out *ou* been published.
publiquement [pyblikmɑ̃] *adv* publicly.
puce [pys] *nf* flea. **cela m'a mis la** ~ **à l'oreille** that started me thinking; **les** ~**s, le marché aux** ~**s** the flea market; **oui, ma** ~* yes, pet*; **jeu de** ~**s** tiddlywinks. ♦ **puceron** *nm* greenfly.
pudeur [pydœR] *nf* (*sexuelle*) sense of modesty *ou* decency; (*délicatesse*) sense of propriety. ♦ **pudibond, e** *adj* prudish. ♦ **pudibonderie** *nf* prudishness. ♦ **pudique** *adj* (*chaste*) modest; (*discret*) discreet. ♦ **pudiquement** *adv* modestly; discreetly.
puer [pɥe] (1) **1** *vi* to stink, reek. **2** *vt* to stink *ou* reek of.
puéricultrice [pɥeRikyltRis] *nf* paediatric nurse. ♦ **puériculture** *nf* paediatric nursing.
puéril, e [pɥeRil] *adj* puerile, childish. ♦ **puérilité** *nf* (*caractère*) puerility, childishness; (*acte*) childish act.
pugilat [pyʒila] *nm* (fist)fight.
puis [pɥi] *adv* then. (*en outre*) **et** ~ and besides; **et** ~ **c'est tout** and that's all; **et** ~ **après?** (*ensuite*) and what next?, and then what?; (*et alors?*) so what?, what of it?
puisard [pɥizaR] *nm* cesspool.
puiser [pɥize] (1) *vt* to draw (*dans* from). ~ **dans son sac** to dip into one's bag.
puisque [pɥisk(ə)] *conj* as, since, seeing that. (*intensif*) ~ **je te le dis!** I'm telling you (so)!
puissance [pɥisɑ̃s] *nf* (*gén, fig, Pol, Sci*) power; *[vent]* strength, force. **avoir une grande** ~ **de travail** to have a great capacity for work; **avoir une grande** ~ **d'imagination** to have a very powerful imagination *ou* great powers of imagination; (*Aut*) ~ **fiscale** engine rating; (*Jur*) ~ **paternelle** parental authority; (*Math*) **10** ~ **4** 10 to the power of 4, 10 to the 4th; **exister en** ~ to have a potential existence; **c'est là en** ~ it is potentially present. ♦ **puissamment** *adv* (*fortement*) powerfully; (*beaucoup*) greatly. ♦ **puissant, e 1** *adj* (*gén*) powerful. **2** *nm*: **les** ~**s** the mighty *ou* powerful.
puits [pɥi] *nm [eau, pétrole]* well; (*Min*) shaft; (*Constr*) well, shaft. ~ **d'aération/d'extraction** ventilation/winding shaft; (*Min*) ~ **à ciel ouvert** opencast mine; ~ **de science** well of learning.
pull(-over) [pul(ɔvœR)] *nm* sweater, jersey, pullover.
pulluler [pylyle] (1) *vi* (*se reproduire*) to proliferate, multiply; (*grouiller*) to swarm (*de* with); *[erreurs]* to abound.
pulmonaire [pylmɔnɛR] *adj* pulmonary, lung.
pulpe [pylp(ə)] *nf* pulp.

pulsation [pylsɑsjɔ̃] *nf* (*action*) beating. ~s heartbeats.
pulsion [pylsjɔ̃] *nf* (*Psych*) drive, urge.
pulvériser [pylveʀize] (1) *vt solide, adversaire* to pulverize; *liquide* to spray; *record* to smash*. ♦ **pulvérisateur** *nm* spray. ♦ **pulvérisation** *nf* pulverization; spraying. (*Méd*) **ordonner des ~s** to prescribe a nasal spray.
puma [pyma] *nm* puma.
punaise [pynɛz] *nf* (*Zool*) bug; (*clou*) drawing pin, thumbtack (*US*).
punir [pyniʀ] (2) *vt* (*gén*) to punish (*pour* for). **être puni de prison** to be sentenced to prison; **c'est puni par la loi** it is punishable by law. ♦ **punissable** *adj* punishable (*de* by). ♦ **punitif, -ive** *adj expédition* punitive. ♦ **punition** *nf* punishment (*de qch* for sth). **pour ta ~** for your punishment.
pupille[1] [pypij] *nf* (*Anat*) pupil.
pupille[2] [pypij] *nmf* (*enfant*) ward. **~ de la Nation** war orphan.
pupitre [pypitʀ(ə)] *nm* (*Scol*) desk; (*Rel*) lectern; *[musicien]* music stand; *[piano]* music rest; *[chef d'orchestre]* rostrum.
pur, e [pyʀ] *adj* **(a)** (*gén, fig*) pure; *personne* pure-hearted; *ciel* clear; *vin* undiluted; *whisky, gin* neat, straight. **(b)** (*intensif*) **c'est de la folie ~e** it's pure *ou* sheer madness; **c'est de l'insubordination ~e et simple** it's insubordination pure and simple; **par ~ hasard** by sheer chance, purely by chance; **c'est la ~e vérité** it's the plain *ou* simple truth; **en ~e perte** for absolutely nothing, fruitlessly. ♦ **purement** *adv* purely. **~ et simplement** purely and simply. ♦ **pureté** *nf* purity. ♦ **pur-sang** *nm inv* thoroughbred, purebred.
purée [pyʀe] *nf [tomates etc]* purée. **~ (de pommes de terre)** mashed potatoes; **être dans la ~**ː to be in the soup*.
purgatoire [pyʀgatwaʀ] *nm* (*Rel, fig*) purgatory.
purge [pyʀʒ(ə)] *nf* (*Méd, Pol*) purge. ♦ **purgatif, -ive** *adj, nm* purgative. ♦ **purger** (3) **1** *vt radiateur* to flush (out), drain; *freins* to bleed; (*Méd, fig*) to purge; (*Jur*) *peine* to serve. **2 se ~** *vpr* to take a purgative.
purifier [pyʀifje] (7) **1** *vt* (*gén*) to purify, cleanse; *métal* to refine. **2 se ~** *vpr* to cleanse o.s. ♦ **purification** *nf* purification, cleansing; refinement.
purin [pyʀɛ̃] *nm* liquid manure.
puritain, e [pyʀitɛ̃, ɛn] **1** *adj* puritan(ical). **2** *nm,f* puritan. ♦ **puritanisme** *nm* puritanism.
pus [py] *nm* pus.
pustule [pystyl] *nf* pustule.
putainː [pytɛ̃] *nf* whore. **ce ~ de réveil!** that goddamnː alarm clock!
putois [pytwa] *nm* polecat.
putréfier *vt*, **se ~** *vpr* [pytʀefje] (7) to putrefy. ♦ **putréfaction** *nf* putrefaction.
putsch [putʃ] *nm* putsch.
puzzle [pœzl(ə)] *nm* jigsaw (puzzle).
pygmée [pigme] *nm* pygmy, pigmy.
pyjama [piʒama] *nm* pyjamas, pajamas (*US*). **un ~** a pair of pyjamas.
pylône [pilon] *nm* pylon.
pyramide [piʀamid] *nf* (*gén*) pyramid.
pyromane [piʀɔman] *nmf* arsonist, fire-raiser.
python [pitɔ̃] *nm* python.

Q

Q, q [ky] *nm* (*lettre*) Q, q.
qu' [k(ə)] *V* **que.**
quadragénaire [kwadʀaʒenɛʀ] *adj*: **être ~** to be forty years old.
quadrilatère [kadʀilatɛʀ] *nm* (*Géom, Mil*) quadrilateral.
quadriller [kadʀije] (1) *vt* (*Mil, Police*) to cover, control. ♦ **quadrillage** *nm* **(a)** (*Mil, Police*) covering, control. **(b)** *[papier]* square *ou* grid pattern. ♦ **quadrillé, e** *adj papier* squared.
quadrimoteur [kadʀimɔtœʀ] *nm* four-engined plane.
quadripartite [kwadʀipaʀtit] *adj* (*Pol*) **conférence ~** four-power conference.
quadriréacteur [kadʀiʀeaktœʀ] *nm* four-engined jet.
quadrupède [kadʀypɛd] *adj, nm* quadruped.
quadruple [kadʀypl(ə)] **1** *adj quantité* quadruple. **en ~ partie** in four parts. **2** *nm* (*Math, gén*) quadruple. **je l'ai payé le ~** I paid four times as much for it; **augmenter au ~** to increase fourfold. ♦ **quadrupler** (1) *vti* to quadruple, increase fourfold. ♦ **quadruplés, -ées** *nm,fpl* quadruplets, quads*.
quai [ke] *nm [port]* quay; (*pour marchandises*) wharf; *[gare]* platform; *[rivière]* embankment. **être à ~** *[bateau]* to be alongside (the quay); *[train]* to be in (the station).
qualifier [kalifje] (7) **1** *vt* **(a)** (*décrire*) to describe (*de* as). **~ qn de menteur** to call *ou* label sb a liar. **(b)** (*Sport, gén: rendre apte*) to qualify (*pour* for). **(c)** (*Gram*) to qualify. **2 se ~** *vpr* (*Sport*) to qualify (*pour* for). (*hum*) **il se qualifie d'artiste** he labels *ou* calls himself an artist. ♦ **qualificatif, -ive 1** *adj adjectif* qualifying. **2** *nm* (*Gram*) qualifier; (*fig: terme*) term. ♦ **qualification** *nf* description; label; qualification. (*Sport*) **obtenir sa ~** to qualify. ♦ **qualifié, e** *adj* **(a)** (*compétent*) qualified; *ouvrier* skilled. **non ~** unskilled. **(b)** *vol* aggravated. (*fig*) **c'est du vol ~** it's daylight *ou* sheer robbery.
qualité [kalite] *nf* **(a)** (*gén*) quality. **de mauvaise ~** of bad *ou* poor quality; **produits de ~** high-quality products; **il a les ~s requises pour faire ce travail** he has the necessary skills for this job. **(b)** (*fonction*) position; (†:*noblesse*) quality; (*Admin: métier*) occupation. **en sa ~ de maire** in his capacity as mayor; (*Jur*) **avoir ~ pour** to have authority to. ♦ **qualitatif, -ive** *adj* qualitative.
quand [kɑ̃] **1** *conj* when. **~ ce sera fini, nous irons prendre un café** when it's finished we'll go and have a coffee; **~ je te le disais!** didn't I tell you so!, I told you so!; **~ bien même** even though *ou* if; **malgré tous ses défauts elle est ~ même gentille** in spite of all her faults she's still nice; **~ même, il exagère!** really, he overdoes it!; **tu aurais pu venir ~ même** even so you could have come, you could have come all the same. **2** *adv* when. **~ pars-tu?** when are you leaving?; **c'est pour ~?** *[devoir]* when is it for?; *[rendez-vous]* when is it?; *[naissance]* when is it to be?; **ça date de ~?** *[événement]* when did it take place?
quant [kɑ̃] *adv*: **~ à** as for, as to; **~ à moi** as for me; **~ à cela, je n'en sais rien** as to that *ou* as regards that, I know nothing about it.
quantité [kɑ̃tite] *nf* quantity, amount. **la ~ de gens qui** the number of people who; **en ~s industrielles** in massive *ou* huge amounts; **(une) ~ de** *argent, eau* a great deal of, a lot of; *gens, objets* a great many, a lot of, a great number of; **des fruits en ~** fruit in plenty; (*fig*) **considérer qn comme ~ négligeable** to consider sb as totally insignificant. ♦ **quantifier** (7) *vt* to quantify. ♦ **quantitatif, -ive** *adj* quantitative.
quarante [kaʀɑ̃t] *adj, nm inv* forty; *V* **soixante.** ♦ **quarantaine** *nf* **(a)** (*nombre*) about forty; *V* **soixantaine. (b)** (*Méd*) quarantine. **mettre en ~** (*lit*) to quarantine; (*fig*) to send to Coventry. ♦ **quarantième** *adj, nmf* fortieth.
quart [kaʀ] *nm* **(a)** (*fraction*) quarter. **un ~ de poulet** a quarter chicken; **un ~ de vin** a quarter-litre bottle of wine; (*Sport*) **~s de finale** quarter finals; **un kilo un ~** *ou* **et ~** a kilo and a quarter; **on n'a pas fait le ~ du travail** we haven't done a quarter of the work; **donner un ~ de tour à un bouton** to give a knob a quarter turn; (*Aut*) **partir au ~ de tour** to start first time. **(b)** (*Mil: gobelet*) beaker (*of 1/4 litre capacity*). **(c) ~ d'heure** quarter of an hour; **3 heures moins le ~** (a) quarter to 3; **3 heures et ~** *ou* **un ~** (a) quarter past 3; **il est le ~/moins le ~** it's (a) quarter past/(a) quarter to; **passer un mauvais ~ d'heure** to have a bad *ou* nasty time of it. **(d)** (*Naut*) watch. **être de ~** to keep the watch; **de ~** *homme* on watch.
quartette [kwaʀtɛt] *nm* (*Mus*) jazz quartet(te).
quartier [kaʀtje] *nm* **(a)** *[ville]* district, area, quarter. **les gens du ~** the local people, the people of the area; **de ~** *cinéma, épicier* local; **le ~ est de la ville** the east end of (the) town. **(b)** (*Mil*) **~(s)** quarters; **avoir ~(s) libre(s)** to be free *ou* off (for a few hours); (*lit, fig*) **prendre ses ~s d'hiver** to go into winter quarters; **grand ~ général** general headquarters. **(c)** *[bœuf]* quarter; *[viande]* chunk; *[fruit]* piece, segment. (*lit, fig*) **mettre en ~s** to tear to pieces; **ne pas faire de ~** to give no quarter.
quartz [kwaʀts] *nm* quartz.
quasi [kazi] **1** *adv* almost, nearly. **2** *préf* near. **~-certitude** near certainty; **la ~-totalité de** the near total of. ♦ **quasiment** *adv* almost, nearly.
quatorze [katɔʀz(ə)] *adj, nm inv* fourteen. **la guerre de ~** the First World War. ♦ **quatorzième** *adj, nmf* fourteenth; *V* **sixième.**
quatrain [katʀɛ̃] *nm* quatrain.
quatre [katʀ(ə)] *adj, nm inv* four. **une robe de ~ sous** a cheap dress; (*lit, fig*) **aux ~ coins de** in the four corners of; **à ~ pattes** on all fours; **être tiré à ~ épingles** to be dressed up to the nines; **un de ces ~ (matins)*** one of these (fine) days; **faire les ~ cents coups** to be a real troublemaker; **faire ses ~ volontés** to do exactly as one pleases; **dire à qn ses ~ vérités** to tell sb a few plain *ou* home truths; **monter (l'escalier) ~ à ~** to rush up the stairs four at a time; **manger comme ~** to eat like a wolf; **se mettre en ~ pour qn** to go out of one's way for sb, put o.s. out for sb; **ne pas y aller par ~ chemins** not to beat about the bush. ♦ **quatre heures** *nm inv* afternoon tea *ou* snack. ♦ **quatre-quarts** *nm inv* (*Culin*) pound cake. ♦ **quatre-vingt-dix** *adj, nm inv* ninety. ♦ **quatre-vingt-dixième** *adj, nmf* ninetieth. ♦ **quatre-vingt-onze**

adj, nm inv ninety-one. ♦ **quatre-vingts** *adj, nm inv* eighty. ♦ **quatrième** **1** *adj* fourth. (*fig*) **en ~ vitesse*** at great speed. **2** *nmf* (*Jeux*) fourth player. **3** *nf* (*Aut*) fourth gear; *V* **sixième.** ♦ **quatrièmement** *adv* fourthly, in the fourth place.

quatuor [kwatɥɔʀ] *nm* quartet(te).

que [k(ə)] **1** *conj* **(a)** (*introduisant subordonnée*) that. **elle sait ~ tu es prêt** she knows (that) you're ready; **je veux qu'il vienne** I want him to come; **venez que nous causions** come along so that we can have a chat. **(b)** (*remplaçant si, quand etc: non traduit*) **si vous êtes sages et qu'il fasse beau** if you are good and the weather is fine; **quand il rentrera et qu'il aura déjeuné** when he comes home and he's had a meal. **(c)** (*temps*) **elle venait à peine de sortir qu'il se mit à pleuvoir** she had no sooner gone out than *ou* she had hardly gone out when it started raining; **ça fait 2 ans qu'il est là** he has been here (for) 2 years; **ça fait 2 ans qu'il est parti** it is 2 years since he left, he left 2 years ago. **(d)** (*ordre, souhait etc*) **qu'il le veuille ou non** whether he likes it or not; **~ la guerre finisse!** if only *ou* I wish the war would end!; **qu'il vienne!** let him come!; **~ m'importe!** what do I care?, I don't care! **(e)** (*comparaison*) (*avec plus, moins*) than; (*avec aussi, autant, tel*) as. **il est plus petit qu'elle** he's smaller than her *ou* than she is; **elle est tout aussi capable ~ vous** she's just as capable as you (are).

2 *adv*: **ce ~ tu es lent!*** you're so slow!, how slow you are!; **~ de monde!** what a crowd (there is)!, what a lot of people!; **~ n'es-tu venu me voir?** why didn't you come to see me?

3 *pron* **(a)** (*relatif direct*) (*personne*) that, whom; (*chose, animal*) which, that (*gén omis*); (*temps*) when. **les enfants ~ tu vois dans la rue** the children that *ou* whom you see in the street; **la raison qu'il a donnée** the reason (that *ou* which) he gave; **un jour ~** one day when. **(b)** (*attribut*) **quel homme charmant ~ votre voisin!** what a charming man your neighbour is; **distrait qu'il est, il n'a rien vu** dreamy as he is, he didn't notice anything; **c'est un inconvénient ~ de ne pas avoir de voiture** it's inconvenient not having a car; **en bon fils qu'il est** being the good son (that) he is. **(c)** (*interrog*) what; (*discriminatif*) which. **~ fais-tu?** what are you doing?; **qu'est-ce qu'il y a?** what's the matter?; **je pense ~ non** I don't think so; **mais il n'a pas de voiture! — il dit ~ si** but he has no car! — he says he has; **qu'est-ce ~ tu préfères, le rouge ou le noir?** which (one) do you prefer, the red or the black? **(d) je ne l'y ai pas autorisé, ~ je sache** I didn't give him permission to do so, as far as I know, I'm not aware that I gave him permission to do so; **qu'il dit!*** that's what he says!; **~ oui!** yes indeed!; **~ non!** certainly not!

quel, quelle [kɛl] **1** *adj* **(a)** (*interrog*) what; (*être animé: attribut*) who. **~ est cet auteur?** who is that author?; **sur ~ auteur/sujet va-t-il parler?** what author/subject is he going to talk about? **(b)** (*discriminatif*) which. **~ acteur préférez-vous?** which actor do you prefer? **(c)** (*excl*) what. **quelle surprise!** what a surprise!; **j'ai remarqué avec quelle attention ils écoutaient** I noticed how attentively they were listening. **(d)** (*relatif*) (*être animé*) whoever; (*chose*) whatever; (*discriminatif*) whichever, whatever. **~ que soit le train que vous preniez** whichever *ou* whatever train you take; **les hommes, ~s qu'ils soient** men, whoever they may be. **2** *pron interrog* which. **des deux solutions quelle est la meilleure?** of the two solutions, which (one) is better?

quelconque [kɛlkɔ̃k] *adj* **(a)** (*n'importe quel*) some (or other), any; (*moindre*) any. **pour une raison ~** for some reason (or other); **à partir d'un point ~ du cercle** from any point on the circle; **il n'a pas manifesté un désir ~ d'y aller** he didn't show the slightest *ou* least desire *ou* any desire to go. **(b)** (*médiocre*) poor, indifferent; (*laid*) plain-looking; (*ordinaire*) ordinary.

quelque [kɛlk(ə)] **1** *adj indéf* **(a)** (*sans pl*) some. **cela fait ~ temps que je ne l'ai vu** I haven't seen him for some time *ou* for a while; **avez-vous ~ idée de?** have you any idea about?; **j'ai ~ peine à croire cela** I find it rather *ou* somewhat difficult to believe; **par ~ temps qu'il fasse** whatever the weather (may be *ou* is like); **en ~ sorte** (*pour ainsi dire*) as it were, so to speak; (*bref*) in a word. **(b)** (*pl*) a few, some. **reste-t-il ~s places?** are there any *ou* some *ou* a few seats left?; **les ~s enfants qui étaient venus** the few children who had come. **2** *adv* **(a)** (*environ*) some, about. **ça a augmenté de ~ 50 F** it's gone up by about *ou* by some 50 francs; **20 kg et ~(s)*** a bit over 20 kg*. **(b) ~ peu déçu** rather *ou* somewhat disappointed; **il est ~ peu menteur** he is something of *ou* a bit of a liar; **~ lourde que soit la tâche** however heavy the task may be.

♦ **quelque chose** *pron indéf* something; (*avec interrog*) anything. **~ d'autre** something else; **il a ~ qui ne va pas** there's something the matter with him; **ça y est pour ~** it has got something to do with it; **il y a ~ comme une semaine** something like a week ago; **il a plu ~!*** it rained something dreadful!*, it didn't half rain!*; (*lit, fig*) **faire ~ à qn** to have an effect on sb; **ça alors, c'est ~!** that's a bit stiff! ♦ **quelquefois** *adv* sometimes, occasionally, at times. ♦ **quelque part** *adv* somewhere. ♦ **quelques-uns, -unes** *pron indéf pl* some, a few. ♦ **quelqu'un** *pron indéf* somebody, someone; (*avec interrog*) anybody, anyone. **c'est ~ de sûr** he's a reliable person, he's someone reliable; **c'est ~** *[savant]* he is (a) somebody; (*excl*) that's a bit stiff!

quémander [kemɑ̃de] (1) *vt* to beg for.

qu'en-dira-t-on [kɑ̃diʀatɔ̃] *nm inv* gossip.

quenelle [kənɛl] *nf* (*Culin*) quenelle.

quenotte* [kənɔt] *nf* tooth, toothy-peg*.

querelle [kəʀɛl] *nf* quarrel. **~ d'amoureux** lovers' tiff; **chercher une mauvaise ~ à qn** to pick a quarrel with sb for nothing. ♦ **quereller** (1) **1** *vt* to scold. **2 se ~** *vpr* to quarrel (with one another). ♦ **querelleur, -euse** *adj* quarrelsome.

question [kɛstjɔ̃] *nf* **(a)** (*demande*) (*gén*) question; (*pour lever un doute*) query, question. **~ subsidiaire** reserve question (to decide the winner); (*Pol*) **poser la ~ de confiance** to ask for a vote of confidence. **(b)** (*problème*) question, matter, issue. **la ~ sociale** the social question *ou* issue; **la ~ n'est pas là** that's not the point; **c'est une ~ de temps** it's a question *ou* matter of time. **(c)** (*locutions*) **~ argent** as far as money goes, money-wise*; **de quoi est-il ~?** what is it about?; **il fut d'abord ~ du budget** first they spoke about *ou* discussed the budget; **il est ~ de lui comme ministre** there's some question of his being *ou* becoming a minister; **il n'en est pas ~!** there's no question of it!; **hors de ~** out of the question; **la personne en ~** the person in question; **remettre en ~** *autorité* to question, challenge; *science* to question, call into question; *projets* to put a question mark over, cast doubt over; **c'est notre vie même qui est en ~** it's our very lives that are at stake. ♦ **questionnaire** *nm* questionnaire. ♦ **questionner** (1) *vt* (*interroger*) to question, ask (*sur* about).

quête [kɛt] *nf* (*collecte*) collection. (*littér: recherche*) *[Graal]* quest; *[absolu]* pursuit. **en ~ de** (*gén*) in search of; **être en ~ de travail** to be looking for work. ♦ **quêter** (1) **1** *vi* (*à l'église*) to take the collection; (*dans la rue*) to collect money. **2** *vt* to seek. ♦ **quêteur, -euse** *nm,f* collector.

queue [kø] **1** *nf* **(a)** (*gén*) tail; *[classement]* bottom; *[poêle]* handle; *[fruit, feuille]* stalk; *[fleur]* stem; *[train]* rear. **commencer par la ~** to begin at the end. **(b)** (*file*) queue, line (*US*). **(c)** (*locutions*) **la ~ entre les jambes*** with one's tail between one's legs; **à la ~ leu leu** *marcher* in single file; *se plaindre* one after the other; **il n'y en avait pas la ~ d'un*** there wasn't the sniff of one*; (*Aut*) **faire une ~ de poisson à qn** to cut in front of sb; **finir en ~ de poisson** to finish up in the air; **histoire sans ~ ni tête*** cock-and-bull story. **2: ~ de billard** billiard cue; **~ de cheval** ponytail; **~-de-pie** *nf, pl* **~s-~-~** tails.

qui [ki] **1** *pron* **(a)** (*interrog*) (*sujet*) who; (*objet*) who, whom. **~ (est-ce) ~ l'a vu?** who saw him?; **~ d'entre eux/parmi vous?** which of them/of you?; **~ a-t-elle vu?** who *ou* whom did she see?; **à ~ voulez-vous parler?** who do you wish to speak to?, who is it you want to speak to?; **à ~ est ce sac?** whose bag is this?, whose is this bag?; **elle ne sait à ~ se plaindre** she doesn't know who to complain to *ou* to whom to complain. **(b)** (*relatif sujet*) (*être animé*) who, that*; (*chose*) which, that. **Paul, ~ traversait le pont, trébucha** Paul, who was crossing the bridge, tripped; **il a un perroquet ~ parle** he's got a talking parrot, he's got a parrot which *ou* that talks; **je la vis ~ nageait vers le rivage** I saw her (as she was) swimming towards the bank. **(c)** (*relatif avec prép*) **le patron pour ~ il travaille** the employer (that *ou* who* *ou* whom) he works for, the employer for whom he works. **(d)** (*relatif sans antécédent*) whoever, anyone who. **amenez ~ vous voulez** bring along whoever *ou* anyone you like; **~ vous savez** you-know-who*; **c'est à ~ des deux mentira le plus** each tries to outdo the other in lying *ou* in lies; **je le dirai à ~ de droit** I will tell whoever is concerned; **j'interdis à ~ que ce soit d'entrer ici** I forbid anyone to come in here; **à ~ mieux mieux** (*gén*) each one more so than the other; *crier* each one louder than the other; **ils ont pris tout ce qu'ils ont pu: ~ une chaise, ~ une radio** they took whatever they could: some took a chair, others a radio. **(e) ~ va lentement va sûrement** more haste less speed; **~ vivra verra** what will be will be; **~ a bu boira** once a thief always a thief; **~ se ressemble s'assemble** birds of a feather flock together; **~ veut la fin veut les moyens** he who wills the end wills the means. **2: qui-vive?** *excl* who goes there?; **être sur le ~** to be on the alert.

quiconque [kikɔ̃k] **1** *pron rel* whoever, anyone who. **2** *pron indéf* anyone, anybody.

quiétude [kjetyd] *nf [lieu]* quiet; *[personne]* peace (of mind). **en toute ~** in (complete) peace.

quille [kij] *nf* (*jouet*) skittle; (*:*jambe*) pin*; (*Naut*) keel. **(jeu de) ~s** ninepins, skittles.

quincaillerie [kɛ̃kɑjʀi] *nf* (*ustensiles, métier*) hardware, ironmongery; (*magasin*) hardware shop *ou* store, ironmonger's (shop); (*fig péj: bijoux*) jewellery. ♦ **quincaillier, -ière** *nm,f* hardware dealer, ironmonger.

quinconce [kɛ̃kɔ̃s] *nm*: **en ~** in staggered rows.

quinine [kinin] *nf* quinine.

quinquagénaire [kɛ̃kaʒenɛʀ] *adj*: **être ~** to be fifty years old.

quinquennal, e *mpl* **-aux** [kɛ̃kenal, o] *adj* five-year, quinquennial.

quintal, *pl* **-aux** [kɛ̃tal, o] *nm* quintal (*100 kg*).

quinte [kɛ̃t] *nf* **(a)** (*Méd*) **~ (de toux)** coughing fit. **(b)** (*Mus*) fifth; (*Escrime*) quinte; (*Cartes*) quint.

quintessence [kɛ̃tesɑ̃s] *nf* quintessence.

quintette [kɛ̃tɛt] *nm* quintet(te).

quintuple [kɛ̃typl(ə)] **1** *adj* quintuple. **en ~ partie** in five parts. **2** *nm* quintuple (*de* of). **je l'ai payé le ~** I paid five times as much for it. ♦ **quintupler** (1) *vti* to quintuple, increase fivefold. ♦ **quintuplés, -ées** *nm,fpl* quintuplets, quins*.

quinze [kɛ̃z] **1** *nm inv* fifteen; *V* **six**. **2** *adj inv* fifteen. **le ~ août** Assumption; **demain/lundi en ~** a fortnight *ou* two weeks tomorrow/on Monday; **dans ~ jours** in a fortnight, in two weeks. ♦ **quinzaine** *nf* about fifteen, fifteen or so. **une ~ (de jours)** a fortnight, two weeks; **~ publicitaire** (two-week) sale; *V* **soixantaine.** ♦ **quinzième** *adj, nmf* fifteenth; *V* **sixième.**

quiproquo [kipʀɔko] *nm* (*sur personne*) mistake; (*sur sujet*) misunderstanding.

quittance [kitɑ̃s] *nf* (*reçu*) receipt; (*facture*) bill.

quitte [kit] *adj*: **être ~ (envers qn)** to be quits *ou* all square (with sb); **tu es ~ *ou* je t'en tiens ~ pour cette fois** I'll let you off this time; **être ~ d'une dette** to be rid *ou* clear of a debt; **nous en sommes ~s pour la peur** we got off with a fright; **~ à s'ennuyer, ils préfèrent rester chez eux** they prefer to stay (at) home even if it means *ou* although it may mean getting bored; (*fig*) **c'est du ~ ou double** it's a big gamble.

quitter [kite] (1) *vt* **(a)** *lieu, personne* to leave. **ne pas ~ la chambre** to be confined to one's room; **les clients sont priés de ~ la chambre avant midi** guests are requested to vacate their rooms before midday; **se ~** to part. **(b)** *espoir* to give up. *[crainte, énergie]* **~ qn** to leave *ou* desert sb. **(c)** *vêtement* to take off. **(d) si je le quitte des yeux une seconde** if I take my eyes off him for a second; (*Téléc*) **ne quittez pas** hold the line.

quoi [kwa] *pron* **(a)** (*interrog*) what. **de ~ parles-tu?** what are you talking about?; **en ~ puis-je vous aider?** how can I help you?; **c'est fait en ~?** what is it made of?; **~ faire?** what are we (going) to do?; **à ~ bon?** what's the use? (*faire* of doing); **et puis ~ encore!** what next! **(b)** (*relatif*) **la chose à ~ tu fais allusion** what you're referring to; **c'est en ~ tu te trompes** that's where you're wrong. **(c) il n'y a pas de ~ rire** it's no laughing matter, there's nothing to laugh about; **il n'y a pas de ~ fouetter un chat** it's not worth making a fuss about; **ils ont de ~ occuper leurs vacances** they've got enough *ou* plenty to occupy their holiday; **avoir de ~ écrire** to have sth to write with; **il n'a pas de ~ se l'acheter** he can't afford it, he hasn't the means to buy it; **si vous avez besoin de ~ que ce soit** if there's anything (at all) you need; **merci beaucoup! — il n'y a pas de ~** many thanks! — don't mention it *ou* (it's) a pleasure *ou* not at all. **(d) ~ qu'il arrive** whatever happens; **~ qu'il en soit** be that as it may, however that may be; **~ qu'on en dise** whatever *ou* no matter what people say.

quoique [kwak(ə)] *conj* (*bien que*) although, though. **quoiqu'il soit malade** although he is ill.

quolibet† [kɔlibɛ] *nm* gibe, jeer.

quote-part, *pl* **~s-~s** [kɔtpaʀ] *nf* (*lit, fig*) share.

quotidien, -ienne [kɔtidjɛ̃, jɛn] **1** *adj* (*journalier*) daily; (*banal*) everyday; *existence* humdrum. **dans la vie ~ienne** in everyday *ou* daily life. **2** *nm* daily (paper). ♦ **quotidiennement** *adv* daily, every day.

quotient [kɔsjɑ̃] *nm* quotient.

R

R, r [ɛʀ] *nm* (*lettre*) R, r.
rabâcher [ʀabɑʃe] (1) **1** *vt* to harp on, keep (on) repeating. **2** *vi* to keep repeating o.s. ♦ **rabâcheur, -euse** *nm,f* repetitive bore.
rabais [ʀabɛ] *nm* reduction, discount. **au ~** *vendre* at a reduced price, (on the) cheap; (*péj*) *enseignement* third-rate.
rabaisser [ʀabese] (1) **1** *vt* (*dénigrer*) to belittle, disparage; (*réduire*) to reduce. **2 se ~** *vpr* to belittle o.s.
rabattre [ʀabatʀ(ə)] (41) **1** *vt* **(a)** *capot* to close; *col* to turn down; *strapontin* (*ouvrir*) to pull down; (*fermer*) to put up. **le vent rabat la fumée** the wind blows the smoke back down; **les cheveux rabattus sur les yeux** with his hair brushed down over his eyes; **~ les couvertures** (*se couvrir*) to pull the blankets up; (*se découvrir*) to push back the blankets. **(b)** (*diminuer*) to reduce; (*déduire*) to deduct, take off. **~ l'orgueil de qn** to humble sb's pride; *[prétentieux]* **en ~** to climb down. **(c)** *gibier* to drive; *terrain* to beat. **~ des clients*** to tout for customers. **2 se ~** *vpr* **(a)** *[voiture, coureur]* to cut in. **se ~ devant qn** to cut in front of sb. **(b) se ~ sur** *marchandise, personne* to fall back on, make do with. **(c)** *[porte]* to fall *ou* slam shut; *[couvercle]* to close. ♦ **rabat** *nm* *[table, poche]* flap. ♦ **rabat-joie** *nm inv* killjoy, spoilsport*. ♦ **rabattage** *nm* (*Chasse*) beating. ♦ **rabatteur, -euse** *nm,f* (*Chasse*) beater; (*fig péj*) tout.
rabbin [ʀabɛ̃] *nm* rabbi. **grand ~** chief rabbi.
rabibocher* [ʀabibɔʃe] (1) **1** *vt* to reconcile. **2 se ~** *vpr* to make it up (*avec* with).
rabiot‡ [ʀabjo] *nm* *[nourriture]* extra (food); *[temps]* extra time. **5 minutes de ~** 5 minutes' extra time, 5 minutes extra. ♦ **rabioter‡** (1) *vt* *nourriture* to scrounge* (*à qn* from sb); *temps, argent* to fiddle* (*à qn* off sb).
râblé, e [ʀɑble] *adj* well-set, stocky.
rabot [ʀabo] *nm* plane. ♦ **raboter** (1) *vt* (*Menuiserie*) to plane (down); (*:égratigner*) to scrape. ♦ **raboteux, -euse** *adj* uneven, rough.
rabougri, e [ʀabugʀi] *adj* (*chétif*) stunted, puny; (*desséché*) shrivelled.
rabrouer [ʀabʀue] (1) *vt* to snub, rebuff.
racaille [ʀakɑj] *nf* rabble, riffraff.
raccommoder [ʀakɔmɔde] (1) **1** *vt* **(a)** (*réparer*) to mend, repair; *chaussette* to darn. **(b)** (*) *ennemis* to reconcile. **2 se ~*** *vpr* to make it up. ♦ **raccommodage** *nm* **(a)** (*action*) mending, repairing; darning. **(b)** (*endroit réparé*) mend, repair; darn.
raccompagner [ʀakɔ̃paɲe] (1) *vt* to take *ou* see back (*à* to). **~ qn en voiture** to drive sb back (home).
raccord [ʀakɔʀ] *nm* **(a)** *[papier peint]* join. **~ (de maçonnerie)** pointing; **~ (de peinture)** touch up. **(b)** *[discours]* link, join; (*Ciné*) (*scène*) link scene. **(c)** (*pièce, joint*) link.
raccorder [ʀakɔʀde] (1) *vt* (*gén*) to link up, join (up); (*Téléc*) to connect (*à* with, to). (*fig*) **~ à** *faits* to link (up) with, tie up with. ♦ **raccordement** *nm* (*action*) linking; joining; connecting; (*résultat*) join; connection.
raccourcir [ʀakuʀsiʀ] (2) **1** *vt* (*gén*) to shorten; *vacances, textes* to curtail, cut short. **2** *vi* *[jours]* to get shorter; (*au lavage*) to shrink. ♦ **raccourci** *nm* (*chemin*) short cut; (*résumé*) summary. **en ~** (*en miniature*) in miniature; (*en bref*) in a nutshell. ♦ **raccourcissement** *nm* shortening.
raccrocher [ʀakʀɔʃe] (1) **1** *vi* (*Téléc*) to hang up, ring off. **2** *vt* *vêtement* to hang back up; *écouteur* to put down; *personne, bonne affaire* to grab *ou* get hold of; *wagons, faits* to link, connect (*à* to, with). **3 se ~** *vpr*: **se ~ à** *branche* to catch *ou* grab (hold of); *espoir, personne* to cling to, hang on to.
race [ʀas] *nf* (*ethnique*) race; (*Zool*) breed. **de ~** (*gén*) pedigree, purebred; *cheval* thoroughbred; **de ~ noble** of noble stock *ou* race; (*péj*) **lui et les gens de sa ~** him and people of his type. ♦ **racé, e** *adj animal* purebred, pedigree; *cheval, personne, voiture* thoroughbred.
racheter [ʀaʃte] (5) **1** *vt* **(a)** *objet qu'on possédait avant* to buy back; *nouvel objet* to buy another; *pain, lait* to buy some more; *firme* to take over; *parts de société* to buy up; *objet d'occasion* to buy (*à* from); *dette* to redeem; *otage* to ransom; (*Rel*) *pécheur* to redeem. **(b)** *crime* to atone for, expiate; *faute, imperfection* to make up for (*par* by). **2 se ~** *vpr* *[pécheur]* to redeem o.s.; *[criminel, fautif]* to make amends. ♦ **rachat** *nm* buying (back); takeover; redemption; ransom; atonement, expiation.
rachitisme [ʀaʃitism(ə)] *nm* rickets (*sg*). **faire du ~** to have rickets. ♦ **rachitique** *adj* (*Méd*) rickety; (*péj*) scraggy, scrawny.
racial, e, mpl -aux [ʀasjal, o] *adj* racial.
racine [ʀasin] *nf* (*gén, Math, fig*) root. **prendre ~** to take root; **~ carrée** square root.
racisme [ʀasism(ə)] *nm* racialism, racism. ♦ **raciste** *adj, nmf* racialist, racist.
raclée* [ʀɑkle] *nf* (*coups*) hiding, thrashing; (*défaite*) thrashing*, licking*.
racler [ʀɑkle] (1) *vt* (*gén*) to scrape; *tache* to scrape away; *écailles* to scrape off. **se ~ la gorge** to clear one's throat.
racoler [ʀakɔle] (1) *vt* *[prostituée]* to solicit; *[vendeur]* to solicit, tout for. ♦ **racolage** *nm* soliciting; touting.
raconter [ʀakɔ̃te] (1) *vt* *histoire* to tell, relate, recount; *malheurs* to tell about, recount. **~ qch à qn** to tell sb sth, relate sth to sb; **~ ce qui s'est passé** to say *ou* relate *ou* recount what happened; **qu'est-ce que tu racontes?** what are you talking about? *ou* saying?; **~ des histoires** to tell stories. ♦ **racontar** *nm* story, lie.
racorni, e [ʀakɔʀni] *adj* (*durci*) hardened; (*desséché*) shrivelled (up).
radar [ʀadaʀ] *nm* radar.
rade [ʀad] *nf* (natural) harbour, roads. **en ~ de Brest** in Brest harbour; **laisser en ~*** *personne* to leave stranded *ou* in the lurch; *projet* to drop, shelve; *voiture* to leave behind.
radeau, pl ~x [ʀado] *nm* raft.
radiateur [ʀadjatœʀ] *nm* (*à eau, huile, Aut*) radiator; (*à gaz*) heater.
radiation [ʀadjɑsjɔ̃] *nf* **(a)** (*Phys*) radiation. **(b)** *[nom]* crossing *ou* striking off.
radical, e, mpl -aux [ʀadikal, o] *adj, nm* (*gén*) radical. ♦ **radicalement** *adv* (*gén*) radically. **~ faux** completely wrong. ♦ **radicaliser** *vt*, **se ~** *vpr* (1) *position* to toughen, harden.

radier [ʀadje] (7) *vt* to cross off, strike off (a list).
radieux, -euse [ʀadjø, øz] *adj personne* beaming *ou* radiant with joy; *air* radiant, beaming; *soleil* radiant; *journée, temps* brilliant, glorious.
radin, e* [ʀadɛ̃, in] **1** *adj* stingy, tight-fisted. **2** *nm,f* skinflint. ♦ **radinerie*** *nf* stinginess.
radio [ʀadjo] **1** *nf* **(a)** (*poste*) radio (set). **mets la ~** turn *ou* put on the radio. **(b)** (*radiodiffusion*) **la ~** (the) radio; **avoir la ~** to have a radio; **parler à la ~** to speak on the radio, broadcast. **(c)** (*radiographie*) X-ray (photograph). **passer une ~** to have an X-ray (taken), be X-rayed. **2** *nm* (*opérateur*) radio operator; (*message*) radiogram, radiotelegram. ♦ **radioactif, -ive** *adj* radioactive. ♦ **radioactivité** *nf* radioactivity. ♦ **radiodiffuser** (1) *vt* to broadcast (*by radio*). ♦ **radiodiffusion** *nf* broadcasting (*by radio*). ♦ **radiographie** *nf* (*technique*) radiography, X-ray photography; (*photographie*) X-ray (photograph), radiograph. ♦ **radiographier** (7) *vt* to X-ray. ♦ **radiographique** *adj* X-ray. ♦ **radioguidage** *nm* (*Aviat*) radio control. ♦ **radiologie** *nf* radiology. ♦ **radiologue** *nmf* radiologist. ♦ **radiophonie** *nf* radiotelephony. ♦ **radiophonique** *adj* radio. ♦ **radioreportage** *nm* radio report. ♦ **radioreporter** *nm* radio reporter. ♦ **radioscopie** *nf* radioscopy. ♦ **radiotélévisé, e** *adj* broadcast and televised.
radis [ʀadi] *nm* radish; (*‡: sou*) penny (*Brit*), cent (*US*). **~ noir** horseradish.
radium [ʀadjɔm] *nm* radium.
radoter [ʀadɔte] (1) *vi* (*péj*) to ramble on *ou* drivel (on). ♦ **radotage** *nm* (*péj*) **~(s)** drivel. ♦ **radoteur, -euse** *nm,f* (*péj*) (old) driveller.
radoucir [ʀadusiʀ] (2) **1** *vt ton* to soften. **2 se ~** *vpr* [*personne*] to calm down; [*voix*] to soften; [*temps*] to become milder. ♦ **radoucissement** *nm* (*Mét*) **le ~** the milder weather; **un ~** a milder spell (of weather).
rafale [ʀafal] *nf* [*vent, pluie*] gust; [*mitrailleuse*] burst. **en** *ou* **par ~s** in gusts; **~s de balles** hail of bullets; **~ de vent** squall.
raffermir [ʀafɛʀmiʀ] (2) **1** *vt* (*gén*) to strengthen; *voix* to steady. **2 se ~** *vpr* (*gén*) to grow stronger; [*voix*] to become steadier.
raffiner [ʀafine] (1) **1** *vt* (*gén*) to refine; *langage* to polish. **2** *vi* to be meticulous. ♦ **raffinage** *nm* refining. ♦ **raffiné, e** *adj* (*gén*) refined; *mœurs* polished, sophisticated. ♦ **raffinement** *nm* (*caractère*) refinement, sophistication; (*détail*) refinement. ♦ **raffinerie** *nf* refinery. ♦ **raffineur, -euse** *nm,f* refiner.
raffoler [ʀafɔle] (1) **~ de** *vt indir* to be very keen on.
raffut* [ʀafy] *nm* row, racket, din. **faire du ~** to kick up* a row.
rafiot [ʀafjo] *nm* (*péj: bateau*) (old) tub (*péj*).
rafistoler* [ʀafistɔle] (1) *vt* to patch up, botch up.
rafle [ʀɑfl(ə)] *nf* (police) roundup *ou* raid. ♦ **rafler*** (1) *vt* to swipe*.
rafraîchir [ʀafʀeʃiʀ] (2) **1** *vt* **(a)** (*refroidir*) to cool, make cooler. **(b) ~ qn** [*bain*] to freshen sb (up); [*boisson*] to refresh sb. **(c)** *vêtement, couleur* to brighten up; *appartement* to do up; *connaissances* to brush up. **se faire ~ les cheveux** to have a trim; **~ la mémoire de qn** to jog *ou* refresh sb's memory. **2** *vi* [*vin etc*] to cool (down). **mettre à ~** to chill. **3 se ~** *vpr* **(a)** [*temps*] to get cooler *ou* colder. **(b)** (*en se lavant*) to freshen (o.s.) up; (*en buvant*) to refresh o.s. ♦ **rafraîchissant, e** *adj* refreshing. ♦ **rafraîchissement** *nm* **(a)** [*température*] cooling. **(b)** (*boisson*) cool *ou* cold drink. (*glaces, fruits*) **~s** refreshments.
ragaillardir [ʀagajaʀdiʀ] (2) *vt* to perk up*, buck up*.
rage [ʀaʒ] *nf* **(a)** (*colère*) rage, fury. **mettre qn en ~** to infuriate *ou* enrage sb; **ivre de ~** mad with rage. **(b)** (*manie*) maddening habit. (*passion*) **avoir la ~ de faire/de qch** to have a mania for doing/for sth. **(c) faire ~** [*incendie, tempête*] to rage. **(d)** (*Méd*) **la ~** rabies (*sg*). **(e) ~ de dents** raging toothache. ♦ **rager** (3) *vi* to fume. **ça (me) fait ~!** it makes me fume! *ou* mad! ♦ **rageur, -euse** *adj* (*coléreux*) bad-tempered; (*furieux*) furious. ♦ **rageusement** *adv* angrily.
ragot* [ʀago] *nm* piece of gossip. **~s** gossip, tittle-tattle.
ragoût [ʀagu] *nm* stew.
ragoûtant, e [ʀagutɑ̃, ɑ̃t] *adj* (*lit, fig*) **peu ~** unsavoury, unappetising.
raid [ʀɛd] *nm* (*Mil*) raid, hit-and-run attack. (*Sport*) **~ automobile** long-distance car rally.
raide [ʀɛd] **1** *adj* **(a)** (*rigide*) (*gén*) stiff; *cheveux* straight; *câble* taut, tight. **(b)** (*abrupt*) steep, abrupt. **(c)** *morale* rigid, inflexible; *manières, démarche* stiff. **(d)** *alcool* rough; (*fig: osé*) *propos* daring, bold. **elle est ~ celle-là*** (*incrédulité*) that's a bit hard to swallow, that's a bit far-fetched; (*indignation*) that's a bit steep *ou* stiff. **(e) être ~ (comme un passe-lacet)*** to be (stony *ou* flat) broke*. **2** *adv* **(a) ça montait ~** [*ascension*] it was a steep climb; [*pente*] it climbed steeply. **(b) tomber ~** to drop to the ground; **~ mort** stone dead; **il l'a étendu ~ (mort)*** he laid him out cold*. ♦ **raideur** *nf* stiffness; straightness; tautness, tightness; steepness, abruptness; rigidity, inflexibility. **avec ~** stiffly. ♦ **raidillon** *nm* (steep) rise *ou* incline.
raidir [ʀediʀ] (2) **1** *vt* (*gén*) to stiffen; *corde* to tighten; (*fig*) *position* to harden, toughen. **2 se ~** *vpr* **(a)** [*tissu*] to stiffen; [*corde*] to grow taut; [*position*] to harden. **(b)** [*personne*] (*perdre sa souplesse*) to become stiff(er); (*bander ses muscles*) to tense *ou* stiffen o.s.; (*s'entêter*) to take a hard *ou* tough line. ♦ **raidissement** *nm* (*gén*) stiffening; [*prise de position*] hard line.
raie [ʀɛ] *nf* **(a)** (*trait*) line; (*éraflure*) mark, scratch. **(b)** (*bande*) stripe. **(c)** (*Coiffure*) parting. **(d)** (*Zool*) skate, ray.
raifort [ʀɛfɔʀ] *nm* horseradish.
rail [ʀɑj] *nm* rail. (*voie*) **les ~s** the rails; **~ conducteur** live rail; (*transport*) **le ~** the railway, the railroad (*US*); (*lit, fig*) **remettre sur les ~s** to put back on the rails.
railler [ʀɑje] (1) *vt* to scoff at, mock at. ♦ **raillerie** *nf* (*action*) mockery; (*parole*) mocking remark. ♦ **railleur, -euse 1** *adj* mocking. **2** *nmpl*: **les ~s** the mockers.
rainure [ʀenyʀ] *nf* groove; (*courte*) slot. ♦ **rainurer** (1) *vt* to groove.
raisin [ʀɛzɛ̃] *nm* (*espèce*) grape. **le ~, les ~s** grapes; **~s de Corinthe** currants; **~s secs** raisins; **~s de table** dessert grapes.
raison [ʀɛzɔ̃] **1** *nf* **(a)** (*faculté*) reason. **il a perdu la ~** he has lost his reason, he has taken leave of his senses, he is not in his right mind; **boire plus que de ~** to drink more than is sensible *ou* more than is good for one. **(b)** (*motif*) reason. **pour quelles ~s l'avez-vous renvoyé?** on what grounds did you sack him?, what were your reasons for sacking him?; **il n'y a pas de ~ de s'arrêter** there's no reason to stop; **ce n'est pas une ~!** that's no excuse! *ou* reason!; **avec (juste) ~** with good reason; **~ de plus** all the more reason (*pour faire* for doing); **comme de ~** as one might expect; **non sans ~** not without reason. **(c) avoir ~** to be right (*de faire* in doing, to do); **avoir ~ de qn/qch** to get the better of sb/sth; **donner ~ à qn** [*événement*] to prove sb right; [*personne*] to side with sb; **se faire une ~** to put up with it; **en ~ du froid** because of *ou* owing to the cold weather; **payé en ~ du travail fourni** paid according to the work produced; **à ~ de 5 F par caisse** at the rate of 5 francs per crate; (*Math*) **~ directe/indirecte** direct/inverse ratio *ou* proportion. **2: ~ d'État** reason of

State; ~ **d'être** raison d'être; (*Comm*) ~ **sociale** corporate name.

raisonnable [ʀɛzɔnabl(ə)] *adj* **(a)** (*sensé*) *personne* sensible, reasonable; *conseil* sensible, sound, sane. **(b)** (*décent*) reasonable, fair. ♦ **raisonnablement** *adv* sensibly, reasonably; *dépenser* moderately.

raisonner [ʀɛzɔne] (1) **1** *vi* (*penser*) to reason; (*discourir, ergoter*) to argue (*sur* about). **il raisonne juste** his reasoning is sound. **2** *vt* **(a)** ~ **qn** to reason with sb, make sb see reason. **(b)** *conduite* to reason out. **explication bien raisonnée** well-reasoned explanation. **3 se** ~ *vpr* to reason with o.s., try to be reasonable.
♦ **raisonné, e** *adj* (*gén*) reasoned. ♦ **raisonnement** *nm* **(a)** (*façon de réfléchir*) reasoning. **ses** ~**s m'étonnent** his reasoning surprises me. **(b)** (*argumentation*) argument. **un** ~ **logique** a logical argument, a logical line of reasoning. **(c)** (*péj: ergotages*) ~s argument, quibbling. ♦ **raisonneur, -euse** (*péj*) **1** *adj* argumentative. **2** *nm,f* arguer, quibbler.

rajeunir [ʀaʒœniʀ] (2) **1** *vt* **(a)** ~ **qn** *[cure]* to rejuvenate sb; *[repos, expérience etc]* to make sb feel (*ou* look) younger. **(b)** *manuel* to update, bring up to date; *institution* to modernize; *installation, vieux habits* to give a new look to, brighten up; *personnel* to recruit younger people into; *thème* to inject new life into. **2** *vi* *[personne]* to feel (*ou* look) younger; *[quartier]* to be modernized. **3 se** ~ *vpr* (*se prétendre moins âgé*) to make o.s. younger. ♦ **rajeunissant, e** *adj* *traitement, crème* rejuvenating. ♦ **rajeunissement** *nm* rejuvenation; updating; modernization.

rajouter [ʀaʒute] (1) *vt* *sel* to add (some) more; *commentaire* to add another. **il rajouta que ...** he added that ...; (*fig*) **en** ~* to overdo it. ♦ **rajout** *nm* addition.

rajuster [ʀaʒyste] (1) **1** *vt* *mécanisme* to readjust; *vêtement* to straighten, tidy. **2 se** ~ *vpr* *[personne]* to tidy *ou* straighten o.s. up, rearrange o.s. ♦ **rajustement** *nm* adjustment.

râle [ʀɑl] *nm* **(a)** *[blessé]* groan; *[mourant]* death rattle. **(b)** (*Méd*) rale. **(c)** (*Orn*) rail.

ralentir [ʀalɑ̃tiʀ] (2) **1** *vt* to slow down. ~ **sa marche** to slacken one's pace, slow down. **2** *vi* *[marcheur]* to slow down, slacken one's pace; *[automobiliste]* to slow down, reduce speed. **3 se** ~ *vpr* *[production]* to slow down *ou* up, slacken off; *[ardeur]* to flag. ♦ **ralenti, e 1** *adj* slow. **2** *nm* (*Ciné*) slow motion; (*Aut*) tick-over. **au** ~ slow motion; (*Aut, Ind*) **tourner au** ~ to tick over, idle; **vivre au** ~ to live at a slower pace. ♦ **ralentissement** *nm* slowing down; slackening off; flagging.

râler [ʀɑle] (1) *vi* **(a)** *[blessé]* to groan, moan; *[mourant]* to give the death rattle. **(b)** (*: *rouspéter*) to grouse*, moan*. **faire** ~ **qn** to infuriate sb, make sb fume. ♦ **râleur, -euse** *nm,f* grouser*, moaner*.

rallier [ʀalje] (7) **1** *vt* (*grouper*) to rally; (*unir*) to unite; (*rejoindre*) to rejoin; *suffrages* to bring in, win. ~ **qn à son avis** to bring sb round *ou* win sb over to one's opinion. **2 se** ~ *vpr* (*se regrouper*) to rally. **se** ~ **à** *parti* to join; *ennemi* to go over to; *chef* to rally round; *avis* to come round to. ♦ **ralliement** *nm* rallying. **son** ~ **à notre cause** his joining *ou* the fact that he joined our cause; **cri de** ~ rallying cry.

rallonger [ʀalɔ̃ʒe] (3) **1** *vt* (*gén*) to lengthen, make longer; *vacances, bâtiment* to extend. **2** *vi* (*) *[jours]* to get longer. ♦ **rallonge** *nf* *[table]* (extra) leaf; *[fil électrique]* extension cord *ou* flex; *[perche]* extension piece. **une** ~ **d'argent/de temps** some extra money/time.

rallumer [ʀalyme] (1) **1** *vt* *feu* to light (up) again, relight; *courage, conflit* to revive, rekindle. ~ **(la lumière)** to switch *ou* turn the light(s) on again. **2 se** ~ *vpr* *[incendie, guerre]* to flare up again; *[lampe]* to come on again; *[haine, courage]* to revive, be revived.

rallye [ʀali] *nm*: ~ **(automobile)** (car) rally.

ramage [ʀamaʒ] *nm* (*chant*) song. (*branchages, dessin*) ~**(s)** foliage.

ramasser [ʀamɑse] (1) **1** *vt* (*lit, fig: prendre*) to pick up; *copies, ordures* to collect; *fruits* to gather; *objets épars* to gather up *ou* together; *pommes de terre* to dig up; *maladie, amende* to get, pick up. ~ **une bûche*** to come a cropper*. **2 se** ~ *vpr* (*se pelotonner*) to curl up; (*pour bondir*) to crouch; (‡: *tomber, échouer*) to come a cropper*. ♦ **ramassage** *nm* picking up; collection; gathering. ~ **scolaire** school bus service. ♦ **ramassé, e** *adj* (*trapu*) squat, stocky; (*concis*) compact, condensed. ♦ **ramasseur, -euse** *nm,f* (*gén*) collector. ~ **de balles (de tennis)** ballboy; ~ **de pommes de terre** potato-picker. ♦ **ramassis** *nm* (*péj*) ~ **de** *voyous* pack *ou* bunch of; *doctrines, objets* jumble of.

rambarde [ʀɑ̃baʀd(ə)] *nf* guardrail.

ramdam‡ [ʀamdam] *nm* row, racket. **faire du** ~ to kick up* a row.

rame [ʀam] *nf* (*aviron*) oar; (*Rail*) train; (*Typ*) ream; (*Agr*) stake, stick.

rameau, *pl* ~**x** [ʀamo] *nm* (small) branch. (*Rel*) les **R**~**x** Palm Sunday.

ramener [ʀamne] (5) **1** *vt* **(a)** (*lit, fig: faire revenir*) to bring back; *paix* to restore. **je vais te** ~ **(en voiture)** I'll drive *ou* take you back (home); ~ **à la vie** to bring back to *ou* restore to life. **(b)** *couverture* to pull. ~ **ses cheveux en arrière** to brush one's hair back; ~ **ses jambes en arrière** to draw back one's legs. **(c)** (*réduire à*) ~ **qch à** to reduce sth to. **2 se** ~ *vpr* **(a)** *[problèmes]* **se** ~ **à** to come down to, boil down to. **(b)** (‡: *arriver*) to roll up‡, turn up*.

ramer [ʀame] (1) *vi* to row. ♦ **rameur, -euse** *nm,f* (*sportif*) oarsman (*ou* oarswoman), rower.

ramier [ʀamje] *nm*: **(pigeon)** ~ woodpigeon.

ramifier (se) [ʀamifje] (7) *vpr* *[veines]* to ramify; *[routes, branches]* to branch out (*en* into). ♦ **ramification** *nf* (*gén*) ramification.

ramollir [ʀamɔliʀ] (2) **1** *vt* to soften. **2 se** ~ *vpr* to get *ou* go soft. ♦ **ramolli, e** *adj* soft. ♦ **ramollissement** *nm* softening.

ramoner [ʀamɔne] (1) *vt* *cheminée* to sweep. ♦ **ramonage** *nm* chimney-sweeping. ♦ **ramoneur** *nm* (chimney) sweep.

rampe [ʀɑ̃p] *nf* **(a)** (*voie d'accès*) ramp; (*côte*) slope. ~ **de lancement** launching pad. **(b)** *[escalier]* banister(s); *[chemin]* handrail. **(c)** (*projecteurs*) **la** ~ the footlights.

ramper [ʀɑ̃pe] (1) *vi* *[serpent]* to crawl, creep; *[homme]* to crawl; *[plante, ombre]* to creep; *[sentiment]* to lurk. (*péj*) ~ **devant qn** to grovel before *ou* crawl to sb.

ramure [ʀamyʀ] *nf* *[cerf]* antlers; *[arbre]* boughs, foliage.

rancard‡ [ʀɑ̃kaʀ] *nm* (*tuyau*) tip; (*rendez-vous*) date. **donner** ~ **à qn** to make a date with sb. ♦ **rancarder**‡ (1) *vt* to tip off.

rancart‡ [ʀɑ̃kaʀ] *nm*: **mettre au** ~ to chuck out‡, scrap.

rance [ʀɑ̃s] *adj* *beurre* rancid; *odeur* rank, rancid. ♦ **rancir** (2) *vi* to go rancid.

rancœur [ʀɑ̃kœʀ] *nf* rancour, resentment.

rançon [ʀɑ̃sɔ̃] *nf* (*lit*) ransom. **la** ~ **de la gloire** the price of fame. ♦ **rançonner** (1) *vt* *voyageurs* to demand *ou* exact a ransom from; (*fig*) *contribuables* to fleece.

rancune [ʀɑ̃kyn] *nf* grudge, rancour. **garder** ~ **à qn** to hold a grudge against sb, bear sb a grudge (*de qch* for sth); **sans** ~**!** no hard feelings! ♦ **rancunier, -ière** *adj*: **être** ~ to bear a grudge.

randonnée [ʀɑ̃dɔne] *nf*: ~ **(en voiture)** drive, ride; ~ **(à bicyclette)** ride; ~ **(à pied)** walk, ramble;

(*grande*) hike; **faire une ~** to go for a drive (*ou* a ride *etc*).

rang [Rɑ̃] *nm* **(a)** (*rangée*) row, line; (*Mil, fig*) rank. **en ~ d'oignons** in a row *ou* line; **en ~s serrés** in close order, in serried ranks; **en ~ par 2** 2 abreast; **sur 4 ~s** 4 deep; **se mettre sur un ~** to get into *ou* form a line; **se mettre en ~s par 4** to get into *ou* form rows of 4. **(b)** (*noblesse*) station, rank. **(c)** (*hiérarchique*) rank; *[classement]* place. **avoir ~ de** to hold the rank of; **par ~ d'âge** in order of age; **mettre qn au ~ de** to count *ou* rank sb among; **c'est au premier ~ de mes préoccupations** that's uppermost in *ou* in the forefront of my mind. ♦ **rangée**[1] *nf* row, line.

ranger [Rɑ̃ʒe] (3) **1** *vt* **(a)** (*mettre en ordre*) *maison, papiers* to tidy (up); *mots* to arrange, order. **(b)** (*mettre à sa place*) (*gén*) to put away; *véhicule* to park. **où se rangent les tasses?** where do the cups go? *ou* belong?; **je le range parmi les meilleurs** I rank it among the best. **(c)** *écoliers* to line up, put into rows; *invités* to place. **2 se ~** *vpr* **(a)** *[automobiliste]* (*stationner*) to park; (*venir s'arrêter*) to pull in; *[piéton]* to step *ou* stand aside. **(b)** (*se mettre en rang*) to line up, get into rows. **(c)** (*se rallier à*) **se ~ à** *décision, avis* to fall in with; **se ~ du côté de qn** to side with sb. **(d)** (*: *se marier*) to settle down. ♦ **rangé, e**[2] *adj pièce* tidy; *vie* well-ordered; *personne* (*ordonné*) orderly; (*sans excès*) settled. **il est ~ maintenant** he has settled down now; **mal ~** untidy. ♦ **rangement** *nm* **(a)** *[objets]* putting away. **faire du ~** to do some tidying (up). **(b)** (*espace*) *[appartement]* cupboard space; *[remise]* storage space. **(c)** (*arrangement*) arrangement.

ranimer [Ranime] (1) **1** *vt blessé* to revive, bring round*; *souvenir, querelle, douleur* to revive; *feu, sentiment* to rekindle; *forces, ardeur* to revive, restore. **2 se ~** *vpr* to revive; to come round; to rekindle; to be restored.

rapace [Rapas] **1** *nm* (*Orn*) bird of prey. **2** *adj* (*Orn*) predatory; (*fig*) rapacious, grasping. ♦ **rapacité** *nf* (*lit, fig*) rapaciousness, rapacity.

rapatrier [RapatRije] (7) *vt personne* to repatriate; *objet* to bring back (home). ♦ **rapatrié, e** *nm,f* repatriate. ♦ **rapatriement** *nm* repatriation.

râper [Rɑpe] (1) *vt* (*Culin*) to grate; *bois* to rasp. ♦ **râpe** *nf* grater; rasp. ♦ **râpé, e 1** *adj* (*usé*) threadbare; (*Culin*) grated. **2** *nm* (*fromage*) grated cheese.

rapetisser [Raptise] (1) **1** *vt* (*raccourcir*) to shorten; (*dénigrer*) to belittle. (*faire paraître plus petit*) **~ qch** to make sth seem *ou* look small(er). **2** *vi*, **se ~** *vpr [vieillard]* to shrink, get smaller; *[jours]* to get shorter.

râpeux, -euse [Rɑpø, øz] *adj* (*gén*) rough.

raphia [Rafja] *nm* raffia.

rapiat, e [Rapja, at] **1** *adj* niggardly, tight-fisted. **2** *nm,f* niggard, skinflint.

rapide [Rapid] **1** *adj* (*gén*) quick, rapid, swift; *coureur* fast; *guérison* speedy; *mouvement* brisk; *intelligence* lively; *pente* steep, abrupt. **~ comme l'éclair** (as) quick as a flash. **2** *nm* **(a)** (*train*) express (train), fast train. **(b)** *[rivière]* rapid. ♦ **rapidement** *adv* (*gén*) fast, quickly, rapidly, swiftly, speedily; *marcher* briskly; *descendre en pente* steeply, abruptly. ♦ **rapidité** *nf* (*gén*) speed, rapidity, speediness, swiftness, quickness; *[mouvement]* briskness; *[intelligence]* liveliness.

rapiécer [Rapjese] (3 *et* 6) *vt* to patch (up).

rappel [Rapɛl] *nm* **(a)** *[ambassadeur, réservistes]* recall; (*Théât*) curtain call. **(b)** (*évocation, avertissement*) reminder; (*Comm: référence*) quote; (*somme due*) back pay; (*vaccination*) booster. **~ à l'ordre** call to order. **(c)** (*Alpinisme*) **faire un ~** to abseil, rope down.

rappeler [Raple] (4) **1** *vt* **(a)** (*faire revenir*) to call back; *réservistes, diplomate* to recall. **(b) ~ qch** (*mentionner*) to mention sth; (*Comm*) *référence* to quote sth; (*être similaire*) to be reminiscent of sth; **~ qch à qn** to remind sb of sth; **cela ne te rappelle rien?** doesn't that remind you of anything?, doesn't that ring a bell? **(c) ~ qn à la vie** to bring sb back to life, revive sb; **~ qn à l'ordre** to call sb to order; **~ qn à son devoir** to remind sb of his duty. **(d)** (*retéléphoner à*) to call *ou* ring *ou* phone back. **2 se ~** *vpr* to remember, recollect, recall.

rappliquer* [Raplike] (1) *vi* (*revenir*) to come back; (*arriver*) to turn up*, show up*.

rapport [RapɔR] *nm* **(a)** (*lien*) connection, relationship, link. **avoir beaucoup de ~/n'avoir aucun ~ avec qch** to have a lot to do/nothing to do with sth, be closely related/be unrelated to sth. **(b)** (*relations*) **~s** relations, relationships; **entretenir de bons/mauvais ~s avec qn** to be on good/bad terms *ou* have good/bad relations with sb; **~s (sexuels)** sexual relations. **(c)** (*compte rendu*) report; (*Mil*) conference. **~ de police** police report. **(d)** (*profit*) yield, return. **être d'un bon ~** to give a good profit *ou* return; **immeuble de ~** block of flats (used as a letting concern). **(e)** (*Math, Tech*) ratio. **~ de 1 à 100** ratio of 1 to 100. **(f)** (*locutions*) **être en ~ avec qch** (*en harmonie*) to be in keeping *ou* in line with sth; **être en ~ avec qn** to have connections *ou* dealings with sb; **mettre/se mettre en ~ avec qn** to put/get in touch *ou* contact with sb; **par ~ à** in relation to; **sous le ~ de l'honnêteté** from the point of view of honesty; **sous tous les ~s** in every respect; (*équilibre*) **le ~ des forces** the balance of power; (*lutte*) **des ~s de force** power struggle.

rapporter [RapɔRte] (1) **1** *vt* **(a)** *objet, réponse* to bring *ou* take back (*à* to). **(b)** (*Fin, fig*) *profit* to bring in. **placement qui rapporte 5%** investment that yields (a return of) 5% *ou* that brings in (a yield *ou* revenue of) 5%. **(c)** *fait* (*gén*) to report; (*mentionner*) to mention; (*citer*) to quote. **on nous a rapporté que** we were told that, it was reported to us that. **(d)** (*ajouter*) to add. **c'est un élément rapporté** this element has been added on. **(e)** (*établir un lien entre*) **~ qch à** to relate sth to. **(f)** (*annuler*) to revoke. **2** *vi* **(a)** (*Chasse*) to retrieve. **(b)** (*Fin*) to give a good return *ou* yield. **ça rapporte gros** it brings in a lot of money, it pays very well. **(c)** (*arg Scol: moucharder*) **~ (sur ses camarades)** to tell on* *ou* sneak on* one's friends. **3 se ~** *vpr* **(a) se ~ à qch** to relate to sth; **ça se rapporte à ce que je disais tout à l'heure** that ties up with *ou* links up with *ou* relates to what I was saying just now. **(b) s'en ~ à qn/au jugement de qn** to rely on sb/on sb's judgment.

rapporteur, -euse [RapɔRtœR, øz] **1** *nm,f* (*mouchard*) telltale, sneak*. **2** *nm* (*Admin*) reporter; (*Géom*) protractor.

rapprocher [RapRɔʃe] (1) **1** *vt* **(a)** (*approcher*) to bring closer *ou* nearer (*de* to). **~ sa chaise (de la table)** to pull *ou* draw one's chair up (to the table). **(b)** (*réconcilier, réunir*) to bring together. **(c)** *indices, textes* (*confronter*) to put *ou* bring together; (*assimiler*) to establish a connection *ou* link between. **c'est à ~ de ce qu'on disait tout à l'heure** that ties up *ou* connects with what was being said earlier. **2 se ~** *vpr* **(a)** (*approcher*) to get closer *ou* nearer (*de* to). **rapproche-toi** come *ou* move *ou* draw closer; **se ~ de la vérité** to get near *ou* close to the truth. **(b)** (*en fréquence*) to become more frequent. **(c)** *[ennemis]* to come together; *[points de vue]* to draw closer together. **se ~ de** to move *ou* draw closer to. **(d)** (*s'apparenter à*) to be close to. **ça se rapproche de ce qu'on disait** that's close to *ou* that ties up with what was being said. ♦ **rapproché, e** *adj*: **être ~** (*proche*) to be close *ou* near (*de* to); (*répété*) to be frequent. ♦ **rapprochement** *nm* (*réconciliation*) reconciliation; (*comparaison*) comparison; (*rapport*) link, connection. **le ~ des 2 objets** (*action*) bringing the 2 objects (closer) together; (*résultat*) the fact that the 2 objects are close together.

rapt [ʀapt] *nm* (*enlèvement*) abduction.

raquette [ʀakɛt] *nf* (*Tennis*) racket; (*Ping-Pong*) bat; (*à neige*) snowshoe.

rare [ʀaʀ] *adj* **(a)** (*peu commun*) (*gén*) rare; *énergie* exceptional; *imprudence* singular. **ça n'a rien de ~** there's nothing uncommon *ou* unusual about it; **il était ~ qu'il ne sache pas** he rarely *ou* seldom did not know. **(b)** (*peu nombreux*) few, rare. **les ~s voitures qui passaient** the few *ou* odd cars that went by; **les clients sont ~s** customers are scarce *ou* are few and far between. **(c)** (*peu abondant*) (*gén*) scarce; *barbe* thin; *végétation* sparse; *gaz* rare. *[légumes]* **se faire ~** to become scarce, be in short supply. ♦ **se raréfier** (7) *vpr* (*gén*) to become scarce; *[air]* to rarefy, get thin. ♦ **rarement** *adv* rarely, seldom. ♦ **rareté** *nf* **(a)** *[objet, cas]* rarity; *[vivres, argent]* scarcity; *[visites]* infrequency. **(b)** (*objet*) rarity; (*événement*) rare *ou* unusual occurrence. ♦ **rarissime** *adj* extremely rare.

ras, e [ʀɑ, ʀɑz] *adj* **(a)** *poil, herbe* short; *cheveux* close-cropped; *mesure* full. **à poil ~** *chien* short-haired; *étoffe* with a short pile; **cheveux coupés (à) ~** hair cut short. **(b)** (*locutions*) **à ~ de terre** level with the ground; **coupé à ~ de terre** cut down to the ground; **voler au ~ de l'eau** to skim the water; **à ~ bords** to the brim; **en ~e campagne** in open country; **pull ~ du cou** crew-neck jumper, round-neck jumper; **j'en ai ~ le bol*** I'm fed up to the back teeth‡.

rasade [ʀɑzad] *nf* glassful.

raser [ʀɑze] (1) **1** *vt* **(a)** *barbe* to shave off; *menton, malade etc* to shave. **(b)** *[projectile]* to graze, scrape; *[oiseau, balle de tennis]* to skim (over). **~ les murs** to hug the walls. **(c)** (*abattre*) to raze (to the ground). **(d)** (*: *ennuyer*) to bore. **2 se ~** *vpr* **(a)** (*toilette*) to shave. **se ~ les jambes** to shave one's legs. **(b)** (*: *s'ennuyer*) to be bored stiff *ou* to tears. ♦ **rasage** *nm* shaving. ♦ **rasant, e** *adj* **(a)** (*: *ennuyeux*) boring. **(b)** *lumière* low-angled. **tir ~** grazing fire. ♦ **rasé, e** *adj menton* (clean-)shaven; *tête* shaven. **mal ~** unshaven; **~ de près** close-shaven. ♦ **rase-mottes** *nm inv*: **faire du ~** to hedgehop. ♦ **raseur, -euse*** *adj, nm,f* bore. ♦ **rasoir** *nm* **(a)** razor. **~ électrique** (electric) shaver, electric razor. **(b)** (*: *importun*) bore.

rassasier [ʀasazje] (7) **1** *vt faim, désirs* to satisfy. **~ qn** to satisfy sb *ou* sb's hunger (*de* with); **être rassasié** to be satisfied, have eaten one's fill; (*dégoûté*) to have had more than enough (*de* of). **2 se ~** *vpr* to satisfy one's hunger. **je ne me rassasierai jamais de ...** I'll never tire of ... .

rassembler [ʀasɑ̃ble] (1) **1** *vt* (*gén*) to gather, assemble; *troupes* to rally; *troupeau* to round up; *objets, notes* to gather together, collect; (*après démontage*) to put back together, reassemble; *idées* to collect; *courage* to summon up. **2 se ~** *vpr* to gather, assemble. ♦ **rassemblement** *nm* **(a)** gathering, assembling *etc.* (*Mil*) **~!** fall in! **(b)** (*groupe*) gathering; (*parti*) union.

rasseoir [ʀaswaʀ] (26) **1** *vt bébé* to sit back up (straight); *objet* to put back up straight. **2 se ~** *vpr* to sit down again.

rasséréner (se) [ʀaseʀene] (6) *vpr* to become serene again.

rassir *vi*, **se ~** *vpr* [ʀasiʀ] (2) to go stale. ♦ **rassis, e** *adj* (*lit, péj*) stale.

rassurer [ʀasyʀe] (1) **1** *vt*: **~ qn** to put sb's mind at ease, reassure sb. **2 se ~** *vpr* to put one's mind at ease, reassure o.s. ♦ **rassurant, e** *adj* reassuring, comforting, cheering.

rat [ʀa] *nm* rat. **il est fait comme un ~** he's cornered, he has no escape; **~ de bibliothèque** bookworm; **~ des champs** fieldmouse; **~ d'hôtel** hotel thief; **~ musqué** muskrat, musquash; **(petit) ~ de l'Opéra** pupil of the Opéra ballet class.

ratatiner [ʀatatine] (1) **1** *vt* **(a)** *pomme* to dry up, shrivel; *visage* to wrinkle. **(b)** (‡: *détruire*) to wreck. **se faire ~** (*battre*) to get thrashed; (*tuer*) to get done in‡. **2 se ~** *vpr [pomme]* to shrivel *ou* dry up; *[visage, personne]* to become wrinkled *ou* shrivelled.

rate [ʀat] *nf* (*Anat*) spleen.

râteau, *pl* **~x** [ʀɑto] *nm* (*Agr, Roulette*) rake.

râtelier [ʀɑtəlje] *nm* rack; (*: *dentier*) set of dentures.

rater [ʀate] (1) **1** *vi [coup]* to misfire, fail to go off; *[projet]* to fail, go wrong, backfire. **tout faire ~** to ruin everything; **ça ne va pas ~*** it's dead certain*. **2** *vt* (*) *cible, occasion, train* to miss; *gâteau, travail* to mess up*, spoil, botch; *examen* to fail, flunk*. **raté!** missed!; (*iro*) **il n'en rate pas une** he's always putting his foot in it*; **je ne te raterai pas!** you won't get away with it!; **~ son effet** to spoil one's effect; **il a raté son coup** he didn't pull it off. ♦ **raté, e 1** *nm,f* (*personne*) failure. **2** *nm* (*Aut*) *[arme]* misfire. **avoir des ~s** to misfire.

ratiboiser‡ [ʀatibwaze] (1) *vt maison* to wreck; *personne* to do in*. **~ qch à qn** (*au jeu*) to clean sb out of sth*; (*en le volant*) to nick‡ *ou* pinch* sth from sb.

ratifier [ʀatifje] (7) *vt* to ratify. ♦ **ratification** *nf* (*Admin, Jur*) ratification.

ration [ʀɑsjɔ̃] *nf* (*gén*) ration; (*fig: part*) share; *[soldat]* rations.

rationaliser [ʀasjɔnalize] (1) *vt* to rationalize. ♦ **rationnel, -elle** *adj* rational. ♦ **rationnellement** *adv* rationally.

rationner [ʀasjɔne] (1) **1** *vt charbon, personne* to ration. **2 se ~** *vpr* to ration o.s. ♦ **rationnement** *nm* rationing.

ratisser [ʀatise] (1) *vt gravier* to rake; *feuilles* to rake up; (*Mil, Police*) to comb; (*: *au jeu*) to clean out*, fleece*. ♦ **ratissage** *nm* raking; combing.

raton [ʀatɔ̃] *nm*: **~ laveur** racoon.

rattacher [ʀataʃe] (1) *vt prisonnier* to tie up again; *lacets* to do up *ou* fasten again; *territoire, service* to join (*à* to), unite (*à* with); *problème* to link, connect, tie up (*à* with); *fait* to relate (*à* to). **rien ne le rattache plus à sa famille** nothing binds *ou* ties him to his family any more. ♦ **rattachement** *nm* uniting (*à* with), joining (*à* to).

rattraper [ʀatʀape] (1) **1** *vt* **(a)** *prisonnier* to recapture; *objet, enfant qui tombe* to catch (hold of); *voiture, coureur, (fig) leçon en retard* to catch up with. **on ne m'y rattrapera plus** I won't be caught (at it) again. **(b)** *mayonnaise* to salvage; *erreur, temps perdu* to make up for; *argent perdu* to recover, get back, recoup; *sommeil* to catch up on. **(c)** (*Scol: repêcher*) **~ qn** to allow sb to pass, let sb get through. **2 se ~** *vpr* (*reprendre son équilibre*) to stop o.s. falling; (*fig: récupérer*) to make up for it, make good (one's losses *ou* one's mistakes). **se ~ à une branche** to catch hold of a branch to stop o.s. falling. ♦ **rattrapage** *nm [candidat]* passing. **le ~ d'un oubli/du retard** making up for an omission/for lost time; **~ scolaire** remedial teaching.

raturer [ʀatyʀe] (1) *vt* (*corriger*) to make an alteration to; (*barrer*) to erase, delete. ♦ **rature** *nf* alteration; erasure, deletion.

rauque [ʀok] *adj voix* (*enrouée*) hoarse; (*éraillée*) husky; *cri* raucous.

ravage [ʀavaʒ] *nm*: **faire des ~s** to wreak havoc (*dans* in). ♦ **ravagé, e‡** *adj* nuts*, bonkers‡. ♦ **ravager** (3) *vt pays* to lay waste, ravage, devastate; *visage [maladie]* to ravage; *[soucis]* to harrow. ♦ **ravageur, -euse** *adj* devastating.

ravaler [ʀavale] (1) *vt* **(a)** (*nettoyer*) to clean, give a face lift* to; (*réparer*) to restore. **(b)** *sanglots, colère* to choke back. **(c)** *dignité, personne* to

lower. ♦ **ravalement** *nm* cleaning; restoration; face lift*.
ravauder [ʀavode] (1) *vt vêtement* to repair, mend; *chaussette* to darn.
rave [ʀav] *nf (Bot)* rape.
ravi, e [ʀavi] *adj (enchanté)* delighted.
ravier [ʀavje] *nm* hors d'œuvres dish.
ravigoter* [ʀavigɔte] (1) *vt* to buck up*.
ravin [ʀavɛ̃] *nm (gén)* gully; *(encaissé)* ravine. ♦ **ravinement** *nm* gullying. ♦ **raviner** (1) *vt (Géog)* to gully; *visage* to furrow.
ravir [ʀaviʀ] (2) *vt* **(a)** *(charmer)* to delight. **cela lui va à ~** that suits her beautifully. **(b)** *(enlever)* **~ qch à qn** to rob sb of sth, take sth (away) from sb. ♦ **ravissant, e** *adj* ravishing, delightful. ♦ **ravissement** *nm* rapture. **plongé dans le ~** in raptures; **regarder qn avec ~** to look at sb rapturously. ♦ **ravisseur, -euse** *nm,f* kidnapper, abductor.
raviser (se) [ʀavize] (1) *vpr* to change one's mind, decide otherwise, think better of it.
ravitailler [ʀavitɑje] (1) **1** *vt (en vivres)* to provide with fresh supplies; *(en carburant)* to refuel. **2 se ~** *vpr [armée]* to get fresh supplies; *[ménagère]* to stock up *(à* at); *[véhicule]* to refuel. ♦ **ravitaillement** *nm (action)* resupplying; refuelling; *(réserves)* supplies. **aller au ~** to go for fresh supplies.
raviver [ʀavive] (1) *vt feu, sentiment* to revive, rekindle; *couleur* to brighten up.
ravoir [ʀavwaʀ] *vt (recouvrer)* to have *ou* get back; *(obtenir davantage)* to get more *ou* another; (*: *nettoyer)* to get clean.
rayer [ʀeje] (8) *vt (marquer)* to rule, line; *(érafler)* to scratch; *(biffer)* to cross *ou* score out, delete. **~ qn d'une liste** to cross sb *ou* sb's name off a list, delete sb's name from a list. ♦ **rayé, e** *adj tissu, pelage* striped.
rayon [ʀɛjɔ̃] *nm* **(a)** *(gén, Opt, Phys: faisceau)* ray; *[jour]* ray, beam; *[phare]* beam. *(radiations)* **~s** radiation; **~s X** X-rays; **~ laser** laser beam; *(lit, fig)* **~ de soleil** ray of sunshine; **~ de lune** moonbeam; **~ d'espoir** ray *ou* gleam of hope. **(b)** *[roue]* spoke. **(c)** *(planche)* shelf; *[bibliothèque]* (book)shelf. **(d)** *(Comm) (section)* department; *(comptoir)* counter. **c'est son ~** *(spécialité)* that's his line; *(responsabilité)* that's his concern *ou* responsibility *ou* department*. **(e)** *[ruche]* (honey)comb. **(f)** *(Math, fig)* radius. **dans un ~ de 10 km** within a radius of 10 km *ou* a 10-km radius; **~ d'action** *(lit)* range; *(fig)* scope, range; **à grand ~ d'action** long-range; *(Aut)* **~ de braquage** lock. ♦ **rayonnage** *nm*: **~(s)** set of shelves, shelving.
rayonne [ʀɛjɔn] *nf* rayon.
rayonner [ʀɛjɔne] (1) *vi* **(a)** *[influence, joie, astre]* to radiate. *[prestige etc]* **~ sur/dans** to extend over/in; **~ de bonheur** to be radiant *ou* glowing with happiness. **(b)** *(Phys) [chaleur, énergie]* to radiate. **(c) ~ dans une région** *[touristes]* to tour around a region (from a base); *[cars]* to service a region. **(d)** *[avenues, lignes]* to radiate *(autour de* from, out from). ♦ **rayonnant, e** *adj (Phys, fig)* radiant. ♦ **rayonnement** *nm [culture]* influence; *[influence]* extension; *[personnalité, beauté, astre]* radiance; *(Phys: radiation)* radiation.
rayure [ʀejyʀ] *nf (dessin)* stripe; *(éraflure)* scratch. **papier à ~s** striped paper.
raz-de-marée [ʀɑdmaʀe] *nm inv (Géog, fig)* tidal wave. **~ électoral** landslide.
razzia [ʀazja] *nf* raid, foray. *(fig)* **faire une ~ dans qch*** to raid *ou* plunder sth.
ré [ʀe] *nm (Mus)* D; *(en chantant)* re.
réaccoutumer [ʀeakutyme] (1) **1** *vt* to reaccustom. **2 se ~** *vpr* to reaccustom o.s. *(à* to).
réacteur [ʀeaktœʀ] *nm (Aviat)* jet engine; *(Chim, Phys nucléaire)* reactor.
réaction [ʀeaksjɔ̃] *nf (gén)* reaction. **être sans ~** to show no reaction; **~ en chaîne** chain reaction; *(Aviat)* **moteur à ~** jet engine. ♦ **réactionnaire** *adj, nmf* reactionary.
réadapter [ʀeadapte] (1) **1** *vt personne* to readjust *(à* to); *(Méd)* to rehabilitate; *muscle* to re-educate. **2 se ~** *vpr* to readjust *(à* to). ♦ **réadaptation** *nf* readjustment; rehabilitation; re-education.
réaffirmer [ʀeafiʀme] (1) *vt* to reaffirm, reassert.
réagir [ʀeaʒiʀ] (2) *vi* to react *(à* to, *contre* against, *sur* upon).
réaliser [ʀealize] (1) **1** *vt* **(a)** *rêve* to achieve, fulfil; *effort* to make, exercise; *exploit* to achieve, carry off; *projet* to carry out. **(b)** (*: *se rendre compte de)* to realize. **(c)** *(Ciné)* to produce. **(d)** *vente, bénéfice* to make. **(e)** *(Fin) capital* to realize. **2 se ~** *vpr [rêve]* to come true; *[personnalité]* to fulfil o.s. ♦ **réalisateur, -trice** *nm,f (Ciné, Rad, TV)* director. ♦ **réalisation** *nf* **(a)** *(action)* realization; fulfilment, achievement. **(b)** *(ouvrage)* achievement, creation. **(c)** *(Ciné)* production.
réalisme [ʀealism(ə)] *nm* realism. ♦ **réaliste** **1** *adj* realistic. **2** *nmf* realist.
réalité [ʀealite] *nf* reality. **en ~** in (actual) fact, in reality; **la ~ dépasse la fiction** truth is stranger than fiction; **son rêve est devenu (une) ~** his dream became (a) reality *ou* came true.
réanimer [ʀeanime] (1) *vt* to resuscitate, revive. ♦ **réanimation** *nf* resuscitation.
réapparaître [ʀeapaʀɛtʀ(ə)] (57) *vi* to reappear. ♦ **réapparition** *nf* reappearance.
réapprendre [ʀeapʀɑ̃dʀ(ə)] (58) *vt (gén)* to relearn, learn again. **~ qch à qn** to teach sth to sb again.
réapprovisionner [ʀeapʀɔvizjɔne] (1) **1** *vt* to restock. **2 se ~** *vpr* to stock up again *(en* with).
réarmer [ʀeaʀme] (1) **1** *vt fusil, appareil-photo* to reload; *bateau* to refit. **2** *vi,* **se ~** *vpr [pays]* to rearm. ♦ **réarmement** *nm (Pol)* rearmament.
réassortir [ʀeasɔʀtiʀ] (2) **1** *vt magasin* to restock *(en* with); *stock* to replenish; *verres* to match (up). **2 se ~** *vpr (Comm)* to stock up again *(de* with). ♦ **réassortiment** *nm* replenishment.
rébarbatif, -ive [ʀebaʀbatif, iv] *adj mine* forbidding, unprepossessing; *sujet, tâche* daunting, forbidding.
rebâtir [ʀ(ə)bɑtiʀ] (2) *vt* to rebuild.
rebattre [ʀ(ə)batʀ(ə)] (41) *vt*: **~ les oreilles de qn de qch** to keep harping about sth*. ♦ **rebattu, e** *adj citation* hackneyed.
rebelle [ʀəbɛl] **1** *adj soldat* rebel; *enfant, esprit* rebellious; *maladie* stubborn; *cheveux* unruly. **~ à** *discipline* unamenable to; **il est ~ à la poésie** poetry is a closed book to him. **2** *nmf* rebel. ♦ **se rebeller** (1) *vpr* to rebel *(contre* against). ♦ **rébellion** *nf (révolte)* rebellion. *(rebelles)* **la ~** the rebels.
rebiffer (se)* [ʀ(ə)bife] (1) *vpr* to hit *ou* strike back *(contre* at).
reboiser [ʀ(ə)bwaze] (1) *vt* to reafforest.
rebondir [ʀ(ə)bɔ̃diʀ] (2) *vi* **(a)** *(sur le sol)* to bounce; *(contre un mur etc)* to rebound. **(b)** *[conversation, action]* to get going *ou* moving again, spring to life again; *[scandale]* to take a new turn. **faire ~** to set *ou* get going again. ♦ **rebond** *nm* bounce; rebound. ♦ **rebondi, e** *adj objet* potbellied; *croupe* rounded; *ventre* fat; *visage* chubby; *porte-monnaie* well-lined. ♦ **rebondissement** *nm [affaire]* (sudden new) development *(de* in).
rebord [ʀ(ə)bɔʀ] *nm [assiette, pot]* rim; *[puits, falaise, table]* edge. **le ~ de la fenêtre** the windowsill, the window ledge.
rebours [ʀ(ə)buʀ] *nm*: **à ~** *(à rebrousse-poil)* the wrong way; *(à l'envers)* the other way round; **compter à ~** to count backwards; **faire tout à ~** to

do everything the wrong way round; (*à l'opposé de*) **à ~ de** against.
rebouteux, -euse [R(ə)butø, øz] *nm,f* bonesetter.
rebrousser [R(ə)bRuse] (1) *vt poil* to brush up. **~ chemin** to turn back, retrace one's steps; (*lit, fig*) **à rebrousse-poil** the wrong way.
rebuffade [R(ə)byfad] *nf* rebuff.
rébus [Rebys] *nm* rebus.
rebut [Rəby] *nm* (*déchets*) scrap. **mettre au ~** to scrap, throw out, discard; (*péj: racaille*) **le ~ de la société** the scum *ou* dregs of society; (*Poste*) **~s** dead letters.
rebuter [R(ə)byte] (1) **1** *vt* (*décourager*) to put off, dishearten, discourage; (*répugner*) to repel; (*repousser*) to repulse. **2 se ~** *vpr* to be discouraged. ♦ **rebutant, e** *adj* repellent; off-putting; disheartening.
récalcitrant, e [Rekalsitrɑ̃, ɑ̃t] *adj, nm,f* recalcitrant.
recaler [R(ə)kale] (1) *vt* (*Scol*) to fail. **se faire ~ (en histoire)** to fail *ou* flunk* (history).
récapituler [Rekapityle] (1) *vt* to recapitulate, sum up. ♦ **récapitulatif, -ive** *adj* recapitulatory, summary. ♦ **récapitulation** *nf* recapitulation, summing up.
recauser* [R(ə)koze] (1) *vi*: **~ de qch** to talk about sth again.
receler [Rəs(ə)le] (5) *vt objet volé* to receive; *voleur* to harbour; *trésor* to conceal. ♦ **recel** *nm*: **~ (d'objets volés)** (*action*) receiving stolen goods, receiving; (*résultat*) possession of stolen goods. ♦ **receleur, -euse** *nm,f* receiver.
récemment [Resamɑ̃] *adv* recently. **l'as-tu vu ~?** have you seen him lately? *ou* recently?
recenser [R(ə)sɑ̃se] (1) *vt population* to take a census of; *objets* to make an inventory of; (*Mil*) to compile a register of. ♦ **recensement** *nm* census; inventory; registration. ♦ **recenseur** *adj m, nm*: **(agent) ~** census taker.
récent, e [Resɑ̃, ɑ̃t] *adj événement* recent; *propriétaire* new.
récépissé [Resepise] *nm* receipt.
réception [Resɛpsjɔ̃] *nf* **(a)** (*gala*) reception. **(b)** (*accueil*) reception, welcome. **discours de ~** welcoming speech. **(c)** (*salon*) reception room; *[hôtel]* (*hall*) entrance hall, lobby; (*bureau*) reception desk. **salle de ~** function room. **(d)** *[paquet, lettre]* receipt; (*Bio, Rad, TV*) reception. **(e)** (*Sport*) *[ballon]* trapping, catching; *[sauteur]* landing. ♦ **récepteur, -trice 1** *adj* receiving. **2** *nm* (*gén, Téléc*) receiver. ♦ **réceptif, -ive** *adj* receptive (*à* to). ♦ **réceptionnaire** *nmf [marchandises]* receiving clerk. ♦ **réceptionner** (1) *vt marchandises* to receive, take delivery of; *ballon* to trap, catch. ♦ **réceptionniste** *nmf* receptionist. ♦ **réceptivité** *nf* (*gén*) receptivity, receptiveness.
récession [Resesjɔ̃] *nf* recession. ♦ **récessif, -ive** *adj* recessive.
recette [R(ə)sɛt] *nf* **(a)** (*Culin*) recipe; (*Chim*) formula; (*fig: truc*) formula, recipe (*de* for). **(b)** (*recouvrement*) collection; (*encaisse*) takings. **faire ~** to be a big success, be a winner; (*rentrées d'argent*) **~s** receipts; (*Impôts*) **~-perception** tax office.
recevabilité [Rəsvabilite] *nf* (*Jur*) admissibility. ♦ **recevable** *adj* admissible.
receveur, -euse [Rəsvœr, øz] *nm,f* (*Méd*) recipient. **~ (d'autobus)** bus conductor (*ou* conductress); **~ (des contributions)** tax collector *ou* officer; **~ (des postes)** postmaster (*ou* mistress).
recevoir [RəsvwaR] (28) **1** *vt* **(a)** (*gén*) to receive, get; *refus* to meet with. **nous avons bien reçu votre lettre du 15 courant** we acknowledge receipt of your letter of the 15th instant; **je n'ai d'ordre à ~ de personne** I don't take orders from anyone; **il a reçu un coup de pied/de poing** he got kicked/punched; **c'est lui qui a tout reçu** he got the worst of it; **recevez l'expression de mes sentiments distingués** yours faithfully *ou* sincerely. **(b)** *invité* (*accueillir*) to receive, welcome, greet; (*à dîner*) to entertain; (*pour coucher*) to take in; (*Admin*) *demandeur* to see. **le docteur reçoit de 10h à 12h** the doctor's surgery *ou* office (*US*) is from 10 a.m. till noon; **~ la visite de qn** to receive *ou* have a visit from sb. **(c)** *candidat* to pass. **être reçu à un examen** to pass an exam; **il a été reçu premier** he came first. **(d)** (*contenir*) *[hôtel]* to take, hold, accommodate; (*récolter*) *[gouttière]* to collect. **2 se ~** *vpr* (*en sautant*) to land.
rechange [R(ə)ʃɑ̃ʒ] *nm* **(a) ~ (de vêtements)** change of clothes. **(b) de ~** *solution* alternative; *outil* spare; **j'ai apporté des chaussures de ~** I brought a spare *ou* an extra pair of shoes.
réchapper [Reʃape] (1) *vi*: **~ de** *ou* **à** *accident* to come through.
recharge [R(ə)ʃaRʒ(ə)] *nf [arme]* reload; *[stylo]* refill. ♦ **recharger** (3) *vt véhicule, arme, appareil-photo* to reload; *briquet* to refill; *accumulateur* to recharge. ♦ **rechargement** *nm* reloading; refilling; recharging.
réchauffer [Reʃofe] (1) **1** *vt* **(a)** (*Culin*) **(faire** *ou* **mettre à) ~** to reheat, heat *ou* warm up again. **(b)** *personne* to warm up; *cœur* to warm; *courage* to revive, rekindle. **(c)** *[soleil]* to heat up, warm up. **2 se ~** *vpr [temps]* to get warmer; *[personne]* to warm o.s. (up). ♦ **réchaud** *nm* stove. ♦ **réchauffé, e** *adj* (*lit*) reheated, warmed-up; (*péj: fig*) rehashed (*péj*); *plaisanterie* stale, old hat. ♦ **réchauffement** *nm* warming (up). **un ~ de la température** a rise *ou* an increase in the temperature.
rêche [Rɛʃ] *adj* rough, harsh.
rechercher [R(ə)ʃɛRʃe] (1) *vt* **(a)** *objet égaré* to look for, search for, hunt for; *honneurs, danger* to seek; *succès, plaisir* to pursue; *cause d'accident* to look for, try to determine. **~ comment** to try to find out how; **'on recherche femme de ménage'** 'cleaning lady required'; **recherché pour meurtre** wanted for murder; **~ la perfection** to strive for *ou* seek perfection; **~ l'amitié de qn** to seek sb's friendship. **(b)** (*chercher à nouveau*) to search for *ou* look for again. ♦ **recherche** *nf* **(a)** (*gén*) search (*de* for); *[plaisirs, gloire]* pursuit (*de* of); *[perfection]* quest (*de* for). **se mettre à la ~ de qch** to go in search of sth, look *ou* hunt *ou* search for sth; (*enquête*) **faire des ~s** to make investigations. **(b)** (*Scol, Univ*) **la ~** research; **faire des ~s sur un sujet** to do *ou* carry out research into a subject; **travail de ~** piece of research. **(c)** *[tenue, ameublement]* meticulousness, studied elegance; (*péj: affectation*) affectation. ♦ **recherché, e** *adj* (*très demandé*) in great demand, much sought-after; (*de qualité*) choice, exquisite; *style* mannered; *tenue* meticulous; (*péj*) affected, studied.
rechigner [R(ə)ʃiɲe] (1) *vi* to balk, jib (*à qch* at sth, *à faire* at doing).
rechute [R(ə)ʃyt] *nf* (*Méd*) relapse. **faire une ~** to have a relapse. ♦ **rechuter** (1) *vi* to have a relapse.
récidive [Residiv] *nf* (*Jur*) second *ou* subsequent offence; (*Méd*) recurrence; (*fig*) repetition. ♦ **récidiver** (1) *vi* (*Jur*) to commit a second *ou* subsequent offence; (*fig*) to do it again; (*Méd*) to recur. ♦ **récidiviste** *nmf* recidivist.
récif [Resif] *nm* reef.
récipient [Resipjɑ̃] *nm* container, receptacle.
réciproque [ResipRɔk] **1** *adj* reciprocal. **2** *nf*: **la ~** (*l'inverse*) the opposite, the reverse; (*la pareille*) the same. ♦ **réciprocité** *nf* reciprocity. ♦ **réciproquement** *adv* (*l'un l'autre*) each other, one another; (*vice versa*) vice versa.
récit [Resi] *nm* (*action, histoire*) account; (*genre*) narrative; (*Théât*) monologue. **faire le ~ de** to give an account of.

récital, *pl* ~**s** [ʀesital] *nm* recital.

réciter [ʀesite] (1) *vt* to recite. ♦ **récitation** *nf* (*poème*) recitation; (*action*) recital.

réclamation [ʀeklamɑsjɔ̃] *nf* complaint. **faire une** ~ to make *ou* lodge a complaint; (*Téléc*) **téléphonez aux** ~**s** ring the engineers.

réclame [ʀeklam] *nf* (*annonce*) advertisement, advert. (*publicité*) **la** ~ advertising; **faire de la** ~ **pour** to advertise; **article (en)** ~ special offer.

réclamer [ʀeklame] (1) **1** *vt aide, argent etc* to ask for; *droit, part* to claim; *patience, soin* to call for, require, demand. ~ **l'indulgence de qn** to beg *ou* crave sb's indulgence; **je réclame la parole!** I ask *ou* beg to speak!; **il se réclame de l'école romantique** he claims to draw his inspiration from the romantic school. **2** *vi* to complain.

reclasser [ʀ(ə)klɑse] (1) *vt chômeur* to redeploy; *ex-prisonnier* to rehabilitate.

reclus, e [ʀəkly, yz] **1** *adj* cloistered. **2** *nm,f* recluse. ♦ **réclusion** *nf*: ~ **(criminelle)** imprisonment.

recoiffer [ʀ(ə)kwafe] (1) **1** *vt*: ~ **qn** to do sb's hair. **2 se** ~ *vpr* to do one's hair.

recoin [ʀəkwɛ̃] *nm* nook.

récolter [ʀekɔlte] (1) *vt* (*Agr*) to harvest, gather (in); *signatures, argent* to collect; (*) *coups* to get, collect*. ♦ **récoltant, e** *nm,f* grower. ♦ **récolte** *nf* (*action*) harvesting, gathering (in); (*lit, fig: produit*) crop; *[blé]* harvest.

recommander [ʀ(ə)kɔmɑ̃de] (1) **1** *vt* **(a)** (*gén*) to recommend (*à* to). ~ **à qn de faire** to recommend *ou* advise sb to do; **il est recommandé de** it's advisable to, you would be well-advised to. **(b)** *lettre* (*pour attester sa remise*) to record; (*pour assurer sa valeur*) to register. **2 se** ~ *vpr*: **se** ~ **de qn** to give sb's name as a reference; **il se recommande par son talent** his talent commends him. ♦ **recommandable** *adj* commendable. ♦ **recommandation** *nf* recommendation; recording; registration. ♦ **recommandé, e** *adj* **(a) envoyer qch en** ~ to send sth recorded delivery (*ou* by registered mail). **(b)** (*conseillé*) recommended.

recommencer [ʀ(ə)kɔmɑ̃se] (3) **1** *vt récit, travail* to begin *ou* start (over) again; *erreur* to make again, repeat; *combat* to renew. **2** *vi* (*gén*) to begin *ou* start again; *[combat]* to start afresh, resume. ~ **à** *ou* **de faire** to begin *ou* start to do *ou* doing again. ♦ **recommencement** *nm* new beginning, renewal.

recomparaître [ʀ(ə)kɔ̃paʀɛtʀ(ə)] (57) *vi* (*Jur*) to appear (in court) again.

récompense [ʀekɔ̃pɑ̃s] *nf* reward; (*prix*) award. **en** ~ **de** in return for. ♦ **récompenser** (1) *vt* to reward (*de* for).

recompter [ʀ(ə)kɔ̃te] (1) *vt* to count again, recount.

réconcilier [ʀekɔ̃silje] (7) **1** *vt* to reconcile. **2 se** ~ *vpr* to be *ou* become reconciled (*avec* with). ♦ **réconciliation** *nf* reconciliation.

reconduire [ʀ(ə)kɔ̃dɥiʀ] (38) *vt* **(a)** *politique, bail* to renew. **(b)** ~ **qn chez lui** to see *ou* take sb (back) home; **il m'a reconduit à la porte** he showed me to the door. ♦ **reconductible** *adj* renewable. ♦ **reconduction** *nf* renewal.

réconfort [ʀekɔ̃fɔʀ] *nm* comfort. ♦ **réconfortant, e** *adj parole* comforting; *aliment* fortifying. ♦ **réconforter** (1) *vt* to comfort; to fortify.

reconnaître [ʀ(ə)kɔnɛtʀ(ə)] (57) **1** *vt* **(a)** (*gén: identifier*) to recognize. **ces jumeaux sont impossibles à** ~ these twins are impossible to tell apart; **on reconnaît un fumeur à ses doigts jaunis** you can tell *ou* recognize *ou* spot a smoker by his stained fingers; **je le reconnais bien là** that's just like him *ou* typical of him, that's him all over! **(b)** (*admettre*) (*gén*) to recognize; *torts* to admit; *supériorité, dette* to acknowledge. **il faut** ~ **qu'il faisait très froid** admittedly it was very cold, you must admit it was very cold; **il a reconnu s'être trompé** he admitted making a mistake; (*Jur*) ~ **qn coupable** to find sb guilty; **il ne reconnaît à personne le droit d'intervenir** he doesn't recognize in anyone the right *ou* acknowledge that anyone has the right to intervene. **(c)** *terrain* to reconnoitre. ~ **les lieux** to see how the land lies, reconnoitre (the ground). **2 se** ~ *vpr* (*dans la glace*) to recognize o.s.; (*entre personnes*) to recognize each other; (*lit, fig: trouver son chemin*) to find one's way about *ou* around. **je ne m'y reconnais plus** I'm completely lost; **je commence à me** ~ I'm beginning to find my bearings; **le pêcher se reconnaît à ses fleurs roses** the peach tree is recognizable by its pink flowers, you can tell a peach tree by its pink flowers; **se** ~ **vaincu** to admit *ou* acknowledge defeat. ♦ **reconnaissable** *adj* recognizable (*à* by, from). ♦ **reconnaissance** *nf* **(a)** (*gratitude*) gratitude, gratefulness (*à qn* to *ou* towards sb). **(b)** (*gén, Pol: fait de reconnaître*) recognition; (*Jur: d'un droit*) recognition, acknowledgement; (*littér: aveu*) acknowledgement, admission. **signe de** ~ sign of recognition; ~ **de dette** note of hand. **(c)** (*exploration*) reconnaissance, survey; (*Mil*) reconnaissance, recce*. **partir en** ~ to make a reconnaissance, go on a recce*; **mission de** ~ reconnaissance mission. ♦ **reconnaissant, e** *adj* grateful (*à qn de qch* to sb for sth). **je vous serais** ~ **de me dire** I would be grateful if you could tell me. ♦ **reconnu, e** *adj* recognized.

reconquérir [ʀ(ə)kɔ̃keʀiʀ] (21) *vt* (*Mil*) to reconquer; *liberté* to recover, win back. ♦ **reconquête** *nf* reconquest; recovery.

reconsidérer [ʀ(ə)kɔ̃sideʀe] (6) *vt* to reconsider.

reconstituer [ʀ(ə)kɔ̃stitɥe] (1) *vt parti, texte* to reconstitute; *fortune* to build up again; *crime, édifice* to reconstruct; *faits, puzzle* to piece together; (*Bio*) *organisme* to regenerate. ♦ **reconstituant, e 1** *adj* energizing. **2** *nm* tonic. ♦ **reconstitution** *nf* reconstitution; rebuilding; reconstruction; piecing together; regeneration. ~ **historique** reconstruction of history.

reconstruire [ʀ(ə)kɔ̃stʀɥiʀ] (38) *vt* to rebuild, reconstruct. ♦ **reconstruction** *nf* reconstruction.

reconvertir [ʀ(ə)kɔ̃vɛʀtiʀ] (2) **1** *vt usine* to reconvert (*en* to); *personnel* to redeploy. **2 se** ~ *vpr [personne]* to move into *ou* turn to a new type of employment. **nous nous sommes reconvertis dans le textile** we have moved (over) into textiles. ♦ **reconversion** *nf* reconversion; redeployment.

recopier [ʀ(ə)kɔpje] (7) *vt* to copy out *ou* write out (again). ~ **ses notes au propre** to make a fair copy of one's notes.

record [ʀ(ə)kɔʀ] *nm, adj inv* record. **en un temps** ~ in record time. ♦ **recordman** [ʀ(ə)kɔʀdman], *pl* **recordmen** [ʀ(ə)kɔʀdmɛn] *nm* record holder.

recoucher [ʀ(ə)kuʃe] (1) **1** *vt enfant* to put back to bed. **2 se** ~ *vpr* to go back to bed.

recouper [ʀ(ə)kupe] (1) **1** *vt* (*à nouveau*) to cut again; (*davantage*) to cut more; *route* to intersect; *témoignage* to tie up *ou* match up with. **2 se** ~ *vpr [faits]* to tie *ou* match up. ♦ **recoupement** *nm* cross-check. **faire un** ~ to cross-check.

recourbé, e [ʀ(ə)kuʀbe] *adj* (*gén*) curved; *bec* hooked. **nez** ~ hooknose.

recourir [ʀ(ə)kuʀiʀ] (11) ~ **à** *vt indir moyen* to resort to; *personne* to turn to, appeal to. ♦ **recours** *nm* resort, recourse; (*Jur*) appeal. **en dernier** ~ as a last resort; **la situation est sans** ~ there's no solution to the situation; **avoir** ~ **à** *moyen* to resort to; *personne* to turn to, appeal to; ~ **en grâce** appeal for mercy.

recouvrer [ʀ(ə)kuvʀe] (1) *vt santé* to recover; *cotisation* to collect. ♦ **recouvrement** *nm* recovery; collection.

recouvrir [ʀ(ə)kuvʀiʀ] (18) **1** *vt* (*gén, fig*) to

cover; (*à nouveau*) to re-cover. **recouvert d'eau** covered in *ou* with water; **~ une casserole** to put a lid on a saucepan. **2 se ~** *vpr* (*se superposer*) to overlap.

récréation [ʀekʀeasjɔ̃] *nf* **(a)** (*lycée*) break; (*école primaire*) playtime, break. **aller/être en ~** to go out for/have one's break. **(b)** (*amusement*) recreation, relaxation.

recréer [ʀ(ə)kʀee] (1) *vt* to re-create.

récrier (se) [ʀekʀije] (7) *vpr* to exclaim.

récriminer [ʀekʀimine] (1) *vi* to recriminate (*contre* against). ♦ **récrimination** *nf* recrimination.

récrire [ʀekʀiʀ] (39) *vt* (*à nouveau*) to rewrite; (*davantage*) to write again.

recroqueviller (se) [ʀ(ə)kʀɔkvije] (1) *vpr* *[papier]* to shrivel up, curl up; *[personne]* to huddle *ou* curl o.s. up.

recrudescence [ʀ(ə)kʀydesɑ̃s] *nf* upsurge, new wave *ou* outburst.

recrue [ʀ(ə)kʀy] *nf* recruit. ♦ **recrutement** *nm* recruitment. ♦ **recruter** (1) *vt* to recruit.

rectangle [ʀɛktɑ̃gl(ə)] *nm* rectangle. ♦ **rectangulaire** *adj* rectangular.

rectifier [ʀɛktifje] (7) *vt* (*corriger*) to correct; (*ajuster*) to adjust; *erreur* to rectify, put right; *tracé* to straighten. **~ le tir** (*lit*) to adjust the fire; (*fig*) to adjust one's sights. ♦ **rectificatif** *nm* correction. ♦ **rectification** *nf* rectification; correction.

rectiligne [ʀɛktiliɲ] *adj* (*gén*) straight; *mouvement* rectilinear; (*Géom*) rectilinear.

rectitude [ʀɛktityd] *nf* (*morale*) rectitude; *[ligne]* straightness.

recto [ʀɛkto] *nm* front (of a page), first side. **~ verso** on both sides (of the page).

reçu, e [ʀ(ə)sy] **1** *adj usages* accepted; *candidat* successful. **2** *nm* (*quittance*) receipt.

recueil [ʀ(ə)kœj] *nm* (*gén*) book, collection.

recueillir [ʀ(ə)kœjiʀ] (12) **1** *vt suffrages etc* to get; *graines* to gather, collect; *argent* to collect; *réfugié* to take in; *déposition* to take down, take note of; *opinion* to record. **2 se ~** *vpr* (*Rel, gén*) to collect *ou* gather one's thoughts. **se ~ sur la tombe de qn** to meditate at sb's grave. ♦ **recueillement** *nm* (*Rel, gén*) meditation, contemplation. **écouter avec ~** to listen reverently. ♦ **recueilli, e** *adj* meditative.

recul [ʀ(ə)kyl] *nm* **(a)** (*lit, fig: retraite*) retreat. **avoir un mouvement de ~** to recoil, start *ou* shrink back (*par rapport à* from). **(b)** *[maladie]* recession; *[civilisation, valeur boursière]* decline. **être en ~** (*gén*) to be on the decline; *[monnaie]* to be falling; *[parti]* to be losing ground; (*Pol*) **~ de la majorité** fall *ou* drop in government support. **(c)** (*éloignement*) distance. **avec le ~** (*du temps*) with the passing of time; (*dans l'espace*) from a distance, from further away; **prendre du ~** to stand back (*par rapport à* from); **cette salle n'a pas assez de ~** there isn't enough room to move back in this room. **(d)** *[arme à feu]* recoil, kick. **(e)** *[échéance]* deferment. **(f)** *[véhicule]* backward movement. ♦ **reculade** *nf* retreat.

reculer [ʀ(ə)kyle] (1) **1** *vi* **(a)** *[personne]* to move *ou* step back; (*par peur*) to draw back, back away; *[automobiliste]* to reverse; (*Mil*) to retreat. **~ de 2 pas** to take 2 paces back, retreat 2 paces; **faire ~** *foule* to move *ou* force back; *cheval* to move back; *ennemi* to push *ou* force back. **(b)** (*hésiter*) to shrink back; (*changer d'avis*) to back out. **~ devant la dépense** to shrink from the expense; **rien ne me fera ~** I'll stop *ou* stick at nothing, nothing will stop me. **(c)** (*diminuer*) (*gén*) to decline; *[incendie]* to subside; *[eaux]* to subside, recede, go down. **faire ~ l'épidémie** to reduce the epidemic. **(d)** *[arme à feu]* to recoil. **2** *vt meuble, frontière* to push back; *véhicule* to reverse; *date, décision* to postpone; *échéance* to defer. **3 se ~** *vpr* to step back, retreat. **se ~ d'horreur** to draw back *ou* back away in horror. ♦ **reculé, e** *adj époque* remote, distant; *ville* remote, out-of-the-way. ♦ **reculons** *loc adv*: **aller à ~** to go backwards; **sortir à ~ d'une pièce** to back out of a room.

récupérer [ʀekypeʀe] (6) **1** *vt argent, forces* to recover, get back; *ferraille* to salvage; *chiffons* to reprocess; *délinquant* to rehabilitate; *journées de travail* to make up; (*Pol: péj*) *mouvement* to take over; (*: *prendre*) to get. **regarde si tu peux ~ qch dans ces vieux habits** have a look and see if there's anything you can rescue *ou* retrieve from among these old clothes. **2** *vi [coureur]* to recover, recuperate. ♦ **récupération** *nf* recovery; salvage; reprocessing; rehabilitation; takeover; recuperation.

récurer [ʀekyʀe] (1) *vt* to scour.

récuser [ʀekyze] (1) **1** *vt* (*Jur*) to challenge. **2 se ~** *vpr* to decline to give an opinion. ♦ **récusation** *nf* challenge.

recycler [ʀ(ə)sikle] (1) **1** *vt élève* to reorientate; *ingénieur* (*perfectionner*) to send on a refresher course; (*reconvertir*) to retrain; *matière* to recycle. **2 se ~** *vpr* to retrain; to go on a refresher course. ♦ **recyclage** *nm* reorientation; retraining; recycling.

rédaction [ʀedaksjɔ̃] *nf* **(a)** *[contrat]* drafting; *[thèse]* writing; *[dictionnaire]* compilation. **(b)** (*Presse*) (*personnel*) editorial staff; (*bureaux*) editorial offices. **(c)** (*Scol*) essay, composition. ♦ **rédacteur, -trice** *nm,f* (*Presse*) (sub)-editor; *[article]* writer; *[loi]* drafter; *[encyclopédie]* compiler. **~ en chef** chief editor.

reddition [ʀedisjɔ̃] *nf* (*Mil*) surrender.

redemander [ʀədmɑ̃de] (1) *vt adresse* to ask again for; *aliment* to ask for more.

rédemption [ʀedɑ̃psjɔ̃] *nf* redemption. ♦ **rédempteur, -trice** **1** *adj* redemptive, redeeming. **2** *nm,f* redeemer.

redescendre [ʀ(ə)desɑ̃dʀ(ə)] (41) **1** *vt* (*avec aux avoir*) *escalier* to go *ou* come (back) down again; *objet* to take downstairs again. **2** *vi* (*avec aux être*) *[personne]* to go *ou* come (back) down again; *[ascenseur, chemin]* to go down again; *[baromètre, fièvre]* to fall again.

redevable [ʀədvabl(ə)] *adj*: **être ~ à qn de** *argent* to owe sb; *aide* to be indebted to sb for.

redevance [ʀədvɑ̃s] *nf* (*gén: impôt*) tax; (*Rad, TV*) licence fee; (*Téléc*) rental charge; (*bail, rente*) dues, fees.

rédhibitoire [ʀedibitwaʀ] *adj défaut* damning.

rédiger [ʀediʒe] (3) *vt lettre* to write; *dictionnaire* to compile, write; *contrat* to draw up, draft.

redire [ʀ(ə)diʀ] (37) *vt* to repeat. **~ qch à qn** to say sth to sb again, tell sb sth again, repeat sth to sb; **elle ne se le fait pas ~ deux fois** she doesn't need telling *ou* to be told twice; **trouver à ~ à qch** to find fault with sth; **je ne vois rien à ~ (à cela)** I've no complaint with that, I can't see anything wrong with that.

redite [ʀ(ə)dit] *nf* (needless) repetition.

redondance [ʀ(ə)dɔ̃dɑ̃s] *nf*: **la ~** superfluity. ♦ **redondant, e** superfluous.

redonner [ʀ(ə)dɔne] (1) *vt objet* to give back, return; *confiance, énergie* to restore; *renseignement* to give again; *pain* to give more; *couche, tranche* to give another. **cela te redonnera des forces** that will build your strength back up *ou* put new strength into you.

redoubler [ʀ(ə)duble] (1) **1** *vt joie, douleur* to increase, intensify; *efforts* to step up, redouble. **frapper à coups redoublés** to bang twice as hard; **~ (une classe)** to repeat a year *ou* a grade (*US*). **2 ~ de** *vt indir*: **~ d'efforts** to step up *ou* redouble one's efforts; **~ de prudence** to be extra *ou* doubly careful; **~ de larmes** to cry even harder.

3 *vi* (*gén*) to increase, intensify; *[vent]* to become twice as strong; *[cris]* to get even louder *ou* twice as loud. ♦ **redoublant, e** *nm,f* pupil who is repeating a year at school. ♦ **redoublement** *nm* increase (*de* in), intensification (*de* of). **avec un ~ d'attention** with increased attention; (*Scol*) **le ~** repeating a year.
redouter [ʀ(ə)dute] (1) *vt* to dread. ♦ **redoutable** *adj* fearsome, formidable.
redoux [ʀ(ə)du] *nm* spell of milder weather.
redresser [ʀ(ə)dʀese] (1) **1** *vt* **(a)** *poteau* to set upright; *tige* to straighten (up); *tôle cabossée* to straighten out; (*Élec*) *courant* to rectify; (*Opt*) *image* to straighten; *personne couchée* to sit *ou* prop up. **~ la tête** (*lit*) to hold up *ou* lift one's head; (*être fier*) to hold one's head up high; (*se révolter*) to show signs of rebellion. **(b)** *bateau* to right; *avion, voiture* to straighten up. **(c)** *situation, économie* to redress. **~ le pays** to get *ou* put the country on its feet again. **(d)** *erreur, torts, abus* to right, redress. **2 se ~** *vpr* **(a)** (*se mettre assis*) to sit up; (*se mettre droit*) to stand up straight; (*être fier*) to hold one's head up high. **(b)** *[bateau]* to right itself; *[avion; voiture]* to straighten up; *[économie]* to recover; *[situation]* to correct itself. **(c)** *[cheveux]* to stick up. ♦ **redressement** *nm [économie, situation]* recovery. **~ fiscal** payment of back taxes. ♦ **redresseur** *nm* (*Élec*) rectifier. **~ de torts** righter of wrongs.
réduire [ʀedɥiʀ] (38) **1** *vt* **(a)** (*diminuer*) (*gén*) to reduce; *prix* to cut, bring down; *pression* to lessen; *texte* to shorten, cut; *production* to cut (back), lower; *dépenses* to cut down *ou* back (on); *inflation* to curb; *dessin* to scale down; *photographie* to make smaller. **(b) ~ à** (*contraindre à*) to reduce to; (*ramener à*) to bring down to, reduce to; (*limiter à*) to limit *ou* confine to; **il en est réduit à mendier** he has been reduced to begging; **~ qch à néant** to reduce sth to nothing. **(c) ~ en** *poudre etc* to reduce to; **~ qch en morceaux** to smash sth to pieces; **~ qch en bouillie** to crush *ou* reduce sth to (a) pulp; **réduit en cendres** reduced to ashes, burnt to a cinder. **(d)** (*Méd*) to set, reduce; (*Chim*) to reduce. **(e)** *place forte* to capture; *rebelles* to quell. **~ l'opposition** to silence the opposition. **2** *vi* (*Culin*) *[sauce]* to reduce. **faire ~** to reduce. **3 se ~** *vpr* (*financièrement*) to cut down on *ou* reduce one's spending. **se ~ à** *[incident]* to boil down to, amount to; *[somme, quantité]* to amount to; **je me réduirai à quelques exemples** I'll limit *ou* confine myself to a few examples; **se ~ en cendres** to be burnt to a cinder, be reduced to ashes.
♦ **réduction** *nf* (*gén, Culin, Sci*) reduction; (*diminution*) reduction, cut (*de* in); (*rabais*) discount, reduction; (*Mil*) *[ville]* capture; *[rebelles]* quelling. **un monde en ~** a world in miniature.
♦ **réduit, e 1** *adj* **(a)** *objet* (*à petite échelle*) small-scale, scaled-down; (*en miniature*) miniature; (*miniaturisé*) miniaturized. **(b)** *prix, vitesse* reduced; *moyens, débouchés* limited. **livres à prix ~s** cut-price books, books at reduced prices. **2** *nm* (*pièce*) tiny room; (*péj*) cubbyhole; (*recoin*) recess; (*Mil*) *[maquisards]* hideout.
rééditer [ʀeedite] (1) *vt* (*Typ*) to republish; (* *fig*) to repeat. ♦ **réédition** *nf* (*Typ*) new edition; (* *fig*) repetition, repeat.
rééduquer [ʀeedyke] (1) *vt* (*gén*) to re-educate; *délinquant, malade* to rehabilitate. ♦ **rééducation** *nf* re-education; rehabilitation. **faire de la ~ (fonctionnelle)** to have physiotherapy.
réel, -elle [ʀeɛl] **1** *adj* (*gén*) real; *plaisir, amélioration* real, genuine; (*Fin*) *valeur, salaire* real, actual. **dans la vie ~elle** in real life; **faire de ~elles économies** to make genuine *ou* real savings. **2** *nm*: **le ~** reality. ♦ **réellement** *adv* really.
réélire [ʀeeliʀ] (43) *vt* to re-elect. ♦ **réélection** *nf* re-election. ♦ **rééligible** *adj* re-eligible.
réescompter [ʀeɛskɔ̃te] (1) *vt* to rediscount. ♦ **réescompte** *nm* rediscount.
réévaluer [ʀeevalɥe] (1) *vt* to revalue. ♦ **réévaluation** *nf* revaluation.
réexaminer [ʀeɛgzamine] (1) *vt* to re-examine. ♦ **réexamen** *nm* re-examination.
réexpédier [ʀeɛkspedje] (7) *vt* (*à l'envoyeur*) to return, send back; (*au destinataire*) to send on, forward.
refaire [ʀ(ə)fɛʀ] (60) **1** *vt* **(a)** (*recommencer*) (*gén*) to redo, make *ou* do again; *pansement* to renew; *devoir* to rewrite; *nœud* to do up again, tie again. **~ sa vie** to start a new life; **il m'a refait une visite** he paid me another call; **il va falloir ~ de la soupe** we'll have to make some more soup; **son éducation est à ~** he'll have to be re-educated; **si c'était à ~!** if I had to do it again! *ou* begin again! **(b)** *toit* to redo, renew; *meuble, chambre* to do up, renovate. **~ qch à neuf** to do sth up like new; (*fig*) **~ ses forces** to recover one's strength. **(c)** (*: *duper*) to take in. **je me suis fait ~ de 5 F** he did me out of 5 francs*. **2 se ~** *vpr* (*santé*) to recover; (*argent*) to make up one's losses. **on ne se refait pas!** you can't change your own character!
réfection [ʀefɛksjɔ̃] *nf* (*action*) repairing; (*résultat*) repairs.
réfectoire [ʀefɛktwaʀ] *nm* (*Scol*) dining hall, canteen; (*Rel*) refectory; *[usine]* canteen.
référence [ʀefeʀɑ̃s] *nf* **(a)** (*renvoi*) reference; (*en bas de page*) footnote. **par ~ à** in reference to; **ouvrage de ~** reference book; **point de ~** point of reference; **faire ~ à** to refer to, make reference to. **(b)** *[employé]* reference, testimonial. (*iro*) **ce n'est pas une ~** that's no recommendation.
référendum [ʀefeʀɛ̃dɔm] *nm* referendum.
référer [ʀefeʀe] (6) **1 en ~ à** *vt indir*: **en ~ à qn** to refer *ou* submit a matter to sb. **2 se ~** *vpr*: **se ~ à** (*consulter*) to consult; (*s'en remettre à*) to refer to.
refermer [ʀ(ə)fɛʀme] (1) **1** *vt* to close *ou* shut again. **2 se ~** *vpr* to close up. **le piège se referma sur lui** the trap closed *ou* shut on him.
refiler* [ʀ(ə)file] (1) *vt* (*gén*) to give; *maladie* to pass on (*à* to); *fausse pièce* to palm off* (*à* on).
réfléchir [ʀefleʃiʀ] (2) **1** *vi* to think (*à* about). **prends le temps de ~** take time to think about it *ou* to consider it; **cela donne à ~** that makes you think; (*péj*) **sans ~** thoughtlessly, without thinking; **réfléchissez-y** think about it, think it over. **2** *vt* **(a) ~ que** to realize that. **(b)** *lumière, son* to reflect. **3 se ~** *vpr* to be reflected. ♦ **réfléchi, e** *adj* (*Gram*) reflexive; (*Opt*) reflected; *action* well thought-out; *personne, air* thoughtful. **tout bien ~** after careful consideration *ou* thought; **c'est tout ~** my decision is made, my mind is made up. ♦ **réfléchissant, e** *adj* reflective. ♦ **réflecteur, -trice 1** *adj* reflecting. **2** *nm* (*gén*) reflector.
reflet [ʀ(ə)flɛ] *nm* **(a)** (*éclat*) (*gén*) reflection; *[cheveux]* (*naturel*) light; (*artificiel*) highlight. **~s du soleil sur la mer** reflection *ou* glint *ou* flash of the sun on the sea. **(b)** (*lit, fig: image*) reflection. **c'est le ~ de son père** he's the image of his father. ♦ **refléter** (6) **1** *vt* to reflect. **2 se ~** *vpr* to be reflected.
réflexe [ʀeflɛks(ə)] **1** *adj* reflex. **2** *nm* reflex. **~ conditionné** conditioned reflex; **il eut le ~ de couper l'électricité** he instinctively switched off the electricity.
réflexif, -ive [ʀeflɛksif, iv] *adj* (*Math*) reflexive; (*Psych*) introspective.
réflexion [ʀeflɛksjɔ̃] *nf* **(a)** (*méditation*) thought. **la ~** reflection; **ceci donne matière à ~** this gives (you) food for thought; *[offre]* **ceci mérite ~** this is worth thinking about *ou* considering; **avec ~** thoughtfully; **~ faite** on reflection, on second thoughts; **à la ~** when you think about it. **(b)**

(*remarque*) remark, comment, reflection; (*idée*) thought; (*plainte*) complaint. **(c)** (*Phys*) reflection.

refluer [R(ə)flye] (1) *vi [liquide]* to flow back; *[foule]* to pour *ou* surge back; *[sang]* to rush back. ♦ **reflux** *nm [foule]* backward surge; *[marée]* ebb.

refondre [R(ə)fɔ̃dR(ə)] (41) *vt cloche, texte* to recast. ♦ **refonte** *nf* (*gén*) recasting; *[enseignement]* restructuring.

réforme [RefɔRm(ə)] *nf* reform; (*Rel*) reformation. **mettre à la ~** *objets* to scrap; *soldat* to discharge. ♦ **réformateur, -trice 1** *adj* reforming. **2** *nm,f* reformer. ♦ **réformé, e 1** *adj* (*Rel*) reformed; (*Mil*) *appelé* declared unfit for service; *soldat* discharged. **2** *nm,f* (*Rel*) Protestant. ♦ **réformer** (1) **1** *vt loi, mœurs, administration* to reform; *abus* to (put) right; *jugement* to reverse; (*Mil*) *appelé* to declare unfit for service; *soldat* to discharge; *matériel* to scrap. **2 se ~** *vpr* to change one's ways, turn over a new leaf. ♦ **réformisme** *nm* reformism. ♦ **réformiste** *adj, nmf* reformist.

reformer *vt*, **se ~** *vpr* [R(ə)fɔRme] (1) to reform.

refouler [R(ə)fule] (1) *vt envahisseur* to drive back, repulse; *immigrant* to turn back; *larmes, liquide* to force back; *désir, colère* to repress. ♦ **refoulé, e** *adj personne* frustrated, inhibited. ♦ **refoulement** *nm* driving (*ou* turning *ou* forcing) back; (*Psych: complexe*) repression.

réfractaire [RefRaktɛR] **1** *adj* **(a) ~ à** *autorité, virus* resistant to; *musique* impervious to. **(b)** *métal* refractory; *brique* fire; *plat* ovenproof, heat-resistant. **2** *nm* (*Mil*) draft evader.

réfracter [RefRakte] (1) *vt* to refract. ♦ **réfraction** *nf* refraction.

refrain [R(ə)fRɛ̃] *nm* refrain, chorus. **c'est toujours le même ~*** it's always the same old story.

refréner [R(ə)fRene] (6) *vt* to curb, (hold in) check.

réfrigérateur [RefRiʒeRatœR] *nm* refrigerator, fridge*. ♦ **réfrigérant, e** *adj fluide* refrigerating; *accueil* icy, frosty. ♦ **réfrigération** *nf* refrigeration; (*Tech*) cooling. ♦ **réfrigérer** (6) *vt* (*gén*) to refrigerate; (*Tech*) to cool; *enthousiasme* to put a damper on, cool. **je suis réfrigéré*** I'm frozen stiff*.

refroidir [R(ə)fRwadiR] (2) **1** *vt nourriture* to cool (down); *zèle* to cool, put a damper on; *personne* (*dégouter*) to put off; (**‡**: *tuer*) to do in**‡**, bump off**‡**. **2** *vi* to cool (down); (*devenir trop froid*) to get cold. **faire ~** to let cool. **3 se ~** *vpr [ardeur]* to cool (off); *[temps]* to get cooler *ou* colder; *[personne]* to get *ou* catch cold. ♦ **refroidissement** *nm [air, liquide]* cooling; (*Méd*) chill. **~ de la température** drop in the temperature.

refuge [R(ə)fyʒ] *nm* (*gén*) refuge; (*pour piétons*) (traffic) island; (*en montagne*) mountain hut *ou* shelter. ♦ **réfugié, e** *adj, nm,f* refugee. ♦ **se réfugier** (7) *vpr* (*lit, fig*) to take refuge.

refuser [R(ə)fyze] (1) **1** *vt* **(a)** (*gén*) to refuse; *offre* to decline, turn down, reject; *marchandise, routine* to refuse to accept. **~ de faire** to refuse to do; **~ le risque** to refuse to take risks; **~ à qn la permission de faire** to refuse sb permission to do; **~ l'entrée à qn** to refuse admittance *ou* entry to sb; **je lui refuse toute compétence** I deny him any ability. **(b)** *client* to turn away; *candidat* (*à un examen*) to fail; (*à un poste*) to turn down. **2 se ~** *vpr plaisir* to refuse o.s., deny o.s. **ça ne se refuse pas** it is not to be refused, I wouldn't say no (to it); **se ~ à** *solution* to refuse (to accept), reject; *commentaire* to refuse to make; **se ~ à faire qch** to refuse to do sth. ♦ **refus** *nm* refusal. **ce n'est pas de ~*** I won't say no (to that).

réfuter [Refyte] (1) *vt* to refute. ♦ **réfutation** *nf* refutation.

regagner [R(ə)gaɲe] (1) *vt amitié* to regain; *argent* to win *ou* get back; *lieu* to get back to. **~ le temps perdu** to make up for lost time; (*Mil, fig*) **~ du terrain** to regain ground.

regain [R(ə)gɛ̃] *nm* **(a) ~ de** *jeunesse* renewal of; *popularité* revival of. **(b)** (*Agr*) second crop of hay.

régaler [Regale] (1) **1** *vt personne* to treat to a delicious meal. **2 se ~** *vpr* (*bien manger*) to have a delicious meal; (*fig: profiter*) to make a handsome *ou* fat* profit. **on s'est bien régalé** it was delicious; **se ~ de qch** to have a feast on sth. ♦ **régal,** *pl* **~s** *nm* delight, treat.

regard [R(ə)gaR] *nm* **(a)** (*vue*) eye, glance, gaze; (*fixe*) stare. **parcourir qch du ~** to cast a glance *ou* an eye over sth; **soustraire qch aux ~s** to hide sth from sight *ou* view; **cela attire les ~s** it catches people's eye *ou* attention. **(b)** (*expression*) look *ou* expression (in one's eye). **(c)** (*coup d'œil*) look, glance. **lancer un ~ de colère à qn** to cast an angry look *ou* glare *ou* glance at sb. **(d)** *[égout]* manhole; *[four]* peephole, window. **(e) au ~ de la loi** in the eyes of the law; **texte avec photos en ~** text with photos on the opposite page *or* with photos facing; **en ~ de ce qu'il gagne** in comparison with what he earns.

regardant, e [R(ə)gaRdɑ̃, ɑ̃t] *adj* careful with money. **il n'est pas ~** he's quite free with his money.

regarder [R(ə)gaRde] (1) **1** *vt* **(a)** *paysage, objet* to look at; *action en déroulement* to watch. **~ la télévision** to watch television; **~ le journal** to look at *ou* have a look at the paper; **~ par la fenêtre** to look out of the window; **regarde où tu marches*** watch *ou* look where you're going; **regarde voir dans l'armoire** have a look in the wardrobe; **regardez-moi ça!*** just (take a) look at that!; **vous ne m'avez pas regardé!‡** what do you take me for!*; **regardez-le faire** watch him do it; **elles sont allées ~ les vitrines** they've gone to do some window-shopping; **sans ~** *traverser* without looking; *payer* regardless of the expense. **(b)** (*rapidement*) to glance at; (*longuement*) to gaze at; (*fixement*) to stare at. **~ (qch) par le trou de la serrure** to peep (at sth) through the keyhole; **~ de près** to have a close look at; **~ bouche bée** to gape at; **~ à la dérobée** to steal a glance at; **~ qn avec colère** to glare angrily at sb; **~ qn de travers** to scowl at sb; **~ qch d'un bon/mauvais œil** to look on sth *ou* view sth favourably/unfavourably; **~ qn de haut** to give sb a scornful look, look scornfully at sb; (*lit, fig*) **~ qn/qch en face** to look sb/sth in the face. **(c)** (*vérifier*) to (have a) look at; *essence* to check. **~ un mot dans le dictionnaire** to look up *ou* check a word in the dictionary. **(d)** (*envisager*) *problème, avenir* to view. **ne ~ que son propre intérêt** to be only concerned with one's own interests; **~ qn comme un ami** to look upon *ou* regard *ou* consider sb as a friend. **(e)** (*concerner*) to concern. **la suite me regarde** what happens next is my concern *ou* business; **mêlez-vous de ce qui vous regarde** mind your own business. **(f)** *[maison]* **~ (vers)** to face.

2 ~ à *vt indir*: **y ~ à deux fois avant de faire qch** to think twice before doing sth; **il n'y regarde pas de si près** he's not that fussy *ou* particular; **à y bien ~** on thinking it over; **c'est qn qui va ~ à 2 F** he's the sort of person who worries about 2 francs; **il ne regarde pas à la dépense** he doesn't worry how much he spends, he spares no expense.

3 se ~ *vpr* (*dans une glace*) to look at o.s.; (*l'un l'autre*) to look at each other *ou* at one another. (*iro*) **il ne s'est pas regardé!*** he should take a look at himself!

régate [Regat] *nf*: **~(s)** regatta.

régence [Reʒɑ̃s] *nf* regency.

régénérer [ReʒeneRe] (6) *vt* (*Bio, Rel*) to regenerate; *personne, forces* to revive, restore.

régent, e [Reʒɑ̃, ɑ̃t] *nm,f* regent. ♦ **régenter** (1) *vt* (*gén*) to rule over; *personne* to dictate to.

régie [ʀeʒi] *nf* (*Ciné, Théât, TV*) production department. (*compagnie*) ~ **(d'État)** state-owned company.

regimber [ʀ(ə)ʒɛ̃be] (1) *vi* (*gén*) to baulk, jib (*contre* at).

régime [ʀeʒim] *nm* **(a)** (*Pol*) (*mode*) system (of government); (*gouvernement*) government; (*péj*) régime. **(b)** (*Admin*) (*système*) system; (*règlements*) regulations. ~ **(matrimonial)** marriage settlement. **(c)** (*Méd*) diet. **être au** ~ to be on a diet. **(d)** *[moteur]* (engine *ou* running) speed. (*Tech, fig*) **marcher à plein** ~ to go (at) full speed; (*fig*) **à ce** ~ at this rate. **(e)** (*Gram*) object. **(f)** *[dattes, bananes]* bunch.

régiment [ʀeʒimɑ̃] *nm* regiment. **être au** ~* to be doing (one's) military service.

région [ʀeʒjɔ̃] *nf* (*gén, fig*) region; (*limitée*) area. ♦ **régional, e,** *mpl* **-aux** *adj* regional. ♦ **régionalisme** *nm* regionalism. ♦ **régionaliste** *adj, nmf* regionalist.

régir [ʀeʒiʀ] (2) *vt* (*gén*) to govern.

régisseur [ʀeʒisœʀ] *nm* **(a)** (*Théât*) stage manager; (*Ciné, TV*) assistant director. **(b)** *[propriété]* steward.

registre [ʀəʒistʀ(ə)] *nm* (*gén, Ling, Mus*) register. ~ **de l'état civil** register of births, marriages and deaths.

réglage [ʀeglaʒ] *nm* adjustment; *[moteur]* tuning. ♦ **réglable** *adj* adjustable.

règle [ʀɛgl(ə)] *nf* (*gén, Rel: loi*) rule; (*instrument*) ruler. (*lit, fig*) **c'est la** ~ **du jeu** those are the rules of the game; ~ **de conduite/de 3** rule of conduct/of 3; ~ **à calculer** slide rule; **avoir pour** ~ **de faire** to make it a rule to do; (*menstruation*) **avoir ses** ~**s** to have one's period(s); **il est de** ~ **qu'on fasse un cadeau** it's usual *ou* it's standard practice *ou* the done thing to give a present; **en** ~ *comptabilité* in order; *réclamation* made according to the rules; **bataille en** ~ proper *ou* right old* fight; **je ne suis pas en** ~ my papers *etc* are not in order; **en** ~ **générale** as a (general) rule; (*hum*) **dans les** ~**s de l'art** according to the rule book.

réglé, e [ʀegle] *adj vie* (well-)ordered, regular; *personne* steady, stable; *papier* ruled, lined.

règlement [ʀɛgləmɑ̃] *nm* **(a)** (*règle*) regulation; (*réglementation*) rules, regulations. **(b)** *[conflit, facture]* settlement. ~ **par chèque** payment by cheque; (*fig*) ~ **de compte(s)** settling of scores; (*de gangsters*) gangland killing. ♦ **réglementaire** *adj uniforme* regulation; *procédure* statutory. **dans le temps** ~ in the prescribed time; **ce n'est pas** ~ it doesn't conform to the regulations.

réglementer [ʀɛgləmɑ̃te] (1) *vt* to regulate, control. ♦ **réglementation** *nf* (*règles*) regulations; (*contrôle*) control, regulation.

régler [ʀegle] (6) *vt* **(a)** *conflit* to settle; *problème* to settle, sort out. **(b)** *dette* to settle (up), pay; *compte* to settle; *commerçant* to settle up with, pay; *travaux* to settle up for, pay for. ~ **par chèque** to pay by cheque; **j'ai un compte à** ~ **avec lui** I've got a score to settle with him; **on lui a réglé son compte*** they've settled his hash‡. **(c)** *débit, machine* to regulate, adjust; *tir, poste de T.V.* to adjust; *moteur* to tune; *thermostat* to set. **(d)** (*fixer*) *modalités* to settle (on), fix, decide on; *conduite* to determine. ~ **le sort de qn** to decide *ou* determine sb's fate. **(e)** (*imiter*) ~ **qch sur** to model sth on; **se** ~ **sur qn d'autre** to model o.s. on sb else. **(f)** *papier* to rule (lines on).

réglisse [ʀeglis] *nf ou nm* liquorice.

règne [ʀɛɲ] *nm* (*Pol, fig*) reign; (*Bot, Min, Zool*) kingdom. **sous le** ~ **de Louis XIV** (*période*) in the reign of Louis XIV; (*domination*) under the reign *ou* rule of Louis XIV. ♦ **régner** (6) *vi* (*Pol, fig*) to reign; (*exercer sa domination*) to rule; *[silence]* to reign; *[confiance, confusion]* to prevail (*sur* over). **faire** ~ **l'ordre** to maintain law and order; **faire** ~ **la terreur** to make terror reign. ♦ **régnant, e** *adj* reigning; prevailing.

regorger [ʀ(ə)gɔʀʒe] (3) *vi*: ~ **de** *[pays]* to abound in, overflow with; *[magasin]* to be packed *ou* crammed with; **le marché regorge de fruits** there is plenty of fruit *ou* there is an abundance of fruit on the market.

régresser [ʀegʀese] (1) *vi [science, enfant]* to regress; *[épidémie]* to recede, diminish, decrease. ♦ **régressif, -ive** *adj* regressive. ♦ **régression** *nf* (*gén*) regression. **en (voie de)** ~ on the decline *ou* decrease.

regret [ʀ(ə)gʀɛ] *nm [décision, faute]* regret (*de* for); *[passé]* regret (*de* about). **le** ~ **d'avoir échoué** the regret that he had failed *ou* at having failed; **j'ai le** ~ **de vous le dire, c'est avec** ~ **que je vous le dis** I'm sorry *ou* I regret to have to tell you this; **sans** ~ with no regrets; **à** ~ *partir* with regret, regretfully; *donner* with regret, reluctantly. ♦ **regrettable** *adj* regrettable, unfortunate. ♦ **regretter** (1) *vt* (*gén*) to regret; (*être désolé*) to be sorry; *personne, jeunesse* to miss. **notre regretté président** our late lamented president; **on le regrette beaucoup dans le village** he is greatly *ou* sadly missed in the village; **je ne regrette rien** I have no regrets; **je regrette mon geste** I'm sorry I did that, I regret doing that; **je regrette de ne pas lui avoir écrit** I'm sorry *ou* I regret that I didn't write to him, I regret not writing *ou* not having written to him.

regrouper [ʀ(ə)gʀupe] (1) **1** *vt* (*gén*) to group *ou* gather together; (*de nouveau*) *armée* to reassemble; *parti* to regroup; *bétail* to round up. **2 se** ~ *vpr* to gather (together), assemble (*autour de* round). ♦ **regroupement** *nm* grouping *ou* gathering together; reassembly; round-up.

régulariser [ʀegylaʀize] (1) *vt position* to regularize, straighten out, sort out; *passeport* to put in order; *débit* to regulate. ♦ **régularisation** *nf* regularization; straightening out; putting in order; regulation.

régularité [ʀegylaʀite] *nf* (*V* **régulier**) regularity; steadiness; evenness. **contester la** ~ **d'une opération** to question the lawfulness *ou* legality of an operation.

régulation [ʀegylɑsjɔ̃] *nf* (*gén*) regulation; *[circulation, naissances]* control. ♦ **régulateur, -trice 1** *adj* regulating. **2** *nm* (*Tech, fig*) regulator.

régulier, -ière [ʀegylje, jɛʀ] **1** *adj* **(a)** (*gén, Mil, Rel*) regular; *élève, qualité, vitesse* steady; *répartition, ligne, paysage* even; *humeur* equable. **à intervalles** ~**s** at regular intervals; **il est** ~ **dans son travail** he's steady in his work; (*Aviat*) **ligne** ~**ière** scheduled service; **armée** ~**ière** regular *ou* standing army; **il faut que la pression soit bien** ~**ière** the pressure must be evenly distributed. **(b)** *gouvernement* legitimate; *élection, procédure* in order; *tribunal* legal, official; *opération, homme d'affaires* aboveboard, on the level. **être en situation** ~**ière** to be in line with the law; **ce n'est pas très** ~ it is not quite on the level *ou* aboveboard; ~ **en affaires** straight *ou* honest in business. **2** *nm* (*Mil, Rel*) regular. ♦ **régulièrement** *adv* **(a)** regularly; steadily; evenly. **élu** ~ properly elected. **(b)** (*normalement*) normally.

réhabiliter [ʀeabilite] (1) **1** *vt condamné* to rehabilitate; *art* to restore to favour; *mémoire, droits de qn* to restore. ~ **qn dans ses fonctions** to reinstate sb (in his job). **2 se** ~ *vpr [criminel]* to rehabilitate o.s.; *[candidat etc]* to redeem o.s. ♦ **réhabilitation** *nf* rehabilitation; restoring; reinstatement.

rehausser [ʀəose] (1) *vt mur, plafond* to raise, heighten; *beauté, couleur* to set off, enhance; *goût, détail* to emphasize, bring out; *mérite* to enhance, increase; *tableau, robe* to brighten up, liven up. **rehaussé de** embellished with.

réimprimer [ʀeɛ̃pʀime] (1) *vt* to reprint. ♦ **réimpression** *nf* (*action*) reprinting; (*livre*) reprint.

rein [ʀɛ̃] *nm* **(a)** (*organe*) kidney. ~ **artificiel** kidney machine. **(b)** (*région*) ~s (small of the) back; **avoir mal aux** ~s to have backache; (*fig*) **avoir les** ~**s solides** to be on a sound financial footing; (*fig*) **casser les** ~**s à qn** to ruin *ou* break sb.

réincarner (se) [ʀeɛ̃kaʀne] (1) *vpr* to be reincarnated. ♦ **réincarnation** *nf* reincarnation.

reine [ʀɛn] 1 *nf* (*Échecs, Pol, Zool, fig*) queen. **la** ~ **d'Angleterre** the Queen of England; **la** ~ **Élisabeth** Queen Elizabeth; ~ **de beauté** beauty queen. **2:** ~**-claude** *nf, pl* ~(s)-~s greengage; ~**-marguerite** *nf, pl* ~s-~s (China) aster.

reinette [ʀɛnɛt] *nf* rennet, pippin. ~ **grise** russet.

réinscrire [ʀeɛ̃skʀiʀ] (39) **1** *vt nom* to put down again; *élève* to re-enrol, reregister. **2 se** ~ *vpr* to re-enrol, reregister. ♦ **réinscription** *nf* re-enrolment, reregistration.

réinsérer [ʀeɛ̃seʀe] (6) *vt publicité* to reinsert; *délinquant* to reintegrate, rehabilitate. ♦ **réinsertion** *nf* reinsertion; reintegration, rehabilitation.

réinstaller [ʀeɛ̃stale] (1) **1** *vt objet* to put back, reinstall; (*dans ses fonctions*) to reinstate. **2 se** ~ *vpr* (*dans un fauteuil*) to settle down again (*dans* in); (*dans une maison*) to settle back (*dans* into). ♦ **réinstallation** *nf* putting back; reinstallation; settling back.

réintégrer [ʀeɛ̃tegʀe] (6) *vt* **(a)** (*dans ses fonctions*) to reinstate. **(b)** *lieu* to return to, go back to. ♦ **réintégration** *nf* reinstatement (*dans* in); return (*de* to).

réitérer [ʀeiteʀe] (6) *vt ordre, question* to reiterate, repeat; *exploit* to repeat.

rejaillir [ʀ(ə)ʒajiʀ] (2) *vi [liquide]* to splash back *ou* up (*sur* onto, at). ~ **sur qn** *[scandale]* to rebound on sb; *[gloire]* to be reflected on sb; *[bienfaits]* to fall upon sb.

rejeter [ʀəʒte] (4) **1** *vt* **(a)** (*relancer*) to throw back (*à* to). **(b)** *nourriture* to bring *ou* throw up, vomit; *lave* to spew *ou* throw out; *déchets, fumée* to discharge. **cadavre rejeté par la mer** corpse cast up *ou* washed up by the sea. **(c)** *envahisseur* to drive back, repulse; *indésirable* to cast out, expel; *domination, projet de loi* to reject; *offre* to turn down; *hypothèse* to dismiss. **la machine rejette les mauvaises pièces de monnaie** the machine rejects *ou* refuses invalid coins. **(d)** ~ **une faute sur qn/qch** to shift *ou* transfer the blame *ou* responsibility for a mistake onto sb/sth. **(e)** (*placer*) **la préposition est rejetée à la fin** the preposition is put at the end; ~ **en arrière** *tête* to throw *ou* toss back; *cheveux* to push (*ou* comb *ou* brush) back; *épaules* to pull back; *chapeau* to tilt back.

2 se ~ *vpr*: **se** ~ **sur qch** to fall back on sth.

♦ **rejet** *nm* **(a)** (*action*) bringing *ou* throwing up *etc*; discharge; repulsion; expulsion; rejection; dismissal. **(b)** (*Bot*) shoot; (*Littérat*) enjambment; (*Méd*) *[greffe]* rejection. ♦ **rejeton** *nm* (*: *enfant*) kid*; (*Bot*) shoot.

rejoindre [ʀ(ə)ʒwɛ̃dʀ(ə)] (49) **1** *vt* **(a)** (*retrouver*) *lieu* to get (back) to; *personne* to (re)join, meet (again); *poste* to rejoin, return to. **la route rejoint la voie ferrée à X** the road meets (up with) *ou* joins the railway line at X. **(b)** (*rattraper*) to catch up (with). **(c)** (*se rallier à*) *parti* to join; *point de vue* to agree with. **mon idée rejoint la vôtre** my idea is closely akin to yours *ou* is very similar to yours. **(d)** (*réunir*) to bring together (again). **2 se** ~ *vpr [routes]* to join, meet; *[idées]* to be similar *ou* closely akin to each other; *[personnes] (pour rendez-vous)* to meet (up) (again); (*sur point de vue*) to agree.

rejouer [ʀ(ə)ʒwe] (1) **1** *vt* (*gén*) to play again; *match* to replay; *pièce* to perform again. **on rejoue une partie?** shall we have *ou* play another game? **2** *vi* to play again; *[musicien]* to perform again.

réjouir [ʀeʒwiʀ] (2) **1** *vt* to delight. **ça ne me réjouit pas beaucoup** I don't find it particularly appealing. **2 se** ~ *vpr* to be delighted *ou* thrilled (*de faire* to do, *de qch* about *ou* at sth). **se** ~ **du malheur de qn** to take delight in *ou* rejoice over sb's misfortunes; **je m'en réjouis pour vous** I'm delighted for you; **je me réjouis à l'avance de les voir** I am greatly looking forward to seeing them; **réjouissez-vous!** rejoice! ♦ **réjoui, e** *adj air* joyful, joyous. ♦ **réjouissance** *nf* rejoicing. ~s festivities. ♦ **réjouissant, e** *adj histoire* amusing, entertaining; *nouvelle* cheering; (*iro*) *perspective* delightful, heartening. (*iro*) **c'est** ~**!** that's great!* (*iro*).

relâche [ʀ(ə)lɑʃ] **1** *nm ou nf* **(a)** (*littér: répit*) respite, rest. **sans** ~ without a break, non-stop. **(b)** (*Théât*) closure. **faire** ~ to be closed. **2** *nf* (*Naut*) port of call. **faire** ~ **dans un port** to put in at *ou* call at a port.

relâcher [ʀ(ə)lɑʃe] (1) **1** *vt* **(a)** *étreinte, muscle* to relax; *lien* to loosen, slacken (off); *ressort* to release; *discipline, effort* to relax, slacken. **(b)** (*libérer*) *prisonnier, otage, gibier* to release, let go, set free. **(c)** (*refaire tomber*) to let go of again. **2** *vi* (*Naut*) ~ **(dans un port)** to put into port. **3 se** ~ *vpr* **(a)** *[courroie]* to go loose *ou* slack; *[muscle]* to relax. **(b)** *[surveillance, discipline, mœurs]* to become *ou* get lax; *[style]* to become loose; *[attention]* to flag; *[effort, zèle]* to slacken, flag. **ne te relâche pas maintenant!** don't let up *ou* slacken off now!; **il se relâche dans son travail** he's growing lax *ou* slack in his work. ♦ **relâché, e** *adj style* loose; *mœurs* loose, lax; *discipline* lax, slack. ♦ **relâchement** *nm* relaxation; loosening; slackening; release; laxity; flagging.

relais [ʀ(ə)lɛ] *nm* (*Sport*) relay (race); (*Ind: équipe*) shift; (*Téléc*) (*action*) relaying; (*dispositif*) relay; (*chevaux*) relay; (*restaurant*) restaurant; (*Hist: auberge*) coaching inn. **prendre le** ~ to take over (*de* from); ~ **de télévision** television relay station.

relancer [ʀ(ə)lɑ̃se] (3) *vt ballon* to throw back (again); *idée* to revive, relaunch; *économie* to boost, stimulate; *débiteur* to pester, badger. ♦ **relance** *nf* boosting, stimulation; revival, relaunching. (*résultat*) **la** ~ **de l'économie** the boost (given) to the economy.

relater [ʀ(ə)late] (1) *vt* to relate, recount.

relatif, -ive [ʀ(ə)latif, iv] **1** *adj* (*gén*) relative; *silence, luxe* relative, comparative. ~ **à** relative *ou* relating to, connected with. **2** *nm* (*Gram*) relative pronoun. **3** *nf* (*Gram*) relative clause.

relation [ʀ(ə)lasjɔ̃] *nf* **(a)** (*gén, Math, Philos*) relation(ship). **c'est sans** ~ **avec** it has no connection with, it bears no relation to. **(b)** (*rapports*) ~s (*gén*) relations; ~**s amoureuses** love affair; **avoir de bonnes** ~**s avec qn** to be on good terms with sb, have a good relationship with sb; **être en** ~**s d'affaires avec qn** to have business relations *ou* dealings with sb; **être en** ~**(s) avec qn** to be in touch *ou* contact with sb; **entrer** *ou* **se mettre en** ~**(s) avec qn** to get in touch *ou* make contact with sb. **(c)** (*connaissance*) acquaintance. **avoir des** ~s to have (influential) connections. **(d)** (*récit*) account, report.

relativement [ʀ(ə)lativmɑ̃] *adv* relatively, comparatively. ~ **à** (*par comparaison*) in relation to, compared to; (*concernant*) with regard to, concerning.

relativité [ʀ(ə)lativite] *nf* relativity.

relaxer [ʀ(ə)lakse] (1) **1** *vt* **(a)** (*acquitter*) to acquit, discharge; (*relâcher*) to release. **(b)** *muscles* to relax. **2 se** ~ *vpr* to relax. ♦ **relaxation** *nf* relaxation. ♦ **relaxe**[1] *nf* acquittal, discharge; release. ♦ **relaxe**[2]* *adj* (*gén*) relaxed; *tenue* informal, casual.

relayer [R(ə)leje] (8) **1** *vt ouvrier etc* to relieve, take over from; (*Téléc*) to relay. **se faire** ~ to hand over to somebody else. **2 se** ~ *vpr* to take turns (*pour faire* to do); (*Sport*) to take over from one another. ♦ **relayeur, -euse** *nm,f* relay runner.

reléguer [R(ə)lege] (6) *vt* to relegate (*en, à* to). ♦ **relégation** *nf* relegation.

relent [R(ə)lɑ̃] *nm* foul smell, stench. **des** ~**s de** the stench *ou* reek of.

relever [Rəlve] (5) **1** *vt* **(a)** *meuble* to stand up again; *véhicule* to right; *personne* to help (back) up, help (back) to his feet; *blessé* to pick up. (*lit, fig*) ~ **la tête** to raise one's head. **(b)** (*gén*), *niveau* to raise; *col* to turn up; *chaussettes* to pull up; *jupe* to raise, lift; *manche* to roll up; *vitre* (*en poussant*) to push up; (*avec manivelle*) to wind up; *siège* to tip up. ~ **les yeux** to lift *ou* raise one's eyes, look up. **(c)** *mur en ruines* to rebuild; *pays, économie* to put back on its feet. **(d)** *salaire, note* to raise, increase, put up; *niveau de vie* to raise. **(e)** *sauce* to season, add seasoning *ou* spice to; *goût* to bring out. **(f)** *sentinelle* to relieve, take over from. ~ **la garde** to change the guard. **(g)** (*remarquer*) (*gén*) to find; *faute* to pick out. **(h)** (*inscrire*) *renseignement* to take down, note (down); *plan* to copy out, sketch; (*Naut*) *point* to plot; *compteur* to read. ~ **une cote** to plot an altitude. **(i)** *injure* to react to; *défi* to accept, take up, answer. **je n'ai pas relevé cette insinuation** I ignored this insinuation. **(j)** (*ramasser*) *copies* to collect (in), take in. **(k)** ~ **qn de** *promesse* to release sb from; *fonctions* to relieve sb of.

2 ~ **de** *vt indir* (*être du ressort de*) to be a matter for, be the concern of; (*être sous la tutelle de*) to come under. **ça relève de l'imagination la plus fantaisiste** that is a product of the wildest imagination; ~ **de maladie** to recover from *ou* get over an illness.

3 *vi [vêtement]* to pull up, go up.

4 se ~ *vpr* **(a)** (*se remettre debout*) to stand *ou* get up (again), get back (on)to one's feet; (*sortir du lit*) to get up (again). **(b)** *[col]* to turn up; *[strapontin]* to tip up; *[couvercle]* to lift up. **(c)** *[pays, économie]* to pick up again, recover. **se** ~ **de** *chagrin* to recover from, get over; *ruines* to rise from.

♦ **relève** *nf* (*gén*) relief; (*troupe*) relief (troops). **la** ~ **de la garde** the changing of the guards; (*lit, fig*) **prendre la** ~ to take over (*de* from). ♦ **relevé, e 1** *adj virage* banked; *sauce* spicy, highly seasoned; *style* elevated, lofty, refined. **chapeau à bords** ~**s** hat with a turned-up brim. **2** *nm [dépenses]* summary, statement; *[cote]* plotting; *[adresses]* list; *[compteur]* reading; (*facture*) bill. ~ **de compte** bank statement; ~ **de notes** ≃ (school) report. ♦ **relèvement** *nm [note, prix]* (*action*) raising, increasing, putting up; (*résultat*) rise, increase (*de* in); *[pays, économie]* recovery (*de* of); (*Naut*) *[position]* plotting (*de* of). ♦ **releveur** *nm* (gas *ou* electricity *etc*) meter man.

relief [Rəljɛf] *nm* **(a)** (*gén, Art, Géog*) relief. **au** ~ **accidenté** hilly; (*lit, fig*) **manquer de** ~ to be flat; **portrait qui a beaucoup de** ~ portrait which has plenty of depth. **(b) en** ~ *motif* in relief; *caractères* raised, embossed; *photographie* three-dimensional; **carte en** ~ relief map; **mettre en** ~ *intelligence, détail* to bring out; *qualités* to set off, enhance; *point à débattre* to underline, stress, emphasize; **essayer de se mettre en** ~ to try to get o.s. noticed. **(c)** (†: *restes*) ~**s** remains, left-overs.

relier [Rəlje] (7) *vt* (*gén*) to link (*à* to); (*ensemble*) to link *ou* join up *ou* together; *faits* to connect *ou* link together; *livre* to bind. **livre relié** bound volume, hard-back (book). ♦ **relieur, -euse** *nm,f* (book)binder.

religion [R(ə)liʒjɔ̃] *nf* (*gén, fig*) religion; (*foi*) (religious) faith; (*vie monastique*) monastic life. **se faire une** ~ **de qch** to make a religion of sth; **entrer en** ~ to take one's vows. ♦ **religieusement** *adv* religiously. ♦ **religieux, -euse 1** *adj* (*gén*) religious; *art* sacred; *école, mariage, musique* church. **l'habit** ~ the monk's (*ou* nun's) habit. **2** *nm* monk. **3** *nf* **(a)** (*nonne*) nun. **(b)** (*Culin*) cream bun (*made with choux pastry*).

reliquaire [R(ə)likɛR] *nm* reliquary.

reliquat [R(ə)lika] *nm [compte]* balance; *[somme]* remainder.

relique [R(ə)lik] *nf* (*Rel, fig*) relic. **garder qch comme une** ~ to treasure sth.

relire [R(ə)liR] (43) *vt* to read again, reread.

reliure [RəljyR] *nf* (*couverture*) binding; (*art, action*) (book)binding.

reloger [R(ə)lɔʒe] (3) *vt* to rehouse. ♦ **relogement** *nm* rehousing.

reluire [RəlɥiR] (38) *vi* to shine, gleam; (*sous la pluie*) to glisten. **faire** ~ **qch** to polish *ou* shine sth up, make sth shine. ♦ **reluisant, e** *adj* shining, shiny, gleaming (*de* with). (*iro*) **peu** ~ *avenir, résultat* far from brilliant; *personne* despicable.

reluquer‡ [R(ə)lyke] (1) *vt* to eye (up)*.

remâcher [R(ə)maʃe] (1) *vt [ruminant]* to ruminate; *échec* to ruminate *ou* brood over.

remanger [R(ə)mɑ̃ʒe] (3) **1** *vt* (*de nouveau*) to have again; (*davantage*) to have *ou* eat some more. **2** *vi* to eat again.

remanier [R(ə)manje] (7) *vt* (*gén*) to revise; *livre* to reshape, recast; *programme* to reorganize; *ministère* to reshuffle. ♦ **remaniement** *nm* revision; reshaping, recasting; reorganization; reshuffle.

remarier *vt*, **se** ~ *vpr* [R(ə)maRje] (7) to remarry. ♦ **remariage** *nm* second marriage, remarriage.

remarquable [R(ə)maRkabl(ə)] *adj personne, exploit* remarkable, outstanding; *fait* striking, noteworthy. ~ **par sa taille** notable for his height. ♦ **remarquablement** *adv doué* remarkably, outstandingly; *jouer* remarkably *ou* outstandingly well.

remarque [R(ə)maRk(ə)] *nf* (*observation*) remark, comment; (*critique*) critical remark; (*annotation*) note. **il m'en a fait la** ~ he remarked *ou* commented on it to me, he made a remark *ou* a comment about it to me.

remarquer [R(ə)maRke] (1) *vt* **(a)** (*apercevoir*) to notice. **sans se faire** ~ unnoticed, without being noticed, without attracting attention; **cette tache se remarque beaucoup/à peine** this stain is quite/hardly noticeable; **se faire** ~ to make o.s. conspicuous, draw attention to o.s.; **je remarque que vous avez une cravate** I see *ou* note that you are wearing a tie. **(b)** (*faire une remarque*) to remark, observe, comment. **remarquez (bien) que je n'en sais rien** mark you *ou* mind you I don't know; **faire** ~ *détail, erreur* to point out (*à qn* to sb).

remballer [Rɑ̃bale] (1) *vt* to pack (up) again; (*dans du papier*) to rewrap.

rembarquer *vti*, **se** ~ *vpr* [Rɑ̃baRke] (1) to re-embark.

rembarrer [Rɑ̃baRe] (1) *vt* to rebuff.

remblai [Rɑ̃blɛ] *nm* (*Rail, pour route*) embankment; (*Constr*) cut. **(terre de)** ~ (*Rail*) ballast; (*pour route*) hard core; (*Constr*) backfill; (*Aut*) ~**s récents** soft verges. ♦ **remblayer** (8) *vt route, voie ferrée* to bank up; *fossé* to fill in *ou* up.

rembobiner [Rɑ̃bɔbine] (1) *vt* to rewind.

remboîter [Rɑ̃bwate] (1) *vt tuyaux* to fit together again; *os* to put back into place.

rembourrer [Rɑ̃buRe] (1) *vt fauteuil* to stuff; *vête-*

ment to pad. ♦ **rembourrage** *nm* stuffing; padding.
rembourser [ʀɑ̃buʀse] (1) *vt* (*gén*) to reimburse, repay, pay back; *dette* to settle; *billet* to refund. **se faire ~** to get one's money back, get reimbursed; **je veux être remboursé** I want my money back; **~ qn de ses dépenses** to refund *ou* reimburse sb's expenses; **je te rembourserai demain** I'll pay you back *ou* square up with you* tomorrow. ♦ **remboursable** *adj billet* refundable; *emprunt* repayable. ♦ **remboursement** *nm* reimbursement, repayment; settlement; refund. **envoi contre ~** cash with order.
rembrunir (se) [ʀɑ̃bʀyniʀ] (2) *vpr [visage]* to darken; *[ciel]* to darken, cloud over.
remède [ʀ(ə)mɛd] *nm* (*Méd, fig: traitement*) remedy, cure; (*médicament*) medicine. **~ de bonne femme** old wives' *ou* folk cure *ou* remedy; **~ universel** cure-all; **porter ~ à qch** to cure *ou* remedy sth; **la situation est sans ~** the situation cannot be remedied *ou* is beyond remedy. ♦ **remédier à** (7) *vt indir maladie* to cure; *situation* to remedy, put right; *difficulté* to solve.
remembrer [ʀ(ə)mɑ̃bʀe] (1) *vt terres* to regroup. ♦ **remembrement** *nm* regrouping of lands.
remémorer (se) [ʀ(ə)memɔʀe] (1) *vpr* to recall, recollect.
remercier [ʀ(ə)mɛʀsje] (7) *vt* **(a)** (*dire merci*) to thank (*de qch* for sth, *d'avoir fait* for doing). **il me remercia d'un sourire** he thanked me with a smile, he smiled his thanks; **je vous remercie** thank you, thanks. **(b)** (*refuser*) **vous voulez boire? – je vous remercie** would you like a drink? – no thank you. **(c)** *employé* to dismiss (*from his job*). ♦ **remerciement** *nm* **(a)** **~s** thanks; (*dans un livre*) acknowledgements. **(b)** (*action*) thanking. **lettre de ~** thank-you letter.
remettre [ʀ(ə)mɛtʀ(ə)] (56) **1** *vt* **(a)** (*à nouveau*) *objet* to put back; *vêtement* to put back on, put on again; *radio, chauffage* to put *ou* turn *ou* switch on again. **~ un bouton à une veste** to sew *ou* put a button back on a jacket; **~ un enfant insolent à sa place** to put an insolent child in his place; **~ un appareil en marche** to restart a machine, start a machine (up) again; **~ en question** *autorité* to (call into) question, challenge; *accord* to cast doubt over, throw back into question; **~ une pendule à l'heure** to put *ou* set a clock right; **~ qch à neuf** to make sth as good as new again; **~ qch en état** to repair *ou* mend sth; **le repos l'a remise (sur pied)** the rest has set her back on her feet; **~ de l'ordre dans qch** to sort sth out. **(b)** (*davantage*) *chaise* to add; *tricot* to put on another; *sel, argent* to put in some more. **~ de l'huile dans le moteur** to top up the engine with oil. **(c)** *lettre, rançon, criminel* to hand over; *devoir, clefs* to hand in, give in; *objet prêté ou volé* to return; *récompense* to present; *démission* to hand in, tender (*à* to). **il s'est fait ~ les clefs** he got *ou* had the keys given to him; **~ un enfant à ses parents** to return a child to his parents; **~ son sort entre les mains de qn** to put one's fate into sb's hands. **(d)** *réunion* to put off, postpone (*à* until); *date* to put back (*à* to). **il ne faut jamais ~ au lendemain ce qu'on peut faire le jour même** never put off till tomorrow what you can do today. **(e)** (*se rappeler*) to remember. **~ qch en mémoire à qn** to remind sb of sth, recall sth to sb. **(f)** *peine, péché* to remit. **~ une dette à qn** to remit sb's debt, let sb off a debt. **(g) ~ ça*** (*démarches*) to go through it all again; (*au café*) to have another drink; (*travail*) to get down to it again; (*bruit*) **les voilà qui remettent ça!** there they go again!, they're at it again!*
2 se ~ *vpr* **(a)** (*recouvrer la santé*) to recover, get better, pick up*. **se ~ d'une maladie** to recover from *ou* get over an illness; **remettez-vous!** pull yourself together! **(b)** (*recommencer*) **se ~ à (faire) qch** (*gén*) to start (doing) sth again; (*sport, habitude*) to take up sth again; **il se remet à faire froid** the weather *ou* it is getting *ou* turning cold again; **se ~ debout** to get back to one's feet. **(c)** (*se confier*) **se ~ entre les mains de qn** to put o.s. in sb's hands; **je m'en remets à vous** I'll leave it (up) to you. **(d)** (*se réconcilier*) **se ~ avec qn** to make it up with sb; **ils se sont remis ensemble** they've come back together again.
réminiscence [ʀeminisɑ̃s] *nf* reminiscence. **quelques ~s de** some vague recollections of.
remise [ʀ(ə)miz] **1** *nf* **(a)** *[lettre]* delivery; *[rançon, clefs]* handing over; *[récompense]* presentation; *[devoir]* handing in. **(b)** *[péchés, dette]* remission; *[peine]* reduction (*de* of, in). **(c)** (*rabais*) discount, reduction. **(d)** (*local*) shed. **(e)** (*ajournement*) postponement, putting off *ou* back. **2: ~ en cause** calling into question; **~ en état** *[machine]* repair(ing); *[tableau]* restoration; **~ en jeu** throw-in; **~ à jour** updating; **~ en marche** restarting; **~ en ordre** reordering; **~ en place** putting back in place.
remiser [ʀ(ə)mize] (1) *vt* (*ranger*) to put away.
rémission [ʀemisjɔ̃] *nf* (*gén*) remission. **sans ~** *travailler* unremittingly, relentlessly; *mal* irremediable.
remontage [ʀ(ə)mɔ̃taʒ] *nm [montre]* rewinding, winding up; *[meuble]* reassembly, putting back together.
remontant, e [ʀ(ə)mɔ̃tɑ̃, ɑ̃t] **1** *adj* **(a)** *boisson* invigorating, fortifying. **(b)** *rosier* remontant; *fraisier* double-cropping *ou* -fruiting. **2** *nm* tonic, pick-me-up*.
remontée [ʀ(ə)mɔ̃te] *nf [côte, rivière]* ascent; *[prix]* rise; *[candidat]* recovery. (*Sport*) **~ mécanique** skilift.
remonte-pente, *pl* **~-~s** [ʀ(ə)mɔ̃tpɑ̃t] *nm* skilift.
remonter [ʀ(ə)mɔ̃te] (1) **1** *vi* **(a)** (*à nouveau*) *[personne]* to go *ou* come back up; *[marée]* to come in again; *[prix, baromètre, route]* to rise again, go up again. **il remonta sur la table** he climbed back (up) onto the table; **~ en voiture** to get back into one's car, get into one's car again; **il est remonté de la 7e à la 3e place** he has come up *ou* recovered from 7th to 3rd place. **(b)** *[vêtement]* to go up, pull up. **(c)** (*revenir*) *[souvenir]* to come back; *[odeur]* to come up. **~ jusqu'au coupable** to trace back to the guilty man; **~ à la source** to go back *ou* return to the source; **aussi loin que remontent ses souvenirs** as far back as he can remember; **cette histoire remonte à plusieurs années** this story dates back *ou* goes back several years; **tout cela remonte au déluge!** all that's as old as the hills!
2 *vt* **(a)** *étage, côte* to go *ou* climb back up; *rue* to go *ou* come back up. **~ le courant** (*en barque*) to sail *ou* row (back) upstream; (*fig*) to begin to get back on one's feet again. **(b)** *adversaire* to catch up with. **il a 15 points à ~** he has 15 marks to catch up. **(c)** *mur, jupe, note* to raise; *vitre* (*en poussant*) to push up; (*avec manivelle*) to wind up; *manche* to roll up; *col* to turn up. **(d)** (*reporter*) *objet* to take *ou* bring back up. **(e)** *montre* to wind up. **(f)** (*réinstaller*) *machine, meuble* to put together again, put back together (again), reassemble; *usine* to set up again. **(g)** (*réassortir*) *garde-robe* to renew; *magasin* to restock. **(h)** (*remettre en état*) *personne* (*physiquement*) to set up (again); (*moralement*) to cheer *ou* buck* up (again); *entreprise* to put *ou* set back on its feet.
3 se ~ *vpr* **(a)** **se ~ en boîtes de conserves** to get in (further) stocks of tinned food; **se ~ en chaussures** to get some new shoes. **(b)** (*physiquement*) to set o.s. up (again); (*moralement*) to cheer *ou* buck* o.s. up.
remontoir [ʀ(ə)mɔ̃twaʀ] *nm* winder.
remontrance [ʀ(ə)mɔ̃tʀɑ̃s] *nf* **(a)** reproof, reprimand. **faire des ~s à qn** to reprimand sb. **(b)** (*Hist*) remonstrance.
remontrer [ʀ(ə)mɔ̃tʀe] (1) *vt* **(a)** (*de nouveau*) to

show again. **(b) en ~ à qn: il pourrait t'en ~** he could teach you a thing or two; **il a voulu m'en ~** he wanted to show he knew better than me.

remords [ʀ(ə)mɔʀ] *nm*: **le ~, les ~** remorse; **avoir un** *ou* **des ~** to feel remorse, be conscience-stricken; **j'ai eu un ~ de conscience** I had second thoughts.

remorque [ʀ(ə)mɔʀk(ə)] *nf* (*véhicule*) trailer; (*câble*) tow-rope, towline. **prendre une voiture en ~** to tow a car; **avoir qn en ~** to have sb in tow; (*lit, fig*) **être à la ~ de** to tag behind. ♦ **remorquer** (1) *vt voiture, bateau* to tow; *train* to pull, haul; (*fig*) *personne* to have in tow, trail *ou* drag along. ♦ **remorquage** *nm* towing; pulling, hauling. ♦ **remorqueur** *nm* tug(boat).

remous [ʀ(ə)mu] *nm*: **le ~, les ~** *[bateau]* the (back)wash; *[eau]* the swirl, the eddies; *[air]* the eddy; *[foule]* the bustle; *[scandale]* the stir.

rempailler [ʀɑ̃pɑje] (1) *vt chaise* to reseat, rebottom (*with straw*).

rempart [ʀɑ̃paʀ] *nm* (*Mil, fig*) rampart. **sur les ~s** on the ramparts *ou* battlements; **faire à qn un ~ de son corps** to shield sb with one's (own) body.

remplacer [ʀɑ̃plase] (3) *vt* (*gén*) to replace (*par* with); *objet usagé* to change (*par* for); *directeur à la retraite* to take over from; *professeur malade* to stand in for, substitute for. **se faire ~** to find o.s. a stand-in *ou* replacement; **le miel peut ~ le sucre** honey can be used in place of *ou* as a substitute for sugar. ♦ **remplaçable** *adj* replaceable. ♦ **remplaçant, e** *nm,f* (*gén*) replacement, substitute; (*Méd*) locum; (*Sport*) reserve; (*pendant un match*) substitute; (*Scol*) supply teacher, stand-in. ♦ **remplacement** *nm* replacement. (*intérim*) **assurer le ~ de qn** to stand in *ou* deputize for sb; **faire des ~s** to do temporary (replacement) work; **en ~ de qch** instead of sth, as a replacement *ou* substitute for sth; **solution de ~** alternative solution; **produit de ~** substitute (product).

remplir [ʀɑ̃pliʀ] (2) **1** *vt* **(a)** (*gén*) to fill (*de* with); *récipient* to fill (up); (*à nouveau*) to refill; *questionnaire* to fill in. **~ qch à moitié** to half fill sth, fill sth half full. **(b)** *promesse, fonction, condition* to fulfil; *travail* to carry out, do; *rôle* to fill, play; *besoin* to fulfil, meet, satisfy. **~ ses fonctions** to carry out *ou* perform one's duties. **2 se ~** *vpr [récipient, salle]* to fill (up) (*de* with). **se ~ les poches*** to line one's pockets. ♦ **rempli, e** *adj* (*gén*) full (*de* of), filled (*de* with); *visage* full, plump; *journée, vie* full, busy. **avoir l'estomac bien ~** to have a full stomach, have eaten one's fill; **texte ~ de fautes** text riddled *ou* packed with mistakes. ♦ **remplissage** *nm [tonneau]* filling (up); *[discours]* padding.

remplumer* **(se)** [ʀɑ̃plyme] (1) *vpr* (*physiquement*) to fill out again; (*financièrement*) to get back on one's feet.

remporter [ʀɑ̃pɔʀte] (1) *vt* **(a)** *objet* to take away (again), take back. **(b)** *victoire* to win; *prix* to carry off; *succès* to achieve.

remuer [ʀ(ə)mɥe] (1) **1** *vt* **(a)** *tête, bras* to move; *oreille* to twitch; *hanches* to sway. **~ la queue** *[vache]* to flick its tail; *[chien]* to wag its tail; (*fig*) **il n'a pas remué le petit doigt** he didn't lift a finger (to help). **(b) (faire) ~** *branches* to stir; *objet* (*déplacer*) to move, shift; (*secouer*) to shake. **(c)** *café, sauce* to stir; *salade* to toss; *terre* to dig *ou* turn over; *souvenirs* to stir up, arouse. **~ de l'argent (à la pelle)** to handle a great deal of money; **~ ciel et terre pour** to move heaven and earth (in order) to. **(d)** (*émouvoir*) to move. **2** *vi [personne]* to move; *[dent, tuile]* to be loose. **cesse de ~!** keep still!, stop fidgeting! **3 se ~** *vpr* **(a)** (*bouger*) to move; (*se déplacer*) to move about. **(b)** (*: *s'activer*) to bestir o.s., get a move on*. ♦ **remuant, e** *adj* restless. ♦ **remue-ménage** *nm inv* (*bruit*) commotion; (*activité*) hurly-burly. **faire du ~** to make a commotion.

rémunérer [ʀemyneʀe] (6) *vt personne* to remunerate, pay. **~ le travail de qn** to remunerate *ou* pay sb for his work. ♦ **rémunérateur, -trice** *adj emploi* remunerative, lucrative. ♦ **rémunération** *nf* remuneration, payment (*de* for).

renâcler [ʀ(ə)nɑkle] (1) *vi [animal]* to snort; *[personne]* to grumble, show (one's) reluctance. **~ à faire qch** to jib at having to do sth, do sth reluctantly.

renaissance [ʀ(ə)nɛsɑ̃s] **1** *nf* (*Rel, fig*) rebirth. (*Hist*) **la R~** the Renaissance. **2** *adj inv mobilier* Renaissance.

renaître [ʀ(ə)nɛtʀ(ə)] (59) *vi* **(a)** *[sentiment, intérêt]* to be revived (*dans* in); *[plante, conflit]* to spring up again; *[difficulté]* to recur, crop up again; *[économie]* to revive, recover; *[sourire]* to return (*sur* to); *[jour]* to dawn, break. **faire ~** to bring back, revive. **(b)** (*revivre*) to come to life again. **~ de ses cendres** to rise from one's ashes; **je me sens ~** I feel as if I've been given a new lease of life; (*littér*) **~ au bonheur** to find happiness again.

rénal, e, *mpl* **-aux** [ʀenal, o] *adj* renal, kidney.

renard [ʀ(ə)naʀ] *nm* (*Zool*) fox. (*fig*) **fin ~** crafty *ou* sly fox *ou* dog. ♦ **renarde** *nf* vixen.

renchérir [ʀɑ̃ʃeʀiʀ] (2) *vi* **(a)** *[personne]* to go further. **~ sur ce que qn dit** to add something to what sb says, go further *ou* one better (*péj*) than sb. **(b)** *[prix]* to get dearer *ou* more expensive. ♦ **renchérissement** *nm [marchandises]* rise *ou* increase in the price (*de* of).

rencontre [ʀɑ̃kɔ̃tʀ(ə)] *nf* (*gén*) meeting; (*imprévue*) encounter; (*Mil*) encounter; *[éléments]* conjunction; *[routes]* junction. **faire la ~ de qn** to meet sb; **aller à la ~ de qn** to go and meet sb, go to meet sb; **faire une mauvaise ~** to have an unpleasant encounter; **~ de boxe** boxing match.

rencontrer [ʀɑ̃kɔ̃tʀe] (1) **1** *vt* **(a)** (*gén*) to meet; (*par hasard*) to run *ou* bump into; (*en réunion*) to have a meeting with. **(b)** (*trouver*) *expression, village, passant* to find, come across; *occasion* to meet with; *obstacle* to meet with, encounter, come up against. **(c)** (*heurter*) to strike; (*toucher*) to meet (with). **(d)** *équipe* to meet, play (against); *boxeur* to meet, fight (against). **2 se ~** *vpr* **(a)** (*gén*) to meet; (*en réunion*) to have a meeting; *[équipes]* to meet, play (each other); *[véhicules]* to collide (with each other). **(b)** (*avoir les mêmes idées*) to be at one (*avec* with), be of the same opinion *ou* mind (*avec* as). **(c)** *[coïncidence, curiosité]* to be found.

rendement [ʀɑ̃dmɑ̃] *nm [champ]* yield; *[machine, personne]* output; *[entreprise]* (*productivité*) productivity; (*production*) output (*de* of); *[investissement]* return (*de* on); (*Phys*) efficiency.

rendez-vous [ʀɑ̃devu] *nm inv* **(a)** (*rencontre*) appointment; (*d'amoureux*) date. **donner un ~ à qn** to make an appointment with sb, arrange to see *ou* meet sb; **~ spatial** docking (in space). **(b)** (*lieu*) meeting place. **~ de chasse** meet.

rendormir (se) [ʀɑ̃dɔʀmiʀ] (16) *vpr* to go back to sleep, fall asleep again.

rendre [ʀɑ̃dʀ(ə)] (41) **1** *vt* **(a)** *objet, argent* to give back, return; (*Scol*) *devoir* to hand *ou* give in; *réponse* to give. **~ à qn sa parole** to release sb from a promise, let sb off (his promise); **~ la liberté à qn** to set sb free, give sb his freedom; **~ la santé à qn** to restore sb to health; **~ la vue à qn** to restore sb's sight. **(b)** *justice* to administer, dispense; *jugement* to pronounce, render; *verdict* to return. (*fig*) **~ justice à qn** to do justice to sb. **(c)** *hospitalité, invitation* to return, repay; *salut, coup* to return. **il m'a joué un sale tour, mais je le lui rendrai** he played a dirty trick on me, but I'll get even with him *ou* I'll pay him back; **il la déteste, et elle le lui rend bien** he hates her and she feels exactly the same about him; **~ la mon-**

naie à qn to give sb his change; (*fig*) ~ **à qn la monnaie de sa pièce** to pay sb back in his own coin. **(d)** (+ *adj*) to make. ~ **qn heureux** *etc* to make sb happy *etc*; **c'est à vous ~ fou!** it's enough to drive you mad! **(e)** *expression, traduction* to render. **(f)** (*produire*) *liquide* to give out; *son* to produce. (*fig*) **l'enquête n'a rien rendu** the inquiry drew a blank *ou* didn't come to anything. **(g)** (*vomir*) to vomit, bring up. **(h)** (*locutions*) ~ **l'âme** *ou* **le dernier soupir** to breathe one's last, give up the ghost; ~ **les armes** to lay down one's arms; ~ **des comptes à qn** to be accountable to sb; ~ **compte de qch à qn** to give sb an account of sth; ~ **gloire à Dieu** to glorify God; ~ **grâces à** to give thanks to; ~ **hommage à** to pay tribute to; ~ **la pareille à qn** to do the same for sb, pay sb back the same way; (*Sport*) *[cheval]* ~ **du poids** to have a weight handicap; ~ **service à qn** to be of service *ou* help to sb; ~ **visite à qn** to visit sb, call on sb, pay sb a visit.

2 *vi* **(a)** *[arbres, terre]* to yield, be productive. **la pêche a bien rendu** we have got a good catch (of fish). **(b)** (*vomir*) to be sick, vomit.

3 se ~ *vpr* **(a)** (*céder*) *[soldat, criminel]* to give o.s. up, surrender. **se ~ à l'avis de qn** to bow to sb's opinion; **se ~ à l'évidence** to face (the) facts; **se ~ aux prières de qn** to give in *ou* yield to sb's pleas. **(b)** (*aller*) **se ~ à** to go to; **alors qu'il se rendait à ...** as he was on his way to ... *ou* going to ... . **(c) se ~ compte de qch** to realize sth, be aware of sth; **se ~ compte que** to realize that, be aware that; **rendez-vous compte!** just imagine! *ou* think! **(d)** (+*adj*) to make o.s. **se ~ ridicule** to make o.s. ridiculous, make a fool of o.s.

rendu, e [Rɑ̃dy] **1** *adj* **(a)** (*arrivé*) **être ~** to have arrived. **(b)** (*remis*) ~ **à domicile** delivered to the house. **(c)** (*fatigué*) exhausted, tired out, worn out. **2** *nm* (*Comm*) return.

rêne [Rɛn] *nf* rein. **tenir les ~s du gouvernement** to hold the reins of government, be in the saddle.

renégat, e [Rənega, at] *nm,f* renegade.

renfermer [Rɑ̃fɛRme] (1) **1** *vt* to contain, hold. **2 se** ~ *vpr*: **se ~ (en soi-même)** to withdraw (into o.s.). ♦ **renfermé, e 1** *adj* withdrawn. **2** *nm*: **odeur de** ~ fusty *ou* stale smell.

renflé, e [Rɑ̃fle] *adj* bulging. ♦ **renflement** *nm* bulge.

renflouer [Rɑ̃flue] (1) *vt entreprise, bateau* to refloat; *personne* to set back on his feet.

renfoncement [Rɑ̃fɔ̃smɑ̃] *nm* recess.

renforcer [Rɑ̃fɔRse] (3) **1** *vt objet, argument, équipe* to reinforce; *paix* to consolidate; *effort* to add to, intensify; *position, amitié* to strengthen. ~ **qn dans une opinion** to confirm sb in an opinion. **2 se** ~ *vpr [craintes, amitié]* to strengthen; *[pression]* to intensify.

renfort [Rɑ̃fɔR] *nm* **(a)** (*Mil*) ~**s** (*hommes*) reinforcements; (*matériel*) (further) supplies. **(b)** (*Tech*) reinforcement, strengthening piece. **(c) de ~** *barre, toile* strengthening; *armée* back-up, supporting; *personnel* extra, additional; **envoyer qn en ~** to send sb as an extra; **à grand ~ de gestes** accompanied by a great many gestures.

renfrogner (se) [Rɑ̃fRɔɲe] (1) *vpr* to scowl. ♦ **renfrogné, e** *adj* sullen, sulky.

rengager [Rɑ̃gaʒe] (3) **1** *vt discussion* to start up again; *fonds* to reinvest; *combat, ouvrier* to re-engage. **2 se** ~ *vpr* (*Mil*) to join up again, re-enlist.

rengaine [Rɑ̃gɛn] *nf*: **(vieille)** ~ (old) folk song; **c'est toujours la même ~*** it's always the same old song*.

rengainer [Rɑ̃gene] (1) *vt épée* to sheathe, put up; *revolver* to put back in its holster; (*) *compliment* to save, withhold.

rengorger (se) [Rɑ̃gɔRʒe] (3) *vpr [oiseau]* to puff out its throat; *[personne]* to puff o.s. up.

renier [Rənje] (7) **1** *vt foi, Dieu* to renounce; *signature* to disown, repudiate; *promesse* to go back on, break. **2 se** ~ *vpr* to go back on what one has said *ou* done. ♦ **reniement** *nm* renunciation; disowning, repudiation; breaking.

renifler [R(ə)nifle] (1) **1** *vt* to sniff (at). **2** *vi [personne]* to sniff; *[cheval]* to snort. ♦ **reniflement** *nm* (*action*) sniffing; (*bruit*) sniff.

renne [Rɛn] *nm* reindeer.

renom [R(ə)nɔ̃] *nm* (*notoriété*) renown, fame; (*réputation*) reputation. **de grand ~, en ~** renowned, famous; **avoir du ~** to be famous. ♦ **renommé, e**[1] *adj* celebrated, famous. ~ **pour** renowned *ou* famed for. ♦ **renommée**[2] *nf* **(a)** (*célébrité*) fame, renown. **de ~ mondiale** world-famous. **(b)** (*opinion publique*) public report. **(c)** (*réputation*) reputation. **bonne/mauvaise ~** good/bad reputation *ou* name.

renoncer [R(ə)nɔ̃se] (3) ~ **à** *vt indir* (*gén*) to give up, renounce. ~ **à qn** to give sb up; **je** *ou* **j'y renonce** I give up. ♦ **renoncement** *nm* renunciation. ♦ **renonciation** *nf* giving up, renunciation.

renouer [Rənwe] (1) **1** *vt lacet* to tie (up) again, re-tie; *conversation* to renew. **2** *vi*: ~ **avec** *habitude* to take up again; ~ **avec qn** to take up with sb again.

renouveau, *pl* ~**x** [R(ə)nuvo] *nm* (*transformation*) revival. (*regain*) ~ **de succès/faveur** renewed success/favour.

renouveler [R(ə)nuvle] (4) **1** *vt* (*gén*) to renew; *stock* to replenish; *conseil d'administration* to re-elect; *congé* to re-grant; *offre, exploit, erreur* to repeat; *douleur, théorie* to revive. ~ **l'air d'une salle** to air a room; ~ **sa confiance à qn** to reassert one's confidence in sb. **2 se** ~ *vpr* (*se répéter*) *[erreur, fait]* to recur, be repeated; (*être remplacé*) *[personnel]* to be renewed; (*innover*) *[auteur]* to try sth new. ♦ **renouvelable** *adj passeport* renewable; *assemblée* that must be re-elected. ♦ **renouvellement** *nm* renewal; replenishment; repetition; revival; recurrence. (*Pol*) **solliciter le ~ de son mandat** to stand for re-election.

rénover [Renɔve] (1) *vt maison* to renovate, modernize; *meuble* to restore; *institutions, méthodes* to reform, regenerate; *science* to renew. ♦ **rénovateur, -trice** *adj, nm,f*: **être ~** to have a reforming *ou* regenerative influence. ♦ **rénovation** *nf* renovation, modernization; restoration; reform; renewal.

renseignement [Rɑsɛɲmɑ̃] *nm*: ~**(s)** information; **un ~ intéressant** an interesting piece of information, some interesting information; **demander des ~s sur qn** to make inquiries *ou* ask for information *ou* for particulars about sb; **avoir de bons ~s sur qn** to have good reports about *ou* on sb; **pourriez-vous me donner un ~?** could you give me some information?, could you tell me something?; '~**s**' (*panneau*) 'inquiries', 'information'; (*Téléc*) directory inquiries. **(b)** (*Mil*) ~**(s)** intelligence; **agent de ~s** intelligence agent.

renseigner [Rɑ̃seɲe] (1) **1** *vt* to give information to. **qui pourrait me ~ sur lui?** who could tell me sth about him?, who could give me some information *ou* particulars about him?; **il a l'air bien renseigné** he seems to be well informed; **on vous a mal renseigné** you have been misinformed. **2 se** ~ *vpr* to make inquiries, ask for information *ou* particulars (*sur* about). **je vais me ~ auprès de lui** I'll ask him about it; **j'essaierai de me ~** I'll try to find out.

rentable [Rɑ̃tabl(ə)] *adj* profitable. **c'est très ~** it really pays. ♦ **rentabilité** *nf* profitability.

rente [Rɑ̃t] *nf* (*pension*) annuity, pension; (*fournie par la famille*) allowance; (*emprunt d'État*) government stock *ou* bond. **avoir des ~s** to have a private income, have private *ou* independent means. ♦ **rentier, -ière** *nm,f* person of independent *ou* private means.

rentrant, e [rɑ̃trɑ̃, ɑ̃t] *adj train d'atterrissage* retractable; (*Math*) *angle* reflex.

rentrée [rɑ̃tre] *nf* **(a)** (*Scol*) start of the new school year; (*Univ*) start of the new academic year; (*du trimestre*) start of the new term. **la ~ aura lieu lundi** the new term begins on Monday, school starts again on Monday; **à la ~ de Noël** at the start of (the) term after the Christmas holidays. **(b)** *[tribunaux]* reopening; *[parlement]* reassembly; *[députés]* return. **c'est la ~ des théâtres parisiens** it's the start of the theatrical season in Paris; **on verra ça à la ~** we'll see about that after the holidays. **(c)** *[acteur, sportif]* comeback. **faire sa ~ politique** to make a *ou* one's political comeback. **(d)** (*retour*) return. **à l'heure des ~s dans Paris** when everyone is coming back into Paris *ou* returning to Paris; (*Espace*) **~ dans l'atmosphère** re-entry into the atmosphere; **effectuer sa ~ dans l'atmosphère** to re-enter the atmosphere. **(e)** (*Comm*) **~s** income; **~ d'argent** (incoming) sum of money.

rentrer [rɑ̃tre] (1) **1** *vi* **(a)** (*à nouveau*) (*aller*) to go back in; (*venir*) to come back in. **~ (chez soi)** to return home, go (*ou* get *ou* come) back home; **est-ce qu'il est rentré?** is he (back) home?; **~ à Paris/de Paris** to go back *ou* come back *ou* return to Paris/from Paris; **je rentre en voiture** I'm driving back, I'm going back by car. **(b)** (*reprendre ses activités*) *[élèves]* to go back to school, start school again; *[université]* to start again; *[tribunaux]* to reopen; *[parlement]* to reassemble; *[députés]* to return. **le trimestre prochain, on rentrera un lundi** next term we start on a Monday. **(c)** (*entrer*) *[personne]* to go in; to come in; *[chose]* to go in. **nous sommes rentrés dans un café** we went into a café; **cette clef ne rentre pas dans la serrure** this key doesn't fit (into) the lock. **(d) ~ dans** (*travailler dans*) to join, go into; (*s'écraser contre*) to crash into, collide with; (*être compris dans*) to be included in, be part of; **il l'a fait ~ dans la firme** he helped him to get a job in the firm; **furieux, il lui est rentré dedans**‡ he was furious and he pitched* *ou* laid* into him; **~ dans une catégorie** to fall into *ou* come into a category. **(e)** *[argent]* to come in. **faire ~ l'argent** to get the money in. **(f)** (*) *[connaissances]* **les maths, ça ne rentre pas** he can't take maths in, he can't get the hang of maths*; **faire ~ qch dans la tête de qn** to drum *ou* get sth into sb's head. **(g)** (*locutions*) **~ dans sa coquille** to go back into one's shell; **~ dans son argent** to recover *ou* get back one's money; **tout est rentré dans l'ordre** (*dans son état normal*) everything is back to normal again; (*dans le calme*) order has been restored; (*tout a été clarifié*) everything is sorted out now; **~ dans le rang** to come *ou* fall back into line; **~ en grâce auprès de qn** to get back into sb's good graces.

2 *vt* **(a)** *foins, marchandises, animaux* to bring in. **~ sa voiture au garage** to put the car away in the garage. **(b)** *train d'atterrissage* to raise; (*lit, fig*) *griffes* to draw in. **~ sa chemise (dans son pantalon)** to tuck one's shirt in (one's trousers); **ne me rentre pas ton coude dans le ventre** don't jab *ou* stick your elbow in(to) my stomach; **~ le ventre** to pull one's stomach in; **~ sa rage** to hold back *ou* suppress one's unger.

renverser [rɑ̃vɛrse] (1) **1** *vt* **(a)** (*faire tomber*) *personne* to knock over *ou* down; *objet* to knock over, upset, overturn; *liquide* to spill, upset; *grains* to scatter. **(b)** (*mettre à l'envers*) to turn upside down. **(c)** (*abattre*) *obstacles* (*lit*) to knock down; (*fig*) to overcome; *ordre établi, royauté* to overthrow. **~ le gouvernement** (*coup d'État*) to overthrow *ou* overturn the government; (*vote*) to defeat the government. **(d) ~ la tête en arrière** to tip *ou* tilt one's head back; **~ le corps en arrière** to lean back. **(e)** (*inverser*) *ordre des mots, courant* to reverse; (*Opt*) *image* to invert, reverse. **~ la situation** to reverse the situation; **~ la vapeur** (*lit*) to reverse steam; (*fig*) to change course. **(f)** (*: *étonner*) to bowl over, stagger. **2 se ~** *vpr* **(a) se ~ en arrière** to lean back. **(b)** *[voiture]* to overturn; *[bateau]* to overturn, capsize; *[vase]* to fall over, be overturned. ♦ **renversant, e*** *adj nouvelle* staggering, astounding; *personne* amazing, incredible. ♦ **renverse** *nf*: **tomber à la ~** to fall backwards. ♦ **renversement** *nm [ordre des mots]* inversion, reversal; *[situation, valeurs]* reversal; (*Pol*) (*par un coup d'État*) overthrow; (*par vote*) defeat.

renvoi [rɑ̃vwa] *nm* **(a)** (*V* **renvoyer**) dismissal; expulsion; suspension; return; discharge; referral; postponement. **(b)** (*référence*) cross-reference; (*en bas de page*) footnote. **(c)** (*rot*) belch. **ça me donne des ~s** it gives me wind, it makes me belch.

renvoyer [rɑ̃vwaje] (8) *vt* **(a)** (*congédier*) *employé* to dismiss; *élève* (*définitivement*) to expel; (*temporairement*) to suspend. **se faire ~** to be dismissed (*ou* expelled). **(b)** *lettre, ballon, personne* to send back; *cadeau* to return. **~ les soldats dans leurs foyers** to discharge soldiers, send soldiers back home; **~ la balle** (*Sport*) to return the ball; **il m'a renvoyé la balle** (*argument*) he threw the *ou* my argument back at me; (*responsabilité*) he tried to pass the buck (to me)*. **(c)** (*référer*) *lecteur* to refer (*à* to). **(d)** (*différer*) *rendez-vous* to postpone, put off (*à plus tard* until later). (*Jur*) **l'affaire a été renvoyée à huitaine** the case was postponed *ou* deferred for a week. **(e)** (*réfléchir*) *son* to echo; *lumière, chaleur, image* to reflect.

réorganiser [reɔrganize] (1) **1** *vt* to reorganize. **2 se ~** *vpr [pays, parti]* to be reorganized. ♦ **réorganisation** *nf* reorganization.

réouverture [reuvɛrtyr] *nf* reopening.

repaire [r(ə)pɛr] *nm* (*Zool*) den, lair; (*fig*) den, hideout. **~ de brigands** thieves' den.

repaître (se) [rəpɛtr(ə)] (57) *vpr*: **se ~ de** *aliments* to gorge o.s. on; *lectures* to revel in.

répandre [repɑ̃dr(ə)] (41) **1** *vt* **(a)** (*accidentellement*) *liquide* to spill; *grains* to scatter. **(b)** (*gén, fig*) (*volontairement*) to spread; *dons* to lavish; *sang, larmes, lumière* to shed; *odeur* to give off; *chaleur, fumée* to give out. **2 se ~** *vpr [liquide]* to spill, be spilled; *[grains]* to scatter, be scattered; *[odeur, lumière, doctrine]* to spread (*sur* over); *[son]* to carry (*dans* through); *[opinion, méthode]* to become widespread (*dans* among). **la foule se répand dans les rues** the crowd spills out *ou* pours out into the streets; **la nouvelle se répandit comme une traînée de poudre** the news spread like wildfire; **se ~ en menaces** *etc* to pour out threats *etc.* ♦ **répandu, e** *adj opinion* widespread. **idée très ~e** widely held *ou* widespread idea.

reparaître [r(ə)parɛtr(ə)] (57) *vi* to reappear.

réparer [repare] (1) *vt* **(a)** (*remettre en état*) (*gén*) to mend, repair, fix*; *forces, santé* to restore. (*lit, fig*) **~ les dégâts** to repair the damage; **faire ~ qch** to get *ou* have sth mended *ou* repaired; **~ qch sommairement** to patch sth up. **(b)** (*corriger*) *erreur, négligence* to put right. **(c)** (*compenser*) *faute* to make up for, make amends for; *perte* to make good, make up for, compensate for. ♦ **réparable** *adj objet* repairable, which can be repaired; *erreur* which can be put right. ♦ **réparateur, -trice 1** *adj sommeil* refreshing. **2** *nm,f* repairer. **~ de télévision** television repairman *ou* engineer. ♦ **réparation** *nf* **(a)** (*remise en état*) mending, repairing, fixing*; restoration; (*résultat*) repair. **en ~** under repair; **faire des ~s** to do some repairs; **l'atelier de ~** the repair shop. **(b)** (*correction*) putting right. **(c)** (*compensation*) compensation (*de* for). **en ~ du dommage** to make up for *ou* to compensate for the harm; **obtenir ~ (d'un affront)** to obtain redress (for an insult). **(d)** (*dommages-intérêts*) damages, compensation. (*Hist*) ~s reparations.

reparler [R(ə)parle] (1) *vi*: ~ **de qch** to talk about sth again; ~ **à qn** to speak to sb again.

repartie [Rəparti] *nf* retort. **avoir de la** ~ to be good *ou* quick at repartee.

repartir [R(ə)partiR] (16) *vi [voyageur]* to set off *ou* leave again; *[machine]* to start (up) again; *[affaire]* to get going again. ~ **chez soi** to go back home; ~ **à zéro** to start from scratch again; *[discussion]* **c'est reparti!*** they're off again!*

répartir [RepartiR] (2) **1** *vt* **(a)** (*diviser*) *somme, travail* to share out, divide up (*en* into, *entre* among), distribute (*entre* among). ~ **les joueurs en 2 groupes** to divide *ou* split (up) the players into 2 groups. **(b)** (*égaliser*) *masses, chaleur* to distribute; (*étaler*) *paiement, horaire* to spread (*sur* over). **les troupes sont réparties le long de la frontière** troops are spread out *ou* distributed *ou* scattered along the frontier.

2 se ~ *vpr* (*se diviser*) to be divided (up); (*s'égaliser*) to be distributed. **se** ~ **le travail** to share out the work (among themselves *ou* ourselves *etc*).

♦ **répartition** *nf* (*action*) sharing out, division, distribution; spreading; (*résultat*) distribution.

repas [R(ə)pɑ] *nm* meal. ~ **léger** light meal, snack; ~ **de noces** wedding breakfast; **aux heures des** ~ at mealtimes; **panier** ~ picnic basket; **plateau** ~ meal tray.

repasser [R(ə)pɑse] (1) **1** *vt* **(a)** *frontière* to cross again; *examen* to resit, take again; *film* to show again. ~ **un plat au four** to put a dish in the oven again *ou* back in the oven. **(b)** (*au fer*) to iron. **ça ne se repasse pas** it doesn't need ironing; **planche à** ~ ironing board. **(c)** *couteau, lame* to sharpen (up). **(d)** *leçon* to go (back) over, go over again (*dans son esprit* in one's mind). **(e)** (*: *transmettre*) *affaire* to hand over *ou* on; *maladie* to pass on (*à qn* to sb). (*au téléphone*) **je te repasse ta mère** I'm handing you back to your mother. **2** *vi* (*dans un endroit*) to come back, go back; (*devant un même lieu*) to go *ou* come past again; (*sur un même trait*) to go over again, go back over. **tu peux toujours** ~‡ nothing doing‡, you've got a hope*. ♦ **repassage** *nm [linge]* ironing; *[couteau]* sharpening.

repayer [R(ə)peje] (8) *vt* to pay again.

repêcher [R(ə)peʃe] (1) *vt* **(a)** *corps* to recover, fish out. **(b)** (*Scol*) *candidat* to let through, pass (*with less than the official pass mark*); *athlète* to give a second chance to. ♦ **repêchage** *nm* recovery, fishing out; passing. **question de** ~ question to give candidates a second chance.

repeindre [R(ə)pɛ̃dR(ə)] (52) *vt* to repaint.

repenser [R(ə)pɑ̃se] (1) **1** ~ **à** *vt indir*: ~ **à qch** to think about sth again. **2** *vt concept* to rethink; *question* to think out again.

repentir[1] **(se)** [R(ə)pɑ̃tiR] (16) *vpr* (*Rel*) to repent. **se** ~ **de qch/d'avoir fait qch** to regret sth/having done sth, be sorry for sth/for having done sth; (*Rel*) to repent of sth/of having done sth. ♦ **repentant, e** *ou* **repenti, e** *adj* repentant, penitent. ♦ **repentir**[2] *nm* (*Rel*) repentance; (*regret*) regret.

répercuter [RepɛRkyte] (1) **1** *vt son* to echo; *écho* to send *ou* throw back; *lumière* to reflect. ~ **une augmentation sur le client** to pass an increase in cost on to the customer. **2 se** ~ *vpr [son]* to reverberate, echo; *[lumière]* to be reflected, reflect. (*fig*) **se** ~ **sur** to have repercussions on. ♦ **répercussion** *nf* (*gén*) repercussion (*sur, dans* on).

repérer [R(ə)peRe] (6) **1** *vt* (*Mil*) to locate; (*) *personne, erreur* to spot, pick out; *coin tranquille* to discover, locate, find. **se faire** ~ to be spotted, be picked out. **2 se** ~ *vpr* (*se diriger*) to find one's way about *ou* around; (*lit, fig: savoir où l'on est*) to find *ou* get one's bearings. ♦ **repérable** *adj* which can be spotted. ♦ **repérage** *nm* (*Aviat, Mil*) location. **le** ~ **d'un point sur la carte** locating a point on the map. ♦ **repère** *nm* (*marque*) line, mark; (*jalon*) marker, indicator; (*monument etc*) landmark; (*fig*) landmark.

répertoire [RepɛRtwaR] *nm* **(a)** (*carnet*) index notebook; (*liste*) (alphabetical) list; (*catalogue*) catalogue. ~ **des rues** street index. **(b)** (*Théât*) repertoire, repertory; *[chanteur]*, (*fig*) repertoire. **pièce du** ~ stock play.

répertorier [RepɛRtɔRje] (7) *vt* to itemize, list.

répéter [Repete] (6) **1** *vt* **(a)** *parole, essai etc* to repeat. **je l'ai répété/je te l'ai répété dix fois** I've said that/I've told you that a dozen times; **il ne se l'est pas fait** ~ he didn't have to be told *ou* asked twice; **tentatives répétées** repeated attempts. **(b)** *pièce de théâtre* to rehearse; *rôle, leçon* to learn, go over; *morceau de piano* to practise. **2 se** ~ *vpr [personne]* to repeat o.s.; *[événement]* to be repeated, recur. **que cela ne se répète pas!** (just) don't let that happen again! ♦ **répétition** *nf* repetition; (*Théât*) rehearsal. ~ **générale** (final) dress rehearsal; **fusil à** ~ repeater rifle.

repeupler [Rəpœple] (1) **1** *vt région* to repopulate; *bassin, chasse* to restock (*de* with); *forêt* to replant (*de* with). **2 se** ~ *vpr* to be *ou* become repopulated. ♦ **repeuplement** *nm* repopulation; restocking; replanting.

repiquer [R(ə)pike] (1) *vt* **(a)** (*Bot*) to plant out. **plantes à** ~ bedding plants. **(b)** *disque* to record, tape. **(c)** *[moustique]* to bite again; *[épine]* to prick again. ♦ **repiquage** *nm* planting out; recording.

répit [Repi] *nm* (*rémission*) respite; (*repos*) respite, rest; (*pour payer*) respite, breathing space. **sans** ~ *travailler* continuously, without respite; *harceler* relentlessly.

replacer [R(ə)plase] (3) *vt objet* to replace, put back (in its place).

replanter [R(ə)plɑ̃te] (1) *vt plante* to replant, plant out; *forêt, arbre* to replant.

replâtrer [R(ə)plɑtRe] (1) *vt* **(a)** *mur* to replaster. **(b)** (*) *amitié, gouvernement* to patch up. ♦ **replâtrage** *nm* patching up.

replet, -ète [Rəplɛ, ɛt] *adj personne* podgy, fat; *visage* chubby.

repleuvoir [R(ə)plœvwaR] (23) *vb impers* to rain again, start raining again.

replier [R(ə)plije] (7) **1** *vt* **(a)** *journal* to fold up, fold back up; *manche* to roll up, fold up; *coin de feuille* to fold over; *ailes* to fold; *jambes* to tuck up. **(b)** *troupes* to withdraw. **2 se** ~ *vpr* (*Mil*) to fall back, withdraw (*sur* to). **se** ~ **(sur soi-même)** to withdraw into oneself. ♦ **repli** *nm [terrain, papier]* fold; *[conscience]* hidden *ou* innermost recess; (*Mil*) withdrawal, falling back. ~ **sur soi-même** withdrawal into oneself.

réplique [Replik] *nf* **(a)** (*réponse*) reply, retort. **et pas de** ~! and don't answer back!; **argument sans** ~ unanswerable *ou* irrefutable argument. **(b)** (*contre-attaque*) counter-attack. **(c)** (*Théât*) line; (*signal*) cue. **donner la** ~ **à qn** (*pour répéter*) to give sb his cue; (*dans une scène*) to play opposite sb; (*fig*) **je saurai lui donner la** ~ I can match him (in an argument). **(d)** (*Art, objet identique*) replica. (*fig*) **il est la** ~ **de son jumeau** he is the image of his twin brother. ♦ **répliquer** (1) **1** *vt* to reply. ~ **que** to reply *ou* retort that; **il n'y a rien à** ~ **à cela** there's no answer to that. **2** *vi* (*répondre*) to reply; (*protester*) to protest; (*être insolent*) to answer back; (*contre-attaquer*) to counter-attack, retaliate.

répondant, e [Repɔ̃dɑ̃, ɑ̃t] **1** *nm,f* guarantor, surety. (*Fin*) **servir de** ~ **à qn** to stand surety for sb, be sb's guarantor. **2** *nm*: **avoir du** ~ to have a lot of money.

répondeur [repɔ̃dœʀ] *nm* (telephone) answering machine, Ansafone ®.

répondre [repɔ̃dʀ(ə)] (41) **1** *vt bêtise, insulte* to reply with. ~ **que** to answer *ou* reply that; **il m'a répondu qu'il viendrait** he told me (in reply) *ou* he replied that he would come; ~ **présent à l'appel** (*lit*) to answer present at roll call; (*fig*) to come forward, volunteer; **bien répondu!** well said!; **qu'est-ce que vous voulez ~ à cela?** what can you reply *ou* say to that?

2 *vi* **(a)** to answer, reply. ~ **à qn/à une question** *etc* to reply to *ou* answer sb/a question *etc*; ~ **à une invitation** to reply to *ou* acknowledge an invitation; ~ **(à la porte/à la sonnette)** to answer the door/the bell; ~ **(au téléphone)** to answer the telephone; **il répond au nom de Dick** he answers to the name of Dick; ~ **par oui** to reply *ou* answer *ou* say yes; ~ **par un sourire** to smile in reply; ~ **par des injures** to reply with a string of insults. **(b)** (*être impertinent*) to answer back. **(c)** (*réagir*) *commandes, membres* to respond (*à* to).

3 ~ **à** *vt indir* **(a)** *besoin* to answer; *signalement* to answer, fit; *désirs* to meet. **ça répond à mon attente** it comes up to *ou* meets my expectations. **(b)** *attaque, avances, appel* to respond to; *amour, salut* to return; *politesse, invitation* to repay, pay back. **s'ils lancent une attaque, nous saurons y ~** if they launch an attack we'll fight back *ou* retaliate. **(c)** *dessin, façade* to match. **les 2 ailes du bâtiment se répondent** the 2 wings of the building match (each other).

4 ~ **de** *vt indir* (*garantir*) to answer *ou* vouch for. **il viendra, je vous en réponds!** he'll come all right, you can take it from me!* *ou* you can take my word for it!; **si vous agissez ainsi, je ne réponds plus de rien** if you behave like that, I'll accept no further responsibility; (*Jur*) ~ **de ses crimes** to answer for one's crimes.

réponse [repɔ̃s] *nf* (*gén*) answer, reply; (*Physiol, Tech, fig*) response (*à, de* to). **en ~ à votre question** in answer *ou* reply to your question; **ma lettre est restée sans ~** my letter remained unanswered; **sa demande est restée sans ~** there has been no reply *ou* response to his request; **coupon-~** reply coupon; **avoir ~ à tout** to have an answer for everything; **c'est la ~ du berger à la bergère** it's tit for tat; ~ **de Normand** evasive answer.

report [ʀ(ə)pɔʀ] *nm* (*V* **reporter**[1]) postponement, deferment; transfer; carrying over; (*sur livre de compte*) '~' (*en bas de page*) 'carried forward'; (*en haut de page*) 'brought forward'.

reportage [ʀ(ə)pɔʀtaʒ] *nm* report (*sur* on); (*métier*) (news) reporting. ~ **en direct** live commentary; **faire le ~ d'une cérémonie** to cover a ceremony, do the coverage of a ceremony.

reporter[1] [ʀ(ə)pɔʀte] (1) **1** *vt* **(a)** *objet* to take back; (*par la pensée*) to take back (*à* to). **(b)** *match* to postpone, put off; *date* to put back, defer (*à* until). **(c)** *indications, vote, affection* to transfer (*sur* to). ~ **une somme sur la page suivante** to carry an amount over to the next page. **2 se ~** *vpr*: **se ~ à** to refer to; (*par la pensée*) to think back to; **reportez-vous à la page 5** turn to *ou* refer to *ou* see page 5.

reporter[2] [ʀ(ə)pɔʀtɛʀ] *nm* reporter.

repos [ʀ(ə)po] *nm* **(a)** (*détente*) rest. **prendre du ~** to take *ou* have a rest; **rester en ~** to rest; **après une journée de ~** after a day's rest. **(b)** (*congé*) **jour de ~** day off; **le médecin lui a donné du ~** the doctor has given him some time off. **(c)** (*tranquillité*) peace and quiet; (*moral*) peace of mind; (*littér: sommeil, mort*) rest, sleep. **avoir la conscience en ~** to have an easy *ou* a clear conscience; **pour avoir l'esprit en ~** to put my (*ou* your *etc*) mind at rest; **laisse ton frère en ~** leave your brother in peace. **(d)** (*pause*) *[discours]* pause; *[vers]* rest; (*Mus*) cadence. **(e)** (*locutions*) (*Mil*) ~! (stand) at ease!; **au ~** *machine, animal* at rest; **sans ~** *poursuivre* relentlessly; *quête* relentless; **de tout ~** *situation, entreprise* secure, safe; *placement* gilt-edged, safe.

reposer [ʀ(ə)poze] (1) **1** *vt* **(a)** *verre etc* to put back down, put down again; *objet démonté* to refit, put back. (*Mil*) **reposez armes!** order arms! **(b)** *yeux, membres* to rest; *esprit* to rest, relax. ~ **sa tête sur un coussin** to rest one's head on a cushion; **elle avait le visage reposé** she looked rested. **(c)** *question* to repeat, ask again; *problème* to bring up again, raise again. **2 ~ sur** *vt indir [bâtiment]* to be built on; *[supposition]* to rest on. **3** *vi* **(a)** (*littér*) (*être étendu, enterré, endormi*) to rest. **l'épave repose par 20 mètres de fond** the wreck is lying 20 metres down. **(b) laisser ~** *liquide* to leave to settle; *pâte à crêpes* to leave to stand; **laisser ~ la terre** to let the land lie fallow; **faire ~ son cheval** to rest one's horse. **4 se ~** *vpr* **(a)** (*se délasser*) to rest. **(b) se ~ sur qn** to rely on sb. **(c)** (*à nouveau*) *[oiseau]* to settle again; *[problème]* to crop up again. ♦ **reposant, e** *adj sommeil* refreshing; *lieu, couleur* restful; *vacances* restful, relaxing. ♦ **repose-pieds** *nm inv* footrest. ♦ **repose-tête,** *pl* **~-~s** *nm* headrest.

repousser [ʀ(ə)puse] (1) **1** *vt* **(a)** *objet encombrant, personne* to push away; *ennemi* to repel, drive back; *coups* to ward off; *quémandeur* to turn away, repulse. **(b)** (*fig: refuser*) (*gén*) to reject; *demande, aide* to turn down; *hypothèse* to reject, dismiss, rule out. **(c)** (*remettre en place*) *meuble* to push back; *tiroir* to push back in; *porte* to push to. **(d)** (*différer*) *date* to put back; *réunion* to put off, postpone (*à plus tard* until later). **(e)** (*dégoûter*) to repel, repulse. **(f)** (*Tech*) *cuir, métal* to emboss (by hand). **en cuir repoussé** in repoussé leather. **2** *vi [feuilles, cheveux]* to grow again. ♦ **repoussant, e** *adj* repulsive.

répréhensible [ʀepʀeɑ̃sibl(ə)] *adj acte, personne* reprehensible. **ce n'est pas ~!** there's nothing wrong with that!

reprendre [ʀ(ə)pʀɑ̃dʀ(ə)] (58) **1** *vt* **(a)** (*récupérer*) *ville, prisonnier* to recapture; *employé, objet prêté* to take back; *espoir, forces* to regain, recover. ~ **des couleurs** to get some colour back in one's cheeks; ~ **sa place** (*à table*) to go back to one's seat, resume one's seat; (*dans un groupe*) to take one's place again; **j'irai ~ mon manteau chez le teinturier** I'll go and get *ou* fetch my coat (back) from the cleaner's. **(b)** (*Comm*) *marchandises* to take back; (*contre un nouvel achat*) to take in part exchange; *usine* to take over. **les articles en solde ne sont pas repris** sale goods cannot be returned *ou* exchanged. **(c)** *pain, viande* to have *ou* take (some) more; *légumes* to have a second helping of. **(d)** *travaux, récit etc* to resume; *livre* to pick up again, go back to; *hostilités* to reopen, start again; *lutte, habitudes, idée* to take up again; *pièce de théâtre* to put on again; *refrain* to take up; *argument, critique* to repeat. **reprenez votre histoire au début** start your story from the beginning again; **reprenons les faits un par un** let's go over the facts one by one again; ~ **le travail** to go back to work, start work again; ~ **la route** to go on *ou* set off on one's way again. **(e)** (*saisir à nouveau*) (*gén*) to catch again. **son mal de gorge l'a repris** he's suffering from a sore throat again; (*iro*) **voilà que ça le reprend!** there he goes again!, he's off again!*; **ses doutes le reprirent** he was seized with doubts once more. **(f)** (*fig*) **on ne m'y reprendra plus** I won't let myself by caught (out) *ou* had* again; (*menace*) **que je ne t'y reprenne pas!** don't let me catch you doing that again! **(g)** (*Sport: rattraper*) *balle* to catch. **(h)** (*retoucher*) *tableau* to touch up; *chapitre* to go over again; *manteau* (*gén*) to alter; (*trop grand*) to take in; (*trop petit*) to let out; (*trop long*) to take up; (*trop court*) to let down. **il y a beaucoup de choses à ~ dans ce travail** there are lots of improvements to be made to this work. **(i)** (*réprimander*) to reprimand, tell off*; (*pour faute de langue*) to pull up; (*corriger*) to correct.

2 *vi* **(a)** (*retrouver la vigueur*) *[plante]* to take again; *[affaires]* to pick up. **(b)** (*recommencer*) to start again. **(c)** (*dire*) **'ce n'est pas moi' reprit-il** 'it's not me' he went on.

3 se ~ *vpr* **(a)** (*se corriger*) to correct o.s.; (*s'interrompre*) to stop o.s. **(b)** (*recommencer*) **se ~ à plusieurs fois pour faire qch** to make several attempts to do sth *ou* at doing sth; **se ~ à espérer** to find o.s. hoping again. **(c)** (*réagir*) to take a grip on o.s., pull o.s. together (again), take o.s. in hand. **le coureur s'est bien repris sur la fin** the runner made a good recovery towards the end.

représailles [ʀ(ə)pʀezɑj] *nfpl* (*Pol, fig*) reprisals, retaliation. **user de ~** to take reprisals (*envers* against); **en ~** as a reprisal, in retaliation (*de* for).

représenter [ʀ(ə)pʀezɑ̃te] (1) **1** *vt* **(a)** *[peintre, romancier]* to depict, portray, show; *[photographie]* to represent, show. **~ fidèlement les faits** to describe the facts faithfully. **(b)** (*symboliser, signifier*) to represent. **ça va ~ beaucoup de travail** that will mean *ou* represent *ou* involve a lot of work. **(c)** (*Théât*) (*jouer*) to perform, play; (*mettre à l'affiche*) to perform, put on; *adaptation* to stage. **(d)** (*agir au nom de*) to represent. **il s'est fait ~ par son notaire** he was represented by his solicitor, he sent his solicitor to represent him. **(e)** (*littér: insister sur*) **~ qch à qn** to point sth out to sb. **2** *vi* (*en imposer*) **il représente bien** he cuts a fine figure. **3 se ~** *vpr* **(a)** (*s'imaginer*) to imagine. **(b)** (*survenir à nouveau*) *[idée, situation]* to occur again; *[occasion]* to present itself again, arise again; *[problème]* to crop up again. **(c) se ~ à un examen** to resit an exam; **se ~ à une élection** to stand for election again.

♦ **représentant, e** *nm,f* (*gén*) representative. **~ de commerce** sales representative *ou* rep*, travelling salesman. ♦ **représentatif, -ive** *adj* (*gén*) representative (*de* of). ♦ **représentation** *nf* **(a)** (*notation*) (*gén, fig*) representation; *[paysage, société]* portrayal; *[faits]* description. **(b)** (*Théât*) performance. **(c)** *[pays, mandant]* representation; (*groupe de délégués*) representatives. **(d)** (*Comm*) (*métier*) commercial travelling. **faire de la ~** to be a (sales) representative *ou* a commercial traveller. **(e)** (*réception*) **avoir des frais de ~** to get an entertainment allowance. ♦ **représentativité** *nf* representativeness.

répression [ʀepʀesjɔ̃] *nf* repression. ♦ **répressible** *adj* repressible. ♦ **répressif, -ive** *adj* repressive.

réprimande [ʀepʀimɑ̃d] *nf* reprimand, rebuke. ♦ **réprimander** (1) *vt* to reprimand, rebuke.

réprimer [ʀepʀime] (1) *vt* (*gén*) to suppress; *insurrection* to quell, put down; *larmes, colère* to hold back, swallow.

repris de justice [ʀ(ə)pʀidʒystis] *nm inv* ex-prisoner, ex-convict.

reprise [ʀ(ə)pʀiz] *nf* **(a)** *[activité]* resumption; *[hostilités]* re-opening, renewal; *[froid]* return; (*Théât*) revival; (*Ciné*) rerun; (*Rad, TV: rediffusion*) repeat. **les ouvriers ont décidé la ~ du travail** the men have decided to go back *ou* return to work; **~ (économique)** (economic) revival *ou* recovery. **(b)** (*Aut*) **avoir de bonnes ~s** to have good acceleration. **(c)** (*Boxe*) round. (*Ftbl*) **à la ~** at the start of the second half. **(d)** (*Comm*) *[marchandise]* taking back; (*pour nouvel achat*) part exchange. **valeur de ~ d'une voiture** part-exchange value *ou* trade-in value of a car; **~ des bouteilles vides** return of empties. **(e)** *[chaussette]* darn; *[drap, chemise]* mend. **(f) à 2 ou 3/à plusieurs ~s** on 2 or 3/on several occasions, 2 or 3/several times.

repriser [ʀ(ə)pʀize] (1) *vt chaussette, lainage* to darn; *drap, accroc* to mend.

réprobation [ʀepʀɔbɑsjɔ̃] *nf* reprobation. ♦ **réprobateur, -trice** *adj* reproving.

reproche [ʀ(ə)pʀɔʃ] *nm* reproach. **faire des ~s à qn** to reproach *ou* blame sb; **conduite qui mérite des ~s** reprehensible behaviour; **avec ~** reproachfully; **ton de ~** reproachful tone; **homme sans ~** man beyond *ou* above reproach.

reprocher [ʀ(ə)pʀɔʃe] (1) *vt* **(a) ~ qch à qn** to reproach sb for sth; **~ à qn de faire qch** to reproach sb for *ou* with doing sth; **je ne te reproche rien** I'm not blaming you for anything; **je n'ai rien à me ~** I've nothing to reproach myself with. **(b)** (*critiquer*) **qu'as-tu à ~ à mon plan/à ce tableau?** what have you got against my plan/this picture?; **je reproche à ce tissu d'être salissant** the fault I find with that material is that it gets dirty; **il n'y a rien à ~ à cela** there's nothing wrong with that.

reproduire [ʀ(ə)pʀɔdɥiʀ] (38) **1** *vt* (*gén*) to reproduce; *modèle* to copy; *erreur* to repeat. **2 se ~** *vpr* (*Bio, Bot*) to reproduce, breed; *[phénomène]* to recur. **et que ça ne se reproduise plus!** and don't let that happen again! ♦ **reproducteur, -trice** *adj* reproductive. ♦ **reproduction** *nf* (*action*) reproduction; copy; repeat; (*photo*) reproduction. **organes de ~** reproductive organs; (*sur un livre*) **'~ interdite'** 'all rights (of reproduction) reserved'.

réprouver [ʀepʀuve] (1) *vt personne* to reprove; *action* to condemn; *projet* to disapprove of; (*Rel*) to damn, reprobate. ♦ **réprouvé, e** *nm,f* reprobate.

reptile [ʀɛptil] *nm* (*Zool*) reptile; (*serpent*) snake; (*péj: personne*) creep* (*péj*).

repu, e [ʀəpy] *adj animal* sated, satisfied. **je suis ~** I'm full, I've eaten my fill.

république [ʀepyblik] *nf* republic. ♦ **républicain, e** *adj, nm,f* republican; (*US Pol*) Republican.

répudier [ʀepydje] (7) *vt conjoint* to repudiate; *foi, engagement* to renounce. ♦ **répudiation** *nf* repudiation; renouncement.

répugnance [ʀepyɲɑ̃s] *nf* **(a)** (*répulsion*) repugnance, disgust (*pour* for), loathing (*pour* of). **avoir de la ~ pour les épinards** to loathe spinach. **(b)** (*hésitation*) reluctance (*à faire qch* to do sth). **éprouver de la ~ à faire** to be loath *ou* reluctant to do; **avec ~** reluctantly, unwillingly. ♦ **répugnant, e** *adj individu* repugnant; *laideur* revolting; *travail, odeur, nourriture* disgusting, revolting, loathsome. ♦ **répugner** (1) **~ à** *vt indir* **(a)** (*dégoûter*) to repel, disgust, be repugnant to. **ça me répugne** I am repelled by *ou* disgusted with it, I find it disgusting. **(b)** (*hésiter*) **~ à faire qch** to be loath *ou* reluctant to do sth.

répulsion [ʀepylsjɔ̃] *nf* (*gén, Phys*) repulsion (*pour* for). ♦ **répulsif, -ive** *adj* repulsive.

réputation [ʀepytɑsjɔ̃] *nf* (*honneur*) reputation, good name; (*renommée*) reputation. **avoir bonne/mauvaise ~** to have a good/bad reputation; **connaître qn de ~** to know sb by repute; **il a la ~ d'être avare** he has a reputation for being miserly, he is reputed to be miserly. ♦ **réputé, e** *adj* **(a)** (*célèbre*) reputable, renowned. **hautement ~** of great repute *ou* renown; **~ pour** renowned *ou* famous for. **(b)** (*prétendu*) **remède ~ infaillible** cure which is reputed *ou* supposed *ou* said to be infallible.

requérir [ʀəkeʀiʀ] (21) *vt* (*exiger*) to call for, require; (*solliciter*) to request; *police* to call on; (*Jur*) *peine* to call for, demand.

requête [ʀəkɛt] *nf* (*Jur*) petition; (*supplique*) request, petition. **adresser une ~ à un juge** to petition a judge; **à** *ou* **sur la ~ de qn** at sb's request.

requiem [ʀekɥijɛm] *nm inv* requiem.

requin [ʀ(ə)kɛ̃] *nm* (*Zool, fig*) shark.

requinquer* [R(ə)kɛ̃ke] (1) **1** *vt* to pep up*, buck up*. **2 se** ~ *vpr* to perk up*.

requis, e [Rəki, iz] *adj conditions* requisite, required. (*réquisitionné*) **les** ~ labour conscripts (*civilians*).

réquisitionner [Rekizisjɔne] (1) *vt biens* to requisition, commandeer; *hommes* to requisition, conscript. ♦ **réquisition** *nf* requisition; conscription.

réquisitoire [RekizitwaR] *nm* (*plaidoirie*) closing speech for the prosecution; (*fig*) indictment (*contre* of).

rescapé, e [Rɛskape] **1** *adj personne* surviving. **2** *nm,f* survivor (*de* of).

rescousse [Rɛskus] *nf*: **venir à la** ~ to come to the rescue; **appeler qn à la** ~ to call on *ou* to sb for help.

réseau, *pl* ~**x** [Rezo] *nm* (*gén, fig*) network. ~ **fluvial** river system, network of rivers; ~ **d'espionnage** spy network *ou* ring; ~ **d'intrigues** web of intrigue; ~ **d'habitudes** pattern of habits.

réservation [RezɛRvɑsjɔ̃] *nf* (*à l'hôtel*) reservation; (*des places*) reservation, booking.

réserve [RezɛRv(ə)] *nf* **(a)** (*provision*) reserve. **faire des** ~**s de sucre** to get in *ou* lay in a stock of *ou* reserves of sugar; **mettre qch en** ~ to put sth by, put sth in reserve; **avoir/tenir qch en** ~ (*gén*) to have/keep sth in reserve; (*Comm*) to have/keep sth in stock. **(b)** (*restriction*) reservation, reserve. **émettre des** ~**s sur qch** to have reservations *ou* reserves about sth; **sous toutes** ~**s** *publier* with all reserve; *dire* with reservations; **sous** ~ **de** subject to; **sans** ~ *admiration* unreserved; *approuver* unreservedly. **(c)** (*prudence, discrétion*) reserve. **(d)** (*Mil*) **la** ~ the reserve; **armée de** ~ reserve army. **(e)** (*territoire*) *[nature, animaux]* reserve; *[Indiens]* reservation. ~ **de pêche/chasse** fishing/hunting preserve. **(f)** *[bibliothèque]* reserve collection. **(g)** (*entrepôt*) storehouse, storeroom.

réserver [RezɛRve] (1) **1** *vt* **(a)** (*mettre à part*) (*gén*) to keep, save, reserve; *marchandises* to put aside *ou* on one side (*à, pour* for). ~ **le meilleur pour la fin** to keep *ou* save the best till last. **(b)** (*louer*) *place, table* to book, reserve. **(c)** (*fig: destiner*) *accueil, châtiment* to have in store, reserve (*à* for). **nous ne savons pas ce que l'avenir nous réserve** we don't know what the future has in store for us *ou* holds for us; **il lui était réservé de mourir jeune** he was destined to die young. **(d)** (*retarder*) *réponse, opinion* to reserve. **2 se** ~ *vpr*: **se** ~ **le meilleur morceau** to keep *ou* save *ou* reserve the best bit for o.s.; **se** ~ **pour plus tard** to save *ou* reserve o.s. for later; **se** ~ **pour une autre occasion** to wait for another opportunity; **se** ~ **le droit/la possibilité de faire qch** to reserve the right to do sth/the possibility of doing sth. ♦ **réservé, e** *adj place* reserved (*à* for); *personne, caractère* reserved. **pêche** ~**e** private fishing; **les médecins sont très** ~**s à son sujet** the doctors are very guarded *ou* cautious in their opinions about him; **tous droits** ~**s** all rights reserved.

réserviste [RezɛRvist(ə)] *nm* reservist.

réservoir [RezɛRvwaR] *nm* (*cuve*) tank; (*plan d'eau*) reservoir; *[poissons]* fishpond; *[usine à gaz]* gasometer, gasholder.

résider [Rezide] (1) *vi [personne]* to live, reside; *[problème]* to lie, reside (*dans* in). ♦ **résidant, e** *adj* resident. ♦ **résidence** *nf* (*gén*) residence. **changer de** ~ to move (house); **en** ~ **surveillée** under house arrest; (*Diplomatie*) **la** ~ the residency; ~ **principale** main home; ~ **secondaire** second home, weekend cottage; ~ **universitaire** (university) hall of residence. ♦ **résident, e** *nm,f* (*étranger*) foreign national *ou* resident; (*diplomate*) resident. ♦ **résidentiel, -ielle** *adj* residential.

résidu [Rezidy] *nm* **(a)** (*reste*) (*Chim, fig*) residue; (*Math*) remainder. **(b)** (*déchets*) ~**s** remnants, residue; ~**s industriels** industrial waste. ♦ **résiduel, -elle** *adj* residual.

résigner (se) [Reziɲe] (1) *vpr* to resign o.s. (*à* to). **il faudra s'y** ~ we'll have to resign ourselves to it *ou* put up with it. ♦ **résignation** *nf* resignation (*à* to). **avec** ~ with resignation, resignedly. ♦ **résigné, e** *adj* resigned (*à* to).

résilier [Rezilje] (7) *vt contrat* to terminate. ♦ **résiliation** *nf* termination.

résine [Rezin] *nf* resin. ♦ **résineux, -euse 1** *adj* resinous. **2** *nm* coniferous tree.

résistance [Rezistɑ̃s] *nf* **(a)** (*gén*) resistance (*à* to). **en appuyant, je sentis une** ~ when I pressed I felt some resistance; **opposer une** ~ **farouche à un projet** to put up fierce resistance to a project, make a very determined stand against a project; **il a une grande** ~ he has great resistance *ou* stamina; **coureur qui a de la** ~ runner who has lots of staying power; **ça offre une grande** ~ **au feu/aux chocs** it is very heat-/shock-resistant. **(b)** (*Élec*) (*mesure*) resistance; *[réchaud, radiateur]* element. ♦ **resistant, e 1** *adj personne* robust, tough; *plante* hardy; *tissu* strong, hard-wearing; *couleur* fast; *métal* resistant, strong. ~ **à la chaleur** heatproof, heat-resistant. **2** *nm,f* (*Hist*) (French) Resistance worker *ou* fighter. ♦ **résister** (1) ~ **à** *vt indir* (*gén*) to resist; *fatigue, sécheresse* to stand up to, withstand; *douleur* to stand; *attaque* to hold out against. ~ **au courant d'une rivière** to hold one's own against the current of a river; ~ **à l'épreuve du temps** to stand the test of time; **le plancher ne pourra pas** ~ **au poids** the floor won't support *ou* take the weight; **ça n'a pas résisté longtemps** it didn't resist *ou* hold out for long; **couleur qui résiste au lavage** colour which is fast in the wash; **cette vaisselle résiste au feu** this crockery is heat-resistant *ou* heatproof; **ça ne résiste pas à l'analyse** it does not stand up to analysis.

résolu, e [Rezɔly] *adj personne, air* resolute. ~ **à faire** resolved *ou* determined to do, set on doing. ♦ **résolument** *adv* resolutely. ♦ **résolution** *nf* (*gén, Pol: décision*) resolution; (*énergie*) resolve, resolution; (*solution*) solution. **prendre la** ~ **de faire** to make a resolution to do, resolve to do, make up one's mind to do.

résonner [Rezɔne] (1) *vi [son]* to resonate, reverberate, resound; *[salle]* to be resonant; *[objet]* to resound. **ça résonne** the noise resonates *ou* reverberates *ou* echoes; ~ **de** to resound *ou* ring *ou* resonate with. ♦ **résonance** *nf* (*gén, Élec, Phys*) resonance; (*fig*) echo; **être en** ~ to be resonating. ♦ **résonateur** *nm* resonator. ♦ **résonnant, e** *adj* resonant.

résorber [RezɔRbe] (1) **1** *vt* (*Méd*) to resorb; *chômage* to bring down, reduce gradually; *surplus* to absorb; *inflation* to curb. **2 se** ~ *vpr* to be resorbed; to be brought down *ou* reduced; to be absorbed. ♦ **résorption** *nf* resorption; gradual reduction (*de* in); absorption.

résoudre [RezudR(ə)] (51) **1** *vt* **(a)** *problème etc* to solve; *difficultés* to resolve, settle, sort out. **(b)** (*décider*) *exécution* to decide on, determine on. ~ **de faire qch** to decide *ou* resolve to do sth, make up one's mind to do sth; ~ **qn à faire qch** to induce sb to do sth. **2 se** ~ *vpr* **(a) se** ~ **à faire qch** (*se décider*) to resolve *ou* decide to do sth, make up one's mind to do sth; (*se résigner*) to bring o.s. to do sth. **(b) se** ~ **en pluie** to resolve into rain.

respect [Rɛspɛ] *nm* **(a)** respect (*de, pour* for). **il n'a aucun** ~ **pour le bien d'autrui** he has no respect *ou* consideration *ou* regard for other people's property; **sauf votre** ~ with all due respect; ~ **de soi** self-respect. **(b)** (*formule de politesse*) **présentez mes** ~**s à votre femme** give my regards *ou* pay my respects† to your wife; **mes** ~**s, mon colonel** good day to you, sir. **(c)**

tenir qn en ~ (*avec une arme*) to keep sb at a respectful distance *ou* at bay. ♦ **respectabilité** *nf* respectability. ♦ **respectable** *adj* (*honorable*) respectable; (*important*) respectable, sizeable. ♦ **respecter** (1) **1** *vt* to respect, have respect for. **se faire ~** to be respected (*par* by), command respect (*par* from); **la jeunesse ne respecte rien** young people show no respect for anything *ou* do not respect anything; **~ l'ordre alphabétique** to keep things in alphabetical order; **faire ~ la loi** to enforce the law; **~ les termes d'un contrat** to abide by the terms of a contract. **2 se ~** *vpr* to respect o.s. (*hum*) **le professeur qui se respecte** any self-respecting teacher.

respectif, -ive [ʀɛspɛktif, iv] *adj* respective. ♦ **respectivement** *adv* respectively.

respectueux, -euse [ʀɛspɛktɥø, øz] *adj* respectful (*envers* to, *de* of). **se montrer ~ du bien d'autrui** to show respect *ou* consideration for other people's property; **~ de la loi** respectful of the law, law-abiding; **veuillez agréer mes salutations ~euses** yours respectfully. ♦ **respectueusement** *adv* respectfully.

respirer [ʀɛspiʀe] (1) **1** *vi* **(a)** (*lit, Bio*) to breathe. **~ par le nez** to breathe through one's nose; **~ profondément** to breathe deeply, take a deep breath. **(b)** (*fig*) (*se détendre*) to get one's breath, have a break; (*se rassurer*) to breathe again. **2** *vt* **(a)** (*inhaler*) to breathe (in), inhale. **faire ~ qch à qn** to make sb inhale sth. **(b)** *calme, bonheur* to radiate; *honnêteté* to exude, emanate; *joie* to glow with. ♦ **respirable** *adj* (*lit, fig*) breathable. ♦ **respiration** *nf* (*fonction*) breathing, respiration; (*souffle*) breath. **avoir la ~ difficile** to have difficulty (in) breathing; **retenir sa ~** to hold one's breath; **faites 3 ~s complètes** breathe in and out 3 times. ♦ **respiratoire** *adj* breathing, respiratory.

resplendir [ʀɛsplɑ̃diʀ] (2) *vi* (*gén, fig*) to shine; *[astre]* to beam; *[surface métallique]* to gleam; *[lac, neige]* to glisten, glitter. **~** *ou* **être resplendissant de bonheur** to be aglow *ou* radiant with happiness; **soleil resplendissant** radiant *ou* beaming sun.

responsable [ʀɛspɔ̃sabl(ə)] **1** *adj* **(a)** (*de dégâts*) liable, responsible (*de* for); (*de délits*) responsible (*de* for); (*moralement*) responsible, accountable (*de* for, *devant qn* to sb). **civilement ~** liable in civil law. **(b)** (*chargé de*) **~ de** responsible for, in charge of. **(c)** (*coupable*) responsible. **les freins défectueux sont ~s (de l'accident)** the faulty brakes are to blame *ou* are responsible for the accident. **(d)** (*sérieux*) *attitude, étudiant* responsible. **2** *nmf* **(a)** (*coupable*) **le ~** the person responsible *ou* who is to blame, the culprit; **le seul ~ est l'alcool** alcohol alone is to blame. **(b)** (*chef*) *[service]* person in charge; *[parti, syndicat]* official. **des ~s de l'industrie** representatives *ou* leaders of industry. ♦ **responsabilité** *nf* (*gén*) responsibility (*de* for). **de lourdes ~s** heavy responsibilities; **avoir la ~ de qch** to be responsible for sth; **~ civile** civil liability.

resquiller [ʀɛskije] (1) *vi* (*dans l'autobus*) to fiddle* a free seat; (*au cinéma*) to get in on the sly; (*ne pas faire la queue*) to jump the queue. ♦ **resquilleur, -euse** *nm,f* (*gén*) fiddler*; (*dans une queue*) queue-jumper; (*dans l'autobus*) fare-dodger.

ressac [ʀəsak] *nm*: **le ~** (*mouvement*) the backwash, the undertow; (*vague*) the surf.

ressaisir [ʀ(ə)seziʀ] (2) **1** *vt* **(a)** *objet* to catch hold of again; *fuyard* to recapture; *prétexte* to seize on again. **(b)** *[peur]* to grip (once) again; *[désir]* to take hold of again. **2 se ~** *vpr* **(a)** to regain one's self-control; *[athlète]* to rally. **ressaisissez-vous!** pull yourself together! **(b) se ~ de** *pouvoir* to seize again.

ressasser [ʀ(ə)sase] (1) *vt pensées* to keep turning over; *conseil* to keep trotting out.

ressembler [ʀ(ə)sɑ̃ble] (1) **1 ~ à** *vt indir* to resemble, be *ou* look like. **à quoi ressemble-t-il?*** what does he look like?, what's he like?; **ça ne ressemble à rien!*** (*attitude*) it makes no sense at all; (*peinture*) it's like nothing on earth!*; **à quoi ça ressemble de crier comme ça!*** what do you mean by shouting like that!; **cela lui ressemble bien, de dire ça** it's just like him *ou* it's typical of him to say that. **2 se ~** *vpr* to look *ou* be alike, resemble each other. **ils se ressemblent comme deux gouttes d'eau** they're as like as two peas (in a pod). ♦ **ressemblance** *nf* (*visuelle*) resemblance, likeness; (*de composition*) similarity. **avoir une ~ avec qch** to bear a resemblance *ou* likeness to sth. ♦ **ressemblant, e** *adj photo* lifelike, true to life.

ressemeler [ʀ(ə)səmle] (4) *vt* to resole. ♦ **ressemelage** *nm* resoling.

ressentiment [ʀ(ə)sɑ̃timɑ̃] *nm* resentment (*contre* against, *de* at). **éprouver du ~** to feel resentful (*envers* towards).

ressentir [ʀ(ə)sɑ̃tiʀ] (16) **1** *vt* (*gén*) to feel; *sensation* to experience. **2 se ~** *vpr*: **se ~ de** *[travail, qualité]* to show the effects of; *[personne]* to feel the effects of.

resserre [ʀ(ə)sɛʀ] *nf* (*cabane*) shed; (*réduit*) storeroom.

resserrer [ʀ(ə)seʀe] (1) **1** *vt* (*gén*) to tighten; *amitié* to strengthen; *crédits* to squeeze. **2 se ~** *vpr [étreinte]* to tighten; *[liens affectifs]* to grow stronger; *[groupe]* to draw in; *[pores, mâchoire]* to close; *[vallée]* to narrow. **le filet se resserrait autour de lui** the net was closing in on him. ♦ **resserré, e** *adj vallée* narrow. **maison ~e entre des immeubles** house squeezed between high buildings. ♦ **resserrement** *nm* **(a)** (*action*) strengthening; narrowing. **le ~ du crédit** the tightening of *ou* squeeze on credit. **(b)** (*partie étroite*) narrow part.

resservir [ʀ(ə)sɛʀviʀ] (14) **1** *vt plat* to serve (up) again (*à* to); *dîneur* to give a second helping to (*de, en* of); (*fig*) *histoire* to trot out again* (*péj*). **2** *vi [vêtement, outil]* to serve again, do again, be useful again. **3 se ~** *vpr [dîneur]* to help o.s. again (*de* to), take another helping (*de* of). **se ~ de** *outil* to use again.

ressort [ʀ(ə)sɔʀ] *nm* **(a)** (*de métal*) spring. **~ à boudin** spiral spring; **faire ~** to spring back; **à ~** spring-loaded. **(b)** (*énergie*) spirit. **avoir du ~** to have spirit. **(c)** (*littér: motivation*) **les ~s qui le font agir** the motivating forces behind his actions. **(d)** (*Jur: circonscription*) jurisdiction. (*compétence*) **être du ~ de** to fall within the competence of; (*fig*) **ce n'est pas de mon ~** this is not my responsibility.

ressortir [ʀ(ə)sɔʀtiʀ] (2) **1** *vi* **(a)** (*à nouveau*) *[personne]* to go out again, leave again; *[objet]* to come out again. **souvenirs qui ressortent** memories which resurface. **(b)** (*contraster*) *[détail, qualité]* to stand out. **faire ~ qch** to make sth stand out, bring out sth. **2 ~ de** *vt indir* (*résulter*) to emerge from, be the result of. **3 ~ à** *vt indir* (*Jur*) to come under the jurisdiction of. **4** *vt vêtements, outil etc* to take *ou* bring out again; (*Comm*) *modèle* to bring out again.

ressortissant, e [ʀ(ə)sɔʀtisɑ̃, ɑ̃t] *nm,f* national.

ressouder [ʀ(ə)sude] (1) **1** *vt objet* to solder together again; *amitié* to patch up. **2 se ~** *vpr [os]* to knit, mend.

ressource [ʀ(ə)suʀs(ə)] *nf* **(a) ~s** (*gén*) resources; *[art, technique]* possibilities; (*finances personnelles*) means; **famille sans ~s** family with no means of support *ou* no resources; **~s en hommes** manpower resources; **être à bout de ~s** to have exhausted all the possibilities, be at the end of one's resources; **homme de ~(s)** man of resource, resourceful man. **(b)** (*recours*) **n'ayant pas la ~ de lui parler** having no means *ou* possibility of speaking to him; **sa seule ~ était de** the only way *ou* course open to him was to; **vous êtes ma dernière ~** you are my last resort. **(c) avoir de la ~** *[sportif, cheval]* to have strength in reserve.

ressouvenir (se) [R(ə)suvniR] (22) *vpr*: **se ~ de** to remember, recall; **faire se ~ qn de qch** to remind sb of sth.

ressusciter [Resysite] (1) **1** *vi* (*Rel*) to rise (from the dead); (*fig*) to come back to life, revive. **2** *vt* (*Rel*) to raise (from the dead); (*fig*) to bring back to life, revive; *mourant* to resuscitate; (*péj*) *passé, coutume* to resurrect (*péj*).

restant, e [Restɑ̃, ɑ̃t] **1** *adj* remaining. **2** *nm* **(a)** (*l'autre partie*) **le ~** the rest, the remainder. **(b)** (*ce qui est en trop*) **faire une écharpe dans un ~ de tissu** to make a scarf out of some left-over material.

restaurant [RestɔRɑ̃] *nm* restaurant. **on va au ~?** shall we have a meal out?; **~ d'entreprise** staff canteen *ou* dining room; **~ libre-service** self-service restaurant; **~ universitaire** university refectory *ou* canteen.

restaurer [RestɔRe] (1) **1** *vt* to restore. **2 se ~** *vpr* to have sth to eat. ♦ **restaurateur, -trice** *nm,f* **(a)** (*Art, Pol*) restorer. **(b)** (*aubergiste*) restaurant owner. ♦ **restauration** *nf* **(a)** (*Art, Pol*) restoration. **(b)** (*hôtellerie*) catering.

reste [Rest(ə)] *nm* **(a)** (*l'autre partie*) **le ~** the rest; **le ~ du lait** the rest *ou* remainder *ou* remains of the milk, what is left of the milk. **(b)** (*ce qui est en trop*) **il y a un ~ de fromage** there's some cheese left over; **s'il y a un ~ de laine** if there's some spare wool *ou* some wool to spare; **un ~ de tendresse le poussa à rester** a last trace *ou* a remnant of tenderness moved him to stay. **(c) les ~s** (*nourriture*) the left-overs; (*dépouille mortelle*) the (mortal) remains; **les ~s de** the remains of, what is left of. **(d)** (*Math: différence*) remainder. **(e) avoir de l'argent/du temps de ~** to have money/time left over *ou* in hand *ou* to spare; **il ne voulait pas être en ~ avec eux** he didn't want to be outdone by them *ou* indebted to them; **au ~, du ~** besides, moreover; **partir sans demander son ~** to leave without further ado; **pour le ~** (as) for the rest; **et (tout) le ~** and everything else, and all the rest.

rester [Reste] (1) **1** *vi* **(a)** (*dans un lieu*) to stay, remain; (*: *habiter*) to live. **~ à la maison** to stay *ou* remain indoors; **~ (à) dîner** to stay for *ou* to dinner; **je ne peux ~ que 10 minutes** I can only stay *ou* stop* 10 minutes; **un os lui est resté dans la gorge** a bone was caught *ou* got stuck in his throat; **~ à regarder la télévision** to stay watching television; **naturellement ça reste entre nous** of course we shall keep this to ourselves *ou* this is just between ourselves. **(b)** (*dans un état*) to stay, remain. **~ sans rien dire** to stay *ou* keep *ou* remain silent; **~ dans l'ignorance** to remain in ignorance; **~ debout** to stand, remain standing; (*ne pas se coucher*) to stay up; **je suis resté assis toute la journée** I spent the whole day sitting; **ne reste pas là les bras croisés** don't just stand there with your arms folded; **~ en carafe**‡ to be left stranded. **(c)** (*subsister*) to be left, remain. **rien ne reste de l'ancien château** nothing is left *ou* remains of the old castle; **le seul parent qui leur reste** their only remaining relative; **l'argent qui leur reste** the money they have left; **10 km restaient à faire** there were still 10 km to go. **(d)** (*durer*) *[sentiments, œuvre]* to last, live on. **le surnom lui est resté** the nickname stayed with him, the nickname stuck*. **(e) ~ sur une impression** to retain an impression; (*lit, fig*) **~ sur sa faim** to be left unsatisfied; **ça m'est resté sur le cœur** I still feel sore about it*, it still rankles with me. **(f) ils en sont restés à des discussions préliminaires** they have got no further than *ou* they are still at the stage of preliminary discussions; **où en étions-nous restés?** where did we leave off?; **restons-en là** let's leave off there, let's leave it at that. **(g)** (*: *mourir*) **y ~** to meet one's end.

2 *vb impers*: **il reste encore un peu de pain** there's still a little bread left; **il me reste à faire ceci** I still have this to do; **il reste beaucoup à faire** much remains *ou* there's a lot left to do *ou* to be done; **il ne me reste que toi** you're all I have left; **il ne me reste qu'à vous remercier** it only remains for me to thank you; **il restait à faire 50 km** there were 50 km still *ou* left to go; **reste à savoir si** it remains to be seen whether; **il n'en reste pas moins que** the fact remains (nonetheless) that.

restituer [Restitɥe] (1) *vt objet volé* to return, restore (*à qn* to sb); *somme d'argent* to return, refund (*à qn* to sb); *texte reconstitué* to restore; (*Tech*) *énergie, chaleur* to release; *sons* to reproduce. ♦ **restitution** *nf* return; restoration; release; reproduction.

restreindre [RestRɛ̃dR(ə)] (52) **1** *vt* (*gén*) to restrict, limit; *dépenses* to cut down. **2 se ~** *vpr* **(a)** (*dans ses dépenses*) to cut down. **(b)** *[production]* to decrease, go down; *[espace]* to decrease, diminish; *[ambition, champ d'action]* to narrow; *[sens d'un mot]* to become more restricted. ♦ **restreint, e** *adj* limited, restricted (*à* to).

restriction [RestRiksjɔ̃] *nf* **(a)** (*limitation*) restriction, limiting, limitation. **~s** restrictions. **(b)** (*condition*) qualification. (*réticence*) **~ (mentale)** mental reservation. ♦ **restrictif, -ive** *adj* restrictive.

résultat [Rezylta] *nm* (*gén*) result. **cette tentative a eu des ~s désastreux** this attempt had disastrous results *ou* a disastrous outcome; **c'est un ~ remarquable** it's a remarkable result *ou* achievement; **~s sportifs** sports results. ♦ **résultante** *nf* (*Sci*) resultant; (*fig: conséquence*) outcome, result, consequence. ♦ **résulter** (1) **1** *vi*: **~ de** to result from; **rien de bon ne peut en ~** no good can come of it *ou* result from it. **2** *vb impers*: **il résulte de tout ceci que** the result of all this is that; **qu'en résultera-t-il?** what will be the result? *ou* outcome?

résumer [Rezyme] (1) **1** *vt* (*abréger*) to summarize; (*récapituler, aussi Jur*) to sum up; (*reproduire en petit*) to epitomize, typify. **2 se ~** *vpr* **(a)** *[personne]* to sum up (one's ideas). **(b)** (*se réduire à*) **se ~ à** to amount to, come down to, boil down to*. ♦ **résumé** *nm* summary, résumé. **en ~** (*en bref*) in short, in brief; (*pour conclure*) to sum up; (*en miniature*) in miniature.

résurrection [RezyRɛksjɔ̃] *nf* (*Rel*) resurrection; (*fig*) revival.

rétablir [RetabliR] (2) **1** *vt* (*gén*) to restore; *fait, vérité* to re-establish. **~ qn dans son emploi** to reinstate sb in *ou* restore sb to his post; (*guérir*) **~ qn** to restore sb to health, bring about sb's recovery. **2 se ~** *vpr [malade]* to recover; *[calme]* to return, be restored; (*faire un rétablissement*) to pull o.s. up (*onto a ledge etc*). ♦ **rétablissement** *nm* (*action*) restoring; re-establishment; (*guérison*) recovery. (*Sport*) **faire un ~** to do a pull-up (*onto a ledge etc*).

rétamer [Retame] (1) *vt* **(a)** *casseroles* to re-coat, re-tin. **(b)** (‡) (*fatiguer*) to wear out*; (*rendre ivre*) to knock out‡; (*démolir*) to wipe out; (*au jeu*) to clean out*. **se ~ (par terre)** to take a dive*, crash to the ground.

retape‡ [R(ə)tap] *nf*: **faire (de) la ~** to tout for business.

retaper [R(ə)tape] (1) **1** *vt* **(a)** (*) *maison, vêtement* to do up; *voiture* to fix up; *lit* to straighten; *malade* to set up (again), buck up*. **(b)** (*dactylographier*) to retype, type again. **2 se ~** *vpr* **(a)** (*: *guérir*) to get back on one's feet. **(b)** (‡: *à* *nouveau*) to do again. **se ~ un verre** to have o.s. another drink*.

retapisser [ʀ(ə)tapise] (1) *vt* to re-paper.

retard [ʀ(ə)taʀ] *nm* **(a)** *[personne attendue]* lateness. **être/mettre qn en ~** to be/make sb late; **vous avez 2 heures de ~** you're 2 hours late; **après plusieurs ~s** after being late several times. **(b)** *[train etc]* delay. **en ~ sur l'horaire** behind schedule; **combler son ~** to make up for the delay; (*Sport*) **être en ~ (de 2 km) sur le peloton** to be (2 km) behind the pack. **(c)** *[montre]* **cette montre a du ~** this watch is slow; **prendre un ~ de 3 minutes par jour** to lose 3 minutes a day. **(d)** (*sur des délais*) delay. **paiement en ~** (*effectué*) late payment; (*non effectué*) overdue payment; **il est toujours en ~ sur les autres pour payer** he is always behind the others *ou* later than the others in paying; **sans ~** without delay. **(e)** (*sur un programme*) delay. **en ~ sur le programme** behind schedule; **j'ai du courrier en ~** I'm behind *ou* behind-hand with my mail, I have a backlog of mail; **il doit combler son ~ en anglais** he has to make up for the ground he has lost in English. **(f)** (*infériorité*) *[peuple, pays]* backwardness. **il est en ~ pour son âge** he's backward for his age; **~ de croissance** slow development; **pays qui a un siècle de ~ économique** country whose economy is a century behind; **être en ~ sur son temps** to be behind the times. **(g)** (*Aut*) **~ à l'allumage** retarded ignition.

♦ **retardataire 1** *adj arrivant* late; *théorie* obsolete, outmoded. **2** *nmf* latecomer. ♦ **retardement** *nm*: **à ~** *dispositif* delayed action; (*Phot*) *mécanisme* self-timing; *comprendre* after the event; **bombe à ~** time bomb.

retarder [ʀ(ə)taʀde] (1) **1** *vt* **(a)** (*mettre en retard*) (*gén*) to delay; *opération, automobiliste* to hold up; *programme* to hinder, set back. **ne te retarde pas** don't make yourself late; **ça l'a retardé dans ses études** this has set him back in *ou* hindered him in his studies. **(b)** (*remettre*) *opération* to delay; *date* to put back. **~ son départ d'une heure** to put back one's departure by an hour, delay one's departure for an hour. **(c)** *montre* to put back. **~ l'horloge d'une heure** to put the clock back an hour. **2** *vi [montre]* to be slow; (*d'habitude*) to lose. **je retarde de 10 minutes** I'm 10 minutes slow; (*fig*) *[personne]* **~ (sur son époque)** to be behind the times, be out of touch. ♦ **retardé, e** *adj enfant* backward.

retéléphoner [ʀ(ə)telefɔne] (1) *vi* to phone again, call back.

retenir [ʀətniʀ] (22) **1** *vt* **(a)** (*empêcher de tomber, de passer etc*) to hold back; *cheval, chien* to check. **la timidité le retenait** shyness held him back; **~ qn de faire qch** to keep sb from *ou* stop sb doing sth. **(b)** (*garder*) *personne* to keep. **~ qn à dîner** to have sb stay for dinner, keep sb for dinner; **j'ai été retenu** I was kept back *ou* detained *ou* held up; **~ qn prisonnier** to hold sb prisoner. **(c)** *humidité, odeur, chaleur* to retain. **(d)** (*fixer*) *[clou, nœud etc]* to hold. (*fig*) **~ l'attention de qn** to hold sb's attention. **(e)** (*réserver*) *place, table* to book, reserve. **(f)** (*se souvenir de*) *leçon, nom* to remember; *impression* to retain. **j'en retiens qu'il est borné** the thing that stands out *ou* that sticks in my mind *ou* the thing I've learnt is that he's narrow-minded; **celui-là, je le retiens!*** I'll remember him all right!, I shan't forget him in a hurry!* **(g)** (*réprimer*) *larmes, cri* to hold *ou* choke back *ou* in; *colère* to hold back, restrain. **~ son souffle** to hold one's breath; **il ne put ~ un sourire** he could not hold back a smile, he could not help smiling. **(h)** (*garder*) *salaire* to stop, withhold; *bagages d'un client* to retain; (*prélever*) *somme d'argent* to deduct, keep back. (*Math*) **je pose 4 et je retiens 2** put down 4 and carry 2. **(i)** (*accepter*) *proposition, plan* to accept.

2 se ~ *vpr* (*s'accrocher*) to hold o.s. back; (*se contenir*) to restrain o.s.; (*besoins naturels*) to hold on. **se ~ de pleurer** to stop o.s. crying; **se ~ à qch** to hold *ou* cling on to sth.

rétention [ʀetɑ̃sjɔ̃] *nf* (*Jur, Méd*) retention.

retentir [ʀ(ə)tɑ̃tiʀ] (2) *vi [sonnerie]* to ring. **~ de** to ring *ou* resound with; (*affecter*) **~ sur** to have an effect upon, affect. ♦ **retentissant, e** *adj voix* ringing; *claque, bruit, succès* resounding; *scandale* tremendous; *discours* which causes a great stir. ♦ **retentissement** *nm [nouvelle, œuvre]* stir, effect. (*répercussions*) **~s** repercussions.

retenue [ʀətny] *nf* **(a)** (*prélèvement*) deduction, stoppage*. **(b)** (*modération*) self-control, (self-) restraint; (*réserve*) reserve. **avoir de la ~** to be reserved; **sans ~** without restraint, unrestrainedly. **(c)** (*Math*) **n'oublie pas la ~** don't forget what to carry (over). **(d)** (*Scol*) detention. **être en ~** to be in detention, be kept in.

réticence [ʀetisɑ̃s] *nf* reluctance. **~s** hesitations, reservations; **avec ~** reluctantly; **sans ~** without (any) hesitation *ou* reservation(s). ♦ **réticent, e** *adj* (*hésitant*) hesitant, reluctant; (*réservé*) reticent, reserved.

rétif, -ive [ʀetif, iv] *adj* restive.

rétine [ʀetin] *nf* retina.

retirer [ʀ(ə)tiʀe] (1) **1** *vt* **(a)** (*lit, fig: enlever*) *manteau etc* to take off, remove; *candidature* to withdraw; *plainte* to withdraw, take back. **il retira vite sa main** he quickly took away *ou* removed *ou* withdrew his hand; **~ qch à qn** (*gén*) to take sth away from sb; *emploi, amitié* to deprive sb of sth; **je retire ce que j'ai dit** I take back what I said; **retire-lui ses chaussures** take his shoes off (for him); **~ son permis de conduire à qn** to disqualify sb from driving; **~ à qn sa confiance** to withdraw one's confidence in sb; **~ à qn l'envie de recommencer** to stop sb wanting to start again. **(b)** (*faire sortir*) to take out, remove (*de* from). **~ un bouchon** to pull out *ou* take out *ou* remove a cork; **je ne peux pas ~ la clef de la serrure** I can't get the key out of the lock; **on ne peut pas lui ~ ça de la tête** we can't get it out of his head. **(c)** *bagages, billets réservés* to collect, pick up; *argent en dépôt* to withdraw, take out; *gage* to redeem. **(d)** (*obtenir*) **~ des avantages de qch** to get *ou* gain *ou* derive advantages from sth; **il n'en a retiré que des ennuis** it brought him nothing but worry. **(e)** (*extraire*) *minerai, huile* to obtain.

2 se ~ *vpr* (*partir*) to retire, withdraw; (*se coucher*) to retire (to bed); (*prendre sa retraite*) to retire; (*ôter sa candidature*) to withdraw, stand down (*en faveur de* in favour of); (*pour laisser passer qn etc*) to move out of the way; (*Mil*) *[troupes]* to withdraw; *[marée]* to recede, go back, ebb; *[eaux d'inondation]* to recede, go down. **se ~ de** *compétition etc* to withdraw from.

♦ **retiré, e** *adj lieu* remote, out-of-the-way; *vie* secluded. **il vivait ~ du reste du monde** he lived withdrawn *ou* cut off from the rest of the world; **~ des affaires** retired from business.

retombée [ʀ(ə)tɔ̃be] *nf* **(a)** *[invention etc]* spin-off. **~s** *[bombe, scandale]* fallout. **(b)** (*Archit*) spring, springing.

retomber [ʀ(ə)tɔ̃be] (1) *vi* **(a)** (*à nouveau*) *[personne, neige]* to fall again. **~ dans** *erreur, guerre* to lapse into; *oubli* to sink into; **~ en enfance** to lapse into second childhood; **~ amoureux/malade** to fall in love/fall ill again. **(b)** (*redescendre*) *[fusée, personne]* to land; *[chose lancée, liquide]* to come down; *[capot]* to fall back down; *[conversation, intérêt]* to fall away. (*lit, fig*) **~ sur ses pieds** to fall *ou* land on one's feet; (*fig*) **ça lui est retombé sur le nez** it has rebounded on him; **se laisser ~ sur son oreiller** to fall back *ou* sink back onto one's pillow. **(c)** (*pendre*) *[cheveux, rideaux]* to fall, hang (down) (*sur* onto). **(d)** *[responsabilité]* **~ sur qn** to fall *ou* land on sb; **les**

frais retombèrent sur nous we were landed* *ou* saddled* with the expense; **faire ~ sur qn la responsabilité de qch** to pass the responsibility for sth on to sb.

rétorquer [RetɔRke] (1) *vt* to retort.

rétorsion [RetɔRsjɔ̃] *nf* (*Jur, Pol*) retortion, retaliation.

retoucher [R(ə)tuʃe] (1) **1** *vt* **(a)** *photo, peinture* to touch up; *vêtement, texte* to alter, make alterations to. **(b)** (*toucher de nouveau*) to touch again; (*blesser de nouveau*) to hit again. **2** *vi*: ~ **à qch** to lay hands on sth again, touch sth again. ♦ **retouche** *nf [texte, vêtement]* alteration. **faire une ~ *ou* des ~s à une photo** to touch up a photograph.

retour [R(ə)tuR] **1** *nm* **(a)** (*gén, Comm, Tech*) return; (*billet*) return (ticket). **être sur le (chemin du) ~** to be on one's way back; **pendant le ~** on the way *ou* journey back, during the return journey; **à leur ~ (d'Afrique), ils trouvèrent la maison vide** when they got back *ou* on their return (from Africa) they found the house empty; **de ~ à la maison** back home; **le ~ à une vie normale** the return *ou* reversion to (a) normal life; **le ~ (périodique) de ce phénomène/thème** the recurrence of this phenomenon/theme; **on prévoit un ~ du froid** a return of the cold weather is forecast; **un ~ offensif de la grippe** a renewed outbreak of flu; **~ à l'envoyeur** return to sender. **(b) en ~** in return; **choc *ou* effet en ~** backlash; **c'est un juste ~ des choses** it's poetic justice; **par ~ (du courrier)** by return (of post); **sans ~** *partir* for ever; *voyage* final; **faire un ~ sur soi-même** to take stock of o.s., do some soul-searching. **2:** ~ **d'âge** change of life; ~ **en arrière** (*Littérat, Ciné*) flashback; (*souvenir*) look back; (*mesure rétrograde*) retreat; ~ **de flamme** blowback; ~ **en force** return in strength; ~ **de manivelle** (*lit*) kick; (*fig*) backlash.

retourner [R(ə)tuRne] (1) **1** *vt* **(a)** (*dans l'autre sens*) *caisse* to turn upside down; *matelas* to turn (over); *carte* to turn up; *viande, omelette* to turn over. ~ **un tableau contre le mur** to turn a picture against the wall; (*fig*) **elle l'a retourné comme une crêpe*** she soon changed his mind for him; ~ **la situation** to reverse the situation. **(b)** (*en remuant*) *foin, terre* to turn over; *salade* to toss. ~ **qch dans sa tête** to turn sth over in one's mind; ~ **le couteau dans la plaie** to twist the knife in the wound. **(c)** (*mettre l'intérieur à l'extérieur*) *sac, gant* to turn inside out; (*Couture*) *col* to turn. (*fig*) ~ **sa veste** to turn one's coat; **son col est retourné** (*par mégarde*) his collar is turned up. **(d)** (*dans le sens opposé*) *phrase* to turn round; *argument* to turn back (*contre* against); *compliment, critique* to return. **il retourna le pistolet contre lui-même** he turned the gun on himself. **(e)** (*renvoyer*) *marchandise, lettre* to return, send back. **(f)** (*fig**: *bouleverser*) *pièce, maison* to turn upside down; *personne* to shake. **ce spectacle m'a retourné*** the sight of this shook me *ou* gave me quite a turn*.

2 *vi* to return, go back (*à, chez* to). ~ **sur ses pas** to turn back, retrace one's steps.

3 *vb impers*: **nous voudrions bien savoir de quoi il retourne** we should really like to know what is going on.

4 se ~ *vpr* **(a)** *[personne couchée]* to turn over; *[véhicule]* to turn over, overturn. **se ~ dans son lit** to toss and turn in bed; **il doit se ~ dans sa tombe** he must be turning in his grave; (*fig*) **laissez-lui le temps de se ~** give him time to sort himself out *ou* find his feet; (*fig*) **il sait se ~** he knows how to cope. **(b)** (*tourner la tête*) to turn round; (*tourner les yeux*) to look back. **(c)** (*fig*) **se ~ contre qn** *[personne]* to turn against sb; *[situation]* to backfire on sb, rebound on sb; **il ne savait vers qui se ~** he didn't know who to turn to. **(d)** (*tordre*) *pouce* to wrench, twist. **(e)** (*partir*) **s'en ~** to go back.

retracer [R(ə)tRase] (3) *vt vie, histoire* to relate, recount; *trait effacé* to redraw, draw again.

rétracter [RetRakte] (1) **1** *vt griffe* to draw in, retract; *parole* to retract, withdraw. **2 se ~** *vpr [griffe, antenne]* to retract; (*se dédire*) to retract, back down. ♦ **rétractation** *nf* retraction. ♦ **rétractile** *adj* retractile. ♦ **rétraction** *nf* retraction.

retrait [R(ə)tRɛ] *nm* **(a)** *[mer]* ebb; *[eaux, glacier]* retreat; *[troupes, candidat, somme d'argent]* withdrawal; *[bagages]* collection; *[objet en gage]* redemption. **~ du permis de conduire** disqualification from driving. **(b) situé en ~** set back (*de* from); **se tenant en ~** standing back; (*fig*) **rester en ~** to stand aside.

retraite [R(ə)tRɛt] *nf* **(a)** (*fuite*) retreat. **~ aux flambeaux** torchlight tattoo. **(b)** *[travailleur]* (*état*) retirement; (*pension*) retirement pension. **être en ~** to be retired *ou* in retirement; **mettre qn à la ~** to pension sb off; **mise à la ~** retirement; **prendre sa ~** to retire, go into retirement; **prendre une ~ anticipée** to retire early; **~ complémentaire** supplementary pension. **(c)** (*littér: refuge*) retreat; *[animal]* lair; *[voleurs]* hideout, hiding place. **(d)** (*Rel*) retreat. **faire une ~** to be in retreat. ♦ **retraité, e 1** *adj* retired. **2** *nm,f* (old age) pensioner.

retranchement [R(ə)tRɑ̃ʃmɑ̃] *nm* (*Mil*) entrenchment, retrenchment. (*fig*) **poursuivre qn jusque dans ses derniers ~s** to drive sb into a corner.

retrancher [R(ə)tRɑ̃ʃe] (1) **1** *vt quantité, nombre* to take away, subtract; *somme d'argent* to deduct, dock, take off; *passage, mot* to take out, remove, omit (*de* from). (*littér*) **son argent le retranchait des autres** his money cut him off from other people. **2 se ~** *vpr* (*Mil*) **se ~ derrière/dans** to entrench o.s. behind/in; **se ~ dans son mutisme/derrière la loi** to take refuge in silence/behind the law.

retranscrire [R(ə)tRɑ̃skRiR] (39) *vt* to retranscribe. ♦ **retranscription** *nf* retranscription.

retransmettre [R(ə)tRɑ̃smɛtR(ə)] (56) *vt* to broadcast, relay. ♦ **retransmission** *nf* broadcast. **~ en direct/différé** live/recorded broadcast.

rétrécir [RetResiR] (2) **1** *vt vêtement* to take in; *tissu* to shrink; *pupille* to contract; *rue, orifice* to make narrower; *bague* to tighten, make smaller; *esprit* to narrow. **faire ~** *tissu* to shrink. **2** *vi*, **se ~** *vpr [tissu]* to shrink; *[pupilles]* to contract; *[vallée]* to narrow, get narrower; *[esprit]* to grow narrow; *[cercle d'amis]* to grow smaller, dwindle. ♦ **rétrécissement** *nm [tricot]* shrinkage; *[pupille]* contraction; *[vallée]* narrowing.

rétribuer [RetRibɥe] (1) *vt ouvrier* to pay. **~ le travail de qn** to pay sb for his work. ♦ **rétribution** *nf* payment.

rétro [RetRo] *adj inv*: **la mode ~** the Twenties fashion.

rétroactif, -ive [RetRɔaktif, iv] *adj* retrospective; (*Jur*) retroactive. (*Admin*) **augmentation avec effet ~** backdated pay rise. ♦ **rétroaction** *nf* retrospective effect. ♦ **rétroactivement** *adv* (*gén*) retrospectively; (*Jur*) retroactively. ♦ **rétroactivité** *nf* retroactivity.

rétrofusée [RetRɔfyze] *nf* retrorocket.

rétrograde [RetRɔgRad] *adj idées, politique* retrograde, reactionary; *mouvement, sens* backward, retrograde.

rétrograder [RetRɔgRade] (1) **1** *vi* (*Aut*) to change down; (*dans une hiérarchie*) to regress, move down; (*perdre son avance*) to fall back; (*reculer*) to move back. **2** *vt fonctionnaire* to demote, downgrade.

rétrospectif, -ive [RetRɔspɛktif, iv] *adj, nf* retrospective. ♦ **rétrospectivement** *adv* in retrospect.

retrousser [R(ə)tRuse] (1) **1** *vt jupe* to hitch up,

tuck up; *manche* to roll up; *lèvres* to curl up. **2 se ~** *vpr [bords]* to turn outwards. ♦ **retroussé, e** *adj nez* turned-up, retroussé; *moustaches* curled up.

retrouvailles [ʀ(ə)tʀuvɑj] *nfpl* reunion.

retrouver [ʀ(ə)tʀuve] (1) **1** *vt* **(a)** (*récupérer*) *objet, situation, chemin* to find again; *santé, calme* to regain; *secret, recette* to rediscover; *nom, date* to think of, remember. **on a retrouvé le corps** the body has been found; **une telle occasion ne se retrouvera jamais** an opportunity like this will never occur again *ou* crop up again; **une chienne n'y retrouverait pas ses petits** it's in absolute chaos. **(b)** (*rencontrer*) *personne* to meet (up with) again; (*pour rendez-vous*) to join, meet *ou* see again; *endroit* to be back in, see again; *caractéristique, phénomène* to find, encounter. **et que je ne te retrouve pas ici!** and don't let me catch *ou* find you here again!; **on retrouve chez Jacques le sourire de son père** you can see *ou* recognize his father's smile in Jacques; **je retrouve bien là mon fils!** that's my son all right!; **on retrouve sans cesse les mêmes tournures dans ses romans** you are constantly coming across *ou* meeting the same expressions in his novels.

2 se ~ *vpr* **(a)** (*se réunir*) to meet; (*après une absence*) to meet again. **on se retrouvera!** I'll get even with you!; **comme on se retrouve!** fancy meeting *ou* seeing you here! **(b)** (*dans même endroit, situation*) to find o.s. back (*dans* in). **(c)** (*: *finir*) **il s'est retrouvé en prison/dans le fossé** he ended up *ou* landed (up)* in prison/in the ditch. **(d) s'y ~** (*trouver son chemin*) to find one's way; (*: *rentrer dans ses frais*) to break even; (*: *tirer un profit*) to make a profit; **on a de la peine à s'y ~, dans ces digressions** it's hard to find one's way through *ou* to make sense of these digressions; **je ne m'y retrouve plus** I'm completely lost.

rétroviseur [ʀetʀɔvizœʀ] *nm* rear-view mirror, (driving) mirror. **~ (d'aile)** wing mirror.

réunir [ʀeyniʀ] (2) **1** *vt* **(a)** *objets* to gather *ou* collect (together); *preuves* to put together; *fonds* to raise; *pièces de collection* to collect; *tendances, styles* to combine. **(b)** *participants* to gather, collect; *membres d'un parti* to call together, call a meeting of; *amis, famille* to entertain, have round*; *personnes brouillées* to bring together, reunite. **(c)** (*raccorder*) *[couloir, fil]* to join, link. **~ deux fils** to tie *ou* join two threads together; **~ à** *province etc* to unite to. **2 se ~** *vpr* **(a)** (*se rencontrer*) to meet, get together*. **se ~ entre amis** to have a friendly get-together*. **(b)** *[compagnies]* to combine; *[états]* to unite; *[fleuves]* to merge. ♦ **réuni, e** *adj*: **~s** (*pris ensemble*) (put) together; (*Comm: associés*) associated. ♦ **réunification** *nf* reunification. ♦ **réunifier** (7) *vt* to reunify. ♦ **réunion** *nf* **(a)** (*action*) collection, gathering; raising; combination; reunion. **~ d'une province à un état** union of a province with a state. **(b)** (*séance*) meeting. **~ cycliste** cycle rally; **~ hippique** gymkhana, horse show; **~ de famille** family gathering; **~ sportive** sports meeting.

réussir [ʀeysiʀ] (2) **1** *vi* **(a)** *[projet]* to succeed, be a success, be successful; *[culture]* to thrive, do well. **tout lui réussit** everything goes *ou* comes right for him, everything works for him; **cela ne lui a pas réussi** that didn't do him any good. **(b)** *[personne]* to succeed, be successful, be a success; (*à un examen*) to pass; (*dans les affaires, ses études*) to do well (*dans* in). **ont-ils réussi?** did they succeed?, did they pull it off?*; **il a réussi à son examen** he passed his exam; **il réussit bien en maths** he does well *ou* he's a success at maths; **~ à faire** to succeed in doing, manage to do. **(c)** *[climat, aliment]* **~ à qn** to agree with sb. **2** *vt entreprise, plat* to make a success of, make a good job of; *but* to bring off, pull off*; *photo* to manage successfully. **~ son coup*** to pull it off*. ♦ **réussi, e** *adj* (*gén*) successful; *mouvement* good, well executed. **c'était très ~** it was a great success *ou* very successful. ♦ **réussite** *nf* (*succès*) success; (*Cartes*) patience. **faire une ~** *ou* **des ~s** to play patience.

revaloir [ʀ(ə)valwaʀ] (29) *vt*: **je te revaudrai ça** (*hostile*) I'll pay you back for this; (*reconnaissant*) I'll repay you some day.

revaloriser [ʀ(ə)valɔʀize] (1) *vt monnaie* to revalue; *salaire* to raise; *méthode* to promote again. ♦ **revalorisation** *nf* revaluation; raising; fresh promotion.

revanche [ʀ(ə)vɑ̃ʃ] *nf* revenge; (*Jeux, Sport*) return match; (*Boxe*) return fight *ou* bout. **prendre sa ~ (sur qn)** to take one's revenge (on sb), get one's own back (on sb)*; **en ~** on the other hand.

rêvasser [ʀɛvase] (1) *vi* to daydream. ♦ **rêvasserie** *nf*: **~(s)** daydreaming.

rêve [ʀɛv] *nm* (*lit, fig*) dream; (*éveillé*) daydream. **faire des ~s** to dream, have dreams; **il est dans un ~** he's (day)dreaming; **voiture/silence de ~** dream car/silence; **son ~ de jeunesse** his youthful dream; **la femme de ses ~s** the woman of his dreams, his dream woman; **disparaître comme dans un ~** to disappear in a trice; **ça, c'est le ~*** that would be ideal, that would be (just) perfect.

revêche [ʀəvɛʃ] *adj* surly, sour-tempered.

réveil [ʀevɛj] *nm* **(a)** *[dormeur]* waking (up), wakening; (*retour à la réalité*) awakening; *[nature, sentiment, souvenir]* reawakening; *[volcan]* fresh stirrings; *[douleur]* return. **dès le ~, il chante** as soon as he's awake *ou* he wakes up he starts singing. **(b)** (*Mil*) reveille. **(c)** (*réveille-matin*) alarm (clock).

réveiller [ʀeveje] (1) **1** *vt dormeur* to wake (up), waken; *personne évanouie* to bring round, revive; *appétit, courage, sentiment* to rouse, awaken; *douleur* (*physique*) to start up again; (*mentale*) to revive, reawaken. **2 se ~** *vpr [dormeur]* to wake (up), awake; *[personne évanouie]* to come round, regain consciousness; *[appétit, courage, sentiment]* to be roused; *[douleur, souvenir]* to return; *[nature]* to reawaken; *[volcan]* to stir again. **se réveillant de sa torpeur** rousing himself from his lethargy. ♦ **réveillé, e** *adj* awake; (*: *dégourdi*) bright. **à moitié ~** half asleep. ♦ **réveille-matin** *nm inv* alarm clock.

réveillon [ʀevɛjɔ̃] *nm* Christmas Eve *ou* New Year's Eve dinner. ♦ **réveillonner** (1) *vi* to celebrate Christmas *ou* New Year's Eve (*with a dinner and a party*).

révéler [ʀevele] (6) **1** *vt* **(a)** *secret* to disclose, reveal; *opinion* to make known. **(b)** *aptitude, caractère* to reveal, display; *sentiments* to show. **(c)** *artiste [impresario]* to discover; *[œuvre]* to bring to fame. **2 se ~** *vpr [vérité, talent, tendance]* to be revealed, reveal itself; (*Rel*) to reveal o.s.; *[artiste]* to show *ou* display one's talent. **se ~ cruel** to show o.s. *ou* prove to be cruel; **se ~ difficile** to prove difficult. ♦ **révélateur, -trice 1** *adj indice* revealing. **c'est ~ d'un malaise** it reveals a malaise. **2** *nm* (*Phot*) developer; (*expérience*) revelation. ♦ **révélation** *nf* revelation; disclosure. **ce jeune auteur a été la ~ de l'année** this young author was the discovery of the year; **faire des ~s** to make disclosures *ou* revelations. ♦ **révélé, e** *adj* (*Rel*) revealed.

revenant, e [ʀəvnɑ̃, ɑ̃t] *nm,f* ghost. **tiens, un ~!*** hello stranger!*

revendeur, -euse [ʀ(ə)vɑ̃dœʀ, øz] *nm,f* (*détaillant*) retailer; (*d'occasion*) secondhand dealer.

revendiquer [ʀ(ə)vɑ̃dike] (1) *vt droits* to claim, demand; *responsabilité* to claim. ♦ **revendicatif, -ive** *adj mouvement etc* of protest. ♦ **revendication** *nf* (*action*) claiming; (*demande*) claim, demand.

revendre [R(ə)vɑ̃dR(ə)] (41) *vt* (*d'occasion*) to resell; (*au détail*) to sell. (*davantage*) **j'en ai revendu 4** I sold another 4; **avoir de l'énergie à ~** to have energy enough and to spare; **des tableaux, on en a à ~** pictures, we've got them by the score.

revenir [Rəvnir] (22) **1** *vi* **(a)** *[personne]* (*repasser de nouveau*) to come back, come again; (*rentrer*) to come back, return; *[saison, mode, lettre]* to come back, return; *[fête, date]* to come (round) again; *[calme, soleil]* to return. **cette expression revient souvent dans sa conversation** that expression often crops up in his conversation; **~ chez soi/de voyage/dans son pays** to come back *ou* return home/from a journey/to one's country; **~ en bateau/avion** to sail/fly back; **je reviens dans un instant** I'll be back in a minute, I'll be right back*. **(b) ~ à** *études, sujet* to go back to, return to; *méthode* to revert to; **~ à la charge** to return to the attack; **revenons à nos moutons** let's get back to the subject; **nous y reviendrons dans un instant** we'll come back to that in a moment; **il n'y a pas à y ~** there's no going back on it. **(c) ~ à** (*équivaloir à*) to come down to, amount to, boil down to*; (*coûter*) to amount to, come to; **cela revient à dire que** that amounts to saying that; **cela revient au même** it amounts to *ou* comes to the same thing; **ça revient cher** it's expensive; **à combien est-ce que cela va vous ~?** how much will that cost you? **(d) ~ à qn** *[souvenir oublié]* to come back to sb; *[courage, appétit, parole]* to come back to sb, return (to sb); *[prérogative, honneur]* to fall to sb; *[héritage]* to come *ou* go *ou* pass to sb; *[ragots]* to reach sb's ears; **il a une tête qui ne me revient pas** I don't like the look of him; **tout le mérite vous revient** all the credit goes to you, the credit is all yours; **il lui revient de décider** it's for him *ou* it's up to him to decide; **ce titre lui revient de droit** this title is his by right; **là-dessus, 100 F me reviennent** 100 francs of that comes to me. **(e) ~ sur** *passé, problème* to go back over; *promesse* to go back on; **ne revenons pas là-dessus** let's not go back over that. **(f) ~ de** *maladie* to recover from, get over; *syncope* to come round from; *surprise* to get over; *illusions* to lose, shake off; *erreurs, théories* to leave behind, cast aside; **elle est revenue de tout** she's seen it all before; **crois-tu qu'il en reviendra?** do you think he'll pull through?; **il revient de loin** it's a miracle he's still with us; **je n'en reviens pas!** I can't get over it! **(g) ~ à soi** to come round; **~ à la vie** to come back to life. **(h)** (*Culin*) **faire ~** to brown. **2 s'en ~** *vpr* to come back (*de* from).

revente [R(ə)vɑ̃t] *nf* resale.

revenu [Rəvny] *nm [particulier]* income; *[état]* revenue (*de* from); *[investissement]* yield, revenue (*de* from, on).

rêver [Reve] (1) **1** *vi* **(a)** (*gén, fig*) to dream (*de, à* of, about); (*rêvasser*) to daydream. **tu m'as appelé? – moi? tu rêves!** did you call me? – me? you must have been dreaming! *ou* you're imagining things!; **on croit ~!*** I can hardly believe it!, the mind boggles!* **(b)** (*désirer*) **~ de qch/de faire** to dream of sth/of doing; **~ de réussir** to long to succeed, long for success. **2** *vt* (*en dormant*) to dream; (*imaginer*) to dream up; (*désirer*) to dream of. **il se rêve conquérant** he dreams of being a conqueror.

réverbérer [RevɛRbeRe] (6) *vt son* to send back, reverberate; *chaleur, lumière* to reflect. ♦ **réverbération** *nf* reverberation. ♦ **réverbère** *nm* street lamp *ou* light.

révérence [ReveRɑ̃s] *nf* **(a)** *[homme]* bow; *[femme]* curtsey. **faire une ~** to bow; to curtsey (*à qn* to sb); (*fig: partir*) **tirer sa ~ (à qn)** to take one's leave (of sb). **(b)** (*respect*) reverence (*envers* for). ♦ **révérencieux, -ieuse** *adj* reverent.

révérend, e [ReveRɑ̃, ɑ̃d] *adj, nm* reverend.

révérer [ReveRe] (6) *vt* to revere.

rêverie [RɛvRi] *nf* (*état*) daydreaming; (*rêve, chimère*) daydream.

revers [R(ə)vɛR] *nm* **(a)** *[papier, main]* back; *[étoffe]* wrong side; *[médaille]* reverse side. **prendre l'ennemi à ~** to take the enemy from *ou* in the rear; (*fig*) **c'est le ~ de la médaille** that's the other side of the coin; **d'un ~ de main** with the back of one's hand. **(b)** (*Tennis*) backhand. **faire un ~** to play a backhand shot. **(c)** *[veste]* lapel; *[pantalon]* turn-up, cuff (*US*); *[bottes]* top; *[manche]* (turned-back) cuff. **(d)** (*coup du sort*) **~ (de fortune)** reverse (of fortune); **~ économiques** economic setbacks *ou* reverses.

reverser [R(ə)vɛRse] (1) *vt liquide* to pour out some more; *somme* to put back, pay back (*dans, sur* into).

réversible [RevɛRsibl(ə)] *adj* reversible; (*Jur*) revertible (*sur* to). ♦ **réversion** *nf* (*Bio, Jur*) reversion.

revêtir [R(ə)vetiR] (20) **1** *vt* **(a)** *habit* to don, put on. **(b)** *caractère, importance, forme* to assume, take on. **(c) ~ qn de** *habit* to array sb in; *autorité, dignité* to endow *ou* invest sb with; (*déguiser*) **~ qch de** to cloak sth in, cover sth with; **~ un document de sa signature** to append one's signature to a document. **(d)** (*enduire*) to coat; *route* to surface; *mur, sol* to cover (*de* with). **~ de plâtre** to plaster; **montagnes revêtues de neige** mountains covered in snow, snow-covered mountains. **2 se ~** *vpr* (*mettre*) **se ~ de** *habit* to array o.s. in, don, dress o.s. in; *neige, feuilles* to be covered in. ♦ **revêtement** *nm* (*enduit*) coating; *[route]* surface; *[mur extérieur]* facing; *[mur intérieur]* covering; *[sol]* flooring, floor-covering. ♦ **revêtu, e** *adj [personne]* **~ de** dressed in, wearing.

rêveur, -euse [RɛvœR, øz] **1** *adj air* dreamy. **ça vous laisse ~*** the mind boggles*, it makes you wonder. **2** *nm,f* (*lit, péj*) dreamer. ♦ **rêveusement** *adv* dreamily.

revigorer [R(ə)vigɔRe] (1) *vt [vent]* to invigorate; *[repas]* to revive, buck up*; *[discours]* to cheer. **ça revigore** it's bracing *ou* invigorating.

revirement [R(ə)viRmɑ̃] *nm* (*gén*) reversal (*de* of); *[goûts]* (abrupt) change (*de* in); *[opinions]* change, turnaround (*de* in).

réviser [Revize] (1) *vt procès, règlement* to review; *opinion* to review, reappraise; *comptes* to audit; *liste, leçons, manuscrit* to revise; *moteur* to overhaul, service; *montre* to service. ♦ **révision** *nf* (*action*) review; reappraisal; auditing; revision; overhauling; servicing. (*Scol*) **faire ses ~s** to do one's revision; (*Aut*) **prochaine ~ après 10 000 km** next major service after 10,000 km.

revivifier [R(ə)vivifje] (7) *vt* to revive.

revivre [RəvivR(ə)] (46) **1** *vi* (*être ressuscité*) to live again; (*être revigoré*) to come alive again; *[coutumes]* to be revived. **faire ~** (*ressusciter*) to bring back *ou* restore to life; (*revigorer*) to revive, put new life into; *mode, époque* to revive. **2** *vt* to relive, live again.

révocation [Revɔkɑsjɔ̃] *nf [fonctionnaire]* removal (from office), dismissal; *[contrat]* revocation, repeal. ♦ **révocable** *adj* removable, dismissible; revocable.

revoici* [R(ə)vwasi] *prép*, **revoilà*** [R(ə)vwala] *prép*: **~ Paul!** Paul's back (again)!, here's Paul again!; **le ~ qui se plaint!** there he goes complaining again!

revoir [R(ə)vwaR] (30) *vt* **(a)** (*gén, fig*) to see again; *photos* to have another look at. **quand le revois-tu?** when are you seeing *ou* meeting him again?, when are you meeting again?; **au ~ Monsieur** goodbye Mr X; **dire au ~ à qn** to say goodbye to sb; **faire au ~ de la main** to wave goodbye; **ce n'est qu'un au ~** it's only a temporary goodbye.

(b) (*réviser*) **édition** to revise; (*Scol*) **leçons** to revise, go over again.

révolter [ʀevɔlte] (1) **1** *vt* to revolt, outrage, appal. **2 se ~** *vpr* (*s'insurger*) to revolt, rise up (*contre* against); (*protester*) to rebel (*contre* against); (*s'indigner*) to be revolted *ou* outraged *ou* appalled (*contre* by). ♦ **révoltant, e** *adj* revolting, outrageous, appalling. ♦ **révolte** *nf* revolt. **en ~ contre** in revolt *ou* up in arms against. ♦ **révolté, e 1** *adj* **(a)** rebellious, in revolt. **(b)** (*outré*) outraged, appalled. **2** *nm,f* rebel.

révolu, e [ʀevɔly] *adj* past. **des jours ~s** past *ou* bygone days, days gone by; (*Admin*) **âgé de 20 ans ~s** over 20 years of age; **après 2 ans ~s** when two full years had (*ou* have) passed.

révolution [ʀevɔlysjɔ̃] *nf* (*gén*) revolution. *[rue]* **être en ~** to be in an uproar. ♦ **révolutionnaire** *adj, nmf* revolutionary. ♦ **révolutionner** (1) *vt* (*transformer radicalement*) to revolutionize; (*: *bouleverser*) to stir up.

revolver [ʀevɔlvɛʀ] *nm* (*gén*) gun; (*à barillet*) revolver.

révoquer [ʀevɔke] (1) *vt* **fonctionnaire** to remove from office, dismiss; **contrat, édit** to revoke, repeal.

revue [ʀ(ə)vy] *nf* **(a)** (*gén, Mil: examen*) review. **~ de presse** review of the press; (*lit, fig*) **passer en ~** to pass in review. **(b)** (*magazine*) magazine; (*spécialisée*) journal; (*érudite*) review. **(c)** (*spectacle*) (*satirique*) revue; (*de variétés*) variety show *ou* performance. **~ à grand spectacle** revue spectacular.

révulser (se) [ʀevylse] (1) *vpr [visage]* to contort; *[yeux]* to roll upwards. ♦ **révulsif, -ive** *adj, nm* revulsant.

rez-de-chaussée [ʀedʃose] *nm inv* ground floor, first floor (*US*). **habiter un ~** to live in a ground-floor flat.

rhabiller [ʀabije] (1) **1** *vt*: **~ qn** to dress sb again; (*lui racheter des habits*) to fit sb out again, reclothe sb. **2 se ~** *vpr* to put one's clothes back on, dress (o.s.) again. **tu peux aller te ~!‡** you've had it!*

rhapsodie [ʀapsɔdi] *nf* rhapsody.

rhésus [ʀezys] *nm* (*Méd*) Rhesus.

rhétorique [ʀetɔʀik] **1** *nf* rhetoric. **2** *adj* rhetorical.

Rhin [ʀɛ̃] *nm*: **le ~** the Rhine.

rhinocéros [ʀinɔseʀɔs] *nm* rhinoceros.

rhinopharyngite [ʀinɔfaʀɛ̃ʒit] *nf* sore throat, throat infection.

rhododendron [ʀɔdɔdɛ̃dʀɔ̃] *nm* rhododendron.

rhubarbe [ʀybaʀb(ə)] *nf* rhubarb.

rhum [ʀɔm] *nm* rum.

rhumatisme [ʀymatism(ə)] *nm*: **~(s)** rheumatism. ♦ **rhumatisant, e** *adj, nm,f* rheumatic. ♦ **rhumatismal, e,** *mpl* **-aux** *adj* rheumatic. ♦ **rhumatologie** *nf* rheumatology. ♦ **rhumatologue** *nmf* rheumatologist.

rhume [ʀym] *nm* cold. **attraper un ~** to catch a cold; **~ de cerveau** head cold; **~ des foins** hay fever.

riant, e [ʀijɑ̃, ɑ̃t] *adj* **paysage** smiling; **atmosphère, perspective** cheerful, pleasant, happy.

ribambelle [ʀibɑ̃bɛl] *nf*: **~ de** *enfants* swarm *ou* herd *ou* flock of; *noms* string of.

ribouldingue*† [ʀibuldɛ̃g] *nf* spree, binge*. **faire la ~** to go on the spree *ou* the binge*.

ricain, e‡ [ʀikɛ̃, ɛn] *adj,* **R~(e)** *nm(f)* (*péj*) Yank(ee)* (*péj*).

ricaner [ʀikane] (1) *vi* (*méchamment*) to snigger; (*bêtement*) to giggle. ♦ **ricanement** *nm* snigger; giggle.

riche [ʀiʃ] **1** *adj* (*gén, fig*) rich; **personne** rich, wealthy, well-off. **~ à millions** enormously wealthy; **faire un ~ mariage** to marry (into) money; **ce n'est pas un ~ cadeau** it's not much of a gift; **ça fait ~*** it looks plush(y)* *ou* expensive *ou* posh*; **c'est une ~ idée** that's a great* *ou* grand idea; **il y a une documentation très ~ sur ce sujet** there is a wealth of *ou* a vast amount of information on this subject; **~ en** *calories, gibier* rich in; **~ de** *possibilités, espérances* full of; **~ en protéines** with a high protein content, rich in protein; **je ne suis pas ~ en sucre** I'm not very well-off for sugar. **2** *nmf* rich *ou* wealthy person. **les ~s** the rich, the wealthy. ♦ **richard, e*** *nm,f* (*péj*) moneybags*. ♦ **richement** *adv* richly. ♦ **richesse** *nf* **(a)** *[personne, pays]* wealth; *[ameublement, décor]* richness; *[sol, texte, collection]* richness. **la ~ en calcium de cet aliment** the high calcium content of this food; **la ~ en pétrole du pays** the country's abundant *ou* vast oil resources; **la santé est une ~** good health is a great blessing *ou* is a boon. **(b) ~s** (*argent*) riches, wealth; (*ressources*) wealth; (*fig: trésors*) treasures; **~s naturelles** natural resources. ♦ **richissime** *adj* fabulously rich *ou* wealthy.

ricin [ʀisɛ̃] *nm* castor oil plant.

ricocher [ʀikɔʃe] (1) *vi [balle de fusil]* to rebound, ricochet; *[pierre etc]* to rebound; (*sur l'eau*) to bounce (*sur qch* off sth). ♦ **ricochet** *nm* rebound; ricochet; bounce. **faire ~** to rebound *ou* ricochet *ou* bounce (*sur* off); (*fig*) to rebound; **faire des ~s** to skim pebbles, play ducks and drakes.

rictus [ʀiktys] *nm* (*moqueur, cruel*) grin; *[animal, dément]* grimace.

ride [ʀid] *nf [peau, pomme]* wrinkle (*de* in); *[eau, sable]* ripple (*de* on, in), ridge (*de* in).

rideau, *pl* **~x** [ʀido] *nm* (*gén, Théât*) curtain; *[boutique]* shutter; *[cheminée]* blower; *[classeur]* roll shutter; *[appareil-photo]* shutter. **tirer les ~x** to draw the curtains *ou* drapes (*US*); **~ de** *arbres* screen of; *pluie* sheet of; **~ de fer** *[boutique]* metal shutter(s); *[théâtre]* (metal) safety curtain; (*Pol*) **le ~ de fer** the Iron Curtain.

rider [ʀide] (1) **1** *vt* **peau, fruit** to wrinkle; **eau** to ripple; **sable** to ruffle the surface of. **2 se ~** *vpr* to become wrinkled; to become rippled.

ridicule [ʀidikyl] **1** *adj* (*gén*) ridiculous; **personne, vêtement** ludicrous, absurd; **prétentions** laughable; **quantité** ridiculously small. **se rendre ~** to make o.s. (look) ridiculous, make a fool of o.s. **2** *nm* **(a) le ~** (*grotesque*) ridicule; (*absurdité*) **le ~ de qch** the ridiculousness *ou* the absurdity of sth; **se donner le ~ de ...** to be ridiculous enough to ...; **tomber dans le ~** to become ridiculous; **le ~ ne tue pas** ridicule never killed anyone. **(b)** (*travers*) **~s** ridiculous *ou* silly ways, absurdities. ♦ **ridiculement** *adv* ridiculously. ♦ **ridiculiser** (1) **1** *vt* to ridicule, hold up to ridicule. **2 se ~** *vpr* to make o.s. (look) ridiculous, make a fool of o.s.

rien [ʀjɛ̃] **1** *pron indéf* **(a)** (*avec ne*) nothing. **je n'ai ~ entendu** I didn't hear anything, I didn't hear a thing, I heard nothing; **il n'y a plus ~** there's nothing left. **(b) ~ de** + *adj, ptp* nothing; **~ de plus** nothing more *ou* else *ou* further; **il n'est ~ de tel qu'une bonne pêche** there's nothing like *ou* nothing to beat a good peach; **~ de plus facile** nothing easier. **(c) ~ que la chambre coûte très cher** the room alone costs a great deal; **la vérité, ~ que la vérité** the truth and nothing but the truth; **je voudrais vous voir, ~ qu'une minute** could I see you just for a minute. **(d)** (= *quelque chose*) anything. **as-tu jamais lu ~ de plus drôle?** have you ever read anything funnier? **(e)** (*intensif*) **~ au monde** nothing on earth *ou* in the world; **~ du tout** nothing at all; **~ de ~*** nothing, absolutely nothing; **trois fois ~** next to nothing. **(f)** (*Sport*) nil, nothing. **~ partout** nothing all; (*Tennis*) **15 à ~** 15 love. **(g)** (*avec avoir, être, faire*) **n'avoir ~ contre qn** to have nothing against sb; **il n'a ~ d'un dictateur** he's got nothing of the dictator about him; **n'être ~** *[personne]* to be a nobody; *[chose]* to be nothing; **il ne nous est ~**

he's nothing to do with us; **n'être pour ~ dans une affaire** to have no hand in *ou* have nothing to do with an affair; **il n'en est ~** it's not so at all, it's nothing of the sort; **élever 4 enfants, ça n'est pas ~** bringing up 4 children is no mean feat; **il ne fait (plus) ~** he doesn't work (any more); **il ne nous a ~ fait** he hasn't done anything to us; **cela ne lui fait ~** he doesn't mind, it doesn't matter to him; **ça ne fait ~*** it doesn't matter, never mind; **~ à faire!** it's no good!, nothing doing!* **(h)** (*locutions*) **je vous remercie - de ~*** thank you - you're welcome *ou* don't mention it *ou* not at all; **c'est cela ou ~** it's that or nothing; **c'est mieux que ~** it's better than nothing; **c'est à moi, ~ qu'à moi** it's mine and mine alone; **une blessure de ~ (du tout)** a trifling *ou* trivial injury; **une fille de ~** a worthless girl; **cela ne nous gêne en ~ (du tout)** it doesn't bother us in any way *ou* at all; **pour ~** (*peu cher*) for a song, for next to nothing; (*inutilement*) for nothing; **ce n'est pas pour ~ que ...** it is not without cause *ou* good reason *ou* it's not for nothing that ...; **il ne s'agit de ~ moins qu'un crime** it's nothing less than a crime.

2 *nm* **(a)** (*néant*) nothingness. **(b) un ~** a mere nothing; **des ~s** trivia; **il a peur d'un ~** every little thing *ou* anything frightens him; **avec un ~ d'ironie** with a hint *ou* touch of irony; **en un ~ de temps** in no time (at all), in next to no time; **c'est un ~ bruyant ici** it's a bit *ou* a shade noisy in here.

3 *adv* (ꜩ) (*très*) not halfꜩ. **il fait ~ froid ici** it isn't half cold hereꜩ.

rieur, rieuse [ʀijœʀ, ʀijøz] **1** *adj personne* cheerful, merry; *expression* cheerful, laughing **2** *nm,f*: **les ~s** people who are (*ou* were) laughing.

rigide [ʀiʒid] *adj armature* rigid, stiff; *muscle, carton* stiff; *règle, politique* strict, rigid. **livre à couverture ~** hardback (book). ♦ **rigidement** *adv* strictly, rigidly. ♦ **rigidité** *nf* rigidity, stiffness; strictness.

rigole [ʀigɔl] *nf* (*canal*) channel; (*filet d'eau*) rivulet; (*Agr: sillon*) furrow. **~ d'irrigation** irrigation channel; **~ d'écoulement** drain.

rigoler* [ʀigɔle] (1) *vi* (*rire*) to laugh; (*s'amuser*) to have fun, have a laugh*; (*plaisanter*) to joke. (*iro*) **tu me fais ~** you make me laugh; **on a bien rigolé** we had great fun *ou* a good laugh*; **tu rigoles!** you're kidding!ꜩ *ou* joking!; **il ne faut pas ~ avec ce genre de maladie** you mustn't fool around with an illness like this*; **j'ai dit ça pour ~** it was only a joke, I only said it in fun *ou* for a laugh*. ♦ **rigolade*** *nf*: **aimer la ~** to like a bit of fun *ou* a laugh*; **il prend tout à la ~** he thinks everything's a big joke *ou* laugh*, he makes a joke of everything; **c'est de la ~** (*c'est facile*) it's child's play *ou* a cinch*; (*c'est une parodie*) it's a big joke* *ou* farce; (*c'est un attrape-nigaud*) it's a complete conꜩ. ♦ **rigolo, -ote* 1** *adj personne, histoire* funny, killing*. **ce n'est pas ~** it's no joke, it's not funny; **c'est ~, je n'avais jamais remarqué cela** that's funny *ou* odd, I had never noticed that. **2** *nm,f* (*amusant*) comic, wag; (*péj: fumiste*) fraud, phoney.

rigueur [ʀigœʀ] *nf* **(a)** *[discipline, climat]* harshness, rigour. **les ~s du sort/de l'hiver** the rigours of fate/winter. **(b)** *[morale, personne]* strictness. **(c)** *[définition, classification]* strictness, rigour. **manquer de ~** to lack rigour. **(d) tenir ~ à qn de n'être pas venu** to hold it against sb that he didn't come; **à la ~** (*si nécessaire*) at a pinch, if need be; (*peut-être*) possibly; **il est de ~ d'envoyer un mot de remerciement** it is the done thing to send a note of thanks; **'tenue de soirée de ~'** 'evening dress', 'dress: formal'. ♦ **rigoureusement** *adv punir* harshly; *démontrer* rigorously; *appliquer* rigorously, strictly; *exact* rigorously; *interdit, vrai* strictly. ♦ **rigoureux, -euse** *adj* (*gén*) rigorous; *punition, climat* harsh; *moraliste, interdiction, définition* strict.

rime [ʀim] *nf* rhyme. **faire qch sans ~ ni raison** to do sth without either rhyme or reason. ♦ **rimer** (1) **1** *vi [mot]* to rhyme (*avec* with); *[poète]* to write verse. (*fig*) **cela ne rime à rien** it does not make sense, there's no sense *ou* point in it. **2** *vt* to put into verse.

rimmel [ʀimɛl] *nm* ® mascara.

rincer [ʀɛ̃se] (3) **1** *vt* to rinse (out). **se faire ~*** (*par la pluie*) to get drenched *ou* soaked; (*au jeu*) to get cleaned out*. **2 se ~** *vpr*: **se ~ la bouche** to rinse out one's mouth; **se ~ l'œilꜩ** to get an eyeful*. ♦ **rinçage** *nm* (*action*) rinsing (out). **cette machine à laver fait 3 ~s** this washing machine does 3 rinses. ♦ **rince-doigts** *nm inv* finger-bowl.

ring [ʀiŋ] *nm* (boxing) ring.

riper [ʀipe] (1) *vi* to slip. **faire ~** to slide along.

riposter [ʀipɔste] (1) **1** *vi* **(a)** (*répondre*) to answer back, retaliate. **~ à une insulte** to reply to an insult; **~ par une insulte** to retort *ou* retaliate with an insult. **(b)** (*contre-attaquer*) to counter-attack, retaliate. **~ à une attaque** to counter an attack (*par* by). **2** *vt*: **~ que** to retort *ou* answer back that. ♦ **riposte** *nf* (*réponse*) retort, riposte; (*contre-attaque*) counter-attack, reprisal.

riquiqui* [ʀikiki] *adj inv portion* tiny, mean, stingy*; *vêtement, objet* tiny.

rire [ʀiʀ] (36) **1** *vi* **(a)** to laugh. **~ aux éclats** to roar with laughter, laugh one's head off; **~ bruyamment** to guffaw; **~ dans sa barbe** to laugh to o.s.; **~ jaune** to laugh on the other side of one's face; (*iro*) **laissez-moi ~!** don't make me laugh!, you make me laugh! (*iro*); **c'est à mourir de ~** it's hilarious, it's awfully funny; **ça ne me fait pas ~** I don't find it funny; **nous avons bien ri** we had a good laugh*; **il a pris les choses en riant** (*avec bonne humeur*) he saw the funny side of it; (*à la légère*) he laughed it off; **rira bien qui rira le dernier** he who laughs last laughs longest. **(b)** *[yeux, visage]* to shine with happiness. **(c)** (*s'amuser*) to have fun, have a laugh*. **il aime bien ~** he likes a bit of fun *ou* a good laugh*. **(d)** (*plaisanter*) **vous voulez ~!** you must be joking!; **il a dit cela pour ~** he was only joking, he said it in fun; **il a fait cela pour ~** he did it for a joke *ou* laugh*; **c'était une bagarre pour ~** it wasn't a real fight.

2 ~ de *vt indir* to laugh *ou* scoff at. **il fait ~ de lui** he makes himself a laughing stock.

3 se ~ *vpr*: **se ~ de** *difficultés* to make light of; *menaces, personne* to laugh at.

4 *nm* (*façon, éclat*) laugh. **le ~** laughter; **un gros ~** a loud laugh, a guffaw; **un petit ~ de satisfaction** a little chuckle of satisfaction; **un petit ~ bête** a stupid giggle *ou* titter; **il y eut des ~s** there was laughter; **elle eut un ~ méchant** she gave a wicked laugh, she laughed wickedly.

ris [ʀi] *nm*: **~ de veau** calf sweetbread.

risée [ʀize] *nf*: **s'exposer à la ~ générale** to lay o.s. open to ridicule; **être la ~ de toute l'Europe** to be *ou* make o.s. the laughing stock of Europe.

risette [ʀizɛt] *nf*: **faire (une) ~ à qn** to give sb a nice *ou* little smile.

risible [ʀizibl(ə)] *adj* (*ridicule*) ridiculous, silly; *aventure* laughable, funny.

risque [ʀisk(ə)] *nm* **(a)** (*gén, Jur: danger*) risk. **le goût du ~** a taste for danger; **prendre tous les ~s** to take any number of risks; **à cause du ~ d'incendie** because of the fire risk *ou* the risk of fire; **~ pour la santé** health hazard *ou* risk. **(b) ce sont les ~s du métier** that's an occupational hazard (*hum*); **il n'y a pas de ~ qu'il refuse** there's no risk *ou* chance of his refusing; **au ~ de le mécontenter** at the risk of displeasing him; **c'est à tes ~s et périls** it's at your own risk.

risquer [ʀiske] (1) **1** *vt* **(a)** *réputation, vie* to risk. **~ le tout pour le tout** to risk *ou* chance the lot; **risquons le coup*** let's chance it; **qui ne risque rien n'a rien** nothing ventured, nothing gained.

(b) *prison, ennuis* to risk. **tu risques gros** you're taking a big risk; **tu risques qu'on te le vole** you risk having it stolen; **bien emballé, ce vase ne risque rien** packed like this the vase is quite safe *ou* won't come to any harm; **ce vieux pantalon ne risque rien** these old trousers don't matter at all. **(c)** *allusion, regard* to venture, hazard. **(d) tu risques de le perdre** (*éventualité*) you might (well) *ou* could (well) lose it; (*probabilité*) you're likely to lose it; **pourquoi ~ de tout perdre?** why should we risk losing *ou* take the risk of losing everything?; **ça ne risque pas d'arriver!** there's no chance *ou* danger of that happening!, that's not likely to happen. **2 se ~** *vpr*: **se ~ dans** *grotte* to venture into; *entreprise* to venture (up)on, launch o.s. into; **se ~ à faire qch** to venture *ou* dare to do sth, have a try *ou* a go at doing sth. ♦ **risqué, e** *adj* (*hasardeux*) risky; (*licencieux*) risqué, daring. ♦ **risque-tout** *nmf inv* daredevil.

rissoler [risɔle] (1) *vti* (*aussi*: **faire ~**) to brown.

ristourne [risturn(ə)] *nf* rebate, discount. ♦ **ristourner** (1) *vt* to give a rebate of.

rite [rit] *nm* (*gén, Rel*) rite; (*fig: habitude*) ritual.

ritournelle [riturnɛl] *nf* (*Mus*) ritornello. (*fig*) **c'est toujours la même ~** it's always the same (old) story *ou* tune.

rituel, -elle [ritɥɛl] *adj, nm* (*gén*) ritual. ♦ **rituellement** *adv* ritually; (*invariablement*) invariably, unfailingly.

rivage [rivaʒ] *nm* shore.

rival, e, *mpl* **-aux** [rival, o] *adj, nm,f* rival. **sans ~** unrivalled. ♦ **rivaliser** (1) *vi*: **~ avec** *[personne]* to rival, compete *ou* vie with; *[chose]* to rival, hold its own against; **ils rivalisaient de générosité** they vied with each other *ou* they tried to outdo each other in generosity. ♦ **rivalité** *nf* rivalry.

rive [riv] *nf [mer, lac]* shore; *[rivière]* bank.

river [rive] (1) *vt clou* to clinch; *plaques* to rivet together. **~ son clou à qn*** to shut sb up*; **~ qch au sol** to nail sth to the floor. ♦ **rivé, e** *adj*: **~ à** (*gén*) riveted to; *travail* tethered *ou* tied to; **~ sur place** rooted to the spot.

riverain, e [rivrɛ̃, ɛn] **1** *adj* (*d'un lac*) waterside. (*d'une route*) **les propriétés ~es** the houses along the road. **2** *nm,f* lakeside (*ou* riverside) resident. *[rue]* **les ~s** the residents of *ou* in the street; **'interdit sauf aux ~s'** 'no entry except for access'.

rivet [rivɛ] *nm* rivet. ♦ **rivetage** *nm* riveting. ♦ **riveter** (4) *vt* to rivet (together).

rivière [rivjɛr] *nf* (*lit, fig*) river; (*Équitation*) water jump. **~ de diamants** diamond rivière.

rixe [riks(ə)] *nf* brawl, fight, scuffle.

riz [ri] *nm* rice. **~ au lait** rice pudding. ♦ **rizière** *nf* paddy-field, ricefield.

robe [rɔb] *nf [femme, fillette]* dress, frock; *[magistrat, prélat]* robe; *[professeur]* gown; *[cheval, fauve]* coat; (*couleur*) *[vin]* colour. **~ bain de soleil** sundress; **~ de chambre** dressing gown; **pommes de terre en ~ de chambre *ou* des champs** jacket potatoes; **~ de grossesse** maternity dress; **~ de mariée** wedding dress *ou* gown; **~ du soir** evening dress *ou* gown.

robinet [rɔbinɛ] *nm* tap, faucet (*US*). ♦ **robinetterie** *nf* (*installations*) taps; (*usine*) tap factory; (*commerce*) tap trade.

robot [rɔbo] *nm* (*lit, fig*) robot. **~ ménager** food-processor; **avion ~** remote-controlled aircraft.

robuste [rɔbyst(ə)] *adj personne, voiture* robust, sturdy; *santé* robust, sound; *plante* robust, hardy; *foi* firm, strong. ♦ **robustesse** *nf* robustness; sturdiness; soundness; hardiness; firmness, strength.

roc [rɔk] *nm* (*lit, fig*) rock.

rocade [rɔkad] *nf* (*route*) bypass.

rocaille [rɔkaj] *nf* (*cailloux*) loose stones; (*terrain*) rocky *ou* stony ground; (*jardin*) rockery, rock garden. ♦ **rocailleux, -euse** *adj terrain* rocky, stony; *voix* harsh, grating.

rocambolesque [rɔkɑ̃bɔlɛsk(ə)] *adj* fantastic, incredible.

roche [rɔʃ] *nf* rock. ♦ **rocher** *nm* rock. ♦ **rocheux, -euse** *adj* rocky. **paroi ~euse** rock face.

rock (and roll) [rɔk(ɛnrɔl)] *nm* (*musique*) rock-'n'-roll; (*danse*) jive.

roder [rɔde] (1) *vt moteur, spectacle etc* to run in, break in (*US*); *soupape* to grind. **il faut ~ ce spectacle** we have to let this show get into its stride; *[personne]* **il n'est pas encore rodé** he is not yet broken in. ♦ **rodage** *nm* running in, breaking in (*US*); grinding.

rôder [rode] (1) *vi* (*au hasard*) to roam *ou* wander about; (*de façon suspecte*) to lurk *ou* prowl about. **~ autour d'un magasin** to hang *ou* lurk around a shop. ♦ **rôdeur, -euse** *nm,f* prowler.

rogne* [rɔɲ] *nf* anger. **être/se mettre en ~** to be/get (hopping) mad*.

rogner [rɔɲe] (1) *vt ongle, page* to trim; *aile* to clip; *salaire* to cut *ou* whittle down. **~ sur** *dépense* to cut down *ou* back on.

rognon [rɔɲɔ̃] *nm* (*Culin*) kidney.

rognures [rɔɲyr] *nfpl [métal, ongles]* clippings; *[viande]* scraps.

roi [rwa] *nm* king. **les R~s mages** the Magi, the Three Wise Men; **le R~-Soleil** the Sun-King; **le jour des R~s** (*gén*) Twelfth Night; (*Rel*) Epiphany; **tirer les ~s** to eat Twelfth Night cake; **un des ~s de la presse** one of the press barons *ou* kings *ou* magnates *ou* tycoons; **X, le ~ des fromages** X, the leading *ou* first name in cheese(s); **c'est le ~ de la resquille!*** he's a master *ou* an ace at getting something for nothing; **tu es le ~ (des imbéciles)!*** you're the world's biggest idiot!*

roide [rwad], **roideur** [rwadœr], **roidir** [rwadir] = **raide, raideur, raidir.**

roitelet [rwatlɛ] *nm* (*péj*) kinglet; (*Orn*) wren.

rôle [rol] *nm* **(a)** (*Théât, fig*) role, part. **premier/petit ~** leading/minor role *ou* part; **jouer un ~** to play a part, act a role; (*fig*) **il joue les seconds ~s** he plays second fiddle; **ce n'est pas mon ~ de vous sermonner mais ...** it isn't my job *ou* place to lecture you but ...; **la télévision a pour ~ de ...** the role *ou* function of television is to ... . **(b)** (*registre*) roll, list.

romain, e [rɔmɛ̃, ɛn] **1** *adj* (*gén*) Roman. **2** *nm(f)* **R~(e)** Roman. **3** *nf*: **(laitue) ~e** cos (lettuce); **(balance) ~e** steelyard.

roman¹ [rɔmɑ̃] *nm* (*livre*) novel; (*genre médiéval*) romance; (*fig: récit*) story. **ils ne publient que des ~s** they only publish novels *ou* fiction; (*lit, fig*) **~ d'amour** love story; **~ d'aventures** adventure story; **~ de cape et d'épée** historical romance; **~ de chevalerie** tale of chivalry; **~ courtois** courtly romance; **~ d'épouvante** horror story; **~ d'espionnage** spy story; **~-feuilleton** (*lit*) serialized novel, serial; (*fig*) saga; **~ policier** detective novel *ou* story; **~ de science-fiction** science fiction novel; **~ (de) série noire** thriller.

roman², e [rɔmɑ̃, an] *adj* (*Ling*) Romance, Romanic; (*Archit*) Romanesque.

romance [rɔmɑ̃s] *nf* sentimental ballad, lovesong.

romancer [rɔmɑ̃se] (3) *vt* (*sous forme de roman*) to make into a novel; (*agrémenter*) to romanticize.

romancier, -ière [rɔmɑ̃sje, jɛr] *nm,f* novelist.

romanesque [rɔmanɛsk(ə)] **1** *adj histoire* fabulous, fantastic; *amours, aventures* storybook; *personne, imagination* romantic; *mode littéraire* novelistic. **œuvres ~s** novels, fiction. **2** *nm [personne]* romantic side; (*imagination*) fancy.

romanichel, -elle [rɔmaniʃɛl] *nm,f* gipsy.

romantique [rɔmɑ̃tik] *adj, nmf* romantic. ♦ **romantisme** *nm* romanticism.

romarin [rɔmarɛ̃] *nm* rosemary.

rompre [rɔ̃pr(ə)] (41) **1** *vt* (*gén, fig*) to break; *fian-*

çailles, pourparlers to break off. ~ **l'équilibre** to upset the balance; ~ **le front de l'ennemi** to break through the enemy front; ~ **qn à un exercice** to break sb in to an exercise; ~ **des lances contre qn** to cross swords with sb; (*Mil*) ~ **les rangs** to fall out, dismiss. **2** *vi [corde]* to break, snap; *[digue]* to burst, break; *[fiancés]* to break it off; (*Boxe, Escrime]* to break. (*Mil*) ~ **le combat** to withdraw from the engagement; ~ **avec** *personne, habitude* to break with. **3 se** ~ *vpr [corde, branche]* to break, snap; *[digue]* to burst, break; *[veine]* to burst, rupture. **il va se** ~ **le cou** he's going to break his neck. ♦ **rompu, e** *adj* **(a)** (*fourbu*) exhausted, worn-out, tired out. **(b)** (*expérimenté*) ~ **à qch** experienced in sth; ~ **aux affaires** with wide business experience; ~ **aux privations** accustomed *ou* inured to deprivation.

romsteck [ʀɔmstɛk] *nm* (*viande*) rumpsteak; (*tranche*) piece of rumpsteak.

ronce [ʀɔ̃s] *nf* (*branche*) bramble branch. (*buissons*) ~s brambles.

ronchonner* [ʀɔ̃ʃɔne] (1) *vi* to grumble, grouse*, grouch* (*après* at). ♦ **ronchon* 1** *adj* grumpy, grouchy*. **2** *nm* grumbler, grouch(er)*, grouser*. ♦ **ronchonnement*** *nm*: ~(s) grumbling, grousing*, grouching*.

rond, e [ʀɔ̃, ʀɔ̃d] **1** *adj* **(a)** *forme* round. **(b)** (*gras*) *visage* round, chubby, plump; *mollet, poitrine* (well-)rounded; *ventre, personne* plump, tubby. **(c)** (*net*) round. **chiffre** ~ round number *ou* figure; **ça fait 50 F tout** ~ it comes to a round 50 francs; **pour faire un compte** ~ to make a round figure; **être** ~ **en affaires** to be straight(forward) *ou* on the level* in business matters. **(d)** (*: *soûl*) drunk, tight*.

2 *nm* **(a)** (*cercle dessiné*) circle, ring; (*tranche*) slice; (*objet*) ring. ~ **de serviette** serviette *ou* napkin ring; **en** ~ in a circle *ou* ring. **(b)** (*: *sou*) ~s lolly‡, cash; **il n'a pas le** *ou* **un** ~ he hasn't got a penny *ou* a cent; **il n'a plus le** ~ he's broke*; **ça doit valoir des** ~**s!** that must cost a lot! *ou* a packet!*

3 *nf* **(a)** *[gardien, soldats]* rounds; *[policier]* beat, patrol, rounds; (*patrouille*) patrol. **faire sa** ~**e** to be on one's rounds *ou* on the beat *ou* on patrol. **(b)** (*danse*) round (dance), dance in a ring; (*danseurs*) circle, ring. **faites la** ~**e** dance round in a circle *ou* ring. **(c)** (*Mus: note*) semibreve, whole note (*US*). **(d)** (*Écriture*) roundhand. **(e) à des kilomètres à la** ~**e** for miles around; **passer qch à la** ~**e** to pass sth round.

♦ **rondelet, -ette** *adj femme* plumpish; *somme* tidy. ♦ **rondelle** *nf* (*tranche*) slice; (*disque*) disc; *[boulon]* washer. ♦ **rondement** *adv* (*efficacement*) briskly; (*franchement*) frankly. ♦ **rondeur** *nf* **(a)** *[forme]* (*gén*) roundness; *[bras, visage]* plumpness, chubbiness. (*hum*) **les** ~**s d'une femme** (*formes*) a woman's curves; (*embonpoint*) a woman's plumpness. **(b)** (*bonhomie*) friendly straightforwardness, easygoing directness. ♦ **rondin** *nm* log. ♦ **rondouillard, e*** *adj* (*péj*) tubby, podgy, pudgy (*US*). ♦ **rond-point,** *pl* ~**s-**~**s** *nm* (*carrefour*) roundabout, traffic circle (*US*).

ronéoter [ʀɔneɔte] (1) *vt* to duplicate, roneo.

ronfler [ʀɔ̃fle] (1) *vi* **(a)** *[dormeur]* to snore; *[toupie]* to hum; *[poêle]* (*sourdement*) to hum; (*fort*) to roar; *[moteur]* (*sourdement*) to purr, throb; (*fort*) to roar. **faire** ~ **son moteur** to rev up one's engine. **(b)** (*: *dormir*) to snore away. ♦ **ronflant, e** *adj* (*péj*) *promesse* high-flown; *titre* pompous, grand(-sounding). ♦ **ronflement** *nm*: ~**(s)** snore(s); hum; roar; purr, throb. ♦ **ronfleur, -euse** *nm,f* snorer.

ronger [ʀɔ̃ʒe] (3) **1** *vi [souris, chagrin]* to gnaw *ou* eat away at; *[acide, vers]* to eat into; *[mer]* to wear away, eat into. ~ **un os** to gnaw (at) a bone; **rongé par les vers** worm-eaten; **rongé par la rouille** rust-eaten; (*lit, fig*) ~ **son frein** to champ (at) the bit; **rongé par la maladie** sapped by illness. **2 se** ~ *vpr*: **se** ~ **les ongles** to bite one's nails; **se** ~ **les sangs** to worry o.s., eat one's heart out. ♦ **rongeur, -euse** *adj, nm* rodent.

ronronner [ʀɔ̃ʀɔne] (1) *vi [chat]* to purr; *[moteur]* to purr, hum. ♦ **ronronnement** *nm*: ~**(s)** purr; hum.

roquet [ʀɔkɛ] *nm* (*péj*) (nasty little) dog.

roquette [ʀɔkɛt] *nf* (*Mil*) rocket.

rosace [ʀozas] *nf [cathédrale]* rose window; *[plafond]* (ceiling) rose; (*Géom*) rosette.

rosaire [ʀozɛʀ] *nm* rosary.

rosbif [ʀɔsbif] *nm*: **du** ~ (*rôti*) roast beef; (*à rôtir*) roasting beef; **un** ~ a joint of (roast) beef.

rose [ʀoz] **1** *nf* (*fleur*) rose; (*vitrail*) rose window; (*diamant*) rose diamond. **pas de** ~**s sans épines** no rose without a thorn; ~ **de Noël** Christmas rose; ~ **pompon** button rose; ~ **des sables** gypsum flower; ~ **trémière** hollyhock; ~ **des vents** compass card. **2** *nm* (*couleur*) pink. **3** *adj* (*gén*) pink; (*plein de santé*) rosy. ~ **bonbon** candy-pink; **tout n'est pas** ~ it's not all roses *ou* all rosy, it's not a bed of roses; **voir la vie en** ~ to see everything through rose-coloured spectacles.

rosé, e¹ [ʀoze] **1** *adj couleur* pinkish; *vin* rosé. **2** *nm* rosé (wine).

roseau, *pl* ~**x** [ʀozo] *nm* reed.

rosée² [ʀoze] *nf* dew.

roseraie [ʀozʀɛ] *nf* rose garden.

rosette [ʀozɛt] *nf* (*nœud*) bow; (*insigne, Archit, Bot*) rosette.

rosier [ʀozje] *nm* rosebush, rose tree. ~ **nain/grimpant** dwarf/climbing rose.

rosir [ʀoziʀ] (2) *vti* to turn pink.

rosse [ʀɔs] **1** *nf* **(a)** († *péj: cheval*) nag. **(b)** (**péj*) (*homme*) beast*, swine‡; (*femme*) beast*, bitch‡. **2** *adj* (*péj*) horrid, nasty, rotten*. ♦ **rosserie** *nf* nastiness; (*propos*) nasty remark; (*acte*) nasty trick.

rosser [ʀɔse] (1) *vt* to thrash. **se faire** ~ to get a (good) hiding *ou* a thrashing.

rossignol [ʀɔsiɲɔl] *nm* **(a)** (*Orn*) nightingale. **(b)** (*: *invendu*) unsaleable article. **(c)** (*clef*) picklock.

rot [ʀo] *nm* belch, burp*; *[bébé]* burp.

rotation [ʀɔtɑsjɔ̃] *nf* **(a)** (*mouvement*) rotation. **mouvement de** ~ rotating *ou* rotary movement. **(b)** *[matériel]* turnover; *[avions, bateaux]* frequency (of service); *[cultures, équipes de travail]* rotation. **par** ~ in rotation. ♦ **rotatif, -ive 1** *adj* rotary. **2** *nf* rotary press. ♦ **rotatoire** *adj* rotary.

roter* [ʀɔte] (1) *vi* to burp*, belch.

rotin [ʀɔtɛ̃] *nm* rattan (cane). **chaise de** ~ cane chair.

rôtir [ʀotiʀ] (2) **1** *vt* (*Culin: aussi* **faire** ~) to roast. **agneau rôti** roast lamb. **2** *vi* (*lit, fig*) to roast. **3 se** ~ *vpr*: **se** ~ **au soleil** to bask in the sun. ♦ **rôti** *nm*: **du** ~ roasting meat; (*cuit*) roast meat; **un** ~ a joint. ♦ **rôtisserie** *nf* (*restaurant*) steakhouse, grill and griddle; (*boutique*) shop selling roast meat. ♦ **rôtisseur, -euse** *nm,f* seller of roast meat; steakhouse proprietor. ♦ **rôtissoire** *nf* (roasting) spit.

rotonde [ʀɔtɔ̃d] *nf* (*Archit*) rotunda.

rotor [ʀɔtɔʀ] *nm* rotor.

rotule [ʀɔtyl] *nf* (*Anat*) kneecap. **être sur les** ~**s*** to be dead beat* *ou* all in.

rouage [ʀwaʒ] *nm [engrenage]* cog(wheel), gearwheel; *[montre]* part; (*fig*) cog. **les** ~**s** *[montre]* the works *ou* parts; *[organisme]* the workings; **les** ~**s de l'État** the wheels of State.

roublard, e* [ʀublaʀ, aʀd(ə)] *adj* crafty, wily, artful.

roucouler [ʀukule] (1) **1** *vi [oiseau]* to coo; *[amoureux]* to bill and coo; *[chanteur]* to warble. **2** *vt* (*péj*) *chanson* to warble; *mots d'amour* to coo.

♦ **roucoulade** *nf ou* ♦ **roucoulement** *nm*: **~(s)** cooing, warbling.
roue [ʀu] *nf (gén)* wheel; *[engrenage]* cog(wheel), (gear)wheel. **~ à aubes** paddle wheel; **~ de secours** spare wheel; **véhicule à deux ~s** two-wheeled vehicle; **faire la ~** *[paon]* to spread *ou* fan its tail; *[personne] (se pavaner)* to strut about; *(Gymnastique)* to do a cartwheel; **faire ~ libre** to freewheel.
roué, e [ʀwe] *adj* cunning, wily, sly.
rouer [ʀwe] (1) *vt* **(a) ~ qn de coups** to give sb a beating *ou* thrashing. **(b)** *(supplice)* to put on the wheel.
rouerie [ʀuʀi] *nf* cunning, wiliness, slyness; *(tour)* cunning *ou* wily *ou* sly trick.
rouet [ʀwɛ] *nm (à filer)* spinning wheel.
rouflaquettes* [ʀuflakɛt] *nfpl* sideburns.
rouge [ʀuʒ] **1** *adj (gén)* red; *(porté à l'incandescence) fer* red-hot. **~ de colère/honte** red *ou* flushed with anger/shame; **devenir ~ comme une cerise** to blush, go red in the face; **il est ~ comme une pivoine** he's as red as a beetroot *ou* a lobster. **2** *nm (couleur)* red; *(vin)* red wine; *(fard)* rouge. **~ à lèvres** lipstick; *(Pol)* **voter ~** to vote Communist; *(Aut)* **le feu est au ~** the lights are red; **le ~ lui monta aux joues** his cheeks flushed, he blushed, he went red in the face; **fer porté au ~** red-hot iron. **3** *nmf (péj: communiste)* Red* *(péj)*, Commie* *(péj)*. ♦ **rougeâtre** *adj* reddish. ♦ **rougeaud, e** *adj* red-faced. ♦ **rouge-gorge,** *pl* **~s-~s** *nm* robin (redbreast).
rougeole [ʀuʒɔl] *nf*: **la ~** (the) measles *(sg)*; **une ~** a bout of measles.
rougeoyer [ʀuʒwaje] (8) *vi [feu]* to glow red; *[ciel]* to turn red. ♦ **rougeoiement** *nm* red *ou* reddish glow. ♦ **rougeoyant, e** *adj ciel* reddening; *cendres* glowing.
rouget [ʀuʒɛ] *nm*: **~ (barbet)** red mullet; **~ (grondin)** gurnard.
rougeur [ʀuʒœʀ] *nf (teinte)* redness; *(Méd: tache)* red blotch *ou* patch; *[visage]* redness. **sa ~ a trahi sa gêne** her red face *ou* her blushes betrayed her embarrassment.
rougir [ʀuʒiʀ] (2) **1** *vi* **(a)** *[personne] (gén)* to go red, redden; *(émotion)* to flush; *(honte)* to blush *(de* with). **~ jusqu'aux oreilles** to go bright red, blush to the roots of one's hair; *(lit, fig)* **faire ~ qn** to make sb blush; **dire qch sans ~** to say sth without blushing *ou* unblushingly. **(b)** *(fig: avoir honte)* **~ de** to be ashamed of. **(c)** *[ciel, tomate, feuille]* to go *ou* turn red, redden; *[métal]* to get red-hot. **2** *vt ciel, feuilles* to turn red; *métal* to make red-hot. ♦ **rougissant, e** *adj visage* blushing; *feuille, ciel* reddening. ♦ **rougissement** *nm (de honte etc)* blush; *(d'émotion)* flush.
rouille [ʀuj] **1** *nf* rust. **2** *adj inv* rust(-coloured), rusty. ♦ **rouillé, e** *adj métal* rusty, rusted; *mémoire, athlète* rusty; *muscles* stiff. **tout ~** rusted over. ♦ **rouiller** (1) **1** *vi* to rust, go *ou* get rusty. **2** *vt métal, esprit* to make rusty. **3 se ~** *vpr [métal]* to go *ou* get rusty, rust; *[athlète, mémoire]* to become rusty; *[muscles]* to get stiff.
roulade [ʀulad] *nf* **(a)** *(Mus)* roulade, run; *[oiseau]* trill. **(b)** *(Culin)* rolled meat. **(c)** *(Sport)* roll.
roulant, e [ʀulɑ̃, ɑ̃t] **1** *adj* **(a)** *meuble* on wheels. *(Rail)* **matériel ~** rolling stock; **personnel ~** train crews. **(b)** (‡: *drôle)* killing*. **2** *nf (arg Mil)* field kitchen.
roulé, e [ʀule] **1** *adj* **(a) être bien ~*** to have a good *ou* shapely figure. **(b)** *bord de chapeau* curved; *bord de foulard, morceau de boucherie* rolled. **2** *nm (gâteau)* Swiss roll; *(pâte)* ≃ turnover; *(viande)* rolled meat. ♦ **roulé-boulé,** *pl* **~s-~s** *nm* roll.
rouleau, *pl* **~x** [ʀulo] *nm (gén, Sport)* roll; *(outil, vague)* roller; *[machine à écrire]* platen, roller; *(pour se coiffer)* curler, roller. **~ compresseur** steamroller, roadroller; **~ à pâtisserie** rolling pin; **~ de papier** roll of paper; **passer une pelouse au ~** to roll a lawn.
roulement [ʀulmɑ̃] *nm* **(a)** *(rotation)* rotation. **travailler par ~** to work on a rota system, work in rotation. **(b) avoir des ~s d'épaules/de hanches** to sway one's shoulders/wiggle one's hips; **faire des ~s d'yeux** to roll one's eyes. **(c)** *(circulation)* movement. **pneu usé par le ~** tyre worn through use. **(d)** *(bruit) [train, camion]* rumble; *[charrette]* rattle. **~ de tonnerre** rumble *ou* peal *ou* roll of thunder; **~ de tambour** drum roll. **(e)** *[capitaux]* circulation. **(f) ~ (à billes)** ball bearings.
rouler [ʀule] (1) **1** *vt* **(a)** *meuble, tonneau* to roll along; *brouette* to wheel along, trundle along. **~ qch dans la farine** to roll sth in flour; **~ des projets dans sa tête** to turn plans over (and over) in one's mind. **(b)** *tapis, manches* to roll up; *cigarette* to roll; *ficelle* to wind up, roll up. **~ qn dans une couverture** to wrap *ou* roll sb (up) in a blanket. **(c)** *(Culin) pâte* to roll out. **(d)** (*: *duper)* to con‡; *(sur le prix, le poids)* to diddle* *(sur* over). **(e)** *épaules* to sway; *hanches* to wiggle; *yeux* to roll. **il a roulé sa bosse** he has knocked about the world*; *(Ling)* **~ les 'r'** to roll one's r's.
2 *vi* **(a)** *[voiture, train]* to go, run; *[conducteur]* to drive. **cette voiture a très peu roulé** this car has a very low mileage; **les voitures ne roulent pas bien sur le sable** cars don't run well on sand; **le véhicule roulait à gauche** the vehicle was driving (along) on the left; **~ au pas** *(prudence)* to go dead slow; *(dans un embouteillage)* to crawl along; **~ à 80 km à l'heure** to do 80 km per hour, drive at 80 km per hour; **on a bien roulé*** we kept up a good speed; **ça roule bien** the traffic is flowing well; **il roule en Rolls** he drives around in a Rolls. **(b)** *[bille, dé]* to roll. **une larme roula sur sa joue** a tear rolled down his cheek; **un coup de poing l'envoya ~ dans la poussière** a punch sent him rolling in the dust; **faire ~** *boule* to roll; *cerceau* to roll along. **(c)** *[bateau]* to roll. **(d)** *[tambour]* to roll; *[tonnerre]* to roll, rumble, peal. **(e)** *(fig) [aventurier]* to knock about, drift around. *[conversation]* **~ sur** to turn on, be centred on; **~ sur l'or** to be rolling in money*, have pots of money*.
3 se ~ *vpr*: **se ~ par terre** to roll on the ground; *(fig)* to fall about* (laughing); **se ~ dans une couverture** to roll *ou* wrap o.s. up in a blanket; **se ~ en boule** to roll o.s. (up) into a ball.
roulette [ʀulɛt] *nf* **(a)** *[meuble]* castor. **ça a été comme sur des ~s*** it went very smoothly. **(b) ~ de dentiste** dentist's drill. **(c)** *(jeu)* roulette; *(instrument)* roulette wheel. **~ russe** Russian roulette.
roulis [ʀuli] *nm* roll(ing). **il y a du ~** the ship is rolling a lot.
roulotte [ʀulɔt] *nf* caravan, trailer *(US)*.
Roumanie [ʀumani] *nf* Rumania, Romania. ♦ **roumain, e** *adj, nm,* **R~(e)** *nm(f)* Rumanian, Romanian.
roupie [ʀupi] *nf (Fin)* rupee.
roupiller* [ʀupije] (1) *vi (dormir)* to sleep; *(faire un somme)* to have a snooze *ou* a kip‡; *(fig)* to doze, be half asleep. **je vais ~** I'll be turning in*. ♦ **roupillon*** *nm* snooze, kip‡.
rouquin, e* [ʀukɛ̃, in] **1** *adj personne* red-haired; *cheveux* red, carroty*. **2** *nm,f* redhead.
rouspéter* [ʀuspete] (6) *vi* to grouse*, grouch* *(après* at). ♦ **rouspétance*** *nf* grousing*, grouching*. ♦ **rouspéteur, -euse*** **1** *adj* grumpy. **2** *nm,f* grouser*, grouch*.
roussir [ʀusiʀ] (2) **1** *vt [fer à repasser]* to scorch, singe; *[flamme]* to singe. *[chaleur]* **~ l'herbe** to scorch the grass. **2** *vi* **(a)** *[feuilles]* to turn brown *ou* russet. **(b)** *(Culin)* **faire ~** to brown. ♦ **rousse** *adj f V* **roux.** ♦ **rousseur** *nf [cheveux]* redness; *[feuilles]* russet colour. *(sur la peau)* **~s** brownish

marks. ♦ **roussi** *nm*: **ça sent le** ~! (*lit*) there's a smell of burning; (*fig**) I can smell trouble.

route [ʀut] *nf* **(a)** road. ~ **nationale/départementale** ≃ trunk *ou* main/secondary road; **faire de la** ~ to do a lot of mileage; **accidents de la** ~ road accidents. **(b)** (*chemin à suivre*) way; (*Naut: cap*) course. **montrer la** ~ **à qn** to show the way to sb; **la** ~ **sera longue** (*gén*) it'll be a long journey; (*en voiture*) it'll be a long drive; **ce n'est pas ma** ~ it's not on my way. **(c)** (*ligne de communication*) route. ~ **aérienne/maritime** air/sea route; **la** ~ **de l'opium** the opium route *ou* trail. **(d)** (*fig*) path, road, way. **être sur la bonne** ~ (*dans la vie*) to be on the right road *ou* path; (*dans un problème*) to be on the right track. **(e)** (*locutions*) **faire** ~ **vers** (*gén*) to head towards *ou* for; *[bateau]* **en** ~ **pour** bound for; **faire** ~ **avec qn** to travel with sb; **prendre la** ~, **se mettre en** ~ to set off *ou* out; **en** ~ on the way; **en** ~! let's go!, let's be off!; **bonne** ~! have a good journey! *ou* trip!; **mettre en** ~ *moteur* to start (up); *affaire* to set in motion, get under way; **mise en** ~ starting up; setting in motion; **carnet de** ~ travel diary; **tenir bien la** ~ to hold the road well. ♦ **routier, -ière 1** *adj* road. **2** *nm* (*camionneur*) long-distance lorry *ou* truck (*US*) driver; (*restaurant*) ≃ transport café.

routine [ʀutin] *nf* routine. **visite de** ~ routine visit. ♦ **routinier, -ière** *adj travail, vie* humdrum, routine; *personne* routine-minded.

rouvrir *vti*, **se** ~ *vpr* [ʀuvʀiʀ] (18) to reopen, open again.

roux, rousse [ʀu, ʀus] **1** *adj personne* red-haired; *cheveux* red, auburn; (*orangé*) ginger; *pelage, feuilles* russet, reddish-brown. **2** *nm* **(a)** (*couleur*) red, auburn; ginger; russet, reddish-brown. **(b)** (*Culin*) roux. **3** *nm,f* redhead.

royal, e, *mpl* **-aux** [ʀwajal, o] *adj* (*lit*) royal; *magnificence* kingly, regal; *repas, cadeau* fit for a king; *salaire* princely; *mépris* majestic, regal; *paix* blissful. ♦ **royalement** *adv vivre, traiter* royally. **il s'en moque** ~* he couldn't care less*; (*iro*) **il m'a** ~ **offert 3 F d'augmentation*** he offered me a princely 3-franc rise (*iro*). ♦ **royaliste** *adj, nmf* royalist. ♦ **royaume** *nm* (*lit*) kingdom, realm; (*fig*) realm. **le R~-Uni** the United Kingdom. ♦ **royauté** *nf* (*régime*) monarchy; (*fonction, dignité*) kingship.

ruade [ʀyad] *nf* kick (*of a horse's hind legs*). **lancer une** ~ to lash *ou* kick out.

ruban [ʀybɑ̃] *nm* (*gén, fig*) ribbon; *[téléscripteur]* tape; *[ourlet]* binding, tape. ~ **d'acier** steel band *ou* strip; ~ **adhésif** adhesive tape, sticky tape; ~ **de chapeau** hat band.

rubéole [ʀybeɔl] *nf* German measles (*sg*), rubella.

rubis [ʀybi] **1** *nm* (*pierre, couleur*) ruby; *[montre]* jewel. **2** *adj inv* ruby(-coloured).

rubrique [ʀybʀik] *nf* (*article*) column; (*titre, catégorie*) heading, rubric.

ruche [ʀyʃ] *nf* (*lit, fig*) (bee)hive.

rude [ʀyd] *adj* **(a)** (*au toucher*) rough; (*à l'ouïe*) harsh. **(b)** *métier, climat, adversaire* tough; *montée* stiff. **être mis à** ~ **épreuve** *[personne]* to be put through the mill; *[tissu]* to get rough treatment; **il a été à** ~ **école** he learned life the hard way; **en faire voir de** ~**s à qn** to give sb a hard *ou* tough time. **(c)** (*fruste*) *manières* unpolished, crude; *traits* rugged; *montagnards* rugged, tough. **(d)** (*bourru*) *personne* harsh, hard; *manières* rough. **(e)** (*intensif*) *gaillard, appétit* hearty; *peur, coup* real. ♦ **rudement** *adv* **(a)** *frapper* hard; *répondre* harshly; *traiter* roughly, harshly. **(b)** (*) *content, mauvais, cher* terribly*, awfully*; *travailler* terribly *ou* awfully hard*. ~ **bien** terribly *ou* awfully well*; **ça change** ~ it's a real change; **il est** ~ **plus généreux** he's a great deal *ou* darned sight* more generous; **j'ai eu** ~ **peur** I had a dreadful *ou* an awful fright.

♦ **rudesse** *nf* roughness; harshness; toughness; crudeness; ruggedness.

rudiments [ʀydimɑ̃] *nmpl [discipline]* rudiments; *[théorie]* principles. **avoir quelques** ~ **d'anglais** to have a smattering of English *ou* some basic knowledge of English. ♦ **rudimentaire** *adj* rudimentary.

rudoyer [ʀydwaje] (8) *vt* to treat harshly.

rue [ʀy] *nf* street. (*péj: populace*) **la** ~ the mob; ~ **à sens unique** one-way street; **être à la** ~ to be out on the street.

ruée [ʀɥe] *nf* rush; (*péj*) stampede, (mad) scramble. **la** ~ **vers l'or** the gold rush.

ruelle [ʀɥɛl] *nf* (*rue*) alley(-way).

ruer [ʀɥe] (1) **1** *vi [cheval]* to kick (out). (*fig*) ~ **dans les brancards** to rebel. **2 se** ~ *vpr*: **se** ~ **sur** to pounce on; **se** ~ **vers/dans** to dash *ou* rush towards/into; **se** ~ **à l'assaut** to hurl *ou* fling o.s. into the attack.

rugby [ʀygbi] *nm* Rugby (football), rugger*. ~ **à quinze** Rugby Union; ~ **à treize** Rugby League. ♦ **rugbyman,** *pl* **rugbymen** *nm* rugby player.

rugir [ʀyʒiʀ[(2) **1** *vi* (*gén*) to roar (*de* with); *[vent]* to howl, roar. **2** *vt* to roar out. ♦ **rugissement** *nm* roar; howl.

rugueux, -euse [ʀygø, øz] *adj* (*gén*) rough; (*grossier*) coarse; *sol* rugged, bumpy. ♦ **rugosité** *nf* roughness; coarseness; ruggedness, bumpiness; (*aspérité*) rough patch, bump.

ruine [ʀɥin] *nf* (*lit, fig*) ruin. (*péj*) ~ **(humaine)** (human) wreck; **en** ~ in ruins, ruined; **c'est la** ~ **de tous mes espoirs** that puts paid to *ou* that means the ruin of all my hopes; **menacer** ~ to be threatening to collapse; **tomber en** ~ to fall in ruins; (*financièrement*) **cette voiture est une vraie** ~ that car will ruin me. ♦ **ruiner** (1) **1** *vt* (*lit, fig*) to ruin. **ça ne va pas te** ~!* it won't break* *ou* ruin you! **2 se** ~ *vpr* to ruin *ou* bankrupt o.s.; (*fig: dépenser trop*) to spend a fortune. ♦ **ruineux, -euse** *adj goût* ruinously expensive; *dépense* ruinous.

ruisseau, *pl* ~**x** [ʀɥiso] *nm* (*cours d'eau*) stream, brook; (*lit, fig: caniveau*) gutter. **des** ~**x de** *larmes* floods of; *lave, sang* streams of.

ruisseler [ʀɥisle] (4) *vi [liquide]* to flow, stream; *[mur]* to run with water, stream (with water). ~ **de** *eau, lumière etc* to stream with. ♦ **ruissellement** *nm*: **le** ~ **de la pluie sur le mur** the rain streaming *ou* running *ou* flowing down the wall; ~ **de lumière** stream of light.

rumeur [ʀymœʀ] *nf* **(a)** (*nouvelle imprécise*) rumour. **selon certaines** ~**s, elle ...** rumour has it that she ..., it is rumoured that she ... . **(b)** *[vagues, vent]* murmur, murmuring; *[rue, conversation]* hum; *[émeute]* hubbub. **(c)** (*protestation*) rumblings. ~ **de mécontentement** rumblings of discontent.

ruminer [ʀymine] (1) **1** *vt* (*Zool*) to ruminate; *projet* to ruminate *ou* chew over; *chagrin* to brood over; *vengeance* to ponder, meditate. **2** *vi* (*Zool*) to ruminate, chew the cud. ♦ **ruminant** *nm* ruminant. ♦ **rumination** *nf* rumination.

rumsteck [ʀɔmstɛk] *nm* = **romsteck.**

rupin, e‡ [ʀypɛ̃, in] *adj quartier* ritzy‡, plush(y)*; *personne* stinking *ou* filthy rich‡.

rupture [ʀyptyʀ] *nf* **(a)** (*annulation*) *[contrat]* breach (*de* of); *[relations diplomatiques]* severance, rupture (*de* of); *[pourparlers]* breakdown (*de* of, in). (*action*) **la** ~ **des pourparlers entre les 2 pays** the breaking off of talks between the 2 countries. **(b)** (*séparation amoureuse*) break-up, split. **(c)** *[câble, poutre]* breaking; *[digue]* bursting; *[organe]* rupture; *[tendon]* tearing. **limite de** ~ breaking point; ~ **entre le passé et le présent** break between the past and the present; ~ **de rythme** (sudden) break in (the) rhythm; ~ **d'équilibre** (*lit*) loss of balance; (*fig*) upsetting of the balance; ~ **d'essieu** broken axle.

rural, e, *mpl* **-aux** [ʀyʀal, o] **1** *adj* country, rural. **2** *nm,f* country person.
ruse [ʀyz] *nf* **(a)** **la ~** (*pour gagner*) cunning, craftiness, slyness; (*pour tromper*) trickery, guile. **(b)** (*subterfuge*) trick, ruse. (*lit, fig*) **~ de guerre** stratagem, tactics. ♦ **rusé, e** *adj personne* cunning, crafty, sly. ♦ **ruser** (1) *vi* to use cunning; to use trickery.
russe [ʀys] *adj, nm,* **R~** *nmf* Russian. ♦ **Russie** *nf* Russia.
rustaud, e [ʀysto, od] **1** *adj* coarse. **2** *nm,f* country bumpkin, yokel.
rustine [ʀystin] *nf* ® rubber repair, patch (*for bicycle tyre*).
rustique [ʀystik] **1** *adj* (*gén*) rustic; *vie* country; (*Agr*) hardy. **2** *nm* (*style*) rustic style.
rustre [ʀystʀ(ə)] **1** *nm* lout, boor. **2** *adj* boorish.
rut [ʀyt] *nm [mâle]* rut; *[femelle]* heat; (*période*) rutting *ou* heat period. **être en ~** to be rutting; to be in *ou* on heat.
rutabaga [ʀytabaga] *nm* swede, rutabaga (*US*).
rutiler [ʀytile] (1) *vi* to gleam, shine brightly. ♦ **rutilant, e** *adj* brightly shining, gleaming. ♦ **rutilement** *nm* gleam.
rythme [ʀitm(ə)] *nm* **(a)** (*Art, fig: cadence*) rhythm. (*Mus*) **au ~ de** to the beat *ou* rhythm of; (*Théât*) **pièce qui manque de ~** play which lacks tempo, slow-moving play. **(b)** (*vitesse*) (*gén*) rate; *[vie, travail]* tempo, pace. **~ cardiaque** (rate of) heartbeat; **à ce ~-là** at that rate; **suivre le ~** to keep up (the pace); **au ~ de 1 000 par jour** at the rate of 1,000 a *ou* per day. ♦ **rythmé, e** *adj* rhythmic(al). ♦ **rythmer** (1) *vt* to give rhythm to, punctuate. ♦ **rythmique** **1** *adj* rhythmic(al). **danse ~** rhythmics (*sg*). **2** *nf* rhythmics (*sg*).

S

S, s [ɛs] *nm* (*lettre*) S, s. **en s** *route* zigzagging, winding; *barre* S-shaped.
s' [s] *V* **se, si**[1].
sa [sa] *adj poss V* **son**[1].
sabbat [saba] *nm* (*Rel*) Sabbath; (*: *bruit*) racket, row*.
sable [sɑbl(ə)] **1** *nm* sand. **de ~** *dune, vent* sand; *plage* sandy; **~s mouvants** quicksands. **2** *adj inv* sandy, sand-coloured. ♦ **sablage** *nm [allée]* sanding; *[façade]* sandblasting. ♦ **sablé** *nm* shortbread biscuit *ou* cookie (*US*). ♦ **sabler** (1) *vt* **(a)** *route* to sand; *façade* to sandblast. **(b) ~ le champagne** to drink *ou* have champagne. ♦ **sableux, -euse** *ou* ♦ **sablonneux, -euse** *adj* sandy. ♦ **sablier** *nm* (*gén*) hourglass, sandglass; (*Culin*) egg timer. ♦ **sablière** *nf* (*carrière*) sand quarry.
sabord [sabɔʀ] *nm* scuttle (*Naut*). ♦ **sabordage** *nm* (*Naut*) scuttling; (*fig*) winding up, shutting down. ♦ **saborder** (1) **1** *vt navire, projet* to scuttle; *entreprise* to wind up, shut down. **2 se ~** *vpr* (*Naut*) to scuttle one's ship; (*fig*) to wind up, shut down.
sabot [sabo] *nm* (*chaussure*) clog; (*Zool*) hoof; (*péj: machine*) useless heap*. **il travaille comme un ~** he's a hopeless worker; **~ de frein** brake shoe; **~ de Denver** Denver shoe.
saboter [sabɔte] (1) *vt* **(a)** (*Mil, Pol, fig*) to sabotage. **(b)** (*bâcler*) to make a (proper) mess of, botch; (*abîmer*) to mess up, ruin. ♦ **sabotage** *nm* **(a)** (*Mil, Pol, fig*) sabotage; (*acte*) act of sabotage. **(b)** (*bâclage*) botching. ♦ **saboteur, -euse** *nm,f* (*Mil, Pol*) saboteur; (*bâcleur*) shoddy worker, botcher.
sabre [sɑbʀ(ə)] *nm* sabre. **~ d'abordage** cutlass; **mettre ~ au clair** to draw one's sword. ♦ **sabrer** (1) *vt* (*Mil*) to sabre, cut down; (*: *recaler à l'examen*) to plough*; (*: *critiquer*) to tear to pieces; (*: *biffer*) to score out. **cette nouvelle m'a sabré (le moral)** I was really shattered by the news*.
sac [sak] **1** *nm* **(a)** (*gén*) bag; (*de grande taille, en toile*) sack; (*cartable*) (school) bag; (*à bretelles*) satchel. **(b)** (*contenu*) bag, bagful; sack, sackful. **(c)** (ᵻ: *argent*) ten francs. **(d)** *[ville]* sack(ing). **mettre à ~** *ville* to sack; *maison* to ransack. **(e)** (*locutions*) **mettre dans le même ~*** to lump together; **l'affaire est dans le ~*** it's in the bag*. **2: ~ de couchage** sleeping bag; **~ à dos** rucksack, knapsack; **~ à main** handbag; **~ à provisions** shopping bag; (*en papier*) (paper) carrier; **~ de voyage** overnight *ou* travelling bag.
saccade [sakad] *nf* jerk. **par ~s** in fits and starts, jerkily. ♦ **saccadé, e** *adj gestes, style* jerky; *respiration* spasmodic, halting; *bruit* staccato; *sommeil* fitful.
saccager [sakaʒe] (3) *vt* **(a)** (*dévaster*) *pièce* to turn upside down; *jardin* to create havoc in, wreck. **saccagé par la grêle** devastated by the hail. **(b)** (*piller*) *ville* to sack, lay waste; *maison* to ransack. ♦ **saccage** *nm* havoc (*de* in).
saccharine [sakaʀin] *nf* saccharin(e).
sacerdoce [sasɛʀdɔs] *nm* (*Rel*) priesthood; (*fig*) calling, vocation. ♦ **sacerdotal, e, *mpl* -aux** *adj* priestly, sacerdotal.
sachet [saʃɛ] *nm [bonbons]* bag; *[poudre]* sachet. **~ de thé** tea bag.
sacoche [sakɔʃ] *nf* (*gén*) bag; (*pour outils*) toolbag; *[cycliste]* (*de selle*) saddlebag; (*de porte-bagages*) pannier; *[écolier]* (school)bag; (*à bretelles*) satchel.
sacquer* [sake] (1) *vt* **(a)** *employé* to give the sack* *ou* pushᵻ to. **se faire ~** to get the sack*, get fired*. **(b)** *élève* (*mauvaise note*) to give a lousy mark toᵻ; (*recaler*) to plough*, fail.
sacrer [sakʀe] (1) **1** *vt roi* to crown; *évêque* to consecrate. **2** *vi* (*†) to curse, swear. ♦ **sacraliser** (1) *vt* to regard as sacred. ♦ **sacre** *nm [roi]* coronation; *[évêque]* consecration. ♦ **sacré, e** **1** *adj* **(a)** (*Rel*) sacred, holy; *art, droit, repas* sacred; *terreur* holy. **(b)** (*) (*maudit*) blasted*, confounded*, damnedᵻ. (*considérable*) **c'est un ~ menteur** he's one heck* *ou* hellᵻ of a liar; **ce ~ Paul a encore gagné** that devil Paul has gone and won again*. **2** *nm*: **le ~** the sacred. ♦ **sacrement** *nm* sacrament. ♦ **sacrément*** *adv froid etc* fearfully, damnedᵻ. **ça m'a ~ plu** I liked it ever so much*.
sacrifice [sakʀifis] *nm* (*Rel, fig*) sacrifice. **faire le ~ de sa vie** to sacrifice one's life. ♦ **sacrifier** (7) **1** *vt* (*gén*) to sacrifice (*à* to, *pour* for); (*Comm*) *marchandises* to give away (at a knockdown price). **2 ~ à** *vt indir mode* to conform to. **3 se ~** *vpr* to sacrifice o.s.
sacrilège [sakʀilɛʒ] **1** *adj* (*Rel, fig*) sacrilegious. **2** *nm* sacrilege. **3** *nmf* sacrilegious person.
sacripant [sakʀipɑ̃] *nm* (†, *hum*) rogue, scoundrel.
sacristie [sakʀisti] *nf* (*catholique*) sacristy; (*protestante*) vestry. ♦ **sacristain** *nm [sacristie]* sacristan; *[église]* sexton.
sacro-saint, e [sakʀɔsɛ̃, ɛ̃t] *adj* (*lit, iro*) sacrosanct.
sacrum [sakʀɔm] *nm* sacrum.
sadique [sadik] **1** *adj* sadistic. **2** *nmf* sadist. ♦ **sadiquement** *adv* sadistically. ♦ **sadisme** *nm* sadism.
safari [safaʀi] *nm* safari. **faire un ~** to go on safari; **~-photo** photographic safari.
safran [safʀɑ̃] *nm, adj inv* saffron.
sagace [sagas] *adj* (*littér*) sagacious, shrewd. ♦ **sagacité** *nf* sagacity, shrewdness.
sagaie [sagɛ] *nf* assegai.
sage [saʒ] **1** *adj* (*avisé*) wise, sensible; (*chaste*) good, proper; (*docile*) good, well-behaved; (*modéré*) *goûts etc* sober, moderate. **~ comme une image** (as) good as gold. **2** *nm* wise man; (*Antiq*) sage. ♦ **sage-femme, *pl* ~s-~s** *nf* midwife. ♦ **sagement** *adv* wisely, sensibly; properly; moderately. **il est resté ~ assis** he sat quietly, he sat like a good child *ou* boy. ♦ **sagesse** *nf* wisdom, (good) sense; properness; good behaviour; moderation.
Sagittaire [saʒitɛʀ] *nm*: **le ~** Sagittarius; **être (du) ~** to be Sagittarius *ou* a Sagittarian.
sagouinᵻ [sagwɛ̃] *nm* (*sale*) dirty *ou* filthy pig*; (*salopard*) swineᵻ, slobᵻ, bastardᵻ.
saigner [seɲe] (1) **1** *vi* to bleed. **il saignait du nez** he had (a) nosebleed, his nose was bleeding. **2** *vt* to bleed. **~ qn à blanc** to bleed sb white. **3 se ~** *vpr*: **se ~ (aux quatre veines) pour qn** to bleed o.s. white for sb. ♦ **saignant, e** *adj plaie* (*lit*) bleeding; (*fig*) raw; *viande* rare, underdone; (ᵻ) *critique,*

mésaventure damned nasty‡. ♦ **saignée** *nf* **(a)** (*Méd*) bleeding. **faire une ~ à qn** to bleed sb, let sb's blood. **(b)** *[budget]* savage cut (*à, dans* in). **les ~s faites par la guerre** the heavy losses incurred by the war. **(c)** (*Anat*) **la ~ du bras** the bend of the arm. **(d)** (*sillon*) *[sol]* trench, ditch; *[mur]* groove. ♦ **saignement** *nm* bleeding. **~ de nez** nosebleed.

saillir [sajiʀ] (2) **1** *vi [corniche]* to jut out, stick out, project; *[menton, veine, muscle]* to protrude; *[pommette]* to be prominent; *[yeux]* to bulge. **2** *vt* (*Zool*) to cover, serve. ♦ **saillant, e** *adj* jutting, projecting; protruding; prominent; bulging; *événement* salient, outstanding. ♦ **saillie** *nf* **(a)** (*aspérité*) projection. **faire ~** to project, jut out. **(b)** (*boutade*) witticism. **(c)** (*Zool*) covering, serving.

sain, saine [sɛ̃, sɛn] *adj* **(a)** *personne* healthy; *constitution, dents* healthy, sound. **~ et sauf** safe and sound. **(b)** *climat, nourriture* healthy, wholesome. **il est ~ de faire** it is good for you *ou* healthy to do. **(c)** *fondations, fruit* sound; *viande* good; *gestion* healthy. **(d)** (*moralement*) *personne* sane; *politique, jugement* sound, sane; *goûts* healthy; *lectures* wholesome. ♦ **sainement** *adv* healthily; soundly; wholesomely; sanely.

saindoux [sɛ̃du] *nm* lard.

saint, e [sɛ̃, sɛ̃t] **1** *adj* **(a)** (*sacré*) holy. **la ~e Famille** the Holy Family; **le vendredi ~** Good Friday; **le jeudi ~** Maundy Thursday; **le mardi ~** Tuesday of Holy Week; **toute la ~e journée*** the whole blessed day*; **avoir une ~e terreur de qch*** to have a holy terror of sth*. **(b)** (*devant prénom*) Saint. (*apôtre*) **~ Pierre** Saint Peter; (*église*) **S~-Pierre** Saint Peter's; (*fête*) **la S~-Pierre** the feast of Saint Peter; (*jour*) **à la S~-Pierre** on Saint Peter's day. **(c)** *personne* saintly, godly; *action* pious, saintly, holy.

2 *nm,f* (*lit, fig*) saint; (*statue*) statue of a saint.

3: ~-bernard *nm inv* (*chien*) St Bernard; (*fig*) good Samaritan; **le S~-Esprit** the Holy Spirit *ou* Ghost; **~-frusquin*** clobber*, gear*; **et tout le ~-frusquin*** and the whole caboodle; **à la ~-glinglin*** never in a month of Sundays*; **jusqu'à la ~-glinglin*** till the cows come home*; (*péj*) **~e nitouche** (pious) hypocrite; **~ patron** patron saint; **S~-Père** Holy Father; **le ~ sacrement** the Blessed Sacrament; **le S~ des S~s** the Holy of Holies; **le S~-Siège** the Holy See; **la S~-Sylvestre** New Year's Eve; **la S~e Vierge** the Blessed Virgin.

♦ **saintement** *adv* like a saint. ♦ **sainteté** *nf [personne]* saintliness; *[Évangile, Vierge]* holiness; *[lieu, mariage]* sanctity. **Sa S~ (le pape)** His Holiness (the Pope).

saisir [seziʀ] (2) **1** *vt* **(a)** (*prendre*) to take hold of, catch hold of; (*s'emparer de*) to seize, grab (hold of); *prétexte* to seize. **~ qn à la gorge** to grab *ou* seize sb by the throat; **~ une occasion au vol** to jump at the opportunity. **(b)** *mot, nom* to catch, get*; *explications* to grasp, understand, get*. **(c)** *[sentiment]* to take hold of, seize, grip; *[malaise]* to come over. (*surprendre*) **~ qn** to bring sb up with a start; **saisi de joie** overcome with joy; **saisi de panique** seized with panic, panic-stricken; **être saisi par** *horreur* to be gripped by; *ressemblance, froid* to be struck by; **elle fut tellement saisie que ...** she was so overcome that ... . **(d)** (*Jur*) *personne, chose* to seize; *juridiction* to submit *ou* refer to. **(e)** (*Culin*) to fry briskly. **2 se ~** *vpr*: **se ~ de qch/qn** to seize *ou* grab sth/sb. ♦ **saisie** *nf [biens, journal]* seizure. **~-arrêt** distraint. ♦ **saisissant, e** *adj spectacle* gripping; *ressemblance* startling, striking. ♦ **saisissement** *nm* (*froid*) sudden chill; (*émotion*) (rush of) emotion; (*surprise*) surprise.

saison [sɛzɔ̃] *nf* season; (*cure*) cure. **la belle ~** the summer months; **en cette ~** at this time of year; **en toutes ~s** all (the) year round; **temps de ~** seasonable weather; **la ~ des pluies** the rainy *ou* wet season; (*Tourisme*) **haute/basse ~** high/low *ou* off-season; **hors ~** *plante* out of season. ♦ **saisonnier, -ière 1** *adj* seasonal. **2** *nm,f* seasonal worker.

salade [salad] *nf* **(a)** (*laitue*) lettuce; (*scarole*) endive; (*plat*) green salad. **~ de tomates** *etc* tomato *etc* salad; **~ niçoise** salade niçoise; **haricots en ~** bean salad. **(b)** (**fig*) (*confusion*) tangle, muddle. (*mensonges*) **~s** stories*. ♦ **saladier** *nm* salad bowl.

salaire [salɛʀ] *nm* **(a)** wage(s), salary, pay. **(b)** (*fig: récompense, châtiment*) reward (*de* for).

salaison [salɛzɔ̃] *nf* (*procédé*) salting; (*aliment*) salt meat (*ou* fish).

salamandre [salamɑ̃dʀ(ə)] *nf* (*Zool*) salamander; (*poêle*) slow-combustion stove.

salami [salami] *nm* salami.

salarié, e [salaʀje] **1** *adj travailleur* salaried, wage-earning; *travail* paid. **2** *nm,f* salaried employee, wage-earner.

salaud‡ [salo] *nm* bastard, swine‡.

sale [sal] *adj* **(a)** (*crasseux*) dirty. **~ comme un cochon** filthy (dirty). **(b)** (*ordurier*) dirty, filthy. **(c)** (*: *avant n: mauvais*) (*gén*) nasty; *temps, caractère* rotten*, foul, lousy*. **~ tour** dirty trick; **faire une ~ tête*** to be damned annoyed‡.

salé, e [sale] **1** *adj* **(a)** *saveur, mer* salty; *amande, plat, beurre* salted; (*conservé au sel*) *poisson, viande* salt. **(b)** (*: *grivois*) spicy*, juicy*. **(c)** (*) *punition* stiff*; *facture* steep*. **2** *nm* (*nourriture*) salty food; (*porc salé*) salt pork. **3** *adv*: **manger ~** to like a lot of salt on one's food.

salement [salmɑ̃] *adv* dirtily; (‡: *très*) damned‡. **j'ai eu ~ peur** I had a hell of a fright‡, I was damned scared‡.

saler [sale] (1) *vt* **(a)** (*lit*) to put salt in, salt. **(b)** (*) *client* to do*, fleece; *facture* to bump up*; *inculpé* to be tough on*.

saleté [salte] *nf* **(a)** (*malpropreté*) *[lieu, personne]* dirtiness; (*crasse*) dirt, filth. **il y a une ~ par terre** there's some dirt on the floor; **tu as fait des ~s** *ou* **de la ~ partout** you've made a mess all over the place. **(b)** (*) **de la ~, une ~** (*objet*) rubbish, junk; (*nourriture*) rubbish, muck*; **ce réfrigérateur est une ~** *ou* **de la ~** this fridge is a load of old rubbish*; **acheter une ~** to buy some (old) junk *ou* rubbish *ou* trash. **(c)** (*) (*maladie*) nasty bug*; (*obscénité*) dirty *ou* filthy remark; (*méchanceté*) dirty *ou* filthy trick*; (*salaud*) nasty piece of work*, nasty character.

salière [saljɛʀ] *nf* saltcellar.

saligaud‡ [saligo] *nm* (*malpropre*) dirty *ou* filthy pig*; (*salaud*) swine‡, bastard‡.

salin, e [salɛ̃, in] *adj* saline.

salir [saliʀ] (2) **1** *vt lieu* to (make) dirty, mess up. **~ qn** to soil *ou* tarnish sb's reputation. **2 se ~** *vpr [tissu]* to get dirty *ou* soiled; *[personne]* to get dirty, dirty o.s. (*lit, fig*) **se ~ les mains** to get one's hands dirty, dirty one's hands.

♦ **salissant, e** *adj étoffe* which shows the dirt; *travail* dirty, messy.

salive [saliv] *nf* saliva, spittle. ♦ **saliver** (1) *vi* to salivate.

salle [sal] **1** *nf* **(a)** *[musée, café]* room; *[château]* hall; *[restaurant]* (dining) room; *[hôpital]* ward. **(b)** (*Ciné, Théât*) (*auditorium*) auditorium, theatre; (*public*) audience; (*cinéma*) cinema, movie theater (*US*). **faire ~ comble** to have a full house. **2: ~ d'attente** waiting room; **~ de bain(s)** bathroom; **~ de classe** classroom; **~ de concert** concert hall; **~ d'eau** shower-room; **~ des fêtes** village hall; **~ à manger** (*pièce*) dining room; (*meubles*) dining room suite; **~ d'opération** operating theatre; **~ des professeurs** staff room; **~ de rédaction** (newspaper) office; **~ de séjour** living room; **~ de spectacle** theatre; cinema; **~ des ventes** saleroom, auction room.

salon [salɔ̃] **1** *nm* **(a)** *[maison]* lounge, sitting room; *[hôtel]* lounge; *[navire]* saloon, lounge. **(b)** (*meubles*) lounge *ou* living-room suite. **(c)** (*exposition*) exhibition, show. **(d)** (*cercle littéraire*) salon. **2: S~ de l'Auto** Motor Show; **~ de coiffure** hairdressing salon; **~ de thé** tearoom.
salopard‡ [salɔpaʀ] *nm* bastard‡, swine‡.
salope‡ [salɔp] *nf* (*méchante*) bitch‡; (*dévergondée*) tart‡; (*sale*) slut.
saloper‡ [salɔpe] (1) *vt* (*bâcler*) to botch, bungle; (*salir*) to mess up*, muck up*.
saloperie‡ [salɔpʀi] *nf* **(a) de la ~** (*nourriture*) rubbish, muck*; (*objet*) trash, junk, rubbish; **acheter une ~** to buy some (old) trash *ou* junk *ou* rubbish. **(b)** (*maladie*) nasty bug*; (*action*) dirty trick*; (*obscénité*) dirty *ou* filthy remark. **(c)** (*crasse*) filth. **ça fait de la ~** *ou* **des ~s partout** it makes a mess everywhere.
salopette [salɔpɛt] *nf* (*gén*) dungarees; *[ouvrier]* overall(s).
salpêtre [salpɛtʀ(ə)] *nm* saltpetre.
salsifis [salsifi] *nm* salsify, oyster-plant.
saltimbanque [saltɛ̃bɑ̃k] *nmf* (travelling) acrobat.
salubre [salybʀ(ə)] *adj* healthy, salubrious. ♦ **salubrité** *nf* healthiness, salubrity. **~ publique** public health.
saluer [salɥe] (1) *vt* (*gén, fig*) to greet; (*Mil, Naut*) to salute. (*dire au revoir*) **~ qn** to take one's leave of sb; **~ qn de la main** to wave (one's hand) to sb (in greeting); **~ qn d'un signe de tête** to nod (a greeting) to sb; **saluez-le de ma part** give him my regards; **~ (le public)** to bow to the audience; **'je vous salue, Marie'** 'Hail, Mary'.
salut [saly] **1** *nm* **(a)** (*de la main*) wave (of the hand); (*de la tête*) nod (of the head); (*du buste*) bow; (*Mil, Naut*) salute. **(b)** (*sauvegarde*) safety. **mesures de ~ public** measures for the protection of the public. **(c)** (*Rel: rédemption*) salvation. **2** *excl* **(a)** (*) (*bonjour*) hi (there)!*, hello!; (*au revoir*) see you!*, bye!*. **(b)** (*littér*) **~ (à toi)** (all) hail (to thee).
salutaire [salytɛʀ] *adj* (*gén*) salutary; *air* healthy; *remède* beneficial. **ça m'a été ~** it did me good *ou* was good for me.
salutation [salytɑsjɔ̃] *nf* salutation, greeting. **veuillez agréer, Monsieur, mes ~s distinguées** yours faithfully *ou* truly.
salve [salv(ə)] *nf* salvo.
samedi [samdi] *nm* Saturday. **~ nous irons** on Saturday we'll go; **~ qui vient** this Saturday, next Saturday; **un ~ sur deux** every other *ou* second Saturday; **~, le 18 décembre** Saturday December 18th; **le ~ 23 janvier** on Saturday January 23rd; **~ soir** Saturday evening *ou* night.
sanatorium [sanatɔʀjɔm] *nm* sanatorium, sanitarium (*US*).
sanctifier [sɑ̃ktifje] (7) *vt* to sanctify, hallow. ♦ **sanctification** *nf* sanctification.
sanction [sɑ̃ksjɔ̃] *nf* **(a)** (*condamnation*) sanction, penalty; (*Scol*) punishment; (*fig: conséquence*) penalty (*de* for). **(b)** (*ratification*) sanction, approval. ♦ **sanctionner** (1) *vt* (*punir*) to punish; (*consacrer*) to sanction, approve.
sanctuaire [sɑ̃ktɥɛʀ] *nm* sanctuary.
sandale [sɑ̃dal] *nf* sandal. ♦ **sandalette** *nf* sandal.
sandow [sɑ̃do] *nm* ® (*attache*) luggage elastic; (*Aviat*) catapult.
sandwich [sɑ̃dwitʃ] *nm* sandwich. **(pris) en ~ (entre)*** sandwiched (between).
sang [sɑ̃] *nm* (*lit, fig*) blood. **animal à ~ froid/chaud** cold-blooded/warm-blooded animal; **être en ~** to be bleeding; **du même ~** of the same flesh and blood; **avoir le ~ chaud** to be hot-blooded; **il a le jeu dans le ~** he's got gambling in his blood; **mon ~ n'a fait qu'un tour** (*peur*) my heart missed *ou* skipped a beat; (*colère*) I saw red; **se ronger les ~s** to worry (o.s.), fret. ♦ **sang-froid** *nm inv* sangfroid, self-control. **garder/perdre son ~-~** to keep/lose one's head; **faire qch de ~-~** to do sth in cold blood *ou* cold-bloodedly; **répondre avec ~-~** to reply coolly *ou* calmly. ♦ **sanglant, e** *adj* (*gén*) bloody; *insulte, défaite* savage.
sangle [sɑ̃gl(ə)] *nf* (*gén*) strap; *[selle]* girth. *[siège]* **~s** webbing. ♦ **sangler** (1) *vt cheval* to girth; *colis, corps* to strap up.
sanglier [sɑ̃glije] *nm* (wild) boar.
sanglot [sɑ̃glo] *nm* sob. ♦ **sangloter** (1) *vi* to sob.
sangsue [sɑ̃sy] *nf* (*lit, fig*) leech.
sanguin, e [sɑ̃gɛ̃, in] **1** *adj caractère* fiery, passionate; *visage* ruddy; (*Anat*) blood. **2** *nf* (*Bot*) blood orange; (*dessin*) red pencil drawing.
sanguinaire [sɑ̃ginɛʀ] *adj personne* bloodthirsty; *combat* bloody.
sanguinolent, e [sɑ̃ginɔlɑ̃, ɑ̃t] *adj linge* streaked with blood; *plaie* slightly bleeding.
sanitaire [sanitɛʀ] **1** *adj* **(a)** (*Méd*) *services, mesures* health; *conditions* sanitary. **(b)** (*Plomberie*) **l'installation ~** the bathroom plumbing; **appareil ~** bathroom *ou* sanitary appliance. **2** *nmpl*: **les ~s** (*lieu*) the bathroom; (*appareils*) the bathroom suite; (*plomberie*) the bathroom plumbing.
sans [sɑ̃] **1** *prép* **(a)** (*gén*) without. **je suis sorti ~ chapeau ni manteau** I went out without a hat or coat *ou* with no hat or coat; **repas à 60 F ~ le vin** meal at 60 francs exclusive of wine *ou* not including wine; **manger ~ fourchette/faim** to eat without a fork/without feeling hungry; **non ~ mal** not without difficulty; **marcher ~ chaussures** to walk barefoot; **marcher ~ but** to walk aimlessly; **il est ~ scrupules** he is unscrupulous, he has no scruples, he is devoid of scruples; **robe ~ manches** sleeveless dress; **~ père** fatherless, with no father; **dictée ~ fautes** error-free dictation; **demain ~ faute** tomorrow without fail; **je le connais, ~ plus** I know him but no more that that. **(b)** (*cause négative*) but for. **~ cette réunion, il aurait pu partir ce soir** if it had not been for *ou* were it not for *ou* but for this meeting he could have left tonight. **(c)** (*avec infin ou subj*) without. **vous n'êtes pas ~ savoir que** you must be aware that; **je n'irai pas ~ être invité** *ou* **~ que je sois invité** I won't go without being invited; **~ plus attendre** without further delay; **j'y crois ~ y croire** I believe it and I don't; **je ne suis pas ~ avoir des doutes** I have my doubts *ou* I am not without some doubts; **il ne se passe pas de jour ~ qu'il lui écrive** not a day passes without his writing to him; **il va ~ dire que** it goes without saying that. **(d)** (*) **~ ça, ~ quoi** otherwise; if not; **sois sage, ~ ça ...!** be good or else ...!, be good – otherwise ...! **2** *adv* (*) **votre parapluie! vous alliez partir ~** your umbrella! you were going to go off without it. **3: ~-abri** *nmf inv* homeless person; **~-gêne** (*adj inv*) inconsiderate; (*nm inv*) lack of consideration (for others); (*nmf inv*) inconsiderate type; **~-soin** (*adj inv*) careless; (*nmf inv*) careless person; **~-le-sou** *adj inv* penniless; **~-souci** *adj inv* carefree; **~-travail** *nmf inv* unemployed person.
santé [sɑ̃te] *nf* health. **avoir la ~** to be healthy, be in good health; **meilleure ~** get well soon; (*Admin*) **services de ~** health services; (*en trinquant*) **à votre ~!** cheers!*; **à la ~ de Paul!** here's to Paul!; **boire à la ~ de qn** to drink (to) sb's health.
saoul, e [su, sul] = **soûl**.
sape [sap] *nf* **(a)** (*lit, fig: action*) undermining, sapping; (*tranchée*) approach *ou* sapping trench. **(b)** (*habits*) **~s‡** gear*, clobber‡. ♦ **saper** (1) **1** *vt* (*lit, fig*) to undermine, sap. **2 se ~‡** *vpr* to do o.s. up*. **bien sapé** well turned out *ou* got up*. ♦ **sapeur** *nm* (*Mil*) sapper. **~-pompier** fireman.
saphir [safiʀ] *nm* (*pierre*) sapphire; (*aiguille*) sapphire, needle.
sapin [sapɛ̃] *nm* (*arbre*) fir (tree); (*bois*) fir. **~ de**

Noël Christmas tree. ♦ **sapinière** *nf* fir plantation *ou* forest.

saquer* [sake] (1) *vt* = **sacquer***.

sarabande [saʀabɑ̃d] *nf* (*danse*) saraband; (*: *tapage*) racket*, hullabaloo*. **faire la ~*** to make a racket*; **~ de chiffres** jumble of figures.

sarbacane [saʀbakan] *nf* (*arme*) blowpipe, blowgun; (*jouet*) peashooter.

sarcasme [saʀkasm(ə)] *nm* (*ironie*) sarcasm; (*remarque*) sarcastic remark. ♦ **sarcastique** *adj* sarcastic.

sarcler [saʀkle] (1) *vt* *jardin* to weed; *mauvaise herbe* to pull up. ♦ **sarcloir** *nm* spud, weeding hoe.

sarcophage [saʀkɔfaʒ] *nm* (*cercueil*) sarcophagus.

Sardaigne [saʀdɛɲ] *nf* Sardinia.

sardine [saʀdin] *nf* sardine.

sardonique [saʀdɔnik] *adj* sardonic. ♦ **sardoniquement** *adv* sardonically.

sarment [saʀmɑ̃] *nm*: **~ (de vigne)** vine shoot.

sarrasin [saʀazɛ̃] *nm* (*Bot*) buckwheat.

sas [sɑ] *nm* **(a)** (*Espace, Naut*) airlock; *[écluse]* lock. **(b)** (*tamis*) sieve, screen.

Satan [satɑ̃] *nm* Satan. ♦ **satané, e*** *adj* blasted*, confounded*. ♦ **satanique** *adj* satanic.

satellite [satelit] *nm* (*lit, fig*) satellite. ♦ **satelliser** (1) *vt* *fusée* to put into orbit; *pays* to make into a satellite.

satiété [sasjete] *nf* satiety, satiation. **à ~** *manger* to satiety *ou* satiation; *répéter* ad nauseam; **j'en ai à ~** I've more than enough.

satin [satɛ̃] *nm* satin. ♦ **satiné, e** *adj* *tissu, aspect* satiny, satin-like; *peinture* with a silk finish. ♦ **satiner** (1) *vt* *étoffe* to put a satin finish on; *photo* to put a silk finish on.

satire [satiʀ] *nf* satire. ♦ **satirique** *adj* satirical. ♦ **satiriquement** *adv* satirically. ♦ **satiriser** (1) *vt* (*gén*) to satirize.

satisfaction [satisfaksjɔ̃] *nf* satisfaction; *[désir]* satisfaction, gratification. **je vois avec ~ que** I'm gratified to see that; **à la ~ de tous** to everybody's satisfaction; **leur fils ne leur a donné que des ~s** their son has been a (source of) great satisfaction to them; **donner ~ à qn/obtenir ~** to give sb/get satisfaction (*de qch* for sth). ♦ **satisfaire** (60) **1** *vt* (*gén*) to satisfy; *désir, besoin* to satisfy, gratify; *demande* to satisfy, meet. **2 ~ à** *vt indir* to satisfy; to gratify; to meet; *promesse, condition* to fulfil. **3 se ~** *vpr* to be satisfied (*de* with); (*euph*) to relieve o.s. ♦ **satisfaisant, e** *adj* (*acceptable*) satisfactory; (*qui fait plaisir*) satisfying. ♦ **satisfait, e** *adj* satisfied. **être ~ de** *décision* to be satisfied with, be happy with *ou* about; *soirée* to be pleased with; **~ de soi** self-satisfied.

saturer [satyʀe] (1) *vt* (*gén, Sci*) to saturate (*de* with). **saturé d'eau** *terre* waterlogged; (*lit, fig*) **j'en suis saturé** I've had my fill of it. ♦ **saturation** *nf* (*gén, Sci*) saturation. **être à ~** to be at saturation point.

Saturne [satyʀn(ə)] *nm* (*Astron, Myth*) Saturn.

satyre [satiʀ] *nm* (*: *obsédé*) sex maniac*; (*Myth*) satyr.

sauce [sos] *nf* (*Culin*) sauce; *[salade]* dressing; (*jus de viande*) gravy. **~ blanche** *etc* white *etc* sauce; **à quelle ~ allons-nous être mangés?** I wonder what Fate has in store for us; **mettre de la ~ dans un discours** to pad out *ou* add some padding to a speech; **mettre un exemple à toutes les ~s** to turn *ou* adapt an example to fit any case; **recevoir la ~*** to get soaked *ou* drenched. ♦ **saucer** (3) *vt* *assiette* to wipe (the sauce off). **se faire ~*** to get soaked *ou* drenched. ♦ **saucière** *nf* sauceboat; *[jus de viande]* gravy boat.

saucisse [sosis] *nf* sausage. **~ de Francfort** ≃ frankfurter. ♦ **saucisson** *nm* (slicing) sausage.

sauf¹, sauve [sof, sov] *adj* *personne* unharmed, unhurt; *honneur* saved, intact. ♦ **sauf-conduit,** *pl* **~-~s** *nm* safe-conduct.

sauf² [sof] *prép* (*à part*) except; (*à moins de*) unless. **tout le monde ~ lui** everyone except *ou* but him; **~si** except if, unless; **~ avis contraire** unless you hear otherwise *ou* to the contrary.

sauge [soʒ] *nf* (*Culin*) sage; (*ornementale*) salvia.

saugrenu, e [sogʀəny] *adj* preposterous, ludicrous.

saule [sol] *nm* willow (tree). **~ pleureur** weeping willow.

saumâtre [somɑtʀ(ə)] *adj* *goût* briny; (*fig*) unpleasant.

saumon [somɔ̃] **1** *nm* salmon. **2** *adj inv* salmon pink.

saumure [somyʀ] *nf* brine.

sauna [sona] *nm* sauna.

saupoudrer [sopudʀe] (1) *vt* (*gén*) to sprinkle; (*Culin*) to dredge, dust, sprinkle (*de* with).

saut [so] *nm* (*lit, fig: bond*) jump, leap; (*Sport: épreuve, spécialité*) jumping. **faire qch au ~ du lit** to do sth on getting up *ou* getting out of bed; **faire un ~ chez qn** to pop *ou* nip over *ou* round to sb's (place)*; **il a fait un ~ jusqu'à Bordeaux** he paid a flying visit to Bordeaux; **~ avec/sans élan** running/standing jump; **~ en hauteur** high jump; **~ en longueur** long jump; **~ en parachute** (*sport*) parachuting, parachute jumping; (*bond*) parachute jump; **~ à la perche** (*sport*) pole vaulting; (*bond*) (pole) vault; **~ périlleux** somersault. ♦ **saute** *nf*: **~ de** *humeur* sudden change of; *température* jump in; **~ de vent** (sudden) change of wind direction. ♦ **sauté, e** *adj, nm* sauté.

sauter [sote] (1) **1** *vi* **(a)** (*gén, fig*) to jump, leap; *[oiseau]* to hop. **~ à pieds joints** to make a standing jump; **~ à cloche-pied** to hop; **~ à la corde** to skip (*with a rope*); **~ en parachute** to parachute; **il sauta de la table** he jumped *ou* leapt (down) off *ou* from the table; **~ en l'air** to jump *ou* leap *ou* spring up; (*de colère*) to hit the roof*; (*de peur*) to jump, start; **~ de joie** to jump for joy; **~ à la gorge/au cou de qn** to fly at sb's throat/into sb's arms; (*fig*) **~ sur une occasion** to jump *ou* leap at an opportunity; **~ d'un sujet à l'autre** to jump *ou* leap *ou* skip from one subject to another; **il m'a sauté dessus** he pounced on me, he leapt at me; **va faire tes devoirs, et que ça saute!*** go and do your homework and get a move on!* *ou* be quick about it!; **cela saute aux yeux** it sticks out a mile, it's (quite) obvious. **(b)** *[bouchon]* to pop *ou* fly off; *[chaîne de vélo]* to come off; *[bombe, pont]* to blow up, explode; (*Élec*) *[circuit]* to fuse; *[fusible]* to blow; (*) *[employé, ministère]* to get the sack*, get kicked out‡; *[cours]* to be cancelled. **(c) faire ~** *train, caserne* to blow up; (*Élec*) *plombs* to blow; *crêpe* to toss; *serrure* to break open; (*: *annuler*) to cancel; (*Culin*) to sauté, shallow-fry; **faire ~ un enfant sur ses genoux** to bounce *ou* dandle a child on one's knee; (*Casino*) **faire ~ la banque** to break the bank; **se faire ~ la cervelle*** to blow one's brains out.

2 *vt* *obstacle* to jump (over), leap (over); *page, repas* to skip, miss (out). (*fig*) **~ le pas** to take the plunge; **on la saute ici!‡** we're starving to death here!*

♦ **saute-mouton** *nm* leapfrog. ♦ **sauterelle** *nf* (*Zool*) grasshopper. **(grande) ~*** beanpole. ♦ **sauterie** *nf* party. ♦ **sauteur, -euse 1** *nm,f* jumper. **~ à la perche** pole-vaulter. **2** *nf* (*Culin*) high-sided frying pan.

sautiller [sotije] (1) *vi* *[oiseau]* to hop; *[enfant]* to skip; (*sur un pied*) to hop. ♦ **sautillant, e** *adj* *mouvement* hopping, skipping; *musique* bouncy, bouncing. ♦ **sautillement** *nm*: **~(s)** hopping, skipping.

sautoir [sotwaʀ] *nm* (*Bijouterie*) chain. **porter qch en ~** to wear sth (on a chain) round one's neck.

sauvage [sovaʒ] **1** *adj* **(a)** (*gén*) wild; *peuplade,* *combat* savage; (*fig: insociable*) unsociable. **vivre à l'état ~** to live wild. **(b)** *camping, vente* unauthorized; *concurrence* unfair; *grève, école* unofficial. **2** *nmf* (*solitaire*) unsociable type, recluse; (*brute*) brute, savage; (*indigène*) savage. ♦ **sauvagement** *adv* savagely, wildly. ♦ **sauvagerie** *nf* savagery.

sauve [sov] *adj f V* **sauf**[1]. ♦ **sauvegarde** *nf* safeguard. **sous la ~ de** under the protection of. ♦ **sauvegarder** (1) *vt* to safeguard.

sauve-qui-peut [sovkipø] *nm inv* (*panique*) stampede, mad rush.

sauver [sove] (1) **1** *vt* (*gén*) to save; (*en portant secours*) to rescue (*de* from); (*en retirant des décombres*) *meubles* to salvage. **ce sont les illustrations qui sauvent le livre** it's the illustrations which save *ou* redeem the book; **~ la vie à qn** to save sb's life; (*fig*) **~ les meubles** to salvage *ou* save sth from the wreckage (*fig*); **~ la mise** to retrieve the situation; **~ les apparences** to keep up appearances. **2 se ~** *vpr* **(a) se ~ de** *danger* to save o.s. from. **(b)** (*s'enfuir*) to run away (*de* from); (*: *partir*) to be off, get going*; *[lait]* to boil over. ♦ **sauvetage** *nm* rescue; (*moral*) salvation; *[biens]* salvaging. **~ en montagne** mountain-rescue; **cours de ~** life-saving lessons. ♦ **sauveteur** *nm* rescuer. ♦ **sauveur** *adj m, nm* saviour.

sauvette* [sovɛt] *nf*: **à la ~** hastily, hurriedly; **vendre à la ~** to hawk *ou* peddle on the streets (*without authorization*).

savane [savan] *nf* savannah.

savant, e [savɑ̃, ɑ̃t] **1** *adj* (*érudit*) learned, scholarly; (*habile*) clever, skilful; *chien, puce* performing. (*hum*) **c'est trop ~ pour moi** it's too learned *ou* highbrow for me. **2** *nm* (*sciences*) scientist; (*lettres*) scholar. ♦ **savamment** *adv* learnedly; skilfully, cleverly. (*par expérience*) **j'en parle ~** I speak knowingly.

savate* [savat] *nf* worn-out old shoe.

saveur [savœʀ] *nf* flavour; (*fig*) savour.

savoir [savwaʀ] (32) **1** *vt* **(a)** *adresse, nom, leçon* to know; *nouvelle* to hear, learn of. **je la savais malade** I knew (that) she was ill, I knew her to be ill; **elle sait cela par** *ou* **de son boucher** she heard it from her butcher; **personne ne savait sur quel pied danser/où se mettre** nobody knew what to do/where to put themselves; **je crois ~ que** I believe *ou* understand that; **il ment - qu'en savez-vous?** he is lying - how do you know? *ou* what do you know about it?; **il nous a fait ~ que** he informed us *ou* let us know that; **ça finira bien par se ~** it will surely end up getting out *ou* getting known. **(b)** (*avec infin: être capable de*) to know how to. **elle sait lire** she can read, she knows how to read; **~ plaire** to know how to please; **il sait parler aux enfants** he's good at talking to children; **elle saura bien se défendre** she'll be quite able to look after herself *ou* quite capable of looking after herself; **~ y faire** *ou* **s'y prendre** to know how to go about things (the right way); **il faut ~ attendre** you have to learn to be patient; **je ne saurais pas vous répondre** I'm afraid I couldn't answer you. **(c)** (*se rendre compte*) to know. **il ne sait plus ce qu'il dit** he doesn't know *ou* realize what he's saying, he isn't aware of what he's saying; **il se savait très malade** he knew he was very ill; **sans le ~** unknowingly. **(d)** (*locutions*) **qui sait?** who knows?; **et que sais-je encore** and I don't know what else; **il nous a emmenés je ne sais où** he took us goodness knows where; **elle ne sait pas quoi faire pour l'aider** she's at a loss to know how to help him; **on ne sait jamais** you never know, you can never tell; **pas que je sache** not as far as I know, not to my knowledge; **sachez que** you should know that, let me tell you that; (*énumération*) **à ~** that is, namely, i.e.; (*hum*) **la personne que vous savez** you-know-who; **vous n'êtes pas sans ~ que** you are not unaware (of the fact) that; **il ne savait à quel saint se vouer** he didn't know which way to turn; **elle ne savait où donner de la tête** she didn't know what to do first; **si j'avais su** had I known, if I had known. **2** *nm* learning, knowledge. **~-faire** savoir-faire, know-how*; **avoir du ~-vivre** to know how to behave.

savon [savɔ̃] *nm* (*matière*) soap; (*morceau*) bar *ou* cake of soap. **~ à barbe/de Marseille** shaving/household soap; **~ en poudre** soap powder; **il m'a passé un ~*** he gave me a ticking-off* *ou* dressing-down*. ♦ **savonnage** *nm* soaping. ♦ **savonner** (1) *vt* to soap. ♦ **savonnette** *nf* bar *ou* cake of (toilet) soap. ♦ **savonneux, -euse** *adj* soapy.

savourer [savuʀe] (1) *vt* to savour. ♦ **savoureux, -euse** *adj plat* tasty, flavoursome; *anecdote* juicy*, spicy.

saxophone [saksɔfɔn] *nm* saxophone. ♦ **saxophoniste** *nmf* saxophonist.

sbire [sbiʀ] *nm* (*péj*) henchman (*péj*).

scabreux, -euse [skabʀø, øz] *adj* (*indécent*) improper, shocking; (*dangereux*) risky.

scalp [skalp] *nm* (*action*) scalping; (*chevelure*) scalp. ♦ **scalper** (1) *vt* to scalp.

scalpel [skalpɛl] *nm* scalpel.

scandale [skɑ̃dal] *nm* **(a)** (*fait choquant*) scandal. **ce livre a fait ~** that book scandalized people *ou* provoked an uproar; **crier au ~** to cry out in indignation; **à ~** *livre, couple* controversial. **(b)** (*tapage*) scene, fuss. **faire un** *ou* **du ~** to make a scene, kick up a fuss*. ♦ **scandaleusement** *adv* scandalously, outrageously. ♦ **scandaleux, -euse** *adj* scandalous, outrageous, shocking. ♦ **scandaliser** (1) *vt* to scandalize. **se ~ de qch** to be scandalized by sth.

scander [skɑ̃de] (1) *vt vers* to scan; *nom, slogan* to chant.

Scandinavie [skɑ̃dinavi] *nf* Scandinavia. ♦ **scandinave** *adj*, **S~** *nmf* Scandinavian.

scaphandre [skafɑ̃dʀ(ə)] *nm [plongeur]* diving suit; *[cosmonaute]* space-suit. **~ autonome** aqualung. ♦ **scaphandrier** *nm* (underwater) diver.

scarabée [skaʀabe] *nm* beetle.

scarlatine [skaʀlatin] *nf* scarlet fever.

scarole [skaʀɔl] *nf* curly endive.

sceau, *pl* **~x** [so] *nm* seal; (*fig*) stamp, mark. **sous le ~ du secret** under the seal of secrecy.

scélérat, e [seleʀa, at] **1** *adj* (†) villainous, wicked. **2** *nm,f* (†) villain, blackguard†. **petit ~!*** (you) little rascal!

sceller [sele] (1) *vt pacte, sac* to seal; (*Constr*) to embed. ♦ **scellement** *nm* sealing; embedding. ♦ **scellés** *nmpl* seals.

scénario [senaʀjo] *nm* (*Ciné, fig: plan*) scenario; (*dialogues*) screenplay, (film) script, scenario. (*fig*) **ça s'est déroulé selon le ~ habituel** it followed the usual pattern. ♦ **scénariste** *nmf* (*Ciné*) scriptwriter.

scène [sɛn] *nf* **(a)** (*gén*) scene. (*Théât*) **dans la première ~** in the first scene, in scene one; **changement de ~** scene change; **la ~ se passe à Rome** the action takes place in Rome, the scene is set in Rome; **sur la ~ internationale** on the international scene; **j'ai assisté à toute la ~** I was present at *ou* during the whole scene; **~ de ménage** domestic fight *ou* scene; **faire une ~ (à qn)** to make a scene. **(b)** (*estrade*) stage. **en ~, sur ~** on stage; (*le théâtre*) **la ~** the stage; **mettre en ~** *personnage* to present; *pièce de théâtre* to stage, direct; *film* to direct.

sceptique [sɛptik] **1** *adj* sceptical. **2** *nmf* sceptic. ♦ **scepticisme** *nm* scepticism. ♦ **sceptiquement** *adv* sceptically.

sceptre [sɛptʀ(ə)] *nm* (*lit, fig*) sceptre.

schéma [ʃema] *nm* (*diagramme*) diagram, sketch; (*résumé*) outline. ♦ **schématique** *adj*

dessin diagrammatic(al), schematic; (*péj*) *conception* oversimplified. ♦ **schématiquement** *adv* diagrammatically, schematically. **expliquer qch** ~ to outline sth. ♦ **schématisation** *nf* schematization; (*péj*) (over)simplification. ♦ **schématiser** (1) *vt* to schematize; (*péj*) to (over)simplify.
schisme [ʃism(ə)] *nm* schism.
schiste [ʃist(ə)] *nm* schist.
schizophrène [skizɔfʀɛn] *adj, nmf* schizophrenic. ♦ **schizophrénie** *nf* schizophrenia.
schnoque‡ [ʃnɔk] *nm*: **vieux** ~ old fathead‡.
sciage [sjaʒ] *nm [bois, métal]* sawing.
sciatique [sjatik] **1** *nf* sciatica. **2** *adj* sciatic.
scie [si] *nf* **(a)** saw. ~ **à découper** fretsaw; (*mécanique*) jigsaw; ~ **à métaux** hacksaw; ~ **à ruban** bandsaw. **(b)** (*péj*) (*chanson*) catch-tune; (*personne*) bore.
sciemment [sjamɑ̃] *adv* knowingly, wittingly.
science [sjɑ̃s] *nf* **(a)** (*domaine*) science. ~**s appliquées/humaines** applied/social sciences; (*Scol*) ~**s naturelles** biology. **(b)** (*art*) art. **sa** ~ **des couleurs** his skill *ou* technique in the use of colour. **(c)** (*érudition*) knowledge. **avoir la** ~ **infuse** to have innate knowledge. ♦ **science-fiction** *nf* science fiction. ♦ **scientifique 1** *adj* scientific. **2** *nmf* scientist. ♦ **scientifiquement** *adv* scientifically.
scier [sje] (7) *vt* (*gén*) to saw; *bûche* to saw (up); *partie en trop* to saw off. **ça m'a scié!*** it bowled me over!, it staggered me! ♦ **scierie** *nf* sawmill. ♦ **scieur** *nm* sawyer.
scinder *vt*, **se** ~ *vpr* [sɛ̃de] (1) to split (up) (*en* in, into).
scintiller [sɛ̃tije] (1) *vi [diamant, lumières]* to sparkle, glitter; *[étoile]* to twinkle; *[yeux]* to sparkle; *[goutte d'eau]* to glisten; *[esprit]* to sparkle, scintillate. ♦ **scintillement** *nm*: ~**(s)** sparkling; glittering; twinkling; glistening; scintillating.
scission [sisjɔ̃] *nf* split, scission. **faire** ~ to split away, secede. ♦ **scissionniste** *adj, nmf* secessionist.
sciure [sjyʀ] *nf*: ~ **(de bois)** sawdust.
sclérose [skleʀoz] *nf* (*Méd*) sclerosis; (*fig*) ossification. ~ **en plaques** multiple sclerosis. ♦ **scléroser (se)** (1) *vpr* (*Méd*) to become sclerosed, sclerose; (*fig*) to become ossified.
scolaire [skɔlɛʀ] *adj* (*gén*) school; (*péj*) schoolish. **ses succès** ~**s** his success in *ou* at school, his scholastic achievements. ♦ **scolarisation** *nf* schooling. ♦ **scolariser** (1) *vt* to provide with schooling. ♦ **scolarité** *nf* (*gén*) schooling; (*âge limite*) school-leaving age. **pendant mes années de** ~ during my school years; ~ **obligatoire** compulsory school attendance *ou* schooling.
scoliose [skɔljoz] *nf* scoliosis.
sconse [skɔ̃s] *nm* skunk (fur).
scooter [skutœʀ] *nm* (motor) scooter.
scorbut [skɔʀbyt] *nm* scurvy.
score [skɔʀ] *nm* (*Sport*) score.
scories [skɔʀi] *nfpl* (*Ind*) slag; (*Géol*) (volcanic) scoria.
scorpion [skɔʀpjɔ̃] *nm* **(a)** (*Zool*) scorpion. **(b)** (*Astron*) **le S**~ Scorpio, the Scorpion; **être (du) S**~ to be Scorpio.
scotch [skɔtʃ] *nm* **(a)** (*boisson*) scotch (whisky). **(b)** ® sellotape ®, Scotchtape ® (*US*).
scout, e [skut] *adj, nm* (boy) scout. ♦ **scoutisme** *nm* (*mouvement*) (boy) scout movement; (*activités*) scouting.
scribe [skʀib] *nm* (*Hist*) scribe. ♦ **scribouillard, e** *nm,f* (*péj*) penpusher (*péj*).
script [skʀipt] *nm*: **(écriture)** ~ printing. ♦ **script-girl**, *pl* ~**-**~**s** *nf* continuity girl.
scrupule [skʀypyl] *nm* scruple. **avoir des** ~**s à faire qch** to have scruples *ou* misgivings *ou* qualms about doing sth; **sans** ~**s** *personne* unscrupulous, without scruples; *agir* without scruple, unscrupulously; **par un** ~ **d'honnêteté** in scrupulous regard for honesty. ♦ **scrupuleusement** *adv* scrupulously. ♦ **scrupuleux, -euse** *adj* scrupulous. **peu** ~ unscrupulous.
scrutateur, -trice [skʀytatœʀ, tʀis] **1** *adj regard* searching. **2** *nm* (*Pol*) scrutineer, canvasser (*US*).
scruter [skʀyte] (1) *vt* to scrutinize, examine; *pénombre* to peer into, search.
scrutin [skʀytɛ̃] *nm* (*vote*) ballot; (*élection*) poll; (*système*) (election) system. **au** ~ **secret** by secret ballot; **au 3e tour de** ~ on *ou* at the third ballot *ou* round; **dépouiller le** ~ to count the votes; **le jour du** ~ polling day; ~ **majoritaire** election on a majority basis; ~ **uninominal** uninominal system.
sculpter [skylte] (1) *vt marbre* to sculpture, sculpt; *bois* to carve (*dans* out of). ♦ **sculpteur** *nm* (*homme*) sculptor; (*femme*) sculptress. ~ **sur bois** woodcarver. ♦ **sculptural, e**, *mpl* **-aux** *adj* (*Art*) sculptural; *beauté* statuesque. ♦ **sculpture** *nf* sculpture. ~ **sur bois** woodcarving.
se [s(ə)] *pron* **(a)** (*réfléchi*) (*sg*) (*indéfini*) oneself; (*mâle*) himself; (*femelle*) herself; (*non humain*) itself; (*pl*) themselves. ~ **regarder dans la glace** to look at o.s. in the mirror; ~ **raser/laver** to shave/wash; ~ **mouiller/salir** to get wet/dirty. **(b)** (*réciproque*) each other, one another. **deux personnes qui s'aiment** two people who love each other *ou* one another. **(c)** (*possessif*) ~ **casser la jambe** to break one's leg; **il** ~ **lave les mains** he is washing his hands. **(d)** (*passif*) **cela ne** ~ **fait pas** that's not done; **cela** ~ **répare facilement** it can easily be repaired again; **l'anglais** ~ **parle dans le monde entier** English is spoken throughout the world; **cela** ~ **vend bien** it sells well. **(e)** (*impersonnel*) **il** ~ **peut que** it may be that; **comment** ~ **fait-il que ...?** how is it that ...? **(f)** (*changement*) **s'améliorer** to get better; ~ **boucher** to become *ou* get blocked; *V aussi le verbe en question.*
séance [seɑ̃s] *nf* **(a)** *[conseil municipal]* meeting, session; *[tribunal, parlement]* session, sitting. **être en** ~ to be in session, sit. **(b)** (*période*) session. ~ **de gymnastique** gymnastics session; ~ **de pose** sitting. **(c)** (*Théât*) performance. ~ **de cinéma** film show; (*Ciné*) **première/dernière** ~ first/last showing. **(d)** ~ **tenante** forthwith.
séant[1] [seɑ̃] *nm* (*hum*) posterior (*hum*). **se mettre sur son** ~ to sit up.
séant[2], **e** [seɑ̃, ɑ̃t] *adj* (*convenable*) seemly, fitting.
seau, *pl* ~**x** [so] *nm* (*récipient*) bucket, pail; (*contenu*) bucket(ful), pail(ful). **il pleut à** ~**x** it's pouring down in buckets*; ~ **hygiénique** slop pail.
sébile [sebil] *nf* (offering) bowl.
sec, sèche [sɛk, sɛʃ] **1** *adj* (*gén, fig*) dry; *raisins, figue* dried; (*maigre*) *bras, personne* thin; *cœur* hard, cold; *réponse* curt; (*sans eau*) *alcool* neat, straight. (*fig*) **avoir la gorge sèche*** to be parched *ou* dry; **il est** ~ **comme un coup de trique*** he's as thin as a rake; (*Sport*) **placage** ~ hard tackle; **bruit** ~ sharp snap; **je suis** ~ **sur ce sujet*** I draw a blank on that subject. **2** *adv frapper, boire* hard. **démarrer** ~ (*sans douceur*) to start (up) with a jolt *ou* jerk; (*fig*) **ça démarre** ~ **ce soir** it's getting off to a good start this evening; **aussi** ~‡ straight away. **3** *nm*: **au** ~ *conserver* in a dry place; *rester* in the dry; **être à** ~ *[torrent, puits]* to be dry *ou* dried-up; (*: *sans argent*) *[personne]* to be broke*; *[caisse]* to be empty; **mettre à** ~ **un étang** to drain a pond. **4** *nf* (*: *cigarette*) fag*.
sécateur [sekatœʀ] *nm* (pair of) secateurs, (pair of) pruning shears.
sécession [sesesjɔ̃] *nf* secession. **faire** ~ to secede. ♦ **sécessionniste** *adj, nmf* secessionist.

sécher [seʃe] (6) **1** *vt* **(a)** (*gén*) to dry; *flaque* to dry (up). **se ~ au soleil** to dry o.s. in the sun. **(b)** (*arg Scol*) *cours* to skip*. **2** *vi* **(a)** *[surface, peinture]* to dry (off); *[pâte, éponge]* to dry (out); *[linge]* to dry; *[fleur]* to dry up *ou* out. **faire** *ou* **laisser ~ qch** to leave sth to dry (off *ou* out); *fruits, viande* to dry sth; **le caoutchouc a séché** the rubber has dried up *ou* gone dry. **(b)** (*arg Scol*) (*rester sec*) to be stumped*, dry up*; (*être absent*) to skip classes. ♦ **sèche-cheveux** *nm inv* hair-drier. ♦ **sèche-linge** *nm inv* drying cabinet. ♦ **sèchement** *adv* (*gén*) drily; *répondre* curtly. ♦ **sécheresse** *nf* (*gén*) dryness; *[réponse]* curtness; *[cœur]* coldness, hardness; (*absence de pluie*) drought. ♦ **séchoir** *nm* (*local*) drying shed; (*appareil*) drier; (*pliant*) clothes-horse. **~ à cheveux** hair-drier.

second, e[1] [s(ə)gɔ̃, ɔ̃d] **1** *adj* **(a)** (*gén*) second. **en ~ lieu** second(ly), in the second place; **de ~e main** secondhand; **de ~ choix** (*péj*) low-quality, low-grade; (*Comm*) class two; **voyager en ~e classe** to travel second-class; **passer en ~** to come second; **commander en ~** to be second in command; **chez lui, c'est une ~e nature** with him it's second nature; **doué de ~e vue** gifted with second sight; **être dans un état ~** to be in a sort of trance. **(b)** (*dérivé*) *cause* secondary. **2** *nm,f* second. **3** *nm* **(a)** (*adjoint*) second in command; (*Naut*) first mate. **(b)** (*étage*) second floor, third floor (*US*). **4** *nf* (*transport*) second class; (*billet*) second-class ticket; (*Scol*) ≃ fifth form, tenth grade (*US*); (*Aut*) second (gear).

secondaire [s(ə)gɔ̃dɛʀ] **1** *adj* (*gén*) secondary. (*gén, Méd*) **effets ~s** side effects. **2** *nm* (*Scol*) **le ~** secondary *ou* high-school (*US*) education.

seconde[2] [s(ə)gɔ̃d] *nf* (*gén, Géom*) second.

seconder [s(ə)gɔ̃de] (1) *vt* (*lit, fig*) to assist, aid, help.

secouer [s(ə)kwe] (1) **1** *vt* **(a)** (*lit*) to shake; *poussière, paresse, oppression* to shake off; *tapis* to shake (out). **~ la tête** (*pour dire oui*) to nod (one's head); (*pour dire non*) to shake one's head; **on est drôlement secoué** (*dans un autocar*) you're terribly shaken about; (*dans un bateau*) you're terribly tossed about. **(b)** *[deuil, professeur]* **~ qn** to shake sb up; **~ les puces à qn*** (*réprimander*) to give sb a ticking-off* *ou* telling-off; (*stimuler*) to give sb a good shake(-up)*. **2 se ~** *vpr* (*lit*) to shake o.s.; (**fig*) to shake o.s. up*.

secours [s(ə)kuʀ] *nm* **(a)** (*aide*) help, aid, assistance. **crier au ~** to shout *ou* call (out) for help; **au ~!** help!; **porter ~ à qn** to give sb help *ou* assistance; (*en montagne etc*) to rescue sb; **~ aux blessés** aid *ou* assistance for the wounded; **le ~ en mer** sea rescue; **équipe de ~** rescue party *ou* team; **cela m'a été d'un grand ~** this has been a *ou* of great help to me; **sortie de ~** emergency exit; **roue de ~** spare wheel.

(b) (*Mil*) **le ~, les ~** relief.

(c) (*aumône*) **un ~, des ~** aid.

♦ **secourable** *adj personne* helpful. ♦ **secourir** (11) *vt* to help, assist, aid. ♦ **secourisme** *nm* first aid. ♦ **secouriste** *nmf* first-aid worker.

secousse [s(ə)kus] *nf* (*choc*) jerk, jolt; (*traction*) tug, pull; (*morale*) jolt, shock. **sans une ~** smoothly; **~ sismique** earth tremor; **~ politique** political upheaval.

secret, -ète [səkʀɛ, ɛt] **1** *adj* (*gén*) secret; (*renfermé*) *personne* reserved. **garder qch ~** to keep sth secret *ou* (in the) dark*.

2 *nm* **(a)** secret. **~ de fabrication/d'État/de Polichinelle** trade/state/open secret; **ce n'est un ~ pour personne que ...** it's no secret that ...; **une sauce dont il a le ~** a sauce of which he (alone) has the secret; **mettre qn dans le ~** to let sb into *ou* in on the secret, let sb in on it*; **être dans le ~ des dieux** to share the secrets of the powers that be; **en ~** secretly; (*Prison*) **au ~** in solitary confinement. **(b)** (*discrétion, silence*) secrecy. **promettre le ~ (absolu)** to promise (absolute) secrecy; **le ~ professionnel** professional secrecy; **le gouvernement a gardé le ~ sur les négociations** the government has maintained silence *ou* remained silent about the negotiations.

secrétaire [s(ə)kʀetɛʀ] **1** *nmf* (*gén*) secretary. **~ médicale/commerciale** medical/business *ou* commercial secretary; **~ de direction** executive secretary; **~ d'État** junior minister; (*US Pol*) state secretary; **~ général** Secretary-General. **2** *nm* (*meuble*) writing desk, secretaire, secretary (*US*). ♦ **secrétariat** *nm* **(a)** *[club, organisme]* (*fonction officielle*) secretaryship; (*bureau*) secretariat. **~ d'État** office of junior minister. **(b)** (*profession, travail*) secretarial work; (*bureaux*) *[école]* (secretary's) office; *[firme]* secretarial offices; (*personnel*) secretarial staff. **école de ~** secretarial college.

sécréter [sekʀete] (6) *vt* (*Bio*) to secrete; *ennui* to exude. ♦ **sécrétion** *nf* secretion.

secte [sɛkt(ə)] *nf* sect. ♦ **sectaire** *adj, nmf* sectarian. ♦ **sectarisme** *nm* sectarianism.

secteur [sɛktœʀ] *nm* **(a)** (*Écon, Mil*) sector; (*Admin*) district; (*gén: zone*) area; (*fig*) (*domaine*) area; (*partie*) part. **dans le ~*** (*ici*) round here; (*là-bas*) round there; (*Écon*) **~ primaire** *etc* primary *etc* sector. **(b)** (*Élec*) (*zone*) local supply area. (*circuit*) **le ~** the mains (supply).

section [sɛksjɔ̃] *nf* (*gén*) section; (*Admin*) section, department; (*en autobus*) fare stage; (*Mil*) platoon. ♦ **sectionnement** *nm* severance. ♦ **sectionner** (1) **1** *vt* to sever. **2 se ~** *vpr* to be severed.

séculaire [sekylɛʀ] *adj* (*très vieux*) age-old. **forêts 4 fois ~s** 4-century-old forests.

séculier, -ière [sekylje, jɛʀ] *adj* secular.

sécuriser [sekyʀize] (1) *vt* to give (a feeling of) security to.

sécurité [sekyʀite] *nf* (*absence de danger*) safety; (*absence de troubles*) security. **être en ~** to be safe, be secure; **la ~ de l'emploi** security of employment, job security; **mesures de ~** strict security measures; (*contre accident*) safety measures; (*contre attentat*) **de ~** *dispositif* safety; **la ~ routière** road safety; **la S~ sociale** ≃ Social Security.

sédatif, -ive [sedatif, iv] *adj, nm* sedative.

sédentaire [sedɑ̃tɛʀ] *adj* sedentary. ♦ **sédentariser** (1) *vt* to settle.

sédiment [sedimɑ̃] *nm* sediment. ♦ **sédimentaire** *adj* sedimentary. ♦ **sédimentation** *nf* sedimentation.

séditieux, -euse [sedisjø, øz] **1** *adj troupes* insurrectionary; *propos* seditious. **2** *nm,f* insurrectionary. ♦ **sédition** *nf* insurrection; sedition.

séduire [sedɥiʀ] (38) *vt* **(a)** (*abuser de*) to seduce. **(b)** *[femme]* to charm, captivate; *[charlatan]* to win over, charm; *[style, qualité, projet]* to appeal to. ♦ **séducteur, -trice 1** *adj* seductive. **2** *nm* seducer; (*péj: Don Juan*) womanizer (*péj*). **3** *nf* seductress. ♦ **séduction** *nf* **(a)** seduction, seducing; charming; captivation; winning over. **(b)** (*attirance*) appeal; charm. **les ~s de la vie estudiantine** the attractions *ou* appeal of student life. ♦ **séduisant, e** *adj femme, beauté* enticing, seductive; *homme, visage* (very) attractive; *projet* appealing, attractive.

segment [sɛgmɑ̃] *nm* (*gén*) segment. ♦ **segmentation** *nf* segmentation. ♦ **segmenter** *vt,* **se ~** (1) *vpr* to segment.

ségrégation [segʀegasjɔ̃] *nf* segregation. ♦ **ségrégationnisme** *nm* segregationism. ♦ **ségrégationniste** *adj, nmf* segregationist.

seiche [sɛʃ] *nf* (*Zool*) cuttlefish.

seigle [sɛgl(ə)] *nm* rye.

seigneur [seɲœʀ] *nm* lord. (*Rel*) **le S~** the Lord. ♦ **seigneurial, e** *mpl* **-aux** *adj château* seigniorial; *allure* lordly, stately. ♦ **seigneurie** *nf* **(a) votre/sa S~** your/his Lordship. **(b)** (*terre*) seigniory.

sein [sɛ̃] *nm* (*mamelle*) breast; (*littér, fig*) (*giron*) bosom (*littér*); (*matrice*) womb. **donner le ~ à un bébé** to breast-feed (a baby); **dans le ~ de la terre** in the bosom of the earth; **au ~ de** *équipe* within; *bonheur, flots* in the midst of.

séisme [seism(ə)] *nm* (*Géog*) earthquake.

seize [sɛz] *adj inv, nm* sixteen; *V* **six.** ♦ **seizième** *adv, nmf* sixteenth. ♦ **seizièmement** *adv* in the sixteenth place.

séjour [seʒuʀ] *nm* **(a)** (*arrêt*) stay. **faire un ~ forcé** to have an enforced stay. **(b)** (*salon*) living room. **(c)** (*littér: endroit*) abode (*littér*), dwelling place. ♦ **séjourner** (1) *vi [personne]* to stay; *[neige, eau]* to lie.

sel [sɛl] *nm* (*gén, Chim*) salt; (*humour*) wit; (*piquant*) spice. **~s de bain** bath salts; **~ fin** *ou* **de table** table salt; **~ gemme** rock salt.

select* [selɛkt] *adj inv* posh*.

sélectionner [selɛksjɔne] (1) *vt* to select, pick. *[joueur international]* **3 fois sélectionné** capped *ou* selected 3 times. ♦ **sélecteur** *nm* selector. ♦ **sélectif,-ive** *adj* selective. ♦ **sélection** *nf* selection. **faire une ~ parmi** to make a selection from among; **épreuve de ~** (selection) trial. ♦ **sélectionné, e 1** *adj* specially selected. **2** *nm,f* selected player *ou* competitor. ♦ **sélectionneur, -euse** *nm,f* (*Sport*) selector.

self(-service) [sɛlf(sɛʀvis)] *nm* self-service (restaurant).

selle [sɛl] *nf* **(a)** saddle. **se mettre en ~** to mount, get into the saddle. **(b)** (*Méd*) **~s** stools, motions; **êtes-vous allé à la ~ ?** have you had a motion? ♦ **seller** (1) *vt* to saddle. ♦ **sellerie** *nf* saddlery. ♦ **sellier** *nm* saddler.

sellette [sɛlɛt] *nf* (*support*) stand. (*fig*) **être/mettre qn sur la ~** to be/put sb on the carpet.

selon [s(ə)lɔ̃] *prép* (*conformément à*) in accordance with; (*en fonction de, suivant l'opinion de*) according to. **vivre ~ ses moyens** to live according to one's means; **c'est ~ le cas** it all depends on the individual case; **~ moi** in my opinion, to my mind, according to me; **~ toute vraisemblance** in all probability; **~ que** according to *ou* depending on whether.

semailles [s(ə)mɑj] *nfpl* (*opération*) sowing; (*période*) sowing period.

semaine [s(ə)mɛn] *nf* (*gén*) week; (*salaire*) week's *ou* weekly pay. **en ~** during the week, on weekdays; **dans 2 ~s** in 2 weeks *ou* a fortnight; **~ publicitaire** publicity week; **la ~ sainte** Holy Week; **il te le rendra la ~ des quatre jeudis** he'll never give it back to you in a month of Sundays; **faire la ~ anglaise** to work *ou* do a five-day week; **officier de ~** officer on duty (*for the week*).

sémantique [semɑ̃tik] **1** *adj* semantic. **2** *nf* semantics (*sg*).

sémaphore [semafɔʀ] *nm* (*Naut*) semaphore.

semblable [sɑ̃blabl(ə)] **1** *adj* **(a)** (*similaire*) similar. **~ à** like, similar to. **(b)** (*tel*) such. **de ~s erreurs sont inacceptables** such errors *ou* errors of this kind are unacceptable. **(c)** (*qui se ressemblent*) *[jumeaux, objets]* **être ~s** to be alike. **2** *nm* fellow creature, fellow man. (*péj*) **toi et tes ~s** you and your kind (*péj*), you and people like you (*péj*).

semblant [sɑ̃blɑ̃] *nm* **(a) un ~ de** *calme, vie, vérité* a semblance of; *soleil* a glimmer of; **un ~ de réponse** some vague attempt at a reply. **(b) faire ~ de faire qch** to pretend to do sth; **il fait ~** he's pretending.

sembler [sɑ̃ble] (1) **1** *vb impers*: **il semble** it seems; **il me semble que** (*j'estime*) it seems *ou* appears to me that, it looks to me as though; (*je crois*) I think that, I have a feeling that; **comme bon te semble** as you see fit, as you think best; **prenez ce que bon vous semble** take what you please *ou* wish; **il me semble revoir mon grand-père** it's as though I see my grandfather again. **2** *vi* to seem (*à qn* to sb). **il semblait content** he seemed (to be) *ou* appeared happy; **vous me semblez pessimiste** you sound *ou* seem *ou* look pessimistic.

semelle [s(ə)mɛl] *nf* sole. **~s intérieures** insoles; **~s compensées** platform soles; **leur viande était de la vraie ~*** their meat was like leather; **il n'a pas reculé d'une ~** he hasn't moved back an inch; **il ne m'a pas quitté d'une ~** he never left me by so much as an inch.

semence [s(ə)mɑ̃s] *nf* (*Agr, fig*) seed; (*sperme*) seed; (*clou*) tack. **blé de ~** seed corn.

semer [s(ə)me] (5) *vt* **(a)** *graines, peur* to sow; *clous* to scatter, strew; *faux bruits* to spread. **(b)** (*: *perdre*) to lose, shed*; *poursuivant* to shake off. ♦ **semé, e** *adj*: **~ de pièges** bristling with; *difficultés* plagued with; *anecdotes* interspersed *ou* sprinkled with; *arbres* dotted with; *fleurs, diamants, étoiles* studded with; **la vie est ~e de joies et de peines** life is strewn with joys and troubles. ♦ **semeur, -euse** *nm,f* sower.

semestre [s(ə)mɛstʀ(ə)] *nm* (*période*) half-year, six-month period; (*loyer*) half-yearly rent; (*Univ*) semester. **payé par ~** paid half-yearly; **le premier ~** the first half of the year. ♦ **semestriel, -elle** *adj* half-yearly, six-monthly; semestral.

semi- [səmi] *préf inv* semi-. **~-automatique** semiautomatic; **~-circulaire** semicircular; **~-conducteur, -trice** (*adj*) semiconducting; (*nm*) semiconductor; **~-remorque** (*nf: remorque*) trailer, semitrailer (*US*); (*nm: camion*) articulated lorry, trailer truck (*US*).

sémillant, e [semijɑ̃, ɑ̃t] *adj* (*vif*) vivacious; (*fringant*) dashing.

séminaire [seminɛʀ] *nm* (*Rel*) seminary; (*Univ*) seminar. ♦ **séminariste** *nm* seminarist.

semis [s(ə)mi] *nm* (*plante*) seedling; (*opération*) sowing; (*terrain*) seedbed.

semonce [səmɔ̃s] *nf* reprimand. (*Naut, fig*) **coup de ~** shot across the bows.

semoule [s(ə)mul] *nf* semolina.

sempiternel, -elle [sɛ̃pitɛʀnɛl] *adj* eternal, never-ending.

sénat [sena] *nm* senate. ♦ **sénateur** *nm* senator. ♦ **sénatorial, e,** *mpl* **-aux** *adj* senatorial.

sénile [senil] *adj* senile. ♦ **sénilité** *nf* senility.

sens [sɑ̃s] *nm* **(a)** (*instinct, conscience*) sense. **les 5 ~** the 5 senses; **reprendre ses ~** to regain consciousness; **avoir le ~ des réalités** to be a realist; **avoir le ~ de l'orientation** to have a (good) sense of direction. **(b)** (*raison, avis*) sense. **c'est plein de ~** it is very sensible; **cela n'a pas de ~** that doesn't make (any) sense; **~ commun** common sense; **à mon ~** to my mind, in my opinion. **(c)** (*signification*) meaning. **au ~ propre/figuré** in the literal/figurative sense *ou* meaning; **dépourvu de ~** meaningless; **en un ~** in a way *ou* sense; **en ce ~ que** in the sense that. **(d)** (*direction*) direction. **aller dans le mauvais ~** to go in the wrong direction, go the wrong way; **dans le ~ de la longueur/largeur** lengthwise *ou* lengthways/widthwise; **dans le ~ (du bois)** with the grain (of the wood); **venir en ~ contraire** to come from the opposite direction; **dans le ~ des aiguilles d'une montre** clockwise; **dans le ~ contraire des aiguilles d'une montre** anticlockwise, counterclockwise (*US*); **dans le ~ de la marche** facing the engine; **il a retourné la boîte dans tous les ~** he turned the box this way and that; (*lit, fig*) **mettre ~ dessus dessous** to turn upside down. **(e)** (*ligne directrice*) line. **il a agi dans le même ~** he acted along the same lines; **j'ai donné des directives dans ce ~** I've given instructions to that effect *ou* end. **(f)** (*Aut*) **être en ~ giratoire** to form a roundabout *ou* traffic circle (*US*); **~ interdit** *ou* **unique** one-way street; '**~ interdit**' 'no entry'; **à ~ unique** (*Aut*) one-way; (*fig: concession*) one-sided.

sensation [sɑ̃sɑsjɔ̃] *nf* feeling, sensation. **j'ai la ~ de l'avoir déjà vu** I have a feeling I've seen him before; **faire ~** to cause *ou* create a sensation; **roman à ~** sensational novel; **la presse à ~** the gutter press. ♦ **sensationnel, -elle** *adj* (*: *merveilleux*) fantastic*, terrific*, sensational*; (*qui fait sensation*) sensational.

sensé, e [sɑ̃se] *adj* sensible.

sensibiliser [sɑ̃sibilize] (1) *vt*: **~ qn** to make sb sensitive *ou* alive (*à* to). ♦ **sensibilisation** *nf*: **la ~ de l'opinion publique à ce problème est récente** public opinion has only become sensitive *ou* alive to this problem in recent years.

sensible [sɑ̃sibl(ə)] *adj* **(a)** *personne, blessure, balance etc* sensitive (*à* to). **pas recommandé aux personnes ~s** not recommended for people of (a) nervous disposition; **elle a le cœur ~** she is tenderhearted; **être ~ au froid** to feel the cold, be sensitive to the cold. **(b)** (*perceptible*) (*gén*) perceptible (*à* to); *progrès, différence* appreciable, noticeable. ♦ **sensibilité** *nf* (*gén, Tech*) sensitivity. ♦ **sensiblement** *adv* (*presque*) approximately, more or less; (*notablement*) appreciably, noticeably. ♦ **sensiblerie** *nf* (*sentimentalité*) sentimentality, mawkishness; (*impressionnabilité*) squeamishness.

sensitif, -ive [sɑ̃sitif, iv] **1** *adj* (*Anat*) sensory. **2** *nf* (*Bot*) sensitive plant.

sensoriel, -elle [sɑ̃sɔʀjɛl] *adj* sensory.

sensuel, -elle [sɑ̃sɥɛl] *adj* sensuous; (*sexuellement*) sensual. ♦ **sensualité** *nf* sensuousness; sensuality. ♦ **sensuellement** *adv* sensuously; sensually.

sentence [sɑ̃tɑ̃s] *nf* (*verdict*) sentence; (*adage*) maxim. ♦ **sentencieux, -euse** *adj* sententious.

senteur [sɑ̃tœʀ] *nf* scent, perfume.

senti, e [sɑ̃ti] *adj*: **bien ~** *sentiment, discours* heartfelt; *mots* well-chosen; **quelques vérités bien ~es** a few home truths.

sentier [sɑ̃tje] *nm* (*lit*) (foot)path; (*fig*) path. (*lit, fig*) **hors des ~s battus** off the beaten track; (*lit, fig*) **sur le ~ de la guerre** on the warpath.

sentiment [sɑ̃timɑ̃] *nm* **(a)** (*émotion, opinion*) feeling. **~ de culpabilité** guilt *ou* guilty feeling. **(b)** (*sensibilité*) **le ~** feeling, emotion; (*péj*) sentiment; (*péj*) **faire du ~** to sentimentalize, be sentimental. **(c)** (*conscience*) **avoir le ~ de** to be aware of; **avoir le ~ que qch va arriver** to have a feeling that sth is going to happen. **(d)** (*formules de politesse*) **recevez, Monsieur, mes ~s distingués** yours faithfully; **transmettez-lui nos meilleurs ~s** give him our best wishes. ♦ **sentimental, e,** *mpl* **-aux 1** *adj* (*gén*) sentimental; (*péj*) soppy*; *aventure* love. **il a des problèmes ~aux** he has problems with his love life. **2** *nm,f* sentimentalist. ♦ **sentimentalement** *adv* sentimentally. ♦ **sentimentalité** *nf* sentimentality.

sentinelle [sɑ̃tinɛl] *nf* sentry. **être en ~** (*Mil*) to be on sentry duty; (*fig*) to stand guard at the window.

sentir [sɑ̃tiʀ] (16) **1** *vt* **(a)** (*par l'odorat*) to smell; (*au goût*) to taste; (*au toucher, contact*) to feel. **il ne peut pas ~ la différence** he can't tell (*ou* taste *ou* smell) the difference; **elle sentit une odeur de brûlé** she smelt burning; (*fatigue*) **je ne sens plus mes jambes** my legs are dropping off*; **il ne peut pas le ~*** he can't stand *ou* bear (the sight of) him. **(b)** (*dégager une odeur*) to smell. **~ bon/mauvais** to smell good *ou* nice/bad; **~ des pieds** to have smelly feet; **ce thé sent le jasmin** (*goût*) this tea tastes of jasmine; (*odeur*) this tea smells of jasmine; **la pièce sent le renfermé/le moisi** the room smells stale/musty; **ça ne sent pas la rose!*** it's not a very nice smell, is it? **(c)** (*fig: dénoter*) *autoritarisme, hypocrisie* to smack of. **ça sent le piège** there's a trap *ou* catch in it; **ça sent la pluie** it looks *ou* feels like rain; **ça sent l'orage** there's a storm in the air; **ça sent le roussi*** there's going to be trouble. **(d)** *changement, fatigue* to feel, be aware *ou* conscious of; *beauté de qch* to appreciate; *danger, difficulté* to sense. **~ que** to feel *ou* be aware *ou* conscious that; (*pressentir*) to sense that; **il ne sent pas sa force** he doesn't know *ou* realize his own strength. **(e) faire ~ son autorité** to make one's authority felt; **faire ~ la beauté de qch** to bring out *ou* demonstrate *ou* show the beauty of sth; **les effets commencent à se faire ~** the effects are beginning to be felt *ou* to make themselves felt.

2 se ~ *vpr* **(a) se ~ mieux** *etc* to feel better *etc*; **se ~ revivre** to feel o.s. coming alive again; **il ne se sent pas le courage de le lui dire** he doesn't feel brave enough to tell him. **(b)** (*effet, changements*) to be felt, show. **(c) ne pas se ~ de joie** to be beside o.s. with joy; **il ne se sent plus!*** he's off his head!* *ou* out of his mind!*

seoir [swaʀ] (26) **1** *vi*: **~ à qn** to become sb. **2** *vb impers*: **il sied de/que** it is proper *ou* fitting to/that.

séparer [sepaʀe] (1) **1** *vt* (*gén*) to separate (*de* from); *combattants* to pull apart, part; *questions, aspects* to distinguish between. **~ l'écorce du tronc** to pull the bark off *ou* away from the trunk; **~ qch en 2** to split *ou* divide sth in 2; **~ les cheveux par une raie** to part one's hair; **ils avaient séparé l'enfant de sa mère** they had separated *ou* parted the child from its mother; **un seul obstacle le séparait du but** only one obstacle stood between him and his goal.

2 se ~ *vpr* **(a) se ~ de** *employé, objet* to part with. **(b)** (*s'écarter*) to divide, part (*de* from); (*se détacher*) to split off, separate off (*de* from). **le second étage de la fusée s'est séparé** the second stage of the rocket has split off *ou* separated (off); **le fleuve se sépare en deux** the river divides in(to) two. **(c)** *[adversaires]* to separate, break apart; *[manifestants]* to disperse; *[assemblée]* to break up; *[convives]* to leave each other, part; *[époux]* to part, split up*, separate. **se ~ de sa femme** to part *ou* separate from one's wife. ♦ **séparable** *adj* separable (*de* from). ♦ **séparation** *nf* **(a)** (*gén, Jur, Pol*) separation. **au moment de la ~** *[manifestants]* when they dispersed; *[convives]* when they parted; **mur de ~** separating *ou* dividing wall; **~ de corps** legal separation; **des ~s déchirantes** heartrending partings. **(b)** (*cloison*) division, partition. (*fig*) **faire une ~ nette entre 2 problèmes** to draw a clear dividing line between 2 problems. ♦ **séparatisme** *nm* separatism. ♦ **séparatiste** *adj, nmf* separatist. ♦ **séparé, e** *adj sons, notions* separate; *personnes* (*Jur: désuni*) separated; (*gén: éloigné*) apart. **vivre ~** to live apart (*de* from). ♦ **séparément** *adv* separately.

sept [sɛt] *adj inv, nm inv* seven; *V* **six.**

septante [sɛptɑ̃t] *adj inv* († *ou dial*) seventy.

septembre [sɛptɑ̃bʀ(ə)] *nm* September. **arriver le premier ~** to arrive on the first of September; **en ~** in September; **à la mi-~** in mid-September; **vers la fin de ~** in late September; **en ~ prochain/dernier** next/last September.

septennat [sɛptena] *nm* seven-year term (of office).

septentrional, e, *mpl* **-aux** [sɛptɑ̃tʀijɔnal, o] *adj* northern.

septicémie [sɛptisemi] *nf* blood poisoning, septicaemia.

septième [sɛtjɛm] *adj, nmf* seventh. **le ~ art** the cinema; **être au ~ ciel** to be in (the) seventh heaven; *V* **sixième.** ♦ **septièmement** *adv* seventhly; *V* **sixièmement.**

septuagénaire [sɛptɥaʒenɛʀ] *adj, nmf* septuagenarian.
sépulcre [sepylkʀ(ə)] *nm* sepulchre. ♦ **sépulcral, e,** *mpl* **-aux** *adj* sepulchral.
sépulture [sepyltyʀ] *nf* (*tombeau*) burial place.
séquelles [sekɛl] *nfpl [maladie]* after-effects; *[guerre]* aftermath.
séquence [sekɑ̃s] *nf* sequence.
séquestrer [sekɛstʀe] (1) *vt personne* to confine illegally. ♦ **séquestration** *nf* illegal confinement. ♦ **séquestre** *nm*: **mettre sous** ~ to sequester.
sérail [seʀaj] *nm* seraglio.
séraphin [seʀafɛ̃] *nm* seraph.
serein, e [səʀɛ̃, ɛn] *adj ciel* serene, clear; *visage* serene, calm; *jugement* calm, dispassionate. ♦ **sereinement** *adv* serenely; clearly; calmly; dispassionately. ♦ **sérénissime** *adj* Serene. ♦ **sérénité** *nf* serenity; clarity; calmness; dispassionateness.
sérénade [seʀenad] *nf* **(a)** (*Mus*) serenade. **donner une** ~ **à qn** to serenade sb. **(b)** (**hum: vacarme*) racket*, hullabaloo*.
serf, serve [sɛʀ(f), sɛʀv(ə)] *nm,f* serf.
sergent [sɛʀʒɑ̃] *nm* (*Mil*) sergeant. ~**-chef** staff sergeant; ~ **de ville**† policeman; ~**-major** ≈ quartermaster sergeant.
série [seʀi] *nf* **(a)** *[objets, timbres]* set; *[ennuis]* series, string*. (*beaucoup*) **(toute) une** ~ **de*** ... a (whole) series *ou* string* of ...; **ouvrages de** ~ **noire** crime thrillers. **(b)** (*catégorie*) (*Naut*) class; (*Sport*) rank; (*éliminatoire*) qualifying heat *ou* round. **(c)** (*Ind, fig*) **fabrication en** ~ mass production; **article de** ~ standard article. **(d)** (*Chim, Math, Mus*) series. (*Élec*) **monté en** ~ connected in series.
sérieux, -euse [seʀjø, øz] **1** *adj* **(a)** *personne* (*ne plaisantant pas*) serious, earnest; (*réfléchi*) serious-minded; (*digne de confiance*) reliable, dependable; (*moralement*) *jeune fille* responsible, trustworthy. ~ **comme un pape** sober as a judge; **ce n'est vraiment pas** ~! it's not taking a very responsible *ou* serious attitude. **(b)** *acquéreur, promesses, menace* genuine, serious. **non, il était** ~ no, he was serious *ou* he meant it; **'pas** ~ **s'abstenir'** 'only genuine inquirers need apply'. **(c)** *conversation, situation, maladie, travail* serious. **(d)** (*intensif*) *raison, avance, chances* strong, good; *coup* serious; *différence* serious, considerable. **2** *nm* seriousness; earnestness; serious-mindedness; dependability. **garder son** ~ to keep a straight face; **(se) prendre au** ~ to take (o.s.) seriously. ♦ **sérieusement** *adv* seriously; responsibly; genuinely; considerably. **il l'a dit** ~ he meant it seriously, he was in earnest.
serin [s(ə)ʀɛ̃] *nm* (*Orn*) canary.
seriner [s(ə)ʀine] (1) *vt* (*péj*) ~ **qch à qn** to drum *ou* din sth into sb.
seringue [s(ə)ʀɛ̃g] *nf* syringe.
serment [sɛʀmɑ̃] *nm* **(a)** (*solennel*) oath. **faire un** ~ to take an oath; **sous** ~ on *ou* under oath. **(b)** (*promesse*) pledge. **des** ~**s (d'amour)** vows *ou* pledges of love; **je te fais le** ~ **de venir** I swear to you that I'll come.
sermon [sɛʀmɔ̃] *nm* (*Rel, fig*) sermon. ♦ **sermonner** (1) *vt*: ~ **qn** to lecture sb.
serpe [sɛʀp(ə)] *nf* billhook, bill. **visage taillé à coups de** ~ craggy *ou* rugged face.
serpent [sɛʀpɑ̃] *nm* (*Zool*) snake, serpent; (*fig: ruban*) ribbon. ~ **à sonnettes** rattlesnake. ♦ **serpenter** (1) *vi [rivière, chemin]* to snake, meander, wind; *[vallée]* to wind. ♦ **serpentin** *nm* (*ruban*) streamer; (*Chim*) coil.
serpillière [sɛʀpijɛʀ] *nf* floorcloth.
serpolet [sɛʀpɔlɛ] *nm* wild thyme.
serre [sɛʀ] *nf* **(a)** (*Agr*) (*gén*) greenhouse, glasshouse; (*attenant à une maison*) conservatory. ~ **chaude** hothouse. **(b)** (*griffe*) talon, claw.
serrer [seʀe] (1) **1** *vt* **(a)** (*avec la main*) to grip, hold tight. ~ **qn dans ses bras** to clasp sb in one's arms; ~ **la main à qn** (*la donner à qn*) to shake sb's hand, shake hands with sb; (*presser*) to squeeze *ou* press sb's hand; **se** ~ **la main** to shake hands; ~ **qn à la gorge** to grab sb by the throat. **(b)** *poing, mâchoires* to clench; *lèvres* to set. **les lèvres serrées** with tight lips; **avoir la gorge serrée par l'émotion** to be choked by emotion; **cela serre le cœur** it wrings your heart; ~ **les dents** (*lit*) to clench one's teeth; (*fig*) to grit one's teeth. **(c)** *[chaussures, vêtements]* (*comprimer*) to be too tight; (*mouler*) to fit tightly. **(d)** *vis* to tighten; *joint* to clamp; *robinet* to turn off tight; *nœud, ceinture* to tighten, pull tight. ~ **qch dans un étau** to grip sth in a vice; ~ **le frein à main** to put on the handbrake; ~ **la vis à qn*** to crack down harder on sb*. **(e)** *véhicule, piéton* (*par derrière*) to keep close behind; (*latéralement*) to squeeze (*contre* up against). ~ **qn dans un coin** to wedge sb in a corner; ~ **le trottoir** to hug the kerb; (*fig*) ~ **une question de plus près** to study a question more closely; (*Naut*) ~ **la côte** to sail close to the shore, hug the shore. **(f)** (*rapprocher*) *objets, mots* to close up, put close together; *convives* to squeeze up *ou* together. (*Mil*) ~ **les rangs** to close ranks. **(g)** (†: *ranger*) to put away.
2 *vi* (*Aut*) ~ **à droite** to move in to the right.
3 se ~ *vpr*: **se** ~ **contre qn** to huddle (up) against sb; (*tendrement*) to cuddle up to sb; **se** ~ **autour du feu** to squeeze *ou* crowd round the fire; **serrez-vous un peu** squeeze up a bit; **son cœur se serra** he felt a pang of anguish; **se** ~ **les coudes** to back one another up; **se** ~ **la ceinture** to tighten one's belt.
♦ **serrage** *nm [vis]* tightening; *[joint]* clamping.
♦ **serré, e 1** *adj* **(a)** *vêtement* tight. **(b)** *spectateurs* (tightly) packed. **(c)** *tissu* closely woven; *réseau, herbe* dense; *mailles, écriture* close. **(d)** (*bloqué*) **trop** ~ too tight; **pas assez** ~ not tight enough. **(e)** (*contracté*) **avoir le cœur** ~ to feel a pang of anguish; **avoir la gorge** ~**e** to feel a tightening *ou* a lump in one's throat. **(f)** *discussion* closely conducted, closely argued; *lutte, match* tight, close-fought; *budget* tight. **2** *adv*: **écrire** ~ to write a cramped hand; (*fig*) **jouer** ~ to play a tight game. ♦ **serrement** *nm*: ~ **de main** handshake; ~ **de cœur** pang of anguish.
serrure [seʀyʀ] *nf* lock. ♦ **serrurerie** *nf* (*métier*) locksmith's trade; (*travail*) ironwork. ♦ **serrurier** *nm* locksmith.
sertir [sɛʀtiʀ] (2) *vt bijou* to set.
sérum [seʀɔm] *nm* serum.
servant [sɛʀvɑ̃] *nm* (*Rel, Mil*) server. ♦ **servante** *nf* (maid) servant.
serveur [sɛʀvœʀ] *nm [restaurant]* waiter; *[bar]* barman. ♦ **serveuse** *nf* waitress; barmaid.
serviable [sɛʀvjabl(ə)] *adj* obliging, willing to help. ♦ **serviabilité** *nf* obligingness.
service [sɛʀvis] **1** *nm* **(a)** (*travail*) duty. **heures de** ~ hours of duty; **prendre son/être de** ~ to come on/be on duty; **pompier de** ~ duty fireman, fireman on duty; (*Admin, Mil*) **en** ~ **commandé** on an official assignment; **avoir 25 ans de** ~ to have completed 25 years' service. **(b)** (*gén, Écon: prestations*) ~**s** services; **offrir ses** ~**s à qn** to offer sb one's services. **(c)** (*domesticité*) (domestic) service. **entrer en** ~ **chez qn** to go into service with sb; **être au** ~ **de** to be in the service of; **escalier de** ~ backstairs, servants' stairs; **entrée de** ~ service *ou* tradesman's entrance. **(d)** (*Mil*) **le** ~ **(militaire)** military *ou* national service; **faire son** ~ to do one's military *ou* national service; ~ **armé** combatant service. **(e)** (*organisme public*) service; (*section*) department, section. **les** ~**s postaux** the postal services; ~ **des achats/des urgences** buying/casualty department. **(f)** (*Rel*) service. ~ **funèbre** funeral

service. **(g)** (*faveur, aide*) service. **rendre un ~ à qn** to do sb a favour *ou* a service; **rendre ~ à qn** (*aider*) to do sb a service *ou* a good turn; (*s'avérer utile*) to come in useful *ou* handy for sb, be of use to sb; **il aime rendre ~** he likes to be helpful; **rendre un mauvais ~ à qn** to do sb a disservice; **qu'y-a-t-il pour votre ~?** how can I be of service to you?; **je suis à votre ~** I am at your service. **(h)** (*au restaurant*) service; (*pourboire*) service (charge). **~ compris/non compris** service included/not included, inclusive/exclusive of service; **premier/deuxième ~** first/second sitting. **(i)** *[vaisselle, linge]* service, set. **~ à liqueurs** set of liqueur glasses. **(j)** (*fonctionnement*) **mettre en ~** to put *ou* bring into service; **hors de ~** out of order *ou* commission. **(k)** (*transport*) service. **~ d'autobus/d'hiver** bus/winter service. **(l)** (*Tennis*) service. **être au ~** to have the service. **2: ~ après-vente** after-sales service; **~ d'ordre** (*policiers*) police patrol; (*manifestants*) team of stewards (*responsible for crowd control etc*); **~s secrets** secret service.

serviette [sɛʀvjɛt] *nf* **(a) ~ (de toilette)** (hand) towel; **~ (de table)** serviette, (table) napkin; **~ de bain** bath towel; **~-éponge** towel; **~ périodique** sanitary towel. **(b)** (*cartable*) briefcase.

servile [sɛʀvil] *adj homme, obéissance* servile, cringing; *imitation* slavish. ♦ **servilement** *adv* servilely, cringingly; slavishly. ♦ **servilité** *nf* servility; slavishness.

servir [sɛʀviʀ] (14) **1** *vt* **(a)** (*être au service de*) to serve. **~ qn** (*dans un magasin*) to attend to *ou* serve sb; (*au restaurant*) to wait on *ou* serve sb; **~ la messe** to serve Mass; **elle aime se faire ~** she likes to be waited on; **le boucher m'a bien servi** the butcher has sold me good meat; **'Madame est servie'** 'dinner is served'; **il sert dans un café** he is a waiter in a café; **ils voulaient la pluie, ils ont été servis!** they wanted rain – well, they've got what they asked for *ou* wanted!; **en fait d'ennuis, elle a été servie** as regards troubles, she's had her share (and more). **(b)** *plat* to serve. **~ qch à qn** to serve sb with sth, help sb to sth; **'~ frais'** 'serve cool'; **~ à boire à qn** to serve a drink to sb; **à table, c'est servi!** come and sit down now, it's ready!; **il nous sert toujours les mêmes plaisanteries** he always trots out the same old jokes. **(c)** (*aider*) *personne, ambitions* to serve (well), aid. **sa prudence l'a servi** his caution served him well (*auprès de* with); **il a été servi par une bonne mémoire** he was aided by a good memory. **(d)** (*être utile*) **~ à** *personne* to be of use *ou* help to; *usage* to be of use in, be useful for; **~ à faire** to be used for doing; **ça m'a servi à réparer le lit** I used it to mend the bed; **cela ne sert à rien** it's no use, it's useless; **cela ne sert à rien de pleurer** it's no use crying, crying doesn't help; **à quoi sert cet objet?** what is this object used for?; **à quoi servirait de réclamer?** what use would complaining be?, what would be the point of complaining? **(e) ~ de qch** *[objet]* to serve as sth, be used as sth; *[personne]* **elle lui a servi d'interprète** she acted as his interpreter; **~ de leçon à qn** to be a lesson to sb. **(f)** (*verser*) to pay. **~ des intérêts à qn** to pay sb interest. **(g)** (*Cartes*) to deal; (*Tennis*) to serve; (*Mil*) *canon* to serve.

2 se ~ *vpr* **(a)** (*distribution*) to help o.s. (*chez un fournisseur*) **se ~ chez X** to shop at X's. **(b) se ~ de qch** to use sth; **se ~ de ses relations** to make use of *ou* use one's contacts.

serviteur [sɛʀvitœʀ] *nm* (*gén*) servant.

servitude [sɛʀvityd] *nf* **(a)** (*esclavage*) servitude. **(b)** (*gén pl: contrainte*) constraint.

servofrein [sɛʀvɔfʀɛ̃] *nm* (*Tech*) servo(-assisted) brake.

ses [se] *adj poss V* **son**[1].

session [sesjɔ̃] *nf* (*Jur, Parl*) session. **~ (d'examen)** university exam session.

seuil [sœj] *nm* (*marche*) doorstep; (*entrée*) doorway, threshold†; (*fig*) threshold; (*Géog, Tech*) sill. (*fig*) **au ~ de la mort** on the threshold *ou* brink of death.

seul, e [sœl] **1** *adj* **(a)** (*non accompagné*) alone, on one's (*ou* its *etc*) own, by oneself (*ou* itself *etc*); (*isolé*) lonely. **ils se retrouvèrent enfin ~s** they were alone (together) *ou* on their own *ou* by themselves at last; **une femme ~e peut très bien se débrouiller** a woman on her own *ou* a single woman can manage perfectly well. **(b)** (*avant n: unique*) **un ~ livre** (*et non plusieurs*) one book, a single book; (*à l'exception de tout autre*) only one book; **le ~ homme** the one man, the only man, the sole man; **pour cette ~e raison** for this reason alone *ou* only, for this one reason; **une ~e fois** only once. **(c)** (*en apposition*) only, alone. **~ le résultat compte** the result alone counts, only the result counts. **(d)** (*locutions*) **~ et unique** one and only; **c'est la ~e et même personne** it's one and the same person; **d'un ~ coup** (*subitement*) suddenly; (*ensemble, à la fois*) in *ou* at one go; **d'un ~ tenant** *terrain* all in one piece; **vous êtes ~ juge** you alone can judge; **à ~e fin de** with the sole purpose of; **du ~ fait que ...** by the mere *ou* very fact that ...; **parler à qn ~ à ~** to speak to sb in private *ou* privately *ou* alone; **se retrouver ~ à ~ avec qn** to find o.s. alone with sb; (*fig*) **comme un ~ homme** as one man.

2 *adv parler, rire* to oneself; *vivre* alone, by oneself, on one's own. (*sans aide*) **faire qch (tout) ~** to do sth (all) on one's own *ou* unaided *ou* single-handed.

3 *nm,f*: **un ~** (*gén*) only one; **le ~ que j'aime** the only one I love; **il n'en reste pas un ~** there isn't a single one left.

seulement [sœlmɑ̃] *adv* **(a)** (*gén*) only; (*exclusivement*) only, solely; (*toutefois*) only, but. **nous serons ~ 4** there will be only 4 of us; **on ne vit pas ~ de pain** you can't live on bread alone *ou* only *ou* solely on bread; **ce n'est pas ~ sa maladie qui le déprime** it's not only *ou* just his illness that depresses him; **il vient ~ d'entrer** he's only just (now) come in; **c'est bien, ~ c'est cher** it's fine only *ou* but it's expensive. **(b)** (*locutions*) **non ~ il a plu, mais (encore) il a fait froid** it didn't only rain but it was cold too; **on ne nous a pas ~ donné un verre d'eau** we were not even given a glass of water, we were not given so much as a glass of water; **si ~** if only.

sève [sɛv] *nf* sap.

sévère [sevɛʀ] *adj* (*gén*) severe; *juge, climat* harsh; *parent, ton* stern. ♦ **sévèrement** *adv* severely; harshly; sternly. ♦ **sévérité** *nf* severity; harshness; sternness.

sévices [sevis] *nmpl* (physical) cruelty, ill treatment.

sévir [seviʀ] (2) *vi* **(a)** (*punir*) to act ruthlessly. **~ contre** to deal ruthlessly with. **(b)** *[fléau, doctrine]* to rage, hold sway; *[pauvreté]* to be rampant *ou* rife.

sevrer [səvʀe] (5) *vt nourrisson* to wean. (*fig*) **~ qn de qch** to deprive sb of sth. ♦ **sevrage** *nm* weaning.

sexe [sɛks(ə)] *nm* sex; (*organes*) sex organs. **enfant du ~ masculin** child of male sex, male child; **le beau ~** the fair sex. ♦ **sexualité** *nf* sexuality. ♦ **sexué, e** *adj* sexual. ♦ **sexuel, -elle** *adj* (*gén*) sexual; *éducation, hormone, organe* sexual, sex. ♦ **sexuellement** *adv* sexually. ♦ **sexy*** *adj inv* sexy*.

sextant [sɛkstɑ̃] *nm* sextant.

seyant, e [sɛjɑ̃, ɑ̃t] *adj vêtement* becoming.

shah [ʃa] *nm* shah.

shakespearien, -ienne [ʃɛkspiʀjɛ̃, jɛn] *adj* Shakespearian.

shampooing [ʃɑ̃pwɛ̃] *nm* shampoo. **faire un ~ à qn** to shampoo sb's hair; **~ colorant** tint, rinse.

shérif [ʃeʀif] *nm* sheriff.
shooter [ʃute] (1) *vi* (*Ftbl*) to shoot, make a shot. ♦ **shoot** *nm* shot.
short [ʃɔʀt] *nm*: ~**(s)** pair of shorts, shorts.
si[1] [si] **1** *conj* **(a)** (*hypothèse*) if. ~ **j'avais de l'argent** if I had any money, had I any money; ~ **j'étais riche** if I were rich; ~ **j'avais su!** if I had only known!, had I only *ou* but known!; **et s'il refusait?** and what if he refused?; ~ **tu lui téléphonais?** how *ou* what about phoning him?, supposing you phoned him? **(b)** (*répétition*) if, when. ~ **je sors sans parapluie, il pleut** if *ou* when(ever) I go out without an umbrella, it always rains. **(c)** (*opposition*) while. ~ **lui est aimable, sa femme est arrogante** while *ou* whereas he is very pleasant, his wife is arrogant. **(d)** (*exposant un fait*) **c'est un miracle** ~ **la voiture n'a pas pris feu** it's a miracle (that) the car didn't catch fire; **excusez-nous** ~ **nous n'avons pas pu venir** please excuse us for not being able to come. **(e)** (*interrogation indirecte*) if, whether. **il demande** ~ **elle viendra** he is asking whether *ou* if she will come; **vous imaginez s'ils étaient fiers!** you can imagine how proud they were!; ~ **je veux y aller! quelle question!** do I want to go! what a question! **(f) qui peut le savoir,** ~ **ce n'est lui?** who will know if not him? *ou* apart from him? *ou* but him?; ~ **ce n'était la crainte de les décourager** if it were not *ou* were it not for the fear of putting them off; **une des plus belles,** ~ **ce n'est la plus belle** one of the most beautiful, if not the most beautiful; **elle va bien,** ~ **ce n'est qu'elle est fatiguée** she's quite well apart from the fact that she is tired. **(g)** (*locutions*) **il te répondra** ~ **tant est qu'il le sache** he'll tell you, that is if he knows; **s'il te** *ou* **vous plaît** please; ~ **je ne me trompe** if I am not mistaken, unless I'm mistaken; ~ **j'ose dire** if I may say so, if I may put it like that; ~ **l'on peut dire** so to speak; ~ **l'on veut** in a way; ~ **c'est ça*, je m'en vais** if that's how it is, I'm off*. **2** *nm inv* if. **avec des** ~ **on mettrait Paris en bouteille** if ifs and ands were pots and pans there'd be no need for tinkers.
si[2] [si] *adj* **(a)** (*affirmatif*) **vous ne venez pas?** – ~**/mais** ~ aren't you coming? – yes I am/of course I am; ~**,**~**, il faut venir** oh but you must come!; **il n'a pas voulu, moi** ~ he didn't want to, but I did. **(b)** (*tellement*) so. **un ami** ~ **gentil** such a kind friend; **j'ai** ~ **faim** I'm so hungry. **(c)** ~ **bien que** so that. **(d)** (*concessif*) however. ~ **bête qu'il soit, il comprendra** stupid as he is *ou* however stupid he is he will understand; ~ **peu que ce soit** however little it may be. **(e)** (*égalité*) as, so. **elle n'est pas** ~ **timide que vous croyez** she's not so *ou* as shy as you think.
si[3] [si] *nm inv* (*Mus*) B; (*en chantant*) ti, te.
siamois, e [sjamwa, waz] **1** *adj* Siamese. **2** *nm,fpl*: ~,~es Siamese twins. **3** *nm* (*chat*) Siamese.
sic [sik] *adv* sic.
Sicile [sisil] *nf* Sicily.
sidéral, e *mpl* **-aux** [sideʀal, o] *adj* sidereal.
sidérer* [sideʀe] (6) *vt* to stagger, shatter*.
sidérurgie [sideʀyʀʒi] *nf* (*fabrication*) iron and steel metallurgy; (*industrie*) iron and steel industry. ♦ **sidérurgique** *adj procédé* (iron and) steel-making. ♦ **sidérurgiste** *nmf* (iron and) steel worker.
siècle [sjɛkl(ə)] *nm* century; (*époque*) age, century. **être de son** ~**/d'un autre** ~ to live with the times/be behind the times; **le** ~ **de Périclès** the age of Pericles; **il y a des** ~**s que nous ne nous sommes vus*** it's years *ou* ages since we last saw each other.
siege [sjɛʒ] *nm* **(a)** (*objet*) seat. ~ **de jardin** garden chair; **prenez un** ~ take a seat; ~ **éjectable** ejector seat. **(b)** (*Méd: postérieur*) seat. **(c)** (*Pol: fonction*) seat. **(d)** (*Jur*) *[magistrat]* bench. **(e)** *[firme]* head office; *[parti]* headquarters; *[assemblée]* seat. ~ **social** registered office; ~ **épiscopal** episcopal see. **(f)** *[maladie, rébellion]* seat; *[faculté, sensation]* centre. **(g)** *[place forte]* siege. (*lit, fig*) **faire le** ~ **de** to lay siege to; **lever le** ~ (*lit*) to raise the siege; (*fig*) to get up and go. ♦ **siéger** (3 et 6) *vi [assemblée]* to sit. **voilà où siège le mal** that's where the trouble lies.
sien, sienne [sjɛ̃, sjɛn] **1** *pron poss*: **le** ~**, la sienne, les** ~**s, les siennes** *[homme]* his (own); *[femme]* hers, her own; *[chose]* its own; (*indéf*) one's own; **ce sac est le** ~ this bag is hers; **mes enfants sont sortis avec les 2** ~s my children have gone out with her 2. **2** *nm* **(a) y mettre du** ~ to give and take. **(b) les** ~s (*famille*) one's family; (*partisans*) one's own people. **3** *nf*: **il a encore fait des siennes*** he has (gone and) done it again*. **4** *adj poss* (*littér*) **un** ~ **cousin** a cousin of his *ou* hers; **faire sienne une théorie** to adopt a theory, make a theory one's own.
sieste [sjɛst(ə)] *nf* (*gén*) nap, snooze*; (*en Espagne etc*) siesta. **faire la** ~ to have a nap *ou* siesta.
siffler [sifle] (1) **1** *vi* (*gén, fig*) to whistle; (*avec un sifflet*) to blow one's *ou* a whistle; *[gaz, serpent]* to hiss; *[respiration]* to wheeze. **2** *vt* **(a)** (*appeler*) *chien* to whistle for; (*pour infraction*) to blow one's whistle at; *départ, faute* to blow one's whistle for. (*Ftbl*) ~ **la fin du match** to blow the final whistle, blow for time. **(b)** *acteur, pièce* to hiss, boo. **(c)** *chanson* to whistle. **(d)** (*ᵗ: avaler*) to guzzle*, knock backᵗ. ♦ **sifflant, e** *adj sonorité* whistling; *toux* wheezing; *prononciation* hissing, whistling. **(consonne)** ~e sibilant. ♦ **sifflement** *nm*: ~**(s)** whistling; hissing; wheezing. **un** ~ a whistle; ~ **d'oreilles** whistling in the ears. ♦ **sifflet** *nm* whistle. (*huées*) ~s hissing, booing, cat calls. ♦ **siffleur, -euse 1** *adj merle* whistling; *serpent* hissing. **2** *nm,f* whistler; hisser, booer. ♦ **sifflotement** *nm* whistling. ♦ **siffloter** (1) *vti* to whistle.
sigle [sigl(ə)] *nm* abbreviation, acronym.
sigma [sigma] *nm* sigma.
signal, *pl* **-aux** [siɲal, o] *nm* signal. **donner le** ~ **de** (*lit*) to give the signal for; (*fig: déclencher*) to be the signal *ou* sign for, signal; **à mon** ~ **tous se levèrent** when I gave the signal *ou* sign everyone got up; ~ **de détresse** distress signal; (*Aut*) **signaux (lumineux)** traffic signals *ou* lights; **tirer le** ~ **d'alarme** to pull the alarm. ♦ **signalé, e** *adj service* signal. ♦ **signalement** *nm* description, particulars. ♦ **signaler** (1) **1** *vt* (*être l'indice de*) to indicate, be a sign of; (*avertir*) to signal; (*mentionner*) to indicate; *fait, vol* to report; *erreur, détail* to point out. **signalez que vous allez tourner à droite** indicate *ou* signal that you are turning right; **rien à** ~ nothing to report; ~ **qn à l'attention de qn** to bring sb to sb's attention; **nous vous signalons que ...** we would point out to you that ... . **2 se** ~ *vpr* (*s'illustrer*) to distinguish o.s., stand out; (*attirer l'attention*) to draw attention to o.s. **se** ~ **à l'attention de qn** to attract sb's attention, bring o.s. to sb's attention.
signaliser [siɲalize) (1) *vt route* to put up (road) signs on; *voie* to put signals on. ♦ **signalisation** *nf* **(a)** (*action*) erection of (road)signs (*ou* signals) (*de* on). **erreur de** ~ signposting (*ou* signalling) error; **panneau de** ~ roadsign; **moyens de** ~ means of signalling. **(b)** (*signaux*) signals. ~ **routière** roadsigns.
signature [siɲatyʀ] *nf* (*action*) signing; (*marque*) signature. ♦ **signataire** *nmf* signatory.
signe [siɲ] **1** *nm* **(a)** (*gén*) sign. **un** ~ **de tête affirmatif/négatif** a nod/a shake of the head; **c'est un** ~ **de pluie** it's a sign it's going to rain; **c'est bon/mauvais** ~ it's a good/bad sign; (*lit, fig*) **ne pas donner** ~ **de vie** to give no sign of life; **en** ~ **de respect** as a sign *ou* mark *ou* token of respect; '~**s particuliers: néant**' 'special peculiarities: none'; (*fig*) **rencontre placée sous le** ~ **de l'amitié franco-britannique** meeting where the keynote

ou where the dominant theme was Franco-British friendship. **(b) faire ~ à qn** (*lit*) to make a sign to sb, sign to sb (*de faire* to do); (*fig: contacter*) to get in touch with sb, contact sb; **faire ~ du doigt à qn** to beckon (to) sb with one's finger; (*de la tête*) **faire ~ que oui** to nod in agreement; **faire ~ que non** to shake one's head. **2: ~ de croix/du zodiaque** *etc* sign of the cross/of the Zodiac *etc*; **~s extérieurs de richesse** outward signs of wealth; (*clin d'œil*) **~ d'intelligence** knowing look; **~ de ponctuation** punctuation mark; **~ précurseur** omen, portent; **~ de ralliement** rallying symbol.

signer [siɲe] (1) **1** *vt* to sign. **tableau non signé** unsigned painting; (*fig*) **c'est signé!*** it's written all over it!* **2 se ~** *vpr* (*Rel*) to cross o.s.

signet [siɲɛ] *nm* bookmark.

signifier [siɲifje] (7) *vt* **(a)** (*avoir pour sens*) to mean, signify. **bonté ne signifie pas forcément faiblesse** kindness does not necessarily mean *ou* signify *ou* imply weakness; **qu'est-ce que cela signifie?** what's the meaning of this? **(b)** (*faire connaître*) to make known; (*Jur*) to serve notice of (*à* on), notify (*à* to). **~ sa volonté à qn** to make one's wishes known to sb, inform sb of one's wishes; **~ son congé à qn** to give sb his notice.

silence [silɑ̃s] *nm* **(a)** silence. (*lit, fig*) **garder le ~** to keep silent (*sur* on); **faire ~** to be silent; **passer qch sous ~** to pass over sth in silence; **en ~** in silence; **sortez vos cahiers et en ~!** get out your books and no talking! **(b)** (*dans la conversation, un récit*) pause; (*Mus*) rest. **à son entrée il y eut un ~** there was a hush when he came in. **(c)** (*paix*) silence, stillness. ♦ **silencieusement** *adv* silently; noiselessly. ♦ **silencieux, -euse 1** *adj* (*gén*) silent; (*paisible*) still; *moteur* noiseless. **2** *nm* (*Tech*) silencer.

silex [silɛks] *nm* flint.

silhouette [silwɛt] *nf* (*profil*) outline, silhouette; (*allure, dessin*) figure. **~s de tir** figure targets.

silice [silis] *nf* silica.

silicium [silisjɔm] *nm* silicon.

silicone [silikon] *nf* silicone.

sillage [sijaʒ] *nm* [*bateau*] wake; [*avion*] slipstream. (*lit, fig*) **dans son ~** in his (*ou* its *etc*) wake *ou* trail.

sillon [sijɔ̃] *nm* (*Agr, fig*) furrow; [*disque*] groove. ♦ **sillonner** (1) *vt* [*bateau, routes*] to cut across, cross; [*rides, ravins*] to furrow.

silo [silo] *nm* silo.

simagrées [simagʀe] *nfpl* fuss. **faire des ~** to make a fuss *ou* a to-do*.

simiesque [simjɛsk(ə)] *adj* (*V* **singe**) monkey-like; ape-like.

similaire [similɛʀ] *adj* similar. ♦ **simili** *préf* imitation. ♦ **similitude** *nf* similarity.

simple [sɛ̃pl(ə)] **1** *adj* **(a)** (*non complexe*) simple; (*non multiple*) *billet, fleur* single; (*facile*) straightforward. **en ~ épaisseur** in a single thickness; **réduit à sa plus ~ expression** reduced to a minimum; **~ comme bonjour*** easy as pie*. **(b)** (*modeste*) plain, simple. **il a su rester ~** he has managed to stay unaffected *ou* simple; (*hum*) **dans le plus ~ appareil** in one's birthday suit. **(c)** (*naïf*) simple. **~ d'esprit** (*adj*) simple-minded; (*nmf*) simpleton. **(d)** (*restrictif*) simple. **un ~ particulier** an ordinary citizen; **un ~ soldat** a private; **une ~ formalité** a simple *ou* mere formality; **un ~ regard la déconcertait** just a *ou* a mere look would upset her. **2** *nm* **(a) passer du ~ au double** to double. **(b)** († *Bot*) simple†. **(c)** (*Tennis*) singles. **~ dames** ladies' singles. ♦ **simplement** *adv* simply; straightforwardly; plainly; unaffectedly. **je veux ~ dire que ...** I simply *ou* merely *ou* just want to say that ... . ♦ **simplet, -ette** *adj personne* simple; *raisonnement* simplistic. ♦ **simplicité** *nf* simplicity; straightforwardness; plainness; unaffectedness; (*naïveté*) simpleness. ♦ **simplification** *nf* simplification. ♦ **simplifier** (7) *vt* (*gén, Math*) to simplify. **trop ~** to oversimplify. ♦ **simpliste** *adj* (*péj*) simplistic.

simuler [simyle] (1) *vt* (*gén, Tech*) to simulate; *sentiment, attaque* to feign, sham. **~ une maladie** to feign illness, pretend to be ill. ♦ **simulacre** *nm* (*action simulée*) enactment. (*péj*) **un ~ de justice** a pretence of justice; **un ~ de procès** a sham trial, a mockery of a trial. ♦ **simulateur, -trice 1** *nm,f* shammer, pretender; (*Mil: faux malade*) malingerer. **2** *nm*: **~ de vol** flight simulator. ♦ **simulation** *nf* simulation, feigning. **c'est de la ~** it's all sham, it's all put on. ♦ **simulé, e** *adj* feigned, sham.

simultané, e [simyltane] *adj* simultaneous. ♦ **simultanéité** *nf* simultaneity. ♦ **simultanément** *adv* simultaneously.

sinapisme [sinapism(ə)] *nm* mustard plaster.

sincère [sɛ̃sɛʀ] *adj* (*gén*) sincere; *partisan, sentiment* sincere, genuine, true. ♦ **sincèrement** *adv* sincerely; genuinely; truly; (*pour parler franchement*) honestly, really. ♦ **sincérité** *nf* sincerity; genuineness.

sinécure [sinekyʀ] *nf* sinecure. **ce n'est pas une ~*** it's not exactly a rest cure.

singe [sɛ̃ʒ] *nm* (*Zool*) monkey; (*de grande taille*) ape; (*personne laide*) horror; (*enfant espiègle*) monkey. **faire le ~** to monkey about; **malin comme un ~** as crafty *ou* artful as a monkey. ♦ **singer** (3) *vt attitude* to ape, mimic, take off*; *sentiments* to feign. ♦ **singeries** *nfpl* (*pitreries*) antics, clowning; (*simagrées*) airs and graces. **faire des ~** to clown about, play the fool.

singulier, -ière [sɛ̃gylje, jɛʀ] **1** *adj* (*Ling*) singular; (*étonnant*) remarkable, singular. **2** *nm* (*Ling*) singular. ♦ **singulariser** (1) **1** *vt* to mark out, make conspicuous. **2 se ~** *vpr* to call attention to o.s., make o.s. conspicuous. ♦ **singularité** *nf* **(a)** remarkable nature; singularity. **(b)** (*exception*) peculiarity. ♦ **singulièrement** *adv* remarkably, singularly; peculiarly; (*en particulier*) particularly, especially.

sinistre [sinistʀ(ə)] **1** *adj* sinister, ominous. (*avant n: intensif*) **un ~ imbécile** an utter idiot. **2** *nm* (*catastrophe*) disaster; (*incendie*) blaze; (*Assurances: cas*) accident. **déclarer un ~** to put in *ou* submit an accident claim. ♦ **sinistré, e 1** *adj* (disaster-)stricken. **2** *nm,f* disaster victim. ♦ **sinistrement** *adv* in a sinister way.

sinon [sinɔ̃] *conj* **(a)** (*sauf*) except, other than. **à quoi sert cette manœuvre ~ à nous intimider?** what is the purpose of this manoeuvre other than to intimidate us?; **je ne sais pas grand-chose, ~ qu'il a démissionné** I don't know much about it, except that *ou* only that he has resigned. **(b)** (*concession*) if not. **il avait leur approbation, ~ leur enthousiasme** he had their approval, if not their enthusiasm. **(c)** (*autrement*) otherwise, or else. (*menace*) **fais-le, ~ ...** do it, or else ... .

sinueux, -euse [sinɥø, øz] *adj route* winding; *rivière* winding, meandering; *ligne* sinuous; *pensée* tortuous. ♦ **sinuosité** *nf* (*aspect*) winding; (*courbe*) curve, loop.

sinus [sinys] *nm* (*Anat*) sinus; (*Math*) sine. ♦ **sinusite** *nf* sinusitis. ♦ **sinusoïdal, e, *mpl* -aux** *adj* sinusoidal. ♦ **sinusoïde** *nf* sinusoid.

sionisme [sjɔnism(ə)] *nm* Zionism. ♦ **sioniste** *adj, nmf* Zionist.

siphon [sifɔ̃] *nm* (*tube, bouteille*) siphon; [*évier, W.-C.*] U-bend; (*Spéléologie*) sump. ♦ **siphonné, e*** *adj* cracked*. ♦ **siphonner** (1) *vt* to siphon.

sire [siʀ] *nm* **(a)** (*au roi*) **S~** Sire. **(b)** (*seigneur*) lord. **(c) triste ~** unsavoury individual.

sirène [siʀɛn] *nf* **(a)** (*Myth, fig*) siren, mermaid. **(b)** [*bateau, ambulance*] siren; [*usine*] hooter. (*incendie*) **~ d'alarme** fire alarm.

sirop [siʀo] *nm* (*pharmaceutique*) syrup, mixture;

(*pour boisson*) syrup, cordial. ~ **de menthe** mint cordial; ~ **d'érable** maple syrup.
siroter [siʀɔte] (1) *vt* to sip.
sirupeux, -euse [siʀypø, øz] *adj* (*lit, péj*) syrupy.
sis, sise [si, siz] *adj* (*Admin, Jur*) located.
sismique [sismik] *adj* seismic. ♦ **sismographe** *nm* seismograph.
site [sit] *nm* (*environnement*) setting; (*endroit pittoresque*) beauty spot; (*Constr: emplacement*) site. ~ **naturel/classé** natural/listed site; **la protection des** ~**s** the conservation of places of interest.
sitôt [sito] **1** *adv*: ~ **(après qu'elle fut) couchée, elle s'endormit** as soon as *ou* immediately she was in bed she fell asleep, she was no sooner in bed than she fell asleep; ~ **dit,** ~ **fait** no sooner said than done; ~ **qu'il sera guéri** as soon as he is better; ~ **après la guerre** straight *ou* immediately after the war; **il ne reviendra pas de** ~ he won't be back for quite a while *ou* for (quite) some time; (*hum*) he won't be back in a hurry. **2** *prép*: ~ **les vacances, elle partait** she went away as soon as the holidays started.
situation [sitɥɑsjɔ̃] *nf* (*circonstances*) situation; (*emplacement*) situation, position, location; (*emploi*) job, position, situation; (*Fin: état*) statement of finances. **être en** ~ **de faire** to be in a position to do; ~ **de fait** de facto situation; ~ **de famille** marital status; **se faire une belle** ~ to work up to a good position.
situer [sitɥe] (1) **1** *vt* (*construire*) to site, situate, locate; (*par la pensée: localiser*) to set, place; (*: *catégoriser*) *personne* to place, pin down*. **2 se** ~ *vpr* **(a)** (*emploi réfléchi*) to place o.s. (*par rapport à* in relation to). **(b)** (*dans l'espace*) to be situated; (*dans le temps*) to take place; (*par rapport à des notions*) to stand. **bien/mal situé** well/badly situated; **l'action se situe à Paris** the action is set *ou* takes place in Paris.
six [sis], *devant consonne* [si], *devant voyelle ou h muet* [siz] **1** *adj cardinal inv* six. ~ **mille** six thousand; **les** ~ **huitièmes de cette somme** six eighths of this sum; **il a** ~ **ans** he is six (years old); **un enfant de** ~ **ans** a six-year-old (child), a child of six; **un objet de** ~ **F** a six-franc article; **à** ~ **faces** six-sided; **il est trois heures moins** ~ it is six minutes to three; **cinq fois sur** ~ five times out of six; **tous les** ~ all six of them; **ils ont porté la table à eux** ~ the six of them carried the table; **ils viennent à** ~ **pour déjeuner** there are six coming to lunch; **on peut s'asseoir à** ~ **autour de cette table** this table can seat six (people); **se battre à** ~ **contre un** to fight six against one; **entrer** ~ **par** ~ to come in six at a time *ou* six by six; **se mettre en rangs par** ~ to form rows of six.
2 *adj ordinal inv* sixth, six. **arriver le** ~ **septembre** to arrive on the sixth of September *ou* (on) September (the) sixth; **Louis** ~ Louis the Sixth; **page** ~ page six; **il habite au numéro** ~ he lives at number six; **il est** ~ **heures du soir** it's six in the evening *ou* p.m.
3 *nm inv* six. **quarante-**~ forty-six; **quatre et deux font** ~ four and two are *ou* make six; **il fait mal ses** ~ he writes his sixes badly; (*numéro*) **le** ~ number six; **il habite** ~ **rue de Paris** he lives at six Rue de Paris; **nous sommes le** ~ **aujourd'hui** it's the sixth today; (*Cartes*) **le** ~ **de cœur** the six of hearts; (*Dominos*) **le** ~ **et deux** the six-two.
4: (*Mus*) ~**-huit** *nm inv* six-eight (time); **mesure à** ~**-huit** bar in six-eight (time); (*Naut*) ~**-mâts** *nm inv* six-master.
♦ **sixième 1** *adj* sixth. **vingt-**~ twenty-sixth; **dans le** ~ **(arrondissement)** in the sixth arrondissement (*in Paris*); **au** ~ **(étage)** on the sixth floor. **2** *nmf* (*gén*) sixth (person). **se classer** ~ to come sixth. **3** *nm* (*portion*) sixth. **calculer le** ~ **d'un nombre** to work out the sixth of a number; **recevoir le** ~ **d'une somme** to receive a sixth of a sum; **(les) deux** ~**s du budget** two sixths of the budget. **4** *nf* (*Scol*) ≃ first year *ou* form, ≃ sixth grade (*US*). **entrer en (classe de)** ~ ≃ to go into the first form; **élève de** ~ ≃ first form pupil. ♦ **sixièmement** *adv* in the sixth place, sixthly.
skaï [skɑj] *nm* ® Skai (fabric) ®, leatherette.
sketch, *pl* ~**es** [skɛtʃ] *nm* (variety) sketch.
ski [ski] *nm* (*objet*) ski; (*sport*) skiing. ~ **alpin** Alpine skiing; ~ **de fond** langlauf; ~ **nautique** water-skiing; **faire du** ~ to ski, go skiing; **chaussures de** ~ ski boots. ♦ **skier** (7) *vi* to ski. ♦ **skieur, -euse** *nm,f* skier.
slalom [slalɔm] *nm* slalom; (*fig*) zigzag. ♦ **slalomer** (1) *vi* (*Ski*) to slalom; (*fig: obstacles*) to zigzag. ♦ **slalomeur, -euse** *nm,f* slalom skier.
slave [slav] **1** *adj* Slavic, Slavonic. **2** *nmf*: **S**~ Slav.
slip [slip] *nm* briefs, pants. ~ **de bain** *[homme]* (bathing) trunks; (*du bikini*) bikini briefs; **2** ~**s** 2 pairs of briefs *ou* pants.
slogan [slɔgɑ̃] *nm* slogan.
slow [slo] *nm* slow number.
smala* [smala] *nf* (*troupe*) tribe*.
smicard, e* [smikaʀ, aʀd(ə)] *nm,f* minimum wage earner.
smoking [smɔkiŋ] *nm* (*costume*) dinner suit, (*veston*) dinner jacket, tuxedo (*US*).
snack(-bar) [snak(baʀ)] *nm* snack bar.
snob [snɔb] **1** *nmf* snob. **2** *adj* snobby, posh*. ♦ **snober** (1) *vt*: ~ **qn** to snub sb, give sb the cold shoulder. ♦ **snobisme** *nm* snobbery.
sobre [sɔbʀ(ə)] *adj personne* sober, temperate, abstemious; *style* sober. ~ **de paroles** sparing of words; ~ **comme un chameau** as sober as a judge. ♦ **sobrement** *adv* soberly, temperately; frugally. ♦ **sobriété** *nf* sobriety, temperance; frugality.
sobriquet [sɔbʀikɛ] *nm* nickname.
sociable [sɔsjabl(ə)] *adj caractère* sociable; *milieu* hospitable. ♦ **sociabilité** *nf* sociability; hospitality.
social, e, *mpl* **-aux** [sɔsjal, o] *adj* (*gén*) social. **prestations** ~**es** social security benefits. ♦ **social-démocrate,** *mpl* **sociaux-démocrates** *adj, nmf* Social Democrat. ♦ **socialement** *adv* socially. ♦ **socialisation** *nf* socialization. ♦ **socialiser** (1) *vt* to socialize. ♦ **socialisme** *nm* socialism. ♦ **socialiste** *adj, nmf* socialist.
société [sɔsjete] *nf* **(a)** (*groupe*) society. **la** ~ society; **la bonne/haute** ~ polite/high society; **la** ~ **de consommation** the consumer society. **(b)** (*club*) (*littéraire*) society; (*sportive*) club. **la S**~ **protectrice des animaux** ≃ the Royal Society for the Prevention of Cruelty to Animals. **(c)** (*Comm*) company, firm. ~ **par actions/anonyme** joint stock/limited company. **(d)** (*assemblée*) company, gathering. **une** ~ **d'artistes** a company *ou* gathering of artists; **toute la** ~ **se leva** the whole company rose. **(e)** (*compagnie*) company. **rechercher la** ~ **de qn** to seek sb's company. ♦ **sociétaire** *nmf* member (*of a society*).
socio- [sɔsjɔ] *préf* socio. ~**-éducatif/-économique** *etc* socioeducational/economic *etc.*
sociologie [sɔsjɔlɔʒi] *nf* sociology. ♦ **sociologique** *adj* sociological. ♦ **sociologiquement** *adv* sociologically. ♦ **sociologue** *nmf* sociologist.
socle [sɔkl(ə)] *nm [statue]* plinth, pedestal; *[lampe]* base.
socquette [sɔkɛt] *nf* ankle sock.
soda [sɔda] *nm* fizzy drink. ~ **à l'orange** orangeade.
sodium [sɔdjɔm] *nm* sodium.
sœur [sœʀ] *nf* (*gén, Rel*) sister. **avec un dévouement de** ~ with a sister's *ou* with sisterly devotion; **et ta** ~**?‡** get lost‡; ~ **Jeanne** Sister Jeanne; **mis en pension chez les** ~**s** sent to a convent (boarding) school.
sofa [sɔfa] *nm* sofa.
soi [swa] **1** *pron pers* (*gén*) oneself. **n'aimer que** ~ to love only oneself; **il faut regarder devant** ~

you must look in front of you; **il n'agit que pour ~** he is only acting for himself; **se rendre service entre ~** to help each other *ou* one another (out); **cela va de ~** it's obvious, it stands to reason, it goes without saying (*que* that); **en ~** (*intrinsèquement*) in itself; **~-même** oneself; **le respect de ~-même** self-respect; (*hum*) **Monsieur X? – ~-même!** Mr X? – in person! **2** *nm* (*Philos*) self; (*Psych*) id. ♦ **soi-disant 1** *adj inv* so-called. **2** *adv* supposedly. **il était ~ parti** he had supposedly left, he was supposed to have left.

soie [swa] *nf* (*Tex*) silk; *[sanglier etc]* bristle. ♦ **soierie** *nf* (*tissu*) silk; (*commerce*) silk trade.

soif [swaf] *nf* **(a)** (*lit*) **avoir ~** to be thirsty; **le sel donne ~** salt makes you thirsty, salt gives one a thirst; **jusqu'à plus ~*** till one can take no more. **(b)** (*fig: désir*) **~ de qch** thirst *ou* craving for sth; **~ de faire qch** craving to do sth.

soigné, e [swaɲe] *adj* **(a)** *personne, tenue, chevelure* tidy, well-groomed, neat; *ongles* well-groomed, well-kept; *mains* well-cared-for; *travail, présentation* neat, careful, meticulous; *jardin* well-kept, neat; *repas* carefully-prepared. **peu ~** *personne* untidy; *cheveux* unkempt, untidy. **(b)** (*: *intensif*) *note* massive*, whopping*; *punition* stiff*. **avoir un rhume ~** to have a whopper* of a cold.

soigner [swaɲe] (1) **1** *vt* **(a)** *[médecin]* to treat; *[infirmière]* to look after, nurse. **se faire ~** to have treatment; **il faut te faire ~!*** you need your head examined!* **(b)** *plantes, invité, ongles* to look after, take (good) care of; *tenue, travail, repas* to take care over. **2 se ~** *vpr* (*lit, fig*) *[personne]* to take good care of o.s, look after o.s. **cette maladie se soigne** this disease can be treated. ♦ **soigneur** *nm* (*Boxe*) second; (*Cyclisme, Ftbl*) trainer.

soigneux, -euse [swaɲø, øz] *adj* *personne* tidy, neat; *travail* careful, meticulous. **~ de sa personne/de ses vêtements** careful about one's appearance/with one's clothes. ♦ **soigneusement** *adv* tidily, neatly; carefully, meticulously. **~ préparé** carefully prepared.

soin [swɛ̃] *nm* **(a)** (*application*) care; (*ordre et propreté*) tidiness, neatness. **sans ~** (*adj*) careless; untidy; (*adv*) carelessly; untidily; **avec (grand) ~** with (great) care, (very) carefully. **(b)** (*charge*) care. **confier à qn le ~ de faire** to entrust sb with the job of doing; **je vous laisse ce ~** I leave this to you, I leave you to take care of this; **son premier ~ fut de faire ...** his first concern was to do ... . **(c) ~s** care; (*traitement*) attention, treatment; **les ~s du ménage** the care of the home; **les ~s du visage** face-care, care of the complexion; **le blessé a reçu les premiers ~s** the injured man has been given first aid; **confier qn/qch aux (bons) ~s de** to leave sb/sth in the hands *ou* care of; (*sur lettre*) **aux bons ~s de** care of, c/o; **être aux petits ~s pour qn** to wait on sb hand and foot. **(d) avoir** *ou* **prendre ~ de faire** to take care to do; **avoir** *ou* **prendre ~ de qn/qch** to take care of *ou* look after sb/sth; **prenez ~ d'éteindre** take care *ou* be sure to turn out the lights.

soir [swaʀ] *nm* evening. **journal du ~** evening paper; **5 heures du ~** 5 (o'clock) in the afternoon *ou* evening, 5 p.m.; **11 heures du ~** 11 (o'clock) at night, 11 p.m.; **le ~** in the evening; **j'y vais ce ~** I'm going this evening *ou* tonight; **hier ~** last night, yesterday evening; **la veille au ~** the previous evening, in the evening of the previous day. ♦ **soirée** *nf* (*soir*) evening; (*réception*) party; (*Théât*) evening performance. **~ dansante** dance.

soit [swa] **1** *adv* (*oui*) very well, well and good. **2** *conj* **(a)** (*d'alternative*) **~ l'un ~ l'autre** (either) one or the other; **~ avant ~ après** (either) before or after; **~ qu'il soit fatigué, ~ qu'il en ait assez** whether he is tired or whether he has had enough. **(b)** (*à savoir*) that is to say. **(c)** (*Math: posons*) **~ un rectangle ABCD** let ABCD be a rectangle.

soixante [swasɑ̃t] *adj inv, nm inv* sixty. **les années ~** the sixties, the 60s; **~ et un** sixty-one; **~ et unième** sixty-first; **~-dix** seventy; **~-dixième** seventieth; **~ et onze** seventy-one. ♦ **soixantaine** *nf* **(a)** (*environ soixante*) sixty or so, (round) about sixty, sixty-odd*. **la ~ de spectateurs qui étaient là** the sixty or so *ou* the sixty-odd* people there; **ils étaient une bonne ~** there were a good sixty of them; **ça doit coûter une ~ de mille (francs)** that must cost sixty thousand or so francs *ou* (round) about sixty thousand francs. **(b)** (*soixante*) sixty. **(c)** (*âge*) sixty. **d'une ~ d'années** *personne* of about sixty; *arbre* sixty or so years old; **elle a la ~** she is sixtyish *ou* in her sixties. ♦ **soixantième** *adj, nmf* sixtieth.

soja [sɔʒa] *nm* (*plante*) soya.

sol[1] [sɔl] **1** *nm* (*gén*) ground; (*d'une maison*) floor; (*Agr, Géol*) soil. **sur le ~ français** on French soil; **vitesse au ~** ground speed; (*Sport*) **exercices au ~** floor exercises. **2:** (*Mil*) **~-air** *adj inv* ground-to-air; **~-~** *adj inv* ground-to-ground.

sol[2] [sɔl] *nm inv* (*Mus*) G; (*en chantant*) so(h).

solaire [sɔlɛʀ] *adj* (*Astrol, Astron*) solar; *crème* sun.

soldat [sɔlda] *nm* (*gén*) soldier. **simple ~** private; **~ d'infanterie** infantryman; **le S~ inconnu** the Unknown Soldier *ou* Warrior; **~ de plomb** tin soldier.

solde[1] [sɔld(ə)] *nf* (*salaire*) pay. (*péj*) **être à la ~ de** to be in the pay of.

solde[2] [sɔld(ə)] *nm* **(a)** (*Fin*) balance; (*à payer*) balance outstanding. **~ créditeur** credit balance; **pour ~ de tout compte** in settlement. **(b) (article en) ~** sale(s) article; **~ de lainages** sale of woollens, woollen sale; **acheter qch en ~** to buy sth at sale price; **les ~s** the sales.

solder [sɔlde] (1) **1** *vt* **(a)** *compte* (*arrêter*) to wind up; (*acquitter*) to settle, balance. **(b)** *marchandises* to sell (off) at sale price. **je vous le solde à 10 F** I'll let you have it for 10 francs. **2 se ~** *vpr* (*Fin*) **se ~ par un bénéfice** to show a profit; (*fig*) **se ~ par un échec** to end in failure.

sole [sɔl] *nf* (*poisson*) sole.

solécisme [sɔlesism(ə)] *nm* solecism (*in language*).

soleil [sɔlɛj] *nm* **(a)** (*astre*) sun; (*lumière*) sunshine, sunlight; (*chaleur*) sunshine. **le ~ levant/couchant/de minuit** the rising/setting/midnight sun; **se mettre au ~** to go out into the sun(shine) *ou* sunlight; **il fait du ~** the sun is shining, it's sunny; **il fait un ~ de plomb** the sun is blazing down; **des jours sans ~** sunless days. **(b)** (*feu d'artifice*) Catherine wheel; (*acrobatie*) grand circle; (*fig: culbute*) somersault; (*fleur*) sunflower. **(c)** (*locutions*) **rien de nouveau sous le ~** there's nothing new under the sun; **avoir du bien au ~** to be the owner of property; (*fig*) **se faire une place au ~** to find o.s a place in the sun.

solennel, -elle [sɔlanɛl] *adj* (*gén*) solemn; *séance* ceremonial. ♦ **solennellement** *adv* solemnly; ceremonially. ♦ **solennité** *nf* solemnity.

solfège [sɔlfɛʒ] *nm* musical theory.

solidaire [sɔlidɛʀ] *adj* **(a)** (*mutuellement liés*) **être ~s** to show solidarity, stand *ou* stick together; **être ~ de** to stand by, back, support. **(b)** *mécanismes* interdependent. **être ~ de** to be dependent on. **(c)** (*Jur*) *engagement* binding all parties; *débiteurs* jointly liable. ♦ **solidairement** *adv* jointly. ♦ **se solidariser** (1) *vpr*: **se ~ avec** to show solidarity with. ♦ **solidarité** *nf* solidarity; interdependence; joint liability. **faire une grève de ~** to come out in sympathy *ou* stop work in sympathy with the strikers.

solide [sɔlid] **1** *adj* **(a)** (*non liquide*) solid. **(b)** (*robuste*) *objet, muscles* solid, sturdy, strong; *qualité, connaissances, santé, esprit* sound; *personne* sturdy; (*sérieux*) reliable, solid. **c'est du ~**

it's solid stuff; **être ~ sur ses jambes** to be steady on one's legs; **cela ne repose sur rien de ~** it has no solid *ou* sound foundation; **avoir la tête ~** (*lit*) to have a hard head; (*fig: équilibré*) to have a good head on one's shoulders. **(c)** *coup de poing* hefty*; *revenus* substantial; *repas* (good) solid. **2** *nm* (*Géom, Phys*) solid. ♦ **solidement** *adv fixer* firmly; *fabriquer* solidly; *s'installer* securely. ♦ **solidification** *nf* solidification. ♦ **solidifier** *vt*, **se ~** *vpr* (7) to solidify. ♦ **solidité** *nf* solidity; sturdiness; soundness; reliability.

soliloque [sɔlilɔk] *nm* soliloquy.

soliste [sɔlist(ə)] *nmf* soloist.

solitaire [sɔlitɛʀ] **1** *adj* (*gén*) solitary, lonely; *caractère* solitary. **un passant ~** a solitary *ou* lone passer-by. **2** *nmf* (*ermite*) recluse; (*fig: ours*) lone wolf, loner. **travailler en ~** to work on one's own. **3** *nm* (*sanglier*) old boar; (*diamant*) solitaire; (*jeu*) solitaire. ♦ **solitude** *nf* **(a)** (*tranquillité*) solitude; (*manque de compagnie*) loneliness; *[endroit]* loneliness. **(b)** (*désert*) solitude.

solliciter [sɔlisite] (1) *vt faveur, audience* to seek, request, solicit (*de qn* from sb); *poste* to seek; *curiosité* to appeal to; *attention* to attract; *cheval, voiture* to coax forward. **il est très sollicité** he's very much in demand; **les attractions qui sollicitent le touriste** the attractions that are there to tempt the tourist. ♦ **sollicitation** *nf* (*démarche*) entreaty, appeal; (*tentation*) temptation, solicitation. ♦ **solliciteur, -euse** *nm,f* supplicant.

sollicitude [sɔlisityd] *nf* concern, solicitude.

solo [sɔlo] *adj inv, nm* solo.

solstice [sɔlstis] *nm* solstice.

soluble [sɔlybl(ə)] *adj substance* soluble; *problème* soluble, solvable. **café ~** instant coffee. ♦ **solubilité** *nf* solubility.

solution [sɔlysjɔ̃] *nf* (*réponse*) solution (*de* to); (*Math, Chim*) solution. **c'est une ~ de facilité** that's an easy answer *ou* the easy way out; **~ de continuité** solution of continuity.

solvable [sɔlvabl(ə)] *adj* (*Fin*) solvent. ♦ **solvabilité** *nf* solvency.

solvant [sɔlvɑ̃] *nm* (*Chim*) solvent.

sombre [sɔ̃bʀ(ə)] *adj* **(a)** (*foncé*) dark. **il fait ~** it's dark; **bleu ~** dark blue. **(b)** *pensées, avenir* sombre, gloomy, dark, dismal. **(c) ~ idiot** utter idiot; **une ~ histoire d'enlèvement** a murky story of abduction. ♦ **sombrement** *adv* darkly; sombrely, gloomily, dismally.

sombrer [sɔ̃bʀe] (1) *vi [bateau]* to sink, go down, founder; *[raison]* to give way; *[empire]* to founder. **~ dans le désespoir** to sink into despair; **~ corps et biens** to go down with all hands.

sommaire [sɔmɛʀ] **1** *adj exposé, réponse* brief, summary; *examen* cursory; *réparation, repas* basic; *tenue, décoration* scanty; *justice* summary. **2** *nm* summary. ♦ **sommairement** *adv* briefly; summarily; cursorily; basically; scantily.

sommation [sɔmɑsjɔ̃] *nf* (*Jur*) summons; (*injonction*) demand; (*Mil*) warning.

somme[1] [sɔm] *nm* nap, snooze*. **faire un ~** to have a nap *ou* a snooze*.

somme[2] [sɔm] *nf* (*Math*) sum; (*quantité*) amount. **la ~ totale** the grand total, the total sum; **faire la ~ de** to add up; **~ (d'argent)** sum *ou* amount (of money); **en ~** in sum, in short; **~ toute** when all's said and done.

sommeil [sɔmɛj] *nm* (*gén, fig*) sleep; (*envie de dormir*) drowsiness, sleepiness. **avoir ~** to be *ou* feel sleepy; **8 heures de ~** 8 hours' sleep; **~ de plomb** heavy *ou* deep sleep; **premier ~** first hours of sleep; **nuit sans ~** sleepless night; **laisser une affaire en ~** to leave a matter (lying) dormant, leave a matter in abeyance; (*littér*) **le ~ éternel** eternal rest. ♦ **sommeiller** (1) *vi [personne]* to doze; *[qualité, nature]* to lie dormant.

sommelier [sɔməlje] *nm* wine waiter.

sommer [sɔme] (1) *vt*: **~ qn de faire** to charge *ou* enjoin sb to do.

sommet [sɔmɛ] *nm* **(a)** (*gén*) top; *[montagne]* summit; *[vague]* crest; *[crâne]* crown; *[angle]* vertex. **les ~s de la gloire** the summits *ou* heights of fame. **(b)** (*montagne*) summit, mountain top.

sommier [sɔmje] *nm* bedsprings; (*avec pieds*) divan base.

sommité [sɔmite] *nf* leading light (*de* in).

somnambule [sɔmnɑ̃byl] *nmf* sleepwalker, somnambulist. ♦ **somnambulisme** *nm* sleepwalking, somnambulism.

somnifère [sɔmnifɛʀ] **1** *nm* sleeping drug, soporific; (*pilule*) sleeping pill *ou* tablet. **2** *adj* soporific.

somnolence [sɔmnɔlɑ̃s] *nf* sleepiness, drowsiness, somnolence. ♦ **somnolent, e** *adj* sleepy, drowsy, somnolent. ♦ **somnoler** (1) *vi* (*lit*) to doze; (*fig*) to lie dormant.

somptueux, -euse [sɔ̃ptɥø, øz] *adj habit, résidence* sumptuous, magnificent; *train de vie* lavish; *cadeau* handsome; *repas* sumptuous, lavish. ♦ **somptueusement** *adv* sumptuously, magnificently; lavishly; handsomely. ♦ **somptuosité** *nf* sumptuousness, magnificence; lavishness; handsomeness.

son[1] [sɔ̃], **sa** [sa], **ses** [se] *adj poss* **(a)** *[homme]* his; *[femme]* her; *[objet]* its. **Sa Majesté** *(roi)* His Majesty; (*reine*) Her Majesty; **ce n'est pas ~ genre** he (*ou* she) is not that sort, it's not like him (*ou* her); (*emphatique*) **~ jardin à lui est une vraie jungle** HIS *ou* his own garden is a real jungle; **à sa vue, elle poussa un cri** she screamed at the sight of him (*ou* her) *ou* on seeing him (*ou* her); **un de ses amis** one of his (*ou* her) friends, a friend of his (*ou* hers); **~ idiote de sœur*** that stupid sister of hers (*ou* his); **ça a ~ importance** that has its *ou* a certain importance. **(b)** (*à valeur d'indéfini*) one's. **faire ses études** to study; **être satisfait de sa situation** to be satisfied with one's situation; **chacun selon ses possibilités** each according to his (own) capabilities. **(c)** (*: *valeur intensive*) **il doit gagner ~ million par an** he must be earning a million a year; **il a passé tout ~ dimanche à travailler** he spent the whole of *ou* all Sunday working.

son[2] [sɔ̃] *nm* (*gén, Ling, Phys*) sound. **défiler au ~ d'une fanfare** to march past to the music of a band; **le ~ d'une cloche** the sound *ou* ringing of a bell; (*fig*) **entendre un autre ~ de cloche** to hear another side of the story; **(spectacle) ~ et lumière** son et lumière (display).

son[3] [sɔ̃] *nm* (*Agr*) bran.

sonate [sɔnat] *nf* sonata.

sonde [sɔ̃d] *nf* (*Naut*) sounding line; (*Tech: de forage*) borer, drill; (*Méd*) probe; (*à canal central*) catheter; (*d'alimentation*) feeding tube; (*Mét*) sonde; (*spatiale*) probe. **mettre une ~ à qn** to put a catheter in sb. ♦ **sondage** *nm* boring, drilling; sounding; probing; catheterization. **~ (d'opinion)** (opinion) poll. ♦ **sonder** (1) *vt* **(a)** (*Naut*) to sound; (*Mét*) to probe; *terrain* to bore, drill; *plaie* to probe; *vessie* to catheterize. **(b)** *personne* to sound out; *avenir* to probe.

songer [sɔ̃ʒe] (3) **1** *vi* (*littér*) to dream. **2** *vt*: **~ que** (*réfléchir*) to reflect *ou* consider that; (*imaginer*) to imagine that; **songe que ...** remember that ... . **3 ~ à** *vt indir* (*évoquer*) to think over, reflect upon; (*s'occuper de*) to think of. **songez-y** think it over, consider it; **~ à faire qch** to contemplate doing sth, think of doing sth. ♦ **songe** *nm* (*littér*) dream. ♦ **songerie** *nf* (*littér*) reverie. ♦ **songeur, -euse 1** *adj* pensive. **cela me laisse ~** I just don't know what to think. **2** *nm,f* dreamer.

sonner [sɔne] (1) **1** *vt* **(a)** *cloche* to ring; *glas* to sound, toll; *clairon, réveil, retraite* to sound; *infirmière* to ring for. **~ l'alarme** to sound the alarm; **la pendule sonne 3 heures** the clock strikes 3 (o'clock); **on ne t'a pas sonné!*** nobody asked you!; **se faire ~ les cloches*** to get a good telling-off*. **(b)** (*: *étourdir*) *[chute]* to knock out; *[nouvelle]* to stagger*, take aback. **2** *vi [cloches, téléphone]* to ring; *[réveil]* to ring, go off; *[clairon]* to sound; *[glas]* to sound, toll; *[heure]* to strike; *[clefs, monnaie]* to jangle, jingle. **~ creux** (*lit*) to sound hollow; (*fig*) to ring hollow; **~ faux** (*lit*) to sound out of tune; (*fig*) to ring false; (*fig*) **~ bien/mal** to sound good/bad; **~ à toute volée** to peal out; **on a sonné** the bell has just gone, sb just rang (the bell). **3 ~ de** *vt indir clairon, cor* to sound. ♦ **sonnant, e** *adj*: **à 4 heures ~(es)** on the stroke of 4. ♦ **sonné, e** *adj* **(a) il est midi ~** it's gone twelve; **avoir trente ans bien ~s*** to be on the wrong side of thirty*. **(b)** (*: *fou*) cracked*. **(c)** (*: *assommé*) groggy. ♦ **sonnerie** *nf* **(a)** (*son*) *[cloche]* ringing; *[téléphone]* bell; *[clairon]* sound. **(b)** (*Mil: air*) call. **(b)** (*mécanisme*) *[réveil]* alarm (mechanism); *[pendule]* chimes; (*sonnette*) bell. ♦ **sonnette** *nf* bell. **~ de nuit** night-bell; **~ d'alarme** alarm bell. ♦ **sonneur** *nm*: **~ (de cloches)** bell ringer.

sonore [sɔnɔʀ] *adj objet* resonant; *voix* resonant, ringing, sonorous; *baiser, gifle* resounding; *salle, voûte* echoing; (*Ling*) voiced; (*Acoustique*) *vibrations* sound. **onde ~** sound wave; **fond ~** background noise; **bande ~** sound track. ♦ **sonorisation** *nf ou* ♦ **sono*** *nf* (*équipement*) public address system, P.A. system. ♦ **sonorité** *nf [instrument de musique]* tone; *[salle]* acoustics (*pl*); *[grotte]* resonance. **~s** tones.

sophistiqué, e [sɔfistike] *adj* (*gén*) sophisticated.

soporifique [sɔpɔʀifik] *adj, nm* soporific.

soprano [sɔpʀano] *nmf* soprano.

sorbet [sɔʀbɛ] *nm* water ice, sorbet. ♦ **sorbetière** *nf* ice cream churn.

sorcellerie [sɔʀsɛlʀi] *nf* witchcraft, sorcery. **c'est de la ~!** it's magic! ♦ **sorcier** *nm* (*lit*) sorcerer. **il ne faut pas être ~ pour ...** you don't have to be a wizard to ... . ♦ **sorcière** *nf* witch, sorceress; (*fig péj*) (old) witch, (old) hag.

sordide [sɔʀdid] *adj quartier* sordid, squalid; *action* base, sordid; *gains* sordid. ♦ **sordidement** *adv* sordidly; squalidly; basely.

sornettes† [sɔʀnɛt] *nfpl* twaddle, balderdash.

sort [sɔʀ] *nm* **(a)** (*condition*) lot. **envier le ~ de qn** to envy sb's lot. **(b)** (*destinée*) fate. **le (mauvais) ~** fate; **abandonner qn à son triste ~** to abandon sb to his sad fate; **faire un ~ à un plat*** to polish off a dish*. **(c)** (*hasard*) fate. **le ~ est tombé sur lui** he was chosen by fate, it fell to his lot; **tirer (qch) au ~** to draw lots (for sth). **(d)** (*sorcellerie*) curse, spell. **jeter un ~ sur** to put a curse *ou* spell on.

sortable* [sɔʀtabl(ə)] *adj*: **tu n'es pas ~!** you're not presentable!

sorte [sɔʀt(ə)] *nf* **(a)** (*espèce*) sort, kind. **toutes ~s de gens** all kinds *ou* sorts of people; **une ~ de** a sort *ou* kind of; (*péj*) **une ~ de médecin** a doctor of sorts. **(b) accoutré de la ~** dressed in that fashion *ou* way; **il n'a rien fait de la ~** he did nothing of the kind *ou* no such thing; **de ~ à** so as to, in order to; **en quelque ~** in a way, as it were; **de (telle) ~ que** (*de façon à ce que*) so that, in such a way that; (*si bien que*) so much so that; **faites en ~ d'avoir fini demain** see to it *ou* arrange it so that you will have finished tomorrow; **faire en ~ que** to see to it that.

sortie [sɔʀti] *nf* **(a)** (*action*) *[personne]* leaving, exit; *[véhicule]* departure; (*Théât*) exit. **à sa ~** when he went out *ou* left; **faire une ~ discrète** to leave discreetly, make a discreet exit; **faire une ~** (*Mil*) to make a sortie; *[gardien de but]* to leave the goal mouth; **attention! ~ d'usine** caution, factory exit; **à la ~ de l'école** after school; **c'est sa première ~ depuis sa maladie** it's his first day *ou* time out since his illness. **(b)** (*promenade etc*) outing; (*le soir: au théâtre etc*) evening *ou* night out. **jour de ~** *[domestique]* day off; *[pensionnaire]* day out. **(c)** (*lieu*) exit. (*lit, fig*) **(porte de) ~** way out; **~ de secours** emergency exit; **~ des artistes** stage door; **les ~s de Paris** the roads out of Paris. **(d)** (*paroles*) (*indignée*) outburst; (*drôle*) sally; (*incongrue*) odd remark. **(e)** (*Comm*) *[voiture, modèle]* launching; *[livre]* appearance; *[disque, film]* release; (*pour l'exportation*) export. **(f)** (*somme dépensée*) outlay. **~s** outgoings. **(g) ~ de bain** bathrobe.

sortilège [sɔʀtilɛʒ] *nm* (magic) spell.

sortir [sɔʀtiʀ] (16) **1** *vi* **(a)** *[personne]* (*aller*) to go out, leave; (*venir*) to come out, leave; (*à pied*) to walk out; (*le soir*) to go out; (*Théât*) to exit, leave (the stage). **~ acheter du pain** to go out to buy some bread *ou* for some bread; **faites ~ ces gens** make these people go *ou* leave, get these people out; **sors (d'ici)!** get out (of here)!; **laisser ~ qn** to let sb out *ou* leave. **(b)** *[objet]* (*gén*) to come out; *[disque, film]* to be released; (*à la loterie*) to come up *ou* out. (*Comm*) **tout ce qui sort (du pays) doit être déclaré** everything going out *ou* leaving (the country) must be declared. **(c)** (*dépasser*) to stick out; (*pousser*) *[plante]* to come up; *[dent]* to come through. **(d)** (*quitter*) **~ de** *lieu* to go *ou* come out of, leave; *indifférence* to overcome; *silence* to break out of; **~ de l'eau** to come out of the water; **~ du lit** to get out of bed; *[fleuve]* **~ de son lit** to overflow its banks; **~ des rails** to go off the rails. **(e)** (*passé immédiat*) **on sortait de l'hiver** it was getting near the end of winter; **il sort d'ici/du lit** he's just left/just got up. **(f)** (*s'écarter de*) **~ de** *légalité, limites* to go beyond, overstep; *compétences* to be outside; **~ du sujet** to go *ou* get off the subject; **~ du jeu** *[balle]* to go out of play; **cela sort de l'ordinaire** that's out of the ordinary; **il n'y a pas à ~ de là, nous avons besoin de lui** there's no getting away from it — we need him; **il ne veut pas ~ de là** he won't budge. **(g)** (*provenir de*) **~ de** *lieu, bonne famille* to come from; **il sort du Lycée X** he was educated at the Lycée X; **sait-on ce qui sortira de ces entrevues!** who knows what'll come (out) of these talks!; **de la fumée sortait par les fenêtres** smoke was pouring out of the windows; (*lit, fig*) **d'où sors-tu!** where have you been! **(h)** (*locutions*) **~ de ses gonds** (*lit*) to come off its hinges; (*fig*) to fly off the handle; **je sors d'en prendre*** I've had quite enough thank you (*iro*); **il est sorti d'affaire** he has got over it; **on n'est pas sorti de l'auberge*** we're not out of the wood yet; **se croire sorti de la cuisse de Jupiter*** to think a lot of o.s.; **cela lui est sorti de la mémoire** that slipped his mind.

2 *vt* (*gén*) to take out; (*expulser*) to throw out; (*mettre en vente*) to bring out; *film* to release; (*Aviat*) *train d'atterrissage* to lower. **~ qch de sa poche** to take *ou* bring *ou* pull sth out of one's pocket; (*dire*) **qu'est-ce qu'il va encore nous ~?*** what will he come out with next?*

3 se ~ *vpr* to go out. **tu crois qu'il va s'en ~?** (*travail*) do you think he'll ever see the end of it?; (*procès, maladie*) do you think he'll come through all right?

4 *nm*: **au ~ de l'hiver** as winter draws (*ou* drew) to a close.

sosie [sozi] *nm* double (*person*).

sot, sotte [so, sɔt] *adj* silly, foolish, stupid. ♦ **sottement** *adv* foolishly, stupidly. ♦ **sottise** *nf* stupidity, foolishness; (*parole, action*) silly *ou* foolish remark (*ou* action).

sou [su] *nm* (*monnaie*) sou; (*fig*) penny. **machine à ~s** (*jeu*) one-armed bandit, fruit-machine; (*distributeur*) slot machine; **économiser ~ à** *ou* **par ~** to save penny by penny; **il est sans le ~** he's penniless; **il n'a pas pour un ~ de bon sens** he hasn't an ounce of common sense (in him); **il n'est pas menteur pour un ~** he isn't the least bit

untruthful; **propre comme un ~ neuf** (as) neat as a new pin.
soubassement [subasmɑ̃] *nm [maison]* base.
soubresaut [subʀəso] *nm* (*cahot*) jolt; (*de peur*) start; (*d'agonie*) convulsive movement. **avoir un ~** to give a start; to make a convulsive movement.
soubrette [subʀɛt] *nf* (†, *hum*) maid.
souche [suʃ] *nf* **(a)** *[arbre]* stump; *[vigne]* stock. **rester planté comme une ~** to stand stock-still. **(b)** *[famille]* founder. **de vieille ~** of old stock. **(c)** (*Ling*) root. **(d)** *[microbes]* colony, clone. **(e)** (*talon*) counterfoil, stub. **carnet à ~s** counterfoil book.
souci [susi] *nm* **(a)** (*tracas*) worry. **donner du ~ à, se faire du ~** to worry; **être sans ~** to be free of worries *ou* care(s); **~s d'argent** money worries. **(b)** (*préoccupation*) concern (*de* for). **avoir ~ du bien-être de son prochain** to have concern for the well-being of one's neighbour; **c'est le cadet de mes ~s** that's the least of my worries. **(c)** (*fleur*) marigold. ♦ **se soucier** (7) *vpr*: **se ~ de** *chose* to care about; *personne* to care about, show concern for; **il s'en soucie comme de l'an quarante*** he doesn't give *ou* care a fig (about it)*, he couldn't care less (about it). ♦ **soucieux, -euse** *adj* (*inquiet*) concerned, worried. **peu ~** unconcerned; **être ~ de qch** to be concerned about sth; **être ~ de faire** to be anxious to do.
soucoupe [sukup] *nf* saucer. **~ volante** flying saucer.
soudain, e [sudɛ̃, ɛn] **1** *adj* (*gén*) sudden; *mort* sudden, unexpected. **2** *adv* (*tout à coup*) suddenly, all of a sudden. ♦ **soudainement** *adv* suddenly. ♦ **soudaineté** *nf* suddenness.
soude [sud] *nf* (*industrielle*) soda. **~ caustique** caustic soda.
souder [sude] (1) **1** *vt métal* to solder; (*soudure autogène*) to weld; *os* to knit; *organismes* to fuse (together); *êtres* to bind together. **soudé au sol** glued to the spot. **2 se ~** *vpr [os]* to knit together. ♦ **soudeur** *nm* solderer; welder. ♦ **soudure** *nf* (*opération*) soldering; welding; knitting; (*endroit*) soldered joint; weld; (*substance*) solder. **~ à l'arc** arc welding; **~ autogène** welding; **faire la ~ (entre)** to bridge the gap (between).
soudoyer [sudwaje] (8) *vt* to bribe, buy over.
souffle [sufl(ə)] *nm* **(a)** (*expiration*) (*en soufflant*) blow, puff; (*en respirant*) breath. **murmurer un nom dans un ~** to breathe a name; **le dernier ~ d'un agonisant** the last breath of a dying man. **(b)** (*respiration*) breathing; (*capacité*) breath. **~ régulier** regular breathing; **manquer de/être à bout de ~** to be short of/be out of breath; **avoir le ~ court** to be short-winded; **reprendre son ~** to get one's breath back; **n'avoir plus de ~, être à bout de ~** to be out of breath; (*lit*) **avoir le ~ coupé** to be winded; (*fig*) **il en a eu le ~ coupé** it took his breath away. **(c)** *[ventilateur, explosion]* blast. **(d)** (*vent*) puff *ou* breath of air, puff of wind. **un ~ d'air** a slight breeze. **(e)** (*inspiration*) inspiration. **(f) ~ au cœur** cardiac *ou* heart murmur.
souffler [sufle] (1) **1** *vi* **(a)** *[vent, personne]* to blow. **le vent soufflait en rafales** the wind was blowing in gusts. **(b)** (*respirer avec peine*) to puff (and blow). **(c)** (*se reposer*) to get one's breath back. **laisser ~ qn** to give sb a breather, let sb get his breath back. **2** *vt* **(a)** *bougie, feu* to blow out. **(b) ~ de la fumée au nez de qn** to blow smoke in(to) sb's face. **(c)** (*: *prendre*) to pinch*, nick‡. **(d)** *[bombe, explosion]* to destroy. **(e)** *conseil, réponse* to whisper (*à qn* to sb). (*Théât*) **~ son rôle à qn** to prompt sb; **ne pas ~ mot** not to breathe a word. **(f)** (*: *étonner*) to flabbergast*, stagger. **(g)** (*Tech*) **~ le verre** to blow glass. ♦ **soufflé** *nm* (*Culin*) soufflé. ♦ **soufflerie** *nf [orgue, forge]* bellows; (*d'aération*) ventilating fan; (*Ind*) blowing engine; (*Aviat*) wind tunnel. ♦ **soufflet** *nm* **(a)** *[forge, appareil photo]* bellows; (*Rail*) vestibule; (*Couture*) gusset. **(b)** (†: *gifle*) slap (in the face). ♦ **souffleur, -euse** *nm,f* (*Théât*) prompter. **~ de verre** glass-blower.
souffrir [sufʀiʀ] (18) **1** *vi* (*gén, fig*) to suffer (*de* from). **il souffre beaucoup** he is suffering a great deal, he is in great pain; **faire ~ qn** (*physiquement*) to hurt sb; (*moralement*) to make sb suffer; *[événement]* to cause sb pain; **ça fait ~** it hurts, it is painful; **~ de l'estomac** to have stomach trouble; **je souffre de le voir si affaibli** it pains *ou* grieves me to see him so weakened. **2** *vt* **(a)** *pertes, mépris, tourments* to endure, suffer. **~ le martyre** to go through agonies. **(b)** (*supporter*) to bear. **il ne peut pas ~ les épinards/cet individu** he can't stand *ou* bear spinach/that individual. **(c)** (*permettre*) *retard, exception* to admit of, allow of. **~ que** to allow *ou* permit that; **je ne souffrirai pas que mon fils en pâtisse** I will not allow my son to suffer from it. ♦ **souffrance** *nf* **(a)** (*douleur*) suffering. **(b) être en ~** *[colis]* to be awaiting delivery, be held up; *[dossier]* to be pending. ♦ **souffrant, e** *adj personne* unwell. **l'humanité ~e** suffering humanity. ♦ **souffre-douleur** *nmf inv* whipping boy, underdog. ♦ **souffreteux, -euse** *adj* sickly.
soufre [sufʀ(ə)] *nm* sulphur. (*fig*) **sentir le ~** to smack of heresy.
souhait [swɛ] *nm* wish. **les ~s de bonne année** New Year greetings; **à tes ~s!** bless you!; **tout marchait à ~** everything went as well as one could wish *ou* went perfectly. ♦ **souhaitable** *adj* desirable. ♦ **souhaiter** (1) *vt réussite, changements* to wish for. **~ que** to hope that; **je souhaite réussir** I hope to succeed; **je souhaiterais vous aider** I wish I could help you; **~ à qn le bonheur** to wish sb happiness; **je vous souhaite bien des choses** all good wishes; **~ la bonne année/bonne chance à qn** to wish sb a happy New Year/luck.
souiller [suje] (1) *vt* (*littér*) *vêtement, atmosphère* to dirty; *réputation, âme* to sully, tarnish. **souillé de boue** spattered with mud; (*fig*) **~ ses mains** to stain one's hands. ♦ **souillon** *nf* slattern, slut. ♦ **souillure** *nf* (*lit, fig*) stain.
soûl, soûle [su, sul] **1** *adj* drunk. **~ comme un Polonais*** (as) drunk as a lord. **2** *nm*: **manger tout son ~** to eat one's fill; **elle a ri tout son ~** she laughed till she could laugh no more.
soulager [sulaʒe] (3) **1** *vt* (*gén*) to relieve (*de* of); *douleur* to relieve, soothe; *conscience* to ease. **buvez, ça vous soulagera** drink this — it'll give you relief *ou* make you feel better. **2 se ~** *vpr* to find relief; (*apaiser sa conscience*) to ease one's conscience; (*: *euph*) to relieve o.s. ♦ **soulagement** *nm* relief.
soûler [sule] (1) **1** *vt*: **~ qn** *[personne]* to get sb drunk; *[boisson]* to make sb drunk; *[fatigue, vitesse etc]* to make sb's head spin *ou* reel; **~ qn de** *théories, promesses* to intoxicate sb with, make sb's head spin *ou* reel with. **2 se ~** *vpr* to get drunk. (*fig*) **se ~ de** *bruit, vent* to intoxicate o.s. with. ♦ **soûlard, e‡** *nm,f ou* ♦ **soûlaud, e‡** *nm,f* drunkard. ♦ **soûlerie** *nf* (*péj*) drunken binge.
soulever [sulve] (5) **1** *vt* **(a)** *poids* to lift (up); *poussière* to raise. **cela me soulève le cœur** it makes me feel sick; **le bateau soulevait de grosses vagues** the boat was sending up great waves. **(b)** *foule* to stir up, rouse; *enthousiasme, colère* to arouse; *protestations, applaudissements* to raise; *difficultés, problème* to raise, bring up. **2 se ~** *vpr [malade]* to lift o.s. up; *[véhicule, couvercle, rideau]* to lift; *[vague]* to swell (up); *[rebelles]* to rise up. **à cette vue, son cœur se souleva** his stomach turned at the sight. ♦ **soulèvement** *nm* (*révolte*) uprising; (*Géol*) upthrust.
soulier [sulje] *nm* shoe. **~s montants** boots; **être dans ses petits ~s** to feel awkward.

souligner [suliɲe] (1) *vt* (*lit*) to underline; *silhouette* to emphasize; *détail, problème* to underline, stress, emphasize.
soumettre [sumɛtʀ(ə)] (56) **1** *vt* **(a)** (*asservir, astreindre*) (*gén*) to subject (*à* to); *rebelles* to put down, subdue, subjugate. **(b)** *idée, cas* to submit (*à* to). **2 se ~** *vpr* (*gén*) to submit (*à* to). **se ~ à un régime** to submit o.s. to a diet. ♦ **soumis, e** *adj* submissive. ♦ **soumission** *nf* submission (*à* to). **faire sa ~** to submit.
soupape [supap] *nf* valve. (*lit, fig*) **~ de sûreté** safety valve.
soupçon [supsɔ̃] *nm* **(a)** (*suspicion*) suspicion. **avoir des ~s** to have one's suspicions; **au-dessus de tout ~** above suspicion; **difficultés dont il n'avait pas ~** difficulties of which he had no inkling *ou* no suspicion. **(b)** *[assaisonnement, vulgarité]* hint, touch, suggestion; *[vin, lait]* drop. ♦ **soupçonner** (1) *vt* to suspect (*de* of). **vous ne soupçonnez pas ce que ça demande comme travail** you haven't an inkling *ou* you've no idea how much work that involves. ♦ **soupçonneux, -euse** *adj* suspicious.
soupe [sup] *nf* soup. **~ aux légumes** vegetable soup; **à la ~!**‡ grub's up!‡; **il est ~ au lait** he's very quick-tempered; **~ populaire** soup kitchen.
souper [supe] **1** *nm* supper. **2** *vi* (1) to have supper. **j'en ai soupé de ces histoires!*** I'm sick and tired* of all this fuss!
soupeser [supəze] (5) *vt* (*lit*) to weigh in one's hands; (*fig*) to weigh up.
soupière [supjɛʀ] *nf* (soup) tureen.
soupir [supiʀ] *nm* **(a)** sigh. **~ de soulagement** sigh of relief. **(b)** (*Mus*) crotchet rest. ♦ **soupirant** *nm* suitor. ♦ **soupirer** (1) *vi* (*lit*) to sigh. (*littér*) **~ après qch** to sigh *ou* yearn for sth.
soupirail, *pl* **-aux** [supiʀaj, o] *nm* (small) basement window.
souple [supl(ə)] *adj membres* supple; *tige* pliable, supple; *caractère, discipline* flexible; *silhouette, démarche, taille* lithe. ♦ **souplesse** *nf* suppleness; pliability; flexibility; litheness.
source [suʀs(ə)] *nf* **(a)** (*point d'eau*) spring; (*début de cours d'eau*) source. **~ thermale** thermal spring; **prendre sa ~ dans** to have its source in. **(b)** (*fig*) source. **~ de** *ridicule, chaleur etc* source of; **l'argent est la ~ de tous nos maux** money is the root of all our ills; **tenir qch de ~ sûre** to have sth on good authority, get sth from a reliable source; **de ~ autorisée** from an official source.
sourcil [suʀsi] *nm* (eye)brow. ♦ **sourciller** (1) *vi*: **il n'a pas sourcillé** he didn't turn a hair *ou* bat an eyelid. ♦ **sourcilleux, -euse** *adj* (*pointilleux*) finicky.
sourd, e [suʀ, suʀd(ə)] **1** *adj* **(a)** *personne* deaf. **être ~ comme un pot*** to be as deaf as a post; **faire la ~e oreille** to turn a deaf ear; **~ à** *conseils* deaf to; *vacarme* oblivious to. **(b)** *son* muffled, muted; *couleur* toned-down, subdued; (*Phonétique*) *consonne* voiceless; *douleur* dull; *désir, inquiétude* gnawing; *hostilité* veiled; *lutte, manigances* silent, hidden. **2** *nm,f* deaf person. **les ~s** the deaf; **taper comme un ~** to bang with all one's might; **crier comme un ~** to yell at the top of one's voice. ♦ **sourdement** *adv* (*avec un bruit assourdi*) dully; (*secrètement*) silently. ♦ **sourdine** *nf* mute. **jouer en ~** to play softly *ou* quietly; (*fig*) **mettre une ~ à** *enthousiasme* to moderate. ♦ **sourd-muet,** *f* **~e-~ette 1** *adj* deaf-and-dumb. **2** *nm,f* deaf-mute.
sourdre [suʀdʀ(ə)] *vi [source]* to rise.
souriant, e [suʀjɑ̃, ɑ̃t] *adj visage* smiling; *personne* cheerful; (*fig*) *pensée, philosophie* benign, agreeable.
souricière [suʀisjɛʀ] *nf* (*lit*) mousetrap; (*fig*) trap.
sourire [suʀiʀ] **1** *nm* smile. **avec le ~** (*accueillir qn*) with a smile; (*travailler*) cheerfully; **gardez le ~!** keep smiling!; **faire un ~ à qn** to give sb a smile. **2** *vi* (36) to smile (*à qn* at sb). **faire ~ qn** to make sb smile; **cette idée ne me sourit guère** that idea doesn't appeal to me, I don't fancy that idea*; **la chance lui souriait** luck smiled on him.
souris [suʀi] *nf* **(a)** (*Zool*) mouse. **~ blanche** white mouse. **(b)** (‡: *femme*) bird*, broad* (*US*).
sournois, e [suʀnwa, waz] *adj personne, regard, air* sly, shifty; *méthode, propos* sly, underhand. ♦ **sournoisement** *adv* slyly; shiftily; in an underhand manner. ♦ **sournoiserie** *nf* slyness; shiftiness; underhand manner.
sous [su] **1** *prép* **(a)** (*position*) under, underneath, beneath. **s'abriter ~ un arbre** to shelter under *ou* underneath *ou* beneath a tree; **se promener ~ la pluie** to take a walk in the rain; **le pays était ~ la neige** the country was covered with *ou* in snow; **dormir ~ la tente** to sleep under canvas *ou* in a tent; **~ terre** underground, under the ground; **cela s'est passé ~ nos yeux** it happened before *ou* under our very eyes; **~ le feu de l'ennemi** under enemy fire; **~ une apparence paisible** beneath his (*ou* her *etc*) peaceful exterior. **(b)** (*à l'époque de*) under, during; (*dans un délai de*) within. **~ le règne de** under *ou* during the reign of; **~ peu** shortly, before long; **~ huitaine** within the *ou* a week. **(c)** (*cause, dépendance etc*) under. **~ l'influence/les ordres/la direction de** under the influence/orders/management of; **~ l'empire de la terreur** in the grip of terror; **examiner une question ~ tous ses angles** to look at a question from every angle; **~ certaines conditions** on certain conditions; **voir qch ~ un jour nouveau** to see sth in a new light; **~ ce rapport** on that score, in this respect; **il a été peint ~ les traits d'un berger** he was painted as a shepherd *ou* in the guise of a shepherd; **l'affaire est ~ sa responsabilité** the affair is his responsibility. **(d)** (*Méd*) **~ anesthésie** under anaesthetic; **malade ~ perfusion** patient on the drip. **(e)** (*Tech*) **(emballé) ~ plastique** plastic-wrapped; **~ tube** in (a) tube; **(emballé) ~ vide** vacuum-packed.
2 *préf* **(a)** (*infériorité*) **c'est du ~-art** it's pseudo-art; **~-homme** subhuman. **(b)** (*subordination*) sub-. **~-directeur** assistant *ou* sub-manager; **~-chef de bureau** deputy chief clerk; **~-officier** non-commissioned officer, N.C.O; **~-secrétaire d'État** Undersecretary of State; **~-louer** to sublet; **~-titrer** to subtitle; **~-agence** sub-branch. **(c)** (*insuffisance*) under. **~-alimenté** undernourished, underfed; **~-équipé** underequipped; **~-équipement** lack of equipment; **~-développement** underdevelopment; **pays ~-développés** underdeveloped *ou* developing *ou* emergent countries; **~-évaluer** to underestimate, underrate; **~-peuplé** underpopulated.
♦ **sous-bois** *nm inv* undergrowth. ♦ **sous-entendre** (41) *vt* to imply, infer. ♦ **sous-entendu, e 1** *adj* implied, understood. **2** *nm* innuendo, insinuation. ♦ **sous-estimer** *vt* to underestimate, underrate. ♦ **sous-fifre*** *nm* underling. ♦ **sous-jacent, e** *adj* underlying. ♦ **sous-main** *nm inv* desk blotter. (*fig*) **en ~-main** secretly. ♦ **sous-marin, e 1** *adj chasse* underwater; *faune* submarine. **2** *nm* submarine. ♦ **sous-sol** *nm [terre]* subsoil, substratum; *[maison]* basement. ♦ **sous-tendre** *vt* (*Géom*) to subtend; (*fig*) to underlie. ♦ **sous-vêtement** *nm* undergarment. **~-vêtements** underwear, undergarments.
souscrire [suskʀiʀ] (39) **1 ~ à** *vt indir* (*Fin, fig*) to subscribe to. **~ pour 100 F à qch** to subscribe 100 francs to sth. **2** *vt* (*Comm*) *billet* to sign. ♦ **souscripteur, -trice** *nm,f* subscriber (*de* to). ♦ **souscription** *nf* subscription. **ouvrir une ~ en faveur de ...** to start a fund in aid of ... .
soussigné, e [susiɲe] *adj, nm,f* undersigned. **je ~**

X déclare que ... I the undersigned, X, certify that ... .
soustraire [sustʀɛʀ] (50) **1** *vt* (*défalquer*) to subtract, take away (*de* from); (*dérober*) to remove, abstract; (*cacher*) to conceal, shield (*à* from). **2 se** ~ *vpr*: se ~ **à** *devoir* to shirk; *autorité* to elude, escape from; *curiosité* to conceal o.s. from. ♦ **soustraction** *nf* (*Math*) subtraction; (*vol*) removal, abstraction.
soutane [sutan] *nf* cassock, soutane.
soute [sut] *nf [navire]* hold. ~ **(à bagages)** baggage hold; ~ **à charbon** coal-bunker; ~ **à mazout** oil-tank.
souteneur [sutnœʀ] *nm* procurer.
soutenir [sutniʀ] (22) **1** *vt* **(a)** (*physiquement*) to support, hold up; *[médicament etc]* to sustain. **(b)** *parti, candidat* to support, back; *famille* to support. (*moralement*) **il m'a beaucoup soutenu** he was a real support *ou* prop to me; **elle soutient les enfants contre leur père** she takes the children's part *ou* she stands up for the children against their father. **(c)** *attention, effort* to keep up, sustain; *réputation* to keep up, maintain. **(d)** *assaut, choc* to stand up to, withstand; *regard* to bear, support. ~ **la comparaison avec** to bear *ou* stand comparison with. **(e)** *opinion* to uphold, support. (*Univ*) ~ **sa thèse** to attend one's viva; ~ **que** to maintain that. **2 se** ~ *vpr* (*sur ses jambes*) to hold o.s. up, support o.s.; (*s'entraider*) to stand by each other. (*fig*) **ça peut se** ~ it's a tenable point of view. ♦ **soutenu, e** *adj style* elevated; *effort* sustained, unflagging.
souterrain, e [sutɛʀɛ̃, ɛn] **1** *adj* underground, subterranean. **2** *nm* underground *ou* subterranean passage.
soutien [sutjɛ̃] *nm* support. ♦ **soutien-gorge,** *pl* ~**s-**~ *nm* bra.
soutirer [sutiʀe] (1) *vt* **(a)** ~ **qch à qn** to squeeze *ou* get sth out of sb, extract sth from sb. **(b)** *vin* to decant.
souvenir [suvniʀ] **1** *nm* **(a)** (*réminiscence*) memory, recollection; (*fait de se souvenir*) recollection, remembrance. **mauvais** ~ bad memory; **vague** ~ vague recollection; ~**s d'enfance** childhood memories; **avoir le** ~ **de qch** to have a memory of sth; **je n'ai pas** ~ **d'avoir** ... I have no recollection of having ...; **en** ~ **de** in memory *ou* remembrance of. **(b)** (*mémoire*) memory. **(c)** (*objet*) keepsake, memento; (*trace, pour touristes*) souvenir. **magasin de** ~**s** souvenir shop. **(d)** (*formules de politesse*) **amical** ~ yours (ever); **mon bon** ~ **à X** remember me to X, (my) regards to X.
2 se ~ (22) *vpr*: se ~ **de qn** to remember sb; **se** ~ **de qch/d'avoir fait qch/que** ... to remember *ou* recall *ou* recollect sth/doing sth/that ...; **il s'en souviendra!** he won't forget it!; **souvenez-vous qu'il est très puissant** bear in mind *ou* remember that he is very powerful; **souviens-toi de ta promesse!** remember your promise!; **tu m'as fait me** ~ **que** ... you have reminded me that ... .
3 *vb impers* (*littér*) **il me souvient d'avoir fait** I recollect *ou* recall *ou* remember having done.
souvent [suvɑ̃] *adv* often. **le plus** ~ more often than not; **peu** ~ seldom.
souverain, e [suvʀɛ, ɛn] **1** *adj* (*Pol*) sovereign; *juge, mépris* supreme. **le** ~ **pontife** the Supreme Pontiff; **remède** ~ **contre qch** sovereign remedy against sth. **2** *nm,f* (*Pol, fig*) sovereign. ♦ **souverainement** *adv* (*intensément*) supremely, intensely; (*en tant que souverain*) with sovereign power. ♦ **souveraineté** *nf* sovereignty.
soviet [sɔvjɛt] *nm* soviet. ♦ **soviétique 1** *aaj* Soviet. **2** *nmf*: **S**~ Soviet citizen.
soyeux, -euse [swajø, øz] **1** *adj* silky. **2** *nm* (Lyons) silk manufacturer.
spacieux, -euse [spasjø, øz] *adj* spacious, roomy.
sparadrap [spaʀadʀa] *nm* adhesive *ou* sticking plaster.
spartiate [spaʀsjat] *adj*, **S**~ *nmf* Spartan.
spasme [spasm(ə)] *nm* spasm. ♦ **spasmodique** *adj* spasmodic.
spatial, e, *mpl* **-aux** [spasjal, o] *adj* spatial; (*Espace*) space.
spatule [spatyl] *nf* spatula.
speaker [spikœʀ] *nm* (*Rad, TV*) announcer. ♦ **speakerine** *nf* (woman) announcer.
spécial, e, *mpl* **-aux** [spesjal, o] *adj* (*gén*) special; (*bizarre*) peculiar. ♦ **spécialement** *adv* (*particulièrement*) especially, particularly; (*exprès*) specially.
spécialiser (se) [spesjalize] (1) *vpr* to specialize (*dans* in). ♦ **spécialisation** *nf* specialization. ♦ **spécialisé, e** *adj travail, personne* specialized. **être** ~ **dans** *[personne]* to be a specialist in; *[firme]* to specialize in. ♦ **spécialiste** *nmf* (*gén, Méd*) specialist. ♦ **spécialité** *nf* (*gén, Culin*) speciality; (*Univ etc: branche*) specialism, special field. **il a la** ~ **de faire** ...* he has a special *ou* particular knack of doing ... .
spécieux, -euse [spesjø, øz] *adj* specious.
spécifier [spesifje] (7) *vt* to specify, state. ♦ **spécification** *nf* specification. ♦ **spécificité** *nf* specificity. ♦ **spécifique** *adj* specific. ♦ **spécifiquement** *adv* (*tout exprès*) specifically; (*typiquement*) typically.
spécimen [spesimɛn] *nm* (*gén*) specimen; (*publicitaire*) specimen copy, sample copy.
spectacle [spɛktakl(ə)] *nm* **(a)** (*vue*) sight; (*grandiose*) spectacle. **au** ~ **de** at the sight of; (*péj*) **se donner en** ~ **(à qn)** to make a spectacle *ou* an exhibition of o.s. (in front of sb). **(b)** (*Ciné, Théât*) (*représentation*) show. (*branche*) **le** ~ show business, entertainment; (*rubrique*) '~**s**' 'entertainment'; **aller au** ~ to go to a show. ♦ **spectaculaire** *adj* spectacular, dramatic. ♦ **spectateur, -trice** *nm,f [événement]* onlooker, witness; (*Sport*) spectator; (*Ciné, Théât*) member of the audience. **les** ~**s** the audience.
spectre [spɛktʀ(ə)] *nm* (*fantôme*) spectre; (*Phys*) spectrum. ♦ **spectral, e,** *mpl* **-aux** *adj* (*gén*) spectral.
spéculer [spekyle] (1) *vi* (*Philos*) to speculate (*sur* on, about); (*Fin*) to speculate (*sur* in). (*fig: tabler sur*) ~ **sur** to bank on, rely on. ♦ **spéculateur, -trice** *nm,f* speculator. ♦ **spéculatif, -ive** *adj* (*Fin, Philos*) speculative. ♦ **spéculation** *nf* speculation.
spéléologie [speleɔlɔʒi] *nf* (*étude*) speleology; (*exploration*) potholing. ♦ **spéléologique** *adj* speleological; potholing. ♦ **spéléologue** *nmf* speleologist; potholer.
sperme [spɛʀm(ə)] *nm* semen, sperm.
sphère [sfɛʀ] *nf* (*Astron, fig*) sphere. ♦ **sphérique** *adj* spherical.
sphincter [sfɛ̃ktɛʀ] *nm* sphincter.
sphinx [sfɛ̃ks] *nm* sphinx.
spirale [spiʀal] *nf* spiral.
spirite [spiʀit] *adj, nmf* spiritualist. ♦ **spiritisme** *nm* spiritualism, spiritism. ♦ **spiritualité** *nf* spirituality.
spirituel, -elle [spiʀitɥɛl] *adj* **(a)** (*fin*) witty. **(b)** (*Philos, Rel, gén*) spiritual. **concert** ~ concert of sacred music. ♦ **spirituellement** *adv* wittily; spiritually.
spiritueux [spiʀitɥø] *nm* (*alcool*) spirit.
splendeur [splɑ̃dœʀ] *nf* (*gén*) splendour. **c'est une** ~ it is quite magnificent *ou* splendid; (*iro*) **dans toute sa** ~ in all its glory. ♦ **splendide** *adj* splendid, magnificent. ♦ **splendidement** *adv* splendidly, magnificently.
spolier [spɔlje] (7) *vt* to despoil. ♦ **spoliation** *nf* despoilment (*de* of).
spongieux, -euse [spɔ̃ʒjø, øz] *adj* spongy.
spontané, e [spɔ̃tane] *adj* spontaneous.

♦ **spontanéité** *nf* spontaneity. ♦ **spontanément** *adv* spontaneously.
sporadique [spɔradik] *adj* sporadic. ♦ **sporadiquement** *adv* sporadically.
sport [spɔʀ] **1** *nm* sport. **~s d'équipe** team sports; **faire du ~** to do sport; **aller aux ~s d'hiver** to go on a winter sports holiday, go winter sporting; **voiture** *etc* **de ~** sports car *etc*; **il va y avoir du ~!*** we'll see some fun!* *ou* action!* **2** *adj inv vêtement* casual. ♦ **sportif, -ive 1** *adj épreuve, résultats* sports; *pêche* competitive; *jeunesse, allure* athletic; *mentalité* sporting, sportsmanlike. **2** *nm* sportsman. **3** *nf* sportswoman. ♦ **sportivement** *adv* sportingly. ♦ **sportivité** *nf* sportsmanship.
spot [spɔt] *nm* (*Phys*) light spot; (*Théât etc*) spotlight, spot. **~ (publicitaire)** commercial, advert*.
square [skwaʀ] *nm* public garden(s).
squelette [skəlɛt] *nm* (*lit, fig*) skeleton. ♦ **squelettique** *adj personne, arbre* scrawny, skeleton-like; *exposé* sketchy, skimpy; (*Anat*) skeletal; *effectifs* minimal. **d'une maigreur ~** all skin and bone.
stable [stabl(ə)] *adj* (*gén*) stable; *position, échelle* steady. ♦ **stabilisateur, -trice 1** *adj* stabilizing. **2** *nm [véhicule]* anti-roll device; *[navire, vélo]* stabilizer; *[avion]* (*horizontal*) tailplane; (*vertical*) fixed fin; (*Chim*) stabilizer. ♦ **stabilisation** *nf* stabilization. ♦ **stabiliser** *vt*, **se ~** *vpr* (1) to stabilize. ♦ **stabilité** *nf* stability.
stade [stad] *nm* **(a)** (*sportif*) stadium. **(b)** (*période*) stage.
stage [staʒ] *nm* (*période*) training period; (*cours*) training course. **faire un ~** to go on a (training) course. ♦ **stagiaire** *nmf, adj* trainee.
stagner [stagne] (1) *vi* (*lit, fig*) to stagnate. ♦ **stagnant, e** *adj* stagnant. ♦ **stagnation** *nf* stagnation.
stalactite [stalaktit] *nf* stalactite.
stalagmite [stalagmit] *nf* stalagmite.
stand [stɑ̃d] *nm [exposition]* stand; *[foire]* stall. **~ (de tir)** (*Sport*) shooting range; (*Mil*) firing range; **~ de ravitaillement** pit.
standard [stɑ̃daʀ] **1** *nm* (*Téléc*) switchboard. **~ de vie** standard of living. **2** *adj inv* standard. ♦ **standardisation** *nf* standardization. ♦ **standardiser** (1) *vt* to standardize. ♦ **standardiste** *nmf* switchboard operator.
standing [stɑ̃diŋ] *nm* standing. **immeuble de grand ~** block of luxury flats *ou* apartments (*US*).
star [staʀ] *nf* (*Ciné*) star. ♦ **starlette** *nf* starlet.
starter [staʀtɛʀ] *nm* (*Aut*) choke. **mettre le ~** to pull the choke out.
station [stɑsjɔ̃] *nf* **(a) ~ (de métro)** (underground *ou* subway (*US*)) station; **~ (d'autobus)** (bus) stop; **~ (de chemin de fer)** halt; **~ de taxis** taxi rank. **(b)** (*poste, lieu*) station. **~ radiophonique** radio station; **~-service** service *ou* petrol *ou* filling station. **(c)** (*de vacances*) resort. **~ balnéaire** sea *ou* seaside resort; **~ thermale** thermal spa. **(d)** (*posture*) posture, stance. **la ~ debout** an upright posture *ou* stance. **(e)** (*halte*) stop. ♦ **stationnaire** *adj* stationary.
stationner [stasjɔne] (1) *vi* (*être garé*) to be parked; (*se garer*) to park. ♦ **stationnement** *nm* (*Aut*) parking. '**~ interdit**' 'no parking'; (*sur autoroute*) 'no stopping'.
statique [statik] *adj* static. ♦ **statiquement** *adv* statically.
statistique [statistik] **1** *nf* (*science*) statistics (*sg*). (*données*) **des ~s** statistics; **une ~** a statistic. **2** *adj* statistical. ♦ **statisticien, -ienne** *nm,f* statistician. ♦ **statistiquement** *adv* statistically.
statue [staty] *nf* statue. ♦ **statuette** *nf* statuette.
statuer [statɥe] (1) *vi*: **~ sur** to rule on.
statu quo [statykwo] *nm* status quo.
stature [statyʀ] *nf* stature.
statut [staty] *nm* (*position*) status. (*règlement*) **~s** statutes. ♦ **statutaire** *adj* statutory. ♦ **statutairement** *adv* in accordance with the statutes *ou* regulations.
stencil [stɛnsil] *nm* (*Typ*) stencil.
sténo(dactylo) [steno(daktilo)] *nf* (*personne*) shorthand typist; (*travail*) shorthand typing. ♦ **sténo(graphie)** *nf* shorthand. ♦ **sténographier** (7) *vt* to take down in shorthand. ♦ **sténographique** *adj* shorthand.
stentor [stɑ̃tɔʀ] *nm*: **une voix de ~** a stentorian voice.
steppe [stɛp] *nf* steppe.
stère [stɛʀ] *nm* stere.
stéréo [steʀeo] *nf, adj* stereo. ♦ **stéréophonie** *nf* stereophony. ♦ **stéréophonique** *adj* stereophonic.
stéréotype [steʀeɔtip] *nm* (*lit, fig*) stereotype. ♦ **stéréotypé, e** *adj* stereotyped.
stérile [steʀil] *adj* (*gén*) sterile; *terre* barren; *discussion, effort* fruitless. ♦ **stérilet** *nm* coil, loop. ♦ **stérilisateur** *nm* sterilizer. ♦ **stérilisation** *nf* sterilization. ♦ **stériliser** (1) *vt* to sterilize. ♦ **stérilité** *nf* sterility; barrenness; fruitlessness.
sternum [stɛʀnɔm] *nm* breastbone, sternum.
stéthoscope [stetɔskɔp] *nm* stethoscope.
steward [stiwaʀt] *nm* (*Aviat*) steward.
stigmate [stigmat] *nm* (*marque*) mark. (*Rel*) **~s** stigmata. ♦ **stigmatisation** *nf* stigmatization. ♦ **stigmatiser** (1) *vt* to stigmatize.
stimuler [stimyle] (1) *vt* to stimulate. ♦ **stimulant, e 1** *adj* stimulating. **2** *nm* (*physique*) stimulant; (*intellectuel*) stimulus, spur, incentive. ♦ **stimulation** *nf* stimulation. ♦ **stimulus,** *pl* **stimuli** *nm* stimulus.
stipuler [stipyle] (1) *vt* to stipulate. ♦ **stipulation** *nf* stipulation.
stock [stɔk] *nm* stock. ♦ **stockage** *nm* stocking. ♦ **stocker** (1) *vt* (*Comm*) to stock; (*péj*) to stockpile.
stoïque [stɔik] *adj* stoical, stoic. ♦ **stoïquement** *adv* stoically.
stomacal, e, *mpl* **-aux** [stɔmakal, o] *adj* stomach, gastric.
stop [stɔp] **1** *excl* stop. **2** *nm* (*panneau*) stop sign; (*feu arrière*) brake-light. **faire du ~*** to hitch-hike, hitch*. ♦ **stoppage** *nm* invisible mending. ♦ **stopper** (1) **1** *vti* to halt, stop. **2** *vt* (*Couture*) *bas* to stop from running. **faire ~ un vêtement** to get a garment (invisibly) mended. ♦ **stoppeur, -euse** *nm,f* invisible mender.
store [stɔʀ] *nm [fenêtre]* blind, shade; (*voilage*) net curtain; *[magasin]* awning, shade. **~ vénitien** Venetian blind.
strabisme [stʀabism(ə)] *nm* squint.
strapontin [stʀapɔ̃tɛ̃] *nm* jump seat, foldaway seat.
stratagème [stʀataʒɛm] *nm* stratagem.
strate [stʀat] *nf* stratum.
stratège [stʀatɛʒ] *nm* (*Mil, fig*) strategist. ♦ **stratégie** *nf* strategy. ♦ **stratégique** *adj* strategic.
stratifier [stʀatifje] (7) *vt* to stratify. ♦ **stratification** *nf* stratification.
stratosphère [stʀatɔsfɛʀ] *nf* stratosphere.
strict, e [stʀikt(ə)] *adj discipline, maître, sens* strict; *costume* plain; *interprétation* literal. **c'est la ~e vérité** it is the plain *ou* simple truth; **c'est son droit le plus ~** it is his most basic right; **le ~ nécessaire/minimum** the bare essentials/minimum; **dans la plus ~e intimité** strictly in private. ♦ **strictement** *adv* strictly; plainly.
strident, e [stʀidɑ̃, ɑ̃t] *adj* shrill, strident.
strie [stʀi] *nf* (*de couleur*) streak; (*en relief*) ridge; (*Anat, Géol*) stria. ♦ **strier** (7) *vt* to streak; to ridge; to striate.

strophe [stRɔf] *nf* verse, stanza.
structure [stRyktyR] *nf* structure. ~**s d'accueil** reception facilities. ♦ **structural, e,** *mpl* **-aux** *adj* structural. ♦ **structuralement** *adv* structurally. ♦ **structurel, -elle** *adj* structural. ♦ **structurer** (1) *vt* to structure.
stuc [styk] *nm* stucco.
studieux, -euse [stydjø, øz] *adj personne* studious; *vacances* study. ♦ **studieusement** *adv* studiously.
studio [stydjo] *nm* (*d'artiste, de prise de vues*) studio; (*auditorium*) film theatre, arts cinema; (*d'habitation*) bedsitter, studio apartment (*US*).
stupéfaire [stypefɛR] (60) *vt* to stun, astound, dumbfound. ♦ **stupéfaction** *nf* stupefaction, amazement. ♦ **stupéfait, e** *adj* stunned, dumbfounded, astounded (*de qch* at sth).
stupéfier [stypefje] (7) *vt* to stun, stagger, astound. ♦ **stupéfiant, e 1** *adj* stunning, astounding, staggering. **2** *nm* drug, narcotic. ♦ **stupeur** *nf* astonishment, amazement; (*Méd*) stupor.
stupide [stypid] *adj* (*inepte*) stupid, silly, foolish; (*hébété*) stunned. ♦ **stupidement** *adv* stupidly. ♦ **stupidité** *nf* stupidity; (*parole, acte*) stupid *ou* silly *ou* foolish remark (*ou* action).
style [stil] *nm* **(a)** (*genre, classe*) style. **meubles de** ~ period furniture. **(b)** (*pointe*) style, stylus. **(c)** (*Ling*) ~ **direct/indirect** direct/indirect *ou* reported speech; ~ **journalistique** journalistic style, journalese (*péj*); ~ **télégraphique** telegraphese. ♦ **styler** (1) *vt domestique etc* to train. **(bien) stylé** well-trained. ♦ **stylisation** *nf* stylization. ♦ **styliser** (1) *vt* to stylize.
stylo [stilo] *nm* pen. ~**(-bille** *ou* **à bille**) ball-point (pen); ~ **(à encre)** (fountain) pen.
su [sy] *nm*: **au** ~ **de** with the knowledge of.
suaire [sɥɛR] *nm* (*littér*) shroud.
suant, e* [sɥɑ̃, ɑ̃t] *adj* (*ennuyeux*) deadly (dull)*.
suave [sɥav] *adj personne, manières* suave, smooth; *musique, parfum* sweet; *couleurs* mellow; *formes* smooth. ♦ **suavement** *adv s'exprimer* suavely. ♦ **suavité** *nf* suavity; smoothness; sweetness; mellowness.
subalterne [sybaltɛRn(ə)] **1** *adj rôle* subordinate, subsidiary; *employé, poste* junior. **officier** ~ subaltern. **2** *nmf* subordinate, inferior.
subconscient, e [sypkɔ̃sjɑ̃, ɑ̃t] *adj, nm* subconscious.
subdiviser [sybdivize] (1) **1** *vt* to subdivide (*en* into). **2 se** ~ *vpr* to be subdivided (*en* into). ♦ **subdivision** *nf* subdivision.
subir [sybiR] (2) *vt attaque, critique* to undergo, suffer, be subjected to; *perte, défaite* to suffer, sustain; *corvée, importun* to put up with, endure; *examen, modifications* to undergo, go through; *peine de prison, opération* to undergo; *charme* to be subject to, be under the influence of; *influence* to be under. ~ **les effets de qch** to experience the effects of sth; **faire** ~ **à qn** *torture* to subject sb to; *défaite* to inflict upon sb; *influence* to exert over sb; *examen* to put sb through.
subit, e [sybi, it] *adj* sudden. ♦ **subitement** *adv* suddenly, all of a sudden.
subjectif, -ive [sybʒɛktif, iv] *adj* subjective. ♦ **subjectivement** *adv* subjectively. ♦ **subjectivité** *nf* subjectivity.
subjonctif, -ive [sybʒɔ̃ktif, iv] *adj, nm* subjunctive.
subjuguer [sybʒyge] (1) *vt auditoire* to captivate, enthrall; *esprits* to render powerless; *vaincu* to subjugate.
sublime [syblim] *adj* sublime. ♦ **sublimation** *nf* sublimation. ♦ **sublimement** *adv* sublimely. ♦ **sublimer** (1) *vt* to sublimate.
submerger [sybmɛRʒe] (3) *vt terres* to flood, submerge; *barque* to submerge. ~ **qn** *[foule]* to engulf sb; *[ennemi, émotion]* to overcome *ou* overwhelm sb; **submergé de** *travail, commandes* snowed under *ou* swamped with. ♦ **submersible** *adj, nm* submarine. ♦ **submersion** *nf* flooding, submersion.
subordonner [sybɔRdɔne] (1) *vt*: ~ **qn/qch à** to subordinate sb/sth to; (*faire dépendre de*) **leur départ est subordonné au résultat des examens** their departure is subject to *ou* depends on the exam results. ♦ **subordination** *nf* subordination. ♦ **subordonné, e 1** *adj* subordinate (*à* to). **2** *nm,f* subordinate. **3** *nf* (*Ling*) subordinate clause.
suborner [sybɔRne] (1) *vt témoins* to bribe; *jeune fille* to seduce.
subreptice [sybRɛptis] *adj* surreptitious. ♦ **subrepticement** *adv* surreptitiously.
subside [sypsid] *nm* grant. ~**s** allowance.
subsidiaire [sypsidjɛR] *adj* subsidiary. ♦ **subsidiairement** *adv* subsidiarily.
subsistance [sybzistɑ̃s] *nf* subsistence. **assurer la** ~ **de qn** to support *ou* maintain *ou* keep sb; **ma** ~ **était assurée** I had enough to live on; **moyen de** ~ means of subsistence. ♦ **subsistant, e** *adj* remaining. ♦ **subsister** (1) *vi* (*ne pas périr*) to live on, survive; (*se nourrir*) to subsist; *[doute, vestiges]* to remain, subsist.
substance [sypstɑ̃s] *nf* substance. **en** ~ in substance; ~ **alimentaire** food. ♦ **substantiel, -elle** *adj* substantial. ♦ **substantiellement** *adv* substantially.
substantif [sypstɑ̃tif] *nm* noun, substantive.
substituer [sypstitɥe] (1) **1** *vt*: ~ **qch/qn à** to substitute sth/sb for. **2 se** ~ *vpr*: **se** ~ **à qn** (*en évinçant*) to substitute o.s. for sb; (*en le représentant*) to substitute for sb. ♦ **substitut** *nm* (*magistrat*) deputy public prosecutor; (*succédané*) substitute (*de* for). ♦ **substitution** *nf* (*intentionnelle*) substitution (*à* for); (*accidentelle*) mix-up (*de* of, in).
subterfuge [syptɛRfyʒ] *nm* subterfuge.
subtil, e [syptil] *adj* (*sagace*) *esprit, réponse* subtle; *distinction* subtle, fine, nice. ♦ **subtilement** *adv* subtly. ♦ **subtilité** *nf* subtlety; nicety.
subtiliser [syptilize] (1) *vt* to spirit away (*hum*). ♦ **subtilisation** *nf* spiriting away.
subvenir [sybvəniR] (22) ~ **à** *vt indir besoins* to provide for, meet; *frais* to meet, cover. ~ **à ses besoins** to support o.s.
subvention [sybvɑ̃sjɔ̃] *nf* (*gén*) grant; (*aux agriculteurs, à un théâtre*) subsidy. ♦ **subventionner** (1) *vt* to grant funds to; to subsidize.
subversion [sybvɛRsjɔ̃] *nf* subversion. ♦ **subversif, -ive** *adj* subversive.
suc [syk] *nm* (*gén, Anat*) juice.
succédané [syksedane] *nm* substitute (*de* for).
succéder [syksede] (6) **1** ~ **à** *vt indir* (*gén*) to succeed, follow; *roi* to succeed; *titres* to succeed to. **2 se** ~ *vpr* to follow *ou* succeed one another.
succès [syksɛ] *nm* (*gén*) success; (*livre*) best-seller; (*disque*) hit; (*film, pièce*) box-office success, hit. (*conquête*) ~ **(féminin)** conquest; **avoir du** ~ to be a success, be successful (*auprès de* with); **avec** ~ successfully; **sans** ~ unsuccessfully, without success; **à** ~ *auteur* successful; **chanson à** ~ hit (song).
succession [syksesjɔ̃] *nf* (*gén*) succession; (*Jur: patrimoine*) estate, inheritance. **prendre la** ~ **de** *directeur* to succeed, take over from; *roi* to succeed; *maison de commerce* to take over. ♦ **successeur** *nm* successor. ♦ **successif, -ive** *adj* successive. ♦ **sucessivement** *adv* successively.
succinct, e [syksɛ̃, ɛ̃t] *adj écrit* succinct; *repas* frugal. ♦ **succinctement** *adv* succinctly; frugally.
succion [syksjɔ̃] *nf* suction. **bruit de** ~ sucking noise.
succomber [sykɔ̃be] (1) *vi* (*mourir*) to die, suc-

cumb. ~ **sous le nombre** to be overcome by numbers; ~ **à** *tentation, fatigue etc* to succumb to.
succulent, e [sykylɑ̃, ɑ̃t] *adj* delicious, succulent.
succursale [sykyʀsal] *nf* (*Comm*) branch.
sucer [syse] (3) *vt* to suck. ♦ **sucette** *nf* (*bonbon*) lollipop; (*tétine*) dummy.
sucre [sykʀ(ə)] *nm* (*substance*) sugar; (*morceau*) lump of sugar. **cet enfant n'est pas en ~ quand même!** for goodness sake, the child won't break!; **être tout ~ tout miel** to be all sweetness and light; ~ **de canne** cane sugar; ~ **cristallisé** coarse grained sugar; ~ **en morceaux** lump sugar, ~ **d'orge** (*substance*) barley sugar; (*bâton*) stick of barley sugar; ~ **en poudre** castor sugar; ~ **semoule** granulated sugar. ♦ **sucré, e 1** *adj fruit, saveur* sweet; *jus de fruits* sweetened; (*péj*) *ton* sugary, honeyed. **trop** ~ too sweet; **bien** ~ well-sweetened; **non** ~ unsweetened. **2** *nm*: **le** ~ sweet things. ♦ **sucrer** (1) **1** *vt* **(a)** *boisson* to sugar, put sugar in, sweeten. ~ **les fraises**‡ to be a bit doddery*. **(b)** (‡: *supprimer*) *argent, avantage* to stop. **2 se** ~ *vpr* (*lit*) to help o.s. to sugar; (‡*fig: s'enrichir*) to line one's pocket(s)*. ♦ **sucrerie** *nf* **(a)** ~**s** sweets, sweet things; **aimer les** ~**s** to have a sweet tooth. **(b)** (*usine*) sugar house; (*raffinerie*) sugar refinery. ♦ **sucrier, -ière 1** *adj industrie, betterave* sugar; *région* sugar-producing. **2** *nm* **(a)** (*récipient*) sugar basin *ou* bowl. ~ **(verseur)** sugar shaker. **(b)** (*industriel*) sugar producer.
sud [syd] **1** *nm* south. **vent du** ~ south(erly) wind; **regarder vers le** ~ to look south(wards) *ou* towards the south; **au** ~ **de** (to the) south of; **l'Europe du** ~ Southern Europe; **le S**~ **de la France** the South of France. **2** *adj inv région, partie* southern; *entrée* south; *côte* south(ern); *côté* south(ward); *direction* southward, southerly (*Mét*). **3:** ~**-africain** *etc* South African *etc*; ~**-est/-ouest** south-east/-west. ♦ **sudiste** (*Hist US*) **1** *nmf* Southerner. **2** *adj* Southern.
Suède [sɥɛd] **1** *nf* Sweden. **2** *nm* (*peau*) **s**~ suede. ♦ **suédine** *nf* suedette. ♦ **suédois, e 1** *adj, nm* Swedish. **2** *nm(f)*: **S**~**(e)** Swede.
suer [sɥe] (1) **1** *vi* (*transpirer*) to sweat; (*fig: peiner*) to sweat* (*sur* over). ~ **à grosses gouttes** to sweat profusely; **faire** ~ **qn** (*lit*) to make sb sweat; **tu me fais** ~* you're a pain (in the neck)*; **on se fait** ~ **ici*** what a drag it is here*. **2** *vt sueur* to sweat; *humidité* to ooze; *pauvreté* to exude. ~ **sang et eau pour faire qch** to sweat blood to do sth. ♦ **suée*** *nf* sweat. **prendre une bonne** ~ to work up a good sweat*; **quelle** ~! what a drag!* *ou* pain!* ♦ **sueur** *nf* sweat. **en** ~ in a sweat, sweating; **j'en avais des** ~**s froides** I was in a cold sweat.
suffire [syfiʀ] (37) **1** *vi* to be enough, be sufficient, suffice. ~ **à** *besoins* to meet; *personne* to be enough for; **5 hommes me suffisent (pour ce travail)** 5 men will do me *ou* will be sufficient (for me) (for this job); **il ne peut** ~ **à tout** he can't manage (to do) everything, he can't cope with everything; **ça suffit** that's enough, that'll do; **ça ne te suffit pas de l'avoir cassé?** isn't it enough for you to have broken it?

2 *vb impers:* **il suffit de s'inscrire pour devenir membre** enrolling is enough *ou* sufficient to become a member, you just *ou* only have to enrol to become a member; **il suffit d'un rien pour l'inquiéter** it only takes the smallest thing to worry him, the smallest thing is enough to worry him; **il suffit d'une fois** once is enough.

3 se ~ *vpr* (*Écon*) **se** ~ **(à soi-même)** to be self-sufficient.

♦ **suffisamment** *adv* sufficiently, enough. ~ **fort** sufficiently strong, strong enough; **être** ~ **vêtu** to have sufficient *ou* enough clothes on, be adequately dressed; ~ **de nourriture** sufficient *ou* enough food. ♦ **suffisance** *nf* **(a)** (*vanité*) self-importance, bumptiousness. **(b) avoir qch en** ~ to have sth in plenty, have a sufficiency of sth. ♦ **suffisant, e** *adj* **(a)** (*adéquat*) sufficient; (*Scol*) *résultats* satisfactory. **c'est** ~ **pour qu'il se mette en colère** it's enough to make him lose his temper; **je n'ai pas la place** ~**e** I haven't got sufficient *ou* enough room. **(b)** (*prétentieux*) self-important, bumptious.
suffixe [syfiks(ə)] *nm* suffix.
suffoquer [syfɔke] (1) **1** *vi* (*lit*) to choke, suffocate, stifle. (*fig*) ~ **de** to choke with. **2** *vt [fumée]* to suffocate, choke, stifle; *[colère, joie]* to choke; (*étonner*) *[nouvelle]* to stagger. ♦ **suffocant, e** *adj* suffocating, stifling; staggering. ♦ **suffocation** *nf* (*sensation*) suffocating feeling.
suffrage [syfʀaʒ] *nm* (*Pol: voix*) vote; (*approbation*) approval, approbation. ~**s exprimés** valid votes; ~ **universel** universal suffrage *ou* franchise; **remporter tous les** ~**s** to meet with universal approval *ou* approbation.
suggérer [sygʒeʀe] (6) *vt* (*gén*) to suggest; *solution* to suggest, put forward. **j'ai suggéré d'aller** *ou* **que nous allions au cinéma** I suggested going *ou* that we went to the cinema.
suggestion [sygʒɛstjɔ̃] *nf* suggestion. ♦ **suggestif, -ive** *adj* suggestive.
suicide [sɥisid] *nm* (*lit, fig*) suicide. ♦ **suicidaire** *adj* suicidal. ♦ **suicidé, e** *nm,f* (*personne*) suicide. ♦ **se suicider** (1) *vpr* to commit suicide.
suie [sɥi] *nf* soot.
suif [sɥif] *nm* tallow.
suinter [sɥɛ̃te] (1) *vi* to ooze. ♦ **suintement** *nm*: ~**(s)** oozing.
Suisse [sɥis] **1** *nf* (*pays*) Switzerland. ~ **romande** French-speaking Switzerland. **2** *nmf* (*habitant*) Swiss. **3** *adj*: **s**~ Swiss. **4** *nm*: **s**~ (*bedeau*) ≈ verger; (*fromage*) **(petit-)**~ petit-suisse. ♦ **Suissesse** *nf* Swiss (woman).
suite [sɥit] *nf* **(a)** (*escorte*) retinue, suite. **(b)** (*nouvel épisode*) continuation, following episode; (*second roman, film*) sequel; (*rebondissement d'une affaire*) follow-up; (*reste*) remainder, rest. **la** ~ **au prochain numéro** to be continued (in the next issue); ~ **et fin** concluding *ou* final episode; **la** ~ **des événements devait lui donner raison** what followed was to prove him right; **attendons la** ~ let's see what comes next. **(c)** (*aboutissement*) result. (*prolongements*) ~**s** *[maladie]* after-effects; *[accident]* results; *[incident]* consequences, repercussions; **la** ~ **logique de** the logical result of. **(d)** (*succession*) (*Math*) series. ~ **de** *maisons etc* succession *ou* string *ou* series of; *événements* train of; (*Comm*) **article sans** ~ discontinued line. **(e)** (*cohérence*) coherence. **des propos sans** ~ disjointed talk; **avoir de la** ~ **dans les idées** to show great singleness of purpose, not to be easily put off. **(f)** (*appartement*) suite. **(g)** (*Mus*) suite. **(h)** (*locutions*) **(comme)** ~ **à votre lettre** further to your letter; **à la** ~ (*successivement*) one after the other; (*derrière*) **mettez-vous à la** ~ join on at the back; **à la** ~ **de** (*derrière*) behind; (*en conséquence de*) following; **de** ~ (*immédiatement*) at once; **pendant 3 jours de** ~ (for) 3 days on end *ou* in a row *ou* running; **par** ~ **de** owing to, as a result of; (*par conséquent*) **par** ~ consequently, therefore; **par la** ~**, dans la** ~ afterwards, subsequently; **donner** ~ **à** to follow up; **faire** ~ **à** to follow; **prendre la** ~ **de** *firme, directeur* to succeed, take over from.
suivant[1]**, e** [sɥivɑ̃, ɑ̃t] **1** *adj* following, next. **le mardi** ~ the following *ou* next Tuesday; **voir page** ~**e** see next page; **faites l'exercice** ~ do the following exercise. **2** *nm,f* following (one), next (one). **(au)** ~! next (please)!
suivant[2] [sɥivɑ̃] *prép* (*selon*) according to. ~ **l'usage** in keeping with the custom; ~ **l'expression** as the saying goes; ~ **les jours** according to *ou* depending on the day; **découper** ~ **le pointillé**

cut (out) along the dotted line; ~ **que** according to whether.

suivi, e [sɥivi] *adj travail* steady; *correspondance* regular; *qualité* consistent; *conversation, politique* consistent; (*Comm*) *article* in general production. **très** ~ *cours* well-attended; *mode* widely adopted; *feuilleton* widely followed.

suivre [sɥivʀ(ə)] (40) **1** *vt* **(a)** (*espace, temps, série*) to follow. **il me suit comme mon ombre** he follows me about like my shadow; **je ne peux pas vous** ~ I can't keep up (with you); (*iro*) **certains députés, suivez mon regard, ont ...** certain deputies, without mentioning any names, have ...; **faire** ~ **qn** to have sb followed; **suivez le guide!** this way, please!; **suivez la N7 sur 10 km** keep to *ou* follow the N7 (road) for 10 km; (*Police*) ~ **une piste** to follow up a clue. **(b)** *exemple, instinct, conseil* to follow. ~ **un traitement** to follow a course of treatment; ~/**faire** ~ **un régime** to be/put on a diet; **l'enquête suit son cours** the inquiry is running *ou* taking its course; ~ **le mouvement** to follow the crowd. **(c)** (*Scol*) (*être inscrit à*) to attend, go to; (*être attentif à*) to follow, attend to; (*assimiler*) *programme* to keep up with. **(d)** *affaire, match* to follow; *feuilleton, actualité* to follow, keep up with. ~ **un élève** to follow the progress of a pupil; **il est suivi par un médecin** he's having treatment from a doctor; **à** ~ to be continued. **(e)** (*Comm*) *article* to (continue to) stock. **(f)** (*comprendre*) *argument, personne* to follow. **jusqu'ici je vous suis** I'm with you* *ou* I follow you so far.

2 *vi* **(a)** *[élève]* (*être attentif*) to attend, pay attention; (*assimiler le programme*) to keep up, follow. **(b) faire** ~ **son courrier** to have one's mail forwarded; **'faire** ~**'** 'please forward'. **(c)** (*venir après*) to follow. **ce qui suit** what follows.

3 *vb impers*: **il suit que ...** it follows that ...; **comme suit** as follows.

4 se ~ *vpr [personnes, événements]* to follow one behind the other; *[pages, nombres]* to be in (the right) order; *[argument, pensée]* to be coherent, be consistent. **3 démissions qui se suivent** 3 resignations running *ou* in a row *ou* in quick succession.

sujet, -ette [syʒɛ, ɛt] **1** *adj*: ~ **à** *maladie etc* liable to, subject to, prone to; ~ **à faire** liable *ou* prone to do; **il n'est pas** ~ **à faire des imprudences** he is not one to do anything imprudent; ~ **à caution** *nouvelle* unconfirmed; *moralité* questionable. **2** *nm,f* (*gouverné*) subject. **3** *nm* **(a)** (*matière*) subject (*de* for). ~ **de conversation** topic of conversation, subject (for conversation); **c'était devenu un** ~ **de plaisanterie** it had become a standing joke *ou* sth to joke about; ~ **d'examen** examination question. **(b)** (*motif*) ~ **de** *mécontentement etc* cause for, ground(s) for; **avoir** ~ **de faire** to have cause *ou* grounds for doing; **ayant tout** ~ **de croire à sa bonne foi** having every reason to believe in his good faith. **(c)** (*individu*) subject. (*Scol*) **brillant** ~ brilliant pupil; **un mauvais** ~ (*enfant*) a bad boy; (*jeune homme*) a bad lot. **(d)** (*Ling, Mus, Philos*) subject. **(e)** (*à propos de*) **au** ~ **de** about, concerning; **à ce** ~**, je voulais vous dire que ...** on that subject I wanted to tell you that ... .

sujétion [syʒesjɔ̃] *nf* (*asservissement*) subjection; (*contrainte*) constraint.

sulfamides [sylfamid] *nmpl* sulpha drugs.

sulfate [sylfat] *nm* sulphate.

sulfure [sylfyʀ] *nm* sulphide. ♦ **sulfureux, -euse** *adj* sulphurous. ♦ **sulfurique** *adj* sulphuric. ♦ **sulfurisé, e** *adj*: **papier** ~ greaseproof paper.

sultan [syltɑ̃] *nm* sultan. ♦ **sultane** *nf* sultana (*sultan's wife*).

summum [sɔmɔm] *nm* height.

super [sypɛʀ] **1** *nm*: ~**(carburant)** super, four-star (petrol), premium (*US*). **2** *préf* (*) ~ **chic** fantastically smart*; (*Pol*) **les** ~**-grands** the super-powers. **3** *adj inv* (*) terrific*, great*.

superbe [sypɛʀb(ə)] *adj* (*gén*) superb, magnificent. ♦ **superbement** *adv* superbly, magnificently.

supercherie [sypɛʀʃəʀi] *nf* trick. **la** ~ trickery.

superficie [sypɛʀfisi] *nf* (*gén*) area.

superficiel, -ielle [sypɛʀfisjɛl] *adj* (*gén*) superficial; *esprit* shallow; *blessure* superficial, skin-deep. ♦ **superficiellement** *adv* superficially.

superflu, e [sypɛʀfly] **1** *adj* superfluous. **2** *nm*: le ~ (*excédent*) the surplus; (*accessoire*) the superfluity.

supérieur, e [sypeʀjœʀ] **1** *adj* **(a)** (*les plus importants*) *niveaux, branches, classes etc* upper; *planètes* superior; *animaux, végétaux* higher. **la partie** ~**e de l'objet** the upper *ou* top part of the object; **montez à l'étage** ~ go to the next floor up *ou* to the floor above; (*Rel*) **Père** ~ Father Superior. **(b)** (*plus important*) (*gén*) higher; *intelligence, qualité* superior; *nombre, vitesse* greater; *quantité, somme* larger. **forces** ~**es en nombres** forces superior in number(s); ~ **à** *nombre* greater *ou* higher than, above; *production* superior to; **intelligence** ~**e à la moyenne** above-average *ou* higher than average intelligence; **hiérarchiquement** ~ **à qn** above sb in the hierarchy. **(c)** (*hautain*) superior. **(d)** (*à la hauteur*) ~ **à sa tâche** more than equal to the task; **restant** ~ **à la situation** remaining master of the situation. **2** *nm,f* superior. ~ **hiérarchique** immediate superior, senior. ♦ **supérieurement** *adv* exceptionally well. ~ **doué** exceptionally gifted. ♦ **supériorité** *nf* (*gén*) superiority. **nous avons la** ~ **du nombre** we outnumber them.

superlatif, -ive [sypɛʀlatif, iv] *adj, nm* superlative.

supermarché [sypɛʀmaʀʃe] *nm* supermarket.

superposer [sypɛʀpoze] (1) **1** *vt objets* to superpose (*à* on); *clichés*, (*fig*) *visions* to superimpose. **2 se** ~ *vpr* to be superposed; to be superimposed (on one another). ♦ **superposition** *nf* superposition; superimposition.

superproduction [sypɛʀpʀɔdyksjɔ̃] *nf* (*Ciné*) spectacular.

supersonique [sypɛʀsɔnik] *adj* supersonic.

superstition [sypɛʀstisjɔ̃] *nf* superstition. ♦ **superstitieusement** *adv* superstitiously. ♦ **superstitieux, -euse** *adj* superstitious.

superstructure [sypɛʀstʀyktyʀ] *nf* (*gén*) superstructure.

superviser [sypɛʀvize] (1) *vt* to supervise.

supplanter [syplɑ̃te] (1) *vt* to supplant.

suppléance [sypleɑ̃s] *nf* (*poste*) supply post; (*action*) temporary replacement. ♦ **suppléant, e** **1** *adj* supply; deputy. **médecin** ~ locum. **2** *nm,f* (*professeur*) supply teacher; (*juge*) deputy (judge); (*député*) deputy (M.P.); (*médecin*) locum.

suppléer [syplee] (1) **1** *vt* **(a)** (*ajouter*) to supply. **(b)** *lacune* to fill; *défaut* to make up for. **(c)** (*remplacer*) (*gén*) to replace; *professeur* to stand in for; *juge* to deputize for. **2** ~ **à** *vt indir défaut, manque* to make up for; *qualité, faculté* to substitute for.

supplément [syplemɑ̃] *nm* (*gén*) supplement; (*au restaurant*) extra charge; (*dans le train*) excess fare. **un** ~ **de travail** extra *ou* additional work; **un** ~ **d'information** supplementary *ou* additional information; **payer un** ~ **pour excès de bagages** to pay extra for excess luggage; **le fromage est en** ~ cheese is extra. ♦ **supplémentaire** *adj crédits, retards* additional, further; *travail* additional, extra; *trains* relief; *angle* supplementary.

suppliant, e [sypljɑ̃, ɑ̃t] **1** *adj* beseeching, imploring. **2** *nm,f* suppliant, supplicant. ♦ **supplication** *nf* (*gén*) plea, entreaty; (*Rel*) supplication.

supplice [syplis] *nm* **(a)** (*peine*) le ~ torture; **un** ~ a form of torture; le ~ **de la roue** torture on the wheel; ~ **chinois** Chinese torture; ~ **de Tantale** torment of Tantalus. **(b)** (*souffrance*) torture. ~**s moraux** moral tortures *ou* torments; **le** ~ **de l'incertitude** the ordeal *ou* torture of uncertainty; **être au** ~ (*appréhension*) to be in agonies; (*douleur*) to be in misery; **mettre qn au** ~ to torture sb. ♦ **supplicié, e** *nm,f* torture victim. ♦ **supplicier** (7) *vt* (*lit, fig*) to torture.

supplier [syplije] (7) *vt* to beseech, implore, entreat (*de faire* to do). **n'insistez pas, je vous en supplie** I beg of you not to insist.

supplique [syplik] *nf* petition.

supporter[1] [sypɔʀte] (1) *vt* **(a)** (*soutenir*) to support, hold up. **(b)** (*subir, endurer*) (*gén*) to bear; *conséquences, malheur* to suffer; *maladie, solitude* to endure; *conduite* to tolerate, put up with. **elle supporte tout de son fils** she puts up with *ou* takes anything from her son; **je ne peux pas** ~ **l'hypocrisie** I can't bear *ou* abide hypocrisy; **je ne peux pas les** ~ I can't bear *ou* stand them; **je ne supporte pas qu'elle fasse cela** I won't stand for *ou* tolerate her doing that; **on supporte un gilet, par ce temps*** you can do with a cardigan in this weather. **(c)** (*résister à*) *température, épreuve* to withstand. **verre qui supporte la chaleur** heat-proof *ou* heat-resistant glass; **il a bien supporté l'opération** he took the operation well; **il ne supporte pas l'alcool** he can't take alcohol; **il ne supporte pas la chaleur/les épinards** heat/spinach doesn't agree *ou* disagrees with him, he can't stand *ou* bear the heat/spinach; **lait facile à** ~ easily-digested milk.

♦ **support** *nm* **(a)** (*soutien*) (*gén*) support; (*béquille*) prop. **(b)** (*moyen*) medium. ~ **publicitaire** advertising medium; **conférence faite à l'aide d'un** ~ **écrit** lecture given with the help of a written text; ~ **audio-visuel** audio-visual aid. ♦ **supportable** *adj douleur, chaleur* bearable; *conduite* tolerable.

supporter[2] [sypɔʀtɛʀ] *nm* (*Sport*) supporter.

supposer [sypoze] (1) *vt* **(a)** (*présumer*) to suppose, assume. **à** ~ **que** supposing *ou* assuming (that); **je suppose que tu es contre** I take it *ou* I assume *ou* I suppose you are against it. **(b)** (*présupposer*) to presuppose; (*suggérer*) to imply. **ta réponse suppose que tu n'as rien compris** your reply implies that you haven't understood a thing. ♦ **supposé, e** *adj auteur* supposed; *nombre* estimated. ♦ **supposition** *nf* supposition.

suppositoire [sypozitwaʀ] *nm* suppository.

supprimer [sypʀime] (1) **1** *vt objet, obstacle* to remove (*de* from); *mot, paragraphe* to delete (*de* from); *trains* to cancel; *permis de conduire* to withdraw, take away (*de* from); *emplois, témoin gênant* to do away with; *douleur, fatigue* to eliminate; *loi, concurrence* to abolish; *publication, effets nocifs* to suppress; *abus* to put an end to; *allocation* to stop. ~ **qch à qn** to deprive sb of sth; **cette technique supprime des opérations inutiles** this technique does away with *ou* cuts out some useless operations. **2 se** ~ *vpr* to do away with o.s., take one's own life. ♦ **suppression** *nf* removal; deletion; cancellation; withdrawal; elimination; abolition; suppression. **faire des** ~**s dans un texte** to make some deletions in a text.

suppurer [sypyʀe] (1) *vi* to suppurate. ♦ **suppuration** *nf* suppuration.

supputer [sypyte] (1) *vt* to calculate. ♦ **supputation** *nf* calculation.

supra ... [sypʀa] *préf* supra ... .

suprême [sypʀɛm] **1** *adj* (*gén*) supreme. **2** *nm* (*Culin*) supreme. ♦ **suprématie** *nf* supremacy. ♦ **suprêmement** *adv* supremely.

sur[1] [syʀ] **1** *prép* **(a)** (*position*) on, upon; (*sur le haut de*) on (top of); (*avec mouvement*) on, onto; (*dans*) on, in; (*par-dessus*) over; (*au-dessus*) above. **il y a un sac** ~ **la table** there's a bag on the table; ~ **ma route** on my way; **elle rangea ses chapeaux** ~ **l'armoire** she put her hats away on top of the wardrobe; **elle a jeté son sac** ~ **la table** she threw her bag onto the table; **une chambre (qui donne)** ~ **la rue** a room that looks out onto the street; **il n'est jamais monté** ~ **un bateau** he's never been in *ou* on a boat; ~ **la place** in the square; **lire qch** ~ **le journal** to read sth in the paper; **un pont** ~ **la rivière** a bridge across *ou* on *ou* over the river; **l'avion est passé** ~ **nos têtes** the aircraft flew over *ou* above our heads; **retire tes livres de** ~ **la table** take your books (from) off the table; **je n'ai pas d'argent** ~ **moi** I haven't (got) any money on *ou* with me; **elle a acheté des poires** ~ **le marché** she bought pears at the market.

(b) (*direction*) to, towards. **tourner** ~ **la droite** to turn (to the) right; **l'église est** ~ **votre gauche** the church is on *ou* to your left; **travaux** ~ **5 km** roadworks for 5 km; **fermez bien la porte** ~ **vous** be sure and close the door behind *ou* after you.

(c) (*temps*) **il est arrivé** ~ **les 2 heures** he came (at) about *ou* (at) around 2; **il va** ~ **ses quinze ans** he's getting on for fifteen; **l'acte s'achève** ~ **une réconciliation** the act ends with a reconciliation; **il est** ~ **le départ** he's just going, he's (just) about to leave; ~ **ce, il est sorti** whereupon *ou* upon which he went out; ~ **ce, il faut que je vous quitte** and now I must leave you; **boire du café** ~ **de la bière** to drink coffee on top of beer.

(d) (*cause*) on, by. ~ **commande** by order; ~ **la recommandation de X** on X's recommendation.

(e) (*manière*) on. **ils vivent** ~ **son traitement** they live on *ou* off* his salary; **ne le prends pas** ~ **ce ton** don't take it like that; **chanter qch** ~ **l'air de** to sing sth to the tune of.

(f) (*sujet*) on, about. **causerie** ~ **la Grèce** talk on *ou* about Greece; **être** ~ **un travail** to be occupied with *ou* (in the process of) doing a job; **être** ~ **une bonne affaire/une piste** to be on to a bargain/on a trail.

(g) (*proportion*) out of, in; (*mesure*) by; (*accumulation*) after. ~ **12 verres, 6 sont ébréchés** out of 12 glasses 6 are chipped; **un homme** ~ **10** one man in (every) *ou* out of 10; (*note*) **9** ~ **10** 9 out of 10; **la cuisine fait 2 mètres** ~ **3** the kitchen is *ou* measures 2 metres by 3; **un vendredi** ~ **trois** every third Friday; **un jour** ~ **deux** every other day; **faire faute** ~ **faute** to make one mistake after another.

(h) (*influence*) over, on. **elle ne peut rien** ~ **lui** she has no control over him; **savoir prendre** ~ **soi** to keep a grip on o.s.; **prendre** ~ **soi de faire qch** to take it upon o.s. to do sth.

2 *préf* over. ~**excité** overexcited; ~**production** overproduction.

3: ~**-le-champ** *adv* immediately.

sur[2], **e** [syʀ] *adj* (*aigre*) sour.

sûr, e [syʀ] *adj* **(a)** (*certain*) certain, sure (*de* of, about). **il est** ~ **de son fait** he's sure *ou* confident he'll do it; ~ **de soi** self-assured, self-confident; **j'en étais** ~! I knew it!, just as I thought!; **j'en suis** ~ **et certain** I'm positive (about it), I'm absolutely certain (of it); **la chose est** ~**e** that's certain, that's for sure *ou* certain. **(b)** (*sans danger*) safe. **peu** ~ unsafe; **le plus** ~ **est de ...** the safest thing is to ...; **en lieu** ~ in a safe place. **(c)** (*digne de confiance*) (*gén*) reliable; *personne, firme* trustworthy; *instinct, raisonnement* sound; *remède, moyen* safe, sure. **avoir la main** ~**e** to have a steady hand; **peu** ~ (*gén*) unreliable; *allié* untrustworthy; *méthode* unsafe; *bases* unsound.

surabonder [syʀabɔ̃de] (1) *vi* to be overabundant, be superabundant. ♦ **surabondance** *nf* overabundance, superabundance. ♦ **surabondant, e** *adj* overabundant, superabundant.

surannné, e [syʀane] *adj* outmoded, outdated.

surcharger [syʀʃaʀʒe] (3) *vt voiture* to overload.

~ qn de travail to overload *ou* overburden sb with work; **manuscrit surchargé de corrections** manuscript covered *ou* littered with corrections. ♦ **surcharge** *nf* **(a)** (*action*) overloading; (*poids en excédent*) extra load, excess load. **une tonne de ~** an extra *ou* excess load of a ton; **prendre des passagers en ~** to take on excess *ou* extra passengers; **une ~ de travail** extra work. **(b)** *[document]* alteration.

surchauffer [syrʃofe] (1) *vt pièce* to overheat; (*Phys, Tech*) to superheat.

surchoix [syrʃwa] *adj inv* top-quality.

surclasser [syrklɑse] (1) *vt* to outclass.

surcroît [syrkrwa] *nm*: **donner un ~ de travail** to give extra *ou* additional work; **par (un) ~ d'honnêteté** through an excess of honesty; **pour ~ de malheur ...** to add to his (*ou* her *etc*) misfortune ...; **avare et paresseux de** *ou* **par ~** miserly and idle to boot.

surdité [syrdite] *nf* deafness.

sureau, *pl* **~x** [syro] *nm* elder (tree).

surélever [syrɛlve] (5) *vt* to raise, heighten (*de* by). **rez-de-chaussée surélevé** raised ground floor.

sûrement [syrmɑ̃] *adv* **(a)** *progresser* in safety; *attacher* securely; *fonctionner* safely. **(b)** (*certainement*) certainly. **~ pas!** surely not!; **il viendra ~** he'll certainly come, he's sure to come.

surenchère [syrɑ̃ʃɛr] *nf* (*sur prix fixé*) overbid; (*enchère plus élevée*) higher bid. **une ~ de violence** an increasing build-up of violence; (*fig*) **faire de la ~** to use outbidding tactics. ♦ **surenchérir** (2) *vi* to bid higher (*sur* than); (*élection etc*) to try to outmatch *ou* outbid each other (*de* with). **~ sur qn** to bid higher than sb, outbid sb.

surestimer [syrɛstime] (1) *vt importance* to overestimate; *maison à vendre* to overvalue. ♦ **surestimation** *nf* overestimation; overvaluation.

sûreté [syrte] *nf* **(a)** (*sécurité*) safety; (*précaution*) precaution. **la ~ de l'État** state security; **pour plus de ~** as an extra precaution, to be on the safe side; **être en ~** to be in safety, be safe; **mettre en ~** to put in a safe *ou* secure place; **serrure** *etc* **de ~** safety lock *etc*. **(b)** (*exactitude*) (*gén*) reliability; *[coup d'œil, geste]* steadiness; *[jugement]* soundness. **il a une grande ~ de main** he has a very sure hand; **~ d'exécution** sureness of touch. **(c)** (*dispositif*) safety device. **(d)** (*garantie*) assurance, guarantee. **(e)** (*Police*) **la S~ (nationale)** = the CID (*Brit*), = the FBI (*US*).

surévaluer [syrevalɥe] (1) *vt* to overvalue.

surexciter [syrɛksite] (1) *vt* to overexcite. ♦ **surexcitation** *nf* overexcitement.

surface [syrfas] *nf* (*gén*) surface; *[champ, chambre]* surface area. **faire ~** to surface; **en ~** *nager* at the surface, near the surface; *apprendre* superficially; (*Ftbl*) **~ de réparation** penalty area.

surfait, e [syrfɛ, ɛt] *adj* overrated.

surfin, e [syrfɛ̃, in] *adj* superfine.

surgelé, e [syrʒəle] *adj* deep-frozen. **(aliments) ~s** (deep-)frozen food.

surgir [syrʒir] (2) *vi* (*lit*) to appear suddenly; *[difficultés]* to arise, crop up. *[plante, immeuble]* **~ de terre** to shoot up, spring up.

surhomme [syrɔm] *nm* superman. ♦ **surhumain, e** *adj* superhuman.

surir [syrir] (2) *vi* to turn *ou* go sour.

surlendemain [syrlɑ̃dmɛ̃] *nm*: **le ~ de son arrivée** two days after his arrival; **il est mort le ~** he died two days later.

surmener [syrməne] (5) **1** *vt* to overwork. **2 se ~** *vpr* to overwork (o.s.). ♦ **surmenage** *nm* (*action*) overworking; (*état*) overwork. **le ~ intellectuel** mental fatigue, brain-fag*.

surmonter [syrmɔ̃te] (1) **1** *vt* (*dans l'espace*) to surmount, top; (*vaincre*) to overcome, get over, surmount. **2 se ~** *vpr* to master o.s., control o.s.

surnager [syrnaʒe] (3) *vi [objet]* to float (on the surface); *[souvenir]* to linger on.

surnaturel, -elle [syrnatyrɛl] **1** *adj* supernatural; (*ambiance inquiétante*) uncanny. **2** *nm*: **le ~** the supernatural.

surnom [syrnɔ̃] *nm* nickname; (*d'un héros*) name.

surnombre [syrnɔ̃br(ə)] *nm*: **en ~** too many; **j'étais en ~** I was one too many.

surnommer [syrnɔme] (1) *vt*: **~ qn 'le gros'** to nickname sb 'fatty'; **le roi Richard surnommé 'le Courageux'** King Richard known as *ou* named 'the Brave'.

surpasser [syrpɑse] (1) **1** *vt* (*gén*) to surpass; *rival* to surpass, outdo (*en* in). **2 se ~** *vpr* to surpass o.s.

surpeuplé, e [syrpœple] *adj* overpopulated. ♦ **surpeuplement** *nm* overpopulation.

surplis [syrpli] *nm* surplice.

surplomb [syrplɔ̃] *nm* overhang. **en ~** overhanging. ♦ **surplomber** (1) *vt* to overhang.

surplus [syrply] *nm* **(a)** (*gén, Comm*) surplus. **marchandises en ~** surplus goods; **il me reste un ~ de clous** I've got some nails left over *ou* some surplus nails; **avec le ~ (du bois)** with the leftover *ou* surplus (wood). **(b)** (*d'ailleurs*) **au ~** moreover, what is more.

surpopulation [syrpɔpylɑsjɔ̃] *nf* overpopulation.

surprendre [syrprɑ̃dr(ə)] (58) *vt* **(a)** *ennemi* to surprise; *voleur* to surprise, catch in the act; (*par visite imprévue*) to catch unawares *ou* on the hop*. **se ~ à faire qch** to find o.s. doing sth; **je vais aller le ~ au travail** I'm going to drop in (unexpectedly) on him at work. **(b)** *secret* to discover; *conversation* to overhear; *regard* to intercept. **(c)** *[pluie, marée, nuit]* to catch out. **se laisser ~ par la nuit** to be overtaken by nightfall. **(d)** (*étonner*) to amaze, surprise. ♦ **surprenant, e** *adj* amazing, surprising. ♦ **surpris, e**[1] *adj* surprised. **~ de qch** surprised *ou* amazed at sth. ♦ **surprise**[2] *nf* (*gén*) surprise. **avoir la ~ de voir que** to be surprised to see that; **prix sans ~s** (all-)inclusive price; **par ~** *attaquer* by surprise; **il m'a pris par ~** he caught me off guard. ♦ **surprise-partie,** *pl* **~s-~s** *nf* party.

surproduction [syrprɔdyksjɔ̃] *nf* overproduction.

surréalisme [syrrealism(ə)] *nm* surrealism. ♦ **surréaliste 1** *adj* (*Art*) surrealist; (*bizarre*) surrealistic. **2** *nmf* surrealist.

sursaut [syrso] *nm* start, jump. (*fig*) **~ d'énergie** (sudden) burst *ou* fit of energy; **se réveiller en ~** to wake up with a start. ♦ **sursauter** (1) *vi* to start, jump, give a start. **faire ~ qn** to make sb start *ou* jump, startle sb.

surseoir [syrswar] (26) **~ à** *vt indir publication* to defer, postpone; (*Jur*) *jugement etc* to stay. **~ à l'exécution d'un condamné** to grant a reprieve to a condemned man. ♦ **sursis** *nm [condamnation à mort]*, (*fig*) reprieve. **peine avec ~** suspended sentence; **il a eu 2 ans avec ~** he was given a 2-year suspended sentence; **~ (d'incorporation)** deferment. ♦ **sursitaire** *adj* (*Mil*) deferred.

surtaxe [syrtaks(ə)] *nf* surcharge. ♦ **surtaxer** (1) *vt* to surcharge.

surtout [syrtu] *adv* (*avant tout*) above all; (*spécialement*) especially, particularly. **j'aime ~ les romans** I particularly like novels, I like novels above all; **dernièrement, j'ai ~ lu des romans** I have read mostly *ou* mainly novels of late; **~ que*** especially as *ou* since; **~ pas (maintenant)** certainly not (now); **~ ne vous mettez pas en frais** please *ou* above all don't go to any expense.

surveiller [syrveje] (1) **1** *vt* (*gén*) to watch, keep an eye on; *prisonnier, malade, territoire* to (keep) watch over; *locaux, ennemi* to keep watch on; *études de qn* to supervise; *réparation* to supervise; oversee; (*Scol*) *examen* to invigilate. ~ **sa ligne** to watch one's figure. **2 se** ~ *vpr* to keep a check *ou* a watch on o.s. ♦ **surveillance** *nf* watch; supervision; invigilation. **sous la** ~ **de la police** under police surveillance; **mission de** ~ surveillance mission; ~ **médicale** medical supervision. ♦ **surveillant, e** *nm,f [prison]* warder; *[usine, chantier]* supervisor, overseer; *[magasin]* shopwalker; *[hôpital]* nursing officer; (*Scol*) (*pion*) supervisor; (*aux examens*) invigilator. (*Scol*) ~ **d'internat** supervisor of boarders.

survenir [syʀvəniʀ] (22) *vi [événement]* to take place; *[incident, retards]* to occur, arise.

survêtement [syʀvɛtmɑ̃] *nm* (*sportif*) tracksuit; *[skieur]* overgarments.

survivre [syʀvivʀ(ə)] (46) *vi* (*lit, fig*) to survive. ~ **à** *accident, humiliation* to survive; *personne, époque* to outlive; **se** ~ **dans** *œuvre, enfant* to live on in. ♦ **survie** *nf* survival. (*Rel*) **la** ~ afterlife. ♦ **survivance** *nf* survival. ♦ **survivant, e 1** *adj* surviving. **2** *nm,f* survivor.

survoler [syʀvɔle] (1) *vt* (*lit*) to fly over; *livre* to skim *ou* skip through; *question* to skim over. ♦ **survol** *nm*: **le** ~ **de** flying over; skimming *ou* skipping through; skimming over.

survolté, e [syʀvɔlte] *adj* **(a)** (*surexcité*) worked up, wrought up. **(b)** (*Élec*) stepped up, boosted.

sus [sy(s)] *adv* (*Admin*) **en** ~ in addition (*de* to).

susceptible [sysɛptibl(ə)] *adj* **(a)** (*ombrageux*) touchy, thin-skinned, sensitive. **(b) être** ~ **de faire qch** (*aptitude*) to be in a position *ou* be able to do sth; (*éventualité*) to be likely *ou* liable to do sth; ~ **d'être démontré** susceptible of proof; **texte** ~ **d'améliorations** text open to improvement *ou* that can be improved upon; **il est** ~ **de gagner** he may well win, he is liable to win. ♦ **susceptibilité** *nf* touchiness, sensitiveness. ~**s** susceptibilities, sensibilities.

susciter [sysite] (1) *vt intérêt* to arouse; *passions* to arouse, incite; *controverse* to give rise to, provoke; *obstacles* to create.

suspect, e [syspɛ(kt), ɛkt(ə)] **1** *adj individu, conduite* suspicious; *opinion, citoyen* suspect. **être** ~ **de qch** to be suspected of sth. **2** *nm,f* suspect. ♦ **suspecter** (1) *vt personne* to suspect (*de faire* of doing); *bonne foi* to have (one's) suspicions about, question.

suspendre [syspɑ̃dʀ(ə)] (41) **1** *vt* **(a)** *vêtements* to hang up (*à* on); *lampe* to hang, suspend (*à* from); *hamac* to sling (up). **(b)** (*interrompre*) (*gén*) to suspend; *récit* to break off; *séance* to adjourn. **(c)** *jugement* to suspend, defer; *décision* to postpone, defer. **(d)** *fonctionnaire, joueur* to suspend. ~ **qn de ses fonctions** to suspend sb from office. **2 se** ~ *vpr*: **se** ~ **à qch** to hang from sth. ♦ **suspendu, e** *adj* **(a)** ~ **à qch** *vêtement, lustre* hanging *ou* suspended from sth; (*fig*) **être** ~ **aux lèvres de qn** to hang upon sb's every word; (*fig*) **chalets** ~**s au-dessus d'une gorge** chalets suspended *ou* perched over a gorge. **(b)** (*Aut*) **voiture bien/mal** ~**e** car with good/poor suspension.

suspens [syspɑ̃] *nm*: **en** ~ *affaire, projet* in abeyance; *poussière* in suspension; (*dans l'incertitude*) in suspense; **tenir les lecteurs en** ~ to keep the reader in suspense; **en** ~ **dans l'air** suspended in the air.

suspense [syspɑ̃s] *nm* suspense.

suspension [syspɑ̃sjɔ̃] **1** *nf* **(a)** (*action: V* **suspendre**) hanging; suspending; breaking off; adjournment; suspension, deferment; postponement. **(b)** (*Aut*) suspension. **(c)** (*lustre*) chandelier. **(d)** (*Chim*) suspension. **(e) en** ~ *poussière* in suspension; **en** ~ **dans l'air** suspended in the air. **2:** ~ **d'armes** suspension of fighting; ~ **de paiement** suspension of payment(s); ~ **de séance** adjournment.

suspicion [syspisjɔ̃] *nf* suspicion.

susurrer [sysyʀe] (1) *vti* to whisper, murmur.

suture [sytyʀ] *nf* suture. ♦ **suturer** (1) *vt* to suture (*Méd*), stitch up.

suzerain, e [syzʀɛ̃, ɛn] *adj, nm,f* suzerain. ♦ **suzeraineté** *nf* suzerainty.

svelte [svɛlt(ə)] *adj* slender. ♦ **sveltesse** *nf* slenderness.

sycomore [sikɔmɔʀ] *nm* sycamore (tree).

syllabe [silab] *nf* syllable. ♦ **syllabique** *adj* syllabic.

syllogisme [silɔʒism(ə)] *nm* syllogism.

sylviculture [silvikyltyʀ] *nf* forestry.

symbole [sɛ̃bɔl] *nm* (*gén*) symbol. ♦ **symbolique** *adj* (*gén*) symbolic(al); (*fig: très modique*) token, nominal. **geste** ~ symbolic *ou* token gesture. ♦ **symboliquement** *adv* symbolically. ♦ **symbolisation** *nf* symbolization. ♦ **symboliser** (1) *vt* to symbolize.

symétrie [simetʀi] *nf* (*gén*) symmetry. ♦ **symétrique** *adj* symmetrical (*de* to, *par rapport à* in relation to). ♦ **symétriquement** *adv* symmetrically.

sympa* [sɛ̃pa] *adj inv* (*abrév de* **sympathique**) nice, friendly. **sois** ~, **prête-le-moi** be a pal* and lend it to me.

sympathie [sɛ̃pati] *nf* **(a)** (*inclination*) liking; (*affinité*) fellow feeling. **j'ai beaucoup de** ~ **pour lui** I have a great liking for him, I like him a great deal; **des relations de** ~ **les unissaient** they were united by a fellow feeling. **(b)** (*compassion*) sympathy. **croyez à notre** ~ you have our deepest sympathy. ♦ **sympathique** *adj* **(a)** (*agréable*) nice, friendly; *ambiance* pleasant; *plat* good. **je le trouve** ~ I like him, I find him likeable. **(b)** (*Anat*) sympathetic. ♦ **sympathiquement** *adv accueillir* in a friendly manner. ♦ **sympathisant, e** *nm,f* (*Pol*) sympathizer. ♦ **sympathiser** (1) *vi* (*bien s'entendre*) to get on (well) (*avec* with); (*se prendre d'amitié*) to make friends (*avec* with). (*fréquenter*) **ils ne sympathisent pas avec les voisins** they don't have much contact with the neighbours; **ils ont tout de suite sympathisé** they took to each other immediately.

symphonie [sɛ̃fɔni] *nf* symphony. ♦ **symphonique** *adj* symphonic; *orchestre* symphony.

symposium [sɛ̃pozjɔm] *nm* symposium.

symptôme [sɛ̃ptom] *nm* (*Méd*) symptom; (*signe*) sign, symptom. ♦ **symptomatique** *adj* (*Méd*) symptomatic; (*révélateur*) significant. ~ **de** symptomatic of.

synagogue [sinagɔg] *nf* synagogue.

synchronie [sɛ̃kʀɔni] *nf* synchrony. ♦ **synchronique** *adj* synchronic. ♦ **synchronisation** *nf* synchronization. ♦ **synchronisé, e** *adj* synchronized. ♦ **synchroniser** (1) *vt* to synchronize. ♦ **synchronisme** *nm* synchronism.

syncope [sɛ̃kɔp] *nf* **(a)** (*évanouissement*) blackout, fainting fit. **tomber en** ~ to faint, pass out. **(b)** (*Mus*) syncopation. ♦ **syncopé, e** *adj* (*Mus*) syncopated.

syndic [sɛ̃dik] *nm*: ~ **(d'immeuble)** managing agent.

syndicat [sɛ̃dika] *nm [travailleurs]* (trade) union; *[employeurs]* union, syndicate; *[producteurs agricoles]* union; (*non professionnel*) association. ~ **d'initiative** tourist (information) office *ou* bureau; ~ **de propriétaires** association of property owners. ♦ **syndical, e,** *mpl* **-aux** *adj* (trade-) union. ♦ **syndicalisme** *nm* (*mouvement*) trade unionism. (*activité*) **faire du** ~ to participate in unionist activities. ♦ **syndicaliste 1** *nmf* trade unionist. **2** *adj chef* trade-union; *doctrine* unionist. ♦ **syndiqué, e 1** *adj*: **être** ~ to be a union member; **travailleurs non** ~**s** non-union workers. **2** *nm,f* union member. ♦ **syndiquer** (1) **1** *vt* to unionize. **2 se** ~ *vpr* (*se grouper*) to form a trade union; (*adhérer*) to join a trade union.

syndrome [sɛ̃dʀom] *nm* syndrome.

synode [sinɔd] *nm* synod.

synonyme [sinɔnim] **1** *adj* synonymous (*de* with). **2** *nm* synonym. ♦ **synonymie** *nf* synonymy.
syntaxe [sɛ̃taks(ə)] *nf* syntax. ♦ **syntactique** *adj ou* ♦ **syntaxique** *adj* syntactic.
synthèse [sɛ̃tɛz] *nf* synthesis. **faire la ~ de qch** to synthesize sth. ♦ **synthétique** *adj* synthetic. ♦ **synthétiquement** *adv* synthetically. ♦ **synthétiser** (1) *vt* to synthesize.
syphilis [sifilis] *nf* syphilis. ♦ **syphilitique** *adj, nmf* syphilitic.
Syrie [siʀi] *nf* Syria. ♦ **syrien, -ienne** *adj*, **S~(ne)** *nm(f)* Syrian.
système [sistɛm] *nm* (*gén*) system. **~ métrique/nerveux** metric/nervous system; **il connaît le ~** he knows the system; **il me tape sur le ~*** he gets on my nerves*; **le ~ D*** resourcefulness. ♦ **systématique** *adj* (*gén*) systematic. **il est trop ~** he's too rigid *ou* dogmatic in his thinking. ♦ **systématiquement** *adv* systematically. ♦ **systématisation** *nf* systematization. ♦ **systématiser** (1) **1** *vt* to systematize. **2 se ~** *vpr* to become the rule.

T

T, t [te] *nm* (*lettre*) T, t. **en T** *table etc* T-shaped.
t' [t(ə)] *V* **te, tu.**
ta [ta] *adj poss V* **ton**[1].
tabac [taba] **1** *nm* **(a)** (*produit*) tobacco; (*couleur*) tobacco brown; (*magasin*) tobacconist's (shop). ~ **blond/brun** light/dark tobacco; ~ **à priser** snuff. **(b)** (*) **passer qn à** ~ to beat sb up; (*arg Théât*) **faire un** ~ to be a great hit; **c'est toujours le même** ~ it's always the same old thing. **2** *adj inv* buff.
tabasser* [tabase] (1) **1** *vt*: ~ **qn** to beat sb up. **2 se** ~ *vpr* to have a punch-up*.
tabatière [tabatjɛʀ] *nf* **(a)** (*boîte*) snuffbox. **(b)** (*lucarne*) skylight.
tabernacle [tabɛʀnakl(ə)] *nm* tabernacle.
table [tabl(ə)] **1** *nf* **(a)** (*meuble*) table. (*fig*) **faire** ~ **rase** to make a clean sweep (*de* of). **(b)** (*pour le repas*) table. **être à** ~ to be having a meal, be at table; **à** ~! come and eat!; **mettre la** ~ to lay *ou* set the table; **se mettre à** ~ to sit down to eat, sit down at the table; (*arg Police*) to talk, come clean*; **toute la** ~ **éclata de rire** the whole table burst out laughing; **avoir une bonne** ~ to keep a good table; **aimer (les plaisirs de) la** ~ to enjoy one's food. **(c)** (*gén, Math: liste*) table. ~ **alphabétique** alphabetical table. **(d)** (*Géol: plateau*) tableland, plateau. **2:** ~ **de conférence** conference table; ~ **à dessin** drawing board; ~ **d'écoute** wire-tapping set; ~ **des matières** (table of) contents; ~ **de nuit** bedside table; ~ **d'opération** operating table; ~ **d'orientation** viewpoint indicator; ~ **à repasser** ironing board; (*lit, fig*) ~ **ronde** round table; ~ **roulante** trolley; ~ **de travail** work table *ou* desk.
tableau, *pl* ~**x** [tablo] *nm* **(a)** (*peinture*) painting; (*reproduction, gravure*) picture. (*lit, fig*) ~ **de chasse** bag; ~ **de maître** masterpiece. **(b)** (*fig*) (*scène*) picture, scene; (*description*) picture. **un** ~ **tragique** a tragic picture *ou* scene; **pour compléter le** ~* to cap it all; **gagner sur les 2/sur tous les** ~**x** to win on both/all counts. **(c)** (*Théât*) scene. **(d)** (*Scol*) ~ **(noir)** (black)board. **(e)** (*panneau*) (*gén*) board; *[fusibles]* box; *[clefs]* rack, board. ~ **des horaires** timetable; ~ **d'affichage** notice board; ~ **de bord** dashboard, instrument panel; ~ **d'honneur** list of merit; ~ **de service** duty roster. **(f)** (*carte, graphique*) table, chart; (*Admin: liste*) register, roll, list.
tablée [table] *nf* table (*of people*).
tabler [table] (1) *vi*: ~ **sur qch** to count *ou* reckon *ou* bank on sth.
tablette [tablɛt] *nf* **(a)** *[chocolat]* bar; *[chewing-gum]* stick; *[métal]* block. **(b)** *[lavabo, étagère]* shelf; *[secrétaire]* flap. **(c)** (*Hist: pour écrire*) tablet. (*hum*) **marquer qch sur ses** ~**s** to make a note of sth.
tablier [tablije] *nm* **(a)** (*gén*) apron; *[ménagère]* apron, pinafore; *[écolier]* overall, smock. **(b)** *[pont]* roadway. **(c)** *[cheminée]* (flue-)shutter; *[magasin]* (iron *ou* steel) shutter.
tabou [tabu] *nm, adj* taboo.
tabouret [tabuʀɛ] *nm* stool; (*pour les pieds*) footstool.
tac [tak] *nm* **(a)** (*bruit*) tap. **(b) répondre du** ~ **au** ~ to answer pat.
tache [taʃ] *nf* **(a)** *[fruit]* mark; *[plumage, pelage]* spot; *[peau]* blotch, mark. ~ **de rousseur** freckle; (*fig*) **faire** ~ to jar, stick out like a sore thumb*. **(b)** (*salissure*) stain, mark. ~ **d'encre** ink stain; (*sur le papier*) ink blot *ou* blotch; ~ **d'huile** oily mark, oil stain; (*fig*) **faire** ~ **d'huile** to spread, gain ground; ~ **de sang** bloodstain; **sa robe n'avait pas une** ~ her dress was spotless. **(c)** (*sur réputation*) blot, stain. **sans** ~ *conduite* spotless, unblemished. **(d)** (*impression visuelle*) ~ **de couleur/d'ombre** patch of colour/shadow. **(e)** (*Peinture*) spot, dot, blob.
tâche [tɑʃ] *nf* (*travail*) task, work; (*mission*) task, job. **mourir à la** ~ to die in harness; **à la** ~ *payer* by the piece; **travail à la** ~ piecework.
tacher [taʃe] (1) **1** *vt* **(a)** *[encre, vin]* to stain; *[graisse]* to mark, stain. **taché de sang** bloodstained. **(b)** (*colorer*) *pré, robe* to spot, dot; *peau, fourrure* to spot, mark. **(c)** *réputation* to stain. **2 se** ~ *vpr [personne]* to get stains on one's clothes; *[tissu]* to get stained *ou* marked; (*s'abîmer*) *[fruits]* to become marked.
tâcher [tɑʃe] (1) *vi*: ~ **de faire** to try to do; **tâchez de venir avant samedi** try to *ou* try and come before Saturday; **et tâche de ne pas recommencer*** and see to it that *ou* mind it doesn't happen again.
tacheter [taʃte] (4) *vt* to spot, dot, speckle.
tacite [tasit] *adj* tacit. ♦ **tacitement** *adv* tacitly.
taciturne [tasityʀn(ə)] *adj* taciturn, silent.
tacot* [tako] *nm* (*voiture*) banger*, crate*.
tact [takt] *nm* tact. **avoir du** ~ to have tact, be tactful; **avec** ~ tactfully; **sans** ~ (*adj*) tactless; (*adv*) tactlessly.
tactile [taktil] *adj* tactile.
tactique [taktik] **1** *adj* tactical. **2** *nf* (*gén*) tactics.
taie [tɛ] *nf* **(a)** ~ **(d'oreiller)** pillowcase, pillowslip; ~ **de traversin** bolster case. **(b)** (*Méd*) opaque spot.
taillader [tɑjade] (1) *vt* to slash, gash.
taille[1] [tɑj] **(a)** *[personne, cheval]* height. **homme de haute/petite** ~ tall/short man; **ils sont de la même** ~ they are the same height. **(b)** *[objet, maison]* size. **de petite/moyenne** ~ small-/medium-sized; **c'est de la** ~ **d'un crayon** it's the size of a pencil. **(c)** (*Comm: mesure*) size. **la** ~ **40** size 40; **ce pantalon n'est pas à sa** ~ these trousers aren't his size; **si je trouvais qn de ma** ~ if I found sb my size. **(d)** (*fig*) **c'est un poste à sa** ~ it's a job in keeping *ou* in line with his capabilities; **être de** ~ **à faire** to be up to doing, be quite capable of doing; **il n'est pas de** ~ (*face à un concurrent*) he doesn't measure up; **de** ~ *erreur, enjeu* considerable, sizeable. **(e)** (*ceinture*) waist. **avoir la** ~ **fine** to have a slim waist, be slim-waisted; **avoir la** ~ **mannequin** to have a perfect figure; **ils se tenaient par la** ~ they had their arms round each other's waist; **pantalon (à)** ~ **basse** low-waisted trousers, hipsters.
taille[2] [tɑj] *nf* (*action: V* **tailler**) cutting; carving; pruning; trimming; clipping. (*résultat*) **de** ~ **hexagonale** with a six-sided cut. ♦ **taille-crayon(s)** *nm inv* pencil sharpener.
tailler [tɑje] (1) **1** *vt* **(a)** *pierre* to cut; *bois* to carve; *crayon* to sharpen; *tissu* to cut (out); *arbre* to prune, cut back; *haie* to trim, clip, cut; *barbe* to trim. ~ **qch en biseau** to bevel sth; ~ **qch en pointe** to cut sth to a point. **(b)** *vêtement* to make;

statue to carve; *tartines* to cut, slice. **rôle taillé à sa mesure** tailor-made role; **~ une bavette*** to have a natter*; **~ une armée en pièces** to hack an army to pieces. **2** *vi*: **~ dans la chair** to cut into the flesh. **3 se ~** *vpr* **(a)** (‡: *partir*) to beat it‡, clear off‡. **(b) se ~ un franc succès** to be a great success; **se ~ la part du lion** to take the lion's share; **se ~ un empire** to carve out an empire for o.s. ♦ **taillé, e** *adj personne* **bien ~** well-built; **il est ~ en athlète** he has an athletic build; (*fig*) **être ~ pour qch/pour faire qch** to be cut out for sth/to do sth. ♦ **tailleur** *nm* **(a)** (*couturier*) tailor. **en ~** *assis* cross-legged. **(b)** (*costume*) (woman's) suit. **(c) ~ de pierre(s)** stone-cutter.

taillis [taji] *nm* copse, coppice.

tain [tɛ̃] *nm [miroir]* silvering. **glace sans ~** two-way mirror.

taire [tɛʀ] (54) **1 se ~** *vpr* **(a)** *[personne]* to be silent *ou* quiet; *[nature, forêt]* to be silent; *[bruit]* to disappear. **ils ne voulaient pas se ~** they wouldn't stop talking *ou* keep quiet; **l'orchestre s'était tu** the orchestra had fallen silent. **(b)** (*être discret*) to keep quiet, remain silent (*sur qch* about sth). **tais-toi!*** (*ne m'en parle pas*) don't talk to me about it! **2** *vt fait, vérité* to hush up, not to tell; *raisons* to conceal, say nothing about; *chagrin* to stifle, keep to o.s. **une personne dont je tairai le nom** a person who shall remain nameless *ou* whose name I shan't mention. **3** *vi*: **faire ~** *opposition* to silence; **fais ~ les enfants** make the children keep *ou* be quiet, make the children shut up*.

talc [talk] *nm* talcum powder, talc.

talent [talɑ̃] *nm* talent. (*hum*) **montrez-nous vos ~s*** show us what you can do; **avoir du ~** to have talent, be talented; **encourager les jeunes ~s** to encourage young talent; (*iro*) **il a le ~ de se faire des ennemis** he has a gift for making enemies. ♦ **talentueux, -euse** *adj* talented.

taler [tale] (1) *vt fruits* to bruise.

talisman [talismɑ̃] *nm* talisman.

taloche* [talɔʃ] *nf* clout*, cuff. ♦ **talocher*** (1) *vt* to cuff.

talon [talɔ̃] *nm* (*gén, Anat*) heel; *[chèque]* stub, counterfoil; (*Cartes*) talon. **tourner les ~s** to turn on one's heel and leave; **être sur les ~s de qn** to be (hot) on sb's heels; **~ d'Achille** Achilles' heel. ♦ **talonner** (1) *vt fugitifs* to follow (hot) on the heels of; *débiteur* to hound; *[cheval]* to kick; *[faim]* to gnaw at. (*Rugby*) **~ (le ballon)** to heel (the ball). ♦ **talonneur** *nm* (*Rugby*) hooker.

talquer [talke] (1) *vt* to put talcum powder *ou* talc on.

talus [taly] *nm [route]* embankment; *[rivière]* bank.

tambouille* [tɑ̃buj] *nf* grub*. **faire la ~** to cook the grub*.

tambour [tɑ̃buʀ] *nm* **(a)** (*instrument*) drum. **~ de basque** tambourine; **~ battant** briskly; **sans ~ ni trompette** without any fuss. **(b)** (*musicien*) drummer. **~-major** drum major. **(c)** (*à broder*) embroidery hoop. **(d)** (*porte*) (*sas*) tambour; (*à tourniquet*) revolving door. **(e)** *[machine à laver]* drum; *[moulinet]* spool. **~ de frein** brake drum. ♦ **tambourin** *nm* tambourine. ♦ **tambouriner** (1) **1** *vi [personne, pluie]* to drum (*sur* on). **2** *vt musique* to drum out; (*fig*) *nouvelle* to broadcast.

tamis [tami] *nm* (*gén*) sieve; (*à sable*) riddle, sifter. **passer au ~** (*lit*) to sieve; to riddle, sift; *personne* to screen; *dossier* to sift through. ♦ **tamiser** (1) *vt farine* to sieve; *sable* to riddle, sift; (*fig*) *lumière* to filter. ♦ **tamisage** *nm* sieving; sifting, riddling; filtering. ♦ **tamisé, e** *adj lumière* (*artificielle*) subdued; (*du jour*) soft, softened.

Tamise [tamiz] *nf*: **la ~** the Thames.

tampon [tɑ̃pɔ̃] *nm* **(a)** (*pour boucher*) (*gén*) plug; (*en coton*) wad; (*pour nettoyer une plaie*) swab; (*pour étendre un liquide*) pad. **~ buvard** blotter; **~ encreur** inking-pad; **~ à récurer** scouring pad; **rouler qch en ~** to roll sth (up) into a ball. **(b)** (*timbre*) stamp. **le ~ de la poste** the postmark. **(c)** (*Rail, fig: amortisseur*) buffer. **état ~** buffer state. ♦ **tamponner** (1) **1** *vt* **(a)** (*essuyer*) to mop up, dab; *yeux* to dab (at). **(b)** (*collision*) to ram (into), crash into. **(c)** (*avec un timbre*) to stamp. **2 se ~** *vpr* **(a)** *[trains]* to crash into each other, ram each other. **(b) se ~ de qch‡** not to give a damn about sth‡.

tam-tam, *pl* **~s-~s** [tamtam] *nm* tomtom. **faire du ~ autour de*** *affaire* to make a lot of fuss *ou* a hullaballoo about.

tancer [tɑ̃se] (3) *vt* (*littér*) to berate (*littér*).

tandem [tɑ̃dɛm] *nm* (*bicyclette*) tandem; (*fig: duo*) pair, duo.

tandis [tɑ̃di] *conj*: **~ que** (*simultanéité*) while; (*opposition*) whereas, while.

tangage [tɑ̃gaʒ] *nm* (*Naut*) pitching.

tangent, e [tɑ̃ʒɑ̃, ɑ̃t] **1** *adj* (*Géom*) tangent, tangential (*à* to). (*: *juste*) **c'était ~** it was a close thing, it was touch-and-go*; **il était ~** he was a borderline case. **2** *nf* (*Géom*) tangent. **prendre la ~e*** (*partir*) to make off*; (*éluder*) to dodge the issue.

tangible [tɑ̃ʒibl(ə)] *adj* tangible.

tanguer [tɑ̃ge] (1) *vi [navire, avion]* to pitch; (*fig*) to reel.

tanière [tanjɛʀ] *nf* (*lit, fig*) den, lair.

tank [tɑ̃k] *nm* tank.

tanker [tɑ̃kɛʀ] *nm* tanker.

tanner [tane] (1) *vt cuir* to tan; *visage* to weather. **~ le cuir à qn‡** to tan sb's hide*; **~ qn*** to pester sb. ♦ **tannage** *nm* tanning. ♦ **tannant, e*** *adj* (*ennuyeux*) maddening*. ♦ **tannerie** *nf* (*endroit*) tannery; (*activité*) tanning. ♦ **tanneur** *nm* tanner.

tant [tɑ̃] *adv* **(a)** (*intensité: avec vb*) so much. **il mange ~!** he eats so much! *ou* such a lot!; **vous m'en direz ~!** is that really so! **(b)** (*quantité*) **~ de** *temps, eau* so much; *arbres, gens* so many; *habileté* such, so much; **~ de fois** so many times, so often. **(c)** (*avec adj, participe*) so. **il est rentré ~ le ciel était menaçant** he went home (because) the sky looked so overcast; **cet enfant ~ désiré** this child they had longed for so much; **~ il est vrai que ...** which only goes to show *ou* prove that ... ; **le jour ~ attendu** the long-awaited day. **(d)** (*quantité imprécise*) so much. **gagner ~ par mois** to earn so much a month; **~ pour cent** so many per cent. **(e)** (*comparaison*) **ce n'est pas ~ leur maison qui me plaît que leur jardin** it's not so much their house that I like as their garden; **il criait ~ qu'il pouvait** he shouted as much as he could; **~ filles que garçons** both girls and boys, girls as well as boys, girls and boys alike. **(f) ~ que** (*aussi longtemps que*) as long as; (*pendant que*) while; **~ qu'elle aura de la fièvre** while *ou* as long as she has a temperature; **~ que vous y êtes*** while you are about it. **(g) ~ bien que mal** so-so, after a fashion; **s'il est ~ soit peu intelligent** if he is at all *ou* in the least bit intelligent; **~ mieux** so much the better, that's fine; **~ mieux pour lui** good for him; **~ pis** (*conciliant*) never mind, (that's) too bad; (*indifférent*) (that's just) too bad; **~ pis pour lui** (that's just) too bad for him; **~ et si bien que** to such an extent that, so much so that; **il y en a ~ et plus** (*eau*) there is ever so much; (*objets*) there are ever so many; **il a protesté ~ et plus** he protested for all he was worth; **~ qu'à faire, on va payer maintenant** we might *ou* may as well pay now; **~ qu'à marcher, allons en forêt** if we have to walk let's go to the forest; **~ que ça?*** as much as that?; **pas ~ que ça*** not that much*; **~ s'en faut** far from it.

tante [tɑ̃t] *nf* (*parente*) aunt, aunty*; (‡: *homosexuel*) poof‡, queer‡.

tantinet* [tɑ̃tinɛ] *nm*: **un ~ fatigant** a tiny *ou* weeny* bit tiring.
tantôt [tɑ̃to] *adv* **(a)** (*cet après-midi*) this afternoon. **(b)** (*parfois*) **~ à pied, ~ en voiture** sometimes on foot, sometimes by car.
taon [tɑ̃] *nm* horsefly, gadfly.
tapage [tapaʒ] *nm* **(a)** (*vacarme*) din, uproar, row. **faire du ~** to create a din *ou* an uproar, make a row; **~ nocturne** disturbance of the peace (*at night*). **(b)** (*battage*) fuss, talk (*autour de* about, over). ♦ **tapageur, -euse** *adj* **(a)** (*bruyant*) noisy, rowdy. **(b)** *publicité* obtrusive; *toilette* flashy, loud, showy.
tapant, e* [tapɑ̃, ɑ̃t] *adj*: **à 8 heures ~(es)** at 8 o'clock sharp *ou* on the dot*.
tape [tap] *nf* (*coup*) slap.
taper [tape] (1) **1** *vt* **(a)** *tapis* to beat; *enfant* to slap, clout*; *porte* to bang, slam. **~ un coup à la porte** to knock once at the door, give a knock at the door. **(b) ~ (à la machine)** *lettre* to type (out); **tapé à la machine** typed, typewritten. **(c)** (ᵻ: *emprunter*) **~ qn (de 10 F)** to touch sb* (for 10 francs), cadge (10 francs) off sb*.
2 *vi* **(a) ~ sur** *clou* to hit; *table* to bang *ou* rap on; **~ sur qn*** (*coups*) to thump sb*; (*critiques*) to run sb down*; **~ à la porte** to knock on the door; **~ dans un ballon** to kick a ball about; **~ dur** to hit hard. **(b)** (ᵻ: *entamer*) **~ dans** *provisions, caisse* to dig into*. **(c)** *[soleil]* to beat down. **(d) ~ des pieds** to stamp one's feet; **~ des mains** to clap one's hands; (*fig*) **se faire ~ sur les doigts*** to be rapped over the knuckles; **il a tapé à côté*** he was wide of the mark; **~ sur les nerfs de qn*** to get on sb's nerves*; **~ dans l'œil de qn*** to take sb's fancy*; **~ dans le tas** (*bagarre*) to pitch into the crowd; (*repas*) to tuck in*, dig in*.
3 se ~ *vpr* **(a)** (ᵻ: *s'envoyer*) *repas* to put away*; *marche* to do; *corvée* to get landed with*. **(b) c'est à se ~ la tête contre les murs** it's enough to drive you up the wall*; **se ~ la cloche*** to feed one's face*.
♦ **tape-à-l'œil 1** *adj inv* flashy, showy. **2** *nm* show, flash*.
tapette [tapɛt] *nf* **(a)** (*pour tapis*) carpet beater; (*pour mouches*) flyswatter; (*pour souris*) mousetrap. **(b)** (*langue*) **elle a une (bonne) ~** she's a real chatterbox*. **(c)** (ᵻ: *homosexuel*) poofᵻ, queer*.
tapeur, -euse* [tapœʀ, øz] *nm,f* (*emprunteur*) cadger*.
tapinᵻ [tapɛ̃] *nm*: **faire le ~** to walk the streets (*for prostitution*), hustleᵻ.
tapinois [tapinwa] *nm*: **en ~** furtively.
tapioca [tapjɔka] *nm* tapioca.
tapir (se) [tapiʀ] (2) *vpr* (*se blottir*) to crouch; (*se cacher*) to hide away; (*s'embusquer*) to lurk.
tapis [tapi] *nm* **(a)** (*gén, fig*) carpet; (*petit*) rug; (*natte*) mat; (*sur un meuble*) cloth. **~ vert** (*tissu*) green baize; (*table de jeu*) gambling table; **~-brosse** doormat; **~ roulant** (*pour colis etc*) conveyor belt; (*pour piétons*) moving walkway, travelator. **(b) aller au ~** to go down for the count; **envoyer qn au ~** to floor sb; **mettre sur le ~** *affaire* to lay on the table, bring up for discussion; **revenir sur le ~** to come back up for discussion. ♦ **tapisser** (1) *vt* **(a)** *[personne]* (*de papier peint*) to (wall)paper; (*de tentures*) to hang, cover; (*d'affiches*) to plaster, cover (*de* with). **(b)** *[tenture, papier]* to cover, line; *[mousse, neige]* to carpet, cover; (*Anat, Bot*) to line. **tapissé de lierre** ivy-clad, covered in ivy. ♦ **tapisserie** *nf* **(a)** (*tenture*) tapestry; (*papier peint*) wallpaper; (*activité*) tapestry-making. *[danseur]* **faire ~** to sit out. **(b)** (*broderie*) tapestry; (*activité*) tapestry-work. ♦ **tapissier, -ière** *nm,f* (*fabricant*) tapestry-maker; (*commerçant*) upholsterer; (*décorateur*) interior decorator.
taquin, e [takɛ̃, in] **1** *adj* teasing. **il est ~** he is a tease *ou* teaser. **2** *nm,f* tease, teaser. ♦ **taquiner** (1) *vt [personne]* to tease; *[fait, douleur]* to bother, worry. ♦ **taquinerie** *nf*: **~(s)** teasing.
tarabiscoté, e [taʀabiskɔte] *adj* (over-)ornate, fussy.
tarabuster [taʀabyste] (1) *vt [personne]* to badger, pester; *[fait, idée]* to bother, worry.
taratata [taʀatata] *excl* nonsense!, rubbish!
tard [taʀ] **1** *adv* late. **il se fait ~** it's getting late; **~ dans la matinée** late in the morning, in the late morning; **plus ~** later (on); **jeudi au plus ~** on Thursday at the latest; **pas plus ~ qu'hier** only yesterday; **remettre qch à plus ~** to put sth off till later (on). **2** *nm*: **sur le ~** (*dans la vie*) late (on) in life. ♦ **tarder** (1) **1** *vi* **(a) ~ à entreprendre qch** to put off *ou* delay starting sth; **ne tardez pas (à le faire)** don't be long doing it; **~ en chemin** to loiter on the way; **sans (plus) ~** without (further) delay. **(b)** *[réaction, moment, lettre]* to be a long time coming. **ça n'a pas tardé** it wasn't long (in) coming; **ils ne vont pas ~** they won't be long (now); **il n'a pas tardé à s'en apercevoir** it didn't take him long to notice, he noticed soon enough. **2** *vb impers*: **il me tarde de le revoir** I am longing *ou* I can't wait to see him again. ♦ **tardif, -ive** *adj* (*gén*) late; *regrets, remords* belated. ♦ **tardivement** *adv rentrer* late; *s'apercevoir* belatedly.
tare [taʀ] *nf* **(a)** (*contrepoids*) tare. **faire la ~** to allow for the tare. **(b)** *[personne]* defect (*de* in, of); *[système]* flaw (*de* in), defect (*de* of). ♦ **taré, e 1** *adj régime* tainted, corrupt; *enfant* with a defect. **2** *nm,f* (*Méd*) degenerate; (*péj*) cretin*.
targette [taʀʒɛt] *nf* bolt (*on a door*).
targuer (se) [taʀge] (1) *vpr*: **se ~ de qch/de faire qch** to boast about sth/that one can do sth, pride *ou* preen o.s. on sth/on doing sth.
tarif [taʀif] *nm* (*tableau*) price list, tariff; (*barème*) rate, tariff; (*taux*) rate. **les ~s postaux vont augmenter** postage rates are going up; **voyager à plein ~/à ~ réduit** to travel at full/reduced fare; (*hum*) **50 F d'amende, c'est le ~!*** a 50-franc fine is what you get! ♦ **tarifaire** *adj* tariff. ♦ **tarifer** (1) *vt* to fix the price *ou* rate for. **marchandises tarifées** fixed-price goods.
tarir [taʀiʀ] (2) **1** *vi* (*gén*) to dry up; *[imagination, puits]* to run dry, dry up. **il ne tarit pas sur ce sujet** he can't stop talking about that. **2** *vt* (*lit, fig*) to dry up. **3 se ~** *vpr* to run dry, dry up. ♦ **tarissement** *nm* drying up.
tartare [taʀtaʀ] **1** *adj* (*Hist*) Tartar; (*Culin*) tartar(e). **2** *nmf*: **T~** Tartar.
tarte [taʀt(ə)] **1** *nf* (*Culin*) tart; (ᵻ: *gifle*) clout*. **c'est pas de la ~ᵻ** it's no easy matter. **2** *adj inv* (*) (*bête*) daft*, stupid; (*laid*) ugly. ♦ **tartelette** *nf* tartlet, tart.
tartine [taʀtin] *nf* **(a)** slice of bread; (*beurrée*) slice of bread and butter. **(b)** (**fig: lettre, article*) screed. ♦ **tartiner** (1) *vt pain* to spread (*de* with); *beurre* to spread. **fromage à ~** cheese spread.
tartre [taʀtʀ(ə)] *nm [dents]* tartar; *[chaudière]* fur.
tas [tɑ] *nm* **(a)** (*amas*) pile, heap. **mettre en ~** to put into a heap, heap *ou* pile up; **~ de fumier** manure heap. **(b)** (*: *beaucoup de*) **un** *ou* **des ~ de** loads of*, heaps of*, lots of; **un ~ de mensonges** a pack of lies; **~ de crétins*** you load of idiots!* **(c) tirer dans le ~** to fire into the crowd; **dans le ~, il n'y en a que 3 de bons** out of that lot there are only 3 that are any good; **former qn sur le ~** to train sb on the job*.
tasse [tɑs] *nf* cup. **~ à thé** teacup; **~ de thé** cup of tea; (*fig*) **boire une ~*** to swallow a mouthful (*when swimming*).
tasser [tɑse] (1) **1** *vt* (*gén*) to pack; *passagers* to pack, cram; *sol* to pack down. **2 se ~** *vpr* **(a)** *[terrain]* to settle, sink; *[vieillard]* to shrink. **(b)** (*se serrer*) to bunch *ou* squeeze up. **(c)** (*) **ça va se ~**

things will settle down. ♦ **tassé, e** *adj*: **bien ~*** (*café*) good and strong; *demi de bière* well-filled. ♦ **tassement** *nm* packing; settling. **~ de la colonne (vertébrale)** compression of the spinal cord.

tata [tata] *nf* (*: *tante*) auntie*; (‡: *homosexuel*) poof‡, queer‡.

tâter [tɑte] (1) **1** *vt* (*palper*) to feel; (*fig: sonder*) to sound out. **marcher en tâtant les murs** to feel *ou* grope one's way along the walls; (*fig*) **~ le terrain** to see how the land lies. **2** *vi*: **~ de** (*gén*) to try; *mets* to taste; *prison* to sample. **3 se ~** *vpr* to feel o.s.; (*: *hésiter*) to be in two minds.

tatillon, -onne [tatijɔ̃, ɔn] *adj* finicky, pernickety.

tâtonner [tɑtɔne] (1) *vi* (*lit, fig*) to grope around; (*par méthode*) to proceed by trial and error. ♦ **tâtonnement** *nm*: **~(s)** trial and error, experimentation. ♦ **tâtons** *adv* (*lit, fig*) **avancer à ~** to grope along; **chercher qch à ~** to grope *ou* feel around for sth.

tatouage [tatwaʒ] *nm* (*action*) tattooing; (*dessin*) tattoo. ♦ **tatouer** (1) *vt* to tattoo.

taudis [todi] *nm* hovel. **quartier de ~** slum area.

taule‡ [tol] *nf* (*prison*) nick‡, clink‡. **il a fait de la ~** he's done time, he has been inside*.

taupe [top] *nf* (*animal*) mole; (*fourrure*) moleskin. (*péj*) **vieille ~** old crone. ♦ **taupinière** *nf* molehill.

taureau, *pl* **~x** [tɔʀo] *nm* (*Zool*) bull. (*Astron*) **le T~** Taurus, the Bull; (*fig*) **prendre le ~ par les cornes** to take the bull by the horns; **être (du) T~** to be Taurus *ou* a Taurean.

tautologie [tɔtɔlɔʒi] *nf* tautology. ♦ **tautologique** *adj* tautological.

taux [to] *nm* (*gén, Fin, Statistique*) rate; [*infirmité*] degree; [*cholestérol*] level. **~ de change** exchange rate, rate of exchange.

taverne [tavɛʀn(ə)] *nf* inn, tavern.

taxe [taks(ə)] *nf* (*impôt*) tax; (*à la douane*) duty. **toutes ~s comprises** inclusive of tax; **~ à la valeur ajoutée** value added tax, VAT. ♦ **taxable** *adj* taxable. ♦ **taxer** (1) *vt* **(a)** (*imposer*) to tax. **(b)** *produit* to fix the price of. **(c) ~ qn de qch** (*qualifier de*) to call sb sth; (*accuser de*) to accuse sb of sth. ♦ **taxation** *nf* taxing, taxation; fixing the price.

taxi [taksi] *nm* (*voiture*) taxi, (taxi)cab; (*: *chauffeur*) cabby*, taxi driver.

taximètre [taksimɛtʀ(ə)] *nm* (taxi)meter.

taxiphone [taksifɔn] *nm* pay phone, public (tele)phone.

Tchécoslovaquie [tʃekɔslɔvaki] *nf* Czechoslovakia. ♦ **tchécoslovaque** *adj* Czechoslovak(ian). ♦ **tchèque** *adj, nm*, **T~** *nmf* Czech.

te [t(ə)] *pron* you; (*réfléchi*) yourself.

technique [tɛknik] **1** *nf* technique. **2** *adj* technical. ♦ **technicien, -ienne** *nm,f* technician. ♦ **technicité** *nf* technical nature. ♦ **techniquement** *adv* technically.

technocrate [tɛknɔkʀat] *nmf* technocrat. ♦ **technocratie** *nf* technocracy. ♦ **technocratique** *adj* technocratic. ♦ **technologie** *nf* technology. ♦ **technologique** *adj* technological. ♦ **technologue** *nmf* technologist.

teck [tɛk] *nm* teak.

teckel [tekɛl] *nm* dachshund.

teigne [tɛɲ] *nf* (*Méd*) ringworm; (*péj: personne*) pest.

teindre [tɛ̃dʀ(ə)] (52) **1** *vt* to dye. **2 se ~** *vpr*: **se ~ (les cheveux)** to dye one's hair. ♦ **teint** *nm* (*permanent*) complexion, colouring; (*momentané*) colour. ♦ **teinte** *nf* (*nuance*) shade, tint; (*couleur*) colour; (*fig*) tinge, hint. ♦ **teinter** (1) *vt* (*gén*) to tint; *bois* to stain; (*fig*) to tinge. ♦ **teinture** *nf* (*colorant*) dye; (*action*) dyeing; (*Pharm*) tincture. (*fig*) **une ~ de maths** a smattering of maths. ♦ **teinturerie** *nf* (*métier*) dyeing; (*magasin*) (dry) cleaner's. ♦ **teinturier, -ière** *nm,f* (*qui nettoie*) dry cleaner; (*qui teint*) dyer.

tel, telle [tɛl] **1** *adj* **(a)** (*similitude, quantité*) such; (*dans comparaison*) like. **une telle ignorance/réponse** such ignorance/such an answer; **~ père, ~ fils** like father like son; **as-tu jamais rien vu de ~?** have you ever seen such a thing? *ou* anything like it?; **en tant que ~, comme ~** as such; **~ il était enfant, ~ je le retrouve** so he was as a child and so he has remained; (*littér*) **le lac ~ un miroir** the lake like a mirror. **(b)** (*indéfini*) such-and-such. **venez ~ jour** come on such-and-such a day; **telle quantité d'alcool** a given quantity of alcohol; **telle ou telle personne vous dira que** someone or other will tell you that. **(c) ~ que** like, such as; **il est resté ~ que je le connaissais** he is still the same *ou* just as he used to be; **un homme ~ que lui** a man like him, such a man; **~ que je le connais, il ne viendra pas** if I know him, he won't come; **~ que vous me voyez, j'ai 72 ans** you wouldn't think it to look at me but I'm 72; **les métaux ~s que l'or et le platine** metals like *ou* such as gold and platinum; **laissez tous ces dossiers ~s quels** *ou* **~s que*** leave all those files as they are *ou* as you find them. **(d)** (*conséquence*) **de telle façon que** in such a way that; **de telle sorte que** so that; **à telle(s) enseigne(s) que** so much so that. **2** *pron indef*: **~ vous dira oui, ~ autre ...** one will say yes, another ...; **~ ou ~** somebody (or other); **~ est pris qui croyait prendre** (it's) the biter bitten.

télé* [tele] *nf* (*abrèv de* **télévision**) TV*, telly*.

télécommande [telekɔmɑ̃d] *nf* remote control. ♦ **télécommander** (1) *vt* (*Tech*) to operate by remote control. (*fig*) **ça a été télécommandé** it was initiated from elsewhere.

télécommunications [telekɔmynikɑsjɔ̃] *nfpl* telecommunications.

téléenseignement [teleɑ̃sɛɲmɑ̃] *nm* television teaching, teaching by television.

téléférique [telefeʀik] *nm* (*installation*) cableway; (*cabine*) cable-car.

télégramme [telegʀam] *nm* telegram, wire, cable.

télégraphe [telegʀaf] *nm* telegraph. ♦ **télégraphie** *nf* telegraphy. ♦ **télégraphier** (7) **1** *vt message* to telegraph, wire, cable. **2** *vi*: **~ à qn** to wire *ou* cable sb. ♦ **télégraphique** *adj fils* telegraph; *alphabet* Morse; *message, adresse,* (*fig*) *style* telegraphic. ♦ **télégraphiste** *nmf* (*messager*) telegraph boy.

téléguidage [telegidaʒ] *nm* radio control. ♦ **téléguider** (1) *vt* (*Tech*) to radio-control. (*fig*) **ça a été téléguidé** it was initiated from elsewhere.

téléobjectif [teleɔbʒɛktif] *nm* telephoto lens.

télépathie [telepati] *nf* telepathy. ♦ **télépathique** *adj* telepathic.

téléphone [telefɔn] *nm* (*système*) telephone; (*appareil*) (tele)phone. **avoir le ~** to be on the (tele)phone; **~ arabe** bush telegraph; **~ automatique** automatic telephone system; (*Pol*) **~ rouge** hot line. ♦ **téléphoner** (1) **1** *vt* to (tele)phone. **téléphone-lui de venir** phone *ou* call him and tell him to come. **2** *vi* to phone, be on the phone. **~ à qn** to telephone sb, phone *ou* ring *ou* call sb (up). ♦ **téléphonique** *adj* telephone. ♦ **téléphoniste** *nmf* (telephone) operator.

télescope [telɛskɔp] *nm* telescope. ♦ **télescopique** *adj* (*gén*) telescopic.

télescoper [telɛskɔpe] (1) **1** *vt véhicule* to smash up. **2 se ~** *vpr* to telescope, concertina. ♦ **télescopage** telescoping, concertinaing.

téléscripteur [teleskʀiptœʀ] *nm* teleprinter.

télésiège [telesjɛʒ] *nm* chairlift.

téléski [teleski] *nm* ski tow.

téléspectateur, -trice [telespɛktatœʀ, tʀis] *nm,f* (television *ou* TV) viewer.

télétype [teletip] *nm* teleprinter.

télévision [televizjɔ̃] *nf* (*gén*) television; (*appareil*) television (set). **à la ~** on television.

♦ **téléviser** (1) *vt* to televise. ♦ **téléviseur** *nm* television (set).

telex [telɛks] *nm* telex.

tellement [tɛlmɑ̃] *adv* **(a)** (*si*) so; (*avec comp*) so much. **il est ~ gentil** he's so (very) nice (*que* that); **~ mieux** so much better (*que l'autre* than the other). **(b)** (*tant*) so much. **~ de gens** so many people; **~ de temps** so much time, so long; **on ne le comprend pas, ~ il parle vite** he talks so quickly (that) you can't understand him; **il dort à peine, ~ il travaille** he hardly sleeps, he works so much *ou* hard. **(c)** (*avec nég*) **pas ~ fort** not (all) that strong, not so (very) strong; **il ne travaille pas ~** he doesn't work (all) that much *ou* so (very) much; **tu aimes le cinéma? - pas ~** do you like the cinema? - not (all) that much *ou* - not (very) much; **on ne la voit plus ~** we don't really see (very) much of her any more.

téméraire [temerɛr] *adj action, personne* rash, reckless, foolhardy; *jugement* rash. ♦ **témérairement** *adv* rashly; recklessly; foolhardily. ♦ **témérité** *nf* rashness; recklessness; foolhardiness.

témoignage [temwaɲaʒ] *nm* **(a)** (*gén, Jur*) testimony, evidence; (*fig: récit, reportage*) account, testimony. **ces ~s sont contradictoires** these are contradictory pieces of evidence. **(b)** (*preuve*) **~** *de bonne conduite* evidence *ou* proof of; *confiance* expression of; **~ d'amitié** (*geste*) expression of friendship; (*cadeau*) token *ou* mark *ou* sign of friendship; **en ~ de ma reconnaissance** as a token *ou* mark of my gratitude.

témoigner [temwaɲe] (1) **1** *vi* (*Jur*) to testify, give evidence. **2** *vt* **(a)** *goût, intérêt* to show, display. **(b) ~ que** *[témoin]* to testify that; *[attitude, situation]* to attest *ou* reveal *ou* show that. **3 ~ de** *vt indir [conduite, évolution]* to attest, show. *[personne]* **je peux en ~** I can testify *ou* bear witness to that.

témoin [temwɛ̃] **1** *nm* **(a)** (*gén, Jur*) witness; *[duel]* second. **~ oculaire** eyewitness; **~ à charge/à décharge** witness for the prosecution/for the defence; **être ~ de** to witness, be a witness to; **prendre qn à ~ (de qch)** to call sb to witness (to *ou* of sth); **faire qch sans ~** to do sth unwitnessed. **(b)** (*preuve*) evidence, testimony. **les ~s d'une époque révolue** the surviving evidence of a bygone age. **(c)** (*Sport*) baton. **passer le ~** to hand on *ou* pass the baton. **2** *adj sujet, échantillon* control. **appartement ~** show-flat; **réalisation ~** pilot *ou* test development; **lampe ~** warning light.

tempe [tɑ̃p] *nf* (*Anat*) temple.

tempérament [tɑ̃peramɑ̃] *nm* **(a)** (*physique*) constitution; (*caractère*) disposition, temperament, nature. **(b)** (*Comm*) **vente à ~** sale on deferred (payment) terms; **achat à ~** ≈ hire purchase, installment plan (*US*); **acheter qch à ~** to buy sth on hire purchase *ou* on an installment plan (*US*).

tempérance [tɑ̃perɑ̃s] *nf* temperance. ♦ **tempérant, e** *adj* temperate.

température [tɑ̃peratyr] *nf* temperature. **avoir** *ou* **faire de la ~** to have a temperature; **prendre la ~ de** *malade* to take the temperature of; *auditoire, public* to gauge the temperature of.

tempérer [tɑ̃pere] (16) *vt climat, ardeur, sévérité* to temper; *douleur* to soothe, ease. ♦ **tempéré, e** *adj climat* temperate.

tempête [tɑ̃pɛt] *nf* (*lit, fig*) storm. **~ de sable** sandstorm; **vent qui souffle en ~** gale force wind; **une ~ dans un verre d'eau** a storm in a teacup; **une ~ d'applaudissements** a storm of applause, thunderous applause. ♦ **tempêter** (1) *vi* to rant and rave, rage. ♦ **tempétueux, -euse** *adj* tempestuous, stormy.

temple [tɑ̃pl(ə)] *nm* (*Hist, littér*) temple; (*protestant*) (Protestant) church.

temporaire [tɑ̃pɔrɛr] *adj* temporary. ♦ **temporairement** *adv* temporarily.

temporel, -elle [tɑ̃pɔrɛl] *adj* **(a)** (*Rel*) (*non spirituel*) worldly, temporal; (*non éternel*) temporal. **(b)** (*Ling, Philos*) temporal.

temporiser [tɑ̃pɔrize] (1) *vi* to temporize, stall, play for time. ♦ **temporisateur, -trice 1** *adj* temporizing, stalling. **2** *nm,f* temporizer. ♦ **temporisation** *nf* temporization, stalling, playing for time.

temps[1] [tɑ̃] *nm* **(a)** (*durée*) **le ~** time; **il a mis beaucoup de ~ à se préparer** he took a long time to get ready; **avec le ~** with *ou* in time; **la jeunesse n'a qu'un ~** youth will not endure; **travailler à plein ~/à ~ partiel** to work full-time/part-time; **peu de ~ avant/après** shortly before/after, a short while *ou* time before/after; **dans quelque ~** before too long, in a (little) while; **pour un ~** for a time *ou* while; **durant (tout) ce ~ (là)** all this time; **je ne le vois plus depuis quelque ~** I haven't seen him for a (little) while *ou* some (little) time.

(b) (*portion de temps*) time. **~ d'arrêt** pause, halt; **marquer un ~ d'arrêt** to pause momentarily; **~ mort** (*dans le travail*) slack period; (*dans la conversation*) lull; **s'accorder un ~ de réflexion** to give o.s. time for reflection; **la plupart du ~** most of the time; **avoir le ~ (de faire)** to have time (to do); **prenez votre ~** take your time; **passer son ~ à lire** to spend one's time reading; **donnez-moi le ~ de m'habiller** just give me time to get dressed; **je me suis arrêté juste le ~ de prendre un verre** I stopped just long enough for a drink; **le ~ perdu ne se rattrape jamais** time and tide wait for no man; *[soldat, prisonnier]* **faire son ~** to serve one's time; (*fig*) *[personne]* **il a fait son ~** he has had his day.

(c) (*moment précis*) time. **il est grand ~ qu'il parte** it's high time he went, it's time for him to go; **le ~ est venu de ...** the time has come to ...; **il était ~!** none too soon!, not before time!; **il n'est plus ~ de se lamenter** the time for bemoaning one's lot is past *ou* over.

(d) (*époque*) time, times, days. **en ~ de guerre** in wartime; **en ~ de crise** in times of crisis; **par les ~ qui courent** these days, nowadays; **c'était le bon ~** those were good times, those were the days; **dans le ~** at one time; **dans le bon vieux ~** in the good old days; **en ce ~ là** at that time; **en ~ normal** in normal circumstances; **les premiers ~** at the beginning, at first; **ces derniers ~** lately, latterly; **au ~ des Tudors** in Tudor times, in the days of the Tudors; **de mon ~** in MY day *ou* time; **dans mon jeune ~** in my younger days; **être de son ~** to move with the times; **les jeunes de notre ~** young people of our time *ou* (of) today; **le ~ des vacances** holiday time.

(e) (*Mus*) beat; (*Gym*) *[mouvement]* stage. **~ fort/faible** strong/weak beat; (*fig*) **les ~ forts d'un roman** the powerful moments of a novel; **à deux/trois ~** in double/triple time.

(f) (*Ling*) *[verbe]* tense. **~ simple/composé** simple/compound tense.

(g) (*Tech*) stroke. **moteur à 4 ~** 4-stroke engine.

(h) (*Sport*) *[coureur]* time.

(i) (*locutions*) **à ~** in time; **de ~ en ~, de ~ à autre** from time to time, now and again; **de tout ~** from time immemorial; **au ~ où** in the days when, at the time when; **en ~ voulu** *ou* **utile** in due time *ou* course; **à ~ perdu** in one's spare time; **cela fait passer le ~** it passes the time; **le ~ c'est de l'argent** time is money.

temps[2] [tɑ̃] *nm* (*conditions atmosphériques*) weather. **quel ~ fait-il?** what's the weather like?; **il fait beau/mauvais ~** the weather's fine/bad; **avec le ~ qu'il fait!** in this weather!, with the weather we are having!; **~ de chien*** rotten* *ou* lousy* weather; **le ~ est lourd aujourd'hui** it's close today; (*fig*) **prendre le ~ comme il vient** to take things as they come.

tenable [t(ə)nabl(ə)] *adj*: **ce n'est pas ~** it's unbearable.

tenace [tənas] *adj* **(a)** (*persistant*) (*gén*) stubborn, persistent; *volonté* tenacious, stubborn. **(b)** *colle* firmly adhesive, strong. ♦ **tenacement** *adv* stubbornly; persistently; tenaciously. ♦ **ténacité** *nf* stubbornness; persistence; tenacity.

tenaille [t(ə)nɑj] *nf*: **~(s)** *[menuisier]* pincers; *[forgeron]* tongs; (*Mil*) **prendre en ~** to catch in a pincer movement.

tenailler [tənɑje] (1) *vt [inquiétude]* to torture, torment. **la faim le tenaillait** he was gnawed by hunger.

tenancier [tənɑ̃sje] *nm [bar]* manager. ♦ **tenancière** *nf [bar]* manageress.

tenant [tənɑ̃] *nm* **(a)** *[doctrine]* supporter, upholder (*de* of); (*Sport*) *[titre]* holder. **(b) les ~s et (les) aboutissants d'une affaire** the ins and outs of a question; **d'un (seul) ~** *terrain* all in one piece.

tendance [tɑ̃dɑ̃s] *nf* **(a)** (*inclination, Psych*) tendency. **~ à l'exagération** tendency to exaggerate. **(b)** (*opinions*) *[parti, artiste]* leanings; *[livre]* drift, tenor. **quelle est sa ~ (politique)?** what are his (political) leanings? *ou* sympathies? **(c)** (*évolution*) *[art, économie, public]* trend. **~ à la hausse** upward trend. **(d) avoir ~ à faire qch** to have a tendency *ou* tend *ou* be inclined to do sth.

tendancieux, -ieuse [tɑ̃dɑ̃sjø, jøz] *adj* tendentious.

tendon [tɑ̃dɔ̃] *nm* tendon, sinew. **~ d'Achille** Achilles' tendon.

tendre[1] [tɑ̃dʀ(ə)] (41) **1** *vt* **(a)** (*raidir*) *corde* to tighten, tauten; *ressort* to set; *muscles* to tense, brace; *pièce de tissu* to stretch, pull *ou* draw tight. **(b)** (*installer*) *tenture* to hang; *piège, filet* to set. **~ une bâche sur une remorque** to stretch *ou* pull a tarpaulin over a trailer; **~ un fil entre deux points** to stretch a thread between two points; **~ une pièce de tentures** to hang a room with draperies. **(c)** (*avancer*) *cou* to crane; *joue* to offer; *main* to hold out; *bras* to stretch out (*à* to). **~ une main secourable** to hold out *ou* offer a helping hand; **~ l'oreille** to prick up one's ears. **(d) ~ qch à qn** (*donner*) to hold sth out to sb; (*offrir*) to offer sth to sb; (*fig*) **~ une perche à qn** to throw sb a line. **2 se ~** *vpr [corde]* to become taut, tighten; *[rapports]* to become strained. **3** *vi*: **~ à qch/à faire** (*avoir tendance à*) to tend towards sth/to do; (*viser à*) to aim at sth/to do; (*Math*) **~ vers l'infini** to tend towards infinity.

tendre[2] [tɑ̃dʀ(ə)] *adj* **(a)** *peau, pierre* soft; *haricots, viande* tender. **l'herbe ~** the sweet grass; **depuis sa plus ~ enfance** from his earliest days; **c'est ~ comme la rosée** it melts in the mouth. **(b)** (*affectueux*) *personne* tender, loving; *amour, regard* fond, tender. **ne pas être ~ pour qn** to be hard on sb. **(c)** *couleurs* soft, delicate. ♦ **tendrement** *adv* tenderly; lovingly; fondly. ♦ **tendresse** *nf* tenderness; fondness. **~ maternelle** maternal love; **combler qn de ~s** to overwhelm sb with tenderness *ou* with tokens of (one's) love; **n'avoir aucune ~ pour** to have no fondness for. ♦ **tendreté** *nf [viande]* tenderness; *[bois, métal]* softness.

tendu, e [tɑ̃dy] *adj corde, toile* tight, taut; *muscles* tensed, braced; *rapports* strained; *personne* tense, strained; *situation* tense. **les bras ~s** with arms outstretched; **~ de** *velours, soie* hung with.

ténèbres [tenɛbʀ(ə)] *nfpl* darkness, gloom. ♦ **ténébreux, -euse** *adj* (*obscur*) dark, gloomy; (*mystérieux*) dark; *époque* obscure.

teneur [tənœʀ] *nf* (*gén*) content; *[lettre]* content, terms. **~ en alcool** alcohol content.

tenir [t(ə)niʀ] (22) **1** *vt* **(a)** (*maintenir*) (*avec les mains, une ficelle*) to hold; (*en position*) to hold, keep; (*dans un état*) to keep; (*Mus*) *note* to hold. **~ les yeux fermés** to keep one's eyes shut; **une robe qui tient chaud** a dress which keeps you warm; **elle tient ses enfants très propres** she keeps her children very neat; **~ qch en place** to hold *ou* keep sth in place; **ses affaires le tiennent** he is tied by his business; **l'envie me tenait de ...** I was gripped by the desire to ... . **(b)** *voleur,* (*) *rhume etc* to have, have got; *vérité, preuve* to hold, have. (*menace*) **si je le tenais!** if I could get my hands on him! *ou* lay hands on him!; **nous le tenons** we've got him; **nous tenons un bon filon** we're on to a good thing; **mieux vaut ~ que courir** a bird in the hand is worth two in the bush. **(c)** (*avec autorité*) *enfant, classe* to have *ou* keep under control, control; *pays* to have under one's control. **(d)** *hôtel, magasin* to run, keep; *registre* to keep; *emploi* to hold; (*Comm*) *marchandise* to stock, keep; *conférence* to hold; *maison, ménage* to keep. **(e) ~ de qn** *renseignement* to have from sb; *bijou* to have got from sb; **il tient cela de son père** he gets that from his father. **(f)** (*occuper*) *place, largeur* to take up. **tu tiens trop de place!** you are taking up too much room!; (*Aut*) **il ne tenait pas sa droite** he was not keeping to the right. **(g)** (*contenir*) *[récipient]* to hold. **(h)** (*résister*) *[souliers]* **~ l'eau** to keep out the water; (*Naut*) **~ la mer** to be seaworthy; (*Aut*) **~ la route** to hold the road. **(i)** *promesse* to keep; *pari* (*accepter*) to take on; (*respecter*) to keep to, honour. **(j)** *discours* to give; *langage* to use. **~ des propos désobligeants à l'égard de qn** to make *ou* pass offensive remarks about sb, say offensive things about sb. **(k) ~ qn/qch pour** to regard sb/sth as, consider sb/sth (as), hold sb/sth to be; **~ pour certain que ...** to regard it as certain that ... . **(l) tiens!** (*en donnant*) take this, here (you are); (*de surprise*) ah!; (*pour attirer l'attention*) look!; **tiens, tiens*** well, well!, fancy that!; **tenez, ça m'écœure** you know, that sickens me.

2 *vi* **(a)** *[objet, fixe, nœud]* to hold; *[échafaudage]* to stay up, hold (up). **l'armoire tient au mur** the cupboard is held *ou* fixed to the wall; **ce chapeau ne tient pas sur ma tête** this hat won't stay on (my head); **il n'y a pas de bal qui tienne** there's no question of going to any dance; **ça tient toujours, notre pique-nique?*** is our picnic still on?*, does our picnic still stand? **(b)** *[personne]* **~ debout** to stand up; **il tient bien sur ses jambes** he is very steady on his legs; **cet enfant ne tient pas en place** this child cannot keep *ou* stay still. **(c)** (*Mil, gén: résister*) **~ (bon** *ou* **ferme)** to hold *ou* stand firm; **je n'ai pas pu ~** (*chaleur*) I couldn't stand it; (*colère*) I couldn't contain myself. **(d)** (*être contenu dans*) **~ dans** to fit in(to); **nous tenons à 4 à cette table** this table seats 4, we can get 4 round this table; **son discours tient en quelques pages** his speech is just a few pages long. **(e)** *[accord, beau temps]* to hold; *[couleur]* to be fast; *[mariage]* to last; *[fleurs]* to last (well); *[mise en plis]* to hold, stay in.

3 ~ à *vt indir* **(a)** (*aimer*) *réputation* to value, care about; *objet, personne* to be attached to, be fond of; *vie* to care about. **un peu de vin? — je n'y tiens pas** would you like some wine? — not really, not particularly. **(b)** (*vouloir*) **il tient beaucoup à vous connaître** he is very anxious to meet you, he is very keen *ou* eager to meet you; **il tient à ce que nous sachions ...** he insists *ou* is anxious that we should know ...; **si vous y tenez** if you really want to. **(c)** (*avoir pour cause*) to be due to, stem from.

4 ~ de *vt indir* (*ressembler à*) *parent* to take after. **il a de qui ~** it runs in the family; **sa réussite tient du prodige** his success is something of a miracle.

5 *vb impers* to depend. **il ne tient qu'à elle** it's up to her, it depends on her; **à quoi cela tient-il qu'il**

n'écrive pas? how is it *ou* why is it that he doesn't write?; **qu'à cela ne tienne** never mind (that), that needn't matter.

6 se ~ *vpr* **(a) se ~ la tête** to hold one's head; **se ~ par la main** to hold hands; **se ~ à qch** to hold on to sth; **se ~ debout/couché/à genoux** to be standing (up)/lying (down)/kneeling (down); **tenez-vous prêts à partir** be ready to leave; **elle se tenait à sa fenêtre** she was standing at her window; **tiens-toi tranquille** keep still; **tiens-toi droit** (*debout*) stand up straight; (*assis*) sit up (straight). **(b)** (*se conduire*) to behave. **tiens-toi bien!** behave yourself! **(c)** (*réunion etc: avoir lieu*) to be held. **(d)** *[faits etc]* (*être liés*) to hang *ou* hold together. **(e)** (*se retenir*) **il ne peut se ~ de rire** he can't help laughing; **il ne se tenait pas de joie** he couldn't contain his joy; **se ~ à quatre pour ne pas faire qch** to struggle to stop o.s. (from) doing sth. **(f) s'en ~ à qch** (*se limiter à*) to confine o.s. to sth; (*se satisfaire de*) to content o.s. with sth; **nous nous en tiendrons là pour aujourd'hui** we'll leave it at that for today; **il aimerait savoir à quoi s'en ~** he'd like to know where he stands. **(g)** (*se considérer*) **il ne se tient pas pour battu** he doesn't consider himself beaten; **tenez-vous le pour dit** consider yourself told *ou* warned once and for all.

tennis [tenis] **1** *nm* **(a)** (*Sport*) tennis. **~ sur gazon/terre battue** lawn/hard-court tennis; **~ de table** table tennis. **(b)** (*terrain*) (tennis) court. **2** *nfpl* (*chaussures*) gym shoes, sneakers; (*pour jouer au tennis*) tennis shoes. ♦ **tennisman,** *pl* **tennismen** *nm* tennis player.

ténor [tenɔʀ] **1** *nm* (*Mus*) tenor; (*fig*) big name*. **2** *adj* tenor.

tension [tɑ̃sjɔ̃] *nf* **(a)** *[ressort etc]* tension. **(b)** (*Élec*) voltage, tension. **à haute/basse ~** high-/low-voltage *ou* tension; **sous ~** (*lit*) live; (*fig*) under stress; **chute de ~** voltage drop. **(c)** (*Méd*) **~ (artérielle)** blood pressure; **avoir de la ~** to have (high) blood pressure; **~ nerveuse** nervous tension; (*fig*) **~ d'esprit** sustained mental effort. **(d)** (*fig*) *[relations]* tension (*de* in); *[situation]* tenseness (*de* of).

tentacule [tɑ̃takyl] *nm* (*Zool, fig*) tentacle. ♦ **tentaculaire** *adj* (*Zool*) tentacular; (*fig*) sprawling.

tente [tɑ̃t] *nf* (*gén*) tent. **coucher sous la ~** to sleep under canvas; **~ à oxygène** oxygen tent.

tenter [tɑ̃te] (1) *vt* **(a)** (*séduire*) to tempt. **se laisser ~** to yield to temptation; **~ le diable** to tempt fate, ask for trouble. **(b)** (*essayer*) to try, attempt. **~ l'impossible pour ...** to attempt the impossible to ...; **~ sa chance** to try one's luck; **~ le coup*** to have a go*, give it a try; **~ de faire** to attempt *ou* try to do. ♦ **tentant, e** *adj* (*gén*) tempting; *offre* attractive, enticing. ♦ **tentateur, -trice 1** *adj* (*gén*) tempting; *beauté* alluring, enticing. **2** *nm* tempter. **3** *nf* temptress. ♦ **tentation** *nf* temptation. ♦ **tentative** *nf* (*gén*) attempt, endeavour; (*sportive, style journalistique*) bid, attempt. **~ de meurtre** murder attempt, attempted murder.

tenture [tɑ̃tyʀ] *nf* (*tapisserie*) hanging; (*rideau*) curtain.

tenu, e[1] [t(ə)ny] *adj* **(a) bien/mal ~** *enfant* well/poorly turned out; *maison* well/poorly kept *ou* looked after. **(b)** (*surveillé*) **leurs filles sont très ~es** their daughters are kept on a tight rein. **(c)** (*obligé*) **être ~ de faire** to be obliged to do; **être ~ au secret professionnel** to be bound by professional secrecy.

tenue[2] [t(ə)ny] *nf* **(a)** *[maison]* upkeep, running; *[magasin]* running; *[classe]* handling, control; *[séance]* holding. **la ~ des livres de comptes** the book-keeping. **(b)** (*conduite*) (good) manners, good behaviour. **un peu de ~!** behave yourself!, watch your manners! **(c)** (*qualité*) *[journal]* standard, quality. **publication de haute ~** quality publication. **(d)** (*maintien*) posture. **(e)** (*apparence*) appearance; (*vêtements*) dress, clothes; (*uniforme*) uniform. **~ d'intérieur** indoor clothes; **en ~ légère** (*d'été*) wearing light clothing; (*osée*) scantily dressed; **en grande ~** in full dress (uniform); **~ de combat/de soirée** battle/evening dress. **(f)** (*Aut*) **~ de route** road holding.

ténu, e [teny] *adj point, fil* fine; *brume, voix* thin; *raisons, nuances* tenuous.

ter [tɛʀ] *adj* (*numéro*) **10 ~** (number) 10 B.

térébenthine [teʀebɑ̃tin] *nf* turpentine.

tergal [tɛʀgal] *nm* ® Terylene ®.

tergiverser [tɛʀʒivɛʀse] (1) *vi* to procrastinate. ♦ **tergiversations** *nfpl* procrastinations.

terme [tɛʀm(ə)] *nm* **(a)** (*mot*) term. **en ~s clairs** in clear terms; **en d'autres ~s** in other words. **(b)** *[équation, contrat]* term. **(c)** (*date limite*) time limit, deadline; *[vie, voyage, récit]* end, term. **arriver à ~** *[délai]* to expire; *[opération]* to reach its conclusion; *[paiement]* to fall due; **mettre un ~ à qch** to put an end *ou* a stop to sth; **mener qch à ~** to bring sth to completion; **à court/long ~** *emprunt, projet* short-/long-term; (*Bourse*) **marché à ~** forward market. **(d)** (*Méd*) **à ~** *accouchement* full-term; *naître* at term; **avant ~** *naître* prematurely; *naissance* premature; **un bébé né 2 mois avant ~** a baby born 2 months premature. **(e)** *[loyer]* (*date*) term; (*période*) quarter (year); (*somme*) (quarterly) rent. **(f)** (*relations*) **~s** terms; **en bons/mauvais ~s avec qn** on good/bad terms with sb.

terminer [tɛʀmine] (1) **1** *vt* **(a)** *séance* to bring to an end *ou* to a close, terminate; *travail* to finish (off), complete; *repas, récit* to finish, end. **~ un repas par un café** to finish off *ou* end a meal with a coffee; **j'en ai terminé avec eux** I am *ou* have finished with them, I have done with them. **(b)** (*dernier élément*) **le café termina le repas** the meal finished *ou* ended with coffee; **un bourgeon termine la tige** the stalk ends in a bud. **2 se ~** *vpr* (*gén*) to end (*par* with, *en* in); *[repas, vacances]* to (come to an) end. **se ~ en pointe** to end in a point. ♦ **terminaison** *nf* ending. ♦ **terminal, e,** *mpl* **-aux** *adj* terminal, final. (*Scol*) **(classe) ~e** ≃ Upper Sixth, 12th grade (*US*).

terminologie [tɛʀminɔlɔʒi] *nf* terminology.

terminus [tɛʀminys] *nm* terminus.

termite [tɛʀmit] *nm* termite, white ant. ♦ **termitière** *nf* ant-hill.

terne [tɛʀn(ə)] *adj* (*gén*) dull, drab; *regard* lifeless.

ternir [tɛʀniʀ] (2) **1** *vt métal* to tarnish; *glace* to dull; *réputation* to tarnish. **2 se ~** *vpr* to become tarnished; to become dull.

terrain [teʀɛ̃] **1** *nm* **(a)** (*relief*) ground; (*sol*) soil, ground; (*Géol: formation*) formation. **~ lourd** heavy soil *ou* ground. **(b)** (*Ftbl, Rugby*) pitch, field; (*avec les installations*) ground; (*Courses, Golf*) course; (*Basketball*) basketball court. **(c)** (*parcelle*) plot (of land), piece of land; (*à bâtir*) site. **maison avec 2 hectares de ~** house with 2 hectares of land; **le prix du ~** the price of land. **(d)** (*Mil*) (*lieu d'opérations*) terrain; (*gagné ou perdu*) ground. (*lit, fig*) **gagner/perdre du ~** to gain/lose ground; **reconnaître le ~** (*lit*) to reconnoitre the terrain; (*fig*) to see how the land lies; (*fig*) **tâter le ~** to test the ground; **préparer/déblayer le ~** to prepare/clear the ground; (*Sociol etc*) **sur le ~** in the field. **(e)** (*fig: sujet*) ground. **être sur son ~** to be on home ground *ou* territory; **trouver un ~ d'entente** to find an area of agreement; **je ne le suivrai pas sur ce ~** I can't go along with him there *ou* on that; **sur un ~ glissant** on slippery *ou* dangerous ground. **(f)** *[épidémie]* breeding ground. **2: ~ d'aviation** airfield; **~ de camping** campsite, camping ground; **~ de sport** sports ground; **un ~ vague** a piece of *ou* some waste ground.

terrasse [tɛʀas] *nf [parc, appartement]* terrace; (*sur le toit*) terrace roof; *[café]* pavement (area). **à la ~ (du café)** outside (the café).

terrasser [tɛʀase] (1) *vt* **(a)** *[adversaire]* to floor, bring down; *[fatigue]* to overcome; *[attaque]* to bring down; *[émotion]* to overwhelm; *[maladie]* to strike down. **(b)** (*Tech*) to excavate, dig out. ♦ **terrassement** *nm* (*action*) excavation. (*remblais*) ~s earthworks; *[voie ferrée]* embankments. ♦ **terrassier** *nm* navvy.

terre [tɛʀ] **1** *nf* **(a) la ~** (*planète*) the earth; (*monde*) the world; **parcourir la ~ entière** to travel the world over *ou* all over the globe; **sur la ~** on (the) earth, in the world; (*fig*) **redescendre sur ~** to come back to earth. **(b)** (*sol*) ground; (*matière*) earth, soil; (*pour poterie*) clay. **vase en ~** clay vase; **à** *ou* **par ~** *poser* (down) on the ground; *jeter* to the ground; **cela fiche tous nos projets par ~*** that really messes up all our plans*; **mettre qn en ~** to bury sb; **(5 mètres) sous ~** (5 metres) underground. **(c)** (*étendue, campagne*) land. **une langue de ~** a strip of land; **aimer la ~** to love the land; **des ~s à blé** corn-growing land; **lopin de ~** piece *ou* patch *ou* plot of land. **(d)** (*opp à mer*) land. **sur la ~ ferme** on dry land; (*Naut*) **aller à ~** to go ashore; **dans les ~s** inland; **voyager par voie de ~** to travel by land *ou* overland. **(e)** (*domaine*) **la ~** land; **une ~** an estate. **(f)** (*pays*) land, country. **la T~ promise** the Promised Land. **(g)** (*Élec*) earth, ground (*US*). **mettre à la ~** to earth.

2: ~ battue hard-packed surface; **politique de la ~ brûlée** scorched earth policy; **~ de bruyère** heath-peat; **~ cuite** (*pour tuiles*) baked clay; (*pour statuettes*) terracotta; **~ glaise** clay; **la T~ Sainte** the Holy Land.

♦ **Terre-Neuve 1** *nf* Newfoundland. **2** *nm inv*: **t~-n~** (*chien*) Newfoundland. ♦ **terre-plein,** *pl* **~-~s,** *nm* (*Mil*) terreplein; (*Constr*) platform. ♦ **terre-à-terre** *adj inv esprit* down-to-earth, matter-of-fact.

terreau [tɛʀo] *nm* compost. **~ de feuilles** leaf mould.

terrer (se) [tɛʀe] (1) *vpr [criminel, renard]* (*en fuite*) to crouch down; (*dans une tanière*) to go to ground *ou* earth; *[timide, insociable]* to hide (o.s.) away.

terrestre [tɛʀɛstʀ(ə)] *adj faune, transports* land; *surface* earth's, terrestrial; *biens, plaisirs, vie* earthly, terrestrial.

terreur [tɛʀœʀ] *nf* terror. **avec ~** with terror *ou* dread; **vaines ~s** empty fears; (**hum*) **jouer les ~s** to play the tough guy*.

terreux, -euse [tɛʀø, øz] *adj goût* earthy; *sabots* muddy; *mains, salade* dirty; *teint* sallow.

terrible [tɛʀibl(ə)] *adj* (*: *excellent*) terrific*, tremendous*; (*horrible*) terrible, dreadful. **c'est ~ ce qu'il peut manger*** it's incredible what he can eat*; **ce film n'est pas ~*** this film is nothing special. ♦ **terriblement** *adv* terribly, dreadfully.

terrien, -ienne [tɛʀjɛ̃, jɛn] **1** *adj propriétaire* landed; *origine* country. **2** *nm* (*paysan*) countryman; (*habitant de la Terre*) Earthman; (*non-marin*) landsman. **3** *nf* countrywoman; Earthwoman; landswoman.

terrier [tɛʀje] *nm* **(a)** *[lapin]* burrow, hole. **(b)** (*chien*) terrier.

terrifier [tɛʀifje] (7) *vt* to terrify. ♦ **terrifiant, e** *adj* (*effrayant*) terrifying; *progrès, appétit* fearsome, incredible.

terrine [tɛʀin] *nf* (*récipient*) terrine; (*pâté*) pâté.

territoire [tɛʀitwaʀ] *nm* (*gén, Pol, Zool*) territory; *[commune]* area; *[évêque, juge]* jurisdiction. ♦ **territorial, e,** *mpl* **-aux 1** *adj* territorial. **2** *nf* Territorial Army.

terroir [tɛʀwaʀ] *nm* (*Agr*) soil. **accent du ~** country *ou* rural accent.

terroriser [tɛʀɔʀize] (1) *vt* to terrorize. ♦ **terrorisme** *nm* terrorism. ♦ **terroriste** *adj, nmf* terrorist.

tertiaire [tɛʀsjɛʀ] *adj* (*Géol, Méd*) tertiary. (*Écon*) **(secteur) ~** service industries, tertiary sector.

tertio [tɛʀsjo] *adv* third(ly).

tertre [tɛʀtʀ(ə)] *nm* mound.

tes [te] *adj poss V* **ton^1**.

tesson [tesɔ̃] *nm*: **~ (de bouteille)** piece of broken bottle.

test [tɛst] **1** *nm* (*gén*) test. **faire passer un ~ à qn** to give sb a test, put sb through a test. **2** *adj*: **région-~** test area. ♦ **tester^1** (1) *vt* to test.

testament [tɛstamɑ̃] *nm* (*Jur*) will, testament; (*fig*) testament. **ceci est mon ~** this is my last will and testament; (*Rel*) **Ancien/Nouveau T~** Old/New Testament. ♦ **testamentaire** *adj*: **dispositions ~s** provisions of a will. ♦ **testateur** *nm* testator. ♦ **testatrice** *nf* testatrix. ♦ **tester^2** (1) *vi* to make (out) one's will.

testicule [tɛstikyl] *nm* testicle.

tétanos [tetanos] *nm* (*Méd*) tetanus, lockjaw; (*Physiol*) tetanus.

têtard [tɛtaʀ] *nm* tadpole.

tête [tɛt] **1** *nf* **(a)** *[homme, animal, objet, plante]* head. **être ~ nue** to be bareheaded; **avoir la ~ sale** to have dirty hair; **de la ~ aux pieds** from head to foot; **gagner d'une ~** to win by a head; **20 ~s de bétail** 20 head of cattle; **50 F par ~** 50 francs a head *ou* apiece *ou* per person. **(b)** (*fig: vie*) head, neck. **risquer sa ~** to risk one's neck. **(c)** (*visage*) face. **il a une ~ sympathique** he has a friendly face; **faire une drôle de ~** to pull a (wry *ou* long) face; **faire la ~** to sulk, have the sulks*; **c'est une ~ à claques*** he has got the sort of face you itch to smack. **(d)** (*début*) *[train, procession]* front, head; (*Mil*) *[colonne]* head; *[page, liste, classe]* top, head. **en ~ de phrase** at the head of the sentence; (*Rail*) **monter en ~** to get on at the front; *[coureur etc]* **être en/prendre la ~** to be in/take the lead; **être en ~** *ou* **à la ~ de qch** to be at the head of sth, head sth. **(e)** (*facultés mentales*) **avoir (toute) sa ~** to have (all) one's wits about one; **n'avoir rien dans la ~** to be empty-headed; **où ai-je la ~?** whatever am I thinking of?; **avoir une petite ~** to be dim-witted; **~ sans cervelle** *ou* **en l'air** *ou* **de linotte** scatterbrain; **avoir la ~ sur les épaules** to be level-headed; **femme de ~** capable woman; **calculer qch de ~** to work sth out in one's head; **je n'ai plus le nom en ~** the name has gone (clean) out of my head; **chercher qch dans sa ~** to search one's memory for sth; **mettre qch dans la ~ de qn** to put *ou* get sth into sb's head; **se mettre dans la ~ que** (*s'imaginer*) to get it into one's head that; **se mettre dans la** *ou* **en ~ de faire qch** (*se décider*) to take it into one's head to do sth; **avoir la ~ ailleurs** to have one's mind elsewhere; **se creuser la ~** to rack one's brains; **ils ne se sont pas cassé la ~!** they didn't exactly overexert themselves!; **n'en faire qu'à sa ~** to do (exactly) as one pleases; **faire qch à ~ reposée** to do sth in a more leisurely moment; **c'est lui la ~ du complot** he's the brains *ou* mind behind the plot. **(f)** (*tempérament*) **avoir la ~ chaude/froide/dure** to be hot-/cool-/thick-headed; **il fait sa mauvaise ~** he's being awkward; **c'est une forte ~** he's self-willed. **(g)** (*Ftbl*) header. **faire une ~** to head the ball. **(h)** (*locutions*) **marcher la ~ haute** to walk with one's head held high; **avoir la ~ basse** to hang one's head; (*lit, fig*) **courir ~ baissée** to rush headlong (*dans* into); **tomber la ~ la première** to fall headfirst; **jeter** *ou* **lancer à la ~ de qn que ...** to hurl in sb's face that ...; **en avoir par-dessus la ~** to be fed up to the teeth*; **j'en donnerais ma ~ à couper** I would stake my life on it; **ne plus savoir où donner de la ~** not to know which way to turn; **tenir ~ à** to stand up to; **mettre la ~ de qn à prix** to put a price on sb's head; **se trouver à la ~ d'une**

petite fortune to find o.s. the possessor of a small fortune.

2 (*Théât*) ~ **d'affiche** top of the bill; (*Aut*) ~ **de bielle** big end; ~ **brûlée** wild adventurer; ~ **chaude** hothead; ~ **chercheuse** homing device; (*Aut*) ~ **de Delco** ® distributor head; ~ **d'épingle** pinhead; ~ **de lard*** *ou* **de mule*** pigheaded so and so*; ~ **de lecture** *[pick-up]* pickup head; *[magnétophone]* recording head; ~ **de ligne** terminus, end of the line (*Rail*); ~ **de mort** (*emblème*) death's-head; *[pavillon]* skull and crossbones, Jolly Roger; (*Culin*) Gouda cheese; ~ **nucléaire** nuclear warhead; ~ **de pont** (*fleuve*) bridgehead; (*mer*) beachhead; ~ **de Turc** whipping boy, Aunt Sally.

♦ **tête-bêche** *adv* head to foot *ou* tail. ♦ **tête-de-nègre** *adj inv* dark brown. ♦ **tête-à-queue** *nm inv* (*Aut*) spin. ♦ **tête-à-tête** *nm inv* (*conversation*) tête-a-tête, private conversation. **en** ~-~-~ alone together; **dîner en** ~-~-~ intimate dinner for two.

téter [tete] (6) *vt lait, pouce* to suck; *biberon, sein, pipe* to suck at. ~ **sa mère** to suck at one's mother's breast; **donner à** ~ **à un bébé** to feed a baby. ♦ **tétée** *nf* (*action*) sucking; (*repas*) feed; (*moment*) feeding time. ♦ **tétine** *nf [vache, biberon]* teat; (*sucette*) dummy, pacifier (*US*). ♦ **teton*** *nm* breast.

têtu, e [tety] *adj* stubborn, pigheaded.

texte [tɛkst(ə)] *nm* (*gén*) text; (*morceau choisi*) passage, piece; (*énoncé de devoir*) subject, topic. **erreur dans le** ~ textual error; (*Théât*) **apprendre son** ~ to learn one's lines. ♦ **textuel, -elle** *adj traduction* literal, word for word; *citation* verbatim, exact. ♦ **textuellement** *adv* literally, word for word; exactly, verbatim. **il me l'a dit** ~ those were his very words.

textile [tɛkstil] **1** *nm* **(a)** (*matière*) textile. ~**s synthétiques** synthetic *ou* man-made fibres. **(b)** (*Ind*) **le** ~ the textile industry, textiles. **2** *adj* textile.

texture [tɛkstyʀ] *nf* (*lit, fig*) texture.

thé [te] **1** *nm* tea; (*plante*) tea plant; (*réunion*) tea party. ~ **à la menthe** mint tea. **2** *adj inv*: **rose** ~ tea rose.

théâtre [teɑtʀ(ə)] *nm* **(a) le** ~ (*technique*) the theatre; (*profession*) the stage *ou* theatre; **faire du** ~ to be on the stage, be an actor; **s'intéresser au** ~ to be interested in drama *ou* the theatre; **je n'aime pas le** ~ **à la télévision** I do not like stage productions on television; ~ **d'essai** experimental theatre *ou* drama; ~ **d'amateurs** amateur dramatics *ou* theatricals; **roman adapté pour le** ~ novel adapted for the stage. **(b)** (*lieu*) theatre. ~ **de marionnettes/de verdure** puppet/open-air theatre; **il ne va jamais au** ~ he never goes to the theatre, he is not a theatregoer; **le** ~ **était plein** there was a full house. **(c) homme de** ~ man of the theatre *ou* stage; **accessoires de** ~ stage props; **directeur de** ~ theatrical *ou* stage director; **troupe de** ~ theatre *ou* drama company. **(d)** (*genre littéraire*) theatre. **le** ~ **de Sheridan** Sheridan's plays *ou* dramatic works, the theatre of Sheridan; **le** ~ **classique** the classical theatre, classical drama; **le** ~ **de boulevard** light theatrical entertainment. **(e)** (*fig péj*) (*exagération*) theatricals, histrionics; (*simulation*) playacting. **(f)** *[crime]* scene. (*Mil*) **le** ~ **des opérations** the theatre of operations.

♦ **théâtral, e,** *mpl* **-aux** *adj* **(a)** *œuvre* theatrical, dramatic; *rubrique, saison* theatre; *représentation* stage, theatrical. **(b)** (*péj*) *attitude* theatrical, histrionic. ♦ **théâtralement** *adv* theatrically, histrionically.

théière [tejɛʀ] *nf* teapot.

thème [tɛm] *nm* **(a)** (*sujet*) theme. **(b)** (*Scol: traduction*) prose (composition).

théologie [teɔlɔʒi] *nf* theology. ♦ **théologien** *nm* theologian. ♦ **théologique** *adj* theological.

théorème [teɔʀɛm] *nm* theorem.

théorie [teɔʀi] *nf* theory. **en** ~ in theory. ♦ **théoricien, -ienne** *nm,f* theoretician, theorist. ♦ **théorique** *adj* theoretical. ♦ **théoriquement** *adv* theoretically.

thérapeutique [teʀapøtik] **1** *adj* therapeutic. **2** *nf* (*science*) therapeutics (*sg*); (*traitement*) therapy.

thermal, e, *mpl* **-aux** [tɛʀmal, o] *adj*: **cure** ~**e** water cure; **établissement** ~ hydropathic *ou* water-cure establishment; **source** ~**e, eaux** ~**es** thermal *ou* hot springs; **station** ~**e** spa.

thermique [tɛʀmik] *adj unité* thermal; *énergie* thermic. **centrale** ~ thermal power station.

thermoélectrique [tɛʀmɔelɛktʀik] *adj* thermoelectric(al).

thermomètre [tɛʀmɔmɛtʀ(ə)] *nm* thermometer. ~ **médical** clinical thermometer; (*fig*) **le** ~ **de l'opinion publique** the barometer *ou* gauge of public opinion.

thermonucléaire [tɛʀmɔnykleɛʀ] *adj* thermonuclear.

thermos [tɛʀmos] *nm ou nf* (®: *aussi* **bouteille** ~) vacuum *ou* Thermos ® flask.

thermostat [tɛʀmɔsta] *nm* thermostat.

thésauriser [tezɔʀize] (1) **1** *vi* to hoard money. **2** *vt* to hoard (up).

thèse [tɛz] *nf* (*gén*) thesis; (*Univ*) ≃ Ph.D. thesis.

thon [tɔ̃] *nm* tunny (fish), tuna(-fish).

thorax [tɔʀaks] *nm* thorax. ♦ **thoracique** *adj cavité* thoracic. **cage** ~ rib-cage; **capacité** ~ respiratory *ou* vital capacity.

thrombose [tʀɔ̃boz] *nf* thrombosis.

thym [tɛ̃] *nm* thyme.

thyroïde [tiʀɔid] *adj, nf* thyroid. ♦ **thyroïdien, -ienne** *adj* thyroid.

tiare [tjaʀ] *nf* tiara.

tibia [tibja] *nm* shinbone, tibia.

tic [tik] *nm* (*nerveux*) twitch, tic; (*manie*) mannerism.

ticket [tikɛ] *nm* ticket. ~ **de quai** platform ticket; ~ **de rationnement** (ration) coupon.

tic-tac [tiktak] *nm* ticking, tick-tock. **faire** ~ to tick, go tick tock.

tiède [tjɛd] **1** *adj liquide, foi, accueil* lukewarm; *vent, temps* mild, warm. **2** *nmf* (*péj*) lukewarm *ou* half-hearted individual. **3** *adv*: **boire qch** ~ to drink sth when it's lukewarm *ou* not very hot *ou* not very cold. ♦ **tièdement** *adv* (*péj*) in a lukewarm way, half-heartedly. ♦ **tiédeur** *nf* lukewarmness, half-heartedness; mildness, warmth. ♦ **tiédir** (2) **1** *vi* **(a)** (*devenir moins chaud*) to cool (down); (*se réchauffer*) to grow warm(er). **faire** ~ **de l'eau** to warm *ou* heat up some water. **(b)** *[foi, ardeur]* to cool (off). **2** *vt [soleil]* to warm (up); *[air frais]* to cool (down).

tien, tienne [tjɛ̃, tjɛn] **1** *pron poss*: **le** ~**, la tienne, les** ~**s, les tiennes** yours, your own; **à la tienne** your (good) health, cheers*. **2** *nm*: **le** ~ what's yours; **les** ~**s** (*famille*) your family; (*groupe*) your set. **3** *adj poss*: **un** ~ **cousin** a cousin of yours; *V* **sien.**

tiens [tjɛ̃] *excl V* **tenir**; **un** ~ **vaut mieux que deux tu l'auras** a bird in the hand is worth two in the bush.

tiers, tierce [tjɛʀ, tjɛʀs(ə)] **1** *adj* third. **une tierce personne** a third party; **le T~-Monde** the Third World; le **T~-État** the third estate. **2** *nm* **(a)** (*fraction*) third. **j'ai lu un** ~**/les deux** ~ **du livre** I have read a third/two thirds of the book. **(b)** (*personne*) third party. **3** *nf* (*Mus*) third; (*Cartes, Escrime*) tierce. ♦ **tiercé** *nm* tiercé, *French system of forecast betting.*

tif‡ [tif] *nm* hair. ~**s** hair.

tige [tiʒ] *nf [fleur]* stem; *[céréales]* stalk; *[botte, chaussette]* leg (part); (*en métal*) shaft.

tignasse* [tiɲas] *nf* shock of hair, mop (of hair).

tigre [tigʀ(ə)] *nm* tiger. ♦ **tigré, e** *adj* (*tacheté*) spotted; (*rayé*) striped, streaked. ♦ **tigresse** *nf* tigress.

tilleul [tijœl] *nm* (*arbre*) lime (tree); (*infusion*) lime tea.

timbale [tɛ̃bal] *nf* **(a)** (*Mus*) **les** ~s the timpani, the kettledrums. **(b)** (*gobelet*) (metal) cup *ou* tumbler; (*Culin*) timbale. ♦ **timbalier** *nm* timpanist.

timbre [tɛ̃bʀ(ə)] *nm* **(a)** (*objet, vignette*) stamp. **~(-poste)** (postage) stamp; ~ **fiscal** excise stamp. **(b)** (*marque*) stamp; (*cachet de la poste*) postmark. **(c)** (*son*) timbre, tone. **(d)** (*sonnette*) bell. ♦ **timbrage** *nm* stamping; postmarking. **dispensé de** ~ postage paid. ♦ **timbré, e*** *adj* (*fou*) cracked*, dotty*. ♦ **timbrer** (1) *vt* (*apposer un cachet sur*) *acte* to stamp; *lettre* to postmark; (*affranchir*) to stamp, put a stamp on.

timide [timid] *adj* (*timoré*) timid, timorous; (*emprunté*) shy, timid; *amoureux* bashful. **faussement** ~ coy; **c'est un grand** ~ he's very shy. ♦ **timidement** *adv* timidly; timorously; shyly; bashfully. ♦ **timidité** *nf* timidity; timorousness; shyness; bashfulness.

timonier [timɔnje] *nm* (*Naut*) helmsman, steersman.

timoré, e [timɔʀe] *adj* timorous.

tintamarre [tɛ̃tamaʀ] *nm* din, racket*. **faire du** ~ to make a din *ou* racket*.

tinter [tɛ̃te] (1) *vi [cloche]* to ring, chime; *[clochette]* to tinkle; *[objets métalliques]* to jingle, chink; *[verres]* to chink. **faire** ~ *cloche* to ring; *verres* to make chink; **les oreilles me tintent** my ears are ringing. ♦ **tintement** *nm*: **~(s)** ringing; chiming; tinkling; jingling; chinking.

tintin‡ [tɛ̃tɛ̃] *excl* nothing doing!*, no go!‡ **faire** ~ to go without.

tintouin* [tɛ̃twɛ̃] *nm* bother.

tique [tik] *nf* (*Zool*) tick.

tiquer [tike] (1) *vi* to pull a face. **sans** ~ without turning a hair.

tir [tiʀ] *nm* **(a)** (*Sport*) shooting. ~ **au pistolet** pistol shooting; ~ **à l'arc** archery. **(b)** (*action*) firing. **déclencher le** ~ to open the firing. **(c)** (*trajectoire*) fire. **régler le** ~ to regulate the fire; ~ **groupé** grouped fire; **angle de** ~ angle of fire. **(d)** (*rafales*) fire. **un** ~ *ou* **des** ~**s de barrage/d'artillerie** barrage/artillery fire. **(e)** (*Boules, Ftbl*) shot. **(f)** (*stand*) ~ **(forain)** shooting gallery, rifle range.

tirade [tiʀad] *nf* soliloquy.

tirage [tiʀaʒ] *nm* **(a)** (*Phot*) (*action*) printing; (*photo*) print. **(b)** *[journal]* circulation; *[livre]* edition. **quel est le** ~ **de cet ouvrage?** how many copies of this work were printed?; ~ **de 2.000 exemplaires** run *ou* impression of 2,000 copies; ~ **à part** off-print. **(c)** *[cheminée]* draught. **(d)** (*Loterie*) draw. **le** ~ **des numéros gagnants** the draw for the winning numbers; **procéder par** ~ **au sort** to draw lots. **(e)** (*: *désaccord*) friction.

tirailler [tiʀɑje] (1) **1** *vt* **(a)** *corde, manche* to pull at, tug at. **(b)** *[douleurs]* to gnaw at, stab at; *[doutes]* to plague. **tiraillé entre plusieurs possibilités** torn between several possibilities. **2** *vi* (*Mil*) to fire. ♦ **tiraillement** *nm* (*douleur*) gnawing *ou* stabbing pain; (*doute*) doubt. **~(s)** (*conflit*) friction; (*sur une corde*) tugging. ♦ **tirailleur** *nm* (*Mil, fig*) skirmisher.

tirant [tiʀɑ̃] *nm*: ~ **d'eau** draught; **avoir 6 mètres de** ~ **d'eau** to draw 6 metres of water.

tire[1]**‡** [tiʀ] *nf* (*voiture*) car.

tire[2] [tiʀ] *nf*: **voleur à la** ~ pick-pocket; *V aussi* **tirer.**

tiré, e[1] [tiʀe] *adj traits, visage* drawn, haggard. ~ **à quatre épingles** done up *ou* dressed up to the nines*; (*fig*) ~ **par les cheveux** far-fetched.

tirée[2]***** [tiʀe] *nf* (*trajet*) long haul* *ou* trek. (*quantité*) **une** ~ **de** a load* of, heaps* of.

tirelire [tiʀliʀ] *nf* **(a)** moneybox, piggy bank. **(b)** (‡) (*tête*) nut*; (*visage*) face.

tirer [tiʀe] (1) **1** *vt* **(a)** *poignée, corde* to pull; *manche, robe* to pull down; *chaussette* to pull up; *véhicule, charge* to pull, draw; *remorque, navire* to tow. ~ **qn par la manche** to tug at sb's sleeve; ~ **qn à l'écart** to draw sb aside; **ne tire pas** don't pull; ~ **les cheveux à qn** to pull sb's hair. **(b)** *rideaux* to draw, pull; *verrou* to slide to, shoot. **tire la porte** pull the door to. **(c)** *vin, idée etc* to draw; *épée* to draw, pull out; *plaisir* to draw, get, derive; *jus, substance* to extract; *mot, citation, passage* to take (*de* from). ~ **un son d'un instrument** to get a sound out of *ou* draw a sound from an instrument; ~ **un objet d'un tiroir** to pull an object out of a drawer; ~ **son chapeau à qn** to raise one's hat to sb; ~ **de l'argent d'une activité** to make money from an activity; ~ **son origine de qch** to have sth as its origin; ~ **son nom de qch** to take its name from sth; ~ **qn du sommeil** to arouse sb from sleep; ~ **qn du lit** to get *ou* drag sb out of bed; **on ne peut rien en** ~ you can't get anything out of him; **encore une heure à** ~ **avant la fin*** another hour to get through before the end. **(d)** (*délivrer*) ~ **qn de** *prison etc* to get sb out of; *misère* to rescue sb from; ~ **qn du doute** to remove *ou* dispel sb's doubts; ~ **qn de l'erreur** to disabuse sb; **il faut le** ~ **de là** we'll have to help him out. **(e)** *numéro* to draw; *carte* to take, draw. **(f)** (*Phot, Typ*) to print. **se faire** ~ **le portrait*** to have one's picture taken. **(g)** (*tracer*) *trait* to draw; *plan* to draw up. **(h)** *coup de feu* to fire; *feu d'artifice* to set off; *gibier* to shoot. **il a tiré plusieurs coups de revolver sur l'agent** he shot *ou* fired at the policeman several times; ~ **le canon** to fire the cannon. **(i)** *chèque* to draw.

2 *vi* **(a)** (*faire feu*) to fire, shoot; (*Ftbl*) to shoot; (*Boules*) to throw. ~ **à vue** to shoot on sight; ~ **à balles/à blanc** to fire bullets/blanks; **apprendre à** ~ to learn to shoot. **(b)** (*Presse*) ~ **à 10.000 exemplaires** to have a circulation of 10,000. **(c)** *[cheminée]* to draw; *[voiture]* to pull. **(d)** ~ **au flanc*** to skive*; ~ **dans les jambes** *ou* **pattes* de qn** to make life difficult for sb.

3 ~ **sur** *vt indir* **(a)** *corde, poignée* to pull *ou* tug at. (*fig*) ~ **sur la ficelle*** to push one's luck*. **(b)** *couleur* to border on, verge on; *âge* to be getting on for *ou* verging on. **(c)** (*faire feu sur*) to shoot at, fire at. **(d)** *pipe* to pull at, draw on; *cigarette* to puff at, draw on.

4 ~ **à** *vt indir*: ~ **à sa fin** to be drawing to a close; ~ **à conséquence** to matter.

5 se ~ *vpr* **(a) se** ~ **de** *danger, situation* to get (o.s.) out of; *travail, examen* to manage, cope with, get through; **s'en** **~*** *[malade]* to pull through; *[délinquent]* to get away with it; (*financièrement*) to manage, get by; **il s'en est bien tiré** (*procès*) he got off lightly; (*épreuve*) he coped well with it, he made a good job of it; **il s'en est tiré avec une amende** he got off with a fine. **(b)** (‡: *déguerpir*) to push off‡, clear off‡. **(c)** (*: *toucher à sa fin*) to drag towards its close. **(d)** *[traits, visage]* to become drawn.

♦ **à tire d'ailes** *loc adv voler* swiftly. ♦ **tire-bouchon,** *pl* ~-~**s** *nm* corkscrew. **en** ~ in a corkscrew. ♦ **tire-fesses*** *nm inv* ski tow. ♦ **tire-au-flanc*** *nmf inv* skiver*. ♦ **à tire-larigot*** *loc adv* to one's heart content.

tiret [tiʀɛ] *nm* (*trait*) dash; (*en fin de ligne*) hyphen.

tireur [tiʀœʀ] *nm* **(a)** ~ **isolé** sniper; ~ **d'élite** marksman, sharpshooter; **c'est un bon** ~ he is a good shot. **(b)** (*Fin*) drawer.

tireuse [tiʀøz] *nf* **(a)** ~ **de cartes** fortuneteller. **(b)** (*pompe*) (hand) pump.

tiroir [tiʀwaʀ] *nm* drawer. ♦ **~-caisse** *pl* **~s-~s** *nm* till.

tisane [tizan] *nf* herb(al) tea. ~ **de menthe** mint tea.

tison [tizɔ̃] *nm* brand. ♦ **tisonner** (1) *vt* to poke. ♦ **tisonnier** *nm* poker.

tisser [tise] (1) *vt* (*lit, fig*) to weave; *[araignée]* to spin. ♦ **tissage** *nm* weaving. ♦ **tisserand, e** *nm,f* *ou* ♦ **tisseur, -euse** *nm,f* weaver.

tissu [tisy] *nm* (*Tex*) cloth, fabric, material; (*Anat*) tissue. (*péj*) **un** ~ **de** *mensonges, intrigues* a web of; *obscénités, inepties* a farrago of. ♦ **tissu-éponge,** *pl* ~**s-**~ *nm* (terry) towelling.

titre [titʀ(ə)] *nm* **(a)** *[livre etc]* title; *[chapitre]* heading, title. (*Presse*) **les (gros)** ~**s** the headlines. **(b)** (*honorifique, sportif etc*) title; (*appellation*) title, name. ~ **de noblesse** title; (*Admin*) **en** ~ titular. **(c)** (*document*) title. ~ **de propriété** title deed; ~ **de transport** ticket. **(d)** (*Bourse*) security. ~**s** securities, stocks; ~ **au porteur** bearer bond. **(e)** (*diplôme*) qualification. **avoir les** ~**s requis** to be fully qualified, have all the necessary qualifications. **(f)** (*littér: prétentions*) **ses** ~**s de gloire** his claims to fame. **(g)** *[or, argent]* fineness; *[solution]* titre. ~ **d'alcool** alcohol content. **(h) à ce** ~ (*en cette qualité*) as such; (*pour cette raison*) therefore; **à quel** ~**?** on what grounds?; **au même** ~ in the same way (*que* as); **à aucun** ~ on no account; **à double** ~ on two accounts; **à** ~ **privé/personnel** in a private/personal capacity; **à** ~ **permanent/provisoire** on a permanent/temporary basis; **à** ~ **exceptionnel** in exceptional cases; **à** ~ **d'ami** as a friend; **à** ~ **gratuit** *ou* **gracieux** free of charge; **à** ~ **d'exemple** as an example, by way of example; **à** ~ **indicatif** for information only; **à** ~ **d'indemnité** by way of indemnity, as an indemnity. ♦ **titré, e** *adj personne* titled. ♦ **titrer** (1) *vt* **(a)** (*ennoblir*) to confer a title on. **(b)** (*Presse*) to run as a headline. **(c)** (*Chim*) *solution* to titrate. ~ **10°** to be 10° proof (*on the Gay Lussac scale*).

tituber [titybe] (1) *vi* to stagger *ou* totter *ou* stumble (along); (*d'ivresse*) to reel (along).

titulaire [titylɛʀ] **1** *adj professeur* tenured. **être** ~ to have tenure; **être** ~ **de** *poste, permis* to hold. **2** *nmf* *[poste]* incumbent; *[carte]* holder. ♦ **titulariser** (1) *vt* to give tenure to.

toast [tost] *nm* (*pain*) slice *ou* piece of toast; (*discours*) toast. **porter un** ~ **en l'honneur de qn** to toast sb.

toboggan [tɔbɔgɑ̃] *nm* (*jeu*) slide; (*traîneau*) toboggan; (*Aut*) flyover, overpass (*US*).

toc [tɔk] **1** *excl* (*bruit*) ~ ~! knock knock!, rat-a-tat! **2** *nm*: **c'est du** ~* (*faux*) it's a fake; (*camelote*) it's rubbish *ou* trash*; **en** ~ imitation, fake.

tocsin [tɔksɛ̃] *nm* alarm (bell), tocsin.

toge [tɔʒ] *nf* (*Hist*) toga; (*Jur, Scol*) gown.

Togo [tɔgo] *nm* Togo.

tohu-bohu [tɔybɔy] *nm* hubbub.

toi [twa] *pron pers* **(a)** (*sujet, objet*) you. **si j'étais** ~ if I were you; **il a accepté,** ~ **non** he accepted but you didn't *ou* but not you; ~**, tu n'as pas à te plaindre** YOU have no cause to complain; ~**, je te connais** I know YOU. **(b)** (*avec vpr*) **assieds-**~ sit down; **tais-**~**!** you be quiet! **(c)** (*avec prép*) **cette maison est-elle à** ~**?** is this house yours?; **tu n'as même pas une chambre à** ~ **tout seul?** you haven't even a room of your own? *ou* a room to yourself?

toile [twal] **1** *nf* **(a)** (*tissu*) cloth; (*morceau*) piece of cloth. **grosse** ~ (rough *ou* coarse) canvas; ~ **de lin/coton** linen/cotton (cloth); **en** ~**, de** ~ *draps* linen; *pantalon* (heavy) cotton; *sac* canvas; ~ **imprimée** printed cotton. **(b)** (*Art*) (*support*) canvas; (*œuvre*) canvas, painting. **(c)** *[araignée]* web. **la** ~ **de l'araignée** the spider's web; **plein de** ~**s d'araignées** full of cobwebs. **2:** ~ **cirée** oilcloth; ~ **émeri** emery cloth; (*Théât, fig*) ~ **de fond** backdrop; ~ **de jute** hessian; ~ **à matelas** ticking; ~ **de tente** tent canvas.

toilette [twalɛt] *nf* **(a)** (*action*) washing; *[voiture]* cleaning; (*chien*) grooming. **faire sa** ~ to have a wash, get washed; *[chat]* to wash itself; ~ **intime** intimate hygiene; **elle passe des heures à sa** ~ she spends hours getting ready *ou* washing and dressing; **la** ~ **des enfants prend toujours du temps** children always take a long time washing; **nécessaire de** ~ toilet bag; **faire la** ~ **de** *voiture* to clean; *chien* to groom. **(b)** (*meuble*) washstand. **(c)** (*vêtements*) clothes; (*costume*) outfit. **en** ~ **de bal** dressed for a dance; ~ **de mariée** wedding *ou* bridal dress *ou* gown. **(d)** (*W.-C.*) ~**s** toilet; (*publiques*) public conveniences *ou* lavatory, restroom (*US*); **aller aux** ~**s** to go to the toilet.

toiser [twaze] (1) *vt* to eye scornfully (up and down).

toison [twazɔ̃] *nf* **(a)** *[mouton]* fleece. **(b)** (*chevelure*) (*épaisse*) mop; (*longue*) mane. **(c)** (*poils*) abundant growth.

toit [twa] *nm* (*lit*) roof; (*fig: maison*) home, roof. **habiter sous les** ~**s** to live under the eaves; (*fig*) **crier qch sur les** ~**s** to shout sth from the rooftops; **voiture à** ~ **ouvrant** car with a sunshine roof; **vivre sous le** ~ **paternel** to live in the parental home. ♦ **toiture** *nf* roof.

tôle [tol] *nf* (*matériau*) sheet metal; (*morceau*) steel (*ou* iron) sheet. ~ **ondulée** corrugated iron.

tolérer [tɔleʀe] (6) *vt* (*gén, Méd, Tech*) to tolerate; *comportement* to put up with; *douleur* to bear, endure, stand; *excédent de bagages etc* to allow. **il ne tolère pas qu'on le contredise** he won't stand (for) *ou* tolerate being contradicted. ♦ **tolérable** *adj* tolerable, bearable. ♦ **tolérance** *nf* (*gén*) tolerance; (*religieuse*) toleration. **c'est une** ~**, pas un droit** it is tolerated rather than allowed as of right; (*Douane*) **il y a une** ~ **de 200 cigarettes** there's an allowance of 200 cigarettes. ♦ **tolérant, e** *adj* tolerant.

tôlerie [tolʀi] *nf* (*commerce*) sheet metal trade; (*atelier*) sheet metal workshop; (*carcasse*) plates, steel-work. ♦ **tôlier** *nm* sheet metal worker. ~ **en voitures** panel beater.

tollé [tɔle] *nm*: ~ **(général)** general outcry.

tomahawk [tɔmaok] *nm* tomahawk.

tomate [tɔmat] *nf* tomato.

tombe [tɔ̃b] *nf* (*gén, fig*) grave; (*avec monument*) tomb; (*pierre*) gravestone, tombstone. **suivre qn dans la** ~ to follow sb to the grave. ♦ **tombale** *adj f*: **pierre** ~ tombstone. ♦ **tombeau,** *pl* ~**x** *nm* (*lit*) tomb; (*fig*) grave. **mettre au** ~ to entomb; **mise au** ~ entombment; **à** ~ **ouvert** at breakneck speed.

tombée [tɔ̃be] *nf*: **(à) la** ~ **de la nuit** (at) nightfall; **(à) la** ~ **du jour** (at) the close of the day.

tomber [tɔ̃be] (1) **1** *vi* **(a)** *[personne, objet]* to fall (over *ou* down). ~ **de vélo/d'un arbre** to fall off one's bike/down from a tree; ~ **par terre** to fall down, fall to the ground; ~ **raide mort** to fall down *ou* drop (down) dead; ~ **à genoux** to fall on(to) one's knees; (*fig*) ~ **aux pieds de qn** to fall at sb's feet; ~ **de tout son long** to fall headlong, go sprawling; **faire** ~ **qn/qch** to knock sb/sth over *ou* down; ~ **de fatigue** to drop from exhaustion; ~ **de sommeil** to be falling asleep on one's feet; (*fig*) ~ **(bien) bas** to sink (very) low; **la nouvelle vient de** ~ the news has just broken *ou* come through. **(b)** *[feuilles, lumière, nuit]* to fall; *[cheveux]* to fall (out); *[pluie]* to fall, come down; *[foudre]* to strike; *[brouillard]* to come down. **il tombe de la neige** snow is falling. **(c)** *[soldat, régime, garnison]* to fall. **faire** ~ **le gouvernement** to bring down the government. **(d)** *[température, prix, nombre]* to drop, fall; *[vent, fièvre]* to drop; *[baromètre]* to fall; *[jour]* to draw to a close; *[voix]* to drop, fall away; *[colère, conversation]* to die down; *[enthousiasme]* to fall away. **faire** ~ *vent, prix etc* to bring down. **(e)** *[obstacle, objection]* to disappear; *[projet]* to fall through. **(f)** *[draperie, robe, chevelure]* to fall, hang; *[moustaches, épaules]* to droop. **ce pantalon tombe bien** these trousers hang well. **(g)** *[date, choix, sort]* to fall (*sur* on). **Noël tombe un mardi** Christmas falls on a Tuesday; **et il a fallu que ça tombe sur moi** it (just) had to be me. **(h)** (*inopinément*) **il est tombé en pleine réunion** he walked in right in the middle of a meeting. **(i)** (*devenir: V aussi noms etc en question*) ~ **malade** *etc* to fall ill *etc.* **(j)** (*se trouver: V aussi noms en question*) ~ **dans un piège** *etc* to fall into a trap *etc.* **(k) laisser** ~ *objet,* (*) *amis, activité* to drop. **laisse** ~**!*** give it a rest!*; **se laisser** ~ **dans un fauteuil** to drop *ou* fall into an armchair. **(l)** (*locutions*) *[projets etc]* ~ **à l'eau** to fall through; **bien/mal** ~ (*avoir de la chance/malchance*) to be lucky/unlucky; (*se produire au bon/mauvais moment*) to come at the right/wrong moment; ~ **de Charybde en Scylla** to jump out of the frying pan into the fire; ~ **juste** (*en devinant*) to be right; *[calculs]* to come out right; ~ **de haut** to be bitterly disappointed; **il n'est pas tombé de la dernière pluie** he wasn't born yesterday; **ce n'est pas tombé dans l'oreille d'un sourd** it didn't fall on deaf ears; **il est tombé sur la tête!*** he's got a screw loose!*; *[aubaine]* ~ **du ciel** to be heaven-sent; ~ **des nues** to be completely taken aback; *[projet]* ~ **à l'eau** to fall through; *[plaisanterie]* ~ **à plat** to fall flat; **cela tombe sous le sens** it's obvious, it stands to reason.

2 ~ **sur** *vt indir* **(a)** *ami* to run into; *détail* to come across. **(b)** *[regard]* to fall *ou* light upon; *[conversation]* to come round to. **(c)** (*: *attaquer, critiquer*) to go for*. (*: *s'inviter*) **il nous est tombé dessus hier** he landed on us yesterday.

3 *vt*: ~ **la veste*** to slip off one's jacket.

tombereau, *pl* ~**x** [tɔ̃bʀo] *nm* (*charrette*) tipcart; (*contenu*) cartload.

tombola [tɔ̃bɔla] *nf* tombola.

tome [tɔm] *nm* (*division*) part, book; (*volume*) volume.

ton[1] [tɔ̃], **ta** [ta], **tes** [te] *adj poss* your, your own.

ton[2] [tɔ̃] *nm* **(a)** (*hauteur de la voix*) pitch; (*timbre*) tone. ~ **aigu** shrill pitch; ~ **nasillard** nasal tone; **hausser/baisser le** ~ to raise/lower one's voice; (*fig*) **il devra changer de** ~ he'll have to sing a different tune; **ne le prenez pas sur ce** ~ don't take it that way *ou* like that; (*fig*) **dire qch sur tous les** ~**s** to say sth in every possible way. **(b)** (*Mus*) (*intervalle*) tone; (*clef*) key. **donner le** ~ to give the pitch; **être dans le** ~ to be in tune. **(c)** (*Ling*) tone. **(d)** (*manière de s'exprimer*) tone. **des plaisanteries de bon** ~ jokes in good taste; **il est de bon** ~ **de faire** it is good form to do; **être dans le** ~ to fit in; **donner le** ~ to set the tone; (*mode*) to set the fashion. **(e)** (*couleur*) shade, tone. **être dans le** ~ to tone in, match; **la ceinture n'est pas du même** ~ **que la robe** the belt does not match the dress. ♦ **tonalité** *nf* (*gén*) tone; (*Mus: système*) tonality; (*Mus: clef*) key; (*Téléc*) dialling tone.

tondre [tɔ̃dʀ(ə)] (41) *vt* **(a)** *mouton,* (*hum*) *personne* to shear; *gazon* to mow; *haie* to clip, cut; *caniche* to clip; *cheveux* to crop. **(b)** (*: *escroquer*) to fleece*. ♦ **tondeuse** *nf* (*à cheveux*) clippers; (*pour les moutons*) shears. ~ **(à gazon)** (lawn)mower. ♦ **tondu, e** *adj cheveux, pelouse* closely-cropped.

tonifier [tɔnifje] (7) *vt muscles* to tone up; *esprit* to invigorate, stimulate. ♦ **tonifiant, e** *adj air* bracing, invigorating; *lotion* toning; *lecture* invigorating, stimulating. ♦ **tonique 1** *adj boisson* tonic; *lotion* toning; *air, froid* invigorating, bracing; *lecture* invigorating, stimulating; (*Ling*) tonic. **2** *nm* (*Méd, fig*) tonic; (*lotion*) toning lotion.

tonitruant, e [tɔnitʀyɑ̃, ɑ̃t] *adj voix* thundering, booming.

tonnage [tɔnaʒ] *nm* tonnage.

tonnant, e [tɔnɑ̃, ɑ̃t] *adj voix* thunderous, thundering.

tonne [tɔn] *nf* (metric) ton, tonne. **des** ~**s de*** tons of*, loads of*.

tonneau, *pl* ~**x** [tɔno] *nm* **(a)** (*récipient*) barrel, cask. **(b)** (*Aviat*) hestitation flick roll; (*Aut*) somersault. **faire un** ~ to somersault, roll over. **(c)** (*Naut*) ton. ♦ **tonnelet** *nm* keg, (small) cask. ♦ **tonnelier** *nm* cooper.

tonnelle [tɔnɛl] *nf* bower, arbour.

tonner [tɔne] (1) **1** *vi [canon]* to thunder, boom, roar; *[personne]* to thunder, rage (*contre* against). **2** *vb impers*: **il tonne** it is thundering.

tonnerre [tɔnɛʀ] **1** *nm* **(a)** thunder. **le** ~ **gronde** there is a rumble of thunder; **un bruit de** ~ a noise like thunder, a thunderous noise; **un** ~ **d'applaudissements** thunderous applause, a thunder of applause. **(b) du** ~***** terrific*, fantastic*. **2** *excl*: ~**!*** hell's bells!*

tonsure [tɔ̃syʀ] *nf* (*Rel*) tonsure; (*: *calvitie*) bald patch.

tonte [tɔ̃t] *nf [moutons]* shearing; *[haie]* clipping; *[gazon]* mowing; (*époque*) shearing-time.

tonton* [tɔ̃tɔ̃] *nm* uncle.

tonus [tɔnys] *nm* (*musculaire*) tone; (*fig: dynamisme*) energy, dynamism.

top [tɔp] **1** *nm* pip. (*Rad*) **au 4e** ~ at the 4th stroke. **2** *adj*: ~ **secret** top secret.

topaze [tɔpaz] *nf* topaz.

topinambour [tɔpinɑ̃buʀ] *nm* Jerusalem artichoke.

topo* [tɔpo] *nm* (*exposé*) spiel*.

topographie [tɔpɔgʀafi] *nf* topography. ♦ **topographique** *adj* topographic(al).

toquade [tɔkad] *nf* (*péj*) (*pour qn*) infatuation; (*pour qch*) fad, craze.

toque [tɔk] *nf [femme]* fur hat; *[juge, jockey]* cap. ~ **de cuisinier** chef's hat.

toqué, e* [tɔke] **1** *adj* crazy*, cracked*, nuts* (*de* about). **2** *nm,f* nutcase*.

torche [tɔʀʃ(ə)] *nf* torch. ~ **électrique** (electric) torch; (*Parachutisme*) **se mettre en** ~ to candle. ♦ **torchère** *nf* (*Ind*) flare.

torcher* [tɔʀʃe] (1) *vt* to wipe.

torchis [tɔʀʃi] *nm* cob (*for walls*).

torchon [tɔʀʃɔ̃] *nm* **(a)** (*gén*) cloth; (*pour épousseter*) duster; (*à vaisselle*) tea towel, dish towel. **le** ~ **brûle entre eux** they're at daggers drawn. **(b)** (*péj*) (*devoir mal présenté*) mess; (*mauvais journal*) rag.

tordant, e* [tɔʀdɑ̃, ɑ̃t] *adj* killing*, screamingly funny*. **il est** ~ he's a scream* *ou* a kill*.

tordre [tɔʀdʀ(ə)] (41) **1** *vt* (*gén*) to wring; (*pour essorer*) to wring (out); *barre de fer, bras* to twist; (*déformer*) *visage* to contort, twist. **je vais lui** ~ **le cou** I'll wring his neck (for him). **2 se** ~ *vpr* **(a)** *[personne]* (*de douleur, de rire*) to be doubled up (*de* with). **se** ~ **le bras** to sprain *ou* twist one's arm. **(b)** *[barre]* to bend; *[roue]* to buckle, twist. ♦ **tordu, e 1** *adj jambes* bent, crooked; *tronc* twisted; *barre* bent; *roue* buckled, twisted; *esprit* warped. (*péj*) **être** ~***** to be round the bend*. **2** *nm,f* (*: *fou*) nut case*.

toréador [tɔʀeadɔʀ] *nm* toreador, bullfighter.

tornade [tɔʀnad] *nf* tornado.

torpeur [tɔʀpœʀ] *nf* torpor.

torpille [tɔʀpij] *nf* (*Mil, Zool*) torpedo. ♦ **torpillage** *nm* torpedoing. ♦ **torpiller** (1) *vt* to torpedo. ♦ **torpilleur** *nm* torpedo boat.

torréfier [tɔʀefje] (7) *vt café* to roast.

torrent [tɔʀɑ̃] *nm* (*lit, fig*) torrent. **il pleut à** ~**s** the rain is coming down in torrents; (*fig*) **des** ~**s de** streams *ou* floods of. ♦ **torrentiel, -elle** *adj* torrential.

torride [tɔʀid] *adj région* torrid; *chaleur* scorching.

torsade [tɔʀsad] *nf [fils]* twist. ♦ **torsader** (1) *vt* to twist.

torse [tɔʀs(ə)] *nm* (*gén*) chest; (*Anat, Sculp*) torso. ~ **nu** stripped to the waist.

torsion [tɔʀsjɔ̃] *nf* (*action*) twisting; (*Phys, Tech*) torsion. **exercer une ~ sur qch** to twist sth.
tort [tɔʀ] *nm* **(a)** (*action blâmable*) fault. **il a le ~ d'être trop jeune** his trouble is that he's too young; **ils ont tous les ~s de leur côté** the fault *ou* wrong is entirely on their side, they're entirely at fault *ou* in the wrong; **avoir des ~s envers qn** to have wronged sb; **regretter ses ~s** to be sorry for one's wrongs; **vous avez refusé? c'est un ~** did you refuse? — you were wrong (to do so). **(b)** (*préjudice*) wrong. **faire (du) ~ à qn** to harm sb, do sb harm; **ça va faire du ~ aux produits laitiers** it will harm *ou* be harmful to *ou* be detrimental to the dairy industry. **(c) à ~** wrongly; **c'est à ~ qu'on l'avait dit malade** he was wrongly *ou* mistakenly said to be ill; **à ~ ou à raison** rightly or wrongly; **dépenser à ~ et à travers** to spend wildly; **parler à ~ et à travers** to talk wildly. **(d) être/se mettre dans son ~** to be/put o.s. in the wrong; **être en ~** to be in the wrong *ou* at fault; **avoir ~** to be wrong (*de faire* to do); **donner ~ à qn** *[témoin]* to lay the blame on sb, blame sb; *[événements]* to show sb to be wrong, prove sb wrong.
torticolis [tɔʀtikɔli] *nm* stiff neck.
tortiller [tɔʀtije] (1) **1** *vt mouchoir* to twist; *moustache* to twirl. **2** *vi*: **~ des hanches** to wiggle one's hips; **il n'y a pas à ~*** there's no wriggling round it. **3 se ~** *vpr [serpent]* to writhe; *[ver, personne]* to wiggle, squirm.
tortionnaire [tɔʀsjɔnɛʀ] *nm* torturer.
tortue [tɔʀty] *nf* (*Zool, fig: lent*) tortoise. **~ de mer** turtle; **avancer comme une ~** to crawl along at a snail's pace.
tortueux, -euse [tɔʀtɥø, øz] *adj chemin, rivière* winding; *discours* tortuous; *manœuvres* devious.
torture [tɔʀtyʀ] *nf*: **~(s)** torture. ♦ **torturer** (1) *vt* to torture. **se ~ l'esprit** to rack *ou* cudgel one's brains.
tôt [to] *adv* **(a)** (*au début*) early. **il se lève ~** he is an early riser, he gets up early; **~ dans la matinée** early in the morning, in the early morning. **(b)** (*après peu de temps*) soon, early. **il est un peu ~ pour le juger** it's a little too soon *ou* early to judge him; **~ ou tard** sooner or later; **il a eu ~ fait de s'en apercevoir!** he was quick to notice it!, it wasn't long before he noticed it!; **si seulement vous me l'aviez dit plus ~!** if only you had told me sooner! *ou* earlier!; **ce n'est pas trop ~!** it's not a moment too soon!, it's not before time!; **il n'était pas plus ~ parti que la voiture est tombée en panne** no sooner had he set off than the car broke down. **(c) venez le plus ~ possible** come as early *ou* as soon as you can; **le plus ~ sera le mieux** the sooner the better; **il peut venir jeudi au plus ~** Thursday is the earliest *ou* soonest he can come.
total, e, *mpl* **-aux** [tɔtal, o] **1** *adj* (*gén*) total; *ruine, désespoir* utter, complete. **2** *adv*: **~, il a tout perdu*** the net result *ou* outcome was he lost everything. **3** *nm* total. **le ~ de la population** the total (number of the) population; (*fig*) **si on fait le ~** if you add it all up *ou* together; **au ~** (*lit*) in total; (*fig*) on the whole, all in all. ♦ **totalement** *adv* totally, completely. ♦ **totaliser** (1) *vt* to total. ♦ **totalitaire** *adj* (*Pol*) *régime* totalitarian. ♦ **totalitarisme** *nm* totalitarianism. ♦ **totalité** *nf* **(a)** (*gén*) **la ~ de** all of; **la ~ de son salaire** his whole *ou* entire salary, all of his salary; **vendu en ~ aux États-Unis** all sold to the USA; **pris dans sa ~** taken as a whole *ou* in its entirety. **(b)** (*Philos*) totality.
toubib* [tubib] *nm* doctor, doc*.
toucan [tukɑ̃] *nm* toucan.
touchant[1] [tuʃɑ̃] *prép* concerning.
touchant[2]**, e** [tuʃɑ̃, ɑ̃t] *adj* (*émouvant*) touching, moving.
touche [tuʃ] *nf* **(a)** *[piano etc]* key. **(b)** (*de couleur*) touch, stroke; (*d'ironie*) touch. **une ~ de gaieté** a touch *ou* note of gaiety. **(c)** (*Pêche*) bite; (*Escrime*) hit. **faire une ~** (*lit*) to have a bite; (*: *flirter*) to make a hit. **(d)** (*Ftbl, Rugby*) (*ligne*) touchline; (*sortie*) touch; (*remise en jeu*) (*Ftbl*) throw-in; (*Rugby*) line-out. **sortir en ~** to go into touch; **rester sur la ~** (*lit*) to stay on the touchlines; (*fig*) to be left on the sidelines. **(e)** (*: *allure*) **quelle drôle de ~!** what a sight!*, what DOES he (*ou* she *etc*) look like!*
touche-à-tout [tuʃatu] *nmf inv* (*gén enfant*) (little) meddler; (*inventeur*) dabbler.
toucher [tuʃe] (1) **1** *vt* **(a)** (*gén*) to touch; (*pour palper*) *tissu etc* to feel. **~ qch du doigt** to touch sth with one's finger; **je n'avais pas touché une raquette depuis 6 mois** I hadn't had a racket in my hands for 6 months; **il ne faut pas que ça touche (le mur)** it mustn't touch (the wall); **~ le fond** to touch the bottom; **~ terre** to land; **l'avion toucha le sol** the plane touched down. **(b)** (*jouxter*) to adjoin. **son jardin touche le nôtre** his garden (ad)joins ours *ou* is adjacent to ours. **(c)** *adversaire, objectif* to hit. **touché d'une balle en plein cœur** hit by a bullet in the heart. **(d)** (*contacter*) to reach, get in touch with, contact. **(e)** (*faire escale à*) *port* to put in at, call at. **(f)** *salaire* to draw, get, be paid; *prime* to get, receive; *chèque* to cash; *gros lot* to win. **(g)** (*émouvoir*) *[drame, deuil]* to affect; *[cadeau, bonté]* to touch, move; *[reproche]* to have an effect on. **~ qn au vif** to cut sb to the quick. **(h)** (*concerner*) *[problème]* to affect, concern. **touché par la dévaluation** affected *ou* hit* by devaluation. **(i) je vais lui en ~ un mot** I'll have a word with him about it, I'll mention it to him; **touchons du bois!*** touch wood!*, let's keep our fingers crossed!
2 se ~ *vpr [lignes, cercles]* to touch; *[terrains]* to be adjacent (to each other), adjoin.
3 ~ à *vt indir* **(a)** *objet* to touch; *économies* to break into, touch. **~ à tout** (*lit*) to meddle with everything; (*faire plusieurs métiers*) to dabble in everything; **on n'a pas touché au fromage** we haven't touched the cheese, the cheese has been left untouched. **(b)** (*malmener*) *enfant* to touch, lay a finger on; *réputation* to question. **(c)** (*modifier*) *règlement* to meddle with; *mécanisme* to tamper with; *monument* to touch. **(d)** (*concerner*) *intérêts* to affect; *problème, domaine* to touch, have to do with. **(e)** (*aborder*) *période, but* to near, approach; *sujet* to broach, come onto; *activité* to try one's hand at. (*fig*) **sans avoir l'air d'y ~** looking as if butter wouldn't melt in his (*ou* her *etc*) mouth; **l'hiver touche à sa fin** winter is nearing its end. **(f)** (*être en contact avec*) to touch; (*être contigu à*) to border on, adjoin. **cela touche à la folie** that verges *ou* borders on madness.
4 *nm* (*sens*) (sense of) touch; (*impression produite*) feel. **doux au ~** soft to the touch.
touffe [tuf] *nf [herbe, poils]* tuft; *[arbres, fleurs]* clump.
touffu, e [tufy] *adj barbe* bushy; *arbres* leafy; *haie, bois* thick; *roman, style* complex.
touiller* [tuje] (1) *vt* to stir.
toujours [tuʒuʀ] *adv* **(a)** (*continuité*) always; (*répétition*) forever, always. **~ à l'heure** always on time; **la vie se déroule ~ pareille** life goes on the same as ever *ou* forever the same; **il est ~ en train de critiquer** he is always *ou* forever criticizing, he keeps on criticizing; **comme ~** as ever, as always; **ce sont des amis de ~** they are lifelong friends; **il est parti pour ~** he's gone forever *ou* for good. **(b)** (*encore*) still. **il travaille ~** he is still working; **j'espère ~ qu'elle viendra** I keep hoping she'll come; **ils n'ont ~ pas répondu** they still haven't replied, they have not yet replied. **(c)** (*intensif*) anyway, anyhow. **écrivez ~, il vous répondra peut-être** write anyway *ou* anyhow, he (just) might answer you; **où est-elle?**

— **pas chez moi** ~! where is she? — not at my place anyway! *ou* at any rate!; **je trouverai** ~ **(bien) une excuse** I can always think up an excuse; **tu trouveras** ~ **(bien) une poste** you're sure *ou* bound to find a post office; **tu peux** ~ **courir!*** you've got some hope! (*iro*); **vous pouvez** ~ **crier, il n'y a personne** shout as much as you like, there's no one about; ~ **est-il que** the fact remains that, that does not alter the fact that.

toupet [tupɛ] *nm* **(a)** ~ **(de cheveux)** quiff. **(b)** (*: *culot*) sauce*, nerve, cheek. **avoir du** ~ to have a nerve *ou* a cheek.

toupie [tupi] *nf* (*jouet*) (spinning) top. **vieille** ~‡ silly old trout‡.

tour¹ [tuʀ] *nf* **(a)** tower; (*immeuble*) tower block, high-rise block. ~ **de contrôle** control tower. **(b)** (*Échecs*) castle, rook.

tour² [tuʀ] *nm* **(a)** (*parcours autour de*) **faire le** ~ **de** *parc etc* to go round; *possibilités* to explore; *magasins* to go round, look round; *problème* to consider from all angles; ~ **de ville** (*pour touristes*) city tour; **si on faisait le** ~? shall we go round (it)?; (*fig*) **faire le** ~ **du cadran** to sleep (right) round the clock; **faire le** ~ **du monde** to go round the world; **faire un** ~ **d'Europe** to tour Europe; ~ **d'horizon** (general) survey; ~ **de chant** song recital; ~ **de piste** (*Sport*) lap; (*Cirque*) circuit; **la bouteille a fait le** ~ **de la table** the bottle went round the table.

(b) (*excursion*) trip, outing; (*balade*) (*à pied*) walk, stroll; (*en voiture*) run, drive. **faire un** ~ **de manège** to have a ride on a merry-go-round; **faire un** ~ **en ville** to go for a walk round town; **je vais te faire faire le** ~ **du propriétaire** I'll show you over *ou* round the place.

(c) (*succession*) turn. ~ **de garde** spell *ou* turn of duty; **c'est votre** ~ it's your turn; **attendre son** ~ to wait one's turn; **chacun son** ~ everyone will have his turn; **nous le faisons chacun à notre** ~ *ou* ~ **à** ~ *ou* **à** ~ **de rôle** we do it in turn, we take turns at it; **à qui le** ~? whose turn is it?, who is next?

(d) (*Pol*) ~ **(de scrutin)** ballot; **au premier** ~ in the first ballot *ou* round.

(e) *[partie du corps]* measurement; *[tronc, colonne]* girth; *[visage]* contour, outline; *[surface]* circumference. ~ **de taille** *etc* waist *etc* measurement; **la table fait 3 mètres de** ~ the table measures 3 metres round (the edge).

(f) (*rotation*) turn; (*Tech*) revolution. **un** ~ **de vis** a (turn of a) screw; (*Aut*) **régime de 2.000** ~**s** speed of 2,000 revs *ou* revolutions; **donner un** ~ **de clef** to turn the key, give the key a turn; **faire un** ~ **sur soi-même** to spin round once; **souffrir d'un** ~ **de reins** to suffer from a sprained back; **à** ~ **de bras** *frapper* with all one's strength; *produire* prolifically.

(g) (*tournure*) *[situation, conversation]* turn. ~ **d'esprit** turn *ou* cast of mind; ~ **(de phrase)** turn of phrase.

(h) *[acrobate]* feat, stunt; *[jongleur, escroc, plaisantin]* trick. ~ **d'adresse/de cartes** skilful/card trick; ~ **de force** (*lit*) feat of strength; (*fig*) amazing feat; **en un** ~ **de main** in next to no time; **et le** ~ **est joué!** and there you have it!; **par un** ~ **de passe-passe** by sleight of hand; **c'est un** ~ **à prendre** it's just a knack one picks up; **avoir plus d'un** ~ **dans son sac** to have more than one trick up one's sleeve; **jouer un** ~ **à qn** to play a trick on sb; **un** ~ **de cochon*** a dirty *ou* lousy trick*.

(i) (*Tech*) lathe. ~ **de potier** potter's wheel.

tourbe [tuʀb(ə)] *nf* peat. ♦ **tourbeux, -euse** *adj* peaty. ♦ **tourbière** *nf* peat bog.

tourbillon [tuʀbijɔ̃] *nm* (*dans l'eau*) whirlpool; (*de vent*) whirlwind; ~ **de fumée/neige** swirl *ou* eddy of smoke/snow; ~ **de plaisirs** whirl of pleasure; **le** ~ **de la vie** the hurly-burly *ou* hustle and bustle of life. ♦ **tourbillonnement** *nm* whirling, swirling, eddying. ♦ **tourbillonner** (1) *vi [poussière etc]* to whirl, swirl, eddy; *[danseurs, idées]* to swirl *ou* whirl round.

tourelle [tuʀɛl] *nf* (*gén*) turret; *[sous-marin]* conning tower.

tourisme [tuʀism(ə)] *nm*: **le** ~ tourism; **le** ~ **d'hiver** the winter tourist trade *ou* industry; **avion/voiture de** ~ private plane/car; **office du** ~ tourist office; **agence de** ~ tourist agency; **faire du** ~ to do some touring *ou* sightseeing. ♦ **touriste** *nmf* tourist. ♦ **touristique** *adj* (*gén*) tourist; *région* popular with (the) tourists, touristic (*péj*).

tourment [tuʀmɑ̃] *nm* agony, torment.

tourmente [tuʀmɑ̃t] *nf* (*lit*) storm, gale; (*fig*) storm. ~ **de neige** blizzard.

tourmenter [tuʀmɑ̃te] (1) **1** *vt* (*gén*) to torment; *[remords, doute]* to rack, plague. **2 se** ~ *vpr* to fret, worry (o.s.). ♦ **tourmenté, e** *adj personne, visage* tormented, tortured; *formes* tortured; *vie, mer* stormy.

tournage [tuʀnaʒ] *nm* (*Ciné*) shooting; (*Menuiserie*) turning.

tournant, e [tuʀnɑ̃, ɑ̃t] **1** *adj fauteuil* swivel; *scène* revolving; (*Mil*) *mouvement* encircling; *escalier* spiral. **2** *nm* (*virage*) bend. (*fig*) ~ **décisif** watershed, turning point; **avoir qn au** ~* to get even with sb; **attendre qn au** ~* to wait for the chance to catch sb out.

tourné, e¹ [tuʀne] *adj* **(a) bien** ~ *personne, jambes* shapely; *taille* neat, trim; *compliment* well-turned; **mal** ~ *lettre* badly phrased; **avoir l'esprit mal** ~ to have a nasty turn of mind. **(b)** *lait, vin* sour. **(c)** (*Menuiserie*) turned.

tournebouler* [tuʀnəbule] (1) *vt personne* to put in a whirl.

tournebroche [tuʀnəbʀɔʃ] *nm* roasting jack.

tourne-disque, *pl* ~-~**s** [tuʀnədisk(ə)] *nm* record player.

tournedos [tuʀnədo] *nm* tournedos.

tournée² [tuʀne] *nf* **(a)** *[conférencier, artiste]* tour; *[inspecteur, livreur]* round. **être en** ~ to be on tour; to be on one's rounds; **faire la** ~ **de** *magasins* to do the rounds of, go round; **faire la** ~ **des grands ducs** to go out on a spree*. **(b)** (*consommations*) round (of drinks).

tournemain [tuʀnəmɛ̃] *nm*: **en un** ~ in next to no time.

tourner [tuʀne] (1) **1** *vt* **(a)** *clef, regard etc* to turn; *sauce* to stir; *page* to turn (over). ~ **et retourner** to turn over and over; **quand il m'a vu, il a tourné la tête** when he saw me he looked away *ou* he turned his head away; (*lit, fig*) ~ **le dos à** to turn one's back on; **le dos tourné à la fenêtre** with one's back to the window; ~ **ses pensées/efforts vers** to turn one's thoughts/efforts towards *ou* to. **(b)** *armée* to turn, outflank; *obstacle* to round; *difficulté* to get round *ou* past. **(c)** *phrase, compliment* to turn; *demande, lettre* to phrase, express. **(d)** (*Ciné*) *scène* to shoot, film; *film* (*faire les prises de vue*) to shoot; (*en être producteur ou acteur*) to make. **ils ont dû** ~ **en studio** they had to do the filming in the studio. **(e)** *bois, ivoire* to turn; *pot* to throw. **(f)** (*locutions*) ~ **qch en ridicule** to ridicule sth, hold sth up to ridicule; **il a tourné l'incident en plaisanterie** he made a joke out of the incident; **il tourne tout à son avantage** he turns everything to his (own) advantage; (*fig*) ~ **la page** to turn over a new leaf; **se** ~ **les pouces** to twiddle one's thumbs; ~ **la tête à qn** *[vin]* to go to sb's head; *[succès]* to go to *ou* turn sb's head.

2 *vi* **(a)** (*gén*) to turn; *[aiguilles]* to go round; (*Tech*) *[roue]* to revolve; *[toupie]* to spin; *[taximètre]* to tick away; *[usine, moteur]* to run. ~ **sur soi-même** to turn round on o.s.; (*très vite*) to spin round; **l'heure tourne** time is passing *ou* is going on; **j'ai vu tout** ~ my head began to spin *ou* swim; **faire** ~ **le moteur** to run the engine; ~ **au ralenti** to tick over. **(b)** ~ **autour de** (*gén*) to revolve *ou* go round; *[oiseau, mouches]* to fly round; ~ **autour de qn** (*péj: importuner*) to hang round sb; (*par curiosité*) to hover round sb; *[enquête, conversation]* ~ **autour de qch** to centre on sth. **(c)** (*changer*) *[vent, opinion]* to turn, shift, veer (round); *[chemin, promeneur]* to turn; *[chance]* to change. **bien/mal** ~ to turn out well/badly; **ça va mal** ~* that'll lead to trouble; ~ **au froid/au rouge** to turn cold/red; ~ **à l'avantage de qn** to turn to sb's advantage; ~ **à la bagarre** to turn *ou* degenerate into a fight; **sa bronchite a tourné en pneumonie** his bronchitis has turned *ou* developed into pneumonia; ~ **au drame** to take a dramatic turn. **(d)** *[lait]* to turn (sour). **faire** ~ to turn sour. **(e)** (*locutions*) ~ **à l'aigre** to turn sour; ~ **court** to come to a sudden end; ~ **de l'œil*** to pass out*, faint; ~ **en rond** to go round in circles; ~ **rond** to run smoothly; **elle ne tourne pas rond*** she must be a bit touched*; **qu'est-ce qui ne tourne pas rond?*** what's the matter?, what's wrong?, what's up?*; ~ **autour du pot*** to beat about the bush; **faire** ~ **qn en bourrique** to drive sb round the bend*.

3 se ~ *vpr* (*lit, fig*) **se** ~ **vers** to turn to; **se** ~ **contre qn** to turn against sb; **tourne-toi (de l'autre côté)** turn round *ou* the other way.

tournesol [turnəsɔl] *nm* sunflower.

tourneur [turnœr] *nm* (*Tech*) turner.

tournevis [turnəvis] *nm* screwdriver.

tourniquet [turnikɛ] *nm* (*barrière*) turnstile; (*porte*) revolving door; (*d'arrosage*) sprinkler hose; (*présentoir*) revolving stand; (*Méd*) tourniquet.

tournis* [turni] *nm*: **donner le** ~ **à qn** to make sb feel dizzy *ou* giddy.

tournoi [turnwa] *nm* tournament.

tournoyer [turnwaje] (8) *vi [eau, fumée]* to whirl, swirl, eddy; *[oiseaux]* to wheel (round); *[feuilles mortes]* to swirl around. **faire** ~ **qch** to whirl sth round. ♦ **tournoiement** *nm*: ~**(s)** whirling; swirling; eddying; wheeling.

tournure [turnyr] *nf* **(a)** (*tour de phrase*) turn of phrase; (*forme*) form. ~ **négative** negative form. **(b)** *[événements]* turn. **la situation a pris une mauvaise/meilleure** ~ the situation took a turn for the worse/for the better; **prendre** ~ to take shape. **(c)** ~ **d'esprit** turn *ou* cast of mind.

tourteau, *pl* ~**x** [turto] *nm* (sort of) crab.

tourterelle [turtərɛl] *nf* turtledove.

tous [tu] *V* **tout.**

Toussaint [tusɛ̃] *nf*: **la** ~ All Saints' Day.

tousser [tuse] (1) *vi [personne]* to cough; *[moteur]* to splutter, cough, hiccup. ♦ **toussoter** (1) *vi* to cough, have a slight cough.

tout [tu], **toute** [tut], *mpl* **tous** [tu] (*adj*) *ou* [tus] (*pron*), *fpl* **toutes** [tut] **1** *adj* **(a)** (*complet*) all (of), the whole (of). ~ **le, toute la** all (the), the whole (of the); **lire** ~ **Balzac** to read the whole of *ou* all (of) Balzac; **il a plu toute la nuit/toute une nuit** it rained the whole (of the) night *ou* all night (long)/for a whole night; ~ **le monde** everybody, everyone; ~ **le reste** (all) the rest; ~ **le temps** all the time; **toute la France** the whole of *ou* all France; **donner toute satisfaction** to give complete satisfaction; **en toute franchise** in all sincerity; **c'est toute une affaire** it's quite a business.

(b) (*tout à fait*) **c'est** ~ **le contraire** it's quite the opposite *ou* the very opposite; **lui** ~ **le premier** him *ou* he first of all; **c'est** ~ **autre chose** that's quite another matter; **c'est** ~ **le portrait de son père** he is the spitting image of his father.

(c) (*seul*) **c'est** ~ **l'effet que cela lui fait** that's all the effect *ou* the only effect it has on him; **c'est là** ~ **le problème** that's the whole problem; **cet enfant est toute ma joie** this child is all my joy.

(d) (*n'importe quel*) any, all. **toute personne** any person, everyone; **toute trace d'agitation a disparu** all *ou* any trace of agitation has gone; **à** ~ **instant** at any moment; **à** ~ **âge** at any age, at all ages; **pour** ~ **renseignement, téléphoner** ... for all information, ring ... .

(e) (*complètement*) **il était** ~ **à son travail** he was entirely taken up by his work; **habillé** ~ **en noir** dressed all in black; **un style** ~ **en nuances** a very subtle style.

(f) tous, toutes (*l'ensemble*) all, every; **toutes les personnes** all the people, everyone; **courir dans tous les sens** to run in all directions *ou* in every direction; **toutes sortes de** all sorts of, every kind of.

(g) tous *ou* **toutes les** (*chaque*) every; **tous les ans** every year; **tous les deux jours** every other day, every two days; **tous les 10 mètres** every 10 metres; **tous les trente-six du mois** once in a blue moon; **tous (les) deux** both (of them), the two of them; **tous (les) 3/4** all 3/4 (of them).

(h) (*locutions*) **en** ~ **bien** ~ **honneur** with the most honourable (of) intentions; **à** ~ **bout de champ** every now and then; **en** ~ **cas** in any case, at any rate; ~ **un chacun** every one of us; **de** ~ **côté** *chercher* on all sides, everywhere; **à tous égards** in every respect; **en** ~ **état de cause, de toute façon** in any case, anyway, anyhow; **à** ~ **instant** continually, constantly; **à toutes jambes** as fast as one's legs can carry one; **en tous lieux** everywhere; **faire** ~ **son possible** to do one's utmost; **toutes proportions gardées** relatively speaking, making due allowances; **à** ~ **propos** every other minute; **de** ~ **cœur** wholeheartedly; **de toute beauté** most beautiful, of the utmost beauty; **de** ~ **temps, de toute éternité** from time immemorial, since the beginning of time; **de** ~ **repos** easy; **à** ~ **prix** at all costs; **à toute vitesse** at full *ou* top speed; **il a une patience/un courage à toute épreuve** his patience/courage will stand any test, he has limitless patience/unshakeable courage; **selon toute apparence** to all appearances.

2 *pron indéf* **(a)** (*gén*) everything, all; (*n'importe quoi*) anything. **il a** ~ **organisé** he organized everything, he organized it all; **il vend de** ~ he sells everything; **c'est** ~ **ou rien** it's all or nothing; ~ **ce que** everything (that); all that.

(b) tous, toutes all; **vous tous** all of you; **tous ensemble** all together.

(c) (*locutions*) ~ **est bien qui finit bien** all's well that ends well; ... **et** ~ **et** ~* ... and all that sort of thing, ... and so on and so forth; ~ **est là** that's the whole point; **c'est** ~ that's all; **c'est** ~ **dire** I need say no more; **ce n'est pas** ~ **de partir, il faut arriver** it's not enough to set off, one must arrive as well; **il y avait des gens** ~ **ce qu'il y a de plus distingué** there were the most distinguished people there; **à** ~ **prendre,** ~ **bien considéré** all things considered, taking everything into consideration; (*Comm*) ~ **compris** inclusive, all-in; **avoir** ~ **d'un brigand** to be an absolute *ou* a real outlaw; **en** ~ in all; ~ **ce qui brille n'est pas or** all that glitters is not gold.

3 *adv* **(a)** *surpris, déçu* very, most; *cru* quite, completely. **les toutes premières années** the very first *ou* early years; **c'est une** ~ **autre histoire** that's quite another story; **c'est** ~ **naturel** it's perfectly *ou* quite natural; **la ville** ~ **entière** the whole town; ~ **nu** stark naked; ~ **neuf** brand new.

(b) (*quoique*) ~ **médecin qu'il soit** even though *ou* although he is a doctor; **toute malade qu'elle se dise** however *ou* no matter how ill she says she is.

(c) (*intensif*) ~ **près** very near *ou* close; ~ **là-bas/au bout** right over there/at the end; ~ **simplement** quite simply; **parler** ~ **bas** to speak very low; **il était** ~ **en sueur** he was running with sweat; **elle était** ~ **en larmes** she was in floods of tears; **le jardin est** ~ **en fleurs** the garden is a mass of flowers.

(d) ~ **en** + *participe présent*: ~ **en marchant** as *ou* while you walk, while walking.

(e) (*avec n*) **être** ~ **yeux/oreilles** to be all eyes/ears; **être** ~ **sucre** ~ **miel** to be all sweetness and light; ~ **laine** all wool; **être** ~ **feu** ~ **flammes** to be fired with enthusiasm.

(f) (*locutions*) ~ **à coup** all of a sudden, suddenly; ~ **à fait** quite, entirely; ~ **à l'heure** (*futur*) in a moment; (*passé*) a moment ago; **tous risques** *assurance etc* all-risks; ~ **de suite** straightaway, at once, immediately; (*Aut*) ~ **terrain** all-roads; ~ **au plus** at the (very) most; ~ **au moins** at (the very) least; ~ **d'abord** first of all, in the first place; ~ **de même** all the same, for all that; ~ **de même!** well really!; **idées toutes faites** ready-made ideas; **vendu** ~ **cuit** sold ready-cooked; **c'est du** ~ **cuit*** it's a cinch* *ou* a pushover*; **il est gentil** ~ **plein*** he is really very *ou* really awfully* nice; ~ **nouveau** ~ **beau** (just) wait till the novelty wears off; **c'est** ~ **comme*** it comes to the same thing really; **c'est** ~ **un** it's one and the same thing; **c'est** ~ **vu*** it's a foregone conclusion.

4 *nm* **(a)** (*ensemble*) whole. **vendre le** ~ to sell the (whole) lot.

(b) le ~ **est qu'il arrive à temps** the main *ou* most important thing is that he arrives in time; **du** ~ **au** ~ completely, utterly, entirely; **ce n'est pas le** ~***, il faut se dépécher** this isn't good enough, we'll have to hurry; **pas du** ~ not at all; **il n'y a plus du** ~ **de pain** there's no bread left at all. ♦ **tout-à-l'égout** *nm inv* mains drainage. ♦ **tout-petit,** *pl* ~**-**~**s** *nm* little one. ♦ **toute-puissance** *nf* omnipotence. ♦ **tout-puissant,** *f* ~**e-**~**e** *adj* omnipotent, all-powerful. **le T~-P~** the Almighty.

toutefois [tutfwa] *adv* however.

toutou* [tutu] *nm* doggie*, bow-wow*. **obéir à qn comme un** ~ to obey sb as meekly as a lamb.

toux [tu] *nf* cough.

toxique [tɔksik] **1** *adj* toxic, poisonous. **2** *nm* toxin, poison. ♦ **toxicologie** *nf* toxicology. ♦ **toxicologique** *adj* toxicological. ♦ **toxicologue** *nmf* toxicologist. ♦ **toxicomane** *nmf* drug addict. ♦ **toxicomanie** *nf* drug addiction. ♦ **toxine** *nf* toxin.

trac [tʀak] *nm* (*Théât, en public*) stage fright; (*aux examens etc*) nerves. **avoir le** ~ to get stage fright; to get nerves; **donner le** ~ **à qn** to give sb a fright.

tracas [tʀaka] *nm* worry. **donner du** *ou* **des** ~ **à qn** to give sb trouble, worry sb. ♦ **tracasser** (1) **1** *vt* to worry, bother. **2 se** ~ *vpr* to worry, fret.

trace [tʀas] *nf* **(a)** (*gén, fig: marque*) mark; (*empreinte d'animal, de pneu*) tracks; (*vestige de civilisation*) trace; (*indice*) sign. ~**s de pas** footprints; ~**s de doigt** finger marks; ~**s d'effraction** signs of a break-in. **(b)** (*quantité minime*) *[poison, substance]* trace. **sans une** ~ **d'accent étranger** without a *ou* any trace of a foreign accent. **(c) disparaître sans laisser de** ~**s** to disappear without trace; **il n'y avait pas** ~ **des documents** there was no trace of the documents; **être sur la** ~ **de** to be on the track of; **perdre la** ~ **d'un fugitif** to lose track of *ou* lose the trail of a fugitive; (*fig*) **marcher sur les** ~**s de qn** to follow in sb's footsteps.

tracé [tʀase] *nm* **(a)** (*plan*) layout, plan. **(b)** (*parcours*) *[autoroute]* route; *[rivière]* line, course; *[côte, crête]* line. **(c)** (*graphisme*) line.

tracer [tʀase] (3) *vt* (*dessiner*) to draw; (*écrire*) to trace; (*frayer*) *route* to open up. (*fig*) ~ **la voie à qn** to show sb the way.

trachée [tʀaʃe] *nf*: ~**(-artère)** windpipe.

tract [tʀakt] *nm* leaflet.

tractations [tʀaktɑsjɔ̃] *nfpl* dealings, bargaining, negotiations.

tracteur [tʀaktœʀ] *nm* tractor.

traction [tʀaksjɔ̃] *nf* (*gén*) traction. (*Aut*) ~ **avant** car with front-wheel drive.

tradition [tʀadisjɔ̃] *nf* (*gén*) tradition. **il est de** ~ **que** it is a tradition *ou* traditional that. ♦ **traditionnel, -elle** *adj* traditional; (*: *habituel*) **sa** ~**elle robe noire*** her good old* *ou* usual black dress. ♦ **traditionnellement** *adv* traditionally; (*: *habituellement*) as usual.

traduire [tʀadɥiʀ] (38) **1** *vt* **(a)** *texte, auteur* to translate (*en* into); *sentiment* to convey, render, express. **cela traduit notre inquiétude** this shows *ou* conveys our anxiety. **(b)** ~ **qn en justice** to bring sb before the courts. **2 se** ~ *vpr* (*gén*) to be translated. **ça va se** ~ **par une augmentation des impôts** the visible outcome will be an increase in taxes, it will be translated into an increase in taxes. ♦ **traducteur, -trice** *nm,f* translator. ♦ **traduction** *nf* translation; rendering; expression. **la** ~ **de ce texte en anglais** the translation of *ou* translating this text into English. ♦ **traduisible** *adj* translatable.

trafic [tʀafik] *nm* **(a)** (*péj*) traffic; (†: *commerce*) trade (*de* in). ~ **d'armes** arms dealing, gunrunning; ~ **de la drogue** drug trafficking. **(b)** (*activités suspectes*) dealings; (*: *micmac*) funny business*, goings-on*. **(c)** (*Aut, Aviat, Rail*) traffic. ♦ **trafiquant, e** *nm,f* (*péj*) trafficker. ~ **d'armes** arms dealer, gunrunner. ♦ **trafiquer** (1) **1** *vi* (*péj*) to traffic, trade (illicitly). **2** *vt* (*: *péj*) *moteur, vin* to doctor*.

tragédie [tʀaʒedi] *nf* (*gén, Théât*) tragedy. ♦ **tragédien, -ienne** *nm,f* tragic actor *ou* actress. ♦ **tragique 1** *adj* (*Théât, fig*) tragic. **ce n'est pas** ~ it's not the end of the world*. **2** *nm* (*auteur*) tragic author; (*tragédie*) tragedy. **prendre qch au** ~ to make a tragedy out of sth. ♦ **tragiquement** *adv* tragically.

trahir [tʀaiʀ] (2) *vt ami, patrie* to betray; *secret, émotion* to betray, give away. **ses nerfs l'ont trahi** his nerves failed him; **ces mots ont trahi ma pensée** those words misrepresented my thoughts. ♦ **trahison** *nf* (*gén*) betrayal; (*Jur, Mil: crime*) treason.

train [tʀɛ̃] *nm* **(a)** (*Rail*) train. ~ **omnibus/direct** slow *ou* stopping/fast *ou* non-stop train; ~ **de marchandises/voyageurs** goods/passenger train; ~ **auto-couchettes** car-sleeper train; **prendre le** ~ to take the train; **prendre le** ~ **en marche** (*lit*) to get on the moving train; (*fig*) to jump on the bandwagon. **(b)** (*allure*) pace. **aller son petit** ~ to go along at one's own pace; **aller bon** ~ *[affaire, voiture]* to make good progress; *[commentaires]* to be rife; **il allait à un** ~ **d'enfer** he was going hell for leather; **au** ~ **où il travaille** (at) the rate he is working; **au** *ou* **du** ~ **où vont les choses** at THIS rate. **(c) être en** ~ (*en forme*) to be in good form; (*gai*) to be in good spirits; **mettre un travail en** ~ to get a job under way *ou* started off; **mise en** ~ *[travail]* starting (up), start; (*exercices de gym*) warm-up; **elle ne se sent pas très en** ~ she doesn't feel too good *ou* too bright*. **(d) être en** ~ **de faire qch** to be doing sth; **être en** ~ **de manger** to be (busy) eating. **(e)** (*ensemble*) *[bateaux, mulets]* train, line; *[réformes, mesures]* set, batch. ~ **de pneus** set of (four) tyres; (*Aut*) ~ **avant/arrière** front/rear wheel-axle unit; *[animal]* ~ **de devant** forequarters; ~ **de derrière** hindquarters; ~ **d'atterrissage** undercarriage, landing gear. **(f)** ~ **de vie** style of living, life style.

traînant, e [tʀɛnɑ̃, ɑ̃t] *adj voix* drawling.

traînard, e [tʀɛnaʀ, aʀd(ə)] *nm,f* (*en marchant*) straggler; (*: *au travail*) slowcoach*.

traîne [tʀɛn] *nf [robe]* train. (*fig*) **être à la** ~ (*en remorque*) to be in tow; (*: *en retard*) to lag behind.

traîneau, *pl* ~**x** [tʀɛno] *nm* sleigh, sledge, sled (*US*).

traînée [tʀene] *nf* (*sur le sol*) trail, tracks; (*sur un*

mur, dans le ciel) streak. **se répandre comme une ~ de poudre** to spread like wildfire.
traîner [tʀene] (1) **1** *vt objet lourd, personne* to drag (along). **~ les pieds** to drag one's feet, shuffle along; **~ la jambe** to limp, hobble; **~ qn dans la boue** to drag sb through the mud; (*fig*) **~ un boulet** to have a millstone round one's neck; **elle est obligée de ~ ses enfants partout** she has to trail *ou* drag her children round (with her) everywhere; **elle traîne un mauvais rhume** she has a bad cold she can't get rid of. **2** *vi* **(a)** *[personne]* (*rester en arrière*) to lag *ou* trail behind; (*péj: errer, s'attarder*) to hang about. **~ en chemin** to dawdle on the way. **(b)** *[chose]* (*être éparpillé*) to lie about *ou* around. **des idées qui traînent partout** ideas that float around everywhere. **(c)** *[conversation, procès, maladie]* **~ (en longueur)** to drag on; **ça n'a pas traîné!*** that wasn't long coming!; **faire ~ qch** to drag sth out; **doctrine où traînent des relents de fascisme** doctrine with a lingering whiff of fascism about it. **(d)** *[robe]* to trail. **~ par terre** to trail *ou* hang *ou* drag on the ground. **3 se ~** *vpr* **(a)** *[personne]* to drag o.s. (about *ou* along). **se ~ par terre** to crawl on the ground; (*fig*) **se ~ aux pieds de qn** to grovel at sb's feet. **(b)** *[conversation, journée, hiver]* to drag on.
train-train [tʀɛ̃tʀɛ̃] *nm* humdrum routine.
traire [tʀɛʀ] (50) *vt vache* to milk; *lait* to draw.
trait [tʀɛ] *nm* **(a)** (*ligne*) line. **faire un ~** to draw a line; **~ de plume/de crayon** stroke of the pen/of the pencil; **~ d'union** (*Typ*) hyphen; (*fig*) link; **biffer qch d'un ~** to score *ou* cross sth out; (*lit, fig*) **à grands ~s** roughly. **(b)** (*caractéristique*) feature, trait; (*acte*) act. **avoir des ~s de ressemblance avec** to have certain features in common with; **~ de courage** act of courage. **(c)** (*physionomie*) **~s** features. **(d)** (†: *projectile*) arrow, dart; (*littér: critique*) taunt, gibe. **filer comme un ~** to be off like an arrow *ou* a shot; **~ d'esprit** flash *ou* shaft of wit; **~ de génie** brainwave, flash of genius. **(e)** (*courroie*) trace. **animal de ~** draught animal. **(f)** (*gorgée*) draught, gulp. **d'un ~** *boire* in one gulp; *dormir* uninterruptedly, without a break. **(g)** (*rapport*) **avoir ~ à** to relate to, have to do with, concern.
traite [tʀɛt] *nf* **(a)** (*trafic*) **~ des Noirs** slave trade. **(b)** (*Comm: billet*) draft, bill. **(c)** (*parcours*) stretch. **d'une (seule) ~** at a stretch. **(d)** *[vache]* milking.
traité [tʀete] *nm* (*livre*) treatise; (*convention*) treaty.
traitement [tʀɛtmɑ̃] *nm* **(a)** *[personne]* treatment; (*Méd*) course of treatment. **mauvais ~s** ill-treatment. **(b)** (*rémunération*) salary. **(c)** *[matières premières]* processing, treating.
traiter [tʀete] (1) **1** *vt* **(a)** *personne, animal* to treat; (*Méd*) to treat; (†) *invités* to entertain. **~ qn bien/mal** to treat sb well/badly; **~ qn durement** to be hard with *ou* on sb; **~ qn en enfant** to treat sb as *ou* like a child; **se faire ~ pour** to undergo treatment for, be treated for. **(b)** (*qualifier*) to call. **~ qn de menteur** to call sb a liar. **(c)** *question* to treat, deal with; (*Art*) *thème* to treat; (*Comm*) *affaire* to handle, deal with. **(d)** (*Tech*) to treat, process. **non traité** untreated. **2 ~ de** *vt indir sujet, problème* to deal with, treat of. **3** *vi* (*négocier*) to deal, have dealings (*avec* with).
traiteur [tʀɛtœʀ] *nm* caterer.
traître, traîtresse [tʀɛtʀ(ə), tʀɛtʀɛs] **1** *adj* (*lit, fig*) treacherous. **ne pas dire un ~ mot** not to breathe a (single) word. **2** *nm* (*gén*) traitor; (*Théât*) villain. **prendre/attaquer qn en ~** to play an underhand trick/make an insidious attack on sb. **3** *nf* traitress. ♦ **traîtreusement** *adv* treacherously. ♦ **traîtrise** *nf*: **la ~** treacherousness; **une ~** a treachery.
trajectoire [tʀaʒɛktwaʀ] *nf* trajectory.
trajet [tʀaʒɛ] *nm* (*à parcourir*) distance; (*itinéraire*) route; (*voyage*) journey; (*par mer*) voyage; (*Anat*) *[nerf, artère]* course. **quel ~ il a parcouru depuis son dernier roman!** what a long way he has come since his last novel!
tralala* [tʀalala] *nm* (*luxe, apprêts*) fuss.
trame [tʀam] *nf [tissu]* weft, woof; *[roman]* framework; *[vie]* web. **usé jusqu'à la ~** threadbare.
tramer [tʀame] (1) *vt évasion* to plot; *complot* to hatch. **il se trame qch** there's sth brewing.
tramway [tʀamwɛ] *nm* (*moyen de transport*) tram(way); (*voiture*) tram(car).
tranchant, e [tʀɑ̃ʃɑ̃, ɑ̃t] **1** *adj* **(a)** *couteau, arête* sharp. **du côté ~** with the cutting edge. **(b)** *personne* sharp, cutting. **2** *nm* cutting edge.
tranche [tʀɑ̃ʃ] *nf* **(a)** *[pain, jambon]* slice; *[bacon]* rasher. **~ de bœuf** beefsteak; **couper en ~s** to slice. **(b)** (*bord*) *[livre, planche]* edge. **(c)** (*section*) section. (*Admin*) **~ d'âge/de salaires** age/wage bracket.
trancher [tʀɑ̃ʃe] (1) **1** *vt* **(a)** *corde* to cut, sever. **~ le cou à qn** to cut off sb's head; **~ la gorge à qn** to cut *ou* slit sb's throat. **(b)** *discussion* to conclude, bring to a close; *question, difficulté* to settle, decide. **~ court *ou* net** to bring to a firm conclusion; **il faut ~** we have to take a decision. **2** *vi [couleur]* to stand out clearly (*sur, avec* against); *[trait, qualité]* to contrast strongly *ou* sharply (*sur, avec* with). ♦ **tranché, e**[1] *adj couleurs* clear, distinct; *opinion, limite* clear-cut, definite. ♦ **tranchée**[2] *nf* (*fossé*) trench.
tranquille [tʀɑ̃kil] *adj* **(a)** (*calme*) quiet, tranquil (*littér*); (*paisible*) peaceful. **aller d'un pas ~** to walk calmly; **se tenir ~** to be quiet; **nous étions bien ~s** we were having a nice quiet time; **j'aime être ~** I like (to have) some peace; **laisser qn ~** to leave sb alone, to leave sb in peace; **laisser qch ~** to leave sth alone. **(b)** (*rassuré*) **être ~** to be easy in one's mind; **tu peux être ~** you needn't worry; **pour avoir l'esprit ~** to set my (*ou* his *etc*) mind at rest *ou* at ease; **avoir la conscience ~** to be at peace with one's conscience, have a clear conscience; **tu peux être ~ que ...** you may be sure that ..., rest assured that ... . ♦ **tranquillement** *adv* quietly; tranquilly; peacefully. ♦ **tranquillisant, e 1** *adj nouvelle* reassuring; *effet, produit* soothing, tranquillizing. **2** *nm* (*Méd*) tranquillizer. ♦ **tranquilliser** (1) *vt*: **~ qn** to reassure sb; **se ~** to set one's mind at rest. ♦ **tranquillité** *nf* quietness; tranquillity; peacefulness. **en toute ~** *agir* without being bothered *ou* disturbed; *partir* with complete peace of mind; **troubler la ~ publique** to disturb the peace; **travailler dans la ~** to work in peace (and quiet); **~ (d'esprit)** peace of mind; **~ matérielle** material security.
trans ... [tʀɑ̃z] *préf* trans ... .
transaction [tʀɑ̃zaksjɔ̃] *nf* (*Comm*) transaction.
transatlantique [tʀɑ̃zatlɑ̃tik] **1** *adj* transatlantic. **2** *nm* (*paquebot*) transatlantic liner; (*fauteuil*) deckchair.
transbahuter* [tʀɑ̃zbayte] (1) *vt* to shift, lug along*.
transborder [tʀɑ̃sbɔʀde] (1) *vt* (*Naut*) to tran(s)ship; (*Rail*) to transfer. ♦ **transbordement** *nm* tran(s)shipment; transfer. ♦ **transbordeur** *nm*: **pont ~** transporter bridge.
transcendance [tʀɑ̃sɑ̃dɑ̃s] *nf* transcendence. ♦ **transcendant, e** *adj* (*sublime*) transcendent; (*Philos, Math*) transcendental. ♦ **transcendental, e,** *mpl* **-aux** *adj* transcendental. ♦ **transcender** (1) **1** *vt* to transcend. **2 se ~** *vpr* to transcend o.s.
transcrire [tʀɑ̃skʀiʀ] (39) *vt* (*copier*) to copy out; (*Mus, Ling*) to transcribe. ♦ **transcription** *nf* copying out; transcription.
transe [tʀɑ̃s] *nf* **(a)** (*état second*) trance. **être/entrer en ~** to be in/to go into a trance. **(b)** (*affres*) **~s** agony; **dans les ~s** in agony; **dans**

les ~s de l'attente in agonies of anticipation.

transférer [tʀɑ̃sfeʀe] (6) *vt* to transfer. ♦ **transfert** *nm* transfer; (*Psych*) transference.

transfigurer [tʀɑ̃sfigyʀe] (1) *vt* to transfigure.

transformer [tʀɑ̃sfɔʀme] (1) **1** *vt* (*gén*) to change, alter; (*radicalement*) to transform; *magasin, essai de rugby* to convert; *matière première* to convert, process. **le bonheur l'a transformé** happiness has transformed him *ou* made a new man of him; **~ qch en** to turn *ou* convert sth into; **elle a fait ~ son manteau en jaquette** she's had her coat made *ou* converted into a jacket. **2 se ~** *vpr [embryon]* to be transformed, transform itself; *[énergie, matière]* to be converted; *[personne, pays]* to change, alter; (*radicalement*) to be transformed (*en* into). ♦ **transformable** *adj structure, canapé* convertible; *aspect* transformable. ♦ **transformateur** *nm* transformer. ♦ **transformation** *nf* change; alteration; transformation; conversion; processing. **industries de ~** processing industries.

transfuge [tʀɑ̃sfyʒ] *nmf* (*Mil, Pol*) renegade.

transfusion [tʀɑ̃sfyzjɔ̃] *nf*: **~ (sanguine)** (blood) transfusion.

transgresser [tʀɑ̃sgʀese] (1) *vt règle* to infringe, contravene; *ordre* to disobey, go against. ♦ **transgression** *nf* infringement, contravention; disobedience.

transiger [tʀɑ̃ziʒe] (3) *vi* to compromise (*avec* with).

transir [tʀɑ̃ziʀ] (2) *vt [froid]* to chill to the bone, numb; *[peur]* to paralyze, numb. ♦ **transi, e** *adj* numb (with cold).

transistor [tʀɑ̃zistɔʀ] *nm* transistor. ♦ **transistorisé, e** *adj* transistorized.

transit [tʀɑ̃zit] *nm* transit. **en ~** in transit; **de ~** transit. ♦ **transiter** (1) *vti* to pass in transit.

transitif, -ive [tʀɑ̃zitif, iv] *adj* transitive.

transition [tʀɑ̃zisjɔ̃] *nf* transition. **de ~** *période, mesure* transitional; **sans ~** without any transition.

transitoire [tʀɑ̃zitwaʀ] *adj* transitional.

translucide [tʀɑ̃slysid] *adj* translucent.

transmettre [tʀɑ̃smɛtʀ(ə)] (56) *vt* **(a)** (*lit, fig: léguer*) to transmit, pass on; *biens* to hand down; *fonctions, titre* to hand over. **(b)** *message* to pass on, convey; *lettre* to send on, forward; (*Téléc*) to transmit; (*Rad, TV*) to broadcast. **(c)** (*Sport*) *ballon* to pass; *témoin, flambeau* to hand over, pass on. **(d)** (*Sci*) *énergie, impulsion* to transmit; (*Méd*) *maladie* to pass on, transmit. ♦ **transmetteur** *nm* transmitter. ♦ **transmissible** *adj* transmissible, transmittable. ♦ **transmission** *nf* transmission; passing on; handing down; handing over; sending on, forwarding; broadcasting. (*Pol*) **~ des pouvoirs** handing over *ou* transfer of power; (*Mil: service*) **~s** ≃ Signals (corps); **~ de pensée** thought transfer, telepathy.

transparaître [tʀɑ̃spaʀɛtʀ(ə)] (57) *vi* to show (through). ♦ **transparent, e** *adj* (*lit, fig*) transparent; *eau, ciel, yeux* transparent, limpid, clear. ♦ **transparence** *nf* transparency, transparence; limpidity, clearness. **regarder qch par ~** to look at sth against the light; **voir qch par ~** to see sth showing through.

transpercer [tʀɑ̃spɛʀse] (3) *vt* (*lit, fig*) to go through, pierce; (*d'un coup de couteau*) to stab. **~ qn du regard** to give sb a piercing look.

transpirer [tʀɑ̃spiʀe] (1) *vi* **(a)** (*lit*) to perspire, sweat. **il transpire des mains** his hands perspire *ou* sweat, he has sweaty hands; **~ à grosses gouttes** to be running *ou* streaming with sweat; **~ sur un devoir*** to sweat over an exercise*. **(b)** *[secret]* to come to light, leak out. ♦ **transpiration** *nf* perspiration. **être en ~** to be perspiring *ou* sweating *ou* in a sweat.

transplanter [tʀɑ̃splɑ̃te] (1) *vt* (*Bot, Méd, fig*) to transplant. ♦ **transplantation** *nf* (*action*) transplantation; (*Méd: intervention*) transplant. **~ cardiaque** heart transplant.

transport [tʀɑ̃spɔʀ] *nm* **(a)** (*action*) (*gén*) carrying; (*par véhicule*) transport(ation), conveyance. **un train se chargera du ~ des bagages** the luggage will be taken by train; **endommagé pendant le ~** damaged in transit; **~ par train** rail transport(ation); **entreprise de ~(s)** transport business; **frais de ~** transportation costs. **(b) les ~s** transport; **~s publics** *ou* **en commun** public transport; **~(s) routier(s)** road haulage *ou* transport; **~s aériens** air transport. **(c)** (*émotion*) transport. **avec des ~s de joie** with transports of delight; **~ au cerveau** seizure, stroke.

transporter [tʀɑ̃spɔʀte] (1) **1** *vt* **(a)** (*gén, fig*) to carry; (*avec véhicule*) to transport, carry, convey; *énergie, son* to carry. **transporté d'urgence à l'hôpital** rushed to hospital; **ils ont dû ~ le matériel à bras** they had to move the equipment by hand; **cette musique nous transporte dans un autre monde** this music transports us into another world. **(b)** (*exalter*) to carry away, send into raptures. **~ qn de joie** to send sb into raptures; **être transporté de joie** to be in transports of delight, be carried away with delight. **2 se ~** *vpr* (*littér: se déplacer*) to betake o.s., repair (*à, dans* to). ♦ **transporteur** *nm* (*entrepreneur*) haulage contractor, carrier; (*appareil*) conveyor.

transposer [tʀɑ̃spoze] (1) *vt* to transpose. ♦ **transposition** *nf* transposition.

transvaser [tʀɑ̃svɑze] (1) *vt* to decant.

transversal, e, *mpl* **-aux** [tʀɑ̃svɛʀsal, o] *adj coupe, barre* cross; *mur, rue* which runs across; *vallée* transverse. ♦ **transversalement** *adv* across, crosswise.

trapèze [tʀapɛz] *nm* **(a)** (*Géom*) trapezium, trapezoid (*US*). **(b)** (*Sport*) trapeze. **~ volant** flying trapeze. ♦ **trapéziste** *nmf* trapeze artist.

trappe [tʀap] *nf* trap door; (*Tech*) hatch; (*pour parachute*) exit door; (*piège*) trap.

trappeur [tʀapœʀ] *nm* trapper, fur trader.

trapu, e [tʀapy] *adj* **(a)** *personne* squat, stocky, thickset; *maison* squat. **(b)** (*arg Scol*) *élève* brainy*; *problème* rough, tough. **~ en maths** terrific at maths*.

traquenard [tʀaknaʀ] *nm* (*lit*) trap; (*fig*) pitfall, trap.

traquer [tʀake] (1) *vt gibier, fugitif* to track down, hunt down; *abus* to hunt down; *débiteur, vedette* to hound, pursue. **bête traquée** hunted animal.

traumatiser [tʀomatize] (1) *vt* to traumatize. ♦ **traumatisme** *nm* traumatism.

travail, *pl* **-aux** [tʀavaj, o] *nm* **(a)** (*activité*) **le ~** work; **~ manuel/scolaire** manual/school work; **c'est le ~ de l'électricien** that's the electrician's job; **observer qn au ~** to watch sb at work *ou* working; **séance de ~** working session; **avoir du ~/beaucoup de ~** to have (some) work/a lot of work to do; **se mettre au ~** to set to *ou* get down to work. **(b)** (*tâche*) **un ~** work, a job; **c'est un ~ de spécialiste** (*difficile à faire*) it's work for a specialist, it's a specialist's job; (*bien fait*) it's the work of a specialist; **commencer un ~** to start a piece of work *ou* a job; **un ~ de Romain** a Herculean task. **(c) ~aux** work; **~aux pratiques/scientifiques/de réparation/de plomberie** practical/scientific/repair/plumbing work; **~aux d'approche** (*Mil*) sapping *ou* approach works; (*fig*) manœuvres; **faire faire des ~aux dans la maison** to have some work *ou* some jobs done in the house; **les ~aux des champs** farm work; **les ~aux pénibles** the heavy work *ou* tasks; **~aux ménagers** housework; (*Scol*) **~aux manuels** handicrafts; (*Admin*) **~aux publics** public works; (*Comm*) **'pendant les ~aux'** 'during alterations'; **attention! ~aux!** caution! work in progress!; (*sur la route*) road works ahead! **(d)** (*métier*) **le ~** work; **un ~** a job, an occupation;

être sans ~ to be out of work *ou* without a job *ou* unemployed; **accident du** ~ industrial accident; ~ **d'équipe/en usine** team/factory work; ~ **à la pièce** piecework; ~ **à la chaîne** assembly line *ou* production line work; ~ **au noir*** moonlighting*; **cesser le** ~ to stop work, down tools; **reprendre le** ~ to go back to work. **(e)** (*Écon: opposé au capital*) labour. **(f)** *[pierre, bois, cuir]* (*façonnage*) working; (*facture*) work. **dentelle d'un** ~ **très fin** finely-worked lace; **c'est un très joli** ~ it's a very nice piece of craftsmanship *ou* work. **(g)** *[machine, organe]* (*fonctionnement*) working(s); (*opération*) operation. ~ **musculaire** work of the muscles. **(h)** *[gel, érosion]* work; *[bois]* warp, warping; *[vin, cidre]* working. **le** ~ **du temps** the work of time. **(i)** (*Phys*) work. **unité de** ~ unit of work. **(j)** (*Méd*) *[femme]* labour; **femme en** ~ woman in labour. **entrer en** ~ to go into *ou* start labour; **salle de** ~ labour ward. **(k)** ~**aux forcés** hard labour.

travaillé, e [tʀavaje] *adj bois, cuivre* worked, wrought; *style* polished; *meuble, ornement* finely-worked. (*tourmenté*) ~ **par** tormented by.

travailler [tʀavaje] (1) **1** *vi* **(a)** (*gén*) to work; *[artiste]* (*s'exercer*) to practise, train. **commencer à/finir de** ~ to start/stop work; **je vais** ~ **un peu** I'm going to do some work; **faire** ~ **sa tête** to set one's mind to work; **faire** ~ **ses bras** to exercise one's arms; **va** ~ (go and) get on with your work; **sa femme travaille** his wife works/ *ou* goes out to work; **le temps travaille pour/contre eux** time is on their side/against them. **(b)** *[métal, bois]* to warp; *[vin, imagination]* to work. **2** *vt* **(a)** (*façonner*) *verre, cuir* to work; *discipline, style* to work on. ~ **la terre** to work the land; (*Culin*) ~ **la pâte** to work the mixture; ~ **le chant/piano** to practise singing/the piano; ~ **les esprits** to work on people's minds. **(b)** *[doutes]* to distract, worry; *[douleur]* to distract, torment. **cette idée le travaille** this idea is on his mind *ou* is preying on his mind. **3** ~ **à** *vt indir projet* to work on; *but* to work for. ~ **à la perte de qn** to work towards sb's downfall.

travailleur, -euse [tʀavajœʀ, øz] **1** *adj* hard-working. **2** *nm,f* worker. **les** ~**s** the workers, working people; ~**s étrangers** immigrant workers; ~ **agricole** agricultural *ou* farm worker; ~ **de force** labourer; ~ **indépendant** self-employed person.

travailliste [tʀavajist(ə)] **1** *adj* Labour. **2** *nmf* Labour Party member. **il est** ~ he is Labour; **les** ~**s** Labour.

travée [tʀave] *nf* **(a)** (*section*) *[mur]* bay; *[pont]* span. **(b)** (*rangée*) row (of benches *ou* seats).

travers[1] [tʀavɛʀ] *nm* (*défaut*) failing, fault, shortcoming.

travers[2] [tʀavɛʀ] *nm* **(a) en** ~ across, crosswise; **en** ~ **de** across; **le véhicule se mit en** ~ **de la route** the vehicle stopped sideways on *ou* stopped across the road; **se mettre en** ~ **des projets de qn** to stand in the way of sb's plans; **en** ~**, par le** ~ *navire* abeam, on the beam. **(b) au** ~ **(de)** through; **le vent passe au** ~ the wind comes (right) through; (*fig*) **passer au** ~ to get away with it. **(c) de** ~ *nez* crooked; **comprendre de** ~ to misunderstand; **marcher de** ~ (*lit*) to stagger *ou* totter along; (*fig*) to be going wrong; **il répond toujours de** ~ he never gives a proper answer; **elle a mis son chapeau de** ~ she has put her hat on crooked, her hat is not on straight; **il a l'esprit un peu de** ~ he's slightly odd; **il l'a regardé de** ~ he looked askance at him, he gave him a funny look; **il a avalé sa soupe de** ~ his soup has gone down the wrong way; **prendre qch de** ~ to take sth the wrong way, take sth amiss. **(d) à** ~ (*lit, fig*) through; *campagne* across, through; **à** ~ **le grillage/les siècles** through the fence/the centuries; **à** ~ **champs** through *ou* across the fields.

traverse [tʀavɛʀs(ə)] *nf* (*Rail*) sleeper; (*barre transversale*) strut, crosspiece.

traversée [tʀavɛʀse] *nf* (*gén*) crossing. **la** ~ **de la ville en voiture** going through *ou* crossing the town by car; **faire la** ~ **d'un fleuve à la nage** to swim across a river.

traverser [tʀavɛʀse] (1) *vt* **(a)** *rue, pont, mer* to cross; *forêt, tunnel,* (*fig*) *crise* to go through. ~ **une rivière à la nage** to swim across a river; ~ **la foule** to make one's way through the crowd. **(b)** *[pont, route]* to cross, run across; *[tunnel]* to cross under; *[barre, trait]* to run across; *[projectile, infiltration]* to go *ou* come through. ~ **qch de part en part** to go right through sth; **une idée lui traversa l'esprit** an idea passed through his mind *ou* occurred to him.

traversin [tʀavɛʀsɛ̃] *nm [lit]* bolster.

travestir [tʀavɛstiʀ] (2) *vt personne* to dress up; *vérité, paroles* to travesty, misrepresent. ♦ **travesti** *nm* (*acteur*) drag artist; (*Psych: déséquilibré*) transvestite; (*déguisement*) fancy dress.

trébucher [tʀebyʃe] (1) *vi* (*lit, fig*) to stumble. **faire** ~ **qn** to trip sb up; ~ **sur** *ou* **contre** *pierre* to stumble over, trip against; *mot* to stumble over.

trèfle [tʀɛfl(ə)] *nm* (*Bot*) clover; (*Cartes*) clubs. ~ **à quatre feuilles** four-leaf clover.

tréfonds [tʀefɔ̃] *nm*: **le** ~ **de** the inmost depths of; **dans le** ~ **de mon cœur** deep down in my heart.

treillage [tʀɛjaʒ] *nm* (*sur un mur*) lattice work, trellis(work); (*clôture*) trellis fence.

treille [tʀɛj] *nf* (*tonnelle*) vine arbour; (*vigne*) climbing vine.

treillis [tʀeji] *nm* **(a)** (*en bois*) trellis; (*en métal*) wire-mesh; (*Constr*) lattice work. **(b)** (*Tex*) canvas; (*Mil: tenue*) combat uniform.

treize [tʀɛz] *adj inv, nm inv* thirteen; *V* **six.** ♦ **treizième** *adj, nmf* thirteenth; *V* **sixième.** ♦ **treizièmement** *adv* in the thirteenth place.

tréma [tʀema] *nm* dieresis. **i** ~ i dieresis.

tremble [tʀɑ̃bl(ə)] *nm* aspen.

tremblement [tʀɑ̃bləmɑ̃] *nm* (*frisson*) shiver. ~**(s)** trembling; **avec des** ~**s dans la voix** with a trembling *ou* quavering voice; **tout le** ~* the whole caboodle*; ~ **de terre** earthquake.

trembler [tʀɑ̃ble] (1) *vi* to tremble; (*de froid, fièvre*) to shiver (*de* with); *[feuille]* to flutter; *[lumière]* to flicker; *[voix]* to quaver. **tremblant de tout son corps** shaking *ou* trembling all over; **faire** ~ **le sol** to make the ground tremble; **la terre a tremblé** there has been an earth tremor; (*fig: avoir peur*) ~ **pour qn/qch** to fear for *ou* tremble for sb/sth. ♦ **tremblote*** *nf*: **avoir la** ~ (*froid*) to have the shivers*; (*peur*) to have the jitters*; (*vieillesse*) to have the shakes*. ♦ **tremblotement** *nm*: ~**(s)** trembling. ♦ **trembloter** (1) *vi* to tremble *ou* shake *ou* flutter *ou* flicker slightly.

trémolo [tʀemɔlo] *nm [instrument]* tremolo; *[voix]* quaver. **avec des** ~**s dans la voix** with a tremor in one's voice.

trémousser (se) [tʀemuse] (1) *vpr* (*sur sa chaise*) to jig about, wriggle; (*en marchant*) to wiggle.

trempe [tʀɑ̃p] *nf* **(a)** *[acier]* (*processus*) quenching; (*qualité*) temper. **(b)** *[personne, âme]* calibre. **(c)** (*) (*gifle*) slap; (*râclée*) hiding*.

tremper [tʀɑ̃pe] (1) **1** *vt* **(a)** *[pluie]* to soak, drench. **se faire** ~ to get drenched. **(b)** (*plus gén faire* ~) *linge* to soak; *aliments* to soak, steep; *papier* to damp, wet; *tiges de fleurs* to stand in water. **(c)** (*plonger*) to dip (*dans* into, in). ~ **sa main dans l'eau** to dip one's hand in the water. **(d)** (*Tech*) *métal, lame* to quench; (*littér*) *caractère* to steel, strengthen. **2** *vi* **(a)** *[tige de fleur]* to stand in water; *[linge, graines]* to soak. **(b)** (*péj*) ~ **dans** *crime* to take part in, have a hand in, be involved in. **3 se** ~ *vpr* (*bain rapide*) to have a quick dip; (*se mouiller*) to get (o.s.) soaked, get drenched. ♦ **trempé, e** *adj* **(a)** (*mouillé*) soaked, drenched. ~ **de sueur** bathed in perspiration; ~ **jusqu'aux os** wet through, soaked to the skin. **(b)** (*Tech*) tempered. ♦ **trempette*** *nf* (*baignade*) (quick) dip. **faire** ~ to have a (quick) dip.

tremplin [tʀɑ̃plɛ̃] *nm [piscine]* diving-board, spring-board; *[gymnase]* springboard; *[ski]* ski-jump; (*fig*) springboard.

trente [tʀɑ̃t] *adj inv, nm inv* thirty. **il y en a ~-six modèles*** there are umpteen* models; **il n'y a pas ~-six possibilités*** there aren't all that many choices; **voir ~-six chandelles*** to see stars; **se mettre sur son ~ et un*** to put on one's Sunday best; *V* **six, soixante.** ♦ **trentaine** *nf* about thirty, thirty or so; *V* **soixantaine.** ♦ **trentième** *adj, nmf* thirtieth; *V* **sixième, soixantième.**

trépan [tʀepɑ̃] *nm* trepan. ♦ **trépanation** *nf* trepanation. ♦ **trépaner** (1) *vt* to trepan.

trépas [tʀepɑ] *nm* (*littér*) demise, death. ♦ **trépassé, e** *adj, nm,f* (*littér*) deceased. ♦ **trépasser** (1) *vi* (*littér*) to pass away.

trépider [tʀepide] (1) *vi* to vibrate, reverberate. ♦ **trépidant, e** *adj* vibrating; *rythme* pulsating; *vie* hectic, busy. ♦ **trépidation** *nf* vibration, reverberation.

trépied [tʀepje] *nm* tripod.

trépigner [tʀepiɲe] (1) *vi* to stamp one's feet (*de* with). ♦ **trépignement** *nm*: ~**(s)** stamping (of feet).

très [tʀɛ] *adv* very; (*avec ptp*) (very) much. ~ **difficile** very *ou* most difficult; ~ **admiré** greatly *ou* highly *ou* (very) much admired; ~ **peu de gens** very few people; **avoir ~ peur** to be very much afraid *ou* very frightened; **c'est ~ nécessaire** it's most essential; **ils sont ~ amis** they are great friends; **il est ~ en avant** (*sur le chemin*) he is well *ou* a long way ahead; ~ **bien, si vous insistez** all right *ou* very well, if you insist.

trésor [tʀezɔʀ] *nm* **(a)** (*gén, fig*) treasure. **chasse au** ~ treasure hunt; **des ~s de** *renseignements, patience* a wealth of; **dépenser des ~s d'ingéniosité** to expend boundless ingenuity. **(b)** (*musée*) treasure-house, treasury. **(c)** (*Fin*) *[roi, état]* exchequer, finances. (*service*) **T~ (public)** public revenue department. ♦ **trésorerie** *nf* (*bureaux*) *[Trésor public]* public revenue office; *[firme]* accounts department; (*gestion*) accounts; (*argent disponible*) finances, funds. ♦ **trésorier, -ière** *nm,f* treasurer. (*Admin*) **~-payeur général** paymaster.

tressaillir [tʀesajiʀ] (13) *vi* **(a)** (*de plaisir*) to thrill, quiver; (*de peur*) to shudder, shiver; (*de douleur*) to wince. **son cœur tressaillait** his heart was fluttering. **(b)** (*sursauter*) to start, give a start. **faire ~ qn** to startle sb, make sb jump. **(c)** (*s'agiter*) *[personne, animal]* to quiver, twitch; *[plancher, véhicule]* to shake, vibrate. ♦ **tressaillement** *nm* thrill, quiver; shudder; wince; start; twitch; vibration.

tressauter [tʀesote] (1) *vi* **(a)** (*sursauter*) to start, give a start. **faire ~ qn** to startle sb, make sb jump. **(b)** (*être secoué*) *[voyageurs]* to be jolted *ou* tossed about; *[objets]* to shake about, jump about. ♦ **tressautement** *nm* start; jump; jolt.

tresser [tʀese] (1) *vt cheveux, rubans* to plait, braid; *paille* to plait; *panier, guirlande* to weave; *câble* to twist. ♦ **tressage** *nm* plaiting; braiding; weaving; twisting. ♦ **tresse** *nf* (*cheveux*) plait, braid; (*cordon*) braid.

tréteau, *pl* **~x** [tʀeto] *nm* trestle. (*Théât fig*) **les ~x** the boards, the stage.

treuil [tʀœj] *nm* winch, windlass.

trêve [tʀɛv] *nf* (*Mil, Pol*) truce; (*fig: répit*) respite, rest. ~ **de plaisanteries** enough of this joking; **sans** ~ unremittingly, unceasingly, relentlessly.

tri [tʀi] *nm* (*classement*) sorting (out); (*sélection*) selection. **faire le ~ de** to sort (out); to select; (*Poste*) **le (bureau de)** ~ the sorting office. ♦ **triage** *nm* (*gén*) sorting (out); *[wagons]* marshalling. **gare de** ~ marshalling yard.

tri ... [tʀi] *préf* tri ... .

triangle [tʀijɑ̃gl(ə)] *nm* (*Géom, Mus*) triangle. **en** ~ in a triangle. ♦ **triangulaire** *adj* (*gén*) triangular; *débat, tournoi* three-cornered.

tribal, e, *mpl* **-aux** [tʀibal, o] *adj* tribal.

tribord [tʀibɔʀ] *nm* starboard. **à** ~ to starboard.

tribu [tʀiby] *nf* tribe.

tribulations [tʀibylɑsjɔ̃] *nfpl* tribulations, troubles.

tribunal, *pl* **-aux** [tʀibynal, o] *nm* court. ~ **pour enfants/de police** juvenile/police court; ~ **militaire** military tribunal; **porter une affaire devant les ~aux** to bring a case before the courts; (*fig*) **le ~ des hommes** the justice of men.

tribune [tʀibyn] *nf* **(a)** (*pour le public*) gallery; (*sur un stade*) stand. ~ **d'honneur** grandstand. **(b)** (*pour un orateur*) platform, rostrum. **(c)** (*fig: débat*) forum. ~ **libre d'un journal** opinion column of a newspaper.

tribut [tʀiby] *nm* (*lit, fig*) tribute.

tributaire [tʀibytɛʀ] *adj* (*dépendant*) **être ~ de** to be dependant *ou* reliant on.

tricentenaire [tʀisɑ̃tnɛʀ] **1** *adj* three-hundred-year-old. **2** *nm* tercentenary, tricentennial.

tricher [tʀiʃe] (1) *vi* (*gén*) to cheat. ~ **sur son âge** to lie about *ou* cheat over one's age. ♦ **triche*** *nf* cheating. ♦ **tricherie** *nf*: **la** ~ cheating; **une** ~ a trick. ♦ **tricheur, -euse** *nm,f* cheater, cheat*.

tricolore [tʀikɔlɔʀ] *adj* three-coloured. **le drapeau** ~ the (French) tricolour; (*Sport*) **l'équipe ~*** the French team.

tricot [tʀiko] *nm* **(a)** (*vêtement*) jumper, sweater. ~ **de corps** vest, undershirt (*US*). **(b)** (*technique*) knitting. **faire du** ~ to knit. **(c)** (*tissu*) knitted fabric. **en** ~ knitted. ♦ **tricoter** (1) *vti* to knit.

tricycle [tʀisikl(ə)] *nm* tricycle.

trident [tʀidɑ̃] *nm* trident.

trier [tʀije] (7) *vt* (*classer*) to sort (out); (*sélectionner*) to select, pick; (*en calibrant*) to grade; (*en tamisant*) to sift. (*fig*) **trié sur le volet** hand-picked. ♦ **trieur, -euse** *nm,f* sorter; grader.

trilogie [tʀilɔʒi] *nf* trilogy.

trimbal(l)er [tʀɛ̃bale] (1) **1** *vt* (*) *bagages* to lug* *ou* cart* around; (*péj*) *personne* to trail along. **2 se ~‡** *vpr* to trail along.

trimer* [tʀime] (1) *vi* to slave away. **faire ~ qn** to drive sb hard, keep sb hard at it*.

trimestre [tʀimɛstʀ(ə)] *nm* **(a)** (*période*) quarter; (*Scol*) term. **(b)** (*loyer*) quarter, quarter's rent; (*frais de scolarité*) term's fees; (*salaire*) quarter's income. ♦ **trimestriel, -elle** *adj publication* quarterly; *paiement* three-monthly, quarterly; (*Scol*) *bulletin, examen* end-of-term.

tringle [tʀɛ̃gl(ə)] *nf* rod. ~ **à rideaux** curtain rod *ou* rail.

trinité [tʀinite] *nf* trinity. **à la T~** on Trinity Sunday.

trinquer [tʀɛ̃ke] (1) *vi* **(a)** (*porter un toast*) to clink glasses. ~ **à qch** to drink to sth. **(b)** (*: *écoper*) to cop it‡.

triomphe [tʀijɔ̃f] *nm* (*gén*) triumph; *[maladie, mode]* victory. **en** ~ in triumph; **air de** ~ air of triumph, triumphant air; **remporter un** ~ to have *ou* be a triumphant success. ♦ **triomphal, e,** *mpl* **-aux** *adj succès* triumphal; *entrée, air* triumphant. ♦ **triomphalement** *adv saluer* in triumph; *annoncer* triumphantly. ♦ **triomphant, e** *adj* triumphant. ♦ **triomphateur, -trice** *nm,f* triumphant victor. ♦ **triompher** (1) **1** *vi* **(a)** (*gén, Mil*) to triumph; *[raison]* to prevail, be triumphant; *[maladie]* to claim its victory. **faire ~ une cause** to bring *ou* give victory to a cause. **(b)** (*crier victoire*) to exult, rejoice. **2 ~ de** *vt indir* (*gén*) to triumph over.

tripatouiller* [tʀipatuje] (1) *vt* (*péj*) (*toucher*) to fiddle about with*; (*truquer*) to fiddle*.

tripes [tʀip] *nfpl* (*Culin*) tripe; (*: *intestins*) guts*. **rendre ~s et boyaux** to be as sick as a dog*. ◆ **triperie** *nf* (*boutique*) tripe shop; (*commerce*) tripe trade. ◆ **tripier, -ière** *nm,f* tripe butcher.

tripette* [tʀipɛt] *nf*: **ça ne vaut pas ~** that's a load of rubbish*.

triple [tʀipl(ə)] *adj* **(a)** triple. (*péj*) **~ menton** row of chins; (*Sport*) **~ saut** triple jump; **au ~ galop** hell for leather*; **faire qch en ~ exemplaire** to make three copies of sth, do sth in triplicate; **l'inconvénient en est ~** there are three disadvantages, the disadvantages are threefold; **prendre une ~ dose (de)** to take a triple dose (of). **(b)** (*intensif*) **~ idiot/sot** prize idiot/fool. **2** *nm*: **manger le ~ (de qn)** to eat three times as much (as sb); **9 est le ~ de 3** 9 is three times 3; **c'est le ~ du prix normal** it's three times *ou* treble the normal price. ◆ **triplé, e 1** *nm* (*Sport*) treble. **2 ~(e)s** *nm(f)pl* (*bébés*) triplets. ◆ **triplement 1** *adv* (*pour trois raisons*) in three ways; (*à un degré triple*) trebly. **2** *nm* trebling, tripling (*de* of); threefold increase (*de* in). ◆ **tripler** (1) **1** *vt* to treble, triple. **2** *vi* to triple, treble, increase threefold (*de* in).

triporteur [tʀipɔʀtœʀ] *nm* delivery tricycle.

tripot [tʀipo] *nm* (*péj*) dive*, joint*.

tripoter* [tʀipɔte] (1) (*péj*) **1** *vt* to fiddle with. **se ~ le nez** to fiddle with one's nose. **2** *vi* (*fouiller*) to root about, rummage about (*dans* in). (*trafiquer*) **~ dans qch** to get involved in sth. ◆ **tripotage*** *nm* (*manigances*) **~(s)** jiggery-pokery*. ◆ **tripotée*** *nf* **(a)** (*correction*) belting**, hiding*. **(b)** (*grand nombre*) **une ~ de ...** loads* of ...; lots of ... . ◆ **tripoteur, -euse*** *nm,f* (*affairiste*) shark*, shady dealer*.

trique [tʀik] *nf* cudgel. **mener qn à la ~** to bully sb along; **donner des coups de ~** to cudgel, thrash; **sec comme un coup de ~** as skinny as a rake.

triste [tʀist(ə)] *adj* **(a)** (*gén*) sad; *personne, sort* unhappy; *regard, sourire* sorrowful; *nécessité, devoir* painful; *pensée* gloomy; *couleur, temps, paysage* dreary, dismal, miserable. **chanson ~** sad *ou* melancholy song; **il est ~ comme un bonnet de nuit** he's as miserable as sin; **faire ~ figure** *ou* **mine** to look downcast, look sorry for o.s.; **être dans un ~ état** to be in a sad *ou* sorry state. **(b)** (*péj: lamentable*) *résultats* wretched, deplorable; *affaire, époque* dreadful; *réputation* sorry. **un ~ sire** *ou* **personnage** an unsavoury individual. ◆ **tristement** *adv* sadly; sorrowfully; gloomily. **se rendre ~ célèbre par ses crimes** to gain an unenviable reputation because of one's crimes. ◆ **tristesse** *nf* (*gén*) sadness; *[pensée]* gloominess; *[paysage]* bleakness, dreariness; (*chagrin*) sorrow.

triturer [tʀityʀe] (1) *vt pâte* to knead; *objet* to manipulate. **se ~ la cervelle*** to rack one's brains.

trivial, e, *mpl* **-aux** [tʀivjal, o] *adj* (*vulgaire*) coarse, crude; (*littér: ordinaire*) mundane, commonplace. ◆ **trivialement** *adv* coarsely, crudely; in a mundane *ou* commonplace way. ◆ **trivialité** *nf* coarseness, crudeness; mundane *ou* commonplace nature; (*remarque*) coarse *ou* crude remark.

troc [tʀɔk] *nm* (*échange*) exchange; (*système*) barter. **faire un ~ avec qn** to make an exchange with sb.

troène [tʀɔɛn] *nm* privet.

troglodyte [tʀɔglɔdit] *nm* cave dweller.

trogne* [tʀɔɲ] *nf* (*péj: visage*) mug** (*péj*), face.

trognon [tʀɔɲɔ̃] *nm* *[fruit]* core; *[chou]* stalk, core. **il s'est fait avoir jusqu'au ~**** he was well and truly had*; **mon petit ~*** sweetie pie*.

trois [tʀwa] *adj, nm* three. **~ fois rien** hardly anything, next to nothing; **en ~ coups de cuiller à pot*** in next to no time; **à ~ dimensions** three-dimensional; *V* **six.** ◆ **trois étoiles** *nm inv* three-star hotel (*ou* restaurant). ◆ **trois-mâts** *nm inv* three-master. ◆ **trois-pièces** *nm inv* (*complet*) three-piece suit; (*appartement*) three-room flat. ◆ **trois-quarts 1** *nmpl* three-quarters. **manteau ~-~** three-quarter (length) coat; **les ~-~ du travail** three-quarters of the work; **aux ~-~ détruit** almost totally destroyed. **2** *nm inv* (*Rugby*) three-quarter. ◆ **troisième** *adj, nmf* third. **le ~ âge** (*période*) the years of retirement; (*groupe social*) senior citizens; *V* **sixième.** ◆ **troisièmement** *adv* third(ly), in the third place.

trolleybus [tʀɔlɛbys] *nm* trolley bus.

trombe [tʀɔ̃b] *nf* (*Mét*) waterspout. (*fig: pluie*) **des ~s d'eau** a cloudburst, a downpour; **entrer en ~** to sweep in like a whirlwind.

trombine** [tʀɔ̃bin] *nf* (*visage*) face, mug** (*péj*); (*tête*) nut*.

trombone [tʀɔ̃bɔn] *nm* **(a)** (*Mus*) (*instrument*) trombone; (*artiste*) trombonist, trombone (player). **~ à coulisse/à pistons** slide/valve trombone. **(b)** (*agrafe*) paper clip.

trompe [tʀɔ̃p] *nf* **(a)** (*Mus*) horn. **~ de chasse** hunting horn. **(b)** *[éléphant]* trunk; *[insecte]* proboscis. (*Anat*) **~ d'Eustache** Eustachian tube.

tromper [tʀɔ̃pe] (1) **1** *vt* **(a)** (*duper*) (*gén*) to deceive (*sur* about, over); (*sans le faire exprès*) to mislead; *poursuivant, vigilance* to elude; *époux* to be unfaithful to, deceive. **mari trompé** husband who has been deceived; **cette manœuvre les a trompés** this move tricked *ou* fooled them; **les apparences trompent** appearances are deceptive; **c'est ce qui vous trompe** that's where you are mistaken *ou* wrong. **(b)** *attente* to while away; *faim, soif* to stave off; *espoirs* to fall short of, fail to come up to, disappoint. **2 se ~** *vpr* to make a mistake, be mistaken. **se ~ de 5 F dans un calcul** to be 5 francs out in one's reckoning; **on pourrait s'y ~** you'd hardly know the difference; **si je ne me trompe** if I am not mistaken; **se ~ de route** to take the wrong road; **se ~ de jour** to get the day wrong, make a mistake about the day. ◆ **trompe-l'œil** *nm inv* (*Art*) trompe-l'œil; (*fig*) eye-wash*. ◆ **tromperie** *nf* (*duperie*) deception, deceit. ◆ **trompeur, -euse 1** *adj personne, paroles* deceitful; *apparences* deceptive, misleading; *distance, profondeur* deceptive. **2** *nm,f* deceiver. ◆ **trompeusement** *adv* deceitfully; deceptively.

trompette [tʀɔ̃pɛt] **1** *nf* trumpet. **2** *nm* trumpeter, trumpet (player). ◆ **trompettiste** *nmf* trumpet player, trumpeter.

tronc [tʀɔ̃] *nm* (*gén*) trunk; (*pour aumônes*) (collection) box. (*Scol*) **~ commun** common-core syllabus.

tronche** [tʀɔ̃ʃ] *nf* (*visage*) mug** (*péj*), face; (*tête*) nut*.

tronçon [tʀɔ̃sɔ̃] *nm* section. ◆ **tronçonner** (1) *vt* to cut into sections. ◆ **tronçonneuse** *nf* chain saw.

trône [tʀon] *nm* throne. **monter sur le ~** to come to *ou* ascend the throne. ◆ **trôner** (1) *vi [roi, invité]* to sit enthroned; *[chose]* to sit imposingly.

tronquer [tʀɔ̃ke] (1) *vt colonne* to truncate; *texte* to truncate, curtail, cut down.

trop [tʀo] **1** *adv* **(a)** (*devant adv, adj*) too; (*avec vb*) (*gén*) too much; *attendre, durer* (for) too long. **il a ~ bu** he has had too much to drink, he has drunk too much; **un ~ grand effort l'épuiserait** too great an effort would exhaust him; **c'est ~ loin pour que j'y aille à pied** it's too far for me to walk there; **c'est ~ beau pour être vrai** it's too good to be true; **elle en a déjà bien** *ou* **beaucoup** *ou* **par ~ dit** she has said far *ou* much too much already; **vous êtes ~ (nombreux)/~ peu (nombreux)** there are too many/too few of you; **une ~ forte dose** an overdose; **insister ~** to be overinsistent *ou* too pressing; **c'est ~ chauffé** it's overheated.

(b) ~ de *pain, eau* too much; *objets* too many;

gentillesse, sévérité excessive; **s'il te reste ~ de dollars, vends-les-moi** if you have dollars left over *ou* to spare, sell me them; **nous avons ~ de personnel/de travail** we are overstaffed/overworked; **il y a ~ de monde dans la salle** the hall is overcrowded *ou* overfull.

(c) (*superl, intensif*) too, so (very). **c'est ~ bête/drôle** how stupid/funny, it's too stupid/funny for words; **nous n'avons pas ~ de place chez nous** we haven't got (so) very much room *ou* (all) that much room at our place; **vous êtes ~ aimable** you are too *ou* most kind; **il n'aime pas ~ ça*** he isn't too keen *ou* overkeen (on it), he doesn't like it overmuch *ou* (all) that much; **je ne le sais que ~** I know only too well; **c'est ~!** that's going too far!, enough is enough!; **cela ne va pas ~ bien** things are not going so *ou* terribly well; **je n'en sais ~ rien** I don't really know.

(d) de ~, en ~: il y a une personne de ~ *ou* **en ~ dans l'ascenseur** there is one person too many in the lift; **s'il y a du pain en ~, j'en emporterai** if there is any bread (left) over *ou* any bread extra I'll take some away; **il m'a rendu 2 F de ~** he gave me back 2 francs too much; **l'argent versé en ~** the excess payment; **il pèse 3 kg de ~** he is 3 kg overweight; **si je suis de ~, je peux m'en aller!** if I'm in the way *ou* not welcome I can always leave!; **cette remarque est de ~** that remark is uncalled for; **il a bu un verre de ~** he's had a drink too many.

2 *nm* (*excédent*) excess; (*reste*) extra. **le ~ d'importance accordé à** the excessive importance attributed to.

♦ **trop-perçu,** *pl* **~-~s** *nm* excess (tax) payment. ♦ **trop-plein,** *pl* **~-~s** *nm* excess; (*d'eau*) overflow. **~ d'énergie** surplus *ou* boundless energy.

trophée [tʀɔfe] *nm* trophy.

tropique [tʀɔpik] *nm* tropic. **~ du cancer/capricorne** tropic of Cancer/Capricorn; **les ~s** the tropics. ♦ **tropical, e,** *mpl* **-aux** *adj* tropical.

troquer [tʀɔke] (1) *vt*: **~ qch contre qch d'autre** to swap sth for sth else; (*Écon*) to barter *ou* trade sth for sth else.

troquet‡ [tʀɔkɛ] *nm* small café.

trot [tʀo] *nm* trot. **petit/grand ~** jog/full trot; **course de ~** trotting race; (*fig*) **au ~*** at the double. ♦ **trotte*** *nf*: **il y a une ~ (d'ici au village)** it's a fair distance (from here to the village). ♦ **trotter** (1) *vi [cheval, cavalier]* to trot; *[personne]* (*à petits pas*) to trot along; (*beaucoup*) to run around; *[souris, enfants]* to scurry *ou* scamper (about). **un air/une idée qui vous trotte dans la tête** a tune/an idea which keeps running through your head. ♦ **trotteur, -euse 1** *nm,f* (*cheval*) trotter, trotting horse. **2** *nf* (*aiguille*) (sweep) second hand. ♦ **trottiner** (1) *vi [cheval]* to jog along; *[personne]* to trot along; *[souris]* to scurry *ou* scamper along. ♦ **trottinette** *nf* (child's) scooter.

trottoir [tʀɔtwaʀ] *nm* pavement, sidewalk (*US*). **~ roulant** moving walkway, travellator; (*péj*) **faire le ~*** to walk the streets, be on the game*.

trou [tʀu] *nm* **(a)** (*lit*) hole. **~ d'aération** airhole, air vent; **~ d'air** air pocket; **le ~ de la serrure** the keyhole; (*Théât*) **le ~ du souffleur** the prompt box; **faire un ~** (*gén*) to dig *ou* make a hole; (*déchirure*) to tear a hole; (*usure*) to wear a hole. **(b)** (*moment de libre*) gap; (*déficit*) deficit. **un ~ dans ses économies** a hole in his savings; **~ (de mémoire)** lapse of memory. **(c)** (*péj: localité*) place, hole* (*péj*), dump* (*péj*). **il n'est jamais sorti de son ~** he has never been out of his own backyard.

troubadour [tʀubaduʀ] *nm* troubadour.

troublant, e [tʀublɑ̃, ɑ̃t] *adj* (*gén*) disturbing.

trouble[1] [tʀubl(ə)] **1** *adj* **(a)** *eau, vin* unclear, cloudy; *regard, image* blurred, misty. **(b)** *affaire* shady, murky; *désir* dark. **2** *adv*: **voir ~** to have blurred vision.

trouble[2] [tʀubl(ə)] *nm* **(a)** (*remue-ménage*) tumult, turmoil; (*désunion*) discord, trouble. (*émeute*) **~s** disturbances, troubles; **~s politiques** political unrest *ou* disturbances. **(b)** (*émoi*) (inner) turmoil, agitation; (*inquiétude*) distress; (*gêne, perplexité*) confusion, embarrassment. **(c)** (*gén pl: Méd*) disorder. **~s psychiques** psychological trouble *ou* disorders.

trouble-fête [tʀubləfɛt] *nmf inv* spoilsport.

troubler [tʀuble] (1) **1** *vt* **(a)** *ordre etc* to disturb, disrupt; *esprit* to cloud. **en ces temps troublés** in these troubled times. **(b)** *personne* (*impressionner*) to disturb; (*inquiéter, gêner*) to trouble, bother. **(c)** (*brouiller*) *eau* to make cloudy; *atmosphère, ciel* to cloud. **les larmes lui troublaient la vue** tears clouded *ou* blurred her vision. **2 se ~** *vpr* **(a)** *[eau]* to cloud, become cloudy. **(b)** *[personne]* to become flustered. **sans se ~** unperturbed.

trouer [tʀue] (1) *vt* **(a)** *vêtement* (*usure*) to wear a hole in; (*déchirure*) to tear a hole in; (*brûlure*) to burn a hole in. **sac troué** bag with a hole *ou* with holes in it; **tout troué** full of holes. **(b)** (*fig: traverser*) *silence, nuit* to pierce. ♦ **trouée** *nf [haie, nuages]* gap, break; (*Mil*) breach (*dans* in).

troufion* [tʀufjɔ̃] *nm* soldier.

trouille‡ [tʀuj] *nf*: **avoir la ~** to be scared stiff; **flanquer la ~ à qn** to put the wind up sb*. ♦ **trouillard, e**‡ **1** *adj* chicken*, yellow-bellied‡. **2** *nm,f* chicken, yellowbelly‡.

troupe [tʀup] *nf* **(a)** (*Mil*) troop. **la ~** (*l'armée*) the army; (*les simples soldats*) the troops. **(b)** *[chanteurs, danseurs]* troupe. *[acteurs]* **~ (de théâtre)** (theatrical) company. **(c)** *[gens, animaux]* band, group, troop.

troupeau, *pl* **~x** [tʀupo] *nm [bœufs, chevaux]* (*dans un pré*) herd; (*transhumant*) drove; *[moutons]* flock; *[oies]* gaggle; (*péj*) *[touristes]* herd (*péj*).

trousse [tʀus] *nf* **(a)** (*étui*) (*gén*) case, kit; *[médecin]* instrument case; *[écolier]* pencil case *ou* wallet. **~ de maquillage** vanity case; **~ à outils** toolkit; **~ de toilette** (*sac*) toilet bag, sponge bag; (*mallette*) travelling case. **(b) aux ~s de** (hot) on the heels of, on the tail of.

trousseau, *pl* **~x** [tʀuso] *nm* **(a) ~ de clefs** bunch of keys. **(b)** *[mariée]* trousseau; *[écolier]* outfit.

trouvaille [tʀuvaj] *nf* (*objet*) find; (*fig: idée, métaphore, procédé*) stroke of inspiration.

trouver [tʀuve] (1) **1** *vt* **(a)** (*en cherchant*) to find; (*par hasard*) to find, come upon *ou* across; *difficultés* to meet with, come up against. **~ un emploi à qn** to find sb a job, find a job for sb; **je ne le trouve pas** I can't find it; **où peut-on le ~?** where can he be found?, where is he to be found?; **aller/venir ~ qn** to go/come and see sb; **j'ai trouvé!** I've got it!; **formule bien trouvée** clever *ou* happy phrase; **où est-il allé ~ ça?** where (on earth) did he get that idea from?, whatever gave him that idea? **(b)** (*avec à + infin*) **~ à redire (à tout)** to find sth to criticize (in everything); **~ à manger** to find sth to eat; **~ à se distraire** to find a way to amuse o.s. **(c)** (*éprouver*) **~ du plaisir à qch/à faire qch** to take pleasure in sth/in doing sth; **~ de la difficulté à faire** to find *ou* have difficulty in doing. **(d)** (*estimer*) **~ que** to find *ou* think that; **je le trouve fatigué** I think he looks tired, I find him tired-looking; **vous trouvez?** (do) you think so?; **il a trouvé bon de nous écrire** he thought *ou* saw fit to write to us. **(e)** (*locutions*) **~ à qui parler** to meet one's match; **~ son maître** to find one's master; **cet objet n'avait pas trouvé preneur** the object had had no takers; **~ la mort** to meet one's death; **je la trouve mauvaise!*** I think it's a bit off*, I don't like it at all; **~ le sommeil** to get to sleep; **~ chaussure à son pied** to find a suitable match; ~ **son compte à faire qch** to be better (off) doing sth; **il a trouvé le moyen de s'égarer** he managed *ou* contrived to get (himself) lost.

2 se ~ *vpr* **(a)** (*être placé*) to be; (*soudainement*) to find o.s. **où se trouve la poste?** where is the post office?; **ça ne se trouve pas sur la carte** it isn't *ou* doesn't appear on the map; **je me trouvais près de l'entrée** I was (standing *ou* sitting *etc*) near the entrance; **je me suis trouvé dans l'impossibilité de répondre** I found myself unable to reply. **(b)** (*se sentir*) to feel. **se** ~ **bien** (*dans un fauteuil etc*) to feel comfortable; (*dans une atmosphère*) to feel happy *ou* at ease; (*santé*) **se** ~ **bien/mieux** to feel well/better; **se** ~ **mal** to faint, pass out; **se** ~ **bien/mal d'avoir fait qch** to be pleased/displeased at having done sth, have reason to be glad/to regret having done sth. **(c)** (*coïncidence*) **se** ~ **être/avoir ...** to happen to be/have ...; **elles se trouvaient avoir le même chapeau** it turned out that they had *ou* they happened to have the same hat.

3 *vpr impers* **(a)** (*le fait est*) **il se trouve que c'est moi** it happens *ou* it turns out to be me, it's me as it happens; **comme il se trouve parfois** as is sometimes the case, as sometimes happens. **(b)** (*il y a*) **il se trouve toujours des gens pour dire ...** you'll always find people who will say ... . **(c)** (*) **ils sont sortis, si ça se trouve** they may well be out, they're probably out.

truand [tʀyɑ̃] *nm* gangster. ♦ **truander**‡ (1) *vt* to swindle, do‡.

trublion [tʀyblijɔ̃] *nm* troublemaker, agitator.

truc* [tʀyk] *nm* (*moyen*) way; (*tour, artifice*) trick; (*dispositif*) thingummy*, whatsit*. **trouver le** ~ **(pour faire)** to find a way (of doing). **(b)** (*chose, idée*) thing. **j'ai pensé (à) un** ~ I've thought of sth, I've had a thought; **il y a un tas de** ~**s à faire** there's a heap of things to do*; **méfie-toi de ces** ~**s-là** be careful of those things. **(c)** (*personne*) **(Machin-)**~ what's-his-(*ou* -her-name*. ♦ **trucage** *nm* = **truquage**.

truchement [tʀyʃmɑ̃] *nm*: **par le** ~ **de qn** through (the intervention of) sb; **par le** ~ **de qch** by means of sth.

truculent, e [tʀykylɑ̃, ɑ̃t] *adj* colourful. ♦ **truculence** *nf* colourfulness.

truelle [tʀyɛl] *nf* trowel.

truffe [tʀyf] *nf* (*Culin*) truffle; (*nez du chien*) nose. ♦ **truffer** (1) *vt* to garnish with truffles. (*fig*) **truffé de** *citations* peppered *ou* larded with; *pièges* bristling with.

truie [tʀɥi] *nf* (*Zool*) sow.

truite [tʀɥit] *nf* trout.

truquer [tʀyke] (1) *vt* (*gén*) to fix*; *élections* to rig; *comptes* to fiddle*. ♦ **truquage** *nm* **(a)** fixing; rigging*; fiddling*. **(b)** (*Ciné*) effect, trick.

trust [tʀœst] *nm* (*Écon: cartel*) trust; (*grande entreprise*) corporation. ♦ **truster** (1) *vt* (*lit, fig*) to monopolize.

tsar [dzaʀ] *nm* tsar.

tsé-tsé [tsetse] *nf*: **(mouche)** ~ tsetse fly.

tsigane [tsigan] **1** *adj* (Hungarian) gypsy, tzigane. **2** *nmf*: **T**~ (Hungarian) Gypsy, Tzigane.

tu [ty] *pron pers* you (*used to address a child, close relation or friend*); (*Rel*) thou†. **dire** ~ **à qn** to address sb as 'tu'; **être à** ~ **et à toi avec qn*** to be on first-name terms with sb.

tuant, e [tɥɑ̃, ɑ̃t] *adj* (*fatigant*) exhausting; (*énervant*) exasperating.

tuba [tyba] *nm* (*Mus*) tuba; (*Sport*) snorkel, breathing tube.

tube [tyb] *nm* **(a)** (*gén*) tube; (*canalisation*) pipe. ~ **de rouge (à lèvres)** lipstick; ~ **digestif** digestive tract. **(b)** (*: *chanson à succès*) hit song *ou* record.

tubercule [tybɛʀkyl] *nm* (*Anat, Méd*) tubercle; (*Bot*) tuber.

tuberculose [tybɛʀkyloz] *nf* tuberculosis. ♦ **tuberculeux, -euse 1** *adj* tuberculous, tubercular. **être** ~ to have tuberculosis *ou* TB. **2** *nm,f* tuberculosis *ou* tubercular *ou* TB patient.

tubulure [tybylyʀ] *nf* (*tube*) pipe. ♦ **tubulaire** *adj* tubular.

tuer [tɥe] (1) **1** *vt* (*gén*) to kill; (*à la chasse*) to shoot; (*fig: exténuer*) to exhaust, wear out. ~ **qn à coups de couteau** to stab *ou* knife sb to death; ~ **qn d'une balle** to shoot sb dead; **l'alcool tue** alcohol can kill *ou* is a killer; **cet enfant me tuera** this child will be the death of me; ~ **la poule aux œufs d'or** to kill the goose that lays the golden eggs; ~ **qch dans l'œuf** to nip sth in the bud; ~ **le temps** to kill time. **2 se** ~ *vpr* (*accident*) to be killed; (*suicide*) to kill o.s. **se** ~ **à travailler** to work o.s. to death, kill o.s. with work; **se** ~ **à répéter qch à qn** to wear o.s. out repeating sth to sb. ♦ **tué, e** *nm,f* person killed. **les** ~**s** the dead. ♦ **tuerie** *nf* (*carnage*) slaughter, carnage. ♦ **tue-tête** *adv*: **crier à** ~ to shout at the top of one's voice, shout one's head off*. ♦ **tueur, -euse 1** *nm,f* killer. ~ **(à gages)** hired killer, hitman. **2** *nm* (*d'abattoir*) slaughterman, slaughterer.

tuile [tɥil] *nf* **(a)** (*Constr*) tile. **(b)** (*: *malchance*) blow. **quelle** ~! what a blow! **(c)** (*Culin*) wafer.

tulipe [tylip] *nf* tulip.

tuméfié, e [tymefje] *adj* puffed-up, swollen.

tumeur [tymœʀ] *nf* tumour.

tumulte [tymylt(ə)] *nm* **(a)** (*bruit*) *[foule, rue]* commotion; *[voix]* hubbub; *[acclamations]* thunder, tumult. **(b)** (*agitation*) *[affaires]* hurly-burly; *[passions]* turmoil, tumult. ♦ **tumultueux, -euse** *adj séance, époque* stormy, turbulent; *foule* turbulent, agitated; *passion* tumultuous, turbulent.

tunique [tynik] *nf* tunic.

Tunisie [tynizi] *nf* Tunisia. ♦ **tunisien, -ienne** *adj*, **T**~**(ne)** *nm(f)* Tunisian.

tunnel [tynɛl] *nm* tunnel.

turban [tyʀbɑ̃] *nm* turban.

turbine [tyʀbin] *nf* turbine.

turboréacteur [tyʀbɔʀeaktœʀ] *nm* turbojet.

turbulent, e [tyʀbylɑ̃, ɑ̃t] *adj enfant* boisterous; (*Sci*) turbulent. ♦ **turbulence** *nf* (*Sci: remous*) ~**(s)** turbulence.

turc, turque [tyʀk(ə)] **1** *adj* Turkish. **2** *nm* **(a)** (*personne*) **T**~ Turk; (*fig*) **jeune T**~ Young Turk. **(b)** (*Ling*) Turkish. **3** *nf*: **Turque** Turkish woman.

turfiste [tyʀfist(ə)] *nmf* racegoer.

turlupiner* [tyʀlypine] (1) *vt* to bother, worry.

turne [tyʀn(ə)] *nf* (*arg Scol: chambre*) room.

Turquie [tyʀki] *nf* Turkey.

turquoise [tyʀkwaz] *nf, adj inv* turquoise.

tutelle [tytɛl] *nf* (*Jur*) guardianship; (*Pol*) trusteeship. **mettre qn en** ~ to put sb in the care of a guardian; **sous la** ~ **de qn** (*dépendance*) under sb's supervision; (*protection*) in sb's tutelage *ou* guardianship.

tuteur, -trice [tytœʀ, tʀis] **1** *nm,f* (*Jur*) guardian. **2** *nm* (*Agr*) stake, support, prop.

tutoyer [tytwaje] (8) *vt*: ~ **qn** to address sb as 'tu', ≃ be on first-name terms with sb. ♦ **tutoiement** *nm* use of (the familiar) 'tu'.

tutu [tyty] *nm* tutu, ballet skirt.

tuyau, *pl* ~**x** [tɥijo] *nm* **(a)** (*gén, rigide*) pipe, length of piping; (*flexible*) length of rubber (*ou* plastic *etc*) tubing; *[pipe]* stem. ~ **d'arrosage** hosepipe, garden hose; ~ **de cheminée** chimney pipe; ~ **d'échappement** exhaust (pipe); (*fig*) **dans le** ~ **de l'oreille*** in sb's ear. **(b)** (*: *conseil*) tip. ♦ **tuyauter*** (1) *vt*: ~ **qn** (*conseiller*) to give sb a tip; (*mettre au courant*) to put sb in the know*. ♦ **tuyauterie** *nf*: ~**(s)** piping; *[orgue]* pipes.

tympan [tɛ̃pɑ̃] *nm* (*Anat*) eardrum.

type [tip] **1** *nm* **(a)** (*modèle*) type. **une pompe du** ~ **réglementaire** a regulation-type pump; **avoir le** ~ **oriental** to be Oriental-looking, have

Oriental looks; **ce** *ou* **il n'est pas mon ~*** he is not my type *ou* sort; **c'est le ~ (parfait** *ou* **même) de l'intellectuel** he's a perfect *ou* classic example *ou* he's the epitome of the intellectual. **(b)** (*: *individu*) bloke*, guy*. **quel sale ~!** what a nasty customer *ou* piece of work! **2** *adj inv* typical, classic; (*Statistique*) standard. **l'exemple ~** the typical *ou* classic example.

typhoïde [tifɔid] *adj* typhoid. **la (fièvre) ~** typhoid (fever).

typhon [tifɔ̃] *nm* typhoon.

typhus [tifys] *nm* typhus (fever).

typique [tipik] *adj* typical. **sa réaction est ~** his reaction is typical (of him). ♦ **typiquement** *adv* typically.

typographe [tipɔgʀaf] *nmf* typographer. ♦ **typographie** *nf* typography. ♦ **typographique** *adj opérations, art* typographic(al). **erreur ~** typographic(al) *ou* printer's error, misprint.

typologie [tipɔlɔʒi] *nf* typology.

tyran [tiʀɑ̃] *nm* (*lit, fig*) tyrant. ♦ **tyrannie** *nf* tyranny. **exercer sa ~ sur qn** to tyrannize sb. ♦ **tyrannique** *adj* tyrannical. ♦ **tyranniser** (1) *vt* to tyrannize.

U

U, u [y] *nm (lettre)* U, u.
ulcère [ylsɛʀ] *nm* ulcer. ♦ **ulcération** *nf* ulceration. ♦ **ulcérer** (6) **1** *vt (révolter)* to sicken, appal; *(Méd)* to ulcerate. **2 s'~** *vpr* to ulcerate. ♦ **ulcéreux, -euse** *adj* ulcerated, ulcerous.
ultérieur, e [ylteʀjœʀ] *adj* later, subsequent, ulterior. **à une date ~e** at a later *ou* subsequent date. ♦ **ultérieurement** *adv* later, subsequently.
ultimatum [yltimatɔm] *nm* ultimatum.
ultime [yltim] *adj* ultimate, final.
ultra [yltʀa] *préf* ultra. **~-moderne** *etc* ultramodern *etc*; **~-son** ultrasonic sound; **~-violet** *(adj)* ultraviolet; *(nm)* ultraviolet ray.
un, une [œ̃, yn] **1** *adj indéf* **(a)** a, an *(devant voyelle)*; *(un, une quelconque)* some; *(avec noms abstraits) non traduit.* **ne venez pas ~ dimanche** don't come on a Sunday; **retrouvons-nous dans ~ café** let's meet in a café *ou* in some café (or other); **~ jour, tu comprendras** one day *ou* some day you'll understand; **avec une grande sagesse** with great wisdom; **cet enfant sera ~ Paganini** this child will be another Paganini; **ce n'est pas ~ génie** he's no genius. **(b)** *(intensif)* **elle a fait une de ces scènes!** she made a dreadful scene! *ou* such a scene!; **j'ai une de ces faims!** I'm so hungry!; **il est d'~ sale!** he's so dirty! **(c) ~ autre** another, another one. **Monsieur Un tel** Mr So-and-So; **~ certain Mr X** a (certain) Mr X, one Mr X; **~ (petit) peu** a little.

2 *pron* **(a)** one. **prêtez-m'en ~** lend me one (of them); **j'en connais ~ qui sera content!** I know someone *ou* somebody *ou* ONE person who'll be pleased! **(b)** *(avec art déf)* **l'~** one; **les ~s** some; **l'une et l'autre solution sont acceptables** either solution is acceptable, both solutions are acceptable; **ils se regardaient l'~ l'autre** they looked at one another *ou* at each other; *(à tout prendre)* **l'~ dans l'autre** on balance, by and large.

3 *adj inv* one. **~ seul** one only, only one; **pas ~ (seul)** not one; *(emphatique)* not a single one; **sans ~ sou*** penniless, broke*.

4 *nm,f* one. **j'ai tiré le (numéro) ~** I picked (number) one; **(d'abord) et d'une!*** for a start!; **il n'a fait ni une ni deux, il a accepté** he accepted without a second's hesitation; *(Presse)* **la une** the front page, page one.
unanime [ynanim] *adj* unanimous. ♦ **unanimement** *adv* unanimously. ♦ **unanimité** *nf* unanimity. **élu à l'~** elected unanimously; **cette décision a fait l'~** this decision was approved unanimously.
uni, e [yni] *adj* **(a)** *tissu* plain, self-coloured; *couleur* plain. **(b)** *couple, amis* close; *famille* close(-knit). **présenter un front ~ contre** to present a united front to. **(c)** *surface* smooth, even.
unième [ynjɛm] *adj*: **vingt/trente et ~** twenty-/thirty-first.
unifier [ynifje] (7) **1** *vt (gén)* to unify. **2 s'~** *vpr [pays]* to become unified. ♦ **unificateur, -trice** *adj* unifying. ♦ **unification** *nf* unification.
uniforme [ynifɔʀm(ə)] **1** *adj (gén)* uniform; *surface* even. **2** *nm (vêtement)* uniform. **en (grand) ~** in (dress) uniform. ♦ **uniformément** *adv* uniformly; evenly. ♦ **uniformisation** *nf* standardization. ♦ **uniformiser** (1) *vt (standardiser)* to standardize; *teinte* to make uniform. ♦ **uniformité** *nf* uniformity; evenness.
unijambiste [yniʒɑ̃bist(ə)] **1** *adj* one-legged. **2** *nmf* one-legged man (*ou* woman).
unilatéral, e, *mpl* **-aux** [ynilateʀal, o] *adj* unilateral. ♦ **unilatéralement** *adv* unilaterally.
unilingue [ynilɛ̃g] *adj* unilingual.
union [ynjɔ̃] **1** *nf (alliance, mariage)* union; *(groupe)* association, union; *[éléments, couleurs]* combination, blending. **l'~ fait la force** strength through unity. **2: ~ de consommateurs** consumers' association; **l'U~ Soviétique** the Soviet Union.
unique [ynik] *adj* **(a)** *(seul)* only. **mon ~ espoir** my only *ou* sole *ou* one hope; **fils ~** only son; **route à voie ~** single-lane road; **tiré par un cheval ~** drawn by only one *ou* by a single horse; **~ en France** the only one of its kind in France; **deux aspects d'un même et ~ problème** two aspects of one and the same problem. **(b)** *(après n: exceptionnel) livre, talent* unique. **~ en son genre** unique of its kind; **~ au monde** absolutely unique. **(c)** (*: *impayable*) priceless*. ♦ **uniquement** *adv* **(a)** *(exclusivement)* only, solely. **pas ~** not only *ou* not just that; **il pense ~ à l'argent** he thinks only of money. **(b)** *(simplement)* only, merely, just. **c'était ~ par curiosité** it was only *ou* just *ou* merely out of curiosity.
unir [yniʀ] (2) **1** *vt* **(a)** *(associer)* to unite (*à* with). **le sentiment qui les unit** the feeling which binds them together *ou* unites them; **~ en mariage** to unite *ou* join in marriage. **(b)** *(combiner) couleurs, qualités* to combine (*à* with). **(c)** *(relier) continents, villes* to link, join up. **2 s'~** *vpr (s'associer)* to unite (*à, avec* with, *contre* against); *(se marier)* to be joined in marriage; *(se combiner)* to combine (*à, avec* with).
unisexe [ynisɛks] *adj inv* unisex.
unisson [ynisɔ̃] *nm*: **à l'~** in unison.
unitaire [ynitɛʀ] *adj (Comm, Math, Phys)* unitary; *(Pol)* unitarian.
unité [ynite] *nf* **(a)** *(cohésion)* unity. **~ de vues** unity of views. **(b)** *(Comm, Math: élément)* unit. **~ de mesure** unit of measure. **(c)** *(troupe)* unit; *(navire)* (war)ship. **(d)** (*: *10 000 F*) ten thousand francs.
univers [ynivɛʀ] *nm* *(gén)* universe. ♦ **universalité** *nf* universality. ♦ **universel, -elle** *adj* *(gén)* universal; *réputation* world-wide. ♦ **universellement** *adv* universally.
universitaire [ynivɛʀsitɛʀ] **1** *adj vie, restaurant* university; *études, milieux, diplôme* university, academic. **2** *nmf* academic.
université [ynivɛʀsite] *nf* university.
uranium [yʀanjɔm] *nm* uranium.
urbain, e [yʀbɛ̃, ɛn] *adj* **(a)** *(de la ville)* urban, city. **(b)** *(littér: poli)* urbane. ♦ **urbanisation** *nf* urbanization. ♦ **urbaniser** (1) **1** *vt* to urbanize. **2 s'~** *vpr* to become urbanized. ♦ **urbanisme** *nm* town planning. ♦ **urbaniste** *nmf* town planner. ♦ **urbanité** *nf (littér)* urbanity.
urée [yʀe] *nf* urea. ♦ **urémie** *nf* uraemia.
urgence [yʀʒɑ̃s] *nf* **(a)** *[décision, situation]* urgency. **y a-t-il ~ à ce que nous fassions ...?** is it urgent for us to do ...?; **d'~** *mesures, situation* emergency; **faire qch d'~** to do sth as a matter of urgency; **transporté d'~ à l'hôpital** rushed to hos-

pital; **à envoyer d'~** to be sent immediately; **le patron l'a convoqué d'~** the boss requested to see him urgently *ou* immediately. **(b)** (*cas urgent*) emergency. **salle des ~s** emergency ward. ♦ **urgent, e** *adj* urgent. **rien d'~** nothing urgent; **l'~ est de** the most urgent thing is to. ♦ **urger*** (3) *vi*: **ça urge!** it's urgent!

urine [yʀin] *nf*: **~(s)** urine. ♦ **uriner** (1) *vi* to urinate. ♦ **urinoir** *nm* (public) urinal.

urne [yʀn(ə)] *nf* **(a)** (*Pol*) **~ (électorale)** ballot box; **aller aux ~s** to vote, go to the polls. **(b)** (*vase*) urn.

urticaire [yʀtikɛʀ] *nf* nettle rash, hives, urticaria.

us [ys] *nmpl*: **~ (et coutumes)** (habits and) customs.

usage [yzaʒ] *nm* **(a)** (*utilisation*) use. **outil à ~s multiples** multi-purpose tool; **faire ~ de** (*gén*) to use, make use of; *droit* to exercise; **faire un bon/mauvais ~ de qch** to put sth to good/bad use; **avoir l'~ de qch** to have the use of sth; **ces souliers ont fait de l'~** I've (*ou* we've *etc*) had good use out of these shoes; **à l'~** with use; **à l'~ de** for; **en ~** in use. **(b)** (*coutume, habitude*) custom. **c'est l'~** it's the custom, it's what's done; **entrer dans l'~ (courant)** *[objet, mot]* to come into common *ou* current use; *[mœurs]* to become common practice; **contraire aux ~s** contrary to common practice *ou* to custom; **il était d'~ de** it was customary *ou* a custom *ou* usual to; **formule d'~** set formula; **après les compliments d'~** after the usual *ou* customary compliments. **(c)** (*Ling*) **l'~** usage; **l'~ écrit** written usage. ♦ **usagé, e** *adj* worn, old. ♦ **usager, -ère** *nm,f* user. **~ de la route** roaduser.

user [yze] (1) **1** *vt* **(a)** (*détériorer*) *outil, roches* to wear away; *vêtements, personne* to wear out; *nerfs* to wear down. **(b)** (*consommer*) (*gén*) to use; *essence, charbon* to use, burn. **il use 2 paires de chaussures par mois** he goes through 2 pairs of shoes (in) a month. **2** *vi* (*littér*) **en ~ bien/mal avec qn** to deal well/badly by sb, treat sb well/badly. **3 ~ de** *vt indir* (*gén*) to make use of, use; *droit* to exercise. **il en a usé et abusé** he has used and abused it. **4 s'~** *vpr [tissu]* to wear out. **s'~ les yeux** to strain one's eyes (*à faire* by doing). ♦ **usé, e** *adj* **(a)** *objet* worn; (*fig*) *personne* worn-out. **~ jusqu'à la corde** threadbare. **(b)** (*banal*) *thème* hackneyed, trite; *plaisanterie* well-worn, stale.

usine [yzin] *nf* (*gén*) factory; (*importante*) plant; (*textile*) mill; (*métallurgique*) works. **~ à gaz** gasworks. ♦ **usiner** (1) *vt* (*traiter*) to machine; (*fabriquer*) to manufacture.

usité, e [yzite] *adj* in common use, common.

ustensile [ystɑ̃sil] *nm* (*gén*) implement. **~ (de cuisine)** (kitchen) utensil.

usuel, -elle [yzɥɛl] **1** *adj* *objet* everyday, ordinary; *mot* everyday; *nom* common. **2** *nm* (*livre*) book on the open shelf.

usufruit [yzyfʀɥi] *nm* usufruct. ♦ **usufruitier, -ière** *adj, nm,f* usufructuary.

usure¹ [yzyʀ] *nf* **(a)** (*processus*) *[vêtement]* wear (and tear); *[roche]* wearing away; *[forces]* wearing out. **on l'aura à l'~** we'll wear him down in the end. **(b)** (*état*) *[objet]* worn state.

usure² [yzyʀ] *nf* (*intérêt*) usury. ♦ **usuraire** *adj* usurious. ♦ **usurier, -ière** *nm,f* usurer.

usurper [yzyʀpe] (1) *vt* to usurp. ♦ **usurpateur, -trice** **1** *adj* usurping. **2** *nm,f* usurper. ♦ **usurpation** *nf* usurpation.

ut [yt] *nm* (*Mus*) (the note) C.

utérus [yteʀys] *nm* womb.

utile [ytil] *adj* (*gén*) useful; *conseil* useful, helpful (*à qn* to *ou* for sb). **livre ~ à lire** useful book to read; **cela vous sera ~** that'll be of use to you; **ton parapluie m'a été bien ~ ce matin** your umbrella came in very handy this morning; **est-il vraiment ~ que j'y aille?** do I really need to go?; **puis-je vous être ~?** can I be of help?, can I do anything for you? ♦ **utilement** *adv* profitably, usefully.

utiliser [ytilize] (1) *vt* (*gén*) to use, make use of. ♦ **utilisable** *adj* usable. ♦ **utilisateur, -trice** *nm,f* user. ♦ **utilisation** *nf* use.

utilitaire [ytilitɛʀ] *adj* utilitarian.

utilité [ytilite] *nf* usefulness, use. **cet outil peut avoir son ~** this tool has its uses *ou* may come in handy *ou* useful; **d'aucune ~** (of) no use *ou* help, useless; **déclaré d'~ publique** state-approved.

utopie [ytɔpi] *nf* utopian view (*ou* idea *etc*). **c'est de l'~** that's sheer utopianism. ♦ **utopique** *adj* utopian.

V

V, v [ve] *nm* (*lettre*) V, v. **en V** V-shaped.
vacance [vakɑ̃s] **1** *nf* (*Admin: poste*) vacancy. **2** *nfpl*: ~s holidays, vacation (*US*). **les ~s de Noël** the Christmas holidays; **partir/être en ~s** to go/be away on holiday; **prendre ses ~s en une fois** to take (all) one's holiday(s) at once; **j'ai besoin de ~s** I need a holiday *ou* vacation; **~s de neige** winter sports holiday; **lieu de ~s** holiday place. ♦ **vacancier, -ière** *nm,f* holiday-maker, vacationist (*US*).
vacant, e [vakɑ̃, ɑ̃t] *adj* (*gén*) vacant; *appartement* unoccupied.
vacarme [vakaʀm(ə)] *nm* din, racket, row. **faire du ~** to make a din.
vaccin [vaksɛ̃] *nm* (*substance*) vaccine. (*vaccination*) **faire un ~ à qn** to give sb a vaccination. ♦ **vaccination** *nf* vaccination. ♦ **vacciner** (1) *vt* (*Méd*) to vaccinate (*contre* against). **se faire ~** to have a vaccination, get vaccinated.
vache [vaʃ] **1** *nf* **(a)** (*Zool*) cow; (*cuir*) cowhide. **~ laitière** dairy cow. **(b)** (*: *méchant*) (*femme*) bitch*, cow*; (*homme*) swine*. **(c) ~ à eau** canvas waterbag. **(d)** (*locutions*) **période de ~s grasses/maigres** fat/lean years; **c'est une ~ à lait*** he's a mug* *ou* sucker*; **il parle français comme une ~ espagnole** he absolutely murders the French language; **manger de la ~ enragée** to go through hard *ou* lean times; **faire un coup en ~ à qn** to do the dirty on sb*; **ah la ~!*** (*douleur, indignation*) hell!*, damn!*; **une ~ de surprise*** a hell of a surprise*. **2** *adj* (*: *méchant*) rotten*, mean. ♦ **vachement*** *adv* **(a)** *crier etc* like mad*. **~ bon/difficile** damned* good/hard. **(b)** (*méchamment*) in a rotten* *ou* mean way. ♦ **vacher** *nm* cowherd. ♦ **vacherie** *nf* **(a)** (*: *méchanceté*) rottenness*, meanness. **une ~** (*action*) a dirty trick*; (*remarque*) a nasty remark. **(b)** (*: *intensif*) **quelle ~ de temps** *etc*! what damned* awful weather *etc*!
vaciller [vasije] (1) *vi* **(a)** (*lit*) *[personne, mur]* to sway (to and fro); *[bébé, meuble]* to wobble. **~ sur ses jambes** to stand shakily *ou* unsteadily on one's legs; **s'avancer en vacillant** to totter *ou* reel along. **(b)** *[lumière]* to flicker; *[voix]* to shake; *[résolution, courage]* to falter, waver; *[raison, santé, mémoire]* to be shaky, be failing. ♦ **vacillant, e** *adj* *démarche* shaky, wobbly; *flamme* flickering; *santé, mémoire, raison* shaky, failing; *caractère* indecisive. ♦ **vacillement** *nm*: **~(s)** swaying; wobbling, flickering; faltering, wavering.
vadrouille* [vadʀuj] *nf* ramble. **être en ~** to be out on a ramble. ♦ **vadrouiller*** (1) *vi* to ramble *ou* rove around *ou* about.
va-et-vient [vaevjɛ̃] *nm inv [personnes etc]* comings and goings, to-ings and fro-ings; *[piston]* to and fro (motion), backwards and forwards motion. **faire le ~ entre** to go to and fro between; (*Élec*) **(interrupteur de) ~** two-way switch.
vagabond, e [vagabɔ̃, ɔ̃d] **1** *adj* *peuple, vie* wandering; *imagination, humeur* restless. **2** *nm,f* (*péj: rôdeur*) tramp, vagrant, vagabond. ♦ **vagabondage** *nm* wandering, roaming; (*Jur, péj*) vagrancy. ♦ **vagabonder** (1) *vi [personne, imagination]* to roam, wander.
vagin [vaʒɛ̃] *nm* vagina.
vagir [vaʒiʀ] (2) *vi [bébé]* to cry, wail. ♦ **vagissement** *nm* cry, wailing.
vague[1] [vag] **1** *adj* (*gén*) vague; *idée* hazy; *regard* faraway; *robe, manteau* loose(-fitting). **un ~ cousin** some distant cousin; **il avait un ~ diplôme** he had a degree of sorts *ou* some kind of degree. **2** *nm* vagueness. **il est resté dans le ~** he kept it all rather vague; **regarder dans le ~** to gaze (vacantly) into space; **avoir du ~ à l'âme** to feel vaguely melancholic. ♦ **vaguement** *adv* vaguely.
vague[2] [vag] *nf* (*lit, fig*) wave. **~(s) de fond** ground swell; **~ d'enthousiasme** wave *ou* surge of enthusiasm; **premières ~s de touristes** first influxes of tourists; **~ de chaleur** heatwave; **~ de froid** cold spell *ou* snap.
vaillant, e [vajɑ̃, ɑ̃t] *adj* **(a)** (*courageux*) brave, courageous; (*au combat*) valiant, gallant. **(b)** (*vigoureux*) vigorous, robust. **je ne me sens pas très ~** I don't feel particularly great today*. ♦ **vaillamment** *adv* bravely, courageously; valiantly, gallantly. ♦ **vaillance** *nf* courage, bravery; valour, gallantry.
vain, e [vɛ̃, vɛn] *adj* **(a)** *promesse, espoir* vain, empty; *tentative, attente* vain, futile, fruitless; *regrets, discussion* vain, useless, idle. **en ~** in vain; **son sacrifice n'aura pas été ~** his sacrifice will not have been in vain; **il est ~ d'essayer de ...** it is futile to try to ... . **(b)** (*vaniteux*) vain. ♦ **vainement** *adv* vainly.
vaincre [vɛ̃kʀ(ə)] (42) *vt* *rival* to defeat; *ennemi* to defeat, vanquish, conquer; *obstacle etc* to overcome; *timidité, sentiment, maladie* to overcome, triumph over, conquer. **nous vaincrons** we shall overcome. ♦ **vaincu, e** *adj* defeated, vanquished. **s'avouer ~** to admit defeat; **les ~s** the vanquished, the defeated. ♦ **vainqueur** **1** *nm* (*à la guerre*) conqueror, victor; (*en sport*) winner. **2** *adj m* victorious, triumphant.
vaisseau, *pl* ~x [vɛso] *nm* **(a)** (*Naut*) ship, vessel. **~ amiral** flagship; **~ de guerre** warship; (*Aviat*) **~ spatial** spaceship. **(b)** (*Anat*) vessel.
vaisselle [vɛsɛl] *nf* (*plats*) crockery; (*plats à laver*) dishes; (*lavage*) washing-up, dishes. **faire la ~** to wash up, do the washing-up *ou* the dishes. ♦ **vaisselier** *nm* dresser.
val, *pl* ~s *ou* vaux [val, vo] *nm* valley.
valable [valabl(ə)] *adj* *contrat, passeport, raison, motif* valid; *œuvre, solution, équipements* decent, worthwhile. ♦ **valablement** *adv* validly. **pour en parler ~** ... to be able to say anything worthwhile *ou* valid about it ... .
valdinguer* [valdɛ̃ge] (1) *vi*: **aller ~** *[personne]* to go sprawling; *[objet]* to come crashing down; **envoyer ~ qch** to send sth flying*.
valet [valɛ] *nm* (*domestique*) (man)servant; (*Cartes*) jack, knave. **~ de chambre** manservant, valet; **~ de ferme** farmhand; **~ de pied** footman; (*cintre*) **~ (de nuit)** valet.
valeur [valœʀ] *nf* **(a)** (*commerciale*) value, worth; (*Fin*) *[devise, action]* value, price. **~ marchande/vénale** market/monetary value; **prendre/perdre de la ~** to go up/down in value, lose/gain in value; **ça a beaucoup de/n'a aucune ~** it is worth a lot/worthless. **(b)** (*titre boursier*) security. **~s** securities, stocks and shares; **~s (mobilières)** transferable securities. **(c)**

(*qualité*) *[personne]* worth, merit; *[roman]* value, merit; *[science, théorie]* value. **acteur de ~** actor of considerable merit; **juger qn/qch à sa (juste) ~** to judge sb/sth at his/its true value; **~s morales** moral values. **(d)** (*mesure*) value. **~ relative/absolue d'un terme** relative/absolute value of a term; **en ~ absolue/relative** in absolute/relative terms; **donnez-lui la ~ d'une cuiller à café** give him the equivalent of a teaspoonful, give him a teaspoon's worth. **(e)** (*locutions*) **objets de ~** valuables, articles of value; **sans ~** *objet* valueless, worthless; *témoignage* invalid, valueless; **mettre en ~** *terrain* to exploit; *détail* to bring out, highlight; *objet décoratif* to set off; **mettre qn en ~** *[conversation, esprit]* to show sb (off) to advantage, bring out sb's personal qualities.

valeureux, -euse [valœʀø, øz] *adj* valorous. ♦ **valeureusement** *adv* valorously.

valide [valid] *adj* **(a)** (*non blessé*) able-bodied; (*en bonne santé*) fit, well; *membre* good. **(b)** *billet, carte d'identité* valid. ♦ **valider** (1) *vt passeport, billet* to validate; *document* to authenticate. ♦ **validation** *nf* validation; authentication. ♦ **validité** *nf* validity.

valise [valiz] *nf* (suit)case. (*lit, fig*) **faire ses ~s** to pack one's bags; **la ~ (diplomatique)** the diplomatic bag.

vallée [vale] *nf* valley. ♦ **vallon** *nm* small valley. ♦ **vallonné, e** *adj* undulating. ♦ **vallonnement** *nm* undulation.

valoir [valwaʀ] (29) **1** *vi* **(a)** *[objet]* **~ qch** to be worth sth; **ça vaut 10 F** it's worth 10 francs; **~ cher** to be worth a lot, be expensive; **accompte à ~ sur ...** deposit to be deducted from ...; **cette montre vaut-elle plus cher que l'autre? — elles se valent à peu près** is this watch worth more than the other one? — they are worth about the same (amount). **(b)** (*qualité*) **que vaut cet auteur/cette pièce?** is this author/this play any good?; **ils ne valent pas mieux l'un que l'autre** there's nothing to choose between them, they are two of a kind; **il ne vaut pas cher!** *ou* **pas grand-chose!** he's a bad lot; **il a conscience de ce qu'il vaut** he is aware of his worth, he knows his worth; **ça ne vaut rien** *ou* **pas un clou*** (*gén*) it's no good (*pour* for); *[marchandise]* it's rubbish; *[argument]* it's worthless; *[outil]* it's useless *ou* no use; **ne faire rien qui vaille** to do nothing useful *ou* worthwhile *ou* of any use; **cela ne me dit rien qui vaille** I don't like the look of that, it seems rather ominous to me. **(c)** (*s'appliquer*) to hold, apply, be valid. **ceci ne vaut que dans certains cas** this only holds *ou* applies *ou* is only valid in certain cases. **(d)** (*être aussi bon*) **~ qn/qch** to be as good as sb/sth; (*revenir au même*) **~ qch** to be equivalent to sth, be worth sth; **rien ne vaut la mer** there's nothing like *ou* nothing to beat the sea; **cette méthode en vaut une autre** it's as good a method as any (other); (*en mal*) **ces deux frères se valent** these two brothers are two of a kind; **ça se vaut*** it's six of one and half a dozen of the other*. **(e)** (*justifier*) to be worth. **le musée valait le détour/d'être vu** the museum was worth the detour/was worth seeing; **cela vaut la peine** *ou* **le coup*** it's worth it, it's worth the trouble. **(f) faire ~** *domaine* to exploit; *droits* to assert; *fait, argument* to emphasize; (*mettre en vedette*) *caractéristique* to highlight, bring out; *personne* to show off to advantage; **je lui fis ~ que ...** I impressed upon him that ... . **(g) il vaut/vaudrait mieux refuser, mieux vaut/vaudrait refuser** it is better/would be better to refuse; **il vaudrait mieux que vous refusiez** you had better refuse, you would do better to refuse; **mieux vaut trop de travail que pas assez** too much work is better than not enough.

2 *vt*: **ceci lui a valu des reproches** *etc* this earned *ou* brought him reproaches *etc*; **qu'est ce qui nous vaut l'honneur de cette visite?** to what do we owe the honour of this visit?

valoriser [valɔʀize] (1) *vt* to enhance the value of. ♦ **valorisation** *nf* valorization.

valse [vals(ə)] *nf* (*danse*) waltz; (*fig: carrousel*) musical chairs. **~ hésitation** pussyfooting*. ♦ **valser** (1) *vi* **(a)** (*danser*) to waltz. **(b)** (**fig*) **envoyer ~ qch/qn** to send sth/sb flying; **il est allé ~ contre le mur** he went flying against the wall; **faire ~ l'argent** to spend money like water. ♦ **valseur, -euse** *nm,f* waltzer.

valve [valv(ə)] *nf* valve.

vampire [vɑ̃piʀ] *nm* (*gén*) vampire; (*Zool*) vampire bat.

vandale [vɑ̃dal] *adj, nmf* vandal. ♦ **vandalisme** *nm* vandalism.

vanille [vanij] *nf* vanilla.

vanité [vanite] *nf* **(a)** (*amour-propre*) pride, vanity, conceit. **sans ~** without false modesty; **tirer ~ de** to pride o.s. on. **(b)** (*futilité*) *[promesse, espoir]* emptiness, vanity; *[tentative]* futility, fruitlessness; *[regrets, discussion]* uselessness, idleness. ♦ **vaniteusement** *adv* vainly, conceitedly. ♦ **vaniteux, -euse** *adj* vain, conceited.

vanne [van] *nf* (*canalisation*) gate; *[écluse, digue]* (sluice) gate.

vanner [vane] (1) *vt* **(a)** (*Agr*) to winnow. **(b)** (‡: *fatiguer*) to exhaust, do in*. **je suis vanné** I'm dead-beat*.

vannerie [vanʀi] *nf* basketwork. ♦ **vannier** *nm* basket maker.

vantail, *pl* **-aux** [vɑ̃taj, o] *nm [porte]* leaf. **porte à double ~** Dutch door.

vanter [vɑ̃te] (1) **1** *vt auteur, endroit, qualités* to praise, speak highly of, speak in praise of; *méthode, avantages, marchandises* to vaunt. **2 se ~** *vpr* **(a)** (*fanfaronner*) to boast, brag. **sans me ~** without false modesty, without wishing to boast *ou* brag. **(b)** (*se targuer*) **se ~ de qch/d'avoir fait qch** to pride o.s. on sth/on having done sth; **se ~ de (pouvoir) faire ...** to boast one can do ...; **il n'y a pas de quoi se ~** there's nothing to be proud of *ou* to boast about. ♦ **vantard, e 1** *adj* boastful, bragging, boasting. **2** *nm,f* braggart, boaster. ♦ **vantardise** *nf* (*caractère*) boastfulness; (*propos*) boast.

va-nu-pieds [vanypje] *nmf inv* (*péj*) tramp, beggar.

vapes‡ [vap] *nfpl*: **tomber dans les ~** to fall into a dead faint, pass out; **être dans les ~** (*évanoui*) to be out cold*; (*drogué, après un choc*) to be woozy* *ou* in a daze.

vapeur [vapœʀ] *nf* **(a)** (*brouillard*) haze, vapour; (*Chim: émanation*) vapour. **~s d'essence** petrol fumes; **~ (d'eau)** steam, (water) vapour; **machine** *etc* **à ~** steam engine *etc*; **(cuit à la) ~** steamed; **aller à toute ~** to go full steam ahead. **(b)** (†: *malaises*) **~s** vapours†.

vaporeux, -euse [vapɔʀø, øz] *adj tissu* filmy; *atmosphère* misty, vaporous; *cheveux* gossamer.

vaporiser [vapɔʀize] (1) **1** *vt* to spray. **2 se ~** *vpr* (*Phys*) to vaporize. ♦ **vaporisateur** *nm* spray.

vaquer [vake] (1) **1 ~ à** *vt indir* to attend to, see to. **~ à ses occupations** to go about one's business. **2** *vi* (*Admin: être en vacances*) to be on vacation.

varappe [vaʀap] *nf* rock climbing.

varech [vaʀɛk] *nm* wrack.

vareuse [vaʀøz] *nf* *[marin]* pea jacket; (*d'uniforme*) tunic.

varice [vaʀis] *nf* varicose vein.

varicelle [vaʀisɛl] *nf* chickenpox.

varier [vaʀje] (7) *vti* to vary. ♦ **variable 1** *adj* (*gén*) variable; *temps* changeable, unsettled; *humeur* changeable. **le baromètre est au ~** the barometer reads 'change'; **les réactions sont très ~s** reactions are very varied *ou* vary greatly. **2** *nf* variable. ♦ **variante** *nf* (*gén*) variant (*de* of).

♦ **variation** *nf* variation (*de* in). ♦ **varié, e** *adj* **(a)** (*non monotone*) *style, paysage, menu* varied. **un travail très ~** a very varied job. **(b)** (*divers*) *opinions, sujets, objets* various, divers. **hors-d'œuvre ~s** selection of hors d'œuvres. ♦ **variété** *nf* (*gén*) variety. (*Music-hall*) **(spectacle de) ~s** variety show.

variole [vaʀjɔl] *nf* smallpox.

vase[1] [vɑz] *nm* vase. (*fig*) **en ~ clos** in isolation *ou* seclusion; **~s communicants** communicating vessels; **~ de nuit** chamberpot.

vase[2] [vɑz] *nf* silt, mud, sludge.

vaseline [vazlin] *nf* vaseline, petroleum jelly.

vaseux, -euse [vɑzø, øz] *adj* **(a)** (*) (*fatigué*) washed out*; (*confus*) woolly*, hazy. **(b)** (*boueux*) silty, muddy, sludgy.

vasistas [vazistɑs] *nm* fanlight.

vasque [vask(ə)] *nf* (*bassin*) basin; (*coupe*) bowl.

vassal, e, mpl -aux [vasal, o] *nm,f* (*Hist, fig*) vassal.

vaste [vast(ə)] *adj* (*gén*) vast, huge, immense. **c'est une ~ fumisterie*** it's a huge *ou* gigantic hoax.

Vatican [vatikɑ̃] *nm*: **le ~** the Vatican.

va-tout [vatu] *nm*: **jouer son ~** to stake *ou* risk one's all.

vaudeville [vodvil] *nm* vaudeville, light comedy.

vau-l'eau [volo] *adv*: **aller à ~** to be on the road to ruin.

vaurien, -ienne [voʀjɛ̃, jɛn] *nm,f* (*voyou*) good-for-nothing; (*garnement*) little devil*.

vautour [votuʀ] *nm* (*Zool, fig*) vulture.

vautrer (se) [votʀe] (1) *vpr*: **se ~ dans** *boue, vice* to wallow in; *fauteuil* to loll in; **se ~ sur** *tapis* to sprawl on; **vautré dans l'herbe** sprawling *ou* sprawled in the grass.

va-vite* [vavit] *adv*: **à la ~** in a rush *ou* hurry.

veau, *pl* **~x** [vo] *nm* **(a)** (*Zool*) calf; (*Culin*) veal; (*cuir*) calfskin. **côte de ~** veal chop; **foie de ~** calf's liver. **(b)** (**péj*) (*personne*) lump* (*péj*); (*voiture*) tank* (*péj*).

vecteur [vɛktœʀ] *nm* (*Bio, Math*) vector.

vécu, e [veky] **1** *adj* real(-life). **2** *nm*: **le ~** real-life experience.

vedette [vədɛt] *nf* **(a)** *[spectacle]* star. **une ~ de la politique** a leading light *ou* figure in politics; **produit-~** leading product; **avoir la ~** *[artiste]* to top the bill, have star billing; *[événement, criminel]* to be in the spotlight, make the headlines; *[orateur etc]* to be in the limelight; **mettre qn en ~** (*Ciné*) to give sb star billing; (*fig*) to push sb into the limelight, put the spotlight on sb; **en ~ américaine** as a special guest star. **(b)** (*embarcation*) launch; (*Mil*) patrol boat.

végétal, e, mpl -aux [veʒetal, o] **1** *adj graisses, teintures* vegetable; *biologie, cellules* plant. **2** *nm* vegetable, plant.

végétarien, -ienne [veʒetaʀjɛ̃, jɛn] *adj, nm,f* vegetarian.

végéter [veʒete] (6) *vi* (*péj*) *[personne]* to vegetate; *[affaire]* to stagnate. ♦ **végétatif, -ive** *adj* vegetative. ♦ **végétation** *nf* **(a)** (*Bot*) vegetation. **(b)** (*Méd*) **~s** adenoids.

véhémence [veemɑ̃s] *nf* vehemence. ♦ **véhément, e** *adj* vehement.

véhicule [veikyl] *nm* **(a)** (*Aut*) vehicle. **~ automobile/utilitaire** motor/commercial vehicle. **(b)** *[pensée]* vehicle, medium. ♦ **véhiculer** (1) *vt* (*Aut*) to convey, transport; *substance, idées* to convey.

veille [vɛj] *nf* **(a)** (*état*) wakefulness. **en état de ~** in the waking state, awake. **(b)** (*garde*) (night) watch. **(c)** (*jour précédent*) **la ~** the day before; **la ~ au soir** the previous evening, the evening before; **la ~ de cet examen** the day before that exam; **la ~ de Noël/du jour de l'an** Christmas/New Year's Eve; **la ~ de sa mort** on the eve of his death, on the day before his death. **(d)** (*fig*) **à la ~ de guerre** on the eve of; **être à la ~ de faire qch** to be on the brink *ou* point of doing sth.

veiller [veje] (1) **1** *vi* (*rester éveillé*) to stay up, sit up; (*être de garde*) to be on watch; (*rester vigilant*) to be watchful; (*faire la veillée*) to spend the evening in company. **2** *vt mort, malade* to watch over, sit up with. **3** *vt indir* **(a) ~ à** *intérêts, approvisionnement etc* to attend to, see to, look after. **~ à ce que ...** to see to it that ..., make sure that ...; **~ au grain** to keep an eye open for trouble. **(b) ~ sur** to watch over, keep a watchful eye on. ♦ **veillée** *nf* (*réunion*) evening gathering. **~ (funèbre)** wake, watch. ♦ **veilleur** *nm* **(a) ~ (de nuit)** (night) watchman. **(b)** (*Mil*) look-out. ♦ **veilleuse** *nf* (*lampe*) night light; (*Aut*) sidelight. (*fig*) **mettre qch en ~** to soft-pedal on sth; **mets-la en ~!‡** belt up!‡

veine [vɛn] *nf* **(a)** (*gén, Anat, Méd*) vein; *[houille]* seam, vein; *[minerai de fer]* lode, vein. **(b)** (*fig: inspiration*) inspiration. **de la même ~** in the same vein; **être en ~** to be inspired; **être en ~ de patience** to be in a patient mood *ou* frame of mind. **(c)** (*: *chance*) luck. **c'est une ~** that's a bit of luck; **coup de ~** stroke of luck; **pas de ~!** hard *ou* bad *ou* rotten* luck!; **avoir de la ~** to be lucky; **il n'a pas eu de ~ aux examens** his luck was out at the exams; (*iro*) **c'est bien ma ~** that's just my (rotten*) luck. ♦ **veinard, e*** **1** *adj* lucky. **2** *nm,f* lucky devil*. ♦ **veiner** (1) *vt* (*donner l'aspect du bois*) to grain; (*donner l'aspect du marbre*) to vein.

vêler [vele] (1) *vi* to calve. ♦ **vêlage** *nm* calving.

vélin [velɛ̃] *nm* vellum.

velléité [veleite] *nf* vague desire, vague impulse. ♦ **velléitaire** **1** *adj* irresolute, wavering. **2** *nmf* waverer.

vélo [velo] *nm* bike, cycle. **~ de course** racing cycle; **venir en ~** to come by bike; **faire du ~** to cycle, do some cycling; **il sait faire du ~** he can ride a bike. ♦ **vélodrome** *nm* velodrome. ♦ **vélomoteur** *nm* moped.

vélocité [velɔsite] *nf* swiftness.

velours [v(ə)luʀ] *nm* **(a)** (*tissu*) velvet. **~ côtelé** corduroy, cord. **(b)** (*velouté*) (*gén*) velvet; *[pêche]* bloom. **peau de ~** velvet(y) skin.

velouté, e [vəlute] **1** *adj joues, crème, vin* smooth, velvety; *lumière, voix* mellow. **2** *nm* **(a)** (*douceur*) velvetiness, smoothness. **(b)** (*sauce*) velouté sauce; (*potage*) velouté. **~ de tomates** cream of tomato soup.

velu, e [vəly] *adj* hairy.

venaison [vənɛzɔ̃] *nf* venison.

vénal, e, mpl -aux [venal, o] *adj* venal. ♦ **vénalité** *nf* venality.

vendange [vɑ̃dɑ̃ʒ] *nf*: **~(s)** grape harvest, vintage; **faire la ~** to harvest *ou* pick the grapes. ♦ **vendanger** (3) **1** *vt vigne* to harvest *ou* pick grapes from; *raisins* to harvest. **2** *vi* to harvest *ou* pick the grapes. ♦ **vendangeur, -euse** *nm,f* grape-picker.

vendetta [vɑ̃deta] *nf* vendetta.

vendre [vɑ̃dʀ(ə)] (41) **1** *vt* **(a)** (*lit, fig*) to sell (*à* to). **~ qch à qn** to sell sb sth *ou* sth to sb; **il m'a vendu un tableau 500 F** he sold me a picture for 500 francs; **il vend cher** he is expensive *ou* dear, his prices are high; **~ qch aux enchères** to sell sth by auction; **maison à ~** house for sale. **(b)** (*: *trahir*) to sell. **(c)** (*locutions*) **~ chèrement sa vie** to sell one's life dearly; **~ la peau de l'ours (avant de l'avoir tué)** to count one's chickens (before they are hatched); **~ la mèche*** to give the game away*.

2 se ~ *vpr* **(a)** *[marchandise]* **se ~ à la pièce/douzaine** to be sold singly/by the dozen; **ça se vend bien/comme des petits pains** that sells well/like hot cakes. **(b)** (*se trahir*) to give o.s. away. ♦ **vendeur, -euse** *nm,f* (*gén*) salesman (*ou* saleswoman), shop *ou* sales assistant;

(*Jur*) vendor, seller. ~ **de journaux** newsvendor; **je ne suis pas** ~ I'm not selling. ♦ **vendu** *nm* (*péj*) Judas.

vendredi [vɑ̃dʀədi] *nm* Friday. ~ **saint** Good Friday; *V* **samedi.**

vénéneux, -euse [venenø, øz] *adj* poisonous.

vénérer [veneʀe] (6) *vt* to venerate, revere. ♦ **vénérable** *adj* venerable. ♦ **vénération** *nf* veneration, reverence.

vengeance [vɑ̃ʒɑ̃s] *nf* vengeance, revenge. **ce forfait crie** ~ this crime cries out for revenge; **de petites** ~**s** petty acts of vengeance *ou* revenge. ♦ **venger** (3) **1** *vt* to avenge (*de qch* for sth). **2 se** ~ *vpr* to take (one's) revenge *ou* vengeance; (*pour son honneur*) to avenge o.s. **se** ~ **de qn** to take revenge on sb; **se** ~ **de qch** to take one's revenge for sth. ♦ **vengeur, -geresse 1** *adj personne* (re)vengeful; *bras, lettre* avenging. **2** *nm,f* avenger.

véniel, -elle [venjɛl] *adj* venial.

venin [vənɛ̃] *nm* (*lit, fig*) venom. ♦ **venimeux, -euse** *adj* (*lit, fig*) venomous.

venir [v(ə)niʀ] (22) **1** *vi* **(a)** *[personne]* to come. **ils viennent de Lyon** they are coming from Lyons; **il vint vers moi** he came up to me *ou* towards me; **ils sont venus en voiture** they came by car, they drove (here); **je viens!** I'm coming!, I'm on my way!*; **je viens dans un instant** I'll be there in a moment; **le voisin est venu** the man from next door came round *ou* called; **il vient chez nous tous les jeudis** he comes (round) to our house *ou* to us every Thursday. **(b) faire** ~ *médecin* to call, send for; **tu nous as fait** ~ **pour rien** you got us to come *ou* you made us come for nothing; **faire** ~ **son vin de Provence** to get one's wine sent from Provence. **(c)** (*fig*) to come. **le bruit est venu jusqu'à nous que ...** word has reached us *ou* come to us that ...; **ça ne me serait pas venu à l'idée** that would never have occurred to me *ou* entered my head, I should never have thought of that; **la semaine qui vient** the coming week; **cette plante vient bien** this plant is coming along *ou* is doing well *ou* nicely; **les années à** ~ the years to come, future years. **(d)** (*provenance, cause*) ~ **de** to come from; **l'épée lui vient de son oncle** the sword has been passed down to him by his uncle; **ces troubles viennent du foie** this trouble stems *ou* comes from the liver; **d'où vient cette hâte soudaine?** what's the reason for this sudden haste?, how come* *ou* why this sudden haste?; **ça vient de ce que ...** it comes *ou* results *ou* stems from the fact that ... . **(e)** (*atteindre*) ~ **(jusqu')à** (*vers le haut*) to come up to, reach (up to); (*vers le bas*) to come down to, reach (down to); (*en longueur, en superficie*) to come out to, reach; **l'eau nous vient aux genoux** the water comes up to *ou* reaches (up to) our knees; ~ **au monde** to come into the world, be born; ~ **à bout de** *travail, gâteau* to get through; *adversaire* to get the better of, overcome; **je n'en viendrai jamais à bout** I'll never manage it, I'll never get through it. **(f) en** ~ **à: j'en viens maintenant à votre question** I shall now come *ou* turn to your question; **venons-en au fait** let's get to the point; **j'en viens à la conclusion que ...** I have come to *ou* reached the conclusion that ...; **j'en viens à leur avis** I'm coming round to their opinion; **j'en viens à me demander si ...** I'm beginning to wonder if ...; **comment les choses en sont-elles venues là?** how did things come to this? *ou* get to this stage?; **en** ~ **aux mains** to come to blows; **où voulez-vous en** ~? what are you getting *ou* driving at?

2 *vb aux* **(a)** (*se déplacer pour*) **je suis venu travailler** I have come to work; **il va** ~ **la voir** he's going to come to *ou* and see her; **viens m'aider** come and help me; **ne viens pas te plaindre!** don't (you) come and complain *ou* come complaining. **(b)** (*passé récent*) **il vient d'arriver** he has just arrived; **elle venait de se lever** she had just got up. **(c)** (*éventualité*) **s'il venait à mourir** if he were to die *ou* if he should (happen to) die.

3 *vb impers* **(a) il vient beaucoup d'enfants** a lot of children are coming; **il lui est venu des boutons** he came out in spots; **il ne lui viendrait pas à l'idée que ...** it wouldn't occur to him *ou* enter his head that ...; **il vient une heure où ...** the hour is coming when ... . **(b)** (*éventualité*) **s'il vient à pleuvoir** if it should (happen to) rain.

4 s'en ~ *vpr* (*littér*) to come.

vent [vɑ̃] *nm* **(a)** wind. ~ **du nord** North wind; ~ **coulis** draught; **un** ~ **de révolte** a wind of revolt; (*Naut*) ~ **contraire** headwind; **au** ~**/sous le** ~ **(de)** to windward/to leeward (of); **être en plein** ~ to be exposed to the wind; **il y a** *ou* **il fait du** ~ it is windy; **coup de** ~ gust of wind. **(b)** (*Méd*) **avoir des** ~**s** to have wind. **(c)** (*locutions*) (*lit, fig*) **observer d'où vient le** ~ to see how the wind blows; **le** ~ **est à l'optimisme** there is optimism in the air; (*fig*) **il a le** ~ **en poupe** he has the wind in his sails; **à tous les** ~**s, aux quatre** ~**s** to the four winds; **être dans le** ~* to be with it*, be trendy*; **jeune fille dans le** ~* trendy girl*; (*péj*) **c'est du** ~* it's all wind *ou* hot air*; **avoir** ~ **de** to get wind of; **quel bon** ~ **vous amène?** to what do I (*ou* we) owe the pleasure of seeing you?; **elle l'a fait contre** ~**s et marées** she did it against all the odds *ou* despite all the obstacles.

ventail, *pl* **-aux** [vɑ̃taj, o] *nm* ventail.

vente [vɑ̃t] *nf* sale. **bureau/promesse de** ~ sales office/agreement; **être en** ~ **libre** (*gén*) to be freely sold, have no sales restrictions; **en** ~ **chez votre libraire** available *ou* on sale at your local bookshop; **mettre en** ~ *produit* to put on sale; *maison* to put up for sale; **nous n'en avons pas la** ~ we have no demand *ou* sale for that; **la livre vaut 10 F à la** ~ the selling rate for sterling is 10 francs; ~ **(aux enchères)** (auction) sale, auction; ~ **de charité** charity bazaar, jumble sale, sale of work.

venter [vɑ̃te] (1) *vb impers*: **il vente** the wind blows. ♦ **venté, e** *adj* windswept, windy.

ventiler [vɑ̃tile] (1) *vt* **(a)** (*aérer*) to ventilate. **(b)** *total* to break down; *crédits, travail* to allocate. ♦ **ventilateur** *nm* (*gén*) fan; (*dans un mur, une fenêtre*) ventilator, fan. ♦ **ventilation** *nf* ventilation; breaking down; allocation.

ventouse [vɑ̃tuz] *nf* (*Méd*) cupping glass; (*Zool*) sucker; (*dispositif adhésif*) suction pad. **faire** ~ to cling, adhere.

ventre [vɑ̃tʀ(ə)] *nm* **(a)** (*abdomen*) stomach, tummy*. **être étendu sur le** ~ to be lying on one's stomach *ou* front; **avoir/prendre du** ~ to have/be getting rather a paunch; (*fig*) **passer sur le** ~ **de qn** to ride roughshod over sb; **courir** ~ **à terre** to run at top speed. **(b)** (*estomac*) stomach. **avoir le** ~ **creux** to have an empty stomach; **avoir le** ~ **plein** to be full; **avoir mal au** ~ to have stomach ache *ou* (a) tummy ache*; (*fig*) **ça me ferait mal au** ~* it would make me sick; (*fig*) **voyons ce que ça a dans le** ~* let's see what's inside it; (*courage*) **il n'a rien dans le** ~* he's got no guts*. **(c)** (*utérus*) womb. **(d)** *[animal]* (under)belly; *[vase]* bulb; *[bateau, avion]* belly. ♦ **ventricule** *nm* ventricle. ♦ **ventriloque** *nmf* ventriloquist. ♦ **ventripotent, e** *adj* potbellied. ♦ **ventru, e** *adj personne* potbellied; *objet* bulbous.

venu, e [v(ə)ny] *adj* **(a) être bien** ~ **de faire** to have (good) grounds for doing; **être mal** ~ **de faire** to have no grounds for doing, be in no position to do. **(b)** *remarque* **bien** ~ timely, apposite; **mal** ~ untimely, inapposite; **il serait mal** ~ **de lui poser cette question** it would be unseemly to ask him this question. **(c) bien** ~ *enfant* sturdy; *plante* sturdy, well-developed, fine. **(d)** (*arrivé*) **tard** ~ late; **tôt** ~ early. ♦ **venue** *nf* coming. **lors de ma** ~ **au monde** when I came into the world.

vêpres [vɛpʀ(ə)] *nfpl* vespers.
ver [vɛʀ] *nm* (*gén*) worm; (*larve*) grub; *[viande, fruits]* maggot. *[bois]* ~s woodworm; ~ **luisant** glow-worm; ~ **à soie** silkworm; ~ **solitaire** tapeworm; ~ **de terre** earthworm; **tirer les ~s du nez à qn*** to worm information out of sb*.
véracité [veʀasite] *nf* veracity, truthfulness.
véranda [veʀɑ̃da] *nf* veranda(h).
verbal, e, *mpl* **-aux** [vɛʀbal, o] *adj* (*gén*) verbal. ♦ **verbalement** *adv* verbally.
verbaliser [vɛʀbalize] (1) *vi*: **l'agent a dû** ~ the officer had to book* *ou* report him (*ou* me *etc*).
verbe [vɛʀb(ə)] *nm* **(a)** (*Gram*) verb. ~ **d'action/d'état** verb of action/state; ~ **fort** strong verb. **(b)** (*Rel, littér: langage*) **le** ~ the word; **avoir le** ~ **haut** to speak in a high and mighty tone.
verbiage [vɛʀbjaʒ] *nm* verbiage.
verdâtre [vɛʀdɑtʀ(ə)] *adj* greenish.
verdeur [vɛʀdœʀ] *nf* **(a)** (*jeunesse*) vigour, vitality. **(b)** *[fruit]* tartness, sharpness; *[vin]* acidity. **(c)** *[langage]* forthrightness.
verdict [vɛʀdik(t)] *nm* (*Jur, gén*) verdict.
verdir [vɛʀdiʀ] (2) *vti* to turn green.
verdoyant, e [vɛʀdwajɑ̃, ɑ̃t] *adj* green, verdant (*littér*).
verdure [vɛʀdyʀ] *nf* (*végétation*) greenery; (*légumes verts*) green vegetables.
véreux, -euse [veʀø, øz] *adj* **(a)** *aliment* maggoty, worm-eaten. **(b)** *financier, affaire* dubious, shady.
verge [vɛʀʒ(ə)] *nf* (*baguette*) rod; (*Anat*) penis.
verger [vɛʀʒe] *nm* orchard.
verglas [vɛʀgla] *nm* (black) ice (*on road etc*). ♦ **verglacé, e** *adj* icy, iced-over.
vergogne [vɛʀgɔɲ] *nf*: **sans** ~ (*adj*) shameless; (*adv*) shamelessly.
vergue [vɛʀg(ə)] *nf* (*Naut*) yard.
véridique [veʀidik] *adj* ***récit, témoin*** truthful, veracious; ***repentir*** genuine, authentic.
vérifier [veʀifje] (7) *vt* **(a)** (*contrôler*) (*gén*) to check, verify; (*Fin*) *comptes* to audit. **cela a été vérifié et revérifié** it has been checked and double-checked. **(b)** (*prouver*) to establish *ou* confirm (the truth of), prove to be true; (*confirmer*) to bear out, confirm. **cet accident a vérifié mes craintes** this accident has borne out *ou* confirmed my fears; **ça peut se** ~ **tous les jours** it is borne out every day. ♦ **vérifiable** *adj* verifiable. ♦ **vérificateur, -trice 1** *adj* checking, verifying. **2** *nm,f* controller, checker, inspector. ♦ **vérification** *nf* **(a)** (*action*) checking; verification; auditing. ~ **faite** on checking. **(b)** (*contrôle*) check; (*preuve*) proof; (*confirmation*) confirmation. ~ **d'identité** identity check.
vérin [veʀɛ̃] *nm* jack.
véritable [veʀitabl(ə)] *adj* (*gén*) real; *raisons, sentiment, ami* true, genuine; *cuir, perles* genuine. **sous son jour** ~ in its (*ou* his *etc*) true light; **un** ~ **coquin** a real *ou* a downright rogue; **c'est une** ~ **folie** it's absolute madness. ♦ **véritablement** *adv* really; truly; genuinely. **il l'a** ~ **fait** he actually *ou* really did it; **c'est** ~ **délicieux** it's absolutely *ou* positively *ou* really delicious.
vérité [veʀite] *nf* **(a) la** ~ (*connaissance du vrai*) truth; (*conformité aux faits*) the truth; **nul n'est dépositaire de la** ~ no one has a monopoly of truth; **c'est l'entière** ~ it is the whole truth; **dire la** ~ to tell *ou* speak the truth; **la** ~**, c'est qu'il est paresseux** the truth (of the matter) is, he's lazy. **(b)** (*ressemblance*) *[portrait]* lifelikeness, trueness to life; *[tableau]* trueness to life. **(c)** (*sincérité*) truthfulness, sincerity. **un air de** ~ an air of sincerity *ou* truthfulness, a truthful *ou* sincere look. **(d)** (*fait vrai*) truth. ~**s éternelles/premières** eternal/first truths. **(e) c'est peu de chose, en** ~ it's really *ou* actually nothing very much; **à la** ~ *ou* **en** ~ **il préfère s'amuser** to tell the truth *ou* to be honest he prefers to enjoy himself.
vermeil, -eille [vɛʀmɛj] **1** *adj* ***tissu*** vermilion, bright red; ***bouche*** ruby, cherry; ***teint*** rosy. **2** *nm* vermeil.
vermicelle [vɛʀmisɛl] *nm*: ~**(s)** vermicelli.
vermifuge [vɛʀmifyʒ] *adj, nm* vermifuge.
vermillon [vɛʀmijɔ̃] *nm, adj inv* vermilion.
vermine [vɛʀmin] *nf* (*lit, fig*) vermin.
vermoulu, e [vɛʀmuly] *adj* worm-eaten.
vernir [vɛʀniʀ] (2) *vt* to varnish; ***poterie*** to glaze. ♦ **verni, e** *adj* **(a)** *bois* varnished; (*luisant*) shiny, glossy. **souliers** ~**s** patent (leather) shoes. **(b)** (*: *chanceux*) lucky. ♦ **vernis** *nm* varnish; glaze; (*éclat*) shine, gloss. ~ **(à ongles)** nail varnish *ou* polish; ~ **de culture** veneer of culture. ♦ **vernissage** *nm* **(a)** varnishing; glazing. **(b)** (*exposition*) preview (*at art gallery*).
vérole‡ [veʀɔl] *nf* pox‡.
verre [vɛʀ] **1** *nm* **(a)** (*substance*) glass. **cela se casse comme du** ~ it's as brittle as glass. **(b)** *[vitre, cadre]* glass; *[lunettes]* lens. **mettre qch sous** ~ to put sth under glass; **porter des** ~**s** to wear glasses. **(c)** (*récipient, contenu*) glass. ~ **à bière** beer glass; ~ **de bière** glass of beer. **(d)** (*boisson*) drink. **boire** *ou* **prendre un** ~ to have a drink; **un petit** ~* a quick one*, a dram*; **avoir bu un** ~ **de trop*, avoir un** ~ **dans le nez*** to have had one too many*, have had a drop too much*. **2:** ~ **blanc** plain glass; ~**s de contact** contact lenses; ~ **à dents** tooth mug *ou* glass; ~ **dépoli** frosted glass; ~**s fumés** tinted lenses; ~ **de montre** watch glass; ~ **à pied** stemmed glass. ♦ **verrerie** *nf* (*usine*) glassworks, glass factory; (*objets*) glassware; (*commerce*) glass trade *ou* industry. ♦ **verrier** *nm* (*ouvrier*) glassworker; (*artiste*) glass artist. ♦ **verrière** *nf* (*fenêtre*) window; (*toit vitré*) glass roof; (*paroi vitrée*) glass wall. ♦ **verroterie** *nf*: **bijoux en** ~ glass jewellery.
verrou [vɛʀu] *nm [porte]* bolt. **mettre le** ~ to bolt the door; **mettre qn sous les** ~**s** to put sb behind bars *ou* under lock and key; **être sous les** ~**s** to be behind bars. ♦ **verrouiller** (1) *vt* ***porte*** to bolt; ***culasse*** to lock. ♦ **verrouillage** *nm* (*action*) bolting; locking; (*dispositif*) locking mechanism.
verrue [vɛʀy] *nf* wart. ~ **plantaire** verruca.
vers[1] [vɛʀ] *prép* **(a)** (*direction*) toward(s), to. **en allant** ~ **la gare** going to *ou* towards the station; **il tendit la main** ~ **la bouteille** he reached out for the bottle, he stretched out his hand toward(s) the bottle. **(b)** (*approximation*) around, about. **c'est** ~ **Aix que nous avons eu une panne** it was (somewhere) near Aix *ou* round about Aix that we broke down; ~ **quelle heure doit-il venir?** (at) around *ou* (at) about what time is he due?; **il était** ~ **(les) 3 heures** it was about *ou* around 3; ~ **le début du siècle** toward(s) *ou* about the turn of the century.
vers[2] [vɛʀ] *nm* **(a)** (*sg: ligne*) line. **au 3e** ~ in line 3, in the 3rd line. **(b)** (*pl: poésie*) verse. **traduction en** ~ verse translation; **faire des** ~ to write verse; ~ **blancs/libres** blank/free verse.
versant [vɛʀsɑ̃] *nm [vallée]* side; *[massif]* slopes.
versatile [vɛʀsatil] *adj* fickle, changeable. ♦ **versatilité** *nf* fickleness, changeability.
verse [vɛʀs(ə)] *adv*: **à** ~ in torrents; **il pleut à** ~ it is pouring down.
versé, e [vɛʀse] *adj*: ~**/peu** ~ **dans qch** (well-) versed/ill-versed in sth.
Verseau [vɛʀso] *nm* (*Astron*) **le** ~ Aquarius, the Water-carrier; **être (du)** ~ to be Aquarius *ou* an Aquarian.
versement [vɛʀsəmɑ̃] *nm* payment (*sur un compte* into an account); (*échelonné*) instalment.
verser [vɛʀse] (1) **1** *vt* **(a)** ***liquide, grains*** to pour, tip (*dans* into, *sur* onto); (*servir*) ***thé etc*** to pour (out) (*dans* into). **verse-toi à boire** pour yourself a drink. **(b)** ***larmes, sang, clarté*** to shed. **(c)** (*classer*) ~ **une pièce à un dossier** to add an item to a

file. **(d)** (*payer*) to pay. ~ **qch à qn** to pay sb sth; ~ **une somme à un compte** to pay a sum of money into an account; ~ **des arrhes** to put down *ou* pay a deposit. **(e)** (*incorporer*) ~ **qn dans** to assign *ou* attach sb to. **2** *vi* **(a)** *[véhicule]* to overturn. **il va nous faire ~ dans le fossé** he'll tip us into the ditch. **(b)** ~ **dans** *sentimentalité* to lapse into. ♦ **verseur, -euse 1** *adj*: **bec** ~ (pouring) lip; **bouchon** ~ pour-through stopper. **2** *nm* pourer.

verset [vɛʀsɛ] *nm* (*Rel*) verse.

version [vɛʀsjɔ̃] *nf* **(a)** (*traduction*) translation (*into the mother tongue*), unseen (translation). ~ **anglaise** English unseen (translation), translation from English. **(b)** (*variante*) version. **film en** ~ **originale** film in the original language *ou* version; **film italien en** ~ **française** Italian film dubbed in French. **(c)** (*interprétation*) version.

verso [vɛʀso] *nm* back. **au** ~ on the back (of the page); **'voir au** ~**'** 'see over(leaf)'.

vert, verte [vɛʀ, vɛʀt(ə)] **1** *adj* **(a)** (*couleur*) green. ~ **de peur** green with fear. **(b)** *céréale, fruit* unripe, green; *vin* young; *bois* green. **(c)** *vieillard* sprightly, spry. **(d)** *réprimande* sharp, stiff. **(e)** *propos* spicy, saucy. **il en a dit des vertes (et des pas mûres)*** he said some pretty spicy *ou* saucy things. **2** *nm* green. ~ **olive** *etc* olive *etc* (-green); **mettre un cheval au** ~ to put a horse out to grass *ou* to pasture; **se mettre au** ~ to hole up* in the country. ♦ **vert-de-gris 1** *nm inv* verdigris. **2** *adj inv* grey(ish)-green. ♦ **vertement** *adv réprimander* sharply.

vertèbre [vɛʀtɛbʀ(ə)] *nf* vertebra. ♦ **vertébral, e,** *mpl* **-aux** *adj* vertebral. ♦ **vertébré, e** *adj, nm* vertebrate.

vertical, e, *mpl* **-aux** [vɛʀtikal, o] **1** *adj* (*gén*) vertical; *position du corps* upright. **2** *nf* (*ligne*) vertical line. (*direction*) **la** ~**e** the vertical; **à la** ~**e** *s'élever* vertically. ♦ **verticalement** *adv monter* vertically, straight up; *descendre* vertically, straight down. ♦ **verticalité** *nf* verticalness, verticality.

vertige [vɛʀtiʒ] *nm* **(a)** (*peur du vide*) **le** ~ vertigo; **avoir le** ~ to suffer from vertigo, get dizzy; **être pris de** ~ to feel dizzy *ou* giddy, have a fit of vertigo; **cela me donne le** ~ it makes me feel dizzy *ou* giddy, it gives me vertigo. **(b)** (*étourdissement*) dizzy *ou* giddy spell *ou* turn. **(c)** (*fig: égarement*) fever. **gagné par le** ~ **de l'expansion ...** having caught the expansion fever ... . ♦ **vertigineusement** *adv*: ~ **haut** breathtakingly high, of a dizzy height; **les prix montent** ~ prices are rising at a dizzy *ou* breathtaking rate, prices are rocketing. ♦ **vertigineux, -euse** *adj* (*gén*) breathtaking; *précipice* breathtakingly high; *hauteur* dizzy, giddy.

vertu [vɛʀty] *nf* (*gén: morale*) virtue; (*littér: pouvoir*) virtue (*littér*), power. **en** ~ **de** in accordance with. ♦ **vertueusement** *adv* virtuously. ♦ **vertueux, -euse** *adj* virtuous.

vésicule [vezikyl] *nf* vesicle. **la** ~ **(biliaire)** the gall-bladder.

vespasienne [vɛspazjɛn] *nf* urinal.

vessie [vesi] *nf* bladder. **prendre des** ~**s pour des lanternes** to believe that the moon is made of green cheese.

veste [vɛst(ə)] *nf* jacket. ~ **droite/croisée** single-/double-breasted jacket; ~ **de pyjama** pyjama jacket *ou* top; **retourner sa** ~* to turn one's coat; **ramasser une** ~* to come a cropper*.

vestiaire [vɛstjɛʀ] *nm [théâtre, restaurant]* cloakroom; *[stade, piscine]* changing-room. **(armoire-)**~ locker.

vestibule [vɛstibyl] *nm* hall, vestibule.

vestige [vɛstiʒ] *nm* (*objet*) relic; (*fragment*) trace; *[coutume, gloire]* vestige, remnant, relic. ~**s** *[ville]* remains, vestiges; *[passé]* vestiges, remnants, relics.

vestimentaire [vɛstimɑ̃tɛʀ] *adj*: **élégance** ~ sartorial elegance; **fantaisies** ~**s** eccentricities of dress; **détails** ~**s** details of one's dress.

veston [vɛstɔ̃] *nm* jacket.

vêtement [vɛtmɑ̃] *nm* **(a)** (*article d'habillement*) garment, item *ou* article of clothing. (*tenue*) **son** ~ his clothes; (*Comm: industrie*) **le** ~ the clothing industry. **(b)** ~**s** clothes; ~**s de sport** sports clothes; (*dans magasin*) sportswear; ~**s de dessous** underclothes.

vétéran [veteʀɑ̃] *nm* (*Mil*) veteran; (*fig*) veteran, old hand*.

vétérinaire [veteʀinɛʀ] **1** *nm* vet, veterinary surgeon. **2** *adj* veterinary.

vétille [vetij] *nf* trifle, triviality.

vêtir [vetiʀ] (20) **1** *vt* (*habiller*) to clothe, dress. **2 se** ~ *vpr* to dress (o.s.). ♦ **vêtu, e** *adj* dressed. **bien/mal** ~ well-/badly-dressed; ~ **de** dressed in, wearing.

veto [veto] *nm* (*Pol, gén*) veto. **opposer son** ~ **à qch** to veto sth.

vétuste [vetyst(ə)] *adj* ancient, dilapidated. ♦ **vétusté** *nf* dilapidation.

veuf, veuve [vœf, vœv] **1** *adj* widowed. **il est deux fois** ~ he has been twice widowed, he is a widower twice over. **2** *nm* widower. **3** *nf* (*gén*) widow. ♦ **veuvage** *nm* widowhood.

vexer [vɛkse] (1) **1** *vt* to hurt, upset. **être vexé par qch** to be hurt by sth, be upset at sth. **2 se** ~ *vpr* to be hurt (*de* by), be upset (*de* at). ♦ **vexant, e** *adj* (*contrariant*) annoying; (*blessant*) hurtful. ♦ **vexation** *nf* humiliation.

via [vja] *prép* via.

viabilité [vjabilite] *nf* **(a)** *[chemin]* practicability. **avec/sans** ~ *terrain* with/without services (laid on). **(b)** *[entreprise]* viability. ♦ **viable** *adj* (*gén*) viable.

viaduc [vjadyk] *nm* viaduct.

viager, -ère [vjaʒe, ɛʀ] **1** *adj*: **rente** ~**ère** life annuity. **2** *nm* (*rente*) life annuity; (*bien*) *property mortgaged for a life annuity.* **mettre un bien en** ~ *to sell a property in return for a life annuity.*

viande [vjɑ̃d] *nf* meat. ~ **rouge/blanche** red/white meat; ~ **de boucherie** (butcher's *ou* fresh) meat.

vibrer [vibʀe] (1) *vi* (*gén, Phys*) to vibrate; *[voix]* to quiver, be vibrant; *[personne]* to thrill (*de* with), be stirred (*de* by). **faire** ~ *objet* to vibrate; *auditoire* to stir, thrill; ~ **d'enthousiasme** to be vibrant with enthusiasm. ♦ **vibrant, e** *adj membrane* vibrating; *voix* vibrant, resonant; *discours, nature* emotive. ~ **de** vibrant with. ♦ **vibration** *nf* (*gén, Phys*) vibration. ♦ **vibratoire** *adj* vibratory.

vicaire [vikɛʀ] *nm [paroisse]* curate. *[évêque]* ~ **général** vicar-general.

vice [vis] *nm* **(a)** (*moral*) vice. **vivre dans le** ~ to live a life of vice. **(b)** (*défectuosité*) fault, defect. ~ **de construction** fault *ou* defect in construction; ~ **de forme** legal flaw *ou* irregularity.

vice- [vis] *préf* vice-. ~**-amiral** *nm, pl* ~**-**~**aux** vice-admiral; ~**-président, e** *nm,f, mpl* ~**-**~**s** vice-president, vice-chairman; ~**-roi** *nm, pl* ~**-**~**s** viceroy.

vice versa [visevɛʀsa] *adv* vice versa.

vicier [visje] (7) *vt atmosphère* to pollute, taint; *sang* to contaminate, taint; *rapports* to taint. ♦ **vicieusement** *adv* pervertedly. ♦ **vicieux, -euse 1** *adj personne, penchant* perverted, depraved; *cheval* restive, unruly; *attaque, balle* well-disguised, nasty*; *prononciation, expression* incorrect, wrong. **2** *nm,f* pervert.

vicinal, e, *mpl* **-aux** [visinal, o] *adj*: **chemin** ~ by-road, byway.

vicissitudes [visisityd] *nfpl* (*gén*) vicissitudes.

vicomte [vikɔ̃t] *nm* viscount. ♦ **vicomtesse** *nf* viscountess.

victime [viktim] *nf* (*gén*) victim; *[accident]* casualty, victim. **être** ~ **de** to be the victim of.

victoire [viktwaʀ] *nf* (*gén*) victory; (*Sport*) win, victory. ~ **aux points** win on points; **crier** ~ to crow (over one's victory). ♦ **victorieusement** *adv* victoriously; triumphantly. ♦ **victorieux, -euse** *adj armée* victorious; *équipe* winnning, victorious; *air* triumphant.

victuailles [viktɥɑj] *nfpl* provisions.

vidange [vidɑ̃ʒ] *nf* **(a)** *[réservoir]* emptying; (*Aut*) oil change. (*Aut*) **faire la ~** to change the oil. **(b)** (*dispositif*) *[lavabo]* waste outlet. ♦ **vidanger** (3) *vt réservoir* to empty; *liquide* to empty out.

vide [vid] **1** *adj* (*lit, fig*) empty; *appartement* empty, vacant. **avoir l'estomac** *ou* **le ventre ~** to have an empty stomach; (*Comm*) **bouteilles ~s** empty bottles, empties*; **sa vie était ~** his life was empty *ou* a void; **~ de** (*gén*) empty *ou* (de)void of; **~ de sens** *mot* meaningless; **les rues ~s de voitures** the streets empty *ou* devoid of cars. **2** *nm* **(a) le ~** (*l'espace*) the void; (*le néant*) emptiness; **suspendu au-dessus du ~** hanging over the void; **avoir peur du ~** to have no head for heights; **faire le ~ dans** to create a vacuum in; **sous ~** under vacuum; **emballé sous ~** vacuum-packed; **regarder dans le ~** to gaze into space *ou* emptiness; **le ~ de l'existence** the emptiness of existence. **(b)** (*trou*) (*entre deux objets*) gap, (empty) space; **un ~ dans son cœur** an emptiness *ou* a void in one's heart; **~ sanitaire** underfloor space. **(c) à ~** *repartir etc* empty; **faire le ~ dans son esprit** to make one's mind a blank; **parler dans le ~** (*sans objet*) to talk vacuously; (*personne n'écoute*) to waste one's breath; *V aussi* **vider**.

vidéocassette [videokasɛt] *nf* video-cassette.

vider [vide] (1) **1** *vt* **(a)** *récipient, meuble, pièce* to empty; *étang, citerne* to empty, drain; *contenu* to empty (out). **~ un appartement de ses meubles** to empty *ou* clear a flat of its furniture; **il vida son verre** he emptied *ou* drained his glass; **ils ont vidé tous les tiroirs** they cleaned out *ou* emptied all the drawers. **(b)** *poisson, poulet* to gut, clean out; *pomme* to core. **(c)** *querelle* to settle. **(d)** *cavalier* to throw. **~ les étriers** to leave the stirrups. **(e)** (*: *expulser*) to throw out*, chuck out* (*de* of). **(f)** (*: *épuiser*) to wear out. **(g)** (*locutions*) **~ son sac*** to come out with it*; **~ l'abcès** to root out the evil; **~ son cœur** to pour out one's heart; **~ les lieux** to quit *ou* vacate the premises. **2 se ~** *vpr* to empty. ♦ **vide-ordures** *nm inv* (rubbish) chute. ♦ **vide-poches** *nm inv* tidy; (*Aut*) glove compartment.

vie [vi] *nf* **(a)** (*gén*) life. **être en ~** to be alive; **être bien en ~** to be well and truly alive, be alive and kicking*; **donner la ~** to give birth (*à* to); **plein de ~** full of life; **rappeler qn à la ~** to bring sb back to life; **attends de connaître la ~ pour juger** wait until you know (something) about life before you pass judgment; **sa présence met de la ~ dans la maison** he brings some life *ou* a bit of life into the house. **(b)** (*activités*) life. **dans la ~ courante** in everyday life; **(mode de) ~** way of life, life style; **la ~ de garçon** a bachelor's life *ou* existence; **la ~ d'un professeur n'est pas toujours drôle** a teacher's life *ou* the life of a teacher isn't always fun; **la ~ des animaux** animal life; **~ de bohème** bohemian way of life *ou* life style; **~ de château** life of luxury. **(c)** (*moyens matériels*) living. **(le coût de) la ~** the cost of living; **la ~ chère** the high cost of living. **(d)** (*durée*) life(time). **toute sa ~** all his life; **ça n'arrive qu'une seule fois dans la ~** it only happens once in a lifetime. **(e)** (*biographie*) life (story). **elle m'a raconté sa ~** she told me her life story *ou* the story of her life. **(f)** (*locutions*) **à ~, pour la ~** for life; **passer de ~ à trépas** to pass on; **faire passer qn de ~ à trépas** to dispatch sb into the next world; **une question de ~ ou de mort** a matter of life and death; **c'est la belle ~!** this is the life!; **ce n'est pas une ~!** it's a rotten* *ou* hard life!; **c'est une ~ de chien!*** it's a dog's life!*; **c'est la ~!** that's life!; **jamais de ma ~** never in my life; **jamais de la ~!** never!, not on your life!*; **être entre la ~ et la mort** to be at death's door; **avoir la ~ dure** *[personne]* to have nine lives; *[superstitions]* to die hard; **mener la ~ dure à qn** to give sb a hard time of it; **sans ~** (*mort*) lifeless; (*évanoui*) unconscious; (*amorphe*) lifeless, listless; **refaire sa ~ (avec qn)** to make a new life (with sb); **faire la ~** (*se débaucher*) to lead a life of pleasure; (*: *faire une scène*) to kick up a row*, make a scene; **laisser la ~ sauve à qn** to spare sb's life; **voir la ~ en rose** to see life through rose-coloured glasses, take a rosy view of life.

vieillesse [vjɛjɛs] *nf [personne]* old age; *[chose]* age, oldness. **aide à la ~** help for the old *ou* the elderly *ou* the aged. ♦ **vieil, vieille** *V* **vieux.** ♦ **vieillard** *nm* old man. **les ~s** the elderly, old people. ♦ **vieillerie** *nf* old-fashioned thing. ♦ **vieillir** (2) **1** *vi* (*prendre de l'âge*) to grow old; (*paraître plus vieux*) to age; *[mot, doctrine]* to become (out)dated; *[vin, fromage]* to age. **je la trouve très vieillie** I find she has aged a lot. **2** *vt*: **~ qn** *[coiffure, maladie]* to age sb, put years on sb; (*par fausse estimation*) to make sb older than he (really) is. **3 se ~** *vpr* to make o.s. older. ♦ **vieillissant, e** *adj* ageing. ♦ **vieillissement** *nm [personne, vin]* ageing; *[doctrine, œuvre]* becoming (out)dated. ♦ **vieillot, -otte** *adj* (*démodé*) antiquated, quaint.

vierge [vjɛʀʒ(ə)] **1** *nf* **(a)** virgin. **la (Sainte) V~** the (Blessed) Virgin. **(b)** (*Astron*) **la V~** Virgo, the Virgin; **être de la V~** to be Virgo *ou* a Virgoan. **2** *adj* **(a)** *personne* virgin. **être ~** to be a virgin. **(b)** *feuille de papier* blank, virgin; *film* unexposed; *casier judiciaire* clean; *terre, neige* virgin. **(c) ~ de** free from.

Viet-Nam [vjɛtnam] *nm* Vietnam. ♦ **vietnamien, -ienne** *adj, nm,* **V~(ne)** *nm(f)* Vietnamese.

vieux [vjø], *f* **vieille** [vjɛj], *msg* **vieil** [vjɛj] *devant voyelle ou h muet, mpl* **vieux** [vjø] **1** *adj* **(a)** (*âgé*) old. **très ~** ancient, very old; **la vieille génération** the older generation; **les vieilles gens** old people, old folk*, the aged *ou* elderly; **il est plus ~ que moi** he is older than I am; **~ comme le monde** as old as the hills; **il commence à se faire ~** he is getting on (in years), he's beginning to get old; **sur ses ~ jours** in his old age; **il n'a pas fait de ~ os** he didn't last *ou* live long. **(b)** (*de longue date*) *ami, habitude* old, long-standing; *coutumes, famille* old, ancient. **de vieille race** of ancient lineage; **connaître qn de vieille date** to have known sb for a very long time. **(c)** (*précédent*) old, former, previous. **ma vieille voiture était plus rapide que la nouvelle** my old *ou* previous car was quicker than the new one.

2 *nm* **(a)** old man. **les ~** the old *ou* aged *ou* elderly, old people, old folk*; **un ~ de la vieille*** one of the old brigade; (*père*) **le ~‡** my old man‡; (*parents*) **ses ~‡** his folks*; **mon ~*** old man* *ou* chap* *ou* boy*. **(b) préférer le ~ au neuf** to prefer old things to new.

3 *nf* old woman. (*mère*) **la vieille‡** my old woman‡ *ou* lady‡; **ma vieille*** old girl*; (*à un homme*) old man* *ou* chap* *ou* boy*.

4 *adv vivre* to a ripe old age; *s'habiller* old.

5: vieille bique* old bag‡; (*hum*) **vieille branche** old bean*; **de la vieille école** old-fashioned, traditional; **vieille fille** spinster, old maid; **~ garçon** bachelor; **~ gâteux** old dodderer*; **~ jeton*** *ou* **schnock‡** old misery*; **~ jeu** *adj inv* old-fashioned, old hat; **vieille noix*** (silly) old twit‡ *ou* fathead‡.

vif, vive[1] [vif, viv] **1** *adj* **(a)** *personne* (*plein de vie*) lively, vivacious; (*alerte*) sharp, quick; *rythme* lively; *imagination, intelligence* lively, keen. **il a l'œil ~** he has a sharp *ou* keen eye; **à l'esprit ~** quick-witted. **(b)** (*emporté*) *personne* sharp, brusque, quick-tempered; *ton, propos* sharp, brusque. **(c)** (*intense*) *émotion, plaisir, déception etc* keen, intense; *souvenirs, impres-*

sion vivid; *satisfaction* deep, great; *impatience* great; *penchant* strong; *lumière, éclat* bright, brilliant; *couleur* vivid, brilliant; *froid* biting, bitter; *douleur* sharp; *vent* keen. **à vive allure** at a brisk pace; **avec mes plus ~s remerciements** with my most profound thanks; **c'est avec un ~ plaisir que ...** it is with very great pleasure that ...; **l'air ~ les revigorait** the bracing *ou* sharp air gave them new life. **(d)** (*à nu*) *pierre* bare; *joints* dry; (*acéré*) *arête* sharp. **(e)** (*locutions*) **brûler ~ qn** to burn sb alive; **de vive voix** *renseigner* by word of mouth; *remercier* personally, in person.

2 *nm* **(a)** **à ~** *chair* bared; *plaie* open; **avoir les nerfs à ~** to be on edge; **piqué au ~** cut *ou* hurt to the quick; **couper dans le ~** to cut into the living flesh; **entrer dans le ~ du sujet** to get to the heart of the matter; **prendre qn en photo sur le ~** to photograph sb in a real-life situation. **(b)** (*Pêche*) **pêcher au ~** to fish with live bait. **(c)** (*Jur: personne*) living person. **donation entre ~s** donation inter vivos.

vigie [viʒi] *nf* (*matelot*) look-out, watch; (*poste*) look-out post.

vigilant, e [viʒilɑ̃, ɑ̃t] *adj personne, œil* vigilant, watchful; *soins* vigilant. ♦ **vigilance** *nf* vigilance; watchfulness.

vigile [viʒil] *nm* (*Hist*) watch; (*veilleur de nuit*) (night) watchman.

vigne [viɲ] *nf* (*plante*) vine; (*vignoble*) vineyard. **~ vierge** Virginia creeper. ♦ **vigneron, -onne** *nm,f* wine grower. ♦ **vignoble** *nm* vineyard.

vignette [viɲɛt] *nf* (*Art: motif*) vignette; (*illustration*) illustration; (*Comm: timbre*) label. (*Aut*) **la ~** ≃ the (road) tax disc.

vigoureux, -euse [viguʀø, øz] *adj* (*gén*) vigorous, robust; *bras, mains* strong, powerful; *style* vigorous, energetic; *résistance* vigorous, strenuous. ♦ **vigoureusement** *adv* vigorously. ♦ **vigueur** *nf* **(a)** vigour; robustness; strength; energy. **(b) en ~** *loi* in force; *formule* current, in use; **entrer en ~** to come into force *ou* effect; **cesser d'être en ~** to cease to apply.

vil, e [vil] *adj* **(a)** (*méprisable*) vile, base. **(b) à ~ prix** at a very low price.

vilain, e [vilɛ̃, ɛn] **1** *adj* **(a)** (*laid*) *personne, vêtement* ugly(-looking); *couleur* nasty. **(b)** *temps* nasty, bad, lousy*; *odeur, blessure, affaire* nasty, bad. **(c)** (*méchant*) *enfant, conduite* naughty; *action, pensée* wicked. **jouer un ~ tour à qn** to play a nasty *ou* mean trick on sb; **c'est un ~ monsieur** he's a nasty customer. **2** *nm* **(a)** (*Hist*) villain. **(b)** (*) **il va y avoir du ~** it's going to turn nasty.

vilebrequin [vilbʀəkɛ̃] *nm* (*outil*) (bit-)brace; (*Aut*) crankshaft.

villa [villa] *nf* (detached) house.

village [vilaʒ] *nm* village. **~ de toile** tent village. ♦ **villageois, e 1** *adj* village. **2** *nm,f* villager.

ville [vil] **1** *nf* **(a)** town; (*plus importante*) city. **en ~, à la ~** in town, in the city; **aller en ~** to go into town; **les gens de la ~** townspeople; (*vie*) **aimer la ~** to like town *ou* city life; (*quartier*) **la vieille ~** the old (part of) town. **(b)** (*municipalité*) ≃ local authority, (town) council. **2: ~ champignon** mushroom town; **~ d'eaux** spa (town); **~ satellite** satellite town.

villégiature [vileʒjatyʀ] *nf*: **aller en/être en ~ quelque part** to go on/be on holiday *ou* vacation (*US*) somewhere; **(lieu de) ~** (holiday) resort.

vin [vɛ̃] *nm* wine. **~ chaud** mulled wine; **~ cuit** liqueur wine; (*réunion*) **~ d'honneur** reception (*where wine is served*); **être entre deux ~s** to be tipsy.

vinaigre [vinɛgʀ(ə)] *nm* vinegar. **tourner au ~*** to turn sour. ♦ **vinaigré, e** *adj*: **trop** *etc* **~** with too much *etc* vinegar. ♦ **vinaigrette** *nf* French dressing, vinaigrette, oil and vinegar dressing.

vindicatif, -ive [vɛ̃dikatif, iv] *adj* vindictive.

vingt [vɛ̃] ([vɛ̃t] *en liaison et dans les nombres de 22 à 29*) *adj inv, nm inv* twenty. **je te l'ai dit ~ fois** I've told you a hundred times; **il n'avait plus ses jambes de ~ ans** he no longer had the legs of a young man; **~-quatre heures sur ~-quatre** round the clock, twenty-four hours a day; *V* **six, soixante.** ♦ **vingtaine** *nf*: **une ~** about twenty, twenty or so, (about) a score. ♦ **vingtième** *adj, nmf* twentieth. ♦ **vingtièmement** *adv* in the twentieth place.

vinicole [vinikɔl] *adj industrie* wine; *région* wine-growing, wine-producing; *établissement* wine-making.

vinyle [vinil] *nm* vinyl.

viol [vjɔl] *nm [femme]* rape; *[temple]* violation, desecration.

violacé, e [vjɔlase] *adj* purplish, mauvish.

violent, e [vjɔlɑ̃, ɑ̃t] *adj* (*gén*) violent; *effort* violent, strenuous; *besoin* intense, urgent. ♦ **violemment** *adv* violently. ♦ **violence** *nf* violence. **commettre des ~s contre qn** to assault sb, commit acts of violence against sb; **se faire ~** to force o.s.; **faire ~ à** to do violence to. ♦ **violenter** (1) *vt femme* to assault (sexually).

violer [vjɔle] (1) *vt* (*gén*) to violate; *promesse* to break; *temple* to desecrate; *femme* to rape. ♦ **violation** *nf* (*gén*) violation; *[promesse]* breaking; *[sépulture]* desecration. (*Jur*) **~ de domicile** forcible entry (*into a person's home*); **~ du secret professionnel** breach *ou* violation of professional secrecy.

violet, -ette [vjɔlɛ, ɛt] **1** *adj* purple; (*pâle*) violet. **2** *nm* (*couleur*) purple. **3** *nf* (*Bot*) violet.

violon [vjɔlɔ̃] *nm* **(a)** (*instrument, musicien*) violin, fiddle*. (*personne*) **premier ~** leader. **(b)** (*: *prison*) lock-up*, jug‡. **(c) ~ d'Ingres** (artistic) hobby. ♦ **violoniste** *nmf* violonist, violin-player, fiddler*.

violoncelle [vjɔlɔ̃sɛl] *nm* cello. ♦ **violoncelliste** *nmf* cellist, cello-player.

vipère [vipɛʀ] *nf* adder, viper. **langue de ~** viper's tongue.

virage [viʀaʒ] *nm [véhicule, coureur]* turn; *[politique]* change in policy *ou* direction; (*Aut: tournant*) bend. **prendre un ~ à la corde** to hug the bend; **~ en épingle à cheveux** hairpin bend; **~ relevé** banked corner.

virée* [viʀe] *nf* (*en voiture*) drive, run; (*à pied*) walk; (*en vélo*) run; (*de plusieurs jours*) trip; (*dans les cafés etc*) tour. **faire une ~** to go for a run (*ou* walk, drive *etc*).

virement [viʀmɑ̃] *nm*: **~ (bancaire)** credit transfer; **~ postal** ≃ (National) Giro transfer.

virer [viʀe] (1) **1** *vi* **(a)** (*changer de direction*) to turn. **~ sur l'aile** to bank; **~ de bord** to tack. **(b)** *[couleur]* to turn, change; (*Phot*) *[épreuves]* to tone; (*Méd*) *[cuti-réaction]* to come up positive. **bleu qui vire au violet** blue which is turning purple *ou* changing to purple; **~ à l'aigre** to turn sour. **2** *vt* **(a)** (*Fin*) to transfer (*à un compte* (in)to an account). **(b)** (*: *expulser*) to kick out*, chuck out*. **se faire ~** to get (o.s.) kicked* *ou* chucked out*. **(c)** (*Méd*) **il a viré sa cuti** he gave a positive skin test.

virevolter [viʀvɔlte] (1) *vi [danseuse]* to twirl around; *[cheval]* to do a demivolt. ♦ **virevolte** *nf* twirl; demivolt.

virginité [viʀʒinite] *nf [femme]* virginity, maidenhood; *[âme]* purity.

virgule [viʀgyl] *nf* (*de ponctuation*) comma; (*Math*) (decimal) point. **5 ~ 2** 5 point 2; **~ flottante** floating decimal.

viril, e [viʀil] *adj attributs* male, masculine; *attitude, traits* manly, virile; *prouesses* virile. ♦ **virilement** *adv* in a manly *ou* virile way. ♦ **virilité** *nf* masculinity; manliness; virility.

virtuel, -elle [viʀtɥɛl] *adj* (*gén*) potential; (*Philos, Phys*) virtual. ♦ **virtuellement** *adv* (*en puis-*

sance) potentially; (*pratiquement*) virtually.
virtuose [viRtɥoz] *nmf* (*Mus*) virtuoso; (*fig: artiste*) master. ♦ **virtuosité** *nf* virtuosity.
virulence [viRylɑ̃s] *nf* virulence. ♦ **virulent, e** *adj* virulent.
virus [viRys] *nm* (*lit*) virus. (*fig*) **le ~ du jeu** the gambling bug.
vis [vis] *nf* screw. **escalier à ~** spiral staircase; **~ sans fin** worm, endless screw; (*Aut*) **~ platinées** (contact) points.
visa [viza] *nm* (*gén*) stamp; *[passeport]* visa. **~ de censure** (censor's) certificate; (*fig*) **~ pour ...** passport to ... .
visage [vizaʒ] *nm* face. **au ~ pâle** pale-faced; **V~ pâle** paleface; **agir à ~ découvert** to act openly; **faire bon ~ à qn** to put on a show of friendliness for sb.
vis-à-vis [vizavi] **1** *prép*: **~ de** (*en face de*) opposite, vis-à-vis; (*comparé à*) beside, vis-à-vis, next to; (*envers*) towards, vis-à-vis; **sincère ~ de soi-même** frank with o.s.; **j'en ai honte ~ de lui** I'm ashamed of it in front of *ou* before him. **2** *adv* (*face à face*) face to face. **se faire ~** to be facing *ou* opposite each other. **3** *nm inv* (*personne*) person opposite; (*maison*) house opposite. **immeuble sans ~** building with an open *ou* unimpeded outlook.
viscères [visɛR] *nmpl* intestines. ♦ **viscéral, e, *mpl* -aux** *adj* (*Anat*) visceral; *peur* deep-seated, deep-rooted.
viscosité [viskozite] *nf* viscosity.
viser [vize] (1) **1** *vt* **(a)** *cible, effet, carrière* to aim at. **(b)** (*concerner*) *[mesure, remarque]* to be aimed at, be directed at. **se sentir visé** to feel one is being got at*. **(c)** (*: regarder*) to take a look at. **(d)** (*Admin*) *passeport* to visa; *document* to stamp. **faire ~ un passeport** to have a passport visaed. **2** *vi [tireur]* to aim, take aim. **~ juste** to aim accurately; **~ à la tête** to aim for the head; (*fig: ambitionner*) **~ haut** to set one's sights high, aim high. **3 ~ à** *vt indir*: **~ à qch/à faire** *[personne]* to aim at sth/at doing *ou* to do; *[mesures]* to be aimed at sth/at doing. ♦ **visée** *nf* **(a)** (*avec une arme*) aiming. **pour faciliter la ~** to help one's aim, help in taking aim. **(b)** (*desseins*) **~s** aims, designs; **avoir des ~s sur** to have designs on. ♦ **viseur** *nm [arme]* sights; *[caméra]* viewfinder; (*Astron: lunette*) telescopic sight.
visible [vizibl(ə)] *adj* (*gén*) visible; *embarras* obvious, evident, visible; *progrès* clear, perceptible. **il est ~ que ...** it is obvious *ou* apparent *ou* clear that ...; **Monsieur est-il ~?** is Mr X seeing *ou* is Mr X receiving visitors?; **elle n'est pas ~ le matin** she's not at home to visitors in the morning. ♦ **visibilité** *nf* visibility. **sans ~** *pilotage, virage* blind. ♦ **visiblement** *adv* obviously, clearly.
visière [vizjɛR] *nf [casquette]* peak; (*en celluloïd*) eyeshade; *[armure]* visor.
vision [vizjɔ̃] *nf* **(a)** (*vue*) (eye)sight, vision. **champ de ~** field of view *ou* vision; **~ nette** clear vision; **porter des lunettes pour la ~ de loin** to wear glasses for seeing at a distance. **(b)** (*conception*) vision. **(c)** (*apparition*) vision. **tu as des ~s*** you're seeing things. ♦ **visionnaire** *adj, nmf* visionary. ♦ **visionner** (1) *vt* to view. ♦ **visionneuse** *nf* (*Ciné, Phot*) viewer.
visite [vizit] *nf* **(a)** (*action*) *[pays etc]* visiting; *[bagages]* examination, inspection. (*à l'hôpital*) **heures de ~** visiting hours; **la ~ du château a duré 2 heures** it took 2 hours to go round the castle. **(b)** (*tournée*) (*gén*) visit; *[ami, représentant]* visit, call; *[inspecteur]* visit, inspection. **~ guidée** guided tour; **en ~ officielle en France** on an official visit to France; **rendre ~ à qn** to pay sb a visit, call on sb, visit sb; **avoir la ~ de qn** to have a visit from sb. **(c)** (*visiteur*) visitor. **nous attendons de la ~ *ou* des ~s** we are expecting visitors *ou* company *ou* guests. **(d)** (*Méd*) **~ médicale** medical examination; **~ (à domicile)** (house)call, visit; **~ de contrôle** follow-up visit; **la ~** (*chez le médecin*) (medical) consultations; (*Mil*) sick parade; (*Mil*) **passer la ~** (*d'entrée*) to have one's medical. ♦ **visiter** (1) *vt* **(a)** *pays* to visit; *château* to go round, visit; *maison à vendre* to go *ou* look over, view. **il nous a fait ~ la maison** he showed us round the house. **(b)** *bagages* to examine, inspect; *recoins* to search (in); *navire* to inspect; (*hum*) *coffre-fort* to visit. **(c)** *[médecin, représentant]* to visit, call on. ♦ **visiteur, -euse** *nm,f* visitor.
vison [vizɔ̃] *nm* mink; (*manteau*) mink (coat).
visqueux, -euse [viskø, øz] *adj* (*gén*) viscous; *surface* sticky; (*fig*) *personne, manière* smarmy, slimy.
visser [vise] (1) *vt* **(a)** to screw on. **ce n'est pas bien vissé** it's not screwed down *ou* up properly; (*fig*) **rester vissé sur sa chaise** to be rooted *ou* glued to one's chair. **(b)** (*: surveiller*) *élève, employé* to keep a tight rein on.
visu [vizy] *adv*: **de ~** with one's own eyes.
visuel, -elle [vizɥɛl] *adj* (*gén*) visual. **troubles ~s** eye trouble. ♦ **visuellement** *adv* visually.
vital, e, *mpl* -aux [vital, o] *adj* vital. ♦ **vitalité** *nf* vitality.
vitamine [vitamin] *nf* vitamin. ♦ **vitaminé, e** *adj* with added vitamins.
vite [vit] *adv* **(a)** (*rapidement*) quickly, fast; (*en hâte*) in a rush *ou* hurry. **c'est ~ fait** it doesn't take long, it's done in a jiffy*; **ça ne va pas ~** it's slow work; **fais ~!** be quick about it!; **le temps passe ~** time flies; **aller ~ en besogne*** to be a fast worker*; **aller plus ~ que la musique** to jump the gun. **(b)** (*tôt*) soon, in no time. **on a ~ fait de dire que ...** it's easy to say that ...; **il eut ~ fait de découvrir que ...** he soon *ou* quickly discovered that ..., he discovered in no time that ... . **(c)** (*toute de suite*) quick. **lève-toi ~!** get up quick!; **eh, pas si ~!** hey, not so fast!, hey, hold on (a minute)!; **~! un médecin** quick! a doctor; **et plus ~ que ça!** and get a move on!*, and be quick about it!
vitesse [vitɛs] *nf* **(a)** (*promptitude*) speed, quickness. **en ~** (*rapidement*) quickly; (*en hâte*) in a hurry *ou* rush; **faites-moi ça en ~** do this for me quickly; **faites-moi ça, et en ~!** do this for me and be quick about it!; **écrire un petit mot en ~** to scribble a hasty note; **à toute ~, en quatrième ~** at full *ou* top speed. **(b)** *[véhicule, courant]* speed. **~ acquise** momentum; **~ de croisière** cruising speed; **à quelle ~ allait-il?** what speed was he going at? *ou* doing?; **faire de la ~** to go *ou* drive fast; **prendre de la ~** to pick up *ou* gather speed; **gagner qn de ~** (*lit*) to beat sb; (*fig*) to beat sb to it; (*Rail*) **expédier un colis en petite/grande ~** to send a parcel by slow/express goods service. **(c)** (*Aut*) gear. **changer de ~** to change gear; **en 2e/4e ~** in 2nd/4th gear; **passer les ~s** to go *ou* run through the gears.
viticole [vitikɔl] *adj industrie* wine; *région* wine-growing *ou* -producing; *établissement* wine-making. ♦ **viticulteur** *nm* wine grower. ♦ **viticulture** *nf* wine growing.
vitre [vitR(ə)] *nf [fenêtre, vitrine]* (window) pane; *[voiture]* window. **les camions font trembler les ~s** the lorries make the window panes *ou* the windows rattle; **casser une ~** to break a window (pane). ♦ **vitrage** *nm* (*vitres*) windows; (*cloison*) glass partition. ♦ **vitrail, *pl* -aux** *nm* stained-glass window. ♦ **vitré, e** *adj* glass. ♦ **vitrer** (1) *vt* to glaze, put glass in. ♦ **vitrerie** *nf* (*activité*) glaziery, glazing; (*marchandise*) glass. ♦ **vitreux, -euse** *adj* (*Anat, Géol*) vitreous; *yeux* glassy, dull; *eau* dull. ♦ **vitrier** *nm* glazier.
vitrifier [vitRifje] (7) *vt* (*par fusion*) to vitrify; (*par enduit*) to glaze, put a glaze on. ♦ **vitrification** *nf* vitrification; glazing.
vitrine [vitRin] *nf* **(a)** (*devanture*) (shop) window.

en ~ in the window. **(b)** (*armoire*) display cabinet.
vitriol [vitʀijɔl] *nm* vitriol.
vitupérer [vitypeʀe] (6) *vi* to vituperate (*contre* against), rant and rave (*contre* about). ♦ **vitupérations** *nfpl* vituperations.
vivable [vivabl(ə)] *adj personne* livable-with*; *milieu, monde* fit to live in.
vivace [vivas] *adj arbre* hardy; *préjugé* inveterate, indestructible. **plante ~** (hardy) perennial.
vivacité [vivasite] *nf* **(a)** (*joie de vivre*) liveliness, vivacity; (*agilité*) sharpness, quickness; *[rythme, imagination]* liveliness; *[intelligence]* liveliness, keenness. **~ d'esprit** quick-wittedness. **(b)** (*brusquerie*) **~ d'humeur** brusqueness, quick-temperedness. **(c)** *[lumière, couleur]* brightness, brilliance. **(d)** *[émotion]* keenness, intensity; *[souvenir, impression]* vividness.
vivant, e [vivɑ̃, ɑ̃t] **1** *adj* **(a)** (*en vie*) living. **il est encore ~** he's still alive *ou* living; **expériences sur des animaux ~s** experiments on live *ou* living animals. **(b)** (*plein de vie*) *enfant, rue, récit* lively; *portrait* lifelike. **c'est le portrait ~ de sa mère** he's the (living) image of his mother. **(c)** (*en usage*) *expression, croyance* living. **expression encore très ~e** expression which is still very much alive. **2** *nm* (*personnes*) **les ~s** the living; (*vie*) **de son ~** in his lifetime, while he was alive.
vivats [viva] *nmpl* cheers.
vive² [viv] *excl*: **~ le roi!** long live the king!; **~ les vacances!** three cheers for *ou* hurrah for the holidays!
vivement [vivmɑ̃] *adv* **(a)** (*avec brusquerie*) sharply, brusquely. **(b)** *regretter* deeply, greatly; *désirer* keenly. **s'intéresser ~ à** to take a keen *ou* deep interest in. **(c)** *éclairer etc* brilliantly, vividly, brightly. **(d)** (*souhait*) **~ les vacances!** roll on the holidays!*; **~ que ce soit fini!** I'll be glad when it's all over!
viveur [vivœʀ] *nm* high liver, pleasure-seeker.
vivier [vivje] *nm* (*étang*) fishpond; (*réservoir*) fish-tank.
vivifier [vivifje] (7) *vt* to invigorate. ♦ **vivifiant, e** *adj air* invigorating, bracing.
vivisection [vivisɛksjɔ̃] *nf* vivisection.
vivoter [vivɔte] (1) *vi [personne]* to rub *ou* get along (somehow).
vivre [vivʀ(ə)] (46) **1** *vi* **(a)** (*être vivant*) to live, be alive. **il avait cessé de ~** he was dead; **~ vieux/centenaire** to live to a ripe old age/to be a hundred; **ce manteau a vécu*** this coat is finished *ou* has had its day; **il fait bon ~** it's good to be alive, it's a good life. **(b)** (*habiter*) to live. **~ à Londres** to live in London; **~ avec qn** to live with sb. **(c)** (*se comporter*) to live. **se laisser ~** to take life as it comes; **être facile/difficile à ~** to be easy/difficult to live with *ou* to get on with; **il a beaucoup vécu** he has seen a lot of life; **elle ne vit plus depuis que son fils est pilote** she lives on her nerves since her son became a pilot. **(d)** (*subsister*) to live; *de laitages, son traitement* to live on. **avoir (juste) de quoi ~** to have (just) enough to live on; **travailler pour ~** to work for a living; **faire ~ qn** to provide (a living) for sb, support sb; **~ de l'air du temps** to live on air. **(e)** *[idée, rue]* to be alive; *[portrait]* to be lifelike *ou* lively. **2** *vt*: **~ des jours heureux** to live through *ou* spend happy days; **nous vivons des temps troublés** we are living in *ou* through troubled times; **il vivait une belle aventure** he was living out an exciting adventure; **~ sa vie** to live one's own life. **3** *nm*: **le ~ et le couvert** board and lodging; **~s** supplies, provisions.
vlan, v'lan [vlɑ̃] *excl* wham!, bang!
vocabulaire [vɔkabylɛʀ] *nm* vocabulary. (*péj*) **quel ~!** what language!
vocal, e, *mpl* **-aux** [vɔkal, o] *adj* vocal. ♦ **vocalement** *adv* vocally.
vocation [vɔkɑsjɔ̃] *nf* vocation. **avoir la ~ de l'enseignement** to be cut out to be a teacher, have a vocation for teaching; **la ~ industrielle du Japon** the industrial vocation of Japan.
vociférer [vɔsifeʀe] (6) **1** *vi* to utter cries of rage, vociferate. **~ contre qn** to scream at sb. **2** *vt* to shout (out), scream. ♦ **vocifération** *nf* cry of rage, vociferation.
vœu, *pl* **~x** [vø] *nm* **(a)** (*promesse*) vow. **faire (le) ~ de faire** to vow to do, make a vow to do. **(b)** (*souhait*) wish. **faire un ~** to make a wish; **tous nos ~x (de bonheur)** all good wishes for your happiness; **meilleurs ~x** best wishes.
vogue [vɔg] *nf* fashion, vogue. **être en ~** to be in fashion *ou* vogue; **c'est la grande ~ maintenant** it's all the rage now.
voguer [vɔge] (1) *vi* (*littér*) to sail; *[pensées]* to drift, wander. **~ au fil de l'eau** to float *ou* drift along.
voici [vwasi] *prép* **(a)** here *ou* this is; (*pl*) here *ou* these are. **~ mon bureau** here is *ou* this is my office; **~ vos livres** here *ou* these are your books; **~ la pluie** here comes the rain; **me** *etc* **~** here I am *etc*; **les ~ prêts à partir** they're ready to leave; **la maison que ~** this (particular) house; **M Dupont, que ~** M Dupont here; **il m'a raconté l'histoire que ~** he told me the following story; **~ qu'il se met à pleuvoir maintenant** and now it's starting to rain; **~ pourquoi je l'avais supprimé** that was why I'd eliminated it. **(b)** (*il y a*) **~ 5 ans que je ne l'ai pas vu** it's 5 years (now) since I last saw him, I haven't seen him for the past 5 years; **il est parti ~ une heure** he left an hour ago, it's an hour since he left.
voie [vwa] *nf* **(a)** (*chemin*) way; (*Admin: route*) road. **par la ~ des airs** by air; **~ d'accès** access; **~s de communication** communication routes; **~s navigables** waterways; **la ~ publique** the public highway; **~ de raccordement** slip road; **~ sans issue** no through road, cul-de-sac. **(b)** (*partie d'une route*) lane. **route à ~ unique** single-lane *ou* single-track road; **route à 3/4 ~s** 3-/4-lane road. **(c)** (*Rail*) **~(s)** track, line. **~ ferrée** railway *ou* railroad (*US*) line; **~ de garage** siding; (*fig*) **mettre sur une ~ de garage** *affaire* to shelve; *personne* to shunt to one side; **ligne à ~ unique** single-track line; **ligne à ~ étroite** narrow-gauge line; **le train est annoncé sur la ~ 2** the train will arrive at platform 2. **(d)** (*Anat*) **~s digestives** *etc* digestive *etc* tract; **par ~ orale** orally. **(e)** (*fig*) way. **la ~ du bien** the path of good; **montrer la ~** to show the way; **l'affaire est en bonne ~** the matter is shaping *ou* going well; **mettre qn sur la ~** to put sb on the right track. **(f)** (*filière*) **par des ~s détournées** by devious *ou* roundabout means; **par la ~ hiérarchique/diplomatique** through official/diplomatic channels; **par ~ de conséquence** in consequence, as a result. **(g) en ~ d'exécution** in (the) process of being carried out; **pays en ~ de développement** developing country; **en ~ de guérison** getting better; **en ~ d'achèvement** (well) on the way to completion, nearing completion. **(h) ~ d'eau** leak; **se livrer à des ~s de fait sur qn** to assault sb; **la ~ lactée** the Milky Way.
voilà [vwala] **1** *prép* **(a)** (*même sens que voici*) here *ou* this is; (*pl*) here *ou* these are; (*opposé à voici*) there *ou* that is; (*pl*) there *ou* those are. **~ mon frère** this is *ou* here is my brother; **voici mon frère et ~ ma sœur** this is my brother and that is my sister, here is my brother and there is my sister; **voici mes valises et ~ les vôtres** here *ou* these are my bags and there *ou* those are yours; **~ le printemps** here comes spring; **le ~, c'est lui** there he is, that's him; **le ~ prêt à partir** he's ready to leave; **~ ce dont il s'agit** that's *ou* this is what it's all about; **~ comment il faut faire** that's how it's done; **l'homme que ~** that man (there); **M**

Dupont que ~ M Dupont there; **il m'a raconté l'histoire que** ~ he told me the following story; ~ **qu'il se met à pleuvoir** it's starting to rain; ~ **qui est louche** that's a bit odd *ou* suspicious. **(b)** (*il y a*) ~ **5 ans que je ne l'ai pas vu** it's 5 years since I last saw him, I haven't seen him for the past 5 years; **il est parti** ~ **une heure** he left an hour ago, it's an hour since he left. **(c)** (*locutions*) **en** ~ **une histoire/blague!** what a story/joke!; **en** ~ **assez!** that's enough!, that'll do!; **veux-tu de l'argent? – en** ~ do you want some money? – here's some *ou* here you are; ~ **le hic** there's *ou* that's the hitch; ~ **tout** that's all; ~ **bien les Français!** how like the French!, isn't that just like the French!, that's the French all over!* **2** *excl*: ~**! j'arrive!** there – I'm coming!; **ah!** ~**! je comprends!** oh, (so) that's it; ~**! ça devait arriver!** there you are, it was bound to happen!; ~**, je vais vous expliquer** right (then), I'll explain to you.

voilage [vwalaʒ] *nm* (*rideau*) net curtain. (*tissu*) **acheter du** ~ to buy some net.

voile[1] [vwal] *nf* **(a)** *[bateau]* sail. **faire** ~ **vers** to sail towards; **toutes** ~**s dehors** with full sail on; **mettre les** ~**s**‡ to clear off‡, push off‡. **(b)** (*sport*) sailing. **faire de la** ~ to sail, go sailing.

voile[2] [vwal] *nm* **(a)** (*gén*) veil. (*Rel*) **prendre le** ~ to take the veil; **sous le** ~ **de** under the veil of; ~ **de brume** veil of mist; **avoir un** ~ **devant les yeux** to have a film before one's eyes. **(b)** (*tissu*) net. ~ **de tergal** ® Terylene ® net. **(c)** (*Méd*) ~ **au poumon** shadow on the lung; (*Anat*) ~ **du palais** soft palate, velum. ♦ **voilé, e** *adj* **(a)** *femme, allusion* veiled. **(b)** *lumière, ciel, contour* misty, hazy; *éclat* dimmed; *regard* misty. **avoir la voix** ~**e** to have a husky voice. ♦ **voiler**[1] (1) **1** *vt* (*lit, fig*) to veil. **2 se** ~ *vpr* **(a)** *[musulmane]* **se** ~ **le visage** to wear a veil; (*fig*) **se** ~ **la face** to hide one's face. **(b)** *[horizon, soleil, regard]* to mist over; *[ciel]* to grow hazy *ou* misty. ♦ **voilette** *nf* (hat) veil.

voiler[2] *vt*, **se** ~ *vpr* [vwale] (1) *[roue]* to buckle; *[planche]* to warp.

voilier [vwalje] *nm* sailing ship; (*de plaisance*) sailing boat. ♦ **voilure** *nf [bateau]* sails. **une** ~ **de 1 000m²** 1,000m² of sail.

voir [vwaʀ] (30) **1** *vt* **(a)** to see. **on n'y voit rien** you can't see a thing; ~ **double** to see double; **c'est un film à** ~ it's a film worth seeing; **il a vu du pays** he has been around *ou* knocked about a bit; ~ **qn faire qch** to see sb do sth; **j'ai vu bâtir ces maisons** I saw these houses being built; **je l'ai vu naître** I've known him since he was born; **le pays qui l'a vu naître** his native country; **il a vu deux guerres** he has lived through *ou* seen two wars. **(b)** (*se représenter*) to see. **je le vois mal habitant la banlieue** I (somehow) can't see *ou* imagine him living in the suburbs; **ne** ~ **que par qn** to see only *ou* see everything through sb's eyes; ~ **la vie en rose/les choses en noir** to take a rosy/black view of things; ~ **loin** to see ahead; ~ **le problème sous un autre jour** to see *ou* view the problem in a different light; **on n'en voit pas le bout** there seems to be no end to it; **façon de** ~ view of things, outlook; **il a vu petit/grand** he planned things on a small/big scale; **ne** ~ **que son intérêt** to consider only one's own interest. **(c)** (*étudier*) *problème* to look into; *dossier* to look at; *leçon* to go over; *circulaire* to see, read. **je verrai** I'll have to see, I'll think about it; **c'est à vous de** ~ it's up to you to see *ou* decide. **(d)** (*découvrir*) to see, find (out). **aller** ~ **s'il y a quelqu'un** to go and see *ou* go and find out if there is anybody there; **vous verrez que ce n'est pas leur faute** you will see *ou* find that it's not their fault; **c'est à** ~ (*à prouver*) that remains to be seen. **(e)** (*rendre visite à*) *médecin, avocat* to see. **aller** ~ **qn** (*gén*) to go and see sb; *ami* to call on *ou* visit sb. **(f)** (*faire l'expérience de*) **il en a vu de dures** *ou* **de toutes les couleurs** he has been through the mill *ou* through some hard times; **en faire** ~ **(de dures) à qn** to give sb a hard time; **j'en ai vu d'autres!** I've been through *ou* seen worse!; **on n'a jamais vu ça!** did you ever see *ou* hear the like?; **il ne voit pas ce que vous voulez dire** he doesn't see *ou* grasp what you mean. **(g) laisser** ~**, faire** ~ to show; **faites-moi** ~ **ce dessin** let me see *ou* show me this picture; **elle ne peut pas le** ~* she can't stand him; **se faire mal** ~ **(de qn)** to be frowned on (by sb); **se faire bien** ~ **(de qn)** to make o.s. popular (with sb); **vous aurez du mal à lui faire** ~ **que ...** you will find it difficult to make him see *ou* realise that ... . **(h)** (*locutions*) **voyons** (*réflexion*) let's see now; (*irritation*) come (on) now, come, come; **dis-moi** ~ tell me; **je voudrais t'y** ~ I'd like to see you try; **essaie** ~**!*** just you try it!; **regarde** ~ **ce qu'il a fait*** just look what he has done!; **pour** ~ just to see; **qu'il aille se faire** ~**!‡** he can go to hell!‡; **il ferait beau** ~ **qu'il ...** it would be a fine thing if he ...; **cela n'a rien à** ~ **avec ...** this has got nothing to do with ...; **n'y** ~ **que du feu** to be completely hoodwinked *ou* taken in; ~ **trente-six chandelles** to see stars; **ne pas** ~ **plus loin que le bout de son nez** to see no further than the end of one's nose; ~ **venir** to wait and see; **je te vois venir*** I can see what you're leading up to *ou* getting at.

2 ~ **à** *vt indir* to make sure that, see (to it) that. **voyez à être à l'heure** see *ou* make sure that you are on time.

3 se ~ *vpr* **(a)** (*être visible*) *[tache etc]* to show. **cela se voit!** that's obvious! **(b) se** ~ **forcé de** to find o.s. forced to; **cela se voit tous les jours** it happens *ou* can be seen *ou* found every day; **il s'est vu interdire l'accès** he found himself *ou* he was refused admission.

voire [vwaʀ] *adv* or even.

voirie [vwaʀi] *nf* (*enlèvement des ordures*) refuse collection; (*entretien des routes*) highway maintenance.

voisin, e [vwazɛ̃, in] **1** *adj* **(a)** (*proche*) neighbouring; (*adjacent*) next. **les rues** ~**es** the neighbouring streets; **une maison** ~**e de l'église** a house next to *ou* adjoining the church. **(b)** *idées, espèces, cas* connected. ~ **de** akin to, related to; **dans un état** ~ **de la folie** in a state bordering on *ou* akin to madness. **2** *nm,f* neighbour. **nos** ~**s d'à-côté** our next-door neighbours, the people next door; **mon voisin de dortoir** the person in the next bed to mine (in the dormitory). ♦ **voisinage** *nm* **(a)** (*voisins*) neighbourhood. **être en bon** ~ **avec qn** to be on neighbourly terms with sb. **(b)** (*environs*) vicinity; (*proximité*) proximity, closeness. **les villages du** ~ the villages in the vicinity; **le** ~ **de la montagne** the proximity *ou* closeness of the mountains. ♦ **voisiner** (1) *vi*: ~ **avec qch** to be (placed) side by side with sth.

voiture [vwatyʀ] *nf* **(a)** (*automobile*) (motor)car. ~ **de sport** sportscar; ~ **de tourisme** saloon, sedan (*US*), private car. **(b)** (*wagon*) carriage, coach, car (*US*). **en** ~**!** all aboard! **(c)** (*attelée ou poussée*) (*pour marchandises*) cart; (*pour voyageurs*) carriage, coach. ~ **à bras** handcart; ~ **d'enfant** pram, perambulator, baby carriage (*US*).

voix [vwa] *nf* **(a)** voice. **à** ~ **basse/haute** in a low *ou* hushed/loud voice; **à haute et intelligible** ~ loud and clear; **rester sans** ~ to be speechless; *[chien]* **donner de la** ~ to bay, give tongue; **la** ~ **du sang** the call of the blood. **(b)** (*opinion*) voice; (*Pol: suffrage*) vote. **avoir** ~ **consultative** to have consultative powers *ou* a consultative voice; **donner sa** ~ **à qn** to vote for sb; **avoir** ~ **au chapitre** to have a say in the matter. **(c)** (*Mus*) voice. **chanter à 2/3** ~ to sing in 2/3 parts; **chanter d'une** ~ **juste** to sing in tune; **être en** ~ to be in good voice. **(d)** (*Ling*) voice.

vol[1] [vɔl] *nm* **(a)** (*gén*) flight. **il y a 8 heures de** ~ **entre** ... it's an 8-hour flight between ...; **condi-**

tions de ~ flying conditions; ~ **à voile** gliding. **(b)** **un** ~ **de perdrix** a covey *ou* flock of partridges; **un** ~ **de moucherons** a cloud of gnats. **(c)** (*locutions*) **en (plein)** ~ in (full) flight; **prendre son** ~ to take wing, fly off *ou* away; **attraper au** ~ *autobus* to leap onto as it moves off; *ballon* to catch as it flies past; *occasion* to leap at, seize; **à** ~ **d'oiseau** as the crow flies. ♦ **voler**[1] (1) *vi* (*lit, fig*) to fly. ~ **de ses propres ailes** to fend for o.s.; ~ **en éclats** to fly into pieces; ~ **au vent** to fly in the wind, float on the wind; ~ **vers qn/au secours de qn** to fly to sb/to sb's assistance.

vol[2] [vɔl] *nm* theft. (*fig*) **c'est du** ~! it's daylight robbery!; ~ **à l'étalage** shoplifting; ~ **à main armée** armed robbery; ~ **à la tire** pickpocketing. ♦ **voler**[2] (1) *vt* **(a)** ~ **qch à qn** to steal sth from sb; **se faire** ~ **ses bagages** to have one's luggage stolen; (*fig*) **il ne l'a pas volé!** he asked for it! **(b)** ~ **qn** to rob sb; ~ **les clients sur le poids** to cheat customers over (the) weight, give customers short measure; **on n'est pas volé*** you get your money's worth all right*. ♦ **voleur, -euse 1** *adj*: **être** ~ to be a thief. **2** *nm,f* (*malfaiteur*) thief; (*commerçant*) swindler. ~ **de grand chemin** highwayman; **au** ~! stop thief!

volage [vɔlaʒ] *adj* *époux* flighty, fickle.

volaille [vɔlɑj] *nf*: **une** ~ a fowl; **la** ~ poultry. ♦ **volailler** *nm* poulterer.

volant[1] [vɔlɑ̃] *nm* **(a)** (*Aut*) steering wheel. **prendre le** ~ to take the wheel; **un brusque coup de** ~ a sharp turn of the wheel; **as du** ~ crack *ou* ace driver. **(b)** (*Tech*) (*régulateur*) flywheel; (*de commande*) (hand)wheel. **(c)** *[rideau, robe]* flounce. **jupe à** ~**s** flounced skirt. **(d)** (*Badminton*) shuttlecock.

volant[2]**, e** [vɔlɑ̃, ɑ̃t] *adj* flying. (*Aviat*) **le personnel** ~ the flight *ou* flying staff.

volatil, e[1] [vɔlatil] *adj* (*Chim*) volatile. ♦ **volatiliser** (1) **1** *vt* (*Chim*) to volatilize. **2 se** ~ *vpr* (*Chim*) to volatilize; (*fig*) to vanish (into thin air).

volatile[2] [vɔlatil] *nm* (*volaille*) fowl; (*oiseau*) bird.

vol-au-vent [vɔlovɑ̃] *nm inv* vol-au-vent.

volcan [vɔlkɑ̃] *nm* (*Géog*) volcano; (*personne*) spitfire; (*situation*) powder keg. ♦ **volcanique** *adj* (*lit, fig*) volcanic.

volée [vɔle] *nf* **(a)** ~ **de** *moineaux* flock *ou* flight of; *enfants* swarm of; *flèches* flight *ou* volley of; *coups* volley of; **recevoir une bonne** ~ to get a sound thrashing *ou* beating. **(b)** (*Ftbl, Tennis*) volley. **de** ~ on the volley. **(c)** ~ **d'escalier** flight of stairs. **(d) jeter qch à la** ~ to fling sth about; **semer à la** ~ to sow broadcast; **à toute** ~ *gifler, lancer* vigorously, with full force; **les cloches sonnaient à toute** ~ the bells were pealing out.

voler [vɔle] *V* **vol**[1]**, vol**[2].

volet [vɔlɛ] *nm* **(a)** (*persienne*) shutter; (*Aut: panneau articulé*) flap. **(b)** *[triptyque]* volet, wing; *[carte]* section; *[reportage]* part.

voleter [vɔlte] (4) *vi* to flutter about.

voleur, -euse [vɔlœr, øz] *V* **vol**[2].

volière [vɔljɛʀ] *nf* (*cage*) aviary. (*fig*) **c'est une** ~ it's a proper henhouse*.

volley-ball [vɔlɛbol] *nm* volleyball. ♦ **volleyeur, -euse** *nm,f* volleyball player.

volontaire [vɔlɔ̃tɛʀ] **1** *adj* **(a)** (*voulu*) (*gén*) voluntary; *oubli* intentional. **(b)** (*décidé*) *personne* self-willed; *expression, menton* determined. **2** *nmf* (*Mil, gén*) volunteer. ♦ **volontairement** *adv* (*de son plein gré*) voluntarily, of one's own free will; (*exprès*) intentionally, deliberately; (*d'une manière décidée*) determinedly.

volonté [vɔlɔ̃te] *nf* **(a)** (*intention*) wish, will. **manifester sa** ~ **de faire qch** to show one's intention of doing sth; **respecter la** ~ **de qn** to respect sb's wishes; **la** ~ **nationale** the will of the nation; ~ **de puissance/de réussir** will for power/to succeed. **(b) bonne** ~ goodwill, willingness; **mauvaise** ~ unwillingness; **il y met de la mauvaise** ~ he does it unwillingly *ou* grudgingly *ou* with a bad grace; **avec la meilleure** ~ **du monde** with the best will in the world. **(c)** (*énergie*) willpower, will. **une** ~ **de fer** a will of iron; **réussir à force de** ~ to succeed through sheer willpower *ou* determination. **(d) à** ~ at will; **servez-vous de pain à** ~ take as much bread as you like; **'sucrer à** ~**'** 'sweeten to taste'.

volontiers [vɔlɔ̃tje] *adv* **(a)** (*de bonne grâce*) with pleasure, gladly, willingly. **voulez-vous dîner chez nous?** – ~ would you like to eat with us? – I'd love to *ou* with pleasure. **(b)** (*naturellement*) readily. **on croit** ~ **que ...** people readily believe that ... .

volt [vɔlt] *nm* volt. ♦ **voltage** *nm* voltage.

volte-face [vɔltəfas] *nf inv* **(a)** (*lit*) **faire** ~ to turn round. **(b)** (*fig*) volte-face, about-turn.

voltige [vɔltiʒ] *nf* (*Équitation*) trick riding; (*Aviat*) aerobatics.

voltiger [vɔltiʒe] (3) *vi* to flutter about.

volubile [vɔlybil] *adj* voluble. ♦ **volubilité** *nf* volubility.

volubilis [vɔlybilis] *nm* convolvulus, morning glory.

volume [vɔlym] *nm* (*gén*) volume. *[gros objets]* **faire du** ~ to be bulky, take up space. ♦ **volumineux, -euse** *adj* voluminous, bulky.

volupté [vɔlypte] *nf* sensual *ou* voluptuous pleasure. ♦ **voluptueusement** *adv* voluptuously. ♦ **voluptueux, -euse** *adj* voluptuous.

volute [vɔlyt] *nf* (*Archit*) volute; *[fumée]* curl.

vomir [vɔmiʀ] (2) *vt* *aliments* to vomit, bring up; *flammes, injures* to spew out; (*fig: détester*) to loathe, abhor. **avoir envie de** ~ to want to be sick; (*fig*) **c'est à** ~ it's enough to make you sick. ♦ **vomi** *nm* vomit. ♦ **vomissement** *nm*: ~**(s)** vomiting.

vorace [vɔʀas] *adj* voracious. ♦ **voracement** *adv* voraciously. ♦ **voracité** *nf* voracity, voraciousness.

vos [vo] *adj poss* *V* **votre.**

voter [vɔte] (1) **1** *vi* to vote. **2** *vt* *projet de loi* to vote for; *loi* to pass; *crédits* to vote. ♦ **votant, e** *nm,f* voter. ♦ **vote** *nm* **(a)** (*action*) (*gén*) voting (*de* for); *[loi]* passing. **(b)** (*suffrage*) vote. ~ **de confiance** vote of confidence; ~ **à main levée** vote by a show of hands; ~ **secret/par correspondance/par procuration** secret/postal/proxy vote.

votre [vɔtʀ(ə)], *pl* **vos** [vo] *adj poss* your; *V* **son**[1]**, ton**[1].

vôtre [votʀ(ə)] **1** *pron poss*: **le** ~**, la** ~**, les** ~**s** yours, your own; **à la (bonne)** ~! your (good) health!, cheers!* **2** *nmf* **(a) j'espère que vous y mettrez du** ~ I hope you'll pull your weight. **(b) les** ~**s** your family; (*péj*) **vous et tous les** ~**s** you and your ilk *ou* all those like you; **nous pourrons être des** ~**s ce soir** we shall be able to join you tonight; *V* **sien. 3** *adj poss* yours; *V* **sien.**

vouer [vwe] (1) *vt* *temps, argent* to devote; *amour, fidélité* to vow; (*Rel*) to dedicate (à to). **se** ~ **à une cause** to dedicate o.s. *ou* devote o.s. to a cause; **projet voué à l'échec** plan doomed to *ou* destined for failure.

vouloir [vulwaʀ] (31) **1** *vt* **(a)** (*gén*) to want. **je veux de vous une réponse** I want an answer from you; *[vendeur]* **j'en veux 10 F** I want 10 francs for it; **je veux que tu te laves les mains/que tes mains soient lavées** I want you to wash your hands/your hands to be washed; **que lui voulez-vous?** what do you want with him?; **qu'il le veuille ou non** whether he likes *ou* wants it or not; **il veut absolument venir** he is absolutely set on coming, he is determined to come.

(b) (*sens affaibli: désirer*) **voulez-vous à boire?** would you like *ou* do you want a drink?; **je voudrais/j'aurais voulu du pain** I would like/I would have liked some bread; **je voudrais bien y aller** I'd love to go; **elle voulut se lever mais retomba** she tried to get up but fell back; **je voulais vous dire/lui écrire** I meant to tell you/to write to him; **ça va comme tu veux?*** is everything going all right *ou* O.K. (for you)?*; ~ **du bien à qn** to wish sb well; **je voudrais que vous voyiez sa tête!** I wish you could see his face!; **si tu veux** if you like; **s'il voulait, il pourrait être ministre** if he wanted (to), he could be a minister; **comme vous voulez** as you like *ou* wish *ou* please.

(c) (*consentir*) **ils ne voulurent pas nous recevoir** they wouldn't see us, they weren't willing to see us; **le moteur ne veut pas partir** the engine won't start; **il joue bien quand il veut** he plays well when he wants to *ou* has a mind (to); **voudriez-vous avoir l'obligeance de** would you be so kind as to; **veuillez croire à toute ma sympathie** please accept my deepest sympathy; **voulez-vous me prêter ce livre?** will you lend me this book?; **voudriez-vous fermer la fenêtre?** would you mind closing the window?; **veux-tu (bien) te taire!** will you be quiet!; **veuillez quitter la pièce immédiatement** please leave the room at once; **je veux bien le faire/qu'il vienne** (*volontiers*) I'm happy *ou* I'll be happy to do it/for him to come; (*s'il le faut vraiment*) I don't mind doing it/if he comes; **moi je veux bien le croire mais ...** I'm quite willing *ou* prepared to believe him but ...; **moi je veux bien, mais ...** fair enough*, but ... .

(d) *[choses]* (*requérir*) to want, require. **ces plantes veulent de l'eau** these plants want *ou* need water; **l'usage veut que ...** custom requires that ...; **le hasard voulut que ...** chance decreed that ..., as fate would have it ... .

(e) (*s'attendre à*) to expect. **comment voulez-vous que je sache?** how do you expect me to know?, how should I know?; **et vous voudriez que nous acceptions?** and you expect us to agree?, and you would have us agree?

(f) en ~ à qn to have sth against sb, have a grudge against sb; **en ~ à qn de qch** to hold sth against sb; **il m'en veut d'avoir fait cela** he holds a grudge against me for having done that; **ne m'en veuillez pas** don't hold it against me; **tu ne m'en veux pas?** no hard feelings?; **en ~ à qch** to be after sth; **il en veut à mon argent** he is after my money.

(g) ~ dire (*signifier*) to mean; **qu'est-ce que cela veut dire?** what does that mean?

(h) (*locutions*) **que voulez-vous (qu'on y fasse)!** what can we do?, it can't be helped!; **je veux être pendu si ...** I'll be hanged *ou* damned if ...; **sans le ~** unintentionally, inadvertently; **tu l'as voulu** you asked for it; **tu l'auras voulu** it'll have been your own fault; **il y a eu des discours en veux-tu en voilà** there were speeches galore; **elle fait de lui ce qu'elle veut** she twists him round her little finger.

2 ~ de *vt indir*: **~ de qn/qch** to want sb/sth; **on ne veut plus de lui au bureau** they don't want him *ou* won't have him in the office any more.

3 *nm* will. **bon ~** goodwill; **mauvais ~** ill will; **attendre le bon ~ de qn** to wait on sb's pleasure.

voulu, e [vuly] *adj* **(a)** (*requis*) required, requisite. **l'argent ~** the required *ou* requisite money, the money required. **(b)** (*volontaire*) deliberate, intentional. **c'est ~*** it's done on purpose, it's intentional.

vous [vu] **1** *pron pers* **(a)** you. **si j'étais ~** if I were you; **eux ont accepté, ~ pas** they accepted but you didn't *ou* but not you; **~ parti** once you've gone; **qui l'a vu?, ~?** who saw him?, (did) you? *ou* was it you?; **pourquoi ne le ferais-je pas: ~ l'avez bien fait, ~!** why shouldn't I do it – YOU did (it)!; **~ tous qui m'écoutez** all of you listening to me; **cette maison est-elle à ~?** does this house belong to you?, is this house yours? *ou* your own?; **vous ne pensez qu'à ~** you think only of yourself (*ou* yourselves). **(b)** (*dans comparaisons*) you. **il est aussi fort que ~** he is as strong as you (are); **je vais faire comme ~** I'll do the same as you (do). **(c)** (*avec vpr*) **~ êtes-~ bien amusé(s)?** did you have a good time?; **je crois que ~ ~ connaissez** I believe you know each other; **servez-~ donc** do help yourself (*ou* yourselves); **ne ~ disputez pas** don't fight. **2** *nm*: **le ~** the 'vous'. form; **dire ~ à qn** to call sb 'vous'.

voûte [vut] *nf* (*Archit*) vault; (*porche*) archway. **la ~ céleste** the vault *ou* canopy of heaven; **~ plantaire** arch of the foot. ♦ **voûter** (1) *vt* **(a)** (*Archit*) to arch, vault. **(b)** *personne, dos* to make stooped. **dos voûté** bent back; **il s'est voûté** he has become stooped.

vouvoyer [vuvwaje] (8) *vt*: **~ qn** to address sb as 'vous'. ♦ **vouvoiement** *nm* addressing sb as 'vous'.

voyage [vwajaʒ] *nm* journey, trip; (*par mer*) voyage. (*action*) **le ~, les ~s** travelling; **il revient de ~** he's just come back from a journey *ou* a trip; **il est en ~** he's away; **au moment de partir en ~** just as he was setting off on his journey *ou* travels; **frais/souvenirs de ~** travel expenses/souvenirs; **~ d'affaires** *etc* business *etc* trip; **~ de noces** honeymoon; **~ organisé** package tour *ou* holiday. ♦ **voyager** (3) *vi* to travel. **aimer ~** to be fond of travelling; **cette malle a beaucoup voyagé** this trunk has travelled a great deal *ou* has done a lot of travelling. ♦ **voyageur, -euse 1** *adj tempérament* wayfaring. **2** *nm,f* traveller. **~ de commerce** commercial traveller.

voyant, e [vwajɑ̃, ɑ̃t] **1** *adj couleurs* loud, gaudy, garish. **2** *nm* (*signal*) light. **~ d'huile** oil warning light. **3** *nf*: **~e (extra-lucide)** clairvoyant.

voyelle [vwajɛl] *nf* vowel.

voyeur, -euse [vwajœʀ, øz] *nm,f* (*péj*) peeping Tom, voyeur.

voyou [vwaju] **1** *nm* (*enfant*) rascal; (*adulte*) lout, hoodlum, hooligan. **2** *adj inv air* loutish.

vrac [vʀak] *adv*: **en ~** (*sans emballage*) (*au détail*) loose; (*en gros*) in bulk; (*fig: en désordre*) in a jumble.

vrai, vraie [vʀɛ] **1** *adj* (*gén*) true; (*réel*) real; (*authentique*) genuine. **c'est dangereux, c'est ~, mais ...** it's dangerous, it's true *ou* certainly, but ...; **ce sont ses ~s cheveux** that's his real *ou* own hair; **un ~ Picasso** a real *ou* genuine Picasso; **son ~ nom est Charles** his real *ou* true name is Charles; **un ~ de ~*** the real thing, the genuine article; **c'est un ~ fou!** he's really mad!, he's downright mad!; **c'est une vraie mère pour moi** she's a real mother to me. **2** *nm*: **le ~** the truth; **il y a du ~ dans ce qu'il dit** there's some truth in what he says; **être dans le ~** to be right. **3** *adv*: **il dit ~** he's right, what he says is right *ou* true; **à dire ~, à ~ dire** to tell (you) the truth, in (actual) fact; **pour de ~*** for real*; *[décor, perruque]* **faire ~** to look real *ou* like the real thing. ♦ **vraiment** *adv* (*gén*) really. **nous voulons ~ la paix** we really (and truly) want peace; **il est ~ idiot** he's a real idiot.

vraisemblable [vʀɛsɑ̃blabl(ə)] *adj hypothèse* likely; *intrigue* plausible, convincing. **peu ~** *histoire* improbable, unlikely; **il est ~ que** it's likely *ou* probable that. ♦ **vraisemblablement** *adv* in all likelihood *ou* probability, probably. ♦ **vraisemblance** *nf [hypothèse]* likelihood; *[situation romanesque]* plausibility. **selon toute ~** in all likelihood *ou* probability.

vrille [vʀij] *nf* (*Tech*) gimlet; (*spirale*) spiral; (*Aviat*) (tail)spin. **escalier en ~** spiral staircase.

vrombir [vʀɔ̃biʀ] (2) *vi* to hum. ♦ **vrombissement** *nm*: **~(s)** humming.

vu, vue[1] [vy] **1** *adj* **(a)** (*: *compris*) **c'est ~?** all right?, got it?*, understood? **(b)** (*considéré*) **bien**

~ *personne* well thought of; *chose* good form; **mal** ~ *personne* poorly thought of; *chose* bad form. **2** *nm*: **au ~ et au su de tous** openly and publicly. **3** *prép* in view of. **~ la situation** in view of *ou* considering the situation. **4** *conj* (*) **~ que** in view of the fact that, seeing that.

vue² [vy] *nf* **(a)** (*sens*) (eye)sight. **il a la ~ basse** he is short-sighted. **(b)** (*regard*) **détourner la ~** to look away; **s'offrir à la ~ de tous** to present o.s. for all to see; (*lit, fig*) **perdre de ~** to lose sight of; **il lui en a mis plein la ~*** he dazzled him (*ou* her). **(c)** (*panorama*) view. **avec ~ imprenable** with an open *ou* unobstructed view *ou* outlook; **cette pièce a ~ sur la mer** this room looks out onto the sea. **(d)** (*spectacle*) sight. **la ~ du sang l'a fait s'évanouir** the sight of the blood made him faint; **à sa ~ elle s'est mise à rougir** when she saw him she began to blush. **(e)** (*image*) view; (*photo*) photograph, photo. **(f)** (*conception*) view. **c'est une ~ de l'esprit** that's a purely theoretical view;**~s** (*opinion*) views; (*projet*) plans; (*sur qn ou ses biens*) designs (*sur* on). **(g)** (*locutions*) **je le connais de ~** I know him by sight; **à ~** *payable etc* at sight; *atterrir* visually; *atterrissage* visual; **à ~ d'œil** *diminuer etc* before one's very eyes; **à ~ de nez*** roughly, at a rough guess; **en ~** (*lit, fig: proche*) in sight; (*en évidence*) **(bien) en ~** conspicuous; (*célèbre*) **très en ~** very much in the public eye; **avoir un poste en ~** to have one's sights on a job; **avoir un collaborateur en ~** to have an associate in mind; **avoir en ~ de faire** to have it in mind to do, plan to do; **il a acheté une maison en ~ de son mariage** he has bought a house with his marriage in mind; **il a dit cela en ~ de le décourager** he said that with the idea of *ou* with a view to discouraging him.

vulgaire [vylgɛʀ] *adj* (*grossier*) vulgar, coarse; (*commun*) common. **de la ~ matière plastique** ordinary *ou* common or garden plastic. ♦ **vulgairement** *adv* vulgarly, coarsely. ♦ **vulgarisation** *nf* popularization. ♦ **vulgariser** (1) *vt* to popularize. ♦ **vulgarité** *nf* vulgarity, coarseness. **des ~s** vulgarities.

vulnérable [vylneʀabl(ə)] *adj* vulnerable. ♦ **vulnérabilité** *nf* vulnerability.

vulve [vylv(ə)] *nf* vulva.

WXYZ

W, w [dubləve] *nm* (*lettre*) W, w.
wagon [vagɔ̃] *nm* (*de marchandises*) truck, wagon, freight car (*US*); (*de voyageurs*) carriage, car (*US*); (*contenu*) truckload, wagonload. ~ **à bestiaux** cattle truck ~**-citerne** *nm, pl* ~**s**-~**s** tanker, tank wagon; ~ **frigorifique** refrigerated van; ~**-lit** *nm, pl* ~**s**-~**s** sleeping car, sleeper; ~**-restaurant** *nm, pl* ~**s**-~**s** restaurant *ou* dining car. ♦ **wagonnet** *nm* small truck.
water-polo [watɛʀpɔlo] *nm* water polo.
waters [watɛʀ] *nmpl* toilet, lavatory.
watt [wat] *nm* watt.
week-end, *pl* ~**-**~**s** [wikɛnd] *nm* weekend. **partir en** ~ to go away for the weekend.
western [wɛstɛʀn] *nm* western.
whisky, *pl* ~**ies** [wiski] *nm* whisky.

X, x [iks] *nm* (*lettre*) X, x. **ça fait x temps que je ne l'ai pas vu*** I haven't seen him for n months; **plainte contre X** action against person or persons unknown.
xénophobe [ksenɔfɔb] **1** *adj* xenophobic. **2** *nmf* xenophobe. ♦ **xénophobie** *nf* xenophobia.
xérès [gzeʀɛs] *nm* (*vin*) sherry.
xylophone [ksilɔfɔn] *nm* xylophone.

Y, y¹ [igʀɛk] *nm* (*lettre*) Y, y.
y² [i] **1** *adv* there. **restez-**~ stay there; **il avait une feuille de papier et il** ~ **dessinait un bateau** he had a sheet of paper and he was drawing a ship on it; **j'**~ **suis, j'**~ **reste** here I am and here I stay. **2** *pron pers* it. **elle s'**~ **connaît** she knows all about it, she's an expert; **il faudra vous** ~ **faire** you'll just have to get used to it; **je n'**~ **suis pour rien** it is nothing to do with me.
yacht [jɔt] *nm* yacht.
yaourt [jauʀ(t)] *nm* yog(h)urt.
yeux [jø] *nmpl de* **œil.**
yoga [jɔga] *nm* yoga.
yoghourt [jɔguʀ(t)] *nm* = **yaourt.**
Yougoslavie [jugɔslavi] *nf* Yugoslavia. ♦ **yougoslave** *adj,* **Y**~ *nmf* Yugoslav(ian).
youyou [juju] *nm* dinghy.
yo-yo [jojo] *nm inv* yo-yo.

Z, z [zɛd] *nm* (*lettre*) Z, z.
zèbre [zɛbʀ(ə)] *nm* (*Zool*) zebra; (*: *individu*) bloke*, guy*. **courir comme un** ~ to run like a hare *ou* the wind.
zébrer [zebʀe] (6) *vt* to stripe, streak (*de* with).
zébu [zeby] *nm* zebu.
zèle [zɛl] *nm* zeal. (*péj*) **faire du** ~ to be overzealous, overdo it. ♦ **zélé, e** *adj* zealous.
zénith [zenit] *nm* (*lit, fig*) zenith.
zéro [zeʀo] **1** *nm* **(a)** (*gén, Math*) zero, nought; (*dans un numéro de téléphone*) O. **recommencer à** ~ to start from scratch again, go back to square one; **3 degrés au-dessus de** ~ 3 degrees above freezing (point) *ou* above zero. **(b)** (*Ftbl*) nil; (*Tennis*) love. **(c)** (*Scol*) zero, nought. ~ **de conduite** bad mark for behaviour *ou* conduct; (*fig*) **mais en cuisine,** ~ **(pour la question)*** but as far as cooking goes he's (*ou* she's) useless* *ou* a dead loss*. **(d)** (*: *personne*) nonentity. **2** *adj*: ~ **heure** zero hour; **il a fait** ~ **faute** he didn't make any mistakes; **ça m'a coûté** ~ **franc** ~ **centime*** I got it for precisely *ou* exactly nothing.
zeste [zɛst(ə)] *nm*: ~ **de citron** piece of lemon peel.
zézayer [zezeje] (8) *vi* to lisp. ♦ **zézaiement** *nm* lisp.
zibeline [ziblin] *nf* sable.
zig* [zig] *nm,* **zigomar*** [zigɔmaʀ] *nm,* **zigoto*** [zigɔto] *nm* bloke*, guy*.
zigouiller* [ziguje] (1) *vt* to do in*.
zigzag [zigzag] *nm* zigzag. **route en** ~ winding *ou* zigzagging road. ♦ **zigzaguer** (1) *vi* to zigzag (along).
zinc [zɛ̃g] *nm* (*métal*) zinc; (*: *avion*) plane; (*: *comptoir*) bar, counter.
zinzin* [zɛ̃zɛ̃] **1** *adj* cracked*, nuts*, barmy*. **2** *nm* what's-it*.
zizanie [zizani] *nf* ill-feeling, discord.
zizi* [zizi] *nm* willy*.
zodiaque [zɔdjak] *nm* zodiac.
zona [zona] *nm* shingles (*sg*).
zone [zon] *nf* zone, area. ~ **bleue** ≃ restricted parking zone *ou* area; ~ **dangereuse** danger zone; ~ **franche** free zone; ~ **franc** franc area; (*fig*) **de deuxième/troisième** ~ second-/third-rate; (*bidonville*) **la** ~ the slum belt.
zoo [zoo] *nm* zoo. ♦ **zoologie** *nf* zoology. ♦ **zoologique** *adj* zoological. ♦ **zoologiste** *nmf ou* ♦ **zoologue** *nmf* zoologist.
zoom [zum] *nm* (*objectif*) zoom lens; (*effet*) zoom.
zouave [zwav] *nm* Zouave, zouave. **faire le** ~* to play the fool, fool around.
zozoter [zɔzɔte] (1) *vi* to lisp.
zut* [zyt] *excl* (*c'est embêtant*) dash (it)!*; (*tais-toi*) (do) shut up!*

ENGLISH–FRENCH DICTIONARY
DICTIONNAIRE ANGLAIS–FRANÇAIS

A

A, a^1 [eɪ] *n* A, a *m*; (*Mus*) la *m*. **to know sth from A to Z** connaître qch de A à Z; (*houses*) **24a** le 24 bis; (*Aut*) **on the A4** ≃ sur la nationale 4. ♦ **A-1,** (*US*) **A number 1** *adj* champion*. ♦ **ABC** *n* abc *m*, alphabet *m*; **as easy as ABC** simple comme bonjour. ♦ **A-bomb** *n* bombe *f* atomique. ♦ **A-levels** *npl* ≃ baccalauréat *m*.

a^2 [eɪ, ə], **an** *indef art* un, une. ~ **tree** un arbre; **an apple** une pomme; **he smokes ~ pipe** il fume la pipe; ~ **third of the book** le tiers du livre; ~ **woman hates violence** les femmes détestent la violence; **she was ~ doctor** elle était médecin; **as ~ soldier** en tant que soldat; **my uncle, ~ sailor** mon oncle, qui est marin; **what ~ pleasure!** quel plaisir!; **I have heard of ~ Mr Martin** j'ai entendu parler d'un certain M. Martin; **they are of ~ size** ils sont de la même grandeur; **at ~ blow** d'un seul coup; **£4 ~ person** 4 livres par personne; **3 francs ~ kilo** 3 F le kilo; **twice ~ month** deux fois par mois; **80 km an hour** 80 kilomètres-heure.

aback [ə'bæk] *adv*: **to be taken ~** être interloqué (*by* par), en rester tout interdit.

abacus ['æbəkəs] *n* boulier *m* (compteur).

abandon [ə'bændən] **1** *vt* (*gen*) abandonner; *right* renoncer à; *lawsuit* se désister de. **to ~ ship** abandonner le navire. **2** *n*: **with (gay) ~** avec (une belle) désinvolture. ♦ **abandoned** *adj* abandonné; (*dissolute*) débauché.

abase [ə'beɪs] *vt* abaisser; (*humiliate*) humilier. **to ~ o.s. so far as to do** s'abaisser jusqu'à faire.

abashed [ə'bæʃt] *adj* confus.

abate [ə'beɪt] *vi [storm, emotions, pain]* s'apaiser; *[flood, fever, noise]* baisser; *[pollution]* diminuer; *[wind]* se modérer. ♦ **abatement** *n [noise, pollution]* suppression *f*, réduction *f*.

abattoir ['æbətwɑːʳ] *n* abattoir *m*.

abbey ['æbɪ] *n* abbaye *f*.

abbot ['æbət] *n* abbé *m*, supérieur *m*.

abbreviate [ə'briːvɪeɪt] *vt* abréger. ♦ **abbreviation** *n* abréviation *f*.

abdicate ['æbdɪkeɪt] **1** *vt right* abdiquer; *responsibility, post* se démettre de. **to ~ the throne** abdiquer. **2** *vi* abdiquer. ♦ **abdication** *n [monarch]* abdication *f*.

abdomen ['æbdəmen] *n* abdomen *m*. ♦ **abdominal** [æb'dɒmɪnl] *adj* abdominal.

abduct [æb'dʌkt] *vt* enlever, kidnapper. ♦ **abduction** *n* enlèvement *m*. ♦ **abductor** *n* ravisseur *m*.

abed† [ə'bed] *adv* au lit. **to lie ~** rester couché.

aberrant [ə'berənt] *adj* aberrant, anormal. ♦ **aberration** *n* aberration *f*.

abet [ə'bet] *vt* encourager (*sb in a crime* qn à commettre un crime).

abeyance [ə'beɪəns] *n* suspension *f* temporaire. **to be in ~** rester en suspens.

abhor [əb'hɔːʳ] *vt* abhorrer, avoir en horreur. ♦ **abhorrence** *n* horreur *f* (*of* de). ♦ **abhorrent** *adj* odieux (*to* à).

abide [ə'baɪd] *vt* supporter, souffrir.

abide by *vt fus rule, decision* se conformer à; *promise* rester fidèle à; *resolve* s'en tenir à. ♦ **abiding** *adj* éternel.

ability [ə'bɪlɪtɪ] *n* aptitude *f* (*to do* à faire), compétence *f* (*in* en; *to do* pour faire); (*skill*) talent *m*, don *m*. **to the best of one's ~** de son mieux; **a person of great ~** une personne très douée; **a certain artistic ~** un certain talent artistique.

abject ['æbdʒekt] *adj person, action* abject; *state* misérable; *apology* servile; *poverty* extrême. ♦ **abjectly** *adv* abjectement; avec servilité.

abjure [əb'dʒʊəʳ] *vt* renoncer (publiquement) à.

ablaze [ə'bleɪz] *adj, adv*: **to be ~** flamber; **~ with** *anger* enflammé de; *light* resplendissant de.

able ['eɪbl] *adj* (*having means*) capable (*to do* de faire); (*clever*) capable, compétent; (*physically*) valide. **to be ~ to do** (*be capable of*) pouvoir faire; (*know how to*) savoir faire; **~ to pay** en mesure de payer; **you are better ~ to do it** (*easier for you*) vous êtes mieux à même de le faire; (*better qualified*) vous êtes mieux désigné pour le faire; **I was ~ to catch the bus** j'ai réussi à attraper l'autobus. ♦ **able-bodied** *adj* robuste. ♦ **able(-bodied) seaman** *n* matelot breveté. ♦ **ably** *adv* habilement, de façon très compétente.

abnormal [æb'nɔːməl] *adj* anormal. ♦ **abnormality** *n* (*state*) caractère anormal; (*instance: gen, Bio, Psych*) anomalie *f*; (*Med*) malformation *f*. ♦ **abnormally** *adv formed* d'une manière anormale; *long, quiet etc* exceptionnellement.

aboard [ə'bɔːd] **1** *adv* (*Aviat, Naut*) à bord. **to go ~** monter à bord; **to take ~** embarquer; **all ~!** (*Rail*) en voiture!; (*Naut*) tout le monde à bord! **2** *prep* (*Aviat, Naut*) à bord de. **~ the train** dans le train.

abode [ə'bəʊd] *n* demeure *f*; (*Jur*) domicile *m*.

abolish [ə'bɒlɪʃ] *vt death penalty, law* abolir; *practice, custom, ignorance* supprimer. ♦ **abolishment** *or* ♦ **abolition** *n* abolition *f*; suppression *f*.

abominable [ə'bɒmɪnəbl] *adj* abominable. ♦ **abominably** *adv* abominablement.

abominate [ə'bɒmɪneɪt] *vt* abominer, exécrer. ♦ **abomination** *n* abomination *f*.

aborigine [ˌæbə'rɪdʒɪnɪ] *n* aborigène *mf*. ♦ **aboriginal** *adj, n* aborigène (*mf*).

abort [ə'bɔːt] **1** *vi* (*Med, fig*) avorter; (*Mil, Space*) échouer. **2** *vt* (*Med, fig*) faire avorter; (*Mil, Space*) abandonner (pour raisons de sécurité). ♦ **abortion** *n* (*Med*) avortement *m*; **to have an ~ion** avorter; **to get an ~ion** se faire avorter. ♦ **abortionist** *n* avorteur *m*, -euse *f*. ♦ **abortive** *adj plan, invasion, coup* manqué, raté; *attempt* infructueux. ♦ **abortively** *adv* en vain.

abound [ə'baʊnd] *vi* abonder (*in* en).

about [ə'baʊt] **1** *adv* **(a)** (*approximately*) vers, à peu près, environ. **~ 11 o'clock** vers 11 heures; **it's ~ 11 o'clock** il est environ 11 heures; **it's ~ time to go** il est presque temps de partir; **there are ~ 30** il y en a une trentaine; **she's ~ as old as you** elle est à peu près de votre âge; **I've had ~ enough!*** je commence à en avoir marre!* **(b)** (*here and there*) çà et là, ici et là, de tous côtés. **shoes lying ~** des chaussures dans tous les coins *or* traînant çà et là. **(c)** (*near*) près, par ici, par là. **there was nobody ~** il n'y avait personne; **he's somewhere ~** il est par ici quelque part; **there's a lot of flu ~** il y a beaucoup de cas de grippe en ce moment. **(d)** (*all round*) autour. **to glance ~** jeter un coup d'œil autour de soi. **(e)** (*opposite direc-*

tion) à l'envers. (*fig*) **it's the other way ~** c'est tout le contraire; (*Mil*) **~ turn!** demi-tour, marche!; (*Naut*) **to go ~** virer de bord vent debout (*or* vent devant). **(f) to be ~ to do** être sur le point de faire, aller faire.

2 *prep* **(a)** (*concerning*) au sujet de, à propos de. **I heard nothing ~ it** je n'en ai pas entendu parler; **what is it ~?** de quoi s'agit-il?; **I know what it's all ~** je sais de quoi il retourne; **to speak ~ sth** parler de qch; **how ~*** *or* **what ~* going to the pictures?** si on allait au cinéma? **(b)** (*near to*) vers, près de; (*somewhere in*) en, dans. **~ here** par ici, près d'ici; **~ the house** quelque part dans la maison; **to wander ~ the town/the streets** errer dans la ville/par les rues. **(c)** (*occupied with*) **what are you ~?** que faites-vous?; **while we're ~ it** pendant que nous y sommes; **mind what you're ~!** faites un peu attention!; **how does one go ~ it?** comment est-ce qu'on s'y prend? **(d)** (*with, on*) **I've got it ~ me somewhere** je l'ai quelque part sur moi; **there is something interesting ~ him** il a un côté intéressant. **(e) (round) ~** autour de.

♦ **about-face** *or* ♦ **about-turn 1** *n* (*Mil*) demi-tour *m*; (*fig*) volte-face *f*; **2** *vi* faire un demi-tour; faire volte-face.

above [əˈbʌv] **1** *adv* **(a)** (*overhead, higher up*) au-dessus, en haut. **from ~** d'en haut; **the flat ~** l'appartement au-dessus *or* du dessus; (*fig*) **a warning from ~** un avertissement (venu) d'en haut. **(b)** (*more*) **boys of 6 and ~** les garçons à partir de 6 ans. **(c)** (*earlier: in document etc*) ci-dessus, plus haut. **the address ~** l'adresse ci-dessus. **2** *prep* **(a)** (*higher or better than*) au-dessus de. **~ all** surtout. **(b)** (*more than*) plus de. **children ~ 7 years of age** les enfants de plus de 7 ans *or* au-dessus de 7 ans; **over and ~ the cost of ...** en plus de ce que coûte ... . **(c)** (*beyond*) au-delà de. **to get ~ o.s.** avoir des idées de grandeur; **~ one's means** au-delà de *or* au-dessus de ses moyens; **that is quite ~ me*** c'est trop compliqué pour moi; **he is ~ such behaviour** il est au-dessus d'une pareille conduite; **he's not ~ stealing** il irait jusqu'à voler; **he's not ~ playing with the children** il ne dédaigne pas de jouer avec les enfants. **3** *adj* (*in text*) ci-dessus mentionné.

♦ **aboveboard 1** *adj person* franc, loyal; *action, decision* loyal; **it's all quite ~board** (*not unfair*) c'est franc jeu; (*not illegal*) c'est régulier; **2** *adv* cartes sur table, ouvertement. ♦ **aboveground** *adv* au-dessus du sol, à la surface. ♦ **above-mentioned** *adj* ci-dessus mentionné. ♦ **above-named** *adj* susnommé.

abrasion [əˈbreɪʒən] *n* frottement *m*; (*Med*) écorchure *f*; (*Geol*) érosion *f*; (*Tech*) abrasion *f*. ♦ **abrasive** *adj substance* abrasif; *voice* caustique; *wit* corrosif.

abreast [əˈbrest] *adv* de front. **3 ~** 3 de front; (*Naut*) **in line ~** en ligne de front; **~ of** (*at level of*) à la hauteur de; (*aware of*) au courant de; **to be ~ of the times** marcher avec son temps.

abridge [əˈbrɪdʒ] *vt book, edition, speech* abréger; *interview* écourter; *text* réduire. ♦ **abridgement** *n* (*short version*) abrégé *m*.

abroad [əˈbrɔːd] *adv* **(a)** (*in foreign land*) à l'étranger. **news from ~** nouvelles de l'étranger. **(b)** (*far and wide*) au loin; (*in all directions*) de tous côtés, dans toutes les directions. **there is a rumour ~ that ...** le bruit circule que ... .

abrupt [əˈbrʌpt] *adj person, conduct, turn* soudain; *style, speech* heurté; *slope* raide. ♦ **abruptly** *adv turn, move* brusquement; *speak, behave* avec brusquerie; *rise* en pente raide. ♦ **abruptness** *n [person]* brusquerie *f*; *[departure]* soudaineté *f*; (*steepness*) raideur *f*.

abscess [ˈæbsɪs] *n* abcès *m*.

abscond [əbˈskɒnd] *vi* s'enfuir (*from* de). ♦ **absconder** *n* évadé(e) *m(f)*. **to be an ~er** être en cavale*.

abseil [ˈæpsaɪl] **1** *vi* descendre en rappel. **2** *n* rappel *m*.

absence [ˈæbsəns] *n* **(a)** absence *f*. (*Jur*) **sentenced in his ~** condamné par contumace. **(b)** (*lack*) manque *m*, défaut *m*. **in the ~ of information** faute de renseignements.

absent [ˈæbsənt] **1** *adj* absent; (*absent-minded*) distrait. (*Mil*) **~ without leave** absent sans permission. **2** [æbˈsent] *vt*: **to ~ o.s.** s'absenter (*from* de). ♦ **absentee 1** *n* absent(e) *m(f)*; (*habitual*) absentéiste *mf*; **2** *adj* absentéiste. ♦ **absenteeism** *n* absentéisme *m*. ♦ **absently** *adv* distraitement. ♦ **absent-minded** *adj person* distrait; *air, manner* absent, distrait. ♦ **absent-mindedly** *adv* d'un air distrait *or* absent. ♦ **absent-mindedness** *n* distraction *f*, absence *f*.

absolute [ˈæbsəluːt] **1** *adj* (*gen*) absolu. **the divorce was made ~** le jugement en divorce a été prononcé; **it's an ~ scandal** c'est un véritable scandale; **~ idiot*** parfait crétin*; **it's an ~ fact that ...** c'est un fait indiscutable que ...; **~ proof** preuve *f* irréfutable. **2** *n* absolu *m*. ♦ **absolutely** *adv* absolument.

absolution [ˌæbsəˈluːʃən] *n* absolution *f*.

absolve [əbˈzɒlv] *vt* (*from sin etc*) absoudre (*from, of* de); (*Jur*) acquitter (*of* de); (*from obligation, oath*) délier (*from* de).

absorb [əbˈsɔːb] *vt* (*lit, fig*) absorber; *sound, shock* amortir. **to become ~ed in one's work/in a book** s'absorber dans son travail/dans la lecture d'un livre; **to be ~ed in a book** être plongé dans un livre; **to be completely ~ed in one's work** être tout entier à son travail. ♦ **absorbed** *adj* absorbé (*in* dans). ♦ **absorbency** *n* pouvoir absorbant; (*Chem, Phys*) absorptivité *f*. ♦ **absorbent** *adj* absorbant; (*US*) **~ent cotton** coton *m* hydrophile. ♦ **absorbing** *adj book, film* captivant; *work* absorbant. ♦ **absorption** *n* absorption *f*.

abstain [əbˈsteɪn] *vi* s'abstenir (*from* de; *from doing* de faire); (*be teetotaller*) s'abstenir complètement des boissons alcoolisées. ♦ **abstainer** *n* (*Pol*) abstentionniste *mf*; (*teetotaller*) personne *f* qui ne boit pas d'alcool.

abstemious [əbˈstiːmɪəs] *adj* frugal. ♦ **abstemiousness** *n* frugalité *f*.

abstention [əbˈstenʃən] *n* abstention *f* (*from* de).

abstinent [ˈæbstɪnənt] *adj* sobre, tempérant. ♦ **abstinence** *n* abstinence *f*.

abstract [ˈæbstrækt] **1** *adj* abstrait. **2** *n* (*summary*) résumé *m*; (*work of art*) œuvre abstraite. **in the ~** dans l'abstrait. **3** [æbˈstrækt] *vt* (*remove*) retirer (*from* de); (*summarize*) résumer. ♦ **abstracted** *adj* préoccupé. ♦ **abstraction** *n* (*removing*) extraction *f*; (*abstract concept*) abstraction *f*.

abstruse [æbˈstruːs] *adj* abstrus.

absurd [əbˈsɜːd] *adj, n* absurde (*m*). ♦ **absurdity** *n* absurdité *f*. ♦ **absurdly** *adv* absurdement.

abundant [əˈbʌndənt] *adj* abondant. **there is ~ proof that he is guilty** les preuves de sa culpabilité abondent. ♦ **abundance** *n* abondance *f*; **in abundance** en abondance. ♦ **abundantly** *adv supply etc* abondamment; *grow* à foison; *clear* tout à fait; **he made it ~ly clear to me that ...** il m'a bien fait comprendre que ... .

abuse [əˈbjuːz] **1** *vt privilege* abuser de; *person* (*insult*) injurier; (*ill-treat*) maltraiter. **2** [əˈbjuːs] *n* (*gen*) abus *m*; (*curses, insults*) insultes *fpl*, injures *fpl*. ♦ **abusive** *adj language* injurieux, offensant; *person* grossier.

abut [əˈbʌt] *vi*: **to ~ on** être contigu à.

abysmal [əˈbɪzməl] *adj ignorance* sans bornes; *mistake* énorme; *work* exécrable. ♦ **abysmally** *adv* abominablement, atrocement.

abyss [əˈbɪs] *n* abîme *m*, gouffre *m*.

acacia [əˈkeɪʃə] *n* acacia *m*.

academic [ˌækəˈdemɪk] **1** *adj affairs, career* universitaire; *freedom* de l'enseignement;

(*scholarly*) *style, approach* intellectuel; (*theoretical*) théorique. ~ **year** année *f* universitaire; **that's quite** ~ c'est purement théorique; **it's** ~ **now** ça n'a plus d'importance. **2** *n* (*person*) universitaire *mf*.
academy [ə'kædəmɪ] *n* académie *f*; (*Scol etc*) école *f*, collège *m*. **the Royal A**~ l'Académie Royale (*de Londres*); **military** ~ école militaire. ♦ **academician** *n* académicien(ne) *m(f)*.
accede [æk'si:d] *vi*: **to** ~ **to a request** agréer une demande; **to** ~ **to the throne** monter sur le trône.
accelerate [æk'seləreɪt] **1** *vt movement* accélérer; *work* activer; *events* précipiter. **2** *vi* (*esp Aut*) accélérer. ♦ **acceleration** *n* accélération *f*. ♦ **accelerator** *n* accélérateur *m*.
accent ['æksənt] **1** *n* (*all senses*) accent *m*. **2** [æk'sent] *vt* accentuer. ♦ **accentuate** *vt* accentuer. ♦ **accentuation** *n* accentuation *f*.
accept [ək'sept] *vt* (*gen*) accepter; *goods* prendre livraison de. **I** ~ **that** ... je conviens que ... . ♦ **acceptable** *adj gift, suggestion* acceptable; **the money was most** ~**able** l'argent était vraiment le bienvenu. ♦ **acceptance** *n* acceptation *f*. ♦ **accepted** *adj fact, method, principle* reconnu; *idea* courant; *behaviour, pronunciation* admis; *sense, meaning* usuel.
access ['ækses] **1** *n* accès *m* (*to sth* à qch; *to sb* auprès de qn); (*Jur: in divorce*) droit *m* de visite. **2** *adj*: ~ **road** route *f* d'accès; (*to motorway*) bretelle *f* d'accès. ♦ **accessibility** *n* accessibilité *f*. ♦ **accessible** *adj* accessible (*to* à).
accession [æk'seʃən] *n [monarch]* avènement *m*.
accessory [æk'sesərɪ] **1** *adj* accessoire, auxiliaire. **2** *n* **(a)** (*Dress, Theat, Comm etc*) accessoire *m*. **toilet accessories** objets *mpl* de toilette. **(b)** (*Jur*) complice *mf* (*before the fact* par instigation; *after the fact* par assistance).
accident ['æksɪdənt] **1** *n* accident *m*. **by** ~ *injure etc* accidentellement; *meet etc* par hasard. **2** *adj statistics etc* des accidents; *insurance* contre les accidents. ~ **prevention** prévention *f* des accidents; (*Aut*) prévention routière. ♦ **accidental** *adj death* accidentel; *meeting* fortuit; *effect, benefit* accessoire. ♦ **accidentally** *adv meet etc* par hasard; *injure etc* accidentellement; **it was done quite** ~**ally** on ne l'a pas fait exprès. ♦ **accident-prone** *adj* prédisposé aux accidents.
acclaim [ə'kleɪm] **1** *vt* (*applaud*) acclamer; (*proclaim*) proclamer. **2** *n* acclamations *fpl*. ♦ **acclamation** *n* acclamation *f*.
acclimatize [ə'klaɪmətaɪz], (*US*) **acclimate** [ə'klaɪmət] **1** *vt* acclimater (*to* à); (*fig*) accoutumer (*to* à). **2** *vi* (*also* **become** ~**d**) s'acclimater; (*fig*) s'accoutumer. ♦ **acclimatization,** (*US*) **acclimation** *n* acclimatation *f*; (*fig*) accoutumance *f* (*to* à).
accommodate [ə'kɒmədeɪt] *vt* **(a)** (*lodge*) *[landlady, town council]* loger; *[car, house]* contenir; *[hotel]* recevoir. **(b)** (*supply*) fournir (*sb with sth* qch à qn). **to** ~ **sb with a loan** consentir un prêt à qn. **(c)** (*reconcile*) *differences* concilier; (*adapt*) *plans, wishes* adapter (*to* à). ♦ **accommodating** *adj* accommodant, obligeant.
accommodation [əˌkɒmə'deɪʃən] **1** *n* **(a)** (*also US* ~**s**) logement *m*. '~ **(to let)**' 'chambres *fpl* à louer'; **we have no** ~ **available** nous n'avons pas de place; **there is no** ~ **for children** on n'accepte pas les enfants. **(b)** (*compromise*) compromis *m*. **2** *adj*: ~ **address** *adresse utilisée pour la correspondance*; ~ **bureau** agence *f* de logement; ~ **officer** responsable *mf* de l'hébergement; (*US*) ~ **train** (train *m*) omnibus *m*.
accompany [ə'kʌmpənɪ] *vt* accompagner (*Mus: on* à). **accompanied by** accompagné de. ♦ **accompaniment** *n* accompagnement *m*. ♦ **accompanist** *n* accompagnateur *m*, -trice *f*.
accomplice [ə'kʌmplɪs] *n* complice *mf* (*in a crime* d'un crime).
accomplish [ə'kʌmplɪʃ] *vt* accomplir, exécuter; *task, mission* accomplir, achever; *desire* réaliser; *aim* arriver à; *journey* effectuer. ♦ **accomplished** *adj* accompli. ♦ **accomplishment** *n* (*achievement*) œuvre accomplie; (*skill*) talent *m*; (*completion*) réalisation *f*, accomplissement *m*.
accord [ə'kɔ:d] **1** *vt* accorder (*to* à). **2** *vi* s'accorder (*with* avec). **3** *n* **(a)** (*agreement*) consentement *m*, accord *m*. **of his own** ~ de lui-même, de son propre chef; **with one** ~ d'un commun accord. **(b)** (*treaty*) traité *m*. ♦ **accordance** *n* accord *m* (*with* avec); **in** ~**ance with** conformément à.
according [ə'kɔ:dɪŋ] *adv*: ~ **to** selon, suivant; **everything went** ~ **to plan** tout s'est passé comme prévu; ~ **to what he says** d'après ce qu'il dit; ~ **to him** selon lui. ♦ **accordingly** *adv* **(a)** (*and so*) en conséquence; **(b) to act** ~**ly** faire le nécessaire.
accordion [ə'kɔ:dɪən] *n* accordéon *m*. ♦ **accordionist** *n* accordéoniste *mf*.
accost [ə'kɒst] *vt* accoster.
account [ə'kaʊnt] **1** *n* **(a)** (*reckoning, bill*) compte *m*. **put it on my** ~ vous le mettrez sur mon compte; **in** ~ **with** en compte avec; **to** ~ **rendered** facture non payée; **on** ~ à compte; **to pay £50 on** ~ verser un acompte de 50 livres; (*Advertising*) **they have the Michelin** ~ ce sont eux qui détiennent la publicité de Michelin; **to keep the** ~**s** tenir la comptabilité *or* les comptes. **(b)** (*benefit*) profit *m*, avantage *m*. **to turn sth to** ~ mettre qch à profit. **(c)** (*report*) compte rendu *m*. **to give an** ~ **of** faire le compte rendu de; **to call sb to** ~ **for having done** demander des comptes à qn pour avoir fait; **he gave a good** ~ **of himself** il s'en est bien tiré; **by all** ~**s** d'après l'opinion générale; **by her own** ~ d'après ce qu'elle dit. **(d)** (*phrases*) **of no** ~ sans importance; **to take sth into** ~ prendre qch en considération, tenir compte de qch; **on** ~ **of** à cause de; **on no** ~ en aucun cas, sous aucun prétexte; **on her** ~ à cause d'elle, pour elle. **2** *adj*: ~ **book** livre *m* de comptes; ~**s department** (service *m* de) comptabilité *f*. **3** *vt* estimer, juger. **to** ~ **o.s. lucky** s'estimer heureux.
account for *vt fus expenses* rendre compte de; *one's conduct* justifier; *circumstances* expliquer; (*Hunting etc: kill*) tuer. **there's no** ~**ing for tastes** chacun son goût; **everyone is** ~**ed for** on n'a oublié personne; (*after air crash etc*) tous les passagers ont été retrouvés.
♦ **accountable** *adj*: **to be** ~**able for sth** avoir à répondre de qch (*to sb* devant qn). ♦ **accountancy** *n* comptabilité *f*. ♦ **accountant** *n* comptable *mf*; ~**ant's office** agence *f* comptable. ♦ **accounting** *n* comptabilité *f*.
accoutrements [ə'ku:trəmənts], (*US*) **accouterments** [ə'ku:tərments] *npl* (*gen*) attirail *m*; (*Mil*) équipement *m*.
accredit [ə'kredɪt] *vt* accréditer (*to* auprès de).
accretion [ə'kri:ʃən] *n* accroissement *m*.
accrue [ə'kru:] *vi [money, advantages]* revenir (*to* à); *[interest]* courir.
accumulate [ə'kju:mjʊleɪt] **1** *vt* accumuler. **2** *vi* s'accumuler. ♦ **accumulation** *n* (*act*) accumulation *f*; (*heap of objects etc*) tas *m*. ♦ **accumulator** *n* accumulateur *m*.
accurate ['ækjʊrɪt] *adj figures, clock* exact; *report, story, shot* précis; *aim, judgment, assessment* juste; *memory, translation* fidèle. ♦ **accuracy** *n* exactitude *f*; précision *f*; justesse *f*; fidélité *f*. ♦ **accurately** *adv* exactement; avec précision; avec justesse; fidèlement.
accursed, accurst [ə'kɜ:st] *adj* (*liter*) (*damned*) maudit; (*hateful*) détestable, exécrable.
accusative [ə'kju:zətɪv] *adj, n* accusatif (*m*). **in the** ~ à l'accusatif.
accuse [ə'kju:z] *vt* accuser (*of* de; *of doing* de faire). ♦ **accusal** *or* ♦ **accusation** *n* accusation *f*. ♦ **accused** *n* accusé(e) *m(f)*. ♦ **accuser** *n*

accusateur *m*, -trice *f*. ♦ **accusing** *adj* accusateur. ♦ **accusingly** *adv* d'une manière accusatrice.

accustom [əˈkʌstəm] *vt* habituer, accoutumer (*to* à, *to doing* à faire). ♦ **accustomed** *adj* **(a)** (*used*) habitué, accoutumé (*to* à; *to do, to doing* à faire). **to become ~ed to** s'habituer *or* s'accoutumer à; **I am not ~ed to such treatment** je n'ai pas l'habitude qu'on me traite (*subj*) de cette façon. **(b)** (*usual*) *kindness etc* habituel, coutumier.

ace [eɪs] *n* as *m* (*also fig: of sportsman etc*). (*fig*) **to keep an ~ up one's sleeve** avoir un atout dans sa manche; (*fig*) **to play one's ~** jouer sa meilleure carte; **within an ~ of** à deux doigts de.

acerbity [əˈsɜːbɪtɪ] *n* âpreté *f*, aigreur *f*.

acetate [ˈæsɪteɪt] *n* acétate *m*.

acetic [əˈsiːtɪk] *adj* acétique.

acetone [ˈæsɪtəʊn] *n* acétone *f*.

acetylene [əˈsetɪliːn] **1** *n* acétylène *m*. **2** *adj*: **~ burner** chalumeau *m* à acétylène; **~ welding** soudure *f* autogène.

ache [eɪk] **1** *vi* faire mal, être douloureux. **my head ~s** j'ai mal à la tête; **to be aching all over** (*after exercise*) être courbaturé; (*from illness*) avoir mal partout; **it makes my heart ~** cela me fend le cœur; (*fig*) **to be aching to do** mourir d'envie de faire. **2** *n* douleur *f*, souffrance *f*. **stomach ~** mal *m* de ventre; **I've got stomach ~** j'ai mal au ventre; **all his ~s and pains** toutes ses douleurs. ♦ **aching** *adj* douloureux; *tooth, limb* malade; **to have an aching heart** avoir le cœur gros.

achieve [əˈtʃiːv] *vt task* accomplir, exécuter; *aim* atteindre, arriver à; *success* obtenir; *fame* parvenir à. **I feel I've ~d sth** je crois que j'ai fait qch d'utile. ♦ **achievement** *n* réussite *f*, exploit *m*.

acid [ˈæsɪd] **1** *n* acide *m*. **2** *adj* acide; (*fig*) *person* revêche; *voice* aigre; *remark* mordant. (*fig*) **~ test** épreuve décisive. ♦ **acidity** *n* acidité *f*.

acknowledge [əkˈnɒlɪdʒ] *vt* **(a)** avouer, admettre (*that* que); *child, error* reconnaître. **to ~ sb as leader** reconnaître qn pour chef. **(b)** *greeting* répondre à; (*also* **~ receipt of**) *letter, parcel* accuser réception de; *sb's action, services, help* manifester sa gratitude pour; *source of quotation etc* mentionner; *applause, cheers* saluer pour répondre à. **I smiled at him but he didn't even ~ me** je lui ai souri mais il a fait comme s'il ne me voyait pas. ♦ **acknowledged** *adj* reconnu. ♦ **acknowledgement** *n [money]* reçu *m*; *[letter]* accusé *m* de réception; (*in preface etc*) remerciements *mpl*. **in ~ment of your help** en reconnaissance de votre aide.

acme [ˈækmɪ] *n* point *m* culminant.

acne [ˈæknɪ] *n* acné *f*.

acorn [ˈeɪkɔːn] *n* (*Bot*) gland *m*.

acoustic [əˈkuːstɪk] *adj* acoustique. ♦ **acoustics** *n* (*sg or pl*) acoustique *f*.

acquaint [əˈkweɪnt] *vt* aviser (*sb with sth* qn de qch), renseigner (*sb with sth* qn sur qch). **to ~ sb with the situation** mettre qn au courant de la situation; **to be ~ed with** *person, subject* connaître; *fact* savoir, être au courant de; **to become ~ed with** *person* faire la connaissance de; *facts* prendre connaissance de. ♦ **acquaintance** *n* connaissance *f*; **to make sb's ~ance** faire la connaissance de qn; **to improve upon ~ance** gagner à être connu; **old ~ances** de vieilles connaissances; **she's an ~ance of mine** c'est une de mes relations.

acquiesce [ˌækwɪˈes] *vi* consentir, acquiescer (*in* à). ♦ **acquiescence** *n* consentement *m*. ♦ **acquiescent** *adj* consentant.

acquire [əˈkwaɪəʳ] *vt knowledge, money, fame* acquérir; *language* apprendre; *habit* prendre; *reputation* se faire; *car, house* faire l'acquisition de. **to ~ a taste for** prendre goût à. ♦ **acquired** *adj characteristic* acquis; *taste* qui s'acquiert. ♦ **acquirement** *n* acquisition *f* (*of* de); (*skill*) connaissance *f*.

acquisition [ˌækwɪˈzɪʃən] *n* acquisition *f*. ♦ **acquisitive** *adj* (*for money*) âpre au gain; (*greedy*) avide (*of* de). ♦ **acquisitiveness** *n* instinct *m* de possession.

acquit [əˈkwɪt] *vt* **(a)** (*Jur*) acquitter (*of* de). **(b) to ~ o.s. well** bien s'en tirer. ♦ **acquittal** *n* acquittement *m*.

acre [ˈeɪkəʳ] *n* ≃ demi-hectare *m*. **a few ~s of land** quelques hectares de terrain; (*fig*) **~s of*** des kilomètres et des kilomètres de.

acrid [ˈækrɪd] *adj smell* âcre; *remark* acerbe.

Acrilan [ˈækrɪlæn] *n* ® Acrilan *m* ®.

acrimonious [ˌækrɪˈməʊnɪəs] *adj* acrimonieux. ♦ **acrimony** *n* acrimonie *f*.

acrobat [ˈækrəbæt] *n* acrobate *mf*. ♦ **acrobatic** *adj* acrobatique. ♦ **acrobatics** *npl [gymnast etc]* acrobatie *f*; *[child etc]* acrobaties *fpl*.

acronym [ˈækrənɪm] *n* sigle *m*.

across [əˈkrɒs] **1** *prep* **(a)** (*from one side to other of*) d'un côté à l'autre de. **bridge ~ the river** pont sur le fleuve; **to walk ~ the road** traverser la route. **(b)** (*on other side of*) de l'autre côté de. **the shop ~ the road** le magasin d'en face, le magasin de l'autre côté de la rue; **lands ~ the sea** terres d'outre-mer. **(c)** (*crosswise over*) en travers de, à travers. **to go ~ the fields** *or* **~ country** aller à travers champs; **plank ~ a door** planche en travers d'une porte; **~ his chest** sur la poitrine. **2** *adv*: **the river is 5 km ~** le fleuve a 5 km de large; **to help sb ~** aider qn à traverser; (*fig*) **to get sth ~ to sb*** faire comprendre qch à qn; **~ from** en face de.

acrylic [əˈkrɪlɪk] *adj* acrylique.

act [ækt] **1** *n* **(a)** (*deed*) acte *m*. **in the ~ of doing** en train de faire; **caught in the ~** pris en flagrant délit; **A~s of the Apostles** Actes des Apôtres. **(b)** (*Jur*: **~ of Parliament**) loi *f*. **(c)** *[play]* acte *m*; (*in circus etc*) numéro *m*. **he's just putting on an ~** il joue la comédie; **to get in on the ~*** (parvenir à) participer aux opérations.

2 *vi* **(a)** (*gen*) agir. **to ~ like a fool** agir comme un imbécile; *[drug]* **to ~ on sth** agir sur qch; **the table ~s as a desk** la table sert de bureau; **he ~s as my assistant** il me fait office d'assistant. **(b)** (*Theat*) jouer. **have you ever ~ed before?** avez-vous déjà fait du théâtre?; (*fig*) **she's only ~ing** elle joue la comédie.

3 *vt* (*Theat*) *part* jouer. (*Theat, fig*) **to ~ the part of** tenir le rôle de; (*fig*) **to ~ the fool*** faire l'idiot(e).

act out *vt sep event* faire un récit mimé de; *fantasies* vivre.

act up* *vi [person]* se conduire mal; *[car etc]* faire des caprices.

act (up)on *vt fus advice* suivre, se conformer à; *order* exécuter. **I ~ed (up)on your letter** j'ai fait le nécessaire quand j'ai reçu votre lettre.

acting [ˈæktɪŋ] **1** *adj* suppléant, par intérim. **2** *n*: **his ~ is very good** il joue très bien; **I like his ~** j'aime son jeu; **he has done some ~** il a fait du théâtre (*or* du cinéma).

action [ˈækʃən] **1** *n* **(a)** action *f*. **to put into ~** *plan* mettre à exécution; *principles, suggestion* mettre en action; *machine* mettre en marche; **the time has come for ~** il est temps d'agir; **to take ~** agir; **to go into ~** passer à l'action; **out of ~** *machine etc* en dérangement, détraqué; *person* hors de combat; **to put out of ~** *machine* mettre hors d'usage, détraquer; *person* mettre hors de combat. **(b)** (*deed*) acte *m*, action *f*. **to suit the ~ to the word** joindre le geste à la parole; **~s speak louder than words** les actes sont plus éloquents que les paroles. **(c)** (*Jur*) procès *m*, action *f* en justice. **to bring an ~ against sb** intenter une action *or* un procès contre qn. **(d)** (*Tech*) mécanisme *m*; *[clock etc]* mécanique *f*. **(e)** (*Mil*)

combat *m*, engagement *m*. **to go into ~** *[unit, person]* aller au combat; *[army]* engager le combat; **to see ~** combattre; **killed in ~** tué à l'ennemi. **2** *adj*: (*TV*) **~ replay** répétition immédiate (*d'une séquence*); **~ stations!** à vos postes! ♦ **actionable** *adj* (*Jur*) donnant matière à procès.
activate ['æktıveıt] *vt* activer.
active ['æktıv] *adj person, life, imagination* actif; *file, case* en cours; *volcano* en activité. **to take an ~ part in** prendre une part active à; **we're giving it ~ consideration** nous l'examinons sérieusement; (*Mil*) **on ~ service** en campagne; **on the ~ list** en activité; (*Gram*) **in the ~** à l'actif. ♦ **actively** *adv* activement. ♦ **activist** *n* activiste *mf*. ♦ **activity** *n* (*gen*) activité *f*; *[town, port]* mouvement *m*.
actor ['æktəʳ] *n* acteur *m*. ♦ **actress** *n* actrice *f*.
actual ['æktjʊəl] *adj figures, result* réel, véritable; *example* concret; *fact* positif. **in ~ fact** en fait; **his ~ words were ...** il a dit très exactement ... . ♦ **actuality** *n* réalité *f*. ♦ **actually** *adv* **(a)** (*in reality*) effectivement, véritablement, en fait; **the person ~ly in charge is ...** la personne véritablement responsable *or* responsable en fait, c'est ...; **~ly I don't know him** à vrai dire *or* en fait, je ne le connais pas; **what did he ~ly say?** qu'est-ce qu'il a dit exactement *or* au juste? **(b)** (*even*) même; **he ~ly beat her** il est même allé jusqu'à la battre.
actuary ['æktjʊərı] *n* actuaire *mf*.
actuate ['æktjʊeıt] *vt* faire agir. **~d by** animé de.
acumen ['ækjʊmen] *n* flair *m*. **business ~** sens *m* aigu des affaires.
acupuncture ['ækjʊpʌŋktʃəʳ] *n* acupuncture *f*. ♦ **acupuncturist** *n* acupuncteur *m*.
acute [ə'kju:t] *adj pain, accent, angle* aigu (*f* -guë); *remorse* intense; *shortage, situation* critique, grave; *person, mind* pénétrant, perspicace; *hearing* fin. ♦ **acutely** *adv* **(a)** (*intensely*) *suffer* vivement, intensément; **~ly aware that** profondément conscient du fait que; **(b)** (*shrewdly*) *observe* avec perspicacité.
ad* [æd] *n abbr of* **advertisement.**
Adam ['ædəm] *n* Adam *m*. **~'s apple** pomme *f* d'Adam; **I don't know him from ~*** je ne le connais ni d'Ève ni d'Adam.
adamant ['ædəmənt] *adj* inflexible.
adapt [ə'dæpt] **1** *vt* adapter (*to* à, *for* pour). **2** *vi* s'adapter. ♦ **adaptability** *n* faculté *f* d'adaptation. ♦ **adaptable** *adj* adaptable; **he's very ~able** il s'adapte à tout. ♦ **adaptation** *n* adaptation *f* (*of* de, *to* à). ♦ **adapter** *or* ♦ **adaptor** *n* (*person*) adaptateur *m*, -trice *f*; (*device*) adaptateur *m*; (*Elec*) prise *f* multiple.
add [æd] *vt* **(a)** ajouter (*to* à, *that* que). **~ some more pepper** rajoutez un peu de poivre; **to ~ insult to injury** porter l'insulte à son comble; **~ed to which ...** ajoutez à cela que ... . **(b)** (*Math*) *figures* additionner; *column of figures* totaliser.
add in *vt sep* inclure, ajouter.
add to *vt fus* ajouter à, accroître.
add together *vt sep* additionner.
add up 1 *vi* (*fig*) **it all ~s up*** tout s'explique; **it doesn't ~ up*** il y a qch qui cloche*. **2** *vt sep figures* additionner; *column of figures* totaliser; *advantages, reasons* faire la somme de.
add up to *vt fus [figures]* s'élever à; (* *fig: mean*) signifier.
♦ **adding machine** *n* calculatrice *f*, machine *f* à calculer. ♦ **additive** *n* additif *m*.
adder ['ædəʳ] *n* vipère *f*.
addict ['ædıkt] *n* intoxiqué(e) *m(f)*. **heroin ~** héroïnomane *mf*; **he's an ~** il ne peut plus s'en passer; **he's a yoga ~*** c'est un fanatique du yoga. ♦ **addicted** *adj* adonné (*to* à); **to become ~ed to** s'adonner à; **he's ~ed to cigarettes** c'est un fumeur invétéré. ♦ **addiction** *n* penchant *m* très fort (*to* pour); (*Med*) dépendance *f* (*to* à). ♦ **addictive** *adj* qui crée une dépendance.
addition [ə'dıʃən] *n* (*Math etc*) addition *f*; (*fact of adding*) adjonction *f*; (*increase*) augmentation *f* (*to* de); (*to tax, income, profit*) surcroît *m* (*to* de). **in ~** de plus; **in ~ to** en plus de; **there's been an ~ to the family** la famille s'est agrandie; **this is a welcome ~ to the series** ceci enrichit la série. ♦ **additional** *adj* additionnel; (*extra*) de plus, supplémentaire. ♦ **additionally** *adv* de plus, en sus.
address [ə'dres] **1** *n* **(a)** [(*US*) 'ædres] (*on letter etc*) adresse *f*. **(b)** (*talk*) discours *m*, allocution *f*. **2** *vt* **(a)** (*direct*) *letter, speech, writing* adresser (*to* à). **this is ~ed to you** *[letter etc]* ceci vous est adressé; *[words, comment]* ceci s'adresse à vous; **to ~ o.s. to sth** se mettre à qch. **(b)** (*speak to*) s'adresser à. **he ~ed the meeting** il a pris la parole (devant l'assistance); **don't ~ me as 'Colonel'** ne m'appelez pas 'Colonel'. ♦ **addressee** *n* destinataire *mf*.
adenoids ['ædınɔıdz] *npl* végétations *fpl* (adénoïdes). ♦ **adenoidal** *adj*: **in an adenoidal voice** en parlant du nez.
adept ['ædept] **1** *n* expert *m* (*in, at* en). **2** [ə'dept] *adj* expert (*in, at* à, en, dans; *at doing* à faire).
adequate ['ædıkwit] *adj amount, supply, reward, description* suffisant (*for* pour, *to do* pour faire); *tool etc* adapté (*to* à); *essay, performance* satisfaisant; *person* compétent. ♦ **adequately** *adv warm* suffisamment; *do etc* convenablement.
adhere [əd'hıəʳ] *vi* adhérer (*to* à). **to ~ to** *party* adhérer à; *rule* obéir à; *promise* tenir; *resolve* persister dans. ♦ **adherence** *n* adhésion *f* (*to* à). ♦ **adherent** *n* adhérent(e) *m(f)*; (*Rel*) adepte *mf*. ♦ **adhesion** *n* adhérence *f*. ♦ **adhesive** *adj, n* adhésif (*m*). **adhesive plaster** pansement adhésif; **adhesive tape** (*Med*) sparadrap *m*; (*stationery*) ruban adhésif.
adieu [ə'dju:] *n, excl* adieu *m*.
ad infinitum [,ædınfı'naıtəm] *adv* à l'infini.
adjacent [ə'dʒeısənt] *adj* (*gen*) voisin (*to* de); (*Math*) adjacent.
adjective ['ædʒektıv] *n* adjectif *m*. ♦ **adjectival** *adj* adjectival.
adjoin [ə'dʒɔın] *vt* être contigu à. ♦ **adjoining** *adj* voisin.
adjourn [ə'dʒɜ:n] **1** *vt* ajourner, reporter (*to, until* à; *for a month* à un mois); (*Jur*) *case* renvoyer (*to* à). **to ~ a meeting** (*break off*) suspendre la séance; (*close*) lever la séance. **2** *vi* (*break off*) suspendre la séance; (*close*) lever la séance; *[Parliament]* s'ajourner. **to ~ to the drawing room** passer au salon. ♦ **adjournment** *n* ajournement *m*; renvoi *m*; suspension *f*.
adjudicate [ə'dʒu:dıkeıt] *vt case, competition* juger; *claim* décider. ♦ **adjudication** *n* jugement *m*; décision *f*. ♦ **adjudicator** *n* juge *m*.
adjunct ['ædʒʌŋkt] *n* accessoire *m*.
adjust [ə'dʒʌst] **1** *vt wages, prices* ajuster (*to* à); *instrument, tool* régler; *tie, picture* arranger; *dress* rajuster. **2** *vi* s'adapter (*to* à). ♦ **adjustable** *adj* qui peut s'ajuster; *tool, fastening* réglable; **~able spanner** clef *f* à molette. ♦ **adjustment** *n [prices, wages etc]* rajustement *m*; (*Opt, Tech*) réglage *m*; *[person]* adaptation *f*.
ad lib [æd'lıb] **1** *adv continue* à volonté. **there was food ~** il y avait à manger à discrétion. **2** *n* improvisation *f*. **3 ad-lib** *adj* improvisé. **4 ad-lib** *vti* improviser.
adman* ['ædmæn] *n* publicitaire *m*.
admass ['ædmæs] **1** *n* masses *fpl*. **2** *adj* de masse.
admin* ['ædmın] *n abbr of* **administration.**
administer [əd'mınıstəʳ] *vt* (*gen*) administrer (*to* à). **to ~ an oath to sb** faire prêter serment à qn. ♦ **administration** *n* administration *f*; (*Pol*) **under previous administrations** sous des gouvernements précédents. ♦ **administrative** *adj*

administratif. ♦ **administrator** *n* administrateur *m*, -trice *f*.
admiral ['ædmərəl] *n* amiral *m* (d'escadre). **A~ of the Fleet** amiral (à cinq étoiles). ♦ **Admiralty Board** *n* (*Brit*) ≃ ministère *m* de la Marine.
admire [əd'maɪəʳ] *vt* admirer. ♦ **admirable** ['ædmərəbl] *adj* admirable. ♦ **admirably** *adv* admirablement. ♦ **admiration** *n* admiration *f* (*of, for* pour). **to be the admiration of** faire l'admiration de. ♦ **admirer** *n* admirateur *m*, -trice *f*; (†: *suitor*) soupirant† *m*. ♦ **admiring** *adj* admiratif. ♦ **admiringly** *adv* avec admiration.
admissible [əd'mɪsəbl] *adj plan* acceptable; *evidence* recevable.
admission [əd'mɪʃən] *n* **(a)** (*entry*) admission *f*, entrée *f* (*to* à). **~ free** entrée gratuite; **to gain ~ to** *person* trouver accès auprès de; *place* être admis dans. **(b)** (*confession*) aveu *m*. **by one's own ~** de son propre aveu.
admit [əd'mɪt] *vt* **(a)** (*let in*) laisser entrer. **children not ~ted** entrée interdite aux enfants; **this ticket ~s 2** ce billet est valable pour 2 personnes. **(b)** (*acknowledge*) reconnaître, admettre (*that* que); *crime* reconnaître avoir commis; *one's guilt* reconnaître. **I must ~ that ...** je dois avouer *or* admettre que ...; **I was wrong I ~** j'ai eu tort, j'en conviens.
admit of *vt fus* admettre, permettre.
admit to *vt fus crime* reconnaître avoir commis. **to ~ to having done** reconnaître avoir fait; **to ~ to a feeling of** avouer avoir un sentiment de.
♦ **admittance** *n* droit *m* d'entrée, admission *f* (*to sth* à qch); accès *m* (*to sth* à qch; *to sb* auprès de qn); **I gained ~tance** on m'a laissé entrer; **no ~tance except on business** accès interdit à toute personne étrangère au service. ♦ **admittedly** *adv*: **~tedly this is true** je reconnais *or* il faut reconnaître que c'est vrai.
admonish [əd'mɒnɪʃ] *vt* (*reprove*) réprimander (*for doing* pour avoir fait; *about, for* pour, à propos de); (*warn*) avertir (*against doing* de ne pas faire); (*exhort*) exhorter (*to do* à faire). ♦ **admonition** *n* réprimande *f*; avertissement *m*.
ad nauseam [ˌæd'nɔːsɪæm] *adv* à satiété.
ado [ə'duː] *n*: **much ~ about nothing** beaucoup de bruit pour rien; **without more ~** sans plus de cérémonies.
adolescent [ˌædəʊ'lesnt] *adj, n* adolescent(e) *m(f)*. ♦ **adolescence** *n* adolescence *f*.
adopt [ə'dɒpt] *vt child, method,* (*Pol*) *motion* adopter; *candidate, career* choisir. ♦ **adopted** *adj child* adopté; *country* d'adoption; *son, family* adoptif. ♦ **adoption** *n* adoption *f*; choix *m*. ♦ **adoptive** *adj parent, child* adoptif; *country* d'adoption.
adore [ə'dɔːʳ] *vt* adorer. ♦ **adorable** *adj* adorable. ♦ **adoration** *n* adoration *f*. ♦ **adoringly** *adv* avec adoration.
adorn [ə'dɔːn] *vt room* orner; *dress* parer (*with* de). **to ~ o.s.** se parer. ♦ **adornment** *n* ornement *m*; parure *f*.
adrenalin(e) [ə'drenəlɪn] *n* adrénaline *f*. (*fig*) **he felt the ~ rising** il a senti son pouls s'emballer.
Adriatic (Sea) [ˌeɪdrɪ'ætɪk('siː)] *n* (mer *f*) Adriatique *f*.
adrift [ə'drɪft] *adv, adj* (*Naut*) à la dérive. **to turn ~** *boat* abandonner à la dérive; (*fig*) *person* laisser se débrouiller tout seul; **to come ~*** *[wire etc]* se détacher; *[plans]* tomber à l'eau.
adroit [ə'drɔɪt] *adj* adroit. ♦ **adroitly** *adv* adroitement. ♦ **adroitness** *n* adresse *f*.
adulate ['ædjʊleɪt] *vt* aduler. ♦ **adulation** *n* adulation *f*.
adult ['ædʌlt] **1** *n* adulte *mf*. (*Cine etc*) **~s only** interdit aux moins de 18 ans. **2** *adj person, animal* adulte; *film, book, classes* pour adultes. **~ education** enseignement *m* post-scolaire.
adulterate [ə'dʌltəreɪt] *vt* frelater.
adultery [ə'dʌltərɪ] *n* adultère *m*. ♦ **adulterous** *adj* adultère.
advance [əd'vɑːns] **1** *n* **(a)** (*gen, Mil*) avance *f*. **to make ~s in technology** faire des progrès *mpl* en technologie; **to make ~s to sb** faire des avances à qn; **in ~** *prepare, thank, book* à l'avance; *decide, announce* d'avance; **to be in ~ of one's time** être en avance sur son époque; **a week in ~** une semaine à l'avance; **luggage in ~** bagages enregistrés. **(b)** (*sum of money*) avance *f* (*on* sur). **2** *adj payment* anticipé; *copy of speech etc* distribué à l'avance. **~ guard** avant-garde *f*; **~ notice** préavis *m*; (*Mil*) **~ party** pointe *f* d'avant-garde; **~ post** poste avancé. **3** *vt* (*gen*) avancer; *work* faire avancer. **4** *vi* avancer, s'avancer (*on* sur, *towards* vers); *[troops]* se porter en avant; *[work, civilization, mankind]* progresser, faire des progrès. **he ~d upon me** il est venu vers *or* a marché sur moi. ♦ **advanced** *adj ideas, age, child* avancé; *studies, class* supérieur; *work* poussé; **~d mathematics** hautes études *fpl* mathématiques. ♦ **advancement** *n* avancement *m*.
advantage [əd'vɑːntɪdʒ] *n* avantage *m*. **to have an ~ over sb** avoir un avantage sur qn; **to have the ~ of numbers** avoir l'avantage du nombre; **to take ~ of** *occasion* profiter de; *person* exploiter; **to turn sth to ~** tourner qch à son avantage; **I find it to my ~** j'y trouve mon compte; **it is to his ~ to do it** il a tout intérêt à le faire; **this dress shows her off to ~** cette robe l'avantage. ♦ **advantageous** *adj* avantageux (*to* pour).
advent ['ædvənt] *n* avènement *m*. (*Rel*) **A~** l'Avent *m*.
adventure [əd'ventʃəʳ] **1** *n* aventure *f*. **2** *adj story, film* d'aventures. ♦ **adventurer** *n* aventurier *m*. ♦ **adventuress** *n* aventurière *f*. ♦ **adventurous** *adj* aventureux.
adverb ['ædvɜːb] *n* adverbe *m*. ♦ **adverbial** *adj* adverbial.
adversary ['ædvəsərɪ] *n* adversaire *mf*.
adverse ['ædvɜːs] *adj factor, report, circumstances* défavorable; *wind* contraire. ♦ **adversity** *n* adversité *f*.
advert* ['ædvɜːt] *n abbr of* **advertisement.**
advertise ['ædvətaɪz] **1** *vt* (*Comm etc*) *goods* faire de la publicité *or* de la réclame pour. **I've seen that ~d on television** j'ai vu une publicité pour ça à la télévision; **to ~ a flat for sale** mettre une annonce pour vendre un appartement; **try not to ~ the fact that ...** essaie de ne pas trop laisser voir que ...; **don't ~ your ignorance!** inutile d'afficher votre ignorance! **2** *vi* (*Comm*) faire de la publicité *or* de la réclame. **it pays to ~** la publicité paie; **to ~ for a flat** faire paraître une annonce pour trouver un appartement. ♦ **advertiser** *n* annonceur *m* (publicitaire). ♦ **advertising 1** *n* publicité *f*. **2** *adj* (*gen*) publicitaire; *agency* de publicité.
advertisement [əd'vɜːtɪsmənt] *n* **(a)** (*Comm*) réclame *f*, publicité *f*; (*TV*) spot *m* publicitaire. (*Cine, Press, Rad, TV*) **~s** publicité; (*TV*) **during the ~s** pendant que passait la publicité; **he's not a good ~ for his school** il ne constitue pas une bonne réclame pour son école. **(b)** (*private: in paper etc*) annonce *f*. **~ column** petites annonces; **to put an ~ in a paper** mettre une annonce dans un journal.
advice [əd'vaɪs] *n* avis *m*, conseils *mpl*; (*Comm: notification*) avis. **a piece of ~** un avis, un conseil; **to seek ~ from sb** demander conseil à qn; **to take medical ~** consulter un médecin; **to follow sb's ~** suivre le(s) conseil(s) de qn.
advise [əd'vaɪz] *vt* **(a)** (*give advice to*) conseiller (*sb on/about sth* qn sur/à propos de qch). **to ~ sb to do** conseiller à qn de faire; **to ~ sb against sth** déconseiller qch à qn; **to ~ sb against doing** conseiller à qn de ne pas faire; **you would be well/ill ~d to do that** vous feriez bien de/vous auriez tort de faire cela. **(b)** (*recommend*) *course*

of action recommander. **(c)** (*inform*) aviser (*sb of sth* qn de qch). ♦ **advisability** *n* opportunité *f* (*of* de, *of doing* de faire). ♦ **advisable** *adj* recommandé, conseillé; **I do not think it advisable for you to come** je ne vous conseille pas de venir. ♦ **advisedly** *adv* en toute connaissance de cause. ♦ **adviser** *n* conseiller *m*, -ère *f*. ♦ **advisory** *adj* consultatif; **in an advisory capacity** à titre consultatif.

advocate ['ædvəkɪt] **1** *n* **(a)** *[cause etc]* défenseur *m*, avocat(e) *m(f)*. **to be an ~ of** être partisan de. **(b)** (*Scot Jur*) avocat *m* (plaidant). **2** ['ædvəkeɪt] *vt* recommander, préconiser.

Aegean (Sea) [iː'dʒiːən('siː)] *n* mer *f* Égée.

aegis ['iːdʒɪs] *n*: **under the ~ of** sous l'égide *f* de.

aeons ['iːənz] *npl* éternités *fpl*.

aerate ['ɛəreɪt] *vt liquid* gazéifier; *blood* oxygéner; *room* aérer; *soil* retourner. **~d water** eau *f* gazeuse.

aerial ['ɛərɪəl] **1** *adj* aérien. **~ railway** téléphérique *m*. **2** *n* (*Telec etc*) antenne *f*.

aero... ['ɛərəʊ] *pref* aéro... . ♦ **aerobatics** *npl* acrobatie *f* aérienne. ♦ **aerodrome** *n* aérodrome *m*. ♦ **aerodynamic** *adj* aérodynamique. ♦ **aerodynamics** *nsg* aérodynamique *f*. ♦ **aero-engine** *n* aéromoteur *m*. ♦ **aeronaut** *n* aéronaute *mf*. ♦ **aeronautic(al)** *adj* aéronautique. ♦ **aeronautics** *nsg* aéronautique *f*. ♦ **aeroplane** *n* avion *m*. ♦ **aerosol** **1** *n* (*system*) aérosol *m*; (*spray*) bombe *f*; **2** *adj* en bombe. ♦ **aerospace** *adj*: **~space industry** industrie aérospatiale.

aesthete ['iːsθiːt] *n* esthète *mf*. ♦ **aesthetic(al)** *adj* esthétique. ♦ **aesthetically** *adv* esthétiquement. ♦ **aestheticism** *n* esthétisme *m*. ♦ **aesthetics** *nsg* esthétique *f*.

afar [ə'fɑːʳ] *adv* au loin. **from ~** de loin.

affable ['æfəbl] *adj* affable. ♦ **affability** *n* affabilité *f*. ♦ **affably** *adv* avec affabilité.

affair [ə'fɛəʳ] *n* (*gen*) affaire *f*; (*love ~*) liaison *f* (*with* avec). **the Suez ~** l'affaire de Suez; **this is not her ~** ce n'est pas son affaire, cela ne la regarde pas; **state of ~s** situation *f*; **~s of state** affaires d'État.

affect [ə'fekt] *vt* **(a)** *person* (*concern*) toucher; (*sadden*) affecter; *situation, belief, attitude* influer sur; *health, results, numbers* avoir un effet sur. **it does not ~ the way I do it** cela ne change rien à ma façon de le faire. **(b)** *[disease]* affecter; *[drug]* agir sur. **(c)** (*feign*) *ignorance, indifference* affecter. **(d)** (*have a liking for*) aimer, affectionner. ♦ **affectation** *n* affectation *f*. ♦ **affected** *adj* affecté. ♦ **affectedly** *adv* avec affectation.

affection [ə'fekʃən] *n* affection *f* (*for* pour). **I have a great ~ for her** j'ai beaucoup d'affection pour elle. ♦ **affectionate** *adj* affectueux; (*letter-ending*) **your ~ate daughter** votre fille affectionnée. ♦ **affectionately** *adv* affectueusement; **yours ~ately** (bien) affectueusement à vous.

affidavit [ˌæfɪ'deɪvɪt] *n* (*Jur*) déclaration *f* par écrit sous serment. **to swear an ~ to the effect that** déclarer sous serment que.

affiliate [ə'fɪlɪeɪt] *vt* affilier (*to, with* à). **~d company** filiale *f*. ♦ **affiliation** *n* affiliation *f*.

affinity [ə'fɪnɪtɪ] *n* (*gen*) affinité *f* (*with, to* avec; *between* entre). *[people]* **there is a certain ~ between them** ils ont des affinités.

affirm [ə'fɜːm] *vt* affirmer (*that* que). ♦ **affirmation** *n* affirmation *f*. ♦ **affirmative** *adj, n* affirmatif (*m*); **in the ~ative** (*Gram*) à l'affirmatif; *answer* affirmativement. ♦ **affirmatively** *adv* affirmativement.

affix [ə'fɪks] **1** *vt seal, signature* apposer (*to* à); *stamp* coller (*to* à). **2** ['æfɪks] *n* affixe *m*.

afflict [ə'flɪkt] *vt* affliger. **~ed with** affligé de. ♦ **affliction** *n* affliction *f*.

affluent ['æflʊənt] *adj person* riche; *society* d'abondance. ♦ **affluence** *n* (*wealth*) richesse *f*; (*plenty*) abondance *f*.

afford [ə'fɔːd] *vt* **(a)** (*gen*) avoir les moyens (*to do* de faire); *object, car* s'offrir, se payer*. **he can't ~ (to make) a mistake** il ne peut pas se permettre (de faire) une erreur; **I can't ~ the time to do it** je n'ai pas le temps de le faire. **(b)** (*provide*) *opportunity* fournir; *pleasure* procurer.

afforestation [æˌfɒrɪs'teɪʃən] *n* (re)boisement *m*.

affray [ə'freɪ] *n* échauffourée *f*.

affront [ə'frʌnt] **1** *vt* (*insult*) faire un affront à; (*face*) affronter. **2** *n* affront *m*.

afield [ə'fiːld] *adv*: **far ~** très loin; **further ~** plus loin.

afloat [ə'fləʊt] *adv* à flot (*also fig*); (*Naut: on board ship*) en mer. **to stay ~** *[ship]* rester à flot; *[person]* (*in water*) surnager; (*fig*) rester à flot.

afoot [ə'fʊt] *adv*: **there is sth ~** il se prépare qch; **there is a plan ~ to do** on envisage de faire.

afraid [ə'freɪd] *adj*: **to be ~ of sb/sth** avoir peur de qn/qch, craindre qn/qch; **don't be ~** n'ayez pas peur, ne craignez rien; **I am ~ of hurting him** j'ai peur *or* je crains de lui faire mal; **I am ~ he will hurt me** je crains *or* j'ai peur qu'il (ne) me fasse mal; **I am ~ to go** je n'ose pas y aller, j'ai peur d'y aller; **he is not ~ of work** le travail ne lui fait pas peur; (*regret*) **I'm ~ I can't do it** je regrette *or* je suis désolé, mais je ne pourrai pas le faire; **I'm ~ that ...** je regrette de vous dire que ...; **I'm ~ not/so** hélas non/oui; **there are too many people, I'm ~** je regrette, mais il y a trop de monde.

afresh [ə'freʃ] *adv* de nouveau. **to start ~** recommencer.

Africa ['æfrɪkə] *n* Afrique *f*. ♦ **African** **1** *n* Africain(e) *m(f)*; **2** *adj* (*gen*) africain; *elephant* d'Afrique.

Afrikaans [ˌæfrɪ'kɑːns] *n* afrikaans *m*. ♦ **Afrikaaner** *n* Afrikander *mf*.

afro* ['æfrəʊ] *adj* afro* *inv*.

Afro-Asian ['æfrəʊ'eɪʃən] *adj* afro-asiatique.

aft [ɑːft] *adv* (*Naut*) sur *or* à *or* vers l'arrière.

after ['ɑːftəʳ] **1** *prep* après. **~ dinner** après le dîner; **the day ~ tomorrow** après-demain; **shortly ~ 10 o'clock** peu après 10 heures; **it was ~ 2 o'clock** il était plus de 2 heures; (*US*) **it was 20 ~ 3** il était 3 heures 20; **~ all** après tout; **~ hours*** après la fermeture; **~ seeing her** après l'avoir vue; **~ you** après vous; **~ you with the salt*** passez-moi le sel, s'il vous plaît; **to run ~ sb** courir après qn; **he shut the door ~ her** il a refermé la porte sur elle; **shut the door ~ you** fermez la porte (derrière vous); **day ~ day** jour après jour; **for kilometre ~ kilometre** sur des kilomètres et des kilomètres; **you tell me lie ~ lie** tu me racontes mensonge sur mensonge; **time ~ time** maintes et maintes fois; **they went out one ~ the other** ils sont sortis (*individually*) les uns après les autres *or* (*in a line*) à la file; (*according to*) **~ El Greco** d'après Le Gréco; **she takes ~ her mother** elle tient de sa mère; **to name a child ~ sb** donner à un enfant le nom de qn; **to be ~ sb/sth** chercher qn/qch; (*after loss, robbery etc*) rechercher qn/qch; **the police are ~ him** il est recherché par la police; **what are you ~?** (*want*) qu'est-ce que vous désirez?; (*thinking of*) où voulez-vous en venir?; (*nagging*) **she's always ~ her children*** elle est toujours après ses enfants*.

2 *adv* après, ensuite. **for years ~** pendant des années après cela; **soon ~** bientôt après; **the week ~** la semaine d'après, la semaine suivante.

3 *conj* après (que). **~ he had closed the door, she spoke** après qu'il eut fermé la porte, elle parla; **~ he had closed the door, he spoke** après avoir fermé la porte, il a parlé.

4 *adj*: **in ~life** *or* **~ years** plus tard (dans la vie).

5 *npl* (*dessert*) **~s*** dessert *m*.

♦ **afterbirth** *n* placenta *m*. ♦ **aftercare** *n* *[convalescent]* post-cure *f*; *[ex-prisoner]* surveillance *f* (après libération). ♦ **after-dinner**

drink *n* digestif *m*. ♦ **after-dinner speaker** *n* orateur *m* (de fin de banquet). ♦ **after-effect** *n* *[events etc]* suite *f*, répercussion *f*; *[treatment]* réaction *f*; *[illness]* séquelle *f*; (*Psych*) after-effect *m*. ♦ **afterlife** *n* vie future. ♦ **after-lunch** *adj*: **to have an ~-lunch nap** faire la sieste. ♦ **aftermath** *n* suites *fpl*, séquelles *fpl*. ♦ **afternoon 1** *n* après-midi *m or f*; **in the ~noon** l'après-midi; **at 3 o'clock in the ~noon** à 3 heures de l'après-midi; **on Sunday ~noon(s)** le dimanche après-midi; **on the ~noon of December 2nd** l'après-midi du 2 décembre, le 2 décembre dans l'après-midi; **good ~noon!** (*on meeting sb*) bonjour!; (*on leaving sb*) au revoir!; **2** *adj lecture, class, train, meeting* (de) l'après-midi; **~noon performance** matinée *f*; **~noon tea** thé *m* (de cinq heures). ♦ **after-sales service** *n* service *m* après-vente. ♦ **after-shave** *n* lotion *f* après-rasage. ♦ **aftertaste** *n* arrière-goût *m*. ♦ **afterthought** *n* pensée *f* après coup; **I had an ~thought** cela m'est venu après coup; **I had ~thoughts about my decision** j'ai eu après coup des doutes sur ma décision; **added as an ~thought** ajouté après coup. ♦ **afterwards** *adv* après, plus tard, par la suite.

again [ə'gen] *adv* de nouveau, encore une fois, une fois de plus. **here we are ~!** nous revoilà!; **~ and ~, time and ~** maintes et maintes fois; **I've told you ~ and ~** je te l'ai dit et répété; **she is home ~** elle est rentrée chez elle; **what's his name ~?** comment s'appelle-t-il déjà?; **to begin ~** recommencer; **I won't do it ~** je ne le ferai plus; **never ~** plus jamais; **never ~!** c'est bien la dernière fois!; (*iro*) **not ~!** encore! (*iro*); **as much ~** deux fois autant; **then ~, and ~** d'autre part, d'un autre côté; **~ it is not certain that** et d'ailleurs il n'est pas sûr que.

against [ə'genst] *prep* **(a)** (*opposition etc*) contre. **to be ~ capital punishment** être contre la peine de mort; **I'm ~ helping him at all** je ne suis pas d'avis qu'on l'aide (*subj*); **I've got nothing ~ him** je n'ai rien contre lui; **to be dead ~ sth** s'opposer absolument à qch; (*Pol*) **to run ~ sb** se présenter contre qn; **now we're up ~ it!** nous voici au pied du mur!, c'est maintenant qu'on va s'amuser!*; **~ my will** malgré moi; **to work ~ the clock** travailler contre la montre; **(as) ~** contre, en comparaison de; **~ that, it might be said ...** en revanche *or* par contre on pourrait dire .... **(b)** (*support, impact*) contre. **to lean ~ a wall** s'appuyer contre un mur; **to hit one's head ~ the mantelpiece** se cogner la tête contre la cheminée; **the truck ran ~ a tree** le camion s'est jeté sur un arbre. **(c)** (*in contrast to*) sur. **~ the light** à contre-jour; **the trees stood out ~ the sunset** les arbres se détachaient sur le couchant; **it shows up ~ the white background** cela ressort sur le fond blanc. **(d) tickets are available ~ this voucher** on peut obtenir des billets contre remise de ce bon.

age [eɪdʒ] **1** *n* **(a)** âge *m*. **what's her ~?, what ~ is she?** quel âge a-t-elle?; **he is 10 years of ~** il a 10 ans; **you don't look your ~** vous ne faites pas votre âge; **of an ~** du même âge; **to come of ~** atteindre sa majorité; **to be of ~** être majeur; **to be under ~** être mineur. **(b) I haven't seen him for ~s** il y a une éternité que je ne l'ai vu; **she stayed for ~s** elle est restée un temps fou. **2** *vti* vieillir. **3** *adj*: **the 40-50 ~ group** la tranche d'âge de 40 à 50 ans, les 40 à 50 ans; **~ limit** limite *f* d'âge. ♦ **aged** [eɪdʒd] **1** *adj* **(a)** âgé de; **a boy ~d 10** un garçon (âgé) de 10 ans; **(b)** ['eɪdʒɪd] (*old*) âgé, vieux; **2** *npl*: **the ~d** les personnes âgées; **the ~d and infirm** les gens âgés et infirmes. ♦ **ageing 1** *adj person* vieillissant; *hairstyle, dress* qui fait paraître vieux; **2** *n* vieillissement *m*. ♦ **ageless** *adj* toujours jeune. ♦ **age-old** *adj* séculaire.

agency ['eɪdʒənsɪ] *n* **(a)** agence *f*. **tourist ~** agence de tourisme. **(b) through the ~ of friends** par l'intermédiaire *m* d'amis, grâce à des amis. ♦ **agent** *n* (*gen*) agent *m* (*of, for* de); (*dealer*) **the Citroën ~** le concessionnaire Citroën.

agenda [ə'dʒendə] *n* ordre *m* du jour. **on the ~** à l'ordre du jour.

agglomeration [əˌglɒmə'reɪʃən] *n* agglomération *f*.

aggravate ['ægrəveɪt] *vt* aggraver; (*annoy*) exaspérer, agacer. ♦ **aggravating** *adj* exaspérant, agaçant. ♦ **aggravation** *n* aggravation *f*; (*annoyance*) exaspération *f*, agacement *m*.

aggregate ['ægrɪgɪt] **1** *n* ensemble *m*, total *m*. **in the ~** dans l'ensemble. **2** *adj* global, total.

aggression [ə'greʃən] *n* agression *f*; (*aggressiveness*) agressivité *f*. ♦ **aggressive** *adj* agressif. ♦ **aggressively** *adv* d'une manière agressive, agressivement. ♦ **aggressiveness** *n* agressivité *f*. ♦ **aggressor** *n* agresseur *m*.

aggrieved [ə'griːvd] *adj* chagriné (*at, by* par).

aggro* ['ægrəʊ] *n* (*abbr of* **aggression**) (*emotion*) agressivité *f*; (*physical violence*) grabuge* *m*.

aghast [ə'gɑːst] *adj* atterré (*at* de).

agile ['ædʒaɪl] *adj* agile. ♦ **agility** *n* agilité *f*.

agitate ['ædʒɪteɪt] **1** *vt* agiter. **2** *vi* (*Pol etc*) mener une campagne (*for* en faveur de; *against* contre). ♦ **agitated** *adj* agité. ♦ **agitation** *n* agitation *f*; (*campaign*) campagne *f* (*for* pour; *against* contre). ♦ **agitator** *n* agitateur *m*, -trice *f*.

agnostic [æg'nɒstɪk] *adj,n* agnostique (*mf*). ♦ **agnosticism** *n* agnosticisme *m*.

ago [ə'gəʊ] *adv*: **a week ~** il y a huit jours; **how long ~?** il y a combien de temps?; **a little while ~** tout à l'heure; **as long ~ as 1950** déjà en 1950.

agog [ə'gɒg] *adj*: **to be (all) ~** être en émoi; **to be ~ to do** brûler de faire; **~ for news** impatient d'avoir des nouvelles.

agonize ['ægənaɪz] *vi* avoir des doutes déchirants (*over* sur). ♦ **agonized** *adj* déchirant. ♦ **agonizing** *adj situation* angoissant; *cry* déchirant; **agonizing reappraisal** révision déchirante.

agony ['ægənɪ] **1** *n* (*mental pain*) angoisse *f*; (*physical pain*) douleur *f* atroce. **death ~** agonie *f*; **to suffer agonies, to be in ~** souffrir le martyre; **to be in an ~ of impatience** se mourir d'impatience. **2** *adj*: **~ column** courrier *m* du cœur.

agrarian [ə'grɛərɪən] *adj* agraire.

agree [ə'griː] **1** *vt* **(a)** (*consent*) consentir (*to do* à faire), accepter (*to do* de faire); (*accept*) *statement, report* accepter (la véracité de); (*fix*) *price, date* se mettre d'accord sur. **(b)** (*admit*) reconnaître, admettre (*that* que). **(c)** (*come to agreement*) convenir (*to do* de faire), se mettre d'accord (*to do* pour faire). **everyone ~s that we should stay** tout le monde s'accorde à reconnaître que nous devrions rester; **it was ~d** c'était convenu; **to ~ to differ** rester sur ses positions.

2 *vi* **(a)** (*be in agreement*) être d'accord (*with* avec), être du même avis (*with* que). **they all ~d in finding the play dull** tous ont été d'accord pour trouver la pièce ennuyeuse; **she ~s with me that it is unfair** elle trouve comme moi que c'est injuste; **I quite ~** je suis tout à fait d'accord; **I can't ~ with you there** je ne suis absolument pas d'accord avec vous sur ce point. **(b)** (*come to terms*) se mettre d'accord (*with sb* avec qn; *about, on sth* sur qch); (*get on well*) s'entendre (bien). **(c)** (*consent*) consentir (*to sth* à qch; *to doing* à faire). **to ~ to a proposal** accepter une proposition; **I ~ to your going** je consens à ce que vous y alliez. **(d)** *[ideas, stories]* concorder (*with* avec). **(e)** (*Gram*) s'accorder (*with* avec). **(f)** (*suit the health of*) réussir à. **onions don't ~ with me** les oignons ne me réussissent pas.

♦ **agreeable** *adj* (*pleasant*) *person* agréable; (*willing*) **to be ~able to (doing) sth** consentir volontiers à (faire) qch. ♦ **agreeably** *adv* agréablement. ♦ **agreed** *adj* **(a) to be ~d** être d'accord (*about* au sujet de; *on* sur); **(b)** *time, place, amount* convenu; **it's all ~d** c'est tout décidé; **it's ~d that** il est convenu que + *indic;* **~d!** entendu!, d'accord! ♦ **agreement** *n* (*all senses*) accord *m*; **to be in ~ment on** être d'accord sur; **to come to an ~ment** parvenir à un accord; **by mutual ~ment** d'un commun accord; (*without quarrelling*) à l'amiable.

agriculture [ˈægrɪkʌltʃəʳ] *n* agriculture *f*. **Ministry of A~** ministère *m* de l'Agriculture. ♦ **agricultural** *adj* (*gen*) agricole; *engineer, expert* agronome; **agricultural college** école *f* d'agriculture. ♦ **agricultur(al)ist** *n* (*scientist*) agronome *mf*; (*farmer*) agriculteur *m*.

aground [əˈgraʊnd] *adj* échoué. **to run ~** s'échouer.

ahead [əˈhed] *adv* **(a)** (*in space*) en avant, devant. **to draw ~** gagner de l'avant; **I'll go on ~** moi, je vais en avant; (*lit, fig*) **to get ~** prendre de l'avance. **(b)** (*in time*) *book, plan* à l'avance. **~ of time** *decide, announce* d'avance; *arrive, be ready* avant l'heure, en avance; **2 hours ~ of the next car** en avance de 2 heures sur la voiture suivante; **he's 2 hours ~ of you** il a 2 heures d'avance sur vous; (*fig*) **~ of one's time** en avance sur son époque; **to plan ~** faire des projets à l'avance; **to think ~** penser à l'avenir.

ahoy [əˈhɔɪ] *excl* ohé! **ship ~!** ohé du navire!

aid [eɪd] **1** *n* **(a)** (*help*) aide *f*. **with the ~ of** *sb* avec l'aide de; *sth* à l'aide de; **in ~ of the blind** au profit des aveugles; (*fig*) **what is the meeting in ~ of?*** c'est dans quel but, cette réunion? **(b)** (*helper*) aide *mf*, assistant(e) *m(f)*; (*apparatus*) aide *f*, moyen *m*. **audio-visual ~s** support audio-visuel, moyens audio-visuels. **2** *vt person* aider (*to do* à faire); *progress, recovery* contribuer à. (*Jur*) **to ~ and abet sb** être complice de qn.

aide [eɪd] *n* aide *mf*.

ailing [ˈeɪlɪŋ] *adj* souffrant. ♦ **ailment** *n* ennui *m* de santé.

aim [eɪm] **1** *n* **(a) to miss one's ~** manquer son coup; **to take ~** viser (*at sb/sth* qn/qch); **his ~ is bad** il vise mal. **(b)** (*purpose*) but *m*. **with the ~ of doing** dans le but de faire; **her ~ is to do** elle a pour but de faire. **2** *vt gun* braquer (*at* sur); *stone* lancer (*at* sur); *blow* décocher (*at* à); *remark* diriger (*at* contre). **3** *vi* viser. **to ~ at sth** viser qch; **to ~ at doing** *or* **to do** viser à faire, (*less formally*) avoir l'intention de faire. ♦ **aimless** *adj* sans but. ♦ **aimlessly** *adv wander* sans but; *stand around* sans trop savoir que faire; *chat, kick ball about* pour passer le temps.

air [ɛəʳ] **1** *n* **(a)** air *m*. **to go out for a breath of (fresh) ~** sortir prendre l'air; **by ~** par avion; **to throw sth (up) into the ~** jeter qch en l'air; **the balloon rose up into the ~** le ballon s'est élevé (dans les airs); (*fig*) **there's sth in the ~** il se prépare qch; **it's still all in the ~** ce ne sont encore que des projets en l'air; **all her plans were up in the ~** (*vague*) tous ses projets étaient vagues; (*destroyed*) tous ses projets étaient tombés à l'eau; **to be up in the ~ about*** être (*angry*) en rogne* *or* (*excited*) très excité à l'idée de; **I can't live on ~** je ne peux pas vivre de l'air du temps; **to walk on ~** être aux anges. **(b)** (*Rad, TV*) **on the ~** à l'antenne; **you're on the ~** vous avez l'antenne; **he's on the ~ every day** il parle à la radio tous les jours; **the station is on the ~** la station émet; **the programme goes on the ~ every week** l'émission passe (sur l'antenne) toutes les semaines; **to go off the ~** quitter l'antenne. **(c)** (*manner*) air *m*. **with an ~ of bewilderment** d'un air perplexe; **she has an ~ about her** elle a de l'allure; **to put on ~s** se donner de grands airs; **~s and graces** minauderies *fpl*. **(d)** (*Mus*) air *m*.

2 *vt linen, room, bed* aérer; *anger* exhaler; *opinion* faire connaître; *idea* mettre sur le tapis.

3 *adj bubble* d'air; *hole* d'aération; *cushion, mattress* pneumatique; *pressure, current* atmosphérique; (*Mil*) *superiority, base* aérien. **~ bed** matelas *m* pneumatique; **~ brake** (*Aut*) frein *m* à air comprimé; (*Aviat*) aérofrein *m*; **~ force** armée *f* de l'air; **by ~ freight** par voie aérienne; **~ lane** couloir aérien; **~ letter** lettre *f* par avion; **~ pocket** trou *m* d'air; **~ pump** compresseur *m*; **~ show** (*Comm etc*) salon *m* de l'aéronautique; (*flying display*) meeting *m* d'aviation; **~ terminal** aérogare *f*; **~ traffic control** contrôle *m* de la navigation aérienne; **~ traffic controller** contrôleur *m*, -euse *f* de la navigation aérienne. ♦ **airborne** *adj*: **~borne troops** troupes aéroportées; **the plane was ~borne** l'avion avait décollé. ♦ **airbus** *n* airbus *m*. ♦ **air-conditioned** *adj* climatisé. ♦ **air-conditioner** *n* climatiseur *m*. ♦ **air-conditioning** *n* climatisation *f*. ♦ **air-cooled** *adj* à refroidissement par air. ♦ **aircraft** *n* (*pl inv*) avion *m*. ♦ **aircraft-carrier** *n* porte-avions *m inv*. ♦ **aircrew** *n* équipage *m* (*d'un avion*). ♦ **airdrome** *n* aérodrome *m*. ♦ **airdrop 1** *vt* parachuter; **2** *n* parachutage *m*. ♦ **airfield** *n* terrain *m* d'aviation. ♦ **airgun** *n* fusil *m* à air comprimé. ♦ **airily** *adv* d'un ton dégagé, avec désinvolture. ♦ **airing** *n [linen]* aération *f*; **to give an idea an ~ing** mettre une idée sur le tapis. ♦ **airing cupboard** *n* placard-séchoir *m*. ♦ **airless** *adj room* privé d'air. ♦ **air-hostess** *n* hôtesse *f* de l'air. ♦ **airlift 1** *n* pont aérien; **2** *vt* transporter par avion. ♦ **airline** *n* (*Aviat*) compagnie *f* d'aviation. ♦ **airliner** *n* avion *m* (de ligne). ♦ **airlock** *n [spacecraft, caisson etc]* sas *m*; (*in pipe*) bouchon *m* d'air. ♦ **airmail 1** *n*: **by ~mail** par avion; **2** *adj letter, edition* par avion; **3** *vt* expédier par avion. ♦ **airman** *n* aviateur *m*; (*in Air Force*) soldat *m* (de l'armée de l'air). ♦ **airplane** *n* avion *m*. ♦ **airport** *n* aéroport *m*. ♦ **air-raid** *n* attaque aérienne, raid aérien. ♦ **air-sea rescue** *n* sauvetage *m* en mer (*par hélicoptère etc*). ♦ **airship** *n* (ballon *m*) dirigeable *m*. ♦ **airsick** *adj*: **to be ~sick** avoir le mal de l'air. ♦ **airstrip** *n* piste *f* d'atterrissage. ♦ **airtight** *adj* hermétique, étanche (à l'air). ♦ **air-to-air** *adj* avion-avion *inv*. ♦ **air-to-ground** *or* ♦ **air-to-surface** *adj* air-sol *inv*. ♦ **airway** *n* (*route*) voie aérienne; (*company*) compagnie *f* d'aviation. ♦ **airwoman** *n* aviatrice *f*; (*in Air Force*) auxiliaire *f* (de l'armée de l'air). ♦ **airworthiness** *n* navigabilité *f*. ♦ **airworthy** *adj* en état de navigation. ♦ **airy** *adj room* clair; *manner* désinvolte, dégagé; *promise* en l'air. ♦ **airy-fairy*** *adj* farfelu.

aisle [aɪl] *n [church]* nef latérale; (*between pews*) allée centrale; *[theatre]* allée *f*; *[train, coach]* couloir *m* (central).

ajar [əˈdʒɑːʳ] *adj* entrouvert.

akimbo [əˈkɪmbəʊ] *adj*: **with arms ~** les poings sur les hanches.

akin [əˈkɪn] *adj*: **~ to** qui tient de, qui ressemble à.

alabaster [ˈæləbɑːstəʳ] *n* albâtre *m*.

alacrity [əˈlækrɪtɪ] *n* empressement *m*.

alarm [əˈlɑːm] **1** *n* (*gen*) alarme *f*; (*clock*) réveil *m*. **to raise the ~** donner l'alarme *or* l'alerte. **2** *vt person* alarmer; *animal, bird* effaroucher. **to become ~ed** prendre peur. **3** *adj bell, signal, call* d'alarme. **~ clock** réveil *m*, réveille-matin *m inv*. ♦ **alarming** *adj* alarmant. ♦ **alarmingly** *adv* d'une manière alarmante. ♦ **alarmist** *adj, n* alarmiste (*mf*).

alas [əˈlæs] *excl* hélas!

Albania [ælˈbeɪnɪə] *n* Albanie *f*.

albatross [ˈælbətrɒs] *n* albatros *m*.

albino [ælˈbiːnəʊ] *n* albinos *mf*. **~ rabbit** lapin *m* albinos.

album [ˈælbəm] *n* album *m*. **photo/stamp ~** album de photos/de timbres.

albumen, albumin [ˈælbjʊmɪn] *n* albumen *m*; (*Physiol*) albumine *f*.

alchemy ['ælkɪmɪ] *n* alchimie *f.* ♦ **alchemist** *n* alchimiste *m.*
alcohol ['ælkəhɒl] *n* alcool *m.* ♦ **alcoholic 1** *adj* (*gen*) alcoolique; *drink* alcoolisé; **2** *n* alcoolique *mf.* ♦ **alcoholism** *n* alcoolisme *m.*
alcove ['ælkəʊv] *n* alcôve *f.*
alder ['ɔːldəʳ] *n* aulne *m.*
alderman ['ɔːldəmən] *n* ≃ conseiller *m*, -ère *f* municipal(e).
ale [eɪl] *n* bière *f*, ale *f.*
alert [ə'lɜːt] **1** *n* alerte *f.* **to give the ~** donner l'alerte; **on the ~** *person* sur le qui-vive; *troops* en état d'alerte. **2** *adj* (*watchful*) vigilant; (*acute*) éveillé. **3** *vt* alerter (*to* sur). **we are now ~ed to ...** notre attention est maintenant éveillée sur ... . ♦ **alertness** *n* vigilance *f*; esprit éveillé.
alfalfa [æl'fælfə] *n* luzerne *f.*
alfresco [æl'freskəʊ] *adj, adv* en plein air.
algae ['ældʒiː] *npl* algues *fpl.*
algebra ['ældʒɪbrə] *n* algèbre *f.*
Algeria [æl'dʒɪərɪə] *n* Algérie *f.* ♦ **Algiers** *n* Alger.
alias ['eɪlɪæs] **1** *adv* alias. **2** *n* faux nom *m.*
alibi ['ælɪbaɪ] *n* alibi *m.*
alien ['eɪlɪən] **1** *n* (*foreign*) étranger *m*, -ère *f*; (*non human*) extra-terrestre *mf.* **2** *adj* étranger (*to* à); extra-terrestre. ♦ **alienate** *vt* aliéner; **this has ~ated his friends** ceci a aliéné ses amis; **she has ~ated her friends** elle s'est aliéné ses amis (*by doing* en faisant). ♦ **alienation** *n* aliénation *f.*
alight¹ [ə'laɪt] *vi [person]* descendre (*from* de); *[bird]* se poser (*on* sur).
alight² [ə'laɪt] *adj, adv fire* allumé; *building* en feu. **to set sth ~** mettre le feu à qch.
align [ə'laɪn] **1** *vt* aligner (*on, with* sur). **non-~ed** non-aligné. **2** *vi [persons]* s'aligner; *[object]* être aligné. ♦ **alignment** *n* alignement *m.*
alike [ə'laɪk] **1** *adj* semblable. **to be ~** se ressembler; **it's all ~ to me** cela m'est tout à fait égal. **2** *adv dress, treat* de la même façon. **winter and summer ~** été comme hiver; **they think ~** ils sont souvent du même avis.
alimentary [ˌælɪ'mentərɪ] *adj* alimentaire. **~ canal** tube *m* digestif.
alimony ['ælɪmənɪ] *n* (*Jur*) pension *f* alimentaire.
alive [ə'laɪv] *adj* (*living*) vivant, en vie. **to bury sb ~** enterrer qn vivant; **to burn ~** brûler vif; **it's good to be ~** il fait bon vivre; **no man ~** personne au monde; **as well as anyone ~** aussi bien que n'importe qui; **to keep ~** *person* maintenir en vie; *tradition* préserver; *memory* garder; **to stay ~** rester en vie, survivre; **~ to** *honour* sensible à; *danger* conscient de; **~ and kicking*** (*living*) bien en vie; (*energy*) plein de vie; **look ~!*** remuez-vous!*; **~ with insects** grouillant d'insectes.
alkali ['ælkəlaɪ] *n* base *f.* ♦ **alkaline** *adj* basique.
all [ɔːl] **1** *adj* tout. **~ the country** tout le pays, le pays tout entier; **~ my life** toute ma vie; **~ the others** tous (*or* toutes) les autres; **~ you boys** vous (tous) les garçons; **~ three** tous les trois; **~ three men** les trois hommes; **~ day** toute la journée; **~ that** tout cela; **why me of ~ people?** pourquoi moi?; **with ~ (possible) care** avec tout le soin possible.

2 *pron* **(a)** tout *m.* **~ is well** tout va bien; **that is ~** c'est tout; **if that's ~ then it's not important** s'il n'y a que cela, ce n'est pas important; **and I don't know what ~*** et je ne sais quoi encore; **~ of it was lost** (le) tout a été perdu; **he drank ~ of it** il a tout bu, il l'a bu en entier; **~ of Paris** Paris tout entier; **that is ~ he said** c'est tout ce qu'il a dit; **~ that is in the box** tout ce qui est dans la boîte; **bring it ~** apportez le tout. **(b)** (*pl*) tous *mpl*, toutes *fpl.* **we ~ sat down** nous nous sommes tous assis (*or* toutes assises); **~ of the boys came** tous les garçons sont venus, les garçons sont tous venus; **one and ~** tous sans exception; **~ who knew him** tous ceux qui l'ont connu; **the score was two ~** le score était (*Tennis*) deux partout *or* (*other sports*) deux à deux. **(c)** (*in phrases*) **if she comes at ~** si tant est qu'elle vienne; **very rarely if at ~** très rarement (si tant est); **I don't know at ~** je n'en sais rien; **if there is any water at ~** si seulement il y a de l'eau; **if at ~ possible** dans la mesure du possible; **not at ~** pas du tout; (*after thanks*) il n'y a pas de quoi; **it was ~ I could do not to laugh** c'est à peine *or* tout juste si j'ai pu m'empêcher de rire; **it's not as bad as ~ that** ce n'est pas si mal que ça; **that's ~ very well but ...** tout cela est bien beau mais ...; **taking it ~ in ~** à tout prendre; **she is ~ in ~ to him** elle est tout pour lui; **~ but** presque; **he ~ but lost it** il a bien failli le perdre; **for ~ I know** autant que je sache; **for ~ his wealth he was unhappy** malgré sa fortune il était malheureux; **for ~ he may say** quoi qu'il en dise; **once and for ~** une fois pour toutes; **most of ~** surtout.

3 *adv* **(a)** tout, tout à fait. **~ of a sudden** tout à coup, soudain; **~ too soon it was time to go** malheureusement il a bientôt fallu partir; **dressed ~ in white** habillé tout en blanc; **~ along the road** tout le long de la route; **I feared that ~ along** je l'ai craint depuis le début; **he won the race ~ the same** il a néanmoins *or* tout de même gagné la course; **it's ~ the same** *or* **~ one to me** cela m'est tout à fait égal; **~ over** (*everywhere*) partout, d'un bout à l'autre; (*finished*) fini; **to be ~ for sth*** être tout à fait en faveur de qch; **to be ~ there*** avoir toute sa tête; **she's not quite ~ there*** il lui manque une case*; **it is ~ up with him*** il est fichu*; **~ the better!** tant mieux!; **~ the more so since ...** d'autant plus que ... . **(b) ~ right** (très) bien; (*in approval, exasperation*) ça va!*; (*in agreement*) entendu!, c'est ça!; **it's ~ right** ça va*, tout va bien; **he's ~ right** (*doubtful*) il n'est pas mal*; (*approving*) c'est un type bien*; (*reassuring*) il est très bien; (*healthy*) il va bien; (*safe*) il est sain et sauf; **I'm ~ right Jack*** moi en tout cas je suis peinard*; (*comfortably off*) **we're ~ right for the rest of our lives** nous sommes tranquilles pour le restant de nos jours.

4 *n* : **my ~** tout ce que j'ai.

♦ **all-American** *adj* cent pour cent américain. ♦ **all-day** *adj* qui dure toute la journée. ♦ **all-embracing** *adj* compréhensif. ♦ **all-important** *adj* de la plus haute importance, capital. ♦ **all-in** *adj* (*exhausted*) éreinté; (*inclusive*) *price* net; *cost* tout compris; *insurance policy* tous risques *inv*; *tariff* inclusif. ♦ **all-night** *adj*: **~-night service** permanence *f* de nuit. ♦ **all-out 1** *adj effort* maximum; **2** *adv*: **to go ~-out** aller à la limite de ses forces. ♦ **allover** *adj* (qui est) sur toute la surface. ♦ **all-powerful** *adj* tout-puissant. ♦ **all-purpose** *adj* qui répond à tous les besoins; *knife, spanner* universel. ♦ **all-round** *adj sportsman* complet; *improvement* général, sur toute la ligne. ♦ **all-rounder** *n*: **to be a good ~-rounder** être bon en tout. ♦ **allspice** *n* poivre *m* de la Jamaïque. ♦ **all-star** *adj*: (*Theat*) **~-star show** plateau *m* de vedettes. ♦ **all-time** *adj record* sans précédent; **an ~-time low** un record de médiocrité. ♦ **all-weather** *adj* de toute saison, tous temps *inv.* ♦ **all-the-year-round** *adj sport* que l'on pratique toute l'année; *resort* ouvert toute l'année.
Allah ['ælə] *n* Allah *m.*
allay [ə'leɪ] *vt* (*gen*) apaiser. **to ~ suspicion** dissiper les soupçons.
allege [ə'ledʒ] *vt* alléguer, prétendre (*that* que). **to ~ illness** prétexter *or* alléguer une maladie; **he is ~d to have said** il aurait dit. ♦ **allegation** *n* allégation *f.* ♦ **alleged** *adj reason* allégué; *thief, author* présumé. ♦ **allegedly** *adv* à ce que l'on prétend.
allegiance [ə'liːdʒəns] *n* allégeance *f* (*to* à).
allegory ['ælɪgərɪ] *n* allégorie *f.* ♦ **allegoric(al)** *adj* allégorique.
allergy ['ælədʒɪ] *n* allergie *f* (*to* à). ♦ **allergic** *adj* allergique (*to* à).

alleviate [ə'liːvɪeɪt] *vt pain* soulager; *sorrow* adoucir; *thirst* apaiser.

alley ['ælɪ] 1 *n* (*between buildings: also* **~way**) ruelle *f*; (*in garden*) allée *f*. **this is right up my ~*** (*my speciality*) c'est tout à fait mon rayon; (*just what I wanted*) c'est tout à fait ce que j'espérais. 2 *adj*: **~ cat** chat *m* de gouttière.

alliance [ə'laɪəns] *n* alliance *f*.

allied ['ælaɪd] *adj* (*gen, Pol*) allié (*to* à, *with* avec); (*Bio*) de la même famille *or* espèce. **history and ~ subjects** l'histoire et sujets apparentés.

alligator ['ælɪgeɪtə^r] *n* alligator *m*.

alliteration [əˌlɪtə'reɪʃən] *n* allitération *f*.

allocate ['æləʊkeɪt] *vt money, task* allouer, attribuer (*to sb* à qn); *money* affecter (*to sth* à qch). ◆ **allocation** *n* allocation *f*.

allot [ə'lɒt] *vt* attribuer, assigner (*sth to sb* qch à qn). **in the time ~ted** dans le temps qui est assigné. ◆ **allotment** *n* parcelle *f* de terre (*louée pour la culture*).

allow [ə'laʊ] *vt* **(a)** (*permit*) permettre (*sb sth* qch à qn; *sb to do* à qn de faire), autoriser (*sb to do* qn à faire); (*tolerate*) tolérer (*sb to do* que qn fasse). **she was not ~ed to do it** elle n'était pas autorisée à le faire; **to ~ sb in** *etc* permettre à qn d'entrer *etc*; **to ~ sth to happen** laisser se produire qch; **smoking/dogs not ~ed** interdit de fumer/aux chiens. **(b)** (*grant*) *money* accorder, allouer; (*Jur*) accorder. **to ~ sb a discount** consentir une remise à qn; **~ an hour to cross the city** comptez une heure pour traverser la ville; **~ 5 cm for shrinkage** prévoyez 5 cm de plus pour le cas où le tissu rétrécirait. **(c)** (*concede*) admettre, reconnaître (*that* que); *claim* admettre. **~ing that ...** en admettant que ... + *subj*.

allow for *vt fus* tenir compte de. **~ing for the circumstances** compte tenu des circonstances; **to ~ for all possibilities** parer à toute éventualité.

allow of *vt fus* admettre, souffrir.

allowable [ə'laʊəbl] *adj* permis, admissible; (*Tax*) *expenses* déductible.

allowance [ə'laʊəns] *n* **(a)** (*money given to sb*) pension *f*, rente *f*; (*for lodgings, food etc*) indemnité *f*, (*Admin*) allocation *f*; (*from separated husband*) pension *f* alimentaire; (*salary*) appointements *mpl*; (*food*) ration *f*. **rent ~** allocation de logement; **she has a dress ~** (*from father*) elle reçoit une certaine somme pour ses vêtements; (*from employers*) elle touche une allocation vestimentaire. **(b)** (*Comm, Fin: discount*) réduction *f*, rabais *m*. **tax ~s** sommes *fpl* déductibles. **(c) you must learn to make ~s** tu dois apprendre à faire la part des choses; **to make ~(s) for** (*excuse*) *person, fault* se montrer indulgent envers; (*allow for*) *shrinkage etc* tenir compte de.

alloy ['ælɔɪ] *n* alliage *m*.

allude [ə'luːd] *vi* faire allusion (*to* à).

allure [ə'ljʊə^r] 1 *vt* attirer. 2 *n* charme *m*, attrait *m*. ◆ **alluring** *adj* attrayant, séduisant.

allusion [ə'luːʒən] *n* allusion *f*.

alluvial [ə'luːvɪəl] *adj ground* alluvial; *deposit* alluvionnaire.

ally [ə'laɪ] 1 *vt*: **to ~ o.s. with** s'allier avec. 2 ['ælaɪ] *n* allié(e) *m(f)*.

almanac ['ɔːlmənæk] *n* almanach *m*.

almighty [ɔːl'maɪtɪ] 1 *adj* tout-puissant. **A~ God** Dieu Tout-Puissant; **he is an ~ fool*** c'est un sacré* imbécile; **an ~ din*** un vacarme du diable. 2 *n*: **the A~** le Tout-Puissant.

almond ['ɑːmənd] *n* amande *f*; (**~ tree**) amandier *m*. ◆ **almond-shaped** *adj* en amande.

almost ['ɔːlməʊst] *adv* presque. **it is ~ midnight** il est presque *or* bientôt minuit; **he ~ fell** il a failli tomber.

alms [ɑːmz] *n* aumône *f*. **to give ~** faire l'aumône; **~ box** tronc *m* pour les pauvres.

aloft [ə'lɒft] *adv* (**up ~**) en l'air; (*Naut*) dans la mâture.

alone [ə'ləʊn] *adj, adv* seul. **all ~** tout(e) seul(e); **leave them ~ together** laissez-les seuls ensemble; **he ~ could tell you** lui seul pourrait vous le dire; **we are not ~ in thinking** nous ne sommes pas les seuls à penser; **he lives on bread ~** il ne vit que de pain; **to let** *or* **leave ~** *person* laisser tranquille; *book etc* ne pas toucher à; *business, scheme* ne pas se mêler de; **he can't read, let ~ write** il ne sait pas lire, encore moins écrire.

along [ə'lɒŋ] 1 *adv*: **come ~!** venez donc!; (*remonstrating*) allons, allons!; **she'll be ~ tomorrow** elle viendra demain; **come ~ with me** venez avec moi; **bring your friend ~** amène ton camarade (avec toi); **~ here** dans cette direction-ci, par ici; **get ~ with you!*** (*go away*) fiche le camp!*; (*you can't mean it*) allons donc!; **all ~** (*space*) d'un bout à l'autre; (*time*) depuis le début. 2 *prep* le long de. **to walk ~ the beach** se promener le long de la plage; **the trees ~ the road** les arbres qui sont au bord de la route; **somewhere ~ the way** quelque part en chemin; (*fig: at some time*) à un moment donné; **~ the lines suggested** conformément à la ligne d'action proposée. ◆ **alongside** 1 *prep* (*along*) le long de; (*beside*) à côté de; **to come ~side the quay** accoster le quai; **the railway runs ~side the beach** la ligne de chemin de fer longe la plage; 2 *adv* (*Naut*) bord à bord. **to come ~side** accoster.

aloof [ə'luːf] *adj* distant (*towards* à l'égard de). ◆ **aloofness** *n* réserve *f*, attitude *f* distante.

aloud [ə'laʊd] *adv read* à haute voix; *think, wonder* tout haut.

alphabet ['ælfəbet] *n* alphabet *m*. ◆ **alphabetic(al)** *adj* alphabétique. ◆ **alphabetically** *adv* par ordre alphabétique. ◆ **alphabetize** *vt* classer par ordre alphabétique.

Alps [ælps] *npl* Alpes *fpl*. ◆ **alpine** *adj* des Alpes, alpestre; **alpine hut** (chalet-)refuge *m*. ◆ **alpinism** *n* alpinisme *m*. ◆ **alpinist** *n* alpiniste *mf*.

already [ɔːl'redɪ] *adv* déjà.

alright ['ɔːlˌraɪt] = **all right; V all 3b.**

Alsatian [æl'seɪʃən] *n* (*dog*) berger *m* allemand.

also ['ɔːlsəʊ] *adv* **(a)** (*too*) aussi, également. **her cousin ~ came** son cousin aussi est venu *or* est venu également. **(b)** (*moreover*) de plus, en outre, également. **~ I must explain** de plus *or* en outre, je dois expliquer, je dois également expliquer. ◆ **also-ran** *n* (*Horse-racing*) cheval non classé; (*: *person*) perdant(e) *m(f)*.

altar ['ɒltə^r] *n* autel *m*.

alter ['ɒltə^r] 1 *vt* **(a)** (*gen*) changer, modifier; *plans* modifier; *painting, poem, speech etc* remanier; *garment* retoucher, (*stronger*) transformer. **to ~ one's attitude** changer d'attitude (*to* envers); **that ~s the case** voilà qui change tout; **to ~ sth for the better/worse** changer qch en mieux/en mal. **(b)** (*falsify*) *date, evidence* falsifier; *text* altérer. 2 *vi* changer. ◆ **alteration** *n* **(a)** (*act of altering*) changement *m*, modification *f*, remaniement *m*, retouchage *m*, transformation *f*; **timetable subject to ~ation** horaire sujet à des modifications; **(b)** (*to plan, rules etc*) modification *f*, changement *m* (*to, in* apporté à); (*to painting etc*) retouche *f*, (*major*) remaniement *m*; (*to garment*) retouche, (*major*) transformation *f*; (*Archit*) transformation (*to* apportée à); **they're having ~ations made to their house** ils font des travaux dans leur maison.

altercation [ˌɒltə'keɪʃən] *n* altercation *f*.

alter ego ['æltər'iːgəʊ] *n* alter ego *m*.

alternate [ɒl'tɜːnɪt] 1 *adj* (*by turns*) alterné; (*every second*) tous les deux. **on ~ days** tous les deux jours, un jour sur deux; **they work on ~ days** ils travaillent un jour sur deux à tour de rôle. 2 ['ɒltɜːneɪt] *vt* faire alterner; *crops* alterner. 3 *vi* alterner (*with* avec). ◆ **alternately** *adv* alternativement, tour à tour; **~ly with** en alternance avec. ♦ **alternating** *adj* alternant; (*Elec*) alternatif.

alternative [ɒl'tɜːnətɪv] **1** *adj possibility, answer* autre; (*Philos*) *proposition* alternatif; (*Mil*) *position* de repli; (*Tech*) de rechange. ~ **proposal** contre-proposition *f*; **the only** ~ **method** la seule autre méthode; ~ **theatre** anti-théâtre *m*; (*Aut*) ~ **route** itinéraire *m* de délestage. **2** *n* (*choice*) (*between two*) alternative *f*, choix *m*; (*among several*) choix; (*solution*) (*only one*) alternative, seule autre solution; (*one of several*) autre solution. **she had no** ~ **but to accept** elle n'avait pas d'autre solution que d'accepter; **there is no** ~ il n'y a pas le choix. ♦ **alternatively** *adv* comme alternative.

although [ɔːl'ðəʊ] *conj* bien que + *subj*, quoique + *subj*. ~ **it's raining** bien qu'il pleuve, malgré la pluie; **even** ~ **he might agree to go** quand bien même il accepterait d'y aller.

altimeter ['æltɪmiːtəʳ] *n* altimètre *m*.

altitude ['æltɪtjuːd] *n* altitude *f*. **at these** ~**s** à cette altitude.

alto ['æltəʊ] *n* (*female*) contralto *m*; (*male*) haute-contre *f*; (*instrument*) alto *m*. ~ **saxophone** saxophone *m* alto.

altogether [ˌɔːltə'geðəʳ] **1** *adv* **(a)** (*wholly*) entièrement, tout à fait, complètement. **it is** ~ **out of the question** il n'en est absolument pas question. **(b)** (*on the whole*) somme toute, tout compte fait. ~ **it wasn't very pleasant** somme toute ce n'était pas très agréable. **(c)** (*with everything included*) en tout. **what do I owe you** ~? je vous dois combien en tout?; **taken** ~ à tout prendre. **2** *n* (*hum*) **in the** ~**‡** tout nu, à poil‡.

altruism ['æltrʊɪzəm] *n* altruisme *m*. ♦ **altruist** *n* altruiste *mf*. ♦ **altruistic** *adj* altruiste.

aluminium [ˌæljʊ'mɪnɪəm], (*US*) **aluminum** [ə'luːmɪnəm] *n* aluminium *m*.

alveolar [æl'vɪələʳ] *adj* alvéolaire.

always ['ɔːlweɪz] *adv* toujours. **as** ~ comme toujours; **for** ~ pour toujours; **office** ~ **open** bureau ouvert en permanence.

amalgam [ə'mælgəm] *n* amalgame *m*. ♦ **amalgamate 1** *vt metals* amalgamer; *companies* fusionner. **2** *vi* s'amalgamer; fusionner. ♦ **amalgamation** *n* amalgamation *f*; fusion *f*.

amanuensis [əˌmænjʊ'ensɪs] *n, pl* **-enses** secrétaire *mf*.

amass [ə'mæs] *vt* amasser.

amateur ['æmətəʳ] **1** *n* amateur *m*. **2** *adj painter, player, sport* amateur *inv*; *photography etc* d'amateur; (*pej*) *work* d'amateur. ~ **dramatics** théâtre *m* amateur; ~ **status** statut *m* d'amateur. ♦ **amateurish** *adj* (*pej*) d'amateur.

amaze [ə'meɪz] *vt* stupéfier, ébahir. **to be** ~**d at (seeing) sth** être stupéfait *or* stupéfié de (voir) qch. ♦ **amazement** *n* stupéfaction *f*, ébahissement *m*. ♦ **amazing** *adj* stupéfiant, ahurissant; *bargain, offer* sensationnel. ♦ **amazingly** *adv* étonnamment; **amazingly enough, he ...** chose étonnante *or* par miracle, il ... .

Amazon ['æməzən] *n* (*river*) Amazone *m*; (*woman*) Amazone *f*.

ambassador [æm'bæsədəʳ] *n* (*lit, fig*) ambassadeur *m*. **French** ~ ambassadeur de France; ~**-at-large** ambassadeur extraordinaire. ♦ **ambassadorial** *adj* d'ambassadeur. ♦ **ambassadress** *n* ambassadrice *f*.

amber ['æmbəʳ] **1** *n* ambre *m*. **2** *adj* (*colour*) couleur d'ambre *inv*. (*Aut*) ~ **light** feu *m* orange. ♦ **ambergris** *n* ambre *m* gris.

ambidextrous [ˌæmbɪ'dekstrəs] *adj* ambidextre.

ambiguous [æm'bɪgjʊəs] *adj phrase* ambigu (*f* -uë); *past* équivoque. ♦ **ambiguity** *n* ambiguïté *f*. ♦ **ambiguously** *adv* de façon ambiguë.

ambition [æm'bɪʃən] *n* ambition *f*. **it is my** ~ **to do** mon ambition est de faire. ♦ **ambitious** *adj* ambitieux; **to be ambitious to do** ambitionner de faire. ♦ **ambitiously** *adv* ambitieusement.

ambivalent [æm'bɪvələnt] *adj* ambivalent. ♦ **ambivalence** *n* ambivalence *f*.

amble ['æmbl] *vi [horse]* aller l'amble; *[person]* aller d'un pas tranquille *or* sans se presser.

ambulance ['æmbjʊləns] **1** *n* ambulance *f*. **2** *adj*: ~ **driver** ambulancier *m*, -ière *f*.

ambush ['æmbʊʃ] **1** *n* embuscade *f*, guet-apens *m*. **to lie in** ~ se tenir en embuscade; **to lie in** ~ **for sb** tendre une embuscade à qn. **2** *vt* tendre une embuscade à.

ameliorate [ə'miːlɪəreɪt] **1** *vt* améliorer. **2** *vi* s'améliorer. ♦ **amelioration** *n* amélioration *f*.

amen ['ɑː'men] *excl* amen.

amenable [ə'miːnəbl] *adj* maniable, conciliant. ~ **to argument** prêt à se laisser convaincre; ~ **to kindness** sensible à la douceur; ~ **to reason** raisonnable; ~ **to treatment** guérissable.

amend [ə'mend] *vt law, document* amender; *text, wording* modifier; *habits* réformer. ♦ **amendment** *n* amendement *m*. ♦ **amends** *npl*: **to make** ~**s** (*apologize*) faire amende honorable; (*by doing sth*) se racheter; **to make** ~**s to sb for sth** (*apologize*) s'excuser auprès de qn de qch; (*compensate*) dédommager qn de qch.

amenity [ə'miːnɪtɪ] **1** *n* (*gen*) agrément *m*. **amenities** *[town etc]* aménagements *mpl* (socio-culturels); (*courtesies*) politesses *fpl*. **2** *adj*: (*Brit Med*) ~ **bed** lit 'privé' (dans un hôpital).

America [ə'merɪkə] *n* Amérique *f*. ♦ **American 1** *adj* américain; ~**n English** anglais américain; ~**n Indian** Indien(ne) *m(f)* d'Amérique; **2** *n* Américain(e) *m(f)*; (*Ling*) américain *m*. ♦ **americanism** *n* américanisme *m*. ♦ **americanize** *vt* américaniser.

amethyst ['æmɪθɪst] **1** *n* améthyste *f*. **2** *adj* (*colour*) violet d'améthyste *inv*.

amiable ['eɪmɪəbl] *adj* aimable. ♦ **amiability** *n* amabilité *f* (*to, towards* envers). ♦ **amiably** *adv* aimablement.

amicable ['æmɪkəbl] *adj* amical; (*Jur*) *settlement* à l'amiable. ♦ **amicably** *adv* amicalement; (*Jur*) à l'amiable.

amid(st) [ə'mɪd(st)] *prep* parmi, au milieu de. ♦ **amidships** *adv* au milieu du navire.

amiss [ə'mɪs] **1** *adv*: **to take sth** ~ prendre qch de travers, s'offenser de qch; **nothing comes** ~ **to him** il tire parti de tout; **a little courtesy wouldn't come** ~ un peu de politesse ne ferait pas de mal. **2** *adj*: **there's sth** ~ il y a qch qui ne va pas; **to say sth** ~ dire qch mal à propos.

ammonia [ə'məʊnɪə] *n* (*gas*) ammoniac *m*; (*liquid*) ammoniaque *f*.

ammunition [ˌæmjʊ'nɪʃən] **1** *n* munitions *fpl*. **2** *adj*: ~ **belt** ceinturon *m*; ~ **dump** dépôt *m* de munitions.

amnesia [æm'niːzɪə] *n* amnésie *f*.

amnesty ['æmnɪstɪ] **1** *n* amnistie *f*. **under an** ~ en vertu d'une amnistie. **2** *vt* amnistier.

amoeba [ə'miːbə] *n* amibe *f*. ♦ **amoebic** *adj* amibien.

amok [ə'mɒk] *adv* = **amuck**.

among(st) [ə'mʌŋ(st)] *prep* entre, parmi. **this is** ~ **the things we must do** ceci fait partie des choses que nous avons à faire; ~ **yourselves** entre vous; ~ **other things** entre autres (choses); **to count sb** ~ **one's friends** compter qn parmi *or* au nombre de ses amis; ~ **friends** entre amis.

amoral [eɪ'mɒrəl] *adj* amoral.

amorous ['æmərəs] *adj* amoureux. ♦ **amorously** *adv* amoureusement.

amorphous [ə'mɔːfəs] *adj* amorphe.

amount [ə'maʊnt] *n* **(a)** (*total*) montant *m*; (*sum of money*) somme *f*. **the** ~ **of a bill** le montant d'une facture; **there is a small** ~ **still to pay** il reste une petite somme à payer. **(b)** (*quantity*) quantité *f*. **an enormous** ~ **of, any** ~ **of** énormément de; **any** ~ **of time** tout le temps qu'il faut.

amount to *vt fus [sums, debts]* s'élever à; (*fig*) revenir à, représenter. **it ~s to the same thing** cela revient au même; **it ~s to stealing/a change in policy** cela revient à du vol/un changement de politique; **this ~s to very little** cela ne représente pas grand-chose; **he will never ~ to much** il ne fera jamais grand-chose.

amp(ère) ['æmp(ɛəʳ)] *n* ampère *m*. **a 13-amp plug** une fiche de 13 ampères.

ampersand ['æmpəsænd] *n* esperluète *f*.

amphetamine [æm'fetəmiːn] *n* amphétamine *f*.

amphibian [æm'fɪbɪən] **1** *adj* amphibie. **2** *n* (*Zool*) amphibie *m*; (*car/tank etc*) voiture *f*/char *m* amphibie. ♦ **amphibious** *adj* amphibie.

amphitheatre, (*US*) **-ter** ['æmfɪˌθɪətəʳ] *n* (*gen*) amphithéâtre *m*; (*in mountains*) cirque *m*.

ample ['æmpl] *adj* **(a)** (*enough*) *money etc* bien *or* largement assez de; *reason, motive* solide; *means, resources* gros. **there is ~ room for** il y a largement la place pour; (*fig*) **there is ~ room for improvement** il y a encore bien des progrès à faire; **to have ~ time** avoir largement le temps (*to do* de *or* pour faire). **(b)** (*large*) *garment* ample. ♦ **amply** *adv* amplement.

amplify ['æmplɪfaɪ] *vt sound, story* amplifier; *statement, idea* développer. ♦ **amplifier** *n* amplificateur *m*.

amputate ['æmpjʊteɪt] *vt* amputer. **to ~ sb's leg** amputer qn de la jambe. ♦ **amputation** *n* amputation *f*.

amuck [ə'mʌk] *adv*: **to run ~** être pris d'un accès de folie meurtrière; *[crowd]* se déchaîner.

amuse [ə'mjuːz] *vt* **(a)** (*cause mirth to*) amuser, divertir, faire rire. **it ~d us** cela nous a fait rire; **to be ~d at** *or* **by** s'amuser de; **he was not ~d** il n'a pas trouvé ça drôle. **(b)** (*entertain*) amuser, distraire. **to ~ o.s. with sth/by doing** s'amuser avec qch/à faire; **you'll have to ~ yourselves** il va vous falloir trouver de quoi vous distraire *or* vous occuper. ♦ **amusement 1** *n* **(a)** amusement *m*; **to my ~ment** à mon grand amusement; **look of ~ment** regard amusé; **to hide one's ~ment** dissimuler son envie de rire; **(b)** (*diversion*) distraction *f*, amusement *m*; **a town with plenty of ~ments** une ville qui offre beaucoup de distractions; **2** *adj*: **~ment arcade** ≃ luna-park *m*; **~ment park** parc *m* d'attractions. ♦ **amusing** *adj* amusant, drôle. ♦ **amusingly** *adv* d'une manière amusante.

an [æn, ən, n] *indef art V* **a**[2].

anachronism [ə'nækrənɪzəm] *n* anachronisme *m*. ♦ **anachronistic** *adj* anachronique.

anaemia [ə'niːmɪə] *n* anémie *f*. ♦ **anaemic** *adj* anémique.

anaesthesia [ˌænɪs'θiːzɪə] *n* anesthésie *f*. ♦ **anaesthetic** [ˌænɪs'θetɪk] **1** *n* anesthésique *m*; **under the anaesthetic** sous anesthésie; **2** *adj* anesthésique. ♦ **anaesthetist** [æ'niːsθɪtɪst] *n* anesthésiste *mf*. ♦ **anaesthetize** [æ'niːsθɪtaɪz] *vt* anesthésier.

anagram ['ænəgræm] *n* anagramme *f*.

analgesia [ˌænæl'dʒiːzɪə] *n* analgésie *f*. ♦ **analgesic** *adj, n* analgésique (*m*).

analog, analogue ['ænəlɒg] *n* analogue *m*. **~ computer** calculateur *m* analogique. ♦ **analogic(al)** *adj* analogique. ♦ **analogous** *adj* analogue (*to, with* à). ♦ **analogy** *n* analogie *f*.

analyse, (*US*) **analyze** ['ænəlaɪz] *vt* analyser, faire l'analyse de; (*Psych*) psychanalyser. ♦ **analysis** *n, pl* **analyses** analyse *f*; (*Psych*) psychanalyse *f*; **in the last** *or* **final analysis** en dernière analyse. ♦ **analyst** *n* (*Psych*) (psych)analyste *mf*. ♦ **analytic(al)** *adj* analytique.

anarchy ['ænəkɪ] *n* anarchie *f*. ♦ **anarchic(al)** *adj* anarchique. ♦ **anarchism** *n* anarchisme *m*. ♦ **anarchist** *n* anarchiste *mf*.

anathema [ə'næθɪmə] *n* anathème *m*. **it was ~ to him** il l'avait en abomination.

anatomy [ə'nætəmɪ] *n* (*Sci*) anatomie *f*; *[country etc]* structure *f*. **he had spots all over his ~** il avait des boutons partout. ♦ **anatomical** *adj* anatomique. ♦ **anatomist** *n* anatomiste *mf*.

ancestor ['ænsɪstəʳ] *n* ancêtre *m*. ♦ **ancestral** *adj* ancestral; **ancestral home** château ancestral. ♦ **ancestry** *n* ascendance *f*; (*ancestors collectively*) ancêtres *mpl*.

anchor ['æŋkəʳ] **1** *n* ancre *f*. **to be at ~** être à l'ancre. **2** *vt* (*Naut*) mettre à l'ancre; (*fig*) ancrer. **3** *vi* (*Naut*) jeter l'ancre. **4** *adj*: **~ man** (*Rad, TV*) présentateur-réalisateur *m*; (*in team, organization*) pilier *m*. ♦ **anchorage** *n* ancrage *m*.

anchovy ['æntʃəvɪ] *n* anchois *m*.

ancient ['eɪnʃənt] **1** *adj* **(a)** *world, painting* antique; *document, custom, history* ancien; *monument* historique; *rock etc* très vieux. **in ~ days** dans les temps anciens; **~ Rome** la Rome antique. **(b)** *person* très vieux; *clothes, object* antique, très vieux. **this is positively ~** cela remonte à Mathusalem. **2** *n*: **the ~s** les anciens *mpl*.

ancillary [æn'sɪlərɪ] *adj* (*gen*) auxiliaire. **~ to** subordonné à; **~ workers** personnel *m* des services auxiliaires.

and [ænd, ənd, nd, ən] *conj* et. **his table ~ chair** sa table et sa chaise; **~?** et alors?; **on Saturday ~/or Sunday** (*Admin*) samedi et/ou dimanche; (*gen*) samedi ou dimanche ou les deux; **three hundred ~ ten** trois cent dix; **two thousand ~ eight** deux mille huit; **two pounds ~ six pence** deux livres (et) six pence; **an hour ~ twenty minutes** une heure vingt (minutes); **five ~ three quarters** cinq trois quarts; **try ~ come** tâchez de venir; **for hours ~ hours** pendant des heures et des heures; **I rang ~ rang** j'ai sonné et resonné; **he talked ~ talked** il a parlé pendant des heures; **~ so on, ~ so forth** et ainsi de suite; **uglier ~ uglier** de plus en plus laid; **eggs ~ bacon** œufs au bacon; **summer ~ winter (alike)** été comme hiver.

Andes ['ændiːz] *n* Andes *fpl*.

anecdote ['ænɪkdəʊt] *n* anecdote *f*.

anemia *etc* = **anaemia** *etc*.

anemone [ə'nemənɪ] *n* anémone *f*.

anesthesia *etc* = **anaesthesia** *etc*.

aneurism ['ænjʊrɪzəm] *n* anévrisme *m*.

anew [ə'njuː] *adv* de nouveau. **to begin ~** recommencer.

angel ['eɪndʒəl] *n* ange *m*. **be an ~ and fetch me my gloves** apporte-moi mes gants, tu seras un ange. ♦ **angelic** *adj* angélique.

angelica [æn'dʒelɪkə] *n* angélique *f*.

angelus ['ændʒɪləs] *n* (*prayer, bell*) angélus *m*.

anger ['æŋgəʳ] **1** *n* colère *f*. **in ~** sous le coup de la colère. **2** *vt* mettre en colère

angina [æn'dʒaɪnə] *n* angine *f*; *[heart]* angine de poitrine.

angle[1] ['æŋgl] **1** *n* (*also Math*) angle *m*. **at an ~ of** formant un angle de; **at an ~** en biais (*to* par rapport à); **cut at an ~** coupé en biseau; **to study a topic from every ~** étudier un sujet sous tous les angles; **from the parents' ~** du point de vue des parents; **let's have your ~ on it*** dites-nous votre point de vue là-dessus. **2** *vt lamp* diriger la lumière de (*towards* sur); (*) *information, report* présenter sous un certain angle. ♦ **Angle-poise ® lamp** *n* lampe *f* d'architecte.

angle[2] ['æŋgl] *vi* (*lit*) pêcher à la ligne. **to ~ for** *trout* pêcher; *compliments* chercher; **to ~ for an invitation** chercher à se faire inviter. ♦ **angler** *n* pêcheur *m*, -euse *f* (à la ligne). ♦ **angling** *n* pêche *f* (à la ligne).

Anglican ['æŋglɪkən] *adj, n* anglican(e) *m(f)*. ♦ **Anglicanism** *n* anglicanisme *m*.

anglicism ['æŋglɪsɪzəm] *n* anglicisme *m*. ♦ **anglicist** *n* angliciste *mf*. ♦ **anglicize** *vt* angliciser.

Anglo- ['æŋgləʊ] *pref* anglo-. **~-French** *adj* anglo-français; **~-Catholic** *adj* des anglicans (proches du catholicisme); **~-Saxon** *adj, n* anglo-saxon (*m*).
anglophile ['æŋgləʊfaɪl] *adj, n* anglophile (*mf*).
anglophobe ['æŋgləʊfəʊb] *adj, n* anglophobe (*mf*).
angora [æŋ'gɔːrə] **1** *n* angora *m*. **2** *adj* angora *inv*.
angry ['æŋgrɪ] *adj person* en colère (*with sb* contre qn, *at sth* à cause de qch, *about sth* à propos de qch); (*annoyed*) irrité, fâché (*with sb* contre qn, *at sth* de qch, *about sth* à cause de qch); *look, reply* irrité, plein de colère; (*fig*) *sea* mauvais; *wound* enflammé. **to get ~** se fâcher, se mettre en colère; **to make sb ~** mettre qn en colère; **he was ~ at being dismissed** il était furieux qu'on l'ait renvoyé; **you won't be ~ if I tell you?** vous n'allez pas vous fâcher si je vous le dis?; **an ~ mark on his forehead** une vilaine meurtrissure au front. ♦ **angrily** *adv leave* en colère; *talk* avec colère, avec emportement.
anguish ['æŋgwɪʃ] *n* angoisse *f*. ♦ **anguished** *adj* angoissé.
angular ['æŋgjʊləʳ] *adj* anguleux.
animal ['ænɪməl] **1** *n* animal *m*; (**pej: person*) brute *f*. **2** *adj* (*gen*) animal. **~ husbandry** élevage *m*; **~ kingdom** règne animal; **~ spirits** entrain *m*.
animate ['ænɪmɪt] **1** *adj* animé. **2** ['ænɪmeɪt] *vt* animer. ♦ **animated** *adj* animé; **to become ~d** s'animer; **~d cartoon** dessin(s) animé(s). ♦ **animatedly** *adv talk* d'un ton animé, avec animation; *behave* avec entrain. ♦ **animation** *n* (*gen, Cine*) animation *f*; *[person]* entrain *m*. ♦ **animator** *n* (*Cine*) animateur *m*, -trice *f*.
animosity [ˌænɪ'mɒsɪtɪ], **animus** ['ænɪməs] *n* animosité *f* (*against, towards* contre).
aniseed ['ænɪsiːd] **1** *n* graine *f* d'anis. **2** *adj* à l'anis.
ankle ['æŋkl] **1** *n* (*Anat*) cheville *f*. **2** *adj*: **~ sock** socquette *f*; **~ strap** bride *f*. ♦ **anklebone** *n* astragale *m*. ♦ **anklet** *n* bracelet *m* de cheville.
annals ['ænəlz] *npl* annales *fpl*.
annex [ə'neks] **1** *vt* annexer. **2** ['æneks] *n* (*also* **annexe**) annexe *f*. ♦ **annexation** *n* annexation *f* (*of* de).
annihilate [ə'naɪəleɪt] *vt army, fleet* anéantir; *effect, argument* annihiler. ♦ **annihilation** *n* anéantissement *m*.
anniversary [ˌænɪ'vɜːsərɪ] **1** *n* anniversaire *m* (*d'une date*). **2** *adj*: **~ dinner** dîner commémoratif.
Anno Domini ['ænəʊ'dɒmɪnaɪ] (*abbr* **A.D.**): **in 53 ~** en 53 après Jésus-Christ (*abbr* ap. J.-C.); **it's just ~*** c'est le poids des ans (*hum*).
annotate ['ænəʊteɪt] *vt* annoter. ♦ **annotation** *n* annotation *f*.
announce [ə'naʊns] *vt* (*gen*) annoncer. **to ~ the birth/death of** faire part de la naissance de/du décès de; **it is ~d from London** on apprend de Londres. ♦ **announcement** *n* (*gen*) annonce *f*; (*esp Admin*) avis *m*; *[birth, marriage, death]* avis; (*privately inserted or circulated*) faire-part *m inv*. ♦ **announcer** *n* (*Rad, TV*) (*linking programmes*) speaker(ine) *m(f)*; (*within a programme*) présentateur *m*, -trice *f*.
annoy [ə'nɔɪ] *vt* (*vex*) agacer, ennuyer, contrarier; (*deliberately irritate*) agacer, énerver; (*inconvenience*) ennuyer. **to be/get ~ed with sb** être/se mettre en colère contre qn; **to be ~ed about** *or* **over sth** être contrarié par qch; **to be ~ed with sb about sth** être mécontent de qn à propos de qch; **to get ~ed with a machine** se mettre en colère *or* s'énerver contre une machine; **don't get ~ed!** ne vous fâchez pas!; **I am very ~ed that he hasn't come** je suis très ennuyé *or* contrarié qu'il ne soit pas venu. ♦ **annoyance** *n* **(a)** contrariété *f*, mécontentement *m*; **with a look of ~ance** d'un air contrarié; **to his great ~ance** à son grand mécontentement; **(b)** (*cause of ~ance*) ennui *m*. ♦ **annoying** *adj* agaçant, énervant; (*stronger*) ennuyeux, fâcheux. ♦ **annoyingly** *adv* d'une façon agaçante *etc*.
annual ['ænjʊəl] **1** *adj* annuel. **~ general meeting** assemblée générale annuelle. **2** *n* (*Bot*) plante annuelle; (*book*) publication annuelle; (*children's comic book*) album *m*. ♦ **annually** *adv* annuellement, tous les ans; **£5 ~ly** 5 livres par an.
annuity [ə'njuːɪtɪ] *n* (*income*) rente *f*; (*for life*) rente viagère; (*investment*) viager *m*.
annul [ə'nʌl] *vt* (*gen*) annuler; *law* abroger. ♦ **annulment** *n* annulation *f*; abrogation *f*.
Annunciation [əˌnʌnsɪ'eɪʃən] *n* Annonciation *f*.
anode ['ænəʊd] *n* anode *f*.
anodyne ['ænəʊdaɪn] *adj* (*Med*) analgésique; (*fig*) apaisant.
anoint [ə'nɔɪnt] *vt* oindre (*with* de). **to ~ sb king** sacrer qn.
anomalous [ə'nɒmələs] *adj* anormal. ♦ **anomaly** *n* anomalie *f*.
anon [ə'nɒn] *adj abbr of* **anonymous.**
anonymous [ə'nɒnɪməs] *adj* anonyme. **to remain ~** garder l'anonymat. ♦ **anonymity** [ænə'nɪmɪtɪ] *n* anonymat *m*. ♦ **anonymously** *adv* anonymement.
anorak ['ænəræk] *n* anorak *m*.
anorexia [ænə'reksɪə] *n* anorexie *f*.
another [ə'nʌðəʳ] **1** *adj* **(a)** (*one more*) un ... de plus, encore un. **~ 10** 10 de plus, encore 10; **not ~ minute!** pas une minute de plus!; **without ~ word** sans ajouter un mot; **and ~ thing, ...** et de plus, ..., et d'ailleurs, ... ; **in ~ 20 years** dans 20 ans d'ici. **(b)** (*similar*) un autre, un second. **there is not ~ book like it** ce livre est unique dans son genre; **~ Hitler** un second Hitler. **(c)** (*different*) un autre. **that's quite ~ matter** c'est une tout autre question. **2** *pron* **(a)** un(e) autre, encore un(e). **many ~** bien d'autres. **(b) one ~ = each other;** *V* **each.**
answer ['ɑːnsəʳ] **1** *n* **(a)** (*reply*) réponse *f*; (*to prayer*) exaucement *m* (*to* de). **there's no ~** (*gen*) on ne répond pas; (*Telec*) ça ne répond pas; **in ~ to your letter** en réponse à votre lettre; **she's always got an ~** elle a réponse à tout; (*hum*) **it's the ~ to a maiden's prayer*** c'est ce dont j'ai toujours rêvé; **the poor man's ~ to caviar** le caviar du pauvre. **(b)** (*solution*) solution *f*. **there is no easy ~** c'est un problème difficile à résoudre. **2** *vt* **(a)** *question* répondre à; *charge, argument* réfuter. **~ me** répondez-moi; **to ~ the bell** *or* **door** aller ouvrir. **(b)** *description, need* répondre à; *prayer* exaucer; *problem* résoudre. **it ~s the purpose** cela fait l'affaire. **3** *vi* répondre.
answer back *vi* répondre (avec impertinence) (*to* à).
answer for *vt fus sb's safety etc* répondre de; *truth of sth* garantir. **he has a lot to ~ for** il a bien des comptes à rendre.
answer to *vt fus name, description* répondre à.
♦ **answerable** *adj* **(a)** *question* susceptible de réponse; *charge, argument* réfutable; *problem* soluble; **(b)** (*responsible*) responsable (*to sb* devant qn, *for sth* de qch); **I am ~able to no one** je n'ai de comptes à rendre à personne.
ant [ænt] *n* fourmi *f*. ♦ **anteater** *n* fourmilier *m*. ♦ **anthill** *n* fourmilière *f*.
antagonize [æn'tægənaɪz] *vt* éveiller l'hostilité de, contrarier. **I don't want to ~ him** je ne veux pas le contrarier *or* me le mettre à dos. ♦ **antagonism** *n* antagonisme *m* (*between* entre), opposition *f* (*to* à). ♦ **antagonist** *n* antagoniste *mf*. ♦ **antagonistic** *adj* opposé (*to sth* à qch).
Antarctic [ænt'ɑːktɪk] **1** *n* Antarctique *m*. **2** *adj* antarctique. **~ Circle/Ocean** cercle *m*/océan *m* Antarctique. ♦ **Antarctica** *n* Antarctique *m*.
ante... ['æntɪ] *pref* anté..., anti... . ♦ **antechamber** *n* antichambre *f*. ♦ **antedate** *vt document* antidater; *event* précéder. ♦ **antediluvian** *adj* antédiluvien. ♦ **antenatal** *adj* prénatal; **~natal clinic** service *m* de consultation prénatale. ♦ **anteroom** *n* antichambre *f*.

antecedent [ˌæntɪ'si:dənt] **1** *adj* antérieur (*to* à). **2** *n* antécédent *m*.
antelope ['æntɪləʊp] *n* antilope *f*.
antenna [æn'tenə] *n, pl* **-ae** antenne *f*.
anterior [æn'tɪərɪə^r] *adj* antérieur (*to* à).
anthem ['ænθəm] *n* motet *m*.
anthology [æn'θɒlədʒɪ] *n* anthologie *f*. ♦ **anthologist** *n* anthologiste *mf*.
anthracite ['ænθrəsaɪt] *n* anthracite *m*.
anthropoid ['ænθrəʊpɔɪd] *adj, n* anthropoïde (*m*).
anthropology [ˌænθrə'pɒlədʒɪ] *n* anthropologie *f*. ♦ **anthropological** *adj* anthropologique. ♦ **anthropologist** *n* anthropologiste *mf*.
anti... ['æntɪ] *pref* anti..., contre... . **he's rather ~*** il est plutôt contre. ♦ **anti-aircraft** *adj gun* antiaérien. ♦ **antibiotic** *adj, n* antibiotique (*m*). ♦ **antibody** *n* anticorps *m*. ♦ **Antichrist** *n* Antéchrist *m*. ♦ **anticlerical** *adj* anticlérical. ♦ **anticlimax** *n [style, thought]* chute *f* (dans le trivial); **it was an ~climax** cela n'a pas répondu à l'attente; **what an ~climax!** quelle retombée! ♦ **anticlockwise** *adv* dans le sens inverse des aiguilles d'une montre. ♦ **anticyclone** *n* anticyclone *m*. ♦ **antidote** *n* antidote *m* (*for, to* à, contre). ♦ **antifreeze** *n* antigel *m*. ♦ **antigen** *n* antigène *m*. ♦ **antihistamine** *n* antihistaminique *m*. ♦ **antipodes** [æn'tɪpədi:z] *npl* antipodes *mpl*. ♦ **anti-rust** *adj* antirouille *inv*. ♦ **anti-semitic** *adj* antisémite, antisémitique. ♦ **anti-semitism** *n* antisémitisme *m*. ♦ **antisepsis** *n* antisepsie *f*. ♦ **antiseptic** *adj, n* antiseptique (*m*). ♦ **anti-skid** *adj* antidérapant. ♦ **antislavery** *adj* antiesclavagiste. ♦ **antisocial** *adj tendency, behaviour* antisocial; **don't be ~social*** ne sois pas si sauvage. ♦ **anti-tank** *adj* antichar. ♦ **antitheft** *adj*: **~-theft device** (*Aut*) antivol *m*; (*gen*) dispositif *m* antivol. ♦ **antithesis** *n, pl* **-eses** (*direct opposite*) opposé *m*, contraire *m* (*to, of* de); (*contrast*) antithèse *f*. ♦ **antivivisectionist** *n* adversaire *mf* de la vivisection.
antic ['æntɪk] *n [child, animal]* cabriole *f*; *[clown]* bouffonnerie *f*. (*pej*) **all his ~s** tout le cinéma* qu'il a fait.
anticipate [æn'tɪsɪpeɪt] *vt* **(a)** (*expect, foresee*) prévoir, s'attendre à; *question, attack* prévoir. **we don't ~ any trouble** nous ne prévoyons pas d'ennuis; **I ~ that he will come** je m'attends à ce qu'il vienne; **I ~ seeing him tomorrow** je pense le voir demain; **as ~d** comme prévu. **(b)** (*use etc before due time*) *pleasure* savourer à l'avance; *event, profits, income* anticiper sur; *grief, pain* souffrir à l'avance; *success* escompter; *wishes, objections, command, needs* aller au-devant de. **they ~d Columbus' discovery of America** ils ont découvert l'Amérique avant Christophe Colomb. ♦ **anticipation** *n*: **in anticipation** par anticipation; (*Comm*) **thanking you in anticipation** avec mes remerciements anticipés; **in anticipation of** en prévision de; **with growing anticipation** avec une impatience grandissante.
antimony ['æntɪmənɪ] *n* antimoine *m*.
antipathetic [ˌæntɪpə'θetɪk] *adj* antipathique (*to* à). ♦ **antipathy** [æn'tɪpəθɪ] *n* antipathie *f*.
antiquarian [ˌæntɪ'kwɛərɪən] **1** *adj* d'antiquaire. **~ bookseller** libraire *mf* spécialisé(e) dans le livre ancien. **2** *n* amateur *m* d'antiquités; (*Comm*) antiquaire *mf*. ♦ **antiquary** *n* (*Comm*) antiquaire *mf*.
antiquated ['æntɪkweɪtɪd] *adj* vieillot; *person* vieux jeu *inv*; *building* vétuste.
antique [æn'ti:k] **1** *adj* (*very old*) ancien; (*pre-medieval*) antique; (*: *hum*) antédiluvien*. **2** *n* (*sculpture, ornament etc*) objet *m* d'art (ancien); (*furniture*) meuble *m* ancien. **~ dealer** antiquaire *mf*; **~ shop** magasin *m* d'antiquités; **it's a genuine ~** c'est un objet (*or* un meuble) d'époque. ♦ **antiquity** *n* antiquité *f*.
antirrhinum [ˌæntɪ'raɪnəm] *n* gueule-de-loup *f*.
antler ['æntlə^r] *n* merrain *m*. **the ~s** les bois *mpl*.
antonym ['æntənɪm] *n* antonyme *m*.
anus ['eɪnəs] *n* anus *m*.
anvil ['ænvɪl] *n* enclume *f*.
anxiety [æŋ'zaɪətɪ] *n* (*anxiousness: also Psych*) anxiété *f*. **deep ~** angoisse *f*; **this is a great ~ to me** ceci m'inquiète énormément; **in his ~ to be gone** dans son souci de partir au plus vite; **his biggest ~ was** son plus grand sujet d'inquiétude était; **~ to do well** grand désir *m* de réussir.
anxious ['æŋkʃəs] *adj* **(a)** (*troubled*) anxieux, (très) inquiet, angoissé. **to be over-~** être d'une anxiété maladive; **she is ~ about my health** mon état de santé la préoccupe *or* l'inquiète beaucoup. **(b)** (*causing anxiety*) *news* inquiétant, angoissant; *moment* d'anxiété. **(c)** (*desirous*) anxieux, impatient (*for* de). **~ to start** pressé *or* impatient de commencer; **he is ~ to see you** il tient beaucoup à vous voir; **I am ~ that he should do it** je tiens beaucoup à ce qu'il le fasse; **I am not very ~ to do** j'ai peu envie de faire. ♦ **anxiously** *adv* (*with concern*) avec inquiétude, anxieusement; (*eagerly*) avec impatience.
any ['enɪ] **1** *adj* **(a)** (*neg etc*) **I haven't ~ money/books** je n'ai pas d'argent/de livres; **without ~ difficulty** sans la moindre difficulté. **(b)** (*interrog etc*) **have you ~ butter?** avez-vous du beurre?; **can you see ~ birds?** voyez-vous des oiseaux?; **are there ~ others?** y en a-t-il d'autres?; **if you see ~ children** si vous voyez des enfants; **if you have ~ money** si vous avez de l'argent. **(c)** (*no matter which*) n'importe quel, quelconque; (*each and every*) tout. **take ~ two points** prenez deux points quelconques; **take ~ dress you like** prenez n'importe quelle robe; **come at ~ time** venez à n'importe quelle heure; **~ day now** d'un jour à l'autre; **at ~ hour of the day** à toute heure du jour; **~ amount** *or* **number of** n'importe quelle quantité de; (*fig: a lot*) beaucoup de; **~ person who** toute personne qui.
2 *pron* **(a) I haven't ~** je n'en ai pas; **I have hardly ~ left** il ne m'en reste presque plus; **have you got ~?** en avez-vous? **(b) if ~ of you can sing** si quelqu'un parmi vous sait chanter; **few, if ~** peu de gens, et peut-être même personne; **~ of those books will do** n'importe lequel de ces livres fera l'affaire.
3 *adv*: **I can't hear him ~ more** je ne l'entends plus; **not ~ further** pas plus loin; **not ~ longer** pas plus longtemps; **they didn't behave ~ too well** ils ne se sont pas tellement bien conduits; **are you feeling ~ better?** vous sentez-vous un peu mieux?; **do you want ~ more soup?** voulez-vous encore de la soupe?; **it didn't help them ~*** cela ne leur a pas servi à grand-chose.
anybody ['enɪbɒdɪ] *pron* **(a)** (*neg etc*) **I can't see ~** je ne vois personne; **there is hardly ~ there** il n'y a presque personne; **without ~ seeing him** sans que personne le voie. **(b)** (*interrog etc*) quelqu'un. **did ~ see you?** est-ce que quelqu'un t'a vu?; **~ want my sandwich?*** quelqu'un veut mon sandwich?* **(c)** (*no matter who*) **~ could tell you** n'importe qui pourrait vous le dire; **~ would have thought he had lost** on aurait pu croire qu'il avait perdu; **bring ~ you like** amenez qui vous voudrez; **~ who had heard him speak** quiconque l'a entendu parler; **~ with any sense would know that!** le premier venu saurait cela pourvu qu'il ait un minimum de bon sens!; **~ but Robert** n'importe qui d'autre que Robert; **~ else would have refused** un autre aurait refusé; **bring ~ else you like** amenez n'importe qui d'autre; **is there ~ else I can talk to?** est-ce qu'il y a quelqu'un d'autre à qui je puisse parler?; **work harder if you want to be ~** il faut travailler plus si vous voulez devenir quelqu'un; **he's not just ~** ce n'est pas n'importe qui.
anyhow ['enɪhaʊ] *adv* **(a)** (*any way whatever*)

n'importe comment. **do it ~ you like** faites-le comme vous voulez; **I couldn't get in ~** je n'avais aucun moyen d'entrer; **I finished my essay ~** j'ai bâclé* la fin de ma dissertation; **the books were all ~* on the floor** les livres étaient tous en désordre *or* en vrac *or* n'importe comment par terre. **(b)** (*in any case*) en tout cas, de toute façon, quand même. **whatever you say, they'll do it ~** vous pouvez dire ce que vous voulez, ils le feront de toute façon *or* quand même; **you can try ~** vous pouvez toujours essayer.

anyone ['enɪwʌn] *pron* = **anybody.**

anyplace* ['enɪpleɪs] *adv* (*US*) = **anywhere.**

anything ['enɪθɪŋ] *pron* **(a)** (*neg etc*) **we haven't seen ~** nous n'avons rien vu; **hardly ~** presque rien; **this is ~ but pleasant** ceci n'a vraiment rien d'agréable; (*reply to question*) **~ but!** pas du tout! **(b)** (*interrog etc*) **did you see ~?** avez-vous vu quelque chose?; **is there ~ in this idea?** peut-on tirer quoi que ce soit de cette idée?; **can ~ be done?** peut-on faire quelque chose?; **~ else?** c'est tout?; **is there ~ more tiring than ...** y a-t-il rien de plus fatigant que ...; **~ between 15 and 20 apple trees** quelque chose comme 15 ou 20 pommiers; **if ~ it's an improvement** ce serait plutôt une amélioration. **(c)** (*no matter what*) **say ~ (at all)** dites n'importe quoi; **take ~ you like** prenez ce que vous voudrez; **~ else would disappoint her** s'il en était autrement elle serait déçue; **I'll try ~ else** j'essaierai n'importe quoi d'autre; **I'd give ~ to know the secret** je donnerais n'importe quoi pour connaître le secret; (*intensive*) **he ran** *etc* **like ~*** il a drôlement* couru *etc.*

anyway ['enɪweɪ] *adv* = **anyhow (b).**

anywhere ['enɪwεəʳ] *adv* **(a)** (*affirmative*) n'importe où, partout. **I'd live ~ in France** j'habiterais n'importe où en France; **put it down ~** pose-le n'importe où; **you can find that soap ~** ce savon se trouve partout; **go ~ you like** allez où vous voulez; **~ you go it's the same** où que vous alliez c'est la même chose; **~ else** partout ailleurs. **(b)** (*neg*) nulle part. **they didn't go ~** ils ne sont allés nulle part; **~ else** ailleurs; **not ~ else** nulle part ailleurs; (*fig*) **it won't get you ~** cela ne vous mènera à rien. **(c)** (*interrog*) quelque part. **have you seen it ~?** l'avez-vous vu quelque part?

aorta [eɪ'ɔːtə] *n* aorte *f.*

apace [ə'peɪs] *adv* rapidement.

apart [ə'pɑːt] *adv* **(a)** (*separated*) **2 houses a long way ~** 2 maisons à une grande distance l'une de l'autre; **birthdays 2 days ~** anniversaires à 2 jours d'intervalle; **to stand with one's feet ~** se tenir les jambes écartées. **(b)** (*on one side*) à part, à l'écart. **to hold o.s. ~** se tenir à l'écart (*from* de); **~ from these difficulties** en dehors de *or* à part ces difficultés, ces difficultés mises à part; **~ from the fact that** outre que. **(c)** (*separately*) séparément. **they are living ~** ils sont séparés; **he lives ~ from his wife** il est séparé de sa femme; **to tell ~** distinguer l'un(e) de l'autre; **to keep ~** séparer; **to come ~** *[two objects]* se séparer, se détacher; *[small object]* se défaire; *[furniture]* se démonter; (*break*) s'en aller en morceaux; **to take ~** démonter; (*fig*) **they are in a class ~** ils sont tout à fait à part.

apartheid [ə'pɑːteɪt] *n* apartheid *m.*

apartment [ə'pɑːtmənt] *n* **(a)** (*Brit: room*) pièce *f.* **a 5-~ house** une maison de 5 pièces; **'~s'** 'chambres *fpl* à louer'; **furnished ~(s)** meublé *m.*

(b) (*US: flat*) appartement *m,* logement *m.* **~ building, ~ house** immeuble *m* (*de résidence*).

apathy ['æpəθɪ] *n* apathie *f,* indifférence *f.* ♦ **apathetic** *adj* apathique.

ape [eɪp] **1** *n* (grand) singe *m.* **2** *vt* singer.

aperient [ə'pɪərɪənt] *adj, n* laxatif (*m*).

aperitif [ə'perɪtɪv] *n* apéritif *m.*

aperture ['æpətʃjʊəʳ] *n* ouverture *f* (*also Phot*).

apex ['eɪpeks] *n* sommet *m.*

aphid ['eɪdɪd] *n* puceron *m* (des plantes).

aphis ['eɪfɪs] *n, pl* **aphides** ['eɪfɪdiːz] aphis *m.*

aphorism ['æfərɪzəm] *n* aphorisme *m.*

aphrodisiac [ˌæfrəʊ'dɪzɪæk] *n* aphrodisiaque *m.*

apiary ['eɪpɪərɪ] *n* rucher *m.*

apiece [ə'piːs] *adv* chacun(e).

aplomb [ə'plɒm] *n* sang-froid *m.*

Apocalypse [ə'pɒkəlɪps] *n* Apocalypse *f.* ♦ **apocalyptic** *adj* apocalyptique.

Apocrypha [ə'pɒkrɪfə] *npl* apocryphes *mpl.* ♦ **apocryphal** *adj* apocryphe.

apogee ['æpəʊdʒiː] *n* apogée *m.*

apolitical [ˌeɪpə'lɪtɪkəl] *adj* apolitique.

apologetic [əˌpɒlə'dʒetɪk] *adj smile etc* d'excuse. **she was very ~ for not coming/about her mistake** elle s'est beaucoup excusée de n'être pas venue/de son erreur. ♦ **apologetically** *adv* en s'excusant, pour s'excuser.

apologize [ə'pɒlədʒaɪz] *vi* s'excuser (*to sb for sth* de qch auprès de qn; *for having done* d'avoir fait). **to ~ profusely** se confondre en excuses.

apology [ə'pɒlədʒɪ] *n* **(a)** (*regrets*) excuses *fpl.* **to make an ~ for sth/for having done** faire ses excuses pour qch/pour avoir fait; **to send one's apologies** envoyer une lettre d'excuse; (*pej*) **it was an ~ for a bed** comme lit c'était plutôt minable*. **(b)** (*defence: for beliefs etc*) apologie *f* (*for* de).

apoplexy ['æpəpleksɪ] *n* apoplexie *f.* ♦ **apoplectic** *adj* apoplectique; **apoplectic fit** attaque *f* d'apoplexie.

apostle [ə'pɒsl] *n* apôtre *m.* **A~s' Creed** Credo *m.* ♦ **apostolic** *adj* apostolique.

apostrophe [ə'pɒstrəfɪ] *n* apostrophe *f.*

appal, (*US*) **appall** [ə'pɔːl] *vt* consterner; (*stronger*) épouvanter. ♦ **appalling** *adj destruction* épouvantable; *ignorance* consternant. ♦ **appallingly** *adv* épouvantablement.

apparatus [ˌæpə'reɪtəs] *n* (*for heating etc: also Anat*) appareil *m*; *[laboratory]* instruments *mpl*; *[gym]* appareils *mpl*; *[filming, camping etc]* équipement *m.*

apparent [ə'pærənt] *adj* **(a)** (*obvious*) évident, apparent, manifeste. **(b)** (*not real*) apparent. **his ~ weakness** son air de faiblesse. ♦ **apparently** *adv* apparemment.

apparition [ˌæpə'rɪʃən] *n* apparition *f.*

appeal [ə'piːl] **1** *vi* **(a)** (*request publicly*) lancer un appel (*on behalf of* en faveur de; *for sb* pour qn; *for sth* pour obtenir qch). (*Fin*) **to ~ for funds** faire un appel de fonds; **he ~ed for silence** il a demandé le silence; (*Pol*) **to ~ to the country** en appeler au pays. **(b)** (*beg*) faire appel (*to sb's generosity* à la générosité de qn). **to ~ to sb for money/help** demander de l'argent/des secours à qn; **I ~ to you!** je vous en supplie! **(c)** (*Jur*) se pourvoir en appel. **to ~ to the supreme court** se pourvoir en cassation; **to ~ against** *judgment* appeler de; *decision* faire opposition à. **(d)** (*attract*) **to ~ to** plaire à; **it doesn't ~ to me** cela ne me dit rien*; **it ~s to the imagination** cela parle à l'imagination.

2 *n* **(a)** (*public call*) appel *m.* (*Fin*) **~ for funds** appel de fonds; **he made a public ~ for the blind** il a lancé un appel au profit des aveugles. **(b)** (*by individual: for help etc*) appel *m* (*for* à); (*for money*) demande *f* (*for* de). **with a look of ~** d'un air suppliant. **(c)** (*Jur*) appel *m.* **acquitted on ~** acquitté en sèconde instance; **A~ Court** cour *f* d'appel. **(d)** (*attraction*) *[person, object]* attrait *m,* charme *m*; *[plan, idea]* intérêt *m.*

♦ **appealing** *adj* (*moving*) émouvant; *look* pathétique; (*begging*) suppliant; (*attractive*) attirant. ♦ **appealingly** *adv* de façon émouvante; d'un air suppliant; (*charmingly*) avec beaucoup de charme.

appear [ə'pɪəʳ] *vi* **(a)** *[person, sun etc]* apparaître, se montrer; *[ghost, vision]* apparaître, se manifester (*to sb* à qn); *[publication]* paraître. (*Theat*) **to ~ in 'Hamlet'** jouer dans 'Hamlet'; **to ~ as Hamlet** jouer Hamlet; **to ~ on TV** passer à la télévision. **(b)** (*arrive*) arriver, se présenter. **he ~ed from nowhere** il est apparu comme par miracle. **(c)** (*Jur etc*) comparaître (*before* devant). **to ~ on a charge of** être jugé pour; **to ~ for sb** plaider pour qn. **(d)** (*physical aspect*) paraître, avoir l'air. **they ~ (to be) ill** ils ont l'air malades. **(e)** (*on evidence*) paraître (*that* que + *indic*). **so it ~s, so it would ~** à ce qu'il paraît; (*iro*) on dirait! **(f)** (*by surmise*) sembler (*that* que *gen* + *subj*), sembler bien (*that* que + *indic*). **there ~s to be a mistake** il semble qu'il y ait une erreur; **it ~s he did say that** il semble bien qu'il a dit cela; **it ~s to me they are mistaken** il me semble qu'ils ont tort; **how does it ~ to you?** qu'en pensez-vous?

appearance [ə'pɪərəns] *n* **(a)** (*act*) apparition *f*; (*arrival*) arrivée *f*; (*Jur*) comparution *f*; *[publication]* parution *f*. **to make a personal ~** apparaître en personne; **to put in an ~** faire acte de présence; (*Theat*) **in order of ~** par ordre d'entrée en scène. **(b)** (*look*) apparence *f*; *[house etc]* aspect *m*. **his ~ worried us** la mine qu'il avait nous a inquiétés; **~s are deceptive, you shouldn't go by ~s** il ne faut pas se fier aux apparences; **in order to keep up ~s** pour sauver les apparences; **to all ~s** selon toute apparence.

appease [ə'pi:z] *vt* apaiser. ♦ **appeasement** *n* apaisement *m*.

append [ə'pend] *vt document* joindre; *signature* apposer. ♦ **appendage** *n* appendice *m*.

appendix [ə'pendɪks] *n, pl* **-ices** **(a)** (*Anat*) appendice *m*. **to have one's ~ out** se faire opérer de l'appendicite. **(b)** *[book]* appendice *m*; *[document]* annexe *f*. ♦ **append(ic)ectomy** *n* appendicectomie *f*. ♦ **appendicitis** *n* appendicite *f*.

appertain [ˌæpə'teɪn] *vi* se rapporter (*to* à).

appetite ['æpɪtaɪt] *n* appétit *m*; (*fig*) goût *m* (*for* pour). **to have a good ~** avoir bon appétit. ♦ **appetizer** *n* (*drink*) apéritif *m*; (*food*) amuse-gueule* *m inv*. ♦ **appetizing** *adj* appétissant.

applaud [ə'plɔ:d] *vt person, victory* applaudir; *decision, efforts* approuver. ♦ **applause** *n* applaudissements *mpl*.

apple ['æpl] **1** *n* pomme *f*; (*~ tree*) pommier *m*. **he's the ~ of my eye** je tiens à lui comme à la prunelle de mes yeux. **2** *adj*: **~ blossom** fleur *f* de pommier; **~ core** trognon *m* de pomme; **~ orchard** champ *m* de pommiers; **~ pie** tourte *f* aux pommes; **in ~-pie order** en ordre parfait; **~ sauce** compote *f* de pommes.

apply [ə'plaɪ] **1** *vt paint, ointment, dressing* appliquer, mettre (*to* sur); *theory, rule, law* appliquer (*to* à). **to ~ a match to sth** allumer qch avec une allumette; **to ~ the brakes** actionner les freins; **to ~ one's mind** *or* **o.s. to (doing) sth** s'appliquer à (faire) qch; **applied sciences** sciences appliquées. **2** *vi* s'adresser (*to sb for sth* à qn pour obtenir qch). **~ at the office** adressez-vous au bureau.

apply for *vt fus scholarship, money, assistance* demander. **to ~ for a job** faire une demande d'emploi (*to sb* auprès de qn); **to ~ for a divorce** formuler une demande en divorce.

apply to *vt fus* s'appliquer à. **this does not ~ to you** ceci ne s'applique pas à vous.

♦ **appliance** *n* appareil *m*; (*smaller*) dispositif *m*. ♦ **applicable** *adj* applicable (*to* à). ♦ **applicant** *n* (*for job*) candidat(e) *m(f)* (*for* à); (*Admin: for benefits etc*) demandeur *m*, -euse *f*. ♦ **application** *n* **(a)** (*act of applying*) application *f* (*to* à); (*request*) demande *f*; **application for a job** demande d'emploi, candidature *f* à un poste; **on application** sur demande; **details may be had on application to the secretary** s'adresser au secrétaire pour tous renseignements; **application form** formulaire *m* de demande; **(b)** (*diligence*) application *f*, attention *f*. ♦ **applicator** *n* applicateur *m*.

appliqué [æ'pli:keɪ] **1** *vt* coudre (en application). **2** *n* (*~ work*) travail *m* d'application.

appoint [ə'pɔɪnt] *vt* nommer (*sb to a post* qn à un emploi *or* poste); (*fix*) *date, place* fixer; (*ordain*) prescrire (*that* que + *subj*). **at the ~ed time** à l'heure dite *or* convenue; **to ~ sb manager** nommer qn directeur; **to ~ a new secretary** engager une nouvelle secrétaire; **a well-~ed house** une maison bien aménagée.

appointment [ə'pɔɪntmənt] *n* **(a)** (*arrangement to meet*) rendez-vous *m*. **to make an ~ with sb** prendre rendez-vous avec qn; **to keep an ~** aller à un rendez-vous; **have you an ~?** avez-vous pris rendez-vous?; **to meet sb by ~** rencontrer qn sur rendez-vous. **(b)** (*act of appointing*) nomination *f* (*to a post* à un emploi *or* poste); (*office assigned*) emploi *m*, (*more impressive*) poste *m*. (*Comm*) **'By ~ to Her Majesty the Queen'** 'fournisseur de S.M. la Reine'; (*Press*) **'~s (vacant)'** 'offres *fpl* d'emploi'; **~s bureau** agence *f* de placement.

apposite ['æpəzɪt] *adj* juste, pertinent. ♦ **apposition** *n* apposition *f*.

appraise [ə'preɪz] *vt* évaluer, estimer. ♦ **appraisal** *n* évaluation *f*, estimation *f*.

appreciate [ə'pri:ʃɪeɪt] **1** *vt* **(a)** (*be aware of*) *difficulty, fact, sb's attitude* se rendre compte de, être conscient de. **to ~ sth at its true value** estimer qch à sa juste valeur; **yes, I ~ that** oui, je m'en rends bien compte. **(b)** (*value*) *help, music, person* apprécier; *honour* être sensible à; *sb's help, work, kindness* être reconnaissant de. **he felt that nobody ~d him** il ne se sentait pas apprécié à sa juste valeur. **2** *vi [currency]* monter; *[object, property]* prendre de la valeur. ♦ **appreciable** *adj* appréciable. ♦ **appreciably** *adv* de façon appréciable. ♦ **appreciation** *n* estimation *f*; (*gratitude*) reconnaissance *f*; (*Art etc: critique*) critique *f*; (*Fin*) hausse *f*. ♦ **appreciative** *adj person* sensible (*of* à); (*admiring*) admiratif; (*grateful*) reconnaissant; *comment* élogieux; **an appreciative glance** un regard connaisseur *or* admiratif.

apprehend [ˌæprɪ'hend] *vt* (*arrest*) appréhender, arrêter; (*fear*) redouter, appréhender. ♦ **apprehension** *n* (*fear*) appréhension *f*; (*arrest*) arrestation *f*. ♦ **apprehensive** *adj* plein d'appréhension. ♦ **apprehensively** *adv* avec appréhension.

apprentice [ə'prentɪs] **1** *n* apprenti(e) *m(f)*. **~ plumber, plumber's ~** apprenti plombier. **2** *vt* mettre en apprentissage (*to sb* chez qn). **to be ~d to** être en apprentissage chez. ♦ **apprenticeship** *n* apprentissage *m*.

apprise [ə'praɪz] *vt* informer (*sb of sth* qn de qch).

appro* ['æprəʊ] *n* (*Comm*) *abbr of* **approval**.

approach [ə'prəʊtʃ] **1** *vi [person, vehicle]* (s')approcher; *[date, season, death, war]* approcher, être proche. **2** *vt place* s'approcher de, s'avancer vers; *topic* aborder; (*fig*) *perfection etc* atteindre presque à. **it all depends on how one ~es it** tout dépend de la façon dont on s'y prend; **to ~ sb about sth** s'adresser à qn à propos de qch; **a man ~ed me in the street** un homme m'a abordé dans la rue; **I saw him ~ing me** je l'ai vu qui venait vers moi; **she is ~ing 30** elle approche de la trentaine; **it was ~ing midnight** il était près de *or* presque minuit.

3 *n [person, vehicle]* approche *f*. **at the ~ of** à l'approche de; **his ~ to the problem** sa façon d'aborder le problème; **a new ~ to teaching French** une nouvelle façon d'enseigner le français; **to make ~es to sb** faire des avances à qn; **to make an ~ to sb** faire une proposition à qn; **all the ~es to the town** tous les abords *mpl or* toutes les approches de la ville; **the ~ to the top of the hill** le

chemin qui mène au sommet de la colline; **the station ~** les abords de la gare.
4 *adj*: (*Aviat*) **~ lights** balisage *m*; **~ road** (*to city*) voie *f* de dégagement urbain; (*to motorway*) route *f* d'accès, bretelle *f*.
♦ **approachable** *adj* approchable. ♦ **approaching** *adj date, car* qui approche; *oncoming car* venant en sens inverse.
approbation [ˌæprəˈbeɪʃən] *n* approbation *f*. **a nod of ~** un signe de tête approbateur.
appropriate [əˈprəʊprɪɪt] **1** *adj moment, decision, ruling* opportun; *remark* opportun, juste; *word* juste, propre; *name* bien choisi; *authority, department* compétent. **~ for** *or* **to** propre à, approprié à; **it would not be ~ for me to comment** ce n'est pas à moi de faire des commentaires; **he is the ~ person to ask** c'est à lui qu'il faut le demander. **2** [əˈprəʊprɪeɪt] *vt* s'approprier.
♦ **appropriately** *adv speak, comment* pertinemment; *design* convenablement; *situated* au bon endroit; **~ly named** au nom bien choisi.
♦ **appropriation** *n* (*act: also Jur*) appropriation *f*; (*funds assigned*) dotation *f*; (*US Pol*) crédit *m* budgétaire.
approve [əˈpruːv] *vt* (*gen*) approuver; *decision* ratifier; *request* agréer.
approve of *vt fus behaviour, idea* approuver, être partisan de; *person* avoir bonne opinion de. **she doesn't ~ of drinking** elle n'approuve pas qu'on boive; **he doesn't ~ of me** il désapprouve ma façon d'être; **we ~ of our new neighbours** nos nouveaux voisins nous plaisent.
♦ **approval** *n* approbation *f*, assentiment *m*; (*Comm*) **on approval** sous condition, à l'essai; **a nod of approval** un signe de tête approbateur; **has it got your approval?** l'approuvez-vous?
♦ **approving** *adj* approbateur. ♦ **approvingly** *adv* d'un air *or* d'un ton approbateur.
approximate [əˈprɒksɪmɪt] **1** *adj* approximatif. **~ to** proche de. **2** [əˈprɒksɪmeɪt] *vi* s'approcher (*to* de). ♦ **approximately** *adv* approximativement.
♦ **approximation** *n* approximation *f*.
apricot [ˈeɪprɪkɒt] *n* abricot *m*; (**~ *tree***) abricotier *m*.
April [ˈeɪprəl] **1** *n* avril *m*; *for phrases V* **September. 2** *adj*: **to make an ~ fool of sb** faire un poisson d'avril à qn; **~ Fools' Day** le premier avril; **~ showers** ≈ giboulées *fpl* de mars.
apron [ˈeɪprən] **1** *n* tablier *m*; (*Aviat*) aire *f* de stationnement. **2** *adj*: **tied to his mother's ~ strings** pendu aux jupes de sa mère; (*Theat*) **~ stage** avant-scène *f*.
apropos [ˌæprəˈpəʊ] *adj, adv* à propos (*of* de).
apse [æps] *n* abside *f*.
apt [æpt] *adj* **(a)** *person* enclin, porté, disposé (*to do* à faire); *thing* susceptible (*to do* de faire). **one is ~ to believe that ...** on a tendance à croire que ...; **he's ~ to be out in the afternoons** il a tendance à ne pas être chez lui l'après-midi. **(b)** *comment, reply* approprié, juste; *pupil* doué. ♦ **aptitude** *n* aptitude *f* (*for* à), disposition *f* (*for* pour). ♦ **aptly** *adv answer* avec justesse; *behave* avec propos.
♦ **aptness** *n* à-propos *m*, justesse *f*.
aqualung [ˈækwəlʌŋ] *n* scaphandre *m* autonome.
aquamarine [ˌækwəməˈriːn] **1** *n* aigue-marine *f*. **2** *adj* (*colour*) bleu vert *inv*.
aquaplane [ˈækwəpleɪn] *vi* (*Sport*) faire de l'aquaplane; (*Aut*) faire de l'aquaplaning.
aquarium [əˈkwɛərɪəm] *n* aquarium *m*.
Aquarius [əˈkwɛərɪəs] *n* le Verseau.
aquatic [əˈkwætɪk] *adj animal, plant* aquatique; *sport* nautique.
aqueduct [ˈækwɪdʌkt] *n* aqueduc *m*.
aquiline [ˈækwɪlaɪn] *adj* aquilin.
Arab [ˈærəb] **1** *n* Arabe *mf*; (*horse*) (cheval *m*) arabe *m*. **2** *adj* arabe. ♦ **Arabia** *n* Arabie *f*.
♦ **Arabian** *adj* arabe; *desert, sea* d'Arabie; **~ian Gulf** golfe *m* Arabique; **the ~ian Nights** les Mille et Une Nuits. ♦ **Arabic 1** *n* arabe *m*; **2** *adj* arabe; **~ic numerals** chiffres *mpl* arabes.
arable [ˈærəbl] *adj* arable.
arbitrary [ˈɑːbɪtrərɪ] *adj* arbitraire. ♦ **arbitrarily** *adv* arbitrairement.
arbitrate [ˈɑːbɪtreɪt] *vti* arbitrer. ♦ **arbitration 1** *n* arbitrage *m*; **to go to arbitration** recourir à l'arbitrage; **2** *adj*: **arbitration tribunal** instance *f* chargée d'arbitrer les conflits sociaux.
♦ **arbitrator** *n* arbitre *m* (*Ind, Jur*).
arc [ɑːk] **1** *n* arc *m*. **2** *adj*: **~ light** lampe *f* à arc, (*Cine, TV*) sunlight *m*; **~ welding** soudure *f* à l'arc voltaïque.
arcade [ɑːˈkeɪd] *n* (*arches*) arcade *f*; (*shopping precinct*) galerie *f* marchande.
arch[1] [ɑːtʃ] **1** *n* [*church etc*] arc *m*, voûte *f*; [*bridge etc*] arche *f*; [*eyebrows*] arcade *f*; [*foot*] voûte *f* plantaire. **2** *vt* arquer. **~ed** *foot, back* cambré; *window* cintré. ♦ **archway** *n* voûte *f* (d'entrée), porche *m*.
arch[2] [ɑːtʃ] *adj* (*teasing*) coquin.
arch[3] [ɑːtʃ] **1** *adj* (*chief*) *hypocrite etc* grand (*before n*). **an ~ villain** un scélérat achevé; **the ~ villain** le principal scélérat. **2** *pref* arch(i)... .
♦ **archangel** [ˈɑːkˌeɪndʒəl] *n* archange *m*.
♦ **archbishop** *n* archevêque *m*. ♦ **archduke** *n* archiduc *m*. ♦ **arch-enemy** *n* ennemi *m* par excellence. ♦ **arch-priest** *n* archiprêtre *m*.
archaeology [ˌɑːkɪˈɒlədʒɪ] *n* archéologie *f*.
♦ **archaeological** *adj* archéologique.
♦ **archaeologist** *n* archéologue *mf*.
archaic [ɑːˈkeɪɪk] *adj* archaïque. ♦ **archaism** *n* archaïsme *m*.
archeology *etc* (*US*) = **archaeology** *etc*.
archer [ˈɑːtʃəʳ] *n* archer *m*. ♦ **archery** *n* tir *m* à l'arc.
archetype [ˈɑːkɪtaɪp] *n* archétype *m*.
♦ **archetypal** *adj* archétype.
archipelago [ˌɑːkɪˈpelɪgəʊ] *n* archipel *m*.
architect [ˈɑːkɪtekt] *n* architecte *m*.
♦ **architectural** *adj* architectural.
♦ **architecture** *n* architecture *f*.
archives [ˈɑːkaɪvz] *npl* archives *fpl*. ♦ **archivist** *n* archiviste *mf*.
Arctic [ˈɑːktɪk] **1** *adj* arctique. (*fig: very cold*) **a~** glacial; **~ Circle/Ocean** cercle *m*/océan *m* Arctique. **2** *n*: **the ~** l'Arctique *m*.
ardent [ˈɑːdənt] *adj* ardent; *admirer* fervent.
♦ **ardently** *adv* ardemment.
ardour, (*US*) **ardor** [ˈɑːdəʳ] *n* ardeur *f*.
arduous [ˈɑːdjʊəs] *adj* ardu. ♦ **arduously** *adv* laborieusement. ♦ **arduousness** *n* difficulté *f*.
area [ˈɛərɪə] **1** *n* **(a)** (*surface measure*) aire *f*, superficie *f*. **an ~ of 800 m²** une superficie de 800 m², 800 m² de superficie. **(b)** (*region*) région *f*; (*Mil, Pol*) territoire *m*, (*smaller*) secteur *m*, zone *f*; (*fig: of knowledge, enquiry*) domaine *m*, champ *m*. **the ~s of disagreement** les zones *fpl* de désaccord; (*fig*) **in this ~** à ce propos; **dining/sleeping ~** coin *m* salle-à-manger/chambre. **2** *adj*: **~ manager** directeur régional; **~ office** agence régionale.
arena [əˈriːnə] *n* arène *f*.
Argentina [ˌɑːdʒənˈtiːnə] *n* (*also* **the Argentine**) Argentine *f*. ♦ **Argentinian 1** *n* Argentin(e) *m(f)*; **2** *adj* argentin.
argue [ˈɑːgjuː] **1** *vi* **(a)** (*dispute*) se disputer (*with sb* avec qn, *about sth* au sujet de qch). **don't ~!** pas de discussion! **(b)** (*reason*) argumenter (*about* sur; *against sb* contre qn). **he ~d against going** il a donné les raisons qu'il avait de ne pas vouloir y aller; **to ~ from sth** tirer argument de qch; **it ~s in favour of** c'est un argument en faveur de. **2** *vt* **(a) to ~ sb into/out of doing** persuader/dissuader qn de faire. **(b)** (*debate*) *case* discuter, débattre; (*maintain*) soutenir, affirmer (*that* que). **a well-~d case** un cas étayé de bons arguments; **to ~ the toss*** discuter le

coup*. **(c)** (*show evidence of*) dénoter, indiquer. **it ~s a certain lack of feeling** cela dénote *or* indique une certaine insensibilité. ♦ **arguable** *adj*: **it is arguable that** on peut soutenir que. ♦ **arguably** *adv*: **it is arguably ...** on peut soutenir que c'est ... .

argument ['ɑːgjʊmənt] *n* **(a)** (*debate*) discussion *f*, débat *m*. **one side of the ~** une seule version de l'affaire; **for ~'s sake** à titre d'exemple; **it is open to ~ that** on peut soutenir que. **(b)** (*dispute*) dispute *f*, discussion *f*. **to have an ~** se disputer (*with sb* avec qn). **(c)** (*reasons*) argument *m*. **his ~ is that ...** il soutient que ... . ♦ **argumentative** *adj* raisonneur, ergoteur (*pej*).

argy-bargy* ['ɑːdʒɪ'bɑːdʒɪ] *n* discutailleries* *fpl*.

aria ['ɑːrɪə] *n* aria *f*.

arid ['ærɪd] *adj* aride. ♦ **aridity** *n* aridité *f*.

Aries ['ɛəriːz] *n* le Bélier.

aright [ə'raɪt] *adv* bien, correctement.

arise [ə'raɪz] *pret* **arose**, *ptp* **arisen** [ə'rɪzn] *vi* **(a)** *[difficulty]* survenir, surgir; *[question]* se présenter, se poser; *[cry]* s'élever; *[occasion]* se présenter. **should the need ~** en cas de besoin. **(b)** (*result*) résulter, provenir (*from* de). **(c)** (†: *rise*) se lever.

aristocracy [ˌærɪs'tɒkrəsɪ] *n* aristocratie *f*. ♦ **aristocrat** ['ærɪstəkræt] *n* aristocrate *mf*. ♦ **aristocratic** [ˌærɪstə'krætɪk] *adj* aristocratique.

arithmetic [ə'rɪθmətɪk] *n* arithmétique *f*. ♦ **arithmetical** *adj* arithmétique.

ark [ɑːk] *n* arche *f*. **Noah's ~** l'arche de Noé; (*fig*) **it's out of the ~*** ça date du déluge.

arm[1] [ɑːm] *n* (*gen*) bras *m*; *[garment]* manche *f*. **in one's ~s** dans ses bras; **he had a coat over his ~** il avait un manteau sur le bras; **take my ~** prenez mon bras; **on her husband's ~** au bras de son mari; **to put one's ~ round sb** passer son bras autour des épaules de qn; **~ in ~** bras dessus bras dessous; **within ~'s reach** à portée de la main; **at ~'s length** à bout de bras; (*fig*) à distance; **the (long) ~ of the law** le bras de la loi; (*fig*) **to have a long ~** avoir le bras long. ♦ **armband** *n* brassard *m*. ♦ **armchair 1** *n* fauteuil *m*; **2** *adj*: **~chair general** *etc* général *m etc* en chambre. ♦ **armful** *n* brassée *f*. ♦ **armhole** *n* emmanchure *f*. ♦ **armlet** *n* brassard *m*. ♦ **armpit** *n* aisselle *f*. ♦ **armrest** *n* accoudoir *m*.

arm[2] [ɑːm] **1** *n* **(a)** (*weapon*) arme *f*. **under ~s** sous les armes; **in ~s** armé; **to ~s!** aux armes!; **to be up in ~s against** *sb, the authorities* être en rébellion ouverte contre; *decision etc* partir en guerre contre; **she was up in ~s about it** cela la mettait hors d'elle-même. **(b)** (*Her*) **~s** armes *fpl*.

2 *adj*: **~s factory** fabrique *f* d'armes; **~s manufacturer** fabricant *m* d'armes; **~s race** course *f* aux armements.

3 *vt person, nation* armer; *missile* munir d'une (tête d')ogive.

4 *vi* (s')armer (*against* contre).

♦ **armaments** *npl* armement *m*; **~aments race** course *f* aux armements. ♦ **armed** *adj* (*lit, fig*) armé (*with* de); *missile* muni d'une (tête d')ogive; *conflict, neutrality* armé; **~ed to the teeth** armé jusqu'aux dents; **the ~ed forces** les (forces) armées *fpl*; **~ed robbery** vol *m* à main armée.

armistice ['ɑːmɪstɪs] *n* armistice *m*. (*Brit*) **A~ Day** le onze novembre.

armour, (*US*) **armor** ['ɑːmər] *n* **(a)** *[knight]* armure *f*. **in full ~** armé de pied en cap. **(b)** (*Mil: ~-plating*) blindage *m*; (*vehicles*) blindés *mpl*; (*forces*) forces blindées. ♦ **armour-clad** *or* ♦ **armour-plated** *adj* blindé. ♦ **armoured car** *n* voiture blindée. ♦ **armour-piercing** *adj shell, bullet* perforant. ♦ **armour-plate** *or* ♦ **armour-plating** *n* (*Mil*) blindage *m*; (*Naut*) cuirasse *f*. ♦ **armoury** *n* dépôt *m* d'armes; (*US: factory*) fabrique *f* d'armes.

army ['ɑːmɪ] **1** *n* armée *f* (de terre); (*fig*) foule *f*, armée. **to be in the ~** être dans l'armée, être militaire; **to join the ~** s'engager; **to go into the ~** *[professional]* devenir militaire *m* (de carrière); *[conscript]* partir au service. **2** *adj life, nurse, uniform* militaire. **~ corps** corps *m* d'armée; **~ officer** officier *m* (de l'armée de terre).

aroma [ə'rəʊmə] *n* arôme *m*. ♦ **aromatic** *adj* aromatique.

arose [ə'rəʊz] *pret of* **arise**.

around [ə'raʊnd] **1** *adv* **(a)** autour. **all ~** tout autour, de tous côtés; **for miles ~** sur un rayon de plusieurs kilomètres. **(b)** (*nearby*) dans les parages. **he is somewhere ~** il est dans les parages; **is he ~?*** est-ce qu'il est là?; **there's a lot of flu ~** il y a beaucoup de cas de grippe en ce moment; **he's been ~*** (*travelled*) il a pas mal roulé sa bosse*; (*experienced*) il n'est pas né d'hier. **2** *prep* **(a)** (*round*) autour de. **~ the fire** autour du feu; **to go ~ an obstacle** contourner un obstacle; **the country ~ the town** les environs *mpl or* alentours *mpl* de la ville; **~ the corner** après le coin. **(b)** (*about*) **to wander ~ the city** errer dans la ville; **they are somewhere ~ the house** ils sont quelque part dans la maison. **(c)** (*approximately*) environ, à peu près, vers. **~ 2 kilos** environ *or* à peu près 2 kilos; **~ 10 o'clock/1890** vers 10 heures/1890.

arouse [ə'raʊz] *vt* **(a)** (*awaken*) réveiller; (*stir to action*) pousser à agir. **that ~d him to protest** cela l'a poussé à protester. **(b)** (*cause*) *suspicion, curiosity etc* éveiller; *contempt, anger* provoquer.

arrange [ə'reɪndʒ] **1** *vt* **(a)** (*order*) *room, clothing, hair, flowers* arranger; (*Mus*) arranger (*for* pour); *books, objects* ranger, mettre en ordre. **room ~d as a laboratory** pièce aménagée en laboratoire. **(b)** (*decide on*) *meeting* arranger, organiser; *date* fixer; *plans, programme* arrêter, convenir de. **it was ~d that** il a été arrangé *or* décidé *or* convenu que; **I have sth ~d for tonight** j'ai qch de prévu pour ce soir; **to ~ a marriage** faire un mariage. **2** *vi* s'arranger (*to do* pour faire; *for sb to do* pour que qn fasse; *with sb about sth* avec qn au sujet de qch). **to ~ for sb's luggage to be sent up** faire monter les bagages de qn; **to ~ with sb to do** s'entendre avec qn pour faire.

arrangement [ə'reɪndʒmənt] *n* (*gen: also Mus*) arrangement *m*; (*plan*) décision *f*, arrangement. **larger sizes by ~** tailles supérieures sur demande; **price by ~** prix *m* à débattre; **by ~ with Covent Garden** avec l'autorisation *f* de Covent Garden; **to make ~s to do** s'arranger pour faire; **to make ~s for a holiday** faire des préparatifs *mpl* pour des vacances; **to make ~s for sth to be done** prendre des mesures *fpl or* dispositions *fpl* pour faire faire qch.

array [ə'reɪ] **1** *vt*: **~ed in** revêtu de. **2** *n [objects]* ensemble impressionnant; *[people]* assemblée *f*.

arrears [ə'rɪəz] *npl* arriéré *m*. **rent in ~** (loyer) arriéré; **to get into ~** s'arriérer; **to be 3 months in ~ with the rent** devoir 3 mois de loyer.

arrest [ə'rest] **1** *vt* **(a)** *[police etc]* arrêter. **(b)** *growth etc* (*stop*) arrêter; (*hinder*) entraver; (*retard*) retarder; *disease* enrayer. (*Psych*) **~ed development** atrophie *f* de la personnalité. **2** *n [police etc]* arrestation *f*. **under ~** en état d'arrestation; (*Mil*) aux arrêts; **to put sb under ~** arrêter qn; (*Mil*) mettre qn aux arrêts; **to make an ~** procéder à une arrestation. ♦ **arresting** *adj* (*fig*) frappant, saisissant.

arrival [ə'raɪvəl] *n* **(a)** (*gen*) arrivée *f*; (*Comm*) *[goods in bulk]* arrivage *m*. **on ~** à l'arrivée. **(b)** (*consignment*) arrivage *m*. (*person*) **the first ~** le premier arrivé; **a new ~** un nouveau venu; (*baby*) un(e) nouveau-né(e).

arrive [ə'raɪv] *vi* arriver (*at* à); (*succeed*) arriver, réussir. **to ~ on the scene** arriver; **the moment**

has ~d when we must go le moment est venu pour nous de partir.
arrive at *vt fus decision, solution* aboutir à, parvenir à; *perfection* atteindre. **to ~ at a price** *[one person]* fixer un prix; *[2 people]* se mettre d'accord sur un prix; **they finally ~d at the idea of doing** ils en sont finalement venus à l'idée de faire.
arrogant ['ærəgənt] *adj* arrogant. ♦ **arrogance** *n* arrogance *f*.
arrow ['ærəʊ] **1** *n* flèche *f*. **2** *vt route, direction* flécher; *item on list etc* cocher. ♦ **arrowhead** *n* pointe *f* de flèche.
arsenal ['ɑːsɪnl] *n* arsenal *m*.
arsenic ['ɑːsnɪk] *n* arsenic *m*.
arson ['ɑːsn] *n* incendie *m* volontaire. ♦ **arsonist** *n* incendiaire *mf*.
art [ɑːt] **1** *n* art *m*. **~ for ~'s sake** l'art pour l'art; **to study ~** (*gen*) faire des études d'art; (*Univ*) faire les beaux-arts; **~s and crafts** artisanat *m*; (*Univ*) **Faculty of A~s** faculté *f* des Lettres; **he's doing A~s** il fait des lettres. **2** *adj*: **~ collection** collection *f* de tableaux (*or* d'objets d'art *etc*); **~ exhibition** exposition *f* (de peinture *or* de sculpture); **~ form** moyen *m* d'expression artistique; **~ gallery** (*museum*) musée *m* d'art; (*shop*) galerie *f* (de tableaux *or* d'art); **~ paper** papier couché; **~ school** école *f* des beaux-arts; (*Univ*) **A~s degree** licence *f* ès lettres; **~ student** étudiant(e) *m(f)* des *or* en beaux-arts; **A~s student** étudiant(e) *m(f)* en *or* de Lettres.
♦ **artful** *adj* rusé, astucieux; **he's an ~ful one*** c'est un petit malin*; **~ful dodger** roublard(e)* *m(f)*. ♦ **artfully** *adv* (*cunningly*) astucieusement; (*skilfully*) habilement. ♦ **artfulness** *n* (*cunning*) astuce *f*; (*skill*) habileté *f*. ♦ **artless** *adj* naturel. ♦ **artlessly** *adv* ingénument. ♦ **arty*** *adj person* qui a le genre artiste *or* bohème; *clothes* de style bohème; *decoration, style* (d'un art) apprêté. ♦ **art(s)y-craft(s)y*** *adj* (*pej*) *object, style* exagérément artisanal; *person* qui affiche un genre artiste *or* bohème.
artefact ['ɑːtɪfækt] *n* objet *m* fabriqué.
artery ['ɑːtərɪ] *n* artère *f* (*also fig: road*). ♦ **arterial** *adj* (*Anat*) artériel; **arterial road** route *f* à grande circulation. ♦ **arteriosclerosis** *n* artériosclérose *f*.
artesian [ɑː'tiːzɪən] *adj*: **~ well** puits *m* artésien.
arthritis [ɑː'θraɪtɪs] *n* arthrite *f*. ♦ **arthritic** *adj, n* arthritique (*mf*).
artichoke ['ɑːtɪtʃəʊk] *n* (*globe ~*) artichaut *m*; (*Jerusalem ~*) topinambour *m*.
article ['ɑːtɪkl] *n* (*Admin, Jur, Gram, Press etc*) article *m*; (*Comm*) article, marchandise *f*; (*object*) objet *m*. **~s of clothing** vêtements *mpl*; **~ of food** denrée *f*; **~s of value** objets de valeur.
articulate [ɑː'tɪkjʊlɪt] **1** *adj speech* bien articulé; *person* qui s'exprime bien; *book* clair; (*Anat*) articulé. **2** [ɑː'tɪkjʊleɪt] *vti* articuler. **~d lorry** semi-remorque *m*. ♦ **articulately** *adv* avec facilité. ♦ **articulation** *n* articulation *f*.
artifact ['ɑːtɪfækt] *n* = **artefact**.
artifice ['ɑːtɪfɪs] *n* (*stratagem*) artifice *m*; (*cunning*) adresse *f*.
artificial [ˌɑːtɪ'fɪʃəl] *adj* artificiel (*also fig*). **~ teeth** fausses dents; **it was a very ~ situation** la situation manquait de naturel. ♦ **artificiality** *n* manque *m* de naturel. ♦ **artificially** *adv* artificiellement.
artillery [ɑː'tɪlərɪ] *n* artillerie *f*.
artisan ['ɑːtɪzæn] *n* artisan *m*.
artist ['ɑːtɪst] *n* artiste *mf*. ♦ **artiste** *n* (*Cine, Theat, TV*) artiste *mf*. ♦ **artistic** *adj arrangement, activity, sense* artistique; *temperament* artiste; *person* qui a un sens artistique très développé. ♦ **artistically** *adv* artistiquement, avec art. ♦ **artistry** *n* art *m*, talent *m* artistique.
Aryan ['ɛərɪən] *adj* aryen.

as [æz, əz] **1** *conj* **(a)** (*when, while*) comme, alors que, tandis que, pendant que. **~ she was resting she heard it** tandis qu'elle *or* comme elle se reposait elle l'entendit; **I saw him ~ he came out** je l'ai vu comme *or* au moment où il sortait; **he got deafer ~ he got older** il devenait plus sourd à mesure qu'il vieillissait. **(b)** (*since, because*) comme, puisque. **(c)** (*in comparisons*) **as tall ~** aussi grand que; **not so** *or* **not as tall ~** pas aussi *or* pas si grand que; **as much ~** autant que; **twice as rich ~** deux fois plus riche que; **by day (as well) ~ by night** de jour comme de nuit. **(d)** (*concessive*) **big ~ the box is ...** si grande que soit la boîte ...; **try ~ he would, he couldn't do it** il a eu beau essayer, il n'y est pas arrivé. **(e)** (*manner*) comme. **do ~ you like** faites comme vous voudrez; **M ~ in Marcel** M comme Marcel; **~ usual** comme d'habitude; **~ often happens** comme il arrive souvent; **~ is her brother** comme son frère, ainsi que son frère, de même que son frère; **~ it were** pour ainsi dire; **~ it is, I can't come** les choses étant ce qu'elles sont, je ne peux pas venir; **leave it ~ it is** laisse ça tel quel. **(f)** (*in the capacity of*) comme, en tant que. **sold ~ a slave** vendu comme esclave; **~ a bachelor he ...** en tant que célibataire il ...; **Olivier ~ Hamlet** Olivier dans le rôle de Hamlet. **(g) to treat sb ~ a child** traiter qn comme un enfant *or* en enfant; **to acknowledge sb ~ leader** reconnaître qn pour chef; **such people ~ knew him** les gens qui le connaissaient; **such a book ~ you gave him** un livre comme celui que tu lui as donné; **the same day ~** le même jour que; **a man such ~ he is** un homme tel que lui; **~ if, ~ though** comme (si); **~ if he'd been drinking** comme s'il avait bu; **he rose ~ if to go out** il s'est levé comme pour sortir; **~ for, ~ to, ~ regards** quant à. **(h) so ~ to** + *infin* pour, de façon à, afin de + *infin*. **2** *adv* aussi, si. **~ tall as** aussi grand que; **not ~ tall as** pas si *or* pas aussi grand que.
asbestos [æz'bestəs] *n* amiante *f*. **~ mat** plaque *f* d'amiante. ♦ **asbestosis** *n* asbestose *f*.
ascend [ə'send] **1** *vi* monter, (*esp Rel*) s'élever (*to* à, jusqu'à). **2** *vt ladder* monter à; *mountain* gravir, faire l'ascension de; *river* remonter; *staircase* monter; *throne* monter sur. ♦ **ascendancy** *n* ascendant *m* (*over* sur). ♦ **ascendant** *adj, n* ascendant (*m*). ♦ **ascension** *n* ascension *f*. ♦ **ascent** *n* ascension *f*, (*in rank*) montée *f*.
ascertain [ˌæsə'teɪn] *vt* s'assurer, vérifier (*that* que); *truth, what happened* établir; *sb's age, name, address etc* vérifier.
ascetic [ə'setɪk] **1** *adj* ascétique. **2** *n* ascète *mf*. ♦ **asceticism** *n* ascétisme *m*.
ascribe [ə'skraɪb] *vt virtue, work* attribuer (*to* à); *fault* imputer (*to* à).
aseptic [eɪ'septɪk] *adj* aseptique.
asexual [eɪ'seksjʊəl] *adj* asexué.
ash[1] [æʃ] *n* (*~ tree*) frêne *m*.
ash[2] [æʃ] **1** *n* cendre *f*. **~es to ~es, dust to dust** tu es poussière et tu retourneras en poussière. **2** *adj*: **~ blond(e)** blond cendré *inv*; **A~ Wednesday** mercredi *m* des Cendres. ♦ **ashcan** *n* boîte *f* à ordures, poubelle *f*. ♦ **ashen** *adj face* terreux. ♦ **ashtray** *n* cendrier *m*.
ashamed [ə'ʃeɪmd] *adj* honteux, confus. **to be** *or* **feel ~ (of o.s.)** avoir honte; **to be ~ of** avoir honte de; **I am ~ to say** à ma honte je dois dire.
ashore [ə'ʃɔːʳ] *adv* à terre. **to go ~** descendre à terre; **to put sb ~** débarquer qn.
Asia ['eɪʃə] *n* Asie *f*. ♦ **Asian** *or* ♦ **Asiatic** **1** *adj* asiatique; **2** *n* Asiatique *mf*.
aside [ə'saɪd] **1** *adv* de côté, à l'écart, à part. **to put sth ~** mettre qch de côté; **to take sb ~** prendre qn à part; **joking ~** plaisanterie *or* blague* à part; **~ from** à part. **2** *n* (*esp Theat*) aparté *m*. **in an ~** en aparté.
asinine ['æsɪnaɪn] *adj* stupide, idiot.
ask [ɑːsk] **1** *vt* **(a)** (*inquire*) demander (*sb sth* qch

à qn). **to ~ sb about sth** interroger qn *or* poser des questions à qn au sujet de qch; **to ~ (sb) a question** poser une question (à qn); **~ him if he has seen her** demande-lui s'il l'a vue; **don't ~ me!*** allez savoir!*; **I ~ you!*** je vous demande un peu!* **(b)** (*request*) demander (*sb to do* à qn de faire; *that sth be done* que qch soit fait; *sb for sth* qch à qn). **to ~ sb a favour** demander une faveur à qn; **he ~ed to go on the picnic** il a demandé s'il pouvait se joindre au pique-nique; **that's ~ing a lot!** c'est beaucoup en demander!; (*Comm*) **he is ~ing £50,000 for the house** il demande 50 000 livres *or* veut 50 000 livres pour la maison; **~ing price** prix *m* de départ. **(c)** (*invite*) inviter (*sb to sth* qn à qch; *sb to do* qn à faire). **to ~ sb in/out** *etc* inviter qn à entrer/sortir *etc*.

2 *vi* demander. **to ~ about sth** s'informer de qch, se renseigner sur qch; **it's there for the ~ing** il suffit de le demander (pour l'obtenir).

ask after *vt fus person* demander des nouvelles de; *sb's health* s'informer de.

ask along *vt sep* inviter.

ask back *vt sep* (*for a second visit*) réinviter; (*on reciprocal visit*) rendre son invitation à.

ask for *vt fus help, permission, money* demander; *person* demander à voir. **he ~ed for his pen back** il a demandé qu'on lui rende son stylo; **they are ~ing for trouble*** ils cherchent les ennuis *or* les embêtements*; **she was ~ing for it!*** elle l'a bien cherché!*

askance [əˈskɑːns] *adv*: **to look ~ at** (*sideways*) regarder de côté; (*suspiciously etc*) *person* regarder d'un air soupçonneux; *sb's hat/work etc* regarder d'un œil désapprobateur; *suggestion* se formaliser de.

askew [əˈskjuː] *adv* de travers.

asleep [əˈsliːp] *adj* endormi. **to be ~** dormir, être endormi; **to be fast *or* sound ~** dormir profondément *or* à poings fermés; **my finger is ~** j'ai le doigt engourdi; **to fall ~** s'endormir.

asparagus [əsˈpærəgəs] *n* (*Bot*) asperge *f*; (*Culin*) asperges. **~ fern** asparagus *m*; **~ tips** pointes *fpl* d'asperges.

aspect [ˈæspekt] *n* **(a)** (*gen; also Gram*) aspect *m*. **to study every ~ of a question** étudier une question sous tous ses aspects; **seen from this ~** vu sous cet angle. **(b)** *[building etc]* exposition *f*. **house with a southerly ~** maison exposée au midi.

asperity [æsˈperɪtɪ] *n* rudesse *f*.

aspersion [əsˈpɜːʃən] *n* calomnie *f*. **to cast ~s on sth/sb** dénigrer qch/qn.

asphalt [ˈæsfælt] **1** *n* asphalte *m*. **2** *vt* asphalter. **3** *adj* asphalté.

asphyxia [æsˈfɪksɪə] *n* asphyxie *f*. ♦ **asphyxiate 1** *vt* asphyxier; **2** *vi* s'asphyxier. ♦ **asphyxiation** *n* asphyxie *f*.

aspic [ˈæspɪk] *n*: **chicken in ~** aspic *m* de volaille.

aspidistra [ˌæspɪˈdɪstrə] *n* aspidistra *m*.

aspirate [ˈæspərɪt] **1** *n* aspirée *f*. **2** *adj* aspiré.

aspire [əsˈpaɪəʳ] *vi* aspirer (*to sth* à qch; *to do* à faire). **we can't ~ to that** nos prétentions ne vont pas jusque-là. ♦ **aspiration** *n* aspiration *f*. ♦ **aspiring** *adj* ambitieux.

aspirin [ˈæsprɪn] *n* aspirine *f*.

ass [æs] *n* (*Zool*) âne *m*; (*fool*) idiot(e) *m(f)*, imbécile *mf*. **to make an ~ of o.s.** se rendre ridicule; **don't be an ~!** (*action*) ne fais pas l'imbécile!; (*speech*) ne dis pas de sottises!

assail [əˈseɪl] *vt* assaillir (*with* de). ♦ **assailant** *n* agresseur *m*.

assassin [əˈsæsɪn] *n* assassin *m* (*Pol etc*). ♦ **assassinate** *vt* assassiner. ♦ **assassination** *n* assassinat *m*.

assault [əˈsɔːlt] **1** *n* (*Mil*) assaut *m* (*on* de); (*Jur*) agression *f*. **the ~ on the man** l'agression dont l'homme a été victime; **~ and battery** coups *mpl* et blessures *fpl*. **2** *vt* (*Jur*) agresser; (*sexually*) violenter; (*Mil*) donner l'assaut à. **3** *adj*: (*Mil*) **~ course** parcours *m* du combattant.

assemble [əˈsembl] **1** *vt objects, ideas* assembler; *people* rassembler; (*Tech*) *machine* monter. **2** *vi* s'assembler; se rassembler; se monter. ♦ **assemblage** *n [things]* collection *f*; *[people]* assemblée *f*. ♦ **assembly 1** *n* **(a)** (*meeting*) assemblée *f*; (*Scol*) rassemblement *m* des élèves; **in open assembly** en séance publique; **the general assembly of the U.N.** l'assemblée générale de l'ONU; **(b)** (*Tech*) montage *m*; **the engine assembly** le bloc moteur; **2** *adj*: **assembly line** chaîne *f* de montage.

assent [əˈsent] **1** *n* assentiment *m*. **2** *vi* donner son assentiment (*to* à).

assert [əˈsɜːt] *vt* affirmer, soutenir (*that* que); *one's innocence* protester de; *claim* défendre; *one's rights* faire valoir. ♦ **assertion** *n* affirmation *f*, assertion *f*. ♦ **assertive** *adj* assuré.

assess [əˈses] *vt* (*gen*) estimer, évaluer; *payment, damages, tax* déterminer le montant de; *rateable property* calculer la valeur imposable de; *situation, time, amount* évaluer; *candidate* juger (la valeur de). ♦ **assessment** *n* estimation *f*; évaluation *f*; détermination *f* (du montant); calcul *m* (de la valeur imposable); jugement *m* (*of* sur); (*Scol, Univ*) **continuous ~ment** contrôle *m* continu. ♦ **assessor** *n [property]* expert *m*; (*US*) **~or of taxes** contrôleur *m* des contributions directes.

asset [ˈæset] **1** *n*: **~s** (*Fin*) actif *m*; (*gen*) biens *mpl*; **~s and liabilities** actif et passif *m*; (*fig*) **his greatest ~** son meilleur atout. **2** *adj*: **~-stripping** cannibalisation *f* (d'une compagnie).

assiduous [əˈsɪdjʊəs] *adj* assidu. ♦ **assiduity** *n* assiduité *f*. ♦ **assiduously** *adv* assidûment.

assign [əˈsaɪn] *vt task, office, date* assigner (*to* à); *meaning* attribuer (*to* à); *employee* affecter (*to* à); (*Jur*) *property, right* céder (*to sb* à qn). ♦ **assignation** *n* (*appointment*) rendez-vous *m inv*. ♦ **assignment** *n* (*task*) mission *f*.

assimilate [əˈsɪmɪleɪt] *vt* assimiler (*to* à). ♦ **assimilation** *n* assimilation *f*.

assist [əˈsɪst] **1** *vt* aider, assister (*to do, in doing* à faire). **to ~ sb in/out** *etc* aider qn à entrer/sortir *etc*; **~ed by** avec le concours de; (*Travel*) **~ed passage** billet subventionné. **2** *vi* aider, prêter secours (*in* à). ♦ **assistance** *n* assistance *f*; **to come to sb's ~ance** venir à l'aide de qn; **can I be of ~ance?** puis-je vous aider? ♦ **assistant 1** *n* aide *mf*, auxiliaire *mf*; (*Scol, US Univ*) assistant(e) *m(f)*; **2** *adj* adjoint; **~ant librarian** bibliothécaire *mf* adjoint(e); (*Scol*) **~ant master *or* mistress** professeur *m* (*de lycée etc*); *[primary school]* instituteur *m*, -trice *f*.

assizes [əˈsaɪzɪz] *npl* (*Jur*) assises *fpl*.

associate [əˈsəʊʃɪɪt] **1** *adj* associé, allié. **2** *n* **(a)** associé(e) *m(f)*, collègue *mf*; (*accomplice*) complice *mf*. **(b)** *[a society]* associé *m*; *[learned body]* (membre *m*) correspondant *m*. **3** [əˈsəʊʃɪeɪt] *vt* associer (*with* avec). (*in undertaking etc*) **to be ~ed with sth** être associé à qch; **I should like to ~ myself with what has been said** je voudrais me faire l'écho de cette opinion; **I don't wish to be ~d with it** je préfère que mon nom ne soit pas mêlé à ceci. **4** *vi*: **to ~ with sb** fréquenter qn. ♦ **association** [əˌsəʊsɪˈeɪʃən] **1** *n* (*most senses*) association *f*; **full of historic associations** riche en souvenirs historiques; **2** *adj*: **association football** football *m* (association).

assorted [əˈsɔːtɪd] *adj* assorti. **well-/ill-~** bien/mal assortis; **in ~ sizes** de différentes tailles. ♦ **assortment** *n [objects]* assortiment *m*; **this shop has a good assortment** ce magasin a un grand choix; **an assortment of people** des gens (très) divers.

assuage [əˈsweɪdʒ] *vt* calmer.

assume [əˈsjuːm] *vt* **(a)** (*suppose*) supposer, présumer, admettre. **let us ~ that** admettons *or* supposons que + *subj*; **you resigned, I ~** vous avez démissionné, je suppose *or* présume; **you are assuming a lot** vous faites bien des suppositions. **(b)** (*take*) (*gen*) prendre; *responsibility, burden, role* assumer; *title, right, authority* s'approprier; *name, air, attitude* adopter; *innocence, indifference* affecter un air de. **to ~ control of** prendre en main la direction de; **under an ~d name** sous un nom d'emprunt. ♦ **assumption** *n* **(a)** (*supposition*) supposition *f*, hypothèse *f*; **on the assumption that** en supposant que + *subj*; **to go on the assumption that** présumer que; **(b)** *[power etc]* appropriation *f*; *[indifference]* affectation *f*; (*Rel*) **A~** Assomption *f*.

assure [əˈʃʊəʳ] *vt* (*all senses*) assurer (*sb of sth* qn de qch). ♦ **assurance** *n* (*all senses*) assurance *f*; **in the assurance that** avec l'assurance que; **you have my assurance that** je vous promets formellement que. ♦ **assuredly** *adv* assurément.

aster [ˈæstəʳ] *n* aster *m*.

asterisk [ˈæstərɪsk] *n* astérisque *m*.

astern [əˈstɜːn] *adv* (*Naut*) à *or* sur l'arrière.

asteroid [ˈæstərɔɪd] *n* astéroïde *m*.

asthma [ˈæsmə] *n* asthme *m*. ♦ **asthmatic** *adj* asthmatique.

astigmatism [æsˈtɪgmətɪzəm] *n* astigmatisme *m*. ♦ **astigmatic** *adj* astigmate.

astonish [əˈstɒnɪʃ] *vt* étonner; (*stronger*) ahurir. **you ~ me!** non! pas possible! ♦ **astonished** *adj* étonné; ahuri; **I am ~ed that** cela m'étonne *or* m'ahurit que + *subj*. ♦ **astonishing** *adj* étonnant; ahurissant. ♦ **astonishingly** *adv* incroyablement. ♦ **astonishment** *n* étonnement *m*; ahurissement *m*; **look of ~ment** regard stupéfait; **to my ~ment** à mon grand étonnement.

astound [əˈstaʊnd] *vt* stupéfier, abasourdir. ♦ **astounded** *adj* abasourdi, sidéré*. ♦ **astounding** *adj* stupéfiant, ahurissant.

astrakhan [ˌæstrəˈkæn] *n* astrakan *m*.

astray [əˈstreɪ] *adv*: **to go ~** s'égarer; **to lead sb ~** détourner qn du droit chemin.

astride [əˈstraɪd] **1** *adv* à califourchon, à cheval. **2** *prep* à califourchon *or* à cheval sur.

astringent [əsˈtrɪndʒənt] **1** *adj* astringent; (*fig*) dur. **2** *n* astringent *m*.

astrology [əsˈtrɒlədʒɪ] *n* astrologie *f*. ♦ **astrologer** *n* astrologue *m*. ♦ **astrological** *adj* astrologique.

astronaut [ˈæstrənɔːt] *n* astronaute *mf*.

astronomy [əsˈtrɒnəmɪ] *n* astronomie *f*. ♦ **astronomer** *n* astronome *m*. ♦ **astronomic(al)** *adj* (*lit, fig*) astronomique.

astrophysics [ˈæstrəʊˈfɪzɪks] *nsg* astrophysique *f*.

astute [əsˈtjuːt] *adj* fin, astucieux. ♦ **astutely** *adv* avec finesse, astucieusement. ♦ **astuteness** *n* finesse *f*, astuce *f*.

asylum [əˈsaɪləm] *n* asile *m*.

at [æt] *prep* **(a)** (*place*) à. **~ the table** à la table; **~ my brother's** chez mon frère; **~ home** à la maison, chez soi; **to dry o.s. ~ the fire** se sécher devant le feu; **to stand ~ the window** se tenir à *or* devant la fenêtre. **(b)** (*time*) à. **~ 10 o'clock** à 10 heures; **3 ~ a time** 3 par 3, 3 à la fois, (*stairs*) 3 à 3; **~ a time like this** à un moment pareil; **~ my time of life** à mon âge. **(c)** (*activity*) **to play ~ football** jouer au football; **while we are ~ it*** pendant que nous y sommes; **let me see you ~ it again!*** que je t'y reprenne!; **they are ~ it all day*** ils font ça toute la journée; **she was (on) ~ her husband to buy a new car*** elle a harcelé son mari pour qu'il achète (*subj*) une nouvelle voiture; **he's always (on) ~ me*** il est toujours après moi*; **good ~ languages** bon en langues; **~ war** en guerre. **(d)** (*manner*) **~ full speed** à toute allure; **~ 80 km/h** à 80 km/h; **he drove ~ 80 km/h** il faisait du 80 (à l'heure). **(e)** (*cause*) **surprised ~** étonné de; **annoyed ~** contrarié par; **angry ~** en colère contre. **(f)** (*rate, value, degree*) à, dans, en. **he sells them ~ 2 francs a kilo** il les vend 2 F le kilo; **let's leave it ~ that** restons-en là!; **~ a stroke** d'un seul coup; **he's only a teacher and a poor one ~ that** ce n'est qu'un professeur et encore assez piètre. ♦ **at-home** *n* réception *f* (*chez soi*).

ate [et, (*US*) eɪt] *pret of* **eat.**

atheism [ˈeɪθɪɪzəm] *n* athéisme *m*. ♦ **atheist** *n* athée *mf*. ♦ **atheistic(al)** *adj* athée.

Athens [ˈæθɪnz] *n* Athènes.

athlete [ˈæθliːt] *n* (*in competitions*) athlète *mf*. (*gen*) **he's a fine ~** il est très sportif; (*Med*) **~'s foot** mycose *f*. ♦ **athletic** [æθˈletɪk] *adj activity* athlétique; *meeting* sportif, d'athlétisme; *person* (*sporty*) sportif; (*muscular*) athlétique. ♦ **athletics** *nsg* (*Brit*) athlétisme *m*; (*US*) sport *m*.

Atlantic [ətˈlæntɪk] *adj winds, currents* de l'Atlantique. **the ~ (Ocean)** l'Atlantique *m*, l'océan *m* Atlantique; **~ liner** translantique *m*.

atlas [ˈætləs] *n* atlas *m*.

atmosphere [ˈætməsfɪəʳ] *n* atmosphère *f*. ♦ **atmospheric** [ˌætməsˈferɪk] *adj* atmosphérique. ♦ **atmospherics** *nsg* (*Telec*) parasites *mpl*.

atom [ˈætəm] **1** *n* atome *m*. (*fig*) **smashed to ~s** réduit en miettes; **not an ~ of truth** pas un grain de vérité. **2** *adj*: **~ bomb** *n* bombe *f* atomique. ♦ **atomic** *adj* atomique. ♦ **atomize** *vt* atomiser. ♦ **atomizer** *n* atomiseur *m*.

atone [əˈtəʊn] *vi*: **to ~ for** *sin* expier; *mistake* réparer. ♦ **atonement** *n* expiation *f* (*Rel*); réparation *f*.

atrocious [əˈtrəʊʃəs] *adj* atroce. ♦ **atrociously** *adv* atrocement. ♦ **atrocity** [əˈtrɒsɪtɪ] *n* atrocité *f*.

atrophy [ˈætrəfɪ] **1** *n* atrophie *f*. **2** *vi* s'atrophier. **3** *vt* atrophier.

attach [əˈtætʃ] *vt* (*gen*) attacher (*to* à); *document* joindre (*to* à); *troops* affecter (*to* à); *employee* attacher (*to* à). **the ~ed letter** la lettre ci-jointe; **to ~ credence to** ajouter foi à; **to ~ o.s. to a group** se joindre à un groupe; (*fond of*) **to be ~ed to sb/sth** être attaché à qn/qch; **he's ~ed*** (*married etc*) il n'est pas libre. ♦ **attaché** [əˈtæʃeɪ] *n* attaché(e) *m(f)*; **~é case** mallette *f*, attaché-case *m*. ♦ **attachment** *n* (*for tool etc: accessory*) accessoire *m*; (*affection*) attachement *m* (*to* à); (*temporary transfer*) stage *m* (*to* chez).

attack [əˈtæk] **1** *n* **(a)** (*gen, also Mil*) attaque *f* (*on* contre). **to return to the ~** revenir à la charge; **~ on sb's life** attentat *m* contre qn; **to leave o.s. open to ~** prêter le flanc à la critique; **to be under ~** (*Mil*) être attaqué (*from* par); (*fig*) être en butte aux attaques (*from* de). **(b)** (*Med*) crise *f*. **~ of fever** accès *m* de fièvre; **an ~ of migraine** une migraine. **2** *vt person, enemy* attaquer; *task, problem* s'attaquer à; (*Chem*) *metal* attaquer. ♦ **attacker** *n* attaquant *m*, agresseur *m*.

attain [əˈteɪn] *vti* **(a)** *aim, rank, age* atteindre, parvenir à. **(b)** (*also* **~ to**) *knowledge* acquérir; *happiness* atteindre à; *perfection etc* toucher à; *power, prosperity* parvenir à. ♦ **attainable** *adj* accessible (*by* à), à la portée (*by* de). ♦ **attainment** *n* réussite *f*, résultat *m* obtenu.

attempt [əˈtempt] **1** *vt* essayer, tenter (*to do* de faire); *task* entreprendre. **~ed escape/murder** *etc* tentative *f* d'évasion/de meurtre *etc*; **to ~ suicide** tenter de se suicider. **2** *n* tentative *f* (*at sth* de qch), effort *m*; (*unsuccessful*) essai *m*. **first ~** coup *m* d'essai; **to make an ~ at doing** essayer de faire; **to be successful at the first ~** réussir du premier coup; **to make an ~ on the record** essayer de battre le record; **it was a good ~ on his part** il a vraiment essayé; **~ on sb's life** attentat *m* contre qn.

attend [əˈtend] **1** *vt* **(a)** *meeting, lecture* assister à; *classes, course* suivre; *church, school* aller à. **the meeting was well ~ed** il y avait beaucoup de monde à la réunion. **(b)** *[lady-in-waiting]* accompagner; *[doctor]* soigner. **method ~ed by great risks** méthode qui comporte de grands risques.

2 *vi* (*pay attention*) faire attention (*to* à); (*be present*) être présent *or* là.
attend to *vt fus speech, lesson* écouter attentivement; *advice* prêter attention à; *business, customer* s'occuper de.
♦ **attendance** 1 *n* (*being present*) présence *f*; (*number of people present*) assistance *f*; **he was in ~ance on the queen** il escortait la reine; **to be in ~ance** être de service; (*Med*) **~ance on a patient** visites *fpl* à un malade. 2 *adj*: (*Scol*) **~ance officer** ≈ inspecteur *m* (chargé de faire respecter l'obligation scolaire). ♦ **attendant** 1 *n [museum etc]* gardien(ne) *m(f)*; (*servant*) serviteur *m*; **the prince and his ~ants** le prince et sa suite. 2 *adj* qui accompagne (qch); **old age and its ~ant ills** la vieillesse et les infirmités qui l'accompagnent.
attention [əˈtenʃən] 1 *n* attention *f*. **to pay ~ to** faire attention à; **to call (sb's) ~ to sth** attirer l'attention (de qn) sur qch; **it has come to my ~ that** je me suis aperçu que; **for the ~ of** à l'attention de; **it needs daily ~** il faut s'en occuper tous les jours; (*kindness*) **~s** attentions *fpl*; (*Mil*) **~!** garde-à-vous!; **to stand at/come to ~** être/se mettre au garde-à-vous; **to jump** *or* **spring to ~** se mettre vivement au garde-à-vous.
2 *adj*: **his ~ span is too short** il ne peut pas se concentrer assez longtemps.
♦ **attention-seeking** *adj* cherchant à se faire remarquer. ♦ **attentive** *adj* prévenant (*to sb* envers qn); soucieux (*to sth* de qch); *audience, spectator* attentif; **attentive to sb's advice** attentif aux conseils de qn. ♦ **attentively** *adv* attentivement. ♦ **attentiveness** *n* attention *f*.
attenuate [əˈtenjʊeɪt] *vt* atténuer.
attest [əˈtest] *vt* attester. ♦ **attestation** *n* attestation *f* (*that* que).
attic [ˈætɪk] *n* grenier *m*. **~ room** mansarde *f*.
attire [əˈtaɪəʳ] 1 *vt* vêtir (*in* de). 2 *n* vêtements *mpl*.
attitude [ˈætɪtjuːd] *n* attitude *f* (*towards* envers, à l'égard de). **~ of mind** état *m* d'esprit; **if that's your ~** si c'est ainsi que vous le prenez. ♦ **attitudinize** *vi* se donner des attitudes.
attorney [əˈtɜːnɪ] *n* mandataire *m*; (*US: lawyer*) avoué *m*. **A~ General** (*Brit*) ≈ Procureur Général; (*US*) ≈ Ministre *m* de la Justice.
attract [əˈtrækt] *vt* attirer. ♦ **attraction** *n [magnet]* attraction *f*; *[plan]* attrait *m*; *[person, place]* attraits, charmes *mpl*. ♦ **attractive** *adj person, manner* attrayant, attirant; *price, idea, offer* attrayant, intéressant. ♦ **attractively** *adv* d'une manière attrayante; **~ively dressed woman** femme élégamment habillée.
attribute [əˈtrɪbjuːt] 1 *vt* attribuer (*to* à). 2 [ˈætrɪbjuːt] *n* attribut *m*; (*Gram*) épithète *f*. ♦ **attributable** *adj* attribuable (*to* à). ♦ **attribution** *n* attribution *f*. ♦ **attributive** 1 *adj* attributif; (*Gram*) qualificatif; 2 *n* attribut *m*; (*Gram*) épithète *f*.
attrition [əˈtrɪʃən] *n* usure *f* (*par frottement*). **war of ~** guerre *f* d'usure.
attuned [əˈtjuːnd] *adj*: **~ to** *person* habitué à; *methods, tastes* en accord avec.
aubergine [ˈəʊbəʒiːn] *n* aubergine *f*.
auburn [ˈɔːbən] *adj* auburn *inv*.
auction [ˈɔːkʃən] 1 *n* (vente *f* aux) enchères *fpl*. 2 *vt* vendre aux enchères. 3 *adj*: **~ bridge** bridge *m* aux enchères; **~ room** salle *f* des ventes; **~ sale** (vente *f* aux) enchères *fpl*. ♦ **auctioneer** *n* commissaire-priseur *m*.
audacious [ɔːˈdeɪʃəs] *adj* audacieux. ♦ **audacity** *n* audace *f*.
audible [ˈɔːdɪbl] *adj sound* audible, perceptible; *voice* distinct. **she was hardly ~** on l'entendait à peine; **there was ~ laughter** des rires se firent entendre. ♦ **audibility** *n* audibilité *f*. ♦ **audibly** *adv* distinctement.
audience [ˈɔːdɪəns] 1 *n* **(a)** (*Theat*) spectateurs *mpl*, public *m*; *[speaker]* auditoire *m*; (*Mus, Rad*) auditeurs *mpl*; (*TV*) téléspectateurs *mpl*. **the whole ~ applauded** toute la salle a applaudi; **those in the ~** les gens dans la salle. **(b)** (*formal interview*) audience *f*. 2 *adj*: **~ participation** participation *f* de l'assistance (*à ce qui se passe sur scène*); (*Rad, TV*) **~ rating** indice *m* d'audience; **~ research** études *fpl* d'opinion.
audio-visual [ˌɔːdɪəʊˈvɪzjʊəl] *adj* audio-visuel. **~ aids** (support *m*) audio-visuel *m*.
audit [ˈɔːdɪt] 1 *n* vérification *f* des comptes. 2 *vt accounts* vérifier; (*US Univ*) *lecture course* assister comme auditeur libre à. ♦ **auditor** *n* expert-comptable *m*, vérificateur *m* (de comptes).
audition [ɔːˈdɪʃən] 1 *n* audition *f*. 2 *vti* auditionner (*for a part* pour un rôle).
auditorium [ˌɔːdɪˈtɔːrɪəm] *n* salle *f*.
aught [ɔːt] *n*: **for ~ I know** (pour) autant que je sache; **for ~ I care** pour ce que cela me fait.
augment [ɔːgˈment] *vti* augmenter (*by* de). ♦ **augmentation** *n* augmentation *f*.
augur [ˈɔːgəʳ] 1 *vi*: **to ~ well/ill** être de bon/de mauvais augure (*for* pour). 2 *vt* présager. ♦ **augury** *n* augure *m*.
August [ˈɔːgəst] *n* août *m*; *for phrases V* **September.**
august [ɔːˈgʌst] *adj* auguste.
auk [ɔːk] *n* pingouin *m*.
aunt [ɑːnt] *n* tante *f*. **yes ~** oui, ma tante; **A~ Sally** (*game*) jeu *m* de massacre; (*person*) tête *f* de Turc. ♦ **auntie*, aunty*** *n* tata* *f*.
au pair [ˈəʊˈpɛə] 1 *adj, adv* au pair. 2 *n* jeune fille *f* au pair.
aura [ˈɔːrə] *n* (*lit*) aura *f*; (*fig: of place*) atmosphère *f*. **he has an ~ of** il donne une impression de.
aurora borealis [ɔːˈrɔːrəbɔːrɪˈeɪlɪs] *n* aurore *f* boréale.
auspices [ˈɔːspɪsɪz] *npl*: **under the ~ of** sous les auspices *mpl* de. ♦ **auspicious** [ɔːsˈpɪʃəs] *adj sign* de bon augure; *occasion* propice; *start* bon. ♦ **auspiciously** *adv* sous d'heureux auspices; *start* bien.
Aussie* [ˈɒzɪ] = **Australian.**
austere [ɒsˈtɪəʳ] *adj* austère. ♦ **austerely** *adv* avec austérité. ♦ **austerity** *n* austérité *f*; **years of austerity** années *fpl* de restrictions.
Australasia [ˌɔːstrəˈleɪsjə] *n* Australasie *f*.
Australia [ɒsˈtreɪlɪə] *n* Australie *f*. ♦ **Australian** 1 *n* Australien(ne) *m(f)*; 2 *adj* australien.
Austria [ˈɒstrɪə] *n* Autriche *f*. ♦ **Austrian** 1 *n* Autrichien(ne) *m(f)*; 2 *adj* autrichien.
authentic [ɔːˈθentɪk] *adj* authentique. ♦ **authenticate** *vt* établir l'authenticité de. ♦ **authenticity** *n* authenticité *f*.
author [ˈɔːθəʳ] *n* auteur *m*. ♦ **authoress** *n* femme *f* auteur.
authority [ɔːˈθɒrɪtɪ] *n* (*power*) autorité *f*; (*permission*) autorisation *f*. **I'm in ~ here** c'est moi qui commande ici; **to be in ~ over sb** avoir autorité sur qn; **those in ~** ceux qui nous gouvernent; **he did it without ~, he had no ~ to do it** il l'a fait sans autorisation; **he has no ~ to do it** il n'a pas le droit de le faire; **on her own ~** de sa propre autorité; **the proper authorities** les autorités compétentes; **the health authorities** les services *mpl* de la santé publique; *[person, book]* **to be an ~** faire autorité (*on* en matière de); **I have it on good ~ that ...** je sais de source sûre que ... . ♦ **authoritarian** *adj* autoritaire. ♦ **authoritative** *adj opinion, source* autorisé; *person* autoritaire; *treatise, edition* qui fait autorité. ♦ **authorization** *n* autorisation *f* (*of*, *for* pour; *to do* de faire). ♦ **authorize** *vt* autoriser (*sb to do* qn à faire); **the Authorized Version** la Bible de 1611.
autism [ˈɔːtɪzəm] *n* autisme *m*. ♦ **autistic** *adj* autistique.

auto ['ɔːtəʊ] *n* (*US*) auto *f*. ♦ **autocade** *n* cortège *m* d'automobiles.
autobiography [ˌɔːtəʊbaɪ'ɒgrəfɪ] *n* autobiographie *f*. ♦ **autobiographic(al)** *adj* autobiographique.
autocrat ['ɔːtəʊkræt] *n* autocrate *m*. ♦ **autocratic** *adj* autocratique.
autocue ['ɔːtəʊkjuː] *n* autocue *m or f*.
autocycle ['ɔːtəʊsaɪkl] *n* cyclomoteur *m*; (*bigger*) vélomoteur *m*.
autograph ['ɔːtəgrɑːf] **1** *n* autographe *m*. **2** *adj*: ~ **album** album *m* d'autographes; ~ **hunter** collectionneur *m*, -euse *f* d'autographes. **3** *vt* dédicacer.
automat ['ɔːtəmæt] *n* cafétéria *f* à distributeurs automatiques.
automatic [ˌɔːtə'mætɪk] **1** *adj* automatique. **on** ~ **pilot** en pilotage automatique. **2** *n* (*gun*) automatique *m*; (*car*) voiture *f* (à transmission) automatique. ♦ **automatically** *adv* automatiquement. ♦ **automation** *n* automatisation *f*. ♦ **automaton** [ɔː'tɒmətən] *n*, *pl* **-ta** automate *m*.
automobile ['ɔːtəməbiːl] *n* automobile *f*, auto *f*.
automotive [ˌɔːtə'məʊtɪv] *adj* (*Aut*) (de l')automobile; (*self-propelled*) automoteur.
autonomy [ɔː'tɒnəmɪ] *n* autonomie *f*. ♦ **autonomous** *adj* autonome.
autopsy ['ɔːtɒpsɪ] *n* autopsie *f*.
autosuggestion ['ɔːtəʊsə'dʒestʃən] *n* autosuggestion *f*.
autumn ['ɔːtəm] **1** *n* automne *m*. **in** ~ en automne. **2** *adj* d'automne. ~ **leaves** feuilles mortes. ♦ **autumnal** *adj* d'automne.
auxiliary [ɔːg'zɪlɪərɪ] **1** *adj* auxiliaire. **2** *n* (*person*) auxiliaire *mf*; (*verb*) auxiliaire *m*.
avail [ə'veɪl] **1** *vt*: **to** ~ **o.s. of** *opportunity* profiter de; *right* user de; *service* utiliser. **2** *n*: **to no** ~ sans résultat; **it is of no** ~ cela ne sert à rien. ♦ **availability** *n* disponibilité *f*. ♦ **available** *adj* disponible; **to make sth** ~**able to sb** mettre qch à la disposition de qn; **every** ~**able means** tous les moyens possibles; **he is not** ~**able just now** il n'est pas libre en ce moment; **he is not** ~**able for comment** il se refuse à toute déclaration.
avalanche ['ævəlɑːnʃ] **1** *n* avalanche *f*. **2** *adj* *precautions* anti-avalanche *inv*; *warning* aux avalanches.
avant-garde ['ævɑ̃ŋ'gɑːd] **1** *n* avant-garde *f*. **2** *adj* d'avant-garde.
avarice ['ævərɪs] *n* avarice *f*. ♦ **avaricious** *adj* avare.
avenge [ə'vendʒ] *vt* venger. **to** ~ **o.s. on** se venger de. ♦ **avenger** *n* vengeur *m*. ♦ **avenging** *adj* vengeur (*f* -geresse).
avenue ['ævənjuː] *n* avenue *f*; (*fig*) route *f*.
aver [ə'vɜːʳ] *vt* déclarer.
average ['ævərɪdʒ] **1** *n* moyenne *f*. **on** ~ en moyenne; **above/below** ~ au-dessus/en-dessous de la moyenne. **2** *adj* moyen. **3** *vt* (*find the* ~ *of*) établir *or* faire la moyenne de; (*reach an* ~ *of*) atteindre la moyenne de. **we** ~ **8 hours' work** *or* **our working hours** ~ **(out at) 8 per day** nous travaillons en moyenne 8 heures par jour; **the sales** ~ **200 copies a month** la vente moyenne est de 200 exemplaires par mois; (*Aut*) **we** ~**d 50 the whole way** nous avons fait (du) 50 de moyenne pendant tout le trajet.
averse [ə'vɜːs] *adj* opposé (*to* à). **to be** ~ **to doing** répugner à *or* (*less formal*) avoir horreur de faire; **I am not** ~ **to an occasional drink** je ne refuse pas un verre de temps en temps. ♦ **aversion** *n* aversion *f*, répugnance *f*. **to take an aversion to** se mettre à détester; **my greatest** *or* **pet aversion** ce que je déteste le plus.
avert [ə'vɜːt] *vt* *danger, accident* prévenir, éviter; *blow, eyes, thoughts* détourner (*from* de).
aviary ['eɪvɪərɪ] *n* volière *f*.
aviation [ˌeɪvɪ'eɪʃən] *n* aviation *f*. ~ **fuel** kérosène *m*; ~ **industry** aéronautique *f*. ♦ **aviator** *n* aviateur *m*, -trice *f*.
avid ['ævɪd] *adj* avide (*for* de). ♦ **avidity** *n* avidité *f*. ♦ **avidly** *adv* avidement.
avocado [ˌævə'kɑːdəʊ] *n*: ~ **(pear)** avocat *m* (*fruit*).
avoid [ə'vɔɪd] *vt* (*gen*) éviter (*doing* de faire). **to** ~ **tax** (*legally*) se soustraire à l'impôt; (*illegally*) frauder le fisc; ~ **being seen** évitez qu'on ne vous voie; **to** ~ **sb's eye** fuir le regard de qn; **to** ~ **notice** échapper aux regards; **I can't** ~ **going now** je ne peux plus me dispenser d'y aller; ~ **it like the plague** il faut fuir cela comme la peste. ♦ **avoidable** *adj* évitable. ♦ **avoidance** *n*: **his** ~**ance of me** le soin qu'il met à m'éviter; **tax** ~**ance** fraude *f* fiscale.
avoirdupois [ˌævədə'pɔɪz] *n* poids commercial; (*: *overweight*) embonpoint *m*.
avow [ə'vaʊ] *vt* avouer. **he is an** ~**ed atheist** il avoue être athée; ~**ed enemy** ennemi déclaré. ♦ **avowal** *n* aveu *m*. ♦ **avowedly** *adv* de son propre aveu.
await [ə'weɪt] *vt* attendre. **long-**~**ed** longtemps attendu.
awake [ə'weɪk] *pret* **awoke** *or* ~**d**, *ptp* **awoken** *or* ~**d** **1** *vi* s'éveiller, se réveiller. (*fig*) **to** ~ **to sth** prendre conscience de qch; **to** ~ **to the fact that** se rendre compte que. **2** *vt* *person* éveiller, réveiller; *suspicion, hope, curiosity* éveiller; *memories* réveiller. **3** *adj* **(a)** (*not asleep*) éveillé, réveillé. **he was still** ~ il ne s'était pas encore endormi; **to lie** ~ ne pas pouvoir dormir; **to stay** ~ **all night** (*deliberately*) veiller toute la nuit; (*involuntarily*) passer une nuit blanche; **it kept me** ~ cela m'a empêché de dormir. **(b)** (*alert*) en éveil, vigilant. **to be** ~ **to** avoir conscience de. ♦ **awaken** *vti* = **awake**. ♦ **awakening** **1** *n* réveil *m*; **a rude** ~**ning** un réveil brutal; **2** *adj* *interest* naissant.
award [ə'wɔːd] **1** *vt* *prize etc* décerner (*to* à); *money* attribuer (*to* à); *dignity, honour* conférer (*to* à); *damages* accorder (*to* à). **2** *n* prix *m*; (*scholarship*) bourse *f*.
aware [ə'wɛəʳ] *adj* **(a)** (*conscious*) conscient (*of* de); (*informed*) au courant (*of* de). **to become** ~ **of sth/that sth is happening** prendre conscience *or* se rendre compte de qch/que qch se passe; **to be** ~ **of/that** être conscient de/que; **I am quite** ~ **of it** je m'en rends bien compte; **as far as I am** ~ autant que je sache; **not that I am** ~ **of** pas que je sache; **to make sb** ~ **of sth** rendre qn conscient de qch. **(b)** (*knowledgeable*) informé. **politically** ~ politisé; **socially** ~ au courant des problèmes sociaux. ♦ **awareness** *n* conscience *f* (*of* de).
awash [ə'wɒʃ] *adj* inondé (*with* de).
away [ə'weɪ] **1** *adv* **(a)** au loin, loin. ~ **from** loin de; **far** ~ au loin, très loin; **the lake is 3 km** ~ le lac est à 3 km de distance *or* à une distance de 3 km; ~ **back** (*distance*) très loin derrière; ~ **back in prehistoric times** dans les temps reculés de la préhistoire; ~ **back in 1600** il y a bien longtemps en 1600; ~ **back in the 40s** il y a longtemps déjà dans les années 40; ~ **over there** là-bas au loin, loin là-bas. **(b)** (*absent*) **he's** ~ **just now** il n'est pas là en ce moment; **he is** ~ **in London** il est (parti) à Londres; **when I have to be** ~ lorsque je dois m'absenter; **she was** ~ **before I could speak** elle était partie avant que j'aie pu parler; ~ **with you!** allez-vous-en! **(c)** (*continuously*) sans arrêt. **to work** ~ travailler sans arrêt. **(d)** (*loss etc*) **to gamble** ~ **one's money** perdre son argent au jeu; **the snow has melted** ~ la neige a fondu complètement. **2** *adj* (*Sport*) ~ **match** match *m* à l'extérieur.
awe [ɔː] **1** *n* crainte *f* révérentielle. **to be in** ~ **of sb** être intimidé par qn. **2** *vt* inspirer un respect mêlé de crainte à. ♦ **awed** *adj* respectueux et intimidé. ♦ **awe-inspiring** *or* ♦ **awesome** *adj*

impressionnant, imposant. ♦ **awe-struck** *adj* (*frightened*) frappé de terreur; (*astounded*) stupéfait.

awful ['ɔːfəl] *adj* affreux, terrible; (*stronger*) épouvantable; (*imposing*) imposant. **an ~ lot of** *cars, dogs, people* un nombre incroyable de; *butter, flowers* une quantité incroyable de. ♦ **awfully** *adv* vraiment, très, terriblement; **thanks ~ly*** merci infiniment; **~ly sorry** vraiment désolé; **an ~ly big house** une très grande maison.

awhile [ə'waɪl] *adv* (pendant) quelque temps. **wait ~** attendez un peu.

awkward ['ɔːkwəd] *adj* **(a)** *tool, shape* peu commode; *path* difficile; (*Aut*) *bend* difficile à négocier; *problem, task, question, situation* délicat; *silence* embarrassé. **at an ~ time** au mauvais moment; **an ~ moment** (*embarrassing*) un moment gênant; **he's an ~ customer*** c'est un type pas facile*; **it's a bit ~** (*inconvenient*) ce n'est pas très commode; (*annoying*) c'est un peu ennuyeux; **he's being ~ about it** il ne se montre pas très coopératif à ce sujet. **(b)** (*clumsy*) *person, movement* maladroit; *style* gauche. **the ~ age** l'âge ingrat. ♦ **awkwardly** *adv speak* d'un ton embarrassé; *behave, handle, move* maladroitement, peu élégamment; *place* à un endroit difficile; *express* gauchement. ♦ **awkwardness** *n* *[person, movement]* maladresse *f*; *[situation etc]* côté *m* délicat; (*embarrassment*) embarras *m*.

awl [ɔːl] *n* alêne *f*, poinçon *m*.

awning ['ɔːnɪŋ] *n* (*Naut*) taud *m*; *[shop]* banne *f*; *[hotel door]* marquise *f*; *[tent]* auvent *m*.

awoke(n) [ə'wəʊk(ən)] *pret* (*ptp*) *of* **awake**.

awry [ə'raɪ] *adv* de travers. **to go ~** *[plan etc]* s'en aller à vau-l'eau; *[undertaking]* mal tourner.

ax (*US*), **axe** [æks] **1** *n* hache *f*. (*fig*) **I've no ~ to grind** ce n'est pas mon intérêt personnel que j'ai en vue; (*fig*) **when the ~ fell** quand le coup fut porté. **2** *vt* **to ~ expenditure** réduire les dépenses, faire *or* opérer des coupes sombres dans le budget; **to ~ sb** mettre qn à la porte (*pour raisons économiques*).

axiom ['æksɪəm] *n* axiome *m*. ♦ **axiomatic** *adj* axiomatique; (*clear*) évident.

axis ['æksɪs] *n, pl* **axes** axe *m* (*Geom etc*).

axle ['æksl] **1** *n [wheel]* axe *m*; (*Aut:* **~*-tree***) essieu *m*. **front/rear ~** essieu avant/arrière. **2** *adj*: **~ grease** graisse *f* à essieux; **~ pin** clavette *f* d'essieu.

ay(e) [aɪ] **1** *particle* oui. **2** *n* oui *m*. (*in voting*) **the ~s and noes** les voix *fpl* pour et contre; **the ~s have it** les oui l'emportent.

azalea [ə'zeɪlɪə] *n* azalée *f*.

azure ['eɪʒə^r] **1** *n* azur *m*. **2** *adj* d'azur.

B

B, b [bi:] *n* B, b *m*; (*Mus*) si *m*. (*house numbers*) **24b** le 24 ter.
babble [ˈbæbl] **1** *n [voices]* rumeur *f*; *[baby, stream]* gazouillement *m*. **2** *vi* (*indistinctly*) bredouiller; (*chatter*) bavarder; *[baby, stream]* gazouiller. **3** *vt* bredouiller. ♦ **babbling** *adj* babillard.
babe [beɪb] *n* bébé *m*, petit(e) enfant *m(f)*. **~ in arms** enfant au berceau.
babel [ˈbeɪbəl] *n* brouhaha *m*.
baboon [bəˈbu:n] *n* babouin *m*.
baby [ˈbeɪbɪ] **1** *n* bébé *m*. **~ of the family** benjamin(e) *m(f)*; **don't be such a ~!** ne fais pas l'enfant!; (*fig*) **he was left holding the ~** tout lui est retombé dessus; (*fig*) **to throw out the ~ with the bathwater** jeter l'enfant avec l'eau du bain; **come on, ~!*** (*to woman*) viens ma belle!; (*to man*) viens mon gars!*; **the new system is his ~** le nouveau système est son affaire. **2** *vt* (*) *person* dorloter. **3** *adj clothes etc* de bébé; *rabbit etc* bébé-. **~ boy** petit garçon; **~ girl** petite fille; (*US*) **~ carriage** voiture *f* d'enfant; **~ face** visage *m* poupin; **~ grand (piano)** (piano *m*) demi-queue *m*; **~ linen** layette *f*; **~ scales** pèse-bébé *m*; **~ talk** langage *m* de bébé. ♦ **baby-batterer** *n* bourreau *m* d'enfants. ♦ **baby-battering** *n* mauvais traitements infligés aux enfants. ♦ **babyhood** *n* petite enfance *f*. ♦ **babyish** *adj clothes* de bébé; *behaviour, speech* puéril. ♦ **baby-minder** *n* nourrice *f* (*gardant les enfants dont les mères travaillent*). ♦ **baby-sit** *vi* garder les bébés *or* les enfants. ♦ **baby-sitter** *n* baby-sitter *mf*. ♦ **baby-sitting** *n* baby-sitting *m*; **to go ~-sitting** faire du baby-sitting. ♦ **baby-walker** *n* trotte-bébé *m inv*.
baccalaureate [ˌbækəˈlɔ:rɪɪt] *n* (*US*) licence *f*.
baccara(t) [ˈbækərɑ:] *n* baccara *m*.
bachelor [ˈbætʃələʳ] *n, adj* célibataire (*m*). **B~ of Arts/of Science/of Law** licencié(e) *m(f)* ès lettres/ès sciences/en droit; **~ flat** garçonnière *f*; **~ girl** célibataire *f*.
bacillus [bəˈsɪləs] *n, pl* **-illi** bacille *m*.
back [bæk] **1** *n* **(a)** *[person, animal, book]* dos *m*; *[chair]* dossier *m*. **to fall on one's ~** tomber à la renverse; (*fig*) **behind his mother's ~** derrière le dos de sa mère; (*lit, fig*) **~ to ~** dos à dos; **with one's ~ to the light** le dos à la lumière; **he had his ~ to the houses** il tournait le dos aux maisons; **he stood with his ~ (up) against the wall** il était adossé au mur; (*fig*) **to have one's ~ to the wall** être au pied du mur; **to put one's ~ into doing** mettre toute son énergie à faire; **to put sb's ~ up** braquer qn; **to get off sb's ~** laisser qn en paix. **(b)** (*as opp to front*) (*gen*) dos *m*, derrière *m*; *[hand, hill, medal]* revers *m*; *[record]* deuxième face *f*; *[dress]* dos; *[head, house]* derrière; *[page, cheque]* verso *m*; *[material]* envers *m*. **~ to front** (sens) devant derrière; **at the ~ of the book** à la fin du livre; **to have an idea at the ~ of one's mind** avoir une idée derrière la tête; **in the ~ (of a car)** à l'arrière (d'une voiture); **I know Paris like the ~ of my hand** je connais Paris comme ma poche. **(c)** (*furthest from front*) *[cupboard, garden, stage]* fond *m*. **at the very ~** tout au fond; **at the ~ of beyond*** au diable vert*. **(d)** (*Ftbl etc*) arrière *m*.
2 *adj* **(a)** (*not front*) *seat, wheel* arrière *inv*; *door, garden* de derrière; (*Ling*) *vowel* postérieur. (*fig*) **to enter through the ~ door** entrer par la petite porte; **~ room** chambre *f* du fond; (*fig*) **the ~room boys*** ceux qui restent dans la coulisse; (*fig*) **to take a ~ seat*** passer au second plan; (*fig*) **he's a ~seat driver*** il est toujours à donner des conseils au conducteur; **~ streets** (*lit*) petites rues; **he grew up in the ~ streets of Leeds** il a grandi dans les quartiers pauvres de Leeds; **~ tooth** molaire *f*; **~ number** *[magazine etc]* vieux numéro; (*fig*) **to be a ~ number*** ne plus être dans le coup. **(b)** (*overdue*) *taxes* arriéré. **~ pay** rappel *m* de salaire *or* (*Mil*) de solde; **~ rent** arriéré *m* de loyer.
3 *adv* **(a)** (*to the rear*) en arrière, à *or* vers l'arrière. **(stand) ~!** rangez-vous!, reculez!; **far ~** loin derrière; **the house stands ~ from the road** la maison est en retrait par rapport à la route; **~ and forth** en allant et venant; (*in mechanism*) par un mouvement de va-et-vient. **(b)** (*in return*) **to give ~** rendre. **(c)** (*again: often re- + vb in French*) **to come ~** revenir; **to be ~** être de retour, être rentré; **he's not ~ yet** il n'est pas encore rentré *or* revenu; **he went to Paris and ~** il a fait le voyage de Paris aller et retour; **to go there and ~** faire l'aller et retour. **(d)** (*in time phrases*) **as far ~ as 1800** déjà en 1800; **a week ~** il y a une semaine.
4 *vt* **(a)** (*support*) *wall, map* renforcer; *book* endosser; *picture* maroufler; (*fig*) *singer* accompagner; *person* soutenir; *candidate* pistonner*; (*finance*) *person, enterprise* financer; *bill* endosser. **(b)** (*bet on*) *horse* parier sur. **to ~ a horse each way** jouer un cheval gagnant et placé; **to ~ a loser** (*Sport, fig*) parier sur un perdant; (*Comm*) mal placer son argent. **(c)** (*reverse*) *horse, cart* faire reculer; *train* refouler. **he ~ed the car out** il a sorti la voiture en marche arrière; **to ~ the oars** culer.
5 *vi [person, animal]* reculer; *[vehicle]* faire marche arrière. **to ~ in/out** *etc [vehicle]* entrer/sortir *etc* en marche arrière; *[person]* entrer/sortir *etc* à reculons.
back away *vi* reculer (*from* devant).
back down *vi* (*fig*) se dégonfler*.
back on to *vt fus [house etc]* donner par derrière sur.
back out *vi* (*of duty*) se dérober (*of* à); (*of deal*) se dégager (*of* de).
back up 1 *vi* (*Aut*) faire marche arrière. **2** *vt sep* (*support*) soutenir; (*reverse*) *vehicle* faire reculer.
♦ **backache** *n* mal *m* de *or* aux reins. ♦ **backbencher** *n* membre *m* du Parlement sans portefeuille; **the ~benchers** le gros des députés. ♦ **backbiting** *n* médisance *f*. ♦ **backbone** *n* colonne vertébrale; *[fish]* arête centrale; **English to the ~bone** anglais jusqu'à la moelle (des os); **to be the ~bone of an organisation** être le pivot d'une organisation; **he's got no ~bone** c'est un mollusque. ♦ **back-breaking** *adj work* éreintant. ♦ **backchat*** *n* impertinence *f*. ♦ **backcloth** *n* toile *f* de fond. ♦ **backcomb** *vt* crêper. ♦ **backdate** *vt cheque etc* antidater; (*increase etc*) **~dated to** avec rappel à compter de. ♦ **backdrop** *n* = **backcloth**. ♦ **backer** *n* (*supporter*) partisan *m*; *[play etc]* commanditaire *m*. ♦ **backfire** *vi* (*Aut*) avoir un raté (d'allumage);

[plan etc] échouer. ♦ **backgammon** *n* trictrac *m*. ♦ **background** *V below*. ♦ **backhand 1** *adj blow* en revers; *writing* penché à gauche; **2** *n* (*Tennis*) revers *m*. ♦ **backhanded** *adj* (*fig*) *action* déloyal; *compliment* équivoque. ♦ **backing** *n* (*gen, Fin, Pol*) soutien *m*; (*Mus*) accompagnement *m*; *[picture]* marouflage *m*. ♦ **back-kitchen** *n* arrière-cuisine *f*. ♦ **backlash** *n* (*fig*) réaction *f* (brutale). ♦ **backlog** *n [rent etc]* arriéré *m*; **~log of work** accumulation *f* de travail (en retard). ♦ **backpacking** *n*: **to go ~packing** faire de la randonnée (sac au dos). ♦ **backpedal** *vi* pédaler en arrière; (*fig*) faire marche arrière (*fig*). ♦ **backrest** *n* dossier *m*. ♦ **back-shop** *n* arrière-boutique *f*. ♦ **backside** *n* arrière *m*; (*: *buttocks*) postérieur* *m*. ♦ **backslapping*** *n* grandes démonstrations d'amitié. ♦ **backslide** *vi* ne pas tenir bon. ♦ **backspace** *vi* (*Typ*) rappeler le chariot. ♦ **backstage** *adv, adj* dans les coulisses. ♦ **backstairs 1** *n* escalier *m* de service; **2** *adj* (*fig*) *gossip, plot* d'antichambre. ♦ **backstroke** *n* (*Swim*) dos *m* crawlé. ♦ **back-to-back** *adj*: **~-to-~ houses** maisons adossées les unes aux autres. ♦ **backtrack** *vi* faire marche arrière (*fig*). ♦ **backup 1** *n* appui *m*; **2** *adj vehicle etc* supplémentaire; *person* remplaçant. ♦ **backward** *V below*. ♦ **backwash** *n* (*lit, fig*) remous *m* (*from* provoqué par). ♦ **backwater** *n [river]* bras mort; (*fig*) petit coin tranquille; (*pej*) trou perdu (*pej*). ♦ **backwoods** *npl* région (forestière) inexploitée; (*pej*) **in the ~woods** en plein bled*. ♦ **backyard** *n* arrière-cour *f*.

background ['bækgraʊnd] **1** *n* **(a)** *[picture, fabric]* fond *m*; *[photograph]* arrière-plan *m*; (*Theat*) arrière *m* du décor; (*fig*) arrière-plan. **in the ~** dans le fond, à l'arrière-plan; **on a blue ~** sur fond bleu; **to keep sb in the ~** tenir qn à l'écart. **(b)** (*circumstances etc*) antécédents *mpl*; (*Soc*) milieu *m* (socioculturel); (*Pol*) climat *m* politique; (*basic knowledge*) éléments *mpl* de base; (*experience*) formation *f*. **family ~** milieu familial; **what is his ~?** (*social*) de quel milieu est-il?; (*professional*) qu'est-ce qu'il a comme formation?; (*to case etc*) **to fill in the ~** compléter la documentation; **what is the ~ to these events?** quel est le contexte de ces événements? **2** *adj music, noise* de fond. **~ reading** lectures générales (autour du sujet).

backward ['bækwəd] **1** *adj look, step* en arrière; (*retarded*) arriéré; (*reluctant*) lent, peu disposé (*in doing* à faire). **2** *adv* (*also* **~s**) *look* en arrière; *fall* à la renverse. **to walk ~ and forwards** aller et venir; **to walk ~** marcher à reculons; **I know the poem ~*** je sais le poème sur le bout des doigts; **I know this road ~*** je connais cette route comme ma poche. ♦ **backward-looking** *adj project* rétrograde. ♦ **backwardness** *n* (*Med*) arriération *f* mentale; (*Econ*) état *m* arriéré; (*reluctance, shyness*) manque *m* d'empressement (*in doing* à faire).

bacon ['beɪkən] *n* bacon *m*. **fat ~** lard *m*; **~ and eggs** œufs *mpl* au jambon; (*fig*) **to bring home the ~*** décrocher la timbale*. ♦ **bacon-slicer** *n* coupe-jambon *m inv*.

bacteria [bæk'tɪərɪə] *npl of* **bacterium** bactéries *fpl*. ♦ **bacterial** *adj* bactérien. ♦ **bacteriological** *adj* bactériologique. ♦ **bacteriologist** *n* bactériologiste *mf*. ♦ **bacteriology** *n* bactériologie *f*.

bad [bæd] **1** *adj, comp* **worse**, *superl* **worst** (*gen*) mauvais; *person* méchant; *child, dog* vilain; *tooth* carié; *coin, money* faux; *mistake, accident, wound* grave. **~ language** gros mots; **he's a ~ lot*** c'est un sale type*; **it was a ~ thing to do** ce n'était pas bien de faire cela; **you ~ boy!** vilain!; **it is not so ~** ce n'est pas si mal; **too ~!** (*indignant*) c'est un peu fort!; (*sympathetic*) quel dommage!; **it's too ~ of you** ce n'est vraiment pas bien de votre part; **how is he? – not so ~** comment va-t-il? – pas trop mal; **~ for the health** mauvais pour la santé; **this is ~ for you** cela ne vous vaut rien; (*Med*) **to feel ~** se sentir mal; **I feel very ~ about it*** ça m'embête*; **from ~ to worse** de mal en pis; **business is ~** les affaires vont mal; **she speaks ~ English** elle parle un mauvais anglais; **to go ~** *[food]* se gâter; *[milk]* tourner; *[bread etc]* moisir; *[teeth]* se carier; (*fig*) **~ blood** animosité *f*; **it's a ~ business** (*sad*) c'est une triste affaire; (*unpleasant*) c'est une mauvaise histoire; **a ~ cold** un gros rhume; **to come to a ~ end** mal finir; **~ headache** violent mal *m* de tête; **her ~ leg** sa jambe malade; (*Ling*) **in a ~ sense** dans un sens péjoratif; **there is a ~ smell** ça sent mauvais; **it wouldn't be a ~ thing (to do)** ce ne serait pas une mauvaise idée (de faire); **to have a ~ time of it** (*poverty*) manger de la vache enragée; (*pain*) avoir très mal; (*trouble*) être dans une mauvaise passe; **to be in a ~ way** (*in a fix*) être dans le pétrin; (*very ill*) être très mal. **2** *n*: **the ~** le mauvais; **he's gone to the ~*** il a mal tourné. **3** *adv*: **he's got it ~** (*hobby etc*) c'est une marotte chez lui; (*person*) il l'a dans la peau*.
♦ **baddie‡** *n* méchant *m*. ♦ **baddish** *adj* pas fameux. ♦ **badly** *adv* **(worse, worst) (a)** mal; **he did ~ly** ça a mal marché (pour lui); **things are going ~ly** les choses vont mal; **he took it ~ly** il a mal pris la chose; **to be ~ly off** être dans la gêne; **he is ~ly off for space** il manque de place; **(b)** (*seriously*) *wound* grièvement; **~ly defeated** battu à plate couture; **the ~ly disabled** les grands invalides; **(c)** (*very much*) **to want sth ~ly** avoir grande envie de qch; **I need it ~ly** j'en ai absolument besoin; **he ~ly needs a beating*** il a sérieusement besoin d'une correction. ♦ **bad-mannered** *adj* mal élevé. ♦ **badness** *n* (*wickedness*) méchanceté *f*. ♦ **bad-tempered** *adj*: **to be ~-tempered** avoir mauvais caractère; (*in bad temper*) être de mauvaise humeur.

bade [bæd, beɪd] *pret of* **bid.**

badge [bædʒ] *n* (*gen, also Mil*) insigne *m*; *[an order, police]* plaque *f*; (*sew-on, stick-on*) badge *m*; (*fig*) signe *m* (distinctif). **his ~ of office** l'insigne de sa fonction.

badger ['bædʒəʳ] **1** *n* blaireau *m* (*animal*). **2** *vt* harceler (*sb to do* qn pour qu'il fasse; *with* de).

badminton ['bædmɪntən] *n* badminton *m*.

baffle ['bæfl] *vt person* déconcerter; *pursuers* semer*; *description* défier. ♦ **baffling** *adj* déconcertant.

bag [bæg] **1** *n* sac *m*. **~s** (*luggage*) bagages *mpl*, valises *fpl*; **~s of*** des masses de*; **paper ~** sac en papier; **~s under the eyes*** poches *fpl* sous les yeux; **with ~ and baggage** avec armes et bagages; **the whole ~ of tricks*** tout le bataclan*; (*fig*) **it's in the ~*** c'est dans le sac*; (*pej*) **she's an old ~‡** (*ugly*) c'est un vieux tableau*; (*grumpy*) c'est une vieille teigne. **2** *vt* **(a)** (*Hunting*) tuer; (*: *get, grab*) empocher. **I ~s that!‡** c'est à moi! **(b)** (**~ up**) *flour, goods* mettre en sac. **3** *vi [garment]* goder. ♦ **bagful** *n* sac *m* plein. ♦ **baggy** *adj jacket* flottant; *trousers* ample, (*pej*) trop ample. ♦ **bagpipes** *npl* cornemuse *f*. ♦ **bag-snatching** *n*: **to be accused of ~-snatching** être accusé d'avoir arraché son sac à qn.

baggage ['bægɪdʒ] **1** *n* bagages *mpl*; (*Mil*) équipement *m*. **2** *adj*: (*esp US*) **~ car** fourgon *m*; **~ check** bulletin *m* de consigne; **~ handler** bagagiste *m*; **~ room** consigne *f*.

Bahamas [bə'hɑːməz] *npl*: **the ~** les Bahamas *fpl*.

bail¹ [beɪl] **1** *n* (*Jur*) caution *f*. **on ~** sous caution; **to free** *or* **release sb on ~** mettre qn en liberté provisoire sous caution; **to stand ~ for sb** se porter garant de qn; **to ask for ~** demander la mise en liberté sous caution. **2** *vt* (**~ out**) (*Jur*) faire mettre en liberté provisoire sous caution; (*fig*) sortir d'affaire.

bail² [beɪl] *vt* (**~ out**) *boat* écoper; *water* vider.

bailiff ['beɪlɪf] *n* (*Jur*) huissier *m*; *[estate]* régisseur *m*.
bait [beɪt] **1** *n* appât *m*; (*fig*) appât, leurre *m*. (*lit, fig*) **to swallow the ~** mordre à l'hameçon. **2** *vt hook, trap* appâter; (*torment*) *animal, person* tourmenter.
baize [beɪz] *n* serge *f*. **~ door** porte matelassée.
bake [beɪk] **1** *vt* (*Culin*) faire cuire au four; *bricks etc* cuire. **to ~ a cake** (*make*) faire un gâteau; (*actually cook*) faire cuire un gâteau; **~d potatoes** pommes *fpl* de terre au four; **~d beans** haricots blancs à la sauce tomate.
2 *vi [bread, cakes]* cuire (au four). **she ~s every Tuesday** elle fait du pain (*or* de la pâtisserie *etc*) tous les mardis.
♦ **baker** *n* boulanger *m*, -ère *f*; **~r's shop** boulangerie *f*; **~r's dozen** treize à la douzaine. ♦ **bakery** *or* ♦ **bakehouse** *n* boulangerie(-pâtisserie) *f*. ♦ **baking 1** *n* cuisson *f*; **the bread is our own baking** nous faisons le pain nous-mêmes; **2** *adj*: **baking dish** plat *m* allant au four; **baking powder** ≃ levure alsacienne; **baking sheet** *or* **tray** plaque *f* à gâteau; **baking soda** bicarbonate *m* de soude; **baking-tin** *[cakes]* moule *m* (à gâteaux); *[tarts]* tourtière *f*; **it's baking (hot)!*** il fait une de ces chaleurs!
balaclava [ˌbælə'klɑːvə] *n*: **~ (helmet)** passe-montagne *m*.
balance ['bæləns] **1** *n* **(a)** (*equilibrium*) équilibre *m*; (*scales*) balance *f*. (*fig*) **to hang in the ~** être en balance; (*fig*) **to hold the ~** faire pencher la balance; **to keep/lose one's ~** garder/perdre son équilibre; (*lit, fig*) **off ~** mal équilibré; **to throw sb off ~** (*lit*) faire perdre l'équilibre à qn; (*fig*) couper le souffle à qn; **the ~ of power** l'équilibre des forces; **to strike a ~** trouver le juste milieu; **on ~** tout compte fait; (*Jur*) **when the ~ of his mind was disturbed** alors qu'il n'était pas responsable de ses actes; **a nice ~ of humour and pathos** un délicat dosage d'humour et de pathétique. **(b)** (*Comm, Fin*) (*equality*) balance *f*; (*difference*) solde *m*; (*remainder: of holidays etc*) reste *m*. **credit ~, ~ in hand** solde créditeur; **~ carried forward** solde reporté *or* à reporter; (*Econ*) **~ of trade/payments** balance commerciale/des paiements; **sterling ~s** balances sterling; **(bank) ~** état *m* de compte (bancaire).
2 *adj*: **~ sheet** bilan *m*.
3 *vt* **(a)** tenir en équilibre; (*fig: counterbalance*) équilibrer, compenser. *[2 objects]* **they ~ each other** ils se font contrepoids. **(b)** (*weigh up*) balancer, peser; *arguments, solutions* comparer. **this must be ~d against that** il faut peser le pour et le contre. **(c)** *account* balancer; *budget* équilibrer. **to ~ the books** dresser le bilan; **to ~ the cash** faire la caisse.
4 *vi [acrobat etc]* se maintenir en équilibre; *[scales, accounts]* être en équilibre; (*waver*) balancer (*between* entre). **to ~ on one foot** se tenir en équilibre sur un pied.
♦ **balanced** *adj person, diet* équilibré; *views* judicieux. ♦ **balancing** *adj*: (*fig*) **to do a balancing act** jongler (*fig*).
balcony ['bælkənɪ] *n* balcon *m*; (*Theat*) fauteuils *mpl* de deuxième balcon.
bald [bɔːld] *adj person* chauve; *tyre* lisse; *lie* flagrant, non déguisé. **~ patch** *[person]* (petite) tonsure *f*; *[animal]* place *f* dépourvue de poils; *[carpet etc]* coin *m* pelé; **a ~ statement** une simple exposition de faits. ♦ **bald-headed** *adj* chauve. ♦ **baldly** *adv* abruptement. ♦ **baldness** *n [person]* calvitie *f*; *[tyre]* état *m* lisse.
balderdash ['bɔːldədæʃ] *n* balivernes *fpl*.
bale[1] [beɪl] *n* balle *f* (*de coton etc*).
bale[2] [beɪl] *vi*: **to ~ out** (*Aviat*) sauter (en parachute).
Balearic [ˌbælɪ'ærɪk] *adj*: **the ~ Islands** les (îles *fpl*) Baléares *fpl*.
baleful ['beɪlfʊl] *adj* sinistre. **to give sb/sth a ~ look** regarder qn/qch d'un œil torve. ♦ **balefully** *adv* sinistrement; *look* d'un œil torve.
balk [bɔːk] **1** *vt person, plan* contrecarrer. **2** *vi [person]* regimber (*at* contre); *[horse]* se dérober (*at* devant).
Balkan ['bɔːlkən] *n*: **the ~s** les Balkans *mpl*.
ball[1] [bɔːl] *n* **(a)** (*gen*) balle *f*; (*inflated: Ftbl etc*) ballon *m*; (*Billiards*) bille *f*, boule *f*; (*Croquet*) boule. **as round as a ~** rond comme une boule; **cat curled up in a ~** chat pelotonné (en boule); (*fig*) **to keep the ~ rolling** soutenir la conversation (*or* l'intérêt *etc*); **to start the ~ rolling*** faire démarrer une affaire (*or* une conversation *etc*); (*fig*) **the ~ is in your court** (c'est) à vous de jouer; **to be on the ~*** (*competent*) être à la hauteur; (*alert*) ouvrir l'œil et le bon*; **~ of fire** globe *m* de feu; (*fig*) **he's a real ~ of fire*** il est débordant d'activité; **~ of the foot** plante *f* du pied; **~ and chain** boulet *m*. **(b)** *[wool, string]* pelote *f*, peloton *m*. **(c)** *[meat, fish]* boulette *f*; *[potato]* croquette *f*.
♦ **ball bearings** *npl* roulement *m* à billes. ♦ **ballcock** *n* robinet *m* à flotteur. ♦ **ball game** *n* (*US*) partie *f* de baseball. ♦ **ballpark** *n* (*US*) stade *m* de baseball. ♦ **ballpoint (pen)** *n* stylo *m* à bille.
ball[2] [bɔːl] *n* (*dance*) bal *m*. (*fig*) **to have a ~*** faire la bringue*. ♦ **ballroom** *n* salle *f* de bal; **~room dancing** danse *f* (de salon).
ballad ['bæləd] *n* (*Mus*) romance *f*; (*Literat*) ballade *f*.
ballast ['bæləst] *n* (*Naut etc*) lest *m*.
ballerina [ˌbælə'riːnə] *n* ballerine *f*.
ballet ['bæleɪ] **1** *n* ballet *m*. **2** *adj*: **~ dancer** danseur *m*, -euse *f* de ballet.
ballistic [bə'lɪstɪk] *adj* balistique. **~ missile** engin *m* balistique. ♦ **ballistics** *nsg* balistique *f*.
balloon [bə'luːn] **1** *n* ballon *m*. **to go up in a ~** monter en ballon; (*fig*) **the ~ went up*** l'affaire a éclaté; **weather ~** ballon-sonde *m*. **2** *adj*: **~ glass** verre *m* ballon; **~ tyre** pneu *m* ballon. **3** *vi*: **to go ~ing** faire une *or* des ascension(s) en ballon.
♦ **balloonist** *n* aéronaute *mf*.
ballot ['bælət] **1** *n* (*Pol etc*) scrutin *m*; (*drawing lots*) tirage *m* au sort. **first ~** premier tour de scrutin. **2** *vi* (*Pol etc*) voter au scrutin secret; (*draw lots*) tirer au sort. **3** *adj*: **~ box** urne *f* (électorale); **~ paper** bulletin *m* de vote.
ballyhoo* [ˌbælɪ'huː] *n* balivernes *fpl*.
balm [bɑːm] *n* baume *m*. ♦ **balmy** *adj* (*mild*) doux; (*: *silly*) timbré*.
baloney* [bə'ləʊnɪ] *n* balivernes *fpl*.
balsa ['bɔːlsə] *n*: **~ (wood)** balsa *m*.
Baltic ['bɔːltɪk] *adj port* de la Baltique; *state* balte. **the ~ (Sea)** la (mer) Baltique.
balustrade [ˌbæləs'treɪd] *n* balustrade *f*.
bamboo [bæm'buː] *n* bambou *m*.
bamboozle* [bæm'buːzl] *vt* (*deceive*) avoir*, embobiner*; (*perplex*) déboussoler*.
ban [bæn] **1** *n* interdit *m*. **2** *vt* (*gen*) interdire (*sth* qch, *sb from doing* à qn de faire); *person* exclure (*from* de); (*Rel*) *book etc* mettre à l'index.
banal [bə'nɑːl] *adj* banal. ♦ **banality** *n* banalité *f*.
banana [bə'nɑːnə] **1** *n* banane *f*; (*tree*) bananier *m*. **2** *adj*: **~ boat** bananier *m* (*cargo*); **~ republic** république *f* bananière; **~ skin** peau *f* de banane.
band[1] [bænd] *n* (*gen*) bande *f*; *[cigar]* bague *f*; *[hat]* ruban *m*; *[gramophone record]* plage *f*. **elastic ~** élastique *m*.
band[2] [bænd] *n* **(a)** (*group*) bande *f*, troupe *f*. **(b)** (*Mus*) orchestre *m*; (*Mil*) fanfare *f*.
band together *vi* former une bande.
♦ **bandsman** *n* musicien *m*. ♦ **bandstand** *n* kiosque *m* (à musique). ♦ **bandwagon** *n*: (*fig*) **to climb on the ~wagon** prendre le train en marche*.
bandage ['bændɪdʒ] **1** *n* (*strip*) bande *f*; (*dressing*) bandage *m*, (*of gauze*) pansement *m*; *[blindfolding]* bandeau *m*. **2** *vt* (**~ up**) *limb* bander;

wound mettre un pansement *or* un bandage sur.
bandan(n)a [bæn'dænə] *n* foulard *m* (à pois).
bandit ['bændɪt] *n* bandit *m*. ◆ **banditry** *n* banditisme *m*.
bandolier [ˌbændə'lɪəʳ] *n* cartouchière *f*.
bandy[1] ['bændɪ] *vt ball, reproaches* se renvoyer; *blows, jokes* échanger. **to ~ words** discuter.
bandy about *vt sep story, report* faire circuler. **to ~ sb's name about** parler de qn.
bandy[2] ['bændɪ] *adj leg* arqué; (*also* **~-legged**) *person* bancal; *horse* arqué.
bane [beɪn] *n*: **he's the ~ of my life*** il m'empoisonne la vie*. ◆ **baneful** *adj* funeste.
bang [bæŋ] **1** *n* (*noise*) *[gun, explosives]* détonation *f*, fracas *m*; (*Aviat*) bang *m* (supersonique); *[door]* claquement *m*; (*blow*) coup *m* (violent). **2** *excl* pan! **3** *adv* (*) **to go ~** éclater; **~ in the middle** en plein milieu; **his answer was ~ on** sa réponse est tombée pile; **~ on time** à l'heure pile; **~ went a £10 note!** et pan, voilà un billet de 10 livres fichu!* **4** *vt* frapper violemment. **to ~ one's fist on the table** frapper la table du poing; **to ~ one's head against sth** se cogner la tête contre qch; (*fig*) **you're ~ing your head against a brick wall** tu perds ton temps!; **to ~ the door** (faire) claquer la porte. **5** *vi [door]* claquer, battre; *[fireworks]* éclater; *[gun]* détoner. **to ~ on the door** donner de grands coups dans la porte; **to ~ into sth** heurter qch; **to ~ about** *or* **around** faire du bruit.
bang down *vt sep* poser brusquement; *lid* rabattre violemment. (*Telec*) **to ~ down the receiver** raccrocher brutalement.
bang together *vt sep objects* cogner l'un(e) contre l'autre. **I could have ~ed their heads together!*** j'en aurais pris un pour taper sur l'autre!
banger* ['bæŋəʳ] *n* **(a)** (*sausage*) saucisse *f*. **~s and mash** saucisses à la purée. **(b)** (*old car*) (vieux) tacot* *m*.
Bangladesh ['bæŋglə'deʃ] *n* Bangladesh *m*.
bangle ['bæŋgl] *n* bracelet *m*, (*rigid*) jonc *m*.
banish ['bænɪʃ] *vt person* exiler (*from* de; *to* en, à), bannir (*from* de); *cares* bannir. ◆ **banishment** *n* bannissement *m*, exil *m*.
banister ['bænɪstəʳ] *n* = **bannister.**
banjo ['bændʒəʊ] *n* banjo *m*.
bank[1] [bæŋk] **1** *n* **(a)** (*mound*) *[earth, snow]* talus *m*; (*embankment*) remblai *m*; (*on road, racetrack*) bord relevé; *[sand, sea, river]* banc *m*. **(b)** (*edge*) *[river, lake]* bord *m*, rive *f*; *[canal]* bord. *[Paris]* **the Left B~** la Rive gauche. **2** *vt* (**~ up**) *road* relever (*dans un virage*); *earth* amonceler; *fire* couvrir. **3** *vi* (*Aviat*) virer (sur l'aile).
bank[2] [bæŋk] *n [oars, switches]* rangée *f*.
bank[3] [bæŋk] **1** *n* (*Fin, Betting, Med*) banque *f*. **the B~ of France** la Banque de France; **it is as safe as the B~ of England** ça ne court aucun risque; **to break the ~** faire sauter la banque. **2** *adj*: **~ account** compte *m* en banque; **~ balance** état *m* de compte (bancaire); **~ book** livret *m* de banque; **~ card** carte *f* d'identité bancaire; **~ charges** frais *mpl* de banque; **~ clerk** employé(e) *m(f)* de banque; **~ holiday** jour férié; **~ note** billet *m* de banque; **~ rate** taux *m* d'escompte; **~ statement** relevé *m* de compte. **3** *vt* déposer en banque. **4** *vi*: **to ~ with Lloyds** avoir un compte à la Lloyds; **where do you ~?** quelle est votre banque?
bank (up)on *vt fus* (*fig*) compter sur.
◆ **banker** *n* banquier *m*; **~er's card** carte *f* d'identité bancaire; **~er's order** ordre *m* de virement bancaire (*pour paiements réguliers*). ◆ **banking** **1** *n*: **to study ~ing** faire des études bancaires; **he's in ~ing** il est banquier; **2** *adj*: **~ing hours** heures *fpl* d'ouverture des banques; **~ing house** banque *f*. ◆ **bankrupt** **1** *n* failli(e) *m(f)*; **2** *adj* (*Jur*) failli; (**fig: penniless*) fauché*; **to go ~rupt** faire faillite; **to be ~rupt** être en faillite; **3** *vt* mettre en faillite; (*: *fig*) ruiner. ◆ **bankruptcy** **1** *n* faillite *f*; **2** *adj*: **B~ruptcy Court** ≃ tribunal *m* de commerce; **~ruptcy proceedings** procédure *f* de faillite.
banner ['bænəʳ] *n* bannière *f*. (*Press*) **~ headline** manchette *f*.
bannister ['bænɪstəʳ] *n* rampe *f* (d'escalier). **to slide down the ~(s)** descendre sur la rampe.
banns [bænz] *npl* bans *mpl* (*de mariage*). **to call the ~** publier les bans.
banquet ['bæŋkwɪt] *n* banquet *m*; (*fig: lavish meal*) festin *m*. ◆ **banquet(ing) hall** *n* salle *f* des banquets.
banshee ['bæn'ʃiː] *n* fée *f* (*aux cris funestes*).
bantam ['bæntəm] *n* coq *m* nain, poule *f* naine.
banter ['bæntəʳ] **1** *n* badinage *m*. **2** *vi* badiner. ◆ **bantering** *adj* badin.
baptize [bæp'taɪz] *vt* baptiser. ◆ **baptism** *n* baptême *m*. ◆ **baptismal** *adj* baptismal. ◆ **baptist** *n, adj* (*Rel*) **B~** baptiste (*mf*).
bar[1] [bɑːʳ] **1** *n* **(a)** (*slab*) *[metal]* barre *f*; *[wood]* planche *f*; *[gold]* lingot *m*; *[chocolate]* tablette *f*. **~ of soap** savonnette *f*. **(b)** (*rod*) *[window, cage]* barreau *m*; *[grate, door, also Sport]* barre *f*. **behind ~s** sous les verrous; **to be a ~ to progress** faire obstacle au progrès. **(c)** (*Jur*) barreau *m*. **to be called** *or* (*US*) **admitted to the ~** s'inscrire au barreau; **the prisoner at the ~** l'accusé(e) *m(f)*. **(d)** (*in hotel etc*) bar *m*; (*at open-air shows etc*) buvette *f*; (*counter*) comptoir *m*. **to have a drink at the ~** prendre un verre au comptoir; (*Comm*) **stocking ~** rayon *m* des bas. **(e)** (*Mus*) mesure *f*. **the opening ~s** les premières mesures.
2 *vt* **(a)** *road* barrer; *door* mettre la barre à. **to ~ sb's way** barrer le passage à qn, couper la route à qn; (*lit, fig*) **to ~ the door against sb** barrer la porte à qn; **five-~red gate** barrière *f* à cinq barreaux. **(b)** (*exclude*) *person* exclure (*from* de); *action, thing* défendre.
◆ **barmaid** *n* serveuse *f* (*de bar*). ◆ **barman** *or* ◆ **bartender** *n* barman *m*.
bar[2] [bɑːʳ] *prep* sauf. **~ none** sans exception.
barb [bɑːb] *n [fish hook]* barbillon *m*; *[arrow]* barbelure *f*; *[feather]* barbe *f*; (*fig*) *[wit etc]* trait *m*. ◆ **barbed** *adj arrow* barbelé; *words, wit* acéré; **~(ed) wire** fil *m* de fer barbelé; **~(ed)-wire fence** haie *f* barbelée.
Barbados [bɑː'beɪdɒs] *n* Barbade *f*.
barbarian [bɑː'bɛərɪən] *adj, n* barbare (*mf*). ◆ **barbaric** *adj* barbare, de barbare. ◆ **barbarism** *n* (*Ling*) barbarisme *m*. ◆ **barbarity** *n* barbarie *f*. ◆ **barbarous** *adj* barbare. ◆ **barbarously** *adv* cruellement.
barbecue ['bɑːbɪkjuː] **1** *n* barbecue *m*. **2** *vt steak* griller au charbon de bois; *animal* rôtir tout entier. **3** *adj*: **~ sauce** sauce *f* barbecue.
barber ['bɑːbəʳ] *n* coiffeur *m* (*pour hommes*). **~'s pole** enseigne *f* de coiffeur.
barbiturate [bɑː'bɪtjʊrɪt] *n* barbiturique *m*. **~ poisoning** dose *f* excessive de barbituriques.
bard[1] [bɑːd] *n* barde *m*; (*poet*) poète *m*.
bard[2] [bɑːd] *vt* (*Culin*) barder.
bare [bɛəʳ] **1** *adj* (*gen*) nu; *hill* pelé; *countryside, tree, style* dépouillé; (*Elec*) *wire* dénudé; *cupboard, room* vide; *wall* nu. **with his ~ hands** à mains nues; **~ patch** *[grass]* place pelée; *[carpet]* coin pelé; **with his head ~** nu-tête *inv*; **to sleep on ~ boards** coucher sur la dure; **to lay ~** mettre à nu; **~ statement of facts** simple énoncé *m* des faits; **the ~ necessities/minimum** le strict nécessaire/minimum; **to earn a ~ living** gagner tout juste de quoi vivre; **~ majority** faible majorité *f*. **2** *vt* mettre à nu. **to ~ one's teeth** montrer les dents (*at* à); **to ~ one's head** se découvrir (la tête).
◆ **bareback** *adv* à cru. ◆ **barefaced** *adj* éhonté. ◆ **barefoot(ed)** *adv* nu-pieds; *adj* aux pieds nus. ◆ **bareheaded** *adv* nu-tête *inv*; *adj* nu-tête *inv*; *woman* en cheveux. ◆ **barelegged** *adj* aux

jambes nues. ♦ **barely** *adv* à peine. ♦ **bareness** *n* *[person]* nudité *f*; *[room]* dénuement *m*.

bargain ['bɑːgɪn] **1** *n* **(a)** (*transaction*) marché *m*, affaire *f*. **to make a** ~ conclure un marché (*with* avec); **it's a** ~**!*** c'est convenu!; **a bad** ~ une mauvaise affaire; (*fig*) **into the** ~ par-dessus le marché. **(b)** (*good buy*) occasion *f*. **it's a (real)** ~**!** c'est une véritable occasion! **2** *adj offer, price* avantageux. ~ **basement** coin *m* des (bonnes) affaires; ~ **hunter** chercheur *m*, -euse *f* d'occasions; ~ **sale** soldes *mpl*. **3** *vi*: **to** ~ **with sb** (*haggle*) marchander avec qn; (*negotiate*) négocier avec qn; (*fig*) **I did not** ~ **for that** je ne m'attendais pas à cela; **I got more than I** ~**ed for** j'ai eu du fil à retordre. ♦ **bargaining 1** *n* marchandage *m*; **2** *adj*: **that gives us more** ~**ing power** ceci nous donne plus d'atouts dans les négociations.

barge [bɑːdʒ] **1** *n* (*on river, canal*) chaland *m*; (*large*) péniche *f*; (*with sail*) barge *f*; *[admiral]* vedette *f*; (*ceremonial*) barque *f*. **2** *adj*: **I wouldn't touch it with a** ~ **pole*** (*revolting*) je n'y toucherais pas avec des pincettes; (*risky*) je ne m'y frotterais pas. **3** *vi*: **to** ~ **into a room** faire irruption dans une pièce, entrer sans façons dans une pièce.

barge in *vi* (*enter*) faire irruption; (*interrupt*) interrompre; (*interfere*) se mêler de ce qui ne vous regarde pas.

♦ **bargee** *or* ♦ **bargeman** *n* batelier *m*, marinier *m*.

baritone ['bærɪtəʊn] **1** *n* baryton *m*. **2** *adj* de baryton.

barium ['bɛərɪəm] *n*: ~ **meal** sulfate *m* de baryum.

bark[1] [bɑːk] **1** *n [tree]* écorce *f*. **to strip the** ~ **off a tree** écorcer un arbre. **2** *vt*: **to** ~ **one's shins** s'écorcher les jambes.

bark[2] [bɑːk] **1** *n [dog]* aboiement *m*; *[fox]* glapissement *m*. **the** ~ **of a gun** un coup de canon; **his** ~ **is worse than his bite** il fait plus de bruit que de mal. **2** *vi [dog]* aboyer (*at* après); *[fox]* glapir; *[gun]* aboyer, tonner; (*speak sharply*) crier. (*fig*) **to** ~ **up the wrong tree** faire fausse route.

bark out *vt sep order* glapir.

♦ **barker** *n [fairground]* bonimenteur *m*. ♦ **barking 1** *n* aboiements *mpl*; **2** *adj*: ~**ing cough** toux *f* sèche.

barley ['bɑːlɪ] **1** *n* orge *f*. **2** *adj*: ~ **sugar** sucre *m* d'orge; ~ **water** orgeat *m*.

barmy* ['bɑːmɪ] *adj* timbré*.

barn [bɑːn] *n* grange *f*; (*US*) *[horses]* écurie *f*; *[cattle]* étable *f*; (*huge house*) énorme bâtisse *f*. ~ **dance** soirée *f* de danses paysannes. ♦ **barnyard** *n* basse-cour *f*; ~**yard fowls** volaille *f*.

barnacle ['bɑːnəkl] *n* anatife *m*.

barometer [bə'rɒmɪtəʳ] *n* baromètre *m*. ♦ **barometric** *adj* barométrique.

baron ['bærən] *n* baron *m*; (*fig*) magnat *m*. ♦ **baroness** *n* baronne *f*. ♦ **baronet** *n* baronnet *m*. ♦ **baronial hall** *n* demeure *f* seigneuriale.

baroque [bə'rɒk] *adj, n* baroque (*m*).

barrack ['bærək] **1** *n*: ~**s** caserne *f*; **in** ~**s** à la caserne. **2** *adj*: ~ **square** cour *f* de caserne. ♦ **barrack room 1** *n* chambrée *f*; **2** *adj language* de caserne; (*fig*) **to be a** ~**-room lawyer** se promener toujours avec le code sous le bras.

barracuda [ˌbærə'kjuːdə] *n* barracuda *m*.

barrage ['bærɑːʒ] **1** *n* **(a)** *[river]* barrage *m*. **(b)** (*Mil*) tir *m* de barrage; *[questions]* pluie *f*; *[words]* flot *m*. **2** *adj*: ~ **balloon** ballon *m* de barrage.

barrel ['bærəl] **1** *n* **(a)** *[wine, beer]* tonneau *m*; *[cider]* futaille *f*; *[herring]* caque *f*; *[oil, tar]* baril *m*. **(b)** *[firearm, key]* canon *m*; *[fountain pen]* corps *m*. **to give sb both** ~**s*** lâcher ses deux coups sur qn*. **2** *adj*: ~ **organ** orgue *m* de Barbarie.

barren ['bærən] *adj* stérile; (*fig*) aride. ♦ **barrenness** *n* stérilité *f*.

barricade [ˌbærɪ'keɪd] **1** *n* barricade *f*. **2** *vt* barricader.

barrier ['bærɪəʳ] **1** *n* barrière *f*; (*in station*) portillon *m* (d'accès); (*fig*) obstacle *m* (*to* à). **2** *adj*: ~ **cream** crème *f* isolante.

barring ['bɑːrɪŋ] *prep* excepté, sauf.

barrister ['bærɪstəʳ] *n* avocat *m*.

barrow[1] ['bærəʊ] *n* (*wheel*~) brouette *f*; (*coster's*) voiture *f* des quatre saisons; (*Rail: luggage* ~) diable *m*; (*Min*) wagonnet *m*. ♦ **barrow-boy** *n* marchand *m* des quatre saisons.

barrow[2] ['bærəʊ] *n* (*Archeol*) tumulus *m*.

barter ['bɑːtəʳ] **1** *n* échange *m*, troc *m*. **2** *vt* échanger, troquer (*for* contre).

barter away *vt sep rights* vendre (*for* pour).

basalt ['bæsɔːlt] *n* basalte *m*.

base[1] [beɪs] **1** *n* (*gen; also Mil*) base *f*; *[tree]* pied *m*; (*of paint*: ~ *coat*) première couche.

2 *vt opinion* baser (*on* sur); *troops* baser (*at* à). **post** ~**d on London** poste centré sur Londres; **London-**~**d** dont le centre d'opérations est Londres; **I am** ~**d on Glasgow** j'opère à partir de Glasgow.

♦ **baseball** *n* base-ball *m*. ♦ **baseless** *adj* sans fondement.

base[2] [beɪs] *adj* **(a)** (*vile: gen*) bas; *behaviour, motive* ignoble; *metal* vil. **(b)** (*US*) = **bass**[1]. ♦ **basely** *adv* bassement; ignoblement. ♦ **baseness** *n* bassesse *f*.

bash [bæʃ] **1** *n* coup *m*. **the bumper has had a** ~ le pare-choc est cabossé; **I'll have a** ~ **(at it)*** je vais essayer un coup*. **2** *vt* frapper, cogner. **to** ~ **sb on the head** assommer qn.

bash in *vt sep door* enfoncer; *car* cabosser; *cover* défoncer. **to** ~ **sb's head in** défoncer le crâne à qn*.

bash up *vt sep car* bousiller*; *person* tabasser*.

bashful ['bæʃfʊl] *adj* timide. ♦ **bashfully** *adv* timidement. ♦ **bashfulness** *n* timidité *f*.

basic ['beɪsɪk] **1** *adj* (*fundamental*) *principle, problem, French* fondamental; *salary, vocabulary* de base; (*elementary*) *rules, precautions* élémentaire. **2** *n*: **the** ~**s** l'essentiel *m*. ♦ **basically** *adv* au fond, essentiellement.

basil ['bæzl] *n* (*Bot*) basilic *m*.

basilica [bə'zɪlɪkə] *n* basilique *f*.

basin ['beɪsn] *n* (*gen*) cuvette *f*, bassine *f*; (*for food*) saladier *m*, (*smaller*) bol *m*; (*wash*~) cuvette, (*plumbed in*) lavabo *m*; *[fountain]* vasque *f*; *[river]* bassin *m*.

basis ['beɪsɪs] *n, pl* **bases** base *f*. **on that** ~ dans ces conditions; **on the** ~ **of what you've told me** par suite de ce que vous m'avez dit.

bask [bɑːsk] *vi* (*in sun*) se dorer (*in* à). **to** ~ **in sb's favour** jouir de la faveur de qn; ~**ing shark** requin *m* pèlerin.

basket ['bɑːskɪt] **1** *n* (*gen*) corbeille *f*; (*one-handled; also for bicycle etc*) panier *m*. **2** *adj*: ~ **chair** chaise *f* en osier. ♦ **basketball** *n* basket(-ball) *m*. ♦ **basketwork** *n* vannerie *f*.

Basque [bæsk] **1** *n* Basque *mf*; (*Ling*) basque *m*. **2** *adj* basque. ~ **Country** Pays *m* basque.

bass[1] [beɪs] (*Mus*) **1** *n* basse *f*. **2** *adj* bas; *clef* de fa. ~ **baritone** basse chantante; ~ **drum** grosse caisse.

bass[2] [bæs] *n* (*freshwater*) perche *f*; (*sea*) bar *m*.

basset ['bæsɪt] *n*: ~ **(hound)** basset *m*.

bassoon [bə'suːn] *n* basson *m*.

bastard ['bɑːstəd] **1** *n* bâtard(e) *m(f)*; (*‡pej*) salaud‡ *m*. **poor** ~‡ pauvre type*. **2** *adj child* bâtard; *language* abâtardi.

baste [beɪst] *vt* (*Culin*) arroser; (*Sewing*) bâtir.

bat[1] [bæt] *n* (*Zool*) chauve-souris *f*. (*fig*) **to have** ~**s in the belfry*** avoir une araignée au plafond*.

bat[2] [bæt] **1** *n* (*Baseball, Cricket*) batte *f*; (*Table Tennis*) raquette *f*. (*fig*) **off one's own** ~ de sa propre initiative. **2** *vi* manier la batte.

bat[3] [bæt] *vt*: **he didn't** ~ **an eyelid** il n'a pas

sourcillé; **without ~ting an eyelid** sans sourciller.
batch [bætʃ] *n [loaves]* fournée *f*; *[people]* groupe *m*; *[letters]* paquet *m*; *[goods]* lot *m*.
bated ['beɪtəd] *adj*: **with ~ breath** en retenant son souffle.
bath [bɑːθ] **1** *n, pl* **~s** [bɑːðz] (*gen*) bain *m*; (**~***tub*) baignoire *f*. **to have a ~** prendre un bain; **to give sb a ~** donner un bain à qn; **room with ~** chambre *f* avec salle de bains; **~s** (*washing*) (établissement *m* de) bains-douches *mpl*; (*swimming*) piscine *f*. **2** *vt* donner un bain à. **3** *vi* prendre un bain. **4** *adj towel, sheet, salts* de bain. ♦ **bathchair** *n* fauteuil roulant. ♦ **bathmat** *n* tapis *m* de bain. ♦ **bathrobe** *n* peignoir *m* de bain. ♦ **bathroom 1** *n* salle *f* de bains; **2** *adj*: **~room cabinet** armoire *f* de toilette; **~room scales** pèse-personne *m*. ♦ **bathtub** *n* baignoire *f*. ♦ **bathwater** *n* eau *f* du bain.
bathe [beɪð] **1** *vt* baigner; *wound* laver. **~d in sweat** en nage; **~d in light** baigné de lumière. **2** *vi* se baigner (*dans la mer etc*); (*US*) prendre un bain (*dans une baignoire*). **3** *n*: **to have a ~** se baigner. ♦ **bather** *n* baigneur *m*, -euse *f*. ♦ **bathing 1** *n* baignade *f*; **2** *adj*: **bathing beauty** belle baigneuse; **bathing cap** bonnet *m* de bain; **bathing costume** *or* **suit** *or* **trunks** maillot *m* (de bain).
baton ['bætən] *n* (*Mil, Mus, French Police*) bâton *m*; (*Brit Police*) matraque *f*; *[relay race]* témoin *m*. **~ charge** charge *f* à la matraque.
bats* [bæts] *adj* toqué*, timbré*.
battalion [bə'tælɪən] *n* (*Mil, fig*) bataillon *m*.
batten¹ ['bætn] *n* (*Carpentry*) latte *f*.
batten² ['bætn] *vi* s'engraisser (*on sb* aux dépens de qn; *on sth* de qch).
batter ['bætəʳ] **1** *n* (*Culin*) (*for frying*) pâte *f* à frire; (*for pancakes*) pâte à crêpes. **fried fish in ~** poisson frit (enrobé de pâte à frire). **2** *vt* battre; *baby* martyriser. **3** *vi*: **to ~ at the door** cogner à la porte à coups redoublés.
batter down, batter in *vt sep* défoncer.
♦ **battered** *adj hat, car* cabossé; *face* meurtri; *furniture, house* délabré; **~ed babies** enfants martyrs. ♦ **battering** *adj*: **~ing ram** bélier *m*.
battery ['bætərɪ] **1** *n* **(a)** (*guns*) batterie *f*. **(b)** *[torch, radio]* pile *f*; *[vehicle]* accumulateurs *mpl*. **(c)** (*row of similar objects*) batterie *f*; *[questions etc]* pluie *f*. **(d)** (*Agr*) batterie *f*. **2** *adj radio* à piles; *farming* intensif; *hen* de batterie. (*Elec*) **~ charger** chargeur *m*.
battle ['bætl] **1** *n* bataille *f*, combat *m*; (*fig*) lutte *f*, combat (*for sth* pour obtenir qch; *to do* pour faire). **killed in ~** tué à l'ennemi; (*fig*) **to fight sb's ~s** se battre à la place de qn; **we are fighting the same ~** nous nous battons pour la même cause; **~ royal** bataille en règle; **that's half the ~*** c'est déjà pas mal*. **2** *adj cry* de guerre; *zone* de combat. **~ dress** tenue *f* de campagne. **3** *vi* se battre, lutter (*for sth* pour obtenir qch; *to do* pour faire). ♦ **battle-axe*** *n* (*woman*) virago *f*. ♦ **battlefield** *or* ♦ **battleground** *n* champ *m* de bataille. ♦ **battlements** *npl* remparts *mpl*. ♦ **battle-scarred** *adj* marqué par les combats. ♦ **battleship** *n* cuirassé *m*.
bauble ['bɔːbl] *n* babiole *f*.
baulk [bɔːlk] = **balk**.
bauxite ['bɔːksaɪt] *n* bauxite *f*.
bawdy ['bɔːdɪ] *adj* paillard.
bawl [bɔːl] *vti* brailler (*at* contre).
bawl out* *vt sep* (*scold*) engueuler*.
bay¹ [beɪ] *n* (*Geog: gen*) baie *f*. **the B~ of Biscay** le golfe de Gascogne.
bay² [beɪ] *n* (**~** *tree*) laurier(-sauce) *m*. **~ leaf** feuille *f* de laurier.
bay³ [beɪ] *n* (*for parking*) lieu *m* de stationnement (autorisé). **~ window** fenêtre *f* en saillie.
bay⁴ [beɪ] **1** *n*: **to be at ~** être aux abois; **to keep sb/sth at ~** tenir qn/qch en échec. **2** *vi [dog]* aboyer (*at* à, après).
bay⁵ [beɪ] *adj horse* bai.
bayonet ['beɪənɪt] **1** *n* baïonnette *f*. **2** *vt* passer à la baïonnette. **3** *adj charge* à la baïonnette.
bazaar [bə'zɑːʳ] *n* (*market; shop*) bazar *m*; (*sale of work*) vente *f* de charité.
bazooka [bə'zuːkə] *n* bazooka *m*.
be [biː] *pret* **was, were,** *ptp* **been 1** *copulative vb* **(a)** être. **he is a soldier** il est soldat; **she is an Englishwoman** c'est une Anglaise, elle est anglaise; **who is that? – it's me!** qui est-ce? – c'est moi!; **~ good** sois sage. **(b)** (*health*) aller. **how are you?** comment allez-vous?; **I am better** je vais mieux; **she is well** elle va bien. **(c)** (*age*) **how old is he?** quel âge a-t-il?; **he is 3** il a 3 ans; **I would take her to ~ 40** je lui donnerais 40 ans. **(d)** (*cost*) coûter. **how much is it?** combien cela coûte-t-il?, ça fait combien?*; **it is 10 francs** cela coûte 10F. **(e)** (*Math*) faire. **2 and 2 are 4** 2 et 2 font 4.
2 *aux vb* **(a)** (+ *prp* = *continuous tense*) **what are you doing? – I am reading a book** qu'est-ce que vous faites? – je lis *or* je suis en train de lire un livre; **what have you been doing this week?** qu'avez-vous fait cette semaine?; **I have been waiting for you for an hour** je t'attends depuis une heure. **(b)** (+ *ptp* = *passive*) être. **he was killed** il a été tué, on l'a tué; **he is to ~ pitied** il est à plaindre; **the car is to ~ sold** la voiture doit être vendue; **peaches are sold by the kilo** les pêches se vendent au kilo. **(c)** (*in tag questions, short answers*) **he's always late, isn't he? – yes, he is** il est toujours en retard, n'est-ce pas? – oui, toujours; **it's all done, is it?** tout est fait, alors? **(d)** (+ *to* + *infin*) **he is to do it** il doit le faire; **they are to ~ married** ils vont se marier; **she was never to return** elle ne devait jamais revenir; **the telegram was to warn us** le télégramme était pour nous avertir; **I am not to speak to him** je ne dois pas lui parler, on m'a défendu de lui parler; **I wasn't to tell you** je ne devais pas vous le dire; **it is not to ~ opened** il est interdit de l'ouvrir. **(e)** (*modal 'were'*) **if we were in London** si nous étions à Londres; **if I were to tell him** et à supposer (même) que je lui dise; **if I were you** à votre place, si j'étais vous.
3 *vi* **(a)** être, exister. **to ~ or not to ~** être ou ne pas être; **the best artist that ever was** le meilleur peintre qui ait jamais existé; **that may ~** cela se peut; **~ that as it may** quoi qu'il en soit; **how is it that ...?** comment se fait-il que + *indic or subj*; **let me ~** laissez-moi tranquille; **the bride-/mother-to-be** la future mariée/maman. **(b) there is, there are** il y a; **there was once a castle here** il y avait autrefois un château ici; **there will ~ dancing** on dansera; **there were three of us** nous étions trois; **there is no knowing ...** il est impossible de savoir ...; **let there ~ light** que la lumière soit. **(c)** (*presenting, pointing out*) **here is, here are** voici; **there is, there are** voilà; **there he was, sitting at the table** il était là, assis à la table. **(d)** (*come, go: esp in perfect tense*) aller, venir, être. **I have been to see my aunt** je suis allé voir ma tante; **I have already been to Paris** j'ai déjà été *or* je suis déjà allé à Paris; **he has been and gone** il est venu et reparti.
4 *impers vb* **(a)** (*time*) être. **it is morning** c'est le matin; **it is 6 o'clock** il est 6 heures; **it is the 14th June today** nous sommes *or* c'est aujourd'hui le 14 juin; **it is a long time since I saw you** il y a longtemps que je ne vous ai vu; **it is you who did it** c'est vous qui l'avez fait; **were it not that** si ce n'était que; **were it not for my friendship for him** sans mon amitié pour lui; **had it not been for him we ...** sans lui, nous ...; **as it were** pour ainsi dire. **(b)** (*weather etc*) faire. **it is fine/cold** il fait beau/froid; **it is windy** il fait du vent.
♦ **be-all** *n*: **the ~-all and end-all** le but suprême

(*of* de). ♦ **being** *n* **(a)** existence *f*; **to come into ~ing** *[idea]* prendre naissance; *[society]* être créé; **to bring into ~ing** faire naître; **then in ~ing** qui existait alors; **(b)** être *m*; **human ~ings** êtres humains; **all my ~ing revolts at** tout mon être se révolte à.

beach [biːtʃ] **1** *n [sea]* plage *f*; (*shore*) grève *f*; *[lake]* rivage *m*. **2** *vt* échouer. **3** *adj*: **~ ball** ballon *m* de plage; **~ buggy** buggy *m*; **~ umbrella** parasol *m*. ♦ **beachcomber** *n* ramasseur *m* d'épaves. ♦ **beachhead** *n* tête *f* de pont. ♦ **beachwear** *n* tenue *f* de plage.

beacon [ˈbiːkən] *n* (*gen, fig*) phare *m*; (*Aviat, Naut*) balise *f*; (*on hills*) feu *m* (d'alarme). **Belisha ~** lampadaire *m* (*indiquant un passage clouté*).

bead [biːd] *n* (*gen*) perle *f*; *[rosary]* grain *m*; *[dew]* perle; *[sweat]* goutte *f*. **(string of) ~s** collier *m*. ♦ **beady-eyed** *adj* (*glittering*) aux yeux en boutons de bottines; (*pej*) aux yeux de fouine.

beak [biːk] *n* bec *m*; (꞉: *nose*) nez *m* crochu.

beaker [ˈbiːkəʳ] *n* gobelet *m*; (*Chem*) vase *m* à bec.

beam [biːm] **1** *n* **(a)** (*Archit*) poutre *f*. **(b)** (*Naut*) **on the port ~** à bâbord. **(c)** *[light, sunlight]* rayon *m*, trait *m*; *[headlight, searchlight, etc]* faisceau *m* (lumineux); (*Phys*) faisceau; (*Aviat, Naut*) chenal *m* de radio-guidage. (*fig*) **to be on (the) ~*** être sur la bonne voie; (*fig*) **to be off (the) ~*** dérailler*. **(d)** (*smile*) sourire *m* épanoui. **2** *vi* *[sun]* rayonner. **she ~ed** son visage s'est épanoui en un large sourire; **she ~ed at me** elle a levé vers moi un visage épanoui; **face ~ing with joy** visage rayonnant de joie. **3** *vt* (*Rad, Telec*) *message* transmettre par émission dirigée; *programme* diffuser (*to* à l'intention de). ♦ **beam-ends** *npl*: **on one's ~-ends*** dans la gêne.

bean [biːn] *n* haricot *m*; (*green ~*) haricot vert; (*broad ~*) fève *f*; *[coffee]* grain *m*. **full of ~s*** en pleine forme; **he hasn't a ~**꞉ il n'a pas le sou. ♦ **beanshoots** *or* ♦ **beansprouts** *npl* germes *mpl* de soja.

bear[1] [bɛəʳ] *pret* **bore**, *ptp* **borne** **1** *vt* **(a)** (*carry*) *burden, message, signature, name* porter. **to ~ away** emporter; **to ~ back** rapporter; **to ~ no relation to** être sans rapport avec; **he bore himself like a soldier** (*carried himself*) il avait une allure militaire *or* de soldat; (*conducted himself*) il se comportait en soldat; **it was borne in on me that ...** il m'est apparu de plus en plus évident que ...; **the love he bore her** l'amour qu'il lui portait; **to ~ sb ill-will** *or* **a grudge** garder rancune à qn. **(b)** (*support*) *weight* supporter; *comparison* soutenir; *responsibility* assumer; (*endure*) supporter, tolérer. **I cannot ~ that man** je ne peux pas souffrir cet homme; **she cannot ~ being laughed at** elle ne supporte pas qu'on se moque (*subj*) d'elle. **(c)** (*produce*) *child* donner naissance à; *crop* produire; (*Fin*) *interest* rapporter. (*lit, fig*) **to ~ fruit** porter des fruits.

2 *vi* **(a) to ~ right** prendre à droite; **~ towards the church** allez vers l'église; **~ north at the windmill** prenez la direction nord au moulin. **(b)** *[ice etc]* porter, supporter. **(c)** *[fruit tree etc]* donner, produire. **(d) to bring to ~** *pressure* exercer (*on sth* sur qch); *gun* pointer (*on* sur); *energy* consacrer (*on* à); **to bring one's mind to ~ on sth** porter son attention sur qch.

bear down *vi [ship]* venir (*on* sur); (*fig*) *[person]* foncer (*on* sur); (*press*) appuyer fermement, peser (*on* sur).

bear out *vt sep suspicions* confirmer; *statement* corroborer. **to ~ sb out** corroborer ce que qn dit.

bear up *vi* ne pas se laisser abattre, tenir le coup*. **~ up!*** courage!; **how are you? – ~ing up!*** comment ça va? – on fait aller*.

bear with *vt fus* supporter patiemment. **~ with me** je vous demande un peu de patience.

♦ **bearable** *adj* supportable, tolérable. ♦ **bearer** *n [letter, coffin, title, cheque]* porteur *m*, -euse *f*; *[passport]* titulaire *mf*; (*servant*) serviteur *m*. ♦ **bearing** *n* **(a)** (*posture*) maintien *m*; **noble ~ing** maintien noble; **(b)** (*relation*) rapport *m*; **to have a ~ing on** avoir un rapport avec; **(c) to take a compass ~ing** prendre un relèvement au compas; **to take a ship's ~ings** faire le point; (*fig*) **to get one's ~ings** se repérer; (*fig*) **to lose one's ~ings** être désorienté; **(d)** (*Tech*) palier *m*, coussinet *m*.

bear[2] [bɛəʳ] **1** *n* ours(e) *m(f)*; (*St Ex*) baissier *m*. **like a ~ with a sore head*** d'une humeur massacrante; (*Astron*) **the Great B~** la Grande Ourse. **2** *adj*: **~ cub** ourson *m*; (*fig*) **~ garden** pétaudière *f*.

beard [bɪəd] **1** *n* barbe *f*. **to have a ~** porter la barbe; **a man with a ~** un (homme) barbu. **2** *vt* braver. (*fig*) **to ~ the lion in his den** aller braver le lion dans sa tanière. ♦ **bearded** *adj* barbu; **a ~ed man** un barbu; **the ~ed lady** la femme à barbe. ♦ **beardless** *adj* imberbe.

beast [biːst] *n* bête *f*, animal *m*; (*cruel person*) brute *f*; (*: *disagreeable*) chameau* *m*. **the king of the ~s** le roi des animaux; **~ of burden** bête de somme; (*Agr*) **~s** bétail *m*; *[greedy person]* **to make a ~ of o.s.** se goinfrer. ♦ **beastly** *adj person, conduct* brutal; *language* obscène; *food, sight* dégoûtant; (*: *less strong*) *weather, person* infect*; *child, trick, business* sale (*before n*).

beat [biːt] (*vb: pret* **beat**, *ptp* **beaten**) **1** *n* **(a)** *[heart, drums]* battement *m*; (*Mus*) mesure *f*; *[conductor]* battement; (*Jazz*) rythme *m*. (*Mus*) **strong ~** temps fort. **(b)** *[policeman, sentry]* ronde *f*. **on the ~** faisant sa (*etc*) ronde.

2 *adj* **(a)** (*: **dead-~**) éreinté, claqué*. **(b) the ~* generation** la génération beatnik.

3 *vt* **(a)** (*strike*) battre. **to ~ sb with a stick** donner des coups de bâton à qn; **to ~ a drum** battre du tambour; **to ~ a retreat** battre en retraite; **~ it!**꞉ fiche le camp!*; **to ~ one's breast** se frapper la poitrine; **to ~ time** battre la mesure; **off the ~en track** hors des sentiers battus. **(b)** (*defeat*) battre, vaincre. **to be ~en** être vaincu; **to ~ sb to the top of a hill** arriver au sommet d'une colline avant qn; (*fig*) **to ~ sb to it*** devancer qn; **to ~ sb hollow** battre qn à plates coutures; **coffee ~s tea any day*** le café vaut tout le thé du monde; **that ~s me, that's got me ~en** *or* **~*** ça me dépasse complètement; **it ~s me how ...** ça me dépasse que* + *subj*; **that takes some ~ing!*, can you ~ it!*** faut le faire!*

4 *vi* (*gen*) battre. **to ~ at the door** cogner à la porte; **he doesn't ~ about the bush** il n'y va pas par quatre chemins; (*Naut*) **to ~ (to windward)** louvoyer au plus près.

beat back *vt sep* repousser.

beat down **1** *vi [sun]* taper*. **the rain was ~ing down** il pleuvait à torrents. **2** *vt sep prices* faire baisser; *person* faire baisser ses prix à. **I ~ him down to £2** je l'ai fait descendre à 2 livres.

beat in *vt sep door* défoncer. **to ~ sb's brains in** défoncer le crâne à qn*.

beat off *vt sep* repousser.

beat out *vt sep fire* étouffer; *metal* marteler; *rhythm* marquer.

beat up *vt sep eggs, cream* battre; (*assault*) *person* passer à tabac; (*find*) *recruits, customers* racoler.

♦ **beater** *n* (*carpet ~*) tapette *f*; (*egg whisk*) fouet *m*; (*rotary*) batteur *m*. ♦ **beating** *n* **(a)** (*whipping*) correction *f*; **to give/get a ~ing** flanquer/recevoir une correction; **(b)** *[drums, wings, heart]* battement *m*; **(c)** (*defeat*) défaite *f*; **the car takes a ~ing on that road*** la voiture en voit de dures* sur cette route. ♦ **beatnik** *n, adj* beatnik (*mf*). ♦ **beat-up*** *adj* bousillé*.

beatify [biːˈætɪfaɪ] *vt* béatifier. ♦ **beatific** [ˌbiːəˈtɪfɪk] *adj* béatifique; *smile* béat.

beauty [ˈbjuːtɪ] **1** *n* beauté *f*. **~ is only skin-deep** la beauté n'est pas tout; ~ **is in the eye of the beholder** il n'y a pas de laides amours; **the ~ of it is that*** ... ce qui est formidable, c'est que*...; **she is no ~*** ce n'est pas une beauté; **B~ and the Beast** la Belle et la Bête; **isn't this car a ~!*** quelle merveille que cette voiture!

2 *adj cream, preparations, salon* de beauté. ~ **competition** *or* **contest** concours *m* de beauté; ~ **queen** reine *f* de beauté; **you need your ~ sleep** tu as besoin de bien dormir; ~ **specialist** esthéticien(ne) *m(f)*; ~ **spot** (*on skin*) grain *m* de beauté; (*in countryside*) site *m* superbe; (*in tourist guide etc*) site *m* touristique; ~ **treatment** soins *mpl* de beauté.

♦ **beauteous** *adj* (*liter*) = **beautiful.** ♦ **beautician** *n* esthéticien(ne) *m(f)*. ♦ **beautiful** *adj* (*gen*) beau (*f* belle); *weather, dinner* magnifique. ♦ **beautifully** *adv* (*very well*) *work, sew* à la perfection; *fit, adapt* parfaitement; (*pleasantly*) *hot, calm* merveilleusement. ♦ **beautify** *vt* embellir.

beaver ['bi:vəʳ] *n* castor *m*. **to work like a ~** travailler d'arrache-pied.

becalmed [bɪ'kɑ:md] *adj* encalminé.

became [bɪ'keɪm] *pret of* **become.**

because [bɪ'kɒz] *conj* (*gen*) parce que. **the more surprising ~** d'autant plus surprenant que; ~ **he lied, he was punished** il a été puni pour avoir menti; ~ **of** à cause de, en raison de.

beck [bek] *n*: **to be at sb's ~ and call** être (constamment) à la disposition de qn; **to have sb at one's ~ and call** faire marcher qn au doigt et à l'œil.

beckon ['bekən] *vti* faire signe (*to sb* à qn; *to do* de faire). **he ~ed me in/over** *etc* il m'a fait signe d'entrer/d'approcher *etc*.

become [bɪ'kʌm] *pret* **became,** *ptp* **become 1** *vi* devenir. **to ~ famous** devenir célèbre; **to ~ a doctor** devenir *or* se faire médecin; **to ~ thin** maigrir; **to ~ accustomed to** s'accoutumer à. **2** *impers vb*: **what has ~ of him?** qu'est-il devenu? **3** *vt*: **it does not ~ him** cela ne lui sied pas. ♦ **becoming** *adj behaviour* bienséant; *clothes* seyant.

bed [bed] **1** *n* **(a)** lit *m*. **room with 2 ~s** chambre *f* à 2 lits; **to go to ~** se coucher; **to go to ~ with sb*** coucher avec qn*; **to get out of ~** se lever; (*fig*) **to get out of ~ on the wrong side** se lever du pied gauche; **to put to ~** *person* coucher; *newspaper* boucler; **to make the ~** faire le lit; **to be in ~** être couché; (*through illness*) garder le lit; **to give sb a ~ for the night** loger qn pour la nuit; **before ~** avant de se coucher; ~ **of sickness** lit de douleur; '**~ and breakfast**' 'chambres'; **to book in for ~ and breakfast** prendre une chambre avec le petit déjeuner; **we stayed at ~-and-breakfast places** nous avons pris une chambre chez des particuliers; ~ **and board** le vivre et le couvert; **it's not a ~ of roses** ce n'est pas une partie de plaisir; ~ **of nails** lit à clous. **(b)** (*layer*) *[coal, ore]* gisement *m*; *[clay]* couche *f*; *[coral, oysters]* banc *m*; *[mortar]* bain *m*. **(c)** (*bottom*) *[sea]* fond *m*; *[river]* lit *m*. **(d)** *[vegetables]* planche *f*; (*square*) carré *m*; *[flowers]* parterre *m*; (*strip*) plate-bande *f*. **2** *adj*: ~ **bath** grande toilette *f* (d'un malade); ~ **jacket** liseuse *f*; ~ **linen** draps *mpl* de lit (et taies *fpl* d'oreillers).

bed down *vi* (aller) se coucher; (*spend nights*) coucher.

bed out *vt sep plants* repiquer.

♦ **bed-bug** *n* punaise *f*. ♦ **bedclothes** *npl* couvertures *fpl* et draps *mpl* (de lit). ♦ **bedcover** *n* couvre-lit *m*. ♦ **bedding** *n* literie *f*; (*Mil etc*) matériel *m* de couchage; *[animals]* litière *f*. ♦ **bedfellow** *n*: (*fig*) **they are queer ~fellows** ils font une drôle d'association*. ♦ **bedhead** *n* tête *f* de lit. ♦ **bedpan** *n* bassin *m* (hygiénique). ♦ **bedpost** *n* colonne *f* de lit. ♦ **bedridden** *adj* alité, cloué au lit. ♦ **bedrock** *n* (*Geol*) soubassement *m*; (*fig*) base *f*. ♦ **bedroom 1** *n* chambre *f* (à coucher); **2** *adj*: (*Theat*) **~room farce** comédie *f* de boulevard; **~room slipper** pantoufle *f*; **~room suite** chambre *f* à coucher (*mobilier*). ♦ **bedsettee** *n* divan-lit *m*. ♦ **bedside 1** *n*: **at his ~side** à son chevet; **2** *adj book, lamp* de chevet; **~side rug** descente *f* de lit; *[doctor]* **he has a good ~side manner** il sait parler à ses malades. ♦ **bed-sitter** *or* ♦ **bed-sitting room** *or* ♦ **bedsit*** *n* chambre meublée. ♦ **bedsocks** *npl* chaussettes *fpl* (de lit). ♦ **bedsore** *n* escarre *f*. ♦ **bedspread** *n* dessus-de-lit *m inv*. ♦ **bedstead** *n* bois *m* de lit. ♦ **bedtime 1** *n*: **it is ~time** il est l'heure d'aller se coucher; **his ~time is 7 o'clock** il se couche à 7 heures; **it's past your ~time** tu devrais être déjà couché; **2** *adj*: **to tell a child a ~time story** raconter une histoire à un enfant avant qu'il ne s'endorme. ♦ **bedwetting** *n* incontinence *f* nocturne.

bedeck [bɪ'dek] *vt* parer (*with* de).

bedevil [bɪ'devl] *vt* embrouiller. **~led by** *person* accablé par; *plan* qui a souffert de.

bedlam ['bedləm] *n* ramdam‡ *m*, chahut* *m*.

bedraggled [bɪ'drægld] *adj clothes, person* débraillé; *hair* embroussaillé; (*wet*) trempé.

bee [bi:] *n* **(a)** abeille *f*. **to have a ~ in one's bonnet*** avoir une idée fixe (*about* en ce qui concerne); **like ~s round a honeypot** comme des mouches sur un pot de confiture. **(b) to have a sewing ~** se réunir pour coudre. ♦ **beehive** *n* ruche *f*. ♦ **beekeeper** *n* apiculteur *m*, -trice *f*. ♦ **beeline** *n*: **to make a ~line for** filer droit sur. ♦ **beeswax** *n* cire *f* d'abeille.

beech [bi:tʃ] *n* hêtre *m*. ♦ **beechnut** *n* faine *f*.

beef [bi:f] **1** *n* (*Culin*) bœuf *m*. **roast ~** rosbif *m*. **2** *adj*: ~ **cattle** bœufs *mpl* de boucherie; ~ **olive** paupiette *f* de bœuf; ~ **tea** bouillon *m* (de viande). **3** *vi* (‡: *complain*) râler* (*about* contre). ♦ **beefeater** *n* hallebardier *m* (*de la Tour de Londres*). ♦ **beefsteak** *n* bifteck *m*, steak *m*. ♦ **beefy*** *adj* costaud* *f inv*.

been [bi:n] *ptp of* **be.**

beer [bɪəʳ] **1** *n* bière *f*. **life's not all ~ and skittles** tout n'est pas qu'une partie de rigolade* en ce monde. **2** *adj*: ~ **bottle** canette *f*; ~ **can** boîte *f* de bière; ~ **glass** bock *m*, chope *f*.

beet [bi:t] **1** *n* betterave *f*. **2** *adj sugar* de betterave. ♦ **beetroot** *n* betterave *f* (potagère).

beetle ['bi:tl] **1** *n* (*Zool*) coléoptère *m*; (*black ~*) cafard *m*, blatte *f*; (*scarab*) scarabée *m*. **there's a huge ~ in the bath!** il y a un énorme cafard dans la baignoire! **2** *vi* (‡) **to ~ in/out** *etc* entrer/sortir *etc* en vitesse. ♦ **beetle-browed** *adj* aux sourcils broussailleux.

befall [bɪ'fɔ:l] *pret* **befell,** *ptp* **befallen 1** *vi* arriver, advenir. **2** *vt* arriver à.

befit [bɪ'fɪt] *vt* (*impers*) convenir à. **it ill ~s him** il lui sied mal (*to do* de faire). ♦ **befitting** *adj* convenable.

before [bɪ'fɔ:ʳ] **1** *prep* **(a)** (*time, order, rank*) avant. ~ **Christ** avant Jésus-Christ; **the year ~ last** il y a deux ans; **not ~ next week** pas avant la semaine prochaine; ~ **then** avant, auparavant; ~ **now** déjà; ~ **long** avant peu, d'ici peu; ~ **doing** avant de faire. **(b)** (*place, position*) devant. **he stood ~ me** il était là devant moi; **the question ~ us** la question qui nous occupe; **the task ~ him** la tâche qu'il a devant lui; **to appear ~ a judge** comparaître devant un juge. **(c)** (*rather than*) plutôt que. **to put death ~ dishonour** préférer la mort au déshonneur; **he would die ~ betraying** ... il mourrait plutôt que de trahir ...

2 *adv* **(a)** (*time*) avant, auparavant. **the day ~** la veille; **the evening ~** la veille au soir; **the week ~** la semaine d'avant *or* précédente; **I have read it ~** je l'ai déjà lu; **it has never happened ~** cela n'est jamais arrivé jusqu'ici; **it had never happened ~** cela n'était jamais arrivé jusqu'alors;

long ~ longtemps auparavant; **to continue as** ~ faire comme par le passé. **(b)** (*place*) en avant, devant. **(c)** (*order*) avant. **that chapter and the one** ~ ce chapitre et celui d'avant.

3 *conj* **(a)** (*time*) avant de + *infin*, avant que + ne + *subj*. **I did it** ~ **going out** je l'ai fait avant de sortir; **go and see him** ~ **he goes** allez le voir avant son départ *or* avant qu'il ne parte; **it will be 6 weeks** ~ **the boat returns** le bateau ne reviendra pas avant 6 semaines; ~ **I forget ...** avant que je n'oublie (*subj*) .... . **(b)** (*rather than*) plutôt que de + *infin*. **he will die** ~ **he surrenders** il mourra plutôt que de se rendre.

♦ **beforehand** *adv* à l'avance.

befriend [bɪ'frend] *vt* donner son amitié à.

befuddled [bɪ'fʌdld] *adj* (*confused*) embrouillé; (*tipsy*) éméché.

beg [beg] **1** *vt* **(a)** *money, food* mendier; *favour* solliciter. **to** ~ **sb's pardon** demander pardon à qn; **I** ~ **your pardon** (*apologizing*) je vous demande pardon; (*not having heard*) pardon?; **I** ~ **to state that** je me permets de faire remarquer que; **I** ~ **to differ** permettez-moi d'être d'un autre avis; **I** ~ **to inform you that** j'ai l'honneur de vous faire savoir que; **to** ~ **leave to do** solliciter l'autorisation de faire; **to** ~ **sb to do** supplier qn de faire; **I** ~ **you!** je vous en supplie! **(b) this** ~**s the question** c'est présumer la question résolue. **2** *vi* mendier. **to** ~ **for money** mendier; **to** ~ **for food** mendier de la nourriture; **to** ~ **for help** demander de l'aide; *[dog]* **to sit up and** ~ faire le beau; **it's going** ~**ging*** personne n'en veut.

beg off* *vi* se faire excuser (*from* de).

♦ **beggar 1** *n* mendiant(e) *m(f)*; ~**gars can't be choosers** nécessité fait loi; ~**gar's opera** opéra *m* de quat' sous; **poor** ~**gar!*** pauvre diable!*; a **lucky** ~**gar** un veinard*; **a queer little** ~**gar*** un drôle de petit bonhomme; **2** *vt* (*fig: ruin*) ruiner; **to** ~**gar description** défier toute description. ♦ **beggarly** *adj amount, meal* piètre (*before n*); *wage* dérisoire. ♦ **beggar-my-neighbour** *n* bataille *f* (*Cartes*).

began [bɪ'gæn] *pret of* **begin.**

beget [bɪ'get] *pret* **begot,** *ptp* **begotten** *vt* engendrer.

begin [bɪ'gɪn] *pret* **began,** *ptp* **begun 1** *vt* commencer (*to do, doing* à faire, de faire), se mettre (*to do, doing* à faire); *work, song, bottle, book* commencer; *conversation* engager; *quarrel, rumour* faire naître; *reform, war, series of events* déclencher; *fashion* lancer; *custom, policy* inaugurer. **to** ~ **a journey** partir en voyage; **he began the day with a glass of milk** il a bu un verre de lait pour bien commencer la journée; **to** ~ **life as** débuter dans la vie comme; **that doesn't even** ~ **to compare with ...** c'est loin d'être comparable à ...; **it soon began to rain** il n'a pas tardé à pleuvoir; **to** ~ **again** recommencer (*to do* à faire).

2 *vi* commencer (*with* par; *by doing* par faire), s'y mettre; *[river]* prendre sa source; *[road]* partir (*at* de); *[political party, movement, custom]* commencer, naître. **to** ~ **at the beginning** commencer par le commencement; **it's** ~**ning rather well** cela s'annonce plutôt bien; **just where the hair** ~**s** à la naissance des cheveux; **before October** ~**s** avant le début d'octobre; **to** ~ **again** recommencer; *[classes]* reprendre; ~**ning from Monday** à partir de lundi; **he began in the sales department** il a débuté dans le service des ventes; **he began as a Marxist** il a commencé par être marxiste; **he began with the intention of writing a thesis** au début son intention était d'écrire une thèse; **to** ~ **with, there were only 3 of them** d'abord, ils n'étaient que 3; ~ **on a new page** prenez une nouvelle page; **to** ~ **on sth** commencer qch; **since the world began** depuis que le monde est monde.

♦ **beginner** *n* débutant(e) *m(f)*; **it's just** ~**ner's luck** aux innocents les mains pleines. ♦ **beginning** *n* commencement *m*, début *m*; **to make a** ~**ning** commencer, débuter; **the** ~**ning of the academic year** la rentrée (universitaire *or* scolaire); **in the** ~**ning** au commencement, au début; **to start again at** *or* **from the** ~**ning** recommencer au commencement; **the** ~**ning of negotiations** l'ouverture *f* des négociations; **the** ~**ning of the end** le commencement de la fin; **the** ~**nings of science** les rudiments *mpl* de la science; **the shooting was the** ~**ning of the rebellion** la fusillade a été à l'origine de la révolte; **fascism had its** ~**nings ...** le fascisme prit naissance ... .

begone [bɪ'gɒn] *excl* partez!

begonia [bɪ'gəʊnɪə] *n* bégonia *m*.

begot(ten) [bɪ'gɒt(n)] *pret* (*ptp*) of **beget.**

begrudge [bɪ'grʌdʒ] *vt* = **grudge.**

beguile [bɪ'gaɪl] *vt* (*deceive*) tromper; (*entertain*) distraire; (*charm*) captiver. ♦ **beguiling** *adj* séduisant.

begun [bɪ'gʌn] *ptp of* **begin.**

behalf [bɪ'hɑːf] *n*: **on** ~ **of sb** *attend, accept* de la part de qn, pour qn; *plead* en faveur de qn; **he was worried on my** ~ il s'inquiétait pour moi.

behave [bɪ'heɪv] *vi* (~ **o.s.**) (*conduct o.s.*) se conduire; (*conduct o.s. well*) bien se tenir; *[child]* être sage; *[machine]* marcher. **to** ~ **well towards sb** bien agir envers qn; ~ **yourself!** tiens-toi bien! ♦ **behaviour,** (*US*) **behavior** *n* conduite *f*, comportement *m* (*to, towards* envers); *[machine]* fonctionnement *m*; **to be on one's best behaviour** se conduire de son mieux; *[child]* se montrer d'une sagesse exemplaire. ♦ **behavio(u)ral** *adj sciences, studies* behavioriste; *problem, pattern* de comportement. ♦ **behavio(u)rism** *n* behaviorisme *m*. ♦ **behavio(u)rist** *adj, n* behavioriste (*mf*).

behead [bɪ'hed] *vt* décapiter.

beheld [bɪ'held] *pret, ptp of* **behold.**

behest [bɪ'hest] *n*: **at the** ~ **of** sur l'ordre de.

behind [bɪ'haɪnd] **1** *adv come* derrière; *stay, look* en arrière. **to leave** ~ laisser derrière soi; **to be** ~ **with sth** être en retard dans qch. **2** *prep* derrière. **from** ~ **the door** de derrière la porte; **walk close** ~ **me** suivez-moi de près; (*fig*) **to put sth** ~ **one** oublier qch, refuser de penser à qch; (*fig*) **what is** ~ **this?** qu'y a-t-il là-dessous?; **he is** ~ **the other pupils** il est en retard sur les autres élèves; ~ **time** en retard; ~ **the times** en retard sur son temps. **3** *n* (*: *buttocks*) derrière *m*, postérieur* *m*. ♦ **behindhand** *adv, adj* en retard (*with sth* dans qch).

behold [bɪ'həʊld] *pret, ptp* **beheld** *vt* voir, apercevoir. ~! voici!

beholden [bɪ'həʊldən] *adj* redevable (*to* à, *for* de).

behove [bɪ'həʊv], (*US*) **behoove** [bɪ'huːv] *impers vt* incomber (*sb to do* à qn de faire).

beige [beɪʒ] *adj, n* beige (*m*).

bejewelled, (*US*) **bejeweled** [bɪ'dʒuːəld] *adj* couvert de bijoux.

belabour, (*US*) **-or** [bɪ'leɪbə^r] *vt* rouer de coups.

belated [bɪ'leɪtɪd] *adj* tardif.

belch [beltʃ] **1** *vi* faire un renvoi. **2** *vt* (~ **forth**) *smoke etc* vomir. **3** *n* renvoi *m*.

beleaguered [bɪ'liːgəd] *adj city* assiégé; *army* cerné.

belfry ['belfrɪ] *n* beffroi *m*.

Belgium ['beldʒəm] *n* Belgique *f*. ♦ **Belgian 1** *n* Belge *mf*; **2** *adj* belge.

belie [bɪ'laɪ] *vt* démentir.

belief [bɪ'liːf] *n* **(a)** croyance *f* (*in* en, à). ~ **in God/in ghosts** croyance en Dieu/aux revenants; **beyond** ~ (*adj*) incroyable; **wealthy beyond** ~ incroyablement riche. **(b)** conviction *f*. **in the** ~ **that** persuadé que; **it is my** ~ **that** je suis convaincu que; **to the best of my** ~ autant que je sache.

believe [bɪ'liːv] **1** *vt statement, evidence, person* croire (*that* que). **I don't ~ a word of it** je n'en crois pas un mot; **don't you ~ it!** ne va pas croire ça!; **he could hardly ~ his eyes** il en croyait à peine ses yeux; **if he is to be ~d** à l'en croire; **I ~ I'm right** je crois avoir raison; **I don't ~ he will come** je ne crois pas qu'il viendra *or* qu'il vienne; **he is ~d to be ill** on le croit malade; **I ~ so/not** je crois que oui/non. **2** *vi* croire. **to ~ in** *God* croire en; *ghosts, promises, antibiotics* croire à; *friend* avoir confiance en; *method* être partisan de; **I don't ~ in borrowing** je ne suis pas d'avis qu'il faille faire des emprunts. ◆ **believable** *adj* croyable. ◆ **believer** *n* (*Rel*) croyant(e) *m(f)*; (*gen*) **he is a great ~er in** il est très partisan de.

belittle [bɪ'lɪtl] *vt* déprécier.

bell [bel] *n [church, school, cows]* cloche *f*; (*hand~*) clochette *f*; *[toys, cats etc]* grelot *m*; *[goats, sheep]* clochette; *[door]* sonnette *f*; (*electric, also telephone*) sonnerie *f*; *[cycle, typewriter]* timbre *m*. **there's the ~!** on sonne!; (*Naut*) **eight ~s** huit coups piqués. ◆ **bell-bottomed** *adj*: **~-bottomed trousers** pantalon *m* de marine. ◆ **bellboy** *or* ◆ **bellhop** *n* groom *m*. ◆ **bell-push** *n* bouton *m* de sonnette. ◆ **bell-ringer** *n* sonneur *m*. ◆ **bell-tent** *n* tente *f* conique. ◆ **bell-tower** *n* clocher *m*.

belladonna [ˌbelə'dɒnə] *n* belladonne *f*.

belle [bel] *n* beauté *f*. **the ~ of the ball** la reine du bal.

bellicose ['belɪkəʊs] *adj* belliqueux.

belligerent [bɪ'lɪdʒərənt] *adj, n* belligérant(e) *m(f)*. ◆ **belligerence** *or* ◆ **belligerency** *n* belligérance *f*.

bellow ['beləʊ] **1** *vi [animals]* mugir; *[person]* brailler, beugler* (*with* de). **2** *vt* (**~ out**) *song, order* brailler, beugler*. **3** *n* mugissement *m*; beuglement* *m*.

bellows ['beləʊz] *npl [forge, organ]* soufflerie *f*; *[fire]* soufflet *m*.

belly ['belɪ] **1** *n* ventre *m*. **2** *vi* (**~ out**) se gonfler. **3** *adj*: **~ button** nombril *m*; **~ dancer** danseuse orientale; **~ laugh** gros rire gras. ◆ **bellyache 1** *n* mal *m* de *or* au ventre; **2** *vi* (‡: *complain*) ronchonner*. ◆ **bellyflop** *n* (*Swimming*) plat-ventre *m*. ◆ **bellyful** *n*: **he had had a ~ful‡** il en avait plein le dos*. ◆ **belly-landing*** *n* (*Aviat*) atterrissage *m* sur le ventre.

belong [bɪ'lɒŋ] *vi* appartenir (*to* à). **this book ~s to me** ce livre m'appartient, ce livre est à moi; **the lid ~s to this box** le couvercle va avec cette boîte; **to ~ to a society** faire partie *or* être membre d'une société; **to ~ to a town** *[native]* être originaire d'une ville; *[inhabitant]* habiter une ville; **to feel that one doesn't ~** se sentir étranger; **to ~ together** aller ensemble; **put it back where it ~s** remets-le à sa place. ◆ **belongings** *npl* affaires *fpl*, possessions *fpl*; **personal ~ings** objets personnels.

beloved [bɪ'lʌvɪd] *adj, n* bien-aimé(e) *m(f)*.

below [bɪ'ləʊ] **1** *prep* (*under*) sous; (*lower than*) au-dessous de. **~ the bed** sous le lit; **on the bed and ~ it** sur le lit et en dessous; **skirt well ~ the knee** jupe bien au-dessous du genou; **~ average** au-dessous de la moyenne; **the Thames ~ Oxford** la Tamise en aval d'Oxford. **2** *adv* en bas, en dessous, plus bas; (*Naut*) en bas. **the tenants ~** les locataires du dessous; **they live 2 floors ~** ils habitent 2 étages en dessous; **voices from ~** des voix venant d'en bas; **the road ~** la route en contre-bas; (*on earth*) **here ~** ici-bas; (*in hell*) **down ~** en enfer; *[documents]* **see ~** voir ci-dessous.

belt [belt] **1** *n* **(a)** (*gen*) ceinture *f*; (*Tech*) courroie *f*; (*corset*) gaine *f*. **(shoulder) ~** baudrier *m*; **that was below the ~** c'était un coup bas; **he's got 10 years' experience under his ~** il a 10 ans d'expérience à son acquis; (*fig*) **to tighten one's ~** se serrer la ceinture; (*Judo*) **to be a Black B~** être ceinture noire. **(b)** (*Geog*) zone *f*; (*Agr*) région *f*. **industrial ~** zone industrielle; **the cotton ~** la région de culture du coton. **2** *vt* (*thrash*) administrer une correction à. **she ~ed him one in the eye‡** elle lui a flanqué un gnon‡ dans l'œil. **3** *vi* (‡: *rush*) **to ~ in/out/across** *etc* entrer/sortir/traverser *etc* à toutes jambes.

belt out* *vt sep song* chanter à pleins poumons.

belt up *vi* **(a)** (*seat belts*) attacher sa ceinture. **(b)** (‡: *quiet*) la boucler‡. **~ up!** boucle-la!‡

bemoan [bɪ'məʊn] *vt* pleurer, déplorer.

bemuse [bɪ'mjuːz] *vt* stupéfier, hébéter.

bench [bentʃ] *n* (*gen, Parl*) banc *m*; (*in tiers*) gradin *m*; (*padded*) banquette *f*; *[workshop, factory]* établi *m*. **to be on the B~** (*permanent office*) être juge (*or* magistrat); (*when in court*) siéger au tribunal.

bend [bend] (*vb: pret, ptp* **bent**) **1** *n [river, tube, pipe]* coude *m*; *[arm, knee]* pli *m*; *[road]* coude, virage *m*. **~s for 8 km** virages sur 8 km; *[car]* **to take a ~** prendre un virage; (*fig*) **round the ~‡** cinglé*; (*Med*) **the ~s*** la maladie des caissons.

2 *vt* **(a)** *back, body, head, branch, rail* courber; *leg, arm* plier; *bow* bander. **to ~ at right angles** couder; **to ~ out of shape** fausser; **to go down on ~ed knee** se mettre à genoux. **(b) to be bent on doing** vouloir absolument faire.

3 *vi [person]* se courber; *[branch, instrument etc]* être courbé; *[river, road]* faire un coude. **to ~ backward/forward** se pencher en arrière/en avant.

bend back *vt sep* replier, recourber.

bend down *vi* se courber.

bend over 1 *vi* se pencher. (*fig*) **to ~ over backwards to help sb*** se mettre en quatre pour aider qn. **2** *vt sep* replier.

beneath [bɪ'niːθ] **1** *prep* (*under*) sous; (*lower than*) au-dessous de. **~ the table** sous la table; **town ~ the castle** ville (située) au-dessous du château; **it is ~ my notice** cela ne mérite pas mon attention; **it is ~ her to interfere** elle ne daignerait pas intervenir. **2** *adv*: **the flat ~** l'appartement au-dessous *or* du dessous.

benediction [ˌbenɪ'dɪkʃən] *n* bénédiction *f*.

benefactor ['benɪfæktə[r]] *n* bienfaiteur *m*. ◆ **benefactress** *n* bienfaitrice *f*.

benefice ['benɪfɪs] *n* bénéfice *m* (*Rel*).

beneficent [bɪ'nefɪsənt] *adj person* bienfaisant; *thing* salutaire. ◆ **beneficence** *n* bienfaisance *f*.

beneficial [ˌbenɪ'fɪʃəl] *adj* salutaire (*to* pour). **~ to the health** bon pour la santé. ◆ **beneficially** *adv* avantageusement.

beneficiary [ˌbenɪ'fɪʃərɪ] *n* bénéficiaire *mf*.

benefit ['benɪfɪt] **1** *n* **(a)** (*advantage*) avantage *m*. **for the ~ of your health** dans l'intérêt de votre santé; **it is for his ~ that ...** c'est pour lui que ... ; **it is to your ~** c'est dans votre intérêt; **it wasn't (of) much ~ to me** cela ne m'a pas beaucoup aidé; **he's just crying for your ~*** il pleure pour se faire remarquer; **to give sb the ~ of the doubt** laisser à qn le bénéfice du doute; **the ~s of a good education** les bienfaits *mpl or* les avantages d'une bonne éducation. **(b)** (*money*) allocation *f*, prestation *f*. **unemployment ~** allocation de chômage. **2** *vt* faire du bien à, profiter à. **3** *vi* gagner (*from, by doing* à faire). **he will ~ from a holiday** des vacances lui feront du bien. **4** *adj* (*Sport*) **~ match** match *m* au profit d'un joueur.

Benelux ['benɪlʌks] *adj*: **the ~ countries** les pays *mpl* du Bénélux.

benevolent [bɪ'nevələnt] *adj* (*kind*) bienveillant (*to* envers); (*charitable*) bienfaisant, charitable (*to* envers); *society* de bienfaisance. ◆ **benevolence** *n* (*kindness*) bienveillance *f*; (*generosity*) bienfaisance *f*.

benign [bɪ'naɪn], **benignant** [bɪ'nɪgnənt] *adj* bienveillant; (*Med*) bénin.

bent[1] [bent] (*pret, ptp of* **bend**) *adj wire, pipe* tordu; (*: *dishonest*) véreux; (*: *homosexual*) homosexuel. ♦ **bentwood** *adj hatstand* en bois courbé; *chair* bistrot *inv*.
bent[2] [bent] *n* (*aptitude*) dispositions *fpl* (*for* pour); (*liking*) penchant *m* (*for* pour). **to follow one's ~** suivre son inclination *f*.
benumbed [bɪ'nʌmd] *adj limb* engourdi; *person* (*cold, fear*) transi; (*shock*) paralysé.
Benzedrine ['benzɪdriːn] *n* ® benzédrine *f*.
benzine ['benziːn] *n* benzine *f*.
bequeath [bɪ'kwiːð] *vt* léguer (*to* à). ♦ **bequest** *n* legs *m*.
berate [bɪ'reɪt] *vt* réprimander.
bereave [bɪ'riːv] *pret, ptp* **bereft** *vt* (*deprive*) priver (*of* de). ♦ **bereaved 1** *adj* endeuillé; **2** *n*: **the ~d** la famille du disparu. ♦ **bereavement** *n* deuil *m*; **owing to a recent ~ment** en raison d'un deuil récent.
beret ['bereɪ] *n* béret *m*.
Berlin [bɜː'lɪn] *n* Berlin. **East/West ~** Berlin Est/Ouest.
Bermuda [bɜː'mjuːdə] *n* Bermudes *fpl*. **~ shorts** bermuda *m*.
berry ['berɪ] *n* baie *f*.
berserk [bə'sɜːk] *adj* fou furieux (*f* folle furieuse). **to go ~** (*lit*) devenir fou furieux; (*fig: with anger*) se mettre en rage.
berth [bɜːθ] **1** *n* **(a)** (*in plane, train, ship*) couchette *f*. (*easy job*) **a soft ~*** une bonne planque*. **(b)** (*place for ship*) poste *m* d'amarrage. (*fig*) **to give sb a wide ~** éviter qn à tout prix. **2** *vi* s'amarrer. **3** *vt* amarrer.
beryl ['berɪl] *n* béryl *m*.
beseech [bɪ'siːtʃ] *pret, ptp* **besought** *vt* implorer (*sb to do* qn de faire). ♦ **beseeching** *adj* implorant. ♦ **beseechingly** *adv* d'un air implorant.
beset [bɪ'set] *pret, ptp* **beset** *vt [difficulties, doubts]* assaillir; *[temptations]* entourer. **enterprise ~ with difficulties** entreprise hérissée de difficultés. ♦ **besetting** *adj*: **his ~ting sin** son plus grand défaut.
beside [bɪ'saɪd] *prep* (*at the side of*) à côté de, auprès de; (*compared with*) à côté de, comparé à. **that's ~ the point** cela n'a rien à voir avec la question; **it's quite ~ the point to suggest that ...** il est tout à fait inutile de suggérer que ...; **to be ~ o.s.** (*with anger*) être hors de soi; (*with excitement*) ne plus se posséder; **~ himself with joy** fou de joie.
besides [bɪ'saɪdz] **1** *adv* **(a)** (*in addition*) en outre, en plus. **many more ~** bien d'autres encore; **there is nothing ~** il n'y a rien de plus *or* d'autre. **(b)** (*moreover*) d'ailleurs, du reste, en outre. **2** *prep* **(a)** (*in addition to*) en plus de. **others ~ ourselves** d'autres que nous; **there were 3 of us ~ Mary** nous étions 3 sans compter Marie; **~ which ...** et par-dessus le marché ... . **(b)** (*except*) excepté, hormis, en dehors de. **no one ~ you** personne en dehors de vous, personne d'autre que vous; **who ~ them** qui si ce n'est eux.
besiege [bɪ'siːdʒ] *vt* assiéger; (*fig*) assaillir.
besom ['biːzəm] *n* balai *m* de bouleau.
besotted [bɪ'sɒtɪd] *adj* (*drunk*) hébété (*with* de); (*infatuated*) entiché (*with* de).
besought [bɪ'sɔːt] *pret, ptp of* **beseech.**
bespatter [bɪ'spætəʳ] *vt* éclabousser (*with* de).
bespectacled [bɪ'spektɪkld] *adj* à lunettes.
bespoke [bɪ'spəʊk] *adj garment* fait sur commande; *tailor* à façon.
best [best] **1** *adj* (*superl of* **good**) le meilleur, la meilleure. **the ~ pupil in the class** le meilleur élève de la classe; **the ~ thing about her is ...** ce qu'il y a de meilleur chez elle c'est ...; **the ~ thing to do is to wait** le mieux c'est d'attendre; **the ~ years of one's life** les plus belles années de sa vie; **in one's ~ clothes** vêtu de ses plus beaux vêtements; **may the ~ man win!** que le meilleur gagne!; **her ~ friend** sa meilleure amie; (*biggest*) **the ~ part of** la plus grande partie de; **for the ~ part of an hour** pendant près d'une heure; **~ man** (*at wedding*) garçon *m* d'honneur.
2 *n*: **to do one's ~** faire tout son possible (*to do* pour faire); **do the ~ you can** faites de votre mieux; **to get the ~ out of** tirer le maximum de; **to get the ~ of it** l'emporter; **he wants the ~ of both worlds** il veut tout avoir; **to make the ~ of sth** profiter au maximum de qch; **to make the ~ of a bad job** faire contre mauvaise fortune bon cœur; **the ~ of it is that ...** le plus beau de l'affaire c'est que ...; **it's all for the ~** c'est pour le mieux; **to the ~ of my knowledge/recollection** *etc* autant que je sache/que je me souvienne *etc*; **to look one's ~** être resplendissant; *[woman]* être en beauté; (*on form*) **to be at one's ~** être en pleine forme*; **that is Racine at his ~** voilà du meilleur Racine; **even at the ~ of times he's not very patient but ...** il n'est jamais particulièrement patient mais ...; **at ~** au mieux; **he can sing with the ~ of them** il sait chanter comme pas un*.
3 *adv* (*superl of* **well**) le mieux, le plus. **the ~ dressed** le mieux habillé; **the ~ loved** le plus aimé; **I like strawberries ~** je préfère les fraises; **as ~ I can** *or* **could** de mon mieux; **to think it ~ to do** croire qu'il vaudrait mieux faire; **do as you think ~** faites pour le mieux; **you know ~** c'est vous le mieux placé pour en décider; **you had ~ go** tu ferais mieux de t'en aller.
4 *vt* battre, l'emporter sur.
♦ **bestseller** *n* (*book, goods*) best-seller *m*; (*author*) auteur *m* à succès.
bestial ['bestɪəl] *adj* bestial. ♦ **bestiality** *n* bestialité *f*.
bestow [bɪ'stəʊ] *vt* (*gen*) accorder (*on* à); *title* conférer (*on* à).
bet [bet] *pret, ptp* **bet** *or* **betted 1** *vi* parier (*against* contre; *on* sur; *with* avec). **to ~ 10 to 1** parier (à) 10 contre 1; **to ~ on horses** parier *or* jouer aux courses; **to ~ on a horse** jouer un cheval. **2** *vt* (*fig*) **I ~ he'll come!*** je te parie qu'il viendra!; **you ~!*** tu parles!;* **~ you can't!*** chiche!*; **you can ~ your life that*** ... tu peux parier tout ce que tu veux que ... . **3** *n* pari *m* (*on* sur). ♦ **better**[1] *or* ♦ **bettor** *n* parieur *m*, -euse *f*; (*at races*) turfiste *mf*. ♦ **betting 1** *n* paris *mpl*; **the ~ting was 2 to 1** la cote était 2 contre 1; (*fig*) **the ~ting is that ...** il y a des chances que ...; **2** *adj*: **~ting shop** ≈ bureau *m* de P.M.U.; **~ting slip** ≈ P.M.U. *m*.
betel ['biːtəl] *n* bétel *m*.
bethink [bɪ'θɪŋk] *pret, ptp* **bethought** *vt*: **to ~ o.s. of sth/to do/that ...** s'aviser de qch/de faire/que ... .
betimes [bɪ'taɪmz] *adv* (*early*) tôt; (*quickly*) promptement.
betoken [bɪ'təʊkən] *vt* être signe de.
betray [bɪ'treɪ] *vt* (*gen*) trahir; (*disclose*) *age, fears etc* révéler (*to* à), trahir. **to ~ sb to the police** livrer qn à la police; **his speech ~ed the fact that ...** on devinait à l'écouter que ... . ♦ **betrayal** *n* trahison *f*; **~al of trust** abus *m* de confiance.
betrothal [bɪ'trəʊðəl] *n* (*liter*) fiançailles *fpl* (*to* avec). ♦ **betrothed** *adj, n* fiancé(e) *m(f)*.
better[2] ['betəʳ] **1** *adj* (*comp of* **good**) meilleur (*than* que). **she is ~ at dancing than at singing** elle danse mieux qu'elle ne chante; **he's a ~ man than his brother** il est mieux que son frère; (*hum*) **you're a ~ man than I am!** vous êtes plus doué que moi!*; **he's no ~ than a thief** c'est un voleur ni plus ni moins; **he's no ~ than he should be!** ce n'est pas l'honnêteté qui l'étouffe!*; (*Med*) **he is much ~ now** il va bien mieux maintenant; **to get ~** (*gen*) s'améliorer; (*Med*) se remettre (*from* de); **~ and ~!** de mieux en mieux!; **that's ~!** voilà qui est mieux!; **it couldn't be ~** ça ne pourrait pas

mieux tomber; **it would be ~ to stay at home** il vaudrait mieux rester à la maison; **a ~ class of hotel** un hôtel de catégorie supérieure; **his ~ nature** ses bons sentiments; **to go one ~ than sb** damer le pion à qn; **the ~ part of a year** près d'un an; **to hope for ~ things** espérer mieux.

2 *adv* (*comp of* **well**) mieux (*than* que). **he sings ~ than he dances** il chante mieux qu'il ne danse; **all the ~, so much the ~** tant mieux (*for* pour); **he was all the ~ for it** il s'en est trouvé mieux; **it would be all the ~ for a drop of paint** un petit coup de peinture ne lui ferait pas de mal; **they are ~ off than we are** (*richer*) ils ont plus d'argent que nous; (*more fortunate*) ils sont dans une meilleure position que nous; **he is ~ off at his sister's** il est mieux chez sa sœur; **I had ~ go** il faudrait que je m'en aille; **hadn't you ~ speak to him?** ne vaudrait-il pas mieux que tu lui parles (*subj*)?; **~ dressed** mieux habillé; **~ known** plus connu.

3 *n*: **a change for the ~** une amélioration, un changement en mieux; **for ~ or worse** pour le meilleur ou pour le pire; **to get the ~ of sb** triompher de qn; **one's ~s** ses supérieurs *mpl*.

4 *vt sb's achievements* dépasser; *record, score* améliorer. **to ~ o.s.** améliorer sa condition.

between [bɪ'twiːn] **1** *prep* (*gen*) entre. **no one can come ~ us** personne ne peut nous séparer; **~ the wars** entre les deux guerres; **the ferry goes ~ Dover and Calais** le ferry fait la navette entre Douvres et Calais; **~ here and London** d'ici (à) Londres; **~ now and next week** d'ici la semaine prochaine; **the match ~ A and B** le match qui oppose A à B; **they have 5 oranges ~ them** ils ont 5 oranges en tout; **~ ourselves, he ...** entre nous, il ...; **the 2 boys managed to lift the box ~ them** à eux deux les garçons sont arrivés à soulever la caisse. **2** *adv* au milieu, dans l'intervalle. **few and far ~** très espacés, très rares; **rows of trees with grass in ~** des rangées d'arbres séparées par de l'herbe.

betwixt [bɪ'twɪkst] *adv*: **~ and between** entre les deux.

bevel ['bevəl] **1** *n* (**~** *edge*) biseau *m*; (*tool*: **~** *square*) fausse équerre *f*. **2** *vt* biseauter.

beverage ['bevərɪdʒ] *n* boisson *f*.

bevy ['bevɪ] *n* bande *f*, troupe *f*.

bewail [bɪ'weɪl] *vt* se lamenter sur.

beware [bɪ'wɛəʳ] *vti*: **to ~ (of)** prendre garde (*sb/sth* à qn/à qch; *doing* de faire), se garder (*doing* de faire), se méfier (*sth* de qch); **~ of falling** prenez garde de tomber; **~ of listening to him** gardez-vous de l'écouter; **'~ of the dog!'** 'attention, chien méchant'; **'~ of pickpockets!'** 'attention aux pickpockets!'; **'~ of imitations'** 'se méfier des contrefaçons'.

bewilder [bɪ'wɪldəʳ] *vt* dérouter; (*stronger*) confondre. ♦ **bewildered** *adj person* dérouté, ahuri; *look* perplexe. ♦ **bewildering** *adj* déroutant; (*stronger*) ahurissant. ♦ **bewilderingly** *adv* d'une façon déroutante *or* ahurissante. ♦ **bewilderment** *n* confusion *f*; (*stronger*) ahurissement *m*.

bewitch [bɪ'wɪtʃ] *vt* ensorceler; (*fig*) charmer. ♦ **bewitching** *adj* charmant. ♦ **bewitchingly** *adv* d'une façon séduisante; **~ingly beautiful** belle à ravir.

beyond [bɪ'jɒnd] **1** *prep* (*in space*) au-delà de, de l'autre côté de; (*in time*) plus de; (*exceeding*) au-dessus de; (*except*) sauf. **this work is quite ~ him** ce travail le dépasse complètement; **it's ~ me* why he hasn't left her** ça me dépasse* qu'il ne l'ait pas quittée; **~ my reach** hors de ma portée; **he is ~ caring** il ne s'en fait plus du tout; **that's ~ a joke** cela dépasse les bornes; **~ his means** au-dessus de ses moyens; **he gave her no answer ~ a grunt** il ne lui a répondu que par un grognement. **2** *adv* au-delà, plus loin, là-bas. **the room ~** la pièce d'après; **the lands ~** les terres lointaines.

bezique [bɪ'ziːk] *n* bésigue *m*.

bi... [baɪ] *pref* bi... . ♦ **biannual** *adj* semestriel. ♦ **bicentenary** *adj, n* bicentenaire (*m*). ♦ **biennial** *adj* biennal. ♦ **bifocals** *npl* verres *mpl* à double foyer. ♦ **bilateral** *adj* bilatéral. ♦ **bilingual** *adj* bilingue. ♦ **bimonthly** *adj* bimensuel. ♦ **biped** *adj, n* bipède (*m*). ♦ **biplane** *n* biplan *m*. ♦ **bisexual** *adj* (*Bio*) bisexué; (*Psych*) (sexuellement) ambivalent. ♦ **biweekly** *adj* bihebdomadaire.

bias ['baɪəs] **1** *n* **(a)** (*inclination*) tendance *f* (*towards* à); (*prejudice*) préjugé *m* (*towards* pour; *against* contre). **(b)** (*Sewing*) **on the ~** dans le biais; **~ binding** biais *m* (*ruban*). **2** *vt* influencer, (*pej*) prévenir (*towards* en faveur de; *against* contre). ♦ **bias(s)ed** *adj* partial; **to be ~(s)ed against** avoir un préjugé contre.

bib [bɪb] *n [child]* bavoir *m*; *[apron]* bavette *f*. **in her best ~ and tucker*** sur son trente et un.

Bible ['baɪbl] **1** *n* Bible *f*. **2** *adj oath* sur la Bible; *story* tiré de la Bible. **~ thumper*** évangéliste *m* de carrefour. ♦ **biblical** ['bɪblɪkəl] *adj* biblique.

bibliography [ˌbɪblɪ'ɒgrəfɪ] *n* bibliographie *f*. ♦ **bibliographer** *n* bibliographe *mf*. ♦ **bibliographic(al)** *adj* bibliographique. ♦ **bibliomaniac** *n* bibliomane *mf*.

bibulous ['bɪbjʊləs] *adj* adonné à la boisson; *look* aviné; *evening* bien arrosé.

bicarbonate [baɪ'kɑːbənɪt] *n*: **~ of soda** bicarbonate *m* de soude.

biceps ['baɪseps] *n* biceps *m*.

bicker ['bɪkəʳ] *vi* se chamailler*. ♦ **bickering** *n* chamailleries* *fpl*.

bicycle ['baɪsɪkl] **1** *n* bicyclette *f*, vélo *m*. **to ride a ~** faire de la bicyclette *or* du vélo. **2** *adj bell, chain* de bicyclette; *pump* à bicyclette; *path* cyclable; *race* cycliste. **~ rack** râtelier *m* à bicyclettes. **~ shed** abri *m* à bicyclettes.

bid [bɪd] *pret* **bade** *or* **bid**, *ptp* **bidden** *or* **bid** **1** *vt* **(a)** (*command*) ordonner (*sb to do* à qn de faire). **(b)** (*say*) dire. **to ~ sb good morning** dire bonjour à qn; **to ~ sb welcome** souhaiter la bienvenue à qn. **(c)** (*offer*) *amount* offrir; (*at auction*) faire une enchère de; (*Cards*) demander. **2** *vi* faire une offre *or* (*at auction*) une enchère (*for* pour). **to ~ against sb** renchérir sur qn; **to ~ for power** viser le pouvoir; **to ~ fair to do** promettre de faire. **3** *n* **(a)** offre *f*; (*at auction*) enchère *f*; (*Cards*) demande *f*. **'no ~'** 'parole'. **(b)** (*attempt*) tentative *f*. **suicide ~** tentative de suicide; **to make a ~ for power/freedom** tenter de s'emparer du pouvoir/de s'évader. ♦ **biddable** *adj child* docile; (*Cards*) *suit* demandable. ♦ **bidder** *n* enchérisseur *m*, offrant *m*; **the highest ~der** le plus offrant. ♦ **bidding** *n* **(a)** (*at sale, also Cards*) enchère(s) *f(pl)*; **the ~ding is closed** l'enchère est faite; **(b) I did his ~ding** j'ai fait ce qu'il m'a dit.

bide [baɪd] *vt*: **to ~ one's time** attendre le bon moment.

bidet ['biːdeɪ] *n* bidet *m*.

bier [bɪəʳ] *n* bière *f* (*pour enterrement*).

biff* [bɪf] *vt* flanquer* un coup de poing à.

big [bɪg] **1** *adj* (*in height, age*) *person, building, tree* grand; (*in bulk, amount*) *fruit, parcel, book, lie* gros (*f* grosse). **my ~ brother** mon grand frère, mon frère aîné; (*Aut*) **~ end** tête *f* de bielle; **a ~ man** un homme grand et fort; (*important*) un grand homme, un homme marquant; (*Pol*) **the B~ Four** les quatre Grands; **~ game** gros gibier; **~ game hunter** chasseur *m* de gros gibier; **~ game hunting** chasse *f* au gros gibier; **~ toe** gros orteil; **~ top** (*circus*) cirque *m*; (*main tent of it*) grand chapiteau *m*; **to grow ~** *or* **~ger** grandir (*or* grossir); **to look ~** faire l'important; **~ noise*, ~ shot*** grosse légume*; **~ business** les grosses affaires; **to have ~ ideas** voir grand; **what's the ~ idea?*** ça ne va pas, non?*; **to do things in a ~ way** faire les choses en grand; **that's rather a ~ word**

c'est un bien grand mot; ~ **talk** beaux discours (*pej*); **he's too ~ for his boots** il a des prétentions; **he's got a ~ head*** il est crâneur*; **he's got a ~ mouth*** il ne sait pas se taire; **why can't you keep your ~ mouth shut!*** tu aurais mieux fait de la boucler!‡; **to make the ~ time*** réussir; (*iro*) ~ **deal!*** tu parles!*; (*iro*) **that's ~ of you!*** quelle générosité! **2** *adv*: **to talk ~*** fanfaronner, se faire mousser*; **to go over ~‡** avoir un succès monstre*; **his speech went down ~* with his audience** ses auditeurs ont été emballés* par son discours.
◆ **big-boned** *adj* fortement charpenté. ◆ **bighead*** *n* crâneur* *m*, -euse* *f*. ◆ **bigheaded*** *adj* crâneur*. ◆ **big-hearted** *adj* au grand cœur; to be **~-hearted** avoir du cœur. ◆ **bigmouth*** *n* hâbleur *m*, -euse *f*. ◆ **big-sounding** *adj idea, plan etc* prometteur, faramineux*; *name* ronflant. ◆ **bigwig‡** *n* grosse légume* *f*.

bigamy ['bɪgəmɪ] *n* bigamie *f*. ◆ **bigamist** *n* bigame *mf*. ◆ **bigamous** *adj* bigame.

bigot ['bɪgət] *n* (*Rel*) bigot(e) *m(f)*; (*Pol etc*) fanatique *mf*. ◆ **bigoted** *adj* bigot; fanatique. ◆ **bigotry** *n* bigoterie *f*; fanatisme *m*.

bike [baɪk] **1** *n* (*) vélo *m*. **2** *vi* (‡) aller à vélo.

bikini [bɪ'kiːnɪ] *n* bikini *m*.

bilberry ['bɪlbərɪ] *n* myrtille *f*.

bile [baɪl] *n* (*Anat*) bile *f*; (*anger*) mauvaise humeur. ~ **stone** calcul *m* biliaire.

bilge [bɪldʒ] *n* (*water*) eau *f* de cale; (*: *nonsense*) idioties *fpl*.

bilious ['bɪlɪəs] *adj* bilieux. ~ **attack** crise *f* de foie. ◆ **biliousness** *n* affection *f* hépatique.

bill[1] [bɪl] **1** *n* **(a)** (*account*) facture *f*; *[hotel, also gas etc]* note *f*; *[restaurant]* addition *f*. **have you paid the milk ~?** as-tu payé le lait?; **a pile of ~s in the post** une pile de factures dans le courrier; **may I have the ~ please** l'addition (*or* la note) s'il vous plaît. **(b)** ~ **of fare** menu *m*, carte *f* (du jour); ~ **of indictment** acte *m* d'accusation; ~ **of lading** connaissement *m*; ~ **of rights** déclaration *f* des droits; ~ **of exchange** lettre *f* de change; ~ **of sale** acte *m* de vente. **(c)** (*US: banknote*) billet *m* (de banque). **5-dollar ~** billet de 5 dollars. **(d)** (*Parl*) projet *m* de loi. **(e)** (*poster*) placard *m*; (*Theat etc*) affiche *f*. **to top the ~** être en tête d'affiche.
2 *vt* **(a)** *goods* facturer. **to ~ sb for sth** envoyer la facture de qch à qn. **(b) he is ~ed to play Hamlet** il est à l'affiche dans le rôle de Hamlet.
◆ **billboard** *n* panneau *m* d'affichage. ◆ **billfold** *n* portefeuille *m*. ◆ **billing**[1] *n* (*Theat*) **to get top/second ~ing** figurer en tête d'affiche/en deuxième place à l'affiche. ◆ **billposter** *or* ◆ **billsticker** *n* colleur *m* d'affiches.

bill[2] [bɪl] **1** *n [bird]* bec *m*. **2** *vi*: **to ~ and coo** roucouler. ◆ **billing**[2] *n*: **~ing and cooing** roucoulements *mpl* (d'amoureux).

billet ['bɪlɪt] (*Mil*) **1** *n* cantonnement *m* (chez l'habitant). **2** *vt* cantonner (*on sb* chez qn).

billhook ['bɪlhʊk] *n* serpette *f*.

billiard ['bɪljəd] **1** *n*: **~s** (jeu *m* de) billard *m*. **2** *adj*: ~ **ball/cue** boule *f*/queue *f* de billard; **~(s) saloon** (café-)billard *m*; ~ **table** (table *f* de) billard *m*.

billion ['bɪljən] *n* (*Brit*) billion *m*; (*US*) milliard *m*.

billow ['bɪləʊ] **1** *n* flot *m*. **2** *vi [sea]* se soulever; *[sail]* se gonfler; *[cloth]* onduler.

billy can ['bɪlɪkæn] *n* gamelle *f*.

billy goat ['bɪlɪgəʊt] *n* bouc *m*.

billy-ho* ['bɪlɪhəʊ] *n*: **like ~** *laugh* très fort; *run* très vite.

bin [bɪn] *n [coal, corn]* coffre *m*; *[bread]* boîte *f*, (*larger*) huche *f*; *[wine]* casier *m* (à bouteilles); (*dust~, rubbish ~*) boîte *f* à ordures, poubelle *f*.

binary ['baɪnərɪ] *adj* binaire.

bind [baɪnd] *pret, ptp* **bound 1** *vt* **(a)** (*fasten*) *thing* attacher; *2 or more things* attacher, lier; *person, animal* lier, attacher (*to* à); *prisoner* ligoter; (*Culin*) lier. **bound hand and foot** pieds et poings liés. **(b)** (*encircle*) entourer (*with* de); *artery* ligaturer; *wound* bander; *material, hem* border (*with* de); *book* relier (*in* en). **(c)** (*oblige*) obliger (*sb to do* qn à faire). **2** *vi* **(a)** *[agreement]* engager. **(b)** (‡: *complain*) rouspéter*. **3** *n* (‡: *nuisance*) scie* *f*.

bind over *vt sep* (*Jur*) mettre en liberté conditionnelle.

bind together *vt sep sticks* lier; (*fig*) *people* unir.

bind up *vt sep wound* bander. **to be totally bound up with** *person* se dévouer entièrement à; *work, hobby* se donner corps et âme à; **it's all bound up with whether ...** tout dépend si ... .
◆ **binder** *n* (*Agr*) lieuse *f*; (*for papers*) classeur *m*; (*Med etc*) bandage *m*. ◆ **binding 1** *n [book]* reliure *f*; *[skis]* fixation *f*; (*tape*) extra-fort *m*; **2** *adj rule* obligatoire; *agreement, promise* qui lie; **to be ~ing on sb** lier qn. ◆ **bindweed** *n* liseron *m*.

binge‡ [bɪndʒ] *n*: **to have a ~** faire la bombe*.

bingo ['bɪŋgəʊ] *n* loto *m* (*joué collectivement pour de l'argent*).

binoculars [bɪ'nɒkjʊləz] *npl* jumelles *fpl*.

biochemistry ['baɪəʊ'kemɪstrɪ] *n* biochimie *f*. ◆ **biochemical** *adj* biochimique. ◆ **biochemist** *n* biochimiste *mf*.

biodegradable ['baɪəʊdɪ'greɪdəbl] *adj* biodégradable.

biography [baɪ'ɒgrəfɪ] *n* biographie *f*. ◆ **biographer** *n* biographe *mf*. ◆ **biographic(al)** *adj* biographique.

biology [baɪ'ɒlədʒɪ] *n* biologie *f*. ◆ **biologist** *n* biologiste *mf*. ◆ **biological** *adj reason, warfare* biologique; *soap powder* aux enzymes.

biophysics [ˌbaɪəʊ'fɪzɪks] *nsg* biophysique *f*. ◆ **biophysical** *adj* biophysique. ◆ **biophysicist** *n* biophysicien(ne) *m(f)*.

biopsy ['baɪɒpsɪ] *n* biopsie *f*.

birch [bɜːtʃ] **1** *n* (*tree, wood*) bouleau *m*; (*for whipping*) verge *f*, fouet *m*. **2** *vt* fouetter. ◆ **birching** *n* peine *f* du fouet.

bird [bɜːd] **1** *n* oiseau *m*; (*game*) pièce *f* de gibier (à plume); (*Culin*) volaille *f*; (‡: *fellow*) type* *m*; (‡: *girl*) nana‡ *f*. ~ **of passage/prey** oiseau de passage/proie; **~'s nest** nid *m* d'oiseau; **a ~ in the hand is worth two in the bush** un tiens vaut mieux que deux tu l'auras; **they're ~s of a feather** ils sont à mettre dans le même sac; **a little ~ told me*** mon petit doigt me l'a dit; **to give sb the ~‡** envoyer paître qn‡; **that's strictly for the ~s‡** ça c'est bon pour les imbéciles. **2** *adj*: ~ **bath** vasque *f* pour les oiseaux; ~ **brain‡** tête *f* de linotte; ~ **cage** cage *f* à oiseaux; ~ **call** cri *m* d'oiseau; **to go ~ nesting** aller dénicher les oiseaux; ~ **sanctuary** réserve *f* d'oiseaux; **a ~'s eye view of Paris** Paris (vu) à vol d'oiseau; (*fig*) **~'s-eye view** vue *f* d'ensemble; ~ **watcher** ornithologue *mf* amateur; **to go ~ watching** aller observer les oiseaux.

Biro ['baɪərəʊ] *n* ® ≃ (pointe *f*) Bic *m* ®.

birth [bɜːθ] **1** *n [baby, idea etc]* naissance *f*; (*childbirth*) accouchement *m*. **during the ~** pendant l'accouchement; **to give ~ to** *[woman]* donner naissance à; *[animal]* mettre bas; **from ~, by ~** de naissance; **of good ~** de bonne famille. **2** *adj*: ~ **certificate** acte *m* de naissance; ~ **control** contrôle *m* des naissances; ~ **pill** pilule *f* (anticonceptionnelle); ~ **rate** (taux *m* de) natalité *f*. ◆ **birthday 1** *n* anniversaire *m*; **2** *adj cake, card, present* d'anniversaire; **she is having a ~day party** on a organisé une petite fête pour son anniversaire; (*hum*) **in one's ~day suit*** dans le costume d'Adam (*or* d'Ève)*. ◆ **birthmark** *n* tache *f* de vin (*sur la peau*). ◆ **birthplace** *n* (*gen, Admin*) lieu *m* de naissance; (*house*) maison natale; (*fig: of civilisation etc*) berceau *m*. ◆ **birthright** *n* droit *m* acquis en naissant.

biscuit ['bɪskɪt] **1** *n* (*Brit*) petit gâteau sec, biscuit *m*; (*US*) petit pain au lait. **he takes the ~!**: il est marrant!: **2** *adj* (*colour*) biscuit *inv*.

bisect [baɪ'sekt] *vt* couper en deux (parties égales).

bishop ['bɪʃəp] *n* évêque *m*; (*Chess*) fou *m*. ♦ **bishopric** *n* évêché *m*.

bismuth ['bɪzməθ] *n* bismuth *m*.

bison ['baɪsn] *n* bison *m*.

bit[1] [bɪt] **1** *pret of* **bite**. **2** *n* **(a)** *[horse]* mors *m*. **to take the ~ between one's teeth** prendre le mors aux dents. **(b)** *[tool]* mèche *f*.

bit[2] [bɪt] **1** *n [bread]* morceau *m*; *[paper, string]* bout *m*; *[book, talk etc]* passage *m*. **a ~ of** (*gen*) un peu de; **a ~ of garden** un bout de jardin; **a tiny little ~** un tout petit peu; **a ~ of advice** un petit conseil; **a ~ of news** une nouvelle; **a ~ of luck** une chance; **he's got a ~ of money put aside** il a un peu d'argent en réserve; **the ~ of money he had left** le peu d'argent qui lui restait; **a ~/a little ~/a good ~ late** un peu/un petit peu/très en retard; **a good ~ bigger** bien *or* beaucoup plus grand; **I'm a ~ of a socialist*** je suis plutôt socialiste; **it was a ~ of a shock** ça nous a plutôt fait un choc; **not a ~** pas du tout; **bring all your ~s and pieces** apporte toutes tes petites affaires; **in ~s and pieces** (*broken*) en morceaux, en miettes; (*dismantled*) en pièces détachées; (*fig*) *plan, scheme* en ruines; **to come to ~s** (*break*) s'en aller en morceaux; (*dismantle*) se démonter; (*fig*) **he went to ~s*** il a craqué*; **~ by ~** petit à petit; **to do one's ~** fournir sa part d'effort; **when it comes to the ~** en fin de compte; (*of time*) **after a good ~** après un bon bout de temps*; **wait a ~** attendez un instant; **to pay a good ~ for sth** payer qch assez cher. **2** *adj* (*Theat*) **~ part** petit rôle. ♦ **bitty*** *adj* décousu.

bitch [bɪtʃ] **1** *n [dog]* chienne *f*; *[canines generally]* femelle *f*; (:*pej: woman*) garce: *f*. **terrier ~** terrier *m* femelle. **2** *vi* (:: *complain*) râler* (*about* contre). ♦ **bitchy:** *adj* rosse*, vache:.

bite [baɪt] (*vb: pret* **bit**, *ptp* **bitten**) **1** *n [dog, snake etc]* morsure *f*; *[insect]* piqûre *f*; (*Fishing*) touche *f*; (*piece bitten off*) bouchée *f*; (*something to eat*) morceau *m*. **in two ~s** en deux bouchées; **there's not a ~ to eat** il n'y a rien à manger; **come and have a ~** venez manger un morceau. **2** *vt* (*gen*) mordre; *[insect]* piquer. **to ~ one's nails** se ronger les ongles; **to ~ one's tongue/fingers** se mordre la langue/les doigts; **to ~ the dust** mordre la poussière; (*fig*) **to ~ the hand that feeds you** être d'une ingratitude monstrueuse; **once bitten twice shy** chat échaudé craint l'eau froide; **to be bitten with* the desire to do** mourir d'envie de faire; **what's biting you?**: qu'est-ce que tu as à râler?* **3** *vi* (*gen*) mordre; *[insect]* piquer; *[cogs]* s'engrener. **to ~ into sth** *[person]* mordre (dans) qch; *[acid]* mordre sur qch.

bite off *vt sep* couper d'un coup de dents. **she bit off a piece of apple** elle a mordu dans la pomme; (*fig*) **he has bitten off more than he can chew** il a eu les yeux plus grands que le ventre; (*fig*) **to ~ sb's head off*** rembarrer qn (brutalement).

bite through *vt fus lip* mordre (de part en part); *thread* couper avec les dents.

♦ **biting** *adj cold* perçant; *wind* cinglant; *wit, remarks* mordant. ♦ **bitingly** *adv speak* d'un ton mordant.

bitter ['bɪtə[r]] **1** *adj* **(a)** *taste* amer, âpre. (*fig*) **it was a ~ pill to swallow** la pilule était amère; **~ lemon** Schweppes *m* ® au citron; **~ orange** (*fruit*) orange *f* amère. **(b)** *weather* glacial; *winter* rude. **(c)** *person, reproach, tears* amer; *critic, criticism* acerbe; *fate, sorrow, suffering* cruel; *hatred* acharné; *opposition, protest* violent; *remorse* cuisant. **to the ~ end** jusqu'au bout; **I feel very ~ about the whole business** toute cette histoire m'a rempli d'amertume. **2** *n* (*Brit: beer*) bière anglaise (*pression*). (*drink*) **~s** bitter *m*. ♦ **bitterly** *adv speak, complain, weep* amèrement; *criticize, reproach* âprement; *oppose, resist* avec acharnement; *disappointed* cruellement; *jealous* profondément; (*Met*) **it was ~ly cold** il faisait un froid de loup. ♦ **bitterness** *n* amertume *f*. ♦ **bittersweet** *adj* aigre-doux.

bitumen ['bɪtjʊmɪn] *n* bitume *m*.

bivouac ['bɪvʊæk] **1** *n* bivouac *m*. **2** *vi* bivouaquer.

bizarre [bɪ'zɑːʳ] *adj* bizarre.

blab [blæb], **blabber** ['blæbə] **1** *vi* (*tell secret*) tout raconter; (*chatter*) jaser. **2** *vt* (**~ out**) aller raconter.

black [blæk] **1** *adj* (*lit, fig*) noir. **~ and blue** couvert de bleus; **~ art(s), ~ magic** magie noire; **~ beetle** cafard *m*; (*Aviat*) **~ box** boîte noire; **the B~ Country** le Pays Noir (de l'Angleterre); **the B~ Death** la peste noire; **~ eye** œil *m* au beurre noir*; **to give sb a ~ eye** pocher l'œil à qn; **~ ice** verglas *m*; **B~ Maria*** panier *m* à salade*; **on the ~ market** au marché noir; **~ marketeer** profiteur *m*, -euse *f*; **~ mass** messe noire; **the B~ Prince** le Prince Noir; **~ pudding** boudin *m*; **B~ Sea** mer Noire; **~ sheep (of the family)** brebis galeuse (de la famille); **(accident) ~ spot** point noir (*Aut*); '**~ tie**' (*on invitation*) 'smoking'; **~ man** Noir *m*; **~ woman** Noire *f*; **the ~ Americans** les Américains noirs; '**~ is beautiful**' ≈ 'nous sommes fiers d'être noirs'; (*fig*) **~list** liste *f* noire (*V below*); **B~ Power** (*movement*) Black Power *m*; **it is as ~ as pitch** il fait noir comme dans un four; **his hands were ~** il avait les mains noires; (*fig*) **he looked as ~ as thunder** il avait l'air furibond; **you can scream till you're ~ in the face but ...** tu peux toujours t'égosiller, mais ...; **a ~ deed** un crime; **things are looking ~** les choses se présentent très mal; **a ~ day on the roads** une sombre journée sur les routes; **a ~ day for England** un jour bien triste *or* (*stronger*) un jour de deuil pour l'Angleterre; (*during strike*) **to declare a cargo ~** boycotter une cargaison; **~ goods** marchandises boycottées.

2 *n* (*colour*) noir *m*; (*person*) Noir(e) *m(f)*; (*darkness*) obscurité *f*. **dressed in ~** habillé de noir; **there it is in ~ and white** c'est écrit noir sur blanc; **two ~s don't make a white** la faute de l'un n'excuse pas celle de l'autre; **to swear that ~ is white** *[obstinate person]* se refuser à l'évidence; *[liar]* mentir effrontément.

3 *vt* (*gen*) noircir; *shoes* cirer; (*Ind*) *goods, firm* boycotter. **to ~ sb's eye (for him)** pocher l'œil à qn.

black out **1** *vi* (*Med*) s'évanouir. **2** *vt sep* (*in wartime*) *town, building* faire le black-out dans; *[power cut]* plonger dans l'obscurité totale; (*Theat*) *stage* faire l'obscurité sur.

♦ **black-ball** **1** *n* vote *m* contraire; **2** *vt* blackbouler. ♦ **blackberry** **1** *n* mûre *f*; (*bush*) mûrier *m*; **2** *vi*: **to go ~berrying** aller cueillir des mûres. ♦ **blackbird** *n* merle *m*. ♦ **blackboard** *n* tableau *m* (noir). ♦ **blackcurrant** *n* cassis *m*. ♦ **blacken** *vti* noircir. ♦ **blackguard** ['blægɑːd] *n* fripouille *f*. ♦ **blackguardly** *adj* ignoble. ♦ **blackhead** *n* point noir (*sur la peau*). ♦ **black-hearted** *adj* mauvais. ♦ **blacking** *n [shoes]* cirage *m* (noir); *[stoves]* pâte *f* à noircir; *[cargo etc]* boycottage *m*. ♦ **blackish** *adj* tirant sur le noir, noirâtre (*pej*). ♦ **blackjack** *n* (*flag*) pavillon noir (*des pirates*); (*weapon*) matraque *f*; (*Cards*) vingt-et-un *m*. ♦ **blacklead** *vt* frotter à la mine de plomb. ♦ **blackleg** (*Ind*) **1** *n* jaune *m*; **2** *vi* briser la grève. ♦ **blacklist** *vt person* mettre sur la liste noire; *book* mettre à l'index. ♦ **blackmail** **1** *n* chantage *m*; **2** *vt* faire chanter; **to ~mail sb into doing** forcer qn par le chantage à faire. ♦ **blackmailer** *n* maître-chanteur *m*. ♦ **blackness** *n [colour, substance]* couleur noire, noirceur *f*; (*darkness*) obscurité *f*; (*dirtiness*) saleté *f*. ♦ **blackout** *n [lights]* panne *f* d'électricité; (*during war*) black-out *m*; (*amnesia*) trou *m* de mémoire; (*fainting*) évanouissement *m.* ♦ **blackshirt** *n* (*Pol*) chemise noire (*fasciste*). ♦ **blacksmith** *n* (*shoes horses*) maréchal-ferrant *m*; (*forges iron*) forgeron *m.*

bladder ['blædəʳ] *n* vessie *f*; (*Bot*) vésicule *f.*

blade [bleɪd] *n [knife, tool, weapon, razor]* lame *f*; *[chopper, guillotine]* couperet *m*; *[tongue, oar]* plat *m*; *[spade]* fer *m*; *[propeller]* pale *f*; *[windscreen wiper]* caoutchouc *m*; *[grass]* brin *m.*

blah‡ [blɑː] *n* blablabla* *m.*

blame [bleɪm] **1** *vt* **(a)** (*fix responsibility on*) **to ~ sb for sth, to ~ sth on sb*** rejeter la responsabilité de qch sur qn, mettre qch sur le dos de qn*; **I'm not to ~** ce n'est pas ma faute; **you have only yourself to ~** tu l'as bien cherché; **whom/what are we to ~ for this accident?** à qui/à quoi attribuer cet accident? **(b)** (*censure*) reprocher (*sb for doing* à qn de faire; *sb for sth* qch à qn), blâmer (*sb for doing* qn de faire; *sb for sth* qn de qch). **to ~ o.s. for sth/for having done** se reprocher qch/d'avoir fait; **he was greatly to ~ for doing that** il a eu grand tort de faire cela. **2** *n* **(a)** (*responsibility*) responsabilité *f.* **to put** *or* **lay the ~ for sth on sb** rejeter la responsabilité de qch sur qn. **(b)** (*censure*) blâme *m.* ♦ **blamable** *adj* blâmable. ♦ **blameless** *adj* irréprochable. ♦ **blamelessly** *adv* d'une manière irréprochable. ♦ **blameworthy** *adj* blâmable.

blanch [blɑːntʃ] **1** *vt vegetables* blanchir; *almonds* monder. **2** *vi [person]* blêmir.

blancmange [blə'mɒnʒ] *n* blanc-manger *m.*

bland [blænd] *adj air, flavour* doux; *manner* affable. ♦ **blandly** *adv* avec affabilité.

blandishments ['blændɪʃmənts] *npl* flatteries *fpl.*

blank [blæŋk] **1** *adj paper, page* blanc; *map* muet; *cheque* en blanc; *cartridge* à blanc; *wall* aveugle; *silence, darkness* profond; *refusal, denial* absolu; *life etc* dépourvu d'intérêt, vide; *face, look* (*expressionless*) sans expression, vide; (*puzzled*) déconcerté, dérouté. (*fig*) **to give sb a ~ cheque (to do)** donner à qn carte blanche (pour faire); **~ space** blanc *m*, espace *m* vide; **~ form** formulaire *m* (à remplir); (*on form*) **please leave ~** laisser en blanc s.v.p.; **a look of ~ astonishment** un regard ébahi; **his mind went ~** il a eu un passage à vide; **~ verse** vers *mpl* blancs. **2** *n* **(a)** (*void*) blanc *m*, espace *m* vide. **she left several ~s in her answers** elle a laissé plusieurs de ses réponses en blanc; **my mind was a ~** j'avais la tête vide. **(b)** (**~** *form*) formulaire *m*, fiche *f*; *[coin, medal, record]* flan *m.* (*fig*) **to draw a ~** faire chou blanc. ♦ **blankly** *adv say, announce* carrément; *look* (*expressionlessly*) sans expression; (*without understanding*) sans comprendre.

blanket ['blæŋkɪt] **1** *n* couverture *f*; *[snow etc]* couche *f*; *[fog]* nappe *f*; *[smoke]* nuage *m.* **2** *adj statement, condemnation etc* global. *[insurance policy]* **to give ~ cover** être tous risques.

blare [blɛəʳ] **1** *n* vacarme *m.* **2** *vi [music, horn etc]* retentir; *[loud voice]* claironner; *[radio]* beugler. **3** *vt music* faire retentir.

blarney* ['blɑːnɪ] *n* boniment* *m.*

blasé ['blɑːzeɪ] *adj* blasé.

blaspheme [blæs'fiːm] *vti* blasphémer (*against* contre). ♦ **blasphemer** *n* blasphémateur *m*, -trice *f.* ♦ **blasphemous** ['blæsfɪməs] *adj person* blasphémateur; *words* blasphématoire. ♦ **blasphemously** *adv* avec impiété. ♦ **blasphemy** ['blæsfɪmɪ] *n* blasphème *m.*

blast [blɑːst] **1** *n* **(a)** (*sound*) *[bomb, quarrying]* explosion *f*; *[space rocket]* grondement *m*; *[trumpets etc]* fanfare *f.* **~ on the siren** coup *m* de sirène; **to blow a ~ on the bugle** donner un coup de clairon; **the radio was going at full ~** la radio marchait à plein volume. **(b)** (*shock wave*) *[bomb, furnace etc]* souffle *m.* (*lit, fig*) **at full ~** à plein; **~ of air/steam** jet *m* d'air/de vapeur; **~ of wind** coup *m* de vent, rafale *f*; (*wind*) **the icy ~** le souffle glacé (du vent). **2** *adj*: **~ furnace** haut fourneau *m.* **3** *vt rocks* faire sauter; *[lightning]* foudroyer; *hopes, future* anéantir. **4** *excl* (*) la barbe!* **~ him!** il est embêtant!*

blast off *vi [rocket etc]* être mis à feu.

♦ **blasted*** *adj* fichu* (*before n*). ♦ **blasting** *n* (*Tech*) minage *m*; **'~ing in progress'** 'attention, tir de mines'. ♦ **blast-off** *n* (*Space*) lancement *m.*

blatant ['bleɪtənt] *adj injustice, lie etc* criant, flagrant; *bully, social climber* éhonté; *coward, thief, liar* fieffé (*before n*). ♦ **blatantly** *adv* d'une manière flagrante.

blather ['blæðəʳ] *vi* raconter des bêtises.

blaze¹ [bleɪz] **1** *n* (*fire*) feu *m*, flambée *f*; (*conflagration*) incendie *m*; *[gems, beauty etc]* éclat *m.* **~ of light** torrent *m* de lumière; **~ of colour** flamboiement *m* de couleur(s); **a ~ of anger** une explosion de colère; **go to ~s!*** va te faire voir!*; **how the ~s!*** comment diable!; **like ~s*** comme un fou (*f* une folle). **2** *vi [fire]* flamber; *[sun, colour]* flamboyer; *[jewel, light]* resplendir; *[anger]* éclater. **blazing with colour** resplendissant de couleur.

blaze away *vi [soldiers, guns]* maintenir un feu nourri (*at* contre).

blaze up *vi [fire]* s'enflammer; *[person, anger]* éclater.

♦ **blazing** *adj* **(a)** *building etc* en feu, en flammes; *torch* enflammé; *sun* éclatant, ardent; (*fig*) *eyes* qui jette des éclairs; *jewel* étincelant; *colour* très vif; **(b)** (*: *angry*) furibard*; **(c)** (*fig*) *indiscretion, lie* flagrant.

blaze² [bleɪz] **1** *n* (*mark*) *[horse etc]* étoile *f*; *[tree]* marque *f.* **2** *vt*: **to ~ a trail** (*lit*) frayer un chemin; (*fig*) montrer la voie.

blazer ['bleɪzəʳ] *n* blazer *m.*

bleach [bliːtʃ] **1** *n* décolorant *m*; (*liquid*) eau *f* oxygénée. **(household) ~** eau de Javel. **2** *vt linen, bones etc* blanchir; *hair* décolorer. **to ~ one's hair** se décolorer (les cheveux).

bleach out *vt sep colour* enlever.

bleak [bliːk] *adj country, landscape* exposé au vent, désolé; *room* nu, austère; *weather, wind* froid; *existence* sombre; *prospect* lugubre; *smile* triste. **things look rather ~ for him** les choses se présentent plutôt mal pour lui. ♦ **bleakly** *adv look* sombrement; *speak* d'un ton morne. ♦ **bleakness** *n* aspect désolé; austérité *f*; froid *m*; aspect sombre; tristesse *f.*

bleary ['blɪərɪ] *adj eyes* (*from sleep, fatigue*) voilé; (*from illness*) chassieux; (*from tears*) larmoyant. ♦ **bleary-eyed** *adj* aux yeux voilés *etc.*

bleat [bliːt] **1** *vi* bêler; (‡: *complain*) se plaindre (*about* de). **2** *n* bêlement *m.*

bleed [bliːd] *pret, ptp* **bled** [bled] **1** *vi* saigner. **his nose is ~ing** il saigne du nez; **he is ~ing to death** il perd tout son sang; (*iro*) **my heart ~s for you** tu me fends le cœur. **2** *vt* saigner. **to ~ sb white** saigner qn à blanc. ♦ **bleeding 1** *n* saignement *m*; (*more serious*) hémorragie *f*; **2** *adj wound* saignant; *person* qui saigne; (*fig*) *heart* brisé.

bleep [bliːp] **1** *n* (*Rad, TV*) top *m*; *[pocket call radio]* bip *m.* **2** *vi* émettre des signaux. **3** *vt* biper. ♦ **bleeper** *n* bip *m.*

blemish ['blemɪʃ] *n* défaut *m*; (*on fruit, reputation*) tache *f.*

blench [blentʃ] *vi* (*flinch*) sursauter; (*turn pale*) blêmir. **without ~ing** sans broncher.

blend [blend] **1** *n* (*gen*) mélange *m*; *[qualities]* alliance *f.* **excellent ~ of tea** thé *m* d'excellente qualité; *[coffee]* **Brazilian ~** café *m* du Brésil; **'our own ~'** 'mélange (spécial de la) maison'. **2** *vt* (*gen*) mélanger (*with* à, avec); *qualities* joindre (*with* à); *colours, styles* fondre. **3** *vi* (**~ in**) (*gen*) se mélanger (*with* à, avec); *[voices, perfumes]* se confondre; *[styles]* se marier; *[ideas, political parties, races]* fusionner; *[colours]* (*shade in*) se fondre; (*go together*) aller bien ensemble.

♦ **blender** *n* (*Tech*) malaxeur *m*; (*Culin*) mixeur *m*.

bless [bles] *pret, ptp* **blessed** [blest] *or* **blest** *vt* bénir. **God ~ the king!** Dieu bénisse le roi!; **I was never ~ed with children** je n'ai jamais connu le bonheur d'avoir des enfants; (*iro*) **she'll ~ you for this!** elle va te bénir!; **~ you!** vous êtes un ange!; (*sneezing*) à vos souhaits!; **and Paul, ~ his heart, had no idea that ...** et ce brave Paul dans son innocence ne savait pas que ...; **~ his little heart!** qu'il est mignon!; **~ my soul!*, well I'm blest!*** ça alors!* ♦ **blessed** ['blesɪd] *adj* **(a)** (*Rel*) (*holy*) béni, saint; (*happy*) bienheureux; **B~ed Virgin** Sainte Vierge; **B~ed Sacrament** Saint Sacrement; **the B~ed Antony Bennet** le bienheureux Antony Bennet; **(b)** (*) fichu* (*before n*), satané (*before n*); **that ~ed child** ce fichu* gosse; **the whole ~ed day** toute la sainte journée; **every ~ed evening** tous les soirs que le bon Dieu fait*. ♦ **blessing** *n* **(a)** (*prayer*) bénédiction *f*; **with God's ~ing** par la grâce de Dieu; **the plan had his ~ing*** il avait donné sa bénédiction à ce projet; (*at meal*) **to ask a ~ing** dire le bénédicité; **(b)** (*benefit*) bienfait *m*; **the ~ings of civilization** les bienfaits *or* les avantages *mpl* de la civilisation; **what a ~ing that ...** quelle chance que ... + *subj*; **this rain has been a real ~ing*** cette pluie a été une vraie bénédiction*; **it was a ~ing in disguise** c'était malgré les apparences un bien.

blew [blu:] *pret of* **blow**[1].

blight [blaɪt] **1** *n [cereals, plants]* rouille *f*, charbon *m*; *[fruit trees]* cloque *f*; (*fig*) fléau *m*. **2** *vt plants* rouiller; *hopes* anéantir; *career, life, future* gâcher.

blighter* ['blaɪtəʳ] *n* type* *m*, bonne femme. **silly ~** imbécile *mf*; **lucky ~!** quel(le) veinard(e)*!; **you ~!** espèce de chameau!*

blimey‡ ['blaɪmɪ] *excl* mince alors!*

blind [blaɪnd] **1** *adj person, obedience* aveugle; *corner, flying* sans visibilité; *passage* sans issue; *door, window* faux. **a ~ man/woman** un/une aveugle; **~ man's buff** colin-maillard *m*; **a ~ boy** un jeune aveugle; **~ in one eye** borgne; **as ~ as a bat** myope comme une taupe*; **it was approaching on his ~ side** cela approchait dans son angle mort; **~ spot** (*Med*) point *m* aveugle; (*Aut, Aviat*) angle *m* mort; (*fig*) **that was his ~ spot** sur ce point il refusait d'y voir clair; **she was ~ to his faults** elle ne voyait pas ses défauts; **to turn a ~ eye to** fermer les yeux sur; **~ alley** impasse *f*; **a ~-alley job** une situation sans avenir; **~ date** rendez-vous *m* avec qn qu'on ne connaît pas; **not a ~ bit of use**‡ qui ne sert strictement à rien.

2 *vt* aveugler; (*fig*) aveugler (*to* sur). **the war-~ed** les aveugles *mpl* de guerre.

3 *n* **(a) the ~** les aveugles *mpl*; **it's the ~ leading the ~** c'est comme l'aveugle qui conduit l'aveugle. **(b)** *[window]* store *m*. **(c)** (*pretence*) feinte *f*, masque *m*. **(d) to go on a ~**‡ (aller) se soûler la gueule‡.

4 *adv fly* sans visibilité. **~ drunk**‡ complètement rond*.

♦ **blindfold 1** *vt* bander les yeux à *or* de; **2** *n* bandeau *m*; **3** *adj* aux yeux bandés; **4** *adv* les yeux bandés. ♦ **blinding** *adj* aveuglant. ♦ **blindly** *adv* aveuglément. ♦ **blindness** *n* cécité *f*; (*fig*) aveuglement *m* (*to* devant); **~ness to the truth** refus *m* de voir la vérité.

blink [blɪŋk] **1** *n* clignotement *m* (des yeux). **my telly's on the ~*** ma télé est détraquée. **2** *vi* cligner des yeux; *[light]* vaciller. **3** *vt*: **to ~ one's eyes** cligner des yeux; **to ~ back the tears** refouler les larmes (d'un battement de paupières). ♦ **blinkers** *npl* œillères *fpl*. ♦ **blinking*** *adj* fichu* (*before n*); **~ing idiot** espèce *f* d'idiot.

bliss [blɪs] *n* (*Rel*) béatitude *f*; (*gen*) félicité *f*. **what ~!*, it's ~!*** c'est merveilleux!, c'est divin! ♦ **blissful** *adj* (*Rel, gen*) bienheureux, (*) divin, merveilleux. ♦ **blissfully** *adv smile* d'un air béat; *happy, unaware* parfaitement.

blister ['blɪstəʳ] **1** *n [skin]* ampoule *f*; *[paint]* boursouflure *f*; *[metal, skin]* soufflure *f*; (‡ *pej: person*) plaie* *f*. **2** *vi* former une *or* des ampoule(s); *[paint]* se boursoufler. ♦ **blistering** *adj heat, day* étouffant; *sun* brûlant; *attack* cinglant. ♦ **blister-pack** *n* (*Comm*) plaquette *f*.

blithe [blaɪð] *adj* joyeux. ♦ **blithely** *adv* joyeusement.

blithering* ['blɪðərɪŋ] *adj*: **~ idiot** espèce *f* d'idiot(e).

blitz [blɪts] **1** *n* (*Mil*) attaque *f* éclair *inv*; (*Aviat*) bombardement *m* (aérien). **the B~** le Blitz; (*fig*) **to have a ~ on sth** s'attaquer à qch. **2** *vt* bombarder. ♦ **blitzkrieg** *n* guerre-éclair *f*.

blizzard ['blɪzəd] *n* tempête *f* de neige.

bloated ['bləʊtɪd] *adj* (*gen*) gonflé; *face* bouffi; *stomach* ballonné; (*with pride etc*) bouffi (*with* de).

bloater ['bləʊtəʳ] *n* (hareng *m*) bouffi *m*.

blob [blɒb] *n* (*drop*) grosse goutte *f*; (*spot, stain*) tache *f*.

bloc [blɒk] *n* bloc *m* (*Pol*). **en ~** en bloc.

block [blɒk] **1** *n* **(a)** *[stone]* bloc *m*; *[wood]* bille *f*; *[butcher, blacksmith, executioner]* billot *m*; *[chocolate]* plaque *f*. (*toys*) **~s** (jeu *m* de) cubes *mpl*. **(b)** *[buildings]* pâté *m* (de maisons). **a ~ of flats, an apartment ~** un immeuble; **to walk round the ~** faire le tour du pâté de maisons; (*US*) **3 ~s away** 3 rues plus loin. **(c)** (*obstruction*) *[traffic]* embouteillage *m*, encombrement *m*; *[pipe]* obstruction *f*; (*Med, Psych*) blocage *m*. **(d)** (*unit*) *[tickets]* série *f*; *[shares]* tranche *f*; *[seats]* groupe *m*. **(e)** (*Tech*) **~ and tackle** palan *m*. **2** *adj*: **in ~ capitals** *or* **letters** en majuscules *fpl* d'imprimerie. **3** *vt* (*gen*) bloquer; *pipe etc* boucher; (*Ftbl*) *opponent* gêner. **to ~ sb's way** barrer le chemin à qn.

block off *vt sep part of road etc* interdire; (*accidentally*) obstruer.

block out *vt sep* **(a)** (*obscure*) *view* boucher; (*censor*) *passage* caviarder. **(b)** (*sketch roughly*) *scheme* ébaucher.

block up *vt sep gangway* encombrer; *pipe* bloquer; *window, entrance* murer, condamner; *hole* boucher, bloquer.

♦ **blockade 1** *n* blocus *m*; **2** *vt* bloquer. ♦ **blockage** *n* (*gen*) obstruction *f*; (*Med, Psych*) blocage *m*; (*fig*) bouchon *m*. ♦ **blockbuster*** *n* bombe *f* de gros calibre; (*film, TV series*) superproduction *f*; (*argument*) argument *m* massue *inv*. ♦ **blockhead*** *n* imbécile *mf*. ♦ **blockhouse** *n* blockhaus *m*.

bloke* [bləʊk] *n* type* *m*.

blond(e) [blɒnd] *adj, n* blond(e) *m(f)*.

blood [blʌd] **1** *n* sang *m*. **till the ~ comes** jusqu'au sang; **it's like trying to get ~ out of a stone** c'est comme si on parlait à un mur; **bad ~** désaccord *m*; **his ~ will be on your head** vous aurez sa mort sur la conscience; **my ~ was boiling** je bouillais (de rage); **his ~ is up** il est très monté; **he's out for ~*** il cherche qn sur qui passer sa colère; **she is out for his ~*** elle veut sa peau*; **his ~ ran cold** son sang s'est figé *or* s'est glacé dans ses veines; **~ is thicker than water** la voix du sang est la plus forte; **it's in his ~** il a cela dans le sang; **of Irish ~** de sang irlandais; (*fig*) **new ~** sang nouveau.

2 *adj temperature* du sang; *group, plasma, transfusion* sanguin. **~ bank** banque *f* du sang; **~ bath** massacre *m*; **~ blister** pinçon *m*; **~ brother** frère *m* de sang; **~ cell** globule *m* (sanguin); **~ count** numération *f* globulaire; **~ donor** donneur *m*, -euse *f* de sang; **~ grouping** recherche *f* du groupe sanguin; **~ heat** température *f* du sang (37°); **~ lust** soif *f* de sang; **~ money** prix *m* du

sang; ~ **orange** (orange *f*) sanguine *f*; ~ **poisoning** empoisonnement *m* du sang; ~ **pressure** tension *f* (artérielle); **to have high/low** ~ **pressure** faire de l'hypertension/hypotension; **to take sb's** ~ **pressure** prendre la tension de qn; **his** ~ **pressure went up** sa tension a monté; (*fig*) il a failli avoir une attaque; ~ **relation** parent(e) *m(f)* par le sang; ~ **sports** sports *mpl* sanguinaires; ~ **test** analyse *f* du sang; ~ **vessel** vaisseau *m* sanguin.
♦ **blood-and-thunder** *adj novel* à sensation; **a ~-and-thunder play** *or* **film** un sombre mélodrame.
♦ **bloodcurdling** *adj* à vous figer le sang.
♦ **bloodhound** *n* limier *m*. ♦ **bloodless** *adj complexion* anémié; *victory* sans effusion de sang.
♦ **bloodlessly** *adv* sans effusion de sang.
♦ **bloodletting** *n* saignée *f* (*Med*). ♦ **blood-red** *adj* rouge sang *inv*. ♦ **bloodshed** *n* effusion *f* de sang. ♦ **bloodshot** *adj* injecté (de sang); **to become ~shot** s'injecter. ♦ **bloodstain** *n* tache *f* de sang. ♦ **bloodstained** *adj* taché de sang, ensanglanté. ♦ **bloodstock** *n* bêtes *fpl* de sang.
♦ **bloodstream** *n* sang *m*, système *m* sanguin.
♦ **bloodthirsty** *adj* sanguinaire.

bloody ['blʌdɪ] **1** *adj* **(a)** *hands, weapon* taché de sang, ensanglanté; *battle* sanglant; *nose* en sang. **(b)** (ꞎ) foutuꞎ (*before n*); (*horrible*) emmerdantꞎ. **2** *adv* (ꞎ) vachementꞎ. **not ~ likely!** tu te fous de moi!ꞎ ♦ **bloody-mindedꞎ** *adj* mauvais coucheur. ♦ **bloody-mindedness** *n*: **out of sheer ~-mindednessꞎ** (rien que) pour emmerder le mondeꞎ.

bloom [blu:m] **1** *n* **(a)** (*flower*) fleur *f*. **in ~ flower** éclos; *tree* en fleurs; **in full ~ flower** épanoui; *tree* en pleine floraison. **(b)** *[fruit, skin]* velouté *m*. **2** *vi [flower]* éclore; *[tree]* fleurir; *[person]* être florissant. **~ing with health** resplendissant de santé. ♦ **bloomer** *n* **(a)** (ꞎ: *mistake*) gaffe *f*; **(b)** (*Dress*) **~ers** culotte *f* bouffante. ♦ **blooming*** *adj* fichu* (*before n*).

blossom ['blɒsəm] **1** *n* fleurs *fpl*; (*one flower*) fleur *f*. **a spray of** ~ une petite branche fleurie; **peach** ~ fleur de pêcher. **2** *vi* fleurir; (*fig*) s'épanouir. (*fig*) **to ~ (out) into** devenir.

blot [blɒt] **1** *n* tache *f*. **a ~ on his character** une tache à sa réputation; **to be a ~ on the landscape** déparer le paysage. **2** *vt* **(a)** (*spot with ink*) tacher d'encre. (*fig*) **to ~ one's copybook** faire un accroc à sa réputation. **(b)** (*dry*) *ink, page* sécher.
blot out *vt sep words* rayer; *memories* effacer; *[fog etc] view* masquer; (*destroy*) *city* annihiler.
♦ **blotter** *n* buvard *m*; (*desk pad*) sous-main *m inv*; (*US: record*) registre *m*. ♦ **blotting paper** *n* (papier *m*) buvard *m*.

blotch [blɒtʃ] **1** *n* tache *f*. **2** *vt* tacher. ♦ **blotchy** *adj face* marbré; *paint* couvert de taches.

blottoꞎ ['blɒtəʊ] *adj* bourréꞎ, rondꞎ.

blouse [blaʊz] *n* chemisier *m*.

blow¹ [bləʊ] *pret* **blew**, *ptp* **blown 1** *vt* **(a)** *[wind] ship* pousser; *leaves* chasser. **the wind blew the ship off course** le vent a fait dévier le navire; **the wind blew the door open** un coup de vent a ouvert la porte. **(b)** *fire* souffler sur; *bellows* faire marcher; *egg* vider. **to ~ one's nose** se moucher. **(c)** *bubbles* faire; *glass* souffler; *kiss* envoyer. **(d)** *trumpet, horn* jouer de, souffler dans. **to ~ a whistle** siffler; **to ~ one's own trumpet** chanter ses propres louanges. **(e)** *fuse, safe* faire sauter. **to ~ a gasket** griller un joint de culasse; **the whole plan has been ~n sky-high** tout le projet a sauté; **I blew £5 on a new hat*** j'ai claqué* 5 livres pour un nouveau chapeau. **(f)** (*phrases*) **to ~ one's topꞎ** piquer une colère*; **to ~ the gaffꞎ** vendre la mèche; **he realized he was ~nꞎ** il a compris qu'il était brûlé*; ~ **the expense!*** tant pis pour la dépense!; **well, I'm ~ed!*** ça alors!*; ~ **it!*** la barbe!*, zut!*
2 *vi* **(a)** *[wind, person, animal]* souffler. **to ~ on one's fingers/one's soup** souffler dans ses doigts/sur sa soupe; **it was ~ing a gale** le vent soufflait en tempête; **it's ~ing great guns*** il fait un vent à décorner les bœufs*; (*fig*) **to see which way the wind ~s** regarder de quel côté souffle le vent; **to ~ hot and cold** *[person]* souffler le chaud et le froid; *[enthusiasm]* avoir des hauts et des bas; **the door blew open** un coup de vent a ouvert la porte; **his hat blew out of the window** son chapeau s'est envolé par la fenêtre. **(b)** *[trumpet]* sonner; *[whistle]* retentir; *[foghorn]* mugir. **when the whistle ~s** au coup de sifflet. **(c)** *[fuse, light bulb]* sauter; *[tyre]* éclater.
blow down 1 *vi [tree etc]* être abattu par le vent. **2** *vt sep [person]* abattre (en soufflant); *[wind]* faire tomber.
blow in 1 *vi* (*: *arrive*) débarquer*. **2** *vt sep door, window* enfoncer. **look what the wind's ~n in!*** regardez qui s'amène!*
blow off 1 *vi [hat]* s'envoler. **2** *vt sep hat* emporter. **that blew the lid off the whole business*** c'est cela qui a fait découvrir le pot aux roses; **to ~ off steam** lâcher de la vapeur; (*: *fig*) se défouler*.
blow out 1 *vi [lamp]* s'éteindre; *[tyre]* éclater; *[fuse]* sauter. **2** *vt sep lamp* éteindre; *candle* souffler; *one's cheeks* gonfler. **to ~ one's brains out** se brûler la cervelle.
blow over 1 *vi [storm, dispute]* passer. **2** *vt sep tree* renverser.
blow up 1 *vi [bomb]* exploser; (*: *get angry*) sauter au plafond; *[wind]* se lever; *[storm]* (*gather*) se préparer; (*begin*) éclater. **2** *vt sep building* faire sauter; *tyre* gonfler; *photo* agrandir; *event* exagérer; (ꞎ: *reprimand*) passer un (bon) savon à*.
♦ **blowerꞎ** *n* (*loudspeaker*) haut-parleur *m*; (*telephone*) téléphone *m*. ♦ **blowfly** *n* mouche *f* à viande. ♦ **blowhole** *n* évent *m*. ♦ **blowlamp** *n* lampe *f* à souder. ♦ **blow-out** *n [tyre]* éclatement *m*; (*Elec*) court-circuit *m*; (ꞎ: *feast*) gueuletonꞎ *m*.
♦ **blowtorch** *n* lampe *f* à souder. ♦ **blow-up** *n* explosion *f*; (ꞎ: *quarrel*) engueuladeꞎ *f*; (*Phot**) agrandissement *m*. ♦ **blowy** *adj* éventé.

blow² [bləʊ] *n* (*gen*) coup *m*; (*with fist*) coup de poing. **to come to ~s** en venir aux mains; **at one ~** du premier coup; **he gave me a ~-by-~ account** il ne m'a fait grâce d'aucun détail; **it was a terrible ~ for him** cela a été un coup terrible pour lui.

blowzy ['blaʊzɪ] *adj hair* mal peigné; *woman* débraillé.

blubber ['blʌbəʳ] **1** *n [whale]* blanc *m* de baleine. **2** *vi* (*weep*) pleurer comme un veau.

bludgeon ['blʌdʒən] **1** *n* matraque *f*. **2** *vt* matraquer. (*fig*) **he ~ed me into doing it** il m'a forcé la main (pour que je le fasse).

blue [blu:] **1** *adj* **(a)** bleu. ~ **with cold** bleu de froid; **you may talk till you are ~ in the face*** tu peux toujours parler; ~ **baby** enfant bleu; ~ **blood** sang bleu; ~ **cheese** (fromage *m*) bleu *m*; ~ **jeans** blue-jean *m*; **once in a ~ moon*** tous les trente-six du mois; **like a ~ streak*** au triple galop; **to have a ~ fitꞎ** piquer une crise*; (*fig*) **to feel ~*** avoir le cafard*; **to be in a ~ funk*** avoir la frousse*. **(b)** (*obscene*) *talk* grivois; *book, film* porno* *inv*.
2 *n* (*colour*) bleu *m*. **the ~** (*sky*) l'azur *m*; (*sea*) les flots *mpl*; (*fig*) **to come out of the ~** être complètement inattendu; **to go off into the ~** (*into the sky*) disparaître dans le ciel; (*into the unknown*) partir à l'aventure; (*out of touch*) disparaître de la circulation*; **the ~s*** (*depression*) le cafard*; (*Mus*) le blues; (*Univ*) **he is a rugby ~** il a représenté son université au rugby.
3 *vt* (*: *squander*) gaspiller, claquerꞎ.
♦ **bluebell** *n* jacinthe *f* des bois. ♦ **bluebird** *n* oiseau *m* bleu. ♦ **bluebottle** *n* mouche *f* bleue.
♦ **blue-eyed** *adj* aux yeux bleus; (*fig*) **the ~-eyed boy** le chouchou*. ♦ **blueprint** *n* (*fig*) plan *m*,

schéma *m* directeur (*for* de). ♦ **bluestocking** *n* bas-bleu *m*.

bluff[1] [blʌf] **1** *adj person* direct. **2** *n* (*headland*) falaise *f* avancée.

bluff[2] [blʌf] **1** *vti* bluffer*. **2** *n* bluff* *m*. **to call sb's ~** prouver que qn bluffe*. ♦ **bluffer** *n* bluffeur* *m*, -euse* *f*.

blunder ['blʌndəʳ] **1** *n* gaffe *f*; (*error*) grosse faute. **2** *vi* (*make mistake*) faire une gaffe *or* une grosse faute. **to ~ in/out** *etc* entrer/sortir *etc* à l'aveuglette; **to ~ against** *or* **into sth** se cogner contre qch. ♦ **blunderer** *n* gaffeur *m*, -euse *f*. ♦ **blundering** *adj* maladroit.

blunt [blʌnt] **1** *adj* **(a)** *blade, knife, point, needle* émoussé; *pencil* mal taillé. (*Jur*) **with a ~ instrument** avec un instrument contondant. **(b)** (*outspoken*) *person, speech* carré, brusque (*slightly pej*); *fact* brutal. **he was very ~** il n'a pas mâché ses mots. **2** *vt blade, pencil etc* émousser; *palate, feelings* blaser. ♦ **bluntly** *adv speak* carrément. ♦ **bluntness** *n* état émoussé *etc*; (*outspokenness*) franc-parler *m*, brusquerie *f* (*slightly pej*).

blur [blɜːʳ] **1** *n* (*vague form*) masse *f* confuse, tache *f* floue; (*mist: on mirror etc*) buée *f*. **2** *vt shining surface* embuer, troubler; *inscription, view, outline* estomper. **eyes ~red with tears** yeux voilés de larmes. ♦ **blurred** *adj* (*TV, Phot etc*) flou.

blurb [blɜːb] *n* (*gen*) baratin* *m* publicitaire; (*on book jacket*) texte *m* de présentation *or* de couverture.

blurt [blɜːt] *vt* (**~ out**) *word* lâcher; *information* laisser échapper.

blush [blʌʃ] **1** *vi* rougir (*with* de). **I ~ for him** j'ai honte pour lui; **I ~ to say so** je rougis de le dire. **2** *n* rougeur *f*. **with a ~** en rougissant; **without a ~** sans rougir. ♦ **blushing** *adj* (*with shame*) le rouge au front; (*from embarrassment*) le rouge aux joues; *bride* rougissant.

bluster ['blʌstəʳ] *vi [wind, storm]* faire rage; *[person]* (*rage*) tempêter, fulminer (*at sb* contre qn); (*boast*) fanfaronner. ♦ **blustering 1** *adj* fanfaron; **2** *n* fanfaronnades *fpl*. ♦ **blustery** *adj wind* qui souffle en rafales; *weather, day* à bourrasques.

boa ['bəʊə] *n* boa *m*. **~ constrictor** boa constricteur *m*.

boar [bɔːʳ] *n* (*wild*) sanglier *m*; (*male pig*) verrat *m*. **~'s head** hure *f*. ♦ **boarhound** *n* vautre *m*.

board [bɔːd] **1** *n* **(a)** (*piece of wood*) planche *f*. (*Theat*) **the ~s** les planches, la scène; (*fig*) **above ~** tout ce qu'il y a de plus régulier; (*fig*) **across the ~** (*adv*) systématiquement; (*adj*) de portée générale. **(b)** (*meals*) pension *f*. **~ and lodging** (chambre *f* avec) pension; **full ~** pension complète. **(c)** (*group of officials*) conseil *m*, commission *f*. **~ of directors** conseil d'administration; **he has a seat on the ~** il siège au conseil d'administration; (*Brit*) **B~ of Trade** ministère *m* du Commerce; **medical ~** commission *f* médicale; (*Mil*) conseil de révision; **~ of inquiry** commission *f* d'enquête; **~ of examiners** jury *m* (d'examen). **(d)** (*Aviat, Naut*) **to go on ~** monter à bord (*a ship etc* d'un navire *etc*); **to take on ~** embarquer;(*fig*) prendre note de; **on ~ (ship)** à bord; **to go by the ~** *[plan, attempt]* échouer; *[business]* aller à vau-l'eau; *[principles, dreams]* être abandonné. **(e)** (*cardboard*) carton *m*; (*for games*) tableau *m*. **2** *adj*: **~ game** jeu *m* de société; **~ room** salle *f* de conférence; **~walk** passage *m* en planches. **3** *vt* **(a)** *ship, plane* monter à bord de; *train, bus* monter dans; (*Naut*) (*in attack*) monter à l'abordage de, prendre à l'abordage; (*for inspection*) arraisonner. **(b)** (*lodge*) prendre en pension. **4** *vi*: **to ~ with sb** être en pension chez qn.

board out *vt sep person* mettre en pension (*with* chez).

board up *vt sep window* boucher, clouer des planches en travers de.

♦ **boarder** *n* pensionnaire *mf*. ♦ **boarding** *adj*: **~ing card** *or* **pass** carte *f* d'embarquement; **~ing house** pension *f* (de famille); **~ing school** pension *f*, pensionnat *m*; **to send a child to ~ing school** mettre un enfant en pension.

boast [bəʊst] **1** *n* fanfaronnade *f*. **it is their ~ that they succeeded** ils se vantent d'avoir réussi. **2** *vi* se vanter (*about, of* de). **3** *vt* (être fier de) posséder.

♦ **boaster** *n* vantard(e) *m(f)*. ♦ **boastful** *adj* vantard. ♦ **boastfully** *adv* en se vantant. ♦ **boasting** *n* vantardise *f*.

boat [bəʊt] **1** *n* (*gen*) bateau *m*; (*small, light*) embarcation *f*; (*ship*) navire *m*; (*rowing ~*) barque *f*, canot *m*; (*ship's ~*) canot, chaloupe *f*; (*sailing ~*) voilier *m*; (*barge*) péniche *f*. **to go by ~** prendre le bateau; **to cross by ~** traverser en bateau; (*fig*) **we're all in the same ~** nous sommes tous logés à la même enseigne. **2** *vi*: **to go ~ing** aller faire une partie de canot. **3** *adj*: **~ hook** gaffe *f*; **~ people** gens *mpl* de la mer (*réfugiés du Vietnam etc*); **~ race** course *f* d'aviron; **~ train** *train qui assure la correspondance avec le ferry*. ♦ **boatbuilder** *n* constructeur *m* de bateaux. ♦ **boatbuilding** *n* construction *f* de bateaux. ♦ **boater** *n* (*hat*) canotier *m*. ♦ **boathouse** *n* abri *m* à bateaux. ♦ **boating 1** *n* canotage *m*; **2** *adj club, accident* de canotage; *holiday, trip* en bateau. ♦ **boatload** *or* ♦ **boatful** *n [goods etc]* cargaison *f*; *[people]* plein bateau *m*. ♦ **boatswain** ['bəʊsn] *n* maître *m* d'équipage. ♦ **boatyard** *n* chantier *m* de construction de bateaux.

bob[1] [bɒb] **1** *vi* monter et descendre. **to ~ up and down** (*in the air*) pendiller; (*in water*) danser sur l'eau; **he ~bed* up again in London** il s'est repointé* à Londres. **2** *n* (*curtsy*) petite révérence *f*.

bob[2]*† [bɒb] *n, pl inv* (*Brit*) shilling *m*.

bob[3] [bɒb] **1** *n* (*haircut*) coiffure courte; (*straight*) coiffure à la Jeanne d'Arc. **2** *vt* couper court.

bob[4] [bɒb] *n* (**~sled, ~sleigh**) bobsleigh *m*.

bobbin ['bɒbɪn] *n* (*gen*) bobine *f*; *[lace]* fuseau *m*.

bobby* ['bɒbɪ] *n* (*policeman*) flic* *m*.

bod‡ [bɒd] *n* type* *m*.

bode [bəʊd] *vi*: **to ~ well/ill** être de bon/mauvais augure (*for* pour).

bodice ['bɒdɪs] *n* corsage *m* (*d'une robe*).

bodkin ['bɒdkɪn] *n* grosse aiguille *f*.

body ['bɒdɪ] *n* **(a)** corps *m*. **(dead) ~** cadavre *m*, corps; **just enough to keep ~ and soul together** juste assez pour subsister; **he's a pleasant little ~** c'est un gentil petit bonhomme; **~ of troops** corps de troupes; **the main ~ of the army** le gros de l'armée; **the great ~ of readers** la masse des lecteurs; **a large ~ of people** une masse de gens; **in a ~** en masse; **the ~ politic** le corps politique; **legislative ~** corps législatif; **a large ~ of water** une grande masse d'eau; (*Phys*) **heavenly ~** corps céleste. **(b)** *[car]* carrosserie *f*; *[plane]* fuselage *m*; *[ship]* coque *f*; *[speech, document]* fond *m*. **in the ~ of the hall** au centre de la salle. **(c)** *[wine, paper]* corps *m*. **to give one's hair ~** donner du volume à ses cheveux.

♦ **bodily 1** *adv carry* dans ses bras; *lift* à bras-le-corps; **2** *adj need, comfort* matériel; *pain* physique; **bodily harm** blessure *f*. ♦ **bodybuilder** *n* (*food*) aliment *m* énergétique. ♦ **body-building** *n* culturisme *m*. ♦ **bodyguard** *n* (*group*) gardes *mpl* du corps; (*person*) garde *m* du corps. ♦ **bodywork** *n* (*Aut*) carrosserie *f*.

boffin* ['bɒfɪn] *n* chercheur *m* (*scientifique*).

bog [bɒg] *n* marécage *m*; *[peat]* tourbière *f*; (‡: *lavatory*) W.-C. *mpl*.

bog down *vt sep*: **to get ~ged down** s'enliser (*in* dans).

♦ **boggy** *adj* marécageux, tourbeux.

bogey ['bəʊgɪ] *n* (*frightening*) épouvantail *m*, démon *m*; (*bugbear*) bête *f* noire. (*fig*) **it is a ~ for them** cela leur fait peur. ♦ **bogeyman** *n* croque-mitaine *m*.
boggle ['bɒgl] *vi* (*be amazed*) être ahuri (*at* par); (*hesitate*) hésiter (*at* à). **the mind ~s!** c'est ahurissant!; **his mind ~d when he heard the news** la nouvelle l'a plongé dans l'ahurissement.
bogus ['bəʊgəs] *adj* faux (*before n*), simulé.
bohemian [bəʊ'hiːmɪən] *adj, n* (*gipsy*) bohémien(ne) *m(f)*; (*artist, writer etc*) bohème *mf*.
boil[1] [bɔɪl] *n* (*Med*) furoncle *m*.
boil[2] [bɔɪl] **1** *vi* **(a)** *[water etc]* bouillir. **the kettle is ~ing** l'eau bout (dans la bouilloire); **to ~ fast/gently** bouillir à gros bouillons/à petits bouillons; **to let the kettle ~ dry** laisser s'évaporer complètement l'eau de la bouilloire. **(b)** *[sea]* bouillonner; *[person]* bouillir (*with* de). **2** *vt water* faire bouillir; *food* (faire) cuire à l'eau, (faire) bouillir. **3** *n*: **on the ~** bouillant, qui bout; **off the ~** qui ne bout plus.
boil away *vi* s'évaporer.
boil down 1 *vi* (*fig*) revenir (*to* à). **2** *vt sep sauce etc* faire réduire; *text* réduire.
boil over *vi* déborder.
boil up *vi [milk]* monter. **they are ~ing up* for a row (*or* confrontation *etc*) le torchon brûle!**
♦ **boiled** *adj bacon, beef* bouilli; *ham* cuit; *egg* à la coque; *vegetables* cuit à l'eau; *potatoes* à l'anglaise, à l'eau; *sweet* à sucer. ♦ **boiler 1** *n* (*gen*) chaudière *f*; (*for clothes*) lessiveuse *f*; (*pan*) casserole *f*; **2** *adj*: **~er house** bâtiment *m* des chaudières; **~er room** salle *f* des chaudières; (*Naut*) chaufferie *f*; **~er suit** bleu(s) *m(pl)* de travail. ♦ **boilermaker** *n* chaudronnier *m*. ♦ **boilermaking** *n* grosse chaudronnerie *f*. ♦ **boiling** *adj water, oil* bouillant; *beef* pour pot-au-feu; *chicken* à faire au pot; **at ~ing point** (*lit*) au point d'ébullition; (*fig*) à ébullition; **it's ~ing (hot)** il fait une chaleur terrible; **I'm ~ing hot*** je crève* de chaleur!; **he is ~ing (with rage)** il bout de colère.
boisterous ['bɔɪstərəs] *adj sea, meeting* houleux; *wind* violent; *person, evening* (gai et) bruyant. ♦ **boisterously** *adv* bruyamment.
bold [bəʊld] *adj* **(a)** (*brave*) *person, action, look* hardi, audacieux, intrépide. **to grow ~** s'enhardir. **(b)** (*impudent*) hardi, effronté. **to be ~ enough to do** avoir l'audace de faire; **as ~ as brass** d'une impudence peu commune. **(c)** (*Art, Literat: striking*) hardi, vigoureux. **to paint in ~ strokes** avoir une touche puissante; **~ type** caractères *mpl* gras. ♦ **boldly** *adv* hardiment, avec audace; effrontément; avec vigueur. ♦ **boldness** *n* hardiesse *f*, audace *f*; effronterie *f*; vigueur *f*.
bolero [(*Mus*) bə'lɛərəʊ, (*Dress*) 'bɒlərəʊ] *n* boléro *m*.
bollard ['bɒləd] *n* borne *f*.
boloney‡ [bə'ləʊnɪ] *n* idioties *fpl*.
Bolshevik ['bɒlʃəvɪk], **Bolshevist** ['bɒlʃəvɪst] **1** *n* Bolchevique *mf*. **2** *adj* bolchevique. ♦ **Bolshevism** *n* bolchevisme *m*. ♦ **bolshie*** *adj* (*Pol*) rouge; (*gen*) querelleur.
bolster ['bəʊlstə^r] **1** *n* traversin *m*. **2** *vt* (**~ up**) soutenir (*with* par).
bolt [bəʊlt] **1** *n* **(a)** *[door, window]* verrou *m*; *[lock]* pêne *m*; (*for nut*) boulon *m*; *[cloth]* rouleau *m*; (*lightning*) éclair *m*. (*fig*) **a ~ from the blue** un coup de tonnerre dans un ciel bleu. **(b)** (*dash*) **he made a ~ for the door** il a fait un bond vers la porte; **to make a ~ for it*** se sauver à toutes jambes. **2** *adv*: **~ upright** droit comme un piquet. **3** *vi* **(a)** (*run away*) *[horse]* s'emballer; *[person]* se sauver. **(b)** (*move quickly*) se précipiter. **to ~ in/out** *etc* entrer/sortir *etc* comme un ouragan. **4** *vt* **(a)** *food* engouffrer. **(b)** *door, window* verrouiller. **~ the door!** mettez les verrous! **(c)** (*Tech*: **~ together**) *beams* boulonner.
bomb [bɒm] **1** *n* bombe *f*. **letter/parcel ~** lettre *f*/paquet *m* piégé(e); **his party went like a ~*** sa réception a été (un succès) du tonnerre*; **this car goes like a ~*** elle file, cette bagnole*; **it cost a ~*** cela a coûté les yeux de la tête. **2** *adj*: **~ crater** entonnoir *m*; **~ disposal squad** équipe *f* de désamorçage; **~ shelter** abri *m* (anti-aérien); **~ site** lieu *m* bombardé. **3** *vt town* bombarder.
bomb out *vt sep house* détruire par un bombardement. **the family was ~ed out** la famille a dû abandonner sa maison bombardée.
♦ **bomber** *n* (*aircraft*) bombardier *m*; (*terrorist*) plastiqueur *m*. ♦ **bombing 1** *n* bombardement *m*; *[terrorists]* attentat *m* au plastic *or* à la bombe; **2** *adj raid, plane* de bombardement. ♦ **bomb-proof** *adj* blindé. ♦ **bombshell** *n* (*Mil*) obus *m*; (*fig*) **to come like a ~shell** faire l'effet d'une bombe; **she's a real ~shell!*** c'est une fille sensass!*
bombard [bɒm'bɑːd] *vt* bombarder (*with* de). ♦ **bombardment** *n* bombardement *m*.
bombast ['bɒmbæst] *n* (*pej*) grandiloquence *f*. ♦ **bombastic** *adj* grandiloquent. ♦ **bombastically** *adv* avec grandiloquence.
bona fide ['bəʊnə'faɪdɪ] *adj traveller* véritable; *offer* sérieux. ♦ **bona fides** *n* bonne foi *f*.
bonanza [bə'nænzə] *n* (*money etc*) filon *m*, mine *f* d'or; (*boon*) aubaine *f*.
bond [bɒnd] **1** *n* **(a)** (*agreement*) engagement *m*. **to enter into a ~** s'engager (*to do* à faire). **(b)** (*link*) lien(s) *m(pl)*. **~s** (*chains*) fers *mpl*, chaînes *fpl*; (*fig: ties*) liens. **(c)** (*Fin*) bon *m*, titre *m*. **(d)** (*Comm*) **to put sth into ~** entreposer qch en douane. **(e)** (*adhesion between surfaces*) adhérence *f*. **2** *vt bricks* liaisonner; *[strong glue]* coller, souder. **~ed warehouse** entrepôt *m* des douanes. ♦ **bondage** *n* esclavage *m*. ♦ **bondsman** *n* esclave *m*.
bone [bəʊn] **1** *n* (*gen*) os *m*; *[fish]* arête *f*; *[corset]* baleine *f*. **chilled to the ~** glacé jusqu'à la moelle (des os); **I feel it in my ~s** j'en ai le pressentiment; **~ of contention** pomme *f* de discorde; **to have a ~ to pick with sb** avoir un compte à régler avec qn; **he made no ~s about saying what he thought** il n'a pas hésité à dire ce qu'il pensait; **there are no ~s broken** il n'y a rien de cassé; (*fig*) il n'y a rien de grave; **(made) of ~** en os. **2** *adj buttons etc* en os. **~ china** porcelaine *f* tendre; **~ meal** engrais *m* (de cendres d'os). **3** *vt meat, fowl* désosser; *fish* ôter les arêtes de.
bone up‡ *vt sep*, **bone up on**‡ *vt fus* potasser*.
♦ **boned** *adj meat* désossé; *fish* sans arêtes; *corset* baleiné. ♦ **bone-dry** *adj* absolument sec. ♦ **bonehead**‡ *n* crétin(e) *m(f)*. ♦ **bone-idle*** *or* ♦ **bone-lazy*** *adj* fainéant. ♦ **bone-shaker*** *n* (*car*) vieille guimbarde *f*. ♦ **bony** *adj tissue* osseux; *knee, person* anguleux; *fish* plein d'arêtes; *meat* plein d'os.
bonfire ['bɒnfaɪə^r] *n* feu *m* (de joie); (*for rubbish*) feu (de jardin).
bonkers‡ ['bɒŋkəz] *adj* cinglé*.
bonnet ['bɒnɪt] *n* bonnet *m*; (*Brit*) *[car]* capot *m*.
bonny ['bɒnɪ] *adj* (*esp Scot*) joli.
bonus ['bəʊnəs] *n* prime *f*, gratification *f*. **~ of 500 francs** 500 F de prime; (*fig*) **as a ~** en prime; (*Fin*) **~ issue** émission *f* d'actions gratuites.
boo [buː] **1** *excl* hou!, peuh! **he wouldn't say ~ to a goose*** il n'ose jamais ouvrir le bec*. **2** *vti* huer. **to be ~ed off the stage** sortir de scène sous les huées. **3** *n*: **~s** (*also* **~ing**) huées *fpl*.
boob‡ [buːb] **1** *n* (*mistake*) gaffe *f*; (*breast*) sein *m*, nichon‡ *m*. **2** *vi* gaffer.
booby ['buːbɪ] **1** *n* nigaud(e) *m(f)*. **2** *adj*: **~ prize** prix *m* de consolation (*décerné au dernier*); **~ trap** traquenard *m*; (*Mil*) objet *m* piégé.
book [bʊk] **1** *n* livre *m*, bouquin* *m*; *[Bible etc]*

livre; (*exercise* ~) cahier *m*; (*libretto*) livret *m*; *[samples etc]* album *m*; *[tickets etc]* carnet *m*; *[matches]* pochette *f*. **(account)** ~**s** livre *m* de comptes; **to keep the** ~**s** tenir la comptabilité; **to be on the** ~**s of an organization** être inscrit à une organisation; **to take one's name off the** ~**s** donner sa démission; (*Betting*) **to make (a)** ~ inscrire les paris; **to bring sb to** ~ obliger qn à rendre des comptes; **by the** ~ selon les règles; **to go by the** ~**, to stick to the** ~ se conformer à la règle; **to be in sb's good/bad** ~**s** être bien/mal vu de qn; (*fig*) **in my** ~* à mon avis; **that's one for the** ~**!*** c'est à marquer d'une pierre blanche!

2 *adj*: ~ **club** club *m* du livre; ~ **learning** connaissances *fpl* livresques; ~ **lover** bibliophile *mf*; ~ **post** tarif *m* imprimés *inv*; ~ **token** bon-cadeau *m* (*négociable en librairie*).

3 *vt* **(a)** *seat* louer; *room, sleeper* retenir, réserver; *ticket* prendre. (*Theat*) **we're fully** ~**ed** on joue à guichets fermés; **the hotel is fully** ~**ed** l'hôtel est complet; **I'm** ~**ed for lunch*** je suis pris à déjeuner; (*Rail*) **to** ~ **sb through to Birmingham** assurer à qn une réservation jusqu'à Birmingham. **(b)** (*Comm, Fin*) *order* inscrire, enregistrer. **(c)** (*Police*) *driver etc* donner un procès-verbal *or* P.-V.* à; (*Ftbl*) *player* prendre le nom de. **to be** ~**ed for speeding** attraper une contravention pour excès de vitesse.

book in 1 *vi* (*at hotel etc*) prendre une chambre. **2** *vt sep person* réserver une chambre *etc* à.

book up *vt sep* retenir, réserver. **the tour is** ~**ed up** on ne prend plus d'inscriptions pour l'excursion; **the hotel is** ~**ed up** l'hôtel est complet; **I'm very** ~**ed up*** je suis très pris.

♦ **bookable** *adj seat etc* qu'on peut retenir; **all seats** ~**able in advance** toutes les places peuvent être retenues à l'avance; **seats** ~**able from 6th June** location ouverte dès le 6 juin. ♦ **bookbinder** *n* relieur *m*, -euse *f*. ♦ **bookcase** *n* bibliothèque *f* (*meuble*). ♦ **bookends** *npl* presse-livres *m inv*. ♦ **bookie*** *n* bookmaker *m*. ♦ **booking 1** *n* réservation *f*; **2** *adj*: ~**ing clerk** préposé(e) *m(f)* aux réservations; ~**ing office** (bureau *m* de) location *f*. ♦ **bookish** *adj* qui aime les livres. ♦ **book-keeper** *n* comptable *mf*. ♦ **book-keeping** *n* comptabilité *f*. ♦ **booklet** *n* petit livre, brochure *f*. ♦ **bookmaker** *n* bookmaker *m*. ♦ **bookmark** *n* signet *m*. ♦ **bookmobile** *n* (*US*) bibliothèque *f* circulante. ♦ **bookplate** *n* ex-libris *m inv*. ♦ **bookrest** *n* support *m* à livres. ♦ **bookseller** *n* libraire *mf*. ♦ **bookshelf** *n* rayon *m* (de bibliothèque). ♦ **bookshop** *n* librairie *f*. ♦ **bookstall** *n [station etc]* kiosque *m* à journaux; *[second-hand* ~*s]* étalage *m* de bouquiniste. ♦ **bookstore** *n* librairie *f*. ♦ **bookworm** *n* rat *m* de bibliothèque.

boom[1] [bu:m] *n* **(a)** (*across river etc*) barrage *m*. **(b)** *[mast]* gui *m*; *[crane]* flèche *f*; *[microphone, camera]* perche *f*.

boom[2] [bu:m] **1** *n* (*sound*) *[sea, waves, wind]* mugissement *m*; *[guns, thunder, voices, storm]* grondement *m*; *[organ]* ronflement *m*. **sonic** ~ bang *m* supersonique. **2** *vi [wind]* mugir; *[thunder, sea, guns]* gronder; *[organ]* ronfler; *[voice]* retentir; *[person]* tonitruer. **3** *vt* (~ **out**) dire d'une voix tonitruante.

♦ **booming** *adj sound, noise* retentissant; *voice* tonitruant.

boom[3] [bu:m] **1** *vi [trade]* être en expansion; *[business, sales]* être en plein essor; *[books, goods]* se vendre comme des petits pains; *[prices]* être en forte hausse.

2 *n [business, prices, shares]* montée *f* en flèche, forte hausse *f*; *[product]* popularité *f*; *[sales]* progression *f*; (*Econ:* ~ **period**) boom *m*. ~ **town** ville *f* en plein développement.

boomerang ['bu:məræŋ] **1** *n* boomerang *m*. **2** *vi* faire boomerang.

boon [bu:n] **1** *n* (*godsend*) bénédiction* *f*; (*good luck*) aubaine *f*. **2** *adj*: ~ **companion** joyeux compère.

boor [bʊəʳ] *n* rustre *m*. ♦ **boorish** *adj* rustre, grossier. ♦ **boorishly** *adv behave* en rustre; *speak* grossièrement. ♦ **boorishness** *n* rudesse *f*, manque *m* de savoir-vivre.

boost [bu:st] **1** *n*: **to give sb a** ~ **(up)** (*help him up*) soulever qn par derrière *or* par en dessous; (*raise his morale*) remonter le moral à qn; (*do publicity for him*) faire de la réclame pour qn. **2** *vt* (*Elec*) survolter; *engine* suralimenter; *spacecraft* propulser; *price* faire monter; *output, productivity* accroître; *sales* augmenter; *product* promouvoir; *the economy* donner du tonus à; *confidence etc* renforcer. ♦ **booster** *n* (*Elec*) survolteur *m*; (*Rad*) amplificateur *m*; (~*er rocket*) booster *m*; (~*er shot,* ~*er dose*) (piqûre *f* de) rappel *m*.

boot[1] [bu:t] *n*: **to** ~ par-dessus le marché.

boot[2] [bu:t] **1** *n* **(a)** (*gen*) botte *f*; (*ankle* ~) bottillon *m*; *[soldier]* brodequin *m*; *[workman etc]* grosse chaussure (montante). (*fig*) **the** ~ **is on the other foot** les rôles sont renversés; **to give sb the** ~**‡** flanquer* qn à la porte. **(b)** *[car]* coffre *m*. **2** *vt*: **to** ~ **sb out** flanquer* qn à la porte. ♦ **bootee** *n* petit chausson. ♦ **bootlace** *n* lacet *m* (de chaussure). ♦ **bootleg* 1** *vi* faire la contrebande de l'alcool; **2** *adj* de contrebande. ♦ **bootlegger** *n* bootlegger *m*. ♦ **bootlicker** *n* lèche-bottes* *mf inv*. ♦ **bootmaker** *n* bottier *m*. ♦ **bootpolish** *n* cirage *m*. ♦ **bootstrap** *n*: **to pull o.s. up by one's (own)** ~**straps** s'élever à la force du poignet.

booth [bu:ð] *n [fair]* baraque *f* (foraine); *[language lab, telephone etc]* cabine *f*; (*voting* ~) isoloir *m*.

booty ['bu:tɪ] *n* butin *m*.

booze* [bu:z] **1** *n* alcool *m* (*boissons*). **to buy some** ~ acheter à boire. **2** *vi* biberonner*. ♦ **boozer‡** *n* (*drunkard*) pochard(e)‡ *m(f)*; (*pub*) bistro* *m*. ♦ **booze-up‡** *n* soûlographie* *f*. ♦ **boozy‡** *adj person* qui a la dalle en pente‡; *evening* où l'on boit beaucoup.

borage ['bɒrɪdʒ] *n* bourrache *f*.

borax ['bɔ:ræks] *n* borax *m*. ♦ **boracic** *adj* borique.

Bordeaux [bɔ:'dəʊ] *n* (*wine*) bordeaux *m*.

border ['bɔ:dəʳ] **1** *n* **(a)** *[lake, carpet, dress]* bord *m*; *[woods]* lisière *f*; *[picture]* bordure *f*; (*in garden*) bordure. **(b)** (*frontier*) frontière *f*. **to escape over the** ~ s'enfuir en passant la frontière; (*Brit*) **the B**~**s** la région frontière (*entre l'Écosse et l'Angleterre*). **2** *adj*: ~ **dispute** différend *m* sur une question de frontière(s); ~ **incident** incident *m* de frontière; ~ **raid** incursion *f*; ~ **town** ville *f* frontière. **3** *vt [trees etc]* border.

border (up)on *vt fus [country]* être limitrophe de; *[estate]* toucher; (*fig: come near to being*) être voisin de, frôler.

♦ **borderer** *n* frontalier *m*, -ière *f*. ♦ **borderland** *n* (*fig*) **on the** ~**land of** aux frontières de. ♦ **borderline** *n* ligne *f* de démarcation; ~**line case** cas *m* limite.

bore[1] [bɔ:ʳ] **1** *vt hole, tunnel* percer; *well, rock* forer. **to** ~ **one's way through** se frayer un chemin en creusant à travers. **2** *n [tube, gun]* calibre *m*. **a 12-**~ **shotgun** un fusil de (calibre) 12. ♦ **borehole** *n* trou *m* de sonde.

bore[2] [bɔ:ʳ] **1** *n* (*person*) raseur* *m*, -euse* *f*; (*event, situation*) ennui *m*, corvée *f*. **2** *vt* ennuyer, raser*. ♦ **bored** *adj person* qui s'ennuie; *look* d'ennui; **to be** ~**d stiff** *or* **to death** *or* **to tears** s'ennuyer ferme *or* à mourir; **he was** ~**d with reading** il en avait assez de lire. ♦ **boredom** *n* ennui *m*. ♦ **boring** *adj* ennuyeux, rasant*.

bore[3] [bɔ:ʳ] *pret of* **bear**[1].

bore[4] [bɔ:ʳ] *n* (*tidal wave*) mascaret *m*.

born [bɔ:n] *adj* né. **to be** ~ naître; **to be** ~ **again** renaître; **he was** ~ **in 1920** il est né *or* il naquit en 1920; **3 sons** ~ **to her** 3 fils nés d'elle; **every baby** ~ **into the world** tout enfant qui vient au monde; **a**

Parisian ~ and bred un vrai Parisien de Paris; **he wasn't ~ yesterday*** il n'est pas né de la dernière pluie; **in all my ~ days*** de toute ma vie; **poets are ~, not made** on naît poète, on ne le devient pas; **a ~ poet** un poète né; **~ fool** parfait idiot; **misfortunes ~ of war** malheurs dûs à la guerre; **Chicago-~** natif de Chicago, né à Chicago; **Australian-~** d'origine australienne.

borne [bɔːn] *ptp of* **bear**[1].

borough ['bʌrə] *n* municipalité *f*; (*in London*) ≃ arrondissement *m*; (*Brit Parl*) circonscription *f* électorale urbaine.

borrow ['bɒrəʊ] *vt* emprunter (*from* à). **a ~ed word** un mot d'emprunt; (*Math*) **~ 10** ≃ j'ajoute 10. ♦ **borrower** *n* emprunteur *m*, -euse *f*. ♦ **borrowing** *n* emprunt *m*.

Borstal ['bɔːstl] *n* (*Brit*) maison *f* de redressement.

bosh* [bɒʃ] *n* blague(s)* *f(pl)*, bêtises *fpl*.

bos'n ['bəʊsn] *n* = **bosun**.

bosom ['bʊzəm] *n [person]* poitrine *f*, seins *mpl*; *[dress]* corsage *m*; (*fig*) sein. **in the ~ of the family** au sein de la famille; **~ friend** ami(e) *m(f)* intime.

boss* [bɒs] **1** *n* patron(ne) *m(f)*, chef *m*; *[gang etc]* caïd‡ *m*. **2** *vt* mener.

boss about*, boss around* *vt sep* mener à la baguette, régenter.

♦ **bossy*** *adj* autoritaire.

boss-eyed [bɒs'aɪd] *adj* qui louche.

bosun ['bəʊsn] *n* maître *m* d'équipage.

botany ['bɒtənɪ] *n* botanique *f*. ♦ **botanic(al)** *adj* botanique. ♦ **botanist** *n* botaniste *mf*. ♦ **botanize** *vi* herboriser.

botch [bɒtʃ] *vt* (**~ up**) (*repair*) rafistoler*; (*bungle*) saboter, bousiller*.

both [bəʊθ] **1** *adj* les deux, l'un(e) et l'autre. **~ (the) books are his** les deux livres sont à lui; **you can't have it ~ ways*** il faut choisir.

2 *pron* tous *or* toutes (les) deux, l'un(e) et l'autre. **~ (of them) were there, they were ~ there** ils étaient là tous les deux; **~ of us agree** nous sommes d'accord tous les deux; **~ alike** l'un comme l'autre.

3 *adv*: **~ this and that** non seulement ceci mais aussi cela, aussi bien ceci que cela; **~ you and I saw him** nous l'avons vu vous et moi, vous et moi (nous) l'avons vu; **~ Paul and I came** Paul et moi sommes venus tous les deux; **she was ~ laughing and crying** elle riait et pleurait à la fois.

bother ['bɒðə[r]] **1** *vt* (*annoy*) ennuyer, embêter*; (*pester*) harceler; (*worry*) inquiéter, ennuyer. **don't ~ me!** laisse-moi tranquille!; **I'm sorry to ~ you** excusez-moi de vous déranger; **does it ~ you if I smoke?** ça vous dérange que je fume (*subj*) *or* si je fume?; **to ~ o.s.** *or* **one's head about sth** se tracasser au sujet de qch; **to get (all hot and) ~ed*** se mettre dans tous ses états (*about* au sujet de); **I can't be ~ed going out** *or* **to go out** je n'ai pas le courage de sortir; **his leg ~s him** sa jambe le fait pas mal* souffrir.

2 *vi* se donner la peine (*to do* de faire). **you needn't ~ to come** ce n'est pas la peine de venir; **don't ~ about me/about my lunch** ne vous occupez pas de moi/de mon déjeuner; **please don't ~** ce n'est pas la peine.

3 *n* ennui *m*, barbe* *f*. **what a ~ it all is!** quel ennui *or* quelle barbe* que tout cela!; (*excl*) **~!** zut*, la barbe!*; **she's having a spot of ~** elle a des ennuis; **we had a bit of ~ with the car** on a eu un petit embêtement* avec la voiture.

♦ **botheration*** *excl* zut!* ♦ **bothersome** *adj* ennuyeux, embêtant*.

bottle ['bɒtl] **1** *n* bouteille *f*; (*small*) flacon *m*; (*wide-mouthed*) bocal *m*; (*of stone*) cruche *f*; (*for beer*) canette *f*; (*baby's* ~) biberon *m*. **wine ~** bouteille à vin; **~ of wine** bouteille de vin; **to take to the ~*** se mettre à boire. **2** *adj*: **~ party** surprise-party *f* où chacun apporte une bouteille; **~ rack** casier *m* à bouteilles. **3** *vt wine* mettre en bouteilles; *fruit* mettre en bocaux.

bottle up *vt sep feelings etc* refouler.

♦ **bottlebrush** *n* rince-bouteilles *m inv*. ♦ **bottled** *adj beer* en canette; *wine* en bouteilles; *fruit* en bocaux. ♦ **bottle-fed** *adj* nourri au biberon. ♦ **bottle-green** *adj* vert bouteille *inv*. ♦ **bottleneck** *n [road]* rétrécissement *m* de la chaussée; *[traffic]* bouchon *m*; *[production etc]* goulet *m* d'étranglement. ♦ **bottle-opener** *n* ouvre-bouteille(s) *m*.

bottom ['bɒtəm] **1** *n [box]* (*outside*) bas *m*, (*inside*) fond *m*; *[well, garden, sea]* fond; *[dress, heap, page]* bas *m*; *[tree, hill]* pied *m*; *[table]* bout *m*; *[chair]* siège *m*; *[ship]* carène *f*; (*buttocks*) derrière *m*; (*fig: origin*) base *f*, fondement *m*. **at the ~ of page 10** en *or* au bas de la page 10; **at the ~ of the hill** au pied *or* au bas de la colline; **the name at the ~ of the list** le nom en bas de la liste; **he's at the ~ of the list** il est en queue de liste; **to be ~ of the class** être le dernier de la classe; **~s up!‡** cul sec!; **from the ~ of my heart** du fond de mon cœur; **at ~** au fond; **to knock the ~ out of an argument** démolir un argument; **the ~ fell out of his world*** son monde s'est effondré; (*fig*) **to be at the ~ of sth** être à l'origine de qch; **we can't get to the ~ of it** impossible de découvrir le fin fond de cette histoire.

2 *adj shelf* du bas, inférieur; *step, gear* premier; *part of garden etc* du fond. (*fig*) **her ~ drawer** son trousseau; **~ half** *[box]* partie *f* inférieure; *[class, list]* deuxième moitié *f*.

♦ **bottomless** *adj pit* sans fond; *mystery* insondable; *supply* inépuisable. ♦ **bottommost** *adj* le plus bas.

botulism ['bɒtjʊlɪzəm] *n* botulisme *m*.

bouclé [buː'kleɪ] *adj* en bouclette.

bougainvill(a)ea [ˌbuːgən'vɪlɪə] *n* bougainvillée *f*.

bough [baʊ] *n* rameau *m*, branche *f*.

bought [bɔːt] *pret, ptp of* **buy**.

boulder ['bəʊldə[r]] *n* rocher *m* (rond), grosse pierre.

bounce [baʊns] **1** *vi [ball]* rebondir; *[child, car]* faire des bonds; (*) *[cheque]* être sans provision. *[person]* **to ~ in/out** *etc* entrer/sortir *etc* avec entrain. **2** *vt ball* faire rebondir; (*) *cheque* refuser; (‡) *rowdy customer* vider‡, flanquer* à la porte. **3** *n [ball]* rebond *m*. (*fig*) **he's got plenty of ~*** il est très dynamique.

♦ **bouncer‡** *n* videur‡ *m*. ♦ **bouncing** *adj*: **bouncing baby** beau bébé *m* (florissant de santé). ♦ **bouncy** *adj ball, mattress* élastique; *hair* vigoureux; *person* dynamique.

bound[1] [baʊnd] **1** *n*: **~s** limite(s) *f(pl)*, bornes *fpl*; **to know no ~s** être sans bornes; **to keep within ~s** rester dans la juste mesure; **within the ~s of possibility** dans les limites du possible; **out of ~s** dont l'accès est interdit; (*Scol*) défendu aux élèves. **2** *vt*: **~ed by** borné *or* limité par. ♦ **boundless** *adj space* infini; *trust* illimité; *devotion* sans bornes.

bound[2] [baʊnd] **1** *n* bond *m*, saut *m*. **2** *vi [person, horse]* bondir, faire un bond *or* des bonds. **to ~ in/away** *etc* entrer/partir *etc* d'un bond; **the horse ~ed over the fence** le cheval a sauté la barrière (d'un bond).

bound[3] [baʊnd] (*pret, ptp of* **bind**) *adj* **(a)** *prisoner* lié, attaché. **(b)** *book* relié. **(c) I am ~ to confess** je suis forcé d'avouer; **you're ~ to do it** (*obliged to*) vous êtes tenu *or* obligé de le faire; (*sure to*) vous le ferez sûrement; **it was ~ to happen** cela devait arriver, c'était à prévoir. **(d)** (*destined*) **~ for** *person* en route pour; *parcel, train* à destination de; *ship, plane* en route pour, (*about to leave*) en partance pour; **where are you ~ for?** où allez-vous?; **Australia-~** à destination de l'Australie. ♦ **bounden** *adj duty* impérieux.

boundary ['baʊndərɪ] *n* limite *f*, frontière *f*; (*Sport*) limites *fpl* du terrain.
bounty ['baʊntɪ] *n* (*generosity*) générosité *f*; (*gift*) don *m*; (*Mil*) prime *f*. ♦ **bounteous** *or* ♦ **bountiful** *adj harvest* abondant; *rain* bienfaisant; *person* généreux.
bouquet ['bʊkeɪ] *n* bouquet *m*.
bourbon ['bɜːbən] *n* (*whisky*) bourbon *m*.
bourgeois ['bʊəʒwɑː] *adj, n* bourgeois(e) *m(f)*. ♦ **bourgeoisie** *n* bourgeoisie *f*.
bout [baʊt] *n* **(a)** *[fever, malaria etc]* accès *m*; *[rheumatism]* crise *f*. **a ~ of flu** une grippe; **he's had several ~s of illness** il a été malade plusieurs fois; **a ~ of work** une période de travail intensif; **drinking ~** beuverie *f*. **(b)** (*Boxing, Wrestling*) combat *m*; (*Fencing*) assaut *m*.
boutique [buː'tiːk] *n* boutique *f* (*de mode etc*).
bovine ['bəʊvaɪn] *adj* bovin.
bow[1] [bəʊ] **1** *n* (*weapon*) arc *m*; (*Mus*) archet *m*; *[rainbow etc]* arc; (*knot*) nœud *m*.
2 *adj*: **~ tie** nœud *m* papillon; **~ window** fenêtre *f* en saillie.
♦ **bow-legged** *adj* aux jambes arquées. ♦ **bowstring** *n* corde *f*.
bow[2] [baʊ] **1** *n* salut *m*. **to make one's ~ (as a pianist etc)** faire ses débuts (de pianiste etc); **to take a ~** saluer. **2** *vi* **(a)** (*in greeting*) saluer, incliner la tête. **to ~ to sb** saluer qn; **~ing and scraping** salamalecs *mpl*. **(b)** (**~ down**) *[branch etc]* fléchir, se courber; *[person]* se courber; (*fig: submit*) s'incliner (*before, to* devant; *under* sous). **3** *vt back* courber; *head* pencher. **to ~ one's back** courber le dos; **to ~ one's knee** fléchir le genou.
bow out *vi* (*fig*) tirer sa révérence.
bow[3] [baʊ] *n [ship]* **~(s)** avant *m*, proue *f*. **in the ~s** à l'avant, en proue; **on the port ~** par bâbord devant.
bowdlerize ['baʊdləraɪz] *vt* expurger.
bowels ['baʊəlz] *npl* intestins *mpl*. **~ of the earth** entrailles *fpl* de la terre.
bowl[1] [bəʊl] *n* bol *m*, jatte *f*; (*for water, washing up*) cuvette *f*; (*for fruit*) coupe *f*; (*for salad*) saladier *m*; (*for punch*) bol; (*for sugar*) sucrier *m*; *[spoon]* creux *m*; *[lamp]* globe *m*; *[lavatory, sink]* cuvette.
bowl[2] [bəʊl] **1** *n* boule *f*. (*game*) **~s** (*Brit*) (jeu *m* de) boules; (*US: skittles*) bowling *m*. **2** *vi* **(a) to go ~ing** jouer aux boules (*or* au bowling). **(b)** *[person, car]* **to go ~ing down the street** descendre la rue à bonne allure. **3** *vt bowl, ball* lancer; *hoop* faire rouler; (*Cricket*) *ball* servir; *batsman* (**~ out**) mettre hors jeu.
bowl down* *vt sep* renverser.
bowl over *vt sep* renverser. (*fig*) **to be ~ed over by** (*surprise*) rester stupéfait devant; (*emotion*) être bouleversé par.
♦ **bowler** *n* joueur *m*, -euse *f* de boules (*or* de bowling); (*Cricket*) lanceur *m*, -euse *f* (de la balle); (*hat*) (chapeau *m*) melon *m*. ♦ **bowling 1** *n* (*Brit*) jeu *m* de boules; (*US*) bowling *m*; **2** *adj*: **~ing alley** bowling *m*; **~ing green** terrain *m* de boules (*sur gazon*); **~ing match** concours *m* de boules (*or* de bowling).
box[1] [bɒks] **1** *n* **(a)** boîte *f*; (*crate; also for cash*) caisse *f*; (*cardboard* **~**) carton *m*. (*TV*) **on the ~*** à la télé*. **(b)** (*Theat*) loge *f*; (*Jur*) *[jury, press]* banc *m*; *[witness]* barre *f*; *[stable]* box *m*. **2** *adj*: **~ calf** box(-calf) *m*; **~ number** numéro *m* d'annonce; **~ office** bureau *m* de location; **it's good ~ office** cela fait recette; **~-office attraction** *or* **success** spectacle *m* à (grand) succès; **~ room** (cabinet *m* de) débarras *m*. **3** *vt goods* mettre en boîte *or* en caisse *etc*. (*Naut*) **to ~ the compass** réciter les aires du vent.
box in *vt sep bath, sink* encastrer. (*fig*) **to feel ~ed in** se sentir confiné *or* à l'étroit.
♦ **Boxing Day** *n* le lendemain de Noël.
box[2] [bɒks] **1** *vi* (*Sport*) faire de la boxe. **2** *vt* (*Sport*) boxer avec. **to ~ sb's ears** gifler qn. **3** *n*: **a ~ on the ear** une gifle. ♦ **boxer** *n* (*Sport*) boxeur *m*; (*dog*) boxer *m*. ♦ **boxing 1** *n* boxe *f*; **2** *adj gloves, match* de boxe; **~ing ring** ring *m*.
box[3] [bɒks] *n* (**~** *wood*) buis *m*.
boy [bɔɪ] *n* garçon *m*. **little ~** petit garçon, garçonnet *m*; **English ~** petit *or* jeune Anglais *m*; **come, my ~** viens ici, mon petit *or* mon grand; **the Jones ~** le petit Jones; **when I was a ~** quand j'étais petit *or* enfant; **~s will be ~s!** les garçons, on ne les changera jamais!; **he was as much a ~ as ever** il était toujours aussi gamin; **my dear ~** mon cher (ami); **a night out with the ~s** une sortie avec les copains*; (*excl*) **~!*** bigre!* ♦ **boyfriend** *n* petit ami. ♦ **boyhood** *n* enfance *f*, adolescence *f*. ♦ **boyish** *adj behaviour* d'enfant, de garçon, (*pej*) puéril; *smile, look* gamin; *girl* garçonnier.
boycott ['bɔɪkɒt] **1** *vt* boycotter. **2** *n* boycottage *m*.
bra [brɑː] *n* soutien-gorge *m*.
brace [breɪs] **1** *n* **(a)** (*gen*) attache *f*; (*Med*) appareil *m* orthopédique; (*dental*) appareil (dentaire *or* orthodontique); (*Constr*) entretoise *f*. (*Brit Dress*) **~s** bretelles *fpl*; **~ and bit** vilebrequin *m* (*à main*). **(b)** (*pl inv: pair*) *[animals etc]* paire *f*. **2** *vt* (*support*) soutenir, consolider; *beam* armer. **to ~ o.s.** s'arc-bouter; (*fig*) rassembler ses forces (*to do* pour faire); **~ yourself for the news!** tenez-vous bien que je vous raconte (*subj*) la nouvelle! ♦ **bracing** *adj air, climate* tonifiant; *wind* vivifiant.
bracelet ['breɪslɪt] *n* bracelet *m*.
bracken ['brækən] *n* fougère *f*.
bracket ['brækɪt] **1** *n* **(a)** (*angled support*) support *m*; (*for shelf*) tasseau *m*; (*shelf itself*) (petite) étagère *f*; (*for lamp*) fixation *f*. **~ lamp** applique *f*. **(b)** (*Typ*) (*round*) parenthèse *f*; (*square*) crochet *m*; (*Mus, Typ*) **brace ~** accolade *f*; **in ~s** entre parenthèses; **the lower income ~** la tranche des petits revenus. **2** *vt* (*Typ*) mettre entre parenthèses *etc*; (*fig*: **~ together**) *names, persons* mettre dans le même groupe; *candidates etc* mettre ex aequo. (*Scol, Sport etc*) **~ed first** premiers ex aequo.
brackish ['brækɪʃ] *adj* saumâtre.
bradawl ['brædɔːl] *n* poinçon *m* (*de menuisier*).
brag [bræg] *vti* se vanter (*about, of* de; *about or of doing* de faire; *that one has done* d'avoir fait). ♦ **braggart** *n* vantard(e) *m(f)*. ♦ **bragging 1** *n* vantardise *f*; **2** *adj* vantard.
braid [breɪd] **1** *vt hair* tresser. **2** *n* (*on dress*) ganse *f*; (*Mil*) galon *m*; *[hair]* tresse *f*.
Braille [breɪl] *n, adj* braille (*m*) *inv*.
brain [breɪn] **1** *n* (*Anat, fig*) cerveau *m*. **~s** (*Anat, Culin*) cervelle *f*; (*fig*) **he's got that on the ~*** il ne pense qu'à ça!*; **his ~ reeled** la tête lui a tourné; **he's got ~s** il est intelligent; **he's the ~(s) of the family** c'est le cerveau de la famille. **2** *adj* (*Med*) *disease, operation* cérébral. **~ drain** émigration *f* des chercheurs (européens); **~s trust** réunion-débat *f*; (*US*) **~ trust** brain-trust *m*. **3** *vt* (*: *knock out*) assommer. ♦ **brain-child** *n* invention *f* personnelle. ♦ **brainless** *adj* sans cervelle, stupide. ♦ **brainstorm** *n* (*Med*) congestion cérébrale; (*fig*) idée *f* géniale. ♦ **brainstorming** *n* remue-méninges *m* (*hum*), brain-storming *m*. ♦ **brainwash** *vt* faire un lavage de cerveau à; (*fig*) **he was ~washed into believing that ...** on a réussi à lui faire croire que .... ♦ **brainwashing** *n* lavage *m* de cerveau; *[the public etc]* bourrage *m* de crâne*. ♦ **brainwave** *n* idée *f* géniale. ♦ **brainwork** *n* travail *m* intellectuel. ♦ **brainy*** *adj* intelligent, doué.
braise [breɪz] *vt* (*Culin*) braiser.
brake[1] [breɪk] *n* (*vehicle*) break *m*.
brake[2] [breɪk] **1** *n* (*Aut etc*) frein *m*. (*fig*) **to act as a ~ on** mettre un frein à. **2** *vi* freiner. **3** *adj pedal, drum, lining* de frein. **~ fluid** liquide *m* pour freins (hydrauliques); **~ light** feu *m* rouge (*des*

freins), stop *m*. ♦ **braking 1** *n* freinage *m*; **2** *adj distance, power* de freinage.
bramble ['bræmbl] *n* (*thorny shrub*) roncier *m*; (*blackberry bush*) mûrier *m* sauvage; (*berry*) mûre *f* (sauvage).
bran [bræn] *n* son *m* (*de blé*). ~ **mash** son mouillé.
branch [brɑːntʃ] **1** *n* **(a)** (*gen: lit, fig*) branche *f*; *[river]* bras *m*; *[mountain chain]* ramification *f*; *[road, pipe, railway]* embranchement *m*; (*Ling*) rameau *m*; (*Admin*) section *f*. (*Mil*) **their ~ of the service** leur arme *f*. **(b)** *[store, company, bank]* succursale *f*. **2** *adj* (*Rail*) ~ **line** ligne *f* secondaire; ~ **office** succursale *f* (locale). **3** *vi* se ramifier. **the road ~es off the main road** la route quitte la grand-route.
branch out *vi [businessman, company]* étendre ses activités (*into* à).
brand [brænd] **1** *n* **(a)** (*Comm: of goods*) marque *f*. **(b)** (*mark*) *[cattle, property]* marque *f*; *[prisoner]* flétrissure *f*. **(c)** (*burning wood*) tison *m*. **2** *vt cattle, property* marquer (au fer rouge). **~ed goods** produits *mpl* de marque; (*fig: stigmatize*) **to ~ sb a criminal** flétrir qn du nom de criminel. **3** *adj*: ~ **image** image *f* de marque; ~ **name** (nom *m* de) marque *f*. ♦ **branding-iron** *n* fer *m* à marquer. ♦ **brand-new** *adj* flambant neuf (*f* flambant neuve).
brandish ['brændɪʃ] *vt* brandir.
brandy ['brændɪ] *n* cognac *m*. ~ **and soda** fine *f* à l'eau; **plum** ~ eau-de-vie *f* de prune.
brash [bræʃ] *adj* (*reckless*) impétueux; (*impudent*) effronté; (*tactless*) indiscret.
brass [brɑːs] **1** *n* **(a)** (*metal*) cuivre *m* (jaune); (*ː: money*) pognonː *m*. **(b)** (*tablet*) plaque *f* (en cuivre); (*object/ornament*) objet *m*/ornement *m* en cuivre. **to clean the ~** astiquer les cuivres; (*Mus*) **the ~** les cuivres *mpl*; (*Mil*) **the (top) ~*** les huiles* *fpl*. **2** *adj ornament etc* en *or* de cuivre. ~ **band** fanfare *f*; **it's not worth a ~ farthing*** cela ne vaut pas un clou*; (*Mil*) ~ **hat*** huile* *f*; **he's got a ~ neck*** il a du toupet*; ~ **plate** plaque *f* de cuivre; ~ **rubbing** (*activity*) décalque *m* et frottement; (*object*) décalque; **to get down to ~ tacks*** en venir aux choses sérieuses. ♦ **brassware** *n* chaudronnerie *f* d'art. ♦ **brassy** *adj* cuivré.
brassière ['bræsɪəʳ] *n* soutien-gorge *m*; (*strapless*) bustier *m*.
brat [bræt] *n* (*pej*) moutard* *m*, gosse* *mf*.
bravado [brə'vɑːdəʊ] *n* bravade *f*.
brave [breɪv] **1** *adj* courageux, brave. **be ~!** du courage!; **be ~ and tell her** prends ton courage à deux mains et va lui dire; (*iro*) **it's a ~ new world!** on n'arrête pas le progrès! **2** *vt* braver. **to ~ it out** faire face à la situation. ♦ **bravely** *adv* courageusement, bravement. ♦ **bravery** *n* courage *m*.
bravo ['brɑː'vəʊ] *excl, n* bravo (*m*).
bravura [brə'vʊərə] *n* bravoure *f*.
brawl [brɔːl] **1** *vi* se bagarrer*. **2** *n* rixe *f*, bagarre *f*. ♦ **brawling 1** *adj* bagarreur*; **2** *n* rixe *f*, bagarre *f*.
brawn [brɔːn] *n* muscle *m*; (*Culin*) fromage *m* de tête. ♦ **brawny** *adj arm* musculeux; *person* musclé.
bray [breɪ] **1** *n* braiement *m*. **2** *vi* braire.
brazen ['breɪzn] **1** *adj* (~*-faced*) effronté. **2** *vt*: **to ~ it out** payer d'effronterie. ♦ **brazenly** *adv* effrontément.
brazier ['breɪzɪəʳ] *n* brasero *m*.
Brazil [brə'zɪl] *n* Brésil *m*. ~ **nut** noix *f* du Brésil. ♦ **Brazilian 1** *n* Brésilien(ne) *m(f)*; **2** *adj* brésilien, du Brésil.
breach [briːtʃ] **1** *n* **(a)** *[law, secrecy]* violation *f*; *[rules]* infraction *f* (*of* à); *[friendship, manners]* manquement *m* (*of* à). ~ **of contract** rupture *f* de contrat; ~ **of the peace** attentat *m* à l'ordre public; ~ **of promise** violation de promesse de mariage; ~ **of trust** abus *m* de confiance. **(b)** (*gap: in wall etc*) brèche *f*; (*estrangement*) brouille *f* (*between* entre). **2** *vt wall* ouvrir une brèche dans; *enemy lines, defences* percer.
bread [bred] **1** *n* pain *m*; (*ː: money*) fricː *m*. ~ **and milk** pain au lait; ~ **and butter** tartine *f* (beurrée *or* de beurre); (*fig*) **it's his ~ and butter** c'est son gagne-pain; **he knows which side his ~ is buttered** il sait où est son intérêt; **to put sb on ~ and water** mettre qn au pain et à l'eau; (*Rel*) **the ~ and wine** les (deux) espèces *fpl*. **2** *adj*: **to be on the ~ line*** être sans le sou; ~ **sauce** sauce *f* à la mie de pain. ♦ **bread-and-butter letter** *n* lettre *f* de remerciements (*pour hospitalité reçue*). ♦ **breadbasket** *n* corbeille *f* à pain. ♦ **breadbin** *n* boîte *f* à pain, (*larger*) huche *f* à pain. ♦ **breadboard** *n* planche *f* à pain. ♦ **breadcrumbs** *npl* miettes *fpl* de pain; (*Culin*) chapelure *f*; **fried in ~crumbs** pané. ♦ **breadfruit** *n* fruit *m* de l'arbre à pain. ♦ **breadknife** *n* couteau *m* à pain. ♦ **breadwinner** *n* soutien *m* (de famille).
breadth [bretθ] *n* largeur *f* (*also fig: of thought etc*). **this field is 100 metres in ~** ce champ a 100 mètres de large. ♦ **breadthwise** *adv* dans la *or* en largeur.
break [breɪk] (*vb: pret* **broke**, *ptp* **broken**) **1** *n* **(a)** (*gen*) cassure *f*; *[relationship]* rupture *f*, brouille *f*; *[wall]* trouée *f*; *[line, conversation, transmission]* interruption *f*; *[journey]* arrêt *m*; (*Scol*) récréation *f*. **to take a ~** (*few minutes*) s'arrêter cinq minutes; (*holiday*) prendre des vacances; (*change*) se changer les idées; **6 hours without a ~** 6 heures de suite; (*Elec*) ~ **in circuit** rupture *f* de circuit; **a ~ in the clouds** une éclaircie; **a ~ in the weather** un changement de temps; **with a ~ in her voice** d'une voix entrecoupée; **at ~ of day** au point du jour; **to make a ~ for it*** (*escape*) prendre la fuite; **to have a good/bad ~*** avoir une période de veine/de déveine*; **give me a ~!*** donnez-moi ma chance! **(b)** (*vehicle*) break *m*.
2 *vt* **(a)** (*gen*) casser; (*into small pieces*) briser; *stick* casser, rompre; *bone, limb* casser, fracturer; *skin* écorcher. **to ~ one's leg/back** se casser la jambe/la colonne vertébrale; (*fig*) **to ~ the back of a task** faire le plus dur d'une tâche; **to ~ open** *door* enfoncer; *packet* ouvrir; *lock, safe* fracturer; (*fig*) **to ~ new ground** faire œuvre de pionnier; **to ~ cover** *[animal]* débusquer; *[hunted person]* sortir à découvert; **to ~ ranks** rompre les rangs; (*Aviat*) **to ~ the sound barrier** franchir le mur du son; (*Sport etc*) **to ~ a record** battre un record; **to ~ one's heart over sth** avoir le cœur brisé par qch; **to ~ sb's heart** briser le cœur à *or* de qn; (*lit, fig*) **to ~ the ice** briser la glace. **(b)** *promise* manquer à; *vow* rompre; *treaty, law, the sabbath* violer; *commandment* désobéir à. **to ~ faith with sb** manquer de parole à qn; **to ~ an appointment with sb** faire faux bond à qn. **(c)** *health* détériorer; *strike, rebellion, courage, spirit* abattre, briser; *horse* dresser. **to ~ sb** (*morally*) causer la perte de qn; (*financially*) ruiner qn; **to ~ sb of a habit** faire perdre une habitude à qn; (*Betting*) **to ~ the bank** faire sauter la banque. **(d)** *silence, spell, fast* rompre; *journey* interrompre; (*Elec*) couper. **(e)** *fall, blow* amortir. **the wall ~s the force of the wind** le mur coupe le vent. **(f)** *news* annoncer (*to* à). **try to ~ it to her gently** essayez de le lui annoncer avec ménagement.
3 *vi* **(a)** (*gen*) se casser, se briser; *[stick, rope]* se casser, se rompre; *[bone, limb]* se casser, se fracturer; *[wave]* déferler; *[clouds]* se dissiper; *[ranks]* se rompre; *[heart]* se briser. **to ~ into little pieces** se casser en mille morceaux; (*fig*) **to ~ with a friend** rompre avec un ami; **to ~ even** s'y retrouver; **to ~ free** *or* **loose** se libérer (*from* de). **(b)** *[dawn, day]* poindre; *[news, story, storm]* éclater. **(c)** *[health, weather]* se détériorer; *[heatwave etc]* toucher à sa fin; *[voice]* (*boy's*)

muer; (*in emotion*) se briser (*with* de). **he broke under torture** il a craqué sous la torture; **his spirit broke** son courage l'a abandonné.

break away 1 *vi* (*gen*) se détacher (*from* de); (*Ftbl, Racing*) s'échapper. **to ~ away from routine** sortir de la routine. **2** *vt sep* détacher (*from* de).

break down 1 *vi [vehicle, machine]* tomber en panne; *[health]* se détériorer; *[argument]* s'effondrer; *[resistance]* céder; *[negotiations, plan]* échouer; (*weep*) éclater en sanglots. **2** *vt sep* **(a)** (*demolish*) démolir; *door* enfoncer; *opposition* briser. **(b)** (*analyse: gen*) décomposer (*into* en); *accounts* détailler; (*Chem*) *substance* décomposer.

break in 1 *vi* **(a)** (*interrupt*) interrompre. **to ~ in on sb/sth** interrompre qn/qch. **(b)** *[burglar]* entrer par effraction. **2** *vt sep* **(a)** *door* enfoncer. **(b)** (*train*) *horse* dresser. **it will take you 6 months before you're broken in*** vous mettrez 6 mois à vous faire au métier.

break into *vt fus house* entrer par effraction dans; *safe, cashbox* forcer; *savings, new box* entamer. **he broke into a long explanation** il s'est lancé dans une longue explication; **to ~ into a trot** se mettre à trotter.

break off 1 *vi* **(a)** *[twig etc]* se détacher net. **(b)** (*stop*) s'arrêter (*doing* de faire). **to ~ off from work** interrompre le travail; **to ~ off with sb** rompre avec qn. **2** *vt sep piece of chocolate etc* casser, détacher; *engagement, negotiations* rompre; *habit* se défaire de; *work* interrompre.

break out *vi* **(a)** *[epidemic, fire, storm, war]* éclater. **to ~ out into a sweat** commencer à suer. **(b)** (*escape*) s'évader (*of* de).

break through 1 *vi* (*Mil*) faire une percée; *[sun]* percer (les nuages). **2** *vt fus defences, obstacles, sb's reserve* percer; *crowd* se frayer un passage à travers; *sound barrier* franchir.

break up 1 *vi [ice]* craquer; *[road]* être défoncé; *[ship in storm]* se disloquer; *[partnership]* prendre fin; *[marriage]* se briser; *[health, weather]* se détériorer; *[clouds, crowd, group, meeting]* se disperser; *[friends]* se quitter; *[school, college]* entrer en vacances. **the schools ~ up tomorrow** les vacances (scolaires) commencent demain. **2** *vt sep object* mettre en morceaux; *house* démolir; *ground* ameublir; *road* défoncer; *coalition* briser; *empire* démembrer; *marriage* désunir; *crowd, meeting* disperser.

♦ **breakable 1** *adj* cassable, fragile; **2** *n*: **~ables** objets *mpl* fragiles. ♦ **breakage** *n* casse *f*, bris *m*; **to pay for ~ages** payer la casse. ♦ **breakaway 1** *n [group, movement]* rupture *f*; (*Sport*) échappée *f*; (*Boxing*) dégagement *m*; **2** *adj group, movement* séparatiste, dissident; *state* dissident. ♦ **breakdown 1** *n [machine, vehicle, electricity]* panne *f*; *[communications etc]* rupture *f*; *[railway system etc]* interruption *f* (subite) de service; (*in health*) délabrement *m*; (*mental*) dépression nerveuse; (*analysis*) analyse *f*; (*into categories etc*) décomposition *f* (*into* en); **2** *adj*: **~down gang/service** équipe *f*/service *m* de dépannage; **~down truck** dépanneuse *f*. ♦ **breaker** *n* **(a)** (*wave*) brisant *m*; **(b) to send to the ~er's** *ship* envoyer à la démolition; *car* envoyer à la casse. ♦ **breakfast** ['brekfəst] **1** *n* petit déjeuner *m*; **2** *vi* déjeuner (*off, on* de); **3** *adj*: **~fast cereals** céréales *fpl*, flocons *mpl* d'avoine (*or* de maïs *etc*); **~fast cup** déjeuner *m* (*tasse*); **~fast room** petite salle à manger. ♦ **break-in** *n* cambriolage *m*. ♦ **breaking 1** *n [cup, chair, seal]* bris *m*; *[bone, limb]* fracture *f*; *[promise]* manquement *m* (*of* à); *[treaty, law]* violation *f* (*of* de); *[commandment]* désobéissance *f* (*of* à); *[silence, spell]* rupture *f*; *[journey]* interruption *f* (*of* de); (*Jur*) **~ing and entering** effraction *f*; **2** *adj*: **at ~ing point** *rope, political situation* au point de rupture; *person, sb's patience* à bout. ♦ **breakneck** *adj*: **at ~neck speed** à fond de train. ♦ **breakout** *n* évasion *f* (*de prison*). ♦ **breakthrough** *n* (*Mil*) percée *f*; *[research etc]* découverte *f* sensationnelle. ♦ **break-up** *n [ship]* bris *m*; *[ice, political party]* débâcle *f*; *[friendship]* rupture *f*; *[empire]* démembrement *m*. ♦ **breakwater** *n* brise-lames *m inv*.

bream [bri:m] *n* brème *f*.

breast [brest] **1** *n [woman]* sein *m*; (*chest*) poitrine *f*; (*Culin*) *[chicken etc]* blanc *m*. **2** *vt hill* atteindre le sommet de. ♦ **breast-fed** *adj* nourri au sein. ♦ **breast-feed** *vt* allaiter. ♦ **breast-feeding** *n* allaitement *m* au sein. ♦ **breast-pocket** *n* poche *f* de poitrine. ♦ **breast-stroke** *n*: **to swim ~-stroke** nager la brasse.

breath [breθ] *n* haleine *f*, souffle *m*. **bad ~** mauvaise haleine; **to get one's ~ back** reprendre haleine; **out of ~** essoufflé, hors d'haleine; **to take a deep ~** respirer à fond; **to take sb's ~ away** couper le souffle à qn; **save your ~!** inutile de gaspiller ta salive!; **to be short of ~** avoir le souffle court; **under one's ~** tout bas; **in the same ~** dans la même seconde; **all in one ~** tout d'un trait; **with one's dying ~** en mourant; **there wasn't a ~ of air** *or* **wind** il n'y avait pas un souffle d'air; **to go out for a ~ of air** sortir prendre l'air. ♦ **breathalyse,** (*US*) **-ze** *vt* faire subir l'alcootest à. ♦ **breathalyser,** (*US*) **-zer** *n* alcootest *m*. ♦ **breathless** *adj* (*from exertion*) hors d'haleine; (*through illness*) qui a de la peine à respirer; (*with excitement*) le souffle coupé par l'émotion; *silence* ému. ♦ **breathlessly** *adv* en haletant; (*fig*) en grande hâte. ♦ **breathtaking** *adj* stupéfiant, à vous couper le souffle.

breathe [bri:ð] **1** *vi* respirer. **to ~ deeply** *or* **hard** (*after running*) souffler (fort); (*in illness*) respirer péniblement; **to ~ freely, to ~ again** (pouvoir) respirer; **she is still breathing** elle vit encore. **2** *vt air* respirer; *sigh* laisser échapper; *prayer* murmurer. **to ~ air into sth** insuffler de l'air dans qch; **don't ~ a word (about it)!** n'en dis rien à personne!

breathe in *vi, vt sep* aspirer, inspirer.

breathe out *vi, vt sep* expirer.

♦ **breather*** *n* moment *m* de répit; **to give sb a ~r** laisser souffler qn; **to go out for a ~r** sortir prendre l'air. ♦ **breathing 1** *n* respiration *f*; **heavy breathing** respiration bruyante; **2** *adj apparatus* respiratoire; **a breathing space** un moment de répit.

bred [bred] (*pret, ptp of* **breed**) *adj*: **well-/ill-~** bien/mal élevé.

breech [bri:tʃ] **1** *n [gun]* culasse *f*. **2** *adj*: **~ birth** accouchement *m* par le siège.

breeches ['brɪtʃɪz] *npl* (*riding ~*) culotte *f* (de cheval); (*knee ~*) haut-de-chausses *m*. **his wife wears the ~** c'est sa femme qui porte la culotte.

breed [bri:d] *pret, ptp* **bred 1** *vt animals* élever, faire l'élevage de; *hate, suspicion* faire naître, engendrer. **to ~ sth in/out** faire acquérir/perdre qch (*par la sélection*). **2** *vi* se reproduire, se multiplier. **3** *n* race *f*, espèce *f*; (*fig*) espèce. ♦ **breeder** *n* **(a)** (*Phys: ~er reactor*) générateur *m or* réacteur *m* nucléaire; **(b)** (*Agr etc: person*) éleveur *m*, -euse *f*. ♦ **breeding** *n* **(a)** (*Agr*) élevage *m*; (*reproduction*) reproduction *f*; **~ing season** saison *f* des accouplements; **(b) (good) ~ing** (bonne) éducation *f*, savoir-vivre *m*.

breeze [bri:z] **1** *n* (*wind*) brise *f*. **gentle ~** petite brise; **stiff ~** vent frais. **2** *vi*: **to ~ in/out** entrer/sortir (*jauntily*) d'un air dégagé *or* (*briskly*) en coup de vent. ♦ **breezily** *adv* (*jauntily*) d'un air dégagé; (*briskly*) brusquement; (*jovially*) jovialement. ♦ **breezy** *adj weather, day* frais; *corner, spot* éventé; *person* (*jaunty*) dégagé; (*brisk*) brusque; (*jovial*) jovial.

breeze-block ['bri:zblɒk] *n* parpaing *m*.

Bren gun ['bren gʌn] *n* fusil *m* mitrailleur.
brethren ['breðrɪn] *npl* (*Rel*) *pl of* **brother.**
Breton ['bretən] **1** *adj* breton. **2** *n* Breton(ne) *m(f)*; (*Ling*) breton *m.*
brevity ['brevɪtɪ] *n* brièveté *f*; (*conciseness*) concision *f.*
brew [bru:] **1** *n* décoction *f.* **witch's ~** brouet *m* de sorcière. **2** *vt beer* brasser; *tea, scheme, mischief* préparer. **3** *vi [brewer]* brasser; *[beer]* fermenter; *[tea]* infuser; *[storm]* se préparer; *[plot]* se tramer. **there's trouble ~ing** il y a de l'orage dans l'air (*fig*); **sth's ~ing** il se trame qch.
brew up *vi* **(a)** (*: *make tea*) faire du thé. **(b)** *[storm, dispute]* se préparer.
♦ **brewer** *n* brasseur *m.* ♦ **brewery** *n* brasserie *f* (*fabrique*). ♦ **brewing** *n* brassage *m.*
briar ['braɪə^r] *n* = **brier.**
bribe [braɪb] **1** *n* pot-de-vin *m.* **to take/offer a ~** accepter/offrir un pot-de-vin (*from sb* de qn; *to* à). **2** *vt* suborner, soudoyer; *witness* suborner. **to ~ sb to do sth** soudoyer qn pour qu'il fasse qch.
♦ **bribery** *n* corruption *f.*
brick [brɪk] *n* brique *f*; (*toy*) cube *m* (*de construction*). **you can't make ~s without straw** à l'impossible nul n'est tenu; **he came down on me like a ton of ~s*** il m'a passé un de ces savons!*; **you might as well talk to a ~ wall*** autant parler à un mur; **to come up against a ~ wall** se heurter à un mur; **a ~ of ice cream** une glace pour plusieurs personnes; **he's a ~*** il est sympa*.
brick in, brick up *vt sep* murer.
♦ **brickbat** *n* (*fig*) critique *f.* ♦ **brick-built** *adj* en brique(s). ♦ **bricklayer** *n* ouvrier-maçon *m.* ♦ **brick-red** *adj* (rouge) brique *inv.* ♦ **brickwork** *n* briquetage *m.* ♦ **brickworks** *npl* briqueterie *f.*
bride [braɪd] *n* (future *or* jeune) mariée *f.* **the ~ and groom** les mariés. ♦ **bridal** *adj feast* de noce; *procession* nuptial; *veil, gown* de mariée; *suite* réservé aux jeunes mariés. ♦ **bridegroom** *n* (futur *or* jeune) marié *m.* ♦ **bridesmaid** *n* demoiselle *f* d'honneur.
bridge[1] [brɪdʒ] **1** *n* (*gen*) pont *m* (*across* sur); (*Naut*) passerelle *f* (de commandement); *[nose]* arête *f*; (*Dentistry*) bridge *m.* **2** *vt river* construire un pont sur. (*fig*) **to ~ a gap** établir un contact (*between* entre); (*in knowledge*) combler une lacune (*in* dans); (*in budget*) combler un trou (*in* dans). ♦ **bridge-building** *n* (*fig*) efforts *mpl* de rapprochement. ♦ **bridgehead** *n* tête *f* de pont.
♦ **bridging** *adj*: **bridging loan** crédit *m* de relais.
bridge[2] [brɪdʒ] *n* (*Cards*) bridge *m.* ♦ **bridge-player** *n* bridgeur *m*, -euse *f.*
bridle ['braɪdl] **1** *n* bride *f.* **~ path** sentier *m* (*pour chevaux*). **2** *vt* mettre la bride à. **3** *vi* (*in anger*) regimber; (*in scorn*) lever le menton (*de mépris*).
brief [bri:f] **1** *adj life, meeting* bref; *interval, period, stay* court; *speech* bref, concis, laconique (*pej*); *account* sommaire. **in ~** *or* **to be ~, he didn't come** bref *or* en deux mots, il n'est pas venu. **2** *n* **(a)** (*Jur*) dossier *m*, affaire *f.* (*fig*) **I hold no ~ for him** je ne prends pas sa défense; **to have a watching ~ for** veiller (en justice) aux intérêts de. **(b)** (*Mil: instructions*) briefing *m*; (*gen*) instructions *fpl.* **(c)** (*Dress*) **~s** slip *m.* **3** *vt barrister* confier une cause à; *pilots, soldiers* donner des instructions à; *person* mettre au fait (*on sth* de qch).
♦ **briefcase** *n* serviette *f.* ♦ **briefing** *n* briefing *m.* ♦ **briefly** *adv visit* en coup de vent; *reply* laconiquement; *speak* brièvement. ♦ **briefness** *n* brièveté *f*; courte durée *f*; concision *f*, laconisme *m.*
brier ['braɪə^r] *n* (racine *f* de) bruyère *f*; (**~ *pipe***) pipe *f* de bruyère.
brigade [brɪ'geɪd] *n* brigade *f.* **one of the old ~** un vieux de la vieille*. ♦ **brigadier (general)** *n* général *m* de brigade.
brigand ['brɪgənd] *n* brigand *m.*

bright [braɪt] *adj* **(a)** *eyes, star, gem* brillant; *light, fire* vif; *sunshine* éclatant; *day, weather, room* clair; *colour* vif, éclatant; *metal* poli. (*Met*) **to become ~(er)** s'éclaircir; (*Met*) **~ intervals** éclaircies *fpl*; **the outlook is ~er** (*Met*) on prévoit une amélioration (du temps); (*fig*) l'avenir se présente mieux. **(b)** (*cheerful*) *person* gai, animé; *face, expression* gai, radieux; *prospects, future* brillant, splendide. **as ~ as a button** gai comme un pinson; **~ and early** de bon matin; **to look on the ~ side** essayer d'être optimiste. **(c)** (*intelligent*) *person* intelligent, doué; *child* éveillé. **he's a ~ spark*** il est vraiment futé.
♦ **brighten 1** *vt* (**~ up**) *metal* faire reluire; *colour* aviver; *room, person* égayer; *prospects, situation* améliorer; **2** *vi [weather, sky]* se dégager; *[eyes, expression]* s'éclairer; *[person]* s'animer; *[prospects, future]* s'améliorer. ♦ **brightly** *adv shine* avec éclat; *behave* gaiement; *say* avec animation; **the sun shone ~ly** le soleil brillait d'un vif éclat.
♦ **brightness** *n* (*gen*) éclat *m*; *[light]* intensité *f*; (*intelligence*) intelligence *f.*
brilliant ['brɪljənt] *adj light* éclatant; *person, idea, wit* brillant. ♦ **brilliance** *n* éclat *m*; *[person]* intelligence *f* supérieure. ♦ **brilliantly** *adv shine* avec éclat; *suggest etc* brillamment.
brim [brɪm] *n* bord *m.*
brim over *vi* (*lit, fig*) déborder (*with* de).
♦ **brimful** *adj* plein à déborder; (*fig*) débordant (*with* de).
brine [braɪn] *n* eau *f* salée; (*Culin*) saumure *f.*
bring [brɪŋ] *pret, ptp* **brought** *vt object, news, information* apporter; *person, animal, vehicle, storm, consequences* amener; *evidence* fournir. **to ~ sb up/down** *etc* faire monter/faire descendre *etc* qn (avec soi); **to ~ sth up/down** monter/descendre qch; **it brought him a good income** cela lui rapportait bien; (*Jur*) **to ~ an action against sb** intenter un procès à qn; **to ~ luck** porter bonheur; **to ~ tears to sb's eyes** faire venir les larmes aux yeux de qn; **to ~ sth (up)on o.s.** s'attirer qch; **to ~ sth to a close** *or* **an end** mettre fin à qch; **to ~ sth to light** mettre qch en lumière; **he brought him to understand that ...** il l'a amené à comprendre que ...; **I cannot ~ myself to speak to him** je ne peux me résoudre à lui parler.
bring about *vt sep* **(a)** *reforms, review* amener, provoquer; *war, accident* causer, provoquer. **(b)** *boat* faire virer de bord.
bring along *vt sep object* apporter; *person, car* amener.
bring back *vt sep* **(a)** *person* ramener; *object* rapporter; *spacecraft* récupérer. **(b)** (*call to mind*) rappeler (à la mémoire).
bring down *vt sep kite etc* ramener au sol; *plane* faire atterrir; *animal, bird, enemy plane* descendre; *tree, opponent* abattre; *dictator, government* faire tomber; *temperature, prices* faire baisser; *swelling* réduire. **the play brought the house down*** la pièce a fait crouler la salle sous les applaudissements.
bring forward *vt sep person* faire avancer; *chair etc* avancer; *witness* produire; *evidence* avancer; (*advance time of*) *meeting* avancer; (*Book-keeping*) *figure* reporter.
bring in *vt sep person* faire entrer; *chair* rentrer; *police, troops* faire intervenir; *fashion* lancer; *custom, legislation* introduire; *income, interest* rapporter; *[jury] verdict* rendre; (*Parl*) *bill* présenter.
bring off *vt sep people from wreck* sauver; *plan, aim* réaliser; *deal* mener à bien; *attack, hoax* réussir. **he didn't ~ it off** il n'a pas réussi son coup.
bring on *vt sep illness, quarrel* provoquer, causer; *crops, flowers* faire pousser; (*Theat*) *person* amener; *thing* apporter sur la scène.
bring out *vt sep person* faire sortir; *object*

sortir; *meaning, colour* faire ressortir; *qualities* mettre en valeur; *book* publier, faire paraître; *new product* lancer.
bring round *vt sep person* amener; *object* apporter; *conversation* ramener (*to* sur); *unconscious person* ranimer; (*convert*) convertir (*to* à).
bring together *vt sep people* (*introduce*) faire se rencontrer; (*reconcile*) réconcilier.
bring up *vt sep person* faire monter; *object* monter; (*vomit*) vomir, rendre; (*mention*) *fact, problem* mentionner; *question* soulever; (*rear*) *child, animal* élever. **well brought-up** bien élevé; **to ~ sb up short** arrêter qn net; **to ~ sb up before a court** faire comparaître qn devant un tribunal. ♦ **bring-and-buy sale** *n* vente *f* de charité.
brink [brɪŋk] *n* bord *m*. **on the ~ of (doing) sth** à deux doigts de (faire) qch. ♦ **brinkmanship*** *n* stratégie *f* du bord de l'abîme.
brisk [brɪsk] *adj person, voice* vif, animé, (*abrupt*) brusque; *movement* vif, rapide; *attack* vigoureux; *trade, trading* actif; *air* frais. **at a ~ pace** d'un bon pas; **business is ~** les affaires marchent (bien). ♦ **briskly** *adv move* vivement; *walk* d'un bon pas; *speak* brusquement; *act* sans tarder; *sell* très bien. ♦ **briskness** *n* vivacité *f*; animation *f*; brusquerie *f*; rapidité *f*; activité *f*; fraîcheur *f*.
bristle ['brɪsl] **1** *n [beard, brush, plant]* poil *m*; *[boar etc]* soie *f*. **brush with nylon ~s** brosse en nylon; **pure ~ brush** brosse pur sanglier *inv*. **2** *vi [animal, hair, person]* se hérisser (*at* à). **bristling with** *pins, difficulties* hérissé de; *policemen* grouillant de. ♦ **bristly** *adj chin* qui pique; *hair, beard* hérissé.
Britain ['brɪtən] *n*: **(Great) ~** Grande-Bretagne *f*. ♦ **Briticism** *n* (*US*) anglicisme *m*. ♦ **British 1** *adj economy, team* britannique, anglais; *ambassador* de Grande-Bretagne; **the British Commonwealth** le Commonwealth; (*US*) **British English** l'anglais d'Angleterre; **British Isles** îles *fpl* Britanniques; **2** *n*: **the British** les Britanniques *mpl*, les Anglais *mpl*. ♦ **Britisher** *or* ♦ **Briton** *n* Britannique *mf*, Anglais(e) *m(f)*.
Brittany ['brɪtənɪ] *n* Bretagne *f*.
brittle ['brɪtl] *adj* cassant, fragile.
broach [brəʊtʃ] *vt* entamer.
broad [brɔːd] *adj road, smile* large; *hint* transparent; *mind, ideas* large, libéral; *accent* prononcé. **to grow ~(er)** s'élargir; **to make ~(er)** élargir; **~ bean** fève *f*; (*fig*) **he's got a ~ back** il a bon dos; **the lake is 200 metres ~** le lac a 200 mètres de largeur *or* de large; (*fig*) **it's as ~ as it is long** c'est du pareil au même*; **in ~ daylight** au grand jour; **the ~ outlines** les grandes lignes; **in the ~est sense** au sens le plus large. ♦ **broadcast** *V below*. ♦ **broaden** (**~ out**) **1** *vt* élargir; **2** *vi* s'élargir. ♦ **broadly** *adv*: **~ly (speaking)** en gros. ♦ **broad-minded** *adj* qui a les idées (très) larges. ♦ **broad-mindedness** *n* largeur *f* d'esprit. ♦ **broadness** *n* largeur *f*. ♦ **broadsheet** *n* placard *m*. ♦ **broad-shouldered** *adj* large d'épaules. ♦ **broadside** *n* (*Naut*) bordée *f*; (*fig: insults etc*) bordée d'injures *etc*; **~side on** par le travers. ♦ **broadways** *or* ♦ **broadwise** *adv* en largeur.
broadcast ['brɔːdkɑːst] *pret, ptp* **broadcast 1** *vt* (*Rad*) (radio)diffuser, émettre, (*TV*) téléviser, émettre. (*fig*) **don't ~ it!*** ne va pas le crier sur les toits! **2** *vi [station]* émettre; *[actor, interviewee]* participer à une émission; *[interviewer]* faire une émission. **3** *n* émission *f*. **4** *adj* (*Rad*) (radio)diffusé; (*TV*) télévisé. ♦ **broadcaster** *n* personnalité *f* de la radio *or* de la télévision. ♦ **broadcasting** *n* (*Rad*) radiodiffusion *f*; (*TV*) télévision *f*; (*broadcasts*) émissions *fpl*.
brocade [brəʊ'keɪd] *n* brocart *m*.
broccoli ['brɒkəlɪ] *n* brocoli *m*.
brochure ['brəʊʃjʊəʳ] *n* (*Scol etc*) prospectus *m*; (*Tourism*) brochure *f*, dépliant *m*.
brogue [brəʊg] *n* (*shoe*) chaussure *f* de marche; (*accent*) accent *m* irlandais.
broil [brɔɪl] *vti* (*also fig*) griller.
broke [brəʊk] (*pret of* **break**) *adj* (*: *penniless*) à sec*, fauché*. **to go ~*** faire faillite.
broken ['brəʊkən] (*ptp of* **break**) *adj* **(a)** *window, rib* cassé; *neck, leg* fracturé, cassé; *heart, marriage* brisé; *promise* rompu, violé; *appointment* manqué. **~ bones** fractures *fpl*; **~ home** foyer brisé; **he is a ~ reed** on ne peut jamais compter sur lui; **a spell of ~ weather** un temps variable. **(b)** (*uneven*) *ground* accidenté; *road* défoncé; *surface* raboteux; *line* brisé; *coastline* dentelé. **(c)** (*interrupted*) *journey* interrompu; *sleep* (*disturbed*) interrompu, (*restless*) agité; *gestures* incohérent; *voice* brisé; *words* haché. **to speak ~ English** parler un mauvais anglais; **~ nights** mauvaises nuits. **(d)** (*spoilt*) *health* délabré; *spirit* abattu. **he is a ~ man** il est brisé. ♦ **broken-down** *adj car* en panne; *machine* détraqué; *house* délabré, en ruines. ♦ **broken-hearted** *adj* au cœur brisé. ♦ **brokenly** *adv say* d'une voix entrecoupée; *sob* par à-coups.
broker ['brəʊkəʳ] *n* courtier *m*.
bromide ['brəʊmaɪd] *n* bromure *m*; (*fig*) banalité *f* euphorisante.
bronchial ['brɒŋkɪəl] *adj infection* des bronches. **~ tubes** bronches *fpl*.
bronchitis [brɒŋ'kaɪtɪs] *n* bronchite *f*.
bronze [brɒnz] **1** *n* bronze *m*. **2** *vi* se bronzer. **3** *vt skin* faire bronzer. **4** *adj* (*made of* ~) en bronze; (*colour*) bronze *inv*. **B~ Age** âge *m* du bronze. ♦ **bronzed** *adj* bronzé.
brooch [brəʊtʃ] *n* broche *f* (*bijou*).
brood [bruːd] **1** *n* nichée *f*. **2** *vi [storm, danger]* couver; *[person]* broyer du noir. *[person]* **to ~ on** *misfortune* remâcher; *plan* ruminer; *the past* ressasser. ♦ **broody** *adj person* distrait; (*depressed*) cafardeux*. **~ hen** couveuse *f*.
brook[1] [brʊk] *n* (*stream*) ruisseau *m*.
brook[2] [brʊk] *vt* (*tolerate*) souffrir, admettre.
broom [brʊm] *n* **(a)** (*Bot*) genêt *m*. **(b)** (*brush*) balai *m*. (*fig*) **this firm needs a new ~** cette compagnie a besoin de sang nouveau. ♦ **broomstick** *n* (manche *m* à) balai *m*.
broth [brɒθ] *n* bouillon *m* de viande et de légumes.
brothel ['brɒθl] *n* bordel‡ *m*.
brother ['brʌðəʳ] **1** *n* (*gen, Rel*) frère *m*; (*in trade unions etc*) camarade *m*. **2** *adj*: **his ~ officers** ses compagnons *mpl* d'armes. ♦ **brotherhood** *n* fraternité *f*; (*association*) confrérie *f*. ♦ **brother-in-law** *n* beau-frère *m*. ♦ **brotherly** *adj* fraternel.
brought [brɔːt] *pret, ptp of* **bring.**
brow [braʊ] *n* (*forehead*) front *m*; (*arch above eye*) arcade *f* sourcilière; (*eyebrow*) sourcil *m*; *[hill]* sommet *m*; *[cliff]* bord *m*. ♦ **browbeat** (*pret* **~beat**, *ptp* **~beaten**) *vt* intimider, brusquer; **to ~beat sb into doing sth** forcer qn à faire qch par l'intimidation.
brown [braʊn] **1** *adj* (*gen*) brun; *hair* châtain; *shoes, material, leather* marron *inv*; (*tanned*) bronzé, bruni; (*dusky-skinned*) brun de peau. **~ ale** bière brune; **~ bread** pain bis; **~ bear** ours brun; **~ paper** papier *m* d'emballage; **in a ~ study** plongé dans ses pensées; **~ sugar** cassonade *f*, sucre brun; **to go ~** *[person]* brunir; *[leaves]* roussir; **as ~ as a berry** tout bronzé. **2** *n* brun *m*, marron *m*. **3** *vt [sun]* bronzer, brunir; (*Culin*) *meat, potatoes* faire dorer; *sauce* faire roussir. **to be ~ed off‡** en avoir marre*. ♦ **brownie** *n* lutin *m*; **B~ie (Guide)** jeannette *f*. ♦ **brownish** *adj* qui tire sur le brun, brunâtre (*pej*). ♦ **brownout** *n* (*US Elec*) panne *f* partielle. ♦ **brownstone (house)** *n* (*US*) bâtiment *m* de grès brun.
browse [braʊz] *vi [animal]* brouter; *[person in bookshop]* feuilleter les livres; (*in other shops*) regarder.
bruise [bruːz] **1** *vt person* faire un bleu à; *fruit*

abîmer, taler; *lettuce* froisser. **to ~ one's foot** se faire un bleu au pied; **to be ~d all over** être couvert de bleus. **2** *n [person]* bleu *m*, ecchymose *f*; *[fruit]* talure *f*. **body covered with ~s** corps couvert d'ecchymoses. ♦ **bruiser‡** *n* malabar‡ *m*.
brunch [brʌntʃ] *n* (grand) petit déjeuner *m*.
brunt [brʌnt] *n*: **the ~** *[attack, blow]* le choc; *[argument, displeasure]* le poids; *[work, expense]* le (plus) gros; **he bore the ~ of it all** c'est lui qui a porté le poids de l'affaire.
brush [brʌʃ] **1** *n* **(a)** (*gen*) brosse *f*; (*paint~*) pinceau *m*, brosse; (*broom*) balai *m*; (*hearth ~ etc*) balayette *f*; (*scrubbing ~*) brosse (dure); (*shaving ~*) blaireau *m*. **hair/shoe ~** brosse à cheveux/à chaussures; **give your coat a ~** donne un coup de brosse à ton manteau. **(b)** (*light touch*) effleurement *m*. **~ with the law** ennuis *mpl* avec la police; (*quarrel*) **to have a ~ with sb** avoir un accrochage avec qn. **(c)** (*undergrowth*) broussailles *fpl*. **2** *vt* **(a)** *carpet* balayer; *clothes, hair etc* brosser. **to ~ one's teeth** se laver les dents; **to ~ one's hair** se brosser les cheveux; **hair ~ed back** cheveux ramenés en arrière. **(b)** (*touch lightly*) effleurer; *the ground* raser. **(c)** (*Tex*) *wool* gratter. **~ed nylon** nylon gratté. **3** *vi*: **to ~ against sb/sth** effleurer *or* frôler qn/qch; **to ~ past sb/sth** frôler qn/qch en passant.
brush aside *vt sep* (*fig*) écarter.
brush away *vt sep mud, dust* (*on clothes*) brosser, (*on floor*) balayer; *tears* essuyer; *insects* chasser.
brush down *vt sep person, garment* donner un coup de brosse à; *horse* brosser.
brush off *vt sep mud, snow, fluff* enlever; *insect* balayer.
brush up *vt sep crumbs, dirt* ramasser avec une brosse *or* à la balayette; (*: *revise*) se remettre à, réviser.
♦ **brush-off‡** *n*: **to give sb the ~-off‡** envoyer promener* qn; **to get the ~-off‡** se faire envoyer promener*. ♦ **brush-stroke** *n* coup *m* de pinceau. ♦ **brushwood** *n* (*undergrowth*) broussailles *fpl*; (*cuttings*) brindilles *fpl*. ♦ **brushwork** *n* (*Art*) facture *f*.
brusque [bru:sk] *adj* brusque. ♦ **brusquely** *adv* avec brusquerie. ♦ **brusqueness** *n* brusquerie *f*.
Brussels ['brʌslz] *n* Bruxelles. **~ sprouts** choux *mpl* de Bruxelles.
brute [bru:t] **1** *n* (*animal*) brute *f*, bête *f*; (*person*) brute. **this machine is a ~!*** quelle vache que cette machine!‡ **2** *adj strength, passion* brutal; *matter* brut. **by (sheer) ~ force** par la force. ♦ **brutal** *adj* brutal, cruel. ♦ **brutality** *n* brutalité *f*. ♦ **brutally** *adv* brutalement. ♦ **brutish** *adj* (*animal-like*) bestial; (*unfeeling*) grossier.
bubble ['bʌbl] **1** *n* bulle *f*; (*in hot liquid*) bouillon *m*. **to blow ~s** faire des bulles; **soap ~** bulle de savon. **2** *adj*: **~ bath** bain moussant. **3** *vi [liquid]* bouillonner; *[champagne]* pétiller; *[gas]* barboter; (*gurgle*) faire glouglou, glouglouter. **to ~ out** sortir à gros bouillons; **to ~ up** monter en bouillonnant; (*lit, fig*) **to ~ over** déborder (*with* de). ♦ **bubble-car** *n* petite voiture (*à toit transparent*). ♦ **bubble-gum** *n* chewing-gum *m* (qui fait des bulles).
bubonic [bju:'bɒnɪk] *adj* bubonique.
buccaneer [ˌbʌkə'nɪəʳ] *n* boucanier *m*.
buck [bʌk] **1** *n* **(a)** (*Zool*) mâle *m*. **(b)** (*US**) dollar *m*. **(c) to pass the ~** refiler* la responsabilité aux autres. **(d)** (*Gymnastics*) cheval *m* d'arçons. **2** *adj rabbit* mâle. **3** *vi [horse]* lancer une ruade.
buck up* **1** *vi* (*hurry up*) se grouiller*; (*cheer up*) se secouer. **2** *vt sep* remonter le moral de.
♦ **bucked‡** *adj* tout content. ♦ **buckshot** *n* chevrotines *fpl*. ♦ **buckskin** *n* peau *f* de daim. ♦ **buck-toothed** *adj*: **to be ~-toothed** avoir des dents de lapin.
bucket ['bʌkɪt] **1** *n* (*gen*) seau *m*; *[dredger etc]* godet *m*. **~ of water** seau d'eau; **chain of ~s** pompe *f* à chapelet; **to weep ~s*** pleurer toutes les larmes de son corps. **2** *vi*: **the rain is ~ing (down)‡** il pleut à seaux, il tombe des cordes*. **3** *adj*: **~ seat** (siège-)baquet *m*. ♦ **bucketful** *n* plein seau; **I've had a ~ful‡** j'en ai ras le bol‡ (*of* de).
buckle ['bʌkl] **1** *n* boucle *f*. **2** *vt* **(a)** *belt* boucler, attacher. **(b)** *wheel* voiler; *metal* gauchir. **3** *vi* **(a)** se boucler. **(b)** se voiler; gauchir.
buckle down* *vi* se coller au boulot*. **to ~ down to a job** s'atteler à un boulot*.
buckle on *vt sep armour* revêtir; *sword* ceindre.
buckram ['bʌkrəm] *n* bougran *m*.
bucksheeǂ [bʌk'ʃi:] *adj, adv* gratis (*inv*).
bud [bʌd] **1** *n [tree, plant]* bourgeon *m*; *[flower]* bouton *m*. **in ~** *tree* bourgeonnant; *flower* en bouton. **2** *vi [tree]* bourgeonner; *[flower]* être en bouton. ♦ **budding** *adj plant* bourgeonnant; *flower* en bouton; *poet etc* en herbe; *passion* naissant.
Buddha ['bʊdə] *n* Bouddha *m*. ♦ **Buddhism** *n* bouddhisme *m*. ♦ **Buddhist** **1** *n* Bouddhiste *mf*; **2** *adj monk* bouddhiste; *religion* bouddhique.
buddy* ['bʌdɪ] *n* (*US*) copain* *m*, copine* *f*.
budge [bʌdʒ] **1** *vi* bouger; (*fig*) changer d'avis. **2** *vt* faire bouger; (*fig*) faire changer d'avis.
budge over*, budge up* *vi* se pousser.
budgerigar ['bʌdʒərɪgɑ:ʳ] *n* perruche *f*.
budget ['bʌdʒɪt] **1** *n* budget *m*. **2** *adj* (*Comm*) **~ account** compte-crédit *m*; (*Parl*) **~ day** jour *m* de la présentation du budget; (*US Comm*) **~ plan** système *m* de crédit. **3** *vi* dresser un budget. **to ~ for sth** (*Econ*) porter qch au budget; (*gen*) inscrire qch à son budget. **4** *vt* budgétiser. ♦ **budgetary** *adj* budgétaire; **~ary year** exercice *m* budgétaire.
budgie* ['bʌdʒɪ] *n abbr of* **budgerigar**.
buff[1] [bʌf] **1** *n* (*for polishing*) polissoir *m*; (*colour*) (couleur *f*) chamois *m*. **in the ~‡** à poil‡. **2** *adj* (*~-coloured*) (couleur) chamois *inv*. **3** *vt metal* polir.
buff[2]* [bʌf] *n* (*enthusiast*) mordu(e)* *m(f)*. **film ~** mordu(e)* du cinéma.
buffalo ['bʌfələʊ] *n, pl ~ or ~es* (*wild ox*) buffle *m*, bufflesse *f*; (*esp in US*) bison *m*.
buffer ['bʌfəʳ] **1** *n* (*gen, also Rail*) tampon *m*; (*US Aut*) pare-chocs *m inv*. **2** *adj*: **~ state** état *m* tampon.
buffet[1] ['bʌfɪt] **1** *n* gifle *f*. (*fig*) **the ~s of fate** les coups *mpl* du sort. **2** *vt [waves]* battre, ballotter; *[wind]* secouer. ♦ **buffeting** **1** *n [wind, rain etc]* assaut *m*; **2** *adj wind* violent.
buffet[2] ['bʊfeɪ] **1** *n* buffet *m* (*repas*). (*in menu*) **cold ~** viandes froides. **2** *adj* (*Rail*) **~ car** voiture-buffet *f*, buffet *m*; **~ lunch** lunch *m*; **~ supper** souper-buffet *m*.
buffoon [bə'fu:n] *n* bouffon *m*. ♦ **buffoonery** *n* bouffonneries *fpl*.
bug [bʌg] **1** *n* **(a)** punaise *f*; (*: *any insect*) insecte *m*, bestiole* *f*; (*: *germ*) microbe *m*. **the flu ~** le virus de la grippe. **(b)** (*: *microphone*) micro *m* (caché). **2** *vt* **(a)** (*) *phone* brancher sur table d'écoute; *room etc* poser des micros dans. **(b)** (‡: *annoy*) embêter*. ♦ **bugbear** *n* épouvantail *m*, cauchemar *m*. ♦ **bug-eyed‡** *adj* aux yeux à fleur de tête. ♦ **bugging*** *adj*: **~ging device** appareil *m* d'écoute (*clandestine*). ♦ **bug-ridden** *adj* infesté de punaises.
buggy ['bʌgɪ] *n* (*for beach*) buggy *m*; (*for moon*) jeep *f* lunaire; (‡: *car*) bagnole* *f*; (*pram*) voiture *f* d'enfant.
bugle ['bju:gl] *n* clairon *m*. **~ call** sonnerie *f* de clairon. ♦ **bugler** *n* (joueur *m* de) clairon *m*.
build [bɪld] (*vb: pret, ptp* **built**) **1** *n [person]* carrure *f*. **2** *vt house, town* bâtir, construire; *bridge, ship, machine* construire; *temple* bâtir, édifier; *nest* faire, bâtir; *theory, plan, empire* bâtir; (*Games*) *words* former. **the house is being built** la

maison se bâtit; **to ~ sth into a wall** encastrer qch dans un mur; *[person]* **to be solidly built** être puissamment charpenté; **pine-built house** maison en bois de pin; **French-built ship** navire de construction française.

build in *vt sep wardrobe* encastrer; *safeguards* intégrer (*into* à).

build on *vt sep* ajouter (*to* à).

build up 1 *vi [pressure]* s'accumuler; *[interest]* monter. **2** *vt sep* **(a)** (*establish*) *reputation* bâtir; *business* créer, monter; *theory* échafauder; (*increase*) *production, forces* accroître; *pressure* accumuler; *tension, excitement* faire monter. **(b)** (*cover with houses*) *area, land* urbaniser. ♦ **builder** *n [houses etc]* maçon *m*, (*large-scale*) entrepreneur *m*; *[ships, machines]* constructeur *m*; (*fig*) fondateur *m*, -trice *f*; **~er's labourer** ouvrier-maçon *m*. ♦ **building 1** *n* bâtiment *m*, construction *f*; (*imposing*) édifice *m*; (*habitation or offices*) immeuble *m*; **2** *adj*: **~ing contractor** entrepreneur *m* (de bâtiment); **~ing industry** (industrie *f* du) bâtiment *m*; **~ing land** terrain *m* à bâtir; **~ing materials** matériaux *mpl* de construction; **~ing site** chantier *m* (de construction); **~ing society** ≃ société *f* d'investissement immobilier. ♦ **build-up** *n [pressure, gas]* accumulation *f*; (*Mil*) *[troops]* rassemblement *m*; *[tension, excitement]* montée *f*; (*fig*) **to give sb/sth a good ~-up** faire une bonne publicité pour qn/qch. ♦ **built-in** *adj bookcase* encastré; *desire* inné. ♦ **built-up** *adj* urbanisé; **~-up area** agglomération *f* (urbaine).

bulb [bʌlb] *n* **(a)** *[plant]* bulbe *m*, oignon *m*. **~ of garlic** tête *f* d'ail. **(b)** (*Elec*) ampoule *f*; *[thermometer]* cuvette *f*. ♦ **bulbous** *adj* bulbeux.

Bulgaria [bʌl'gɛərɪə] *n* Bulgarie *f*.

bulge [bʌldʒ] **1** *n [surface, metal]* bombement *m*; *[cheek]* gonflement *m*; *[plaster]* bosse *f*; *[tyre]* hernie *f*; *[pocket, jacket]* renflement *m*; *[numbers]* augmentation *f* temporaire; *[sales, birth rate]* poussée *f*. **the postwar ~** l'explosion *f* démographique de l'après-guerre. **2** *vi* (**~ out**) (*swell*) bomber; (*stick out*) faire saillie; *[plaster]* être bosselé; *[pocket, sack, cheek]* être gonflé (*with* de). ♦ **bulging** *adj forehead, wall* bombé; *stomach, eyes* protubérant; *pockets, suitcase* bourré (*with* de).

bulk [bʌlk] *n [thing]* grosseur *f*, grandeur *f*; *[person]* corpulence *f*. **the ~ of** *[people, community]* la plus grande partie de; *[work]* le plus gros de; **in ~** (*in large quantities*) en gros; (*not pre-packed*) en vrac. ♦ **bulk-buying** *n* achat *m* en gros. ♦ **bulkiness** *n [parcel, luggage]* grosseur *f*; *[person]* corpulence *f*. ♦ **bulky** *adj parcel, suitcase* volumineux; *book* épais; *person* corpulent.

bull[1] [bʊl] **1** *n* **(a)** taureau *m*; (*male of elephant etc*) mâle *m*; (*St Ex*) haussier *m*. (*fig*) **to take the ~ by the horns** prendre le taureau par les cornes; **like a ~ in a china shop** comme un éléphant dans un magasin de porcelaine; **it's like a red rag to a ~** ça lui (*etc*) fait monter la moutarde au nez; **to go at it like a ~ at a gate** foncer tête baissée. **(b)** (*Mil sl*) fourbissage *m*. **2** *adj elephant etc* mâle.
♦ **bulldog 1** *n* bouledogue *m*; **2** *adj*: **~dog clip** pince *f* (à dessin). ♦ **bulldoze** *vt* passer au bulldozer; (*fig*) **to ~doze sb into doing sth*** employer les grands moyens pour faire faire qch à qn. ♦ **bulldozer** *n* bulldozer *m*. ♦ **bullfight** *n* course *f* de taureaux, corrida *f*. ♦ **bullfighter** *n* matador *m*, torero *m*. ♦ **bullfighting** *n* courses *fpl* de taureaux; (*art*) tauromachie *f*. ♦ **bullfinch** *n* bouvreuil *m*. ♦ **bullfrog** *n* grosse grenouille *f* d'Amérique. ♦ **bull-necked** *adj* au cou de taureau. ♦ **bullock** *n* bœuf *m*; (*young*) bouvillon *m*. ♦ **bullring** *n* arène *f* (*pour courses de taureaux*). ♦ **bull's-eye** *n* centre *m* (de la cible); **to hit the ~'s-eye** mettre dans le mille. ♦ **bullterrier** *n* bull-terrier *m*.

bull[2] [bʊl] *n* (*Rel*) bulle *f*.

bullet ['bʊlɪt] *n* balle *f*. **~ hole** trou *m* d'une balle; **~ wound** blessure *f* par balle. ♦ **bulletheaded** *adj* à (la) tête ronde. ♦ **bulletproof 1** *adj garment etc* pare-balles *inv*; *car etc* blindé; **2** *vt* blinder.

bulletin ['bʊlɪtɪn] *n* bulletin *m*.

bullion ['bʊljən] *n* (*gold*) or *m* en lingot(s); (*silver*) argent *m* en lingot(s).

bully ['bʊlɪ] **1** *n* brute *f*. **2** *vt* persécuter, brutaliser, brimer. **to ~ sb into doing sth** contraindre qn par la menace à faire qch. ♦ **bullying 1** *adj* brutal; **2** *n* brimades *fpl*, brutalités *fpl*.

bully-beef ['bʊlɪbi:f] *n* corned-beef *m*.

bulrush ['bʊlrʌʃ] *n* jonc *m*.

bulwark ['bʊlwək] *n* rempart *m*.

bum [bʌm] **1** *n* **(a)** (*) (*vagrant*) clochard* *m*; (*good-for-nothing*) bon à rien *m*. **(b)** (‡: *bottom*) derrière *m*. **2** *vi* (**~ about** *or* **around**) fainéanter. **3** *vt*: **to ~ a meal off sb*** taper* qn d'un repas.

bumblebee ['bʌmblbi:] *n* (*Zool*) bourdon *m*.

bumf [bʌmf] *n* (*: *forms etc*) paperasses *fpl*; (‡: *toilet paper*) papier *m* de cabinets.

bump [bʌmp] **1** *n* **(a)** (*blow*) choc *m*, heurt *m*; (*jolt*) cahot *m*, secousse *f*; (*Boat-racing*) heurt. **(b)** (*swelling etc: on road, car, head etc*) bosse *f*. **~ of locality*** sens *m* de l'orientation. **2** *vt car, boat* heurter. **to ~ one's head** se cogner la tête (*against* contre). **3** *vi*: **to ~ along** cahoter; **to ~ into** *[vehicle]* entrer en collision avec, rentrer dans*; *[person]* se cogner contre; (*: *meet*) rencontrer par hasard, tomber sur; **the car ~ed up onto the pavement** la voiture a grimpé sur le trottoir.
bump off‡ *vt sep* liquider*, supprimer.
♦ **bumper 1** *n [car]* pare-chocs *m inv*; **2** *adj crop* exceptionnel. ♦ **bumping** *adj*: **~ing cars** autos *fpl* tamponneuses. ♦ **bumpy** *adj road* bosselé, inégal; **we had a ~y flight/crossing** nous avons été très secoués pendant le vol/la traversée.

bumptious ['bʌmpʃəs] *adj* suffisant, prétentieux.

bun [bʌn] *n* (*Culin*) petit pain au lait; *[hair]* chignon *m*. ♦ **bun-fight*** *n* thé *m* (*servi pour un grand nombre de gens*).

bunch [bʌntʃ] *n [flowers]* bouquet *m*; *[bananas]* régime *m*; *[feathers]* touffe *f*; *[radishes, asparagus]* botte *f*; *[twigs]* paquet *m*; *[keys]* trousseau *m*; *[ribbons]* nœud *m*, flot *m*; *[people]* groupe *m*, bande *f*. **~ of grapes** grappe *f* de raisin; *[hair]* **~es** couettes *fpl*; (*fig*) **the pick** *or* **the best of the ~** le *or* la meilleur(e), les meilleur(e)s; **the best of a bad ~*** le *or* les moins médiocre(s); **what a ~!** quelle équipe!*
bunch together 1 *vi* se grouper. **2** *vt sep* grouper.

bundle ['bʌndl] **1** *n [clothes, goods]* paquet *m*, ballot *m*; *[hay]* botte *f*; *[letters, papers]* liasse *f*; *[linen]* paquet; *[firewood]* fagot *m*; *[rods, sticks]* poignée *f*, paquet. **he is a ~ of nerves** c'est un paquet de nerfs; **a ~ of mischief** un sac à malices; (*money*) **to make a ~*** faire son beurre*.
2 *vt* **(a)** (**~ up**) mettre en paquet; *clothes* faire un ballot de; *papers* mettre en liasse. **(b) to ~ sth into a corner** fourrer qch dans un coin; **to ~ sb into the house** pousser qn dans la maison sans cérémonie; **he was ~d off to Australia** on l'a expédié* en Australie.

bung [bʌŋ] **1** *n* bonde *f*. **2** *vt* **(a)** (**~ up**) *pipe etc* boucher, obstruer. **~ed up*** *nose* bouché; *person* très enrhumé. **(b)** (‡: *throw*) envoyer*, jeter.

bungalow ['bʌŋgələʊ] *n* bungalow *m*, petit pavillon *m*. ♦ **bungaloid growth** *n* (*hum, pej*) extension *f* pavillonnaire.

bungle ['bʌŋgl] *vt* bousiller*, saboter. ♦ **bungler** *n* bousilleur* *m*, -euse* *f*. ♦ **bungling 1** *adj* maladroit; **2** *n* gâchis *m*.

bunion ['bʌnjən] *n* (*Med*) oignon *m*.

bunk [bʌŋk] *n* **(a)** (*bed*) couchette *f*. **(b) to do a ~‡**

mettre les voiles*. **(c)** (**:** *also* **bunkum**) blagues* *fpl*, balivernes *fpl*. ♦ **bunk-beds** *npl* lits *mpl* superposés. ♦ **bunk-up*** *n*: **to give sb a ~-up*** soulever qn par derrière *or* par en dessous.

bunker ['bʌŋkəʳ] *n [coal]* coffre *m*, (*Naut*) soute *f* (à charbon); (*Mil*) blockhaus *m*; (*Golf*) bunker *m*.

bunny ['bʌnɪ] *n* (~ **rabbit**) Jeannot *m* lapin; (~ **girl**) hôtesse *f* (*du Club Playboy*).

Bunsen ['bʌnsn] *n*: ~ **burner** bec *m* Bunsen.

bunting ['bʌntɪŋ] *n* (*flags etc*) drapeaux *mpl*, pavoisement *m*.

buoy [bɔɪ] *n* bouée *f*, balise *f* flottante.

buoy up *vt sep* maintenir à flot; (*fig*) soutenir. ♦ **buoyancy** *n [ship, object]* flottabilité *f*; *[liquid]* poussée *f*; (*lightheartedness*) entrain *m*; **~ancy aid** gilet *m* de sauvetage. ♦ **buoyant** *adj ship, object* flottable; *liquid* dans lequel les objets flottent; *person* plein d'entrain; *mood* optimiste; *step* léger; (*Fin*) *market* ferme. ♦ **buoyantly** *adv walk, float* légèrement; *answer* avec entrain, avec optimisme.

bur [bɜ:ʳ] *n* **(a)** (*Bot*) bardane *f*. **(b) to speak with a ~** grasseyer.

burble ['bɜ:bl] *vi [stream]* murmurer; *[person]* marmonner.

burden ['bɜ:dn] **1** *n* fardeau *m*, charge *f*; *[taxes, years]* poids *m*. **to be a ~ to** être un fardeau pour; **to make sb's life a ~** rendre la vie intenable à qn; **the ~ of the expense** les frais *mpl* à charge; **the ~ of proof lies with him** la charge de la preuve lui incombe; **the ~ of their complaint** leur principal sujet de plainte. **2** *vt person* accabler (*with* de); *object, memory, essay* surcharger (*with* de). ♦ **burdensome** *adj* pénible.

bureau [bjʊə'rəʊ] *n* (*writing desk*) secrétaire *m* (*bureau*); (*chest of drawers*) commode *f*; (*office*) bureau *m*; (*government department*) service *m* (gouvernemental). ♦ **bureaucracy** *n* bureaucratie *f*. ♦ **bureaucrat** *n* bureaucrate *mf*. ♦ **bureaucratic** *adj* bureaucratique.

burglar ['bɜ:gləʳ] **1** *n* cambrioleur *m*, -euse *f*. **2** *adj*: ~ **alarm** sonnerie *f* d'alarme. ♦ **burglarize** *vt* (*US*) cambrioler. ♦ **burglar-proof 1** *vt house* munir d'un dispositif d'alarme; **2** *adj lock* incrochetable. ♦ **burglary** *n* cambriolage *m*. ♦ **burgle** *vt* cambrioler.

Burgundy ['bɜ:gəndɪ] *n* Bourgogne *f*. (*wine*) **b~** bourgogne *m*.

burial ['berɪəl] **1** *n* enterrement *m*. **2** *adj*: ~ **ground** cimetière *m*; ~ **place** lieu *m* de sépulture.

burlesque [bɜ:'lesk] **1** *n* (*Literat*) burlesque *m*; (*Theat*) revue *f*; *[book, poem etc]* parodie *f*; *[society, way of life]* caricature *f*. **2** *vt* tourner en ridicule; (*parody*) parodier.

burly ['bɜ:lɪ] *adj* de forte carrure. **a ~ policeman** un grand gaillard d'agent.

burn [bɜ:n] (*vb: pret, ptp* **burned** *or* **burnt**) **1** *n* (*gen*) brûlure *f*; *[space rocket]* mise *f* à feu. **2** *vt* (*gen*) brûler; *town, building* incendier; *meat, toast* laisser brûler. **~t to a cinder** carbonisé; **to be ~t to death** *or* **~t alive** être brûlé vif; **to ~ one's fingers** se brûler les doigts; **~t offering** holocauste *m*; **~t orange** orange foncé *inv*; **money ~s a hole in my pocket** l'argent me fond dans les mains; (*fig*) **to ~ one's boats** brûler ses vaisseaux; **to ~ the candle at both ends** brûler la chandelle par les deux bouts. **3** *vi* (*gen*) brûler; *[wound]* cuire. **you left all the lights ~ing** vous avez laissé toutes les lumières allumées; **a ~ing question** une question brûlante; **he was ~ing for revenge** il brûlait du désir de se venger.

burn down 1 *vi [house etc]* brûler complètement; *[fire, candle]* baisser. **2** *vt sep building* incendier.

burn off *vt sep paint etc* brûler (au chalumeau).

burn out 1 *vi [fire, candle]* s'éteindre; *[light bulb]* griller. **2** *vt sep*: **to be ~t out** *[candle]* être mort; *[student]* être usé (à force de travail).

burn up 1 *vi [fire etc]* flamber, monter; *[rocket in atmosphere]* se désintégrer. **2** *vt sep rubbish* brûler. **~ed up with envy** dévoré d'envie. ♦ **burner** *n [cooker]* brûleur *m*; *[lamp, science lab]* bec *m* (de gaz). ♦ **burning 1** *adj town, forest* en flammes, incendié; *fire, candle* allumé; *coals, faith* ardent; *feeling* cuisant; *thirst, fever, question, topic* brûlant; *indignation* violent; *words* véhément; **the ~ing bush** le buisson ardent; **with a ~ing face** (*shame*) le rouge au front; (*embarrassment*) le rouge aux joues; **it's a ~ing* shame that ...** c'est un scandale que + *subj*; **2** *n* (*setting on fire*) incendie *m*; **there is a smell of ~ing** ça sent le brûlé *or* le roussi; **I could smell ~ing** je sentais une odeur de brûlé.

burnish ['bɜ:nɪʃ] *vt* polir.

burp* [bɜ:p] **1** *vi* faire un rot*. **2** *vt baby* faire faire son rot* à. **3** *n* rot* *m*.

burr [bɜ:ʳ] *n* = **bur**.

burrow ['bʌrəʊ] **1** *n* terrier *m*. **2** *vi [rabbits]* creuser un terrier; *[dog]* creuser. *[person]* **to ~ under** (*in earth*) se creuser un chemin sous; (*under blanket etc*) se réfugier sous.

bursar ['bɜ:səʳ] *n [small institution]* économe *mf*; *[large institution]* administrateur *m*, -trice *f*. ♦ **bursary** *n* bourse *f* (d'études).

burst [bɜ:st] (*vb: pret, ptp* **burst**) **1** *n [shell, anger, indignation]* explosion *f*; *[laughter]* éclat *m*; *[affection, eloquence, enthusiasm]* élan *m*; *[activity]* vague *f*; *[applause]* salve *f*; *[flames]* jaillissement *m*. **~ of rain** averse *f*; **to put on a ~ of speed** faire une pointe de vitesse; **~ of gunfire** rafale *f* de tir.

2 *vi* **(a)** *[bomb, shell, boiler]* éclater; *[bubble, balloon, abscess]* crever; *[tyre]* (*blow out*) éclater; (*puncture*) crever. **to ~ open** *[door]* s'ouvrir violemment; *[container]* s'éventrer; *[sack etc]* **to be ~ing at the seams** être plein à crever (*with* de); **filled to ~ing point** rempli à craquer; **she's ~ing out of that dress** elle éclate de partout dans cette robe; **to be ~ing with** *health, joy* déborder de; *impatience* brûler de; *pride* éclater de; **I was ~ing* to tell you** je mourais d'envie de vous le dire. **(b)** (*rush*) **to ~ in/out** *etc* entrer/sortir *etc* en trombe; **he ~ into/out of the room** il s'est précipité dans/hors de la pièce; **to ~ into tears** fondre en larmes; **to ~ out laughing** éclater de rire; **to ~ out singing/crying** se mettre tout d'un coup à chanter/à pleurer; **to ~ into flames** prendre feu (soudain). **3** *vt balloon, bubble, tyre* crever; *bag* crever, (*by blowing*) faire éclater; *boiler* faire sauter. **to ~ open** *door* ouvrir violemment; *container* éventrer; **the river has ~ its banks** le fleuve a rompu ses digues; **to ~ a blood vessel** (se) rompre un vaisseau; (*fig: with anger etc*) en avoir une attaque*.

bury ['berɪ] *vt body, treasure, quarrel* enterrer; (*conceal*) enfouir; *[avalanche etc]* ensevelir; (*plunge*) *hands, knife* enfoncer, plonger (*in* dans). **he was buried at sea** son corps fut immergé en haute mer; (*fig*) **to ~ one's head in the sand** pratiquer la politique de l'autruche; (*fig*) **to ~ the hatchet** enterrer la hache de guerre; **to ~ one's face in one's hands** se couvrir la figure de ses mains; **village buried in the country** village enfoui en pleine campagne; **buried in thought** plongé dans une rêverie *or* dans ses pensées.

bus [bʌs] **1** *n* autobus *m*, bus* *m*; (*long-distance*) autocar *m*, car *m*. **2** *vi* (*) prendre l'autobus *or* le car. **3** *vt*: **to ~ children to school** transporter des enfants à l'école en car. **4** *adj driver, depot, service, ticket* d'autobus. **the house is on a ~ route** la maison est sur un trajet d'autobus; **~ service** réseau *m* or service *m* d'autobus; **~ shelter** abribus *m*; **~ station** gare *f* d'autobus; *[coaches]* gare routière; **~ stop** arrêt *m* d'autobus. ♦ **busload** *n* car entier (*of* de); **by the ~load, in ~loads** par cars entiers. ♦ **busman** *n* (*fig*) **to take a ~man's holiday** passer ses vacances à travailler; **the ~men's strike** la grève des employés des autobus. ♦ **bussing** *n* ramassage *m* scolaire (*comme mesure de déségrégation*).

bush [bʊʃ] *n* (*shrub*) buisson *m*; (*thicket*) taillis *m*, fourré *m*. *[Africa, Australia]* **the ~** la brousse. ♦ **bushed**✱ *adj* (*exhausted*) crevé*, claqué*. ♦ **bushfighting** *n* guérilla *f*. ♦ **bushfire** *n* feu *m* de brousse. ♦ **bush-telegraph*** *n* (*fig*) téléphone *m* arabe. ♦ **bushy** *adj* touffu.

business ['bɪznɪs] **1** *n* **(a)** (*commerce*) affaires *fpl*. **to be in ~** être dans les affaires; **to be in the grocery ~** être dans l'épicerie; **to be in ~ for o.s.** travailler pour son propre compte; **to set up in ~ as a butcher** s'établir boucher; **to do ~ with sb** faire des affaires avec qn; **~ is ~** les affaires sont les affaires; **on ~** pour affaires; (*fig*) **what's his line of ~?*** qu'est-ce qu'il fait (dans la vie)?; **to know one's ~** s'y connaître; **to get down to ~** passer aux choses sérieuses; **now we're in ~!*** tout devient possible!; **he means ~*** il ne plaisante pas; **to mix ~ with pleasure** joindre l'utile à l'agréable; **our ~ has doubled** notre chiffre d'affaires a doublé; **he gets a lot of ~ from the Americans** il travaille beaucoup avec les Américains.

(b) (*commercial enterprise*) commerce *m*. **a grocery ~** un commerce d'alimentation.

(c) (*task, duty*) affaire *f*. **it's all part of the day's ~** cela fait partie de la routine journalière; **to make it one's ~ to do** se charger de faire; **that's none of his ~** ce n'est pas son affaire, cela ne le regarde pas; **it's your ~ to do it** c'est à vous de le faire; **you've no ~ to do that** ce n'est pas à vous de faire cela; **mind your own ~** mêlez-vous de vos affaires *or* de ce qui vous regarde; **finding a flat is quite a ~** c'est toute une affaire de trouver un appartement; **she made a terrible ~ of helping him** elle a fait toute une histoire* pour l'aider; **it's a bad ~** c'est une sale affaire *or* histoire; **I am tired of this protest ~** j'en ai assez de cette histoire de contestation; **there's some funny ~ going on** il se passe qch de louche.

2 *adj lunch, trip, meeting* d'affaires; *college, studies* commercial. **his ~ address** l'adresse *f* de son bureau; **~ centre** centre *m* d'affaires; **the ~ end of a knife** le côté opérant d'un couteau; **~ expenses** frais généraux; **~ girl** jeune femme *f* d'affaires; **~ manager** (*Comm, Ind*) directeur commercial; (*Cine, Sport, Theat*) manager *m*; **to have ~ sense** avoir du flair pour les affaires; **~ suit** complet *m* (veston).

♦ **businesslike** *adj person, method* pratique, efficace; *firm, transaction, manner* sérieux; **this is a very ~like knife!*** ça, c'est un couteau sérieux!* ♦ **businessman** *n* homme *m* d'affaires. ♦ **businesswoman** *n* femme *f* d'affaires.

bust[1] [bʌst] *n* (*Anat, Sculp*) buste *m*. **~ measurement** tour *m* de poitrine.

bust[2]* [bʌst] **1** *adj* (*broken*) fichu*, cassé. (*bankrupt*) **to go ~** faire faillite. **2** *vt* **(a)** = **burst 3. (b)** (*break*) casser.

bust up✱ *vt sep marriage, friendship* briser, flanquer en l'air*.

♦ **bust-up**✱ *n* engueulade✱ *f*; **to have a ~-up**✱ **with sb** s'engueuler✱ avec qn (*et rompre*).

bustle ['bʌsl] **1** *vi*: **to ~ about** s'affairer; **to ~ in/out** *etc* entrer/sortir *etc* d'un air affairé. **2** *n* remue-ménage *m inv*. ♦ **bustling** *adj person* empressé, affairé; *place* bruyant.

busy ['bɪzɪ] **1** *adj* **(a)** (*occupied*) *person* occupé (*with sth* à qch). **she's ~ cooking** elle est en train de faire la cuisine; **he's ~ playing with the children** il est occupé à jouer avec les enfants; **~ at his work** absorbé dans son travail. **(b)** *person* (*active*) énergique; (*having a lot to do*) affairé; *day* chargé; *period* de grande activité; *place, street, town* animé. **as ~ as a bee** très occupé; **to keep o.s. ~** trouver à s'occuper; **to get ~** s'y mettre; **the shop is at its busiest in summer** c'est en été qu'il y a le plus d'affluence dans le magasin. **(c)** (*Telec*) *line* occupé. **~ signal** tonalité *f* occupé *inv*.

2 *vt*: **to ~ o.s.** s'occuper, s'appliquer (*doing* à faire; *with sth* à qch).

♦ **busily** *adv* activement; (*pej*) avec trop de zèle; **to be busily engaged in (doing) sth** être très occupé à (faire) qch. ♦ **busybody** *n* mouche *f* du coche.

but [bʌt] **1** *conj* (*gen*) mais. **never a week passes ~ she is ill** il ne se passe jamais une semaine qu'elle ne soit malade; (*fig*) **it never rains ~ it pours** un malheur n'arrive jamais seul.

2 *adv* seulement, ne ... que. **she's ~ a child** ce n'est qu'une enfant; **I cannot ~ think that ...** je ne peux m'empêcher de penser que ... ; **you can ~ try** vous pouvez toujours essayer.

3 *prep* sauf, excepté. **they've all gone ~ me** ils sont tous partis sauf *or* excepté moi; **no one ~ him** personne d'autre que lui; **anything ~ that** tout mais pas ça; **there was nothing for it ~ to jump** il n'y avait plus qu'à sauter; **the last house ~ one** l'avant-dernière maison; **the next house ~ one** la seconde maison à partir d'ici; **~ for you** sans vous; **it was all ~*** c'était tout juste.

4 *n*: **no ~s about it!** il n'y a pas de mais (qui tienne)!

butane ['bju:teɪn] *n* butane *m*. **~ gas** gaz *m* butane, butagaz *m* ®.

butcher ['bʊtʃəʳ] **1** *n* boucher *m*. **at the ~'s** chez le boucher; **~'s shop** boucherie *f*; **~ meat** viande *f* de boucherie. **2** *vt animal* tuer, abattre; *person* massacrer.

butler ['bʌtləʳ] *n* maître *m* d'hôtel.

butt[1] [bʌt] *n* (*barrel*) (gros) tonneau *m*.

butt[2] [bʌt] *n* (*end*) bout *m*; *[rifle]* crosse *f*. **cigarette ~** mégot *m*.

butt[3] [bʌt] *n* (*Shooting*) **the ~s** le champ de tir; **to be a ~ for ridicule** être un objet de risée, être en butte au ridicule; **the ~ of a practical joker** la victime d'un farceur.

butt[4] [bʌt] **1** *n* coup *m* de tête; *[goat etc]* coup de corne. **2** *vt* donner un coup de tête *or* de corne à.

butt in *vi* intervenir dans les affaires des autres; (*speaking*) dire son mot. **I don't want to ~ in** je ne veux pas m'immiscer dans la conversation.

butter ['bʌtəʳ] **1** *n* beurre *m*. **he looks as if ~ wouldn't melt in his mouth** on lui donnerait le bon Dieu sans confession. **2** *adj*: **~ bean** (gros) haricot blanc; **~ dish** beurrier *m*; **~ knife** couteau *m* à beurre. **3** *vt bread etc* beurrer.

butter up* *vt sep* passer de la pommade à* (*fig*).

♦ **buttercup** *n* bouton *m* d'or. ♦ **butter-fingered** *adj*: **he is ~-fingered** tout lui glisse des mains. ♦ **butterfingers** *n* maladroit(e) *m(f)*; (*excl*) **~fingers!** espèce d'empoté(e)!* ♦ **butterfly 1** *n* papillon *m*; **to have ~flies in the stomach*** avoir le trac; **2** *adj net* à papillons; **~fly nut** papillon *m* (*écrou*); **~fly stroke** brasse *f* papillon *inv*. ♦ **buttermilk** *n* babeurre *m*. ♦ **butterscotch** *n* caramel dur.

buttock ['bʌtək] *n* fesse *f*.

button ['bʌtn] **1** *n* bouton *m*. **chocolate ~s** pastilles *fpl* de chocolat. **2** *vt* (**~ up**) *garment* boutonner. **3** *vi* se boutonner. **4** *adj*: **~ mushroom** (petit) champignon *m* de couche. ♦ **button-down** *adj collar* boutonné. ♦ **buttonhole 1** *n* boutonnière *f*; **to wear a ~hole** avoir une fleur à sa boutonnière; **2** *vt person* accrocher*, attirer l'attention de. ♦ **button-through** *adj*: **~-through dress** robe *f* chemisier.

buttress ['bʌtrɪs] **1** *n* (*Archit*) contrefort *m*; (*flying ~*) arc-boutant *m*. **2** *vt* arc-bouter; (*fig*) étayer.

buxom ['bʌksəm] *adj* bien en chair.

buy [baɪ] *pret, ptp* **bought 1** *vt* acheter (*sth from sb* qch à qn; *sth for sb* qch pour *or* à qn); *petrol, tickets* prendre. **victory dearly bought** victoire chèrement payée; **he won't ~* that explanation** il n'avalera* jamais cette explication; **all right, I'll ~ it*** bon, je marche*; (*die*) **he's bought it‡** il y est resté*. **2** *n*: **a good/bad ~*** une bonne/mauvaise affaire.
buy back *vt sep* racheter.
buy in *vt sep* s'approvisionner en.
buy off *vt sep person* acheter (pour s'en débarrasser).
buy out *vt sep business partner* désintéresser. (*Mil*) **to ~ o.s. out** se racheter.
buy up *vt sep* acheter tout ce qu'il y a de.
♦ **buyer** *n* acheteur *m*, -euse *f*; **~er's market** marché *m* acheteur; **house ~ers** acheteurs de propriétés. ♦ **buying** *n* achat *m*.
buzz [bʌz] **1** *n* bourdonnement *m*; (*Rad etc: extraneous noise*) friture *f*. (*Telec*) **to give sb a ~*** passer un coup de fil* à qn. **2** *adj*: **~ saw** scie *f* mécanique. **3** *vi [insect, ears]* bourdonner. **my head is ~ing** j'ai des bourdonnements; (*fig*) **~ing with** bourdonnant de. **4** *vt* **(a)** *person* appeler (par interphone); (*: *telephone*) passer un coup de fil* à. **(b)** (*Aviat*) *plane, building* raser.
buzz off‡ *vi* ficher le camp*.
♦ **buzzer** *n* (*phone*) interphone *m*; (*hooter*) sirène *f*. ♦ **buzzing 1** *n* bourdonnement *m*; **2** *adj insect* bourdonnant; *sound* confus.
buzzard ['bʌzəd] *n* buse *f*.
by [baɪ] **1** *adv* près. **close** *or* **hard ~** tout près; **to go** *or* **pass ~** passer; **he'll be ~ any minute** il sera là dans un instant; **we'll get ~** on y arrivera; **to put** *or* **lay ~** mettre de côté; **~ and ~** bientôt, (un peu) plus tard; **~ and large** généralement.

2 *prep* **(a)** (*close to*) à côté de, près de. **~ the fire** près du feu; **the house ~ the church** la maison à côté de l'église; **~ the sea** au bord de la mer; **I've got it ~ me** je l'ai sous la main; **(all) ~ himself** (tout) seul.

(b) (*through, along*) par. **I went ~ Dover** j'y suis allé par Douvres; **he came in ~ the window** il est entré par la fenêtre; (*fig*) **~ the way, ~ the by(e)** à propos, au fait.

(c) (*past*) à côté de, devant. **I go ~ the church every day** je passe devant l'église tous les jours; **he went ~ me** il est passé à côté de moi.

(d) (*during*) **~ day** le jour, de jour; **~ night** la nuit, de nuit.

(e) (*not later than*) avant. **I'll be back ~ midnight** je rentrerai avant minuit *or* pas plus tard que minuit; **~ tomorrow I'll be in France** d'ici demain je serai en France; **~ the time I got there** lorsque je suis arrivé; **~ 30th September we had paid ...** au 30 septembre nous avions payé ... ; **~ then I knew** à ce moment-là je savais déjà.

(f) (*amount*) à. **to sell ~ the metre/the kilo** vendre au mètre/au kilo; **~ the hour** à l'heure; **~ degrees** par degrés, graduellement; **one ~ one** un à un; **little ~ little** petit à petit, peu à peu.

(g) (*agent, cause*) par, de. **he was warned ~ his neighbour** il a été prévenu par son voisin; **killed ~ lightning** tué par la foudre; **a painting ~ Van Gogh** un tableau de Van Gogh; **surrounded ~ soldiers** entouré de soldats.

(h) (*method, means, manner*) par. **~ land and sea** par terre et par mer; **~ bus/car** en autobus/voiture; **~ rail** *or* **train** par le train, en train; **~ electric light** à la lumière électrique; **made ~ hand** fait à la main; **to lead ~ the hand** conduire par la main; **~ cheque** par chèque; **a daughter ~ his first wife** une fille de sa première femme.

(i) (*according to*) d'après, suivant, selon. **~ what he says** d'après *or* selon ce qu'il dit; **to judge ~ appearances** juger d'après les apparences; **~ my watch** à ma montre; **to do one's duty ~ sb** remplir son devoir envers qn; **to call sth ~ its proper name** appeler qch de son vrai nom; **it's all right ~ me*** je n'ai rien contre*.

(j) (*measuring difference*) de. **broader ~ a metre** plus large d'un mètre; **it missed me ~ 10 centimetres** cela m'a manqué de 10 centimètres.

(k) (*Math, Measure*) **to divide ~** diviser par; **room 3 metres ~ 4** pièce de 3 mètres sur 4.

(l) (*points of compass*) **south ~ south-west** sud quart sud-ouest.

(m) (*in oaths*) par. **~ all I hold sacred** par tout ce que j'ai de plus sacré; **~ God!*** nom d'un chien!*

♦ **by-election** *n* élection (législative) partielle. ♦ **bygone 1** *adj*: **in ~gone days** jadis; **2** *n*: **let ~gones be ~gones** oublions le passé. ♦ **by-law** *n* arrêté *m* (municipal). ♦ **bypass 1** *n* **(a)** (*road*) route *f* de contournement *m*; **the Carlisle ~pass** la route qui contourne Carlisle; **(b)** (*Tech: pipe etc*) conduit *m* de dérivation; **(c)** (*Elec*) dérivation *f*; **2** *vt town, village* contourner, éviter; *pipe* éviter; *fluid, gas* amener (en dérivation); (*fig*) **he ~passed his foreman and went straight to the manager** il est allé trouver le directeur sans passer par le contremaître. ♦ **by-product** *n* (*Ind etc*) sous-produit *m*, dérivé *m*; (*fig*) conséquence *f* (secondaire). ♦ **by-road** *n* chemin *m* de traverse. ♦ **bystander** *n* spectateur *m*, -trice *f*. ♦ **byway** *n* chemin *m* (écarté). ♦ **byword** *n*: **his name was a ~word for meanness** son nom était devenu synonyme d'avarice.
bye* [baɪ] *excl* (*also* **bye-bye***) salut!* ♦ **bye-law** *n* = **by-law** (*V above*).

C

C, c [siː] *n* C, c *m*; (*Mus*) do *m*, ut *m*.
cab [kæb] **1** *n* **(a)** taxi *m*. **by ~** en taxi. **(b)** *[truck, engine]* cabine *f*. **2** *adj*: **~ rank** station *f* de taxis. ♦ **cabby*** *or* ♦ **cab-driver** *or* ♦ **cabman** *n* chauffeur *m* de taxi, taxi* *m*.
cabal [kəˈbæl] *n* cabale *f*.
cabaret [ˈkæbəreɪ] *n* cabaret *m*.
cabbage [ˈkæbɪdʒ] **1** *n* chou *m*. **she's just a ~*** elle végète. **2** *adj*: **~ lettuce** laitue *f* pommée.
cabin [ˈkæbɪn] **1** *n* (*hut*) cabane *f*, hutte *f*; (*on ship*) cabine *f*; (*driver's ~*) cabine. **2** *adj*: **~ boy** mousse *m*; **~ cruiser** yacht *m* de croisière (à moteur); **~ trunk** malle-cabine *f*.
cabinet [ˈkæbɪnɪt] **1** *n* meuble *m* (de rangement); (*glass-fronted*) vitrine *f*; (*filing ~*) classeur *m*; (*medicine ~*) armoire *f* à pharmacie; (*Parl*) cabinet *m*. **2** *adj* (*Parl*) *crisis, decision* ministériel. **~ minister** ministre *m*, membre *m* du cabinet. ♦ **cabinetmaker** *n* ébéniste *m*. ♦ **cabinetmaking** *n* ébénisterie *f*.
cable [ˈkeɪbl] **1** *n* câble *m*. **by ~** par câble. **2** *vt* câbler (*to* à). **3** *adj*: **~ television** télédistribution *f*. ♦ **cablecar** *n* téléphérique *m*; (*on rail*) funiculaire *m*. ♦ **cablegram** *n* câblogramme *m*. ♦ **cable-laying** **1** *n* pose *f* de câbles; **2** *adj*: **~-laying ship** câblier *m*. ♦ **cable-railway** *n* funiculaire *m*.
caboodle‡ [kəˈbuːdl] *n*: **the whole ~** tout le tremblement*.
cacao [kəˈkɑːəʊ] *n* cacao *m*.
cache [kæʃ] *n* (*place*) cachette *f*. **a ~ of guns** des fusils cachés.
cachet [ˈkæʃeɪ] *n* cachet *m*.
cackle [ˈkækl] **1** *n* *[hen]* caquet *m*; (*laugh*) gloussement *m*; (*talking*) caquetage *m*. **2** *vi* caqueter; glousser.
cacophony [kæˈkɒfənɪ] *n* cacophonie *f*.
cactus [ˈkæktəs] *n*, *pl* **-ti** [-taɪ] cactus *m*.
cadaver [kəˈdeɪvəʳ] *n* cadavre *m*. ♦ **cadaverous** *adj* cadavérique.
caddie [ˈkædɪ] *n* caddie *m*.
caddy [ˈkædɪ] *n* (*tea ~*) boîte *f* à thé.
cadence [ˈkeɪdəns] *n* cadence *f*.
cadet [kəˈdet] *n* (*Mil etc*) élève *m* officier. **~ force** peloton *m* de préparation militaire; **~ school** école *f* militaire.
cadge [kædʒ] *vt*: **to ~ 10 francs from sb** taper* qn de 10 F; **to ~ lunch from sb** se faire inviter par qn; **to ~ a lift from sb** se faire emmener en voiture par qn; **he's always cadging** il est toujours à quémander. ♦ **cadger** *n* parasite *m*; *[money]* tapeur* *m*, -euse* *f*; *[meals]* pique-assiette *mf inv*.
cadre [ˈkædrɪ] *n* (*Mil, fig*) cadre *m*.
Caesarean, Caesarian [siːˈzɛərɪən] *adj*, *n* (*Med*) **~ (section)** césarienne *f*.
café [ˈkæfeɪ] *n* café(-restaurant) *m*; (*snack bar*) snack *m*. ♦ **cafeteria** *n* cafétéria *f*.
caffein(e) [ˈkæfiːn] *n* caféine *f*. **~-free** décaféiné.
caftan [ˈkæftæn] *n* caftan *m*.
cage [keɪdʒ] **1** *n* cage *f*; *[elevator]* cabine *f*; (*Min*) cage. **2** *adj*: **~ bird** oiseau *m* de volière. **3** *vt* (**~ up**) mettre en cage. **~d bird** oiseau *m* en cage.
cagey* [ˈkeɪdʒɪ] *adj* peu communicatif, dissimulé (*pej*). **she is ~ about her age** elle n'aime pas avouer son âge.
cahoots* [kəˈhuːts] *npl*: **in ~** de mèche* (*with* avec).
cairn [kɛən] *n* cairn *m*. ♦ **cairngorm** *n* quartz *m* fumé.
Cairo [ˈkaɪərəʊ] *n* Le Caire.
cajole [kəˈdʒəʊl] *vt* cajoler. **to ~ sb into doing sth** faire faire qch à qn à force de cajoleries. ♦ **cajolery** *n* cajolerie *f*.
cake [keɪk] **1** *n* **(a)** gâteau *m*; (*small*) pâtisserie *f*; (*fruit ~*) cake *m*; (*sponge ~ etc*) génoise *f*. **it's selling like hot ~s*** cela se vend comme des petits pains; **it's a piece of ~*** c'est du gâteau*. **(b)** *[chocolate]* tablette *f*; *[wax, tobacco]* pain *m*. **~ of soap** savonnette *f*. **2** *adj*: **~ shop** pâtisserie *f* (*magasin*). **3** *vi* *[mud]* durcir, faire croûte; *[blood]* se coaguler. ♦ **caked** *adj* *blood* coagulé; *mud* séché; **clothes ~d with mud** vêtements raidis par la boue.
calamity [kəˈlæmɪtɪ] *n* calamité *f*. ♦ **calamitous** *adj* catastrophique.
calcify [ˈkælsɪfaɪ] **1** *vt* calcifier. **2** *vi* se calcifier. ♦ **calcification** *n* calcification *f*.
calcium [ˈkælsɪəm] *n* calcium *m*.
calculate [ˈkælkjʊleɪt] **1** *vt* *cost, numbers, dates* calculer; *distance* évaluer; *chances* estimer. **this was not ~d to reassure me** cela n'était pas fait pour me rassurer. **2** *vi* calculer, faire des calculs. **to ~ for sth** prévoir qch. ♦ **calculable** *adj* calculable. ♦ **calculated** *adj* *action, decision, insult* délibéré; *risk* pris en toute connaissance de cause. ♦ **calculating** *adj* (*scheming*) calculateur; **calculating machine** machine *f* à calculer. ♦ **calculation** *n* calcul *m*. ♦ **calculator** *n* calculatrice *f*. ♦ **calculus** *n* calcul *m*.
calendar [ˈkæləndəʳ] **1** *n* calendrier *m*. **university ~** ≃ guide *m* de l'étudiant. **2** *adj*: **~ month** mois *m* (de calendrier); **~ year** année *f* civile.
calf¹ [kɑːf] **1** *n*, *pl* **calves** (*animal*) veau *m*; (*skin*) veau; (*for shoes, bags*) box(-calf) *m*. **cow in ~** vache pleine; **elephant ~** éléphanteau *m*. **2** *adj*: **~ love** amour *m* juvénile.
calf² [kɑːf] *n*, *pl* **calves** (*Anat*) mollet *m*.
calibre, (*US*) -ber [ˈkælɪbəʳ] *n* (*lit, fig*) calibre *m*. ♦ **calibrate** *vt* calibrer. ♦ **calibration** *n* calibrage *m*.
calipers [ˈkælɪpəz] *npl* (*Math*) compas *m*; (*leg-irons*) appareil *m* orthopédique.
calisthenics [ˌkælɪsˈθenɪks] *nsg* gymnastique *f* suédoise.
call [kɔːl] **1** *n* **(a)** (*shout*) appel *m*, cri *m*; *[bird]* cri; *[duty]* appel; (*Theat*) rappel *m*; (*vocation*) vocation *f*; (*Bridge*) annonce *f*. (*telephone ~*) coup *m* de téléphone, coup de fil*, communication *f* (*Admin*). **within ~** à portée de (la) voix; **a ~ for help** un appel au secours; (*Telec*) **to make a ~** téléphoner, donner *or* passer un coup de fil*; **I'd like a ~ at 7 a.m.** j'aimerais qu'on me réveille (*subj*) à 7 heures; **to be on ~** être de garde; **the ~ of the unknown** l'attrait *m* de l'inconnu; **the ~ of the sea** l'appel du large; **there's not much ~ for these articles** ces articles ne sont pas très demandés; **repayable on ~/ at 3 months' ~** remboursable sur demande/à 3 mois; **I have many ~s on my time** je suis très pris; **I have many ~s on my purse** j'ai beaucoup de dépenses; **there is no ~ for you to worry** vous n'avez pas besoin de

vous inquiéter; **there was no ~ to say that** vous n'aviez aucune raison de dire cela. **(b)** (*visit: also Med*) visite *f*. **to make a ~ on sb** rendre visite à qn, aller voir qn; **I have several ~s to make** j'ai plusieurs visites à faire; **port of ~** (port *m* d')escale *f*.

2 *adj*: **~ girl** call-girl *f*; (*Telec*) **~ sign,** (*US*) **~ letters** indicatif *m* (d'appel).

3 *vt* **(a)** (*gen*) appeler; (*Telec*) téléphoner à; (*waken*) réveiller; (*summon*) appeler, convoquer; *doctor, taxi* appeler, faire venir; (*Bridge*) annoncer, demander. **to ~ sb in/out** *etc* crier à qn d'entrer/de sortir *etc*; **~ me at eight** réveillez-moi à huit heures; (*Rad*) **London ~ing** ici Londres; **duty ~s** le devoir m'appelle; **to ~ a meeting** convoquer une assemblée; **to ~ sb as a witness** (*Jur*) avoir qn comme témoin. **(b)** (*give name to*) appeler. **what are you ~ed?** comment vous appelez-vous?; **he is ~ed after his father** on lui a donné le nom de son père; **he ~s himself a colonel** il se prétend colonel; **are you ~ing me a liar?** dites tout de suite que je suis un menteur; **he ~ed her a liar** il l'a traitée de menteuse; **would you ~ French a difficult language?** diriez-vous que le français est difficile?; **I ~ that a shame** j'estime que c'est une honte; **shall we ~ it £1?** disons 1 livre?; **let's ~ it a day!*** ça suffira (pour aujourd'hui)!*

4 *vi* **(a)** *[person]* appeler, crier; *[birds]* pousser un cri. **to ~ (out) to sb** appeler qn, (*from afar*) héler qn. **(b)** (*visit*: **~ in**) passer. **he was out when I ~ed** il n'était pas là quand je suis passé chez lui; (*Naut*) **to ~ (in) at Dover** faire escale à Douvres.

call aside *vt sep person* prendre à part.

call away *vt sep*: **to be ~ed away on business** être obligé de s'absenter pour affaires; **to be ~ed away from a meeting** devoir quitter une réunion (*pour affaires plus pressantes*).

call back *vi, vt sep* (*Telec*) rappeler.

call for *vt fus* **(a)** (*summon*) *person* appeler; *food, drink* demander; *courage* demander, exiger. **that was not ~ed for** ce n'était pas justifié. **(b)** (*collect*) *person, thing* passer prendre.

call in 1 *vi* = **call 4b. 2** *vt sep* **(a)** *doctor* faire venir, appeler; *police* appeler. **he was ~ed in to arbitrate** on a fait appel à lui pour arbitrer. **(b)** *money, library books* faire rentrer; *banknotes* retirer de la circulation; *faulty machines etc* rappeler.

call off 1 *vi* se décommander. **2** *vt sep* **(a)** *appointment* annuler; *agreement, deal* résilier. **to ~ off a strike** annuler un ordre de grève. **(b)** *dog* rappeler.

call out 1 *vi* pousser un *or* des cri(s). **to ~ out for sth** demander qch à haute voix; **to ~ out to sb** héler qn. **2** *vt sep doctor, troops, fire brigade* appeler. **to ~ workers out (on strike)** donner la consigne de grève.

call round *vi* passer (*to see sb* voir qn).

call up *vt sep* **(a)** (*Mil*) appeler, mobiliser. **(b)** (*esp US: Telec*) téléphoner à. **(c)** *memories* évoquer.

call (up)on *vt fus* **(a)** *person* rendre visite à. **(b) to ~ (up)on sb to do** (*invite*) inviter qn à faire; (*demand*) sommer qn de faire; **I now ~ (up)on Mr Brown to speak** je laisse maintenant la parole à M. Brown.

♦ **callbox** *n* (*Brit*) cabine *f* (téléphonique); (*US*) téléphone *m* de police-secours. ♦ **callboy** *n* (*Theat*) avertisseur *m*. ♦ **caller** *n* (*visitor*) visiteur *m*, -euse *f*; (*Telec*) demandeur *m*, -euse *f*. ♦ **call-in** *n* (*US Rad*) programme *m* à ligne ouverte. ♦ **calling-card** *n* (*US*) carte *f* de visite. ♦ **call-up 1** *n* (*Mil*) appel *m* (sous les drapeaux); **2** *adj*: **~-up papers** feuille *f* de route.

calligraphy [kə'lɪgrəfɪ] *n* calligraphie *f*.

callipers ['kælɪpəz] *npl* = **calipers.**

callisthenics [ˌkælɪs'θenɪks] *n* = **calisthenics.**

callous ['kæləs] *adj* dur, sans cœur. ♦ **callously** *adv act, speak* avec dureté; *decide, suggest* cyniquement. ♦ **callousness** *n* dureté *f*, manque *m* de cœur.

callow ['kæləʊ] *adj* inexpérimenté, novice.

calm [kɑːm] **1** *adj* calme, tranquille. **keep ~!** du calme!; **to grow ~** se calmer; **~ and collected** maître (*f* maîtresse) de soi. **2** *n* période *f* de calme *or* de tranquillité; (*after agitation*) accalmie *f*. **the ~ before the storm** le calme qui précède la tempête. **3** *vt* (**~ down**) calmer, apaiser.

calm down *vi* se calmer.

♦ **calmly** *adv* calmement, avec calme. ♦ **calmness** *n* calme *m*.

Calor ['kælə^r] *n* ® **~ gas** butane *m*, butagaz *m* ®.

calorie ['kælərɪ] *n* calorie *f*. **to be ~-conscious*** avoir la hantise des calories. ♦ **calorific** *adj* calorifique.

calumny ['kæləmnɪ] *n* calomnie *f*; (*Jur*) diffamation *f*.

calve [kɑːv] *vi* vêler.

calves [kɑːvz] *npl of* **calf.**

cam [kæm] *n* (*Tech*) came *f*. **~shaft** arbre *m* à cames.

camber ['kæmbə^r] **1** *n [road]* bombement *m*. **2** *vt* bomber.

came [keɪm] *pret of* **come.**

camel ['kæməl] **1** *n* chameau *m*. **2** *adj* (*colour*) (de couleur) fauve *inv*. ♦ **camel-hair** *adj brush* en poil de chameau.

camellia [kə'miːlɪə] *n* camélia *m*.

cameo ['kæmɪəʊ] *n* camée *m*.

camera ['kæmərə] *n* **(a)** appareil *m* (photographique), appareil-photo *m*; (*movie* **~**) caméra *f*. **(b)** (*Jur*) **in ~** à huis clos. ♦ **cameraman** *n* caméraman *m*, opérateur *m* de prise de vue. ♦ **camerawork** *n* prise *f* de vue.

camomile ['kæməʊmaɪl] *n* camomille *f*.

camouflage ['kæməflɑːʒ] **1** *n* camouflage *m*. **2** *vt* camoufler.

camp[1] [kæmp] **1** *n* camp *m*, (*less permanent*) campement *m*. **to go to ~** partir camper; (*fig*) **in the same ~** du même bord; **a foot in both ~s** un pied dans chaque camp.

2 *adj* (*fig*) **~ follower** sympathisant(e) *m(f)*; **~(ing) chair** chaise pliante (de camping); **~(ing) ground** *or* **site** (*commercialized*) camping *m*; (*clearing etc*) endroit *m* où camper; (*with tent on it*) camp *m*; **~(ing) stool** pliant *m*; **~(ing) stove** réchaud *m* de camping.

3 *vi* camper. **to go ~ing** (aller) faire du camping.

camp out *vi* camper (*also fig*).

♦ **campbed** *n* lit *m* de camp. ♦ **camper** *n* campeur *m*, -euse *f*. ♦ **campfire** *n* feu *m* de camp. ♦ **camping** *n* camping *m* (*activité*).

camp[2]* [kæmp] **1** *adj* (*affected*) maniéré; (*overdramatic*) cabotin; (*homosexual*) *man* (qui fait) pédé‡; *manners, clothes* de pédé‡; (*vulgar*) vulgaire. **2** *vt*: **to ~ it up** cabotiner.

campaign [kæm'peɪn] **1** *n* campagne *f*. **2** *vi* faire campagne (*also fig*: *for* pour, *against* contre). ♦ **campaigner** *n* (*Mil*) **old ~er** vétéran *m*; (*fig*) **a ~er for/against sth** un(e) militant(e) *m(f)* pour/contre qch.

camphor ['kæmfə^r] *n* camphre *m*. ♦ **camphorated** *adj* camphré.

campus ['kæmpəs] *n* campus *m*.

can[1] [kæn] *modal aux vb: neg* **cannot, can't;** *cond and pret* **could. (a)** (*am etc able to*) (je) peux *etc*. **he ~ lift the suitcase** il peut soulever la valise; **he will do what he ~** il fera ce qu'il pourra, il fera son possible; **he will help you all he ~** il vous aidera de son mieux; **he couldn't speak because he had a bad cold** il ne pouvait pas parler parce qu'il était très enrhumé; **he could have helped us** il aurait pu nous aider; **it could be true** cela pourrait être vrai; **you could be making a big mistake** tu es peut-être en train de faire une grosse erreur; **could you be hiding sth from us?** est-il possible que vous nous cachiez (*subj*) qch?; **he could have changed his mind** il aurait pu changer d'avis; **he could have forgotten** il a peut-être oublié; **you can't be serious!** vous ne parlez pas sérieusement!; **he can't have known about it** il est impossible qu'il l'ait su; **she can't be very clever** elle ne doit pas être très intelligente; **where CAN he be?** où peut-il bien être?; **as big as ~ *or* could be** aussi grand que possible; **it ~ be very cold here** il arrive qu'il fasse très froid ici.

(b) (*know how to*) (je) sais *etc.* **he ~ read and write** il sait lire et écrire; **he ~ speak Italian** il parle italien, il sait l'italien; **she could not swim** elle ne savait pas nager.

(c) (*not translated*) **I ~ see you** je vous vois; **they could hear him** ils l'entendaient; **~ you smell it?** tu le sens?

(d) (*have permission to*) (je) peux *etc.* **you ~ go** vous pouvez partir; **~ I have some milk? – yes, you ~** puis-je avoir du lait? – mais oui, bien sûr; **could I have a word with you?** est-ce que je pourrais vous parler un instant?; **I can't go out** je n'ai pas le droit de sortir.

can[2] [kæn] **1** *n [milk, oil, water]* bidon *m*; *[garbage]* boîte *f* à ordures, poubelle *f*; (*for foodstuffs*) boîte *f* (de conserve). **a ~ of fruit/beer** une boîte de fruits/bière. **2** *vt food* mettre en boîte(s) *or* en conserve. ♦ **canned** *adj fruit, salmon* en boîte, en conserve; (*: *recorded*) *music* enregistré; (*: *drunk*) rétamé‡, soûl; **~ned goods** conserves *fpl*. ♦ **cannery** *or* ♦ **canning factory** *n* conserverie *f* (*fabrique*). ♦ **canning industry** *n* conserverie *f* (*industrie*). ♦ **can-opener** *n* ouvre-boîtes *m inv*.

Canada ['kænədə] *n* Canada *m*. ♦ **Canadian 1** *adj* canadien; **2** *n* Canadien(ne) *m(f)*.

canal [kə'næl] *n* canal *m*.

canary [kə'nɛərı] **1** *n* (*bird*) canari *m*. **2** *adj*: **~ yellow** jaune canari *inv*.

cancel ['kænsəl] *vt agreement, contract* résilier; *order, arrangement, meeting, debt* annuler; *cheque* faire opposition à; *taxi, appointment, party* décommander, annuler; *decree, will* révoquer; *train* supprimer; *application* retirer; (*cross out*) barrer, biffer; *stamp* oblitérer; (*Math*) *figures* éliminer.

cancel out *vt sep* (*Math*) *noughts* barrer; *amounts etc* annuler; (*fig*) neutraliser. **they ~ each other out** ils se neutralisent.

♦ **cancellation** *n* résiliation *f*; annulation *f*; révocation *f*; suppression *f*; retrait *m*; biffage *m*; oblitération *f*; (*Math*) élimination *f*; **~lations will not be accepted after ...** (*travel, hotel*) les réservations *or* (*Theat*) les locations ne peuvent être annulées après ...; **I have 2 ~lations for tomorrow** j'ai 2 personnes qui se sont décommandées pour demain.

cancer ['kænsəʳ] **1** *n* cancer *m*; (*Astron, Geog*) **C~** Cancer *m*. **2** *adj*: **~ patient** cancéreux *m*, -euse *f*; **~ research** cancérologie *f*, (*in appeals*) la lutte contre le cancer; **~ specialist** cancérologue *mf*. ♦ **cancerous** *adj* cancéreux. ♦ **cancer-producing** *adj* cancérigène.

candelabra [ˌkændı'lɑːbrə] *n* candélabre *m*.

candid ['kændıd] *adj* franc, sincère. ♦ **candidly** *adv* franchement, sincèrement. ♦ **candidness** *or* ♦ **candour,** (*US*) **-or** *n* franchise *f*, sincérité *f*.

candidate ['kændıdeıt] *n* candidat(e) *m(f)*. ♦ **candidacy** *or* ♦ **candidature** *n* candidature *f*.

candied ['kændıd] *adj* confit. **~ peel** écorce confite.

candle ['kændl] **1** *n [wax]* bougie *f*; *[tallow]* chandelle *f*; (*in church*) cierge *m*. **the game is not worth the ~** le jeu n'en vaut pas la chandelle. **2** *adj*: **~ grease** suif *m*. ♦ **candlelight 1** *n*: **by ~light** à la lueur d'une bougie *etc*; **2** *adj*: **~light dinner** dîner *m* aux chandelles. ♦ **Candlemas** *n* la Chandeleur. ♦ **candlestick** *n* (*flat*) bougeoir *m*; (*tall*) chandelier *m*. ♦ **candlewick** *n* chenille *f* (de coton).

candy ['kændı] *n* sucre *m* candi; (*US: sweets*) bonbon(s) *m(pl)*. ♦ **candy-floss** *n* barbe *f* à papa. ♦ **candy-striped** *adj* à rayures multicolores.

cane [keın] **1** *n* (*gen*) canne *f*; *[officer, rider]* badine *f*; (*for chairs, baskets*) rotin *m*, jonc *m*; (*for punishment*) trique *f*, (*Scol*) verge *f*. **2** *vt* donner des coups de trique à; (*Scol*) fouetter. **3** *adj*: **~ chair** chaise cannée; **~ sugar** sucre *m* de canne. ♦ **caning** *n*: **to get a caning** (*lit*) recevoir la trique *or* (*Scol*) le fouet; (*: *fig*) se faire taper sur les doigts* (*fig*).

canine ['kænaın] **1** *adj* canin. **2** *n* (*tooth*) canine *f*.

canister ['kænıstəʳ] *n* boîte *f* (*en métal*).

cannabis ['kænəbıs] *n* cannabis *m*.

cannibal ['kænıbəl] *adj, n* cannibale (*mf*), anthropophage (*mf*). ♦ **cannibalism** *n* cannibalisme *m*, anthropophagie *f*. ♦ **cannibalize** *vt machine, car* démonter pour en réutiliser les pièces.

cannon ['kænən] **1** *n* canon *m*. **2** *adj*: **~ fodder*** chair *f* à canon*. **3** *vi*: **to ~ into *or* against** *object* percuter; *person* se heurter contre. ♦ **cannonball** *n* boulet *m* de canon.

canoe [kə'nuː] **1** *n* canoë *m*; (*Sport*) kayac *m*. **2** *vi*: **to go ~ing** faire du canoë *or* du kayac. ♦ **canoeing** *n* (sport *m* du) canoë *m*. ♦ **canoeist** *n* canoéiste *mf*.

canon ['kænən] **1** *n* (*Mus, Rel, also gen: law etc*) canon *m*; (*cleric*) chanoine *m*. **2** *adj*: **~ law** droit *m* canon. ♦ **canonization** *n* canonisation *f*. ♦ **canonize** *vt* canoniser.

canoodle‡† [kə'nuːdl] *vi* se faire des mamours*.

canopy ['kænəpı] *n [bed]* baldaquin *m*; *[throne etc]* dais *m*.

cant[1] [kænt] *n* (*pej*) (*insincere talk*) paroles *fpl* hypocrites; (*clichés*) phrases toutes faites; (*jargon*) jargon *m*.

cant[2] [kænt] *vti* (*tilt*) pencher.

can't [kɑːnt] *abbr of* **cannot**; *V* **can**[1].

cantankerous [kæn'tæŋkərəs] *adj* (*ill-tempered*) acariâtre; (*aggressive*) hargneux.

canteen [kæn'tiːn] *n* **(a)** (*restaurant*) cantine *f*. **(b) a ~ of cutlery** une ménagère (*couverts de table*).

canter ['kæntəʳ] **1** *n* petit galop. **2** *vi* aller au petit galop.

Canterbury ['kæntəbərı] *n* Cantorbéry. **~ bell** campanule *f*.

cantilever ['kæntılıːvəʳ] *n*: **~ bridge** pont *m* cantilever *inv*.

canton ['kæntɒn] *n* canton *m*. ♦ **cantonal** *adj* cantonal.

canvas ['kænvəs] *n* toile *f*. **under ~** (*in a tent*) sous la tente; (*Naut*) sous voiles.

canvass ['kænvəs] **1** *vt* **(a)** (*Pol*) *district* faire du démarchage électoral dans; *person* solliciter le suffrage de; (*Comm*) *district* prospecter; (*gen*) *people, opinions* sonder (*about* à propos de). **(b)** *matter, question* examiner à fond. **2** *vi* (*Pol*) solliciter des suffrages; (*Comm*) (*door to door*) faire du démarchage. **to ~ for sb** (*Pol*) solliciter des voix pour qn; (*gen*) faire campagne pour qn. ♦ **canvasser** *n* (*Pol*) agent électoral (*qui sollicite les voix des électeurs*); (*Comm*) démarcheur *m*. ♦ **canvassing** *n* (*Pol*) démarchage électoral (*pour solliciter les suffrages*); (*when applying for job etc*) **no ~ing allowed** ≃ s'abstenir de toute démarche personnelle.

canyon ['kænjən] *n* cañon *m*, gorge *f*.

cap [kæp] **1** *n* **(a)** (*gen*) casquette *f*; *[baby, sailor]* bonnet *m*; *[officer]* képi *m*; *[soldier]* calot *m*. (*fig*) **~ in hand** chapeau bas, humblement; **if the ~ fits, put it on** qui se sent morveux qu'il se mouche; (*Sport*) **he's got his ~ for England** il a été sélectionné pour l'équipe d'Angleterre. **(b)** *[bottle]* capsule *f*; *[fountain pen]* capuchon *m*; *[radiator, tyre-valve]* bouchon *m*. **(c)** (*for toy gun*) amorce *f*. **2** *vt bottle etc* couvrir d'une capsule *etc*; *sb's words* renchérir sur; *achievements* surpasser. **he ~ped this story** il a trouvé une histoire encore meilleure que celle-ci; **to ~ it all*** pour couronner le tout. ♦ **capful** *n*: **one ~ful to 4 litres of water** une capsule pleine pour 4 litres d'eau.

capable ['keɪpəbl] *adj person* capable (*of doing* de faire); *event, situation* susceptible (*of* de); (*competent*) capable. ♦ **capability** *n* capacité *f* (*to do, for doing* de faire); **capabilities** moyens *mpl*. ♦ **capably** *adv* habilement, avec compétence.

capacity [kə'pæsɪtɪ] **1** *n* **(a)** (*gen, Elec, Phys*) capacité *f*; *[factory]* moyens *mpl* de production. **filled to ~** absolument plein; **the hall has a seating ~ of 400** la salle a 400 places assises; *[machine, factory]* **to work at full ~** produire à plein rendement. **(b)** (*ability*) aptitude *f* (*for sth* à qch; *for doing* à faire). **capacities** capacité(s) *f(pl)*, moyens *mpl*. **(c)** (*legal power*) pouvoir légal (*to do* de faire); (*position*) qualité *f*. **in my ~ as a doctor** en ma qualité de médecin; **in his official ~** dans l'exercice de ses fonctions; **in an advisory ~** à titre consultatif; **we must not employ him in any ~ whatsoever** il ne faut pas l'employer à quelque titre que ce soit. **2** *adj*: **there was ~ booking** on jouait à guichets fermés; **there was a ~ crowd** il n'y avait plus une place (de) libre. ♦ **capacious** *adj* d'une grande capacité.

cape[1] [keɪp] *n* (*full length*) cape *f*; (*policeman's, cyclist's*) pèlerine *f*.

cape[2] [keɪp] *n* (*Geog*) cap *m*. (*in South Africa*) **C~ Coloureds** métis sud-africains; **the C~ (of Good Hope)** le cap de Bonne Espérance; **C~ Town** Le Cap.

caper[1] ['keɪpə^r] **1** *vi* (**~ about**) *[child]* gambader; (*fool around*) faire l'idiot. **2** *n* (*pej*) **that was quite a ~*** ça a été toute une histoire*.

caper[2] ['keɪpə^r] *n* (*Culin*) câpre *f*.

capillary [kə'pɪlərɪ] *adj, n* capillaire (*m*).

capital ['kæpɪtl] **1** *adj* **(a)** (*gen, also Jur*) capital. **~ offence** crime capital; **~ punishment** peine capitale; (*excl*) **~!** excellent!; **of ~ importance** d'une importance capitale; **~ A** A majuscule. **(b)** (*Fin*) **~ expenditure** dépenses *fpl* en capital; **~ gains tax** impôt *m* sur les plus-values; **~ goods** biens *mpl* d'équipement; **~ reserves** réserves *fpl* et provisions *fpl*; **~ sum** capital *m*. **2** *n* (**~ *city***) capitale *f*; (**~ *letter***) majuscule *f*; (*Fin*) capital *m*. **~ invested** mise *f* de fonds; (*fig*) **to make ~ out of** tirer parti *or* profit de. ♦ **capitalism** *n* capitalisme *m*. ♦ **capitalist** *adj, n* capitaliste (*mf*). ♦ **capitalization** *n* capitalisation *f*. ♦ **capitalize 1** *vt property, plant* capitaliser; *company* constituer le capital social de (*par émission d'actions*); (*Fin*) **over-/under-~ized** sur-/sous-capitalisé; **2** *vi* (*fig*) **to ~ize on** tirer parti de.

capitulate [kə'pɪtjʊleɪt] *vi* capituler. ♦ **capitulation** *n* capitulation *f*.

caprice [kə'pri:s] *n* caprice *m*. ♦ **capricious** *adj* capricieux, fantasque. ♦ **capriciously** *adv* capricieusement.

Capricorn ['kæprɪkɔ:n] *n* Capricorne *m*.

capsicum ['kæpsɪkəm] *n* (*sweet*) poivron *m*; (*hot*) piment *m*.

capsize [kæp'saɪz] **1** *vi [boat]* chavirer; *[object]* se renverser. **2** *vt* faire chavirer; renverser.

capstan ['kæpstən] *n* cabestan *m*.

capsule ['kæpsju:l] *n* capsule *f*.

captain ['kæptɪn] **1** *n* capitaine *m*. **~ of industry** capitaine d'industrie. **2** *vt team* être le capitaine de; *ship* commander; (*fig*) diriger.

caption ['kæpʃən] **1** *n* (*Press*) (*heading*) sous-titre *m*; (*under illustration*) légende *f*; (*Cine*) sous-titre. **2** *vt* mettre une légende à; sous-titrer.

captious ['kæpʃəs] *adj person* chicanier; *remark* critique.

captivate ['kæptɪveɪt] *vt* captiver. ♦ **captivating** *adj* captivant.

captive ['kæptɪv] **1** *n* captif *m*, -ive *f*. **to take sb ~** faire qn prisonnier; **to hold ~** garder en captivité. **2** *adj* captif. **she had a ~ audience** son auditoire était bien obligé de l'écouter. ♦ **captivity** *n* captivité *f*; **in captivity** en captivité.

capture ['kæptʃə^r] **1** *vt animal, soldier* capturer; *escapee* reprendre; *city* s'emparer de; (*fig*) *attention* captiver; *interest* gagner; (*Art*) rendre. **2** *n [town, treasure, escapee]* capture *f*. ♦ **captor** *n* (*unlawful*) ravisseur *m*; (*lawful*) personne *f* qui capture.

car [kɑ:^r] *n* (*Aut*) voiture *f*, automobile *f*, auto *f*; (*US Rail*) wagon *m*, voiture; (*tramcar*) tramway *m*. **2** *adj*: **~ allowance** indemnité *f* de déplacements (en voiture); **~ transporter** (*Aut*) camion *m* or (*Rail*) wagon *m* pour transport d'automobiles; **~ wash** (*place*) lave-auto *m*. ♦ **car-ferry** *n* ferry *m*. ♦ **carhop** *n* (*US*) serveur *m*, -euse *f*. ♦ **car-park** *n* parking *m*. ♦ **carport** *n* auvent *m* (pour voiture). ♦ **car-sick** *adj*: **to be ~-sick** avoir le mal de la route. ♦ **carworker** *n* (*Ind*) ouvrier *m*, -ière *f* de l'industrie automobile.

caramel ['kærəməl] *n* caramel *m*.

carat ['kærət] *n* carat *m*. **22 ~ gold** or *m* à 22 carats.

caravan ['kærəvæn] *n* (*Aut*) caravane *f*; *[gipsy]* roulotte *f*; (*group: in desert etc*) caravane. **~ site** camping *m* pour caravanes. ♦ **caravanette** *n* auto-camping *f*.

caraway ['kærəweɪ] *n* cumin *m*.

carbohydrate [ˌkɑ:bəʊ'haɪdreɪt] *n* hydrate *m* de carbone. (*in diets etc*) **~s** féculents *mpl*.

carbolic [kɑ:'bɒlɪk] *adj*: **~ acid** phénol *m*.

carbon ['kɑ:bən] **1** *n* carbone *m*. **2** *adj*: **~ copy** *[typing etc]* carbone *m*; (*fig*) réplique *f*; **~ dating** datation *f* au carbone; **~ dioxide** gaz *m* carbonique; **~ monoxide** oxyde *m* de carbone; **~ paper** (papier *m*) carbone *m*. ♦ **carbonate** *n* carbonate *m*. ♦ **carbonic** *adj* carbonique. ♦ **carboniferous** *adj* carbonifère. ♦ **carbonization** *n* carbonisation *f*. ♦ **carbonize** *vt* carboniser.

carborundum [ˌkɑ:bə'rʌndəm] *n* carborundum *m*.

carboy ['kɑ:bɔɪ] *n* bonbonne *f*.

carbuncle ['kɑ:bʌŋkl] *n* (*jewel*) escarboucle *f*; (*Med*) furoncle *m*.

carburet(t)or [ˌkɑ:bjʊ'retə^r] *n* carburateur *m*.

carcass ['kɑ:kəs] *n* carcasse *f*.

carcinogen [kɑ:'sɪnədʒen] *n* substance *f* cancérigène. ♦ **carcinogenic** *adj* cancérigène.

carcinoma ['kɑ:sɪ'nəʊmə] *n* carcinome *m*.

card [kɑ:d] **1** *n* (*gen*) carte *f*; (***index* ~**) fiche *f*; (*cardboard*) carton *m*. **identity ~** carte d'identité; **to play ~s** jouer aux cartes; (*fig*) **to play one's ~s well** manœuvrer habilement; **to put one's ~s on the table** jouer cartes sur table; **it's (quite) on the ~s that*...** il y a de grandes chances pour que ... + *subj*; (*Ind etc*) **to get one's ~s** être mis à la porte; (*Ind etc*) **to ask for one's ~s** quitter son travail.

2 *adj*: **~ game** (*e.g. bridge etc*) jeu *m* de cartes; (*game of cards*) partie *f* de cartes.

3 *vt information* mettre sur fiches.

♦ **cardboard 1** *n* carton *m*; **2** *adj* de *or* en carton; **~board box** (boîte *f* en) carton *m*. ♦ **card-carrying** *adj*: **~-carrying member** membre *m*, adhérent(e) *m(f)*. ♦ **card-index** *n* fichier *m*. ♦ **card-player** *n* joueur *m*, -euse *f* de cartes. ♦ **cardsharp(er)** *n* tricheur *m*, -euse *f* (*professionnel*). ♦ **card-table** *n* table *f* de jeu *or* à jouer. ♦ **card-trick** *n* tour *m* de cartes.

cardamom ['kɑ:dəməm] *n* cardamome *f*.

cardiac ['kɑ:dɪæk] *adj* cardiaque. **~ arrest** arrêt *m* du cœur.

cardigan ['kɑ:dɪgən] *n* cardigan *m*.

cardinal ['kɑ:dɪnl] *adj, n* cardinal (*m*).

cardiology [ˌkɑːdɪˈɒlədʒɪ] *n* cardiologie *f*. ◆ **cardiological** *adj* cardiologique. ◆ **cardiologist** *n* cardiologue *mf*.

care [kɛəʳ] **1** *n* **(a)** (*heed*) attention *f*, soin *m*; (*charge*) charge *f*, garde *f*. **with the greatest ~** avec le plus grand soin; (*on parcels*) **'with ~'** 'fragile'; **take ~ not to catch cold** faites attention de *or* à ne pas prendre froid; **take ~** (fais) attention; (*as good wishes*) fais bien attention (à toi); **to take (great) ~ with sth** faire très attention à qch; **you should take more ~ with your work** vous devriez apporter plus d'attention à votre travail; **you should take more ~ of yourself** tu devrais faire plus attention (à ta santé); (*Jur*) **driving without due ~ and attention** conduite négligente; **he took ~ to explain why ...** il a pris soin d'expliquer pourquoi ...; **to take ~ of** s'occuper de; **to take good ~ of** *person* bien s'occuper de; *object* prendre grand soin de; (*threateningly*) **I'll take ~ of him!** je vais m'occuper de lui!; **he can take ~ of himself** il sait se débrouiller tout seul; **that can take ~ of itself** cela s'arrangera tout seul; **I leave** *or* **put it in your ~** je vous le confie; (*on letters*) **~ of** (*abbr* **c/o**) aux bons soins de; **he was left in his aunt's ~** on l'a laissé à la garde de sa tante; (*Sociol*) **children in ~** enfants retirés de la garde de leurs parents. **(b)** (*anxiety*) souci *m*. **he hasn't a ~ in the world** il n'a pas le moindre souci; **the ~s of State** les responsabilités *fpl* de l'État.

2 *vi* **(a)** se soucier (*about* de), s'intéresser (*about* à). **money is all he ~s about** il n'y a que l'argent qui l'intéresse (*subj*); **to ~ deeply about** *thing* être profondément concerné par; *person* être profondément attaché à; **not to ~ about** se moquer de; **he really ~s about this** c'est vraiment important pour lui; **I don't ~** ça m'est égal; **as if I ~d!** je m'en fiche!*; **what do I ~?** qu'est-ce que cela peut me faire?; **for all I ~** pour ce que cela me fait; **I couldn't ~ less what people say** je me fiche pas mal* de ce que les gens peuvent dire; **he doesn't ~ a damn*** il s'en fiche comme de l'an quarante*; **who ~s!** qu'est-ce que cela peut bien faire! **(b)** (*like*) vouloir, aimer. **would you ~ to sit down?** voulez-vous vous asseoir?; **I shouldn't ~ to meet him** je n'aimerais pas le rencontrer; **I don't much ~ for it** cela ne me dit pas grand-chose; **I don't ~ for him** il ne me plaît pas beaucoup; **would you ~ for a cup of tea?** voulez-vous (prendre) une tasse de thé?

care for *vt fus invalid* soigner; *child* s'occuper de. **well-~d for** *invalid* qu'on soigne bien; *child* dont on s'occupe bien; *hands, hair* soigné; *garden* bien entretenu; *house* bien tenu.

◆ **carefree** *adj* insouciant. ◆ **careful,** ◆ **careless** *V below*. ◆ **caretaker 1** *n* gardien(ne) *m(f)*, concierge *mf*; **2** *adj government* intérimaire. ◆ **careworn** *adj* rongé par les soucis. ◆ **caring** *adj parent* aimant; *teacher* bienveillant; *society* humanitaire; **a child needs a caring environment** un enfant a besoin d'être entouré d'affection.

career [kəˈrɪəʳ] **1** *n* carrière *f*. **journalism is his ~** il fait carrière dans le journalisme; **he is making a ~ (for himself) in advertising** il est en train de faire carrière dans la publicité. **2** *adj soldier, diplomat* de carrière. **~ girl** jeune fille *f* qui veut faire une carrière; **~ guidance** orientation professionnelle; **~s officer** conseiller *m*, -ère *f* d'orientation professionnelle. **3** *vi* (**~ along**) aller à toute allure. ◆ **careerist** *n* carriériste *mf*.

careful [ˈkɛəfʊl] *adj* (*painstaking*) *writer, worker* consciencieux, soigneux; *work* soigné; (*cautious*) prudent, circonspect; (*acting with care*) soigneux. **to be ~** faire attention (*of, with sth* à qch; *to do* à faire); **(be) ~!** (fais) attention!; **be ~ not to let it fall** faites attention à ne pas le laisser tomber; **be ~ to shut the door** n'oubliez pas de fermer la porte; **be ~ what you do** faites attention à ce que vous faites; **be ~ (that) he doesn't hear you** faites attention à ce qu'il ne vous entende pas; **he was ~ to point out that** il a pris soin de faire remarquer que; **you can't be too ~** (*gen*) on n'est jamais trop prudent; (*when double-checking sth*) deux précautions valent mieux qu'une; **he is very ~ with (his) money** il regarde à la dépense. ◆ **carefully** *adv* (*painstakingly*) *work, cut, choose* soigneusement, avec soin; (*cautiously*) *proceed, announce* prudemment, avec précaution; *reply* avec circonspection; (*fig*) **we must go ~ly here** il faut nous montrer prudents là-dessus. ◆ **carefulness** *n* soin *m*, attention *f*.

careless [ˈkɛəlɪs] *adj worker* qui manque de soin; *driver, driving* négligent. **~ mistake** faute *f* d'inattention. ◆ **carelessly** *adv* (*inattentively*) négligemment, sans faire attention; (*in carefree way*) avec insouciance. ◆ **carelessness** *n* manque *m* de soin; négligence *f*; manque d'attention; (*carefreeness*) insouciance *f*.

caress [kəˈres] **1** *n* caresse *f*. **2** *vt* caresser.

cargo [ˈkɑːgəʊ] *n* cargaison *f*. **~ boat** cargo *m*.

Caribbean [ˌkærɪˈbiːən] *adj, n*: **the ~ (Sea)** la mer des Antilles *or* des Caraïbes.

caricature [ˈkærɪkətjʊəʳ] **1** *n* caricature *f*. **2** *vt* caricaturer. ◆ **caricaturist** *n* caricaturiste *mf*.

caries [ˈkɛərɪiːz] *n* carie *f*. ◆ **carious** *adj* carié.

carmine [ˈkɑːmaɪn] *adj, n* carmin (*m*).

carnage [ˈkɑːnɪdʒ] *n* carnage *m*.

carnal [ˈkɑːnl] *adj* (*of the flesh*) charnel; (*sensual*) sensuel; (*sexual*) sexuel.

carnation [kɑːˈneɪʃən] *n* œillet *m*.

carnival [ˈkɑːnɪvəl] *n* carnaval *m*.

carnivore [ˈkɑːnɪvɔːʳ] *n* carnivore *m*. ◆ **carnivorous** [kɑːˈnɪvərəs] *adj* carnivore.

carol [ˈkærəl] *n*: **(Christmas) ~** chant *m* de Noël.

carouse [kəˈraʊz] *vi* faire ribote*. ◆ **carousal** *n* beuverie *f*.

carp¹ [kɑːp] *n* (*fish*) carpe *f*.

carp² [kɑːp] *vi* critiquer sans cesse. **to ~ at sb/sth** critiquer sans cesse qn/qch. ◆ **carping 1** *adj person, manner* chicanier; *criticism* mesquin; *voice* malveillant; **2** *n* critique *f* (malveillante).

carpenter [ˈkɑːpɪntəʳ] *n* charpentier *m*; (*joiner*) menuisier *m*. ◆ **carpentry** *n* charpenterie *f*; menuiserie *f*.

carpet [ˈkɑːpɪt] **1** *n* tapis *m*; (*fitted*) moquette *f*. (*fig*) **to be on the ~*** [*subject*] être sur le tapis; [*person scolded*] être sur la sellette. **2** *adj*: **~ slippers** pantoufles *fpl*; **~ sweeper** (*mechanical*) balai *m* mécanique; (*vacuum cleaner*) aspirateur *m*. **3** *vt floor* recouvrir d'un tapis *or* d'une moquette; (*: *scold*) houspiller. ◆ **carpetbagger*** *n* profiteur *m*, -euse *f*. ◆ **carpeting** *n* moquette *f*.

carriage [ˈkærɪdʒ] *n* **(a)** (*horse-drawn*) voiture *f* (de maître), équipage *m*; (*Rail*) voiture, wagon *m* (de voyageurs). **(b)** (*Comm: conveyance of goods*) transport *m*. **~ free** franco de port; **~ paid** (en) port payé. **(c)** [*person*] (*bearing*) maintien *m*, port *m*.

carrier [ˈkærɪəʳ] *n* **(a)** (*company*) entreprise *f* de transports; (*truck owner etc*) transporteur *m*. **by ~** (*Aut*) par camion; (*Rail*) par chemin de fer. **(b)** (*basket etc: on cycle etc*) porte-bagages *m inv*; (**~ bag**) sac *m* (en plastique). **(c)** (*Med*) porteur *m*, -euse *f*. **(d)** (*aircraft ~*) porte-avions *m inv*; (*troop ~*) (*plane*) appareil *m* transporteur (de troupes); (*ship*) transport *m*. ◆ **carrier-bag** *n* sac *m* (en plastique). ◆ **carrier-pigeon** *n* pigeon *m* voyageur.

carrion [ˈkærɪən] *n* charogne *f*.

carrot [ˈkærət] *n* carotte *f*. ◆ **carroty** *adj hair* carotte *inv*, roux.

carry [ˈkærɪ] **1** *vt* **(a)** (*gen*) porter; *goods, passengers* transporter; *identity card, cigarettes, money* avoir (sur soi); *umbrella, gun* porter; *message, news* porter; [*sea, river*] emporter; [*pillar*] supporter, soutenir; [*pipe*] amener; [*wire*] conduire. **they carried the pipes under the street** ils ont fait passer les tuyaux sous la rue; (*fig*) **to ~ sth too far** pousser qch trop loin; **she carries herself very well** elle se tient très droite; **he carries himself like a soldier** il a le port d'un militaire; **to ~ in one's head** retenir dans sa tête; (*Math*) **and ~ 3** et je retiens 3; (*fig*) **to ~ coals to Newcastle** porter de l'eau à la rivière; **to ~ the can*** (devoir) payer les pots cassés; **he carries his life in his hands** il risque sa vie; **£5 won't ~ you far** on ne va pas loin avec 5 livres; **enough food to ~ us through the winter** assez de provisions pour nous durer tout l'hiver; **he can't ~ his liquor** l'alcool lui monte à la tête.

(b) *consequences* entraîner; (*Fin*) *interest* rapporter; *responsibility, pay* comporter. **it carries a penalty of** cela est passible d'une amende de.

(c) (*Comm*) *goods* stocker. **we don't ~ that article** nous ne faisons pas cet article.

(d) (*win*) gagner, remporter; *fortress* enlever; *motion* voter. **to ~ the day** l'emporter; (*Mil*) être vainqueur; **to ~ all before one** l'emporter sur tous les tableaux.

(e) *[newspaper etc] story, details* rapporter. **all the papers carried (the story of) the murder** tous les journaux ont parlé du meurtre.

2 *vi [voice, sound]* porter.

carry away *vt sep* emporter. (*fig*) **to get carried away by sth*** s'emballer* *or* s'enthousiasmer pour qch.

carry back *vt sep things* rapporter; *person* ramener; (*fig: remind*) reporter (*to* à).

carry forward *vt sep* reporter (*to* à).

carry off *vt sep* (*gen*) emporter, enlever; (*kidnap*) enlever; *prizes* remporter. **to ~ it off** (*succeed*) réussir (son coup).

carry on 1 *vi* continuer (*with sth* qch); (*: *make a scene*) faire des histoires*; (*: *have an affair*) avoir une liaison (*with sb* avec qn). **2** *vt sep* (*conduct*) *business, trade* diriger; *correspondence* entretenir; *conversation* soutenir; *negotiations* mener; (*continue*) continuer (*doing* à *or* de faire).

carry out *vt sep* (*lit*) emporter; (*fig*) *plan, order* exécuter; *idea* mettre à exécution; *one's duty, obligation* s'acquitter de; *experiment* se livrer à; *search, investigation, inquiry* mener; *reform* effectuer; *the law, regulations* appliquer; *promise* tenir.

carry over *vt sep* reporter (*to* à).

carry through *vt sep plan* mener à bonne fin. **his courage carried him through** son courage lui a permis de surmonter l'épreuve.

♦ **carryall** *n* fourre-tout *m inv* (*sac*). ♦ **carrycot** *n* porte-bébé *m*. ♦ **carryings-on** *npl* façons *fpl* de se conduire. ♦ **carry-on*** *n* histoires* *fpl*; **what a ~-on about nothing!*** que d'histoires* pour rien! ♦ **carry-out** *adj meal* à emporter.

cart [kɑːt] **1** *n* (*horse-drawn*) charrette *f*; (*tip ~*) tombereau *m*; (*hand ~*) voiture *f* à bras. (*fig*) **to put the ~ before the horse** mettre la charrue devant *or* avant les bœufs; (*fig*) **to be in the ~*** être dans le pétrin. **2** *vt* (*in truck*) transporter (par camion); (*: *carry*) *shopping, books* trimballer*. ♦ **carter** *n* camionneur *m*. ♦ **cart-horse** *n* cheval *m* de trait. ♦ **cartload** *n* charretée *f*; tombereau *m*; voiturée *f*. ♦ **cart-track** *n* chemin *m* rural. ♦ **cartwheel** *n*: **to turn a ~wheel** faire la roue (*en gymnastique etc*).

cartilage ['kɑːtɪlɪdʒ] *n* cartilage *m*.

cartography [kɑː'tɒgrəfɪ] *n* cartographie *f*. ♦ **cartographer** *n* cartographe *mf*.

carton ['kɑːtən] *n [yogurt, cream]* pot *m*; *[milk, squash]* carton *m*; *[ice cream]* boîte *f*; *[cigarettes]* cartouche *f*.

cartoon [kɑː'tuːn] *n [newspaper etc]* dessin *m* (humoristique); (*Cine, TV*) dessin animé; (*Art: sketch*) carton *m*. ♦ **cartoonist** *n [newspaper etc]* caricaturiste *mf*; (*Cine, TV*) dessinateur *m*, -trice *f* de dessins animés.

cartridge ['kɑːtrɪdʒ] **1** *n [rifle, pen]* cartouche *f*; *[camera]* chargeur *m*. **2** *adj*: **~ paper** papier *m* à cartouche, papier fort.

carve [kɑːv] *vt* tailler (*in, out of* dans); (*sculpt*) sculpter (*in, out of* dans); (*Culin*) découper. **to ~ one's initials on** graver ses initiales sur.

carve out *vt sep piece* découper (*from* dans); *land* prendre (*from* à); *statue, tool* tailler (*of* dans). **to ~ out a career for o.s.** se tailler une carrière.

carve up *vt sep meat* découper; (*fig*) *country* morceler; (*: *disfigure*) *person* amocher‡ (à coups de couteau); *sb's face* taillader.

♦ **carver** *or* ♦ **carving knife** *n* couteau *m* à découper.

cascade [kæs'keɪd] **1** *n* cascade *f*. **2** *vi* tomber en cascade.

cascara [kæs'kɑːrə] *n* cascara sagrada *f*.

case[1] [keɪs] **1** *n* **(a)** (*gen, also Gram, Med, Soc*) cas *m*. **is it the ~ that ...?** est-il vrai que ...?; **that's not the ~** ce n'est pas le cas; **if that's the ~** en ce cas, dans ce cas-là; **put the ~ that** admettons que + *subj*; **as the ~ may be** selon le cas; **a clear ~ of lying** un exemple manifeste de mensonge; **in ~ he comes** au cas où il viendrait; **in ~ of** en cas de; **(just) in ~** à tout hasard; **in any ~** en tout cas; **in this ~** dans *or* en ce cas; **in that ~** dans ce cas-là; **in the ~ in point** en l'occurrence; **here is a ~ in point** en voici un bon exemple; **in nine ~s out of ten** neuf fois sur dix; **that alters the whole ~** cela change tout; **he's a hard ~** c'est un dur*; **she's a real ~!*** c'est un cas* *or* un numéro!*

(b) (*Jur*) affaire *f*, procès *m*. **to try a ~** juger une affaire; **to win one's ~** (*Jur*) gagner son procès; (*fig*) avoir gain de cause; **the ~ for the defendant** les arguments *mpl* en faveur de l'accusé; **there is no ~ against ...** il n'y a pas lieu à poursuites contre ...; **he's working on the Smith ~** il s'occupe de l'affaire Smith.

(c) (*reasoning*) arguments *mpl*. **to make out a good ~ for sth** réunir *or* présenter de bons arguments en faveur de qch; **to make out a good ~ for doing** bien expliquer pourquoi il faudrait faire; **there is a strong ~ for/against ...** il y a beaucoup à dire en faveur de/contre ...; **a ~ of conscience** un cas de conscience; **to have a strong ~** avoir de solides arguments.

2 *adj* (*Jur, Med, Soc*) **~ file** dossier *m*; **~ history** (*Soc*) évolution *f* du cas social; (*Med*) antécédents médicaux; **to have a heavy ~ load** avoir beaucoup de dossiers (sur les bras).

♦ **case-hardened** *adj* endurci. ♦ **casework** *n* (*Soc*) travail *m* avec des cas individuels. ♦ **caseworker** *n* ≈ assistante *f* sociale, auxiliaire *mf* social(e).

case[2] [keɪs] *n* (*suitcase*) valise *f*; (*packing ~, crate*) caisse *f*; (*for lettuce etc*) cageot *m*; (*box*) boîte *f*; (*chest*) coffre *m*; (*for goods on display*) vitrine *f*; (*for jewels*) coffret *m*; (*for watch etc*) écrin *m*; (*for camera, violin etc*) étui *m*; (*covering*) enveloppe *f*; (*Tech*) boîte.

cash [kæʃ] **1** *n* **(a)** (*notes and coins*) argent *m*. **how much ~ is there in the till?** combien d'argent y a-t-il dans la caisse?; **paid in ~ and not by cheque** payé en espèces et non pas par chèque; **ready ~** (argent *m*) liquide *m*; **~ in hand** encaisse *f*. **(b)** (*immediate payment*) **~ down** argent comptant; **to pay ~ (down)** payer comptant *or* cash*; **discount for ~** escompte *m* au comptant; **~ with order** payable à la commande; **~ on delivery** paiement *m* à la livraison. **(c)** (*: *money in general*) argent *m*. **to be short of ~** être à court (d'argent); **I've no ~** je suis sans le rond*.

2 *adj terms, sale, transaction* au comptant; *payment, price* comptant *inv*; *prize* en espèces. **~ flow** cash-flow *m*; **~ offer** offre *f* d'achat avec paiement comptant; **~ receipts** recettes *fpl* de caisse.

3 *vt cheque* encaisser; *banknote* changer. **to ~ sb a cheque** donner à qn de l'argent contre un chèque; *[bank]* payer un chèque à qn.
cash in *vt sep* réaliser.
cash in on* *vt fus* tirer profit de.
♦ **cash-and-carry** *n* supermarché *m* de gros et demi-gros. ♦ **cashbook** *n* livre *m* de caisse. ♦ **cashbox** *n* caisse *f.* ♦ **cashdesk** *n [shop, restaurant]* caisse *f*; *[cinema, theatre]* guichet *m.* ♦ **cash-register** *n* caisse *f* (enregistreuse).
cashew [kæ'ʃuː] *n* (~ *nut*) noix *f* de cajou.
cashier[1] [kæ'ʃɪəʳ] *n* (*Fin etc*) caissier *m*, -ière *f.*
cashier[2] [kæ'ʃɪəʳ] *vt officer* casser.
cashmere [kæʃ'mɪəʳ] *n* cachemire *m.*
casino [kə'siːnəʊ] *n* casino *m.*
cask [kɑːsk] *n* tonneau *m*, fût *m.*
casket ['kɑːskɪt] *n* (*gen*) coffret *m*; (*coffin*) cercueil *m.*
cassava [kə'sɑːvə] *n* manioc *m.*
casserole ['kæsərəʊl] **1** *n* (*utensil*) cocotte *f*; (*food*) ragoût *m* (en cocotte). **2** *vt* faire cuire à la cocotte.
cassette [kæ'set] **1** *n* (*Sound Recording*) cassette *f*; (*Phot*) cartouche *f.* **2** *adj*: ~ **deck** platine *f* à cassettes; ~ **player** lecteur *m* de cassettes; ~ **recorder** magnétophone *m* à cassettes.
cassock ['kæsək] *n* soutane *f.*
cast [kɑːst] (*vb: pret, ptp* **cast**) **1** *n* **(a)** (*Fishing*) lancer *m.* **(b)** (*mould*) moule *m*; (*in plaster, metal etc*) moulage *m*; *[medallion etc]* empreinte *f.* (*Med*) **leg in a ~** jambe *f* dans le plâtre; **~ of features** traits *mpl* (du visage); **~ of mind** tournure *f* d'esprit. **(c)** (*Theat*) (*actors*) acteurs *mpl*; (*list on programme etc*) distribution *f.* **(d)** (*Med: squint*) strabisme *m.* **to have a ~ in one eye** loucher d'un œil.
2 *vt* **(a)** (*throw*) (*gen*) jeter; *net, fishing line, stone* lancer, jeter; *shadow, light* projeter; *horoscope* tirer; *doubt* émettre; *blame* rejeter. **to ~ a vote** voter; **to ~ one's eye(s) towards** porter ses regards du côté de. **(b)** (*shed*) se dépouiller de; *horseshoe* perdre. *[snake]* **to ~ its skin** muer. **(c)** (*Art, Tech*) *plaster, metal* couler; *statue* mouler. **(d)** (*Theat*) *play* distribuer les rôles de. **he was ~ as Hamlet** on lui a donné le rôle de Hamlet.
cast about, cast around *vi*: **to ~ about for sth** chercher qch.
cast away *vt sep* (*Naut*) **to be ~ away** être naufragé.
cast down *vt sep object* jeter par terre; *eyes* baisser. **to be ~ down** (*depressed*) être abattu.
cast off 1 *vi* (*Naut*) larguer les amarres; (*Knitting*) arrêter les mailles. **2** *vt sep* (*Naut*) larguer les amarres de; (*Knitting*) arrêter; *chains* se libérer de.
cast on (*Knitting*) **1** *vi* monter les mailles. **2** *vt sep* monter.
cast up *vt sep* (*reproach*) reprocher (*sth to sb* qch à qn).
♦ **castaway** *n* naufragé(e) *m(f).* ♦ **casting** *adj*: **to have a ~ing vote** avoir voix prépondérante. ♦ **cast-iron 1** *n* fonte *f*; **2** *adj* de *or* en fonte; (*fig*) *case* solide. ♦ **cast-off clothes** *or* ♦ **cast-offs** *npl* vêtements *mpl* dont on ne veut plus, (*pej*) vieilles nippes* *fpl.*
castanets [ˌkæstə'nets] *npl* castagnettes *fpl.*
caste [kɑːst] **1** *n* caste *f.* **2** *adj mark* de caste.
caster ['kɑːstəʳ] *n* (*wheel*) roulette *f.* ♦ **caster sugar** *n* sucre *m* en poudre.
castigate ['kæstɪgeɪt] *vt person* châtier; *book etc* critiquer sévèrement.
castle ['kɑːsl] **1** *n* château *m* (fort); (*Chess*) tour *f.* **~s in the air** châteaux en Espagne. **2** *vi* (*Chess*) roquer.
castor[1] ['kɑːstəʳ] *n* = **caster.**
castor[2] ['kɑːstəʳ] *n*: **~ oil** huile *f* de ricin.
castrate [kæs'treɪt] *vt* (*Anat*) châtrer; (*fig*) *text, film* expurger. ♦ **castration** *n* castration *f.*
casual ['kæʒjʊl] **1** *adj* **(a)** (*by chance*) *error* fortuit; *fall, spark* accidentel; *meeting* de hasard; *glance* jeté au hasard; *walk, stroll* sans but précis; *caller* venu par hasard; *remark* fait en passant. **a ~ acquaintance (of mine)** qn que je connais un peu; **a ~ (love) affair** une aventure; **to have ~ sex** faire l'amour au hasard d'une rencontre. **(b)** (*informal*) *person, manners* sans-gêne *inv*; *tone, voice* désinvolte; *clothes* sport *inv.* **to sound ~** parler avec désinvolture; **he was very ~ about it** il a pris tout ça avec beaucoup de désinvolture. **(c)** *work* intermittent; *worker* temporaire. **~ conversation** conversation *f* à bâtons rompus; **~ labourer** (*on building sites*) ouvrier *m* sans travail fixe; (*on a farm*) journalier *m.*
2 *n* (*shoes*) **~s** chaussures *fpl* de sport.
♦ **casually** *adv* (*by chance*) par hasard, fortuitement; (*informally*) avec sans-gêne, avec désinvolture; *mention* en passant.
casualty ['kæʒjʊltɪ] **1** *n* **(a)** (*Mil*) (*dead*) mort(e) *m(f)*; (*wounded*) blessé(e) *m(f).* **casualties** les morts *mpl* et blessés *mpl*; (*dead*) les pertes *fpl.* **(b)** (*accident victim*) victime *f*; (*accident*) accident *m.* **2** *adj*: **~ list** (*Mil*) état *m* des pertes; (*Aviat, gen*) liste *f* des victimes; **~ ward** salle *f* de traumatologie.
cat [kæt] *n* chat(te) *m(f)*; (*species*) félin *m*; (**pej: woman*) rosse* *f.* **to let the ~ out of the bag** vendre la mèche; **the ~'s out of the bag** ce n'est plus un secret maintenant; **to fight like ~ and dog** s'entendre comme chien et chat; **to be like a ~ on hot bricks** être sur des charbons ardents; **when the ~'s away the mice will play** quand le chat n'est pas là les souris dansent; **that set the ~ among the pigeons** ça a été le pavé dans la mare.
♦ **cat-and-mouse** *adj*: **to play a ~-and-mouse game with sb** jouer avec qn comme un chat avec une souris. ♦ **cat-burglar** *n* monte-en-l'air* *m inv.* ♦ **catcall** *n* (*Theat*) sifflet *m.* ♦ **catfish** *n* poisson-chat *m.* ♦ **catgut** *n* (*Mus, Sport*) boyau *m* (de chat); (*Med*) catgut *m.* ♦ **catlike 1** *adj* félin; **2** *adv* comme un chat. ♦ **catnap** *n*: **to take a ~nap** faire un (petit) somme. ♦ **cat-o'nine-tails** *n* martinet *m.* ♦ **cat's-eyes** *npl* (*Aut*) cataphotes *mpl.* ♦ **cat's-paw** *n* dupe *f* (*qui tire les marrons du feu*). ♦ **catsuit** *n* combinaison-pantalon *f.* ♦ **cattiness** *n* méchanceté *f*, rosserie* *f.* ♦ **catty** *adj* méchant, rosse*; **~ty remark** rosserie* *f*; **to be ~ty about sb/sth** dire des rosseries* de qn/qch. ♦ **catwalk** *n* passerelle *f.*
cataclysm ['kætəklɪzəm] *n* cataclysme *m.*
catalogue, (*US*) **catalog** ['kætəlɒg] **1** *n* catalogue *m.* **2** *vt* cataloguer.
catalyst ['kætəlɪst] *n* catalyseur *m.*
catamaran [ˌkætəmə'ræn] *n* catamaran *m.*
catapult ['kætəpʌlt] **1** *n* (*slingshot*) lance-pierres *m inv*; (*Aviat, Mil*) catapulte *f.* **2** *vt* catapulter.
cataract ['kætərækt] *n* (*Geog, Med*) cataracte *f.*
catarrh [kə'tɑːʳ] *n* catarrhe *m.*
catastrophe [kə'tæstrəfɪ] *n* catastrophe *f.* ♦ **catastrophic** [ˌkætə'strɒfɪk] *adj* catastrophique.
catch [kætʃ] (*vb: pret, ptp* **caught**) **1** *n* (*thing caught*) prise *f*, capture *f*; (*person caught*) capture; (*Fishing*) pêche *f*, (*single fish*) prise; (*drawback*) attrape *f*, entourloupette* *f.* **where's the ~?** qu'est-ce qui se cache là-dessous?; **with a ~ in one's voice** d'une voix entrecoupée.
2 *adj*: **~ question** colle* *f.*
3 *vt* **(a)** (*gen*) attraper; *fish, mice, thief* prendre, attraper. **to ~ sb by the arm** prendre *or* saisir qn par le bras; **you can usually ~ me (in) around noon*** en général on peut m'avoir* *or* me trouver vers midi; **to ~ sb doing sth** surprendre qn à faire qch; **if I ~ you at it again!** que je t'y reprenne!; **you won't ~ me doing that again** il n'y a pas de danger que je recommence (*subj*); **caught in the**

act pris en flagrant délit; **caught in a storm** pris dans un orage; **to get caught by sb** se laisser attraper par qn; **I must ~ the train** il ne faut pas que je manque le train; **he caught his train** il a eu son train; **to ~ the post** arriver à temps pour la levée; **to ~ one's foot in sth** se prendre le pied dans qch. **(b)** (*understand, hear*) saisir, comprendre. **(c)** *flavour* sentir; *sound* percevoir; *tune, disease* attraper; *attention* attirer. **to ~ a cold** attraper un rhume; **to ~ cold** prendre froid; **to ~ one's death**: attraper la crève:; **to ~ one's breath** retenir son souffle (un instant); **to ~ fire** prendre feu; **to ~ sight of** apercevoir; **you'll ~ it!*** tu vas prendre quelque chose!*

4 *vi [fire, wood, ice]* prendre. **her dress caught in the door/on a nail** sa robe s'est prise dans la porte/s'est accrochée à un clou.

catch at *vt fus object* (essayer d')attraper; *opportunity* sauter sur.

catch on *vi [fashion]* prendre; *[song]* marcher; (*understand*) comprendre (*to sth* qch).

catch out *vt sep* (*catch sb napping*) prendre en défaut; (*catch sb in the act*) prendre sur le fait. **to ~ sb out in a lie** surprendre qn en train de mentir.

catch up 1 *vi* (*gen*) se rattraper; (*with news*) se remettre au courant. **to ~ up on one's work** se mettre à jour dans son travail; **to ~ up with sb** rattraper qn. **2** *vt sep* **(a)** *person* rattraper. **(b)** (*pick up quickly*) ramasser vivement.

♦ **catch-22** *adj*: **it's a ~-22* situation** il n'y a pas moyen de s'en sortir. ♦ **catch-as-catch-can** *n* catch *m.* ♦ **catching** *adj* contagieux. ♦ **catchment** *n*: **~ment area** *[hospital]* circonscription *f* hospitalière; *[school]* aire *f* de recrutement. ♦ **catch-phrase** *n* cliché *m*, scie *f*; (*striking phrase*) slogan *m* accrocheur. ♦ **catchword** *n* slogan *m.* ♦ **catchy** *adj*: **~y tune** air entraînant.

catechism ['kætɪkɪzəm] *n* catéchisme *m.* ♦ **catechist** *n* catéchiste *mf.* ♦ **catechize** *vt* catéchiser.

category ['kætɪgərɪ] *n* catégorie *f.* ♦ **categoric(al)** *adj* catégorique. ♦ **categorically** *adv* catégoriquement. ♦ **categorize** *vt* classer par catégories.

cater ['keɪtəʳ] *vi* (*provide food*) préparer un *or* des repas (*for* pour). **to ~ for** *sb's needs* pourvoir à; *sb's tastes* satisfaire; **this magazine ~s for all ages** ce magazine s'adresse à tous les âges. ♦ **caterer** *n* fournisseur *m* (*en alimentation*). ♦ **catering 1** *n* (*providing supplies*) approvisionnement *m*; (*providing meals*) restauration *f*; **the ~ing was done by ...** le buffet a été confié à ...; **2** *adj*: **~ing trade** restauration *f.*

caterpillar ['kætəpɪləʳ] **1** *n* (*Zool, Tech*) chenille *f.* **2** *adj vehicle* à chenilles. **~ tractor** autochenille *f.*

caterwaul ['kætəwɔ:l] *vi [cat]* miauler; *[person]* brailler. ♦ **caterwauling** *n* miaulement *m*; braillements *mpl.*

cathedral [kə'θi:drəl] *n* cathédrale *f.* **~ city** évêché *m.*

catheter ['kæθɪtəʳ] *n* (*Med*) sonde *f* creuse.

cathode ['kæθəʊd] *n* cathode *f.* **~ ray tube** tube *m* cathodique.

catholic ['kæθəlɪk] **1** *adj* **(a)** (*Rel*) **C~** catholique; **the C~ Church** l'Église *f* catholique. **(b)** (*universal*) universel; (*broad-minded*) libéral. **~ tastes** goûts *mpl* éclectiques; **~ views** opinions libérales. **2** *n*: **C~** catholique *mf.* ♦ **Catholicism** *n* catholicisme *m.*

catkin ['kætkɪn] *n* (*Bot*) chaton *m.*

cattle ['kætl] **1** *collective n* bétail *m*, bestiaux *mpl.* **herded like ~** parqués comme du bétail. **2** *adj*: **~ breeder** éleveur *m* (de bétail); **'~ crossing'** 'passage *m* de troupeaux'; **~ shed** étable *f*; **~ show** concours *m* agricole; **~ truck** fourgon *m* à bestiaux. ♦ **cattleman** *n* bouvier *m.*

caucus ['kɔ:kəs] *n* (*US: committee*) comité *m* électoral; (*pej*) coterie *f* politique.

caught [kɔ:t] *pret, ptp of* **catch.**

cauldron ['kɔ:ldrən] *n* chaudron *m.*

cauliflower ['kɒlɪflaʊəʳ] **1** *n* chou-fleur *m.* **2** *adj* (*Culin*) **~ cheese** chou-fleur *m* au gratin; (*fig*) **~ ear** oreille *f* en chou-fleur.

cause [kɔ:z] **1** *n* cause *f.* **~ and effect** la cause et l'effet *m*; **the relation of ~ and effect** la relation de cause à effet; **to be the ~ of** être cause de; **she has no ~ to be angry** elle n'a aucune raison de se fâcher; **there's no ~ for anxiety** il n'y a pas de raison de s'inquiéter *or* pas de quoi s'inquiéter; **with ~** à juste titre; **without good ~** sans raison valable; **~ for complaint** sujet *m* de plainte; **in the ~ of justice** pour (la cause de) la justice; **it's all in a good ~*** c'est pour le bien de la communauté; **to plead sb's ~** plaider la cause de qn. **2** *vt* causer. **to ~ trouble to sb** (*problems*) créer des ennuis à qn; (*disturbance*) déranger qn; **to ~ sb to do sth** faire faire qch à qn; **to ~ sth to be done** faire faire qch. ♦ **causal** *adj* causal. ♦ **causality** *or* ♦ **causation** *n* causalité *f.* ♦ **causative** *adj* causatif.

causeway ['kɔ:zweɪ] *n* chaussée *f.*

caustic ['kɔ:stɪk] *adj* caustique.

cauterize ['kɔ:təraɪz] *vt* cautériser.

caution ['kɔ:ʃən] **1** *n* (*gen*) prudence *f*, circonspection *f*; (*warning*) avertissement *m*; (*rebuke*) réprimande *f.* (*Aut*) **proceed with ~** avancez lentement. **2** *vt* avertir. (*Police*) **to ~ sb** informer qn de ses droits; **to ~ sb against sth/against doing sth** déconseiller qch à qn/à qn de faire qch. ♦ **cautionary** *adj*: **~ary tale** récit *m* édifiant.

cautious ['kɔ:ʃəs] *adj* prudent, circonspect. **to be ~ about doing sth** longuement réfléchir avant de faire qch. ♦ **cautiously** *adv* prudemment, avec circonspection. ♦ **cautiousness** *n* prudence *f*, circonspection *f.*

cavalier [,kævə'lɪəʳ] **1** *n* cavalier *m*; (*Hist*) royaliste *m.* **2** *adj* cavalier.

cavalry ['kævəlrɪ] *n* cavalerie *f.*

cave [keɪv] **1** *n* caverne *f*, grotte *f.* **2** *adj*: **~ painting** peinture *f* rupestre. **3** *vi*: **to go caving** faire de la spéléologie.

cave in *vi [floor, building]* s'effondrer; *[wall, beam]* céder; (*: *yield*) se dégonfler*.

♦ **cave-in** *n* effondrement *m.* ♦ **caveman** *n* homme *m* des cavernes. ♦ **caving** *n* spéléologie *f.*

caveat ['kævɪæt] *n* avertissement *m.*

cavern ['kævən] *n* caverne *f.* ♦ **cavernous** *adj darkness* épais; *eyes* cave; *voice* caverneux; *yawn* profond.

caviar(e) ['kævɪɑ:ʳ] *n* caviar *m.*

cavil ['kævɪl] *vi* ergoter (*about, at* sur).

cavity ['kævɪtɪ] *n* cavité *f.* **~ wall insulation** isolation *f* des murs creux.

cavort* [kə'vɔ:t] *vi* faire des gambades.

caw [kɔ:] **1** *vi* croasser. **2** *n* croassement *m.*

cayenne ['keɪen] *n* (*pepper*) (poivre *m* de) cayenne *m.*

cease [si:s] **1** *vi* cesser, s'arrêter. **2** *vt* cesser, arrêter (*doing* de faire). **to ~ fire** cesser le feu. ♦ **ceasefire** *n* cessez-le-feu *m inv.* ♦ **ceaseless** *adj* incessant. ♦ **ceaselessly** *adv* sans cesse, sans arrêt.

cedar ['si:dəʳ] *n* cèdre *m.*

cede [si:d] *vt* céder.

cedilla [sɪ'dɪlə] *n* cédille *f.*

ceiling ['si:lɪŋ] **1** *n* plafond *m.* **to hit the ~*** (*get angry*) piquer une crise*; *[prices]* crever le plafond.

2 *adj lamp, covering* de plafond; *price* plafond *inv.*

celebrate ['selɪbreɪt] *vt* (*gen*) célébrer; *event* fêter; *anniversary* commémorer; *mass* célébrer. **let's ~!*** il faut fêter ça!; (*with drink*) il faut arroser ça!* ♦ **celebrated** *adj* célèbre.

♦ **celebration** *n* (*occasion*) festivités *fpl*; (*act*) célébration *f*; **we must have a celebration** il faut fêter cela. ♦ **celebrity** *n* célébrité *f*.
celeriac [sə'leriæk] *n* céleri(-rave) *m*.
celery ['seləri] *n* céleri *m* (à côtes). **head/stick of ~** pied *m*/côte *f* de céleri.
celestial [sɪ'lestɪəl] *adj* (*lit, fig*) céleste.
celibacy ['selɪbəsɪ] *n* célibat *m*. ♦ **celibate** *adj, n* célibataire (*mf*).
cell [sel] *n* (*gen*) cellule *f*; (*Elec*) élément *m* (*de pile*). ♦ **cellular** *adj* (*Anat, Bio*) cellulaire; *blanket* en cellular. ♦ **Celluloid** *n* ® celluloïd *m* ®.
cellar ['selə^r] *n [wine, coal]* cave *f*; *[food etc]* cellier *m*.
cello ['tʃeləʊ] *n* violoncelle *m*. ♦ **cellist** *n* violoncelliste *mf*.
cellophane ['seləfeɪn] *n* ® cellophane *f* ®.
cellulose ['seljʊləʊs] *n* cellulose *f*.
Celsius ['selsɪəs] *adj* Celsius *inv*.
Celt [kelt, selt] *n* Celte *mf*. ♦ **Celtic** ['keltɪk, 'seltɪk] **1** *adj* celtique, celte; **2** *n* celtique *m*.
cement [sə'ment] **1** *n* ciment *m*. **2** *vt* cimenter. **3** *adj*: **~ mixer** bétonnière *f*.
cemetery ['semɪtrɪ] *n* cimetière *m*.
cenotaph ['senətɑ:f] *n* cénotaphe *m*.
censor ['sensə^r] **1** *n* censeur *m*. **2** *vt* censurer. ♦ **censorship** *n* censure *f*.
censure ['senʃə^r] **1** *vt* blâmer. **2** *n* blâme *m*.
census ['sensəs] *n* recensement *m*.
cent [sent] *n* **(a) per ~** pour cent. **(b)** (*money*) cent *m*. **not a ~*** pas un sou.
centenary [sen'ti:nərɪ] *adj, n* centenaire (*m*). ♦ **centenarian** *adj, n* centenaire (*mf*).
centennial [sen'tenɪəl] **1** *adj* (*100 years old*) centenaire; (*every 100 years*) séculaire. **2** *n* centenaire *m*.
center ['sentə^r] *n* (*US*) = **centre.**
centigrade ['sentɪgreɪd] *adj* centigrade.
centimetre, (*US*) **-ter** ['sentɪˌmi:tə^r] *n* centimètre *m*.
centipede ['sentɪpi:d] *n* mille-pattes *m inv*.
central ['sentrəl] **1** *adj* central. **C~ America/Europe** Amérique/Europe centrale; **C~ European** (habitant(e) *m(f)*) de l'Europe centrale; **~ heating** chauffage central; (*Aut*) **~ reservation** bande médiane. **2** *n* (*US*) central *m* téléphonique. ♦ **centralization** *n* centralisation *f*. ♦ **centralize** **1** *vt* centraliser; **2** *vi* se centraliser. ♦ **centrally** *adv*: **~ly heated** doté du chauffage central.
centre, (*US*) **-ter** ['sentə^r] **1** *n* centre *m*. **in the ~** au centre. **2** *vt* centrer. **3** *vi* tourner (*on* autour de). ♦ **centre-board** *n* dérive *f* (*d'un bateau*). ♦ **centre-fold** *n* double page *f* (détachable). ♦ **centre-forward** *n* avant-centre *m*. ♦ **centre-half** *n* demi-centre *m*.
centrifugal [sen'trɪfjʊgəl] *adj* centrifuge. ♦ **centrifuge** *n* centrifugeuse *f*.
century ['sentjʊrɪ] *n* siècle *m*. **in the twentieth ~** au vingtième siècle. ♦ **centuries-old** *adj* séculaire.
ceramic [sɪ'ræmɪk] **1** *adj art* céramique; *vase* en céramique. **2** *n*: **~s** céramique *f*.
cereal ['sɪərɪəl] *n* (*plant*) céréale *f*; (*grain*) grain *m* (*de céréale*). **baby ~** blédine *f* ®; **breakfast ~** flocons *mpl* de céréales.
ceremony ['serɪmənɪ] *n* (*event*) cérémonie *f*; (*pomp*) cérémonies *fpl*, façons *fpl*. **to stand on ~** faire des cérémonies *or* des façons; **without ~** sans cérémonies. ♦ **ceremonial** **1** *adj rite* cérémoniel; *dress* de cérémonie; **2** *n* cérémonial *m*. ♦ **ceremonially** *adv* selon le cérémonial d'usage. ♦ **ceremonious** *adj* solennel; (*slightly pej*) cérémonieux. ♦ **ceremoniously** *adv* solennellement; (*slightly pej*) cérémonieusement.
cert* [sɜ:t] *n*: **it's a dead ~** c'est sûr et certain*.
certain ['sɜ:tən] *adj* **(a)** (*sure*) certain, sûr; *death, success* certain, inévitable; *remedy* infaillible. **he is ~ to go** il est certain qu'il ira; **that's for ~*** c'est sûr et certain*; **I cannot say for ~ that ...** je ne peux pas affirmer que ...; **I don't know for ~** je n'en suis pas sûr; **I am ~ he didn't do it** je suis certain qu'il n'a pas fait cela; **be ~ to go** allez-y sans faute, ne manquez pas d'y aller; **you can be ~ of success** vous êtes sûr de réussir; **to make ~ of sth/that ...** s'assurer de qch/que ... **(b)** (*particular*) certain (*before n*). **a ~ gentleman** un certain monsieur. ♦ **certainly** *adv* certainement, sans aucun doute; **~ly!** bien sûr!; **~ly not!** certainement pas!; **I shall ~ly be there** j'y serai sans faute; **you may ~ly leave** vous pouvez partir, bien sûr. ♦ **certainty** *n* certitude *f*.
certify ['sɜ:tɪfaɪ] **1** *vt* **(a)** certifier (*that* que). **certified as a true copy** certifié conforme; **to ~ sb (insane)** déclarer qn atteint d'aliénation mentale. **(b)** (*Comm*) *goods* garantir. (*US*) **to send by certified mail** ≃ envoyer avec avis de réception. **2** *vi*: **to ~ to sth** attester qch. ♦ **certifiable** *adj* qu'on peut certifier; (*: *mad*) bon à enfermer. ♦ **certificate** [sə'tɪfɪkɪt] *n* (*legal*) certificat *m*; (*academic*) diplôme *m*. ♦ **certificated** *adj* diplômé. ♦ **certification** *n* certification *f*.
certitude ['sɜ:tɪtju:d] *n* certitude *f*.
cervix ['sɜ:vɪks] *n* col *m* de l'utérus. ♦ **cervical** *adj*: **cervical smear** frottis *m* vaginal.
cessation [se'seɪʃən] *n* cessation *f*.
cesspit ['sespɪt] *n* fosse *f* à purin.
cesspool ['sespu:l] *n* fosse *f* d'aisance.
chafe [tʃeɪf] **1** *vt* (*rub*) frotter, frictionner; (*rub against*) frotter contre, gratter; (*wear through*) user (en frottant). (*from cold*) **~d lips/hands** lèvres/mains gercées.
2 *vi* s'user; (*fig*) s'impatienter, s'irriter (*at, against* de).
chaff[1] [tʃɑ:f] *n [grain]* balle *f*; (*cut straw*) menue paille *f*.
chaff[2] [tʃɑ:f] *vt* (*tease*) taquiner.
chaffinch ['tʃæfɪntʃ] *n* pinson *m*.
chagrin ['ʃægrɪn] *n* vive déception, vif dépit. **much to my ~** à mon vif dépit.
chain [tʃeɪn] **1** *n* **(a)** (*gen*) chaîne *f*. **in ~s** enchaîné; *[lavatory]* **to pull the ~** tirer la chasse (d'eau). **(b)** *[mountains, atoms, shops]* chaîne *f*; *[ideas]* enchaînement *m*; *[events]* série *f*, suite *f*. *[people]* **to make a ~** faire la chaîne. **2** *adj*: **~ letters** chaîne *f* (de lettres); **~ mail** cotte *f* de mailles; **~ reaction** réaction *f* en chaîne; **~ smoke** fumer cigarette sur cigarette; **~ smoker** fumeur *m*, -euse *f* invétéré(e); **~ store** grand magasin (à succursales multiples). **3** *vt* enchaîner; *dog* mettre à l'attache.
chair [tʃɛə^r] **1** *n* (*gen*) chaise *f*; (*arm~*) fauteuil *m*; (*seat*) siège *m*; (*Univ*) chaire *f*; (*wheel~*) fauteuil roulant. **to take a ~** s'asseoir; **dentist's ~** fauteuil de dentiste; (*US: electric ~*) **to go to the ~** passer à la chaise électrique; (*at meeting*) **to be in the ~** présider; **~! ~!** à l'ordre! **2** *vt meeting* présider; *hero* porter en triomphe. ♦ **chairlift** *n* télésiège *m*. ♦ **chairman** *n* président *m* (*d'un comité etc*). ♦ **chairmanship** *n* présidence *f*. ♦ **chairperson*** *n* président(e) *m(f)*.
chalet ['ʃæleɪ] *n* (*gen*) chalet *m*; *[motel]* bungalow *m*.
chalice ['tʃælɪs] *n* calice *m*.
chalk [tʃɔ:k] **1** *n* craie *f*. **a (piece of) ~** une craie, un morceau de craie; **they're as different as ~ from cheese** c'est le jour et la nuit; **by a long ~** de beaucoup, de loin; **not by a long ~** loin de là. **2** *vt* écrire à la craie; *luggage* marquer à la craie.
chalk up *vt sep achievement, victory* remporter. (*amount owed*) **~ it up** mettez-le sur mon compte; **he ~ed it up to experience** il l'a mis au compte de l'expérience.
♦ **chalkpit** *n* carrière *f* de craie. ♦ **chalky** *adj* crayeux.
challenge ['tʃælɪndʒ] **1** *n* défi *m*; (*by sentry*) sommation *f*. **to put out a ~** lancer un défi; **to take**

up the ~ reveler le défi; **the ~ of new ideas** la stimulation qu'offrent de nouvelles idées; **the ~ of the 20th century** le défi du 20e siècle; **Smith's ~ for leadership** la tentative qu'a faite Smith pour s'emparer du pouvoir; **the job was a great ~ to him** il a pris cette tâche comme une gageure. **2** *vt* défier (*sb to do* qn de faire); (*Sport*) inviter (*sb to a game* qn à faire une partie); *statement* mettre en question, contester; *[sentry]* faire une sommation à; *juror, jury* récuser. **to ~ sb to a duel** provoquer qn en duel; **to ~ sb's authority to do** contester à qn le droit de faire; **to ~ the wisdom of a plan** mettre en question la sagesse d'un projet. ♦ **challenger** *n* provocateur *m*, -trice *f*; (*Sport*) challenger *m*. ♦ **challenging** *adj remark* provocateur; *look, tone* de défi; *book* stimulant; **this is a very challenging situation** cette situation est une véritable gageure.

chamber ['tʃeɪmbəʳ] **1** *n* (*hall*) chambre *f*; (†: *room*) pièce *f*; (*bed~*) chambre. **~s** *[barrister, judge, magistrate]* cabinet *m*; *[solicitor]* étude *f*; **C~ of Commerce** Chambre de commerce; (*Parl*) **the Upper/Lower C~** la Chambre Haute/Basse; **the C~ of Horrors** la Chambre d'épouvante. **2** *adj*: **~ music** musique *f* de chambre. ♦ **chambermaid** *n* femme *f* de chambre (*dans un hôtel*). ♦ **chamberpot** *n* pot *m* de chambre.

chamberlain ['tʃeɪmbəlɪn] *n* chambellan *m*.

chameleon [kə'miːlɪən] *n* caméléon *m*.

chamois ['ʃæmwɑː] *n* **(a)** (*Zool*) chamois *m*. **(b)** ['ʃæmɪ] (*~ cloth*) chamois *m*. **~ leather** peau *f* de chamois.

champ [tʃæmp] *vti* mâchonner. **to ~ at the bit** ronger son frein.

champagne [ʃæm'peɪn] *n* champagne *m*.

champion ['tʃæmpjən] **1** *n* champion(ne) *m(f)*. **world ~** champion(ne) du monde; **skiing ~** champion(ne) de ski. **2** *adj* sans rival, de première classe; *show animal* champion. **~ swimmer** champion(ne) *m(f)* de natation. **3** *vt* défendre, soutenir. ♦ **championship** *n* (*Sport*) championnat *m*; *[cause etc]* défense *f*.

chance [tʃɑːns] **1** *n* **(a)** (*luck*) hasard *m*. **by ~** par hasard; **have you a pen by (any) ~?** auriez-vous par hasard un stylo?; **a game of ~** un jeu de hasard; **he left nothing to ~** il n'a rien laissé au hasard. **(b)** (*possibility*) chances *fpl*, possibilité *f*. **he hasn't much ~ of winning** il n'a pas beaucoup de chances de gagner; **the ~s are that** il y a de grandes chances que + *subj*, il est très possible que + *subj*; **the ~s are against that happening** il y a peu de chances pour que cela arrive (*subj*); **there is little ~ of his coming** il est peu probable qu'il vienne; **you'll have to take a ~ on his coming** vous verrez bien s'il vient ou non; **he's taking no ~s** il ne veut prendre aucun risque. **(c)** (*opportunity*) occasion *f*, chance *f*. **I had the ~ to go *or* of going** j'ai eu l'occasion d'y aller; **if there's a ~ of buying it** s'il y a une possibilité d'achat; **she was waiting for her ~** elle attendait son heure; **now's your ~!** vas-y!, saute sur l'occasion!; **this is his big ~** c'est le grand moment pour lui; **give him another ~** laisse-lui encore sa chance; **he never had a ~ in life** il n'a jamais eu sa chance dans la vie; **give me a ~ to show you ...** donnez-moi la possibilité de vous montrer ... .

2 *adj error, remark* fortuit; *companion* rencontré par hasard; *discovery* accidentel; *meeting* de hasard.

3 *vt* (*happen*) **to ~ to do** faire par hasard; (*risk*) **to ~ doing** prendre le risque de faire; **to ~ it, to ~ one's arm*** risquer le coup*.

chance upon *vt fus person* rencontrer par hasard; *thing* trouver par hasard.

♦ **chancy*** *adj* risqué.

chancel ['tʃɑːnsəl] *n* chœur *m* (*d'une église*).

chancellor ['tʃɑːnsələʳ] *n* chancelier *m*. **C~ of the Exchequer** Chancelier *m* de l'Échiquier.

chandelier [ˌʃændə'lɪəʳ] *n* lustre *m*.

chandler ['tʃɑːndləʳ] *n*: **ship's ~** shipchandler *m*, marchand *m* de fournitures pour bateaux.

change [tʃeɪndʒ] **1** *n* **(a)** changement *m* (*from* de, *into* en). **a ~ for the better/worse** un changement en mieux/en pire; **~ in the weather** changement de temps; **just for a ~** pour changer un peu; **to have a ~ of heart** changer d'avis; **it makes a ~*** ça change un peu; **it will be a nice ~** cela nous fera un changement; **the ~ of life** le retour d'âge; **~ of address** changement d'adresse; **a ~ of clothes** des vêtements de rechange; **~ of air *or* scene** changement d'air; **she likes ~** elle aime le changement *or* la variété.

(b) (*money*) monnaie *f*. **small *or* loose ~** petite monnaie; **can you give me ~ of £1?** pouvez-vous me faire la monnaie d'une livre?; **you don't get much ~ from a fiver** il ne reste pas grand-chose d'un billet de cinq livres; (*fig*) **you won't get much ~ out of him*** tu perds ton temps avec lui.

2 *vt* **(a)** (*by substitution*) *clothes, one's address, trains, one's name* changer de. **to ~ colour** changer de couleur; **to ~ hands** changer de main; **a sum of money ~d hands** une somme d'argent a été échangée; **to ~ the guard** faire la relève de la garde; (*Theat*) **to ~ the scene** changer le décor; **let's ~ the subject** parlons d'autre chose; **to ~ one's tune** changer de ton; **to ~ one's opinion *or* mind** changer d'avis; **to ~ gear** changer de vitesse; (*Aut*) **to ~ a wheel** changer une roue.

(b) (*exchange*) échanger (*sth for sth else* qch contre qch d'autre). **to ~ places (with sb)** changer de place (avec qn); (*fig*) **I wouldn't like to ~ places with you** je n'aimerais pas être à votre place; **to ~ ends** (*Tennis*) changer de côté; (*Ftbl etc*) changer de camp; **to ~ sides** changer de camp.

(c) *banknote, coin* faire la monnaie de, changer; *foreign currency* changer, convertir (*into* en).

(d) (*alter*) changer, transformer (*sth into sth else* qch en qch d'autre). **the witch ~d him into a cat** la sorcière l'a changé en chat.

3 *vi* **(a)** (*become different*) changer (*into* en). **you've ~d a lot** tu as beaucoup changé; **the prince ~d into a swan** le prince s'est changé en cygne.

(b) (*~ clothes*) se changer. **she ~d into an old skirt** elle s'est changée et a mis une vieille jupe.

(c) (*Rail etc*) changer. **all ~!** tout le monde descend!

change down *vi* (*Aut*) rétrograder.

change over *vi* passer (*from* de, *to* à); *[2 people, teams etc]* faire l'échange.

change up *vi* (*Aut*) monter les vitesses.

♦ **changeable** *adj person, character, colour* changeant; *weather* variable. ♦ **changeless** *adj rite* immuable; *character* inaltérable. ♦ **changeling** *n* enfant *mf* changé(e) (*substitué à un enfant volé*). ♦ **changeover** *n* changement *m* (*from* de, *to* à); *[guard]* relève *f*. ♦ **changing 1** *adj wind* variable; *expression* mobile; **2** *n*: **the changing of the guard** la relève de la garde. ♦ **changing-room** *n* vestiaire *m*.

channel ['tʃænl] **1** *n* (*navigable passage*) chenal *m*; (*between land masses*) bras *m* de mer; *[irrigation]* rigole *f*; (*in street*) caniveau *m*; (*groove in surface*) rainure *f*; (*Archit*) cannelure *f*; (*TV*) chaîne *f*. **the (English) C~** la Manche; **he directed the conversation into a new ~** il a fait prendre à la conversation une nouvelle direction; **~ of communication** voie *f* de communication; **to go through the usual ~s** suivre la filière (habituelle). **2** *adj* (*Geog*) **the C~ Isles *or* Islands** les îles Anglo-Normandes; **the C~ tunnel** le tunnel sous la Manche. **3** *vt* canaliser (*into* dans, *towards* vers).

chant [tʃɑːnt] **1** *n* (*Mus*) chant *m*; (*Rel Mus*) psalmodie *f*; *[demonstrators, audience etc]* chant

scandé. **2** *vt* (*gen*) chanter; (*recite*) réciter; (*speak rhythmically*) entonner sur l'air des lampions; (*Rel*) psalmodier; *[demonstrators etc]* scander. **3** *vi* chanter; psalmodier; scander des slogans.
chaos ['keɪɒs] *n* chaos *m*. ♦ **chaotic** *adj* chaotique.
chap[1] [tʃæp] **1** *n* (*in skin*) gerçure *f*. **2** *vi* se gercer.
chap[2]* [tʃæp] *n* (*man*) homme *m*, type* *m*. **old ~** mon vieux*; **a nice ~** un chic type*; **poor little ~** pauvre petit.
chapel ['tʃæpəl] *n* chapelle *f*; (*nonconformist church*) église *f*, temple *m*.
chaperon(e) ['ʃæpərəʊn] **1** *n* chaperon *m*. **2** *vt* chaperonner.
chaplain ['tʃæplɪn] *n* (*gen*) aumônier *m*; (*to nobleman etc*) chapelain *m*.
chapter ['tʃæptəʳ] *n* chapitre *m*. **in ~ 4** au chapitre 4; **to quote ~ and verse** citer ses références; **a ~ of accidents** une succession de mésaventures.
char[1] [tʃɑːʳ] *vt* (*burn black*) carboniser.
char[2]* [tʃɑːʳ] **1** *n* (*~lady, ~woman*) femme *f* de ménage. **2** *vi* faire des ménages.
character ['kærɪktəʳ] **1** *n* (*most senses*) caractère *m*. **he has the same ~ as his brother** il a le même caractère que son frère; **it's very much in ~ (for him)** cela lui ressemble tout à fait; **it takes ~ to do ...** il faut avoir du caractère pour faire ...; **he's quite a ~** c'est un numéro*; **he's a queer ~** c'est un type* curieux; **of good ~** qui a une bonne réputation; **Gothic ~s** caractères gothiques. **2** *adj*: **~ actor/actress** acteur *m*/actrice *f* de genre; **~ comedy** comédie *f* de caractère; **~ part** rôle *m* de composition.
♦ **characteristic 1** *adj* caractéristique, typique; **with (his) ~istic enthusiasm** avec l'enthousiasme qui le caractérise; **2** *n* caractéristique *f*. ♦ **characteristically** *adv* d'une façon caractéristique, typiquement. ♦ **characterization** *n* caractérisation *f*; (*Theat*) représentation *f* des caractères; (*Literat*) peinture *f* des caractères. ♦ **characterize** *vt* caractériser. ♦ **characterless** *adj* sans caractère, fade.
charcoal ['tʃɑːkəʊl] **1** *n* charbon *m* de bois. **2** *adj sketch* au charbon; (*colour*) gris anthracite *inv*.
charge [tʃɑːdʒ] **1** *n* **(a)** (*Jur etc*) accusation *f*. **to bring a ~ against sb** porter plainte contre qn; **arrested on a ~ of murder** arrêté sous l'inculpation de meurtre. **(b)** (*Mil*) charge *f*, attaque *f*. **(c)** (*cost*) prix *m*. **to make a ~ for sth** faire payer qch; **is there a ~?** y a-t-il qch à payer?; **free of ~** gratuit; **at a ~ of ...** moyennant ...; **extra ~** supplément *m*; **~ for admission** droit *m* d'entrée; **~ for delivery** (frais *mpl* de) port *m*. **(d)** (*responsibility*) charge *f*, responsabilité *f*. **he took ~** il a assumé la responsabilité (*or* les fonctions *etc*); **who takes ~ when ...?** qui est-ce qui est responsable quand ...?; **to take ~ of** se charger de; **to be in ~ of** avoir la garde de; **in his ~** à sa garde; **to put sb in ~ of sb/sth** charger qn de la garde de qn/qch; **to leave sb in ~ of sb/sth** confier qn/qch à la garde de qn; **the man in ~** le responsable; **the nurse and her ~s** l'infirmière et ses malades. **(e)** *[firearm, battery etc]* charge *f*.
2 *adj*: **~ account** compte *m*.
3 *vt* **(a) to ~ sb with sth** (*Jur*) inculper qn de qch; (*gen*) accuser qn de qch. **(b)** (*Mil*) charger. **(c)** *customer* faire payer; *amount* prendre, demander (*for* pour); *commission* prélever. **I ~d him £2 for this table** je lui ai fait payer cette table 2 livres; **how much do you ~ for mending shoes?** combien prenez-vous pour réparer des chaussures? **(d)** (**~ up**) *amount owed* mettre sur le compte (*to sb* de qn). **(e)** *firearm, battery* charger. **(f)** (*command*) **to ~ sb to do** sommer qn de faire.
4 *vi* **(a)** (*rush*) **to ~ in/out** entrer/sortir en coup de vent; **to ~ up/down** grimper/descendre à toute vitesse. **(b)** *[battery]* se recharger.
♦ **chargehand** *n* chef *m* d'équipe. ♦ **charger** *n* *[battery]* chargeur *m*; (*horse*) cheval *m* (de bataille).
chariot ['tʃærɪət] *n* char *m*.
charisma [kæ'rɪzmə] *n* charisme *m*, magnétisme *m*. ♦ **charismatic** *adj* charismatique, magnétique.
charity ['tʃærɪtɪ] *n* **(a)** charité *f*. **~ begins at home** charité bien ordonnée commence par soi-même; **to live on ~** vivre d'aumônes; **to collect for ~** faire une collecte pour une œuvre charitable. **(b)** (*charitable society*) œuvre *f* de bienfaisance. ♦ **charitable** *adj* charitable; **charitable institution** fondation *f* charitable. ♦ **charitably** *adv* charitablement.
charm [tʃɑːm] **1** *n* charme *m*. **it worked like a ~** ça a marché à merveille. **2** *adj*: **~ bracelet** bracelet *m* à breloques. **3** *vt* charmer. **to lead a ~ed life** être béni des dieux; **to ~ sth out of sb** obtenir qch de qn par le charme. ♦ **charmer** *n* charmeur *m*, -euse *f*. ♦ **charming** *adj* charmant. ♦ **charmingly** *adv* d'une façon charmante.
chart [tʃɑːt] **1** *n* **(a)** (*map*) carte *f* (marine). **(b)** (*graph etc*) graphique *m*, tableau *m*; (*Med*) courbe *f*. **temperature ~** feuille *f or* courbe *f* de température; **(pop) ~s** hit-parade *m*. **2** *vt route* porter sur la carte; *sales, results* faire le graphique *or* la courbe de. **this graph ~s ...** ce graphique montre ... .
charter ['tʃɑːtəʳ] **1** *n* **(a)** (*document*) charte *f*; *[society, organization]* statuts *mpl*. **(b)** (*hiring*) *[plane, coach etc]* affrètement *m*. **on ~** sous contrat d'affrètement. **2** *adj*: **~ flight** (vol *m* en) charter *m*; **by ~ flight** en charter; **~ plane** charter *m*; **~ train** train affrété. **3** *vt plane etc* affréter. ♦ **chartered** *adj*: **~ed accountant** expert-comptable *m*; **~ed surveyor** expert *m* immobilier.
chary ['tʃɛərɪ] *adj* circonspect. **~ of praise** avare de compliments; **to be ~ of doing** hésiter à faire. ♦ **charily** *adv* avec circonspection.
chase [tʃeɪs] **1** *n* chasse *f*. **to give ~ to** donner la chasse à; **in ~ of** à la poursuite de. **2** *vt* poursuivre, donner la chasse à. **3** *vi*: **to ~ up/down** *etc* monter/descendre *etc* au grand galop; **to ~ after sb** courir après qn.
chase away, chase off *vt sep* chasser, faire partir.
chase up *vt sep information* rechercher; *sth already asked for* réclamer. **to ~ sb up for sth** rappeler à qn de donner qch; **I'll ~ it** *or* **him up for you** je vais essayer d'activer les choses.
chasm ['kæzəm] *n* gouffre *m*, abîme *m*.
chassis ['ʃæsɪ] *n* châssis *m*.
chaste [tʃeɪst] *adj* chaste; *style* sobre. ♦ **chastely** *adv behave* chastement; *dress* avec sobriété. ♦ **chastity** *n* chasteté *f*.
chasten ['tʃeɪsn] *vt* (*punish*) châtier; (*subdue*) assagir. ♦ **chastening** *adj thought* qui fait réfléchir; **it had a very ~ing effect on him** cela l'a fait réfléchir *or* l'a assagi.
chastise [tʃæs'taɪz] *vt* (*punish*) châtier; (*beat*) battre, corriger. ♦ **chastisement** *n* châtiment *m*; correction *f*.
chat [tʃæt] **1** *n* causette *f*, petite conversation. **to have a ~** bavarder, parler (*with, to* avec). **2** *adj* (*Rad/TV*) **~ show** entretien *m* (radiodiffusé/télévisé). **3** *vi* bavarder, causer (*with* avec).
chat up* *vt sep girl* baratiner*.
♦ **chatty*** *adj person* bavard; *style* familier; *letter* plein de bavardages.
chatter ['tʃætəʳ] **1** *vi [people]* bavarder, causer; *[children, monkeys, birds]* jacasser. **his teeth were ~ing** il claquait des dents. **2** *n* bavardage *m*; jacassement *m*. ♦ **chatterbox** *n* moulin *m* à paroles, bavard(e) *m(f)*.
chauffeur ['ʃəʊfəʳ] *n* chauffeur *m* (de maître).

chauvinism ['ʃəʊvɪnɪzəm] *n* chauvinisme *m*. ♦ **chauvinist** *n* chauvin(e) *m(f)*.
cheap [tʃi:p] **1** *adj* bon marché *inv*, peu cher; *tickets* à prix réduit; *fare* réduit; *money* déprécié; (*pej: poor quality*) de mauvaise qualité; *success, joke* facile. **on the ~** à bon marché, pour pas cher; **it's ~ at the price** c'est bon marché à ce prix-là; (*fig*) les choses auraient pu être pires; **~er** meilleur marché, moins cher; **it's ~er in the long run** cela revient moins cher à la longue; **this stuff is ~ and nasty** c'est de la camelote*; **his behaviour was very ~** il s'est très mal conduit; **to feel ~** avoir honte (*about* de). **2** *adv* bon marché; (*cut-price*) au rabais. ♦ **cheapen** *vt* baisser le prix de; (*fig*) déprécier; **to ~ en o.s.** *[woman]* être facile; (*gen*) se déconsidérer. ♦ **cheaply** *adv* à bon marché, pour pas cher; **to get off ~ly** s'en tirer à bon compte. ♦ **cheapness** *n* bas prix *m*; (*fig*) médiocrité *f*.
cheat [tʃi:t] **1** *vt* tromper; (*swindle*) escroquer. **to ~ sb out of sth** escroquer qch à qn. **2** *vi* (*at games*) tricher (*at* à); (*defraud*) frauder. **3** *n* tricheur *m*, -euse *f*; (*crook*) escroc *m*. ♦ **cheating 1** *n* tromperie *f*; escroquerie *f*; tricherie *f*; **2** *adj* tricheur.
check[1] [tʃek] *n* (*US*) = **cheque.**
check[2] [tʃek] **1** *n* **(a)** (*setback*) *[movement]* arrêt *m* brusque; *[plans etc]* empêchement *m*; (*Mil*) revers *m*. **to hold *or* keep in ~** tenir en échec; **to put a ~ on** mettre un frein à; **to act as a ~ upon** freiner. **(b)** (*examination*) *[papers, passport, ticket]* contrôle *m*; *[luggage]* vérification *f*; (*mark*) marque *f* de contrôle. **to keep a ~ on** surveiller. **(c)** (*Chess*) **in ~** en échec; (*excl*) **~!** échec au roi! **(d)** (*receipt*) *[left luggage]* bulletin *m* de consigne; (*Theat*) contremarque *f*; *[restaurant]* addition *f*. **2** *vt* **(a)** (*examine*) *figures, quality* vérifier; *tickets, passports* contrôler. **to ~ a copy against the original** vérifier une copie sur l'original. **(b)** (*stop*) *enemy* arrêter; *advance* enrayer; (*restrain*) maîtriser. **to ~ o.s.** se contrôler. **(c)** (*rebuke*) réprimander.
check in 1 *vi* (*in hotel*) (*arrive*) arriver; (*register*) remplir une fiche (d'hôtel); (*Aviat*) se présenter à l'enregistrement. **2** *vt sep luggage* enregistrer.
check off *vt sep* pointer, cocher.
check on *vt fus* vérifier.
check out 1 *vi* (*from hotel*) régler sa note. **2** *vt sep luggage* retirer.
check over *vt sep* examiner, vérifier.
check up *vi* se renseigner, vérifier. **to ~ up on** *fact* vérifier; *person* se renseigner sur.
♦ **checker** *n* contrôleur *m*, -euse *f*; (*US: in supermarket*) caissier *m*, -ière *f*; (*US: in cloakroom*) préposé(e) *m(f)* au vestiaire. ♦ **check-in** *adj*: (*Aviat*) **your ~-in time is ...** présentez-vous à l'enregistrement des bagages à ... . ♦ **checking** *adj*: (*US*) **~ing account** compte *m* courant. ♦ **checklist** *n* liste *f* de contrôle. ♦ **checkmate 1** *n* (*Chess*) échec et mat *m*; (*fig*) impasse *f*; **2** *vt* faire échec et mat à; (*fig*) coincer. ♦ **check-out** *n* (*Comm*) caisse *f* (*dans un libre-service*). ♦ **checkpoint** *n* contrôle *m*. ♦ **checkroom** *n* (*US*) vestiaire *m*. ♦ **checkup** *n*: (*Med*) **to go for *or* have a ~up** se faire faire un bilan de santé.
check[3] [tʃek] *n*: **~s** (*pattern*) carreaux *mpl*, damier *m*. ♦ **checked** *adj* à carreaux. ♦ **checkerboard** *n* (*US*) damier *m*. ♦ **checkered** *adj* (*US*) = **chequered.** ♦ **checkers** *npl* (*US*) jeu *m* de dames.
cheddar ['tʃedəʳ] *n* (fromage *m* de) cheddar *m*.
cheek [tʃi:k] **1** *n* **(a)** joue *f*. **~ by jowl** côte à côte; **~ by jowl with** tout près de; **to dance ~ to ~** danser joue contre joue; **~bone** pommette *f*. **(b)** (*: *impudence*) toupet *m*, culot* *m*. **to have the ~ to do** avoir le toupet *or* le culot* de faire; **of all the ~!** quel culot!*, quel toupet! **2** *vt* être insolent avec. ♦ **cheekily** *adv* effrontément, avec insolence. ♦ **cheekiness** *n* effronterie *f*, toupet *m*, culot* *m*. ♦ **cheeky** *adj child* effronté, insolent, culotté*; *remark* impertinent.
cheep [tʃi:p] **1** *n* *[bird]* piaulement *m*. **2** *vi* piauler.
cheer [tʃɪəʳ] **1** *n*: **~s** acclamations *fpl*, hourras *mpl*; **to give three ~s for** acclamer; **three ~s for ...!** un ban pour ...!; **three ~s!** hourra!; (*drinking*) **~s!*** à la vôtre!*, à la tienne!* **2** *adj*: **~ leader** meneur *m* (qui rythme les cris des supporters). **3** *vt* **(a)** (**~ up**) (*gladden*) égayer, dérider; (*comfort*) donner du courage à, remonter le moral à; *room* égayer. **(b)** (*applaud*) acclamer, applaudir. **4** *vi* applaudir, pousser des hourras.
cheer on *vt sep person, team* encourager (*par des cris etc*).
cheer up 1 *vi* prendre courage, prendre espoir. **~ up!** courage! **2** *vt sep* = **cheer 3a.**
♦ **cheerful** *adj person, smile, conversation* joyeux, gai; *place, colour* gai, riant; *prospect* attrayant; *news* réconfortant. ♦ **cheerfully** *adv* gaiement, joyeusement. ♦ **cheerfulness** *n* gaieté *f*. ♦ **cheerily** *adv* gaiement, joyeusement. ♦ **cheering 1** *n* acclamations *fpl*, hourras *mpl*; **2** *adj news, sight* réconfortant, qui remonte le moral. ♦ **cheerio*** *excl* (*goodbye*) au revoir!, salut!*; (*your health*) à la vôtre!*, à la tienne!* ♦ **cheerless** *adj* morne, triste. ♦ **cheery** *adj* gai, joyeux.
cheese [tʃi:z] **1** *n* fromage *m*. (*for photograph*) **'say ~'** 'un petit sourire'. **2** *adj sandwich* au fromage. **~ board** plateau *m* à *or* de fromage(s); **~ dip** ≃ fondue *f*. ♦ **cheeseburger** *n* ≃ croque-monsieur *m*. ♦ **cheesecake** *n* flan *m* au fromage blanc. ♦ **cheesecloth** *n* toile *f* à beurre. ♦ **cheesed** *adj*: **to be ~d off*** en avoir marre* (*with* de). ♦ **cheeseparing 1** *n* économies *fpl* de bouts de chandelles; **2** *adj* pingre.
cheetah ['tʃi:tə] *n* guépard *m*.
chef [ʃef] *n* chef *m* (de cuisine).
chemical ['kemɪkəl] **1** *adj* chimique. **2** *n* produit *m* chimique. ♦ **chemically** *adv* chimiquement.
chemist ['kemɪst] *n* (*researcher etc*) chimiste *mf*; (*pharmacist*) pharmacien(ne) *m(f)*. **~'s shop** pharmacie *f*. ♦ **chemistry** *n* chimie *f*.
cheque [tʃek] *n* chèque *m* (*for £10* de 10 livres). **bad ~** chèque sans provision; **~ book** carnet *m* de chèques; **~ card** carte *f* d'identité bancaire.
chequered ['tʃekəd] *adj* à carreaux, à damier; (*fig*) varié. **he had a ~ career** sa carrière a connu des hauts et des bas.
cherish ['tʃerɪʃ] *vt person, memory* chérir; *feelings, opinion* entretenir; *hope, illusions* caresser. ♦ **cherished** *adj* très cher.
cherry ['tʃerɪ] **1** *n* cerise *f*; (**~ *tree***) cerisier *m*. **2** *adj pie, tart* aux cerises. **~ brandy** cherry-brandy *m*; **~ orchard** cerisaie *f*; **~ red** (rouge) cerise *inv*.
cherub ['tʃerəb] *n* chérubin *m*. ♦ **cherubic** *adj* angélique.
chervil ['tʃɜ:vɪl] *n* cerfeuil *m*.
chess [tʃes] *n* échecs *mpl*. ♦ **chessboard** *n* échiquier *m*. ♦ **chessman** *n* pièce *f* (de jeu d'échecs). ♦ **chessplayer** *n* joueur *m*, -euse *f* d'échecs.
chest[1] [tʃest] *n* (*box*) coffre *m*, caisse *f*; (*tea* **~**) caisse. **~ of drawers** commode *f*.
chest[2] [tʃest] **1** *n* (*Anat*) poitrine *f*. **to get something off one's ~*** déballer* ce qu'on a sur le cœur. **2** *adj cold* de poitrine; *specialist* des voies respiratoires. ♦ **chesty** *adj person* fragile de la poitrine; *cough* de poitrine.
chestnut ['tʃesnʌt] **1** *n* châtaigne *f*; (*Culin*) châtaigne, marron *m*; (**~ *tree***) châtaignier *m*, marronnier *m*; (*horse*) alezan *m*; (*old joke etc*) vieille histoire rabâchée. **2** *adj*: **~ hair** cheveux châtains.
chew [tʃu:] *vt* mâcher, mastiquer. **to ~ tobacco** chiquer; **to ~ the cud** ruminer.
chew over *vt sep facts, problem* ruminer.

chew up *vt sep* mâchonner.
♦ **chewing** *adj*: ~**ing gum** chewing-gum *m*.
chic [ʃi:k] *adj, n* chic (*m*) *inv*.
chick [tʃɪk] 1 *n* (*chicken*) poussin *m*; (*nestling*) oisillon *m*. **come here** ~* viens ici mon petit poulet. 2 *adj*: ~ **pea** pois *m* chiche. ♦ **chickweed** *n* mouron *m* des oiseaux.
chicken ['tʃɪkɪn] 1 *n* poulet *m*; (*very young*) poussin *m*. **she's no** ~* elle n'est plus toute jeune. 2 *adj*: ~ **farmer** éleveur *m* de volailles; ~ **farming** élevage *m* de volailles; ~ **liver** foie(s) *m(pl)* de volaille.
chicken out✱ *vi* se dégonfler*.
♦ **chicken-feed** *n* (*fig*) somme *f* dérisoire. ♦ **chicken-hearted** *adj* peureux. ♦ **chickenpox** *n* varicelle *f*. ♦ **chicken-wire** *n* grillage *m*.
chicory ['tʃɪkərɪ] *n [coffee]* chicorée *f*; (*for salads*) endive *f*.
chide [tʃaɪd] *vt* gronder.
chief [tʃi:f] 1 *n* (*gen*) chef *m*; (*boss*) patron *m*. **in** ~ principalement, surtout; ~ **of staff** chef d'état-major. 2 *adj assistant, inspector* principal, en chef. **C**~ **Constable** ≈ Préfet *m* de police; ~ **priest** archiprêtre *m*. ♦ **chiefly** *adv* principalement, surtout. ♦ **chieftain** *n* chef *m* (*de clan*).
chiffon ['ʃɪfɒn] *n* mousseline *f* de soie.
chilblain ['tʃɪlbleɪn] *n* engelure *f*.
child [tʃaɪld] 1 *n, pl* **children** ['tʃɪldrən] enfant *mf*. **don't be such a** ~ ne fais pas l'enfant; **the** ~ **of his imagination** le produit de son imagination. 2 *adj labour* des enfants; *psychology, psychiatry* de l'enfant, infantile; *psychologist, psychiatrist* pour enfants. ~ **care** protection *f* de l'enfance; ~ **guidance centre** centre *m* psycho-pédagogique; ~ **minder** gardienne *f* d'enfants; ~ **prodigy** enfant *mf* prodige; **it's** ~**'s play** c'est un jeu d'enfant (*to sb* pour qn); ~ **welfare** protection *f* de l'enfance. ♦ **child-bearing** *n*: **constant** ~**-bearing** grossesses répétées; **of** ~**-bearing age** en âge d'avoir des enfants. ♦ **childbirth** *n* accouchement *m*; **in** ~**birth** en couches. ♦ **childhood** *n* enfance *f*; **in his** ~**hood he** ... tout enfant il ...; **to be in one's second** ~**hood** retomber en enfance. ♦ **childish** *adj behaviour* puéril (*pej*); *ailment* infantile; *games* d'enfants; **don't be so** ~**ish** ne fais pas l'enfant. ♦ **childishly** *adv* comme un enfant. ♦ **childishness** *n* puérilité *f* (*pej*). ♦ **childless** *adj* sans enfants. ♦ **childlike** *adj* d'enfant, innocent.
Chile ['tʃɪlɪ] *n* Chili *m*.
chill [tʃɪl] 1 *n* froid *m*; (*fig*) froideur *f*; (*Med*) refroidissement *m*. **there's a** ~ **in the air** il fait un peu froid; **to take the** ~ **off** *wine* chambrer; *water* dégourdir; *room* réchauffer un peu; (*fig*) **to cast a** ~ **over** jeter un froid sur; **a** ~ **down one's spine** un frisson; **to catch a** ~ prendre froid. 2 *adj* (assez) froid. 3 *vt person* donner froid à; *wine, melon* faire rafraîchir; *meat* frigorifier, réfrigérer; *dessert* mettre au frais. ~**ed to the bone** *or* **marrow** transi jusqu'aux os *or* jusqu'à la moelle; **to** ~ **sb's blood** glacer le sang de qn. ♦ **chill(i)ness** *n* (*cold*) froid *m*; (*coolness*) fraîcheur *f*; (*fig*) froideur *f*. ♦ **chilling** *adj wind, look* froid; *thought* qui donne le frisson. ♦ **chilly** *adj person* frileux; *weather, wind* froid; *manner, look, smile* glacé, froid; *[person]* **to feel** ~**y** avoir froid; **it's rather** ~**y** il fait frais.
chilli ['tʃɪlɪ] *n* piment *m* (rouge).
chime [tʃaɪm] 1 *n* carillon *m*. 2 *vi [bells, voices]* carillonner; *[clock]* sonner.
chime in *vi [person]* faire chorus.
chimney ['tʃɪmnɪ] 1 *n* cheminée *f*. 2 *adj*: ~ **breast** manteau *m* de (la) cheminée; ~ **corner** coin *m* du feu; ~ **pot** tuyau *m* de cheminée; ~ **stack** *[factory]* tuyau de cheminée (d'usine); ~ **sweep** ramoneur *m*.
chimpanzee [ˌtʃɪmpæn'zi:] *n* chimpanzé *m*.
chin [tʃɪn] *n* menton *m*. **keep your** ~ **up!*** courage!
China ['tʃaɪnə] *n* Chine *f*. ~ **tea** thé *m* de Chine. ♦ **Chinatown** *n* le quartier chinois (*d'une ville*). ♦ **Chinese** 1 *adj* chinois; **Chinese People's Republic** République *f* populaire de Chine; 2 *n* (*person: pl inv*) Chinois(e) *m(f)*; (*Ling*) chinois *m*.
china ['tʃaɪnə] 1 *n* porcelaine *f*. **a piece of** ~ une porcelaine. 2 *adj* de *or* en porcelaine; *industry* de la porcelaine. ♦ **chinaware** *n* (objets *mpl* de) porcelaine *f*.
chink[1] [tʃɪŋk] *n* (*slit*) *[wall]* fente *f*; *[door]* entrebâillement *m*. (*fig*) **the** ~ **in the armour** le défaut de la cuirasse.
chink[2] [tʃɪŋk] 1 *n* (*sound*) tintement *m*. 2 *vt* faire tinter. 3 *vi* tinter.
chintz [tʃɪnts] *n* chintz *m*.
chip [tʃɪp] 1 *n* **(a)** (*gen: piece*) fragment *m*; *[wood, glass, stone]* éclat *m*; (*Electronics*) microplaquette *f*. **he's a** ~ **off the old block** c'est bien le fils de son père; **to have a** ~ **on one's shoulder** être aigri. **(b)** (*Culin*) ~**s** (*Brit*) frites *fpl*; (*US*) chips *fpl*. **(c)** (*break*) *[stone, crockery]* ébréchure *f*; *[furniture]* écornure *f*. **this cup has a** ~ cette tasse est ébréchée. **(d)** (*Poker etc*) jeton *m*. **he's had his** ~**s**✱ il est fichu*; **when the** ~**s are down*** dans les moments cruciaux. 2 *vt* (*damage*) *cup, plate* ébrécher; *furniture, stone* écorner; *varnish, paint* écailler; (*cut deliberately*) tailler. ~**ped potatoes** (pommes *fpl* de terre) frites *fpl*.
chip away, chip off 1 *vi [paint etc]* s'écailler. 2 *vt sep paint etc* enlever petit à petit.
chip in* *vi* (*interrupt*) dire son mot; (*contribute*) contribuer. **he** ~**ped in with 10 francs** il y est allé de (ses) 10 F*.
♦ **chipboard** *n* (*US*) carton *m*; (*Brit*) bois aggloméré. ♦ **chippings** *npl* gravillons *mpl*.
chiropody [kɪ'rɒpədɪ] *n* (*science*) podologie *f*; (*treatment*) soins *mpl* du pied. ♦ **chiropodist** *n* pédicure *mf*.
chirp [tʃɜ:p], **chirrup** ['tʃɪrəp] 1 *vi [birds]* pépier; *[crickets]* chanter. 2 *n* pépiement *m*; chant *m*. ♦ **chirpy*** *adj* gai.
chisel ['tʃɪzl] 1 *n* (*Tech*) ciseau *m*; (*for engraving*) burin *m*. 2 *vt* ciseler; buriner. **finely** ~**led features** traits finement ciselés; **to** ~ **sb out of sth**✱ carotter* qch à qn.
chit[1] [tʃɪt] *n*: **she's a mere** ~ **of a girl** ce n'est qu'une gamine*.
chit[2] [tʃɪt] *n* note *f*, petit mot.
chitchat ['tʃɪttʃæt] *n* bavardage *m*.
chivalry ['ʃɪvəlrɪ] *n* **(a)** (*Hist*) chevalerie *f*. **(b)** (*quality*) générosité *f*, galanterie *f*. ♦ **chivalresque** *adj* chevaleresque. ♦ **chivalrous** *adj* (*courteous*) chevaleresque; (*gallant*) galant. ♦ **chivalrously** *adv* de façon chevaleresque; galamment.
chives [tʃaɪvz] *npl* ciboulette *f*.
chivvy* ['tʃɪvɪ] *vt* (~ **along**) pourchasser; (*pester*) harceler (*sb into doing* qn jusqu'à ce qu'il fasse).
chlorate ['klɔ:reɪt] *n* chlorate *m*.
chloride ['klɔ:raɪd] *n* chlorure *m*.
chlorine ['klɔ:ri:n] *n* chlore *m*. ♦ **chlorinate** *vt water* javelliser; (*Chem*) chlorurer.
chloroform ['klɒrəfɔ:m] 1 *n* chloroforme *m*. 2 *vt* chloroformer.
chlorophyll ['klɒrəfɪl] *n* chlorophylle *f*.
choc-ice ['tʃɒkaɪs] *n* esquimau *m* (*glace*).
chock [tʃɒk] *n* cale *f*. ♦ **chock-a-block** *or* ♦ **chock-full** *adj container* plein à déborder (*with, of* de); *room* plein à craquer (*with, of* de).
chocolate ['tʃɒklɪt] 1 *n* chocolat *m*. 2 *adj egg* en chocolat; *biscuit, éclair* au chocolat; (*colour*) chocolat *inv*.
choice [tʃɔɪs] 1 *n* choix *m*. **a wide** ~ un grand choix; **to take one's** ~ faire son choix; **he had no** ~ il n'avait pas le choix; **he had no** ~ **but to obey** il ne pouvait qu'obéir; **it's Hobson's** ~ c'est à prendre ou à laisser; **from** ~ de préférence; **he did it from**

~ il a choisi de le faire; **this book would be my ~** c'est ce livre que je choisirais. **2** *adj goods, fruit* de choix; *word, phrase* bien choisi.
choir ['kwaɪəʳ] *n* chœur *m*. **to sing in the ~** faire partie du chœur. ♦ **choirboy** *n* jeune choriste *m*. ♦ **choirstall** *n* stalle *f* (du chœur).
choke [tʃəʊk] **1** *vt person* étrangler; *fire, flower* étouffer; (**~ up**) *pipe, tube* boucher. **street ~d with traffic** rue embouteillée. **2** *vi* étouffer, s'étrangler. **3** *n* (*Aut*) starter *m*.
choke back *vt sep feelings, tears* refouler; *words* contenir.
choke off* *vt sep suggestions etc* étouffer dans l'œuf; *discussion* empêcher; *person* envoyer promener*.
♦ **choker** *n* (*scarf*) foulard *m*; (*necklace*) collier *m* (de chien).
cholera ['kɒlərə] *n* choléra *m*.
cholesterol [kə'lestəˌrɒl] *n* cholestérol *m*.
choose [tʃuːz] *pret* **chose,** *ptp* **chosen 1** *vt* **(a)** (*select*) choisir; (*elect*) élire. (*Rel*) **the chosen (people)** les élus *mpl*; **there is nothing to ~ between them** ils se valent; **in a few well-chosen words** en quelques mots choisis. **(b)** décider, juger bon (*to do* de faire). **he chose not to speak** il a jugé bon de se taire, il a préféré se taire. **2** *vi* choisir. **as you ~** comme vous voulez; **if you ~** si cela vous dit; **he'll do it when he ~s** il le fera quand il voudra; **to ~ between** faire un choix entre; **there's not too much to ~ from** il n'y a pas tellement de choix. ♦ **choos(e)y*** *adj* difficile (à satisfaire); **I'm ~y about the people I go out with** je ne sors pas avec n'importe qui.
chop¹ [tʃɒp] **1** *n* **(a)** (*Culin*) côtelette *f*. **pork ~** côtelette de porc. **(b)** (*blow*) coup *m* (de hache *etc*). **to get the ~‡** se faire mettre à la porte. **2** *vt wood* couper; *meat, vegetables* hacher.
chop down *vt sep tree* abattre.
chop off *vt sep* trancher, couper. **they ~ped off his head** on lui a tranché la tête.
chop up *vt sep wood* couper en morceaux; (*Culin*) hacher menu.
♦ **chopper** *n* hachoir *m*; (*Aviat**) hélico* *m*. ♦ **chopping** *adj*: **~ping board** planche *f* à hacher; **~ping knife** hachoir *m* (*couteau*). ♦ **chopsticks** *npl* baguettes *fpl*.
chop² [tʃɒp] *vi*: **to ~ and change** changer constamment d'avis. ♦ **choppy** *adj lake* clapoteux; *sea* un peu agité; *wind* variable.
chopsuey [tʃɒp'suːɪ] *n* ragoût *m* (à la chinoise).
choral ['kɔːrəl] *adj* choral. **~ society** chorale *f*.
chord [kɔːd] *n* (*gen*) corde *f*; (*Mus*) accord *m*. (*fig*) **to touch the right ~** toucher la corde sensible.
chore [tʃɔːʳ] *n* (*everyday*) travail *m* de routine; (*unpleasant*) corvée *f*. **the ~s** les travaux du ménage; **to do the ~s** faire le ménage.
choreography [ˌkɒrɪ'ɒgrəfɪ] *n* chorégraphie *f*. ♦ **choreographer** *n* chorégraphe *mf*.
chorister ['kɒrɪstəʳ] *n* (*Rel*) choriste *mf*.
chortle ['tʃɔːtl] **1** *vi* glousser, rire (*about* de). **2** *n* gloussement *m*.
chorus ['kɔːrəs] **1** *n* **(a)** (*musical work, people*) chœur *m*. **in ~** en chœur; **she's in the ~** (*at concert*) elle chante dans les chœurs; (*Theat*) elle fait partie de la troupe; **a ~ of objections** un concert de protestations. **(b)** (*part of song*) refrain *m*. **to join in the ~** reprendre le refrain. **2** *adj*: **~ girl** girl *f*. **3** *vt song* chanter *or* réciter en chœur. **'yes' they ~sed** 'oui' répondirent-ils en chœur.
chose [tʃəʊz], **chosen** ['tʃəʊzn] *pret, ptp of* **choose.**
chow [tʃaʊ] *n* chow-chow *m*.
chowder ['tʃaʊdəʳ] *n* bouillabaisse *f* américaine.
Christ [kraɪst] *n* (le) Christ, Jésus-Christ. **the ~ Child** l'enfant Jésus. ♦ **Christendom** *n* chrétienté *f*.
christen ['krɪsn] *vt* (*Rel*) baptiser; (*gen: name*) appeler; (*nickname*) surnommer. **he was ~ed Robert but everyone calls him Bob** son nom de baptême est Robert mais tout le monde l'appelle Bob. ♦ **christening** *n* baptême *m*.
Christian ['krɪstɪən] **1** *adj* chrétien; (*fig*) charitable. **~ name** prénom *m*, nom *m* de baptême; **~ scientist** scientiste *mf* chrétien(ne). **2** *n* chrétien(ne) *m(f)*. ♦ **Christianity** *n* christianisme *m*.
Christmas ['krɪsməs] **1** *n* Noël *m*. **at ~** à Noël. **2** *adj card, tree, present, cake* de Noël. **~ box** étrennes *fpl*; **~ Day** le jour de Noël; **~ Eve** la veille de Noël; **~ party** fête *f or* arbre *m* de Noël; **I got it in my ~ stocking** ≃ je l'ai trouvé sous l'arbre (de Noël); **~ time** période *f* de Noël; **at ~ time** à Noël.
chromatic [krə'mætɪk] *adj* chromatique.
chrome [krəʊm] *n* chrome *m*.
chromium ['krəʊmɪəm] *n* acier *m* chromé. ♦ **chromium-plated** *adj* chromé.
chromosome ['krəʊməsəʊm] *n* chromosome *m*.
chronic ['krɒnɪk] *adj disease, state* chronique; *liar, smoker etc* invétéré; (*) *weather, person* épouvantable.
chronicle ['krɒnɪkl] **1** *n* chronique *f*. (*fig*) **a ~ of disasters** une succession de catastrophes. **2** *vt* faire la chronique de.
chronology [krə'nɒlədʒɪ] *n* chronologie *f*. ♦ **chronological** *adj* chronologique; **in chronological order** par ordre chronologique. ♦ **chronologically** *adv* chronologiquement.
chronometer [krə'nɒmɪtəʳ] *n* chronomètre *m*.
chrysalis ['krɪsəlɪs] *n* chrysalide *f*.
chrysanthemum [krɪ'sænθəməm] *n* chrysanthème *m*.
chubby ['tʃʌbɪ] *adj* potelé. **~-cheeked** joufflu.
chuck¹ [tʃʌk] *vt* **(a)** (*: *throw*) lancer, jeter; (‡: **~ in*, ~ up***) *job, girlfriend* laisser tomber*. **(b) he ~ed her under the chin** il lui a pris le menton.
chuck away* *vt sep* (*throw out*) *old clothes, books* jeter, balancer*; (*waste*) *money* jeter par les fenêtres; *opportunity* laisser passer.
chuck out* *vt sep useless article* jeter, balancer*; *person* vider*, sortir*.
chuck² [tʃʌk] *n* (**~ steak**) morceau *m* dans le paleron.
chuckle ['tʃʌkl] **1** *n* gloussement *m*, petit rire. **2** *vi* rire (*over, at* de), glousser.
chuffed‡ [tʃʌft] *adj* tout content (*about* de).
chug [tʃʌg] *vi [machine]* souffler; *[train]* faire teuf-teuf.
chug along *vi [train]* avancer en faisant teuf-teuf.
chum* [tʃʌm] *n* copain* *m*, copine* *f*. ♦ **chummy*** *adj* sociable; **she is very ~my with him** elle est très copine avec lui*.
chunk [tʃʌŋk] *n* (*gen*) gros morceau; *[bread]* quignon *m*. ♦ **chunky** *adj person* trapu; *knitwear* de grosse laine.
church [tʃɜːtʃ] *n* église *f*. **to go to ~** aller à l'église *f*; **in ~** à l'église; **in the ~** dans l'église; **after ~** après l'office; (*for Catholics*) après la messe; **the C~ of England** l'Église anglicane; **he has gone into the C~** il est entré dans les ordres. ♦ **churchgoer** *n* pratiquant(e) *m(f)*. ♦ **church-hall** *n* salle *f* paroissiale. ♦ **churchyard** *n* cimetière *m* (*autour d'une église*).
churlish ['tʃɜːlɪʃ] *adj* (*ill-mannered*) grossier; (*bad-tempered*) hargneux, de mauvaise humeur. ♦ **churlishly** *adv* grossièrement; avec humeur. ♦ **churlishness** *n* grossièreté *f*; mauvaise humeur *f*.
churn [tʃɜːn] **1** *n* baratte *f*; (*milk can*) bidon *m*. **2** *vt butter* baratter; (**~ up**) *water* battre.
churn out *vt sep objects, letters, books* produire en série.
chute [ʃuːt] *n* (*for coal etc*) descente *f*; (*Sport, for toboggans*) piste *f*; (*Brit: children's slide*) toboggan *m*.
chutney ['tʃʌtnɪ] *n* condiment *m* (*à base de fruits*).

cicada [sɪ'kɑːdə] *n* cigale *f*.
cider ['saɪdəʳ] 1 *n* cidre *m*. 2 *adj apple, press* à cidre. ~ **vinegar** vinaigre *m* de cidre.
cigar [sɪ'gɑːʳ] 1 *n* cigare *m*. 2 *adj box etc* à cigares. ~ **case** étui *m* à cigares; ~ **lighter** allume-cigare *m inv*.
cigarette [ˌsɪgə'ret] 1 *n* cigarette *f*. 2 *adj box, paper etc* à cigarettes; *ash* de cigarette. ~ **case** porte-cigarettes *m inv*; ~ **end** mégot *m*; ~ **holder** fume-cigarette *m inv*; ~ **lighter** briquet *m*.
cinch [sɪntʃ] *n*: **it's a** ~* c'est du gâteau*.
cinder ['sɪndəʳ] 1 *n* cendre *f*. **burnt to a** ~ (*gen*) réduit en cendres; *food* carbonisé. 2 *adj*: ~ **track** (piste *f*) cendrée *f*.
Cinderella [ˌsɪndə'relə] *n* Cendrillon *f*.
cinema ['sɪnəmə] *n* cinéma *m*. ♦ **cine-camera** *n* caméra *f*. ♦ **cine-film** *n* film *m*. ♦ **cine-projector** *n* projecteur *m* de cinéma.
cinnamon ['sɪnəmən] *n* cannelle *f*.
cipher ['saɪfəʳ] *n* (*numeral code*) chiffre *m*; (*zero*) zéro *m*. **he's a mere** ~ c'est un zéro; **in** ~ en chiffre, en code.
circle ['sɜːkl] 1 *n* (*gen*) cercle *m*; (*Theat*) balcon *m*. **to stand in a** ~ faire (un) cercle; **an inner** ~ **of advisers** un groupe de proches conseillers; **in political** ~**s** dans les milieux *mpl* politiques; **to come full** ~ revenir à son point de départ. 2 *vt* (*surround*) entourer; (*move round*) tourner autour de. 3 *vi* (~ **about** *or* **around**) *[birds]* décrire des cercles; *[aircraft]* tourner (en rond). ♦ **circular** 1 *adj* circulaire; 2 *n* (*letter*) circulaire *f*; (*as advertisement etc*) prospectus *m*. ♦ **circularize** *vt* envoyer des circulaires *or* des prospectus à.
circuit ['sɜːkɪt] *n* (*journey*) tour *m*, circuit *m*; *[judge, theatre company]* tournée *f*; (*group of cinemas etc*) groupe *m*; (*Elec, Sport*) circuit. **to make a** ~ **of** faire le tour de; **to make a** ~ **round** faire un détour *or* un circuit autour de; (*Jur*) **he is on the eastern** ~ il fait la tournée de l'est. ♦ **circuit-breaker** *n* disjoncteur *m*. ♦ **circuitous** *adj route, method* indirect; *means* détourné. ♦ **circuitously** *adv reach* en faisant un détour; (*fig*) indirectement.
circulate ['sɜːkjʊleɪt] 1 *vi* circuler. 2 *vt* faire circuler. ♦ **circulation** 1 *n* (*gen*) circulation *f*; *[newspaper etc]* tirage *m*; (*Med*) **he has poor circulation** il a une mauvaise circulation; (*Fin*) **to put into circulation** mettre en circulation; **to withdraw from circulation** retirer de la circulation; **in circulation** en circulation; **he's now back in circulation*** il est à nouveau dans le circuit*; 2 *adj* (*Press*) **circulation manager** directeur *m* du service de la diffusion.
circumcise ['sɜːkəmsaɪz] *vt* circoncire. ♦ **circumcision** *n* circoncision *f*.
circumference [sə'kʌmfərəns] *n* circonférence *f*.
circumflex ['sɜːkəmfleks] *n* accent *m* circonflexe.
circumlocution [ˌsɜːkəmlə'kjuːʃən] *n* circonlocution *f*.
circumnavigate [ˌsɜːkəm'nævɪgeɪt] *vt cape* doubler; *globe* faire naviguer tout autour de. ♦ **circumnavigation** *n* circumnavigation *f*.
circumscribe ['sɜːkəmskraɪb] *vt* circonscrire; *powers* limiter.
circumspect ['sɜːkəmspekt] *adj* circonspect. ♦ **circumspection** *n* circonspection *f*. ♦ **circumspectly** *adv* avec circonspection.
circumstance ['sɜːkəmstəns] *n* circonstance *f*. **in the present** ~**s** dans les circonstances actuelles, vu l'état des choses; **under no** ~**s** en aucun cas; (*financial*) ~**s** situation financière; **in easy/poor** ~**s** dans l'aisance/la gêne. ♦ **circumstantial** *adj report, statement* circonstancié; **circumstantial evidence** preuve indirecte. ♦ **circumstantiate** *vt* confirmer en donnant des détails sur.
circus ['sɜːkəs] *n* (*animals etc*) cirque *m*; (*in town*) rond-point *m*.
cirrhosis [sɪ'rəʊsɪs] *n* cirrhose *f*.
cissy* ['sɪsɪ] *n* = **sissy**.
cistern ['sɪstən] *n* citerne *f*; *[WC]* chasse *f* d'eau.
citadel ['sɪtədl] *n* citadelle *f*.
cite [saɪt] *vt* citer. **to** ~ **as an example** citer en exemple; (*Jur*) **to** ~ **sb to appear** citer qn. ♦ **citation** *n* citation *f*.
citizen ['sɪtɪzn] *n* citoyen(ne) *m(f)*; *[town]* habitant(e) *m(f)*. ♦ **citizenship** *n* citoyenneté *f*.
citrus ['sɪtrəs] *n* citrus *mpl*. ~ **fruits** agrumes *mpl*. ♦ **citric** *adj* citrique.
city ['sɪtɪ] 1 *n* (grande) ville *f*, cité *f*. *[London]* **the C**~ la Cité (de Londres); **he's (something) in the C**~* il est dans les affaires. 2 *adj* (*Press*) *editor, page, news* financier. ~ **centre** centre *m* (de la) ville; ~ **dweller** citadin(e) *m(f)*; **the** ~ **fathers** les élus *mpl* locaux; ~ **planner** urbaniste *mf*; ~ **planning** urbanisme *m*; ~ **slicker*** bêcheur *m*, -euse *f* (*venu de la ville*).
civic ['sɪvɪk] *adj rights, virtues* civique; *guard, authorities* municipal. ~ **centre** centre administratif (municipal). ♦ **civics** *n* instruction *f* civique.
civil ['sɪvl] *adj* **(a)** *law, war, marriage* civil. **the American C**~ **War** la guerre de Sécession; ~ **commotion** émeute *f*; ~ **defence** défense passive; ~ **disobedience** résistance passive (*à la loi*); ~ **engineer** ingénieur *m* des travaux publics; ~ **engineering** travaux publics; ~ **liberties** libertés *fpl* civiques; ~ **rights movement** campagne *f* pour les droits *mpl* civiques; ~ **servant** fonctionnaire *mf*; ~ **service** fonction *f* publique, administration *f*. **(b)** (*polite*) civil, poli. ♦ **civilian** *n, adj* civil(e) *m(f)* (*opposé à militaire*). ♦ **civility** *n* civilité *f*. ♦ **civilization** *n* civilisation *f*. ♦ **civilize** *vt* civiliser. ♦ **civilized** *adj* civilisé; **to become** ~**ized** se civiliser. ♦ **civilly** *adv* poliment.
clad [klæd] *adj* habillé (*in* de).
claim [kleɪm] 1 *vt property, prize, right* revendiquer (*from* à); *diplomatic immunity, damages* réclamer (*from* à); *attention* demander, solliciter; (*maintain*) prétendre (*that* que). **to** ~ **acquaintance with sb** prétendre connaître qn.
2 *n* revendication *f*, réclamation *f*; (*Insurance*) demande *f* d'indemnité; (*Min etc*) concession *f*. **to lay** ~ **to** prétendre à; **there are many** ~**s on my time** mon temps est très pris; **there are many** ~**s on my purse** on fait beaucoup appel à ma bourse; **that's a big** ~ **to make!** la prétention est de taille!; **his** ~ **that he acted legally** son affirmation d'avoir agi d'une manière licite; (*Insurance*) **the** ~**s were all paid** les dommages ont été intégralement payés; (*Ind*) **a** ~ **for an extra £5 per week** une demande d'augmentation de 5 livres par semaine; **expenses** ~ note *f* de frais. **his** ~ **to the throne** son titre *or* droit à la couronne.
3 *adj*: ~ **form** (*gen*) formulaire *m* de demande; (*for expenses*) feuille *f* de note de frais.
♦ **claimant** *n [throne]* prétendant(e) *m(f)* (*to* à); *[social benefits]* demandeur *m*, -eresse *f*.
clairvoyant(e) [klɛə'vɔɪənt] 1 *n* voyant(e) *m(f)*. 2 *adj* doué de seconde vue. ♦ **clairvoyance** *n* voyance *f*.
clam [klæm] *n* grosse praire *f*. ~ **chowder** soupe *f* aux praires.
clam up* *vi* se taire. **he** ~**med up on me** il ne m'a plus dit un mot (là-dessus).
clamber ['klæmbəʳ] *vi* grimper (avec difficulté). **to** ~ **over a wall** escalader un mur.
clammy ['klæmɪ] *adj hand* moite (et froid); *wall* suintant; *climate* humide.
clamour, (*US*) **-or** ['klæməʳ] 1 *n* (*shouts*) clameurs *fpl*, vociférations *fpl*; (*demands*) revendications bruyantes. 2 *vi*: **to** ~ **for sth/sb** réclamer qch/qn à grands cris. ♦ **clamorous** *adj*

crowd vociférant; *demand* impérieux.
clamp [klæmp] **1** *n* (*gen*) attache *f*; (*bigger*) crampon *m*; (*Med*) clamp *m*; (*Carpentry*) valet *m* d'établi; *[stone, china]* agrafe *f*; (*Elec*) serre-fils *m inv*. **2** *vt* fixer (*onto* à); *stones, china* agrafer.
clamp down on* *vt fus person* serrer la vis à*; *expenditure* mettre un frein à; *information* supprimer; *the press, opposition* bâillonner.
clan [klæn] *n* clan *m*. ♦ **clannish** *adj group* fermé; *person* qui a l'esprit de clique.
clandestine [klæn'destɪn] *adj* clandestin.
clang [klæŋ] **1** *n* son *m or* (*louder*) fracas *m* métallique. **2** *vi* émettre un son métallique. **the gate ~ed shut** la grille s'est refermée bruyamment. ♦ **clanger*** *n* gaffe *f*. ♦ **clangorous** *adj noise* métallique. ♦ **clangour,** (*US*) **-or** *n* fracas *m* métallique.
clank [klæŋk] **1** *n* cliquetis *m*. **2** *vi* cliqueter.
clap [klæp] **1** *n [hands]* battement *m*; (*action*) tape *f*; (*applause*) applaudissements *mpl*. **a ~ on the back** une tape dans le dos; **a ~ of thunder** un coup de tonnerre. **2** *vt* **(a)** frapper, taper; *dog* donner des tapes amicales à; (*applaud*) applaudir. **to ~ one's hands** battre des mains; **to ~ sb on the back** donner à qn une tape dans le dos; **he ~ped his hand over my mouth** il a mis sa main sur ma bouche. **(b)** mettre, jeter. **to ~ sb into prison** mettre qn en prison; **to ~ eyes on** voir. **3** *vi* applaudir.
clap on *vt sep one's hat* enfoncer sur sa tête. **to ~ on the brakes** freiner brusquement.
♦ **clapped-out*** *adj person, car* crevé*; *horse* fourbu. ♦ **clapping** *n* applaudissements *mpl*. ♦ **claptrap*** *n* boniment* *m*.
claret ['klærət] *n* bordeaux *m* (rouge).
clarify ['klærɪfaɪ] *vt* clarifier. ♦ **clarification** *n* clarification *f*.
clarinet [ˌklærɪ'net] *n* clarinette *f*. ♦ **clarinettist** *n* clarinettiste *mf*.
clarity ['klærɪtɪ] *n* clarté *f*, précision *f*.
clash [klæʃ] **1** *vi [metallic objects]* s'entrechoquer; *[cymbals]* résonner; *[armies]* se heurter; *[interests, personalities]* être incompatible (*with* avec); *[colours]* jurer (*with* avec); *[two events, invitations etc]* tomber en même temps (*or* le même jour *etc*). **they ~ over the question of ...** ils sont en désaccord total en ce qui concerne ...; **the dates ~** les deux événements tombent le même jour. **2** *vt metallic objects* heurter bruyamment; *cymbals* faire résonner; (*Aut*) *gears* faire grincer. **3** *n* (*sound*) choc *m or* fracas *m* métallique; *[armies, weapons]* heurt *m*; (*between people, parties*) accrochage *m*; (*with police, troops*) échauffourée *f*; *[interests]* conflit *m*; *[colours]* discordance *f*; *[dates, events, invitations]* coïncidence *f* (fâcheuse). **a ~ with the police** une échauffourée avec la police; **a ~ of personalities** une incompatibilité de caractères.
clasp [klɑ:sp] **1** *n* (*gen*) fermoir *m*; *[belt]* boucle *f*. **2** *adj*: **~ knife** grand couteau *m* pliant. **3** *vt* étreindre, serrer; *sb's hand* serrer. **to ~ one's hands (together)** joindre les mains; **to ~ sb in one's arms** serrer qn dans ses bras.
class [klɑ:s] **1** *n* (*gen*) classe *f*. **~ of ship** type *m* de vaisseau; **they are just not in the same ~** il n'y a pas de comparaison (possible) entre eux; **in a ~ by itself** hors concours; **a good ~ (of) hotel** un très bon hôtel; **first ~ honours in history** ≈ licence *f* d'histoire avec mention très bien; **to give/attend a ~** faire/suivre un cours; **the French ~** la classe *or* le cours de français; **an evening ~** un cours du soir; (*US*) **the ~ of 1970** la promotion de 1970; **to have ~** avoir de la classe. **2** *vt* classer, classifier. **~ed as** classé comme. **3** *adj*: **~ distinction** distinction sociale; **~ war(fare)** lutte *f* des classes. ♦ **class-conscious** *adj* conscient des distinctions sociales; (*snobbish*) snob *inv*. ♦ **classmate** *n* camarade *mf* de classe. ♦ **classroom** *n* salle *f* de classe. ♦ **classy*** *adj object* chic *inv*; *person* ultra-chic *inv*.
classic ['klæsɪk] **1** *adj* classique. **it was ~!*** c'était le coup classique!* **2** *n* (*author, work*) classique *m*; (*Racing*) classique *f*. **to study ~s** étudier les humanités *fpl*; **a ~ of its kind** un classique du genre. ♦ **classical** *adj* classique; **~al scholar** humaniste *mf*. ♦ **classicism** *n* classicisme *m*.
classify ['klæsɪfaɪ] *vt* classifier. **classified advertisement** petite annonce *f*; **classified information** renseignements *mpl* secrets. ♦ **classifiable** *adj* qu'on peut classifier. ♦ **classification** *n* classification *f*.
clatter ['klætəʳ] **1** *n* cliquetis *m*, (*louder*) fracas *m*. **the ~ of cutlery** le bruit de couverts entrechoqués. **2** *vi [keys, typewriter]* cliqueter; *[large falling object, cymbals]* résonner. **to ~ in/out** entrer/sortir bruyamment. **3** *vt* entrechoquer bruyamment.
clause [klɔ:z] *n* (*Gram*) proposition *f*; *[contract, law, treaty]* clause *f*; *[will]* disposition *f*.
claustrophobia [ˌklɔ:strə'fəʊbɪə] *n* claustrophobie *f*. ♦ **claustrophobic** *adj person* claustrophobe; *feeling* de claustrophobie; *situation, atmosphere* claustrophobique.
claw [klɔ:] **1** *n [cat, lion, small bird etc]* griffe *f*; *[bird of prey]* serre *f*; *[lobster etc]* pince *f*. **2** *vt* (*scratch*) griffer; (*rip*) déchirer avec ses griffes *or* ses serres; (*clutch*) agripper. ♦ **claw-hammer** *n* marteau *m* à pied-de-biche.
clay [kleɪ] **1** *n* argile *f*. **2** *adj*: **~ pigeon shooting** tir *m* au pigeon; **~ pipe** pipe *f* en terre.
clean [kli:n] **1** *adj* (*gen*) propre; *sheet of paper* blanc, neuf; *reputation, shape, line, cut, stroke* net; *joke, story* qui n'a rien de choquant; *contest, game* loyal. **to wipe sth ~** essuyer qch; **keep it ~** ne le salissez pas; (*fig*) pas d'inconvenances!; **as ~ as a new pin** propre comme un sou neuf; **to make a ~ breast of it** dire ce qu'on a sur la conscience; **to make a ~ sweep** faire table rase (*of* de); **~ living** une vie saine; (*Jur*) **a ~ record** un casier judiciaire vierge; **a ~ driving licence** un permis de conduire où n'est portée aucune contravention; **the doctor gave him a ~ bill of health** le médecin l'a trouvé en parfait état de santé; **he's ~*** (*carrying nothing incriminating*) il n'a rien sur lui; (*innocent*) il n'a rien fait.
2 *adv* complètement, tout à fait. **he got ~ away** il a décampé sans laisser de traces; **to cut ~ through sth** couper qch de part en part; **he jumped ~ over the fence** il a sauté la barrière sans la toucher; **the car went ~ through the hedge** la voiture est carrément passée à travers la haie; **to break off ~** casser net; **to come ~ about sth*** tout dire sur qch.
3 *n*: **to give sth a good ~** bien nettoyer qch.
4 *vt clothes, room* nettoyer; *vegetables* laver; *blackboard* essuyer. **to ~ one's teeth** se brosser les dents; **to ~ one's nails** se nettoyer les ongles; **to ~ the windows** faire les vitres.
clean off *vt sep* (*from blackboard*) essuyer; (*from floor, wall*) enlever.
clean out *vt sep* nettoyer à fond; (*: *leave penniless etc*) ruiner, nettoyer*.
clean up **1** *vi* tout nettoyer; (*tidy*) remettre en ordre; (*: *make profit*) faire son beurre* (*on a deal* dans une affaire). **2** *vt sep room* nettoyer; (*fig*) *a town, television etc* épurer. **to ~ o.s. up** se laver, se débarbouiller.
♦ **clean-cut** *adj* bien délimité, net. ♦ **cleaner** *n* (*Comm*) teinturier *m*, -ière *f*; (*charwoman*) femme *f* de ménage; (*device*) appareil *m* de nettoyage; (*household ~er*) produit *m* d'entretien; (*stain-remover*) détachant *m*; **the ~er's shop** la teinturerie. ♦ **cleaning** *n* nettoyage *m*; (*housework*) ménage *m*; **~ing fluid** détachant *m*; **~ing woman** femme *f* de ménage. ♦ **clean-limbed** *adj* bien proportionné. ♦ **cleanliness** ['klenlɪnɪs] *n*

(habitude *f* de la) propreté *f*. ♦ **clean-living** *adj* honnête. ♦ **cleanly** ['kli:nlɪ] **1** *adv* proprement, nettement; **2** ['klenlɪ] *adj* propre. ♦ **cleanness** *n* propreté *f*. ♦ **clean-out** *n* nettoyage *m* à fond. ♦ **clean-shaven** *adj*: **to be ~-shaven** n'avoir ni barbe ni moustache. ♦ **clean-up** *n [room]* nettoyage *m*; *[person]* débarbouillage *m*.

cleanse [klenz] *vt* nettoyer; *ditch, drain etc* curer; (*fig*) laver (*of* de); *soul etc* purifier. ♦ **cleanser** *n* (*detergent*) détergent *m*; (*for complexion*) démaquillant *m*. ♦ **cleansing 1** *adj*: **cleansing cream** crème *f* démaquillante; **cleansing department** service *m* de voirie; **2** *n* nettoyage *m*.

clear [klɪəʳ] **1** *adj* **(a)** *piece of glass, plastic* transparent; *water, lake, stream* limpide; *sky, weather, complexion* clair; *photograph, outline* net; *honey* liquide; *majority, profit* net. **on a ~ day** par temps clair; **~ red** rouge vif; **~ soup** bouillon *m*; **he left with a ~ conscience** il est parti la conscience tranquille. **(b)** *sound* clair; *words* distinct. **you're not very ~** je ne vous entends pas bien. **(c)** *explanation, account, style* clair; *reasoning* clair, lucide; *intelligence* pénétrant; *proof, sign, consequence, motive* évident, clair. **~ thinker** esprit *m* lucide; **I want to be quite ~ on this point** (*understand clearly*) je veux savoir exactement ce qu'il en est; (*explain unambiguously*) je veux bien me faire comprendre; **a ~ case of murder** un cas d'assassinat manifeste; **to make o.s. ~** se faire bien comprendre; **to make it ~ to sb that** bien faire comprendre à qn que; **I wish to make it ~ that** je tiens à préciser que; **as ~ as day** clair comme le jour; **it is ~ to me that** il me paraît hors de doute que. **(d)** *road, path* libre; *route* sans obstacles. **all ~!** fin d'alerte!; **we had a ~ view** rien ne gênait la vue; **we were ~ of the town** nous étions hors de l'agglomération; **~ of debts** libre de dettes; **three ~ days** trois jours entiers.

2 *n*: **to send a message in ~** envoyer un message en clair; **in the ~*** (*above suspicion*) au-dessus de tout soupçon; (*no longer suspected*) blanchi de tout soupçon; (*out of danger*) hors de danger.

3 *adv* **(a) loud and ~** très distinctement. **(b)** entièrement, complètement. **the thief got ~ away** le voleur a disparu sans laisser de traces. **(c) ~ of** à l'écart de, à distance de; **to keep ~ of sth/sb** éviter qch/qn; **to stand ~** s'écarter; **stand ~ of the doors!** dégagez les portes!; **to get ~ of** (*go away from*) s'éloigner *or* s'écarter de; (*rid o.s. of*) se débarrasser de.

4 *vt* **(a)** *liquid* clarifier; *blood* dépurer; *bowels* purger; *situation, account* éclaircir. **to ~ the air** aérer; (*fig*) détendre l'atmosphère; **to ~ one's throat** s'éclaircir la voix; **to ~ one's head** se dégager le cerveau. **(b)** *canal, path, road, railway line* dégager, déblayer; *pipe* déboucher; *land* défricher. **to ~ the table** débarrasser la table; (*fig*) **to ~ the decks** tout déblayer; **to ~ sth of rubbish** déblayer qch; **to ~ the way for** faire place à; (*fig*) ouvrir la voie à; **to ~ a way through** ouvrir un passage à travers; **to ~ a room** (*of people*) faire évacuer une salle; (*of things*) débarrasser une salle; (*Jur*) **to ~ the court** faire évacuer la salle; (*Ftbl*) **to ~ the ball** dégager le ballon. **(c)** (*find innocent etc*) *person* disculper (*of* de). **to ~ o.s.** se disculper; **to ~ sb of suspicion** laver qn de tout soupçon; **you will have to be ~ed by our security department** il faudra que nos services de sécurité donnent (*subj*) le feu vert en ce qui vous concerne; **we've ~ed it with him** nous avons obtenu son accord. **(d)** *hedge, fence* franchir, sauter; *obstacle, rocks* éviter; *harbour* quitter. **he ~ed the gate by 10 cm** il a sauté la barrière avec 10 cm de marge; **raise the car till the wheel ~s the ground** soulevez la voiture jusqu'à ce que la roue ne touche (*subj*) plus le sol. **(e)** *cheque* compenser; *account, goods* liquider; *debt* s'acquitter de; *profit* gagner net; (*Customs*) *goods* dédouaner; *ship* expédier; *one's conscience* décharger; *doubts* dissiper. (*Comm*) **'half price to ~'** 'solde à moitié prix pour liquider'; **I've ~ed £100 on this business** cette affaire m'a rapporté 100 livres net.

5 *vi [weather]* s'éclaircir; *[sky]* se dégager; *[fog]* se dissiper; *[face, expression]* s'éclairer.

clear away 1 *vi [mist etc]* se dissiper; (*clear the table*) desservir. **2** *vt sep* enlever.

clear off 1 *vi* (*) filer*, décamper. **2** *vt sep things on desk* enlever; *debts* s'acquitter de; *stock, goods* liquider.

clear out 1 *vi* (*) = **clear off 1**. **2** *vt sep cupboard* vider; *room* débarrasser; *unwanted objects* enlever. **he ~ed everyone out of the room** il a fait évacuer la pièce.

clear up 1 *vi* (*tidy*) ranger; *[weather]* se lever. **2** *vt sep mystery, matter* éclaircir; *room, clothes* ranger. **to ~ up the mess** (*lit*) tout nettoyer; (*fig*) tout arranger.

♦ **clearance 1** *n [road, path, land]* déblaiement *m*; *[room, court]* évacuation *f*; *[cupboard, passage]* dégagement *m*; *[accused]* disculpation *f*; *[litter, objects, rubbish]* enlèvement *m*; *[cheque]* compensation *f*; (*Customs*) dédouanement *m*; (*permission etc*) autorisation *f*; **sent to the Foreign Office for ~ance** soumis au ministère des Affaires étrangères pour contrôle; (*Aviat*) **~ance for takeoff** autorisation de décoller; **2 metre ~ance** espace *m* de 2 mètres; **2** *adj*: **~ance sale** soldes *mpl*. ♦ **clear-cut** *adj* net. ♦ **clear-headed** *adj* lucide, perspicace. ♦ **clearing 1** *n* (*in forest*) clairière *f*; *[liquid]* clarification *f*; *[bowels]* purge *f*; *[rubbish, objects]* enlèvement *m*; *[land]* défrichement *m*; *[pipe etc]* débouchage *m*; *[road]* dégagement *m*; **2** *adj*: **~ing bank** banque *f* (appartenant à une chambre de compensation); **~ing house** (*Banking*) chambre *f* de compensation; (*for documents etc*) bureau *m* central. ♦ **clearly** *adv* (*distinctly*) *see, state* clairement; *hear* distinctement; *understand* bien; (*obviously*) manifestement. ♦ **clearness** *n [air, glass]* transparence *f*; *[liquid]* limpidité *f*; *[sound, sight, print, thought etc]* clarté *f*, netteté *f*. ♦ **clear-sighted** *adj* (*fig*) clairvoyant. ♦ **clearway** *n* route *f* à stationnement interdit.

cleave [kli:v] *pret* **cleft** *or* **clove**, *ptp* **cleft** *or* **cloven** *vt* fendre. **in a cleft stick** dans une impasse; **cleft palate** palais *m* fendu. ♦ **cleavage** *n*: **a dress which showed her cleavage*** une robe qui laissait voir la naissance des seins. ♦ **cleaver** *n* couperet *m*.

clef [klef] *n* (*Mus*) clef *f*.

cleft [kleft] *n* (*in rock*) crevasse *f* (*V also* **cleave**).

clematis ['klemətɪs] *n* clématite *f*.

clement ['klemənt] *adj* clément. ♦ **clemency** *n* clémence *f*.

clench [klentʃ] *vt object* serrer dans ses mains; *fists, teeth* serrer.

clergy ['klɜ:dʒɪ] *collective n* clergé *m*. ♦ **clergyman** *n* ecclésiastique *m*.

clerical ['klerɪkəl] *adj* **(a)** (*Rel*) clérical; *collar* de pasteur. **(b)** (*Comm etc*) *job* d'employé; *work, worker* de bureau. **~ error** erreur *f* d'écriture.

clerk [klɑ:k, (*US*) klɜ:rk] *n* employé(e) *m(f)* (*de bureau, de commerce*), commis *m*; (*US: shop assistant*) vendeur *m*, -euse *f*. **bank ~** employé(e) de banque; (*in hotel*) **desk ~** réceptionniste *mf*; (*Jur*) **C~ of the Court** greffier *m* (du tribunal); **~ of works** conducteur *m* de travaux.

clever ['klevəʳ] *adj person* intelligent; (*smart*) astucieux; *book* intelligemment écrit; *play, film* intelligemment fait; *machine, invention, trick, explanation* ingénieux; *idea, joke, story* astucieux; (*skilful*) habile (*at doing* à faire). **to be ~ at French** être fort en français; **~ with one's**

hands adroit de ses mains; **he's very ~ with cars** il s'y connaît en voitures; **he was too ~ for me** il m'a eu*; **~ Dick** petit malin *m.* ♦ **cleverly** *adv* intelligemment; astucieusement; ingénieusement; habilement. ♦ **cleverness** *n* intelligence *f*; astuce *f*; ingéniosité *f*; habileté *f* (*at* à).

clew [klu:] *n* (*US*) = **clue.**

click [klɪk] **1** *n* déclic *m*, petit bruit sec; *[tongue]* claquement *m*; *[wheel]* cliquet *m.* **2** *vi [lid, device]* faire un bruit sec; *[heels, typewriter]* cliqueter. **the door ~ed shut** la porte s'est refermée avec un déclic; (*fig*) **suddenly it ~ed*** j'ai compris tout à coup. **3** *vt*: **to ~ one's heels** claquer des talons; **to ~ one's tongue** faire claquer sa langue. ♦ **clicking** *n* cliquetis *m.*

client ['klaɪənt] *n* client(e) *m(f).* ♦ **clientele** *n* clientèle *f.*

cliff [klɪf] *n [seashore]* falaise *f*; *[mountains]* escarpement *m.* ♦ **cliff-hanger*** *n* récit *m* (*or* situation *f etc*) à suspense.

climate ['klaɪmɪt] *n* climat *m.* **the ~ of opinion** les courants *mpl* de l'opinion. ♦ **climatic** *adj* climatique. ♦ **climatology** *n* climatologie *f.*

climax ['klaɪmæks] *n* point *m* culminant; *[career etc]* apogée *m*; (*sexual*) orgasme *m.* **to bring sth to/to come to a ~** porter qch à/atteindre son point culminant; **to work up to a ~** *[story, events]* tendre vers son point culminant; *[speaker]* amener le point culminant.

climb [klaɪm] **1** *vt* (**~ up**) *stairs, steps, slope* monter; *hill* grimper; *tree, ladder* monter sur *or* à; *rope* monter à; *cliff, wall* escalader; *mountain* faire l'ascension de. **2** *vi* **(a)** (**~ up:** *gen*) monter; *[persons, plants]* grimper; *[road, sun]* monter; *[aircraft, rocket]* monter, prendre de l'altitude. **(b) to ~ down sth** descendre de qch; **to ~ over sth** escalader qch; **to ~ into an aircraft** monter à bord d'un avion; **to ~ out of a hole** se hisser hors d'un trou; (*Sport*) **to go ~ing** faire de l'alpinisme. **3** *n [hill]* montée *f*, côte *f*; (*Alpinism, Aviat*) ascension *f.*

climb down *vi* descendre; (*fig*) en rabattre.

♦ **climber** *n* grimpeur *m*, -euse *f*; (*mountaineer*) alpiniste *mf*; (*social etc ~er*) arriviste *mf*; (*plant*) plante *f* grimpante. ♦ **climbing** *n* (*Sport*) alpinisme *m.*

clinch [klɪntʃ] **1** *vt argument* consolider, confirmer; *bargain, deal* conclure. **that ~es it** comme ça c'est réglé. **2** *n* (*embrace*) **in a ~*** enlacés.

cling [klɪŋ] *pret, ptp* **clung** *vi* **(a)** (*hold tight*) **to ~ to** *rope, sb's hand* se cramponner à; *opinion* maintenir envers et contre tout; *belief* se raccrocher à; **to ~ to one another** (*lovingly*) se tenir étroitement enlacés; (*fearfully*) se cramponner l'un à l'autre. **(b)** (*stick*) coller (*to* à). ♦ **clingfilm** *n* scellofrais *m* ®. ♦ **clinging** *adj garment, person* collant; *odour* tenace.

clinic ['klɪnɪk] *n* (*nursing home; teaching session*) clinique *f*; *[G.P., hospital]* service *m* de consultation. ♦ **clinical** *adj* (*Med*) clinique; *thermometer* médical; (*fig*) *attitude, approach* objectif.

clink [klɪŋk] **1** *vt* faire tinter. **to ~ glasses with sb** trinquer avec qn. **2** *vi* tinter. **3** *n* tintement *m.*

clip¹ [klɪp] *n* (*paper ~*) trombone *m*; (*bulldog ~*) pince *f* à dessin; (*for tube*) collier *m*; (*cartridge ~*) chargeur *m*; (*brooch*) clip *m.*

clip on *vt sep brooch* fixer (*to* sur); *document* attacher.

clip together *vt sep* attacher.

clip² [klɪp] **1** *vt* **(a)** (*cut: gen*) couper; *hedge* tailler; *sheep, dog* tondre; *ticket* poinçonner; *article from newspaper* découper. (*fig*) **to ~ sb's wings** rogner les ailes à qn; (*fig*) **in a ~ped voice** en détachant bien les syllabes. **(b)** (*: *hit*) flanquer une taloche à*.

2 *n* (*Cine*) extrait *m.*

♦ **clipper** *n* (*Aviat, Naut*) clipper *m.* ♦ **clippers** *npl* (*for hair*) tondeuse *f*; (*for hedge*) sécateur *m*; (*for nails*) pince *f* à ongles. ♦ **clipping** *n [newspaper etc]* coupure *f* de presse.

clique [kli:k] *n* clique *f*, coterie *f.* ♦ **cliquey** *or* ♦ **cliquish** *adj* qui a l'esprit de clique.

cloak [kləʊk] **1** *n* grande cape. **as a ~ for sth** pour cacher qch. **2** *vt* (*fig*) masquer, cacher. **~ed with mystery** empreint de mystère. ♦ **cloak-and-dagger** *adj* clandestin, mystérieux. ♦ **cloakroom** *n [coats etc]* vestiaire *m*; (*W.C.*) (*public*) toilettes *fpl*; (*in house*) cabinets *mpl*; **~room ticket** numéro *m* de vestiaire.

clock [klɒk] **1** *n* **(a)** (*large*) horloge *f*; (*smaller*) pendule *f.* **by the church ~** à l'horloge *or* au clocher de l'église; **2 hours by the ~** 2 heures d'horloge; **round the ~** vingt-quatre heures d'affilée; **to work against the ~** travailler contre la montre. **(b)** *[taxi]* compteur *m.* (*Aut*) **50,000 miles on the ~** 50 000 milles au compteur. **2** *vt runner* chronométrer. **he ~ed 4 minutes for the mile** il a fait le mille en 4 minutes. **3** *vi*: **to ~ in** *or* **on** pointer (à l'arrivée); **to ~ out** *or* **off** pointer (à la sortie).

clock up *vt sep work, distance* faire.

♦ **clock-golf** *n* jeu *m* de l'horloge. ♦ **clockmaker** *n* horloger *m*, -ère *f.* ♦ **clock-radio** *n* radio-réveil *m.* ♦ **clock-tower** *n* clocher *m.* ♦ **clock-watcher** *n*: **he's a terrible ~-watcher** il ne fait que guetter l'heure de sortie. ♦ **clockwise** *adv, adj* dans le sens des aiguilles d'une montre. ♦ **clockwork** **1** *n*: **to go like ~work** aller comme sur des roulettes; **2** *adj toy* mécanique.

clog [klɒg] **1** *n* sabot *m* (*chaussure*). **2** *vt* (**~ up**) *pipe* boucher; *wheel, passage* bloquer. **3** *vi* (**~ up**) se boucher.

cloister ['klɔɪstəʳ] *n* cloître *m.* ♦ **cloistered** *adj*: **~ed life** vie *f* monacale.

close¹ [kləʊs] **1** *adj* **(a)** (*near*) *date, relative* proche; *friend* intime; *resemblance* exact, fidèle; *connection* étroit; *contact* direct; *encounter* face à face. **house ~ to the shops** maison près *or* proche des magasins; **sit here ~ to me** asseyez-vous ici près de moi; **~ to tears** au bord des larmes; **at ~ quarters** tout près; **to have a ~ call*** *or* **shave*** l'échapper belle, y échapper de justesse; **that was ~!** on l'a échappé belle! **(b)** *handwriting, rank, election, reasoning* serré; *grain* fin; *account* proche de la vérité; *argument* précis; *control, surveillance* étroit; *questioning, investigation* serré, minutieux; *examination, study* attentif; *attention* soutenu; *translation* fidèle; *silence* impénétrable; (*secretive*) *person* peu communicatif. **to keep a ~ watch on** surveiller de près; **~ combat** corps à corps *m*; **in ~ confinement** en détention surveillée; **she was very ~ to her brother** (*in age*) son frère et elle étaient d'âges très rapprochés; (*in friendship*) elle était très proche de son frère. **(c)** (*airless*) *room* mal aéré; *weather* lourd, étouffant. **it's very ~ in here** il n'y a pas d'air ici; **it's ~ today** il fait lourd aujourd'hui. **(d)** (*Sport*) **~ season** chasse *f* *or* pêche *f* fermée.

2 *adv* étroitement, de près. **to hold sb ~** serrer qn dans ses bras; **~ by** tout près, tout proche; **~ by, ~ to, ~ up(on)** tout près de; **~ to the ground** très bas, au ras du sol; **~ by us** tout à côté de nous; **~ at hand** tout près; **he followed ~ behind me** il me suivait de près; **~ together** serrés les uns contre les autres; **to come ~r together** se rapprocher.

3 *n [cathedral]* enceinte *f.*

♦ **close-cropped** *adj* coupé ras. ♦ **close-fisted** *adj* grippe-sou *inv.* ♦ **close-fitting** *adj* ajusté. ♦ **close-knit** *adj* (*fig*) très uni. ♦ **closely** *adv guard* étroitement; *grasp* en serrant fort; *resemble* beaucoup; *watch, follow, study* de près; *listen* attentivement; *connected* étroitement; **they are ~ly related** ils sont proches parents.

♦ **close-mouthed** *adj* taciturne. ♦ **closeness** *n* *[weave]* texture *f* serrée; *[friendship]* intimité *f*; *[resemblance etc]* fidélité *f*; *[pursuers]* proximité *f*; *[weather, atmosphere]* lourdeur *f*; *[room]* manque *m* d'air. ♦ **close-run** *adj*: **~-run race** course très disputée. ♦ **close-set** *adj* *eyes* rapprochés. ♦ **close-shaven** *adj* rasé de près. ♦ **close-up** *n* gros plan *m*; **in ~-up** en gros plan.

close² [kləʊz] **1** *n* (*end*) fin *f*. **to come to a ~** se terminer; **to draw to a ~** tirer à sa fin; **to bring sth to a ~** mettre fin à qch. **2** *vt* **(a)** (*shut: gen*) fermer; *pipe, opening* boucher; *road* barrer. **~d to traffic** interdit à la circulation; **the shop is ~d** le magasin est fermé; **the shop is ~d on Sundays** le magasin ferme le dimanche; **to ~ a gap between 2 objects** réduire l'intervalle qui sépare 2 objets; **to ~ ranks** serrer les rangs. **(b)** (*end*) *proceedings, discussion* terminer, mettre fin à; *account* arrêter, clore; *bargain* conclure. **to ~ the meeting** lever la séance. **3** *vi* **(a)** *[door, box, lid]* fermer, se fermer; *[museum, shop]* fermer; *[eyes]* se fermer. **the door ~d** la porte s'est fermée; **the door ~s badly** la porte ferme mal; **the shop ~s on Sundays** le magasin ferme le dimanche; **his fingers ~d around the pencil** ses doigts se sont refermés sur le crayon; **to ~ with sb** se prendre corps à corps avec qn. **(b)** (*end*) *[meeting etc]* se terminer, prendre fin; *[speaker etc]* terminer. (*St Ex*) **shares ~d at 120p** les actions étaient cotées à 120 pence en clôture.

close down **1** *vi* *[business, shop]* fermer (définitivement); (*Rad, TV*) terminer les émissions. **2** *vt sep* fermer (définitivement).

close in **1** *vi* *[hunters etc]* se rapprocher; *[evening, night]* tomber; *[darkness, fog]* descendre. **the days are closing in** les jours raccourcissent; **to ~ in on sb** cerner qn. **2** *vt sep* *area* clôturer.

close up **1** *vi* *[people in line etc]* se rapprocher; *[wound]* se refermer. **2** *vt sep* *house, shop* fermer (complètement); *pipe, opening* boucher; *wound* refermer.

♦ **closed** *adj* *door, eyes* fermé; *road* barré; *pipe, opening etc* bouché; '**~d**' (*gen*) 'fermé'; (*Theat*) 'relâche'; **maths are a ~d book to me** je suis complètement rebelle aux maths; **~d-circuit television** télévision *f* en circuit fermé; (*Ind*) **~d shop** atelier *m* qui n'admet que des travailleurs syndiqués; **~d-shop policy** exclusion *f* des travailleurs non syndiqués. ♦ **close-down** *n* *[shop etc]* fermeture *f* (définitive); (*Rad, TV*) fin *f* des émissions. ♦ **closing** **1** *n* (*gen*) fermeture *f*; *[meeting]* clôture *f*; **2** *adj* final, dernier; **closing speech** discours *m* de clôture; **when is closing time?** à quelle heure est-ce qu'on ferme?; (*St Ex*) **closing price** cours *m* en clôture. ♦ **closure** *n* fermeture *f*; (*Parl*) **to move the closure** demander la clôture.

closet ['klɒzɪt] **1** *n* (*cupboard*) armoire *f*, placard *m*; (*for clothes*) penderie *f*; (*room*) cabinet *m*; (*W.C.*) cabinets *mpl*. **2** *vt*: **he was ~ed with his father for several hours** son père et lui sont restés plusieurs heures enfermés à discuter.

clot [klɒt] **1** *n* caillot *m*; (*: *fool*) imbécile *mf*. **a ~ on the brain/in the lung** une embolie cérébrale/pulmonaire; **a ~ in the leg** une thrombose. **2** *vti* coaguler. **~ted cream** crème *f* en grumeaux.

cloth [klɒθ] **1** *n* **(a)** (*material*) tissu *m*, étoffe *f*; *[linen, cotton]* toile *f*; *[wool]* drap *m*; (*Bookbinding, Naut*) toile *f*. **(b)** (*tablecloth*) nappe *f*; (*duster*) chiffon *m*; (*dishcloth*) torchon *m*. **2** *adj*: **~ cap** casquette *f* (d'ouvrier).

clothe [kləʊð] *vt* habiller, vêtir (*in, with* de). ♦ **clothes** **1** *npl* vêtements *mpl*; (**bed~s**) draps *mpl* et couvertures *fpl*; **with one's ~s on** tout habillé; **with one's ~s off** déshabillé, tout nu; **to put on one's ~s** s'habiller; **to take off one's ~s** se déshabiller; **2** *adj*: **~s basket** panier *m* à linge; **~s brush** brosse *f* à habits; **~s hanger** cintre *m*; **~s horse** séchoir *m* à linge pliant; **~s line** corde *f* à linge; **~s peg** pince *f* à linge; **~s shop** magasin *m* d'habillement; (*US*) **~s tree** portemanteau *m*. ♦ **clothier** *n* (*clothes seller*) marchand *m* de confection; (*cloth dealer, maker*) drapier *m*. ♦ **clothing** *n* vêtements *mpl*; **an article of clothing** un vêtement; **clothing allowance** indemnité *f* vestimentaire.

cloud [klaʊd] **1** *n* (*Met*) nuage *m*; *[smoke, dust etc]* nuage; *[insects, arrows etc]* nuée *f*; *[gas]* nappe *f*. **to have one's head in the ~s** être dans les nuages; **to be on ~ nine**‡ être aux anges; (*fig*) **under a ~** (*under suspicion*) en butte aux soupçons; (*in disgrace*) en disgrâce. **2** *vt* *liquid* rendre trouble; *mirror* embuer; *mind* obscurcir. **~ed sky** ciel couvert; **to ~ the issue** brouiller les cartes (*fig*). **3** *vi* (**~ over**) *[sky]* se couvrir (de nuages); *[face, expression]* s'assombrir. ♦ **cloudburst** *n* déluge *m* de pluie. ♦ **cloud-cuckoo land** *n*: **she lives in ~-cuckoo land** elle plane complètement. ♦ **cloudiness** *n* *[sky]* aspect *m* nuageux; *[liquid]* aspect trouble; *[mirror]* buée *f*. ♦ **cloudless** *adj* sans nuages. ♦ **cloudy** *adj* *sky* couvert; *liquid* trouble; **it was ~y** le temps était couvert.

clout [klaʊt] **1** *n* coup *m* de poing (*or* de canne *etc*). **2** *vt* donner un coup de poing *etc* à.

clove¹ [kləʊv] *n* clou *m* de girofle. **oil of ~s** essence *f* de girofle; **~ of garlic** gousse *f* d'ail.

clove² [kləʊv] *pret of* **cleave.**

cloven ['kləʊvn] **1** *ptp of* **cleave.** **2** *adj*: **~ hoof** *[animal]* sabot *m* fendu; *[devil]* pied *m* fourchu.

clover ['kləʊvə^r] *n* trèfle *m*. **to be in ~*** être comme un coq en pâte; **~leaf** (*Bot*) feuille *f* de trèfle; (*road intersection*) croisement *m* en trèfle.

clown [klaʊn] **1** *n* clown *m*. **2** *vi* (**~ about, ~ around**) faire le clown *or* le pitre. ♦ **clowning** *n* pitreries *fpl*.

cloy [klɔɪ] *vi* perdre son charme. ♦ **cloying** *adj* écœurant.

club [klʌb] **1** *n* **(a)** (*weapon*) matraque *f*; (*golf* **~**) club *m*. (*Cards*) **~s** trèfles *mpl*; **the ace of ~s** l'as *m* de trèfle; **one ~** un trèfle; **he played a ~** il a joué trèfle. **(b)** (*society*) club *m*. **tennis ~** club de tennis; (*fig*) **join the ~!*** tu n'es pas le seul! **2** *adj*: **~ member** membre *m* du club; **~ sandwich** sandwich *m* à deux étages. **3** *vt* *person* matraquer. **to ~ sb with a rifle** assommer qn d'un coup de crosse.

club together *vi* se cotiser (*to buy* pour acheter).

♦ **club-foot** *n* pied-bot *m*. ♦ **clubhouse** *n* pavillon *m*.

cluck [klʌk] **1** *vi* glousser. **2** *n* gloussement *m*.

clue [kluː] *n* (*gen*) indication *f*; (*police etc*) indice *m*; *[crosswords]* définition *f*. **to find the ~ to sth** découvrir la clef de qch; **to have a ~** être sur une piste; (*fig*) **I haven't a ~!*** je n'en ai pas la moindre idée!

clue up‡ *vt sep* renseigner (*on* sur). **he's very ~d up on politics** il est très calé* en politique.

♦ **clueless*** *adj* qui n'a pas la moindre idée.

clump¹ [klʌmp] *n* *[shrubs]* massif *m*; *[trees]* bouquet *m*; *[flowers, grass]* touffe *f*.

clump² [klʌmp] **1** *n* (*noise*) bruit *m* de pas lourds. **2** *vi* (**~ about**) marcher d'un pas lourd.

clumsy ['klʌmzɪ] *adj* *person, action, painting, forgery* maladroit; *tool etc* peu pratique; *shape, form* lourd; (*tactless*) *person, remark, apology, style* gauche, maladroit. ♦ **clumsily** *adv* maladroitement; gauchement. ♦ **clumsiness** *n* maladresse *f*; caractère *m* peu pratique; gaucherie *f*.

clung [klʌŋ] *pret, ptp of* **cling.**

cluster ['klʌstə^r] **1** *n* *[flowers, blossom, fruit]* grappe *f*; *[bananas]* régime *m*; *[trees]* bouquet *m*; *[persons, houses, islands]* (petit) groupe; *[stars]*

amas *m.* **2** *vi [people]* se rassembler (*around* autour de); *[things]* former un groupe *etc* (*around* autour de).

clutch [klʌtʃ] **1** *n* **(a)** (*Aut*) embrayage *m*; (~ *pedal*) pédale *f* d'embrayage. **to let in the ~** embrayer; **to let out the ~** débrayer; **~ plate** disque *m* d'embrayage. **(b) to fall into sb's ~es** tomber sous les griffes de qn. **2** *vt* (*grasp*) empoigner, saisir; (*hold tightly*) serrer fort; (*hold on to*) se cramponner à. **3** *vi*: **to ~ at** essayer de saisir; (*fig*) **to ~ at a straw** se raccrocher à n'importe quoi.

clutter ['klʌtəʳ] **1** *n* désordre *m*, fouillis *m*. **in a ~** en désordre, en pagaille*. **2** *vt* (~ **up**) encombrer (*with* de).

co- [kəʊ] *pref* co-. ♦ **co-author** *n* co-auteur *m*. ♦ **co-driver** *n* (*in race*) copilote *m*; *[lorry]* deuxième chauffeur *m*. ♦ **coeducation** *n* éducation *f* mixte. ♦ **coeducational** *adj* mixte. ♦ **coexist** *vi* coexister (*with* avec). ♦ **coexistence** *n* coexistence *f*. ♦ **co-pilot** *n* copilote *m* (*Aviat*). ♦ **co-respondent** *n* co-défendeur *m*, -deresse *f* (d'un adultère). ♦ **co-star** *n* (*Cine, Theat*) partenaire *mf*. ♦ **co-worker** *n* collègue *mf* de travail.

coach [kəʊtʃ] **1** *n* **(a)** (*Rail*) voiture *f*, wagon *m*; (*motor* ~) car *m*, autocar *m*; (*horse-drawn*) carrosse *m*. **(b)** (*tutor*) répétiteur *m*, -trice *f*; (*Sport*) entraîneur *m*. **2** *vt* donner des leçons particulières à; (*Sport*) entraîner. **to ~ sb for an exam** préparer qn à un examen; **he had been ~ed in what to say** on lui avait fait répéter ce qu'il aurait à dire. **3** *adj*: **~ trip** excursion *f* en car. ♦ **coachman** *n* cocher *m*. ♦ **coachwork** *n* carrosserie *f*.

coagulate [kəʊ'ægjʊleɪt] **1** *vt* coaguler. **2** *vi* se coaguler. ♦ **coagulant** *n* coagulant *m*. ♦ **coagulation** *n* coagulation *f*.

coal [kəʊl] **1** *n* charbon *m*; (*Ind*) houille *f*. (*fig*) **on hot ~s** sur des charbons ardents. **2** *adj fire, dust* de charbon; *box, stove, cellar* à charbon; *industry* houiller. **~ scuttle** seau *m* à charbon; **~ shed** réserve *f* à charbon. ♦ **coal-black** *adj* noir comme du charbon. ♦ **coal-face** *n* front *m* de taille. ♦ **coalfield** *n* bassin *m* houiller. ♦ **coal-gas** *n* gaz *m* (de houille). ♦ **coalman** *or* ♦ **coal-merchant** *n* charbonnier *m*. ♦ **coalmine** *n* houillère *f*, mine *f* de charbon. ♦ **coalminer** *n* mineur *m*. ♦ **coalmining** *n* charbonnage *m*.

coalesce [ˌkəʊə'les] *vi* se grouper.

coalition [ˌkəʊə'lɪʃən] *n* coalition *f*.

coarse [kɔːs] *adj material, cloth, texture* grossier; *linen, salt, sand* gros; *sandpaper* à gros grain; *skin* rude; *food* fruste; *manners, language, joke* grossier; *laugh* gras; *accent* vulgaire. **~ red wine** gros rouge *m*. ♦ **coarse-grained** *adj* à gros grain. ♦ **coarsely** *adv* grossièrement; grassement; vulgairement; **~ly woven** de texture grossière. ♦ **coarsen 1** *vt* rendre grossier *or* vulgaire *etc*; **2** *vi* devenir rude *or* grossier *or* vulgaire *etc*. ♦ **coarseness** *n* caractère *m* grossier *or* rude; vulgarité *f*; grossièreté *f*.

coast [kəʊst] **1** *n* côte *f*; (*~line*) littoral *m*. **the ~ is clear** la voie est libre. **2** *vi* (*Aut, Cycling*) avancer (*or* descendre) en roue libre. ♦ **coastal** *adj* côtier. ♦ **coaster** *n* (*Naut*) caboteur *m*; (*drip mat*) dessous *m* de verre. ♦ **coastguard 1** *n* garde *m* maritime; (*US*) douanier *m* garde-côte; **2** *adj*: **~guard station** station *f* de garde-côtes; **~guard vessel** garde-côte *m*.

coat [kəʊt] **1** *n* (*gen*) manteau *m*; *[animal]* pelage *m*, poil *m*; *[horse]* robe *f*; *[paint, tar etc]* couche *f*. **~ of arms** armoiries *fpl*. **2** *vt* enduire, couvrir (*with* de); (*with egg*) dorer. **his tongue was ~ed** il avait la langue chargée. ♦ **coat-hanger** *n* cintre *m*. ♦ **coating** *n* couche *f*. ♦ **coatstand** *n* portemanteau *m*.

coax [kəʊks] *vt* enjôler. **to ~ sb into doing** amener qn à force de cajoleries à faire; **to ~ sth out of sb** obtenir qch de qn par des cajoleries. ♦ **coaxing** *n* cajolerie(s) *f(pl)*. ♦ **coaxingly** *adv* d'un ton câlin *or* enjôleur.

cobalt ['kəʊbɒlt] *n* cobalt *m*.

cobble ['kɒbl] *n* (*~***stone**) pavé *m* rond. ♦ **cobbled** *adj*: **~d street** rue pavée.

cobbler ['kɒbləʳ] *n* cordonnier *m*.

cobra ['kəʊbrə] *n* cobra *m*.

cobweb ['kɒbweb] *n* toile *f* d'araignée.

Coca-Cola [ˌkəʊkə 'kəʊlə] *n* ® coca-cola *m inv*.

cocaine [kə'keɪn] *n* cocaïne *f*.

cochineal ['kɒtʃɪniːl] *n* (*Culin*) colorant *m* rouge.

cock [kɒk] **1** *n* coq *m*. **the ~ of the walk** le roi (*fig*). **2** *vt gun* armer. **to ~ one's ear** dresser les oreilles; (*fig*) dresser l'oreille; **to ~ a snook at** faire un pied de nez à; (*fig*) faire fi de. **3** *adj*: **~ bird** (oiseau *m*) mâle *m*. ♦ **cock-a-doodle-doo** *n* cocorico *m*. ♦ **cock-a-hoop 1** *adj* fier comme Artaban; **2** *adv* d'un air de triomphe. ♦ **cock-and-bull** *adj*: **~-and-bull story** histoire *f* à dormir debout. ♦ **cockcrow** *n*: **at ~crow** au premier chant du coq. ♦ **cocked** *adj*: **to knock sb into a ~ed hat*** battre qn à plate couture. ♦ **cockerel** *n* jeune coq *m*. ♦ **cock-eyed** *adj* (*: *cross-eyed*) qui louche; (*: *crooked*) de traviole*; (*: *absurd*) absurde; (‡: *drunk*) soûl*. ♦ **cockfighting** *n* combats *mpl* de coqs. ♦ **cockiness** *n* outrecuidance *f*. ♦ **cockpit** *n* *[aircraft]* poste *m* de pilotage; *[racing car]* poste du pilote; (*fig*) arènes *fpl*. ♦ **cockroach** *n* cafard *m*. ♦ **cocksure** *adj* (trop) sûr de soi. ♦ **cocktail 1** *n* cocktail *m* (*boisson*); **fruit ~tail** salade *f* de fruits; **prawn ~tail** cocktail de crevettes; **2** *adj*: **~tail bar** bar *m* (*dans un hôtel*); **~tail cabinet** bar *m* (*meuble*); **~tail party** cocktail *m* (*réunion*). ♦ **cocky** *adj* trop sûr de soi, outrecuidant.

cockade [kɒ'keɪd] *n* cocarde *f*.

cockatoo ['kɒkə'tuː] *n* cacatoès *m*.

cocker ['kɒkəʳ] *n*: **~ (spaniel)** cocker *m*.

cockle ['kɒkl] *n* (*Zool*) coque *f*. **it warmed the ~s of his heart** cela lui a réchauffé le cœur.

cockney ['kɒknɪ] **1** *n* Cockney *mf* (*personne née dans l'"East End' de Londres*); (*Ling*) cockney *m*. **2** *adj* cockney, londonien.

cocoa ['kəʊkəʊ] *n* cacao *m*.

coconut ['kəʊkənʌt] **1** *n* noix *f* de coco. **2** *adj*: **~ matting** tapis *m* de fibre; **~ palm** cocotier *m*; **~ shy** jeu *m* de massacre.

cocoon [kə'kuːn] *n* cocon *m*.

cod [kɒd] *n,pl inv* morue *f*; (*Culin*) cabillaud *m*, (*salted, dried*) morue. **the C~ War** la guerre de la morue. ♦ **cod-liver oil** *n* huile *f* de foie de morue.

coddle ['kɒdl] *vt* dorloter; (*Culin*) cuire à feu doux.

code [kəʊd] **1** *n* (*all senses*) code *m*. **in ~** en code. **2** *vt* coder. **3** *adj*: **~ letter** chiffre *m*; **~ name** nom *m* codé; (*Tax*) **~ number** ≃ indice *m* des déductions fiscales. ♦ **codify** *vt* codifier. ♦ **coding** *n [message]* mise *f* en code; (*Computers*) codage *m*.

codeine ['kəʊdiːn] *n* codéine *f*.

codicil ['kɒdɪsɪl] *n* codicille *m*.

coefficient [ˌkəʊɪ'fɪʃənt] *n* coefficient *m*.

coerce [kəʊ'ɜːs] *vt* contraindre (*sb into doing* qn à faire). ♦ **coercion** *n* contrainte *f*. ♦ **coercive** *adj* coercitif.

coffee ['kɒfɪ] **1** *n* café *m*. **a ~** un café; **black ~** café noir; **white ~** café au lait; **one white ~, please!** un (café-)crème s'il vous plaît! **2** *adj*: **~ bar** cafétéria *f*; **~ bean** grain *m* de café; **~ break** pause-café *f*; **~ cup** tasse *f* à café, (*smaller; also measure*) tasse à moka; **~ percolator** cafetière *f* (*à pression*); **~ pot** *n* cafetière *f*; **~ spoon** cuiller *f* à moka; **~ table** (petite) table *f* basse; **a ~ table book** un beau livre grand format.

coffer ['kɒfəʳ] *n* coffre *m*.

coffin ['kɒfɪn] *n* cercueil *m*.

cog [kɒg] *n* dent *f* (*d'engrenage*). (*fig*) **a ~ in the wheel** un simple rouage dans la machine.

cogent ['kəʊdʒənt] *adj* (*compelling*) puissant; (*relevant*) pertinent. ♦ **cogency** *n* puissance *f*. ♦ **cogently** *adv* puissamment; pertinemment.
cogitate ['kɒdʒɪteɪt] *vti* méditer (*on* sur). ♦ **cogitation** *n* réflexion *f*.
cognac ['kɒnjæk] *n* cognac *m*.
cohabit [kəʊ'hæbɪt] *vi* cohabiter (*with* avec). ♦ **cohabitation** *n* cohabitation *f*.
coherent [kəʊ'hɪərənt] *adj person, words* cohérent; *account, speech* facile à suivre; *behaviour* logique. ♦ **coherence** *n* (*fig*) cohérence *f*. ♦ **coherently** *adv* d'une façon cohérente.
coil [kɔɪl] **1** *vt* enrouler. **2** *vi [rope]* s'enrouler; *[snake]* se lover. **3** *n* (*roll: gen*) rouleau *m*; (*one loop*) spire *f*; *[snake, smoke]* anneau *m*; *[hair at back of head]* chignon *m*. (*contraceptive*) **the ~** le stérilet.
coin [kɔɪn] **1** *n* pièce *f* de monnaie. **a 10p ~** une pièce de 10 pence. **2** *vt money* frapper; *word* inventer. (*fig*) **he is ~ing money** il fait des affaires d'or; (*hum*) **to ~ a phrase** si je peux m'exprimer ainsi. ♦ **coin-operated** *adj* automatique. ♦ **coin-op*** *n* laverie *f* automatique.
coincide [ˌkəʊɪn'saɪd] *vi* coïncider (*with* avec). ♦ **coincidence** *n* coïncidence *f*. ♦ **coincidental** *adj* de coïncidence.
coke [kəʊk] *n* coke *m*.
Coke [kəʊk] *n* ® coca *m* ®.
colander ['kʌləndəʳ] *n* passoire *f*.
cold [kəʊld] **1** *adj* (*lit, fig*) froid. **as ~ as ice** (*gen*) glacé; *room* glacial; **it's as ~ as charity** il fait un froid de canard*; **it's a ~ morning** il fait froid ce matin; **the tea's ~** le thé est froid; **I am ~** j'ai froid; **my feet are ~** j'ai froid aux pieds; (*fig*) **to have ~ feet** avoir la frousse*; **to get ~** *[weather, room]* se refroidir; *[food]* refroidir; *[person]* commencer à avoir froid, (*catch a chill*) attraper froid; **that's ~ comfort** ce n'est pas tellement réconfortant; **that leaves me ~*** ça ne me fait ni chaud ni froid; **in ~ blood** de sang-froid; **he was out ~*** il était sans connaissance; **~ cream** crème *f* de beauté; **~ sore** herpès *m*; **to put into ~ storage** *food* mettre en chambre froide; *scheme* mettre en attente; **~ store** entrepôt *m* frigorifique; **the ~ war** la guerre froide.
2 *n* **(a)** (*Met etc*) froid *m*. **I am beginning to feel the ~** je commence à avoir froid; **I never feel the ~** je ne suis pas frileux; (*fig*) **to be left out in the ~** rester en plan*. **(b)** (*Med*) rhume *m*. **~ in the head** rhume de cerveau; **a bad ~** un gros rhume; **to have a ~** être enrhumé; **to get a ~** s'enrhumer. ♦ **cold-blooded** *adj animal* à sang froid; *person* sans pitié. ♦ **cold-hearted** *adj* impitoyable. ♦ **coldly** *adv* avec froideur. ♦ **coldness** *n* froideur *f*. ♦ **cold-shoulder*** *vt* se montrer froid envers.
coleslaw ['kəʊlslɔː] *n* salade *f* de chou cru.
colic ['kɒlɪk] *n* coliques *fpl*; (*diarrhoea*) colique.
colitis [kɒ'laɪtɪs] *n* colite *f*.
collaborate [kə'læbəreɪt] *vi* collaborer (*with sb in sth* avec qn à qch). ♦ **collaboration** *n* collaboration *f* (*in* à). ♦ **collaborator** *n* collaborateur *m*, -trice *f*.
collapse [kə'læps] **1** *vi [person, building, roof, floor]* s'écrouler, s'effondrer; *[beam]* fléchir; *[government]* tomber; *[prices, defences, civilization, society]* s'effondrer; *[scheme]* s'écrouler; (*: *with laughter*) être plié en deux (de rire). **he ~d at work** il a eu un grave malaise à son travail. **2** *vt chair* plier; *paragraphs* comprimer. **3** *n* écroulement *m*; effondrement *m*; fléchissement *m*; *[lung etc]* collapsus *m*; *[government]* chute *f*. ♦ **collapsible** *adj* pliant.
collar ['kɒləʳ] **1** *n* col *m*; (*separate*) (*for men*) faux-col *m*; (*for women*) collerette *f*; *[dogs]* collier *m*; (*on pipe etc*) bague *f*. **to get hold of sb by the ~** saisir qn au collet. **2** *vt* (*) *person* accrocher*, intercepter*; *book, object* faire main basse sur. ♦ **collarbone** *n* clavicule *f*. ♦ **collarstud** *n* bouton *m* de col.
collate [kɒ'leɪt] *vt* collationner (*with* avec). ♦ **collation** *n* collation *f*.
collateral [kɒ'lætərəl] *adj* (*parallel*) parallèle; (*corresponding*) concomitant; (*Jur, Med*) collatéral; (*subordinate*) accessoire. (*Fin*) **~ (security)** nantissement *m*.
colleague ['kɒliːg] *n* collègue *mf*.
collect [kə'lekt] **1** *vt* **(a)** (*assemble*) *valuables, wealth* accumuler; *facts, documents* rassembler, recueillir; *group of helpers* rassembler, réunir; *money, subscriptions* recueillir; *taxes, dues, fines* percevoir; *rents* encaisser. (*US*) **~ on delivery** livraison *f* contre remboursement; **the ~ed works of Milton** les œuvres *fpl* complètes de Milton; (*fig*) **to ~ one's thoughts** se recueillir. **(b)** (*pick up*) *books etc* ramasser; *[bus or railway company] luggage etc* prendre à domicile; *[ticket collector]* ramasser. (*Post*) **to ~ letters** faire la levée du courrier; **the rubbish is ~ed twice a week** les ordures sont enlevées deux fois par semaine. **(c)** (*as hobby*) *stamps* collectionner. **she ~s* poets** elle collectionne* les poètes. **(d)** (*call for*) *person, books, one's mail* passer prendre. **the bus ~s the children** l'autobus ramasse les enfants.
2 *vi* **(a)** *[people]* se rassembler; *[things]* s'amasser; *[dust, water]* s'accumuler. **(b) to ~ for the injured** faire la quête pour les blessés.
3 *adv* (*US Telec*) **to call ~** téléphoner en P.C.V. ♦ **collection** *n [information]* rassemblement *m*; *[taxes]* perception *f*; *[refuse]* enlèvement *m*; *[stamps etc]* collection *f*; *[miscellaneous objects]* amas *m*, ramassis *m* (*pej*); (*in church*) quête *f*; (*Post*) levée *f*. ♦ **collective** *adj* collectif; **~ive bargaining** ≃ convention *f* collective du travail. ♦ **collectively** *adv* collectivement. ♦ **collectivism** *n* collectivisme *m*. ♦ **collector** *n [taxes]* percepteur *m*; *[stamps etc]* collectionneur *m*, -euse *f*.
college ['kɒlɪdʒ] *n* (*gen*) collège *m*. **~ of agriculture** institut *m* agronomique; **~ of art** école *f* des beaux-arts; **~ of domestic science** école d'enseignement ménager; **~ of education** ≃ école normale; **~ of music** conservatoire *m* de musique; **technical ~** collège technique; **to go to ~** faire des études supérieures; **C~ of Physicians/Surgeons** Académie *f* de médecine/de chirurgie.
collide [kə'laɪd] *vi* entrer en collision, (*less violently*) se heurter. **to ~ with** entrer en collision avec, heurter. ♦ **collision** *n* collision *f*; **to be on a collision course** être sur une route de collision.
collie ['kɒlɪ] *n* colley *m*.
collier ['kɒlɪəʳ] *n* mineur *m*. ♦ **colliery** *n* mine *f* (de charbon), houillère *f*.
colloquial [kə'ləʊkwɪəl] *adj* familier, parlé. ♦ **colloquialism** *n* expression *f* familière. ♦ **colloquially** *adv* familièrement, dans la langue parlée.
collusion [kə'luːʒən] *n* collusion *f*. **in ~ with** de connivence avec.
colon ['kəʊlən] *n* (*Anat*) côlon *m*; (*Gram*) deux-points *m inv*.
colonel ['kɜːnl] *n* colonel *m*. **C~ Smith** le colonel Smith.
colony ['kɒlənɪ] *n* colonie *f*. ♦ **colonial** *adj* colonial; **Colonial Office** ministère *m* des Colonies. ♦ **colonialism** *n* colonialisme *m*. ♦ **colonialist** *adj, n* colonialiste (*mf*). ♦ **colonist** *n* colon *m*. ♦ **colonization** *n* colonisation *f*. ♦ **colonize** *vt* coloniser.
Colorado beetle [ˌkɒlə'rɑːdəʊ 'biːtl] *n* doryphore *m*.
colossus [kə'lɒsəs] *n* colosse *m*. ♦ **colossal** *adj* colossal.
colour, (*US*) **-or** ['kʌləʳ] **1** *n* couleur *f*. **what ~ is**

it? de quelle couleur est-ce?; **to take the ~ out of sth** décolorer qch; (*fig*) **let's see the ~ of your money*** fais voir la couleur de ton fric*; **under (the) ~ of** sous prétexte de; **to change ~** changer de couleur; **to lose (one's) ~** pâlir; **to get one's ~ back** reprendre des couleurs; **he looks an unhealthy ~** il a très mauvaise mine; **to have a high ~** avoir le teint vif; **to paint sth in bright/dark ~s** (*lit*) peindre qch de couleurs vives/sombres; (*fig*) peindre qch sous de belles couleurs/sous des couleurs sombres; **to see sth in its true ~s** voir qch sous son vrai jour; (*gen, Mil, Naut*) **~s** couleurs *fpl*; **to salute the ~s** saluer le drapeau; (*fig*) **he showed his true ~s** il s'est révélé tel qu'il est vraiment; **his ~ counted against him** sa couleur jouait contre lui; **it is not a question of ~** ce n'est pas une question de race.

2 *adj film, slide, photograph* en couleur; *problem etc* racial. **~ bar** discrimination raciale; **~ scheme** combinaison *f* de(s) couleurs; **to choose a ~ scheme** assortir les couleurs; (*Press*) **~ supplement** supplément illustré; **~ television** télévision *f* (en) couleur; **~ television (set)** téléviseur *m* couleur *inv*.

3 *vt* (*gen: lit, fig*) colorer; (*paint*) peindre; (*crayon*) colorier; (*dye*) teindre; (*tint*) teinter. **to ~ sth red** colorer *etc* qch en rouge; **~ing book** album *m* à colorier.

4 *vi [person]* rougir.

♦ **coloration** *n* coloration *f*. ♦ **colorcast 1** *n* programme *m* (télévisé) en couleur; **2** *vt* téléviser en couleur. ♦ **colour-blind** *adj* daltonien. ♦ **colour-blindness** *n* daltonisme *m*. ♦ **coloured 1** *adj liquid* coloré; *drawing* colorié; *pencil* de couleur; *photograph etc* en couleur; *person, race* de couleur; **a highly ~ed tale** un récit très coloré; **a straw-~ed hat** un chapeau couleur paille; **muddy-~ed** couleur de boue; **2** *n*: **~eds** personnes *fpl* de couleur; (*in South Africa*) métis *mpl*. ♦ **colourful** *adj dress, tale* coloré; *personality* pittoresque. ♦ **colouring** *n* coloration *f*; (*complexion*) teint *m*; **high ~ing** teint coloré. ♦ **colourless** *adj* incolore.

colt [kəʊlt] *n* poulain *m*.

column ['kɒləm] *n* (*all senses*) colonne *f*. ♦ **columnist** *n* journaliste *mf* (*chargé(e) d'une rubrique régulière*).

coma ['kəʊmə] *n* coma *m*. **in a ~** dans le coma. ♦ **comatose** *adj* comateux.

comb [kəʊm] **1** *n* peigne *m*. **to run a ~ through one's hair** se donner un coup de peigne. **2** *vt* **(a)** peigner. **to ~ one's hair** se peigner; **to ~ sb's hair** peigner qn. **(b)** (*search*) *area, town* ratisser; (**~ through**) *file* dépouiller.

combat ['kɒmbæt] **1** *n* combat *m*. **on ~ duty** en service commandé. **2** *vti* combattre (*for* pour, *with, against* contre). ♦ **combatant** *adj, n* combattant(e) *m(f)*.

combine [kəm'baɪn] **1** *vt projects, objectives* combiner (*with* avec); *qualities* allier (*with* à); *forces, efforts* unir. **to ~ business with pleasure** joindre l'utile à l'agréable; **~d clock and radio** combiné *m* radio-réveil; **their ~d wealth** leurs richesses réunies; **a ~d effort** un effort conjugué; **~d forces** forces alliées; **~d operation** (*Mil*) opération *f* interarmes *inv*; (*by allies*) opération alliée; (*fig*) entreprise *f* faite en commun. **2** *vi* (*gen*) s'unir, s'associer; *[parties]* fusionner; *[workers]* se syndiquer; (*Chem*) se combiner; (*fig*) se liguer (*against* contre); *[events]* concourir (*to* à). **3** ['kɒmbaɪn] *n* association *f*; (*Comm, Fin*) trust *m*, cartel *m*; (*Jur*) corporation *f*; (**~ harvester**) moissonneuse-batteuse *f*. ♦ **combination 1** *n* (*gen*) combinaison *f*; *[events]* concours *m*; **(motorcycle) combination** side-car *m*; **2** *adj*: **combination lock** serrure *f* à combinaison.

combustion [kəm'bʌstʃən] *n* combustion *f*. ♦ **combustible** *adj* combustible.

come [kʌm] *pret* **came,** *ptp* **come** *vi* **(a)** (*gen*) venir; (*arrive*) venir, arriver; (*have its place*) venir, se trouver. **~ with me** venez avec moi; **~ and see me soon** venez me voir bientôt; **he has ~ to mend the television** il est venu réparer la télévision; **he has ~ from Edinburgh** il est venu d'Édimbourg; **he has just ~ from Edinburgh** il arrive d'Édimbourg; (*originate from*) **to ~ from** venir de; **he has ~ a long way** il est venu de loin; (*fig*) il a fait du chemin; **they were coming and going all day** ils n'ont fait qu'aller et venir toute la journée; (*TV*) **the picture ~s and goes** l'image saute; **the pain ~s and goes** la douleur est intermittente; **to ~ running** arriver en courant; **to ~ home** rentrer (chez soi *or* à la maison); **to ~ for sb/sth** venir chercher qn/qch, venir prendre qn/qch; **I'll ~ after you** je vous suis; **coming!** j'arrive!; (*excl*) **~, ~!, ~ now!** voyons!; **they came to a town** ils sont arrivés à une ville, ils ont atteint une ville; **help came in time** les secours sont arrivés à temps; **it came into my head that** il m'est venu à l'esprit que; **it came as a shock to him** cela lui a fait un choc; **it came as a surprise to him** cela l'a (beaucoup) surpris; **when it ~s to mathematics** pour ce qui est des mathématiques; **when it ~s to choosing** quand il faut choisir; (*fig*) **he will never ~ to much** il ne sera *or* fera jamais grand-chose; **the time will ~ when ...** il viendra un temps où ...; **May ~s before June** mai vient avant *or* précède juin; **July ~s after June** juillet vient après *or* suit juin; **this passage ~s on page 10** ce passage se trouve à la page 10.

(b) (*happen*) arriver (*to* à), se produire. **~ what may** quoi qu'il arrive (*subj*); **nothing came of it** il n'en est rien résulté; **that's what ~s of disobeying!** voilà ce que c'est que de désobéir!; **no good will ~ of it** il n'en sortira rien de bon; **how do you ~ to be so late?** comment se fait-il que vous soyez si en retard?

(c) (*be, become*) devenir, se trouver. **his dreams came true** ses rêves se sont réalisés; **the handle has ~ loose** le manche s'est desserré; **it ~s less expensive to shop in town** cela revient moins cher de faire ses achats en ville; **that ~s naturally to him** il est doué pour cela; **everything came right in the end** tout s'est arrangé à la fin; **this dress ~s in 3 sizes** cette robe existe en 3 tailles; **I have ~ to believe him** j'en suis venu à le croire; **he came to admit he was wrong** il a fini par reconnaître qu'il avait tort; **now I ~ to think of it** réflexion faite, quand j'y songe; (*liter*) **it came to pass that** il advint que (*liter*); **to ~ undone** se défaire; **to ~ apart** (*come off*) se détacher; (*come unstuck*) se décoller.

(d) (*phrases*) **the life to ~** la vie future; **the years to ~** les années à venir; **if it ~s to that, you shouldn't have done it either** à ce compte-là *or* à ce moment-là*, tu n'aurais pas dû le faire non plus; **I've known him for 3 years ~ January** cela fera 3 ans en janvier que je le connais; **she is coming* 6** elle va sur ses 6 ans; **she had it coming to her*** elle l'a *or* l'avait (bien) cherché; **to ~ between two people** (venir) se mettre entre deux personnes; **she's as clever as they ~*** elle est futée comme pas une*; **you could see that coming*** on voyait venir ça de loin; **~ again?*** comment?, pardon?; **how ~?*** comment ça se fait?; **how ~ you can't find it?*** comment se fait-il que tu n'arrives (*subj*) pas à le trouver?

come about *vi* se faire (*that* que + *subj*), arriver.

come across 1 *vi* (*gen*) traverser; (*be received*) faire de l'effet. **his speech came across very well/badly** son discours a fait beaucoup d'effet/n'a pas fait d'effet; **his true feelings came across** ses vrais sentiments se faisaient sentir. **2** *vt fus* (*find, meet*) tomber sur.

come along *vi* **(a) ~ along!** (*impatiently*) (allons *or* voyons,) dépêchez-vous!; (*in friendly tone*)

(allez,) venez! **(b)** (*accompany*) venir. **(c)** (*progress*) faire des progrès. **how is your broken arm? – it's coming along quite well** comment va votre bras cassé? – il *or* ça se remet bien; **how are your lettuces/plans coming along?** où en sont vos laitues/vos projets?
come away *vi* (*leave*) partir, s'en aller; *[button etc]* se détacher, partir. **~ away from there!** sors de là!, écarte-toi de là!
come back *vi* revenir. **I asked her to ~ back with me** je lui ai demandé de me raccompagner; **to ~ back to what I was saying** pour en revenir à ce que je disais; **I'll ~ back to you on that one*** nous en reparlerons plus tard; **his name is coming back to me** son nom me revient (à la mémoire).
come by *vt fus* (*obtain*) *object* se procurer; *idea, opinion* se faire.
come down *vi* descendre (*from* de, *to* jusqu'à); *[buildings etc]* être démoli; *[prices]* baisser. **to ~ down in the world** descendre dans l'échelle sociale; **he came down on me like a ton of bricks*** il m'est tombé dessus à bras raccourcis; **to ~ down with flu** attraper une grippe.
come forward *vi* se présenter (*as* comme). **to ~ forward with** *help, money, suggestion* offrir; *answer* suggérer.
come in *vi [person]* entrer; *[trains etc]* arriver; *[tide]* monter; (*in race*) arriver. **where does your brother ~ in?** et ton frère là-dedans?; **he came in fourth** il est arrivé quatrième; **the socialists came in at the last election** les socialistes sont arrivés au pouvoir aux dernières élections; **he has £5,000 coming in every year** il touche 5 000 livres chaque année; **to ~ in for** *criticism, reproach* être l'objet de, subir; *praise* recevoir; **to ~ into** (*inherit*) hériter de.
come off 1 *vi* **(a)** *[button]* se détacher; *[stains, marks]* partir. **(b)** *[event etc]* avoir lieu; *[plans etc]* se réaliser; *[attempts, experiments]* réussir. **(c)** (*acquit o.s.*) s'en tirer, s'en sortir. **he came off well by comparison with his brother** il s'en est très bien tiré en comparaison de son frère; **to ~ off best** gagner. **2** *vt fus*: **a button came off his coat** un bouton s'est détaché de son manteau; **he came off his bike** il est tombé de son vélo; **~ off it!*** et puis quoi encore?, vraiment?
come on 1 *vi* **(a)** (*follow*) suivre; (*continue to advance*) continuer d'avancer. **(b)** = **come along (a)**. **(c)** = **come along (c)**. **(d)** (*start*) *[illness]* se déclarer. **the rain came on** il s'est mis à pleuvoir; **I feel a cold coming on** je sens que je m'enrhume. **(e)** (*Theat*) *[actor]* entrer en scène. **'Hamlet' is coming on next week** on donne 'Hamlet' la semaine prochaine. **2** *vt fus* = **come upon.**
come out *vi [person, object, flowers, car, drawer]* sortir (*of* de); *[sun, stars]* paraître; *[spots, rash]* sortir; *[secret, news]* être divulgué; *[truth]* se faire jour; *[books, magazines, films]* paraître, sortir; *[qualities]* se manifester; *[stains]* s'en aller; *[dyes, colours]* (*run*) déteindre; (*fade*) se faner; (*Math*) *[problems]* se résoudre; *[division etc]* tomber juste. **to ~ out on strike** se mettre en grève; **the photo came out well** la photo est très bonne; **the total ~s out at 500** le total s'élève à 500; **he came out third in French** il s'est classé troisième en français; **to ~ out in a rash** avoir une poussée de boutons; **to ~ out for/against sth** se déclarer ouvertement pour/contre qch; **you never know what she's going to ~ out with next*** on ne sait jamais ce qu'elle va dire *or* sortir*.
come over 1 *vi* venir. **he came over to England for a few months** il est venu passer quelques mois en Angleterre; **he came over to our way of thinking** il s'est rangé à notre avis; **she came over faint** elle a failli s'évanouir; **his speech came over well** son discours a fait bonne impression. **2** *vt fus*: **a feeling of shyness came over her** la timidité la saisit; **what's ~ over you?** qu'est-ce qui vous prend?
come round *vi* **(a)** faire le tour *or* un détour. **we had to ~ round by the farm** nous avons dû faire un détour par la ferme. **(b)** venir, passer. **do ~ round and see me one evening** passez me voir un de ces soirs. **(c)** (*recur regularly*) revenir périodiquement. **your birthday will soon ~ round again** ce sera bientôt à nouveau ton anniversaire. **(d)** (*change one's mind*) changer d'avis. **(e)** (*regain consciousness*) reprendre connaissance. **(f)** (*throw off bad mood etc*) **leave her alone, she'll soon ~ round** laissez-la tranquille, elle reviendra bientôt à d'autres sentiments.
come through 1 *vi* (*survive*) s'en tirer. (*Telec*) **the call came through** on a eu la communication. **2** *vt fus* (*survive*) *danger, war* se tirer indemne de; *illness* survivre à.
come to 1 *vi* = **come round (e)**. **2** *vt fus*: **how much does it ~ to?** cela fait combien?; **it ~s to much less per metre if you buy a lot** cela revient bien moins cher le mètre si vous en achetez beaucoup.
come together *vi* (*assemble*) se rassembler; (*meet*) se rencontrer.
come under *vt fus sb's influence, domination* tomber sous; *heading* être classé sous, se trouver sous.
come up *vi* **(a)** monter. **he came up to me with a smile** il m'a abordé en souriant. **(b)** *[accused]* comparaître (*before* devant); *[law suit]* être entendu (*before* par); *[matters for discussion, question]* être soulevé. **he came up against total opposition to his plans** il s'est heurté à une opposition radicale à ses projets; **to ~ up against sb** entrer en conflit avec qn. **(c) the water came up to his knees** l'eau lui venait *or* arrivait jusqu'aux genoux; **my son ~s up to my shoulder** mon fils m'arrive à l'épaule; **his work has not ~ up to our expectation** son travail n'a pas répondu à notre attente.
come up with *vt fus idea, plan* proposer, suggérer; *money, suggestion* offrir.
come upon *vt fus* (*find, meet*) *object, person* tomber sur.
♦ **comeback** *n* (*Theat etc*) rentrée *f*; (*reaction*) réaction *f*; (*response*) réplique *f*. ♦ **comedown*** *n*: **it was rather a ~down for him to have to work** c'était assez humiliant pour lui d'avoir à travailler. ♦ **comer** *n*: **open to all ~rs** ouvert à tous; **the first ~r** le premier venu. ♦ **comehither*** *adj*: **a ~-hither look** un regard aguichant. ♦ **comeuppance*** [ˌkʌmˈʌpəns] *n*: **he got his ~uppance** il a échoué (*or* perdu *etc*) et il ne l'a pas volé. ♦ **coming 1** *n* arrivée *f*, venue *f*; **coming and going** va-et-vient *m*; **comings and goings** allées *fpl* et venues; **2** *adj* (*future*) à venir, futur; (*next*) prochain; (*promising*) qui promet, d'avenir; **a coming politician** un homme politique d'avenir.
comedy [ˈkɒmɪdɪ] *n* comédie *f*. **low ~** farce *f*. ♦ **comedian** *n* (acteur *m*) comique *m*. ♦ **comedienne** *n* actrice *f* comique.
comely [ˈkʌmlɪ] *adj* (*liter*) beau, gracieux. ♦ **comeliness** *n* beauté *f*, grâce *f*.
comet [ˈkɒmɪt] *n* comète *f*.
comfort [ˈkʌmfət] **1** *n* **(a)** confort *m*, bien-être *m*. **to live in ~** vivre dans l'aisance; **every modern ~** tout le confort moderne; **he likes his ~s** il aime ses aises. **(b)** (*consolation*) consolation *f*, réconfort *m*. **to take ~ from sth** trouver du réconfort *or* une consolation dans qch; **you are a great ~ to me** vous êtes pour moi d'un grand réconfort; **if it's any ~ to you** si ça peut te consoler; **it is a ~ to know that ...** il est consolant de savoir que ...; **to take ~ from the fact/the knowledge that** trouver rassurant le fait que/de savoir que; **the fighting was too close for (my) ~** les combats étaient trop près pour mon goût.

2 *adj*: (*US*) ~ **station** toilettes *fpl*.
3 *vt* consoler, soulager.
♦ **comfortable** *adj armchair, bed, win, majority* confortable; *temperature* agréable; *thought, idea, news* réconfortant; *income* très suffisant; **I am quite ~able here** je me trouve très bien ici; **to make o.s. ~able** se mettre à son aise; (*fig*) **I am not very ~able about it** cela m'inquiète un peu. ♦ **comfortably** *adv* confortablement; agréablement; *live* dans l'aisance; **they are ~ably off** ils sont à l'aise. ♦ **comforter** *n* (*person*) consolateur *m*, -trice *f* (*liter*); (*scarf*) cache-nez *m inv*; (*dummy-teat*) tétine *f*; (*quilt*) édredon *m*. ♦ **comforting** *adj words, thoughts* consolant; *news* soulageant; **it is ~ing to think that ...** il est réconfortant de penser que .... ♦ **comfortless** *adj room* sans confort; *prospect* désolant. ♦ **comfy*** *adj chair, room* confortable; **are you comfy?** êtes-vous bien?
comic ['kɒmɪk] **1** *adj* comique. ~ **opera** opéra *m* comique; ~ **relief** moment *m* de détente comique; ~ **verse** poésie *f* humoristique. **2** *n* (*person*) (acteur *m*) comique *m*, actrice *f* comique; (*magazine*) comic *m*. **~s, ~ strip** bande dessinée. ♦ **comical** *adj* comique. ♦ **comically** *adv* comiquement.
comma ['kɒmə] *n* virgule *f*.
command [kə'mɑːnd] **1** *vt* ordonner, commander (*sb to do* à qn de faire; *that* que + *subj*); *army, ship* commander; *money, services, resources* disposer de; *respect etc* imposer. **that ~s a high price** cela se vend très cher. **2** *vi* commander. **3** *n* (*order*) ordre *m*; (*Mil*) commandement *m*. **at** *or* **by the ~ of** sur l'ordre de; **at the word of ~** au commandement; **to be in ~ of** être à la tête de; **to have/take ~ of** avoir/prendre le commandement de; **under the ~ of** sous le commandement *or* les ordres de; **who's in ~ here?** qui est-ce qui commande ici?; **~ of the seas** maîtrise *f* des mers; **he has a ~ of 3 foreign languages** il possède 3 langues étrangères; **his ~ of English** sa maîtrise de l'anglais; **all the money at my ~** tout l'argent à ma disposition. **4** *adj*: ~ **module** module *m* de commande; ~ **performance** ≈ représentation *f* de gala (*à la requête du souverain*); ~ **post** poste *m* de commandement. ♦ **commandant** *n* commandant *m*. ♦ **commandeer** *vt* réquisitionner. ♦ **commander** *n* chef *m*; (*Mil*) commandant *m*; **~er-in-chief** commandant *m* en chef. ♦ **commanding** *adj air* imposant; *look, voice, tone* impérieux; **~ing officer** commandant *m*; **to be in a ~ing position** avoir une position dominante. ♦ **commandment** *n* commandement *m*. ♦ **commando** *n* commando *m*.
commemorate [kə'meməreɪt] *vt* commémorer. ♦ **commemoration** *n* commémoration *f*. ♦ **commemorative** *adj* commémoratif.
commence [kə'mens] *vti* commencer (*sth* qch; *to do, doing* à faire). ♦ **commencement** *n* commencement *m*.
commend [kə'mend] *vt* (*praise*) louer; (*recommend*) recommander; (*entrust*) confier (*to* à). **his scheme did not ~ itself to the public** son projet n'a pas été du goût du public; **his scheme has little to ~ it** son projet n'a pas grand-chose qui le fasse recommander. ♦ **commendable** *adj* louable; recommandable. ♦ **commendably** *adv*: **that was ~ably short** cela avait le mérite de la brièveté. ♦ **commendation** *n* louange *f*; recommandation *f*.
commensurate [kə'menʃərɪt] *adj*: ~ **with** proportionné à.
comment ['kɒment] **1** *n* (*spoken, written*) commentaire *m* (bref), remarque *f*; (*critical*) critique *f*. **he let it pass without ~** il ne l'a pas relevé; **'no ~'** 'je n'ai rien à dire'. **2** *vt* remarquer (*that* que); *text* commenter. **3** *vi* faire des remarques (*on* sur). ♦ **commentary** *n* (*gen*) commentaire *m*; (*Sport*) reportage *m*. ♦ **commentate 1** *vi* (*Rad, TV*) faire un reportage (*on* sur); **2** *vt* (*Rad, TV*) faire un reportage sur; *text* commenter. ♦ **commentator** *n* (*Rad, TV*) reporter *m*.
commerce ['kɒmɜːs] *n* (*Comm*) commerce *m*, affaires *fpl*; **Department of C~** ≈ ministère *m* du Commerce. ♦ **commercial 1** *adj* (*gen*) commercial; *world* du commerce; *value* marchand, commercial; *district* commerçant; **commercial college** école *f* de commerce; **commercial traveller** représentant *m* de commerce; **commercial vehicle** véhicule *m* utilitaire; **2** *n* (*Rad, TV*) annonce *f* publicitaire, spot *m*. ♦ **commercialism** *n* mercantilisme *m*; (*on large scale*) affairisme *m*. ♦ **commercialization** *n* commercialisation *f*. ♦ **commercialize** *vt* commercialiser. ♦ **commercially** *adv* commercialement.
commiserate [kə'mɪzəreɪt] *vi* (*show commiseration for*) témoigner de la sympathie (*with* à); (*feel it*) éprouver de la commisération (*with* pour). ♦ **commiseration** *n* commisération *f*.
commissar ['kɒmɪsɑːʳ] *n* commissaire *m* du peuple. ♦ **commissariat** *n* commissariat *m*.
commission [kə'mɪʃən] **1** *n* **(a)** (*Comm*) commission *f*. **on a ~ basis** à la commission; **he gets 10% ~** il reçoit une commission de 10%. **(b)** (*orders*) instructions *fpl*; (*to artist etc*) commande *f*. **(c)** (*Mil*) brevet *m*. **to get one's ~** être nommé officier. **(d)** (*body of people*) commission *f*, comité *m*. **~ of inquiry** commission d'enquête. **(e) out of ~** *machine, lift etc* en panne, hors service. **2** *vt* **(a)** donner pouvoir à. **he was ~ed to inquire into ...** il a reçu mission de faire une enquête sur ...; **I have been ~ed to say** j'ai été chargé de dire. **(b)** *book, painting* commander. **(c)** (*Mil etc*) **~ed officer** officier *m*; **he was ~ed in 1970** il a été nommé officier en 1970. ♦ **commissionaire** *n* commissionnaire *m* (*d'hôtel*). ♦ **commissioner** *n* membre *m* d'une commission, commissaire *m*; (*Police*) ≈ préfet *m* (de police).
commit [kə'mɪt] *vt* **(a)** *crime etc* commettre. **to ~ suicide** se suicider. **(b)** (*consign*) remettre (*to* à, aux soins de). **to ~ sb to prison** faire incarcérer qn; **to ~ sb for trial** mettre qn en accusation; **to ~ to writing** coucher par écrit; **to ~ to memory** apprendre par cœur. **(c) to ~ o.s.** s'engager (*to* à); **a ~ted writer** un écrivain engagé; **to be ~ted to a policy** s'être engagé à poursuivre une politique. ♦ **commitment** *n* (*gen*) engagement *m*; (*obligation*) responsabilité(s) *f(pl)*; (*Fin*) engagement financier; (*Comm*) **'without ~ment'** 'sans obligation'; **teaching ~ments** (heures *fpl* d') enseignement *m*. ♦ **committal** *n* remise *f* (*to* à, aux soins de); (*to prison*) incarcération *f*; (*burial*) mise *f* en terre.
committee [kə'mɪtɪ] **1** *n* (*gen*) comité *m*, commission *f*; (*Parl*) commission. **to be on a ~** faire partie d'une commission *or* d'un comité; **~ of inquiry** commission d'enquête. **2** *adj*: ~ **meeting** réunion *f* de comité *or* de commission; ~ **member** membre *m* d'un comité *or* d'une commission.
commodious [kə'məʊdɪəs] *adj* spacieux.
commodity [kə'mɒdɪtɪ] *n* produit *m*; (*food*) denrée *f*. **staple commodities** produits de base.
common ['kɒmən] **1** *adj* **(a)** (*affecting many*) *interest, cause, language* commun. **to make ~ cause with sb** faire cause commune avec qn; **by ~ consent** d'un commun accord; (*fig*) **~ ground** terrain *m* d'entente; **it's ~ knowledge that ...** chacun sait que ...; **~ land** terrain communal; **~ lodging house** asile *m* de nuit; **the C~ Market** le Marché commun; **~ wall** mur mitoyen. **(b)** (*usual, universal*) *method* commun, ordinaire; *sight* familier; *occurrence* fréquent; *belief* général; (*pej*) *accent, person* commun, vulgaire; (*Gram, Math*) commun. **it's quite ~** c'est très courant; **it's a ~ experience** cela arrive à tout le monde; **it is only**

~ **courtesy to apologise** la politesse la plus élémentaire veut qu'on s'excuse (*subj*); (*pej*) **the ~ herd** la plèbe; ~ **honesty** la simple honnêteté; **the ~ man** l'homme du commun *or* du peuple; **the ~ people** le peuple; **in ~ parlance** dans le langage courant; **out of the ~ run** hors du commun; ~ **salt** sel *m* (ordinaire); ~ **or garden** ordinaire.

2 *n* **(a)** (*land*) terrain communal. **(b) in ~** en commun (*with* avec); **they have nothing in ~** ils n'ont rien de commun.

♦ **commoner** *n* roturier *m*, -ière *f*. ♦ **common-law** *adj*: **~-law wife** épouse *f* de droit coutumier. ♦ **commonly** *adv* (*V above* **1b**) communément; ordinairement; fréquemment; généralement; (*vulgarly*) d'une façon vulgaire *or* commune. ♦ **commonness** *n* caractère *m* commun *or* ordinaire; fréquence *f*; généralité *f*; vulgarité *f*. ♦ **commonplace 1** *adj* ordinaire; **2** *n* lieu *m* commun. ♦ **commonroom** *n* salle *f* commune; (*staffroom*) salle des professeurs. ♦ **commons** *npl* (*Parl*) **the C~s** les Communes *fpl*; (*gen*) **on short ~s** strictement rationné. ♦ **commonsense 1** *n* sens *m* commun, bon sens; **2** *adj* sensé, plein de bon sens. ♦ **Commonwealth** *n*: **the C~wealth** le Commonwealth; (*Hist*) la république de Cromwell; **Minister of C~wealth Affairs** ministre *m* du Commonwealth.

commotion [kəˈməʊʃən] *n* agitation *f*, commotion *f*. **to make** *or* **cause a ~** semer la perturbation.

commune [kəˈmju:n] **1** *vi* converser intimement (*with* avec). **to ~ with nature** communier avec la nature. **2** [ˈkɒmju:n] *n* (*Admin*) commune *f*; (*community*) communauté *f*. **to live in a ~** vivre en communauté. ♦ **communal** *adj facilities* commun; *life* collectif. ♦ **communally** *adv* en commun, collectivement.

communicate [kəˈmju:nɪkeɪt] **1** *vt* (*gen*) communiquer (*to* à); *illness* transmettre (*to* à). **2** *vi* communiquer, se mettre en rapport (*with* avec); *[rooms]* communiquer; (*Rel*) communier. ♦ **communicant** *n* (*Rel*) communiant(e) *m(f)*. ♦ **communication 1** *n* communication *f*; **to be in communication with sb** être en contact *or* rapport avec qn; **to be in radio communication with sb** communiquer avec qn par radio; **there has been no communication between them** il n'y a eu aucun contact entre eux; **2** *adj* (*Rail*) **communication cord** sonnette *f* d'alarme; **communication satellites** satellites *mpl* de transmission. ♦ **communicative** *adj* communicatif. ♦ **communion** *n* (*gen*) communion *f*; **to take communion** recevoir la communion. ♦ **communiqué** *n* communiqué *m*.

communism [ˈkɒmjʊnɪzəm] *n* communisme *m*. ♦ **communist** *adj*, *n* communiste (*mf*). ♦ **communistic** *adj* communisant.

community [kəˈmju:nɪtɪ] **1** *n* communauté *f*. **the French ~ in Edinburgh** la colonie française d'Édimbourg; **the student ~** les étudiants *mpl*, le monde étudiant. **2** *adj*: ~ **centre** foyer *m* socio-éducatif; (*US*) ~ **chest** fonds *m* commun; ~ **health centre** centre *m* médico-social; ~ **singing** chants *mpl* en chœur (*improvisés*); ~ **spirit** esprit *m* civique; ~ **worker** animateur *m*, -trice *f* socio-culturel(le).

commute [kəˈmju:t] **1** *vt* substituer (*into* à); (*Elec, Jur*) commuer (*into* en). **2** *vi* faire un trajet journalier, faire la navette (*between* entre; *from* de). ♦ **commuter** *n* banlieusard(e) *m(f)*; (*Brit*) **I work in London but I'm a ~r** je travaille à Londres mais je fais la navette; **the ~r belt** la grande banlieue.

compact [kəmˈpækt] **1** *adj* compact, serré. **the house is very ~** la maison n'a pas de place perdue. **2** [ˈkɒmpækt] *n* (*agreement*) contrat *m*, convention *f*; (*powder* ~) poudrier *m*. ♦ **compactly** *adv build, design* sans perte de place. ♦ **compactness** *n [room etc]* économie *f* d'espace.

companion [kəmˈpænjən] **1** *n* compagnon *m*, compagne *f*; (*lady* ~) dame *f* de compagnie; (*one of pair of objects*) pendant *m*; (*handbook*) manuel *m*. **2** *adj*: ~ **volume** volume *m* qui va de pair (*to* avec). ♦ **companionable** *adj person* sociable; *presence* sympathique. ♦ **companionship** *n* compagnie *f*. ♦ **companionway** *n* escalier *m* des cabines.

company [ˈkʌmpənɪ] *n* (*gen, also Mil*) compagnie *f*; (*Comm, Fin*) société *f*, compagnie; *[actors]* troupe *f*, compagnie. **to keep sb ~** tenir compagnie à qn; **to part ~ with** se séparer de; **in ~ with** en compagnie de; **he is good ~** on ne s'ennuie pas avec lui; **it's ~ for her** ça lui fait une compagnie; **we are expecting ~** nous attendons des invités; **to be in good ~** être en bonne compagnie; **to get into bad ~** avoir de mauvaises fréquentations; **she is no fit ~ for your sister** ce n'est pas une fréquentation pour votre sœur; **Smith & C~** Smith et Compagnie; **shipping ~** compagnie de navigation; ~ **car** voiture *f* de fonction; ~ **secretary** secrétaire *m* général (*d'une société*); **National Theatre C~** la troupe du Théâtre National; (*Naut*) **ship's ~** équipage *m*.

compare [kəmˈpɛəʳ] **1** *vt* comparer (*with* à, avec; *to* à), mettre en comparaison (*with* avec). **~d with** en comparaison de, par comparaison avec; (*fig*) **to ~ notes with sb** échanger ses impressions avec qn. **2** *vi* être comparable (*with* à). **how do the cars ~ for speed?** quelles sont les vitesses respectives des voitures?; **how do the prices ~?** est-ce que les prix sont comparables?; **he can't ~ with you** il n'y a pas de comparaison entre vous et lui. **3** *n*: **beyond ~** (*adv*) incomparablement; (*adj*) sans pareil. ♦ **comparable** [ˈkɒmpərəbl] *adj* comparable (*with, to* à). ♦ **comparative** [kəmˈpærətɪv] **1** *adj method* comparatif; *linguistics, literature* comparé; (*Gram*) comparatif; *cost, freedom, luxury* relatif; **he's a comparative stranger** je le connais relativement peu; **2** *n*: **in the comparative** au comparatif. ♦ **comparatively** *adv* relativement. ♦ **comparison** *n* comparaison *f*; **in comparison with** en comparaison de; **by comparison (with)** par comparaison (avec).

compartment [kəmˈpɑ:tmənt] *n* compartiment *m*. ♦ **compartmentalize** *vt* compartimenter.

compass [ˈkʌmpəs] *n* boussole *f*; (*Naut*) compas *m*; (*of powers, voice*) étendue *f*. **within the ~ of** dans les limites *fpl* de; (*Math*) **~es** compas *m*.

compassion [kəmˈpæʃən] *n* compassion *f*. ♦ **compassionate** *adj person* compatissant; *reasons, grounds* de convenance personnelle; *leave* exceptionnel.

compatible [kəmˈpætɪbl] *adj* compatible (*with* avec). ♦ **compatibility** *n* compatibilité *f*.

compatriot [kəmˈpætrɪət] *n* compatriote *mf*.

compel [kəmˈpel] *vt* contraindre (*sb to do* qn à faire). **to be ~led to do** être contraint de faire; **to ~ obedience from sb** contraindre qn à obéir. ♦ **compelling** *adj* irrésistible. ♦ **compellingly** *adv* irrésistiblement.

compendium [kəmˈpendɪəm] *n* (*summary*) abrégé *m*. (*Brit*) ~ **of games** boîte *f* de jeux.

compensate [ˈkɒmpənseɪt] **1** *vi*: **to ~ for sth** compenser qch; **then, to ~ for that, he ...** puis, pour compenser, il ...; **2** *vt* (*gen*) compenser (*sb for sth* qn de qch); (*financially*) dédommager (*sb for sth* qn de qch). ♦ **compensation** *n* compensation *f*; dédommagement *m*; **in compensation** en compensation (*for* de).

compere [ˈkɒmpɛəʳ] **1** *n* animateur *m*, -trice *f*. **2** *vt show* animer.

compete [kəmˈpi:t] *vi* (*gen*) concourir (*for* pour, *to do* pour faire); (*vie*) rivaliser (*with* avec, *in* de); (*Comm*) faire concurrence (*with* à, *for* pour). **to ~ with one another** se faire concurrence.

competent [ˈkɒmpɪtənt] *adj person, court* compétent (*for* pour, *to do* pour faire). **a ~ knowledge of** une connaissance suffisante de. ♦ **competence** *or* ♦ **competency** *n* compétence *f* (*for* pour, *in* en).

♦ **competently** *adv* avec compétence.
competition [ˌkɒmpɪˈtɪʃən] *n* **(a)** compétition *f*, concurrence *f* (*for* pour); (*Comm*) concurrence. **in ~ with** en concurrence avec. **(b)** concours *m* (*for* pour); (*Sport*) compétition *f*; (*Aut*) course *f*. **to go in for a ~** se présenter à un concours; **beauty ~** concours de beauté; **I won it in a newspaper ~** je l'ai gagné en faisant un concours dans le journal. ♦ **competitive** *adj entry, selection* par concours; *person* qui a l'esprit de compétition; *price* concurrentiel; *goods* à prix concurrentiel; **competitive examination** concours *m*. ♦ **competitor** *n* concurrent(e) *m(f)*.
compile [kəmˈpaɪl] *vt material* compiler; *dictionary* composer (par compilation); *list, catalogue* dresser. ♦ **compiler** *n* compilateur *m*, -trice *f*.
complacent [kəmˈpleɪsənt] *adj* satisfait de soi, suffisant. ♦ **complacence** *or* ♦ **complacency** *n* suffisance *f*. ♦ **complacently** *adv* avec suffisance.
complain [kəmˈpleɪn] *vi* se plaindre (*to sb* à qn; *of, about* de; *that* que). ♦ **complaint** *n* (*expression of discontent*) plainte *f*; (*reason for ~*) sujet *m* de plainte; (*Comm*) réclamation *f*; (*Jur*) plainte; (*Med*) maladie *f*. (*Comm*) **to make a ~t** faire une réclamation (*about* au sujet de).
complement [ˈkɒmplɪmənt] **1** *n* (*gen, Gram, Math*) complément *m*; *[staff etc]* effectif *m* complet. **2** [ˈkɒmplɪment] *vt* être le complément de. ♦ **complementary** *adj* complémentaire.
complete [kəmˈpliːt] **1** *adj* **(a)** (*total*) complet, total. **~ works** œuvres *fpl* complètes; **he's a ~ idiot*** il est complètement idiot. **(b)** (*finished*) achevé, terminé. **2** *vt collection* compléter; *misfortune* mettre le comble à; *piece of work* achever, terminer; *form, questionnaire* remplir. **and to ~ his happiness** et pour comble de bonheur; **and just to ~ things** et pour couronner le tout. ♦ **completely** *adv* complètement. ♦ **completeness** *n* état complet. ♦ **completion** *n* *[work]* achèvement *m*; *[contract, sale]* exécution *f*; **near completion** près d'être achevé; **on completion of contract** à la signature du contrat.
complex [ˈkɒmpleks] **1** *adj* (*all senses*) complexe. **2** *n* **(a)** complexe *m*, ensemble *m*. **mining ~** complexe minier; **housing ~** (ensemble de) résidences *fpl*, (*high rise*) grand ensemble. **(b)** (*Psych*) complexe *m*. **he's got a ~ about it** il en fait un complexe. ♦ **complexity** *n* complexité *f*.
complexion [kəmˈplekʃən] *n* *[face]* teint *m*. (*fig*) **that puts a new ~ on it** ça change tout.
complicate [ˈkɒmplɪkeɪt] *vt* compliquer (*with* de; *by doing* en faisant). ♦ **complicated** *adj* compliqué. ♦ **complication** *n* complication *f*.
compliment [ˈkɒmplɪmənt] **1** *n* compliment *m*. **to pay sb a ~** faire un compliment à qn; **give him my ~s** faites-lui mes compliments; **the ~s of the season** tous mes vœux; **'with the ~s of Mr X'** 'avec les hommages *or* les bons compliments de Monsieur X'; **~s slip** ≈ papillon *m* (avec les bons compliments de l'expéditeur). **2** [ˈkɒmplɪment] *vt* faire des compliments à (*on* de, sur); féliciter (*on doing* d'avoir fait). ♦ **complimentary** *adj* (*praising*) flatteur; (*gratis*) à titre gracieux; *ticket* de faveur.
comply [kəmˈplaɪ] *vi*: **to ~ with** *rules* obéir à; *sb's wishes* se conformer à; *request* accéder à. ♦ **compliance** *n*: **in compliance with** conformément à. ♦ **compliant** *adj* accommodant.
component [kəmˈpəʊnənt] **1** *adj* constituant. **2** *n* (*Aut, Tech*) pièce *f*. **~s factory** usine *f* de pièces détachées.
compose [kəmˈpəʊz] *vt* composer. **to be ~d of** se composer de; **to ~ o.s.** se calmer. ♦ **composed** *adj* calme, posé. ♦ **composedly** *adv* avec calme, posément. ♦ **composer** *n* compositeur *m*, -trice *f*. ♦ **composition** **1** *n* (*gen*) composition *f*; (*Scol: essay*) rédaction *f*; *[sentence]* construction *f*; *[word]* composition; **2** *adj rubber* synthétique. ♦ **compositor** *n* (*Typ*) compositeur *m*, -trice *f*. ♦ **composure** *n* calme *m*, sang-froid *m*.
compos mentis [ˈkɒmpɒsˈmentɪs] *adj* sain d'esprit.
compost [ˈkɒmpɒst] *n* compost *m*.
compound [ˈkɒmpaʊnd] **1** *n* (*Chem*) composé; (*Gram*) mot *m* composé; (*Tech*) compound *f*; (*enclosed area*) enclos *m*, enceinte *f*. **2** *adj* (*Chem*) composé; *number, sentence* complexe; *tense, word, interest* composé; *fracture* compliqué. **3** [kəmˈpaʊnd] *vt mixture* composer (*of* de); *ingredients* combiner; (*fig*) *problem, difficulties* aggraver.
comprehend [ˌkɒmprɪˈhend] *vt* comprendre. ♦ **comprehensible** *adj* compréhensible. ♦ **comprehension** *n* compréhension *f*; (*Scol*) exercice *m* de compréhension; (*inclusion*) inclusion *f*. ♦ **comprehensive** **1** *adj description, review* détaillé, complet; *knowledge* étendu; *rule* compréhensif; *measures* d'ensemble; *insurance* tous-risques *inv*; **2** *n*: **comprehensive (school)** ≈ collège *m* d'enseignement secondaire, C.E.S. *m*.
compress [kəmˈpres] **1** *vt substance* comprimer; *facts* condenser. **2** *vi* se comprimer; se condenser. **3** [ˈkɒmpres] *n* (*Med*) compresse *f*. ♦ **compression** *n* compression *f*; condensation *f*. ♦ **compressor** *n* compresseur *m*.
comprise [kəmˈpraɪz] *vt* comprendre, englober.
compromise [ˈkɒmprəmaɪz] **1** *n* compromis *m*. **2** *vi* transiger (*over* sur), aboutir à un compromis. **3** *vt* compromettre. **4** *adj decision, solution* de compromis. ♦ **compromising** *adj* compromettant.
comptometer [kɒmpˈtɒmɪtəʳ] *n* ® machine *f* comptable. **~ operator** mécanographe *mf*.
compulsion [kəmˈpʌlʃən] *n* contrainte *f*. **under ~** sous la contrainte; **you are under no ~** vous n'êtes nullement obligé. ♦ **compulsive** *adj reason, demand* coercitif; *desire, behaviour* compulsif; *smoker, liar* invétéré; **she's a compulsive talker** parler est un besoin chez elle. ♦ **compulsively** *adv drink, smoke, talk* d'une façon compulsive. ♦ **compulsorily** *adv* obligatoirement, de force. ♦ **compulsory** *adj education, military service* obligatoire; *loan* forcé; **compulsory purchase** expropriation *f* pour cause d'utilité publique; **compulsory retirement** mise *f* à la retraite d'office.
compunction [kəmˈpʌŋkʃən] *n* scrupule *m* (*about sth* à propos de qch; *about doing* à faire).
compute [kəmˈpjuːt] *vt* calculer. ♦ **computation** *n* calcul *m*. ♦ **computer** **1** *n* ordinateur *m*; **he is in ~rs** il est dans l'informatique; **2** *adj*: **~r language** langage *m* de programmation; **~r programmer** programmeur *m*, -euse *f*; **~r programming** programmation *f*; **~r science** informatique *f*; **~r scientist** informaticien(ne) *m(f)*. ♦ **computerization** *n* *[facts, figures]* traitement *m* électronique; *[system, process]* automatisation *f* électronique. ♦ **computerize** *vt facts* informatiser; *system* automatiser.
comrade [ˈkɒmrɪd] *n* camarade *mf*. ♦ **comrade-in-arms** *n* compagnon *m* d'armes. ♦ **comradeship** *n* camaraderie *f*.
con* [kɒn] **1** *vt*: **to ~ sb into doing** amener qn à faire en le dupant; **I've been ~ned** je me suis fait avoir*. **2** *n*: **it was all a big ~** c'était une vaste escroquerie. **3** *adj*: **~ man** escroc *m*; **~ game** escroquerie *f*.
concave [ˈkɒnˈkeɪv] *adj* concave.
conceal [kənˈsiːl] *vt object* cacher, dissimuler (*from sb* pour que qn ne le voie pas *etc*); *news, event* cacher (*from sb* à qn), garder secret; *emotions, thoughts* cacher (*from sb* à qn), dissimuler. **~ed lighting** éclairage *m* indirect; (*Aut*) **~ed turning** intersection *f* cachée. ♦ **concealment** *n*

dissimulation *f*; *[facts]* non-divulgation *f*; (*place of ~ment*) cachette *f*.
concede [kən'si:d] *vt* concéder. **to ~ victory** s'avouer vaincu.
conceit [kən'si:t] *n* vanité *f*, suffisance *f*. ♦ **conceited** *adj* vaniteux, suffisant. ♦ **conceitedly** *adv* avec vanité, avec suffisance.
conceive [kən'si:v] **1** *vt child, idea* concevoir. **I cannot ~ why ...** je ne comprends vraiment pas pourquoi ... . **2** *vi*: **to ~ of** concevoir. ♦ **conceivable** *adj* concevable; **it is conceivable that** il est concevable que + *subj*. ♦ **conceivably** *adv*: **she may conceivably be right** il est concevable qu'elle ait raison.
concentrate ['kɒnsəntreɪt] **1** *vt* (*gen*) concentrer (*on* sur); *hopes* reporter (*on* sur). **2** *vi* **(a)** *[troops, people]* se concentrer. **(b)** (*think hard*) se concentrer (*on* sur). **to ~ on doing** s'appliquer à faire; **I just can't ~!** je n'arrive pas à me concentrer!; **the terrorists ~d on the outlying farms** les terroristes ont concentré leurs attaques sur les fermes isolées; **~ on getting well** occupe-toi d'abord de ta santé; *[speaker]* **I shall ~ on the 16th century** je traiterai en particulier le 16e siècle. **3** *adj, n* (*Chem*) concentré (*m*). ♦ **concentration** *n* concentration *f*; **concentration camp** camp *m* de concentration.
concept ['kɒnsept] *n* concept *m*.
conception [kən'sepʃən] *n* conception *f*.
concern [kən'sɜ:n] **1** *vt* (*affect*) concerner; (*be the business of*) être l'affaire de. **as ~s** en ce qui concerne; **that doesn't ~ you** cela ne vous regarde pas, ce n'est pas votre affaire; **'to whom it may ~'** ≈ 'je soussigné(e) certifie que ...'; **as far as he is ~ed** en ce qui le concerne; **the persons ~ed** les intéressés; **the department ~ed** (*under discussion*) le service en question; (*relevant*) le service compétent; **to be ~ed in** avoir un intérêt dans; **to ~ o.s. with** s'occuper de; **we are ~ed only with facts** nous ne nous occupons que des faits; **to be ~ed by** *or* **for** *or* **about** *or* **at** s'inquiéter de, être inquiet de; **I am ~ed about him** je m'inquiète à son sujet; **I am ~ed to hear that ...** j'apprends avec inquiétude que ... .
2 *n* **(a) to have no ~ with** n'avoir rien à voir avec, être sans rapport avec; **it's no ~ of his, it's none of his ~** cela ne le regarde pas; **what ~ is it of yours?** en quoi est-ce que cela vous regarde? **(b)** (*business ~*) entreprise *f*, affaire *f*. **he has a ~ in the business** il a des intérêts dans l'affaire. **(c)** (*anxiety*) inquiétude *f*, souci *m*. **a look of ~** un regard inquiet.
♦ **concerned** *adj* (*worried*) inquiet, soucieux (*for* de); (*affected*) affecté (*about, at, for* de, par). ♦ **concerning** *prep* en ce qui concerne, concernant.
concert ['kɒnsət] **1** *n* concert *m*. **in ~** à l'unisson. **2** *adj ticket, pianist* de concert. **~ performer** concertiste *mf*; **~ tour** tournée *f* de concerts. ♦ **concerted** *adj action, effort* concerté. ♦ **concertgoer** *n* habitué(e) *m(f)* des concerts. ♦ **concert-hall** *n* salle *f* de concert.
concertina [ˌkɒnsə'ti:nə] **1** *n* concertina *m*. **2** *vi* se télescoper.
concerto [kən'tʃɛətəʊ] *n* concerto *m*.
concession [kən'seʃən] *n* concession *f*. **price ~** réduction *f*. ♦ **concessionary** *adj* concessionnaire; *ticket, fare* à prix réduit.
conch [kɒntʃ] *n* conque *f*.
conciliate [kən'sɪlɪeɪt] *vt person* apaiser; *opposing views* concilier. ♦ **conciliation** *n* apaisement *m*; conciliation *f*; (*Ind*) **conciliation board** conseil *m* d'arbitrage. ♦ **conciliator** *n* conciliateur *m*, -trice *f*; (*in negotiations*) médiateur *m*, -trice *f*. ♦ **conciliatory** *adj person, words, manner* conciliant; *spirit* de conciliation; *procedure* conciliatoire.
concise [kən'saɪs] *adj* (*short*) concis; (*shortened*) abrégé. ♦ **concisely** *adv* avec concision. ♦ **conciseness** *or* ♦ **concision** *n* concision *f*.
conclude [kən'klu:d] **1** *vt* (*all senses*) conclure. **'to be ~d'** 'suite et fin au prochain numéro'. **2** *vi* *[events]* se terminer (*with* par, sur); *[speaker]* conclure. ♦ **concluding** *adj* final. ♦ **conclusion** *n* (*all senses*) conclusion *f*; **in conclusion** pour conclure, en conclusion; **to come to the conclusion that** conclure que; **to try conclusions with sb** se mesurer contre qn. ♦ **conclusive** *adj* concluant. ♦ **conclusively** *adv* de façon concluante.
concoct [kən'kɒkt] *vt* (*Culin etc*) confectionner; *scheme, excuse* fabriquer. ♦ **concoction** *n* (*Culin etc*) mélange *m*, mixture *f* (*pej*).
concord ['kɒŋkɔ:d] *n* concorde *f*.
concourse ['kɒŋkɔ:s] *n* (*crowd*) foule *f*; (*place*) lieu *m* de rassemblement; (*US: in park*) carrefour *m*; (*US: in building, station*) hall *m*; (*US: street*) boulevard *m*.
concrete ['kɒnkri:t] **1** *adj* **(a)** *object, proof, advantage* concret; *proposal, offer* précis. **(b)** *building* en béton. **~ mixer** bétonnière *f*. **2** *n* **(a)** (*Constr*) béton *m*. **(b) the ~ and the abstract** le concret et l'abstrait. **3** *vt path* bétonner.
concur [kən'kɜ:ʳ] *vi* (*agree*) être d'accord (*with sb* avec qn, *in sth* sur qch); *[events]* coïncider, arriver en même temps; (*contribute*) concourir (*to* à). ♦ **concurrent** *adj* simultané. ♦ **concurrently** *adv* simultanément.
concussed [kən'kʌst] *adj* commotionné. ♦ **concussion** *n* commotion *f* cérébrale.
condemn [kən'dem] *vt person* condamner (*to* à); *building* condamner; *materials* déclarer inutilisable. **to ~ to death** condamner à mort; **the ~ed man** le condamné; **the ~ed cell** la cellule des condamnés. ♦ **condemnation** *n* condamnation *f*.
condense [kən'dens] *vt* condenser. ♦ **condensation** *n* condensation *f*. ♦ **condenser** *n* condensateur *m*.
condescend [ˌkɒndɪ'send] *vi* daigner (*to do* faire). **to ~ to sb** se montrer condescendant envers qn. ♦ **condescending** *adj* condescendant. ♦ **condescendingly** *adv* avec condescendance. ♦ **condescension** *n* condescendance *f*.
condiment ['kɒndɪmənt] *n* condiment *m*.
condition [kən'dɪʃən] **1** *n* (*all senses*) condition *f*. **on ~ that** à condition que + *fut indic or subj*, à condition de + *infin*; **he made the ~ that no one should accompany him** il a stipulé que personne ne devait l'accompagner; **under** *or* **in the present ~s** dans les conditions actuelles; **working/living ~s** conditions de travail/de vie; **weather ~s** conditions météorologiques; **physical ~** condition *or* état *m* physique; **in ~** *thing* en bon état; *person* en forme; **it's out of ~** c'est en mauvais état; **he's out of ~** il n'est pas en forme; **she was not in a ~** *or* **in any ~ to go out** elle n'était pas en état de sortir. **2** *vt* (*all senses*) conditionner (*into doing* à faire). ♦ **conditional 1** *adj* conditionnel; **to be ~al (up)on** dépendre de; **2** *n* conditionnel *m*; **in the ~al** au conditionnel. ♦ **conditionally** *adv* conditionnellement.
condole [kən'dəʊl] *vi* offrir ses condoléances (*with sb* à qn). ♦ **condolences** *npl* condoléances *fpl*.
condom ['kɒndəm] *n* préservatif *m*.
condone [kən'dəʊn] *vt* (*overlook*) fermer les yeux sur; (*forgive*) pardonner.
conduce [kən'dju:s] *vi*: **to ~ to** conduire à. ♦ **conducive** *adj*: **to be conducive to** conduire à.
conduct ['kɒndʌkt] **1** *n* conduite *f* (*towards* envers). **2** [kən'dʌkt] *vt person, group* conduire, mener; *heat* conduire; *business, orchestra* diriger; *enquiry* conduire. **he ~ed me round the gardens** il m'a fait faire le tour des jardins; **~ed tour** (*gen*) voyage *m* organisé; *[building]* visite *f* guidée; **to ~ o.s.** se conduire, se comporter. ♦ **conduction** *n* conduction *f*. ♦ **conductivity** *n*

conductivité *f.* ♦ **conductor** *n* (*Mus*) chef *m* d'orchestre; *[bus]* receveur *m*; (*US Rail*) chef de train; *[heat etc]* conducteur *m.* ♦ **conductress** *n* receveuse *f.*

cone [kəʊn] *n* (*gen*) cône *m*; *[ice cream]* cornet *m.*

confab* ['kɒnfæb] *n* brin *m* de causette*.

confectioner [kən'fekʃənəʳ] *n* (*sweetmaker*) confiseur *m*, -euse *f*; (*cakemaker*) pâtissier *m*, -ière *f.* ~'s **(shop)** confiserie *f* (-pâtisserie *f*); (*US*) ~'s **sugar** sucre *m* glace. ♦ **confectionery** *n* confiserie *f*; (*cakes etc*) pâtisserie *f.*

confederate [kən'fedərɪt] **1** *adj* confédéré. **2** *n* confédéré(e) *m(f)*; (*in criminal act*) complice *mf.* **3** [kən'fedəreɪt] *vt* confédérer. **4** *vi* se confédérer. ♦ **confederacy** *n* confédération *f*; (*US Hist*) **the Confederacy** les États *mpl* Confédérés. ♦ **confederation** *n* confédération *f.*

confer [kən'fɜːʳ] **1** *vt* conférer (*on* à). **2** *vi* conférer (*with sb* avec qn; *about sth* de qch). ♦ **conference** ['kɒnfərəns] **1** *n* (*meeting*) conférence *f*, réunion *f*, (*especially academic*) congrès *m*; **in ~ence** en conférence; **the ~ence decided ...** les participants à la conférence ont décidé ...; **2** *adj*: **~ence table** table *f* de conférence; **~ence member** congressiste *mf.*

confess [kən'fes] **1** *vt* avouer, confesser (*that* que); *mistake* reconnaître; (*Rel*) confesser. **2** *vi* avouer (*to sth* qch; *to doing* avoir fait); (*Rel*) se confesser. ♦ **confession** *n* aveu *m*, confession *f* (*of* de); (*Rel*) confession; (*Jur*) **a full ~ion** des aveux complets; (*Rel*) **to hear sb's ~ion** confesser qn; **to go to ~ion** aller se confesser; **to make one's ~ion** se confesser. ♦ **confessional** *n* confessionnal *m.* ♦ **confessor** *n* confesseur *m.*

confetti [kən'fetiː] *n* confettis *mpl.*

confide [kən'faɪd] **1** *vt* avouer en confidence (*that* que). **2** *vi*: **to ~ in sb** s'ouvrir à qn, se confier à qn; **to ~ in sb about sth** confier qch à qn; **to ~ in sb about what one is going to do** révéler à qn ce qu'on va faire. ♦ **confidant** *n* confident *m.* ♦ **confidante** *n* confidente *f.*

confidence ['kɒnfɪdəns] **1** *n* **(a)** (*trust*) confiance *f* (*in* en). **to have every ~ in sb** avoir pleine confiance en qn; **I have every ~ that** je suis sûr *or* certain que; **motion of no ~** motion *f* de censure. **(b)** (*self-~*) confiance *f* en soi, assurance *f.* **(c)** (*secret*) confidence *f.* **to take sb into one's ~** faire des confidences à qn; **this is in strict ~** c'est strictement confidentiel; **'write in ~ to X'** 'écrire à X: discrétion garantie'. **2** *adj*: **~ trick** escroquerie *f*; **~ trickster** escroc *m.* ♦ **confident** *adj* (*self~*) sûr de soi, assuré; (*sure*) sûr, persuadé (*of* de; *of doing* de faire; *that* que). ♦ **confidential** *adj letter, remark, information* confidentiel; *servant* de confiance; *secretary* particulier. ♦ **confidentially** *adv* en confidence. ♦ **confidently** *adv* avec confiance.

confine [kən'faɪn] *vt* **(a)** (*imprison*) emprisonner; (*shut up*) enfermer (*in* dans). **to be ~d to the house** être obligé de rester chez soi; (*Mil*) **~d to barracks** consigné. **(b)** (*limit*) limiter, borner. **to ~ o.s. to doing** se borner à faire; **the damage is ~d to the back of the car** seul l'arrière de la voiture est endommagé; **in a ~d space** dans un espace restreint. ♦ **confinement** *n* (*Med*) couches *fpl*; (*imprisonment*) emprisonnement *m*, réclusion *f* (*Jur*).

confirm [kən'fɜːm] *vt* (*gen, also Rel*) confirmer; *one's resolve* raffermir; *treaty, appointment* ratifier. ♦ **confirmation** *n* confirmation *f*; raffermissement *m*; ratification *f.* ♦ **confirmed** *adj smoker, habit, liar* invétéré; *bachelor* endurci; *admirer* fervent.

confiscate ['kɒnfɪskeɪt] *vt* confisquer (*sth from sb* qch à qn). ♦ **confiscation** *n* confiscation *f.*

conflict ['kɒnflɪkt] **1** *n* conflit *m.* **2** [kən'flɪkt] *vi* être *or* entrer en conflit (*with* avec); *[ideas]* s'opposer, se heurter (*with* à). **that ~s with what he told me** ceci est en contradiction avec ce qu'il m'a raconté. ♦ **conflicting** *adj views* incompatible; *reports, evidence* contradictoire.

conform [kən'fɔːm] *vi* se conformer (*to, with* à); *[actions, sayings]* être en conformité (*to* avec). ♦ **conformist** *adj, n* conformiste (*mf*). ♦ **conformity** *n*: **in ~ity with** conformément à.

confound [kən'faʊnd] *vt* confondre. **~ it!*** la barbe!*; **~ him!*** qu'il aille au diable!

confront [kən'frʌnt] *vt* confronter (*sb with sb* qn avec qn); *enemy, danger* affronter. **to ~ sb with sth** présenter qch à qn; **problems which ~ us** problèmes auxquels nous devons faire face. ♦ **confrontation** *n* confrontation *f.*

confuse [kən'fjuːz] *vt* **(a)** (*throw into disorder*) *opponents* confondre; (*perplex*) déconcerter; (*embarrass*) confondre, embarrasser; (*mix up*) *persons, ideas* embrouiller. **you are just confusing me** tu m'embrouilles. **(b)** (*not distinguish between*) confondre (*with* avec). ♦ **confused** *adj person* (*muddled, embarrassed*) confus, (*perplexed*) déconcerté; *opponent* confondu; *mind, sounds, memories, ideas, situation* confus; **to get ~d** (*muddled up*) ne plus savoir où on en est; (*embarrassed*) se troubler. ♦ **confusedly** *adv* confusément. ♦ **confusing** *adj* déroutant. ♦ **confusion** *n* confusion *f*; **he was in a state of confusion** la confusion régnait dans son esprit.

congeal [kən'dʒiːl] *vi [spilt blood, paint]* sécher; *[spilt oil, gravy]* se figer.

congenial [kən'dʒiːnɪəl] *adj* sympathique, agréable.

congenital [kən'dʒenɪtl] *adj* congénital.

congested [kən'dʒestɪd] *adj town, countryside* surpeuplé; *street, corridors* encombré; *telephone lines* embouteillé; (*Med*) congestionné. **~ traffic** encombrements *mpl.* ♦ **congestion** *n* surpeuplement *m*; encombrement *m*; congestion *f.*

congratulate [kən'grætjʊleɪt] *vt* féliciter (*on* de, *on doing* de faire). ♦ **congratulations** *npl* félicitations *fpl* (*on* pour); **congratulations!** toutes mes félicitations!

congregate ['kɒŋgrɪgeɪt] *vi* se rassembler, s'assembler. ♦ **congregation** *n [worshippers]* assemblée *f* (des fidèles); *[cardinals etc]* congrégation *f.* ♦ **congregational** *adj*: **the Congregational Church** l'Église *f* congrégationaliste.

congress ['kɒŋgres] **1** *n* congrès *m.* (*US*) **C~** le Congrès. **2** *adj*: **~ member** congressiste *mf.* ♦ **Congressional** *adj* (*US*) du Congrès; **C~ional Record** Journal *m* Officiel du Congrès. ♦ **congressman** *or* **congresswoman** *n* (*US*) membre *m* du Congrès, ≃ député *m*; **C~man J. Smith said that ...** Monsieur le Député J. Smith a dit que ... .

conic(al) ['kɒnɪk(əl)] *adj* conique.

conifer ['kɒnɪfəʳ] *n* conifère *m.* ♦ **coniferous** *adj tree* conifère; *forest* de conifères.

conjecture [kən'dʒektʃəʳ] **1** *vti* conjecturer. **2** *n* conjecture *f.* ♦ **conjectural** *adj* conjectural.

conjugal ['kɒndʒʊgəl] *adj* conjugal.

conjugate ['kɒndʒʊgeɪt] **1** *vt* conjuguer. **2** *vi* se conjuguer. ♦ **conjugation** *n* conjugaison *f.*

conjunction [kən'dʒʌŋkʃən] *n* conjonction *f.* **in ~ with** conjointement avec.

conjunctivitis [kən,dʒʌŋktɪ'vaɪtɪs] *n* conjonctivite *f.*

conjuncture [kən'dʒʌŋktʃəʳ] *n* conjoncture *f.*

conjure ['kʌndʒəʳ] **1** *vt* faire apparaître (*par la prestidigitation*). **2** *vi* faire des tours de passe-passe; (*juggle*) jongler (*with* avec). **a name to ~ with** un nom prestigieux.

conjure up *vt sep memories* évoquer. **to ~ up visions of ...** évoquer ... .

♦ **conjurer** *or* ♦ **conjuror** *n* prestidigitateur *m*, -trice *f.* ♦ **conjuring** *n* prestidigitation *f*; **conjuring trick** tour *m* de passe-passe.

conk* [kɒŋk] *vi* (~ **out**) tomber *or* rester en panne.
conker* ['kɒŋkə^r] *n* (*Brit*) marron *m*.
connect [kə'nekt] **1** *vt* (*gen*) relier, rattacher (*with, to* à); *[roads, rail link, airline]* relier (*with, to* à); (*Telec*) *caller* mettre en communication (*with* avec); *pipes, drains* raccorder (*to* à); (*install*) *cooker, telephone* brancher, raccorder. (*Telec*) **we are trying to ~ you** nous essayons d'obtenir votre communication; (*Elec*) **to ~ to the mains** brancher sur le secteur; **I always ~ Paris with springtime** j'associe toujours Paris au printemps; **he is ~ed with that firm** il a des rapports *or* des contacts avec cette firme; **it is not ~ed with the murder** cela n'a aucun rapport avec *or* n'a rien à voir avec le meurtre; **well ~ed** de bonne famille. **2** *vi* se relier, se raccorder; *[trains]* assurer la correspondance (*with* avec). (*Aut*) **~ing rod** bielle *f*. ♦ **connected** *adj languages, species* connexe; *events* lié; *rooms* communicants. ♦ **connection** *or* ♦ **connexion** *n* (*gen*) rapport *m* (*with* avec), lien *m* (*between* entre); (*Elec*) contact *m*; (*Telec*) communication *f*; (*Rail*) correspondance *f* (*with* avec); **this has no ~ion with** ceci n'a aucun rapport avec; **in this ~ion** à ce sujet; **in ~ion with** à propos de; **in another ~ion** dans un autre ordre d'idées; **to build up a ~ion with a firm** établir des relations d'affaires avec une firme; **we have no ~ion with any other firm** toute ressemblance avec une autre compagnie est purement fortuite; **they have some family ~ion** ils ont un lien de parenté; (*Rail*) **to miss one's ~ion** manquer la correspondance.
conning tower ['kɒnɪŋ ˌtaʊə^r] *n [submarine]* kiosque *m*; *[warship]* centre *m* opérationnel.
connive [kə'naɪv] *vi*: **to ~ at** (*pretend not to notice*) fermer les yeux sur; (*aid and abet*) être de connivence dans. ♦ **connivance** *n* connivence *f*.
connoisseur [ˌkɒnə'sɜː^r] *n* connaisseur *m*, -euse *f* (*of* de, en).
conquer ['kɒŋkə^r] *vt* (*lit*) *person, enemy* vaincre; *nation, country, castle* conquérir; (*fig*) *feelings, habits* surmonter. ♦ **conquering** *adj* victorieux. ♦ **conqueror** *n* conquérant *m*; (*fig*) vainqueur *m*. ♦ **conquest** *n* conquête *f*.
conscience ['kɒnʃəns] *n* conscience *f*. **to have a clear ~** avoir la conscience tranquille; **to have sth on one's ~** avoir qch sur la conscience; **in (all) ~** en conscience; **for ~' sake** par acquit de conscience. ♦ **conscience-stricken** *adj* pris de remords. ♦ **conscientious** *adj person, work* consciencieux; **conscientious objector** objecteur *m* de conscience. ♦ **conscientiously** *adv* consciencieusement. ♦ **conscientiousness** *n* conscience *f*.
conscious ['kɒnʃəs] *adj* **(a)** conscient, ayant conscience (*of* de); *insult* délibéré; *guilt* ressenti clairement. **to be ~ of doing** avoir conscience de faire; **to become ~ of sth** prendre conscience de qch. **(b)** (*Med*) conscient. **to become ~** revenir à soi, reprendre connaissance. ♦ **consciously** *adv* consciemment. ♦ **consciousness** *n* conscience *f* (*of* de); (*Med*) connaissance *f*; **to lose/regain ~ness** perdre/reprendre connaissance.
conscript [kən'skrɪpt] **1** *vt* recruter (par conscription). **2** ['kɒnskrɪpt] *n* conscrit *m*. ♦ **conscription** *n* conscription *f*.
consecrate ['kɒnsɪkreɪt] *vt* consacrer (*to* à). ♦ **consecration** *n* consécration *f*.
consecutive [kən'sekjʊtɪv] *adj* consécutif, de suite. ♦ **consecutively** *adv* consécutivement; (*Jur*) ... **the sentences to be served ~ly** ... avec cumul *m* de peines.
consensus [kən'sensəs] *n*: **~ of opinion** opinion *f* générale, consensus *m* d'opinion.
consent [kən'sent] **1** *vi* consentir (*to sth* à qch, *to do* à faire). (*Jur*) **~ing adults** adultes consentants. **2** *n* consentement *m*, assentiment *m*. **by common ~** de l'opinion de tous; **by mutual ~** (*general agreement*) d'un commun accord; (*private arrangement*) à l'amiable; **divorce by (mutual) ~** divorce *m* par consentement mutuel; **age of ~** âge *m* nubile légal.
consequence ['kɒnsɪkwəns] *n* (*result*) conséquence *f*. **in ~** par conséquent; **in ~ of which** par suite de quoi; **it's of no ~** cela n'a aucune importance; **he's of no ~** c'est un homme de peu d'importance. ♦ **consequent** *adj* résultant (*on* de). ♦ **consequently** *adv* par conséquent, en conséquence.
conserve [kən'sɜːv] *vt* conserver, préserver; *strength* ménager. ♦ **conservancy** *or* ♦ **conservation** *n* préservation *f*; *[nature]* défense *f* de l'environnement; (*Phys*) conservation *f*. ♦ **conservationist** *n* partisan *m* de la défense de l'environnement. ♦ **conservatism** *n* conservatisme *m*. ♦ **conservative** **1** *adj* (*Pol*) conservateur; (*gen*) *assessment* modeste; *style, behaviour* traditionnel; **at a conservative estimate** au bas mot; **2** *n* conservateur *m*, -trice *f*. ♦ **conservatory** *n* (*greenhouse*) serre *f*; (*Mus etc*) conservatoire *m*.
consider [kən'sɪdə^r] *vt* (*gen*) considérer (*that* que); (*think about*) *problem, possibility* considérer, examiner; *question, matter, subject* réfléchir à; (*take into account*) *facts* prendre en considération; *person's feelings* avoir égard à; *cost, difficulties, dangers* tenir compte de. **I had not ~ed taking it with me** je n'avais pas envisagé de l'emporter; **all things ~ed** tout bien considéré; **it is my ~ed opinion that ...** après avoir mûrement réfléchi je pense que ...; **he is being ~ed for the post** on songe à lui pour le poste; **she ~s him very mean** elle le considère comme très avare, elle estime qu'il est très avare; **~ yourself lucky*** estimez-vous heureux. ♦ **considering** **1** *prep* étant donné, vu (*that* que); **2** *adj*: **he played very well, ~ing** tout compte fait, il a très bien joué.
considerable [kən'sɪdərəbl] *adj* considérable. **to a ~ extent** dans une large mesure; **we had ~ difficulty in finding you** nous avons eu beaucoup de mal à vous trouver. ♦ **considerably** *adv* considérablement.
considerate [kən'sɪdərɪt] *adj* prévenant (*towards* envers), plein d'égards (*towards* pour, envers). ♦ **considerately** *adv act* avec prévenance.
consideration [kənˌsɪdə'reɪʃən] *n* (*all senses*) considération *f*. **out of ~ for** par égard pour; **to show ~ for sb's feelings** ménager les susceptibilités de qn; **to take sth into ~** prendre qch en considération, tenir compte de qch; **taking everything into ~** tout bien considéré; **the matter is under ~** l'affaire est à l'étude; **after due ~** après mûre réflexion; **money is the first ~** il faut considérer avant tout la question d'argent; **it's of no ~** cela n'a aucune importance; **money is no ~** l'argent n'entre pas en ligne de compte; **his age was an important ~** son âge constituait un facteur important; **to do sth for a ~** faire qch moyennant finance.
consign [kən'saɪn] *vt* (*send*) expédier; (*hand over*) remettre. ♦ **consignee** *n* consignataire *mf*. ♦ **consignment** *n* (*incoming*) arrivage *m*; (*outgoing*) envoi *m*.
consist [kən'sɪst] *vi* consister (*of* en; *in doing* à faire; *in sth* dans qch). ♦ **consistency** *n* consistance *f*; (*fig*) **to lack ~ency** manquer de logique *f*. ♦ **consistent** *adj person, behaviour* conséquent, logique; *argument* qui se tient; **~ent with** compatible avec. ♦ **consistently** *adv argue* avec logique; *happen* régulièrement, sans exception; **~ently with** conformément à.
console [kən'səʊl] *vt* consoler (*sb for sth* qn de qch). ♦ **consolation** **1** *n* consolation *f*; **2** *adj*: **consolation prize** prix *m* de consolation. ♦ **consoling** *adj* consolant.

consolidate [kən'sɒlɪdeɪt] *vt* consolider. ♦ **consolidation** *n* consolidation *f.*
consonant ['kɒnsənənt] *n* consonne *f.*
consort ['kɒnsɔːt] **1** *n* époux *m*, épouse *f.* **prince ~** prince *m* consort. **2** [kən'sɔːt] *vi*: **to ~ with sb** fréquenter qn.
consortium [kən'sɔːtɪəm] *n* consortium *m.*
conspicuous [kən'spɪkjʊəs] *adj person, behaviour, clothes* voyant, qui attire la vue; *poster* qui attire les regards; *bravery* insigne; *difference, fact* notable, remarquable. **a ~ lack of ...** un manque manifeste de ...; **he was in a ~ position** il était bien en évidence; (*fig*) il occupait une situation très en vue; **to make o.s. ~** se faire remarquer; **to be ~ by one's absence** briller par son absence. ♦ **conspicuously** *adv behave* d'une manière à se faire remarquer; *angry* visiblement.
conspire [kən'spaɪəʳ] *vi* conspirer (*against* contre). **to ~ to do** *[people]* comploter pour faire; *[events]* conspirer à faire. ♦ **conspiracy** *n* conspiration *f*, conjuration *f.* ♦ **conspirator** *n* conspirateur *m*, -trice *f.*
constable ['kʌnstəbl] *n* (*police ~*) (*in town*) agent *m* de police, gardien *m* de la paix; (*in country*) gendarme *m.* ♦ **constabulary** *n* police *f*; gendarmerie *f.*
constant ['kɒnstənt] **1** *adj quarrels, interruptions* incessant, continuel; *affection* inaltérable, constant; *friend* fidèle. **2** *n* (*Math, Phys*) constante *f.* ♦ **constancy** *n* constance *f.* ♦ **constantly** *adv* constamment, sans cesse.
constellation [ˌkɒnstə'leɪʃən] *n* constellation *f.*
consternation [ˌkɒnstə'neɪʃən] *n* consternation *f.* **filled with ~** frappé de consternation, consterné.
constipate [ˌkɒnstɪpeɪt] *vt* constiper. ♦ **constipated** *adj* constipé. ♦ **constipation** *n* constipation *f.*
constituency [kən'stɪtjʊənsɪ] *n* (*place*) circonscription *f* électorale; (*people*) électeurs *mpl* (d'une circonscription). **~ party** section *f* locale (du parti). ♦ **constituent** **1** *adj* constituant; **2** *n* (*element*) élément constitutif; (*Pol*) électeur *m*, -trice *f* (dans une circonscription).
constitute ['kɒnstɪtjuːt] *vt* constituer. ♦ **constitution** *n* constitution *f.* ♦ **constitutional** **1** *adj* (*Pol etc*) constitutionnel; (*Med*) diathésique. **2** *n* (*) petite promenade *f.* ♦ **constitutionally** *adv* (*Pol etc*) constitutionnellement; (*Med etc*) par nature.
constrain [kən'streɪn] *vt* contraindre (*sb to do* qn à faire). **to be ~ed to do** être contraint de faire. ♦ **constrained** *adj atmosphere* de gêne; *voice, manner* contraint. ♦ **constraint** *n* contrainte *f.*
constrict [kən'strɪkt] *vt* (*gen*) resserrer; *muscle etc* serrer; *movements* gêner. ♦ **constricted** *adj freedom* restreint; *point of view* borné. ♦ **constriction** *n* resserrement *m*; constriction *f* (*esp Med*).
construct [kən'strʌkt] *vt building, novel, play* construire; *theory, one's defence* bâtir. ♦ **construction** *n* construction *f*; **under ~ion** en construction; **to put a wrong ~ion on sb's words** mal interpréter les paroles de qn. ♦ **constructive** *adj* constructif. ♦ **constructively** *adv* d'une manière constructive. ♦ **constructor** *n* constructeur *m*, -trice *f.*
construe [kən'struː] *vt sentence* analyser; *Latin poem* expliquer. **this was ~d as ...** on a interprété ceci comme signifiant ... .
consul ['kɒnsəl] *n* consul *m.* **~ general** consul général. ♦ **consular** *adj* consulaire; **~ar section** service *m* consulaire. ♦ **consulate** *n* consulat *m.*
consult [kən'sʌlt] **1** *vt* consulter (*about* sur, au sujet de). **2** *vi* être en consultation (*with* avec). **to ~ together** se consulter. ♦ **consultant** **1** *n* consultant *m*, expert-conseil *m* (*to sb* auprès de qn); (*Med*) médecin *m* consultant, spécialiste *m*; **2** *adj* consultant. ♦ **consultation** *n* consultation *f.* ♦ **consultative** *adj* consultatif. ♦ **consulting** *adj engineer etc* conseil (*f inv*); **~ing hours** heures *fpl* de consultation; **~ing room** cabinet *m* de consultation.
consume [kən'sjuːm] *vt food, resources, fuel* consommer; *[fire]* consumer. **~d with** *grief* consumé de; *desire* brûlant de; *jealousy* rongé par. ♦ **consumer** **1** *n* consommateur *m*, -trice *f*; *[telephone, gas, electricity]* abonné(e) *m(f)*; **2** *adj protection, resistance* du consommateur; **~r durables** biens *mpl* de consommation durable; **~r goods** biens *mpl* de consommation; **Ministry of C~r Protection** ≃ Secrétariat *m* d'État à la Consommation; **~r research** études *fpl* de marchés; **~r society** société *f* de consommation. ♦ **consuming** *adj passion* dévorant, brûlant.
consummate [kən'sʌmɪt] **1** *adj* consommé. **2** ['kɒnsʌmeɪt] *vt* consommer. ♦ **consummation** *n* consommation *f* (*d'un mariage*).
consumption [kən'sʌmpʃən] *n* **(a)** *[food, fuel]* consommation *f.* **not fit for human ~** non-comestible; (*pej*) immangeable. **(b)** (†: *tuberculosis*) phtisie† *f.*
contact ['kɒntækt] **1** *n* (*all senses*) contact *m.* **to be in ~ with sb** être en contact avec qn; **we have had no ~ with him** nous sommes sans contact avec lui; **I seem to make no ~ with him** je n'arrive pas à communiquer avec lui; **he has some ~s in Paris** il a des relations *fpl* à Paris. **2** *vt* se mettre en contact *or* en rapport avec, contacter. **we'll ~ you soon** nous nous mettrons en rapport avec vous sous peu. **3** *adj*: **~ lenses** verres *mpl* de contact.
contagion [kən'teɪdʒən] *n* contagion *f.* ♦ **contagious** *adj* contagieux.
contain [kən'teɪn] *vt* contenir. **he couldn't ~ himself for joy** il ne se sentait pas de joie. ♦ **container** **1** *n* (*goods transport*) conteneur *m*; (*jug, box etc*) récipient *m*; **2** *adj train, ship* porte-conteneurs *inv*; *dock* pour la manutention de conteneurs; *terminal* à conteneurs; *transport* par conteneurs. ♦ **containerization** *n* conteneurisation *f.* ♦ **containerize** *vt* conteneuriser.
contaminate [kən'tæmɪneɪt] *vt* contaminer. ♦ **contamination** *n* contamination *f.*
contemplate ['kɒntəmpleɪt] *vt* (*look at*) contempler; (*consider*) envisager (*doing* de faire). ♦ **contemplation** *n* contemplation *f.* ♦ **contemplative** *adj* contemplatif.
contemporary [kən'tempərərɪ] *adj, n* contemporain(e) *m(f)* (*with* de).
contempt [kən'tempt] *n* mépris *m.* **to hold in ~** mépriser; **it's beneath ~** c'est au-dessous de tout; **~ of court** outrage *m* à la Cour. ♦ **contemptible** *adj* méprisable. ♦ **contemptuous** *adj person* dédaigneux (*of* de); *manner* méprisant; *gesture* de mépris. ♦ **contemptuously** *adv* avec mépris, dédaigneusement.
contend [kən'tend] **1** *vi*: **to ~ with sb for sth** disputer qch à qn; **to have sth to ~ with** devoir faire face à qch; **to have sb to ~ with** avoir affaire à qn; **he has a lot to ~ with** il a beaucoup de problèmes. **2** *vt* soutenir, prétendre (*that* que). ♦ **contender** *n* concurrent(e) *m(f)*; **~er for** prétendant(e) *m(f)* à. ♦ **contention** *n* (*dispute*) dispute *f*; (*assertion*) assertion *f*; **bone of contention** pomme *f* de discorde. ♦ **contentious** *adj person* querelleur; *issue* contesté.
content[1] [kən'tent] **1** *adj* content, satisfait (*with* de). **to be ~ with** (*accept*) se contenter de; **he is quite ~ to stay** il ne demande pas mieux que de rester. **2** *n* contentement *m.* **3** *vt* contenter. **to ~ o.s. with doing** se contenter de faire. ♦ **contented** *adj* content (*with* de). ♦ **contentedly** *adv* avec contentement. ♦ **contentedness** *or* ♦ **contentment** *n* contentement *m.*
content[2] ['kɒntent] *n [book, play]* contenu *m*; *[document, metal]* teneur *f. [box etc]* **~s** contenu; *[book]* '**~s**' 'table *f* des matières'; **oranges have a**

high vitamin C ~ les oranges sont riches en vitamine C; **gold** ~ teneur en or.

contest [kən'test] **1** *vt matter, result, will* contester; *election, seat* disputer. **2** ['kɒntest] *n* combat *m*, lutte *f*; (*Sport*) lutte; (*Boxing, Wrestling*) rencontre *f*; (*competition*) concours *m*. ♦ **contestant** *n* (*for prize*) concurrent(e) *m(f)*; (*in fight*) adversaire *mf*.

context ['kɒntekst] *n* contexte *m*. **in/out of** ~ dans le/sans contexte.

continent ['kɒntɪnənt] *n* continent *m*. (*Brit*) **the C**~ l'Europe continentale; **on the C**~ en Europe. ♦ **continental** *adj* (*gen*) continental; *drift* des continents; ~**al breakfast** café *m or* thé *m* complet; ~**al quilt** couette *f*.

contingency [kən'tɪndʒənsɪ] **1** *n* événement *m* imprévu, éventualité *f*. **in a** ~ en cas d'imprévu. **2** *adj*: ~ **fund** caisse *f* de prévoyance; ~ **plans** plans *mpl* d'urgence. ♦ **contingent 1** *adj* contingent; **to be contingent upon sth** dépendre de qch; **2** *n* contingent *m*.

continue [kən'tɪnju:] **1** *vt* (*gen*) continuer (*to do* à *or* de faire); *tradition, policy* maintenir; (*after interruption*) reprendre. *[serial]* **to be** ~**d** à suivre; **to be** ~**d on page 10** suite page 10; **to** ~ **one's way** continuer son chemin; (*after pause*) se remettre en marche; **'and so,' he** ~**d** 'et ainsi,' reprit-il *or* poursuivit-il. **2** *vi* (*gen*) continuer; (*after interruption*) reprendre. **the forest** ~**s to the sea** la forêt s'étend jusqu'à la mer; **to** ~ **in one's job** garder *or* conserver son poste; **he** ~**d with his voluntary work** il a poursuivi son travail bénévole; **she** ~**d as his secretary** elle est restée sa secrétaire. ♦ **continual** *adj* continuel. ♦ **continually** *adv* continuellement, sans cesse. ♦ **continuance** *n* (*duration*) durée *f*; (*continuation*) continuation *f*; (*continuity*) continuité *f*. ♦ **continuation** *n* continuation *f*; (*after interruption*) reprise *f*; *[serial story]* suite *f*. ♦ **continuity** *n* continuité *f*; **continuity girl** scripte *f*. ♦ **continuous** *adj* continu; (*Cine*) **continuous performance** spectacle *m* permanent. ♦ **continuously** *adv* (*uninterruptedly*) sans interruption; (*repeatedly*) continuellement, sans arrêt. ♦ **continuum** *n* continuum *m*.

contort [kən'tɔ:t] *vt features* tordre; *words, story* déformer. ♦ **contortion** *n [esp acrobat]* contorsion *f*; *[features]* convulsion *f*. ♦ **contortionist** *n* contorsionniste *mf*.

contour ['kɒntʊəʳ] **1** *n* contour *m*. **2** *adj*: ~ **line** courbe *f* de niveau; ~ **map** carte *f* avec courbes de niveau.

contraband ['kɒntrəbænd] **1** *n* contrebande *f*. **2** *adj* de contrebande.

contraception [ˌkɒntrə'sepʃən] *n* contraception *f*. ♦ **contraceptive** *adj, n* contraceptif (*m*).

contract ['kɒntrækt] **1** *n* contrat *m*. **marriage** ~ contrat de mariage; **to enter into a** ~ **with sb for sth** passer un contrat avec qn pour qch; **to put work out to** ~ mettre du travail à l'entreprise; **by** ~ par *or* sur contrat; (*fig: by killer*) **there's a** ~ **out for him!** sa tête a été mise à prix (*par un rival*). **2** *adj*: ~ **bridge** bridge *m* contrat; ~ **work** travail *m* à l'entreprise. **3** [kən'trækt] *vt* **(a)** *debts, illness, vices, alliance* contracter. **to** ~ **to do** s'engager (par contrat) à faire; **to** ~ **with sb to do** passer un contrat avec qn pour faire. **(b)** *muscles, metal* contracter; *face* crisper; *word, phrase* contracter (*to* en). **4** *vi* se contracter.

contract in *vi* s'engager (par contrat).

contract out *vi* se libérer, se dégager (*of* de). **to** ~ **out of a pension scheme** cesser de cotiser à une caisse de retraite.

♦ **contraction** *n* contraction *f*; (*word*) forme *f* contractée. ♦ **contractor** *n* entrepreneur *m*. ♦ **contractual** *adj* contractuel.

contradict [ˌkɒntrə'dɪkt] *vt* contredire. ♦ **contradiction** *n* contradiction *f*; **a** ~**ion in terms** une contradiction (dans les termes). ♦ **contradictory** *adj* contradictoire.

contralto [kən'træltəʊ] **1** *n* contralto *m*. **2** *adj* de contralto.

contraption* [kən'træpʃən] *n* machin* *m*, truc* *m*.

contrary ['kɒntrərɪ] **1** *adj* **(a)** (*gen*) contraire (*to* à). **in a** ~ **direction** en sens inverse *or* opposé; ~ **to nature** contre nature. **(b)** [kən'trɛərɪ] (*self-willed*) contrariant. **2** *adv* contrairement (*to* à). **3** *n* contraire *m*. **on the** ~ au contraire; **unless you hear to the** ~ sauf contrordre. ♦ **contrariness** *n* esprit *m* de contradiction. ♦ **contrariwise** *adv* (*on the contrary*) au contraire; (*in opposite direction*) en sens opposé.

contrast [kən'trɑ:st] **1** *vt* mettre en contraste, contraster (*with* avec). **2** *vi* contraster, faire contraste (*with* avec). **3** ['kɒntrɑ:st] *n* contraste *m* (*between* entre). **in** ~ par contraste (*to* avec). ♦ **contrasting** *adj opinions* opposé; *colours* contrasté.

contravene [ˌkɒntrə'vi:n] *vt* enfreindre. ♦ **contravention** *n* infraction *f* (*of* à).

contribute [kən'trɪbju:t] **1** *vt* (*gen*) contribuer; *specific sum* offrir, donner, (*Admin*) cotiser; *article to a newspaper* donner, envoyer. **2** *vi*: **to** ~ **to** *collection, charity, misunderstanding* contribuer à; *discussion* prendre part à, participer à; *newspaper* collaborer à; **to** ~ **to doing** contribuer à faire. ♦ **contribution** [ˌkɒntrɪ'bju:ʃən] *n* (*gen*) contribution *f*; (*Admin*) cotisation *f*; (*to publication*) article *m*. ♦ **contributor** *n* (*to publication*) collaborateur *m*, -trice *f*; *[money, goods]* donateur *m*, -trice *f*. ♦ **contributory** *adj cause* accessoire; **it was a contributory factor in ...** cela a contribué à ...; **contributory pension scheme** caisse *f* de retraite (à laquelle cotisent les employés).

contrite ['kɒntraɪt] *adj* contrit. ♦ **contrition** *n* contrition *f*.

contrive [kən'traɪv] *vt plan, scheme* combiner, inventer. **to** ~ **a means of doing** trouver un moyen pour faire; **to** ~ **to do** s'arranger pour faire, trouver le moyen de faire; **can you** ~ **to be here at 3 o'clock?** est-ce que vous pouvez vous arranger pour être ici à 3 heures? ♦ **contrivance** *n* (*gen*) appareil *m*; (*device*) dispositif *m*. ♦ **contrived** *adj* forcé, qui manque de naturel.

control [kən'trəʊl] **1** *n* **(a)** (*gen*) contrôle *m* (*of* de); autorité *f* (*over* sur). **the** ~ **of** *[traffic]* la réglementation de; *[aircraft]* le contrôle de; *[pests]* la suppression de; *[disease, forest fires]* la lutte contre; *[the seas, the air]* la maîtrise de; **he has no** ~ **over his children** il n'a aucune autorité sur ses enfants; **to keep a dog under** ~ se faire obéir d'un chien; **to have a horse under** ~ maîtriser un cheval; **to lose** ~ **of** perdre le contrôle de; **to lose** ~ **of o.s.** perdre tout contrôle de soi; **to be in** ~ **of** être maître de; **to get a fire under** ~ maîtriser un incendie; **the situation is under** ~ on a la situation bien en main; **everything's under** ~* tout est en ordre; **his car went out of** ~ il a perdu le contrôle de sa voiture; **the children are quite out of** ~ les enfants sont déchaînés; **under French** ~ sous contrôle français; **circumstances beyond our** ~ circonstances indépendantes de notre volonté; **who is in** ~ ? qui *or* quel est le responsable?; (*Sport*) **his** ~ **of the ball is not very good** il ne contrôle pas très bien la balle; **price** ~**s** le contrôle des prix. **(b)** ~**s** *[train, car, ship, aircraft]* commandes *fpl*; *[radio, TV]* boutons *mpl* de commande; **to be at the** ~**s** être aux commandes; (*Rad, TV*) **volume** ~ (bouton *m* de) réglage *m* de volume. **(c)** (*Phys, Psych etc: standard of comparison*) cas *m* témoin.

2 *vt emotions* maîtriser; *animal, child* se faire obéir de; *vehicle, machine* manier; *organization, business* diriger; *expenditure, traffic* régler; *prices, wages, immigration* contrôler; *disease* enrayer. **to** ~ **o.s.** se contrôler, se maîtriser; **she**

can't ~ **the children** elle n'a aucune autorité sur les enfants.

3 *adj* (*Med etc*) ~ **case/group** cas *m*/groupe *m* témoin; ~ **knob** bouton *m* de commande *or* de réglage; ~ **panel** *[aircraft, ship]* tableau *m* de bord; *[TV, computer]* pupitre *m* de commande; ~ **room** (*Naut*) poste *m* de commande; (*Mil*) salle *f* de commande; (*Rad, TV*) régie *f*; (*Aviat*) ~ **tower** tour *f* de contrôle.

♦ **controlled** *adj emotion* contenu; **he was very** ~**led** il se dominait très bien; **... he said in a** ~**led voice** ... dit-il en se contrôlant; (*Econ*) ~**led economy** économie dirigée. ♦ **controller** *n* contrôleur *m*. ♦ **controlling** *adj factor* déterminant; ~**ling interest** participation *f* majoritaire.

controversy [kən'trɒvəsɪ] *n* controverse *f*. **there was a lot of** ~ **about it** ça a provoqué beaucoup de controverses. ♦ **controversial** *adj* (*thought-provoking*) *speech, action, decision* discutable, sujet à controverse; (*talked about*) *person, book, suggestion* discuté.

contusion [kən'tju:ʒən] *n* contusion *f*.

conundrum [kə'nʌndrəm] *n* énigme *f*.

conurbation [ˌkɒnɜ:'beɪʃən] *n* conurbation *f*.

convalesce [ˌkɒnvə'les] *vi* se remettre (*d'une maladie*). **to be convalescing** être en convalescence. ♦ **convalescence** *n* convalescence *f*. ♦ **convalescent** *adj, n* convalescent(e) *m(f)*; ~**nt home** maison *f* de convalescence *or* de repos.

convection [kən'vekʃən] *n* convection *f*. ♦ **convection heater** *or* ♦ **convector** *n* radiateur *m* à convection.

convene [kən'vi:n] 1 *vt* convoquer. 2 *vi* s'assembler. ♦ **convener** *or* ♦ **convenor** *n* président(e) *m(f)* (*de commission etc*). ♦ **convening** *adj*: **convening country** pays *m* hôte.

convenient [kən'vi:nɪənt] *adj tool, device* commode; *time* qui convient; *place, position* bon; *event, occurrence* opportun. **if it is** ~ **to you** si vous n'y voyez pas d'inconvénient, si cela ne vous dérange pas; **will it be** ~ **for you to come tomorrow?** est-ce que cela vous arrange *or* vous convient de venir demain?; **is it** ~ **to see him now?** peut-on le voir tout de suite sans le déranger?; **it is not a very** ~ **time** le moment n'est pas très bien choisi; **the house is** ~ **for shops** la maison est bien située pour les magasins; **he put it down on a** ~ **chair** il l'a posé sur une chaise qui se trouvait à portée. ♦ **convenience** 1 *n* **(a)** *[plan, apartment]* commodité *f*; **for convenience' sake** par souci de commodité; (*Comm*) **at your earliest convenience** dans les meilleurs délais; **do it at your own convenience** faites-le quand cela vous conviendra; *[house]* **conveniences** commodités; **(b)** (*lavatory*) W.C. *mpl*; 2 *adj*: **convenience foods** aliments *mpl* à préparation rapide. ♦ **conveniently** *adv happen* fort à propos; *situated etc* bien; **very** ~**ly he arrived late** heureusement il est arrivé en retard.

convent ['kɒnvənt] 1 *n* couvent *m*. **to go into a** ~ entrer au couvent. 2 *adj*: ~ **school** couvent *m*.

convention [kən'venʃən] *n* (*meeting, agreement*) convention *f*; (*accepted behaviour*) usage *m*, convenances *fpl*. **there is a** ~ **that** l'usage veut que + *subj*. ♦ **conventional** *adj person, behaviour* conventionnel (*also slightly pej*); *method* conventionnel, classique; *weapons* classique.

converge [kən'vɜ:dʒ] *vi* converger (*on* sur). ♦ **convergence** *n* convergence *f*. ♦ **convergent** *or* ♦ **converging** *adj* convergent.

conversant [kən'vɜ:sənt] *adj*: **to be** ~ **with** *car, machinery* s'y connaître en; *language, science, laws* connaître; *facts* être au courant de.

conversation [ˌkɒnvə'seɪʃən] 1 *n* conversation *f*, entretien *m*. **in** ~ **with** en conversation avec; **what was your** ~ **about?** de quoi parliez-vous? 2 *adj*: **that was a** ~ **piece*** cela a fourni un grand sujet de conversation; **that was a** ~ **stopper*** cela a arrêté net la conversation. ♦ **conversational** *adj voice, words* de la conversation; *person* qui a la conversation facile. ♦ **conversationalist** *n* causeur *m*, -euse *f*; **she's a great** ~**alist** elle brille dans la conversation. ♦ **conversationally** *adv speak* sur le ton de la conversation; **'nice day' she said** ~**ally** 'il fait beau' dit-elle du ton de quelqu'un qui cherche à entamer une conversation.

converse[1] [kən'vɜ:s] *vi* converser. **to** ~ **with sb about sth** s'entretenir avec qn de qch.

converse[2] ['kɒnvɜ:s] *adj, n* inverse (*m*). ♦ **conversely** [kɒn'vɜ:slɪ] *adv* inversement.

convert ['kɒnvɜ:t] 1 *n* converti(e) *m(f)*. **to become a** ~ **to** se convertir à. 2 [kən'vɜ:t] *vt* convertir (*into* en, *to* à); (*Rugby*) transformer; *house* aménager (*into* en). ♦ **conversion** 1 *n* (*gen*) conversion *f* (*to* à, *into* en); *[house, room etc]* aménagement *m* (*into* en); (*Rugby*) transformation *f*; 2 *adj*: **conversion table** table *f* de conversion. ♦ **converter** *n* (*Elec*) convertisseur *m*. ♦ **convertibility** *n* convertibilité *f*. ♦ **convertible** 1 *adj* convertible; 2 *n* (*Aut*) décapotable *f*.

convex ['kɒn'veks] *adj* convexe.

convey [kən'veɪ] *vt goods, passengers* transporter; *[pipeline etc]* amener; *sound, order, thanks, congratulations* transmettre (*to* à); *ideas* communiquer (*to* à). **to** ~ **to sb that ...** faire comprendre à qn que ...; **words cannot** ~**...** les paroles ne peuvent traduire ...; **what does this music** ~ **to you?** qu'est-ce que cette musique évoque pour vous? ♦ **conveyance** *n [goods]* transport *m*; (*vehicle*) véhicule *m*. ♦ **conveyancing** *n* rédaction *f* d'actes translatifs. ♦ **conveyor** *n* transporteur *m*, convoyeur *m*; ~**or belt** tapis *m* roulant.

convict ['kɒnvɪkt] 1 *n* forçat *m*, bagnard *m*. 2 [kən'vɪkt] *vt* reconnaître coupable (*sb of a crime* qn d'un crime). **a** ~**ed murderer** un homme reconnu coupable de meurtre. 3 *vi [jury]* rendre un verdict de culpabilité. ♦ **conviction** *n* **(a)** (*Jur*) condamnation *f*; **(b)** conviction *f*; **to carry** ~**ion** être convaincant.

convince [kən'vɪns] *vt* convaincre, persuader (*of* de). **he** ~**d her that she should leave** il l'a persuadée de partir, il l'a convaincue qu'elle devait partir. ♦ **convincing** *adj speaker, argument* persuasif, convaincant; *victory* décisif. ♦ **convincingly** *adv speak* d'une façon convaincante; *win* de façon décisive.

convivial [kən'vɪvɪəl] *adj* joyeux.

convoke [kən'vəʊk] *vt* convoquer. ♦ **convocation** *n* (*act*) convocation *f*; (*assembly*) assemblée *f*.

convoluted ['kɒnvəlu:tɪd] *adj shape* contourné; *argument* compliqué.

convolution [ˌkɒnvə'lu:ʃən] *n* circonvolution *f*.

convolvulus [kən'vɒlvjʊləs] *n* liseron *m*.

convoy ['kɒnvɔɪ] 1 *n* convoi *m*. **in** ~ en convoi. 2 *vt* convoyer.

convulse [kən'vʌls] *vt [earthquake, storm]* ébranler; *[war, riots]* bouleverser. **to be** ~**d with laughter** se tordre de rire; ~**d with pain** *etc* convulsé par la douleur *etc*. ♦ **convulsion** *n* convulsion *f*. ♦ **convulsive** *adj* convulsif.

coo [ku:] *vti [doves etc]* roucouler; *[baby]* gazouiller.

cook [kʊk] 1 *n* cuisinier *m*, -ière *f*. **she is a good** ~ elle fait bien la cuisine; **head** ~ **and bottle-washer*** (*in household*) bonne *f* à tout faire; (*elsewhere*) factotum *m*. 2 *vt* **(a)** *food* (faire) cuire. (*fig*) **to** ~ **sb's goose*** faire son affaire à qn. **(b)** (*: *falsify*) *figures* truquer. **to** ~ **the books*** truquer les comptes. 3 *vi [food]* cuire; *[person]* faire la cuisine. (*fig*) **what's** ~**ing?*** qu'est-ce qui se mijote?*

cook up* *vt sep excuse, story* inventer, fabriquer.

♦ **cookbook** *n* livre *m* de cuisine. ♦ **cooker** *n* cuisinière *f* (*fourneau*). ♦ **cookery** *n* cuisine *f* (*activité*); ~**ery book** livre *m* de cuisine.

♦ **cookhouse** *n* cuisine *f* (*endroit*). ♦ **cookie** *n* gâteau *m* sec. ♦ **cooking 1** *n* cuisine *f* (*activité, nourriture*); **2** *adj utensils* de cuisine; *apples, chocolate* à cuire; **~ing foil** papier *m* d'aluminium; **~ing salt** gros sel. ♦ **cookout** *n* repas *m* (cuit) en plein air.

cool [ku:l] **1** *adj* (*gen*) frais (*f* fraîche); *drink* rafraîchissant; *soup, hot drink* qui n'est plus chaud; *dress* léger; (*calm*) calme; (*impertinent*) effronté; (*unfriendly etc*) froid (*towards* envers). (*Met*) **it is ~** il fait frais; **it's turning ~er** le temps se rafraîchit; **to keep in a ~ place** tenir au frais; **I feel quite ~ now** j'ai bien moins chaud maintenant; **to keep ~** ne pas s'échauffer; (*fig: calm*) garder son sang-froid; **keep ~!** du calme!; **play it ~!*** pas de panique!*; **she was as ~ as a cucumber** elle n'avait pas chaud du tout; (*fig*) elle affichait un calme imperturbable; **to be ~ towards sb** traiter qn avec froideur; **he's a ~ customer*** il n'a pas froid aux yeux; **that was very ~* of him** quel toupet!*; **he earns a ~* £10,000 a year** il se fait la coquette somme de 10 000 livres par an.

2 *n*: **in the ~ of the evening** dans la fraîcheur du soir; **to keep sth in the ~** tenir qch au frais; **to keep/lose one's ~*** garder/perdre son sang-froid *or* son calme.

3 *vt air* rafraîchir, (*stronger*) refroidir; *food* laisser refroidir. **to ~ one's heels** attendre, poireauter*; **~ it!*** calme-toi!

4 *vi [air, liquid]* (*from being warm*) (se) rafraîchir, (*from being hot*) refroidir.

cool down 1 *vi* refroidir; *[anger, person]* se calmer; *[critical situation]* se détendre. **2** *vt sep* faire refroidir; (*fig*) calmer.

cool off *vi* (*lose enthusiasm*) perdre son enthousiasme; (*change one's affections*) se refroidir (*towards sb* envers qn); (*become less angry*) se calmer.

♦ **cooler** *n* glacière *f*; (‡: *prison*) taule‡ *f*. ♦ **cooling** *adj* rafraîchissant; **~ing tower** refroidisseur *m*; **~ing-off period** période *f* de détente. ♦ **coolly** *adv* (*calmly*) de sang-froid, calmement; (*unenthusiastically*) avec froideur; (*impertinently*) sans la moindre gêne. ♦ **coolness** *n* fraîcheur *f*; froideur *f*; calme *m*; effronterie *f*.

coop [ku:p] *n* (*hen ~*) poulailler *m*, cage *f* à poules.

coop up *vt sep person* claquemurer; *feelings* refouler.

co-op [ˈkəʊˈɒp] *n* (*abbr of* **cooperative**) coop* *f*.

cooperate [kəʊˈɒpəreɪt] *vi* coopérer (*with sb* avec qn; *in sth* à qch; *to do* pour faire). **I hope he'll ~** j'espère qu'il va se montrer coopératif. ♦ **cooperation** *n* coopération *f*, concours *m*. ♦ **cooperative 1** *adj* coopératif; **2** *n* coopérative *f*.

coopt [kəʊˈɒpt] *vt* coopter (*onto* à).

coordinate [kəʊˈɔ:dnɪt] **1** *n* coordonnée *f*. **2** [kəʊˈɔ:dɪneɪt] *vt* coordonner (*with* avec). ♦ **coordination** *n* coordination *f*. ♦ **coordinator** *n* coordinateur *m*, -trice *f*.

cop* [kɒp] **1** *n* **(a)** (*policeman*) flic* *m*. **to play at ~s and robbers** jouer aux gendarmes et aux voleurs. **(b) it's not much ~*** ça ne vaut pas grand-chose.

2 *vt*: **to ~ it** écoper*, être puni.

cop out‡ *vi* se défiler*, se dérober.

cope [kəʊp] *vi* se débrouiller, s'en tirer. **to ~ with** *task, person* s'occuper de; *situation* faire face à; *difficulties, problems* (*tackle*) affronter, (*solve*) venir à bout de; **they ~ with 500 applications a day** 500 formulaires leur passent entre les mains chaque jour; **can you ~?** ça ira?, vous y arriverez?; **leave it to me, I'll ~** laissez cela, je m'en charge *or* je me débrouillerai; **he's coping pretty well** il se débrouille très bien; **she just can't ~ any more** (*overworked etc*) elle ne s'en sort plus; (*work too difficult*) elle est complètement dépassée.

copious [ˈkəʊpɪəs] *adj food* copieux; *amount, notes, harvest* abondant.

copper [ˈkɒpəʳ] *n* **(a)** cuivre *m*; (*money*) petite pièce *f*. **~s** la petite monnaie. **(b)** (*: *policeman*) flic* *m*. ♦ **copper-coloured** *or* ♦ **coppery** *adj* cuivré. ♦ **copperplate** *adj*: **~plate handwriting** écriture moulée.

coppice [ˈkɒpɪs], **copse** [kɒps] *n* taillis *m*.

copulate [ˈkɒpjʊleɪt] *vi* copuler. ♦ **copulation** *n* copulation *f*. ♦ **copulative** *adj* copulatif.

copy [ˈkɒpɪ] **1** *n* **(a)** *[painting, document]* copie *f*; (*Phot: print*) épreuve *f*; *[book, newspaper]* exemplaire *m*. **(b)** (*material: for advertisement*) texte *m* (*for* de). (*Press*) **it makes good ~** c'est un bon sujet d'article; **he handed in his ~** il a remis son article *m*.

2 *vt* copier.

♦ **copier** *n* machine *f* à polycopier. ♦ **copybook** *n* cahier *m*. ♦ **copying** *adj*: **~ing ink** encre *f* à copier. ♦ **copyright 1** *n* droits *mpl* d'auteur, copyright *m*; **out of ~right** dans le domaine public; **2** *vt* obtenir les droits exclusifs sur. ♦ **copywriter** *n* rédacteur *m*, -trice *f* publicitaire.

coral [ˈkɒrəl] **1** *n* corail *m*. **2** *adj necklace, reef* de corail; *island* coralien.

cord [kɔ:d] **1** *n* **(a)** *[curtains, pyjamas etc]* cordon *m*; *[windows]* corde *f*; *[parcel etc]* ficelle *f*; (*Elec*) cordon *or* fil *m* électrique. **(b)** (*corduroy*) velours *m* côtelé. **~s** *npl* pantalon *m* en velours côtelé.

2 *adj*: **~ carpet** tapis *m* de corde.

♦ **corded** *adj fabric* côtelé.

cordial [ˈkɔ:dɪəl] *adj, n* cordial (*m*). ♦ **cordiality** *n* cordialité *f*. ♦ **cordially** *adv* cordialement.

cordon [ˈkɔ:dn] **1** *n* cordon *m*. **2** *vt* (**~ off**) *crowd* tenir à l'écart; *area* interdire l'accès à.

corduroy [ˈkɔ:dərɔɪ] *n* velours *m* côtelé.

core [kɔ:ʳ] **1** *n [fruit]* trognon *m*; *[earth, cable]* noyau *m*; *[nuclear reactor]* cœur *m*; *[problem etc]* essentiel *m*. (*fig*) **rotten to the ~** pourri jusqu'à l'os; **English to the ~** anglais jusqu'à la moelle (des os).

2 *vt fruit* enlever le trognon de.

♦ **corer** *n* vide-pomme *m*.

coriander [ˌkɒrɪˈændəʳ] *n* coriandre *f*.

cork [kɔ:k] **1** *n* (*substance*) liège *m*; (*in bottle etc*) bouchon *m*. **to pull the ~ out of** déboucher. **2** *vt* (**~ up**) *bottle* boucher. **3** *adj*: **~ oak** chêne-liège *m*. ♦ **corked** *adj wine* qui sent le bouchon. ♦ **corkscrew** *n* tire-bouchon *m*.

corn¹ [kɔ:n] **1** *n* (*gen*) grain *m*; (*Brit: wheat*) blé *m*; (*US: maize*) maïs *m*. **~ on the cob** épi *m* de maïs. **2** *adj oil, cob* de maïs. ♦ **cornfield** *n* (*Brit*) champ *m* de blé; (*US*) champ de maïs. ♦ **cornflakes** *npl* céréales *fpl*, cornflakes *fpl*. ♦ **cornflour** *or* ♦ **cornstarch** (*US*) *n* maïzena *f* ®. ♦ **cornflower** *n* bleuet *m*.

corn² [kɔ:n] *n* (*Med*) cor *m*. **to tread on sb's ~s** toucher qn à l'endroit sensible; **~ plaster** pansement *m* (pour cors).

cornea [ˈkɔ:nɪə] *n* cornée *f*.

corned beef [kɔ:nd ˈbi:f] *n* corned-beef *m*.

cornelian [kɔ:ˈni:lɪən] *n* cornaline *f*.

corner [ˈkɔ:nəʳ] **1** *n* (*gen*) coin *m*; (*Aut*) tournant *m*. (*fig*) **to drive sb into a ~** coincer* qn; **to be in a (tight) ~** être dans le pétrin; **out of the ~ of one's eye** du coin de l'œil; **it's just round the ~** (*lit*) c'est juste après le coin; (*fig: very near*) c'est à deux pas d'ici; (*in time*) c'est pour demain; **in odd ~s** dans des recoins; **in every ~** dans tous les coins et recoins; **in every ~ of Europe** dans toute l'Europe; **in the four ~s of the earth** aux quatre coins du monde; **to make a ~ in wheat** accaparer le marché du blé. **2** *adj*: **~ cupboard** placard *m* de coin; **the ~ house** la maison du coin; (*Rail*) **~ seat** (place *f* de) coin *m*; **~ shop** boutique *f* du coin. **3** *vt hunted animal etc* acculer; (*fig: catch to speak to etc*) coincer*. **to ~ the market** accaparer le marché. **4** *vi* (*Aut*) prendre un virage. ♦ **cornerstone** *n* (*lit, fig*) pierre *f* angulaire; (*foundation stone*) première pierre.

cornet ['kɔ:nɪt] *n* **(a)** (*Mus*) cornet *m* (à pistons). ~ **player** cornettiste *mf*. **(b)** *[sweets, ice cream]* cornet *m*.

Cornwall ['kɔ:nwəl] *n* Cornouailles *f*. ♦ **Cornish** *adj* de Cornouailles.

corny* ['kɔ:nɪ] *adj joke, story* rebattu, banal.

corollary [kə'rɒlərɪ] *n* corollaire *m*.

coronary ['kɒrənərɪ] *adj, n*: ~ **(thrombosis)** infarctus *m*.

coronation [ˌkɒrə'neɪʃən] *n* couronnement *m*.

coroner ['kɒrənəʳ] *n* coroner *m* (*officiel qui détermine les causes d'un décès*).

corporal¹ ['kɔ:pərəl] *n* (*Mil*) caporal-chef *m*.

corporal² ['kɔ:pərəl] *adj* corporel. ~ **punishment** châtiment *m* corporel.

corporate ['kɔ:pərɪt] *adj action, ownership* en commun; *responsibility* collectif. ~ **body** corps *m* constitué. ♦ **corporation** *n [town]* conseil *m* municipal; (*Comm, Fin*) société *f* commerciale.

corps [kɔ:ʳ] *n* corps *m*. ~ **de ballet** corps de ballet.

corpse [kɔ:ps] *n* cadavre *m*, corps *m*.

corpulence ['kɔ:pjʊləns] *n* corpulence *f*. ♦ **corpulent** *adj* corpulent.

corpus [kɔ:pəs] *n* corpus *m*. **C~ Christi** la Fête-Dieu.

corpuscle ['kɔ:pʌsl] *n* corpuscule *m*; *[blood]* globule *m*.

correct [kə'rekt] **1** *adj answer, amount* correct, exact, juste; *temperature, time* exact; *forecast, estimate, dress, behaviour* correct. **the predictions proved** ~ les prédictions se sont avérées justes; **you are** ~ vous avez raison; **it's the** ~ **thing** c'est ce qui se fait; **the** ~ **procedure** la procédure d'usage. **2** *vt work, error, proofs* corriger. **he ~ed me several times during the course of my speech** il m'a repris plusieurs fois pendant mon discours; **I stand ~ed** je reconnais mon erreur. ♦ **correction** *n* correction *f*. ♦ **correctly** *adv* correctement; d'une manière exacte; avec justesse. ♦ **correctness** *n* correction *f*; exactitude *f*; justesse *f*.

correlate ['kɒrɪleɪt] **1** *vi* être en corrélation (*with* avec). **2** *vt* mettre en corrélation (*with* avec). ♦ **correlation** *n* corrélation *f*.

correspond [ˌkɒrɪs'pɒnd] *vi* **(a)** (*agree; be equivalent*) correspondre (*with, to* à). **that does not ~ with what he said** cela ne correspond pas à ce qu'il a dit; **his job ~s roughly to mine** son poste est à peu près l'équivalent du mien. **(b)** (*exchange letters*) correspondre (*with* avec). **they** ~ ils correspondent. ♦ **correspondence** **1** *n* correspondance *f* (*between* entre, *with* avec); **2** *adj*: **~ence card** carte-lettre *f*; **~ence column** courrier *m* (des lecteurs); **~ence course** cours *m* par correspondance. ♦ **correspondent** *n* correspondant(e) *m(f)*; (*Press*) **foreign/sports ~ent** correspondant étranger/sportif. ♦ **corresponding** *adj* (*gen*) correspondant; **~ing to the original** conforme à l'original; **for a ~ing period** pendant une période analogue. ♦ **correspondingly** *adv* (*as a result*) en conséquence; (*proportionately*) proportionnellement.

corridor ['kɒrɪdɔ:ʳ] *n* couloir *m*, corridor *m*. ~ **train** train *m* à couloir.

corroborate [kə'rɒbəreɪt] *vt* corroborer. ♦ **corroboration** *n* corroboration *f*.

corrode [kə'rəʊd] **1** *vt* corroder. **2** *vi* se corroder. ♦ **corrosion** *n* corrosion *f*. ♦ **corrosive** *adj, n* corrosif (*m*).

corrugated ['kɒrəgeɪtɪd] *adj* ondulé. ~ **iron** tôle *f* ondulée.

corrupt [kə'rʌpt] **1** *adj* (*evil*) corrompu; (*dishonest*) vénal. ~ **practices** (*dishonesty*) tractations *fpl* malhonnêtes; (*bribery etc*) trafic *m* d'influence, malversations *fpl*. **2** *vt* corrompre. ♦ **corruption** *n* corruption *f*.

corset ['kɔ:sɪt] *n* (*Dress*) corset *m*, (*lightweight*) gaine *f*; (*Med*) corset.

Corsica ['kɔ:sɪkə] *n* Corse *f*.

cortisone ['kɔ:tɪzəʊn] *n* cortisone *f*.

cosh [kɒʃ] **1** *vt* (*) taper sur. **2** *n* matraque *f*.

cosmetic [kɒz'metɪk] **1** *adj surgery* esthétique; *preparation* cosmétique. **2** *n* cosmétique *m*, produit *m* de beauté.

cosmic ['kɒzmɪk] *adj* cosmique.

cosmographer [kɒz'mɒgrəfəʳ] *n* cosmographe *mf*. ♦ **cosmography** *n* cosmographie *f*.

cosmology [kɒz'mɒlədʒɪ] *n* cosmologie *f*.

cosmonaut ['kɒzmənɔ:t] *n* cosmonaute *mf*.

cosmopolitan [ˌkɒzmə'pɒlɪtən] *adj, n* cosmopolite (*mf*).

cosmos ['kɒzmɒs] *n* cosmos *m*.

cosset ['kɒsɪt] *vt* dorloter.

cost [kɒst] **1** *vt* **(a)** (*pret, ptp* **cost**) coûter. **how much** *or* **what does it ~?** combien est-ce que cela coûte *or* vaut?; **what will it ~ to have it repaired?** combien est-ce que cela coûtera de le faire réparer?; **it ~ him a lot of money** cela lui a coûté cher; **it ~s the earth*** cela coûte les yeux de la tête; **it ~ him a great effort/a lot of trouble** cela lui a coûté un gros effort/causé beaucoup d'ennuis; **it will ~ you a present** vous en serez quitte pour un cadeau; **politeness ~s very little** il ne coûte rien d'être poli; (*fig*) **whatever it ~s** coûte que coûte.

(b) (*pret, ptp* **~ed**) *articles for sale* établir le prix de revient de; *job etc* évaluer le coût de. **the job was ~ed at £200** le devis pour ces travaux s'élevait à 200 livres.

2 *n* coût *m*. ~ **of living** coût de la vie; **to bear the ~ of** faire face aux frais *mpl or* aux dépenses *fpl* de; (*fig*) faire les frais de; (*lit, fig*) **at great** ~ à grands frais; **at ~ (price)** au prix coûtant; (*Jur*) **to be ordered to pay ~s** être condamné aux dépens *mpl*; (*fig*) **at all ~s, at any ~** coûte que coûte, à tout prix; (*fig*) **whatever the ~** quoi qu'il en coûte; **at the ~ of his life/health** au prix de sa vie/santé; (*fig*) **to my ~** à mes dépens.

♦ **cost-effective** *adj* rentable. ♦ **costing** *n* estimation *f* du prix de revient; évaluation *f* du coût. ♦ **costliness** *n* (*value*) grande valeur; (*high price*) cherté *f*. ♦ **costly** *adj furs, jewels* de grande valeur; *undertaking, trip* coûteux; *tastes* dispendieux. ♦ **cost-of-living** *adj*: **~-of-living allowance** indemnité *f* de vie chère; **~-of-living index** index *m* du coût de la vie.

costermonger ['kɒstəˌmʌŋgəʳ] *n* marchand(e) *m(f)* des quatre saisons.

costume ['kɒstju:m] **1** *n* (*gen*) costume *m*; (*lady's suit*) tailleur *m*. **national** ~ costume national; (*fancy dress*) **in** ~ déguisé. **2** *adj*: ~ **ball** bal *m* masqué; ~ **jewellery** bijoux *mpl* fantaisie.

cosy ['kəʊzɪ] **1** *adj room* douillet, confortable; *atmosphere* douillet. **we are very ~ here** nous sommes très bien ici; **it is ~ in here** il fait bon ici; **a ~ little corner** un petit coin intime. **2** *n* (*tea* ~) couvre-théière *m*; (*egg* ~) couvre-œuf *m*. ♦ **cosiness** *n* confort *m*.

cot [kɒt] *n* lit *m* d'enfant; (*folding bed*) lit *m* de camp.

cottage ['kɒtɪdʒ] **1** *n* petite maison (à la campagne), cottage *m*; (*thatched*) chaumière *f*; (*in holiday village etc*) villa *f*.

2 *adj*: ~ **cheese** fromage *m* blanc (*maigre*); ~ **hospital** petit hôpital *m*; ~ **industry** industrie *f* à domicile.

cotton ['kɒtn] **1** *n* (*material*) coton *m*; (*sewing thread*) fil *m* (de coton). **2** *adj shirt, dress* de coton. (*US*) ~ **candy** barbe *f* à papa; ~ **goods** cotonnades *fpl*; ~ **industry** industrie *f* cotonnière; ~ **mill** filature *f* de coton; ~ **wool** ouate *f*, coton *m* hydrophile.

cotton on* *vi* piger*. **to ~ on to sth** piger* qch.

couch [kaʊtʃ] 1 *n* (*gen*) divan *m*; (*in doctor's surgery*) lit *m*. 2 *vt* (*express*) formuler.
cougar ['kuːgəʳ] *n* couguar *m*.
cough [kɒf] 1 *n* toux *f*. **to give a warning ~** tousser en guise d'avertissement; **he has a bad ~** il tousse beaucoup. 2 *adj*: **~ drop** pastille *f* pour la toux; **~ mixture** sirop *m* pour la toux. 3 *vi* tousser.
cough up *vt sep* cracher en toussant; (*: *fig*) *money* cracher*.
could [kʊd] *pret, cond of* **can**[1].
council ['kaʊnsl] 1 *n* conseil *m*. **~ of war** conseil de guerre; **city** *or* **town ~** conseil municipal; **the Security C~** le Conseil de Sécurité. 2 *adj*: **~ flat** *or* **house** ≃ habitation *f* à loyer modéré, H.L.M. *m or f*; **~ housing** logements *mpl* sociaux; **~ housing estate** quartier *m* de logements sociaux. ♦ **councillor** *n* conseiller *m*, -ère *f*.
counsel ['kaʊnsəl] 1 *n* **(a)** (*pl inv: Jur*) avocat(e) *m(f)*. **~ for the defence** avocat de la défense; **~ for the prosecution** avocat du ministère public; **King's** *or* **Queen's C~** avocat de la couronne. **(b)** (*advice*) conseil *m*. **to keep one's own ~** garder ses opinions pour soi. 2 *vt* conseiller (*sb to do* à qn de faire); *caution* recommander. ♦ **counsellor** *n* **(a)** (*Psych*) conseiller *m*, -ère *f*; **(b)** (*Ir, US: Jur*) avocat(e) *m(f)*.
count[1] [kaʊnt] 1 *n* **(a)** compte *m*; *[votes at election]* dépouillement *m*. **at the last ~** la dernière fois qu'on a compté; **to be out for the ~** (*Boxing*) être (mis) knock-out; (*: *gen*) être K.-O.*; **to keep ~ of** tenir le compte de; **you make me lose ~** je ne sais plus où j'en suis. **(b)** (*Jur*) chef *m* d'accusation. **guilty on 3 ~s** coupable à 3 chefs.
2 *vt* **(a)** (*gen*) compter; *inhabitants, injured, causes* compter, dénombrer; *one's change etc* compter, vérifier; (*consider*) estimer. **to ~ the votes** dépouiller le scrutin; **don't ~ your chickens before they're hatched** il ne faut pas vendre la peau de l'ours avant de l'avoir tué; (*fig*) **to ~ sheep** compter les moutons; **to ~ the cost** compter *or* calculer la dépense; (*fig*) faire le bilan; (*lit, fig*) **without ~ing the cost** sans compter; **~ your blessings** estimez-vous heureux. **(b)** (*include*) compter (*among* parmi). **not ~ing the children** sans compter les enfants; **~ing him** lui inclus *or* compris; **will you ~ it against me?** m'en tiendrez-vous rigueur?; **we must ~ ourselves fortunate** nous devons nous estimer heureux; **I ~ it an honour** je m'estime honoré (*to do* de faire; *that* que +*subj*).
3 *vi* compter. **~ing from tonight** à compter de ce soir; **~ing from the left** à partir de la gauche; **two children ~ as one adult** deux enfants comptent pour un adulte; **that doesn't ~** ça ne compte pas; **that ~s against him** cela est un désavantage; **it ~s for very little** ça n'a pas beaucoup de valeur.
count in* *vt sep* compter. **you can ~ me in** je suis de la partie!
count out *vt sep* **(a)** (*Boxing*) **to be ~ed out** être mis knock-out. **(b)** *money* compter pièce par pièce; *small objects* compter. **(c) you can ~ me out of it*** ne comptez pas sur moi là-dedans.
count up *vt sep* faire le compte de, additionner.
count (up)on *vt fus* compter sur. **I'm ~ing (up)on you** je compte sur vous; **to ~ (up)on doing** compter faire.
♦ **countable** *adj* qui peut être compté; **~able noun** substantif *m* distributif. ♦ **countdown** *n* compte *m* à rebours. ♦ **counting** *adj*: **~ing house** comptabilité *f* (*bureau*). ♦ **countless** *adj* innombrable, sans nombre; **on ~less occasions** je ne sais combien de fois.
count[2] [kaʊnt] *n* (*nobleman*) comte *m*. ♦ **countess** *n* comtesse *f*.
countenance ['kaʊntɪnəns] 1 *n* mine *f*, figure *f*. **to keep one's ~** rester impassible. 2 *vt* admettre (*sth* qch; *sb's doing* que qn fasse).
counter[1] ['kaʊntəʳ] 1 *n* **(a)** (*in shop, canteen*) comptoir *m*; (*position: in post office*) guichet *m*. (*fig*) **to buy under the ~** acheter clandestinement. **(b)** (*disc*) jeton *m*. **(c)** (*Tech*) compteur *m*. **Geiger ~** compteur Geiger. 2 *adj*: **~ hand** (*in shop*) vendeur *m*, -euse *f*; (*in snack bar*) serveur *m*, -euse *f*.
counter[2] ['kaʊntəʳ] 1 *adv*: **~ to** à l'encontre de. 2 *vt plans* contrecarrer; *blow* parer. 3 *vi* contre-attaquer, riposter; (*Boxing etc*) riposter (*with* par).
counter... ['kaʊntəʳ] *pref* contre... . ♦ **counteract** *vt* neutraliser, contrebalancer. ♦ **counter-attack** 1 *n* contre-attaque *f*; 2 *vti* contre-attaquer. ♦ **counter-attraction** *n* attraction *f* rivale. ♦ **counterbalance** *vt* faire contrepoids à. ♦ **counter-clockwise** *adv* en sens inverse des aiguilles d'une montre. ♦ **counter-espionage** *or* ♦ **counterintelligence** *n* contre-espionnage *m*. ♦ **counter-measure** *n* contre-mesure *f*. ♦ **counter-offensive** *n* contre-offensive *f*. ♦ **counterpart** *n* contrepartie *f*; *[person]* homologue *mf*. ♦ **counter-productive** *adj* inefficace. ♦ **Counter-Reformation** *n* Contre-Réforme *f*. ♦ **counter-revolution** *n* contre-révolution *f*. ♦ **countersign** *vt* contresigner. ♦ **countertenor** *n* (*singer*) haute-contre *m*; (*voice*) haute-contre *f*.
counterfeit ['kaʊntəfiːt] 1 *adj, n* faux (*m*). 2 *vt* contrefaire.
counterfoil ['kaʊntəfɔɪl] *n* talon *m*, souche *f*.
counterpane ['kaʊntəpeɪn] *n* dessus-de-lit *m inv*.
countersink ['kaʊntəsɪŋk] *vt* noyer (*une vis*).
country ['kʌntrɪ] 1 *n* **(a)** (*gen*) pays *m*; (*native land*) patrie *f*. (*Pol*) **to go to the ~** appeler le pays aux urnes; **to die for one's ~** mourir pour la patrie. **(b)** (*as opposed to town*) campagne *f*; (*region*) pays *m*, région *f*. **in the ~** à la campagne; **there is some lovely ~ to the north** il y a de beaux paysages dans le nord; **mountainous ~** une région montagneuse; (*fig*) **in unknown ~** en terrain inconnu.
2 *adj life, people* de (la) campagne. (*music*) **~ and western** country music *f*; **~ bumpkin** culterreux* *m*; **~ cottage** *[weekenders]* maison *f* de campagne; (*fig*) **~ cousin** cousin(e) *m(f)* de province; **~ dancing** danse *f* folklorique; **~ dweller** campagnard(e) *m(f)*; **~ house** manoir *m*; **~ life** vie *f* de la *or* à la campagne; **~ road** petite route (de campagne); **~ seat** château *m*. ♦ **countrified** *adj* rustique. ♦ **countryman** *n*: **fellow ~man** compatriote *m*, concitoyen *m*. ♦ **countryside** *n* campagne *f*. ♦ **country-wide** *adj* national.
county ['kaʊntɪ] 1 *n* comté *m*, ≃ département *m*. 2 *adj*: **~ town** chef-lieu *m*.
coup [kuː] *n* beau coup *m*; (*Pol*) coup d'État.
couple ['kʌpl] *n [animals, people]* couple *m*. **a ~ of** deux; **a ~ of times** deux ou trois fois; **I did it in a ~ of hours** je l'ai fait en deux heures environ.
coupon ['kuːpɒn] *n [newspaper, advertisements etc]* coupon *m* (*détachable*); *[cigarette packets etc]* bon *m*, vignette *f*; (*offering price reductions*) bon de réduction; (*rationing*) ticket *m*; (*Fin*) coupon.
courage ['kʌrɪdʒ] *n* courage *m*. **I haven't the ~ to refuse** je n'ai pas le courage de refuser, je n'ose pas refuser; **to have the ~ of one's convictions** avoir le courage de ses opinions. ♦ **courageous** *adj* courageux. ♦ **courageously** *adv* courageusement.
courier ['kʊrɪəʳ] *n* (*messenger*) courrier *m*; (*tourist guide*) guide *m*.
course [kɔːs] 1 *n* **(a)** (*duration*) *[life, disease]* cours *m*. **in the ~ of time** à la longue; **in the ordinary ~ of events** normalement, en temps normal *or* ordinaire; **in the ~ of conversation** au cours de la conversation; **in (the) ~ of construction** en cours de construction; **in the ~ of the next**

few months au cours des prochains mois; **in the ~ of the week** dans le courant de la semaine.

(b) of ~ bien sûr, naturellement; **(yes) of ~** (oui) bien sûr; **of ~ not!** (*answering; denying; disagreeing*) bien sûr que non!; (*refusing*) certainement pas!; **of ~ I won't do it** je ne vais évidemment pas faire ça.

(c) (*route*) *[river, planet]* cours *m*; *[ship]* route *f*. **to hold one's ~** poursuivre sa route; (*Naut*) **to set ~ for** mettre le cap sur; (*Naut*) **to change ~** changer de cap; **to go off ~** faire fausse route; **~ of action** ligne *f* de conduite; **we have no other ~ but to ...** nous n'avons d'autre moyen *or* ressource que de ...; **there are several ~s open to us** plusieurs partis s'offrent à nous; **the best ~ would be to leave** le mieux à faire serait de partir; **to let sth take its ~** laisser qch suivre son cours.

(d) (*Scol, Univ*) cours *m*. **to go to a French ~** suivre un cours *or* des cours de français; **a ~ of lectures on Proust** une série de conférences sur Proust; (*Med*) **~ of treatment** traitement *m*.

(e) (*Golf*) terrain *m* de golf; (*Horseracing*) champ *m* de courses.

(f) (*Culin*) plat *m*. **first ~** entrée *f*; **main ~** plat de résistance.

2 *vi [water etc]* couler à flots; *[tears]* ruisseler. **it sent the blood coursing through his veins** cela lui a fouetté le sang.

court [kɔ:t] **1** *n* **(a)** (*Jur*) cour *f*, tribunal *m*; (**~** *room*) salle *f* du tribunal. **~ of appeal(s)** cour d'appel; **~ of inquiry** commission *f* d'enquête; **to settle a case out of ~** arranger une affaire à l'amiable; **to rule out of ~** déclarer inadmissible; **to take sb to ~ over sth** poursuivre qn en justice à propos de qch; **he was brought before the ~s** il est passé en jugement. **(b)** *[monarch]* cour *f* (royale); (*Tennis*) court *m*; (*~yard*) cour *f* (*de maison etc*). **2** *adj*: **~ card** figure *f* (*de jeu de cartes*); **~ shoe** escarpin *m*. **3** *vt woman* faire la cour à; *danger, defeat* aller au-devant de. **4** *vi*: **they are ~ing*** ils sortent ensemble. ♦ **courthouse** *n* palais *m* de justice, tribunal *m*. ♦ **courtier** *n* courtisan *m*, dame *f* de la cour. ♦ **courting** *adj*: **a ~ing couple** un couple d'amoureux. ♦ **court-martial 1** *n, pl* **~s-martial** conseil *m* de guerre; **2** *vt* faire passer en conseil de guerre. ♦ **courtship** *n*: **during their ~ship** au temps où ils sortaient ensemble.

Courtelle [kɔ:'tel] *n* ® Courtelle *m* ®.

courteous ['kɜ:tɪəs] *adj* courtois (*towards* envers). ♦ **courteously** *adv* courtoisement. ♦ **courtesy** ['kɜ:tɪsɪ] **1** *n* courtoisie *f*, politesse *f*; **will you do me the courtesy of reading it?** auriez-vous l'obligeance de le lire?; **exchange of courtesies** échange *m* de politesses; **by courtesy of** avec la permission de; **2** *adj visit* de politesse; *title* de courtoisie; (*free*) *coach etc* gratuit; **courtesy card** carte *f* de priorité (*dans les hôtels etc*); (*Aut*) **courtesy light** plafonnier *m*.

cousin ['kʌzn] *n* cousin(e) *m(f)*.

cove [kəʊv] *n* crique *f*.

covenant ['kʌvɪnənt] **1** *n* (*gen*) convention *f*; (*Fin*) obligation *f* contractuelle. **2** *vt* s'engager (*to do* à faire). **to ~ £10 per annum to a charity** s'engager par obligation contractuelle à verser 10 livres par an à une œuvre.

Coventry ['kɒvəntrɪ] *n*: **to send sb to ~** mettre qn en quarantaine (*fig*).

cover ['kʌvəʳ] **1** *n* **(a)** *[saucepan, bowl, dish]* couvercle *m*; *[table]* nappe *f*; *[furniture, typewriter]* housse *f*; *[merchandise, vehicle etc]* bâche *f*; (*bed~*) dessus-de-lit *m inv*; *[book]* couverture *f*; (*envelope*) enveloppe *f*; *[parcel]* emballage *m*. (*bedclothes*) **the ~s** les couvertures *fpl*; **to read a book from ~ to ~** lire un livre de la première à la dernière page; (*Comm*) **under separate ~** sous pli séparé. **(b)** (*shelter*) abri *m*; (*covering fire*) feu *m* de couverture. **the trees gave him ~** les arbres le cachaient; (*sheltered*) les arbres l'abritaient; **to take ~** (*hide*) se cacher; (*Mil*) s'embusquer; (*shelter*) s'abriter (*from* de); **under ~** à l'abri, à couvert; **under ~ of darkness** à la faveur de la nuit. **(c)** (*Fin, Insurance*) couverture *f*. (*Fin*) **without ~** à découvert; (*Insurance*) **full ~** garantie *f* tous risques; **fire ~** assurance-incendie *f*. **(d)** (*in espionage etc*) identité *f* d'emprunt. **(e)** (*at table*) couvert *m*.

2 *adj [restaurant]* **~ charge** couvert *m*; (*Insurance*) **~ note** ≈ récépissé *m* (d'assurance).

3 *vt* **(a)** (*gen*) couvrir (*with* de). **~ed with confusion** couvert de confusion; **to ~ o.s. with glory** se couvrir de gloire. **(b)** (*hide*) *feelings, facts* dissimuler, cacher; *noise* couvrir. **(c)** (*protect*) *person, retreat* couvrir. (*Insurance*) **~ed against fire** assuré contre l'incendie; **he only said that to ~ himself** il n'a dit cela que pour se couvrir. **(d)** (*point gun at*) braquer un revolver sur. **to keep sb ~ed** tenir qn sous la menace du revolver; **I've got you ~ed!** ne bougez pas ou je tire! **(e)** (*Sport*) *opponent* marquer. **(f)** *distance* parcourir, couvrir. **to ~ a lot of ground** faire beaucoup de chemin; (*fig*) faire du bon travail. **(g)** (*be sufficient for*) couvrir; (*include*) englober, traiter. **his work ~s many fields** son travail englobe *or* embrasse plusieurs domaines; **the book ~s the subject thoroughly** le livre traite le sujet à fond; **in order to ~ all possibilities** pour parer à toute éventualité; **to ~ one's expenses** rentrer dans ses frais; **£5 will ~ everything** 5 livres payeront tout. **(h)** (*Press*) *event* assurer le reportage de.

cover over *vt sep* recouvrir.

cover up 1 *vi* (*warmly*) se couvrir. (*fig*) **to ~ up for sb** couvrir qn, protéger qn. **2** *vt sep child, object* recouvrir, envelopper (*with* de); (*hide*) *truth, facts* dissimuler, cacher. **to ~ up one's tracks** couvrir sa marche.

♦ **coverage** *n* (*Press, Rad, TV*) reportage *m*; **to give full ~age to an event** assurer la couverture complète d'un événement; **the match got nationwide ~age** (*Rad*) le reportage du match a été diffusé *or* (*TV*) le match a été retransmis sur l'ensemble du pays. ♦ **coveralls** *npl* bleus *mpl* de travail. ♦ **covergirl** *n* cover-girl *f*. ♦ **covering 1** *n* couverture *f*; (*of snow, dust etc*) couche *f*; **2** *adj letter* explicatif; (*Mil*) *fire* de couverture. ♦ **coverlet** *n* dessus-de-lit *m inv*. ♦ **cover-up** *n*: **the ~-up** les tentatives *fpl* faites pour étouffer l'affaire.

covert ['kʌvət] *adj* (*gen*) caché; *attack* indirect; *glance* dérobé.

covet ['kʌvɪt] *vt* convoiter. ♦ **covetous** *adj person* avide; *look* de convoitise. ♦ **covetously** *adv* avidement; avec convoitise. ♦ **covetousness** *n* avidité *f*; convoitise *f*.

cow¹ [kaʊ] **1** *n* vache *f*; (**:** *woman*) rosse* *f*, vache**:** *f*. (*fig*) **till the ~s come home*** jusqu'à la Trinité (*fig*); **to wait till the ~s come home*** attendre la semaine des quatre jeudis*. **2** *adj*: **~ elephant/buffalo** *etc* éléphant *m*/buffle *m etc* femelle. ♦ **cowboy** *or* ♦ **cowpuncher*** *n* cow-boy *m*; **to play ~boys and Indians** jouer aux cow-boys. ♦ **cowherd** *or* ♦ **cowman** *n* vacher *m*, bouvier *m*. ♦ **cowhide** *n* (peau *f* de) vache *f*. ♦ **cowpox** *n* variole *f* de la vache. ♦ **cowshed** *n* étable *f*. ♦ **cowslip** *n* (*Bot*) coucou *m*.

cow² [kaʊ] *vt person* intimider. **a ~ed look** un air de chien battu.

coward ['kaʊəd] *n* lâche *mf*. ♦ **cowardice** *or* ♦ **cowardliness** *n* lâcheté *f*. ♦ **cowardly** *adj* lâche.

cower ['kaʊəʳ] *vi* (**~ down**) se recroqueviller.

cowl [kaʊl] *n* capuchon *m*.

cowrie, cowry ['kaʊrɪ] *n* porcelaine *f* (*mollusque*).

cox [kɒks] **1** *n* barreur *m*. **2** *vti* barrer.

coy [kɔɪ] *adj person* qui fait le *or* la timide; *smile* de sainte nitouche (*pej*); (*coquettish*) *woman* qui fait la coquette. ♦ **coyly** *adv* avec une timidité feinte; avec coquetterie. ♦ **coyness** *n* timidité *f* feinte; coquetterie *f*.

cozy ['kəʊzɪ] (*US*) = **cosy.**

crab [kræb] *n* crabe *m*; (~ **apple**) pomme *f* sauvage. ♦ **crabbed** *or* ♦ **crabby** *adj person* grincheux.

crack [kræk] **1** *n* **(a)** (*split, slit*) fente *f*; (*in glass, pottery, bone etc*) fêlure *f*; (*in wall*) fente, lézarde *f*; (*in ground, skin*) crevasse *f*; (*in paint*) craquelure *f*. **through the ~ in the door** (*slight opening*) par l'entrebâillement de la porte; **at the ~ of dawn** au point du jour. **(b)** (*noise*) *[twigs]* craquement *m*; *[whip]* claquement *m*; *[rifle, thunder]* coup *m*. **(c)** (*sharp blow*) **a ~ on the head** un grand coup sur la tête; **that was a ~* at your brother** ça, c'était pour votre frère; **that was a dirty ~*** c'était vache‡ de dire ça; (*try*) **to have a ~ at (doing) sth*** essayer (de faire) qch.

2 *adj sportsman* de première classe. **a ~ tennis player/skier** un as du tennis/du ski; **~ shot** excellent fusil *m*; (*Mil, Police etc*) tireur *m* d'élite.

3 *vt* **(a)** *pottery, glass, bone* fêler; *wall* lézarder; *ground* crevasser; *nut etc* casser; (*) *safe* cambrioler; *bottle* déboucher. **to ~ one's skull** se fendre le crâne; **to ~ sb over the head** assommer qn. **(b)** *whip* faire claquer. **to ~ one's finger joints** faire craquer ses doigts; **to ~ jokes*** faire des astuces*. **(c)** *code etc* déchiffrer; *case* résoudre.

4 *vi [pottery, glass]* se fêler; *[ground, skin]* se crevasser; *[wall]* se lézarder; *[whip]* claquer; *[dry wood]* craquer. **to get ~ing*** s'y mettre, se mettre au boulot*.

crack down on *vt fus person* tomber à bras raccourcis sur; *expenditure, sb's actions* mettre le frein à.

crack up* 1 *vi* **(a)** ne pas tenir le coup, flancher*. (*hum*) **I must be ~ing up!** ça ne tourne plus rond chez moi!* **(b)** (*US*) *[vehicle, plane]* s'écraser. **2** *vt sep*: **he's not all he's ~ed up to be*** il n'est pas aussi sensationnel* qu'on le dit.

♦ **crack-brained** *or* ♦ **cracked*** *or* ♦ **crackers*** *adj* fou, cinglé*. ♦ **cracker** *n* (*biscuit*) craquelin *m*, cracker *m*; (*firework*) pétard *m*; (*at parties etc*) diablotin *m*. ♦ **crackpot*** *n, adj* fou *m*, folle *f*, tordu(e)‡ *m(f)*. ♦ **crack-up*** *n* (*gen*) effondrement *m*; (*mental*) dépression *f* nerveuse; (*US*) accident *m*.

crackle ['krækl] **1** *vi [twigs burning]* crépiter; *[sth frying]* grésiller. **2** *n* crépitement *m*; grésillement *m*; (*on telephone etc*) crépitement(s), friture* *f*; *[china, porcelain etc]* craquelure *f*. ♦ **crackling** *n* (*sound*) crépitement *m*; (*Rad*) friture* *f*; (*Culin*) couenne *f* rissolée (*de rôti de porc*).

cradle ['kreɪdl] **1** *n* berceau *m*; (*Constr*) pont *m* volant; *[telephone]* support *m*; (*Med*) arceau *m*. **2** *vt child* bercer; *object* tenir entre ses mains. ♦ **cradle-snatcher*** *n* personne *f* qui les prend au berceau*. ♦ **cradlesong** *n* berceuse *f*.

craft [krɑːft] *n* **(a)** (*skill*) art *m*, métier *m*; (*job*) métier. **(b)** (*pl inv: boat*) embarcation *f*. **(c)** (*cunning*) astuce *f*, ruse *f* (*pej*). ♦ **craftsman** *n* artisan *m*, homme *m* de métier. ♦ **craftsmanship** *n* connaissance *f* d'un métier; **a superb piece of ~smanship** un travail superbe.

crafty ['krɑːftɪ] *adj* malin, rusé (*pej*); *gadget, action* astucieux. **he's a ~ one*** c'est un malin. ♦ **craftily** *adv* astucieusement, avec ruse (*pej*). ♦ **craftiness** *n* astuce *f*, ruse *f* (*pej*).

crag [kræg] *n* rocher *m* escarpé. ♦ **craggy** *adj rock* escarpé; *features* taillé à la serpe.

cram [kræm] **1** *vt* (*gen*) fourrer (*into* dans), bourrer (*with* de); *people, passengers* faire entrer (*into* dans); *pupil* faire bachoter. **we can ~ in another book** nous pouvons encore y faire tenir un autre livre; **to ~ food into one's mouth** enfourner* de la nourriture; **we were all ~med into one room** nous étions tous entassés dans une seule pièce; **he ~med his hat (down) over his eyes** il a enfoncé son chapeau sur ses yeux; **head ~med with odd ideas** tête farcie d'idées bizarres. **2** *vi [people]* s'entasser, s'empiler (*into* dans). **to ~ for an exam** bachoter. ♦ **cram-full** *adj room, bus* bondé; *case* bourré (*of* de).

cramp [kræmp] **1** *n* crampe *f* (*in* à). **2** *vt* gêner, entraver. **to ~ sb's style** enlever ses moyens à qn. ♦ **cramped** *adj handwriting* en pattes de mouche; *posture* inconfortable; *space* resserré; **we were very ~ed** on était à l'étroit.

cranberry ['krænbərɪ] *n* canneberge *f*. **turkey with ~ sauce** dinde *f* aux canneberges.

crane [kreɪn] **1** *n* (*Orn, Tech*) grue *f*. **2** *adj*: **~ driver** grutier *m*. **3** *vti*: **to ~ forward, to ~ one's neck** tendre le cou.

crank [kræŋk] **1** *n* **(a)** (*eccentric*) excentrique *mf*. **a religious ~** un fanatique religieux. **(b)** (*Tech*) manivelle *f*. **2** *vt* (~ **up**) *car* faire partir à la manivelle; *cine-camera* remonter; *barrel organ* tourner la manivelle de. ♦ **crankcase** *n* carter *m*. ♦ **crankshaft** *n* vilebrequin *m*. ♦ **cranky** *adj* (*eccentric*) excentrique, loufoque*; (*bad-tempered*) revêche.

crap‡ [kræp] *n* merde‡ *f*.

crape [kreɪp] *n* = **crêpe.**

crash [kræʃ] **1** *n* **(a)** (*noise*) fracas *m*; *[thunder]* coup *m*. **~!** patatras! **(b)** (*accident*) accident *m*. **in a car ~** dans un accident de voiture. **(c)** *[company, firm]* faillite *f*; (*St Ex*) krach *m*. **2** *vt car* avoir une collision *or* un accident avec. **he ~ed the car into a tree** il a percuté un arbre; **he ~ed the plane** il s'est écrasé (au sol). **3** *vi* **(a)** *[aeroplane]* s'écraser au sol; *[vehicle]* s'écraser; *[two vehicles]* se percuter, se rentrer dedans*. **to ~ into sth** rentrer dans qch*, percuter qch; **the plate ~ed to the ground** l'assiette s'est fracassée par terre; **the car ~ed through the gate** la voiture a enfoncé la barrière. **(b)** *[bank, firm]* faire faillite; *[stock market]* s'effondrer. **4** *adj*: **~ course** cours *m* intensif; **~ helmet** casque *m* (protecteur); (*Aviat*) **~ landing** atterrissage en catastrophe.

crash in, crash down *vi [roof etc]* s'effondrer (avec fracas).

crass [kræs] *adj* crasse.

crate [kreɪt] *n* (*gen*) caisse *f*; (*for peaches etc*) cageot *m*.

crater ['kreɪtəʳ] *n* (*gen*) cratère *m*; *[bomb, shell]* entonnoir *m*.

crave [kreɪv] *vti* **(a)** (~ **for**) *drink, tobacco etc* avoir un besoin maladif de; *affection* avoir soif de. **(b)** *pardon* implorer; *permission* solliciter. ♦ **craving** *n* besoin *m* maladif (*for* de); *[affection]* soif *f* (*for* de).

crawl [krɔːl] **1** *n* **(a)** (*Aut*) **to go at a ~** avancer au pas. **(b)** (*Swimming*) crawl *m*. **to do the ~** nager le crawl. **2** *vi* (*gen*) ramper; *[vehicles]* avancer au pas; *[child]* se traîner à quatre pattes. **to ~ in/out** *etc* entrer/sortir *etc* en rampant *or* à quatre pattes; (*fig*) **to ~ to sb** s'aplatir devant qn; **the fly ~ed up the wall/along the table** la mouche a grimpé le long du mur/a avancé le long de la table; **to make sb's skin ~** donner la chair de poule à qn; **to ~ with vermin** grouiller de vermine. ♦ **crawler** *adj* (*Aut*) **~er lane** voie *f* pour véhicules lents.

crayfish ['kreɪfɪʃ] *n* (*freshwater*) écrevisse *f*; (*saltwater*) langouste *f*.

crayon ['kreɪən] *n* crayon *m* de couleur; (*Art*) pastel *m*.

craze [kreɪz] **1** *n* engouement *m* (*for* pour), manie *f* (*for* de). **it's all the ~*** cela fait fureur. **2** *vt* rendre fou. ♦ **crazed** *adj person* affolé, fou; *glaze, pottery* craquelé. ♦ **crazily** *adv* follement. ♦ **crazy** *adj* (*mad*) fou (*f* folle), cinglé*; *angle, slope* incroyable; (*: *enthusiastic*) fou, fana* (*f inv*) (*about sb/sth* de qn/qch); **to go crazy** devenir fou; **crazy with anxiety** fou d'inquiétude; **it was a crazy idea** c'était une idée idiote; **you were crazy to do it** tu étais fou de faire ça; **I am not crazy about it** ça ne m'emballe* pas; **he's crazy about her** il l'aime à la folie; **crazy paving** dallage *m* irrégulier.

creak [kri:k] **1** *vi [door hinge]* grincer; *[shoes, floorboard]* craquer. **2** *n* grincement *m*; craquement *m*.
♦ **creaky** *adj* grinçant; qui craque.

cream [kri:m] **1** *n* **(a)** crème *f*. **single/double** ~ crème fraîche liquide/épaisse; **to take the ~ off the milk** écrémer le lait; **the ~ of society** la crème de la société; **chocolate** ~ chocolat *m* fourré; **~ of tartar** crème de tartre; **~ of tomato soup** crème de tomates. **(b)** (*face* ~, *shoe* ~) crème *f*. **2** *adj* (~*-coloured*) crème *inv*; (*made with* ~) à la crème. ~ **cheese** fromage *m* frais; ~ **jug** pot *m* à crème. **3** *vt butter* battre. **to ~ (together) sugar and butter** travailler le beurre en crème avec le sucre; **~ed potatoes** purée *f* de pommes de terre.
cream off *vt sep best talents, part of profits* prélever, écrémer.
♦ **creamery** *n* (*making cream*) laiterie *f*; (*shop*) crémerie *f*. ♦ **creamy** *adj* crémeux.

crease [kri:s] **1** *n* (*gen*) pli *m*; (*unwanted*) faux pli; (*on face*) ride *f*. **~-resistant** infroissable. **2** *vt* plisser. **3** *vi* se froisser, prendre un faux pli. **his face ~d with laughter** le rire a plissé son visage.

create [kri:'eɪt] **1** *vt* (*gen*) créer; *new fashion* lancer; *impression, noise, din* faire; *problem, difficulty* créer, provoquer. **to ~ a sensation** faire sensation; **he was ~d baron** il a été fait baron. **2** *vi* (‡: *fuss*) faire une scène *or* des histoires* (*about* au sujet de). ♦ **creation** *n* création *f*; **since the creation** depuis la création du monde. ♦ **creative** *adj mind, power* créateur; *person, activity* créatif. ♦ **creativity** *n* imagination *f* créatrice, créativité *f*. ♦ **creator** *n* créateur *m*, -trice *f*.
♦ **creature** ['kri:tʃəʳ] **1** *n* (*gen*) créature *f*; **the creatures of the deep** les animaux *mpl* marins; **2** *adj*: **creature comforts** confort *m* matériel.

credentials [krɪ'denʃəlz] *npl* (*identifying papers*) pièce *f* d'identité; *[diplomat]* lettres *fpl* de créance; (*references*) références *fpl*.

credible ['kredɪbl] *adj* (*gen*) plausible; *person* crédible; *witness* digne de foi. ♦ **credibility** **1** *n* crédibilité *f*; **2** *adj*: **credibility gap** manque *m* de crédibilité.

credit ['kredɪt] **1** *n* **(a)** (*Banking etc*) crédit *m*. **to give sb ~** faire crédit à qn; **on ~** à crédit; **you have £10 to your ~** vous avez un crédit de 10 livres. **(b)** honneur *m*. **to his ~ we must point out that ...** il faut faire remarquer à son honneur *or* à son crédit que ...; **he is a ~ to his family** il fait honneur à sa famille, il est l'honneur de sa famille; **to give sb ~ for (doing) sth** reconnaître que qn a fait qch; **I gave him ~ for more sense** je lui supposais plus de bon sens; **to take ~ for sth** s'attribuer le mérite de qch; **it does you ~** cela est tout à votre honneur, cela vous fait grand honneur; (*Cine*) **~s** générique *m*. **(c)** (*Scol*) unité *f* de valeur, U.V. *f*.
2 *vt* **(a)** (*believe*) croire, ajouter foi à. **(b) to be ~ed with having done** passer pour avoir fait; **I ~ed him with more sense** je lui supposais plus de bon sens; **it is ~ed with having magic powers** on lui attribue des pouvoirs magiques. **(c)** (*Banking*) **to ~ £5 to sb, to ~ sb with £5** créditer (le compte de) qn de 5 livres.
3 *adj limits, agency* de crédit. **~ balance** solde *m* créditeur; **~ card** carte *f* de crédit; **~ entry** inscription *f* au crédit; **~ facilities** facilités *fpl* de paiement; **on the ~ side** à l'actif; **~ squeeze** restrictions *fpl* de crédit; **~worthiness** solvabilité *f*.
♦ **creditable** *adj* honorable, estimable. ♦ **creditably** *adv* honorablement. ♦ **creditor** *n* créancier *m*, -ière *f*.

credulity [krɪ'dju:lɪtɪ] *n* crédulité *f*. ♦ **credulous** *adj* crédule. ♦ **credulously** *adv* avec crédulité.

creed [kri:d] *n* credo *m*.

creek [kri:k] *n* crique *f*, anse *f*.

creep [kri:p] *pret, ptp* **crept** **1** *vi* (*gen*) ramper; (*move silently*) se glisser. **to ~ in** *[person]* entrer sans un bruit; *[error]* s'y glisser; **to ~ up on sb** *[person]* s'approcher de qn à pas de loup; *[old age etc]* prendre qn par surprise; **the traffic crept along** les voitures avançaient au pas; **a feeling of peace crept over me** un sentiment de paix me gagnait peu à peu; **it makes my flesh ~** cela me donne la chair de poule. **2** *n*: **it gives me the ~s*** cela me donne la chair de poule; **he's a ~‡** c'est un saligaud‡. ♦ **creeper** *n* (*Bot*) plante rampante; (*US: rompers*) **~ers** barboteuse *f*. ♦ **creeping** *adj plant* grimpant, rampant; (*fig*) *person* lécheur; **~ing paralysis** paralysie progressive. ♦ **creepy** *adj* qui donne la chair de poule. ♦ **creepy-crawly*** *n* petite bestiole.

cremate [krɪ'meɪt] *vt* incinérer (*un cadavre*).
♦ **cremation** *n* incinération *f*. ♦ **crematorium** *or* ♦ **crematory** *n* crématorium *m*.

creosote ['krɪəsəʊt] **1** *n* créosote *f*. **2** *vt* créosoter.

crêpe [kreɪp] **1** *n* crêpe *m*. **2** *adj*: **~ bandage** bande *f* Velpeau ®; **~ paper** papier *m* crêpon; **~(-soled) shoes** chaussures *fpl* à semelles de crêpe.

crept [krept] *pret, ptp of* **creep**.

crescent ['kresnt] *n* (*gen*) croissant *m*; (*street*) rue *f* (*en arc de cercle*). **~ moon** croissant *m* de (la) lune.

cress [kres] *n* cresson *m*.

crest [krest] *n [bird, wave, mountain]* crête *f*; *[helmet]* cimier *m*; *[road]* haut *m* de côte. **family ~** armoiries *fpl* familiales; (*fig*) **he is on the ~ of the wave** tout lui réussit en ce moment.
♦ **crestfallen** *adj person* déçu, déconfit; **to look ~fallen** avoir l'oreille basse.

Crete [kri:t] *n* Crète *f*.

cretin ['kretɪn] *n* crétin(e) *m(f)*. ♦ **cretinous** *adj* crétin.

crevice ['krevɪs] *n* fissure *f*, fente *f*.

crew¹ [kru:] **1** *n* (*Aviat, Naut*) équipage *m*; (*Cine, Rowing etc*) équipe *f*; (*group, gang*) bande *f*, équipe. (*pej*) **what a ~!*** quelle engeance! **2** *vi* (*Sailing*) **to ~ for sb** être l'équipier de qn.
♦ **crew-cut** *n*: **to have a ~-cut** avoir les cheveux en brosse. ♦ **crew-neck** *adj*: **~-neck sweater** pull-over *m* à col ras.

crew² [kru:] *pret of* **crow**².

crib [krɪb] **1** *n* **(a)** (*cot*) lit *m* d'enfant; (*Rel*) crèche *f*; (*manger*) mangeoire *f*. **(b)** (*plagiarism*) plagiat *m*; (*Scol*) traduction *f* (*utilisée illicitement*). **2** *vti* (*Scol*) copier.

crick [krɪk] **1** *n*: **~ in the neck** torticolis *m*; **~ in the back** tour *m* de reins. **2** *vt*: **to ~ one's neck** attraper un torticolis; **to ~ one's back** se faire un tour de reins.

cricket¹ ['krɪkɪt] *n* (*insect*) grillon *m*.

cricket² ['krɪkɪt] **1** *n* (*Sport*) cricket *m*. (*fig*) **that's not ~** ce n'est pas fair-play. **2** *adj ball, match* de cricket.

crime [kraɪm] *n* crime *m*. **minor ~** délit *m*; **~ wave** vague *f* de crimes; **~ is on the increase/decrease** il y a un accroissement/une régression de la criminalité. ♦ **criminal** ['krɪmɪnl] **1** *n* criminel(le) *m(f)*; **2** *adj action, motive, law* criminel; (*fig*) **it's criminal* to stay indoors today** c'est un crime de rester enfermé aujourd'hui; **the Criminal Investigation Department** la police judiciaire, la P.J.; **criminal lawyer** avocat *m* au criminel; **to take criminal proceedings against sb** poursuivre qn au pénal; **Criminal Records Office** identité *f* judiciaire. ♦ **criminologist** *n* criminologiste *mf*. ♦ **criminology** *n* criminologie *f*.

crimp [krɪmp] *vt hair* frisotter; *pastry* pincer.
Crimplene ['krɪmpli:n] *n* ® ≈ crêpe *m* acrylique.
crimson ['krɪmzn] *adj, n* cramoisi (*m*).
cringe [krɪndʒ] *vi* avoir un mouvement de recul (*from* devant); (*fig*) ramper (*before* devant). **the very thought of it makes me ~*** rien qu'à y penser j'ai envie de rentrer sous terre. ♦ **cringing** *adj movement* craintif; *behaviour* servile.
crinkle ['krɪŋkl] *vt* froisser, chiffonner. ♦ **crinkly** *adj paper* gaufré; *hair* crêpelé.
cripple ['krɪpl] **1** *n* (*lame*) estropié(e) *m(f)*; (*disabled*) invalide *mf*; (*maimed*) mutilé(e) *m(f)*. **2** *vt* **(a)** estropier. **~d with rheumatism** perclus de rhumatismes. **(b)** *ship, plane* désemparer; *[strikes etc] production, exports etc* paralyser. **crippling taxes** impôts *mpl* écrasants.
crisis ['kraɪsɪs] *n, pl* **crises** ['kraɪsi:z] crise *f*. **to come to a ~** atteindre un point critique; **we've got a ~ on our hands** nous avons un problème urgent.
crisp [krɪsp] **1** *adj biscuit, bread* croustillant; *vegetables* croquant; *snow, paper* craquant; *linen* apprêté; *weather* vif, piquant; *reply, style* vif, tranchant (*pej*); *tone, voice* acerbe, cassant (*pej*). **2** *n* **(potato) ~s** (pommes) chips *fpl*; **packet of ~s** sachet *m* de chips. ♦ **crispbread** *n* pain *m* scandinave. ♦ **crisply** *adv say etc* d'un ton acerbe *or* cassant (*pej*).
criss-cross ['krɪskrɒs] **1** *adj lines* entrecroisés. **in a ~ pattern** en croisillons. **2** *n* entrecroisement *m*. **3** *vt* entrecroiser (*by* de). **4** *vi* s'entrecroiser.
criterion [kraɪ'tɪərɪən] *n, pl* **-ia** *or* **-s** critère *m*.
critic ['krɪtɪk] *n [books, painting, music, films etc]* critique *m*; (*faultfinder*) détracteur *m*, -trice *f*. **film ~** critique de cinéma. ♦ **critical** *adj* (*all senses*) critique. **to be ~al of** critiquer, trouver à redire à. ♦ **critically** *adv* (*discriminatingly*) *judge, consider, discuss* en critique, d'un œil critique; (*adversely*) *review, report* sévèrement; **~ally ill** gravement malade. ♦ **criticism** *n* critique *f*. ♦ **criticize** *vt* critiquer. ♦ **critique** [krɪ'ti:k] *n* critique *f*.
croak [krəʊk] **1** *vi [frog]* coasser; *[raven]* croasser; *[person]* parler d'une voix rauque. **2** *vt* dire d'une voix rauque. **3** *n* coassement *m*; croassement *m*.
crochet ['krəʊʃeɪ] **1** *n* travail *m* au crochet. **~ hook** crochet *m*. **2** *vt* faire au crochet. **3** *vi* faire du crochet.
crock [krɒk] *n* (*pot*) cruche *f*; (*: *car*) guimbarde* *f*. (*broken pieces*) **~s** débris *mpl* de faïence; **he's an old ~*** c'est un croulant*. ♦ **crockery** *n* (*earthenware*) poterie *f*; (*cups, saucers, plates*) vaisselle *f*.
crocodile ['krɒkədaɪl] *n* crocodile *m*. **~ tears** larmes *fpl* de crocodile; **to walk in a ~** aller deux par deux.
crocus ['krəʊkəs] *n* crocus *m*.
croft [krɒft] *n* petite ferme *f*. ♦ **crofter** *n* petit fermier *m*.
crone [krəʊn] *n* vieille bique *f* (*femme*).
crony* ['krəʊnɪ] *n* copain* *m*, copine* *f*.
crook [krʊk] **1** *n* **(a)** *[shepherd]* houlette *f*; *[bishop]* crosse *f*. **(b)** *[road, river]* angle *m*. **(c)** (*: *thief*) escroc *m*. **2** *vt finger* courber; *arm* plier. ♦ **crooked** ['krʊkɪd] *adj stick* courbé, tordu; *person* tout courbé; *path* tortueux; *smile* contraint; *method, action* malhonnête; **the picture is ~ed** le tableau est de travers. ♦ **crookedness** *n* courbure *f*; malhonnêteté *f*.
croon [kru:n] *vti* chantonner; *[crooner]* chanter. ♦ **crooner** *n* chanteur *m*, -euse *f* de charme.
crop [krɒp] **1** *n* **(a)** (*produce*) culture *f*; (*amount produced: of fruit, vegetables etc*) récolte *f*; *[cereals]* moisson *f*; *[problems, questions]* série *f*, tas* *m*. **the ~s** la récolte; **one of the basic ~s** l'une des cultures de base. **(b)** *[bird]* jabot *m*; *[whip]* manche *m*; (*riding ~*) cravache *f*. **2** *adj*: **~ spraying** pulvérisation *f* des cultures; **~ sprayer** (*device*) pulvérisateur *m*; (*plane*) avion-pulvérisateur *m*. **3** *vt* **(a)** *[animals]* brouter. **(b)** *hair* tondre. **~ped hair** cheveux coupés ras.
crop up *vi [questions, problems, subject]* se présenter. **sth's ~ped up** il s'est passé qch; **ready for anything that might ~ up** prêt à toute éventualité.
cropper* ['krɒpə^r] *n* (*lit, fig*) **to come a ~** se casser la figure*.
croquet ['krəʊkeɪ] *n* croquet *m*.
cross [krɒs] **1** *n* **(a)** croix *f*. **to sign with a ~** signer d'une croix; **we each have our ~ to bear** chacun porte sa croix. **(b)** (*Bio, Zool*) hybride *m*. **it's a ~ between a novel and a poem** cela tient du roman et du poème. **(c) cut on the ~** *material* coupé dans le biais; *skirt* en biais.
2 *adj* **(a)** (*angry*) de mauvaise humeur. **to be ~ with sb** être fâché contre qn; **it makes me ~ when ...** cela m'agace quand ...; **to get ~ with sb** se fâcher contre qn; **don't be ~ with me** ne m'en veuillez pas; **to be as ~ as a bear with a sore head** être d'une humeur massacrante; **they haven't had a ~ word** ils ne se sont pas disputés une seule fois. **(b)** (*diagonal*) transversal, diagonal.
3 *vt* **(a)** *room, street, sea, continent, line* traverser; *river, bridge* traverser, passer; *threshold, fence, ditch* franchir. **the bridge ~es the river** le pont enjambe la rivière; **it ~ed my mind that ...** il m'est venu à l'esprit que ...; **don't ~ your bridges before you come to them** chaque chose en son temps; (*fig*) **to ~ sb's path** se trouver sur le chemin de qn. **(b)** *letter T, cheque* barrer. **to ~ o.s.** se signer, faire le signe de (la) croix; **~ my heart!*** ≈ croix de bois croix de fer!* **(c)** *arms, legs* croiser. **to ~ swords with sb** croiser le fer avec qn; **keep your fingers ~ed for me*** fais une petite prière pour moi (, ça me portera bonheur); (*Telec*) **the lines are ~ed** les lignes sont embrouillées; **they've got their lines ~ed*** il y a un malentendu quelque part. **(d)** (*thwart*) *person, plans* contrecarrer. **(e)** *animals, plants* croiser (*with* avec).
4 *vi* **(a)** (**~ over**) traverser. **to ~ from one place to another** passer d'un endroit à un autre; **to ~ from Newhaven to Dieppe** faire la traversée de Newhaven à Dieppe. **(b)** *[roads, letters, people]* se croiser.
cross off, cross out *vt sep* barrer, rayer.
♦ **crossbar** *n [bicycle]* barre *f*. ♦ **crossbow** *n* arbalète *f*. ♦ **crossbreed** *n* hybride *m*. ♦ **cross-Channel** *adj*: **~-Channel ferry** ferry *m* qui traverse la Manche. ♦ **cross-check 1** *n* contre-épreuve *f*; **2** *vti* vérifier par contre-épreuve. ♦ **cross-country** *adj*: **~-country race** cross-country *m*; **~-country skiing** ski *m* de randonnée. ♦ **cross-examination** *n* contre-interrogatoire *m*. ♦ **cross-examine** *vt* (*Jur*) faire subir un contre-interrogatoire à; (*gen*) interroger (de façon serrée). ♦ **cross-eyed** *adj* qui louche. ♦ **crossfire** *n* feux *mpl* croisés. ♦ **crossing** *n* (*esp by sea*) traversée *f*; *[equator]* passage *m*; (*road junction*) croisement *m*, carrefour *m*; (*level ~*) passage à niveau; (*pedestrian ~*) passage *m* clouté; **school ~ing patrol** contractuel(le) *m(f)* (*qui fait traverser la rue aux enfants*); **cross at the ~ing** traversez sur le passage clouté *or* dans les clous*. ♦ **cross-legged** *adv* les jambes croisées. ♦ **crossly** *adv* avec humeur. ♦ **crosspatch*** *n* grincheux *m*, -euse *f*. ♦ **cross-purposes** *npl*: **to be at ~-purposes with sb** (*misunderstand*) comprendre qn de travers; (*disagree*) être en désaccord avec qn; **we were talking at ~-purposes** notre conversation tournait autour d'un quiproquo. ♦ **cross-question** *vt* faire subir un interrogatoire à. ♦ **cross-refer** *vt* renvoyer (*to* à). ♦ **cross-reference** *n* renvoi *m* (*to* à). ♦ **crossroads** *n* carrefour *m*. ♦ **cross-section** *n* (*Bio etc*) coupe *f* transversale; *[population etc]* échantillon *m*. ♦ **crosswalk** *n* (*US*) passage

m clouté. ♦ **crosswind** *n* vent *m* de travers. ♦ **crosswise** *adv* en travers, en croix. ♦ **crossword puzzle** *n* mots *mpl* croisés.

crotch [krɒtʃ] *n [body, tree]* fourche *f*; *[garment]* entre-jambes *m inv*.

crotchet ['krɒtʃɪt] *n* (*Mus*) noire *f*. ♦ **crotchety** *adj* grincheux.

crouch [kraʊtʃ] *vi* (~ **down**) *[person, animal]* s'accroupir, se tapir; (*before springing*) se ramasser.

croup [kru:p] *n* (*Med*) croup *m*.

crow[1] [krəʊ] *n* (*bird*) corneille *f*. **as the ~ flies** à vol d'oiseau; (*US*) **to eat ~*** faire des excuses humiliantes; (*wrinkles*) **~'s feet** pattes *fpl* d'oie (*rides*); (*Naut*) **~'s nest** nid *m* de pie. ♦ **crowbar** *n* pince *f* à levier.

crow[2] [krəʊ] *vi* **(a)** *pret* **crowed** *or* **crew,** *ptp* **crowed** *[cock]* chanter. **(b)** *pret, ptp* **crowed** *[baby]* gazouiller; *[victor]* chanter victoire (*over sb* sur qn). **he ~ed with delight** il poussait des cris de joie; **it's nothing to ~ about** il n'y a pas de quoi pavoiser.

crowd [kraʊd] **1** *n* foule *f*; (*disorderly*) cohue *f*. **in ~s** en foule, en masse; **a large ~** une foule immense; **there was quite a ~** il y avait beaucoup de monde; **how big was the ~?** est-ce qu'il y avait beaucoup de monde?; (*actors*) **the ~** les figurants *mpl*; **~ scene** scène *f* de foule; **that would pass in a ~*** ça peut passer si on n'y regarde pas de trop près; **~s of books/people** des masses* de livres/de gens; (*fig*) **to follow the ~** suivre la foule *or* le mouvement; **I don't like that ~* at all** je n'aime pas du tout cette bande; **he's one of our ~*** il fait partie de notre bande.

2 *vi*: **to ~ into** s'entasser dans; **to ~ together** se serrer; **to ~ round sth** s'attrouper pour voir qch; **to ~ round sb** se presser autour de qn; **to ~ down/in** *etc* descendre/entrer *etc* en foule.

3 *vt objects* entasser (*into* dans). **the houses are ~ed together** les maisons sont les unes sur les autres; **~ed with** *people, facts, incidents* plein de, bourré de; *objects, furniture* encombré de; **to ~ on sail** mettre toutes voiles dehors.

crowd out *vt sep* empêcher d'entrer (faute de place).

♦ **crowded** *adj room, train, café* bondé, plein; *town, profession* encombré; *streets* plein (de monde); *day* chargé; **the shops are too ~ed** il y a trop de monde dans les magasins; (*Theat*) **~ed house** salle *f* comble.

crown [kraʊn] **1** *n* **(a)** couronne *f*. (*Jur*) **the C~** la Couronne, ≃ le ministère public. **(b)** *[head]* sommet *m* de la tête; *[hat]* fond *m*; *[road]* milieu *m*; *[tooth]* couronne *f*; *[hill]* faîte *m*. **2** *adj* (*Jur*) **C~ court** ≃ cour *f* d'assises; **~ jewels** joyaux *mpl* de la couronne; **~ prince** prince *m* héritier. **3** *vt* (*gen, Dentistry, fig*) couronner (*with* de); *[draughts]* damer; (*: *hit*) flanquer* un coup sur la tête à. **he was ~ed king** il fut couronné roi; **to ~ it all* it began to snow** pour couronner le tout il s'est mis à neiger. ♦ **crowning 1** *n* couronnement *m*; **2** *adj achievement, moment* suprême.

crucial ['kru:ʃəl] *adj* crucial.

crucifix ['kru:sɪfɪks] *n* crucifix *m*. ♦ **crucifixion** *n* crucifixion *f*. ♦ **crucify** *vt* crucifier.

crude [kru:d] *adj materials* brut; *sugar* non raffiné; *drawing* qui manque de fini; *piece of work* mal fini, sommaire; *object, tool* grossier, rudimentaire; *light, colour* cru, vif; *person, behaviour* grossier; *manners* fruste. **~ oil** pétrole *m* brut; **he made a ~ attempt at building ...** il a essayé tant bien que mal de construire ...; **a ~ word** une grossièreté. ♦ **crudely** *adv make, fashion* sommairement; *say, order, explain* grossièrement, brutalement; **to put it ~ly I think he's mad** pour dire les choses crûment je pense qu'il est fou. ♦ **crudeness** *or* ♦ **crudity** *n* état *m* brut, manque *m* de fini; caractère *m* rudimentaire; grossièreté *f*.

cruel ['krʊəl] *adj* cruel (*to* envers). ♦ **cruelly** *adv* cruellement. ♦ **cruelty** *n* cruauté *f* (*to* envers); (*Jur*) sévices *mpl* (*to* sur); **mental ~ty** cruauté mentale.

cruet ['kru:ɪt] *n* (~ *stand*) ≃ huilier *m*; (~ *set*) salière *f* et poivrier *m*.

cruise [kru:z] **1** *vi* **(a)** *[fleet, ship]* croiser; *[holidaymakers]* être en croisière. **(b)** *[cars]* **to ~ at 80 km/h** faire du 80 km/h sans effort; **we were cruising along when suddenly ...** nous roulions tranquillement quand tout à coup ...; (*Aut, Aviat*) **cruising speed** vitesse *f* de croisière. **(c)** *[taxi, patrol car]* marauder. **a cruising taxi** un taxi en maraude. **2** *n* (*Naut*) croisière *f*. **to go on** *or* **for a ~** faire une croisière. ♦ **cruiser** *n* (*Naut*) croiseur *m*.

crumb [krʌm] *n* miette *f*; (*inside of loaf*) mie *f*. (*fig*) **a ~ of** *comfort* un brin de; *information* des miettes de; **~s!*** zut alors!*; **he's a ~*** c'est un pauvre type*. ♦ **crumble 1** *vt bread* émietter; *earth* effriter; **2** *vi [bread]* s'émietter; *[buildings etc]* tomber en ruine; *[plaster, stones]* s'effriter; *[rock, ceiling]* s'ébouler; *[hopes etc]* s'effondrer. ♦ **crumbly** *adj* friable.

crummy* ['krʌmɪ] *adj* minable.

crumple ['krʌmpl] **1** *vt* froisser; (~ **up**) chiffonner. **he ~d the paper into a ball** il a fait une boule de la feuille de papier. **2** *vi* se froisser; se chiffonner.

crunch [krʌntʃ] **1** *vt* (*with teeth*) croquer; (*underfoot*) écraser, faire craquer. **to ~ sth up** broyer qch. **2** *vi*: **he ~ed across the gravel** il a traversé en faisant craquer le gravier sous ses pas. **3** *n [broken glass, gravel]* craquement *m*. (*fig*) **when it comes to the ~*** dans une situation critique, au moment crucial.

♦ **crunchy** *adj* croquant.

crusade [kru:'seɪd] **1** *n* croisade *f*. **2** *vi* (*fig*) faire une croisade (*against* contre, *for* pour). ♦ **crusader** *n* (*Hist*) croisé *m*; (*fig*) champion *m* (*for* de), militant(e) *m(f)* (*against* contre).

crush [krʌʃ] **1** *n* **(a)** (*crowd*) cohue *f*, foule *f*. **there was a great ~ to get in** c'était la bousculade pour entrer. **(b) to have a ~ on sb*** avoir le béguin* pour qn. **(c) orange ~** orange *f* pressée.

2 *adj*: **~ barrier** barrière *f* *or* rampe *f* de sécurité.

3 *vt stones, old cars* broyer; *grapes* écraser; (*crumple*) *clothes* froisser; (*fig*) *enemy, revolution, opponent* écraser; *hope* détruire; (*snub*) rabrouer. **to ~ to a pulp** réduire en pulpe; **to ~ clothes into a bag** fourrer des vêtements dans une valise; **we were very ~ed in the car** nous étions très tassés dans la voiture.

4 *vi [clothes]* se froisser. **to ~ round sb** se presser autour de qn; **they ~ed into the car** ils se sont entassés dans la voiture; **to ~ (one's way) into/through** *etc* se frayer un chemin dans/à travers *etc*.

crush out *vt sep juice etc* presser; *cigarette end, revolt* écraser.

♦ **crushing** *adj defeat* écrasant; *reply* percutant. ♦ **crush-resistant** *adj* infroissable.

crust [krʌst] *n* croûte *f*. **a ~ of ice** une couche de glace; (*Geol*) **the earth's ~** la croûte terrestre. ♦ **crusty** *adj loaf* croustillant; (*) *person* hargneux.

crustacean [krʌs'teɪʃən] *n* crustacé *m*.

crutch [krʌtʃ] *n* **(a)** (*support*) soutien *m*; (*Med*) béquille *f*. **he gets about on ~es** il marche avec des béquilles. **(b)** = **crotch.**

crux [krʌks] *n* (*gen*) point *m* crucial; *[problem]* cœur *m*. **the ~ of the matter** le point capital dans l'affaire.

cry [kraɪ] **1** *n* **(a)** cri *m*. **to give a ~** pousser un cri; **he gave a ~ for help** il a appelé au secours; **'votes for women' was their ~** leur slogan *m* était 'le vote pour les femmes'. **(b)** (*weep*) **she had a good**

~* elle a pleuré un bon coup*. **2** *vt* **(a)** s'écrier, crier. **'here I am' he cried** 'me voici' s'écria-t-il; **'go away' he cried to me** 'allez-vous-en' me cria-t-il. **(b) to ~ o.s. to sleep** s'endormir à force de pleurer; **to ~ one's eyes out** pleurer toutes les larmes de son corps. **3** *vi* **(a)** (*weep*) pleurer (*about, over* sur; *for sth* pour avoir qch; *with rage etc* de rage *etc*). **to laugh till one cries** rire aux larmes; **I'll give him sth to ~ for!*** je vais lui apprendre à pleurnicher!; **it's no use ~ing over spilt milk** ce qui est fait est fait. **(b)** (**~ out**) (*inadvertently*) pousser un cri; (*deliberately*) s'écrier. **he cried out with pain** il a poussé un cri de douleur; **to ~ out for help** appeler à l'aide; **to ~ out for mercy** implorer la pitié; **that floor is just ~ing out to be washed*** ce plancher a grandement besoin d'être lavé.

cry off* **1** *vi* (*from meeting*) se décommander; (*from promise*) se dédire. **I'm ~ing off!** je ne veux plus rien savoir! **2** *vt fus arrangement, deal* annuler; *project* ne plus se mêler à; *meeting* décommander.

♦ **crying 1** *adj child* qui pleure; *injustice* criant, flagrant; *need* pressant, urgent; **it's a ~ing shame** c'est une honte; **2** *n* (*shouts*) cris *mpl*; (*weeping*) pleurs *mpl*.

crypt [krɪpt] *n* crypte *f*.

cryptic(al) ['krɪptɪk(əl)] *adj* (*mysterious*) énigmatique; (*terse*) laconique. ♦ **cryptically** *adv* énigmatiquement; laconiquement.

crystal ['krɪstl] **1** *n* (*gen*) cristal *m*; (*watch glass*) verre *m* de montre. **2** *adj vase, lake* de cristal. **~ ball** boule *f* de cristal. ♦ **crystal-clear** *adj* clair comme le jour. ♦ **crystal-gazing** *n* prédictions *fpl*, prophéties *fpl*. ♦ **crystalline** *adj* cristallin. ♦ **crystallize 1** *vi* se cristalliser; **2** *vt* cristalliser; **~lized fruits** fruits *mpl* confits *or* candis. ♦ **crystallography** *n* cristallographie *f*.

cub [kʌb] *n* petit(e) *m(f)*. **wolf ~** louveteau *m*, jeune loup *m*. **~ reporter** jeune reporter *m*; **~ scout** louveteau *m* (*scout*).

Cuba ['kju:bə] *n* Cuba *m*. **in ~** à Cuba.

cubbyhole ['kʌbɪhəʊl] *n* cagibi *m*; (*Aut*) vide-poches *m inv*.

cube [kju:b] **1** *n* cube *m*. **~ root** racine *f* cubique; (*Culin*) **to cut into ~s** couper en dés. **2** *vt* (*Math*) cuber. ♦ **cubic** *adj shape, volume* cubique; *yard, metre* cube; **cubic capacity** volume *m*. ♦ **cubism** *n* cubisme *m*. ♦ **cubist** *adj, n* cubiste (*mf*).

cubicle ['kju:bɪkəl] *n [hospital, dormitory]* box *m*; *[swimming baths]* cabine *f*.

cuckoo ['kʊku:] **1** *n* (*Orn*) coucou *m*. **~ clock** coucou *m* (*pendule*). **2** *adj* (*) toqué*, fou.

cucumber ['kju:kʌmbə^r] *n* concombre *m*.

cuddle ['kʌdl] **1** *vt* caresser; *child* câliner. **2** *vi* **to ~ down** se pelotonner; **to ~ up to sb** se pelotonner contre qn. ♦ **cuddly** *adj child* caressant; *animal* qui donne envie de le caresser; *toy* doux.

cudgel ['kʌdʒəl] **1** *n* gourdin *m*. **to take up the ~s on behalf of** prendre fait et cause pour. **2** *vt*: **to ~ one's brains** se creuser la cervelle.

cue [kju:] *n* **(a)** (*Theat: verbal*) réplique *f* (*indiquant à un acteur qu'il doit parler*); (*sign: Theat, Mus etc*) signal *m*. (*Theat*) **to give sb his ~** donner la réplique à qn; (*fig*) **to take one's ~ from sb** emboîter le pas à qn (*fig*). **(b)** (*Billiards*) queue *f* de billard.

cue in *vt sep* (*Rad, TV*) donner le signal à; (*Theat*) donner la réplique à.

cuff [kʌf] **1** *n* **(a)** manchette *f*; (*US: trouser turn-up*) revers *m* de pantalon. **~ link** bouton *m* de manchette; (*fig*) **off the ~** impromptu. **(b)** (*blow*) gifle *f*. **2** *vt* (*strike*) gifler.

cul-de-sac ['kʌldə'sæk] *n* cul-de-sac *m*.

culinary ['kʌlɪnərɪ] *adj* culinaire.

cull [kʌl] **1** *vt surplus objects etc* trier (et jeter). **2** *n* tri *m*, sélection *f*. **seal ~** abattage *m* sélectif des phoques.

culminate ['kʌlmɪneɪt] *vi* culminer. **to ~ in** finir *or* se terminer par; (*be cause of*) mener à; **it ~d in his throwing her out** pour finir il l'a mise à la porte.

♦ **culminating** *adj* culminant. ♦ **culmination** *n [success, career]* apogée *m*; *[disturbance, quarrel]* point *m* culminant.

culpable ['kʌlpəbl] *adj* coupable (*of* de).

culprit ['kʌlprɪt] *n* coupable *mf*.

cult [kʌlt] *n* (*Rel, fig*) culte *m*. **to make a ~ of sth** avoir le culte de qch; **~ figure** objet *m* d'un culte, idole *f*.

cultivate ['kʌltɪveɪt] *vt* cultiver. ♦ **cultivable** *adj* cultivable. ♦ **cultivated** *adj land, person* cultivé; *voice* distingué. ♦ **cultivation** *n* culture *f*. ♦ **cultivator** *n* (*machine*) cultivateur *m*; (*power-driven*) motoculteur *m*.

culture ['kʌltʃə^r] *n* (*all senses*) culture *f*. ♦ **cultural** *adj* culturel; (*Agr*) cultural. ♦ **cultured** *adj person* cultivé; *voice* distingué; *pearl* de culture.

cumbersome ['kʌmbəsəm] *adj* (*bulky*) encombrant; (*heavy*) pesant.

cumin ['kʌmɪn] *n* cumin *m*.

cumulative ['kju:mjʊlətɪv] *adj* cumulatif.

cunning ['kʌnɪŋ] **1** *n* astuce *f*, ruse *f* (*pej*). **2** *adj* malin, rusé (*pej*); (*: *clever*) astucieux. ♦ **cunningly** *adv* avec astuce, avec ruse; astucieusement.

cup [kʌp] **1** *n* tasse *f*; (*Sport etc: prize*) coupe *f*; *[brassière]* bonnet *m* (de soutien-gorge). **~ of tea** tasse de thé; **tea ~** tasse à thé; **that's just his ~ of tea*** c'est tout à fait à son goût; **it isn't everyone's ~ of tea*** ça ne plaît pas à tout le monde; **champagne ~** cup *m* au champagne. **2** *vt one's hands* mettre en coupe. **to ~ one's hands round sth** mettre ses mains autour de qch; **to ~ one's hand round one's ear** mettre sa main en cornet. ♦ **cup final** *n* (*Ftbl*) finale *f* de la coupe. ♦ **cupful** *n* tasse *f* (*contenu*). ♦ **cuppa*** *n* tasse *f* de thé. ♦ **cup-tie** *n* (*Ftbl*) match *m* de coupe.

cupboard ['kʌbəd] *n* (*esp Brit*) placard *m*. (*Brit*) **~ love** amour *m* intéressé.

cupidity [kju:'pɪdɪtɪ] *n* cupidité *f*.

cur [kɜ:^r] *n* sale chien *m*, sale cabot* *m*.

curate ['kjʊərɪt] *n* vicaire *m*. **it's like the ~'s egg** il y a du bon et du mauvais.

curator [kjʊə'reɪtə^r] *n* conservateur *m* (*d'un musée etc*).

curb [kɜ:b] **1** *n* (*US*) = **kerb. 2** *vt impatience, passion, tendency* refréner; *expenditure* réduire.

curdle ['kɜ:dl] **1** *vt* cailler. **2** *vi* se cailler. **it made my blood ~** cela m'a glacé le sang dans les veines.

curds [kɜ:dz] *npl* lait *m* caillé. ♦ **curd cheese** *n* fromage *m* blanc.

cure [kjʊə^r] **1** *vt* **(a)** *disease, patient* guérir (*of* de); *poverty, unfairness* éliminer; *injustice* réparer; *an evil* remédier à. **to be ~d (of)** guérir (de); **to ~ sb of a habit** faire perdre une habitude à qn; **to ~ o.s. of smoking** se guérir de l'habitude de fumer. **(b)** *meat, fish* (*salt*) saler; (*smoke*) fumer; (*dry*) sécher; *skins* traiter.

2 *n* (*remedy*) remède *m*, cure *f*; (*recovery*) guérison *f*. **to take a ~** faire une cure; **beyond ~** *person* incurable; *state, injustice, evil* irrémédiable.

♦ **curable** *adj* guérissable, curable. ♦ **curative** *adj* curatif. ♦ **cure-all** *n* (*lit, fig*) panacée *f*.

curfew ['kɜ:fju:] *n* couvre-feu *m*.

curio ['kjʊərɪəʊ] *n* bibelot *m*, curiosité *f*.

curiosity [ˌkjʊərɪ'ɒsɪtɪ] *n* curiosité *f* (*about* de). **~ killed the cat** la curiosité est toujours punie; **~ shop** magasin *m* de curiosités. ♦ **curious** *adj* (*inquisitive*) curieux (*about* de, *to know* de savoir); (*odd*) curieux, bizarre. ♦ **curiously** *adv* (*inquisitively*) avec curiosité; (*oddly*) curieusement, singulièrement; **curiously enough, he ...** chose bizarre, il ... .

curl [kɜːl] 1 *n [hair]* boucle *f*; (*gen*) courbe *f*; *[smoke]* volute *f*. **with a ~ of the lip** avec une moue méprisante. 2 *vt hair* (*loosely*) boucler; (*tightly*) friser. **she ~s her hair** elle frise (*or* boucle) ses cheveux; **he ~ed his lip in disdain** il a fait une moue méprisante. 3 *vi [hair]* boucler; friser. **it's enough to make your hair ~*** c'est à vous faire dresser les cheveux sur la tête.
curl up *vi* (*gen*) s'enrouler; *[paper]* corner; *[person]* se pelotonner; (*: *from shame etc*) rentrer sous terre; *[cat]* se mettre en boule; *[dog]* se coucher en rond; *[leaves, stale bread]* se racornir; *[smoke]* monter en volutes. **he lay ~ed up on the floor** il était couché en boule par terre; **to ~ up with laughter** se tordre de rire.
♦ **curler** *n* rouleau *m*, bigoudi *m*. ♦ **curling tongs** *npl* fer *m* à friser. ♦ **curly** *adj hair* bouclé, (*tightly*) frisé; *eyelashes* recourbé; *lettuce* frisé; **~y-haired, ~y-headed** aux cheveux bouclés (*or* frisés).
curlew ['kɜːluː] *n* courlis *m*.
currant ['kʌrənt] *n* groseille *f*; (*bush*) groseillier *m*; (*dried fruit*) raisin *m* sec *or* de Corinthe. **~ bun** petit pain *m* aux raisins.
currency ['kʌrənsɪ] *n* **(a)** monnaie *f*, devise *f*; (*money*) argent *m*. **the ~ is threatened** la monnaie est en danger; **foreign ~** devise *or* monnaie étrangère; **hard ~** devise forte; **paper ~** billets *mpl*. **(b)** *[ideas etc]* **to gain ~** se répandre, s'accréditer.
current ['kʌrənt] 1 *adj opinion, phrase, price* courant; *fashion, tendency, popularity* actuel; *year, month, week* en cours. **in ~ use** d'usage courant; (*Bank*) **~ account** compte *m* courant; **~ affairs** questions *fpl* d'actualité; **~ events** événements *mpl* actuels, actualité *f*; (*Press*) **~ issue** dernier numéro *m*; **his ~ job** le travail qu'il fait en ce moment; **her ~ boyfriend*** le petit ami du moment. 2 *n [air, water]* courant *m* (*also Elec*); *[events, opinions]* tendance *f*. (*fig*) **to go against the ~** aller à contre-courant. ♦ **currently** *adv* actuellement, en ce moment.
curriculum [kə'rɪkjʊləm] *n* programme *m* (d'études). **~ vitae** curriculum vitae *m*, C.V.*m*.
curry[1] ['kʌrɪ] *n* curry *m*. **beef ~** curry de bœuf; **~ powder** poudre *f* de curry.
curry[2] ['kʌrɪ] *vt*: **to ~ favour with sb** chercher à gagner la faveur de qn.
curse [kɜːs] 1 *n* malédiction *f*; (*swearword*) juron *m*, imprécation *f*. **~s!*** zut!*; **the ~ of poverty** le fléau de la pauvreté; **it has been the ~ of my life** c'est un sort qui m'a poursuivi toute ma vie; (*menstruation*) **she has the ~*** elle a ses règles *fpl*; **the ~ of it is that** l'embêtant*, c'est que. 2 *vt* maudire. (*fig*) **to be ~d with** être affligé de. 3 *vi* jurer, sacrer. ♦ **cursed*** ['kɜːsɪd] *adj* sacré*, maudit (*both before n*).
cursory ['kɜːsərɪ] *adj* (*superficial*) superficiel; (*hasty*) hâtif. **to take a ~ glance at** jeter un coup d'œil à. ♦ **cursorily** *adv* superficiellement; à la hâte.
curt [kɜːt] *adj* (*gen*) brusque, sec; *voice* cassant. **a ~ nod** un bref signe de tête. ♦ **curtly** *adv* sèchement; d'un ton cassant. ♦ **curtness** *n* brusquerie *f*, sécheresse *f*.
curtail [kɜː'teɪl] *vt* (*gen*) écourter; *wages, expenses* réduire. ♦ **curtailment** *n* raccourcissement *m*; réduction *f*.
curtain ['kɜːtn] 1 *n* rideau *m*. **to draw** *or* **pull the ~s** tirer les rideaux. 2 *adj* (*Theat*) **~ call** rappel *m*; **~ hook** crochet *m* de rideau; (*Theat*) **~ raiser** lever *m* de rideau (*pièce*); **~ ring** anneau *m* de rideau; **~ rod** tringle *f* à rideaux.
curtain off *vt sep room* diviser par un rideau; *bed, kitchen area* cacher derrière un rideau.
curts(e)y ['kɜːtsɪ] 1 *n* révérence *f*. 2 *vi* faire une révérence (*to* à).
curvaceous* [kɜː'veɪʃəs] *adj woman* bien balancée*, bien faite.
curve [kɜːv] 1 *n* (*gen*) courbe *f*; *[arch]* voussure *f*; *[beam]* cambrure *f*. **~ in the road** tournant *m*, virage *m*; **a woman's ~s*** les rondeurs *fpl* d'une femme. 2 *vt* (*gen*) courber; *arch, roof* cintrer. 3 *vi [surface, beam]* se courber; *[road, line etc]* faire une courbe. **the river ~s round the town** la rivière fait un méandre autour de la ville. ♦ **curvature** *n* courbure *f*; (*Med*) déviation *f*; **curvature of the spine** déviation de la colonne vertébrale; **the curvature of space** la courbure de l'espace. ♦ **curved** *adj line, space* courbe.
cushion ['kʊʃən] 1 *n* coussin *m*. 2 *vt seat* rembourrer; *shock, sb's fall* amortir. **to ~ sb against sth** protéger qn contre qch. ♦ **cushy*** *adj*: **a cushy job** un petit travail tranquille; **to have a cushy time** se la couler douce*.
cuss* [kʌs] 1 *n* (*oath*) juron *m*. (*person*) **a queer ~** un drôle de type*. 2 *vi* jurer. ♦ **cussed*** ['kʌsɪd] *adj* têtu comme une mule*. ♦ **cussedness*** *n* esprit *m* de contradiction.
custard ['kʌstəd] 1 *n* (*pouring*) crème *f* anglaise; (*set*) crème renversée. 2 *adj*: **~ cream (biscuit)** biscuit *m* fourré; **~ powder** crème instantanée (en poudre); **~ tart** flan *m*.
custody ['kʌstədɪ] *n* **(a)** (*Jur etc*) garde *f*. **in safe ~** sous bonne garde; **in the ~ of** sous la garde de; (*Jur*) **she was given ~ of the children** elle a reçu la garde des enfants. **(b)** (*imprisonment*) emprisonnement *m*. **in ~** en captivité; (*Jur*) en détention préventive; **to take sb into ~** mettre qn en détention préventive.
♦ **custodian** *n* (*gen*) gardien(ne) *m(f)*; *[museum]* conservateur *m*, -trice *f*.
custom ['kʌstəm] 1 *n* **(a)** coutume *f*, usage *m*, habitude *f*. **social ~s** usages sociaux, coutumes sociales; **it was his ~ to rest each morning** il avait l'habitude *or* la coutume de se reposer chaque matin. **(b)** (*Comm*) **to get sb's ~** obtenir la clientèle de qn; **he has lost a lot of ~** il a perdu beaucoup de clients. **(c) the ~s** la douane; **to go through the ~s** passer la douane. 2 *adj*: **~s duty** droits *mpl* de douane; **~s house** *or* **post** (poste *m* *or* bureaux *mpl* de) douane *f*; **~s inspection** visite *f* douanière; **~s officer** douanier *m*; **~s service** service *m* des douanes. ♦ **customary** *adj* habituel, coutumier. ♦ **custom-built** *adj* fait sur commande. ♦ **customer** *n* client(e) *m(f)*; **he's an awkward ~er*** il n'est pas commode; **ugly ~er*** sale type* *m*.
cut [kʌt] (*vb: pret, ptp* **cut**) 1 *n* **(a)** (*stroke*) coup *m*; *[cards]* coupe *f*; (*mark, slit*) coupure *f*; (*notch*) entaille *f*; (*Med*) incision *f*. **a deep ~ in the leg** une profonde coupure à la jambe; **the ~ and thrust of politics** les estocades *fpl* de la politique; **that was a ~ at me** c'était une pierre dans mon jardin; **he is a ~ above the others** il vaut mieux que les autres.
(b) (*reduction*) réduction *f*, diminution *f* (*in* de). **power ~** coupure *f* de courant; **to take a ~ in salary** subir une réduction de salaire; **to make ~s in a book** faire des coupures dans un livre.
(c) *[meat]* (*piece*) morceau *m*; (*slice*) tranche *f*; (*: *share*) **they all want a ~ in the profits*** ils veulent tous leur part du gâteau*.
(d) *[clothes]* coupe *f*; *[jewel]* taille *f*. **I like the ~ of this coat** j'aime la coupe de ce manteau.
2 *adj flowers* coupé; *tobacco* découpé. **~ glass** cristal *m* taillé; **~ prices** prix *mpl* réduits; **it was all ~ and dried** tout était déjà arrangé; **~ and dried opinions** opinions toutes faites.
3 *vt* **(a)** (*gen*) couper; *joint of meat, tobacco* découper; (*Med*) *abscess* inciser; *cards* couper. **to ~ one's finger** se couper le doigt *or* au doigt; **to ~ sb's throat** couper la gorge à qn; (*fig*) **he is ~ting his own throat** il prépare sa propre ruine; **to ~ in half** couper en deux; **to ~ in pieces** couper en morceaux; *army* tailler en pièces; *reputation*

démolir; **to ~ open** ouvrir avec un couteau (*or* avec des ciseaux *etc*); **he ~ his arm open on a nail** il s'est ouvert le bras sur un clou; **to ~ sb free** délivrer qn en coupant ses liens; **it ~ me to the heart** cela m'a profondément blessé; **to ~ short** *story, proceedings* abréger; *visit* écourter; *speaker* couper la parole à; **to ~ a long story short, he came** bref *or* pour en finir, il est venu.

(b) (*shape*) couper; *steps, jewel, key, glass* tailler; *channel* creuser; *figure, statue* sculpter (*out of* dans); (*engrave*) graver; *record* graver. **to ~ one's way through** s'ouvrir un chemin à travers; (*fig*) **to ~ one's coat according to one's cloth** vivre selon ses moyens.

(c) (*clip, trim*) *hedge, trees* tailler; *corn, hay* faucher; *lawn* tondre. **to ~ one's nails/hair** se couper les ongles/les cheveux; **to get one's hair ~** se faire couper les cheveux.

(d) (*: *avoid*) *appointment* manquer exprès; *lecture, class* sécher*. **to ~ sb (dead)** faire semblant de ne pas voir qn.

(e) (*intersect*) couper.

(f) (*reduce*) *profits, wages, prices* réduire; *text, book, play* faire des coupures dans; *film* faire le montage de. (*Sport*) **he ~ 30 seconds off the record** il a amélioré le record de 30 secondes.

(g) (*phrases*) *[child]* **to ~ a tooth** percer une dent; **he is ~ting teeth** il fait ses dents; (*fig*) **to ~ one's teeth on sth** se faire les dents sur qch; **she ~s a fine figure** elle a beaucoup d'allure; **to ~ a dash** faire de l'effet; **to ~ it fine** compter un peu juste, ne pas (se) laisser de marge; **that ~s no ice with me** ça ne m'impressionne guère, ça me laisse froid; **to ~ the ground from under sb's feet** couper l'herbe sous le pied de qn; **to ~ one's losses** sauver les meubles*; (*Aut*) **to ~ a corner** prendre un virage à la corde; (*fig*) **to ~ corners** prendre des raccourcis (*fig*); **to ~ the Gordian knot** trancher le nœud gordien; **~ the cackle!*** assez bavardé comme ça!*

4 *vi* **(a)** *[person, knife]* couper, trancher. **he ~ into the cake** il a entamé le gâteau; **to ~ along the dotted line** découper suivant le pointillé; **that ~s both ways** c'est à double tranchant; **to ~ and run*** filer*; **to ~ loose** couper les amarres (*from* avec); **this piece will ~ into 4** ce morceau peut se couper en 4.

(b) (*hurry*) **to ~ across country** couper à travers champs; **to ~ through the lane** couper par la ruelle; **to ~ along** s'en aller.

(c) (*Cine, TV*) **they ~ from the street to the shop scene** ils ont passé de la rue à la scène du magasin; **~!** coupez!

(d) (*Cards*) couper. **to ~ for deal** tirer pour la donne.

cut away *vt sep branch* élaguer; *unwanted part* enlever (en coupant).

cut back *vt sep plants* tailler; *production, expenditure* réduire.

cut down *vt sep* **(a)** *tree* couper; *corn* faucher; *enemy* abattre. **~ down by pneumonia** terrassé par la *or* une pneumonie. **(b)** (*reduce*) *expenses* réduire; *article, essay* couper. (*fig*) **to ~ sb down to size*** remettre qn à sa place.

cut down on *vt fus food* acheter moins de; *cigarettes* fumer moins de; *expenditure* réduire.

cut in 1 *vi* (*into conversation*) se mêler à la conversation; (*Aut*) se rabattre. (*Aut*) **to ~ in on sb** faire une queue de poisson à qn. **2** *vt sep:* **to ~ sb in on a deal*** faire entrer qn dans une transaction.

cut off *vt sep* **(a)** *piece of cloth, meat* couper (*from* dans); *limb* couper. **to ~ off sb's head** trancher la tête à qn; **to ~ off one's nose to spite one's face** agir contre son propre intérêt par dépit. **(b)** (*disconnect*) *telephone, car engine, gas, electricity* couper. **our water supply has been ~ off** on nous a coupé l'eau; (*Telec*) **we were ~ off** nous avons été coupés. **(c)** (*isolate*) isoler (*sb from sth* qn de qch). **to ~ o.s. off from** rompre ses liens avec; **he feels very ~ off** il se sent très isolé; **to ~ off the enemy's retreat** couper la retraite à l'ennemi; **to ~ sb off with a shilling** déshériter qn.

cut out 1 *vi [engine]* caler.

2 *vt sep* **(a)** *picture, article* découper (*of, from* de); *statue, figure* tailler (*of* dans); *coat* couper (*of, from* dans). **to ~ out a path through the jungle** se frayer un chemin à travers la jungle; **to be ~ out for sth/to do** être fait pour qch/pour faire; **he had his work ~ out for him** il avait du pain sur la planche; **you'll have your work ~ out to do that** vous aurez du mal à faire cela. **(b)** *rival* supplanter. **(c)** (*remove*) enlever, ôter; *unnecessary detail* élaguer. **~ it out!*** ça suffit!; **~ out the tears!*** arrête de pleurnicher! **(d)** (*give up*) *tobacco* supprimer. **to ~ out smoking** arrêter de fumer.

cut up 1 *vi*: **to ~ up rough*** se mettre en rogne* *or* en colère. **2** *vt sep* **(a)** *wood, food* couper; *meat* (*carve*) découper, (*chop up*) hacher; *enemy, army* tailler en pièces. **(b) to be ~ up about sth** (*hurt*) être affecté par qch; (*annoyed*) être très embêté par qch*.

◆ **cutback** *n* (*in expenditure, production, staff*) réduction *f*, diminution *f* (*in* de); (*Cine: flashback*) flashback *m*. ◆ **cutoff** *n* arrêt *m*; **~off switch** interrupteur *m*. ◆ **cut-price** *adj goods* au rabais; *shop* de rabais. ◆ **cutter** *n* **(a)** (*person*) *[clothes]* coupeur *m*, -euse *f*; *[stones]* tailleur *m*; *[films]* monteur *m*, -euse *f*; **(b)** (*tool*) coupoir *m*; **(c)** (*boat*) vedette *f*. ◆ **cut-throat 1** *n* assassin *m*; **2** *adj competition* acharné; *game* à trois; *razor* de coiffeur. ◆ **cutting 1** *n* **(a)** (*gen*) coupe *f*; *[diamond]* taille *f*; *[film]* montage *m*; **(b)** (*cleared way: for road, railway*) tranchée *f*; **(c)** (*press ~*) coupure *f*; **2** *adj knife* coupant, tranchant; *wind, cold* glacial; *rain* cinglant; *words, remark* cinglant, incisif; **the ~ting edge** le tranchant; (*Cine*) **~ting room** salle *f* de montage.

cute* [kjuːt] *adj* (*clever*) futé; (*attractive*) mignon.

cuticle ['kjuːtɪkl] *n [fingernail]* petites peaux *fpl*, envie *f*. **~ remover** repousse-peaux *m inv*.

cutlery ['kʌtlərɪ] *n* couverts *mpl*.

cutlet ['kʌtlɪt] *n* côtelette *f*; (*US: croquette*) croquette *f*.

cuttlefish ['kʌtlfɪʃ] *n* seiche *f*. ◆ **cuttlebone** *n* os *m* de seiche.

cyanide ['saɪənaɪd] *n* cyanure *m*.

cybernetics [ˌsaɪbəˈnetɪks] *n* cybernétique *f*.

cyclamen ['sɪkləmən] *n* cyclamen *m*.

cycle ['saɪkl] **1** *n* **(a)** bicyclette *f*, vélo *m*. **racing ~** vélo de course. **(b)** *[poems, seasons etc]* cycle *m*.

2 *vi* faire de la bicyclette, faire du vélo. **he ~s to school** il va à l'école à bicyclette *or* en vélo.

3 *adj path* cyclable; *race* cycliste. **~ rack** râtelier *m* à bicyclettes; **~ shed** abri *m* à bicyclettes.

◆ **cycling 1** *n* cyclisme *m*; **2** *adj holiday* à bicyclette. **cycling clothes** tenue *f* cycliste. ◆ **cyclist** *n* cycliste *mf*.

cyclone ['saɪkləʊn] *n* cyclone *m*.

cyclostyle ['saɪkləstaɪl] *vt* polycopier (*avec des stencils*).

cygnet ['sɪgnɪt] *n* jeune cygne *m*.

cylinder ['sɪlɪndə^r] **1** *n* (*gen*) cylindre *m*; *[typewriter]* rouleau *m*. **a 6-~ car** une 6-cylindres; **to fire on all 4 ~s** avoir les 4 cylindres qui donnent; (*fig*) fonctionner à pleins gaz*. **2** *adj*: **~ block** bloc-cylindres *m*; **~ head** culasse *f*. ◆ **cylindrical** *adj* cylindrique.

cymbal ['sɪmbəl] *n* cymbale *f*.

cynic ['sɪnɪk] *n* cynique *mf*. ◆ **cynical** *adj* cynique. ◆ **cynically** *adv* cyniquement, avec cynisme. ◆ **cynicism** *n* cynisme *m*.

cypress ['saɪprɪs] *n* cyprès *m*.

Cyprus [ˈsaɪprəs] *n* Chypre *f.* **in** ~ à Chypre. ♦ **Cypriot 1** *adj* cypriote. **2** *n* Cypriote *mf.*
cyst [sɪst] *n* kyste *m.* ♦ **cystitis** *n* cystite *f.*
czar [zɑːʳ] *n* tsar *m.* ♦ **czarina** *n* tsarine *f.*

Czech [tʃek] **1** *adj* tchèque. **2** *n* Tchèque *mf*; (*Ling*) tchèque *m.* ♦ **Czechoslovakia** *n* Tchécoslovaquie *f.* ♦ **Czechoslovak(ian) 1** *adj* tchécoslovaque; **2** *n* Tchécoslovaque *mf.*

D

D, d [diː] *n* D, d *m*; (*Mus*) ré *m*. **in 3-D** en relief; **D and C*** dilatation *f* et curetage *m*; **D-day** le jour J.
dab[1] [dæb] **1** *n* **(a) a ~ of** un petit peu de; *[glue]* une goutte de; *[paint]* un petit coup de. **(b)** (*fingerprints*) **~s‡** empreintes *fpl* digitales. **2** *vt* (*gen*) tamponner. **to ~ iodine** *etc* **on sth** appliquer de la teinture d'iode *etc* à petits coups sur qch.
dab[2] [dæb] *adj*: **to be a ~ hand* at sth/at doing** être doué en qch/pour faire.
dabble ['dæbl] **1** *vt*: **to ~ one's hands in the water** barboter dans l'eau avec les mains. **2** *vi* se mêler un peu (*in* de). **to ~ in politics** donner dans la politique; **to ~ in stocks and shares** boursicoter.
dachshund ['dækshʊnd] *n* teckel *m*.
Dacron ['dækrɒn] *n* ® dacron *m* ®.
dad*, [dæd], **daddy*** ['dædɪ] *n* papa *m*. ♦ **daddy-long-legs** *n, pl inv* (*Zool*) faucheux *m*.
dado ['deɪdəʊ] *n* plinthe *f*; *[pedestal]* dé *m*; *[wall]* lambris *m* d'appui.
daffodil ['dæfədɪl] *n* jonquille *f*. **~ yellow** (jaune) jonquille *inv*.
daft [dɑːft] *adj* stupide, idiot. **to be ~ about sb/sth*** être fou de qn/qch.
dagger ['dægəʳ] *n* poignard *m*, dague *f*; (*Typ*) croix *f*. **to be at ~s drawn with sb** être à couteaux tirés avec qn; **to look ~s at sb** foudroyer qn du regard.
dago ['deɪgəʊ] *n* métèque *m*.
dahlia ['deɪlɪə] *n* dahlia *m*.
daily ['deɪlɪ] **1** *adj task, routine, walk, paper* quotidien; *consumption, output, wage* journalier; (*everyday*) de tous les jours. **our ~ bread** notre pain quotidien; **~ dozen*** gymnastique *f* quotidienne; **the ~ grind*** le train-train (quotidien). **2** *adv* quotidiennement, tous les jours. **3** *n* (**~ paper**) quotidien *m*; (**~ help, ~ woman**) femme *f* de ménage.
dainty ['deɪntɪ] *adj food* de choix, délicat; *figure, person* menu; *handkerchief, blouse, gesture* délicat; *child* mignon; (*difficult to please*) difficile. ♦ **daintily** *adv eat, hold* délicatement; *walk* à petits pas élégants. ♦ **daintiness** *n* délicatesse *f*.
dairy ['dɛərɪ] **1** *n* (*on farm*) laiterie *f*; (*shop*) crémerie *f*. **2** *adj cow, farm, produce* laitier; *herd* de vaches laitières; *ice cream* fait à la crème. **~ butter** beurre *m* fermier; **~ farming** industrie *f* laitière. ♦ **dairymaid** *n* fille *f* de laiterie. ♦ **dairyman** *n* (*on farm etc*) employé *m* de laiterie; (*in shop*) crémier *m*.
daisy ['deɪzɪ] *n* pâquerette *f*; (*cultivated*) marguerite *f*. **~ chain** guirlande *f* de pâquerettes.
dale [deɪl] *n* vallée *f*.
dally ['dælɪ] *vi* (*dawdle*) lanterner (*over sth* dans *or* sur qch). **to ~ with an idea** caresser une idée.
dalmatian [dæl'meɪʃən] *n* (*dog*) dalmatien *m*.
dam[1] [dæm] **1** *n* (*wall*) barrage *m* (de retenue); (*water*) réservoir *m*. **2** *vt river* endiguer; *lake* construire un barrage sur; *flow of words, oaths* endiguer. **to ~ the waters of the Nile** construire un barrage pour contenir les eaux du Nil.
dam[2] [dæm] *n* (*animal*) mère *f*.
damage ['dæmɪdʒ] **1** *n* dommage(s) *m(pl)*; (*visible, eg to car*) dégâts *mpl*; (*to ship, cargo*) avaries *fpl*; (*fig*) préjudice *m*, tort *m*. **~ to property** dégâts matériels; **the bomb did a lot of ~** la bombe a causé des dommages importants *or* a fait de gros dégâts; **there was a lot of ~ to the house** la maison a beaucoup souffert; **there's no ~ done** il n'y a pas de mal; **what's the ~?*** (*how much is it?*) cela se monte à combien?; (*Jur*) **~s** dommages *mpl* et intérêts *mpl*; **liable for ~s** tenu des dommages et intérêts; **war ~** dommages de guerre.
2 *vt furniture, crops, machine* endommager; *food, eyesight, health* abîmer; *good relations, reputation* nuire à, porter atteinte à; *cause* faire du tort à.
♦ **damaging** *adj* nuisible (*to* à); (*Jur*) préjudiciable.
dame [deɪm] *n* dame *f*; (*Theat*) vieille dame (*bouffonne jouée par un homme*); (*US*: ‡) fille *f*, nana‡ *f*.
damfool‡ ['dæm'fuːl] *adj* fichu* (*before n*).
dammit* ['dæmɪt] *excl* mince!* **as near as ~** à un poil* près.
damn [dæm] **1** *excl* (‡) merde!‡ **2** *vt* (*Rel*) damner; *book, person* condamner; *plan* éreinter. **to ~ with faint praise** éreinter sous couleur d'éloge; **~ him!‡** qu'il aille se faire fiche!*; **well I'll be ~ed!‡** ça c'est trop fort!; **~ this machine!‡** au diable cette machine! **3** *n* (‡) **I don't care a ~** je m'en fiche pas mal*; **it's not worth a ~** cela ne vaut pas un clou*. **4** *adj* (‡: *also* **dam', ~ed**) fichu*, sacré* (*before n*). **it is one ~ thing after another** quand ce n'est pas une chose, c'est l'autre. **5** *adv* (‡: *also* **dam', ~ed**) vachement‡, rudement*. **~ all** strictement rien, fichtre* rien. ♦ **damnable*** *adj* détestable. ♦ **damnably*** *adv* rudement*. ♦ **damnation** **1** *n* (*Rel*) damnation *f*; **2** *excl* (‡) merde!‡ ♦ **damnedest‡** *n*: **to do one's ~edest to help** faire l'impossible pour aider. ♦ **damning** *adj* accablant; **~ing criticism** éreintement *m*.
damp [dæmp] **1** *adj* (*gen*) humide; *skin* moite. **that was a ~ squib*** c'est tombé à plat (*fig*). **2** *n* humidité *f*; (*fire~*) grisou *m*. **3** *vt a cloth, ironing* humecter; *enthusiasm, courage* refroidir; (**~ down**) *fire* couvrir. **to ~ sb's spirits** décourager qn. ♦ **damp-course** *n* couche *f* isolante. ♦ **dampen** *vt* = **damp 3**. ♦ **damper** *or* (*US*) ♦ **dampener** *n [chimney]* registre *m*; (*fig*) **to put a ~er on*** jeter un froid sur. ♦ **dampness** *n* humidité *f*; moiteur *f*. ♦ **damp-proof** *adj* imperméable.
damson ['dæmzən] *n* prune *f* de Damas; (*tree*) prunier *m* de Damas.
dance [dɑːns] **1** *n* **(a)** (*movement*) danse *f*. **to lead sb a (pretty) ~** donner à qn du fil à retordre. **(b)** (*event*) bal *m*, soirée *f* dansante. **2** *vt waltz* danser. **to ~ attendance on sb** être aux petits soins pour qn. **3** *vi* danser. **he ~d with her** il l'a fait danser; **she ~d with him** elle a dansé avec lui; (*fig*) **to ~ in/out** *etc* entrer/sortir *etc* joyeusement; **to ~ about** gambader, sautiller. **4** *adj band, music* de danse. **~ hall** dancing *m*. ♦ **dancer** *n* danseur *m*, -euse *f*. ♦ **dancing** **1** *n* danse *f*; **2** *adj master, school* de danse.
dandelion ['dændɪlaɪən] *n* pissenlit *m*.
dandruff ['dændrəf] *n* pellicules *fpl* (*du cuir chevelu*).
dandy ['dændɪ] **1** *n* dandy *m*. **2** *adj* (*) épatant*.
Dane [deɪn] *n* Danois(e) *m(f)*. ♦ **Danish** **1** *adj* danois; **Danish blue cheese** bleu *m* du Danemark; **Danish pastry** feuilleté *m* fourré aux fruits *etc*; **2** *n* danois *m*.
danger ['deɪndʒəʳ] **1** *n* danger *m* (*to* pour). **in ~** en

danger; **he was in little ~** il ne courait pas grand risque; **out of ~** hors de danger; **in ~ of invasion** menacé d'invasion; **he was in ~ of losing his job** il risquait de perdre sa place; **there was no ~ that she would be recognized** elle ne courait aucun risque d'être reconnue; a **~ of fire** un risque d'incendie; '**~ road up**' 'attention travaux'; '**~ keep out**' 'danger: défense d'entrer'. 2 *adj*: **~ area, ~ zone** zone *f* dangereuse; (*Med*) **on the ~ list** dans un état critique; **~ money** prime *f* de risque; **~ point** cote *f* d'alerte; **~ signal** signal *m* d'alarme. ♦ **dangerous** *adj* (*gen*) dangereux; *illness* grave. ♦ **dangerously** *adv* (*gen*) dangereusement; *ill* gravement; *wounded* grièvement.

dangle ['dæŋgl] **1** *vt object on string* balancer; *arm, leg* laisser pendre; *prospect, offer* faire miroiter (*before sb* aux yeux de qn). **2** *vi* pendre.

dank [dæŋk] *adj* humide et froid.

dapper ['dæpəʳ] *adj* fringant.

dare [dɛəʳ] **1** *vt* **(a)** oser (*do, to do* faire); *death* affronter, braver. **~ you do it?** oserez-vous le faire?; **how ~ you!** comment osez-vous?, vous en avez du culot!*; **I ~ say he'll come** il viendra sans doute, j'imagine qu'il va venir; (*iro*) **I ~ say!** c'est bien possible! (*iro*). **(b) to ~ sb to do** mettre qn au défi de faire; **I ~ you!** chiche!*

2 *n* défi *m*. **to do sth for a ~** faire qch pour relever un défi.

♦ **daredevil 1** *n* casse-cou *mf inv*; **2** *adj behaviour* de casse-cou *inv*; *adventure* fou. ♦ **daring 1** *adj* audacieux, hardi; **2** *n* audace *f*, hardiesse *f*. ♦ **daringly** *adv* audacieusement, avec hardiesse.

dark [dɑːk] **1** *adj* **(a)** *room* sombre, obscur; *dungeon* noir, ténébreux. **it is ~** il fait nuit *or* noir; **it is getting ~** il commence à faire nuit; **the sky is getting ~** le ciel s'assombrit; **the ~ side of the moon** la face cachée de la lune; (*Phot*) **~ room** chambre *f* noire. **(b)** *colour* foncé, sombre; *complexion, hair, person* brun. **~ blue** *etc* bleu *etc* foncé *inv*; **~ brown hair** cheveux châtain foncé *inv*; **~ glasses** lunettes *fpl* noires; **~ chocolate** chocolat *m* à croquer. **(c)** (*sinister*) *plan* noir; *hint* sibyllin; *threat* sourd; (*gloomy*) *thoughts* sombre, triste. **to keep sth ~** tenir qch secret; **keep it ~!** pas un mot!; **to look on the ~ side of things** voir tout en noir; (*fig*) **he's a ~ horse** c'est une quantité inconnue; **the D~ Ages** le haut moyen âge.

2 *n* obscurité *f*, noir *m*. **after/until ~** après/ jusqu'à la tombée de la nuit; **to be afraid of the ~** avoir peur du noir; **I am quite in the ~ about it** j'ignore tout de cette histoire; **to leave sb in the ~ about sth** laisser qn dans l'ignorance sur qch; (*fig*) **to work in the ~** travailler à l'aveuglette.

♦ **darken 1** *vt room, landscape* obscurcir, assombrir; *sky, future* assombrir; *colour* foncer; **2** *vi* s'obscurcir; s'assombrir; foncer. ♦ **dark-eyed** *adj* aux yeux noirs. ♦ **darkly** *adv* (*gloomily*) tristement; (*sinisterly*) sinistrement. ♦ **darkness** *n* obscurité *f*; **in total ~ness** dans une complète obscurité; **the house was in ~ness** la maison était plongée dans l'obscurité. ♦ **dark-skinned** *adj person* brun (de peau); *race* de couleur.

darling ['dɑːlɪŋ] **1** *n* favori(te) *m(f)*, bien-aimé(e) *m(f)*. **the ~ of the people** l'idole *f* du peuple; **a mother's ~** un chouchou*, une chouchoute*; **she's a little ~** elle est adorable; **come here, ~** viens, (mon) chéri; **be a ~* ...** sois un ange ... . **2** *adj child* chéri, bien-aimé; (*) *house etc* ravissant, adorable.

darn [dɑːn] **1** *vt socks* repriser; *clothes etc* raccommoder. **2** *n* reprise *f*. **3** *excl* (*) *euph for* **damn**. ♦ **darning 1** *n* reprise *f*, raccommodage *m*; (*things to be darned*) raccommodage *m*; **2** *adj needle, wool* à repriser.

dart [dɑːt] **1** *n* **(a)** fléchette *f*. **~s** (*game*) fléchettes *fpl*; **~ board** cible *f*. **(b)** (*Sewing*) pince *f*. **2** *vi*: **to ~ in/out** *etc* entrer/sortir *etc* comme une flèche; **to ~ at sth** se précipiter sur qch. **3** *vt*: **to ~ a look at sth** jeter un regard sur qch.

dash [dæʃ] **1** *n* **(a) to make a ~** se précipiter, se ruer, foncer* (*at* sur, *towards* vers); **he made a ~ for it*** il s'est enfui; (*Sport*) **the 100 metre ~** le sprint, le 100 mètres. **(b)** (*small amount*) petite quantité *f*; *[vinegar, flavouring]* goutte *f*; *[seasonings etc]* pointe *f*; *[colour]* tache *f*. **a ~ of soda** un peu d'eau de Seltz. **(c)** (*punctuation mark*) tiret *m*; (*Morse*) trait *m*. **2** *vt* **(a)** (*throw*) jeter violemment. **to ~ sth to pieces** casser qch en mille morceaux; **to ~ sth to the ground** jeter qch par terre; **to ~ one's head against** se cogner la tête contre. **(b)** *spirits* abattre; *person* démoraliser; *hopes* anéantir. **3** *vi* **(a)** (*rush*) **to ~ away/back** *etc* s'en aller/revenir *etc* à toute allure; **to ~ into a room** se précipiter dans une pièce; **I must ~*** il faut que je file*. **(b)** (*crash*) *[waves]* se briser (*against* contre); *[car, bird, object]* se jeter (*against* contre). **4** *excl* (*) zut alors!*

dash off *vt sep letter etc* faire en vitesse; *drawing* dessiner en un tour de main.

♦ **dashboard** *n* (*Aut*) tableau *m* de bord. ♦ **dashing** *adj behaviour* plein d'allant; *appearance* fringant, qui a grande allure.

data ['deɪtə] **1** *npl* données *fpl*, information *f* brute. **2** *adj*: **~ bank** banque *f* de données; **~ processing** traitement *m* des données; **~ processor** unité *f* de traitement des données.

date¹ [deɪt] *n* datte *f*; **~ palm** dattier *m*.

date² [deɪt] **1** *n* **(a)** (*gen*) date *f*; (*on coin etc*) millésime *m*. **~ of birth** date de naissance; **what is today's ~?** quelle est la date aujourd'hui?, nous sommes le combien aujourd'hui?; **what ~ is he coming on?** à quelle date vient-il?; **what is the ~ of this letter?** de quand est cette lettre?; **to ~ we have ...** jusqu'ici nous avons ...; **to be out of ~** *[document]* ne plus être applicable; *[building, object]* être démodé; *[person]* retarder; **to be up to ~** *[document]* être à jour; *[building, person]* être moderne; (*in one's work etc*) être à jour; **to bring up to ~** *accounts, correspondence etc* mettre à jour; *method etc* moderniser; **to bring sb up to ~** mettre qn au courant (*about sth* de qch). **(b)** (*: *appointment*) rendez-vous *m*, rancard: *m*; (: *person*) petit(e) ami(e) *m(f)*. **to have/make a ~** avoir/prendre rendez-vous.

2 *vt* **(a)** *document etc* dater; (*with machine*) composter. **letter ~d August 7th** lettre datée du 7 août; **a coin ~d 1390** une pièce au millésime de 1390. **(b)** *manuscripts, ruins etc* donner *or* assigner une date à, fixer la date de. **that ~s him** cela trahit son âge. **(c)** (*) (*go out with*) sortir avec; (*arrange meeting with*) prendre rendez-vous avec.

3 *vi* **(a) to ~ from** remonter à, dater de. **(b)** (*become old-fashioned*) dater.

♦ **dated** *adj* démodé, qui date. ♦ **dateless** *adj* qui ne date jamais. ♦ **date-line** *n* ligne *f* de changement de date. ♦ **date-stamp 1** *n [library etc]* dateur *m*; (*postmark*) cachet *m* de la poste; **2** *vt library book* tamponner; *document* apposer le cachet de la date sur.

dative ['deɪtɪv] *adj, n* datif (*m*). **in the ~** au datif.

daub [dɔːb] *vt* barbouiller (*with* de).

daughter ['dɔːtəʳ] *n* fille *f*. **~-in-law** belle-fille *f*, bru *f*.

daunt [dɔːnt] *vt* intimider, démonter. **nothing ~ed he ...** sans se démonter il ... . ♦ **daunting** *adj task, problem* décourageant; *person* intimidant. ♦ **dauntless** *adj person* intrépide; *courage* indomptable. ♦ **dauntlessly** *adv* avec intrépidité.

dawdle ['dɔːdl] *vi* flâner, traîner (*pej*). **to ~ over one's work** traînasser sur son travail. ♦ **dawdler** *n* flâneur *m*, -euse *f*. ♦ **dawdling 1** *adj* traînard; **2** *n* flânerie *f*.

dawn [dɔːn] **1** *n* aube *f*, point *m* du jour; *[civiliza-*

tion] aube; *[idea, hope]* naissance *f.* **at ~** à l'aube, au point du jour; **from ~ to dusk** du matin au soir; **~ chorus** concert *m* matinal des oiseaux. **2** *vi [day]* poindre, se lever; *[hope]* naître. **the day will ~ when ...** un jour viendra où ...; **an idea ~ed upon him** une idée lui est venue à l'esprit; **the truth ~ed upon him** il a commencé à entrevoir la vérité; **it suddenly ~ed on him that ...** il lui vint tout d'un coup à l'esprit que ... . ♦ **dawning** *adj* naissant, croissant.

day [deɪ] **1** *n* **(a)** (*24 hours*) jour *m.* **3 ~s ago** il y a 3 jours; **what ~ is it today?** quel jour sommes-nous aujourd'hui?; **what ~ of the month is it?** nous sommes le combien?; **the ~ that they ...** le jour où ils ...; **on that ~** ce jour-là; **on a ~ like this** un jour comme aujourd'hui; **twice a ~** deux fois par jour; **the ~ before yesterday** avant-hier *m*; **the ~ before/two ~s before her birthday** la veille/l'avant-veille de son anniversaire; **the ~ after, the following ~** le lendemain; **the ~ after tomorrow** après-demain; **this ~ week** d'aujourd'hui en huit; **2 years ago to the ~** il y a 2 ans jour pour jour; **any ~ now** d'un jour à l'autre; **every ~** tous les jours; **every other ~** tous les deux jours; **one of these ~s** un de ces jours, un jour ou l'autre; **~ by ~** jour après jour; **~ in ~ out** tous les jours que (le bon) Dieu fait; **for ~s on end** pendant des jours et des jours; **to live from ~ to ~** vivre au jour le jour; **the other ~** l'autre jour, il y a quelques jours; **to this ~** encore aujourd'hui; **he's fifty if he's a ~*** il a cinquante ans bien sonnés*; **the ~ of judgment** *or* **reckoning** le jour du jugement dernier; (*fig*) **the ~ of reckoning will come** un jour il faudra rendre des comptes.

(b) (*daylight hours*) jour *m*, journée *f.* **during the ~** pendant la journée; **to work all ~** travailler toute la journée; **to travel by ~** voyager de jour; **to work ~ and night** travailler jour et nuit; **it's a fine ~** il fait beau aujourd'hui; **one summer's ~** un jour d'été; **on a wet ~** par une journée pluvieuse.

(c) (*working hours*) journée *f.* **paid by the ~** payé à la journée; **it's all in the ~'s work** ça fait partie de la routine; **a ~ off** un jour de congé; **to work an 8-hour ~** faire une journée de 8 heures.

(d) (*period*) époque *f*, temps *m.* **these ~s, in the present ~** à l'heure actuelle, de nos jours, actuellement; **in this ~ and age** par les temps qui courent; **in ~s to come** dans l'avenir, dans les jours à venir; **in his working ~s** à l'époque où il travaillait; **in his younger ~s** quand il était plus jeune; **in Napoleon's ~** à l'époque *or* du temps de Napoléon; **famous in her ~** célèbre à son époque; **in the good old ~s** dans le bon vieux temps; **the happiest ~s of my life** les jours les plus heureux de ma vie; **during the early ~s of the war** tout au début *or* pendant les premiers temps de la guerre; **that has had its ~** cela est passé de mode.

2 *adj*: **~ bed** banquette-lit *f*; (*Scol*) **~ boy/girl** externe *m/f*; **~ nursery** crèche *f*; **~ release course** ≈ cours professionnel (*de l'industrie etc*) à temps partiel; **~ return ticket** billet *m* d'aller et retour (*valable pour la journée*); **to go to ~ school** être externe *mf*; **~ shift** (*workers*) équipe *f* *or* poste *m* de jour; **to be on ~ shift** être de jour; **~ trip** excursion *f* (d'une journée); **to go on a ~ trip to Calais** faire une excursion (d'une journée) à Calais; **~-tripper** excursionniste *mf.*

♦ **daybreak** *n*: **at ~break** au point du jour, à l'aube. ♦ **daydream** **1** *n* rêvasserie *f*; **2** *vi* rêvasser. ♦ **daylight** **1** *n*: **in the ~light** à la lumière du jour, au grand jour; **it is still ~light** il fait encore jour; **I begin to see ~light*** (*understand*) je commence à voir clair; (*see the end appear*) j'en aperçois la fin; **2** *adj attack* de jour; **it's ~light robbery*** c'est du vol caractérisé; **~light-saving time** l'heure *f* d'été. ♦ **daytime** **1** *n* jour *m*, journée *f*; **2** *adj* de jour. ♦ **day-to-day** *adj routine* quotidien; *occurrence* journalier; **on a ~-to-~ basis** au jour le jour.

daze [deɪz] **1** *n*: **in a ~** = **dazed.** **2** *vt [drug]* hébéter; *[blow]* étourdir; *[news etc]* abasourdir. ♦ **dazed** *adj* hébété; tout étourdi; abasourdi.

dazzle ['dæzl] *vt* éblouir. ♦ **dazzling** *adj* éblouissant.

deacon ['di:kən] *n* diacre *m.* ♦ **deaconess** *n* diaconesse *f.*

dead [ded] **1** *adj person, animal, plant* mort; *march* funèbre; *matter* inanimé; *limb* engourdi; *fingers* gourd; *custom* tombé en désuétude; *fire, town, language* mort; *cigarette* éteint. **~ or alive** mort ou vif; (*lit, fig*) **~ and buried** mort et enterré; **to drop down ~** tomber mort; **stone ~** raide mort; **as ~ as a doornail** tout ce qu'il y a de plus mort; **to wait for a ~ man's shoes*** attendre que qn veuille bien mourir pour prendre sa place; **over my ~ body!*** pas question!*; **~ men tell no tales** les morts ne parlent pas; **he's a ~ duck*** c'est un homme fini; **he was ~ to the world*** il dormait comme une souche; (*Telec*) **the line is ~** on n'entend rien (sur la ligne); **~ calm** calme plat; **in the ~ centre** au beau milieu, en plein milieu; **it's a ~ cert‡** c'est sûr et certain*; **he's in ~ earnest** il ne plaisante pas; **the race was a ~ heat** ils sont arrivés ex aequo; **that is a ~ loss*** ça ne vaut rien; **to make a ~ set at*** *thing* s'acharner pour avoir; *person* chercher à mettre le grappin sur*; (*Naut*) **by ~ reckoning** à l'estime *f*; **~ season** morte-saison *f*; **~ silence** silence *m* de mort; **~ weight** poids *m* mort.

2 *adv* (*completely*) *certain* absolument, complètement; *stop* net, pile. **~ ahead** tout droit; **~ broke‡** fauché (comme les blés)*; **~ drunk*** ivre mort; **~ on time** juste à l'heure; **to be ~ set on doing*** vouloir faire à tout prix; **to be ~ set against sth*** s'opposer absolument à qch; (*order*) **~ slow** (*Aut*) allez au pas; (*Naut*) en avant lentement; **~ tired** éreinté, crevé*.

3 *n* **(a) the ~** les morts *mpl.* **(b) at ~ of night** au plus profond de la nuit.

♦ **dead-and-alive** *adj town* triste, mort. ♦ **deadbeat*** *adj* (*tired*) crevé*. ♦ **deaden** *vt shock, blow* amortir; *feeling* émousser; *sound* assourdir; *pain* calmer; *nerve* endormir. ♦ **dead-end** *n* impasse *f*; **a ~-end job** un travail sans débouchés. ♦ **deadline** *n* (*Press etc*) dernière limite; **to work to a ~line** travailler en vue d'une date *or* d'une heure limite. ♦ **deadlock** *n* impasse *f.* ♦ **deadly** **1** *adj* (*gen*) mortel; *aim* qui ne rate jamais; *weapon* meurtrier; *pallor* de mort; (*: *boring*) casse-pieds* *inv*, rasoir* *f inv*; **~ly nightshade** belladone *f*; **seven ~ly sins** sept péchés *mpl* capitaux; **in ~ly earnest** tout à fait sérieux; **2** *adv dull* mortellement, terriblement; *pale* comme la mort. ♦ **deadnettle** *n* ortie *f* blanche. ♦ **deadpan** *adj face* sans expression; *humour* pince-sans-rire *inv.* ♦ **deadwood** *n* bois *m* mort.

deaf [def] **1** *adj* sourd. **~ in one ear** sourd d'une oreille; **~ as a door post** sourd comme un pot*; **to be ~ to sth** rester sourd à qch; **to turn a ~ ear to sth** faire la sourde oreille à qch. **2** *n*: **the ~** les sourds *mpl.* ♦ **deaf-aid** *n* appareil *m* acoustique. ♦ **deaf-and-dumb** *adj* sourd-muet; *alphabet* des sourds-muets. ♦ **deafen** *vt* rendre sourd. ♦ **deafening** *adj* assourdissant. ♦ **deaf-mute** *n* sourd(e)-muet(te) *m(f).* ♦ **deafness** *n* surdité *f.*

deal[1] [di:l] *n* (bois *m* de) sapin *m*, bois blanc.

deal[2] [di:l] (*vb: pret, ptp* **dealt**) **1** *n* **(a) a (good** *or* **great) ~ of** beaucoup de, énormément de; **to have a great ~ to do** avoir beaucoup à faire; **a good ~ of the work** une bonne partie du travail; **that's saying a good ~** ce n'est pas peu dire; **there's a good ~ of truth in it** il y a beaucoup de vrai là-dedans; **to think a great ~ of sb** avoir beaucoup d'estime pour qn; **to mean a great ~ to sb** compter beaucoup pour qn; **a good ~ cleverer** beaucoup *or* nettement plus intelligent. **(b)** (*agreement, bargain*) marché *m*, affaire *f*; (*St Ex*) opération *f*, transaction *f*. **business ~** affaire, marché; **to do a ~ with sb** (*Comm*) faire une affaire avec qn; (*gen*) conclure un marché avec qn; **we might do a ~?** on pourrait peut-être s'arranger?; **it's a ~!*** d'accord!; (*Pol etc*) **a new ~** un programme de réformes; **he got a very bad ~ from them** ils se sont très mal conduits envers lui. **(c)** (*Cards*) donne *f*. **it's your ~** à vous de donner.

2 *vt* **(a)** (**~ out**) *cards* donner. **(b) to ~ sb a blow** porter *or* assener un coup à qn.

3 *vi* **(a)** (*Comm*) traiter, négocier (*with sb* avec qn). **I always ~ with that butcher** je vais *or* me fournis toujours chez ce boucher-là; **to ~ in wood** être dans le commerce du bois. **(b) to ~ with** *person, task* s'occuper de, se charger de; *problem* venir à bout de; (*Comm*) *order* régler; *[book, film etc]* traiter de, avoir pour sujet; **I'll ~ with him** je me charge de lui; **I'll ~ with you later!** tu vas avoir affaire à moi tout à l'heure!; **to know how to ~ with sb** savoir s'y prendre avec qn; **he's not very easy to ~ with** il n'est pas commode; **to have to ~ with sb** avoir affaire à qn; **to ~ well/badly by sb** agir bien/mal avec qn.

deal out *vt sep gifts, money* distribuer, partager (*between* entre). **to ~ out justice** rendre la justice.

♦ **dealer** *n* (*Comm*) marchand *m* (*in* de), négociant *m* (*in* en); (*Cards*) donneur *m*. ♦ **dealings** *npl* (*gen*) relations *fpl* (*with sb* avec qn); (*Comm, St Ex*) transactions *fpl* (*in* en); (*trafficking*) trafic *m* (*in sth* de qch).

dean [diːn] *n* doyen *m*.

dear [dɪəʳ] **1** *adj* **(a)** (*loved*) cher; (*lovable*) adorable. **she is very ~ to me** elle m'est très chère; **a ~ friend of mine** un de mes amis les plus chers; **to hold sb/sth ~** chérir qn/qch; **his ~est wish** son plus cher désir; **a ~ little dress** une ravissante petite robe; (*in letter-writing*) **~ Daddy** (mon) cher papa; **~ Sir** Monsieur; **~ Sirs** Messieurs; **~ Mr Smith** cher Monsieur; **~ Mr and Mrs Smith** cher Monsieur, chère Madame. **(b)** (*expensive*) *prices, goods* cher, coûteux; *price* élevé; *shop* cher. **to get ~er** augmenter.

2 *excl*: **oh ~!** (*surprise*) mon Dieu!, pas possible!; (*regret*) oh mon Dieu!

3 *n*: **my ~** mon cher (ami); (*to child*) mon petit; **my ~est** mon chéri, mon amour; **poor ~** (*to child*) pauvre petit, pauvre chou*; (*to woman*) ma pauvre; **she is a ~*** c'est un amour; **give it to me, there's a ~*** sois gentil, donne-le-moi.

4 *adv buy, pay, sell* cher.

♦ **dearly** *adv*: **to love sb/sth ~ly** être très attaché à qn/qch; **I should ~ly like to live here** j'aimerais infiniment habiter ici; **to pay ~ly for sth** payer qch cher.

dearth [dɜːθ] *n [food, ideas]* disette *f*; *[money, resources, water]* pénurie *f*. **there is no ~ of young men** les jeunes gens ne manquent pas.

death [deθ] **1** *n* mort *f*, décès *m* (*Jur, Admin*); *[plans, hopes]* effondrement *m*. **to be burnt to ~** mourir carbonisé; **he drank himself to ~** c'est la boisson qui l'a tué; **at ~'s door** à l'article de la mort; **to sentence sb to ~** condamner qn à mort; **to put to ~** mettre à mort; **a fight to the ~** une lutte à mort; (*fig*) **to be in at the ~** assister au dénouement; (*lit*) **it will be the ~ of him** cela va l'achever; (*fig*) **he will be the ~ of me** il me fera mourir; **to be bored to ~*** crever* d'ennui; **you look tired to ~*** tu as l'air crevé*; **I'm sick to ~*** *or* **tired to ~* of all this** j'en ai par-dessus la tête de tout ceci.

2 *adj*: **~ cell** cellule *f* de condamné à mort; **~ certificate** acte *m* de décès; **~ duties** droits *mpl* de succession; **~ march** marche *f* funèbre; **~ mask** masque *m* mortuaire; **~ penalty** peine *f* de mort; **~ rate** (taux *m* de) mortalité *f*; **~ rattle** râle *m* d'agonie; **~ sentence** arrêt *m* de mort; **~ throes** affres *fpl* de la mort, agonie *f*; **~ toll** chiffre *m* des morts; **~ warrant** ordre *m* d'exécution; **~ wish** désir *m* de mort.

♦ **deathbed 1** *n* lit *m* de mort; **2** *adj repentance* de la dernière heure. ♦ **death-blow** *n* coup *m* mortel *or* fatal. ♦ **deathless** *adj* immortel. ♦ **deathly 1** *adj appearance* cadavérique; *silence* mortel, de mort; **2** *adv*: **~ly pale** d'une pâleur mortelle. ♦ **death's-head** *n* tête *f* de mort. ♦ **deathtrap** *n* endroit *m* (*or* véhicule *m etc*) dangereux; **it's a real ~trap** c'est mortellement dangereux.

debar [dɪˈbɑːʳ] *vt* exclure (*from sth* de qch), interdire (*sb from doing* à qn de faire).

debase [dɪˈbeɪs] *vt* (*Fin*) *coinage* déprécier; *word, object* dégrader; *person* avilir. **to ~ o.s. by doing** s'avilir en faisant. ♦ **debasement** *n* dépréciation *f*; dégradation *f*; avilissement *m*.

debate [dɪˈbeɪt] **1** *vt* discuter, débattre. **2** *vi* discuter (*with* avec, *about* sur). **he was debating with himself whether to refuse or not** il se demandait s'il refuserait ou non. **3** *n* débat *m*, discussion *f*. **after much ~** après un long débat. ♦ **debatable** *adj* discutable, contestable; **it is debatable whether ...** on est en droit de se demander si .... ♦ **debating society** *n* société *f* de conférences contradictoires.

debauch [dɪˈbɔːtʃ] *vt person* débaucher, corrompre; *morals, taste* corrompre. ♦ **debauched** *adj* débauché, corrompu. ♦ **debauchery** *n* débauche *f*.

debilitate [dɪˈbɪlɪteɪt] *vt* débiliter. ♦ **debility** *n* débilité *f*.

debit [ˈdebɪt] **1** *n* (*Comm*) débit *m*. **2** *adj account, balance* débiteur. **on the ~ side** au débit; (*fig*) au passif. **3** *vt*: **to ~ sb's account with a sum, to ~ sb with a sum** porter une somme au débit de qn, débiter qn d'une somme.

debonair [ˌdebəˈnɛəʳ] *adj* jovial.

debrief [ˌdiːˈbriːf] *vt* faire faire un compte rendu (de fin de mission) à; (*Mil*) faire faire un rapport à. (*Mil*) **to be ~ed** faire rapport. ♦ **debriefing** *n* compte rendu *m* (de fin de mission); rapport *m*.

debris [ˈdebriː] *n* débris *mpl*.

debt [det] *n* (*payment owed*) dette *f*, créance *f*. **bad ~s** créances irrécouvrables; **~ of honour** dette d'honneur; **to be in ~** avoir des dettes, être endetté; **I am £5 in ~** je dois 5 livres; **to be out of sb's ~** être quitte envers qn; **to get into ~** faire des dettes, s'endetter; **to get out of ~** s'acquitter de ses dettes; **to be out of ~** n'avoir plus de dettes; **I am greatly in your ~ for sth/for having done** je vous suis très redevable de qch/d'avoir fait. ♦ **debt collector** *n* agent *m* de recouvrements. ♦ **debtor** *n* débiteur *m*, -trice *f*. ♦ **debt-ridden** *adj* criblé de dettes.

debunk* [ˌdiːˈbʌŋk] *vt* (*gen*) démythifier; *person* déboulonner*; *claim* démentir; *institution* discréditer.

decade [ˈdekeɪd] *n* décennie *f*.

decadence [ˈdekədəns] *n* décadence *f*. ♦ **decadent** *adj* décadent.

decamp* [dɪˈkæmp] *vi* décamper*.

decant [dɪˈkænt] *vt wine* décanter. ♦ **decanter** *n* carafe *f*.

decapitate [dɪˈkæpɪteɪt] *vt* décapiter.

decay [dɪˈkeɪ] **1** *vi [work of art, stone]* s'altérer, se détériorer; *[food]* se gâter; *[flowers, vegetation, wood]* pourrir; *[tooth]* se carier; *[building]* se délabrer; *[radioactive nucleus]* se désintégrer; *[hopes]* s'enfuir; *[beauty]* se faner; *[civilization]* décliner; *[race, one's faculties]* s'affaiblir. **2** *n* (*gen*) pourriture *f*; (*Med*) carie *f*; *[building]* délabrement *m*; (*Phys*) désintégration *f*; *[hopes]* ruine *f*; *[civilization]* décadence *f*; *[race, faculties]* affaiblissement *m*. ♦ **decayed** *adj tooth* carié; *wood* pourri; *food* gâté; *building* délabré; (*Phys*) partiellement désintégré; *health, civiliza-*

tion en déclin. ♦ **decaying** *adj flesh* en pourriture; *food* en train de s'avarier; *tooth* qui se carie.

decease [dɪ'si:s] *n* décès *m.* ♦ **deceased 1** *adj* décédé; **2** *n* défunt(e) *m(f).*

deceit [dɪ'si:t] *n* tromperie *f.* ♦ **deceitful** *adj person* faux, trompeur; *words, conduct* trompeur, mensonger. ♦ **deceitfully** *adv* avec duplicité, faussement. ♦ **deceitfulness** *n* fausseté *f,* duplicité *f.*

deceive [dɪ'si:v] *vt* tromper, abuser; *spouse, hopes* tromper. **he ~d me into thinking that ...** il m'a faussement fait croire que ...; **I thought my eyes were deceiving me** je n'en croyais pas mes yeux; **to be ~d by appearances** être trompé par les apparences; **to ~ o.s.** s'abuser. ♦ **deceiver** *n* trompeur *m,* -euse *f,* imposteur *m.*

December [dɪ'sembəʳ] *n* décembre *m; for phrases V* **September.**

decent ['di:sənt] *adj* **(a)** (*respectable*) *person* convenable, bien* *inv; house, shoes* convenable; (*seemly*) *language, behaviour, dress* décent. **(b)** (*: *pleasant*) *person* bon, brave (*before n*). **it was ~ of him** c'était chic* de sa part; **to do the ~ thing*** agir élégamment (*by sb* envers qn); **quite a ~ flat** un appartement qui n'est pas mal; **a ~ meal** un bon repas. ♦ **decency** *n [dress, conversation]* décence *f; [person]* pudeur *f;* **to have a sense of decency** avoir de la pudeur; **the decencies** les convenances *fpl;* **common decency** la simple politesse; **to have the decency to do sth** avoir la décence de faire qch. ♦ **decently** *adv dressed etc* convenablement; (*: *well*) bien. **you can't ~ly ask him that** décemment vous ne pouvez pas lui demander cela.

decentralize [di:'sentrəlaɪz] *vt* décentraliser. ♦ **decentralization** *n* décentralisation *f.*

deception [dɪ'sepʃən] *n* (*deceiving*) tromperie *f;* (*deceitful act*) supercherie *f.* ♦ **deceptive** *adj* trompeur. ♦ **deceptively** *adv*: **it looks deceptively near** *etc* ça donne l'illusion d'être proche *etc.* ♦ **deceptiveness** *n* caractère *m* trompeur.

decibel ['desɪbel] *n* décibel *m.*

decide [dɪ'saɪd] **1** *vt* décider (*to do* de faire; *that* que; *sb to do* qn à faire), se décider (*to do* à faire); *question, quarrel* décider; *piece of business* régler; *difference of opinion* juger; *sb's fate, future* décider de. **2** *vi* se décider (*on, for* pour; *against* contre; *on doing* à faire). **to ~ for/against sb** donner raison/tort à qn. ♦ **decided** *adj improvement* incontestable; *difference* marqué; *refusal* catégorique; *character, person, tone, look* résolu, décidé; *opinion* arrêté. ♦ **decidedly** *adv act, reply* avec décision; *lazy* incontestablement. ♦ **decider** *n* (*goal*) but *m* décisif; (*point*) point *m* décisif; (*factor*) facteur *m* décisif; (*game*) **the ~r** la belle. ♦ **deciding** *adj* décisif.

deciduous [dɪ'sɪdjʊəs] *adj tree* à feuilles caduques.

decimal ['desɪməl] **1** *adj* (*gen*) décimal. **to three ~ places** à la troisième décimale; **~ point** virgule *f* (*de fraction décimale*). **2** *n* décimale *f.* **~s** le calcul décimal. ♦ **decimalization** *n* décimalisation *f.* ♦ **decimalize** *vt* décimaliser.

decimate ['desɪmeɪt] *vt* (*lit, fig*) décimer.

decipher [dɪ'saɪfəʳ] *vt* déchiffrer. ♦ **decipherable** *adj* déchiffrable.

decision [dɪ'sɪʒən] *n* décision *f;* (*Jur*) arrêt *m.* **to come to a ~** arriver à une décision, se décider. ♦ **decisive** *adj battle, victory, factor* décisif; *manner, answer* décidé, catégorique; *person* qui a de la décision. ♦ **decisively** *adv speak* d'un ton décidé; *act* d'une façon décidée. ♦ **decisiveness** *n [person]* décision *f,* fermeté *f.*

deck [dek] **1** *n* **(a)** *[ship]* pont *m.* **to go up on ~** monter sur le pont; **below ~** sous le pont, en bas; **top ~, upper ~** *[bus]* impériale *f; [jumbo jet]* étage *m.* **(b)** *[record player etc]* platine *f.* **(c) ~ of cards** jeu *m* de cartes. **2** *vt* (**~ out**) orner (*with* de). ♦ **deckchair** *n* chaise *f* longue. ♦ **deck-hand** *n* matelot *m.*

declaim [dɪ'kleɪm] *vti* déclamer (*against* contre). ♦ **declamation** *n* déclamation *f.* ♦ **declamatory** *adj* déclamatoire.

declare [dɪ'klɛəʳ] *vt* (*gen*) déclarer (*that* que); *results* proclamer. (*Customs*) **have you anything to ~?** avez-vous qch à déclarer?; **to ~ war** déclarer la guerre (*on* à); **to ~ o.s. for/against** se déclarer en faveur de/contre. ♦ **declaration** *n* déclaration *f.* ♦ **declared** *adj* déclaré, ouvert. ♦ **declaredly** *adv* ouvertement.

declassify [di:'klæsɪfaɪ] *vt* rendre accessible à tous.

declension [dɪ'klenʃən] *n* (*Gram*) déclinaison *f.*

decline [dɪ'klaɪn] **1** *n* (*gen*) déclin *m.* **~ in price** baisse *f* de prix; **these cases are on the ~** ces cas sont de moins en moins fréquents. **2** *vt* (*gen*) refuser (*to do* de faire); *invitation, honour, responsibility* décliner; (*Gram*) décliner. **3** *vi [health, influence]* décliner; *[empire]* tomber en décadence; *[prices, business]* être en baisse; (*Gram*) se décliner. **to ~ in importance** perdre de l'importance. ♦ **declining** *adj*: **in his declining years** au déclin de sa vie.

declutch ['di:'klʌtʃ] *vi* débrayer.

decode ['di:'kəʊd] *vt* décoder.

decoke [di:'kəʊk] **1** *vt* décalaminer. **2** *n* décalaminage *m.*

decompose [ˌdi:kəm'pəʊz] **1** *vt* décomposer. **2** *vi* se décomposer. ♦ **decomposition** *n* décomposition *f.*

decompression [ˌdi:kəm'preʃən] **1** *n* décompression *f.* **2** *adj*: **~ chamber** caisson *m* de décompression; **~ sickness** maladie *f* des caissons.

decontaminate [ˌdi:kən'tæmɪneɪt] *vt* décontaminer. ♦ **decontamination** *n* décontamination *f.*

decontrol [ˌdi:kən'trəʊl] *vt prices* libérer des contrôles gouvernementaux; *butter* lever le contrôle du prix de. **~led road** route *f* non soumise à la limitation de vitesse.

decorate ['dekəreɪt] *vt* **(a)** orner, décorer (*with* de); *cake* décorer; (*paint etc*) *room* peindre (et tapisser). **to ~ with flags** pavoiser. **(b)** *soldier* décorer (*for gallantry* pour acte de bravoure). ♦ **decorating** *n*: **(painting and) decorating** décoration *f* intérieure; **they are doing some decorating** ils sont en train de refaire les peintures. ♦ **decoration** *n* (*state*) décor *m;* (*ornament, medal*) décoration *f;* **Christmas decorations** décorations de Noël. ♦ **decorative** *adj* décoratif. ♦ **decorator** *n* décorateur *m,* -trice *f.*

decorum [dɪ'kɔ:rəm] *n* décorum *m.* **a breach of ~** une inconvenance; **a sense of ~** le sens des convenances. ♦ **decorous** ['dekərəs] *adj* comme il faut. ♦ **decorously** *adv* comme il faut.

decoy ['di:kɔɪ] **1** *n* (*person*) compère *m.* **police ~** policier *m* en civil (*servant à attirer un criminel dans une souricière*). **2** [*also* dɪ'kɔɪ] *vt* attirer dans un piège.

decrease [di:'kri:s] **1** *vi [amount, numbers, supplies, birth rate, population]* diminuer, décroître; *[power, strength, intensity]* s'affaiblir, décroître; *[price, value, enthusiasm]* baisser; (*Knitting*) diminuer. **2** *vt* diminuer; affaiblir; baisser. **3** ['di:kri:s] *n* diminution *f* (*in* de); affaiblissement *m* (*in* de); baisse *f* (*in* de). **~ in speed** ralentissement *m;* **~ in strength** affaiblissement. ♦ **decreasing** *adj* décroissant; qui s'affaiblit; en baisse. ♦ **decreasingly** *adv* de moins en moins.

decree [dɪ'kri:] **1** *n* (*Jur, Rel*) décret *m; [tribunal]* jugement *m;* (*municipal*) arrêté *m.* **by royal ~** par décret du roi; *[divorce]* **~ absolute/nisi** jugement définitif/provisoire de divorce. **2** *vt* décréter, arrêter (*that* que + *indic*).

decrepit [dɪ'krepɪt] *adj structure, building*

délabré; (*) *person* décrépit. ◆ **decrepitude** *n* délabrement *m*; décrépitude *f*.

decry [dɪ'kraɪ] *vt* décrier.

dedicate ['dedɪkeɪt] *vt* dédier (*to* à). **to ~ o.s.** *or* **one's life to sth/to doing** se consacrer à qch/à faire. ◆ **dedication** *n* (*in book*) dédicace *f*; (*devotion*) dévouement *m*.

deduce [dɪ'dju:s] *vt* déduire, conclure (*from* de, *that* que). ◆ **deduction**¹ *n* déduction *f*. ◆ **deductive** *adj* déductif.

deduct [dɪ'dʌkt] *vt amount* déduire (*from* de); *numbers* soustraire (*from* de). **to ~ sth from the price** faire une réduction sur le prix; **to ~ 5% from the wages** faire une retenue de 5% sur les salaires; **after ~ing 5%** déduction faite de 5%. ◆ **deductible** *adj* à déduire (*from* de); *expenses* déductible. ◆ **deduction**² *n* déduction *f* (*from* de); (*from wage*) retenue *f* (*from* sur).

deed [di:d] *n* **(a)** action *f*, acte *m*. **brave ~** exploit *m*. **good ~** bonne action; **in ~** de fait, en fait. **(b)** (*Jur*) acte *m*. **~ of covenant** *or* **gift** (acte de) donation *f*; **by ~ poll** par acte unilatéral.

deem [di:m] *vt* juger, estimer. **to ~ it prudent to do** juger prudent de faire.

deep [di:p] **1** *adj* **(a)** *water, hole, wound* profond; *snow* épais. **the pond was 4 metres ~** l'étang avait 4 mètres de profondeur; (*fig*) **to be in ~ water** être dans de vilains draps; *[swimming pool]* **the ~ end** le grand bain; **to go off (at) the ~ end*** (*excited*) se mettre dans tous ses états; (*angry*) se mettre en colère; (*fig*) **he was thrown in at the ~ end** ça a été le baptême du feu (pour lui); **he was ankle-~ in water** l'eau lui arrivait aux chevilles. **(b)** *shelf, cupboard* large, profond; *edge, border* large, haut. **the spectators stood 10 ~** il y avait 10 rangs de spectateurs debout; **~ space** espace *m* interstellaire. **(c)** *sound, voice, tones* grave; (*Mus*) *note, voice* bas, grave. **(d)** *sorrow, relief, colour, mystery, sleep* profond; *feeling* intense; *interest, concern* vif; *writer, thinker* profond. **~ in thought/in a book** absorbé dans ses pensées/dans un livre; **~ breathing (exercises)** exercices *mpl* respiratoires; (*Ling*) **~ structure** structure *f* profonde; **he's a ~ one*** il est plus malin qu'il n'en a l'air.

2 *adv breathe, penetrate* profondément; *drink* à longs traits. **don't go in too ~ if you can't swim** ne va pas trop loin si tu ne sais pas nager; **~ into the night** tard dans la nuit; **he's in it pretty ~*** il s'est engagé très loin là-dedans, (*pej*) il est dedans jusqu'au cou.

3 *n*: **the ~** (les grands fonds de) l'océan *m*. ◆ **deep-chested** *adj person* large de poitrine; *animal* à large poitrail. ◆ **deepen 1** *vt hole, darkness* approfondir; *sorrow, interest* augmenter; *sound* rendre plus grave; *colour* foncer; **2** *vi* devenir plus profond (*or* plus foncé *etc*); *[night, mystery]* s'épaissir; *[voice]* se faire plus grave. ◆ **deepening** *adj* de plus en plus profond *etc*. ◆ **deep-freeze 1** *n* (*also* **deepfreezer**) congélateur *m*; **2** *vt* surgeler. ◆ **deep-freezing** *n* surgélation *f*. ◆ **deep-frozen** *adj* surgelé. ◆ **deep-fry** *vt* faire frire (en friteuse). ◆ **deeply** *adv dig, cut* profondément; *drink* à longs traits; *consider* profondément; (*very*) *grateful etc* infiniment; *moving, concerned* extrêmement; *offended* profondément; **to regret ~ly** regretter vivement; **to go ~ly into sth** approfondir qch. ◆ **deep-rooted** *adj affection* profond; *prejudice* profondément enraciné; *habit* invétéré. ◆ **deep-sea** *adj animal, plant* pélagique; *diver* sous-marin; *fisherman, fishing* hauturier. ◆ **deep-seated** *adj prejudice, dislike* profondément enraciné; *conviction* fermement ancré; *cough* caverneux. ◆ **deep-set** *adj eyes* très enfoncé.

deer [dɪəʳ] *n, pl inv* cerf *m*, biche *f*; (*red ~*) cerf; (*fallow ~*) daim *m*; (*roe ~*) chevreuil *m*. **certain types of ~** certains types de cervidés *mpl*. ◆ **deerskin** *n* peau *f* de daim. ◆ **deer-stalking** *n* chasse *f* au cerf à pied.

deface [dɪ'feɪs] *vt monument, door* dégrader; *work of art* mutiler; *poster, inscription* barbouiller; *[thing] countryside* mutiler.

defame [dɪ'feɪm] *vt* diffamer. ◆ **defamation** *n* diffamation *f*. ◆ **defamatory** *adj* diffamatoire.

default [dɪ'fɔ:lt] **1** *n*: **in ~ of** à défaut de. **2** *vi* manquer à ses engagements. ◆ **defaulter** *n* délinquant(e) *m(f)*. ◆ **defaulting** *adj* défaillant.

defeat [dɪ'fi:t] **1** *n [army, team]* défaite *f*; *[project, ambition]* échec *m*; *[legal case, appeal]* rejet *m*. **2** *vt opponent* vaincre; *army, team* battre; *hopes* ruiner; *ambitions, plans, efforts* faire échouer; (*Parl*) *party, group* mettre en minorité; *bill, amendment* rejeter. **to ~ one's own ends** aller à l'encontre du but que l'on s'est proposé; **that plan will ~ its own ends** ce plan sera auto-destructeur. ◆ **defeatism** *n* défaitisme *m*. ◆ **defeatist** *adj, n* défaitiste (*mf*).

defecate ['defəkeɪt] *vi* déféquer.

defect ['di:fekt] **1** *n* (*gen*) défaut *m*. **physical ~** vice *m or* défaut de conformation; **mental ~** anomalie *f* mentale; **moral ~** défaut. **2** [dɪ'fekt] *vi* (*Pol*) faire défection. **to ~ from one country to another** s'enfuir d'un pays dans un autre pour raisons politiques; **to ~ to the enemy** passer à l'ennemi. ◆ **defection** *n* (*Pol*) défection *f*. ◆ **defective** *adj machine* défectueux; *reasoning* mauvais; (*Med*) déficient; (*Gram*) défectif; **to be ~ive in sth** manquer de qch. ◆ **defector** *n* transfuge *mf*.

defence [dɪ'fens] **1** *n* (*gen*) défense *f*, protection *f*; *[action, belief]* justification *f*. **in ~ of** à la défense de; **Ministry** *or* **Department of D~** ministère *m* de la Défense nationale; (*Mil*) **~s** ouvrages *mpl* défensifs; **the body's ~s against disease** la défense de l'organisme contre la maladie; **as a ~ against** en guise de défense contre; **in his ~** à sa décharge; (*Jur*) **witness for the ~** témoin *m* à décharge; (*Jur*) **the case for the ~** la défense. **2** *adj* de défense. **the ~ forces** les forces *fpl* défensives, la défense; **~ mechanism** (*Physiol*) système *m* de défense; (*Psych*) défenses *fpl*. ◆ **defenceless** *adj* sans défense.

defend [dɪ'fend] *vt* (*gen*) défendre (*against* contre); *action, decision, opinion* défendre, justifier. **to ~ o.s.** se défendre (*against* contre). ◆ **defendant** *n* (*Jur*) défendeur *m*, -eresse *f*; (*in criminal case*) prévenu(e) *m(f)*, accusé(e) *m(f)*. ◆ **defender** *n* (*gen*) défenseur *m*; *[sport record, title]* détenteur *m*, -trice *f*; **~er of the faith** défenseur de la foi. ◆ **defending** *adj* (*Sport*) **~ing champion** champion(ne) *m(f)* en titre; (*Jur*) **~ing counsel** avocat *m* de la défense.

defense [dɪ'fens] *n* (*US*) = **defence**.

defensive [dɪ'fensɪv] **1** *adj* défensif. **2** *n* défensive *f*. **on the ~** sur la défensive.

defer¹ [dɪ'fɜ:ʳ] *vt* (*gen*) différer, remettre à plus tard (*doing* de faire); *meeting* reporter; *business* renvoyer; **~red payment** paiement *m* par versements échelonnés; (*Mil*) **his call-up's been ~red** il a été mis en sursis d'incorporation. ◆ **deferment** *n* report *m*; renvoi *m*.

defer² [dɪ'fɜ:ʳ] *vi* (*submit*) déférer (*to sb* à qn). **to ~ to sb's knowledge** s'en remettre aux connaissances de qn. ◆ **deference** *n* déférence *f*. ◆ **deferential** *adj person* plein de déférence; *tone* de déférence. ◆ **deferentially** *adv* avec déférence.

defiance [dɪ'faɪəns] *n* défi *m* (*of* à). **in ~ of** au mépris de. ◆ **defiant** *adj attitude, tone* de défi; *reply* provocant; *person* intraitable. ◆ **defiantly** *adv* d'un air *or* ton de défi.

deficiency [dɪ'fɪʃənsɪ] *n* **(a)** *[goods]* manque *m*, insuffisance *f*; *[vitamins etc]* carence *f*; (*of liver etc*) déficience *f* (*of* de). **(b)** (*in character, system*) imperfection *f* (*in* dans). **(c)** (*Fin*) déficit

m, découvert *m*. ♦ **deficient** *adj* insuffisant, faible (*in* en); **to be deficient in sth** manquer de qch.
deficit ['defɪsɪt] *n* (*Fin etc*) déficit *m*.
defile[1] ['di:faɪl] **1** *n* (*procession; place*) défilé *m*. **2** [dɪ'faɪl] *vi* (*march in file*) défiler.
defile[2] [dɪ'faɪl] *vt* (*pollute*) souiller, salir. ♦ **defilement** *n* souillure *f*.
define [dɪ'faɪn] *vt* **(a)** *word, attitude, conditions, powers* définir. **(b)** (*outline*) **the tower was ~d against the sky** la tour se détachait sur le ciel. ♦ **definable** *adj* définissable. ♦ **definition** *n* (*gen*) définition *f*; (*Phot*) netteté *f*; (*TV*) définition *f*. ♦ **definitive** *adj* définitif. ♦ **definitively** *adv* définitivement.
definite ['defɪnɪt] *adj* **(a)** (*exact, clear*) *decision, agreement, plan* bien déterminé, précis; *stain, mark* très visible; *improvement* net, manifeste; *intention, order, sale* ferme. **(b)** (*certain*) certain, sûr; *manner, tone* assuré, positif. **it is ~ that** il est certain que + *indic*; **is it ~ that ...?** est-il certain que ...? + *subj*; **she was very ~ about it** elle a été catégorique *or* très nette sur la question. **(c)** (*Gram*) ~ **article** article *m* défini; **past ~ tense** prétérit *m*. ♦ **definitely** *adv* (*certainly*) sans aucun doute, certainement; (*appreciably*) *better* nettement, manifestement; (*emphatically*) *state* catégoriquement; **~ly!** absolument!, bien sûr!; **she said very ~ly that ...** elle a déclaré catégoriquement que ....
deflate [di:'fleɪt] *vt tyre* dégonfler; *prices* faire baisser; (*) *person* rabattre le caquet à. ♦ **deflation** *n* (*Econ*) déflation *f*. ♦ **deflationary** *adj* (*Econ*) déflationniste.
deflect [dɪ'flekt] **1** *vt ball, projectile* faire dévier; *stream, person* détourner (*from* de). **2** *vi* dévier. ♦ **deflector** *n* déflecteur *m*.
defoliate [di:'fəʊlɪeɪt] *vt* défeuiller. ♦ **defoliant** *n* défoliant *m*. ♦ **defoliation** *n* défoliation *f*.
deforest [di:'fɒrɪst] *vt* déboiser.
deform [dɪ'fɔ:m] *vt* déformer. ♦ **deformation** *n* déformation *f*. ♦ **deformed** *adj limb, body, person* difforme; *mind, structure* déformé. ♦ **deformity** *n* [*body*] difformité *f*; [*mind*] déformation *f*.
defraud [dɪ'frɔ:d] *vt Customs, state* frauder; *person* escroquer. **to ~ sb of sth** escroquer qch à qn.
defray [dɪ'freɪ] *vt cost* couvrir. **to ~ sb's expenses** défrayer qn.
defrock [di:'frɒk] *vt* défroquer.
defrost [di:'frɒst] *vt refrigerator, windscreen* dégivrer; *meat, vegetables* décongeler.
deft [deft] *adj* adroit, preste. ♦ **deftly** *adv* adroitement, prestement. ♦ **deftness** *n* adresse *f*.
defuse [di:'fju:z] *vt* (*lit, fig*) désamorcer.
defy [dɪ'faɪ] *vt person, law, danger, death* braver, défier; *attack, description* défier; *efforts* résister à. **to ~ sb to do** défier qn de faire, mettre qn au défi de faire.
degenerate [dɪ'dʒenəreɪt] **1** *vi* dégénérer (*into* en). **2** [dɪ'dʒenərɪt] *adj, n* dégénéré(e) *m(f)*. ♦ **degeneracy** *or* ♦ **degeneration** *n* dégénérescence *f*.
degrade [dɪ'greɪd] *vt* dégrader. **he felt ~d** il se sentait dégradé; **I wouldn't ~ myself to do that** je n'irais pas m'avilir à faire cela. ♦ **degradation** *n* (*state*) déchéance *f*. ♦ **degrading** *adj* dégradant, avilissant.
degree [dɪ'gri:] *n* **(a)** (*gen, Geog, Math*) degré *m*. **it was 35 ~s in the shade** il faisait 35 (degrés) à l'ombre. **(b) by ~s** par degrés, petit à petit; **to a ~** extrêmement; **to some ~, to a certain ~** jusqu'à un certain point, dans une certaine mesure; **to such a ~ that** à un tel point que; **a high ~ of error** un pourcentage élevé d'erreurs; **a considerable ~ of doubt remains** des doutes considérables subsistent; **third-~ burns** brûlures *fpl* au troisième degré. **(c)** (*Univ*) diplôme *m* (universitaire). **first ~** ≃ licence *f*; **higher ~** ≃ doctorat *m*; **a science ~** une licence de sciences; **to have a ~ in** avoir une licence de; **to get one's ~** avoir sa licence.
dehumanize [di:'hju:mənaɪz] *vt* déshumaniser.
dehydrate [,di:'haɪdreɪt] *vt* déshydrater. ♦ **dehydrated** *adj person, vegetables* déshydraté; *milk, eggs* en poudre. ♦ **dehydration** *n* déshydratation *f*.
de-ice ['di:'aɪs] *vt* dégivrer. ♦ **de-icer** *n* dégivreur *m*.
deify ['di:ɪfaɪ] *vt* déifier. ♦ **deification** *n* déification *f*.
deign [deɪn] *vt* daigner (*to do* faire).
deity ['di:ɪtɪ] *n* divinité *f*. **the D~** Dieu *m*.
dejected [dɪ'dʒektɪd] *adj* découragé. **to become ~** se décourager. ♦ **dejection** *n* découragement *m*.
delay [dɪ'leɪ] **1** *vt person* retarder, retenir; *train, plane, action, event* retarder; *traffic* ralentir, entraver; *payment* différer. **~ed-action bomb** bombe *f* à retardement; **to ~ doing sth** différer à faire qch. **2** *vi* s'attarder (*in doing* à faire). **don't ~!** dépêchez-vous! **3** *n* (*waiting*) délai *m*; (*stop*) arrêt *m*. **with as little ~ as possible** dans les plus brefs délais; **without ~** sans délai; **without further ~** sans plus tarder; **after 2 or 3 ~s** après 2 ou 3 arrêts; **there will be ~s to trains** on prévoit des retards *mpl* pour les trains; **there will be ~s to traffic** la circulation sera ralentie. ♦ **delaying** *adj* dilatoire.
delegate ['delɪgeɪt] **1** *vt* déléguer (*to sb* à qn; *to do* pour faire). **2** ['delɪgɪt] *n* délégué(e) *m(f)* (*to* à). ♦ **delegation** *n* délégation *f*.
delete [dɪ'li:t] *vt* (*gen*) effacer (*from* de); (*score out*) barrer, rayer (*from* de), effacer (*from* de). **'~ where inapplicable'** 'rayer les mentions inutiles'. ♦ **deletion** *n* suppression *f*; (*thing deleted*) rature *f*.
deliberate [dɪ'lɪbərɪt] **1** *adj* (*intentional*) délibéré, voulu; (*cautious, thoughtful*) bien pesé, mûrement réfléchi; (*slow, purposeful*) *air, voice* décidé; *manner, walk* mesuré, posé. **2** [dɪ'lɪbəreɪt] *vi* délibérer (*upon* sur). **3** *vt* (*consider*) considérer, examiner; (*discuss*) délibérer sur. ♦ **deliberately** *adv* (*intentionally*) exprès, délibérément; (*slowly, purposefully*) posément. ♦ **deliberation** *n* (*gen*) délibération *f*; **after due deliberation** après mûre réflexion. ♦ **deliberative** *adj assembly* délibérant.
delicate ['delɪkɪt] *adj* délicat. ♦ **delicacy** *n* délicatesse *f*; (*tasty food*) mets *m* délicat. ♦ **delicately** *adv touch* délicatement; *act, express* avec délicatesse. ♦ **delicatessen** *n* (*shop*) épicerie *f* fine; (*food*) ≃ charcuterie *f*.
delicious [dɪ'lɪʃəs] *adj* délicieux.
delight [dɪ'laɪt] **1** *n* **(a)** (*joy*) grand plaisir *m*, joie *f*. **to my ~** à ma plus grande joie; **with great ~** *watch, taste* avec délices; *learn, wait* avec joie. **(b)** (*pleasant thing etc*) délice *m* (*f in pl*), charme *m*. **the ~s of life in the open** les charmes *or* les délices de la vie en plein air; **this book is a great ~** ce livre est vraiment merveilleux; **a ~ to the eyes** un plaisir pour les yeux; **he's a ~ to watch** il fait plaisir à voir. **2** *vt person* réjouir, enchanter. **3** *vi* prendre plaisir, se délecter (*in sth* à qch; *in doing* à faire). ♦ **delighted** *adj* ravi, enchanté (*with, at, by* de, par; *to do* de faire; *that* que + *subj*); **I shall be ~ed** avec grand plaisir. ♦ **delightful** *adj person* charmant; *character, smile* délicieux, charmant; *place, object* ravissant; **it's ~ful** c'est merveilleux. ♦ **delightfully** *adv* délicieusement.
delineate [dɪ'lɪnɪeɪt] *vt outline* esquisser; *character* décrire.
delinquent [dɪ'lɪŋkwənt] *adj, n* délinquant(e) *m(f)*. ♦ **delinquency** *n* délinquance *f*.
delirious [dɪ'lɪrɪəs] *adj* (*Med, fig*) délirant (*with* de). **to become ~** (*Med*) être pris de délire; (*fig*) entrer en délire; (*Med, fig*) **to be ~** délirer.

◆ **deliriously** *adv* (*Med*) en délire; (*fig*) frénétiquement; ~**ly happy** débordant de joie. ◆ **delirium** *n* délire *m*; **fit of delirium** accès *m* de délire; **delirium tremens** delirium *m* tremens.
deliver [dɪˈlɪvəʳ] *vt* **(a)** (*gen*) *message, object* remettre (*to sb* à qn); *[postman]* distribuer; *goods* livrer. **I will ~ the children to school tomorrow** j'emmènerai les enfants à l'école demain; **to ~ a child into sb's care** confier un enfant aux soins de qn; (*fig*) **he ~ed the goods*** il a fait ce qu'on attendait de lui. **(b)** (*rescue*) délivrer, sauver (*sb from sth* qn de qch). ~ **us from evil** délivrez-nous du mal. **(c)** *speech, sermon* prononcer; *ultimatum* lancer; *blow* porter, asséner. **(d)** *baby* mettre au monde; *woman* (faire) accoucher.
◆ **deliverance** *n* délivrance *f*. ◆ **deliverer** *n* sauveur *m*. ◆ **delivery** **1** *n [goods, parcels]* livraison *f*; *[letters]* distribution *f*; (*Med*) accouchement *m*; *[speaker]* débit *m*; **to take ~y of** prendre livraison de; **2** *adj note, service, truck* de livraison; ~**y man** livreur *m*; (*Med*) ~**y room** salle *f* de travail.
delouse [ˈdiːˈlaʊs] *vt* épouiller.
delta [ˈdeltə] *n* delta *m*. ~**-winged** à ailes en delta.
delude [dɪˈluːd] *vt* tromper, duper (*with* de). **to ~ sb into thinking that** faire croire à qn que; **to ~ o.s.** se faire des illusions. ◆ **deluded** *adj*: **to be ~d** être victime d'illusions; **the poor ~d boy said ...** dans son erreur le pauvre garçon dit ... . ◆ **delusion** *n* (*false belief*) illusion *f*; (*Psych*) fantasme *m*.
deluge [ˈdeljuːdʒ] **1** *n* déluge *m*. **a ~ of protests** un déluge de protestations; **a ~ of letters** une avalanche de lettres. **2** *vt* (*lit, fig*) inonder (*with* de).
delve [delv] *vi* fouiller, creuser.
demagogue [ˈdeməgɒg] *n* démagogue *m*.
demand [dɪˈmɑːnd] **1** *vt* (*gen*) exiger (*to do* de faire; *that* que + *subj*); *money, explanation, help, attention* exiger, réclamer (*from, of* de); *higher pay etc* revendiquer, réclamer. **2** *n* **(a)** *[person, situation etc]* exigence *f*; (*for better pay etc*) revendication *f*, réclamation *f*; (*for help, money*) demande *f*; (*Admin etc*: *letter*) avertissement *m*. **payable on ~** payable sur demande; **final ~ for payment** dernier avertissement d'avoir à payer; **to make great ~s on sb** exiger beaucoup de qn; *[child, work]* accaparer qn; **the ~s of the case** les nécessités *fpl* du cas. **(b)** (*Comm, Econ*) demande *f* (*for* pour). **to be in great ~** être très demandé; **the ~ for this product increases** ce produit est de plus en plus demandé; **there's no ~ for them** ils ne sont pas demandés. **3** *adj* (*Med*) ~ **feeding** alimentation *f* libre.
◆ **demanding** *adj person* exigeant; *work* astreignant; **physically ~ing** qui demande beaucoup de résistance physique.
demarcation [ˌdiːmɑːˈkeɪʃən] *n* démarcation *f*. ~ **line** ligne *f* de démarcation; ~ **dispute** conflit *m* d'attributions.
demean [dɪˈmiːn] *vt*: **to ~ o.s.** s'abaisser (*to do* à faire).
demeanour, (*US*) **-or** [dɪˈmiːnəʳ] *n* attitude *f*; (*bearing*) maintien *m*.
demented [dɪˈmentɪd] *adj* dément, fou. ◆ **dementedly** *adv* comme un fou.
demerara [ˌdeməˈrɛərə] *n* (~ *sugar*) cassonade *f*.
demi... [ˈdemɪ] *pref* demi-. ~**god** demi-dieu *m*; ~**tasse** (*cup*) tasse *f* (à moka); (*coffee*) (tasse de) café *m* noir.
demijohn [ˈdemɪdʒɒn] *n* dame-jeanne *f*.
demilitarize [ˈdiːˈmɪlɪtəraɪz] *vt* démilitariser. ◆ **demilitarization** *n* démilitarisation *f*.
demise [dɪˈmaɪz] *n* décès *m*.
demo* [ˈdeməʊ] *n* (*Brit abbr of* **demonstration**) manif* *f*.
demob* [ˈdiːˈmɒb] *abbr of* **demobilize, demobilization.**
demobilize [diːˈməʊbɪlaɪz] *vt* démobiliser. ◆ **demobilization** *n* démobilisation *f*.
democracy [dɪˈmɒkrəsɪ] *n* démocratie *f*. **people's ~** démocratie populaire; **they are working towards ~** ils sont en train de se démocratiser. ◆ **democrat** *n* démocrate *mf*. ◆ **democratic** *adj institution, spirit* démocratique; (*believing in democracy*) démocrate; (*Pol*) *party* démocrate. ◆ **democratically** *adv* démocratiquement. ◆ **democratize** **1** *vt* démocratiser; **2** *vi* se démocratiser.
demography [dɪˈmɒgrəfɪ] *n* démographie *f*. ◆ **demographer** *n* démographe *mf*. ◆ **demographic** *adj* démographique.
demolish [dɪˈmɒlɪʃ] *vt* (*gen*) démolir; (*) *cake* liquider*. ◆ **demolisher** *n* démolisseur *m*. ◆ **demolition** **1** *n* démolition *f*; **2** *adj*: **demolition squad** équipe *f* de démolition; **demolition zone** zone *f* de démolition.
demon [ˈdiːmən] *n* (*gen*) démon *m*. **to be a ~ for work** être un bourreau de travail. ◆ **demoniac(al)** [ˌdiːməˈnaɪək(əl)] *adj* démoniaque.
demonstrate [ˈdemənstreɪt] **1** *vt truth, need* démontrer; *system* expliquer, décrire; *appliance* faire une démonstration de. **to ~ how sth works** montrer le fonctionnement de qch, faire une démonstration de qch; **to ~ how to do** montrer comment faire. **2** *vi* (*Pol etc*) manifester, faire une manifestation (*for* pour, *against* contre). ◆ **demonstrable** *adj* démontrable. ◆ **demonstrably** *adv* manifestement. ◆ **demonstration** **1** *n* (*gen*) démonstration *f*; (*Pol etc*) manifestation *f*; **to hold a demonstration** manifester; **2** *adj car, model* de démonstration. ◆ **demonstrative** *adj* démonstratif. ◆ **demonstrator** *n* (*Comm*) démonstrateur *m*, -trice *f*; (*Univ*) chargé(e) *m(f)* de travaux pratiques; (*Pol*) manifestant(e) *m(f)*.
demoralize [dɪˈmɒrəlaɪz] *vt* démoraliser. **to become ~d** perdre courage. ◆ **demoralization** *n* démoralisation *f*. ◆ **demoralizing** *adj* démoralisant.
demote [dɪˈməʊt] *vt* rétrograder. ◆ **demotion** *n* rétrogradation *f*.
demur [dɪˈmɜːʳ] **1** *vi* élever des objections (*at sth* contre qch). **2** *n*: **without ~** sans faire de difficultés.
demure [dɪˈmjʊəʳ] *adj* sage, modeste. ◆ **demurely** *adv* sagement, modestement. ◆ **demureness** *n* sagesse *f*, air *m* modeste.
den [den] *n [animal]* antre *m*; *[thieves]* repaire *m*; (*: *room, study*) antre, turne* *f*. ~ **of iniquity** lieu *m* de perdition.
denationalize [diːˈnæʃnəlaɪz] *vt* dénationaliser. ◆ **denationalization** *n* dénationalisation *f*.
denial [dɪˈnaɪəl] *n [rights, guilt, truth]* dénégation *f*; *[authority]* reniement *m*. ~ **of justice** déni *m* de justice; **to issue a ~** publier un démenti; **Peter's ~ of Christ** le reniement du Christ.
denigrate [ˈdenɪgreɪt] *vt* dénigrer.
denim [ˈdenɪm] **1** *n* toile *f* de jean, (*heavier*) treillis *m*. ~**s** (*npl*) (*trousers*) blue-jean *m*; (*overalls*) bleus *mpl* de travail. **2** *adj jacket, skirt* en toile de jean.
Denmark [ˈdenmɑːk] *n* Danemark *m*.
denomination [dɪˌnɒmɪˈneɪʃən] *n* (*Rel*) confession *f* (*secte*); *[money]* valeur *f*.
denominator [dɪˈnɒmɪneɪtəʳ] *n* dénominateur *m*.
denote [dɪˈnəʊt] *vt* (*gen*) dénoter; *[word]* signifier.
denounce [dɪˈnaʊns] *vt* (*gen*) dénoncer (*to* à). **to ~ sb as an impostor** accuser publiquement qn d'imposture.
dense [dens] *adj* (*gen*) dense; (*: *stupid*) bête, bouché*. ◆ **densely** *adv*: ~**ly wooded** couvert de forêts épaisses; ~**ly populated** très peuplé. ◆ **density** *n* densité *f*.
dent [dent] **1** *n* (*in wood*) entaille *f*; (*in metal*) bosse *f*, bosselure *f*; (*: *in savings*) trou *m*. **to have a ~ in the bumper** avoir le pare-choc bosselé *or*

cabossé. **2** *vt hat* cabosser; *car* bosseler, cabosser.

dental ['dentl] *adj* dentaire. ~ **surgeon** chirurgien *m* dentiste; ~ **technician** mécanicien *m* dentiste.

dentifrice ['dentɪfrɪs] *n* dentifrice *m*.

dentist ['dentɪst] *n* dentiste *mf*. ~**'s chair** fauteuil *m* de dentiste; ~**'s surgery** cabinet *m* de dentiste. ♦ **dentistry** *n*: **to study** ~**ry** faire l'école dentaire.

dentures ['dentʃəz] *npl* dentier *m*.

denude [dɪ'nju:d] *vt* dénuder.

denunciation [dɪˌnʌnsɪ'eɪʃən] *n* dénonciation *f*; (*in public*) accusation *f* publique.

deny [dɪ'naɪ] *vt* nier (*having done* avoir fait; *that* que + *indic or subj*); *fact, accusation* nier; *leader, religion* renier. **there is no** ~**ing it** c'est indéniable; **to** ~ **sb sth** refuser qch à qn; **to** ~ **o.s. cigarettes** se priver de cigarettes.

deodorant [di:'əʊdərənt] *adj, n* déodorant (*m*). ♦ **deodorize** *vt* déodoriser.

depart [dɪ'pɑ:t] *vi* (*gen*) partir; (*from rule*) s'écarter (*from* de); (*from custom*) faire une entorse (*from* à). **to** ~ **from a city** quitter une ville, partir *or* s'en aller d'une ville. ♦ **departed 1** *adj* (*dead*) défunt; (*bygone*) *glory, happiness* passé; *friends* disparu; **2** *n, pl inv* défunt(e) *m(f)*. ♦ **departure 1** *n* (*gen*) départ *m*; (*from custom, principle, truth*) entorse *f* (*from* à); (*Comm: new type of goods*) nouveauté *f*; **a** ~**ure from the norm** une exception à la règle; **it's a new** ~**ure in biochemistry** c'est une nouvelle voie qui s'ouvre en biochimie; **2** *adj preparations, gate, time* de départ; ~**ure indicator** horaire *m* des départs; ~**ure lounge** salle *f* de départ.

department [dɪ'pɑ:tmənt] **1** *n* (*Admin*) département *m*; (*Ind*) service *m*; *[shop, store]* rayon *m*; *[smaller shop]* comptoir *m*; (*Scol, Univ*) section *f*; (*French Admin, Geog*) département; (*fig: field of activity*) domaine *m*, rayon. **D~ of Employment** ≃ ministère *m* du Travail; (*US*) **D~ of State** Département d'État; **which government** ~**?** quel ministère?; (*Comm*) **the shoe** ~ le rayon des chaussures; **gardening is my wife's** ~* le jardinage, c'est le rayon de ma femme. **2** *adj*: ~ **store** grand magasin. ♦ **departmental** *adj* d'un *or* du département *or* ministère *or* service; d'une *or* de la section; *[France]* départemental; *[shop]* ~**al manager** chef *m* de rayon.

depend [dɪ'pend] *vi* dépendre (*on sb/sth* de qn/qch). **it all** ~**s** ça dépend; **it** ~**s on whether he will do it or not** ça dépend s'il veut le faire ou non; **it** ~**s what you mean** ça dépend de ce que vous voulez dire (*by* par); ~**ing on what happens tomorrow ...** selon ce qui se passera demain ... .

depend (up)on *vt fus* compter sur. **I'm** ~**ing on you to tell me what he wants** je compte sur vous pour savoir ce qu'il veut; **I'm** ~**ing on you for moral support** je compte sur votre soutien; **you can** ~ **(up)on it** soyez-en sûr, je vous le garantis; **he** ~**s (up)on his father for money** il dépend de son père pour son argent. ♦ **dependability** *n [machine]* sécurité *f* de fonctionnement; *[person]* sérieux *m*; **his** ~**ability is well-known** tout le monde sait qu'on peut compter sur lui. ♦ **dependable** *adj person* sérieux, sur qui on peut compter; *mechanism* fiable; *vehicle* solide; *information* sûr. ♦ **dependant** *n* personne *f* à charge. ♦ **dependence** *n* dépendance *f* (*on* à l'égard de). ♦ **dependency** *n* dépendance *f*. ♦ **dependent 1** *adj* (*gen*) dépendant (*on* de); *child, relative* à charge; **to be** ~**ent on** dépendre de; **2** *n* personne *f* à charge.

depersonalize [di:'pɜ:sənəlaɪz] *vt* dépersonnaliser.

depict [dɪ'pɪkt] *vt* (*in words*) dépeindre; (*in picture*) représenter.

depilatory [dɪ'pɪlətərɪ] *adj, n* dépilatoire (*m*).

deplenish [dɪ'plenɪʃ] *vt* dégarnir.

deplete [dɪ'pli:t] *vt* (*reduce*) réduire; (*exhaust*) épuiser. **our stock is very** ~**d** nos stocks sont très bas; **numbers were greatly** ~**d** les effectifs étaient très réduits. ♦ **depletion** *n* réduction *f*; épuisement *m*.

deplore [dɪ'plɔ:ʳ] *vt* déplorer, regretter vivement. **to** ~ **the fact that** déplorer le fait que + *indic*, regretter vivement que + *subj*. ♦ **deplorable** *adj* déplorable. ♦ **deplorably** *adv* déplorablement.

deploy [dɪ'plɔɪ] *vt* déployer. ♦ **deployment** *n* déploiement *m*.

deponent [dɪ'pəʊnənt] *adj, n* déponent (*m*).

depopulate [ˌdi:'pɒpjʊleɪt] *vt* dépeupler. ♦ **depopulation** *n* dépeuplement *m*; **rural depopulation** exode *m* rural.

deport [dɪ'pɔ:t] *vt* expulser; (*Hist*) *convict* déporter. ♦ **deportation** *n* expulsion *f*; déportation *f*; (*Jur*) ~**ation order** arrêt *m* d'expulsion.

depose [dɪ'pəʊz] *vt king* déposer; *official* destituer. ♦ **deposition** *n* déposition *f*.

deposit [dɪ'pɒzɪt] **1** *vt* (*all senses*) déposer (*in or with the bank* à la banque; *sth with sb* qch chez qn). **2** *n* **(a)** (*in bank*) dépôt *m*. **(b)** (*part payment*) arrhes *fpl*, acompte *m*; (*in hire purchase*) premier versement *m* comptant; (*in hiring goods, against damage etc*) caution *f*; (*on bottle etc*) consigne *f*. **to leave a £2** ~ **on a dress** verser 2 livres d'arrhes *or* d'acompte sur une robe; (*Pol*) **to lose one's** ~ perdre son cautionnement. **(c)** (*Chem, Geol etc*) dépôt *m*; *[mineral, oil]* gisement *m*. **to form a** ~ se déposer. **3** *adj*: ~ **account** compte *m* de dépôt; ~ **slip** bulletin *m* de versement. ♦ **depositor** *n* déposant(e) *m(f)*. ♦ **depository** *n* dépôt *m*.

depot ['depəʊ, (*US*) 'di:pəʊ] *n* dépôt *m*.

deprave [dɪ'preɪv] *vt* dépraver. ♦ **depraved** *adj* dépravé. ♦ **depravity** *n* dépravation *f*.

deprecate ['deprɪkeɪt] *vt* désapprouver. ♦ **deprecating** *adj* (*disapproving*) désapprobateur; (*apologetic*) humble; **a deprecating smile** un sourire d'excuse. ♦ **deprecatingly** *adv* d'un ton désapprobateur; avec l'air de s'excuser.

depreciate [dɪ'pri:ʃɪeɪt] **1** *vt* déprécier. **2** *vi* se déprécier. ♦ **depreciation** *n* dépréciation *f*.

depredations [ˌdeprɪ'deɪʃənz] *npl* déprédations *fpl*.

depress [dɪ'pres] *vt person* déprimer; *trade* réduire; *the market, prices* faire baisser; (*press down*) *lever* abaisser. ♦ **depressant** *adj, n* dépresseur (*m*). ♦ **depressed** *adj industry, area* en déclin, touché par la crise; (*Fin*) *market, trade* en crise; *business* dans le marasme; *class, group* économiquement faible; *person* déprimé; **to feel** ~**ed** se sentir déprimé, avoir le cafard*; **to get** ~**ed** se décourager, se laisser abattre. ♦ **depressing** *adj* déprimant, décourageant; **I find it** ~**ing** ça me donne le cafard*. ♦ **depressingly** *adv* d'une manière déprimante *or* décourageante; ~**ingly monotonous** d'une monotonie déprimante. ♦ **depression** *n* (*gen, Econ, Med, Met etc*) dépression *f*; *[lever, key etc]* abaissement *m*; **the D~ion** la crise de 1929; **the economy was in a state of** ~**ion** l'économie était dans le marasme *or* en crise. ♦ **depressive** *adj, n* dépressif (*m*), -ive (*f*).

deprive [dɪ'praɪv] *vt* priver (*of* de). **to** ~ **o.s. of** se priver de; ~**d child/family** enfant/famille déshérité(e). ♦ **deprivation** *n* privation *f*; (*Psych*) carence *f* affective.

depth [depθ] **1** *n* (*gen*) profondeur *f*; *[shelf, cupboard]* profondeur, largeur *f*; *[snow]* épaisseur *f*; *[edge, border]* largeur, hauteur *f*; *[knowledge, relief]* profondeur; *[feeling, sorrow, colour]* intensité *f*. **at a** ~ **of 3 metres** à 3 mètres de profondeur, par 3 mètres de fond; (*lit, fig*) **to get out of one's** ~ perdre pied; (*fig*) **I am quite out of my** ~ je nage complètement*; **the** ~**s of the ocean** les profondeurs océaniques; **to study in** ~ étudier en profondeur; **to be in the** ~**s of despair** toucher le fond du désespoir; **I would never sink to such ~s as to do that** je ne tomberais jamais assez bas pour faire cela; **in the ~ of** *winter* au plus fort de; *night, forest* au plus profond de. 2 *adj*: **~ charge** grenade *f* sous-marine; **in-~ interview** interview *f* en profondeur.

depute [dɪ'pju:t] *vt power, authority* déléguer; *person* députer (*sb to do* qn pour faire). ♦ **deputation** *n* députation *f*.

deputy ['depjʊtɪ] 1 *n* (*second in command*) adjoint(e) *m(f)*; (*replacement*) suppléant(e) *m(f)*, remplaçant(e) *m(f)*; (*Pol*) député *m*. 2 *adj* adjoint. **~ chairman** vice-président *m*; **~ head** directeur *m* adjoint. ♦ **deputize** *vi* assurer l'intérim (*for sb* de qn).

derail [dɪ'reɪl] *vt* faire dérailler. ♦ **derailment** *n* déraillement *m*.

derange [dɪ'reɪndʒ] *vt plan* déranger; *machine* dérégler; (*Med*) déranger. **~d person/mind** personne *f*/esprit *m* dérangé(e); **to be (mentally) ~d** avoir le cerveau dérangé.

derelict ['derɪlɪkt] *adj* (*abandoned*) abandonné; (*ruined*) en ruines.
♦ **dereliction** *n*: **~ion of duty** négligence *f* (dans le service).

derestricted [,di:rɪ'strɪktɪd] *adj* (*Aut*) sans limitation de vitesse.

deride [dɪ'raɪd] *vt* tourner en ridicule. ♦ **derision** *n* dérision *f*. ♦ **derisive** *adj smile, person* railleur; *amount, offer* dérisoire. ♦ **derisively** *adv* d'un ton railleur *or* de dérision. ♦ **derisory** *adj* dérisoire.

derive [dɪ'raɪv] 1 *vt profit, satisfaction* tirer (*from* de); *comfort, ideas* puiser (*from* dans); *name, origins* tenir (*from* de); *happiness* trouver (*from* dans).
2 *vi*: **to ~ from** (*also* **be ~d from**) dériver de; *[power, fortune]* provenir de; *[idea]* avoir sa source dans; **it all ~s from the fact that** tout cela tient au fait que.
♦ **derivation** *n* dérivation *f*. ♦ **derivative** *adj* (*Chem, Ling, Math*) dérivé; *literary work etc* peu original.

dermatitis [,dɜ:mə'taɪtɪs] *n* dermatite *f*.
♦ **dermatologist** *n* dermatologue *mf*.
♦ **dermatology** *n* dermatologie *f*.

derogatory [dɪ'rɒgətərɪ] *adj* désobligeant (*of, to* à).

derrick ['derɪk] *n* (*Naut*) mât *m* de charge; (*above oil well*) derrick *m*.

derv [dɜ:v] *n* (*Brit*) gas-oil *m*.

descale [di:'skeɪl] *vt* détartrer.

descend [dɪ'send] 1 *vi* (*gen*) descendre (*from* de); *[property, customs, rights]* passer (*from* de, *to* à). (*Mil, fig*) **to ~ on** faire une descente sur; **sadness ~ed upon him** la tristesse l'a envahi; **in ~ing order of importance** par ordre d'importance décroissante; **visitors ~ed upon us** des gens sont arrivés chez nous sans crier gare; **to ~ to (doing) sth** s'abaisser à faire qch.
2 *vt stairs* descendre. **to be ~ed from sb** descendre de qn.
♦ **descendant** *n* descendant(e) *m(f)*. ♦ **descent** *n* (*gen*) descente *f* (*into* dans); (*fig: into crime etc*) chute *f*; (*ancestry*) origine *f*, famille *f*.

describe [dɪs'kraɪb] *vt* **(a)** *scene, person* décrire, faire la description de. **~ what it is like** racontez *or* dites comment c'est; **~ him for us** décrivez-le-nous; **he ~s himself as a doctor** il se dit *or* se prétend docteur.
(b) (*Math*) décrire.
♦ **description** *n* description *f*; (*Police*) signalement *m*; **beyond description** indescriptible; **vehicles of every description** véhicules de toutes sortes. ♦ **descriptive** *adj* descriptif.

descry [dɪs'kraɪ] *vt* discerner, distinguer.

desecrate ['desɪkreɪt] *vt* profaner. ♦ **desecration** *n* profanation *f*.

desegregate [,di:'segrɪgeɪt] *vt* abolir la ségrégation raciale dans. **~d schools** écoles *fpl* où la ségrégation raciale n'est plus pratiquée.
♦ **desegregation** *n* déségrégation *f*.

desert[1] ['dezət] 1 *n* désert *m*. 2 *adj region, climate, animal, plant* désertique. **~ boot** chaussure *f* montante; **~ island** île *f* déserte.

desert[2] [dɪ'zɜ:t] 1 *vt* (*gen*) déserter; *spouse, family, friend* abandonner. **his courage ~ed him** son courage l'a abandonné. 2 *vi* (*Mil*) déserter; (*from one's party*) faire défection. **to ~ to** passer du côté de.
♦ **deserted** *adj place* désert; *wife* abandonné.
♦ **deserter** *n* (*Mil*) déserteur *m*; (*to the enemy*) transfuge *m*. ♦ **desertion** *n* désertion *f*; abandon *m*; défection *f*.

deserts [dɪ'zɜ:ts] *npl*: **according to his ~** selon ses mérites; **to get one's (just) ~** recevoir ce que l'on mérite.

deserve [dɪ'zɜ:v] *vt* mériter (*to do* de faire). **he ~s to be pitied** il mérite qu'on le plaigne, il est digne de pitié; **he got what he ~d** il n'a eu que ce qu'il méritait. ♦ **deservedly** *adv* à juste titre.
♦ **deserving** *adj person* méritant; *action, cause* méritoire; **she's a deserving case** c'est une personne méritante.

desiccate ['desɪkeɪt] *vt* dessécher. **~d coconut** noix *f* de coco séchée.

design [dɪ'zaɪn] 1 *n* **(a)** (*intention*) dessein *m*, intention *f*. **by ~** à dessein, exprès; **to have ~s on sb/sth** avoir des visées sur qn/qch. **(b)** (*plan drawn in detail*) plan *m*, dessin *m* (*of, for* de); (*preliminary sketch*) étude *f* (*for* de). **I like the ~ of this building/car/dress** *etc* j'aime ce type d'immeuble/de voiture/de robe *etc*; **the latest ~ in ...** le dernier modèle de ...; *[art student etc]* **to study ~** étudier le stylisme; **industrial ~** la création industrielle. **(c)** (*pattern: on pottery etc*) motif *m*, dessin *m* (*on* sur).
2 *vt* **(a)** (*think out*) *object, scheme* concevoir. **well-~ed** bien conçu; **~ed as sth** conçu pour être qch; **~ed to hold sth** fait pour contenir qch. **(b)** (*work out plans on paper for*) *object* dessiner; *scheme* élaborer.
♦ **designedly** *adv* à dessein, exprès. ♦ **designer** *n* *[machine, car]* concepteur *m*; *[furniture, household articles]* styliste *mf*; *[building]* architecte *m*; *[theatre sets]* décorateur *m*, -trice *f*. ♦ **designing** *adj* (*scheming*) intrigant.

designate ['dezɪgneɪt] 1 *vt* désigner (*as* comme; *to do* pour faire).
2 ['dezɪgnɪt] *adj* (*après le nom*) désigné.
♦ **designation** *n* désignation *f*.

desire [dɪ'zaɪəʳ] 1 *n* désir *m* (*for* de; *to do* de faire). **I have no ~ to do it** je n'ai nullement envie de le faire.
2 *vt* **(a)** (*want*) désirer, vouloir (*sth* qch; *to do* faire; *that* que + *subj*). **his work leaves much to be ~d** son travail laisse beaucoup à désirer. **(b)** (*request*) prier (*sb to do* qn de faire).
♦ **desirability** *n* *[plan etc]* avantages *mpl*.
♦ **desirable** *adj* désirable; **it is desirable that** il est désirable *or* souhaitable que + *subj*; **'desirable residence'** 'belle propriété'. ♦ **desirous** *adj* désireux (*of* de).

desist [dɪ'zɪst] *vi* cesser (*from sth* qch; *from doing* de faire).

desk [desk] 1 *n* (*gen*) bureau *m*; *[pupil]* pupitre *m*; (*in shop, restaurant*) caisse *f*; (*in hotel, at airport*) réception *f*. (*Press*) **the news ~** le service des informations. 2 *adj lamp, diary* de bureau. **~ clerk** réceptionniste *mf*; **~ job** travail *m* de bureau.

desolate ['desəlɪt] *adj place* désolé, désert; *outlook, future* sombre, morne; *person* (*grief-stricken*) au désespoir; (*friendless*) délaissé; *cry* de désespoir.
♦ **desolately** *adv* d'un air désolé (*or* sombre *etc*).

♦ **desolation** *n* désolation *f*; *[landscape]* aspect *m* désert.

despair [dɪsˈpɛəʳ] **1** *n* désespoir *m* (*about, at, over* au sujet de; *at having done* d'avoir fait). **in ~** désespéré; **to drive sb to ~** réduire qn au désespoir. **2** *vi* (se) désespérer. **don't ~!** ne (te) désespère pas!; **to ~ of (doing) sth** désespérer de (faire) qch; **his life was ~ed of** on désespérait de le sauver. ♦ **despairing** *adj* désespéré; (*) *situation* catastrophique. ♦ **despairingly** *adv say* d'un ton désespéré; *look* d'un air désespéré; *agree, answer* avec désespoir; *look for* désespérément.

despatch [dɪsˈpætʃ] = **dispatch.**

desperate [ˈdespərɪt] *adj* (*gen*) désespéré; *criminal* prêt à tout; (*: *very bad*) atroce*, abominable. **to feel ~** être désespéré; **to do something ~** commettre un acte de désespoir; **I am ~ for money** j'ai désespérément besoin d'argent. ♦ **desperately** *adv struggle, regret* désespérément; *say, look* avec désespoir; *cold, needy* terriblement; *ill* très gravement; **~ly in love** éperdument amoureux. ♦ **desperation** *n* désespoir *m*; **to be in desperation** être au désespoir; **to drive sb to desperation** pousser qn à bout; **in desperation she killed him** poussée à bout elle l'a tué; **in sheer desperation** en désespoir de cause.

despicable [dɪsˈpɪkəbl] *adj* ignoble, méprisable. ♦ **despicably** *adv* d'une façon ignoble *or* méprisable.

despise [dɪsˈpaɪz] *vt* mépriser (*for sth* pour qch; *for doing* pour avoir fait). ♦ **despisingly** *adv* avec mépris.

despite [dɪsˈpaɪt] *prep* malgré, en dépit de.

despondency [dɪsˈpɒndənsɪ] *n* découragement *m*, abattement *m*. ♦ **despondent** *adj* découragé, abattu (*about* par). ♦ **despondently** *adv* avec découragement.

despot [ˈdespɒt] *n* despote *m*. ♦ **despotic** *adj* despotique. ♦ **despotically** *adv* despotiquement. ♦ **despotism** *n* despotisme *m*.

dessert [dɪˈzɜːt] **1** *n* dessert *m*. **2** *adj*: **~ plate** assiette *f* à dessert; **~ spoon** cuiller *f* à dessert.

destination [ˌdestɪˈneɪʃən] *n* destination *f*.

destine [ˈdestɪn] *vt person, object* destiner (*for* à; *to do* à faire). **~d for** *[train etc]* à destination de; *[writer etc]* destiné à. ♦ **destiny** *n* destin *m*, destinée *f*, sort *m*.

destitute [ˈdestɪtjuːt] *adj* indigent, sans ressources. **utterly ~** dans le dénuement le plus complet. ♦ **destitution** *n* dénuement *m*, indigence *f*.

destroy [dɪsˈtrɔɪ] *vt* (*gen*) détruire; *toy, gadget* démolir; *dangerous animal, injured horse* abattre; *cat, dog* faire piquer. **to ~ o.s.** se suicider; **the village was ~ed by a fire** un incendie a ravagé le village. ♦ **destroyer** *n* (*ship*) contre-torpilleur *m*; (*person*) destructeur *m*, -trice *f*. ♦ **destruct** *vt* détruire volontairement. ♦ **destructible** *adj* destructible. ♦ **destruction** *n* destruction *f*; (*from war, fire*) dégâts *mpl*, dommages *mpl*; **destruction by fire** destruction par un incendie *or* par le feu. ♦ **destructive** *adj person, criticism* destructeur; (*potentially so*) *power* destructif. ♦ **destructively** *adv* de façon destructrice. ♦ **destructiveness** *n* (*gen*) caractère *or* effet destructeur; *[child etc]* penchant destructeur. ♦ **destructor** *n* (*refuse ~*) incinérateur *m* (à ordures).

desultory [ˈdesəltərɪ] *adj reading* sans suite; *attempt* peu soutenu; *firing, contact* irrégulier. **to have a ~ conversation** échanger des propos décousus.

detach [dɪˈtætʃ] *vt* détacher (*from* de). ♦ **detachable** *adj* détachable (*from* de); *collar, lining* amovible. ♦ **detached** *adj part, section* détaché; *opinion* objectif; *manner* détaché, indifférent; **~ed house** = pavillon *m*. ♦ **detachment** *n* détachement *m*.

detail [ˈdiːteɪl] **1** *n* **(a)** détail *m*. **in ~** en détail; **in great ~** dans les moindres détails; **his attention to ~** l'attention qu'il apporte au détail; **to go into ~s** entrer dans les détails. **(b)** (*Mil*) détachement *m*. **2** *vt* **(a)** *reasons, facts* exposer en détail; *story, event* raconter en détail; *items, objects* énumérer. **(b)** (*Mil*) *troops* détacher (*for* pour, *to do* pour faire). ♦ **detailed** *adj* détaillé.

detain [dɪˈteɪn] *vt* retenir; (*in prison*) détenir.

detect [dɪˈtekt] *vt culprit, secret* découvrir; *sadness* déceler; *object, movement, noise* distinguer; *mine, gas* détecter. ♦ **detectable** *adj* qu'on peut découvrir *or* discerner *or* détecter. ♦ **detection** *n* découverte *f*; détection *f*; **the ~ion of crime** la chasse aux criminels; **to escape ~ion** *[criminal]* échapper aux recherches; *[mistake]* passer inaperçu. ♦ **detective** *n* agent *m* de la sûreté, policier *m* en civil; (*private ~*) détective *m* (privé); **~ive story** roman *m* policier. ♦ **detector 1** *n* détecteur *m*; **2** *adj* (*TV*) **~or van** voiture *f* gonio.

detention [dɪˈtenʃən] *n [criminal, spy]* détention *f*; (*Mil*) arrêts *mpl*; (*Scol*) retenue *f*. (*Brit Jur*) **~ centre,** (*US*) **~ home** centre *m* de redressement.

deter [dɪˈtɜːʳ] *vt* (*prevent*) détourner (*from sth* de qch), dissuader (*from doing* de faire); (*discourage*) décourager (*from doing* de faire). **a weapon which ~s no one** une arme qui ne dissuade personne.

detergent [dɪˈtɜːdʒənt] *adj, n* détergent (*m*).

deteriorate [dɪˈtɪərɪəreɪt] *vi* (*gen*) se détériorer; *[species, morals]* dégénérer; *[situation]* se dégrader; *[work]* devenir moins bon. ♦ **deterioration** *n* détérioration *f*; dégénération *f*; dégradation *f*.

determine [dɪˈtɜːmɪn] *vt* (*gen*) déterminer; *frontier* délimiter; *sb's character, future* décider de; (*resolve*) décider (*to do* de faire); (*cause to decide*) *person* décider (*to do* à faire).

determine (up)on *vt fus* décider de, résoudre de (*doing* faire); *course of action* se résoudre à; *alternative* choisir.

♦ **determinable** *adj* déterminable. ♦ **determination** *n* détermination *f* (*to do* de faire). ♦ **determinative** *adj* déterminant; (*Gram*) déterminatif. ♦ **determined** *adj* décidé; **to be ~d to do/that** être déterminé *or* décidé à faire/à ce que + *subj*. ♦ **determiner** *n* déterminant *m*. ♦ **determining** *adj* déterminant.

deterrent [dɪˈterənt] *n* force *f* de dissuasion. **to act as a ~** exercer un effet de dissuasion.

detest [dɪˈtest] *vt* détester, avoir horreur de (*doing* faire). ♦ **detestable** *adj* détestable. ♦ **detestably** *adv* détestablement. ♦ **detestation** *n* haine *f*.

dethrone [diːˈθrəʊn] *vt* détrôner.

detonate [ˈdetəneɪt] **1** *vi* détoner. **2** *vt* faire détoner. ♦ **detonation** *n* détonation *f*. ♦ **detonator** *n* détonateur *m*.

detour [ˈdiːˌtʊəʳ] *n* (*gen*) détour *m*; (*for traffic*) déviation *f*. *[person, road]* **to make a ~** faire un détour.

detract [dɪˈtrækt] *vi*: **to ~ from** *quality, pleasure, merit* diminuer; *reputation* porter atteinte à. ♦ **detractor** *n* détracteur *m*, -trice *f*.

detriment [ˈdetrɪmənt] *n* détriment *m*, préjudice *m*. **to the ~ of** au détriment de; **without ~ to** sans porter préjudice à. ♦ **detrimental** *adj* nuisible; **to be ~al to** nuire à.

detritus [dɪˈtraɪtəs] *n* (*Geol*) roches *fpl* détritiques; (*fig*) détritus *m*.

deuce [djuːs] *n* (*Cards etc*) deux *m*; (*Tennis*) égalité *f*.

devalue [ˈdiːˈvæljuː] *vt* dévaluer. ♦ **devaluation** *n* dévaluation *f*.

devastate [ˈdevəsteɪt] *vt place* dévaster, ravager; *opponent, opposition* anéantir; (*astound*) *person* foudroyer. ♦ **devastating** *adj wind, storm, power, passion* dévastateur; *news, grief, argument,* *effect* accablant; ***wit, humour, charm, woman*** irrésistible. ♦ **devastatingly** *adv beautiful, funny* irrésistiblement. ♦ **devastation** *n* dévastation *f*.

develop [dɪˈveləp] **1** *vt* **(a)** (*gen*) développer; (*change and improve*) *district etc* aménager (*as* en). **this ground is to be ~ed** on va bâtir sur ce terrain. **(b)** *habit, taste, cold* contracter; *tendency, talent* manifester. **2** *vi [person, region, plot]* se développer; *[illness, tendency, talent]* se manifester; *[feeling]* se former; (*Phot*) se développer; *[event, situation]* se produire. **to ~ into** devenir; **it later ~ed that ...** plus tard il est devenu évident que ... . ♦ **developer** *n* (*property* ~) promoteur *m* (de construction); (*Phot*) révélateur *m*. ♦ **developing 1** *adj crisis, storm* qui se prépare; *country* en voie de développement; *industry* en expansion; **2** *n* (*Phot*) développement *m*. ♦ **development 1** *n* (*gen*) développement *m* (*of sth* de qch); aménagement *m* (*of sth as* de qch en); (*in situation etc*) **a new ~ment** un fait nouveau; **to await ~ments** attendre la suite des événements; **2** *adj*: **~ment area** zone *f* d'aménagement concerté; **~ment company** société *f* d'exploitation.

deviate [ˈdiːvɪeɪt] *vi* **(a)** (*from truth, former statement etc*) dévier, s'écarter (*from* de). **to ~ from the norm** s'écarter de la norme. **(b)** *[ship, plane, projectile]* dévier. ♦ **deviance** *n* déviance *f* (*from* de). ♦ **deviant 1** *adj behaviour* qui s'écarte de la norme; *development* anormal; (*sexually*) perverti; **2** *n* déviant(e) *m(f)*. ♦ **deviation** *n* déviation *f* (*from* de).

device [dɪˈvaɪs] *n* **(a)** (*mechanical*) appareil *m*, mécanisme *m* (*for* pour). **nuclear ~** engin *m* nucléaire. **(b)** (*scheme*) formule *f* (*to do* pour faire). **to leave sb to his own ~s** laisser qn se débrouiller. **(c)** (*Her*) devise *f*.

devil [ˈdevl] **1** *n* **(a)** diable *m*. **poor ~!*** pauvre diable!; **you little ~!*** petit monstre!; (*hum*) **be a ~!** laisse-toi tenter!; **between the ~ and the deep blue sea** entre Charybde et Scylla; **go to the ~!*** va te faire voir!*; **he is going to the ~*** il court à sa perte; **his work has gone to the ~*** son travail ne vaut plus rien; **talk of the ~!** quand on parle du loup on en voit la queue!; **to be the ~'s advocate** se faire l'avocat du diable; **to give the ~ his due ...** pour être honnête, il faut reconnaître que ...; **the luck of the ~*** une veine de pendu*. **(b)** (*: *also* **dickens**) **it's the ~ of a job to do ...** c'est un travail épouvantable de faire ... ; **he had the ~ of a job to find it** il a eu un mal fou à le trouver; **it's the ~ of a job to ...** c'est toute une affaire pour ...; **why the ~ ...?** pourquoi diable ...?; **to work/run** *etc* **like the ~** travailler/courir *etc* comme un fou; **to be in a ~ of a mess** être dans un sacré pétrin*; **there will be the ~ to pay** ça va faire du grabuge*.

2 *vt* (*Culin*) *kidneys* (faire) griller au poivre et à la moutarde.

♦ **devilish 1** *adj invention* diabolique; (*: *infuriating*) satané* (*before n*); **2** *adv difficult* diablement. ♦ **devilishly** *adv behave* diaboliquement; *difficult* diablement. ♦ **devilishness** *n [invention]* caractère *m* diabolique; *[behaviour]* méchanceté *f* diabolique. ♦ **devil-may-care** *adj* insouciant. ♦ **devilment** *n* (*mischief*) espièglerie *f*; (*spite*) malice *f*. ♦ **devilry** *or* ♦ **deviltry** (*US*) *n* (*daring*) témérité *f*; (*mischief*) espièglerie *f*, (*stronger*) malice *f*.

devious [ˈdiːvɪəs] *adj route, means, method* détourné; *path, mind* tortueux. **he's very ~** il n'est pas franc. ♦ **deviously** *adv act* d'une façon détournée. ♦ **deviousness** *n [person]* sournoiserie *f*; *[scheme, method]* complexités *fpl*.

devise [dɪˈvaɪz] *vt scheme, style* inventer, concevoir; *plot* tramer; *escape* combiner.

devoid [dɪˈvɔɪd] *adj*: **~ of** dénué de, dépourvu de.

devolution [ˌdiːvəˈluːʃən] *n* (*Pol etc*) décentralisation *f*.

devolve [dɪˈvɒlv] *vi [work, responsibility]* retomber (*on* sur); *[property]* passer (*on* à).

devote [dɪˈvəʊt] *vt* consacrer (*to* à). **to ~ o.s. to** *a cause, study, hobby* se consacrer à; *pleasure* se livrer à. ♦ **devoted** *adj* (*gen*) dévoué; *admirer* fervent. ♦ **devotedly** *adv* avec dévouement. ♦ **devotee** *n [doctrine]* partisan *m*; *[religion]* adepte *mf*; *[sport, music, poetry]* passionné(e) *m(f)*. ♦ **devotion** *n* dévouement *m* (*to sth* à qch; *to sb* à *or* envers qn); (*Rel*) dévotion *f*. ♦ **devotional** *adj book* de dévotion.

devour [dɪˈvaʊəʳ] *vt* dévorer. ♦ **devouring** *adj* dévorant.

devout [dɪˈvaʊt] *adj person* pieux, dévot; *prayer, hope* fervent. ♦ **devoutly** *adv pray* avec dévotion; *hope* bien vivement.

dew [djuː] *n* rosée *f*. ♦ **dewdrop** *n* goutte *f* de rosée. ♦ **dewy** *adj* humide de rosée. ♦ **dewy-eyed** *adj* (*tearful*) le regard brillant de larmes; (*innocent*) aux grands yeux ingénus.

dexterity [deksˈterɪtɪ] *n* (*skill: physical, mental*) adresse *f*, dextérité *f* (*in doing* à faire). ♦ **dext(e)rous** *adj* adroit. ♦ **dext(e)rously** *adv* adroitement, avec dextérité.

diabetes [ˌdaɪəˈbiːtiːz] *n* diabète *m*. ♦ **diabetic** *adj, n* diabétique (*mf*).

diabolic(al) [ˌdaɪəˈbɒlɪk(əl)] *adj* (*lit*) diabolique; (*: *dreadful*) épouvantable. ♦ **diabolically** *adv* diaboliquement.

diacritic [ˌdaɪəˈkrɪtɪk] *adj, n* diacritique (*m*).

diadem [ˈdaɪədem] *n* diadème *m*.

diaeresis [daɪˈerɪsɪs] *n* (*sign*) tréma *m*.

diagnose [ˈdaɪəgnəʊz] *vt* diagnostiquer. **it was ~d as bronchitis** on a diagnostiqué une bronchite. ♦ **diagnosis** *n, pl* **-oses** diagnostic *m*. ♦ **diagnostician** *n* diagnostiqueur *m*.

diagonal [daɪˈægənl] **1** *adj* diagonal. **2** *n* diagonale *f*. ♦ **diagonally** *adv cut, fold* en diagonale; *opposite* diagonalement; **to go ~ly across** traverser en diagonale; **ribbon worn ~ly across the chest** ruban porté en écharpe sur la poitrine.

diagram [ˈdaɪəgræm] *n* schéma *m*, diagramme *m*; (*Math*) figure *f*.

dial [ˈdaɪəl] **1** *n* cadran *m*. **2** *vt* (*Telec*) *number* faire. **you must ~ 336-1295** il faut faire le 336-12-95; **to ~ 999** ≃ appeler Police Secours; **can I ~ London from here?** est-ce que d'ici je peux avoir Londres par l'automatique? ♦ **dialling** *adj*: **~ling code** indicatif *m*; **~ling tone** tonalité *f*.

dialect [ˈdaɪəlekt] **1** *n* dialecte *m*. **local ~** patois *m*. **2** *adj word* dialectal.

dialectic(s) [ˌdaɪəˈlektɪk(s)] *nsg* dialectique *f*.

dialogue [ˈdaɪəlɒg] *n* dialogue *m*.

dialysis [daɪˈæləsɪs] *n* dialyse *f*.

diameter [daɪˈæmɪtəʳ] *n* diamètre *m*. **it is one metre in ~** cela a un mètre de diamètre. ♦ **diametrical** *adj* diamétral. ♦ **diametrically** *adv* diamétralement.

diamond [ˈdaɪəmənd] **1** *n* (*stone*) diamant *m*; (*Cards*) carreau *m*; (*Baseball*) terrain *m*. **the ace of ~s** l'as *m* de carreau; **he played a ~** il a joué carreau. **2** *adj clip, ring* de diamant(s). **~ jubilee** soixantième anniversaire *m* (*d'un événement*); **~ merchant** diamantaire *m*; **~ necklace** rivière *f* de diamants; **~ wedding** noces *fpl* de diamant. ♦ **diamond-shaped** *adj* en losange.

diaper [ˈdaɪəpəʳ] *n* (*US*) couche *f* (*de bébé*).

diaphragm [ˈdaɪəfræm] *n* diaphragme *m*.

diarrh(o)ea [ˌdaɪəˈriːə] *n* diarrhée *f*.

diary [ˈdaɪərɪ] *n* (*record*) journal *m* (intime); (*for engagements*) agenda *m*. **I've got it in my ~** je l'ai noté sur mon agenda.

diatribe [ˈdaɪətraɪb] *n* diatribe *f* (*against* contre).

dice [daɪs] **1** *n, pl inv* dé *m* (à jouer). **to play ~** jouer aux dés. **2** *vi* (*fig*) **to ~ with death** jouer avec la mort. **3** *vt vegetables* couper en dés. ♦ **dicey*** *adj* risqué.

dichotomy [dɪˈkɒtəmɪ] *n* dichotomie *f*.

dickens* ['dɪkɪnz] *n* = **devil (b).**
Dictaphone ['dɪktəfəʊn] *n* ® dictaphone *m* ®. ~ **typist** dactylo *f* qui travaille au dictaphone.
dictate [dɪk'teɪt] **1** *vt* dicter (*to* à). **his action was ~d by circumstances** il a agi comme le lui dictaient les circonstances. **2** *vi*: **to ~ to sb** imposer sa volonté à qn. **3** ['dɪkteɪt] *n*: **~s** préceptes *mpl; [conscience]* voix *f*. ♦ **dictation** *n* dictée *f*; **to sb's dictation** sous la dictée de qn; **at dictation speed** à une vitesse de dictée. ♦ **dictator** *n* dictateur *m*. ♦ **dictatorial** *adj* dictatorial. ♦ **dictatorially** *adv* dictatorialement, en dictateur. ♦ **dictatorship** *n* dictature *f*.
diction ['dɪkʃən] *n* diction *f*.
dictionary ['dɪkʃənrɪ] *n* dictionnaire *m*. **French ~** dictionnaire de français.
dictum ['dɪktəm] *n, pl* **dicta** (*maxim*) maxime *f*; (*pronouncement*) affirmation *f*.
did [dɪd] *pret of* **do**[1].
didactic [dɪ'dæktɪk] *adj* didactique.
diddle* ['dɪdl] *vt* rouler*, escroquer. **to ~ sb out of sth** soutirer qch à qn.
die[1] [daɪ] *n, pl* **dice** dé *m* (à jouer). **the ~ is cast** le sort en est jeté.
die[2] [daɪ] *vi* (*gen*) mourir (*of* de); *[engine, motor]* s'arrêter. **to be dying** être à l'agonie *or* à la mort; **to ~ a natural/violent death** mourir de sa belle mort/de mort violente; **he ~d a hero** il est mort en héros; (*fig*) **never say ~!** il ne faut jamais désespérer; **I nearly ~d*** (*laughing*) j'ai failli mourir de rire; (*fear*) j'ai failli mourir de peur; (*embarrassment*) je voulais rentrer sous terre; **to be dying to do*** mourir d'envie de faire; **I'm dying* for a coffee** j'ai une envie folle d'un café; **the secret ~d with him** il a emporté le secret dans la tombe; **bad habits ~ hard** les mauvaises habitudes ont la vie dure.
die away *vi [sound, voice]* s'éteindre.
die down *vi [plant]* se flétrir; *[emotion, protest, wind]* se calmer; *[fire]* (*in blazing building*) diminuer; (*in grate etc*) baisser; *[noise]* diminuer.
die off *vi* mourir les uns après les autres.
die out *vi* disparaître.
♦ **diehard** **1** *n* réactionnaire *mf*; **2** *adj* intransigeant.
diesel ['di:zəl] **1** *n* diesel *m*. **2** *adj*: **~ engine** (*Aut*) moteur *m* diesel; (*Rail*) motrice *f*; **~ fuel, ~ oil** gas-oil *m*; **~ train** autorail *m*.
diet ['daɪət] **1** *n* **(a)** (*restricted food*) régime *m*. **milk ~** régime lacté; **to go on a ~** se mettre au régime. **(b)** (*customary food*) alimentation *f*. **to live on a ~ of** se nourrir de. **2** *vi* suivre un régime. ♦ **dietary** *adj* de régime, diététique. ♦ **dietetic** *adj* diététique. ♦ **dietetics** *nsg* diététique *f*. ♦ **dietician** *n* diététicien(ne) *m(f)*.
differ ['dɪfə[r]] *vi* (*be different*) différer, être différent (*from* de); (*disagree*) ne pas être d'accord (*from sb* avec qn, *on or about sth* sur qch). **I beg to ~** permettez-moi de ne pas partager cette opinion.
difference ['dɪfrəns] *n* différence *f* (*in* de, *between* entre). **that makes a big ~ to me** c'est très important pour moi, cela compte beaucoup pour moi; **to make a ~ in sb/sth** changer qn/qch; **that makes all the ~** voilà qui change tout; **what ~ does it make if ...?** qu'est-ce que cela peut faire que ...? + *subj*; **it makes no ~** cela ne change rien; **it makes no ~ to me** cela m'est égal; **for all the ~ it makes** pour ce que cela change; **with this ~ that** à ceci près que; **a car with a ~** une voiture pas comme les autres*; **~ of opinion** différence d'opinions; (*quarrel*) différend *m*.
different ['dɪfrənt] *adj* **(a)** différent (*from* de), autre. **he wore a ~ tie each day** il portait chaque jour une cravate différente; **go and put on a ~ tie** va mettre une autre cravate; **I feel a ~ person** je me sens tout autre; (*rested etc*) j'ai l'impression d'avoir fait peau neuve; **let's do sth ~** faisons qch de nouveau; **quite a ~ way of doing** une tout autre manière de faire; **that's quite a ~ matter** c'est tout autre chose; **she's quite ~ from what you think** elle n'est pas du tout ce que vous croyez; **he wants to be ~** il veut se singulariser. **(b)** (*various*) différent, divers, plusieurs. **~ people noticed it** plusieurs personnes l'ont remarqué. ♦ **differential** **1** *adj* différentiel; **2** *n* (*Math*) différentielle *f*; (*Econ*) écart *m* salarial; (*Aut*) différentiel *m*. ♦ **differentiate** **1** *vt* différencier (*from* de); **2** *vi* faire la différence (*between* entre). ♦ **differentiation** *n* différenciation *f*. ♦ **differently** *adv* différemment, d'une manière différente (*from* de), autrement (*from* que); **he thinks ~ly** sa façon de penser n'est pas la même; (*doesn't agree*) il n'est pas de cet avis.
difficult ['dɪfɪkəlt] *adj* difficile. **~ to get on with** difficile à vivre; **it is ~ to know** il est difficile de savoir; **it's ~ to deny that ...** on ne peut guère nier que ... + *indic or subj*; **I find it ~ to believe** il m'est difficile de croire, j'ai de la peine à croire (*that* que); **the ~ thing is to begin** le plus difficile *or* dur c'est de commencer. ♦ **difficulty** *n* difficulté *f*; **she has ~y in walking** elle marche avec difficulté, elle a de la difficulté *or* du mal à marcher; **a slight ~y in breathing** un peu de gêne *f* dans la respiration; **there was some ~y in finding him** on a eu du mal à le trouver; **the ~y is to choose** le difficile, c'est de choisir; **to make ~ies for sb** créer des difficultés à qn; **to get into ~ies** se trouver en difficulté; **to get o.s. into ~y** se créer des ennuis; **I am in ~y** j'ai des difficultés, j'ai des problèmes *mpl*; **to be in (financial) ~ies** avoir des ennuis *mpl* d'argent; **he was in ~y over the rent** il était en difficulté pour son loyer; **he was working under great ~ies** il travaillait dans des conditions très difficiles; **I can see no ~y in what you suggest** je ne vois aucun obstacle à ce que vous suggérez; **he's having ~y or ~ies with ...** il a des ennuis *or* des problèmes avec ... .
diffident ['dɪfɪdənt] *adj person* qui manque d'assurance; *smile* embarrassé. **to be ~ about doing** hésiter à faire. ♦ **diffidence** *n* manque *m* d'assurance. ♦ **diffidently** *adv* avec timidité.
diffuse [dɪ'fju:z] **1** *vt* diffuser. **~d lighting** éclairage *m* indirect. **2** [dɪ'fju:s] *adj* diffus.
dig [dɪg] (*vb: pret, ptp* **dug**) **1** *n* **(a) to give sb a ~ in the ribs** donner un coup de coude dans les côtes de qn; (*: *sly remark*) **to have a ~ at sb** donner un coup de patte *or* de griffe à qn; **that's a ~ at Paul** c'est une pierre dans le jardin de Paul. **(b)** (*Archeol*) fouilles *fpl*. **to go on a ~** aller faire des fouilles. **2** *vt* **(a)** (*gen*) creuser; (*with spade*) bêcher; *potatoes* arracher. **(b)** (*thrust*) enfoncer (*sth into sth* qch dans qch). **(c)** (‡) **~ that guy!** vise un peu le type!*; **I ~ that!** ça me botte!*; **he really ~s jazz** il est vraiment fou de jazz; **I don't ~ that** ça me laisse froid. **3** *vi [dog, pig]* fouiller; *[person]* creuser (*into* dans); (*Tech*) fouiller; (*Archeol*) faire des fouilles. **to ~ for minerals** (creuser pour) extraire du minerai; **to ~ into one's pockets/the past** fouiller dans ses poches/le passé.
dig in **1** *vi* (*Mil*) se retrancher; (*: *eat*) attaquer* un repas (*or* un plat *etc*). **~ in!*** allez-y, mangez! **2** *vt sep compost etc* enterrer; *blade, knife* enfoncer. (*fig*) **to ~ one's heels in** se buter.
dig out *vt sep* déterrer. **to ~ sb out of the snow** sortir qn de la neige (à coups de pelles); **where did he ~ out* that old hat?** où a-t-il déniché ce vieux chapeau?
dig up *vt sep weeds, vegetables* arracher; *treasure, body* déterrer; *earth* retourner; *garden* piocher; (*: *find*) *fact, idea* dénicher.
♦ **digger** *n* (*machine*) pelleteuse *f*. ♦ **diggings** *npl* (*Archeol*) fouilles *fpl*.
digest [daɪ'dʒest] **1** *vti* (*lit, fig*) digérer. **it is not easily ~ed** ça se digère mal. **2** ['daɪdʒest] *n* (*summary*) sommaire *m*; (*magazine*) digest *m*.

♦ **digestible** *adj* facile à digérer. ♦ **digestion** *n* digestion *f.* ♦ **digestive** *adj* digestif; **~ive (biscuit)** sablé *m.*
digit ['dɪdʒɪt] *n* (*Math*) chiffre *m*; (*finger*) doigt *m.* ♦ **digital** *adj clock* à affichage numérique; *computer* numérique.
dignify ['dɪgnɪfaɪ] *vt* donner de la dignité à. ♦ **dignified** *adj* digne; **he is very dignified** il a beaucoup de dignité; **that is not very dignified** cela manque de dignité. ♦ **dignitary** *n* dignitaire *m.* ♦ **dignity** *n* dignité *f.*
digress [daɪ'gres] *vi* s'écarter (*from* de), faire une digression. ♦ **digression** *n* digression *f.*
digs* [dɪgz] *npl*: **to be in ~** avoir une chambre chez un particulier; **I took him back to his ~** je l'ai ramené chez lui.
dilapidated [dɪ'læpɪdeɪtɪd] *adj house* délabré; *clothes* dépenaillé; *book* déchiré. ♦ **dilapidation** *n [buildings]* délabrement *m.*
dilate [daɪ'leɪt] **1** *vt* dilater. **2** *vi* se dilater. ♦ **dilation** *n* dilatation *f.*
dilatory ['dɪlətərɪ] *adj person* lent; *action, policy* dilatoire. ♦ **dilatoriness** *n* lenteur *f* (*in doing* à faire).
dilemma [daɪ'lemə] *n* dilemme *m.* **on the horns of a ~** pris dans un dilemme.
diligent ['dɪlɪdʒənt] *adj student, work* appliqué, assidu; *person, search* laborieux. ♦ **diligence** *n* zèle *m*, assiduité *f.* ♦ **diligently** *adv* avec application *or* assiduité.
dill [dɪl] *n* aneth *m.*
dillydally ['dɪlɪdælɪ] *vi* lanterner, lambiner*. **no ~ing!** ne traînez pas!
dilute [daɪ'lu:t] *vt* (*gen, also fig*) diluer; *sauce, colour* délayer. ♦ **dilution** *n* dilution *f.*
dim [dɪm] **1** *adj light, sight, lamp* faible; *room, forest etc* sombre, obscur; *colour, metal* terne, sans éclat; *sound, memory, outline* vague; imprécis; (*: *stupid*) stupide, borné. **to take a ~ view of sb*** avoir une piètre opinion de qn; **she took a ~ view of his selling the car*** elle n'a pas du tout apprécié qu'il ait vendu la voiture.
2 *vt light* baisser; *lamp* mettre en veilleuse; *colours, metals, beauty, glory* ternir; *sound* affaiblir; *memory, outline* effacer; *mind, senses* troubler. (*Theat*) **to ~ the lights** baisser les lumières; (*Aut*) **to ~ the headlights** se mettre en code.
3 *vi [light, sight]* baisser; *[metal, beauty, glory]* se ternir; *[colours]* devenir terne; *[outlines, memory]* s'effacer.
♦ **dimly** *adv shine, light* faiblement; *see, recollect* vaguement. ♦ **dimmer** *n* (*Elec*) interrupteur *m* à gradation de lumière; (*US Aut*) **~mers** phares *mpl* code *inv*; (*parking lights*) feux *mpl* de position. ♦ **dimness** *n* faiblesse *f*; obscurité *f*; imprécision *f*; stupidité *f.* ♦ **dim-sighted** *adj* à la vue faible. ♦ **dimwit*** *n* crétin(e) *m(f).* ♦ **dim-witted*** *adj* idiot.
dime [daɪm] *n* (*Can, US*) pièce *f* de dix cents. **they're a ~ a dozen*** il y en a à la pelle; **~ store** ≃ prisunic *m.*
dimension [daɪ'menʃən] *n* (*gen*) dimension *f*; *[problem, epidemic etc]* étendue *f.* ♦ **dimensional** *adj*: **two-~al** à deux dimensions.
diminish [dɪ'mɪnɪʃ] *vti* diminuer. ♦ **diminished** *adj* (*gen*) diminué; *workforce, staff, value* réduit; (*Jur*) *responsibility* atténué. ♦ **diminishing** *adj amount, importance, speed* qui diminue; *value, price* qui baisse; **law of ~ing returns** loi *f* des rendements décroissants. ♦ **diminutive 1** *adj* tout petit, minuscule; (*Gram*) diminutif; **2** *n* diminutif *m.*
dimple ['dɪmpl] *n* fossette *f* (*on* à); *[water]* ride *f.*
din [dɪn] **1** *n* (*from people*) vacarme *m*, tapage *m*; (*from battle*) fracas *m*; (*from factory, traffic*) vacarme; (*esp in classroom*) chahut *m.* **to kick up* a ~** faire un boucan monstre*, (*esp Scol*) chahuter. **2** *vt*: **to ~ into sb that ...** répéter sans cesse à qn que ... .
dine [daɪn] *vi* dîner (*off, on* de). **to ~ out** dîner en ville. ♦ **diner** *n* (*person*) dîneur *m*, -euse *f*; (*Rail*) wagon-restaurant *m*; (*eating place*) petit restaurant *m.* ♦ **dining** *adj*: **dining car** wagon-restaurant *m*; **dining hall** réfectoire *m*; **dining room** salle *f* à manger.
dinghy ['dɪŋgɪ] *n* youyou *m*; (*rubber* ~) canot *m* pneumatique; (*sailing* ~) dériveur *m.*
dingy ['dɪndʒɪ] *adj* minable, miteux. ♦ **dinginess** *n* aspect minable *or* miteux.
dinner ['dɪnə^r] **1** *n* dîner *m*; (*lunch*) déjeuner *m*; (*for dog, cat*) pâtée *f.* **we're having people to ~** nous avons du monde à dîner; **we had a good ~** nous avons bien dîné; **to go out to ~** (*restaurant*) dîner dehors *or* en ville; (*at friends'*) dîner chez des amis. **2** *adj*: **~ jacket** smoking *m*; **to give a ~ party** avoir du monde à dîner, donner un dîner; **~ plate** (grande) assiette *f*; **~ service** service *m* de table; **at ~ time** à l'heure *f* du dîner.
dinosaur ['daɪnəsɔ:^r] *n* dinosaure *m.*
dint [dɪnt] *n*: **by ~ of (doing) sth** à force de (faire) qch.
diocese ['daɪəsɪs] *n* diocèse *m.* ♦ **diocesan** [daɪ'ɒsɪsən] *adj* diocésain.
dip [dɪp] **1** *vt* (*into liquid*) tremper, plonger (*into* dans); (*into bag etc*) plonger; *sheep* laver. **to ~ the headlights** se mettre en code. **2** *vi* **(a)** *[ground, road]* descendre; *[temperature, prices, sun]* baisser; *[boat, raft]* tanguer. **(b) to ~ into** *pocket, savings* puiser dans; *book* feuilleter. **3** *n* **(a)** (*: *in sea etc*) baignade *f.* **to have a (quick) ~** prendre un bain rapide. **(b)** (*for cleaning animals*) bain *m* parasiticide. **(c)** (*in ground*) déclivité *f.* **(d)** (*cheese* ~) fondue *f* au fromage. ♦ **dipper** *n* (*ladle*) louche *f*; (*at fairground*) montagnes *fpl* russes; (*Aut: for headlamps*) basculeur *m* (de phares); (*Astron*) **the Big D~per** la Grande Ourse. ♦ **dipstick** *or* ♦ **diprod** (*US*) *n* (*Aut*) jauge *f* (de niveau d'huile).
diphtheria [dɪf'θɪərɪə] *n* diphtérie *f.*
diphthong ['dɪfθɒŋ] *n* diphtongue *f.*
diploma [dɪ'pləʊmə] *n* diplôme *m.* **to have a ~ in** être diplômé de *or* en.
diplomacy [dɪ'pləʊməsɪ] *n* (*Pol, fig*) diplomatie *f.* ♦ **diplomat** ['dɪpləmæt] *or* ♦ **diplomatist** [dɪ'pləʊ-] *n* (*Pol, fig*) diplomate *mf.* ♦ **diplomatic** [dɪplə'mæ-] *adj corps, immunity, service* diplomatique; (*tactful*) *person* diplomate; *action, answer* diplomatique; **diplomatic bag** *or* (*US*) **pouch** valise *f* diplomatique; **to be diplomatic in dealing with sth** s'occuper de qch en usant de diplomatie. ♦ **diplomatically** *adv* diplomatiquement.
dipsomania [ˌdɪpsəʊ'meɪnɪə] *n* dipsomanie *f.* ♦ **dipsomaniac** *n* dipsomane *mf.*
dire ['daɪə^r] *adj event* terrible, affreux; *poverty* extrême; *prediction* sinistre; *necessity* dur (*before n*). **in ~ straits** dans une situation désespérée.
direct [daɪ'rekt] **1** *adj* (*gen*) direct; *refusal, denial* catégorique; *danger* immédiat; (*Gram*) *object, speech* direct. **to be a ~ descendant of sb** descendre de qn en ligne directe; (*Elec*) **~ current** courant *m* continu; **~ grant school** ≃ lycée *m* privé (*subventionné*); **keep away from ~ heat** éviter l'exposition directe à la chaleur; **to make a ~ hit** porter un coup au but; *[bomb, projectile]* toucher son objectif.
2 *vt* **(a)** (*address etc*) *remark, letter* adresser (*to* à); *torch* diriger (*on* sur); *efforts* orienter (*towards* vers); *steps* diriger (*towards* vers); *attention* attirer (*to* sur). **can you ~ me to the town hall?** pourriez-vous m'indiquer le chemin de la mairie? **(b)** (*control*) *sb's work, conduct, business* diriger; *movements* guider; (*Theat*) *play* mettre en scène; (*Cine, Rad, TV*) *film, programme* réaliser; *group of actors* diriger.

(c) (*instruct*) charger (*sb to do* qn de faire), ordonner (*sb to do* à qn de faire).
3 *adv go etc* directement.
♦ **directive** *n* directive *f*. ♦ **directly** **1** *adv go, involve, return, write* directement; *descended* en droite ligne; *speak* sans détours, franchement; (*completely*) *opposite* exactement; *opposed* diamétralement, directement; (*immediately*) tout de suite, immédiatement; **2** *conj* aussitôt que, dès que; **he'll come ~ly he's ready** il viendra dès qu'il sera prêt. ♦ **directness** *n* (*frankness*) franchise *f*.

direction [dɪˈrekʃən] **1** *n* **(a)** (*way*) direction *f*, sens *m*; (*fig*) direction, voie *f*. **in every ~** dans toutes les directions, en tous sens; (*fig*) **it's a step in the right ~** voilà un pas dans la bonne direction; **in the opposite ~** en sens inverse; **in the ~ of** dans la direction de, en direction de; **a sense of ~** le sens de l'orientation. **(b)** (*management*) direction *f*; (*Theat*) mise *f* en scène; (*Cine, Rad, TV*) réalisation *f*. **(c)** (*instruction*) indication *f*, instruction *f*. **~s for use** mode *m* d'emploi; **stage ~s** indications scéniques. **2** *adj*: **~ finder** radiogoniomètre *m*. ♦ **directional** *adj* directionnel.

director [dɪˈrektəʳ] *n* (*gen, Comm etc*) directeur *m*, -trice *f*; (*Theat*) metteur *m* en scène; (*Cine, Rad, TV*) réalisateur *m*, -trice *f*. **~ general** directeur général; **~ of music** chef *m* de musique; **D~ of Public Prosecutions** ≃ procureur *m* général.
♦ **directory** **1** *n* *[addresses]* répertoire *m* (d'adresses); (*street* **~**) guide *m* des rues; (*Telec*) annuaire *m* (des téléphones); (*Comm*) annuaire du commerce; **2** *adj* (*Telec*) **~y inquiries** (service *m* des) renseignements *mpl*.

dirge [dɜːdʒ] *n* chant *m* funèbre.

dirt [dɜːt] **1** *n* (*on skin, clothes, objects*) saleté *f*, crasse *f*; (*earth*) terre *f*; (*mud*) boue *f*; (*excrement*) crotte *f*; (*Ind*) impuretés *fpl*; (*on machine, in engine*) encrassement *m*. **dog ~** crotte de chien; **to treat sb like ~*** traiter qn comme un chien; **to spread the ~* about sb** calomnier qn; **what's the ~ on...?*** qu'est-ce qu'on raconte sur ...? **2** *adj*: **~ track** (*gen*) piste *f*; (*Sport*) cendrée *f*.
♦ **dirt-cheap*** *adj, adv* très bon marché (*inv*).

dirty [ˈdɜːtɪ] **1** *adj* **(a)** (*gen*) sale, crasseux; *job* salissant; *machine, plug* encrassé; *cut, wound* infecté. **to get ~** se salir; **to get sth ~** salir qch; **that coat gets ~ very easily** ce manteau est très salissant. **(b)** (*lewd*) *story, thought* sale, cochon*; *remark* ordurier. **to have a ~ mind** avoir l'esprit mal tourné; **~ old man** vieux cochon* *m*; **~ word** mot *m* grossier; (*fig*) **it's a ~ word* these days** ce mot est tabou de nos jours. **(c)** (*unpleasant*) *weather, business, trick* sale (*before n*). **~ crack*** vacherie‡ *f*; **to give sb a ~ look** regarder qn d'un sale œil; **~ money** argent mal acquis; **he's a ~ rat*** c'est un sale type*; **he left the ~ work for me** il m'a laissé le plus embêtant du boulot*.
2 *vt* salir.
♦ **dirtily** *adv eat, live* salement; (*meanly*) *behave* bassement. ♦ **dirtiness** *n* saleté *f*. ♦ **dirty-faced** *adj* à la figure sale. ♦ **dirty-minded** *adj* à l'esprit mal tourné.

disable [dɪsˈeɪbl] *vt [illness, accident, injury]* rendre infirme, (*stronger*) rendre impotent; *tank, gun* mettre hors d'action; *ship* (*gen*) mettre hors d'état, (*by enemy action*) mettre hors de combat; (*Jur: disqualify*) rendre inhabile (*from doing* à faire). ♦ **disability** *n* (*state*) incapacité *f* (*for* à); (*handicap*) infirmité *f*; (*disadvantage*) désavantage *m*; **disability allowance** pension *f* d'invalidité. ♦ **disabled** **1** *adj* infirme; (*Admin: unable to work*) invalide; (*through illness, old age*) impotent; **~d ex-servicemen** invalides *mpl* de guerre; **2** *n*: **the ~d** les invalides *mpl*. ♦ **disablement** *n* invalidité *f*; **~ment pension** pension *f* d'invalidité.

disadvantage [ˌdɪsədˈvɑːntɪdʒ] **1** *n* désavantage *m*. **to be at a ~** être dans une position désavantageuse; **you've got me at a ~** vous avez l'avantage sur moi; **it would be to your ~** cela vous ferait du tort. **2** *vt* désavantager.
♦ **disadvantaged** *adj child, minority* déshérité.
♦ **disadvantageous** *adj* désavantageux (*to* à).

disagree [ˌdɪsəˈgriː] *vi* ne pas être d'accord, être en désaccord (*with sb/sth* avec qn/qch; *over* sur); (*quarrel*) se disputer (*with sb* avec qn; *over* à propos de); *[reports, figures]* ne pas concorder (*with* avec). **I ~** je ne suis pas de cet avis, je ne suis pas d'accord; **to ~ with the suggestion** être contre la suggestion; **she ~s with everything he has done** elle se trouve en désaccord avec tout ce qu'il a fait; *[climate, food]* **to ~ with sb** ne pas convenir à qn; **mutton ~s with him** il ne digère pas le mouton. ♦ **disagreeable** *adj* (*gen*) désagréable; *person* désagréable, désobligeant (*towards* envers). ♦ **disagreeableness** *n [work, experience]* nature *f* désagréable; *[person]* manières *fpl* désagréables. ♦ **disagreeably** *adv* désagréablement. ♦ **disagreement** *n* désaccord *m*; **to have a ~ment with sb** se disputer avec qn (*about* à propos de).

disallow [ˈdɪsəˈlaʊ] *vt* rejeter.

disappear [ˌdɪsəˈpɪəʳ] *vi* disparaître. **he ~ed from sight** on l'a perdu de vue; **the ship ~ed over the horizon** le navire a disparu à l'horizon; **to do a ~ing trick*** s'éclipser*; **to make sth ~** faire disparaître qch; *[conjurer]* escamoter qch.
♦ **disappearance** *n* disparition *f*.

disappoint [ˌdɪsəˈpɔɪnt] *vt* décevoir, désappointer; (*after promising*) manquer de parole à; *hope* décevoir. ♦ **disappointed** *adj person* déçu, désappointé; *hope, ambition* déçu; *plan* contrecarré; **I'm very ~ed with you** vous m'avez beaucoup déçu *or* désappointé. ♦ **disappointing** *adj* décevant. ♦ **disappointment** *n* déception *f*.

disapprove [ˌdɪsəˈpruːv] *vi* désapprouver (*of sb/sth* qn/qch; *of sb's doing* que qn fasse). **your mother would ~** ta mère ne trouverait pas ça bien; **he entirely ~s of drink** il est tout à fait contre la boisson. ♦ **disapproval** *n* désapprobation *f*. ♦ **disapproving** *adj* désapprobateur.
♦ **disapprovingly** *adv* avec désapprobation.

disarm [dɪsˈɑːm] *vti* désarmer. ♦ **disarmament** *n* désarmement *m*; **~ament talks** conférence *f* sur le désarmement. ♦ **disarming** *adj smile* désarmant. ♦ **disarmingly** *adv* d'une manière désarmante.

disarrange [ˈdɪsəˈreɪndʒ] *vt* mettre en désordre.

disarray [ˌdɪsəˈreɪ] *n*: **in (complete) ~** *troops* en déroute; *party, movement* en plein désarroi; *thoughts* très confus; *clothes* en désordre.

disaster [dɪˈzɑːstəʳ] **1** *n* (*gen, also fig*) désastre *m*, catastrophe *f*; (*air ~, sea ~ etc*) catastrophe. **doomed to ~** voué à la catastrophe; **her hair was a ~*** sa coiffure était une catastrophe*. **2** *adj*: **~ area** région *f* sinistrée; **~ fund** collecte *f* au profit des victimes. ♦ **disastrous** *adj* désastreux, catastrophique. ♦ **disastrously** *adv* désastreusement, catastrophiquement.

disband [dɪsˈbænd] **1** *vt* disperser. **2** *vi* se disperser.

disbelieve [ˈdɪsbəˈliːv] *vt person* ne pas croire; *news etc* ne pas croire à. ♦ **disbelief** *n* incrédulité *f*; **in disbelief** avec incrédulité. ♦ **disbelieving** *adj* incrédule.

disc [dɪsk] **1** *n* (*gen*) disque *m*; (*identity* **~**) plaque *f* d'identité. **2** *adj brakes* à disque. **~ jockey** animateur *m*, -trice *f* (de variétés), disc-jockey *m*.

discard [dɪsˈkɑːd] *vt* (*gen*) se débarrasser de; *idea, plan* abandonner; *part of spacecraft* larguer; (*Cards*) se défausser de.

discern [dɪˈsɜːn] *vt* discerner. ♦ **discernible** *adj object* visible; *likeness, fault* perceptible.

♦ **discerning** *adj person, look* perspicace; *taste* délicat. ♦ **discernment** *n* discernement *m*.

discharge [dɪs'tʃɑːdʒ] **1** *vt ship, cargo* décharger; *liquid* déverser; (*Elec*) décharger; *employee* congédier; *soldier* rendre à la vie civile, (*for health reasons*) réformer; *prisoner* libérer; *jury* congédier; *accused* relaxer; *bankrupt* réhabiliter; *debt* acquitter; *obligation, duty* remplir; *patient* renvoyer (guéri) de l'hôpital; *gun* faire partir. **to ~ pus** suppurer. **2** *vi [wound]* suinter. **3** ['dɪstʃɑːdʒ] *n* (*Elec*) décharge *f*; (*pus etc*) suppuration *f*; (*vaginal*) pertes *fpl* (blanches); *[employee, patient]* renvoi *m*; *[prisoner]* libération *f*. **he got his ~** il a été congédié *or* libéré *etc*.

disciple [dɪ'saɪpl] *n* disciple *m*.

discipline ['dɪsɪplɪn] **1** *n* discipline *f*. **2** *vt* (*control*) discipliner; (*punish*) punir. ♦ **disciplinarian** *n* personne *f* stricte en matière de discipline. ♦ **disciplinary** *adj* disciplinaire.

disclaim [dɪs'kleɪm] *vt* désavouer. ♦ **disclaimer** *n* démenti *m*. **to issue a ~er** publier un démenti.

disclose [dɪs'kləʊz] *vt secret, news* divulguer, révéler; *intentions* révéler; *contents* exposer. ♦ **disclosure** *n* révélation *f*.

disco* ['dɪskəʊ] *n* disco *m*.

discolour, (*US*) **-or** [dɪs'kʌlər] **1** *vt* décolorer; *white object* jaunir. **2** *vi* se décolorer; jaunir. ♦ **discoloration** *n* décoloration *f*; jaunissement *m*.

discomfiture [dɪs'kʌmfɪtʃər] *n* embarras *m*.

discomfort [dɪs'kʌmfət] *n* gêne *f*. **I feel some ~ from it but not real pain** ça me gêne mais ça ne me fait pas vraiment mal; **this ~ will pass** cette gêne va passer.

disconcert [ˌdɪskən'sɜːt] *vt* déconcerter. ♦ **disconcerting** *adj* déconcertant, déroutant. ♦ **disconcertingly** *adv* d'une manière déconcertante.

disconnect ['dɪskə'nekt] *vt* (*gen*) détacher; *pipe, radio, television* débrancher; *gas, electricity, water supply, telephone* couper. (*Telec: in mid-conversation*) **we've been ~ed** nous avons été coupés. ♦ **disconnected** *adj speech, thought* sans suite; *facts* sans rapport.

disconsolate [dɪs'kɒnsəlɪt] *adj* inconsolable. ♦ **disconsolately** *adv* inconsolablement.

discontent ['dɪskən'tent] *n* mécontentement *m*; (*Pol*) malaise *m* social. **cause of ~** grief *m*. ♦ **discontented** *adj* mécontent (*with, about* de).

discontinue ['dɪskən'tɪnjuː] *vt* cesser, interrompre; *series* interrompre; *story* interrompre la publication de. (*Comm*) **~d line** série *f* qui ne se fait plus; (*notice*) 'fin de série'. ♦ **discontinuous** *adj* discontinu.

discord ['dɪskɔːd] *n* discorde *f*; (*Mus*) dissonance *f*. ♦ **discordant** *adj* discordant; dissonant.

discotheque ['dɪskəʊtek] *n* discothèque *f* (*dancing*).

discount ['dɪskaʊnt] **1** *n* escompte *m*; (*on article*) remise *f*, rabais *m*. **to give a ~** faire une remise (*on* sur); **to buy at a ~** acheter au rabais; **~ for cash** escompte au comptant; (*fig*) **to be at a ~** être mal coté. **2** [dɪs'kaʊnt] *vt fact, remark* ne pas tenir compte de. **3** *adj*: **~ store** magasin *m* de demi-gros.

discourage [dɪs'kʌrɪdʒ] *vt* **(a)** (*dishearten*) décourager, abattre. **to become ~d** se laisser décourager. **(b)** (*advise against*) décourager, dissuader (*sb from sth/from doing* qn de qch/de faire); *suggestion* déconseiller; *offer of friendship* repousser. ♦ **discouragement** *n* (*act*) désapprobation *f* (*of* de); (*depression*) découragement *m*. ♦ **discouraging** *adj* décourageant, démoralisant.

discourteous [dɪs'kɜːtɪəs] *adj* peu courtois (*towards* envers, avec). ♦ **discourteously** *adv* d'une manière peu courtoise. ♦ **discourtesy** *n* manque *m* de courtoisie.

discover [dɪs'kʌvər] *vt* (*gen*) découvrir; *mistake, loss* s'apercevoir de; (*after search*) *house, book* dénicher. **to ~ that** (*realize*) s'apercevoir que; (*learn*) apprendre que. ♦ **discoverer** *n*: **the ~er of penicillin** celui qui le premier a découvert la pénicilline. ♦ **discovery** *n* (*act*) découverte *f*; (*happy find*) trouvaille *f*.

discredit [dɪs'kredɪt] **1** *vt* discréditer. **2** *n* discrédit *m*. ♦ **discreditable** *adj* peu honorable.

discreet [dɪs'kriːt] *adj* discret. ♦ **discreetly** *adv* discrètement. ♦ **discretion** [dɪs'kreʃən] *n* discrétion *f*; **use your own discretion** faites comme bon vous semblera; **the age of discretion** l'âge de raison. ♦ **discretionary** *adj powers* discrétionnaire.

discrepancy [dɪs'krepənsɪ] *n* contradiction *f*, divergence *f* (*between* entre). **there is a slight ~ between the explanations** les explications divergent légèrement.

discrete [dɪs'kriːt] *adj* discret (*distinct*).

discriminate [dɪs'krɪmɪneɪt] **1** *vi* distinguer, faire un choix (*between* entre); (*unfairly*) établir une discrimination (*against* contre; *in favour of* en faveur de). **2** *vt* distinguer (*from* de). ♦ **discriminating** *adj judgment, mind* judicieux; *taste* fin; *tariff, tax* différentiel; **he's not very discriminating** il n'a aucun discernement. ♦ **discrimination** *n* (*judgment*) discernement *m*; (*bias*) discrimination *f* (*against* contre, *in favour of* en faveur de).

discus ['dɪskəs] *n* disque *m*. **~ thrower** lanceur *m* de disque.

discuss [dɪs'kʌs] *vt* (*examine in detail*) *problem, project, price* discuter; (*talk about*) *topic, personality* discuter de. **we were ~ing him** nous parlions *or* discutions de lui; **I ~ed it with him** j'en ai discuté avec lui. ♦ **discussion** *n* discussion *f* (*of* sur); **under ~ion** en discussion.

disdain [dɪs'deɪn] **1** *vt* dédaigner (*to do* de faire). **2** *n* dédain *m*. ♦ **disdainful** *adj* dédaigneux. ♦ **disdainfully** *adv* dédaigneusement.

disease [dɪ'ziːz] *n* maladie *f*. ♦ **diseased** *adj* malade.

disembark [ˌdɪsɪm'bɑːk] *vti* débarquer. ♦ **disembarkation** *n* débarquement *m*.

disembodied ['dɪsɪm'bɒdɪd] *adj* désincarné.

disenchanted ['dɪsɪn'tʃɑːntɪd] *adj* désenchanté. ♦ **disenchantment** *n* désenchantement *m*.

disengage [ˌdɪsɪn'geɪdʒ] *vt* (*gen*) dégager (*from* de); *machine* débrayer. **to ~ the clutch** débrayer. ♦ **disengaged** *adj* libre, inoccupé; (*Tech*) débrayé. ♦ **disengagement** *n* (*Pol*) désengagement *m*.

disentangle ['dɪsɪn'tæŋgl] *vt* (*gen*) démêler; *plot* dénouer. **to ~ o.s. from** se dépêtrer de.

disfavour, (*US*) **-or** [dɪs'feɪvər] **1** *n* défaveur *f* (*with sb* auprès de qn). **to fall into ~** tomber en défaveur. **2** *vt* désapprouver.

disfigure [dɪs'fɪgər] *vt* défigurer. ♦ **disfigured** *adj* défiguré (*by* par). ♦ **disfigurement** *n* défigurement *m*.

disgorge [dɪs'gɔːdʒ] *vt* dégorger.

disgrace [dɪs'greɪs] **1** *n* (*dishonour*) honte *f*, déshonneur *m*; (*disfavour*) disgrâce *f*. **there is no ~ in doing** il n'y a aucune honte à faire; **to be in ~** *[politician etc]* être en disgrâce; *[child, dog]* être en pénitence; **it's a ~** c'est une honte; **it is a ~ to the country** cela déshonore le pays. **2** *vt family etc* faire honte à; *name, country* déshonorer. **he ~d himself by drinking too much** il s'est très mal conduit en buvant trop; *[officer, politician]* **to be ~d** être disgracié. ♦ **disgraceful** *adj* honteux, scandaleux. ♦ **disgracefully** *adv act* honteusement, scandaleusement; **~fully badly paid** scandaleusement mal payé.

disgruntled [dɪs'grʌntld] *adj person* mécontent (*about, with* à cause de); *expression* maussade.

disguise [dɪsˈgaɪz] **1** *vt* (*gen*) déguiser (*as* en); *building, vehicle, ship* camoufler (*as* en). **to ~ o.s. as a woman** se déguiser en femme; **there is no disguising the fact that ...** on ne peut pas se dissimuler que ... . **2** *n* déguisement *m*. **in ~** déguisé.

disgust [dɪsˈgʌst] **1** *n* dégoût *m* (*for, at* pour). **he left in ~** il est parti dégoûté; **to my ~ he refused** j'ai trouvé dégoûtant qu'il refuse (*subj*). **2** *vt* dégoûter. ◆ **disgusted** *adj* dégoûté (*at* de, par). ◆ **disgustedly** *adv* avec dégoût; **... he said ~edly** ... dit-il, dégoûté. ◆ **disgusting** *adj* (*gen*) dégoûtant; *behaviour* révoltant; *smell* nauséabond; **what a ~ing mess!** c'est dégoûtant! ◆ **disgustingly** *adv* d'une manière dégoûtante; **~ingly dirty** d'une saleté dégoûtante.

dish [dɪʃ] **1** *n* plat *m*; (*in laboratory etc*) récipient *m*; (*Phot*) cuvette *f*; (*food*) plat, mets *m*. **vegetable ~** plat à légumes; **the ~es** la vaisselle; **to do the ~es** faire la vaisselle. **2** *vt food* verser dans un plat; (‡) *sb's chances, hopes* flanquer par terre*.

dish out *vt sep* distribuer.

dish up *vt sep meal* servir; (*) *facts, statistics* sortir tout un tas de*.

◆ **dishcloth** *n* (*for washing*) lavette *f*; (*for drying*) torchon *m* à vaisselle. ◆ **dished wheel** *n* roue *f* désaxée. ◆ **dishmop** *n* lavette *f*. ◆ **dishpan** *n* bassine *f* (à vaisselle). ◆ **dishrack** *n* égouttoir *m* (à vaisselle). ◆ **dishtowel** *n* torchon *m* (à vaisselle). ◆ **dishwasher** *n* (*machine*) lave-vaisselle *m inv*; (*person: in restaurant*) plongeur *m*, -euse *f*. ◆ **dishwater** *n* eau *f* de vaisselle. ◆ **dishy‡** *adj person* excitant, sexy*.

dishearten [dɪsˈhɑːtn] *vt* décourager. **to get ~ed** se décourager. ◆ **disheartening** *adj* décourageant.

dishevelled [dɪˈʃevəld] *adj person, hair* échevelé; *clothes* en désordre.

dishonest [dɪsˈɒnɪst] *adj* (*gen*) malhonnête; (*untruthful*) *person* menteur; *reply* mensonger. **to be ~ with sb** manquer de franchise envers qn. ◆ **dishonestly** *adv act* malhonnêtement; *say* en mentant. ◆ **dishonesty** *n* malhonnêteté *f*.

dishonour, (*US*) **-or** [dɪsˈɒnəʳ] **1** *n* déshonneur *m*. **2** *vt* déshonorer; *cheque* refuser d'honorer. ◆ **dishono(u)rable** *adj* peu honorable.

disillusion [ˌdɪsɪˈluːʒən] **1** *vt* désillusionner. **to grow ~ed** perdre ses illusions. **2** *n* désillusion *f*.

disincentive [ˌdɪsɪnˈsentɪv] *n* effet *m* décourageant. **to be a ~ to sth** décourager qch.

disinclination [ˌdɪsɪnklɪˈneɪʃən] *n* manque *m* d'enthousiasme (*to do* à faire). ◆ **disinclined** *adj* peu disposé, peu enclin (*for* à, *to do* à faire).

disinfect [ˌdɪsɪnˈfekt] *vt* désinfecter. ◆ **disinfectant** *adj, n* désinfectant (*m*). ◆ **disinfection** *n* désinfection *f*.

disingenuous [ˌdɪsɪnˈdʒenjʊəs] *adj* déloyal, peu sincère.

disinherit [ˈdɪsɪnˈherɪt] *vt* déshériter.

disintegrate [dɪsˈɪntɪgreɪt] **1** *vi* se désintégrer. **2** *vt* désintégrer. ◆ **disintegration** *n* désintégration *f*.

disinterested [dɪsˈɪntrɪstɪd] *adj* (*impartial*) désintéressé; (*uninterested*) indifférent. ◆ **disinterestedness** *n* désintéressement *m*; indifférence *f*.

disjointed [dɪsˈdʒɔɪntɪd] *adj* décousu.

disjunctive [dɪsˈdʒʌŋktɪv] *adj* disjonctif.

disk [dɪsk] = **disc.**

dislike [dɪsˈlaɪk] **1** *vt* ne pas aimer (*doing* faire). **I don't ~ it** cela ne me déplaît pas; **I ~ her** je la trouve antipathique, elle ne me plaît pas; **I ~ this intensely** j'ai cela en horreur. **2** *n*: **his ~ of ...** le fait qu'il n'aime pas ...; **one's likes and ~s** ce que l'on aime et ce que l'on n'aime pas; **to take a ~ to sb/sth** prendre qn/qch en grippe.

dislocate [ˈdɪsləʊkeɪt] *vt* (*Med*) se disloquer; *[fall etc]* disloquer; (*fig*) *traffic, business* désorganiser; *plans* bouleverser. **he ~d his shoulder** il s'est disloqué l'épaule. ◆ **dislocation** *n* dislocation *f*; désorganisation *f*; bouleversement *m*.

dislodge [dɪsˈlɒdʒ] *vt stone* déplacer; *cap, screw, nut* débloquer; *enemy* déloger; *person* faire bouger (*from* de).

disloyal [ˈdɪsˈlɔɪəl] *adj* déloyal (*to* à, envers). ◆ **disloyally** *adv* déloyalement. ◆ **disloyalty** *n* déloyauté *f*.

dismal [ˈdɪzməl] *adj prospects, person* sombre, morne; *weather* morne; *failure* lamentable. ◆ **dismally** *adv say* d'un air sombre; *fail* lamentablement.

dismantle [dɪsˈmæntl] *vt* démonter.

dismay [dɪsˈmeɪ] **1** *n* consternation *f*. **in ~** d'un air consterné. **2** *vt* consterner.

dismember [dɪsˈmembəʳ] *vt* démembrer.

dismiss [dɪsˈmɪs] *vt* **(a)** *employee* licencier, congédier; *official, officer* destituer; *class, visitors* congédier; *troops* faire rompre les rangs à. (*Mil*) **~!** rompez (les rangs)!; (*Scol*) **class ~!** partez! **(b)** *thought, suggestion, possibility* écarter; *request* rejeter. **(c)** (*Jur*) *accused* relaxer; *appeal* rejeter; *jury* congédier. **to ~ a case** rendre une fin de non-recevoir; **to ~ a charge** rendre un non-lieu. ◆ **dismissal** *n* licenciement *m*; destitution *f*; congédiement *m*; rejet *m*; **he made a gesture of ~al** d'un geste il les a congédiés.

dismount [dɪsˈmaʊnt] **1** *vi* descendre (*from* de), mettre pied à terre. **2** *vt* démonter.

disobey [ˈdɪsəˈbeɪ] *vt person* désobéir à; *rule* enfreindre. ◆ **disobedience** *n* désobéissance *f* (*to* à). ◆ **disobedient** *adj* désobéissant (*to* à).

disobliging [ˈdɪsəˈblaɪdʒɪŋ] *adj* désobligeant.

disorder [dɪsˈɔːdəʳ] *n [room, plans etc]* désordre *m*, confusion *f*; (*Pol etc: rioting*) désordres *mpl*; (*Med*) troubles *mpl*. **in ~** en désordre; (*Mil*) en déroute. ◆ **disordered** *adj room* en désordre; *imagination, existence* désordonné; (*Med*) *stomach, mind* malade. ◆ **disorderly** *adj room* en désordre; *flight, mind, crowd, behaviour, life* désordonné; *meeting* tumultueux; (*Jur*) **~ly conduct** conduite *f* contraire aux bonnes mœurs.

disorganize [dɪsˈɔːgənaɪz] *vt* désorganiser. **she's very ~d*** elle est très désorganisée. ◆ **disorganization** *n* désorganisation *f*.

disorientate [dɪsˈɔːrɪənteɪt] *vt* désorienter.

disown [dɪsˈəʊn] *vt* renier.

disparage [dɪsˈpærɪdʒ] *vt person, thing* dénigrer. ◆ **disparagement** *n* dénigrement *m*. ◆ **disparaging** *adj* désobligeant (*to* pour); **to be disparaging about** faire des remarques désobligeantes sur. ◆ **disparagingly** *adv* de façon désobligeante.

disparate [ˈdɪspərɪt] *adj* disparate. ◆ **disparity** *n* disparité *f*.

dispassionate [dɪsˈpæʃənɪt] *adj* (*unemotional*) calme; (*unbiased*) impartial. ◆ **dispassionately** *adv* avec calme; impartialement.

dispatch [dɪsˈpætʃ] **1** *vt* **(a)** (*send*) *letter, goods* expédier; *messenger* dépêcher; *troops* faire partir. **(b)** (*finish off*) *job* expédier; *animal* tuer. **2** *n* **(a)** (*sending*) expédition *f*. **(b)** (*report: Mil, Press etc*) dépêche *f*. (*Mil*) **mentioned in ~es** cité à l'ordre du jour. **(c)** (*promptness*) promptitude *f*. **3** *adj*: **~ box** (*in Parliament*) ≃ tribune *f*; (*case*) valise officielle (*à documents*); **~ case** serviette *f*, porte-documents *m inv*; **~ rider** estafette *f*.

dispel [dɪsˈpel] *vt* dissiper, chasser.

dispense [dɪsˈpens] *vt* **(a)** *food* distribuer; *justice, sacrament* administrer; *hospitality* accorder; *medicine, prescription* préparer. **dispensing chemist** (*person*) pharmacien(ne) *m(f)*; (*shop*) pharmacie *f*. **(b)** (*exempt*) dispenser (*sb from sth/from doing* qn de qch/de faire).

dispense with *vt fus* (*do without*) se passer de; (*make unnecessary*) rendre superflu.

◆ **dispensable** *adj* dont on peut se passer. ◆ **dispensary** *n* (*in hospital*) pharmacie *f*; (*in *chemist's*) officine *f*; (*clinic*) dispensaire *m*. ♦ **dispensation** *n* (*Jur, Rel*) dispense *f* (*from* de). ♦ **dispenser** *n* (*person*) pharmacien(ne) *m(f)*; (*device*) distributeur *m*.

disperse [dɪs'pɜːs] **1** *vt* (*gen*) disperser; *sorrow* dissiper; *knowledge* disséminer. **2** *vi* se disperser; se dissiper; se disséminer. ♦ **dispersal** *or* ♦ **dispersion** *n* dispersion *f*.

dispirited [dɪs'pɪrɪtɪd] *adj* découragé, abattu. ♦ **dispiritedly** *adv* avec découragement.

displace [dɪs'pleɪs] *vt* (*move out of place*) *refugees, official* déplacer; (*replace*) remplacer. **~d person** personne déplacée. ♦ **displacement** *n* déplacement *m*; remplacement *m*; (*Psych*) **~ment activity** déplacement *m*.

display [dɪs'pleɪ] **1** *vt* (*gen*) montrer; (*ostentatiously*) faire parade de; *courage, ignorance* faire preuve de; *notice, results* afficher; *goods* exposer; (*Press, Typ*) mettre en vedette; (*Computers, Electronics*) visualiser. **2** *n* (*act*) exposition *f*, déploiement *m*; (*ostentatious*) étalage *m*; *[paintings]* exposition; (*Comm*) étalage; (*Computers, Electronics*) visuel *m*; *[courage, ignorance]* manifestation *f*; *[force etc]* déploiement. **on ~** exposé; **military ~** parade *f* militaire; **air ~** fête *f* aéronautique. **3** *adj goods* d'étalage. **~ cabinet, ~ case** vitrine *f* (*meuble*); **~ window** vitrine *f* (*de magasin*).

displease [dɪs'pliːz] *vt* déplaire à, mécontenter. **~d with** mécontent de. ♦ **displeasing** *adj* déplaisant (*to* pour, à). ♦ **displeasure** [dɪs'pleʒəʳ] *n* mécontentement *m*.

dispose [dɪs'pəʊz] *vt* **(a)** (*arrange*) *papers, ornaments, troops* disposer; *forces* déployer. **(b)** (*make willing*) disposer (*sb to do* qn à faire).

dispose of *vt fus* **(a)** (*get rid of*) se débarrasser de; (*by selling*) écouler; *one's property, money* disposer de; *rubbish etc* (*remove*) enlever, (*destroy*) détruire; *bomb* désamorcer; *meal, question* expédier; (*kill*) liquider*. **(b)** (*control*) *time, money* disposer de.

♦ **disposable** *adj* (*available*) disponible; (*not reusable*) à jeter; *nappy* de cellulose; **disposable wrapping** emballage *m* perdu. ♦ **disposal** *n [rubbish]* enlèvement *m*, destruction *f*; *[bomb]* désamorçage *m*; *[property]* disposition *f*; **at sb's disposal** à la disposition de qn; **(waste) disposal unit** broyeur *m* (d'ordures). ♦ **disposed** *adj* disposé (*to do* à faire); **well ~d towards sb** bien disposé envers qn. ♦ **disposer** *n* (*waste ~*) broyeur *m* (d'ordures). ♦ **disposition** *n* (*temperament*) naturel *m*, tempérament *m*; (*readiness*) inclination *f* (*to do* à faire); (*arrangement*) disposition *f*.

dispossess ['dɪspə'zes] *vt* déposséder (*of* de).

disproportionate [ˌdɪsprə'pɔːʃnɪt] *adj* disproportionné (*to* à, avec). ♦ **disproportionately** *adv*: **~ly large** *etc* d'une grandeur *etc* disproportionnée.

disprove [dɪs'pruːv] *vt* établir la fausseté de.

dispute [dɪs'pjuːt] **1** *n* **(a)** discussion *f*. **beyond ~** incontestable; **without ~** sans contredit; **there is some ~ about** on n'est pas d'accord sur; **in** *or* **under ~** *matter* en discussion; *territory, facts, figures* contesté; (*Jur*) en litige. **(b)** (*quarrel*) dispute *f*; (*argument*) discussion *f*, débat *m*; (*Jur*) litige *m*; (*Ind, Pol*) conflit *m*. **industrial ~** conflit social; **wages ~** conflit salarial. **2** *vt* contester. **I do not ~ the fact that ...** je ne conteste pas (le fait) que ... + *subj*. ♦ **disputable** *adj* discutable, contestable. ♦ **disputably** *adv* de manière contestable. ♦ **disputed** *adj* contesté.

disqualify [dɪs'kwɒlɪfaɪ] *vt* rendre inapte (*from sth* à qch, *from doing* à faire); (*Sport*) disqualifier. **to ~ sb from driving** retirer à qn le permis de conduire (*for sth* pour qch). ♦ **disqualification** *n* disqualification *f* (*also Sport*), exclusion *f* (*from* de); (*from driving*) retrait *m* du permis (de conduire).

disquieting [dɪs'kwaɪətɪŋ] *adj* inquiétant.

disregard ['dɪsrɪ'gɑːd] **1** *vt* (*gen*) ne tenir aucun compte de; *feelings* faire peu de cas de; *authority, rules, duty* passer outre à. **2** *n [difficulty, comments, feelings, money]* indifférence *f* (*for* à); *[danger]* mépris *m* (*for* de); *[safety]* négligence *f* (*for* en ce qui concerne); *[rule, law]* non-observation *f* (*for* de).

disrepair ['dɪsrɪ'pɛəʳ] *n* mauvais état. **in a state of ~** *building* délabré; *road* en mauvais état; **to fall into ~** *[building]* se délabrer; *[road]* se dégrader.

disrepute ['dɪsrɪ'pjuːt] *n* discrédit *m*, déshonneur *m*. **to fall into ~** tomber en discrédit. ♦ **disreputable** [dɪs'repjʊtəbl] *adj person* peu recommandable; *behaviour* honteux; *clothes* miteux; *area* mal famé.

disrespect ['dɪsrɪs'pekt] *n* manque *m* de respect. ♦ **disrespectful** *adj* irrespectueux (*towards, to* envers); **to be ~ful to** manquer de respect envers.

disrupt [dɪs'rʌpt] *vt peace, relations, train service* perturber; *conversation, communications* interrompre; *plans* déranger. ♦ **disruption** *n* perturbation *f*; interruption *f*; dérangement *m*. ♦ **disruptive** *adj* perturbateur; (*Elec*) disruptif.

dissatisfaction ['dɪsˌsætɪs'fækʃən] *n* mécontentement *m* (*at, with* devant, provoqué par). ♦ **dissatisfied** *adj* mécontent (*with* de).

dissect [dɪ'sekt] *vt* disséquer. ♦ **dissection** *n* dissection *f*.

dissemble [dɪ'sembl] *vti* dissimuler.

disseminate [dɪ'semɪneɪt] *vt* disséminer. **~d sclerosis** sclérose *f* en plaques.

dissension [dɪ'senʃən] *n* dissension *f*. ♦ **dissent** **1** *vi* différer (*from* de); (*Rel*) être dissident; **2** *n* dissentiment *m*; (*Rel*) dissidence *f*. ♦ **dissenter** *n* dissident(e) *m(f)*.

dissertation [ˌdɪsə'teɪʃən] *n* mémoire *m* (*on* sur).

disservice ['dɪs'sɜːvɪs] *n* mauvais service *m*. **to do sb a ~** rendre un mauvais service à qn; *[appearance etc]* constituer un handicap pour qn.

dissidence ['dɪsɪdəns] *n* dissidence *f*. ♦ **dissident** *adj, n* dissident(e) *m(f)*.

dissimilar ['dɪ'sɪmɪləʳ] *adj* différent (*to* de). ♦ **dissimilarity** *n* différence *f* (*between* entre).

dissimulate [dɪ'sɪmjʊleɪt] *vti* dissimuler. ♦ **dissimulation** *n* dissimulation *f*.

dissipate ['dɪsɪpeɪt] *vt* (*gen*) dissiper; *energy, efforts* gaspiller. ♦ **dissipated** *adj life, behaviour* déréglé; *person* débauché, dissipé. ♦ **dissipation** *n* dissipation *f*.

dissociate [dɪ'səʊʃɪeɪt] *vt* dissocier (*from* de). ♦ **dissociation** *n* dissociation *f*.

dissolute ['dɪsəluːt] *adj person* débauché; *way of life* dissolu.

dissolution [ˌdɪsə'luːʃən] *n* dissolution *f*.

dissolve [dɪ'zɒlv] **1** *vt* (*gen*) dissoudre; *[person] substance* faire dissoudre. **2** *vi* se dissoudre; (*Cine*) se fondre. **to ~ into thin air** s'en aller en fumée; **to ~ into tears** fondre en larmes.

dissuade [dɪ'sweɪd] *vt* dissuader (*sb from doing* qn de faire). ♦ **dissuasion** *n* dissuasion *f*. ♦ **dissuasive** *adj voice, person* qui cherche à dissuader; *powers* de dissuasion.

distance ['dɪstəns] **1** *n* distance *f* (*between* entre). **the ~ between the houses** la distance qui sépare les maisons; **the ~ between the eyes/rails** *etc* l'écartement *m* des yeux/des rails *etc*; **at a ~** à quelque distance; **at a ~ of 2 metres** à une distance de 2 mètres; **what ~ is it from here to London?** nous sommes à combien de Londres?; **it's a good ~** c'est assez loin; **in the ~** au loin, dans le lointain; **from a ~** de loin; **it's within walking ~** on peut y aller à pied; **a short ~ away** à une faible distance; **it's no ~*** c'est tout près; **at a ~ of 400 years** à 400 ans d'écart; **at this ~ in time** après un tel intervalle de temps; **to keep sb at a ~** tenir qn à distance; **to keep one's ~** garder ses distances.

2 *adj*: ~ **race/runner** épreuve *f*/coureur *m* de fond.

♦ **distant** *adj* (*gen*) éloigné; *recollection, country* lointain; (*reserved*) distant, froid; **we had a distant view of the church** nous avons vu l'église de loin; **the school is 2 km distant from the church** l'école est à une distance de 2 km de l'église; **in the distant future/past** dans un avenir/un passé lointain. ♦ **distantly** *adv resemble* vaguement, un peu; *smile, say* froidement, d'une manière distante; **distantly related** d'une parenté éloignée.

distaste ['dɪs'teɪst] *n* répugnance *f* (*for* pour). ♦ **distasteful** *adj* déplaisant (*to* à).

distemper[1] [dɪs'tempəʳ] 1 *n* (*paint*) détrempe *f*, badigeon *m*. 2 *vt* badigeonner.

distemper[2] [dɪs'tempəʳ] *n* [*dogs*] maladie *f* des jeunes chiens *or* de Carré.

distend [dɪs'tend] 1 *vt* distendre. 2 *vi* se distendre.

distil(l) [dɪs'tɪl] *vt* distiller. ♦ **distiller** *n* distillateur *m*. ♦ **distillery** *n* distillerie *f*.

distinct [dɪs'tɪŋkt] *adj* **(a)** (*clear*) *landmark, voice, memory* distinct, clair; *promise, offer* précis; *preference, likeness, increase, progress* net (*before n*), marqué. **(b)** (*different*) distinct, différent (*from* de). **as ~ from** par opposition à. ♦ **distinction** *n* (*gen*) distinction *f*; (*Scol*) **he got a ~ion in French** il a été reçu en français avec mention *f* très bien. ♦ **distinctive** *adj* distinctif. ♦ **distinctly** *adv speak, hear, see* distinctement, clairement; *promise* sans équivoque; *stipulate* expressément; *better* incontestablement; *cool, friendly* vraiment.

distinguish [dɪs'tɪŋgwɪʃ] 1 *vt* **(a)** (*discern*) *landmark* distinguer, apercevoir; *change* discerner. **(b)** (*make different*) distinguer (*from* de); (*characterize*) caractériser. **to ~ o.s.** se distinguer (*as* en tant que). 2 *vi* distinguer (*between* entre). ♦ **distinguishable** *adj* (*discernible*) visible, perceptible; **easily ~able from each other** faciles à distinguer l'un de l'autre. ♦ **distinguished** *adj* distingué. ♦ **distinguishing** *adj* distinctif; **~ing mark** (*on passport*) signe *m* particulier.

distort [dɪs'tɔːt] *vt* (*gen*) déformer; *judgment* fausser. **a ~ed impression** une idée fausse; **he gave us a ~ed version of the events** il a dénaturé les événements en les racontant. ♦ **distortion** *n* (*gen*) distorsion *f*; [*facts*] déformation *f*.

distract [dɪs'trækt] *vt* distraire (*from* de). ♦ **distracted** *adj* éperdu, égaré; **she was quite ~ed** elle était dans tous ses états. ♦ **distractedly** *adv behave, run* comme un fou; *love, weep* éperdument. ♦ **distracting** *adj* qui empêche de se concentrer, (*pej*) gênant. ♦ **distraction** *n* interruption *f*; **to love to ~ion** aimer à la folie; **to drive sb to ~ion** rendre qn fou.

distraught [dɪs'trɔːt] *adj* éperdu (*with* de), égaré.

distress [dɪs'tres] 1 *n* **(a)** peine *f*, (*stronger*) douleur *f*. **to be in great ~** être bouleversé. **(b)** (*poverty*) détresse *f*, misère *f*. **(c)** (*danger*) péril *m*, détresse *f*. **in ~** *ship* en perdition; *plane* en détresse; **comrades in ~** compagnons *mpl* d'infortune. 2 *vt* affliger, peiner. 3 *adj signal* de détresse. ♦ **distressed** *adj* affligé, peiné (*by* par, de); **very ~ed** bouleversé; **~ed area** zone *f* sinistrée. ♦ **distressing** *adj* pénible, affligeant.

distribute [dɪs'trɪbjuːt] *vt leaflets, prizes* distribuer; *money, load, weight* répartir. ♦ **distribution** *n* distribution *f*; répartition *f*. ♦ **distributive** *adj* distributif; **the distributive trades** le secteur de la distribution. ♦ **distributor** *n* **(a)** (*Comm: agent for goods*) concessionnaire *mf*; [*films*] distributeur *m*; **(b)** (*Aut, Tech*) distributeur *m*.

district ['dɪstrɪkt] 1 *n* (*of a country*) région *f*; (*in town*) quartier *m*, arrondissement *m* (*Admin*). 2 *adj manager etc* régional. (*US*) **~ attorney** ≃ procureur *m* de la République; (*US*) **~ court** cour *f* fédérale; **~ nurse** infirmière *f* visiteuse.

distrust [dɪs'trʌst] 1 *vt* se méfier de. 2 *n* méfiance *f* (*of* à l'égard de). ♦ **distrustful** *adj* méfiant (*of* de).

disturb [dɪs'tɜːb] *vt* (*inconvenience*) déranger; (*worry*) troubler, inquiéter; *silence, sleep, water* troubler; *atmosphere* perturber; *papers* déranger. **sorry to ~ you** excusez-moi de vous déranger; **'please do not ~'** 'prière de ne pas déranger'. ♦ **disturbance** *n* (*political, social*) troubles *mpl*, émeute *f*; (*in house, street*) tapage *m*; **to cause a ~ance** faire du tapage. ♦ **disturbed** *adj* troublé (*at, by* par); (*Psych*) perturbé. ♦ **disturbing** *adj* (*alarming*) inquiétant, troublant; (*distracting*) gênant.

disuse ['dɪs'juːs] *n* désuétude *f*. **to fall into ~** tomber en désuétude. ♦ **disused** ['dɪs'juːzd] *adj* désaffecté, abandonné.

ditch [dɪtʃ] 1 *n* (*gen*) fossé *m*; (*for irrigation*) rigole *f*. 2 *vt* (*: *get rid of*) *person* se débarrasser de, laisser tomber*; *car etc* abandonner.

dither* ['dɪðəʳ] 1 *n*: **to be in a ~** être dans tous ses états. 2 *vi* hésiter. **to ~ over a decision** se tâter pour prendre une décision.

ditto ['dɪtəʊ] *adv* idem.

divan [dɪ'væn] 1 *n* divan *m*. 2 *adj*: **~ bed** divan-lit *m*.

dive [daɪv] 1 *n* [*swimmer, goalkeeper*] plongeon *m*; [*submarine, deep-sea diver*] plongée *f*; [*aircraft*] piqué *m*. 2 *vi* (*gen: often* ~ **in**) plonger; [*aircraft*] descendre en piqué. **he ~d in head first** il a piqué une tête dans l'eau; **to ~ for pearls** pêcher des perles; **he ~d under the table** il s'est jeté sous la table; (*rush*) **to ~ in/out*** *etc* entrer/sortir *etc* tête baissée; **he ~d* for the exit** il a foncé tête baissée vers la sortie; **the goalie ~d for the ball** le gardien de but a plongé pour bloquer le ballon. ♦ **dive-bomb** *vt* bombarder en piqué. ♦ **dive-bombing** *n* bombardement *m* en piqué. ♦ **diver** *n* plongeur *m*; (*in suit*) scaphandrier *m*. ♦ **diving** *adj*: **diving bell** cloche *f* à plongeur; **diving board** plongeoir *m*; **diving suit** scaphandre *m*.

diverge [daɪ'vɜːdʒ] *vi* diverger. ♦ **divergence** *n* divergence *f*. ♦ **divergent** *adj* divergent.

diverse [daɪ'vɜːs] *adj* divers, différent. ♦ **diversification** *n* diversification *f*. ♦ **diversify** *vt* diversifier. ♦ **diversity** *n* diversité *f*.

diversion [daɪ'vɜːʃən] *n* **(a)** [*traffic*] déviation *f*; [*stream*] dérivation *f*. **(b)** (*amusement*) distraction *f*, diversion *f*. **(c)** (*distraction*) diversion *f*. **to create a ~** (*Mil*) opérer une diversion; (*gen*) faire diversion. ♦ **diversionary** *adj* destiné à faire diversion.

divert [daɪ'vɜːt] *vt stream, conversation, attention, eyes* détourner; *train, plane, ship* dérouter; *traffic* dévier; *blow* écarter; (*amuse*) divertir, distraire, amuser. ♦ **diverting** *adj* divertissant.

divest [daɪ'vest] *vt* dépouiller (*of* de).

divide [dɪ'vaɪd] 1 *vt* (*gen*) diviser (*into* en; *between, among* entre); (**~ out**) répartir, distribuer (*among* entre); (**~ off**) séparer (*from* de). **she ~s her time between** elle partage son temps entre; **to ~ 36 by 6** diviser 36 par 6; **policy of ~ and rule** politique *f* consistant à diviser pour régner. 2 *vi* [*river*] se diviser; [*road*] bifurquer; (**~ up**) se diviser (*into* en); (*Math*) être divisible (*by* par). (*Parl*) **the House ~d** la Chambre a procédé au vote. ♦ **divided** *adj* (*lit*) divisé; (*Bot*) découpé; (*fig*) *people* divisés (*about, on* sur); *opinions etc* partagés (*on* sur); *couple, country* désuni; **I feel ~d in my own mind about this** je me sens indécis à cet égard; (*US*) **~d highway** route *f* à chaussées séparées *or* à quatre voies; **~d skirt** jupe-culotte *f*. ♦ **dividing** *adj fence* mitoyen; *line* de démarcation.

dividend ['dɪvɪdend] *n* dividende *m*.

divine[1] [dɪ'vaɪn] *adj* divin. ♦ **divinely** *adv* divine-

ment. ◆ **divinity** *n* divinité *f*; (*Univ*) théologie *f*.
divine[2] [dɪˈvaɪn] *vt the future* prédire; *sb's intentions* deviner; *water, metal* découvrir par la radiesthésie. ◆ **diviner** *n* radiesthésiste *mf*. ◆ **divining rod** *n* baguette *f* de sourcier.
division [dɪˈvɪʒən] *n* (*gen*) division *f* (*into* en, *between, among* entre). ~ **of labour** division du travail; (*Parl*) **to call a** ~ passer au vote. ◆ **divisible** *adj* divisible (*by* par). ◆ **divisive** [dɪˈvaɪsɪv] *adj* qui sème le désaccord. ◆ **divisor** *n* diviseur *m*.
divorce [dɪˈvɔːs] **1** *n* divorce *m* (*from* d'avec). **2** *vt* divorcer avec *or* d'avec; (*fig*) séparer (*from* de). **3** *vi* divorcer. **4** *adj*: ~ **court** ≃ tribunal *m* de grande instance; **to start** ~ **proceedings** demander le divorce. ◆ **divorced** *adj* (*Jur*) divorcé (*from* d'avec); (*fig*) séparé (*from* de). ◆ **divorcee** *n* divorcé(e) *m(f)*.
divulge [daɪˈvʌldʒ] *vt* divulguer, révéler.
dizzy [ˈdɪzɪ] *adj person* pris de vertige; (*heedless*) étourdi; *height, speed, rise in price* vertigineux. **it makes me** ~ cela me donne le vertige. ◆ **dizzily** *adv walk* avec un sentiment de vertige; *rise, fall, spin* vertigineusement. ◆ **dizziness** *n* vertiges *mpl*; **an attack of dizziness** un étourdissement.
do[1] [duː] *3rd person sg pres* **does,** *pret* **did,** *ptp* **done. 1** *aux vb*: ~ **you understand?** (est-ce que) vous comprenez?; **I don't understand** je ne comprends pas; **didn't you speak?** n'avez-vous pas parlé?; **DO come!** venez donc, je vous en prie!; **DO tell him that ...** dites-lui bien que ...; **but I DO like it!** mais si, je l'aime!; **he DID say it** bien sûr qu'il l'a dit; **so you DO know them!** alors c'est vrai que vous les connaissez!; **I DO wish I could come with you** je voudrais tant pouvoir vous accompagner; **you speak better than I** ~ vous parlez mieux que moi; **she says she will go but she never does** elle dit qu'elle ira, mais elle n'y va jamais; **so** ~ **I** moi aussi; **neither** ~ **I** moi non plus; **they said he would go and so he did** on a dit qu'il s'en irait et c'est bien ce qu'il a fait; **you know him, don't you?** vous le connaissez, n'est-ce pas?; **you know him,** ~ **you?** alors vous le connaissez?; **you DO agree, don't you?** vous êtes bien d'accord, n'est-ce pas?; **she said that, did she?** elle a vraiment dit ça?; **she said that, didn't she?** elle a bien dit ça, n'est-ce pas?; **I like them, don't you?** je les aime, pas vous?; ~ **they really?** vraiment?; **may I come in?** – ~! puis-je entrer? – bien sûr!; **who broke the mirror? – I did** qui est-ce qui a cassé le miroir? – c'est moi.

2 *vt* **(a)** (*gen*) faire. **what are you** ~**ing now?** qu'est-ce que tu fais?; **what are you** ~**ing these days?** qu'est-ce que tu deviens?; **what do you** ~ **for a living?** que faites-vous dans la vie?; **I've got plenty to** ~ j'ai beaucoup à faire; **I shall** ~ **nothing of the sort** je n'en ferai rien; **don't** ~ **too much!** n'en faites pas trop!; **he does nothing but complain** il ne fait que se plaindre; **what shall we** ~ **for money?** comment allons-nous faire pour trouver de l'argent?; **what have you done with my gloves?** qu'avez-vous fait de mes gants?; **what am I to** ~ **with you?** qu'est-ce que je vais bien pouvoir faire de toi?; **he didn't know what to** ~ **with himself all day** il ne savait pas quoi faire (de sa peau*) toute la journée; **I shan't know what to** ~ **with all my free time** je ne saurai pas quoi faire de mon temps libre; **I could** ~ **with a cup of tea** je prendrais bien une tasse de thé; **I can't** ~ **with whining children** je ne peux pas supporter les enfants qui pleurnichent; **to** ~ **without sth** se passer de qch.

(b) (*accomplish, produce etc*) *letter, copy, crossword, sum* faire. **I'll** ~ **all I can** je ferai tout mon possible; **what's to be done?** que faire?; **what can I** ~ **for you?** en quoi puis-je vous aider?; **what do you want me to** ~ **about it?** qu'est-ce que vous voulez que j'y fasse?; **to** ~ **sth again** refaire qch; **it's all got to be done again** tout est à refaire; ~ **something for mc, will you?** rends-moi (un) service, veux-tu?; **what's done cannot be undone** ce qui est fait est fait; **that's just not done!, that's not the done thing*** cela ne se fait pas!; **well done!** bravo!, très bien!; **that's done it!*** (*dismay*) il ne manquait plus que ça!; (*satisfaction*) ça y est!; **to** ~ **6 years in jail** faire 6 ans de prison; (*Scol etc*) **to** ~ **Milton/German** faire Milton/de l'allemand; **to** ~ **the flowers** arranger les fleurs (dans les vases); **to** ~ **one's hair** se coiffer; **to** ~ **one's nails** se faire les ongles; **this room needs** ~**ing** cette pièce est à faire; **he's been badly done by** on s'est très mal conduit à son égard; **they** ~ **you very well at that restaurant** on mange rudement* bien à ce restaurant; **she does her lodgers proud** elle dorlote ses pensionnaires; **to** ~ **o.s. well** ne se priver de rien.

(c) (*finished*) **the work's done** le travail est fait; **the soap is done** il ne reste plus de savon; **I haven't done* telling you** je n'ai pas fini de vous dire; **done!** entendu!; **to get done with sth** en finir avec qch; **to be done for*** être fichu*; **to be done in*** (*exhausted*) être éreinté.

(d) (*visit*) *city, museum* visiter, faire*.

(e) (*Aut etc*) **the car was** ~**ing 100** la voiture roulait à 100 à l'heure *or* faisait du 100 à l'heure; **we've done 200 km** nous avons fait *or* parcouru 200 km.

(f) (*suit*) aller à; (*be sufficient for*) suffire à. **that will** ~ **me nicely** (*what I want*) cela fera très bien mon affaire; (*enough*) cela me suffit.

(g) (*play rôle of*) faire, jouer le rôle de; (*pretend to be*) faire; (*mimic*) imiter. **she does the worried mother very convincingly** elle joue à la mère inquiète avec beaucoup de conviction.

(h) (*cheat*) avoir*, refaire*. **you've been done!** on vous a eu* *or* refait!*; **to** ~ **sb out of £10** refaire* qn de 10 livres; **to** ~ **sb out of a job** prendre à qn son travail.

(i) (*cook*) faire; (*prepare*) faire, préparer. **to** ~ **the cooking** faire la cuisine; **how do you like your steak done?** comment aimez-vous votre bifteck?; **steak well done** bifteck bien cuit; **done to a turn** à point.

3 *vi* **(a)** (*gen: act etc*) faire, agir. ~ **as your friends** ~ faites comme vos amis; **he did well to take advice** il a bien fait de demander des conseils; **she was up and** ~**ing at 6 o'clock** elle était à l'ouvrage dès 6 heures du matin.

(b) (*fare*) aller, marcher, être. **how do you** ~? (*greeting: gen*) comment allez-vous?; (*on being introduced*) enchanté de faire votre connaissance; **how are you** ~**ing?*** comment ça va?; **his business is** ~**ing well** ses affaires vont *or* marchent bien.

(c) (*finish*) finir, terminer. **I've done** c'est fini; **I've done with all that** je ne veux plus rien avoir à faire avec tout ça; **have you done with that book?** vous n'avez plus besoin de ce livre?

(d) (*suit*) aller bien, convenir. **that will never** ~! ça ne peut pas aller!; **this room will** ~ cette chambre ira bien *or* fera l'affaire; **will it** ~ **if I come back at 8?** ça va si je reviens à 8 heures?; **it doesn't** ~ **to tell him ...** ce n'est pas la chose à faire que de lui dire ...; **this coat will** ~ **for a cover** ce manteau servira de couverture; **to make** ~ s'arranger, se débrouiller (*with* avec); **to make** ~ **and mend** faire des économies de bouts de chandelle.

(e) (*be sufficient*) suffire (*for* pour). **that will** ~! ça suffit!, assez!

(f) (*phrases*) **there's nothing** ~**ing* in this town** il n'y a rien d'intéressant dans cette ville; **£5? – nothing** ~**ing!*** 5 livres? – rien à faire!* *or* pas question!; **it has to** ~ **with ...** cela concerne ...; **money has a lot to** ~ **with it** c'est surtout une question d'argent; **what has that got to** ~ **with it?** qu'est-ce que cela a à voir?; **that's got a lot to** ~ **with it!** cela y est pour beaucoup!; **that has**

nothing to ~ with the problem cela n'a rien à voir avec le problème; **that has nothing to ~ with you!** cela ne vous regarde pas!; **I won't have anything to ~ with it** je ne veux pas m'en mêler; **to have to ~ with sb** avoir affaire à qn.

4 *n* (*) **(a)** (*party*) soirée *f*; (*ceremony*) fête *f*. **(b) it's a poor ~** c'est plutôt minable; **the ~s and don'ts** ce qu'il faut faire ou ne pas faire.

do away with *vt fus* (*abolish; kill*) supprimer.

do in‡ *vt sep* (*kill*) supprimer.

do out *vt sep room* faire *or* nettoyer (à fond).

do up *vt sep* **(a)** *buttons* boutonner; *zip* fermer; *dress, shoes* attacher; *parcel* faire. **books done up in paper** des livres emballés dans du papier. **(b)** (*renovate*) *house, room* remettre à neuf, refaire; *old dress etc* rafraîchir. **to ~ o.s. up** se faire beau. ♦ **do-gooder*** *n* pilier *m* de bonnes œuvres. ♦ **doing** *n*: **this is your ~ing** c'est vous qui avez fait cela; **that takes some ~ing** il faut le faire!* ♦ **doings** *n* (*pl: deeds*) faits *mpl* et gestes *mpl*; (*sg: thingummy*) machin* *m*, truc* *m*. ♦ **do-it-yourself** *adj shop* de bricolage; **~-it-yourself enthusiast** bricoleur *m*, -euse *f*; **the ~-it-yourself craze** la passion du bricolage.

do² [dəʊ] *n* (*Mus*) do *m*, ut *m*.

docile ['dəʊsaɪl] *adj* docile. ♦ **docility** *n* docilité *f*.

dock¹ [dɒk] **1** *n* dock *m*. (*fig*) **my car is in ~*** ma voiture est en réparation. **2** *vt* mettre à quai. **3** *vi* [*ship*] arriver à quai; [*two spacecraft*] s'amarrer. **the ship has ~ed** le bateau est à quai. ♦ **docker** *n* docker *m*. ♦ **docking** *n* (*Space*) amarrage *m*. ♦ **dockyard** *n* chantier naval.

dock² [dɒk] *n* (*Jur*) banc *m* des accusés.

dock³ [dɒk] *vt tail* couper; (*fig*) *wages* faire une retenue sur. **to ~ 50p off sb's wages** retenir 50 pence sur le salaire de qn.

dock⁴ [dɒk] *n* (*Bot*) patience *f*.

docket ['dɒkɪt] **1** *n* (*on document, parcel*) étiquette *f* (*indiquant le contenu*); (*Customs certificate*) récépissé *m* de douane. **2** *vt contents* résumer; *information etc* consigner sommairement; *packet, document* étiqueter.

doctor ['dɒktəʳ] **1** *n* **(a)** (*Med*) docteur *m*, médecin *m*. **D~ Smith** le docteur Smith; **yes ~** oui docteur; **she is a ~** elle est médecin *or* docteur; **a woman ~** une femme docteur, une femme médecin; (*fig*) **it's just what the ~ ordered*** c'est exactement ce qu'il me fallait. **(b)** (*Univ*) **D~ of Law/of Science** *etc* docteur *m* en droit/ès sciences *etc*; **D~ of Philosophy** (*abbr* **PhD**) docteur ès lettres. **2** *vt* **(a)** *sick person* soigner. **(b)** (*: *castrate*) châtrer (*un animal*). **(c)** (*tamper with*) *wine* frelater; *food* altérer; *text, document* arranger. ♦ **doctorate** *n* doctorat *m* (*in science* ès sciences; *in geography* en géographie).

doctrine ['dɒktrɪn] *n* doctrine *f*. ♦ **doctrinaire** *adj* doctrinaire. ♦ **doctrinal** [dɒk'traɪnl] *adj* doctrinal.

document ['dɒkjʊmənt] **1** *n* document *m*. **~s relating to a case** dossier *m* d'une affaire. **2** ['dɒkjʊment] *vt* documenter. **3** *adj*: **~ case** porte-documents *m inv*. ♦ **documentary** *adj, n* documentaire (*m*). ♦ **documentation** *n* documentation *f*.

dodder ['dɒdəʳ] *vi* ne pas tenir sur ses jambes. ♦ **dodderer** *n* vieux (*or* vieille) gaga* *m(f)*. ♦ **doddering** *adj* gâteux.

dodge [dɒdʒ] **1** *n* (*: *trick, scheme*) truc* *m*. **2** *vt blow, question, difficulty* esquiver; *pursuer* échapper à; *tax* éviter de payer; *work, duty* se dérober à; *acquaintance* éviter. **he ~d the issue** il est volontairement passé à côté de la question. **3** *vi* (*Boxing, Ftbl*) faire une esquive. **to ~ out of the way** s'esquiver; **to ~ behind a tree** disparaître derrière un arbre; **to ~ through the traffic** se faufiler entre les voitures; **to ~ about** aller et venir, remuer. ♦ **dodgems** *npl* autos *fpl* tamponneuses. ♦ **dodgy*** *adj* épineux, douteux; **in a very dodgy situation** dans une mauvaise passe.

doe [dəʊ] *n* (*deer*) biche *f*; (*rabbit*) lapine *f*. ♦ **doeskin** *n* peau *f* de daim.

dog [dɒg] **1** *n* chien(ne) *m(f)*; [*fox etc*] mâle *m*. **to lead a ~'s life** mener une vie de chien; (*Sport*) **the ~s*** les courses *fpl* de lévriers; (*fig*) **to go to the ~s*** [*person*] gâcher sa vie; [*institution, business*] aller à vau-l'eau; **he is being a ~ in the manger** il fait l'empêcheur de tourner en rond; **he hasn't a ~'s chance*** il n'a pas la moindre chance de réussir; **give a ~ a bad name and hang him** qui veut noyer son chien l'accuse de la rage; **lucky ~*** veinard(e)* *m(f)*; **dirty ~*** sale type* *m*. **2** *adj breed, show* canin; *collar* de chien; *food, biscuit* pour chien; *wolf, fox* mâle. **~ licence** permis *m* de posséder un chien. **3** *vt* suivre (de près). **he ~s my footsteps** il ne me lâche pas d'une semelle; **~ged by ill fortune** poursuivi par la malchance. ♦ **dog-eared** *adj* écorné. ♦ **dogged** *adj person* tenace; *courage* opiniâtre. ♦ **doggedly** *adv* avec ténacité *or* opiniâtreté. ♦ **doggo*** *adv*: **to lie ~go** rester tranquille dans son coin. ♦ **doghouse** *n*: **he is in the ~house*** il n'est pas en odeur de sainteté. ♦ **dogleg** *n* (*in road etc*) coude *m*, virage *m*. ♦ **doglike** *adj* de chien. ♦ **dog-paddle** *vi* nager en chien. ♦ **dogsbody*** *n* factotum *m*, bonne *f* à tout faire. ♦ **dog-tired*** *adj* claqué*, éreinté.

doggerel ['dɒgərəl] *n* vers *mpl* de mirliton.

dogma ['dɒgmə] *n* dogme *m*. ♦ **dogmatic** *adj person, attitude* dogmatique (*about* sur); *tone* autoritaire. ♦ **dogmatically** *adv* d'un ton autoritaire.

doh [dəʊ] *n* (*Mus*) = **do²**.

doldrums ['dɒldrəmz] *npl* (*fig*) **to be in the ~** [*person*] avoir le cafard*; [*business*] être dans le marasme.

dole [dəʊl] *n* indemnité *f* de chômage. **on the ~** au chômage.

dole out *vt sep* distribuer au compte-gouttes.

doleful ['dəʊlfʊl] *adj* lugubre, morne. ♦ **dolefully** *adv* d'une manière lugubre *or* morne.

doll [dɒl] *n* **(a)** poupée *f*. **to play with ~s** jouer à la poupée; **~'s house/pram** maison *f*/voiture *f* de poupée. **(b)** (‡: *esp US: girl*) nana‡ *f*, pépée‡ *f*; (*pretty girl*) poupée *f*.

doll up* *vt sep*: **to ~ o.s. up** se faire (tout) beau*.

dollar ['dɒləʳ] **1** *n* dollar *m*. **2** *adj*: **~ area** zone *f* dollar; **~ bill** billet *m* d'un dollar.

dollop* ['dɒləp] *n* [*butter etc*] bon morceau *m*; [*cream, jam*] bonne cuillerée *f*.

dolphin ['dɒlfɪn] *n* (*Zool*) dauphin *m*.

dolt [dəʊlt] *n* idiot(e) *m(f)*. ♦ **doltish** *adj* gourde*, cruche*.

domain [dəʊ'meɪn] *n* domaine *m*.

dome [dəʊm] *n* dôme *m*. ♦ **domed** *adj forehead* bombé; *building* à dôme.

Domesday Book ['du:mzdeɪ,bʊk] *n* Domesday Book *m* (*recueil cadastral établi par Guillaume le Conquérant*).

domestic [də'mestɪk] **1** *adj duty, happiness* familial, de famille; (*Econ, Pol*) *policy, affairs, flights* intérieur; *animal* domestique. **everything of a ~ nature** tout ce qui se rapporte au ménage; **~ chores** ménage *m*; **~ science** arts ménagers; **~ science college** école *f* d'art ménager; **~ science teaching** enseignement *m* ménager; **~ servants** employé(e)s *m(f)pl* de maison; **she was in ~ service** elle était domestique. **2** *n* domestique *mf*. ♦ **domesticate** *vt animal* domestiquer. ♦ **domesticated** *adj person* qui aime son intérieur; *animal* domestiqué; **she's very ~ated** elle est très femme d'intérieur. ♦ **domesticity** *n* (*home life*) vie *f* de famille.

domicile ['dɒmɪsaɪl] *n* domicile *m*. ♦ **domiciled** *adj* domicilié (*at* à). ♦ **domiciliary** *adj* domiciliaire.

dominate ['dɒmɪneɪt] *vti* dominer. ♦ **dominance** *n*

(*gen, Pol*) prédominance *f*; (*Genetics, Psych*) dominance *f*. ♦ **dominant 1** *adj* (*gen*) dominant; (*overbearing*) dominateur; (*Mus*) de dominante; **2** *n* (*Mus*) dominante *f*. ♦ **domination** *n* domination *f*.
domineer [ˌdɒmɪ'nɪəʳ] *vi* se montrer autoritaire (*over* avec). ♦ **domineering** *adj* dominateur, autoritaire.
dominion [də'mɪnɪən] *n* **(a)** (*power*) domination *f*, empire *m* (*over* sur). **(b)** (*territory*) territoire *m*, possessions *fpl*; (*Brit Pol*) dominion *m*.
domino ['dɒmɪnəʊ] *n, pl* **-es** domino *m*. ~**es** (*sg: game*) (jeu *m* de) dominos *mpl*.
don[1] [dɒn] *n* ≈ professeur *m* d'université.
don[2] [dɒn] *vt garment* revêtir, mettre.
donate [dəʊ'neɪt] *vt* faire don de. ♦ **donation** *n* (*act*) donation *f*; (*gift*) don *m*.
done [dʌn] *ptp of* **do**[1].
donkey ['dɒŋkɪ] **1** *n* âne(sse) *m(f)*; (*: *fool*) imbécile *mf*. **she hasn't been here for** ~**'s years*** il y a une éternité qu'elle n'est pas venue ici. **2** *adj*: **the** ~ **work** le gros du travail.
donor ['dəʊnəʳ] *n* (*gen*) donateur *m*, -trice *f*; (*Med*) donneur *m*, -euse *f*.
donut ['dəʊnʌt] *n* (*US*) beignet *m*.
doodle ['du:dl] *vi* griffonner (distraitement).
doom [du:m] **1** *n* (*ruin*) ruine *f*; (*fate*) sort *m*. **2** *vt* condamner (*to* à). ~**ed to failure** voué à l'échec. ♦ **doomed** *adj thing* voué à l'échec; *person* perdu d'avance. ♦ **doomsday** *n* (*fig*) **till** ~**sday** jusqu'à la fin des temps.
door [dɔ:ʳ] *n* (*gen*) porte *f*; *[railway carriage, car]* portière *f*. **he shut the** ~ **in my face** il m'a fermé la porte au nez; **'pay at the** ~**'** 'billets à l'entrée'; **2** ~**s down the street** 2 portes plus loin; **out of** ~**s** (au-)dehors. ♦ **doorbell** *n* sonnette *f*; **there's the** ~**bell!** on sonne à la porte! ♦ **door-handle** *or* ♦ **doorknob** *n* poignée *f* de porte (*or* de portière). ♦ **doorkeeper** *or* ♦ **doorman** *n [hotel]* portier *m*; *[block of flats]* concierge *m*. ♦ **door-knocker** *n* heurtoir *m*. ♦ **doormat** *n* paillasson *m* (d'entrée); (*: *person*) chiffe *f* molle. ♦ **doorstep** *n* pas *m* de porte; **at my** ~**step** à ma porte. ♦ **door-to-door** *adj salesman* à domicile; ~**-to-**~ **selling** porte à porte *m inv*. ♦ **doorway** *n* porte *f*; **in the** ~**way** dans l'embrasure *f* de la porte.
dope [dəʊp] **1** *n* **(a)** (*: *drugs*) drogue *f*; (*for athlete, horse*) dopant *m*. **to take** ~ se droguer, se doper. **(b)** (*information*) tuyaux* *mpl*, renseignements *mpl*. **to give sb the** ~‡ tuyauter* qn. **(c)** (‡: *stupid person*) andouille‡ *f*, idiot(e) *m(f)*. **2** *vt horse, person* doper; *food* mettre une drogue *or* un dopant dans. ♦ **dope-peddler*** *or* ♦ **dope-pusher*** *n* revendeur *m*, -euse *f* de drogue. ♦ **dope-test*** *n* contrôle *m* anti-doping *inv*. ♦ **dopey*** *adj* (*drugged*) drogué; (*sleepy*) à moitié endormi; (*stupid*) abruti*.
dormant ['dɔ:mənt] *adj energy* en veilleuse; (*Bio, Bot*) dormant; *volcano* en sommeil; *rule* inappliqué. **to lie** ~ rester en sommeil *etc*.
dormer window ['dɔ:mə'wɪndəʊ] *n* lucarne *f*.
dormitory ['dɔ:mɪtrɪ] **1** *n* dortoir *m*. **2** *adj suburb, town* dortoir *f inv*.
Dormobile ['dɔ:məbi:l] *n* ® auto-camping *f*.
dormouse ['dɔ:maʊs] *n, pl* **-mice** loir *m*.
dose [dəʊs] **1** *n* **(a)** (*Pharm*) dose *f*. **give him a** ~ **of medicine** donne-lui son médicament; (*fig*) **to give sb a** ~ **of his own medicine** rendre à qn la monnaie de sa pièce; **in small** ~**s** à faible dose; (*: *fig*) à petites doses. **(b)** (*bout of illness*) attaque *f* (*of* de). **a** ~ **of flu** une bonne grippe*. **2** *vt person* administrer un médicament à. **she's always dosing herself** elle se bourre de médicaments. ♦ **dosage** *n* (*on medicine bottle*) posologie *f*.
doss [dɒs] *vi*: **to** ~ **down*** loger quelque part. ♦ **doss-house** *n* asile *m* (de nuit).
dossier ['dɒsɪeɪ] *n* dossier *m*.
dot [dɒt] **1** *n* (*gen*) point *m*; (*on material*) pois *m*. (*Morse*) ~**s and dashes** points et traits *mpl*; (*in punctuation*) ~**s** points de suspension; (*fig*) **on the** ~* à l'heure pile*. **2** *vt* (*fig*) **to** ~ **one's i's and cross one's t's** mettre les points sur les i; **field** ~**ted with flowers** champ parsemé de fleurs; **cars** ~**ted along the route** des voitures échelonnées sur le parcours; ~**ted line** ligne pointillée; **to tear along the** ~**ted line** détacher suivant le pointillé; **to sign on the** ~**ted line** signer sur la ligne pointillée; (*fig*) accepter. ♦ **dotty**‡ *adj* toqué*, fou (*about* de).
dote [dəʊt] *vi*: **to** ~ **on sb/sth** aimer qn/qch à la folie; **her doting father** son père qui l'adore. ♦ **dotage** *n*: **in one's dotage** gâteux.
double ['dʌbl] **1** *adj* (*gen*) double; *door* à deux battants; *room* pour deux personnes; *bed* de deux personnes. ~ **seven five four** (*7754*) deux fois sept cinq quatre, (*telephone number*) soixante-dix-sept cinquante-quatre; **spelt with a** ~ **'p'** écrit avec deux 'p'; (*Aut*) ~ **bend** virage *m* en S; ~ **consonant** consonne *f* double; ~ **chin** double menton *m*; **with a** ~ **meaning** à double sens; ~ **saucepan** casserole *f* à double fond; (*Typ*) **in** ~ **spacing** à double interligne; **a** ~ **whisky** un double whisky; **to lead a** ~ **life** mener une double vie; **to play a** ~ **game** jouer un double jeu; **to earn** ~ **time** être payé double; **to do a** ~ **take*** y regarder à deux fois.

2 *adv* (*twice*) deux fois; (*twofold*) *fold, bend* en deux; *see* double. **I've got** ~ **what you've got** j'en ai deux fois plus que toi, j'ai le double de ce que tu as.

3 *n* **(a)** (*twice sth*) double *m*. (*Tennis*) **mixed/ ladies'** ~**s** double *m* mixte/dames; ~ **or quits** quitte ou double; (*running*) **at the** ~ au pas de course. **(b)** (*exactly similar thing*) réplique *f*; (*person*) sosie *m*; (*Cine: stand-in*) doublure *f*.

4 *vt* (*multiply by two*) doubler; (*fold:* ~ **over**) plier en deux, replier. (*Theat*) **to** ~ **the parts of** jouer les deux rôles de; **to** ~ **sb's part** être la doublure de qn.

5 *vi [prices etc]* doubler; (*Cards*) contrer. (*Bridge*) ~! contre!; (*Theat*) **he** ~**d as ...** il jouait aussi le rôle de ... .
double back 1 *vi* revenir sur ses pas; *[road]* faire un brusque crochet. **2** *vt sep* replier.
double up *vi* **(a)** (*bend: also* ~ **over**) se plier, se courber. **to** ~ **up with laughter/pain** être plié en deux de rire/de douleur. **(b)** (*share room*) partager une chambre (*with* avec).
♦ **double-barrelled** *adj gun* à deux coups; *surname* à rallonges*. ♦ **double bass** *n* contrebasse *f*. ♦ **double-breasted** *adj* croisé (*veston*). ♦ **double-cross*** *vt* trahir, doubler*. ♦ **double-dealer** *n* fourbe *m*. ♦ **double-dealing 1** *n* double jeu *m*, duplicité *f*; **2** *adj* faux (comme un jeton*). ♦ **double-decker** *n* (*bus*) autobus *m* à impériale; (*sandwich*) sandwich *m* à deux garnitures superposées. ♦ **double-declutch** *vi* faire un double débrayage. ♦ **double-dutch*** *n* charabia* *m*. ♦ **double entendre** [ˌdu:blɒn'tɒndrə] *n* ambiguïté *f*. ♦ **double-glaze** *vt*: **to** ~**-glaze a window** poser une double fenêtre. ♦ **double-glazing** *n*: **to put in** ~**-glazing** faire installer des doubles fenêtres. ♦ **double-jointed** *adj* désarticulé. ♦ **double-knitting** *adj wool* sport *inv*. ♦ **double-lock** *vt* fermer à double tour. ♦ **double-park** *vi* stationner en double file. ♦ **double-quick** *adv run etc* au pas de course; *do, finish* en vitesse. ♦ **double-talk** *n* (*pej*) paroles *fpl* trompeuses. ♦ **doubly** *adv* (*gen*) doublement, deux fois plus; **to be doubly careful** redoubler de prudence.
doubt [daʊt] **1** *n* doute *m*. **to be in** ~ *[person]* être dans le doute (*about* au sujet de); *[sb's honesty etc]* être en doute; **there is room for** ~ il est permis de douter; **to cast** ~**(s) on** jeter le doute sur; **there is some** ~ **about** on ne sait pas très bien si + *indic*; **to have one's** ~**s about sth** avoir des

doutes sur qch; **I have my ~s about whether** je doute que + *subj*; **I have no ~(s) about it** je n'en doute pas; **there is no ~ that** il n'y a pas de doute que + *indic*; **no ~** sans doute; **no ~ he will come** sans doute qu'il viendra; **without (a) ~** sans aucun doute; **beyond ~** (*adj*) indubitable; (*adv*) indubitablement; **if in ~** en cas de doute.

2 *vt* **(a)** *person, sb's honesty, statement* douter de. **I ~ it very much** j'en doute fort; **I ~ed my own eyes** je n'en croyais pas mes yeux; **~ing Thomas** Thomas *m* l'incrédule.

(b) douter (*whether, if* que + *subj*). **I don't ~ that he will come** je ne doute pas qu'il vienne; **she didn't ~ that he would come** elle ne doutait pas qu'il viendrait; **I ~ he won't come now** je crains qu'il ne vienne pas maintenant.

♦ **doubter** *n* incrédule *mf*. ♦ **doubtful** *adj* (*undecided*) *person, look* indécis, peu convaincu; *question* douteux, discutable; *result* indécis; (*questionable*) *person, affair* suspect, louche; *taste* douteux; **to be ~ful about sb/sth** avoir des doutes sur qn/qch; **to be ~ful about doing** hésiter à faire; **I'm a bit ~ful** je n'en suis pas sûr; **it is ~ful whether** *or* **that** il est douteux que + *subj*. ♦ **doubtfully** *adv* (*unconvincedly*) d'un air de doute; (*hesitatingly*) d'une façon indécise. ♦ **doubtfulness** *n* (*hesitation*) indécision *f*; (*uncertainty*) incertitude *f*; (*suspicious quality*) caractère *m* louche. ♦ **doubtless** *adv* très probablement.

douche [duːʃ] **1** *n* (*shower bath*) douche *f*; (*Med: internal*) lavage *m* interne. (*fig*) **it was like a cold ~** cela a été une douche froide. **2** *vt* doucher.

dough [dəʊ] *n* **(a)** pâte *f*. **bread ~** pâte à pain. **(b)** (‡: *money*) fric‡ *m*, argent *m*. ♦ **doughnut** *n* beignet *m*. ♦ **doughy** *adj consistency* pâteux; *bread* mal cuit.

dour ['dʊəʳ] *adj* (*hard*) austère; (*stubborn*) buté.

douse [daʊs] *vt* (*drench*) tremper; *flames* éteindre.

dove [dʌv] *n* colombe *f* (*also Pol*). ♦ **dovecote** *n* colombier *m*. ♦ **dove-grey** *adj* gris perle *inv*. ♦ **dovetail 1** *vt plans etc* faire concorder, raccorder; **2** *vi [piece of wood]* se raccorder (*into* à); *[plans]* concorder.

Dover ['dəʊvəʳ] *n* Douvres.

dowager ['daʊədʒəʳ] *n* douairière *f*.

dowdy ['daʊdɪ] *adj* sans chic. ♦ **dowdiness** *n* manque *m* de chic.

down[1] [daʊn] **1** *adv* **(a)** *move* en bas, vers le bas; (*to ground*) à terre, par terre. (*to dog*) **~!** couché!; **~ with traitors!** à bas les traîtres!; **to come** *or* **go ~** descendre; **to fall ~** tomber; **~ and ~** de plus en plus bas; **to run ~** descendre en courant; **he came ~ from London yesterday** il est arrivé de Londres hier; **we're going ~ to the sea tomorrow** demain nous allons à la mer; (*Univ*) **he came ~ from Oxford in 1973** il est sorti d'Oxford en 1973; **from 1700 ~ to the present** depuis 1700 jusqu'à nos jours; **from the biggest ~ to the smallest** du plus grand jusqu'au plus petit.

(b) *stay* en bas. **~ there** en bas (là-bas); **~ here** ici, en bas; **~ under** aux Antipodes (*Australie etc*); **don't hit a man when he is ~** ne frappez pas un homme à terre; **the sun is ~** le soleil est couché; **the blinds were ~** les stores étaient baissés; **Paul isn't ~ yet** Paul n'est pas encore descendu; **I've been ~ with flu** j'ai été au lit avec une grippe; **I'm feeling rather ~*** j'ai un peu le cafard*; **the tyre is ~** le pneu est dégonflé; **his temperature is ~** sa température a baissé; **I'm £2 ~ on what I expected** j'ai 2 livres de moins que je ne pensais; **I've got it ~ in my diary** je l'ai inscrit sur mon agenda; **did you get ~ what he said?** est-ce que vous avez noté ce qu'il a dit?; **let's get it ~ on paper** mettons-le par écrit; **to be ~ for the next race** être inscrit dans la course suivante; **to be ~ on sb*** avoir une dent contre qn; **I am ~ on my luck** je n'ai pas de chance.

2 *prep roll* du haut en bas de; *drip* le long de. **he ran his finger ~ the list** il a parcouru la liste du doigt; **he went ~ the hill** il a descendu la colline; **he's ~ the hill** il est en bas de la côte; **~ the street (from us)** plus bas *or* plus loin (que nous) dans la rue; **he was walking ~ the street** il descendait la rue; **he has gone ~ town** il est allé *or* descendu en ville; **looking ~ this street, you can see ...** si vous regardez le long de cette rue, vous verrez ...; **~ the ages** au cours des siècles.

3 *n*: **to have a ~ on sb*** avoir une dent contre qn.

4 *vt opponent* terrasser, abattre; *enemy plane* descendre*. **to ~ tools** (*stop work*) cesser le travail; (*strike*) se mettre en grève; **he ~ed* a glass of beer** il a vidé un verre de bière.

5 *adj train, platform* en provenance de Londres. (*fig*) **on the ~ grade** sur le déclin; **~ payment** acompte *m*.

♦ **down-and-out 1** *adj* (*Boxing*) hors de combat; (*destitute*) sur le pavé; **2** *n* (*tramp*) clochard *m*; (*penniless*) sans-le-sou *m*. ♦ **down-at-heel** *adj person, appearance* miteux; *shoes* éculé. ♦ **downcast** *adj* (*discouraged*) abattu, démoralisé; *eyes* baissé. ♦ **downfall** *n* chute *f*, ruine *f*. ♦ **downgrade** *vt person* rétrograder; *thing* déclasser. ♦ **downhearted** *adj* découragé; **don't be ~hearted** ne te laisse pas décourager! ♦ **downhill** *adv*: **to go ~hill** *[road]* descendre; *[car]* descendre la pente; (*fig*) *[person]* être sur le déclin; *[business etc]* péricliter. ♦ **down-in-the-mouth** *adj* abattu, démoralisé. ♦ **downpour** *n* pluie *f* torrentielle. ♦ **downright 1** *adj person* franc, direct; *refusal* catégorique; *lie* effronté; *rudeness* flagrant; **it's a ~right lie to say ...** c'est mentir effrontément que de dire ...; **2** *adv rude* carrément; *refuse* catégoriquement; *impossible* purement et simplement. ♦ **downstage** *adv* sur *or* vers le devant de la scène (*from* par rapport à). ♦ **downstairs 1** *adj* (*on the ground floor*) du rez-de-chaussée; (*on the floor underneath*) de l'étage au-dessous; (*below*) d'en bas; **2** *adv* au rez-de-chaussée; à l'étage inférieur; en bas; **to come** *or* **go ~stairs** descendre (l'escalier). ♦ **downstream** *adv* en aval. ♦ **down-to-earth** *adj* terre-à-terre *inv*. ♦ **downtown 1** *adv* en ville; **2** *adj*: **~town Chicago** le centre de Chicago. ♦ **downtrodden** *adj* opprimé, tyrannisé. ♦ **downward 1** *adj movement, pull* vers le bas; *road* qui descend en pente; *glance* baissé; *trend* à la baisse; **2** *adv* (*also* **~wards**) *go, look* vers le bas, en bas; **face ~ward(s)** *person* face contre terre; *object* face en dessous; **from the 10th century ~ward(s)** à partir du 10e siècle; **from the king ~ward(s)** depuis le roi (jusqu'au plus humble). ♦ **downwind** *adv* sous le vent (*of, from* par rapport à).

down[2] [daʊn] *n [bird, person, plant]* duvet *m*; *[fruit]* peau *f* (veloutée). ♦ **downie** *n* (*quilt*) couette *f*. ♦ **downy** *adj skin, leaf* duveté; *softness* duveteux; *peach* velouté.

down[3] [daʊn] *n* (*hill*) colline *f* (*herbeuse*).

dowry ['daʊrɪ] *n* dot *f*.

dowse [daʊz] *vi* faire de la radiesthésie (*for* pour trouver). ♦ **dowser** *n* radiesthésiste *mf*. ♦ **dowsing rod** *n* baguette *f* (de sourcier).

doze [dəʊz] **1** *n* somme *m*. **2** *vi* sommeiller, faire un petit somme. **to be dozing** être assoupi; **to ~ off** s'assoupir. ♦ **dozy** *adj* (*sleepy*) somnolent; (*: *stupid*) pas très dégourdi.

dozen ['dʌzn] *n* douzaine *f*. **a ~ shirts** une douzaine de chemises; **a round ~** une bonne douzaine; **half-a-~** une demi-douzaine; **20p a ~** 20 pence la douzaine; **~s of times** des dizaines *or* douzaines de fois; **~s of people** des dizaines de gens.

drab [dræb] *adj* terne. ♦ **drabness** *n* caractère *m or* aspect *m* terne.

drachm [dræm] *n* **(a)** (*Measure, Pharm*) drachme *f*. **(b)** = **drachma**.

drachma ['dræknə] *n, pl* **-s** *or* **drachmae** (*coin*) drachme *f.*

draconian [drə'kəʊnɪən] *adj* draconien.

draft [drɑːft] **1** *n* **(a)** (*outline*) *[letter]* brouillon *m*; *[novel]* ébauche *f.* **(b)** (*for money*) traite *f.* **(c)** (*Mil: group*) détachement *m*; (*US Mil: conscript intake*) contingent *m.* **(d)** (*US*) = **draught. 2** *adj letter, essay* au brouillon; *version* préliminaire. (*US Mil*) ~ **board** conseil *m* de révision; ~ **dodger** insoumis *m.* **3** *vt* **(a)** (~ **out**) *letter* faire le brouillon de; *speech* écrire, préparer; *bill, contract* rédiger; *plan, diagram* esquisser. **(b)** (*US Mil*) *conscript* appeler (sous les drapeaux). (*esp Mil*) **to ~ sb to a post/to do sth** détacher *or* désigner qn à un poste/pour faire qch.

drag [dræg] **1** *n* **(a)** (*for dredging etc*) drague *f*; (*cluster of hooks*) araignée *f*; (~*net*) drège *f.* **(b)** (*Aviat, Naut: resistance*) résistance *f.* (*nuisance*) **what a ~!*** quelle barbe!* **(c)** (*: *clothing*) travesti *m.* **in ~** en travesti. **2** *adj* (*Theat*) ~ **show*** spectacle *m* de travestis. **3** *vi* (*gen*) traîner (à terre); *[anchor]* chasser. **4** *vt* **(a)** *object* traîner, tirer; *person* traîner, entraîner. **to ~ one's feet** traîner les pieds; (*fig*) traîner (exprès); **to ~ the truth from sb** arracher la vérité à qn. **(b)** *river* draguer (*for* à la recherche de).

drag about 1 *vi* traîner. **2** *vt sep* traîner, trimbaler*. **to ~ o.s. about (in pain** *etc*) se traîner péniblement (sous l'effet de la douleur *etc*).

drag along *vt sep person* entraîner (à contrecœur); *toy etc* tirer. **to ~ o.s. along** se traîner.

drag away *vt sep* arracher (*from* à), emmener de force (*from* de).

drag down *vt sep* entraîner (en bas); *[illness]* affaiblir. (*fig*) **to ~ sb down to one's own level** rabaisser qn à son niveau.

drag in *vt sep subject* tenir à placer.

drag on *vi [meeting, conversation]* s'éterniser.

dragon ['drægən] *n* dragon *m.* ♦ **dragonfly** *n* libellule *f.*

dragoon [drə'guːn] **1** *n* (*Mil*) dragon *m.* **2** *vt*: **to ~ sb into doing** contraindre qn à faire.

drain [dreɪn] **1** *n* **(a)** (*in town*) égout *m*; (*in house*) canalisation *f* sanitaire, tuyau *m* d'écoulement; (*on washing machine etc*) tuyau d'écoulement; (*Agr, Med*) drain *m*; (~ *cover*) (*in street*) bouche *f* d'égout; (*beside house*) puisard *m.* **open ~** canal *m or* égout à ciel ouvert; (*fig*) **to throw one's money down the ~** jeter son argent par les fenêtres; **all his hopes have gone down the ~*** voilà tous ses espoirs à l'eau*. **(b)** (*on resources, manpower*) perte *f* (*on* en); (*on strength*) épuisement *m* (*on* de). **it has been a great ~ on her** cela l'a complètement épuisée. **2** *vt land, marshes* assécher; *vegetables* égoutter; *mine, wound* drainer; *reservoir, boiler* vider; *glass* vider complètement; *wine in glass* boire jusqu'à la dernière goutte. **to ~ a country of resources** saigner un pays. **3** *vi [liquid, stream]* s'écouler (*into* dans); *[vegetables, dishes]* s'égoutter.

drain away, drain off 1 *vi [liquid]* s'écouler; *[strength]* s'épuiser. **2** *vt sep liquid* faire couler.

♦ **drainage 1** *n* (*act of draining*) assèchement *m*, drainage *m*; (*system*) système *m* de fossés (*land*) *or* d'égouts (*town etc*); **2** *adj* (*Geog*) ~**age basin** bassin *m* hydrographique; (*Med*) ~**age tube** drain *m.* ♦ **drainer** *n* égouttoir *m.* ♦ **drain(ing) board** *n* égouttoir *m*, paillasse *f.* ♦ **drainpipe** *n* tuyau *m* d'écoulement *or* de drainage.

drake [dreɪk] *n* canard *m* (mâle).

drama ['drɑːmə] **1** *n* (*gen*) drame *m*; (*dramatic art*) théâtre *m.* **English ~** le théâtre anglais. **2** *adj*: ~ **critic** critique *m* dramatique. ♦ **dramatic** *adj art, criticism* dramatique; *news, situation, event* dramatique; *effect, entry* théâtral; *change* spectaculaire. ♦ **dramatically** *adv* d'une manière dramatique *or* théâtrale *or* spectaculaire. ♦ **dramatics** *npl* art *m* dramatique; (*: *fig*) comédie *f* (*fig*). ♦ **dramatis personae** *npl* personnages *mpl* (*d'une pièce etc*). ♦ **dramatist** *n* auteur *m* dramatique. ♦ **dramatization** *n* adaptation *f* pour la scène *etc.* ♦ **dramatize** *vt* (*gen*) dramatiser; (*adapt*) *novel etc* adapter pour la scène *or* (*Cine*) pour l'écran *or* (*TV*) pour la télévision; *episodes from sb's life* présenter sous forme de sketch.

drank [dræŋk] *pret of* **drink.**

drape [dreɪp] **1** *vt* (*gen*) draper (*with* de); *room, altar* tendre (*with* de). **2** *n*: ~**s** tentures *fpl*; (*US*) rideaux *mpl.* ♦ **draper** *n* marchand(e) *m(f)* de nouveautés. ♦ **drapery** *n* (*material*) draperie *f*, étoffes *fpl*; (*hangings*) tentures *fpl*; (*shop*) magasin *m* de nouveautés.

drastic ['dræstɪk] *adj remedy* énergique; *effect, change* radical; *measures* énergique, draconien; *price reduction* massif. ♦ **drastically** *adv* radicalement.

drat* [dræt] *excl* zut!* ♦ **dratted*** *adj* sacré* (*before n*).

draught [drɑːft] **1** *n* **(a)** courant *m* d'air; (*for fire*) tirage *m*; (*Naut*) tirant *m* d'eau. (*fig*) **to feel the ~** devoir se serrer la ceinture. **(b)** *[medicine]* breuvage *m.* **a ~ of cider** un coup de cidre; **to drink in long ~s** boire à longs traits. **(c) (game of) ~s** (jeu *m* de) dames *fpl.* **2** *adj animal* de trait; *beer* à la pression. ~ **excluder** bourrelet *m* (*de porte etc*). ♦ **draughtboard** *n* damier *m.* ♦ **draughtiness** *n* courants *mpl* d'air. ♦ **draughtproof 1** *adj* calfeutré; **2** *vt* calfeutrer. ♦ **draughtsman** *n* (*Art*) dessinateur *m*, -trice *f*; (*in drawing office*) dessinateur, -trice industriel(le). ♦ **draughtsmanship** *n [artist]* talent *m* de dessinateur; (*in industry*) art *m* du dessin industriel. ♦ **draughty** *adj room* plein de courants d'air; *street corner* exposé à tous les vents.

draw [drɔː] (*vb: pret* **drew,** *ptp* **drawn**) **1** *n* **(a)** (*lottery*) tombola *f*; (*act of* ~*ing*) tirage *m* au sort. **(b)** match *m* nul, partie *f* nulle. **the match ended in a ~** ils ont fini par faire match nul. **(c)** (*attraction*) attraction *f.* **Dirk Bogarde was the big ~** Dirk Bogarde était la grande attraction. **(d) to be quick on the ~** avoir la détente rapide; (*fig*) avoir la repartie facile.

2 *vt* **(a)** (*pull*) *object, bolt, curtains, cart, train* tirer; *caravan, trailer* remorquer. **to ~ a bow** tirer à l'arc; **to ~ one's hand over one's eyes** se passer la main sur les yeux; **I drew her arm through mine** j'ai passé son bras sous le mien; **to ~ one's finger along a surface** passer le doigt sur une surface; **to ~ one's hat over one's eyes** baisser son chapeau sur ses yeux; (*aim*) **to ~ a bead on sth** viser qch.

(b) (*extract*) (*from pocket, bag, tap, pump*) tirer (*from* de); (*from well*) puiser (*from* dans); *sword* dégainer; *teeth* arracher; *cork, money from bank* retirer (*from* de); *cheque* tirer (*on* sur); *salary* toucher; (*Culin*) *fowl* vider. (*fig*) **to ~ sb's teeth** mettre qn hors d'état de nuire; **he drew a gun on me** il a tiré un pistolet et l'a braqué sur moi; **to ~ a bath** faire couler un bain; **the stone drew blood** la pierre l'a fait saigner; **that remark drew blood** cette remarque a porté; **to ~ (a) breath** aspirer; (*fig*) souffler; **to ~ comfort from** puiser une consolation dans; **to ~ a smile from sb** faire sourire qn.

(c) (*attract etc*) *attention, customer, crowd* attirer. **to feel ~n towards sb** se sentir attiré par qn; **to ~ sb into a plan** entraîner qn dans un projet; **he refuses to be ~n** il refuse de réagir.

(d) (*sketch etc*) *picture* dessiner; *plan, line, circle* tracer; *portrait* faire; *map* (*Geog*) dresser, (*Scol*) dessiner; *situation* faire un tableau de; *character* dépeindre. (*fig*) **I ~ the line at (doing) that** je n'irai pas jusqu'à (faire) cela; **it's hard to know where to ~ the line** il n'est pas facile de savoir où fixer les limites.

(e) (*establish*) *conclusion* tirer (*from* de); *comparison, parallel, distinction* établir (*between* entre).

(f) to ~ a match/game faire match nul/partie nulle.

3 *vi* **(a)** (*move*) se diriger (*towards* vers). **to ~ to one side, to ~ apart** s'écarter; **the train drew into the station** le train est entré en gare; **the car drew over towards ...** la voiture a dévié vers ...; **he drew ahead of the other runners** il s'est détaché des autres coureurs; **they drew level** ils sont arrivés à la hauteur l'un de l'autre; **to ~ near (to)** s'approcher (de); *[time, event]* approcher (de); **to ~ to an end** tirer à *or* toucher à sa fin.

(b) (*Cards*) tirer (*for* pour); *[chimney, pipe]* tirer; *[pump]* aspirer; *[tea]* infuser. **to ~ on one's savings** tirer sur ses économies.

(c) (*be equal*) *[two teams]* faire match nul; (*in exams, competitions*) être ex æquo *inv.* **to ~ for second place** remporter la deuxième place ex æquo.

(d) (*Art*) dessiner.

draw along *vt sep cart* tirer, traîner; (*fig*) *person* entraîner.

draw aside 1 *vi [people]* s'écarter. **2** *vt sep person* tirer à l'écart; *object* écarter.

draw away 1 *vi* (*go away*) s'éloigner (*from* de); (*move ahead*) prendre de l'avance (*from* sur). **2** *vt sep person* éloigner, emmener; *object* retirer, ôter.

draw back 1 *vi* se reculer (*from* de); (*fig*) reculer (*at, before, from* devant). **2** *vt sep person* faire reculer; *object, hand* retirer.

draw down *vt sep blind* baisser; *blame* attirer (*on* sur).

draw in 1 *vi* **(a)** (*Aut*) s'arrêter. **(b) the days are ~ing in** les jours raccourcissent. **2** *vt sep air* aspirer; (*pull back in*) *claws etc* rentrer; *reins* tirer sur; *crowds* attirer.

draw off *vt sep gloves, garment* retirer; *pint of beer* tirer; (*Med*) *blood* prendre.

draw on 1 *vi [time]* s'avancer. **2** *vt sep garment* enfiler; *shoes* mettre.

draw out 1 *vi*: **the days are ~ing out** les jours rallongent. **2** *vt sep* **(a)** (*bring out*) *handkerchief, purse* sortir (*from* de); *money from bank* retirer (*from* de); *secret, plan* soutirer (*from* à). **try and ~ him out** essayez de le faire parler. **(b)** (*stretch*) *wire* étirer; *speech, meeting* faire tirer en longueur; *meal* prolonger.

draw up 1 *vi [car etc]* s'arrêter. **2** *vt sep* **(a)** *chair* approcher; *troops* aligner. **to ~ o.s. up (to one's full height)** se redresser (fièrement). **(b)** *contract, agreement, list* dresser; *scheme* formuler, établir.

♦ **drawback** *n* inconvénient *m*, désavantage *m* (*to* à). ♦ **drawbridge** *n* pont-levis *m*. ♦ **drawer** *n* **(a)** [drɔːʳ] *[furniture]* tiroir *m*; **(b)** [ˈdrɔːəʳ] *[cheque etc]* tireur *m*. ♦ **drawing 1** *n* dessin *m*; **to study ~ing** étudier le dessin; **pencil ~ing** dessin au crayon; **rough ~ing** ébauche *f*; **2** *adj*: **~ing board** planche *f* à dessin; (*fig*) **the scheme is still on the ~ing board** le projet est encore à l'étude; **~ing office** bureau *m* de dessin industriel; **~ing pin** punaise *f* (*à papier*); **~ing room** salon *m*. ♦ **drawn** *adj* **(a)** (*haggard*) *features* tiré, crispé (*with pain* par la douleur); **to look ~n** avoir les traits tirés; **(b)** (*equal*) *game, match* nul; *battle* indécis. ♦ **draw-sheet** *n* alaise *f*. ♦ **drawstring** *n* cordon *m*.

drawl [drɔːl] **1** *vi* parler d'une voix traînante. **2** *vt* dire d'une voix traînante. **3** *n* voix traînante. **an American ~** un accent américain.

dread [dred] **1** *vt* redouter (*doing* de faire; *that* que ... ne + *subj*). **2** *n* terreur *f*, effroi *m*, épouvante *f*. **3** *adj* (*liter*) redoutable. ♦ **dreadful** *adj crime, sight, suffering* épouvantable, atroce; *weapon, foe* redoutable; (*: *less strong*) *weather* affreux, atroce; *child* insupportable; **it's a ~ful thing but ...** c'est terrible, mais ...; **I feel ~ful!** (*ill*) je ne me sens pas bien du tout!; (*ashamed*) j'ai vraiment honte! ♦ **dreadfully** *adv* terriblement, horriblement; **~fully sorry** absolument désolé.

dream [driːm] (*vb: pret, ptp* **dreamed** *or* **dreamt**) **1** *n* rêve *m*. **to have a ~ about sth** faire un rêve sur qch, rêver de qch; **to have ~s of doing** rêver de faire; **I've had a bad ~** j'ai fait un mauvais rêve *or* un cauchemar; **it was like a ~ come true** c'était comme dans un rêve; **sweet ~s!** fais de beaux rêves!; **life is but a ~** la vie n'est qu'un songe; **she goes around in a ~*** elle est dans les nuages, elle rêvasse; **the house of his ~s** la maison de ses rêves; **idle ~s** rêvasseries *fpl*; **rich beyond his wildest ~s** plus riche qu'il n'aurait jamais pu rêver de l'être; **isn't he a ~?*** n'est-ce pas qu'il est adorable?

2 *adj*: **a ~ house** une maison de rêve; **his ~ house** la maison de ses rêves; **he lives in a ~ world** il plane complètement.

3 *vi* **(a)** rêver (*about, of* de; *about or of doing* qu'on a fait). **I'm sorry, I was ~ing** excusez-moi, j'étais dans la lune *or* je rêvais. **(b)** (*imagine*) songer, penser (*of* à; *of doing* à faire). **I shouldn't ~ of telling her!** jamais il ne me viendrait à l'idée de lui dire cela!; **I shouldn't ~ of it!** jamais de la vie!, pas question!

4 *vt* **(a)** (*in sleep*) rêver (*that* que). **to ~ a dream** faire un rêve. **(b)** (*imagine*) imaginer. **I didn't ~ that ...** je n'ai jamais imaginé un instant que ... .

dream up* *vt sep idea* imaginer.

♦ **dreamer** *n* rêveur *m*, -euse *f*; (*politically*) utopiste *mf*. ♦ **dreamily** *adv* d'un air rêveur, rêveusement. ♦ **dreamland** *n* pays *m* des rêves. ♦ **dreamy** *adj* (*gen*) rêveur; *music* langoureux; (*: *adorable*) ravissant.

dreary [ˈdrɪərɪ] *adj weather, landscape* morne; *life, work* monotone; *speech, person* ennuyeux. ♦ **dreariness** *n* caractère *m* morne *or* ennuyeux; monotonie *f*.

dredge[1] [dredʒ] **1** *n* drague *f*. **2** *vti* draguer (*for* pour trouver).

dredge up *vt sep* draguer; *unpleasant facts* déterrer.

♦ **dredger** *n* dragueur *m*. ♦ **dredging** *n* dragage *m*.

dredge[2] [dredʒ] *vt sugar* saupoudrer (*with* de; *over* sur).

dregs [dregz] *npl* lie *f* (*also fig*).

drench [drentʃ] *vt* tremper, mouiller. **to get ~ed to the skin** se faire tremper jusqu'aux os. ♦ **drenching** *adj rain* battant.

Dresden [ˈdrezdən] *n* (~ *china*) porcelaine *f* de Saxe. **a piece of ~** un saxe.

dress [dres] **1** *n* (*gown*) robe *f*; (*clothing*) tenue *f*. **in eastern ~** en tenue orientale. **2** *adj shirt* de soirée; *uniform* de cérémonie. (*Theat*) **~ circle** premier balcon *m*; **~ designer** styliste *mf* (*mode*), (*famous*) couturier *m*; **~ designing** stylisme *m*; **~ length** (*of material*) hauteur *f* (de robe); **~ rehearsal** répétition *f* générale. **3** *vt* **(a)** habiller; (*Theat*) *play* costumer. **to ~ o.s.** s'habiller; **well-~ed** bien habillé; **~ed for the country/for tennis** en tenue de sport/de tennis; **~ed in black** habillé de *or* en noir; **~ed to kill‡** sur son trente et un. **(b)** *salad* assaisonner (*d'une vinaigrette etc*); *food for table* apprêter, accommoder; *chicken, crab* préparer; *skins, material* apprêter; *wound* panser. **to ~ sb's wound** faire le pansement de qn; **to ~ a shop window** faire la vitrine; **to ~ sb's hair** coiffer qn. **4** *vi* s'habiller (*in black etc* de *or* en noir *etc*).

dress up 1 *vi* (*smart clothes*) s'habiller, se mettre en grande toilette; (*fancy dress*) se déguiser (*as* en). **2** *vt sep* déguiser (*as* en).

♦ **dresser** *n* **(a)** (*Theat*) habilleur *m*, -euse *f*; (*window ~*) étalagiste *mf*; **(b)** (*sideboard*) vaisselier *m*; **(c)** (*US: dressing table*) coiffeuse *f*. ♦ **dressing 1** *n* habillement *m*; (*Med*) pansement *m*; (*Culin*) assaisonnement *m*; **oil and vinegar ~ing** vinaigrette *f*; **2** *adj*: **~ing case** trousse *f* de toilette; **to give sb a ~ing down*** passer un savon à qn*; **~ing gown** robe *f* de chambre; *[bather, boxer etc]* peignoir *m*; **~ing room** (*in house*) dressing-room *m*; (*Theat*) loge *f* (*d'acteur*); **~ing table** coiffeuse *f*, (table *f* de) toilette *f*. ♦ **dressmaker** *n* couturière *f*. ♦ **dressmaking** *n* couture *f*. ♦ **dressy*** *adj person* chic *inv*, élégant; *party* habillé; *clothes* qui fait habillé.

drew [dru:] *pret of* **draw.**

dribble ['drɪbl] **1** *vi [liquids]* tomber goutte à goutte; *[person]* baver; (*Sport*) dribbler. *[people]* **to ~ back/in** *etc* revenir/entrer *etc* par petits groupes. **2** *vt* **(a)** (*Sport*) dribbler. **(b) he ~d his milk all down his chin** son lait lui dégoulinait le long du menton.

driblet ['drɪblɪt] *n [liquid]* gouttelette *f*. **in ~s** goutte à goutte; (*fig*) petit à petit.

dribs and drabs ['drɪbzən'dræbz] *npl*: **in ~** (*gen*) petit à petit; *arrive* par petits groupes; *pay, give* au compte-gouttes.

dried [draɪd] (*pret, ptp of* **dry**) *adj fruit, beans* sec; *vegetables, flowers* séché; *eggs, milk* en poudre.

drier ['draɪəʳ] *n* = **dryer.**

drift [drɪft] **1** *vi* (*gen*) dériver; (*in wind, current*) être emporté; *[snow, sand etc]* s'amonceler; *[person, nation]* aller à la dérive; *[events]* tendre (*towards* vers). **to ~ downstream** descendre le courant à la dérive; *[person]* **to ~ away/out** *etc* s'en aller/sortir *etc* d'une allure nonchalante; **he was ~ing aimlessly about** il flânait (sans but); **to let things ~** laisser les choses aller à la dérive; **he ~ed into marriage** il s'est retrouvé marié. **2** *n* **(a)** *[snow, leaves]* amoncellement *m*. **(b)** (*deviation from course*) dérive *f*; (*gist: of questions etc*) portée *f*, sens *m* (général); (*direction: of conversation, events*) tournure *f*. **continental ~** dérive des continents. **3** *adj*: **~ ice** glaces *fpl* en dérive. ♦ **drifter** *n* personne *f* qui se laisse aller. ♦ **driftwood** *n* bois *m* flotté.

drill¹ [drɪl] **1** *n* (*cutting part*) mèche *f*, (*complete tool*) perceuse *f*; *[dentist]* roulette *f*; (*in mine, quarry*) foreuse *f*; (*pneumatic ~*) marteau-piqueur *m*; (*for oil well*) trépan *m*. **electric (hand) ~** perceuse électrique. **2** *vt wood etc* forer, percer; *tooth* fraiser; *oil well* forer. **3** *vi* effectuer des forages (*for* pour trouver). ♦ **drilling 1** *n* forages *mpl*; **2** *adj*: **~ing rig** derrick *m*; (*at sea*) plate-forme *f*; **~ing ship** navire *m* de forage.

drill² [drɪl] **1** *n* (*exercises*) exercice(s) *m(pl)*. (*fig*) **what's the ~?*** quelle est la marche à suivre? **2** *vt soldiers* faire faire l'exercice à; *pupils (in grammar etc)* faire faire des exercices à. **to ~ good manners into a child** dresser un enfant à bien se tenir; **I ~ed it into him that ...** je lui ai bien fait entrer dans la tête que ... . **3** *vi* faire l'exercice.

drill³ [drɪl] *n* (*Tex*) coutil *m*, treillis *m*.

drily ['draɪlɪ] *adv* (*coldly*) sèchement; (*with dry humour*) d'un air pince-sans-rire.

drink [drɪŋk] (*vb: pret* **drank,** *ptp* **drunk) 1** *n* **(a)** (*liquid to ~*) boisson *f*. **there's food and ~ in the kitchen** il y a de quoi boire et manger à la cuisine; **may I have a ~?** est-ce que je pourrais boire qch?; **to give sb a ~** donner à boire à qn. **(b)** (*alcoholic*) **a ~** un verre; (*before meal*) un apéritif; (*after meal*) un digestif; **let's have a ~** on va prendre *or* boire un verre; **I need a ~** il me faut à boire; **to ask friends in for ~s** inviter des amis à venir prendre un verre; **to stand a round of ~s** payer une tournée. **(c)** (*alcoholic liquor*) la boisson, l'alcool *m*. **to be under the influence of ~, to be the worse for ~** être en état d'ébriété; **to take to ~** s'adonner à la boisson; **to smell of ~** sentir l'alcool; **to drive sb to ~** pousser qn à la boisson.

2 *adj*: **the ~ problem** le problème de l'alcoolisme; **to have a ~ problem** boire (trop).

3 *vt* (*gen*) boire, prendre; *soup* manger. **would you like sth to ~?** voulez-vous boire qch?; **to ~ sb's health** boire à la santé de qn; **he ~s all his wages** il boit tout ce qu'il gagne; **to ~ sb under the table** faire rouler qn sous la table.

4 *vi* boire. **'don't ~ and drive'** 'attention, au volant l'alcool tue'; **to ~ like a fish*** boire comme un trou*; **to ~ to sb** boire à qn.

drink in *vt sep [plants, soil]* boire; *[person] fresh air* respirer, humer; *story* avaler*. (*fig*) **the children were ~ing it all in** les enfants n'en perdaient pas une miette* (*fig*).

drink up 1 *vi* boire, vider son verre. **~ up** finis ton vin (*or* ton café *etc*). **2** *vt sep* boire (jusqu'au bout), finir.

♦ **drinkable** *adj* (*not poisonous*) potable; (*palatable*) buvable. ♦ **drinker** *n* buveur *m*, -euse *f*; **he's a heavy ~er** il boit sec. ♦ **drinking 1** *n* (*drunkenness*) alcoolisme *m*; **2** *adj*: **~ing bout** beuverie *f*; **~ing fountain** (*in street*) fontaine *f* publique; (*in toilets etc*) jet *m* d'eau potable; **~ing song** chanson *f* à boire; **~ing water** eau *f* potable.

drip [drɪp] **1** *vi [water, sweat, rain]* tomber goutte à goutte; *[tap]* couler, goutter; *[walls]* suinter; *[cheese, washing]* s'égoutter; *[hair, trees etc]* dégoutter (*with* de). **to be ~ping with sweat** ruisseler de sueur; **hands ~ping with blood** mains dégoulinantes de sang; **~ping wet*** trempé. **2** *vt liquid* faire tomber goutte à goutte. **you're ~ping paint all over the floor** tu mets de la peinture partout. **3** *n* **(a)** (*drop*) goutte *f*; (*: *spineless person*) lavette* *f*, mollasson *m*. **(b)** (*Med*) (*liquid*) perfusion *f*; (*device*) goutte-à-goutte *m inv*. **to be on a ~** être sous perfusion.

♦ **drip-dry** *adj shirt* qui ne nécessite aucun repassage; (*on label*) 'ne pas repasser'. ♦ **drip-feed** *vt* (*Med*) alimenter par perfusion. ♦ **drip-mat** *n* dessous-de-verre *m inv*. ♦ **dripping 1** *n* (*Culin*) graisse *f* (de rôti); **2** *adj tap* qui goutte; *washing, coat* trempé.

drive [draɪv] (*vb: pret* **drove,** *ptp* **driven) 1** *n* **(a)** (*Aut: journey*) promenade *f or* trajet *m* en voiture. **to go for a ~** faire une promenade en voiture; **it's one hour's ~ from London** c'est à une heure de voiture de Londres. **(b)** (*private road*) allée *f*. **(c)** (*energy*) dynamisme *m*, énergie *f*; (*Psych etc*) besoin *m*, instinct *m*. **sex ~** pulsions *fpl* sexuelles. **(d)** (*Pol etc*) campagne *f*, propagande *f*; (*Mil*) poussée *f*. **a ~ to boost sales** une promotion systématique de vente; **output ~** effort *m* de production. **(e)** (*Tech*) transmission *f*. (*Aut*) **front-wheel ~** traction *f* avant; **rear-wheel ~** propulsion *f* arrière; **left-hand ~** conduite *f* à gauche.

2 *vt* **(a)** *people, animals* chasser (devant soi); (*Hunting*) *game* rabattre; *clouds, leaves* chasser. **to ~ sb out of the country** chasser qn du pays; (*fig*) **to ~ sb into a corner** mettre qn au pied du mur; **the gale drove the ship off course** la tempête a fait dériver le navire; (*fig*) **to ~ sb hard** surcharger qn de travail; **to ~ sb mad** rendre qn fou; **to ~ sb to despair** réduire qn au désespoir; **to ~ sb to (do) sth** pousser qn à (faire) qch; **I was driven to it** j'y ai été poussé malgré moi, j'y ai été contraint. **(b)** *cart, car, train* conduire; *racing car* piloter; *passenger* conduire (en voiture). **he ~s a taxi** (*for a living*) il est chauffeur de taxi; **he ~s a Peugeot** il a une Peugeot; (*Aut*) **to ~ sb back** *etc* ramener *etc* qn en voiture. **(c)** (*operate*) *machine* actionner, commander. (*Rail*) **steam-driven engine** locomotive *f* à vapeur; **machine driven by electricity** machine fonctionnant à l'électricité. **(d)** *nail, stake* enfoncer; *rivet* poser; (*Golf, Tennis*) driver; *tunnel, well* percer. (*fig*) **to ~ a point home** réussir à faire comprendre un argument; **to ~ sth out of sb's head** faire complètement oublier qch à qn; to ~ **a bargain** conclure un marché.

3 *vi* **(a)** (*Aut*) conduire, aller en voiture. **to ~ away/back** *etc* partir/revenir *etc* en voiture; **can you ~?** savez-vous conduire?; **to ~ at 50 km/h** rouler à 50 km/h; **to ~ on the right** rouler à droite; **by train? – no, we drove** par le train? – non, en voiture; **we have been driving all day** nous avons fait de la route toute la journée; **to ~ over sth** écraser qch. **(b)** (*fig*) **what are you driving at?** où voulez-vous en venir?

drive away, drive off *vt sep* chasser.

drive back *vt sep person, army* faire reculer.

drive in *vt sep nail, idea* enfoncer.

drive on 1 *vi* poursuivre *or* (*after stopping*) reprendre sa route. **2** *vt sep* pousser (*to* à, *to do* à faire).

drive out *vt sep* chasser.

drive up *vi [car]* arriver; *[person]* arriver (en voiture).

♦ **drive-in** *adj, n* drive-in (*m*). ♦ **driver** *n [car, train]* conducteur *m*, -trice *f*; *[taxi, truck, bus]* chauffeur *m*, conducteur, -trice; *[racing car]* pilote *m*; **car ~rs** automobilistes *mpl*; **to be a good ~r** conduire bien; (*US*) **~r's license** permis *m* de conduire; **to be in the ~r's** *or* **driving seat** être au volant; (*fig*) être aux commandes. ♦ **driveshaft** *n* (*Aut*) arbre *m* de transmission. ♦ **driveway** *n* allée *f*. ♦ **driving 1** *n* (*Aut*) conduite *f*; **his driving is awful** il conduit très mal; **2** *adj* **(a)** *necessity* impérieux, pressant; *force* agissant; *rain* battant; **(b)** (*Aut*) *lesson* de conduite; **driving instructor** moniteur *m*, -trice *f* d'auto-école; **driving licence** permis *m* de conduire; **driving mirror** rétroviseur *m*; **driving school** auto-école *f*; **to fail/pass one's driving test** être refusé à/avoir son permis.

drivel ['drɪvl] *n* sornettes *fpl*, imbécillités *fpl*.

drizzle ['drɪzl] **1** *n* bruine *f*. **2** *vi* bruiner. ♦ **drizzly** *adj* de bruine.

dromedary ['drɒmɪdərɪ] *n* dromadaire *m*.

drone [drəʊn] **1** *vi [bee]* bourdonner; *[engine, aircraft]* ronronner, (*louder*) vrombir; (*speak:* **~ away, ~ on**) parler d'une façon monotone. **2** *n* **(a)** (*sound*) bourdonnement *m*; ronronnement *m*, (*louder*) vrombissement *m*; (*speech*) débit *m* monotone. **(b)** (*bee*) abeille *f* mâle; (*idler*) fainéant(e) *m(f)*.

drool [druːl] *vi* baver; (*: *talk*) radoter (*about* au sujet de). (*fig*) **to ~ over sth*** baver d'admiration *or* s'extasier devant qch.

droop [druːp] *vi [body]* s'affaisser; *[shoulders]* tomber; *[head]* pencher; *[eyelids]* s'abaisser; *[flowers]* commencer à se faner; *[feathers, one's hand]* retomber. **his spirits ~ed** il a été pris de découragement; **the heat made him ~** il était accablé par la chaleur.

drop [drɒp] **1** *n* **(a)** goutte *f*. **~ by ~** goutte à goutte; (*fig*) **a ~ in the ocean** une goutte d'eau dans la mer; **he's had a ~ too much*** il a un verre dans le nez. **(b)** (*fall: gen*) baisse *f* (*in* de). (*Elec*) **~ in voltage** chute *f* de tension; (*fig*) **at the ~ of a hat** sans hésitation. **(c)** (*abyss*) précipice *m*; (*fall*) chute *f*; (*distance of fall*) hauteur *f*; (*parachute jump*) saut *m* (en parachute); *[supplies, arms]* parachutage *m*; *[gallows]* trappe *f*. **sheer ~** descente *f* à pic.

2 *vt* **(a)** (*gen*) laisser tomber; (*release, let go*) lâcher; *bomb* lancer, larguer; *liquid* laisser tomber goutte à goutte; *stitch* sauter; *hem* ressortir; *eyes, voice, price* baisser; (*from car*) *person, thing* déposer; (*from boat*) *cargo, passengers* débarquer. **to ~ a letter in the postbox** mettre une lettre à la boîte; **to ~ by parachute** parachuter; **to ~ anchor** jeter l'ancre; (*fig*) **to ~ a brick*** faire une gaffe; **to ~ a curtsy** faire une révérence. **(b)** *remark, clue* laisser échapper. **to ~ a hint about sth** suggérer qch; **to ~ a word in sb's ear** glisser un mot à l'oreille de qn. **(c)** *letter, card* envoyer, écrire (*to* à). **to ~ sb a line** écrire un (petit) mot à qn. **(d)** (*omit*) omettre; (*intentionally*) *thing* supprimer, *person* écarter (*from* de). **to ~ one's h's** ≃ avoir un accent vulgaire. **(e)** (*abandon*) *habit, idea, plan* renoncer à; *work, discussion, conversation* abandonner; *friend, boyfriend* lâcher, laisser tomber. **let's ~ the subject** ne parlons plus de cela; **~ it!*** laisse tomber!* **(f)** (*lose*) *money, game* perdre.

3 *vi* **(a)** *[object]* tomber, retomber; *[liquids]* tomber goutte à goutte; *[person]* se laisser tomber, (*collapse*) s'écrouler. **I'm ready to ~*** je tombe de fatigue, je ne tiens plus debout; **~ dead!‡** va te faire voir!* **(b)** *[wind]* tomber; *[temperature, voice, price]* baisser; *[numbers, attendance]* diminuer, tomber. **(c)** (*end*) *[conversation, correspondence]* en rester là.

drop back, drop behind *vi* rester en arrière; (*in work etc*) prendre du retard.

drop down *vi* tomber.

drop in *vi*: **to ~ in on sb** passer chez qn.

drop off 1 *vi* **(a)** (*fall asleep*) s'endormir; (*doze*) faire un petit somme. **(b)** *[leaves]* tomber; *[sales, interest]* diminuer. **2** *vt sep* (*from car etc*) déposer, laisser.

drop out *vi [contents etc]* tomber; (*fig*) se retirer (*of* de); (*from society*) s'évader de la société (de consommation); (*from college etc*) abandonner.

♦ **drop-leaf table** *n* table *f* anglaise. ♦ **droplet** *n* gouttelette *f*. ♦ **drop-off** *n* (*in sales etc*) diminution *f*. ♦ **dropout** *n* (*from society*) marginal(e) *m(f)*; (*from college etc*) étudiant(e) *m(f)* qui abandonne ses études. ♦ **dropper** *n* (*Med*) compte-gouttes *m inv*. ♦ **droppings** *npl [birds]* fiente *f*; *[animals, flies]* crottes *fpl*.

dross [drɒs] *n* (*fig*) rebut *m*.

drought [draʊt] *n* sécheresse *f*.

drove [drəʊv] (*pret of* **drive**) *n*: **~s of people** des foules *fpl* de gens; **in ~s** en foule.

drown [draʊn] **1** *vt* (*gen: lit, fig*) noyer; *land* inonder. **to be like a ~ed rat*** être trempé jusqu'aux os. **2** *vi* se noyer. ♦ **drowning 1** *adj* qui se noie (*or* noyait *etc*); **2** *n* (*death*) noyade *f*.

drowse [draʊz] *vi* être à moitié endormi. ♦ **drowsily** *adv* d'un air endormi. ♦ **drowsiness** *n* somnolence *f*. ♦ **drowsy** *adj person, smile, look* somnolent; *afternoon, atmosphere* soporifique; **to grow drowsy** s'assoupir; **to feel drowsy** avoir envie de dormir.

drudge [drʌdʒ] *n* bête *f* de somme (*fig*). **the household ~** la bonne à tout faire (*fig*). ♦ **drudgery** *n* corvées *fpl*, travail fastidieux; **it's sheer ~ry** c'est d'un fastidieux!

drug [drʌg] **1** *n* drogue *f*, stupéfiant *m*; (*Med, Pharm*) médicament *m*; (*fig*) drogue. **he's on ~s** (*gen*) il se drogue; (*Med*) il est sous médication; (*fig*) **a ~ on the market** une marchandise invendable. **2** *adj*: **~ addict** drogué(e) *m(f)*, toxicomane *mf*; **~ addiction** toxicomanie *f*; **~ peddler** *or* **pusher** revendeur *m*, -euse *f* de drogue; **~ runner** trafiquant(e) *m(f)* de drogue; **~ running** *or* **traffic** trafic *m* de la drogue *or* des stupéfiants. **3** *vt person* droguer (*also Med*); *food, wine etc* mêler un narcotique à. **to be in a ~ged sleep** dormir sous l'effet d'un narcotique; **~ged with sleep** abruti de sommeil.

♦ **druggist** *n* (*Brit*) pharmacien(ne) *m(f)*; (*US*) droguiste-épicier *m*, -ière *f*. ♦ **drugstore** *n* (*US*) drugstore *m*. ♦ **drug-taker** *n* consommateur *m*, -trice *f* de drogue. ♦ **drug-taking** *n* usage *m* de la drogue.

drum [drʌm] **1** *n* **(a)** (*Mus*) tambour *m*. **the big ~** la grosse caisse; (*Mil Mus, Jazz*) **the ~s** la batterie. **(b)** (*for oil*) bidon *m*; (*cylinder, also machine part*) tambour *m*; (*Computers*) tambour magnétique; (*box of figs, sweets*) caisse *f*. **2** *vi* (*Mus*) battre le tambour; *[person, fingers]* tam-

bouriner (*with* de, avec; *on* sur). **the noise was ~ming in my ears** le bruit me tambourinait aux oreilles. **3** *vt:* **to ~ one's feet on the floor** tambouriner des pieds sur le plancher; **to ~ sth into sb** enfoncer qch dans le crâne de qn.
drum out *vt sep* expulser (à grand bruit) (*of* de).
drum up *vt sep enthusiasm, support* susciter; *supporters* battre le rappel de; *customers* racoler.
♦ **drummer** *n* tambour *m*; (*Jazz*) batteur *m*; **~mer boy** petit tambour. ♦ **drumstick** *n* baguette *f* de tambour; *[chicken]* pilon *m*.
drunk [drʌŋk] (*ptp of* **drink**) **1** *adj* ivre, soûl*; (*fig*) enivré (*with* de, par). **to get ~** s'enivrer, se soûler* (*on* de); (*Jur*) **~ and disorderly** ≃ en état d'ivresse publique; **as ~ as a lord** soûl comme une grive*. **2** *n* (*) ivrogne *m*, homme *or* femme soûl(e)*. ♦ **drunkard** *n* ivrogne *m*, alcoolique *mf*. ♦ **drunken** *adj* (*habitually*) ivrogne; (*intoxicated*) ivre, soûl*; *orgy, quarrel* d'ivrogne(s); *fury* d'ivrogne; *voice* aviné; **~en driving** conduite *f* en état d'ivresse. ♦ **drunkenly** *adv* (*gen*) comme un ivrogne; *sing* d'une voix avinée; *walk* en titubant. ♦ **drunkenness** *n* (*state*) ivresse *f*; (*problem, habit*) ivrognerie *f*. ♦ **drunkometer** *n* (*US*) alcooltest *m*.
dry [draɪ] **1** *adj* **(a)** (*gen*) sec (*f* sèche); *day* sans pluie; *riverbed, well* à sec; *battery* à piles sèches; *bread* sec; *toast etc* sans beurre. **on ~ land** sur la terre ferme; **as ~ as a bone** tout sec; **to keep sth ~** tenir qch au sec; **'to be kept ~'** 'craint l'humidité'; **~ dock** cale *f* sèche; (*Comm*) **~ goods** tissus *mpl*, mercerie *f*; **~ ice** neige *f* carbonique; **~ rot** pourriture *f* sèche (*du bois*); (*fig*) **~ run** essai *m*; **~ ski slope** piste *f* de ski artificielle; **the river ran ~** la rivière s'est asséchée; **his mouth was ~ with fear** la peur lui desséchait la bouche; (*thirsty*) **to be ~*** avoir le gosier sec*.
(b) *humour* pince-sans-rire *inv*; (*dull*) *lecture, subject* aride. **as ~ as dust** ennuyeux comme la pluie. **2** *vt* (*gen*) sécher; *clothes* faire sécher. **to ~ one's eyes** sécher ses larmes; **to ~ the dishes** essuyer la vaisselle; **to ~ o.s.** s'essuyer, se sécher.
3 *vi* sécher.
dry off *vi* sécher.
dry out 1 *vi* sécher; *[alcoholic]* se désintoxiquer. **2** *vt sep* sécher; désintoxiquer.
dry up *vi* **(a)** *[stream, well]* se dessécher; *[moisture]* s'évaporer; *[source of supply]* se tarir. **(b)** (*dry the dishes*) essuyer la vaisselle. **(c)** (*: *fall silent*) se taire; *[actor]* sécher*.
♦ **dry-clean** *vt* nettoyer à sec; **to have sth ~-cleaned** donner qch à nettoyer. ♦ **dry-cleaner** *n* teinturier *m*. ♦ **dry-cleaning** *n* nettoyage *m* à sec. ♦ **dryer** *n* (*gen*) séchoir *m*; (*at hairdresser's*) **under the ~er** sous le casque. ♦ **dry-eyed** *adj*: **to be ~-eyed** avoir les yeux secs. ♦ **drying** *adj*: **~ing cupboard** *or* **room** séchoir *m*; **to do the ~ing-up** essuyer la vaisselle; **~ing-up cloth** torchon *m*. ♦ **dryness** *n* sécheresse *f*. ♦ **drysalter** *n* marchand *m* de couleurs.
dual ['djʊəl] *adj* double, à deux. **~ carriageway** route *f* à chaussées séparées; **~ controls** double commande *f*; **~ national** binational(e) *m(f)*; **~ nationality** double nationalité *f*; **~ personality** dédoublement *m* de la personnalité. ♦ **dual-control** *adj* à double commande. ♦ **dualism** *or* ♦ **duality** *n* dualisme *m*. ♦ **dual-purpose** *adj* à double usage.
dub [dʌb] *vt* **(a) to ~ sb 'Ginger'** qualifier qn de 'Poil de Carotte'. **(b)** (*Cine*) doubler (*dialogue*). ♦ **dubbing** *n* (*Cine*) doublage *m*.
dubious ['dju:bɪəs] *adj* (*gen*) douteux; *person* qui doute, incertain (*of* de); *look, smile* de doute. **he was ~ about whether** il se demandait si; **I'm very ~ about it** j'en doute fort. ♦ **dubiety** *n* doute *m*, incertitude *f*. ♦ **dubiously** *adv* avec doute.
duchess ['dʌtʃɪs] *n* duchesse *f*.
duchy ['dʌtʃɪ] *n* duché *m*.
duck [dʌk] **1** *n* canard *m*; (*female*) cane *f*; (*Mil: vehicle*) véhicule *m* amphibie. **wild ~** canard sauvage; **to play at ~s and drakes** faire des ricochets (sur l'eau); **he took to it like a ~ to water** c'était comme s'il l'avait fait toute sa vie. **2** *vi* (**~ down**) se baisser vivement; (*in fight etc*) esquiver un coup; (*under water*) plonger subitement. **3** *vt* (*also* **give sb a ducking**) plonger dans l'eau: (*as a joke*) faire faire le plongeon à; (*head only*) faire boire la tasse à*. ♦ **duckboard** *n* caillebotis *m*. ♦ **duck-egg blue** *adj* bleu-vert (pâle) *inv*. ♦ **duckling** *n* caneton *m*. ♦ **duckpond** *n* mare *f* aux canards.
duct [dʌkt] *n* conduite *f*; (*Anat*) conduit *m*.
ductile ['dʌktaɪl] *adj metal* ductile; *person* maniable, malléable, docile.
ductless ['dʌktlɪs] *adj*: **~ gland** glande *f* endocrine.
dud [dʌd] **1** *adj shell, bomb* qui a raté; *object, tool* mal fichu*; *note, coin* faux; *cheque* sans provision; *person* nul. **2** *n* (*person*) nullard(e)* *m(f)*. **this coin is a ~** cette pièce est fausse; **this watch is a ~** cette montre ne marche pas.
dudgeon ['dʌdʒən] *n*: **in high ~** offensé dans sa dignité, furieux.
due [dju:] **1** *adj* **(a)** (*owing*) *sum, money* dû (*f* due). **our thanks are ~ to him** nous aimerions le remercier; **to fall ~** venir à échéance; **~ on the 8th** payable le 8; **when is the rent ~?** quand faut-il payer le loyer?; **I am ~ 6 days' leave** on me doit 6 jours de permission; **he is ~ for a rise** il doit recevoir *or* en principe il va recevoir une augmentation; **the train is ~ at midday** le train doit arriver à midi; **I am ~ there tomorrow** je dois être là-bas demain. **(b)** (*proper*) **after ~ consideration** après mûre réflexion; **in ~ course** (*when the time is ripe*) en temps utile; (*in the long run*) à la longue; **with all ~ respect, I believe ...** sans vouloir vous contredire, je crois ... . **(c) ~ to** (*caused by*) dû à, attribuable à; (*because of*) à cause de; (*thanks to*) grâce à; **what's it ~ to?** comment cela se fait-il?
2 *adv*: **to go ~ west** aller droit vers l'ouest; **to face ~ north** être au nord; **~ east of** plein est par rapport à.
3 *n* **(a) to give sb his ~** rendre justice à qn; **to give him his ~, he did try hard** il faut (être juste et) reconnaître qu'il a quand même fait tout son possible. **(b)** (*fees*) **~s** *[club etc]* cotisation *f*; *[harbour]* droits *mpl*.
duel ['djʊəl] **1** *n* duel *m*. **~ to the death** duel à mort. **2** *vi* se battre en duel (*with* contre, avec).
duet [dju:'et] *n* duo *m*. **to sing/play a ~** chanter/jouer en duo; **violin ~** duo de violon; **piano ~** morceau *m* à quatre mains.
duffel, duffle ['dʌfəl] *adj*: **~ bag** sac *m* de paquetage; **~ coat** duffel-coat *m*.
dug [dʌg] *pret, ptp of* **dig.** ♦ **dugout** *n* (*Mil*) tranchée-abri *f*; (*canoe*) pirogue *f*.
duke [dju:k] *n* duc *m*.
dull [dʌl] **1** *adj* **(a)** *sight, hearing* faible; (*slow-witted*) *person, mind* borné, obtus; *pupil* peu doué; (*boring*) *book, evening* ennuyeux; *style, person* terne. **deadly ~*** assommant*, mortel*; **as ~ as ditchwater** ennuyeux comme la pluie. **(b)** (*not bright*) *colour, eyes, mirror, metal* terne; *sound, pain* sourd; *weather, sky* couvert, maussade; *trade, business* lent; *person, mood* déprimé, las. **a ~ day** un jour maussade. **2** *vt senses, pleasure, blade* émousser; *mind* engourdir; *pain, impression, memory* atténuer; *sound* assourdir; *colour, mirror, metal* ternir. ♦ **dullard** *n* lourdaud(e) *m(f)*. ♦ **dullness** *n* (*slow-wittedness*) lourdeur *f* d'esprit; (*boredom*) caractère ennuyeux; **the ~ness of the weather** le temps couvert. ♦ **dully** *adv* (*depressedly*) *behave, walk*

lourdement; *answer, listen* avec lassitude; (*boringly*) *talk, write* d'une manière ennuyeuse.
duly ['dju:lɪ] *adv* (*properly*) comme il faut, ainsi qu'il convient; (*Jur etc*) dûment; (*on time*) en temps voulu; (*in effect*) en effet. **everybody was ~ shocked** tout le monde a bien entendu été choqué.
dumb [dʌm] *adj* **(a)** muet; (*with surprise etc*) muet, abasourdi (*with, from* de). **a ~ person** un(e) muet(te); **~ animals** les animaux *mpl*; **our ~ friends** nos amis les bêtes *fpl*; **to be struck ~** rester muet; **in ~ show** en pantomime. **(b)** (‡: *stupid*) bête. **a ~ blonde** une blonde évaporée; **to act ~** faire l'innocent. ♦ **dumbbell** *n* (*Sport*) haltère *m*. ♦ **dumbfound** *vt* abasourdir. ♦ **dumbfounded** *adj* abasourdi. ♦ **dumbness** *n* (*Med*) mutisme *m*; (‡: *stupidity*) bêtise *f*.
dummy ['dʌmɪ] **1** *n* (*Comm: sham object*) factice *m*; *[book]* maquette *f*; (*model*) mannequin *m*; *[ventriloquist]* pantin *m*; (*Fin etc: person*) prête-nom *m*; (*Bridge*) mort *m*; (*baby's teat*) tétine *f*. **2** *adj* faux, factice. **~ run** (*Aviat*) attaque *f* simulée; (*Comm, Ind*) essai *m*.
dump [dʌmp] **1** *n* (*pile of rubbish*) tas *m* d'ordures; (*place*) décharge *f* publique; (*Mil*) dépôt *m*; (*: *unpleasant place*) trou *m*; (*: *house, hotel*) baraque* *f*. **to be down in the ~s*** avoir le cafard*. **2** *vt* **(a)** (*get rid of*) *rubbish* déposer, jeter; (*Comm*) *goods* écouler à bas prix; (*) *person* plaquer‡; (*) *thing* se débarrasser de. **(b)** (*put down*) *package* déposer; *sand, bricks* décharger, déverser; (*) *passenger* déposer. **~ your bag on the table** plante ton sac sur la table. ♦ **dumper** *or* ♦ **dump truck** *n* tombereau *m* automoteur. ♦ **dumping** *n [load, rubbish]* décharge *f*; (*Ecol: in sea etc*) déversement *m* (de produits nocifs); (*Comm*) dumping *m*. ♦ **dumpy** *adj* courtaud, boulot.
dumpling ['dʌmplɪŋ] *n* (*savoury*) boulette *f* (de pâte). **apple ~** ≃ chausson *m* aux pommes.
dun [dʌn] *vt* harceler (*pour lui faire payer ses dettes*).
dunce [dʌns] *n* (*Scol*) âne *m*, cancre* *m* (*at* en).
dune [dju:n] *n* dune *f*.
dung [dʌŋ] *n* (*gen*) crotte *f*; *[cattle]* bouse *f*; (*manure*) fumier *m*. ♦ **dunghill** *n* (tas *m* de) fumier *m*.
dungarees [ˌdʌŋgə'ri:z] *npl [workman]* bleu *m* (de travail); *[child, woman]* salopette *f*.
dungeon ['dʌndʒən] *n* cachot *m* (souterrain).
dunk [dʌŋk] *vt:* **to ~ one's bread in one's coffee** *etc* faire trempette.
Dunkirk [dʌn'kɜ:k] *n* Dunkerque.
duodenal [ˌdju:əʊ'di:nl] *adj ulcer* du duodénum.
dupe [dju:p] **1** *vt* duper, tromper. **to ~ sb into doing sth** amener qn à faire qch en le dupant. **2** *n* dupe *f*.
duplex ['dju:pleks] *adj, n* duplex (*m*).
duplicate ['dju:plɪkeɪt] **1** *vt* (*gen*) faire un double de; (*on machine*) *document* polycopier; *action etc* répéter exactement. **that is duplicating work already done** cela fait double emploi avec ce qu'on a déjà fait. **2** ['dju:plɪkɪt] *n* double *m*. **in ~** en deux exemplaires. **3** ['dju:plɪkɪt] *adj copy* en double; *coach* supplémentaire. **a ~ key** un double de la clef. ♦ **duplication** *n [efforts, work]* répétition *f*, reproduction *f*. ♦ **duplicator** *or* ♦ **duplicating machine** *n* duplicateur *m*.
duplicity [dju:'plɪsɪtɪ] *n* duplicité *f*, fausseté *f*.
durable ['djʊərəbl] **1** *adj material* solide, résistant; *friendship* durable. **2** *n* (*Comm*) **~s** biens *mpl* de consommation durables. ♦ **durability** *n* solidité *f*, résistance *f*; durabilité *f*.
duration [djʊə'reɪʃən] *n* (*gen*) durée *f*. **for the ~ of the war** jusqu'à la fin de la guerre.
duress [djʊə'res] *n:* **under ~** sous la contrainte.
during ['djʊərɪŋ] *prep* pendant, durant; (*in the course of*) au cours de.
dusk [dʌsk] *n* (*twilight*) crépuscule *m*; (*gloom*) (semi-) obscurité *f*. **at ~** au crépuscule; **in the ~** dans la semi-obscurité. ♦ **dusky** *adj complexion* foncé; *person* au teint foncé.
dust [dʌst] **1** *n* poussière *f*. **thick ~** une épaisse couche de poussière; **I've got a speck of ~ in my eye** j'ai une poussière dans l'œil. **2** *adj cloud* de poussière. (*Geog*) **~ bowl** désert *m* de poussière; **~ cover** (*of book: also* **~ jacket**) jaquette *f* (*d'un livre*); (*of furniture, also* **~ sheet**) housse *f* de protection; **~ storm** tourbillon *m* de poussière. **3** *vt* **(a)** *furniture* épousseter; *room* essuyer la poussière dans. **(b)** (*sprinkle*) saupoudrer (*with* de). ♦ **dustbin** *n* poubelle *f*, boîte *f* à ordures. ♦ **dustcart** *n* tombereau *m* aux ordures. ♦ **duster** *n* chiffon *m* (*à poussière, à effacer*). ♦ **dustheap** *n* poubelle *f*. ♦ **dusting** *adj:* **~ing powder** talc *m*. ♦ **dustman** *n* éboueur *m*. ♦ **dustpan** *n* pelle *f* à poussière. ♦ **dust-up*** *n:* **to have a ~-up with sb*** avoir un accrochage* avec qn. ♦ **dusty** *adj* poussiéreux; **to get ~y** se couvrir de poussière; **not so ~y*** pas mal; **to get a ~y answer*** en être pour ses frais.
Dutch [dʌtʃ] **1** *adj* hollandais, néerlandais, des Pays-Bas. **~ cheese** hollande *m*; (*fig*) **~ auction** enchères *fpl* au rabais; **~ courage** courage *m* puisé dans la bouteille; **~ elm disease** champignon *m* parasite de l'orme; **to go ~** partager les frais. **2** *n* (*Ling*) hollandais *m*, néerlandais *m*. **the ~** les Hollandais *mpl*, les Néerlandais *mpl*; (*fig*) **it's all ~ to me*** c'est du chinois pour moi. ♦ **Dutchman** *n* Hollandais *m*. ♦ **Dutchwoman** *n* Hollandaise *f*.
duty ['dju:tɪ] **1** *n* **(a)** (*moral, legal*) devoir *m* (*to do* de faire; *to, by sb* envers qn). **I feel (in) ~ bound to say that ...** il est de mon devoir de faire remarquer que ...; *[employee, official etc]* **duties** fonctions *fpl*; **on ~** (*Mil*) de service; (*Med*) de garde; (*Admin, Scol*) de jour, de service; **to be off ~** (*gen*) être libre; (*Mil*) avoir quartier libre; **to go on/off ~** prendre/quitter le service (*or* la garde); **to do ~ for sb** remplacer qn; **the box does ~ for a table** la boîte fait fonction de table. **(b)** (*tax*) droit *m*, taxe *f* (indirecte). **to pay ~ on** payer un droit *or* une taxe sur. **2** *adj visit etc* de politesse. **~ officer** (*Mil etc*) officier *m* de service; (*Admin*) officiel *m* de service; **~ rota** tableau *m* de service. ♦ **dutiable** *adj* (*Customs*) soumis à des droits de douane. ♦ **dutiful** *adj child* respectueux; *husband* plein d'égards; *employee* consciencieux. ♦ **dutifully** *adv obey* respectueusement; *work* consciencieusement. ♦ **duty-free** *adj goods etc* exempté de douane; *shop* hors-taxe.
duvet ['du:veɪ] *n* couette *f* (*édredon*). **~ cover** housse *f* de couette.
dwarf [dwɔ:f] **1** *adj, n* nain(e) *m(f)*. **2** *vt [skyscraper, person]* rapetisser, écraser; *[achievement]* éclipser.
dwell [dwel] *pret, ptp* **dwelt** *vi* (*liter*) demeurer. **dwell (up)on** *vt fus* (*think about*) s'arrêter sur; (*talk about*) s'étendre sur; (*emphasize*) appuyer sur. **don't let's ~ upon it** passons là-dessus. ♦ **dweller** *n* habitant(e) *m(f)*; **town ~er** citadin(e) *m(f)*. ♦ **dwelling 1** *n* habitation *f*; **2** *adj:* **~ing house** maison *f* d'habitation.
dwindle ['dwɪndl] *vi* diminuer (peu à peu). ♦ **dwindling** *adj interest, strength* décroissant; *resources* en diminution.
dye [daɪ] **1** *n* teinture *f*, colorant *m*. **hair ~** teinture pour les cheveux; **fast ~** grand teint. **2** *vt* teindre. **to ~ sth red** teindre qch en rouge; **to ~ one's hair** se teindre les cheveux. ♦ **dyed-in-the-wool** *adj* bon teint *inv* (*fig*). ♦ **dyeing** *n* teinture *f*. ♦ **dyer** *n:* **~r's and cleaner's** teinturier *m*. ♦ **dyestuffs** *npl* matières *fpl* colorantes. ♦ **dyeworks** *npl* teinturerie *f*.
dying ['daɪɪŋ] **1** *adj* mourant; *custom etc* en train de disparaître. **to my ~ day** jusqu'à ma dernière

heure. **2** *n* (*death*) mort *f*; (*just before death*) agonie *f*. **the ~** les mourants *mpl*.
dyke [daɪk] *n* **(a)** digue *f*; (*causeway*) levée *f*. **(b)** (‡: *lesbian*) gouine‡ *f*.
dynamic [daɪ'næmɪk] *adj* dynamique. ♦ **dynamics** *nsg* dynamique *f*. ♦ **dynamism** *n* dynamisme *m*.
dynamite ['daɪnəmaɪt] **1** *n* dynamite *f*. **he's ~!*** c'est de la dynamite!*; **that business is ~*** c'est une affaire explosive. **2** *vt* dynamiter.
dynamo ['daɪnəməʊ] *n* dynamo *f*.
dynasty ['dɪnəstɪ] *n* dynastie *f*. ♦ **dynastic** *adj* dynastique.
dysentery ['dɪsɪntrɪ] *n* dysenterie *f*.
dyslexia [dɪs'leksɪə] *n* dyslexie *f*. ♦ **dyslexic** *adj, n* dyslexique (*mf*).
dyspepsia [dɪs'pepsɪə] *n* dyspepsie *f*.
dystrophy ['dɪstrəfɪ] *n* dystrophie *f*.

E

E, e [iː] *n* E, e *m*; (*Mus*) mi *m*.
each [iːtʃ] **1** *adj* chaque. **~ day** chaque jour, tous les jours; **~ one of us** chacun(e) de *or* d'entre nous. **2** *pron* **(a)** chacun(e) *m(f)*. **~ of the boys** chacun des garçons; **~ of us** chacun(e) de *or* d'entre nous; **a little of ~ please** un peu de chaque s'il vous plaît; **we gave them one apple ~** nous leur avons donné une pomme chacun; **they are £2 ~** ils coûtent 2 livres chacun *or* pièce. **(b) ~ other** l'un(e) l'autre *m(f)*; **they love ~ other** ils s'aiment; **they write to ~ other** ils s'écrivent; **they were sorry for ~ other** ils avaient pitié l'un de l'autre; **you must help ~ other** vous devez vous aider les uns les autres; **separated from ~ other** séparés l'un de l'autre.
eager [ˈiːgəʳ] *adj* (*keen*) désireux, avide (*for* de, *to do* de faire); (*impatient*) impatient (*to do* de faire); *scholar, supporter, desire* passionné; *search, glance* avide. **to be ~ for** (*gen*) désirer vivement; *happiness* rechercher avidement; *knowledge, affection* être avide de; *power, vengeance, pleasure* être assoiffé de; **to be ~ to do** (*keen*) désirer vivement faire; (*impatient*) être impatient de faire; **~ beaver*** bourreau *m* de travail. ♦ **eagerly** *adv* avidement; avec impatience; passionnément. ♦ **eagerness** *n* vif désir *m* (*to do* de faire, *for* de); impatience *f* (*to do* de faire).
eagle [ˈiːgl] *n* aigle *mf* (*gen m*). ♦ **eagle-eyed** *adj* qui a des yeux d'aigle.
ear¹ [ɪəʳ] **1** *n* oreille *f*. **to keep one's ~s open** ouvrir l'oreille; **to keep one's ~ to the ground** être aux écoutes; **to be all ~s*** être tout oreilles; **your ~s must have been burning** les oreilles ont dû vous tinter; **it goes in one ~ and out of the other** cela lui *etc* entre par une oreille et lui *etc* sort par l'autre; **to be up to the ~s in work** avoir du travail pardessus la tête; (*Mus*) **to have a good ~** avoir de l'oreille; **to play by ~** jouer à l'oreille; (*fig*) **I'll play it by ~** je déciderai quoi faire le moment venu. **2** *adj operation* à l'oreille. (*Med*) **~, nose and throat department** service *m* d'oto-rhino-laryngologie; **~, nose and throat specialist** oto-rhino-laryngologiste *mf*; **~ wax** cérumen *m*. ♦ **earache** *n* mal *m* d'oreille(s); **to have ~ache** avoir mal à l'oreille *or* aux oreilles. ♦ **eardrum** *n* tympan *m* (*de l'oreille*). ♦ **earmark** *vt object, seat* réserver (*for* à); *funds, person* assigner, destiner (*for* à). ♦ **earphone** *n* (*Rad, Telec etc*) écouteur *m*; **to listen on ~phones** écouter au casque. ♦ **earplugs** *npl* (*for sleeping*) boules *fpl* Quiès ®. ♦ **earring** *n* boucle *f* d'oreille. ♦ **earshot** *n*: **out of ~shot** hors de portée de voix; **within ~shot** à portée de voix. ♦ **ear-splitting** *adj sound, scream* strident; *din* fracassant. ♦ **earwig** *n* perce-oreille *m*.
ear² [ɪəʳ] *n [grain, plant]* épi *m*.
earl [ɜːl] *n* comte *m*.
early [ˈɜːlɪ] **1** *adj man, Church* primitif; *apple, plant* précoce; *death* prématuré. **it's still ~** il est encore tôt, il n'est pas tard; **you're ~!** vous arrivez de bonne heure!; **his ~ arrival** son arrivée de bonne heure, le fait qu'il arrive (*or* est arrivé *etc*) de bonne heure; **an ~ train** un train tôt le matin; **the ~ train** le premier train; **an ~ text** un texte très ancien; **to be an ~ riser** être matinal; **to keep ~ hours** se coucher tôt; **~ to bed, ~ to rise** tôt couché, tôt levé; **~ warning system** dispositif *m* de première alerte; (*Comm*) **it's ~ closing day** les magasins ferment l'après-midi; **it is too ~ yet to say** il est trop tôt pour dire; **~ fruit** *or* **vegetables** primeurs *fpl*; **at an ~ hour** de bonne heure, très tôt; **it was ~ in the morning** c'était tôt le matin; **in the ~ morning** de bon matin; **in the ~ afternoon/spring** au début de l'après-midi/du printemps; **she's in her ~ forties** elle a juste dépassé la quarantaine; **from an ~ age** dès l'enfance; **his ~ youth** sa première jeunesse; **his ~ life** sa jeunesse; **the ~ Victorians** les Victoriens *mpl* du début du règne; **an ~ Victorian table** une table du début de l'époque victorienne; **at the earliest possible moment** le plus tôt possible; (*Comm*) **at your earliest convenience** dans les meilleurs délais; (*Comm*) **to promise ~ delivery** promettre une livraison rapide.
2 *adv* de bonne heure, tôt. **too ~** trop tôt; **as ~ as possible** le plus tôt possible; **she left 10 minutes ~** elle est partie 10 minutes plus tôt; **10 minutes earlier** 10 minutes plus tôt; **not earlier than Thursday** pas avant jeudi; **earlier on** précédemment, plus tôt; **book ~** réservez longtemps à l'avance; **~ in the morning** de bon matin; **~ in the year** au début de l'année.
earn [ɜːn] *vt money* gagner; *salary* toucher; *interest* rapporter; *praise, rest* mériter. **to ~ one's living** gagner sa vie; **~ed income** revenus *mpl* salariaux. ♦ **earnings** *npl [person]* salaire *m*; *[business]* bénéfices *mpl*.
earnest [ˈɜːnɪst] **1** *adj* sérieux, consciencieux; (*sincere*) sincère; *prayer* fervent; *desire, request* pressant. **2** *n*: **in ~** (*with determination*) sérieusement; (*without joking*) sans rire. **I am in ~** je ne plaisante pas; **it is snowing in ~** il neige pour de bon. ♦ **earnestly** *adv speak* avec sérieux; *work* consciencieusement; *beseech* instamment; *pray* avec ferveur. ♦ **earnestness** *n [person]* sérieux *m*; *[effort]* ardeur *f*; *[demand]* véhémence *f*.
earth [ɜːθ] **1** *n* **(a)** (*the world*) terre *f*, monde *m*. **(the) E~** la Terre; **on ~** sur terre; **to the ends of the ~** au bout du monde; **where/why on ~ ...?** mais où/pourquoi ...?; **nothing on ~** rien au monde; **to promise sb the ~** promettre la lune à qn; **it must have cost the ~!*** ça a dû coûter les yeux de la tête!* **(b)** (*ground*) terre *f*, sol *m*; (*soil*) terre; (*Elec*) masse *f*. **to fall to ~** tomber à terre. **(c)** *[fox, badger etc]* terrier *m*, tanière *f*. **to run sth/sb to ~** dépister qch/qn. **2** *adj*: **~ tremor** secousse *f* sismique. **3** *vt* (*Elec*) *apparatus* mettre à la masse. ♦ **earthen** *adj* de terre, en terre. ♦ **earthenware** **1** *n* faïence *f*; **2** *adj* en faïence. ♦ **earthly** *adj* terrestre; **there is no ~ly reason to think** il n'y a pas la moindre raison de croire; **it's no ~ly use** ça ne sert absolument à rien. ♦ **earthquake** *n* tremblement *m* de terre. ♦ **earth-shaking** *adj* (*fig*) stupéfiant. ♦ **earthward(s)** *adv* vers la terre. ♦ **earthwork** *n* (*Constr*) terrassement *m*; (*Mil*) ouvrage *m* de terre. ♦ **earthworm** *n* ver *m* de terre. ♦ **earthy** *adj taste, smell* terreux; *person* terre-à-terre *inv*; *humour* truculent.
ease [iːz] **1** *n* **(a)** (*mental*) tranquillité *f*; (*physical*) bien-être *m*. **at ~** à l'aise; (*Mil*) au repos; **to put sb**

at his ~ mettre qn à l'aise; **to put sb's mind at** ~ tranquilliser qn; **ill at** ~ mal à l'aise; **to take one's** ~ prendre ses aises; **a life of** ~ une vie facile. **(b)** (*lack of difficulty*) aisance *f*, facilité *f*. **with** ~ sans difficulté. **2** *vt pain* soulager; *mind* calmer, tranquilliser; *strap* relâcher; (*alter*) *coat* donner plus d'ampleur à; *pressure, tension* diminuer; *speed* ralentir. **to** ~ **a key into a lock** introduire doucement *or* délicatement une clef dans une serrure; **to** ~ **in the clutch** embrayer en douceur; **he** ~**d himself through the gap in the fence** il s'est glissé par le trou de la barrière. **3** *vi* (~ **off**) (*slow down*) ralentir; (*work less hard*) se relâcher; *[situation]* se détendre; *[pressure, traffic]* diminuer; *[work, business]* devenir plus calme; *[pain]* se calmer; *[demand]* baisser. **the situation has** ~**d** une détente s'est produite.

ease up *vi* se détendre. ~ **up a bit!** vas-y plus doucement!

easel ['i:zl] *n* chevalet *m*.

east [i:st] **1** *n* est *m*. (*Pol*) **the E**~ les pays *mpl* de l'Est; **the mysterious E**~ l'Orient *m* mystérieux; **to the** ~ **of** à l'est de; **in the** ~ **of** dans l'est de; **the wind is in the** ~/**is from the** ~ le vent est à l'est/vient de l'est; **to live in the** ~ habiter dans l'Est. **2** *adj side* est *inv*; *wind* d'est; *coast, door* est *inv*, oriental. (*in London*) **the E**~ **End** les quartiers *mpl* est de Londres (*quartiers pauvres*); **E**~ **Africa** l'Afrique *f* orientale. **3** *adv travel* en direction de l'est, vers l'est. ~ **of the border** à l'est de la frontière; **to go due** ~ aller droit vers l'est. ♦ **eastbound** *adj traffic, vehicles* en direction de l'est; *carriageway* est *inv*. ♦ **easterly** *adj wind* d'est; *situation, aspect* à l'est; **in an** ~**erly direction** en direction de l'est. ♦ **eastern** *adj region* est *inv*, de l'est; *coast* est *inv*, oriental; *wall, side* exposé à l'est; **E**~**ern France** l'Est *m* de la France; (*Pol*) **the E**~**ern bloc** les pays *mpl* de l'Est; (*US*) **E**~**ern Standard Time** l'heure *f* normale de l'Est. ♦ **easterner** *n* homme *m or* femme *f* de l'Est. ♦ **easternmost** *adj* le plus à l'est. ♦ **eastward 1** *adj* à l'est; **2** *adv* (*also* ~**wards**) vers l'est.

Easter ['i:stəʳ] **1** *n* Pâques *msg or fpl*. **at** ~ à Pâques; **Happy** ~! joyeuses Pâques!; ~ **is celebrated between ...** Pâques est célébré entre ... . **2** *adj egg, Monday* de Pâques; *holidays, week* pascal, de Pâques. ~ **Day** le jour de Pâques.

easy ['i:zɪ] **1** *adj* **(a)** (*not difficult*) facile. **it is** ~ **to see that ...** on voit bien que ...; **it is** ~ **for him to do that** il lui est facile de faire cela; **easier said than done!** c'est vite dit!; **you've got an** ~ **time of it** tu as une vie sans problèmes; **it's** ~ **money** c'est comme si on était payé à ne rien faire; **within** ~ **reach of** à distance commode de; **in** ~ **stages** *travel* par petites étapes; *learn* par degrés; **he is** ~ **to work with** il est agréable dans le travail; ~ **to get on with** facile à vivre; **I'm** ~* ça m'est égal; **he came in an** ~ **first** il est arrivé bon premier. **(b)** (*relaxed*) *manners, style* aisé; *life* tranquille; *pace* modéré; *conditions* favorable; *relationship* cordial. **to feel** ~ **in one's mind** être tout à fait tranquille; ~ **chair** fauteuil *m* (rembourré); **in** ~ **circumstances** dans l'aisance; (*Comm*) **on** ~ **terms** avec facilités *fpl* de paiement.

2 *adv*: **to take things** *or* **it** ~ ne pas se fatiguer; **take it** ~! (*calm down*) ne vous en faites pas!; (*relax*) ne vous fatiguez pas!; (*go slow*) ne vous pressez pas!; **go** ~ **with the sugar** vas-y doucement avec le sucre; **to go** ~ **with sb** ne pas être trop dur envers qn; ~ **does it!** allez-y doucement!; (*Mil*) **stand** ~! repos!

♦ **easily** *adv enter, succeed* facilement, sans difficulté; *answer, agree, say* tranquillement; (*unquestionably*) sans aucun doute, de loin; **that's easily 4 km** cela fait facilement 4 km; **he may easily change his mind** il pourrait bien changer d'avis. ♦ **easiness** *n* facilité *f*, aisance *f*. ♦ **easy-going** *adj* accommodant; *attitude* complaisant.

eat [i:t] *pret* **ate**, *ptp* **eaten 1** *vt food* manger. **to** ~ **(one's) lunch** déjeuner; **to** ~ **a meal** prendre un repas; **to have nothing to** ~ n'avoir rien à manger; **to** ~ **one's fill** manger à sa faim; **to** ~ **one's words** ravaler ses paroles; **I'll** ~ **my hat if ...*** je veux bien être pendu si ...; **he won't** ~ **you*** il ne va pas te manger; **what's** ~**ing you?**‡ qu'est-ce qui ne va pas? **2** *vi* manger. **we** ~ **at 8** nous dînons à 20 heures; **to** ~ **like a horse** manger comme quatre; **he is** ~**ing us out of house and home*** son appétit va nous mettre à la rue; (*fig*) **I've got him** ~**ing out of my hand** il fait tout ce que je veux.

eat away *vt sep [sea]* éroder; *[acid, mice]* ronger.

eat into *vt fus [acid, insects]* ronger; *savings* entamer.

eat out 1 *vi* aller au restaurant. **2** *vt sep*: **to** ~ **one's heart out** se ronger d'inquiétude.

eat up *vt sep meal etc* finir. ~**en up with envy** dévoré d'envie; **it** ~**s up the electricity** cela consomme beaucoup d'électricité.

♦ **eatable 1** *adj* (*fit to eat*) mangeable; (*edible*) comestible; **2** *npl*: ~**ables*** comestibles *mpl*. ♦ **eater** *n*: **a big** ~**er** un gros mangeur. ♦ **eatery** *n* café-restaurant *m*. ♦ **eating** *adj apple* à couteau; (*US*) ~**ing hall** réfectoire *m*; ~**ing place** restaurant *m*.

eaves [i:vz] *npl* avant-toit *m*. ♦ **eavesdrop** *vi* écouter en cachette (*on sth* qch). ♦ **eavesdropper** *n* oreille *f* indiscrète.

ebb [eb] **1** *n [tide]* reflux *m*. ~ **and flow** le flux et le reflux; **to be at a low** ~ *[person, spirits]* être bien bas; *[business]* aller mal. **2** *adj*: ~ **tide** marée *f* descendante. **3** *vi* **(a)** *[tide]* descendre. **to** ~ **and flow** monter et baisser. **(b)** (~ **away**) *[enthusiasm etc]* décliner.

ebony ['ebənɪ] *n* ébène *f*.

ebullient [ɪ'bʌlɪənt] *adj* exubérant. ♦ **ebullience** *n* exubérance *f*.

eccentric [ɪk'sentrɪk] *adj, n* excentrique (*mf*). ♦ **eccentrically** *adv* avec excentricité. ♦ **eccentricity** *n* excentricité *f*.

ecclesiastic [ɪˌkli:zɪ'æstɪk] *n* ecclésiastique *m*. ♦ **ecclesiastical** *adj* ecclésiastique.

echo ['ekəʊ] **1** *n* écho *m*. **to cheer to the** ~ applaudir à tout rompre. **2** *vt [hills etc]* répercuter; *[person] sb's words* répéter. **3** *vi [sound]* se répercuter; *[place]* faire écho. **to** ~ **with music** retentir de musique. **4** *adj* (*Rad*) ~ **chamber** chambre *f* sonore. ♦ **echo-sounder** *n* sondeur *m* (à ultra-sons).

eclectic [ɪ'klektɪk] *adj, n* éclectique (*mf*). ♦ **eclecticism** *n* éclectisme *m*.

eclipse [ɪ'klɪps] **1** *n* éclipse *f*. **2** *vt* éclipser.

ecology [ɪ'kɒlədʒɪ] *n* écologie *f*. ♦ **ecological** *adj* écologique. ♦ **ecologist** *n* écologiste *mf*.

economy [ɪ'kɒnəmɪ] **1** *n* (*all senses*) économie *f* (*in* de). **2** *adj*: ~ **class** classe *f* touriste; **to have an** ~ **drive** (s'efforcer de) faire des économies; ~ **pack/size** paquet *m*/taille *f* économique. ♦ **economic** *adj* **(a)** *development, geography, factor* économique; **the economic system of a country** l'économie *f* d'un pays; **(b)** (*profitable*) *business, rent, price* rentable; **it isn't an economic proposition, it doesn't make economic sense** cela n'est pas intéressant (financièrement). ♦ **economical** *adj person* économe; *method, appliance, speed* économique. ♦ **economically** *adv* économiquement; **to use sth economically** économiser qch. ♦ **economics** *n* (*sg: science*) économie *f* politique; **the economics** (*npl*) **of the situation** le côté économique de la situation. ♦ **economist** *n* économiste *mf*. ♦ **economize 1** *vi* économiser (*on* sur), faire des économies; **2** *vt* économiser.

ecstasy ['ekstəsɪ] *n* extase *f*. **to be in ecstasies over** *object* s'extasier sur; *person* être en extase

devant. ♦ **ecstatic** *adj* extasié. ♦ **ecstatically** *adv* avec extase.
Ecuador ['ekwədɔːʳ] *n* Équateur *m*.
ecumenical [ˌiːkjʊ'menɪkəl] *adj* œcuménique.
eczema ['eksɪmə] *n* eczéma *m*.
eddy ['edɪ] **1** *n* tourbillon *m*. **2** *vi [air, smoke, leaves]* tourbillonner; *[people]* tournoyer; *[water]* faire des tourbillons.
edge [edʒ] **1** *n* (*gen*) bord *m*; *[forest]* lisière *f*; *[town]* abords *mpl*; *[coin]* tranche *f*; *[cube, brick]* arête *f*; (*distance round* ~) pourtour *m*; *[knife, razor]* tranchant *m*, fil *m*. **a book with gilt** ~**s** un livre doré sur tranches; **the trees at the** ~ **of the road** les arbres en bordure de la route; **on the** ~ **of disaster** au bord du désastre; **to take the** ~ **off** *knife, sensation* émousser; *appetite* calmer; **it sets my teeth on** ~ cela m'agace les dents; **he is on** ~ il est énervé; (*fig*) **to have the** ~ **on sb/sth** être légèrement supérieur à qn/qch. **2** *vt* (*put a border on*) border (*with* de); (*sharpen*) aiguiser. **to** ~ **one's chair nearer the door** rapprocher sa chaise tout doucement de la porte. **3** *vi*: **to** ~ **through/into** *etc* se glisser à travers/dans *etc*; **to** ~ **forward** avancer petit à petit. ♦ **edgeways** *or* ♦ **edgewise** *adv* de côté; **I couldn't get a word in** ~**ways*** je n'ai pas réussi à placer un mot. ♦ **edginess** *n* nervosité *f*, énervement *m*. ♦ **edging 1** *n* bordure *f*; *[ribbon, silk]* liseré *m*; **2** *adj*: **edging shears** cisaille *f* de jardinier. ♦ **edgy** *adj* énervé.
edible ['edɪbl] *adj* (*not poisonous*) comestible; (*fit to eat*) mangeable.
edict ['iːdɪkt] *n* (*Hist*) édit *m*; (*Jur, Pol*) décret *m*.
edifice ['edɪfɪs] *n* édifice *m*.
edify ['edɪfaɪ] *vt* édifier. ♦ **edification** *n* édification *f*.
Edinburgh ['edɪnbərə] *n* Édimbourg.
edit ['edɪt] *vt newspaper* être le rédacteur (*or* la rédactrice) en chef de; *magazine, review* diriger; *article, tape* mettre au point, (*cut*) couper; *series of texts* diriger la publication de; *text, author* éditer; *dictionary* rédiger; (*Rad, TV*) *programme* réaliser; *film* monter. ♦ **edition** *n* édition *f*. ♦ **editor** *n [daily newspaper]* rédacteur *m*, -trice *f* en chef; *[magazine, review]* directeur *m*, -trice *f*; *[series]* directeur, -trice de la publication; *[text]* éditeur *m*, -trice *f*; *[dictionary]* rédacteur, -trice; *[Rad, TV programme]* réalisateur *m*, -trice *f*; (*Press*) **political** ~**or** rédacteur, -trice politique. ♦ **editorial 1** *adj* de la rédaction; ~**orial staff** rédaction *f*; **2** *n* éditorial *m*.
educate ['edjʊkeɪt] *vt pupil* instruire, donner de l'instruction à; *the public* éduquer; *mind, tastes* former; (*bring up*) *family, children* élever. **to** ~ **sb to believe that ...** enseigner à qn que ...; **he is being** ~**d in Paris** il fait ses études à Paris. ♦ **educable** *adj* éducable. ♦ **educated** *adj person* instruit, cultivé; *handwriting* distingué; *voice* cultivé; **well-**~**d** qui a reçu une bonne éducation. ♦ **educative** *adj* éducatif. ♦ **educator** *n* éducateur *m*, -trice *f*.
education [ˌedjʊ'keɪʃən] *n* éducation *f*; (*teaching*) enseignement *m*, instruction *f*; (*studies*) études *fpl*; (*training*) formation *f*; (*knowledge*) culture *f*; (*Univ etc: subject*) pédagogie *f*. **Ministry of E**~ ministère *m* de l'Éducation nationale; **primary/secondary** ~ enseignement primaire/secondaire; **he had a good** ~ il a reçu une bonne éducation; **physical/political** ~ éducation physique/politique; **his** ~ **was interrupted** ses études ont été interrompues; **literary/professional** ~ formation littéraire/professionnelle; **diploma in** ~ diplôme *m* de pédagogie. ♦ **educational** *adj methods* pédagogique; *establishment, institution* d'enseignement; *system* d'éducation; *supplies* scolaire; *film, games, visit* éducatif; *role, function* éducateur; *experience, event* instructif; ~**al psychology** psychopédagogie *f*. ♦ **education(al)ist** *n* pédagogue *mf*. ♦ **educationally** *adv* (*as regards teaching methods*) du point de vue pédagogique; (*as regards education, schooling*) sous l'angle scolaire; **it is** ~**ally wrong** il est faux d'un point de vue pédagogique; ~**ally subnormal** sous-performant (du point de vue scolaire); ~**ally deprived children** enfants sous-scolarisés.
Edwardian [ed'wɔːdɪən] *adj* (*Brit*) *lady, architect, society* de l'époque du roi Édouard VII; *clothes, manners, design* dans le style 1900. **the** ~ **era** = la Belle Époque.
eel [iːl] *n* anguille *f*.
eerie, eery ['ɪərɪ] *adj* sinistre, qui donne le frisson.
efface [ɪ'feɪs] *vt* effacer.
effect [ɪ'fekt] **1** *n* **(a)** (*result*) effet *m* (*on* sur), conséquence *f*; *[wind, chemical, drug]* action *f* (*on* sur); (*Phys*) effet. **to have an** ~ **on** produire un effet sur; *[wind etc]* agir sur; **to have no** ~ ne produire aucun effet; **it will have the** ~ **of preventing** cela aura pour effet *or* conséquence d'empêcher; **the** ~ **of all this is that ...** il résulte de tout ceci que ...; **to no** ~ en vain; **to such good** ~ **that** si bien que; **to put into** ~ *project* mettre à exécution; *regulation* mettre en vigueur; **to take** ~ *[drug]* agir; *[law]* entrer en vigueur; **in** ~ en fait, en réalité. **(b)** (*impression*) effet *m*. **stage** ~**s** effets scéniques; **sound** ~**s** bruitage *m*; **to make an** ~ faire de l'effet; **he said it for** ~ il l'a dit pour faire de l'effet; **his letter is to the** ~ **that ...** sa lettre nous apprend que ...; **a letter to that** ~ une lettre dans ce sens; **orders to the** ~ **that** ordres suivant lesquels; **or words to that** ~ ou qch d'analogue. **(c)** (*property*) ~**s** biens *mpl*. **2** *vt reform, reduction, payment, sale* effectuer; *cure* obtenir; *improvement* apporter; *transformation* opérer; *saving* réaliser; *reconciliation, reunion* amener. **to** ~ **an entry** entrer de force. ♦ **effective** *adj* **(a)** (*efficient*) *cure, measures, system* efficace; *word, remark, argument* qui porte; (*impressive*) frappant, qui fait de l'effet; **to become** ~**ive** *[regulation]* entrer en vigueur; *[ticket]* être valide; **(b)** (*actual*) *aid, contribution* effectif; **the** ~**ive head of the family** le chef réel de la famille. ♦ **effectively** *adv* (*efficiently*) efficacement; (*usefully*) utilement; (*strikingly*) d'une manière frappante; (*in reality*) effectivement. ♦ **effectiveness** *n* (*efficiency*) efficacité *f*; (*striking quality*) effet frappant. ♦ **effectual** *adj* efficace. ♦ **effectually** *adv* efficacement. ♦ **effectuate** *vt* effectuer.
effeminate [ɪ'femɪnɪt] *adj* efféminé. ♦ **effeminacy** *n* caractère *m* efféminé.
effervesce [ˌefə'ves] *vi [liquids]* être en effervescence; *[drinks]* mousser; *[person]* être tout excité. ♦ **effervescence** *n* effervescence *f*. ♦ **effervescent** *adj liquid, tablet* effervescent; *drink* gazeux; *person* plein d'entrain.
efficacious [ˌefɪ'keɪʃəs] *adj* efficace. ♦ **efficacy** ['efɪkəsɪ] *n* efficacité *f*.
efficient [ɪ'fɪʃənt] *adj person* capable, compétent; *method, system, organization* efficace; *machine* qui fonctionne bien. ♦ **efficiency** *n* capacité *f*, compétence *f*; efficacité *f*; bon fonctionnement *m*. ♦ **efficiently** *adv* avec compétence; efficacement; *[machine]* **to work** ~**ly** bien fonctionner.
effluent ['eflʊənt] *adj, n* effluent (*m*).
effort ['efət] *n* effort *m*. **to make an** ~ **to do** faire un effort pour faire, s'efforcer de faire; **to make every** ~ **to do** faire tout son possible pour faire; **he made no** ~ **to be polite** il ne s'est pas donné la peine d'être poli; **it's not worth the** ~ cela ne vaut pas la peine; **it's an awful** ~ **to get up!** il en faut du courage pour se lever!; **what do you think of his latest** ~**?*** qu'est-ce que tu penses de ce qu'il vient de faire?; **a first** ~ un coup d'essai, une tentative; **that's a good** ~* ça n'est pas mal réussi;

it's a **pretty poor** ~* ça n'est pas une réussite. ♦ **effortless** *adj success* facile; *movement* aisé. ♦ **effortlessly** *adv* sans effort, facilement.
effrontery [ɪ'frʌntərɪ] *n* effronterie *f.*
effusive [ɪ'fju:sɪv] *adj person* expansif; *welcome* chaleureux; *thanks, apologies* sans fin. ♦ **effusion** *n* effusion *f.* ♦ **effusively** *adv* avec effusion.
eft [eft] *n* (*Zool*) triton *m* crêté.
egalitarian [ɪ,gælɪ'tɛərɪən] **1** *n* égalitariste *mf.* **2** *adj person* égalitariste; *principle* égalitaire. ♦ **egalitarianism** *n* égalitarisme *m.*
egg [eg] **1** *n* œuf *m.* **~s and bacon** œufs au bacon; (*fig*) **to put all one's ~s in one basket** mettre tous ses œufs dans le même panier; (*fig*) **to have ~ on one's face*** avoir l'air plutôt ridicule. **2** *adj*: **~ white/yolk** blanc *m*/jaune *m* d'œuf; **~ custard** ≈ crème *f* renversée. **3** *vt* (**~ on**) inciter (*to do* à faire). ♦ **eggbeater** *n* (*rotary*) batteur *m* (à œufs); (*whisk*) fouet *m* (à œufs). ♦ **eggcup** *n* coquetier *m.* ♦ **eggflip** *or* ♦ **eggnog** *n* flip *m.* ♦ **egghead*** *n* intellectuel(le) *m(f)*, cérébral(e) *m(f).* ♦ **eggplant** *n* aubergine *f.* ♦ **egg-shaped** *adj* ovoïde. ♦ **eggshell 1** *n* coquille *f* (d'œuf); **2** *adj paint* presque mat. ♦ **egg-timer** *n* (*sand*) sablier *m*; (*automatic*) minuteur *m.*
ego ['i:gəʊ] **1** *n* (*Psych*) **the ~** le moi, l'ego *m.* **2** *adj*: **~ trip** fête *f* pour soi. ♦ **egocentric(al)** *adj* égocentrique. ♦ **egomania** *n* manie *f* égocentrique. ♦ **ego(t)ism** *n* égotisme *m.* ♦ **ego(t)ist** *n* égotiste *mf.* ♦ **ego(t)istic(al)** *adj* égotiste.
Egypt ['i:dʒɪpt] *n* Égypte *f.* ♦ **Egyptian 1** *adj* égyptien; **2** *n* Égyptien(ne) *m(f).*
eiderdown ['aɪdədaʊn] *n* édredon *m.*
eight [eɪt] *adj, n* huit (*m*) *inv.* **he's had one over the ~*** il a un verre dans le nez*; *for phrases V* **six.** ♦ **eighteen** *adj, n* dix-huit (*m*) *inv.* ♦ **eighteenth 1** *adj* dix-huitième; **2** *n* dix-huitième *mf*; (*fraction*) dix-huitième *m.* ♦ **eighth 1** *adj* huitième; **2** *n* huitième *mf*; (*fraction*) huitième *m.* ♦ **eightieth 1** *adj* quatre-vingtième; **2** *n* quatre-vingtième *mf*; (*fraction*) quatre-vingtième *m.* ♦ **eighty** *adj, n* quatre-vingts (*m*) *inv*; **~y books** quatre-vingts livres; **~y-one** quatre-vingt-un; **~y-first** quatre-vingt-unième; **page ~y** page quatre-vingt.
Eire ['ɛərə] *n* République *f* d'Irlande, Irlande *f* du Sud.
either ['aɪðəʳ] **1** *adj* **(a)** (*one or other*) l'un ou l'autre, n'importe lequel (des deux). **~ day would suit me** l'un ou l'autre jour me conviendrait; **I don't like ~ girl** je n'aime ni l'une ni l'autre de ces filles. **(b)** (*each*) chaque. **in ~ hand** dans chaque main; **on ~ side of the street** des deux côtés *or* de chaque côté de la rue; **on ~ side lay fields** de part et d'autre s'étendaient des champs. **2** *pron* l'un(e) ou l'autre, n'importe lequel (*or* laquelle) (des deux). **which bus will you take? – ~** quel bus prendrez-vous? – l'un ou l'autre *or* n'importe lequel (des deux); **I don't believe ~ of them** je ne les crois ni l'un ni l'autre; **give it to ~ of them** donnez-le soit à l'un soit à l'autre; **if ~ is attacked the other helps her** si l'une des deux est attaquée l'autre l'aide. **3** *adv* non plus. **he can't act ~** il ne sait pas jouer non plus; **no, I haven't ~** moi non plus. **4** *conj*: **~ ... or** ou (bien) ... ou (bien), soit ... soit; (*after neg*) ni ... ni; **~ he or his sister** soit lui soit sa sœur, ou (bien) lui ou (bien) sa sœur; **I have never been ~ to Paris or to Rome** je ne suis jamais allé ni à Paris ni à Rome.
ejaculate [ɪ'dʒækjʊleɪt] *vti* (*cry out*) s'exclamer; (*Physiol*) éjaculer. ♦ **ejaculation** *n* exclamation *f*; éjaculation *f.*
eject [ɪ'dʒekt] *vt* (*Aviat, Tech etc*) éjecter; *tenant, trouble-maker* expulser, vider*; *trespasser* chasser. ♦ **ejection** *n* éjection *f*; expulsion *f.* ♦ **ejector** *n* éjecteur *m*; **~or seat** siège *m* éjectable.
eke [i:k] *vt*: **to ~ out** (*by adding*) augmenter (*by doing* en faisant); (*by saving*) faire durer.
elaborate [ɪ'læbərɪt] **1** *adj* (*complicated*) complexe, compliqué; (*careful*) minutieux; *joke, meal, style, clothes* recherché; *work of art* travaillé. **with ~ care** très soigneusement, minutieusement. **2** [ɪ'læbəreɪt] *vt* élaborer. **3** *vi* donner des détails (*on* sur). ♦ **elaborately** *adv do, prepare, plan* minutieusement; *dress, write* avec recherche.
elapse [ɪ'læps] *vi* s'écouler, (se) passer.
elastic [ɪ'læstɪk] **1** *adj* élastique. **~ band** élastique *m*; **~ stockings** bas *mpl* à varices. **2** *n* élastique *m.* ♦ **elasticity** *n* élasticité *f.*
elate [ɪ'leɪt] *vt* transporter. ♦ **elated** *adj* transporté (de joie). ♦ **elation** *n* allégresse *f.*
elbow ['elbəʊ] **1** *n* coude *m.* **to lean one's ~s on** s'accouder à, être accoudé à; **at his ~** à ses côtés; **out at the ~s** *garment* percé aux coudes; *person* déguenillé. **2** *adj*: **to use a bit of ~ grease*** mettre de l'huile de coude*; **to have enough ~ room** avoir de la place pour se retourner; (*fig*) avoir les coudées franches. **3** *vt*: **to ~ sb aside** écarter qn du coude; **to ~ (one's way) through the crowd** se frayer un passage à travers la foule (en jouant des coudes).
elder[1] ['eldəʳ] *n* (*Bot*) sureau *m.* ♦ **elderberry** *n* baie *f* de sureau; **~berry wine** vin *m* de sureau.
elder[2] ['eldəʳ] **1** *adj* aîné (*de deux*). **my ~ sister** ma sœur aînée; **~ statesman** homme *m* politique chevronné. **2** *n* aîné(e) *m(f).* *[tribe]* **~s** anciens *mpl*; **one's ~s and betters** ses aînés. ♦ **elderly** *adj* assez âgé. ♦ **eldest** *adj* aîné (*de plusieurs*); **their eldest child** l'aîné(e) de leurs enfants; **my eldest brother** l'aîné de mes frères.
elect [ɪ'lekt] **1** *vt* (*by vote*) élire (*to* à); (*more informally*) nommer (*to* à); (*choose*) choisir (*to do* de faire). **he was ~ed chairman** il a été élu président. **2** *adj* futur. **the president ~** le futur président. **3** *npl*: **the ~** les élus *mpl.* ♦ **election 1** *n* élection *f*; **to hold an ~ion** procéder à une élection; **2** *adj campaign, speech, agent* électoral; *day, results* du scrutin. ♦ **electioneer** *vi* mener une campagne électorale. ♦ **elector** *n* électeur *m*, -trice *f.* ♦ **electoral** *adj* électoral; **~oral district** circonscription *f* électorale; **~oral roll** liste *f* électorale. ♦ **electorate** *n* électorat *m.*
electric [ɪ'lektrɪk] *adj* électrique. **~ blanket** couverture *f* chauffante; **~ chair** chaise *f* électrique; **~ fire** radiateur *m* électrique; **~ light** lumière *f* électrique; **~ shock** décharge *f* électrique; **to get an ~ shock** recevoir une décharge électrique; (*Med*) **~ shock treatment*** électrochocs *mpl*; **~ storm** orage *m* magnétique; (*fig*) **the atmosphere was ~** il y avait de l'électricité dans l'air*. ♦ **electrical** *adj* électrique; **~al engineer** ingénieur *m* électricien; **~al engineering** électrotechnique *f*; **~al failure** panne *f* d'électricité. ♦ **electrician** *n* électricien *m.* ♦ **electricity** *n* électricité *f*; **to switch off/on the ~ity** couper/rétablir le courant; **~ity board** office *m* régional de l'électricité. ♦ **electrification** *n* électrification *f.* ♦ **electrify** *vt* (*Rail*) électrifier; (*charge with ~ity*) électriser; (*fig*) *audience* électriser. ♦ **electrifying** *adj* électrisant.
electro... [ɪ'lektrəʊ] *pref* électro... . ♦ **electrocardiogram** *n* électrocardiogramme *m.* ♦ **electrocardiograph** *n* électrocardiographe *m.* ♦ **electrochemical** *adj* électrochimique. ♦ **electrochemistry** *n* électrochimie *f.* ♦ **electroconvulsive** *adj*: **to give sb ~convulsive therapy** traiter qn par électrochocs. ♦ **electrocute** *vt* électrocuter. ♦ **electrocution** *n* électrocution *f.* ♦ **electrodynamics** *nsg* électrodynamique *f.* ♦ **electroencephalogram** *n* électro-encéphalogramme *m.* ♦ **electroencephalograph** *n* électro-encéphalographie *f.* ♦ **electrolysis**

n électrolyse *f.* ♦ **electromagnetic** *adj* électromagnétique. ♦ **electroplated** *adj*: **~plated silver** ruolz *m.* ♦ **electroshock treatment** *n* (*Med*) électrochocs *mpl.*

electrode [ɪ'lektrəʊd] *n* électrode *f.*

electron [ɪ'lektrɒn] **1** *n* électron *m.* **2** *adj microscope etc* électronique. **~ gun** canon *m* à électrons. ♦ **electronic** *adj* (*gen*) électronique; **~ic surveillance** utilisation *f* d'appareils d'écoute. ♦ **electronics** *nsg* électronique *f.*

elegant ['elɪgənt] *adj* élégant. ♦ **elegance** *n* élégance *f.* ♦ **elegantly** *adv* élégamment, avec élégance.

elegy ['elɪdʒɪ] *n* élégie *f.*

element ['elɪmənt] *n* (*gen*) élément *m*; *[heater, kettle]* résistance *f.* **an ~ of danger/truth** une part de danger/de vérité; **the ~ of chance** le facteur chance; **to be in one's ~** être dans son élément; (*Rel*) **the E~s** les Espèces *fpl.* ♦ **elemental** *adj* élémentaire; (*basic*) essentiel. ♦ **elementary** *adj* (*gen*) élémentaire; *school, education* primaire; **~ary science** les rudiments *mpl* de la science.

elephant ['elɪfənt] *n* éléphant *m.* ♦ **elephantine** *adj* éléphantesque.

elevate ['elɪveɪt] *vt object* élever (*also fig, Rel*). ♦ **elevated** *adj position* élevé; *railway* aérien; *rank* éminent; *style* soutenu; *thoughts* noble. ♦ **elevating** *adj* (*fig*) exaltant. ♦ **elevation** *n* (*gen*) élévation *f*; (*altitude*) altitude *f*; (*Archit*) **front elevation** façade *f*; **sectional elevation** coupe *f* verticale. ♦ **elevator** *n* élévateur *m*; (*US: lift*) ascenseur *m*; (*hoist*) monte-charge *m inv.*

eleven [ɪ'levn] *adj, n* onze (*m*) *inv.* (*Scol*) **the ~ plus** ≃ l'examen *m* d'entrée en sixième; (*Sport*) **the first ~** le onze, la première équipe; *for phrases V* **six.** ♦ **elevenses*** *npl* pause-café *f.* ♦ **eleventh 1** *adj* onzième; (*fig*) **at the ~th hour** à la onzième heure; **2** *n* onzième *mf*; (*fraction*) onzième *m.*

elf [elf] *n, pl* **elves** lutin *m.*

elicit [ɪ'lɪsɪt] *vt truth, secret* arracher (*from sb* à qn), découvrir; *facts of a case* tirer au clair, (*from sb*) obtenir (*from* de); *admission, reply, explanation* obtenir (*from* de).

eligible ['elɪdʒəbl] *adj* (*for membership, office*) éligible (*for* à); (*for job*) admissible (*for* à). **to be ~ for** *pension* avoir droit à; *promotion* avoir les conditions requises pour obtenir; **an ~ young man** un beau parti. ♦ **eligibility** *n* éligibilité *f*; admissibilité *f.*

eliminate [ɪ'lɪmɪneɪt] *vt* (*gen*) éliminer (*from* de); *possibility* exclure; *bad language, detail* supprimer; (*kill*) supprimer. ♦ **elimination** *n* élimination *f*; **by the process of elimination** en procédant par élimination.

elision [ɪ'lɪʒən] *n* élision *f.*

élite [eɪ'li:t] *n* élite *f.* ♦ **elitism** *n* élitisme *m.* ♦ **elitist** *adj* élitiste.

elixir [ɪ'lɪksəʳ] *n* élixir *m.*

Elizabethan [ɪˌlɪzə'bi:θən] *adj* élisabéthain.

elliptic(al) [ɪ'lɪptɪk(əl)] *adj* elliptique.

elm [elm] *n* orme *m.*

elocution [ˌelə'kju:ʃən] *n* élocution *f.*

elongate ['i:lɒŋgeɪt] *vt* allonger. ♦ **elongation** *n* allongement *m*; (*Med*) élongation *f.*

elope [ɪ'ləʊp] *vi [couple]* s'enfuir. **to ~ with sb** *[woman]* se laisser enlever par qn; *[man]* enlever qn. ♦ **elopement** *n* fugue *f* (amoureuse).

eloquent ['eləkwənt] *adj* (*gen*) éloquent; *words* entraînant; *silence* qui en dit long. ♦ **eloquence** *n* éloquence *f.* ♦ **eloquently** *adv* avec éloquence.

else [els] *adv* autre, d'autre, de plus. **anybody ~ would have done it** tout autre *or* n'importe qui d'autre l'aurait fait; **is there anybody ~ there?** y a-t-il qn d'autre?; **I'd prefer anything ~** je préférerais n'importe quoi d'autre; **have you anything ~ to say?** avez-vous encore qch à dire?; **anything ~ sir?** *[shop assistant]* et avec ça*, monsieur?; **nothing ~, thank you** plus rien, merci; **anywhere ~ nobody would have noticed, but ...** n'importe où ailleurs personne ne s'en serait aperçu, mais ...; **can you do it anywhere ~?** pouvez-vous le faire ailleurs?; **how ~ can I do it?** comment est-ce que je peux le faire autrement?; **nobody ~, no one ~** personne d'autre; **nothing ~** rien d'autre; **nowhere ~** nulle part ailleurs; **sb ~** qn d'autre; **sth ~** autre chose, qch d'autre; **somewhere ~** ailleurs, autre part; **who ~?** qui encore?; **what ~ could I do?** que pouvais-je faire d'autre?; **and much ~** et bien d'autres choses (encore); **there is little ~ to be done** il n'y a pas grand-chose d'autre à faire; **or ~** ou bien, sinon, autrement; **do it or ~ go away** faites-le, ou bien allez-vous-en; **do it or ~!*** faites-le sinon ...! ♦ **elsewhere** *adv* ailleurs.

elucidate [ɪ'lu:sɪdeɪt] *vt* élucider. ♦ **elucidation** *n* élucidation *f.*

elude [ɪ'lu:d] *vt enemy, pursuit, arrest* échapper à; *the law, question* éluder; *sb's gaze, police, responsibility* se dérober à; *blow* esquiver, éviter. **the name ~s me** le nom m'échappe; **success ~d him** le succès restait hors de sa portée. ♦ **elusive** *adj enemy, prey, thoughts* insaisissable; *word, happiness, success* qui échappe; *glance, personality* fuyant; *answer* évasif; (*gen*) **she's very elusive** il est impossible de la coincer.

emaciated [ɪ'meɪsɪeɪtɪd] *adj person, face* émacié; *limb* décharné. **to become ~** s'émacier, se décharner. ♦ **emaciation** *n* émaciation *f.*

emanate ['eməneɪt] *vi* émaner (*from* de). ♦ **emanation** *n* émanation *f.*

emancipate [ɪ'mænsɪpeɪt] *vt women* émanciper; *slaves* affranchir; (*fig*) émanciper, affranchir (*from* de). ♦ **emancipation** *n* émancipation *f*; affranchissement *m.*

embalm [ɪm'bɑ:m] *vt* embaumer.

embankment [ɪm'bæŋkmənt] *n [path, railway]* talus *m*, remblai *m*; *[canal, dam]* digue *f.* (*fig*) **to sleep on the E~** ≃ coucher sous les ponts.

embargo [ɪm'bɑ:gəʊ] *n* (*Comm, Naut: prohibition*) embargo *m*; (*fig*) interdiction *f.* **to put an ~ on** mettre l'embargo sur; (*fig*) interdire.

embark [ɪm'bɑ:k] **1** *vt* embarquer. **2** *vi* (*Aviat, Naut*) s'embarquer (*on* à bord de, sur). **to ~ on** *journey* commencer; *business, undertaking, explanation* se lancer dans; *discussion* entamer. ♦ **embarkation 1** *n [passengers]* embarquement *m*; *[cargo]* chargement *m*; **2** *adj*: **~ation card** carte *f* d'embarquement.

embarrass [ɪm'bærəs] *vt* embarrasser, gêner. **I feel ~ed about it** j'en suis gêné, cela m'embarrasse; **to be financially ~ed** avoir des embarras *mpl* d'argent. ♦ **embarrassing** *adj* embarrassant, gênant; **to get out of an ~ing situation** se tirer d'embarras. ♦ **embarrassment** *n* embarras *m*, gêne *f* (*at* devant); **to be an ~ment to sb** embarrasser qn.

embassy ['embəsɪ] *n* ambassade *f.* **the French E~** l'ambassade de France.

embed [ɪm'bed] *vt* (*in wood*) enfoncer; (*in cement, stone*) sceller; *jewel* enchâsser; (*Ling*) enchâsser.

embellish [ɪm'belɪʃ] *vt* (*gen*) embellir (*with* de); *manuscript, tale* enjoliver (*with* de); *truth* broder sur. ♦ **embellishment** *n* enjolivement *m.*

embers ['embəz] *npl* braise *f.* **the dying ~** les tisons *mpl.*

embezzle [ɪm'bezl] *vt* détourner (*des fonds*). ♦ **embezzlement** *n* détournement *m* de fonds. ♦ **embezzler** *n* escroc *m.*

embitter [ɪm'bɪtəʳ] *vt person* aigrir; *relations, disputes* envenimer.

emblem ['embləm] *n* emblème *m.*

embody [ɪm'bɒdeu27] *vt spirit, quality* incarner; *one's thoughts, theories* exprimer (*in* dans, en); *[machine] features* réunir. ♦ **embodiment** *n*

incarnation *f*; **he is the embodiment of kindness** c'est la bonté incarnée.
embolism ['embəlɪzəm] *n* embolie *f*.
emboss [ɪm'bɒs] *vt metal* travailler en relief; *leather, cloth* gaufrer. ♦ **embossed** *adj wallpaper* gaufré; *writing paper* à en-tête en relief.
embrace [ɪm'breɪs] **1** *vt person* embrasser, étreindre; *religion, cause, theme, period* embrasser. **2** *vi* s'étreindre, s'embrasser. **3** *n* étreinte *f*.
embrocation [ˌembrəʊ'keɪʃən] *n* embrocation *f*.
embroider [ɪm'brɔɪdə^r] *vt* broder; *facts, truth* broder sur. ♦ **embroidery 1** *n* broderie *f*; **2** *adj silk* à broder.
embroiled [ɪm'brɔɪld] *adj*: ~ **in** entraîné dans; **to get (o.s.)** ~ **in** se laisser entraîner dans.
embryo ['embrɪəʊ] *n* embryon *m*. **in** ~ en germe. ♦ **embryonic** *adj* embryonnaire; (*fig*) en germe.
emend [ɪ'mend] *vt* corriger (*un texte*). ♦ **emendation** *n* correction *f*.
emerald ['emərəld] **1** *n* (*stone*) émeraude *f*; (*colour*) émeraude *m*. **2** *adj necklace* d'émeraudes; (~ **green**) émeraude *inv*.
emerge [ɪ'mɜːdʒ] *vi* (*gen*) apparaître, surgir (*from* de, *from behind* de derrière); (*from water*) émerger, surgir (*from* de); *[truth, facts]* émerger (*from* de), apparaître; *[difficulties]* surgir, s'élever; *[new nation, theory, school of thought]* naître. **it** ~**s that** il ressort que, il apparaît que. ♦ **emergence** *n* apparition *f*; naissance *f*. ♦ **emergent** *adj*: ~**nt nations** pays *mpl* en voie de développement.
emergency [ɪ'mɜːdʒənsɪ] **1** *n* cas *m* urgent. **in an** ~ en cas d'urgence *or* d'imprévu; **prepared for any** ~ prêt à toute éventualité; **in this** ~ dans cette situation critique; **to declare a state of** ~ déclarer l'état d'urgence. **2** *adj measures, operation, repair* d'urgence; *brake, airstrip* de secours; *powers* extraordinaire; *rations* de réserve; (*improvised*) *mast* de fortune. (*Med*) **an** ~ **case** une urgence; ~ **exit** sortie *f* de secours; (*Mil*) ~ **force** force *f* d'intervention; (*Aviat*) ~ **landing** atterrissage forcé; (*Med*) ~ **service** service *m* des urgences; ~ **ward** salle *f* des urgences.
emery ['emərɪ] **1** *n* émeri *m*. **2** *adj*: ~ **cloth/paper** toile *f*/papier *m* d'émeri.
emetic [ɪ'metɪk] *adj, n* émétique (*m*).
emigrate ['emɪgreɪt] *vi* émigrer. ♦ **emigrant** *n* émigrant(e) *m(f)*; (*established*) émigré(e) *m(f)*. ♦ **emigration** *n* émigration *f*.
eminent ['emɪnənt] *adj* (*gen*) éminent; *person* éminent, très distingué. ♦ **eminence** *n* distinction *f*; **to win eminence** acquérir un grand renom; **Your Eminence** Votre Éminence *f*. ♦ **eminently** *adv suited* éminemment; *respectable* parfaitement; *fair* admirablement.
emir [e'mɪə^r] *n* émir *m*. ♦ **emirate** *n* émirat *m*.
emit [ɪ'mɪt] *vt* (*gen*) dégager, émettre; *sparks* jeter; *light, electromagnetic waves, banknotes, sound* émettre; *cry* laisser échapper. ♦ **emission** *n* dégagement *m*, émission *f*.
emolument [ɪ'mɒljʊmənt] *n* émoluments *mpl*.
emotion [ɪ'məʊʃən] *n* **(a)** émotion *f*. **full of** ~ ému. **(b)** (*jealousy, love etc*) sentiment *m*. ♦ **emotional** *adj shock, disturbance* émotif; *reaction, state* émotionnel; *moment* d'émotion profonde; *story, writing* qui fait appel aux sentiments; *person* facilement ému; **he was being very** ~**al about it** il prenait cela très à cœur. ♦ **emotionalism** *n* sensiblerie *f* (*pej*). ♦ **emotionally** *adv speak* avec émotion; ~**ally deprived** privé d'affection; **he is** ~**ally involved** ses sentiments sont en cause. ♦ **emotive** *adj* émotif.
empathy ['empəθɪ] *n* communauté *f* d'âme.
emperor ['empərə^r] *n* empereur *m*.
emphasis ['emfəsɪs] *n* (*in word, phrase*) accentuation *f*, accent *m* d'intensité; (*fig*) accent. **to speak with** ~ parler sur un ton d'insistance; (*fig*) **the** ~ **is on sport** on accorde une importance particulière au sport. ♦ **emphasize** *vt word, fact, point* appuyer sur, insister sur; *[garment etc] sb's height etc* accentuer; **I must emphasize that ...** je dois souligner le fait que .... ♦ **emphatic** *adj tone, manner, person* énergique; *denial, speech, condemnation* catégorique, énergique. ♦ **emphatically** *adv speak* énergiquement; *deny, refuse* catégoriquement; **yes, emphatically!** oui, absolument!; **I must say this emphatically** sur ce point je suis formel.
empire ['empaɪə^r] **1** *n* empire *m*. **2** *adj*: **E**~ *costume, furniture* Empire *inv*. ♦ **empire-builder** *n* bâtisseur *m* d'empires. ♦ **empire-build** *vi*: **he is** ~**-building** il joue les bâtisseurs d'empire.
empiric(al) [em'pɪrɪk(əl)] *adj* empirique. ♦ **empiricism** *n* empirisme *m*. ♦ **empiricist** *adj, n* empiriste (*mf*).
employ [ɪm'plɔɪ] **1** *vt* employer (*as* comme; *to do* pour faire; *in doing* à faire). **to be** ~**ed in doing** être occupé à faire. **2** *n*: **in the** ~ **of** employé par; *domestic staff* au service de. ♦ **employee** *n* employé(e) *m(f)*. ♦ **employer** *n* (*gen*) patron(ne) *m(f)*; (*Admin*) employeur *m*, -euse *f*; (*Ind: collectively*) ~**ers** le patronat; ~**ers' federation/contribution** fédération/cotisation patronale. ♦ **employment 1** *n* emploi *m*; (*a job*) emploi, travail *m*; **full** ~**ment** le plein emploi; **to take up** ~**ment** prendre un emploi; **without** ~**ment** sans emploi, au chômage; **to find** ~**ment** trouver un emploi *or* du travail; **in sb's** ~**ment** employé par qn; *domestic staff* au service de qn; **conditions/place of** ~**ment** conditions *fpl*/lieu *m* de travail; **Ministry of E**~**ment** ministère *m* de l'Emploi; **2** *adj*: ~**ment agency** agence *f* de placement; ~**ment exchange** bourse *f* du travail.
empower [ɪm'paʊə^r] *vt* autoriser (*sb to do* qn à faire).
empress ['emprɪs] *n* impératrice *f*.
empty ['emptɪ] **1** *adj* (*gen*) vide; *house, room* inoccupé, vide; *post, job* vacant; *words* creux; *promise* en l'air; *threat* vain. **on an** ~ **stomach** à jeun. **2** *npl*: **empties** bouteilles *fpl* (*or* boîtes *fpl etc*) vides. **3** *vt* (*gen*) vider; (~**out**) *pocket* vider; *bricks, books* sortir (*of, from* de; *into* dans); *liquid* vider (*from* de), verser (*from* de; *into* dans). **4** *vi [water]* se déverser; *[river]* se jeter (*into* dans); *[building, container]* se vider. ♦ **emptiness** *n* vide *m*; *[pleasures etc]* vanité *f*; **the emptiness of life** le vide de l'existence. ♦ **empty-handed** *adj*: **to be** ~**-handed** avoir les mains vides; **to arrive** ~**-handed** arriver les mains vides. ♦ **empty-headed** *adj* sot.
emu ['iːmjuː] *n* émeu *m*.
emulate ['emjʊleɪt] *vt* (essayer d')égaler.
emulsify [ɪ'mʌlsɪfaɪ] *vt* émulsionner. ♦ **emulsion 1** *n* émulsion *f*; **2** *adj paint* mat.
enable [ɪ'neɪbl] *vt*: **to** ~ **sb to do** permettre à qn de faire, donner à qn (*opportunity*) la possibilité *or* (*means*) le moyen de faire.
enact [ɪ'nækt] *vt* **(a)** (*Jur*) (*make into law*) promulguer; (*decree*) décréter. **(b)** (*perform*) *play* représenter. (*fig*) **the drama which was** ~**ed** le drame qui s'est déroulé.
enamel [ɪ'næməl] **1** *n* (*gen*) émail *m*. **nail** ~ vernis *m* à ongles. **2** *vt* émailler. **3** *adj* en émail. ~ **paint** ripolin *m* ®. ♦ **enamelled** *adj* en émail. ♦ **enamelware** *n* articles *mpl* en métal émaillé.
enamoured, (*US*) **-ored** [ɪ'næməd] *adj*: **to be** ~ **of** aimer beaucoup.
encampment [ɪn'kæmpmənt] *n* campement *m*.
encapsulate [ɪn'kæpsjʊleɪt] *vt* (*fig*) renfermer, résumer.
encase [ɪn'keɪs] *vt* (*contain*) enfermer (*in* dans); (*cover*) recouvrir (*in* de).
encephalitis [ˌensefə'laɪtɪs] *n* encéphalite *f*.
enchant [ɪn'tʃɑːnt] *vt* enchanter, charmer.

♦ **enchanter** *n* enchanteur *m*. ♦ **enchanting** *adj* enchanteur, charmant. ♦ **enchantingly** *adv smile, dance* d'une façon ravissante; **~ingly beautiful** belle à ravir. ♦ **enchantment** *n* enchantement *m*. ♦ **enchantress** *n* enchanteresse *f*.

encircle [ɪn'sɜːkl] *vt* (*gen*) entourer; *[people]* encercler, entourer. ♦ **encircling** *adj*: **encircling movement** manœuvre *f* d'encerclement.

enclose [ɪn'kləʊz] *vt* **(a)** (*fence in*) clôturer; (*surround*) entourer (*with* de). **(b)** (*with letter etc*) joindre (*in, with* à). **letter enclosing a receipt** lettre contenant un reçu; **please find ~d** veuillez trouver ci-joint. ♦ **enclosed** *adj space* clos; (*Rel*) *order* cloîtré; (*in letter*) *cheque etc* ci-joint. ♦ **enclosure** *n* (*act*) clôture *f*; (*piece of land*) enceinte *f*; (*at racecourse*) pesage *m*; (*document* *~d*) pièce *f* jointe.

encompass [ɪn'kʌmpəs] *vt* (*include*) inclure.

encore [ɒŋ'kɔːʳ] **1** *excl* bis! **2** ['ɒŋkɔːʳ] *n* bis *m*. **to give an ~** jouer (*or* chanter *etc*) un bis.

encounter [ɪn'kaʊntəʳ] **1** *vt person* rencontrer (à l'improviste); *enemy, difficulties* affronter, rencontrer; *danger* rencontrer; *opposition* se heurter à; *enemy fire* essuyer. **2** *n* rencontre *f*.

encourage [ɪn'kʌrɪdʒ] *vt* encourager (*sb to do* qn à faire). ♦ **encouragement** *n* encouragement *m*. ♦ **encouraging** *adj* encourageant. ♦ **encouragingly** *adv* d'une manière encourageante.

encroach [ɪn'krəʊtʃ] *vi* (*on sb's land, time, rights*) empiéter (*on* sur). **the sea is ~ing on the land** la mer gagne du terrain.

encrusted [ɪn'krʌstəd] *adj*: **~ with** *earth etc* encroûté de; *jewels* incrusté de.

encumber [ɪn'kʌmbəʳ] *vt* encombrer (*with* de). ♦ **encumbrance** *n* (*thing*) chose *f* gênante.

encyclical [ɪn'sɪklɪkəl] *adj, n* encyclique (*f*).

encyclop(a)edia [ɪn,saɪkləʊ'piːdɪə] *n* encyclopédie *f*. ♦ **encyclop(a)edic** *adj* encyclopédique.

end [end] **1** *n* **(a)** (*farthest part: gen*) bout *m*. **the southern ~ of the town** l'extrémité *f* sud de la ville; **the fourth from the ~** le quatrième avant la fin; **from ~ to ~** d'un bout à l'autre; **on ~** debout (*V also* **1b**); **to stand a box** *etc* **on ~** mettre une caisse *etc* debout; **his hair stood on ~** ses cheveux se dressèrent sur sa tête; **~ to ~** bout à bout; (*Sport*) **to change ~s** changer de côté; (*fig*) **to make (both) ~s meet** joindre les deux bouts; **to keep one's ~ up*** se défendre assez bien.

(b) (*conclusion*) fin *f*. **the ~ of the world** la fin du monde; **it's not the ~ of the world!*** ce n'est pas une catastrophe!; **it succeeded in the ~** cela a réussi à la fin *or* finalement; **he got used to it in the ~** il a fini par s'y habituer; **at the ~ of the day** à la fin de la journée; (*fig*) en fin de compte; **at the ~ of three weeks** au bout de trois semaines; **that was the ~ of my watch** ma montre était fichue*; **that was the ~ of that!** on n'en a plus reparlé; **there is no ~ to it all** cela n'en finit plus; **to be at an ~** *[action]* être terminé; *[time, period]* être écoulé; *[supplies]* être épuisé; *[patience]* être à bout; **at the ~ of one's patience/strength** à bout de patience/forces; **to bring to an ~** *speech, writing* achever; *work* terminer; *relations* mettre fin à; **to come to an ~** prendre fin, se terminer; **to get to the ~ of** *supplies, food* finir; *work, essay* venir à bout de; *holiday* arriver à la fin de; **to come to a bad ~** mal finir; **we shall never hear the ~ of it** on n'a pas fini d'en entendre parler; **no ~* of** une masse* de, énormément de; **no ~*** (*adv*) énormément; **that's the (bitter) ~!*** il ne manquait plus que ça!, c'est la fin de tout!; **he's the ~!*** il est insupportable!; **for two hours on ~** deux heures de suite; **for days on ~** pendant des jours et des jours.

(c) (*remnant*) *[rope, candle]* bout *m*; *[loaf, meat]* reste *m*, restant *m*. **cigarette ~** mégot *m*.

(d) (*purpose*) but *m*, fin *f*. **with this ~ in view** dans ce but, à cette fin; **an ~ in itself** une fin en soi; **to no ~** en vain; **the ~ justifies the means** la fin justifie les moyens.

2 *adj house* dernier (*before n*); *result* final, définitif. **~ product** (*Comm, Ind*) produit fini; (*fig*) résultat *m*.

3 *vt work* finir, achever; *period of service* accomplir; *speech, writing* conclure (*with* avec, par); *broadcast, series* terminer (*with* par); *speculation, rumour, quarrel, war* mettre fin à. **that was the lie to ~ all lies!*** comme mensonge on ne fait pas mieux!*

4 *vi* finir, se terminer (*in* par), s'achever. **the winter is ~ing** l'hiver tire à sa fin; **word ~ing in an s/in -re** mot se terminant par un s/en -re; **it ~ed in failure** ça s'est soldé par un échec.

end up *vi* **(a)** finir, se terminer (*in* en, par); *[road]* aboutir (*in* à). **(b)** (*finally arrive at*) se retrouver (*in* à, en); (*finally become*) finir par devenir.

♦ **ending** *n* (*gen*) fin *f*; (*outcome*) issue *f*; *[speech etc]* conclusion *f*; (*Ling*) terminaison *f*; **story with a happy ~ing** histoire qui finit bien. ♦ **endless** *adj road, wait* interminable, sans fin; (*Tech*) *belt* sans fin; *times, attempts* innombrable; *discussion, argument* continuel, incessant; *patience* infini; *resources, supplies* inépuisable; *possibilities* illimité; **this job is ~less** on n'en voit pas la fin. ♦ **endlessly** *adv stretch out* interminablement, à perte de vue; *chatter, argue* continuellement; *repeat* sans cesse; **~lessly willing** d'une bonne volonté à toute épreuve. ♦ **endpapers** *npl* (*Typ*) gardes *fpl*. ♦ **endways** *or* ♦ **endwise** *adv* (*~ways on*) en long; (*~ to ~*) bout à bout.

endanger [ɪn'deɪndʒəʳ] *vt life, interests* mettre en danger; *future, chances, health* compromettre.

endear [ɪn'dɪəʳ] *vt* faire aimer (*to* de). **what ~s him to me is ...** ce qui me plaît en lui c'est ... . ♦ **endearing** *adj smile* engageant; *personality* attachant; *characteristic* (qui rend) sympathique. ♦ **endearingly** *adv* de façon engageante *or* sympathique. ♦ **endearments** *npl* (*words*) paroles *fpl* affectueuses; (*acts*) marques *fpl* d'affection.

endeavour [ɪn'devəʳ] **1** *n* effort *m*, tentative *f* (*to do* pour faire). **to make an ~ to do** essayer *or* s'efforcer de faire; **to make every ~ to go** faire tout son possible pour y aller. **2** *vi* essayer, s'efforcer (*to do* de faire), (*stronger*) s'appliquer (*to do* à faire).

endemic [en'demɪk] *adj* endémique.

endive ['endaɪv] *n* (*curly*) chicorée *f*; (*smooth, flat*) endive *f*.

endorse [ɪn'dɔːs] *vt* (*sign*) *document, cheque* endosser; (*guarantee*) *bill* avaliser; (*approve*) *claim* appuyer; *opinion* souscrire à; *action, decision* approuver. (*Aut*) **he has had his licence ~d** il a eu une contravention portée à son permis de conduire. ♦ **endorsement** *n* (*on cheque*) endos *m*; (*approval*) approbation *f*; (*on driving licence*) contravention portée à un permis de conduire.

endow [ɪn'daʊ] *vt institution, church* doter (*with* de); *hospital bed, prize, chair* fonder. **~ed with brains** *etc* doté d'intelligence *etc*. ♦ **endowment** **1** *n* dotation *f*; fondation *f*; **2** *adj*: **~ment assurance** assurance *f* à capital différé.

endure [ɪn'djʊəʳ] **1** *vt* (*gen*) supporter (*doing* de faire); *pain* supporter, endurer. **she can't ~ teasing** elle ne peut pas supporter *or* souffrir qu'on la taquine (*subj*). **2** *vi [building, peace, friendship]* durer; *[book, memory]* rester. ♦ **endurable** *adj* supportable. ♦ **endurance** **1** *n* endurance *f*, résistance *f*; **he has come to the end of his endurance** il n'en peut plus; **beyond endurance** intolérable; **tried beyond endurance** excédé; **2** *adj*: **endurance test** (*gen*) épreuve *f* de résistance; (*Aut*) épreuve d'endurance. ♦ **enduring** *adj* durable.

enema ['enɪmə] *n* (*Med*) lavement *m*.
enemy ['enəmɪ] **1** *n* (*gen*) ennemi(e) *m(f)*, adversaire *mf*; (*Mil*) ennemi *m*. **to make an ~ of sb** (se) faire un ennemi de qn; **he is his own worst ~** il est son pire ennemi. **2** *adj tanks, forces, tribes* ennemi; *morale, strategy* de l'ennemi. **~ action** une attaque ennemie; **killed by ~ action** tombé à l'ennemi; **~ alien** ressortissant(e) *m(f)* d'un pays ennemi. ♦ **enemy-occupied** *adj* occupé par l'ennemi.
energy ['enədʒɪ] **1** *n* énergie *f*. **Ministry of E~** ministère *m* de l'Énergie; **to save ~** faire des économies d'énergie; **with all one's ~** de toutes ses forces; **to put all one's ~ into (doing) sth** se consacrer tout entier à faire qch; **I haven't the ~ to go back** je n'ai pas l'énergie *or* le courage de retourner; **don't waste your ~** ne te donne pas du mal pour rien. **2** *adj crisis* énergétique, de l'énergie. ♦ **energetic** *adj* (*gen*) énergique; **I've had a very energetic day** je me suis beaucoup dépensé aujourd'hui; **do you feel energetic enough to come for a walk?** est-ce que tu as assez d'énergie pour faire une promenade? ♦ **energetically** *adv move, behave* énergiquement, avec énergie; *speak* avec force. ♦ **energize** *vt* donner de l'énergie à; (*Elec*) alimenter (en courant). ♦ **energy-giving** *adj* énergétique.
enervate ['enɜːveɪt] *vt* affaiblir. ♦ **enervating** *adj* débilitant.
enforce [ɪn'fɔːs] *vt decision, policy* appliquer; *law* faire respecter; *discipline* imposer. **to ~ obedience** se faire obéir. ♦ **enforced** *adj* forcé, obligé.
enfranchise [ɪn'fræntʃaɪz] *vt* (*give vote to*) accorder le droit de vote à, admettre au suffrage; (*set free*) affranchir. ♦ **enfranchisement** *n* admission *f* au suffrage; affranchissement *m*.
engage [ɪn'geɪdʒ] **1** *vt servant* engager; *workers* embaucher; *lawyer* prendre; *sb's attention, interest* retenir; (*Mil*) *the enemy* attaquer; (*Tech*) engager. **to ~ sb in conversation** lier conversation avec qn; (*Aut*) **to ~ a gear** engager une vitesse; **to ~ gear** mettre en prise; **to ~ the clutch** embrayer. **2** *vi [person]* s'engager (*to do* à faire); *[wheels]* s'engrener. **to ~ in** *politics* se lancer dans; *controversy* s'embarquer dans; **to ~ in a discussion/conversation** entrer en discussion/conversation (*with* avec). ♦ **engaged** *adj* **(a)** (*gen*) *person, seat, phone number etc* occupé; **to be ~d in doing** être occupé à faire; **to be ~d on sth** s'occuper de qch; (*Telec*) **the ~d signal** la tonalité occupé *inv*; **(b)** (*betrothed*) fiancé (*to* à, avec); **to get ~d** se fiancer (*to* à, avec). ♦ **engagement 1** *n* **(a)** (*appointment*) rendez-vous *m inv*; *[actor etc]* engagement *m*; **previous ~ment** engagement *m* antérieur; **I have an ~ment** je ne suis pas libre; **(b)** *[actor etc]* engagement *m*; **(c)** (*betrothal*) fiançailles *fpl*; **to break off one's ~ment** rompre ses fiançailles; **(d)** (*undertaking*) engagement *m*; **to give an ~ment to do sth** s'engager à faire qch; **(e)** (*Mil*) combat *m*, engagement *m*; **2** *adj*: **~ment book** agenda *m*; **~ment ring** bague *f* de fiançailles. ♦ **engaging** *adj smile* engageant; *personality* attirant.
engender [ɪn'dʒendə^r] *vt* engendrer (*fig*).
engine ['endʒɪn] **1** *n* (*Tech*) machine *f*, moteur *m*; *[ship]* machine; (*Rail*) locomotive *f*; (*Aut, Aviat*) moteur. (*Rail*) **facing/with your back to the ~** dans le sens de/le sens contraire à la marche. **2** *adj* (*Rail*) **~ driver** mécanicien *m*; (*Naut*) **~ room** salle *f* des machines; (*Aut*) **~ unit** bloc-moteur *m*. ♦ **-engined** *adj ending*: **twin-~d** à deux moteurs. ♦ **engineer 1** *n* (*gen*) ingénieur *m*; (*Rail, Naut*) mécanicien *m*; (*tradesman*) technicien *m*; (*for domestic appliances etc*) dépanneur *m*; (*Mil*) **the E~ers** le génie; **the TV ~er came** le dépanneur est venu pour la télé*; **2** *vt scheme* manigancer. ♦ **engineering 1** *n* engineering *m*, ingénierie *f*; **to study ~ering** faire des études d'ingénieur; **2** *adj*: **~ering factory** *or* **works** atelier *m* de construction mécanique; **~ering industries** industries *fpl* d'équipement.
England ['ɪŋglənd] *n* Angleterre *f*. ♦ **English 1** *adj* anglais; *king* d'Angleterre; **the English Channel** la Manche; **2** *n* (*Ling*) anglais *m*; (*people*) **the English** les Anglais *mpl*; **the King's** *or* **Queen's English** l'anglais correct; **in plain** *or* **simple English** ≃ en bon français. ♦ **Englishman** *n* Anglais *m*. ♦ **English-speaker** *n* anglophone *mf*. ♦ **English-speaking** *adj* qui parle anglais; *nation etc* anglophone. ♦ **Englishwoman** *n* Anglaise *f*.
engrave [ɪn'greɪv] *vt* graver. ♦ **engraver** *n* graveur *m*. ♦ **engraving** *n* gravure *f*.
engrossed [ɪn'grəʊst] *adj*: **~ in** *work* absorbé par; *reading, thoughts* plongé dans. ♦ **engrossing** *adj* absorbant.
engulf [ɪn'gʌlf] *vt* engouffrer.
enhance [ɪn'hɑːns] *vt attraction, beauty* mettre en valeur; *position, chances* améliorer; *prestige, reputation, powers* accroître.
enigma [ɪ'nɪgmə] *n* énigme *f*. ♦ **enigmatic** *adj* énigmatique. ♦ **enigmatically** *adv* d'une manière énigmatique.
enjoin [ɪn'dʒɔɪn] *vt* prescrire (*sb to do* à qn de faire); *silence, obedience* imposer (*on* à); *discretion* recommander (*on* à).
enjoy [ɪn'dʒɔɪ] *vt* **(a)** (*gen*) aimer (*doing* faire), trouver agréable (*doing* de faire); *meal, wine* apprécier, trouver bon. **I ~ed doing it** cela m'a fait plaisir de le faire; **to ~ life** profiter de la vie; **to ~ a weekend** passer un bon weekend; **did you ~ the concert?** est-ce que le concert vous a plu?; **to ~ one's dinner** bien manger *or* dîner; **to ~ o.s.** (bien) s'amuser; **did you ~ yourself in Paris?** est-ce que tu t'es bien amusé à Paris?; **she always ~s herself in the country** elle se plaît toujours à la campagne. **(b)** (*benefit from*) *income, health* jouir de. ♦ **enjoyable** *adj visit* agréable; *meal* excellent. ♦ **enjoyment** *n* plaisir *m*; **to get ~ment from (doing) sth** trouver du plaisir à (faire) qch.
enlarge [ɪn'lɑːdʒ] **1** *vt* (*gen, also Phot*) agrandir; (*fig*) *empire, circle of friends* étendre. **2** *vi* **(a)** (*grow bigger*) s'agrandir; s'étendre. **(b) to ~ (up)on** s'étendre sur. ♦ **enlarged** *adj edition* augmenté; *majority* accru; (*Med*) *organ* hypertrophié; *pore* dilaté. ♦ **enlargement** *n* (*gen; Phot*) agrandissement *m*. ♦ **enlarger** *n* (*Phot*) agrandisseur *m*.
enlighten [ɪn'laɪtn] *vt* éclairer (*sb on sth* qn sur qch). ♦ **enlightened** *adj* éclairé; **in this ~ed age** à notre époque éclairée. ♦ **enlightening** *adj* révélateur (*about* au sujet de). ♦ **enlightenment** *n* (*explanations*) éclaircissements *mpl* (*on* sur); **the Age of E~ment** le Siècle des lumières.
enlist [ɪn'lɪst] **1** *vi* (*Mil etc*) s'engager (*in* dans). (*US Mil*) **~ed man** simple soldat *m*. **2** *vt supporters* recruter; *sb's support* s'assurer.
enliven [ɪn'laɪvn] *vt* animer.
enmeshed [ɪn'meʃt] *adj*: **to get ~ in** s'empêtrer dans.
enmity ['enmɪtɪ] *n* inimitié *f*, hostilité *f*.
enormous [ɪ'nɔːməs] *adj* (*gen*) énorme; *patience* immense; *strength* prodigieux; *stature* colossal. **an ~ quantity of** énormément de; **an ~ number of** *things* une masse* de; *people* une foule de. ♦ **enormously** *adv* (+ *vb or ptp*) énormément; (+ *adj*) extrêmement; **it has changed ~ly** cela a énormément changé; **an ~ly funny story** une histoire extrêmement drôle.
enough [ɪ'nʌf] **1** *adj, n* assez (de). **~ money/books** assez d'argent/de livres; **~ to eat** assez à manger; **he earns ~ to live on** il gagne de quoi vivre; **I've had ~!** j'en ai marre!*; **I've had ~ of (doing) this** j'en ai assez de (faire) cela; **you can never have ~ of this music** on ne se lasse jamais de cette musique; **it was ~ to show that ...** cela a suffi à

prouver que ...; **that's ~** cela suffit; **it's ~ to drive you mad** c'est à vous rendre fou; **more than ~ wine** un peu trop de vin; **more than ~ for all** largement (assez) *or* plus qu'assez pour tous; **~'s ~!** ça suffit comme ça!

2 *adv* assez, suffisamment. **old ~ to go alone** suffisamment *or* assez grand pour y aller tout seul; **I was fool ~** *or* **~ of a fool to believe him** j'ai été assez bête pour le croire; **he knows well ~** il sait très bien; **he writes well ~** il écrit assez bien, il n'écrit pas mal; **oddly ~, I ...** chose curieuse *or* c'est curieux, je ... .

enquire [ɪn'kwaɪəʳ] *etc* = **inquire** *etc*.

enrage [ɪn'reɪdʒ] *vt* mettre en rage.

enrapture [ɪn'ræptʃəʳ] *vt* enchanter.

enrich [ɪn'rɪtʃ] *vt* (*gen*) enrichir; *soil* fertiliser. ♦ **enrichment** *n* enrichissement *m*; fertilisation *f*.

enrol, (*US*) **enroll** [ɪn'rəʊl] **1** *vt* (*gen*) inscrire; *workers* embaucher; *soldiers* enrôler. **2** *vi* s'inscrire (*in* à; *for* pour); se faire embaucher (*as* comme); s'enrôler (*in* dans).

ensconce [ɪn'skɒns] *vt*: **to ~ o.s.** bien s'installer; **~d** bien installé.

ensign *n* **(a)** ['ensən] (*flag*) drapeau *m*, pavillon *m* (*Naut*). (*Brit*) **red/white ~** pavillon de la marine marchande/de la marine de guerre. **(b)** ['ensaɪn] (*US Naut*) enseigne *m* de vaisseau.

enslave [ɪn'sleɪv] *vt* asservir.

ensue [ɪn'sju:] *vi* s'ensuivre (*from* de). ♦ **ensuing** *adj event, chaos* qui s'ensuit; *year, day* suivant.

ensure [ɪn'ʃʊəʳ] *vt* assurer (*that* que).

entail [ɪn'teɪl] *vt expense, work, delay* occasionner; *disadvantages, risk, difficulty* comporter; *suffering, hardship* entraîner. **it ~ed buying a car** cela nécessitait l'achat d'une voiture.

entangled [ɪn'tæŋgld] *adj thread etc* emmêlé; (*fig*) empêtré.

enter ['entəʳ] **1** *vt* **(a)** (*go into*) *house etc* entrer dans; *vehicle* monter dans; *path, road* s'engager dans; *profession, the army etc* entrer dans; *university* s'inscrire à. **to ~ the Church** se faire prêtre; **the thought never ~ed my head** cette pensée ne m'est jamais venue à l'esprit. **(b)** (*write down*) *amount, name, fact, order* (*on list etc*) inscrire, (*in notebook*) noter; *item in ledger* porter (*in* sur); *pupil, candidate, show dog* présenter (*for* à); *racehorse, runner* inscrire (*for, in* dans). (*Comm*) **~ these purchases to me** mettez ces achats à mon compte; **to ~ a protest** élever une protestation. **2** *vi* **(a)** entrer. (*Theat*) **~ Macbeth** entre Macbeth. **(b)** (*for race, exam etc*) s'inscrire (*for* pour).

enter into *vt fus* **(a)** *explanation, apology* se lancer dans; *correspondence, conversation* entrer en; *plot* prendre part à; *negotiations* entamer; *alliance* conclure. **(b)** *sb's plans, calculations* entrer dans. **her money doesn't ~ into it at all** son argent n'y est pour rien.

enteritis [ˌentə'raɪtɪs] *n* entérite *f*.

enterprise ['entəpraɪz] *n* **(a)** (*undertaking, company*) entreprise *f*. **(b)** (*initiative*) esprit *m* d'initiative. ♦ **enterprising** *adj person* plein d'initiative, entreprenant; *venture* audacieux; **that was enterprising of you!** vous avez fait preuve d'initiative! ♦ **enterprisingly** *adv*: **to do sth enterprisingly** faire qch de sa propre initiative.

entertain [ˌentə'teɪn] *vt* **(a)** *audience* amuser, divertir; *guests* distraire. **to ~ sb to dinner** offrir un dîner à qn; (*at home*) recevoir qn à dîner; **they ~ a lot** ils reçoivent beaucoup. **(b)** *thought* méditer; *intention, doubt* nourrir; *proposal* accueillir favorablement. ♦ **entertainer** *n* artiste *mf* (de music-hall *etc*); **a well-known radio ~er** un(e) artiste bien connu(e) à la radio. ♦ **entertaining 1** *adj* amusant, divertissant; **2** *n*: **she does a lot of ~ing** elle reçoit beaucoup. ♦ **entertainingly** *adv* d'une façon amusante. ♦ **entertainment 1** *n* **(a)** (*amusement*) *[audience]* amusement *m*; *[guests]* divertissement *m*; **for your ~ment we ...** pour vous distraire nous ...; **for my own ~ment** pour mon divertissement personnel; **(b)** (*performance*) spectacle *m*; **musical ~ment** soirée *f* musicale; **2** *adj*: **~ment allowance** frais *mpl* de représentation; **the ~ment world** le monde du spectacle.

enthral(l) [ɪn'θrɔ:l] *vt [book etc]* captiver, passionner; *[beauty]* ensorceler. ♦ **enthralling** *adj* passionnant; ensorcelant.

enthusiasm [ɪn'θu:zɪæzəm] *n* enthousiasme *m* (*for* pour). ♦ **enthuse** *vi*: **to ~ over** parler avec beaucoup d'enthousiasme de.

enthusiast [ɪn'θu:zɪæst] *n* enthousiaste *mf*. **jazz** *etc* **~** passionné(e) *m(f)* de jazz *etc*; **a Vivaldi ~** un(e) fervent(e) de Vivaldi. ♦ **enthusiastic** *adj* (*gen*) enthousiaste; *swimmer etc* passionné; **I'm not very ~ic about it** ça ne me dit pas grand-chose; **to make sb ~ic** enthousiasmer qn; **to grow ~ic over** s'enthousiasmer pour. ♦ **enthusiastically** *adv* avec enthousiasme.

entice [ɪn'taɪs] *vt* attirer (*towards* vers); entraîner (*away from somewhere* à l'écart d'un endroit); éloigner (*sb away from sb* qn de qn); (*with food, prospects*) allécher. **to ~ sb to do** entraîner qn à faire. ♦ **enticing** *adj* alléchant.

entire [ɪn'taɪəʳ] *adj* **(a)** (*whole*) entier, tout. **the ~ week** la semaine entière, toute la semaine. **(b)** (*complete*) entier, complet; (*unreserved*) entier (*before n*), total. **the ~ house** la maison (tout) entière; **my ~ confidence** mon entière confiance, ma confiance totale. ♦ **entirely** *adv* entièrement, tout à fait; *change* du tout au tout. ♦ **entirety** *n*: **in its ~ty** en (son) entier, intégralement.

entitle [ɪn'taɪtl] *vt* **(a)** *book* intituler. **(b) to ~ sb to sth** donner droit à qch à qn; **to ~ sb to do** donner à qn le droit de faire; **to be ~d to sth** avoir droit à qch; **to be ~d to do** (*by position, qualifications*) avoir qualité pour faire; (*by rules*) avoir le droit de faire; **he is quite ~d to believe that ...** (*gen*) il a le droit de penser que ...; (*has good reason*) il a tout lieu de croire que ... .

entity ['entɪtɪ] *n* entité *f*.

entomology [ˌentə'mɒlədʒɪ] *n* entomologie *f*. ♦ **entomological** *adj* entomologique. ♦ **entomologist** *n* entomologiste *mf*.

entrails ['entreɪlz] *npl* entrailles *fpl*.

entrance[1] [ɪn'trɑ:ns] *vt* transporter, ravir. ♦ **entranced** *adj* en extase. ♦ **entrancing** *adj* enchanteur. ♦ **entrancingly** *adv dance, sing* à ravir; *smile* d'une façon ravissante; **entrancingly beautiful** belle à ravir.

entrance[2] ['entrəns] **1** *n* (*act of entering; way in*) entrée *f* (*into* dans, *to* de); (*right to enter*) admission *f*. **to make an ~** faire son entrée; **'no ~'** 'défense d'entrer'; **to gain ~ to** (réussir à) entrer dans; (*to university etc*) être admis à *or* dans. **2** *adj card, ticket, examination* d'entrée. **~ fee** droit *m* d'inscription. ♦ **entrant** *n* (*to profession*) débutant(e) *m(f)* (*to* dans, en); (*in race, competition*) concurrent(e) *m(f)*; (*in exam*) candidat(e) *m(f)*.

entreat [ɪn'tri:t] *vt* supplier, implorer (*sb to do* qn de faire). **I ~ you** je vous en supplie. ♦ **entreaty** *n* prière *f*, supplication *f*; **at his earnest ~y** sur ses vives instances; **a look of ~y** un regard suppliant.

entrenched [ɪn'trentʃt] *adj*: **firmly ~** (*Mil*) solidement retranché; (*fig*) indélogeable.

entrust [ɪn'trʌst] *vt* confier (*sth to sb, sb with sth* qch à qn).

entry ['entrɪ] **1** *n* **(a)** = **entrance**[2] **1**. **(b)** (*item*) *[list]* inscription *f*; *[account book, ledger]* écriture *f*; *[dictionary, ship's log]* entrée *f*; *[encyclopedia]* article *m*. (*Book-keeping*) **single/double ~** comptabilité *f* en partie simple/double; **there are**

only 3 entries (*for race, competition*) il n'y a que 3 concurrents *mpl*; (*for exam*) il n'y a que 3 candidats *mpl*. 2 *adj*: ~ **form** feuille *f* d'inscription; ~ **permit** visa *m* d'entrée.
entwine [ɪn'twaɪn] *vt* (*twist together*) entrelacer; (*twist around*) enlacer (*with* de).
enumerate [ɪ'nju:məreɪt] *vt* énumérer. ♦ **enumeration** *n* énumération *f*.
enunciate [ɪ'nʌnsɪeɪt] *vt sound, word* articuler; *principle, theory* énoncer. ♦ **enunciation** *n* articulation *f*; énonciation *f*.
enuresis [ˌenjʊ'ri:sɪs] *n* énurésie *f*. ♦ **enuretic** *adj* énurétique.
envelop [ɪn'veləp] *vt* envelopper (*in a blanket* dans une couverture; *in clouds/mystery* de nuages/mystère).
envelope ['envələʊp] *n* enveloppe *f*. **to put a letter in an** ~ mettre une lettre sous enveloppe; **in a sealed** ~ sous pli cacheté; **in the same** ~ sous le même pli.
enviable ['envɪəbl] *adj* enviable.
envious ['envɪəs] *adj* envieux. **to be** ~ **of sth** être envieux de qch; **to be** ~ **of sb** envier qn. ♦ **enviously** *adv* avec envie.
environment [ɪn'vaɪərənmənt] *n* (*gen*) milieu *m*; (*Admin, Pol*) environnement *m*. (*fig*) **hostile** ~ climat *m* d'hostilité, ambiance *f* hostile; **his normal** ~ son cadre *or* son milieu normal; **Ministry of the E**~ ministère *m* de l'Environnement. ♦ **environmental** *adj conditions, changes* écologique, du milieu; *influence* exercé par le milieu *or* l'environnement; ~**al studies** l'écologie *f*. ♦ **environmentalist** *n* environnementaliste *mf*.
envisage [ɪn'vɪzɪdʒ] *vt* (*foresee*) prévoir; (*imagine*) envisager.
envoy ['envɔɪ] *n* (*gen*) envoyé(e) *m(f)*; (*diplomat*) ministre *m* plénipotentiaire.
envy ['envɪ] 1 *n* envie *f*. **it was the** ~ **of everyone** cela faisait l'envie de tout le monde. 2 *vt* envier (*sb sth* qch à qn).
enzyme ['enzaɪm] *n* enzyme *f*.
eons ['i:ənz] *npl* = **aeons**.
ephemeral [ɪ'femərəl] *adj* éphémère.
epic ['epɪk] 1 *adj* épique. 2 *n* épopée *f*. **an** ~ **of the screen** un film à grand spectacle.
epicentre ['epɪsentəʳ] *n* épicentre *m*.
epicure ['epɪkjʊəʳ] *n* gourmet *m*. ♦ **epicurean** *adj* épicurien.
epidemic [ˌepɪ'demɪk] 1 *n* épidémie *f*. 2 *adj* épidémique.
epiglottis [ˌepɪ'glɒtɪs] *n* épiglotte *f*.
epigram ['epɪgræm] *n* épigramme *f*.
epigraph ['epɪgrɑ:f] *n* épigraphe *f*.
epilepsy ['epɪlepsɪ] *n* épilepsie *f*. ♦ **epileptic 1** *adj* épileptique; **epileptic fit** crise *f* d'épilepsie; 2 *n* épileptique *mf*.
epilogue ['epɪlɒg] *n* épilogue *m*.
Epiphany [ɪ'pɪfənɪ] *n* Épiphanie *f*, fête *f* des Rois.
episcopal [ɪ'pɪskəpəl] *adj* épiscopal. ♦ **Episcopalian 1** *adj* épiscopal (*de l'Église épiscopale*). 2 *n* membre *m* de l'Église épiscopale.
episode ['epɪsəʊd] *n* épisode *m*.
epistemology [ɪˌpɪstə'mɒlədʒɪ] *n* épistémologie *f*.
epistle [ɪ'pɪsl] *n* épître *f*.
epitaph ['epɪtɑ:f] *n* épitaphe *f*.
epithet ['epɪθet] *n* épithète *f*.
epitome [ɪ'pɪtəmɪ] *n* modèle *m or* type *m* même. ♦ **epitomize** *vt* incarner, personnifier.
epoch ['i:pɒk] *n* époque *f*. ♦ **epoch-making** *adj* qui fait époque, qui fait date.
equable ['ekwəbl] *adj* égal, constant. **he is very** ~ il a un tempérament très égal. ♦ **equably** *adv* tranquillement.
equal ['i:kwəl] 1 *adj* égal (*to* à). ~ **in number** égal en nombre; **to be** ~ **to sth** égaler qch; ~ **pay for** ~ **work** à travail égal salaire égal; **other things being** ~ toutes choses égales d'ailleurs; **an** ~ **sum of money** une même somme d'argent; **with** ~ **indifference** avec la même indifférence; **to talk to sb on** ~ **terms** parler à qn d'égal à égal; **on an** ~ **footing** sur un pied d'égalité (*with* avec); **to be** ~ **to the task** être à la hauteur de la tâche; **she did not feel** ~ **to going out** elle ne se sentait pas capable de sortir; ~**(s) sign** signe *m* d'égalité. 2 *n* égal(e) *m(f)*. **to treat sb as an** ~ traiter qn d'égal à égal; **she has no** ~ elle n'a pas sa pareille. 3 *vt* égaler (*in* en). **there is nothing to** ~ **it** il n'y a rien de comparable. ♦ **equality** *n* égalité *f*. ♦ **equalize** *vti* égaliser. ♦ **equalizer** *n* (*Sport*) but *m or* point *m* égalisateur. ♦ **equally** *adv guilty, clever* également; *divide* en parts *or* parties égales; **it would be** ~**ly wrong to suggest** il serait tout aussi faux de suggérer.
equanimity [ˌekwə'nɪmɪtɪ] *n* sérénité *f*.
equate [ɪ'kweɪt] *vt* (*identify*) assimiler (*with* à); (*compare*) mettre sur le même pied (*with* que); (*make equal*) égaler. ♦ **equation** *n* (*Math*) équation *f*.
equator [ɪ'kweɪtəʳ] *n* équateur *m* (terrestre). **at the** ~ sous l'équateur. ♦ **equatorial** *adj* équatorial.
equestrian [ɪ'kwestrɪən] *adj* équestre.
equidistant ['i:kwɪ'dɪstənt] *adj* équidistant (*from* de).
equilibrium [ˌi:kwɪ'lɪbrɪəm] *n* équilibre *m*.
equine ['ekwaɪn] *adj* chevalin.
equinox ['i:kwɪnɒks] *n* équinoxe *m*.
equip [ɪ'kwɪp] *vt* équiper (*with* de). **to** ~ **a room as a laboratory** aménager une pièce en laboratoire; **to** ~ **a ship with radar** installer le radar sur un bateau; **to be well** ~**ped with** être bien monté *or* pourvu en; (*fig*) **he is well** ~**ped for the job** il a les qualités nécessaires pour ce travail. ♦ **equipment** *n* (*gen*) équipement *m*; (*for laboratory, office, lifesaving, camping etc*) matériel *m*; **electrical** ~**ment** appareillage *m* électrique.
equity ['ekwɪtɪ] *n* équité *f*. (*St Ex*) **equities** actions *fpl* (cotées en bourse). ♦ **equitable** *adj* équitable. ♦ **equitably** *adv* équitablement.
equivalent [ɪ'kwɪvələnt] *adj, n* équivalent (*m*) (*to* à; *in* en). ♦ **equivalence** *n* équivalence *f*.
equivocate [ɪ'kwɪvəkeɪt] *vi* user d'équivoques. ♦ **equivocal** *adj* équivoque. ♦ **equivocally** *adv* d'une manière équivoque. ♦ **equivocation** *n* paroles *fpl* équivoques.
era ['ɪərə] *n* (*Geol, Hist*) ère *f*; (*gen*) époque *f*.
eradicate [ɪ'rædɪkeɪt] *vt* (*gen*) supprimer; *superstition* mettre fin à; *weeds* détruire.
erase [ɪ'reɪz] *vt* (*gen*) effacer; (*with rubber*) gommer. ♦ **eraser** *n* (*rubber*) gomme *f*; (*liquid: for typing*) liquide *m* correcteur. ♦ **erasure** *n* rature *f*.
erect [ɪ'rekt] 1 *adj* (*straight*) bien droit; (*standing*) debout. **with head** ~ la tête haute. 2 *vt temple, statue* ériger; *wall, flats, factory* construire; *machinery, traffic signs* installer; *scaffolding, furniture* monter; *altar, tent, mast, barricade* dresser; *theory, obstacles* édifier. ♦ **erection** *n* érection *f* (*also Physiol*); construction *f*; installation *f*; montage *m*; dressage *m*; édification *f*.
erode [ɪ'rəʊd] *vt* (*gen*) éroder; *[acid]* corroder; (*fig*) ronger. ♦ **erosion** *n* érosion *f*; corrosion *f*. ♦ **erosive** *adj* érosif; corrosif.
erotic [ɪ'rɒtɪk] *adj* érotique. ♦ **eroticism** *n* érotisme *m*.
err [ɜ:ʳ] *vi* (*be mistaken*) se tromper; (*sin*) pécher. **to** ~ **on the side of caution** pécher par excès de prudence. ♦ **erratum** *n, pl* **-ata** erratum *m*. ♦ **erroneous** *adj* erroné. ♦ **erroneously** *adv* erronément. ♦ **error** *n* erreur *f* (*of, in* de); **it would be an** ~**or to ...** on aurait tort de ...; **compass** ~**or** variation *f* du compas; **typing/spelling** ~**or** faute *f* de frappe/d'orthographe; ~**ors and omissions excepted** sauf erreur ou omission; **in** ~**or**

par erreur; **to see the ~or of one's ways** revenir de ses erreurs.

errand ['erənd] *n* commission *f*, course *f*. **to go on** *or* **run ~s** faire des commissions *or* des courses; **~ of mercy** mission *f* de charité; **~ boy** garçon *m* de courses.

erratic [ɪ'rætɪk] *adj person* capricieux; *record, results, performance* irrégulier; *mood* changeant; (*Geol, Med*) erratique. **his driving is ~** il conduit de façon déconcertante. ♦ **erratically** *adv* capricieusement; irrégulièrement; de façon déconcertante.

ersatz ['ɛəzæts] **1** *n* ersatz *m*. **2** *adj*: **~ coffee** de l'ersatz de café.

erudite ['erʊdaɪt] *adj person, work* érudit, savant; *word* savant. ♦ **erudition** *n* érudition *f*.

erupt [ɪ'rʌpt] *vi [volcano]* entrer en éruption; *[spots]* sortir; *[anger]* exploser; *[war, fighting, quarrel]* éclater. **he ~ed into the room** il a fait irruption dans la pièce.
♦ **erupting** *adj volcano* en éruption. ♦ **eruption** *n [volcano, spots]* éruption *f*; *[anger, violence]* explosion *f*, accès *m*.

escalate ['eskəleɪt] **1** *vi [fighting, bombing, violence]* s'intensifier; *[costs]* monter en flèche. **the war is escalating** c'est l'escalade militaire; **prices are escalating** c'est l'escalade des prix. **2** *vt* intensifier; faire monter en flèche ♦ **escalation** *n* intensification *f*; montée *f* en flèche, escalade *f*.
♦ **escalator** *n* escalier *m* roulant, escalator *m*.

escape [ɪs'keɪp] **1** *vi* (*gen*) échapper (*from sb* à qn), s'échapper (*from somewhere* de quelque part), s'enfuir (*to another place* dans un autre endroit); *[prisoner]* s'évader (*from* de); *[water, gas]* s'échapper, (*accidentally*) fuir. **an ~d prisoner** un évadé; (*fig*) **he ~d with a few scratches** il s'en est tiré avec quelques égratignures; **to ~ with a fright** en être quitte pour la peur; **to ~ from o.s.** se fuir.
2 *vt pursuit, danger, death* échapper à; *consequences* éviter; *punishment* se soustraire à. **he narrowly ~d being run over** il a failli être écrasé; **nothing ~s him** rien ne lui échappe; **to ~ notice** passer inaperçu; **it had not ~d her notice that ...** elle n'avait pas été sans s'apercevoir que ... .
3 *n [person, animal]* fuite *f*; *[prisoner]* évasion *f*; *[water, gas]* fuite; *[steam, gas in machine]* échappement *m*. **to plan an ~** combiner un plan d'évasion; **to have a lucky ~** l'échapper belle.
4 *adj valve, pipe* d'échappement; *plan, route* d'évasion; *device* de secours. **~ clause** échappatoire *f*; **~ hatch** sas *m* de secours; (*Space*) **~ velocity** vitesse *f* de libération.
♦ **escapade** *n* (*misdeed*) fredaine *f*; (*adventure*) équipée *f*. ♦ **escapee** *n* évadé(e) *m(f)*. ♦ **escapism** *n* désir *m* d'évasion (de la réalité); **it's sheer escapism!** c'est simplement s'évader du réel! ♦ **escapist** **1** *n* personne *f* qui se complaît dans l'évasion; **2** *adj* d'évasion. ♦ **escapologist** *n* virtuose *m* de l'évasion.

escarpment [ɪs'kɑːpmənt] *n* escarpement *m*.

escort ['eskɔːt] **1** *n* (*Mil, Naut etc*) escorte *f*; (*male companion*) cavalier *m*. **2** *adj duty, vessel* d'escorte. **~ agency** bureau *m* d'hôtesses (et de cavaliers). **3** [ɪs'kɔːt] *vt* (*Mil, Naut, gen*) escorter. **to ~ sb in** (*Mil, Police*) faire entrer qn sous escorte; (*gen: accompany*) faire entrer qn.

Eskimo ['eskɪməʊ] **1** *n* Esquimau(de) *m(f)*; (*Ling*) esquimau *m*. **2** *adj* esquimau.

esoteric [ˌesəʊ'terɪk] *adj* ésotérique.

especial [ɪs'peʃəl] *adj* particulier, spécial. ♦ **especially** *adv* (*particularly*) particulièrement; (*expressly*) exprès; **more ~ly as** d'autant plus que; **~ly as it's so late** d'autant plus qu'il est si tard; **why me ~ly?** pourquoi moi en particulier?; **I came ~ly to see you** je suis venu exprès pour vous voir.

Esperanto [ˌespə'ræntəʊ] **1** *n* espéranto *m*. **2** *adj* en espéranto. ♦ **Esperantist** *n* espérantiste *mf*.

espionage [ˌespɪə'nɑːʒ] *n* espionnage *m*.

espouse [ɪs'paʊz] *vt* épouser (*fig*).

espresso [es'presəʊ] *n* (café *m*) express *m*. **~ bar** ≃ cafétéria *f*.

esquire [ɪs'kwaɪəʳ] *n*: **B. Smith E~** Monsieur B. Smith.

essay ['eseɪ] *n* (*Literat*) essai *m* (*on* sur); (*Scol*) rédaction *f* (*on* sur); (*Univ*) dissertation *f* (*on* sur). ♦ **essayist** *n* essayiste *mf*.

essence ['esəns] *n* essence *f*; (*Culin*) extrait *m*. **in ~** essentiellement; **the ~ of what was said** l'essentiel *m* de ce qui a été dit; **speed is of the ~** la vitesse est essentielle; **the ~ of stupidity*** le comble de la stupidité; **~ of violets** essence de violette; **meat ~** extrait de viande. ♦ **essential** **1** *adj* essentiel (*to* à); **it is essential that ...** il est indispensable *or* essentiel que ... + *subj*; **2** *n* qualité *f* (*or* objet *m etc*) indispensable; **the essentials** (*necessities*) l'essentiel *m*; (*rudiments*) les éléments *mpl*. ♦ **essentially** *adv* essentiellement.

establish [ɪs'tæblɪʃ] *vt* **(a)** (*set up*) *government, society, tribunal* constituer; *state, business, post* créer; *factory* monter; *laws, custom, sb's reputation, list, relations* établir; *power, authority* affermir; *peace, order* faire régner. **to ~ one's reputation as** se faire une réputation de. **(b)** (*prove*) *fact, identity, rights, innocence* établir; *necessity, guilt* prouver. ♦ **established** *adj* (*gen*) établi; *fact* acquis; *government* au pouvoir; **well-~ed business** maison *f* solide; **the ~ed Church** la religion d'État. ♦ **establishment** *n* (*institution etc*) établissement *m*; (*Admin, Mil, Naut etc: personnel*) effectifs *mpl*; **teaching ~ment** établissement d'enseignement; **the E~ment** les pouvoirs *mpl* établis, l'establishment *m*; **the values of the E~ment** les valeurs traditionnelles; **against the E~ment** anticonformiste; **he has joined the E~ment** il s'est rangé; **the literary E~ment** ceux qui font la loi dans le monde littéraire.

estate [ɪs'teɪt] **1** *n* **(a)** (*land*) propriété *f*, domaine *m*. **country ~** terres *fpl*; **housing ~** lotissement *m*, cité *f*. **(b)** (*Jur: on death*) succession *f*. **he left a large ~** il a laissé une grosse fortune. **2** *adj*: **~ agency** agence *f* immobilière; **~ agent** agent *m* immobilier; **~ car** break *m*; **~ duty** droits *mpl* de succession.

esteem [ɪs'tiːm] **1** *vt* (*think highly of*) *person* estimer; *quality* apprécier; (*consider*) estimer, considérer. **I ~ it an honour to do** je considère comme un honneur de faire.
2 *n* estime *f*. **he went up in my ~** il a monté dans mon estime.
♦ **estimable** ['estɪməbl] *adj* estimable.

esthete ['iːsθiːt] *etc* = **aesthete** *etc*.

estimate ['estɪmɪt] **1** *n* évaluation *f*; (*Comm: for work to be done*) devis *m*. **give me an ~ of what your trip will cost** donnez-moi un état estimatif du coût de votre voyage; **this price is only a rough ~** ce prix n'est que très approximatif; **at a rough ~** approximativement; **at the lowest ~** au bas mot; (*Admin, Pol*) **the ~s** le budget. **2** ['estɪmeɪt] *vt* (*all senses*) estimer (*that* que). ♦ **estimation** *n* **(a)** jugement *m*, opinion *f*; **in my estimation** à mon avis, selon moi; **(b)** (*esteem*) estime *f*; **he went up in my estimation** il a monté dans mon estime.

estranged [ɪs'treɪndʒd] *adj*: **to become ~** se brouiller (*from* avec); **the ~ couple** les époux désunis. ♦ **estrangement** *n* brouille *f* (*from* avec).

estrogen ['iːstrəʊdʒən] *n* (*US*) = **oestrogen**.

estuary ['estjʊərɪ] *n* estuaire *m*.

etch [etʃ] *vti* graver à l'eau forte. ♦ **etching** *n* gravure *f* à l'eau forte.

eternal [ɪ'tɜːnl] *adj* (*gen*) éternel; (*pej*) *complaints etc* continuel, perpétuel. (*fig*) **the ~ triangle** ≃ le ménage à trois. ♦ **eternally** *adv* éternellement; continuellement. ♦ **eternity** *n* éternité *f* (*also fig*).

ether ['i:θəʳ] *n* éther *m*. ♦ **ethereal** [ɪ'θɪərɪəl] *adj* éthéré.

ethic ['eθɪk] *n* morale *f*, éthique *f*. **the work ~** l'attitude *f* moraliste envers le travail. ♦ **ethical** *adj* moral, éthique; **not ~al** contraire à la morale. ♦ **ethics** *n* (*sg: study*) éthique *f*; (*pl: system, principles*) morale *f*.

ethnic ['eθnɪk] *adj* ethnique.

ethnology [eθ'nɒlədʒɪ] *n* ethnologie *f*. ♦ **ethnologist** *n* ethnologue *mf*.

ethos ['i:θɒs] *n* génie *m* (*d'un peuple, d'une culture*).

etiquette ['etɪket] *n* étiquette *f*, convenances *fpl*. **diplomatic ~** protocole *m*; **court ~** cérémonial *m* de cour; **that isn't ~** c'est contraire aux convenances, cela ne se fait pas.

etymology [ˌetɪ'mɒlədʒɪ] *n* étymologie *f*. ♦ **etymological** *adj* étymologique. ♦ **etymologically** *adv* étymologiquement.

eucalyptus [ˌju:kə'lɪptəs] *n* eucalyptus *m*.

Eucharist ['ju:kərɪst] *n* Eucharistie *f*.

eugenics [ju:'dʒenɪks] *nsg* eugénique *f*.

eulogy ['ju:lədʒɪ] *n* panégyrique *m*. ♦ **eulogize** *vt* faire le panégyrique de.

eunuch ['ju:nək] *n* eunuque *m*.

euphemism ['ju:fəmɪzəm] *n* euphémisme *m*. ♦ **euphemistic** *adj* euphémique. ♦ **euphemistically** *adv* par euphémisme.

euphonic [ju:'fɒnɪk] *adj* euphonique.

euphonium [ju:'fəʊnɪəm] *n* saxhorn *m*.

euphoria [ju:'fɔ:rɪə] *n* euphorie *f*. ♦ **euphoric** *adj* euphorique.

Eurasia [jʊə'reɪʃə] *n* Eurasie *f*. ♦ **Eurasian 1** *adj population* eurasien; *continent* eurasiatique; **2** *n* Eurasien(ne) *m(f)*.

euro... ['jʊərəʊ] *pref* euro... . ♦ **eurocrat** *n* eurocrate *mf*. ♦ **eurodollar** *n* eurodollar *m*. ♦ **euromarket** *or* ♦ **euromart** *n* Communauté *f* Économique Européenne. ♦ **eurosize 1** *n* (*Comm*) modèle *m* E1. ♦ **Eurovision** *n* (*TV*) Eurovision *f*.

Europe ['jʊərəp] *n* Europe *f*. (*Pol*) **to go into ~, to join ~** entrer dans le Marché commun. ♦ **European 1** *adj* européen; **the ~an Economic Community** (*abbr* **EEC**) la Communauté Économique Européenne (*abbr* CEE *f*); (*US: in hotel*) **~an plan** chambre *f* sans petit déjeuner; **2** *n* Européen(ne) *m(f)*.

euthanasia [ˌju:θə'neɪzɪə] *n* euthanasie *f*.

evacuate [ɪ'vækjʊeɪt] *vt* (*all senses*) évacuer. ♦ **evacuation** *n* évacuation *f*. ♦ **evacuee** *n* évacué(e) *m(f)*.

evade [ɪ'veɪd] *vt blow, obligation, difficulty* éviter, esquiver; *pursuers, punishment* échapper à; *sb's gaze* éviter; *question* éluder; *law* tourner. **to ~ military service** se dérober à ses obligations militaires; **to ~ taxation/customs duty** frauder le fisc/la douane.

evaluate [ɪ'væljʊeɪt] *vt* évaluer (*at* à). ♦ **evaluation** *n* évaluation *f*.

evangelical [ˌi:væn'dʒelɪkəl] *adj, n* évangélique (*mf*). ♦ **evangelist** *n* évangéliste *m*. ♦ **evangelize 1** *vt* prêcher l'Évangile à; **2** *vi* prêcher l'Évangile.

evaporate [ɪ'væpəreɪt] **1** *vt* faire évaporer. **~d milk** lait concentré. **2** *vi* s'évaporer; *[hopes, fear]* s'évanouir. ♦ **evaporation** *n* évaporation *f*.

evasion [ɪ'veɪʒən] *n [prisoner]* fuite *f*; (*excuse*) faux-fuyant *m*. ♦ **evasive** *adj* évasif; **to take evasive action** (*Mil*) se replier; (*gen*) prendre la tangente. ♦ **evasively** *adv* évasivement.

eve [i:v] *n* veille *f*.

even ['i:vən] **1** *adj* **(a)** (*smooth*) *surface* uni, plat. **to make ~** égaliser, aplanir. **(b)** (*regular*) *progress* régulier; *breathing, temper* égal. **(c)** (*equal*) *quantities, values* égal. **they are an ~ match** (*Sport*) la partie est égale; (*fig*) ils sont bien assortis; **to get ~ with sb** se venger de qn; **I will get ~ with you for that** je vous revaudrai ça; **I'll give you ~ money that ...** il y a une chance sur deux que ... + *subj*. **(d)** *number, date* pair.

2 *adv* **(a)** même. **~ in the holidays** même pendant les vacances; **I have ~ forgotten his name** j'ai oublié jusqu'à son nom, j'ai même oublié son nom; **~ if** même si + *indic*; **~ though** quand (bien) même + *cond*, alors même que + *cond*; **if he ~ made an effort** si encore *or* si au moins il faisait un effort; **~ so** quand même, pourtant. **(b)** (+ *comp adj or adv*) encore. **~ better** encore mieux. **(c)** (+ *neg*) même, seulement. **without ~ saying goodbye** sans même *or* sans seulement dire au revoir; **he can't ~ swim** il ne sait même pas nager.

even out 1 *vi* s'égaliser. **2** *vt sep* égaliser.

even up *vt sep* égaliser. **that will ~ things up** cela rétablira l'équilibre; (*financially*) cela compensera.

♦ **evenly** *adv spread, paint etc* de façon égale; *breathe, space* régulièrement; *divide* également. ♦ **even-tempered** *adj* d'humeur égale.

evening ['i:vnɪŋ] **1** *n* soir *m*; (*length of time*) soirée *f*. **in the ~** le soir; **let's have an ~ out** nous devrions sortir (un soir); **6 o'clock in the ~** 6 heures du soir; **on the ~ of the 29th** le 29 au soir; **the warm summer ~s** les chaudes soirées d'été; **all ~** toute la soirée; **to spend one's ~ reading** passer sa soirée à lire. **2** *adj paper, prayers, service* du soir. **~ class** cours *m* du soir; **in ~ dress** *man* en tenue de soirée; *woman* en robe du soir; **~ performance** (représentation *f* en) soirée *f*; **~ star** étoile *f* du berger.

evensong ['i:vənsɒŋ] *n* ≃ vêpres *fpl*.

event [ɪ'vent] *n* **(a)** événement *m*. **course of ~s** suite *f* des événements; **in the course of ~s** par la suite; **in the normal course of ~s** normalement; **after the ~** après coup; **in the ~ of death** en cas de décès; **in the unlikely ~ that ...** s'il arrivait par hasard que ... + *subj*; **in the ~** en fait; **in that ~** dans ce cas; **in any ~, at all ~s** en tout cas, de toute façon; **in either ~** dans l'un ou l'autre cas. **(b)** (*Sport*) épreuve *f*; (*Racing*) course *f*. **field ~s** épreuves d'athlétisme (*à l'exception des épreuves de vitesse*); **track ~s** épreuves de vitesse. ♦ **eventful** *adj* (*busy etc*) mouvementé; (*momentous*) mémorable.

eventual [ɪ'ventʃʊəl] *adj* (*resulting*) qui s'ensuit; (*probably resulting*) éventuel. **it resulted in the ~ disappearance of ...** cela a abouti finalement à la disparition de ... . ♦ **eventuality** *n* éventualité *f*. ♦ **eventually** *adv* finalement, en fin de compte; à la longue; **he ~ly did it** il a fini par le faire.

ever ['evəʳ] *adv* **(a)** jamais. **nothing ~ happens** il ne se passe jamais rien; **if you ~ see her** si jamais vous la voyez; **do you ~ see her?** est-ce qu'il vous arrive de la voir?; **have you ~ seen her?** l'avez-vous jamais *or* déjà vue?; **I haven't ~ seen her** je ne l'ai jamais vue; **seldom if ~** pour ainsi dire jamais; **now if ~ is the moment to ...** c'est le moment ou jamais de ...; **he's a liar if ~ there was one** c'est un menteur ou je ne m'y connais pas; **more beautiful than ~** plus beau que jamais; **the coldest night ~** la nuit la plus froide qu'on ait jamais connue.

(b) (*at all times*) toujours, sans cesse. **~ ready** toujours prêt; **~ increasing anxiety** inquiétude qui va croissant; **they lived happily ~ after** ils vécurent (toujours) heureux; **~ since I was a boy** depuis mon enfance; **for ~** à jamais, pour toujours; **they are for ~ quarrelling** ils ne font que se disputer, ils se disputent sans cesse *or* continuellement; (*in letters*) **yours ~** bien amicalement à vous.

(c) (*intensive*) **as quickly as ~ you can** aussi vite que vous le pourrez; **the first ~** le tout premier; **~ so slightly drunk** tant soit peu ivre; **~ so pretty** vraiment joli; **thank you ~ so much** merci mille fois; **as if I ~ would!** comme si je ferais ça,

moi!; **what ~ shall we do?** qu'est-ce que nous allons bien faire?; **why ~ not?** mais enfin, pourquoi pas?; **did you ~!*** ça par exemple!
♦ **evergreen** *adj, n* (arbre *m or* plante *f*) à feuilles persistantes. ♦ **everlasting** *adj* éternel. ♦ **everlastingly** *adv* éternellement. ♦ **evermore** *adv*: **for ~more** à tout jamais.

every ['evrɪ] *adj* chaque, tout; tous les. **~ shop in the town** tous les magasins de la ville; **not ~ child has the same advantages** les enfants n'ont pas tous les mêmes avantages; **not ~ child has the advantages you have** tous les enfants n'ont pas les avantages que tu as; **I have ~ confidence in him** j'ai entièrement confiance en lui; **we wish you ~ success** nous vous souhaitons très bonne chance; **~ (single) one of them** chacun d'eux; **~ one had brought sth** chacun d'entre eux avait *or* ils avaient tous apporté qch; **from ~ country** de tous (les) pays; **of ~ sort** de toute sorte; **of ~ age** de tout âge; **~ fifth day, ~ five days** tous les cinq jours; **~ second** *or* **other child** un enfant sur deux; **~ quarter of an hour** tous les quarts d'heure; **~ other Wednesday** un mercredi sur deux; **~ few days** tous les deux ou trois jours; **his ~ action** chacune de ses actions; **his ~ wish** son moindre désir; **~ bit of the wall** le mur tout entier; **~ bit as clever as** tout aussi doué que; **~ now and then, ~ now and again, ~ so often** de temps en temps, de temps à autre; **~ time that** chaque fois que; **~ single time** chaque fois sans exception; **~ one of us is afraid of sth** nous craignons tous qch, tous tant que nous sommes nous craignons qch; **~ man for himself** chacun pour soi; (*excl*) sauve qui peut!
♦ **everybody** *pron* tout le monde, chacun; **~body has finished** tout le monde a fini; **~body has his** *or* **their* own ideas about it** chacun a ses (propres) idées là-dessus; **~body else** tous les autres. ♦ **everyday** *adj coat* de tous les jours; *occurrence* banal; *use, experience* ordinaire; **words in ~day use** mots d'usage courant; **it was not an ~day event** c'était un événement hors du commun. ♦ **everyone** *pron* = **everybody.** ♦ **everyplace** *adv* (*US*) = **everywhere.** ♦ **everything** *n* tout; **~thing is ready** tout est prêt; **~thing you have** tout ce que vous avez; **stamina is ~thing** l'essentiel c'est d'avoir de la résistance. ♦ **everywhere** *adv* (*gen*) partout; **~where you go you meet** ... où qu'on aille on rencontre ... .

evict [ɪ'vɪkt] *vt* expulser (*from* de). ♦ **eviction** *n* expulsion *f*; **eviction notice** avis *m* d'expulsion.

evidence ['evɪdəns] *n* (*data*) preuves *fpl*; (*testimony*) témoignage *m* (*of sb* de qn). **the ~ of the senses** le témoignage des sens; **to give ~** témoigner (*for/against sb* en faveur de/contre qn); **to turn King's** *or* **Queen's ~** *or* (*US*) **state's ~** témoigner contre ses complices; **to show ~ of** témoigner de; **to be in ~** être en évidence; **he was nowhere in ~** il n'y avait pas trace de lui.
♦ **evident** *adj* évident, manifeste; **it was evident from the way he walked** cela se voyait à sa démarche; **it is evident from his speech that** ... il ressort de son discours que ... . ♦ **evidently** *adv* (*obviously*) évidemment, manifestement; (*apparently*) à ce qu'il paraît; **he was evidently frightened** il était évident qu'il avait peur; **they are evidently going to change the rule** il paraît qu'ils vont changer le règlement.

evil ['i:vl] **1** *adj deed, person, example, reputation* mauvais; *influence* néfaste; *doctrine, spell, spirit* malfaisant; *hour, course of action, consequence* funeste. **the ~ eye** le mauvais œil. **2** *n* mal *m*. **the lesser ~** le moindre mal; **the ~s of drink** les conséquences *fpl* funestes de la boisson; **one of the great ~s of our time** un des grands fléaux de notre temps. ♦ **evildoer** *n* scélérat(e) *m(f)*. ♦ **evilly** *adv* avec malveillance. ♦ **evil-minded** *adj* malveillant.

evince [ɪ'vɪns] *vt* manifester.

evoke [ɪ'vəʊk] *vt memories* évoquer; *admiration* susciter. ♦ **evocation** *n* évocation *f*. ♦ **evocative** *adj* évocateur.

evolve [ɪ'vɒlv] **1** *vt system, theory, plan* élaborer. **2** *vi [system, plan]* se développer; *[idea, science]* évoluer; *[species]* se développer (*from* à partir de), évoluer. ♦ **evolution** *n* évolution *f* (*from* à partir de).

ewe [ju:] *n* brebis *f*.

ex- [eks] *pref* **(a)** (*former*) ex-. **~president** ancien président, ex-président; **~husband** ex-mari *m*; **~serviceman** ancien combattant. **(b)** (*out of*) ex-. (*Telec*) **his number is ~directory, he has an ~directory number** son numéro ne figure pas à l'annuaire; (*Comm, Ind*) **price ~ works** prix *m* départ usine; **~ officio** (*adj, adv*) ex officio.

exacerbate [eks'æsəbeɪt] *vt pain etc* exacerber; *situation* aggraver; *person* exaspérer.

exact [ɪg'zækt] **1** *adj* (*accurate*) *description, time, measurements, forecast* exact, juste; *copy* exact; (*precise*) *number, value* exact, précis; *meaning, time, place, instructions* précis; *instrument* de précision. **these were his ~ words** voilà textuellement ce qu'il a dit; **he's 44 to be ~** il a très exactement 44 ans; **to be ~ it was 4 o'clock** il était 4 heures, plus exactement; **can you be more ~?** pouvez-vous préciser un peu? **2** *vt* exiger (*from* de). ♦ **exacting** *adj person* exigeant; *profession, task, activity, work* astreignant. ♦ **exactitude** *n* exactitude *f*. ♦ **exactly** *adv answer, work, describe* avec précision; *obey, resemble, know* exactement; **~ly the same thing** exactement *or* précisément la même chose; **that's ~ly what I thought** c'est exactement *or* précisément ce que je pensais; **it is 3 o'clock ~ly** il est 3 heures juste(s). ♦ **exactness** *n* exactitude *f*; justesse *f*; précision *f*.

exaggerate [ɪg'zædʒəreɪt] *vt* (*overstate*) exagérer; (*in one's own mind*) s'exagérer; (*emphasize*) accentuer. **the dress ~d her paleness** la robe accentuait sa pâleur; **he ~s the importance of the task** il s'exagère l'importance de la tâche. ♦ **exaggerated** *adj* exagéré; **to have an ~d opinion of o.s.** avoir trop bonne opinion de soi-même. ♦ **exaggeration** *n* exagération *f*.

exalted [ɪg'zɔ:ltɪd] *adj* (*high*) *position* élevé; *person* haut placé; (*elated*) exalté.

examine [ɪg'zæmɪn] *vt* **(a)** (*gen, Med*) examiner; *machine* inspecter; *passport* contrôler; (*Customs*) *luggage* fouiller. **(b)** *pupil, candidate* examiner (*in* en); (*orally*) interroger (*on* sur); *witness, suspect, accused* interroger.
♦ **examination** *n* (*gen*) examen *m*; *[machine, premises]* inspection *f*; *[passports]* contrôle *m*; (*Customs*) fouille *f*; (*Scol etc: abbr* **exam**) examen; (*one paper*) épreuve *f*; **on examination** après examen. ♦ **examiner** *n* examinateur *m*, -trice *f* (*in* de).

example [ɪg'zɑ:mpl] *n* exemple *m*. **for ~** par exemple; **to set a good ~** donner l'exemple; **to take sb as an ~** prendre exemple sur qn; **to make an ~ of sb** faire un exemple en punissant qn; **to punish sb as an ~ to others** punir qn pour l'exemple; **to quote sth as an ~** citer qch en exemple.

exasperate [ɪg'zɑ:spəreɪt] *vt* exaspérer.
♦ **exasperated** *adj* exaspéré (*at sth* de qch; *with sb* par qn); **to become ~d** s'exaspérer.
♦ **exasperating** *adj* exaspérant. ♦ **exasperatingly** *adv* d'une manière exaspérante; **exasperatingly slow** d'une lenteur exaspérante.
♦ **exasperation** *n* exaspération *f*.

excavate ['ekskəveɪt] **1** *vt ground* creuser; (*Archeol*) fouiller; *remains* déterrer. **2** *vi* (*Archeol*) faire des fouilles. ♦ **excavation** *n* (*gen*) creusement *m*; (*Archeol*) fouilles *fpl*.
♦ **excavator** *n* (*machine*) excavatrice *f*.

exceed [ɪk'si:d] *vt* (*gen*) dépasser (*in* en, *by* de);

powers, instructions outrepasser. **to ~ the speed limit** dépasser la vitesse permise. ♦ **exceedingly** *adv* extrêmement, infiniment.

excel [ɪk'sel] **1** *vi* briller (*at, in* en), exceller (*at or in doing* à faire). **2** *vt* surpasser. **to ~ o.s.** se surpasser. ♦ **excellence** *n* excellence *f*. ♦ **Excellency** *n*: **His E~lency** Son Excellence *f*. ♦ **excellent** *adj* excellent, parfait. ♦ **excellently** *adv* admirablement, parfaitement.

except [ɪk'sept] **1** *prep* sauf, excepté. **~ for** à part, à l'exception de; **~ that/if/when** *etc* sauf que/si/quand *etc*; **what can they do ~ wait?** que peuvent-ils faire sinon attendre?

2 *vt* excepter (*from* de), faire exception de. **present company ~ed** exception faite des personnes présentes; **always ~ing ...** à l'exception bien entendu de ... .

♦ **excepting** *prep* = **except 1.** ♦ **exception** *n* exception *f* (*to* à); **without ~ion** sans exception; **with the ~ion of** à l'exception de, exception faite de; **to take ~ion to** (*demur*) désapprouver; (*be offended*) s'offenser de; **to make an ~ion** faire une exception (*to sth* à qch, *for sb/sth* pour qn/qch); **the ~ion proves the rule** l'exception confirme la règle; **with this ~ion** à cette exception près, à ceci près. ♦ **exceptional** *adj* exceptionnel. ♦ **exceptionally** *adv* exceptionnellement.

excerpt ['eksɜːpt] *n* extrait *m*.

excess [ɪk'ses] **1** *n* excès *m*. **to ~** à l'excès; **to carry to ~** pousser à l'excès; **in ~ of** dépassant; **the ~ of imports over exports** l'excédent *m* des importations sur les exportations. **2** *adj profit, weight, production* excédentaire. **~ fare** supplément *m*; **~ luggage** excédent *m* de bagages. ♦ **excessive** *adj* excessif; **~ive drinking** abus *m* de la boisson. ♦ **excessively** *adv* (*to excess*) *eat, drink, spend* avec excès; *optimistic* par trop; *proud* démesurément; (*extremely*) extrêmement, infiniment.

exchange [ɪks'tʃeɪndʒ] **1** *vt* (*gen*) échanger (*for* contre); *houses, cars, jobs* faire un échange de. **2** *n* **(a)** échange *m*. **in ~** en échange (*for* de); **to lose on the ~** perdre au change. **(b)** (*Fin*) change *m*. **(c)** (*telephone ~*) central *m*. **labour ~** bourse *f* du travail. **3** *adj*: **~ control** contrôle *m* des changes; **~ rate** taux *m* de change. ♦ **exchangeable** *adj* échangeable (*for* contre).

exchequer [ɪks'tʃekəʳ] *n* (*Brit Parl*) Échiquier *m*; (*treasury*) trésorerie *f*; (*funds*) fonds *mpl*.

excise ['eksaɪz] *n* taxe *f* (*on* sur). **the E~** la Régie; **~ duties** = contributions *fpl* indirectes.

excite [ɪk'saɪt] *vt person* (*gen*) exciter, (*rouse enthusiasm in*) passionner; *emotion* provoquer (*in sb* chez qn). **to ~ enthusiasm/interest in sb** enthousiasmer/intéresser qn. ♦ **excitable** *adj person* excitable, nerveux; *temperament* nerveux. ♦ **excited** *adj* (*gen*) excité; *laughter* énervé; *voice* animé; **to get ~d** s'exciter (*about* au sujet de); **don't get ~d!** ne t'énerve pas! ♦ **excitedly** *adv behave, speak* avec agitation; *laugh* d'excitation. ♦ **excitement** *n* excitation *f*; (*exhilaration*) exaltation *f*; **the ~ment of the departure/elections** la fièvre du départ/des élections; **the book caused great ~ment** le livre a fait sensation; **he likes ~ment** il aime les émotions *fpl* fortes *or* l'aventure *f*. ♦ **exciting** *adj events, story, film* passionnant; *account* saisissant; *holiday, experience* excitant.

exclaim [ɪks'kleɪm] **1** *vi* s'exclamer. **to ~ at sth** se récrier devant qch. **2** *vt* s'écrier. ♦ **exclamation 1** *n* exclamation *f*; **2** *adj*: **exclamation mark** *or* **point** point *m* d'exclamation.

exclude [ɪks'kluːd] *vt* (*gen*) exclure (*from* de); (*from list*) écarter (*from* de). **he was ~d from taking part** il n'a pas eu le droit de participer. ♦ **exclusion** *n* exclusion *f* (*of, from* de).

exclusive [ɪks'kluːsɪv] *adj* **(a)** (*excluding others*) *group, gathering* sélect; *club, society* fermé; *person, friendship, interest, occupation* exclusif. **(b)** (*owned by one person, one firm*) *information, design, report* exclusif. **the ~ rights for** l'exclusivité *f* de; **an interview ~ to ...** une interview accordée exclusivement à ... . **(c)** (*not including*) **from 15th to 20th ~** du 15 au 20 exclusivement; **~ of** non compris; **the price is ~ of transport charges** le prix ne comprend pas les frais de transport. ♦ **exclusively** *adv* exclusivement.

excommunicate [ˌekskə'mjuːnɪkeɪt] *vt* excommunier. ♦ **excommunication** *n* excommunication *f*.

excrement ['ekskrɪmənt] *n* excrément *m*.

excrescence [ɪks'kresns] *n* excroissance *f*.

excrete [ɪks'kriːt] *vt* excréter. ♦ **excreta** *npl* excrétions *fpl*.

excruciating [ɪks'kruːʃɪeɪtɪŋ] *adj pain* atroce; *suffering* déchirant; *noise* insupportable; (*: *unpleasant*) épouvantable, atroce. ♦ **excruciatingly** *adv* atrocement, affreusement; **~ly funny*** désopilant.

exculpate ['ekskʌlpeɪt] *vt person* disculper (*from* de).

excursion [ɪks'kɜːʃən] **1** *n* excursion *f*; (*in car, on cycle*) randonnée *f*; (*fig: digression*) digression *f*. **2** *adj*: **~ ticket** billet *m* d'excursion; **~ train** train spécial (*pour excursions*).

excuse [ɪks'kjuːz] **1** *vt* **(a)** (*justify, pardon*) excuser (*sb for having done* qn d'avoir fait). **to ~ o.s.** s'excuser (*for* de, *for doing* de faire), présenter ses excuses; **if you will ~ the expression** passez-moi l'expression; **and now if you will ~ me, ...** maintenant, si vous permettez, ...; **~ me!** excusez-moi! **(b)** (*exempt*) exempter (*sb from sth* qn de qch), dispenser (*sb from sth* qn de qch, *sb from doing* qn de faire), excuser. (*to children*) **you are ~d** vous pouvez vous en aller; **to ask to be ~d** se faire excuser.

2 [ɪks'kjuːs] *n* **(a)** (*reason, justification*) excuse *f*. **that is no ~ for his leaving so abruptly** cela ne l'excuse pas d'être parti si brusquement. **(b)** (*pretext*) excuse *f*, prétexte *m*. **he is only making ~s** il cherche tout simplement des prétextes; **to make an ~ for sth/for doing** trouver une excuse à qch/pour faire; **he gave the bad weather as his ~ for not coming** il a prétexté le mauvais temps pour ne pas venir.

♦ **excusable** *adj* excusable, pardonnable.

execrate ['eksɪkreɪt] *vt* exécrer. ♦ **execrable** *adj* exécrable. ♦ **execrably** *adv* exécrablement. ♦ **execration** *n* exécration *f*.

execute ['eksɪkjuːt] *vt* **(a)** (*put to death*) exécuter. **(b)** (*carry out*) (*gen*) exécuter; *work of art* réaliser; *purpose, sb's wishes, duties, task* accomplir. ♦ **execution** *n* exécution *f*; **in the execution of his duties** dans l'exercice de ses fonctions. ♦ **executioner** *n* bourreau *m*. ♦ **executive** [ɪg'zekjʊtɪv] **1** *adj powers, committee* exécutif; *job* de cadre; *director, secretary* général; *offices* de la direction; *post, car, plane* de directeur; *unemployment* des cadres; **2** *n* (*power*) (pouvoir *m*) exécutif *m*; (*person*) cadre *m*; (*group of managers*) bureau *m*. ♦ **executor** *n* [ɪg'zekjʊtəʳ] exécuteur *m*, -trice *f* testamentaire.

exemplary [ɪg'zemplərɪ] *adj* (*gen*) exemplaire; *pupil etc* modèle.

exemplify [ɪg'zemplɪfaɪ] *vt* (*illustrate*) exemplifier; (*be example of*) servir d'exemple de.

exempt [ɪg'zempt] **1** *adj* exempt (*from* de). **2** *vt* exempter (*from sth* de qch), dispenser (*from doing* de faire). ♦ **exemption** *n* exemption *f* (*from* de), dispense *f*.

exercise ['eksəsaɪz] **1** *n* (*all senses*) exercice *m*. **in the ~ of his duties** dans l'exercice de ses fonctions; **physical ~** exercice physique; **(physical) ~s** la gymnastique; **to take ~** prendre de l'exercice; **a grammar ~** un exercice de grammaire; **NATO ~s** manœuvres *fpl* de l'OTAN. **2** *vt limb,* *rights, influence* exercer; (*use*) *tact, restraint* faire preuve de; (*) *dog etc* promener. **the problem which is exercising my mind** le problème qui me préoccupe. **3** *vi* prendre de l'exercice. ♦ **exercise-book** *n* (*for writing*) cahier *m.*

exert [ɪg'zɜːt] *vt* (*gen*) exercer; *force* employer. **to ~ o.s.** (*physically*) se dépenser; (*take trouble*) se donner du mal; (*iro*) **don't ~ yourself!** ne vous fatiguez pas! ♦ **exertion** *n* effort *m*; **by his own ~ions** par ses propres moyens *mpl*; **the day's ~ions** les fatigues *fpl* de la journée; **it doesn't require much ~ion** cela n'exige pas un grand effort.

exeunt ['eksɪʌnt] *vi* (*Theat*) ils sortent.

exhale [eks'heɪl] *vti* (*Physiol*) expirer.

exhaust [ɪg'zɔːst] **1** *vt* (*all senses*) épuiser. **2** *n* (*~ system*) échappement *m*; (*~ pipe*) pot *m* d'échappement; (*~ fumes*) gaz *m* d'échappement. ♦ **exhausted** *adj* épuisé; **I'm ~ed** je n'en peux plus; **my patience is ~ed** ma patience est à bout. ♦ **exhausting** *adj* épuisant. ♦ **exhaustion** *n* épuisement *m.* ♦ **exhaustive** *adj account, report* complet; *study, description, list* exhaustif; *inquiry, inspection* minutieux. ♦ **exhaustively** *adv search, study* à fond; *list, describe* exhaustivement.

exhibit [ɪg'zɪbɪt] **1** *vt painting, handicrafts* exposer; *merchandise* exposer, étaler; *document, identity card* présenter; *courage, skill, ingenuity* faire preuve de. **2** *n* (*in exhibition*) objet *m* exposé; (*Jur*) pièce *f* à conviction. ♦ **exhibition** *n [paintings etc]* exposition *f*; *[articles for sale]* étalage *m*; **the Van Gogh ~ion** l'exposition Van Gogh; (*fig*) **to make an ~ion of o.s.** se donner en spectacle. ♦ **exhibitionism** *n* exhibitionnisme *m.* ♦ **exhibitionist** *adj, n* exhibitionniste (*mf*). ♦ **exhibitor** *n* exposant(e) *m(f).*

exhilarate [ɪg'zɪləreɪt] *vt [sea air etc]* vivifier; *[music, wine, good company]* stimuler. ♦ **exhilarated** *adj* stimulé. ♦ **exhilarating** *adj* vivifiant; stimulant. ♦ **exhilaration** *n* joie *f*, allégresse *f.*

exhort [ɪg'zɔːt] *vt* exhorter (*to* à, *to do* à faire). ♦ **exhortation** *n* exhortation *f* (*to* à).

exhume [eks'hjuːm] *vt* exhumer. ♦ **exhumation** *n* exhumation *f.*

exile ['eksaɪl] **1** *n* (*person*) exilé(e) *m(f)*; (*condition*) exil *m.* **in(to) ~** en exil. **2** *vt* exiler (*from* de).

exist [ɪg'zɪst] *vi* **(a)** (*be*) exister. **everything that ~s** tout ce qui existe *or* est; **doubt still ~s** le doute subsiste. **(b)** (*live*) vivre (*on* de), subsister. **we cannot ~ without water** nous ne pouvons pas vivre *or* subsister sans eau; **she ~s on very little** elle vit de très peu. ♦ **existence** *n* existence *f*; **to be in ~ence** exister; **to come into ~ence** être créé; **the only one in ~ence** le seul qui existe (*subj*). ♦ **existent** *adj* existant. ♦ **existential** *adj* existentiel. ♦ **existentialism** *n* existentialisme *m.* ♦ **existentialist** *adj, n* existentialiste (*mf*). ♦ **existing** *adj law* existant; *regime* actuel.

exit ['eksɪt] **1** *n* sortie *f.* **2** *vi* (*Theat*) il sort. **3** *adj*: **~ permit/visa** permis *m*/visa *m* de sortie.

exodus ['eksədəs] *n* exode *m.* (*Bible*) **E~** l'Exode; (*fig*) **there was a general ~** beaucoup de gens sont partis.

exonerate [ɪg'zɒnəreɪt] *vt* disculper (*from* de), innocenter. ♦ **exoneration** *n* disculpation *f.*

exorbitant [ɪg'zɔːbɪtənt] *adj price* exorbitant; *demands* exorbitant, démesuré. ♦ **exorbitantly** *adv* démesurément.

exorcize ['eksɔːsaɪz] *vt* exorciser. ♦ **exorcism** *n* exorcisme *m.* ♦ **exorcist** *n* exorciste *m.*

exotic [ɪg'zɒtɪk] *adj* exotique. ♦ **exoticism** *n* exotisme *m.*

expand [ɪks'pænd] **1** *vt gas, metal, lungs* dilater; *business, ideas, notes, muscles* développer; *production* augmenter; *horizons, study* élargir; *influence, knowledge* étendre. **~ed polystyrene** polystyrène *m* expansé. **2** *vi* se dilater; se développer; augmenter; s'élargir; s'étendre. **the market is ~ing** les débouchés se multiplient. ♦ **expanding** *adj industry* en pleine expansion; *universe* en expansion; *bracelet* extensible.

expanse [ɪks'pæns] *n* étendue *f.* ♦ **expansion** *n [gas]* dilatation *f*; *[business]* agrandissement *m*; *[trade, subject, idea]* développement *m*; *[production]* augmentation *f*; (*territorial, economic, colonial*) expansion *f.* ♦ **expansionism** *n* expansionnisme *m.* ♦ **expansive** *adj* expansif, communicatif; **in an expansive mood** en veine d'épanchements. ♦ **expansively** *adv* (*in detail*) avec abondance; (*warmly*) avec chaleur; **to smile expansively** arborer un large sourire; **to gesture expansively** faire de grands gestes.

expatiate [ɪks'peɪʃɪeɪt] *vi* discourir (*upon* sur).

expatriate [eks'pætrɪeɪt] *adj, n* expatrié(e) *m(f).*

expect [ɪks'pekt] *vt* **(a)** (*anticipate*) s'attendre à; (*with confidence*) escompter; (*count on*) compter sur; (*hope for*) espérer. **to ~ to do** penser *or* compter *or* espérer faire, s'attendre à faire; **that was to be ~ed** c'était à prévoir, il fallait s'y attendre; **I ~ed as much** je m'y attendais; **I know what to ~** je sais à quoi m'attendre; **I did not ~ that from him** je n'attendais pas cela de lui; **to ~ that** s'attendre à ce que + *subj*, escompter que + *indic*; **it is ~ed that** il est vraisemblable que + *indic*, il y a des chances pour que + *subj*; **it is not as heavy as I ~ed** ce n'est pas aussi lourd que je le croyais; **as ~ed** comme prévu. **(b)** (*suppose*) penser, supposer. **I ~ so** je crois que oui; **yes, I ~ it is** oui, je m'en doute. **(c)** (*demand*) exiger, attendre (*sth from sb* qch de qn), demander (*sth from sb* qch à qn). **to ~ sb to do sth** exiger *or* demander que qn fasse qch; **you can't ~ too much from him** on ne peut pas trop exiger de lui; **I ~ you to tidy your own room** tu es censé ranger ta chambre toi-même; **what do you ~ me to do about it?** que voulez-vous que j'y fasse?; **England ~s that ...** l'Angleterre compte que + *fut indic.* **(d)** (*await*) attendre. **I am ~ing them for dinner** je les attends à dîner; **we'll ~ you when we see you*** on ne t'attend pas à une heure précise; **she is ~ing a baby, she is ~ing*** elle attend un bébé.
♦ **expectancy** *n* attente *f*; **with eager ~ancy** avec une vive impatience; **look of ~ancy** regard plein d'espoir. ♦ **expectant** *adj person, crowd* qui attend qch; *attitude* d'expectative; *look* de qn qui attend qch; **~ant mother** femme *f* enceinte. ♦ **expectantly** *adv look, listen* avec l'air d'attendre qch; *wait* avec espoir. ♦ **expectation** *n* attente *f*; **in ~ation of** dans l'attente de, en prévision de; **~ation of life** espérance *f* de vie; **contrary to all ~ation** contre toute attente; **to come up to sb's ~ations** répondre à l'attente *or* aux espérances de qn; **beyond ~ation** au-delà de mes *etc* espérances.

expedient [ɪks'piːdɪənt] **1** *adj* (*convenient*) indiqué, opportun; (*politic*) politique, opportun. **it would be ~ to change the rule** il serait opportun de changer le règlement. **2** *n* expédient *m.* ♦ **expedience** *or* ♦ **expediency** *n* (*self-interest*) opportunisme *m*; (*advisability*) opportunité *f.*

expedite ['ekspɪdaɪt] *vt preparations, process* accélérer; *legal or official matters* activer, hâter; *business, deal* pousser; *task* expédier. ♦ **expedition** *n* expédition *f.* ♦ **expeditionary** *adj* expéditionnaire. ♦ **expeditious** *adj* expéditif. ♦ **expeditiously** *adv* promptement.

expel [ɪks'pel] *vt* (*gen*) expulser (*from* de); (*from school*) renvoyer; *enemy* chasser.

expend [ɪks'pend] *vt time, energy* consacrer (*on* à; *on doing* à faire); *money* dépenser (*on* pour; *on doing* à faire); (*use up*) épuiser. ♦ **expendable** *adj equipment* non-réutilisable; *troops* sacrifiable;

(*of little value*) *person, object* facile à remplacer. ♦ **expenditure** *n* dépenses *fpl*; **an item of ~iture** une dépense.

expense [ɪks'pens] **1** *n* dépense *f*, frais *mpl*. **at my ~** à mes frais; (*fig*) à mes dépens; **at great ~** à grands frais; **to go to the ~ of buying a car** faire la dépense d'une voiture; **to go to great ~** faire beaucoup de frais (*to do* pour faire); **to go to some ~** faire des frais; **regardless of ~** sans regarder à la dépense; **to put sb to ~** causer des dépenses à qn; **to meet the ~ of sth** faire face aux frais de qch; **~s** frais; **after all ~s have been paid** tous frais payés. **2** *adj*: **~ account** frais *mpl* de représentation; **to go on sb's ~ account** passer sur la note de frais de qn. ♦ **expensive** *adj* cher; (*costly*) coûteux; *tastes* de luxe; *journey* onéreux; **to be expensive** coûter cher *inv*, valoir cher *inv*. ♦ **expensively** *adv entertain* à grands frais; *dress* de façon coûteuse. ♦ **expensiveness** *n* cherté *f*.

experience [ɪks'pɪərɪəns] **1** *n* **(a)** (*knowledge etc*) expérience *f* (*of* de). **I know by ~** je le sais par expérience; **from my own** *or* **personal ~** d'après mon expérience personnelle; **I know from bitter ~ that ...** j'ai appris à mes dépens que ...; **he has no ~ of grief/of living in the country** il ne sait pas ce que c'est que le vrai chagrin/que de vivre à la campagne; **the greatest disaster in the ~ of this nation** le plus grand désastre que cette nation ait connu. **(b)** (*practice, skill*) pratique *f*, expérience *f*. **practical ~** pratique; **business/teaching/driving ~** expérience des affaires/de l'enseignement/du volant; **have you any previous ~?** avez-vous déjà fait ce genre de travail?; **I've no ~ of doing that** je n'ai jamais fait cela. **(c)** (*event ~d*) expérience *f*, aventure *f*, sensation *f*. **I had a pleasant/frightening ~** il m'est arrivé une chose *or* une aventure agréable/effrayante; **she's had some terrible ~s** elle en a vu de dures*; **it wasn't an ~ I would care to repeat** ça n'est pas une aventure que je tiens à recommencer; **unfortunate ~** mésaventure *f*.

2 *vt misfortune, hardship* connaître; *setbacks, losses* essuyer; *conditions* vivre dans; *ill treatment* subir; *difficulties* rencontrer; *sensation, terror, remorse* éprouver; *emotion* ressentir. **he has never ~d it** il n'en a jamais fait l'expérience, cela ne lui est jamais arrivé; **he ~s some difficulty in speaking** il éprouve de la difficulté à parler.

♦ **experienced** *adj* (*gen*) expérimenté, qui a de l'expérience (*in* en, en matière de); *eye, ear* exercé.

experiment [ɪks'perɪmənt] **1** *n* expérience *f* (*also Chem etc*). **as an ~** à titre d'essai *or* d'expérience. **2** [ɪks'perɪment] *vi* (*gen, fig*) faire une expérience. **to ~ with a new vaccine** expérimenter un nouveau vaccin; **to ~ on guinea pigs** faire des expériences sur des cobayes. ♦ **experimental** *adj* (*gen*) expérimental; *evidence* confirmé par l'expérience; *cinema, period* d'essai; **at the ~al stage** au stade expérimental; **this system is merely ~al** ce système est encore à l'essai; **~al chemist** chimiste *mf* de laboratoire. ♦ **experimentally** *adv prove etc* expérimentalement; *arrange, organize* à titre expérimental. ♦ **experimentation** *n* expérimentation *f*.

expert ['ekspɜːt] **1** *n* spécialiste *mf* (*on, at sth* de qch); (*qualified*) expert *m* (*at sth* en qch; *at doing* à faire). **he is an ~ on wines** il est grand connaisseur en vins; **he is an ~ on the subject** c'est un expert en la matière. **2** *adj person* expert (*in sth* en qch; *in the art of* dans l'art de; *at, in doing* à faire); *knowledge, advice, evidence* d'expert; (*Jur*) *witness* expert. **he is ~** il s'y connaît; **with an ~ eye** *judge* en expert; *look at* d'un œil connaisseur; **with an ~ touch** avec beaucoup d'habileté. ♦ **expertise** *n* compétence *f* (*in* en), adresse *f* (*in* à). ♦ **expertly** *adv* de façon experte, adroitement.

expire [ɪks'paɪəʳ] *vi [document]* expirer; *[period, time limit]* arriver à terme; (*die*) expirer. ♦ **expiration** *or* ♦ **expiry** *n* expiration *f*.

explain [ɪks'pleɪn] *vt* (*gen*) expliquer; *mystery* éclaircir; *reasons, points of view* exposer. **to ~ o.s.** s'expliquer.

explain away *vt sep* trouver une explication convaincante de.

♦ **explainable** *adj* explicable; **that is easily ~able** cela s'explique facilement. ♦ **explanation** *n* explication *f*; éclaircissement *m*; **to find an explanation for sth** trouver l'explication de qch; **has he something to say in explanation of his conduct?** est-ce qu'il peut fournir une explication de sa conduite?; **what have you to say in explanation?** qu'avez-vous à dire pour votre justification? ♦ **explanatory** *adj* explicatif.

expletive [ɪks'pliːtɪv] *n* (*oath*) juron *m*.

explicit [ɪks'plɪsɪt] *adj intention, statement* explicite; *denial* catégorique. ♦ **explicitly** *adv* explicitement; catégoriquement.

explode [ɪks'pləʊd] **1** *vi* exploser. **to ~ with laughter** éclater de rire. **2** *vt* faire exploser; (*fig*) *theory, rumour* montrer la fausseté de. ♦ **explosion** *n* explosion *f*; (*noise of explosion*) détonation *f*. ♦ **explosive 1** *adj gas, matter* explosible; *mixture* détonant; *weapons, force, situation, temper* explosif; **2** *n* explosif *m*.

exploit ['eksplɔɪt] **1** *n* prouesse *f*; (*heroic*) exploit *m*. **~s** aventures *fpl*. **2** [ɪks'plɔɪt] *vt* exploiter. ♦ **exploitation** *n* exploitation *f*.

explore [ɪks'plɔːʳ] *vt* (*gen*) explorer; (*Med*) sonder. **to go exploring** partir en exploration; **to ~ the ground** sonder le terrain; **to ~ every avenue** examiner toutes les possibilités. ♦ **exploration** *n* exploration *f*. ♦ **exploratory** *adj expedition* d'exploration; *step, discussion* préparatoire; (*Med*) **exploratory operation** sondage *m*. ♦ **explorer** *n* explorateur *m*, -trice *f*.

exponent [ɪks'pəʊnənt] *n [ideas]* interprète *m*; *[literary movement etc]* représentant(e) *m(f)*.

export [ɪks'pɔːt] **1** *vt* exporter (*to* vers). **2** ['ekspɔːt] *n* exportation *f*. **for ~ only** réservé à l'exportation. **3** ['ekspɔːt] *adj goods, permit* d'exportation. **~ drive** campagne *f* pour encourager l'exportation; **~ duty** droit *m* de sortie; **~ reject** article *m* impropre à l'exportation. ♦ **exportation** *n* exportation *f*. ♦ **exporter** *n* exportateur *m*; (*country*) pays *m* exportateur.

expose [ɪks'pəʊz] *vt* (*gen, also Phot*) exposer (*to* à); (*uncover*) découvrir; *wire, nerve* mettre à nu; (*display*) *goods, pictures* exposer; *one's ignorance* afficher; (*unmask, reveal*) *vice* mettre à nu; *scandal, plot* révéler, dévoiler; *secret* éventer; *person* dénoncer. **to be ~d to view** s'offrir à la vue; **digging has ~d the remains of a temple** les fouilles ont mis au jour les restes d'un temple; **to ~ o.s. to** s'exposer à. ♦ **exposed** *adj country* (*gen*) battu par les vents; (*Mil*) découvert; (*Tech*) *part* apparent; *wire* à nu; (*fig*) **he is in a very ~d position** il est très exposé. ♦ **exposition** *n* exposition *f*. ♦ **exposure 1** *n* exposition *f* (*to* à); révélation *f*, dénonciation *f*; (*Phot*) pose *f*; **to threaten sb with exposure** menacer qn d'un scandale; **to die of exposure** mourir de froid; **2** *adj* (*Phot*) **exposure meter** posemètre *m*.

expostulate [ɪks'pɒstjʊleɪt] **1** *vt* protester. **2** *vi*: **to ~ with sb about sth** faire des remontrances à qn au sujet de qch. ♦ **expostulation** *n* protestation *f*; remontrances *fpl*.

expound [ɪks'paʊnd] *vt theory, text* expliquer; *one's views* exposer.

express [ɪks'pres] **1** *vt* **(a)** (*gen*) exprimer; *a truth, proposition* énoncer; *wish* formuler. **to ~ o.s.** s'exprimer. **(b)** (*send*) *letter, parcel* expédier par exprès. **2** *adj* **(a)** *instructions* exprès, formel;

intention explicite. **with the ~ purpose of** dans le seul but de. **(b)** (*fast*) *letter, delivery* exprès *inv*; *coach etc* express *inv*. ~ **train** rapide *m*; (*esp US*) ~ **way** voie *f* express. **3** *adv* très rapidement; *post* par exprès. **4** *n* (*train*) rapide *m*. ♦ **expression** *n* (*gen*) expression *f*; (*phrase etc*) expression, tournure *f*; **set ~ion** expression consacrée. ♦ **expressionism** *n* expressionnisme *m*. ♦ **expressionist** *adj*, *n* expressionniste (*mf*). ♦ **expressive** *adj language, face, hands* expressif; *gestures, silence* éloquent; *look, smile* significatif. ♦ **expressively** *adv* d'une manière expressive. ♦ **expressly** *adv* expressément.

expulsion [ɪks'pʌlʃən] *n* expulsion *f*; (*Scol etc*) renvoi *m*. ~ **order** arrêté *m* d'expulsion.

expurgate ['ekspɜ:geɪt] *vt* expurger.

exquisite [ɪks'kwɪzɪt] *adj* (*gen*) exquis; *sensibility* raffiné; *sense of humour* subtil; *satisfaction, pleasure* vif (*f* vive); *pain* aigu (*f* -guë). ♦ **exquisitely** *adv* (*gen*) d'une façon exquise; (*extremely*) extrêmement; **~ly beautiful** d'une beauté exquise.

extant [eks'tænt] *adj* qui existe encore. **a few examples are still ~** quelques exemples subsistent.

extempore [ɪks'tempərɪ] *adv*, *adj* impromptu. ♦ **extemporize** *vti* improviser.

extend [ɪks'tend] **1** *vt* **(a)** (*stretch out*) *arm* étendre; *one's hand* tendre (*to sb* à qn); (*offer*) *help* apporter; *hospitality, friendship* offrir; *thanks, condolences, congratulations* présenter; *welcome* souhaiter; *invitation* faire, lancer. **(b)** (*prolong*) *street, line, visit* prolonger (*by, for* de); (*enlarge*) *house, property* agrandir; *research* pousser plus loin; *powers, limits, business* étendre; *knowledge* accroître; *frontiers* reculer; *vocabulary* enrichir; (*make demands on*) *worker, pupil* faire donner son maximum à. **~ed credit** un long crédit; **an ~ed play record** un disque double (durée).

2 *vi [wall, estate]* s'étendre (*to, as far as* jusqu'à); *[meeting, visit]* se prolonger (*over* pendant; *for* durant).

♦ **extension** **1** *n* extension *f*; prolongation *f*; agrandissement *m*; (*to road, line*) prolongement *m*; (*for table, wire, electric flex*) rallonge *f*; (*to holidays, leave*) prolongation; (*telephone*) *[private house]* appareil *m* supplémentaire; *[office]* poste *m*; **extension 21** poste 21; **to have an extension built on to the house** faire agrandir la maison; **come and see our extension** venez voir nos agrandissements *mpl*; **2** *adj*: **university extension courses** cours *mpl* publics du soir (organisés par l'Université); **extension ladder** échelle *f* coulissante. ♦ **extensive** *adj estate, forest, knowledge* vaste, étendu; *study, research* approfondi; *investments, alterations* considérable; *plans, reforms, business* de grande envergure; *use* répandu. ♦ **extensively** *adv use, travel* beaucoup.

extent [ɪks'tent] *n [estate, knowledge, activities, power]* étendue *f*; *[road etc]* longueur *f*; *[damage, commitments, losses]* importance *f*; (*degree*) mesure *f*, degré *m*. **to open to its fullest ~** ouvrir entièrement; **to what ~** dans quelle mesure; **to a certain ~** jusqu'à un certain point, dans une certaine mesure; **to a large ~** en grande partie; **to a small ~** dans une faible mesure; **to such an ~ that** à tel point que; **to the ~ of doing** au point de faire.

extenuating [ɪk'stenjʊeɪtɪŋ] *adj* atténuant.

exterior [ɪks'tɪərɪəʳ] **1** *adj* extérieur (*to* à). ~ **decoration** peintures *fpl* d'extérieur; **paint for ~ use** peinture *f* pour bâtiment. **2** *n* extérieur *m*. **on the ~** à l'extérieur.

exterminate [ɪks'tɜ:mɪneɪt] *vt pests, group of people* exterminer; *beliefs, ideas* supprimer. ♦ **extermination** *n* extermination *f*.

external [eks'tɜ:nl] **1** *adj surface* externe, extérieur; *wall* extérieur; *influences* du dehors; *factor, trade* extérieur. (*Pharm*) **for ~ use only** pour usage externe; ~ **examiner** examinateur *m* venu de l'extérieur (*d'une autre université*). **2** *n*: **the ~s** l'extérieur *m*, les apparences *fpl*. ♦ **externally** *adv* extérieurement.

extinct [ɪks'tɪŋkt] *adj* (*gen*) éteint; *race, species* disparu. ♦ **extinction** *n* extinction *f*.

extinguish [ɪks'tɪŋgwɪʃ] *vt* (*lit, fig*) éteindre. ♦ **extinguisher** *n* extincteur *m*.

extol [ɪks'təʊl] *vt* louer avec enthousiasme.

extort [ɪks'tɔ:t] *vt money, signature* extorquer (*from* à); *promise, confession, secret* arracher (*from* à). ♦ **extortion** *n* extorsion *f*. ♦ **extortionate** *adj* exorbitant.

extra ['ekstrə] **1** *adj* (*more*) de plus, supplémentaire; (*spare*) en trop. **an ~ chair** une chaise de plus *or* supplémentaire; ~ **money** de l'argent de plus; **the ~ money/chair** l'argent/la chaise supplémentaire; **the chair is ~** (*spare*) la chaise est en trop; (*costs more*) la chaise est en supplément; (*Ftbl*) **after ~ time** après prolongation *f*; **I have had ~ work** j'ai eu plus de travail que d'habitude; **there will be no ~ charge** on ne vous comptera pas de supplément; **take ~ care!** faites particulièrement attention!; ~ **pay** supplément *m* de salaire (*for* de); **for ~ safety** pour plus de sécurité; **postage ~** frais *mpl* de port en sus; **I bought a few ~ tins** j'ai acheté quelques boîtes de réserve.

2 *adv* plus que d'habitude, particulièrement. ~ **kind** plus gentil que d'habitude.

3 *n* (*perk*) à-côté *m*; (*luxury*) agrément *m*; (*in restaurant*: ~ *dish*) supplément *m*; (*Cine, Theat: actor*) figurant(e) *m(f)*. **singing and piano are ~s** les leçons de chant et de piano ne sont pas comprises.

♦ **extrafine** *adj* extra-fin. ♦ **extra-smart** *adj* ultra-chic* *inv*. ♦ **extra-strong** *adj person* extrêmement fort; *material* extra-solide.

extract [ɪks'trækt] **1** *vt* (*gen*) extraire (*from* de); *tooth* arracher (*from* à); (*fig*) *confession, permission, promise* arracher (*from* à); *information, meaning, moral* tirer (*from* de); *money* soutirer (*from* à). **2** ['ekstrækt] *n* extrait *m*. ♦ **extraction** *n* extraction *f* (*also Dentistry*); (*descent*) origine *f*. ♦ **extractor** *adj*: **~or fan** ventilateur *m*.

extracurricular ['ekstrəkə'rɪkjʊləʳ] *adj* en dehors du programme (*Scol*).

extradite ['ekstrədaɪt] *vt* extrader. ♦ **extradition** *n* extradition *f*.

extramarital ['ekstrə'mærɪtl] *adj* en dehors du mariage.

extramural ['ekstrə'mjʊərəl] *adj course* hors faculté; *lecture* public.

extraordinary [ɪks'trɔ:dnrɪ] *adj* (*gen*) extraordinaire; *quality* exceptionnel; *action, speech, behaviour* étonnant, surprenant; *insults, violence* inouï. **an ~ meeting of the shareholders** une assemblée extraordinaire des actionnaires; **I find it ~ that he hasn't replied** je trouve extraordinaire *or* inouï qu'il n'ait pas répondu; **there's nothing ~ about that** cela n'a rien d'étonnant; **it's ~ to think that ...** il semble incroyable que ... + *subj*; **the ~ fact is that he succeeded** ce qu'il y a d'étonnant c'est qu'il a *or* ait réussi. ♦ **extraordinarily** *adv* extraordinairement.

extrasensory ['ekstrə'sensərɪ] *adj*: ~ **perception** perception extra-sensorielle.

extraspecial ['ekstrə'speʃəl] *adj* (*gen*) exceptionnel; *care* tout particulier; *occasion* grand.

extravagance [ɪks'trævəgəns] *n* (*excessive spending*) prodigalité *f*; (*wastefulness*) gaspillage *m*; (*thing bought*) folie *f*. **that hat was a great ~** ce chapeau était une vraie folie. ♦ **extravagant** *adj* (*wasteful*) *person* dépensier, prodigue; *taste* dispendieux; (*exaggerated*) (*gen*) extravagant; *opinions, praise, claims* exagéré; *prices* exorbitant. ♦ **extravagantly** *adv* (*lavishly*) avec prodigalité; (*flamboyantly*) d'une façon extravagante; **to use sth extravagantly** gaspiller qch. ♦ **extravaganza** *n* fantaisie *f*.

extreme [ɪks'tri:m] **1** *adj* (*exceptional, exaggerated*) extrême; (*furthest*) extrême (*before n*). **in ~ danger** en très grand danger; (*Pol*) **the ~ right** l'extrême droite *f*; **at the ~ end of the path** à l'extrémité du chemin; **how ~!** c'est un peu poussé! **2** *n* extrême *m*. **in the ~** à l'extrême, au plus haut degré; **to go to ~s** pousser les choses à l'extrême. ♦ **extremely** *adv* extrêmement. ♦ **extremist 1** *adj opinion* extrême; *person* extrémiste; *party* d'extrémistes; **2** *n* extrémiste *mf*. ♦ **extremity** [ɪks'tremɪtɪ] *n* (*gen*) extrémité *f*; *[despair, happiness]* extrême degré *m*.

extricate ['ekstrɪkeɪt] *vt object* dégager (*from* de). (*fig*) **to ~ o.s.** se tirer (*from* de).

extrovert ['ekstrəʊvɜ:t] **1** *adj* extraverti. **2** *n* extraverti(e) *m(f)*.

exuberance [ɪg'zu:bərəns] *n* exubérance *f*. ♦ **exuberant** *adj* exubérant. ♦ **exuberantly** *adv* avec exubérance.

exude [ɪg'zju:d] *vti* (*lit*) exsuder. (*fig*) **he ~d charm** le charme lui sortait par tous les pores.

exult [ɪg'zʌlt] *vi* (*rejoice*) se réjouir (*in* de; *over* de, à propos de), exulter; (*triumph*) jubiler. ♦ **exultant** *adj expression, shout* de triomphe; *[person]* **to be ~ant** jubiler. ♦ **exultantly** *adv* triomphalement. ♦ **exultation** *n* exultation *f*.

eye [aɪ] **1** *n* œil *m* (*pl* yeux). **girl with blue ~s, blue-~d girl** fille aux yeux bleus; **to have brown ~s** avoir les yeux bruns; **with tears in her ~s** les larmes aux yeux; **with one's ~s closed** les yeux fermés; **to have the sun in one's ~s** avoir le soleil dans les yeux; **before my very ~s** sous mes yeux; **as far as the ~ can see** à perte de vue; **in the ~s of** aux yeux de; **to look at a question through the ~s of an economist** envisager une question du point de vue de l'économiste; **under the ~ of** sous l'œil de; **with my own ~s** de mes propres yeux; **with an ~ to the future** en prévision de l'avenir; **with an ~ to buying** en vue d'acheter; **that's one in the ~ for him*** c'est bien fait pour lui; **to be all ~s** être tout yeux; **to be up to the** *or* **one's ~s in work** être dans le travail jusqu'au cou; **to shut one's ~s to** *sb's shortcomings* fermer les yeux sur; *evidence* se refuser à; *dangers, truth* se dissimuler; **his ~ fell on ...** son regard est tombé sur ...; **to get one's ~ in** ajuster son coup d'œil; **to have one's ~ on sth/sb** avoir qch/qn en vue; **to have an ~ to the main chance** ne jamais perdre de vue ses propres intérêts; **to have an ~ for sth** savoir reconnaître qch; **to keep one's ~ on the ball** fixer la balle; **to keep an ~ on sth/sb** surveiller qch/qn; **to keep an ~ on things*** avoir l'œil (à tout); **to keep one's ~s open** être vigilant, ouvrir l'œil; **to keep one's ~s open for sth** essayer de trouver qch; **he couldn't keep his ~s open*** il dormait debout; (*fig*) **with one's ~s wide open** en connaissance de cause; **to look sb straight in the ~** regarder qn dans les yeux; **to make ~s at*** faire de l'œil à*; **to see ~ to ~ with sb** partager le point de vue de qn; **I've never set ~s on him** je ne l'ai jamais vu de ma vie; **he didn't take his ~s off her** il ne l'a pas quittée des yeux; **he never uses his ~s** il ne sait pas voir; **use your ~s** tu es aveugle?

2 *vt* regarder. **he was ~ing the girls** il reluquait les filles.

♦ **eyeball** *n* globe *m* oculaire. ♦ **eyebath** *n* œillère *f* (*pour bains d'œil*). ♦ **eyebrow 1** *n* sourcil *m*; **2** *adj*: **~brow pencil** crayon *m* à sourcils; **~brow tweezers** pince *f* à épiler. ♦ **eye-catching** *adj dress, colour* qui tire l'œil; *publicity, poster* accrocheur. ♦ **eyedrops** *npl* gouttes *fpl* pour les yeux. ♦ **eyeful** *n*: **he got an ~ful of mud** il a reçu de la boue plein les yeux; **she's quite an ~ful*** on se rince l'œil à la regarder‡. ♦ **eyelash** *n* cil *m*. ♦ **eyelet** *n* œillet *m* (*dans du tissu etc*). ♦ **eye-level** *adj* à hauteur des yeux; **~-level grill** gril *m* surélevé. ♦ **eyelid** *n* paupière *f*. ♦ **eyeliner** *n* eye-liner *m*. ♦ **eye-opener** *n* révélation *f*. ♦ **eyeshade** *n* visière *f*. ♦ **eyeshadow** *n* fard *m* à paupières. ♦ **eyesight** *n* vue *f*. ♦ **eyestrain** *n*: **to have ~strain** avoir la vue fatiguée. ♦ **eye-tooth** *n* canine *f* supérieure. ♦ **eyewash*** *n* (*fig*) fadaises *fpl*. ♦ **eyewitness** *n* témoin *m* oculaire.

eyrie ['ɪərɪ] *n* aire *f* (*d'aigle*).

F

F, f [ef] *n* F, f *m or f*; (*Mus*) fa *m*.
fa [fɑː] *n* (*Mus*) fa *m*.
fable ['feɪbl] *n* fable *f*. ♦ **fabled** *adj* légendaire.
fabric ['fæbrɪk] *n* (*cloth*) tissu *m*, étoffe *f*; *[building, system, society]* structure *f*. ♦ **fabricate** *vt* fabriquer. ♦ **fabrication** *n* fabrication *f*.
fabulous ['fæbjʊləs] *adj* (*gen*) fabuleux; (*: *wonderful*) formidable*, sensationnel*. **a ~ price*** un prix fou.
façade [fə'sɑːd] *n* façade *f*.
face [feɪs] **1** *n* visage *m*, figure *f*; (*expression*) mine *f*; *[building]* façade *f*; *[clock]* cadran *m*; *[cliff]* paroi *f*; *[coin]* côté *m*; *[the earth]* surface *f*; *[document]* recto *m*; *[playing card]* face *f*, dessous *m*. **~ down(wards)** *person* face contre terre; *card* face en dessous; **~ up(wards)** *person* sur le dos; *card* retourné; **to turn sth ~ up** retourner qch à l'endroit; (*Med*) **injuries to the ~** blessures *fpl* à la face; **you can shout till you're black in the ~, he ...** tu auras beau t'exténuer à crier, il ...; **to change the ~ of a town** changer le visage d'une ville; **he vanished off the ~ of the earth** il a complètement disparu de la circulation; **I've got a good memory for ~s** je suis physionomiste; **he laughed in my ~** il m'a ri au nez; **he won't show his ~ here again** il ne se montrera plus ici; **he told him so to his ~** il le lui a dit tout cru; **in the ~ of** *the enemy* face à; *threat, danger* devant; *difficulty* en dépit de; **to set one's ~ against sth** se dresser contre qch; **to set one's ~ against doing** se refuser à faire; **to put a bold** *or* **brave ~ on things** faire bon visage; **to lose ~** perdre la face; **to save (one's) ~** sauver la face; **to make** *or* **pull ~s** faire des grimaces (*at* à); **to make a (disapproving) ~** faire une moue de désapprobation; **on the ~ of it** à première vue; **to have the ~ to do*** avoir le toupet* de faire.
2 *adj*: **~ card** figure *f*; **~ cream** crème *f* pour le visage; **~ cloth** *or* **flannel** gant *m* de toilette; **to have a ~ lift** se faire faire un lifting; **~ pack** masque *m* de beauté; **~ powder** poudre *f* de riz; **~ value** *[coin]* valeur *f* nominale; *[stamp, card]* valeur; (*fig*) **to take sb** *or* **sth at ~ value** se laisser tromper par les apparences.
3 *vt* **(a)** (*also* **be facing**) *person* être en face de; *wall etc* être face à; *[building]* (*be opposite*) être en face de; (*look towards*) donner sur. **problem facing me** problème devant lequel je me trouve; **facing one another** en face l'un de l'autre; **the picture facing page 16** l'illustration en regard de la page 16; **to be ~d with** *possibility, prospect* se trouver devant; *danger, defeat* être menacé par; **to be ~d with the prospect of doing** risquer d'avoir à faire; **~d with the prospect of ...** devant la perspective de ... . **(b)** (*confront*) *enemy, danger* faire face à. **I can't ~ him** (*ashamed*) je n'ose pas le regarder en face; (*fed up*) je n'ai pas le courage de le voir; **to ~ the music** braver l'orage; **to ~ facts** regarder les choses en face; **to ~ the fact that ...** admettre que ...; **I can't ~ doing it** je n'ai pas le courage de le faire.
4 *vi [person]* **to ~/be facing this way** se tourner/être tourné de ce côté; (*fig*) **to ~ both ways** ménager la chèvre et le chou; *[house]* **facing north** orienté au nord; **facing towards the sea** face à la mer.
face up to *vt fus danger, difficulty* faire face à. **to ~ up to the fact that** admettre que.
♦ **faceless** *adj* anonyme. ♦ **face-saving** *adj* qui sauve la face. ♦ **face-to-face** **1** *adv* face à face; **2** *adj*: **~-to-~ discussion** face à face *m inv*. ♦ **facial** **1** *adj* facial; **2** *n* soin *m* du visage. ♦ **facing** *n* (*Constr*) revêtement *m*; (*Sewing*) revers *m*.
facet ['fæsɪt] *n* facette *f*.
facetious [fə'siːʃəs] *adj person* facétieux; *remark* bouffon.
♦ **facetiously** *adv* facétieusement.
facility [fə'sɪlɪtɪ] *n* facilité *f* (*in, for doing* pour faire). **facilities** (*educational, leisure*) équipements *mpl*; (*transport, production*) moyens *mpl*; (*in harbour, airport*) installations *fpl*; **there are no facilities for it** ce n'est pas équipé pour cela.
♦ **facilitate** *vt* faciliter.
facsimile [fæk'sɪmɪlɪ] *n* fac-similé *m*.
fact [fækt] *n* fait *m*. **it is a ~ that** il est de fait que + *indic*; **is it a ~ that** est-il vrai que + *subj* (*often* * *indic*); **to know (it) for a ~ that** savoir de source sûre que; **the ~s of life** (*sex etc*) les choses *fpl* de la vie; (*fig*) les réalités *fpl* de la vie; **~ and fiction** le réel et l'imaginaire; **story founded on ~** histoire basée sur des faits; **in (point of) ~, as a matter of ~** en fait; **the ~ of the matter is that ...** le fait est que ... .
♦ **fact-finding** *adj*: **~-finding committee** commission *f* d'enquête; **they were on a ~-finding mission to the war front** ils étaient partis enquêter au front. ♦ **factual** *adj report, description* basé sur les faits; *error* de fait. ♦ **factually** *adv* en se tenant aux faits.
faction ['fækʃən] *n* faction *f*.
factor ['fæktə^r] *n* facteur *m*. **safety ~** facteur de sécurité; **human ~** élément *m* humain.
factory ['fæktərɪ] **1** *n* usine *f*, (*gen smaller*) fabrique *f*; *[arms, china, tobacco]* manufacture *f*; (*fig*) usine. **shoe ~** usine *or* fabrique de chaussures. **2** *adj work, worker, chimney* d'usine; *inspector* du travail. **~ farming** élevage *m* industriel; **~ ship** navire-usine *m*.
factotum [fæk'təʊtəm] *n* factotum *m*.
faculty ['fækəltɪ] *n* faculté *f*.
fad [fæd] *n* (*habit*) marotte *f*; (*fashion*) folie *f* (*for* de).
♦ **faddy** *adj person* qui a des marottes; *distaste* capricieux.
fade [feɪd] **1** *vi [flower]* se faner; *[colour, material]* passer; (**~ away**) *[daylight, one's faculties]* baisser; *[memory, vision]* s'effacer; *[hopes, smile]* s'évanouir; *[sound]* s'affaiblir; *[person]* dépérir. **the castle ~d from sight** le château disparut aux regards.
2 *vt*: **to ~ in/out** (*Cine, TV*) faire apparaître/disparaître en fondu; (*Rad*) monter/couper par un fondu sonore.
faeces ['fiːsiːz] *npl* fèces *fpl*.
fag [fæg] **1** *n* (‡: *nasty work*) corvée *f*; (‡: *cigarette*) sèche‡ *f*; (*Brit Scol*) petit *m* (*élève au service d'un grand*). **2** *adj*: **~ end** (*remainder*) restant *m*, reste *m*; (‡) *[cigarette]* mégot* *m*. **3** *vt* (**~ out**) éreinter.
fag(g)ot ['fægət] *n* fagot *m*.
fah [fɑː] *n* (*Mus*) fa *m*.

Fahrenheit ['færənhaɪt] *adj* Fahrenheit *inv.*

fail [feɪl] **1** *vi* **(a)** (*gen*) échouer; *[candidate]* échouer, être collé* (*in an exam* à un examen; *in Latin* en latin); *[play, show]* être un four; *[bank, business]* faire faillite. **to ~ to do** ne pas réussir à faire; **to ~ by 5 votes** échouer à 5 voix près; **to ~ in one's duty** manquer à son devoir. **(b)** *[faculty]* baisser; *[person, voice]* s'affaiblir; *[light]* baisser; *[crops]* être perdu; *[power, electricity, water supply]* manquer; *[engine]* tomber en panne; *[brakes]* lâcher.

2 *vt* **(a)** *examination* échouer à, être collé* à; *subject* échouer en; *candidate* refuser, coller*. **(b)** (*let down*) *[person]* décevoir, laisser tomber*; *[memory etc]* trahir. **don't ~ me!** ne me laissez pas tomber!*, je compte sur vous!; **his heart ~ed him** le cœur lui a manqué; **words ~ me!** les mots me manquent! **(c)** (*omit*) manquer, négliger (*to do* de faire). **to ~ to appear** (*Jur*) faire défaut; (*gen*) ne pas se montrer; **I ~ to see why** je ne vois pas pourquoi.

3 *n* (*in exam*) échec *m*. **without ~** *come, do* sans faute; *happen, befall* immanquablement.

♦ **failing 1** *n* défaut *m*; **2** *prep* à défaut de; **~ing this** à défaut. ♦ **failsafe** *adj* à sûreté intégrée. ♦ **failure** *n* (*gen*) échec *m* (*in an exam* à un examen; *in Latin* en latin); *[bank, business]* faillite *f*; *[electricity, engine]* panne *f*; *[crops]* perte *f*; (*unsuccessful person*) raté(e) *m(f)*; **a total ~ure** un fiasco; **his ~ure to convince them** son impuissance *f* à les convaincre; **he's a ~ure as a writer** il ne vaut rien comme écrivain.

faint [feɪnt] **1** *adj breeze, smell, sound, hope, trace* léger, faible; *colour* pâle; *voice, breathing* faible; *idea, smile* vague. **I haven't the ~est idea** je n'en ai pas la moindre idée; **to make a ~ attempt at doing** essayer sans conviction de faire; **to grow ~(er)** s'affaiblir; (*Med*) **to feel ~** être pris d'un malaise; **~ with hunger** défaillant de faim. **2** *n* évanouissement *m*. **3** *vi* s'évanouir (*from* de). **to be ~ing** défaillir (*from* de). ♦ **fainthearted** *adj* craintif, timide. ♦ **faintly** *adv* (*gen*) faiblement; *write, mark* légèrement; *disappointed* légèrement; *smiling, reminiscent* vaguement.

♦ **faintness** *n* faiblesse *f*; légèreté *f*.

fair[1] [fɛəʳ] *n* (*gen*) foire *f*; (*fun ~*) fête *f* foraine. (*Comm*) **Book F~** Foire du livre. ♦ **fairground** *n* champ *m* de foire.

fair[2] [fɛəʳ] **1** *adj* **(a)** *person, decision* juste (*to sb* vis-à-vis de qn), équitable; *deal, exchange* équitable; *fight, competition, match* loyal; *profit, comment* justifié, mérité; *sample* représentatif. **it's not ~** ce n'est pas juste; **to be ~ (to him), he ...** rendons-lui cette justice, il ...; **as is only ~** et ce n'est que justice; **~ enough!** d'accord!, c'est bien normal!; **to give sb a ~ deal** agir équitablement envers qn; **he was ~ game for the critics** c'était une proie rêvée pour les critiques; **by ~ means or foul** par tous les moyens; **~ play** fair-play *m*; **his ~ share of** sa part de; **~ shares for all** à chacun son dû; **~ and square** tout à fait honnête; **through ~ and foul** à travers toutes les épreuves. **(b)** *work, result* passable, assez bon. **(c)** (*quite large*) *sum* considérable; *number* respectable; *speed* bon. **he is in a ~ way to doing** il y a de bonnes chances pour qu'il fasse; **a ~ amount*** pas mal (*of* de). **(d)** (*light-coloured*) *hair, person etc* blond; *complexion, skin* clair. **(e)** (*fine*) *wind* propice, favorable; *weather, promises, words* beau. **it's set ~** le temps est au beau fixe; **the ~ sex** le beau sexe; **~ copy** (*rewritten*) copie *f* au propre; (*model answer etc*) corrigé *m*.

2 *adv*: **to play ~** jouer franc jeu; **to act ~ and square** agir loyalement; **the branch struck him ~ and square in the face** la branche l'a frappé en plein (milieu du) visage.

♦ **fair-haired** *adj* blond. ♦ **fairly** *adv* **(a)** (*justly*) *treat* équitablement; *obtain* honnêtement; **~ly and squarely** = **fair and square**; *V* **fair**[2] **2**; **(b)** (*reasonably*) assez; **I'm ~ly sure that ...** je suis presque sûr que ...; **(c)** (*utterly*) absolument; **he was ~ly beside himself with rage** il était absolument hors de lui. ♦ **fair-minded** *adj* impartial. ♦ **fairness** *n* **(a)** *[hair]* blondeur *f*; *[skin]* blancheur *f*; **(b)** justice *f*, honnêteté *f*; *[decision, judgment]* équité *f*; **in all ~ness** en toute justice; **in ~ness to him** pour être juste envers lui. ♦ **fair-sized** *adj* assez grand. ♦ **fair-skinned** *adj* à la peau claire.

fairy ['fɛərɪ] **1** *n* fée *f*; (*‡: homosexual*) pédé‡ *m*. **2** *adj helper, gift* magique; *child, dance* des fées. **~ footsteps** pas légers de danseuse (*iro*); (*fig*) **~ godmother** marraine *f* gâteau *inv*; **~ lights** guirlande *f* électrique; **~ queen** reine *f* des fées; **~ tale** conte *m* de fées; (*untruth*) conte à dormir debout.

♦ **fairyland** *n* royaume *m* des fées.

faith [feɪθ] **1** *n* (*all senses*) foi *f*. **F~, Hope and Charity** la foi, l'espérance et la charité; **~ in God** la foi en Dieu; **to have ~ in sb** avoir confiance en qn; **to put one's ~ in** mettre tous ses espoirs en; **to keep ~ with sb** tenir ses promesses envers qn; **in all good ~** en toute bonne foi; **in bad ~** de mauvaise foi. **2** *adj*: **~ healer** guérisseur *m*, -euse *f* (mystique); **~ healing** guérison *f* par la foi. ♦ **faithful 1** *adj* fidèle (*to* à); **2** *n* **the ~ful** (*Christians*) les fidèles *mpl*; (*Muslims*) les croyants *mpl*. ♦ **faithfully** *adv* fidèlement; **to promise ~fully that** donner sa parole que; **yours ~fully** veuillez agréer, Monsieur (*or* Madame *etc*) mes salutations distinguées. ♦ **faithfulness** *n* fidélité *f* (*to* à). ♦ **faithless** *adj* perfide. ♦ **faithlessness** *n* perfidie *f*.

fake [feɪk] **1** *n* (*object etc*) objet *m etc* truqué; (*picture*) faux *m*. **he's a ~** il n'est pas ce qu'il prétend être. **2** *adj* **(a)** *[picture]* **to be ~** être un (*or* des) faux. **(b)** (*also* **faked**) *accounts, interview* truqué. **3** *vt* faire un faux de; truquer. **to ~ illness** faire semblant d'être malade. **4** *vi* faire semblant.

falcon ['fɔːlkən] *n* faucon *m*.

fall [fɔːl] (*vb: pret* **fell**, *ptp* **fallen**) **1** *n* **(a)** (*gen*) chute *f*; (*in price, temperature*) baisse *f* (*in* de); (*more drastic*) chute. (*fig*) **to be riding for a ~** courir à l'échec; **the ~ of the Bastille** la prise de la Bastille; **~ of earth** éboulement *m* de terre; **~ of rock** chute de pierres; **a heavy ~ of snow** de fortes chutes de neige; (*waterfall*) **~s** chute d'eau; **the Niagara F~s** les chutes du Niagara. **(b)** (*US: autumn*) automne *m*. **in the ~** en automne.

2 *vi* **(a)** (*gen*) tomber (*into* dans; *out of, off* de); *[temperature, price, level, voice, wind]* tomber; (*less drastically*) baisser; *[building]* s'écrouler. **to ~ flat** *[person]* tomber à plat ventre; *[event etc]* ne pas répondre à l'attente; *[scheme]* faire long feu; *[joke]* tomber à plat; **to ~ to** *or* **on one's knees** tomber à genoux; **to ~ on one's feet** retomber sur ses pieds; **to ~ over a chair** tomber en butant contre une chaise; **he was ~ing over himself to be polite*** il se mettait en quatre pour être poli; **they were ~ing over each other to get it*** ils se battaient pour l'avoir; **to let sth ~** laisser tomber qch; **to let ~ that** laisser entendre que; **his face fell** son visage s'est assombri; **the students ~ into 3 categories** les étudiants se divisent en 3 catégories; **the responsibility ~s on you** la responsabilité retombe sur vous; **Christmas Day ~s on a Sunday** Noël tombe un dimanche; **he fell to wondering if ...** il s'est mis à se demander si ...; **it ~s to me to say** il m'appartient de dire; **to ~ short of** *expectations* ne pas répondre à; *perfection* ne pas atteindre.

(b) (*become etc*) **to ~ asleep** s'endormir; **to ~ into bad habits** prendre de mauvaises habitudes; **to ~ into conversation with sb** entrer en conversation avec qn; (*fig*) **to ~ from grace**

tomber en disgrâce; to ~ **due** venir à échéance; to ~ **heir to sth** hériter de qch; to ~ **ill** *or* **sick** tomber malade; (*lit, fig*) to ~ **into line** s'aligner; (*fig*) to ~ **into line with sb** se ranger à l'avis de qn; **to ~ in love** tomber amoureux (*with* de); **to ~ for*** *person* tomber amoureux de; *idea* s'enthousiasmer pour; (*be taken in by*) se laisser prendre à; **to ~ silent** se taire.

fall about* *vi* (*fig: laugh*) se tordre (de rire).

fall apart *vi* tomber en morceaux; (*fig*) se désagréger.

fall away *vi* [*ground*] descendre en pente; [*plaster*] s'écailler; [*supporters*] déserter.

fall back *vi* (*retreat*) reculer. **to ~ back on sth** avoir recours à qch; **sth to ~ back on** qch en réserve.

fall behind *vi* rester en arrière; (*in race*) se laisser distancer. **to ~ behind with** *work* prendre du retard dans; *rent* être en retard pour.

fall down *vi* (*gen*) tomber; [*building*] s'effondrer; (*fail*) échouer, rater son coup. **to ~ down on the job** ne pas être à la hauteur.

fall in *vi* (*into water*) tomber (dans l'eau); [*building*] s'affaisser; [*troops*] former les rangs.

fall in with *vt fus* (*meet*) *person* rencontrer; (*agree to*) *proposal, sb's view* accepter. **this fell in very well with our plans** ceci a cadré avec nos projets.

fall off *vi* (*lit*) tomber; [*supporters*] déserter; [*numbers*] diminuer; [*interest*] tomber.

fall out *vi* (*quarrel*) se brouiller (*with* avec); (*Mil*) rompre les rangs. **everything fell out as we had hoped** tout s'est passé comme nous l'avions espéré.

fall over *vi* tomber (par terre); *V* **fall 2.**

fall through *vi* [*plans etc*] échouer.

fall (up)on *vt fus* se jeter sur; (*Mil*) *enemy* fondre sur.

♦ **fallen 1** *adj* tombé; (*morally*) perdu; *angel, woman* déchu; **~en leaf** feuille morte; **~en arches** affaissement *m* de la voûte plantaire; **2** *n* (*Mil*) **the ~en** ceux qui sont tombés au champ d'honneur. ♦ **falling** *adj*: **~ing star** étoile *f* filante. ♦ **fall(ing)-off** *n* réduction *f* (*in* de). ♦ **fallout 1** *n* retombées *fpl*; **2** *adj*: **~out shelter** abri *m* antiatomique.

fallacy ['fæləsɪ] *n* (*false belief*) erreur *f*; (*false reasoning*) faux raisonnement *m*. ♦ **fallacious** *adj* trompeur.

fallible ['fæləbl] *adj* faillible. ♦ **fallibility** *n* faillibilité *f*.

fallopian [fə'ləʊpɪən] *adj*: ~ **tube** trompe *f* utérine.

fallow ['fæləʊ] *adj*: **to lie ~** être en jachère.

false [fɔːls] *adj* (*all senses*) faux (*f* fausse). ~ **alarm** fausse alerte; **a ~ step** un faux pas; **~ start** faux départ *m*; **under ~ pretences** (*Jur*) par des moyens frauduleux; (*by lying*) sous des prétextes fallacieux; **with a ~ bottom** à double fond; **~ teeth** fausses dents *fpl*.

♦ **false-hearted** *adj* fourbe. ♦ **falsehood** *n* (*lie*) mensonge *m*; **truth and ~hood** le vrai et le faux. ♦ **falsely** *adv declare* faussement; *accuse* à tort. ♦ **falseness** *or* ♦ **falsity** *n* fausseté *f*. ♦ **falsification** *n* falsification *f*. ♦ **falsify** *vt document* falsifier; *evidence* maquiller; *accounts, figures* truquer.

falsetto [fɔːl'setəʊ] **1** *n* fausset *m*. **2** *adj* de fausset.

falter ['fɔːltəʳ] **1** *vi* [*voice, speaker*] hésiter; (*waver*) vaciller; [*steps*] chanceler; [*courage*] faiblir. **2** *vt words* bredouiller.

fame [feɪm] *n* renommée *f*, gloire *f*. **his ~ as a writer** sa renommée d'écrivain; **he wanted ~** il était avide de gloire; **M. Mitchell of 'Gone with the Wind'** ~ M. Mitchell connue pour son livre 'Autant en emporte le vent'. ♦ **famed** *adj* célèbre (*for* pour).

familiar [fə'mɪljəʳ] *adj* (*gen*) familier; *complaint, event, protest* habituel. **a ~ figure in the town** un personnage bien connu dans la ville; **a ~ feeling** une sensation bien connue; **his face is ~** sa tête me dit quelque chose*; (*fig*) **to be on ~ ground** être sur son terrain; **to be ~ with sth** bien connaître qch; **to make o.s. ~ with** se familiariser avec; (*pej*) **he got much too ~** il s'est permis des familiarités (*with* avec).

♦ **familiarity** *n* [*sight etc*] caractère *m* familier; (*with customs etc*) familiarité *f* (*with* avec); **familiarities** familiarités *fpl*. ♦ **familiarize** *vt* familiariser (*sb with sth* qn avec qch); **to ~ize o.s. with** se familiariser avec. ♦ **familiarly** *adv* familièrement.

family ['fæmɪlɪ] **1** *n* (*all senses*) famille *f*. **has he any ~?** (*relatives*) a-t-il de la famille?; (*children*) a-t-il des enfants?; **it runs in the ~** cela tient de famille; **he's one of the ~** il fait partie de la famille. **2** *adj jewels, likeness, name, life* de famille; *friend* de la famille. (*Admin*) ~ **allowance** allocations *fpl* familiales; ~ **doctor** médecin *m* de famille; ~ **man** bon père *m* de famille; ~ **planning clinic** centre *m* de planning familial; ~ **tree** arbre *m* généalogique.

famine ['fæmɪn] *n* famine *f*.

famished ['fæmɪʃt] *adj* affamé. **I'm absolutely ~*** je meurs de faim.

famous ['feɪməs] *adj* célèbre, (bien) connu (*for* pour). (*iro*) ~ **last words!*** on verra bien!; (*iro*) **that's his ~ motorbike!** voilà sa fameuse moto! ♦ **famously*** *adv* fameusement*, rudement bien*.

fan[1] [fæn] **1** *n* éventail *m*; (*mechanical*) ventilateur *m*. **2** *adj* (*Aut*) ~ **belt** courroie *f* de ventilateur; ~ **heater** radiateur *m* soufflant; ~ **light** imposte *f* (*semi-circulaire*). **3** *vt person* éventer; *fire, quarrel* attiser. (*fig*) **to ~ the flames** jeter de l'huile sur le feu.

fan out *vi* [*troops, searchers*] se déployer (en éventail).

fan[2] [fæn] **1** *n* enthousiaste *mf*; (*Sport*) supporter *m*; [*pop star etc*] fan *mf*, admirateur *m*, -trice *f*. **he is a jazz/bridge/sports/football** *etc* ~ c'est un mordu* du jazz/bridge/sport/football *etc*; **I'm definitely not one of his ~s** je suis loin d'être un de ses admirateurs. **2** *adj*: ~ **club** club *m* de fans; **his ~ mail** les lettres *fpl* de ses admirateurs.

fanatic [fə'nætɪk] *n* fanatique *mf*. ♦ **fanatic(al)** *adj* fanatique. ♦ **fanaticism** *n* fanatisme *m*.

fancy ['fænsɪ] **1** *n* (*whim*) caprice *m*, fantaisie *f*. **a passing ~** un caprice passager, une lubie; **when the ~ takes him** quand cela lui plaît; **he took a ~ to go swimming** il a eu tout à coup envie d'aller se baigner; **to take a ~ to** *person* se prendre d'affection pour; *thing* prendre goût à, se mettre à aimer; **it caught the public's ~** le public l'a tout de suite aimé; **the realm of ~** le domaine de l'imaginaire.

2 *vt* **(a)** (*imagine*) se figurer, s'imaginer; (*rather think*) croire. **I rather ~ he's gone out** je crois bien qu'il est sorti; **~ that!*** tiens!; **~ seeing you here!*** je ne m'imaginais pas vous voir ici! **(b)** (*want*) avoir envie de; (*like*) aimer. **do you ~ going for a walk?** as-tu envie d'aller faire une promenade?; **I don't ~ the idea** cette idée ne me dit rien*; **he fancies himself*** il ne se prend pas pour rien*; **he fancies himself as an actor*** il ne se prend pas pour une moitié d'acteur*; **he fancies her*** il la trouve attirante.

3 *adj hat, buttons, pattern* fantaisie *inv*; (*pej*) *cure* fantaisiste; *price* exorbitant; (*US: extra good*) de qualité supérieure. ~ **cakes** pâtisseries *fpl*; **it was all very ~** c'était très recherché; **with his ~ house and his ~ car ...** avec sa belle maison et sa voiture grand luxe ...; ~ **dress** déguisement *m*; **in ~ dress** déguisé; **~-dress ball** bal *m* masqué; ~ **goods** nouveautés *fpl*; (*pej*) ~ **woman** bonne amie.

♦ **fancied** *adj* imaginaire. ♦ **-fancier** *n ending in cpds, e.g.* **dog-fancier** amateur *m* de chiens. ♦ **fanciful** *adj person* capricieux; *ideas* fantasque; *story, account* imaginaire.

fanfare ['fænfɛəʳ] *n* fanfare *f* (*air*).

fang [fæŋ] *n* (*gen*) croc *m*; *[snake]* crochet *m*.

fantastic [fæn'tæstɪk] *adj* (*gen*) fantastique; *idea* invraisemblable; (*: *excellent*) sensationnel*, fantastique. ♦ **fantastically** *adv* fantastiquement, extraordinairement.

fantasy ['fæntəzɪ] *n* (*gen*) fantaisie *f*; (*idea, wish*) idée *f* fantasque; (*Psych etc*) fantasme *m*. ♦ **fantasize** *vi* (*Psych etc*) faire des fantasmes.

far [fɑːʳ] *comp* **farther** *or* **further,** *superl* **farthest** *or* **furthest 1** *adv* loin. **how ~ is it to ...?** combien y a-t-il jusqu'à ...?; **is it ~?** est-ce loin?; **is it ~ to London?** c'est loin pour aller à Londres?; **not ~ from here** pas loin d'ici; **how ~ are you going?** jusqu'où allez-vous?; (*fig*) **how ~ have you got with your plans?** où en êtes-vous de vos projets?; **to go ~** aller loin; **I would even go so ~ as to say that ...** je dirais même que ...; **that's going too ~** cela dépasse les bornes; **now you're going too ~** alors là vous exagérez; **he has gone too ~ to back out now** il est trop engagé pour reculer maintenant; **he was ~ gone** (*ill*) il était bien bas; (*drunk*) il était bien parti*; **so ~** jusqu'à présent; **so ~ and no further** jusque-là mais pas plus loin; **so ~ so good** jusqu'ici ça va; **~ be it from me to say** loin de moi l'idée de dire; **as ~ as the town** jusqu'à la ville; **we didn't go as** *or* **so ~ as the others** nous ne sommes pas allés aussi loin que les autres; **as** *or* **so ~ as I know** pour autant que je sache; **as ~ as I can** dans la mesure du possible; **as ~ as the eye can see** à perte de vue; **as ~ as that goes** pour ce qui est de cela; **as ~ as I'm concerned** en ce qui me concerne; **as ~ back as I can remember** d'aussi loin que je m'en souvienne; **as ~ back as 1945** déjà en 1945; **~ and away the best** de très loin le meilleur; **~ and wide, ~ and near** partout; **~ above** loin au-dessus (de); (*fig*) de loin supérieur (à); **~ away, ~ off** au loin; **~ away in the distance** dans le lointain; **he wasn't ~ off** il n'était pas loin; **his birthday is not ~ off** c'est bientôt son anniversaire; **~ beyond** bien au-delà (de); **~ from** loin de (*doing* faire); **~ from it!** loin de là!; **~ into** très avant dans; **~ out at sea** au (grand) large; **our calculations are ~ out** nous avons fait une énorme erreur de calcul; **by ~** de loin, beaucoup; **this is ~ better** ceci est beaucoup *or* bien mieux.

2 *adj country* lointain, éloigné. **the F~ East** l'Extrême-Orient *m*; **the F~ North** le Grand Nord; **the F~ West** le Far West; **it's a ~ cry from** ... on est loin de ...; **on the ~ side of** de l'autre côté de; **at the ~ end of** à l'autre bout de; (*Pol*) **the ~ left** l'extrême-gauche *f*.

♦ **faraway** *adj country, voice* lointain; *village* éloigné; *look* perdu dans le vague; *memory* flou. ♦ **far-distant** *adj* lointain. ♦ **far-fetched** *adj idea, scheme* bizarre; *explanation* tiré par les cheveux. ♦ **far-flung** *adj* vaste. ♦ **far-off** *adj* lointain, éloigné. ♦ **far-reaching** *adj* d'une grande portée. ♦ **far-sighted** *adj person* clairvoyant; *decision, measure* fait (*or* pris *etc*) avec clairvoyance.

farce [fɑːs] *n* (*Theat, fig*) farce *f*. **the whole thing's a ~!** tout ça, c'est vraiment grotesque. ♦ **farcical** *adj* grotesque, ridicule.

fare [fɛəʳ] **1** *n* **(a)** (*charge*) (*on bus, in underground*) prix *m* du ticket; (*on boat, plane, train*) prix du billet; (*in taxi*) prix de la course. **~s, please!** les places, s'il vous plaît!; **~s are going up** les transports *mpl* vont augmenter; **let me pay your ~** laissez-moi payer pour vous; **I haven't got the ~** je n'ai pas assez d'argent pour le billet. **(b)** (*passenger*) voyageur *m*, -euse *f*; *[taxi]* client(e) *m(f)*. **(c)** (*food*) nourriture *f*. **hospital ~** régime *m* d'hôpital. **2** *adj [bus]* **~ stage** section *f*. **3** *vi*: **how did you ~?** comment cela s'est-il passé? ♦ **farewell 1** *n, excl* adieu *m*; **to bid ~well to** faire ses adieux à; **2** *adj dinner etc* d'adieu.

farm [fɑːm] **1** *n* (*Agr*) ferme *f*; (*fish ~ etc*) centre *m* d'élevage. **to work on a ~** travailler dans une ferme. **2** *adj*: **~ labourer, ~ worker** ouvrier *m*, -ère *f* agricole; **~ produce** produits *mpl* de ferme. **3** *vt* cultiver. **4** *vi* être fermier.

farm out *vt sep work* céder en sous-traitance; (*: *hum*) *children* parquer* (*on sb* chez qn). ♦ **farmer** *n* fermier *m*; **~er's wife** fermière *f*. ♦ **farmhand** *n* valet *m* *or* fille *f* de ferme. ♦ **farmhouse** *n* (maison *f* de) ferme *f*. ♦ **farming 1** *n* agriculture *f*; **mink ~ing** élevage *m* du vison; **2** *adj*: **~ing communities** collectivités *fpl* rurales; **~ing methods** méthodes *fpl* d'agriculture. ♦ **farmland** *n* terres *fpl* cultivées. ♦ **farmstead** *n* ferme *f*. ♦ **farmyard** *n* cour *f* de ferme.

farrier ['færɪəʳ] *n* maréchal-ferrant *m*.

fart‡ [fɑːt] **1** *n* pet‡ *m*. **2** *vi* péter‡.

farther ['fɑːðəʳ] *comp of* **far 1** *adv* plus loin. **how much ~ is it?** c'est encore à combien?; **it is ~ than I thought** c'est plus loin que je ne pensais; **have you got much ~ to go?** est-ce que vous avez encore loin à aller?; **I got no ~ with him** je ne suis arrivé à rien de plus avec lui; **nothing could be ~ from the truth** rien n'est plus éloigné de la vérité; **to get ~ and ~ away** s'éloigner de plus en plus; **~ back** plus (loin) en arrière; **move ~ back** reculez-vous; **~ back than 1940** avant 1940; **~ away, ~ off** plus éloigné, plus loin; **~ on, ~ forward** plus en avant, plus loin; (*fig*) plus avancé. **2** *adj* plus éloigné, plus lointain. **the ~ end of the room** l'autre bout de la salle.

farthest ['fɑːðɪst] *superl of* **far 1** *adj* le plus lointain, le plus éloigné. **the ~ way** la route la plus longue. **2** *adv* le plus loin.

fascinate ['fæsɪneɪt] *vt* fasciner. ♦ **fascinated** *adj* fasciné (*by* par). ♦ **fascinating** *adj* fascinant. ♦ **fascination** *n* fascination *f*.

fascism ['fæʃɪzəm] *n* fascisme *m*. ♦ **fascist** *adj, n* fasciste (*mf*).

fashion ['fæʃən] **1** *n* **(a)** (*manner*) façon *f*, manière *f*. **in a queer ~** d'une manière *or* façon bizarre; **after a ~** *finish, manage* tant bien que mal; *cook, paint* si l'on peut dire; **in the French ~** à la française; **in his own ~** à sa manière *or* façon. **(b)** (*latest style*) mode *f*, vogue *f*. **in ~** à la mode, en vogue; **in the latest ~** à la dernière mode; **out of ~** démodé; **to set the ~ for** lancer la mode de; **it is the ~ to say** il est bien porté de dire; **it's no longer the ~** ça ne se fait plus. **(c)** (*habit*) coutume *f*, habitude *f*. **2** *vt carving* façonner; *model* fabriquer; *dress* confectionner. **3** *adj editor, magazine* de mode. **~ designer** modéliste *mf*, (*grander*) couturier *m*; **~ house** maison *f* de couture; **~ model** mannequin *m* (*personne*); **~ parade, ~ show** présentation *f* de collections. ♦ **fashionable** *adj dress, subject* à la mode; *district, shop, hotel* chic *inv*. ♦ **fashionably** *adv* à la mode.

fast[1] [fɑːst] **1** *adj* **(a)** (*speedy*) rapide. (*Aut*) **the ~ lane** ≃ la voie la plus à gauche; **~ train** rapide *m*; **he's a ~ thinker** il a l'esprit très rapide; **he's a ~ worker** il va vite en besogne; **to pull a ~ one on sb*** rouler qn*. **(b)** *[clock etc]* **to be ~** avancer; **my watch is 5 minutes ~** ma montre avance de 5 minutes. **(c)** (*dissipated*) *woman* de mœurs légères; *life* dissolu. **one of the ~ set** un viveur. **(d)** (*firm*) *rope, knot* solide; *grip* tenace; *colour* grand teint *inv*; *friend* sûr. **to make a boat ~** amarrer un bateau. **2** *adv* **(a)** (*quickly*) vite, rapidement. **he ran off as ~ as his legs could carry him** il s'est sauvé à toutes jambes; **how ~ can you type?** à quelle vitesse pouvez-vous taper?; **not so ~!** doucement!; **he'll do it ~ enough if ...** il ne se fera pas prier si ... . **(b)** (*firmly, se-*

curely) *tied* solidement. ~ **asleep** profondément endormi.

fast[2] [fɑːst] **1** *vi* (*not eat*) jeûner. **2** *n* jeûne *m*.

fasten [ˈfɑːsn] **1** *vt* (*gen*) attacher (*to* à); (*with nail*) clouer (*to* à); *box, door* fermer (solidement); *seat belt, dress* attacher; *responsibility* attribuer (*on sb* à qn). **to ~ the blame on sb** rejeter la faute sur le dos de qn. **2** *vi* (*gen*) se fermer; *[dress]* s'attacher.

fasten down *vt sep blind, flap* fixer en place; *envelope* coller.

fasten on *vt sep* fixer (en place).

fasten (up)on *vt fus excuse* saisir; *idea* se mettre en tête.

♦ **fastener** *or* ♦ **fastening** *n* attache *f*; *[box, door, garment]* fermeture *f*; *[bag, necklace, book]* fermoir *m*.

fastidious [fæsˈtɪdɪəs] *adj person* difficile (à contenter); (*about cleanliness etc*) exigeant (*about* en ce qui concerne).

fat [fæt] **1** *n* (*Anat*) graisse *f*; (*on meat*) gras *m*; (*for cooking*) matière *f* grasse. **to fry in deep ~** faire cuire à la grande friture; **the ~'s in the fire** le feu est aux poudres; **to live off the ~ of the land** vivre grassement.

2 *adj person, limb* gros (*f* grosse), gras (*f* grasse); *face* joufflu; *cheeks* gros; *meat, bacon* gras; *volume, cheque, salary* gros; **to get ~** grossir, engraisser; (*fig*) **he grew ~ on the profits** il s'est engraissé avec les bénéfices; **a ~ lot of good that did!*** ça a bien avancé les choses! (*iro*); **a ~ lot he knows about it!*** comme s'il en savait quelque chose!

♦ **fathead*** *n* imbécile *mf*, cruche* *f*. ♦ **fatness** *n* embonpoint *m*. ♦ **fatten** *vt* (~ **up**) (*gen*) engraisser; *geese* gaver. ♦ **fattening** *adj food* qui fait grossir. ♦ **fatty** *adj food* gras; *tissue* adipeux.

fatal [ˈfeɪtl] *adj* (*causing death*) *injury, disease etc* mortel; *consequences* fatal; (*disastrous*) *mistake, day, event* fatal; *influence* néfaste; *consequences* désastreux; (*fateful*) *words, decision* fatidique. **it was absolutely ~ to mention that** c'était une grave erreur que de parler de cela. ♦ **fatalism** *n* fatalisme *m*. ♦ **fatalist** *n* fataliste *mf*. ♦ **fatalistic** *adj* fataliste. ♦ **fatality** *n* mort *m*. ♦ **fatally** *adv wounded* mortellement; **~ly ill** condamné, perdu.

fate [feɪt] *n* **(a)** (*force*) destin *m*, sort *m*. **what ~ has in store for us** ce que le destin nous réserve. **(b)** (*one's lot*) sort *m*. **to leave sb to his ~** abandonner qn à son sort. ♦ **fated** *adj* destiné (*to do* à faire); *friendship, person* voué au malheur. ♦ **fateful** *adj words* fatidique; *day, event, moment* fatal.

father [ˈfɑːðəʳ] *n* (*all senses*) père *m*. (*Rel*) **Our F~** Notre Père; **from ~ to son** de père en fils; **there was the ~ and mother of a row*** il y a eu une dispute à tout casser*; **F~ Bennet** le (révérend) père Bennet, l'abbé Bennet; **yes, F~** oui, mon père; **F~ Christmas** le père Noël; **F~'s Day** la Fête des Pères; **~ confessor** directeur *m* de conscience; **Old F~ Time** le Temps.

♦ **father-figure** *n* personne *f* qui joue le rôle du père. ♦ **fatherhood** *n* paternité *f*. ♦ **father-in-law** *n* beau-père *m*. ♦ **fatherland** *n* patrie *f*. ♦ **fatherless** *adj* orphelin de père. ♦ **fatherly** *adj* paternel.

fathom [ˈfæðəm] **1** *n* (*Naut*) brasse *f* (= *1,83m*). **2** *vt* (*fig*: ~ **out**) sonder. **I just can't ~ it out** je n'y comprends absolument rien.

fatigue [fəˈtiːg] **1** *n* fatigue *f*, épuisement *m*; (*Mil*) corvée *f*. **metal ~** fatigue du métal. **2** *vt* fatiguer.

fatuous [ˈfætjʊəs] *adj* stupide. ♦ **fatuity** *or* ♦ **fatuousness** *n* stupidité *f*.

faucet [ˈfɔːsɪt] *n* (*US*) robinet *m*.

fault [fɔːlt] **1** *n* **(a)** (*gen*) défaut *m*; (*Tech*) défaut, anomalie *f*; (*mistake*) erreur *f*; (*Tennis*) faute *f*; (*Geol*) faille *f*. **to find ~ with** *thing* trouver à redire à; *person* critiquer; **I have no ~ to find with him** je n'ai rien à lui reprocher; **generous to a ~** généreux à l'excès; **to be at ~** être fautif; **my memory was at ~** ma mémoire m'a trompé *or* m'a fait défaut. **(b)** (*responsibility*) faute *f*. **whose ~ is it?** qui est fautif?; **whose ~ is it if we're late?** à qui la faute si nous sommes en retard?; **it's not my ~** ce n'est pas de ma faute. **2** *vt*: **to ~ sth/sb** trouver des défauts dans qch/chez qn. ♦ **faultfind** *vi* critiquer. ♦ **faultfinder** *n* mécontent(e) *m(f)*. ♦ **faultfinding 1** *adj* grincheux; **2** *n* critiques *fpl*. ♦ **faultless** *adj person, behaviour* irréprochable; *work, English* impeccable. ♦ **faulty** *adj* défectueux.

fauna [ˈfɔːnə] *n* faune *f*.

favour, (*US*) **-or** [ˈfeɪvəʳ] **1** *n* **(a)** (*act*) service *m*. **to do sb a ~** rendre (un) service à qn; **to ask a ~ of sb** demander un service à qn; **as a ~ to Paul** pour rendre service à Paul; **do me a ~ and ...** sois gentil et ... . **(b)** (*approval*) faveur *f*. **to be in ~** *[person]* être en faveur; *[style]* être à la mode; **to be in ~ with sb** être bien vu de qn, être en faveur auprès de qn; **to find ~ with sb** *[person]* s'attirer les bonnes grâces de qn; *[suggestion]* gagner l'approbation de qn. **(c)** (*advantage*) faveur *f*. **to decide in sb's ~** donner gain de cause à qn; **in ~ of sb** en faveur de qn; **that's a point in his ~** c'est un bon point pour lui. **(d) to be in ~ of sth** être partisan de qch; **I'm not in ~ of doing that** je ne suis pas d'avis de faire cela. **(e)** (*partiality*) faveur *f*. **to show ~ to sb** montrer un *or* des préjugé(s) en faveur de qn.

2 *vt* (*approve*) *political party, scheme, suggestion* être partisan de; *undertaking* favoriser; (*prefer*) *person* préférer; *candidate, pupil* montrer une préférence pour; *team, horse* être pour. **he ~ed us with a visit** il a eu l'amabilité de nous rendre visite.

♦ **favo(u)rable** *adj* (*gen*) favorable (*to* à); *weather, wind* propice (*for, to* à). ♦ **favo(u)rably** *adv receive, impress* favorablement; *consider* d'un œil favorable; *disposed* bien. ♦ **favo(u)red** *adj* favorisé; **the ~ed few** les élus; **ill-~ed** disgracieux. ♦ **favo(u)rite 1** *n* favori(te) *m(f)*; **that song is a great ~ite of mine** cette chanson est une de mes préférées; **he sang a lot of old ~ites** il a chanté beaucoup de vieux succès; **2** *adj* favori (*f* -ite), préféré. ♦ **favo(u)ritism** *n* favoritisme *m*.

fawn[1] [fɔːn] **1** *n* faon *m*. **2** *adj* (*colour*) fauve.

fawn[2] [fɔːn] *vi*: **to ~ (up)on sb** *[dog]* faire fête à qn; *[person]* flatter qn servilement. ♦ **fawning** *adj* flagorneur.

fear [fɪəʳ] **1** *n* (*fright*) crainte *f*, peur *f*; (*awe*) crainte, respect *m*. **grave ~s have arisen for ...** on est dans la plus vive inquiétude en ce qui concerne ...; **there are ~s that ...** on craint fort que ... + ne + *subj*; **have no ~** ne craignez rien; **without ~ nor favour** impartialement; **to live in ~** vivre dans la peur; **to go in ~ of one's life/of being discovered** craindre pour sa vie/d'être découvert; **in ~ and trembling** en tremblant de peur; **for ~ of waking him** de peur de le réveiller; **for ~ (that)** de peur que + ne + *subj*; **~ of heights** vertige *m*; **to put the ~ of God into sb*** faire une peur bleue à qn; **there's not much ~ of his coming** il est peu probable qu'il vienne, il ne risque guère de venir; **there's no ~ of that!** ça ne risque pas d'arriver!; **no ~!*** pas de danger!*

2 *vt* craindre, avoir peur de; *God* craindre. **to ~ the worst** craindre le pire; **to ~ that** avoir peur que + ne + *subj*, craindre que + ne + *subj*.

3 *vi* trembler (*for* pour).

♦ **fearful** *adj* (*frightening*) *spectacle, noise* effrayant, affreux; *accident* épouvantable; (*bad*) *weather* affreux; (*timid*) craintif; **it's a ~ful nuisance** c'est empoisonnant*. ♦ **fearfully** *adv* (*timidly*) craintivement; (*very*) affreusement, terriblement. ♦ **fearfulness** *n* crainte *f*, appréhension *f.* ♦ **fearless** *adj* intrépide. ♦ **fearlessly** *adv* intrépidement. ♦ **fearlessness** *n* intrépidité *f.* ♦ **fearsome** *adj opponent* redoutable; *apparition* effroyable.

feasible ['fi:zəbl] *adj* (*practicable*) *plan, suggestion* faisable, possible; (*likely*) *story, theory* plausible, vraisemblable. ♦ **feasibility** **1** *n* possibilité *f* (*of doing* de faire); **2** *adj*: **feasibility study** *[scheme etc]* étude *f* des possibilités; *[machine etc]* étude des faisabilités.

feast [fi:st] **1** *n* festin *m*; (*Rel*) fête *f.* ~ **day** (jour *m* de) fête. **2** *vi* festoyer. **to ~ on sth** se régaler de qch. **3** *vt*: **to ~ one's eyes on** se délecter à regarder.

feat [fi:t] *n* exploit *m*, prouesse *f.* ~ **of architecture** *etc* triomphe *m or* réussite *f* de l'architecture *etc*; **that was quite a ~** cela a été un exploit.

feather ['feðəʳ] **1** *n* plume *f.* (*fig*) **to make the ~s fly** mettre le feu aux poudres; **that's a ~ in his cap** c'est une réussite dont il peut être fier; **you could have knocked me over with a ~** les bras m'en sont tombés. **2** *vt*: **to ~ one's nest** faire sa pelote, s'enrichir. **3** *adj mattress etc* de plumes; *headdress* à plumes. ~ **duster** plumeau *m.* ♦ **feather-bed** **1** *n* lit *m* de plumes; **2** *vt* protéger. ♦ **featherbrained** *adj* écervelé. ♦ **featherweight** *adj, n* (*Boxing*) poids (*m*) plume *inv*.

feature ['fi:tʃəʳ] **1** *n* **(a)** (*part of the face*) trait *m* (du visage). **(b)** *[countryside, building]* caractéristique *f*; *[person]* (*physical*) trait *m*; (*mental etc*) caractéristique. **(c)** (*Comm etc*) spécialité *f.* **(d)** (~ *film*) grand film, long métrage; (*Press: column*) chronique *f.* (*Press*) ~ **article** article *m* de fond; **it is a regular ~ in ...** cela paraît régulièrement dans ... . **2** *vt* (*give prominence to*) *person, event* mettre en vedette; *[film]* avoir pour vedette; *name, news* faire figurer; (*depict*) représenter. **3** *vi* (*Cine*) figurer (*in* dans). (*gen*) **this ~d prominently in ...** ceci a été un trait frappant dans ... . ♦ **featureless** *adj* anonyme.

February ['februəri] *n* février *m*; *for phrases V* **September.**

feckless ['feklɪs] *adj* inepte.

fed [fed] *pret, ptp of* **feed.** ♦ **fed up** *adj*: **to be ~ up*** en avoir assez, en avoir marre* (*doing* de faire).

federal ['fedərəl] *adj* fédéral.

federate ['fedəreɪt] **1** *vi* se fédérer. **2** ['fedərɪt] *adj* fédéré. ♦ **federation** *n* fédération *f.*

fee [fi:] *n* (*gen*) prix *m* (*for* de); *[professional person]* honoraires *mpl*; *[artist etc]* cachet *m*; *[private tutor]* appointements *mpl.* (*Univ etc*) **tuition ~** frais *mpl* de scolarité; **registration ~** droits *mpl* d'inscription; **membership ~** montant *m* de la cotisation; (*Ftbl*) **(transfer) ~** prix *m* (de transfert); (*gen*) **what's his ~?** combien prend-il?; **on payment of a small ~** contre une somme modique. ♦ **fee-paying** *adj*: **~-paying school** établissement *m* (d'enseignement) privé.

feeble ['fi:bl] *adj* (*gen*) faible; *attempt, excuse* piètre; *joke* piteux. **she's such a ~ sort of person** c'est une fille si molle. ♦ **feeble-minded** *adj* imbécile. ♦ **feeble-mindedness** *n* imbécillité *f.* ♦ **feebleness** *n* faiblesse *f.* ♦ **feebly** *adv stagger, smile* faiblement; *say, explain* piteusement.

feed [fi:d] (*vb: pret, ptp* **fed**) **1** *n* (*food*) nourriture *f*; (*portion of food*) ration *f*; *[baby]* (*breast-~*) tétée *f*; (*bottle*) biberon *m.* **we had a good ~*** on a bien mangé. **2** *vt* **(a)** (*provide food for*) nourrir; (*give food to*) *child, animal, bird* donner à manger à; *army etc* ravitailler; *baby* (*breastfed*) allaiter; (*bottle-fed*) donner le biberon à. **to ~ sth to sb** donner qch à manger à qn. **(b)** *fire, machine, reservoir* alimenter. (*fig*) **to ~ the flames** jeter de l'huile sur le feu; **to ~ the parking meter** rajouter une pièce dans le parcmètre; **to ~ sth into a machine** introduire qch dans une machine; **to ~ data into a computer** alimenter un ordinateur en données. **3** *vi [animal]* manger, se nourrir; *[baby]* manger, (*at breast*) téter. **to ~ on** se nourrir de.

feed back *vt sep results* donner (en retour).

feed in *vt sep tape, wire* introduire (*to* dans).

feed up *vt sep animal* engraisser; *geese* gaver; *person* faire manger davantage.

♦ **feedback** *n* (*Elec*) réaction *f*; (*gen*) feed-back *m*, réactions *fpl.* ♦ **feeder** *n* (*bib*) bavoir *m.* ♦ **feeding** **1** *n* alimentation *f*; **2** *adj*: **~ing bottle** biberon *m*; **~(ing) stuffs** nourriture *f* (pour animaux).

feel [fi:l] (*vb: pret, ptp* **felt**) **1** *n* (*sense of touch*) toucher *m*; (*sensation*) sensation *f.* **at the ~ of** au contact de; **to know sth by the ~ of it** reconnaître qch au toucher; **I don't like the ~ of that** je n'aime pas cette sensation; (*fig*) ça ne me dit rien de bon; **let me have a ~!*** laisse-moi toucher!; **you have to get the ~ of a new car** il faut se faire à une nouvelle voiture.

2 *vt* **(a)** (*touch*) palper, tâter. **to ~ sb's pulse** tâter le pouls à qn; **~ the envelope and see if there's anything in it** palpez l'enveloppe pour voir s'il y a qch dedans; **to ~ one's way** avancer à tâtons (*towards* pour trouver); (*fig*) **I'm still ~ing my way around** j'essaie de m'y retrouver.

(b) (*be aware of*) *blow, caress, pain* sentir; *sympathy, grief* éprouver, ressentir. **I can ~ sth pricking me** je sens qch qui me pique; **to ~ the heat/cold** craindre la chaleur/le froid; **he felt it move** il l'a senti bouger; **he felt a great sense of relief** il a éprouvé *or* ressenti un grand soulagement; **the effects will be felt later** les effets se feront sentir plus tard; **he ~s his position very much** il est très conscient de la difficulté de sa situation; **she felt the loss of her father greatly** elle a été très affectée par la mort de son père.

(c) (*think*) avoir l'impression, estimer. **I ~ that he ought to go** je considère *or* j'estime qu'il devrait y aller; **I ~ it in my bones that ...** qch en moi me dit que ...; **he felt it necessary to point out ...** il a jugé nécessaire de faire remarquer ...; **if you ~ strongly about it** si cela vous semble important; **what do you ~ about this idea?** que pensez-vous de cette idée?

3 *vi* **(a)** (*physical state*) se sentir. **to ~ cold/hungry/sleepy** avoir froid/faim/sommeil; **to ~ ill** se sentir malade; **I ~ much better** je me sens beaucoup mieux; **he doesn't ~ quite himself** il ne se sent pas tout à fait dans son assiette; **I felt as if I was going to faint** j'avais l'impression que j'allais m'évanouir.

(b) (*mental state*) être. **I ~ sure that ...** je suis sûr que ...; **I ~ very bad about leaving you here** cela m'ennuie beaucoup de vous laisser ici; **how do you ~ about him?** que pensez-vous de lui?; **how do you ~ about going for a walk?** est-ce que cela vous dit d'aller vous promener?; **I ~ as if there's nothing we can do** j'ai l'impression que nous ne pouvons rien faire; **what does it ~ like to do that?** quel effet cela vous fait-il de faire cela?; **to ~ like (doing) sth** avoir envie de (faire) qch; **I don't ~ like it** je n'en ai pas envie; **I ~ for you!** comme je vous comprends!

(c) *[objects]* **to ~ hard** être dur au toucher; **the house ~s damp** la maison donne l'impression d'être humide; **the box ~s as if it has been mended** au toucher on dirait que la boîte a été réparée; **it felt like flying** on se serait cru en train de voler; **it ~s like rain** on dirait qu'il va pleuvoir.

(d) (*grope*: **~ about, ~ around**) (*in dark*) tâtonner; (*in pocket, drawer*) fouiller (*for sth* pour trouver qch).

♦ **feeler** *n [insect]* antenne *f*; *[octopus etc]* tentacule *m*; (*fig*) **to put out ~ers** tâter le terrain (*to discover* pour découvrir).

feeling ['fi:lɪŋ] *n* **(a)** (*physical*) sensation *f.* **I've lost all ~ in my right arm** j'ai perdu toute sensation dans le bras droit; **a cold ~** une sensation de froid. **(b)** (*impression*) sentiment *m*. **a ~ of isolation** un sentiment d'isolement; **I've a funny ~ she will succeed** j'ai comme l'impression qu'elle va réussir; **there was a general ~ that ...** le sentiment général a été que ... . **(c)** (*emotions*) **~s** sentiments *mpl*, sensibilité *f*; **you can imagine my ~s** tu t'imagines ce que je ressens; **~s ran high about it** cela a déchaîné les passions; **his ~s were hurt** on l'avait froissé. **(d)** (*sensitivity*) émotion *f*, sensibilité *f*; (*compassion*) sympathie *f*. **a woman of great ~** une femme très sensible; **with ~** *sing* avec sentiment; *speak* avec émotion; **he doesn't show much ~ for her** il ne fait pas preuve de beaucoup de sympathie pour elle; **ill** *or* **bad ~** hostilité *f*.

♦ **feelingly** *adv* avec émotion.

feet [fi:t] *npl of* **foot.**

feign [feɪn] *vt surprise* feindre; *madness* simuler. **to ~ illness** faire semblant d'être malade. ♦ **feint** **1** *n* feinte *f*; **2** *vi* feinter.

felicitous [fɪ'lɪsɪtəs] *adj* heureux. ♦ **felicity** *n* félicité *f*.

feline ['fi:laɪn] *adj, n* félin(e) *m(f)*.

fell[1] [fel] *pret of* **fall.**

fell[2] [fel] *vt tree* abattre.

fell[3] [fel] *n* (*Brit*) (*mountain*) montagne *f*. (*moorland*) **the ~s** la lande.

fellow ['feləʊ] **1** *n* **(a)** homme *m*, type* *m*, garçon *m*. **a nice ~** un brave garçon, un brave type*; **an old ~** un vieux; **some poor ~** un pauvre malheureux; **poor little ~** pauvre petit bonhomme; **my dear ~** mon cher; **this journalist ~** ce journaliste. **(b)** *[association, society etc]* membre *m*, associé *m*; (*Univ*) ≃ professeur *m* (*attaché à un collège*). **(c)** (*comrade*) camarade *m*, compagnon *m*; (*equal, peer*) semblable *m*. **~s in misfortune** compagnons d'infortune.

2 *adj*: **~ citizen** concitoyen(ne) *m(f)*; **~ countryman/-woman** compatriote *mf*; **~ creature** semblable *mf*; **~ feeling** sympathie *f*; **~ men** semblables *mpl*; **~ traveller** (*lit*) compagnon *m* de voyage; (*Pol: with communists*) communisant(e) *m(f)*; (*gen*) sympathisant(e) *m(f)*; **~ worker** (*in office*) collègue *mf*; (*in factory*) camarade *mf* de travail.

♦ **fellowship** *n* (*comradeship*) camaraderie *f*; (*Rel etc*) communion *f*; (*organization*) association *f*; (*Rel*) confrérie *f*.

felon ['felən] *n* (*Jur*) criminel(le) *m(f)*. ♦ **felonious** *adj* criminel. ♦ **felony** *n* crime *m*.

felt[1] [felt] *pret, ptp of* **feel.**

felt[2] [felt] **1** *n* feutre *m*. **2** *adj* de feutre. **a ~ hat** un feutre. ♦ **felt-tip (pen)** *n* feutre *m* (*crayon*).

female ['fi:meɪl] **1** *adj animal, plant* (*also Tech*) femelle; *subject, slave* du sexe féminin; *company, vote* des femmes; *sex, character, quality* féminin. **~ students** étudiantes *fpl*; **~ labour** main-d'œuvre *f* féminine; (*Theat*) **~ impersonator** travesti *m*. **2** *n* (*person*) femme *f*, fille *f*; (*animal, plant*) femelle *f*. (*pej*) **there was a ~ there who ...*** il y avait là une espèce de bonne femme qui ...* (*pej*).

feminine ['femɪnɪn] **1** *adj* féminin. **2** *n* (*Gram*) féminin *m*. **in the ~** au féminin. ♦ **femininity** *n* féminité *f*. ♦ **feminism** *n* féminisme *m*. ♦ **feminist** *n* féministe *mf*.

fen [fen] *n* marais *m*, marécage *m*.

fence [fens] **1** *n* **(a)** barrière *f*, palissade *f*; (*Racing*) obstacle *m*; (*round machine*) barrière. (*fig*) **to sit on the ~** ménager la chèvre et le chou. **(b)** (‡: *of stolen goods*) receleur *m*. **2** *vt* (**~ in**) *land* clôturer. **~d in by restrictions** entravé par des restrictions. **3** *vi* (*Sport*) faire de l'escrime. ♦ **fencer** *n* escrimeur *m*, -euse *f*. ♦ **fencing** **1** *n* **(a)** (*Sport*) escrime *f*; **(b)** (*material*) matériaux *mpl* pour clôture; **2** *adj*: **fencing match** assaut *m* d'escrime.

fend [fend] *vi*: **to ~ for o.s.** se débrouiller (tout seul).

fend off *vt sep blow* parer; *attack* détourner; *attacker* repousser; *awkward question* éluder.

♦ **fender** *n [fire]* garde-feu *m inv*; (*US Aut*) pare-chocs *m inv*; (*US Rail*) chasse-pierres *m inv*.

fennel ['fenl] *n* fenouil *m*.

ferment [fə'ment] **1** *vi* fermenter. **2** *vt* faire fermenter. **3** ['fɜ:ment] *n* ferment *m*. (*fig*) **in a ~** en effervescence. ♦ **fermentation** *n* fermentation *f*.

fern [fɜ:n] *n* fougère *f*.

ferocious [fə'rəʊʃəs] *adj* féroce. ♦ **ferociously** *adv* férocement. ♦ **ferocity** *n* férocité *f*.

ferret ['ferɪt] **1** *n* furet *m*. **2** *vi* (**~ about, ~ around**) fureter.

ferret out *vt sep* dénicher.

ferroconcrete ['fereʊ'kɒŋkri:t] *n* béton *m* armé.

ferrous ['ferəs] *adj* ferreux.

ferry ['ferɪ] **1** *n* **(a)** (**~** *boat*) (*small: for people, cars*) bac *m*; (*larger: for people, cars, trains*) ferry(-boat) *m*. **~man** passeur *m*. **(b)** (*place*) passage *m*. **2** *vt* (**~ across, ~ over**) faire passer; (*fig*) *people* emmener, conduire; *things* porter.

fertile ['fɜ:taɪl] *adj* (*gen*) fertile; *creature, plant* fertile, fécond. ♦ **fertility** **1** *n* fertilité *f*; fécondité *f*; **2** *adj* de fertilité; **fertility drug** médicament *m* contre la stérilité. ♦ **fertilization** *n* fertilisation *f*. ♦ **fertilize** *vt* fertiliser; féconder. ♦ **fertilizer** *n* engrais *m*.

fervent ['fɜ:vənt], **fervid** ['fɜ:vɪd] *adj* fervent. ♦ **fervour**, (*US*) **-or** *n* ferveur *f*.

fester ['festə^r] *vi* (*Med*) suppurer; *[anger]* couver.

festival ['festɪvəl] *n* (*Rel etc*) fête *f*; (*Mus etc*) festival *m*. ♦ **festive** *adj* de fête; **the festive season** la période des fêtes; **in a festive mood** en veine de réjouissances. ♦ **festivity** *n* fête *f*, réjouissances *fpl*.

festoon [fes'tu:n] *vt* festonner (*with* de).

fetch [fetʃ] *vt* **(a)** (*go and get*) *person, thing* aller chercher; (*bring*) *person* amener; *thing* apporter. **to ~ and carry for sb** faire la bonne pour qn; (*to dog*) **~ it!** rapporte! **(b)** (*sell for*) *money* rapporter; *price* atteindre.

fetch in *vt sep person* faire rentrer; *thing* rentrer.

fetch out *vt sep person* faire sortir; *thing* sortir.

fetch up **1** *vi* se retrouver (*at* à; *in* dans). **2** *vt sep object* monter; *person* faire monter; (*vomit*) vomir.

fetching ['fetʃɪŋ] *adj* charmant.

fête [feɪt] **1** *n* fête *f*. **2** *vt* fêter.

fetid ['fetɪd] *adj* fétide, puant.

fetish ['fi:tɪʃ] *n* fétiche *m* (*objet de culte*); (*Psych*) objet *m* de la fétichisation. (*fig*) **she makes a ~ of ...** elle est obsédée par ... . ♦ **fetishist** *n* fétichiste *mf*.

fetter ['fetə^r] **1** *vt person* enchaîner; *horse, slave* (*also fig*) entraver. **2** *npl*: **~s** chaînes *fpl*; entraves *fpl*.

fettle ['fetl] *n*: **in fine ~** en pleine forme.

fetus ['fi:təs] *n* (*US*) = **foetus.**

feud [fju:d] **1** *n* querelle *f*. **family ~s** querelles de famille. **2** *vi* se quereller. **to ~ with sb** être l'ennemi juré de qn.

feudal ['fju:dl] *adj* féodal. ♦ **feudalism** *n* féodalité *f*.

fever ['fi:və^r] *n* fièvre *f*. **a bout of ~** un accès de fièvre; **high ~** forte fièvre; **the gambling ~** le démon du jeu; **a ~ of impatience** une impatience fébrile; **it reached ~ pitch** c'était à son comble. ♦ **feverish** *adj* fiévreux. ♦ **feverishly** *adv* fiévreusement.

few [fju:] *adj, pron* **(a)** (*not many*) peu (de). **~ books** peu de livres; **~ of them** peu d'entre eux; **~ come to see him** peu de gens viennent le voir; **he is one of the ~ people who ...** c'est l'une des rares personnes qui ... + *indic or subj*; **in the past ~ days** ces derniers jours; **the next ~ days** les quelques jours qui viennent; **with ~ exceptions** à de rares exceptions près; **every ~ days** tous les deux ou trois jours; **they are ~ and far between** ils sont rares; **we are very ~** nous sommes peu nombreux; **the remaining ~ minutes** les quelques minutes qui restent; **the ~ who ...** les rares personnes qui ...; (*the minority*) la minorité qui ...; **I have as ~ books as you** j'ai aussi peu de livres que vous; **I have as ~ as you** j'en ai aussi peu que vous; **how ~ there are!** qu'il y en a peu!; **how ~ they are!** qu'ils sont peu nombreux!; **so ~** si peu (de); **too ~** trop peu (de); **there were 3 too ~** il en manquait 3.

(b) (*some, several*) **a ~** quelques(-uns *or* -unes); **a ~ books** quelques livres; **a ~ more** quelques-un(e)s de plus; **quite a ~ books** pas mal* de livres; **quite a ~ (people) believed him** un bon nombre de gens *or* pas mal* de gens l'ont cru; **a ~ of these people** quelques-uns de ces gens; **a ~ of us** quelques-un(e)s d'entre nous; **a good ~ of** bon nombre de; **a ~ more days** encore quelques jours.

♦ **fewer** *adj, pron, comp of* **few** moins (de); **we have sold ~er this year** nous en avons moins vendu cette année; **he has ~er books than you** il a moins de livres que vous; **we are ~er than ...** nous sommes moins nombreux que ...; **no ~er than 37** pas moins de 37; **few came and ~er stayed** peu sont venus et encore moins sont restés. ♦ **fewest** *adj, pron, superl of* **few** le moins (de); **~est in number** le moins nombreux.

fiancé(e) [fɪ'ɑ̃:ŋseɪ] *n* fiancé(e) *m(f)*.

fiasco [fɪ'æskəʊ] *n* fiasco *m*.

fib* [fɪb] **1** *n* blague* *f*, mensonge *m*. **2** *vi* raconter des blagues*, mentir. ♦ **fibber*** *n* menteur *m*, -euse *f*.

fibre, (*US*) **-er** ['faɪbəʳ] *n* fibre *f*. ♦ **fibreboard** *n* panneau *m* fibreux. ♦ **fibreglass** *n* fibre *f* de verre. ♦ **fibroid** *n* (*Med*) fibrome *m*. ♦ **fibrositis** *n* cellulite *f*. ♦ **fibrous** *adj* fibreux.

fickle ['fɪkl] *adj* inconstant, volage.

fiction ['fɪkʃən] *n* **(a)** (*Literat*) **(works of) ~** romans *mpl*; **light ~** romans faciles à lire. **(b)** (*sth made up*) fiction *f*. **legal ~** fiction légale. **(c)** (*the unreal*) le faux. ♦ **fictional** *or* ♦ **fictitious** *adj* fictif.

fiddle ['fɪdl] **1** *n* **(a)** violon *m*. **(b)** (*: *cheating*) truc* *m*, combine* *f*. **it was a ~** c'était une combine*; **tax ~** fraude *f* fiscale. **2** *vi* **(a)** (*Mus*) jouer du violon. **(b) do stop fiddling!** tiens-toi donc tranquille!; **to ~ with a pencil** tripoter un crayon. **3** *vt* (*) *accounts, expenses claim* truquer.

fiddle about, fiddle around *vi* s'occuper vaguement, bricoler. **we just ~d about yesterday** on n'a rien fait de spécial hier.

♦ **fiddler** *n* violoneux* *m*; (*: *cheat*) combinard* *m*. ♦ **fiddlesticks*** *excl* quelle blague!* ♦ **fiddling 1** *adj* insignifiant; **2** *n* (*: *cheating etc*) combines* *fpl*. ♦ **fiddly** *adj task* délicat (et agaçant); *object* embêtant* à manier.

fidelity [fɪ'delɪtɪ] *n* fidélité *f*.

fidget ['fɪdʒɪt] **1** *vi* (**~ about, ~ around**) remuer (continuellement). **stop ~ing!** reste donc tranquille!; **to ~ with sth** tripoter qch. **2** *n*: **to be a ~** ne jamais se tenir tranquille. ♦ **fidgety** *adj* remuant, agité.

field [fi:ld] **1** *n* (*gen*) champ *m*; (*Miner*) gisement *m*; (*Aviat, Sport*) terrain *m*; (*sphere of activity*) domaine *m*. (*fig*) **a year's trial in the ~** un an d'essais sur le terrain; (*Comm*) **to be first in the ~ with sth** être le premier à lancer qch; **~ of battle** champ de bataille; (*Mil*) **to die in the ~** tomber au champ d'honneur; (*Sport*) **to take the ~** entrer en jeu; **it's outside my ~** ce n'est pas de mon domaine; **his particular ~** sa spécialité; **~ of vision** champ de vision. **2** *vt* (*Sport*) *ball* attraper; *team* faire jouer. **3** *adj* (*fig*) **~ day** grande occasion; **they had a ~ day*** cela a été une bonne journée pour eux; **~ glasses** jumelles *fpl*; **~ gun** canon *m* de campagne; **~ hospital** antenne *f* chirurgicale; **~ marshal** maréchal *m*; **~ mouse** mulot *m*; **~ sports** activités *fpl* de plein air (*chasse, pêche*). ♦ **field-test 1** *vt* soumettre aux essais sur le terrain; **2** *n* essai *m* sur le terrain. ♦ **fieldwork** *n* (*Archeol, Geol etc*) recherches *fpl* sur le terrain; (*Sociol etc*) travail *m* avec des cas sociaux.

fiend [fi:nd] *n* démon *m*. **that child's a real ~*** cet enfant est un petit monstre; **tennis ~** mordu(e)* *m(f)* du tennis. ♦ **fiendish** *adj cruelty, smile, delight, plan* diabolique; (*: *unpleasant*) abominable; **I had a ~ish time* doing ...** j'ai eu un mal fou à faire ... . ♦ **fiendishly** *adv* diaboliquement; (*) *difficult etc* abominablement.

fierce [fɪəs] *adj* (*gen*) féroce; *desire* ardent; *attack, wind, speech* violent; *hatred* implacable; *heat* intense; *competition, fighting, opponent, partisan* acharné. ♦ **fiercely** *adv* férocement; violemment; avec acharnement. ♦ **fierceness** *n* férocité *f*; violence *f*; implacabilité *f*; intensité *f*.

fiery ['faɪərɪ] *adj* (*lit*) ardent; *sky* rougeoyant; *person, speech* fougueux; *temper* violent. ♦ **fiery-tempered** *adj* irascible.

fifteen [fɪf'ti:n] *adj, n* quinze (*m*) *inv*. **about ~ books** une quinzaine de livres; **about ~** une quinzaine; (*Rugby*) **the French ~** le quinze de France; *for other phrases V* **six**. ♦ **fifteenth** *adj, n* quinzième (*mf*); (*fraction*) quinzième *m*.

fifth [fɪfθ] *adj, n* cinquième (*mf*); (*fraction*) cinquième *m*. **~ column** cinquième colonne *f*; *for other phrases V* **sixth**.

fifty ['fɪftɪ] *adj, n* cinquante (*m*) *inv*. **about ~ books** une cinquantaine de livres; **about ~** une cinquantaine; **to go ~-~ with sb** partager moitié-moitié avec qn; **we have a ~-~ chance of success** nous avons une chance sur deux de réussir; *for other phrases V* **sixty**. ♦ **fiftieth** *adj, n* cinquantième (*mf*); (*fraction*) cinquantième *m*.

fig [fɪg] *n* figue *f*; (**~ tree**) figuier *m*. **~ leaf** feuille *f* de figuier; (*on statue etc*) feuille de vigne.

fight [faɪt] (*vb: pret, ptp* **fought**) **1** *n* (*between persons*) bagarre* *f*; (*Mil*) combat *m*, bataille *f*; (*Boxing*) combat; (*against disease, poverty etc*) lutte *f* (*against* contre); (*quarrel*) dispute *f*. **he put up a good ~** il s'est bien défendu; **there was no ~ left in him** il n'avait plus envie de lutter.

2 *vi* [*person, animal*] se battre (*with* avec; *against* contre); [*troops, countries*] se battre, combattre (*against* contre); (*fig*) lutter (*for* pour; *against* contre); (*quarrel*) se disputer (*with* avec). **the dogs were ~ing over a bone** les chiens se disputaient un os; **to ~ shy of (doing) sth** tout faire pour éviter (de faire) qch; **to ~ against sleep** lutter contre le sommeil; **to ~ for one's life** lutter pour la vie.

3 *vt person, army* se battre avec *or* contre; *fire, disease, decision, legislation* lutter contre. **to ~ a battle** livrer bataille; **to ~ a losing battle against sth** se battre en pure perte contre qch; **to ~ a duel** se battre en duel; (*Jur*) **to ~ a case** défendre une cause; **to ~ one's way through the crowd** se frayer un passage à travers la foule.

fight back 1 *vi* (*in fight*) rendre les coups; (*Mil; also in argument*) se défendre; (*after illness*) réagir; (*Sport*) se reprendre. **2** *vt sep tears* refouler; *despair* lutter contre; *doubts* vaincre.

fight down *vt sep anxiety, doubts* vaincre; *desire* réprimer.

fight off *vt sep* (*Mil*) *attack* repousser; *disease, sleep* lutter contre.

fight out *vt sep*: **to ~ it out** se bagarrer* (pour régler qch).

♦ **fighter 1** *n* combattant *m*; (*Boxing*) boxeur *m*; (*fig*) lutteur *m*; (*plane*) avion *m* de chasse; **2** *adj*: **~er pilot** pilote *m* de chasse. ♦ **fighter-bomber** *n* chasseur bombardier *m*. ♦ **fighting 1** *n* (*Mil*) combat *m*; (*in streets etc*) échauffourées *fpl*; (*in *classroom, pub*) bagarres *fpl*; **2** *adj person* combatif; *troops* de combat; **~ing spirit** cran* *m*; **a ~ing chance** une assez bonne chance; (*Mil*) **~ing forces** forces *fpl* armées; **~ing line** front *m*; **~ing strength** effectif *m* mobilisable.

figment ['fɪgmənt] *n*: **a ~ of the imagination** une pure invention.

figure ['fɪgəʳ] **1** *n* **(a)** chiffre *m*. **in round ~s** en chiffres ronds; **he's good at ~s** il est doué pour le calcul; **a mistake in the ~s** une erreur de calcul; **to reach three ~s** atteindre la centaine; **a 3-~ number** un nombre *ou* un numéro de 3 chiffres; **he earns well over five ~s** il gagne bien plus de dix mille livres. **(b)** (*drawing*) figure *f*. **a ~ of eight** un huit. **(c)** (*human form*) **I saw a ~ approach** j'ai vu une forme *or* une silhouette s'approcher de moi; **she has a good ~** elle est bien faite; **remember your ~!** pense à ta ligne!; **to lose one's ~** s'épaissir; **a fine ~ of a woman** une belle femme. **(d)** (*person*) figure *f*, personnage *m*. **a ~ of fun** un guignol. **(e)** (*Literat*) figure *f*. (*fig*) **it's just a ~ of speech** ce n'est qu'une façon de parler. **2** *vt* (*imagine*) penser, s'imaginer; (*guess*) penser, supposer. **3** *vi* **(a)** (*appear*) figurer (*on a list* sur une liste); (*in play etc*) jouer un rôle. **(b)** (*: *make sense*) **that ~s** ça s'explique.
figure on *vt fus* (*US*) compter sur. **I ~d on his coming** je comptais qu'il viendrait.
figure out *vt sep* (*understand*) arriver à comprendre; (*calculate*) calculer. **I can't ~ it out** ça me dépasse*.
♦ **figurative** *adj language, meaning* figuré; (*Art*) figuratif.

filament ['fɪləmənt] *n* filament *m*.

filch [fɪltʃ] *vt* voler, chiper*.

file[1] [faɪl] **1** *n* (*tool*) lime *f*. **2** *vt* (**~ away, ~ down**) limer. **to ~ one's nails** se limer les ongles.
♦ **filings** *npl* limaille *f*.

file[2] [faɪl] **1** *n* (*folder*) dossier *m*; (*with hinges*) classeur *m*; (*for drawings: also in filing drawers*) carton *m*; (*papers*) dossier (*on sb/sth* sur qn/qch); (*Computers*) fichier *m*. **to put a document on the ~** joindre une pièce au dossier. **2** *adj* (*US*) **~ clerk** documentaliste *mf*. **3** *vt notes* classer; (*into ~*) joindre au dossier; (*Jur*) *claim, petition* déposer. **to ~ a suit against sb** intenter un procès à qn.
♦ **filing 1** *n*: **to do the filing** s'occuper du classement; **2** *adj*: **filing cabinet** classeur *m* (*meuble*); **filing clerk** documentaliste *mf*.

file[3] [faɪl] **1** *n* file *f*. **in Indian ~** en file indienne; **in single ~** en file. **2** *vi* marcher en file. **to ~ in/out** *etc* entrer/sortir *etc* en file; **the soldiers ~d past the general** les soldats ont défilé devant le général; **they ~d past the ticket collector** ils sont passés un à un devant le poinçonneur.

filial ['fɪlɪəl] *adj* filial.

filibuster ['fɪlɪbʌstəʳ] *n* (*US Pol*) obstructionniste *mf*; (*pirate*) flibustier *m*.

filigree ['fɪlɪgri:] **1** *n* filigrane *m* (*en métal etc*). **2** *adj* en filigrane.

fill [fɪl] **1** *vt* (*gen*) remplir (*with* de); *teeth* plomber; *need* répondre à. **smoke ~ed the room** la pièce s'est remplie de fumée; **the wind ~ed the sails** le vent a gonflé les voiles; **~ed with** *admiration* rempli de; *anger, despair* en proie à; **to ~ a vacancy** *[employer]* pourvoir à un emploi; *[employee]* prendre un poste vacant; **the position is already ~ed** le poste est déjà pris; **that ~s the bill** cela fait l'affaire. **2** *vi* (**~ up**) se remplir (*with* de). **3** *n*: **to eat one's ~** manger à sa faim; **to drink one's ~** boire tout son content; **I've had my ~ of listening to her** j'en ai assez de l'écouter.
fill in 1 *vi*: **to ~ in for sb** remplacer qn (temporairement). **2** *vt sep* **(a)** *form, questionnaire* remplir; *account, report* compléter. **to ~ sb in on sth*** mettre qn au courant de qch. **(b)** *hole* boucher; *door* murer; *gaps* combler; *outline* remplir.
fill out 1 *vi [sails etc]* gonfler; *[person]* forcir. **2** *vt sep form* remplir.
fill up 1 *vi* (*Aut*) faire le plein d'essence; *V also* **fill 2**. **2** *vt sep container, form* remplir; *hole* boucher. (*Aut*) **~ her up!*** faites le plein!
♦ **filler** *n* (*funnel*) entonnoir *m*; (*for cracks in wood etc*) mastic *m*. ♦ **filling 1** *n* (*in tooth*) plombage *m*; (*Culin*) garniture *f*; **2** *adj food* substantiel; **~ing station** station-service *f*.

fillet ['fɪlɪt] **1** *n* filet *m*. **~ steak** tournedos *m*. **2** *vt meat* désosser; *fish* découper en filets. **~ed sole** filets *mpl* de sole.

fillip ['fɪlɪp] *n* coup *m* de fouet (*fig*).

filly ['fɪlɪ] *n* pouliche *f*.

film [fɪlm] **1** *n* (*Phot*) pellicule *f*; (*Cine*) film *m*; (*for wrapping food*) scellofrais *m* ®. **to go to the ~s** aller au cinéma; **the ~ is on at ...** le film passe à ...; **a ~ of dust** une fine couche de poussière. **2** *vt* filmer. **3** *adj*: **~ camera** caméra *f*; **~ fan** cinéphile *mf*; **~ library** cinémathèque *f*; **~ rights** droits *mpl* d'adaptation (cinématographique); **~ script** scénario *m*; **~ star** vedette *f* (de cinéma), star *f*; **~ studio** studio *m* (de cinéma). ♦ **filmstrip** *n* film *m* fixe. ♦ **filmy** *adj* léger, vaporeux.

filter ['fɪltəʳ] **1** *n* filtre *m*. **2** *adj* (*Aut*) **~ lane** ≈ voie *f* de droite; (*Aut*) **~ light** flèche *f*; **~ paper** papier *m* filtre. **3** *vt liquids* filtrer; *air* purifier. **4** *vi* (*Aut*) **to ~ to the left** tourner à la flèche; *[people]* **to ~ back** *etc* revenir *etc* par petits groupes (espacés); **the news began to ~ in** *or* **through** on a commencé petit à petit à avoir des nouvelles.
♦ **filter-tipped** *adj* à bout filtre.

filth [fɪlθ] *n* (*lit*) saleté *f*, crasse *f*; (*excrement*) ordure *f*; (*fig*) saletés *fpl*. **it's sheer ~** c'est plein de saletés *or* de grossièretés. ♦ **filthy** *adj* (*gen*) sale, crasseux; *habit* dégoûtant; *language* ordurier; (*) *weather etc* abominable; **she's got a ~y mind** elle a l'esprit mal tourné.

fin [fɪn] *n [fish, whale]* nageoire *f*; *[shark]* aileron *m*; *[aircraft]* empennage *m*; *[radiator etc]* ailette *f*; *[frogman]* palme *f*.

final ['faɪnl] **1** *adj* (*last*) dernier; (*conclusive*) définitif. (*Fin*) **~ instalment** versement *m* libératoire; **the umpire's decision is ~** la décision de l'arbitre est sans appel; **and that's ~!** un point c'est tout! **2** *n* (*Sport*) finale *f*. (*Univ*) **the ~s** les examens *mpl* de dernière année.
♦ **finale** [fɪ'nɑ:lɪ] *n* finale *m*; (*fig*) **the grand ~e** l'apothéose *f*. ♦ **finalist** *n* finaliste *mf*. ♦ **finality** *n* irrévocabilité *f*; **with an air of ~ity** avec fermeté. ♦ **finalization** *n* dernière mise *f* au point; confirmation *f* définitive. ♦ **finalize** *vt text, report, arrangements, plans* mettre au point les derniers détails de; *preparations* mettre la dernière main à; *decision* confirmer de façon définitive; *date* fixer de façon définitive. ♦ **finally** *adv* (*lastly*) enfin, pour terminer; (*eventually*) enfin, finalement; (*once and for all*) définitivement.

finance [faɪ'næns] **1** *n* finance *f*. **Ministry of F~** ministère *m* des Finances. **2** *vt* (*supply money for*) financer; (*obtain money for*) trouver des fonds pour. **3** *adj company, news, page* financier.
♦ **financial** *adj* (*gen*) financier; *year* budgétaire.
♦ **financier** *n* financier *m*.

finch [fɪntʃ] *n* fringillidé *m* (*pinson, bouvreuil, gros-bec etc*).

find [faɪnd] *pret, ptp* **found 1** *vt* **(a)** (*gen*) trouver; *sth or sb lost* retrouver; *cure* découvrir. **he found himself in Paris** il s'est retrouvé à Paris; **I'll ~ my way about all right** je trouverai très bien mon chemin; **it found its way into my handbag** ça s'est retrouvé dans mon sac; **it found its way into his essay** ça s'est glissé dans sa dissertation; **we left everything as we found it** nous avons tout laissé tel quel; **to ~ that** trouver que, s'apercevoir que, constater que; **I ~ her very pleasant** je la trouve très agréable; **he ~s it difficult to ...** il a du mal à

...; **he ~s it impossible to leave** il ne peut se résoudre à partir; **he ~s it impossible to walk** il lui est impossible de marcher; **you won't ~ it easy** vous ne le trouverez pas facile; **to ~ some difficulty in doing** éprouver une certaine difficulté à faire; (*fig*) **to ~ one's feet** s'adapter; (*Jur*) **to ~ sb guilty** prononcer qn coupable; **the court found that ...** le tribunal a conclu que ... . **(b)** (*supply*) fournir; (*obtain*) obtenir, trouver. **wages all found** *or* (*US*) **and found** salaire logé et nourri; **go and ~ me a needle** va me chercher une aiguille; **there are no more to be found** il n'en reste plus.

2 *vi* (*Jur*) se prononcer (*for* en faveur de; *against* contre).

3 *n* trouvaille *f*.

find out 1 *vi*: **to ~ out about sth** (*enquire*) se renseigner sur qch; (*discover*) découvrir qch, apprendre qch. **2** *vt sep* (*gen*) découvrir (*that* que); *answer* trouver. **to ~ sb out** démasquer qn.

♦ **findings** *npl* conclusions *fpl*.

fine[1] [faɪn] **1** *n* amende *f*, contravention *f* (*esp Aut*). **I got a ~ for ...** j'ai attrapé une contravention pour ... . **2** *vt* condamner à une amende, donner une contravention à. **to be ~d** recevoir une amende *or* une contravention (*£10* de 10 livres; *for sth* pour qch; *for doing* pour avoir fait).

fine[2] [faɪn] **1** *adj* **(a)** (*not coarse*) (*gen*) fin; *metal* pur; *workmanship, feelings, taste* délicat; *distinction* subtil. **not to put too ~ a point on it ...** bref, ...; **he's got it down to a ~ art** il le fait à la perfection; **~ art, the ~ arts** les beaux arts *mpl*. **(b)** *clothes, future, weather* beau (*f* belle); *musician etc* excellent. **it's ~ this afternoon** il fait beau cet après-midi; (*fig*) **one ~ day** un beau jour; **a ~ lady** une grande dame; (*excl*) **~!** entendu!; (*iro*) **a ~ thing!*** c'est du beau!; (*iro*) **you're a ~ one to talk!** c'est bien à toi de le dire! **2** *adv* **(a)** (*excellently*) très bien. **you're doing ~!** tu te débrouilles bien!, ça va!; **I'm feeling ~** je me sens très bien. **(b)** (*finely*) finement, fin; *cut, chop* menu. (*fig*) **you've cut it a bit ~** vous avez calculé un peu juste.

fine down 1 *vi* (*get thinner*) s'affiner. **2** *vt sep* (*reduce*) réduire; (*simplify*) simplifier.

♦ **finely** *adv written* admirablement; *dressed* magnifiquement; *adjust* délicatement; *chop* menu, fin. ♦ **fineness** *n* finesse *f*; pureté *f*; délicatesse *f*; subtilité *f*. ♦ **finery** *n* parure *f*; **in all her ~ry** dans ses plus beaux atours.

finesse [fɪ'nes] *n* finesse *f*; (*Cards*) impasse *f*.

finger ['fɪŋgəʳ] **1** *n* doigt *m*. **index ~** index *m*; **little ~** petit doigt; **middle ~** médius *m*; **ring ~** annulaire *m*; **between ~ and thumb** entre le pouce et l'index; (*fig*) **to put one's ~ on** mettre le doigt sur; **to keep one's ~s crossed** dire une petite prière (*fig*) (*for sb* pour qn); **his ~s are all thumbs** il est très maladroit de ses mains; **she can twist him round her little ~** elle le mène par le bout du nez; **he has a ~ in the pie** il y est pour quelque chose; **he wouldn't lift a ~ to help me** il ne lèverait pas le petit doigt pour m'aider; **to pull one's ~ out*** faire un effort.

2 *vt* toucher, (*pej*) tripoter; *keyboard, keys* toucher; (*feel*) *money, silk* palper.

3 *adj*: **~ board** touche *f* (*de violon etc*); **~ bowl** rince-doigts *m inv*; **~mark** trace *f* de doigt.

♦ **fingernail** *n* ongle *m* (*de la main*). ♦ **fingerprint 1** *n* empreinte *f* digitale; **2** *vt object* relever les empreintes digitales sur; *person* prendre les empreintes digitales de; **3** *adj*: **~print expert** expert *m* en dactyloscopie. ♦ **fingerstall** *n* doigtier *m*. ♦ **fingertip** *n* bout *m* du doigt; **he has the whole matter at his ~tips** il connaît l'affaire sur le bout du doigt; **a machine with ~tip control** une machine d'un maniement (très) léger.

finicky ['fɪnɪkɪ] *adj person* difficile (*about sth* pour qch), pointilleux; *work, job* qui demande de la patience.

finish ['fɪnɪʃ] **1** *n* **(a)** (*end*) fin *f*; (*Sport*) arrivée *f*. (*fig*) **to be in at the ~** assister au dénouement (d'une affaire); **to fight to the ~** se battre jusqu'au bout. **(b)** (*appearance etc*) finitions *fpl*. **it's a solid car but the ~ is not good** la voiture est solide mais les finitions sont mal faites; **paint with a matt ~** peinture *f* mate; **table with an oak ~** table (*stained*) teintée *or* (*veneered*) plaquée chêne.

2 *vt* (*end*) (*gen*) finir (*doing* de faire); *work* finir, terminer, achever; (*use up*) *supplies, cake* finir, terminer. **~ your soup** finis *or* mange ta soupe; **to put the ~ing touch to sth** mettre la dernière main à qch; **that last mile nearly ~ed me*** ces derniers quinze cents mètres ont failli m'achever.

3 *vi* (*gen*) finir; *[book, film, game, meeting]* finir, s'achever, se terminer; *[holiday, contract]* prendre fin. **the meeting was ~ing** la réunion tirait à sa fin; **he ~ed by saying that ...** il a terminé en disant que ...; (*Sport*) **to ~ first** arriver premier; (*Sport*) **~ing line** ligne *f* d'arrivée. **I've ~ed with the paper** je n'ai plus besoin du journal; **I've ~ed with politics** j'en ai fini avec la politique; **she's ~ed with him** elle a rompu avec lui.

finish off 1 *vi* terminer, finir. **2** *vt sep work* terminer, achever; *food, meal* terminer, finir; (*kill*) achever.

finish up 1 *vi*: **it ~ed up as ...** ça a fini par être ...; **he ~ed up in Rome** il s'est retrouvé à Rome. **2** *vt sep food, supplies* finir.

♦ **finished** *adj product* fini; *performance* accompli; (*done for*) fichu*; (*: *tired*) à plat*.

finite ['faɪnaɪt] *adj* **(a)** fini, limité. **a ~ number** un nombre fini. **(b)** (*Gram*) *mood, verb* fini.

Finland ['fɪnlənd] *n* Finlande *f*. ♦ **Finn** *n* Finlandais(e) *m(f)*; (*Finnish speaker*) Finnois(e) *m(f)*. ♦ **Finnish 1** *adj* finlandais; finnois; **2** *n* finnois *m*.

fir [fɜːʳ] *n* sapin *m*. **~ cone** pomme *f* de pin.

fire ['faɪəʳ] **1** *n* **(a)** (*gen, also fig*) feu *m*; (*house-~ etc*) incendie *m*. **house on ~** maison *f* en feu *or* en flammes; **the chimney was on ~** il y avait un feu de cheminée; (*fig*) **he's playing with ~** il joue avec le feu; **forest ~** incendie de forêt; **to insure o.s. against ~** s'assurer contre l'incendie; **to set ~ to sth** mettre le feu à qch; **in front of a roaring ~** devant une belle flambée. **(b)** (*Mil*) feu *m*. **to open ~** ouvrir le feu, faire feu; **~!** feu!; **to come under ~** (*Mil*) essuyer le feu de l'ennemi; (*fig: be criticized*) être vivement critiqué.

2 *adj*: **~ alarm** avertisseur *m* d'incendie; **~ brigade,** (*US*) **~ department** (sapeurs-)pompiers *mpl*; **~ door** porte *f* anti-incendie; **~ drill** répétition *f* des consignes d'incendie; **~ engine** (*vehicle*) voiture *f* de pompiers; (*apparatus*) pompe *f* à incendie; **~ escape** (*staircase*) escalier *m* de secours; (*ladder*) échelle *f* d'incendie; **~ exit** sortie *f* de secours; **~ extinguisher** extincteur *m* (d'incendie); **~ hazard** *or* **risk** danger *m* d'incendie; **~ insurance** assurance- incendie *f*; **~ irons** garniture *f* de foyer; **~ prevention** mesures *fpl* de sécurité contre l'incendie; **~ regulations** consignes *fpl* en cas d'incendie; **~ station** caserne *f* de pompiers.

3 *vt* **(a)** (*set ~ to*) mettre le feu à; *imagination etc* enflammer; *pottery* cuire. **(b)** *gun* décharger; *rocket, shot, salute* tirer (*at* sur). **to ~ a gun at sb** tirer (un coup de fusil) sur qn; **to ~ questions at sb** bombarder qn de questions. **(c)** (*: *dismiss*) renvoyer, flanquer à la porte*. **you're ~d!** vous êtes renvoyé!

4 *vi* (*shoot*) tirer, faire feu (*at* sur). (*fig*) **~ ahead!*, ~ away!*** vas-y, raconte!

♦ **firearm** *n* arme *f* à feu. ♦ **fireball** *n* (*meteor*) bolide *m*; (*lightning, nuclear*) boule *f* de feu; (*fig*) personne *f* très dynamique. ♦ **firebrand** *n* brandon *m*; (*mischief-maker*) brandon de discorde. ♦ **firebreak** *n* pare-feu *m inv.* ♦ **firebug*** *n* pyromane *mf.* ♦ **firecracker** *n* pétard *m.* ♦ **firedogs** *npl* chenets *mpl.* ♦ **fireguard** *n* garde-feu *m inv.* ♦ **firelight** *n*: **by ~light** à la lueur du feu. ♦ **firelighter** *n* allume-feu *m inv.* ♦ **fireman** *n* (sapeur-)pompier *m.* ♦ **fireplace** *n* cheminée *f*, foyer *m.* ♦ **fireproof** *adj material, door* ignifugé; *dish* allant au feu. ♦ **fire-raiser** *n* pyromane *mf.* ♦ **fireside** *n*: **by the ~side** au coin *m* du feu; **~side chair** fauteuil *m* club. ♦ **firewood** *n* bois *m* de chauffage. ♦ **firework** *n* feu *m* d'artifice; **~works (display)** feu d'artifice. ♦ **firing 1** *n [guns]* tir *m*; **2** *adj*: **firing line** ligne *f* de tir; **firing squad** peloton *m* d'exécution.

firm[1] [fɜːm] *n* (*Comm*) compagnie *f*, firme *f.*

firm[2] [fɜːm] *adj* (*gen*) ferme; *faith, friendship* solide; *character, look* résolu. (*fig*) **I'm on ~ ground** je suis sur mon terrain; **as ~ as a rock** ferme comme le *or* un roc; **to be ~ with sb** être ferme avec qn; **to stand ~** tenir bon. ♦ **firmly** *adv* (*gen*) fermement; *speak* avec fermeté. ♦ **firmness** *n* fermeté *f*; solidité *f*; résolution *f.*

first [fɜːst] **1** *adj* premier. **the ~ of May** le premier mai; **the twenty-~ time** la vingt et unième fois; **Charles the F~** Charles Premier, Charles Ier; **in the ~ place** d'abord, en premier lieu; **~ thing in the morning** dès le matin; (*on waking*) dès le réveil; **~ thing tomorrow** dès demain matin; **~ things first!** les choses importantes d'abord!; **to give ~ aid** donner les secours *mpl* d'urgence; (*fig*) **he didn't even get to ~ base*** il n'a même pas franchi le premier obstacle; **~ cousin** cousin(e) *m(f)* germain(e); **~ edition** première édition *f*, (*valuable*) édition originale; **on the ~ floor** (*Brit*) au premier (étage); (*US*) au rez-de-chaussée; (*Scol*) **~ form** ≈ sixième *f*; **~ name** prénom *m*; (*Theat etc*) **~ night** première *f*; (*Jur*) **~ offender** délinquant *m* primaire; **~ performance** (*Cine, Theat*) première *f*; (*Mus*) première audition.

2 *adv* **(a)** (*gen*) d'abord. **~ A then B** d'abord A ensuite B, premièrement A deuxièmement B; **~ of all** tout d'abord; **~ and foremost** en tout premier lieu; **~ come ~ served** les premiers arrivés seront les premiers servis; **ladies ~!** les dames d'abord!; **he arrived ~** il est arrivé le premier; **he came ~ in the exam** il a été reçu premier à l'examen; **he says ~ one thing and then another** il dit tantôt ceci, tantôt cela; **~ and last** avant tout; **I must finish this ~** il faut que je termine (*subj*) ceci d'abord. **(b)** (*for the ~ time*) pour la première fois. **when did you ~ meet him?** quand est-ce que vous l'avez rencontré pour la première fois? **(c)** (*in preference*) plutôt. **I'd die ~!** plutôt mourir!

3 *n* **(a)** premier *m*, -ière *f*. **they were the ~ to come** ils sont arrivés les premiers. **(b) at ~** d'abord, au commencement, au début; **from ~ to last** du début jusqu'à la fin; **from the ~** dès le début. **(c)** (*~ gear*) première *f* (vitesse). **in ~** en première.

♦ **first-aid** *adj*: **~-aid classes** cours *mpl* de secourisme; **~-aid kit** trousse *f* de pharmacie; **~-aid post** poste *m* de secours. ♦ **first-class 1** *adj* (*Rail etc*) de première (classe); (*excellent*) excellent, de première classe; **~-class mail** courrier *m* tarif normal; **~-class honours degree** ≈ licence *f* avec mention très bien; **2** *adv travel* en première (classe). ♦ **first-day** *adj* (*Post*) **~-day cover** émission *f* du premier jour. ♦ **first-generation** *adj*: **he's a ~-generation American** il n'est américain que depuis une génération. ♦ **first-hand** *adj, adv* de première main. ♦ **firstly** *adv* premièrement. ♦ **first-named** *n* premier *m*, -ière *f*. ♦ **first-rate** *adj* excellent, formidable*.

fiscal ['fɪskəl] *adj* fiscal; *year* budgétaire.

fish [fɪʃ] **1** *n, pl ~ or ~es* poisson *m*. **~ and chips** du poisson frit avec des frites; (*fig*) **I've got other ~ to fry** j'ai d'autres chats à fouetter; (*fig*) **it's neither ~ nor fowl nor good red herring** ce n'est ni chair ni poisson; **he's like a ~ out of water** il est complètement dépaysé; **he's a queer ~!*** c'est un drôle de numéro!* **2** *adj*: **~ farm** centre *m* de pisciculture; **~ knife** couteau *m* à poisson; **~ paste** pâte *f* d'anchois (*or* de homard *etc*); **~ shop** poissonnerie *f*; **~ slice** pelle *f* à poisson; **~ tank** aquarium *m*. **3** *vi* pêcher. **to go ~ing** aller à la pêche; **to go salmon ~ing** aller à la pêche au saumon; **to ~ for trout** pêcher la truite; **to ~ for** *compliments* chercher; *information* tâcher d'obtenir. **4** *vt trout, salmon* pêcher; *river, pool* pêcher dans. **they ~ed a cat out of the well** ils ont repêché un chat du puits; **he ~ed a handkerchief out of his pocket** il a extirpé un mouchoir de sa poche.

fish out, fish up *vt sep* (*from water*) repêcher; (*from box, drawer etc*) sortir, extirper (*from* de).

♦ **fish-and-chip shop** *n* débit *m* de fritures. ♦ **fishbone** *n* arête *f* (de poisson). ♦ **fishbowl** *n* bocal *m* à poissons. ♦ **fishcake** *n* croquette *f* de poisson. ♦ **fisherman** *n* pêcheur *m*; **he's a keen ~erman** il aime beaucoup la pêche. ♦ **fishery** *n* pêcherie *f*. ♦ **fish-fingers** *npl* (*US*: **fish-sticks**) bâtonnets *mpl* de poisson. ♦ **fish-hook** *n* hameçon *m*. ♦ **fishing 1** *n* pêche *f*; **2** *adj*: **~ing boat** bateau *m* de pêche; **~ing fleet** flottille *f* de pêche; **~ing grounds** pêches *fpl*; **~ing line** ligne *f* de pêche; **~ing net** (*on ~ing boat*) filet *m* (de pêche); *[angler]* épuisette *f*; **~ing port** port *m* de pêche; **~ing rod** canne *f* à pêche; **~ing tackle** attirail *m* de pêche. ♦ **fishmonger** *n* poissonnier *m*, -ière *f*. ♦ **fishpond** *n* étang *m* à poissons. ♦ **fish-sticks** = **fish-fingers.** ♦ **fishwife** *n*: **she talks like a ~wife** elle a un langage de poissarde. ♦ **fishy** *adj smell* de poisson; (*: *suspect*) suspect, louche.

fission ['fɪʃən] *n* fission *f*.

fissure ['fɪʃəʳ] *n* fissure *f*.

fist [fɪst] *n* poing *m*. **he shook his ~ at me** il m'a menacé du poing. ♦ **fistful** *n* poignée *f*. ♦ **fisticuffs** *npl* coups *mpl* de poing.

fit[1] [fɪt] **1** *adj* **(a)** (*suitable, suited*) *person* capable (*for* de); *time, occasion* propice; (*worthy*) digne (*for* de); (*right and proper*) convenable, correct. **~ to eat** (*palatable*) mangeable; (*not poisonous*) comestible; (*qualified etc*) **to be ~ for a job** avoir la compétence nécessaire pour faire un travail; (*after illness*) **~ for duty** en état de reprendre le travail; **he's not ~ to drive** il n'est pas capable de *or* pas en état de conduire; **I'm not ~ to be seen** je ne suis pas présentable; **~ to wear** mettable; **~ for habitation** habitable; **to see** *or* **think ~ to do** trouver *or* juger bon de faire; **as I think ~** comme bon me semblera; **he's not ~ company for my son** ce n'est pas une compagnie pour mon fils; **she goes on until she's ~ to drop*** elle continue jusqu'à ce qu'elle tombe (*subj*) de fatigue. **(b)** (*in health*) en bonne santé, en pleine forme. **to be as ~ as a fiddle** se porter comme un charme.

2 *n*: **your dress is a very good ~** votre robe est tout à fait à votre taille; **it's rather a tight ~** c'est un peu juste.

3 *vt* **(a)** *[clothes etc]* aller à. **this coat ~s you well** ce manteau est bien à votre taille; **the key doesn't ~ the lock** la clef ne va pas pour la serrure; **it ~s me like a glove** cela me va comme un gant. **(b)** (*match*) *description* répondre à. **it doesn't ~ the facts** cela ne concorde pas avec les faits; **the punishment should ~ the crime** la punition doit être proportionnée à l'offense. **(c)** (*gen*) mettre, fixer (*on sth* sur qch); *garment* ajuster (*on sb* sur qn). **to ~ a key in the lock** engager une clef dans la serrure; **to ~ 2 things together** ajuster 2 objets; **to have a new window ~ted** faire poser une nouvelle fenêtre; **car ~ted with a radio** voiture équipée d'une radio; **he has**

been ~ted with a new hearing aid on lui a mis un nouvel appareil auditif. **(d)** (*make* ~) préparer (*sb for sth* qn à qch; *sb to do* qn à faire).

4 *vi [clothes]* aller, être bien ajusté; *[key, machine, part]* entrer, aller; *[facts etc]* cadrer, correspondre (*with sth* avec qch). **if the description ~s, he must be the thief** si la description est la bonne, ce doit être lui le voleur; **it all ~s now!** tout s'éclaire!

fit in 1 *vi* **(a)** *[fact]* s'accorder (*with* avec). **(b)** *[remark]* être en harmonie (*with* avec). **he left the firm because he didn't ~ in** il a quitté la compagnie parce qu'il n'arrivait pas à s'intégrer. **2** *vt sep object* faire entrer; (*fig*) *appointment, visitor* prendre, caser*; *plans* adapter (*with* à), faire concorder (*with* avec).

fit on *vt sep* fixer, poser.

fit out *vt sep* (*gen*) équiper; *ship* armer.

fit up *vt sep* pourvoir (*with* de).

♦ **fitment** *n* **(a)** (*built-in furniture*) meuble *m* encastré; *[kitchen]* élément *m* (de cuisine); **the table is a ~ment** la table est encastrée; **(b)** (*for vacuum cleaner, mixer etc*) accessoire *m*; **the light ~ment** l'appareil *m* d'éclairage. ♦ **fitness** *n* **(a)** (*health*) santé *f or* forme *f* (physique); **(b)** (*suitability*) *[remark]* à-propos *m*; *[person]* aptitudes *fpl* (*for* pour). ♦ **fitted** *adj garment* ajusté; **~ted carpet** moquette *f*; **~ted sheet** drap-housse *m*; **to be ~ted to (do) sth** être apte à (faire) qch. ♦ **fitter** *n* (*Dress*) essayeur *m*, -euse *f*; (*Tech*) monteur *m*; *[carpet etc]* poseur *m*. ♦ **fitting 1** *adj* approprié (*to* à); **~ting room** salon *m* d'essayage; **2** *n* (*Dress*) essayage *m*; (*in house etc*) **~tings** installations *fpl*; **furniture and ~tings** mobilier *m* et installations. ♦ **fittingly** *adv dress* de façon appropriée; *say* avec à-propos; *happen* à propos.

fit[2] [fɪt] *n* **(a)** (*Med*) accès *m*, attaque *f*. **~ of coughing** quinte *f* de toux. **(b)** (*outburst: of anger etc*) mouvement *m*, accès *m*. **~ of crying** crise *f* de larmes; **to have** *or* **throw* a ~** avoir *or* piquer* une crise; **to be in ~s (of laughter), to get a ~ of the giggles** avoir le fou rire; **~s of enthusiasm** des accès d'enthousiasme; **in ~s and starts** par à-coups. ♦ **fitful** *adj showers* intermittent; *sleep* agité. ♦ **fitfully** *adv move, work* par à-coups; *sleep* de façon intermittente.

five [faɪv] *adj, n* cinq (*m*) *inv*; *for phrases V* **six.** ♦ **five-and-ten-cent store** *n* bazar *m*. ♦ **fivefold 1** *adj* quintuple; **2** *adv* au quintuple. ♦ **fiver*** *n* billet *m* de cinq livres *or* (*US*) de cinq dollars. ♦ **five-star** *adj*: **~-star restaurant** ≈ restaurant *m* (à) trois étoiles. ♦ **five-year** *adj*: **~-year plan** plan *m* quinquennal.

fix [fɪks] **1** *vt* **(a)** (*with nails etc*) fixer; (*with ropes etc*) attacher; (*drive in*) enfoncer; *attention* fixer (*on* sur); *hopes* mettre (*on sth* en qch); *blame* mettre (*on sb* sur le dos de qn; *on sth* sur qch); (*Phot*) fixer. **to ~ one's eyes on** fixer du regard; **to ~ sth in one's mind** graver qch dans son esprit. **(b)** (*arrange, decide*) *details, plans* décider; *time, price, limit* fixer. **on the date ~ed** à la date convenue. **(c)** (*deal with*) arranger; (*mend*) réparer. **I'll ~ it all** je vais tout arranger; **he ~ed it with the police before ...** il s'est arrangé avec la police avant de ...; **I'll soon ~ him*** je vais lui régler son compte; **to ~ one's hair*** se passer un coup de peigne; **can I ~ you a drink?** puis-je vous offrir un verre?; **I'll go and ~ us sth to eat** je vais vite nous faire qch à manger. **(d)** (*: *bribe etc*) *person* acheter; *match, election, trial* truquer.

2 *n* **(a)** (*) ennui *m*, embêtement* *m*. **to be in a ~** être dans le pétrin; **what a ~!** nous voilà dans le pétrin! **(b)** (*Drugs sl*) piqûre *f*. **(c)** (*Aviat, Naut*) position *f*. **to take a ~ on** déterminer la position de.

fix on 1 *vt fus* choisir. **2** *vt sep lid* fixer, attacher.

fix up 1 *vi* s'arranger (*to do* pour faire). **2** *vt sep* arranger. **let's ~ it all up now** décidons tout de suite des détails; **to ~ sb up with sth** obtenir qch pour qn; **we ~ed them up for one night** nous leur avons trouvé à coucher pour une nuit.

♦ **fixation** *n* (*fig*) obsession *f*; **to have a ~ation about** être obsédé par. ♦ **fixative** *n* fixatif *m*. ♦ **fixed** *adj* (*gen*) fixe; *smile* figé; *determination* inébranlable; **of no ~ed abode** sans domicile fixe; **~ed menu** menu *m* à prix fixe; **how are we ~ed for time?*** on a combien de temps?; **how are you ~ed for tonight?** qu'est-ce que vous faites ce soir? ♦ **fixedly** *adv* fixement. ♦ **fixture** *n* **(a)** (*in building etc*) **~tures** installations *fpl*; **sold with ~tures and fittings** vendu avec toutes les installations; (*fig*) **she's a ~ture*** elle fait partie du mobilier*; **(b)** (*Sport*) match *m* (prévu); **~ture list** calendrier *m*.

fizz [fɪz] *vi [champagne etc]* pétiller; *[steam etc]* siffler.

fizz up *vi* mousser.

♦ **fizzy** *adj soft drink* gazeux; *wine* mousseux.

fizzle ['fɪzl] *vi* pétiller.

fizzle out *vi [firework]* rater; *[event, enterprise, plan]* ne rien donner; *[book]* se terminer en queue de poisson; *[enthusiasm, interest]* tomber.

flabbergast* ['flæbəgɑːst] *vt* sidérer*.

flabby ['flæbɪ] *adj* flasque.

flag[1] [flæg] **1** *n* drapeau *m*; (*Naut*) pavillon *m*; (*for charity*) insigne *m* (*d'une œuvre charitable*). **~ of convenience** pavillon de complaisance; (*fig*) **to go down with ~s flying** mener la lutte jusqu'au bout; (*fig*) **to keep the ~ flying** maintenir une implantation. **2** *vt* pavoiser; (**~ down**) faire signe (de s'arrêter) à. **3** *adj*: **~ day** journée *f* de vente d'insignes (*in aid of* pour). ♦ **flagpole** *or* ♦ **flagstaff** *n* mât *m*. ♦ **flagship** *n* vaisseau *m* amiral.

flag[2] [flæg] *vi [plants etc]* dépérir; *[athlete, walker, health]* s'affaiblir; *[worker, zeal, courage etc]* se relâcher; *[conversation]* languir; *[interest]* faiblir; *[enthusiasm]* tomber.

flag[3] [flæg] *n* (**~stone**) dalle *f*.

flagon ['flægən] *n* grande bouteille *f*.

flagrant ['fleɪgrənt] *adj* flagrant.

flair [flɛəʳ] *n* flair *m*. **to have a ~ for** avoir du flair pour.

flake [fleɪk] **1** *n [snow, cereal etc]* flocon *m*; *[metal etc]* paillette *f*. **2** *vi* (**~ off**) *[stone, plaster etc]* s'effriter; *[paint]* s'écailler; *[skin]* peler. **3** *vt* (**~ off**) écailler.

flake out‡ *vi* (*faint*) tourner de l'œil*; (*fall asleep*) s'endormir tout d'une masse.

flamboyant [flæm'bɔɪənt] *adj* flamboyant (*also Archit*); *person* haut en couleur.

flame [fleɪm] **1** *n* flamme *f*. **in ~s** en flammes, en feu; **to go up in ~s** s'enflammer brusquement. **2** *vi [fire]* flamber; *[passion]* brûler. **her cheeks ~d** ses joues se sont empourprées.

flame up *vi [fire]* flamber; *[anger, angry person]* exploser.

♦ **flamethrower** *n* lance-flammes *m inv*. ♦ **flaming** *adj* ardent; (*: *furious*) furibard*; (‡: *annoying*) fichu* (*before n*).

flamingo [flə'mɪŋgəʊ] *n, pl* **~s** *or* **~es** flamant *m* (rose).

flammable ['flæməbl] *adj* inflammable.

flan [flæn] *n* tarte *f*.

Flanders ['flɑːndəz] *n* Flandre(s) *f(pl)*.

flank [flæŋk] **1** *n* (*gen*) flanc *m*; (*Culin*) flanchet *m*. **2** *vt* flanquer. **~ed by 2 policemen** flanqué de 2 gendarmes.

flannel ['flænl] *n* flanelle *f*; (*face* ~) gant *m* de toilette. ♦ **flannelette** *n* pilou *m*.

flap [flæp] **1** *n [pocket, envelope]* rabat *m*; *[counter]* abattant *m*; (*: *panic*) panique *f*. **to be in a ~** être dans tous ses états. **2** *vi [wings, shutters]* battre; *[sails, garment]* claquer; (*: *be panicky*) paniquer*. **3** *vt*: **to ~ its wings** battre des ailes.

flare [flɛəʳ] **1** *n* feu *m*, signal *m* (lumineux); (*Mil*)

fusée *f* éclairante; (*Aviat: for target*) bombe *f* éclairante; (*for runway*) balise *f*.
2 *adj* (*Aviat*) ~ **path** piste *f* balisée.
3 *vi [match]* s'enflammer; *[candle]* briller; *[sunspot]* brûler.
flare up *vi [fire]* s'embraser; *[person, political situation]* exploser; *[anger, fighting]* éclater. ♦ **flared** *adj skirt* évasé. ♦ **flare-up** *n [fire]* flambée *f* (soudaine); *[war, quarrel, fighting]* intensification *f* soudaine; (*outburst of rage*) crise *f* de colère; (*sudden dispute*) altercation *f*.
flash [flæʃ] **1** *n* **(a)** *[flame, jewels]* éclat *m*. ~ **of lightning** éclair *m*; **in a** ~ en un clin d'œil, tout d'un coup; **a** ~ **in the pan** un feu de paille (*fig*); ~ **of inspiration** éclair de génie. **(b)** (*news* ~) flash *m* (d'information). **(c)** (*Phot*) flash *m*. **2** *vi [jewels]* étinceler; *[light]* clignoter; *[eyes]* lancer des éclairs. *[person, vehicle]* **to** ~ **past** *etc* passer *etc* comme un éclair; **the thought** ~**ed through his mind that ...** un instant, il a pensé que ... . **3** *vt* **(a)** *light* projeter; *torch* diriger (*on* sur). **she** ~**ed him a look of contempt** elle lui a jeté un regard de mépris; (*Aut*) **to** ~ **one's headlights** faire un appel de phares (*at sb* à qn). **(b)** (*flaunt*) étaler. **don't** ~ **all that money around** n'étale pas tout cet argent comme ça. **4** *adj*: ~ **bulb** ampoule *f* de flash; ~ **cube** cube-flash *m*; ~ **gun** flash *m*; ~ **point** (*Chem*) point *m* d'ignition; (*fig*) point critique. ♦ **flashback** *n* (*Cine*) flashback *m inv*. ♦ **flasher** *n* (*device*) clignotant *m*. ♦ **flashing** *adj*: ~**ing light** (*or* **indicator** *etc*) clignotant *m*. ♦ **flashlight** *n* (*Phot*) flash *m*; (*torch*) lampe *f* de poche. ♦ **flashy** *adj person, taste* tapageur; *jewellery, car, colour* tape-à-l'œil *inv*.
flask [flɑːsk] *n* (*Pharm*) fiole *f*; (*bottle*) bouteille *f*; (*for pocket*) flasque *f*; (*vacuum* ~) bouteille *f* Thermos ®.
flat[1] [flæt] **1** *adj* **(a)** (*gen*) plat; *tyre* à plat; (*Sport*) *race* de plat. **as** ~ **as a pancake*** *tyre* plat comme une galette; *surface, countryside* tout plat; **a** ~ **dish** un plat creux; ~ **nose** nez épaté; **to have** ~ **feet** avoir les pieds plats; **he was lying** ~ **on the floor** il était étendu à plat par terre; **lay the book** ~ pose le livre à plat; ~ **fish** poisson plat; ~ **racing,** ~ **season** plat *m*; **in a** ~ **spin*** dans tous ses états. **(b)** *taste, style* monotone, plat; *joke, story* qui tombe à plat; *experience* plutôt décevant; *battery* à plat; *beer etc* éventé; (*not shiny*) *colour* mat. **I was feeling rather** ~ je me sentais sans ressort. **(c)** (*Mus*) *voice* faux. **B** ~ si *m* bémol. **(d)** *refusal, denial* net, catégorique. **and that's** ~**!*** un point c'est tout!* **(e)** (*fixed*) fixe. ~ **rate of pay** salaire *m* fixe; ~ **rate** taux *m* fixe.
2 *adv say, tell, refuse* carrément; *sing* faux. ~ **broke**ꜝ fauché (comme les blés)*; **in 10 seconds** ~ en 10 secondes pile*; **to go** ~ **out** *[runner]* donner son maximum; *[person running in street]* courir comme un dératé*; *[car]* rouler à sa vitesse de pointe; **to be working** ~ **out** travailler d'arrache-pied; **to be** ~ **out** (*lying*) être étendu de tout son long; (*: *exhausted*) être à plat*; (*: *asleep*) dormir; (ꜝ: *drunk*) être rétaméꜝ.
3 *n [hand, blade]* plat *m*; (*Mus*) bémol *m*; (*US Aut*) pneu *m* crevé.
♦ **flat-bottomed** *adj* à fond plat. ♦ **flat-chested** *adj* qui n'a pas de poitrine. ♦ **flatfooted** *adj* aux pieds plats. ♦ **flatiron** *n* fer *m* à repasser. ♦ **flatly** *adv deny, refuse* catégoriquement; *say* tout net. ♦ **flatness** *n* égalité *f*, aspect *m* plat; (*dullness*) monotonie *f*. ♦ **flatten** *vt path, road* aplanir; *metal* aplatir; *town, building* raser; *[wind, storm etc] crops* coucher; **to** ~**ten o.s. against** s'aplatir contre. ♦ **flatten out 1** *vi [countryside, road]* s'aplanir; *[aircraft]* se redresser; **2** *vt sep path* aplanir; *metal* aplatir; *map etc* ouvrir à plat.
flat[2] [flæt] *n* (*Brit*) appartement *m*. ♦ **flat-hunting: to go** ~**-hunting** chercher un appartement. ♦ **flatlet** *n* studio *m*. ♦ **flatmate** *n*: **my** ~**mate** la fille (*or* le garçon *etc*) avec qui je partage mon appartement.
flatter [ˈflætəʳ] *vt* flatter. ♦ **flatterer** *n* flatteur *m*, -euse *f*. ♦ **flattering** *adj person, remark* flatteur; *clothes, photograph* qui avantage. ♦ **flatteringly** *adv* flatteusement. ♦ **flattery** *n* flatterie *f*.
flatulence [ˈflætjʊləns] *n* flatulence *f*.
flaunt [flɔːnt] *vt* étaler, afficher.
flautist [ˈflɔːtɪst] *n* flûtiste *mf*.
flavour, (*US*) **-or** [ˈfleɪvəʳ] **1** *n* goût *m*, saveur *f*; *[ice cream]* parfum *m*. **the** ~ **of Paris in the twenties** l'atmosphère *f* du Paris des années vingt. **2** *vt* donner du goût à; (*with fruit, spirits*) parfumer (*with* à). **pineapple-**~**ed** (parfumé) à l'ananas. ♦ **flavo(u)ring** *n* (*in sauce etc*) assaisonnement *m*; (*in cake etc*) parfum *m*; **vanilla** ~**ing** essence *f* de vanille.
flaw [flɔː] *n* (*gen*) défaut *m*; (*in contract, procedure etc*) vice *m* de forme; (*in arrangements, plans*) inconvénient *m*. ♦ **flawed** *adj* imparfait. ♦ **flawless** *adj* parfait.
flax [flæks] *n* lin *m*. ♦ **flaxen-haired** *adj* aux cheveux de lin.
flay [fleɪ] *vt* (*skin*) écorcher; (*beat*) rosser; (*criticize*) éreinter.
flea [fliː] *n* puce *f*. ~ **market** marché *m* aux puces; **to send sb off with a** ~ **in his ear*** envoyer promener* qn. ♦ **fleabite** *n* piqûre *f* de puce; (*fig*) vétille *f*. ♦ **flea-pit**ꜝ *n* ciné* *m* miteux.
fleck [flek] **1** *n [colour]* moucheture *f*; *[sunlight]* petite tache *f*; *[dust]* particule *f*. **2** *vt*: **blue** ~**ed with white** bleu moucheté de blanc; **hair** ~**ed with grey** cheveux *mpl* poivre et sel.
fled [fled] *pret, ptp of* **flee.**
fledged [fledʒd] *adj* (*fig*) **fully-**~ *doctor, architect* diplômé; **a fully-**~ **British citizen** un citoyen britannique à part entière. ♦ **fledg(e)ling** *n* oiselet *m*.
flee [fliː] *pret, ptp* **fled 1** *vi* fuir (*before* devant), s'enfuir (*from* de), se réfugier (*to* auprès de). **they fled** ils se sont enfuis, ils se sont sauvés. **2** *vt town, country* s'enfuir de; *temptation, danger* fuir.
fleece [fliːs] **1** *n* toison *f*. **2** *vt* (*rob*) voler; (*overcharge*) estamper*. ♦ **fleece-lined** *adj* doublé de mouton. ♦ **fleecy** *adj clouds* floconneux; *blanket* laineux.
fleet[1] [fliːt] *n* flotte *f*. (*fig*) **a** ~ **of vehicles** un parc automobile; (*Brit*) **F**~ **Air Arm** aéronavale *f*.
fleet[2] [fliːt] *adj* (~**-footed**) au pied léger.
fleeting [ˈfliːtɪŋ] *adj time, memory* fugitif; *beauty, pleasure* éphémère; *moment, visit* bref.
Fleming [ˈflemɪŋ] *n* Flamand(e) *m(f)*. ♦ **Flemish 1** *adj* flamand; **2** *n* (*Ling*) flamand *m*; **the Flemish** les Flamands *mpl*.
flesh [fleʃ] *n* chair *f*. ~ **wound** blessure *f* superficielle; **to make sb's** ~ **creep** donner la chair de poule à qn; **I'm only** ~ **and blood** je ne suis qu'un homme (*or* une femme) comme les autres; **my own** ~ **and blood** les miens *mpl*; **it is more than** ~ **and blood can stand** c'est plus que la nature humaine ne peut endurer; **in the** ~ en chair et en os; **to demand one's pound of** ~ exiger son dû. ♦ **fleshy** *adj* charnu.
flew [fluː] *pret of* **fly**[2].
flex [fleks] **1** *vt body, knees* fléchir; *muscle* faire jouer. **2** *n [lamp, iron]* fil *m*; *[telephone]* cordon *m*. ♦ **flexible** *adj* flexible; ~**ible working hours** heures *fpl* de travail élastiques. ♦ **flexibility** *n* flexibilité *f*. ♦ **flextime** *n* les horaires *mpl* libres.
flick [flɪk] **1** *n* **(a)** (*with tail, duster*) petit coup; (*with finger*) chiquenaude *f*; (*with wrist*) petit mouvement (rapide). **(b) the** ~**s**ꜝ le ciné*. **2** *adj*: ~ **knife** couteau *m* à cran d'arrêt. **3** *vt* donner un petit coup à.
flick off *vt sep dust, ash* enlever d'une chiquenaude.
flick through *vt fus book* feuilleter.
flicker [ˈflɪkəʳ] **1** *vi [flames, light]* danser; (*before*

going out) vaciller; *[needle on dial]* osciller; *[eyelids]* battre. **2** *n* danse *f*; vacillement *m*. **in the ~ of an eyelid** en un clin d'œil; **without a ~** sans sourciller; **a ~ of hope** une lueur d'espoir. ♦ **flickering** *adj* dansant; vacillant; battant.

flier ['flaɪəʳ] *n* aviateur *m*, -trice *f*.

flight¹ [flaɪt] **1** *n* (*gen*) vol *m*; *[ball]* trajectoire *f*. **in ~** en plein vol; **~ number 776 from/to Madrid** le vol numéro 776 en provenance/à destination de Madrid; **did you have a good ~?** vous avez fait bon voyage?; **a ~ of fancy** une envolée de l'imagination; **in the top ~ of scientists** parmi les scientifiques les plus marquants; **a top-~ firm** une compagnie de pointe; **~ of stairs** escalier *m*; **to climb 3 ~s** monter 3 étages; **he lives three ~s up** il habite au troisième. **2** *adj* (*Aviat*) **~ deck** poste *m* de pilotage; **~ path** trajectoire *f* (de vol); **~ recorder** enregistreur *m* de vol.

flight² [flaɪt] *n* (*act of fleeing*) fuite *f*. **to put to ~** mettre en fuite; **to take (to) ~** prendre la fuite.

flighty ['flaɪtɪ] *adj* frivole.

flimsy ['flɪmzɪ] **1** *adj dress* trop léger; *cloth, paper* mince; *house* peu solide; *excuse, reasoning* pauvre. **2** *n* papier *m* pelure *inv*. ♦ **flimsily** *adv*: **flimsily built** peu solide.

flinch [flɪntʃ] *vi* tressaillir. **to ~ from sth** reculer devant qch; **without ~ing** sans broncher.

fling [flɪŋ] (*vb: pret, ptp* **flung**) **1** *n* (*throw*) lancer *m*. (*fig*) **to have one's ~** se payer du bon temps; **to go on a ~** aller faire la foire*, (*in shops*) faire des folies; (*attempt*) **to have a ~ at doing** essayer de faire. **2** *vt stone etc* jeter, lancer (*at sb* à qn; *at sth* sur *or* contre qch); *remark, accusation* lancer (*at sb* à qn). **to ~ sb into jail** jeter qn en prison; **to ~ the window open** ouvrir toute grande la fenêtre; **to ~ one's arms round sb's neck** se jeter au cou de qn; **to ~ on/off one's coat** enfiler/enlever son manteau d'un geste brusque; **to ~ o.s. into a job** se lancer à corps perdu dans un travail. **3** *vi*: **to ~ off/out** *etc* partir/sortir *etc* brusquement.

fling away *vt sep* (*throw out*) jeter; (*waste*) gaspiller.

fling out *vt sep person* mettre à la porte; *unwanted object* jeter.

fling up *vt sep* jeter en l'air. **to ~ one's arms up** lever les bras au ciel; **he flung up his head** il a brusquement relevé la tête.

flint [flɪnt] *n* (*gen*) silex *m*; (*for spark, lighter*) pierre *f* (à briquet).

flip [flɪp] **1** *adj*: **the ~ side of a record** l'autre face *f* d'un disque. **2** *vt* donner une chiquenaude à. **he ~ped the letter over to me** il m'a passé la lettre d'une chiquenaude.

flip off *vt sep* faire tomber.

flip through *vt fus book* feuilleter.

♦ **flip-flops** *npl* (*sandals*) tongs *fpl* ®.

flippant ['flɪpənt] *adj* désinvolte, irrévérencieux. ♦ **flippancy** *n* désinvolture *f*, irrévérence *f*. ♦ **flippantly** *adv* avec désinvolture.

flipper ['flɪpəʳ] *n [seal etc]* nageoire *f*. *[swimmer]* **~s** palmes *fpl*.

flipping* ['flɪpɪŋ] *adj* fichu* (*before n*).

flirt [flɜːt] **1** *vi* flirter (*with* avec). **to ~ with an idea** caresser une idée. **2** *n*: **he's a great ~** il est très flirteur. ♦ **flirtation** *n* flirt *m*. ♦ **flirtatious** *adj* flirteur.

flit [flɪt] **1** *vi [bats, butterflies etc]* voltiger. **the idea ~ted through his head** l'idée lui a traversé l'esprit; **she ~ted in and out** elle n'a fait qu'entrer et sortir. **2** *n*: **to do a moonlight ~** déménager à la cloche de bois.

float [fləʊt] **1** *n* (*Fishing, Plumbing*) flotteur *m*; (*cork*) bouchon *m*; *[seaplane etc]* flotteur; (*vehicle in a parade*) char *m*. **2** *vi* (*gen*) flotter; *[ship]* être à flot; *[bather]* faire la planche; *[vision etc]* planer. **to ~ down the river** descendre la rivière. **3** *vt boat* faire flotter; (*refloat*) remettre à flot; *currency* laisser flotter; *company* fonder; *share issue* émettre; *loan* lancer.

float away *vi* partir à la dérive.

float off 1 *vi [wreck etc]* se déséchouer. **2** *vt sep* déséchouer.

♦ **floating** *adj dock, rib, vote, currency* flottant; *population* instable; *assets* circulant; **~ing voter** électeur *m*, -trice *f* indécis(e).

flock [flɒk] **1** *n [animals, geese]* troupeau *m*; *[birds]* vol *m*; *[people]* foule *f*; (*Rel*) ouailles *fpl*. **2** *vi* affluer. **to ~ in/out** *etc* entrer/sortir *etc* en foule; **to ~ round sb** s'attrouper autour de qn.

floe [fləʊ] *n* banquise *f*.

flog [flɒg] *vt* **(a)** flageller. **to ~ an idea to death*** rabâcher une idée; (*fig*) **to ~ a dead horse** perdre sa peine et son temps. **(b)** (*: *sell*) vendre. ♦ **flogging** *n* flagellation *f*; (*Jur*) fouet *m* (*sanction*).

flood [flʌd] **1** *n* inondation *f*; *[river]* crue *f*; *[light]* torrent *m*; *[tears, letters]* déluge *m*; (*Bible*) déluge. **~ tide** marée *f* montante. **2** *vt* (*gen; fig*) inonder (*with* de); *carburettor* noyer. **to ~ the market** inonder le marché (*with* de). **3** *vi [river]* déborder; *[people]* affluer. **the crowd ~ed into the streets** la foule a envahi les rues.

flood in *vi [sunshine]* entrer à flots; *[people]* entrer en foule.

flood out *vt sep house* inonder. **the villagers were ~ed out** les inondations ont forcé les villageois à évacuer leurs maisons.

♦ **floodgate** *n* (*fig*) **to open the ~gates** ouvrir les vannes (*to* à). ♦ **flooding** *n* inondations *fpl*. ♦ **floodlight 1** *vt pret, ptp* **floodlit** *buildings* illuminer; *match* éclairer (aux projecteurs); (*fig*) mettre en lumière; **2** *n* (*device*) projecteur *m*; (*light*) lumière *f* (des projecteurs); **to play a match under ~lights** jouer un match en nocturne. ♦ **floodlighting** *n* illumination *f*; éclairage *m*; **let's go and see the ~lighting** allons voir les illuminations. ♦ **floodlit** *adj* illuminé; en nocturne.

floor [flɔːʳ] **1** *n* **(a)** (*gen*) sol *m*; (*~boards*) plancher *m*; (*for dance*) piste *f* (de danse). **stone/tiled ~** sol dallé/carrelé; **on the ~** par terre, sur le sol; **a question from the ~ of the house** une question de l'auditoire; **sea ~** fond *m* de la mer. **(b)** (*storey*) étage *m*. **on the first ~** (*Brit*) au premier étage; (*US*) au rez-de-chaussée. **2** *vt* (*knock down*) terrasser; (*baffle*) couper le sifflet à*. **he was completely ~ed by this** il n'a rien trouvé à répondre. **3** *adj*: **~ covering** revêtement *m* de sol; **~ polish** cire *f*; **~ polisher** cireuse *f*; **~ show** attractions *fpl* (*dans un cabaret etc*). ♦ **floorboard** *n* planche *f* (*de plancher*). ♦ **floorcloth** *n* serpillière *f*. ♦ **floorwalker** *n* chef *m* de rayon.

flop [flɒp] **1** *vi* **(a)** (*drop etc*) s'effondrer, s'affaler (*on* sur; *into* dans). **(b)** *[play]* faire un four; *[scheme etc]* être un fiasco. **2** *n* (*) *[business venture, scheme]* fiasco *m*. **he was a terrible ~** il s'est payé un échec monumental*.

flora ['flɔːrə] *n* flore *f*.

floral ['flɔːrəl] *adj* floral. **~ tribute** fleurs *fpl* et couronnes *fpl*.

florid ['flɒrɪd] *adj person, complexion* rougeaud; *literary style, architecture* tarabiscoté.

florist ['flɒrɪst] *n* fleuriste *mf*.

flounce [flaʊns] *vi*: **to ~ in/out** *etc* entrer/sortir *etc* dans un mouvement d'humeur (*or* d'indignation *etc*).

flounder¹ ['flaʊndəʳ] *n* (*fish*) flet *m*.

flounder² ['flaʊndəʳ] *vi* patauger (péniblement), (*more violently*) se débattre. (*fig*) **he ~ed through the rest of the speech** il a fini le discours en bredouillant.

flour ['flaʊəʳ] *n* farine *f*. **~ mill** minoterie *f*.

flourish ['flʌrɪʃ] **1** *vi [plants etc]* bien venir; *[business etc]* prospérer; *[writer, artist etc]* avoir du succès; *[literature, the arts, painting]* être en plein essor; *[person]* être en pleine forme. **2** *vt*

stick, book etc brandir. **3** *n* (*gen*) fioriture *f*; (*under signature*) parafe *m*. **he took the lid off with a ~** il a enlevé le couvercle avec un grand moulinet du bras; **a ~ of trumpets** une fanfare. ♦ **flourishing** *adj business, plant* florissant; *person* d'une santé florissante.
flout [flaʊt] *vt orders, advice* passer outre à; *conventions, society* se moquer de.
flow [fləʊ] **1** *vi* (*gen*) couler; *[electric current, blood in veins]* circuler; *[hair etc]* flotter; (*fig: result*) découler, résulter (*from* de). *[people]* **to ~ in/out** entrer/sortir en foule; *[liquid]* **to ~ out of** s'écouler de, sortir de; **the money keeps ~ing in** l'argent rentre bien; **to ~ past sth** passer devant qch; **to ~ back** refluer; **the water ~ed over the fields** l'eau s'est répandue dans les champs; **the river ~s into the sea** le fleuve se jette dans la mer; **tears were ~ing down her cheeks** les larmes coulaient sur ses joues. **2** *n [tide]* flux *m*; *[river]* courant *m*; *[electric current, blood in veins]* circulation *f*; *[blood from wound]* écoulement *m*; *[orders, replies, words]* flot *m*; *[music]* déroulement *m*. **3** *adj*: **~ chart, ~ sheet** organigramme *m*. ♦ **flowing** *adj movement* gracieux; *dress, hair* flottant; *style* coulant.
flower ['flaʊəʳ] **1** *n* fleur *f*. **in ~** en fleurs. **2** *vi* fleurir. **to be ~ing** être en fleurs. **3** *adj*: **~ arrangement** (*art*) art *m* du bouquet; (*exhibit*) composition *f* florale; **~ bed** parterre *m*; **~ garden** jardin *m* d'agrément; **~ shop** boutique *f* de fleuriste; **at the ~ shop** chez le *or* la fleuriste; **~ show** floralies *fpl*, (*smaller*) exposition *f* de fleurs. ♦ **flowered** *adj cloth etc* à fleurs. ♦ **flowering 1** *n* floraison *f*; **2** *adj* (*in* ~) en fleurs; (*which ~s*) *shrub etc* à fleurs. ♦ **flowerpot** *n* pot *m* (à fleurs). ♦ **flower-seller** *n* bouquetière *f*. ♦ **flowery** *adj meadow* fleuri; *material* à fleurs; *style, essay, speech* fleuri.
flown [fləʊn] *ptp of* **fly**[2].
flu [flu:] *n* grippe *f*.
fluctuate ['flʌktjʊeɪt] *vi [prices etc]* fluctuer; *[person]* varier (*between* entre). ♦ **fluctuation** *n* fluctuation *f*; variation *f*.
flue [flu:] *n* conduit *m* (de cheminée). **~ brush** hérisson *m* (*de ramoneur*).
fluent ['flu:ənt] *adj style* coulant. **to be a ~ speaker** avoir la parole facile; **he is ~ in Italian** il parle couramment l'italien. ♦ **fluency** *n* facilité *f*, aisance *f*; **his fluency** l'aisance avec laquelle il s'exprime (*in* en). ♦ **fluently** *adv speak a language* couramment; *speak, write* avec facilité.
fluff [flʌf] **1** *n* (*on birds, young animals*) duvet *m*; (*from material*) peluche *f*; (*dust on floors*) moutons *mpl* (*de poussière*). **2** *vt* **(a)** (~ *out*) *feathers* ébouriffer; *pillows, hair* faire bouffer. **(b)** (*: *do badly*) *lines in play etc* rater. ♦ **fluffy** *adj bird* duveteux; *hair* bouffant; *toy* en peluche; *material* pelucheux.
fluid ['flu:ɪd] **1** *adj* fluide. **~ ounce** *mesure de capacité* (= *0,028L*); **my plans are still fairly ~** je n'ai pas encore de plans très fixes. **2** *n* fluide *m* (*also Chem*), liquide *m*. (*as diet*) **he's on ~s only** il ne peut prendre que des liquides. ♦ **fluidity** *n* fluidité *f*.
fluke [flu:k] *n* coup *m* de chance. **by a (sheer) ~** par un hasard extraordinaire.
flummox* ['flʌməks] *vt* couper le sifflet à*.
flung [flʌŋ] *pret, ptp of* **fling.**
fluorescent [flʊə'resnt] *adj lighting* fluorescent. **~ strip** tube *m* fluorescent.
fluoride ['flʊəraɪd] *n* fluor *m*. **~ toothpaste** dentifrice *m* au fluor. ♦ **fluoridation** *n* traitement *m* au fluor.
flurry ['flʌrɪ] *n* rafale *f*; (*fig*) agitation *f*; *[activity, excitement]* accès *m*. ♦ **flurried** *adj*: **to get flurried** s'affoler (*at* pour).
flush[1] [flʌʃ] **1** *n* **(a)** (*in sky*) lueur *f* rouge; *[blood]* flux *m*; (*blush*) rougeur *f*. (*Med*) **hot ~es** bouffées *fpl* de chaleur. **(b)** *[beauty, health, youth]* éclat *m*; *[joy]* élan *m*; *[excitement]* accès *m*. **in the first ~ of victory** dans l'ivresse *f* de la victoire. **2** *vi* rougir (*with* de). **3** *vt* nettoyer à grande eau. **to ~ the lavatory** tirer la chasse (d'eau).
flush away *vt sep* (*down sink/drain*) faire partir par l'évier/par l'égout; (*down lavatory*) faire partir (en tirant la chasse d'eau).
♦ **flushed** *adj* (tout) rouge; **they were ~ed with success** le succès leur tournait la tête.
flush[2] [flʌʃ] **1** *adj* **(a)** au même niveau (*with* que), au *or* à ras (*with* de). **~ with the ground** à ras de terre; **a door ~ with the wall** une porte dans l'alignement du mur; **~ against** tout contre. **(b) to be ~ (with money)‡** être en fonds. **2** *vt*: **to ~ a door** rendre une porte plane.
flush[3] [flʌʃ] *vt* (~ *out*) *game, birds* lever; (*fig*) *person* forcer à se montrer.
fluster ['flʌstəʳ] *vt* énerver, troubler. **to get ~ed** s'énerver.
flute [flu:t] *n* (*Mus*) flûte *f*. ♦ **flutist** *n* (*US*) flûtiste *mf*.
flutter ['flʌtəʳ] **1** *vi [flag, ribbon]* flotter; *[bird, moth]* voleter; *[wings]* battre; *[leaf]* tomber en tourbillonnant; *[person]* aller et venir dans une grande agitation; *[heart]* palpiter; *[pulse]* battre (faiblement). **2** *vt fan, paper* jouer de. **to ~ one's eyelashes** battre des cils (*at sb* dans la direction de qn). **3** *n* (*nervousness*) agitation *f*. **in a ~** tout troublé; (*gamble*) **to have a ~*** parier une petite somme (*on* sur).
flux [flʌks] *n*: **to be in a state of ~** changer sans arrêt.
fly[1] [flaɪ] **1** *n* mouche *f*. **they died like flies** ils mouraient comme des mouches; **he wouldn't hurt a ~** il ne ferait pas de mal à une mouche; (*fig*) **he's the ~ in the ointment** le gros obstacle, c'est lui; **there are no flies on him‡** il n'est pas né d'hier. **2** *adj*: **~ fishing** pêche *f* à la mouche; **~ paper** papier *m* tue-mouches; **~ swat(ter)** tapette *f*; (*Boxing*) **~ weight** poids *m* mouche. ♦ **fly-blown** *adj* défraîchi.
fly[2] [flaɪ] *pret* **flew,** *ptp* **flown 1** *vi* **(a)** (*gen*) voler; *[air passenger]* voyager en avion; *[flag]* flotter. **to ~ over London** survoler Londres; **the planes flew past *or* over at 3 p.m.** les avions sont passés à 15 heures; **to ~ across *or* over the Channel** *[bird, plane, person]* survoler la Manche; *[passenger]* traverser la Manche en avion; **we flew in from Rome** nous sommes venus de Rome par avion; **to ~ away *or* off** s'envoler; (*fig*) **he is ~ing high** il voit grand; (*fig*) **to find that the bird has flown** trouver l'oiseau envolé.
(b) *[time]* passer vite; *[car, people]* filer*. *[person]* **to ~ in** *etc* entrer *etc* à toute vitesse; **I must ~!** il faut que je me sauve!; **to ~ to sb's assistance** voler au secours de qn; **to ~ into a rage, to ~ off the handle** s'emporter; **to let ~ at sb** (*in angry words*) s'en prendre violemment à qn; (*shoot*) tirer sur qn; **to let ~ a stone** jeter une pierre; **to ~ at sb/at sb's throat** sauter sur qn/à la gorge de qn; **the door flew open** la porte s'est ouverte brusquement.
(c) (*flee*) fuir (*before* devant), s'enfuir (*from* de), se réfugier (*to* auprès de). **~ for your life!** fuyez!
2 *vt* **(a)** *aircraft* piloter; *person* emmener par avion; *goods* transporter par avion; *standard, admiral's flag etc* arborer. **to ~ the French flag** battre pavillon français; **to ~ a kite** faire voler un cerf-volant; (*fig*) lancer un ballon d'essai (*fig*); **to ~ the Atlantic** traverser l'Atlantique (en avion); **we will ~ you to Italy for £80** nous vous offrons le voyage d'Italie par avion pour 80 livres.
(b) to ~ the country s'enfuir du pays.
3 *n*: **flies** (*on trousers*) braguette *f*; (*Theat*) cintres *mpl*.
♦ **flying 1** *n* (*action*) vol *m*; (*activity*) aviation *f*;

he likes ~ing il aime l'avion; **2** *adj fish, machine, saucer, doctor* volant; **to take a ~ing jump** sauter avec élan; (*Sport*) **~ing start** départ *m* lancé; (*fig*) **to get off to a ~ing start** prendre un excellent départ; **~ing visit** visite *f* éclair *inv*; **~ing ambulance** avion *m* (*or* hélicoptère *m*) sanitaire; **~ing boat** hydravion *m*; **~ing buttress** arc-boutant *m*; (*Police*) **F~ing Squad** brigade *f* volante de la police judiciaire; **~ing time** heures *fpl* de vol.
♦ **flyleaf** *n* page *f* de garde. ♦ **flyover** *n* (*Aut*) toboggan *m*; (*Aviat: also* **flypast**) défilé *m* aérien. ♦ **flysheet** *n* feuille *f* volante. ♦ **flywheel** *n* volant *m* (*Tech*).

foal [fəʊl] *n* poulain *m*.

foam [fəʊm] **1** *n* (*gen*) mousse *f*; *[sea, animal]* écume *f*. **2** *adj*: **~ bath** bain *m* moussant; **~ plastic** mousse *f* de plastique; **~ rubber** caoutchouc *m* mousse. **3** *vi [sea]* écumer; *[soapy water]* mousser. **to ~ at the mouth** (*lit*) écumer; (*fig*) écumer de rage. ♦ **foam-backed** *adj carpet* à sous-couche de mousse.

fob [fɒb] *vt*: **to ~ sth off on sb** refiler* qch à qn; **to ~ sb off with promises** se débarrasser de qn par de belles promesses.

fo'c'sle ['fəʊksl] *n* gaillard *m* d'avant.

focus ['fəʊkəs] **1** *n, pl* **~es** *or* **foci** (*gen*) foyer *m*; *[interest]* centre *m*. (*Phot*) **in ~** au point; (*fig*) **the ~ of attention** le point de mire (*fig*). **2** *vt instrument, camera* régler (*on* sur), mettre au point; *light* faire converger (*on* sur); *one's efforts, attention* concentrer (*on* sur). **to ~ one's eyes on sth** fixer ses yeux sur qch. **3** *vi [light, rays]* converger (*on* sur); *[eyes, person]* accommoder. **to ~ on sth** fixer son regard sur qch; (*Phot*) faire le réglage sur qch. ♦ **focal** *adj* focal; **focal point** foyer *m*; (*fig*) point *m* de mire.

fodder ['fɒdəʳ] *n* fourrage *m*.

foe [fəʊ] *n* adversaire *mf*.

foetus ['fi:təs] *n* fœtus *m*. ♦ **foetal** *adj* fœtal.

fog [fɒg] **1** *n* brouillard *m*. (*fig*) **to be in a ~** ne plus savoir où l'on en est. **2** *vt person* embrouiller; (*Phot*) voiler. **to ~ the issue** embrouiller la question. **3** *adj*: **~ bank** banc *m* de brume; **~ signal** (*Naut*) signal *m* de brume; (*Rail*) pétard *m*.
♦ **fogbound** *adj* bloqué par le brouillard. ♦ **foggy** *adj weather* brumeux; *day* de brouillard; *ideas* confus; **it's ~gy** il fait du brouillard; **I haven't the ~giest (idea** *or* **notion)!*** pas la moindre idée!
♦ **foghorn** *n* sirène *f* de brume; **a voice like a ~horn** une voix tonitruante. ♦ **foglamp** *or* ♦ **foglight** *n* phare *m* antibrouillard.

fogey* ['fəʊgɪ] *n*: **old ~** vieille baderne* *f*.

foible ['fɔɪbl] *n* petite manie *f*.

foil[1] [fɔɪl] *n* (*metal sheet*) feuille *f* de métal; (*cooking or kitchen ~*) papier *m* d'aluminium, alu* *m*; (*Fencing*) fleuret *m*. **to act as a ~ to sb/sth** mettre qn/qch en valeur.

foil[2] [fɔɪl] *vt plans, attempts* déjouer.

foist [fɔɪst] *vt*: **to ~ sth off on sb** refiler* qch à qn; **to ~ o.s. on to sb** s'imposer à qn *or* (*as guest*) chez qn.

fold [fəʊld] **1** *n* pli *m*. (*Geol*) **~s** plissement *m*. **2** *vt* (*gen*) plier. **to ~ one's arms** croiser les bras. **3** *vi [chair, table]* se (re)plier; (*: *fail*) *[newspaper]* cesser de paraître; *[business]* fermer; *[play]* quitter l'affiche.

fold away 1 *vi [table, bed]* se (re)plier. **2** *vt sep clothes etc* plier et ranger.

fold back *vt sep* rabattre.

fold over *vt sep* replier.

fold up 1 *vi* (*: *fail*) faire fiasco. **2** *vt sep paper etc* plier, replier.
♦ **foldaway** *adj bed etc* pliant. ♦ **folder** *n* (*file*) chemise *f*; (*with hinges*) classeur *m*; (*for drawings*) carton *m*; (*papers*) dossier *m*; (*leaflet*) dépliant *m*. ♦ **folding** *adj bed etc* pliant; *door* en accordéon; **~ing seat** pliant *m*; (*Aut, Theat*) strapontin *m*.

...fold [fəʊld] *suf*: **twenty~** (*adj*) par vingt; (*adv*) vingt fois.

foliage ['fəʊlɪɪdʒ] *n* feuillage *m*.

folio ['fəʊlɪəʊ] *n* (*sheet*) folio *m*; (*volume*) in-folio *m*.

folk [fəʊk] **1** *npl* (*also* **~s**) gens *mpl* (*adj f if before n*). **good ~(s)** de braves gens, de bonnes gens; **old ~(s)** les vieux *mpl*, les vieilles gens; **hullo ~s!*** bonjour tout le monde!*; **what will ~(s) think?** qu'est-ce qu'on va penser?; (*pl: relatives*) **my ~s*** ma famille. **2** *adj dance, tale* folklorique. **~ music** (*gen*) musique *f* folklorique; (*contemporary*) folk *m*; **~ singer** (*gen*) chanteur *m*, -euse *f* de chansons folkloriques *or* (*contemporary*) de folk; **~ song** chanson *f* folklorique, (*modern*) chanson folk *inv*. ♦ **folklore** *n* folklore *m*. ♦ **folksy*** *adj story, humour* populaire; *person* bon enfant *inv*.

follow ['fɒləʊ] **1** *vt* (*gen*) suivre; *suspect* filer; *serial, strip cartoon* lire (régulièrement); *football team* être supporter de; *career* poursuivre. **we're being ~ed** on nous suit; **to have sb ~ed** faire filer qn; **a bodyguard ~ed the president** un garde du corps accompagnait le président; **~ed by** suivi de; **he ~ed his father into the business** il est entré dans l'affaire sur les traces de son père; **to ~ sb's advice** suivre les conseils de qn; **to ~ suit** (*Cards*) fournir (*in clubs etc* à trèfle *etc*); (*fig*) en faire autant; **I don't quite ~ (you)** je ne vous suis pas tout à fait.

2 *vi* **(a)** (*come after*) suivre. **to ~ right behind sb, to ~ hard on sb's heels** être sur les talons de qn; (*fig*) **to ~ in sb's footsteps** marcher sur les traces de qn; **as ~s** comme suit; **his argument was as ~s** son raisonnement était le suivant; **what is there to ~?** qu'est-ce qu'il y a après? **(b)** (*result*) s'ensuivre (*that* que), découler (*from* de). **that doesn't ~** pas forcément. **(c)** (*understand*) suivre, comprendre.

follow about, follow around *vt sep* suivre (partout).

follow on *vi* (*come after*) suivre; (*result*) découler (*from* de).

follow out, follow through *vt sep idea, plan* poursuivre jusqu'au bout.

follow up 1 *vi* (*Ftbl etc*) suivre l'action. **2** *vt sep* **(a)** (*benefit from*) *advantage, success* tirer parti de; *offer* donner suite à. **(b)** (*not lose track of*) *person, case* suivre. **(c)** (*reinforce*) *victory* asseoir; *remark* faire suivre (*with* de). **they ~ed up the broadcast with another equally good** ils ont donné à cette émission une suite qui a été tout aussi excellente.
♦ **follower** *n* partisan *m*; **the ~ers of fashion** ceux qui s'intéressent à la mode. ♦ **following 1** *adj* suivant; **the ~ing day** le jour suivant, le lendemain; **~ing wind** vent *m* arrière; **2** *n* (*supporters*) partisans *mpl*; **a large ~ing** de nombreux partisans; **he said the ~ing** il a dit ceci; (*in documents etc*) **see the ~ing** voir ce qui suit; **3** *prep*: **~ing your letter/our meeting** comme suite à votre lettre/notre entretien. ♦ **follow-through** *n* (*to a project*) suite *f*, continuation *f*. ♦ **follow-up 1** *n* suite *f* (*to* de); **2** *adj*: **~-up letter** rappel *m*; (*Med*) **~-up care** soins *mpl* post-hospitaliers; **~-up survey** étude *f* complémentaire; **~-up visit** visite *f* de contrôle.

folly ['fɒlɪ] *n* folie *f*.

foment [fəʊ'ment] *vt* fomenter. ♦ **fomentation** *n* fomentation *f*.

fond [fɒnd] *adj* **(a) to be ~ of** aimer beaucoup. **(b)** (*loving*) *husband, friend* affectueux; *parent* (trop) bon; *look* tendre; *hope, ambition* cher; (*foolish*) *hope, ambition* naïf. ♦ **fondly** *adv* affectueusement; tendrement; naïvement; **he ~ly believed that ...** il avait la naïveté de croire que ... . ♦ **fondness** *n* (*for things*) prédilection *f* (*for* pour); (*for people*) affection *f* (*for* pour).

fondle ['fɒndl] *vt* caresser.
font [fɒnt] *n* **(a)** (*Rel*) fonts *mpl* baptismaux. **(b)** (*US Typ*) fonte *f*.
food [fu:d] **1** *n* nourriture *f*; *[dogs]* pâtée *f*; *[plants]* engrais *m*. **there was no ~ in the house** il n'y avait rien à manger dans la maison; **to give sb ~** donner à manger à qn; **~s** aliments *mpl*; **to be off one's ~*** avoir perdu l'appétit; **the ~ is very good here** on mange très bien ici; **he likes plain ~** il aime la cuisine simple; **it gave me ~ for thought** cela m'a donné à penser *or* à réfléchir. **2** *adj rationing, chain* alimentaire. **~ parcel** colis *m* de vivres; **~ poisoning** intoxication *f* alimentaire; **~ processor** robot *m* ménager; **~ supplies** vivres *mpl*; **~ value** valeur *f* nutritive. ♦ **foodstuffs** *npl* denrées *fpl* alimentaires.
fool [fu:l] **1** *n* imbécile *mf*, idiot(e) *m(f)*. **don't be a ~!** ne fais pas l'idiot(e)!; **some ~ of a doctor** un imbécile de médecin; **he was a ~ not to accept** il a été idiot *or* stupide de ne pas accepter; **to play the ~** faire l'imbécile; **he's nobody's ~** il n'est pas né d'hier; **more ~ you!*** tu n'avais qu'à ne pas faire l'idiot!; **he made a ~ of himself** il s'est rendu ridicule; **to make a ~ of sb** ridiculiser qn; **I went on a ~'s errand** j'y suis allé pour rien; **to live in a ~'s paradise** planer (*fig*).
2 *vi* (*~ about*) faire l'imbécile *or* l'idiot(e). **I was only ~ing** je plaisantais.
3 *vt* duper.
fool about, fool around *vi* (*waste time*) perdre son temps; (*play the fool*) faire l'idiot(e) *or* l'imbécile (*with* avec).
♦ **foolery** *n* sottises *fpl*, bêtises *fpl*. ♦ **foolhardiness** *n* témérité *f*. ♦ **foolhardy** *adj* téméraire. ♦ **foolish** *adj* idiot, bête; **that was very ~ish of you** ça n'a pas été très malin de votre part, (*more formally*) vous avez vraiment été imprudent; **to make sb look ~ish** rendre qn ridicule. ♦ **foolishly** *adv* sottement, bêtement; **and ~ishly I believed him** et je l'ai cru comme un(e) imbécile. ♦ **foolishness** *n* bêtise *f*. ♦ **foolproof** *adj method* infaillible; *machinery* indétraquable.
foolscap ['fu:lskæp] *n* ≈ papier *m* pot.
foot [fʊt] **1** *n, pl* **feet** (*gen*) pied *m*; *[dog, cat, bird]* patte *f*; *[table]* (bas) bout *m*; *[page, stairs]* bas *m*; (*measure*) pied (= *30 cm environ*); (*Mil*) infanterie *f*. **to be on one's feet** être debout; (*fig: after illness*) être remis sur pied; **to jump to one's feet** sauter sur ses pieds; **to go on ~** aller à pied; **to get *or* to rise to one's feet** se mettre debout; **it brought him to his feet** à cela, il s'est levé d'un bond; (*fig*) **to put *or* set sb on his feet again** (*healthwise*) remettre qn sur pied; **to keep one's feet** garder l'équilibre; **it's very wet under ~** c'est très mouillé par terre; **to trample sb/sth under ~** piétiner qn/qch; (*fig*) **to get under sb's feet** venir dans les jambes de qn; **to put one's ~ down** (*be firm*) faire acte d'autorité; (*stop sth*) y mettre le holà; (*Aut*: accelerate*) appuyer sur le champignon*; **to put one's ~ in it*** gaffer; **to put one's best ~ forward** (*hurry*) se dépêcher; (*do one's best*) faire de son mieux; **he didn't put a ~ wrong** il n'a pas commis la moindre erreur; **to get off on the right/wrong ~** bien/mal commencer; **to get a ~ in the door** établir un premier contact; **to put one's feet up*** (s'étendre pour) se reposer un peu; **he's got one ~ in the grave*** il a un pied dans la tombe; **I've never set ~ there** je n'y ai jamais mis les pieds; **at the ~ of the page** au *or* en bas de la page; **~ soldier** fantassin *m*.
2 *vt*: **to ~ the bill*** payer (la note).
♦ **foot-and-mouth disease** *n* fièvre *f* aphteuse. ♦ **football 1** *n* (*sport*) football *m*; (*ball*) ballon *m* (de football); **2** *adj ground, match, team* de football; *season* du football; **~ball coupon** fiche *f* de pari (sur les matchs de football); **~ball hooliganism** vandalisme *m* (*lors d'un match de football*); **~ball league** championnat *m* de football; **F~ball League** ≈ Fédération française de football; **to do the ~ball pools** parier sur les matchs de football; (*Rail*) **~ball special** train *m* de supporters (*d'une équipe de football*). ♦ **footballer** *n* joueur *m* de football. ♦ **footbrake** *n* frein *m* à pied. ♦ **footbridge** *n* passerelle *f*. ♦ **-footed** *adj ending in cpds*: **light-~ed** au pied léger. ♦ **footfall** *n* (bruit *m* de) pas *m*. ♦ **footgear*** *n* chaussures *fpl*. ♦ **foothills** *npl* contreforts *mpl*. ♦ **foothold** *n* prise *f* (de pied); **to gain a ~hold** prendre pied; (*fig*) se faire une place. ♦ **footing** *n* prise *f* (de pied); (*fig*) position *f*; **to miss one's ~ing** perdre pied *or* l'équilibre; **to be on a friendly ~ing with sb** avoir des relations d'amitié avec qn; **on an equal ~ing** sur un pied d'égalité; **on a war ~ing** sur le pied de guerre; **to put sth on an official ~ing** rendre qch officiel. ♦ **footlights** *npl* (*Theat*) rampe *f*. ♦ **footloose** *adj*: **~loose and fancy-free** libre comme l'air. ♦ **footman** *n* valet *m* de pied. ♦ **footmark** *n* empreinte *f* (de pied). ♦ **footnote** *n* note *f* en bas de la page; (*fig*) post-scriptum *m*. ♦ **footpath** *n* sentier *m*; (*by highway*) chemin *m*. ♦ **footplate 1** *n* (*Rail*) plate-forme *f* (*d'une locomotive*); **2** *adj*: **~plate workers** *npl* agents *mpl* de conduite. ♦ **footprint** *n* = **footmark**. ♦ **footpump** *n* pompe *f* à pied. ♦ **footsore** *adj*: **to be ~sore** avoir mal aux pieds. ♦ **footstep** *n* (bruit *m* de) pas *m*. ♦ **footstool** *n* tabouret *m*. ♦ **footwear** *n* chaussures *fpl*.
footle* ['fu:tl] *vi*: **to ~ about** perdre son temps à des futilités. ♦ **footling** *adj* futile.
for [fɔ:ʳ] **1** *prep* **(a)** (*indicating intention, destination*) pour. **is this ~ me?** c'est pour moi?; **votes ~ women!** le droit de vote pour les femmes!; **it's time ~ dinner** c'est l'heure du dîner; **a job ~ next week** un travail à faire la semaine prochaine; **she's the wife ~ me** c'est la femme qu'il me faut; **a liking ~ work** le goût du travail; **a gift ~ languages** un don pour les langues; **he's got a genius ~ saying the wrong thing** il a le don de dire ce qu'il ne faut pas; **he left ~ Italy** il est parti pour l'Italie; **trains ~ Paris** trains *mpl* en direction de *or* à destination de Paris; **the train ~ Paris** le train pour *or* de Paris; **he swam ~ the shore** il a nagé dans la direction du rivage *or* vers le rivage; **to make ~ home** prendre la direction de la maison.
(b) (*indicating purpose*) pour. **what ~?** pourquoi?; **what did you do that ~?** pourquoi avez-vous fait cela?; **what's this knife ~?** à quoi sert ce couteau?; **it's not ~ cutting wood** ça n'est pas fait pour couper du bois; **it's been used ~ a hammer** ça a servi de marteau; **a room ~ studying in** une pièce réservée à l'étude; **a bag ~ carrying books in** un sac pour porter des livres; **we went there ~ our holidays** nous y sommes allés pour les vacances; **he does it ~ pleasure** il le fait pour son plaisir; **to get ready ~ a journey** se préparer pour un voyage; **fit ~ nothing** bon à rien; **a campaign ~ ...** une campagne pour ... .
(c) (*representing*) **D ~ Daniel** D comme Daniel; (*Parl*) **member ~ Brighton** député *m* de Brighton; **agent ~ Ford cars** concessionnaire *mf* Ford; **I'll see her ~ you** je la verrai à ta place; **what is G.B. ~?** qu'est-ce que G.B. veut dire?
(d) (*in exchange ~*) **I'll give you this book ~ that one** je vous échange ce livre-ci contre celui-là; **to pay 5 francs ~ a ticket** payer 5 F le billet; **I sold it ~ £2** je l'ai vendu 2 livres; **he'll do it ~ £5** il le fera pour 5 livres; **there is one French passenger ~ every 10 English** sur 11 passagers il y a un Français et 10 Anglais; **what's (the) German ~ 'dog'?** comment est-ce qu'on dit 'chien' en allemand?
(e) (*in favour of*) pour. **~ or against** pour ou contre; **I'm all ~ helping him** je suis tout à fait partisan de l'aider; **I'm all ~ it*** je suis tout à fait pour*.

(f) (*because of*) pour, en raison de. ~ **this reason** pour cette raison; ~ **fear of being left behind** de peur d'être oublié; **famous ~ its church** célèbre pour son église; **to shout ~ joy** hurler de joie; **to go to prison ~ theft/~ stealing** aller en prison pour vol/pour avoir volé; ~ **my sake** pour moi; **to choose sb ~ his ability** choisir qn en raison de sa compétence; **if it weren't ~ him, but ~ him** sans lui.

(g) (*considering; with regard to*) pour. **anxious ~ sb** inquiet pour qn; ~ **my part** pour ma part; **as ~ him** quant à lui; **it is warm ~ January** il fait bon pour janvier; **he's tall ~ his age** il est grand pour son âge.

(h) (*in spite of*) ~ **all his wealth** malgré toute sa richesse, tout riche qu'il soit; ~ **all that** malgré tout, néanmoins.

(i) (*in time*) **I have been/had been waiting ~ 2 hours** j'attends/j'attendais depuis 2 heures; **I am off ~ a few days** je pars pour quelques jours; **I shall be away ~ a month** je serai absent (pendant) un mois; **he won't be back ~ a week** il ne sera pas de retour avant huit jours; **that's enough ~ the moment** cela suffit pour le moment; **he went away ~ two weeks** il est parti (pendant) quinze jours; **I have not seen her ~ 2 years** voilà 2 ans *or* cela fait 2 ans que je ne l'ai vue.

(j) (*distance*) pendant. **a road lined with trees ~ 3 km** une route bordée d'arbres pendant *or* sur 3 km; **we drove ~ 50 km** nous avons conduit pendant 50 km; **nothing to be seen ~ miles** rien à voir pendant des kilomètres.

(k) (*with infin phrases*) pour que + *subj*. ~ **this to be possible** pour que cela puisse être; **it's easy ~ him to do it** il lui est facile de le faire; **I brought it ~ you to see** je l'ai apporté pour que vous le voyiez (*subj*); **it's not ~ me to say** ce n'est pas à moi de le dire; **it would be best ~ you to go away** le mieux serait que vous vous en alliez (*subj*); **there is still time ~ him to come** il a encore le temps d'arriver; **their one hope is ~ him to return** leur seul espoir est qu'il revienne.

(l) (*phrases*) **now ~ it!** allons-y!; **you're ~ it!*** qu'est-ce que tu vas prendre!*; **oh ~ a cup of tea!** je donnerais n'importe quoi pour une tasse de thé!

2 *conj* car.

forage ['fɒrɪdʒ] *vi* fourrager (*for* pour trouver).

forbad(e) [fə'bæd] *pret of* **forbid.**

forbear [fɔː'bɛəʳ] *pret* **forbore,** *ptp* **forborne** *vi* s'abstenir (*from doing, to do* de faire). ◆ **forbearance** *n* patience *f*.

forbid [fə'bɪd] *pret* **forbad(e),** *ptp* **forbidden** *vt* défendre, interdire (*sb to do* à qn de faire). **to ~ sb alcohol** interdire l'alcool à qn; **employees are ~den to do this** il est interdit *or* défendu aux employés de faire cela; **"smoking strictly ~den"** "défense absolue de fumer"; **God ~!*** pourvu que non!, j'espère bien que non! ◆ **forbidding** *adj building, cliff, cloud* menaçant; *person, look* sévère.

forbore [fɔː'bɔʳ], **forborne** [fɔː'bɔːn] *pret, ptp of* **forbear.**

force [fɔːs] **1** *n* **(a)** (*gen*) force *f*. ~ **of gravity** pesanteur *f*; **by sheer ~** de vive force; **by ~ of** à force de; **by ~ of habit** par la force de l'habitude; ~ **of a blow** violence *f* d'un coup; **to resort to ~** avoir recours à la force; **I can see the ~ of that** je comprends la force que cela peut avoir; **to come into ~** entrer en vigueur; **the police were there in ~** la police était là en force; **he is a powerful ~ in the party** il exerce une influence puissante dans le parti; **there are several ~s at work** plusieurs influences se font sentir. **(b)** (*body of men*) force *f*. (*Mil*) **the ~s** les forces armées; (*Mil*) **allied ~s** armées alliées; **police ~** forces de police, la police; (*Comm*) **our sales ~** (l'effectif *m* de) nos représentants *mpl* de commerce.

2 *vt* **(a)** (*constrain*) contraindre, forcer (*sb to do* qn à faire). **to be ~d to do** être contraint *or* forcé de faire. **(b)** (*impose*) *conditions, obedience* imposer (*on sb* à qn). **to ~ o.s. on sb** s'imposer à qn. **(c)** (*push, thrust*) pousser. **to ~ books into a box** fourrer des livres dans une caisse; **to ~ one's way into** entrer *or* pénétrer de force dans; **to ~ one's way through** se frayer un passage à travers; **to ~ a bill through Parliament** forcer la Chambre à voter une loi; **we ~d the secret out of him** nous lui avons arraché le secret. **(d)** (*break open*) *lock etc* forcer. **to ~ sb's hand** forcer la main à qn. **(e)** *smile, answer* forcer. **to ~ the pace** forcer l'allure *or* le pas.

force back *vt sep enemy, crowd* faire reculer. **to ~ back one's tears** refouler ses larmes.

force down *vt sep aircraft* forcer à atterrir. **to ~ food down** se forcer à manger.

force out *vt sep* faire sortir (de force); *cork* sortir en forçant. **he ~d out a reply** il s'est forcé à répondre.

◆ **forced** *adj* forcé. ◆ **force-feed** (*pret, ptp* **-fed**) *vt* nourrir de force. ◆ **forceful** *adj person* énergique; *argument* vigoureux; *influence* puissant. ◆ **forcefully** *adv* avec force, avec vigueur. ◆ **forcible** *adj* (*done by ~*) de *or* par force; (*powerful*) *language, style, argument* vigoureux; *personality* puissant. ◆ **forcibly** *adv* (*by ~*) *take, feed* de force; (*vigorously*) *speak, object* avec véhémence. ◆ **forcing** *adj* (*Bridge*) **forcing bid** annonce *f* de forcing.

forceps ['fɔːseps] *npl* forceps *m*.

ford [fɔːd] **1** *n* gué *m*. **2** *vt* passer à gué. ◆ **fordable** *adj* guéable.

fore [fɔːʳ] **1** *adj* antérieur. **2** *n* avant *m*. **to come to the ~** *[person]* se mettre en évidence; *[evidence, fact]* être révélé; **he was well to the ~** il a été très en évidence. **3** *excl* (*Golf*) gare!, attention! ◆ **forearm** *n* avant-bras *m inv*. ◆ **foreboding** *n* pressentiment *m*; **to have a ~boding that** avoir le pressentiment que. ◆ **forecast** *pret, ptp* **forecast 1** *vt* (*also Met*) prévoir; **2** *n* prévision *f*; (*Betting*) pronostic *m*; **sales ~cast** prévisions de vente; **weather ~cast** bulletin *m* météorologique, météo* *f*. ◆ **forecourt** *n* avant-cour *f*. ◆ **forefathers** *npl* aïeux *mpl*. ◆ **forefinger** *n* index *m*. ◆ **forefoot** *n [horse, cow etc]* pied *m* antérieur; *[cat, dog]* patte *f* antérieure. ◆ **forefront** *n*: **in the ~front of** au premier rang de. ◆ **foregather** *vi* se réunir. ◆ **forego** *pret* **-went,** *ptp* **-gone** *vt* renoncer à; **it was a ~gone conclusion** c'était prévu d'avance. ◆ **foregoing** *adj* précédent; **the ~going** ce qui précède. ◆ **foreground** *n* premier plan; **in the ~ground** au premier plan. ◆ **forehead** *n* front *m*. ◆ **foreland** *n* cap *m*. ◆ **foreleg** *n [horse, cow]* jambe antérieure; *[dog, cat]* patte *f* de devant. ◆ **foreman** *n, pl* **~men** contremaître *m*. ◆ **foremost 1** *adj* le plus en vue; **2** *adv*: **first and ~most** tout d'abord. ◆ **forename** *n* prénom *m*. ◆ **forenoon** *n* matinée *f*. ◆ **foreplay** *n* travaux *mpl* d'approche* (*stimulation érotique*). ◆ **forerunner** *n* précurseur *m*. ◆ **foresee** *pret* **-saw,** *ptp* **-seen** *vt* prévoir, présager. ◆ **foreseeable** *adj* prévisible. ◆ **foreshadow** *vt* laisser prévoir. ◆ **foreshore** *n* (*beach*) plage *f*. ◆ **foresight** *n* prévoyance *f*. ◆ **forestall** *vt competitor* devancer; *desire, eventuality, objection* anticiper. ◆ **foretaste** *n* avant-goût *m*. ◆ **foretell** *pret, ptp* **-told** *vt* prédire. ◆ **forethought** *n* prévoyance *f*. ◆ **forewarn** *vt* avertir; **~warned is ~armed** un homme averti en vaut deux. ◆ **foreword** *n* avant-propos *m inv*.

foreign ['fɒrən] *adj language, visitor* étranger; *politics, trade* extérieur; *produce, aid* de l'étranger; *travel, correspondent* à l'étranger. **F~ Ministry,** (*Brit*) **F~ Office** ministère *m* des Affaires étrangères; ~ **agent** agent *m* étranger; ~ **currency** devises *fpl* étrangères; ~ **exchange**

market marché *m* des changes; **F~ Legion** Légion *f* (étrangère); **~ relations** relations *fpl* avec l'étranger *or* l'extérieur; **that is quite ~ to him** cela lui est (complètement) étranger; (*Med*) **~ body** corps *m* étranger. ♦ **foreigner** *n* étranger *m*, -ère *f*.

forensic [fəˈrensɪk] *adj medicine* légal; *evidence, laboratory* médico-légal; *expert* en médecine légale.

forest [ˈfɒrɪst] *n* forêt *f*. ♦ **forester** *n* forestier *m*. ♦ **forestry** *n* sylviculture *f*; **the F~ry Commission** ≃ les Eaux et Forêts *fpl*.

forever [fərˈevəʳ] *adv* (*incessantly*) toujours; (*US: for always*) pour toujours.

forfeit [ˈfɔːfɪt] **1** *vt* perdre. **2** *n* (*in game*) gage *m*. (*game*) **~s** gages.

forgave [fəˈgeɪv] *pret of* **forgive.**

forge [fɔːdʒ] **1** *vt* **(a)** (*counterfeit*) *signature, banknote* contrefaire; *document, picture* faire un faux de. **(b)** *metal, friendship, plan* forger. **2** *vi*: **to ~ ahead** pousser de l'avant. **3** *n* forge *f*. ♦ **forger** *n* faussaire *mf*. ♦ **forgery** *n* (*action*) contrefaçon *f* (frauduleuse); (*thing* **~d**) faux *m*.

forget [fəˈget] *pret* **-got,** *ptp* **-gotten 1** *vt* oublier (*to do* de faire; *that* que). **to ~ how to do** ne plus savoir faire, oublier comment faire; **never-to-be-forgotten** inoubliable; **she never ~s a face** elle a la mémoire des visages; **he quite forgot himself** il s'est tout à fait oublié; **let's ~ it!** passons l'éponge!; **~ it*** (*when thanked*) de rien*; (*let's drop the subject*) ça n'a aucune importance; (*when irritated*) tant pis. **2** *vi* oublier. **I forgot all about it** je l'ai complètement oublié; **~ about it!** n'y pensez plus! ♦ **forgetful** *adj* (*absent-minded*) distrait; (*careless*) étourdi; **he is very ~ful** il a très mauvaise mémoire; **~ful of** oublieux de. ♦ **forgetfulness** *n* manque *m* de mémoire; étourderie *f*. ♦ **forget-me-not** *n* myosotis *m*.

forgive [fəˈgɪv] *pret* **forgave,** *ptp* **forgiven** *vt person, mistake* pardonner (*sb for sth* qch à qn; *sb for doing* à qn de faire). ♦ **forgivable** *adj* pardonnable. ♦ **forgiveness** *n* (*pardon*) pardon *m*; (*compassion*) indulgence *f*. ♦ **forgiving** *adj* indulgent.

forgot(ten) [fəˈgɒt(n)] *pret* (*ptp*) *of* **forget.**

fork [fɔːk] **1** *n* fourchette *f*; (*Agr*) fourche *f*; *[roads]* embranchement *m*. **take the right ~** prenez à droite à l'embranchement. **2** *vi [roads]* bifurquer. **~ left for Oxford** prenez à gauche pour Oxford.

fork out‡ 1 *vi* casquer*, payer. **2** *vt sep money* allonger‡, sortir.

♦ **forked** *adj* fourchu; *lightning* en zigzags. ♦ **fork-lift truck** *n* chariot *m* élévateur.

forlorn [fəˈlɔːn] *adj person* triste, malheureux; *house* abandonné; *attempt* désespéré. **a ~ hope** un mince espoir.

form [fɔːm] **1** *n* **(a)** (*gen*) forme *f*. **a different ~ of life** une autre forme *or* un autre genre de vie; **the various ~s of energy** les différentes formes *or* espèces d'énergie; **a ~ of apology** une sorte d'excuse; **in the ~ of** sous forme de; **it will take the ~ of ...** cela consistera en ...; **the same thing in a new ~** la même chose sous un aspect nouveau; **it took various ~s** cela s'est manifesté de différentes façons; **~ and content** la forme et le fond; **to take ~** prendre forme; **it lacks ~** il n'y a aucun ordre là-dedans; **as a matter of ~** pour la forme; **it's bad ~** cela ne se fait pas; **another ~ of words** une autre tournure; **the correct ~ of address for a bishop** la manière correcte de s'adresser à un évêque; **what's the ~?*** quelle est la marche à suivre?; **on ~** en forme; **in great ~, on top ~** en pleine forme. **(b)** (*document*) (*gen*) formulaire *m*; (*for cheque, telegram*) formule *f*; (*for tax*) feuille *f*. **printed ~** imprimé *m*. **(c)** (*bench*) banc *m*. **(d)** (*Scol*) classe *f*. **in the sixth ~** ≃ en première.

2 *adj*: **~ master, ~ mistress** professeur *m* de classe.

3 *vt shape, character, government* former; *sentence* construire; *habit* contracter; *plan* arrêter; *impression, idea* avoir; (*constitute*) *council, Cabinet* composer, constituer. **he ~ed it out of a piece of wood** il l'a façonné *or* fabriqué dans un morceau de bois; **he ~ed it into a ball** il l'a roulé en boule; **to ~ an opinion** se faire une opinion; **to ~ part of** faire partie de; **those who ~ the group** les gens qui font partie du groupe; (*Mil*) **to ~ fours** se mettre par quatre; **~ a line/queue/circle** mettez-vous en ligne/file/cercle.

4 *vi* se former (*into* en). **~ up behind your teacher** mettez-vous en ligne derrière votre professeur.

♦ **format** *n* format *m*. ♦ **formation 1** *n* formation *f*; **2** *adj*: **~ation flying** vol *m* en formation. ♦ **formative** *adj* formateur.

formal [ˈfɔːməl] *adj person* compassé, formaliste (*pej*); *manner, style* compassé; *language* soigné; *function, announcement* officiel; *dance, dinner* grand; (*official*) *acceptance, surrender* en bonne et due forme; (*specific*) *denial, instructions* formel; (*in form only*) *agreement* de forme. **he is very ~** il est très à cheval sur les convenances; **don't be so ~** pas tant de cérémonies, s'il vous plaît; **~ gardens** jardins *mpl* à la française; **~ dress** tenue *f* de cérémonie; (*evening dress*) tenue de soirée; **she has no ~ training in teaching** elle n'a reçu aucune formation pédagogique. ♦ **formalism** *n* formalisme *m*. ♦ **formalist** *adj, n* formaliste (*mf*). ♦ **formality** *n* (*convention*) formalité *f*; (*stiffness*) raideur *f*; (*ceremoniousness*) cérémonie *f*; **a mere ~ity** une simple formalité. ♦ **formalize** *vt* formaliser. ♦ **formally** *adv* (*ceremoniously*) cérémonieusement; (*officially*) officiellement; **to be ~ly invited** recevoir une invitation officielle; **~ly dressed** en tenue de cérémonie (*or* de soirée).

former [ˈfɔːməʳ] **1** *adj* **(a)** (*previous*) ancien (*before n*), précédent; *life* antérieur. **the ~ mayor** l'ancien maire, le maire précédent; **a ~ mayor** un ancien maire; **my ~ husband** mon ex-mari; **in ~ days** autrefois; **he was very unlike his ~ self** il ne se ressemblait plus du tout. **(b)** (*as opp to later*) premier. **2** *pron* celui-là, celle-là. **the ~ ... the latter** celui-là ... celui-ci. ♦ **formerly** *adv* autrefois.

Formica [fɔːˈmaɪkə] *n* ® Formica *m* ®.

formidable [ˈfɔːmɪdəbl] *adj* (*gen*) terrible; *person, opposition* redoutable.

formula [ˈfɔːmjʊlə] *n, pl* **~s** *or* **~ae** formule *f*; (*US: for baby's feed*) lait *m* en poudre (*pour biberon*). ♦ **formulate** *vt* formuler. ♦ **formulation** *n* formulation *f*.

fornicate [ˈfɔːnɪkeɪt] *vi* forniquer. ♦ **fornication** *n* fornication *f*.

forsake [fəˈseɪk] *pret* **forsook,** *ptp* **forsaken** *vt person* abandonner; *place* quitter; *habit* renoncer à. **my willpower ~s me** la volonté me fait défaut; **an old ~n farmhouse** une vieille ferme abandonnée.

forsythia [fɔːˈsaɪθɪə] *n* forsythia *m*.

fort [fɔːt] *n* (*Mil*) fort *m*.

forte [ˈfɔːtɪ, (*US*) fɔːt] *n*: **his ~** son fort.

forth [fɔːθ] *adv* en avant. **to set ~** se mettre en route; **to go back and ~ between** aller et venir entre; **and so ~** et ainsi de suite. ♦ **forthcoming** *adj book* qui va paraître; *film* qui va sortir; *play* qui va débuter; *event* à venir, futur; **his ~coming film** son prochain film; **if help is ~coming** si on nous *etc* aide; **if funds are ~coming** si on nous *etc* donne de l'argent; **he wasn't ~coming about it** il s'est montré peu disposé à en parler. ♦ **forthright** *adj answer, person* franc. ♦ **forthwith** *adv* sur-le-champ.

fortify [ˈfɔːtɪfaɪ] *vt* fortifier (*against* contre). **have**

a drink to ~ you* prenez un verre pour vous remonter. ♦ **fortification** *n* fortification *f*.

fortitude [ˈfɔːtɪtjuːd] *n* force *f* d'âme.

fortnight [ˈfɔːtnaɪt] *n* quinze jours *mpl*, quinzaine *f*. **a ~'s holiday** quinze jours de vacances; **a ~ tomorrow** demain en quinze. ♦ **fortnightly 1** *adj* bimensuel; **2** *adv* tous les quinze jours.

fortress [ˈfɔːtrɪs] *n* (*prison*) forteresse *f*; (*mediaeval castle*) château *m* fort.

fortuitous [fɔːˈtjuːɪtəs] *adj* fortuit. ♦ **fortuitously** *adv* fortuitement.

fortune [ˈfɔːtʃən] *n* **(a)** (*chance*) chance *f*, fortune *f*. **the ~s of war** la fortune des armes; **by good ~** par chance; **to tell sb's ~** dire la bonne aventure à qn. **(b)** (*riches*) fortune *f*. **to make a ~** faire fortune; **to come into a ~** hériter d'une fortune; **to seek one's ~** aller chercher fortune; **a small ~*** un argent fou*. ♦ **fortunate** *adj person* heureux; *circumstances, meeting, event* propice; *[person]* **to be fortunate** avoir de la chance; **we were fortunate enough to meet him** nous avons eu la chance de le rencontrer. ♦ **fortune-teller** *n* diseur *m*, -euse *f* de bonne aventure. ♦ **fortune-telling** *n* pratique *f* de dire la bonne aventure.

forty [ˈfɔːtɪ] *adj, n* quarante (*m*) *inv*. **about ~ books** une quarantaine de livres; **to have ~ winks*** faire un petit somme; *for other phrases V* **sixty.**

♦ **fortieth** *adj, n* quarantième (*mf*); (*fraction*) quarantième *m*.

forward [ˈfɔːwəd] **1** *adv* (*also* **forwards**) en avant. **to go ~** avancer; **to go straight ~** aller droit devant soi; **~!, ~ march!** en avant, marche!; **from this time ~** désormais; **he went backward(s) and ~(s) between** il allait et venait entre. **2** *adj movement* en avant; (*Aut*) *gears* avant *inv*; *planning* à long terme; *prices, buying* à terme; *season, child* précoce; (*pert*) effronté. **I am ~ with my work** je suis en avance dans mon travail; **this seat is too far ~** cette banquette est trop en avant; **~ line** (*Mil*) première ligne *f*; (*Sport*) ligne des avants. **3** *n* (*Sport*) avant *m*. **4** *vt goods* expédier; (*send on*) *letter, parcel* faire suivre. **please ~** faire suivre S.V.P. ♦ **forwarding address** *n*: **he left no ~ing address** il est parti sans laisser d'adresse. ♦ **forward-looking** *adj* tourné vers les possibilités de l'avenir. ♦ **forwardness** *n [child]* précocité *f*; (*pertness*) effronterie *f*.

fossil [ˈfɒsl] **1** *n* fossile *m*. **2** *adj insect* fossilisé; *fuel* fossile. ♦ **fossilized** *adj* fossilisé.

foster [ˈfɒstəʳ] **1** *vt child* élever (*sans obligation d'adoption*); *friendship, development* favoriser; *idea, hope* entretenir. **2** *adj child* (*officially arranged*) adoptif; (*where wet-nursed*) nourricier, de lait; *father, parents, family* adoptif, nourricier; *brother, sister* adoptif, de lait. **~ home** famille *f* adoptive, famille nourricière; **~ mother** mère *f* adoptive, nourrice *f*.

fought [fɔːt] *pret, ptp of* **fight.**

foul [faʊl] **1** *adj food, meal, taste* infect; *place* immonde; *smell, breath* fétide; *water* croupi; *air* vicié; *weather, temper* sale (*before n*); *calumny, behaviour* vil; *language* ordurier; (*unfair*) déloyal; *blow* en traître. **~ play** (*Sport*) jeu *m* irrégulier; (*fig*) qch de louche; (*Police etc*) un acte criminel; **to fall ~ of sb** se mettre qn à dos. **2** *n* (*Sport*) coup *m* irrégulier; (*Boxing*) coup bas; (*Ftbl*) faute *f*. **3** *vt* (*pollute*) *air* polluer; (*clog*) *pipe etc* obstruer; (*collide with*) *ship* entrer en collision avec; *fishing line* embrouiller; *propeller* s'emmêler dans. **the dog ~ed the path** le chien a fait des saletés sur le chemin. **4** *vi [rope]* s'emmêler.

foul up* *vt sep relationship* gâcher.

♦ **foul-mouthed** *adj* au langage ordurier. ♦ **foul-smelling** *adj* fétide.

found[1] [faʊnd] *pret, ptp of* **find.** ♦ **foundling** *n* enfant *m(f)* trouvé(e).

found[2] [faʊnd] *vt* (*gen*) fonder; *belief* fonder (*on* sur); *suspicions* baser (*on* sur); **~ed on fact** basé sur des faits réels. ♦ **foundation** *n* fondation *f*; (*fig*) base *f*; **to lay the ~ations of** (*lit*) poser les fondations de; (*fig*) poser les bases de; **to lay the ~ation stone** poser la première pierre; **rumour entirely without ~ation** rumeur dénuée de tout fondement. ♦ **foundation cream** *n* fond *m* de teint. ♦ **foundation stone** *n* pierre commémorative. ♦ **founder**[1] *n* fondateur *m*, -trice *f*. ♦ **founding** *adj* (*US*) **~ing fathers** pères *mpl* fondateurs (*qui élaborèrent la Constitution Fédérale*).

founder[2] [ˈfaʊndəʳ] *vi [ship]* sombrer; *[horse]* s'embourber; *[plans, hopes etc]* s'écrouler.

foundry [ˈfaʊndrɪ] *n* fonderie *f*.

fount [faʊnt] *n* (*spring*) source *f*; (*Typ*) fonte *f*.

fountain [ˈfaʊntɪn] **1** *n* fontaine *f*. **drinking ~** jet *m* d'eau potable. **2** *adj*: **~ pen** stylo *m* (*à encre*).

four [fɔːʳ] **1** *adj* quatre *inv*. **to the ~ corners of the earth** aux quatre coins du monde; **it's in ~ figures** c'est dans les milliers. **2** *n* quatre *m inv*. **on all ~s** à quatre pattes; **will you make up a ~ for bridge?** voulez-vous faire le quatrième au bridge?; *for other phrases V* **six.**

♦ **four-door** *adj* (*Aut*) à quatre portes. ♦ **fourfold 1** *adj* quadruple; **2** *adv* au quadruple. ♦ **fourfooted** *adj* à quatre pattes. ♦ **four-leaf(ed) clover** *n* trèfle *m* à quatre feuilles. ♦ **four-letter word** *n* gros mot *m*, ≈ mot de cinq lettres. ♦ **fourposter** *n* lit *m* à colonnes. ♦ **fourscore** *adj, n* quatre-vingts. ♦ **foursome** *n* (*game*) partie *f* à quatre; **we went in a ~some** nous y sommes allés à quatre. ♦ **foursquare** *adj* (*square*) carré; (*firm*) ferme; (*forthright*) franc. ♦ **fourteen** *adj, n* quatorze (*m*) *inv*. ♦ **fourteenth** *adj, n* quatorzième (*mf*); (*fraction*) quatorzième *m*. ♦ **fourth** *adj, n* quatrième (*mf*); (*fraction*) quart *m*; **~th finger** annulaire *m*. ♦ **fourthly** *adv* quatrièmement. ♦ **four-wheel** *adj* (*Aut*) **with ~-wheel drive** à quatre roues motrices.

fowl [faʊl] *n* volaille *f*. **~ pest** peste *f* aviaire.

fox [fɒks] **1** *n* renard *m*. (*fig*) **a sly ~** un fin renard. **2** *vt* (*puzzle*) rendre perplexe; (*deceive*) berner. **3** *adj*: **~ cub** renardeau *m*; **~ terrier** fox-terrier *m*. ♦ **foxglove** *n* digitale *f* (pourprée). ♦ **foxhunt(ing)** *n* chasse *f* au renard. ♦ **foxy** *adj* rusé, finaud.

foyer [ˈfɔɪeɪ] *n* foyer *m* (*de théâtre etc*).

fraction [ˈfrækʃən] *n* fraction *f*. **a ~ of a second** une fraction de seconde. ♦ **fractionally** *adv* un tout petit peu.

fractious [ˈfrækʃəs] *adj* grincheux.

fracture [ˈfræktʃəʳ] **1** *n* fracture *f*. **2** *vt* fracturer. **to ~ one's leg** se fracturer la jambe. **3** *vi* se fracturer.

fragile [ˈfrædʒaɪl] *adj* fragile. ♦ **fragility** *n* fragilité *f*.

fragment [ˈfrægmənt] **1** *n* fragment *m*. **~s of conversation** bribes *fpl* de conversation. **2** [frægˈment] *vt* fragmenter. **3** *vi* se fragmenter. ♦ **fragmentary** *or* ♦ **fragmented** *adj* fragmentaire.

fragrance [ˈfreɪgrəns] *n* parfum *m*. ♦ **fragrant** *adj* parfumé; *memory* doux.

frail [freɪl] *adj person* frêle, faible; *health, happiness, hope* fragile. ♦ **frailty** *n* faiblesse *f*; fragilité *f*.

frame [freɪm] **1** *n [person, animal]* corps *m*, charpente *f*; *[building]* charpente; *[ship]* carcasse *f*; *[car, window]* châssis *m*; *[cycle, picture, racket]* cadre *m*; *[door]* encadrement *m*; *[spectacles]* monture *f*; (*in garden*) châssis; (*Cine*) image *f*. **~ of mind** humeur *f*; **~ of reference** système *m* de référence. **2** *adj*: **~ house** maison *f* à charpente de bois; **~ rucksack** sac *m* à dos à armature. **3** *vt* **(a)** *picture* encadrer. (*fig*) **~d in** encadré par. **(b)** (*construct*) *idea, plan* formuler;

plot combiner; *sentence* construire. **(c) to ~ sb*, to have sb ~d** monter un coup contre qn (*pour faire porter l'accusation contre lui*); **to be ~d** être victime d'un coup monté. ♦ **frame-up‡** *n* coup *m* monté. ♦ **framework** *n* (*V* **frame 1**) charpente *f*; carcasse *f*; châssis *m*; encadrement *m*; *[society, novel]* structure *f*; (*fig*) **in the ~work of** dans le cadre de.

franc [fræŋk] *n* franc *m*.

France [frɑːns] *n* France *f*. **in ~** en France.

franchise ['fræntʃaɪz] *n* **(a)** (*Pol*) droit *m* de vote. **(b)** (*US Comm*) autorisation *f*.

Franco- ['fræŋkəʊ] *pref* franco-. ♦ **Franco-British** *adj* franco-britannique. ♦ **francophile** *adj, n* francophile (*mf*). ♦ **francophobe** *adj, n* francophobe (*mf*).

frank[1] [fræŋk] *adj* franc (*f* franche). ♦ **frankly** *adv* franchement. ♦ **frankness** *n* franchise *f*.

frank[2] [fræŋk] *vt letter* affranchir. **~ing machine** machine *f* à affranchir.

frankfurter ['fræŋk,fɜːtəʳ] *n* (*Culin*) saucisse *f* de Francfort.

frantic ['fræntɪk] *adj activity, cry* frénétique; *need, desire* effréné; *person* hors de soi, dans tous ses états. **~ with** fou (*or* folle *f*) de; **it drives her ~** cela la rend folle. ♦ **frantically** *adv wave* frénétiquement; *rush* comme un fou (*or* une folle).

fraternal [frəˈtɜːnl] *adj* fraternel. ♦ **fraternity** *n* fraternité *f*; (*US Univ*) (*society*) confrérie *f*. ♦ **fraternization** *n* fraternisation *f*. ♦ **fraternize** *vi* fraterniser (*with* avec).

fraud [frɔːd] *n* (*act*) supercherie *f*; (*financial*) escroquerie *f*; (*Jur*) fraude *f*; (*person*) imposteur *m*; (*object*) attrape-nigaud *m*. **he's a ~** c'est un imposteur, (*less serious*) il joue la comédie*; **it's a ~!** c'est de la frime!* ♦ **fraudulence** *n* caractère *m* frauduleux. ♦ **fraudulent** *adj* frauduleux; **~ulent conversion** malversation *f*.

fraught [frɔːt] *adj* (*tense*) *situation* tendu. **~ with** *danger* plein de; *hatred, menace* chargé de; **the whole business is a bit ~*** tout ça c'est un peu risqué*.

fray[1] [freɪ] *n*: **the ~** le combat; (*lit, fig*) **ready for the ~** prêt à se battre.

fray[2] [freɪ] **1** *vt cloth, garment* effilocher; *cuff, trousers* effranger; *rope* user. **tempers were getting ~ed** tout le monde commençait à s'énerver; **my nerves are quite ~ed** je suis à bout de nerfs. **2** *vi* s'effilocher; s'effranger; s'user.

frazzle* ['fræzl] *n*: **worn to a ~** éreinté, crevé*.

freak [friːk] **1** *n* (*person or animal*) phénomène *m*. **~ of nature** accident *m* de la nature; **~ of fortune** caprice *m* de la fortune; **he won by a ~** il a gagné grâce à un hasard extraordinaire; **a health food ~*** un(e) fana* des aliments naturels. **2** *adj storm, weather* anormal; *error* bizarre; *victory* inattendu; (‡) *culture, clothes* hippie *f inv*.

freak out‡ *vi* (*abandon convention*) se défouler*; (*get high on drugs*) se défoncer‡; (*drop out of society*) devenir marginal.

♦ **freakish** *adj weather* anormal; *error, idea* bizarre.

freckle ['frekl] *n* tache *f* de rousseur. ♦ **freckled** *adj* plein de taches de rousseur.

free [friː] **1** *adj* **(a)** (*at liberty*) libre (*to do* de faire). **to get ~** se libérer; **to set ~** libérer; **he left one end of the string ~** il a laissé un bout de la ficelle flotter libre; **~ from** *or* **of** sans; **to be ~ of sb** être débarrassé de qn; **~ of charge** (*adj*) gratuit; (*adv*) gratuitement; **~ of tax, tax ~** hors taxe; **to be a ~ agent** avoir toute liberté d'action; **~ and easy** décontracté; **~ church** église *f* non-conformiste; **~ enterprise** libre entreprise *f*; **in ~ fall** en chute libre; **~ fight** mêlée *f* générale; **to give sb a ~ hand** donner carte blanche à qn (*to do* pour faire); (*Sport*) **~ kick** coup *m* franc; (*Ind*) **~ labour** main-d'œuvre *f* non syndiquée; **~ love** amour *m* libre; **to give ~ rein to** donner libre cours à; **~ speech** liberté *f* de parole; **~ trade** libre-échange *m*; **~ verse** vers *m* libre; **~ will** libre arbitre *m*; **of his own ~ will** de son propre gré.

(b) (*costing nothing*) *object, ticket* gratuit. **~ on board** franco à bord; (*Comm*) **~ sample** échantillon gratuit; **~ gift** prime *f*.

(c) (*not occupied*) *room, seat, hour, person* libre. **there are 2 ~ rooms left** il reste 2 chambres de libre; **I wasn't able to get ~ earlier** je n'ai pas pu me libérer plus tôt; (*lit, fig*) **to have one's hands ~** avoir les mains libres.

(d) (*lavish*) **to be ~ with one's money** dépenser son argent sans compter; **you're very ~ with your advice** pour donner des conseils vous êtes un peu là*; **he makes ~ with all my things** il ne se gêne pas pour se servir de mes affaires; **feel ~!*** je t'en prie!, sers-toi!

2 *adv* (*for nothing*) *get, send* gratuitement.

3 *vt* (*gen*) libérer; *trapped person, animal* dégager; *tangle* débrouiller; (*unblock*) *pipe* déboucher; (*rescue*) sauver (*from* de); (*from burden*) débarrasser (*from* de); (*from tax*) exonérer (*from* de); (*from anxiety*) libérer, délivrer (*from* de). (*lit, fig*) **to ~ o.s. from** se débarrasser de, se libérer de.

♦ **freedom 1** *n* liberté *f*; **~dom of the press/of speech/of worship** liberté de la presse/de la parole/du culte; **~dom of the seas** franchise *f* des mers; **~dom from care/responsibility** le fait d'être dégagé de tout souci/de toute responsabilité; **to give sb the ~dom of a city** nommer qn citoyen d'honneur d'une ville; **he gave me the ~dom of his house** il m'a permis de me servir comme je voulais de sa maison; **2** *adj*: **~dom fighter** guérillero *m*, partisan *m*. ♦ **free-for-all** *n* mêlée *f* générale. ♦ **freehand** *adj, adv* à main levée. ♦ **freehold** *adv* en propriété libre. ♦ **freelance 1** *adj* indépendant; **2** *vi [journalist/designer etc]* faire du journalisme/du dessin *etc* indépendant. ♦ **freely** *adv give* libéralement; *spend, grow* avec luxuriance; *speak* franchement; *act* librement. ♦ **freeman** *n*: **~man of a city** citoyen(ne) *m(f)* d'honneur d'une ville. ♦ **freemason** *n* franc-maçon *m*. ♦ **freemasonry** *n* franc-maçonnerie *f*. ♦ **free-range** *adj*: **~-range eggs/poultry** œufs *mpl*/poulets *mpl* de ferme. ♦ **freestyle** *adj*: **~style swimming** nage *f* libre. ♦ **freethinker** *n* libre-penseur *m*, -euse *f*. ♦ **freethinking 1** *adj* libre-penseur; **2** *n* libre pensée *f*. ♦ **freeway** *n* (*US*) autoroute *f* (*sans péage*). ♦ **freewheel** *vi [cyclist]* être en roue libre; *[motorist]* rouler au point mort. ♦ **free-will** *adj gift, offering* volontaire.

freesia ['friːzɪə] *n* freesia *m*.

freeze [friːz] *pret* **froze**, *ptp* **frozen 1** *vi* (*gen*) geler; (*Culin*) se congeler; (*fig*) se figer. (*Met*) **to ~ hard** geler dur; **I'm freezing** je suis gelé; **my hands are freezing** j'ai les mains gelées; **to ~ to death** mourir de froid; **the lake froze** le lac a gelé; **the lake has frozen** le lac est gelé; **he froze (in his tracks)** il est resté figé sur place; **~!** pas un geste!; **to ~ on to sb*** se cramponner à qn. **2** *vt water etc* geler; *food* congeler; (*industrially*) surgeler; (*Econ*) *assets* geler; *prices, wages* bloquer. **she froze him with a look** elle lui a lancé un regard qui l'a glacé sur place. **3** *n* (*Met*) gel *m*; *[credits]* gel; *[prices, wages]* blocage *m*.

freeze over *vi [lakes, rivers]* geler; (*Aut*) *[windscreen etc]* givrer.

freeze up 1 *vi* **(a)** = **freeze over. (b)** *[pipes]* geler. **2** *vt sep*: **to be frozen up** être gelé. ♦ **freeze-dry** *vt* lyophiliser. ♦ **freezer** *n* (*domestic*) congélateur *m*; (*industrial*) surgélateur *m*; (*part of fridge*) freezer *m*. ♦ **freeze-up** *n* (*Met*) gel *m*. ♦ **freezing** *adj* *weather, look* glacial; **freezing fog** brouillard *m* givrant; **below freezing point** au-dessous de zéro (centigrade).

freight [freɪt] **1** *n* (*goods*) fret *m*, cargaison *f*; (*transport*) transport *m*; (*charge*) fret.
2 *vt goods* transporter.
3 *adj* (*Rail*) *car, train, yard* de marchandises. ~ **plane** avion *m* de fret.
♦ **freighter** *n* (*Naut*) cargo *m*; (*Aviat*) avion *m* de fret.

French [frentʃ] **1** *adj* français; *lesson, teacher, dictionary* de français; *king, embassy* de France. ~ **bean** haricot *m* vert; ~ **Canadian** (*adj*) canadien français; (*n*) Canadien(ne) français(e) *m(f)*; (*Ling*) français *m* canadien; ~ **chalk** craie *f* de tailleur; ~ **door** porte-fenêtre *f*; (*Culin*) ~ **dressing** vinaigrette *f*; ~ **fried potatoes,** ~ **fries** frites *fpl*; (*Mus*) ~ **horn** cor *m* d'harmonie; **to take** ~ **leave** filer à l'anglaise*; ~ **loaf** baguette *f* (*de pain*); ~ **pastry** pâtisserie *f*; ~ **window** porte-fenêtre *f*. **2** *n* (*Ling*) français *m*. **the** ~ les Français *mpl*.
♦ **Frenchman** *n* Français *m*. ♦ **French-speaking** *adj* qui parle français; *nation etc* francophone.
♦ **Frenchwoman** *n* Française *f*.

frenzy ['frenzɪ] *n* frénésie *f*. ~ **of delight** transport *m* de joie. ♦ **frenzied** *adj person* forcené; *joy, shouts* frénétique; *efforts* désespéré.

frequent ['fri:kwənt] **1** *adj* fréquent. **it's quite** ~ cela arrive souvent; **a** ~ **visitor to our house** un habitué de la maison. **2** [frɪ'kwent] *vt* fréquenter.
♦ **frequency 1** *n* fréquence *f*; **2** *adj* (*Statistics*) *distribution* des fréquences; (*Electronics*) *modulation, band* de fréquence. ♦ **frequently** *adv* fréquemment, souvent.

fresco ['freskəʊ] *n* fresque *f*.

fresh [freʃ] **1** *adj* (*gen: not stale*) frais (*f* fraîche); (*additional, different*) *supplies, horse, sheet of paper* nouveau (*f* nouvelle); *clothes* de rechange; (*lively*) *person* plein d'entrain; *horse* fringant; (*cheeky*) trop libre (*with sb* envers qn). **milk** ~ **from the cow** lait fraîchement trait; ~ **butter** (*not stale*) beurre frais; (*unsalted*) beurre sans sel; **bread** ~ **from the oven** pain tout frais; (*fig*) **to break** ~ **ground** faire qch d'entièrement nouveau; **to make a** ~ **start** prendre un nouveau départ; ~ **water** (*not salt*) eau douce; **it is still** ~ **in my memory** j'en ai encore le souvenir tout frais; **to go out for a breath of** ~ **air** sortir prendre l'air; **in the** ~ **air** au grand air; **let's have some** ~ **air!** un peu d'air!; (*Met*) **it is getting** ~ il commence à faire frais; **she was as** ~ **as a daisy** elle était fraîche comme une rose; **don't get** ~ **with me!** pas d'impertinences!
2 *adv*: ~ **from Scotland** nouvellement *or* fraîchement arrivé d'Écosse.
♦ **fresh-air** *adj*: ~**-air fiend*** mordu(e)* *m(f)* du grand air. ♦ **freshen** *vi [wind, air]* fraîchir.
♦ **freshen up 1** *vi* (*wash etc*) faire un brin de toilette; **2** *vt sep* faire un brin de toilette à; **that will** ~**en you up** cela vous requinquera*.
♦ **fresher** *or* ♦ **freshman** *n* étudiant(e)* *m(f)* de première année. ♦ **freshly** *adv* nouvellement, récemment. ♦ **freshness** *n* fraîcheur *f*.
♦ **freshwater** *adj*: ~**water fish** poisson *m* d'eau douce.

fret [fret] **1** *vi* s'agiter; *[baby]* pleurer. **don't** ~! ne t'en fais pas!; **the child is** ~**ting for its mother** le petit pleure parce qu'il veut sa mère. **2** *n*: **to be in a** ~* se faire du mauvais sang.
♦ **fretful** *adj person* agité, énervé; *baby, child* grognon. ♦ **fretfully** *adv* avec agitation, avec énervement. ♦ **fretfulness** *n* irritabilité *f*.

fretsaw ['fretsɔ:] *n* scie *f* à découper.

Freudian ['frɔɪdɪən] *adj* freudien. ~ **slip** lapsus *m*.

friar ['fraɪəʳ] *n* frère *m* (*Rel*).

friction ['frɪkʃən] *n* friction *f*. (*US*) ~ **tape** chatterton *m*.

Friday ['fraɪdɪ] *n* vendredi *m*; *for phrases V* **Saturday.**

fridge [frɪdʒ] *n* frigo* *m*, frigidaire *m* ®.

fried [fraɪd] *pret, ptp of* **fry**[2].

friend [frend] *n* ami(e) *m(f)*; (*schoolmate, workmate etc*) camarade *mf*, copain* *m*, copine* *f*. **a** ~ **of mine** un de mes amis; ~**s of ours** des amis (à nous); **her best** ~ sa meilleure amie; **to make/be** ~**s with sb** devenir/être ami avec qn; (*after quarrel*) **to make** ~**s** faire la paix; **he made a** ~ **of him** il en a fait son ami; **he makes** ~**s easily** il se fait facilement des amis; **let's be** ~**s again** on fait la paix?; **we're just good** ~**s** nous sommes simplement bons amis; **we're all** ~**s here** nous sommes entre amis; (*fig*) **to have** ~**s at court** avoir des amis influents; (*Rel*) **Society of F**~**s** Quakers *mpl*. ♦ **friendliness** *n* attitude *f* amicale.
♦ **friendly** *adj* (*gen*) amical; *child, dog, act* gentil; *advice* d'ami; **people here are so** ~**ly** les gens sont si gentils ici; **I am quite** ~**ly with her** je suis assez ami(e) avec elle; **on** ~**ly terms with** en termes amicaux avec; (*Sport*) ~**ly match** match *m* amical. ♦ **friendship** *n* amitié *f*.

frieze [fri:z] *n* (*Archit*) frise *f*.

frigate ['frɪgɪt] *n* frégate *f* (*Naut*).

fright [fraɪt] *n* peur *f*. **to take** ~ s'effrayer (*at* de); **to get** *or* **have a** ~ avoir peur; **to give sb a** ~ faire peur à qn; **she looks a** ~ elle est à faire peur.
♦ **frightful** *adj* (*gen*) affreux; *results, weather* épouvantable, effroyable. ♦ **frightfully** *adv late, ugly, hot* affreusement; *kind, pretty* terriblement; **I am** ~**fully sorry** je suis absolument désolé. ♦ **frightfulness** *n [crime etc]* atrocité *f*.

frighten ['fraɪtn] *vt* faire peur à, effrayer. **it nearly** ~**ed him out of his wits** cela lui a fait une peur bleue; **to** ~ **sb into doing sth** faire faire qch à qn par intimidation; **he was** ~**ed into doing it** il l'a fait sous le coup de la peur; **to be** ~**ed of (doing) sth** avoir peur de (faire) qch; **to be** ~**ed to death** avoir une peur bleue.
frighten away, frighten off *vt sep birds* effaroucher; *children etc* chasser (en leur faisant peur).
♦ **frightened** *adj* effrayé; **don't be** ~**ed** n'ayez pas peur. ♦ **frightening** *adj* effrayant.
♦ **frighteningly** *adv* épouvantablement.

frigid ['frɪdʒɪd] *adj* (*Geog, Met*) glacial; *manner, welcome* froid; *woman* frigide. ♦ **frigidity** *n* froideur *f*; frigidité *f*.

frill [frɪl] *n* volant *m*, (*smaller*) ruche *f*; (*Culin*) papillote *f*. (*fig*) **without any** ~**s** tout simple.
♦ **frilly** *adj dress* à fanfreluches; (*fig*) *speech* à fioritures.

fringe [frɪndʒ] **1** *n [rug, shawl, hair]* frange *f*; *[forest]* bord *m*, lisière *f*; *[crowd]* derniers rangs *mpl*. (*fig*) **on the** ~ **of society** en marge de la société; **the outer** ~**s** la périphérie. **2** *vt shawl etc* franger (*with* de). (*fig*) **road** ~**d with trees** route bordée d'arbres. **3** *adj group, theatre* marginal. ~ **benefits** avantages *mpl* divers.

frisk [frɪsk] **1** *vi* gambader. **2** *vt criminal, suspect* fouiller. ♦ **frisky** *adj* vif, fringant.

fritter[1] ['frɪtəʳ] *vt* (~ **away**) gaspiller.

fritter[2] ['frɪtəʳ] *n* (*Culin*) beignet *m*.

frivolous ['frɪvələs] *adj* frivole. ♦ **frivolity** *n* frivolité *f*.

frizzle ['frɪzl] *vi* grésiller. ♦ **frizzled (up)** *adj food* calciné. ♦ **frizzly** *or* ♦ **frizzy** *adj hair* crêpelé.

fro [frəʊ] *adv*: **to and** ~ de long en large; **to go to and** ~ **between** faire la navette entre; **journeys to and** ~ **between London and Edinburgh** allers *mpl* et retours *mpl* entre Londres et Édimbourg.

frock [frɒk] *n* robe *f*; *[monk]* froc *m*.

frog [frɒg] *n* grenouille *f*. (*fig*) **to have a** ~ **in one's throat** avoir un chat dans la gorge. ♦ **frogman** *n* homme-grenouille *m*. ♦ **frog-march** *vt*: **to** ~**-march sb in/out** *etc* amener/sortir *etc* qn de force.

frolic ['frɒlɪk] *vi* (~ **about**) folâtrer.

from [frɒm] *prep* **(a)** (*place: starting point*) de. **~ house to house** de maison en maison; **to jump ~ a wall** sauter d'un mur; **~ London to Paris** de Londres à Paris; **where are you ~?** d'où êtes-vous *or* venez-vous?; **~ above** d'en haut; **~ above the clouds** d'au-dessus des nuages; **~ afar** de loin; **she was looking at him ~ over the wall** elle le regardait depuis l'autre côté du mur; **~ under the table** de dessous la table. **(b)** (*time: starting point*) (à partir) de, dès. **(as) ~ the 14th July** à partir du 14 juillet; **~ that day onwards** à partir de ce jour-là; **~ his childhood** dès son enfance. **(c)** (*distance*) de. **the house is 10 km ~ the coast** la maison est à 10 km de la côte. **(d)** (*origin*) de, de la part de. **a letter ~ my mother** une lettre de ma mère; **tell him ~ me** dites-lui de ma part; **an invitation ~ the Smiths** une invitation (de la part) des Smith; **film ~ the novel by ...** film d'après le roman de ... . **(e)** (*with prices, numbers*) à partir de, depuis. **wine ~ 6 francs a bottle** vins à partir de 6 F la bouteille; **dresses ~ 150 francs** robes à partir de *or* depuis 150 F; **~ 10 to 15 people** de 10 à 15 personnes. **(f)** (*source*) **to drink ~ a brook/a glass/straight ~ the bottle** boire à un ruisseau/dans un verre/à même la bouteille; **he took it ~ the cupboard** il l'a pris dans le placard; **take the knife ~ this child!** prenez le couteau à cet enfant!; **he took/stole it ~ them** il le leur a pris/volé; **to pick sb ~ the crowd** choisir qn dans la foule; **a quotation ~ Racine** une citation tirée de Racine; **to speak ~ notes** parler avec des notes; **~ your point of view** de votre point de vue. **(g)** (*change*) de. **~ bad to worse** de mal en pis; **price increase ~ 1 F to 1.50 F** augmentation de prix de 1 F à 1,50 F. **(h)** (*cause, motive*) **to act ~ conviction** agir par conviction; **to die ~ fatigue** mourir de fatigue; **~ what I heard** d'après ce que j'ai entendu; **~ what I can see** à ce que je vois; **~ the look of things** à en juger par les apparences; **~ the way he talks you would think that ...** à l'entendre on penserait que ... .

front [frʌnt] **1** *n* **(a)** (*gen*) devant *m*, avant *m*; *[class]* premier rang *m*; *[building]* façade *f*, devant; *[boat, train, car]* avant; *[garment]* devant; *[book]* début *m*. **in ~** *be, walk, put* devant; *send, move* en avant; **in ~ of the table** devant la table; (*in car*) **in the ~** à l'avant; (*Sport*) **to be in ~** mener; **to sit in the ~ of the train/bus** s'asseoir en tête du train/à l'avant de l'autobus; **the ~ of the cupboard** (*door*) la porte du placard; (*forepart*) le devant du placard; (*fig*) **to put on a bold ~** faire bonne contenance; **it's all just a ~** tout ça n'est que façade. **(b)** (*gen, Met, Mil, Pol*) front *m*. **at the ~** au front; **on all ~s** de tous côtés; **popular ~** front populaire. **(c)** (*sea ~*) (*beach*) plage *f*; (*prom*) front *m* de mer. **along** *or* **on the ~** sur le front de mer.

2 *adj garden, tooth* de devant; *wheel* avant *inv*; *row, page* premier. **~ door** *[house]* porte *f* d'entrée; *[car]* portière *f* avant; **the ~ end** l'avant *m*; (*Parl*) **~ bench** banc *m* des ministres ou celui des membres du cabinet fantôme; (*Mil*) **~ line(s)** front *m*; **it's merely a ~ organization** cette organisation n'est qu'une couverture; (*Press*) **on the ~ page** en première page, à la une*; (*fig*) **in the ~ rank** parmi les premiers; **~ room** pièce *f* de devant; (*lounge*) salon *m*; (*fig*) **a ~ runner for the party leadership** un des favoris pour être leader du parti; **to have a ~ seat** (*lit*) avoir une place au premier rang; (*fig*) être aux premières loges.

3 *vi*: **to ~ on to** donner sur.

4 *vt*: **house ~ed with stone** maison *f* avec façade en pierre.

♦ **frontage** *n* façade *f*. ♦ **frontal** *adj* (*gen*) frontal; *attack* de front; *nude* de face. ♦ **front-page** *adj*: **~-page news** gros titres *mpl*; **it was ~-page news** cela a été à la une* des journaux. ♦ **frontwards** *adv* en avant, vers l'avant. ♦ **front-wheel** *adj*: **~-wheel drive** traction *f* avant; **~-wheel drive car** traction avant.

frontier ['frʌntɪəʳ] **1** *n* frontière *f*. **2** *adj town, zone, part* frontière *inv*; *incident* de frontière.

frontispiece ['frʌntɪspiːs] *n* frontispice *m*.

frost [frɒst] **1** *n* gel *m*; (*hoar~*) givre *m*. **late ~s** gelées *fpl* tardives; **10° of ~** 10° au-dessous de zéro. **2** *vt* (*freeze*) geler; (*US: ice*) *cake* glacer.

♦ **frostbite** *n* gelure *f*; **to get ~bite in one's hands** avoir les mains qui gèlent. ♦ **frostbitten** *adj* gelé. ♦ **frostbound** *adj* gelé. ♦ **frosted** *adj window, windscreen* givré; *nail varnish* nacré; (*opaque*) *glass* dépoli. ♦ **frosting** *n* (*US: icing*) glaçage *m*. ♦ **frosty** *adj* (*gen: also fig*) glacial; *window* couvert de givre; **it is going to be ~y** il va geler.

froth [frɒθ] **1** *n* mousse *f*. **2** *vi* mousser. **the dog was ~ing at the mouth** le chien avait de l'écume à la gueule.

♦ **frothy** *adj water, beer* mousseux; *sea* écumeux; *lace, nightdress* vaporeux; *play, entertainment* léger.

frown [fraʊn] **1** *n* froncement *m* (de sourcils). **2** *vi* froncer les sourcils. **to ~ at sth/sb** regarder qch/qn en fronçant les sourcils; (*fig: also* **~ on sb/sth**) désapprouver qch/qn.

frowsy, frowzy ['fraʊzɪ] *adj room* qui sent le renfermé; *person, clothes* négligé.

froze [frəʊz] *pret of* **freeze**.

frozen ['frəʊzn] (*ptp of* **freeze**) *adj* gelé; *food* congelé. **I am ~** je suis gelé; **my hands are ~** j'ai les mains gelées; **to be ~ stiff** être gelé jusqu'aux os; **~ food** aliments *mpl* congelés; (*industrially* **~**) aliments surgelés.

frugal ['fruːgəl] *adj person* économe (*with* de); *meal* frugal. ♦ **frugality** *n* frugalité *f*. ♦ **frugally** *adv give out* parcimonieusement; *live* simplement.

fruit [fruːt] **1** *n* fruit *m*. **may I have some ~?** puis-je avoir un fruit?; **more ~ is eaten nowadays** on mange actuellement plus de fruits; **~ is good for you** les fruits sont bons pour la santé; (*lit, fig*) **to bear ~** porter fruit; **the ~ of hard work** le fruit d'un long travail. **2** *adj basket* à fruits; *salad* de fruits; *tree* fruitier. **~ cake** cake *m*; **~ cup** boisson *f* aux fruits (*parfois alcoolisée*); **~ dish** (*for dessert*) coupelle *f* à fruits, (*large*) coupe *f* à fruits, (*for holding* **~**) corbeille *f* à fruits; **~ farm** exploitation *f* *or* entreprise *f* fruitière; **~ farming** arboriculture *f* (fruitière); **~ machine** machine *f* à sous.

♦ **fruiterer** *n* fruitier *m*, -ière *f*; **~erer's shop** fruiterie *f*. ♦ **fruitful** *adj* fécond; (*fig*) fructueux. ♦ **fruitfully** *adv* (*fig*) fructueusement, avec profit. ♦ **fruitfulness** *n* fécondité *f*; caractère *m* fructueux. ♦ **fruition** [fruːˈɪʃən] *n*: **to bring to ~ion** réaliser; **to come to ~ion** se réaliser. ♦ **fruitless** *adj* stérile (*fig*). ♦ **fruity** *adj flavour* fruité; *voice* bien timbré.

frump [frʌmp] *n* bonne femme *f* fagotée. ♦ **frumpish** *adj* fagoté.

frustrate [frʌsˈtreɪt] *vt hopes* tromper; *attempts, plans, plot* faire échouer; *person* décevoir. ♦ **frustrated** *adj person* frustré; *effort* vain; **he feels very ~d in his present job** il se sent très insatisfait dans son poste actuel. ♦ **frustrating** *adj* déprimant, irritant. ♦ **frustration** *n* (*emotion*) frustration *f*; (*sth frustrating etc*) déception *f*.

fry¹ [fraɪ] *n*: **the small ~** (*unimportant people*) le menu fretin; (*children*) les gosses* *mfpl*.

fry² [fraɪ] *pret, ptp* **fried 1** *vt* (faire) frire. **to ~ eggs** faire des œufs *mpl* sur le plat; **fried eggs** œufs sur le plat; **fried fish** poisson *m* frit.

2 *vi* frire.

♦ **frying** *n*: **a smell of ~ing** une odeur de friture; **~ing pan** poêle *f* (à frire); **to jump out of the ~ing pan into the fire** tomber de Charybde en Scylla.

fuchsia ['fjuːʃə] *n* fuchsia *m*.

fuddled ['fʌdld] *adj ideas* confus; *person* (*muddled*) désorienté; (*tipsy*) éméché.

fudge [fʌdʒ] **1** *n* (*Culin*) fondant *m*. **2** *vt*: **to ~ an issue** esquiver un problème.

fuel [fjʊəl] **1** *n* (*gen*) combustible *m*; (*for engine*) carburant *m*. (*fig*) **to add ~ to the flames** jeter de l'huile sur le feu; **the statistics gave him ~ for further attacks on ...** les statistiques sont venues alimenter ses attaques contre ... . **2** *vt furnace etc* alimenter; *ships, aircraft etc* ravitailler en carburant. **3** *vi* se ravitailler en combustible *or* en carburant. (*Aviat etc*) **a ~ling stop** une escale technique. **4** *adj*: **~ oil** mazout *m*, fuel *m*; **~ pump** pompe *f* d'alimentation; **~ tank** réservoir *m* à carburant; *[ship]* soute *f* à mazout.

fugitive ['fju:dʒɪtɪv] *adj, n* fugitif (*m*), -ive (*f*).

fulfil, (*US*) **-ll** [fʊl'fɪl] *vt task, prophecy* accomplir; *order* exécuter; *condition* remplir; *plan, ambition* réaliser; *desire, hope* répondre à; *prayer* exaucer; *promise* tenir; *one's duties* s'acquitter de. **to feel ~led** se réaliser dans la vie. ♦ **fulfilling** *adj work etc* profondément satisfaisant. ♦ **fulfil(l)ment** *n [duty, desire]* accomplissement *m*; *[prayer, wish]* exaucement *m*; *[conditions, plans]* réalisation *f*; (*satisfied feeling*) contentement *m*.

full [fʊl] **1** *adj* **(a)** (*gen*) plein (*of* de); *room, theatre* comble, plein; *hotel, bus, train* complet; *day, programme* chargé. **~ to overflowing** plein à déborder; **a ~ life** une vie bien remplie; **his heart was ~** il avait le cœur gros; (*Theat*) **to play to a ~ house** jouer à bureaux fermés; **we are ~ (up) for July** nous sommes complets pour juillet; **you'll work better on a ~ stomach** tu travailleras mieux après avoir mangé; (*not hungry*) **I am ~ up!*** j'ai trop mangé!; **~ of life** débordant d'entrain; **~ of oneself/of one's own importance** imbu de soi-même/de sa propre importance; **the papers were ~ of the murder** les journaux ne parlaient que du meurtre.

(b) (*complete*) *moon, employment* plein (*before n*). **the ~ particulars** tous les détails; **~ information** des renseignements complets; **2 ~ hours** 2 bonnes heures; **to go (at) ~ blast*** *[car etc]* aller à toute pompe*; *[radio, television]* marcher à plein; **in ~ bloom** épanoui; **to pay ~ fare** payer plein tarif; **to fall ~ length** tomber de tout son long; **~ member** membre *m* à part entière; **~ name** nom et prénom(s) *mpl*; **at ~ speed** à toute vitesse; **~ speed ahead!, ~ steam ahead!** en avant toute!; (*Gram*) **~ stop** point *m*; **I'm not going, ~ stop!*** je n'y vais pas, un point c'est tout!; **working at the factory came to a ~ stop** ça a été l'arrêt complet du travail à l'usine; **battalion at ~ strength** bataillon au grand complet; **party in ~ swing** soirée qui bat son plein; **in ~ uniform** en grande tenue.

(c) *lips* charnu; *face* plein, rond; *figure* rondelet; *skirt etc* large.

2 *adv*: **~ well** fort bien; **~ in the face** *hit* en plein visage; *look* droit dans les yeux; **to go ~ out** aller à toute vitesse.

3 *n*: **in ~** *write sth* en toutes lettres; *publish* intégralement; **he paid in ~** il a tout payé; **to the ~** *justify* complètement; *use* au maximum.

♦ **fullback** *n* (*Sport*) arrière *m*. ♦ **full-blooded** *adj* (*vigorous*) *person* vigoureux; (*of unmixed race*) de race pure. ♦ **full-blown** *adj flower* épanoui. ♦ **full-bodied** *adj wine* qui a du corps. ♦ **full-dress** *adj clothes* de cérémonie; *debate* dans les règles. ♦ **full-grown** *adj* adulte. ♦ **full-length** *adj portrait* en pied; *film* (de) long métrage. ♦ **fullness** *n*: **in the ~ness of time** (*eventually*) avec le temps; (*at predestined time*) en temps et lieu. ♦ **full-scale** *adj drawing, replica* grandeur nature *inv*; *search, retreat* de grande envergure; **~-scale fighting** une bataille rangée. ♦ **full-sized** *adj* grandeur nature *inv*. ♦ **full-time 1** *n* (*Sport*) fin *f* de match; **2** *adj, adv* à plein temps; **it's a ~-time job looking after those children** il faut s'occuper de ces enfants 24 heures sur 24. ♦ **fully** *adv* (*completely*) *satisfied* entièrement; *understand* très bien; *justify* complètement; *use* au maximum; (*at least*) au moins, bien. ♦ **fully-fashioned** *adj* entièrement diminué.

fulminate ['fʌlmɪneɪt] *vi* fulminer (*against* contre).

fulsome ['fʊlsəm] *adj praise* exagéré; *manner* plein d'effusions.

fumble ['fʌmbl] *vi* (**~ about, ~ around**) (*in the dark*) tâtonner; (*in one's pockets*) fouiller (*for sth* pour trouver qch). **to ~ with sth** tripoter qch maladroitement.

fume [fju:m] **1** *vi* fumer; (*: *be furious*) être en rage. **2** *n*: **~s** (*gen*) exhalaisons *fpl*, vapeurs *fpl*; (*from factory*) fumées *fpl*.

fumigate ['fju:mɪgeɪt] *vt* désinfecter par fumigation.

fun [fʌn] **1** *n*: **to have (good** *or* **great) ~** bien s'amuser; **to be (good** *or* **great) ~** être très amusant; **what ~!** ce que c'est amusant!; **for ~, in ~** pour rire; **to do sth for the ~ of it** faire qch pour s'amuser; **to spoil sb's ~** empêcher qn de s'amuser; **to spoil the ~** jouer les trouble-fête; **to have ~ and games with sth** bien s'amuser avec qch; (*fig: trouble*) en voir de toutes les couleurs* avec qch; **there'll be ~ and games over this decision*** cette décision va faire du potin*; **to make ~ of** *or* **poke ~ at sb/sth** se moquer de qn/qch. **2** *adj* (‡) marrant*, rigolo*. ♦ **funfair** *n* fête *f* foraine. ♦ **fun-loving** *adj* aimant s'amuser.

function ['fʌŋkʃən] **1** *n* **(a)** (*gen*) fonction *f*. **in his ~ as judge** en sa qualité de juge. **(b)** (*meeting*) réunion *f*; (*reception*) réception *f*; (*official ceremony*) cérémonie *f* publique. **2** *vi* fonctionner. **to ~ as** faire fonction de. ♦ **functional** *adj* fonctionnel. ♦ **functionary** *n* fonctionnaire *mf*.

fund [fʌnd] *n* caisse *f*, fonds *m*. **to start a ~** lancer une souscription; **~s** fonds *mpl*; **in ~s** en fonds; (*Banking*) **no ~s** défaut *m* de provision; (*fig*) **a ~ of** beaucoup de. ♦ **fundraise** *vi* obtenir des contributions bénévoles (*for* pour).

fundamental [ˌfʌndə'mentl] **1** *adj* fondamental. **2** *n*: **the ~s** les principes *mpl* essentiels; **to get down to (the) ~s** en venir à l'essentiel. ♦ **fundamentalism** *n* fondamentalisme *m*. ♦ **fundamentalist** *n, adj* fondamentaliste (*mf*). ♦ **fundamentally** *adv* fondamentalement.

funeral ['fju:nərəl] **1** *n* enterrement *m*; (*in announcement etc*) obsèques *fpl*, (*grander*) funérailles *fpl*. **my uncle's ~** l'enterrement de mon oncle; **Churchill's ~** les funérailles de Churchill; **that's your ~!*** tant pis pour toi! **2** *adj march, oration, service* funèbre. **~ director** entrepreneur *m* des pompes funèbres; **~ home, ~ parlour** dépôt *m* mortuaire; **~ procession** cortège *m* funèbre, (*in car*) convoi *m* mortuaire. ♦ **funereal** [fju:'nɪərɪəl] *adj* funèbre, lugubre.

fungus ['fʌŋgəs] *n, pl* **-gi** (*Bot*) champignon *m*; (*mould*) moisissure *f*; (*Med*) fongus *m*.

funicular [fju:'nɪkjʊləʳ] *adj, n* funiculaire (*m*).

funk* [fʌŋk] **1** *n*: **to be in a blue ~** avoir la frousse*. **2** *vt*: **he ~ed (doing) it** il s'est dégonflé*.

funnel ['fʌnl] *n* (*for pouring through*) entonnoir *m*; *[ship, engine etc]* cheminée *f*.

funny ['fʌnɪ] **1** *adj* **(a)** (*comic*) drôle, amusant. **~ story** histoire *f* drôle; **he was always trying to be ~** il cherchait toujours à faire de l'esprit; **it's not ~** ça n'a rien de drôle. **(b)** (*strange*) curieux, bizarre. **a ~ idea** une drôle d'idée; **he is ~ that way*** il est comme ça; **the meat tastes ~** la viande a un drôle de goût; **there's sth ~** *or* **some ~ business* going on** il se passe qch de louche; **I felt ~*** je me suis senti tout chose*; **it gave me a ~ feeling** ça m'a fait tout drôle; **~!** c'est drôle, c'est curieux; ~ **bone*** petit juif* *m.* **2** *n* (*Press*) **the funnies‡** les bandes dessinées.

♦ **funnily** *adv* (*amusingly*) drôlement; (*strangely*) curieusement, bizarrement; **funnily enough, ...** chose curieuse, ...

fur [fɜːʳ] **1** *n* **(a)** *[animal]* poil *m*, fourrure *f*. **it will make the ~ fly** cela va faire du grabuge*; **she was dressed in ~s** elle portait de la fourrure. **(b)** (*in kettle etc*) tartre *m*. **2** *adj*: **~ coat** manteau *m* de fourrure. ♦ **furred** *adj tongue* chargé. ♦ **furrier** *n* fourreur *m*. ♦ **furry** *adj animal* à poil; *toy* en peluche.

furbish [ˈfɜːbɪʃ] *vt* (*polish*) fourbir; (*smarten*) remettre à neuf.

furious [ˈfjʊərɪəs] *adj person* furieux (*with sb* contre qn; *at having done* d'avoir fait); *storm, sea* déchaîné; *struggle* acharné; *speed* fou. **to get ~** se mettre en rage (*with sb* contre qn); **the fun was fast and ~** la fête battait son plein. ♦ **furiously** *adv* furieusement; avec acharnement; à une allure folle.

furled [fɜːld] *adj flag* en berne.

furlough [ˈfɜːləʊ] *n* permission *f*, congé *m*.

furnace [ˈfɜːnɪs] *n* (*Ind*) fourneau *m*; (*for central heating etc*) chaudière *f*; (*fig: hot place*) fournaise *f*.

furnish [ˈfɜːnɪʃ] *vt* **(a)** *house* meubler (*with* de). **~ed flat** *or* **apartment** appartement *m* meublé; **in ~ed rooms** en meublé. **(b)** (*supply*) *object, information etc* fournir, donner; *person* pourvoir (*with sth* de qch). ♦ **furnishing** *n*: **~ings** mobilier *m*; **with ~ings and fittings** avec objets mobiliers divers; **~ing fabrics** tissus *mpl* d'ameublement.

furniture [ˈfɜːnɪtʃəʳ] **1** *n* meubles *mpl*. **a piece of ~** un meuble; **dining-room ~** des meubles *or* du mobilier de salle à manger. **2** *adj*: **~ polish** encaustique *f*; **~ remover** déménageur *m*; **~ shop** magasin *m* d'ameublement; **~ van** camion *m* de déménagement.

furore [fjʊəˈrɔːrɪ] *n* (*protests*) scandale *m*; (*enthusiasm*) débordement *m* d'enthousiasme.

furrow [ˈfʌrəʊ] **1** *n* (*Agr*) sillon *m*; (*in garden etc*) rayon *m*; (*on brow*) ride *f*. **2** *vt earth* sillonner; *face, brow* rider.

further [ˈfɜːðəʳ] *comp of* **far 1** *adv* **(a)** = **farther 1. (b)** (*more*) davantage, plus. **without troubling any ~** sans se tracasser davantage; **I got no ~ with him** je ne suis arrivé à rien de plus avec lui; **we heard nothing ~ from him** nous n'avons plus rien reçu de lui; **and ~ I believe ...** et de plus je crois ...; (*Comm*) **~ to** par suite à. **2** *adj* **(a)** = **farther 2. (b)** (*additional*) supplémentaire, autre. **~ education** enseignement *m* post-scolaire; **college of ~ education** centre *m* d'enseignement post-scolaire; **until ~ notice** jusqu'à nouvel ordre; **upon ~ consideration** après plus ample réflexion; **awaiting ~ details** en attendant de plus amples détails; **one or two ~ details** un ou deux autres points. **3** *vt interests, cause* servir, favoriser. ♦ **furtherance** *n* avancement *m*; **in ~ance of sth** pour servir qch. ♦ **furthermore** *adv* en outre, de plus. ♦ **furthermost** *adj* le plus éloigné.

furthest [ˈfɜːðɪst] = **farthest.**

furtive [ˈfɜːtɪv] *adj action, look* furtif; *person* sournois. ♦ **furtively** *adv* furtivement.

fury [ˈfjʊərɪ] *n [person]* fureur *f*; *[storm, wind, struggle]* violence *f*. **to be in a ~** être en furie *or* rage; **to fly into a ~** se mettre dans une rage folle; **like ~*** comme un fou (*or* une folle).

furze [fɜːz] *n* ajoncs *mpl*.

fuse [fjuːz] **1** *vt* **(a)** (*unite*) *metal* fondre; (*fig*) fusionner. **(b)** (*Elec*) **to ~ the television (*or* the iron *or* the lights *etc*)** faire sauter les plombs. **2** *vi* **(a)** *[metals]* fondre; (*fig*: **~ together**) fusionner. **(b)** (*Elec*) **the television (*or* the lights *etc*) ~d** les plombs ont sauté. **3** *n* **(a)** (*Elec: wire*) plomb *m*, fusible *m*. **to blow a ~** faire sauter un plomb *or* un fusible; **there's been a ~ somewhere** il y a un plomb de sauté quelque part. **(b)** *[bomb etc]* détonateur *m*; (*Min*) cordeau *m*. **4** *adj*: **~ box** boîte *f* à fusibles; **~ wire** fusible *m*. ♦ **fused** *adj*: **~d plug** prise *f* avec fusible incorporé. ♦ **fusion** *n* fusion *f*.

fuselage [ˈfjuːzəlɑːʒ] *n* fuselage *m*.

fusilier [ˌfjuːzɪˈlɪəʳ] *n* fusilier *m*.

fuss [fʌs] **1** *n* histoires* *fpl*. **a lot of ~ about very little** beaucoup de bruit pour pas grand-chose; **to make a ~** faire un tas d'histoires* (*about or over sth* pour qch); **she was right to make a ~** elle a eu raison de protester; **what a ~ to get a passport!** que d'histoires* pour obtenir un passeport!; **to make a ~ of sb** être aux petits soins pour qn. **2** *vi* (*excitedly*) s'agiter; (*busily*) faire l'affairé(e); (*worriedly*) se tracasser. **to ~ over sb** être aux petits soins pour qn.

fuss about, fuss around *vi* faire l'affairé.

♦ **fusspot*** *n* personne *f* qui fait des histoires pour rien. ♦ **fussy** *adj person* tatillon; *dress, style* tarabiscoté; **she's very ~y about what she eats** elle est très tatillonne sur ce qu'elle mange; **I'm not ~y*** (*don't mind*) ça m'est égal.

fusty [ˈfʌstɪ] *adj smell* de renfermé; *room* qui sent le renfermé.

futile [ˈfjuːtaɪl] *adj remark* futile, vain; *attempt* vain. ♦ **futility** *n* futilité *f*.

future [ˈfjuːtʃəʳ] **1** *n* **(a)** avenir *m*. **in (the) ~** à l'avenir; **in the near ~** dans un proche avenir; **there is a real ~ in this firm** cette firme offre de réelles possibilités d'avenir; **there's no ~ in it*** *[job etc]* cela n'a aucun avenir; (*fig: no good doing that*) ça ne servira à rien. **(b)** (*Gram*) futur *m*. **in the ~** au futur. **2** *adj life, events* futur (*before n*), à venir; *husband* futur. **at some ~ date** à une date ultérieure; (*Gram*) **~ perfect** futur *m* antérieur; **the ~ tense** le futur. ♦ **futuristic** *adj* futuriste. ♦ **futurologist** *n* futurologue *mf*. ♦ **futurology** *n* futurologie *f*.

fuze [fjuːz] (*US*) = **fuse.**

fuzz [fʌz] *n* (*frizzy hair*) cheveux *mpl* crépus; (*on face*) excroissance *f* (*hum*); (*light growth*) duvet *m*. (*collective: police*) **the ~‡** les flics‡ *mpl*.

♦ **fuzzy** *adj hair* crépu; (*Phot*) flou; *ideas* confus; *person* désorienté; (*: *tipsy*) pompette*.

G

G, g [dʒiː] *n* G, g *m*; (*Mus*) sol *m*; (*gravity*) g *m*. (*Med*) **G.P.** = **general practitioner,** *V* **general.** ♦ **G-string** *n* (*garment*) cache-sexe *m inv*.
gabardine [ˌgæbəˈdiːn] *n* gabardine *f*.
gabble [ˈgæbl] **1** *vi* (*indistinctly*) bredouiller; (*unintelligibly*) baragouiner*. **to ~ on about sth** parler avec volubilité de qch. **2** *vt* bredouiller.
gable [ˈgeɪbl] *n* pignon *m*.
gad [gæd] *vi*: **to ~ about** vadrouiller*.
gadget [ˈgædʒɪt] *n* gadget *m*; (*: *thingummy*) petit truc* *m*. ♦ **gadgetry** *n* tous les gadgets *mpl*.
Gaelic [ˈgeɪlɪk] *adj, n* gaélique (*m*).
gaff [gæf] *n* (*Fishing*) gaffe *f*.
gaffe [gæf] *n* gaffe *f*, bévue *f*.
gaffer* [ˈgæfəʳ] *n* (*old man*) vieux *m*; (*foreman*) contremaître *m*; (*boss*) patron *m*.
gag [gæg] **1** *n* **(a)** (*in mouth*) bâillon *m*. **(b)** (*joke*) plaisanterie *f*. **it's a ~ to raise funds** c'est un truc* comique pour ramasser de l'argent. **2** *vt* (*silence*) bâillonner. **3** *vi* (*: *joke*) plaisanter; (*: *retch*) avoir des haut-le-cœur.
gage [geɪdʒ] (*US*) = **gauge.**
gaiety [ˈgeɪɪtɪ] *n* gaieté *f*.
gaily [ˈgeɪlɪ] *adv behave, speak* gaiement; *decorate* de façon gaie. ♦ **gaily-coloured** *adj* aux couleurs vives.
gain [geɪn] **1** *n* (*Comm, Fin*) (*profit*) bénéfice *m*; (*winning*) gain *m*; (*fig*) avantage *m*; (*increase*) augmentation *f*; (*in wealth*) accroissement *m* (*in* de); (*knowledge etc*) acquisition *f* (*in* de); (*St Ex*) hausse *f*. **to do sth for ~** faire qch pour le profit; **his loss is our ~** là où il perd nous gagnons.

2 *vt* (*gen*) gagner; *experience* acquérir; *objective* atteindre; *liberty* conquérir; *friends* se faire; *supporters* s'attirer. **to ~ ground** gagner du terrain; **to ~ popularity** gagner en popularité; **what have you ~ed by doing it?** qu'est-ce que tu as gagné à faire ça? **(b)** (*increase*) (*St Ex*) **these shares have ~ed 3 points** ces valeurs ont enregistré une hausse de 3 points; **to ~ speed/weight** prendre de la vitesse/du poids; **she's ~ed 3 kg** elle a pris 3 kg; **my watch has ~ed 5 minutes** ma montre a pris 5 minutes d'avance; **to ~ the upper hand** prendre le dessus.

3 *vi* gagner (*in* en, *by* à); *[watch]* avancer; *[runners]* prendre de l'avance (*on* sur).
♦ **gainful** *adj occupation etc* rémunérateur; *employment* rémunéré.
gainsay [ˌgeɪnˈseɪ] *pret, ptp* **gainsaid** *vt person* contredire; *fact* nier; *argument* réfuter. **there's no ~ing it** c'est indéniable.
gait [geɪt] *n* démarche *f*, façon *f* de marcher.
gaiter [ˈgeɪtəʳ] *n* guêtre *f*.
gala [ˈgɑːlə] **1** *n* fête *f*, gala *m*; (*sports*) grand concours *m*. **~ occasion** grande occasion *f*.
galaxy [ˈgæləksɪ] *n* galaxie *f*.
gale [geɪl] **1** *n* coup *m* de vent. **it was blowing a ~** le vent soufflait très fort; **there's a ~ blowing in through that window** c'est une véritable bourrasque qui entre par cette fenêtre; **~s of laughter** grands éclats *mpl* de rire. **2** *adj*: **~ force winds** coups *mpl* de vent; **~ warning** avis *m* de coups de vent.
gall¹ [gɔːl] *n* bile *f*; (*bitterness*) fiel *m*; (*: *impertinence*) culot* *m*. ♦ **gall-bladder** *n* vésicule *f* biliaire. ♦ **gallstone** calcul *m* biliaire.
gall² [gɔːl] *vt* (*irritate*) irriter, exaspérer. ♦ **galling** *adj* (*irritating*) irritant; (*humiliating*) humiliant.
gallant [ˈgælənt] *adj* **(a)** (*brave*) brave, vaillant. **(b)** [gəˈlænt] (*attentive to women*) galant. ♦ **gallantly** *adv* bravement; [gəˈlæntlɪ] galamment. ♦ **gallantry** *n* bravoure *f*.
galleon [ˈgælɪən] *n* galion *m*.
gallery [ˈgælərɪ] *n* (*gen*) galerie *f*; (*for spectators, reporters*) tribune *f*; (*Theat*) dernier balcon *m*; (*art: private*) galerie; (*state-owned*) musée *m*. (*fig*) **to play to the ~** poser *or* parler pour la galerie.
galley [ˈgælɪ] *n* **(a)** (*ship*) galère *f*; (*ship's kitchen*) coquerie *f*. **~ slave** galérien *m*. **(b)** (*Typ*) galée *f*. **~ (proof)** placard *m*.
Gallic [ˈgælɪk] *adj* (*of Gaul*) gaulois; (*French*) français; *charm etc* latin. ♦ **gallicism** *n* gallicisme *m*.
gallivant [ˌgælɪˈvænt] *vi* (**~ about, ~ around**) courir le guilledou*.
gallon [ˈgælən] *n* gallon *m* (*Brit* = *4,546 litres, US* = *3,785 litres*).
gallop [ˈgæləp] **1** *n* galop *m*. **to go for a ~** faire un temps de galop; **at full ~** *[horse]* au grand galop; *[rider]* à bride abattue. **2** *vi [horse, rider]* galoper. (*lit, fig*) **to ~ away/back** *etc* partir/revenir *etc* au galop.
♦ **galloping** *adj horse* au galop; *inflation, pneumonia* galopant.
gallows [ˈgæləʊz] *npl* gibet *m*, potence *f*.
galore [gəˈlɔːʳ] *adv* en abondance, à gogo*.
galvanize [ˈgælvənaɪz] *vt* galvaniser. (*fig*) **to ~ sb into action** galvaniser qn. ♦ **galvanic** *adj* (*Elec*) galvanique; *effect* galvanisant. ♦ **galvanization** *n* galvanisation *f*.
gambit [ˈgæmbɪt] *n* (*Chess*) gambit *m*; (*fig*) manœuvre *f*.
gamble [ˈgæmbl] **1** *n* entreprise *f* risquée. **life's a ~** la vie est un jeu de hasard; **it's a pure ~** c'est affaire de chance; **the ~ paid off** ça a payé de prendre ce risque*. **2** *vi* jouer (*on* sur, *with* avec). **to ~ on the stock exchange** jouer à la Bourse; (*fig*) **to ~ on** compter sur, (*less sure*) miser sur.
gamble away *vt sep money etc* perdre au jeu.
♦ **gambler** *n* joueur *m*, -euse *f*. ♦ **gambling 1** *n* jeu *m*; **his gambling** sa passion du jeu; **2** *adj debts* de jeu; *losses* au jeu; **gambling den, gambling house** maison *f* de jeu, tripot *m* (*pej*).
gambol [ˈgæmbəl] *vi* gambader. **to ~ away** *etc* partir *etc* en gambadant.
game¹ [geɪm] **1** *n* **(a)** (*gen*) jeu *m*; *[football, cricket etc]* match *m*; *[tennis, billiards, chess]* partie *f*. **~ of cards** partie de cartes; **card ~** jeu de cartes (*belotte, bridge etc*); **to have a ~ of** faire une partie de, jouer un match de; (*Scol*) **~s** sport *m*, plein air *m*; **to be good at ~s** être sportif; **that's ~** (*Tennis*) ça fait jeu; (*Bridge*) ça fait la manche; (*Tennis*) **~, set and match** jeu, set et match; **he's off his ~** il n'est pas en forme; **to put sb off his ~** troubler qn; **this isn't a ~!** c'est sérieux!; (*fig*) **it's a profitable ~** c'est une entreprise rentable; **the ~ is up** tout est fichu*; **to play sb's ~** entrer dans le jeu de qn; **two can play at that ~** à bon chat bon rat; **what's the ~?*** qu'est-ce qui se passe?; **I wonder what his ~ is** je me demande ce qu'il

mijoté*; **to beat sb at his own ~** battre qn sur son propre terrain; **how long have you been in this ~?*** ça fait combien de temps que vous faites ça?; **the ~ isn't worth the candle** le jeu n'en vaut pas la chandelle; to **make a ~ of** se moquer de. **(b)** (*Culin, Hunting*) gibier *m*. **big ~** gros gibier.

2 *adj*: **~ birds** gibier *m* à plume; **~ laws** réglementation *f* de la chasse; **~ reserve** réserve *f* de gros gibier; **~s master, ~s mistress** professeur *m* d'éducation physique; **~ warden** (*on reserve*) gardien *m*.

3 *vi* jouer, parier.

♦ **gamekeeper** *n* garde-chasse *m*. ♦ **gamesmanship** *n*: **to be good at ~smanship** être rusé; **it's a piece of ~smanship** c'est un truc* pour gagner.

game² [geɪm] *adj* courageux, brave. **to be ~** avoir du cran*; **to be ~ for sth** *or* **to do sth** se sentir de taille à faire qch; **are you ~?** tu t'en sens capable?; **~ for anything** prêt à tout.

game³ [geɪm] *adj* (*lame*) *arm, leg* estropié. **to have a ~ leg** être estropié.

gamma ['gæmə] *n* gamma *m*. **~ rays** rayons *mpl* gamma.

gammon ['gæmən] *n* (*ham*) jambon *m* fumé.

gamut ['gæmət] *n* gamme *f*. **to run the ~ of** passer par toute la gamme de.

gang [gæŋ] *n* *[workmen]* équipe *f*; *[criminals]* bande *f*, gang *m*; *[youths, friends etc]* bande; *[prisoners]* convoi *m*.

gang together*, gang up* *vi* se mettre à plusieurs (*to do* pour faire). **to ~ up on** *or* **against sb‡** se mettre à plusieurs contre qn.

♦ **gangland*** *n* le milieu. ♦ **gangplank** *n* passerelle *f*. ♦ **gangster** *n* gangster *m*. ♦ **gangway** *n* (*gen*) passage *m*; (*Naut*) passerelle *f*; (*in bus etc*) couloir *m*; (*in theatre*) allée *f*; (*excl*) **~way!** dégagez!

gangling ['gæŋglɪŋ] *adj* dégingandé.

ganglion ['gæŋglɪən] *n, pl* **ganglia** ganglion *m*.

gangrene ['gæŋgriːn] *n* gangrène *f*. ♦ **gangrenous** *adj* gangreneux. **to go ~** se gangrener.

gannet ['gænɪt] *n* (*Orn*) fou *m*.

gantry ['gæntrɪ] *n* (*gen*) portique *m*; (*Space*) tour *f* de lancement.

gaol [dʒeɪl] (*Brit*) = **jail**.

gap [gæp] *n* (*gen*) trou *m*; (*in wall, hedge*) trou, ouverture *f*; (*in print, text*) blanc *m*; (*between floorboards, curtains, teeth*) interstice *m*; (*mountain pass*) trouée *f*; (*fig*) vide *m*; (*in education*) lacune *f*; (*in time*) intervalle *m*; (*in conversation, narrative*) interruption *f*, vide. **to stop up** *or* **fill in a ~** boucher un trou, combler un vide; **a ~ in his memory** un trou de mémoire; **he left a ~ which will be hard to fill** il a laissé un vide qu'il sera difficile de combler; **to close the ~ between two points of view** rapprocher deux points de vue; **to close the ~ in the balance of payments** supprimer le déficit dans la balance des paiements.

gape [geɪp] *vi* **(a)** *[person, seam]* bâiller; *[chasm etc]* être béant. **(b)** (*stare*) rester bouche bée (*at* devant). **to ~ at sb/sth** regarder qn/qch bouche bée. ♦ **gaping** *adj hole, chasm, wound* béant; *seam* qui bâille; *person* bouche bée *inv*.

garage ['gærɑːʒ] **1** *n* garage *m*. **2** *vt* mettre au garage. **3** *adj*: **~ mechanic** mécanicien *m*; **~ proprietor** garagiste *m*.

garb [gɑːb] *n* costume *m*.

garbage ['gɑːbɪdʒ] **1** *n* ordures *fpl*, détritus *mpl*; (*in kitchen*) déchets *mpl*; (*fig*) rebut *m*. **2** *adj*: **~ can** boîte *f* à ordures; **~ collector, ~ man** éboueur *m*; **~ disposal unit** broyeur *m* d'ordures; **~ truck** benne *f* des boueurs.

garble ['gɑːbl] *vt story* raconter de travers; *quotation* déformer; *facts* dénaturer; *instructions* embrouiller. ♦ **garbled** *adj account, instructions* embrouillé; *text* altéré; *words, speech* incompréhensible.

garden ['gɑːdn] **1** *n* jardin *m*. **the G~ of Eden** le jardin d'Éden; **~s** (*private*) parc *m*; (*public*) jardin public; (*fig*) **to lead sb up the ~ (path)*** mener qn en bateau*; (*fig*) **everything in the ~'s lovely** tout va pour le mieux. **2** *vi* faire du jardinage. **3** *adj*: **~ centre** pépinière *f*; **~ city** cité-jardin *f*; **~ hose** tuyau *m* d'arrosage; **~ tools** outils *mpl* de jardinage; **~ party** garden-party *f*; **~ produce** produits *mpl* maraîchers; **~ seat** banc *m* de jardin; **~ shears** cisaille *f* de jardinier; **just over the ~ wall from us** juste à côté de chez nous. ♦ **gardener** *n* jardinier *m*, -ière *f*. ♦ **gardening** *n* jardinage *m*.

gardenia [gɑː'diːnɪə] *n* gardénia *m*.

gargle ['gɑːgl] *vi* se gargariser.

gargoyle ['gɑːgɔɪl] *n* gargouille *f*.

garish ['gɛərɪʃ] *adj* (*gen*) voyant, criard; *light* cru.

garland ['gɑːlənd] *n* guirlande *f*.

garlic ['gɑːlɪk] **1** *n* ail *m*. **2** *adj*: **~ salt** sel *m* d'ail; **~ sausage** saucisson *m* à l'ail. ♦ **garlicky** *adj flavour, smell* d'ail; *sauce* à l'ail; *food* aillé; *breath* qui sent l'ail.

garment ['gɑːmənt] *n* vêtement *m*.

garnet ['gɑːnɪt] *n* grenat *m*.

garnish ['gɑːnɪʃ] **1** *vt* garnir (*with* de). **2** *n* garniture *f*.

garret ['gærət] *n* mansarde *f*.

garrison ['gærɪsən] **1** *n* garnison *f*. **2** *vt* placer une garnison dans; *[troops]* être en garnison dans. **3** *adj town, troops, duty* de garnison.

garrulous ['gærʊləs] *adj* loquace. ♦ **garrulity** *n* loquacité *f*. ♦ **garrulously** *adv* avec volubilité.

garter ['gɑːtər] **1** *n* **(a)** (*gen*) jarretière *f*; (*for men's socks*) fixe-chaussette *m*. **(b)** (*US: from belt*) jarretelle *f*. **2** *adj* (*US*) **~ belt** porte-jarretelles *m inv*.

gas [gæs] **1** *n* **(a)** (*gen*) gaz *m inv*; (*anaesthetic*) anesthésique *m*. **Calor ~ ®** ≃ butane *m*; **to cook by** *or* **with ~** faire la cuisine au gaz; **to turn on/off the ~** allumer/fermer le gaz; (*Med etc*) **I had ~** j'ai eu une anesthésie au masque. **(b)** (*US: gasoline*) essence *f*.

2 *vt* asphyxier; (*Mil*) gazer. **to ~ o.s.** s'asphyxier.

3 *vi* (‡) (*talk*) parler; (*chat*) bavarder.

4 *adj industry* du gaz; *engine, oven, pipe* à gaz; *lighting, heating* au gaz. **~ bracket** applique *f* à gaz; **~ burner, ~ jet** brûleur *m* à gaz; **~ chamber** chambre *f* à gaz; **~ cooker** cuisinière *f* à gaz; (*portable*) réchaud *m* à gaz; **~ fire** appareil *m* de chauffage à gaz; **to light the ~ fire** allumer le gaz; **~ fitter** ajusteur-gazier *m*; **~ heater** appareil *m* de chauffage à gaz; (*for heating water*) chauffe-eau *m inv* (à gaz); **~ lighter** (*for cooker etc*) allume-gaz *m inv*; (*for cigarettes*) briquet *m* à gaz; **~ main** canalisation *f* de gaz; **~ meter** compteur *m* à gaz; **~ oil** gas-oil *m*; **~ pipeline** gazoduc *m*; **~ ring** (*part of cooker*) brûleur *m*; (*small stove*) réchaud *m* à gaz; (*US*) **~ station** station-service *f*; **~ stove** (*portable*) réchaud *m* à gaz; (*larger*) cuisinière *f* à gaz; (*US*) **~ tank** réservoir *m* à essence; **~ tap** (*on pipe*) robinet *m* à gaz; (*on cooker*) bouton *m* (de cuisinière à gaz); **~ turbine** turbine *f* à gaz; **~ worker** gazier *m*.

♦ **gaseous** *adj* gazeux. ♦ **gas-fired** *adj* chauffé au gaz; **~-fired central heating** chauffage central au gaz. ♦ **gaslight** *n*: **by ~light** à la lumière du gaz. ♦ **gaslit** *adj* éclairé au gaz. ♦ **gasman*** *n*: **the ~man** l'employé *m* du gaz. ♦ **gasmask** *n* masque *m* à gaz. ♦ **gasoline** *n* (*US*) essence *f*. ♦ **gasometer** *n* gazomètre *m*. ♦ **gassy** *adj* gazeux. ♦ **gasworks** *npl* usine *f* à gaz.

gash [gæʃ] **1** *n* (*in flesh*) entaille *f*; (*on face*) balafre *f*; (*in fabric*) grande déchirure *f*. **2** *vt* entailler; balafrer; déchirer. **3** *adj* (‡) de trop, en surplus. **if that box is ~** si vous n'avez plus besoin de cette boîte.

gasket ['gæskɪt] *n* *[piston]* garniture *f* de piston;

[joint] joint *m* d'étanchéité; *[cylinder head]* joint de culasse.
gasp [gɑːsp] **1** *n* halètement *m*. **to give a ~ of surprise/fear** *etc* avoir le souffle coupé par la surprise/la peur *etc*; **to be at one's last ~** (*lit*) être à l'agonie; (*: *fig*) n'en pouvoir plus. **2** *vi* (*choke*) haleter; (*from astonishment*) avoir le souffle coupé. (*lit, fig*) **to make sb ~** couper le souffle à qn; **to ~ for breath** *or* **air** haleter, suffoquer. **3** *vt*: **'no!' she ~ed** 'pas possible!' souffla-t-elle.
gasp out *vt sep plea* dire dans un souffle; *word* souffler.
gastric ['gæstrɪk] *adj* gastrique; *flu* gastro-intestinal; *ulcer* de l'estomac.
♦ **gastritis** *n* gastrite *f*. ♦ **gastroenteritis** *n* gastro-entérite *f*.
gastronome ['gæstrənəʊm] *n* gastronome *mf*.
♦ **gastronomic** *adj* gastronomique.
♦ **gastronomy** *n* gastronomie *f*.
gate [geɪt] *n* **(a)** *[castle, town]* porte *f*; *[field, level crossing]* barrière *f*; *[garden]* porte, portail *m*; (*of iron*) grille *f* (d'entrée); (*into courtyard etc*) porte cochère; (*Rail: in Underground*) portillon *m*; *[lock, sluice]* vanne *f*; *[sports ground]* entrée *f*. (*at airport*) ~ **5** porte 5. **(b)** (*Sport*) (*attendance*) spectateurs *mpl*; (~ *money*) recette *f*, entrées *fpl*.
♦ **gatecrash*** **1** *vi* (*not paying*) resquiller; **2** *vt party* s'introduire sans invitation dans; *match etc* assister sans payer à. ♦ **gatecrasher*** *n* (*at party etc*) intrus(e) *m(f)*; (*at match etc*) resquilleur* *m*, -euse* *f*. ♦ **gate-leg(ged)** *adj*: **~-leg(ged) table** table *f* anglaise. ♦ **gatepost** *n* montant *m* (de porte); (*fig*) **between you, me and the ~post*** soit dit entre nous. ♦ **gateway** *n* (*to a place*) porte *f* (*to* de); (*to success*) porte ouverte (*to* à).
gather ['gæðəʳ] **1** *vt* **(a)** (**~ together**) *people* rassembler; *objects* rassembler, ramasser. **(b)** (**~ up, ~ in**) *crops* récolter; *flowers* cueillir; *sticks, mushrooms, papers* ramasser; *taxes etc* percevoir; *contributions, information* recueillir; *skirt, hair etc* ramasser; (*Sewing*) *material* froncer; *dust* ramasser; *energies* rassembler. **to ~ one's thoughts** se ressaisir; **to ~ speed** prendre de la vitesse; *[feeling, movement]* **to ~ strength** se renforcer; **he ~ed his cloak around him** il a resserré sa cape contre lui; **to ~ one's brows** froncer les sourcils. **(c)** (*infer*) déduire, conclure (*from sth* de qch; *that* que); croire comprendre (*from sb* d'après ce que dit qn; *from a newspaper* d'après ce que dit le journal; *that* que). **as you will have ~ed** comme vous avez dû le deviner.
2 *vi* (*collect*) *[people]* (**~ together**) se rassembler; *[crowd]* se former; *[troops etc]* s'amasser; *[objects, dust]* s'accumuler, s'amasser; *[clouds]* s'amonceler; *[storm]* se préparer.
gather round *vi* s'approcher.
♦ **gathering** **1** *n* assemblée *f*, réunion *f*; **family ~ing** réunion de famille; **2** *adj force, speed* croissant; *storm* qui se prépare.
gaudy ['gɔːdɪ] *adj* voyant, criard.
gauge [geɪdʒ] **1** *n* (*size: of pipe, gun etc*) calibre *m*; (*Rail*) écartement *m*; (*instrument*) jauge *f*, indicateur *m*. **fuel/petrol/oil ~** jauge de carburant/d'essence/du niveau d'huile; **pressure ~** manomètre *m*; **tyre ~** indicateur de pression des pneus; **wheel ~** écartement des essieux; **it was a ~ of public feeling** cela a permis de jauger le sentiment du public. **2** *vt nut, screw, gun* calibrer; *temperature* mesurer; *oil* jauger; *wind* mesurer la vitesse de; *distance, sb's capabilities* jauger; *course of events* prévoir. **he was trying to ~ how far he should move it** il essayait d'évaluer de combien il devait le déplacer; **to ~ the right moment** calculer le bon moment.
gaunt [gɔːnt] *adj* (*very thin*) émacié; (*grim*) lugubre.
gauntlet ['gɔːntlɪt] *n* gant *m* (à crispin); *[armour]* gantelet *m*. **he had to run the ~ through the crowd** il a dû foncer à travers une foule hostile.
gauze [gɔːz] *n* gaze *f*.
gave [geɪv] *pret of* **give**.
gavel ['gævl] *n* marteau *m* (*de commissaire-priseur etc*).
gay [geɪ] **1** *adj* **(a)** (*gen*) gai; *company, occasion* joyeux; *laughter* enjoué. **to become ~(er)** s'égayer; **with ~ abandon** avec une belle désinvolture; **to have a ~ time** prendre du bon temps. **(b)** (*: *homosexual*) homosexuel. **2** *n* homosexuel(le) *m(f)*.
gaze [geɪz] **1** *n* regard *m* (fixe). **2** *vi* regarder. **to ~ into space** regarder dans le vide; **to ~ at sth** regarder (fixement) qch.
gazette [gəˈzet] *n* (*official publication*) journal *m* officiel; (*newspaper*) gazette *f*. ♦ **gazetteer** *n* index *m* (géographique).
gazump* [gəˈzʌmp] *vi* (*Brit*) *revenir sur une promesse de vente pour accepter un prix plus élevé*.
gear [gɪəʳ] **1** *n* **(a)** (*equipment*) (*gen*) équipement *m*, matériel *m*; (*belongings*) affaires* *fpl*, effets *mpl* (personnels); (*clothing*) vêtements *mpl*; (‡: *modern*) fringues‡ *fpl* à la mode. **fishing** *etc* **~** matériel *or* équipement de pêche *etc*. **(b)** (*apparatus*) mécanisme *m*, dispositif *m*. **safety ~** mécanisme de sécurité. **(c)** (*Tech*) engrenage *m*; (*Aut*) (*mechanism*) embrayage *m*; (*speed*) vitesse *f*. **in ~** en prise; **not in ~** au point mort; **he put the car into ~** il a mis la voiture en prise; **the car slipped out of ~** la vitesse a sauté; **to change** *or* (*US*) **to shift ~** changer de vitesse; **first** *or* **bottom** *or* **low ~** première vitesse; **in second ~** en seconde; **to change into third ~** passer en troisième (vitesse); **production has moved into top ~** la production a atteint sa vitesse maxima.
2 *vt* adapter (*to* à). **they were not ~ed to cope with that** ils n'étaient pas préparés pour cela.
gear up* *vt sep*: **to ~ o.s. up** se préparer (*for* pour); **we're ~ed up to do it** nous sommes tout prêts à le faire.
♦ **gearbox** *n* (*Aut*) boîte *f* de vitesses. ♦ **gear-lever** *or* ♦ **gearshift** (*US*) *n* levier *m* de vitesse.
♦ **gearwheel** *n [bicycle]* pignon *m*.
geese [giːs] *npl of* **goose**.
gel [dʒel] **1** *n* (*Chem*) colloïde *m*; (*gen*) gelée *f*. **2** *vi [jelly etc]* prendre; *[plan etc]* prendre tournure.
♦ **gelatin(e)** *n* gélatine *f*.
gelding ['geldɪŋ] *n* hongre *m*.
gelignite ['dʒelɪgnaɪt] *n* gélignite *f*.
gem [dʒem] **1** *n* gemme *f*, pierre *f* précieuse. (*house, helper*) **a ~** une vraie merveille. **the ~ of the collection** le joyau de la collection; **her aunt's a real ~*** sa tante est un chou*; **I must read you this ~*** il faut que je te lise cette perle.
♦ **gemstone** *n* pierre *f* gemme *inv*.
Gemini ['dʒemɪniː] *npl* (*Astron*) les Gémeaux *mpl*.
gen* [dʒen] (*Brit*) *n* coordonnées* *fpl* (*on* de), renseignements *mpl* (*on* sur). **what's the ~ on this?** qu'est-ce qu'on sait là-dessus?
gen up‡ *vt sep*: **to ~ sb up on sth** donner à qn les coordonnées* de qch.
gender ['dʒendəʳ] *n* (*Gram*) genre *m*.
gene [dʒiːn] *n* gène *m*.
genealogy [ˌdʒiːnɪˈælədʒɪ] *n* généalogie *f*.
♦ **genealogical** *adj* généalogique. ♦ **genealogist** *n* généalogiste *mf*.
general ['dʒenərəl] **1** *adj* (*gen*) général; (*not in detail*) *view, plan, inquiry* d'ensemble. **as a ~ rule** en règle générale; **in ~ use** d'usage courant; **in the ~ direction of** grosso modo* dans la direction de; **the ~ public** le grand public; **the ~ reader** le lecteur moyen; **this type of behaviour is fairly ~** ce genre de comportement est assez répandu; **the rain has been fairly ~** il a plu un peu partout; **to give sb a ~ idea of sth** donner à qn un aperçu d'ensemble sur qch; **I've got the ~ idea** je vois la question; (*US: Post*) **~ delivery** poste *f* restante; **~ election** élections

législatives; (*Mil*) ~ **headquarters** quartier *m* général; ~ **holiday** jour *m* férié; ~ **hospital** centre *m* hospitalier; ~ **knowledge** culture *f* générale; ~ **manager** directeur *m* général; **G~ Post Office** (*building*) poste *f* centrale; (*Med*) **to be in ~ practice** faire de la médecine générale; ~ **practitioner** (*abbr* **G.P.**) (médecin *m*) généraliste *m*; **go to your G.P.** allez voir votre médecin traitant; ~ **secretary** secrétaire général; ~ **shop** magasin *m* qui vend de tout; (*Mil etc*) ~ **staff** état-major *m*; ~ **store** grand magasin *m*. **2** *n* **(a)** général *m*. **in ~** en général. **(b)** (*Mil*) général *m*. ♦ **generality** *n* (*gen pl*) généralité *f*. ♦ **generalization** *n* généralisation *f*. ♦ **generalize** *vti* généraliser. ♦ **generally** *adv* (*usually*) généralement, en général; (*for the most part*) dans l'ensemble; **~ly speaking** en général. ♦ **general-purpose** *adj tool, dictionary* universel.

generate ['dʒenəreɪt] **1** *vt children, hope, fear* engendrer; *electricity, heat* produire; (*Ling*) générer. ♦ **generating** *adj*: **generating station** centrale *f* électrique; **generating unit** groupe *m* électrogène. ♦ **generation** *n* génération *f*; **the younger generation** la jeune génération; **the generation gap** le conflit des générations. ♦ **generative** *adj* (*Ling*) génératif. ♦ **generator** *n* (*Elec*) groupe *m* électrogène.

generic [dʒɪ'nerɪk] *adj* générique.

generous ['dʒenərəs] *adj* (*gen*) généreux (*with* de); *supply* abondant; *meal* copieux; *spoonful* bon; *size* ample. ♦ **generosity** *n* générosité *f*. ♦ **generously** *adv give etc* généreusement; *say* avec générosité; *pardon, reprieve* avec magnanimité.

genesis ['dʒenɪsɪs] *n* genèse *f*.

genetic [dʒɪ'netɪk] *adj* génétique. ~ **code** code *m* génétique; ~ **engineering** sélection *f* eugénique. ♦ **geneticist** *n* généticien(ne) *m(f)*. ♦ **genetics** *nsg* génétique *f*.

Geneva [dʒɪ'ni:və] *n* Genève. **Lake ~** le lac Léman.

genial ['dʒi:nɪəl] *adj person, smile, voice* cordial; *climate* doux; *warmth* réconfortant. ♦ **geniality** *n* cordialité *f*. ♦ **genially** *adv* cordialement.

genie ['dʒi:nɪ] *n, pl* **genii** (*Myth*) génie *m*.

genital ['dʒenɪtl] **1** *adj* génital. **2** *npl*: **~s** organes *mpl* génitaux.

genitive ['dʒenɪtɪv] *adj, n* génitif (*m*). **in the ~** au génitif.

genius ['dʒi:nɪəs] *n* génie *m*. **to have a ~ for (doing) sth** avoir le génie de (faire) qch.

genocide ['dʒenəʊsaɪd] *n* génocide *m*.

gent [dʒent] *n* (*abbr of* **gentleman**) (*Comm*) homme *m*; (*: *man*) monsieur *m*. (*cloakroom*) **the ~s*** les toilettes *fpl* (pour hommes).

genteel [dʒen'ti:l] *adj* qui se veut distingué. ♦ **gentility** *n* prétention *f* à la distinction.

gentle ['dʒentl] *adj person, animal, voice, disposition* doux (*f* douce); *rebuke* gentil; *exercise, heat* modéré; *slope* doux; *breeze, sound, touch* léger; *progress* mesuré; *hint, reminder* discret. ♦ **gentleness** *n* douceur *f*. ♦ **gently** *adv* (*gen*) doucement; *say, smile, rebuke* gentiment; **gently does it!** doucement!; **to go gently with sth** y aller doucement avec qch.

gentleman ['dʒentlmən] **1** *n, pl* **gentlemen** monsieur *m*; (*man of breeding*) homme *m* bien élevé, gentleman *m*; (*at court etc*) gentilhomme *m*. **gentlemen!** messieurs!; **a perfect ~** un vrai gentleman; **~'s agreement** accord *m* reposant sur l'honneur. **2** *adj*: ~ **farmer** gentleman-farmer *m*. ♦ **gentlemanly** *adj* bien élevé; *voice, appearance* distingué.

gentry ['dʒentrɪ] *n* petite noblesse *f*.

genuflect ['dʒenjʊflekt] *vi* faire une génuflexion.

genuine ['dʒenjʊɪn] *adj* **(a)** (*authentic*) *wool, silver, jewel etc* véritable; *manuscript, antique, coin* authentique; (*Comm*) *goods* garanti d'origine. **I'll only buy the ~ article** (*of furniture etc*) je n'achète que de l'authentique; (*of jewellery, cheeses etc*) je n'achète que du vrai. **(b)** (*sincere*) *laughter* franc (*f* franche); *person, tears, emotion, belief* sincère; *simplicity* vrai. (*Comm*) ~ **buyer** acheteur sérieux. ♦ **genuinely** *adv prove, originate* authentiquement; *believe* sincèrement; *sorry, surprised, unable* vraiment.

genus ['dʒenəs] *n, pl* **genera** (*Bio*) genre *m*.

geography [dʒɪ'ɒgrəfɪ] *n* (*gen*) géographie *f*. **I don't know the ~ of the district** je ne connais pas la topographie de la région. ♦ **geographer** *n* géographe *mf*. ♦ **geographic(al)** *adj* géographique.

geology [dʒɪ'ɒlədʒɪ] *n* géologie *f*. ♦ **geological** *adj* géologique. ♦ **geologist** *n* géologue *mf*.

geometry [dʒɪ'ɒmɪtrɪ] *n* géométrie *f*. ♦ **geometric(al)** *adj* géométrique.

geophysics [ˌdʒi:əʊ'fɪzɪks] *nsg* géophysique *f*.

Georgian ['dʒɔ:dʒɪən] *adj* du temps des rois George I-IV (*1714-1830*).

geranium [dʒɪ'reɪnɪəm] *n* géranium *m*.

geriatric [ˌdʒerɪ'ætrɪk] *adj* gériatrique. ~ **medicine** gériatrie *f*; ~ **nursing** soins *mpl* aux vieillards; ~ **social work** aide *f* sociale aux vieillards. ♦ **geriatrics** *nsg* gériatrie *f*.

germ [dʒɜ:m] **1** *n* (*Bio, also fig*) germe *m*; (*Med*) microbe *m*. **2** *adj*: ~ **warfare** guerre *f* bactériologique. ♦ **germ-free** *adj* stérilisé. ♦ **germicidal** *adj* antiseptique. ♦ **germicide** *n* antiseptique *m*. ♦ **germinate 1** *vi* germer; **2** *vt* faire germer. ♦ **germination** *n* germination *f*. ♦ **germ-killer** *n* antiseptique *m*.

Germany ['dʒɜ:mənɪ] *n* Allemagne *f*. **East/West ~** Allemagne de l'Est/de l'Ouest. ♦ **German 1** *adj* allemand; **East-/West-German** est-/ouest-allemand; **German measles** rubéole *f*; **German sheep dog** berger *m* allemand; **2** *n* Allemand(e) *m(f)*; (*Ling*) allemand *m*. ♦ **Germanic** *adj* germanique.

gerontology [ˌdʒerɒn'tɒlədʒɪ] *n* gérontologie *f*. ♦ **gerontologist** *n* gérontologue *mf*.

gerund ['dʒerənd] *n* gérondif *m*.

gestalt [gə'ʃtɑ:lt] *n* gestalt *f*. ~ **psychology** gestaltisme *m*.

gestate [dʒes'teɪt] *vi* être en gestation. ♦ **gestation** *n* gestation *f*.

gesticulate [dʒes'tɪkjʊleɪt] *vi* gesticuler.

gesture ['dʒestʃər] **1** *n* (*lit, fig*) geste *m*. **they did it as a ~ of support** ils l'ont fait pour manifester leur soutien. **2** *vi*: **to ~ to sb to do** faire signe à qn de faire.

get [get] *pret, ptp* **got,** (*US*) *ptp* **gotten 1** *vt* **(a)** (*obtain*) avoir, trouver; (*through effort*) se procurer, obtenir; *permission, result* obtenir (*from* de); (*buy*) acheter; (*Rad*) *station,* (*Telec*) *person, number* avoir; (*Scol*) *marks* obtenir, avoir. **to ~ sth to eat** (*find food*) trouver de quoi manger; (*eat*) manger qch; **where did you ~ that hat?** où as-tu trouvé ce chapeau?; **I don't ~ much from his lectures** je ne tire pas grand-chose de ses cours; **to ~ sth for sb** trouver qch pour *or* à qn; (*fig*) **we'll never ~ anything out of him** nous ne tirerons jamais rien de lui.

(b) (*acquire*) *power, wealth* acquérir; *ideas, reputation* se faire; *salary* recevoir, toucher; *help* recevoir; *prize* gagner; *fame* connaître. (*of collection, set*) **I've still 3 to ~** il m'en manque encore 3; **it got him fame** *etc* cela lui a valu la célébrité *etc*.

(c) (*receive*) *letter, present* recevoir, avoir; *surprise* avoir; *wound, punishment, shock* recevoir. **I didn't ~ much for it** je ne l'ai pas vendu cher; **to ~ 2 years in prison** attraper* 2 ans de prison; **he ~s it from his mother** il le tient de sa mère; **this room ~s all the sun** cette pièce reçoit tout le soleil.

(d) (*catch*) *ball, disease* attraper; *quarry, person* attraper, prendre; (*hit*) *target etc* atteindre, avoir; (*seize*) prendre, saisir. **to ~ sb round the neck/by the throat** saisir *or* prendre qn au cou/à la gorge; **to ~ sb by the arm** attraper *or* saisir qn par le bras; *[pain]* **it ~s me here** cela me prend ici; **got you at last!** enfin je te tiens!; **we'll ~ them yet!** on les aura!; **he'll ~ you for that!*** qu'est-ce que tu vas prendre!*; **he's got it bad (for her)*** il en pince sérieusement pour elle*; **the bullet got him in the arm** il a pris la balle dans le bras.

(e) (*fetch*) *person, doctor* aller chercher, faire venir; *object* chercher, apporter. **(go and) ~ my books** allez chercher mes livres; **can I ~ you a drink?** voulez-vous boire qch?

(f) (*have, possess*) **to have got** avoir, posséder; **I've got toothache** j'ai mal aux dents; **I have got 3 sisters** j'ai 3 sœurs; **how many have you got?** combien en avez-vous?

(g) (*causative etc*) **to ~ sb to do sth** faire faire qch à qn, obtenir que qn fasse qch; **to ~ sth done** faire faire qch; **to ~ one's hair cut** se faire couper les cheveux; **I got him to cut my hair** je me suis fait couper les cheveux par lui; **he knows how to ~ things done!** il sait faire activer les choses!; **she got her arm broken** elle a eu le bras cassé; **to ~ sth ready** préparer qch; **to ~ sb drunk** soûler qn; **to ~ one's hands dirty** se salir les mains; **to ~ sb into trouble** attirer des ennuis à qn; **we got him on to the subject of the war** nous l'avons amené à parler de la guerre.

(h) (*put, take*) faire parvenir. **they got him home somehow** ils l'ont ramené tant bien que mal; **how can we ~ it home?** comment faire pour le rapporter à la maison?; **to ~ sth to sb** faire parvenir qch à qn; **I'll never ~ the car through here** je n'arriverai jamais à faire passer la voiture par ici; **to ~ sth past the customs** passer qch à la douane; **he got the blood off his hand** il a fait disparaître le sang de sa main; **where does that ~ us?** où est-ce que ça nous mène?

(i) (*understand*) comprendre, saisir. **~ it?*** tu saisis?*; **I've got it!** j'y suis!; **I don't ~ it*** je ne comprends pas, je n'y suis pas du tout; **I didn't ~ your name** je n'ai pas saisi votre nom; (*to secretary etc*) **did you ~ that last sentence?** avez-vous pris la dernière phrase?

(j) (*: *annoy*) mettre en rogne*.

(k) (*: *thrill*) **that ~s me** ça me fait qch, (*stronger*) ça m'emballe*.

2 *vi* **(a)** (*go*) aller, se rendre (*to* à, *from* de); (*arrive*) arriver (*at* à). **how do you ~ there?** comment fait-on pour y aller?; **how did that box ~ here?** comment se fait-il que cette boîte se trouve ici?; (*fig*) **he'll ~ there** il arrivera; (*fig*) **now we're ~ting somewhere!*** enfin on avance!; (*fig*) **you won't ~ anywhere if you behave like that** tu n'arriveras à rien en te conduisant comme ça; **we won't ~ anywhere with him** nous n'arriverons à rien *or* nous perdons notre temps avec lui; **where did you ~ to?** où êtes-vous allé?; (*in book, work etc*) **where have you got to?** où en êtes-vous?; **where can he have got to?** où est-il passé?; **I got as far as speaking to him** j'ai réussi à lui parler.

(b) (*become, be*) devenir, se faire. **to ~ old** devenir vieux, vieillir; **to ~ killed** se faire tuer; **it's ~ting late** il se fait tard; **how do people ~ like that?*** comment peut-on en arriver là?; **to ~ with it*** se mettre à la mode *or* dans le vent*; (*excl*) **~ with it!*** sois un peu dans le vent!*; **to ~ to know sb** (*begin*) commencer à connaître qn; (*know better*) arriver à mieux connaître qn; (*meet*) faire la connaissance de qn; **to ~ to like sb** se mettre à aimer qn.

(c) (*begin*) se mettre à. **to ~ going** commencer, s'y mettre; **I got talking to him** je me suis mis à parler avec lui.

(d) (*be allowed to*) **she never ~s to drive the car** on ne la laisse jamais conduire la voiture.

3 (*modal aux usage*) **you've got to come** il faut absolument que vous veniez; **I haven't got to leave** je ne suis pas obligé de partir; **have you got to go and see her?** est-ce que vous êtes obligé d'aller la voir?; *V also* **have 2.**

get about, get around *vi* **(a)** (*move around*) se déplacer. (*after illness*) **he's ~ting about again** il est de nouveau sur pied. **(b)** *[news]* se répandre. **it has got about that ...** le bruit court que ...

get above *vt fus*: **to ~ above o.s.** se prendre pour plus important qu'on n'est.

get across 1 *vi* traverser; (*fig*) *[play]* passer la rampe; *[meaning, message]* passer*. **he didn't ~ across to the audience** il n'a pas réussi à établir la communication avec le public. **2** *vt sep load* traverser; *person* faire traverser; (*fig*) *play, song* faire passer la rampe à. (*fig*) **to ~ sth across to sb** faire comprendre qch à qn. **3** *vt fus* (*annoy*) **to ~ across sb** se faire mal voir de qn.

get along *vi* **(a)** (*go*) s'en aller. **~ along with you!*** (*go away*) va-t'en!; (*stop joking*) ça va, hein!* **(b)** (*manage*) se débrouiller (*without* sans); (*progress*) *[work]* avancer; *[pupil]* faire des progrès. **how is he ~ting along?** (*in health*) comment va-t-il?; (*in studies etc*) comment est-ce qu'il se débrouille? **(c)** (*be on good terms*) s'entendre bien (*with sb* avec qn).

get at *vt fus* **(a)** (*reach*) *place* parvenir à; *object on shelf* atteindre; *person* accéder jusqu'à; *facts, truth* découvrir. **not easy to ~ at** *house* difficile d'accès; *person* d'un abord peu facile; **let me ~ at him!*** que je l'attrape! **(b)** (*fig*) **what are you ~ting at?** où voulez-vous en venir?; **who are you ~ting at?** à qui voulez-vous faire allusion?; **I feel got at*** je me sens visé; **she's always ~ting at her brother** elle est toujours après son frère*. **(c)** (*: *bribe*) acheter, suborner. **(d)** (*start work on*) *task, essay* se mettre à. **I want to ~ at the redecorating** je veux commencer à refaire les peintures.

get away 1 *vi* **(a)** (*leave*) s'en aller, partir; *[vehicle]* partir, démarrer. **to ~ away from** *place, work* quitter; **I couldn't ~ away any sooner** je n'ai pas pu me libérer plus tôt; **~ away (with you)!*** va-t'en!; (*stop joking*) ça va, hein!* **(b)** (*escape*) s'échapper (*from* de). **to ~ away from sb/one's environment** échapper à qn/à son environnement; **to ~ away from it all** partir se reposer loin de tout; **the thief got away with the money** le voleur est parti avec l'argent; **he got away with an apology** il en a été quitte pour une simple excuse; **you'll never ~ away with that!** on ne te laissera pas passer ça!*; **he'd ~ away with murder*** il tuerait père et mère qu'on lui pardonnerait; (*fig*) **there's no ~ting away from it** le fait est là, on ne peut rien y changer. **2** *vt sep* **(a)** faire partir. **you must ~ her away to the country** il faut que vous l'emmeniez à la campagne. **(b) to ~ sth away from sb** arracher qch à qn.

get back 1 *vi* **(a)** (*return*) revenir, retourner. **to ~ back (home)** rentrer chez soi; **to ~ back to bed** se recoucher; **to ~ back to work** (*after pause*) se remettre au travail; (*after illness, holiday*) retourner au travail; **let's ~ back to why** revenons à la question de savoir pourquoi. **(b)** (*move back*) reculer. **~ back!** reculez! **2** *vt sep* **(a)** (*recover*) *sth lent* se faire rendre; *sth lost* retrouver; *possessions* recouvrer; *strength* reprendre. **(b)** (*replace*) remettre, replacer. **(c)** (*return*) *object* renvoyer; *person* raccompagner.

get back at* *vt fus* (*retaliate against*) rendre la monnaie de sa pièce à.

get by *vi* **(a)** (*pass*) passer. **this work just ~s by** ce travail est tout juste passable. **(b)** (*manage*) se débrouiller (*with, on* avec). **he'll ~ by** il s'en sortira*.

get down 1 *vi* descendre (*from, off* de). **~ down!** descends!, (*lie down*) couche-toi! **2** *vt sep* **(a)** *book, plate, child* descendre (*off* de); *hat, picture* décrocher. **(b)** (*swallow*) avaler. **(c)** (*make note of*) noter. **(d)** (*: *depress*) déprimer. **he ~s me down** il me fiche le cafard*; **don't let it ~ you down!** ne vous laissez pas abattre!

get down to *vt fus*: **to ~ down to (doing) sth** se mettre à (faire) qch; **to ~ down to work** se mettre au travail; **let's ~ down to the facts** venons-en aux faits; (*fig*) **when you ~ down to it there's ...** à bien regarder les faits il y a ... .

get in 1 *vi* **(a)** (*enter*) (réussir à) entrer; (*reach home*) rentrer; *[sunshine, air, water]* pénétrer. **to ~ in between ...** se glisser entre ... . **(b)** *[train, bus, plane]* arriver. **(c)** (*Parl*) *[member]* être élu; *[party]* accéder au pouvoir. **2** *vt sep* **(a)** *thing, harvest* rentrer; *person* faire entrer; *taxes* recouvrer. **(b)** (*plant*) planter. **(c)** (*buy, obtain*) *groceries, coal* acheter, faire rentrer. **to ~ in supplies** faire des provisions. **(d)** (*summon*) *police etc* faire venir. **(e)** (*insert*) glisser. **to ~ a word in edgeways** glisser *or* placer un mot.

get into *vt fus* **(a)** *house, park* entrer dans, pénétrer dans; *car, train* monter dans; *club, school* être accepté dans. (*fig*) **how did I ~ into all this?** comment me suis-je fourré dans un pareil pétrin? **(b)** *clothes* mettre.

get in with *vt fus* (*gain favour of*) se faire bien voir de; (*become friendly with*) se mettre à fréquenter.

get off 1 *vi* **(a)** (*from vehicle*) descendre. (*fig*) **to tell sb where to ~ off*** envoyer qn sur les roses*. **(b)** (*depart*) partir; *[car]* démarrer; *[plane]* décoller. **to ~ off to a good start** prendre un bon départ; **to ~ off (to sleep)** s'endormir. **(c)** (*escape*) s'en tirer. **to ~ off lightly** s'en tirer à bon compte; **to ~ off with a fine** en être quitte pour une amende. **(d)** (*leave work*) s'en aller; (*have free time*) se libérer. **2** *vt sep* **(a)** (*remove*) *clothes, stains* enlever. **(b)** (*despatch*) *mail, child to school* expédier. **to ~ sb off to work** faire partir qn au travail; **to ~ sb off to sleep** endormir qn. **(c)** (*save from punishment*) tirer d'affaire. **(d)** (*learn*) apprendre (*by heart* par cœur). **(e)** *boat* renflouer; *crew, passengers* débarquer. **3** *vt fus* **(a)** *bus, cycle, horse* descendre de; *chair* se lever de; *subject* s'éloigner de. **(b)** (*: *avoid etc*) se faire dispenser (*sth* de qch; *doing* de faire). **to ~ off work** se libérer.

get off with* *vt fus*: **he got off with a blonde** il a eu la touche* avec une blonde.

get on 1 *vi* **(a)** (*on bus etc*) monter. **(b)** (*make progress*) faire des progrès. **how are you ~ting on?** comment ça marche?*; **to be ~ting on (in years)** se faire vieux; **he's ~ting on for forty** il frise la quarantaine; **time is ~ting on** il se fait tard; **~ting on for 500** près de 500. **(c)** (*succeed*) réussir, faire son chemin (*in life etc* dans la vie *etc*). **(d)** (*continue*) continuer (*with sth* qch). **~ on with it!** allez, au travail!; **this will do to be ~ting on with** ça ira pour le moment. **(e)** (*agree*) bien s'entendre (*with sb* avec qn). **2** *vt sep clothes, lid* mettre. **3** *vt fus horse, bicycle* monter sur; *bus, train* monter dans.

get on to *vt fus* **(a)** = **get on 3. (b)** (*recognize*) *truth, person responsible* découvrir. **(c)** (*nag*) être après*. **(d)** (*get in touch with*) se mettre en rapport avec; (*speak to*) parler à; (*Telec*) téléphoner à.

get out 1 *vi* **(a)** sortir (*of* de); (*from vehicle*) descendre (*of* de). **(b)** (*escape*) s'échapper (*of* de). (*fig*) **to ~ out of** *habit* perdre; *obligation* se dérober à; *duty* se soustraire à; *difficulty* se tirer de. **(c)** *[news etc]* se répandre; *[secret]* être éventé. **2** *vt sep object* sortir; *person* faire sortir (*of* de); *plug, stain* enlever; *tooth, nail* arracher; (*fig*) *words* prononcer; *book* sortir; (*prepare*) *scheme* préparer; *list* dresser; (*solve*) *problem, puzzle* venir à bout de.

get over 1 *vi* traverser; *[message, meaning]* passer*.

2 *vt fus* **(a)** (*cross*) *river, road* traverser; *fence* passer par-dessus. **(b)** (*recover from*) *illness, loss* se remettre de; *surprise* revenir de; *lost lover* oublier. **I can't ~ over the fact that ...** je n'en reviens pas que ... + *subj*; **you'll ~ over it!** tu n'en mourras pas! **(c)** (*overcome*) *obstacle* surmonter; *objections, difficulties* venir à bout de.

3 *vt sep* **(a)** *person, vehicle* faire passer. **(b)** (*swallow*) avaler. **(c)** (*have done with*) en finir avec. **let's ~ it over (with)** finissons-en. **(d)** (*Theat*) *play* faire passer la rampe à; *song etc* faire accepter; (*gen: communicate*) faire comprendre (*to sb* à qn; *that* que).

get round 1 *vi* **(a)** = **get about. (b) to ~ round to doing sth** arriver à faire qch, trouver le temps de faire qch; **if I ~ round to it** si j'y arrive. **2** *vt fus obstacle* contourner; *difficulty, regulation* tourner. **he knows how to ~ round her** il sait la prendre; **she got round him in the end** elle a fini par l'entortiller*.

get through 1 *vi* **(a)** *[message, news]* parvenir (*to* à); *[signal, candidate]* être reçu; *[motion, bill]* passer. *[football team etc]* **to ~ through to the third round** se classer pour le troisième tour; **to ~ through to sb** (*Telec*) avoir qn, obtenir la communication avec qn; (*contact*) contacter qn; (*fig: communicate with*) se faire comprendre de qn. **(b)** (*finish*) terminer, finir. **to ~ through with sth*** en finir avec qch.

2 *vt fus* **(a)** *hole, window* passer par; *hedge* passer à travers; *crowd* se frayer un chemin à travers; *enemy lines* franchir. **(b)** (*finish*) *task, book, supplies* venir au bout de. **he got through a lot of work** il a abattu de la besogne; **how can I ~ through the week without you?** comment vais-je pouvoir vivre une semaine sans toi? **(c)** (*consume, use*) *food, supplies* consommer. **we ~ through 10 bottles/£50 a week** il nous faut 10 bouteilles/50 livres par semaine.

3 *vt sep* **(a)** *person, object* faire passer; *message* faire parvenir (*to* à). **I can't ~ it through to him that ...** je n'arrive pas à lui faire comprendre que ... . **(b)** *law, motion* faire adopter. (*exam*) **he got them through** ils ont été reçus grâce à lui.

get together 1 *vi* se rassembler, se réunir. **let's ~ together on Thursday** on se retrouve jeudi; **you'd better ~ together with him** vous feriez bien de le consulter. **2** *vt sep* rassembler.

get under 1 *vi* (*pass underneath*) passer par-dessous. **2** *vt fus fence, rope* passer sous.

get up 1 *vi* **(a)** (*rise*) se lever (*from* de). **~ up out of bed!** sors du lit! **(b)** (*on horse*) monter. **2** *vt fus tree, ladder* monter à; *hill* gravir. **3** *vt sep* **(a)** *person* (*on to ladder etc*) faire monter; (*from chair, bed*) faire lever; (*wake*) réveiller; *thing* monter; *sail* hisser. **(b)** (*organize*) *play, plot* monter; *story* fabriquer; *petition* organiser. **(c)** (*prepare, arrange*) *article for sale* préparer. **to ~ o.s. up as** se déguiser en; **beautifully got up** *person* très bien habillé; *book* très bien présenté. **(d)** (*study*) *history etc* travailler, bûcher*; *speech, lecture* préparer.

get up to *vt fus* (*catch up with*) rattraper; (*reach*) arriver à. **I've got up to page 17** j'en suis à la page 17; **to ~ up to mischief** faire des bêtises; **you never know what he'll ~ up to next** on ne sait jamais ce qu'il va encore inventer.

♦ **get-at-able*** *adj* accessible. ♦ **getaway 1** *n* *[criminals]* fuite *f*; **to make a ~away** filer; **2** *adj*: **a ~away car** une voiture pour filer. ♦ **get-together** *n* (petite) réunion *f*. ♦ **getup*** *n* (*clothing*) mise *f*, tenue *f*; (*presentation*) présentation *f*. ♦ **get-well card** *n* carte *f* de vœux de bon rétablissement.

geyser ['gi:zəʳ] *n* geyser *m*; (*water-heater*) chauffe-bain *m inv*.
ghastly ['gɑ:stlı] *adj* (*pale*) blême, livide; (*horrible*) horrible, affreux.
gherkin ['g3:kın] *n* (*Culin*) cornichon *m*.
ghost [gəʊst] **1** *n* fantôme *m*, revenant *m*. (*fig*) **the ~ of a smile** un pâle sourire; **the ~ of a chance** l'ombre *f* d'une chance. **2** *vt sb else's book etc* écrire. **3** *adj film, story* de revenants; *ship, train* fantôme; *town* mort. ♦ **ghostly** *adj* spectral, fantomatique.
ghoul [gu:l] *n* goule *f*, vampire *m*. (*fig*) **he's a ~** il est morbide. ♦ **ghoulish** *adj* morbide.
giant ['dʒaıənt] **1** *n* géant *m*. **2** *adj tree, packet* géant; *strides* de géant; *amount, task* gigantesque.
gibber ['dʒıbəʳ] *vi* baragouiner*; (*with rage*) bégayer. ♦ **gibberish** *n* charabia* *m*, baragouin* *m*.
gibe [dʒaıb] **1** *vi* **(a) to ~ at sb** railler qn. **(b)** *[boat]* virer lof pour lof. **2** *n* raillerie *f*.
giblets ['dʒıblıts] *npl* abattis *mpl* (*de volaille*).
Gibraltar [dʒı'brɔ:ltəʳ] *n* Gibraltar *m*.
giddy ['gıdı] *adj* (*dizzy*) pris de vertige; *height* vertigineux; (*heedless*) écervelé; (*not serious*) léger. **I feel ~** la tête me tourne; **to go ~** être pris de vertige; **to make sb ~** donner le vertige à qn. ♦ **giddiness** *n* (*Med*) vertige *m*; **a bout of giddiness** un vertige.
gift [gıft] **1** *n* **(a)** cadeau *m*; (*Comm*) prime *f*. **it was a ~** on me l'a offert; (*: *fig: easy*) c'était du gâteau*; **I wouldn't have it as a ~** on m'en ferait cadeau que je n'en voudrais pas; **to make sb a ~ of sth** faire don *or* cadeau de qch à qn. **(b)** (*talent*) don *m*. **to have the ~ of the gab*** avoir la langue bien pendue. **2** *vt* (*esp Jur*) donner. (*fig*) **to be ~ed with patience** *etc* être doué de patience *etc*. **3** *adj* (*Comm*) **~ coupon** *or* **voucher** bon-prime *m*; **~ token** chèque-cadeau *m*. ♦ **gifted** *adj* doué (*for* pour, *with* de); **the ~ed child** l'enfant surdoué. ♦ **giftwrap** *vt*: **to ~wrap a package** faire un paquet-cadeau. ♦ **gift-wrapping** *n* emballage-cadeau *m*.
gig* [gıg] *n* (*Theat etc*) gig *f*.
gigantic [dʒaı'gæntık] *adj* gigantesque.
giggle ['gıgl] **1** *vi* rire (sottement), avoir le fou rire. **2** *n* petit rire sot. **to have/get the ~s** avoir/attraper le fou rire. ♦ **giggly** *adj* qui pouffe de rire.
gild [gıld] *vt* dorer. **to ~ the lily** renchérir sur la perfection.
gill[1] [gıl] *n [mushroom]* lamelle *f*. *[fish]* **~s** ouïes *fpl*. (*fig*) **green around the ~s*** vert (*de peur etc*).
gill[2] [dʒıl] *n = 0,142 litre*.
gilt [gılt] (*ptp of* **gild**) **1** *adj* doré. **2** *n* dorure *f*. **to take the ~ off the gingerbread** gâter le plaisir. ♦ **gilt-edged** *adj*: **~-edged securities** valeurs *fpl* de tout repos.
gimlet ['gımlıt] *n* vrille *f*.
gimmick ['gımık] *n* truc* *m*, astuce *f*. **advertising/sales ~** truc* publicitaire/promotionnel; **he put on an accent as a ~** il a pris un accent pour l'effet. ♦ **gimmickry** *n* trucs* *mpl*. ♦ **gimmicky** *adj photography* à trucs*; *presentation* à astuces.
gin [dʒın] *n* gin *m*. **~ and tonic** gin-tonic *m*.
ginger ['dʒındʒəʳ] **1** *n* gingembre *m*. (*nickname*) **G~** Poil de Carotte. **2** *adj hair* roux, rouquin*; *biscuit etc* au gingembre. **~ ale** *or* **beer** boisson *f* gazeuse au gingembre; (*esp Pol*) **~ group** groupe *m* de pression.
ginger up* *vt sep person* secouer; *event* mettre de l'entrain dans.
♦ **gingerbread** *n* pain *m* d'épice. ♦ **gingerly** *adv* avec précaution. ♦ **gingernut** *or* ♦ **gingersnap** *n* gâteau *m* sec au gingembre.
gingham ['gıŋəm] *n* (*Tex*) vichy *m*.
gipsy ['dʒıpsı] **1** *n* (*gen*) bohémien(ne) *m(f)*; (*Spanish*) gitan(e) *m(f)*; (*Central European*) Tsigane *mf*; (*pej*) romanichel(le) *m(f)*. **2** *adj* (*gen*) de bohémien, de gitan; *music* des gitans, tsigane.
giraffe [dʒı'rɑ:f] *n* girafe *f*. **baby ~** girafeau *m*.
girder ['g3:dəʳ] *n* poutre *f*.
girdle ['g3:dl] *n* (*belt*) ceinture *f*; (*corset*) gaine *f*.
girl [g3:l] **1** *n* (jeune *or* petite) fille *f*. **a little ~** une petite fille, une fillette; **an English ~** une jeune *or* petite Anglaise; **poor little ~** pauvre petite; **the Smith ~s** les filles des Smith; **~s' school** école *f or* lycée *m* de filles; **yes, old ~!** oui, ma vieille*; **the old ~* next door** la vieille d'à côté. **2** *adj*: **~ Friday** aide *f* de bureau; **~ scout** éclaireuse *f*, guide *f*.
♦ **girlfriend** *n [boy]* petite amie *f*; *[girl]* amie *f*, copine* *f*. ♦ **girlhood** *n* enfance *f*, jeunesse *f*. ♦ **girlie** *adj magazine* déshabillé. ♦ **girlish** *adj* (*of woman*) de jeune fille; (*of man, boy*) efféminé.
giro ['dʒaırəʊ] *n*: **bank ~ system** système *m* de virement bancaire; **National G~** ≃ Comptes Chèques Postaux, C.C.P. *mpl*.
girth [g3:θ] *n [tree]* circonférence *f*; *[waist etc]* tour *m* (de taille *etc*). **his (great) ~** sa corpulence.
gist [dʒıst] *n* (*gen*) essentiel *m*. **give me the ~ of what he said** mettez-moi au courant de ce qu'il a dit, en deux mots.
give [gıv] *pret* **gave**, *ptp* **given** **1** *vt* **(a)** (*gen*) donner (*to* à); (*as gift*) faire cadeau *or* don de, offrir (*to* à); *honour, title* conférer (*to* à); *help, support* prêter (*to* à); *food, hospitality, meal* offrir (*to* à); (*dedicate*) *one's life, fortune*, consacrer (*to* à); *message* remettre (*to* à); *description, particulars* donner, fournir (*to* à); *pain, pleasure* occasionner (*to* à); *punishment* infliger (*to* à). **one must ~ and take** il faut faire des concessions; **~ or take a few minutes** à quelques minutes près; **he gave as good as he got** il a rendu coup pour coup; **to ~ sb sth to eat/drink** donner à manger/boire à qn; **can you ~ him sth to do?** pouvez-vous lui trouver qch à faire?; **you've ~n me your cold** tu m'as passé ton rhume; (*Telec*) **~ me Moordown 231** passez-moi le 231 à Moordown; **I'll ~ him something to cry about!*** je lui apprendrai à pleurer!; **I don't ~ a damn*** je m'en fiche*; **the judge gave him 5 years** le juge l'a condamné à 5 ans de prison; (*in age*) **I can ~ him 10 years** il est de 10 ans mon cadet; **how long do you ~ that marriage?** combien de temps crois-tu que ce mariage tiendra?; *[creditor]* **I can't ~ you any longer** je ne peux plus vous accorder de délai; (*agreeing*) **I'll ~ you that** je vous accorde cela; **~ me time** laissez-moi du temps; **~ me Mozart every time!*** pour moi, rien ne vaut Mozart; **to ~ sb to understand that** donner à entendre à qn que; **to ~ sb to believe sth** faire croire qch à qn; **~ him my love** faites-lui mes amitiés; **what will you ~ me for it?** combien m'en donnez-vous?; **what did you ~ for it?** combien l'avez-vous payé?; **I'd ~ anything to know** je donnerais n'importe quoi pour savoir.
(b) (*perform etc*) *jump, gesture* faire; *answer, lecture, party, performance* donner; *sigh, cry, laugh* pousser. **to ~ sb a look** lancer un regard à qn; **~ us a song** chantez-nous qch.
(c) (*produce, supply*) donner, rendre; *sound* rendre; (*Math etc*) *result* donner. **this lamp ~s a poor light** cette lampe éclaire mal; **5 times 4 ~s 20** 5 fois 4 font 20; **it ~s a total of 100** cela fait 100 en tout.
(d) to ~ way *[building, ceiling, ground]* s'affaisser; *[plaster]* s'effriter; *[cable, rope, ladder etc]* casser; *[legs]* fléchir; *[health]* s'altérer; (*yield*) *[person]* céder (*to sb* devant qn; *to a demand* à une revendication; *under* sous); (*agree*) consentir; (*make room for*) céder la place (*to* à); (*Aut*) céder la priorité (*to* à); *[troops]* battre en retraite. (*Aut*) '**~ way**' 'cédez la priorité'.
2 *vi [road, beam etc]* céder (*to* à; *under* sous); *[cloth, elastic etc]* prêter.
give away *vt sep* **(a)** *money, goods* donner;

prizes distribuer; *bride* conduire à l'autel. **(b)** (*betray*) *names, details* révéler; *person* trahir. **to ~ o.s. away** se trahir; **don't ~ anything away** ne dis rien; **to ~ the game** *or* **show away*** vendre la mèche*.
give back *vt sep* (*gen*) rendre (*to* à); *property* restituer (*to* à); *echo, image* renvoyer.
give in 1 *vi* (*yield*) renoncer, abandonner. **to ~ in to sb** céder à qn; **I ~ in!** je renonce!; (*in guessing*) je donne ma langue au chat!* **2** *vt sep parcel, document* remettre; *essay* rendre; *one's name* donner.
give off *vt sep heat, smell* émettre; *gas* dégager.
give on to *vt fus [door, window]* donner sur.
give out 1 *vi [supplies]* s'épuiser; *[car, engine]* tomber en panne. **my patience is giving out** ma patience est à bout; **my patience gave out** la patience m'a manqué. **2** *vt sep* **(a)** (*distribute*) *books, food etc* distribuer. **(b)** (*announce*) *news* annoncer; *list etc* faire connaître.
give over 1 *vt sep* (*devote*) consacrer (*to* à); (*transfer*) affecter (*to* à). **building ~n over to offices** bâtiment affecté à des bureaux. **2** *vt fus* (*: *stop*) cesser (*doing* de faire). **~ over!** arrête!
give up 1 *vi* abandonner, renoncer. **don't ~ up!** tenez bon!; **I ~ up** je renonce; (*in guessing*) je donne ma langue au chat*. **2** *vt sep* **(a)** (*devote*) consacrer (*to* à). **to ~ o.s. up to sth** se livrer à qch. **(b)** (*renounce*) renoncer (*doing* à faire); *friends, interests, habit, idea* abandonner; *seat, place* céder; *job* quitter; *appointment* démissionner de; *business* se retirer de; *subscription* cesser. **he'll never ~ her up** il n'acceptera jamais qu'elle le quitte (*subj*); **I gave it up as a bad job** j'ai laissé tomber*. **(c)** (*hand over*) *prisoner* livrer (*to* à); *authority* se démettre de; *keys of city etc* rendre. **to ~ o.s. up** se livrer (*to the police* à la police), se rendre. **(d)** (*abandon hope for*) *patient* condamner; *expected visitor* ne plus espérer voir; *problem, riddle* renoncer à résoudre. **to ~ sb up for lost** considérer qn comme perdu.
♦ **give-and-take** *n* concessions *fpl* mutuelles. ♦ **giveaway 1** *n* révélation *f* involontaire; (*Comm: free gift*) prime *f*; **2** *adj fact, expression* révélateur; *price* dérisoire. ♦ **given** *adj time, size* donné, déterminé; **~n name** prénom *m*; **to be ~n to (doing) sth** être enclin à (faire) qch; **~n that he is ...** supposé qu'il soit ... . ♦ **giver** *n* donateur *m* -trice *f*.
glacé ['glæseı] *adj fruit* confit.
glacial ['gleısıəl] *adj* glacial; (*Geol*) glaciaire.
glacier ['glæsıə^r] *n* glacier *m*.
glad [glæd] *adj person* content, heureux (*of, about* de; *to do* de faire; *that* que + *subj*); *news* heureux; *occasion* joyeux. **I am ~ about it** cela me fait plaisir, j'en suis bien content, j'en suis ravi; **he's only too ~ to do it** il ne demande pas mieux que de le faire. ♦ **gladden** *vt person* rendre heureux; *heart, occasion* réjouir. ♦ **gladly** *adv* (*joyfully*) avec joie; (*willingly*) avec plaisir, volontiers. ♦ **gladness** *n* joie *f*.
glade [gleıd] *n* clairière *f*.
gladiolus [ˌglædı'əuləs] *n, pl* **-oli** [-əulaı] glaïeul *m*.
glamour ['glæmə^r] *n [person]* séductions *fpl*, fascination *f*; *[occasion]* éclat *m*; *[situation]* prestige *m*. **to lend ~ to sth** prêter de l'éclat à qch; **~ boy*** beau gars* *m*; **~ girl*** pin-up‡ *f inv*.
♦ **glamorize** *vt place, event* présenter sous des couleurs séduisantes. ♦ **glamorous** *adj spectacle, life* brillant; *production* à grand spectacle; *dress, photo* splendide; *person* séduisant, fascinant; *job* prestigieux.
glance [glɑ:ns] **1** *n* coup *m* d'œil, regard *m*. **at a ~** d'un coup d'œil; **at first ~** à première vue; **without a backward ~** sans se retourner; (*fig*) sans plus de cérémonies. **2** *vi* **(a)** (*look*) jeter un coup d'œil (*at* sur, à), lancer un regard (*at* à). **to ~ away** détourner le regard; **he ~d over the paper** il a jeté un coup d'œil sur le journal. **(b) to ~ off sth** dévier sur qch; **to ~ off** dévier. ♦ **glancing** *adj blow* oblique.
gland [glænd] *n* glande *f*. ♦ **glandular** *adj* glandulaire; **~ular fever** mononucléose *f* infectieuse.
glare [glɛə^r] **1** *vi* **(a)** lancer un regard furieux (*at* à). **(b)** *[sun, lights]* briller d'un éclat éblouissant. **2** *n* **(a)** regard furieux. **(b)** *[light]* éclat éblouissant; (*Aut*) éblouissement *m*; *[publicity]* feux *mpl*.
♦ **glaring** *adj light* éblouissant; *sun* aveuglant; *colour* criard; *fact, mistake* qui crève les yeux; *injustice, lie* flagrant.
glass [glɑ:s] **1** *n* (*substance; tumbler*) verre *m*; (*~ware*) verrerie *f*; (*mirror*) glace *f*; (*magnifying ~*) loupe *f*; (*telescope*) longue-vue *f*; (*barometer*) baromètre *m*. **pane of ~** vitre *f*; **window ~** verre à vitre; **a ~ of wine** un verre de vin; **a wine ~** un verre à vin; **grown under ~** cultivé sous verre; **displayed under ~** exposé en vitrine; **~es** (*spectacles*) lunettes *fpl*; (*binoculars*) jumelles *fpl*. **2** *adj bottle, ornament* de verre, en verre; *slipper, eye* de verre; *industry* du verre; *door* vitré. **~ case** vitrine *f*; **to keep sth in a ~ case** garder qch sous verre; **~ fibre** fibre *f* de verre; **~ wool** laine *f* de verre. ♦ **glasscloth** *n* essuie-verres *m inv*. ♦ **glasscutter** *n* (*tool*) diamant *m*. ♦ **glassful** *n* (plein) verre *m*. ♦ **glasshouse** *n* (*for plants*) serre *f*. ♦ **glasspaper** *n* papier *m* de verre. ♦ **glassware** *n* verrerie *f*. ♦ **glassworks** *n* verrerie *f* (*fabrique*). ♦ **glassy** *adj substance, eye, look* vitreux; *surface, sea* uni (comme un miroir).
glaucoma [glɔ:'kəumə] *n* glaucome *m*.
glaze [gleız] **1** *vt door, window* vitrer; *picture* mettre sous verre; *pottery, tiles* vernisser; *cake, meat* glacer. **2** *n* vernis *m*; glaçage *m*. ♦ **glazed** *adj door* vitré; *pottery* vernissé; *paper, photograph* brillant; *eyes* vitreux. ♦ **glazier** *n* vitrier *m*.
gleam [gli:m] **1** *n* lueur *f* (*also fig*); *[metal]* reflet *m*; *[water]* miroitement *m*. **2** *vi* (*gen*) luire; *[metal, shoes etc]* reluire; *[water]* miroiter.
♦ **gleaming** *adj* (*gen*) brillant; (*clean*) reluisant.
glean [gli:n] *vti* (*lit, fig*) glaner.
glee [gli:] *n* joie *f*. **~ club** chorale *f*. ♦ **gleeful** *adj* joyeux, jubilant. ♦ **gleefully** *adv* joyeusement.
glen [glen] *n* vallon *m*.
glib [glıb] *adj excuse, lie* désinvolte; *person* qui a la parole facile. ♦ **glibly** *adv speak* avec aisance; *reply* sans hésiter; *make excuses, lie* avec désinvolture.
glide [glaıd] *vi* **(a)** *[door, drawer]* glisser (en douceur). **to ~ in** *etc [waiter, car etc]* entrer *etc* silencieusement; *[woman etc]* entrer *etc* avec grâce. **(b)** *[birds, aircraft]* planer. ♦ **glider** *n* (*Aviat*) planeur *m*; (*US: swing*) balançoire *f*. ♦ **gliding** *n* (*Aviat*) vol *m* plané.
glimmer ['glımə^r] **1** *vi* (*gen*) luire faiblement; *[water]* miroiter. **2** *n* faible lueur *f* (*also fig*); *[water]* miroitement *m*.
glimpse [glımps] **1** *n* vision *f* momentanée (*of* de); *[truth etc]* aperçu *m*. **2** *vt* (*also* **catch a ~ of**) entrevoir.
glint [glınt] **1** *n [light]* trait *m* de lumière; *[metal]* reflet *m*. **2** *vi* luire, briller.
glisten ['glısn] *vi [water]* miroiter; *[wet surface]* luire; *[metal object]* briller; *[eyes]* être brillant (*with* de).
glitter ['glıtə^r] **1** *vi* (*gen*) scintiller; *[eyes]* briller (de haine *or* de convoitise *etc*). **2** *n* scintillement *m*; (*fig*) éclat *m*.
♦ **glittering** *adj* scintillant, brillant; (*fig*) resplendissant.
gloat [gləut] *vi* exulter, jubiler*; (*maliciously*) se réjouir avec malveillance (*over, upon* de). **to ~ over** *money, possessions* jubiler* à la vue *or* à l'idée de; *beaten enemy* triompher de; *success* savourer.

globe [gləʊb] *n* globe *m.* (*Geog*) **all over the ~** sur toute la surface du globe. ♦ **global** *adj* (*worldwide*) mondial; (*comprehensive*) global. ♦ **globe-trotter** *n* globe-trotter *m.* ♦ **globe-trotting** *n* voyages *mpl* à travers le monde.

globule [ˈglɒbjuːl] *n* globule *m*; *[water etc]* gouttelette *f*.

gloom [gluːm] *n* (*darkness*) ténèbres *fpl*; (*melancholy*) tristesse *f*. **to cast a ~ over** *event* jeter une ombre sur; *person* attrister. ♦ **gloomily** *adv* tristement, d'un air triste *or* lugubre. ♦ **gloomy** *adj person, voice, place* triste, morne, (*stronger*) lugubre; *prospects, day, thoughts, weather* sombre; **he took a ~y view of everything** il voyait tout en noir; **to feel ~y** avoir des idées noires.

glory [ˈglɔːrɪ] **1** *n* gloire *f* (*also Rel*); (*magnificence*) splendeur *f*. **Rome at the height of its ~** Rome à l'apogée de sa gloire; **there she was in all her ~*** elle était là dans toute sa splendeur; **she was in her ~*** elle était tout à fait à son affaire; **~ be!*** Seigneur!; **the city's greatest ~** le principal titre de gloire de la ville. **2** *vi*: **to ~ in sth** être très fier (*proud*) *or* très heureux (*glad*) de qch. **3** *adj*: **~ hole*** capharnaüm* *m.* ♦ **glorify** *vt God* rendre gloire à; *person* exalter; **it was nothing but a glorified ...** ce n'était guère que ... . ♦ **glorious** *adj martyr* glorieux; *person* illustre; *victory* éclatant; *clothes, view, weather etc* magnifique; **glorious deed** action *f* d'éclat.

gloss[1] [glɒs] **1** *n* (*shine*) lustre *m*, brillant *m.* **2** *adj paint* laqué; *paper* glacé. **~ finish** brillant *m*, (*Phot*) glaçage *m.* ♦ **glossy** *adj fur, material* lustré; *paper* glacé; *paint* laqué; *hair, metal* brillant; *leaves* vernissé; *magazine* de luxe.

gloss[2] [glɒs] **1** *n* (*interpretation*) paraphrase *f*. **2** *vi*: **to ~ over sth** (*play down*) glisser sur qch; (*hide*) dissimuler qch. ♦ **glossary** *n* glossaire *m.*

glove [glʌv] **1** *n* gant *m.* (*fig*) **the ~s are off** j'y vais (*or* il y va *etc*) sans prendre de gants. **2** *adj*: (*Aut*) **~ compartment** boîte *f* à gants; **~ puppet** marionnette *f* (à gaine).

glow [gləʊ] **1** *vi [fire, metal, sky]* rougeoyer; *[cigarette end, lamp]* luire; *[colour, jewel]* rutiler; *[complexion, eyes]* rayonner; *[cheeks]* être en feu; (*fig*) brûler (*with* de). **it makes your body ~** cela vous fouette le sang. **2** *n [coal, metal]* rougeoiement *m*, incandescence *f*; *[sun, complexion, colour]* éclat *m*; *[lamp]* lueur *f*; *[passion]* feu *m*; *[enthusiasm]* élan *m.* ♦ **glowing** *adj* (*V* **glow 1**) rougeoyant; luisant; rutilant; rayonnant; *person* (*with health*) florissant (de santé); (*with pleasure*) radieux; *words* chaleureux; *description* enthousiaste; (*fig*) **to paint sth in ~ing colours** présenter qch en rose. ♦ **glow-worm** *n* ver *m* luisant.

glower [ˈglaʊəʳ] *vi*: **to ~ at sb/sth** lancer à qn/qch des regards noirs. ♦ **glowering** *adj look* noir; *person* à l'air mauvais.

glucose [ˈgluːkəʊs] *n* glucose *m.*

glue [gluː] **1** *n* colle *f*, glu *f*. **2** *vt* coller (*to, on* à). **to ~ sth together** recoller qch; **to keep one's eyes ~d to sb/sth*** ne pas détacher les yeux de qn/qch; **he stood there ~d to the spot*** il était là comme s'il avait pris racine; **he was ~d to television*** il est resté cloué devant la télévision.

glum [glʌm] *adj* triste, (*stronger*) lugubre. ♦ **glumly** *adv walk* d'un air triste; *answer* d'un ton triste; *look* d'un regard morne.

glut [glʌt] *n* surabondance *f*, surplus *m.*

glutton [ˈglʌtn] *n* glouton(ne) *m(f)*. **a ~ for work** un bourreau de travail; **a ~ for punishment** un(e) masochiste (*fig*). ♦ **gluttony** *n* gloutonnerie *f*.

glycerin(e) [ˌglɪsəˈriːn] *n* glycérine *f*.

gnarled [nɑːld] *adj* noueux.

gnash [næʃ] *vt*: **to ~ one's teeth** grincer des dents.

gnat [næt] *n* moucheron *m.*

gnaw [nɔː] **1** *vi* ronger. **to ~ through** couper à force de ronger. **2** *vt* ronger. ♦ **gnawing** *adj remorse, anxiety, hunger* tenaillant; *pain* harcelant.

gnome [nəʊm] *n* gnome *m.*

go [gəʊ] *pret* **went**, *ptp* **gone** **1** *vi* **(a)** (*gen*) aller (*to* à, en; *from* de). **to ~ on a journey** faire un *or* partir en voyage; **to ~ up/down** monter/descendre; **to ~ swimming** (*in general*) faire de la natation; (*on one occasion*) (aller) nager; **to ~ looking for sth** aller *or* partir à la recherche de qch; **we can talk as we ~** nous pouvons parler en chemin; **~ after him!** poursuivez-le!; **there he ~es!** le voilà!; **there he ~es again!** (*fig: he's at it again*) le voilà qui recommence!; **here ~es!*** allez, on y va!; **who ~es there?** qui va là?; **you ~ first** passe devant; **you ~ next** à toi après; **~ and shut the door** va fermer la porte; **she went and broke a cup** elle a trouvé le moyen de casser une tasse; **to ~** *or* **be ~ing to do** aller faire; **to be just ~ing to do** être sur le point de faire; **the child went to his mother** l'enfant est allé vers sa mère; **to ~ to the doctor** aller voir le médecin; **to ~ to sb for sth** aller demander qch à qn; **the train ~es at 90 km/h** le train fait du *or* roule à 90 km/h; **we had gone only 3 km** nous n'avions fait que 3 km; **I wouldn't ~ as far as to say that** je n'irais pas jusqu'à dire cela. **that's ~ing too far!** c'est un peu poussé!; **you've gone too far!** tu exagères!

(b) (*depart*) partir, s'en aller; *[train]* partir; (*disappear*) disparaître; *[time]* passer; *[money]* disparaître, filer; *[strength]* manquer; *[hearing, sight etc]* baisser; *[health]* se détériorer. **his mind is ~ing** il n'a plus toute sa tête; **the coffee has all gone** il n'y a plus de café; **my voice has gone** je n'ai plus de voix; **he is gone** (*dead*) il n'est plus; **we must be ~ing** il faut partir; **gone with the wind** autant en emporte le vent; (*Sport*) **~!** partez!; (*fig*) **from the word ~** dès le départ; (*US*) **it's ~ing on 3** il va être 3 heures; **it's just gone 3 o'clock** il vient de sonner 3 heures; **it was gone 4** il était plus de 4 heures; **to let ~** *or* **leave ~** lâcher prise; **to let ~** *or* **leave ~ of sth/sb** lâcher qch/qn; **to let o.s. ~** se laisser aller; **they have let their garden ~** ils ont laissé leur jardin à l'abandon; **I've let my music ~** je n'ai pas travaillé ma musique; **we'll let it ~ at that** ça ira comme ça; **he/it will have to ~** il va falloir se débarrasser de lui/se passer de cela; **'X must ~!'** 'à bas X!'; **it was ~ing cheap** cela se vendait à bas prix; **~ing, ~ing, gone!** un fois, deux fois, adjugé!; (*fig*) **7 down and 3 to ~** 7 de faits, il n'en reste plus que 3; (*pregnant*) **6 months gone*** enceinte de 6 mois.

(c) (*start up*) démarrer; (*function*) marcher, fonctionner. **it ~es on petrol** ça marche *or* fonctionne à l'essence; *[machine]* **to be ~ing** être en marche; **to set** *or* **get ~ing** *machine* mettre en marche; *work, business* mettre en train; **to keep ~ing** *[person]* se maintenir en activité; *[business]* se maintenir à flot; *[machine]* continuer à marcher; **to keep the fire ~ing** entretenir le feu; **she needs it to keep her ~ing** elle en a besoin pour tenir le coup; **to keep sb ~ing in money** *etc* donner à qn ce qu'il lui faut d'argent *etc*; **to make the party ~** animer la soirée; **to get things ~ing** faire démarrer les choses; **to make things ~** faire marcher les choses; **to get ~ing on** *or* **with sth** se mettre à faire qch, s'attaquer à qch; **once he gets ~ing ...** une fois lancé ... .

(d) (*progress*) aller, marcher. **the evening went very well** la soirée s'est très bien passée; **the project was ~ing well** le projet était en bonne voie; **how's it ~ing?** comment ça va?*; **how does the story ~?** comment c'est* cette histoire?; **the tune ~es like this** voici l'air; **let's wait and see how things ~** attendons de voir ce qui va se passer; **as things ~** dans l'état actuel des choses; **all will ~ well** tout ira bien; **all went well for him** tout a bien marché (pour lui).

(e) (*be, become*) devenir, se faire. *[person]* **to ~**

unpunished s'en tirer sans châtiment; **to ~ hungry** avoir faim; **to ~ red** rougir; **the constituency went Labour** la circonscription est passée aux travaillistes.

(f) (*be accepted*) **the story ~es that ...** le bruit court que ...; **anything ~es*** tout est permis; **that ~es without saying** cela va sans dire; **what he says ~es** c'est lui qui commande; **that ~es for me too** (*applies to me*) cela s'applique à moi aussi; (*I agree*) je suis aussi de cet avis.

(g) (*break etc*) *[rope]* céder; *[fuse, lamp]* sauter; *[material]* s'user. **the skirt went at the seams** la jupe a craqué aux coutures; **this jacket has gone at the elbows** cette veste est percée aux coudes; **there ~es another button!** voilà encore un bouton de sauté!

(h) (*extend*) aller, s'étendre. **the garden ~es as far as the river** le jardin va *or* s'étend jusqu'à la rivière; **as far as that ~es** pour ce qui est de cela; **this book is good, as far as it ~es** c'est un bon livre, compte tenu de ses limites; **he's not bad, as boys ~** il n'est pas trop mal, pour un garçon; **it's a fairly good garage as garages ~** comme garage ça peut aller; **money does not ~ very far** l'argent ne va pas loin.

(i) (*be contained*) aller. **it won't ~ into my case** je ne peux pas le mettre dans ma valise; **4 into 12 ~es 3 times** 12 divisé par 4 égale 3; **2 won't ~ exactly into 11** 11 n'est pas exactement divisible par 2; **4 into 3 won't ~** 3 divisé par 4 il n'y va pas; **the books ~ in that cupboard** les livres se mettent *or* vont dans ce placard-là.

(j) *[prize, reward]* aller, être donné (*to* à); *[inheritance]* passer (*to* à).

(k) (*be available*) **are there any jobs ~ing?** est-ce qu'on peut trouver du travail?; **is there any coffee ~ing?** est-ce qu'il y a du café?; **I'll have what's ~ing** je prendrai de ce qu'il y a.

(l) (*contribute*) contribuer (*to* à). **that will ~ to make him happy** cela contribuera à le rendre heureux; **the qualities that ~ to make a great man** les qualités qui font un grand homme; **the money will ~ towards** on mettra l'argent de côté pour.

(m) (*make sound or movement*) faire; *[bell, clock]* sonner. **~ like that with your foot** faites comme ça du pied; **to ~ bang** faire 'pan'; **he went 'psst'** 'psst' fit-il.

2 *vt*: **to ~ it alone** (*gen*) se débrouiller tout seul; (*Pol etc*) faire cavalier seul; **to ~ one better** faire (*or* dire) mieux (*than sb* que qn); (*Cards*) **he went 3 spades** il a annoncé 3 piques.

3 *n, pl* **~es (a)** (*energy*) énergie *f*, dynamisme *m*. **he is always on the ~** il ne s'arrête jamais; **to keep sb on the ~** ne pas laisser souffler qn; **he has 2 books on the ~** il a 2 livres en train; **it's all ~!*** ça n'arrête pas!

(b) (*attempt*) coup *m*, essai *m*. **to have a ~** essayer (*at (doing) sth* de faire qch); **to have another ~** essayer une nouvelle fois; **at one ~** d'un seul coup; (*in games*) **it's your ~** c'est à toi.

(c) (*success*) **to make a ~ of sth** réussir qch; **no ~!*** rien à faire!

4 *adj* (*fig*) **all systems are ~*** tout est O.K.

go about 1 *vi* **(a)** circuler; *[rumour]* courir. **to ~ about with** *friends* fréquenter; *boyfriend etc* sortir avec. **(b)** (*Naut*) virer de bord.

2 *vt fus* **(a)** (*set to work at*) *task* se mettre à. **he knows how to ~ about it** il sait s'y prendre; **how does one ~ about getting seats?** comment fait-on pour avoir des places? **(b)** (*be occupied with*) *business* s'occuper de. **to ~ about one's normal work** vaquer à ses occupations habituelles.

go across *vi, vt fus* traverser.

go after *vt fus job, prize* essayer d'avoir.

go against *vt fus* **(a)** (*prove hostile to*) *[luck, events etc]* être contraire à; *[appearance, evidence]* nuire à; *[decision]* être défavorable à. **(b)** (*oppose*) *public opinion* aller à l'encontre de; *sb's wishes* aller contre. **it ~es against my conscience** ma conscience s'y oppose.

go ahead *vi*: **~ ahead!** allez-y!; **to ~ ahead with a scheme** mettre un projet à exécution; **they went ahead with it** ils l'ont fait.

go along *vi* aller, avancer. **I'll tell you as we ~ along** je vous le dirai en chemin; **to ~ along with sb** (*lit*) accompagner qn; (*fig*) être d'accord avec qn; **I check as I ~ along** je vérifie au fur et à mesure.

go around *vi* = **go about 1 a.**

go at *vt fus* (*attack*) *person* attaquer; (*undertake*) *task* s'attaquer à.

go away *vi* s'en aller, partir.

go back *vi* **(a)** (*return*) revenir, retourner. **to ~ back to a subject** revenir sur un sujet; **to ~ back to the beginning** recommencer. **(b)** (*retreat*) reculer. **(c)** *[memory, family]* remonter (*to* à). **(d)** (*revert*) revenir (*to* à). **(e)** (*extend*) *[garden etc]* s'étendre (*to* jusqu'à). **the cave ~es back 300 metres** la grotte a 300 mètres de profondeur.

go back on *vt fus decision, promise* revenir sur; *friend* laisser tomber.

go before *vi* aller au devant. (*fig*) **all that has gone before** tout ce qui s'est passé avant.

go below *vi* (*Naut*) descendre dans l'entrepont.

go by 1 *vi [person, period of time]* passer. **we've let the opportunity ~ by** nous avons laissé échapper l'occasion; **as time ~es by** à mesure que le temps passe. **2** *vt fus appearances* juger d'après; *instructions* suivre. **that's nothing to ~ by** ça ne prouve rien; **I ~ by what I'm told** je me fonde sur ce qu'on me dit; **the only thing we've got to ~ by** la seule chose sur laquelle nous puissions nous baser.

go down *vi* **(a)** (*descend*) descendre; (*fall*) *[person]* tomber; *[building]* s'écrouler; (*sink*) *[ship, person]* couler; *[sun, moon]* se coucher. **~ down to the bottom of the page** continuez jusqu'au bas de la page; **to ~ down to posterity** passer à la postérité; **to ~ down with flu** attraper la grippe; (*swallowed*) **it went down the wrong way** j'ai (*or* il a *etc*) avalé de travers; (*fig*) **that won't ~ down with me** ça ne prend pas avec moi; **his speech didn't ~ down well** son discours a été très mal reçu. **(b)** (*drop etc*) *[wind, floods, temperature, curtain]* tomber; *[tide]* descendre; *[balloon, tyre, swelling]* se dégonfler; *[standards, price]* baisser. **to ~ down in value** perdre de sa valeur; **this neighbourhood has gone down** ce quartier n'est plus ce qu'il était. **(c)** (*be defeated, fail*) être battu (*to* par); (*Bridge*) chuter; (*fail examination*) échouer (*in* en).

go for *vt fus* **(a)** (*attack*) *person* s'élancer sur; (*verbally*) s'en prendre à; (*in newspaper*) attaquer. (*to dog*) **~ for him!** mors-le! **(b)** (*: *admire*) *person, object* adorer*. **I don't ~ much for that** ça ne me dit pas grand-chose. **(c)** (*strive for*) essayer d'avoir; (*choose*) choisir.

go forward *vi [person, vehicle]* avancer. **to let a suggestion ~ forward** transmettre une proposition.

go in *vi* (*enter*) entrer, rentrer; *[troops]* attaquer; *[sun, moon]* se cacher (*behind* derrière). **what time does the theatre ~ in?** à quelle heure commence la pièce?

go in for *vt fus* **(a)** *examination* se présenter à; *appointment* poser sa candidature à; *competition, race* prendre part à. **(b)** *sport, hobby, politics* faire; *style, principle, cause* adopter; *lectures* suivre; *profession* se consacrer à. **we don't ~ in for that sort of thing** nous n'aimons pas beaucoup ce genre de chose; **he's ~ing in for science** il va se spécialiser dans les sciences.

go into *vt fus* **(a)** (*join, take up*) entrer à *or* dans. **(b)** (*embark on*) *explanation* se lancer dans. **let's not ~ into that now** laissons cela pour le moment; **to ~ into fits of laughter** être pris de fou rire.

(c) (*investigate*) *question, problem* examiner, étudier.
go in with *vt fus* se joindre à (*in* dans; *to do* pour faire); (*to buy sth*) se cotiser avec.
go off 1 *vi* **(a)** (*leave*) partir, s'en aller; (*Theat*) quitter la scène. **to ~ off with sth** emporter qch; **to ~ off with sb** partir avec qn. **(b)** *[alarm clock]* sonner; *[gun]* partir. **the gun didn't ~ off** le coup n'est pas parti; **the pistol went off in his hand** le pistolet lui est parti dans la main. **(c)** (*stop*) *[light, heating etc]* s'éteindre. **(d)** (*spoil*) *[meat, fish etc]* se gâter; *[milk]* tourner; *[sportsman]* perdre de sa forme; *[woman]* perdre de sa beauté. **(e)** *[feeling, effect]* passer. **(f)** (*go to sleep*) s'endormir. **(g)** *[event]* se passer. **the evening went off very well** la soirée s'est très bien passée.
2 *vt fus food etc* perdre le goût de. **I've gone off Dickens** je n'ai plus envie de lire Dickens.
go on 1 *vi* **(a)** *[lid]* aller. **these shoes won't ~ on** je n'entre pas dans ces chaussures. **(b)** (*proceed*) poursuivre son chemin. **to ~ on to another matter** passer à une autre question; **he went on to say that ...** il a dit ensuite que ... . **(c)** (*continue*) continuer (*with sth* qch; *doing* de *or* à faire). **~ on trying!** essaie encore!; **~ on (with you)!*** allons donc!; **you have enough to be ~ing on with** tu as de quoi faire* pour le moment; **he ~es on and on about it*** il ne finit pas d'en parler. **(d)** (*happen*) se passer; *[game, argument]* être en train; (*last*) durer. **while this was ~ing on** au même moment; **what's ~ing on here?** qu'est-ce qui se passe ici? **(e)** (*pass*) *[time, years]* passer. **as the years went on he ...** avec le passage des années, il ... . **(f)** (*behave*) se conduire. **(g)** (*Theat*) entrer en scène; (*Sport*) *[substitute]* entrer en jeu. **(h)** (*progress*) *[patient]* se porter; *[life, affairs]* continuer. 2 *vt fus* (*judge by*) se fonder sur. **what have you to ~ on?** sur quoi vous fondez-vous?; **we don't have much to ~ on** nous ne pouvons pas nous fonder sur grand-chose.
go on at *vt fus* (*nag*) s'en prendre (continuellement) à.
go on for *vt fus*: **to be ~ing on for** approcher de; **it's ~ing on for 5 o'clock** il est presque 5 heures.
go out *vi* (*leave*) sortir; (*depart*) partir (*to* pour, à); *[tide]* descendre; *[sea]* se retirer; *[fashion]* se démoder; *[custom]* disparaître; *[fire, light]* s'éteindre; (*Cards etc*) terminer; *[pamphlet, circular]* être distribué (*to* à). **to ~ out of a room** quitter une pièce; **to ~ out riding** faire une sortie à cheval; **to ~ out for a meal** manger en ville (*or* chez des amis); **he ~e out a lot** il sort beaucoup; **she doesn't ~ out with him any more** elle ne sort plus avec lui; **to ~ out to work** travailler au dehors.
go over 1 *vi* **(a)** (*cross*) **to ~ over to America** aller aux États-Unis; (*fig*) **his speech went over well** son discours a été très bien reçu. **(b)** (*change allegiance*) passer (*to* à). **to ~ over to the enemy** passer à l'ennemi. **(c)** (*be overturned*) *[vehicle, boat]* se retourner.
2 *vt fus* **(a)** (*examine*) *accounts, report* vérifier; *house* visiter; *[doctor] patient* examiner. **(b)** (*rehearse, review*) *lesson, rôle* revoir; *facts etc* récapituler; *events* retracer; *sb's faults, evidence* passer au crible. **to ~ over sth in one's mind** repasser qch dans son esprit; **let's ~ over it again** reprenons les faits; **(c)** (*touch up*) retoucher.
go round *vi* **(a)** *[wheel etc]* tourner. **my head is ~ing round** j'ai la tête qui tourne. **(b)** (*make a detour*) faire un détour (*by* par). **(c) to ~ round to sb's house/to see sb** passer chez qn/voir qn. **(d)** (*be sufficient*) suffire (pour tout le monde). **enough food to ~ round** assez de nourriture pour tout le monde. **(e)** (*circulate*) *[rumour etc]* circuler.
go through 1 *vi [law, bill]* être voté; *[business deal]* être conclu. 2 *vt fus* **(a)** (*suffer*) subir. **we've all gone through it** nous avons tous passé par là. **(b)** (*examine*) *list, book* éplucher; *mail* dépouiller; *subject* examiner à fond; *clothes, wardrobe* trier; *one's pockets* fouiller dans; (*Customs*) fouiller. **to ~ through sb's pockets** faire les poches à qn*. **(c)** (*use up*) *money* dépenser; *a fortune* engloutir; (*wear out*) *garment, shoes* user. **it has already gone through 13 editions** il y en a déjà eu 13 éditions. **(d)** (*perform*) *lesson* réciter; *formalities* remplir; *programme, entertainment* exécuter; *course of study* suivre; *apprenticeship* faire.
go through with *vt fus* (*complete*) *plan, crime, undertaking* exécuter. **she couldn't ~ through with it** elle n'a pas pu aller jusqu'au bout.
go together *vi* (*gen*) aller bien ensemble; *[events, conditions]* aller de pair.
go under *vi* (*sink*) *[ship, person]* couler; (*fail*) *[person]* être vaincu; *[business etc]* couler.
go up 1 *vi* **(a)** (*rise*) *[price, value, temperature]* monter, être en hausse; *[curtain]* se lever. **to ~ up in price** augmenter. **(b)** (*ascend*) monter; (*to bed*) monter se coucher. **(c)** (*explode*) exploser. 2 *vt fus hill* monter.
go with *vt fus* **(a)** (*accompany*) *[circumstances, event, conditions]* aller de pair avec. **the house ~es with the job** le logement va avec le poste; **to ~ with the crowd** suivre la foule. **(b)** (*suit*) *[colours]* s'assortir avec; *[furnishings]* être assorti à; *[behaviour, opinions]* s'accorder avec. **(c)** (*: *also* **~ steady with**) sortir avec.
go without 1 *vi* s'en passer. **2** *vt fus* se passer de.
♦ **go-ahead 1** *adj* dynamique; **2** *n*: **to give sb the ~-ahead*** donner à qn le feu vert (*for* pour; *to do* pour faire). ♦ **go-between** *n* intermédiaire *mf*. ♦ **go-by*** *n*: **to give sb/sth the ~-by*** laisser tomber qn/qch. ♦ **go-getter** *n* arriviste *mf*. ♦ **going 1** *n* (*pace*) **that was good ~ing** ça a été rapide; **it was slow ~ing** on n'avançait pas; (*conditions*) **it's rough ~ing** (*walking*) on marche mal; (*Aut etc*) la route est mauvaise; **while the ~ing was good** au bon moment; **2** *adj price* actuel; **a ~ing concern** une affaire qui marche. ♦ **going-over** *n [accounts, patient]* examen *m*; (*fig: beating -up*) passage *m* à tabac*. ♦ **goings-on*** *npl* (*behaviour*) activités *fpl*. ♦ **go-kart** *n* kart *m*. ♦ **go-slow (strike)** *n* grève *f* perlée.
goad [gəʊd] *vt* (*lit, fig*) aiguillonner. **to ~ sb into doing** talonner qn jusqu'à ce qu'il fasse.
goal [gəʊl] *n* but *m*, objectif *m*; (*Sport*) but. **to play in ~** être gardien de but; **to win by 3 ~s to 2** gagner par 3 buts à 2. ♦ **goalie*** *n* goal* *m*. ♦ **goalkeeper** *n* gardien *m* de but. ♦ **goal-kick** *n* coup *m* de pied de but. ♦ **goalmouth** *n*: **in the ~mouth** juste devant les poteaux. ♦ **goal-post** *n* poteau *m* de but.
goat [gəʊt] *n* chèvre *f*; (*he-~*) bouc *m*. **to act the ~*** faire l'andouille*; **he/it gets my ~*** il/ça me tape sur les nerfs*.
gobble ['gɒbl] *vt* (**~ down, ~ up**) engloutir. ♦ **gobbledegook*** *n* charabia* *m*.
goblet ['gɒblɪt] *n* coupe *f*; (*modern*) verre *m* à pied.
goblin ['gɒblɪn] *n* lutin *m*.
god [gɒd] *n* dieu *m* (*also fig*). **G~** Dieu *m*; **G~ save the Queen** que Dieu bénisse la reine; **for G~'s sake!‡** nom d'un chien!*; **(my) G~!‡** bon Dieu!‡; **G~ knows*** Dieu seul le sait; **G~ forbid!*** Dieu m'en garde!; **G~ willing** s'il plaît à Dieu; (*Theat*) **the ~s*** le poulailler*. ♦ **godchild** *n* filleul(e) *m(f)*. ♦ **goddamn(ed)‡** *adj* foutu‡ (*before n*). ♦ **goddaughter** *n* filleule *f*. ♦ **goddess** *n* déesse *f*. ♦ **godfather** *n* parrain *m*. ♦ **god-fearing** *adj* très croyant. ♦ **godforsaken** *adj place* perdu; *existence* misérable. ♦ **godhead** *n* divinité *f*. ♦ **godless** *adj* impie. ♦ **godlike** *adj* divin. ♦ **godly** *adj* pieux. ♦ **godmother** *n* marraine *f*. ♦ **godparents** *npl*: **his ~parents** son par-

rain et sa marraine. ♦ **godsend** *n* bénédiction *f*, don *m* du ciel (*to* pour). ♦ **godson** *n* filleul *m*.

goggle ['gɒgl] **1** *vi* rouler de gros yeux ronds. **to ~ at sb/sth** regarder qn/qch en roulant de gros yeux ronds. **2** *npl*: **~s** (*gen*) lunettes protectrices; *[skindiver]* lunettes de plongée.

gold [gəʊld] **1** *n* or *m*. **in ~** en or; **heart of ~** cœur *m* d'or. **2** *adj watch, tooth* en or; *coin, cloth, reserves, mine* d'or; (~ *-coloured*) or *inv*. **~ braid** galon *m* d'or; **~ dust** poudre *f* d'or; **~ leaf** or *m* en feuille; **~ plate** vaisselle *f* d'or; **~ rush** ruée *f* vers l'or; **~ standard** étalon-or *m*. ♦ **gold-digger*** *n* aventurière *f*. ♦ **golden** *adj hair* doré; *jewellery, voice* d'or, en or; *era* idéal; *afternoon* merveilleux; *opportunity* magnifique; *remedy* souverain; *rule, age* d'or; **~en eagle** aigle *m* royal; (*fig*) **~en handshake** gratification *f* de fin de service; **~en jubilee** fête *f* du cinquantième anniversaire; **the ~en mean** le juste milieu; (*Bot*) **~en rod** gerbe *f* d'or; **~en syrup** mélasse *f* raffinée; **~en wedding (anniversary)** noces *fpl* d'or. ♦ **goldfinch** *n* chardonneret *m*. ♦ **goldfish** *n* poisson *m* rouge; **~fish bowl** bocal *m* (à poissons). ♦ **gold-plated** *adj* plaqué or. ♦ **goldsmith** *n* orfèvre *m*.

golf [gɒlf] **1** *n* golf *m*. **2** *vi*: **to go ~ing** jouer au golf. **3** *adj*: **~ ball** balle *f* de golf; **~ club** (*stick, place*) club *m* de golf; **~ course** terrain *m* de golf *m*. ♦ **golfer** *n* joueur *m*, -euse *f* de golf.

gone [gɒn] *ptp of* **go**. ♦ **goner‡** *n*: **to be a ~r** être fichu* *or* foutu‡.

gong [gɒŋ] *n* gong *m*.

gonorrhoea [ˌgɒnəˈrɪə] *n* blennorragie *f*.

goo* [guː] *n* matière *f* gluante; (*sentimentality*) sentimentalité *f* mièvre. ♦ **gooey*** *adj substance* gluant; *cake* qui colle aux dents; (*fig*) sentimental.

good [gʊd] **1** *adj, comp* **better**, *superl* **best** **(a)** (*gen*) bon (*f* bonne); (*well-behaved*) *child, animal* sage; (*kind*) bon, gentil. **a ~ man** un homme bien, un brave homme, (*holy*) un saint homme; **he's a ~ man** il est bon; **to lead a ~ life** mener une vie vertueuse; **as ~ as gold** sage comme une image; **be ~!** sois sage!; **be ~ to him** soyez gentil avec lui; **that's very ~ of you** vous êtes bien aimable *or* gentil; **would you be ~ enough to tell me** seriez-vous assez aimable pour me dire; **G~ Friday** Vendredi saint; **~ sort*** brave type* *m or* fille *f*; **~ old Charles!*** ce bon vieux Charles!; **my ~ friend** mon cher ami; **my ~ man** mon brave; **very ~, sir!** très bien, monsieur!; **to do ~ works** faire de bonnes œuvres; **a ~ dress** une robe de qualité; **her ~ dress** sa robe bien; **nothing was too ~ for** rien n'était trop beau pour; (*in shop*) **I want sth ~** je veux qch de bien; **that's not ~ enough** c'est déplorable; **that's ~ enough for me** cela me suffit; **~ for you!** bravo!; **~!** très bien!; (*joke, story*) **that's a ~ one!** elle est bien bonne celle-là!; (*iro*) à d'autres!*; **he's as ~ as you** il vaut autant que vous; **it's as ~ a way as any other** c'est une façon comme une autre; **he was as ~ as his word** il a tenu sa promesse.

(b) (*beneficial*) bon (*for* pour). **it's ~ for you** ça te fait du bien; (*fig*) **if you know what's ~ for you** si tu as le moindre bon sens; **the shock was ~ for him** le choc lui a été salutaire; **to drink more than is ~ for one** boire plus qu'on ne le devrait; *[food]* **to stay ~** (bien) se conserver.

(c) (*efficient, competent*) bon (*at* en). **~ at French** bon *or* fort en français; **she's ~ with children** elle sait s'y prendre avec les enfants; **he's ~ at telling stories** il sait bien raconter les histoires; **he's not ~ enough to do it alone** il ne s'y connaît pas assez pour le faire tout seul; **he's too ~ for that** il mérite mieux que cela.

(d) (*agreeable*) bon; *visit, holiday* bon, agréable; *weather, day* beau (*f* belle); *news* bon, heureux. **we had a ~ time** nous nous sommes bien amusés; **I've had a ~ life** j'ai eu une belle vie; **too ~ to be true** trop beau pour être vrai; **it's ~ to be alive** il fait bon vivre; **it's ~ to be here** cela fait plaisir d'être ici; **I feel ~** je me sens bien; **I don't feel too ~ about that*** (*worried*) cela m'inquiète un peu; (*ashamed*) j'en ai un peu honte; **Robert sends his ~ wishes** Robert envoie ses amitiés; **with every ~ wish, with all ~ wishes** tous mes meilleurs vœux.

(e) (*in greetings*) **~ afternoon** (*early*) bonjour, (*later, on leaving*) bonsoir; **~ evening** bonsoir; **~ morning** bonjour; **~bye**, **~night** *V below*.

(f) (*handsome*) *appearance* beau, joli. **~ looks** beauté *f*; **you look ~ in that, that looks ~ on you** ça vous va bien; **she's got a ~ figure** elle est bien faite; **~ legs** jambes bien faites.

(g) (*favourable*) *terms, contract, deal* avantageux; *offer* favorable, bon; *omen, chance, opportunity* bon; *marriage* beau; *address* chic *inv*. **you've never had it so ~!*** vous n'avez jamais eu la vie si belle!; **he's on to a ~ thing*** il a trouvé un filon*; **to make a ~ thing out of sth*** tirer bon parti de qch; **it would be a ~ thing to ask him** il serait bon de lui demander; **it's a ~ thing I was there** heureusement que j'étais là; **that's a ~ thing!** tant mieux!; **this is as ~ a time as any to do it** autant le faire maintenant.

(h) (*reliable, valid*) *car, tools, machinery* bon, sûr; *cheque* bon; *reason, excuse* bon, valable. **ticket ~ for 3 months** billet bon *or* valable 3 mois; **he's ~ for another 20 years yet** il en a encore bien pour 20 ans.

(i) (*considerable, not less than*) *mile, hour etc* bon. **a ~ deal (of), a ~ many** beaucoup (de); **a ~ way** un bon bout de chemin; **a ~ while** assez longtemps; **a ~ 8 kilometres** 8 bons kilomètres; **that was a ~ 10 years ago** il y a bien 10 ans de cela; **a ~ thrashing** une bonne correction; **to give sth a ~ clean*** nettoyer qch à fond.

(j) (*phrases*) **as ~ as** pour ainsi dire, pratiquement; **as ~ as new** comme neuf; **she as ~ as told me that ...** elle m'a dit à peu de chose près que ...; **it's as ~ as saying that ...** autant dire que ...; **it was as ~ as a play!** c'était une vraie comédie!; **to make ~** (*vi*) (*succeed*) faire son chemin; *[ex-criminal etc]* se refaire une vie; (*vt*) *deficit* combler; *deficiency, losses* compenser; *expenses* rembourser; *injustice, damage* réparer; *promise* tenir; *escape* réussir.

2 *adv* bien. **a ~ strong stick** un bâton bien solide; **a ~ long walk** une bonne promenade; **we had a ~ long talk** nous avons discuté bien longuement; **~ and hot** bien chaud.

3 *n* **(a)** (*virtue*) bien *m*. **to do ~** faire du bien; **she's up to no ~*** elle prépare quelque mauvais coup; **there's some ~ in him** il a du bon; **for ~ or bad** que ce soit un bien ou un mal; **he'll come to no ~** il finira mal.

(b) (*people*) **only the ~ die young** seuls les bons *mpl* meurent jeunes.

(c) (*advantage, profit*) bien *m*, avantage *m*. **the common ~** l'intérêt *m* commun; **for your own ~** pour votre bien; **for the ~ of his health** pour sa santé; **that will do you ~** cela vous fera du bien; **what ~ will that do you?** ça t'avancera à quoi?; **what's the ~?** à quoi bon?; **what's the ~ of hurrying?** à quoi bon se presser?; **a (fat) lot of ~ that will do you!*** tu seras bien avancé!; **much ~ may it do you!** grand bien vous fasse!; **we were £5 to the ~** cela nous a fait 5 livres de gagnées; **that's all to the ~!** tant mieux!; **it's no ~** ça ne sert à rien; **that's no ~** cela ne va pas; **that won't be much ~** cela ne servira pas à grand-chose; **if that is any ~ to you** si ça peut vous être utile; **it's no ~ saying that** ce n'est pas la peine de dire cela.

(d) (*adv phrase*) **for ~** pour de bon; **for ~ and all** une fois pour toutes.

♦ **goodbye** *excl* au revoir. ♦ **good-for-nothing**

adj, n propre à rien (*mf*). ♦ **good-hearted** *adj* qui a bon cœur. ♦ **good-humoured** *adj* bon enfant *inv*. ♦ **good-humouredly** *adv* avec bonhomie. ♦ **good-looker*** *n* beau garçon *m*, jolie fille *f*. ♦ **good-looking** *adj* beau, bien *inv*. ♦ **goodly** *adj* († *or liter*) *appearance* beau; *size* grand; *number* considérable. ♦ **good-natured** *adj person* facile à vivre; *smile, laughter* bon enfant *inv*. ♦ **goodness** *n [person]* bonté *f*; *[thing]* (bonne) qualité *f*; **(my) ~ness!***, **~ness gracious!*** Seigneur!; **~ness knows*** Dieu sait; **for ~ness' sake*** par pitié. ♦ **goodnight** *excl* bonsoir, bonne nuit. ♦ **goods** *npl* marchandises *fpl*, articles *mpl*; **leather/knitted ~s** articles de cuir/en tricot; **all his ~s and chattels** tous ses biens et effets *mpl*; **~s train** train *m* de marchandises; **~s yard** dépôt *m* de marchandises. ♦ **good-tempered** *adj person* qui a bon caractère; *smile, look* aimable. ♦ **good-time girl*** *n* fille *f* qui ne pense qu'à s'amuser. ♦ **goodwill** *n* bonne volonté; **to gain sb's ~will** se faire bien voir de qn; (*Pol*) **~will mission** mission *f* de conciliation; (*Comm*) **the ~will goes with the business** les incorporels *mpl* sont vendus avec le fonds de commerce. ♦ **goody*** **1** *excl* chic!*; **2** *n* (*Cine*) **the ~ies and the baddies*** les bons *mpl* et les méchants *mpl*; (*Culin*) **~ies*** friandises *fpl*. ♦ **goody-goody*** *n* modèle *m* de vertu (*iro*).

goose [guːs] *n,pl* **geese** oie *f*. **the ~ that lays the golden eggs** la poule aux œufs d'or; **don't be such a ~*** ne sois pas si dinde*. ♦ **gooseberry** *n* groseille *f* à maquereau; (**~***berry bush*) groseiller *m*. ♦ **gooseflesh** *n or* ♦ **goosepimples** *npl or* ♦ **goosebumps** *npl* la chair de poule. ♦ **goose-step** *vi* faire le pas de l'oie.

gore [gɔːʳ] *vt [bull etc]* blesser d'un coup de corne.

gorge [gɔːdʒ] **1** *n* (*Anat, Geog*) gorge *f*. **it makes my ~ rise** cela me soulève le cœur. **2** *vt*: **to ~ o.s.** se gorger (*on* de).

gorgeous [ˈgɔːdʒəs] *adj* magnifique, splendide; (*) *holiday etc* sensationnel*, formidable*. **we had a ~ time*** on a passé un moment sensationnel*.

gorilla [gəˈrɪlə] *n* gorille *m*.

gormless* [ˈgɔːmlɪs] *adj* bête.

gorse [gɔːs] *n* ajoncs *mpl*. **~ bush** ajonc *m*.

gory [ˈgɔːrɪ] *adj wound, battle etc* sanglant; *person* ensanglanté. **all the ~ details** tous les détails les plus horribles.

gosh* [gɒʃ] *excl* ça alors!*

gospel [ˈgɒspəl] *n* évangile *m*. **it's the ~ truth*** c'est parole d'évangile.

gossip [ˈgɒsɪp] **1** *n* **(a)** (*chatter*) commérages *mpl*, potins *mpl*; (*in newspaper*) échos *mpl*. **a piece of ~** un ragot; **we had a good old ~** nous nous sommes raconté tous les potins. **(b)** (*person*) commère *f*. **he's a real ~** c'est une vraie commère. **2** *vi* bavarder; (*maliciously*) potiner, faire des commérages (*about* sur). **3** *adj* (*Press*) **~ column** échos *mpl*; **~ columnist** *or* **writer** échotier *m*, -ière *f*. ♦ **gossiping 1** *adj* bavard, cancanier (*pej*); **2** *n* bavardage *m*, commérage *m* (*pej*).

got [gɒt], (*US*) **gotten** [ˈgɒtn] *pret, ptp of* **get**.

Gothic [ˈgɒθɪk] *adj, n* gothique (*m*).

gouge [gaʊdʒ] *vt* (**~ out**) (*with gouge*) gouger; (*with knife etc*) évider.

goulash [ˈguːlæʃ] *n* goulache *f*.

gourd [gʊəd] *n* gourde *f*.

gourmand [ˈgʊəmənd] *n* gourmand(e) *m(f)*.

gourmet [ˈgʊəmeɪ] *n* gourmet *m*.

gout [gaʊt] *n* (*Med*) goutte *f*.

govern [ˈgʌvən] **1** *vt country* gouverner; *province, city, business* administrer; *emotions etc* maîtriser; (*Tech*) régler; (*influence*) *events, speed* déterminer; (*Gram*) gouverner. **2** *vi* (*Pol*) gouverner. ♦ **governess** *n* gouvernante *f*. ♦ **governing** *adj* (*Pol etc*) gouvernant; *belief etc* dominant; **~ing body** conseil *m* d'administration. ♦ **government 1** *n* gouvernement *m*; (*the State*) l'État *m*; **local ~ment** administration *f* locale; **2** *adj policy, decision, department* gouvernemental; *responsibility, loan, spending* de l'État, public. ♦ **governmental** *adj* gouvernemental. ♦ **governor** *n [state, bank]* gouverneur *m*; *[prison]* directeur *m*, -trice *f*; *[school, institution etc]* administrateur *m*, -trice *f*.

gown [gaʊn] *n* robe *f*; (*Jur, Univ*) toge *f*.

grab [græb] **1** *n* **(a) to make a ~ for** *or* **at sth** faire un geste vif pour saisir qch. **(b)** (*Tech*) benne *f* preneuse. **2** *vt object, opportunity* saisir; *land* se saisir de; *power* prendre. **to ~ sth from sb** arracher qch à qn.

grace [greɪs] *n* grâce *f*. **by the ~ of God** par la grâce de Dieu; (*fig hum*) **to fall from ~** tomber en disgrâce; **to say ~** (*before meals*) dire le bénédicité; (*after meals*) dire les grâces; **to be in sb's good ~s** être bien vu de qn; **to do sth with good/bad ~** faire qch de bonne/mauvaise grâce; **he had the ~ to apologize** il a eu la bonne grâce de s'excuser; **his saving ~** ce qui le rachète; **a day's ~** un jour de grâce *or* de répit; **His G~** (*archbishop*) Monseigneur l'Archevêque; (*duke*) Monsieur le duc. ♦ **graceful** *adj* (*gen*) gracieux; *apology* élégant. ♦ **gracefully** *adv* (*gen*) gracieusement; *apologize* avec élégance. ♦ **gracefulness** *n* grâce *f*.

gracious [ˈgreɪʃəs] *adj person, smile* gracieux, bienveillant (*to* envers); *action* courtois; *God* miséricordieux (*to* envers); *house, gardens* d'une élégance raffinée. **~ living** vie élégante; **(good) ~!*** juste ciel! ♦ **graciously** *adv smile, consent* gracieusement; *agree* avec bonne grâce; *live* élégamment. ♦ **graciousness** *n* bienveillance *f* (*towards* envers).

gradate [grəˈdeɪt] **1** *vt* graduer. **2** *vi* être gradué. ♦ **gradation** *n* gradation *f*.

grade [greɪd] **1** *n* **(a)** (*in hierarchy*) catégorie *f*; (*on scale*) échelon *m*, grade *m*; (*Mil: rank*) rang *m*; (*of steel, butter, goods etc*) qualité *f*; (*size: of eggs, anthracite nuts etc*) calibre *m*; (*US: level*) niveau *m*. **the lowest ~ of skilled worker** la catégorie la plus basse des ouvriers qualifiés; **~ B milk** lait *m* de qualité B; **high-~** de première qualité; (*fig*) **to make the ~** avoir les qualités requises. **(b)** (*US*) (*class*) classe *f*; (*mark*) note *f*. **(c)** (*slope*) rampe *f*, pente *f*.

2 *adj* (*US*) **~ crossing** passage *m* à niveau; (*US*) **~ school** école *f* primaire.

3 *vt* **(a)** (*sort into groups: gen*) classer; (*by size*) *apples etc* calibrer. **exercises ~d according to difficulty** exercices classés selon leur degré de difficulté. **(b)** (*make progressively easier, darker etc*) *exercises, colours etc* graduer. **(c)** (*US Scol: mark*) noter.

gradient [ˈgreɪdɪənt] *n* rampe *f*, inclinaison *f*. **a ~ of one in ten** une inclinaison de dix pour cent.

gradual [ˈgrædjʊəl] *adj change* graduel, progressif; *slope* doux. ♦ **gradually** *adv* graduellement, petit à petit.

graduate [ˈgrædjʊeɪt] **1** *vt* **(a)** *jug* graduer (*in* en; *according to* selon). **(b)** (*US Scol, Univ*) conférer un diplôme à. **2** *vi* **(a)** (*Univ*) ≃ obtenir sa licence (*or* son diplôme *etc*); (*US Scol*) ≃ obtenir son baccalauréat. **he ~d as an architect** *etc* il a eu son diplôme d'architecte *etc*. **(b)** *[colours etc]* se changer graduellement (*into* en). **3** [ˈgrædjʊɪt] *n* (*Univ*) ≃ licencié(e) *m(f)*, diplômé(e) *m(f)*. **4** [ˈgrædjʊɪt] *adj* (*Univ*) ≃ licencié, diplômé. **~ course** ≃ études *fpl* de troisième cycle. ♦ **graduation** *n* (*Univ, also US Scol: ceremony*) remise *f* des diplômes *etc*.

graffiti [grəˈfiːtɪ] *npl* graffiti *mpl*.

graft [grɑːft] **1** *n* **(a)** (*Agr, Med*) greffe *f*. **they did a kidney/skin ~ on him** on lui a greffé un rein/fait une greffe de la peau. **(b)** (*bribery etc*) corruption *f*. **2** *vt* greffer (*on* sur).

grain [greɪn] **1** *n* **(a)** (*cereals in gen*) grain *m*, céréale *f*; (*wheat*) blé *m*. **(b)** (*single* ~: *of wheat, salt, sense*) grain *m*. **(c)** (*in leather; also Phot*) grain *m*; (*in wood, meat*) fibre *f*; (*in stone*) veine *f*. **with/against the** ~ dans le sens de/en travers de la fibre (*or* de la veine *etc*); **it goes against the** ~ **for him to apologize** cela va à l'encontre de sa nature de s'excuser; **I'll do it, but it goes against the** ~ je le ferai, mais pas de bon cœur. **2** *adj exports, prices, alcohol* de grain. (*US*) ~ **elevator** silo *m* à céréales.

gram(me) [græm] *n* gramme *m*.

grammar ['græmə^r^] **1** *n* grammaire *f*. **that is bad** ~ cela n'est pas grammatical. **2** *adj*: ~ **school** (*Brit*) ≈ lycée *m*; (*US*) ≈ cours *m* moyen. ♦ **grammarian** *n* grammairien(ne) *m(f)*. ♦ **grammatical** *adj* grammatical. ♦ **grammatically** *adv* grammaticalement.

gramophone ['græməfəʊn] **1** *n* phonographe *m*. **2** *adj needle* de phonographe. ~ **record** disque *m*.

granary ['grænərɪ] *n* grenier *m* (*à blé etc*).

grand [grænd] **1** *adj* (*gen*) grand; *person* magnifique, splendide; *character* grand, noble; *style, scenery, house* grandiose, splendide; *job, post* important; *chorus, concert* grand; (*excellent*) magnifique, formidable*. ~ **duke** grand duc; ~ **jury** jury *m* d'accusation; ~ **opera** grand opéra; ~ **piano** piano *m* à queue; ~ **staircase** escalier *m* d'honneur; ~ **total** résultat final; **a** ~ **tour** le tour complet; **the** ~ **old man of ...** le patriarche de ... ; **we had a** ~ **time** nous nous sommes formidablement* amusés. **2** *n* (*US*‡) mille dollars *mpl*. ♦ **grandchild** *n* petit(e)-enfant *m(f)*, petit-fils *m*, petite-fille *f*. ♦ **grandchildren** *npl* petits-enfants *mpl*. ♦ **grand(d)ad*** *or* ♦ **grand(pa)pa*** *n* grand-papa* *m*. ♦ **granddaughter** *n* petite-fille *f*. ♦ **grandeur** *n* grandeur *f*, splendeur *f*. ♦ **grandfather** *n* grand-père *m*; ~**father clock** ≈ horloge *f* de parquet. ♦ **grand(ma)ma*** *n* grand-maman* *f*. ♦ **grandmother** *n* grand-mère *f*. ♦ **grandparents** *npl* grands-parents *mpl*. ♦ **grandson** *n* petit-fils *m*. ♦ **grandstand** *n* (*Sport*) tribune *f*; (*fig*) **to have a** ~**stand view** être aux premières loges (*of sth* pour voir qch).

grandiose ['grændɪəʊz] *adj* grandiose.

granite ['grænɪt] *n* granit *m*.

granny* ['grænɪ] *n* grand-maman* *f*; (~ *knot*) nœud *m* de vache.

grant [grɑːnt] **1** *vt* (*gen*) accorder; *prayer* exaucer; *request* accéder à; (*admit*) admettre, reconnaître (*that* que). ~**ed that this is true** en admettant que ce soit vrai; **I** ~ **you that** je vous l'accorde; ~**ed!** d'accord!; **he takes her for** ~**ed** il la considère comme faisant partie du décor; **to take details/sb's agreement** *etc* **for** ~**ed** considérer les détails/l'accord de qn *etc* comme convenu(s) *or* certain(s); **you take too much for** ~**ed** vous prenez vos désirs pour des réalités. **2** *n* (*subsidy*) subvention *f*; (*scholarship*) bourse *f*. **he is on a** ~ **of £900** il a une bourse de 900 livres. ♦ **grant-aided** *adj* subventionné par l'État.

granule ['grænjuːl] *n* granule *m*. ♦ **granular** *adj* granuleux. ♦ **granulated sugar** *n* sucre *m* semoule.

grape [greɪp] **1** *n* (grain *m* de) raisin *m*. ~**s** du raisin, des raisins; **to harvest the** ~**s** vendanger. **2** *adj juice* de raisin. ~ **harvest** vendange *f*. ♦ **grapefruit** *n* pamplemousse *m*. ♦ **grapevine** *n* (*fig*) **I hear on the** ~**vine that ...** j'ai appris par le téléphone arabe que ... .

graph [grɑːf] *n* graphique *m*. ~ **paper** ≈ papier *m* millimétré. ♦ **graphic** *adj* (*gen*) graphique; *description* vivant. ♦ **graphics** *n* (*sg: art of drawing*) art *m* graphique; (*pl: process*) procédés *mpl* graphiques; (*pl: sketches*) représentations *fpl* graphiques; (*TV etc*) ~**ics by ...** art graphique (de) ... .

graphology [græ'fɒlədʒɪ] *n* graphologie *f*. ♦ **graphologist** *n* graphologue *mf*.

grapple ['græpl] *vi*: **to** ~ **with** *person* se bagarrer* avec; *problem* essayer de résoudre; *difficult subject* essayer de comprendre.

grasp [grɑːsp] **1** *vt* **(a)** (*seize*) *object* saisir; *power, opportunity, territory* s'emparer de. (*fig*) **to** ~ **the nettle** aborder de front la difficulté. **(b)** (*understand*) saisir, comprendre. **2** *n*: **a strong** ~ une forte poigne; **to lose one's** ~ **on** *or* **of sth** lâcher qch; (*lit, fig*) **within one's** ~ à portée de la main; (*fig*) **in one's** ~ en son pouvoir; (*fig*) **within everyone's** ~ à la portée de chacun; **a good** ~ **of mathematics** une solide connaissance des mathématiques; **it is beyond my** ~ cela me dépasse. ♦ **grasping** *adj* cupide.

grass [grɑːs] **1** *n* **(a)** herbe *f*; (*lawn*) gazon *m*; (*grazing*) herbage *m*. **'keep off the** ~**'** 'défense de marcher sur le gazon'; (*fig*) **to let the** ~ **grow under one's feet** laisser traîner les choses; **to put out to** ~ *horse* mettre au vert; (*fig*) *person* mettre au repos; (*Agr*) **under** ~ en pré; (*Tennis*) **on** ~ sur gazon; (*Bot*) ~**es** graminées *fpl*. **(b)** (*Drugs sl: marijuana*) herbe *f* (*sl*). **(c)** (*Prison sl: informer*) mouchard* *m*. **2** *adj tennis court* en gazon; ~ **cutter** grosse tondeuse *f* à gazon; (*fig*) ~ **roots** (*n*) base *f*; (*adj*) *candidate, movement* populaire, de la masse; ~ **snake** couleuvre *f*; (*US*) ~ **widow** divorcée *f*. **3** *vi* (*Prison sl*) moucharder*. **to** ~ **on sb** vendre qn. ♦ **grasshopper** *n* sauterelle *f*. ♦ **grassland** *n* herbages *mpl*. ♦ **grassy** *adj* herbeux.

grate[1] [greɪt] *n* (*metal part*) grille *f* de foyer; (*fireplace*) foyer *m*. ♦ **grating**[1] *n* grille *f*.

grate[2] [greɪt] **1** *vt* **(a)** *cheese, carrot etc* râper. **(b)** *metallic object, chalk* faire grincer. **to** ~ **one's teeth** grincer des dents. **2** *vi* grincer (*on* sur). **to** ~ **on the ears** écorcher les oreilles; **it** ~**d on his nerves** cela lui tapait sur les nerfs*. ♦ **grater** *n* râpe *f*; **cheese** ~**r** râpe à fromage. ♦ **grating**[2] *adj sound* grinçant; *voice* discordant; (*annoying*) énervant.

grateful ['greɪtfʊl] *adj* reconnaissant (*to* à; *towards* envers; *for* de); *letter* plein de reconnaissance; (*fig*) *warmth* réconfortant. **I am most** ~ **to you** je vous suis très reconnaissant; **I should be** ~ **if you would come** je vous serais reconnaissant de venir; **with** ~ **thanks** avec mes plus sincères remerciements. ♦ **gratefully** *adv* avec reconnaissance.

gratify ['grætɪfaɪ] *vt person* faire plaisir à, être agréable à; *desire etc* satisfaire. ♦ **gratification** *n* satisfaction *f*. ♦ **gratified** *adj* content; **I was gratified to hear ...** j'ai appris avec grand plaisir ... . ♦ **gratifying** *adj* (*gen*) agréable; *attentions etc* flatteur.

gratis ['grætɪs] *adv, adj* gratis *inv*.

gratitude ['grætɪtjuːd] *n* reconnaissance *f*, gratitude *f* (*towards* envers; *for* de).

gratuitous [grə'tjuːɪtəs] *adj* gratuit. ♦ **gratuitously** *adv* gratuitement. ♦ **gratuity** *n* (*Mil etc*) prime *f* de démobilisation; (*tip*) gratification *f*.

grave[1] [greɪv] **1** *n* tombe *f*, (*more elaborate*) tombeau *m*. **someone is walking over my** ~* j'ai eu un frisson. ♦ **gravedigger** *n* fossoyeur *m*. ♦ **gravestone** *n* pierre *f* tombale. ♦ **graveyard** *n* cimetière *m*.

grave[2] [greɪv] *adj* **(a)** (*serious: gen*) grave, sérieux; *symptoms* grave, inquiétant. **(b)** [grɑːv] (*Ling*) *accent* grave. ♦ **gravely** *adv* gravement, sérieusement; *ill* gravement; *wounded* grièvement; *displeased* extrêmement. ♦ **graveness** *n* gravité *f*.

gravel ['grævəl] **1** *n* gravier *m*, (*finer*) gravillon *m*. **2** *adj*: ~ **path** chemin *m* de gravier; ~ **pit** carrière *f* de cailloux.

gravity ['grævɪtɪ] *n* **(a)** (*Phys*) pesanteur *f*. **the law of** ~ la loi de la pesanteur; ~ **feed** alimentation *f* par gravité. **(b)** (*seriousness*) gravité *f*, sérieux *m*. ♦ **gravitate** *vi* (*fig*) être attiré (*towards* vers). ♦ **gravitation** *n* gravitation *f*. ♦ **gravitational** *adj* de gravitation.

gravy ['greɪvɪ] *n* jus *m* de viande. ~ **boat** saucière *f*.

gray [greɪ] = **grey.**

graze[1] [greɪz] **1** *vi* brouter, paître. **2** *vt grass, cattle* paître; *field* pâturer (dans).

graze[2] [greɪz] **1** *vt* (*touch lightly*) frôler, effleurer; (*scrape*) *skin, hand etc* érafler. **to ~ one's knees** s'érafler les genoux. **2** *n* éraflure *f*.

grease [gri:s] **1** *n* (*gen*) graisse *f*; (*Aut, Tech*) lubrifiant *m*, graisse; (*dirt*) crasse *f*. **to get the ~ out of sth** dégraisser qch. **2** *vt* graisser. **like ~d lightning*** en quatrième vitesse*. ♦ **grease-gun** *n* (pistolet *m*) graisseur *m*. ♦ **greasepaint** *n* fard *m* gras; **stick of ~paint** crayon *m* gras. ♦ **greaseproof paper** *n* papier *m* sulfurisé. ♦ **grease-stained** *adj* graisseux. ♦ **greasiness** *n* graisse *f*; *[road etc]* surface *f* glissante. ♦ **greasy** *adj* (*gen*) graisseux; *hair, food, ointment* gras; (*slippery*) *surface, road etc* glissant; *clothes, collar* sale, crasseux; (*fig*) **a greasy character** un personnage fuyant.

great [greɪt] **1** *adj* (*gen*) grand; *heat, pain* fort, intense; *determination, will-power* fort; (*: *excellent*) *holiday, results etc* magnifique, sensationnel*. **Alexander the G~** Alexandre le Grand; **G~ Britain** Grande-Bretagne *f*; **G~er London** le grand Londres; **the G~ War** la Grande Guerre; **a ~ man** un grand homme; **the ~ masters** les grands maîtres; **a ~ deal (of), a ~ many** beaucoup (de); **to reach a ~ age** parvenir à un âge avancé; ~ **big** énorme; **he has a ~ future** il a beaucoup d'avenir; **at a ~ pace** à vive allure; **a ~ while ago** il y a bien longtemps; **you look ~!** tu as de l'allure!; **you were ~*** tu as été magnifique!*; **it was ~*** c'était formidable* *or* terrible*; **we had a ~ time** nous nous sommes rudement* bien amusés; **he's a ~ angler** (*keen*) il est passionné de pêche; (*expert*) c'est un pêcheur émérite; **he's ~* at football** il est doué pour le football; **he's a ~ one* for cathedrals** il adore visiter les cathédrales; **he's a ~ one* for criticizing others** il ne rate pas une occasion de critiquer les autres; **he's ~* on jazz** il connaît à fond le jazz; **~ Scott!;*** grands dieux!; (*excl*) ~! formidable!

2 *n*: **the ~** les grands *mpl*.

♦ **great-aunt** *n* grand-tante *f*. ♦ **greatcoat** *n* pardessus *m*; (*Mil*) capote *f*. ♦ **great-grandchild** *n* arrière-petit(e)-enfant *m(f)*. ♦ **great-granddaughter** *n* arrière-petite-fille *f*. ♦ **great-grandfather** *n* arrière-grand-père *m*. ♦ **great-grandmother** *n* arrière-grand-mère *f*. ♦ **great-grandson** *n* arrière-petit-fils *m*. ♦ **great-great-grandfather** *n* arrière-arrière-grand-père *m*. ♦ **great-hearted** *adj* au grand cœur. ♦ **greatly** *adv* (*gen*) *love* beaucoup; *loved* très; *superior, prefer* de beaucoup; *improve, increase, contribute* considérablement; **you're ~ly mistaken** vous vous trompez grandement; **it is ~ly to be feared** il est fort à craindre. ♦ **great-nephew** *n* petit-neveu *m*. ♦ **greatness** *n* grandeur *f*. ♦ **great-niece** *n* petite-nièce *f*. ♦ **great-uncle** *n* grand-oncle *m*.

Greece [gri:s] *n* Grèce *f*. ♦ **Greek 1** *adj* grec (*f* grecque); **Greek Orthodox Church** Église *f* orthodoxe grecque; **2** *n* Grec(que) *m(f)*; (*Ling*) grec *m*; **ancient/modern Greek** grec classique/moderne; (*fig*) **that's (all) Greek to me*** tout ça c'est de l'hébreu pour moi*.

greed [gri:d] *n*, **greediness** ['gri:dɪnɪs] *n* (*gen*) avidité *f*; (*for food*) gloutonnerie *f*. ♦ **greedily** *adv* avidement; *eat* gloutonnement; *drink* avec avidité; *eye food, lick lips* d'un air vorace. ♦ **greedy** *adj* avide (*for* de), cupide; (*for food*) vorace, glouton; **don't be ~y!** (*gen*) n'en demande pas tant!; (*at table*) ne sois pas si gourmand!

green [gri:n] **1** *adj* (*colour*) vert; *corn* en herbe; *bacon* non fumé; *memory* vivace; (*inexperienced*) inexpérimenté; (*naïve*) naïf. ~ **bean** haricot *m* vert; (*Planning*) ~ **belt** zone *f* de verdure; (*fig*) **he's got ~ fingers** *or* **a ~ thumb** il a un don pour faire pousser les plantes; (*Aut; fig*) ~ **light** feu *m* vert; ~ **peas** petits pois *mpl*; ~ **pepper** poivron *m* vert; (*Econ*) **the ~ pound** la livre verte; (*Theat*) ~ **room** foyer *m* des artistes; ~ **salad** salade *f* (*plat*); ~ **vegetables** légumes *mpl* verts; **to turn ~** verdir; ~ **with envy** vert de jalousie; **to make sb ~ with envy** faire pâlir qn de jalousie; (*fig*) **I'm not as ~ as I look!*** je ne suis pas si naïf que j'en ai l'air!

2 *n* (*colour*) vert *m*; (*grass*) pelouse *f*, gazon *m*. **village ~** = place *f* (du village) (*gazonnée*); (*Culin*) **~s** légumes *mpl* verts.

♦ **greenback** *n* (*US*) billet *m* (de banque). ♦ **greenery** *n* verdure *f*. ♦ **greenfinch** *n* verdier *m*. ♦ **greenfly** *n* puceron *m* (des plantes). ♦ **greengage** *n* reine-claude *f*. ♦ **greengrocer** *n* marchand(e) *m(f)* de légumes; **~grocer's (shop)** fruiterie *f*. ♦ **greenhouse** *n* serre *f*. ♦ **greenish** *adj* verdâtre. ♦ **greenness** *n* vert *m*; *[countryside etc]* verdure *f*; *[wood, fruit etc]* verdeur *f*. ♦ **greenstick fracture** *n* fracture *f* incomplète. ♦ **greenstuff** *n* verdure *f*.

Greenland ['gri:nlənd] *n* Groenland *m*.

Greenwich ['grɪnɪdʒ] *n*: ~ **(mean) time** heure *f* de Greenwich.

greet [gri:t] *vt person* accueillir (*with songs etc* avec des chansons *etc*), saluer; *announcement* accueillir. **he ~ed me with the news that ...** il m'a accueilli en m'apprenant que .... ♦ **greeting** *n* salut *m*, salutation *f*; (*welcome*) accueil *m*; **~ings** compliments *mpl*, salutations; **Xmas ~ings** vœux *mpl* de Noël; **~ing(s) card** carte *f* de vœux; **my mother sends you her ~ings** ma mère vous envoie son bon souvenir.

gregarious [grɪ'gɛərɪəs] *adj animal, instinct* grégaire; *person* sociable.

grenade [grɪ'neɪd] *n* (*Mil*) grenade *f*.

grew [gru:] *pret of* **grow.**

grey [greɪ] **1** *adj* gris; *hair* gris, grisonnant; *complexion* blême; *outlook, prospect* morne. **to go ~** (*from fear etc*) blêmir; *[hair]* grisonner; ~ **skies** ciel gris *or* morne; **a ~ day** un jour gris; (*fig*) un jour triste; (*fig*) ~ **matter*** matière *f* grise, cervelle* *f*; (*fig*) **a ~ area** une zone d'incertitude (*between* entre). **2** *n* (*colour*) gris *m*; (*horse*) cheval gris. **3** *vi [hair]* grisonner. ♦ **greybeard** *n* vieil homme. ♦ **grey-haired** *adj* aux cheveux gris. ♦ **greyhound** *n* lévrier *m*. ♦ **greyish** *adj* grisâtre; *hair, beard* grisonnant.

grid [grɪd] *n* (*gen*) grille *f*; (*Culin: utensil*) gril *m*; (*Aut: on roof*) galerie *f*; (*Elec: system*) réseau *m*. (*Elec*) **the national ~** le réseau électrique national. ♦ **grid(iron)** *n* (*utensil*) gril *m*; (*US Sport*) terrain *m* de football.

griddle ['grɪdl] *n* plaque *f* en fonte (*pour cuire*).

grief [gri:f] *n* chagrin *m*, douleur *f*. **to come to ~** (*gen*) avoir des ennuis; *[vehicle, rider, driver]* avoir un accident; *[plan, marriage etc]* tourner mal; **good ~!*** grands dieux! ♦ **grief-stricken** *adj* accablé de douleur.

grieve [gri:v] **1** *vt* peiner, chagriner, (*stronger*) désoler. **it ~s us to see** nous sommes peinés de voir. **2** *vi* avoir de la peine *or* du chagrin (*at, about, over* à cause de), (*stronger*) se désoler (*at, about, over* de). **to ~ for sb/sth** pleurer qn/qch. ♦ **grievance** *n* (*ground for complaint*) grief *m* (*against* contre); (*complaint*) doléance *f*; (*Ind*) différend *m*, conflit *m*; **to have a grievance against sb** en vouloir à qn. ♦ **grievous** *adj pain, loss, blow* cruel; *injury, fault, wrongs* grave; *crime, offence* odieux; *news* pénible; (*Jur*) **grievous bodily harm** coups *mpl* et blessures *fpl*.

◆ **grievously** *adv* cruellement; gravement; *wounded* grièvement.
grill [grɪl] **1** *n* **(a)** (*cooking utensil*) gril *m*; (*food*) grillade *f*; (~ *room*) grill *m*. **under the ~** au gril. **(b)** (*also* **grille**) (*grating*) grille *f*; (*Aut: radiator* ~) calandre *f*.
2 *vt* **(a)** faire griller. **~ed fish** poisson grillé. **(b)** (*: *interrogate*) faire subir un interrogatoire serré à, cuisiner*.
3 *vi* griller. **it's ~ing in here*** on grille ici*.
grim [grɪm] *adj* (*gen*) sinistre; *landscape, building* lugubre; *joke* macabre; *smile* sardonique; *face* sévère; *reality, necessity* dur (*before n*); *truth* brutal; (*: *unpleasant*) désagréable. **with ~ determination** avec une volonté inflexible; **to hold on to sth like ~ death** rester cramponné à qch de toutes ses forces; **life is rather ~*** la vie n'est pas drôle; **she's feeling pretty ~*** (*ill*) elle ne se sent pas bien du tout; (*depressed*) elle n'a pas le moral*. ◆ **grimly** *adv frown, look* d'un air mécontent; *continue, hold on* inexorablement; *fight, struggle* avec acharnement; *pledge* d'un air résolu.
grimace [grɪˈmeɪs] **1** *n* grimace *f*. **2** *vi* (*from disgust etc*) faire la grimace; (*for fun*) faire des grimaces.
grime [graɪm] *n* crasse *f*, saleté *f*. ◆ **grimy** *adj* crasseux, sale.
grin [grɪn] **1** *vi* sourire; (*broadly*) avoir un grand sourire. **we must just ~ and bear it** il faut le prendre avec le sourire. **2** *n* (grand) sourire *m*.
grind [graɪnd] (*vb: pret, ptp* **ground**) **1** *n* (*) boulot* *m* pénible. **the daily ~** le boulot* quotidien; **I find maths a dreadful ~** pour moi les maths sont une vraie corvée. **2** *vt corn, coffee etc* moudre; (*crush*) écraser; *gems, lens* polir; *knife, blade* aiguiser (à la meule); *handle, pepper mill* tourner; *barrel organ* jouer de. **to ~ one's teeth** grincer des dents. **3** *vi* grincer. **to ~ to a halt** *[vehicle]* s'arrêter dans un grincement de freins; *[process, production]* s'arrêter progressivement.
grind down *vt sep substance* pulvériser; (*fig: oppress*) écraser.
grind up *vt sep* pulvériser.
◆ **grinder** *n* (*apparatus*) broyeur *m*; (*in kitchen*) moulin *m*; (*for knives*) affûteuse *f*. ◆ **grinding 1** *n* (*sound*) grincement *m*; **2** *adj poverty* accablant.
grip [grɪp] **1** *n* **(a)** (*handclasp*) poigne *f*; (*hold*) prise *f*, étreinte *f*. **to hold sth in a vice-like ~** tenir qch comme un étau; **to get a ~ on sth** empoigner qch; (*fig*) **to get a ~ on o.s.*, to keep a ~ on o.s.** se contrôler; **to lose one's ~** lâcher prise; (*: *grow less efficient etc*) baisser*; **he lost his ~ on the rope** il a lâché la corde; **the tyres lost their ~ on the icy road** les pneus ont perdu leur adhérence sur la chaussée gelée; **he has a good ~ of his subject** il possède bien son sujet; **to come** *or* **get to ~s with** *person* en venir aux prises avec; *problem, situation* s'attaquer à; **in the ~ of winter/a strike** paralysé par l'hiver/par une grève. **(b)** (*suitcase*) valise *f*; (*bag*) sac *m* (de voyage). **2** *vt* (*grasp*) saisir; (*hold*) serrer, tenir serré; *[fear etc]* saisir; *[film, story]* empoigner. **to ~ the road** *[tyres]* adhérer à la chaussée; *[car]* coller à la route. **3** *vi* *[wheels]* adhérer; *[vice, brakes]* mordre; *[anchor]* crocher. ◆ **gripping** *adj story, play* passionnant.
gripe [graɪp] **1** *n* (*Med*) coliques *fpl*. **2** *vt* (*: *anger*) mettre en boule*. **3** *vi* (*: *grumble*) rouspéter* (*at* contre). ◆ **griping 1** *adj pain* lancinant; **2** *n* (*: *grumbling*) rouspétance* *f*.
grisly [ˈgrɪzlɪ] *adj* macabre.
gristle [ˈgrɪsl] *n* tendons *mpl* (*dans la viande cuite*). ◆ **gristly** *adj meat* tendineux.
grit [grɪt] **1** *n* (*sand*) sable *m*; (*gravel*) gravillon *m*; (*for fowl*) gravier *m*; (*: *courage*) cran* *m*. **a piece of ~ in the eye** une poussière dans l'œil; **he's got ~*** il a du cran*; (*US*) **~s** gruau *m* de maïs. **2** *vt* **(a) to ~ one's teeth** serrer les dents. **(b)** *road* sabler. ◆ **gritty** *adj path etc* couvert de gravier; *fruit* graveleux.
grizzle [ˈgrɪzl] *vi* (*whine*) pleurnicher.
grizzled [ˈgrɪzld] *adj* grisonnant.
grizzly [ˈgrɪzlɪ] *n* (~ *bear*) ours *m* gris.
groan [grəʊn] **1** *n* (*of pain etc*) gémissement *m*; (*of disapproval, dismay*) grognement *m*. **2** *vi* gémir (*with* de); grogner; *[planks etc]* gémir.
grocer [ˈgrəʊsəʳ] *n* épicier *m*. **at the ~'s (shop)** à l'épicerie, chez l'épicier. ◆ **grocery** *n* (*shop*) épicerie *f*; **~ies** (*goods*) provisions *fpl*.
groggy* [ˈgrɒgɪ] *adj* (*weak*) faible; (*unsteady, also from blow etc*) groggy*.
grogram [ˈgrɒgrəm] *n* gros-grain *m*.
groin [grɔɪn] *n* aine *f*.
groom [gruːm] **1** *n* (*for horses*) valet *m* d'écurie; (*bridegroom*) (futur *or* jeune) marié *m*. **2** *vt horse* panser. **the animal was ~ing itself** l'animal faisait sa toilette; **well-~ed** *person* très soigné; (*fig*) **to ~ sb for a post** former qn pour un poste.
groove [gruːv] *n* (*for sliding door etc*) rainure *f*; (*in column, screw*) cannelure *f*; (*in record*) sillon *m*; (*in penknife blade*) onglet *m*. **in the ~*** (*up-to-date*) dans le vent*; **he's in a ~*** il est pris dans la routine.
grope [grəʊp] *vi* (~ **about,** ~ **around**) tâtonner, aller à l'aveuglette. **to ~ for sth** chercher qch à tâtons; **to ~ for words** chercher ses mots; **to ~ (one's way) in** *etc* entrer *etc* à tâtons.
gross [grəʊs] **1** *adj* **(a)** (*coarse*) grossier; (*fat*) obèse; *injustice* flagrant; *abuse* choquant; *negligence* grave; *ignorance* crasse. **(b)** *weight, income* brut. **~ national product** revenu *m* national brut. **2** *n* **(a) in ~** (*wholesale*) en gros; (*fig*) en général. **(b)** (*pl inv: twelve dozen*) grosse *f*. **3** *vt* (*Comm etc*) faire une recette brute de. ◆ **grossly** *adv exaggerate etc* énormément; *unfair* extrêmement.
grotesque [grəʊˈtesk] *adj* grotesque.
grotto [ˈgrɒtəʊ] *n* grotte *f*.
grotty* [ˈgrɒtɪ] *adj room, food* minable*, affreux. **he was feeling ~** il ne se sentait pas bien.
grouch* [graʊtʃ] *vi* rouspéter*. ◆ **grouchy*** *adj* maussade.
ground[1] [graʊnd] **1** *n* **(a)** terre *f*, sol *m*; (*US Elec*) masse *f*. **(down) on the ~** par terre, sur le sol; **above ~** en surface (*du sol*); **to fall to the ~** tomber à *or* par terre; **to get off the ~** *[plane]* décoller; *[scheme etc]* démarrer*. **(b)** (*soil*) sol *m*, terre *f*, terrain *m*. **stony ~** sol *or* terrain caillouteux. **(c)** (*area, piece of land*) terrain *m*, (*larger*) domaine *m*, terres *fpl*; (*territory*) territoire *m*; **hilly ~** pays *m* vallonné; **on French ~** en territoire français; **to hold** *or* **stand one's ~** ne pas lâcher pied; (*fig*) **to change** *or* **shift one's ~** changer son fusil d'épaule; **to gain ~** (*Mil*) gagner du terrain; *[idea etc]* faire son chemin; (*Mil, fig*) **to lose ~** perdre du terrain; (*fig*) **on dangerous ~** sur un terrain glissant; (*fig*) **to go over the same ~** reprendre les mêmes points; (*fig*) **on his own ~** sur son propre terrain; **football ~** terrain de football; (*gardens etc*) **~s** parc *m*. **(d)** (*reason*) **~s** raison *f*; **on medical ~s** pour (des) raisons médicales; **~s for divorce** motifs *mpl* de divorce; **on what ~s?** à quel titre?; **on the ~(s) of** pour raison de. **(e) (coffee) ~s** marc *m* (de café).
2 *vt* **(a)** *plane, pilot* interdire de voler à; (*keep on* ~) retenir au sol. **(b)** (*US Elec*) mettre une prise de terre à.
3 *adj attack, control, staff* au sol. (*Aviat*) **~ crew** équipe *f* au sol; **~ floor** rez-de-chaussée *m*; (*Mil*) **~ forces** armée *f* de terre; **~ frost** gelée *f* blanche; **at ~ level** au ras du sol; (*US Elec*) **~ wire** fil *m* neutre.
◆ **grounding** *n* **(a)** *[plane]* interdiction *f* de vol; **(b)** (*in education*) connaissances *fpl* fondamentales, base *f*; **a good ~ing in French** une base

solide en français. ♦ **groundless** *adj fear etc* sans fondement. ♦ **groundnut 1** *n* arachide *f*; **2** *adj oil* d'arachide. ♦ **groundsheet** *n* tapis *m* de sol. ♦ **groundsman** *or* ♦ **groundkeeper** *n* gardien *m* de stade. ♦ **groundspeed** *n* (*Aviat*) vitesse-sol *f*. ♦ **groundswell** *n* lame *f* de fond. ♦ **ground-to-air** *adj* sol-air *inv*. ♦ **ground-to-ground** *adj* sol-sol *inv*. ♦ **groundwork** *n [undertaking]* base *f*, travail *m* préparatoire; *[novel, play etc]* plan *m*.

ground² [graʊnd] (*pret, ptp of* **grind**) *adj coffee etc* moulu.

group [gru:p] **1** *n* (*gen*) groupe *m*; (*literary etc*) cercle *m*. **in ~s** par groupes. **2** *adj*: **~ dynamics** dynamique *f* de groupe(s); (*Med*) **~ practice** cabinet *m* collectif; (*Psych*) **~ therapy** psychothérapie *f* de groupe. **3** *vi [people]* se grouper. **4** *vt* (**~ together**) grouper.

grouse¹ [graʊs] *n, pl inv* (*Orn*) grouse *f*.

grouse²* [graʊs] **1** *vi* (*grumble*) râler* (*at, about* contre). **2** *n* grief *m*.

grovel ['grɒvl] *vi* être à plat ventre (*to, before* devant). ♦ **grovelling** *adj* rampant.

grow [grəʊ] *pret* **grew**, *ptp* **grown 1** *vi [plant, hair]* pousser; *[person, animal, friendship]* grandir; *[numbers, amount]* augmenter; *[club, group]* s'agrandir; *[love, influence, knowledge]* augmenter, s'accroître. **to ~ into a man** devenir un homme; **we have ~n away from each other** nous nous sommes éloignés l'un de l'autre avec les années; **to ~ to like** finir par aimer; **to ~ big(ger)** grandir; **to ~ angry** se fâcher. **2** *vt plants* cultiver, faire pousser; *one's hair etc* laisser pousser.

grow in *vi [hair]* repousser.

grow into *vt fus clothes* devenir assez grand pour mettre; *habit* acquérir (avec le temps).

grow on *vt fus [habit etc]* s'imposer petit à petit à. **his paintings ~ on one** plus on voit ses tableaux plus on les apprécie.

grow out of *vt fus clothes* devenir trop grand pour mettre; *habit* perdre (avec le temps).

grow up *vi* **(a)** devenir adulte. **when I ~ up** quand je serai grand; **~ up!*** ne sois pas si enfant! **(b)** *[friendship, custom]* naître.

♦ **grower** *n* cultivateur *m*, -trice *f*. ♦ **growing** *adj plant* qui pousse; *child* qui grandit; *amount, friendship, feeling* grandissant; *group* qui s'agrandit; *opinion* de plus en plus répandu; **to have a ~ing desire to do sth** avoir de plus en plus envie de faire qch; **fast-~ing** *plant* à croissance rapide; *conviction, group* croissant; **~ing pains*** (*Med*) douleurs *fpl* de croissance; *[business, project]* difficultés *fpl* de croissance. ♦ **grown** *adj* (*fully* **~n**) adulte; **he's a ~n man** il est adulte. ♦ **grown-up 1** *n* grande personne *f*; **2** *adj* de grande personne; **she's very ~n-up** elle fait très grande personne. ♦ **growth 1** *n* **(a)** (*gen*) croissance *f*; *[numbers, amount etc]* augmentation *f* (*in* de); **the ~th of interest in ...** l'intérêt croissant pour ...; **a 5 days' ~th of beard** une barbe de 5 jours; **a new ~th of hair** une nouvelle poussée de cheveux; **(b)** (*Med*) grosseur *f* (*on* à); **2** *adj market, industry etc* en (pleine) expansion.

growl [graʊl] **1** *vi* grogner (*at* contre); *[thunder]* gronder. **2** *vt* grogner. **3** *n* grognement *m*.

groyne [grɔɪn] *n* brise-lames *m inv*.

grub [grʌb] **1** *n* **(a)** (*larva*) larve *f*. **(b)** (*: food*) bouffe: *f*. **2** *vi* (**~ about, ~ around**) fouiller (*in, among* dans; *for* pour trouver).

grubby ['grʌbɪ] *adj* sale. ♦ **grubbiness** *n* saleté *f*.

grudge [grʌdʒ] **1** *vt*: **to ~ sb sth** en vouloir à qn de qch; **she ~s paying £2** cela lui fait mal au cœur de payer 2 livres; **it's not the money I ~ but the time** ce n'est pas sur la dépense mais sur le temps que je rechigne. **2** *n* rancune *f*. **to bear a ~ against sb** en vouloir à qn, garder rancune à qn (*for* de). ♦ **grudging** *adj person* mesquin, peu généreux; *contribution* parcimonieux; *gift, praise etc* accordé à contrecœur; *admiration* réticent. ♦ **grudgingly** *adv* de mauvaise grâce.

gruelling ['grʊəlɪŋ] *adj* exténuant.

gruesome ['gru:səm] *adj* horrible, épouvantable.

gruff [grʌf] *adj* bourru. ♦ **gruffly** *adv* d'un ton bourru.

grumble ['grʌmbl] **1** *vi* grogner, ronchonner* (*at, about* contre), se plaindre (*about, at* de). **2** *npl* (*also* **grumblings**) **~s** lamentations *fpl*; **without a ~** sans murmurer.

grumpy ['grʌmpɪ] *adj* maussade, grincheux. ♦ **grumpily** *adv* d'une façon maussade.

grunt [grʌnt] **1** *vti* grogner. **2** *n* grognement *m*. **to give a ~** pousser un grognement; (*in reply*) répondre par un grognement.

guarantee [ˌgærən'ti:] **1** *n* garantie *f* (*against* contre). **there is a year's ~ on this watch** cette montre a une garantie d'un an; **'money-back ~ with all items'** 'remboursement garanti sur tous articles'; **there's no ~ that it will happen** il n'est pas garanti que cela arrivera; **there's no ~ that it actually happened** il n'est pas certain que cela soit arrivé. **2** *adj*: **~ form** garantie *f* (*fiche*). **3** *vt goods etc* garantir (*against* contre; *for 2 years* pendant 2 ans); *behaviour, loan* se porter garant de. **I ~ that he will do it** je garantis *or* certifie qu'il le fera; **I can't ~ that he will come** je ne peux pas certifier qu'il viendra; **I can't ~ that he did it** je ne peux pas certifier qu'il l'ait fait. ♦ **guarantor** *n* garant(e) *m(f)*.

guard [gɑ:d] **1** *n* **(a)** (*gen, also Mil, Boxing etc*) garde *f*. **to go on/come off ~** prendre/finir son tour de garde; **to be on ~** être de garde; **to keep** *or* **stand ~** monter la garde; **to keep** *or* **stand ~ on sb/sth** *V 3 below*; **he was taken under ~ to ...** il a été emmené sous escorte à ...; **to keep sb under ~** garder qn sous surveillance; **to put a ~ on sb/sth** faire surveiller qn/qch; **to be on one's ~** se tenir sur ses gardes (*against* contre); **to put sb on his ~** mettre qn en garde (*against* contre); **to catch sb off his ~** prendre qn au dépourvu. **(b)** (*Mil etc: squad*) garde *f*; (*one man*) garde *m*. **~ of honour** garde *f* d'honneur; (*on either side*) haie *f* d'honneur; **one of the old ~** un vieux de la vieille*; (*Mil*) **the G~s** les régiments *mpl* de la garde royale. **(c)** (*Brit Rail*) chef *m* de train. (*Brit Rail*) **~'s van** fourgon *m* du chef de train. **(d)** (*on machine*) dispositif *m* de sûreté; (*fire* **~**) garde-feu *m inv*.

2 *adj*: **~ dog** chien *m* de garde; (*Mil*) **on ~ duty** de garde.

3 *vt* (*defend*) défendre (*against* contre); (*protect*) protéger (*from* contre); (*also* **keep** *or* **stand ~ on**) *treasure, president* garder; *prisoner, suspect car* surveiller.

guard against *vt fus infection etc* se protéger contre; *anger, reaction* se tenir sur ses gardes contre. **to ~ against doing** se garder de faire; **to ~ against sth happening** empêcher que qch ne se produise.

♦ **guarded** *adj remark, tone etc* circonspect. ♦ **guardedly** *adv* avec circonspection. ♦ **guardhouse** *n* (*Mil*) corps *m* de garde; (*for prisoners*) salle *f* de police. ♦ **guardian** *n* (*gen*) gardien(ne) *m(f)*; *[child]* tuteur *m*, -trice *f*; **~ian angel** ange *m* gardien. ♦ **guardrail** *n* barrière *f* de sécurité. ♦ **guardroom** *n* (*Mil*) corps *m* de garde. ♦ **guardsman** *n* (*Brit Mil*) garde *m* (*de la garde royale*); (*US*) soldat *m* de la garde nationale.

guava ['gwɑ:və] *n* goyave *f*.

gudgeon ['gʌdʒən] *n* (*fish*) goujon *m*; (*Tech*) tourillon *m*.

Guernsey ['gɜ:nzɪ] *n* Guernesey *m or f*.

guerrilla [gə'rɪlə] **1** *n* guérillero *m*. **2** *adj tactics* de guérilla; *strike* sauvage. **~ group** guérilla *f* (*troupe*); **~ war(fare)** guérilla *f* (*guerre*).

guess [ges] **1** *n* supposition *f*, conjecture *f*. **to have** *or* **make a ~** essayer de deviner (*at sth* qch), (*more formally*) hasarder une conjecture; **have a ~!** essaie de deviner!; **that was a good ~ but ...** c'était une bonne intuition mais ...; **it was just a lucky ~** j'ai deviné juste, c'est tout; **at a (rough) ~** à vue de nez, grosso modo; **my ~ is that he refused** d'après moi il aura refusé; **your ~ is as good as mine!*** je n'en sais pas plus que toi!; **it's anyone's ~* who will win** impossible de prévoir qui va gagner; **by ~ and by God*** Dieu sait comment. **2** *vt* **(a)** *answer, sb's age, name etc* deviner; *height, numbers etc* estimer, évaluer. **I ~ed him to be about 20** j'estimais qu'il avait à peu près 20 ans; **~ how heavy he is** devine combien il pèse; **I ~ed as much** je m'en doutais; **~ who!*** devine qui c'est! **(b)** (*surmise*) supposer (*that* que); (*US: believe*) croire, penser. **I ~ so** probablement; **I ~ not** je ne crois pas. **3** *vi* deviner. **to ~ right** deviner juste; **to ~ wrong** tomber à côté*; **to keep sb ~ing** laisser qn dans le doute; **to ~ at** = **guess 2a.** ♦ **guesswork** *n*: **it was sheer ~work** ce n'étaient que des conjectures *fpl*; **by ~work** en devinant, par flair.

guest [gest] **1** *n* (*at home*) invité(e) *m(f)*, hôte *mf*; (*at table*) convive *mf*; (*in hotel*) client(e) *m(f)*; (*in boarding house*) pensionnaire *mf*. **~ of honour** invité(e) d'honneur; **be my ~!*** fais comme chez toi!* **2** *adj* (*Theat*) *artist, speaker etc* invité; *list* des invités. **~ room** chambre *f* d'amis. ♦ **guest house** *n* pension *f* de famille.

guffaw [gʌ'fɔ:] **1** *vi* rire bruyamment. **2** *n* gros rire *m*.

guide [gaɪd] **1** *n* **(a)** (*gen*) guide *m*; (*fig*) indication *f*. **let reason be your ~** il faut vous laisser guider par la raison; **this figure is only a ~** ce chiffre n'est qu'une indication; **as a rough ~** en gros, à peu près. **(b)** (*~book*) guide *m* (*to* de); (*instructions*) manuel *m*. **beginner's ~ to sailing** manuel d'initiation à la voile. **(c)** (*girl ~*) éclaireuse *f*, guide *f*. **2** *vt*: **to be ~d by** se laisser guider par. **3** *adj*: **~ dog** chien *m* d'aveugle. ♦ **guidance 1** *n* **(a)** conseils *mpl* (*about* quant à); **for your guidance** à titre d'information; **(b)** *[rocket etc]* guidage *m*; **2** *adj system* de guidage. ♦ **guided** *adj missile etc* téléguidé; **~d tour** visite *f* guidée. ♦ **guidelines** *npl* lignes *fpl* directrices. ♦ **guiding** *adj principle* directeur; **guiding star** guide *m*; **he needs a guiding hand** il faut l'aider de temps en temps.

guild [gɪld] *n* (*gen*) association *f*; (*Hist*) guilde *f*.

guile [gaɪl] *n* (*deceit*) fourberie *f*; (*cunning*) ruse *f*. ♦ **guileless** *adj* franc (*f* franche), sincère.

guillotine [ˌgɪlə'ti:n] **1** *n* guillotine *f*; (*for paper-cutting*) massicot *m*; (*Parl*) limite *f* de temps. **2** *vt* guillotiner; massicoter.

guilt [gɪlt] *n* culpabilité *f*. **tormented by ~** torturé par un sentiment de culpabilité; (*Psych*) **~ feelings** sentiments *mpl* de culpabilité (*about sth* quant à qch; *about sb* vis-à-vis de qn). ♦ **guiltless** *adj* innocent (*of* de). ♦ **guilty** *adj* coupable (*of* de); **~y person** *or* **party** coupable *mf*; **to plead ~y/not ~y** plaider coupable/non coupable; **verdict of ~y/not ~y** verdict *m* de culpabilité/d'acquittement; **I have been ~y of that myself** j'ai moi-même commis la même erreur; **I feel very ~y about not writing to her** je suis plein de remords de ne pas lui avoir écrit.

guinea-pig ['gɪnɪpɪg] *n* cochon *m* d'Inde. (*fig*) **to be a ~** servir de cobaye *m* (*for sth* pour qch).

guitar [gɪ'tɑ:ʳ] *n* guitare *f*. ♦ **guitarist** *n* guitariste *mf*.

gulf [gʌlf] *n* (*lit, fig*) gouffre *m*; (*in ocean*) golfe *m*. **the Persian G~** le golfe Persique; **G~ Stream** Gulf Stream *m*.

gull [gʌl] *n* mouette *f*, goéland *m*.

gullet ['gʌlɪt] *n* gosier *m*.

gullible ['gʌlɪbl] *adj* crédule. ♦ **gullibility** *n* crédulité *f*.

gully ['gʌlɪ] *n* ravine *f*.

gulp [gʌlp] **1** *n*: **to swallow sth at one ~** avaler qch d'un seul coup; **'yes' he replied with a ~** 'oui' répondit-il la gorge serrée; **he took a ~ of milk** il a avalé une gorgée de lait. **2** *vt* (**~ down**) *food* avaler à grosses bouchées; *drink* avaler à pleine gorge. **3** *vi* essayer d'avaler. **he ~ed** (*from emotion etc*) sa gorge s'est serrée.

gum¹ [gʌm] *n* (*Anat*) gencive *f*. ♦ **gumboil** *n* fluxion *f* dentaire.

gum² [gʌm] **1** *n* (*glue*) gomme *f*, colle *f*; (*for chewing*) chewing-gum *m*; (*sweet: fruit ~*) boule *f* de gomme. **by ~!*** nom d'un chien!*; (*fig*) **to be up a ~ tree‡** être dans le lac* (*fig*). **2** *vt* (*put ~ on*) (**~ down**) coller. **~med label** étiquette *f* gommée.

gum down *vt sep* coller (et fermer).

gum up‡ *vt sep* (*spoil*) abîmer, bousiller‡.

♦ **gumboots** *npl* bottes *fpl* de caoutchouc.

gumption* ['gʌmpʃən] *n* jugeote* *f*, bon sens *m*.

gun [gʌn] **1** *n* (*small*) pistolet *m*, revolver *m*; (*rifle*) fusil *m*; (*cannon*) canon *m*. **he's got a ~!** il est armé!; **he was carrying a ~** il avait une arme (à feu); **to draw a ~ on sb** braquer une arme sur qn; **a 21-~ salute** une salve de 21 coups de canon; (*Mil*) **the ~s** les canons, l'artillerie *f*; **the big ~s** (*Mil*) les gros canons; (*: *people*) les grosses légumes‡; **to be going great ~s‡** *[business]* marcher à pleins gaz‡; *[person]* être en pleine forme; **paint ~** pistolet *m* à peinture. **2** *adj* (*Mil*) **~ crew** peloton *m* de pièce; **~ dog** chien *m* de chasse; **~ licence** permis *m* de port d'armes. **3** *vt* **(a)** (**~ down**) abattre. **(b)** (*Aut*) **to ~ the engine** faire ronfler le moteur. **4** *vi* (*fig*) **to be ~ning for sb*** chercher qn, essayer d'avoir qn. ♦ **gunboat** *n* canonnière *f*. ♦ **gunfight** *n* échange *m* de coups de feu. ♦ **gunfire** *n [rifles etc]* fusillade *f*; *[cannons]* tir *m* d'artillerie. ♦ **gunman** *n* bandit *m* armé; (*Pol etc*) terroriste *m*. ♦ **gunner** *n* artilleur *m*. ♦ **gunnery 1** *n* (*science etc*) tir *m* au canon; (*guns*) artillerie *f*; **2** *adj officer* de tir. ♦ **gunpoint** *n*: **at ~point** *hold sb* sous son pistolet, au bout de son fusil; *do sth, force sb* sous la menace du pistolet. ♦ **gunpowder** *n* poudre *f* à canon. ♦ **gunrunner** *n* trafiquant *m* d'armes. ♦ **gunrunning** *n* trafic *m* d'armes. ♦ **gunshot 1** *n* (*sound*) coup *m* de feu; **2** *adj*: **~shot wound** blessure *f* de balle. ♦ **gunsmith** *n* armurier *m*.

gurgle ['gɜ:gl] **1** *n [water]* glouglou *m*; *[stream]* murmure *m*; *[laughter]* gloussement *m*; *[baby]* gazouillis *m*. **2** *vi* glouglouter; murmurer; glousser; gazouiller.

guru ['gʊru:] *n* gourou *m*.

gush [gʌʃ] **1** *n* flot *m*. **2** *vi* **(a)** (**~ out**) jaillir. *[water]* **to ~ in** *etc* entrer *etc* en bouillonnant. **(b)** *[person]* se répandre en compliments (*over* sur; *about* à propos de). ♦ **gushing** *adj water etc* bouillonnant; *person* trop démonstratif.

gust [gʌst] *n [wind]* coup *m* de vent, rafale *f*; *[smoke]* bouffée *f*; *[rage etc]* accès *m*. **~ of rain** averse *f*; **a ~ of laughter** un grand éclat de rire.

gusto ['gʌstəʊ] *n* enthousiasme *m*. **with ~** *say* vivement; *eat* avec grand appétit.

gut [gʌt] **1** *n* (*Anat*) boyau *m*, intestin *m*; (*Med: for stitching*) catgut *m*; (*Mus etc*) corde *f* de boyau. **~s** (*Anat*) boyaux; (**fig: courage*) cran* *m*; **I hate his ~s‡** je ne peux pas le sentir*. **2** *vt* (*Culin*) vider. **fire ~ted the house** le feu n'a laissé que les quatre murs de la maison. **3** *adj*: **~ feeling** sentiment *m* instinctif; **~ reaction** réaction *f* viscérale.

♦ **gutless*** *adj* qui manque de cran*. ♦ **gutsy‡** *adj* qui a du punch.

gutter ['gʌtəʳ] **1** *n [roof]* gouttière *f*; *[road* caniveau *m*. (*fig*) **language of the ~** langage *m* de corps de garde; **to rise from the ~** sortir du ruisseau (*fig*). **2** *vi [candle]* couler; *[flame]* vaciller. **3** *adj*: **the ~ press** la presse à scandale. ♦ **guttersnipe** *n* gamin(e) *m(f)* des rues.

guttural ['gʌtərəl] *adj* guttural.

guy[1] [gaɪ] **1** *n* (*) type* *m*, individu *m*. **nice ~** type bien*; **smart** *or* **wise ~** malin *m*; **tough ~** dur* *m*. **2** *vt person* tourner en ridicule; (*Theat*) *part* travestir.

guy[2] [gaɪ] *n* (**~-rope**) corde *f* de tente.

guzzle ['gʌzl] **1** *vi* s'empiffrer*. **2** *vt food* bâfrer*; *drink* siffler*.

gym [dʒɪm] **1** *n* (*gymnastics*) gym* *f*; (*gymnasium*) gymnase *m*; (*Scol*) salle *f* de gym*. **2** *adj*: **~ shoes** (chaussures *fpl* de) tennis *fpl*.

gymnasium [dʒɪm'neɪzɪəm] *n* gymnase *m*. ♦ **gymnast** *n* gymnaste *mf*. ♦ **gymnastic** *adj* gymnastique. ♦ **gymnastics** *n* (*sg: art*) gymnastique *f*; (*pl: activity*) **to do gymnastics** faire de la gymnastique.

gynaecology, (*US*) **gyne-** [ˌgaɪnɪ'kɒlədʒɪ] *n* gynécologie *f*. ♦ **gyn(a)ecological** *adj* gynécologique. ♦ **gyn(a)ecologist** *n* gynécologue *mf*.

gypsy ['dʒɪpsɪ] = **gipsy.**

gyrate [ˌdʒaɪə'reɪt] *vi* décrire des girations. ♦ **gyration** *n* giration *f*.

gyro ... ['dʒaɪərəʊ] *pref* gyro ... . ♦ **gyrocompass** *n* gyrocompas *m*. ♦ **gyroscope** *n* gyroscope *m*. ♦ **gyrostabilizer** *n* gyrostabilisateur *m*.

H

H, h [eɪtʃ] *n* H, h *m or f.* **aspirate/silent h** h aspiré/muet. ♦ **H-bomb** *n* bombe *f* H.

haberdasher ['hæbədæʃəʳ] *n* (*Brit*) mercier *m*, -ière *f*; (*US*) chemisier *m*, -ière *f*. ♦ **haberdashery** *n* mercerie *f*; chemiserie *f*.

habit ['hæbɪt] *n* **(a)** (*custom*) habitude *f*, coutume *f*. **to be in the ~ *or* to make a ~ *or* to have a ~ of doing** avoir l'habitude *or* la manie (*slightly pej*) de faire; **I don't make a ~ of it** je le fais rarement, je ne le fais pas souvent; **don't make a ~ of it!** et ne recommence pas!; **to get *or* fall into bad ~s** prendre *or* contracter de mauvaises habitudes; **to get into/out of the ~ of doing** prendre/perdre l'habitude de faire; **to get sb into the ~ of doing** habituer qn à faire; **from (sheer) ~** par (pure) habitude. **(b)** (*costume*) habit *m*. ♦ **habit-forming** *adj* qui crée une accoutumance.

habitable ['hæbɪtəbl] *adj* habitable. ♦ **habitat** *n* habitat *m*. ♦ **habitation** *n* habitation *f*; **fit for habitation** habitable.

habitual [hə'bɪtjʊəl] *adj* (*gen*) habituel; *liar, drinker etc* invétéré. ♦ **habitually** *adv* habituellement, d'habitude. ♦ **habituate** *vt* habituer (*to* à).

hack[1] [hæk] *vt* **(a)** (*cut*: **~ up**) hacher, tailler. **to ~ sth to pieces** tailler qch en pièces. **(b)** (*strike*) frapper; (*kick*) donner des coups de pied à.

hack down *vt sep* abattre (à coups de couteau *etc*).

♦ **hacking**[1] *adj*: **~ing cough** toux *f* sèche (et opiniâtre). ♦ **hacksaw** *n* scie *f* à métaux.

hack[2] [hæk] **1** *n* **(a)** (*worn-out horse*) haridelle *f*; (*ride*) promenade *f* à cheval. **to go for a ~** (aller) se promener à cheval. **(b)** (**~** *writer*) nègre *m* (*écrivain*). **he was just a (literary) ~** il ne faisait que de la littérature alimentaire. **2** *vi*: **to go ~ing** (aller) se promener à cheval. ♦ **hacking**[2] *adj*: **~ing jacket** veste *f* de cheval. ♦ **hackwork** *n* travail *m* de nègre. ♦ **hack-writing** *n* écrits *mpl* alimentaires.

hackney ['hæknɪ] *adj*: **~ carriage** voiture *f* de louage.

♦ **hackneyed** *adj subject* rebattu; *phrase* galvaudé; **~ed expression** cliché *m*.

had [hæd] *pret, ptp of* **have**.

haddock ['hædək] *n* églefin *m*. **smoked ~** haddock *m*.

haem(a)..., (*US*) **hem(a)...** ['hi:m(ə)] *pref* hém(a)... . ♦ **h(a)ematology** *n* hématologie *f*. ♦ **h(a)emoglobin** *n* hémoglobine *f*. ♦ **h(a)emophilia** *n* hémophilie *f*. ♦ **h(a)emophiliac** *adj, n* hémophile (*mf*). ♦ **h(a)emorrhage** *n* hémorragie *f*. ♦ **h(a)emorrhoids** *npl* hémorroïdes *fpl*.

hag [hæg] *n* (*ugly*) vieille sorcière *f*; (*: *nasty*) chameau* *m*. ♦ **hag-ridden** *adj* tourmenté.

haggard ['hægəd] *adj face* hâve, émacié; *look* hagard, égaré.

haggle ['hægl] *vi* marchander. **to ~ about *or* over sth** chicaner sur qch. ♦ **haggling** *n* marchandage *m*.

Hague [heɪg] *n*: **The ~** La Haye.

hail[1] [heɪl] **1** *n* grêle *f* (*also fig: of missiles etc*). **2** *vi* grêler. ♦ **hailstone** *n* grêlon *m*. ♦ **hailstorm** *n* averse *f* de grêle.

hail[2] [heɪl] **1** *vt* **(a)** (*acknowledge*) acclamer (*as* comme); (*greet*) saluer. (*excl*) **~!** je vous salue!; **the H~ Mary** l'Avé Maria *m*. **(b)** *ship, taxi, person* héler. **2** *vi* (*Naut*) être en provenance (*from* de); *[person]* être originaire (*from* de). **where do you ~ from?** d'où êtes-vous? **3** *n* appel *m*. **within ~** à portée de voix. ♦ **hail-fellow-well-met** *adj* liant, exubérant.

hair [hɛəʳ] **1** *n* **(a)** *[person]* cheveux *mpl*; (*on body*) poils *mpl*; *[animal]* pelage *m*. **he has black ~** il a les cheveux noirs; **a man with long ~, a long-~ed man** un homme aux cheveux longs; **a fine head of ~** une belle chevelure; **to wash one's ~** se laver les cheveux *or* la tête; **to do one's ~** se coiffer; **she always does my ~ very well** elle me coiffe toujours très bien; **her ~ is always very nice** elle est toujours très bien coiffée; **to have one's ~ done** se faire coiffer; **to get one's ~ cut** se faire couper les cheveux; **to make sb's ~ stand on end** faire dresser les cheveux sur la tête à qn; (*fig*) **to let one's ~ down*** se défouler*; **keep your ~ on!*** du calme!; **he gets in my ~*** il me tape sur les nerfs*. **(b)** (*single ~*) *[head]* cheveu *m*; *[body, animal]* poil *m*. **not a ~ of his head was harmed** on ne lui a pas touché un cheveu; **it was hanging by a ~** cela ne tenait qu'à un cheveu; **to remove unwanted ~ from one's legs** *etc* s'épiler les jambes *etc*; **he's got him by the short ~s*** il lui tient le couteau sur la gorge; **try a ~ of the dog that bit you*** reprends un petit verre pour faire passer ta gueule de bois*.

2 *adj* **(a)** *sofa, mattress etc* de crin. **(b) ~ appointment** rendez-vous *m* chez le coiffeur; **~ clippers** (*npl*) tondeuse *f*; **~ cream** brillantine *f*; **~ lacquer** laque *f*; **~ oil** huile *f* capillaire; **~ remover** crème *f* épilatoire; **~ restorer** régénérateur *m* des cheveux; **~ roller** rouleau *m*; **~ set** mise *f* en plis; **~ spray** laque *f* (en bombe *etc*); **a can of ~ spray** une bombe de laque; **~ style** coiffure *f* (*arrangement des cheveux*); **~ stylist** coiffeur *m*, -euse *f*.

♦ **hairband** *n* bandeau *m*. ♦ **hairbreadth** *or* ♦ **hairsbreadth** *n*: **by a ~breadth** de justesse; **he was within a ~breadth of doing** il a failli faire. ♦ **hairbrush** *n* brosse *f* à cheveux. ♦ **haircut** *n*: **to have *or* get a ~cut** se faire couper les cheveux; **I like your ~cut** j'aime ta coupe de cheveux. ♦ **hairdo*** *n* coiffure *f*. ♦ **hairdresser** *n* coiffeur *m*, -euse *f*; **~dresser's (shop *or* salon)** salon *m* de coiffure. ♦ **hairdressing** *n* coiffure *f* (*métier*). ♦ **hair-drier** *n* séchoir *m* à cheveux. ♦ **hair-grip** *n* pince *f* à cheveux. ♦ **hairline 1** *n* naissance *f* des cheveux; **he has a receding ~line** son front se dégarnit; **2** *adj*: **~line fracture** fêlure *f*; **~line crack** légère fêlure. ♦ **hairnet** *n* résille *f*. ♦ **hairpiece** *n* postiche *m*. ♦ **hairpin 1** *n* épingle *f* à cheveux; **2** *adj*: **~pin bend** virage *m* en épingle à cheveux. ♦ **hair-raising** *adj* à vous faire dresser les cheveux sur la tête. ♦ **hair-splitting 1** *n* ergotage *m*, chicanerie *f*; **2** *adj* ergoteur, chicanier. ♦ **hairy** *adj body, animal* velu, poilu; *scalp* chevelu; *person* hirsute; (*Bot*) velu; (*: *frightening*) à vous faire dresser les cheveux sur la tête.

hake [heɪk] *n* colin *m*.

hale [heɪl] *adj*: **~ and hearty** en pleine santé.

half [hɑ:f] *pl* **halves 1** *n* **(a)** moitié *f*; demi(e) *m(f)*. **to cut/break in ~** couper/casser en deux; **one ~ of the apple** une *or* la moitié de la pomme; **to take ~**

of prendre la moitié de; **two halves make a whole** deux demis font un tout; **he doesn't do things by halves** il ne fait pas les choses à moitié; **to go halves in sth with sb** se mettre de moitié avec qn pour qch; **bigger by** ~ moitié plus grand; **too clever by** ~ un peu trop malin; **and that's not the** ~ **of it!*** et ce n'est pas le mieux!; (*fig*) **to see how the other** ~ **lives*** aller voir comment vivent les autres; *[rail ticket]* **outward/return** ~ billet *m* aller/retour. **(b)** (*Sport*) (*player*) demi *m*; (*part of match*) mi-temps *f*; (*Scol: term*) semestre *m*.

2 *adj* demi. **a** ~ **cup,** ~ **a cup** une demi-tasse; **two and a** ~ **hours** deux heures et demie; **two and a** ~ **kilos** deux kilos et demi; (*fig*) **in** ~ **a second*** en moins de rien; **to listen with** ~ **an ear** n'écouter que d'une oreille; **I don't like** ~ **measures** je n'aime pas faire les choses à moitié.

3 *adv* **(a)** à moitié, à demi. ~ **asleep/full/done** à moitié endormi/plein/fait; ~ **dressed/open** à demi vêtu/ouvert; ~ **French** ~ **English** mi-français mi-anglais; ~ **laughing** ~ **crying** moitié riant moitié pleurant; **he** ~ **rose to his feet** il s'est levé à demi; **I** ~ **think** je serais tenté de penser; **I** ~ **suspect that ...** je soupçonne presque que ...; **I'm** ~ **afraid that** j'ai un peu peur que +ne +*subj*; **not** ~‡ **rich** drôlement* riche; **she didn't** ~‡ **like it** ça lui a drôlement* plu; **not** ~**!**‡ et comment!*; **it is** ~ **past three** il est trois heures et demie. **(b)** ~ **as big as** moitié moins grand que; ~ **as big again** moitié plus grand; ~ **as much as** moitié moins que; ~ **as much again** moitié plus.

◆ **half-and-half** *adv* moitié-moitié. ◆ **half-back** *n* (*Sport*) demi *m*. ◆ **half-baked** *adj* (*fig*) à la manque*. ◆ **half-brother** *n* demi-frère *m*. ◆ **half-caste** *adj, n* métis(se) *m(f)*. ◆ **half-circle** *n* demi-cercle *m*. ◆ **half-dead** *adj* à moitié mort (*with* de). ◆ **half-dozen** *or* ◆ **half-a-dozen** *n* demi-douzaine *f*. ◆ **half-fare 1** *n* demi-tarif *m*; **2** *adv* à demi-tarif. ◆ **half-fill** *vt* remplir à moitié. ◆ **half-hearted** *adj manner, person* tiède; *attempt* sans conviction; *welcome* peu enthousiaste. ◆ **half-heartedly** *adv* avec tiédeur; sans conviction; sans enthousiasme. ◆ **half-holiday** *n* demi-journée *f* de congé. ◆ **half-hour** *or* ◆ **half-an-hour** *n* demi-heure *f*. ◆ **half-hourly** *adv, adj* toutes les demi-heures. ◆ **half-light** *n* demi-jour *m*. ◆ **half-mast** *n*: **at** ~**-mast** en berne. ◆ **half-moon** *n* demi-lune *f*; (*on fingernail*) lunule *f*. ◆ **half-open 1** *adj* entrouvert; **2** *vt* entrouvrir. ◆ **half-pay** *n*: **on** ~**-pay** à demi-salaire; (*Mil*) en demi-solde. ◆ **halfpenny** ['heɪpnɪ] *n* demi-penny *m*; **he hasn't got a** ~**penny** il n'a pas le sou. ◆ **half-price** *n*: **at** ~**-price** à moitié prix; **the goods were reduced to** ~**-price** le prix des articles était réduit de moitié; **children admitted at** ~**-price** les enfants paient demi-tarif. ◆ **half-seas over**‡ *adj* dans les vignes du Seigneur. ◆ **half-sister** *n* demi-sœur *f*. ◆ **half-term (holiday)** *n* congé *m* de demi-trimestre. ◆ **half-time 1** *n* (*Sport, Ind*) mi-temps *f*; **2** *adv, adj* à mi-temps. ◆ **halfway** *adv, adj* à mi-chemin (*to* de; *between* entre); ~**way up** *or* **down (the hill)** à mi-côte, à mi-pente; **we're** ~**way there** nous n'avons plus que la moitié du chemin à faire; **to meet sb** ~**way** aller à la rencontre de qn; (*fig*) couper la poire en deux; ~**way through sth** à la moitié de qch. ◆ **half-wit** *n* idiot(e) *m(f)*. ◆ **half-witted** *adj* idiot. ◆ **half-yearly 1** *adj* semestriel; **2** *adv* tous les six mois.

halibut ['hælɪbət] *n* flétan *m*.

halitosis [ˌhælɪ'təʊsɪs] *n* mauvaise haleine.

hall [hɔːl] **1** *n* **(a)** (*public room*) (grande) salle *f*. **(b)** (*mansion*) manoir *m*. (*Univ*) ~/~**s of residence** pavillon *m*/cité *f* universitaire. **(c)** (*entrance way*) entrée *f*, hall *m*; (*corridor*) couloir *m*. **2** *adj*: ~ **porter** concierge *mf*. ◆ **hallmark** *n* poinçon *m*; (*fig*) marque *f*. ◆ **hallstand** *n or* ◆ **hall-tree** (*US*) *n* portemanteau *m*. ◆ **hallway** *n* vestibule *m*; (*corridor*) couloir *m*.

hallo [hə'ləʊ] *excl* (*in greeting*) bonjour!; (*Telec*) allô!; (*to attract attention*) hé!; (*in surprise*) tiens!

Hallowe'en ['hæləʊ'iːn] *n* veille *f* de la Toussaint.

hallucination [həˌluːsɪ'neɪʃən] *n* hallucination *f*.

halo ['heɪləʊ] *n* auréole *f*; (*Astron*) halo *m*.

halt [hɔːlt] **1** *n* halte *f*, arrêt *m*. **5 minutes'** ~ 5 minutes d'arrêt; **to come to a** ~ s'arrêter; **to call a** ~ (*order a stop*) commander halte; (*stop*) faire halte; (*fig*) **to call a** ~ **to sth** mettre fin à qch. **2** *vi* s'arrêter. ~! halte! **3** *vt vehicle* faire arrêter; *process* interrompre. ◆ **halting** *adj* hésitant. ◆ **haltingly** *adv* de façon hésitante.

halter ['hɔːltəʳ] *n* licou *m*.

halve [hɑːv] *vt apple etc* partager en deux (moitiés égales); *expense, time* réduire de moitié.

halves [hɑːvz] *npl of* **half**.

ham [hæm] **1** *n* **(a)** jambon *m*. ~ **and eggs** œufs *mpl* au jambon. **(b)** (*Theat**: *pej*) cabotin(e)* *m(f)*; (*Rad**) radio-amateur *m*. **2** *adj sandwich* au jambon. **3** *vti* (*Theat**: *also* ~ **it up**) forcer son rôle. ◆ **ham-fisted** *or* ◆ **ham-handed** *adj* maladroit. ◆ **hamstring** *vt* (*fig*) couper ses moyens à.

hamburger ['hæmˌbɜːgəʳ] *n* hamburger *m*.

hamlet ['hæmlɪt] *n* hameau *m*.

hammer ['hæməʳ] **1** *n* marteau *m*. **the** ~ **and sickle** la faucille et le marteau; **to go at sth** ~ **and tongs** faire qch avec acharnement; **to come under the** ~ être mis aux enchères. **2** *vt* marteler; (*: *defeat*) battre à plate couture; (*criticize severely*) *film etc* éreinter. **to** ~ **a nail into a plank** enfoncer un clou dans une planche (à coups de marteau); **to** ~ **into shape** *metal* façonner au marteau; *plan* mettre au point; **to** ~ **an idea into sb's head** faire entrer de force une idée dans la tête de qn. **3** *vi* (*lit*) frapper (au marteau). (*fig*) **he was** ~**ing at the door** il frappait à la porte à coups redoublés.

hammer down *vt sep nail* enfoncer; *plank* fixer.

hammer out *vt sep plan, agreement* élaborer (avec difficulté).

hammock ['hæmək] *n* hamac *m*.

hamper¹ ['hæmpəʳ] *n* (*basket*) panier *m* d'osier.

hamper² ['hæmpəʳ] *vt* (*hinder*) gêner.

hamster ['hæmstəʳ] *n* hamster *m*.

hand [hænd] **1** *n* **(a)** main *f*. **on (one's)** ~**s and knees** à quatre pattes; **to have in one's** ~ *book* tenir à la main; *money* avoir dans la main; *victory* tenir entre ses mains; **give me your** ~ donne-moi la main; **to take sb's** ~ prendre la main de qn; **by the** ~ par la main; **with** *or* **in both** ~**s** à deux mains; ~**s up!** (*at gunpoint*) haut les mains!; (*in school etc*) levez la main!; ~**s off!** bas les pattes!‡; ~**s off the sweets!** ne touche pas aux bonbons!; ~**s off our village** laissez notre village tranquille; (*lit*) ~ **over** ~ *or* **fist** main sur main; (*fig*) **he's making money** ~ **over fist** il fait des affaires d'or; **good with his** ~**s** adroit de ses mains.

(b) (*phrases*) **at** ~ *object* à portée de la main; *money, information* disponible; *summer, date* tout proche; **at first** ~ de première main; **by** ~ à la main; **from** ~ **to** ~ de main en main; **to live from** ~ **to mouth** vivre au jour le jour; **pistol in** ~ pistolet *m* au poing; **to put in(to) sb's** ~**s** remettre entre les mains de qn; **in good** ~**s** en bonnes mains; **I have this matter in** ~ je suis en train de m'occuper de cette affaire; **he had £6,000 in** ~ il avait 6000 livres de disponibles; **cash in** ~ encaisse *f*; **the matter in** ~ l'affaire en question; **he had the situation well in** ~ il avait la situation bien en main; **she took the child in** ~ elle a pris l'enfant en main; **to keep o.s. well in** ~ se contrôler; **work in** ~ travail *m* en cours; **to have sth on one's** ~**s** avoir qch sur les bras; **on the right/left** ~ du côté droit/gauche; **on my right** ~ à ma droite; **on every** ~**, on all** ~**s** de tous côtés; **on the one** ~ **... on the other** ~ d'une part ... d'autre part; **to get sth off one's** ~**s** se débarrasser de qch; **it/she was off his** ~**s** il n'avait plus à s'en occuper/à s'occuper d'elle; **out of ~** *condemn* sans jugement; *execute* sommairement; **to get out of ~** devenir impossible; **to ~** sous la main; **they are ~ in glove** ils s'entendent comme larrons en foire; **~ in glove with** de mèche avec; **he never does a ~'s turn** il ne remue pas le petit doigt; **to eat out of sb's ~** manger dans la main de qn; (*fig*) marcher au doigt et à l'œil; **to get one's ~ in** se faire la main; **to keep one's ~s off sth** s'empêcher de toucher à qch; **to have one's ~s full** avoir fort à faire (*with* avec); **to have a ~ in** *piece of work, decision* être pour qch dans; *crime, plot* être mêlé à; **she had a ~ in it** elle y était pour qch; **I will have no ~ in it** je ne veux rien avoir à faire là-dedans; **to take a ~ in (doing) sth** contribuer à (faire) qch; **to give sb a ~** donner un coup de main à qn (*to do* pour faire); **to get/have the upper ~ of sb** prendre/avoir le dessus sur qn; **to put** *or* **set one's ~ to sth** entreprendre qch; **empty-~ed** les mains vides; **to win sth ~s down** gagner qch haut la main; **to be waited on ~ and foot** se faire servir comme un prince; *[horse]* **13 ~s high** de 13 paumes.

(c) (*worker*) travailleur *m*, -euse *f* manuel(le), ouvrier *m*, -ière *f*. **~s** (*Ind etc*) main-d'œuvre *f*; (*Naut*) hommes *mpl*; **all ~s on deck** tout le monde sur le pont; (*Naut*) **lost with all ~s** perdu corps et biens; **he's a great ~ at (doing) that** il est vraiment doué pour (faire) cela; **he's an old ~ at it** il n'en est pas à son coup d'essai.

(d) *[clock etc]* aiguille *f*.

(e) (*Cards*) main *f*; (*game etc*) partie *f*. **I've got a good ~** j'ai une belle main; **we played a ~ of bridge** nous avons fait une partie de bridge.

2 *adj cream etc* pour les mains.

3 *vt* passer, donner (*to* à). (*fig*) **you've got to ~ it to him*** c'est une justice à lui rendre; **it was ~ed to him on a plate*** ça lui a été apporté sur un plateau.

hand back *vt sep* rendre (*to* à).

hand down *vt sep object* passer (*de haut en bas); heirloom, tradition* transmettre (*to* à).

hand in *vt sep* remettre (*to* à).

hand on *vt sep* transmettre (*to* à).

hand out *vt sep* distribuer.

hand over *vt sep object* remettre (*to* à); *prisoner* livrer (*to* à); *powers* (*transfer*) transmettre (*to* à), (*surrender*) céder (*to* à); *property, business* céder.

hand round *vt sep bottles, papers* faire circuler; *cakes* faire passer, *[hostess]* offrir.

hand up *vt sep* passer (*de bas en haut*).

♦ **handbag** *n* sac *m* à main. ♦ **handball** *n* handball *m*. ♦ **handbasin** *n* lavabo *m*. ♦ **handbell** *n* sonnette *f*. ♦ **handbill** *n* prospectus *m*. ♦ **handbook** *n* (*instructions*) manuel *m*; *[tourist]* guide *m*; *[museum]* livret *m*. ♦ **handbrake** *n* frein *m* à main. ♦ **handclasp** *n* poignée *f* de main. ♦ **handcuff 1** *n* menotte *f*; **2** *vt* passer les menottes à; **to be ~cuffed** avoir les menottes aux poignets. ♦ **handful** *n* poignée *f*; **in ~fuls** à *or* par poignées; (*fig*) **the children are a ~ful*** les enfants ne me laissent pas une minute de répit. ♦ **hand grenade** *n* grenade *f* (à main). ♦ **handicraft** *n* (*work*) artisanat *m*; (*skill*) habileté *f* manuelle; **exhibition of ~icrafts** exposition *f* d'objets artisanaux. ♦ **hand-in-hand** *adv* la main dans la main; (*fig*) ensemble; (*fig*) **to go ~-in-~ with** aller de pair avec. ♦ **handiwork** *n* ouvrage *m*; (*fig*) œuvre *f*. ♦ **handkerchief** ['hæŋkətʃɪf] *n* mouchoir *m*. ♦ **hand-knitted** *adj* tricoté à la main. ♦ **hand-luggage** *n* bagages *mpl* à main. ♦ **handmade** *adj* fait à la main. ♦ **hand-me-downs*** *npl* vêtements *mpl* d'occasion. ♦ **handout** *n* (*leaflet*) prospectus *m*; (*at meeting*) documentation *f*; (*press release*) communiqué *m*; (*money*) aumône *f*. ♦ **hand-picked** *adj* trié sur le volet. ♦ **handrail** *n [stairs etc]* rampe *f*; *[bridge, quay]* garde-fou *m*. ♦ **handsaw** *n* scie *f* à main. ♦ **handshake** *n* poignée *f* de main. ♦ **handspring** *n* saut *m* de mains. ♦ **handstand** *n*: **to do a ~stand** faire l'arbre droit. ♦ **hand-to-hand 1** *adv* corps à corps; **2** *adj*: **~-to-~ fighting** corps à corps *m*. ♦ **handwork** *n* = **handiwork**. ♦ **hand-woven** *adj* tissé à la main. ♦ **handwriting** *n* écriture *f*. ♦ **handwritten** *adj* manuscrit, écrit à la main.

handicap ['hændɪkæp] **1** *n* handicap *m*. **his appearance is a great ~** son aspect physique le handicape beaucoup. **2** *vt* handicaper. ♦ **handicapped 1** *adj* handicapé; **mentally/physically ~ped** handicapé mentalement/physiquement; **2** *npl*: **the ~ped** les handicapés *mpl*; **the mentally/physically ~ped** les handicapés mentaux/physiques.

handle ['hændl] **1** *n [basket, bucket]* anse *f*; *[broom, spade, knife]* manche *m*; *[door, drawer, suitcase, tap]* poignée *f*; *[saucepan]* queue *f*; *[pump, stretcher, wheelbarrow]* bras *m*. *[car]* **(starting) ~** manivelle *f*.

2 *vt* **(a)** (*wield*) *bow, weapon* manier; (*shift etc: esp Ind*) manipuler; (*touch*) *goods etc* toucher à; (*Sport*) *ball* toucher de la main. '**~ with care**' 'fragile'. **(b)** (*fig*) *ship, car* manœuvrer; *person, animal* manier, s'y prendre avec. **he knows how to ~ a gun/his son** il sait se servir d'un pistolet/s'y prendre avec son fils; **he ~d the situation very well** il a très bien conduit l'affaire; **I'll ~ this** je m'en charge; **we don't ~ that type of product** nous ne faisons pas ce genre de produit; **we don't ~ that type of business** nous ne nous occupons pas de ce type d'affaires; **Orly ~s 5 million passengers a year** 5 millions de passagers passent par Orly chaque année; **can the port ~ big ships?** le port peut-il recevoir les gros bateaux? ♦ **handlebars** *npl* guidon *m*. ♦ **handler** *n* (*dog ~*) dresseur *m*, -euse *f* (de chiens). ♦ **handling** *n [ship]* manœuvre *f*; *[car]* maniement *m*; *[goods, objects]* (*Ind*) manutention *f*; (*fingering*) maniement; **his handling of the matter** la façon dont il a traité l'affaire; *[person, object]* **to get some rough handling** se faire malmener.

handsome ['hænsəm] *adj* (*good-looking*) beau; *conduct, compliment, gift* généreux; *apology* honorable; *amount, fortune, profit* considérable. ♦ **handsomely** *adv* (*elegantly*) *construct* avec élégance; (*generously*) *contribute* généreusement; *apologize* avec bonne grâce; *behave* élégamment.

handy ['hændɪ] *adj* **(a)** *person* adroit (de ses mains). **to be ~ with sth** savoir se servir de qch. **(b)** (*at hand*) *tool* sous la main, prêt; *place* commode; (*nearby*) *shops etc* accessible. **(c)** (*convenient*) *tool, method* pratique. (*fig*) **that's ~!** ça tombe bien!; **that would come in very ~** cela tomberait bien.

♦ **handyman** *n* (*servant*) homme *m* à tout faire; (*do-it-yourself*) bricoleur *m*.

hang [hæŋ] *pret, ptp* **hung 1** *vt* **(a)** (*suspend*) *lamp* suspendre (*on* à); *curtains, hat, picture* accrocher (*on* à); *door* monter; *clothes* pendre (*on, from* à); *wallpaper* poser; *dangling object* laisser pendre. **to ~ one's head** baisser la tête; **trees hung with lights** arbres chargés de lumières; **room hung with paintings** pièce aux murs couverts de tableaux; **to ~ fire** *[guns]* faire long feu; *[plans etc]* traîner (en longueur). **(b)** (*pret, ptp* **hanged**) *criminal* pendre (*for* pour).

2 *vi* **(a)** *[rope, dangling object]* pendre, être accroché *or* suspendu (*on, from* à); *[drapery]* pendre, tomber; *[hair]* tomber; *[picture]* être accroché (*on* à); *[criminal etc]* être pendu. **he'll ~ for it** cela lui vaudra la corde; **to ~ out of the window** *[person]* se pencher par la fenêtre; *[thing]* pendre à la fenêtre; (*fig*) **to ~ by a hair** ne tenir qu'à un cheveu. **(b)** *[fog, threat]* planer, peser (*over* sur); *[hawk]* être comme suspendu.

3 *n*: **to get the ~* of doing sth** attraper le coup* pour faire qch.
hang about, hang around 1 *vi [loiterer]* traîner. **to keep sb ~ing about** faire attendre qn. **2** *vt fus person* coller à; *place* hanter.
hang back *vi* (*in walking etc*) hésiter à aller de l'avant; (*fig*) être réticent (*from doing* pour faire).
hang down *vi, vt sep* pendre.
hang on 1 *vi* **(a)** (*: *wait*) attendre. **~ on!** attendez!; (*on phone*) ne quittez pas! **(b)** (*hold out*) tenir bon, résister. **(c) to ~ on to sth*** (*keep hold of*) ne pas lâcher qch; (*keep*) garder qch. **2** *vt fus* (*depend on*) dépendre de.
hang out 1 *vi* (*gen*) pendre; (*: *live*) percher*, habiter; (*: *resist*) tenir bon. **2** *vt sep streamer* suspendre (dehors); *washing* étendre (dehors); *flag* arborer.
hang together *vi [argument, details]* se tenir; *[story]* tenir debout; *[statements]* concorder.
hang up 1 *vi* (*Telec: also* **~ up on sb**) raccrocher. **2** *vt sep* accrocher (*on* à, sur). (*fig*) **he's hung up about it*** il en fait tout un complexe.
◆ **hangdog expression** *n* air *m* de chien battu. ◆ **hanger** *n* (*clothes ~*) cintre *m*. ◆ **hanger-on** *n* parasite *m* (*personne*). ◆ **hang-glider** *n* aile *f* volante. ◆ **hang-gliding** *n*: **to go ~-gliding** faire du vol libre. ◆ **hanging 1** *n* (*execution*) pendaison *f*; **2** *adj bridge* suspendu; *lamp, light* pendant. ◆ **hangman** *n* bourreau *m*. ◆ **hangover** *n*: **to have a ~over** avoir une *or* la gueule de bois*; **a ~over from the previous administration** un reliquat de l'administration précédente. ◆ **hang-up*** *n* complexe *m* (*about* en ce qui concerne).
hangar ['hæŋəʳ] *n* (*Aviat*) hangar *m*.
hank [hæŋk] *n [wool etc]* écheveau *m*.
hanker ['hæŋkəʳ] *vi*: **to ~** *or* **have a ~ing for** *or* **after** avoir envie de.
hankie* ['hæŋkɪ] *n abbr of* **handkerchief.**
hanky-panky* ['hæŋkɪ'pæŋkɪ] *n* entourloupette* *f*. **there's some ~ going on** il y a une entourloupette* là-dessous.
ha'penny ['heɪpnɪ] *n* = **halfpenny.**
haphazard [ˌhæp'hæzəd] *adj* (fait) au hasard; *arrangement* fortuit. ◆ **haphazardly** *adv* au hasard.
happen ['hæpən] *vi* arriver, se passer, se produire. **sth ~ed** il est arrivé *or* il s'est passé qch; **what's ~ed?** qu'est-ce qui s'est passé *or* est arrivé?; **as if nothing had ~ed** comme si de rien n'était; **whatever ~s** quoi qu'il arrive; **don't let it ~ again!** et que ça ne se reproduise pas!; **these things ~** ce sont des choses qui arrivent; **what has ~ed to him?** (*befallen*) qu'est-ce qui lui est arrivé?; (*become of*) qu'est-ce qu'il est devenu?; **a funny thing ~ed to me this morning** il m'est arrivé qch de bizarre ce matin; **how does it ~ that?** comment se fait-il que? + *subj*; **it might ~ that** il pourrait se faire que + *subj*; **it so ~s that I'm going there** il se trouve que j'y vais justement; **do you ~ to have a pen?** aurais-tu par hasard un stylo?; **if he does ~ to see her** s'il lui arrive de la voir. ◆ **happening** *n* événement *m*; (*Theat*) happening *m*. ◆ **happenstance*** *n* (*US*) événement *m* fortuit.
happy ['hæpɪ] *adj* heureux (*to do* de faire). **I'm not ~ about the plan** je ne suis pas très heureux de ce projet; **I'm not ~ about leaving him alone** je ne suis pas tranquille de le laisser seul; **I'll be quite ~ to do it** je le ferai volontiers; **she was quite ~ to stay there** cela ne l'ennuyait pas de rester là; **I'm ~ here reading** je suis très bien ici à lire; **it has a ~ ending** cela se termine bien; **the ~ few** les rares privilégiés *mpl*; **~ birthday!** bon *or* joyeux anniversaire!; **~ Christmas!** joyeux Noël!; **~ New Year!** bonne année!; **a ~ thought** une heureuse inspiration; **a ~ medium** un moyen terme. ◆ **happily** *adv* (*contentedly*) *play, walk, talk* tranquillement; *say, smile* joyeusement; (*fortunately*) heureusement; (*felicitously*) *word, choose* avec bonheur; **to live happily** vivre heureux; **they lived happily (for) ever after** après cela ils vécurent toujours heureux. ◆ **happiness** *n* bonheur *m*. ◆ **happy-go-lucky** *adj person* insouciant; *arrangement* fait au petit bonheur.
harangue [hə'ræŋ] **1** *vt* haranguer (*about* à propos de). **he ~d her into doing it** il n'a eu de cesse qu'elle ne le fasse. **2** *n* harangue *f*.
harass ['hærəs] *vt* (*harry*) *troops, the enemy etc* harceler; (*worry*) tracasser, (*stronger*) harceler. ◆ **harassed** *adj* tracassé, harcelé.
harbour, (*US*) **-or** ['hɑːbəʳ] **1** *n* port *m*. **2** *adj*: **~ master** capitaine *m* de port. **3** *vt refugee* héberger, abriter; *criminal* receler; *suspicions, fear* entretenir. **to ~ a grudge against sb** garder rancune à qn.
hard [hɑːd] **1** *adj* **(a)** *substance* dur; *mud, snow* durci; *muscle* ferme. **~ hat** casque *m*, (*riding hat*) bombe *f*; **to grow ~** durcir; **a ~ nut to crack** (*problem etc*) un gros problème; (*person*) un(e) dur(e) à cuire*; **he is as ~ as nails** (*physically*) c'est un paquet de muscles; (*mentally*) il est dur. **(b)** (*difficult*) *problem, examination* difficile; *task* pénible, dur. **~ to understand** difficile *or* dur à comprendre; **I find it ~ to explain** j'ai du mal à l'expliquer; **I find it ~ to believe that ...** j'ai du mal à croire que ... + *subj*; **~ to please** exigeant, difficile; **~ to get on with** difficile à vivre; **that is ~ to beat** on peut difficilement faire mieux; **~ of hearing** dur d'oreille. **(c)** (*severe*) dur, sévère (*on, to* avec; *towards* envers); *heart* dur, impitoyable. **he's a ~ man** il est dur, c'est un homme impitoyable; **to grow ~** s'endurcir; **~ sell** promotion *f* de vente agressive. **(d)** (*harsh*) *life* dur, difficile; *words, work* dur; *climate, winter* rude; *fall* mauvais; *rule, decision, treatment* sévère; (*tough*) *battle, fight* acharné; *match* âprement disputé; *study* assidu; *worker* dur à la tâche. **it's ~ work!** c'est dur!; **he drives a ~ bargain** il ne fait pas de cadeaux (*fig*); **a ~ blow** un coup dur, un rude coup; (*Brit*) **~ luck!*, ~ lines!*** pas de veine!*; **it's ~ luck on him*** il n'a pas de veine*; **~ liquor** boisson *f* fortement alcoolisée; **~ drinker** gros buveur *m*; **a ~ core of offenders** un noyau irréductible de délinquants; (*Pol*) **the ~ core of the party** les inconditionnels *mpl* parmi les membres du parti; **the ~ facts** la réalité brutale; **~ feeling** amertume *f*; **no ~ feelings!** sans rancune!; **~ frost** forte gelée *f*; **it was ~ going** ça a été dur*; (*Jur*) **~ labour** travaux *mpl* forcés; **she had a ~ time of it** elle a traversé des moments difficiles; **you'll have a ~ time of it persuading ...** vous allez avoir du mal à persuader ...; **these are ~ times** les temps sont durs. **(e)** (*fig*) *light, line, colour, drug* dur; *water* calcaire; (*Fin*) *market* ferme. **~ cash** espèces *fpl*; **~ news** de l'information *f* sérieuse.

2 *adv pull* fort; *hit* dur, fort; *fall down* durement; *run* à toutes jambes; *think* sérieusement; *work, study* d'arrache-pied; *drink* beaucoup. **as ~ as one can** de toutes ses forces; **it's raining ~** il pleut à verse; **it's snowing ~** il neige dru; **it's freezing ~** il gèle dur; **frozen ~** *lake* profondément gelé; *ground* durci par le gel; **to hold on ~** tenir bon *or* ferme; **to look ~ at** *person* dévisager; *thing* regarder de près; **to try ~** faire un gros effort; **to be ~ hit** être sérieusement touché; **~ at it*** attelé à la tâche; **~ by** tout près; **to follow ~ upon sb's heels** suivre qn de très près; **to be ~ put to it to do** avoir beaucoup de mal à faire; **~ pressed** (*for time*) débordé; (*for money*) à court; **she took it pretty ~** elle a été très affectée; **~ done by*** traité injustement.
◆ **hard-and-fast** *adj* inflexible; *rule* absolu. ◆ **hardback** *n* livre *m* cartonné. ◆ **hard-bitten** *adj* dur à cuire*. ◆ **hardboard** *n* Isorel *m* ®. ◆ **hard-boiled** *adj egg* dur; (*fig*) *person* dur à cuire*. ◆ **hard-core** *adj support, opposition*

inconditionnel; *pornography* dur. ♦ **hard-earned** *adj money* durement gagné; *holiday* bien mérité. ♦ **harden 1** *vt* (*gen*) durcir; *person* endurcir; to **~en one's heart** s'endurcir; **2** *vi [substances]* durcir; *[voice]* se faire dur; *[prices]* être en hausse; *[market]* s'affermir. ♦ **hardened** *adj* durci; *criminal* endurci; *sinner* invétéré; **I'm ~ened to it** j'ai l'habitude. ♦ **hardening** *n* durcissement *m*. ♦ **hard-fought** *adj* âprement disputé. ♦ **hard-headed** *adj* réaliste. ♦ **hard-hearted** *adj* impitoyable, au cœur dur. ♦ **hard-liner** *n* inconditionnel(le) *m(f)*. ♦ **hardly** *adv* **(a)** (*scarcely*) à peine, ne ... guère; **he can ~ly write** il sait à peine écrire; **it's ~ly his business if ...** ce n'est guère son affaire si ...; **you'll ~ly believe it** vous aurez de la peine à le croire; **I need ~ly point out that** je n'ai pas besoin de faire remarquer que; **I ~ly know** je n'en sais trop rien; **~ly anyone/anywhere/ever** presque personne/nulle part/jamais; **~ly!** (*not at all*) certainement pas!; (*not exactly*) pas précisément!; **(b)** (*harshly*) durement, sévèrement. ♦ **hardness** *n* dureté *f*; fermeté *f*; difficulté *f*; sévérité *f*. ♦ **hardship** *n* épreuves *fpl*; (*suffering*) souffrance *f*; **there's a certain amount of ~ship involved** ce sera assez dur; **a life of ~ship** une vie pleine d'épreuves; **it's no great ~ship to go and see her** ce n'est tout de même pas une épreuve d'aller la voir; **~ships** épreuves *fpl*, privations *fpl*. ♦ **hard-up*** *adj* fauché*. ♦ **hardware 1** *n* (*Comm*) quincaillerie *f*; (*Mil, Police etc*) matériel *m*; (*Computers, Space*) hardware *m*; **2** *adj*: **~ware dealer** quincailler *m*; **~ware shop** quincaillerie *f*; (*Computers*) **~ware specialist** technicien(ne) *m(f)* du hardware. ♦ **hard-wearing** *adj* solide, résistant. ♦ **hardwood** *n* bois *m* dur. ♦ **hard-working** *adj* travailleur.

hardy ['hɑːdɪ] *adj* (*strong*) robuste; (*bold*) hardi; *plant* résistant (au gel); *tree* de plein vent. ♦ **hardihood** *n* hardiesse *f*. ♦ **hardiness** *n* force *f*, vigueur *f*.

hare [hɛəʳ] **1** *n* lièvre *m*. **2** *vi*: **to ~ in*** *etc* entrer *etc* en trombe. ♦ **harebell** *n* campanule *f*. ♦ **hare-brained** *adj person* écervelé; *plan* insensé. ♦ **hare-coursing** *n* chasse *f* au lièvre. ♦ **harelip** *n* bec-de-lièvre *m*.

haricot ['hærɪkəʊ] *n*: **~ (bean)** haricot *m* blanc.

hark [hɑːk] *excl* écoutez!

hark back *vi* revenir (*to* sur).

harm [hɑːm] **1** *n* (*gen*) mal *m*; (*to reputation, interests*) tort *m*. **to do sb ~** faire du mal *or* du tort à qn; **no ~ done** il n'y a pas de mal; **he means no ~** il n'a pas de mauvaises intentions; **he meant no ~ by what he said** il ne l'a pas dit méchamment; **he doesn't mean us any ~** il ne nous veut pas de mal; **you will come to no ~** il ne t'arrivera rien; **I don't see any ~ in it** je n'y vois aucun mal; **there's no ~ in it** cela ne peut pas faire de mal; **there's no ~ in doing that** il n'y a pas de mal à faire cela; **out of ~'s way** en sûreté. **2** *vt person* faire du mal *or* du tort à; *crops* endommager; *object* abîmer; *reputation* salir; *interests, a cause* causer du tort à. ♦ **harmful** *adj* nuisible (*to* à). ♦ **harmless** *adj animal, joke* inoffensif; *person* sans méchanceté; *action, game* innocent; *suggestion, conversation* anodin.

harmony ['hɑːmənɪ] *n* harmonie *f*. ♦ **harmonica** *n* harmonica *m*. ♦ **harmonics** *n* (*Mus: sg: science*) harmonie *f*; (*pl: overtones*) harmoniques *mpl*. ♦ **harmonious** *adj* harmonieux. ♦ **harmonium** *n* harmonium *m*. ♦ **harmonize 1** *vt* harmoniser; **2** *vi* (*Mus*) chanter en harmonie; *[colours etc]* s'harmoniser (*with* avec); *[person, facts]* s'accorder (*with* avec).

harness ['hɑːnɪs] **1** *n* harnais *m*. (*fig*) **to get back into ~** reprendre le collier; (*fig*) **to die in ~** mourir à la tâche. **2** *vt horse* harnacher; (*to carriage*) atteler (*to* à); (*fig*) *resources etc* exploiter.

harp [hɑːp] **1** *n* harpe *f*. **2** *vi*: **to ~ on (about) sth*** rabâcher qch, revenir toujours sur qch.

harpoon [hɑː'puːn] **1** *n* harpon *m*. **2** *vt* harponner.

harpsichord ['hɑːpsɪkɔːd] *n* clavecin *m*.

harrow ['hærəʊ] *n* herse *f*. ♦ **harrowing** *adj story* poignant; *cry* déchirant.

harsh [hɑːʃ] *adj* **(a)** *punishment, person* dur (*with sb* avec *or* envers qn), sévère; *words, tone* cassant, dur; *fate* cruel; *climate* rigoureux. **(b)** (*discordant etc*) *sound* discordant; *voice, colour* criard; *contrast* heurté; *taste* âpre. ♦ **harshly** *adv reply* (*gen*) durement; *treat* sévèrement. ♦ **harshness** *n* dureté *f*; sévérité *f*; cruauté *f*; discordance *f*; aspect criard *or* heurté; âpreté *f*.

harum-scarum ['hɛərəm'skɛərəm] *adj, n* écervelé(e) *m(f)*.

harvest ['hɑːvɪst] **1** *n* (*gen*) moisson *f*; *[fruit]* récolte *f*; *[grapes]* vendange *f*. **2** *vt* moissonner (*also fig*); récolter; vendanger. **3** *vi* faire la moisson. **4** *adj*: **~ festival** fête *f* de la moisson; **~ moon** pleine lune (de l'équinoxe d'automne); **at ~ time** à la moisson. ♦ **harvester** *n* (*person*) moissonneur *m*, -euse *f*; (*machine*) moissonneuse *f*.

has [hæz] *V* **have**. ♦ **has-been*** *n* (*person*) homme *m* fini, femme *f* finie; (*object*) vieillerie *f*.

hash [hæʃ] *n* (*Culin*) hachis *m*; (**fig*) gâchis *m*. **to make a ~* of sth** saboter qch; **a ~(-up)* of old ideas** un réchauffé de vieilles idées.

hashish ['hæʃɪʃ] *n* hachisch *m*.

hassle* ['hæsl] *n* (*squabble*) bagarre* *f*; (*fuss, trouble*) histoire* *f* (*to do* pour faire).

haste [heɪst] *n* hâte *f*. **in ~** à la hâte; **in great ~** en toute hâte; **to make ~** se hâter (*to do* de faire). ♦ **hasten** ['heɪsn] *vi* (*gen*) se hâter (*to do* de faire); **I ~n to add ...** je m'empresse d'ajouter ...; **to ~n away** *etc* partir *etc* à la hâte. ♦ **hastily** *adv* (*speedily*) à la hâte; (*too speedily*) précipitamment; (*without thinking*) trop hâtivement; **he suggested hastily** il s'est empressé de suggérer. ♦ **hasty** *adj departure, marriage* précipité; *visit, glance, meal* hâtif; *sketch* fait à la hâte; *action, decision, words* irréfléchi; **don't be so hasty!** ne va pas si vite!

hat [hæt] **1** *n* chapeau *m*. **~ in hand** (*lit*) chapeau bas; (*fig*) obséquieusement; (*fig*) **to take off one's ~ to** tirer son chapeau à; **to keep sth under one's ~*** garder qch pour soi; **to talk through one's ~*** dire n'importe quoi; (*fig*) **to pass round the ~ for sb** faire la quête pour qn; **that's old ~!*** c'est vieux tout ça! **2** *adj*: **to get a ~ trick** réussir trois coups (*or* gagner trois matchs *etc*) consécutifs. ♦ **hatcheck girl** *n* (*US*) dame *f* du vestiaire.

hatch[1] [hætʃ] **1** *vt chick, egg* faire éclore; *plot* ourdir, tramer; *plan* couver. **2** *vi* (**~ out**) *[chick, egg]* éclore.

hatch[2] [hætʃ] *n* **(a)** (*Naut: ~way*) écoutille *f*. (*drinks*) **down the ~!*** à la bonne vôtre! **(b)** (*service ~*) passe-plats *m inv*. ♦ **hatchback** *n* (*Aut*) (*two-door*) coupé *m or* (*four-door*) berline *f* avec hayon arrière.

hatchet ['hætʃɪt] **1** *n* hachette *f*. **2** *adj*: **~ man*** (*killer*) tueur *m* (à gages); (*fig*) homme *m* de main. ♦ **hatchet-faced** *adj* au visage en lame de couteau.

hate [heɪt] **1** *vt person* haïr, (*weaker*) détester; *thing* détester, avoir horreur de. **to ~ to do** *or* **doing** détester faire, avoir horreur de faire; **he ~s to be** *or* **being ordered about** il a horreur qu'on lui donne (*subj*) des ordres; **I ~ to say so** cela m'ennuie beaucoup de devoir le dire; **I should ~ to keep you waiting** je ne voudrais surtout pas vous faire attendre; **I should ~ him to think ...** je ne voudrais surtout pas qu'il pense (*subj*) ... . **2** *n* (*hatred*) haine *f*. **pet ~*** bête *f* noire. ♦ **hateful** *adj* haïssable, détestable. ♦ **hatred** *n* haine *f*.

haughty ['hɔːtɪ] *adj* hautain, arrogant. ♦ **haughtily** *adv* avec hauteur, avec arrogance.

♦ **haughtiness** *n* hauteur *f*, arrogance *f*.
haul [hɔːl] **1** *n* **(a)** (*Aut etc: journey*) voyage *m*. (*lit, fig*) **it's a long ~** la route est longue. **(b)** *[fishermen]* prise *f*; *[thieves]* butin *m*. **they made a good ~ of jewels** ils ont eu un beau butin en bijoux; (*fig*) **a good ~* of presents** une bonne récolte de cadeaux.
2 *vt* **(a)** (*pull*) traîner, tirer. (*fig*) **to ~ sb over the coals** passer un savon* à qn. **(b)** (*transport by truck*) camionner.
haul down *vt sep flag, sail* amener; (*gen*) *object* descendre (*en tirant*).
haul in, haul out *vt sep* (*from water*) *line, catch* amener; *drowning man* tirer (de l'eau).
haul up *vt sep flag, sail* hisser; (*gen*) *object* monter (*en tirant*).
♦ **haulage** *n* (*road transport*) transport *m* routier. ♦ **haulage contractor** *or* ♦ **haulier** *n* entrepreneur *m* de transports (routiers).
haunch [hɔːntʃ] *n* hanche *f*; (*Culin*) cuissot *m*. **squatting on his ~es** *person* accroupi; *dog* assis (sur son derrière).
haunt [hɔːnt] **1** *vt* (*lit, fig*) hanter. **2** *n [criminals]* repaire *m*. **one of his favourite ~s** un des lieux où on le trouve souvent. ♦ **haunted** *adj house* hanté; *expression* égaré; *face* hagard. ♦ **haunting 1** *adj* obsédant; **2** *n* apparition *f*.
have [hæv] *pret, ptp* **had 1** *aux vb* avoir; être. **to ~ been** avoir été; **to ~ eaten** avoir mangé; **to ~ gone** être allé; **to ~ got up** s'être levé; **I ~ just seen him** je viens de le voir; **I had just seen him** je venais de le voir; **I've just come from London** j'arrive à l'instant de Londres; **you've seen her, ~n't you?** vous l'avez vue, n'est-ce pas?; **you ~n't seen her, ~ you?** vous ne l'avez pas vue, je suppose?; **you ~n't seen her - yes I ~!** vous ne l'avez pas vue - si!; **you've made a mistake - no I ~n't!** vous vous êtes trompé - mais non!; **you've dropped your book - so I ~!** vous avez laissé tomber votre livre - en effet!; **~ you been there? if you ~/~n't ...** y êtes-vous allé? si oui/non ...; **~ got** *V 2 and 3 below*.
2 *modal aux vb* (*be obliged*) **I ~ (got) to speak to you at once** je dois vous parler *or* il faut que je vous parle (*subj*) immédiatement; **I ~n't got to do it, I don't ~ to do it** je ne suis pas obligé de le faire; **do you ~ to make such a noise?** tu ne pourrais pas faire un peu moins de bruit?; **you didn't ~ to tell her!** tu n'avais pas besoin de le lui dire!; **~n't you got to write to your mother?** est-ce que tu ne dois pas écrire à ta mère?; **if you go through Dijon you ~n't got to** *or* **you don't ~ to go to Lyons** si vous passez par Dijon vous n'avez pas besoin d'aller à Lyon; **you ~n't (got) to say a word about it!*** tu ne dois pas en dire un mot!; (*US*) **it's got to be** *or* **it has to be the biggest** c'est sûrement le plus grand.
3 *vt* **(a)** (*possess*) avoir, posséder. **she has (got) blue eyes** elle a les yeux bleus; **all I ~ (got)** tout ce que je possède; **I ~n't (got) any more** je n'en ai plus; **I've got an idea** j'ai une idée; **I ~ (got) no German** je ne parle pas un mot d'allemand.
(b) *meals etc* avoir, prendre. **he has had lunch** il a déjeuné; **to ~ tea with sb** prendre le thé avec qn; **what will you ~? - I'll ~ an egg** qu'est-ce que vous voulez? - je prendrai un œuf; **he had eggs for breakfast** il a mangé des œufs au petit déjeuner; **I ~ had some more** j'en ai repris; **he had a cigarette** il a fumé une cigarette.
(c) (*receive, obtain, take*) avoir, recevoir. **I had a telegram from him** j'ai reçu un télégramme de lui; **to ~ a child** avoir un enfant; **I ~ it from my sister that ...** je tiens de ma sœur que ...; **I must ~ more time** il me faut davantage de temps; **I must ~ them by this afternoon** il me les faut pour cet après-midi; **which one will you ~?** lequel voulez-vous?; **let me ~ your address** donnez-moi votre adresse; **I shall let you ~ it for 10 francs** je vous le laisse pour 10 F; **there are no newspapers to be had** on ne trouve pas de journaux.
(d) (*hold*) tenir. **he had (got) me by the throat/the hair** il me tenait à la gorge/par les cheveux; **I ~ (got) him where I want him!*** je le tiens (à ma merci)!
(e) (*maintain, allow*) **he will ~ it that Paul is guilty** il soutient que Paul est coupable; **he won't ~ it that Paul is guilty** il n'admet pas que Paul soit coupable; **rumour has it that ...** le bruit court que ...; **as gossip has it** selon les racontars; **I won't ~ this nonsense/him hurt** je ne tolérerai pas cette absurdité/qu'on lui fasse du mal.
(f) (*causative etc*) **to ~ one's hair cut** se faire couper les cheveux; **I had my luggage brought up** j'ai fait monter mes bagages; **~ it mended** faites-le réparer; **I had him clean the car** je lui ai fait nettoyer la voiture; **what would you ~ me say?** que voulez-vous que je dise?; **he had his car stolen** on lui a volé sa voiture.
(g) (*phrases*) **I had better go** je devrais partir; **you'd better not tell him that!** tu ferais mieux de ne pas lui dire ça!; **I had as soon not see him** j'aimerais autant ne pas le voir; **I had rather do it myself** j'aimerais mieux *or* je préférerais le faire moi-même; **to ~ a walk** faire une promenade; **to ~ a good time** bien s'amuser; **to ~ a pleasant evening** passer une bonne soirée; **he has (got) flu** il a la grippe; **I've (got) a headache** j'ai mal à la tête; **I've (got) £6 left** il me reste 6 livres; **to ~ (got) sth to do/to read** *etc* avoir qch à faire/à lire *etc*; **I ~ (got) nothing to do with it** je n'y suis pour rien; **there you ~ me!** ça je n'en sais rien!; **I ~ it!** j'y suis!, ça y est, j'ai trouvé!; **you've been had*** tu t'es fait avoir*; **he's had it!*** il est fichu!*; **I'm not having any‡** ça ne prend pas*.
4 *n*: **the ~s and the ~-nots** les riches *mpl* et les pauvres *mpl*; **the ~-nots** les déshérités *mpl*.
have in *vt sep* **(a)** *sb waiting outside* faire entrer; *doctor, employee* faire venir. **we had him in for the evening** il est venu passer la soirée chez nous. **(b) to ~ it in for sb*** avoir une dent contre qn.
have on *vt sep* **(a)** *clothes* porter. **he had (got) nothing on** il était tout nu. **(b)** (*be busy*) **I've got so much on this week that ...** j'ai tant à faire cette semaine que ...; **I ~ got nothing on (for) this evening** je ne suis pas pris ce soir. **(c)** (*trick*) **to ~ sb on*** faire marcher* qn.
have out *vt sep*: **to ~ a tooth out** se faire arracher une dent; **to ~ it out with sb** s'expliquer avec qn.
have up *vt sep person* faire venir; (*from below*) faire monter. **he was had up by the headmaster** il a été appelé chez le proviseur; **to be had up by the police** être arrêté (*for doing* pour avoir fait).
haven ['heɪvn] *n* (*fig*) havre *m*, abri *m*.
haversack ['hævəsæk] *n* musette *f*.
havoc ['hævək] *n* ravages *mpl*. **to wreak ~ in** ravager; (*fig*) **to play ~ with** désorganiser complètement.
haw [hɔː] *n* (*Bot*) cenelle *f*.
hawk [hɔːk] *n* faucon *m* (*also Pol fig*). **to have eyes like a ~** avoir des yeux de lynx.
hawker ['hɔːkəʳ] *n* (*street*) colporteur *m*; (*door-to-door*) démarcheur *m*.
hawthorn ['hɔːθɔːn] *n* aubépine *f*.
hay [heɪ] **1** *n* foin *m*. (*fig*) **to make ~ while the sun shines** profiter de l'occasion. **2** *adj*: **~ fever** rhume *m* des foins.
♦ **haycock** *n* meulon *m* (de foin). ♦ **haymaker** *n* faneur *m*, -euse *f*. ♦ **haymaking** *n* fenaison *f*. ♦ **hayrick** *or* ♦ **haystack** *n* meule *f* de foin. ♦ **haywire*** *adj*: **to go ~wire** *[person]* perdre la tête; *[plans etc]* mal tourner; *[equipment etc]* se détraquer.
hazard ['hæzəd] **1** *n* (*chance*) hasard *m*, chance *f*; (*risk*) risque *m*, (*stronger*) danger *m*. **natural/professional ~** risque naturel/du métier; **a nasty ~ for pedestrians** un danger pour les piétons. **2** *vt life, reputation, attempt* risquer; *remark, forecast* hasarder. **to ~ a guess** risquer

une hypothèse; **'I could do it' she ~ed** 'moi je pourrais le faire' se risqua-t-elle à dire. ♦ **hazardous** *adj* hasardeux.

haze [heɪz] *n* brume *f*; *[smoke etc]* vapeur *f*. (*fig*) **to be in a ~** être dans le brouillard. ♦ **hazy** *adj day, weather* brumeux; *outline, photograph* flou; *idea* vague; **to be hazy about sth** avoir une idée très vague de qch.

hazel ['heɪzl] **1** *n* noisetier *m*. **2** *adj* (*colour*) (couleur) noisette *inv*. ♦ **hazelnut** *n* noisette *f*.

he [hi:] *pers pron* **(a)** (*unstressed*) il. **~ has come** il est venu; **here ~ is** le voici; **~ is a doctor** il est médecin, c'est un médecin. **(b)** (*stressed*) lui. **younger than ~** plus jeune que lui; **HE didn't do it** ce n'est pas lui qui l'a fait. **(c)** (+*rel pron*) celui. **~ who can** celui qui peut. **(d) it's a ~*** (*animal*) c'est un mâle; (*baby*) c'est un garçon. ♦ **he-bear** *etc n* ours *m etc* mâle. ♦ **he-man*** *n* (vrai) mâle *m*.

head [hed] **1** *n* **(a)** tête *f*. **~ of hair** chevelure *f*; **covered** *etc* **from ~ to foot** couvert *etc* de la tête aux pieds; **~ down** (*upside down*) la tête en bas; (*looking down*) la tête baissée; **~ downwards** la tête en bas; **~ first, ~ foremost** la tête la première; **my ~ aches, I've got a bad ~** j'ai mal à la tête; **to hit sb on the ~** frapper qn à la tête; **to stand on one's ~** faire le poirier; **I could do it standing on my ~*** c'est bête comme chou*; (*fig*) **he stands ~ and shoulders above everybody else** il surpasse tout le monde; **she is a ~ taller than her sister** elle dépasse sa sœur d'une tête; *[horse]* **to win by a (short) ~** gagner d'une (courte) tête; **~ over ears in debt** dans les dettes jusqu'au cou; **to turn** *or* **go ~ over heels** (*accidentally*) faire la culbute; (*on purpose*) faire une galipette; **~ over heels in love with** éperdument amoureux de; (*fig*) **to keep one's ~ above water** se maintenir à flot; **he was talking his ~ off*** il n'arrêtait pas de parler; **to sing/shout one's ~ off*** chanter/crier à tue-tête; **I'm saying that off the top of my ~*** je dis ça sans savoir exactement; **to give a horse its ~/sb his ~** lâcher la bride à un cheval/à qn; **on your ~ be it!** à vos risques et périls!; **10 francs a ~** 10 F par tête.

(b) (*mind, intellect*) tête *f*. **to get sth into one's ~** se mettre qch dans la tête; **to take it into one's ~ to do** se mettre en tête de faire; **it didn't enter his ~ that/to do** il ne lui est pas venu pas à l'idée que/de faire; **you never know what's going on in his ~** on ne sait jamais ce qui lui passe par la tête; **what put that idea into his ~?** qu'est-ce qui lui a mis cette idée-là dans la tête?; **I can't get it out of my ~** je ne peux pas me sortir ça de la tête; **it's gone right out of my ~** ça m'est tout à fait sorti de la tête; **that tune has been running through my ~ all day** cet air m'a trotté par la tête toute la journée; **he has a good ~ for mathematics** il a des dispositions *fpl* pour les mathématiques; **he has a good ~ for heights** il n'a jamais le vertige; **he has a good business ~** il a le sens des affaires; **he has a good ~ (on his shoulders)** il a de la tête; **he's got his ~ screwed on right*** il a la tête sur les épaules; **two ~s are better than one** deux avis valent mieux qu'un; **we put our ~s together** nous nous sommes consultés; **I can't do it in my ~** je ne peux pas faire ça de tête; **he gave orders over my ~** il a donné des ordres sans me consulter; **it's quite above my ~** cela me dépasse complètement; **to keep one's ~** garder son sang-froid; **to lose one's ~** perdre la tête; **it went to his ~** cela lui est monté à la tête; **he has gone** *or* **he is off his ~*** il a perdu la boule*; **weak** *or* **soft* in the ~** faible *or* simple d'esprit.

(c) *[flower, lettuce, nail, hammer, abscess]* tête *f*; *[arrow]* pointe *f*; *[celery]* pied *m*; *[bed]* chevet *m*; *[tape recorder]* tête magnétique; *[page, staircase]* haut *m*; *[river]* source *f*; *[beer]* mousse *f*; *[lake, pier]* extrémité *f*. **~ of steam** pression *f*; **at the ~ of** (*in charge of*) à la tête de; (*in front row of, at top of*) en tête de; **at the ~ of the queue** en tête de file, au début de la queue; **at the ~ of the table** au haut bout de la table; **to come to a ~** *[abscess etc]* mûrir; *[situation etc]* devenir critique; **to bring things to a ~** précipiter une crise.

(d) (*leader*) *[family, business etc]* chef *m*. (*Scol*) **the ~** le directeur, la directrice; **~ of department** *[business firm]* chef de service; *[shop]* chef de rayon; *[school, college etc]* chef de section; (*Pol*) **~ of state** chef d'État.

(e) (*title*) titre *m*; (*subject ~ing*) (*in newspaper*) rubrique *f*; (*in essay, speech, article*) tête *f* de chapitre. **this comes under the ~ of** ceci se classe sous la rubrique de.

(f) *[coin]* face *f*. **to toss ~s or tails** jouer à pile ou face; **~s or tails?** pile ou face?; **~s I win!** face je gagne!; **he called ~s** il a annoncé 'face'; **I can't make ~ nor tail of what he's saying** je ne comprends rien à ce qu'il dit.

2 *adj* **(a)** *typist, assistant etc* principal. **~ clerk** chef *m* de bureau; **~ gardener** jardinier *m* en chef; **~ office** bureau *m or* siège *m* central; **~ waiter** maître *m* d'hôtel. **(b) ~ cold** rhume *m* de cerveau; **to have a ~ start** avoir une grosse avance (*over, on* sur).

3 *vt* **(a)** *procession, list, poll* être en tête de; *group of people* être à la tête de. **(b)** (*direct*) **he ~ed the car towards town** il a pris la direction de la ville. **(c)** (*entitle*) intituler. **~ed writing paper** papier *m* à en-tête. **(d)** (*Ftbl*) **to ~ the ball** faire une tête.

4 *vi* se diriger. **to ~ for** *[person, car etc]* se diriger vers; *[ship]* mettre le cap sur; **he ~ed up the hill** il s'est mis à monter la colline; **he was ~ing home** il était sur le chemin du retour; **he's ~ing for a disappointment** il va vers une déception; **he's ~ing for a fall** il court à un échec.

head off 1 *vi* partir (*for* pour; *towards* vers). **he ~ed off on to the subject of ...** il est passé à la question de ... . **2** *vt sep enemy* forcer à se rabattre; *person* (*lit*) détourner de son chemin; (*fig*) détourner (*from* de); *questions* parer.

♦ **headache** *n* mal *m* de tête, (*worse*) migraine *f*; **to have a ~ache** avoir mal à la tête, avoir la migraine; (*fig*) **that's his ~ache** c'est son problème à lui; **the whole business was a ~ache from beginning to end** nous n'avons connu que des ennuis avec cette affaire. ♦ **headband** *n* bandeau *m*. ♦ **headdress** *n* (*feathers etc*) coiffure *f*; (*lace*) coiffe *f*. ♦ **header*** *n* (*dive, fall*) plongeon *m*; (*Ftbl*) (coup *m* de) tête *f*; **to take a ~er into the water** piquer une tête dans l'eau. ♦ **headgear** *n* couvre-chef *m*; **I haven't any ~gear** je n'ai rien à me mettre sur la tête. ♦ **heading** *n* (*gen*) titre *m*; (*subject title*) rubrique *f*; (*chapter ~ing*) tête *f* de chapitre; (*printed: on document etc*) en-tête *m*; **essay divided into several ~ings** dissertation divisée en plusieurs têtes de chapitre. ♦ **headlamp** *or* ♦ **headlight** *n* (*Aut*) phare *m*. ♦ **headland** *n* promontoire *m*. ♦ **headline 1** *n* *[newspaper]* manchette *f*, gros titre *m*; (*TV*) grand titre; **it's in the ~lines in the papers** c'est en gros titre *or* en manchette dans les journaux; **to hit the ~lines*** faire les gros titres; **2** *vt* mettre en manchette. ♦ **headlong 1** *adv fall* la tête la première; *run, rush* à toute allure; **2** *adj fall etc* la tête la première; **~long flight** débandade *f*; **a ~long dash for** une ruée générale vers. ♦ **headman** *n* chef *m*. ♦ **headmaster** *n [school]* directeur *m*; *[lycée]* proviseur *m*. ♦ **headmistress** *n* directrice *f*. ♦ **head-on 1** *adj collision* de plein fouet; *confrontation* en face à face; **2** *adv collide* de plein fouet; *meet* face à face. ♦ **headphones** *npl* casque *m* (à écouteurs). ♦ **headquarters** *n* (*gen, Comm*) siège *m* central; (*Mil*) quartier *m* général. ♦ **headrest** *n* appui-tête *m*. ♦ **headroom** *n*: **there is not enough ~room** le toit n'est pas assez haut. ♦ **headscarf** *or*

♦ **headsquare** *n* foulard *m*. ♦ **headstand** *n*: **to do a ~stand** faire le poirier. ♦ **headstone** *n [grave]* pierre *f* tombale. ♦ **headstrong** *adj* (*obstinate*) têtu; (*rash*) impétueux. ♦ **headway** *n*: **to make ~way** (*gen*) faire des progrès (*with* avec); *[ship]* faire route. ♦ **headwind** *n* vent *m* contraire. ♦ **heady** *adj wine, perfume* capiteux; *success, pleasure* grisant.

heal [hi:l] **1** *vi* (**~ over, ~ up**) *[wound]* se cicatriser. **2** *vt* (*gen*) *person* guérir (*of* de); *wound* cicatriser; *differences* régler; *troubles* apaiser. ♦ **healer** *n* guérisseur *m*, -euse *f*. ♦ **healing 1** *n* guérison *f*; **2** *adj ointment* cicatrisant; *hands* de guérisseur.

health [helθ] **1** *n* santé *f*. **in good/bad ~** en bonne/mauvaise santé; **mental ~** santé mentale; **Ministry of H~** ministère *m* de la Santé publique; **to drink (to) sb's ~** boire à la santé de qn; **your ~!, good ~!** à votre santé! **2** *adj*: **~ centre** ≈ centre *m* médico-social; **~ foods** aliments *mpl* naturels; **~ food shop** magasin *m* diététique; **~ hazard** *or* **risk** risque *m* pour la santé; **~ insurance** assurance *f* maladie; **the H~ Service** ≈ la Sécurité sociale; **I got my specs on the H~ Service*** la Sécurité sociale m'a remboursé mes lunettes; **H~ Service doctor/nursing home** médecin/clinique conventionné(e); **~ visitor** ≈ infirmière *f* visiteuse. ♦ **healthful** *or* ♦ **health-giving** *adj air* salubre; *exercise etc* salutaire. ♦ **healthily** *adv* sainement. ♦ **healthy** *adj person, animal, plant* en bonne santé; *climate, air* salubre; *food, skin, surroundings* sain; *appetite* robuste; *exercise* salutaire; (*fig*) *economy, interest, attitude* sain; *respect, doubts* salutaire; **to make sth ~y** *or* **healthier** assainir qch.

heap [hi:p] **1** *n* tas *m*, monceau *m*. **~s of*** *money, books, jobs, people* des tas* de, des masses* de; **we've got ~s* of time** nous avons largement le temps. **2** *vt* (**~ up**) entasser, empiler (*on sth* sur qch). **to ~ gifts/praises** *etc* **on sb** couvrir qn de cadeaux/d'éloges *etc*; (*fig*) **to ~ coals of fire on sb** rendre le bien pour le mal à qn; **she ~ed (up) her plate with cakes** elle a empilé des gâteaux sur son assiette; (*Culin*) **~ed spoonful** grosse cuillerée.

hear [hɪəʳ] *pret, ptp* **heard** [hɜ:d] **1** *vt* **(a)** entendre. **I can't ~ you** je ne vous entends pas; **I heard him say** je l'ai entendu dire; **I heard sb come in** j'ai entendu qn entrer; **he was heard to say** on l'a entendu dire; **to make o.s. heard** se faire entendre; **he likes to ~ himself talk** il aime s'écouter parler; **to ~ him (talk), you'd think he was ...** à l'entendre, vous le prendriez pour ... . **(b)** (*learn*) entendre dire (*that* que); *news, facts* apprendre. **have you heard the rumour that ...?** avez-vous entendu dire que ...?; **I ~ you've been ill** il paraît que vous avez été malade; **I have heard it said that** j'ai entendu dire que; **I've heard tell of** j'ai entendu parler de; **have you heard the one about the Scotsman who ...** tu connais l'histoire de l'Écossais qui ... . **(c)** (*listen to*) *lecture etc* assister à; *mass, law case* entendre. **to ~ a child's lessons** faire répéter ses leçons à un enfant; (*excl*) **~, ~!** bravo!

2 *vi* (*gen*) entendre; (*get news*) recevoir *or* avoir des nouvelles (*from sb* de qn). **I ~ about him from his mother** j'ai de ses nouvelles par sa mère; **I've never heard of him** je ne le connais pas; **everyone has heard of him** tout le monde a entendu parler de lui; **he was never heard of again** on n'a jamais plus entendu parler de lui; **that's the first I've heard of it!** c'est la première fois que j'entends parler de ça!; **I won't ~ of you going there** je ne veux absolument pas que tu y ailles; **I wouldn't ~ of it!** pas question!

hear out *vt sep* écouter jusqu'au bout.

♦ **hearer** *n* auditeur *m*, -trice *f*. ♦ **hearing 1** *n* **(a)** (*sense*) ouïe *f*; **to have good ~ing** avoir l'oreille fine; **within ~ing (distance)** à portée de voix; **in my ~ing** en ma présence; **(b)** *[witness, evidence]* audition *f*; **give him a ~ing!** laissez-le parler!, écoutez ce qu'il a à dire!; **he was refused a ~ing** on a refusé de l'entendre; **(c)** (*meeting: of committee etc*) séance *f*; **2** *adj person* qui entend (bien); **~ing aid** appareil *m* acoustique. ♦ **hearsay 1** *n* ouï-dire *m inv*; **from ~say** par ouï-dire; **it's only ~say** ce ne sont que des rumeurs; **2** *adj report, account* fondé sur des ouï-dire; *evidence* sur la foi d'un tiers.

hearse [hɜ:s] *n* corbillard *m*.

heart [hɑ:t] **1** *n* **(a)** cœur *m* (*also fig*). **to have a weak ~** être cardiaque; **at ~** au fond; **a man after my own ~** un homme selon mon cœur; **he knew in his ~** il savait instinctivement; **in his ~ (of ~s) he thought ...** en son for intérieur il pensait ...; **with all my ~** de tout mon cœur; **from (the bottom of) one's ~** du fond du cœur; **to take sth to ~** prendre qch à cœur; **I hadn't the ~ to tell him** je n'ai pas eu le courage *or* le cœur de lui dire; **have a ~!*** pitié!*; **to eat/sleep to one's ~'s content** manger/dormir tout son content; **it did my ~ good to see them** cela m'a réchauffé le cœur de les voir; **~ and soul** corps et âme; **his ~ isn't in his work** il n'a pas le cœur à l'ouvrage; **to lose/take ~** perdre/prendre courage; **to be in good ~** avoir bon moral; **a ~ of gold/stone** un cœur d'or/de pierre; **his ~ is in the right place** il a bon cœur; **to lose one's ~ to sb** tomber amoureux de qn; **it is close to his ~** cela lui tient à cœur; **to set one's ~ on (doing) sth** vouloir à tout prix (faire) qch; **to wear one's ~ on one's sleeve** laisser voir ses sentiments; **his ~ was in his boots** il avait la mort dans l'âme; **my ~ sank** j'ai eu un coup au cœur; **she had her ~ in her mouth** son cœur battait la chamade; **to learn/know by ~** apprendre/savoir par cœur; **in the ~ of winter/the forest** au cœur de l'hiver/de la forêt; **the ~ of the matter** le fond du problème; **in the ~ of the country** en pleine campagne.

(b) (*Cards*) **~s** cœur *m*; **queen of ~s** dame *f* de cœur; **have you any ~s?** avez-vous du cœur?; **he played a ~** il a joué cœur.

2 *adj disease* de cœur; *surgery* du cœur. **~ attack** crise *f* cardiaque; (*Med*) **~ case** cardiaque *mf*; **~ complaint** maladie *f* de cœur; **to have a ~ condition** être cardiaque; **~ failure** arrêt *m* du cœur; **~ surgeon** chirurgien *m* cardiologue; **~ transplant** greffe *f* du cœur; **~ trouble** troubles *mpl* cardiaques.

♦ **heartache** *n* chagrin *m*. ♦ **heartbeat** *n* battement *m* de cœur. ♦ **heartbreak** *n* immense chagrin *m*. ♦ **heartbreaking** *adj* déchirant. ♦ **heartbroken** *adj*: **to be ~broken** avoir un immense chagrin, (*stronger*) avoir le cœur brisé; *[child]* avoir un gros chagrin. ♦ **heartburn** *n* (*Med*) brûlures *fpl* d'estomac. ♦ **heartburning** *n* (*ill feeling*) rancœur *f*; (*regret*) regrets *mpl*. ♦ **hearten** *vt* encourager. ♦ **heartening** *adj* encourageant. ♦ **heartfelt** *adj* sincère. ♦ **heartily** *adv say, welcome* chaleureusement; *laugh, work* de tout son cœur; *eat* avec appétit; *agree* absolument; *glad, tired* extrêmement. ♦ **heartless** *adj person* sans cœur; *treatment* cruel. ♦ **heartlessness** *n* manque *m* de cœur; cruauté *f*. ♦ **heart-lung machine** *n* cœur-poumon *m* (artificiel). ♦ **heartrending** *adj* déchirant, qui fend le cœur. ♦ **heart-searching** *n*: **after much ~-searching he ...** après s'être longuement interrogé, il ... . ♦ **heart-throb*** *n* idole *f*. ♦ **heart-to-heart 1** *adj, adv* à cœur ouvert; **2** *n*: **to have a ~-to-~*** parler à cœur ouvert. ♦ **heartwarming** *adj* qui réchauffe le cœur. ♦ **hearty** *adj welcome, approval* chaleureux; *laugh* franc; *meal* copieux; *appetite* solide; *kick, slap* bien senti; *person* (*healthy*) vigoureux, (*cheerful*) jovial; **to have a ~y dislike of sth** détester qch de tout son cœur.

hearth [hɑ:θ] *n* foyer *m*. **~ rug** devant *m* de foyer.

heat [hi:t] **1** *n* **(a)** (*gen, Phys*) chaleur *f*; *[fire,* *flames, sun]* ardeur *f*; **I can't stand ~** je ne supporte pas la chaleur; (*Culin*) **at low ~** à feu doux; (*Culin*) **lower the ~** réduire la chaleur; **in the ~ of** *day, afternoon* au plus chaud de; *battle, argument* dans le feu de; *departure etc* dans l'agitation de; **in the ~ of the moment** dans le feu de l'action; **to speak with some ~** parler avec feu; **in** *or* **on ~** *animal* en chaleur; **we had no ~ all day** nous avons été sans chauffage toute la journée; (*fig*) **to put the ~ on sb*** faire pression sur qn. **(b)** (*Sport*) éliminatoire *f*.

2 *adj*: **~ exhaustion** épuisement *m* dû à la chaleur; **~ haze** brume *f* de chaleur; **~ loss** perte *f* calorifique; (*Med*) **~ rash** irritation *f* (due à la chaleur); (*Med*) **~ treatment** thermothérapie *f*.

3 *vt* (**~ up**) chauffer; (*reheat*) réchauffer.

4 *vi* (**~ up**) *[liquids etc]* chauffer; *[room]* se réchauffer.

♦ **heated** *adj* (*lit*) chauffé; (*fig*) *argument* passionné; *words* vif; *person* échauffé; **to grow ~ed** s'échauffer. ♦ **heatedly** *adv* avec passion. ♦ **heater** *n* appareil *m* de chauffage. ♦ **heating** *n* chauffage *m*. ♦ **heatproof** *or* ♦ **heat-resistant** *adj material* résistant à la chaleur; *dish* allant au four. ♦ **heatstroke** *n* (*Med*) coup *m* de chaleur. ♦ **heatwave** *n* vague *f* de chaleur.

heath [hi:θ] *n* (*moorland*) lande *f*; (*plant*) bruyère *f*.

heathen ['hi:ðən] *adj, n* païen(ne) *m(f)*. ♦ **heathenish** *adj* (*pej*) de païen.

heather ['heðə^r] *n* bruyère *f*.

heave [hi:v] **1** *vt* (*lift*) lever *or* (*pull*) tirer *or* (*drag*) traîner avec effort; (*throw*) lancer. **to ~ a sigh** pousser un (gros) soupir. **2** *vi* **(a)** (*pant*) haleter; (*retch*) avoir des haut-le-cœur; (*vomit*) vomir; *[sea, chest, stomach]* se soulever. **(b)** (*pret, ptp* hove) *[ship]* **to ~ in(to) sight** poindre (à l'horizon), paraître; **to ~ to** se mettre en panne.

heaven ['hevn] *n* ciel *m*, paradis *m*. **to go to ~** aller au ciel *or* au paradis; **in ~** au ciel, au paradis; **in the seventh ~** au septième ciel; **~ forbid!*** surtout pas!; **~ knows what/when*** Dieu sait quoi/quand; **~ knows!*** Dieu seul le sait!; **(good) ~s!*** Seigneur!; **for ~'s sake*** (*pleading*) pour l'amour du ciel*; (*protesting*) zut alors!*; **it was ~*** c'était divin; **~ on earth** paradis sur terre; **the ~s opened** le ciel s'est mis à déverser des trombes d'eau. ♦ **heavenly** *adj* céleste; (*delightful*) divin. ♦ **heaven-sent** *adj* providentiel.

heavy ['hevɪ] **1** *adj* (*gen, also fig*) lourd (*with* de); *crop* abondant; *loss, sigh, sea, rain* gros (*before n*); *fog, features, underlining* épais; *eyes* battu; *day* chargé; *blow* violent; *book, film* indigeste; *humour, irony* peu subtil; *population, traffic* dense; *silence* pesant; *sky* couvert; *task* pénible. **~ vehicle** poids lourd *m*; **~ luggage** gros bagages *mpl*; **to make heavier** alourdir; **how ~ are you?** combien pesez-vous?; **to be a ~ drinker/smoker** *etc* boire/fumer *etc* beaucoup; **to be a ~ sleeper** avoir le sommeil profond; **the car is ~ on petrol** la voiture consomme beaucoup; **~ fighting** combats *mpl* acharnés; **~ gunfire** feu *m* nourri; **there were ~ casualties** il y a eu de nombreuses victimes *fpl*; (*Med*) **~ cold** gros rhume *m*; (*fig*) **it's ~ going** ça n'avance pas; **with a ~ heart** le cœur gros; (*fig*) **he made ~ weather of doing it** il a fait toute une histoire* pour le faire; **the ~ work** le gros travail; (*Ind etc*) **~ workers** travailleurs *mpl* de force.

2 *adv weigh, lie* lourd.

♦ **heavily** *adv load, tax, walk* lourdement; *underline* fortement; *sleep, sigh* profondément; *breathe* bruyamment; *move* avec difficulté; *lean* de tout son poids; *say* d'une voix accablée; *rain, snow* très fort; *drink, smoke* beaucoup; **to lose heavily** *[team]* se faire écraser; *[gambler]* perdre gros. ♦ **heavily-built** *adj* solidement bâti. ♦ **heavily-laden** *adj* (très) lourdement chargé. ♦ **heaviness** *n* pesanteur *f*, poids *m*. ♦ **heavy-duty** *adj* très résistant. ♦ **heavy-handed** *adj* (*clumsy*) maladroit; (*harsh*) dur. ♦ **heavy-hearted** *adj*: **to be ~-hearted** avoir le cœur gros. ♦ **heavyweight 1** *n* (*Boxing*) poids lourd; (*: *influential person*) personne *f* de poids; **2** *adj* (*Boxing*) poids lourd *inv*; *cloth* lourd.

Hebrew ['hi:bru:] **1** *adj* hébreu (*m only*), hébraïque. **2** *n* Hébreu *m*; (*Ling*) hébreu *m*.

Hebrides ['hebrɪdi:z] *n* Hébrides *fpl*.

heckle ['hekl] *vti* (*shout*) chahuter (*pour troubler l'orateur*); (*interrupt*) interrompre bruyamment. ♦ **heckler** *n* interrupteur *m*, -trice *f*. ♦ **heckling** *n* chahut *m*; interpellations *fpl*.

hectic ['hektɪk] *adj life, day (busy)* très bousculé, (*eventful*) très mouvementé; *traffic* terrible; *journey* très mouvementé. **I've had a ~ rush** ça a vraiment été une course folle.

hector ['hektə^r] *vt* rudoyer. ♦ **hectoring** *adj* autoritaire.

hedge [hedʒ] **1** *n* haie *f*. **beech ~** haie *f* de hêtres. **2** *vi* (*in answering*) répondre évasivement; (*in explaining etc*) expliquer *etc* avec des détours. **3** *vt*: **~d with difficulties** entouré de difficultés; **to ~ one's bet** se couvrir (*fig*). ♦ **hedgehog** *n* hérisson *m*. ♦ **hedgehop** *vi* (*Aviat*) voler en rase-mottes. ♦ **hedgerow** *n* haie *f*.

hedonism ['hi:dənɪzəm] *n* hédonisme *m*. ♦ **hedonist** *adj, n* hédoniste (*mf*).

heebie-jeebies* ['hi:bɪ'dʒi:bɪz] *npl*: **to have the ~** (*shaking*) avoir la tremblote*; (*fright, nerves*) avoir la frousse*; **it gives me the ~** (*revulsion*) ça me donne la chair de poule; (*fright*) ça me donne la frousse*.

heed [hi:d] **1** *vt* faire attention à, tenir compte de. **2** *n*: **to take ~ of, to pay ~ to** faire attention à, tenir compte de. ♦ **heedless** *adj* (*not thinking*) étourdi; (*not caring*) insouciant; **~less of** sans se soucier de. ♦ **heedlessly** *adv* étourdiment; avec insouciance.

heel[1] [hi:l] **1** *n* **(a)** talon *m*. **at** *or* **on sb's ~s** sur les talons de qn; **to take to one's ~s** prendre ses jambes à son cou; **to turn on one's ~** tourner les talons; (*to dog*) **~!** au pied!; **to come to ~** venir au pied; (*fig*) **to bring sb to ~** rappeler qn à l'ordre. **(b)** (*: *unpleasant person*) chameau* *m*. **2** *vt ball* talonner. (*fig*) **well-~ed*** plein de sous*.

heel[2] [hi:l] *vi* (**~ over**) *[ship]* gîter; *[truck, structure]* pencher dangereusement.

hefty* ['heftɪ] *adj person* costaud*; *parcel* lourd; *part, piece, price* gros (*before n*).

heifer ['hefə^r] *n* génisse *f*.

height [haɪt] *n* **(a)** *[building]* hauteur *f*; *[person]* taille *f*; *[mountain, plane]* altitude *f*. **what ~ are you?** combien mesurez-vous?; **he is 1 metre 80 in ~** il fait 1 m 80; **of average ~** de taille moyenne; **he drew himself up to his full ~** il s'est dressé de toute sa hauteur; **a building 40 metres in ~** un bâtiment de 40 mètres de haut; **~ above sea level** altitude au-dessus du niveau de la mer; (*high ground*) **the ~s** les sommets *mpl*. **(b)** *[success]* apogée *m*; *[absurdity, ill manners]* comble *m*. **at the ~ of** *storm, battle etc* au cœur de; **at the ~ of his power** au summum de sa puissance; **at the ~ of summer/the season** en plein été/pleine saison; **the ~ of fashion** la toute dernière mode; **to be at its ~** *[fair, party]* battre son plein; *[excitement etc]* être à son maximum. ♦ **heighten** *vt* (*gen*) intensifier; *flavour* relever.

heir [ɛə^r] *n* héritier *m* (*to* de). **~ apparent** héritier présomptif. ♦ **heiress** *n* héritière *f*. ♦ **heirloom** *n* héritage *m*; (*picture/jewel etc*) **a family ~loom** un tableau/bijou *etc* de famille.

held [held] *pret, ptp of* **hold**.

helicopter ['helɪkɒptə^r] **1** *n* hélicoptère *m*. **2** *adj patrol, rescue* en hélicoptère; *pilot* d'hélicoptère. ♦ **heliport** *n* héliport *m*.

helium ['hi:lɪəm] *n* hélium *m*.

hell [hel] *n* enfer *m*. **in ~** en enfer; **all ~ was let loose** ça a été infernal; **come ~ or high water** quoi qu'il arrive; **to go ~ for leather** aller à un train d'enfer; **a ~ of a noise*** un boucan du diable*; **a ~ of a lot of*** tout un tas de; **we had a ~ of a time*** (*bad*) ça n'a pas été marrant*; (*good*) ça a été du tonnerre*; **to run** *etc* **like ~*** courir *etc* comme un fou; **to give sb ~*** (*make his life a misery*) faire mener une vie infernale à qn; (*scold*) passer une engueulade‡ à qn; **oh ~!*** flûte!*; **to ~ with it!*** la barbe!*; **go to ~!*** va te faire voir!*; **what the ~ does he want?*** qu'est-ce qu'il peut bien vouloir?; **why/where** *etc* **the ~*** ... mais bon sang*, pourquoi/où est-ce que ... . ♦ **hellbent*** *adj* acharné (*on doing* à faire). ♦ **hellish** *adj* diabolique; (*: *unpleasant*) infernal. ♦ **hellishly*** *adv* vachement‡.

hello [hə'ləʊ] *excl* = **hallo.**

helm [helm] *n* (*Naut*) barre *f*. **to be at the ~** (*also fig*) tenir la barre. ♦ **helmsman** *n* timonier *m*.

helmet ['helmɪt] *n* casque *m*.

help [help] **1** *n* **(a)** aide *f*, secours *m*. (*excl*) **~!** au secours!, (*in dismay*) mon Dieu!; **thanks for your ~** merci de votre aide; **with the ~ of** *person* avec l'aide de; *tool etc* à l'aide de; **to shout for ~** appeler au secours *or* à l'aide; **to go to sb's ~** aller au secours de qn; **to be of ~ to sb** rendre service à qn; **he's a great ~ to me** il m'aide beaucoup; **she has no ~ in the house** elle n'a pas de femme de ménage; **we need more ~ in the shop** il nous faut davantage de personnel au magasin; **he's beyond ~** on ne peut plus rien pour lui; **there's no ~ for it** il n'y a rien à faire. **(b)** (*servant*) domestique *mf*; (*charwoman*) femme *f* de ménage; (*in shop etc*) employé(e) *m(f)*.

2 *vt* **(a)** aider (*sb to do* qn à faire; *sb with sth* qn à faire qch). **to ~ sb with his luggage** aider qn à porter ses bagages; **he got his brother to ~ him** il s'est fait aider par son frère; **that doesn't ~ much** cela ne sert pas à grand-chose; **that won't ~ you** cela ne vous servira à rien; **so ~ me God!** je le jure devant Dieu!; **this money will ~ to save the church** cet argent contribuera à sauver l'église; (*in shops etc*) **can I ~ you?** vous désirez?; **he is ~ing the police with their inquiries** il est en train de répondre aux questions de la police; **to ~ sb across/down** *etc* aider qn à traverser/à descendre *etc*; **to ~ sb on/off with his coat** aider qn à mettre/à enlever son manteau. **(b)** servir. **she ~ed him to potatoes** elle l'a servi de pommes de terre; **~ yourself** servez-vous (*to* de); **he's ~ed himself to my pencil*** il m'a piqué* mon crayon. **(c) I couldn't ~ laughing** je n'ai pas pu m'empêcher de rire; **it can't be ~ed** tant pis!, on n'y peut rien!; **I can't ~ it if ...** je n'y peux rien si ...; **not if I can ~ it!** sûrement pas!; **he won't come if I can ~ it** je vais faire tout mon possible pour l'empêcher de venir; **he can't ~ being stupid** ce n'est pas de sa faute s'il est idiot; **don't say more than you can ~** n'en dites pas plus qu'il ne faut.

help out 1 *vi* aider, donner un coup de main. **2** *vt sep*: **would £5 ~ you out?** est-ce que 5 livres pourraient vous être utiles?

♦ **helper** *n* aide *mf*, assistant(e) *m(f)*. ♦ **helpful** *adj person* (*willing*) obligeant, (*useful*) qui est d'un grand secours; *book, gadget, advice* utile. ♦ **helpfully** *adv* avec obligeance. ♦ **helpfulness** *n* obligeance *f*. ♦ **helping 1** *n* portion *f*; **to take a second ~ing of sth** reprendre de qch; **I've had three ~ings** j'en ai repris deux fois; **2** *adj:* **to lend a ~ing hand** donner un coup de main (*to* à). ♦ **helpless** *adj* (*mentally, morally*) impuissant; (*physically*) impotent; (*powerless*) sans ressource; **she is a ~less invalid** elle est complètement impotente; **~less with laughter** malade de rire. ♦ **helplessly** *adv struggle* en vain; *try, agree* désespérément; *lie, remain* sans pouvoir bouger; *say* d'un ton d'impuissance; **to laugh ~lessly** être pris d'un fou rire. ♦ **helplessness** *n* impuissance *f*; impotence *f*.

helter-skelter ['heltə'skeltəʳ] **1** *adv* à la débandade. **2** *n* (*rush*) débandade *f*; (*in fairground*) toboggan *m*.

hem [hem] **1** *n* (*part doubled over*) ourlet *m*; (*edge*) bord *m*. **I've let the ~ down on my skirt** j'ai rallongé ma jupe.

2 *vt* ourler.

hem in *vt sep* (*physically*) cerner; *[rules etc]* entraver. **I feel ~med in** ça m'oppresse.

hem(a) ... ['hiːm(ə)] *pref* (*esp US*) = **hæm(a)...** .

hemisphere ['hemɪsfɪəʳ] *n* hémisphère *m*. **the northern/southern ~** l'hémisphère nord/sud.

hemlock ['hemlɒk] *n* ciguë *f*.

hemp [hemp] *n* chanvre *m*.

hen [hen] **1** *n* poule *f*; (*female bird*) femelle *f*. **2** *adj*: **~ bird** oiseau *m* femelle; **~ party*** réunion *f* de femmes *or* filles. ♦ **henhouse** *n* poulailler *m*. ♦ **henpecked** *adj* dominé par sa femme.

hence [hens] *adv* (*therefore*) d'où, de là; (*from now on*) d'ici. ♦ **henceforth** *or* ♦ **henceforward** *adv* dorénavant, désormais.

henchman ['hentʃmən] *n* acolyte *m* (*pej*).

henna ['henə] *n* henné *m*.

hepatitis [ˌhepə'taɪtɪs] *n* hépatite *f*.

her [hɜːʳ] **1** *pers pron* **(a)** (*direct*) (*unstressed*) la; (*before vowel*) l'; (*stressed*) elle. **I see ~** je la vois; **I have seen ~** je l'ai vue; **I have never seen HER** elle, je ne l'ai jamais vue. **(b)** (*indirect*) lui. **I give ~ the book** je lui donne le livre; **I'm speaking to ~** je lui parle. **(c)** (*after prep etc*) elle. **I am thinking of ~** je pense à elle; **without ~** sans elle; **if I were ~** si j'étais elle; **it's ~** c'est elle; **younger than ~** plus jeune qu'elle. **2** *poss adj* son, sa, ses. **~ book** son livre; **~ table** sa table; **~ friend** son ami(e); **~ clothes** ses vêtements.

♦ **hers** *poss pron* le sien, la sienne, les siens, les siennes; **this book is ~s** ce livre est à elle, ce livre est le sien; **a friend of ~s** un de ses amis (à elle); **is this poem ~s?** ce poème est-il d'elle?; (*pej*) **that car of ~s** sa fichue* voiture. ♦ **herself** *pers pron* (*reflexive: direct and indirect*) se; (*emphatic*) elle-même; (*after prep*) elle; **she has hurt ~self** elle s'est blessée; **she said to ~self** elle s'est dit; **she told me ~self** elle me l'a dit elle-même; **she kept 3 for ~self** elle s'en est réservé 3; **he asked her for a photo of ~self** il lui a demandé une photo d'elle; **(all) by ~self** toute seule; **she is not ~self** elle n'est pas dans son état normal.

herald ['herəld] **1** *n* héraut *m*. **2** *vt* annoncer. ♦ **heraldic** [he'rældɪk] *adj* héraldique. ♦ **heraldry** ['herəldrɪ] *n* héraldique *f*.

herb [hɜːb] *n* herbe *f*. (*Culin*) **~s** fines herbes. **2** *adj*: **~ garden** jardin *m* d'herbes aromatiques. ♦ **herbaceous** *adj* herbacé; **~aceous border** bordure *f* de plantes herbacées. ♦ **herbal 1** *adj* d'herbes; **2** *n* herbier *m*. ♦ **herbalist** *n* herboriste *mf*. ♦ **herbivorous** *adj* herbivore.

herd [hɜːd] **1** *n* (*lit, fig*) troupeau *m*. **2** *adj*: **~ instinct** instinct *m* grégaire. **3** *vt* diriger.

herd together 1 *vi* s'attrouper. **2** *vt sep* rassembler en troupeau.

here [hɪəʳ] **1** *adv* **(a)** (*place*) ici. **come ~** venez ici; (*at roll call*) **~!** présent!; **~ I am** me voici; **~ is my brother** voici mon frère; **~ are the others** voici les autres; (*bringing sth*) **~ we are!** voici!; (*giving sth*) **~ you are!** tenez!; **~ come my friends** voici mes amis qui arrivent; **he's ~ at last** il est enfin arrivé; **spring is ~** c'est le printemps; **my sister ~ says ...** ma sœur que voici dit ...; **this man ~ saw it** cet homme-ci l'a vu; **~'s to you!** à la vôtre!; **~'s to your success!** à votre succès!; **about** *or* **around ~** par ici; **put it in ~** mettez-le ici; **come in ~ please** par ici s'il vous plaît; **over ~** ici; **it's cold up ~** il fait froid ici; **up to** *or* **down to ~** jusqu'ici; **from ~ to there** d'ici jusqu'à là-bas; **it's 10 km from ~ to Paris** il y a 10 km d'ici à Paris; **Mr Smith**

is not ~ **just now** M. Smith n'est pas là *or* ici en ce moment; **are you there? – yes I'm ~** vous êtes là? – oui je suis là; ~ **and there** par-ci par-là; ~, **there and everywhere** un peu partout; (*fig*) **it's neither ~ nor there** tout cela n'a aucune importance; ~ **goes!*** allons-y!; ~ **and now** en ce moment précis; **the ~ and now** le présent; ~ **below** ici-bas; ~ **lies** ci-gît. **(b)** (*time*) alors, à ce moment-là.

2 *excl* tenez!; (*protesting*) écoutez!

♦ **hereabouts** *adv* près d'ici. ♦ **hereafter 1** *adv* après; **2** *n* au-delà *m*. ♦ **hereby** *adv* par la présente. ♦ **hereupon** *adv* là-dessus. ♦ **herewith** *adv*: **I am sending you ~with** je vous envoie ci-joint *or* sous ce pli.

heredity [hɪ'redɪtɪ] *n* hérédité *f*. ♦ **hereditary** *adj* héréditaire.

heresy ['herəsɪ] *n* hérésie *f*. **an act of ~** une hérésie. ♦ **heretic** *n* hérétique *mf*. ♦ **heretical** [hɪ'retɪkəl] *adj* hérétique.

heritage ['herɪtɪdʒ] *n* patrimoine *m*.

hermetic [hɜː'metɪk] *adj* hermétique. ♦ **hermetically** *adv* hermétiquement; **~ally sealed** fermé hermétiquement.

hermit ['hɜːmɪt] *n* ermite *m*.

hernia ['hɜːnɪə] *n* hernie *f*.

hero ['hɪərəʊ] *n* héros *m*. ♦ **heroic** [hɪ'rəʊɪk] *adj* héroïque. ♦ **heroically** *adv* héroïquement. ♦ **heroics** *npl* (*pej*) (*words*) grandiloquence *f*; (*deeds*) comédie* *f*. ♦ **heroine** ['herəʊɪn] *n* héroïne *f* (*femme*). ♦ **heroism** ['herəʊɪzəm] *n* héroïsme *m*. ♦ **hero-worship 1** *n* culte *m*; **2** *vt* avoir un culte pour.

heroin ['herəʊɪn] *n* héroïne *f* (*drogue*). ~ **addict** héroïnomane *mf*.

heron ['herən] *n* héron *m*.

herpes ['hɜːpiːz] *n* herpès *m*.

herring ['herɪŋ] *n* hareng *m*. ♦ **herringbone (pattern)** *n* chevrons *mpl*.

hesitate ['hezɪteɪt] *vi* hésiter (*over, about, at* sur, devant; *to do* à faire). ♦ **hesitancy** *n* hésitation *f*. ♦ **hesitant** *adj* hésitant; **to be hesitant about doing** hésiter à faire. ♦ **hesitantly** *adv* avec hésitation; *speak, suggest* d'une voix hésitante. ♦ **hesitation** *n* hésitation *f*; **I have no hesitation in saying** je n'hésite pas à dire.

hessian ['hesɪən] *n* toile *f* de jute.

heterogeneous ['hetərəʊ'dʒiːnɪəs] *adj* hétérogène.

heterosexual ['hetərəʊ'seksjʊəl] *adj, n* hétérosexuel(le) *m(f)*.

het up* ['het'ʌp] *adj* agité (*about* par).

hew [hjuː] *pret* **hewed**, *ptp* **hewn** *or* **hewed** *vt stone* tailler; *wood* couper; *coal* abattre. **to ~ sth out of wood** *etc* tailler qch dans du bois *etc*.

hex [heks] **1** *n* sort *m*. **2** *vt* jeter un sort sur.

hexagon ['heksəgən] *n* hexagone *m*. ♦ **hexagonal** [heks'ægənəl] *adj* hexagonal.

heyday ['heɪdeɪ] *n [thing]* âge *m* d'or. **in his ~** à l'apogée de sa gloire.

hi* [haɪ] *excl* hé!; (*: *greeting*) salut!*

hiatus [haɪ'eɪtəs] *n* lacune *f*.

hibernate ['haɪbəneɪt] *vi* hiberner. ♦ **hibernation** *n* hibernation *f*.

hiccough, hiccup ['hɪkʌp] **1** *n* hoquet *m*. **to have ~s** avoir le hoquet. **2** *vi* hoqueter.

hide[1] [haɪd] *pret* **hid**, *ptp* **hidden 1** *vt* (*gen*) cacher (*from sb* à qn); *feelings* dissimuler (*from sb* à qn). **to ~ one's face** se cacher le visage; **hidden from sight** dérobé aux regards, caché; (*fig*) **to ~ one's light under a bushel** cacher ses talents. **2** *vi* (**~ away, ~ out**) se cacher (*from sb* de qn). (*fig*) **he's hiding behind his boss** il se réfugie derrière son patron. ♦ **hide-and-(go-)seek** *n* cache-cache *m*. ♦ **hideaway** *or* ♦ **hideout** *n* cachette *f*. ♦ **hiding**[1] **1** *n*: **to be in hiding** se tenir caché; **to go into hiding** se cacher; **2** *adj*: **hiding place** cachette *f*.

hide[2] [haɪd] **1** *n* (*skin*) peau *f*; (*leather*) cuir *m*. **2** *adj chair etc* de cuir. ♦ **hidebound** *adj* borné.

hideous ['hɪdɪəs] *adj sight, person* hideux; *crime* atroce; *disappointment* terrible. ♦ **hideously** *adv* hideusement; atrocement; terriblement.

hiding[2] ['haɪdɪŋ] *n* correction *f*, raclée *f*. **to give sb a good ~** donner une bonne correction à qn.

hierarchy ['haɪərɑːkɪ] *n* hiérarchie *f*.

hieroglyph ['haɪərəglɪf], **hieroglyphic** [ˌhaɪərə'glɪfɪk] *n* hiéroglyphe *m*.

hi-fi ['haɪ'faɪ] (*abbr of* **high fidelity**) **1** *n* **(a)** hi-fi *f inv*, haute fidélité *inv*. **(b)** (*gramophone/radio*) chaîne *f*/radio *f* hi-fi *inv*.

2 *adj* hi-fi *inv*. ~ **equipment** *or* **system** chaîne *f* (hi-fi).

higgledy-piggledy* ['hɪgldɪ'pɪgldɪ] *adv* pêle-mêle.

high [haɪ] **1** *adj* **(a)** (*gen*) haut. **building 40 metres ~** bâtiment de 40 mètres de haut, bâtiment qui a *or* fait 40 mètres de haut; **how ~ is that tower?** quelle est la hauteur de cette tour?; **when he was so ~*** quand il était grand comme ça; ~ **cheekbones** pommettes saillantes; (*Sport*) ~ **jump** saut *m* en hauteur; **he's for the ~ jump*** il est bon pour une engueulade‡; ~ **chair** chaise *f* haute (*d'enfant*); (*fig*) **on one's ~ horse** sur ses grands chevaux; **at ~ tide** *or* **water** à marée haute.

(b) *frequency, latitude, tension, pressure, official* haut (*before n*); *speed, value, respect* grand (*before n*); *fever* fort (*before n*); *complexion, colour* vif; *polish* brillant; *wind* violent; *salary, number, rent, price* élevé; *sound, voice* aigu; (*Mus*) *note* haut; *character, ideal* noble; (*Culin*) *game, meat* faisandé; *butter* rance; (‡: *intoxicated*) parti*. ~‡ **on drugs/hashish** défoncé‡ par la drogue/au hachisch; **in the ~est degree** au plus haut degré; **to buy sth at a ~ price** acheter qch cher; (*lit, fig*) **to pay a ~ price for sth** payer qch cher; **to have a ~ old time*** s'amuser follement; ~ **altar** maître-autel *m*; **H~ Church** Haute Église *f*; **H~ Mass** grand-messe *f*; ~ **priest** grand prêtre *m*; (*fig*) **to leave sb ~ and dry** laisser qn en plan*; **to be ~ and mighty*** se donner de grands airs; (*Mil*) ~ **command** haut commandement *m*; ~ **commissioner** haut commissaire *m*; (*Jur*) ~ **court** cour *f* suprême; ~ **explosive** explosif *m* puissant; **to have ~ jinks*** se payer du bon temps*; ~ **life** grande vie *f*; ~ **noon** plein midi; ~ **school** (*Brit*) lycée *m*; (*US*) collège *m* d'enseignement secondaire; **on the ~ seas** en haute mer; ~ **society** haute société *f*; ~ **spirits** entrain *m*; **the ~ spot** *[evening, show]* le clou; *[visit, holiday]* le grand moment; **to hit the ~ spots*** faire la noce* (*dans un night-club etc*); (*lit, fig*) **to play for ~ stakes** jouer gros jeu; ~ **street** *[village]* grand-rue *f*; *[town]* rue principale; **in ~ summer** au cœur de l'été; ~ **table** table *f* d'honneur; (*Univ*) table des professeurs; ~ **tea** goûter *m* dînatoire; ~ **treason** haute trahison *f*.

2 *adv rise, float, be, aim* haut; *fly etc* à haute altitude. ~ **up** en haut; **~er up** plus haut; **~er and ~er** de plus en plus haut; ~ **above our heads** bien au-dessus de nos têtes; **to go as ~ as 200 francs** monter jusqu'à 200 F; **to hunt ~ and low** chercher partout; **to hold one's head up ~** avoir la tête haute; (*fig*) **to fly ~** voir grand, viser haut.

3 *n* **(a) on ~** en haut. **(b)** (*record*) **a new ~** un nouveau record.

♦ **highball** *n* whisky *m* à l'eau (avec de la glace). ♦ **highbrow 1** *n* intellectuel(le) *m(f)*; **2** *adj interests* intellectuel; *music* pour intellectuels. ♦ **high-class** *adj hotel, food* de premier ordre; *neighbourhood, flat, publicity* (de) grand standing; *person* du grand monde. ♦ **higher 1** *adj* supérieur (*than* à); **2** *adv* plus haut. ♦ **high-fidelity** *adj* haute fidélité *inv*. ♦ **high-flier** *n* ambitieux *m*, -euse *f*; (*gifted*) doué(e) *m(f)*. ♦ **high-flown** *adj* ampoulé. ♦ **high-flying** *adj aircraft* volant à haute altitude; *person* ambitieux. ♦ **high-frequency** *adj* de *or* à haute fréquence.

♦ **high-grade** *adj* de haute qualité. ♦ **high-handed** *adj* tyrannique. ♦ **high-handedly** *adv* très autoritairement. ♦ **high-heeled** *adj* à hauts talons. ♦ **highjack** *etc* = **hijack** *etc*. ♦ **highlands** *npl* régions *fpl* montagneuses. ♦ **high-level** *adj talks* à très haut niveau. ♦ **highlight** **1** *n* (*Art*) rehaut *m*; (*in hair*) reflet *m*; (*fig: evening etc*) clou *m*; *[match etc]* instant *m* le plus marquant; **2** *vt* mettre en lumière. ♦ **highly** *adv pleased, interesting* extrêmement; *recommended* chaudement; *pay* très bien; *season* fortement; **~ly coloured** *object* haut en couleur; *description etc* exagéré; **~ly strung** nerveux; **to speak/think ~ly of** dire/penser beaucoup de bien de. ♦ **high-minded** *adj person* de caractère élevé; *ambition* noble. ♦ **high-necked** *adj* à col haut. ♦ **highness** *n*: **Your H~ness** Votre Altesse *f*. ♦ **high-pitched** *adj* aigu. ♦ **high-powered** *adj car* très puissant; *person* très important. ♦ **high-pressure** *adj* à haute pression; (*Met*) de hautes pressions; (*fig*) *salesman* de choc*. ♦ **high-priced** *adj* coûteux, cher. ♦ **high-principled** *adj* qui a des principes élevés. ♦ **high-ranking official** *n* haut fonctionnaire *m*. ♦ **high-rise block** *n* tour *f* (d'habitation). ♦ **highroad** *n* grand-route *f*. ♦ **high-sounding** *adj* sonore, grandiloquent (*pej*). ♦ **high-speed** *adj* ultra-rapide; *lens* à obturation ultra-rapide. ♦ **high-spirited** *adj person* plein d'entrain; *horse* fougueux. ♦ **high-up** **1** *adj person, post* haut placé; **2** *n* (*) grosse légume* *f*. ♦ **highway** *n* grande route *f*; **public ~way, the king's** *or* **queen's ~way** la voie publique; **through the ~ways and byways of Sussex** par tous les chemins du Sussex; **the ~way code** le code de la route. ♦ **highwayman** *n* bandit *m* de grand chemin.

hijack ['haɪdʒæk] **1** *vt* détourner (*par la force*). **2** *n* détournement *m*. ♦ **hijacker** *n [plane]* pirate *m* (de l'air); *[coach, train, truck]* gangster *m*. ♦ **hijacking** *n* détournement *m*.

hike [haɪk] **1** *n* excursion *f* à pied; (*Mil, Sport*) marche *f* à pied. **to go on** *or* **for a ~** faire une excursion à pied. **2** *vi* aller à pied (*to* à). **to go hiking** faire des excursions. ♦ **hiker** *n* excursionniste *mf* (*à pied*).

hilarious [hɪ'lɛərɪəs] *adj* (*merry*) hilare; (*funny*) désopilant. ♦ **hilarity** *n* hilarité *f*.

hill [hɪl] *n* colline *f*; (*slope*) côte *f*, pente *f*. **up ~ and down dale** par monts et par vaux; **as old as the ~s** vieux comme les chemins; **this car is not good on ~s** cette voiture ne grimpe pas bien. ♦ **hillbilly music** *n* musique *f* folk *inv*. ♦ **hillock** *n* petite colline. ♦ **hillside** *n* coteau *m*; **on the ~side** à flanc de coteau. ♦ **hilltop** *n*: **on the ~top** en haut de la colline. ♦ **hilly** *adj* accidenté.

hilt [hɪlt] *n [sword]* poignée *f*, garde *f*. **up to the ~** *be in trouble, debt, involved* jusqu'au cou; *back sb* quoiqu'il arrive; *mortgage* au maximum.

him [hɪm] *pers pron* **(a)** (*direct*) (*unstressed*) le; (*before vowel*) l'; (*stressed*) lui. **I see ~** je le vois; **I have seen ~** je l'ai vu; **I've never seen HIM** lui, je ne l'ai jamais vu. **(b)** (*indirect*) lui. **I give ~ the book** je lui donne le livre; **I'm speaking to ~** je lui parle. **(c)** (*after prep etc*) lui. **I am thinking of ~** je pense à lui; **without ~** sans lui; **if I were ~** si j'étais lui; **it's ~** c'est lui; **younger than ~** plus jeune que lui. ♦ **himself** *pers pron* (*reflexive: direct and indirect*) se; (*emphatic*) lui-même; (*after prep*) lui. **he has hurt ~self** il s'est blessé; **he said to ~self** il s'est dit; **he told me ~self** il me l'a dit lui-même; **he kept 3 for ~self** il s'en est réservé 3; **she asked him for a photo of ~self** elle lui a demandé une photo de lui; **(all) by ~self** tout seul; **he is not ~self** il n'est pas dans son état normal.

hind [haɪnd] *adj*: **~ legs, ~ feet** pattes *fpl* de derrière; **she would talk the ~ legs off a donkey*** c'est un vrai moulin à paroles*. ♦ **hindquarters** *npl* arrière-train *m*. ♦ **hindsight** *n*: **with the benefit of ~sight** rétrospectivement.

hinder ['hɪndəʳ] *vt* (*obstruct*) gêner; (*delay*) retarder; (*prevent*) empêcher (*sb from doing* qn de faire). ♦ **hindrance** *n*: **to be a hindrance to sb/sth** gêner qn/qch.

Hindu ['hɪn'du:] **1** *adj* hindou. **2** *n* Hindou(e) *m(f)*. ♦ **Hinduism** *n* hindouisme *m*.

hinge [hɪndʒ] **1** *n [door]* gond *m*; *[box, stamp]* charnière *f*. **the door came off its ~s** la porte est sortie de ses gonds. **2** *vi* (*fig*) dépendre (*on* de). ♦ **hinged** *adj lid* à charnières; *counter flap* relevable.

hint [hɪnt] **1** *n* allusion *f*, insinuation *f* (*pej*). **to drop a ~** faire une allusion (*that* que); **he dropped me a ~ that** il m'a fait comprendre que; **gentle/broad ~** allusion discrète/à peine voilée; **he knows how to take a ~** il comprend à demi-mot; **I can take a ~** (ça va) j'ai compris; (*in guessing etc*) **give me a ~** donne-moi une indication; **he gave no ~ of his feelings** il n'a donné aucune indication sur ce qu'il ressentait; **~s for travellers/on maintenance** conseils *mpl* aux voyageurs/d'entretien; **a ~ of garlic** un soupçon d'ail; **there was not the slightest ~ of a dispute** il n'y a pas eu l'ombre d'une dispute; **a ~ of sadness** un je ne sais quoi de mélancolique. **2** *vt* insinuer, laisser comprendre (*that* que). **he ~ed to me that** il m'a laissé comprendre que. **3** *vi*: **to ~ at sth** faire (une) allusion à qch; **what are you ~ing at?** qu'est-ce que vous voulez dire par là?

hip¹ [hɪp] **1** *n* (*Anat*) hanche *f*. **with one's hands on one's ~s** les mains sur les hanches; **to break one's ~** se casser le col du fémur. **2** *adj*: **~ bath** bain *m* de siège. **~ flask** flacon *m* plat (pour la poche), flasque *f*; **~ joint** articulation *f* iliaque; **~ pocket** poche *f* revolver; **~ size** tour *m* de hanches. ♦ **hipbone** *n* os *m* iliaque. ♦ **hipsters** *npl* pantalon *m* taille basse.

hip² [hɪp] *n* (*Bot*) gratte-cul *m*.

hippie* ['hɪpɪ] *adj, n* hippie (*mf*).

hippopotamus [,hɪpə'pɒtəməs] *n*, *pl* **-mi** [-maɪ] hippopotame *m*.

hire ['haɪəʳ] **1** *n* location *f*; (*price*) prix *m* de la location. **for ~** à louer; (*on taxi*) 'libre'; **on ~** en location. **2** *adj*: **~ purchase** achat *m* à crédit; **on ~ purchase** à crédit. **3** *vt* **(a)** *thing* louer; *person* engager. **~d man** ouvrier *m* payé à l'heure; **~d car** voiture *f* louée. **(b)** (**~ out**) donner en location.

his [hɪz] **1** *poss adj* son, sa, ses. **~ book** son livre; **~ table** sa table; **~ friend** son ami(e); **~ clothes** ses vêtements. **2** *poss pron* le sien, la sienne, les siens, les siennes. **this book is ~** ce livre est à lui; **a friend of ~** un de ses amis (à lui); **is this poem ~?** ce poème est-il de lui?; (*pej*) **that car of ~** sa fichue* voiture.

hiss [hɪs] **1** *vti* siffler. **2** *n* sifflement *m*; (*Theat etc*) sifflet *m*.

history ['hɪstərɪ] *n* histoire *f*. **to make ~, to go down in ~** *[person]* entrer dans l'histoire (*for* pour); *[event, day, decision]* être historique; **he has a ~ of psychiatric disorders** il a dans son passé des désordres psychiatriques; **medical ~** passé *m* médical. ♦ **historian** *n* historien(ne) *m(f)*. ♦ **historic(al)** *adj* historique.

histrionic [,hɪstrɪ'ɒnɪk] *adj* (*pej*) de cabotin; (*gen*) théâtral; *talent* dramatique. ♦ **histrionics** *npl* (*pej*) airs *mpl* dramatiques.

hit [hɪt] (*vb: pret, ptp* **hit**) **1** *n* **(a)** (*stroke, blow*) coup *m*; (*Baseball/Tennis etc*) coup de batte/raquette *etc*. (*fig*) **that's a ~ at me** c'est moi qui suis visé. **(b)** (*as opp to miss*) coup *m* réussi, beau coup. **3 ~s and 3 misses** 3 succès *mpl* et 3 échecs; **direct ~** coup dans le mille. **(c)** (*song/book/film etc*) chanson *f*/livre *m*/film *m* à succès. **to make a ~ of sth*** réussir (pleinement) qch; **to make a ~ with sb*** faire une grosse impression sur qn; **to be**

a big ~ avoir un énorme succès.

2 *adj song, show* à succès. ~ **parade** hit parade *m*.

3 *vt* **(a)** (*strike*) frapper; (*knock against*) heurter, cogner; (*collide with*) heurter, entrer en collision avec; (*reach*) atteindre; (*hurt, annoy*) affecter, toucher. **he** ~ **me!** il m'a frappé!; **his father used to** ~ **him** son père le battait; **to** ~ **sb a blow** porter un coup à qn; (*fig*) **to** ~ **a man when he's down** frapper un homme à terre; **to** ~ **one's head against sth** se cogner *or* se heurter la tête contre qch; **his head** ~ **the pavement** sa tête a donné contre le trottoir; (*fig*) **it** ~**s you in the eye** cela saute aux yeux; **he** ~ **the nail with a hammer** il a tapé sur le clou avec un marteau; (*fig*) **to** ~ **the nail on the head** mettre dans le mille, y être; (*fig*) **to** ~ **the mark** atteindre son but; (*fig*) **that** ~ **home!** le coup a porté!; **to be** ~ **by a stone/bullet/bomb** recevoir une pierre/une balle/une bombe; *[plane]* **to be** ~ être touché; (*fig*) **to be** ~ **by a strike/price rise** être touché par une grève/hausse des prix; (*realization*) **then it** ~ **me*** alors j'ai réalisé* d'un seul coup!; **you've** ~ **it!*** ça y est*, tu as trouvé!; *[news, story]* **to** ~ **the papers** *or* **the front page** être à la une* des journaux; **to** ~ **the bottle*** picoler*; (*fig*) **to** ~ **the ceiling*** sortir de ses gonds; **to** ~ **the hay**‡ se coucher; **to** ~ **the road*** *or* **the trail*** mettre les voiles*. **(b)** (*find*) trouver, tomber sur; *problems, difficulties* rencontrer; (*: *arrive at*) *town etc* débarquer à *or* dans. **at last we** ~ **the right road** nous sommes tombés enfin sur la bonne route.

4 *vi* (*collide*) se heurter, se cogner (*against* à, contre).

hit back 1 *vi* (*fig*) riposter. **to** ~ **back at sb** riposter, répondre à qn. **2** *vt sep*: **to** ~ **sb back** rendre son coup à qn.

hit off *vt sep likeness* saisir. **he** ~ **him off beautifully** il l'a imité à la perfection; **to** ~ **it off with sb** bien s'entendre avec qn.

hit out at *vt fus* décocher un coup à; (*fig*) attaquer.

hit (up)on *vt fus* tomber sur, trouver.

◆ **hit-and-run driver** *n* chauffard* *m* (coupable du délit de fuite). ◆ **hit-and-run raid** *n* raid *m* éclair *inv*. ◆ **hit-or-miss 1** *adv* au petit bonheur; **2** *adj work* fait au petit bonheur; *attitude* désinvolte.

hitch [hɪtʃ] **1** *n* anicroche *f* (*in* dans). **without a** ~ sans anicroche; **technical** ~ incident *m* technique. **2** *vt* **(a)** (~ **up**) *trousers* remonter (d'une saccade). **(b)** (*fasten*) accrocher (*to* à); *carriages, horses* atteler (*to* à). **to get** ~**ed**‡ se marier. **(c)** (*) **to** ~ **a lift to Paris** faire du stop* jusqu'à Paris; **I** ~**ed a lift to Paris with my father** je me suis fait emmener en voiture jusqu'à Paris par mon père. **3** *vi* (*) = **hitch-hike.** ◆ **hitch-hike** *vi* faire du stop* *or* de l'auto-stop (*to* jusqu'à). ◆ **hitch-hiker** *n* auto-stoppeur *m*, -euse *f*. ◆ **hitch-hiking** *n* auto-stop *m*.

hither ['hɪðəʳ] *adv* (†) ici. (*not* †) ~ **and thither** çà et là.

hive [haɪv] *n* ruche *f*. **a** ~ **of industry** une vraie ruche.

hive off* 1 *vi* se séparer (*from* de). **2** *vt sep* séparer (*from* de).

hoard [hɔːd] **1** *n* réserves *fpl*, provision *f*; (*treasure*) trésor *m*. **a** ~ **of food** des provisions, des réserves; **a squirrel's** ~ **of nuts** les réserves *or* provisions de noisettes d'un écureuil; **a** ~ **of money** un trésor, un magot; ~**s* of things** un tas* de choses. **2** *vt* (~ **up**) *food etc* amasser, mettre en réserve; *money* amasser.

hoarding ['hɔːdɪŋ] *n* (*fence*) palissade *f*; (*for advertisements*) panneau *m* d'affichage.

hoarfrost ['hɔː'frɒst] *n* givre *m*.

hoarse [hɔːs] *adj* enroué. ◆ **hoarsely** *adv* d'une voix enrouée. ◆ **hoarseness** *n* enrouement *m*.

hoary ['hɔːrɪ] *adj hair* blanc neigeux *inv*; *person* chenu, (*fig*) vénérable; *joke* éculé.

hoax [həʊks] **1** *n* canular *m*. **2** *vt* faire un canular à. **we were** ~**ed** on nous a eus*.

hobble ['hɒbl] *vi* clopiner. **to** ~ **in/out** *etc* entrer/sortir *etc* en clopinant.

hobby ['hɒbɪ] *n* passe-temps *inv* favori, hobby *m*. ◆ **hobby-horse** *n* (*fig*) dada *m*; **he's off on his** ~**-horse** le voilà reparti (sur son dada).

hobnob ['hɒbnɒb] *vi* frayer (*with* avec).

hobo ['həʊbəʊ] *n* (*US*) vagabond *m*.

hock[1] [hɒk] *n [animal, beef]* jarret *m*.

hock[2] [hɒk] *n* (*wine*) vin *m* du Rhin.

hockey ['hɒkɪ] *n* hockey *m*.

hocus-pocus ['həʊkəs'pəʊkəs] *n* (*trickery*) supercherie *f*; (*talk*) charabia* *m*.

hoe [həʊ] **1** *n* houe *f*, binette *f*. **2** *vt ground* biner; *plants* sarcler.

hog [hɒg] **1** *n* cochon *m*, porc *m*. **he's a greedy** ~ c'est un vrai goinfre*; (*fig*) **to go the whole** ~ aller jusqu'au bout. **2** *vt* (*) *food* se goinfrer* de; (*take selfishly*) *best chair etc* accaparer. **don't** ~ **all the sweets** ne garde pas tous les bonbons pour toi.

hoi polloi [ˌhɔɪpə'lɔɪ] *n* gens *mpl* du commun.

hoist [hɔɪst] **1** *vt* hisser. **2** *n* appareil *m* de levage; (*for goods*) monte-charge *m inv*.

hold [həʊld] (*vb: pret, ptp* **held**) **1** *n* **(a)** prise *f*. **to catch** *or* **get** ~ **of** saisir, s'emparer de; (*fig: contact*) **to get** ~ **of sb** contacter *or* joindre qn; **he caught** ~ **of her arm** il lui a saisi le bras; (*fig*) **can you get** ~ **of a piece of wire?** est-ce que tu peux trouver un morceau de fil de fer?; **to get (a)** ~ **of o.s.** se contrôler; **to have** ~ **of** tenir; **I've got a firm** ~ **on the rope** je tiens bien la corde; **to keep** ~ **of** *object* ne pas lâcher; *idea* s'accrocher à; (*fig*) **to have a** ~ **over sb** avoir prise sur qn; (*fig*) **no** ~**s barred*** tous les coups sont permis.

(b) (*Naut*) cale *f*.

2 *vt* **(a)** (*gen*) tenir; (*contain*) contenir; (*fig*) *audience* tenir; *sb's interest, attention* retenir; *opinion* avoir. **to** ~ **in one's hand** *book* tenir à la main; *coin* tenir dans la main; **they were** ~**ing hands** il se tenaient par la main; **he held my arm** il me tenait le bras; **to** ~ **sb tight** (*in embrace*) serrer qn très fort; (*to prevent fall etc*) bien tenir qn; **the bottle** ~**s one litre** la bouteille contient un litre; **the room** ~**s 20 people** 20 personnes peuvent tenir dans la salle; **the ladder won't** ~ **you** l'échelle ne supportera pas ton poids; **the nails** ~ **the carpet in place** les clous maintiennent la moquette en place; **to** ~ **o.s. upright/ready** se tenir droit/prêt; **to** ~ **one's head high** porter la tête haute; (*fig*) **he was left** ~**ing the baby*** tout est retombé sur sa tête; **to** ~ **one's breath** retenir son souffle; **to** ~ **one's tongue** se taire; **to** ~ **one's own** *[invalid]* se maintenir; (*in conversation etc*) se débrouiller; (*Telec*) **to** ~ **the line** attendre; ~ **the line!** ne quittez pas!; **this car** ~**s the road well** cette voiture tient bien la route; **what the future** ~**s** ce que l'avenir nous réserve.

(b) *meeting, election, conversation etc* tenir; *examination* organiser; *check, count* faire. **the exhibition is always held here** l'exposition a toujours lieu ici; (*Rel*) **to** ~ **a service** célébrer un office; *[employer]* **to** ~ **an interview** recevoir des candidats.

(c) (*believe*) considérer, maintenir (*that* que). **to** ~ **in high esteem** tenir en haute estime; **to** ~ **sb responsible for sth** considérer qn responsable de qch; **all that he** ~**s dear** tout ce qui lui est cher.

(d) (*restrain*) *person* retenir; (*keep*) *object, money* garder. **to** ~ **a train** empêcher un train de partir; ~ **the letter until ...** n'envoyez pas la lettre avant que ... + *subj*; **the police held him for 2 days** la police l'a gardé (à vue) pendant 2 jours; **there's no** ~**ing him** il n'y a pas moyen de le retenir; ~ **it!*** arrêtez!, minute!*

(e) (*possess*) avoir, posséder; (*Mil*) tenir

(*against* contre); *post, position* avoir, occuper; *ticket, permit, shares* avoir, détenir; (*Sport*) *record* détenir. (*Parl*) **to ~ office** avoir *or* tenir un portefeuille; (*fig*) **to ~ the fort** monter la garde; (*fig*) **to ~ the stage** tenir le devant de la scène.

3 *vi [rope, nail etc]* tenir, être solide; *[weather]* se maintenir; *[statement, promise]* (*also* **~ good**) être valable. **to ~ firm** *or* **tight** *or* **fast** tenir bon *or* ferme.

hold back 1 *vi* (*fig*) se retenir (*from sth* de qch; *from doing* de faire). **2** *vt sep* **(a)** *fears, emotions* maîtriser; *crowd* contenir. **to ~ sb back from doing** retenir qn de faire. **(b)** (*not disclose*) *facts, name* ne pas donner. **he was ~ing sth back from me** il me cachait qch.

hold down *vt sep* **(a)** (*keep on ground*) maintenir à terre; (*keep in place*) maintenir en place. **to ~ one's head down** tenir la tête baissée. **(b)** *job* (*have*) avoir, occuper; (*keep*) garder.

hold forth *vi* pérorer (*on* sur).

hold in *vt sep* retenir; *stomach* rentrer. (*fig*) **to ~ o.s. in** se retenir.

hold off 1 *vi* (*fig*) **the rain has held off so far** jusqu'ici il n'a pas plu. **2** *vt sep enemy* tenir à distance; (*fig*) *visitor etc* faire patienter.

hold on 1 *vi* (*endure*) tenir bon, tenir le coup; (*wait*) attendre. **~ on!** attendez!; (*Telec*) ne quittez pas! **2** *vt sep lid etc* tenir en place.

hold on to *vt fus* (*cling to*) *rope, branch* se cramponner à; *hope, idea* se raccrocher à; (*keep*) *object, money* garder; *used clothes etc* conserver. **~ on to this for me** tiens-moi ça.

hold out 1 *vi* **(a)** *[supplies etc]* durer. **(b)** (*endure*) tenir bon, tenir le coup. **to ~ out against** *enemy, attacks* tenir bon devant; *change, progress, threats* résister à; **they are ~ing out for more pay** ils tiennent bon pour avoir une augmentation; **you've been ~ing out on me!*** tu m'as caché qch! **2** *vt sep* tendre, offrir (*sth to sb* qch à qn); *one's arms* ouvrir; (*fig*) *hope* offrir.

hold over *vt sep meeting etc* remettre (*until* à).

hold together 1 *vi [objects]* tenir (ensemble); *[people]* rester unis. **2** *vt sep objects* maintenir (ensemble); *a group* maintenir l'union de.

hold up 1 *vi [building]* tenir debout. **2** *vt sep* **(a)** (*raise*) lever, élever. **~ up your hand** levez la main; **to ~ sth up to the light** élever qch à la lumière. **(b)** (*support*) *roof etc* soutenir. **(c)** (*stop*) arrêter; (*delay*) *traffic* retarder; *person* retenir. **(d)** *[robber] bank, shop* faire un hold-up dans; *coach, person* attaquer (à main armée).

hold with* *vt fus*: **she doesn't ~ with people smoking** elle désapprouve que l'on fume (*subj*).

♦ **holdall** *n* fourre-tout *m inv*. ♦ **holder** *n* **(a)** *[ticket, card, record, title, stocks]* détenteur *m*, -trice *f*; *[passport, post]* titulaire *mf*; **(b)** (*object*) support *m*; **pen ~er** porte-plume *m inv*. ♦ **holding** *n* (*farm*) propriété *f*, ferme *f*; (*Fin*) **~ings** (*lands*) avoirs *mpl* fonciers; (*stocks*) intérêts *mpl*; (*Fin*) **~ing company** holding *m*. ♦ **hold-up** *n* (*robbery*) hold-up *m inv*, attaque *f* à main armée; (*delay*) retard *m*; (*in traffic*) bouchon *m*.

hole [həʊl] *n* **(a)** (*gen*) trou *m*; *[rabbit, fox]* terrier *m*; (*in defences, dam*) brèche *f*; (*in argument etc*) faille *f*. **to wear a ~ in a garment** trouer un vêtement; *[sock etc]* **to go into ~s** se trouer; (*fig*) **it made a ~ in his savings** cela a fait un trou dans ses économies; **to be in a (nasty) ~*** avoir des ennuis, être dans l'embarras; **he got me out of a ~*** il m'a tiré d'embarras*. **(b)** (**pej*) (*town*) bled* *m*; (*room, house*) bouge *m*.

hole up *vi [animal, wanted man]* se terrer.

♦ **hole-and-corner** *adj* (*furtive*) furtif; (*underhand*) fait en douce*. ♦ **hole-in-the-heart** *n* (*Med*) communication *f* interventriculaire. ♦ **holey** *adj* plein de trous.

holiday ['hɒlədɪ] **1** *n* (*vacation*) vacances *fpl*; (*day off*) jour *m* de congé. **on ~** en vacances, en congé; **to take a month's ~** prendre un mois de vacances; **~s with pay** congés *mpl* payés; **school ~s** vacances scolaires. **2** *vi* passer ses vacances. **3** *adj camp, clothes, atmosphere* de vacances; *mood etc* gai, joyeux. **~ resort** villégiature *f*; **~ season** saison *f* des vacances; **~ spirit** esprit *m* de vacances; **~ traffic** circulation *f* des départs (*or* des rentrées) de vacances. ♦ **holiday-maker** *n* vacancier *m*, -ière *f*; (*in summer*) estivant(e) *m(f)*.

Holland ['hɒlənd] *n* Hollande *f*.

holler* ['hɒləʳ] **1** *n* braillement *m*. **2** *vti* brailler.

hollow ['hɒləʊ] **1** *adj* (*gen*) creux; *eyes* cave; *sound* (*from box etc*) creux, (*from cave etc*) caverneux; *voice* caverneux; *sympathy, victory* faux; *promise* vain. **to give a ~ laugh** rire jaune. **2** *n [back, hand, tree]* creux *m*; (*in ground*) dénivellation *f*; (*valley*) cuvette *f*. **3** *vt* (**~ out**) creuser. ♦ **hollow-cheeked** *adj* aux joues creuses. ♦ **hollow-eyed** *adj* aux yeux caves.

holly ['hɒlɪ] *n* houx *m*. **~ bush** buisson *m* de houx.

hollyhock ['hɒlɪhɒk] *n* rose *f* trémière.

holocaust ['hɒləkɔːst] *n* holocauste *m*.

holster ['həʊlstəʳ] *n* étui *m* de revolver.

holy ['həʊlɪ] **1** *adj place, life, poverty* saint (*after n*); *person, oil, Bible, Communion, Trinity* saint (*before n*); *bread, water* bénit; *ground* sacré. **the H~ Father** le Saint-Père; **the H~ Ghost** *or* **Spirit** le Saint-Esprit; **the H~ Land** la Terre Sainte; **~ orders** ordres *mpl* (majeurs); **H~ Week** la Semaine Sainte; **he's a ~ terror*** c'est un vrai démon. **2** *n*: **the ~ of holies** le Saint des Saints.

♦ **holiness** *n* sainteté *f*; **His Holiness** Sa Sainteté.

homage ['hɒmɪdʒ] *n* hommage *m*. **to pay ~ to** rendre hommage à.

home [həʊm] **1** *n* **(a)** maison *f*; (*Bot, Zool*) habitat *m*. **he left ~ in 1978** il a quitté la maison en 1978; **he was glad to see his ~ again** il était content de revoir sa maison; **it is quite near my ~** c'est tout près de chez moi; **my ~ is in London** (*live there*) j'habite Londres; (*was born there*) je suis de Londres; **~ for me is Edinburgh** c'est à Édimbourg que j'ai mes racines; **for some years he made his ~ in France** pendant quelques années il a habité en France; **refugees who made their ~ in Britain** les réfugiés qui se sont installés en Grande-Bretagne; **he is far from ~** il est loin de chez lui; **there's no place like ~** on n'est vraiment bien que chez soi; **to have a ~ of one's own** avoir un foyer *or* un chez-soi; **to give sb a ~** recueillir qn chez soi; **she made a ~ for her brothers** elle a fait un (vrai) foyer pour ses frères; **it's a ~ from ~** c'est un second chez-soi; **she has a lovely ~** elle a un joli intérieur; **he comes from a good ~** il a une famille comme il faut; **'good ~ wanted for kitten'** 'cherche foyer accueillant pour chaton'; **a broken ~** un foyer désuni; **safety in the ~** prudence à la maison; **at ~** chez soi, à la maison; (*Ftbl*) **Celtic are playing Rangers at ~** le Celtic reçoit les Rangers; (*fig*) **Mrs Smith is not at ~ to anyone** Mme Smith ne reçoit personne; **to feel at ~** se sentir à l'aise (*with sb/sth* avec qn/qch); **to make o.s. at ~** faire comme chez soi.

(b) pays *m* natal, patrie *f*. **at ~ and abroad** chez nous et à l'étranger; (*fig*) **let us consider sth nearer ~** considérons qch qui nous intéresse plus directement.

(c) (*institution*) maison *f*, institution *f*. **children's ~** maison pour enfants.

2 *adv* **(a)** chez soi, à la maison. **to go** *or* **get ~** rentrer (chez soi *or* à la maison); **I'll be ~ at 5 o'clock** je rentrerai à 5 heures; **on the journey ~** sur le chemin du retour; **to see sb ~** accompagner qn jusque chez lui; **I must write ~** il faut que j'écrive à la maison; **it's nothing to write ~ about*** ça ne casse rien*; (*fig*) **~ and dry** sauvé.

(b) (*from abroad*) **he came ~** il est rentré de

l'étranger; **to send sb ~** rapatrier qn; **to go** *or* **return ~** rentrer dans son pays.

(c) (*right in etc*) *hammer, drive* à fond. (*fig*) **to bring sth ~ to sb** faire comprendre qch à qn; **the situation was brought ~ to him when** la situation lui est apparue pleinement quand.

3 *adj atmosphere, life* de famille, familial; *troubles* de famille, domestique; *comforts* du foyer; *cooking* familial; *[doctor etc] visit* à domicile; (*Econ, Pol etc*) du pays, national; *policy, market, sales etc* intérieur; (*Sport*) *team etc* qui reçoit; *match* joué à domicile. **~ address** domicile *m* (permanent); (*as opp to business address*) adresse *f* personnelle; **the ~ country** le vieux pays; **~ economics** économie *f* domestique; (*Pol etc*) **on the ~ front** à l'intérieur; **~ help** aide *f* ménagère; **~ leave** congé *m* de longue durée; **~ news** (*gen*) nouvelles *fpl* de chez soi; (*Pol*) nouvelles de l'intérieur; (*Brit*) **H~ Office** ≈ ministère *m* de l'Intérieur; (*Naut*) **~ port** port *m* d'attache; **~ rule** autonomie *f*; (*Brit*) **H~ Secretary** ≈ ministre *m* de l'Intérieur; (*fig*) **to be in the ~ straight** voir la lumière au bout du tunnel; **my ~ town** (*place of birth*) ma ville natale; (*where I grew up*) la ville où j'ai grandi; **~ truths** vérités *fpl* bien senties.

4 *vi [pigeons]* revenir au colombier.

home in on, home on to *vt fus* se diriger (automatiquement) vers *or* sur.

♦ **home-baked** *or* **-brewed** *or* **-cooked** *etc adj* fait à la maison. ♦ **homecoming** *n* retour *m* au foyer (*or* au pays). ♦ **home-grown** *adj* (*not foreign*) du pays; (*from own garden*) du jardin. ♦ **homeland** *n* patrie *f*. ♦ **homeless 1** *adj* sans abri; **2** *npl*: **the ~less** les sans-abri *mpl*. ♦ **homelike** *adj* accueillant, confortable. ♦ **home-lover** *n* casanier *m*, -ière *f*. ♦ **home-loving** *adj* casanier. ♦ **homely** *adj* **(a)** *food, person* simple; *atmosphere* confortable; **(b)** (*US: plain*) laid. ♦ **home-made** *adj* fait à la maison. ♦ **homesick** *adj* nostalgique; **to be ~sick** avoir la nostalgie (*for sth* de qch); (*abroad*) avoir le mal du pays. ♦ **homesickness** *n* nostalgie *f* (*for* de), mal *m* du pays. ♦ **homespun** *adj* (*fig*) simple. ♦ **homestead** *n* (*house etc*) propriété *f*; (*farm*) ferme *f*. ♦ **homeward 1** *adj* du retour; **~ward journey** retour *m*; **2** *adv* (*also* **~wards**) vers la maison; **~ward bound** sur le chemin du retour. ♦ **homework** *n* devoirs *mpl* (à la maison). ♦ **homing** *adj missile* à tête chercheuse; **homing pigeon** pigeon voyageur.

homicide ['hɒmɪsaɪd] *n* homicide *m*. ♦ **homicidal** *adj* homicide.

homoeopath, (*US*) **homeopath** ['həʊmɪəʊpæθ] *n* homéopathe *mf*.

♦ **hom(o)eopathic** *adj medicine, methods* homéopathique; *doctor* homéopathe. ♦ **hom(o)eopathy** *n* homéopathie *f*.

homogeneity [ˌhɒməʊdʒəˈniːɪtɪ] *n* homogénéité *f*. ♦ **homogeneous** [ˌhɒməˈdʒiːnɪəs] *adj* homogène. ♦ **homogenize** [həˈmɒdʒənaɪz] *vt* homogénéiser.

homonym ['hɒmənɪm] *n* homonyme *m*.

homosexual ['hɒməʊˈseksjʊəl] *adj, n* homosexuel(le) *m(f)*. ♦ **homosexuality** *n* homosexualité *f*.

hone [həʊn] *vt* aiguiser.

honest ['ɒnɪst] *adj person, action* honnête; *opinion* sincère; *face* franc; *means, method* légitime; *money, profit* honnêtement acquis. **the ~ truth** la pure vérité; **tell me your ~ opinion of it** dites-moi sincèrement ce que vous en pensez; **to be ~ with you, I don't like it** à vous dire la vérité, je n'aime pas ça; **be ~!** parle franchement!; (*be objective*) sois objectif!; **you've not been ~ with me** tu n'as pas été franc avec moi; **an ~ day's work** une bonne journée de travail; **~ to goodness!*** ça alors! ♦ **honestly** *adv act, behave* honnêtement; **~ly, I don't care** franchement, ça m'est égal; **I didn't do it, ~ly!** je ne l'ai pas fait, je vous le jure!; **~ly?** c'est vrai?; (*exasperated*) **~ly!** ça alors! ♦ **honesty** *n* **(a)** honnêteté *f*; **in all ~y** en toute sincérité; **(b)** (*Bot*) monnaie-du-pape *f*.

honey ['hʌnɪ] *n* miel *m*. **clear/thick ~** miel liquide/solide; **yes, ~*** oui, chéri(e); **she's a ~*** elle est adorable. ♦ **honeybee** *n* abeille *f*. ♦ **honeycomb 1** *n* rayon *m* de miel; (*Tex*) nid *m* d'abeille; (*Metal*) soufflure *f*; **2** *adj pattern* en nid d'abeille; **3** *vt* (*fig*) cribler (*with* de). ♦ **honeyed** *adj words* mielleux. ♦ **honeymoon 1** *n* lune *f* de miel; **2** *vi* passer sa lune de miel; **3** *adj*: **the ~moon couple** les nouveaux mariés *mpl*. ♦ **honeysuckle** *n* chèvrefeuille *m*.

honk [hɒŋk] *vi [car]* klaxonner; *[geese]* cacarder.

honor *etc* (*US*) = **honour** *etc*.

honorary ['ɒnərərɪ] *adj person* honoraire; *duties* honorifique. **~ degree** grade *m* honoris causa.

honour, (*US*) **-or** ['ɒnəʳ] **1** *n* honneur *m*. **in ~ of** en l'honneur de; **on my ~!** parole d'honneur!; **to put sb on his ~ to do** engager qn sur l'honneur à faire; **to be (in) ~ bound to do** être tenu par l'honneur de faire; **to have the ~ to do** *or* **of doing** avoir l'honneur de faire; **Your H~** Votre Honneur; **to do the ~s** faire les présentations (*entre invités*); (*Univ*) **he got first-/second-class ~s in English** ≈ il a eu sa licence d'anglais avec mention très bien/mention bien. **2** *vt* honorer (*with* de). ♦ **hono(u)rable** *adj* honorable. ♦ **hono(u)rably** *adv* honorablement.

hooch‡ [huːtʃ] *n* gnôle* *f*.

hood [hʊd] *n* (*gen*) capuchon *m*; (*Ku Klux Klan type*) cagoule *f*; (*rain-~*) capuche *f*; (*Brit Aut*) capote *f*; (*US Aut*) capot *m*; *[pram]* capote; (*over cooker etc*) hotte *f*.

♦ **hooded** *adj* encapuchonné; *prisoner, gunman* au visage couvert. ♦ **hoodlum** *n* (*US*) voyou *m*. ♦ **hoodwink** *vt* tromper.

hooey‡ ['huːɪ] *n* blagues* *fpl*.

hoof [huːf] *n, pl* **~s** *or* **hooves** sabot *m* (*d'animal*).

hoo-ha* ['huːˌhɑː] *n* (*noise*) brouhaha *m*; (*excitement*) animation *f*; (*pej: publicity*) baratin* *m*. **there was a great ~ about it** on en a fait tout un plat*.

hook [hʊk] **1** *n* (*gen*) crochet *m*; (*for coats*) patère *f*; (*on dress*) agrafe *f*; (*Fishing*) hameçon *m*; (*Agr*) faucille *f*; (*Boxing*) crochet. (*Sewing*) **~s and eyes** agrafes; (*fig*) **he swallowed it ~, line and sinker*** il a gobé tout ce qu'on lui a raconté; **by ~ or by crook** par tous les moyens; **to get sb off the ~*** tirer qn d'affaire. **2** *vt* accrocher (*to* à); (*Fishing*) prendre; *dress* agrafer. **she finally ~ed him*** elle a fini par lui passer la corde au cou.

hook on 1 *vi* s'accrocher (*to* à). **2** *vt sep* accrocher (*to* à).

hook up *vt sep dress etc* agrafer; (*: *TV etc*) faire un duplex entre.

♦ **hooked** *adj* (*hook-shaped*) recourbé; (*having hooks*) muni de crochets; (*fig*) **he's ~ed* on it** il ne peut plus s'en passer; **to get ~ed* on drugs** se droguer; **to get ~ed* on jazz** devenir enragé* de jazz; **he's really ~ed* on her** il en est fou. ♦ **hook-nosed** *adj* au nez recourbé. ♦ **hook-up*** *n* (*TV etc*) relais *m* temporaire. ♦ **hooky‡** *n*: **to play ~y‡** sécher les cours.

hooligan ['huːlɪgən] *n* voyou *m*. ♦ **hooliganism** *n* vandalisme *m*.

hoop [huːp] *n [barrel]* cercle *m*; (*toy; in circus; for skirt*) cerceau *m*; (*Croquet*) arceau *m*. (*fig*) **they put him through the ~*** ils l'ont mis sur la sellette. ♦ **hoopla** *n* jeu *m* d'anneaux.

hoot [huːt] **1** *vi [owl]* hululer; (*Aut*) klaxonner; *[siren]* mugir; *[train]* siffler; (*jeer*) huer; (*with laughter*) s'esclaffer. **2** *n* hululement *m*; coup *m* de klaxon; mugissement *m*; sifflement *m*; huée *f*. **I don't care a ~*** je m'en fiche* éperdument; **it was a ~‡** c'était tordant* *or* marrant‡. ♦ **hooter** *n [factory]* sirène *f*; (*Aut*) klaxon *m*.

hoover ['huːvəʳ] ® **1** *n* aspirateur *m*. **2** *vt* passer l'aspirateur sur *or* dans.

hop[1] [hɒp] **1** *n* (*gen*) saut *m*; *[bird]* sautillement *m*; (*: *dance*) sauterie *f*; (*Aviat*) étape *f*. (*fig*) **to catch sb on the ~** prendre qn au dépourvu. **2** *vi* sauter; (*on one foot*) sauter à cloche-pied; *[bird]* sautiller. **he ~ped over to the window** il est allé à cloche-pied jusqu'à la fenêtre; (*in car etc*) **~ in!** montez!; **to ~ off, to ~ it*** ficher le camp*. ♦ **hopscotch** *n* marelle *f*.

hop[2] [hɒp] *n* (*also* **~s**) houblon *m*. ♦ **hopfield** *n* houblonnière *f*. ♦ **hop-picker** *n* cueilleur *m*, -euse *f* de houblon.

hope [həʊp] **1** *n* espoir *m*. **past** *or* **beyond (all) ~** sans espoir; **to live in ~** vivre d'espoir; **in the ~ of (doing) sth** dans l'espoir de (faire) qch; **to have ~s of doing** avoir l'espoir de faire; **I haven't much ~ of succeeding** je n'ai pas beaucoup d'espoir de réussir; **there is no ~ of that** on ne peut pas y compter; **with high ~s** avec l'espoir de faire de grandes choses; **to raise sb's ~s** donner de l'espoir à qn; **you're my last ~** tu es mon dernier espoir; **what a ~!*, some ~!*** tu parles!*

2 *vti* espérer (*that* que; *to do* faire). **to ~ for success** espérer avoir du succès; **don't ~ for too much** n'en attendez pas trop; **to ~ for the best** être optimiste; **to ~ against hope** espérer en dépit de tout; **hoping to hear from you** dans l'espoir d'avoir de vos nouvelles; **I ~ so/not** j'espère que oui/non.

♦ **hopeful 1** *adj person* plein d'espoir; *situation* qui promet; *response, sign* encourageant; *future* qui se présente bien; **we are ~ful about the results** nous attendons avec confiance les résultats; **I am ~ful that ...** j'ai bon espoir que ...; **I'm not too ~ful** je n'ai pas tellement d'espoir; **2** *n*: **a young ~ful** un jeune loup (*fig*). ♦ **hopefully** *adv* **(a)** *speak, smile* avec optimisme; *develop, progress* d'une façon encourageante; **(b)** (*esp US*) **~fully* it won't rain** on espère qu'il ne va pas pleuvoir. ♦ **hopeless** *adj person, situation, outlook* désespéré; *task* impossible; (*: *bad*) *work* qui ne vaut rien; *liar, drunkard etc* invétéré, incorrigible; **it's ~less!** c'est désespérant; **he's a ~less* teacher** il est nul comme professeur; **I'm ~less* at maths** je suis nul en maths; **he's ~less*** c'est un cas désespéré. ♦ **hopelessly** *adv act* sans espoir; *speak* avec désespoir; *lost etc* complètement; *in love* éperdument.

horde [hɔːd] *n* foule *f*, horde *f* (*pej*).

horizon [həˈraɪzn] *n* horizon *m* (*also fig*). **on the ~** à l'horizon. ♦ **horizontal 1** *adj* horizontal; **2** *n* horizontale *f*. ♦ **horizontally** *adv* horizontalement.

hormone [ˈhɔːməʊn] *n* hormone *f*.

horn [hɔːn] *n* (*gen*) corne *f*; (*Mus*) cor *m*; (*Aut*) klaxon *m*; (*Naut*) sirène *f*. **to draw in one's ~s** (*back down*) diminuer d'ardeur; (*spend less*) restreindre son train de vie. ♦ **horn-rimmed spectacles** *npl* lunettes *fpl* à monture d'écaille. ♦ **horny** *adj hands* calleux.

hornet [ˈhɔːnɪt] *n* frelon *m*.

horoscope [ˈhɒrəskəʊp] *n* horoscope *m*.

horrible [ˈhɒrɪbl] *adj sight, murder* horrible; *holiday, weather etc* affreux, atroce. ♦ **horribly** *adv* horriblement; affreusement.

horrid [ˈhɒrɪd] *adj person* méchant; *thing* affreux.

horrify [ˈhɒrɪfaɪ] *vt* horrifier. ♦ **horrific** *adj* horrible. ♦ **horrifying** *adj* horrifiant.

horror [ˈhɒrəʳ] **1** *n* horreur *f*. **to have a ~ of (doing) sth** avoir horreur de (faire) qch; **that child is a ~*** cet enfant est un petit monstre; **that gives me the ~s*** cela me donne le frisson. **2** *adj film, comic* d'épouvante. ♦ **horror-stricken** *adj* glacé d'horreur.

horse [hɔːs] **1** *n* cheval *m*; (*Gymnastics*) cheval *m* d'arçons. (*fig*) **straight from the ~'s mouth** de source sûre. **2** *adj race* de chevaux; *meat* de cheval. **~ brass** médaillon *m* de cuivre (d'une martingale); **~ chestnut** marron *m* (d'Inde); (*tree*) marronnier *m* (d'Inde); (*Cine, TV*) **~ opera*** western *m*; **~ show** *or* **trials** concours *m* hippique. ♦ **horseback** *n*: **on ~back** à cheval. ♦ **horse-box** *n* (*Aut*) fourgon *m* à chevaux. ♦ **horse-dealer** *n* maquignon *m*. ♦ **horse-drawn** *adj* à chevaux. ♦ **horseflesh** *n* (*horses*) chevaux *mpl*; (*Culin*) viande *f* de cheval. ♦ **horsefly** *n* taon *m*. ♦ **horsehair** *n* crin *m* (de cheval). ♦ **horse-laugh** *n* gros rire *m*. ♦ **horseman** *n* cavalier *m*. ♦ **horsemanship** *n* (*activity*) équitation *f*; (*skill*) talent *m* de cavalier. ♦ **horseplay** *n* jeux *mpl* brutaux. ♦ **horsepower** *n* puissance *f* (en chevaux). ♦ **horse-racing** *n* courses *fpl* de chevaux. ♦ **horseradish** *n* raifort *m*. ♦ **horse-sense*** *n* gros bon sens *m*. ♦ **horseshoe 1** *n* fer *m* à cheval; **2** *adj* en fer à cheval. ♦ **horse-trader** *n* (*lit, fig*) maquignon *m*. ♦ **horse-trading** *n* maquignonnage *m*. ♦ **horsewhip** *vt* cravacher. ♦ **horsey*** *adj person* féru de cheval; *appearance* chevalin.

horticulture [ˈhɔːtɪkʌltʃəʳ] *n* horticulture *f*. ♦ **horticultural** *adj* horticole. ♦ **horticulturist** *n* horticulteur *m*, -trice *f*.

hose [həʊz] **1** *n* **(a)** (*also* **~pipe**) tuyau *m*. **(b)** (*pl: stockings*) bas *mpl*. **2** *vt* (*in garden*) arroser au jet; *[firemen]* arroser à la lance. **to ~ sth down** *or* **out** laver qch au jet.

♦ **hosiery** *n* bonneterie *f*.

hospice [ˈhɒspɪs] *n* hospice *m*.

hospitable [hɒsˈpɪtəbl] *adj* hospitalier. ♦ **hospitably** *adv* avec hospitalité. ♦ **hospitality** [ˌhɒspɪˈtælɪtɪ] *n* hospitalité *f*.

hospital [ˈhɒspɪtl] **1** *n* hôpital *m*. **in ~** à l'hôpital. **2** *adj treatment, staff* hospitalier; *bed etc* d'hôpital. **~ case** patient *m* hospitalisé; **the ~ doctors** les médecins *mpl* des hôpitaux; **the ~ facilities** *or* **service** le service hospitalier. ♦ **hospitalize** *vt* hospitaliser.

host[1] [həʊst] **1** *n* hôte *m*. **2** *adj plant, animal* hôte; *town etc* qui reçoit. ♦ **hostess** *n* hôtesse *f*; (*in night club*) entraîneuse *f*.

host[2] [həʊst] *n [people]* foule *f*; *[reasons]* tas* *m*.

host[3] [həʊst] *n* (*Rel*) hostie *f*.

hostage [ˈhɒstɪdʒ] *n* otage *m*. **to take sb ~** prendre qn comme otage.

hostel [ˈhɒstəl] **1** *n* (*gen*) foyer *m*. **(youth) ~** auberge *f* de jeunesse. **2** *vi*: **to go (youth) ~ling** passer ses vacances dans des auberges de jeunesse.

♦ **hosteller** *n* ajiste *mf*.

hostile [ˈhɒstaɪl] *adj* hostile (*to* à). ♦ **hostility** *n* hostilité *f*.

hot [hɒt] **1** *adj* **(a)** (*gen*) chaud; *sun* brûlant. **to be ~** *[person]* avoir (très *or* trop) chaud; *[thing]* être (très) chaud; (*Met*) faire (très) chaud; **this room is ~** il fait (très *or* trop) chaud dans cette pièce; **to get ~** *[person]* s'échauffer; (*in guessing*) brûler; *[thing]* chauffer; (*Met*) commencer à faire chaud; **~ spring** source *f* chaude; **in the ~ weather** pendant les chaleurs; **I can't drink ~ things** je ne supporte pas le chaud; (*fig*) **in the ~ seat** sur la sellette; (*Med*) **~ flush** bouffée *f* de chaleur; (*fig*) **to be in/get into ~ water** être/se mettre dans le pétrin; **to be ~ and bothered** (*perspiring*) être en nage; (*flustered*) être dans tous ses états (*about* au sujet de); **to be/get ~ under the collar*** être/se mettre dans tous ses états (*about* au sujet de); (*fig*) **~ air*** blablabla* *m*; (*Culin*) **~ dog** hot-dog *m*; (*Telec*) **~ line** téléphone *m* rouge (*to* avec); (*fig*) **~ potato*** sujet *m* brûlant; **he dropped the idea like a ~ potato*** il a laissé tomber comme si ça lui brûlait les doigts; **~ spot*** (*trouble area*) point *m* *or* coin *m* névralgique; (*night club*) boîte *f* (de nuit); **to be ~ stuff*** être sensationnel*.

(b) *curry, spices etc* fort; *news, report* tout frais; *struggle, dispute* acharné; *temperament, supporter* passionné. **~ jazz** hot *m*; **he's got a ~ temper** il est très colérique; (*Pol*) **a ~ war*** une guerre ouverte; ~ **favourite** grand favori *m*; ~ **tip** tuyau *m* sûr; **news ~ from the press** informations de dernière minute; **to make things ~ for sb*** mener la vie dure à qn; **not so ~*** pas formidable*; **he's pretty ~* at maths** il a la bosse* des maths; **he's pretty ~* at football** il est très calé en football; (*stolen*) **it's ~‡** ça a été volé.

2 *adv*: **to be ~ on the trail** être sur la bonne piste; **~ on sb's trail** sur les talons de qn; **he went at it ~ and strong** il n'y est pas allé de main morte*; **to give it to sb ~ and strong*** sonner les cloches à qn*.

hot up* 1 *vi [food etc]* se réchauffer; *[situation, party]* chauffer*. 2 *vt sep food* réchauffer; *evening* mettre de l'animation dans; *music* faire balancer*; *car engine* gonfler*. **a ~ted-up Mini** une Mini au moteur gonflé.

♦ **hot-air balloon** *n* ballon *m* (*Aviat*). ♦ **hotbed** *n* foyer *m* (*de vice etc*). ♦ **hot-blooded** *adj* passionné. ♦ **hotfoot 1** *adv* à toute vitesse; **2** *vt*: **to ~foot it*** galoper. ♦ **hothead** *n* tête *f* brûlée. ♦ **hotheaded** *adj* impétueux. ♦ **hothouse** *n* serre *f* (chaude). ♦ **hotly** *adv* passionnément, violemment. ♦ **hotplate** *n* plaque *f* chauffante. ♦ **hotpot** *n* ragoût *m*. ♦ **hotrod*** *n* (*Aut*) voiture *f* gonflée*. ♦ **hot-tempered** *adj* colérique. ♦ **hot-water bottle** *n* bouillotte *f*.

hotchpotch ['hɒtʃpɒtʃ] *n* fatras *m*.

hotel [həʊ'tel] **1** *n* hôtel *m*. **2** *adj prices, porter, room* d'hôtel. **the ~ industry** l'industrie hôtelière; **he's looking for ~ work** il cherche un travail dans l'hôtellerie; **~ workers** le personnel hôtelier. ♦ **hotelier** *or* ♦ **hotelkeeper** *n* hôtelier *m*, -ière *f*.

hound [haʊnd] **1** *n* chien *m* courant. **the ~s** la meute; **to ride to ~s** chasser à courre. **2** *vt debtor etc* traquer (*for sth* pour obtenir qch). **to ~ sb out of town** chasser qn hors de la ville; **to ~ sb down** (traquer et) capturer qn.

hour ['aʊəʳ] **1** *n* heure *f*. **~ by ~** heure par heure; **80 km an ~** 80 km à l'heure; **to pay sb by the ~** payer qn à l'heure; **she is paid £2 an ~** elle est payée 2 livres (de) l'heure; (*lit, fig*) **she's been waiting for ~s** elle attend depuis des heures; **on the ~** toutes les heures à l'heure juste; **his ~ has come** son heure est venue; **in the early** *or* **small ~s (of the morning)** au petit matin; **at all ~s (of the day and night)** à toute heure (du jour et de la nuit); **at this ~** à cette heure-ci; (*fig*) **at this late ~** à ce stade avancé; **in the ~ of danger** à l'heure du danger; **to keep regular ~s** avoir une vie réglée; **to work long ~s** avoir une journée très longue; **after ~s** après l'heure de fermeture; **out of ~s** en dehors des heures d'ouverture. **2** *adj [watch etc]* **~ hand** petite aiguille *f*. ♦ **hourglass** *n* sablier *m*. ♦ **hourly 1** *adj* (*every hour*) *bus service etc* toutes les heures; (*per hour*) *rate* horaire; (*incessant*) *fear* constant; **2** *adv* toutes les heures; (*fig*) continuellement; **~ly paid workers** ouvriers payés à l'heure.

house [haʊs] **1** *n* **(a)** maison *f*. **at** *or* **to my ~** chez moi; (*fig*) **they got on like a ~ on fire** ils s'entendaient comme larrons en foire; **the children were playing at ~(s)** les enfants jouaient à papa et maman; **~ of cards** château *m* de cartes; **she looks after the ~ herself** c'est elle qui s'occupe de son ménage; **she needs more help in the ~** il faudrait qu'elle soit plus aidée à la maison; **to keep ~** tenir la maison (*for sb* de qn); (*fig*) **to put one's ~ in order** mettre de l'ordre dans ses affaires. **(b)** (*Parl*) **the H~** la Chambre; **H~ of Commons/of Lords** Chambre des communes/des lords; (*US*) **H~ of Representatives** Chambre des députés; **the H~s of Parliament** le Palais de Westminster. **(c)** (*Theat etc*) salle *f*, spectateurs *mpl*. **in the front of the ~** parmi les spectateurs; **a full** *or* **good ~** une salle pleine; **to play to full ~s** jouer à guichets fermés; **'~ full'** 'complet'; **the second ~** la deuxième séance; (*fig*) **to bring the ~ down** faire crouler la salle sous les applaudissements. **(d)** (*Comm, Rel etc*) maison *f*. **the H~ of Windsor** la maison des Windsors; **banking ~** établissement *m* bancaire; **business ~** maison de commerce; **publishing ~** maison d'édition; (*fig: free*) **on the ~** aux frais de la maison.

2 *adj prices, sale* immobilier.

3 [haʊz] *vt [person, town council etc]* loger; *[building]* abriter. **the freezer is ~d in the basement** on garde le congélateur au sous-sol.

♦ **house agent** *n* agent *m* immobilier. ♦ **house arrest** *n*: **to put sb under ~ arrest** assigner qn à domicile. ♦ **houseboat** *n* péniche *f* (aménagée). ♦ **housebound 1** *adj* confiné chez soi; **2** *npl*: **the ~bound** les personnes isolées. ♦ **housebreaking** *n* cambriolage *m*. ♦ **housebroken** *adj animal* propre. ♦ **housecleaning** *n* ménage *m*. ♦ **housecoat** *n* peignoir *m*. ♦ **housefather/-mother** *n* responsable *m/f* (de groupe) (*dans une institution*). ♦ **housefly** *n* mouche *f* (commune). ♦ **houseful** *n*: **a ~ful of people** une pleine maisonnée de gens. ♦ **houseguest** *n* invité(e) *m(f)*. ♦ **household 1** *n* (*persons*) (gens *mpl* de la) maison *f*; (*Admin, Econ etc*) ménage *m*; **there were 7 people in his ~hold** sa maison était composée de 7 personnes; **2** *adj accounts, expenses, equipment* de *or* du ménage; **~hold ammonia** ammoniaque *f*; **~hold linen** linge *m* de maison; (*fig*) **it's a ~hold word** c'est un mot que tout le monde connaît. ♦ **householder** *n* occupant(e) *m(f)*; (*head of house*) chef *m* de famille. ♦ **househunt** *vi* chercher un appartement *or* une maison. ♦ **housekeeper** *n* (*in sb else's house*) gouvernante *f*; (*in institution*) économe *f*; **his wife is a good ~keeper** sa femme est bonne ménagère. ♦ **housekeeping 1** *n* (*work*) ménage *m*; **2** *adj*: **~keeping money** argent *m* du ménage. ♦ **housemaid** *n* bonne *f*. ♦ **house-painter** *n* peintre *m* en bâtiments. ♦ **house-party** *n* partie *f* de campagne. ♦ **house physician** *n* ≃ interne *mf* en médecine. ♦ **house-proud** *adj* très méticuleux. ♦ **houseroom** *n*: **I wouldn't give it ~room** je n'en voudrais pas chez moi. ♦ **house surgeon** *n* ≃ interne *mf* en chirurgie. ♦ **house-to-house 1** *adv* porte à porte *inv*; **2** *adj*: **to make a ~-to-~ search for sb** aller de porte en porte à la recherche de qn. ♦ **housetop** *n*: **to proclaim sth from the ~tops** crier qch sur les toits. ♦ **house-trained** *adj animal* propre. ♦ **housewarming** *n*: **to give a ~warming (party)** pendre la crémaillère. ♦ **housewife** *n, pl* **~wives** ménagère *f*; (*as opposed to career woman*) femme *f* au foyer. ♦ **housewifely** *adj* de ménagère. ♦ **housework** *n* (travaux *mpl* de) ménage *m*; **to do the ~work** faire le ménage.

housing ['haʊzɪŋ] **1** *n* logement *m*. **Ministry of H~** ministère *m* du Logement. **2** *adj shortage, crisis* du logement. **housing estate** *or* **scheme** *or* **project** cité *f*, lotissement *m*.

hove [həʊv] *pret, ptp of* **heave**.

hovel ['hɒvəl] *n* taudis *m*.

hover ['hɒvəʳ] *vi* (*gen*) planer (*above* au-dessus de); *[insect, small bird]* voltiger; *[person]* (**~ about, ~ around**) rôder; *[smile]* errer. **he was ~ing between life and death** il restait suspendu entre la vie et la mort. ♦ **hovercraft** *n* aéroglisseur *m*. ♦ **hoverport** *n* hoverport *m*.

how [haʊ] **1** *adv* **(a)** (*gen*) comment. **~ did you come?** comment êtes-vous venu?; **~ are you?** comment allez-vous?; **~ do you do?** (*greeting*) bonjour; (*on being introduced*) (enchanté) Monsieur (*etc*); **to learn ~ to do sth** apprendre à faire qch; **I know ~ to do it** je sais le faire; **~ was the play?** comment avez-vous trouvé la pièce?; **~ is it that ...?** comment se fait-il que ...? + *subj*; **~ come?*** comment ça se fait?*; **~ come you aren't going out?*** comment ça se fait que tu ne sors pas?*; **~ about going for a walk?** si on allait se promener?; **and ~!*** et comment!* **(b)** que, comme. **~ big he is!** comme *or* qu'il est grand!, ce qu'il est grand!; **~ splendid!** c'est merveilleux!; **~ very kind of you!** c'est très aimable à vous; **~ long is the boat?** quelle est la longueur du bateau?; **~ tall is he?** combien mesure-t-il?; **~ old is he?** quel âge a-t-il?; **~ soon can you come?** quand pouvez-vous venir?; **~ much, ~ many** combien; **~ many days?** combien de jours? **(c)** (*that*) que. **she told me ~ she had seen the child lying on the ground** elle m'a raconté qu'elle avait vu l'enfant couché par terre. **2** *n*: **the ~ and the why of it** le comment et le pourquoi de cela.

♦ **however 1** *adv*: **~ever you may do it, it will never be right** de quelque manière que vous le fassiez, ce ne sera jamais bien fait; **~ever that may be** quoi qu'il en soit; **~ever tall he may be** *or* is quelque *or* si grand qu'il soit; **~ever little** si peu que ce soit; **~ever did you do it?*** comment avez-vous bien pu faire ça?; **2** *conj* pourtant, cependant, toutefois, néanmoins.

howl [haʊl] **1** *vi [person, animal]* hurler (*with pain etc* de douleur *etc*); (*cry*) pleurer; *[wind]* mugir. **to ~ with laughter** rire aux éclats. **2** *vt* hurler. **3** *n* hurlement *m*; mugissement *m*. ♦ **howler*** *n* gaffe *f*; **schoolboy ~er** perle *f* d'écolier. ♦ **howling** *adj* (*lit*) hurlant; **a ~ing gale** une violente tempête; **~ing success*** succès *m* fou*.

hub [hʌb] *n* moyeu *m*; (*fig*) pivot *m*. (*Aut*) **~ cap** enjoliveur *m*.

hubbub ['hʌbʌb] *n* brouhaha *m*.

huddle ['hʌdl] **1** *n* petit groupe *m* (compact). **to go into a ~*** se réunir en petit comité (*fig*). **2** *vi* se blottir (les uns contre les autres).

huddle down *vi* (*crouch*) se recroqueviller; (*snuggle*) se blottir.

huddle together *vi* (*for warmth*) se blottir les uns contre les autres; (*for discussion*) se réunir en petit groupe.

♦ **huddled** *adj* (*under blanket etc*) blotti, pelotonné; **~d over his books** penché sur ses livres.

hue¹ [hju:] *n*: **to raise a ~ and cry** crier haro (*against* sur).

hue² [hju:] *n* (*colour*) teinte *f*, nuance *f*.

huff* [hʌf] *n*: **in a ~** froissé; **to take the ~, to get into a ~** prendre la mouche. ♦ **huffily*** *adv leave* avec humeur; *say* d'un ton froissé. ♦ **huffiness*** *n* mauvaise humeur *f*. ♦ **huffy*** *adj* froissé.

hug [hʌg] **1** *vt* serrer dans ses bras, étreindre; *[bear, gorilla]* écraser entre ses bras; *[car etc] coast, kerb* serrer. **2** *n* étreinte *f*.

huge [hju:dʒ] *adj object, sum of money, helping* énorme; *house* immense, vaste; *man* énorme, gigantesque; *success* fou. ♦ **hugely** *adv* énormément; (*very*) extrêmement. ♦ **hugeness** *n* immensité *f*.

hulk [hʌlk] *n* (*ship*) épave *f*; (*vehicle, building etc*) carcasse *f*. **big ~ of a man** malabar* *m*. ♦ **hulking** *adj* lourdaud.

hull [hʌl] *n* coque *f*.

hullabaloo* [,hʌləbə'lu:] *n* (*noise*) raffut* *m*; (*fuss*) histoire* *f*.

hullo [hʌ'ləʊ] *excl* = **hallo.**

hum [hʌm] **1** *vi [insect, wire]* bourdonner; *[person]* fredonner; *[aeroplane, engine]* vrombir; *[wireless etc]* ronfler. (*fig*) **to make things ~*** mener les choses rondement; **things began to ~*** les choses ont commencé à s'animer. **2** *vt tune* fredonner. **3** *n* bourdonnement *m*; vrombissement *m*; ronflement *m*. ♦ **hummingbird** *n* colibri *m*.

human ['hju:mən] **1** *adj* humain. **~ being** être *m* humain; **~ nature** nature *f* humaine; **it's only ~ nature to want revenge** c'est humain de chercher à se venger; **he's only ~** il n'est pas un saint. **2** *n* être *m* humain. ♦ **humane** *adj person* plein d'humanité; *method* humain. ♦ **humanely** *adv* avec humanité. ♦ **humanism** *n* humanisme *m*. ♦ **humanist** *n* humaniste *mf*. ♦ **humanitarian** *adj, n* humanitaire (*mf*). ♦ **humanity** *n* humanité *f*. ♦ **humanize** *vt* humaniser. ♦ **humanly** *adv* humainement. ♦ **humanoid** *adj, n* humanoïde (*mf*).

humble ['hʌmbl] **1** *adj* humble. **of ~ origin** d'origine modeste; **in my ~ opinion** à mon humble avis; **to eat ~ pie** faire des excuses humiliantes. **2** *vt* humilier. ♦ **humbly** *adv* humblement.

humbug ['hʌmbʌg] *n* (*person*) fumiste* *mf*; (*behaviour, talk*) fumisterie* *f*.

humdinger‡ ['hʌmdɪŋəʳ] *n* qn *or* qch de sensationnel*. **it's a ~!** c'est sensass!‡

humdrum ['hʌmdrʌm] *adj* monotone.

humid ['hju:mɪd] *adj* humide. ♦ **humidifier** *n* humidificateur *m*. ♦ **humidity** *n* humidité *f*.

humiliate [hju:'mɪlɪeɪt] *vt* humilier. ♦ **humiliating** *adj* humiliant. ♦ **humiliation** *n* humiliation *f*.

humility [hju:'mɪlɪtɪ] *n* humilité *f*.

humour, (*US*) **-or** ['hju:məʳ] **1** *n* **(a)** (*sense of fun*) humour *m*. **he has no sense of ~** il n'a pas le sens de l'humour. **(b)** (*temper*) humeur *f*. **to be in a good/bad ~** être de bonne/mauvaise humeur; **he is in no ~ for working** il n'est pas d'humeur à travailler. **2** *vt person* faire plaisir à; *sb's wishes* se prêter à. ♦ **humorist** *n* humoriste *mf*. ♦ **humorous** *adj book, story, writer* humoristique; *person, remark, tone* plein d'humour. ♦ **humorously** *adv* avec humour. ♦ **humo(u)rless** *adj* qui manque d'humour. ♦ **humo(u)rlessly** *adv* sans humour.

hump [hʌmp] **1** *n* bosse *f*. (*fig*) **we're over the ~*** le plus difficile est fait; **he's got the ~‡** il a le cafard*. **2** *vt back, shoulders* voûter; (*: *carry*) porter. ♦ **humpbacked** *adj person* bossu; *bridge* en dos d'âne.

humus ['hju:məs] *n* humus *m*.

hunch [hʌntʃ] **1** *vt* (**~ up**) *back, shoulders* voûter. **~ed (up) over his books** courbé sur ses livres. **2** *n* **(a)** (*hunk*) gros morceau *m*. **(b)** (*: *premonition*) intuition *f*. **to have a ~ that** avoir idée que, soupçonner que; **you should follow your ~** il faut suivre son intuition; **it's only a ~** ce n'est qu'une idée. ♦ **hunchback** *n* bossu(e) *m(f)*. ♦ **hunchbacked** *adj* bossu.

hundred ['hʌndrɪd] *adj, n* cent (*m*). **a ~ books/chairs** cent livres/chaises; **two ~ chairs** deux cents chaises; **about a ~ books** une centaine de livres; **about a ~** une centaine; **~s of** des centaines de; **a ~ and one** cent un; **the ~ and first** le *or* la cent unième; **it was a ~ per cent successful** cela a réussi à cent pour cent; **to live to be a ~** devenir centenaire; **they came in (their) ~s** ils sont venus par centaines. ♦ **hundredth 1** *adj* centième; **2** *n* centième *mf*; (*fraction*) centième *m*. ♦ **hundredweight** *n* (*Brit, Can*) = *50,7 kg*, (*US*) = *45,3 kg*.

hung [hʌŋ] *pret, ptp of* **hang.**

Hungary ['hʌŋgərɪ] *n* Hongrie *f*.

hunger ['hʌŋgəʳ] **1** *n* (*lit, fig*) faim *f* (*for* de). **2** *adj*: **~ strike** grève *f* de la faim. **3** *vi* avoir faim (*for* de).

hungry ['hʌŋgrɪ] *adj*: **to be** *or* **feel ~** avoir faim; **to be very ~** avoir très faim, être affamé; **to make sb ~** donner faim à qn; **to go ~** (*starve*) souffrir de la faim; (*miss a meal*) se passer de manger; **you look ~** tu as l'air d'avoir faim; (*fig*) **~ for** avide de. ♦ **hungrily** *adv* avidement.

hunk [hʌŋk] *n* gros morceau *m*.

hunt [hʌnt] **1** *n* (*gen*) chasse *f*; (*for sth or sb missing*) recherche *f* (*for* de); (*huntsmen*) chasseurs *mpl*. **tiger ~** chasse au tigre; **the ~ for the murderer** la chasse au meurtrier; **I've had a ~ for my gloves** j'ai cherché mes gants partout. **2** *vt* (*Sport*) chasser, faire la chasse à; (*pursue*) poursuivre; (*seek*) chercher. **we ~ed the town for that** nous avons fait* toute la ville pour trouver ça;

I've ~ed my desk for it j'ai retourné tout mon bureau pour le trouver. **3** *vi* (*Sport*) chasser. **to go ~ing** aller à la chasse; **to ~ for** *game* chasser; *object, facts* rechercher (partout); **he ~ed in his pocket for his pen** il a fouillé dans sa poche pour trouver son stylo.
hunt down *vt sep animal* forcer; *person* traquer; *object, quotation* dénicher.
hunt up *vt sep* rechercher.
♦ **hunter** *n* (*Sport*) chasseur *m*; (*gen*) poursuivant *m*; (*horse*) cheval *m* de chasse. ♦ **hunting 1** *n* (*Sport*) chasse *f* (à courre); **fox-~ing** chasse au renard; **2** *adj*: **~ing lodge** pavillon *m* de chasse. ♦ **huntsman** *n* chasseur *m*.
hurdle ['hɜːdl] *n* (*for fences*) claie *f*; (*Sport*) haie *f*; (*fig*) obstacle *m*. (*Sport*) **the 100-metre ~s** le 100 mètres haies.
hurl [hɜːl] *vt stone* jeter *or* lancer (avec violence) (*at* contre); *abuse etc* lancer (*at* à). **they were ~ed to the ground by the blast** ils ont été précipités à terre par le souffle de l'explosion; **to ~ o.s.** se jeter; **to ~ o.s. at sb/sth** se ruer sur qn/qch; (*fig*) **to be ~ed into** être précipité dans.
hurrah [hʊ'rɑː] *n*, **hurray** [hʊ'reɪ] *n* hourra *m*. **hip, hip, ~!** hip, hip, hip, hourra!; **~ for Richard Thomas!** vive Richard Thomas!
hurricane ['hʌrɪkən] *n* ouragan *m*. **~ lamp** lampe-tempête *f*.
hurry ['hʌrɪ] **1** *n* (*haste*) hâte *f*; (*eagerness*) empressement *m*. **to be in a ~** être pressé; **to be in a ~ to do** avoir hâte de faire; **done in a ~** fait à la hâte; **I won't do that again in a ~!*** je ne suis pas près de recommencer!; **are you in a ~ for this?** vous le voulez très vite?; **what's the ~?** qu'est-ce qui presse?; **there's no ~** rien ne presse; **there's no ~ for it** ça ne presse pas.
2 *vi* se dépêcher, se presser (*to do* de faire). **do ~** dépêchez-vous; **don't ~ over that essay** prenez votre temps pour faire cette dissertation; **to ~ over a meal** manger rapidement; **to ~ in/out** *etc* entrer/sortir *etc* à la hâte *or* précipitamment; **he hurried after her** il a couru pour la rattraper.
3 *vt person* faire presser, faire se dépêcher; *piece of work* presser. **don't ~ your meal** ne mangez pas trop vite; **I don't want to ~ you** je ne veux pas vous bousculer; **you can't ~ him, he won't be hurried** vous ne le ferez pas se dépêcher; **it can't be hurried** cela exige d'être fait sans hâte; **to ~ sb in/out** *etc* faire entrer/sortir *etc* qn à la hâte; **they hurried him to a doctor** ils l'ont emmené d'urgence chez un médecin; **troops were hurried to the spot** des troupes ont été envoyées d'urgence sur place.
hurry along 1 *vi* marcher d'un pas pressé. **~ along!** pressons un peu! **2** *vt sep* = **hurry up 2.**
hurry back *vi* se presser de revenir (*or* de retourner).
hurry on 1 *vi* continuer à la hâte. **they hurried on to the next question** ils sont vite passés à la question suivante. **2** *vt sep* = **hurry up 2.**
hurry up 1 *vi* se dépêcher, se presser. **~ up!** dépêchez-vous! **2** *vt sep person* faire se dépêcher; *work* activer.
♦ **hurried** *adj steps, departure* précipité; *remark* dit à la hâte; *reading, work* fait à la hâte; **to have a hurried meal** manger à la hâte. ♦ **hurriedly** *adv* précipitamment, à la hâte.
hurt [hɜːt] *pret, ptp* **hurt 1** *vt* **(a)** (*physically*) faire mal à, blesser. **to ~ o.s.** se faire mal, se blesser; **to ~ one's arm** se blesser au bras; **I hope I haven't ~ you** j'espère que je ne vous ai pas fait mal?; **where does it ~ you?** où avez-vous mal?; **to get ~** se faire mal. **(b)** (*mentally etc*) faire de la peine à. **sb is bound to get ~** il y a toujours qn qui écope*; **what ~ most was ...** ce qui faisait le plus mal c'était ...; **to ~ sb's feelings** froisser *or* blesser qn; **his feelings were ~** cela l'a froissé. **(c)** *thing, material* abîmer, endommager; *reputation, trade* nuire à. **it wouldn't ~ the grass to water it** ça ne ferait pas de mal au gazon d'être arrosé.
2 *vi* faire mal. **that ~s** ça fait mal; **my arm ~s** mon bras me fait mal; **where does it ~?** où avez-vous mal?; **it won't ~ for being left** il n'y aura pas de mal à laisser cela de côté.
3 *n* (*physical*) mal *m*, blessure *f*. (*fig*) **the real ~ lay in** ce qui lui (*etc*) faisait vraiment mal c'était.
4 *adj* blessé; (*offended*) froissé, blessé.
♦ **hurtful** *adj* (*harmful*) nuisible (*to* à); *remark etc* blessant.
hurtle ['hɜːtl] *vi*: **to ~ along** *etc* avancer *etc* à toute vitesse *or* allure.
husband ['hʌzbənd] **1** *n* mari *m*; (*spouse*) époux *m*. **they were living as ~ and wife** ils vivaient maritalement. **2** *vt* ménager.
hush [hʌʃ] **1** *n* silence *m*, calme *m*. **~!** chut!, silence! **2** *adj*: **to pay sb ~ money*** acheter le silence de qn. **3** *vt* (*silence*) faire taire; (*soothe*) calmer.
hush up *vt sep scandal* étouffer; *fact* cacher; *person* faire taire.
♦ **hushed** *adj voice, conversation* étouffé; *silence* grand, profond. ♦ **hush-hush*** *adj* (ultra-)secret.
husk [hʌsk] *n [grain]* balle *f*; *[nut]* écale *f*.
husky ['hʌskɪ] *adj* **(a)** (*hoarse*) *person* enroué; *voice* rauque; *singer's voice* voilé. **(b)** (*burly*) costaud* *f inv*. ♦ **huskily** *adv* d'une voix rauque; d'une voix voilée. ♦ **huskiness** *n* enrouement *m*.
hustle ['hʌsl] **1** *vt*: **to ~ sb in/out** *etc* (*push*) pousser *or* (*hurry*) bousculer qn pour le faire entrer/sortir *etc*; **to ~ things along** faire activer les choses. **2** *vi*: **to ~ in/out** *etc* entrer/sortir *etc* à la hâte. **3** *n*: **~ and bustle** tourbillon *m* (d'activité).
hut [hʌt] *n* hutte *f*; (*shed*) cabane *f*; (*Mil*) baraquement *m*; (*in mountains*) refuge *m*.
hutch [hʌtʃ] *n* clapier *m*.
hyacinth ['haɪəsɪnθ] *n* jacinthe *f*.
hybrid ['haɪbrɪd] *adj, n* hybride (*m*).
hydrangea [haɪ'dreɪndʒə] *n* hortensia *m*.
hydrant ['haɪdrənt] *n* prise *f* d'eau. **fire ~** bouche *f* d'incendie.
hydraulic [haɪ'drɒlɪk] *adj* hydraulique. ♦ **hydraulics** *nsg* hydraulique *f*.
hydr(o)... ['haɪdr(əʊ)] *pref* hydr(o) .... ♦ **hydrochloric** *adj* chlorhydrique. ♦ **hydroelectric** *adj* hydro-électrique. ♦ **hydrofoil** *n* hydrofoil *m*. ♦ **hydrophobia** *n* hydrophobie *f*. ♦ **hydroplane** *n* hydroglisseur *m*.
hydrogen ['haɪdrɪdʒən] *n* hydrogène *m*. **~ bomb** bombe *f* à hydrogène; **~ peroxide** eau *f* oxygénée.
hyena [haɪ'iːnə] *n* hyène *f*.
hygiene ['haɪdʒiːn] *n* hygiène *f*. ♦ **hygienic** *adj* hygiénique.
hymn [hɪm] *n* hymne *m*, cantique *m*. ♦ **hymnal** *n* ['hɪmnəl] livre *m* de cantiques.
hyper... ['haɪpə^r] *pref* hyper.... ♦ **hypercritical** *adj* hypercritique. ♦ **hypermarket** *n* hypermarché *m*. ♦ **hypersensitive** *adj* hypersensible. ♦ **hypertension** *n* hypertension *f*.
hyphen ['haɪfən] *n* trait *m* d'union. ♦ **hyphenate** *vt* mettre un trait d'union à; **~ated word** mot *m* à trait d'union.
hypnosis [hɪp'nəʊsɪs] *n* hypnose *f*. **under ~** en état d'hypnose. ♦ **hypnotic** *adj* hypnotique. ♦ **hypnotism** *n* hypnotisme *m*. ♦ **hypnotist** *n* hypnotiseur *m*, -euse *f*. ♦ **hypnotize** *vt* hypnotiser; **to hypnotize sb into doing sth** faire faire qch à qn sous hypnose.
hypochondria [ˌhaɪpəʊ'kɒndrɪə] *n* hypocondrie *f*. ♦ **hypochondriac 1** *adj* hypocondriaque; **2** *n* malade *mf* imaginaire.
hypocrisy [hɪ'pɒkrɪsɪ] *n* hypocrisie *f*. ♦ **hypocrite** *n* hypocrite *mf*. ♦ **hypocritical** *adj* hypocrite. ♦ **hypocritically** *adv* hypocritement.
hypodermic [ˌhaɪpə'dɜːmɪk] **1** *adj* hypodermique. **2** *n* seringue *f* hypodermique.

hypothermia [ˌhaɪpəʊˈθɜːmɪə] *n* hypothermie *f.*
hypothesis [haɪˈpɒθɪsɪs] *n, pl* **-eses** hypothèse *f.* ♦ **hypothetic(al)** *adj* hypothétique. ♦ **hypothetically** *adv* hypothétiquement.
hysterectomy [ˌhɪstəˈrektəmɪ] *n* hystérectomie *f.*
hysteria [hɪsˈtɪərɪə] *n* (*Psych*) hystérie *f;* (*gen*) crise *f* de nerfs. ♦ **hysterical** *adj* (*Psych*) hystérique; (*gen*) *person* surexcité; *laugh, sobs* convulsif; **to become hysterical** avoir une violente crise de nerfs. ♦ **hysterically** *adv* (*Psych*) hystériquement; (*gen*) *laugh* convulsivement; *shout, argue* comme un(e) hystérique. ♦ **hysterics** *npl* violente crise *f* de nerfs; (*: *laughter*) fou rire *m*; **to have hysterics** avoir une violente crise de nerfs; (*laughing*) attraper un fou rire.

I

I[1], i [aɪ] *n* (*letter*) I, i *m*.
I[2] [aɪ] *pers pron* (*unstressed*) je, (*before vowel*) j'; (*stressed*) moi. **he and ~ are going to sing** lui et moi allons chanter; **I'LL do it** c'est moi qui vais le faire; **it's ~** c'est moi.
ice [aɪs] **1** *n* **(a)** glace *f*; (*on road*) verglas *m*. **my hands are like ~** j'ai les mains glacées; (*fig*) **to be on thin ~** s'aventurer en terrain glissant; (*fig*) **to put sth on ~** mettre qch en attente; **'Cinderella on ~'** 'Cendrillon, spectacle sur glace'. **(b)** (**~** *cream*) glace *f*. **raspberry ~** glace à la framboise.
2 *adj*: **~ age** période *f* glaciaire; **~ axe** piolet *m*; **~ bucket** seau *m* à glace; **~ cube** glaçon *m* (*cube*); **~ floe** banquise *f*; **~ hockey** hockey *m* sur glace; **~ rink** patinoire *f*; **~ show** spectacle *m* sur glace.
3 *vt cake* glacer.
4 *vi*: **to ~ over** *or* **up** *[wings, windscreen]* givrer; *[river]* geler.
♦ **iceberg** *n* iceberg *m*. ♦ **icebox** *n* (*US: refrigerator*) frigidaire *m* ®; (*Brit: part of refrigerator*) freezer *m*; (*insulated box*) glacière *f* (*also fig: of room etc*). ♦ **icebreaker** *n* (*Naut*) brise-glaces *m inv*. ♦ **ice-cold** *adj drink, hands* glacé; *room, manners, person* glacial. ♦ **ice cream** *n* glace *f*. ♦ **ice-cream soda** *n* ice-cream soda *m*. ♦ **iced** *adj tea, coffee* glacé; *martini* avec des glaçons; *champagne* frappé; *melon* rafraîchi. ♦ **ice(d) lolly** *n* glace *f* (sur bâtonnet). ♦ **ice-skate** *vi* patiner (sur glace). ♦ **ice-skating** *n* patinage *m* (sur glace). ♦ **ice-tray** *n* bac *m* à glaçons. ♦ **icily** *adv* d'un air (*or* d'un ton) glacial. ♦ **icing** *n* (*Culin*) glaçage *m*; **icing sugar** sucre *m* glace; **chocolate icing** glaçage au chocolat. ♦ **icy** *adj* **(a)** (**~ cold**) *wind, weather, stare* glacial; *ground, hands* glacé; **(b)** *road* verglacé.
Iceland ['aɪslənd] *n* Islande *f*.
icicle ['aɪsɪkl] *n* glaçon *m* (*naturel*).
icon ['aɪkɒn] *n* icône *f*.
id [ɪd] *n* (*Psych*) ça *m*.
idea [aɪ'dɪə] *n* idée *f*. **brilliant ~** idée géniale; **good ~!** bonne idée!; **I can't bear the ~ (of it)** je n'ose pas y penser; **it might not be a bad ~ to wait** ce ne serait pas une mauvaise idée d'attendre; **the ~ is to sell the car to him** il s'agit de lui vendre la voiture; **it wasn't my ~!** ce n'est pas moi qui en ai eu l'idée!; **where did you get that ~?** où est-ce que tu as pris cette idée-là?; **what gave you the ~ that ...?** qu'est-ce qui t'a fait penser que ...?; **don't get any ~s!*** ce n'est pas la peine de t'imaginer des choses!*; **to put ~s into sb's head** mettre des idées dans la tête de qn; **according to his ~** selon sa façon de penser; **if that's your ~ of fun** si c'est ça que tu appelles t'amuser; **I've got some ~ of physics** j'ai quelques notions de physique; **I haven't the least** *or* **slightest** *or* **foggiest* ~** je n'en ai pas la moindre idée; **I have an ~ that ...** j'ai idée *or* j'ai dans l'idée que ...; **I had no ~ that ...** j'ignorais absolument que ...; **can you give me a rough** *or* **general ~ of how many you want?** pouvez-vous m'indiquer en gros combien vous en voulez?; **you're getting the ~!*** tu y es!; **I've got the general ~*** je vois à peu près (ce dont il s'agit); **that's the ~!*** c'est ça!; **what's the big ~?*** qu'est-ce que c'est que cette histoire?
ideal [aɪ'dɪəl] *adj, n* idéal (*m*). ♦ **idealism** *n* idéalisme *m*. ♦ **idealist** *adj, n* idéaliste (*mf*). ♦ **idealistic** *adj* idéaliste. ♦ **idealize** *vt* idéaliser. ♦ **ideally** *adv suited* idéalement; *placed, equipped, shaped* d'une manière idéale; **~ly the house should have ...** l'idéal serait que la maison ait ... .
identical [aɪ'dentɪkəl] *adj* identique (*to* à); *twins* vrais. ♦ **identically** *adv* identiquement.
identify [aɪ'dentɪfaɪ] **1** *vt* identifier (*as* comme étant; *with* avec, à). **2** *vi* s'identifier (*with* avec, à). ♦ **identification 1** *n* identification *f*; (*document*) pièce *f* d'identité; **2** *adj mark* d'identification; *papers, tag* d'identité. ♦ **identikit** *n* portrait-robot *m*. ♦ **identity 1** *n* identité *f*; **a case of mistaken identity** une erreur d'identité; **2** *adj card, disc, papers* d'identité; **identity parade** séance *f* d'identification (d'un suspect).
ideology [ˌaɪdɪ'ɒlədʒɪ] *n* idéologie *f*. ♦ **ideological** *adj* idéologique.
idiom ['ɪdɪəm] *n* (*phrase*) expression *f* idiomatique; (*language*) idiome *m*. ♦ **idiomatic** *adj* idiomatique. ♦ **idiomatically** *adv* de façon idiomatique.
idiosyncrasy [ˌɪdɪə'sɪŋkrəsɪ] *n* particularité *f*. ♦ **idiosyncratic** *adj* particulier, caractéristique.
idiot ['ɪdɪət] *n* idiot(e) *m(f)*, imbécile *mf*. ♦ **idiocy** *n* idiotie *f*. ♦ **idiotic** *adj* idiot, bête, stupide. ♦ **idiotically** *adv say, do* bêtement, stupidement; *behave* en idiot *or* en imbécile.
idle ['aɪdl] **1** *adj* **(a)** (*doing nothing*) oisif, désœuvré; (*unemployed*) en chômage; (*lazy*) paresseux; *life* oisif; *machine* au repos. **the ~ rich** l'élite oisive; **in my ~ moments** à mes moments de loisir; (*Ind*) **to make sb ~** réduire qn au chômage; **the whole factory stood ~** l'usine entière était arrêtée. **(b)** *speculation, question, threat* oiseux, vain; *promises, words* en l'air; *fears* sans fondement; *pleasures* futile. **out of ~ curiosity** par curiosité pure et simple; **it is ~ to hope that ...** il est inutile d'espérer que ... . **2** *vi* **(a)** (**~ about, ~ around**) paresser. **(b)** *[engine]* tourner au ralenti. ♦ **idleness** *n* oisiveté *f*, désœuvrement *m*; chômage *m*; paresse *f*. ♦ **idler** *n* oisif *m*, -ive *f*, désœuvré(e) *m(f)*; paresseux *m*, -euse *f*. ♦ **idly** *adv* (*without working*) sans travailler; (*lazily*) paresseusement; *say, suggest* négligemment.
idol ['aɪdl] *n* idole *f*. ♦ **idolize** *vt* idolâtrer.
idyll ['ɪdɪl] *n* idylle *f*. ♦ **idyllic** *adj* idyllique.
if [ɪf] **1** *conj* **(a)** si. **I'll go ~ you come with me** j'irai si tu m'accompagnes; **~ I were you** si j'étais vous; **even ~ I knew** même si je le savais; **~ I'm not mistaken** si je ne me trompe, à moins que je ne me trompe (*subj*); **~ only I'd known!** si seulement j'avais su!; **~ necessary** s'il le faut, au besoin; **~ anything, this one is bigger** c'est plutôt celui-ci qui est le plus grand; **~ so** s'il en est ainsi; **~ not** sinon; **~ only for a moment** ne serait-ce que pour un instant; **~ it isn't Smith!** par exemple! Smith!; **~ I know HER, she'll refuse** telle que je la connais, elle refusera. **(b)** (*whenever*) si. **~ I asked him he helped me** si je le lui demandais il m'aidait. **(c)** (*although, admitting that*) **(even) ~ it takes me all day** même si cela doit *or* quand bien même cela devrait me prendre toute la journée; **nice weather, ~ rather cold** temps agréable, bien qu'un peu froid; **even ~ it is a good film it's rather**

long c'est un bon film bien qu'il soit un peu long. **(d)** (*whether*) si. **do you know ~ they have gone?** savez-vous s'ils sont partis? **(e) as ~** comme (si). **he acts as ~ he were rich** il se conduit comme s'il était riche; **as ~ by chance** comme par hasard.

2 *n*: **~s and buts** les si *mpl* et les mais *mpl*; **it's a big ~** c'est un grand point d'interrogation.

igloo [ˈɪgluː] *n* igloo *m*.

ignite [ɪgˈnaɪt] **1** *vt* mettre le feu à. **2** *vi* prendre feu. ♦ **ignition 1** *n* (*gen*) ignition *f*; (*Aut*) allumage *m*; **to switch on the ignition** mettre le contact; **2** *adj*: **ignition key** clef *f* de contact; **ignition switch** contact *m*.

ignoble [ɪgˈnəʊbl] *adj* ignoble.

ignominious [ˌɪgnəˈmɪnɪəs] *adj* ignominieux. ♦ **ignominiously** *adv* ignominieusement. ♦ **ignominy** *n* ignominie *f*.

ignoramus [ˌɪgnəˈreɪməs] *n* ignare *mf*.

ignorance [ˈɪgnərəns] *n* ignorance *f* (*of a fact* d'un fait; *of geography etc* en matière de géographie *etc*). **to be in ~ of sth** ignorer qch; **to keep sb in ~ of sth** laisser ignorer qch à qn; **~ of the law is no excuse** nul n'est censé ignorer la loi; **don't show your ~!** ce n'est pas la peine d'étaler ton ignorance! ♦ **ignorant** *adj person* ignorant (*of* de); *words* qui trahit l'ignorance; **to be ignorant of sth** ignorer qch. ♦ **ignorantly** *adv* par ignorance.

ignore [ɪgˈnɔːʳ] *vt remark, objection, awkward fact* ne tenir aucun compte de; *sb's behaviour* faire semblant de ne pas s'apercevoir de; *person* faire semblant de ne pas reconnaître; *invitation, letter* ne pas répondre à; *rule, prohibition* ne pas respecter; *facts* méconnaître. **I shall ~ your impertinence** je ne relèverai pas votre impertinence; **we cannot ~ this behaviour any longer** nous ne pouvons plus fermer les yeux sur ces agissements.

ill [ɪl] **1** *adj, comp* **worse**, *superl* **worst (a)** (*sick*) malade, (*less serious*) souffrant. **to be ~** être malade *or* souffrant; **to fall** *or* **be taken ~** tomber malade; **he's seriously ~ in hospital** il est à l'hôpital dans un état grave; **~ with anxiety** malade d'inquiétude. **(b)** (*bad*) *deed, health, omen* mauvais (*before n*). **~ effects** conséquences *fpl* désastreuses; **~ feeling** ressentiment *m*; **no ~ feeling!** sans rancune!; **~ humour,** *or* **temper** mauvaise humeur *f*; **~ luck** malchance *f*; **~ nature** méchanceté *f*; **~ will** malveillance *f*; **I bear him no ~ will** je ne lui en veux pas; **it's an ~ wind that blows nobody any good** à quelque chose malheur est bon.

2 *n* mal *m*. **to speak ~ of** dire du mal de; (*misfortunes*) **~s** malheurs *mpl*.

3 *adv nourished, prepared etc* mal. **he can ~ afford to do it** il peut difficilement se permettre de le faire; **to go ~ with sb** aller mal pour qn.

♦ **ill-advised** *adj decision, remark* peu judicieux (*V also* **advise**). ♦ **ill-bred** *adj* mal élevé. ♦ **ill-considered** *adj* irréfléchi. ♦ **ill-fated** *adj person* infortuné; *day* néfaste; *action, effort* malheureux. ♦ **ill-favoured** *adj* laid. ♦ **ill-gotten gains** *npl* biens *mpl* mal acquis. ♦ **ill-humoured** *adj* maussade. ♦ **ill-informed** *adj person* mal renseigné; *essay, speech* plein d'inexactitudes. ♦ **ill-judged** *adj* peu judicieux. ♦ **ill-mannered** *adj person* mal élevé; *behaviour* impoli. ♦ **ill-natured** *adj* désagréable. ♦ **illness** *n* maladie *f*; **to have a long ~ness** faire une longue maladie. ♦ **ill-tempered** *adj* (*habitually*) qui a mauvais caractère; (*on one occasion*) de mauvaise humeur. ♦ **ill-timed** *adj* inopportun, intempestif. ♦ **ill-treat** *or* ♦ **ill-use** *vt* maltraiter. ♦ **ill-treatment** *n* mauvais traitements *mpl*.

illegal [ɪˈliːgəl] *adj* illégal. ♦ **illegality** *n* illégalité *f*. ♦ **illegally** *adv* illégalement.

illegible [ɪˈledʒəbl] *adj* illisible. ♦ **illegibly** *adv* illisiblement.

illegitimate [ˌɪlɪˈdʒɪtɪmɪt] *adj action, child* illégitime; *conclusion* injustifié. ♦ **illegitimacy** *n* illégitimité *f*. ♦ **illegitimately** *adv* illégitimement.

illicit [ɪˈlɪsɪt] *adj* illicite. ♦ **illicitly** *adv* illicitement.

illiterate [ɪˈlɪtərɪt] **1** *adj person* illettré, analphabète; *letter, sentence* plein de fautes. **2** *n* illettré(e) *m(f)*, analphabète *mf*. ♦ **illiteracy** *n* analphabétisme *m*.

illogical [ɪˈlɒdʒɪkəl] *adj* illogique. ♦ **illogicality** *n* illogisme *m*. ♦ **illogically** *adv* illogiquement.

illuminate [ɪˈluːmɪneɪt] *vt* (*gen, also fig*) éclairer; (*for special occasion or effect*) *building etc* illuminer; *manuscript* enluminer. **~d sign** enseigne *f* lumineuse. ♦ **illuminating** *adj* éclairant. ♦ **illumination** *n* éclairage *m*; illumination *f*; **illuminations** illuminations *fpl*.

illusion [ɪˈluːʒən] *n* illusion *f*. **to be under the ~ that** avoir l'illusion que +*indic*; **to have no ~s** ne se faire aucune illusion (*about* sur). ♦ **illusive** *or* ♦ **illusory** *adj* illusoire.

illustrate [ˈɪləstreɪt] *vt* (*lit, fig*) illustrer. **~d paper** *or* **journal** illustré *m*. ♦ **illustration** *n* illustration *f*; (*fig*) **by way of illustration** à titre d'exemple. ♦ **illustrative** *adj* explicatif. ♦ **illustrator** *n* illustrateur *m*, -trice *f*.

illustrious [ɪˈlʌstrɪəs] *adj* illustre. ♦ **illustriously** *adv* glorieusement.

image [ˈɪmɪdʒ] *n* (*gen*) image *f*; (*reflection*) réflexion *f*. (*fig*) **he is the ~ of his father** c'est tout le portrait de son père; **I had a sudden (mental) ~ of her** soudain je l'ai vue en imagination; **they had quite the wrong ~ of him** ils se faisaient une idée tout à fait fausse de lui; *[politician, town etc]* **(public) ~** image de marque (*fig*); **he's got the wrong ~ for that** son image de marque ne convient guère à cela. ♦ **imagery** *n* images *fpl*.

imagine [ɪˈmædʒɪn] *vt* **(a)** (*picture to o.s.*) (s')imaginer. **~ that you were at school** imagine que tu sois à l'école; **I can't ~ myself at 60** je ne m'imagine pas du tout à 60 ans; **just ~!** tu (t')imagines!; **I can ~!** je m'en doute!; **you can ~ how I felt!** imaginez-vous ce que j'ai pu ressentir!; **you can ~ how pleased I was!** vous pensez si j'étais content!; **you can't ~ how difficult it is** vous ne pouvez pas vous imaginer *or* vous figurer combien c'est difficile; **he's always imagining things** il se fait des idées. **(b)** (*suppose, believe*) imaginer, supposer (*that* que). **don't ~ that I can help you** n'allez pas croire *or* vous imaginer que je puisse vous aider; **I didn't ~ he would come** je ne me doutais pas qu'il viendrait. ♦ **imaginable** *adj* imaginable; **the quietest person imaginable** la personne la plus silencieuse qu'on puisse imaginer. ♦ **imaginary** *adj* imaginaire. ♦ **imagination** *n* imagination *f*; **to have a vivid imagination** avoir l'imagination fertile; **he's got imagination** il a de l'imagination; **she lets her imagination run away with her** elle se laisse emporter par son imagination; **in imagination** en imagination; **it is all (your) imagination!** vous vous faites des idées!; **use your imagination!** aie donc un peu d'imagination! ♦ **imaginative** *adj* plein d'imagination.

imbalance [ɪmˈbæləns] *n* déséquilibre *m*.

imbecile [ˈɪmbəsiːl] *adj, n* imbécile (*mf*). **you ~!** espèce d'imbécile! ♦ **imbecility** *n* imbécillité *f*.

imbibe [ɪmˈbaɪb] *vt* (*drink*) boire; (*absorb: also fig*) absorber.

imitate [ˈɪmɪteɪt] *vt* imiter. ♦ **imitation 1** *n* imitation *f*; **in imitation of** à l'imitation de; **2** *adj jewellery etc* faux; *precious stone* artificiel; **imitation leather/marble** *etc* imitation *f* cuir/marbre *etc*. ♦ **imitative** *adj* imitatif. ♦ **imitator** *n* imitateur *m*, -trice *f*.

immaculate [ɪˈmækjʊlɪt] *adj* (*gen*) impeccable; *behaviour* irréprochable. **the I~ Conception** l'Immaculée Conception *f*. ♦ **immaculately** *adv*

dress avec un soin impeccable; *behave* de façon irréprochable.
immaterial [ˌɪməˈtɪərɪəl] *adj* peu important. **it is ~ whether** il importe peu que +*subj*; **that's quite ~** la question n'est pas là; **that is quite ~ to me** cela m'est indifférent.
immature [ˌɪməˈtjʊəʳ] *adj fruit* qui n'est pas mûr; *animal, tree* jeune; *person* qui manque de maturité. ♦ **immaturity** *n* manque *m* de maturité.
immeasurable [ɪˈmeʒərəbl] *adj* (*lit*) incommensurable; (*fig*) infini. ♦ **immeasurably** *adv* (*fig*) infiniment.
immediate [ɪˈmiːdɪət] *adj* (*gen*) immédiat; *knowledge* immédiat, direct; *measures, need* immédiat, urgent. **to take ~ action** agir immédiatement (*to do* pour faire); **in the ~ future** dans un avenir immédiat; **my ~ object** mon premier but; **the ~ area** les environs immédiats. ♦ **immediacy** *n* caractère *m* immédiat. ♦ **immediately 1** *adv* (*at once*) immédiatement, tout de suite; (*directly*) *affect, concern* directement; **~ly after** aussitôt après; **2** *conj* (*gen*) dès que; **~ly I returned** dès mon retour.
immense [ɪˈmens] *adj* immense. ♦ **immensely** *adv rich* immensément, extrêmement; *enjoy o.s.* énormément. ♦ **immensity** *n* immensité *f*.
immerse [ɪˈmɜːs] *vt* plonger (*in* dans), immerger. **~d in one's work** plongé dans son travail. ♦ **immersion 1** *n* immersion *f*; **2** *adj*: **immersion heater** chauffe-eau *m inv* électrique.
immigrant [ˈɪmɪgrənt] *adj, n* (*newly arrived*) immigrant(e) *m(f)*; (*established*) immigré(e) *m(f)*. ♦ **immigrate** *vi* immigrer. ♦ **immigration** *n* immigration *f*; **immigration authorities** service *m* de l'immigration.
imminent [ˈɪmɪnənt] *adj* imminent. ♦ **imminence** *n* imminence *f*.
immobile [ɪˈməʊbaɪl] *adj* immobile. ♦ **immobility** *n* immobilité *f*. ♦ **immobilize** *vt* immobiliser.
immoderate [ɪˈmɒdərɪt] *adj* immodéré. ♦ **immoderately** *adv* immodérément.
immodest [ɪˈmɒdɪst] *adj* (*indecent*) immodeste; (*bumptious*) présomptueux.
immoral [ɪˈmɒrəl] *adj* immoral. ♦ **immorality** *n* immoralité *f*.
immortal [ɪˈmɔːtl] *adj, n* immortel(le) *m(f)*. ♦ **immortality** *n* immortalité *f*. ♦ **immortalize** *vt* immortaliser.
immovable [ɪˈmuːvəbl] *adj object* fixe; *courage* inébranlable; *person* insensible.
immune [ɪˈmjuːn] *adj* immunisé (*from, to, against* contre). ♦ **immunity** *n* immunité *f*. ♦ **immunization** *n* immunisation *f*. ♦ **immunize** *vt* immuniser (*against* contre).
immutable [ɪˈmjuːtəbl] *adj* immuable. ♦ **immutably** *adv* immuablement.
imp [ɪmp] *n* diablotin *m*; (*child*) petit(e) espiègle *m(f)*.
impact [ˈɪmpækt] *n* (*lit, fig*) impact *m* (*on* sur). **to make an ~ on sb** faire une forte impression sur qn.
impair [ɪmˈpɛəʳ] *vt abilities, faculties* diminuer; *negotiations, relations* porter atteinte à; *health* détériorer; *sight, hearing* affaiblir.
impart [ɪmˈpɑːt] *vt* (*make known*) *news, knowledge* communiquer; (*bestow*) transmettre.
impartial [ɪmˈpɑːʃəl] *adj* impartial. ♦ **impartiality** *n* impartialité *f*. ♦ **impartially** *adv* impartialement.
impassable [ɪmˈpɑːsəbl] *adj barrier, river* infranchissable; *road* impraticable.
impassioned [ɪmˈpæʃnd] *adj* passionné.
impassive [ɪmˈpæsɪv] *adj* impassible. ♦ **impassively** *adv* impassiblement.
impatient [ɪmˈpeɪʃənt] *adj* **(a)** impatient (*to do* de faire). **to grow ~** s'impatienter. **(b)** intolérant (*of sth* à l'égard de qch; *with sb* vis-à-vis de qn). ♦ **impatience** *n* impatience *f* (*to do* de faire); intolérance *f* (*with sb* vis-à-vis de qn). ♦ **impatiently** *adv* avec impatience.
impeach [ɪmˈpiːtʃ] *vt public official* mettre en accusation; *sb's character* attaquer; *motives, honesty* mettre en doute.
impeccable [ɪmˈpekəbl] *adj* impeccable. ♦ **impeccably** *adv* impeccablement.
impecunious [ˌɪmpɪˈkjuːnɪəs] *adj* impécunieux.
impede [ɪmˈpiːd] *vt* gêner, entraver.
impediment [ɪmˈpedɪmənt] *n* obstacle *m*. **speech ~** défaut *m* d'élocution.
impel [ɪmˈpel] *vt* (*compel*) obliger, forcer (*to do* à faire); (*drive forward*) pousser.
impending [ɪmˈpendɪŋ] *adj birth, arrival* imminent, prochain (*after n*); *danger, storm* imminent, menaçant.
impenetrable [ɪmˈpenɪtrəbl] *adj* impénétrable.
impenitent [ɪmˈpenɪtənt] *adj* impénitent. ♦ **impenitently** *adv* sans repentir.
imperative [ɪmˈperətɪv] **1** *adj need, voice, manner* impérieux; *order* impératif; (*Gram*) impératif. **silence is ~** le silence s'impose; **it is ~ that** il faut absolument que +*subj*. **2** *n* impératif *m*. **in the ~** à l'impératif.
imperceptible [ˌɪmpəˈseptəbl] *adj* imperceptible. ♦ **imperceptibly** *adv* imperceptiblement.
imperfect [ɪmˈpɜːfɪkt] **1** *adj reasoning* imparfait; *car, machine* défectueux; (*Gram*) imparfait. **2** *n* imparfait *m*. **in the ~** à l'imparfait. ♦ **imperfection** *n* imperfection *f*. ♦ **imperfectly** *adv* imparfaitement.
imperial [ɪmˈpɪərɪəl] *adj* (*gen*) impérial; (*lordly*) *splendour* majestueux; *gesture* impérieux; (*Brit*) *weight, measure* légal. ♦ **imperialism** *n* impérialisme *m*. ♦ **imperialist** *adj, n* impérialiste (*mf*). ♦ **imperially** *adv* impérieusement.
imperil [ɪmˈperɪl] *vt* mettre en péril.
imperious [ɪmˈpɪərɪəs] *adj* impérieux. ♦ **imperiously** *adv* impérieusement.
impermanent [ɪmˈpɜːmənənt] *adj* éphémère.
impermeable [ɪmˈpɜːmɪəbl] *adj* imperméable.
impersonal [ɪmˈpɜːsnl] *adj* impersonnel. ♦ **impersonally** *adv* impersonnellement.
impersonate [ɪmˈpɜːsəneɪt] *vt* (*gen*) se faire passer pour; (*Theat*) imiter. ♦ **impersonation** *n* (*Theat*) imitation *f*. ♦ **impersonator** *n* (*Theat*) imitateur *m*, -trice *f*.
impertinent [ɪmˈpɜːtɪnənt] *adj* impertinent (*to sb* envers qn). ♦ **impertinence** *n* impertinence *f*. ♦ **impertinently** *adv* avec impertinence.
imperturbable [ˌɪmpəˈtɜːbəbl] *adj* imperturbable.
impervious [ɪmˈpɜːvɪəs] *adj* imperméable; (*fig*) sourd (*to* à).
impetigo [ˌɪmpɪˈtaɪgəʊ] *n* impétigo *m*.
impetuous [ɪmˈpetjʊəs] *adj* impétueux. ♦ **impetuosity** *n* impétuosité *f*. ♦ **impetuously** *adv* avec impétuosité.
impetus [ˈɪmpɪtəs] *n [object]* force *f* d'impulsion; *[runner]* élan *m*; (*fig*) impulsion *f*.
impiety [ɪmˈpaɪətɪ] *n* impiété *f*.
impinge [ɪmˈpɪndʒ] *vi*: **to ~ on sb/sth** (*gen*) affecter qn/qch; **it suddenly ~d on him** il en a brusquement pris conscience; **to ~ on sb's rights** empiéter sur les droits de qn.
impious [ˈɪmpɪəs] *adj* impie.
implacable [ɪmˈplækəbl] *adj* implacable (*towards* envers). ♦ **implacably** *adv* implacablement.
implant [ɪmˈplɑːnt] *vt* implanter (*in* dans).
implausible [ɪmˈplɔːzəbl] *adj* peu plausible.
implement [ˈɪmplɪmənt] **1** *n* outil *m*, instrument *m*; (*fig*) instrument. **~s** matériel *m*, outils; (*for cooking*) ustensiles *mpl*. **2** [ˈɪmplɪment] *vt contract, decision* exécuter; *promise* accomplir; *law* appliquer; *plan* réaliser; *ideas* mettre en pratique.
implicate [ˈɪmplɪkeɪt] *vt* impliquer, compromettre (*in* dans). ♦ **implication**[1] *n* implication *f*.

implication² [ˌɪmplɪˈkeɪʃən] *n* (*V* **imply**) insinuation *f*, implication *f*; **by implication** implicitement; **I know only from implication** je ne sais que d'après ce qui a été insinué; **the full implications of his words** la portée de ses paroles; **we shall have to study all the implications** il nous faudra étudier toutes les conséquences possibles.
implicit [ɪmˈplɪsɪt] *adj* **(a)** (*implied*) *threat, acceptance* implicite (*in* dans). **(b)** (*unquestioning*) *belief, faith* absolu; *obedience* aveugle. ♦ **implicitly** *adv* **(a)** implicitement. **(b)** absolument; aveuglément.
implore [ɪmˈplɔːʳ] *vt* implorer, supplier (*sb to do* qn de faire); *sb's help etc* implorer. ♦ **imploring** *adj* suppliant. ♦ **imploringly** *adv* d'un air *or* d'un ton suppliant.
imply [ɪmˈplaɪ] *vt* **(a)** *[person]* laisser entendre; (*insinuate*) insinuer (*pej*). **it is implied that ...** il faut sous-entendre que ... . **(b)** *[fact, event]* suggérer, impliquer. ♦ **implied** *adj* sous-entendu.
impolite [ˌɪmpəˈlaɪt] *adj* impoli (*to, towards* envers). ♦ **impolitely** *adv* impoliment. ♦ **impoliteness** *n* impolitesse *f*.
imponderable [ɪmˈpɒndərəbl] *adj, n* impondérable (*m*).
import [ˈɪmpɔːt] **1** *n* **(a)** (*Comm*) importation *f*. **(b)** (*meaning: gen*) sens *m*; *[document]* teneur *f*. **(c)** (*importance*) importance *f*. **2** *adj duty, licence, surcharge* d'importation. **3** [ɪmˈpɔːt] *vt* importer. ♦ **importation** *n* importation *f*. ♦ **importer** *n* importateur *m*.
important [ɪmˈpɔːtənt] *adj* important (*to sth* pour qch; *to sb* à qn). **it is ~ that** il est important que +*subj*; **that's not ~** ça n'a pas d'importance; **he was trying to look ~** il se donnait des airs importants. ♦ **importance** *n* importance *f*; **to be of importance** avoir de l'importance; **it is of the highest importance that ...** il est de la plus haute importance que ... +*subj*; **of no importance** sans importance; **full of his own importance** plein de lui-même. ♦ **importantly** *adv* (*pej*) *say etc* d'un air important; **but, more ~ly, ...** mais, ce qui est plus important, ...
importune [ˌɪmpɔːˈtjuːn] *vt* *[questioner etc]* importuner; *[creditor]* harceler; *[prostitute etc]* racoler. ♦ **importunate** *adj* importun. ♦ **importuning** *n* (*Jur*) racolage *m*.
impose [ɪmˈpəʊz] **1** *vt task, conditions* imposer (*on* à); *sanctions, fine* infliger (*on* à); *tax* mettre (*on* sur). **to ~ o.s. on sb** s'imposer à qn. **2** *vi*: **to ~ on sb** abuser de la gentillesse de qn. ♦ **imposing** *adj* imposant, impressionnant. ♦ **imposition** *n* imposition *f*; **it's rather an imposition on her** c'est abuser de sa gentillesse.
impossible [ɪmˈpɒsəbl] **1** *adj* impossible. **it is ~ for him to leave** il lui est impossible de partir; **he made it ~ for me to accept** il m'a mis dans l'impossibilité d'accepter; **it is/is not ~ that** il est/n'est pas impossible que +*subj*. **2** *n*: **the ~** l'impossible *m*. ♦ **impossibility** *n* impossibilité *f* (*of sth* de qch; *of doing* de faire). ♦ **impossibly** *adv behave* de façon impossible; *late etc* épouvantablement; *stubborn* incroyablement; **if, impossibly, he were to succeed** si, par impossible, il réussissait; **impossibly difficult** d'une difficulté insurmontable.
impostor [ɪmˈpɒstəʳ] *n* imposteur *m*. ♦ **imposture** *n* imposture *f*.
impotent [ˈɪmpətənt] *adj* (*gen; also sexual*) impuissant; (*Med gen*) impotent. ♦ **impotence** *n* impuissance *f*; impotence *f*.
impound [ɪmˈpaʊnd] *vt* confisquer.
impoverished [ɪmˈpɒvərɪʃt] *adj* appauvri. ♦ **impoverishment** *n* appauvrissement *m*.
impracticable [ɪmˈpræktɪkəbl] *adj* impraticable. ♦ **impracticability** *n* impraticabilité *f*.
impractical [ɪmˈpræktɪkəl] *adj person* qui manque d'esprit pratique; *plan, idea* peu réaliste, pas pratique. ♦ **impracticality** *n* manque *m* de réalisme.
imprecise [ˌɪmprɪˈsaɪs] *adj* imprécis.
impregnable [ɪmˈpregnəbl] *adj* (*Mil*) imprenable; (*fig*) *position* inattaquable, irréfutable.
impregnate [ˈɪmpregneɪt] *vt* (*fertilize*) féconder; (*saturate: also fig*) imprégner (*with* de).
impresario [ˌɪmpreˈsɑːrɪəʊ] *n* impresario *m*.
impress [ɪmˈpres] *vt* **(a)** *person* impressionner. **how did he ~ you?** quelle impression vous a-t-il faite?; **he ~ed me favourably** il m'a fait une bonne impression; **I am not ~ed** ça ne m'impressionne pas. **(b)** *seal, imprint* imprimer (*on* sur). (*fig*) **to ~ sth on sb** faire bien comprendre qch à qn; **to ~ on sb that** faire bien comprendre à qn que. ♦ **impression** *n* impression *f*; **to make an ~ion** faire de l'effet (*on sb* à qn); **the water made no ~ion on the stains** l'eau n'a fait aucun effet sur les taches; **I am under the ~ion that ...** j'ai l'impression que ...; **that wasn't my ~ion!** ce n'est pas l'impression que j'ai eue! ♦ **impressionable** *adj* impressionnable; *age* où l'on est impressionnable. ♦ **impressionism** *n* impressionnisme *m*. ♦ **impressionist** *adj, n* impressionniste (*mf*). ♦ **impressionistic** *adj* impressionniste. ♦ **impressive** *adj* impressionnant. ♦ **impressively** *adv* de façon impressionnante.
imprint [ɪmˈprɪnt] **1** *vt* imprimer (*on* sur). **2** [ˈɪmprɪnt] *n* empreinte *f*. **published under the Collins ~** édité chez Collins.
imprison [ɪmˈprɪzn] *vt* emprisonner; *[judge]* condamner à la prison. **he had been ~ed for 3 months when ...** il avait été en prison 3 mois quand ... . ♦ **imprisonment** *n* (*action, state*) emprisonnement *m*; **one month's ~ment** un mois de prison.
improbable [ɪmˈprɒbəbl] *adj event* improbable; *story, excuse* invraisemblable. **it is ~ that** il est improbable que +*subj*. ♦ **improbability** *n* improbabilité *f*; invraisemblance *f*.
impromptu [ɪmˈprɒmptjuː] *adv, adj, n* impromptu (*m*).
improper [ɪmˈprɒpəʳ] *adj* (*unsuitable*) déplacé; (*indecent*) indécent; (*dishonest*) malhonnête; (*wrong*) incorrect. ♦ **improperly** *adv* d'une manière déplacée; indécemment; malhonnêtement; incorrectement. ♦ **impropriety** *n* inconvenance *f*.
improve [ɪmˈpruːv] **1** *vt* (*gen*) améliorer; *physique* développer; *machine, invention* améliorer, perfectionner; *site* embellir; *soil, land* amender. **to ~ sb's looks** embellir qn; **that should ~ his chances of success** ceci devrait lui donner de meilleures chances de réussir; **to ~ one's mind** se cultiver; **to ~ one's French** se perfectionner en français; **to ~ the occasion** tirer parti de l'occasion. **2** *vi* s'améliorer; se développer; être amélioré, être perfectionné; s'amender. **to ~ on acquaintance** gagner à être connu; **the invalid is improving** l'état du malade s'améliore; **his maths have ~d** il a fait des progrès en maths; **business is improving** les affaires reprennent; **things are improving** les choses vont mieux; **to ~ on sth** faire mieux que qch; **to ~ on sb's offer** enchérir sur qn. ♦ **improvement** *n* amélioration *f*; développement *m*; perfectionnement *m*; embellissement *m*; amendement *m*; **there's been quite an ~ment** il y a du mieux; **to show some ~ment in French** faire quelques progrès en français; **this model is an ~ment on the previous one** ce modèle marque un progrès sur le précédent; **there is room for ~ment** cela pourrait être mieux; **to carry out ~ments to sth** apporter des améliorations à qch; **~ment grant** subvention *f* pour l'amélioration de l'habitat. ♦ **improving** *adj book etc* édifiant.
improvident [ɪmˈprɒvɪdənt] *adj* imprévoyant.
improvise [ˈɪmprəvaɪz] *vti* improviser.

♦ **improvisation** *n* improvisation *f*.
imprudent [ɪm'pru:dənt] *adj* imprudent. ♦ **imprudence** *n* imprudence *f*. ♦ **imprudently** *adv* imprudemment.
impudent ['ɪmpjʊdənt] *adj* impudent. ♦ **impudence** *n* impudence *f*. ♦ **impudently** *adv* impudemment.
impulse ['ɪmpʌls] **1** *n* impulsion *f*. **rash ~** coup *m* de tête; **on a sudden ~ he ...** pris d'une impulsion soudaine il ...; **to act on (an) ~** agir par impulsion. **2** *adj*: **~ buying** tendance *f* à faire des achats sur un coup de tête.
♦ **impulsion** *n* impulsion *f*. ♦ **impulsive** *adj movement, action* impulsif; *temperament* primesautier; *remark* irréfléchi. ♦ **impulsively** *adv* par impulsion. ♦ **impulsiveness** *n* caractère *m* impulsif.
impunity [ɪm'pju:nɪtɪ] *n*: **with ~** impunément.
impure [ɪm'pjʊə^r] *adj* impur. ♦ **impurity** *n* impureté *f*.
impute [ɪm'pju:t] *vt* imputer (*to* à). ♦ **imputation** *n* imputation *f*.
in [ɪn] **1** *prep* **(a)** (*place*) dans, en, à. **~ the garden** dans le *or* au jardin; **~ the country** à la campagne; **~ town** en ville; **~ here** ici; **~ there** là-dedans; **~ school** à l'école; **~ the school** dans l'école; **~ a friend's house** chez un ami; **~ London** à Londres; **~ Yorkshire** dans le Yorkshire; **~ Provence** en Provence; **~ France** en France; **~ Denmark** au Danemark; **~ the United States** aux États-Unis; **~ the army** dans l'armée; **he's ~ the motor trade** il travaille dans l'industrie automobile.
(b) (*people, works*) chez, en, dans. **we find it ~ Dickens** nous le trouvons chez *or* dans Dickens; **rare ~ a child of that age** rare chez un enfant de cet âge; **he has got it ~ him to succeed** il est capable de réussir; **they've got a great leader ~ him** ils ont en lui un excellent dirigeant.
(c) (*time: during*) **~ 1989** en 1989; **~ the sixties** dans les années soixante; **~ the reign of** sous le règne de; **~ June** en juin, au mois de juin; **~ spring** au printemps; **~ summer/autumn/winter** en été/automne/hiver; **~ the morning** le matin, dans la matinée; **~ the mornings** le matin; **~ the daytime** pendant la journée; **~ the evening** le soir, pendant la soirée; **~ the night** la nuit, pendant la nuit; **3 o'clock ~ the afternoon** 3 heures de l'après-midi; **~ those days** à cette époque-là; **~ these days** de nos jours; **I haven't seen him ~ years** cela fait des années que je ne l'ai pas vu.
(d) (*time: in the space of*) en. **I did it ~ 2 hours** je l'ai fait en 2 heures, j'ai mis 2 heures à le faire.
(e) (*time: at the end of*) dans, au bout de. **~ a moment** dans une minute; **he will arrive ~ a week** il arrivera dans une semaine; **he returned ~ a week** il est rentré au bout d'une semaine.
(f) (*manner etc*) **~ a loud voice** d'une voix forte; **~ a soft voice** à voix basse; **~ a whisper** en chuchotant; **~ ink** à l'encre; **~ pencil** au crayon; **~ French** en français; **~ writing** par écrit; **to paint ~ oils** peindre à l'huile; **to stand ~ a row** être en ligne; **~ large/small quantities** en grande/petite quantité; **~ some measure** dans une certaine mesure; **~ part** en partie; **~ hundreds** par centaines; **dressed ~ white** habillé en *or* vêtu de blanc; **~ slippers** en pantoufles; **you look nice ~ that dress** tu es jolie avec cette robe.
(g) (*material*) en. **~ silk** en soie; **~ marble** en marbre.
(h) (*circumstances*) **~ the rain** sous la pluie; **~ the sun** au soleil; **~ the shade** à l'ombre; **~ darkness** dans l'obscurité; **~ the moonlight** au clair de lune; **~ all weathers** par tous les temps.
(i) (*state, condition*) **~ good health** en bonne santé; **~ tears** en larmes; **~ despair** au désespoir; **to be ~ a rage** être en rage; **~ good repair** en bon état; **to live ~ luxury** vivre dans le luxe; **~ private** en privé; **~ secret** en secret.
(j) (*ratio*) **one man ~ ten** un homme sur dix; **once ~ a hundred years** une fois tous les cent ans; **a day ~ a thousand** un jour entre mille; **15 pence ~ the pound** 15 pence par livre sterling.
(k) (*in respect of*) **blind ~ the left eye** aveugle de l'œil gauche; **poor ~ maths** faible en maths; **10 metres ~ height by 30 ~ length** 10 mètres de haut sur 30 de long; **5 ~ number** au nombre de 5; **~ that, he resembles his father** en cela, il ressemble à son père.
(l) (*after superlative*) de. **the best pupil ~ the class** le meilleur élève de la classe.
(m) ~ that there are 5 of them étant donné qu'il y en a 5; **~ so** *or* **as far as** dans la mesure où; **~ all** en tout.
2 *adv*: **to be ~** (*at home, office etc*) être là; *[fire]* brûler encore; *[train]* être arrivé; *[harvest]* être rentré; (*in season*) *[fruit etc]* être en saison; (*in fashion*) *[colour, style]* être à la mode; (*in power*) *[political party]* être au pouvoir; *[candidate]* être élu. **there is nobody ~** il n'y a personne (à la maison); **we were asked ~** on nous a invités à entrer; (*Pol*) **to put sb ~** porter qn au pouvoir; **~ between** (*space*) entre, au milieu; (*time*) entretemps; **we are ~ for trouble** nous allons avoir des ennuis; **he's ~ for it!*** il va en prendre pour son grade!*; **you don't know what you're ~ for!*** tu ne sais pas ce qui t'attend!; **are you ~ for the race?** est-ce que tu es inscrit pour la course?; **he's ~ for the job of ...** il est candidat au poste de ...; **to have it ~ for sb*** avoir une dent contre qn; **to be ~ on a plan/secret** être au courant d'un plan/d'un secret; **to be (well) ~ with sb** être bien avec qn; **day ~ day out** jour après jour.
3 *adj*: **'~' tray** corbeille *f* du courrier du jour; **it's the ~* thing to do that** c'est très dans le vent* de faire ça; **an ~* joke** une plaisanterie qui n'est comprise que des initiés.
4 *n*: **the ~s and outs** les tenants et les aboutissants *mpl*.
♦ **in-between 1** *n*: **the ~-betweens** ceux qui sont entre les deux; **2** *adj*: **it's ~-between** c'est entre les deux; **~-between times** dans les intervalles. ♦ **in-fighting** *n* (*fig: within group etc*) querelles *fpl* internes. ♦ **in-flight** *adj* en vol. ♦ **in-group** *n* noyau *m* (fermé). ♦ **in-laws*** *npl* (*parents-in-law*) beaux-parents *mpl*; (*others*) belle-famille *f*. ♦ **in-patient** *n* malade *mf* hospitalisé(e). ♦ **in-service training** *n* stage *m* de formation professionnelle continue.
inability [,ɪnə'bɪlɪtɪ] *n* incapacité *f* (*to do* de faire), impuissance *f* (*to do* à faire).
inaccessible [,ɪnæk'sesəbl] *adj* inaccessible (*to* à). ♦ **inaccessibility** *n* inaccessibilité *f*.
inaccurate [ɪn'ækjʊrɪt] *adj* (*gen*) inexact; *word, expression* impropre; *story, report, translation* manquant de précision. ♦ **inaccuracy** *n* inexactitude *f*; impropriété *f*; manque *m* de précision. ♦ **inaccurately** *adv* avec inexactitude, inexactement; *multiply* incorrectement.
inactive [ɪn'æktɪv] *adj person* inactif; *life* peu actif; *volcano* qui n'est pas en activité. ♦ **inaction** *n* inaction *f*. ♦ **inactivity** *n* inactivité *f*.
inadequate [ɪn'ædɪkwɪt] *adj* (*gen*) insuffisant; *piece of work* médiocre; *person* incompétent, inadéquat; (*Psych*) mal adapté (sur le plan socio-affectif). **he felt totally ~** il ne se sentait absolument pas à la hauteur. ♦ **inadequacy** *n* insuffisance *f*; médiocrité *f*; incompétence *f*; (*Psych*) inadaptation *f* socio-affective. ♦ **inadequately** *adv* insuffisamment.
inadmissible [,ɪnəd'mɪsəbl] *adj* inadmissible; (*Jur*) *evidence* irrecevable.
inadvertent [,ɪnəd'vɜ:tənt] *adj* fait (*or* dit *etc*) par inadvertance *or* par mégarde. ♦ **inadvertently** *adv* par inadvertance, par mégarde.
inadvisable [,ɪnəd'vaɪzəbl] *adj* peu sage, à déconseiller. **it is ~ to ...** il est déconseillé de ... + *infin*.

♦ **inadvisability** *n* inopportunité *f* (*of doing* de faire).
inane [ɪˈneɪn] *adj* inepte, stupide. ♦ **inanity** *n* ineptie *f*.
inanimate [ɪnˈænɪmɪt] *adj* inanimé.
inapplicable [ɪnˈæplɪkəbl] *adj* inapplicable (*to* à).
inappropriate [ˌɪnəˈprəʊprɪɪt] *adj* (*gen*) inopportun; *word* impropre; *name* mal choisi. ♦ **inappropriately** *adv* inopportunément; improprement.
inarticulate [ˌɪnɑːˈtɪkjʊlɪt] *adj person* qui s'exprime avec difficulté; *speech* indistinct; (*Anat, Bot*) inarticulé. ~ **with anger** bafouillant de colère.
inartistic [ˌɪnɑːˈtɪstɪk] *adj work* peu artistique; *person* dépourvu de sens artistique. ♦ **inartistically** *adv* de façon peu artistique.
inattention [ˌɪnəˈtenʃən] *n* manque *m* d'attention (*to* accordée à). ♦ **inattentive** *adj* (*not paying attention*) inattentif; (*neglectful*) peu attentionné (*towards sb* envers qn). ♦ **inattentively** *adv* sans prêter attention.
inaudible [ɪnˈɔːdəbl] *adj* inaudible. **he was** ~ on ne l'entendait pas. ♦ **inaudibly** *adv* de manière inaudible.
inaugurate [ɪˈnɔːgjʊreɪt] *vt* (*gen*) inaugurer; *person* investir de ses fonctions. ♦ **inaugural** *adj* inaugural; (*Univ*) **inaugural lecture** leçon *f* inaugurale. ♦ **inauguration** *n* inauguration *f*; investiture *f*.
inauspicious [ˌɪnɔːsˈpɪʃəs] *adj beginning, sign* de mauvais augure; *occasion* peu propice; *circumstances* malencontreux. ♦ **inauspiciously** *adv* d'une façon peu propice; malencontreusement.
inborn [ˌɪnˈbɔːn] *adj*, **inbred** [ˌɪnˈbred] *adj* inné.
incalculable [ɪnˈkælkjʊləbl] *adj* incalculable.
incandescent [ˌɪnkænˈdesnt] *adj* incandescent. ♦ **incandescence** *n* incandescence *f*.
incantation [ˌɪnkænˈteɪʃən] *n* incantation *f*.
incapable [ɪnˈkeɪpəbl] *adj* incapable (*of doing* de faire). ♦ **incapability** *n* incapacité *f* (*of doing* de faire).
incapacity [ˌɪnkəˈpæsɪtɪ] *n* incapacité *f* (*to do* de faire). ♦ **incapacitate** *vt* rendre incapable (*for work etc* de travailler *etc*).
incarcerate [ɪnˈkɑːsəreɪt] *vt* incarcérer.
incarnate [ɪnˈkɑːnɪt] *adj* incarné. ♦ **incarnation** *n* incarnation *f*.
incautious [ɪnˈkɔːʃəs] *adj* imprudent.
incendiary [ɪnˈsendɪərɪ] **1** *adj* incendiaire. **2** *n* (*bomb*) engin *m* incendiaire.
incense[1] [ɪnˈsens] *vt* mettre en fureur. ♦ **incensed** *adj* outré (*at, by* de).
incense[2] [ˈɪnsens] *n* encens *m*.
incentive [ɪnˈsentɪv] **1** *n* objectif *m*. **there is no** ~ **to hard work** il n'y a rien qui incite (*subj*) à travailler dur; **he has no** ~ **to do it** il n'a rien qui l'incite (*subj*) à le faire; **it gave me an** ~ cela m'a encouragé. **2** *adj*: ~ **bonus** prime *f* d'encouragement.
inception [ɪnˈsepʃən] *n* commencement *m*.
incertitude [ɪnˈsɜːtɪtjuːd] *n* incertitude *f*.
incessant [ɪnˈsesnt] *adj* incessant. ♦ **incessantly** *adv* sans cesse, incessamment.
incest [ˈɪnsest] *n* inceste *m*. ♦ **incestuous** *adj* incestueux.
inch [ɪntʃ] **1** *n* pouce *m* (= *2,54 cm*). **a few** ~**es** ≃ quelques centimètres; **not an** ~ **of** ≃ pas un centimètre de; **every** ~ **of the ...** tout le (*or* toute la) ...; **he wouldn't budge an** ~ il n'a pas voulu (*lit*) bouger *or* (*fig*) céder d'un pouce; **he's every** ~ **a soldier** c'est un vrai soldat; **within an** ~ **of (doing) sth** à deux doigts de (faire) qch; ~ **by** ~ petit à petit. **2** *vi*: **to** ~ **(one's way) forward/out** *etc* avancer/sortir *etc* petit à petit. ♦ **inchtape** *n* centimètre *m* (de couturière).
incidence [ˈɪnsɪdəns] *n* fréquence *f*, taux *m*. **the high** ~ **of** le taux élevé de; **the low** ~ **of** la faible fréquence de.
incident [ˈɪnsɪdənt] **1** *n* (*gen*) incident *m*; (*in book, play etc*) épisode *m*. **2** *adj* (*Police etc*) ~ **room** salle *f* d'opérations. ♦ **incidental** [ˌɪnsɪˈdentl] **1** *adj* (*accompanying*) accessoire; (*secondary*) d'importance secondaire; (*unplanned*) accidentel; ~**al expenses** faux frais *mpl*; ~**al music** musique *f* d'accompagnement; **2** *n*: ~**als** (*expenses*) frais *mpl* accessoires. ♦ **incidentally** *adv happen etc* accidentellement; (*by the way*) à propos, entre parenthèses.
incinerate [ɪnˈsɪnəreɪt] *vt* incinérer. ♦ **incineration** *n* incinération *f*. ♦ **incinerator** *n* incinérateur *m*.
incipient [ɪnˈsɪpɪənt] *adj* naissant, qui commence.
incise [ɪnˈsaɪz] *vt* inciser; (*Art*) graver. ♦ **incision** *n* incision *f*. ♦ **incisive** *adj* (*trenchant*) incisif; (*acute*) pénétrant. ♦ **incisively** *adv* d'une façon incisive *or* pénétrante. ♦ **incisor** *n* incisive *f*.
incite [ɪnˈsaɪt] *vt* pousser, inciter (*sb to sth* qn à qch; *sb to do* qn à faire). ♦ **incitement** *n* incitation *f*.
incivility [ˌɪnsɪˈvɪlɪtɪ] *n* incivilité *f*.
inclement [ɪnˈklemənt] *adj* inclément.
incline [ɪnˈklaɪn] **1** *vt* (*lean*) incliner, pencher. ~**d plane** plan *m* incliné; **to** ~ **sb to do** incliner qn *or* rendre qn enclin à faire; *[person]* **to be** ~**d to do** incliner à faire; **he is** ~**d to be lazy** il incline à *or* il est enclin à la paresse; **it's** ~**d to break** cela se casse facilement; **he's that way** ~**d** il a tendance à être comme ça; **if you feel** ~**d** si le cœur vous en dit; **well** ~**d towards sb** bien disposé à l'égard de qn. **2** *vi* **(a)** (*slope*) s'incliner. **(b)** *[colour, beliefs etc]* tendre (*towards* vers). **to** ~ **to an opinion** *etc* pencher pour une opinion *etc*. **3** [ˈɪnklaɪn] *n* inclinaison *f*. ♦ **inclination** *n* (*all senses*) inclination *f*; **my inclination is to leave** j'incline à partir; **I have no inclination to help him** je n'ai aucune envie de l'aider.
include [ɪnˈkluːd] *vt* inclure, comprendre. **it is not** ~**d** (*on list*) cela n'est pas inclus; (*in bill*) ce n'est pas compris *or* inclus; **everything** ~**d** tout compris; **does that** ~ **me?** est-ce que cela s'applique aussi à moi?; **the invitation** ~**s everybody** l'invitation s'adresse à tout le monde; **the children** ~**d** y compris les enfants. ♦ **including** *prep* y compris, compris, inclus; **including the kitchen** la cuisine comprise, y compris la cuisine; **including the service charge** service compris; **not including tax** taxe non comprise; **up to and including 4th May** jusqu'au 4 mai inclus. ♦ **inclusion** *n* inclusion *f*. ♦ **inclusive** *adj charge, sum* global; **from 1st to 6th May inclusive** du 1er au 6 mai inclus; **to be inclusive of** inclure, comprendre. ♦ **inclusively** *adv* inclusivement.
incognito [ɪnˈkɒgnɪtəʊ] **1** *adv* incognito. **2** *adj*: **to remain** ~ garder l'incognito.
incoherent [ˌɪnkəʊˈhɪərənt] *adj* incohérent. ♦ **incoherence** *n* incohérence *f*. ♦ **incoherently** *adv* d'une façon incohérente.
incombustible [ˌɪnkəmˈbʌstəbl] *adj* incombustible.
income [ˈɪnkʌm] **1** *n* (*gen*) revenu *m*. **private** ~ rentes *fpl*; **to live beyond/within one's** ~ dépasser/ne pas dépasser son revenu. **2** *adj*: **the lowest** ~ **group** les économiquement faibles *mpl*; **the middle/upper** ~ **group** la classe à revenus moyens/élevés; ~**s policy** politique *f* des revenus; ~ **tax** impôt *m* sur le revenu; ~ **tax return** déclaration *f* d'impôts.
incomer [ˈɪnˌkʌməʳ] *n* arrivant(e) *m(f)*. ♦ **incoming** *adj crowd* qui entre; *tide* montant; *tenant, mayor* nouveau (*before n*).
incommunicado [ˌɪnkəmjʊnɪˈkɑːdəʊ] *adj* tenu au secret.
incomparable [ɪnˈkɒmpərəbl] *adj* incomparable. ♦ **incomparably** *adv* incomparablement.

incompatible [ˌɪnkəmˈpætəbl] *adj* incompatible. ♦ **incompatibility** *n* incompatibilité *f*; (*in divorce*) incompatibilité d'humeur.
incompetent [ɪnˈkɒmpɪtənt] *adj* incompétent. ♦ **incompetence** *or* ♦ **incompetency** *n* incompétence *f*.
incomplete [ˌɪnkəmˈpliːt] *adj* incomplet. ♦ **incompletely** *adv* incomplètement.
incomprehensible [ɪnˌkɒmprɪˈhensəbl] *adj* incompréhensible. ♦ **incomprehensibly** *adv* de manière incompréhensible.
inconceivable [ˌɪnkənˈsiːvəbl] *adj* inconcevable. ♦ **inconceivably** *adv*: **inconceivably stupid** d'une stupidité inconcevable.
inconclusive [ˌɪnkənˈkluːsɪv] *adj* *result, discussion* peu concluant; *evidence, argument* peu convaincant; *action* sans résultat concluant; *fighting* indécis. ♦ **inconclusively** *adv* d'une manière peu concluante *or* peu convaincante; sans résultat concluant.
incongruous [ɪnˈkɒŋgrʊəs] *adj* (*out of place*) *remark, act* incongru, déplacé; (*absurd*) absurde, grotesque. ♦ **incongruity** [ˌɪnkɒŋˈgruːɪtɪ] *n* incongruité *f*; absurdité *f*.
inconsequent [ɪnˈkɒnsɪkwənt] *adj* inconséquent. ♦ **inconsequential** *adj* **(a)** (*illogical*) inconséquent. **(b)** (*unimportant*) sans conséquence.
inconsiderable [ˌɪnkənˈsɪdərəbl] *adj* insignifiant.
inconsiderate [ˌɪnkənˈsɪdərɪt] *adj* *person* qui manque d'égards; *action, reply* inconsidéré. **you were very ~** tu as agi sans aucun égard.
inconsistent [ˌɪnkənˈsɪstənt] *adj* *speech, person* inconsistant. **~ with** incompatible avec. ♦ **inconsistency** *n* inconsistance *f*.
inconsolable [ˌɪnkənˈsəʊləbl] *adj* inconsolable.
inconspicuous [ˌɪnkənˈspɪkjʊəs] *adj* qui passe inaperçu, qui ne se fait pas remarquer. **to make oneself ~** essayer de passer inaperçu. ♦ **inconspicuously** *adv* *behave, move* sans se faire remarquer; *dress* de façon discrète.
inconstant [ɪnˈkɒnstənt] *adj* inconstant. ♦ **inconstancy** *n* inconstance *f*.
incontestable [ˌɪnkənˈtestəbl] *adj* incontestable.
incontinent [ɪnˈkɒntɪnənt] *adj* incontinent. ♦ **incontinence** *n* incontinence *f*.
incontrovertible [ɪnˌkɒntrəˈvɜːtəbl] *adj* *fact* indéniable; *argument, explanation* irréfutable; *sign, proof* irrécusable.
inconvenient [ˌɪnkənˈviːnɪənt] *adj* *time, place* mal choisi; *house, equipment* incommode, peu pratique; *visitor* gênant, importun. **if it is not ~** si cela ne vous dérange pas; **it is most ~** c'est très gênant. ♦ **inconvenience 1** *n* (*annoying thing*) inconvénient *m*; **to put sb to great inconvenience** causer beaucoup de dérangement à qn; **he went to a great deal of inconvenience to help me** il s'est donné beaucoup de mal pour m'aider; **2** *vt* déranger, incommoder, (*stronger*) gêner. ♦ **inconveniently** *adv* *design* incommodément; *happen, arrive* à contretemps.
incorporate [ɪnˈkɔːpəreɪt] *vt* (*put in*) incorporer (*into* dans; (*Culin*) *into* à); (*include, contain*) contenir; (*Comm, Jur*) se constituer en société unique avec. **~d company** société *f* (*enregistrée*).
incorrect [ˌɪnkəˈrekt] *adj* *wording, calculation, dress, behaviour* incorrect; *statement, opinion, report, time, text* inexact. **he is ~ in stating that ...** il se trompe quand il affirme que ...; **it would be ~ to say** il serait inexact de dire. ♦ **incorrectly** *adv* incorrectement; inexactement.
incorrigible [ɪnˈkɒrɪdʒəbl] *adj* incorrigible.
incorruptible [ˌɪnkəˈrʌptəbl] *adj* incorruptible.
increase [ɪnˈkriːs] **1** *vi* augmenter; *[demand, strength, supply, population, speed]* augmenter, s'accroître; *[joy, rage, effort, pain]* augmenter, s'intensifier; *[sorrow, surprise, possessions, trade]* s'accroître, augmenter; *[noise, pride]* grandir; *[business firm, institution]* s'agrandir, se développer. **to ~ in volume/weight** prendre du volume/poids; **to ~ in width** s'élargir; **to ~ in height** *[person]* grandir; *[tree]* pousser. **2** *vt* augmenter; accroître; intensifier; agrandir; développer. **to ~ (one's) speed** accélérer. **3** [ˈɪnkriːs] *n* augmentation *f* (*in, of* de); accroissement *m*; intensification *f*; agrandissement *m*; développement *m*. **there has been an ~ in police activity** la police a redoublé d'activité; **an ~ in pay** une hausse de salaire, une augmentation; **to be on the ~** = **to ~**, *V* **1**. ♦ **increasing** *adj* croissant. ♦ **increasingly** *adv* de plus en plus.
incredible [ɪnˈkredəbl] *adj* incroyable. ♦ **incredibly** *adv* incroyablement.
incredulous [ɪnˈkredjʊləs] *adj* incrédule. ♦ **incredulity** *n* incrédulité *f*. ♦ **incredulously** *adv* d'un air *or* d'un ton incrédule.
increment [ˈɪnkrɪmənt] *n* augmentation *f*.
incriminate [ɪnˈkrɪmɪneɪt] *vt* incriminer, compromettre. ♦ **incriminating** *adj* compromettant; (*Jur: exhibits etc*) **incriminating evidence** pièces *fpl* à conviction.
incubate [ˈɪnkjʊbeɪt] **1** *vt* *eggs, scheme* couver; *disease* incuber. **2** *vi* couver; être en incubation. ♦ **incubation 1** *n* incubation *f*; **2** *adj* d'incubation. ♦ **incubator** *n [chicks, eggs, infants]* couveuse *f*; *[bacteria, cultures]* incubateur *m*; **in an incubator** en couveuse.
inculcate [ˈɪnkʌlkeɪt] *vt* inculquer (*sth into sb* qch à qn).
incumbent [ɪnˈkʌmbənt] **1** *adj*: **to be ~ upon sb to do sth** incomber à qn de faire qch. **2** *n* (*Rel etc*) titulaire *m*. ♦ **incumbency** *n* charge *f* (*Rel*).
incur [ɪnˈkɜːʳ] *vt* *anger, blame* s'attirer, encourir; *risk* courir; *obligation, debts* contracter; *loss* subir; *expenses* encourir.
incurable [ɪnˈkjʊərəbl] *adj, n* incurable (*mf*). ♦ **incurably** *adv* incurablement.
incurious [ɪnˈkjʊərɪəs] *adj* sans curiosité.
incursion [ɪnˈkɜːʃən] *n* incursion *f*.
indebted [ɪnˈdetɪd] *adj* redevable (*to sb for sth* à qn de qch; *to sb for doing* à qn d'avoir fait).
indecent [ɪnˈdiːsnt] *adj* (*offensive*) indécent; (*unseemly*) inconvenant. (*Jur*) **~ assault** attentat *m* à la pudeur (*on* sur); **~ exposure** outrage *m* public à la pudeur. ♦ **indecency** *n* indécence *f*; inconvenance *f*; (*Jur*) outrage *m* public à la pudeur. ♦ **indecently** *adv* indécemment; de façon inconvenante.
indecipherable [ˌɪndɪˈsaɪfərəbl] *adj* indéchiffrable.
indecisive [ˌɪndɪˈsaɪsɪv] *adj* (*gen*) indécis; *discussion, argument* peu concluant. ♦ **indecision** *n* indécision *f*. ♦ **indecisively** *adv* de façon indécise.
indecorous [ɪnˈdekərəs] *adj* peu convenable.
indeed [ɪnˈdiːd] *adv* en effet, vraiment. **and ~ he did so** et en effet il l'a bien fait; **I feel, ~ I know ...** je sens, et même je sais ...; **I may ~ come** il se peut effectivement que je vienne; **yes ~!** mais certainement, (mais) bien sûr!; **~?** vraiment?, c'est vrai?; **very pleased ~** extrêmement content, vraiment très content; **very grateful ~** infiniment reconnaissant; **thank you very much ~** merci mille fois.
indefatigable [ˌɪndɪˈfætɪgəbl] *adj* infatigable. ♦ **indefatigably** *adv* infatigablement.
indefensible [ˌɪndɪˈfensəbl] *adj* (*gen*) indéfendable; *crime* injustifiable.
indefinable [ˌɪndɪˈfaɪnəbl] *adj* indéfinissable.
indefinite [ɪnˈdefɪnɪt] *adj* *intentions, doubts, feelings* incertain, indéfini, vague; *answer* vague; *outline* indistinct; *size, number, duration* indéterminé; *period* indéfini, indéterminé; *plan* mal défini, peu précis; (*Gram*) indéfini. ♦ **indefinitely** *adv* *wait etc* indéfiniment; **postponed ~ly** remis à une date indéterminée.
indelible [ɪnˈdeləbl] *adj* indélébile; (*fig*) ineffa-

çable. ♦ **indelibly** *adv* de façon indélébile; ineffaçablement.

indelicate [ɪn'delɪkɪt] *adj* (*gen*) indélicat; (*tactless*) indiscret. ♦ **indelicacy** *n* indélicatesse *f*; manque *m* de discrétion.

indemnify [ɪn'demnɪfaɪ] *vt* (*compensate*) indemniser, dédommager (*for* de); (*safeguard*) garantir (*against* contre). ♦ **indemnity** *n* indemnité *f*; garantie *f*.

indent [ɪn'dent] **1** *vt border* denteler; (*Typ*) mettre en retrait. **2** *vi* (*Comm*) **to ~ for sth** commander qch (*on sb* à qn). **3** ['ɪndent] *n* (*Comm*) commande *f*. ♦ **indentation** *n* (*hollow impression*) empreinte *f* (en creux). ♦ **indented** *adj border* dentelé; *coast* échancré; (*Typ*) en retrait. ♦ **indentures** *npl* contrat *m* d'apprentissage.

independent [ˌɪndɪ'pendənt] **1** *adj* indépendant (*of* de); (*unrelated*) *reports* émanant de sources différentes. (*Pol*) **I ~** non-inscrit; **an ~ thinker** un penseur original; **to ask for an ~ opinion** demander l'avis d'un tiers. **2** *n* (*Pol*) **I~** non-inscrit *m*, non-affilié *m*. ♦ **independence 1** *n* indépendance *f* (*from* par rapport à); **the country got its independence** le pays est devenu indépendant; **2** *adj* (*US*) **Independence Day** fête *f* de l'Indépendance américaine (*le 4 juillet*). ♦ **independently** *adv* de façon indépendante; **~ly of** indépendamment de.

indescribable [ˌɪndɪs'kraɪbəbl] *adj* indescriptible. ♦ **indescribably** *adv* indescriptiblement.

indestructible [ˌɪndɪs'trʌktəbl] *adj* indestructible.

indeterminate [ˌɪndɪ'tɜːmɪnɪt] *adj* indéterminé.

index ['ɪndeks] **1** *n* **(a)** (*pl* **~es**) (*in book etc*) index *m*; (*in library etc*) catalogue *m* (alphabétique). (*Rel*) **to put a book on the I~** mettre un livre à l'Index. **(b)** (*pl* **indices**) indice *m*. **cost-of-living ~** indice du coût de la vie; (*fig*) **it is an ~ of how much ...** c'est un signe révélateur qui permet de se rendre compte combien ... . **2** *adj*: **~ card** fiche *f*; **~ finger** index *m*. **3** *vt book* faire l'index de; *library books, information* cataloguer (alphabétiquement); *item, article* classer (*under* sous, à).

♦ **index-linked** *adj* indexé.

India ['ɪndɪə] *n* Inde *f*. ♦ **Indian 1** *n* Indien(ne) *m(f)*; **2** *adj* indien, de l'Inde; (*Brit Hist*) des Indes; *elephant* d'Asie; *ink* de Chine; *tea* indien; **(American) ~n** indien, des Indiens (d'Amérique); **~n Ocean** océan *m* Indien; (*fig*) **~n summer** été *m* de la Saint-Martin. ♦ **indiarubber** *n* (*substance*) caoutchouc *m*; (*eraser*) gomme *f* (*à effacer*).

indicate ['ɪndɪkeɪt] *vt* (*gen*) indiquer (*that* que); *intentions* manifester. (*Aut*) **he was indicating left** il avait mis son clignotant gauche. ♦ **indication** *n* indication *f*; **there is every indication that** tout porte à croire que +*indic*; **there is no indication that** rien ne porte à croire que +*subj*; **it is some indication of** cela permet de se rendre compte de. ♦ **indicative** *adj, n* indicatif (*m*); **in the indicative** à l'indicatif. ♦ **indicator** *n* (*gen*) indicateur *m*; (*needle on scale etc*) aiguille *f*; (*Aut*) clignotant *m*; (*plan*) **town indicator** table *f* d'orientation; (*Rail*) **arrival indicator** tableau *m* des arrivées.

indict [ɪn'daɪt] *vt* accuser (*for, on a charge of* de). ♦ **indictable** *adj*: **~able offence** délit pénal. ♦ **indictment** *n* mise *f* en accusation (*for, of* de).

Indies ['ɪndɪz] *npl* Indes *fpl*. **East ~** Indes orientales; **West ~** Antilles *fpl*.

indifferent [ɪn'dɪfrənt] *adj* indifférent (*to* à); (*mediocre*) médiocre, quelconque. ♦ **indifference** *n* indifférence *f* (*to* à; *towards* envers); médiocrité *f*. ♦ **indifferently** *adv* indifféremment; médiocrement.

indigenous [ɪn'dɪdʒɪnəs] *adj* indigène (*to* de).

indigestion [ˌɪndɪ'dʒestʃən] *n*: **to have ~** (*acute*) avoir une indigestion; (*chronic*) avoir une mauvaise digestion.

♦ **indigestible** *adj* indigeste.

indignant [ɪn'dɪgnənt] *adj* indigné (*about* à propos de; *at sth* de *or* devant qch; *with sb* contre qn). **to grow ~** s'indigner; **to make sb ~** indigner qn. ♦ **indignantly** *adv* avec indignation. ♦ **indignation** *n* indignation *f*; **indignation meeting*** réunion *f* de protestation.

indignity [ɪn'dɪgnɪtɪ] *n* indignité *f*.

indigo ['ɪndɪgəʊ] **1** *n* indigo *m*. **2** *adj* indigo *inv*.

indirect [ˌɪndɪ'rekt] *adj* (*gen*) indirect; *route, means etc* détourné. ♦ **indirectly** *adv* indirectement.

indiscreet [ˌɪndɪs'kriːt] *adj* indiscret. ♦ **indiscreetly** *adv* indiscrètement. ♦ **indiscretion** *n* indiscrétion *f*.

indiscriminate [ˌɪndɪs'krɪmɪnɪt] *adj punishment, blows* distribué au hasard; *killings* commis au hasard; *person* manquant de discernement; *admiration* aveugle. ♦ **indiscriminately** *adv choose, kill* au hasard; *watch TV* sans aucun sens critique; *accept, admire* aveuglément.

indispensable [ˌɪndɪs'pensəbl] *adj* indispensable (*to* à). **you're not ~!** on peut se passer de toi!

indisposed [ˌɪndɪs'pəʊzd] *adj* (*unwell*) indisposé, souffrant; (*disinclined*) peu disposé (*to do* à faire). ♦ **indisposition** *n* indisposition *f*.

indisputable [ˌɪndɪs'pjuːtəbl] *adj* incontestable. ♦ **indisputably** *adv* incontestablement.

indistinct [ˌɪndɪs'tɪŋkt] *adj object, voice, words* indistinct; *memory* vague; *noise* confus. (*on telephone*) **you're very ~** je ne vous entends pas bien. ♦ **indistinctly** *adv* indistinctement.

indistinguishable [ˌɪndɪs'tɪŋgwɪʃəbl] *adj* indifférenciable (*from* de); (*slight*) imperceptible.

individual [ˌɪndɪ'vɪdjʊəl] **1** *adj* (*separate*) *portion, attention* individuel; (*characteristic*) *style* original, particulier. **2** *n* individu *m*. ♦ **individualism** *n* individualisme *m*. ♦ **individualist** *n* individualiste *mf*. ♦ **individualistic** *adj* individualiste. ♦ **individuality** *n* individualité *f*. ♦ **individually** *adv* individuellement.

indivisible [ˌɪndɪ'vɪzəbl] *adj* indivisible.

Indo- ['ɪndəʊ] *pref* indo-. ♦ **Indo-China** *n* Indochine *f*. ♦ **Indo-European** *adj, n* indo-européen (*m*).

indoctrinate [ɪn'dɒktrɪneɪt] *vt* endoctriner. **to ~ sb with sth** inculquer qch à qn. ♦ **indoctrination** *n* endoctrinement *m*.

indolent ['ɪndələnt] *adj* indolent. ♦ **indolence** *n* indolence *f*. ♦ **indolently** *adv* indolemment.

indomitable [ɪn'dɒmɪtəbl] *adj* indomptable.

Indonesia [ˌɪndəʊ'niːzɪə] *n* Indonésie *f*.

indoor ['ɪndɔːʳ] *adj shoes, film scene, photography* d'intérieur; *aerial* intérieur; *plant* d'appartement; *swimming pool, tennis court* couvert; *hobby, game, job,* pratiqué en intérieur; *athletics* en salle. ♦ **indoors** *adv* (*in building*) à l'intérieur; (*at home*) à la maison; (*under cover*) à l'abri; **to go ~s** entrer, rentrer.

indubitable [ɪn'djuːbɪtəbl] *adj* indubitable. ♦ **indubitably** *adv* indubitablement.

induce [ɪn'djuːs] *vt* (*gen*) persuader (*sb to do* qn de faire); *reaction, sleep* provoquer (*in sb* chez qn). (*Med*) **to ~ labour** déclencher l'accouchement (*artificiellement*). ♦ **inducement** *n* (*gen*) encouragement *m* (*to do* à faire); (*pej: bribe*) pot-de-vin *m*; **there is an ~ment/no ~ment to work hard** il y a qch qui incite (*indic*)/il n'y a rien qui incite (*subj*) à travailler dur; **as an added ~ment we are offering ...** comme avantage *m* supplémentaire nous offrons ...; **he received £100 as an ~ment** il a reçu 100 livres à titre de gratification *f*.

induct [ɪn'dʌkt] *vt clergyman, president* installer. ♦ **induction** *n* installation *f*; (*Elec, Philos*) induction *f*; **~ion course** stage *m* préparatoire.

indulge [ɪn'dʌldʒ] **1** *vt person* (*spoil*) gâter; (*give way to*) céder à; *sb's wishes* se prêter à; *one's own desires* satisfaire; *one's own laziness* se laisser aller à. **to ~ o.s.** se passer tous ses caprices. **2** *vi*: **to ~ in** *emotion etc* s'adonner à; **to ~ in a cigarette** se permettre une cigarette; **to ~ in sth to excess** abuser de qch.

indulgent [ɪn'dʌldʒənt] *adj* indulgent (*to* envers). ♦ **indulgence** *n* indulgence *f* (*also Rel*); **his little indulgences** les petites faiblesses *fpl* qu'il se permet. ♦ **indulgently** *adv* avec indulgence.

industry ['ɪndəstrɪ] *n* **(a)** industrie *f*. **tourist ~** tourisme *m*, industrie touristique; **Department of I~** ministère *m* de l'Industrie. **(b)** (*industriousness*) assiduité *f* (au travail). ♦ **industrial** *adj* (*gen*) industriel; *worker* de l'industrie; *disease* professionnel; *accident, medicine* du travail; *dispute* ouvrier; **industrial action** action *f* revendicative; **industrial estate** *or* (*US*) **park** zone *f* industrielle; **industrial rehabilitation** réadaptation *f* fonctionnelle; **industrial unrest** agitation *f* ouvrière. ♦ **industrialism** *n* industrialisme *m*. ♦ **industrialist** *n* industriel *m*. ♦ **industrialization** *n* industrialisation *f*. ♦ **industrialize** *vt* industrialiser. ♦ **industrious** *adj* industrieux. ♦ **industriously** *adv* industrieusement. ♦ **industriousness** *n* assiduité *f* (au travail).

inedible [ɪn'edɪbl] *adj* (*not to be eaten*) non comestible; (*not fit to be eaten*) immangeable.

ineffective [ˌɪnɪ'fektɪv] *adj*, **ineffectual** [ˌɪnɪ'fektjʊəl] *adj remedy, measures* inefficace; *attempt* vain (*before n*); *person* incompétent. ♦ **ineffectively** *or* ♦ **ineffectually** *adv use* inefficacement; *try* vainement.

inefficient [ˌɪnɪ'fɪʃənt] *adj* (*gen*) inefficace; *person* incompétent; *use* mauvais. ♦ **inefficiency** *n* inefficacité *f*; *[person]* incompétence *f*. ♦ **inefficiently** *adv* inefficacement; sans compétence; **work ~ly done** travail mal exécuté.

inelegant [ɪn'elɪgənt] *adj* inélégant. ♦ **inelegantly** *adv* inélégamment.

ineligible [ɪn'elɪdʒəbl] *adj candidate* inéligible. **to be ~ for sth/to do** ne pas avoir droit à qch/le droit de faire.

inept [ɪ'nept] *adj* inepte, stupide. ♦ **ineptitude** *n* ineptie *f*, stupidité *f*.

inequality [ˌɪnɪ'kwɒlɪtɪ] *n* inégalité *f*.

ineradicable [ˌɪnɪ'rædɪkəbl] *adj* indéracinable.

inert [ɪ'nɜːt] *adj* inerte. ♦ **inertia** *n* inertie *f*; (*Aut*) **~ia reel belts** ceintures *fpl* de sécurité à enrouleurs.

inescapable [ˌɪnɪs'keɪpəbl] *adj* inéluctable.

inestimable [ɪn'estɪməbl] *adj* inestimable.

inevitable [ɪn'evɪtəbl] *adj* (*gen*) inévitable; *consequence, result* inévitable, fatal. **it was ~ that she should discover ...** elle devait inévitablement *or* fatalement découvrir ...; (*hum*) **his ~ camera** son inévitable appareil-photo. ♦ **inevitability** *n* caractère *m* inévitable. ♦ **inevitably** *adv* inévitablement, fatalement.

inexact [ˌɪnɪg'zækt] *adj* inexact. ♦ **inexactly** *adv* inexactement.

inexcusable [ˌɪnɪks'kjuːzəbl] *adj* inexcusable. ♦ **inexcusably** *adv* inexcusablement.

inexhaustible [ˌɪnɪg'zɔːstəbl] *adj* inépuisable.

inexorable [ɪn'eksərəbl] *adj* inexorable. ♦ **inexorably** *adv* inexorablement.

inexpensive [ˌɪnɪks'pensɪv] *adj* bon marché *inv*, peu coûteux. ♦ **inexpensively** *adv buy* à bon marché; *live* à peu de frais.

inexperience [ˌɪnɪks'pɪərɪəns] *n* inexpérience *f*. ♦ **inexperienced** *adj* inexpérimenté; **to be ~d in** avoir peu d'expérience en.

inexpert [ɪn'ekspɜːt] *adj* maladroit (*in* en). ♦ **inexpertly** *adv* maladroitement.

inexplicable [ˌɪnɪks'plɪkəbl] *adj* inexplicable. ♦ **inexplicably** *adv* inexplicablement.

inexpressible [ˌɪnɪks'presəbl] *adj* inexprimable.

inextricable [ˌɪnɪks'trɪkəbl] *adj* inextricable. ♦ **inextricably** *adv* inextricablement.

infallible [ɪn'fæləbl] *adj* infaillible. ♦ **infallibility** *n* infaillibilité *f*. ♦ **infallibly** *adv* infailliblement.

infamous ['ɪnfəməs] *adj* infâme.

infant ['ɪnfənt] **1** *n* (*baby*) bébé *m*; (*young child*) tout(e) petit(e) enfant *m(f)*; (*Jur*) mineur(e) *m(f)*; (*Brit Scol*) petit(e) *m(f)* (*de 5 à 7 ans*). **2** *adj disease, mortality* infantile. (*Brit*) **~ school** classes *fpl* préparatoires. ♦ **infancy** *n* toute petite enfance *f*, bas âge *m*; (*Jur*) minorité *f*; (*fig*) **still in its infancy** encore à ses débuts. ♦ **infanticide** *n* infanticide *m*. ♦ **infantile** *adj* infantile.

infantry ['ɪnfəntrɪ] *n* infanterie *f*. ♦ **infantryman** *n* fantassin *m*.

infatuated [ɪn'fætjʊeɪtɪd] *adj*: **~ with** *person* entiché de; *idea etc* engoué de; **to become ~ with** s'enticher de, s'engouer pour; **he was ~d** il avait la tête tournée. ♦ **infatuation** *n* entichement *m*; engouement *m* (*with* pour).

infect [ɪn'fekt] *vt* **(a)** (*Med*) infecter; (*fig*) *person* corrompre. **to ~ sb with a disease/one's enthusiasm** communiquer une maladie/son enthousiasme à qn; **~ed with leprosy** atteint de la lèpre. ♦ **infected** *adj* infecté. ♦ **infection** *n* infection *f*; **to have a slight ~ion** être légèrement souffrant. ♦ **infectious** *adj disease* infectieux; *person* contagieux; *laughter* contagieux.

infer [ɪn'fɜːʳ] *vt* déduire, inférer (*from* de; *that* que). ♦ **inference** ['ɪnfərəns] *n* déduction *f*, inférence *f*; **by ~ence** par déduction.

inferior [ɪn'fɪərɪəʳ] **1** *adj* inférieur (*to* à); *work, goods* de qualité inférieure. **he makes me feel ~** il me donne un sentiment d'infériorité. **2** *n* inférieur(e) *m(f)*; (*in rank*) subordonné(e) *m(f)*. ♦ **inferiority** *n* infériorité *f* (*to* par rapport à); **~ity complex** complexe *m* d'infériorité.

infernal [ɪn'fɜːnl] *adj* infernal. ♦ **infernally** *adv* abominablement.

inferno [ɪn'fɜːnəʊ] *n* enfer *m* (*fig*).

infertile [ɪn'fɜːtaɪl] *adj* infertile; *person* stérile. ♦ **infertility** *n* infertilité *f*; stérilité *f*.

infest [ɪn'fest] *vt* infester (*with* de). ♦ **infestation** *n* infestation *f*.

infidelity [ˌɪnfɪ'delɪtɪ] *n* infidélité *f*; (*Jur: in divorce*) adultère *m*.

infiltrate ['ɪnfɪltreɪt] **1** *vi* s'infiltrer (*into* dans). **2** *vt enemy lines* s'infiltrer dans; *group* noyauter; (*put in*) *troops* faire s'infiltrer (*into* dans). ♦ **infiltration** *n* infiltration *f*; noyautage *m*.

infinite ['ɪnfɪnɪt] *adj, n* infini (*m*). ♦ **infinitely** *adv* infiniment. ♦ **infiniteness** *n* infinitude *f*. ♦ **infinitesimal** *adj* infinitésimal. ♦ **infinitive** *n* infinitif *m*; **in the infinitive** à l'infinitif. ♦ **infinitude** *n* infinité *f*. ♦ **infinity** *n* (*as opp to time and space*) infini *m*; (*infinite quantity etc*) infinité *f* (*of* de); (*infiniteness*) infinitude *f*; (*Math*) infini *m*; **to infinity** à l'infini.

infirm [ɪn'fɜːm] *adj* infirme. ♦ **infirmary** *n* hôpital *m*. ♦ **infirmity** *n* infirmité *f*.

inflame [ɪn'fleɪm] *vt* (*Med*) enflammer; (*fig*) attiser. ♦ **inflammable** *adj* inflammable. ♦ **inflammation** *n* inflammation *f*. ♦ **inflammatory** *adj speech etc* incendiaire.

inflate [ɪn'fleɪt] *vt tyre* gonfler (*with* de); *prices* faire monter; *bill, account* grossir. ♦ **inflatable** *adj* pneumatique. ♦ **inflated** *adj tyre etc* gonflé; *lung* dilaté; *value, prices* exagéré; **an ~d sense of** une idée exagérée de. ♦ **inflation** *n* (*Econ*) inflation *f*. ♦ **inflationary** *adj* inflationniste.

inflect [ɪn'flekt] **1** *vt* (*Ling*) modifier la désinence de; *voice* moduler. **2** *vi* (*Ling*) prendre une désinence. ♦ **inflection** *or* ♦ **inflexion** *n* (*Ling: affix*) désinence *f*; *[voice]* inflexion *f*.

inflexible [ɪn'fleksəbl] *adj object* rigide; *person, attitude* inflexible, rigide. ♦ **inflexibility** *n* rigidité *f*; inflexibilité *f*.

inflict [ɪn'flɪkt] *vt* infliger (*on* à). **to ~ o.s. on sb** imposer sa compagnie à qn.

influence ['ɪnflʊəns] **1** *n* influence *f* (*on* sur). **under the ~ of** *person* sous l'influence de; *drugs* sous l'effet *m* de; (*Jur*) **driving under the ~ of drink** conduite *f* en état d'ivresse; **he was a bit under the ~*** il avait bu un coup de trop*; **to use one's ~ with sb to get sth** user de son influence auprès de qn pour obtenir qch; **to be a good ~ on sb** exercer une bonne influence sur qn. **2** *vt* (*gen*) influencer; *attitude, decision* influencer, influer sur. **to be ~d by** (*gen*) se laisser influencer par; *[artist, writer]* être influencé par; **easily ~d** très influençable.

♦ **influential** *adj* influent; **to be influential** avoir de l'influence; **influential friends** amis *mpl* haut placés.

influenza [ˌɪnflʊ'enzə] *n* grippe *f*.

influx ['ɪnflʌks] *n [people]* afflux *m*, flot *m*; *[new ideas, attitudes]* flot, flux *m*.

inform [ɪn'fɔːm] **1** *vt* informer, avertir (*of* de), renseigner (*about* sur); *police* avertir. **to ~ sb of sth** informer *or* avertir qn de qch, faire part de qch à qn; **keep me ~ed** tenez-moi au courant (*of* de).

2 *vi*: **to ~ against sb** dénoncer qn.

♦ **informant** *n* informateur *m*, -trice *f*; (*Ling: native ~ant*) informant(e) *m(f)*. ♦ **information 1** *n* renseignements *mpl*, information(s) *f(pl)*; **a piece of ~ation** un renseignement, une information; **to get ~ation about** se renseigner sur; **more ~ation** des renseignements plus complets, des informations plus complètes; **until more ~ation is available** jusqu'à plus ample informé; **his ~ation on the subject is astonishing** ses connaissances *fpl* en la matière sont stupéfiantes; **for your ~ation, he** je dois vous prévenir qu'il; **for your ~ation** à titre d'information; **2** *adj bureau* de renseignements; *content* informationnel; *theory* de l'information; **~ation processing** informatique *f*; **~ation retrieval** retrouve *f* de l'information. ♦ **informative** *adj book, meeting* instructif; **he's not very ~ative about it** il n'en dit pas grand-chose. ♦ **informed** *adj person* informé, renseigné (*about* sur); *opinion* bien informé; *guess* bien fondé. ♦ **informer** *n* dénonciateur *m*, -trice *f*; **police ~er** indicateur *m*, -trice *f* (de police); **to turn ~er** dénoncer ses complices.

informal [ɪn'fɔːməl] *adj tone, manner, style* simple, familier; *language* de la conversation; *person* simple, qui ne fait pas de façons; *announcement, acceptance, arrangement* officieux; *instructions, invitation, meeting* dénué de caractère officiel; *welcome, visit, discussion* dénué de formalité; *dance, dinner* entre amis. **'dress ~'** 'tenue de ville'; **we had an ~ talk about it** nous en avons discuté entre nous; **it will be quite ~** ce sera sans cérémonie *or* en toute simplicité.

♦ **informality** *n [person, manner]* simplicité *f*; *[visit, welcome etc]* simplicité, absence *f* de formalité; *[arrangement, agreement etc]* caractère *m* officieux; *[meeting]* absence *f* de cérémonie. ♦ **informally** *adv invite* sans cérémonie; *arrange, agree, meet* officieusement; *behave, speak, dress* de façon toute simple.

infra dig* ['ɪnfrə'dɪg] *adj* au-dessous de sa (*or* ma *etc*) dignité.

infrared ['ɪnfrə'red] *adj* infrarouge.

infrastructure ['ɪnfrəˌstrʌktʃəʳ] *n* infrastructure *f*.

infrequent [ɪn'friːkwənt] *adj* peu fréquent, rare. ♦ **infrequency** *n* rareté *f*. ♦ **infrequently** *adv* rarement.

infringe [ɪn'frɪndʒ] **1** *vt* contrevenir à. **2** *vi*: **to ~ on** empiéter sur. ♦ **infringement** *n* infraction *f* (*of* à).

infuriate [ɪn'fjʊərɪeɪt] *vt* rendre furieux, exaspérer. ♦ **infuriating** *adj* exaspérant. ♦ **infuriatingly** *adv* de façon exaspérante; **infuriatingly slow** d'une lenteur exaspérante.

infuse [ɪn'fjuːz] *vt* infuser (*into* dans); *tea, herbs* faire infuser; (*fig*) insuffler (*into* à). ♦ **infusion** *n* infusion *f*.

ingenious [ɪn'dʒiːnɪəs] *adj* ingénieux. ♦ **ingeniously** *adv* ingénieusement. ♦ **ingenuity** *n* ingéniosité *f*.

ingenuous [ɪn'dʒenjʊəs] *adj* ingénu. ♦ **ingenuousness** *n* ingénuité *f*.

inglorious [ɪn'glɔːrɪəs] *adj defeat etc* déshonorant.

ingot ['ɪŋgət] *n* lingot *m*.

ingrained ['ɪn'greɪnd] *adj habit* invétéré; *prejudice* enraciné; *hatred* tenace. **~ dirt** crasse *f*; **~ with dirt** encrassé.

ingratiate [ɪn'greɪʃɪeɪt] *vt*: **to ~ o.s. with sb** s'insinuer dans les bonnes grâces de qn. ♦ **ingratiating** *adj* insinuant, doucereux.

ingratitude [ɪn'grætɪtjuːd] *n* ingratitude *f*.

ingredient [ɪn'griːdɪənt] *n* (*Culin etc*) ingrédient *m*; *[character, success etc]* élément *m*.

ingrowing [ˌɪn'grəʊɪŋ], (*US*) **ingrown** [ˌɪn'grəʊn] *adj* incarné.

inhabit [ɪn'hæbɪt] *vt town, country* habiter; *house* habiter (dans). ♦ **inhabitable** *adj* habitable. ♦ **inhabitant** *n* habitant(e) *m(f)*. ♦ **inhabited** *adj* habité.

inhale [ɪn'heɪl] **1** *vt vapour, gas etc* inhaler; *[smoker]* avaler; *perfume* aspirer. **2** *vi [smoker]* avaler la fumée. ♦ **inhalant** *n* inhalant *m*. ♦ **inhalation** *n* inhalation *f*. ♦ **inhaler** *or* ♦ **inhalator** *n* inhalateur *m*.

inherent [ɪn'hɪərənt] *adj* inhérent (*in, to* à). ♦ **inherently** *adv difficult etc* en soi; *curious, lazy* fondamentalement.

inherit [ɪn'herɪt] *vt* hériter (de); *title* succéder à; *qualities, characteristics* tenir (*from sb* de qn). **to ~ a house** hériter (d')une maison; **to ~ a house from sb** hériter une maison de qn. ♦ **inheritance** *n* (*gen*) héritage *m*; **our national ~ance** notre patrimoine *m* national.

inhibit [ɪn'hɪbɪt] *vt [person] impulse, desire* dominer, maîtriser; (*Psych*) inhiber; *[situation, sb's presence]* entraver, gêner. **to ~ sb from doing** empêcher qn de faire. ♦ **inhibited** *adj* refoulé*; (*Psych*) qui a beaucoup d'inhibitions. ♦ **inhibiting** *adj* gênant; (*Psych*) inhibiteur. ♦ **inhibition** *n* inhibition *f*.

inhospitable [ˌɪnhɒs'pɪtəbl] *adj* inhospitalier.

inhuman [ɪn'hjuːmən] *adj* inhumain. ♦ **inhumanity** *n* inhumanité *f*.

inimical [ɪ'nɪmɪkəl] *adj* (*hostile*) hostile (*to* à).

inimitable [ɪ'nɪmɪtəbl] *adj* inimitable. ♦ **inimitably** *adv* d'une façon inimitable.

iniquitous [ɪ'nɪkwɪtəs] *adj* inique. ♦ **iniquitously** *adv* iniquement. ♦ **iniquity** *n* iniquité *f*.

initial [ɪ'nɪʃəl] **1** *adj* initial, premier. **in the ~ stages** au début, au commencement. **2** *n* initiale *f*. **~s** initiales *fpl*; (*as signature*) parafe *m*. **3** *vt* parafer. ♦ **initially** *adv* initialement.

initiate [ɪ'nɪʃɪeɪt] **1** *vt* **(a)** *reform* promouvoir; *negotiations* amorcer; *enterprise* se lancer dans; *scheme, programme* instaurer; *fashion* lancer. (*Jur*) **to ~ proceedings against sb** intenter une action à qn. **(b)** (*Rel etc*) *person* initier (*into a secret* à un secret). **to ~ sb into a society** admettre qn au sein d'une société secrète. **2** [ɪ'nɪʃɪɪt] *adj, n* initié(e) *m(f)*. ♦ **initiation 1** *n* initiation *f*; admission *f*; **2** *adj rite* d'initiation.

♦ **initiative** *n* initiative *f*; **to take the initiative** prendre l'initiative (*in doing sth* de faire qch); **on one's own initiative** de sa propre initiative; **he's got initiative** il a de l'initiative. ♦ **initiator** *n [plan etc]* auteur *m*.

inject [ɪn'dʒekt] *vt* injecter (*sth into sth* qch dans qch); (*fig*) insuffler (*into* à). **to ~ sb with sth** faire une piqûre *or* une injection de qch à qn.

♦ **injection** *n* injection *f*; (*Med*) injection, piqûre *f*.
injudicious [ˌɪndʒʊ'dɪʃəs] *adj* peu judicieux. ♦ **injudiciously** *adv* peu judicieusement.
injunction [ɪn'dʒʌŋkʃən] *n* (*gen*) ordre *m*; (*court order*) ordonnance *f* (*to do* de faire). **to give sb strict ~s to do** enjoindre formellement à qn de faire.
injure ['ɪndʒəʳ] *vt* **(a)** (*Med*) blesser. **to ~ one's leg** se blesser à la jambe. **(b)** (*wrong, damage*) *person, interests, reputation* nuire à; (*offend*) blesser, offenser. **to ~ sb's feelings** offenser qn. ♦ **injured 1** *adj* (*Med*) blessé; (*in accident*) accidenté; (*offended*) offensé; (*Jur*) **the ~d party** la partie lésée; **2** *npl*: **the ~d** les blessés *mpl*. ♦ **injurious** *adj* nuisible (*to* à). ♦ **injury** *n* (*Med*) blessure *f*; (*wrong*) (*to person*) tort *m*; (*to reputation*) atteinte *f*; (*Ftbl*) **injury time** arrêts *mpl* de jeu.
injustice [ɪn'dʒʌstɪs] *n* injustice *f*. **to do sb an ~** être injuste envers qn.
ink [ɪŋk] **1** *n* encre *f*. **in ~** à l'encre. **2** *adj bottle* d'encre; *eraser* à encre. **3** *vt* encrer. **to ~ sth in** repasser qch à l'encre. ♦ **inkpad** *n* tampon *m* encreur. ♦ **inkpot** *or* ♦ **inkwell** *n* encrier *m*. ♦ **inky** *adj book, hand* taché d'encre; *pad* encré; *darkness etc* noir comme de l'encre.
inkling ['ɪŋklɪŋ] *n* petite idée *f*, soupçon *m*. **I had no ~ that ...** je n'avais pas la moindre idée que ...; **there was no ~ of the disaster** rien ne laissait présager le désastre.
inlaid ['ɪn'leɪd] *adj* (*gen*) incrusté (*with* de); *box, table* marqueté. **~ floor** parquet *m*.
inland ['ɪnlænd] **1** *adj* **(a)** *sea, town* intérieur; *navigation* fluvial. **~ waterways** canaux *mpl* et rivières *fpl*. **(b)** (*domestic*) *mail, trade* intérieur. **the ~ revenue** le fisc. **2** [ɪn'lænd] *adv* à l'intérieur. **to go ~** pénétrer dans les terres.
inlet ['ɪnlet] **1** *n* **(a)** *[sea]* bras *m* de mer; *[river]* bras de rivière. **(b)** (*Tech*) arrivée *f*; *[ventilator]* prise *f* (d'air). **2** *adj pipe* d'arrivée.
inmate ['ɪnmeɪt] *n [prison]* détenu(e) *m(f)*; *[asylum]* interné(e) *m(f)*; *[hospital]* malade *mf*.
inmost ['ɪnməʊst] *adj part* le plus profond; *thoughts, feelings* le plus secret. **one's ~ being** le fin fond de son être; **in one's ~ heart** dans le fond de son cœur.
inn [ɪn] *n* (*small, wayside*) auberge *f*; (*larger, wayside*) hostellerie *f*; (*in town*) hôtel *m*; (†: *tavern*) cabaret† *m*. ♦ **innkeeper** *n* aubergiste *mf*; hôtelier *m*, -ière *f*.
innards* ['ɪnədz] *npl* entrailles *fpl*.
innate [ɪ'neɪt] *adj* inné, naturel.
inner ['ɪnəʳ] *adj room, court* intérieur, de dedans; *ear* interne; *shoe sole* intérieur; *emotions, thoughts* intime, secret, profond; *life* intérieur. **an ~ circle within the society** un petit cercle fermé à l'intérieur de la société; **~ city** centre *m* d'une zone urbaine; **~ city schools** établissements *mpl* scolaires situés dans le centre de la zone urbaine; **~ harbour** arrière-port *m*; *[tyre]* **~ tube** chambre *f* à air. ♦ **innermost** = **inmost**.
innings ['ɪnɪŋz] *n* (*Cricket*) tour *m* de batte. (*fig*) **I've had a good ~** j'ai bien profité de l'existence (*or* de la situation *etc*).
innocent ['ɪnəsnt] **1** *adj* innocent (*of* de). **as ~ as a newborn babe** innocent comme l'enfant qui vient de naître; **to put on an ~ air** faire l'innocent; **~ of any desire to ...** dénué de tout désir de ... . **2** *n* innocent(e) *mf*. ♦ **innocence** *n* innocence *f*. ♦ **innocently** *adv* innocemment.
innocuous [ɪ'nɒkjʊəs] *adj* inoffensif.
innovate ['ɪnəʊveɪt] *vti* innover. ♦ **innovation** *n* innovation *f* (*in* en matière de); **to make innovations in** apporter des innovations à. ♦ **innovator** *n* innovateur *m*, -trice *f*.
innuendo [ˌɪnjʊ'endəʊ] *n* insinuation *f* malveillante.
innumerable [ɪ'njuːmərəbl] *adj* innombrable, sans nombre. **I've told you ~ times** je te l'ai dit cent fois.
inoculate [ɪ'nɒkjʊleɪt] *vt* inoculer (*against* contre; *sb with sth* qch à qn). ♦ **inoculation** *n* inoculation *f*.
inoffensive [ˌɪnə'fensɪv] *adj* inoffensif.
inoperable [ɪn'ɒpərəbl] *adj* inopérable.
inoperative [ɪn'ɒpərətɪv] *adj* inopérant.
inopportune [ɪn'ɒpətjuːn] *adj* (*gen*) inopportun; *remark* déplacé. ♦ **inopportunely** *adv* inopportunément.
inordinate [ɪ'nɔːdɪnɪt] *adj sum of money, price* exorbitant; *size* démesuré; *quantity, demands* excessif; *passion* immodéré. **an ~ amount of** énormément de. ♦ **inordinately** *adv* démesurément; excessivement; immodérément.
inorganic [ˌɪnɔː'gænɪk] *adj* inorganique.
input ['ɪnpʊt] *n* (*Elec*) énergie *f*, puissance *f*; *[computer]* données *fpl*.
inquest ['ɪnkwest] *n* enquête *f* (criminelle).
inquire [ɪn'kwaɪəʳ] **1** *vi* s'informer (*about, after* de), se renseigner (*about* sur). **to ~ for sb** demander qn; **to ~ into** *subject* faire des recherches sur; *possibilities* se renseigner sur; (*Admin, Jur*) faire une enquête sur; *truth of sth* vérifier; **'~ at the information desk'** 's'adresser aux renseignements'. **2** *vt* demander (*sth from sb* qch à qn). **he ~d how to get to the theatre** il a demandé le chemin du théâtre; **he ~d what she wanted** il a demandé ce qu'elle voulait. ♦ **inquiring** *adj attitude, mind* curieux; *look* interrogateur. ♦ **inquiringly** *adv* avec curiosité; d'un air interrogateur.
inquiry [ɪn'kwaɪərɪ] **1** *n* **(a)** (*from individual*) demande *f* de renseignements. **to make inquiries about sb/sth** se renseigner sur qn/qch (*of sb* auprès de qn); **on ~ he found that ...** renseignements pris, il a découvert que ...; **'all inquiries to ...'** 'pour tous renseignements s'adresser à ...'; (*sign*) **'Inquiries'** 'Renseignements'. **(b)** (*Admin, Jur*) enquête *f*. **committee of ~** commission *f* d'enquête; **to hold an ~ into** enquêter *or* faire une enquête sur; **a fruitful line of ~** une bonne direction dans laquelle pousser les recherches; **the police are making inquiries** la police enquête. **2** *adj*: **~ desk, ~ office** bureau *m* de renseignements.
inquisition [ˌɪnkwɪ'zɪʃən] *n* investigation *f*. (*Rel*) **the I~** l'Inquisition *f*. ♦ **inquisitive** *adj* (trop) curieux. ♦ **inquisitively** *adv* (trop) curieusement. ♦ **inquisitiveness** *n* curiosité *f* (indiscrète).
inroad ['ɪnrəʊd] *n* (*Mil*) incursion *f* (*into* en, dans). (*fig*) **to make ~s into** entamer.
insane [ɪn'seɪn] **1** *adj* (*Med*) aliéné; (*gen*) *person* fou; *desire* insensé; *project* démentiel. **to become ~** perdre la raison; **to drive sb ~** rendre qn fou. **2** *npl* (*Med*) **the ~** les aliénés *mpl*. ♦ **insanely** *adv laugh* comme un fou (*or* une folle); *behave* de façon insensée; *jealous* follement. ♦ **insanity** *n* (*Med*) aliénation *f* mentale; (*gen*) folie *f*, démence *f*.
insanitary [ɪn'sænɪtərɪ] *adj* insalubre.
insatiable [ɪn'seɪʃəbl] *adj* insatiable.
inscribe [ɪn'skraɪb] *vt* (*write*) inscrire (*in* dans); (*engrave*) graver (*on* sur); (*dedicate*) dédicacer (*to* à). **watch ~d with his name** montre gravée à son nom. ♦ **inscription** *n* inscription *f*; dédicace *f*.
inscrutable [ɪn'skruːtəbl] *adj* impénétrable (*fig*).
insect ['ɪnsekt] **1** *n* insecte *m*. **2** *adj bite* d'insecte; *powder, spray* insecticide. **~ eater** insectivore *m*; **~ repellent** crème *f* (*or* bombe *f etc*) anti-insecte *inv*. ♦ **insecticide** *n* insecticide *m*.
insecure [ˌɪnsɪ'kjʊəʳ] *adj nail, rope, padlock* peu solide, qui tient mal; *structure, ladder* branlant; *lock* peu sûr; *door* qui ferme mal; *career, future* incertain; (*worried*) *person* anxieux; (*Psych etc*) insécurisé. ♦ **insecurity** *n* insécurité *f*.

insemination [ɪnˌsemɪ'neɪʃən] *n* insémination *f*.

insensible [ɪn'sensəbl] *adj* (*gen*) insensible (*of* à); (*unconscious*) sans connaissance. ♦ **insensibility** *n* insensibilité *f*. ♦ **insensibly** *adv* insensiblement.

insensitive [ɪn'sensɪtɪv] *adj* insensible (*to* à). ♦ **insensitivity** *n* insensibilité *f*.

inseparable [ɪn'sepərəbl] *adj* inséparable (*from* de). ♦ **inseparably** *adv* inséparablement.

insert [ɪn'sɜːt] **1** *vt* insérer. **2** ['ɪnsɜːt] *n* (*gen*) insertion *f*; (*page*) encart *m*. ♦ **insertion** *n* insertion *f*.

inshore ['ɪn'ʃɔːʳ] **1** *adj* (*gen*) côtier; *wind* de mer. **2** *adv fish* près de la côte; *move* vers la côte.

inside ['ɪn'saɪd] **1** *adv* **(a)** dedans, au dedans, à l'intérieur. ~ **and outside** au dedans et au dehors; **come** ~! entrez (donc)!; **it is warmer** ~ il fait plus chaud à l'intérieur *or* dedans. **(b)** (‡: *in jail*) en taule‡.

2 *prep* **(a)** (*of place*) à l'intérieur de, dans. ~ **the house** à l'intérieur (de la maison). **(b)** (*of time*) en moins de. ~ **10 minutes** en moins de 10 minutes; **he was well** ~ **the record time** il avait largement battu le record.

3 *n* **(a)** intérieur *m*. **on the** ~ au dedans, à l'intérieur; **on the** ~ **of the pavement** sur le trottoir du côté maisons; (*fig*) **I see the firm from the** ~ je vois la compagnie de l'intérieur. **(b) your coat is** ~ **out** ton manteau est à l'envers; **the wind blew the umbrella** ~ **out** le vent a retourné le parapluie; **I turned the bag** ~ **out** j'ai retourné le sac entièrement; **to know** ~ **out** *subject* connaître à fond; *district* connaître comme sa poche. **(c)** (*: *stomach*) ventre *m*, intestins *mpl*.

4 *adj* **(a)** intérieur. ~ **leg measurement** hauteur *f* de l'entrejambes; **to get** ~ **information** obtenir des renseignements *mpl* à la source; **'the** ~ **story of the plot'** 'le complot raconté par un des participants'; (*of theft etc*) **an** ~ **job*** un coup monté de l'intérieur. **(b)** (*Aut*) *wheel, headlight etc* (*Brit*) gauche; (*US, Europe etc*) droit. **the** ~ **lane** (*Brit*) la voie de gauche; (*US, Europe etc*) la voie de droite; (*Sport*) **to be on the** ~ **track** tenir la corde.

♦ **inside-forward** *n* intérieur *m*. ♦ **inside-left/-right** *n* intérieur *m* gauche/droit.

insidious [ɪn'sɪdɪəs] *adj* insidieux. ♦ **insidiously** *adv* insidieusement.

insight ['ɪnsaɪt] *n* (*discernment*) pénétration *f*, perspicacité *f*. **I gained an** ~ **into ...** cela m'a permis de comprendre ... .

insignia [ɪn'sɪgnɪə] *npl* insignes *mpl*.

insignificant [ˌɪnsɪg'nɪfɪkənt] *adj* insignifiant. ♦ **insignificance** *n* insignifiance *f*.

insincere [ˌɪnsɪn'sɪəʳ] *adj* peu sincère. ♦ **insincerity** *n* manque *m* de sincérité.

insinuate [ɪn'sɪnjʊeɪt] *vt* insinuer (*into* dans; *sth to sb* qch à qn; *that* que). ♦ **insinuation** *n* insinuation *f*.

insipid [ɪn'sɪpɪd] *adj* insipide, fade.

insist [ɪn'sɪst] **1** *vi* insister (*on doing* pour faire). **he** ~**ed on my waiting for him** il a tenu à ce que *or* insisté pour que je l'attende; **to** ~ **on silence** exiger le silence; **if you** ~ si vous insistez, si vous y tenez; **he** ~**s on the justice of his claim** il affirme *or* soutient que sa revendication est juste. **2** *vt* **(a)** insister. **I** ~ **that you let me help** j'insiste pour que tu me permettes d'aider. **(b)** affirmer, soutenir. **he** ~**s that he has seen her before** il affirme *or* soutient qu'il l'a déjà vue. ♦ **insistence** *n* insistance *f*; **at his** ~**ence** parce qu'il a insisté. ♦ **insistent** *adj* insistant, pressant. ♦ **insistently** *adv* avec insistance.

insolent ['ɪnsələnt] *adj* insolent (*to* envers). ♦ **insolence** *n* insolence *f*. ♦ **insolently** *adv* insolemment.

insoluble [ɪn'sɒljʊbl] *adj* insoluble.

insolvent [ɪn'sɒlvənt] *adj* insolvable; (*bankrupt*) en faillite. ♦ **insolvency** *n* insolvabilité *f*.

insomnia [ɪn'sɒmnɪə] *n* insomnie *f*. ♦ **insomniac** *adj, n* insomniaque (*mf*).

inspect [ɪn'spekt] *vt* (*gen*) inspecter; *document, object* examiner; (*Customs*) *luggage* visiter; *ticket* contrôler; *troops etc* (*check*) inspecter, (*review*) passer en revue. ♦ **inspection 1** *n* inspection *f*; examen *m*; visite *f*; contrôle *m*; revue *f*; **2** *adj* (*Aut*) ~**ion pit** fosse *f* à réparations. ♦ **inspector** *n [schools, police etc]* inspecteur *m*, -trice *f*; (*on bus, train*) contrôleur *m*, -euse *f*.

inspire [ɪn'spaɪəʳ] *vt* inspirer (*sth in sb, sb with sth* qch à qn). **he was** ~**d by her beauty to write ...** inspiré par sa beauté il a écrit ...; **what** ~**d you to offer to help?** qu'est-ce qui vous a donné l'idée de proposer votre aide?; **an** ~**d idea** une inspiration. ♦ **inspiration** *n* inspiration *f*; **to be an inspiration to sb** être une source d'inspiration pour qn. ♦ **inspired** *adj book, poet* inspiré; *moment* d'inspiration. ♦ **inspiring** *adj book, poem* qui suscite l'inspiration; **it isn't inspiring** ça n'a rien d'inspirant.

instability [ˌɪnstə'bɪlɪtɪ] *n* instabilité *f*.

install [ɪn'stɔːl] *vt* installer. ♦ **installation** *n* installation *f*. ♦ **instalment** *or* (*US*) ♦ **installment 1** *n [payment]* versement *m* partiel, acompte *m*; *[story, serial]* épisode *m*; *[book]* fascicule *m*, livraison *f*; **to pay an** ~**ment** verser un acompte, faire un versement partiel; **by** ~**ments** en plusieurs versements, par acomptes; **2** *adj*: ~**ment plan** système *m* de crédit; **to buy on the** ~**ment plan** acheter à tempérament.

instance ['ɪnstəns] **1** *n* exemple *m*, cas *m*. **for** ~ par exemple; **in the present** ~ dans le cas présent; **in many** ~**s** dans bien des cas; **in the first** ~ en premier lieu; **as an** ~ **of** comme exemple de. **2** *vt* (*cite*) donner en exemple; (*exemplify*) illustrer.

instant ['ɪnstənt] **1** *adj obedience, relief* immédiat, instantané; *coffee* soluble; *potatoes* déshydraté; *food* à préparation rapide; *soup* en poudre. **your letter of the 10th inst(ant)** votre lettre du 10 courant. **2** *n* instant *m*, moment *m*. **come here this** ~ viens ici tout de suite *or* immédiatement; **in an** ~ (+*past tense*) en un instant; (+*future tense*) dans un instant; **the** ~ **he heard the news** dès qu'il a appris la nouvelle. ♦ **instantaneous** *adj* instantané. ♦ **instantaneously** *adv* instantanément. ♦ **instantly** *adv* immédiatement, tout de suite.

instead [ɪn'sted] *adv* au lieu de cela. **do that** ~ faites plutôt cela; **if he isn't going, I shall go** ~ s'il n'y va pas, j'irai à sa place; **I went to the pictures** ~ au lieu de cela je suis allé au cinéma; ~ **of (doing) sth** au lieu de (faire) qch; ~ **of sb** à la place de qn; ~ **of him** à sa place; **this is** ~ **of a present** ceci tient lieu de cadeau.

instep ['ɪnstep] *n* (*Anat*) cou-de-pied *m*; *[shoe]* cambrure *f*.

instigate ['ɪnstɪgeɪt] *vt* inciter (*sb to do* qn à faire); *rebellion etc* fomenter. ♦ **instigation** *n*: **at his instigation** à son instigation.

instil [ɪn'stɪl] *vt courage etc* insuffler (*into sb* à qn); *knowledge, principles* inculquer (*into sb* à qn); *idea, fact* faire comprendre (*into sb* à qn). **to** ~ **into sb that** faire pénétrer dans l'esprit de qn que.

instinct ['ɪnstɪŋkt] *n* instinct *m*. **by** ~ d'instinct; **business** ~ l'instinct des affaires. ♦ **instinctive** *adj* instinctif. ♦ **instinctively** *adv* instinctivement.

institute ['ɪnstɪtjuːt] **1** *vt system, rules* instituer, établir; *post, organization* fonder, créer; (*Jur etc*) *inquiry* ouvrir; *proceedings* entamer (*against sb* contre qn). **2** *n* institut *m*.

institution [ˌɪnstɪ'tjuːʃən] *n* **(a)** (*organization, school etc*) établissement *m*; (*mental hospital*) hôpital *m* psychiatrique. **he has been in** ~**s all his adult life** il a passé toute sa vie d'adulte dans des collectivités. **(b)** (*custom etc*) institution *f*. **it is too much of an ~ to abolish** c'est une telle institution qu'il serait impossible de le supprimer. ♦ **institutional** *adj reform etc* institutionnel; (*fig pej*) *food* d'internat; *furniture* d'hospice; **~al life** la vie réglementée d'un établissement (*social, médical ou pédagogique*). ♦ **institutionalized** *adj* marqué par la vie en collectivité.

instruct [ɪnˈstrʌkt] *vt* **(a)** (*teach*) instruire. **to ~ sb in sth** instruire qn en qch, enseigner qch à qn; **to ~ sb in how to do sth** enseigner à qn comment faire qch. **(b)** (*order: also Jur*) donner des instructions à. **to ~ sb to do** ordonner à qn de faire. ♦ **instruction 1** *n* instruction *f*; **~ions** (*Mil*) consigne *f*; (*Pharm, Tech*) indications *fpl*; **'~ions for use'** 'mode *m* d'emploi'; (*Comm, Tech*) **the ~ions are on the back of the box** le mode d'emploi est indiqué au dos de la boîte; **he gave me ~ions not to leave until ...** il m'a donné des instructions selon lesquelles je ne devais pas partir avant ...; **to give ~ions** donner des instructions (*for sb to do* pour que qn fasse); **driving ~ion** leçons *fpl* de conduite; **2** *adj*: **~ion book** manuel *m* d'entretien. ♦ **instructive** *adj* instructif. ♦ **instructor** *n* (*gen*) professeur *m*; (*Mil*) instructeur *m*; (*Ski*) moniteur *m*; **driving ~or** moniteur *m* d'auto-école. ♦ **instructress** *n* (*gen*) professeur *m* (*femme*); (*Ski*) monitrice *f*.

instrument [ˈɪnstrʊmənt] **1** *n* instrument *m*. **2** *adj flying* aux instruments (de bord). **~ board** *or* **panel** tableau *m* de bord. ♦ **instrumental** *adj* **(a) to be ~al in (doing) sth** contribuer à (faire) qch; **(b)** (*Mus*) instrumental. ♦ **instrumentalist** *n* instrumentiste *mf*.

insubordinate [ˌɪnsəˈbɔːdənɪt] *adj* insubordonné. ♦ **insubordination** *n* insubordination *f*.

insufferable [ɪnˈsʌfərəbl] *adj* insupportable. ♦ **insufferably** *adv* insupportablement.

insufficient [ˌɪnsəˈfɪʃənt] *adj* insuffisant. ♦ **insufficiently** *adv* insuffisamment.

insular [ˈɪnsjələʳ] *adj climate* insulaire; (*fig pej*) *outlook* borné; *person* aux vues étroites.

insulate [ˈɪnsjʊleɪt] *vt* (*gen, also Elec*) isoler; (*against sound*) insonoriser; *water tank* calorifuger; *person* (*separate*) séparer (*from* de); (*protect*) protéger (*against* de). ♦ **insulated** *adj* isolant. ♦ **insulating** *adj*: **insulating material** isolant *m*; **insulating tape** chatterton *m*. ♦ **insulation** *n* isolation *f*; insonorisation *f*; calorifugeage *m*; (*material*) isolant *m*. ♦ **insulator** *n* (*device*) isolateur *m*; (*material*) isolant *m*.

insulin [ˈɪnsjʊlɪn] **1** *n* insuline *f*. **2** *adj treatment* à l'insuline; *injection* d'insuline; *shock* insulinique.

insult [ɪnˈsʌlt] **1** *vt* insulter. **2** [ˈɪnsʌlt] *n* insulte *f*. **to hurl ~s at sb** injurier qn. ♦ **insulting** *adj* insultant, injurieux; **~ing language** paroles *fpl* injurieuses *or* insultantes. ♦ **insultingly** *adv* d'une voix *or* d'une manière insultante.

insuperable [ɪnˈsuːpərəbl] *adj* insurmontable.

insure [ɪnˈʃʊəʳ] *vt* **(a)** *car, house* assurer (*against* contre). **to ~ o.s.** *or* **one's life** prendre une assurance-vie; **the ~d** l'assuré(e) *m(f)*; (*fig*) **we ~d (ourselves) against possible disappointment** nous avons paré aux déceptions possibles; **in order to ~ against any delay ...** pour nous (*or* les *etc*) garantir contre les délais .... **(b)** (*make sure*) s'assurer (*that* que + *subj*); (*make sure of*) *success* assurer. **this will ~ that you ...** grâce à ceci vous êtes assuré de .... ♦ **insurance 1** *n* assurance *f*; **to take out (an) insurance against** s'assurer contre; **it's an insurance against inflation** cela protège de l'inflation; **2** *adj agent, company* d'assurances; *certificate, policy, premium* d'assurance; **insurance scheme** régime *m* d'assurances; (*Admin*) **insurance stamp** timbre *m* de contribution à la Sécurité sociale.

insurgent [ɪnˈsɜːdʒənt] *adj, n* insurgé(e) *m(f)*.

insurmountable [ˌɪnsəˈmaʊntəbl] *adj* insurmontable.

insurrection [ˌɪnsəˈrekʃən] *n* insurrection *f*.

intact [ɪnˈtækt] *adj* intact.

intake [ˈɪnteɪk] **1** *n* **(a)** *[water]* adduction *f*; *[gas, air, steam]* admission *f*. **(b)** (*Scol, Univ*) admissions *fpl*; (*Mil*) contingent *m*. **(c)** *[protein, liquid etc]* consommation *f*. **food ~** *[animals]* ration *f* alimentaire; *[person]* consommation de nourriture. **2** *adj*: **~ class** cours *m* préparatoire.

intangible [ɪnˈtændʒəbl] **1** *adj* intangible. **2** *n* impondérable *m*.

integral [ˈɪntɪgrəl] *adj* **(a)** *part* intégrant, constituant. **to be an ~ part of** faire partie intégrante de. **(b)** (*whole*) *payment* intégral. **(c) ~ calculus** calcul *m* intégral.

integrate [ˈɪntɪgreɪt] **1** *vt* (*gen*) intégrer, incorporer (*in, into* dans). **2** *vi* **(a)** (*US: racially*) *[school, neighbourhood etc]* pratiquer la déségrégation raciale. **(b)** *[person, religious or ethnic group etc]* s'intégrer (*into* dans). ♦ **integrated** *adj personality* bien intégré; (*US*) *school* où se pratique la déségrégation raciale. ♦ **integration** *n* (*gen*) intégration *f*; **racial integration** déségrégation *f* raciale.

integrity [ɪnˈtegrɪtɪ] *n* intégrité *f*. **man of ~** homme *m* intègre.

intellect [ˈɪntɪlekt] *n* intellect *m*, intelligence *f*; (*person*) intelligence *f*, esprit *m*. ♦ **intellectual** *adj, n* intellectuel(le) *m(f)*. ♦ **intellectually** *adv* intellectuellement.

intelligence [ɪnˈtelɪdʒəns] **1** *n* (*cleverness*) intelligence *f*; (*information*) informations *fpl*. **Military I~** service *m* de renseignements de l'armée de Terre; **he's in I~** il est dans les services de renseignements. **2** *adj agent, officer, service* de renseignements. **~ quotient** quotient *m* intellectuel; **~ test** test *m* d'aptitude intellectuelle. ♦ **intelligent** *adj* intelligent. ♦ **intelligently** *adv* intelligemment. ♦ **intelligentsia** *n* intelligentsia *f*.

intelligible [ɪnˈtelɪdʒəbl] *adj* intelligible. ♦ **intelligibility** *n* intelligibilité *f*. ♦ **intelligibly** *adv* intelligiblement.

intemperate [ɪnˈtempərɪt] *adj climate* sévère; *haste* excessif; *person* immodéré.

intend [ɪnˈtend] *vt* avoir l'intention, se proposer (*to do, doing* de faire), penser (*to do* faire); *gift, remark etc* destiner (*for* à). **I ~ him to go with me** j'ai l'intention qu'il m'accompagne (*subj*); **I fully ~ to punish him** j'ai la ferme intention de le punir; **this scheme is ~ed to help ...** ce projet est destiné à aider ...; **I ~ it as a present for Robert** c'est un cadeau que je destine à Robert; **I ~ed it as a compliment** dans mon esprit cela voulait être un compliment; **he ~ed no harm** il l'a fait sans mauvaise intention; **did you ~ that?** est-ce que vous avez fait cela exprès? ♦ **intended** *adj* (*deliberate*) *insult etc* intentionnel; (*planned*) *journey* projeté; *effect* voulu.

intense [ɪnˈtens] *adj* (*gen*) intense; *enthusiasm, interest* énorme, vif; *person, tone* véhément; *expression* (*interested*) concentré, (*fervent*) exalté. ♦ **intensely** *adv live, look* intensément; *moved* profondément; *cold* extrêmement. ♦ **intensify 1** *vt* intensifier; **2** *vi* s'intensifier. ♦ **intensity** *n* intensité *f*; véhémence *f*. ♦ **intensive** *adj* (*gen*) intensif; (*Med*) **intensive care unit** service *m* de réanimation; **in intensive care** en réanimation. ♦ **intensively** *adv* intensivement.

intent [ɪnˈtent] **1** *n* intention *f*, dessein *m*. **to all ~s and purposes** en fait, pratiquement; **with good ~** dans une bonne intention; **with criminal ~** dans un but délictueux. **2** *adj* absorbé. **~ stare** regard *m* fixe; **~ on his work** absorbé par son travail; **~ on leaving** bien décidé à partir; **he was so ~ on doing it that he forgot ...** dans sa préoccupation de

le faire, il a oublié ... . ♦ **intently** *adv* avec une vive attention.
intention [ɪn'tenʃən] *n* intention *f*. **to have the ~ of doing** avoir l'intention de faire; **to have no ~ of doing** n'avoir aucune intention de faire; **with the ~ of doing** dans l'intention de faire. ♦ **intentional** *adj* intentionnel, voulu; **it wasn't ~al** ce n'était pas fait exprès. ♦ **intentionally** *adv* (*gen*) intentionnellement; *do, say* exprès.
inter [ɪn'tɜːʳ] *vt* enterrer. ♦ **interment** *n* enterrement *m*.
inter... ['ɪntəʳ] *pref* inter... . ♦ **inter-city** *adj*: **~-city link** *or* **train** ligne *f* interurbaine. ♦ **inter-schools** *adj* interscolaire. ♦ **inter-war** *adj*: **the ~-war period** l'entre-deux-guerres *m*.
interact [ˌɪntər'ækt] *vi* avoir une action réciproque. ♦ **interaction** *n* interaction *f*.
intercede [ˌɪntə'siːd] *vi* intercéder (*with* auprès de; *for* pour, en faveur de).
intercept [ˌɪntə'sept] *vt* (*Mil etc*) *ship, message, messenger* intercepter; (*gen*) *person* arrêter au passage. ♦ **interception** *n* interception *f*.
intercession [ˌɪntə'seʃən] *n* intercession *f*.
interchange ['ɪntəˌtʃeɪndʒ] **1** *n* [*motorway*] échangeur *m*. **2** [ˌɪntə'tʃeɪndʒ] *vt* (*exchange*) *letters, ideas* échanger (*with sb* avec qn); (*alternate*) faire alterner (*with* avec); (*change positions of*) changer de place. ♦ **interchangeable** *adj* interchangeable.
intercom* ['ɪntəkɒm] *n* interphone *m*.
intercontinental ['ɪntəˌkɒntɪ'nentl] *adj* intercontinental.
intercourse ['ɪntəkɔːs] *n* **(a)** relations *fpl*, rapports *mpl*. **(b)** **(sexual) ~** rapports *mpl* (sexuels); **to have ~** avoir des rapports (*with* avec).
interdenominational ['ɪntədɪˌnɒmɪ'neɪʃənl] *adj* interconfessionnel.
interdepartmental ['ɪntəˌdiːpɑːt'mentl] *adj* (*within firm*) entre services; (*within ministry*) entre départements.
interdependent [ˌɪntədɪ'pendənt] *adj* interdépendant.
interest ['ɪntrɪst] **1** *n* **(a)** intérêt *m*. **to take an ~ in** s'intéresser à; **to show an ~ in** manifester de l'intérêt pour; **to be of ~ to sb** intéresser qn; **of little ~** présentant peu d'intérêt; **I'm doing it for ~'s sake** je le fais parce que cela m'intéresse; **my main ~ is reading** ce qui m'intéresse le plus c'est la lecture. **(b)** (*advantage*) intérêt *m*, avantage *m*, profit *m*. **it is in your ~ to do so** il est dans votre intérêt d'agir ainsi; **you have an ~ in doing so** vous avez intérêt à agir ainsi; **to act in sb's ~(s)** agir dans l'intérêt de qn; **in the ~ of peace** dans l'intérêt de la paix. **(c)** (*share, concern*) intérêts *mpl*. **I have an ~ in a hairdressing business** j'ai des intérêts dans un salon de coiffure; **British ~s in Africa** les intérêts britanniques en Afrique; **shipping ~s** les intérêts maritimes. **(d)** (*Fin*) intérêt(s) *m(pl)*. **simple/compound ~** intérêts simples/composés; **~ on an investment** intérêts d'un placement; **at an ~ of 10%** à un taux d'intérêt de 10%.
2 *adj*: **~ rate** taux *m* d'intérêt.
3 *vt* intéresser. **to be** *or* **become ~ed in** s'intéresser à; **I am ~ed in going** ça m'intéresse d'y aller; **can I ~ you in contributing to ...?** est-ce que cela vous intéresserait de contribuer à ...?
♦ **interested** *adj person* intéressé; *look, attitude* d'intérêt; **the ~ed parties** les intéressés *mpl*.
♦ **interesting** *adj* intéressant. ♦ **interestingly** *adv speak* de façon intéressante; **~ingly enough I ...** ce qui est très intéressant, c'est que je ... .
interfere [ˌɪntə'fɪəʳ] *vi* s'ingérer (*in* dans), se mêler des affaires des autres. **stop interfering!** ne vous mêlez pas de mes (*or* leurs *etc*) affaires!; **he's always interfering** il se mêle toujours de tout; [*circumstances etc*] **to ~ with sb's plans** contrecarrer les projets de qn; **he never allows his hobbies to ~ with his work** il ne laisse jamais ses distractions empiéter sur son travail. ♦ **interference** *n* ingérence *f* (*in* dans); (*Rad*) parasites *mpl*. ♦ **interfering** *adj* importun, qui se mêle toujours des affaires des autres.
interim ['ɪntərɪm] **1** *n* intérim *m*. **2** *adj government, arrangements* provisoire; *post, holder of post, dividend* intérimaire.
interior [ɪn'tɪərɪəʳ] **1** *adj* (*gen*) intérieur. **~ decoration/decorator** décoration *f*/décorateur *m*, -trice *f* d'intérieurs. **2** *n* intérieur *m*. **Ministry of the I~** ministère *m* de l'Intérieur.
interject [ˌɪntə'dʒekt] *vt* placer. **'yes' he ~ed** 'oui' réussit-il à placer. ♦ **interjection** *n* interjection *f*.
interloper ['ɪntələʊpəʳ] *n* intrus(e) *m(f)*.
interlude ['ɪntəluːd] *n* intervalle *m*; (*Theat*) intermède *m*. **musical ~** interlude *m*.
intermarry ['ɪntə'mærɪ] *vi*: **they do not ~** ils ne se marient pas entre eux; **they do not ~ with their neighbours** ils ne se marient pas avec leurs voisins.
intermediary [ˌɪntə'miːdɪərɪ] *adj, n* intermédiaire (*mf*).
intermediate [ˌɪntə'miːdɪət] *adj* (*gen*) intermédiaire; (*Scol etc*) moyen.
interminable [ɪn'tɜːmɪnəbl] *adj* interminable.
intermission [ˌɪntə'mɪʃən] *n* (*in work, session*) interruption *f*; (*in hostilities*) trêve *f*; (*Cine, Theat*) entracte *m*; (*Med*) intermission *f*.
intermittent [ˌɪntə'mɪtənt] *adj* intermittent. ♦ **intermittently** *adv* par intermittence.
intern [ɪn'tɜːn] **1** *vt* (*Pol etc*) interner (*pour raisons de sécurité*). **2** ['ɪntɜːn] *n* (*US Med*) interne *mf*. ♦ **internee** *n* (*Pol*) interné(e) *m(f)*. ♦ **internment** *n* internement *m*.
internal [ɪn'tɜːnl] *adj* (*Med, Tech*) interne; (*Ind, Pol*) *dispute, reorganization* intérieur, interne; *evidence* intrinsèque; *belief, conviction* intime. **~ combustion engine** moteur *m* à combustion interne *or* à explosion; **~ injuries** lésions *fpl* internes; (*Pol*) **~ quarrels** querelles intestines; (*US*) **~ revenue** fisc *m*. ♦ **internally** *adv* intérieurement.
international [ˌɪntə'næʃnəl] **1** *n* international. **2** *n* (*match, player*) international *m*. ♦ **internationally** *adv* internationalement, dans le monde entier.
internist [ɪn'tɜːnɪst] *n* (*US Med*) ≃ spécialiste *mf* des maladies organiques.
interplay ['ɪntəpleɪ] *n* effet *m* réciproque.
interpolate [ɪn'tɜːpəleɪt] *vt* interpoler. ♦ **interpolation** *n* interpolation *f*.
interpose [ˌɪntə'pəʊz] *vt* intercaler.
interpret [ɪn'tɜːprɪt] *vti* interpréter. ♦ **interpretation** *n* interprétation *f*. ♦ **interpreter** *n* interprète *mf*.
interrelated [ˌɪntərɪ'leɪtəd] *adj* en corrélation.
interrogate [ɪn'terəgeɪt] *vt* (*gen*) interroger; (*Police*) soumettre à un interrogatoire. ♦ **interrogation** **1** *n* interrogation *f*; interrogatoire *m*; **2** *adj* **interrogation mark** point *m* d'interrogation. ♦ **interrogative** **1** *adj* interrogateur; (*Ling*) interrogatif; **2** *n*: **in the interrogative** à l'interrogatif *m*. ♦ **interrogatively** *adv* d'un air interrogateur; (*Ling*) interrogativement. ♦ **interrogator** *n* interrogateur *m*, -trice *f*.
interrupt [ˌɪntə'rʌpt] *vt* interrompre. ♦ **interruption** *n* interruption *f*.
intersect [ˌɪntə'sekt] **1** *vt* couper; (*Math*) intersecter. **2** *vi* [*lines, wires, roads etc*] s'entrecouper; (*Math*) s'intersecter. ♦ **intersection** *n* (*crossroads*) croisement *m*; (*Math*) intersection *f*.
interspersed [ˌɪntə'spɜːsd] *adj*: **~ with ...** avec, de temps en temps, ...
interval ['ɪntəvəl] *n* intervalle *m*; (*Scol*) récréation *f*; (*Sport*) mi-temps *f*; (*Theat*) entracte *m*;

(*Mus*) intervalle. **at ~s** par intervalles; **at frequent/regular ~s** à intervalles rapprochés/réguliers; **there was an ~ for discussion** il y eut une pause pour la discussion; (*Met*) **bright ~s** belles éclaircies *fpl*.

intervene [ˌɪntəˈviːn] *vi [person]* intervenir (*in* dans); *[event, circumstances etc]* survenir, intervenir; *[time, years]* s'écouler (*between* entre). ♦ **intervening** *adj event* survenu; *period* intermédiaire; *years* qui s'écoulent entre-temps. ♦ **intervention** *n* intervention *f*.

interview [ˈɪntəvjuː] **1** *n* (*gen*) entrevue *f*; (*Press, Rad, TV*) interview *f*. **to call** *or* **invite sb to an ~** convoquer qn; **I had an ~ with the manager** j'ai eu une entrevue avec le directeur; **the ~s will be held next week** les entrevues auront lieu la semaine prochaine.

2 *vt* **(a)** (*for job etc*) avoir une entrevue avec. **he is being ~ed on Monday** on le convoque pour lundi. **(b)** (*Press, Rad, TV*) interviewer. ♦ **interviewer** *n* (*Press, Rad, TV*) interviewer *m*; (*in market research, opinion poll*) enquêteur *m*, -euse *f*; (*for job etc*) **the ~er asked me ...** la personne qui me faisait passer mon entrevue m'a demandé ... .

intestine [ɪnˈtestɪn] *n* intestin *m*.

intimate [ˈɪntɪmɪt] **1** *adj* (*gen*) intime; *knowledge, analysis* approfondi. **they became ~** ils sont devenus amis intimes; (*sexually*) ils ont eu des rapports intimes. **2** *n* intime *mf*. **3** [ˈɪntɪmeɪt] *vt* (*make known officially*) annoncer, faire connaître (*that* que); (*indirectly*) laisser entendre. ♦ **intimacy** *n* **(a)** intimité *f*. **(b)** (*sexual*) rapports *mpl* intimes *or* sexuels. **(c) intimacies** familiarités *fpl*. ♦ **intimately** *adv know, talk* intimement; *connected* étroitement; **~ly involved in sth** mêlé de près à qch. ♦ **intimation** *n* (*gen*) annonce *f*; *[death]* avis *m*; (*hint, sign*) indication *f*.

intimidate [ɪnˈtɪmɪdeɪt] *vt* intimider. ♦ **intimidation** *n* intimidation *f*.

into [ˈɪntʊ] *prep* dans; en. **to come** *or* **go ~ a room** entrer dans une pièce; **to go ~ town** aller en ville; **to get ~ a car** monter dans une voiture *or* en voiture; **he helped her ~ the car** il l'a aidée à monter en voiture; **to change traveller's cheques ~ francs** changer des chèques de voyage contre des francs; **far ~ the night** très avant dans la nuit; **4 ~ 12 goes 3 times** 12 divisé par 4 donne 3; **the children are ~ everything*** les enfants touchent à tout; (*fig*) **she's ~* health foods** *etc* elle donne à fond* dans les aliments naturels *etc*.

intolerable [ɪnˈtɒlərəbl] *adj* intolérable (*that* que + *subj*). ♦ **intolerably** *adv* intolérablement. ♦ **intolerance** *n* intolérance *f*. ♦ **intolerant** *adj* intolérant (*of* de; (*Med*) *of* à). ♦ **intolerantly** *adv* avec intolérance.

intonation [ˌɪntəʊˈneɪʃən] *n* (*Ling*) intonation *f*.

intoxicate [ɪnˈtɒksɪkeɪt] *vt* (*lit, fig*) enivrer. ♦ **intoxicated** *adj* (*lit*) ivre; (*Jur*) en état d'ivresse; (*fig*) ivre (*with* de), grisé (*with* par). ♦ **intoxication** *n* ivresse *f*.

intra... [ˈɪntrə] *pref* intra... . ♦ **intramuscular** *adj* intramusculaire. ♦ **intravenous** *adj* intraveineux.

intractable [ɪnˈtræktəbl] *adj child* intraitable; *problem* insoluble; *illness* opiniâtre.

intransigence [ɪnˈtrænsɪdʒəns] *n* intransigeance *f*. ♦ **intransigent** *adj, n* intransigeant(e) *m(f)*.

intransitive [ɪnˈtrænsɪtɪv] *adj, n* (*Gram*) intransitif (*m*).

intrepid [ɪnˈtrepɪd] *adj* intrépide.

intricate [ˈɪntrɪkɪt] *adj plot, problem* complexe; *mechanism, pattern, style* compliqué. ♦ **intricacy** *n* complexité *f*; complication *f*. ♦ **intricately** *adv* de façon complexe *or* compliquée.

intrigue [ɪnˈtriːg] **1** *vt* intriguer. **2** *vi* intriguer (*with sb* avec qn; *to do* pour faire). **3** *n* intrigue *f*. ♦ **intriguer** *n* intrigant(e) *m(f)*. ♦ **intriguing** **1** *adj* fascinant; **2** *n* intrigues *fpl*.

intrinsic [ɪnˈtrɪnsɪk] *adj* intrinsèque. ♦ **intrinsically** *adv* intrinsèquement.

introduce [ˌɪntrəˈdjuːs] *vt* **(a)** (*bring in*) *reform, innovation* introduire; *subject, question* amener, présenter; *practice* faire adopter, introduire; (*Rad, TV*) *programme* présenter; (*Parl*) *bill* déposer. **to ~ sb into a firm** faire entrer qn dans une compagnie. **(b)** (*make acquainted*) présenter (*to sb* à qn). **he ~d me to the delights of skiing** il m'a initié aux plaisirs du ski; **I was ~d to Shakespeare too young** on m'a fait connaître Shakespeare quand j'étais trop jeune; **who ~d them?** qui les a présentés l'un à l'autre?; **may I ~ Mr Martin?** puis-je (me permettre de) vous présenter M. Martin? **(c)** (*insert*) *key etc* introduire (*into* dans). ♦ **introduction** *n* (*gen*) introduction *f* (*into* dans; *to* à); présentation *f* (*of sb to sb* de qn à qn); **my introduction to life in London** mon premier contact avec la vie londonienne; **letter of introduction** lettre *f* de recommandation (*to sb* auprès de qn). ♦ **introductory** *adj remarks, words* préliminaire, d'introduction; (*Comm*) *offer* de lancement.

introspective [ˌɪntrəʊˈspektɪv] *adj* introspectif. ♦ **introspection** *n* introspection *f*.

introvert [ˈɪntrəʊvɜːt] *adj, n* introverti(e) *m(f)*. ♦ **introversion** *n* introversion *f*.

intrude [ɪnˈtruːd] *vi [person]* être importun, s'imposer; *[feeling, emotion]* se manifester. **to ~ on** *person* s'imposer à; *conversation* s'immiscer dans; **am I intruding?** est-ce que je vous gêne? ♦ **intruder** *n* intrus(e) *m(f)*. ♦ **intrusion** *n* intrusion *f* (*into* dans), imposition *f* (*on* à). ♦ **intrusive** *adj* importun, gênant; (*Ling*) **the intrusive 'r'** *le 'r' rajouté en anglais en liaison abusive*.

intuition [ˌɪntjuːˈɪʃən] *n* intuition *f*. ♦ **intuitive** *adj* intuitif. ♦ **intuitively** *adv* intuitivement.

inundate [ˈɪnʌndeɪt] *vt* (*lit, fig*) inonder (*with* de). **~d with work** débordé (de travail); **~d with visits** inondé de visiteurs.

inure [ɪnˈjʊəʳ] *vt* habituer, aguerrir (*to* à).

invade [ɪnˈveɪd] *vt* (*Mil, gen, fig*) envahir; *privacy* violer; *sb's rights* empiéter sur. ♦ **invader** *n* envahisseur *m*, -euse *f*. ♦ **invading** *adj army, troops* d'invasion.

invalid¹ [ˈɪnvəlɪd] **1** *n* (*sick person*) malade *mf*; (*with disability*) invalide *mf*, infirme *mf*. **2** *adj* (*ill*) malade; (*with disability*) invalide, infirme; *car* d'infirme; **~ chair** fauteuil *m* d'infirme.

invalid out *vt sep* (*Mil*) réformer (pour blessures *or* pour raisons de santé).

invalid² [ɪnˈvælɪd] *adj* non valide, non valable.

invalidate [ɪnˈvælɪdeɪt] *vt* (*gen*) invalider; *will* rendre nul et sans effet; *contract etc* vicier.

invaluable [ɪnˈvæljʊəbl] *adj* inestimable, inappréciable.

invariable [ɪnˈvɛərɪəbl] *adj* invariable. ♦ **invariably** *adv* invariablement.

invasion [ɪnˈveɪʒən] *n* invasion *f*. **it is an ~ of his privacy** c'est une incursion dans sa vie privée.

invective [ɪnˈvektɪv] *n* invective *f*. **stream of ~** flot *m* d'invectives.

inveigh [ɪnˈveɪ] *vi* fulminer (*against* contre).

inveigle [ɪnˈviːgl] *vt* entraîner (par la ruse *etc*) (*into sth* dans qch; *into doing* à faire).

invent [ɪnˈvent] *vt* (*lit, fig*) inventer. ♦ **invention** *n* invention *f*. ♦ **inventive** *adj* inventif. ♦ **inventiveness** *n* esprit inventif. ♦ **inventor** *n* inventeur *m*, -trice *f*.

inventory [ˈɪnvəntrɪ] *n* inventaire *m*.

inverse [ˈɪnˈvɜːs] *adj* inverse. **in ~ proportion** *or* **ratio** en raison inverse (*to* de). ♦ **inversely** *adv* inversement. ♦ **inversion** *n* inversion *f*; (*Mus*) renversement *m*; *[values, roles etc]* renversement.

invert [ɪnˈvɜːt] **1** *vt* (*gen*) inverser, intervertir;

cup, object retourner; *process* renverser. **in ~ed commas** entre guillemets *mpl.* **2** ['ɪnvɜːt] *n* inverti(e) *m(f).*

invertebrate [ɪn'vɜːtɪbrɪt] *adj, n* invertébré (*m*).

invest [ɪn'vest] **1** *vt capital, funds* investir (*in* dans); *money* placer (*in* dans, en); *time* consacrer (*in* à); (*endow*) revêtir, investir (*sb with sth* qn de qch). **2** *vi* placer son argent (*in* en). **I've ~ed in a new car*** je me suis payé* une nouvelle voiture. ♦ **investiture** *n* investiture *f.* ♦ **investment** **1** *n* investissement *m,* placement *m;* **2** *adj bank etc* d'investissement. ♦ **investor** *n* (*gen*) investisseur *m;* (*in a company*) actionnaire *mf.*

investigate [ɪn'vestɪgeɪt] *vt question, possibilities* étudier; *motive, reason* scruter; *crime* enquêter sur. ♦ **investigation** *n [researcher]* investigation *f; [policeman etc]* enquête *f;* **the matter under investigation** la question à l'étude. ♦ **investigator** *n* investigateur *m,* -trice *f;* (*Police*) enquêteur *m;* **private investigator** detective *m.*

inveterate [ɪn'vetərɪt] *adj* invétéré.

invidious [ɪn'vɪdɪəs] *adj* (*gen*) injuste; *comparison* blessant.

invigilate [ɪn'vɪdʒɪleɪt] **1** *vi* être de surveillance (*at* à). **2** *vt examination* surveiller. ♦ **invigilator** *n* surveillant(e) *m(f)* (*à un examen*).

invigorate [ɪn'vɪgəreɪt] *vt [drink, food, thought]* fortifier; *[fresh air, snack]* revigorer; *[climate, air, exercise]* donner du tonus à. ♦ **invigorating** *adj* vivifiant, tonifiant; *speech* stimulant.

invincible [ɪn'vɪnsəbl] *adj* invincible.

invisible [ɪn'vɪzəbl] *adj* (*gen*) invisible; *ink* sympathique. **~ mending** stoppage *m.* ♦ **invisibility** *n* invisibilité *f.* ♦ **invisibly** *adv* invisiblement.

invite [ɪn'vaɪt] *vt person* inviter (*to do* à faire); *opinions, subscriptions etc* demander; *doubts, ridicule* appeler; *discussion* inviter à; *trouble, defeat* chercher. **to ~ sb to dinner** inviter qn à dîner; **to ~ sb in/up** *etc* inviter qn à entrer/monter *etc.*

invite out *vt sep* inviter (à sortir). **I've been ~d out to dinner** j'ai été invité à dîner.

invite over *vt sep* inviter (à venir). **they often ~ us over for a drink** ils nous invitent souvent à venir prendre un verre chez eux.

♦ **invitation** *n* invitation *f;* **at sb's invitation** à *or* sur l'invitation de qn; **by invitation only** sur invitation seulement; **it is an invitation to burglars** c'est une invite aux cambrioleurs. ♦ **inviting** *adj appearance, goods* attrayant; *gesture* encourageant; *meal, odour* appétissant. ♦ **invitingly** *adv describe* d'une manière attrayante; *speak* d'un ton encourageant.

invoice ['ɪnvɔɪs] **1** *n* facture *f.* **2** *vt* facturer. **3** *adj*: **~ clerk** facturier *m,* -ière *f.*

invoke [ɪn'vəʊk] *vt* invoquer.

involuntary [ɪn'vɒləntərɪ] *adj* involontaire. ♦ **involuntarily** *adv* involontairement.

involve [ɪn'vɒlv] *vt* **(a)** (*gen*) mêler (*in* à), entraîner (*in* dans); (*implicate, associate*) impliquer (*in* dans). **to be ~d in a quarrel** être mêlé à une querelle; **we would prefer not to ~ Robert** nous préférerions ne pas mêler Robert à l'affaire *or* ne pas impliquer Robert; **to ~ sb in expense** entraîner qn à faire des frais; **how did you come to be ~d?** comment vous êtes-vous trouvé impliqué?; **he was so ~d in politics that ...** il était tellement engagé dans la politique que ...; **the police became ~d** la police est intervenue; **a question of principle is ~d** c'est une question de principe qui est en jeu; **the factors ~d** les facteurs en jeu; **the person ~d** la personne en question; **to feel personally ~d** se sentir concerné; **we are all ~d** nous sommes tous concernés; **to get ~d with sb** (*gen*) se trouver mêlé aux affaires de qn; (*socially*) se trouver lié intimement à qn; (*fall in love with*) tomber amoureux de qn. **(b)** (*entail*) *expense, trouble* entraîner. **the job ~s living in the country** le poste nécessite qu'on réside (*subj*) à la campagne; **there's a good deal of work ~d** cela nécessite un gros travail. ♦ **involved** *adj* compliqué. ♦ **involvement** *n* **(a)** rôle *m* (*in* dans), participation *f* (*in* à); **we don't know the extent of his ~ment** nous ne savons pas dans quelle mesure il est impliqué; **his ~ment in politics** son engagement *m* dans la politique; **(b)** (*difficulty*) difficulté *f;* **financial ~ments** difficultés financières; **(c)** *[style etc]* complications *fpl.*

invulnerable [ɪn'vʌlnərəbl] *adj* invulnérable. ♦ **invulnerability** *n* invulnérabilité *f.*

inward ['ɪnwəd] **1** *adj movements* vers l'intérieur; *happiness, peace* intérieur; *thoughts, conviction* intime. **2** *adv* (*also* **~s**) vers l'intérieur. ♦ **inwardly** *adv* **(a)** (*in the inside*) à l'intérieur; **(b)** (*secretly*) *feel, think, know* en son (*or* mon *etc*) for intérieur.

iodine ['aɪədiːn] *n* iode *m;* (*Med*) teinture *f* d'iode.

ion ['aɪən] *n* ion *m.*

iota [aɪ'əʊtə] *n* iota *m; [truth]* brin *m; [sense]* grain *m.*

IOU [ˌaɪəʊ'juː] *n* (*abbr of* **I owe you**) reconnaissance *f* de dette (*for* pour).

Iran [ɪ'rɑːn] *n* Iran *m.*

Iraq [ɪ'rɑːk] *n* Irak *m.*

irascible [ɪ'ræsɪbl] *adj* irascible. ♦ **irascibility** *n* irascibilité *f.* ♦ **irascibly** *adv* irasciblement.

irate [aɪ'reɪt] *adj* furieux.

Ireland ['aɪələnd] *n* Irlande *f.* **Northern ~** Irlande du Nord; **Republic of ~** République *f* d'Irlande. ♦ **Irish** **1** *adj* irlandais; **Irish Sea** mer *f* d'Irlande; **2** *n* **(a) the Irish** les Irlandais *mpl;* **(b)** (*Ling*) irlandais *m.* ♦ **Irishman** *n* Irlandais *m.* ♦ **Irishwoman** *n* Irlandaise *f.*

iris ['aɪərɪs] *n* (*Anat, Bot*) iris *m.*

irksome ['ɜːksəm] *adj* ennuyeux.

iron ['aɪən] **1** *n* (*metal*) fer *m;* (*for laundry*) fer (à repasser). **scrap ~** ferraille *f;* **to strike while the ~ is hot** battre le fer pendant qu'il est chaud; **electric ~** fer électrique; (*fig*) **to have too many ~s in the fire** mener trop d'affaires de front; **I've got a lot of ~s in the fire** j'ai des quantités d'affaires en train; (*fetters*) **~s** fers *mpl.* **2** *adj tool, bridge* de *or* en fer; (*fig*) *determination, will, constitution* de fer. **the I~ Age** l'âge *m* de fer; **the ~ and steel industry** l'industrie *f* sidérurgique; (*Pol*) **~ curtain** rideau *m* de fer; **an ~ fist** *or* **hand in a velvet glove** une main de fer dans un gant de velours; **~ foundry** fonderie *f* de fonte; (*Med*) **~ lung** poumon *m* d'acier; **~ ore** minerai *m* de fer; **~ rations** vivres *mpl* de réserve. **3** *vt clothes etc* repasser. **4** *vi [clothes etc]* se repasser.

iron out *vt sep creases* faire disparaître au fer; *difficulties* aplanir; *problems* faire disparaître.

♦ **ironing** **1** *n* repassage *m;* **2** *adj*: **~ing board** planche *f* à repasser. ♦ **ironmonger** *n* quincaillier *m.* ♦ **ironmongery** *n* quincaillerie *f.* ♦ **ironworks** *n* usine *f* sidérurgique.

irony ['aɪərənɪ] *n* ironie *f.* **the ~ of it is that ...** ce qu'il y a d'ironique là-dedans c'est que ... . ♦ **ironic(al)** *adj* ironique. ♦ **ironically** *adv* ironiquement.

irradiate [ɪ'reɪdɪeɪt] *vt* (*illuminate*) illuminer; (*Phys*) irradier. ♦ **irradiation** *n* illumination *f;* irradiation *f.*

irrational [ɪ'ræʃənl] *adj person* qui n'est pas rationnel; *belief* déraisonnable; *behaviour* irrationnel. **she had become quite ~ about it** elle n'était plus du tout capable d'y penser rationellement. ♦ **irrationally** *adv* déraisonnablement; irrationnellement.

irreconcilable [ɪˌrekən'saɪləbl] *adj enemies* irréconciliable; *hatred* implacable; *belief* inconciliable (*with* avec).

irredeemable [ˌɪrɪ'diːməbl] *adj person* incorrigible; *error* irréparable; *disaster* irrémédiable.

irrefutable [ˌɪrɪˈfjuːtəbl] *adj* irréfutable.

irregular [ɪˈregjʊləʳ] *adj* (*gen*) irrégulier; *surface* inégal. ♦ **irregularity** *n* irrégularité *f*.

irrelevant [ɪˈreləvənt] *adj factor, detail* sans rapport; *question, remark* hors de propos. **that's ~** cela n'a rien à voir avec la question. ♦ **irrelevance** *n* manque *m* de rapport, manque d'à-propos (*to* avec).

irreligious [ˌɪrɪˈlɪdʒəs] *adj* irréligieux.

irreparable [ɪˈrepərəbl] *adj* irréparable. ♦ **irreparably** *adv* irréparablement.

irreplaceable [ˌɪrɪˈpleɪsəbl] *adj* irremplaçable.

irrepressible [ˌɪrɪˈpresəbl] *adj laughter etc* irrépressible, irrésistible. **she's quite ~** elle est d'une vitalité débordante; (*of child*) c'est un vrai petit diable.

irreproachable [ˌɪrɪˈprəʊtʃəbl] *adj* irréprochable.

irresistible [ˌɪrɪˈzɪstəbl] *adj* irrésistible. ♦ **irresistibly** *adv* irrésistiblement.

irresolute [ɪˈrezəluːt] *adj* irrésolu, indécis.

irrespective [ˌɪrɪˈspektɪv] *adj*: **~ of sth** sans tenir compte de qch; **~ of whether it's useful or not** que ce soit utile ou non.

irresponsible [ˌɪrɪsˈpɒnsəbl] *adj* irréfléchi.

irretrievable [ˌɪrɪˈtriːvəbl] *adj loss, damage* irréparable; *object* introuvable.

irreverent [ɪˈrevərənt] *adj* irrévérencieux. ♦ **irreverence** *n* irrévérence *f*. ♦ **irreverently** *adv* irrévérencieusement.

irrevocable [ɪˈrevəkəbl] *adj* irrévocable. ♦ **irrevocably** *adv* irrévocablement.

irrigate [ˈɪrɪgeɪt] *vt* irriguer. ♦ **irrigation** *n* irrigation *f*.

irritable [ˈɪrɪtəbl] *adj* (*cross*) irritable; (*irascible*) irascible. ♦ **irritability** *n* irritabilité *f*; irascibilité *f*. ♦ **irritably** *adv behave, nod* avec humeur; *speak* d'un ton irrité.

irritate [ˈɪrɪteɪt] *vt* (*gen, Med*) irriter. ♦ **irritant** *adj, n* irritant (*m*). ♦ **irritating** *adj* irritant. ♦ **irritation** *n* irritation *f*.

irruption [ɪˈrʌpʃən] *n* irruption *f*.

Islam [ˈɪzlɑːm] *n* Islam *m*. ♦ **Islamic** *adj* islamique.

island [ˈaɪlənd] **1** *n* **(a)** île *f*. **(b)** (*traffic or street* **~**) refuge *m* (*pour piétons*). **2** *adj people, community* insulaire. ♦ **islander** *n* insulaire *mf*.

isle [aɪl] *n* (*liter*) île *f*. ♦ **islet** *n* îlot *m*.

isolate [ˈaɪsəʊleɪt] *vt* isoler (*from* de). ♦ **isolated** *adj* isolé. ♦ **isolation** **1** *n* (*action*) isolation *f*; (*state*) isolement *m*; **2** *adj hospital* d'isolement; *ward* des contagieux. ♦ **isolationism** *n* isolationnisme *m*. ♦ **isolationist** *adj, n* isolationniste (*mf*).

isotope [ˈaɪsəʊtəʊp] *adj, n* isotope (*m*).

Israel [ˈɪzreɪl] *n* Israël *m*. ♦ **Israeli** **1** *adj* israélien; **2** *n* Israélien(ne) *m(f)*.

issue [ˈɪʃuː] **1** *n* **(a)** (*matter, question*) question *f*, problème *m*. **he raised several new ~s** il a soulevé plusieurs points nouveaux; **the ~ is whether ...** la question consiste à savoir si ...; **to confuse** *or* **obscure the ~** brouiller les cartes; **to face the ~** regarder le problème en face; **to force the ~** forcer une décision; **to avoid the ~** prendre la tangente; **to make an ~ of sth** faire un problème de qch; **I don't want to make an ~ of it** je ne veux pas trop insister là-dessus; **the factors at ~** les facteurs en jeu; **the point at ~** le point controversé; **to be at ~** être en cause; **to take ~ with sb** engager une controverse avec qn; **I must take ~ with you on this** je me permets de ne pas partager votre avis là-dessus. **(b)** (*outcome*) résultat *m*, issue *f*. **(c)** (*act*) *[goods, tickets]* distribution *f*; *[passport, document]* délivrance *f*; *[banknote, cheque, shares, stamp]* émission *f*; *[warrant, writ, summons]* lancement *m*. **these coins are a new ~** ces pièces viennent d'être émises. **(d)** (*copy*) *[newspaper, magazine]* numéro *m*. **back ~** vieux numéro. **(e)** (*offspring*) descendance *f*.
2 *vt book* publier; *order* donner; *goods, tickets* distribuer; *passport, document* délivrer; *banknote, cheque, shares, stamps* émettre; *proclamation* faire; *warrant, warning, writ* lancer. **to ~ a statement** faire une déclaration; **to ~ sth to sb, to ~ sb with sth** fournir qch à qn.

isthmus [ˈɪsməs] *n* isthme *m*.

it [ɪt] *pron* **(a)** (*specific*) (*nominative*) il, elle; (*accusative*) le, la, (*before vowel*) l'; (*dative*) lui. **where is the book? – ~'s on the table** où est le livre? – il est sur la table; **my machine is old but ~ works** ma machine est vieille mais elle marche; **here's the pencil – give ~ to me** voici le crayon – donne-le-moi; **if you can find the watch give ~ to him** si tu trouves la montre donne-la-lui; **of ~, from ~, about ~, for ~, out of ~** *etc* en; **he's afraid of ~** il en a peur; **he didn't speak to me about ~** il ne m'en a pas parlé; (*following French verbs with 'de'*) **I doubt ~** j'en doute; **in ~, to ~, at ~** *etc* y; (*meeting etc*) **he'll be at ~** il y sera; (*following French verbs with 'à'*) **taste ~!** goûtez-y!; **above ~, over ~** (au-)dessus; **below ~, beneath ~, under ~** (au-)dessous, (en-)dessous.
(b) (*impersonal*) (*nominative*) il, ce, cela, ça; (*accusative*) le; (*dative*) y. **~ is raining** il pleut; **~ frightens me** cela *or* ça m'effraie; **~'s pleasant here** c'est agréable ici; **I've done it** je l'ai fait; **I've thought about it** j'y ai pensé; **~'s Wednesday 16th October** nous sommes le mercredi 16 octobre; **~'s 3 o'clock** il est 3 heures; **who is ~?** qui est-ce?; **~'s me** c'est moi; **what is ~?** qu'est-ce que c'est?; **that's ~!** (*approval, agreement*) c'est ça!; (*achievement, dismay*) ça y est!; **~'s difficult to understand** c'est difficile à comprendre; **~'s difficult to understand why** il est difficile de comprendre pourquoi; **I considered ~ pointless to protest** j'ai jugé (qu'il était) inutile de protester; **~ was your father who phoned** c'est ton père qui a téléphoné.
(c) (*in games*) **you're ~!** c'est toi le chat!
♦ **its** **1** *poss adj* son, sa, ses; **2** *poss pron* le sien, la sienne, les siens, les siennes. ♦ **it's = it is, it has.** ♦ **itself** *pron* (*emphatic*) lui-même *m*, elle-même *f*; (*reflexive*) se; **in the theatre ~self** dans le théâtre même; **the door closes by ~self** la porte se ferme automatiquement *or* toute seule.

italic [ɪˈtælɪk] **1** *adj* (*Typ*) italique. **2** *npl*: **~s** italique *m*. **in ~s** en italique.

Italy [ˈɪtəlɪ] *n* Italie *f*. ♦ **Italian** [ɪˈtæljən] **1** *adj* italien, d'Italie; **2** *n* **(a)** Italien(ne) *m(f)*; **(b)** (*Ling*) italien *m*.

itch [ɪtʃ] **1** *n* démangeaison *f*. (*fig*) **I've got an ~* to travel** l'envie de voyager me démange. **2** *vi [person]* éprouver des démangeaisons. **his legs ~** ses jambes le démangent; (*fig*) **to be ~ing* to do sth** avoir une envie qui vous démange de faire qch; **I am ~ing to tell him the news** la langue me démange de lui annoncer la nouvelle. ♦ **itching** *adj*: **~ing powder** poil *m* à gratter. ♦ **itchy** *adj* qui démange; **I've got an ~y back** j'ai le dos qui me démange; (*fig*) **he's got ~y feet*** il a la bougeotte*; (*fig*) **he's got ~y fingers*** il est chapardeur*.

item [ˈaɪtəm] *n* (*on agenda, at meeting*) question *f*; (*in programme*) numéro *m*; (*in catalogue, newspaper, shopping list; also Comm*) article *m*; (*Jur: in contract*) article; (*Book-keeping*) poste *m*. **~s on the agenda** questions à l'ordre du jour; (*Rad, TV*) **the main ~ in the news** la grosse nouvelle, le fait du jour; **an important ~ in our policy** un point important de notre politique. ♦ **itemize** *vt* détailler, spécifier.

itinerary [aɪˈtɪnərərɪ] *n* itinéraire *m*. ♦ **itinerant** *adj preacher* itinérant; *actors etc* ambulant.

ivory [ˈaɪvərɪ] **1** *n* ivoire *m*. **2** *adj statue, figure* en ivoire, d'ivoire; (*also* **~-coloured**) ivoire *inv*. (*fig*) **~ tower** tour *f* d'ivoire.

ivy [ˈaɪvɪ] *n* lierre *m*. (*US*) **I~ League** (*n*) *ensemble des grandes universités du nord-est*.

J

J, j [dʒeɪ] *n* J, j *m*.
jab [dʒæb] **1** *vti* enfoncer, planter (*into* dans). **to ~ (at) sth with sth, to ~ sth into sth** enfoncer qch dans qch, planter qch dans *or* sur qch. **2** *n* coup *m* (*donné avec un objet pointu*); (*: *injection*) piqûre *f*.
jabber [ˈdʒæbəʳ] **1** *vt* bafouiller, bredouiller. **2** *vi* (**~ away**) (*chatter*) jacasser; (*talk unintelligibly*) baragouiner*.
jack [dʒæk] *n* (*Aut*) cric *m*; (*Bowling*) cochonnet *m*; (*Cards*) valet *m*. **before you could say J~ Robinson*** en moins de temps qu'il n'en faut pour le dire; **~ tar** matelot *m*; **every man ~** chacun.
jack in‡ *vt sep* plaquer‡.
jack up *vt sep car* soulever avec un cric; (*: *raise*) *prices* faire grimper. **~ed up** *car* sur le cric.
◆ **jackass** *n* (*lit, fig*) âne *m*. ◆ **jackboots** *npl* bottes *fpl* à l'écuyère. ◆ **jackdaw** *n* choucas *m*. ◆ **jack-in-office*** *n* gratte-papier *m inv* (qui joue à l'important). ◆ **jack-in-the-box** *n* diable *m* (à ressort). ◆ **jack-knife 1** *n* couteau *m* de poche; **2** *vi*: **the lorry ~-knifed** la remorque (du camion) s'est mise en travers. ◆ **jack-of-all-trades** *n* bricoleur *m*. ◆ **jackpot** *n*: **to hit the ~pot** *[person]* gagner le gros lot; *[song, disc]* faire un malheur*.
jackal [ˈdʒækɔːl] *n* chacal *m*.
jacket [ˈdʒækɪt] *n [man]* veston *m*; *[woman]* veste *f*; *[child]* paletot *m*; *[book]* couverture *f*. **potatoes baked in their ~s** pommes *fpl* de terre au four.
Jacobean [ˌdʒækəˈbiːən] *adj* de l'époque de Jacques Ier (*1603–1625*).
jade [dʒeɪd] **1** *n* jade *m*. **2** *adj* (*colour*) jade *inv*. **~-green** vert jade *inv*.
jaded [ˈdʒeɪdɪd] *adj person* las (*with* de), blasé; *palate* blasé.
jagged [ˈdʒægɪd] *adj* irrégulier, déchiqueté.
jaguar [ˈdʒægjʊəʳ] *n* jaguar *m*.
jail [dʒeɪl] **1** *n* prison *f*. **in ~** en prison; **to be in ~ for 5 years** faire 5 ans de prison; **to send sb to ~/to ~ for 5 years** condamner qn à la prison/à 5 ans de prison. **2** *vt* mettre en prison (*for murder etc* pour meurtre *etc*). **~ed for life** condamné à perpétuité. ◆ **jailbird** *n* récidiviste *mf*. ◆ **jailbreak** *n* évasion *f* (de prison). ◆ **jailbreaker** *n* évadé(e) *m(f)*. ◆ **jailer** *n* geôlier *m*, -ière *f*.
jam¹ [dʒæm] **1** *n* **(a)** *[people]* foule *f*, cohue *f*; *[logs, vehicles etc]* embouteillage *m*. **(b) to get into a ~*** se mettre dans le pétrin; **to get sb out of a ~*** tirer qn du pétrin. **2** *vt* **(a)** (*cram*) (*into box, drawer, suitcase*) enfoncer, tasser (*into* dans); (*into room, vehicle*) entasser (*into* dans); *hat* enfoncer (*on* sur); (*wedge*) coincer (*between* entre). **he ~med his finger in the door** il s'est coincé le doigt dans la porte. **(b)** (*block*) *brake* bloquer; *door* coincer; *gun, machine* enrayer; (*Rad*) *station, broadcast* brouiller; (*Telec*) *line* encombrer; *[crowd, cars etc] street, corridor* encombrer, embouteiller. **street ~med with cars** rue embouteillée; **street ~med with people** rue noire de monde. **3** *vi* **(a)** *[crowd]* s'entasser (*into* dans). **(b)** (*V 2 b above*) se bloquer; se coincer; s'enrayer.
jam in *vt sep* (*into box etc*) serrer; *car, person* coincer.
jam on *vt sep hat* enfoncer. (*Aut*) **to ~ on the brakes** freiner à mort*.
◆ **jam-full** *or* ◆ **jam-packed** *adj vehicle, place* plein à craquer; *container* plein à ras bord. ◆ **jamming** *n* (*Rad*) brouillage *m*.
jam² [dʒæm] **1** *n* confiture *f*. **cherry ~** confiture de cerises; (*fig*) **you want ~ on it!*** et quoi encore! **2** *adj tart* à la confiture. (*Mus*) **~ session** séance *f* de jazz improvisé. ◆ **jamjar** *or* ◆ **jampot** *n* pot *m* à confitures.
Jamaica [dʒəˈmeɪkə] *n* Jamaïque *f*. **in ~** à la Jamaïque.
jamb [dʒæm] *n* montant *m* (*de porte etc*).
jamboree [ˌdʒæmbəˈriː] *n* festivités *fpl*.
jangle [ˈdʒæŋgl] **1** *vi [bells]* retentir; *[bracelets, chains]* cliqueter. **2** *vt* faire retentir; faire cliqueter. ◆ **jangled** *adj nerves* en pelote. ◆ **jangling** *adj bells* discordant; *chains* cliquetant.
janitor [ˈdʒænɪtəʳ] *n* concierge *m*.
January [ˈdʒænjʊərɪ] *n* janvier *m*; *for phrases V* **September**.
Japan [dʒəˈpæn] *n* Japon *m*. ◆ **Japanese 1** *adj* japonais; **2** *n* (*person: pl inv*) Japonais(e) *m(f)*; (*Ling*) japonais *m*.
japonica [dʒəˈpɒnɪkə] *n* cognassier *m* du Japon.
jar¹ [dʒɑːʳ] **1** *n* (*jolt: lit, fig*) secousse *f*, choc *m*. **2** *vi* (*vibrate*) vibrer, trembler; (*be wrong*) *[note]* détonner; *[colours]* jurer (*with* avec); *[ideas, opinions]* ne pas s'accorder (*with* avec). **to ~ on sb's nerves** porter sur les nerfs à qn; **to ~ on sb's ears** écorcher les oreilles à qn. **3** *vt structure* ébranler; *person* heurter; (*fig*) secouer. **you ~red my elbow** tu m'as cogné le coude. ◆ **jarring** *adj sound* discordant; (*fig*) **to strike a ~ring note** être plutôt choquant.
jar² [dʒɑːʳ] *n* (*of earthenware*) pot *m*, jarre *f*; (*for jam etc*) pot; (*for pickles etc*) bocal *m*.
jargon [ˈdʒɑːgən] *n* jargon *m*.
jasmine [ˈdʒæzmɪn] *n* jasmin *m*.
jaundice [ˈdʒɔːndɪs] *n* jaunisse *f*. ◆ **jaundiced** *adj* (*bitter*) amer; (*critical*) désapprobateur; **to have a ~d view of things** voir les choses en noir; **to give sb a ~d look** jeter un regard noir à qn.
jaunt [dʒɔːnt] *n* balade* *f*. **to go for a ~** aller se balader*.
jaunty [ˈdʒɔːntɪ] *adj* (*sprightly*) enjoué, vif; (*carefree*) désinvolte; (*swaggering*) crâneur*. ◆ **jauntily** *adv* d'un pas vif; de façon désinvolte; d'un air crâneur*.
javelin [ˈdʒævlɪn] **1** *n* javelot *m*. **2** *adj* (*Sport*) **~ throwing** lancement *m* du javelot.
jaw [dʒɔː] *n* mâchoire *f*. **the ~s of death** l'étreinte *f* de la mort; **the ~s of hell** les portes *fpl* de l'enfer. ◆ **jawbone** *n* maxillaire *m*.
jay [dʒeɪ] *n* geai *m*. ◆ **jaywalker** *n* piéton *m* indiscipliné.
jazz [dʒæz] **1** *n* (*Mus*) jazz *m*. (*fig*) **he gave them a lot of ~* about his marvellous job** il leur a fait tout un baratin* sur sa magnifique situation; **... and all that ~‡** ... et tout le bataclan*. **2** *adj band, music* de jazz.
jazz up *vt sep* **(a)** (*Mus*) (*play*) jouer en jazz; (*arrange*) adapter pour le jazz. **(b)** (‡) *party* mettre de l'entrain dans; *old dress etc* égayer.
jealous [ˈdʒeləs] *adj* jaloux (*of* de). ◆ **jealously** *adv* (*enviously*) jalousement; (*watchfully*) d'un œil jaloux. ◆ **jealousy** *n* jalousie *f*.

jeans [dʒi:nz] *npl* blue-jean *m*, jean *m*.
jeep [dʒi:p] *n* jeep *f*.
jeer [dʒɪəʳ] **1** *vi [individual]* railler; *[crowd]* huer. **to ~ at sb** railler qn. **2** *vt* huer. **3** *n* raillerie *f*; huée *f*. ♦ **jeering 1** *adj* railleur; **2** *n* railleries *fpl*; huées *fpl*.
Jehovah [dʒɪˈhəʊvə] *n* Jéhovah *m*.
jell [dʒel] *vi [jelly etc]* épaissir, prendre; (*) *[plan etc]* prendre tournure. ♦ **jello** *n* ® (*US*) gelée *f*. ♦ **jelly** *n* gelée *f*. ♦ **jellyfish** *n* méduse *f*.
jemmy [ˈdʒemɪ] *n* pince-monseigneur *f*.
jeopardy [ˈdʒepədɪ] *n* danger *m*, péril *m*. **in ~** *life* en danger; *happiness* menacé, en péril; *business* en mauvaise posture. ♦ **jeopardize** *vt* mettre en danger, compromettre.
jerk [dʒɜ:k] **1** *n* (*gen*) secousse *f*; (*mechanical*) à-coup *m*; (*Med*) crispation nerveuse; (‡*pej: person*) pauvre type* *m*. **2** *vt* (*pull*) tirer brusquement; (*shake*) donner une secousse à. **he ~ed the book out of my hand** d'une secousse il m'a fait lâcher le livre. **3** *vi [person, muscle]* se crisper. ♦ **jerkily** *adv move* par à-coups; *speak* d'une voix saccadée. ♦ **jerky** *adj motion* saccadé; (*fig*) *style* heurté.
jerkin [ˈdʒɜ:kɪn] *n* blouson *m*; (*Hist*) justaucorps *m*.
jerry-building [ˈdʒerɪˌbɪldɪŋ] *n* construction *f* bon marché. ♦ **jerry-built** *adj* en carton-pâte (*fig*).
jerry-can [ˈdʒerɪˌkæn] *n* jerrycan *m*.
Jersey [ˈdʒɜ:zɪ] *n* Jersey *f*. ♦ **jersey** *n* (*garment*) tricot *m*; (*material*) jersey *m*.
jest [dʒest] **1** *n* plaisanterie *f*. **in ~** pour rire. **2** *vi* plaisanter. ♦ **jester** *n* bouffon *m*.
Jesuit [ˈdʒezjʊɪt] *n* Jésuite *m*.
Jesus [ˈdʒi:zəs] *n* Jésus *m*. **~ Christ** Jésus-Christ.
jet¹ [dʒet] **1** *n [liquids, gas]* jet *m*; (*~ plane*) avion *m* à réaction, jet *m*; (*nozzle*) brûleur *m*; (*Aut*) gicleur *m*. **2** *adj* (*Aviat*) *travel* en jet; *engine, fighter* à réaction; *propulsion* par réaction. **~ fuel** kérosène *m*; **~ lag** (troubles *mpl* dûs au) décalage *m* horaire; **to have ~ lag** souffrir du décalage horaire; **the ~ set*** le monde des playboys. ♦ **jet-propelled** *adj* à réaction.
jet² [dʒet] *n* jais *m*. **~-black** noir comme jais.
jettison [ˈdʒetɪsn] *vt* (*gen*) *burden* se délester de; (*Naut*) jeter par-dessus bord; (*Aviat*) *bombs* larguer; *hopes* abandonner.
jetty [ˈdʒetɪ] *n* (*breakwater*) jetée *f*, digue *f*; (*landing pier*) embarcadère *m*.
Jew [dʒu:] *n* Juif *m*. **~'s harp** guimbarde *f*. ♦ **Jewess** *n* Juive *f*. ♦ **Jewish** *adj* juif. ♦ **Jewry** *n* les Juifs *mpl*.
jewel [ˈdʒu:əl] *n* bijou *m*, joyau *m*; (*in watch*) rubis *m*; (*fig*) bijou *m*. ♦ **jewel-case** *n* coffret *m* à bijoux. ♦ **jewelled,** (*US*) **jeweled** *adj* orné de bijoux. ♦ **jewel(l)er** *n* bijoutier *m*, joaillier *m*; **~ler's (shop)** bijouterie *f*, joaillerie *f*. ♦ **jewel(l)ery** *n* bijoux *mpl*, joyaux *mpl*; **a piece of ~lery** un bijou.
jib [dʒɪb] **1** *n* (*Naut*) foc *m*; *[crane]* flèche *f*. **2** *vi [person]* regimber (*at sth* devant qch), se refuser (*at doing* à faire); *[horse]* regimber.
jibe [dʒaɪb] = **gibe**.
jiffy* [ˈdʒɪfɪ] *n*: **wait a ~** attends une seconde; **in a ~** en moins de deux*.
jig [dʒɪg] *n* (*dance*) gigue *f*; (*Tech*) calibre *m*. ♦ **jigsaw (puzzle)** *n* puzzle *m*.
jilt [dʒɪlt] *vt* laisser tomber* *[un(e) fiancé(e)]*.
jingle [ˈdʒɪŋgl] **1** *n [keys etc]* tintement *m*. **advertising ~** couplet *m* publicitaire. **2** *vi* tinter. **3** *vt* faire tinter.
jinx* [dʒɪŋks] *n* porte-poisse* *m inv*. **there's a ~ on ...** on a jeté un sort à ... .
jitters* [ˈdʒɪtəz] *npl* frousse* *f*. **to have the ~** avoir la frousse*. ♦ **jittery*** *adj* froussard*.
jiujitsu [dʒu:ˈdʒɪtsu:] *n* jiu-jitsu *m*.
job [dʒɒb] **1** *n* **(a)** (*piece of work*) travail *m*, boulot* *m*. **I have a little ~ for you** j'ai un petit travail pour vous; **he has made a good/bad ~ of it** il a fait du bon/du sale boulot*; **he's done a good ~ of work** il a fait du bon travail; **this new airliner is a lovely ~*** ce nouvel avion c'est vraiment du beau travail*. **(b)** (*post, situation*) travail *m*, emploi *m*, boulot* *m*. **he found a ~ as a librarian** il a trouvé un poste de bibliothécaire; **to look for a ~** chercher du travail *or* un emploi; **to be out of a ~** être au chômage; **he has a very good ~** il a une belle situation; **~s for the boys*** des planques *fpl* pour les petits copains*. **(c)** (*duty*) travail *m*, boulot* *m*. **he's only doing his ~** il ne fait que son boulot*; **he knows his ~** il connaît son affaire; **that's not his ~** ce n'est pas à lui de faire ça; **I had the ~ of telling them** c'est moi qui ai été obligé de le leur dire. **(d) it's a good ~ that ...** c'est heureux que + *subj*; **a good ~ too!** à la bonne heure!; **it's a bad ~** c'est une sale affaire; **to give sth/sb up as a bad ~** renoncer à qch/qn en désespoir de cause; **this is just the ~*** c'est exactement ce qu'il faut; **to have a ~ to do sth** *or* **doing sth** avoir du mal à faire qch; **it's been quite a ~ finding it** ça a été toute une affaire pour le trouver; **a put-up ~*** un coup monté; **remember that bank ~?*** tu te rappelles le coup de la banque?
2 *adj* **(a)** (*Ind*) **~ analysis** analyse *f* des tâches; **~ centre** agence *f* pour l'emploi; **~ creation** création *f* d'emplois nouveaux; **~ evaluation** qualification *f* du travail; **~ hunting** chasse *f* à l'emploi; **~ satisfaction** satisfaction *f* au travail. **(b) ~ lot** lot *m* d'articles divers.
♦ **jobber** *n* (*St Ex*) *intermédiaire m qui traite directement avec l'agent de change*. ♦ **jobbing** *adj gardener* à la journée; *workman* à la tâche. ♦ **jobless 1** *adj* sans travail, au chômage; **2** *npl*: **the ~less** les chômeurs *mpl*.
Job's comforter [ˈdʒəʊbzˈkʌmfətəʳ] *n* piètre consolateur *m*, -trice *f*.
jockey [ˈdʒɒkɪ] **1** *n* jockey *m*. **2** *vi*: **to ~ about** se bousculer; **to ~ for position** manœuvrer pour se placer avantageusement. **3** *vt*: **to ~ sb into doing** manœuvrer qn pour qu'il fasse.
jockstrap [ˈdʒɒkstræp] *n* suspensoir *m*.
jocular [ˈdʒɒkjʊləʳ] *adj* jovial; (*joking*) badin.
jodhpurs [ˈdʒɒdpɜ:z] *npl* jodhpurs *mpl*.
jog [dʒɒg] **1** *n* **(a)** (*nudge*) légère poussée *f*; (*with elbow*) coup *m* de coude. **(b)** (*~-trot*) petit trot. **2** *vt sb's elbow* pousser; *sb's memory* rafraîchir. (*fig*) **to ~ sb into action** secouer qn. **3** *vi* (*Sport*) faire du jogging.
jog along *vi [vehicle]* aller son petit bonhomme de chemin; (*bumpily*) aller en bringuebalant; (*fig*) *[person]* aller cahin-caha*; *[piece of work]* aller tant bien que mal.
♦ **jogging** *n* (*Sport*) jogging *m*.
joggle [ˈdʒɒgl] *vt* secouer.
join [dʒɔɪn] **1** *vt* **(a)** (*~ together*) (*gen*) joindre, unir; (*link*) relier (*to* à); *broken halves* raccorder; *batteries* connecter. **to ~ battle** engager le combat (*with* avec); **to ~ hands** se donner la main; (*Mil, fig*) **to ~ forces** unir leurs forces; (*fig*) **to ~ forces (with sb) to do** s'unir (à qn) pour faire. **(b)** *club* devenir membre de; *political party* adhérer à; *university* entrer à; *procession* se joindre à; *army* s'engager dans; *one's regiment, ship* rejoindre; *religious order, business firm* entrer dans; *queue* prendre. **(c)** *person* rejoindre, retrouver. **Paul ~s me in wishing you ...** Paul se joint à moi pour vous souhaiter ...; **will you ~ us?** (*come with us*) voulez-vous venir avec nous?; (*be one of us*) voulez-vous être des nôtres?; (*in club, restaurant etc*) voulez-vous vous joindre à nous?; **will you ~ me in a drink?** vous prendrez un verre avec moi? **(d)** *[river, road]* rejoindre. **2** *vi* (*~ together; V* **1a**) se joindre, s'unir (*with* à); *[lines]* se rencontrer; *[roads, rivers]* se rejoindre; *[club member]* devenir membre. **3** *n* (*in mended*

crockery etc) ligne *f* de raccord; (*seam*) couture *f*.
join in 1 *vi* participer. (*in singing etc*) ~ **in!** chantez *etc* avec nous! **2** *vt fus game, activity, conversation* prendre part à; *protest, shouts* joindre sa voix à; *thanks, wishes* s'associer à.
join on 1 *vi* (*in queue*) prendre son rang dans la queue; *[links, parts of structure]* se joindre (*to* à). **2** *vt sep* fixer; (*by tying*) attacher.
join up 1 *vi* (*Mil*) s'engager. **2** *vt sep* (*gen*) joindre; *wires etc* connecter.
♦ **joiner** *n* menuisier *m*. ♦ **joinery** *n* menuiserie *f*.
joint [dʒɔɪnt] **1** *n* **(a)** (*Anat*) articulation *f*. **out of** ~ *shoulder* déboîté; *wrist* luxé; (*fig*) de travers; **to put out of** ~ *one's shoulder* se déboîter; *one's wrist* se luxer. **(b)** (*Carpentry*) jointure *f*; articulation *f*. **(c)** (*Culin*) rôti *m*. **a cut off the** ~ une tranche de rôti. **(d)** (‡: *place*) boîte* *f*. **(e)** (*Drugs sl: reefer*) joint *m* (*sl*). **2** *adj decision, account* commun; *committee* mixte; *consultations* bilatéral; *effort* commun. ~ **author** coauteur *m*; ~ **ownership** copropriété *f*; ~ **responsibility** coresponsabilité *f*. **3** *vt* (*Culin*) découper (aux jointures). ♦ **jointed** *adj doll etc* articulé; *tent pole etc* démontable. ♦ **jointly** *adv* en commun, conjointement. ♦ **joint-stock company** *n* société *f* par actions.
joist [dʒɔɪst] *n* solive *f*.
joke [dʒəʊk] **1** *n* **(a)** plaisanterie *f*, blague* *f*. **for a** ~ pour rire; **to make a** ~ **about** plaisanter sur; **he can't take a** ~ il ne comprend pas la plaisanterie; **it's no** ~ ce n'est pas drôle (*doing* de faire); **what a** ~! ce que c'est drôle!; **it's beyond a** ~* ça cesse d'être drôle; **the** ~ **is that ...** le plus drôle c'est que ...; **he is the** ~ **of the village** il est la risée du village. **(b)** (*practical* ~) tour *m*. **to play a** ~ **on sb** jouer un tour à qn. **2** *vi* plaisanter, blaguer*. **you're joking!** vous voulez rire!, sans blague!*; **I was only joking** ce n'était qu'une plaisanterie; **to** ~ **about sth** plaisanter sur qch; (*mock*) se moquer de qch. ♦ **joker** *n* blagueur* *m*, -euse* *f*; (‡: *person*) type* *m*; (*Cards*) joker *m*. ♦ **joking 1** *adj tone* de plaisanterie; **2** *n* plaisanteries *fpl*, blagues* *fpl*. ♦ **jokingly** *adv* en plaisantant; **it was jokingly called a luxury hotel** on l'avait baptisé, avec le plus grand sérieux, hôtel de luxe.
jolly ['dʒɒlɪ] **1** *adj* (*merry*) enjoué, jovial; (*: *pleasant*) agréable, amusant. **2** *adv* (*) drôlement*, rudement*. **you are** ~ **lucky** tu as une drôle de veine*; **you** ~ **well will go!** pas question que tu n'y ailles pas!
♦ **jollification*** *n* réjouissances *fpl*. ♦ **jollity** *n* joyeuse humeur *f*.
jolt [dʒəʊlt] **1** *vi [vehicle]* cahoter. **to** ~ **along** avancer en cahotant. **2** *vt* (*lit, fig*) secouer, cahoter. (*fig*) **to** ~ **sb into action** secouer qn, inciter qn à agir. **3** *n* (*jerk*) secousse *f*, à-coup *m*; (*fig*) choc *m*. **it gave me a** ~ ça m'a fait un coup*.
Jordan ['dʒɔːdn] *n* (*country*) Jordanie *f*; (*river*) Jourdain *m*.
joss stick ['dʒɒsstɪk] *n* bâton *m* d'encens.
jostle ['dʒɒsl] **1** *vi* se bousculer. **he** ~**d against me** il m'a bousculé; **to** ~ **for sth** jouer des coudes pour obtenir qch. **2** *vt* bousculer.
jot [dʒɒt] **1** *n* brin *m*, iota *m*. **not a** ~ **of truth** pas un grain de vérité. **2** *vt* (~ **down**) *details* noter; *notes* prendre. ♦ **jotter** *n* (*book*) cahier *m* (de brouillon); (*pad*) bloc-notes *m*. ♦ **jottings** *npl* notes *fpl*.
journal ['dʒɜːnl] *n* (*periodical*) revue *f*; (*newspaper*) journal *m*; (*Naut*) livre *m* de bord; (*Comm*) livre de comptes; (*Jur*) compte rendu *m*; (*diary*) journal *m*. ♦ **journalese** *n* jargon *m* journalistique. ♦ **journalism** *n* journalisme *m*. ♦ **journalist** *n* journaliste *mf*. ♦ **journalistic** *adj* journalistique.
journey ['dʒɜːnɪ] **1** *n* (*travelling, trip*) voyage *m*; (*distance covered*) trajet *m*. **a 2 days'** ~ un voyage de 2 jours; **a 10 mile** ~ un trajet de 10 miles; **to go on a** ~ partir en voyage; **to reach one's** ~**'s end** arriver à destination; **the** ~ **from home to office** le trajet de la maison au bureau; **the return** ~ le (voyage de) retour; **the** ~ **there and back** le voyage *or* trajet aller et retour; **a car** ~ un voyage en voiture; **a long bus** ~ un long trajet en autobus. **2** *vi* voyager.
jovial ['dʒəʊvɪəl] *adj* jovial. ♦ **joviality** *n* jovialité *f*.
joy [dʒɔɪ] *n* **(a)** joie *f*. **to my great** ~ à ma grande joie; (*iro*) **I wish you** ~ **of it!** je vous souhaite du plaisir! **(b)** (*gen pl*) ~**s** plaisirs *mpl*; **it's a** ~ **to hear him** c'est un vrai plaisir de l'entendre. ♦ **joyful** *adj* joyeux. ♦ **joyfully** *adv* joyeusement. ♦ **joyous** *adj* (*liter*) joyeux. ♦ **joyride** *n*: **to go for a** ~**ride** faire une virée* en voiture (*parfois volée*). ♦ **joystick** *n* manche *m* à balai (*Aviat*).
jubilant ['dʒuːbɪlənt] *adj* débordant de joie. *[person]* **to be** ~ jubiler. ♦ **jubilation** *n* **(a)** (*emotion*) allégresse *f*, jubilation *f*; **(b)** (*celebration*) réjouissance(s) *f(pl)*.
jubilee ['dʒuːbɪliː] *n* jubilé *m*.
judge [dʒʌdʒ] **1** *n* juge *m*. **to be a good** ~ **of** *character* savoir juger; *wine* s'y connaître en. **2** *vt* juger. **to** ~ **it necessary to do** juger *or* estimer nécessaire de faire; **he** ~**d the moment well** il a bien su choisir son moment (*to do* pour faire). **3** *vi* juger. **to** ~ **for oneself** juger par soi-même; **as far as one can** ~ autant qu'on puisse en juger; **judging by** *or* **from** à en juger par *or* d'après. ♦ **judg(e)ment** *n* jugement *m*; **to pass** ~**ment** prononcer un jugement (*on* sur); (*fig*) **to give one's** ~**ment** donner son avis (*on* sur).
judicial [dʒuː'dɪʃəl] *adj* **(a)** (*Jur*) *power, proceedings, inquiry* judiciaire; *murder* juridique. **(b)** (*critical*) *mind, faculty* critique.
judiciary [dʒuː'dɪʃɪərɪ] *n* magistrature *f*.
judicious [dʒuː'dɪʃəs] *adj* judicieux. ♦ **judiciously** *adv* judicieusement.
judo ['dʒuːdəʊ] *n* judo *m*.
jug [dʒʌg] *n* **(a)** (*for milk etc*) pot *m*; (*of earthenware*) cruche *f*. **(b)** (*prison*) **in** ~‡ en taule‡ *f*. ♦ **jugged** *adj*: ~**ged hare** civet *m* de lièvre.
juggernaut ['dʒʌgənɔːt] *n* (*Aut*) mastodonte *m*.
juggle ['dʒʌgl] **1** *vi* jongler (*with* avec). **2** *vt* jongler avec. ♦ **juggler** *n* jongleur *m*, -euse *f*; (*conjurer*) prestidigitateur *m*, -trice *f*.
jugular ['dʒʌgjʊləʳ] *adj* (*Anat*) jugulaire.
juice [dʒuːs] *n [fruit, meat]* jus *m* (*also fig: petrol etc*). (*Physiol*) ~**s** sucs *mpl*. ♦ **juicer** *n* (*US*) centrifugeuse *f*. ♦ **juiciness** *n* juteux *m*. ♦ **juicy** *adj fruit* juteux; *meat* moelleux; *story* savoureux.
jujitsu [dʒuː'dʒɪtsuː] *n* jiu-jitsu *m*.
jukebox ['dʒuːkbɒks] *n* juke-box *m*.
July [dʒuː'laɪ] *n* juillet *m*; *for phrases V* **September**.
jumble ['dʒʌmbl] **1** *vt* (~ **up**) *objects* mélanger; *facts, details* brouiller, embrouiller. ~**d (up)** pêle-mêle. **2** *n* **(a)** mélange *m*, fouillis *m*. **(b)** (*at* ~ *sale*) bric-à-brac *m*. **3** *adj*: ~ **sale** vente *f* de charité (*d'objets d'occasion*).
jumbo ['dʒʌmbəʊ] **1** *n* (*) éléphant *m*. **2** *adj*: ~ **jet** jumbo-jet *m*.
jump [dʒʌmp] **1** *n* **(a)** saut *m*; (*of fear*) sursaut *m*. **to give a** ~ faire un saut, sauter; (*nervously*) sursauter; **at one** ~ d'un (seul) bond; **the** ~ **in prices** la hausse brutale des prix. **(b)** (*show-jumping*) saut *m*; (*fence*) obstacle *m*.
2 *vi* (*leap*) sauter, bondir; (*nervously*) sursauter; *[prices]* faire un bond, monter en flèche. **to** ~ **up and down** sautiller; **to** ~ **in/out** *etc* entrer/sortir *etc* d'un bond; **to** ~ **off sth** sauter de qch; **to** ~ **on(to) a bus** sauter dans un autobus; **to** ~ **on(to) a bicycle** sauter sur un vélo; ~ **in!** (*into vehicle*) montez vite!; (*into swimming pool*) sautez!; (*onto truck, bus*) ~ **on!** montez vite!; **to** ~ **out of bed** sauter (à bas) du lit; **to** ~ **out of the window** sauter

par la fenêtre; to ~ **out of a car** sauter d'une voiture; (*from car etc*) ~ **out!** sortez *or* descendez vite!; ~ **to it!*** et que ça saute!*; (*fig*) **to** ~ **at sth** sauter sur qch; (*fig*) **to** ~ **on sb*** prendre qn à partie; **to** ~ **to a conclusion** conclure hâtivement; **you mustn't** ~ **to conclusions** il ne faut pas tirer des conclusions trop hâtives; **to** ~ **down sb's throat*** rabrouer qn; **it almost made him** ~ **out of his skin*** ça l'a fait sauter au plafond*.

3 *vt ditch etc* sauter, franchir (d'un bond); *horse* faire sauter. *[train]* **to** ~ **the rails** dérailler; **to** ~ **the points** dérailler à l'aiguillage; *[pickup]* **to** ~ **a groove** sauter; (*Jur*) **to** ~ **bail** ne pas comparaître; (*fig*) **to** ~ **the gun*** agir prématurément; (*Aut*) **to** ~ **the lights** passer au rouge; **to** ~ **the queue** resquiller; **to** ~ **ship** déserter le navire; **to** ~ **sb‡** rouler qn*.

jump about, jump around *vi* sautiller.

jump down *vi* descendre (d'un bond).

jump up *vi* se lever d'un bond. (*to fallen child*) ~ **up now!** lève-toi!

♦ **jumped-up*** *adj* (*pushing*) parvenu; (*conceited*) prétentieux. ♦ **jumper** *n* pull(over) *m*. ♦ **jumpy*** *adj person* nerveux.

junction [ˈdʒʌŋkʃən] *n* **(a)** (*meeting place*) *[pipes]* raccordement *m*; *[roads]* bifurcation *f*; *[rivers]* confluent *m*; *[railway lines]* embranchement *m*. **(b)** (*crossroads*) carrefour *m*; (*station*) gare *f* de jonction.

juncture [ˈdʒʌnktʃəʳ] *n* (*joining place*) point *m* de jonction; (*state of affairs*) conjoncture *f*. **at this** ~ à ce moment-là.

June [dʒuːn] *n* juin *m*; *for phrases V* **September.**

jungle [ˈdʒʌŋgl] **1** *n* jungle *f*. **2** *adj animal* de la jungle; *warfare* de jungle.

junior [ˈdʒuːnɪəʳ] **1** *adj* (*younger*) (plus) jeune, cadet; (*Sport*) ≃ cadet; *employee, officer, job* subalterne. **John Smith J**~ John Smith fils *or* junior; (*Brit*) ~ **school** école *f* primaire (*de 8 à 11 ans*), cours moyen; (*Comm*) ~ **miss** fillette *f* (*de 11 à 14 ans*); (*US*) ~ **high school** collège *m* d'enseignement secondaire (*de 12 à 15 ans*); ~ **executive** jeune cadre *m*; (*Parl*) **J**~ **Minister** ≃ secrétaire *m* d'État; ~ **partner** associé(-adjoint) *m*. **2** *n* cadet(te) *m(f)*; (*Brit Scol*) petit(e) élève *m(f)* (*de 8 à 11 ans*).

juniper [ˈdʒuːnɪpəʳ] *n* genévrier *m*. ~ **berries** du genièvre.

junk[1] [dʒʌŋk] **1** *n* (*rubbish*) bric-à-brac *m inv*; (*metal*) ferraille *f*; (*: *bad quality goods*) camelote* *f*; (‡: *nonsense*) âneries *fpl*; (*Drugs sl*) came *f* (*sl*).

2 *adj*: ~ **heap,** ~ **yard** dépotoir *m*.

♦ **junkie** *n* (*Drugs sl*) drogué(e) *m(f)*. ♦ **junkshop** *n* boutique *f* de brocanteur.

junk[2] [dʒʌŋk] *n* (*boat*) jonque *f*.

junket [ˈdʒʌŋkɪt] *n* **(a)** (*Culin*) lait *m* caillé. **(b)** (*also* **junketing**) (*merrymaking*) bombance *f*; (*: *trip at public expense*) voyage *m* aux frais de la princesse*.

junta [ˈdʒʌntə] *n* junte *f*.

Jupiter [ˈdʒuːpɪtəʳ] *n* (*Myth*) Jupiter *m*; (*Astron*) Jupiter *f*.

jurisdiction [ˌdʒʊərɪsˈdɪkʃən] *n* juridiction *f*. **it comes within our** ~ c'est de notre compétence.

jury [ˈdʒʊərɪ] **1** *n* (*Jur*) jury *m*, jurés *mpl*; *[exhibition etc]* jury *m*. **to be on the** ~ faire partie du jury. **2** *adj*: ~ **box** banc *m* des jurés. ♦ **juror** *n* juré *m*; **woman juror** femme *f* juré. ♦ **juryman** *n* juré *m*.

just[1] [dʒʌst] *adv* **(a)** (*exactly*) juste, exactement. **it's** ~ **on 9** il est tout juste 9 heures; **it cost** ~ **on 50 francs** cela a coûté tout juste 50 F; ~ **what did he say?** qu'est-ce qu'il a dit exactement *or* au juste?; (*fig*) **come** ~ **as you are** venez comme vous êtes; ~ **as I thought, you ...** c'est bien ce que je pensais, tu ...; ~ **as you wish** comme vous voulez; ~ **at that moment** à ce moment-là; ~ **when everything is going so well!** juste quand tout va si bien!; **that's** ~ **it!, that's** ~ **the point!** justement!; **that's** ~ **Robert, always late** c'est bien Robert, toujours en retard; ~ **so!** exactement!; **everything was** ~ **so*** tout était bien en ordre.

(b) (*at this or that moment*) juste. **we're** ~ **off** nous partons; **(I'm)** ~ **coming!** j'arrive!; **we're** ~ **about to start** nous sommes sur le point de commencer; **to have** ~ **done** venir de faire; ~ **this minute,** ~ **this instant** à l'instant.

(c) (*almost not*) juste, de justesse. **we (only)** ~ **caught the train** c'est tout juste si nous avons eu le train; **we only** ~ **missed the train** nous avons manqué le train de très peu; **you're** ~ **in time** vous arrivez juste à temps; **I have only** ~ **enough money** j'ai tout juste assez d'argent; **he passed the exam but only** ~ il a été reçu à l'examen mais de justesse.

(d) (*with expressions of place*) juste. ~ **here** juste ici; ~ **over there/here** juste là/ici; ~ **by the church** juste à côté de l'église.

(e) (*almost*) ~ **about** à peu près, presque. **I've had** ~ **about enough!*** j'en ai par-dessus la tête!*

(f) (*in comparison*) ~ **as** tout aussi; **you sing** ~ **as well as I do** vous chantez tout aussi bien que moi.

(g) (+*imper*) donc, un peu. ~ **taste this!** goûte un peu à ça!*; ~ **look at that!** regarde-moi ça!*; ~ **shut up!*** veux-tu te taire!; ~ **let me get my hands on him!*** que je l'attrape (*subj*) un peu!*

(h) (*slightly, immediately*) (un) peu, juste. ~ **over/under £10** un peu plus/moins de 10 livres; ~ **after 9 o'clock he came in** peu après 9 heures il est entré; **it's** ~ **after 9 o'clock** il est un peu plus de 9 heures; ~ **after he came** juste après son arrivée; ~ **before it rained** juste avant la pluie; **that's** ~ **over the kilo** cela fait tout juste un peu plus du kilo; **it's** ~ **to the left** c'est juste à gauche.

(i) (*only*) juste. ~ **a moment please** un instant s'il vous plaît; **he's** ~ **a lad** ce n'est qu'un gamin; **don't go yet, it's** ~ **9 o'clock** ne partez pas encore, il n'est que 9 heures; **I've come** ~ **to see you** je suis venu exprès pour te voir; **he did it** ~ **for a laugh*** il l'a fait histoire de rire*; ~ **a line to let you know that ...** juste un petit mot pour vous dire que ... .

(j) (*simply*) (tout) simplement, seulement. **I** ~ **told him to go away** je lui ai tout simplement dit de s'en aller; **you should** ~ **send it back** vous n'avez qu'à le renvoyer; **I would** ~ **like to say this** je voudrais seulement *or* simplement dire ceci; **I** ~ **can't imagine what's happened to him** je ne peux vraiment pas m'imaginer *or* je n'arrive pas à imaginer ce qui lui est arrivé; **we shall** ~ **drop in on him** nous ne ferons que passer chez lui; **it's** ~ **one of those things*** c'est la vie.

(k) (*emphatic*) absolument, tout simplement. **it's** ~ **fine!** c'est parfait!; **did you enjoy it? – did we** ~**!*** *or* **I should** ~ **say we did!*** cela vous a plu? – et comment!*

(l) (*phrases*) **it's** ~ **as well it's insured** heureusement que c'est assuré; **it would be** ~ **as well if he took it** il ferait aussi bien de le prendre; **I'm busy** ~ **now** je suis occupé pour l'instant; **I saw him** ~ **now** je l'ai vu tout à l'heure; **not** ~ **yet** pas tout de suite; **I'm taking my umbrella,** ~ **in case** je prends mon parapluie on ne sait jamais *or* à tout hasard; ~ **the same*, you ...** tout de même, tu ...; **I'd** ~ **as soon you kept quiet about it** j'aimerais autant que vous n'en disiez rien à personne.

just[2] [dʒʌst] *adj* (*fair: gen*) juste (*to, towards* envers, avec). **it is only** ~ **to point out that ...** ce n'est que justice de faire remarquer que ... .

♦ **justice** *n* **(a)** (*Jur*) justice *f*; **to bring sb to** ~**ice** amener qn devant les tribunaux; (*US*) **Department of Justice** ministère *m* de la Justice; **(b)** (*fairness*) équité *f*; **in** ~**ice to him he..., to do him**

~ice he ... pour être juste envers lui il ...; **this photo doesn't do him ~ice** cette photo ne l'avantage pas; **she never does herself ~ice** elle ne se montre jamais à sa juste valeur; **to do ~ice to a meal** faire honneur à un repas; **(c)** (*judge*) juge *m*; (*Brit*) **Justice of the Peace** juge de paix. ♦ **justly** *adv* avec raison, tout à fait justement. ♦ **justness** *n [cause]* justice *f*; *[decision etc]* justesse *f*.

justify ['dʒʌstɪfaɪ] *vt* (*gen*) justifier; *decision* prouver le bien-fondé de. **to be justified in doing** être en droit de faire; **am I justified in thinking ...?** est-ce que j'ai raison de penser ...? ♦ **justifiable** *adj* justifiable. ♦ **justifiably** *adv* légitimement, avec raison. ♦ **justification** *n* justification *f* (*of* de, *for* à, pour).

jut [dʒʌt] *vi* (~ **out**) (*gen*) faire saillie; *[hidden object]* dépasser; *[cliff]* avancer. **to ~ (out) over sth** surplomber qch.

jute [dʒu:t] *n* jute *m*.

juvenile ['dʒu:vənaɪl] *adj* juvénile; (*pej*) puéril; *books, court* pour enfants. **~ delinquency** délinquance *f* juvénile; **~ delinquent** jeune délinquant(e) *m(f)*.

juxtaposition [ˌdʒʌkstəpə'zɪʃən] *n* juxtaposition *f*. **to be in ~** se juxtaposer.

K

K, k [keɪ] *n* K, k *m*.
kaftan ['kæftæn] *n* kaftan *m*.
kail, kale [keɪl] *n* chou *m* frisé.
kaleidoscope [kə'laɪdəskəʊp] *n* kaléidoscope *m*.
kangaroo [,kæŋgə'ruː] *n* kangourou *m*.
kaolin ['keɪəlɪn] *n* kaolin *m*.
kapok ['keɪpɒk] *n* kapok *m*.
kaputꜝ [kə'pʊt] *adj* fichu*, kaputꜝ *inv*.
karate [kə'rɑːtɪ] *n* karaté *m*.
kart [kɑːt] **1** *n* kart *m*. **2** *vi*: **to go ~ing** faire du karting.
kayak ['kaɪæk] *n* kayak *m*.
kebab [kə'bæb] *n* kébab *m*, brochette *f*.
kedgeree [,kedʒə'riː] *n* ≃ pilaf *m* de poisson.
keel [kiːl] *n* (*Naut*) quille *f*. **on an even ~** (*Naut*) dans ses lignes, à égal tirant d'eau; (*fig*) stable, en équilibre.
keel over *vi* (*Naut*) chavirer; *[person]* tomber dans les pommes*, s'évanouir.
keen [kiːn] *adj* **(a)** *blade, appetite* aiguisé; *point* aigu; *wind, cold* piquant; *air, interest* vif; *pleasure, desire, feeling* intense; *eye* perçant; *hearing, ear* fin; *price, competition* serré; *intelligence, judgment* pénétrant. **(b)** (*enthusiastic*) *person* enthousiaste, ardent. **to be as ~ as mustard** déborder d'enthousiasme; **a ~ footballer** un passionné du football; **a very ~ socialist** un socialiste passionné; **to be ~ on** *music* avoir la passion de; *idea, suggestion* être enthousiasmé par; *person* avoir un béguin pour; **to grow ~ on sth/sb** se passionner pour qch/qn; **I'm not too ~ on him** il ne me plaît pas beaucoup; **he's very ~ on Mozart/football** *etc* c'est un passionné de Mozart/du football *etc*; **he's not ~ on her coming** il ne tient pas tellement à ce qu'elle vienne; **to be ~ to do** tenir absolument à faire. ♦ **keenly** *adv* **(a)** (*acutely*) *interest, feel* vivement; *desire* ardemment; *observe* astucieusement; *look* d'un regard pénétrant; **(b)** (*enthusiastically*) avec enthousiasme. ♦ **keenness** *n* enthousiasme *m*.
keep [kiːp] *pret, ptp* **kept 1** *vt* **(a)** (*gen*) garder. **you must ~ the receipt** il faut garder *or* conserver le reçu; **they ~ themselves to themselves** *[group]* ils font bande à part; *[couple]* ils se tiennent à l'écart; **to ~ sth clean** tenir *or* garder qch propre; **to ~ o.s. clean** être toujours propre; **exercise will ~ you fit** l'exercice physique vous maintiendra en forme; **the garden was well kept** le jardin était bien entretenu; **he kept them working** *or* **at it** il les a forcés à continuer de travailler; **to ~ sb waiting** faire attendre qn; **she kept him to his promise** elle l'a forcé à tenir sa promesse; **to ~ a piece of news from sb** cacher une nouvelle à qn; **~ it to yourself, ~ it under your hat*** garde-le pour toi. **(b)** (*put aside*) garder, mettre de côté. **I've kept some for him** je lui en ai gardé; **I'm ~ing some sugar just in case** j'ai du sucre en réserve à tout hasard; **~ it somewhere safe** mettez-le en lieu sûr; **you must ~ it in a cold place** il faut le garder *or* le conserver au froid. **(c)** (*detain*) garder, retenir. **to ~ sb in prison** garder qn en prison; **what kept you?** qu'est-ce qui vous a retenu? **(d)** (*own, have*) *shop, hotel, servants* avoir; (*Comm: stock*) vendre, avoir. (*Agr*) *animals* élever. **(e)** *accounts, diary* tenir. **to ~ a note of** noter. **(f)** (*support*) *family* faire vivre. **I earn enough to ~ myself** je gagne assez pour vivre; **to ~ sb in food/clothing** nourrir/habiller qn. **(g)** (*restrain*) **to ~ sb from doing** empêcher qn de faire; **~ him from school** ne l'envoyez pas à l'école. **(h)** (*fulfil*) *promise* tenir; *law, rule, Lent* observer; *treaty* respecter; *vow* rester fidèle à; *obligations* remplir; *feast day* célébrer; *sb's birthday* fêter. **to ~ an appointment** se rendre à un rendez-vous.

2 *vi* **(a)** (*continue*) continuer, suivre; (*remain*) rester, se tenir. **~ on this road until ...** suivez cette route jusqu'à ...; **to ~ (to the) left/right** garder sa gauche/droite; (*Aut*) tenir sa gauche/droite; **to ~ straight on** continuer tout droit; **to ~ to** *promise* tenir; *subject* ne pas s'écarter de; *text* serrer; **to ~ doing** continuer à faire, ne pas cesser de faire; **she ~s talking** elle n'arrête pas de parler; **I ~ hoping that ...** j'espère toujours que ...; **~ going!** allez-y!; **~ smiling!** gardez le sourire!; **to ~ fit** se maintenir en forme; **he ~s in good health** il est toujours en bonne santé; **to ~ still** rester *or* se tenir tranquille; **~ at it!** continuez!; **she ~s at him all the time** elle le harcèle, elle est toujours après lui; **'~ off the grass'** 'défense de marcher sur les pelouses'; **to ~ from doing** s'abstenir *or* se retenir de faire; **to ~ in with sb*** rester en bons termes avec qn, (*for one's own purposes*) cultiver qn; **to ~ to one's room/bed** garder la chambre/le lit; **they ~ to themselves** *[group]* ils font bande à part; *[couple]* ils se tiennent à l'écart. **(b)** (*in health*) aller. **how are you ~ing?** comment allez-vous?; **she's not ~ing very well** elle ne va pas très bien; **he's ~ing better** il va mieux. **(c)** *[food etc]* se garder, se conserver. **apples that ~ all winter** des pommes qui se gardent *or* se conservent tout l'hiver; **this business can ~*** cette affaire peut attendre.

3 *n* **(a)** (*food etc*) **to earn one's ~** gagner sa vie; **I got £15 a week and my ~** j'ai gagné 15 livres par semaine logé et nourri; **he's not worth his ~** il ne vaut pas ce qu'on dépense pour l'entretenir. **(b)** (*Archit*) donjon *m*. **(c) for ~s*** pour de bon.
keep away 1 *vi* (*lit*) ne pas s'approcher (*from* de). (*fig*) **to ~ away from drink** s'abstenir de boire, ne pas boire. **2** *vt sep person* empêcher de s'approcher (*from* de).
keep back 1 *vi* rester en arrière, ne pas approcher. **2** *vt sep* **(a)** (*withhold*) *part of wages etc* retenir. **(b)** (*conceal*) *facts, names* ne pas dire, ne pas révéler; *secrets* taire. **(c)** (*make late*) retarder. **(d)** *crowd* empêcher de s'approcher.
keep down 1 *vi* rester assis (*or* allongé *etc*). **2** *vt sep* **(a)** (*control*) *revolt, one's anger* réprimer, contenir; *dog* retenir, maîtriser. **you can't ~ a good man down** un homme de valeur reprendra toujours le dessus. **(b)** *spending* restreindre, limiter; *prices* empêcher de monter. **(c)** (*Scol*) *pupil* faire redoubler une classe à. **(d) the sick man can't ~ anything down** le malade ne garde rien.
keep in *vt sep* **(a)** *anger, feelings* contenir, réprimer. **(b)** *person* empêcher de sortir; (*Scol*) *pupil* garder en retenue; *stomach, elbows* rentrer.
keep off 1 *vi [person]* rester à l'écart. **~ off!** n'approchez pas!; **if the rain ~s off** s'il ne pleut pas.

2 *vt sep dog, person* empêcher de s'approcher. ~ **your hands off!** ne touchez pas!
keep on 1 *vi* continuer (*to do* à faire), ne pas arrêter (*to do* de faire). **don't ~ on so!** arrête!; **she does ~ on about ...** elle n'arrête pas de parler de ...; **~ on past the church till ...** continuez après l'église jusqu'à ...; **if you ~ on as you're doing now** si tu continues comme ça; to **~ on at sb** harceler qn. **2** *vt sep* garder.
keep out 1 *vi* rester en dehors. '**~ out**' 'défense d'entrer'; **to ~ out of danger** rester à l'abri du danger; **to ~ out of a quarrel** ne pas se mêler à une dispute; **~ out of this!** mêlez-vous de ce qui vous regarde! **2** *vt sep person, dog* empêcher d'entrer. **to ~ out the cold** protéger du froid.
keep together 1 *vi [people]* rester ensemble. **2** *vt sep* garder ensemble.
keep up 1 *vi* **(a)** (*continue*) continuer; *[prices]* se maintenir. **(b) to ~ up with sb** (*in race, walk etc*) aller aussi vite que qn; (*in work, achievement*) se maintenir au niveau de qn; (*in comprehension*) suivre qn; (*fig*) **to ~ up with the Joneses** ne pas se trouver en reste avec les voisins. **(c)** (*stay friends with*) **to ~ up with sb** rester en relations avec qn. **2** *vt sep* **(a)** (*gen*) continuer, ne pas abandonner; *correspondence* entretenir; *subscription, custom* maintenir; *one's French etc* entretenir. **~ it up!** continuez! **(b)** (*maintain*) *house, paintwork, road* entretenir.
♦ **keeper** *n* (*gen*) gardien(ne) *m(f)*; (*in museum etc*) conservateur *m*, -trice *f*; (*game~*) garde-chasse *m*. ♦ **keep-fit** *adj*: **~-fit classes** cours *mpl* de culture physique; **~-fit exercises** culture *f* physique. ♦ **keeping** *n* **(a)** (*care*) garde *f*; **to put in sb's ~ing** confier à qn; **(b) to be in ~ing with** s'accorder avec; **in ~ing with** en accord avec. ♦ **keepsake** *n* souvenir *m* (*objet*).
keg [keg] *n* tonnelet *m*; *[fish]* caque *f*. **~ beer** bière *f* en tonnelet.
kelp [kelp] *n* varech *m*.
ken [ken] *n*: **that is beyond my ~** cela dépasse mes connaissances.
kennel ['kenl] *n [dog]* niche *f*; *[hound]* chenil *m*. **to put a dog in ~s** mettre un chien en chenil.
kept [kept] *pret, ptp of* **keep**.
kerb [kɜːb] *n* (*Brit*) bord *m* du trottoir. **along the ~** le long du trottoir.
kernel ['kɜːnl] *n* amande *f* (*de noyau*).
kerosene ['kerəsiːn] **1** *n* kérosène *m*. **2** *adj* à pétrole.
kestrel ['kestrəl] *n* crécerelle *f*.
ketchup ['ketʃəp] *n* ketchup *m*.
kettle ['ketl] *n* bouilloire *f*. **the ~'s boiling** l'eau bout; **I'll just put the ~ on** je vais mettre l'eau à chauffer.
key [kiː] **1** *n* **(a)** (*gen*) clef *f* or clé *f*; *[clockwork toy etc]* remontoir *m*; *[textbook]* (*answers*) solutions *fpl*; (*translation*) traduction *f*; *[mystery etc]* clef (*to* de). **to turn the ~** donner un tour de clef. **(b)** *[piano, typewriter etc]* touche *f*; *[wind instrument]* clef *f*. **(c)** (*Mus*) ton *m*. **to be in/off ~** être/n'être pas dans le ton; **to sing in/off ~** chanter juste/faux; **in the ~ of C** en do. **2** *adj* **(a)** (*vital*) clef or clé (*f inv*). **~ industry** industrie *f* clef; **~ jobs** postes *mpl* clefs; **~ man** pivot *m* (*fig*). **(b)** (*Mus*) **~ signature** armature *f*. ♦ **keyboard** *n* clavier *m*. ♦ **keyhole** *n*: **through the ~hole** par le trou de la serrure. ♦ **keynote 1** *n* (*Mus*) tonique *f*; *[speech etc]* note *f* dominante; **2** *adj* (*Pol etc*) **~note speech** discours-programme *m*. ♦ **key-ring** *n* porte-clefs *m inv*. ♦ **keystone** *n* clef *f* de voûte.
khaki ['kɑːkɪ] *adj* kaki *inv*.
kibbutz [kɪ'bʊts] *n, pl* **-im** kibboutz *m*.
kibosh‡ ['kaɪbɒʃ] *n*: **to put the ~ on**‡ mettre le holà à.
kick [kɪk] **1** *n* **(a)** coup *m* de pied. **to give sth a ~** donner un coup de pied à *or* dans qch; **to take a ~ at** lancer un coup de pied à; **to give sb a ~ in the pants*** botter* le derrière à *or* de qn; (*fig*) **it was a ~ in the teeth**‡ **for her** cela a été pour elle une gifle en pleine figure; (*fig*) **he gets a ~ out of it*** il trouve ça stimulant, (*pej*) il y prend un malin plaisir; **he did it for ~s*** il l'a fait pour le plaisir. **(b)** *[gun]* recul *m*; *[starting handle]* retour *m*. **2** *vi* donner *or* lancer un coup de pied; *[baby]* gigoter*; *[horse etc]* ruer; *[gun]* reculer. **to ~ at** lancer un coup de pied à; (*fig: object to*) se rebiffer* contre; (*fig*) **to ~ over the traces** ruer dans les brancards. **3** *vt [person]* donner un coup de pied à *or* dans; *[horse etc]* lancer une ruade à. **to ~ sb downstairs** faire descendre qn à coups de pied dans le derrière; **to ~ sth away** repousser qch du pied; **to ~ a goal** marquer un but; (*fig*) **to ~ the bucket**‡ casser sa pipe*, mourir; **I could have ~ed myself*** je me serais flanqué* des coups; (*fig*) **to ~ one's heels** poireauter*.
kick about, kick around 1 *vi* (‡) *[objects, person]* traîner. **2** *vt sep*: **to ~ a ball about** s'amuser avec un ballon.
kick back 1 *vi [engine]* avoir un retour de manivelle. **2** *vt sep ball etc* renvoyer (du pied).
kick down *vt sep* démolir à coups de pied.
kick in *vt sep door* enfoncer à coups de pied. (*fig*) **to ~ sb's teeth in*** casser la figure* à qn.
kick off *vi* (*Ftbl*) donner le coup d'envoi; (*) *[meeting etc]* démarrer*.
kick out 1 *vi [horse]* ruer; *[person]* envoyer de grands coups de pied (*at* à). **2** *vt sep* (**fig*) mettre à la porte.
kick up *vt sep* (*fig*) **to ~ up a row*** *or* **a din*** faire du tapage; **to ~ up a fuss*** faire toute une histoire.
♦ **kick-off** *n* (*Ftbl etc, also fig**) coup *m* d'envoi. ♦ **kick-stand** *n* béquille *f* (*de moto*). ♦ **kick-start(er)** *n* démarreur *m* au pied.
kid [kɪd] **1** *n* (*goat, leather*) chevreau *m*; (*: *child*) gosse* *mf*. **2** *adj* **(a)** (*) *brother etc* petit. **(b)** *gloves etc* de chevreau. (*fig*) **to handle with ~ gloves** *person* prendre des gants avec*; *subject* traiter avec précaution. **3** *vt* (*) **to ~ sb (on)** faire marcher qn*; **no ~ding!** sans blague!*; **don't ~ yourself!** ne te fais pas d'illusions!; **he was ~ding on that he was hurt** il essayait de faire croire qu'il était blessé. **4** *vi* (*: **~ on**) raconter des blagues*. **I was only ~ding (on)** j'ai dit ça pour rigoler*. ♦ **kiddy*** *n* gosse* *mf*, mioche* *mf*.
kidnap ['kɪdnæp] *vt* kidnapper, enlever. ♦ **kidnapper** *n* kidnappeur *m*, -euse *f*, ravisseur *m*, -euse *f*. ♦ **kidnapping** *n* enlèvement *m*, rapt *m*.
kidney ['kɪdnɪ] **1** *n* (*Anat*) rein *m*; (*Culin*) rognon *m*. (*fig*) **of the same ~** du même acabit. **2** *adj disease etc* rénal; *transplant* du rein. **to be on a ~ machine** être sous rein artificiel; **~ stone** calcul *m* du rein. ♦ **kidney-bean** *n* haricot *m* rouge. ♦ **kidney-shaped** *adj* en forme de haricot.
kill [kɪl] **1** *n* (*at bullfight, hunt*) mise *f* à mort. (*fig*) **to be in at the ~** assister au coup de grâce. **2** *vt* **(a)** (*gen*) tuer; (*murder*) assassiner; *[huntsman, slaughterer]* abattre. **to be ~ed in action** tomber au champ d'honneur; (*fig*) **to ~ two birds with one stone** faire d'une pierre deux coups; **it was ~ or cure** c'était un remède de cheval; (*iro*) **don't ~ yourself!*** surtout ne te surmène pas!; **this heat is ~ing me*** cette chaleur me tue; **my feet are ~ing me*** j'ai affreusement mal aux pieds; **she was ~ing herself (laughing)*** elle était pliée en deux de rire. **(b)** (*fig*) *proposal, attempt* faire échouer; *paragraph etc* supprimer; *story* interdire la publication de; *rumour* mettre fin à; *feeling, hope* détruire; *flavour, smell* tuer; *sound* amortir; *engine, motor* arrêter; (*) *bottle* liquider*. **to ~ time** tuer le temps.
kill off *vt sep* exterminer; (*fig*) éliminer.
♦ **killer 1** *n* tueur *m*, -euse *f*; (*murderer*) assassin *m*, meurtrier *m*, -ière *f*; (*lit*) **that's a ~er** cela tue; **2** *adj disease* qui tue; *instinct* qui pousse à tuer;

(*fig*) **he's got the ~er instinct** il sait se montrer impitoyable; **~er whale** épaulard *m*. ♦ **killing 1** *n* [*person*] meurtre *m*; [*people, group*] tuerie *f*, massacre *m*; (*during disturbances etc*) **there were 3 ~ings** 3 personnes ont été tuées; (*Fin*) **to make a ~ing** réussir un beau coup (de filet); **2** *adj blow, disease* meurtrier; (*: *exhausting*) *work* tuant; (‡: *funny*) tordant*. ♦ **killjoy** *n* rabat-joie *m inv*.
kiln [kɪln] *n* four *m* (*de potier*).
kilo ['ki:ləʊ] *n* kilo *m*. ♦ **kilogram(me)** *n* kilogramme *m*. ♦ **kilometre,** (*US*) **kilometer** ['kɪləˌmi:təʳ, kɪ'lɒmɪtəʳ] *n* kilomètre *m*. ♦ **kilowatt** *n* kilowatt *m*.
kilt [kɪlt] *n* kilt *m*. ♦ **kilted** *adj* en kilt.
kilter* ['kɪltəʳ] *n*: **out of ~** détraqué.
kin [kɪn] *n* parents *mpl*, famille *f*. **his next of ~** son parent le plus proche. ♦ **kinship** *n* parenté *f*. ♦ **kinsman** *n* parent *m*. ♦ **kinswoman** *n* parente *f*.
kind [kaɪnd] **1** *n* **(a)** (*type: gen*) genre *m*, espèce *f*, sorte *f*; (*make: of car, coffee etc*) marque *f*. **what ~ do you want?** vous en (*or* le *or* la *etc*) voulez de quelle sorte?; **what ~ of car is it?** quelle marque de voiture est-ce?; **what ~ of dog is he?** qu'est-ce que c'est comme (race de) chien?; **what ~ of man is he?** quel genre d'homme est-ce?; **he is not the ~ of man to refuse** ce n'est pas le genre d'homme à refuser; **he's not that ~ of person** ce n'est pas son genre; **he's the ~ that will cheat** il est du genre à tricher; **I know his ~!** je connais les gens de son espèce; **that's the ~ of person I am** c'est comme ça que je suis; **what ~ of people does he think we are?** pour qui nous prend-il?; **what ~ of an answer do you call that?** vous appelez ça une réponse?; **and all that ~ of thing** et autres choses du même genre, et tout ça*; **you know the ~ of thing I mean** vous voyez ce que je veux dire; **it's my ~ of film** c'est le genre de film que j'aime; **sth of the ~** qch de ce genre(-là); **nothing of the ~!** absolument pas!; (*pej*) **it was beef of a ~** c'était qch qui pouvait passer pour du bœuf; **a ~ of** une sorte *or* espèce de, un genre de; **I was ~ of* frightened that** j'avais comme peur* que + ne + *subj*; **I ~ of* thought that he would come** j'avais un peu l'idée qu'il viendrait; **he was ~ of* worried-looking** il avait l'air un peu inquiet. **(b)** (*race, species*) genre *m*, espèce *f*. **they're two of a ~** ils se ressemblent; **it's the only one of its ~** c'est unique en son genre. **(c) to pay/payment in ~** payer/paiement *m* en nature; (*fig*) **I shall repay you in ~** (*after good deed*) je vous le rendrai; (*after bad deed*) je vous rendrai la monnaie de votre pièce.

2 *adj person* gentil (*to sb* avec qn), bon (*to sb* envers qn), aimable. **would you be ~ enough to open the door?** voulez-vous être assez aimable *or* gentil pour ouvrir la porte?; **he was ~ enough to say** il a eu la gentillesse *or* l'amabilité de dire; **it was very ~ of you to help me** vous avez été bien aimable de m'aider; **that's very ~ of you** c'est très aimable *or* gentil de votre part; **that wasn't a very ~ thing to say** ce n'était pas très gentil de dire cela.
♦ **kind-hearted** *adj* bon, qui a bon cœur. ♦ **kind-heartedness** *n* bonté *f*, bon cœur. ♦ **kindliness** *n* bienveillance *f*, bonté *f*. ♦ **kindly 1** *adv* **(a)** *speak, act* avec bonté, avec gentillesse; **(b) will you ~ly shut the door** voulez-vous avoir la bonté de fermer la porte; **(c) I don't take ~ly to his doing that** je n'aime pas du tout qu'il fasse cela; **she didn't take it ~ly when ...** elle ne l'a pas bien pris quand ...; **2** *adj person, advice* bienveillant; *voice* plein de bonté; *letter* gentil; *treatment* plein de gentillesse. ♦ **kindness** *n* bonté *f* (*towards* pour), gentillesse *f* (*towards* envers); (*kind act*) gentillesse *f*, service *m*; **out of the ~ness of his heart** par bonté d'âme; **to do sb a ~ness** rendre service à qn; **it would be a ~ness to tell him** so ce serait lui rendre service que de le lui dire.
kindergarten ['kɪndəˌgɑ:tn] *n* jardin *m* d'enfants.
kindle ['kɪndl] *vt fire* allumer; *wood, emotion* enflammer. ♦ **kindling** *n* petit bois *m*.
kindred ['kɪndrɪd] **1** *n* parents *mpl*, famille *f*. **2** *adj languages, tribes* apparenté. **~ spirits** âmes *fpl* sœurs; **to have a ~ feeling for sb** sympathiser avec qn.
king [kɪŋ] *n* roi *m* (*also Cards, Chess*); (*Draughts*) dame *f*. **K~ David** le roi David; **an oil ~** un roi *or* un magnat du pétrole. ♦ **kingdom** *n* royaume *m*; (*Bot, Zool*) règne *m*; **the K~dom of Heaven** le royaume des cieux; **till ~dom come*** jusqu'à la fin des siècles. ♦ **kingfisher** *n* martin-pêcheur *m*. ♦ **kingly** *adj* royal, de roi. ♦ **kingpin** *n* (*lit, fig*) cheville *f* ouvrière. ♦ **king-size(d)** *adj* (*Comm*) *cigarette* long; *packet* géant; (*gen*) *object, headache* de première grandeur.
kink [kɪŋk] **1** *n* (*in rope etc*) entortillement *m*; (*fig*) aberration *f*. **2** *vi* s'entortiller. ♦ **kinky*** *adj hair* crépu; *person* bizarre, (*unpleasantly so*) malade (*fig pej*), (*sexually*) qui a des goûts spéciaux; *idea, dress, fashion* bizarre.
kiosk ['ki:ɒsk] *n* (*gen*) kiosque *m*; (*Brit: telephone ~*) cabine *f* téléphonique.
kipper ['kɪpəʳ] *n* hareng *m* fumé et salé, kipper *m*.
kirk [kɜ:k] *n* (*Scot*) église *f*.
kiss [kɪs] **1** *n* baiser *m*. (*Med*) **~ of life** bouche à bouche *m*; (*fig*) **~ of death** coup *m* fatal; (*in letter*) **love and ~es** bons baisers *mpl*. **2** *vt* embrasser, donner un baiser à. **to ~ sb's cheek** embrasser qn sur la joue; **to ~ sb's hand** baiser la main de qn; **to ~ sb good night** embrasser qn en lui souhaitant bonne nuit. **3** *vi* s'embrasser.
kit [kɪt] *n* **(a)** (*equipment: gen*) matériel *m*, équipement *m*; (*Mil*) fourniment *m*; (*tools*) outils *mpl*; (*luggage*) bagages *mpl*; (*belongings*) affaires *fpl*. **fishing ~** matériel *or* équipement de pêche; **got your football ~?** tu as tes affaires de football? **(b)** (*set of items*) trousse *f*. **repair/tool ~** trousse de réparations/à outils; **first-aid ~** trousse de premiers secours. **(c)** (*parts for assembly*) kit *m*. **sold in ~ form** vendu en kit; **model aeroplane ~** maquette *f* d'avion à assembler.
kit out, kit up *vt sep* équiper (*with* de).
♦ **kitbag** *n* sac *m* (*de sportif, de marin etc*).
kitchen ['kɪtʃɪn] **1** *n* cuisine *f* (*pièce*). **2** *adj table, salt etc* de cuisine. **~ cabinet** buffet *m* de cuisine; **~ foil** papier *m* d'aluminium; **~ garden** potager *m*; **~ sink** évier *m*; **everything but the ~ sink*** tout sauf les murs; **~-sink* drama** théâtre *m* naturaliste; **~ soap** savon *m* de Marseille; **~ unit** élément *m* de cuisine. ♦ **kitchenette** *n* kitchenette *f*. ♦ **kitchenmaid** *n* fille *f* de cuisine. ♦ **kitchenware** *n* (*dishes*) vaisselle *f* (*de cuisine*); (*equipment*) ustensiles *mpl* de cuisine.
kite [kaɪt] *n* (*bird*) milan *m*; (*toy*) cerf-volant *m*.
kith [kɪθ] *n*: **~ and kin** amis *mpl* et parents *mpl*.
kitsch [kɪtʃ] *adj, n* kitsch (*m*) *inv*.
kitten ['kɪtn] *n* chaton *m*, petit chat *m*. (*fig*) **to have ~s‡** piquer une crise*.
kitty ['kɪtɪ] *n* **(a)** (*Cards, also fig*) cagnotte *f*. **(b)** (*: *cat*) minet* *m*.
kiwi ['ki:wi:] *n* kiwi *m*.
kleptomania [ˌkleptəʊ'meɪnɪə] *n* kleptomanie *f*. ♦ **kleptomaniac** *adj, n* kleptomane (*mf*).
knack [næk] *n* tour *m* de main. **to learn the ~ of doing** attraper le tour de main pour faire; **to have the ~ of doing** avoir le chic pour faire.
knapsack ['næpsæk] *n* sac *m* à dos, havresac *m*.
knave [neɪv] *n* filou *m*; (*Cards*) valet *m*.
knead [ni:d] *vt dough etc* pétrir; *muscles* masser.
knee [ni:] *n* genou *m*. **on one's ~s** à genoux; **to go (down) on one's ~s** s'agenouiller, se mettre à genoux (*to sb* devant qn). ♦ **kneecap** *n* rotule *f*. ♦ **knee-deep** *adj*: **the water was ~-deep** l'eau arrivait aux genoux. ♦ **knee-high** *adj* à hauteur de genou. ♦ **kneepad** *n* genouillère *f*.

kneel [niːl] *pret, ptp* **knelt** *vi* (~ **down**) s'agenouiller, se mettre à genoux.
knell [nel] *n* glas *m.* **to toll the** ~ sonner le glas.
knew [njuː] *pret of* **know.**
knickers [ˈnɪkəz] *npl* slip *m* (*de femme*).
knick-knack [ˈnɪknæk] *n* bibelot *m.*
knife [naɪf] 1 *n, pl* **knives** (*gen*) couteau *m*; (*pocket* ~) canif *m.* ~**, fork and spoon** couvert *m*; (*fig*) **he's got his** ~ **into me*** il a une dent contre moi; (*fig*) **it's war to the** ~ **between them** ils sont à couteaux tirés. 2 *vt person* donner un coup de couteau à; (*kill*) tuer à coups de couteau. 3 *adj box* à couteaux. (*fig*) **on a** ~ **edge** *person* sur des charbons ardents; *result* qui ne tient qu'à un fil. ♦ **knife-grinder** *n* rémouleur *m.* ♦ **knife-sharpener** *n* aiguisoir *m.*
knight [naɪt] 1 *n* chevalier *m*; (*Chess*) cavalier *m.* 2 *vt* (*Brit*) **he was** ~**ed for services to industry** il a été fait chevalier pour services rendus dans l'industrie. ♦ **knighthood** *n*: **to receive a** ~**hood** recevoir le titre de chevalier.
knit [nɪt] *pret, ptp* **knitted** *or* **knit** 1 *vt* tricoter; (*fig:* ~ **together**) lier. **to** ~ **one's brows** froncer les sourcils. 2 *vi* tricoter; *[bone etc]* se souder. ♦ **knitted** *adj* en tricot. ♦ **knitting** 1 *n* tricot *m*; 2 *adj needle, wool, machine* à tricoter. ♦ **knitwear** *n* tricots *mpl.*
knob [nɒb] *n* (*gen*) bouton *m* (*de porte, de radio etc*); *[cane etc]* pommeau *m.* ~ **of butter** noix *f* de beurre. ♦ **knobb(l)y** *adj* noueux.
knock [nɒk] 1 *n* (*blow*) coup *m*; (*in engine etc*) cognement *m.* **there was a** ~ **at the door** on a frappé (à la porte); **I heard a** ~ j'ai entendu frapper; ~, ~! toc, toc, toc!; **I'll give you a** ~ **at 7 o'clock** je viendrai taper à la porte à 7 heures; **he got a** ~ **on the head** il a reçu un coup sur la tête; (*criticism*) ~**s*** critiques *fpl*; (*fig*) **to take a** ~ en prendre un coup.

2 *vt* **(a)** (*hit, strike*) frapper. **to** ~ **a nail into a plank** planter *or* enfoncer un clou dans une planche; **he** ~**ed the ball into the hedge** il a envoyé la balle dans la haie; **to** ~ **holes in sth** faire des trous dans qch; **to** ~ **the bottom out of** *box* défoncer; *argument* démolir; **to** ~ **sb on the head** frapper qn sur la tête, (*stun*) assommer qn; **to** ~ **sb to the ground** jeter qn à terre; **to** ~ **sb unconscious** assommer qn; **she** ~**ed the knife out of his hand** elle lui a fait tomber le couteau des mains; **to** ~ **a glass off a table** faire tomber un verre d'une table; **to** ~ **spots off sb*** battre qn à plates coutures; (*astonish*) **to** ~ **sb sideways*** ébahir qn; **to** ~ **some sense into sb** ramener qn à la raison. **(b)** (*collide with*) heurter. **to** ~ **one's head on** *or* **against** se cogner la tête contre; **he** ~**ed his foot against a stone** il a donné du pied contre une pierre. **(c)** (ː: *denigrate*) dire du mal de; (*in advertising*) faire de la contre-publicité à.

3 *vi* **(a)** (*strike*) frapper, cogner (*at* à). **he** ~**ed on the table** il a frappé la table, il a cogné sur la table; **his knees were** ~**ing** il tremblait de peur. **(b)** (*bump*) **to** ~ **into** se cogner *or* se heurter contre, heurter; (*: *meet*) tomber sur; **to** ~ **about the world** vagabonder de par le monde. **(c)** *[car engine etc]* cogner.

knock about, knock around 1 *vi* (*travel*) vagabonder; *[sailor]* bourlinguer. 2 *vt sep* (*ill-treat*) maltraiter, malmener.
knock back *vt sep* **(a)** (*: *drink*) s'envoyer*, avaler. **(b)** (ː: *cost*) **it** ~**ed me back £20** ça a fait un trou de 20 livres dans mes finances. **(c)** (**fig: shock*) sonner*, ahurir.
knock down *vt sep* **(a)** *object* renverser; *building etc* démolir; *tree* abattre; *door* enfoncer; *person* jeter à terre; (*Aut*) *pedestrian* renverser, *gatepost* faire tomber. **you could have** ~**ed me down with a feather!** les bras m'en sont tombés! **(b)** *price* baisser, abaisser. **(c)** *lot at auction* adjuger (*to sb* à qn).
knock in *vt sep nail* enfoncer.
knock off 1 *vi* (*: *stop work*) s'arrêter (de travailler); *[striker]* débrayer*. 2 *vt sep* **(a)** *vase from shelf etc* faire tomber. (*fig*) **to** ~ **off £10** baisser le prix de 10 livres. **(b)** (*: *do quickly*) *piece of work* expédier; (ː: *steal*) piquerː, voler; (ː: *stop*) arrêter (*doing* de faire).
knock out *vt sep* **(a)** *nail etc* faire sortir (*of* de); *one's pipe* débourrer. **(b)** (*stun*) assommer; (*Boxing*) mettre knock-out; (*: *shock*) sonner*. **(c)** (*from competition etc*) éliminer (*of* de).
knock over *vt sep* (*gen*) renverser; (*Aut*) *pedestrian* renverser; *gatepost* faire tomber.
knock together 1 *vi [glasses, knees]* s'entrechoquer. 2 *vt sep* **(a)** *two objects* cogner l'un contre l'autre. **(b)** (*make hurriedly*) bricoler à la hâte.
knock up *vt sep* **(a)** *lever* faire lever d'un coup; *sb's arm* faire voler en l'air. **(b)** (*Brit: waken*) réveiller (en frappant à la porte). **(c)** (*make hurriedly*) *meal* préparer en vitesse; *shed* construire à la va-vite; *furniture, toy* fabriquer en un rien de temps. **(d)** (*Brit*: exhaust*) *person* éreinter. **(e)** (*Brit*: make ill*) rendre malade. **(f)** (ː: *make pregnant*) faire un gosse à*.
♦ **knockdown** *adj* **(a)** *price* imbattable; **(b)** *table, shed* démontable. ♦ **knocker** *n* (*door-* ~) marteau *m* (de porte). ♦ **knocking** *n* coups *mpl*; (*in engine*) cognement *m*; **I can hear** ~**ing** j'entends frapper; (*Aut*) il y a qch qui cogne. ♦ **knocking-off time*** *n* heure *f* de la sortie. ♦ **knock-kneed** *adj*, ♦ **knock-knees** *npl*: **to be** ~**-kneed, to have** ~**-knees** avoir les genoux cagneux. ♦ **knockout** 1 *n* **(a)** (*Boxing etc*) knock-out *m*; (*fig: success*) **to be a** ~**out*** être sensationnel*; **(b)** (*Sport*) compétition *f* (avec épreuves éliminatoires); 2 *adj*: ~**out drops*** soporifique *m.* ♦ **knock-up** *n* (*Tennis*) **to have a** ~**-up** faire des balles.
knoll [nəʊl] *n* tertre *m.*
knot [nɒt] 1 *n* **(a)** nœud *m.* **to tie a** ~ faire un nœud. **(b)** (*Naut*) nœud *m.* **to make 20** ~**s** filer 20 nœuds. 2 *vt rope* faire un nœud à, nouer. **to** ~ **together** nouer. ♦ **knotty** *adj wood, hand* noueux; *problem* épineux.
know [nəʊ] *pret* **knew,** *ptp* **known** 1 *vt* **(a)** *facts, a language, dates, results* savoir (*that* que; *why* pourquoi). **to** ~ **a lot about** en savoir long sur; **I don't** ~ **much about** je ne sais pas grand-chose sur; **to get to** ~ **sth** apprendre qch; **to** ~ **how to do sth** savoir faire qch; **he** ~**s all the answers** il s'y connaît, (*pej*) c'est un je-sais-tout*; **to** ~ **the difference between** connaître la différence entre; **to** ~ **one's mind** savoir ce qu'on veut; **he** ~**s what he's talking about** il sait de quoi il parle, il connaît son sujet; **you** ~ **what I mean ...** tu vois ce que je veux dire ...; **that's worth** ~**ing** c'est bon à savoir; **for all I** ~ (autant) que je sache; **not that I** ~ **(of)** pas que je sache; **there's no** ~**ing what he'll do** impossible de savoir ce qu'il va faire; **what do you** ~**!*** eh bien!, ça alors!; **not if I** ~ **it!*** c'est ce qu'on va voir!; **she** ~**s all about sewing** elle s'y connaît *or* elle est très forte en couture; **that's all you** ~**!*** c'est ce que tu crois!; **I** ~ **nothing about it** je n'en sais rien, je ne suis pas au courant; **it soon became** ~**n that ...** on a bientôt appris que ...; **it is well** ~**n that ...** tout le monde sait que ...; **to make sth** ~**n to sb** faire savoir qch à qn; **he is** ~**n to have been there** on sait qu'il y a été; **I've** ~**n such things to happen** j'ai déjà vu cela se produire.

(b) (*be acquainted with*) *person, place, book, subject, plan, route* connaître. **to** ~ **sb by sight/by name** connaître qn de vue/de nom; **I don't** ~ **her to speak to** je ne la connais pas assez pour lui parler; **to get to** ~ **sb** *V* **get 2b**; **to make o.s.** ~**n to sb** se présenter à qn; **he is** ~**n as ...** on le connaît sous le nom de ... .

(c) (*recognize*) reconnaître (*sb by his voice* qn à sa voix). **I knew him at once** je l'ai reconnu tout de suite; **he** ~**s a good horse when he sees one** il sait reconnaître un bon cheval; **I wouldn't ~ it from a screwdriver** je ne sais pas le reconnaître d'un tournevis; **he doesn't ~ one end of a hammer from the other** c'est à peine s'il sait ce que c'est qu'un marteau; **you wouldn't ~ him from his brother** on le prendrait pour son frère.

2 *vi* savoir. **as far as I ~** à ma connaissance; **how should I ~?** comment voulez-vous que je le sache?; **there's no ~ing** on ne peut pas savoir; **Mummy ~s best!** maman a toujours raison!; **you ~ best** tu sais ce que tu dis; **to ~ about** *or* **of sth** savoir qch, connaître qch, avoir entendu parler de qch; **she ~s about cats** elle s'y connaît en (matière de) chats; **do you ~ about Paul?** tu es au courant pour Paul?*; **there were 5 'don't ~s'** il y avait 5 'sans opinion'; **to ~ better than to do** ne pas avoir la stupidité de faire; **you ought to have ~n better** tu aurais dû réfléchir; **they don't ~ any better** ils ne savent pas ce qu'ils font; **he says he didn't do it but I ~ better** il dit que ce n'est pas lui mais je ne suis pas assez stupide pour le croire; **to ~ of** connaître, avoir entendu parler de.

3 *n*: **to be in the ~*** être au courant.

♦ **knowable** *adj* connaissable. ♦ **know-all*** *n* je-sais-tout *mf*. ♦ **know-how*** *n* technique *f*, compétence *f*. ♦ **knowing** *adj* (*shrewd*) fin, malin; (*wise*) sage; *look, smile* entendu. ♦ **knowingly** *adv* (*consciously*) sciemment; (*in ~ing way*) *look, smile* d'un air entendu. ♦ **known** *adj thief etc* connu; *expert* reconnu; *fact* établi.

knowledge ['nɒlɪdʒ] *n* **(a)** (*understanding, awareness*) connaissance *f*. **to have no ~ of** ne pas savoir, ignorer; **to (the best of) my ~** à ma connaissance; **without his ~** à son insu; **to bring sth to sb's ~** signaler qch à qn; **it has come to my ~ that ...** j'ai appris que ...; **it's common** *or* **public ~ that ...** chacun sait que ... . **(b)** (*learning, facts learnt*) connaissances *fpl*, savoir *m*. **my ~ of English** mes connaissances d'anglais; **he has a working ~ of Japanese** il possède les éléments *mpl* de base du japonais; **he has a thorough ~ of geography** il possède la géographie à fond.

♦ **knowledgeable** *adj person* bien informé; *report* bien documenté.

knuckle ['nʌkl] *n* articulation *f* du doigt.

knuckle under* *vi* céder.

♦ **knuckleduster** *n* coup-de-poing *m* américain.

koala [kəʊ'ɑːlə] *n* (**~ bear**) koala *m*.

Koran [kɒ'rɑːn] *n* Coran *m*.

kosher ['kəʊʃəʳ] *adj* kascher *inv*.

kowtow ['kaʊ'taʊ] *vi* se prosterner (*to sb* devant qn).

kudos* ['kjuːdɒs] *n* gloire *f*, lauriers *mpl*.

L

L, l [el] *n* L, l *m or f.* (*Aut*) **L-plate** plaque *f* d'apprenti conducteur.

lab* [læb] *n* (*abbr of* **laboratory**) labo* *m.*

label ['leɪbl] **1** *n* étiquette *f.* **record on the Deltaphone ~** disque sorti chez Deltaphone. **2** *vt* coller une *or* des étiquette(s) sur; (*Comm*) *goods for sale* étiqueter; (*fig*) *person* étiqueter (*as* comme). **the bottle was not ~led** il n'y avait pas d'étiquette sur la bouteille; **it was ~led poison** il y avait marqué poison.

laboratory [lə'bɒrətərɪ, (*US*) 'læbrəˌtɔːrɪ] **1** *n* laboratoire *m.* **2** *adj assistant, equipment* de laboratoire.

labour, (*US*) **labor** ['leɪbəʳ] **1** *n* **(a)** (*hard work; task*) travail *m.* **~ of love** travail fait par plaisir. **(b)** (*Ind: workers*) main-d'œuvre *f,* ouvriers *mpl.* **Ministry** *or* (*US*) **Department of L~** ministère *m* du Travail. **(c)** (*Pol*) **L~** les travaillistes *mpl*; **he votes L~** il vote travailliste. **(d)** (*Med*) travail *m.* **in ~** en travail.

2 *adj* (*Ind*) *dispute, trouble* ouvrier; *relations* ouvriers-patronat *inv*; (*Brit Pol*) **L~** *leader, party* travailliste. **~ camp** camp *m* de travaux forcés; **L~ Day** fête *f* du Travail; **L~ Exchange** ≃ Agence *f* nationale pour l'emploi; (*Ind*) **~ force** (*numbers*) effectifs *mpl* en ouvriers; (*personnel*) main-d'œuvre *f*; (*US*) **~ laws** législation *f* du travail; (*Med*) **~ pains** douleurs *fpl* de l'accouchement; (*US*) **~ union** syndicat *m.*

3 *vi* (*with effort*) travailler dur (*at* à; *to do* pour faire); (*with difficulty*) peiner (*at* sur; *to do* pour faire); *[engine, motor]* peiner; *[ship]* fatiguer. **to ~ under a delusion** être victime d'une illusion; **to ~ up a hill** *[person]* monter péniblement une côte; *[car]* peiner dans une montée.

4 *vt*: **I won't ~ the point** je n'insisterai pas lourdement sur ce point.

♦ **laborious** *adj* laborieux. ♦ **laboriously** *adv* laborieusement. ♦ **labo(u)red** *adj style* laborieux; *breathing* pénible. ♦ **labo(u)rer** *n* (*gen*) ouvrier *m*; (*on roads, building sites*) manœuvre *m.* ♦ **labo(u)r-intensive** *adj* qui nécessite l'emploi de beaucoup de main-d'œuvre. ♦ **labo(u)rite** *n* (*Pol*) travailliste *mf.* ♦ **labo(u)r-saving** *adj* qui allège le travail; (*in household*) **~-saving device** appareil *m* ménager.

laburnum [lə'bɜːnəm] *n* cytise *m.*

labyrinth ['læbɪrɪnθ] *n* labyrinthe *m.*

lace [leɪs] **1** *n* **(a)** (*Tex*) dentelle *f.* **(b)** *[shoe etc]* lacet *m.* **2** *adj collar, curtains* de *or* en dentelle. **3** *vt* **(a)** (**~ up**) *shoe* lacer. **(b)** *drink* arroser (*with* de), corser. ♦ **lacemaker** *n* dentellière *f.* ♦ **lacemaking** *n* fabrication *f* de la dentelle. ♦ **lace-up shoes** *npl* chaussures *fpl* à lacets. ♦ **lacy** *adj* qui ressemble à la dentelle; **the frost made a lacy pattern** il y avait une dentelle de givre.

lacerate ['læsəreɪt] *vt* lacérer; (*fig*) fendre le cœur de. ♦ **laceration** *n* (*Med*) déchirure *f.*

lack [læk] **1** *n* manque *m.* **for ~ of** faute de. **2** *vt* manquer de. **3** *vi*: **to be ~ing** manquer, faire défaut; **to be ~ing in, to ~ for** manquer de. ♦ **lackadaisical** *adj* nonchalant. ♦ **lacking*** *adj* (*stupid*) simplet, débile*. ♦ **lacklustre,** (*US*) **-ter** *adj* terne.

lackey ['lækɪ] *n* laquais *m.*

laconic [lə'kɒnɪk] *adj* laconique. ♦ **laconically** *adv* laconiquement.

lacquer ['lækəʳ] **1** *n* (*substance*) laque *f*; (*object*) laque *m.* **2** *vt wood* laquer; *hair* mettre de la laque sur.

lad [læd] *n* garçon *m,* gars* *m.* **he's only a ~** ce n'est qu'un gamin*; **to have a drink with the ~s*** boire un pot avec les copains*; **come on ~s!** allez les gars!*; **he's a bit of a ~*** il est un peu noceur*.

ladder ['lædəʳ] **1** *n* échelle *f.* (*lit, fig*) **at the top of the ~** au sommet de l'échelle; **to have a ~ in one's stocking** avoir un bas filé. **2** *vti* filer. ♦ **ladderproof** *adj* indémaillable.

laden ['leɪdn] *adj* chargé (*with* de). **fully ~** *truck, ship* en pleine charge.

la-di-da* ['lɑːdɪ'dɑː] *adj person* bêcheur*; *voice* maniéré.

ladle ['leɪdl] **1** *n* louche *f.* **2** *vt* (**~ out**) servir (à la louche); (**fig*) *money, advice* prodiguer à foison.

lady ['leɪdɪ] **1** *n* dame *f.* **the ~ of the house** la maîtresse de maison; **Ladies and Gentlemen!** Mesdames, (Mesdemoiselles,) Messieurs!; **good morning, ladies and gentlemen** bonjour mesdames, bonjour mesdemoiselles, bonjour messieurs; **young ~** (*married*) jeune femme *f*; (*unmarried*) jeune fille *f*; **this is the ~/the young ~ who ...** voilà la dame/la demoiselle qui ...; **ladies' hairdresser** coiffeur *m,* -euse *f* pour dames; **~'s umbrella** parapluie *m* de dame; **he's a ladies' man** il plaît aux femmes; (*Rel*) **Our L~** Notre-Dame *f*; **Ladies** (*public lavatory*) Dames; **where is the Ladies?*** où sont les toilettes?; **L~ Smith** lady Smith; **~'s maid** femme *f* de chambre (*d'une dame*). **2** *adj*: **L~ Day** la fête de l'Annonciation; **~ doctor** femme *f* médecin; **~ friend*** petite amie; **L~ Mayoress** femme *f* (*or* fille *f etc*) du Lord Mayor. ♦ **ladybird** *or* ♦ **ladybug** *n* coccinelle *f.* ♦ **lady-in-waiting** *n* dame *f* d'honneur. ♦ **ladykiller** *n* don Juan *m.* ♦ **ladylike** *adj person* bien élevé, distingué; *manners* distingué. ♦ **ladylove** *n* bien-aimée *f.* ♦ **ladyship** *n*: **Her/Your L~ship** Madame *f* (la comtesse *etc*).

lag¹ [læg] **1** *n*: **(time) ~** retard *m*; (*between two events*) décalage *m.* **2** *vi*: **to ~ behind sb** traîner derrière qn; (*in achievements*) avoir du retard sur qn (*in sth* dans qch).

lag² [læg] *vt pipes* calorifuger. ♦ **lagging** *n* (*material*) calorifuge *m.*

lag³ [læg] *n*: **old ~*** récidiviste *mf.*

lager ['lɑːgəʳ] *n* ≃ bière *f* blonde.

lagoon [lə'guːn] *n* lagune *f*; (*coral*) lagon *m.*

lah [lɑː] *n* (*Mus*) la *m.*

laid [leɪd] *pret, ptp of* **lay¹**.

lain [leɪn] *ptp of* **lie¹**.

lair [lɛəʳ] *n* repaire *m.*

laity ['leɪɪtɪ] *collective n*: **the ~** les laïcs *mpl.*

lake [leɪk] *n* lac *m.*

lama ['lɑːmə] *n* lama *m* (*Rel*).

lamb [læm] **1** *n* (*Culin, Zool*) agneau *m.* **poor ~!*** le (*or* la) pauvre!; **he took it like a ~** il n'a pas protesté. **2** *adj*: **~ chop** côtelette *f* d'agneau. ♦ **lambing** *n* agnelage *m.* ♦ **lambswool** *n* laine *f* d'agneau.

lame [leɪm] **1** *adj animal, person, argument* boiteux; *excuse* faible, piètre. **to be ~** boiter (*in one leg* d'une jambe); **~ duck** canard *m* boiteux.

2 *vt* estropier. ♦ **lamely** *adv say etc* maladroitement. ♦ **lameness** *n* (*Med*) claudication *f*.

lament [lə'ment] **1** *n* lamentation *f*. **2** *vt* se lamenter sur. **(late)** ~**ed** regretté (*before n*). **3** *vi* se lamenter (*for, over* sur). ♦ **lamentable** *adj* lamentable, déplorable. ♦ **lamentably** *adv* lamentablement. ♦ **lamentation** *n* lamentation *f*.

laminated ['læmɪneɪtɪd] *adj metal* laminé; *windscreen* en verre feuilleté; *book-jacket* plastifié.

lamp [læmp] **1** *n* (*light*) lampe *f*; (*Aut*) feu *m*; (*bulb*) ampoule *f*. **2** *adj*: ~ **standard** lampadaire *m* (*dans la rue*). ♦ **lamplight** *n*: **by** ~**light** à la lumière de la lampe. ♦ **lamppost** *n* réverbère *m*. ♦ **lampshade** *n* abat-jour *m inv*. ♦ **lampstand** *n* pied *m* de lampe.

lance [lɑːns] **1** *n* (*weapon*) lance *f*; (*Med*) lancette *f*. **2** *vt* (*Med*) ouvrir. ♦ **lancet** *n* (*Med*) lancette *f*.

land [lænd] **1** *n* **(a)** (*gen*) terre *f*. **dry** ~ terre ferme; **on** ~ à terre; **to go by** ~ voyager par voie de terre; **over** ~ **and sea** sur terre et sur mer; **we sighted** ~ nous sommes arrivés en vue d'une terre; (*fig*) **to see how the** ~ **lies** tâter le terrain; **to live off the** ~ vivre de la terre; **to work on the** ~ travailler la terre; **he bought** ~ **in Devon** il a acheté une terre dans le Devon; **my** ~ mes terres, (*smaller*) mon terrain. **(b)** (*country, nation*) pays *m*. **throughout the** ~ dans tout le pays; ~ **of milk and honey** pays de cocagne; **to be in the** ~ **of the living** être encore de ce monde. **2** *adj breeze* de terre; *defences, forces* terrestre; *law, policy, reform* agraire; *tax* foncier. **3** *vt cargo* décharger; *passengers* débarquer; *aircraft* poser; *fish* prendre; *blow* infliger (*on sb* à qn); (*: *obtain*) *job, contract* décrocher*. **to** ~ **sb in trouble*** attirer des ennuis à qn; **to** ~ **sb in debt*** mettre qn dans les dettes; **to be** ~**ed with sth*** (*left with*) avoir qch sur les bras; (*forced to take on*) devoir se coltiner qch*. **4** *vi* **(a)** *[aircraft etc]* atterrir, se poser; (*on sea*) amerrir; (*on ship's deck*) apponter; *[air traveller]* atterrir; (*from boat*) débarquer. **(b)** (*after fall, jump etc*) *[person, object, bomb]* tomber. (*lit, fig*) **to** ~ **on one's feet** retomber sur ses pieds.

land up* *vi* finir par se retrouver.

♦ **landed** *adj* foncier; ~**ed gentry** aristocratie terrienne. ♦ **landfall** *n*: **to make** ~**fall** accoster. ♦ **landing 1** *n* **(a)** *[aircraft etc]* atterrissage *m*; (*on sea*) amerrissage *m*; (*from ship; also Mil*) débarquement *m*; **(b)** (*between stairs*) palier *m*; (*floor*) étage *m*; **2** *adj*: ~**ing card** carte *f* de débarquement; (*Aviat*) ~**ing gear** train *m* d'atterrissage; (*Fishing*) ~**ing net** épuisette *f*; (*Naut*) ~**ing party** détachement *m* de débarquement; ~**ing stage** débarcadère *m*; (*Aviat*) ~**ing strip** piste *f* d'atterrissage. ♦ **landlady** *n [flat etc]* logeuse *f*; *[boarding house etc]* patronne *f*. ♦ **landlocked** *adj* sans accès à la mer. ♦ **landlord** *n [flat etc]* propriétaire *m*, logeur *m*; *[pub, boarding house]* patron *m*. ♦ **landlubber*** *n* terrien(ne) *m(f)*. ♦ **landmark** *n* point *m* de repère; (*fig*) **to be a** ~**mark in** faire date dans. ♦ **landmine** *n* (*Mil*) mine *f* terrestre. ♦ **landowner** *n* propriétaire foncier. ♦ **landscape 1** *n* paysage *m*; **2** *vt garden* dessiner; *dirty place etc* aménager; **3** *adj gardener, gardening* paysagiste; ~**scape painter** paysagiste *m*. ♦ **landscaping** *n* aménagements *mpl* paysagers. ♦ **landslide 1** *n* (*lit: also* ~**slip**) glissement *m* de terrain; (*Pol*) raz-de-marée *m* électoral; **2** *adj* (*Pol etc*) *victory* écrasant. ♦ **land-worker** *n* ouvrier *m*, -ière *f* agricole.

lane [leɪn] *n* **(a)** (*in country*) chemin *m*; (*in town*) ruelle *f*. **(b)** (*Aut*) (*part of road*) voie *f*; (*line of traffic*) file *f*. **'keep in** ~**'** 'ne changez pas de file'; **'get into** ~**'** 'mettez-vous sur la bonne file'; **3-**~ **road** route *f* à 3 voies; **I'm in the wrong** ~ je suis dans la mauvaise file. **(c)** (*for aircraft, ships, runners, swimmers*) couloir *m*. **air/shipping** ~ couloir aérien/de navigation.

language ['læŋgwɪdʒ] **1** *n* (*gen*) langue *f*; (*means of communication; way of expressing things*) langage *m*. **the French** ~ la langue française; **modern** ~**s** langues vivantes; **he studies** ~**s** il fait des langues; **the origin of** ~ l'origine du langage; **speaking is one aspect of** ~ la parole est l'un des aspects du langage; **scientific/legal** ~ langage scientifique/juridique; (*fig*) **they do not speak the same** ~ ils ne parlent pas le même langage; **express it in your own** ~ exprimez cela en votre propre langage; **the** ~ **of official documents** le langage des documents officiels; **bad** ~ gros mots *mpl*; **watch your** ~! surveille ton langage! **2** *adj studies* de langue(s). ~ **laboratory** laboratoire *m* de langues.

languid ['læŋgwɪd] *adj* languissant. ♦ **languidly** *adv* languissamment.

languish ['læŋgwɪʃ] *vi* se languir (*for, over* après). ♦ **languishing** *adj* languissant.

languor ['læŋgə^{r}] *n* langueur *f*. ♦ **languorous** *adj* langoureux.

lank [læŋk] *adj hair* raide et terne.

lanky ['læŋkɪ] *adj* grand et maigre.

lanolin ['lænəʊlɪn] *n* lanoline *f*.

lantern ['læntən] **1** *n* lanterne *f*. **2** *adj*: ~ **slide** plaque *f* de lanterne magique. ♦ **lantern-jawed** *adj* aux joues creuses.

lap[1] [læp] *n* genoux *mpl*. (*fig*) **in the** ~ **of the gods** entre les mains des dieux; **in the** ~ **of luxury** dans le plus grand luxe. ♦ **lapdog** *n* petit chien *m* d'appartement.

lap[2] [læp] *n* (*Sport*) tour *m* de piste. **to run a** ~ faire un tour de piste; **on the 10th** ~ au 10e tour; ~ **of honour** tour d'honneur; (*fig*) **we're on the last** ~ on a fait le plus gros.

lap[3] [læp] **1** *vt milk* laper. **2** *vi [waves]* clapoter.

lap up *vt sep milk etc* laper; (**fig*) *compliments* boire comme du petit-lait*.

lapel [lə'pel] *n* revers *m* (*de veston etc*).

Lapland ['læplænd] *n* Laponie *f*.

lapse [læps] **1** *n* **(a)** (*fault*) faute *f* légère, défaillance *f*; (*in behaviour, from diet*) écart *m*. ~ **of memory** trou *m* de mémoire; **a** ~ **into bad habits** un retour à de mauvaises habitudes. **(b)** (*passage of time*) intervalle *m*. **a** ~ **of time** un laps de temps. **2** *vi* **(a)** (*err*) faire une *or* des erreur(s) passagère(s). **(b)** (*fall gradually*) tomber, retomber (*into* dans). **to** ~ **into silence** se taire; **to** ~ **into unconsciousness** (re)perdre connaissance. **(c)** *[act, law]* devenir caduc (*f* -uque); *[contract]* expirer; *[ticket, passport, insurance policy]* se périmer; *[subscription]* prendre fin. ♦ **lapsed** *adj contract, law* caduc; *ticket, passport* périmé; *Catholic etc* qui n'est plus pratiquant.

lapwing ['læpwɪŋ] *n* vanneau *m*.

larceny ['lɑːsənɪ] *n* (*Jur*) vol *m* simple.

larch [lɑːtʃ] *n* mélèze *m*.

lard [lɑːd] *n* saindoux *m*.

larder ['lɑːdə^{r}] *n* garde-manger *m inv*.

large [lɑːdʒ] **1** *adj* (*gen*) grand; *garden, room* grand, vaste; *person, animal, slice, hand, sum, loss* gros (*f* grosse); *amount* grand, important; *family, population* nombreux; *meal* copieux. **a** ~ **number of them** beaucoup d'entre eux; **to grow** ~**(r)** grandir, s'agrandir, grossir; **to make** ~**r** agrandir. **2** *n*: **at** ~ (*at liberty*) en liberté; (*as a whole*) en général, dans son ensemble; (*at random*) au hasard. **3** *adv*: **by and** ~ généralement. ♦ **large-hearted** *adj* au grand cœur. ♦ **largely** *adv* (*to a great extent*) en grande mesure *or* partie; (*principally*) pour la plupart, surtout; (*in general*) en général. ♦ **largeness** *n* grandeur *f*; grosseur *f*; importance *f*. ♦ **large-scale** *adj drawing, map* à grande échelle; *business activities, reforms, relations* sur une grande échelle; *powers* étendu. ♦ **large-size(d)** *adj* grand.

lark[1] [lɑːk] *n* alouette *f.* ♦ **larkspur** *n* pied *m* d'alouette.

lark[2]* [lɑːk] *n (joke etc)* blague* *f.* **for a ~** pour rigoler*; **what a ~!** quelle rigolade!*

lark about*, lark around* *vi* faire le petit fou (*f* la petite folle)*.

larva ['lɑːvə] *n, pl* **-ae** ['lɑːviː] larve *f* (*Zool*).

larynx ['lærɪŋks] *n* larynx *m.* ♦ **laryngitis** *n* laryngite *f.*

lascivious [lə'sɪvɪəs] *adj* lascif. ♦ **lasciviously** *adv* lascivement.

laser ['leɪzə^r] *n* laser *m.* **~ beam** rayon *m* laser *inv.*

lash [læʃ] **1** *n* **(a)** (*thong*) lanière *f*; (*blow*) coup *m* de fouet. **(b)** (eye~) cil *m.* **2** *vt* **(a)** (*whip*) fouetter violemment; (*flog*) flageller. (*fig*) **to ~ o.s. into a fury** s'emporter violemment; **the rain was ~ing (against) the windows** la pluie cinglait les carreaux; **to ~ its tail** fouetter l'air de sa queue. **(b)** (*fasten*) attacher (*to* à); (**~ down**) *cargo* arrimer. **3** *vi*: **to ~ against** cingler.

lash down 1 *vi [rain]* tomber avec violence. **2** *vt sep cargo* arrimer.

lash out 1 *vi* **(a) to ~ out at sb** envoyer de violents coups de poing à qn; (*verbally*) se répandre en invectives contre qn. **(b)** (*: *spend*) les lâcher*, beaucoup dépenser. **2** *vt sep* (*) *money* lâcher*.

♦ **lashings** *npl*: **~ings of*** énormément de*.

lass [læs] *n* (*esp Scot*) jeune fille *f.*

lassitude ['læsɪtjuːd] *n* lassitude *f.*

lasso [læ'suː] **1** *n* lasso *m.* **2** *vt* prendre au lasso.

last[1] [lɑːst] **1** *adj* **(a)** (*in series*) dernier (*before n*). **the ~ 10 pages** les 10 dernières pages; **~ but one, second ~** avant-dernier; **it's the ~ round but 3** il n'y a plus que 3 rounds après celui-ci. **(b)** (*past, most recent*) dernier (*usually after n*). **~ night** (*evening*) hier soir; (*night*) cette nuit, la nuit dernière; **~ week/year** *etc* la semaine/l'année *etc* dernière; **~ Monday** lundi dernier; **for the ~ few days** ces derniers jours; **for the ~ 2 years** depuis 2 ans; **the day before ~** avant-hier *m*; **the night before ~** avant-hier soir; **the week before ~** l'avant-dernière semaine; **(the) ~ time I saw him** la dernière fois que je l'ai vu; **~ thing at night** juste avant de se coucher; **I'm down to my ~ pound note** il ne me reste plus qu'une seule livre; **he's the ~ person to ask** c'est la dernière personne à qui demander.

2 *adv* **(a)** (*at the end*) *do, arrive etc* en dernier. **(b)** (*most recently*) la dernière fois. **when I ~ saw him** la dernière fois que je l'ai vu. **(c)** (*finally*) finalement, pour terminer.

3 *n* **(a)** dernier *m*, -ière *f.* **this is the ~ of the pears** voici la dernière poire (*or* les dernières poires); **the ~ of the cider** le reste du cidre; **the ~ but one** l'avant-dernier *m*, -ière *f*; **I'd be the ~ to criticize, but ...** j'ai horreur de critiquer, mais .... **(b)** (*phrases*) **at (long) ~** enfin; **to the ~** jusqu'au bout; **that was the ~ I saw of him** c'est la dernière fois que je l'ai vu; **we shall never hear the ~ of this** on n'a pas fini d'en entendre parler; **I shall be glad to see the ~ of this/of him** je serai content de voir tout ceci terminé/de le voir partir.

♦ **last-ditch** *adj* ultime. ♦ **lastly** *adv* pour terminer, en dernier lieu. ♦ **last-minute** *adj* de dernière minute.

last[2] [lɑːst] **1** *vi [pain, film, resources etc]* durer; (**~ out**) *[person]* tenir (le coup); *[money]* suffire. **too good to ~** trop beau pour durer; **no one ~s long in this job** personne ne tient longtemps dans ce poste; **he/it didn't ~ long** il/cela n'a pas fait long feu*. **2** *vt* durer. **he won't ~ the winter (out)** il ne passera pas l'hiver. **it will ~ you 3 years/a lifetime** cela vous durera *or* vous fera 3 ans/jusqu'à la fin de vos jours. ♦ **lasting** *adj* (*gen*) durable; **to his ~ing shame** à sa plus grande honte.

latch [lætʃ] *n* loquet *m.* **the door is on the ~** la porte n'est pas fermée à clef.

latch on to* *vt fus* **(a)** *person* s'accrocher à. **(b)** (*understand*) saisir.

♦ **latchkey** *n* clef *f* (de la porte d'entrée).

late [leɪt] **1** *adj* **(a)** (*not on time*) *person, train* en retard. **your essay is ~** vous rendez votre dissertation en retard; **the ~ arrival of the flight** le retard du vol; **to make sb ~** mettre qn en retard; **I'm ~** je suis en retard; **I'm ~ for work** je ne serai pas au travail à l'heure; **I was ~ for work** je suis arrivé au travail en retard; **I'm 2 hours ~** j'ai 2 heures de retard; **I'm 2 hours ~ for work** j'arriverai au travail avec 2 heures de retard; **I was 2 hours ~ for work** je suis arrivé au travail avec 2 heures de retard; **to be ~ in arriving** arriver en retard; **to be ~ with payments** avoir des paiements en retard. **(b)** (*last or nearly last*) *edition, symphony* dernier (*before n*). **to keep ~ hours** se coucher tard; **at this ~ hour** à cette heure tardive; **at this ~ stage** à ce stade avancé; **Easter is ~** Pâques est tard; **in ~ October** vers la fin d'octobre; **he is in his ~ sixties** il approche des soixante-dix ans; **of ~** récemment, dernièrement. **(c)** (*former*) ancien (*before n*). **the ~ Prime Minister** l'ancien Premier ministre. **(d)** (*dead*) **the ~ Mr Jones** feu M. Jones; **our ~ colleague** notre regretté collègue.

2 *adv* **(a)** (*not on time*) *arrive etc* en retard. **he arrived 10 minutes ~** il est arrivé 10 minutes en retard *or* avec 10 minutes de retard; **better ~ than never** mieux vaut tard que jamais. **(b)** (*far into day etc*) *get up etc* tard. **to work ~ at the office** rester tard au bureau pour travailler; **it's getting ~** il se fait tard; **~ at night** tard le soir; **~ into the night** tard dans la nuit; **~ in 1960** vers la fin de 1960, fin 1960. **(c)** (*recently*) **as ~ as 1950** en 1950 encore.

♦ **latecomer** *n* retardataire *mf.* ♦ **lately** *adv* dernièrement, récemment; **till ~ly** jusqu'à ces derniers temps. ♦ **lateness** *n [person, vehicle]* retard *m.* ♦ **later 1** *adj date, meeting* ultérieur; *edition* postérieur; *stage, point* plus avancé; **a ~r train** un train plus tard; **the ~r train** le deuxième train; **2** *adv* **(a)** (*not on time*) plus en retard; **(b) 2 weeks ~r** 2 semaines plus tard; **~r on** plus tard; **no ~r than** pas plus tard que; **not ~r than Monday** lundi au plus tard; **see you ~r!*** à tout à l'heure! ♦ **latest 1** *adj* (*gen*) dernier (*before n*); *date* dernier, limite; **2** *adv*: **the ~st you may come** l'heure limite à laquelle vous pouvez arriver; **when is the ~st you can come?** quand pouvez-vous venir, au plus tard?; **by noon at the ~st** à midi au plus tard; **3** *n* (*: *news*) **have you heard the ~st?** tu connais la dernière?*; **what's the ~st on ...?** qu'y a-t-il de nouveau sur ...?; (*Rad, TV*) **for the ~st on the riots** pour les dernières informations sur les émeutes; (*joke*) **have you heard his ~st?** tu connais sa dernière?*

latent ['leɪtənt] *adj* latent.

lateral ['lætərəl] *adj* latéral.

latex ['leɪteks] *n* latex *m.*

lath [læθ] *n, pl* **~s** [lɑːðz] latte *f.*

lathe [leɪð] *n* (*Tech*) tour *m.*

lather ['lɑːðə^r] **1** *n [soap]* mousse *f* (de savon). (*sweating*) **in a ~** *horse* couvert d'écume; *person* en nage. **2** *vt one's face etc* savonner. **3** *vi [soap]* mousser.

Latin ['lætɪn] **1** *adj* latin. **~-American** latino-américain, d'Amérique latine. **2** *n* (*Ling*) latin *m.*

latitude ['lætɪtjuːd] *n* **(a)** (*Geog*) latitude *f.* **at a ~ of 48° north** à 48° de latitude Nord. **(b)** (*freedom*) latitude *f.*

latrine [lə'triːn] *n* latrines *fpl.*

latter ['lætə^r] **1** *adj* **(a)** (*second*) deuxième, dernier (*before n*). **the ~ proposition** cette dernière

or la deuxième proposition. **(b)** (*later*) dernier (*before n*), deuxième. **the ~ half** la deuxième moitié; **in the ~ part of the century** vers la fin du siècle. **2** *n*: **of the two the ~ is ...** des deux celui-ci (*f* celle-ci) est ... .
♦ **latter-day** *adj* d'aujourd'hui. ♦ **latterly** *adv* (*recently*) dernièrement, récemment; (*towards the end*) sur le tard.

lattice ['lætɪs] **1** *n* treillis *m*; (*fence*) treillage *m*. **2** *adj window* treillissé.

laudable ['lɔːdəbl] *adj* louable.

laudatory ['lɔːdətərɪ] *adj* élogieux.

laugh [lɑːf] **1** *n* rire *m*; (*brief*) éclat *m* de rire. **with a ~** en riant; **to have the ~ over sb** l'emporter finalement sur qn; **to have a good ~ at** bien rire de; **that got a ~** cela a fait rire; **if you want a ~** si tu veux t'amuser; **what a ~!*** quelle rigolade!*; **just for a ~** histoire de rire*; **he's always good for a ~*** il nous fera toujours bien rire.
2 *vi* rire (*at, about, over* de). (*fig*) **to ~ at danger** se rire du danger; **there's nothing to ~ about** *or* **at** il n'y a pas de quoi rire; **he ~ed to himself** il a ri en lui-même; **he ~ed until he cried** il riait aux larmes; **he (nearly) split his sides ~ing** il se tordait de rire; **to ~ in sb's face** rire au nez de qn; **he'll soon be ~ing on the other side of his face** il n'aura bientôt plus envie de rire; (*fig*) **to ~ up one's sleeve** rire sous cape; **it's all right for him, he's ~ing*** lui il s'en fiche*, il est tranquille.
3 *vt*: **to ~ a jolly laugh** avoir un rire jovial; **to ~ sb to scorn** tourner qn en dérision; **they ~ed him out of it** ils se sont moqués de lui jusqu'à ce qu'il renonce; **to be ~ing one's head off*** rire comme un fou.
laugh off *vt sep accusation* écarter d'une plaisanterie. **you can't ~ this one off** cette fois tu ne t'en tireras pas par la plaisanterie.
♦ **laughable** *adj suggestion* ridicule; *amount* dérisoire. ♦ **laughing** *adj* riant, rieur; **this is no ~ing matter** il n'y a pas de quoi rire; **~ing gas** gaz *m* hilarant. ♦ **laughingly** *adv say etc* en riant; **it is ~ingly called ...** on l'appelle par plaisanterie ... . ♦ **laughing stock** *n* risée *f*; **to make a ~ing stock of o.s.** se couvrir de ridicule. ♦ **laughter** *n* rires *mpl*; **to roar with ~ter** rire aux éclats.

launch [lɔːntʃ] **1** *n* (*motor ~*) vedette *f*; (*pleasure boat*) bateau *m* de plaisance; (*boat carried by warship*) chaloupe *f*. **2** *vt* (*gen; also fig*) lancer; *shore lifeboat etc* faire sortir; *ship's boat* mettre à la mer. **3** *vi* (*fig*) se lancer (*into, on* dans).
launch out *vi* se lancer (*into, on* dans).
♦ **launcher** *n* lanceur *m*. ♦ **launching 1** *n* lancement *m*; *[shore lifeboat]* sortie *f*; *[ship's boat]* mise *f* à la mer; **2** *adj*: **~ing pad/site** rampe *f*/aire *f* de lancement.

launder ['lɔːndəʳ] *vt* blanchir. ♦ **launderette** *or* ♦ **Laundromat** (*US*) *n* laverie *f* automatique (*à libre-service*). ♦ **laundry 1** *n* (*place*) blanchisserie *f*; (*clothes*) linge *m*; **to do the laundry** faire la lessive; **2** *adj list* de blanchissage; *mark* de la blanchisserie; *basket* à linge.

laurel ['lɒrəl] *n* laurier *m*. **to rest on one's ~s** se reposer sur ses lauriers.

lava ['lɑːvə] *n* lave *f*.

lavatory ['lævətrɪ] **1** *n* toilettes *fpl*, W.-C. *mpl*, cabinets *mpl*. **2** *adj*: **~ paper** papier *m* hygiénique; **~ seat** siège *m* des W.-C.

lavender ['lævɪndəʳ] **1** *n* lavande *f*. **2** *adj* (*colour*) lavande *inv*. **~ bag/water** sachet *m*/eau *f* de lavande.

lavish ['lævɪʃ] **1** *adj* **(a)** *person* prodigue (*with* de). **(b)** *expenditure* très considérable; *amount* gigantesque; *meal* plantureux; *helping, hospitality* généreux; *flat, surroundings* somptueux. **to bestow ~ praise on sb** se répandre en éloges sur qn. **2** *vt* prodiguer (*sth on sb* qch à qn). ♦ **lavishly** *adv spend* sans compter; *give* généreusement; *furnish* somptueusement. ♦ **lavishness** *n* *[surroundings etc]* luxe *m*; (*prodigality*) prodigalité *f*.

law [lɔː] **1** *n* **(a)** (*gen*) loi *f*. **against the ~** contraire à la loi; **the ~ of the land** la législation *or* les lois du pays; **~s of nature** lois de la nature; **~ and order** l'ordre *m* public; **forces of ~ and order** forces *fpl* de l'ordre; **by ~** conformément à la loi; **by** *or* **under French ~** selon la loi française; **above the ~** au-dessus des lois; **to have the ~ on one's side** avoir la loi pour soi; **to keep within the ~** rester dans la légalité; **there's no ~ against it** ce n'est pas interdit; **to take the ~ into one's own hands** faire justice soi-même; **he's a ~ unto himself** il ne connaît d'autre loi que la sienne; **his word is ~** sa parole fait loi; **court of ~** cour *f* de justice, tribunal *m*; **to go to ~** recourir à la justice; **to take to ~** *case* porter devant les tribunaux; *person* faire un procès à; **here's the ~ arriving!‡** voilà les flics!* **(b)** (*science, profession*) droit *m*. **to study ~** faire son *or* du droit; (*Univ*) **Faculty of L~** faculté *f* de Droit; **civil/criminal ~** le droit civil/criminel.
2 *adj*: **~ court** cour *f* de justice, tribunal *m*; (*Univ*) **~ school** faculté *f* de Droit; **~ student** étudiant(e) *m(f)* en droit.
♦ **law-abiding** *adj* respectueux des lois. ♦ **lawbreaker** *n* personne *f* qui transgresse la loi. ♦ **lawful** *adj* légal. ♦ **lawfully** *adv* légalement. ♦ **lawgiver** *or* ♦ **lawmaker** *n* législateur *m*, -trice *f*. ♦ **lawless** *adj country* sans loi; *person* qui n'a foi ni loi. ♦ **lawsuit** *n* procès *m*; **to bring a ~suit against sb** intenter un procès à qn. ♦ **lawyer** *n* (*gen*) homme *m* de loi, juriste *m*; (*for sales, wills etc*) notaire *m*; (*for litigation*) avocat *m*; **I put the matter in the hands of my ~yer** j'ai mis l'affaire entre les mains de mon avocat.

lawn[1] [lɔːn] **1** *n* pelouse *f*. **2** *adj*: **~ tennis** (*gen*) tennis *m*; (*on grass*) tennis sur gazon.

lawn[2] [lɔːn] *n* (*Tex*) linon *m*.

lax [læks] *adj conduct* relâché; *person* négligent.
♦ **laxity** *or* ♦ **laxness** *n* relâchement *m*; négligence *f*.

laxative ['læksətɪv] *adj, n* laxatif (*m*).

lay[1] [leɪ] *pret, ptp* **laid 1** *vt* **(a)** (*put, place, set*) mettre, poser; (*stretch out*) *blanket etc* étendre (*over, on* sur); *tablecloth* mettre; *bricks, carpet, cable, pipe* poser; *road* faire; *[bird] egg* pondre; *tax* mettre (*on* sur); *burden* imposer (*on sb* à qn). (*euph: buried*) **to be laid to rest** être enterré; **I wish I could ~ my hands on ...** si seulement je pouvais mettre la main sur ...; **to ~ a hand on sb** porter la main sur qn; **I didn't ~ a finger on him** je ne l'ai même pas touché; **the scene is laid in Paris** l'action se passe à Paris; **he was laid low with flu** la grippe l'obligeait à garder le lit; **to ~ sb open to criticism** *etc* exposer qn à la critique *etc.* **(b)** (*prepare*) *fire* préparer; *snare, trap* tendre (*for* à); *plans* former. **to ~ the table** mettre le couvert; **to ~ the table for 5** mettre 5 couverts. **(c)** (*wager*) *money* parier, miser (*on* sur). **to ~ a bet** parier (*on* sur). **(d)** (*register*) *accusation* porter; (*Police*) *information* donner. (*Jur*) **to ~ a matter before the court** saisir le tribunal d'une affaire; **he laid his case before the commission** il a porté son cas devant la commission; **to ~ the facts before sb** exposer les faits à qn; **they laid their plan before him** ils lui ont soumis leur projet. **(e)** (*suppress*) *ghost* exorciser; *doubt, fear* dissiper; *dust* faire tomber. **2** *vi [bird etc]* pondre.
lay alongside *vi, vt sep* (*Naut*) accoster.
lay aside, lay by *vt sep* mettre de côté.
lay down *vt sep* **(a)** *parcel, burden* poser, déposer; *one's arms* déposer; *one's cards* étaler; *wine* mettre en cave. **to ~ down one's life for sb** sacrifier sa vie pour qn. **(b)** *rule, policy* établir; *condition, price* imposer, fixer. **he laid it down that ...** il a stipulé que ...; (*fig*) **to ~ down the law** faire la loi (*to sb about sth* à qn sur qch).

lay in *vt sep goods, reserves* amasser. **I must ~ in some fruit** il faut que je m'approvisionne en fruits.
lay into* *vt fus* (*attack physically*) foncer sur; (*verbally*) prendre à partie; (*scold*) passer un savon à*.
lay off 1 *vt sep workers* licencier, débaucher. **2** *vi* (*: *stop*) arrêter. **3** *vt fus* (*) **~ off it!** arrête!; **~ off him!** fiche-lui la paix!*
lay on *vt sep* **(a)** *tax* mettre. **(b)** (*Brit: provide*) *water, gas* installer; *facilities, entertainment* fournir. **a house with water laid on** une maison qui a l'eau courante; **I'll have a car laid on for you** je tiendrai une voiture à votre disposition; **everything will be laid on** il y aura tout ce qu'il faut. **(c)** *varnish, paint* étaler. (*fig*) **he laid it on thick*** (*flattered*) il a passé de la pommade*; (*exaggerated*) il y est allé un peu fort*.
lay out *vt sep* **(a)** (*plan, design*) *garden* dessiner; *house* concevoir le plan de; *essay* faire le plan de; (*Typ*) faire la mise en page de. **well-laid-out flat** appartement bien conçu. **(b)** (*get ready*) *clothes* sortir, préparer; *goods for sale* disposer. **to ~ out a body** faire la toilette d'un mort. **(c)** (*spend*) *money* dépenser (*on* pour). **(d)** (*knock out*) mettre knock-out.
lay over *vi* (*US*) faire une halte.
lay up *vt sep* **(a)** *store, provisions* amasser. **to ~ up trouble for o.s.** se préparer des ennuis. **(b)** *car* remiser; *ship* désarmer. **he is laid up with flu** il est au lit avec la grippe; **you'll ~ yourself up** tu vas te retrouver au lit.
♦ **layabout*** *n* fainéant(e) *m(f)*. ♦ **lay-by** *n* (*Aut*) petite aire *f* de stationnement (*sur bas-côté*). ♦ **lay-off** *n* (*Ind*) licenciement *m*, débauchage *m*. ♦ **layout** *n [building, town]* disposition *f*; *[essay]* plan *m*; *[advertisement, newspaper article etc]* mise *f* en page. ♦ **layover** *n* (*US*) halte *f*.
lay[2] [leɪ] *pret of* **lie**[1].
lay[3] [leɪ] *adj missionary, education* laïque; *brother, sister* convers; (*fig*) *opinion etc* des profanes. (*fig*) **to the ~ mind** pour le profane. ♦ **layman** *n* (*Rel*) laïc *m*; (*fig*) profane *m*.
layer [ˈleɪəʳ] *n* couche *f*.
laze [leɪz] *vi* (**~ about, ~ around**) paresser, traînasser (*pej*). ♦ **lazily** *adv* paresseusement. ♦ **laziness** *n* paresse *f*, fainéantise *f* (*pej*). ♦ **lazy** *adj person* paresseux, fainéant (*pej*); *smile* paresseux; *afternoon* de paresse. ♦ **lazybones*** *n* fainéant(e) *m(f)*.
lead[1] [liːd] (*vb: pret, ptp* **led**) **1** *n* **(a) to be in the ~** (*in match*) mener; (*in race, league*) être en tête; **to take the ~** (*in race*) prendre la tête; (*in match*) mener; **to have a 3-point ~** avoir 3 points d'avance; **to take the ~ in doing sth** être le premier à faire qch; **thanks to his ~** grâce à son initiative; **to follow sb's ~** suivre l'exemple de qn; **to give sb a ~** *[inventor etc]* montrer le chemin à qn (*fig*); *[clue etc]* mettre qn sur la voie; **the police have a ~** la police tient une piste; (*Cards*) **whose ~ is it?** à qui est-ce de jouer? **(b)** (*Theat*) **to play the ~** tenir le rôle principal; **male/female ~** premier rôle masculin/féminin. **(c)** (*leash*) laisse *f*. **on a ~** tenu en laisse. **(d)** (*Elec*) fil *m*; (*extension* **~**) rallonge *f*. **(e)** (*Press:* **~** *story*) article *m* de tête.
2 *vt* **(a)** (*conduct*) mener, conduire (*to* à); *[street]* mener. **to ~ sb in/across** *etc* faire entrer/traverser *etc* qn; **to ~ sb into a room** faire entrer qn dans une pièce; (*fig*) **he is easily led** il est très influençable; (*lit, fig*) **to ~ the way** montrer le chemin; **he led the way to the garage** il nous (*or* les *etc*) a menés jusqu'au garage; **he led the party to victory** il a mené le parti à la victoire. **(b)** (*be ~er of*) *procession* (*in charge*) être à la tête de, (*at head*) être en tête de; *government, team* être à la tête de, diriger; *expedition* être à la tête de, mener; (*Ftbl etc*) *league* être en tête de; *orchestra* (*Brit*) être le premier violon de; (*US*) diriger. (*Sport, fig*) **to ~ the field** venir *or* être en tête; **this country ~s the world in textiles** ce pays est au premier rang mondial pour les textiles. **(c)** (*Cards*) jouer. **(d)** *life, existence* mener. (*fig*) **to ~ sb a dance** faire la vie à qn*. **(e)** (*induce, bring*) amener (*sb to do* qn à faire). **I am led to the conclusion that ...** je suis amené à conclure que ... .
3 *vi* **(a)** (*in match*) mener (*by 4 goals to 3* par 4 buts à 3); (*in race*) être en tête. **to ~ by half a length/3 points** avoir une demi-longueur/3 points d'avance. **(b)** (*go ahead*) aller devant. **you ~, I'll follow** passez devant, je vous suis. **(c)** (*Cards*) jouer. **(d)** *[street, corridor, door]* mener (*to, into* à). **the streets that ~ off the square** les rues qui partent de la place. **(e)** (*result in*) **to ~ to** *war* conduire à; *sb's arrest* aboutir à; *confusion* créer; *change, improvement* amener, causer; **this led to their resigning** ceci les a amenés à démissionner; **one thing led to another and we ...** une chose en amenant une autre, nous ... .
lead away *vt sep* emmener.
lead back *vt sep* ramener.
lead off 1 *vi* (*begin*) commencer. **2** *vt sep* emmener.
lead on 1 *vi*: **~ on!** allez-y, je vous suis! **2** *vt sep* **(a)** (*tease*) taquiner, faire marcher*; (*fool*) avoir*; (*raise hopes of*) donner de faux espoirs à. **(b)** (*induce*) amener (*sb to do* qn à faire).
lead up *vi [road, stair]* conduire (*to* à). **what's all this ~ing up to?** où est-ce qu'on veut en venir avec tout ça?
♦ **leader** *n* **(a)** *[expedition, gang, tribe]* chef *m*; *[club]* dirigeant(e) *m(f)*; (*guide*) guide *m*; *[riot, strike]* meneur *m*, -euse *f*; (*Mil*) commandant *m*; (*Pol*) dirigeant(e), leader *m*; (*Brit Parl*) **L~er of the House** chef de la majorité ministérielle à la Chambre; **he's a born ~er** il est né pour commander; **the ~er of the orchestra** (*Brit*) le premier violon; (*US*) le chef d'orchestre; **one of the ~ers in the scientific field** une des sommités du monde scientifique; **(b)** (*in race*) coureur *m* de tête; (*horse*) cheval *m* de tête; (*in league*) leader *m*; **(c)** (*Press*) (*Brit*) éditorial *m*; (*US*) article *m* de tête. ♦ **leadership** *n* **(a)** direction *f*; **under his ~ership** sous sa direction; **qualities of ~ership** qualités *fpl* de chef; **(b)** (**~ers**) dirigeants *mpl*. ♦ **leader-writer** *n* éditorialiste *mf*. ♦ **lead-in** *n* introduction *f*, entrée *f* en matière. ♦ **leading** *adj horse, car* (*in procession*) de tête, (*in race*) en tête; (*chief*) *person, member, politician* de (tout) premier plan, principal; *part* prépondérant, de premier plan; *theme, idea* principal; **one of the ~ing writers** un des écrivains les plus importants; **one of the ~ing figures of the twenties** un personnage marquant des années vingt; (*Press*) **~ing article** (*Brit*) éditorial *m*; (*US*) article *m* de tête; **the ~ing lady/man** (*Cine*) la vedette féminine/masculine; (*Theat*) l'acteur/l'actrice principal(e); (*fig*) **~ing light** personnalité *f* de premier plan; **~ing question** (*Jur*) question *f* tendancieuse; (*gen*) question insidieuse.
lead[2] [led] **1** *n* (*metal*) plomb *m*; (*black* **~**) mine *f* de plomb; *[pencil]* mine; *[fishing line]* plomb; (*for sounding*) plomb (de sonde). **(window) ~s** plombures *fpl*. **2** *adj object* de *or* en plomb; *paint* à base de plomb. **~ pencil** crayon *m* à mine de plomb; **~ poisoning** saturnisme *m*. ♦ **leaded** *adj window* à tout petits carreaux. ♦ **leaden** *adj colour, sky* de plomb; (*heavy*) pesant; *silence* de mort; *atmosphere* chargé. ♦ **lead-free** *adj* (garanti) sans plomb.
leaf [liːf] *pl* **leaves 1** *n* **(a)** *[plant]* feuille *f*. **in ~** en feuilles. **(b)** *[book]* feuillet *m*, page *f*. (*fig*) **you should take a ~ out of his book** vous devriez prendre exemple sur lui; (*fig*) **to turn over a new ~** changer de conduite. **(c)** *[table]* rabat *m*. **2** *vi*:

to ~ **through a book** feuilleter un livre. ♦ **leaflet** *n* prospectus *m*; (*Pol, Rel*) tract *m*; (*instruction sheet*) mode *m* d'emploi. ♦ **leafy** *adj* feuillu.

league [liːg] *n* **(a)** ligue *f*. **to form a ~ against** se liguer contre; **in ~ with** en coalition avec. **(b)** (*Ftbl etc*) championnat *m*.

leak [liːk] **1** *n* (*gen; also of information*) fuite *f*; (*in boat*) voie *f* d'eau. **to spring a ~** *[boat]* commencer à faire eau; *[bucket, pipe]* se mettre à fuir; **security ~** fuite concernant la sécurité. **2** *vi* **(a)** *[container, roof etc]* fuir; *[ship]* faire eau; *[shoes]* prendre l'eau. **(b)** (~ **out**) *[liquid]* fuir, s'échapper; *[secret, news]* être divulgué. **it ~ed (through) on to the carpet** cela a filtré jusque sur le tapis. **3** *vt liquid* répandre; (*fig*) *information* divulguer (*to* à). ♦ **leakage** *n* (*leak*) fuite *f*; (*amount lost*) perte *f*. ♦ **leaky** *adj container* qui fuit; *roof* qui a une fuite; *boat* qui fait eau.

lean[1] [liːn] *pret, ptp* **leaned** *or* **leant** [lent] **1** *vi* **(a)** *[wall, construction etc]* pencher. (*Pol*) **to ~ towards the left** pencher vers la gauche. **(b)** (*rest*) *[person]* s'appuyer (*against* contre, à; *on* sur). *[person, ladder, cycle]* **to be ~ing** être appuyé (*against* contre, à); **to ~ on sb** (*lit, fig: for support*) s'appuyer sur qn; (*: *put pressure on*) faire pression sur qn. **2** *vt ladder, cycle* appuyer (*against* contre). **to ~ one's head on sb's shoulder** reposer sa tête sur l'épaule de qn.

lean back *vi* se pencher en arrière; (*in armchair*) se laisser aller en arrière. **to ~ back against** s'adosser contre *or* à.

lean forward *vi* se pencher en avant.

lean out *vi* se pencher au dehors. **to ~ out of the window** se pencher par la fenêtre.

lean over *vi [person]* se pencher (*forward*) en avant *or* (*sideways*) sur le côté; *[object, tree]* pencher, être penché. (*fig*) **to ~ over backwards to help sb*** se mettre en quatre pour aider qn. ♦ **leaning 1** *n* tendance *f* (*towards* à); **2** *adj* penché. ♦ **lean-to 1** *n* appentis *m*; **2** *adj* en appentis.

lean[2] [liːn] **1** *adj* maigre. **we had a ~ time** on a mangé de la vache enragée. **2** *n [meat]* maigre *m*. ♦ **leanness** *n* maigreur *f*.

leap [liːp] (*vb: pret, ptp* **leaped** *or* **leapt** [lept]) **1** *n* saut *m*, bond *m*. **at one ~** d'un bond; **by ~s and bounds** à pas de géant; (*fig*) **a ~ in the dark** un saut dans l'inconnu; (*fig*) **a great ~ forward** un bond en avant. **2** *adj*: **~ year** année *f* bissextile. **3** *vi* sauter, bondir. **to ~ out/in** *etc* sortir/entrer *etc* d'un bond; **he leapt into the car** il a sauté dans la voiture; **to ~ over a ditch** franchir un fossé d'un bond; **he leapt for joy** il bondit de joie; **to ~ at an offer** sauter sur une offre. **4** *vt stream, hedge* sauter (par-dessus), franchir d'un bond.

leap up *vi* (*off ground*) sauter en l'air; (*to one's feet*) se lever d'un bond; *[flame]* jaillir; *[prices, etc]* faire un bond.

♦ **leapfrog 1** *n* saute-mouton *m*; **2** *vi*: **to ~frog over sb/sth** sauter par-dessus qn/qch à saute-mouton.

learn [lɜːn] *pret, ptp* **learned** *or* **learnt 1** *vt* apprendre. **to ~ (how) to do sth** apprendre à faire qch; (*fig*) **he's ~t his lesson** cela lui a servi de leçon, il ne recommencera pas de sitôt; **I was sorry to ~ that ...** j'ai appris avec regret que ... ; **that'll ~ you!‡** ça t'apprendra!* **2** *vi* apprendre. **to ~ about sth** (*Scol etc*) étudier qch; (*hear of*) apprendre qch; **to ~ from experience** apprendre par l'expérience; **to ~ from one's mistakes** tirer la leçon de ses erreurs; (*iro*) **he'll ~!** un jour il comprendra!

learn off *vt sep* apprendre par cœur.

learn up *vt sep* (*gen*) apprendre; *school subject* travailler.

♦ **learned** ['lɜːnɪd] *adj* (*gen*) savant; *profession* intellectuel; (*Brit Jur*) **my ~ed friend** mon éminent confrère. ♦ **learner** *n* débutant(e) *m(f)*; **to be a quick ~er** apprendre vite. ♦ **learning** *n* érudition *f*, savoir *m*.

lease [liːs] **1** *n* (*Jur: contract, duration*) bail *m*. **long ~** bail à long terme; (*fig*) **to give sb a new ~ of life** redonner de la vigueur à qn; **to take on a new ~ of life** retrouver une nouvelle jeunesse. **2** *vt [tenant, owner]* louer à bail. ♦ **leasehold 1** *n* bail *m*; **2** *adj* loué à bail.

leash [liːʃ] *n* laisse *f*. **on a ~** en laisse.

least [liːst] *superl of* **little**[2] **1** *adj* (*smallest amount of*) le moins de; (*smallest*) le *or* la moindre, le *or* la plus petit(e). **the ~ money** le moins d'argent; **the ~ thing upsets her** la moindre chose *or* la plus petite chose la contrarie; **that's the ~ of our worries** c'est le cadet de nos soucis. **2** *pron* le moins. **it's the ~ I can do** c'est la moindre des choses; **to say the ~ (of it)!** c'est le moins qu'on puisse dire!; **~ said soonest mended** moins on en dit et mieux ça vaut; **at ~ £5** au moins 5 livres; **at ~ as much as** au moins autant que; **you could at ~ have told me!** tu aurais pu au moins me le dire!; **I can at ~ try** je peux toujours essayer; **... at ~ that's what he says** ... du moins c'est ce qu'il dit; **at the very ~** au moins, au minimum; **not in the ~** pas du tout.

3 *adv* le moins. **the ~ expensive car** la voiture la moins chère; **she is ~ able to afford it** c'est elle qui peut le moins se l'offrir; **~ of all him** surtout pas lui.

♦ **leastways*** *or* ♦ **leastwise*** *adv* du moins, ou plutôt.

leather ['leðə[r]] **1** *n* cuir *m*; (*wash ~*) peau *f* de chamois. **2** *adj* de *or* en cuir. **~ goods** articles *mpl* en cuir, (*handbags etc*) maroquinerie *f*. ♦ **leatherette** *n* similicuir *m*. ♦ **leathering** *n*: **to give sb a ~ing*** tanner le cuir à qn‡. ♦ **leathery** *adj meat, substance* coriace; *skin* parcheminé.

leave [liːv] (*vb: pret, ptp* **left**) **1** *n* **(a)** (*consent*) permission *f*. **without so much as a by-your-~*** sans même demander la permission; **to ask ~ from sb to do** demander à qn la permission de faire. **(b)** (*holiday*) congé *m*; (*Mil*) permission *f*. **on ~** en congé, en permission; **on ~ of absence** en congé exceptionnel, (*Mil*) en permission spéciale. **(c) to take (one's) ~ of sb** prendre congé de qn; **have you taken ~ of your senses?** avez-vous perdu la tête?

2 *vt* **(a)** (*go away from*) *town* quitter, partir de, (*permanently*) quitter; *room, building* sortir de, quitter; *prison, hospital* sortir de; *person, job* quitter. **to ~ school** terminer ses études (secondaires); **he left home in 1979** il est parti de la maison en 1979; **I left home at 6 o'clock** je suis sorti de chez moi à 6 heures; **he has left this address** il n'habite plus à cette adresse; **to ~ the room** (*to lavatory*) sortir (*euph*); **to ~ the table** se lever de table; **to ~ the track** dérailler; **the car left the road** la voiture a quitté la route. **(b)** (*deposit, put*) laisser (*with sb* à qn); (*forget*) laisser, oublier. **to ~ sb a tip** laisser un pourboire à qn; **she left him her house** elle lui a laissé *or* légué sa maison. **(c)** (*allow to remain*) laisser. **to ~ the door open** laisser la porte ouverte; **~ it where it is** laisse-le là où il est; **some things are better left unsaid** il vaut mieux passer certaines choses sous silence; **let's ~ it at that** tenons-nous-en là; **I'll ~ it to you to decide** je te laisse décider; **I'll ~ it to you** je m'en remets à vous; **~ it to me!** je m'en charge!; **I'll ~ you to it*** je vous laisse (continuer); **he was left a widower** il est devenu veuf; **to ~ sb in peace** *or* **to himself** laisser qn tranquille; **left to himself, he ...** tout seul *or* laissé à lui-même, il ...; **take it or ~ it** c'est à prendre ou à laisser; **3 from 6 ~s 3** 3 ôté de 6, il reste 3. **(d) to be left (over)** rester; **what's left?** qu'est-ce qui reste?; **there'll be none left** il n'en restera pas; **how many are (there) left?** combien est-ce qu'il en reste?; **I've no money left** il ne me reste plus d'argent; **there are 3 cakes left** il reste 3 gâteaux;

have you (got) any left? est-ce qu'il vous en reste?; *V also* **left**[1].

3 *vi* partir, s'en aller (*for* pour).

leave about, leave around *vt sep clothes etc* laisser traîner.

leave behind *vt sep person, object* laisser; *opponent in race* distancer; *fellow students* dépasser.

leave in *vt sep* laisser.

leave off 1 *vi* (*: *stop*) s'arrêter. **2** *vt sep* **(a)** (*: *stop*) cesser, arrêter (*doing* de faire). **(b)** *lid, clothes* ne pas mettre; *gas, heating, tap* laisser fermé; *light* laisser éteint.

leave on *vt sep lid, clothes* ne pas enlever; *gas, heating, tap* laisser ouvert; *light* laisser allumé.

leave out *vt sep* **(a)** (*omit*) (*accidentally*) oublier; (*deliberately*) exclure; (*in reading etc*) sauter. **he was feeling left out** il avait l'impression de ne pas être dans le coup. **(b)** *food, note* laisser (*for sb* à qn); (*not put back*) *books, toys* laisser sorti, ne pas ranger.

leave over *vt sep* **(a) to be left over** rester; *V* leave 2d. **(b)** (*postpone*) remettre (à plus tard). ♦ **leavetaking** *n* adieux *mpl.* ♦ **leaving** *n* départ *m.* ♦ **leavings** *npl* restes *mpl.*

leaven ['levn] **1** *n* levain *m.* **2** *vt* faire lever.

Lebanon ['lebənən] *n* Liban *m.*

lecherous ['letʃərəs] *adj* lubrique.

lectern ['lektən] *n* lutrin *m.*

lecture ['lektʃəʳ] **1** *n* **(a)** conférence *f*; (*Univ etc: part of series*) cours *m* (magistral). **to give a ~** faire une conférence *or* un cours (*on* sur). **(b)** (*reproof*) sermon *m.* **to give *or* read sb a ~** sermonner qn. **2** *vi* faire une conférence *or* un cours (*to* à; *on* sur). (*Univ*) **he ~s in law** il est professeur de droit; **he's lecturing at the moment** il fait (son) cours en ce moment. **3** *vt* (*reprove*) sermonner (*sb on sth/for having done* qn pour qch/pour avoir fait). **4** *adj notes* de cours. **~ course** cours *m*; **~ hall** amphithéâtre *m*; **~ room** salle *f* de conférences. ♦ **lecturer** *n* **(a)** (*speaker*) conférencier *m*, -ière *f*; **(b)** (*Brit Univ*) ≃ maître assistant *m*, maître *m* de conférences; **assistant ~r** ≃ assistant(e) *m(f)*; **senior ~r** ≃ chargé(e) *m(f)* d'enseignement.

led [led] *pret, ptp of* **lead**[1].

ledge [ledʒ] *n* (*on wall*) rebord *m*, saillie *f*; (*window ~*) rebord (de la fenêtre); (*on mountain*) saillie.

ledger ['ledʒəʳ] *n* grand livre *m* (*Comptabilité*).

lee [li:] **1** *n* côté *m* sous le vent. **in the ~ of** à l'abri de. **2** *adj* sous le vent. ♦ **leeward 1** *adj, adv* sous le vent; **2** *n* côté *m* sous le vent; **to ~ward** sous le vent. ♦ **leeway** *n* (*Naut*) dérive *f*; (*fig*) **that gives him a certain ~way** cela lui donne une certaine liberté d'action; **a lot of ~way to make up** beaucoup de retard à rattraper.

leech [li:tʃ] *n* sangsue *f.*

leek [li:k] *n* poireau *m.*

leer [lɪəʳ] **1** *vi* lorgner. **to ~ at sb** lorgner qn. **2** *n* (*evil*) regard *m* mauvais; (*lustful*) regard concupiscent.

left[1] [left] *pret, ptp of* **leave.** ♦ **left-luggage** *n* bagages *mpl* en consigne; (*office*) consigne *f.* ♦ **left-luggage locker** *n* casier *m* à consigne automatique. ♦ **left-overs** *npl* restes *mpl.*

left[2] [left] **1** *adj* (*not right*) gauche. **2** *adv* à gauche. **3** *n* **(a)** gauche *f.* **on your ~** à *or* sur votre gauche; **on the ~** *be, stand, see* sur la gauche, à gauche; *drive* à gauche; **the door on the ~** la porte de gauche; **the street on the ~** la rue à gauche; (*Aut*) **to keep to the ~** tenir sa gauche; **to the ~** vers la gauche; (*Pol*) **the L~** la gauche. **(b)** (*Boxing: punch*) gauche *m.* ♦ **left-hand** *adj door, page* de gauche; **~-hand drive** conduite *f* à gauche; **on the ~-hand side** à gauche. ♦ **left-handed** *adj person* gaucher; *screw* fileté à gauche; *scissors* pour gaucher; (*fig*) *compliment* ambigu. ♦ **left-hander** *n* (*person*) gaucher *m*, -ère *f.* ♦ **leftist** *adj* (*Pol*) de gauche. ♦ **left-wing** *adj newspaper, view* de gauche; **he's ~-wing** il est à gauche.

leg [leg] **1** *n* [*person, horse*] jambe *f*; [*other animal, bird, insect*] patte *f*; (*Culin*) [*lamb*] gigot *m*; [*pork, chicken, frog*] cuisse *f*; [*table etc*] pied *m*; [*trousers, stocking etc*] jambe; (*stage*) [*journey*] étape *f*; (*in relay*) relais *m.* **my ~s won't carry me any further!** je ne tiens plus sur mes jambes!; **to be on one's last ~s** [*person, company*] être à bout de ressources; [*machine etc*] être sur le point de rendre l'âme*; **to give sb a ~ up** faire la courte échelle à qn; (**fig*) donner un coup de pouce à qn; **he hasn't got a ~ to stand on** il n'a aucun argument valable; (*fig*) **to pull sb's ~** (*hoax*) faire marcher qn*; (*tease*) taquiner qn. **2** *adj muscle* de la jambe. **~ bone** tibia *m.* **3** *vt*: **to ~ it*** aller à pied, faire le chemin à pied. ♦ **-legged** *adj ending*: **four-~ged** à quatre pattes; **bare-~ged** aux jambes nues. ♦ **leggings** *npl* jambières *fpl*; (*for baby*) culotte *f* (longue). ♦ **leg-pull*** *n* canular *m.* ♦ **leg-pulling*** *n* (*hoaxes*) canulars *mpl*; (*teasing*) taquineries *fpl.* ♦ **leg-room** *n* place *f* pour les jambes. ♦ **leg-warmers** *npl* jambières *fpl.*

legacy ['legəsɪ] *n* (*Jur, also fig*) legs *m.* **to leave a ~ to sb** faire un legs à qn.

legal ['li:gəl] *adj* **(a)** (*lawful*) *act, status, right* légal; *requirements* légitime. **~ currency** monnaie légale; **it's not ~ currency** cela n'a pas cours; **~ document** titre *m* authentique. **(b)** (*concerning the law*) *error, advice* judiciaire; *affairs, question* juridique. **to take ~ action against** intenter un procès à *or* contre; **to take ~ advice** consulter un homme de loi; **~ adviser** conseiller *m*, -ère *f* juridique; (*Brit*) **~ aid** assistance *f* judiciaire; **~ costs** frais *mpl* de justice; **~ department** service *m* du contentieux; **a ~ offence** une infraction à la loi; **~ proceedings** procès *m*, poursuites *fpl*; **the ~ profession** les hommes *mpl* de loi. ♦ **legality** *n* légalité *f.* ♦ **legalization** *n* légalisation *f.* ♦ **legalize** *vt* légaliser. ♦ **legally** *adv* légalement; **to be ~ly binding** lier.

legation [lɪ'geɪʃən] *n* légation *f.*

legend ['ledʒənd] *n* légende *f.* ♦ **legendary** *adj* légendaire.

legible ['ledʒəbl] *adj* lisible. ♦ **legibility** *n* lisibilité *f.* ♦ **legibly** *adv* lisiblement.

legion ['li:dʒən] *n* légion *f.* ♦ **legionary 1** *n* légionnaire *m*; **2** *adj* de la légion.

legionnaire [ˌli:dʒə'nɛəʳ] *n* légionnaire *m.*

legislate ['ledʒɪsleɪt] *vi* faire des lois, légiférer. ♦ **legislation** *n* législation *f*; **to introduce legislation** faire des lois; **a piece of legislation** une loi. ♦ **legislative** *adj* législatif. ♦ **legislator** *n* législateur *m*, -trice *f.* ♦ **legislature** *n* corps *m* législatif.

legitimate [lɪ'dʒɪtɪmɪt] *adj* (*Jur etc*) légitime; *argument, cause, excuse* bon, valable; *complaint* légitime; *reasoning, conclusion* logique. **the ~ theatre** le théâtre littéraire. ♦ **legitimacy** *n* légitimité *f.* ♦ **legitimately** *adv*: **one might ~ly think** on serait en droit de penser. ♦ **legitimize** *vt* légitimer.

leisure ['leʒəʳ] **1** *n* loisir *m*, temps *m* libre. (*hum*) **a lady of ~** une rentière (*fig hum*); **a life of ~** une vie pleine de loisirs; **do it at your ~** faites-le quand vous en aurez le temps; **think about it at ~** réfléchissez-y à tête reposée. **2** *adj*: **in my ~ moments** à mes moments de loisir; **~ time** loisir *m*, temps *m* libre. ♦ **leisured** *adj* qui a beaucoup de loisirs; *classes* oisif. ♦ **leisurely** *adj pace, movement* lent, tranquille; *person* placide; *journey, stroll* fait sans se presser; *occupation* peu fatigant; **in a ~ly way** *walk* sans se presser; *work* sans faire de gros efforts.

lemon ['lemən] **1** *n* (*fruit, colour*) citron *m*; (*tree*) citronnier *m.* **2** *adj* (*colour*) citron *inv.* **~ cheese *or* curd** ≃ crème *f* de citron; **~ drink *or* squash** citronnade *f*; (*fresh lemon*) citron pressé; **~ juice**

jus *m* de citron; ~ **sole** limande-sole *f*; ~ **squeezer** presse-citron *m inv*; ~ **tea** thé *m* au citron; ~ **yellow** jaune citron *inv*. ♦ **lemonade** *n* limonade *f*; (*still*) citronnade *f*.

lemur ['li:mə^r] *n* maki *m*.

lend [lend] *pret, ptp* **lent** *vt* (*gen*) prêter (*to sb* à qn); (*fig*) *importance, one's name* prêter (*to* à); *mystery, dignity, authority* conférer (*to* à). **to ~ an ear** écouter, prêter l'oreille; **to ~ o.s. to sth** se prêter à qch. ♦ **lender** *n* prêteur *m*, -euse *f*. ♦ **lending 1** *n* prêt *m*; **2** *adj library* de prêt.

length [leŋθ] *n* **(a)** (*gen*) longueur *f*; (*duration*) durée *f*. **it was 6 metres in ~** cela avait 6 mètres de long; **what is the ~ of the field?** quelle est la longueur du champ?; **along the whole ~ of** sur toute la longueur de; **what ~ of cloth did you buy?** quel métrage de tissu as-tu acheté?; (*fig*) **over the ~ and breadth of England** dans toute l'Angleterre; **to fall full ~** tomber de tout son long; **what ~ is the film?** combien dure le film?; **~ of life** durée de vie; **~ of time** temps *m*; (*Admin*) **~ of service** ancienneté *f*; **4,000 words in ~** de 4 000 mots; **at ~** (*at last*) enfin, à la fin; **at (great) ~** (*in many words*) fort longuement; (*in detail*) dans le détail; **to go to the ~ of doing** aller jusqu'à faire; **to go to great ~s to do** se donner beaucoup de mal pour faire; **to go to any ~(s) to do** ne reculer devant rien pour faire; **to win by a ~** gagner d'une longueur; **he was 3 car ~s behind me** il était à 3 longueurs de voiture derrière moi. **(b)** (*section: gen*) morceau *m*, bout *m*; *[wallpaper]* lé *m*; *[dress, material]* métrage *m*, hauteur *f*; *[tubing, track]* tronçon *m*. **skirt ~** hauteur de jupe.
♦ **lengthen 1** *vt object* rallonger; *visit, life* prolonger; *vowel* allonger; **2** *vi* rallonger; se prolonger; s'allonger; *[days, nights]* rallonger. ♦ **lengthily** *adv* longuement. ♦ **lengthways** *or* ♦ **lengthwise 1** *adv* dans le sens de la longueur; **2** *adj* en longueur. ♦ **lengthy** *adj* (très) long; (*tedious*) interminable.

lenient ['li:nɪənt] *adj judge, parent* indulgent (*to* envers, pour); *government* clément (*to* envers). ♦ **lenience** *or* ♦ **leniency** *n* indulgence *f*; clémence *f*. ♦ **leniently** *adv* avec indulgence; avec clémence.

lens [lenz] **1** *n* (*for magnifying*) lentille *f*; *[camera]* objectif *m*; *[spectacles]* verre *m*; *[eye]* cristallin *m*. **2** *adj*: **~ holder** porte-objectif *m inv*; **~ hood** parasoleil *m*.

lent [lent] *pret, ptp of* **lend**.

Lent [lent] *n* Carême *m*. **I gave it up for ~** j'y ai renoncé pour le Carême.

lentil ['lentl] *n* lentille *f*. **~ soup** soupe *f* aux lentilles.

Leo ['li:əʊ] *n* (*Astron*) le Lion.

leopard ['lepəd] *n* léopard *m*. **the ~ cannot change its spots** on ne peut pas changer sa nature. ♦ **leopardess** *n* léopard *m* femelle.

leotard ['li:ətɑ:d] *n* collant *m* (*de danseur etc*).

leper ['lepə^r] *n* lépreux *m*, -euse *f* (*also fig*). **~ colony** léproserie *f*. ♦ **leprosy** *n* lèpre *f*. ♦ **leprous** *adj* lépreux.

lesbian ['lezbɪən] **1** *adj* lesbien. **2** *n* lesbienne *f*. ♦ **lesbianism** *n* lesbianisme *m*.

lesion ['li:ʒən] *n* (*Med*) lésion *f*.

less [les] *comp of* **little² 1** *adj, pron* moins (de). **~ butter** moins de beurre; **I have ~ than you** j'en ai moins que vous; **even ~** encore moins; **much ~ milk** beaucoup moins de lait; **a little ~ cream** un peu moins de crème; **~ and ~** de moins en moins; **~ than that** moins que cela; **it costs ~ than** cela coûte moins cher que; **~ than half the audience** moins de la moitié de l'assistance; **he couldn't have done ~** il n'aurait pas pu faire moins; **of ~ importance** de moins d'importance; **I have ~ time for reading** j'ai moins de temps pour lire; **it is ~ than perfect** on ne peut pas dire que ce soit parfait; **~ than a month/a kilo** moins d'un mois/d'un kilo; **~ than you think** moins que vous ne croyez; **can't you let me have it for ~?** vous ne pouvez pas me le laisser à moins?; **no ~ a person than** rien moins que; **he's bought a car, no ~*** il s'est payé une voiture, s'il vous plaît*; **no ~ than 4 months' holiday** au moins 4 mois de vacances; **the ~ said about it the better** mieux vaut ne pas en parler; **the ~ you buy the ~ you spend** moins vous achetez moins vous dépensez; **he's nothing ~ than a thief** il n'est rien moins qu'un voleur; **nothing ~ than a bomb would move them** il faudrait au moins une bombe pour les faire bouger; **it's nothing ~ than disgraceful** le moins qu'on puisse dire, c'est que c'est une honte.
2 *adv* moins. **you must eat ~** vous devez moins manger; **to grow ~** diminuer; **~ and ~** de moins en moins; **~ often** moins souvent; **~ expensive than you think** moins cher que vous ne croyez; **the ~ you say about it the better** le moins vous en parlerez et mieux ça vaudra; **he was none the ~ pleased to see me** il n'en était pas moins content de me voir.
3 *prep* moins. **~ 10%** moins 10%.
♦ **lessen 1** *vt* (*gen*) diminuer; *cost* réduire; *anxiety, pain, effect, shock* atténuer; (*Pol*) *tension* relâcher; **2** *vi* diminuer; s'atténuer; se relâcher. ♦ **lessening** *n* diminution *f*. ♦ **lesser** *adj* moindre; **to a ~er degree** *or* **extent** à un moindre degré; **the ~er of** le *or* la moindre de.

...less [lɪs] *adj ending*: **hatless** sans chapeau; **childless** sans enfants.

lessee [le'si:] *n* preneur *m*, -euse *f* (à bail).

lesson ['lesn] *n* leçon *f* (*also fig*). **a French ~** une leçon de français; **to take/give ~s in** prendre/donner des leçons de; **we have ~s from 9 to midday** nous avons classe *or* cours de 9 heures à midi; **let that be a ~ to you!** que cela vous serve de leçon!

lest [lest] *conj* de peur *or* de crainte de +*infin*, de peur *or* de crainte que (+ne) +*subj*.

let [let] *pret, ptp* **let** *vt* **(a)** laisser (*sb do* qn faire), permettre (*sb do* à qn de faire, que qn fasse). **he wouldn't ~ us** il n'a pas voulu, il ne nous a pas permis; **to ~ sb into the house/into a secret** faire entrer qn dans la maison/dans un secret; **to ~ sb/sth past** *or* **through** laisser passer qn/qch; (*fig*) **to ~ sb off (doing) sth** dispenser qn de (faire) qch; **don't ~ me forget** rappelle-moi; **don't ~ the fire go out** ne laisse pas s'éteindre le feu; **~ me have a look** laissez-moi regarder, faites voir; **when can you ~ me have it?** quand est-ce que je pourrai l'avoir?; **~ him have it** donnez-le-lui; **~ him be!** laisse-le tranquille!; **just you ~ me catch you stealing again*** que je t'y prenne encore à voler; **I ~ myself be persuaded** je me suis laissé convaincre; **to ~ a window into a wall** percer une fenêtre dans un mur; **~ alone** (*used as conj*) *V* **alone**. **(b)** (*in verb forms*) **~ us** *or* **~'s go** allons; **~'s sit down** asseyons-nous; **~ me think** laissez-moi réfléchir; **don't ~ me keep you** que je ne vous retienne pas; **~ him come himself** qu'il vienne lui-même; **~ that be a warning to you** que cela vous serve d'avertissement; **just ~ them try!** qu'ils essaient (*subj*) un peu!; **~ x equal 2** soit x égal à 2. **(c)** (*hire out*) *house etc* louer, mettre en location. **'to ~'** à louer'.

let away *vt sep* (*allow to leave*) laisser partir. (*fig*) **you can't ~ him away with that!** tu ne peux pas le laisser s'en tirer comme ça!

let down *vt sep* **(a)** *window* baisser; *dress* rallonger; *hem* lâcher; *tyre* dégonfler; (*on rope etc*) *person, object* descendre. (*fig*) **he ~ me down gently** il n'a pas été trop sévère avec moi. **(b)** (*fail*) **to ~ sb down** (*gen*) décevoir qn; *[car, watch]* jouer des tours à qn; **don't ~ us down** nous comptons sur vous; **the weather ~ us down** le beau temps n'a pas été de la partie.

let in 1 *vi [shoes, tent]* prendre l'eau; *[roof]*

laisser entrer la pluie. **2** *vt sep person, cat* faire entrer, laisser entrer; *light, rain* laisser entrer. **can you ~ him in?** pouvez-vous lui ouvrir?; **he ~ himself in with a key** il est entré avec une clef; (*fig*) **to ~ sb in for (doing) sth** entraîner qn à (faire) qch; **you don't know what you're ~ting yourself in for** tu ne sais pas à quoi tu t'engages; **to ~ sb in on sth** mettre qn au courant de qch.
let off *vt sep* **(a)** (*explode etc*) *bomb* faire éclater; *firework, firearm* faire partir. **(b)** (*release*) *gas etc* dégager, lâcher. **(c)** (*allow to leave*) *pupils etc* laisser partir. **if you don't want to do it, I'll ~ you off** si tu ne veux pas le faire, je t'en dispense. **(d)** (*not punish*) ne pas punir, faire grâce à. **he ~ me off with a warning** il m'a seulement donné un avertissement; **to ~ sb off lightly** laisser qn s'en tirer à bon compte. **(e)** *rooms etc* louer.
let on* **1** *vi* (*acknowledge*) dire. **I won't ~ on** je ne dirai rien, je garderai ça pour moi. **2** *vt sep* (*acknowledge*) dire, aller raconter (*that* que); (*pretend*) prétendre, raconter (*that* que).
let out *vt sep* **(a)** *person, cat* faire *or* laisser sortir; *prisoner* relâcher; *sheep, cattle* faire sortir (*of* de); *caged bird* lâcher; *water* vider; *fire, candle* laisser s'éteindre; *secret, news* laisser échapper, révéler. **I'll ~ you out** je vais vous ouvrir la porte; **to ~ o.s. out** sortir; **can you ~ yourself out?** vous m'excuserez de ne pas vous reconduire?; **to ~ the air out of a tyre** dégonfler un pneu; **his alibi ~s him out** son alibi le met hors de cause. **(b)** *shout, cry* laisser échapper; *laugh* avoir. **(c)** *dress* élargir; *seam* lâcher; *belt* desserrer. **(d)** *house etc* louer.
let up **1** *vi [rain]* diminuer; *[cold weather]* s'adoucir; *[worker, talker]* s'arrêter (un moment). **2** *vt sep* (*allow to rise*) **to ~ sb up** permettre à qn de se lever.
♦ **let-down*** *n* déception *f*. ♦ **letting** *n [house etc]* location *f*. ♦ **let-up*** *n* (*decrease*) diminution *f*; (*stop*) arrêt *m*; (*respite*) répit *m*.
lethal ['li:θəl] *adj poison, blow* mortel; *effect* fatal; *weapon* meurtrier. **this coffee's ~!*** ce café est atroce!*
lethargy ['leθədʒɪ] *n* léthargie *f*. ♦ **lethargic** [le'θɑ:dʒɪk] *adj* léthargique.
letter ['letə^r] **1** *n* **(a)** (*of alphabet*) lettre *f*. **the ~ L** la lettre L; **in ~s** en lettres; **he's got a lot of ~s after his name*** il a des tas* de diplômes (*or* de décorations *etc*); (*fig*) **the ~ of the law** la lettre de la loi; **to follow sth to the ~** suivre qch à la lettre. **(b)** (*written communication*) lettre *f*. **were there any ~s for me?** y avait-il du courrier *or* des lettres pour moi?; **he was invited by ~** il a reçu une invitation écrite; **~ of introduction** lettre de recommandation. **(c)** (*learning*) **man of ~s** homme *m* de lettres. **2** *vt* (*put ~ on*) inscrire des lettres sur; (*engrave*) graver (des lettres sur).
♦ **letter-bomb** *n* lettre *f* piégée. ♦ **letterbox** *n* boîte *f* à lettres. ♦ **letter-card** *n* carte-lettre *f*. ♦ **letterhead** *n* en-tête *m*. ♦ **lettering** *n* (*engraving*) gravure *f*; (*letters*) caractères *mpl*. ♦ **letter-opener** *n* coupe-papier *m inv*. ♦ **letter-paper** *n* papier *m* à lettres. ♦ **letter-perfect** *adj*: **to be ~-perfect in sth** savoir qch sur le bout du doigt. ♦ **letterpress** *n* (*method*) typographie *f*; (*text*) texte *m* imprimé. ♦ **letter-writer** *n* correspondant(e) *m(f)*.
lettuce ['letɪs] *n* laitue *f*; (*Culin*) laitue, salade *f*.
leuk(a)emia [lu:'ki:mɪə] *n* leucémie *f*.
level ['levl] **1** *n* **(a)** niveau *m*. **at roof ~** au niveau du toit; **to find one's own ~** trouver son niveau; **he came down to their ~** il s'est mis à leur niveau; **it is on a ~ with** (*lit*) c'est du niveau de, c'est à la hauteur de; (*fig*) ça vaut bien; **top-~ talks** conférence *f* au sommet; **at departmental/ministerial ~** à l'échelon départemental/ministériel. **(b)** (*Aut, Rail*) palier *m*. **speed on the ~** vitesse *f* en palier; (*fig*) **is this on the ~?*** est-ce qu'il joue franc jeu? **(c)** (*spirit ~*) niveau *m* à bulle d'air. **(d)** (*flat place*) terrain *m* plat.
2 *adj* **(a)** (*flat*) *surface, ground* plat, uni; *tray* horizontal. (*Brit Rail*) **~ crossing** passage *m* à niveau; **a ~ spoonful** une cuillerée rase; **to do one's ~ best*** faire tout son possible (*to do* pour faire). **(b)** (*equal*) *contestants* à égalité. **to be ~ with** (*in race*) être à la même hauteur que; (*in league*) être à égalité avec; (*in studies, achievements*) être au même niveau que; (*in salary, rank*) être au même échelon que; **to draw ~ with** arriver à la même hauteur *etc* que; **~ with the ground** au niveau du sol. **(c)** (*steady*) *voice, tones* calme, assuré; *judgment* sain. **to keep a ~ head** garder tout son sang-froid.
3 *vt* **(a)** (*make level*) *site, ground* niveler, aplanir; *quantities* répartir également; (*demolish*) *building, town* raser. **(b)** (*aim*) *blow* allonger (*at sb* à qn); *gun* braquer (*at sb* sur qn); *accusation* lancer (*at sb* contre qn).
4 *vi* **(a)** (**~ off**) *[curve on graph, prices etc]* se stabiliser; *[aircraft]* amorcer le vol en palier. **(b)** (*US*) **to ~ with sb*** être franc avec qn.
♦ **level-headed** *adj* équilibré. ♦ **levelling** *adj effect, process* de nivellement.
lever ['li:və^r] **1** *n* (*lit, fig*) levier *m*. **2** *vt*: **to ~ sth out/up** extraire/soulever qch au moyen d'un levier. ♦ **leverage** *n* force *f* (de levier); (*fig: influence*) influence *f* (*on or with sb* sur qn).
levity ['levɪtɪ] *n* manque *m* de sérieux.
levy ['levɪ] **1** *n* (*act, amount*) taxation *f*; (*tax*) impôt *m*, taxe *f*. **2** *vt* **(a)** (*impose*) *tax* prélever, mettre (*on sth* sur qch); *fine* imposer (*on sb* à qn). **(b)** (*collect*) *contributions* percevoir.
lewd [lu:d] *adj* lubrique. ♦ **lewdness** *n* lubricité *f*.
lexical ['leksɪkəl] *adj* lexical.
lexicography [ˌleksɪ'kɒgrəfɪ] *n* lexicographie *f*. ♦ **lexicographer** *n* lexicographe *mf*.
lexicology [ˌleksɪ'kɒlədʒɪ] *n* lexicologie *f*. ♦ **lexicologist** *n* lexicologue *mf*.
lexicon ['leksɪkən] *n* lexique *m*.
liable ['laɪəbl] *adj* **(a)** (*likely*) **it's ~ to explode** cela risque d'exploser; **he's ~ to refuse** il est possible qu'il refuse (*subj*); **we are ~ to get shot at** on risque de se faire tirer dessus; **it's ~ to be hot** il se peut qu'il fasse très chaud. **(b)** (*to illness, tax*) sujet (*to* à); (*to fine*) passible (*to* de). **~ for military service** astreint au service militaire. **(c)** (*responsible*) (civilement) responsable (*for* de).
♦ **liability** *n* (*for accident etc*) responsabilité *f* (*for* de); (*handicap*) handicap *m*; (*person*) poids *m* mort; **liabilities** (*debts*) engagements *mpl*; (*Bookkeeping*) passif *m*.
liaison [li:'eɪzɒn] **1** *n* liaison *f*. **2** *adj committee, officer* de liaison.
liar ['laɪə^r] *n* menteur *m*, -euse *f*.
lib* [lɪb] *n abbr of* **liberation.**
libel ['laɪbəl] **1** *n* diffamation *f* (par écrit). **2** *adj laws* contre la diffamation. **~ proceedings** *or* **suit** procès *m* en diffamation. **3** *vt* (*Jur*) diffamer (par écrit); (*gen*) calomnier, médire de. ♦ **libellous,** (*US*) **libelous** *adj* diffamatoire.
liberal ['lɪbərəl] **1** *adj* (*all senses*) libéral (*with* de). **2** *n* (*Pol*) **L~** libéral(e) *m(f)*. ♦ **liberalism** *n* libéralisme *m*. ♦ **liberality** *n* (*broad-mindedness*) libéralisme *m*; (*generosity*) libéralité *f*. ♦ **liberally** *adv* libéralement.
liberate ['lɪbəreɪt] *vt* libérer. ♦ **liberation** *n* libération *f*. ♦ **liberator** *n* libérateur *m*, -trice *f*.
liberty ['lɪbətɪ] *n* liberté *f*. **at ~** (*not detained*) en liberté; (*not busy*) libre; **at ~ to choose** libre de choisir; **~ of the press** liberté de la presse; **to take liberties** se permettre des libertés (*with* avec); **to take the ~ of doing** se permettre de faire.
libido [lɪ'bi:dəʊ] *n* libido *f*.
Libra ['li:brə] *n* (*Astron*) la Balance.
library ['laɪbrərɪ] **1** *n* bibliothèque *f*. **2** *adj book* de

bibliothèque. ~ **ticket** carte *f* de lecteur. ♦ **librarian** *n* bibliothécaire *mf.* ♦ **librarianship** *n* bibliothéconomie *f.*

libretto [lɪ'bretəʊ] *n* libretto *m,* livret *m.* ♦ **librettist** *n* librettiste *mf.*

Libya ['lɪbɪə] *n* Libye *f.*

lice [laɪs] *npl of* **louse.**

licence ['laɪsəns] **1** *n* **(a)** (*permit*) autorisation *f,* permis *m;* (*for manufacturing, trading*) licence *f;* (*Aut*) (*for driver*) permis; (*for car*) vignette *f;* (*for radio, TV set*) redevance *f.* **driving/export** ~ permis de conduire/d'exporter; **pilot's** ~ brevet *m* de pilote; **married by special** ~ marié avec dispense de bans; **to manufacture under** ~ fabriquer sous licence. **(b)** (*freedom*) liberté *f.* **poetic** ~ licence *f* poétique. **2** *adj [car]* ~ **plate/number** plaque *f*/numéro *m* minéralogique *or* d'immatriculation. ♦ **licentious** *adj* licencieux.

license ['laɪsəns] **1** *n* (*US*) = **licence. 2** *vt* **(a)** (*give licence to*) donner une licence à; *car [licensing authority]* délivrer la vignette de, *[owner]* acheter la vignette de *or* pour. **to be ~d to sell tobacco** détenir une licence de bureau de tabac; **on ~d premises** dans un établissement ayant une licence de débit de boissons. **(b)** (*allow*) autoriser (*sb to do* qn à faire). ♦ **licensee** *n [pub]* patron(ne) *m(f).*

lick [lɪk] **1** *n* **(a)** coup *m* de langue. **to give o.s. a ~ and a promise*** faire un petit brin de toilette; **a ~ of paint** un petit coup de peinture. **(b)** (*speed*) **at full ~*** en quatrième vitesse*. **2** *vt* **(a)** (*gen*) lécher. **to ~ one's lips** se lécher les lèvres; (*fig*) se frotter les mains (*fig*); **to ~ sth clean/off** *etc* nettoyer/enlever *etc* qch à coups de langue; (*fig*) **to ~ sb's boots** jouer les lèche-bottes* envers qn; (*fig*) **to ~ one's wounds** panser ses blessures (*fig*). **(b)** (*) (*defeat*) battre à plates coutures; (*outdo*) battre; (*thrash*) rosser. ♦ **licking*** *n* (*whipping*) rossée* *f;* (*defeat*) déculottée: *f.*

lid [lɪd] *n* (*gen*) couvercle *m;* (*eye~*) paupière *f.* (*fig*) **to take the ~ off sth** étaler qch au grand jour; **that puts the ~ on it!** ça, c'est un comble!

lido ['li:dəʊ] *n* (*resort*) complexe *m* balnéaire; (*swimming pool*) piscine *f* (*en plein air*).

lie[1] [laɪ] *pret* **lay,** *ptp* **lain** *vi* **(a)** *[person etc]* (~ **down**) s'allonger, s'étendre, se coucher; (**be lying**) être allongé *or* étendu *or* couché; *[dead body]* (*at funeral etc*) reposer; (*in grave etc*) être enterré. **he was lying on the floor** (*unable to move*) il était étendu *or* il gisait par terre; **she lay in bed until 10 o'clock** elle est restée au lit jusqu'à 10 heures; **she was lying in bed reading** elle lisait au lit; **he lay dead** il était étendu mort; **he was lying still** il était étendu immobile; ~ **still!** ne bouge pas!; **his body was lying on the ground** son corps gisait sur le sol; (*on tombstone*) **here ~s** ci-gît; (*fig*) **to ~ low** ne pas se faire remarquer; (*hide*) se cacher.

(b) (*be*) *[object]* être; *[place, road]* se trouver, être; *[land, sea etc]* s'étendre; (*remain*) rester, être. **the book lay on the table** le livre était sur la table; **the book lay unopened all day** le livre est resté fermé toute la journée; **to ~ at anchor** être à l'ancre; **the snow lay thick on the ground** il y avait une épaisse couche de neige sur le sol; **the snow will not ~** la neige ne tiendra pas; **to ~ heavy on** peser sur; **the valley lay before us** la vallée s'étendait devant nous; **the years that ~ before us** les années qui sont devant nous; **the difference ~s in the fact that ...** la différence vient de ce que ...; **the real remedy ~s in ...** le vrai remède se trouve dans ... .

lie about, lie around *vi [clothes, books]* traîner; *[person]* traînasser*.

lie back *vi* se renverser (en arrière). (*fig*) ~ **back and enjoy yourself!** laisse-toi donc vivre!

lie down *vi* s'allonger, s'étendre. **to be lying down** être allongé; (*to dog*) ~ **down!** couché!; (*fig*) **to take sth lying down** accepter qch sans protester.

lie in *vi* (*stay in bed*) faire la grasse matinée.

lie up *vi* (*stay in bed*) garder le lit; (*hide*) se cacher.

♦ **lie-down*** *n*: **to have a ~-down** s'allonger, s'étendre. ♦ **lie-in*** *n*: **to have a ~-in** faire la grasse matinée.

lie[2] [laɪ] (*vb: pret, ptp* **lied**) **1** *n* mensonge *m.* **to tell ~s** mentir, dire des mensonges; **to give the ~ to** démentir. **2** *vi* mentir. **3** *vt*: **to ~ one's way out of it** essayer de s'en sortir par des mensonges. **4** *adj*: ~ **detector** détecteur *m* de mensonges.

lieu [lu:] *n*: **in ~ of** au lieu de.

lieutenant [lef'tenənt, (*US*) lu:'tenənt] *n* (*in army*) lieutenant *m;* (*in navy*) [lə'tenənt, (*US*) lu:'tenənt] lieutenant de vaisseau; (*fig*) second *m.* ♦ **lieutenant colonel** *n* lieutenant-colonel *m.* ♦ **lieutenant general** *n* général *m* de corps d'armée.

life [laɪf] *pl* **lives 1** *n* **(a)** (*gen*) vie *f.* **animal and plant** ~ vie animale et végétale; **bird** ~ les oiseaux *mpl;* **insect** ~ les insectes *mpl;* **a matter of ~ and death** une question de vie ou de mort; **to bring sb back to** ~ ranimer qn; **to come to** ~ *[person]* reprendre conscience; *[town etc]* s'éveiller (*fig*).

(b) (*existence*) vie *f; [car, government, battery etc]* durée *f.* **he lived in France all his** ~ il a vécu toute sa vie en France; **for the rest of his** ~ pour le restant de ses jours; **to be sent to prison for ~, to get ~*** être condamné à la prison à vie; **he's doing ~*** il tire une condamnation à perpétuité; **it will last you all your** ~ cela vous durera toute votre vie; **never in all my** ~ jamais de ma vie; **in later** ~ plus tard (dans la vie); **late in** ~ sur le tard; ~ **isn't worth living** la vie ne vaut pas la peine d'être vécue; **tired of** ~ las de vivre; **to take one's (own)** ~ se donner la mort; **to take one's ~ in one's hands** jouer sa vie; **town** ~ la vie à la ville; **it's a good** ~ c'est la belle vie; **to lead a quiet** ~ mener une vie tranquille; **portrait taken from** ~ portrait d'après nature; **it was Paul to the** ~ c'était Paul tout craché*; **I couldn't for the ~ of me*** je ne pouvais absolument pas; **how's ~?*** comment ça va?*; **that's ~!** c'est la vie!; **this is the ~!*** voilà comment je comprends la vie!; **not on your ~!*** jamais de la vie!

(c) (*liveliness*) vie *f.* **full of** ~ plein de vie; **he's the ~ and soul of the party** c'est un boute-en-train; **it put new ~ into me** ça m'a fait revivre; **there isn't much ~ in our village** notre village est plutôt mort.

2 *adj*: ~ **cycle** cycle *m* de (la) vie; ~ **expectancy** espérance *f* de vie; **the ~ force** la force vitale; ~ **imprisonment** prison *f* à vie; ~ **insurance** assurance-vie *f;* ~ **peer/peerage** pair *m*/pairie *f* à vie; ~ **raft** radeau *m* de sauvetage; ~ **sentence** condamnation *f* à perpétuité; ~ **span** durée *f* *or* espérance *f* de vie; ~ **story** biographie *f;* ~ **style** style *m* de vie.

♦ **life-and-death** *adj*: **~-and-death struggle** lutte *f* désespérée. ♦ **lifebelt** *n* bouée *f* de sauvetage. ♦ **lifeblood** *n* élément *m* vital. ♦ **lifeboat** *n* (*shore*) canot *m* de sauvetage; (*from ship*) chaloupe *f* de sauvetage. ♦ **lifebuoy** *n* bouée *f* de sauvetage. ♦ **life-giving** *adj* vivifiant. ♦ **lifeguard** *n* (*on beach*) surveillant *m* de plage *or* de baignade. ♦ **life-jacket** *or* ♦ **life-vest** *n* gilet *m* de sauvetage. ♦ **lifeless** *adj body, matter* inanimé; (*fig*) *style* sans vigueur. ♦ **lifelessness** *n* (*fig*) manque *m* de vigueur. ♦ **lifelike** *adj* qui semble vivant *or* vrai. ♦ **lifeline** *n* (*on ship*) main *f* courante; (*for diver*) corde *f* de sécurité; (*fig*) **it was his ~line** c'était vital pour lui. ♦ **lifelong** *adj ambition* de toute ma (*or* sa *etc*) vie; *friend, friendship* de toujours; *task* de toute une vie. ♦ **life-saver** *n* (*person*) surveillant(e) *m(f)* de baignade; (*fig*) **that money was a ~-saver** cet argent m'a (*or* lui a *etc*) sauvé la vie. ♦ **life-saving 1** *n* (*rescuing*) sauvetage *m*; (*first aid*) secourisme *m*; **2** *adj* de sauvetage. ♦ **life-sized** *adj* grandeur nature *inv*. ♦ **lifetime** *n* vie *f*; **not in my ~time** pas de mon vivant; **once in a ~time** une fois dans la vie; **the work of a ~time** l'œuvre de toute une vie; **it seemed a ~time** cela a semblé une éternité. ♦ **lifework** *n* œuvre *f* de toute une (*or* ma *etc*) vie.

lift [lɪft] **1** *n* **(a)** (*Brit*) (*elevator*) ascenseur *m*; (*for goods*) monte-charge *m inv*. **(b) can I give you a ~?** est-ce que je peux vous déposer quelque part?; **I gave him a ~ to Paris** je l'ai emmené (en voiture) jusqu'à Paris; **he was hoping for a ~** il espérait être pris en stop. **(c) to give sb/sth a ~ up** soulever qn/qch; (*fig*) **to give sb a ~** remonter le moral à *or* de qn.

2 *vt* (*gen*) lever, soulever; (*fig*) *restrictions* supprimer, abolir; *ban, blockade, siege* lever; (*: *steal*) chiper*; *quotation, idea* prendre, voler (*from sb* à qn). **to ~ sth into the air** lever qch en l'air; **to ~ sb/sth onto a table** soulever qn/qch pour le poser sur une table; **to ~ sb over a wall** faire passer qn par-dessus un mur; **he didn't ~ a finger to help** il n'a pas levé le petit doigt pour aider.

3 *vi* [*lid etc*] se soulever; [*fog*] se lever.

lift down *vt sep* descendre (*from* de).

lift off 1 *vi* (*Space*) décoller. **2** *vt sep lid* enlever; *child* descendre.

lift out *vt sep object* sortir; *troops* évacuer par avion (*or* hélicoptère).

lift up 1 *vi* [*drawbridge etc*] se soulever. **2** *vt sep object, person* soulever; *one's eyes, head* lever.

♦ **liftboy** *or* ♦ **liftman** *n* (*Brit*) liftier *m*. ♦ **lift-off** *n* (*Space*) décollage *m*.

light[1] [laɪt] (*vb: pret, ptp* **lit** *or* **lighted**) **1** *n* **(a)** (*gen*) lumière *f*. **electric ~** éclairage *m or* lumière électrique; **to put on the ~** allumer; **to put off the ~** éteindre; **by the ~ of** à la lumière de; **at first ~** au point du jour; **the ~ was beginning to fail** le jour commençait à baisser; **she was sitting with her back to the ~** elle tournait le dos à la lumière; **to stand sth in the ~** mettre qch à la lumière; **you're holding it against the ~** vous le tenez à contre-jour; **you're in my ~** tu me fais de l'ombre; **the ~ isn't good enough** il n'y a pas assez de lumière; (*Art, Phot*) **~ and shade** les clairs *mpl* et les ombres *fpl*; (*fig: understand*) **to see the ~*** comprendre. **(b)** (*fig*) **to bring to ~** mettre en lumière, révéler; **to come to ~** être découvert; **to throw some ~ on sth** éclaircir qch; **it revealed him in a new ~** cela l'a montré sous un jour nouveau; **in the ~ of what you say** tenant compte de ce que vous dites. **(c)** (*single*) lumière *f*; (*Aut*) (*gen*) feu *m*, (*headlamp*) phare *m*; [*cycle*] feu. **there were ~s on in the room** il y avait de la lumière dans la pièce; **~s out** extinction *f* des feux; **the (traffic) ~s were at red** le feu était (au) rouge; (*fig*) **according to his ~s** d'après ce qu'il comprend. **(d)** (*for cigarette etc*) **have you got a ~?** avez-vous du feu?; **to put a ~ to sth, to set ~ to sth** mettre le feu à qch.

2 *adj* **(a)** *evening, room* clair. **while it's ~** pendant qu'il fait jour. **(b)** *hair* blond; *colour, complexion, skin* clair. **~ green** vert clair *inv*. **(c) ~ bulb** ampoule *f*, lampe *f*; (*Phot*) **~ meter** photomètre *m*; **~ wave** onde *f* lumineuse.

3 *vt* **(a)** *candle, cigarette, gas* allumer; *match* frotter. **he lit the fire** il a allumé le feu; **he lit a fire** il a fait du feu. **(b)** *room* éclairer. **lit by electricity** éclairé à l'électricité; **this will ~ your way** ceci vous éclairera le chemin.

4 *vi* [*match*] s'allumer; [*coal, wood*] prendre (feu).

light up 1 *vi* [*lamp*] s'allumer; [*eyes, face*] s'éclairer; (*: *smoke*) allumer une cigarette (*or* une pipe *etc*). **2** *vt sep* [*lighting, sun*] *room* éclairer.

♦ **light-coloured** *adj* clair, de couleur claire. ♦ **lighten[1] 1** *vt darkness, face* éclairer; *colour, hair* éclaircir; **2** *vi* s'éclairer; s'éclaircir. ♦ **lighter 1** *n* (*cigarette ~*) briquet *m*; **2** *adj*: **~er fuel** gaz *m* à briquet. ♦ **light-haired** *adj* blond. ♦ **lighthouse** *n* phare *m* (*sur la côte etc*). ♦ **lighting 1** *n* (*Elec etc*) éclairage *m*; (*Theat*) éclairages; **2** *adj*: **~ing engineer** éclairagiste *m*; **~ing-up time** heure *f* de l'éclairage des véhicules. ♦ **lightness[1]** *n* (*brightness*) clarté *f*. ♦ **lightship** *n* bateau-phare *m*. ♦ **light-year** *n* année-lumière *f*.

light[2] [laɪt] **1** *adj* (*gen: lit, fig*) léger; *rain* fin. **as ~ as a feather** léger comme une plume; **to be ~ on one's feet** avoir le pas léger; **to be a ~ sleeper** avoir le sommeil léger; **~ ale** bière *f* blonde légère; **~ opera** opérette *f*; **~ reading** lecture *f* distrayante; **~ verse** poésie *f* légère; **with a ~ heart** le cœur léger; **'woman wanted for ~ work'** 'on demande employée de maison pour travaux légers'; **to make ~ work of sth** faire qch sans difficulté; **to make ~ of sth** prendre qch à la légère. **2** *adv travel* avec peu de bagages. **3** *npl* (*meat*) **~s** mou *m* (*abats*). ♦ **lighten[2]** *vt* alléger. ♦ **light-fingered** *adj* chapardeur. ♦ **light-headed** *adj* (*dizzy, foolish*) étourdi; (*excited*) exalté. ♦ **light-hearted** *adj person* gai; *laugh, atmosphere* joyeux, gai; *discussion* enjoué. ♦ **lightly** *adv* (*gen*) légèrement; **to sleep ~ly** avoir le sommeil léger; **to get off ~ly** s'en tirer à bon compte. ♦ **lightness[2]** *n* (*in weight*) légèreté *f*. ♦ **lightweight** *adj* (*lit, fig*) léger.

lightning ['laɪtnɪŋ] **1** *n* éclair *m*, foudre *f*. **we saw ~** nous avons vu un éclair *or* des éclairs; **a lot of ~** beaucoup d'éclairs; **a flash of ~** un éclair; **struck by ~** frappé par la foudre; **like ~*** avec la vitesse de l'éclair.

2 *adj attack* foudroyant; *strike* surprise *inv*; *visit* éclair *inv*. **~ conductor**, (*US*) **~ rod** paratonnerre *m*.

like[1] [laɪk] **1** *adj* semblable, du même genre. **to be as ~ as two peas** se ressembler comme deux gouttes d'eau.

2 *prep* **(a)** comme, en. **he behaved ~ a fool** il s'est conduit comme un imbécile *or* en imbécile; **it wasn't ~ that at all** ce n'était pas du tout comme ça; **it was ~ this, I'd just got home ...** voilà, je venais de rentrer ... . **(b)** (*resembling*) comme, pareil à. **to be ~ sb/sth** ressembler à qn/qch; **a house ~ mine** une maison pareille à *or* comme la mienne; **an idiot ~ you** un imbécile comme vous; **~ father, ~ son** tel père, tel fils; **I found one ~ it** j'en ai trouvé un pareil; **I never saw anything ~ it!** je n'ai jamais rien vu de pareil!; **that's just ~ him!** c'est bien de lui!; **it's not ~ him to be late** ça n'est pas son genre d'être en retard; **sth ~ that** qch comme ça*; **I was thinking of giving her sth ~ a necklace** je pensais lui offrir un collier ou qch dans ce genre-là; **that's sth ~ a steak!*** voilà ce que j'appelle un bifteck!; **that's more ~ it!** voilà qui est mieux!; **that's nothing ~ it!** ça n'est pas du tout ça!; **there's nothing ~ real silk** rien ne vaut la soie véritable; **what's he ~?** comment est-il?; **what's the film ~?** comment as-tu trouvé le film?; **what's the weather ~?** quel temps fait-il? **(c)** (*such as*) comme, tel que, par exemple. **the basic necessities of life, ~ food and drink** les éléments indispensables à la vie, tels que *or* comme la nourriture et la boisson.

3 *adv*: **it's nothing ~ as good as ...** c'est loin d'être aussi bon que ... ; **more ~ 30 than 25** plutôt 30 que 25; **~ enough, as ~ as not, very ~** probablement.

4 *conj* (*: *as*) comme. **he did it ~ I did** il l'a fait comme moi.

5 *n*: **did you ever see the ~ of it?** a-t-on jamais vu chose pareille?; **oranges, lemons and the ~** *or*

and such ~ des oranges, des citrons et autres fruits de ce genre; **the** ~ **of which we'll never see again** comme on n'en reverra plus jamais; **his** ~ son pareil; **the** ~**s of him*** des gens comme lui.
♦ **like-minded** *adj* de même opinion. ♦ **liken** *vt* comparer (*to* à). ♦ **likeness** *n* **(a)** (*resemblance*) ressemblance *f* (*to* avec; *between* entre); **a family** ~**ness** un air de famille marqué; **it is a good** ~**ness** c'est très ressemblant; **(b)** (*appearance*) forme *f*; **in the** ~**ness of** sous la forme de.
♦ **likewise** *adv* (*similarly*) de même; (*also*) aussi; (*moreover*) de plus; **to do** ~**wise** en faire autant.

like[2] [laɪk] **1** *vt* **(a)** *person, thing, activity* aimer (bien). **I** ~ **him** (*of relative, friend*) je l'aime bien; (*of acquaintance, colleague etc*) il me plaît; **I** ~ **that hat** j'aime bien ce chapeau, ce chapeau me plaît; **which do you** ~ **best?** lequel préfères-tu?; **this plant doesn't** ~ **sunlight** cette plante ne se plaît pas à la lumière du soleil; **to** ~ **doing** *or* **to do sth** aimer (bien) faire qch; **I** ~ **people to be punctual** j'aime (bien) que les gens soient à l'heure; (*iro*) **well, I** ~ **that!*** ah ça, par exemple!; **how do you** ~ **him?** comment le trouvez-vous?; **how do you** ~ **it here?** vous vous plaisez ici?; **whether he** ~**s it or not** que cela lui plaise ou non.

(b) (*want*) aimer (bien), vouloir (*to do* faire, *sb to do* que qn fasse). **I should** ~ **to go home** j'aimerais (bien) *or* je voudrais (bien) rentrer chez moi; **I didn't** ~ **to disturb you** je ne voulais pas vous déranger; **I thought of asking him but I didn't** ~ **to** j'ai bien pensé à le lui demander mais je n'ai pas osé; **would you** ~ **a drink?** voulez-vous boire qch?; **I would** ~ **you to speak to him** je voudrais que tu lui parles (*subj*); **how would you** ~ **to go to Paris?** est-ce que cela te plairait d'aller à Paris?; **I can do it when I** ~ je peux le faire quand je veux; **whenever you** ~ quand vous voudrez; **you can do as you** ~ vous pouvez faire comme vous voulez; **if you** ~ si vous voulez; **she can do what she** ~**s with him** elle fait tout ce qu'elle veut de lui.

2 *n*: ~**s** goûts *mpl*, préférences *fpl*; **all my** ~**s and dislikes** tout ce que j'aime et tout ce que je n'aime pas.

♦ **likeable** *adj* sympathique, agréable. ♦ **liking** *n* (*for person*) sympathie *f* (*for* pour); (*for thing*) goût *m* (*for* pour); **to take a liking to sb** se prendre d'amitié pour qn; **to take a liking to (doing) sth** se mettre à aimer (faire) qch; **to have a liking for sb/sth** aimer bien qn/qch; **to your liking** à votre goût.

likely ['laɪklɪ] **1** *adj* **(a)** *happening, outcome* probable; *explanation, excuse* plausible. **which is the likeliest time to find him at home?** à quelle heure a-t-on le plus de chances de le trouver chez lui?; **a** ~ **place for mushrooms** un bon endroit pour les champignons; **the likeliest place** le meilleur endroit; (*iro*) **a** ~ **story!** comme si j'allais croire ça!; **the most** ~ **candidates** les candidats qui ont le plus de chances de réussir; **it is** ~ **that** il est probable que + *fut indic*, il y a des chances pour que + *subj*; **it is not** ~ **that** il est peu probable que + *subj*, il y a peu de chances que + *subj*; **it is very** ~ **that** il y a de grandes chances que + *subj*; **it's hardly** ~ **that** il n'est guère probable que + *subj*; **is it** ~ **that he would forget?** risque-t-il d'oublier? **(b)** (*liable*) **to be** ~ **to do** avoir des chances de faire, risquer de faire; **she is** ~ **to arrive at any time** elle va probablement arriver *or* elle risque d'arriver d'une minute à l'autre; **she is not** ~ **to come** il est peu probable *or* il y a peu de chances qu'elle vienne; **the man most** ~ **to succeed** l'homme qui a le plus de chances de réussir.

2 *adv* probablement. **very** *or* **most** ~ très probablement; **as** ~ **as not** sûrement, probablement; **are you going? – not** ~! tu y vas? – pas de danger!*; **I expect he'll let me off with a warning** – (*iro*) **not** ~! je pense qu'il me laissera m'en tirer avec un avertissement – tu crois ça!

♦ **likelihood** *n* probabilité *f*, chance *f*; **there is little likelihood of his coming** *or* **that he will come** il y a peu de chances *or* il est peu probable qu'il vienne; **there is a strong likelihood of his coming** *or* **that he will come** il y a de fortes chances pour qu'il vienne, il est très probable qu'il viendra; **there is no likelihood of that** cela ne risque pas d'arriver; **in all likelihood** selon toute probabilité.

lilac ['laɪlək] **1** *n* lilas *m*. **2** *adj* (*colour*) lilas *inv*.

lilt [lɪlt] *n* [*song*] rythme *m*; [*voice*] cadence *f*.

lily ['lɪlɪ] *n* lis *m*. ~ **of the valley** muguet *m*.

limb [lɪm] *n* (*gen*) membre *m*; [*tree*] grosse branche *f*. **to tear** ~ **from** ~ mettre en pièces; (*fig*) **out on a** ~ (*isolated*) isolé; (*vulnerable*) dans une situation délicate.

limber ['lɪmbəʳ] *adj* souple.
limber up *vi* (*Sport etc*) faire des exercices d'assouplissement.

lime[1] [laɪm] *n* (*Chem*) chaux *f*. ♦ **limestone** *n* pierre *f* à chaux.

lime[2] [laɪm] *n* citron *m* vert.

lime[3] [laɪm] *n* (*tree*) tilleul *m*.

limelight ['laɪmlaɪt] *n*: **in the** ~ (*Theat*) sous les feux de la rampe; (*fig*) en vedette.

limerick ['lɪmərɪk] *n* petit poème *m* humoristique.

limit ['lɪmɪt] **1** *n* (*gen*) limite *f*; (*restriction on amount, number etc*) limitation *f*. **it is true within** ~**s** c'est vrai dans une certaine limite *or* mesure; **weight/speed** ~ limitation de poids/de vitesse; (*US*) **off** ~**s** d'accès interdit; **there is a** ~ **to my patience** ma patience a des limites *or* des bornes; **there are** ~**s!*** il y a une limite à tout!; **there is no** ~ **on the amount** la quantité n'est pas limitée; **there is a** ~ **to what one can do** il y a une limite à ce qu'on peut faire; **that's the** ~!* ça dépasse les bornes!

2 *vt* limiter (*to* à). **to** ~ **o.s. to (doing) sth** se borner à (faire) qch; **to** ~ **o.s. to 10 cigarettes** se limiter à 10 cigarettes; **that plant is** ~**ed to Spain** cette plante ne se trouve qu'en Espagne; **our reorganization plans are** ~**ed to Africa** nos projets de réorganisation se limitent à l'Afrique.

♦ **limitation** *n* limitation *f*, restriction *f*; **he has/knows his** ~**ations** il a/connaît ses limites. ♦ **limited** *adj* (*gen*) restreint, limité; *edition* à tirage limité; (*pej*) *intelligence, person* borné; **to a** ~**ed extent** jusqu'à un certain point; **we are** ~**ed in what we can do** nous sommes limités dans ce que nous pouvons faire; **Smith and Sons L**~**ed** (*abbr* **Ltd**) ≃ Smith et fils, Société anonyme (*abbr* S.A.); ~**ed (liability) company** société *f* à responsabilité limitée. ♦ **limitless** *adj* illimité.

limp[1] [lɪmp] *adj* (*gen*) mou (*f* molle); *person* ramolli; *flesh, skin, body* flasque; *dress, hat* avachi. [*book*] ~ **cover(s)** reliure *f* souple; **let your arm go** ~ décontractez votre bras. ♦ **limply** *adv* mollement. ♦ **limpness** *n* mollesse *f*.

limp[2] [lɪmp] **1** *vi* boiter. **to** ~ **in/out** *etc* entrer/sortir *etc* en boitant; **the plane** ~**ed home** l'avion a regagné sa base tant bien que mal. **2** *n* claudication *f*. **to have a** ~ boiter.

limpet ['lɪmpɪt] *n* patelle *f*. **to stick to sth like a** ~ s'accrocher à qch comme une moule au rocher.

limpid ['lɪmpɪd] *adj* (*lit, fig*) limpide.

line[1] [laɪn] **1** *n* **(a)** (*mark: gen*) ligne *f*; (*pen stroke*) trait *m*; (*wrinkle*) ride *f*; (*boundary*) frontière *f*. **to draw a** ~ **under sth** tirer un trait sous qch; **to put a** ~ **through sth** barrer qch; (*descent*) **in direct** ~ **from** en droite ligne de; **he comes from a long** ~ **of artists** il vient d'une longue lignée d'artistes; (*Bridge*) **above/below the** ~ en points d'honneur/de marche.

(b) (*rope*) corde *f*; (*wire*) fil *m*; (*Elec, Fishing, Telec*) ligne *f*; (*diver's; clothes* ~) corde. **a** ~ **of washing** du linge étendu sur une corde; (*Telec*) **the** ~**'s gone dead** (*cut off*) on nous a coupés; (*no* *dialling tone*) il n'y a plus de tonalité; **Mr Smith is on the** ~ (c'est) M. Smith au téléphone; **he's on the** ~ **to the manager** il téléphone au directeur.

(c) *[print, writing]* ligne *f*; *[poem]* vers *m*; (*: *letter*) mot *m*. (*fig*) **to read between the** ~**s** lire entre les lignes; (*in dictation*) **new** ~ à la ligne; **one of the best** ~**s in 'Hamlet'** l'un des meilleurs vers de 'Hamlet'; (*Theat*) **to learn one's** ~**s** apprendre son texte; **drop me a** ~ envoyez-moi un mot.

(d) (*row*) *[trees, parked cars]* rangée *f*; *[traffic etc]* file *f*; *[hills]* chaîne *f*; *[people]* (*side by side*) rang *m*, rangée; (*behind one another*) file; (*esp US: queue*) queue *f*. (*US*) **to stand in** ~ faire la queue; **they were standing in a** ~ ils étaient alignés; **he got into** ~ (*beside others*) il s'est mis dans le rang; (*behind others*) il s'est mis dans la file; (*fig*) **to bring sb into** ~ mettre qn au pas; (*fig*) **to come** *or* **fall into** ~ se conformer (*with sth* à qch), tomber d'accord (*with sb* avec qn); (*fig*) **he stepped out of** ~ il a refusé de se conformer; (*fig*) **all along the** ~ sur toute la ligne.

(e) (*direction*) ligne *f*, direction *f*. ~ **of fire** ligne de tir; **right in the** ~ **of fire** en plein champ de tir; **to take the** ~ **of least resistance** choisir la solution de facilité; **in the** ~ **of duty** dans l'exercice de ses fonctions; ~ **of attack** (*Mil*) plan *m* d'attaque; (*fig*) plan d'action; ~ **of research** ligne de recherches; **what's your** ~ **of business?** que faites-vous (dans la vie)?; **it's not my** ~ (*not my speciality*) ce n'est pas dans mes cordes; (*not to my taste*) ce n'est pas mon genre; **to take a strong** ~ **on** adopter une attitude ferme sur; **in** ~ **with** en accord avec, conforme à; **he's in** ~ **for the job** on pense à lui pour le poste; **we are all thinking along the same** ~**s** nous pensons tous de la même façon; **your essay is more or less along the same** ~**s** votre dissertation suit plus ou moins le même plan; **sth along those** ~**s** qch dans ce genre-là; **on the right** ~**s** sur la bonne voie.

(f) (*) (*information*) renseignement *m* (*on sth* sur qch); (*clue*) tuyau* *m* (*on sth* pour qch). **we've got a** ~ **on where he's gone to** nous croyons savoir où il est allé.

(g) (*shipping company*) compagnie *f*; (*route*) ligne *f*; (*Rail; also Underground*) ligne; (*track*) voie *f*. **the Brighton** ~ la ligne de Brighton; **the** ~ **was blocked** la voie était bloquée.

(h) (*Mil*) ligne *f*. (*Mil, fig*) **in the front** ~ en première ligne; **behind the enemy** ~**s** derrière les lignes ennemies; ~ **of battle** ligne de combat.

(i) (*Comm*) article *m*. **a new** ~ une nouveauté.

2 *adj*: ~ **drawing** dessin *m* (au trait).

3 *vt paper* régler.

line up 1 *vi* (*stand in row*) s'aligner; (*in queue*) faire la queue. **2** *vt sep people, objects* aligner. **we must** ~ **up a chairman** il faut que nous trouvions (*subj*) un président; **have you got sb** ~**d up?** avez-vous qn en vue?; **I wonder what he's got** ~**d up for us** je me demande ce qu'il nous prépare.

♦ **lined**[1] *adj paper* réglé; *face* ridé. ♦ **linesman** *n* (*Tennis*) juge *m* de ligne; (*Ftbl*) juge de touche. ♦ **line-up** *n* (*row: of people etc*) file *f*; (*Ftbl etc*) (composition *f* de l')équipe *f*; (*Pol: of powers, countries*) front *m*.

line[2] [laɪn] *vt clothes* doubler (*with* de); (*Tech*) revêtir. (*fig*) **to** ~ **one's pockets** se garnir *or* se remplir les poches; **streets** ~**d with trees/people** rues bordées d'arbres/d'une haie de spectateurs; **crowds** ~**d the route** une foule faisait la haie tout le long du parcours; **walls** ~**d with books** murs couverts de livres. ♦ **lined**[2] *adj* doublé. ♦ **lining** *n* doublure *f*; (*Tech*) revêtement *m*; *[brakes]* garniture *f*.

linen ['lɪnɪn] **1** *n* (*material*) (toile *f* de) lin *m*; (*sheets, tablecloths, underwear*) linge *m*. **dirty** ~ linge sale. **2** *adj sheet* de fil; *suit, thread* de lin; *cupboard* à linge. ~ **basket** panier *m* à linge.

liner ['laɪnəʳ] *n* **(a)** (*ship*) paquebot *m* (de grande ligne); (*plane*) avion *m* (de ligne). **(b) dustbin** ~ sac *m* à poubelle.

ling[1] [lɪŋ] *n* (*Bot*) brande *f*.

ling[2] [lɪŋ] *n* (*sea fish*) morue *f* longue; (*freshwater fish*) lotte *f* de rivière.

linger ['lɪŋgəʳ] *vi [person]* (*wait*) s'attarder; (*take one's time*) prendre son temps; (*dawdle*) traîner; *[smell, pain, tradition, memory]* persister; *[doubt]* subsister. **after the accident he** ~**ed (on) for several months** après l'accident il a traîné quelques mois avant de mourir; **he always** ~**s behind everyone else** il est toujours à la traîne; **to** ~ **over a meal** manger sans se presser; **to** ~ **on a subject** s'attarder sur un sujet. ♦ **lingering** *adj look* insistant; *doubt* qui subsiste (encore); *hope* faible; *death* lent.

lingerie ['lænʒəriː] *n* lingerie *f*.

lingo* ['lɪŋgəʊ] *n* (*pej*) (*foreign language etc*) baragouin *m*; (*jargon*) jargon *m* (*pej*).

lingua franca ['lɪŋgwə'fræŋkə] *n* sabir *m*.

linguist ['lɪŋgwɪst] *n* linguiste *mf*. **I'm no** ~ je ne suis pas doué pour les langues. ♦ **linguistic** *adj* linguistique. ♦ **linguistics 1** *nsg* linguistique *f*; **2** *adj* (*gen*) de linguistique; *student* en linguistique.

liniment ['lɪnɪmənt] *n* liniment *m*.

link [lɪŋk] **1** *n [chain]* maillon *m*; (*connection*) lien *m*. **rail** ~ liaison *f* ferroviaire; **there must be a** ~ **between ...** il doit y avoir un lien *or* un rapport entre ...; **he broke off all** ~**s with them** il a cessé toutes relations avec eux. **2** *vt* **(a)** (*connect*) relier; (*fig*) lier. ~**ed by rail** relié par chemin de fer; (*fig*) **closely** ~**ed to** étroitement lié à. **(b)** (*join:* ~ **together**) lier. **to** ~ **arms** se donner le bras.

link up 1 *vi [persons, roads]* se rejoindre; *[firms, organizations etc]* s'associer; *[spacecraft]* opérer l'arrimage. **to** ~ **up with sb** rejoindre qn. **2** *vt sep* (*Rad, Telec, TV*) assurer la liaison entre.

♦ **link-up** *n* (*gen*) lien *m*; (*Rad, TV: connection*) liaison *f*; (*Rad, TV: programme*) émission *f* duplex; (*Space*) jonction *f*.

linoleum [lɪ'nəʊlɪəm] *n* linoléum *m*, lino *m*.

linseed ['lɪnsiːd] *n*: ~ **oil** huile *f* de lin.

lint [lɪnt] *n* **(a)** (*Med*) tissu *m* ouaté. **piece of** ~ compresse *f*. **(b)** (*US: fluff*) peluches *fpl*.

lintel ['lɪntl] *n* linteau *m*.

lion ['laɪən] **1** *n* lion *m*; (*fig: person*) célébrité *f*. (*fig*) **to take the** ~**'s share** se tailler la part du lion; (*fig*) **to put one's head in the** ~**'s mouth** se jeter dans la gueule du loup. **2** *adj*: ~ **cub** lionceau *m*. ♦ **lioness** *n* lionne *f*. ♦ **lion-hearted** *adj* d'un courage de lion. ♦ **lionize** *vt* fêter comme une célébrité. ♦ **lion-tamer** *n* dompteur *m*, -euse *f* de lions.

lip [lɪp] **1** *n* (*Anat*) lèvre *f*; *[jug]* bec *m*; *[cup]* rebord *m*; *[crater, wound]* bord *m*; (*: *insolence*) culot* *m*. **2** *adj*: **he pays** ~ **service to socialism but ...** il prétend être socialiste mais ...; **that was merely** ~ **service on his part** il ne l'a dit que pour la forme.

♦ **lipread** *vti* lire sur les lèvres. ♦ **lip-reading** *n* lecture *f* sur les lèvres. ♦ **lipstick** *n* rouge *m* à lèvres.

liquefy ['lɪkwɪfaɪ] **1** *vt* liquéfier. **2** *vi* se liquéfier.

♦ **liquefaction** *n* liquéfaction *f*.

liqueur [lɪ'kjʊəʳ] *n* liqueur *f*.

liquid ['lɪkwɪd] **1** *adj substance, diet* liquide; *container* pour les liquides; *eyes, voice* limpide. (*Pharm*) ~ **paraffin** huile *f* de paraffine; (*Fin*) ~ **assets** liquidités *fpl*. **2** *n* (*fluid*) liquide *m*.

♦ **liquidate** *vt* liquider. ♦ **liquidation** *n* liquidation *f*; **to go into** ~**ation** déposer son bilan.

♦ **liquidize** *vt* liquéfier; (*Culin*) passer au mixeur. ♦ **liquidizer** *n* (*Culin*) mixeur *m*.

liquor ['lɪkəʳ] *n* (*alcohol*) spiritueux *m*; (*Culin*) liquide *m*. (*US*) ~ **store** marchand *m* de vins et spiritueux.

liquorice ['lɪkərɪs] *n* (*plant*) réglisse *f*; (*sweet*) réglisse *m*.

lisp [lɪsp] **1** *vi* zézayer. **2** *vt* dire en zézayant. **3** *n* zézaiement *m*. **with a ~** en zézayant.

list[1] [lɪst] **1** *n* liste *f*; (*Comm*) catalogue *m*. **at the top/bottom of the ~** en tête/en fin de liste. **2** *adj*: **~ price** prix *m* de catalogue. **3** *vt* (*make ~ of*) faire *or* dresser la liste de; (*enumerate*) énumérer; (*classify*) classer. **your name isn't ~ed** votre nom n'est pas inscrit (sur la liste); **~ed building** monument *m* classé.

list[2] [lɪst] *vi [ship]* gîter (*20°* de 20°).

listen ['lɪsn] *vi* écouter. **to ~ to sb/sth** écouter qn/qch; (*Rad*) **to ~ in** être à l'écoute; **to ~ for sth** essayer d'entendre qch; **to ~ to reason** entendre raison. ♦ **listener** *n* (*to speaker, radio etc*) auditeur *m*, -trice *f*; **she's a good ~er** elle sait écouter (avec patience et sympathie).

listless ['lɪstlɪs] *adj* (*gen*) indolent, sans énergie; (*uninterested*) indifférent. ♦ **listlessly** *adv* avec indolence, sans énergie; avec indifférence. ♦ **listlessness** *n* indolence *f*, manque *m* d'énergie; indifférence *f*.

lit [lɪt] *pret, ptp of* **light**[1].

litany ['lɪtənɪ] *n* litanie *f*.

liter ['li:tə^r] *n* (*US*) = **litre**.

literacy ['lɪtərəsɪ] **1** *n* fait *m* de savoir lire et écrire. **2** *adj*: **~ campaign** campagne *f* d'alphabétisation.

literal ['lɪtərəl] *adj translation* littéral; *interpretation* au pied de la lettre; *meaning* littéral, propre; *person* (*also* **~-minded**) prosaïque. ♦ **literally** *adv* (*gen*) littéralement; *interpret* au pied de la lettre.

literary ['lɪtərərɪ] *adj* (*gen*) littéraire. **a ~ man** un homme de lettres.

literate ['lɪtərɪt] *adj* qui sait lire et écrire.

literature ['lɪtərɪtʃə^r] *n* littérature *f*; (*brochures etc*) documentation *f*.

lithe [laɪð] *adj person* agile; *body* souple.

lithograph ['lɪθəʊgrɑ:f] *n* lithographie *f* (*estampe*). ♦ **lithographer** *n* lithographe *mf*. ♦ **lithography** *n* lithographie *f* (*procédé*).

litigation [ˌlɪtɪ'geɪʃən] *n* litige *m*.

litmus ['lɪtməs] *n*: **~ paper** papier *m* de tournesol.

litre ['li:tə^r] *n* litre *m*.

litter ['lɪtə^r] **1** *n* **(a)** (*rubbish*) détritus *mpl*, (*dirtier*) ordures *fpl*; (*papers*) vieux papiers *mpl*. **to leave ~** jeter des détritus *or* des papiers; **a ~ of books** un fouillis de livres. **(b)** *[puppies etc]* portée *f*. **(c)** (*bed*) litière *f*. **2** *vt [person] countryside* laisser des détritus dans; *[rubbish, papers] street, floor etc* joncher; *desk* couvrir. **there were books ~ed about the room** il y avait des livres qui traînaient dans toute la pièce. ♦ **litter-basket** *or* ♦ **litter-bin** *n* boîte *f* à ordures. ♦ **litterbug** *or* ♦ **litter-lout** *n personne qui jette des détritus dans la rue etc.*

little[1] ['lɪtl] *adj* (*gen*) petit; *stick, piece of string* petit, court; *period, holiday, visit* court, petit; *voice, noise* petit, faible; *smell* petit, léger; (*small-scale*) *shopkeeper* petit. **~ finger** petit doigt; **a tiny ~ baby** un tout petit bébé; **poor ~ thing!** pauvre petit(e)! ♦ **littleness** *n* petitesse *f*.

little[2] ['lɪtl] *comp* less, *superl* least **1** *adj, pron* peu (de). **~ money** peu d'argent; **he reads ~** il lit peu, il ne lit guère; **he did ~ to help** il n'a pas fait grand-chose pour aider; **he did very ~** il a fait très peu de chose; **there was ~ one could do** il n'y avait pas grand-chose à faire; **that has very ~ to do with it!** ça n'a pas grand-chose à voir (avec ça)!; **~ or nothing** rien ou presque rien; **to make ~ of sth** (*belittle*) rabaisser qch; (*fail to understand*) ne pas comprendre grand-chose à qch; **as ~ as possible** le moins possible; **you could pay as ~ as 20 francs for that** vous pourriez ne payer que 20 F pour cela; **very ~** très peu (de); **so ~** si peu (de); **too ~** trop peu (de); **a ~** un peu (de); **the ~** le peu (de); **a ~ milk** un peu de lait; **give me a ~** donne-m'en un peu; **~ by ~** petit à petit, peu à peu; **what ~ I could** le peu que j'ai pu; **for a ~ (time** *or* **while)** un petit moment.

2 *adv* **(a)** (*slightly*) **a ~** un peu; **a ~ big** un peu grand; **he was not a ~ surprised** il n'a pas été peu surpris; **a ~ more/less cream** un peu plus/moins de crème; **a ~ more** encore un peu. **(b)** (*not much*) **it's ~ better** ça n'est guère mieux; **~ more than a month ago** il y a à peine plus d'un mois; **~ did he know that ...** il était bien loin de se douter que ...; **~ do you know!** si seulement vous saviez!; **~-known** peu connu; **I like him as ~ as you do** je ne l'aime guère plus que vous; **as ~ as before** aussi peu qu'auparavant. **(c)** (*rarely*) *happen* rarement, peu souvent.

liturgy ['lɪtədʒɪ] *n* liturgie *f*.

live[1] [lɪv] **1** *vi* **(a)** (*exist*) vivre. **he was still living when ...** il était encore en vie quand ... ; **as long as I ~** tant que je vivrai; **to ~ to be 90** vivre jusqu'à 90 ans; **she'll never ~ to see it** elle ne vivra pas assez longtemps pour le voir; **she has only 6 months to ~** il ne lui reste plus que 6 mois à vivre; **long ~ the King!** vive le roi!; **the doctor said she would ~** le docteur a dit qu'elle s'en sortirait; (*iro*) **you'll ~!*** tu n'en mourras pas!; **she has ~d through two wars** elle a vu deux guerres; **the difficult years he has ~d through** les années difficiles qu'il a vécues; **he can't ~ through the winter** il ne passera pas l'hiver; **to ~ well** *or* **like a lord** vivre sur un grand pied; **they ~d happily ever after** après cela ils vécurent toujours heureux; (*in fairy tales*) ils furent heureux et ils eurent beaucoup d'enfants; **to ~ by journalism** gagner sa vie comme journaliste; **she ~s for her children/for the day when ...** elle ne vit que pour ses enfants/pour le jour où ... ; **I've got nothing left to ~ for** je n'ai plus de raison de vivre; **you must learn to ~ with it** il faut que tu t'y fasses; **he will have to ~ with that awful memory** il lui faudra vivre avec cet horrible souvenir; **~ and let ~** il faut se montrer tolérant; **(we) ~ and learn** on apprend à tout âge. **(b)** (*reside*) vivre, habiter. **to ~ in London** habiter (à) *or* vivre à Londres; **to ~ in a flat** habiter un appartement; **where do you ~?** où habitez-vous?; **she ~s in the rue de la Paix** elle habite rue de la Paix; **this house isn't fit to ~ in** cette maison n'est pas habitable; **he's not an easy person to ~ with** il n'est pas facile à vivre; **he ~s with his mother** il vit *or* habite avec sa mère; (*in her house*) il vit chez sa mère; **he's living with Anne** (*as man and wife*) il vit avec Anne.

2 *vt*: **to ~ a healthy life** mener une vie saine; **to ~ a life of luxury** vivre dans le luxe; **to ~ one's faith** vivre pleinement sa foi; (*Theat, fig*) **to ~ the part** entrer dans la peau du personnage.

live down *vt sep disgrace* faire oublier (avec le temps).

live in *vi [servant]* être logé et nourri; *[student, doctor]* être interne.

live off *vt fus rice etc* vivre de; *one's parents* vivre aux dépens de. **to ~ off the land** vivre du pays.

live on **1** *vi* survivre. **2** *vt fus rice, one's salary* vivre de. **you can't ~ on air*** on ne vit pas de l'air du temps; **to ~ on £3,000 a year** vivre avec 3 000 livres par an; **just enough to ~ on** juste de quoi vivre; **what does he ~ on?** de quoi est-ce qu'il vit?

live out *vi [servant]* ne pas être logé; *[student, doctor]* être externe.

live together *vi* vivre ensemble.

live up *vt sep*: **to ~ it up*** (*in luxury*) mener la grand vie; (*have fun*) mener une vie de bâton de chaise.

live up to *vt fus one's principles* vivre en accord avec; *one's promises* être fidèle à; *sb's hopes, a challenge* se montrer à la hauteur de; *praise, reputation* se montrer digne de. **it didn't ~ up to**

expectations cela n'a pas été ce qu'on avait espéré.

♦ **livable** *adj climate, life* supportable; *house* habitable; **he is not livable-with*** il est invivable*.

♦ **livelihood** *n* moyens *mpl* d'existence, gagne-pain *m inv*; **their principal ~lihood is ...** ils vivent de ... . ♦ **livelong** *adj*: **all the ~long day** toute la journée.

live² [laɪv] **1** *adj* **(a)** *person etc* (*alive*) vivant, (*lively*) dynamique; *issue, problem* brûlant; *broadcast* en direct. **~ bait** vif *m* (*appât*); **a real ~ spaceman** un astronaute en chair et en os; **performed before a ~ audience** joué en public. **(b)** *coal* ardent; *ammunition, shell, cartridge* de combat, (*unexploded*) non explosé. (*Elec*) **that's ~!** c'est branché!; **~ rail** rail *m* conducteur; **~ wire** fil *m* sous tension; (*fig*) **he's a ~ wire*** il a un dynamisme fou; **the drier was ~** le séchoir était mal isolé (et dangereux). **2** *adv broadcast* en direct. ♦ **livestock** *n* bétail *m*.

lively ['laɪvlɪ] *adj person, character, party, discussion* plein d'entrain, animé; *imagination, interest, colour, speed* vif; *description, account, style* vivant; *expression, example, argument* frappant, vigoureux; *campaign* vigoureux; *tune* entraînant, gai; *evening, week* mouvementé. **things are getting ~** ça commence à s'animer; (*pej*) ça commence à barder*. ♦ **liveliness** *n* entrain *m*; animation *f*; vivacité *f*; vigueur *f*; gaieté *f*. ♦ **liven up 1** *vt sep person, room* égayer; *evening, discussion etc* animer; **2** *vi* s'animer.

liver ['lɪvəʳ] **1** *n* foie *m*. **2** *adj disease, pâté* de foie; *sausage* au pâté de foie. ♦ **liverish*** *adj* (*bilious*) qui a mal au foie.

livery ['lɪvərɪ] **1** *n* livrée *f*. **2** *adj*: **~ stable** écurie *f* (de louage *etc*).

livid ['lɪvɪd] *adj* **(a)** (*in colour*) *complexion* livide; *sky* de plomb. **(b)** (*furious*) furieux, furibond.

living ['lɪvɪŋ] **1** *adj* **(a)** (*alive: gen*) vivant; *person* vivant, en vie. **~ or dead** mort ou vif; **the greatest ~ pianist** le plus grand pianiste actuellement vivant; **there wasn't a ~ soul** il n'y avait pas âme qui vive; **a ~ skeleton** un cadavre ambulant; **within ~ memory** de mémoire d'homme. **(b)** *conditions* de vie. **~ quarters** logement *m*; **~ room** salle *f* de séjour; **~ space** espace *m* vital; **~ standards** niveau *m* de vie; **a ~ wage** un salaire permettant de vivre décemment. **2** *n* vie *f*. **to earn** *or* **make a ~** gagner sa vie; **to work for a ~** travailler pour vivre; **gracious ~** vie élégante; (*pl: people*) **the ~** les vivants *mpl*.

lizard ['lɪzəd] **1** *n* lézard *m*. **2** *adj bag etc* en lézard.

llama ['lɑːmə] *n* lama *m* (*Zool*).

load [ləʊd] **1** *n* **(a)** (*gen, Constr, Elec, Tech*) charge *f*; *[lorry]* chargement *m*; *[ship]* cargaison *f*; (*weight, pressure*) poids *m*; (*fig*) (*burden*) fardeau *m*, charge; (*mental strain*) poids. **to take a ~ off sb's mind** débarrasser qn de ce qui lui pèse (*fig*); **that's a ~ off my mind!** quel soulagement! **(b)** (*fig*) **a ~ of*, ~s of*** des tas de*, énormément de, des masses de*; **we've got ~s of time*** on a largement le temps.

2 *vt* (*gen: often* **~ down** *or* **up**) charger (*with* de). **she was ~ed (down) with shopping** elle pliait sous le poids de ses achats; **pockets ~ed with sweets** poches bourrées de bonbons; **to ~ sb (down) with gifts** couvrir qn de cadeaux; **~ed with cares/sorrow** accablé de soucis/chagrin; *[ship etc]* **to ~ coal** *etc* charger du charbon *etc*.

3 *vi* (**~ up**) *[lorry]* prendre un chargement; *[ship]* embarquer une cargaison; *[camera, gun]* se charger.

♦ **loaded** *adj* **(a)** (*gen*) chargé; *dice* pipé; *cane* plombé; *word, question* insidieux; (*fig*) **the dice were ~ed against him** les cartes étaient truquées à son désavantage; **(b)** (*‡: rich*) bourré de fric‡. ♦ **loader** *n* chargeur *m*. ♦ **loading 1** *n* chargement *m*; **2** *adj*: **~ing bay** aire *f* de chargement.

loaf¹ [ləʊf] *n, pl* **loaves (a)** (**~** *of bread*) pain *m*. **half a ~ is better than no bread** mieux vaut peu que pas du tout. **(b) sugar ~** pain *m* de sucre.

loaf² [ləʊf] *vi* (**~ about** *or* **~ around**) traînasser.

loam [ləʊm] *n* terreau *m*.

loan [ləʊn] **1** *n* (*lent*) prêt *m*; (*borrowed*) emprunt *m*. **on ~** *object* prêté (*from* par; *to* à); *employee* détaché (*from* de; *to* à); *library book* sorti; **I have it on ~** je l'ai emprunté; **to ask for the ~ of sth** demander à emprunter qch; **to give sb the ~ of sth** prêter qch à qn. **2** *vt* prêter (*to* à). **3** *adj capital, word* d'emprunt.

loath [ləʊθ] *adj*: **to be ~ to do** ne pas être disposé à faire, (*stronger*) répugner à faire.

loathe [ləʊð] *vt* détester (*doing* faire; *sb's doing* que qn fasse).

♦ **loathing** *n* dégoût *m*. ♦ **loathsome** *adj* détestable, répugnant.

lobby ['lɒbɪ] **1** *n* **(a)** vestibule *m*. **(b)** (*Parl*) (*for public*) ≈ salle *f* des pas perdus; (*division ~*) vestibule *m* (*où l'on vote*); (*pressure group*) groupe *m* de pression, lobby *m*. **2** *adj*: **~ correspondent** journaliste *mf* parlementaire. **3** *vt* (*Pol*) faire pression sur. **4** *vi* (*Pol*) faire pression (*for sth* pour obtenir qch).

lobe [ləʊb] *n* lobe *m*.

lobster ['lɒbstəʳ] *n* homard *m*. **~ pot** casier *m* à homards.

local ['ləʊkəl] **1** *adj* (*gen*) local; *shops, library* du *or* de quartier; *wine, speciality* du pays, local; *pain* localisé. (*Telec*) **a ~ call** une communication urbaine; **what is the ~ situation?** quelle est la situation (*here*) ici? *or* (*there*) là-bas?; **he's a ~ man** il est du pays *or* du coin*; **the ~ doctor** le médecin du quartier (*or* du village *etc*); **~ colour** couleur *f* locale; **~ authority** (*n*) autorité *f* locale; (*adj*) des autorités locales; **~ education authority** ≈ office *m* régional de l'enseignement; **~ government** administration *f* locale; **~ government elections** élections *fpl* municipales; **~ government officer** *or* **official** administrateur *m* local, ≈ fonctionnaire *mf*. **2** *n* **(a)** (*: *person*) personne *f* du pays. **the ~s** les gens *mpl* du pays. **(b)** (*Brit**: *pub*) café *m* du coin. ♦ **locality** *n* (*neighbourhood*) environs *mpl*; (*district*) région *f*; (*place, position*) lieu *m*, endroit *m*. ♦ **localize** *vt* localiser.

♦ **locally** *adv* (*in certain areas; not centrally*) localement; (*nearby*) dans les environs; (*near here*) par ici; (*out there*) là-bas; **showers ~ly** temps localement pluvieux; **~ly appointed staff** personnel recruté localement.

locate [ləʊ'keɪt] *vt* **(a)** (*find*) *place, person, object* repérer, trouver; *noise, leak, cause* localiser. **(b)** (*situate*) *factory, school etc* situer. **to be ~d** être situé, se trouver. ♦ **location** *n* emplacement *m*; (*Cine*) **on location** en extérieur.

loch [lɒx] *n* (*Scot*) lac *m*, loch *m*.

lock¹ [lɒk] **1** *n* **(a)** (*gen*) serrure *f*; (*on steering wheel*) antivol *m*. **under ~ and key** *possessions* sous clef; *prisoner* sous les verrous; (*fig*) **~, stock and barrel** en bloc. **(b)** *[canal]* écluse *f*. **(c)** (*Aut: turning*) rayon *m* de braquage. **2** *vt door, suitcase, safe* fermer à clef; *person* enfermer (*in* dans); *mechanism* bloquer. **behind ~ed doors** à huis clos; **~ed in her arms** serré dans ses bras; **~ed in a close embrace** unis dans une étreinte passionnée; **~ed in combat** aux prises. **3** *vi [door]* fermer à clef; *[wheel, steering wheel]* se bloquer. (*Space*) **to ~ on to sth** s'arrimer à qch.

lock away *vt sep object* mettre sous clef; *criminal* mettre sous les verrous; *mental patient etc* enfermer.

lock in *vt sep* enfermer (à l'intérieur).

lock out *vt sep* (*deliberately*) mettre à la porte; (*by mistake*) enfermer dehors; (*Ind*) *workers* lock-outer. **to ~ o.s. out of one's car** fermer la voiture en laissant les clefs à l'intérieur.

lock up 1 *vi* tout fermer (à clef). **2** *vt sep object*

mettre sous clef; *house* fermer (à clef); *criminal* mettre sous les verrous; *mental patient etc* enfermer; *funds* bloquer (*in* dans).
♦ **locker** *n* casier *m*, petit placard. ♦ **lockjaw** *n* tétanos *m*. ♦ **lock-keeper** *n* éclusier *m*, -ière *f*. ♦ **lockout** *n* (*Ind*) lock-out *m inv*. ♦ **locksmith** *n* serrurier *m*. ♦ **lock-up** *n* (*garage*) box *m*; (*shop*) boutique *f* (*sans logement*); (*prison*) prison *f*; (*cell*) cellule *f* (provisoire).
lock[2] [lɒk] *n [hair]* mèche *f*. ~s chevelure *f*.
locket ['lɒkɪt] *n* médaillon *m* (*bijou*).
locomotion [,ləʊkə'məʊʃən] *n* locomotion *f*. ♦ **locomotive** **1** *n* (*Rail*) locomotive *f*; **2** *adj* locomotif.
locum ['ləʊkəm] *n* remplaçant(e) *m(f)* (*de médecin etc*).
locust ['ləʊkəst] *n* sauterelle *f*.
lodge [lɒdʒ] **1** *n* (*house*) pavillon *m* de gardien; (*porter's rooms*) loge *f*; (*Freemasonry*) loge. **2** *vt person, bullet* loger; *money* déposer; *statement, report* présenter (*with sb* à qn). (*Jur*) **to ~ an appeal** se pourvoir en cassation. **3** *vi [person]* être logé (*with* chez); *[bullet]* se loger. ♦ **lodger** *n* (*room only*) locataire *mf*; (*with meals*) pensionnaire *mf*; **to take (in) ~rs** louer des chambres; (*with meals*) prendre des pensionnaires.
lodging ['lɒdʒɪŋ] **1** *n* **(a)** (*accommodation*) logement *m*. **they gave us a night's ~** ils nous ont logés une nuit. **(b) ~s** (*room*) chambre *f*; (*flatlet*) logement *m*; **he's in ~s** il vit en meublé; **to look for ~s** chercher une chambre meublée (*or* un logement meublé); (*with meals*) chercher à prendre pension.
2 *adj*: **~ house** pension *f*.
loft [lɒft] *n* grenier *m*.
lofty ['lɒftɪ] *adj mountain* très haut; *feelings, aims* élevé; (*haughty*) hautain. ♦ **loftily** *adv* avec hauteur.
log[1] [lɒg] **1** *n* **(a)** (*tree trunk*) rondin *m*; (*for fire*) bûche *f*. **he lay like a ~** il ne bougeait pas plus qu'une souche. **(b)** (*~book*) (*Naut*) livre *m* de bord; (*Aviat*) carnet *m* de vol; *[lorry driver etc]* carnet de route; (*gen*) registre *m*. **2** *adj*: **~ cabin** cabane *f* en rondins; **~ fire** feu *m* de bois. **3** *vt* **(a)** (*record*) (*gen*) noter, consigner; (*Naut*) inscrire au livre de bord; (*Aviat*) inscrire sur le carnet de vol. **(b)** (**~ up**) *distance, speed etc* faire. **to ~ 50 mph** faire 80 km/h. ♦ **logbook** *n* (*Aut*) carte *f* grise (*V also* **log**[1] **1b**).
log[2] [lɒg] *n* (*abbr of* **logarithm**) log* *m*.
logarithm ['lɒgərɪθəm] *n* logarithme *m*.
loggerheads ['lɒgəhedz] *npl*: **at ~** en désaccord complet (*with* avec).
logic ['lɒdʒɪk] *n* logique *f*. ♦ **logical** *adj* logique. ♦ **logically** *adv* logiquement. ♦ **logician** *n* logicien(ne) *m(f)*. ♦ **logistics** *n* logistique *f*.
loin [lɔɪn] **1** *n* **(a) ~s** reins *mpl*. **(b)** (*Culin*) (*gen*) filet *m*; *[veal, venison]* longe *f*; *[beef]* aloyau *m*. **2** *adj*: **~ chop** côte *f* première; **~ cloth** pagne *m*.
loiter ['lɔɪtə[r]] *vi* traîner; (*Police etc*) traîner d'une manière suspecte.
loll [lɒl] *vi [head, tongue]* pendre.
loll about, loll around *vi* fainéanter.
loll back *vi [person]* se prélasser.
lollipop ['lɒlɪpɒp] *n* sucette *f* (*bonbon*).
lolly ['lɒlɪ] *n* **(a)** = **lollipop**. **(b)** (‡: *money*) fric‡ *m*.
London ['lʌndən] **1** *n* Londres *m*. **2** *adj* (*gen*) londonien; *people* de Londres. ♦ **Londoner** *n* Londonien(ne) *m(f)*.
lone [ləʊn] *adj* **person** solitaire; *village, house* isolé; (*unique*) unique. (*fig*) **to play a ~ hand** mener une action solitaire; (*fig*) **~ wolf** solitaire *mf*.
lonely ['ləʊnlɪ], **lonesome** ['ləʊnsəm] *adj* (*gen*) solitaire; *person* seul, solitaire. **to feel ~** se sentir seul; **a small ~ figure** une petite silhouette seule *or* solitaire; **~ hearts' club** club *m* de rencontres (pour personnes seules). ♦ **loneliness** *or* ♦ **lonesomeness** *n [person, life]* solitude *f*; *[house, road]* (*position*) isolement *m*; (*atmosphere*) solitude.
long[1] [lɒŋ] **1** *adj* **(a)** (*in size*) long (*f* longue). **how ~ is the field?** quelle est la longueur du champ?; **10 metres ~** (long) de 10 mètres; **to get ~er** rallonger; **to pull a ~ face** faire une grimace; **~ division** division écrite complète; (*Sport*) **~ jump** saut *m* en longueur; (*fig*) **it's a ~ shot** *or* **chance** c'est très risqué; (*Rad*) **on the ~ wave** sur (les) grandes ondes. **(b)** (*in time*) long. **6 months ~** qui dure 6 mois, de 6 mois; **a ~ time** longtemps; **at ~ last** enfin; **he wasn't ~ in coming** il n'a pas mis longtemps pour venir; **how ~ are the holidays?** les vacances durent combien de temps?; **to take a ~ look at** regarder longuement; (*fig*) regarder bien en face; **a ~ drink of water** une grande gorgée d'eau; **a ~ drink** un long drink; (*fig*) **in the ~ run** à la longue, en fin de compte; **it will be a ~ job** cela demandera du temps; **to have a ~ memory** avoir de la mémoire; **to be ~ on sth*** être doué pour qch, avoir beaucoup de qch.
2 *adv* **(a)** depuis longtemps. **it has ~ been used in industry** c'est employé depuis longtemps dans l'industrie; **~-awaited** (si) longtemps attendu. **(b)** (*a ~ time*) longtemps. **~ ago** il y a longtemps; **how ~ ago?** il y a combien de temps?; **as ~ ago as 1930** déjà en 1930; **~ before** longtemps avant (que + *subj*); **~ before now** il y a longtemps; **not ~ before** peu de temps avant (que + *subj*); **~ since dead** mort depuis longtemps; **how ~ is it since you saw him?** cela fait combien de temps que tu ne l'as pas vu?; **have you been waiting ~?** il y a longtemps que vous attendez?; **I only had ~ enough to buy a paper** je n'ai eu que le temps d'acheter un journal; **wait a little ~er** attendez encore un peu; **will you be ~?** tu en as pour longtemps?; **don't be ~** dépêche-toi; **how ~?** combien de temps?; **as ~ as I live** tant que je vivrai; **before ~** (+ *future*) dans peu de temps; (+ *past*) peu de temps après; **for ~** pour longtemps; **at (the) ~est** au plus. **(c) all night ~** toute la nuit; **so ~ as, as ~ as** pourvu que + *subj*; **so ~!*** à bientôt!, salut!*; **he is no ~er living there** il n'habite plus là.
3 *n*: **the ~ and the short of it is that ...** le fin mot de l'histoire, c'est que ... .
♦ **long-distance** *adj race, runner* de fond; (*Telec*) *call* interurbain; *flight* sur long parcours. ♦ **long-drawn-out** *adj* qui traîne, interminable. ♦ **long-forgotten** *adj* oublié depuis longtemps. ♦ **long-haired** *adj person* aux cheveux longs; *animal* à longs poils. ♦ **longhand** *adj* en écriture normale. ♦ **long johns*** *npl* caleçon *m* long. ♦ **long-legged** *adj person, horse* aux jambes longues; *other animal* à longues pattes. ♦ **long-lived** *adj* d'une grande longévité. ♦ **long-lost** *adj* perdu depuis longtemps. ♦ **long-playing** *adj*: **~-playing record** 33 tours *m inv*. ♦ **long-range** *adj gun* à longue portée; *plane* (*Mil*) à grand rayon d'action, (*civil*) long-courrier; *weather forecast* à long terme. ♦ **longshoreman** *n* débardeur *m*. ♦ **long-sighted** *adj* (*lit*) hypermétrope; (*in old age*) presbyte; (*fig*) *person* prévoyant, qui voit loin; *decision* pris avec prévoyance. ♦ **long-sleeved** *adj* à manches longues. ♦ **long-standing** *adj* de longue date. ♦ **long-suffering** *adj* très patient. ♦ **long-term** *adj* à long terme. ♦ **longways** *adv* en longueur, en long; **~ways on** dans le sens de la longueur. ♦ **long-winded** *adj person* intarissable; *speech* interminable.
long[2] [lɒŋ] *vi* avoir très envie (*to do* de faire; *for sth* de qch; *for sb to do* que qn fasse); **to ~ for sb** se languir de qn.
♦ **longing** **1** *n* (*urge*) désir *m* (*to do* de faire; *for sth* de qch; *for sb* de voir qn); (*nostalgia*) nostalgie *f*; (*for food*) envie *f*; **2** *adj look* plein de désir *or* de nostalgie *or* d'envie. ♦ **longingly** *adv* avec désir *or* nostalgie.

longitude ['lɒŋgɪtju:d] *n* longitude *f*.
loo* [lu:] *n* (*Brit*) cabinets *mpl*, petit coin* *m*. **in the ~** au petit coin*, aux cabinets.
look [lʊk] **1** *n* **(a)** regard *m*, coup *m* d'œil. **to have** *or* **take a ~ at sth** regarder qch, jeter un coup d'œil à qch; (*in order to repair it etc*) s'occuper de qch; **to take a good ~ at sth** (bien) examiner qch; **to take a good ~ at sb** (bien) observer qn; **let me have a ~** faites voir; **to have a ~ round the house** faire un tour dans la maison; **I just want to have a ~ round** (*in town*) je veux simplement faire un tour; (*in shop*) je ne fais que regarder; (*in house etc*) je veux simplement jeter un coup d'œil; **with a nasty ~ in his eye** avec un regard méchant; **we got some very odd ~s** les gens nous regardaient d'un drôle d'air; **if ~s could kill* I'd be dead** il (*or* elle *etc*) m'a fusillé *or* foudroyé du regard; **to have a ~ for sth** chercher qch.
(b) (*appearance etc*) air *m*, allure *f*. **she has a ~ of her mother about her** elle a qch de sa mère; **there was a sad ~ about him** il avait l'air plutôt triste; **I like the ~ of her** je lui trouve l'air sympathique; **I don't like the ~ of him** je n'aime pas son allure *or* son air; **I don't like the ~ of this** ça ne me plaît pas du tout; **you can't go by ~s** on ne peut pas se fier aux apparences; **by the ~ of him** à le voir; **by the ~(s) of it, by the ~(s) of things*** de toute apparence; **(good) ~s** beauté *f*; **she has kept her ~s** elle est restée belle; (*Fashion*) **the leather ~** la mode du cuir.
2 *vi* **(a)** (*see, glance*) regarder. **to ~ at** *person, object* regarder; *situation, problem* considérer; **just ~ at you!** regarde de quoi tu as l'air!; **to ~ at him you would never think that ...** à le voir on ne penserait jamais que ...; **it isn't much to ~ at** ça ne paie pas de mine; **that's one way of ~ing at it** c'est une façon de voir les choses; **I wouldn't ~ at the job** je n'accepterais ce poste pour rien au monde; **will you ~ at the carburettor?** pourriez-vous vérifier le carburateur?; **I'll ~ at it tomorrow** je m'en occuperai demain; **to ~ for sth/sb** chercher qch/qn; **to ~ into** *complaint, matter, possibility* examiner; **I shall ~ into it** je vais me renseigner là-dessus; **I ~ on him as ...** je le considère comme ...; **~ and see if ...** regarde voir si ...; **let me ~** laisse-moi voir; **~ who's here!** regarde qui est là!; **~ here, ...** écoutez, ...; (*protesting*) **~ here!** enfin voyons!; **to ~ the other way** regarder ailleurs; (*fig*) fermer les yeux (*fig*); **~ before you leap** il ne faut pas se lancer à l'aveuglette; **to ~ ahead** (*in front*) regarder devant soi; (*to future*) considérer l'avenir; **to ~ down the list** parcourir la liste; **she ~ed into his eyes** elle a plongé son regard dans le sien; **the house ~s on to the main street** la maison donne sur la grand-rue; **you should have ~ed more carefully** tu aurais dû chercher plus soigneusement *or* mieux regarder.
(b) sembler, avoir l'air. **she ~s (as if she's) tired** elle semble *or* elle a l'air fatiguée; **how pretty you ~!** que vous êtes jolie!; **you ~** *or* **you're ~ing well** vous avez bonne mine; **he doesn't ~ himself, he doesn't ~ very great*** il n'a pas l'air bien; **he ~s about 40/1 metre 80** il a l'air d'avoir 40 ans/de faire 1 mètre 80; **she ~s her age** elle fait son âge; **she's tired and she ~s it** elle est fatiguée et ça se voit; **you must ~ your best** il faut que tu sois à ton avantage; **they made me ~ a fool** *or* **foolish** ils m'ont fait paraître ridicule; (*fig*) **to make sb ~ small** rabaisser qn; (*fig*) **it made me ~ small** j'ai eu l'air fin!* (*iro*); (*fig*) **he just does it to ~ big** il fait cela uniquement pour se donner de l'importance; **ugly-~ing** laid; (*fig*) **to ~ the part** avoir le physique de l'emploi; **don't ~ like that!** ne faites pas cette tête-là!; **try to ~ as if you're glad to see them** essaie d'avoir l'air content de les voir; **~ sharp about it!*** dépêche-toi!; **he ~s good in uniform** l'uniforme lui va bien; **it makes her ~ old** cela la vieillit; **how did she ~?** (*health*) est-ce qu'elle avait bonne mine?; (*on hearing news etc*) quelle tête faisait-elle?; **how do I ~?** est-ce que ça va?; **that ~s good** *[food]* ça a l'air bon; *[picture etc]* ça fait très bien; *[plan, book]* ça a l'air intéressant; **it ~s good on paper** c'est très bien en théorie; **it doesn't ~ right** il y a qch qui ne va pas; **it ~s all right to me** je trouve que ça va; **how does it ~ to you?** ça va à votre avis?; **it ~s promising** c'est prometteur; **it will ~ bad** cela fera mauvais effet.
(c) it ~s as if it's going to snow on dirait qu'il va neiger; **it ~s as if he isn't coming** il n'a pas l'air de venir; **it ~s to me as if he isn't coming** j'ai l'impression qu'il ne va pas venir; **what does it/he ~ like?** comment est-ce/est-il?; **he ~s like his brother** il ressemble à son frère; **he ~s like a soldier** il a l'air d'un soldat; **it ~s like salt** ça a l'air d'être du sel; **it ~s like rain** on dirait qu'il va pleuvoir; **it certainly ~s like it** c'est bien probable; **the evening ~ed like being interesting** la soirée promettait d'être intéressante.
3 *vt* regarder. **she ~ed him full in the face/straight in the eye** elle l'a regardé bien en face/droit dans les yeux; **to ~ sb up and down** regarder qn de haut en bas; **~ where you're going!** regarde où tu vas!
look about, look around *vi* regarder autour de soi. **to ~ about for sth** chercher qch des yeux.
look after *vt fus* (*gen*) s'occuper de; *possessions* faire attention à; *one's car* entretenir; *one's interests* protéger. **she doesn't ~ after herself very well** elle néglige sa santé; **~ after yourself!*** fais bien attention à toi!*; **she's old enough to ~ after herself** elle est assez grande pour se défendre* toute seule; (*take responsibility for*) **to ~ after sth for sb** garder qch pour qn.
look away *vi* détourner les yeux (*from* de).
look back *vi* regarder derrière soi; (*remember*) regarder en arrière. **to ~ back at sth/sb** se retourner pour regarder qch/qn; **to ~ back on** revoir en esprit, penser à; **we can ~ back on 20 years of ...** nous avons derrière nous 20 ans de ...; **after that he never ~ed back*** après, ça n'a fait qu'aller de mieux en mieux.
look down *vi* baisser les yeux; (*from height*) regarder en bas. **to ~ down at sb/sth** regarder qn/qch d'en haut; (*fig*) **to ~ down on sb/sth** mépriser qn/qch.
look forward to *vt fus* attendre avec impatience. **I'm ~ing forward to seeing you** j'attends avec impatience le plaisir de vous voir; (*in letter*) **~ing forward to hearing from you** en espérant avoir bientôt une lettre de vous, dans l'attente de votre réponse; **are you ~ing forward to it?** est-ce que vous êtes content à cette perspective?; **I'm so ~ing forward to it** je m'en réjouis à l'avance.
look in *vi* **(a)** (*~ inside*) regarder à l'intérieur; (*visit*) passer. **to ~ in on sb** passer voir qn; **the doctor will ~ in again** le docteur repassera. **(b)** (*: *watch television*) regarder la télévision.
look on *vi* regarder. **he wrote the letter while I ~ed on** il a écrit la lettre tandis que je le regardais faire.
look out 1 *vi* **(a)** (*outside*) regarder dehors. **to ~ out of the window** regarder par la fenêtre; (*fig*) **to ~ out for sb** (*seek*) chercher qn; (*watch for*) guetter qn. **(b)** (*take care*) faire attention, prendre garde. **~ out!** attention!; **~ out for ice on the road** (faites) attention au verglas, méfiez-vous du verglas. **2** *vt sep* chercher et trouver. **I shall ~ out some old magazines** je vais essayer de trouver quelques vieux magazines.
look over *vt sep essay* jeter un coup d'œil à; *book* parcourir; *town, building* visiter; *person* (*quickly*) jeter un coup d'œil à; (*slowly*) regarder de la tête aux pieds.
look round 1 *vi* **(a)** regarder (autour de soi); (*in shop*) regarder. **to ~ round for sth** chercher qch.

(b) (~ *back*) regarder derrière soi. **to ~ round to see sth** se retourner pour voir qch; **don't ~ round!** ne vous retournez pas! **2** *vt fus town, factory* visiter, faire le tour de.

look through *vt fus papers, book* examiner, (*briefly*) parcourir; (*revise*) revoir.

look to *vt fus* (*look after*) *children* s'occuper de; (*rely on*) compter sur. **I ~ to you for help** je compte sur votre aide; **I always ~ to my mother for advice** quand j'ai besoin d'un conseil je me tourne vers ma mère.

look up 1 *vi* **(a)** regarder en haut; (*from reading etc*) lever les yeux. (*fig*) **to ~ up to sb** respecter qn. **(b)** (*improve*) *[prospects]* s'améliorer; *[business]* reprendre; *[weather]* se lever; *[shares, sales]* remonter. **things are ~ing up** ça a l'air d'aller mieux (*for sb* pour qn). **2** *vt sep* **(a)** (*visit*) *person* passer voir. **(b)** (*in dictionary*) chercher (*in* dans). **3** *vt fus reference book* consulter.

♦ **looker-on** *n* spectateur *m*, -trice *f*. ♦ **look-in*** *n*: **they didn't have** *or* **get a ~-in** ils n'ont jamais eu la moindre chance. ♦ **looking-glass** *n* miroir *m*. ♦ **look-out 1** *n* **(a) to keep a ~-out, to be on the ~-out** guetter (*for sb/sth* qn/qch); **to be on the ~-out for danger** être sur ses gardes à cause d'un danger éventuel; **(b)** (*observer*) (*gen*) guetteur *m*; (*Mil*) homme *m* de guet; (*Naut*) homme de veille; **(c)** (*~-out post*) (*gen, Mil*) poste *m* de guet; (*Naut*) vigie *f*; **(d) it's a poor ~-out for ...** ça s'annonce mal pour ...; **that's your ~-out!** cela vous regarde!, c'est votre affaire!; **2** *adj tower* d'observation.

loom[1] [lu:m] *vi* (~ **up**) *[building, mountain]* apparaître indistinctement; *[figure, ship]* surgir; *[disaster]* menacer; *[event]* paraître imminent.

loom[2] [lu:m] *n* (*Tex*) métier *m* à tisser.

loop [lu:p] **1** *n* (*gen*) boucle *f* (*de ficelle etc*); (*Elec*) circuit *m* fermé; (*by motorway etc*) bretelle *f*; (*curtain fastener*) embrasse *f*; (*contraceptive*) stérilet *m*. **2** *vt string etc* faire une boucle à. **to ~ a rope round a post** passer une corde autour d'un poteau; (*Aviat*) **to ~ the loop** boucler la boucle; **to ~ back a curtain** relever un rideau avec une embrasse. ♦ **loophole** *n* (*in argument, regulations*) point *m* faible; **to find a ~hole** trouver une échappatoire.

loose [lu:s] **1** *adj* **(a)** *knot, shoelace* qui se défait; *screw* desserré; *brick, tooth* qui branle; *page from book* détaché; *hair* dénoué; *animal etc* en liberté. **to be working ~** se défaire, se desserrer, branler, se détacher, se dénouer; *[animal etc]* **to get ~** s'échapper; **to let** *or* **set** *or* **turn ~** lâcher; **a ~ sheet of paper** une feuille volante; *[horse]* **~ box** fourgon *m* à chevaux; (*on roadway*) **~ chippings** gravillons *mpl*; (*Elec*) **~ connection** mauvais contact *m*; *[furniture]* **~ covers** housses *fpl*; **~ end of a rope** bout *m* pendant d'une corde; **to be at a ~ end** ne pas trop savoir quoi faire; (*fig*) **to tie up ~ ends** régler les détails qui restent. **(b)** (*not packed*) *biscuits, carrots etc* en vrac; *butter, cheese* au poids. **just put them ~ into the basket** mettez-les à même dans le panier. **(c)** *coat, dress* (*not close-fitting*) vague, ample; (*not tight enough*) lâche, large; *skin* flasque; *collar* lâche. **(d)** *soil* meuble; (*fig*) *association, link* vague; *discipline, style* relâché; *reasoning, thinking* confus, imprécis; *translation* assez libre. **a ~ weave** un tissu lâche; **~ bowels** intestins relâchés. **(e)** (*pej*) *woman* facile; *morals* relâché. **~ living** vie *f* dissolue.

2 *vt* **(a)** (*undo*) défaire; (*untie*) délier; *screw etc* desserrer; (*free*) *animal* lâcher; *prisoner* relâcher. **to ~ a boat (from its moorings)** larguer les amarres; **they ~d the dogs on him** ils ont lâché les chiens après lui. **(b)** (~ **off**) *gun* décharger (*on or at sb* sur qn); *arrow* tirer (*on or at sb* sur qn); *abuse* lâcher (*on sb* sur qn).

♦ **loose-fitting** *adj* ample. ♦ **loose-leaf(ed)** *adj* à feuilles volantes. ♦ **loose-limbed** *adj* agile. ♦ **loosely** *adv attach, tie, hold* sans serrer; *be fixed, weave* lâchement; *associate* vaguement; *translate* assez librement; *use word* de façon plutôt impropre. ♦ **loosen 1** *vt* (*slacken*) *screw, belt, knot* desserrer; *rope, one's grip* relâcher; (*untie*) défaire; *tongue* délier; *soil* rendre meuble; *bowels* relâcher; **2** *vi [fastening]* se défaire; *[screw]* se desserrer; *[knot]* (*slacken*) se desserrer; (*come undone*) se défaire; *[rope]* se détendre; **to ~n up** (*limber up*) faire des exercices d'assouplissement; (*be less shy*) se dégeler. ♦ **looseness** *n [knot]* desserrement *m*; *[screw, tooth]* jeu *m*; *[rope]* relâchement *m*; *[clothes]* ampleur *f*; *[translation]* imprécision *f*; *[behaviour]* relâchement.

loot [lu:t] **1** *n* butin *m*. **2** *vt* piller. **3** *vi*: **to go ~ing** se livrer au pillage. ♦ **looter** *n* pillard *m*. ♦ **looting** *n* pillage *m*.

lop [lɒp] *vt tree* tailler; *branch* couper.

lop off *vt sep* couper.

♦ **lop-eared** *adj* aux oreilles pendantes. ♦ **lop-sided** *adj* (*not straight*) de travers; (*asymmetric*) disproportionné.

lope [ləʊp] *vi*: **to ~ along/in** *etc* avancer/entrer *etc* en bondissant.

loquacious [lə'kweɪʃəs] *adj* loquace. ♦ **loquacity** *n* loquacité *f*.

lord [lɔ:d] **1** *n* seigneur *m*. **~ of the manor** châtelain *m*; **~ and master** seigneur et maître; **L~ (John) Smith** lord (John) Smith; **the House of L~s** la Chambre des Lords; **my L~** Monsieur le baron (*or* comte *etc*); (*to judge*) Monsieur le Juge; (*to bishop*) Monseigneur; (*Rel*) **Our L~** Notre Seigneur; **the L~'s supper** la sainte Cène; **the L~'s prayer** le Notre-Père; **good L~!*** Seigneur!; **oh L~!*** zut!* **2** *vt*: **to ~ it over sb*** traiter qn de haut. ♦ **lordliness** *n* noblesse *f*; (*pej*) hauteur *f*. ♦ **lordly** *adj* (*dignified*) noble, de grand seigneur; (*arrogant*) hautain. ♦ **lordship** *n* autorité *f* (*over* sur); **Your L~ship** Monsieur le comte (*or* le baron *etc*); (*to judge*) Monsieur le Juge; (*to bishop*) Monseigneur.

lore [lɔ:ʳ] *n* traditions *fpl*. **bird/wood** *etc* **~** connaissance *f* des oiseaux/de la vie dans les forêts *etc*.

lorry ['lɒrɪ] (*Brit*) **1** *n* camion *m*. **2** *adj*: **~ driver** camionneur *m*; (*long-distance*) routier *m*; **~ load** chargement *m*.

lose [lu:z] *pret, ptp* **lost 1** *vt* **(a)** (*gen*) perdre. **he got lost** il s'est perdu *or* égaré; **the key got lost** on a perdu *or* égaré la clef; **get lost!**‡ fiche le camp!*; **I lost my father when I was 10** j'ai perdu mon père à l'âge de 10 ans; **you've nothing to ~** tu n'as rien à perdre, tu ne risques rien (*by doing* à faire); **to ~ one's life** périr, perdre la vie; **100 men** *or* **lives were lost** 100 hommes ont péri, on a perdu 100 hommes; **20 lives were lost** 20 personnes ont péri; **there were no lives lost** il n'y a eu aucun mort *or* aucune victime; **to be lost at sea** périr en mer; **I lost his last sentence** je n'ai pas entendu sa dernière phrase; **to ~ one's breath** perdre haleine; **to have lost one's breath** être hors d'haleine; (*Aut*) **he's lost his licence** on lui a retiré son permis de conduire; **to ~ one's way** perdre son chemin, se perdre; **we mustn't ~ any time** il ne faut pas perdre de temps; **to ~ no time in doing sth** faire qch au plus vite; **there's not a minute to ~** il n'y a pas une minute à perdre; **he managed to ~ the detective who was following him** il a réussi à semer le détective qui le suivait; (*after explanation etc*) **you've lost me there*** je ne vous suis plus. **(b)** (*cause loss of*) faire perdre. **that will ~ you your job** cela va vous faire perdre votre place. **(c)** *[clock etc]* **to ~ 10 minutes a day** retarder de 10 minutes par jour.

2 *vi* **(a)** *[player, team]* perdre. **to ~ to sb** se faire battre par qn; **they lost 6-1** ils ont perdu *or* ils se sont fait battre 6-1; (*fig*) **he lost (out) on the deal** il a été perdant dans l'affaire; **you can't ~*** tu ne risques rien; (*fig*) **it ~s in translation** cela perd à la traduction. **(b)** *[watch, clock]* retarder.

♦ **loser** *n* perdant(e) *m(f)*; **good/bad ~r** bon/mauvais joueur, bonne/mauvaise joueuse; **to come off the ~r** être perdant; **he's a born ~r** il n'a jamais de veine*. ♦ **losing** *adj team, number* perdant; *business, concern* mauvais; **on a losing streak*** en période de déveine*; (*fig*) **a losing battle** une bataille perdue d'avance.

loss [lɒs] *n* **(a)** perte *f*. **without ~ of life** sans qu'il y ait de victimes; (*Mil*) **heavy ~es** pertes sévères; **to sell at a ~** vendre à perte; **he's no great~*** ce n'est pas une grosse perte. **(b) to be at a ~** être perplexe; **at a ~ to explain** incapable d'expliquer; **we are at a ~ to know** nous ne savons absolument pas; **to be at a ~ for words** chercher ses mots.

lost [lɒst] (*pret, ptp of* **lose**) *adj cause, opportunity* perdu; (*fig*) (*bewildered*) perdu, désorienté; (*uncomprehending*) perdu, perplexe; (*absorbed*) perdu (*in* dans), absorbé (*in* par). **several ~ children** plusieurs enfants qui s'étaient perdus; **a ~ soul** une âme en peine; **the ~ sheep** la brebis égarée; **to make up for ~ time** rattraper le temps perdu; **~ property,** (*US*) **~ and found** objets *mpl* trouvés; **~ property office, ~-and-found department** bureau *m* des objets trouvés; **he looked quite ~** il avait l'air complètement désorienté; **to give sb/sth up for ~** considérer qn/qch comme perdu; **my advice/the remark was ~ on him** il n'a pas écouté mes conseils/pas compris la remarque; **~ in thought** perdu dans ses pensées.

lot [lɒt] *n* **(a)** (*destiny*) sort *m*. **the common ~** le sort commun; **it was not his ~ to make a fortune** il n'était pas destiné à faire fortune; **it fell to my ~ to do it** il m'est revenu de le faire; **to throw in one's ~ with sb** partager le sort de qn. **(b)** (*random selection*) **by ~** par tirage au sort; **to draw ~s (for sth)** tirer (qch) au sort. **(c)** (*at auctions; also batch: of people, goods*) lot *m*. **he's a bad ~*** il ne vaut pas cher*. **(d)** (*land*) lot *m* (de terrain), parcelle *f*. **building ~** lotissement *m*; **parking ~** parking *m*. **(e) the ~** (*everything*) (le) tout; (*everyone*) tous *mpl*, toutes *fpl*; **that's the ~** c'est tout; **take the ~** prends tout ce qu'il y a, prends le tout; **the ~ of you** vous tous; **the whole ~ of them went off** ils sont tous partis. **(f)** (*large amount*) beaucoup. **a ~ of, ~s of** beaucoup de; **what a ~ of people!** que de monde! *or* de gens!; **what a ~!** quelle quantité!; **there wasn't a ~ we could do** nous ne pouvions pas faire grand-chose; **I'd give a ~ to know ...** je donnerais cher pour savoir ...; **quite a ~ of** pas mal de; **such a ~ of** tellement de, tant de; **an awful ~ of*** énormément* de; **a ~ better** beaucoup *or* bien mieux; **we don't go out a ~** nous ne sortons pas beaucoup *or* pas souvent; **thanks a ~!*** merci beaucoup!; (*iro*) **a ~** *or* **a fat lot you care!*** comme si ça te faisait qch!

lotion ['ləʊʃən] *n* lotion *f*.

lottery ['lɒtərɪ] *n* loterie *f*.

loud [laʊd] **1** *adj voice* fort, sonore; *laugh* grand, bruyant; *noise, cry* sonore, grand; *music* bruyant; *thunder* fracassant; *applause* vif (*f* vive); *protests* vigoureux; *behaviour* tapageur; *colour, clothes* voyant. **the radio is too ~** la radio joue trop fort; (*Mus*) **~ pedal** pédale *f* forte. **2** *adv speak etc* fort, haut. **out ~** tout haut. ♦ **loudhailer** *n* (*Brit*) mégaphone *m*. ♦ **loudly** *adv shout, speak* fort; *proclaim* vigoureusement; *knock, laugh* bruyamment. ♦ **loud-mouthed** *adj* braillard, fort en gueule‡. ♦ **loudness** *n [voice, music etc]* force *f*; *[applause]* bruit *m*; *[protests]* vigueur *f*. ♦ **loudspeaker** *n* haut-parleur *m*; *[stereo]* baffle *m*.

lounge [laʊndʒ] **1** *n* salon *m* (*d'une maison, d'un hôtel etc*). **2** *adj*: **~ suit** complet(-veston) *m*; (*on invitation*) 'tenue de ville'. **3** *vi* (*on bed etc*) se prélasser; (*in chair*) être vautré; (*stroll*) flâner; (*also* **~ about:** *idle*) paresser, être oisif.

♦ **lounger** *n* (*sun-bed*) lit *m* de plage.

louse [laʊs] *n, pl* **lice** (*insect*) pou *m*; (‡: *person*) salaud‡ *m*.

louse up‡ *vt sep deal, event* bousiller*.

♦ **lousy** *adj* (*lit*) pouilleux; (‡: *terrible*) infect; **he's a lousy teacher** il est nul comme prof*; **a lousy trick** un tour de cochon*; **I feel lousy** je suis mal fichu*.

lout [laʊt] *n* rustre *m*. ♦ **loutish** *adj* de rustre.

love [lʌv] **1** *n* **(a)** amour *m* (*of* de, pour; *for* pour). **to be/fall in ~** être/tomber amoureux (*with* de); **they are in ~** ils s'aiment; **~ at first sight** le coup de foudre; **to make ~** faire l'amour (*with* avec; *to* à); **there's no ~ lost between them** ils ne peuvent pas se sentir*; **for the ~ of God** pour l'amour de Dieu; (*: *indignantly: also* **for the ~ of Mike***) pour l'amour du Ciel; **to marry for ~** faire un mariage d'amour; **for ~ of** par amour pour; **not for ~ nor money** *do* pour rien au monde; *sell* à aucun prix; **give her my ~** dis-lui bien des choses de ma part, (*stronger*) embrasse-la pour moi; **he sends you his ~** il t'envoie bien des choses; (*stronger*) il t'embrasse; (*in letter*) **~ from Jim** affectueusement, Jim, (*stronger*) bons baisers, Jim; **yes (my) ~** oui mon amour; **the theatre was her great ~** le théâtre était sa grande passion; **he studies history for the ~ of it** il étudie l'histoire pour son plaisir. **(b)** (*Tennis etc*) rien *m*, zéro *m*. **~ 30** rien à 30, zéro 30.

2 *vt* **(a)** *spouse, child* aimer; *relative, friend* aimer (beaucoup). **he didn't just like her, he LOVED her** il ne l'aimait pas d'amitié, mais d'amour; **she ~d him dearly** elle l'aimait tendrement. **(b)** *food, activity, place* aimer (beaucoup), (*stronger*) adorer. **to ~ to do** *or* **doing sth** aimer (beaucoup) *or* adorer faire qch; **I'd ~ to come** je serais ravi de venir; **I'd ~ to!** cela me ferait très plaisir!

3 *adj letter, song, story, scene* d'amour. **~ affair** liaison *f* (amoureuse); **how's your ~ life these days?*** comment vont les amours?; **~ match** mariage *m* d'amour.

♦ **lovable** *adj person* très sympathique; *child, animal* adorable. ♦ **loveless** *adj* sans amour. ♦ **lovemaking** *n* amour *m* (*acte sexuel*). ♦ **lover** *n* **(a)** amant *m*; (*romantic*) amoureux *m*; **~rs' vows** promesses *fpl* d'amoureux; **they are ~rs** ils ont une liaison; **(b) theatre ~r** amateur *m* de théâtre; **a ~r of Brahms** un(e) fervent(e) de Brahms. ♦ **lovesick** *adj* qui languit d'amour. ♦ **lovey-dovey*** *adj* (*hum*) (trop) tendre. ♦ **loving** *adj* (*gen*) affectueux; (*tender*) tendre; *wife, son* aimant; **money-loving** qui aime l'argent. ♦ **lovingly** *adv* affectueusement; tendrement; (*stronger*) avec amour.

lovely ['lʌvlɪ] *adj* (*pretty: gen*) (très) joli, ravissant; *baby* mignon, joli; (*pleasant: gen*) charmant; *meal, evening, party, voice* très agréable; *night, sunshine, weather* beau; *holiday* excellent; *idea, suggestion* merveilleux; *smell, food* bon. **we had a ~ time** nous nous sommes bien amusés; **it's been ~ seeing you** j'ai été vraiment content de vous voir; **~ and cool** *etc* délicieusement frais *etc*. ♦ **loveliness** *n* beauté *f*, charme *m*.

low[1] [ləʊ] **1** *adj* (*gen*) bas (*f* basse); *density, groan, income, intelligence* faible; *murmur* étouffé; *stock, supply* presque épuisé; *speed* petit, faible; *standard* bas, faible; *quality* inférieur; *person* (*feeble*) faible, affaibli; (*depressed*) déprimé; (*Bio, Zool: primitive*) inférieur; (*pej*) *taste* mauvais; *café etc* de bas étage; (*shameful*) *behaviour* ignoble. *[person, object, sum]* **to be ~ down** être (bien) bas *inv*; **~er down the hill** plus bas sur la colline; **the L~ Countries** les Pays-Bas; **fog on ~ ground** brouillard *m* à basse altitude;

town on ~ **ground** ville bâtie dans une dépression; **at ~ tide** *or* **water** à marée basse; **in a ~ voice** à voix basse; (*of radio etc*) **it's a bit ~** ça n'est pas assez fort, c'est trop bas; (*Cards*) **a ~ diamond** un petit carreau; (*Aut*) **in ~ gear** en première ou seconde vitesse; (*Culin*) **at a ~ heat** à feu doux; **to become** *or* **get ~er** baisser; **L~ Church** Basse Église (*Anglicane*); **~ flying** vols *mpl* à basse altitude; **L~ Latin** bas latin; **L~ Sunday** dimanche *m* de Quasimodo; **~er** *deck, jaw* inférieur; (*Typ*) **~er case** bas *m* de casse; **~er middle class** (*n*) petite bourgeoisie; (*adj*) petit bourgeois; **the ~er classes** (*socially*) les classes inférieures; (*Scol*) **the ~er school** le premier cycle; **the ~er income groups** les économiquement faibles *mpl*; (*Parl*) **the L~er House** la Chambre basse; **the ~er paid** la tranche inférieure des salariés *or* du salariat; **they were ~ on water** ils étaient à court d'eau; **I'm ~ on funds** je suis à court (d'argent); **to be in ~ spirits, to feel ~** être déprimé, ne pas avoir le moral*; **~ forms of life** les formes de vie inférieures *or* les moins évoluées; **the ~est of the ~** le dernier des derniers; **a ~ trick** un sale tour*.

2 *adv aim, sing* bas; *fly* bas, (*of plane*) à basse altitude; *bow, fall, sink* bien bas. (*Elec*) **to turn sth down ~** baisser qch; **supplies are running ~** les provisions baissent; (*Cards*) **to play ~** jouer une basse carte.

3 *n* **(a)** (*Met*) dépression *f*. **(b)** (*low point*) niveau bas, point bas. **to reach a new ~** atteindre son niveau le plus bas.

♦ **lowbrow 1** *n* personne *f* sans prétentions intellectuelles; **2** *adj* sans prétentions intellectuelles. ♦ **low-budget** *adj* bon marché *inv*. ♦ **low-calorie** *adj* à basses calories. ♦ **low-cost** *adj* bon marché *inv*; **~-cost housing** habitations *fpl* à loyer modéré, H.L.M. *mpl*. ♦ **low-cut** *adj* décolleté. ♦ **low-down 1** *adj* (*mean*) méprisable; (*spiteful*) mesquin; **2** *n*: **to give sb the ~-down on*** mettre qn au courant de. ♦ **lower 1** *vt* (*gen*) baisser; *sail, flag* abaisser; *boat, lifeboat* mettre à la mer; *sb/sth on a rope* descendre; *sb's resistance* diminuer; **to ~er one's guard** (*Boxing*) baisser sa garde; (*fig*) ne plus être sur ses gardes; **to ~er sb's morale** démoraliser qn; **~er your voice!** (parle) moins fort!; **to ~er o.s. to do sth** s'abaisser à faire qch; **2** *vi* (*lit*) baisser. ♦ **lower-class** *adj* de la classe inférieure. ♦ **lowering**[1] **1** *n [window, flag, temperature]* abaissement *m*; *[boat]* mise *f* à la mer; *[price, pressure]* baisse *f*; **2** *adj* abaissant, dégradant. ♦ **low-flying** *adj* volant à basse altitude. ♦ **low-grade** *adj* de qualité *or* de catégorie inférieure. ♦ **low-heeled** *adj* à talons plats. ♦ **low-key** *adj* modéré; *operation* très discret; **to keep sth ~-key** faire qch avec modération. ♦ **lowland** *n* plaine *f*; **the L~lands of Scotland** les Basses-Terres *fpl* d'Écosse. ♦ **low-level** *adj* bas; (*fig*) *job* subalterne. ♦ **lowliness** *n* humilité *f*. ♦ **lowly** *adj* (*humble*) humble; (*low-born*) d'origine modeste. ♦ **low-lying** *adj* à basse altitude. ♦ **low-necked** *adj* décolleté. ♦ **lowness** *n* (*in height*) manque *m* de hauteur; *[price, wages]* modicité *f*; *[temperature]* peu *m* d'élevation. ♦ **low-paid** *adj* mal payé; **the ~-paid workers** les petits salaires. ♦ **low-priced** *adj* à bas prix, bon marché *inv*. ♦ **low-profile** *adj* = **low-key**. ♦ **low-rise** *adj* (*Archit*) de hauteur limitée, bas. ♦ **low-spirited** *adj* déprimé, démoralisé.

low[2] [ləʊ] *vi [cattle]* meugler. ♦ **lowing** *n* meuglement *m*.

lowering[2] ['laʊərɪŋ] *adj* sombre, menaçant.

loyal ['lɔɪəl] *adj* loyal (*to sb* envers qn), fidèle (*to sb* à qn). (*Brit*) **the ~ toast** le toast porté au souverain.

♦ **loyalist** *adj, n* loyaliste (*mf*). ♦ **loyally** *adv* fidèlement, loyalement. ♦ **loyalty** *n* loyauté *f*, fidélité *f*.

lozenge ['lɒzɪndʒ] *n* (*Med*) pastille *f*; (*Her, Math*) losange *m*.

lubricate ['lu:brɪkeɪt] *vt* lubrifier; (*Aut*) graisser. **lubricating oil** huile *f* (de graissage). ♦ **lubricant** *adj, n* lubrifiant (*m*). ♦ **lubrication** *n* lubrification *f*; (*Aut*) graissage *m*. ♦ **lubricator** *n* graisseur *m*.

lucid ['lu:sɪd] *adj* lucide. ♦ **lucidity** *n* lucidité *f*. ♦ **lucidly** *adv* lucidement.

luck [lʌk] *n* **(a)** (*chance, fortune*) chance *f*, hasard *m*. **good ~** (bonne) chance, veine* *f*; **bad ~** malchance *f*, déveine* *f*; **to bring sb good/bad ~** porter bonheur/malheur à qn; **good ~!** bonne chance!; **bad** *or* **hard ~!** pas de chance!; **better ~ next time!** ça ira mieux la prochaine fois!; **yes, worse ~** oui, malheureusement; **as ~ would have it** comme par hasard; (*fig*) **it's the ~ of the draw** c'est une question de chance; **it's good/bad ~ to see a black cat** cela porte bonheur/malheur de voir un chat noir; **to be down on one's ~** être dans une mauvaise passe. **(b)** (*good fortune*) (bonne) chance *f*, veine* *f*. **you're in ~, your ~'s in** tu as de la chance *or* de la veine*; **that's a bit of ~!** quelle chance!, quelle veine!*; **he had the ~ to meet her in the street** il a eu la chance de la rencontrer dans la rue; **no such ~!*** ç'aurait été trop beau!; **with any ~** ... avec un peu de chance ...; (*iro*) **and the best of ~!*** je vous (*or* leur *etc*) souhaite bien du plaisir!* (*iro*); **he's got the ~ of the devil*** il a une veine de pendu*. ♦ **luckily** *adv* heureusement, par bonheur. ♦ **luckless** *adj person* malchanceux; *action* malencontreux. ♦ **lucky** *adj person* qui a de la chance; *day* de chance, de veine*; *shot, guess, coincidence* heureux; *horseshoe, charm* porte-bonheur *inv*; **you are ~y to be alive** tu as de la chance de t'en sortir vivant; **he was ~y enough to get a seat** il a eu la chance *or* la veine* de trouver une place; **you ~y thing!** veinard(e)!*; **it was ~y for him that** ... heureusement pour lui que ...; **how ~y!** quelle chance!; **to have a ~y break*** avoir un coup de veine*; **~y dip** pêche *f* miraculeuse; (*fig*) loterie *f*.

lucrative ['lu:krətɪv] *adj* lucratif.

ludicrous ['lu:dɪkrəs] *adj* ridicule. ♦ **ludicrously** *adv* ridiculement.

ludo ['lu:dəʊ] *n* jeu *m* des petits chevaux.

lug [lʌg] *vt* traîner, tirer.

luggage ['lʌgɪdʒ] **1** *n* bagages *mpl*. **~ in advance** bagages non accompagnés. **2** *adj* (*Brit Aut*) **~ boot** coffre *m*; **~ label** étiquette *f* à bagages; **~ rack** (*Rail*) porte-bagages *m inv*, filet *m*; (*Aut*) galerie *f*; **~ van** fourgon *m* (à bagages).

lugubrious [lu:'gu:brɪəs] *adj* lugubre. ♦ **lugubriously** *adv* lugubrement.

lukewarm ['lu:kwɔ:m] *adj* tiède.

lull [lʌl] **1** *n* (*gen*) arrêt *m*; *[storm]* accalmie *f*; (*in work etc*) moment *m* de calme. **2** *vt* apaiser, calmer. to **~ a child to sleep** endormir un enfant en le berçant *etc*; (*fig*) **to be ~ed into a false sense of security** s'endormir dans une fausse sécurité. ♦ **lullaby** *n* berceuse *f*.

lumbago [lʌm'beɪgəʊ] *n* lumbago *m*.

lumber[1] ['lʌmbər] **1** *n* (*wood*) bois *m* de charpente; (*junk*) bric-à-brac *m inv*. **2** *vt* **(a)** *room* encombrer. **(b)** (*US Forestry*) (*fell*) abattre; (*saw up*) débiter. **(c)** (*Brit*: burden*) **to ~ sb with sth** coller* qch à qn. ♦ **lumberjack** *n* bûcheron *m*. ♦ **lumber-jacket** *n* blouson *m*. ♦ **lumber room** *n* débarras *m*. ♦ **lumber yard** *n* chantier *m* de scierie.

lumber[2] ['lʌmbər] *vi* (**~ about, ~ along**) (*gen*) marcher pesamment; *[vehicle]* rouler pesamment. ♦ **lumbering** *adj* lourd, pesant.

luminous ['lu:mɪnəs] *adj* lumineux.

lump[1] [lʌmp] **1** *n* (*gen*) morceau *m*, (*larger*) gros morceau; *[clay, earth]* motte *f*; (*in sauce etc*) grumeau *m*; (**pej: person*) lourdaud(e) *m(f)*; (*Med*) grosseur *f* (*on* à). (*fig*) **to have a ~ in one's throat** avoir la gorge serrée. **2** *adj*: **~ sugar** sucre

m en morceaux; ~ **sum** somme *f* globale *or* forfaitaire; (*payment*) paiement *m* unique.
lump together *vt sep* (*gen*) réunir; (*fig*) *people, cases* mettre dans la même catégorie.
♦ **lumpy** *adj gravy* grumeleux; *bed* défoncé.
lump²* [lʌmp] *vt* (*endure*) **you'll just have to ~ it** il faut bien que tu acceptes (*subj*) sans rien dire.
lunacy ['lu:nəsɪ] *n* aliénation *f* mentale, folie *f*; (*fig*) folie. **that's sheer ~!** c'est de la pure folie! ♦ **lunatic 1** *n* (*Med*) fou *m*, folle *f*; (*Jur*) dément(e) *m(f)*; (*fig*) fou, folle; **2** *adj person* fou (*f* folle), dément; *idea, action* (*crazy*) absurde, (*stupid*) idiot; **lunatic asylum** asile *m* d'aliénés; **the lunatic fringe** les enragés* *mpl*.
lunar ['lu:nəʳ] *adj* (*gen*) lunaire; *eclipse* de la lune. ~ **landing** alunissage *m*.
lunch [lʌntʃ] **1** *n* déjeuner *m*. **to have ~** déjeuner; **come to** *or* **for ~ on Sunday** venez déjeuner dimanche. **2** *vi* déjeuner (*on, off* de). **3** *vt* offrir un déjeuner à. **4** *adj*: ~ **break** heure *f* du déjeuner; **his ~ hour** l'heure *f* de son déjeuner. ♦ **lunchtime** *n* heure *f* de *or* du déjeuner.
luncheon ['lʌntʃən] **1** *n* déjeuner *m*. **2** *adj*: ~ **meat** ≃ mortadelle *f*; ~ **voucher** ticket-restaurant *m*.
lung [lʌŋ] **1** *n* poumon *m*. (*fig*) **at the top of one's ~s** à pleins poumons.
2 *adj disease* pulmonaire. ~ **cancer** cancer *m* du poumon.
lunge [lʌndʒ] **1** *n* brusque mouvement *m* en avant. **2** *vi* (~ **forward**) faire un mouvement brusque en avant; **to ~ at sb** envoyer un coup à qn.
lurch¹ [lɜ:tʃ] **1** *n [car, ship]* embardée *f*. **2** *vi [person]* tituber; *[car, ship]* faire une embardée. *[person]* **to ~ in** *etc* entrer *etc* en titubant.
lurch² [lɜ:tʃ] *n*: **to leave sb in the ~** faire faux bond à qn.
lure [ljʊəʳ] **1** *n* (*charm: of sea etc*) attrait *m*; (*false attraction*) leurre *m*. **2** *vt* attirer (par la ruse). **to ~ sb into a trap** attirer qn dans un piège; **to ~ sb in** *etc* persuader qn par la ruse d'entrer *etc*.
lurid ['ljʊərɪd] *adj* **(a)** *details* atroce; *account, tale* (*gruesome*) terrifiant; (*sensational*) à sensation; *description* saisissant. **(b)** *colour* criard; *sky, sunset* empourpré.
lurk [lɜ:k] *vi [person]* (*hide*) se cacher, se tapir; (*creep about*) rôder; *[danger]* menacer; *[doubt]* persister. ♦ **lurking** *adj fear etc* vague.
luscious ['lʌʃəs] *adj* succulent.
lush [lʌʃ] *adj vegetation* luxuriant; *pasture* riche; (*) *house etc* luxueux.
lust [lʌst] *n* (*gen*) désir *m* (*sexuel*); (*for power etc*) soif *f* (*for* de).
lustre, (*US*) **luster** ['lʌstəʳ] *n* lustre *m*.
lusty ['lʌstɪ] *adj* vigoureux.
lute [lu:t] *n* luth *m*.
Luxembourg ['lʌksəmbɜ:g] *n* Luxembourg *m*.
luxuriant [lʌg'zjʊərɪənt] *adj* (*gen*) luxuriant; *beard* exubérant; *soil* riche. ♦ **luxuriance** *n* luxuriance *f*; exubérance *f*; richesse *f*. ♦ **luxuriate** *vi* s'abandonner avec délices (*in* à).
luxury ['lʌkʃərɪ] **1** *n* luxe *m*. **it's quite a ~ for me to do that** c'est du luxe pour moi que de faire ça. **2** *adj goods* de luxe; *flat, hotel* de grand luxe. ♦ **luxurious** *adj hotel, surroundings* luxueux, somptueux; *tastes* de luxe. ♦ **luxuriously** *adv furnish* luxueusement; *live* dans le luxe; *yawn, stretch* voluptueusement.
lying ['laɪɪŋ] **1** *n* mensonge(s) *m(pl)*. **2** *adj person* menteur; *statement, story* mensonger, faux (*f* fausse).
lymphatic [lɪm'fætɪk] *adj* lymphatique.
lynch [lɪntʃ] *vt* (*lit, fig*) lyncher. ♦ **lynching** *n* lynchage *m*.
lynx [lɪŋks] *n* lynx *m inv*.
lyre ['laɪəʳ] *n* lyre *f*. ~**bird** oiseau-lyre *m*.
lyric ['lɪrɪk] **1** *n* (*poem*) poème *m* lyrique. (*words of song*) ~**s** paroles *fpl*. **2** *adj poem, poet* lyrique. ♦ **lyrical** *adj* lyrique (*also fig*). ♦ **lyrically** *adv* avec lyrisme. ♦ **lyricism** *n* lyrisme *m*. ♦ **lyric-writer** *n* parolier *m*, -ière *f*.

M

M, m [em] *n* (*letter*) M, m *m or f.* (*abbr of* **motorway**) **on the M6** ≃ sur l'A6.
ma'am [mæm] *n abbr of* **madam (a).**
mac* [mæk] *n* (*Brit:* **mackintosh**) imper* *m.*
macadam [məˈkædəm] *n* macadam *m.* ♦ **macadamize** *vt* macadamiser.
macaroni [ˌmækəˈrəʊnɪ] *n* macaroni *m.* ~ **cheese** macaroni au gratin.
macaroon [ˌmækəˈruːn] *n* macaron *m.*
macaw [məˈkɔː] *n* ara *m.*
mace[1] [meɪs] *n* (*spice*) macis *m.*
mace[2] [meɪs] *n* (*weapon*) massue *f*; (*ceremonial*) masse *f.* ~**bearer** massier *m.*
macerate [ˈmæsəreɪt] *vti* macérer.
Mach [mæk] *n*: **at** ~ **2** à Mach 2.
machete [məˈtʃeɪtɪ] *n* machette *f.*
machine [məˈʃiːn] **1** *n* (*gen, also fig*) machine *f*; (*plane*) appareil *m.* **adding** *etc* ~ machine à calculer *etc*; **the** ~ **of government** la machine politique; (*US Pol*) **the democratic** ~ la machine administrative du parti démocrate. **2** *vt* (*Tech*) usiner; (*Sewing*) piquer à la machine. ♦ **machine-gun 1** *n* mitrailleuse *f*; **2** *vt* mitrailler. ♦ **machine-gunner** *n* mitrailleur *m.* ♦ **machine-made** *adj* fait à la machine. ♦ **machine operator** *n* machiniste *mf*; (*on sewing, knitting machines*) mécanicien(ne) *m(f).* ♦ **machinery** *n* (*machines*) machines *fpl*; (*parts*) mécanisme *m*, rouages *mpl*; **a piece of** ~**ry** un mécanisme; **the** ~**ry of government** les rouages de l'État. ♦ **machine-shop** *n* atelier *m* d'usinage. ♦ **machine-stitch** *vt* piquer à la machine. ♦ **machine-tool** *n* machine-outil *f.* ♦ **machinist** = **machine operator.**
machismo [mæˈkɪzməʊ] *n* machisme *m.*
mackerel [ˈmækrəl] *n, pl inv* maquereau *m.*
mackintosh [ˈmækɪntɒʃ] *n* imperméable *m.*
mad [mæd] *adj person* fou (*f* folle), cinglé*; *bull* furieux; *dog* enragé; (*rash*) *person* fou; *hope, plan* insensé; *race, gallop* effréné; (*: *angry*) furieux (*at, with sb* contre qn). **to go** ~ devenir fou; **to drive sb** ~ (*gen*) rendre qn fou; (*exasperate*) exaspérer qn; (*anger*) mettre qn en fureur; **as** ~ **as a hatter** *or* **a March hare** complètement fou; **stark raving** *or* **staring** ~ fou à lier; ~ **with grief** fou de douleur; **you're** ~ **to think of it!** tu es fou d'y songer!; **are you** ~? ça ne va pas?* (*iro*); (*adv phrase*) **like** ~* comme un fou (*or* une folle); **I'm in a** ~ **rush** c'est une vraie course contre la montre; **to get** ~ **at sb*** s'emporter contre qn; **hopping** *or* **spitting** ~* fou furieux; ~ **(keen)*** **about** *or* **on** fou de, mordu de*; **I'm not** ~ **about it*** ça ne m'emballe pas*. ♦ **madden** *vt* rendre fou; (*infuriate*) exaspérer. ♦ **maddening** *adj* exaspérant. ♦ **maddeningly** *adv* à un degré exaspérant, à vous rendre fou; ~**deningly slow** d'une lenteur exaspérante. ♦ **madhouse** *n* maison *f* de fous. ♦ **madly** *adv behave* comme un fou; *interest, excite* follement; *love sb* à la folie; ~**ly keen on** fou *or* passionné de; **I** ~**ly offered to help her** j'ai eu la folie de lui offrir mon aide. ♦ **madman** *n* fou *m*, aliéné *m.* ♦ **madness** *n* folie *f.* ♦ **madwoman** *n* folle *f*, aliénée *f.*
madam [ˈmædəm] *n* **(a)** madame *f*; (*unmarried*) mademoiselle *f.* (*in letters*) **Dear M**~ Madame (*or* Mademoiselle); **M**~ **Chairman** Madame la Présidente. **(b) a little** ~ une petite pimbêche.
made [meɪd] *pret, ptp of* **make.** ♦ **made-to-measure** *adj* fait sur mesure. ♦ **made-to-order** *adj* fait sur commande. ♦ **made-up** *adj story* inventé, factice; (*pej*) faux (*f* fausse); *face, person* maquillé; *eyes, nails* fait.
Madeira [məˈdɪərə] *n* (*Geog*) Madère *f*; (*wine*) madère *m.*
Madonna [məˈdɒnə] *n* madone *f.*
mafia [ˈmæfɪə] *n* maffia *f.*
magazine [ˌmægəˈziːn] *n* (*Press: abbr* **mag***) revue *f*, magazine *m*; (*Rad, TV:* ~ *programme*) magazine; (*Mil: store*) magasin *m*; (*part of gun etc*) magasin.
maggot [ˈmægət] *n* ver *m*, asticot *m.* ♦ **maggoty** *adj* véreux.
magic [ˈmædʒɪk] **1** *n* magie *f.* **like** ~ comme par enchantement. **2** *adj* magique; (*fig*) merveilleux; *beauty* enchanteur (*f* -teresse). ~ **lantern** lanterne *f* magique; ~ **spell** sortilège *m*; **to say the** ~ **word** prononcer la formule magique. ♦ **magical** *adj* magique. ♦ **magically** *adv* magiquement. ♦ **magician** [məˈdʒɪʃən] *n* magicien(ne) *m(f)*; (*Theat etc*) illusionniste *mf.*
magistrate [ˈmædʒɪstreɪt] *n* magistrat *m.*
magnanimous [mægˈnænɪməs] *adj* magnanime. ♦ **magnanimity** *n* magnanimité *f.* ♦ **magnanimously** *adv* magnanimement.
magnate [ˈmægneɪt] *n* magnat *m.* **industrial** ~ magnat de l'industrie.
magnesia [mægˈniːʃə] *n* magnésie *f.*
magnesium [mægˈniːzɪəm] *n* magnésium *m.*
magnet [ˈmægnɪt] *n* aimant *m.* ♦ **magnetic** *adj* magnétique. ♦ **magnetically** *adv* magnétiquement. ♦ **magnetism** *n* magnétisme *m.* ♦ **magnetize** *vt* magnétiser. ♦ **magneto** *n* magnéto *f.*
magnificent [mægˈnɪfɪsənt] *adj* magnifique, splendide; (*sumptuous*) somptueux. ♦ **magnificence** *n* magnificence *f*, splendeur *f*; somptuosité *f.* ♦ **magnificently** *adv* magnifiquement.
magnify [ˈmægnɪfaɪ] *vt image* grossir; *sound* amplifier; *incident etc* exagérer. ~**ing glass** loupe *f.* ♦ **magnification** *n* grossissement *m*; amplification *f.*
magnitude [ˈmægnɪtjuːd] *n* (*gen*) grandeur *f*; (*Astron*) magnitude *f.*
magnolia [mægˈnəʊlɪə] *n* magnolia *m.*
magnum [ˈmægnəm] *n* magnum *m.*
magpie [ˈmægpaɪ] *n* pie *f.*
mahogany [məˈhɒgənɪ] **1** *n* acajou *m.* **2** *adj* (*made of* ~) en acajou; (~*-coloured*) acajou *inv.*
Mahomet [məˈhɒmɪt] *n* Mahomet *m.* ♦ **Mahometan 1** *adj* mahométan; **2** *n* Mahométan(e) *m(f).*
maid [meɪd] *n* **(a)** (*servant*) bonne *f.* **(b)** (*pej*) **old** ~ vieille fille; (*Hist*) **the M**~ **(of Orleans)** la Pucelle (d'Orléans). ♦ **maid-of-all-work** *n* bonne *f* à tout faire. ♦ **maid-of-honour** *n* demoiselle *f* d'honneur.
maiden [ˈmeɪdn] **1** *n* (*liter*) jeune fille *f.* **2** *adj* **(a)** ~ **aunt** tante *f* célibataire; ~ **lady** demoiselle *f*; ~ **name** nom *m* de jeune fille. **(b)** *flight, voyage* premier (*before n*), inaugural. (*Parl*) ~ **speech** premier discours (*d'un député etc*). ♦ **maidenhair**

(fern) *n* capillaire *m* (*Bot*).

mail [meɪl] **1** *n* poste *f*; (*letters*) courrier *m*. **by ~** par la poste; **here's your ~** voici votre courrier. **2** *vt* poster. **3** *adj* (*US Rail*) **~ car** wagon-poste *m*; (*US*) **~ carrier** facteur *m*, préposé(e) *m(f)*; **~ clerk** préposé(e) *m(f)* au courrier; **~ train** train-poste *m*; (*Brit*) **~ van** (*Aut*) voiture *f or* fourgon *m* des postes; (*Rail*) wagon-poste *m*. ♦ **mailbag** *n* sac postal. ♦ **mailbox** *n* (*US*) boîte *f* aux lettres. ♦ **mailing** *adj*: **~ing list** liste *f* d'adresses. ♦ **mailman** *n* (*US*) facteur *m*, préposé *m*. ♦ **mail-order 1** *n* vente *m or* achat *m* par correspondance; **2** *adj*: **~-order firm** maison *f* de vente par correspondance.

maim [meɪm] *vt* estropier, mutiler.

main [meɪn] **1** *adj feature, objective* principal, essentiel; *door, deck, shop* principal; *pipe, beam* maître (*f* maîtresse). **the ~ body of the army/the crowd** le gros de l'armée/de la foule; **one of his ~ ideas** l'une de ses idées principales; **my ~ idea was ...** mon idée directrice était ...; **the ~ thing is to ...** l'essentiel est de ...; **the ~ thing to remember is ...** ce qu'il ne faut surtout pas oublier c'est ...; (*Aut etc*) **~ bearing** palier *m*; (*Culin*) **~ course** plat *m* de résistance; (*Rail*) **~ line** grande ligne *f*; **a ~ road** une grande route, une route à grande circulation; **the ~ road** la grand-route; **~ street** grand-rue *f*, rue principale.

2 *n* **(a)** (*principal pipe, wire*) canalisation *f or* conduite *f* maîtresse. **electricity ~** conducteur principal; **gas ~** (*in street*) conduite principale; (*house*) conduite de gaz; **~ (sewer)** égout *m* collecteur; **water ~** (*in street or house*) conduite d'eau de la ville; **water from the ~s** eau *f* de la conduite; (*Elec*) **connected to the ~s** branché sur le secteur; **it works by battery or from the ~s** cela marche sur piles ou sur le secteur; **to turn off at the ~(s)** couper au compteur. **(b) in the ~** dans l'ensemble.

♦ **mainland** *n* continent *m* (*opposé à une île*); **the ~land of Greece** la Grèce continentale. ♦ **mainly** *adv* principalement; (*especially*) surtout. ♦ **mainmast** *n* grand mât *m*. ♦ **mainsail** *n* grand-voile *f*. ♦ **mainspring** *n* [*clock etc*] ressort *m* principal; (*fig*) mobile *m* principal. ♦ **mainstay** *n* (*fig*) pilier *m*, soutien *m*.

maintain [meɪn'teɪn] *vt* **(a)** (*continue: gen*) maintenir; *silence* garder; *radio silence* maintenir; *friendship, correspondence* entretenir; *attitude, advantage* conserver; *cause, rights, one's strength* soutenir. **the improvement is ~ed** l'amélioration se maintient. **(b)** (*support*) *army, family* entretenir. **(c)** (*keep in repair*) *road, building, machine* entretenir. **(d)** (*assert*) soutenir, maintenir (*that* que).

♦ **maintenance 1** *n* (*gen*) maintien *m*; [*army, family, road*] entretien *m*; (*after divorce*) pension *f* alimentaire; **2** *adj crew, costs* d'entretien; **maintenance allowance** *or* **grant** [*student*] bourse *f* (d'études); [*worker away from home*] indemnité *f* pour frais de déplacement; (*Jur*) **maintenance order** obligation *f* alimentaire.

maisonette [ˌmeɪzə'net] *n* duplex *m*.

maize [meɪz] *n* maïs *m*.

majesty ['mædʒɪstɪ] *n* majesté *f*. **His M~ the King** Sa Majesté le Roi.

♦ **majestic** *adj* majestueux. ♦ **majestically** *adv* majestueusement.

major ['meɪdʒəʳ] **1** *adj* majeur. (*Mus*) **~ key** ton *m* majeur; **in the ~ key** en majeur; **the ~ part** la majeure partie; **for the ~ part** en grande partie; **~ road** route *f* à priorité; (*Cards*) **~ suit** majeure *f*. **2** *n* **(a)** (*Mil*) commandant *m*. **(b)** (*Jur*) majeur(e) *m(f)*. **(c)** (*US Univ*) matière *f* principale. **3** *vi* (*US Univ*) se spécialiser (*in* en). ♦ **major-general** *n* général *m* de division. ♦ **majority 1** *n* (*all senses*) majorité *f*; **to be in the ~ity** être en majorité; **elected by a ~ity of 9** élu avec une majorité de 9 voix; **the ~ity of people** la plupart des gens; **2** *adj government, verdict* majoritaire.

Majorca [mə'jɔːkə] *n* Majorque *f*. **in ~** à Majorque.

make [meɪk] *pret, ptp* **made 1** *vt* **(a)** (*gen*) faire; (*Comm*) faire, fabriquer; *building* construire; *points, score* marquer. **God made Man** Dieu a créé l'homme; **made in France** fabriqué en France; (*on label*) 'made in France'; **made of gold** en or; (*fig*) **to show what one is made of** donner sa mesure; **as clever as they ~ 'em*** malin comme pas un*; **this business has made him** cette affaire a fait son succès; **that film made her** ce film l'a consacrée; **he was made for life** son avenir était assuré; **to ~ or break sb** assurer ou briser la carrière de qn; **that made my day!*** ça a transformé ma journée!

(b) (*cause to be*) faire; (+*adj*) rendre. **to ~ sb sad** rendre qn triste; **to ~ o.s. ill** *etc* se rendre malade *etc*; **to ~ o.s. understood** se faire comprendre; **to ~ yellow** jaunir; **to ~ sb king** faire qn roi; **he made him his assistant** il en a fait son assistant; **to ~ sth into sth else** transformer qch en qch d'autre; **let's ~ it £3** si on disait 3 livres.

(c) (*force*) faire; (*stronger*) obliger, forcer. **to ~ sb do sth** faire faire qch à qn, obliger *or* forcer qn à faire qch; **to ~ sb wait** faire attendre qn; **I don't know what ~s him do it** je ne sais pas ce qui le pousse à le faire; **you can't ~ me!** tu ne peux pas m'y forcer!; **to ~ believe** faire semblant (*that one is* d'être); **to ~ do with sth/sb** (*be satisfied*) s'arranger de qch/qn; (*manage*) se débrouiller avec qch/qn; (*fig*) **to ~ do and mend** se débrouiller avec ce qu'on a.

(d) (*earn etc*) *money* [*person*] gagner, [*business deal etc*] rapporter; *profits* faire. **he made £500 on it, it made him £500** cela lui a rapporté 500 livres.

(e) (*equal; constitute*) faire. **2 and 2 ~ 4** 2 et 2 font 4; **that ~s 20** ça fait 20; (*in shop etc*) **how much does that ~?** combien ça fait?; **these books ~ a set** ces livres forment une collection; **it ~s pleasant reading** c'est agréable à lire; **they ~ a handsome pair** ils forment un beau couple; **he made a good husband** il s'est montré bon mari; **she made him a good wife** elle a été une bonne épouse pour lui; **he'll ~ a good footballer** il fera un bon joueur de football.

(f) (*reach*) *destination* arriver à; (*catch*) *train etc* attraper, avoir. **will we ~ (it to) Paris before lunch?** est-ce que nous arriverons à Paris avant le déjeuner?; **to ~ port** arriver au port; **he made (it into) the first team** il a réussi à être sélectionné dans la première équipe; **to ~ it** (*arrive*) arriver; (*achieve sth*) parvenir à qch; (*succeed*) réussir, y arriver; **can you ~ it by 3 o'clock?** est-ce que tu peux y être pour 3 heures?; (*Naut*) **to ~ 10 knots** filer 10 nœuds.

(g) (*reckon; believe*) **what time do you ~ it?** quelle heure as-tu?; **I ~ it 100 km from here to Paris** selon moi *or* d'après moi il y a 100 km d'ici à Paris; **what do you ~ of him/of it?** qu'est-ce que tu penses de lui/tu en penses?; **I can't ~ anything of it** je n'y comprends rien.

(h) *cards* battre; *trick* faire.

2 *vi* **(a) to ~ as if to do** faire mine de faire.

(b) (*go*) aller, se diriger (*for, towards* vers); [*ship*] faire route (*for* pour). **they made after him** ils se sont mis à sa poursuite; **to ~ for home** rentrer, prendre le chemin du retour; (*fig*) **to ~ for sth** (*result in*) tendre à qch; (*contribute to*) contribuer à qch; (*conduce to*) être favorable à qch.

3 *n* **(a)** (*Comm*) (*brand*) marque *f*; (*manufacture*) fabrication *f*. **French ~ of car** marque française de voiture; **these are our own ~** ceux-ci sont fabriqués par nous. **(b) he's on the ~*** il veut réussir à tout prix.

make away *vi* = **make off.**
make away with *vt fus* (*kill*) supprimer, tuer.
make off *vi* se sauver, filer*. **to ~ off with sth** filer avec qch.
make out 1 *vi* (*: *get on*) se débrouiller. **2** *vt sep* **(a)** (*draw up*) *list, account* faire, dresser; *cheque, bill, will* faire. **(b)** (*distinguish*) *object, person* distinguer; (*decipher*) *handwriting* déchiffrer; (*understand*) *sb's motives* comprendre. **I can't ~ it out at all** je n'y comprends rien; **how do you ~ that out?** qu'est-ce qui vous fait penser cela? **(c)** (*claim*) prétendre (*that* que); (*imply*) faire paraître. **it ~s her out to be naïve** cela la fait passer pour naïve.
make over *vt sep* **(a)** (*assign*) *money, land* céder (*to* à). **(b)** (*remake*) *garment* refaire.
make up 1 *vi* **(a)** (*~ friends again*) se réconcilier. **(b)** (*apply cosmetics*) se maquiller. **2** *vt sep* **(a)** (*invent*) *story* inventer. **(b)** (*put together*) *packet, parcel, list, bed* faire; *medicine, solution* préparer; *prescription* exécuter. **to ~ sth up into a bundle** faire un paquet de qch. **(c)** (*complete etc*) *loss, deficit* combler; *quantity, total* compléter; *lost time* rattraper; *lost ground* regagner. **he made it up to £100** il a complété les 100 livres; **to ~ it up to sb for sth** compenser qn pour qch. **(d)** (*settle*) *dispute* mettre fin à. **to ~ it up** se réconcilier; **let's ~ it up** faisons la paix. **(e)** (*cosmetics*) maquiller. **(f)** (*form*) *a whole etc* former. **group made up of** groupe fait *or* formé *or* composé de.
make up for *vt fus loss, injury* compenser; *lost time* rattraper; *trouble caused* se faire pardonner; *mistake* se rattraper pour.
make up on *vt fus* (*catch up with*) rattraper.
make up to* *vt fus* (*curry favour with*) essayer de se faire bien voir par.
♦ **make-believe** *n*: **the land of ~-believe** le pays des chimères; **it's just ~-believe** (*activity*) c'est pour faire semblant; (*pej: story*) c'est de l'invention pure. ♦ **maker** *n* (*Comm*) fabricant *m*; (*Rel*) **our M~r** le Créateur. ♦ **makeshift 1** *n* expédient *m*; **2** *adj* de fortune. ♦ **make-up 1** *n* **(a)** (*nature etc*) *[object, group etc]* constitution *f*; *[person]* caractère *m*; **(b)** (*cosmetics*) maquillage *m*; **2** *adj*: **~-up artist** maquilleur *m*, -euse *f*; **~-up bag** trousse *f* de maquillage; **~-up remover** démaquillant *m*. ♦ **making** *n* **(a)** (*Comm, gen*) fabrication *f*; *[dress, food]* confection *f*; **in the making** en formation; **still in the making** encore en cours de développement; **history in the making** l'histoire en train de se faire; **war in the making** la guerre qui se prépare; **troubles of his own making** des ennuis de sa propre faute; **it was the making of him/her** cela en a fait un homme/une femme; **(b) the makings of a library** ce qu'il faut pour faire une bibliothèque; **he has the makings of a footballer** il a l'étoffe d'un joueur de football.
maladjusted [ˌmæləˈdʒʌstɪd] *adj* (*Psych*) inadapté.
maladroit [ˌmæləˈdrɔɪt] *adj* maladroit.
malady [ˈmælədɪ] *n* maladie *f*, mal *m*.
malaria [məˈlɛərɪə] *n* malaria *f*.
male [meɪl] **1** *adj* (*gen*) mâle; *sex* masculin; *clothes* d'homme. **~ chauvinist pig** sale phallocrate‡ *m*. **2** *n* mâle *m*.
malevolent [məˈlevələnt] *adj* malveillant. ♦ **malevolence** *n* malveillance *f*. ♦ **malevolently** *adv* avec malveillance.
malformation [ˌmælfɔːˈmeɪʃən] *n* malformation *f*.
malfunction [ˌmælˈfʌŋkʃən] **1** *n* mauvais fonctionnement *m*. **2** *vi* mal fonctionner.
malice [ˈmælɪs] *n* méchanceté *f*; (*stronger*) malveillance *f*. **to bear sb ~** vouloir du mal à qn; (*Jur*) **~ aforethought** préméditation *f*. ♦ **malicious** *adj* méchant; malveillant; (*Jur*) *damage* causé avec intention de nuire. ♦ **maliciously** *adv* avec méchanceté; avec malveillance.
malign [məˈlaɪn] **1** *adj* pernicieux, nuisible. **2** *vt* calomnier.
♦ **malignancy** [məˈlɪgnənsɪ] *n [look, intention]* malveillance *f*; *[action, effect]* malfaisance *f*; (*Med*) malignité *f*. ♦ **malignant** *adj* malveillant; malfaisant; (*Med*) malin (*f* -igne).
malinger [məˈlɪŋgəʳ] *vi* faire le (*or* la) malade. ♦ **malingerer** *n* faux (*or* fausse) malade *m(f)*.
mallard [ˈmæləd] *n* canard *m* sauvage.
malleable [ˈmælɪəbl] *adj* malléable.
mallet [ˈmælɪt] *n* (*all senses*) maillet *m*.
malnutrition [ˌmælnjʊˈtrɪʃən] *n* sous-alimentation *f*.
malt [mɔːlt] **1** *n* malt *m*. **2** *adj vinegar* de malt. **~ed milk** lait malté; **~ whisky** whisky *m* pur malt.
Malta [ˈmɔːltə] *n* Malte *f*. **in ~** à Malte.
maltreat [ˌmælˈtriːt] *vt* maltraiter. ♦ **maltreatment** *n* mauvais traitement *m*.
mam(m)a [məˈmɑː] *n* maman *f*.
mammal [ˈmæməl] *n* mammifère *m*.
mammoth [ˈmæməθ] **1** *n* mammouth *m*. **2** *adj* monstre.
man [mæn] *pl* **men 1** *n* (*gen*) homme *m*; (*servant*) valet *m*; (*in factory etc*) ouvrier *m*; (*in office, shop etc*) employé *m*; (*Mil*) homme (de troupe), soldat *m*; (*Naut*) homme (d'équipage), matelot *m*; (*Sport: player*) joueur *m*; (*husband*) homme, type* *m*; (*Chess*) pièce *f*; (*Draughts*) pion *m*. **an old ~** un vieillard; **a blind ~** un aveugle; **that ~ Smith** ce Smith; **as one ~** comme un seul homme; **they're communists to a ~** ils sont tous communistes sans exception; **to the last ~** jusqu'au dernier; **every ~ jack of them** tous autant qu'ils sont; **~ and wife** mari et femme; **to live as ~ and wife** vivre maritalement; **he was ~ enough to apologize** il a eu le courage de s'excuser; **he's a Leeds ~** il est *or* vient de Leeds; **he's not the ~ to fail** il n'est pas homme à échouer; **the ~ for the job** l'homme qu'il faut pour ce travail; **a medical ~** un docteur; **the ~ in the street** l'homme de la rue; **~ of the world** homme d'expérience; **~ about town** homme du monde; **the ice-cream ~** le marchand de glaces; (*humanity*) **M~** l'homme; **men say that ...** on dit que ...; **any ~ would have ...** n'importe qui aurait ...; **hurry up, ~!*** (*to friend etc*) dépêche-toi mon vieux!*; **my little ~** mon grand; **good ~!** bravo!
2 *vt ship, fortress, boats, pumps* armer; *guns* servir. **the ship was ~ned by Chinese** l'équipage était composé de Chinois; **the telephone is ~ned 12 hours a day** il y a une permanence au téléphone 12 heures par jour.
♦ **man-eating** *adj animal* mangeur d'hommes; *tribe etc* anthropophage. ♦ **manful** *adj* vaillant. ♦ **manfully** *adv* vaillamment. ♦ **manhandle** *vt* (*treat roughly*) malmener; (*move by hand*) *goods etc* manutentionner. ♦ **manhole** *n* regard *m* (d'égout); **~hole cover** plaque *f* d'égout. ♦ **manhood** *n* **(a)** (*age, state*) âge *m* d'homme; **during his early ~hood** quand il était jeune homme; **(b)** (*manliness*) virilité *f*; **(c)** (*collect n*) **Scotland's ~hood** tous les hommes d'Écosse. ♦ **man-hour** *n* (*Ind*) heure *f* de main-d'œuvre. ♦ **manhunt** *n* chasse *f* à l'homme. ♦ **mankind** *n* l'homme *m*, le genre humain. ♦ **manlike** *adj form, figure* à l'aspect humain; *qualities* humain. ♦ **manliness** *n* virilité *f*. ♦ **manly** *adj* viril. ♦ **man-made** *adj fibre* synthétique; *lake* artificiel. ♦ **mannish** *adj* masculin, hommasse (*pej*). ♦ **manpower** *n* (*gen, Ind*) main-d'œuvre *f*; (*Mil*) effectifs *mpl*. ♦ **manservant** *n* valet *m* de chambre. ♦ **man-sized** *adj* (*fig*) grand, de taille. ♦ **manslaughter** *n* (*Jur*) homicide *m* involontaire. ♦ **man-to-man** *adj, adv* d'homme à homme. ♦ **mantrap** *n* piège *m* à hommes.
manacle [ˈmænəkl] *n* menotte *f* (*de prisonnier*).

manage ['mænɪdʒ] **1** *vt* **(a)** (*direct: gen, Comm*) gérer; *institution, organization* diriger; *farm* exploiter; (*pej*) *election etc* truquer. **(b)** (*deal with*) *boat, vehicle* manœuvrer; *tool* manier; *animal, person* savoir s'y prendre avec. **you ~d the situation very well** tu t'en es très bien tiré. **(c)** (*succeed, contrive*) réussir, arriver (*to do* à faire). **how did you ~ not to spill it?** comment as-tu fait pour ne pas le renverser?; (*iro*) **he ~d to annoy them** il a trouvé le moyen de les mécontenter; **I can't ~ it** je ne peux pas; **I can ~ 10 francs** je peux y mettre 10 F; **can you ~ the suitcases?** pouvez-vous porter les valises?; **can you ~ 8 o'clock?** 8 heures, ça vous convient? **2** *vi* **(a)** (*succeed*) **can you ~?** tu y arrives?; **I can ~** ça va; **to ~ without sth/sb** se passer de qch/qn. **(b)** (*financially*) se débrouiller (*on* avec). ♦ **manageable** *adj vehicle, boat* facile à manœuvrer; *person, animal* docile; *size, proportions* maniable; *hair* souple. ♦ **management 1** *n* **(a)** (*act: V* **manage 1a**) gestion *f*; direction *f*; exploitation *f*; **'under new ~ment'** 'changement de direction'; **(b)** (*people*) *[business, firm]* cadres *mpl*, direction *f*; *[hotel, shop, theatre]* direction; **~ment and workers** les cadres et les ouvriers; **2** *adj committee* de direction; **~ment consultant** conseiller *m* de gestion; **~ment trainee** cadre *m* stagiaire. ♦ **manager** *n* (*gen*) directeur *m*; *[restaurant, shop]* gérant *m*; *[farm]* exploitant *m*; *[actor, singer, boxer etc]* manager *m*; **sales ~r** directeur commercial. ♦ **manageress** *n [hotel, shop]* gérante *f*; *[theatre]* directrice *f*. ♦ **managerial** *adj* directorial; **the ~rial class** les cadres *mpl*. ♦ **managing** *adj* **(a) managing director** directeur général, ≈ P.-D.G. *m*; **(b)** (*bossy*) autoritaire.

mandarin ['mændərɪn] *n* **(a)** (*person*) mandarin *m*. **(b) ~ (orange)** mandarine *f*.

mandate ['mændeɪt] *n* mandat *m* (*to do* de faire). ♦ **mandatory** *adj* obligatoire.

mandolin(e) ['mændəlɪn] *n* mandoline *f*.

mane [meɪn] *n* crinière *f*.

maneuver [mə'nuːvər] *etc* (*US*) = **manœuvre** *etc*.

manganese [ˌmæŋgə'niːz] *n* manganèse *m*.

mange [meɪndʒ] *n* gale *f*.

manger ['meɪndʒər] *n* mangeoire *f*; (*Rel*) crèche *f*.

mangle[1] ['mæŋgl] **1** *n* (*wringer*) essoreuse *f* (*à rouleaux*). **2** *vt* essorer.

mangle[2] ['mæŋgl] *vt* (*mutilate*) *object, body* déchirer; *text* mutiler; *quotation, message* estropier.

mango ['mæŋgəʊ] *n* (*fruit*) mangue *f*; (*tree*) manguier *m*. **~ chutney** condiment *m* à la mangue.

mania ['meɪnɪə] *n* manie *f*. **persecution ~** manie de la persécution; **to have a ~ for (doing) sth*** avoir la manie de (faire) qch. ♦ **maniac 1** *n* (*Psych*) maniaque *mf*; (*: *fig*) fou *m* (folle *f*) à lier; **football ~c*** mordu* *m* du football; **2** *adj* maniaque; fou. ♦ **manic** *adj* (*Psych*) maniaque; **manic depression** cyclothymie *f*. ♦ **manic-depressive** *adj, n* cyclothymique (*mf*).

manicure ['mænɪˌkjʊər] **1** *n* soin *m* des mains. **2** *vt nails* (se) faire. ♦ **manicurist** *n* manucure *mf*.

manifest ['mænɪfest] **1** *adj* manifeste. **2** *vt* manifester. **3** *n* manifeste *m* (*Aviat, Naut*). ♦ **manifestation** *n* manifestation *f*. ♦ **manifestly** *adv* manifestement. ♦ **manifesto** *n* manifeste *m* (*Pol etc*).

manifold ['mænɪfəʊld] **1** *adj* (*varied*) divers; (*numerous*) multiple; *wisdom* infini. **2** *n* (*Aut etc*) **exhaust ~** tubulure *f* d'échappement.

manipulate [mə'nɪpjʊleɪt] *vt tool etc* manipuler; *vehicle, person* manœuvrer; (*pej*) *facts, figures* tripoter*. **to ~ a situation** faire son jeu des circonstances. ♦ **manipulation** *n* manipulation *f*; manœuvre *f*; (*pej*) tripotage* *m*.

manna ['mænə] *n* manne *f*.

mannequin ['mænɪkɪn] *n* mannequin *m*.

manner ['mænər] *n* **(a)** (*mode, way*) manière *f*, façon *f*. **the ~ in which he did it** la manière *or* façon dont il l'a fait; **in such a ~ that** de telle sorte que + *indic* (*actual result*) *or* + *subj* (*intended result*); **in this ~** de cette manière *or* façon; **in a ~ of speaking** pour ainsi dire; **it's a ~ of speaking** c'est une façon de parler; **~ of payment** mode *m* de paiement; **(as) to the ~ born** comme s'il (*or* elle *etc*) avait cela dans le sang. **(b)** (*attitude*) attitude *f* (*to sb* envers qn), comportement *m*. **(c)** (*social*) **~s** manières *fpl*; **it's good/bad ~s** cela se fait/ne se fait pas (*to do* de faire); **road ~s** politesse *f* au volant; **comedy of ~s** comédie *f* de mœurs. **(d)** (*type*) sorte *f*, genre *m*. **all ~ of** toutes sortes de. ♦ **mannered** *adj* maniéré. ♦ **mannerism** *n* **(a)** (*habit*) trait *m* particulier; (*pej*) tic *m*; **(b)** (*Art etc*) maniérisme *m*. ♦ **mannerly** *adj* poli, bien élevé.

man(n)ikin ['mænɪkɪn] *n* **(a)** (*dwarf etc*) nabot *m*. **(b)** (*dummy*) mannequin *m* (*objet*).

manœuvre [mə'nuːvər] **1** *n* manœuvre *f*. (*Mil etc*) **on ~s** en manœuvres. **2** *vt* (*all senses*) manœuvrer (*sth into position* qch pour le mettre en position; *sb into doing* qn pour qu'il fasse). **to ~ sth through** *etc* faire traverser *etc* qch en manœuvrant. **3** *vi* manœuvrer. ♦ **manœuvrability** *n* manœuvrabilité *f*. ♦ **manœuvrable** *adj* facile à manœuvrer.

manor ['mænər] *n* (**~ house**) manoir *m*.

mansion ['mænʃən] *n* (*in town*) hôtel *m* particulier; (*in country*) château *m*, manoir *m*.

mantel ['mæntl] *n* (**~piece, ~shelf**) (tablette *f* de) cheminée *f*.

mantle ['mæntl] *n* (†: *garment*) cape *f*; *[gas lamp]* manchon *m*. **~ of snow** manteau *m* de neige.

manual ['mænjʊəl] **1** *adj* manuel. **~ worker** travailleur manuel. **2** *n* (*book*) manuel *m*; *[organ]* clavier *m*. ♦ **manually** *adv* à la main.

manufacture [ˌmænjʊ'fæktʃər] **1** *n* (*gen*) fabrication *f*; *[clothes]* confection *f*. **2** *vt* fabriquer (*also fig*); confectionner. **~d goods** produits manufacturés; **manufacturing industries** industries *fpl* de fabrication. ♦ **manufacturer** *n* fabricant *m*.

manure [mə'njʊər] **1** *n* fumier *m*; (*artificial*) engrais *m*. **liquid ~** purin *m*. **2** *adj*: **~ heap** tas *m* de fumier. **3** *vt* fumer; répandre des engrais sur.

manuscript ['mænjʊskrɪpt] *adj, n* manuscrit (*m*).

Manx [mæŋks] **1** *adj* de l'île de Man. **2** *n* (*Ling*) mannois *m*.

many ['menɪ] *adj, pron: comp* **more**, *superl* **most** **(a)** beaucoup (de), un grand nombre (de). **~ books** beaucoup de livres, un grand nombre de livres, de nombreux livres; **very ~** un très grand nombre (de); **~ of them/of those books** un grand nombre d'entre eux/de ces livres; **a good ~ of** un bon nombre de; **~ came** beaucoup sont venus; **~ times** bien des fois; **~ years** bien des années, longtemps; **of ~ kinds** de toutes sortes; **a good** *or* **great ~ things** pas mal de choses*; **in ~ cases** dans bien des cas; **~ a man would be ...** il y en a plus d'un qui serait ...; **~ happy returns (of the day)!** bon *or* joyeux anniversaire!

(b) (*in phrases*) **as ~ as** autant que; **as ~ books as** autant de livres que; **as ~ as 100 people** jusqu'à 100 personnes; **how ~?** combien?; **how ~ people?** combien de gens?; **how ~ there are!** qu'ils sont nombreux!; **however ~ books you have** quel que soit le nombre de livres que vous ayez; **so ~** tant (*that* que); **so ~ dresses** tant de robes; **ever so ~ times** je ne sais combien de fois; **too ~** trop; **too ~ cakes** trop de gâteaux; **3 too ~** 3 de trop; (*fig*) **he's had one too ~*** il a bu un coup de trop; **there are too ~ of you** vous êtes trop nombreux.

♦ **many-coloured** *adj* multicolore. ♦ **many-sided** *adj object* qui a de nombreux côtés; (*fig*) *person* aux intérêts (*or* talents) variés; *problem* complexe.

map [mæp] 1 *n* (*gen*) carte *f*; *[town, railway]* plan *m*. (*fig*) **this will put Moordown on the ~** cela fera connaître Moordown; (*fig*) **wiped off the ~** rasé; (*fig*) **off the ~*** à l'autre bout du monde, perdu. 2 *vt* faire la carte *or* le plan de; *route* tracer.
map out *vt sep route* tracer; *book* établir les grandes lignes de; *one's time, career* organiser.
♦ **mapmaker** *n* cartographe *m*. ♦ **mapmaking** *n* cartographie *f*. ♦ **mapping pen** *n* plume *f* à dessin.
maple ['meɪpl] 1 *n* érable *m*. 2 *adj* d'érable.
mar [mɑːʳ] *vt* gâter. **to make or ~ sth** faire la fortune ou la ruine de qch.
maraschino [ˌmærəsˈkiːnəʊ] *n* marasquin *m*.
marathon ['mærəθən] 1 *n* marathon *m*. 2 *adj meeting etc* marathon *inv*; (*Sport*) *runner* du marathon.
maraud [məˈrɔːd] *vi* marauder. **to go ~ing** aller à la maraude. ♦ **marauder** *n* maraudeur *m*, -euse *f*.
♦ **marauding** *adj* maraudeur.
marble ['mɑːbl] 1 *n* **(a)** (*substance, sculpture etc*) marbre *m*. **(b)** (*toy*) bille *f*. **to play ~s** jouer aux billes. 2 *adj staircase* de *or* en marbre; *industry* marbrier. **~ quarry** marbrière *f*.
March [mɑːtʃ] *n* mars *m*; *for phrases V* **September.**
march [mɑːtʃ] 1 *n* (*all senses*) marche *f*. **on the ~** en marche; **quick/slow ~** marche rapide/lente; **a day's ~** une journée de marche. 2 *vi* (*Mil etc*) marcher au pas. **to ~ into battle** marcher au combat; **to ~ past** défiler; **to ~ past sb** défiler devant qn; **~!** marche!; **to ~ in** *etc* (*Mil*) entrer *etc* (au pas); (*gen*) entrer *etc* (*briskly*) d'un pas énergique *or* (*angrily*) d'un air furieux; **he ~ed up to me** il s'est approché de moi d'un air décidé; **to ~ up and down the room** faire les cent pas dans la pièce. 3 *vt* (*Mil*) faire marcher (au pas). (*gen*) **to ~ sb in** *etc* faire entrer *etc* qn tambour battant; **to ~ sb off to prison** embarquer qn en prison*.
♦ **marching** *adj song* de route; **~ing orders** feuille *f* de route; (*fig*) **to give sb his ~ing orders*** flanquer* qn à la porte. ♦ **march-past** *n* défilé *m* (*Mil etc*).
marchioness ['mɑːʃənɪs] *n* marquise *f* (*title*).
mare [mɛəʳ] *n* jument *f*.
margarine [ˌmɑːdʒəˈriːn] *n* (*abbr* **marge***) margarine *f*.
margin ['mɑːdʒɪn] *n* (*gen, also fig*) marge *f*; *[wood]* lisière *f*. **notes in the ~** notes en marge; **do not write in the ~** n'écrivez pas dans la marge; (*fig*) **to win by a wide/narrow ~** gagner de loin/de peu; **elected by a narrow ~** élu avec peu de voix de majorité. ♦ **marginal** *adj* (*gen*) marginal; *ability* très moyen; *importance* secondaire; *case* limite; *existence* précaire; *land* de faible rendement; (*Parl*) **~al seat** siège *m* disputé. ♦ **marginally** *adv* très légèrement.
marguerite [ˌmɑːgəˈriːt] *n* marguerite *f*.
marigold ['mærɪgəʊld] *n* (*Bot*) souci *m*.
marijuana [ˌmærɪˈhwɑːnə] *n* marijuana *f*.
marina [məˈriːnə] *n* marina *f*.
marinade [ˌmærɪˈneɪd] *n* marinade *f*. ♦ **marinate** *vt* mariner.
marine [məˈriːn] 1 *adj plant, animal, life* marin; *products* de mer; *forces, insurance* maritime. **~ engineering** génie *m* maritime. 2 *n* **(a) mercantile** *or* **merchant ~** marine *f* marchande. **(b)** (*Mil*) fusilier *m* marin; (*US*) marine *m* (américain). (*fig*) **tell that to the ~s!*** à d'autres! ♦ **mariner** ['mærɪnəʳ] *n* (*liter*) marin *m*; **~r's compass** boussole *f*.
marionette [ˌmærɪəˈnet] *n* marionnette *f*.
marital ['mærɪtl] *adj problems* matrimonial; *happiness, relations* conjugal. (*Admin*) **~ status** situation *f* de famille.
maritime ['mærɪtaɪm] *adj* maritime.
marjoram ['mɑːdʒərəm] *n* marjolaine *f*.
mark[1] [mɑːk] *n* (*currency*) mark *m*.
mark[2] [mɑːk] 1 *n* **(a)** (*gen*) marque *f*. **to make a ~ on** marquer; **the ~s of his shoes in ...** l'empreinte *f* de ses souliers dans ...; **without a ~ on his body** sans trace *f* de coups sur le corps; (*fig*) **to make one's ~ as** se faire un nom en tant que; **to leave one's ~ on sth** laisser son empreinte sur qch; **the ~ of a good teacher** le signe d'un bon professeur; **the ~ of genius** la marque du génie; **as a ~ of my gratitude** en témoignage de ma gratitude; **punctuation ~** signe *m* de ponctuation; **finger ~** trace *f* de doigt. **(b)** (*Scol*) note *f*. **good/bad ~** bonne/mauvaise note (*in* en); **to fail by 2 ~s** échouer à 2 points; (*fig*) **I give him full ~s for helping** je lui donne un bon point pour son aide; **there are no ~s for guessing his name** il n'y a pas besoin d'être un génie pour savoir de qui on parle. **(c)** (*Sport etc: target*) but *m*, cible *f*. (*fig*) **to hit the ~** mettre le doigt dessus*; (*fig*) **to miss** *or* **be wide of the ~** être loin de la vérité. **(d)** (*Sport*) ligne *f* de départ. **on your ~s! get set! go!** à vos marques! prêts! partez!; (*lit, fig*) **to get off the ~** démarrer; (*fig*) **to be quick off the ~** ne pas perdre de temps (*in doing* pour faire); **up to the ~** (*in health*) en forme; (*in efficiency etc*) *person* à la hauteur; *work* satisfaisant; **to come up to the ~** répondre à l'attente. **(e)** (*Tech*) **M~** série *f*; **Concorde M~ 1** Concorde première série.
2 *vt* **(a)** (*make a ~ on*) marquer; (*stain*) tacher, marquer. **(b)** (*indicate*) *price, score* marquer; *change, improvement* indiquer. **X ~s the spot** l'endroit est marqué d'une croix; **in order to ~ the occasion** pour marquer l'occasion; **to ~ time** (*Mil*) marquer le pas; (*fig*) faire du sur-place; (*by choice: before doing sth*) attendre son heure. **(c)** *exam* corriger. **to ~ sth right/wrong** marquer qch juste/faux. **(d)** (*note*) noter; (*Sport*) *opposing player* marquer. **~ my words** écoutez-moi bien.
3 *vi*: **this material ~s easily** tout marque ce tissu; **this material will not ~** rien ne se voit sur ce tissu.
mark down *vt sep* **(a)** (*write down*) inscrire, noter. **(b)** (*reduce*) *price* baisser; *goods* démarquer. **(c)** (*single out*) désigner (*for* pour).
mark off *vt sep* **(a)** (*separate*) séparer, distinguer (*from* de). **(b)** (*tick off*) *names* cocher.
mark out *vt sep* **(a)** *zone etc* délimiter; *field* borner; *tennis court* tracer les lignes de. **(b)** (*single out*) désigner (*for* pour). **it ~ed him out from the others** cela le distinguait des autres.
mark up *vt sep* **(a)** (*write up*) *price, score* marquer. **(b)** (*increase*) *price* augmenter; *goods* majorer le prix de. **to be ~ed up** augmenter.
♦ **marked** *adj difference, accent, bias* marqué; *improvement, increase* sensible; **a ~ed man** un homme marqué. ♦ **markedly** *adv differ* d'une façon marquée; *improve* sensiblement.
♦ **marker** *n* (*person*) marqueur *m*; (*stake*) jalon *m*; (*book~*) signet *m*; (*tool*) marquoir *m*; (*pen*) marker *m*. ♦ **marking** 1 *n* **(a)** (*Scol*) correction *f* (de copies); **(b)** (*on animal etc*) marques *fpl*; (*on road*) signalisation *f* horizontale; 2 *adj*: **~ing ink** encre *f* à marquer. ♦ **marksman** *n* tireur *m* d'élite. ♦ **marksmanship** *n* adresse *f* au tir.
♦ **mark-up** *n* (*profit*) marge *f* bénéficiaire; (*increase*) hausse *f*.
market ['mɑːkɪt] 1 *n* marché *m*. **to go to ~** aller au marché; **the wholesale ~** le marché de gros; **cattle ~** marché *or* foire *f* aux bestiaux; **the ~ in sugar** le marché du sucre; (*St Ex*) **the ~ is rising** les cours *mpl* sont en hausse; **to have a good ~ for sth** avoir une grosse demande pour qch; **there is a ready ~ for small cars** les petites voitures se vendent bien; **this appeals to the French ~** cela se vend bien en France; **to be in the ~ for sth** être acheteur de qch; **on the ~** sur le marché; **on the open ~** en vente libre. 2 *adj day, analysis* de marché; *square, trends* du marché; *value, price* marchand. **~ garden** jardin *m* maraîcher; **~ gardener** maraîcher *m*, -ère *f*; **~ gardening** cul-

ture *f* maraîchère; (*St Ex*) ~ **prices** cours *m* du marché; ~ **research** étude *f* de marché (*in* de). **3** *vt* (*sell*) vendre; (*launch*) lancer sur le marché; (*find outlet for*) trouver un débouché pour. ♦ **marketable** *adj* vendable. ♦ **marketing** *n* marketing *m*.

marmalade ['mɑːməleɪd] *n* confiture *f* d'orange. ~ **orange** orange *f* amère.

marmoset ['mɑːməʊzet] *n* ouistiti *m*.

marmot ['mɑːmət] *n* marmotte *f*.

maroon[1] [mə'ruːn] *adj* (*colour*) bordeaux *inv*.

maroon[2] [mə'ruːn] *vt*: ~**ed** (*on island*) abandonné; (*by sea, traffic, strike etc*) bloqué (*by* par).

marquee [mɑː'kiː] *n* grande tente *f*.

marquess, marquis ['mɑːkwɪs] *n* marquis *m*.

marriage ['mærɪdʒ] **1** *n* mariage *m*. **by** ~ par alliance. **2** *adj bed* conjugal; *vows* de mariage. ~ **bureau** agence *f* matrimoniale; ~ **certificate** extrait *m* d'acte de mariage; ~ **guidance counsellor** conseiller *m*, -ère *f* conjugal(e); ~ **licence** ≃ certificat *m* de publication des bans. ♦ **marriageable** *adj*: **of** ~**able age** en âge de se marier.

marrow ['mærəʊ] *n* **(a)** *[bone]* moelle *f*. ~**bone** os *m* à moelle; **chilled to the** ~ gelé jusqu'à la moelle des os. **(b)** (*vegetable*) courge *f*. **baby** ~ courgette *f*.

marry ['mærɪ] **1** *vt* (*take in marriage*) épouser, se marier avec; *[priest, parent]* marier. **will you** ~ **me?** voulez-vous m'épouser?; **to get** *or* **be married** se marier. **2** *vi* se marier. **to** ~ **into a family** s'allier à une famille par le mariage; **to** ~ **beneath o.s.** se mésallier; **to** ~ **again** se remarier. ♦ **married** *adj person* marié; *name* de femme mariée; *life, love* conjugal; (*Mil*) **married quarters** appartements *mpl* pour familles.

Mars [mɑːz] *n* (*Astron*) Mars *f*; (*Myth*) Mars *m*.

marsh [mɑːʃ] *n* (*also* ~*land*) marais *m*, marécage *m*. ♦ **marshmallow** *n* guimauve *f*. ♦ **marsh marigold** *n* souci *m* d'eau. ♦ **marshy** *adj* marécageux.

marshal ['mɑːʃəl] **1** *n* (*Mil etc*) maréchal *m*; (*at demonstration, meeting etc*) membre *m* du service d'ordre. **2** *vt troops* rassembler; *crowd* faire entrer *etc* en bon ordre; *wagons* trier; (*fig*) *facts, one's wits* rassembler. ♦ **marshalling yard** *n* gare *f* de triage.

marsupial [mɑː'suːpɪəl] *adj, n* marsupial (*m*).

marten ['mɑːtɪn] *n* martre *f*.

martial ['mɑːʃəl] *adj* martial. ~ **law** loi martiale.

Martian ['mɑːʃɪən] *n* Martien(ne) *m(f)*.

martin ['mɑːtɪn] *n* (*house* ~) hirondelle *f* (de fenêtre).

martinet [ˌmɑːtɪ'net] *n*: **to be a** ~ être impitoyable en matière de discipline.

martyr ['mɑːtə^r] *n* martyr(e) *m(f)*. **he is a** ~ **to migraine** ses migraines lui font souffrir le martyre. ♦ **martyrdom** *n* martyre *m*.

marvel ['mɑːvəl] **1** *n [nature, patience]* merveille *f*; *[science, skill]* prodige *m*. **it will be a** ~ **if ...** ce sera (un) miracle si ...; **it's a** ~ **to me how ...** je ne sais vraiment pas comment ...; **it's a** ~ **to me that** cela me paraît un miracle que + *subj*, je n'en reviens pas que + *subj*; **it's a** ~ **that** c'est un miracle que + *subj*. **2** *vi* s'émerveiller, s'étonner (*at* de; *that* de ce que + *indic or subj*). ♦ **marvellous,** (*US*) **marvelous** *adj* merveilleux. ♦ **marvel(l)ously** *adv* merveilleusement.

Marxism ['mɑːksɪzəm] *n* marxisme *m*. ♦ **Marxist** *adj, n* marxiste (*mf*).

marzipan [ˌmɑːzɪ'pæn] *n* pâte *f* d'amandes.

mascara [mæs'kɑːrə] *n* mascara *m*.

mascot ['mæskət] *n* mascotte *f*.

masculine ['mæskjʊlɪn] *adj, n* masculin (*m*). ♦ **masculinity** *n* masculinité *f*.

mash [mæʃ] **1** *n* (*also* ~**ed potatoes**) purée *f* (de pommes de terre). **2** *vt* (~ **up**) (*Culin*) faire une purée de; (*gen, Tech*) écraser.

mask [mɑːsk] **1** *n* masque *m*. **2** *vt* masquer. ♦ **masking tape** *n* papier-cache *m* adhésif.

masochism ['mæsəʊkɪzəm] *n* masochisme *m*. ♦ **masochist** *n* masochiste *mf*. ♦ **masochistic** *adj* masochiste.

mason ['meɪsn] *n* maçon *m*; (*free*~) franc-maçon *m*. ♦ **masonic** [mə'sɒnɪk] *adj* franc-maçonnique. ♦ **masonry** *n* maçonnerie *f*; franc-maçonnerie *f*.

masquerade [ˌmæskə'reɪd] **1** *n* mascarade. **2** *vi*: **to** ~ **as** se faire passer pour.

mass[1] [mæs] **1** *n* masse *f*. **in the** ~ dans l'ensemble; **he was a** ~ **of bruises** il était couvert de bleus; ~**es of*** des masses de*, des tas de*; (*people*) **the** ~**(es)** la masse, les masses populaires; **Shakespeare for the** ~**es** Shakespeare à l'usage des masses. **2** *adj culture* de masse; *psychology, education* des masses; *resignations* en masse; *demonstration* en masse, massif; *funeral, protest, hysteria* collectif. ~ **grave** fosse *f* commune; ~ **media** mass-media *mpl*; ~ **meeting** (*of everyone concerned*) réunion *f* générale; (*huge*) grand rassemblement *m*; ~ **murders** tueries *fpl*. **3** *vt troops etc* masser. **4** *vi [people]* se masser; *[clouds]* s'amonceler. ♦ **mass-produce** *vt* fabriquer en série. ♦ **mass production** *n* production *f or* fabrication *f* en série.

mass[2] [mæs] *n* (*Rel*) messe *f*. **to say** ~ dire la messe; **to go to** ~ aller à la messe.

massacre ['mæsəkə^r] **1** *n* massacre *m*. **2** *vt* massacrer.

massage ['mæsɑːʒ] **1** *n* massage *m*. **2** *vt* masser. ♦ **masseur** *n* masseur *m*. ♦ **masseuse** *n* masseuse *f*.

massive ['mæsɪv] *adj* massif.

mast [mɑːst] *n [ship, flag]* mât *m*; *[radio]* pylône *m*. **to sail before the** ~ servir comme simple matelot.

master ['mɑːstə^r] **1** *n* **(a)** (*gen*) maître *m*. **the** ~ **of the house** le maître de maison; ~ **in one's own house** maître chez soi; **I am the** ~ **now** c'est moi qui commande maintenant; (*fig*) **he has met his** ~ il a trouvé son maître; **to be** ~ **of the situation** être maître de la situation; ~ **of ceremonies** maître des cérémonies; (*Univ*) **M**~ **of Arts/Science** *etc* titulaire *mf* d'une maîtrise ès lettres/sciences *etc*; **a** ~**'s degree** une maîtrise. **(b)** (*teacher*) professeur *m*. **music** ~ professeur de musique. **(c)** *[ship]* capitaine *m*; *[liner]* (capitaine) commandant *m*; *[fishing boat]* patron *m*. **(d) M**~ **John Smith** Monsieur John Smith (*jeune garçon*).

2 *adj beam, card* maître (*f* maîtresse); *control, switch, bedroom* principal. ~ **baker/butcher** *etc* maître boulanger/boucher *etc*; ~ **builder** entrepreneur *m* (de bâtiments); ~ **class** cours *m* de grand maître; ~ **hand** (*skill*) main *f* de maître; **to be a** ~ **hand at (doing) sth** être maître dans l'art de (faire) qch; ~ **key** passe-partout *m inv*; ~ **mariner** (*foreign-going*) ≃ capitaine *m* au long cours; (*home trade*) ≃ capitaine de la marine marchande; ~ **plan** stratégie *f* d'ensemble; **the** ~ **race** la race supérieure; ~ **stroke** coup *m* de maître.

3 *vt* **(a)** *person, animal, emotion* maîtriser; *difficulty* venir à bout de. **(b)** (*understand*) *theory* saisir; (*learn*) *language, skill* apprendre. **to have** ~**ed sth** posséder qch à fond; **he'll never** ~ **the violin** il ne saura jamais bien jouer du violon. ♦ **masterful** *adj* dominateur, autoritaire. ♦ **masterfully** *adv act, decide* en maître, avec autorité; *speak, announce* sur un ton d'autorité. ♦ **masterly** *adj* magistral; **in a** ~**ly way** magistralement. ♦ **mastermind 1** *n* (*genius*) intelligence *f* supérieure; *[plan, crime etc]* cerveau *m*; **2** *vt operation etc* diriger, organiser. ♦ **masterpiece** *n* chef-d'œuvre *m*. ♦ **mastery** *n [subject, musical instrument]* connaissance *f* approfondie (*of* de); (*skill*) maîtrise *f*; (*of the seas*

etc) maîtrise; (*over opponent etc*) supériorité *f* (*over* sur).
masticate ['mæstɪkeɪt] *vti* mastiquer.
mastiff ['mæstɪf] *n* mastiff *m*.
mastoid ['mæstɔɪd] **1** *adj* mastoïde. **2** *n* (*) mastoïdite *f*. ♦ **mastoiditis** *n* mastoïdite *f*.
masturbate ['mæstəbeɪt] *vi* se masturber. ♦ **masturbation** *n* masturbation *f*.
mat [mæt] *n* **(a)** (*on floor*) (petit) tapis *m*; (*of straw etc*) natte *f*; (*at door*) paillasson *m*. **(b)** (*on table etc*) (*heat-resistant*) dessous-de-plat *m inv*; (*decorative*) set *m* (de table); (*embroidered linen*) napperon *m*. ♦ **matted** *adj hair* emmêlé; *sweater* feutré. ♦ **matting** *n* tapis *m* de corde *etc*.
match[1] [mætʃ] *n* allumette *f*. **box/book of ~es** boîte *f*/pochette *f* d'allumettes; **to put a ~ to** mettre le feu à. ♦ **matchbox** *n* boîte *f* à allumettes. ♦ **matchwood** *n*: **to smash to ~wood** réduire en miettes.
match[2] [mætʃ] **1** *n* **(a)** (*Sport*) match *m*; (*game*) partie *f*. **to play a ~ against sb** disputer un match contre qn; **~ abandoned** match suspendu. **(b)** (*equal*) égal(e) *m(f)*. **to meet one's ~** trouver à qui parler (*in sb* avec qn); **he's a ~ for anybody** il est de taille à faire face à n'importe qui; **he was more than a ~ for Paul** Paul n'était pas à sa mesure. **(c)** *[colours etc]* **to be a good ~** aller bien ensemble. **(d)** (*marriage*) mariage *m*. **2** *vt* **(a)** (*equal*: **~ up** to) *[person]* égaler; *[piece of work]* égaler, valoir. **it didn't ~ our hopes** cela a déçu nos espérances. **(b)** *[clothes, colours etc]* aller bien avec. **his looks ~ his character** son physique s'accorde avec sa personnalité. **(c)** (*find similar to*: **~ up**) *cups etc* assortir. **can you ~ (up) this material?** avez-vous du tissu assorti à celui-ci?; **to ~ sb against sb** opposer qn à qn; **they are well ~ed** *[opponents]* ils sont de force égale; *[married couple etc]* ils sont bien assortis. **3** *vi* *[colours, materials]* être bien assortis. **with a ~ing skirt** avec une jupe assortie. ♦ **matchless** *adj* sans égal. ♦ **matchmake** *vi*: **she's always matchmaking** elle veut toujours marier les gens. ♦ **matchmaker** *n* marieur *m*, -euse *f*.
mate[1] [meɪt] **1** *n* **(a)** (*at work*) camarade *mf* (de travail); (*: *friend*) copain* *m*, copine* *f*. **hey, ~!*** eh mon vieux!* **(b)** (*assistant*) aide *mf*. **plumber's ~** aide-plombier *m*. **(c)** (*animal*) mâle *m*, femelle *f*. **(d)** (*Merchant Navy*) ≈ second *m*. **2** *vt* accoupler (*with* à). **3** *vi* s'accoupler (*with* à, avec). ♦ **mating 1** *n* accouplement *m*; **2** *adj call* du mâle; *season* des amours.
mate[2] [meɪt] (*Chess*) **1** *n* mat *m*. **2** *vt* mettre échec et mat.
material [mə'tɪərɪəl] **1** *adj* **(a)** *success, object, needs* matériel. **(b)** (*important*) essentiel; (*relevant*) qui importe (*to* à); (*Jur*) *fact, evidence* pertinent; *witness* direct. **2** *n* **(a)** (*substance*) matière *f*; (*cloth etc*) tissu *m*, étoffe *f*. **dress ~** tissu pour robes; (*fig*) **he is officer ~** il a l'étoffe d'un officier. **(b)** (*equipment etc*) **~s** fournitures *fpl*; **building ~s** matériaux *mpl* de construction; **have you got any writing ~s?** avez-vous de quoi écrire? **(c)** (*for book, lecture*) matériaux *mpl*, documentation *f*. **~ for a TV programme** des matériaux pour une émission télévisée; **this is the kind of ~ he needs** c'est le genre de documentation dont il a besoin. ♦ **materialism** *n* matérialisme *m*. ♦ **materialist** *adj, n* matérialiste (*mf*). ♦ **materialistic** *adj* matérialiste. ♦ **materialize** *vi* (*gen*) se matérialiser; *[idea]* prendre forme; **at last the bus ~ized*** le bus est enfin arrivé. ♦ **materially** *adv* (*V* 1 *above*) matériellement; essentiellement.
maternity [mə'tɜːnɪtɪ] **1** *n* maternité *f*. **2** *adj clothes* de grossesse. **~ benefit** ≈ allocation *f* de maternité; **~ home** *or* **hospital** maternité *f*; **~ ward** (service *m* de) maternité *f*. ♦ **maternal** *adj* maternel.
mathematics [ˌmæθə'mætɪks] *n* (*abbr* **maths***, (*US*) **math***) mathématiques *fpl*, math(s)* *fpl*. ♦ **mathematical** *adj process etc* mathématique; **I'm not mathematical** je n'ai pas le sens des mathématiques. ♦ **mathematically** *adv* mathématiquement. ♦ **mathematician** *n* mathématicien(ne) *m(f)*.
matinée ['mætɪneɪ] *n* matinée *f* (*Theat*).
matriarch ['meɪtrɪɑːk] *n* femme *f* chef de famille. ♦ **matriarchal** *adj* matriarcal. ♦ **matriarchy** *n* matriarcat *m*.
matricide ['meɪtrɪsaɪd] *n* matricide *m*.
matriculate [mə'trɪkjʊleɪt] *vi* s'inscrire. ♦ **matriculation** *n* inscription *f*.
matrimony ['mætrɪmənɪ] *n* mariage *m*. ♦ **matrimonial** *adj* matrimonial.
matrix ['meɪtrɪks] *n* matrice *f*.
matron ['meɪtrən] *n* (*gen*) matrone *f*; *[hospital]* infirmière *f* en chef; (*in school*) infirmière; *[old people's home etc]* directrice *f*. ♦ **matronly** *adj person* très digne, matrone (*pej*). ♦ **matron-of-honour** *n* dame *f* d'honneur.
matt [mæt] *adj* mat.
matter ['mætə[r]] **1** *n* **(a)** (*physical substance: gen, Philos, Phys etc*) matière *f*; (*Med: pus*) pus *m*. **colouring ~** substance *f* colorante; **reading ~** de quoi lire; **advertising ~** publicité *f*. **(b)** (*content*) fond *m*. **~ and form** le fond et la forme. **(c)** (*affair, concern*) affaire *f*, question *f*. **the ~ in hand** l'affaire en question; **business ~s** (questions d')affaires *fpl*; **there's the ~ of my expenses** il y a la question de mes frais; **that's quite another ~** ça, c'est une autre affaire; **that will only make ~s worse** cela ne fera qu'aggraver la situation; **in this ~** à cet égard; **the ~ is closed** l'affaire est close; **a ~ of great concern to us** une source de profonde inquiétude pour nous; **it's not a laughing ~** il n'y a pas de quoi rire; **there's the small ~ of that £200** il y a la petite question des 200 livres; **it will be no easy ~** cela ne sera pas facile; **in the ~ of** en ce qui concerne; **as ~s stand** dans l'état actuel des choses; **for that ~** d'ailleurs; **as a ~ of course** tout naturellement; **as a ~ of fact** en réalité, en fait; **in a ~ of 10 minutes** en l'affaire de 10 minutes. **(d)** (*importance*) **no ~!** peu importe!; **no ~ how** par n'importe quel moyen; **no ~ when he comes** quelle que soit l'heure (*or* la date) de son arrivée; **no ~ how big it is** si grand qu'il soit; **no ~ what he says** quoi qu'il dise; **no ~ where/who** où/qui que ce soit. **(e)** (*difficulty, problem*) **what's the ~?** qu'est-ce qu'il y a?; **what's the ~ with him?** qu'est-ce qu'il a?; **what's the ~ with my hat?** qu'est-ce qu'il a, mon chapeau?*; **what's the ~ with trying to help him?** quelle objection y a-t-il à ce qu'on l'aide (*subj*)?; **there's sth the ~ with my arm** j'ai qch au bras; **there's sth the ~ with the engine** il y a qch qui ne va pas dans le moteur; **as if nothing was the ~** comme si de rien n'était; **nothing's the ~*** il n'y a rien; **there's nothing the ~ with me!** moi, je vais tout à fait bien!; **there's nothing the ~ with that idea** il n'y a rien à redire à cette idée.

2 *vi* importer (*to* à). **the place doesn't ~** l'endroit n'a pas d'importance; **it doesn't ~** cela ne fait rien (*whether* si); **it doesn't ~ who/where** *etc* peu importe qui/où *etc*; **what does it ~ (to you)?** qu'est-ce que cela peut bien (vous) faire?; **why should it ~ to me?** pourquoi est-ce que cela me ferait qch?
♦ **matter-of-fact** *adj tone, voice* neutre; *style* prosaïque; *attitude, person* terre à terre; *assessment, account* qui se limite aux faits; **in a very matter-of-fact way** sans avoir l'air de rien.
mat(t)ins ['mætɪnz] *n* matines *fpl*.
mattress ['mætrɪs] *n* matelas *m*.
mature [mə'tjʊə[r]] **1** *adj* mûr. **he's much more ~** il a beaucoup mûri. **2** *vi* *[person]* mûrir; *[wine, cheese]* se faire. ♦ **maturity** *n* maturité *f*.

maudlin ['mɔːdlɪn] *adj* larmoyant.
maul [mɔːl] *vt [tiger etc]* lacérer, (*to death*) déchiqueter; *[person]* malmener (*also fig*).
Maundy ['mɔːndɪ] *n*: ~ **Thursday** le jeudi saint.
mausoleum [ˌmɔːsə'lɪəm] *n* mausolée *m*.
mauve [məʊv] *adj* mauve.
maverick ['mævərɪk] *n* dissident(e) *m(f)*, franc-tireur *m* (*fig*).
mawkish ['mɔːkɪʃ] *adj* d'une sentimentalité excessive.
maxi* ['mæksɪ] *n*: ~ **single record** disque *m* double durée.
maxim ['mæksɪm] *n* maxime *f*.
maximum ['mæksɪməm] **1** *n, pl* **-ima** maximum *m*. **2** *adj* maximum (*f inv or* maxima). ~ **prices** prix *mpl* maximums *or* maxima; (*Aut etc*) ~ **speed** (*highest permitted*) vitesse *f* limite *or* maximum; (*highest possible*) vitesse maximale; ~ **temperatures** températures maximales. ♦ **maximize** *vt* porter au maximum.
may[1] [meɪ] *modal aux vb* (*pret and cond* **might**) **(a)** (*possibility*) **he ~ arrive** il va peut-être arriver, il peut arriver; **he might arrive** il pourrait arriver; **you ~ be making a big mistake** tu fais peut-être une grosse erreur; **I might have left it behind** je l'ai peut-être bien oublié; **you might have killed me!** tu aurais pu me tuer!; **as soon as ~ be** aussitôt que possible; **be that as it ~** quoi qu'il en soit; **one might well ask whether ...** on est en droit de demander si ...; **what might your name be?** comment vous appelez-vous? **(b)** (*permission*) ~ **I have a word with you? - you ~** puis-je vous parler un instant? - oui, bien sûr; **might I see it?** est-ce que je pourrais le voir?; **might I suggest that ...?** puis-je me permettre de suggérer que ...?; ~ **I sit here?** vous permettez que je m'assoie ici?; ~ **I?** vous permettez?; **if I ~ say so** si je puis me permettre; **he said I might leave** il a dit que je pouvais partir. **(c)** (*suggestion: 'might' only*) **you might try writing to him** tu pourrais toujours lui écrire; **you might have told me that!** tu aurais (tout de même) pu me le dire! **(d)** (*phrases*) **one might as well say £5** autant dire 5 livres; **I ~** *or* **might as well tell you all about it** je ferais aussi bien de tout vous dire; **you may** *or* **might as well leave now as wait** vous feriez aussi bien de partir tout de suite plutôt que d'attendre; **they might just as well not have gone** ils auraient tout aussi bien pu ne pas y aller; **she blushed, as well she might!** elle a rougi, et pour cause!; ~ **God bless you!** que Dieu vous bénisse!
may[2] [meɪ] **1** *n* **(a)** (*month*) **M~** mai *m*; *for phrases V* **September. (b)** (*hawthorn*) aubépine *f*. **2** *adj*: **M~ Day** le Premier Mai (*fête du Travail*). ♦ **mayday** *n* (*Aviat, Naut*) S.O.S. *m*. ♦ **mayfly** *n* éphémère *m*. ♦ **maypole** *n* ≈ arbre *m* de mai.
maybe ['meɪbiː] *adv* peut-être. ~ **he'll be there** peut-être sera-t-il là, peut-être qu'il sera là, il sera peut-être là.
mayonnaise [ˌmeɪə'neɪz] *n* mayonnaise *f*.
mayor [mɛəʳ] *n* maire *m*. **Lord M~** *titre du maire des principales villes*. ♦ **mayoress** *n* femme *f* du maire.
maze [meɪz] *n* labyrinthe *m*, dédale *m*.
me [miː] *pers pron* **(a)** (*direct*) (*unstressed*) me; (*before vowel*) m'; (*stressed*) moi. **he can see ~** il me voit; **he saw ~** il m'a vu; **you saw** ME! vous m'avez vu, moi! **(b)** (*indirect*) me, moi; (*before vowel*) m'. **he gave ~ the book** il me donna *or* m'a donné le livre; **give it to ~** donnez-le-moi; **he was speaking to ~** il me parlait. **(c)** (*after prep etc*) moi. **without ~** sans moi; **it's ~** c'est moi; **smaller than ~** plus petit que moi; **poor (little) ~!*** pauvre de moi!; **dear ~!*** mon Dieu!
meadow ['medəʊ] *n* pré *m*, prairie *f*. ♦ **meadowsweet** *n* reine *f* des prés.
meagre, (*US*) **-ger** ['miːgəʳ] *adj* maigre (*before n*).
meal[1] [miːl] **1** *n* repas *m*. **to have a ~** manger; **to have a good ~** bien manger; **that was a lovely ~!** nous avons très bien déjeuné (*or* dîné); (*fig*) **to make a ~ of sth*** faire toute une histoire de qch*. **2** *adj*: ~ **ticket** (*lit*) ticket-repas *m*; (**fig: job, person etc*) gagne-pain *m inv*. ♦ **mealtime** *n* heure *f* du repas; **at ~times** aux heures des repas.
meal[2] [miːl] *n* (*flour etc*) farine *f* (*d'avoine etc*). ♦ **mealies** *npl* maïs *m*. ♦ **mealy** *adj* farineux. ♦ **mealy-mouthed** *adj* mielleux.
mean[1] [miːn] *pret, ptp* **meant** [ment] *vt* **(a)** vouloir dire, signifier; (*imply*) vouloir dire. **'homely' ~s something different in America** 'homely' a un sens différent en Amérique; **what do you ~ by that?** que voulez-vous dire par là?; **you don't really ~ that** vous ne parlez pas sérieusement; **I always ~ what I say** je pense toujours ce que je dis; **the name ~s nothing to me** ce nom ne me dit rien; **the play didn't ~ a thing to her** la pièce n'avait aucun sens pour elle; **this ~s war** c'est la guerre à coup sûr; **it will ~ a lot of expense** cela entraînera beaucoup de dépenses; **catching the train ~s getting up early** pour avoir ce train il faut se lever tôt; **a pound ~s a lot to him** une livre représente une grosse somme pour lui; **holidays don't ~ much to me** les vacances comptent peu pour moi; **don't I ~ anything to you at all?** je ne suis donc rien pour toi?
(b) (*intend*) avoir l'intention (*to do* de faire), compter, vouloir (*to do* faire); *gift etc* destiner (*for* à); *remark* adresser (*for* à). **I didn't ~ to break it** je n'ai pas fait exprès de le casser; **I ~ to succeed** j'ai bien l'intention de réussir; **I ~ you** *or* (*US*) **I ~ for you to leave** je veux que vous partiez (*subj*); **he said it as if he meant it** il a dit cela sans avoir l'air de plaisanter; **I meant it as a joke** j'ai dit (*or* fait) cela pour rire; **to be meant to do** être censé faire; **she ~s well** elle est pleine de bonnes intentions; **he ~s trouble** il cherche la bagarre; **it ~s trouble** ça nous annonce des ennuis; **do you ~ me?** (*are you speaking to me*) c'est à moi que vous parlez?; (*about me*) c'est de moi que vous parlez? ♦ **meaning 1** *n [word]* sens *m*; *[phrase, action]* signification *f*; **with a double ~ing** à double sens; **literal ~ing** sens propre *or* littéral; **what is the ~ing of this word?** que signifie ce mot?; (*in anger etc*) **what is the ~ing of this?** qu'est-ce que cela signifie?; **you haven't got my ~ing** vous m'avez mal compris; **2** *adj* significatif, éloquent. ♦ **meaningful** *adj* significatif, éloquent. ♦ **meaningless** *adj word, action* dénué de sens; *waste, suffering* insensé.
mean[2] [miːn] **1** *n* **(a)** (*middle term*) milieu *m*; (*Math*) moyenne *f*. **the golden** *or* **happy ~** le juste milieu. **(b)** (*way*) **~s** moyen *m*; **to find the ~s to do** *or* **of doing** trouver le moyen de faire; **to find a ~s of doing** trouver moyen de faire; **there's no ~s of getting in** il n'y a pas moyen d'y entrer; **the ~s to an end** le moyen d'arriver à ses fins; **by ~s of** *tool etc* au moyen de; *person* par l'entremise de; *hard work etc* à force de; **come in by all ~s!** je vous en prie, entrez!; **by all ~s!** mais certainement!; **by all manner of ~s** par tous les moyens; **by any (manner of) ~s** n'importe comment; **by no ~s** nullement, pas du tout; **by some ~s or other** d'une façon ou d'une autre; **by this ~s** de cette façon. **(c)** (*wealth etc*) **~s** moyens *mpl*; **to live within/beyond one's ~s** vivre selon ses moyens/au-dessus de ses moyens; **private ~s** fortune *f* personnelle; **slender ~s** ressources *fpl* très modestes. **2** *adj distance, temperature* moyen. ♦ **means test** *n* enquête *f* financière sur les ressources (*d'une personne qui demande une aide pécuniaire*). ♦ **meantime** *or* ♦ **meanwhile** *adv* (*also* **in the ~time** *or* **~while**) en attendant, pendant ce temps.
mean[3] [miːn] *adj* **(a)** (*stingy*) avare (*with* de), radin*. **(b)** (*unkind*) mesquin, méchant. **a ~ trick**

un sale tour; **you ~ thing!*** chameau!*; **you were ~ to me** tu n'as vraiment pas été chic* avec moi; **to feel ~ about sth*** avoir un peu honte de qch. **(c)** (*US**: *vicious*) *animal etc* méchant; *person* salaud‡. **(d)** (*poor*) *appearance* misérable. **the ~est citizen** le dernier des citoyens. ♦ **meanness** *n* avarice *f*; mesquinerie *f*, méchanceté *f*; aspect *m* misérable.

meander [mɪ'ændəʳ] **1** *vi [river]* faire des méandres. *[person]* **to ~ in** *etc* entrer *etc* sans se presser. **2** *n* méandre *m*.

measles ['mi:zlz] *n* rougeole *f*.

measly* ['mi:zlɪ] *adj* misérable (*before n*), minable.

measure ['meʒəʳ] **1** *n* **(a)** (*gen*) mesure *f*; (*tape ~ etc*) mètre *m*. **to give good** *or* **full ~** faire bonne mesure; (*fig*) **for good ~** pour faire bonne mesure; **made to ~** fait sur mesure; **a pint ~** une mesure d'un demi-litre; (*fig*) **I've got his ~** je sais ce qu'il vaut; **happiness beyond ~** bonheur sans bornes; **a ~ of success** un certain succès; **in some/large ~** dans une certaine/large mesure. **(b)** (*step*) mesure *f*. **strong/drastic ~s** mesures énergiques/draconiennes. **2** *vt* mesurer (*also fig*). **to ~ off** *or* **out** *or* **up** mesurer; **to be ~d for a dress** faire prendre ses mesures pour une robe; **what does it ~?** quelles sont ses dimensions?; **the carpet ~s 3 metres by 2 metres across** le tapis fait *or* mesure 3 mètres sur 2 mètres de large; (*fall*) **to ~ one's length** tomber de tout son long. **3** *vi*: **to ~ up to** être à la hauteur de. ♦ **measured** *adj* (*gen*) mesuré; (*Sport etc*) **over a ~d kilometre** sur un kilomètre exactement. ♦ **measureless** *adj* incommensurable. ♦ **measurements** *npl* mesures *fpl*. ♦ **measuring** *adj*: **measuring jug** pot *m* gradué; **measuring rod** règle *f*; **measuring tape** mètre *m* à ruban.

meat [mi:t] **1** *n* viande *f*. **~ and drink** de quoi manger et boire; (*fig*) **this is ~ and drink to them** c'est une aubaine pour eux; **one man's ~ is another man's poison** ce qui guérit l'un tue l'autre; **there's not much ~ in his book** son livre n'a pas beaucoup de substance. **2** *adj*: **~ diet** régime *m* carné; **~ extract** concentré *m* de viande; **~ pie** pâté *m* en croûte. ♦ **meatball** *n* boulette *f* de viande. ♦ **meat-eater** *n* (*animal*) carnivore *m*; **he's a big ~-eater** c'est un gros mangeur de viande. ♦ **meat-eating** *adj* carnivore. ♦ **meaty** *adj flavour* de viande; (*fig*) *book* étoffé.

Mecca ['mekə] *n* la Mecque. (*fig*) **a ~ for tourists** un haut lieu du tourisme.

mechanic [mɪ'kænɪk] *n* mécanicien *m*. **motor ~** mécanicien garagiste *or* auto. ♦ **mechanical** *adj* (*lit*) mécanique; (*fig*) *action, reply* machinal, automatique; **~al engineer** ingénieur *m* mécanicien; **~al engineering** (*science*) mécanique *f*; (*industry*) construction *f* mécanique. ♦ **mechanically** *adv* mécaniquement; (*fig*) machinalement. ♦ **mechanics** *n* **(a)** (*sg*: *science*) mécanique *f*; **(b)** (*pl*) (*lit*) mécanisme *m*; (*fig*) **the ~s of running an office** le processus de la gestion d'un bureau. ♦ **mechanism** *n* mécanisme *m*. ♦ **mechanistic** *adj* mécaniste. ♦ **mechanization** *n* mécanisation *f*. ♦ **mechanize** *vt process, industry* mécaniser; *army, troops* motoriser.

medal ['medl] *n* médaille *f*. **swimming ~** médaille de natation. ♦ **medallion** *n* médaillon *m*. ♦ **medallist,** (*US*) **medalist** *n* médaillé(e) *m(f)*; **gold/silver ~(l)ist** médaillé d'or/d'argent.

meddle ['medl] *vi* **(a)** (*interfere*) se mêler (*in* de). **stop meddling!** cesse de te mêler de ce qui ne te regarde pas! **(b)** (*tamper*) toucher (*with* à). ♦ **meddler** *n* (*busybody*) mouche *f* du coche; (*touching things*) touche-à-tout *m inv*. ♦ **meddlesome** *or* ♦ **meddling** *adj* (*interfering*) qui fourre son nez partout; (*touching*) qui touche à tout.

media ['mi:dɪə] **1** *npl of* **medium** (*souvent employé au sg*) (*gen*: *Press, Rad, TV*) media *mpl*. (*journalists*) **the ~ were waiting for him at the airport*** les journalistes et les photographes l'attendaient à l'aéroport. **2** *adj*: **~ man** (*Press, Rad, TV*) reporter *m*; (*Publicity*) agent *m* publicitaire.

mediaeval [ˌmedɪ'i:vəl] *adj* médiéval, du moyen âge; *streets, charm* moyenâgeux (*also pej*).

mediate ['mi:dɪeɪt] **1** *vi* servir d'intermédiaire (*between* entre; *in* dans). **2** *vt settlement* obtenir par médiation. ♦ **mediating** *adj* médiateur. ♦ **mediation** *n* médiation *f*. ♦ **mediator** *n* médiateur *m*, -trice *f*.

medical ['medɪkəl] *adj* (*gen*) médical; *studies, faculty* de médecine; *student* en médecine. **~ board** commission *f* médicale; (*Mil*) conseil *m* de révision; **~ examination** examen *m* médical; (*at work etc*) visite *f* médicale; **~ officer** (*Ind*) médecin *m* du travail; (*Mil*) médecin-major *m* (*or* -colonel *etc*); *[town, country]* directeur *m* de la santé publique; **~ practitioner** généraliste *mf*; **the ~ profession** (*doctors etc*) le corps médical. ♦ **medically** *adv* médicalement; **to be ~ly examined** subir un examen médical.

Medicare ['medɪkɛəʳ] *n* (*US*) assistance *f* médicale aux personnes âgées.

medicated ['medɪkeɪtɪd] *adj* médical, traitant. ♦ **medication** *n* médication *f*.

medicine ['medsn, 'medɪsn] **1** *n* **(a)** (*science*) médecine *f*. **to study ~** faire des études de médecine; **Doctor of M~** docteur *m* en médecine. **(b)** (*drug etc*) médicament *m*. **to take one's ~** prendre son médicament; (*fig*) avaler la pilule; (*fig*) **to give sb a taste of his own ~** rendre à qn la monnaie de sa pièce. **2** *adj*: **~ box** *or* **chest** pharmacie *f* (portative); **~ cabinet** *or* **chest** *or* **cupboard** armoire *f* à pharmacie; **~ man** sorcier *m*. ♦ **medicinal** [me'dɪsɪnl] *adj* médicinal.

medieval [ˌmedɪ'i:vəl] = **mediaeval.**

mediocre [ˌmi:dɪ'əʊkəʳ] *adj* médiocre. ♦ **mediocrity** *n* médiocrité *f*.

meditate ['medɪteɪt] *vti* méditer (*sth* qch; *doing* de faire; *on, about* sur). ♦ **meditation** *n* méditation *f*. ♦ **meditative** *adj* méditatif. ♦ **meditatively** *adv* d'un air méditatif.

Mediterranean [ˌmedɪtə'reɪnɪən] *adj* méditerranéen. **the ~ (Sea)** la (mer) Méditerranée.

medium ['mi:dɪəm] **1** *n, pl* **media (a)** (*gen*) milieu *m*; (*Phys etc*) véhicule *m*; (*fig*) moyen *m*, intermédiaire *m*, voie *f*. (*fig*) **through the ~ of the press** par voie de presse; **advertising ~** organe *m* de publicité; **artist's ~** moyens *mpl* d'expression d'un artiste; **television is the best ~ for this** c'est la télévision qui rend cela le mieux. **(b) the happy ~** le juste milieu. **(c)** (*pl* **-s**: *Spiritualism*) médium *m*. **2** *adj* moyen. (*Rad*) **on the ~ wavelength** sur les ondes moyennes. ♦ **medium-dry** *adj wine* demi-sec. ♦ **medium-sized** *adj* de grandeur *or* de taille moyenne.

medley ['medlɪ] *n* mélange *m*; (*Mus*) pot-pourri *m*.

meek [mi:k] *adj* doux, humble. **~ and mild** doux comme un agneau. ♦ **meekly** *adv* avec douceur, humblement. ♦ **meekness** *n* douceur *f*, humilité *f*.

meet [mi:t] *pret, ptp* **met 1** *vt* **(a)** (*gen*) rencontrer; *sb coming in opposite direction* croiser; (*by arrangement*) retrouver, rejoindre; (*go to ~*) aller *or* venir chercher. **to arrange to ~ sb at 3 o'clock** donner rendez-vous à qn pour 3 heures; **I am being met** on doit venir me chercher *or* m'attendre; **the car will ~ the train** la voiture sera là à l'arrivée du train; **he went out to ~ them** il est allé à leur rencontre. **(b)** (*get to know*) rencontrer, faire la connaissance de. **~ Mr Jones** je vous présente M. Jones; **pleased to ~ you** enchanté (de faire votre connaissance). **(c)** (*encounter*) *team, obstacle* rencontrer; (*face*) *enemy, danger* affronter; (*in duel*) se battre avec. **to ~ one's**

death *or* **end** trouver la mort. **(d)** (*satisfy etc*) *expenses, bill* faire face à; *deficit* combler; *demand* satisfaire à; *need* répondre à; *charge, objection* réfuter. **this will ~ the case** ceci fera l'affaire. **(e) it met his ears** cela a frappé ses oreilles; **the sight which met my eye(s)** le spectacle qui s'est offert à mes yeux; **I dared not ~ her eye** je n'osais pas la regarder en face; **there's more to this than ~s the eye** c'est moins simple que cela n'en a l'air.

2 *vi* **(a)** *[people]* (*by chance*) se rencontrer; (*by arrangement*) se retrouver, se rejoindre; (*more than once*) se voir; (*get to know each other*) se rencontrer, faire connaissance. **to ~ again** se revoir; **until we ~ again!** à la prochaine fois!; **have you met before?** vous vous connaissez déjà?; **they arranged to ~ at 10 o'clock** ils se sont donné rendez-vous pour 10 heures. **(b)** *[committee, Parliament]* se réunir. **the class ~s in the art room** le cours a lieu dans la salle de dessin. **(c)** *[armies, teams, rivers]* se rencontrer.

3 *n* (*Hunting*) rendez-vous *m* (de chasse); (*US Sport etc*) meeting *m*.

meet up *vi* (*by chance*) se rencontrer; (*by arrangement*) se retrouver. **to ~ up with sb** rencontrer *or* retrouver qn.

meet with *vt fus* **(a)** *difficulties, resistance* rencontrer; *refusal, losses, storm* essuyer; *welcome* recevoir. **he met with an accident** il lui est arrivé un accident; **we met with kindness** on nous a traités avec gentillesse. **(b)** (*esp US*) = **meet 1 a.**

♦ **meeting 1** *n* **(a)** *[group of people, club, political party]* réunion *f*, (*formal*) assemblée *f*; (*business ~*) séance *f or* réunion de travail; (*Pol, Sport: rally*) meeting *m*; **to call a ~ing of shareholders** convoquer les actionnaires; **to call a ~ing to discuss sth** convoquer une réunion (*or* une assemblée *etc*) pour débattre qch; **he's in a ~ing** il est en conférence; **(b)** (*between individuals*) rencontre *f*; (*arranged*) rendez-vous *m*, (*formal*) entrevue *f*; **(c)** (*Quakers*) culte *m*; **2** *adj*: **~ing place** lieu *m* de réunion.

mega... ['megə] *pref* méga... . ♦ **megacycle** *n* mégacycle *m*. ♦ **megalith** *n* mégalithe *m*. ♦ **megaton** *n* mégatonne *f*.

megalomania [ˌmegələʊ'meɪnɪə] *n* mégalomanie *f*. ♦ **megalomaniac** *adj, n* mégalomane (*mf*).

megaphone ['megəfəʊn] *n* porte-voix *m inv*.

melamine ['meləmiːn] *n* mélamine *f*.

melancholy ['melənkəlɪ] **1** *n* mélancolie *f*. **2** *adj person* mélancolique; *thing* triste. ♦ **melancholia** *n* mélancolie *f* (*Med*). ♦ **melancholic** *adj* mélancolique. ♦ **melancholically** *adv* mélancoliquement.

mellow ['meləʊ] **1** *adj fruit* bien mûr; *wine, voice* moelleux; *colour, light* velouté; *building* patiné; *person* mûri (et tranquille). **to grow ~** mûrir, s'adoucir. **2** *vi* mûrir; devenir moelleux; se velouter; se patiner; *[person, character]* s'adoucir. **3** *vt*: **the years have ~ed him** il s'est adouci avec les années.

melodrama ['meləʊˌdrɑːmə] *n* mélodrame *m*. ♦ **melodramatic** *adj* mélodramatique. ♦ **melodramatically** *adv* d'un air mélodramatique.

melody ['melədɪ] *n* mélodie *f*. ♦ **melodious** *adj* mélodieux. ♦ **melodiously** *adv* mélodieusement.

melon ['melən] *n* melon *m*.

melt [melt] **1** *vi* **(a)** (*gen*) fondre. **to ~ in the mouth** fondre dans la bouche; (*fig*) **she looks as if butter wouldn't ~ in her mouth** on lui donnerait le bon Dieu sans confession*; (*be too hot*) **to be ~ing*** être en nage. **(b)** *[colours, sounds]* se fondre (*into* dans); *[anger]* tomber; *[resolution, determination]* fléchir. **to ~ into tears** fondre en larmes; **he ~ed into the crowd** il s'est fondu dans la foule. **2** *vt* (*gen*) fondre; *sb's heart* attendrir.

melt away *vi [ice, savings]* fondre; *[anger, fog]* se dissiper; *[confidence]* disparaître; *[crowd]* se disperser; *[person]* se volatiliser.

melt down *vt sep* fondre; *scrap* remettre à la fonte.

♦ **melting 1** *adj snow* fondant; *voice, look* attendri; *words* attendrissant; **~ing point** point *m* de fusion; (*fig*) **a ~ing pot of many nationalities** le creuset de bien des nationalités; **it's back in the ~ing pot** c'est remis en question; **it's still all in the ~ing pot** c'est encore au stade des discussions; **2** *n [snow]* fonte *f*; *[metal]* fusion *f*.

member ['membəʳ] **1** *n* (*gen*) membre *m*; *[club, party]* adhérent(e) *m(f)* (*of* à), membre (*of* de). (*notice*) **'~s only'** 'réservé aux adhérents'; **they treated her like a ~ of the family** ils l'ont traitée comme si elle faisait partie de la famille; **M~ of Parliament** ≈ député *m* (*for* de); **~ of the public** simple particulier *m* (*f* -ère); **a ~ of the staff** (*gen*) un(e) employé(e); (*Scol, Univ*) **a ~ of staff** un professeur. **2** *adj*: **~ nations** les États *mpl* membres. ♦ **membership 1** *n* (*gen*) adhésion *f* (*of* à); **a ~ship of over 800** plus de 800 membres; **2** *adj card* d'adhérent, de membre; **~ship fee** cotisation *f*.

membrane ['membreɪn] *n* membrane *f*.

memento [mə'mentəʊ] *n* souvenir *m* (*objet etc*). **as a ~ of** en souvenir de.

memo ['meməʊ] *n* (*abbr of* **memorandum**) note *f* (de service). ♦ **memo pad** *n* bloc-notes *m*.

memoir ['memwɑːʳ] *n* mémoire *m* (*on* sur); (*biography*) notice *f* biographique. **~s** (*autobiographical*) mémoires; *[learned society]* actes *mpl*.

memory ['memərɪ] *n* **(a)** (*faculty*) mémoire *f*. **to have a good/bad ~** avoir bonne/mauvaise mémoire; **a ~ for faces** la mémoire des visages; **from ~** de mémoire; **loss of ~** perte *f* de mémoire; (*Med*) amnésie *f*. **(b)** (*recollection*) souvenir *m*. **childhood memories** souvenirs d'enfance; **in ~ of** en souvenir de; **sacred to the ~ of** à la mémoire de; **of blessed ~** de glorieuse mémoire. ♦ **memorable** *adj* mémorable. ♦ **memorandum** *n, pl* **-anda** (*gen*) mémorandum *m*; (*informal letter etc*) note *f* (de service). ♦ **memorial 1** *adj* commémoratif; (*US*) **Memorial Day** le jour des morts au champ d'honneur; **2** *n* monument *m* (*to* à); **war memorial** monument *m* aux morts; **this scholarship is a memorial to ...** cette bourse est en mémoire de ... . ♦ **memorize** *vt facts, figures* retenir; *poem* apprendre par cœur.

men [men] *npl of* **man.** ♦ **menfolk*** *npl* hommes *mpl*. ♦ **menswear** *n* (*Comm*) (*clothing*) habillement *m* masculin; (*dept*) rayon *m* hommes.

menace ['menɪs] **1** *n* menace *f*; (*fig: sth or sb annoying*) plaie* *f*. **a public ~** un danger public. **2** *vt* menacer. ♦ **menacing** *adj* menaçant. ♦ **menacingly** *adv* d'un air *or* d'un ton menaçant.

mend [mend] **1** *vt clothes* raccommoder; *other object* réparer; *mistake etc* corriger, rectifier. **to ~ matters** arranger les choses; **to ~ one's ways** *or* **manners** s'amender. **2** *vi* (*darn etc*) faire le raccommodage. **3** *n*: **to be on the ~** (*gen*) s'améliorer; *[invalid]* aller mieux. ♦ **mending** *n* (*act*) raccommodage *m*; (*clothes*) vêtements *mpl* à raccommoder.

menial ['miːnɪəl] *adj person* servile; *task* inférieur; *position* subalterne.

meningitis [ˌmenɪn'dʒaɪtɪs] *n* méningite *f*.

menopause ['menəʊpɔːz] *n* ménopause *f*. ♦ **menopausal** *adj symptom* dû à la ménopause; *woman* à la ménopause.

menstruate ['menstrʊeɪt] *vi* avoir ses règles. ♦ **menstruation** *n* menstruation *f*.

mental ['mentl] *adj* (*gen*) mental; *ability, process* mental, intellectuel; *calculation* mental, de tête; *prayer* intérieur; *treatment* psychiatrique; (*: *mad*) timbré*. **~ arithmetic** calcul *m* mental; **~ defective** débile *mf* mental(e); **~ deficiency** débi-

lité *f* mentale; ~ **home** *or* **hospital** *or* **institution** hôpital *m* psychiatrique; ~ **illness** maladie mentale; ~ **patient** malade *mf* mental(e); ~ **powers** facultés *fpl* intellectuelles; ~ **strain** (*tension*) tension *f* nerveuse; (*overwork*) surmenage *m* intellectuel; **he made a ~ note to do it** il a pris note mentalement de le faire; ~ **reservations** doutes *mpl* (*about* sur).
♦ **mentality** *n* mentalité *f*. ♦ **mentally** *adv calculate* mentalement; **~ly defective** mentalement déficient; **~ly handicapped** handicapé mental; **she is ~ly handicapped** c'est une handicapée mentale; **~ly ill** atteint de maladie mentale; **~ly retarded** (mentalement) arriéré.

menthol ['menθɒl] **1** *n* menthol *m*. **2** *adj* mentholé.

mention ['menʃən] **1** *vt* (*gen*) mentionner (*sth to sb* qch à qn; *that* que); (*quote*) *figures, names, dates* citer. **I'll ~ it to him** je lui en toucherai un mot, je le lui signalerai; **to ~ sb in one's will** coucher qn sur son testament; **he didn't ~ the accident** il n'a pas parlé de *or* fait mention de l'accident; **just ~ my name** dites que c'est de ma part; **too numerous to ~** trop nombreux pour qu'on les mentionne (*subj*); **don't ~ it!** il n'y a pas de quoi!; **I need hardly ~ that...** il va sans dire que ...; **not to ~, without ~ing** sans compter; **it is not worth ~ing** cela ne vaut pas la peine d'en parler; **nothing worth ~ing** pour ainsi dire rien. **2** *n* (*gen*) mention *f*. **it got a ~* in the news** on en a parlé aux informations.

menu ['menju:] *n* menu *m*; (*printed*) menu, carte *f*.

mercenary ['mɜ:sɪnərɪ] *adj, n* mercenaire (*m*).

merchandise ['mɜ:tʃəndaɪz] *n* marchandises *fpl*.
♦ **merchandizing** *n* merchandising *m*.

merchant ['mɜ:tʃənt] **1** *n* (*trader*) négociant *m*; (*shopkeeper*) commerçant *m*. **wine ~** marchand *m* de vins, (*large-scale*) négociant en vins. **2** *adj bank, ship* de commerce. (*US*) **~ marine,** (*Brit*) **~ navy** marine marchande; **~ seaman** marin *m* de la marine marchande.

mercury ['mɜ:kjʊrɪ] *n* mercure *m*. **M~** (*Astron*) Mercure *f*; (*Myth*) Mercure *m*.

mercy ['mɜ:sɪ] **1** *n* pitié *f*, indulgence *f*; (*Rel*) miséricorde *f*. **without ~** sans pitié; **for ~'s sake** par pitié; **no ~ was shown to them** on les a traités sans merci; **to have ~ on** avoir pitié de; **to beg for ~** demander grâce; **to show ~ towards** *or* **to sb** montrer de l'indulgence pour *or* envers qn; **to throw o.s. on sb's ~** s'en remettre à la merci de qn; **at the ~ of** à la merci de; **to leave to the tender ~ of** abandonner aux bons soins de (*iro*); **thankful for small mercies** reconnaissant du peu qui s'offre; **it's a ~ that** heureusement que + *indic*. **2** *adj*: **~ killing** euthanasie *f*. ♦ **merciful** *adj* miséricordieux (*to* pour); **a merciful release** une véritable délivrance. ♦ **mercifully** *adv* miséricordieusement; (*: *fortunately*) par bonheur. ♦ **merciless** *adj* impitoyable.
♦ **mercilessly** *adv* impitoyablement.

mere [mɪəʳ] *adj formality* simple; *thought etc* seul (*before n*); *chance, spite, coincidence* pur (*before n*). **he's a ~ child** ce n'est qu'un enfant; **a ~ clerk** un simple employé de bureau; **the ~ sight of him** sa seule vue; **a ~ nothing** une vétille. ♦ **merely** *adv want, say* simplement, seulement; **he ~ly nodded** il se contenta de faire un signe de tête; **I did it ~ly to please her** je ne l'ai fait que pour lui faire plaisir; **it's ~ly a formality** ce n'est qu'une formalité.

merge [mɜ:dʒ] **1** *vi* [*colours, shapes, sounds*] se mêler (*into, with* à); [*roads*] se rejoindre (*with* avec); [*river*] confluer (*with* avec); [*states*] s'unir (*with* à); [*companies*] fusionner (*with* avec). **2** *vt* (*Comm, Fin*) fusionner.
♦ **merger** *n* fusion *f*.

meringue [mə'ræŋ] *n* meringue *f*.

merino [mə'ri:nəʊ] *n* mérinos *m*.

merit ['merɪt] **1** *n* mérite *m*. **to decide a case on its ~s** décider d'un cas en toute objectivité; **they went into the ~s of the new plan** ils ont discuté le pour et le contre du nouveau projet. **2** *adj*: **~ list** tableau *m* d'honneur. **3** *vt* mériter.
♦ **meritocracy** *n* méritocratie *f*.

mermaid ['mɜ:meɪd] *n* sirène *f* (*Myth*).

merry ['merɪ] *adj* joyeux, gai; (*: *tipsy*) éméché. **M~ Christmas** Joyeux Noël; **M~ England** l'Angleterre du bon vieux temps. ♦ **merrily** *adv* joyeusement, gaiement. ♦ **merriment** *n* gaieté *f*, joie *f*; (*laughter*) hilarité *f*. ♦ **merry-go-round** *n* (*in fairground*) manège *m* (*de foire etc*); (*fig*) tourbillon *m*. ♦ **merrymaker** *n* fêtard *m*.
♦ **merrymaking** *n* réjouissances *fpl*.

mesh [meʃ] **1** *n* **(a)** [*net etc*] maille *f*. **netting with 5-cm ~** filet *m* à mailles de 5 cm; **the ~ of lies/of intrigue** le réseau de mensonges/d'intrigues. **(b)** (*fabric*) tissu *m* à mailles. **nylon ~** tulle *m* de nylon; **wire ~** grillage *m*. **(c)** [*gears etc*] engrenage *m*. **in ~** en prise. **2** *adj stockings* (*net*) filet *inv*; (*non-run*) indémaillable. **~ bag** filet *m* (à provisions). **3** *vi* [*wheels*] s'engrener; [*plans*] concorder.

mesmerize ['mezməraɪz] *vt* hypnotiser; [*snake*] fasciner. (*fig*) **I was ~d** je ne pouvais pas détourner mon regard.

mess [mes] **1** *n* **(a)** (*confusion of objects*) désordre *m*, fouillis *m*; (*dirt*) saleté *f*; (*muddle*) gâchis *m*. **to make a ~** faire du désordre (*or* mettre de la saleté) partout; **the cat has made a ~** le chat a fait des saletés; **get this ~ cleared up!** (*tidy*) range *or* (*clean*) nettoie tout ça!; [*object, room*] **to be (in) a ~** être en désordre (*or* très sale); **to be (in) a terrible ~** être dans un état épouvantable; **you look a ~** tu n'es pas présentable; **to make a ~ of** (*dirty*) salir; (*tear*) déchirer; (*wreck*) saccager; *essay, career, one's life* gâcher; **to make a ~ of things*** tout bousiller*, tout gâcher; [*person*] **to be/get (o.s.) in a ~*** être/se mettre dans de beaux draps; **to get sb/get o.s. out of a ~** sortir qn/se sortir d'un mauvais pas. **(b)** (*Mil*) mess *m*; (*Naut*) carré *m*. **2** *vt* salir, souiller. **3** *vi* manger (*with* avec).

mess about*, mess around* **1** *vi* (*in water, mud*) patauger; (*waste time*) perdre son temps; (*dawdle*) lambiner*; (*hang about*) traîner. **what were you doing? – just ~ing about** que faisais-tu? – rien de particulier; **to ~ about** *or* **around with** *object* tripoter; *person* s'amuser avec; (*sexually*) peloter*. **2** *vt sep person* embêter*; *arrangements* chambouler*.

mess up *vt sep clothes* salir; *room* mettre en désordre; *hair* ébouriffer; *situation, plans, life etc* gâcher.
♦ **mess-up*** *n* gâchis *m*. ♦ **messy** *adj* (*dirty*) sale; (*untidy*) *room* en désordre; *piece of work* pas assez soigné; *text, page* sale; *job* salissant; *situation* compliqué.

message ['mesɪdʒ] *n* message *m*. **telephone ~** message téléphonique; **to leave a ~** laisser un mot (*for sb* à qn); **would you give him this ~?** voudriez-vous lui faire cette commission?; (*fig*) **to get the ~*** comprendre, piger*. ♦ **messenger** **1** *n* messager *m*, -ère *f*; (*in office etc*) coursier *m*; **2** *adj*: **messenger boy** garçon *m* de courses.

Messiah [mɪ'saɪə] *n* Messie *m*.

Messrs ['mesəz] *npl* messieurs *mpl* (*abbr* MM.).

met¹ [met] *pret, ptp of* **meet.**

met² [met] *adj* (*abbr of* **meteorological**) **the M~ Office** ≃ l'O.N.M. *m*; **~ report** bulletin *m* de la météo*.

metabolism [me'tæbəlɪzəm] *n* métabolisme *m*.

metal ['metl] **1** *n* métal *m*. **road ~** empierrement *m*. **2** *adj* en *or* de métal. **~ polish** produit *m* d'entretien (pour métaux). **3** *vt road* empierrer.
♦ **metallic** *adj* métallique. ♦ **metallurgist** *n* métallurgiste *m*. ♦ **metallurgy** *n* métallurgie *f*.

♦ **metalwork** *n* (*articles*) ferronnerie *f*; (*craft*) travail *m* des métaux. ♦ **metalworker** *n* (*Ind*) ouvrier *m* métallurgiste.
metamorphosis [ˌmetəˈmɔːfəsɪs] *n* métamorphose *f*. ♦ **metamorphose** *vi* se métamorphoser (*into* en).
metaphor [ˈmetəfəʳ] *n* métaphore *f*. ♦ **metaphorical** *adj* métaphorique.
metaphysics [ˌmetəˈfɪzɪks] *nsg* métaphysique *f*. ♦ **metaphysical** *adj* métaphysique.
mete [miːt] *vt*: **to ~ out** *punishment* infliger; *reward* décerner; *justice* rendre.
meteor [ˈmiːtɪəʳ] *n* météore *m*. ♦ **meteoric** *adj* météorique; (*fig*) fulgurant; **~ic rise** montée *f* en flèche. ♦ **meteorite** *n* météorite *m or f*.
meteorology [ˌmiːtɪəˈrɒlədʒɪ] *n* météorologie *f*. ♦ **meteorological** *adj* météorologique. ♦ **meteorologist** *n* météorologue *mf*.
meter [ˈmiːtəʳ] **1** *n* **(a)** (*gen*) compteur *m*; (*parking* ~) parcmètre *m*. **electricity/gas/water ~** compteur d'électricité/à gaz/à eau. **(b)** (*US*) = metre. **2** *adj* (*US Aut*) **~ maid** contractuelle *f*; **~ reader** releveur *m* de compteurs.
methane [ˈmiːθeɪn] *n* méthane *m*.
method [ˈmeθəd] *n* **(a)** (*gen*) méthode *f*. **there's ~ in his madness** sa folie ne manque pas d'une certaine logique. **(b)** (*manner*) méthode *f*, façon *f*. **his ~ of working** sa méthode de travail, sa façon de travailler. ♦ **methodical** *adj* méthodique. ♦ **Methodism** *n* méthodisme *m*. ♦ **Methodist** *adj, n* méthodiste (*mf*). ♦ **methodology** *n* méthodologie *f*.
meths* [meθs] *n abbr of* **methylated spirit(s)**.
methyl [ˈmeθɪl] *n* méthyle *m*. ♦ **methylated spirit(s)** *n* alcool *m* à brûler.
meticulous [mɪˈtɪkjʊləs] *adj* méticuleux. ♦ **meticulously** *adv* méticuleusement.
métier [ˈmeɪtɪeɪ] *n* (*trade etc*) métier *m*; (*one's particular work etc*) partie *f*, rayon* *m*; (*strong point*) point *m* fort.
metre [ˈmiːtəʳ] *n* (*all senses*) mètre *m*. ♦ **metric** *adj* métrique; **to go metric*** adopter le système métrique. ♦ **metrication** *n* conversion *f* au système métrique.
metronome [ˈmetrənəʊm] *n* métronome *m*.
metropolis [mɪˈtrɒpəlɪs] *n* métropole *f* (*ville*). ♦ **metropolitan** *adj* métropolitain.
mettle [ˈmetl] *n* fougue *f*. **on one's ~** prêt à donner le meilleur de soi-même; **to show one's ~** montrer ce dont on est capable.
mew [mjuː] **1** *n* miaulement *m*. **2** *vi* miauler.
mews [mjuːz] (*Brit*) *n sg or pl* ruelle *f*. **~ flat** petit appartement *m* assez chic.
Mexico [ˈmeksɪkəʊ] *n* Mexique *m*. **~ City** Mexico. ♦ **Mexican 1** *adj* mexicain; **2** *n* Mexicain(e) *m(f)*.
mezzanine [ˈmezəniːn] *n* mezzanine *f*.
mezzo-soprano [ˌmetsəʊsəˈprɑːnəʊ] *n* (*voice*) mezzo-soprano *m*; (*singer*) mezzo(-soprano) *f*.
mi [miː] *n* (*Mus*) mi *m*.
miaow [miːˈaʊ] **1** *n* miaou *m*. **2** *vi* miauler.
mica [ˈmaɪkə] *n* mica *m*.
mice [maɪs] *npl of* **mouse**.
Michaelmas [ˈmɪklməs] **1** *n* la Saint-Michel. **2** *adj*: **~ daisy** aster *m* d'automne.
mickey* [ˈmɪkɪ] *n*: **to take the ~ out of sb** se payer la tête de qn*.
micro... [ˈmaɪkrəʊ] *pref* micro-. ♦ **microbiology** *n* microbiologie *f*. ♦ **microchip** *n* microplaquette *f*. ♦ **microcircuit** *n* microcircuit *m*. ♦ **microdot** *n* micro-image-point *m*. ♦ **microelectronics** *nsg* micro-électronique *f*. ♦ **microfilm 1** *n* microfilm *m*; **2** *vt* microfilmer. ♦ **microgroove** *n* microsillon *m*. ♦ **micromesh** *adj stockings* super-fin. ♦ **micro-organism** *n* micro-organisme *m*. ♦ **microprocessor** *n* microprocesseur *m*. ♦ **microreader** *n* microlecteur *m*. ♦ **microwave** *n* micro-onde *f*.
microbe [ˈmaɪkrəʊb] *n* microbe *m*.
microcosm [ˈmaɪkrəʊkɒzəm] *n* microcosme *m*.
microphone [ˈmaɪkrəfəʊn] *n* microphone *m*.
microscope [ˈmaɪkrəskəʊp] *n* microscope *m*. **under the ~** au microscope. ♦ **microscopic** *adj* microscopique.
mid [mɪd] *adj*: **in ~ May** à la mi-mai, au milieu de mai; **in ~ morning** au milieu de la matinée; **in ~ air** (*lit*) en plein ciel; (*fig*) *leave sth etc* en suspens; **in ~ course** à mi-course; **in ~ Atlantic** au milieu de l'Atlantique; **~-Victorian** du milieu de l'époque victorienne. ♦ **midday 1** *n* midi *m*; **at ~day** à midi; **2** *adj sun* de midi. ♦ **midland 1** *n*: **the Midlands** les comtés *mpl* du centre de l'Angleterre; **2** *adj* du centre (du pays); *region* central. ♦ **midnight 1** *n* minuit *m*; **at ~night** à minuit; **2** *adj* de minuit; **to burn the ~night oil** travailler (*or* lire *etc*) fort avant dans la nuit. ♦ **midriff** *n* (*diaphragm*) diaphragme *m*; (*stomach*) estomac *m*. ♦ **midshipman** *n* midshipman *m*. ♦ **midst** *n*: **in the ~st of** (*in the middle of*) au milieu de; (*surrounded by*) entouré de; (*among*) parmi; (*during*) pendant; **in our ~st** parmi nous. ♦ **midstream** *n*: **in ~stream** au milieu du courant. ♦ **midsummer 1** *n* (*height of summer*) milieu *m* de l'été; (*solstice*) solstice *m* d'été; **at ~summer** à la Saint-Jean; **2** *adj* de plein été; **Midsummer Day** la Saint-Jean. ♦ **midterm** *n* (*holiday*) ≃ vacances *fpl* de la Toussaint (*or* de février *or* de Pentecôte). ♦ **midway** *adj, adv* à mi-chemin. ♦ **midweek 1** *adv* vers le *or* au milieu de la semaine; **2** *adj* de milieu de semaine. ♦ **Midwest** *n* (*US*) Midwest *m*. ♦ **midwinter 1** *n* (*heart of winter*) milieu *m* de l'hiver; (*solstice*) solstice *m* d'hiver; **in ~winter** en plein hiver; **2** *adj* de plein hiver.
middle [ˈmɪdl] **1** *adj chair, period etc* du milieu; *size, quality* moyen. (*fig*) **to take the ~ course** choisir le moyen terme; **during his ~ age** quand il n'était déjà plus jeune; **he fears ~ age** il a peur de la cinquantaine; **the M~ Ages** le moyen âge; (*Mus*) **~ C** do *m* en dessous du la du diapason; **the ~ classes** les classes moyennes, la bourgeoisie; **in the ~ distance** (*Art etc*) au second plan; (*gen*) à mi-distance; **M~ East** Moyen-Orient *m*; **~ finger** médius *m*, majeur *m*; **~ name** deuxième nom *m*; **~ school** ≃ (*Brit Admin*) cours *m* moyen; (*US*) **M~ West** Middle West *m*. **2** *n* **(a)** milieu *m*. **in the ~ of** au milieu de; **right in the ~** au beau milieu; **it's in the ~ of nowhere*** c'est en plein bled*; **a village in the ~ of nowhere*** un petit trou perdu*; **I was in the ~ of my work** j'étais en plein travail; **I'm in the ~ of reading it** je suis justement en train de le lire. **(b)** (*: *waist*) taille *f*. ♦ **middle-aged** *adj* d'un certain âge. ♦ **middle-class** *adj* bourgeois, des classes moyennes. ♦ **middleman** *n* intermédiaire *m*. ♦ **middle-of-the-road** *adj* modéré. ♦ **middle-sized** *adj tree, building* de grandeur moyenne; *parcel* de grosseur moyenne; *person* de taille moyenne. ♦ **middleweight** *n* poids *m* moyen. ♦ **middling** *adj* moyen.
midge [mɪdʒ] *n* moucheron *m*.
midget [ˈmɪdʒɪt] **1** *n* nain(e) *m(f)*. **2** *adj* minuscule.
midwife [ˈmɪdwaɪf] *n* sage-femme *f*. ♦ **midwifery** [ˈmɪdwɪfərɪ] *n* obstétrique *f*.
might[1] [maɪt] *modal aux vb V* **may**[1]. ♦ **might-have-been** *n* (*thing*) ce qui aurait pu être; (*person*) raté(e) *m(f)*.
might[2] [maɪt] *n* force(s) *f(pl)*. **with ~ and main, with all one's ~** de toutes ses forces.
mighty [ˈmaɪtɪ] **1** *adj* (*gen*) puissant; *achievement* formidable; *ocean* vaste; (*: *very big*) *row, rage* sacré* (*before n*). **2** *adv* (*) rudement*.
migraine [ˈmiːgreɪn] *n* migraine *f*.
migrate [maɪˈgreɪt] *vi* émigrer. ♦ **migrant 1** *adj bird* migrateur; *worker* migrant; **2** *n* (*Agr*) saisonnier *m*. ♦ **migration** *n* migration *f*.
mike* [maɪk] *n* (*microphone*) micro *m*.
mild [maɪld] *adj* (*gen*) doux (*f* douce); *reproach,*

punishment, beer, sedative léger; *exercise, effect* modéré; *sauce* peu épicé; *curry* pas trop fort; *illness* bénin. **it's ~ today** il fait doux aujourd'hui; **a ~ form of polio** la poliomyélite sous une forme bénigne. ♦ **mildly** *adv* (*gently*) doucement; (*slightly*) légèrement; **to put it ~ly*** ... pour ne pas dire plus ...; **that's putting it ~ly*** c'est le moins qu'on puisse dire. ♦ **mildness** *n* douceur *f*; légèreté *f*.

mildew ['mɪldjuː] *n* (*gen*) moisissure *f*; (*on plants*) rouille *f*; (*on vine*) mildiou *m*. ♦ **mildewed** *adj* moisi; piqué de rouille; mildiousé.

mile [maɪl] *n* mile *m or* mille *m* (= *1 609,33 m*). **20 ~s per gallon** ≃ 14 litres aux cent; **~s and ~s** ≃ des kilomètres et des kilomètres; (*fig*) **not a hundred ~s from here** sans aller chercher bien loin; **~s away** à cent lieues d'ici (*or* de là); **you could see it a ~ off** ça se voyait d'une lieue; **~s* bigger than** bien plus grand que. ♦ **mileage 1** *n* (*Aut etc*) (*distance covered*) ≃ kilométrage *m*; (*distance per gallon etc*) ≃ consommation *f* aux cent; **the car had a low ~age** ≃ la voiture avait peu de kilomètres; **2** *adj*: **~age allowance** ≃ indemnité *f* kilométrique. ♦ **mil(e)ometer** *n* ≃ compteur *m* kilométrique. ♦ **milepost** *or* ♦ **milestone** *n* borne *f* (milliaire), ≃ borne kilométrique; (*in career etc*) jalon *m* (*fig*).

milieu ['miːljɜː] *n* milieu *m* (social).

militant ['mɪlɪtənt] *adj, n* militant(e) *m(f)*. ♦ **militarism** *n* militarisme *m*. ♦ **militarist(ic)** *adj* militariste. ♦ **military 1** *adj* (*gen*) militaire; *service* militaire, national; **2** *npl*: **the military** l'armée *f*. ♦ **militate** *vi* militer (*against* contre). ♦ **militia** *collective n* milices *fpl*.

milk [mɪlk] **1** *n* lait *m*. **coconut ~** lait de coco; **~ of magnesia** lait de magnésie; **a land flowing with ~ and honey** un pays de cocagne; (*hum*) **he came home with the ~*** il est rentré à l'aube. **2** *vt cow* traire; (*fig*) *person* exploiter; *strength* saper. **3** *adj product* laitier; *chocolate* au lait; *diet* lacté; *tooth* de lait. **~ bar** milk-bar *m*; **~ churn** bidon *m* à lait; **~ float** voiture *f* de laitier; **~ jug** pot *m* à lait; **~ powder** lait en poudre; **~ pudding** entremets *m* au lait; **~ shake** milk-shake *m*. ♦ **milk-and-water** *adj* insipide. ♦ **milking 1** *n* traite *f*; **2** *adj*: **~ing machine** trayeuse *f* (mécanique). ♦ **milkman** *n* laitier *m*. ♦ **milksop*** *n* chiffe *f* molle* (*fig*). ♦ **milky** *adj diet, product* lacté; *coffee, tea* au lait; *drink* à base de lait; (*fig: in colour etc*) laiteux; **M~y Way** voie *f* lactée.

mill [mɪl] **1** *n* **(a)** (*gen*) moulin *m*; (*Ind: for grain*) minoterie *f*. **wind~** moulin à vent; **pepper-~** moulin à poivre; (*fig*) **to go through the ~** en voir de dures*; **to put sb through the ~** en faire voir de dures à qn*. **(b)** (*factory*) usine *f*, fabrique *f*. **steel ~** aciérie *f*; **paper ~** usine *f* de papeterie; **cotton ~** filature *f* de coton. **2** *adj* **(a) ~ race** bief *m* de moulin; **~ stream** courant *m* du bief; **~ wheel** roue *f* d'un moulin. **(b) ~ girl** ouvrière *f* des filatures; **~ owner** industriel *m* du textile. **3** *vt flour, coffee, pepper* moudre; *screw, nut* moleter. *[coin]* **~ed edge** crénelage *m*. **4** *vi* (**~ about** *or* **around**) *[crowd etc]* grouiller. ♦ **miller** *n* meunier *m*; (*Ind: large-scale*) minotier *m*. ♦ **millhand** *or* ♦ **millworker** *n* ouvrier *m* des filatures. ♦ **milling** *adj crowd* grouillant. ♦ **millpond** *n*: **sea like a ~pond** mer *f* d'huile. ♦ **millstone** *n* meule *f*; (*fig*) **a ~stone round his neck** un boulet qu'il traîne avec lui.

millennium [mɪ'lenɪəm] *n* millénaire *m*; (*Rel, also fig*) millénium *m*.

millet ['mɪlɪt] *n* millet *m*.

milli... ['mɪlɪ] *pref* milli... . ♦ **millibar** *n* millibar *m*. ♦ **milligram(me)** *n* milligramme *m*. ♦ **millimetre,** (*US*) **millimeter** *n* millimètre *m*.

milliner ['mɪlɪnəʳ] *n* modiste *f*. ♦ **millinery** *n* modes *fpl* (*chapeaux*).

million ['mɪljən] *n* million *m*. **a ~ men** un million d'hommes; **he's one in a ~*** c'est la crème des hommes; (*fig*) **~s of*** des milliers de; **thanks a ~!*** merci mille fois!; (*US*) **to feel like a ~ dollars*** se sentir dans une forme époustouflante*. ♦ **millionaire** *n* millionnaire *m*, ≃ milliardaire *m*. ♦ **millionth** *adj, n* millionième (*mf*); (*fraction*) millionième *m*.

millipede ['mɪlɪpiːd] *n* mille-pattes *m inv*.

mime [maɪm] **1** *n* (*Theat*) (*skill, classical play*) mime *m*; (*modern play*) mimodrame *m*; (*fig: gestures etc*) mimique *f*. **2** *vti* mimer.

mimic ['mɪmɪk] **1** *n* imitateur *m*, -trice *f*. **2** *vt* imiter. ♦ **mimicry** *n* imitation *f*.

mimosa [mɪ'məʊzə] *n* mimosa *m*.

mince [mɪns] **1** *n* (*Culin*) bifteck *m* haché. **2** *adj*: **~ pie** tarte *f* aux fruits secs. **3** *vt* (*Culin*: **~ up**) hacher. (*fig*) **to ~ matters** *or* **one's words** mâcher ses mots. **4** *vi* (*in talking*) parler du bout des lèvres; (*in walking*) marcher à petits pas maniérés. ♦ **mincemeat** *n* hachis *m* de fruits secs; (*fig*) **to make ~meat of** pulvériser (*fig*). ♦ **mincer** *n* hachoir *m* (*appareil*). ♦ **mincing** *adj* affecté, minaudier.

mind [maɪnd] **1** *n* **(a)** (*gen*) esprit *m*; (*sanity*) raison *f*; (*memory*) mémoire *f*; (*opinion*) avis *m*. **in one's ~'s eye** en imagination; **his ~ is going** il n'a plus tout à fait sa tête; **his ~ went blank** ça a été le vide complet dans sa tête; **I'm not clear in my own ~ about it** je ne sais pas qu'en penser moi-même; **to be easy in one's ~** avoir l'esprit tranquille; **one of the great ~s of the century** un des grands cerveaux du siècle; **it was a case of ~ over matter** c'était la victoire de l'esprit sur la matière; **to be out of one's ~** ne plus avoir toute sa raison *or* sa tête; **you must be out of your ~!*** tu as perdu la tête!; **he went out of his ~** il a perdu la tête. **(b)** (*phrases*) **with one ~** comme un seul homme; **of one ~** du même avis; **to be in two ~s about (doing) sth** se tâter pour ce qui est de (faire) qch; **I was of the same ~ as my brother** j'étais du même avis que mon frère, je partageais l'opinion de mon frère; **to my ~** à mon avis; **nothing is further from my ~ than doing that** loin de moi la pensée de faire cela; **ecology-~ed** très sensibilisé sur l'écologie; **an industrially-~ed nation** une nation orientée vers l'industrie; **to bear** *or* **keep sth in ~** (*take account of*) tenir compte de qch; (*remember*) penser à qch, ne pas oublier qch; **to bring** *or* **call to ~** rappeler; **you must get it into your ~ that ...** tu dois te mettre dans la tête que ...; **I can't get it out of my ~** je ne peux m'empêcher d'y penser; **to give one's ~ to sth, to keep one's ~ on sth** se concentrer sur qch; **to give sb a piece of one's ~*** dire ses quatre vérités à qn; **it went right** *or* **clean* out of my ~** cela m'est complètement sorti de la tête*; **if you have a ~ to** si vous le voulez vraiment; **to have (it) in ~ to do** avoir dans l'idée de faire; **I've a good ~ to do it*** j'ai bien envie de le faire; **I've half a ~ to do it*** j'ai presque envie de le faire; **to have in ~** *thing* avoir dans l'idée; *person* avoir en vue; **to have sth on one's ~** avoir l'esprit préoccupé de qch; **what's on your ~?** qu'est-ce qui vous préoccupe?; **to know one's own ~** savoir ce que l'on veut; **to let one's ~ run on sth** se laisser aller à penser à qch; **to let one's ~ wander** laisser flotter son attention; **to make up one's ~ about sth/to do** prendre une décision à propos de qch/la décision de faire; **that puts me in ~ of ...** cela me rappelle ...; **to put sth out of one's ~** oublier qch; **to put** *or* **set one's ~ to sth** s'appliquer à qch; **to set one's ~ on (doing) sth** vouloir fermement (faire) qch; **to set sb's ~ at rest** rassurer qn; **this will take her ~ off it** cela lui changera les idées; **the noise takes my ~ off my work** le bruit m'empêche de me concentrer sur mon travail.

2 *vt* **(a)** (*pay attention to*) faire attention à; (*beware of*) prendre garde à. **never ~!** (*don't*

worry) ne t'en fais pas!; (*it makes no odds*) ça ne fait rien!; (*iro*) **don't ~ me!*** ne vous gênez surtout pas pour moi!* (*iro*); **never ~ the expense!** tant pis pour le prix!; **~ your language!** surveille ton langage!; **~ what you're doing!** attention à ce que tu fais!; **~ the step!** attention à la marche!; **~ you don't fall** prenez garde de ne pas tomber; **~ you tell her** n'oublie pas de le lui dire; **~ you*, I ...** remarquez, je ... . **(b)** (*object to*) **do you ~ if I take this book? – I don't ~** cela ne vous ennuie pas que je prenne ce livre? – je vous en prie!; **which? – I don't ~** lequel? – ça m'est égal; **if you don't ~** si cela ne vous fait rien; **did she ~ (it) when he got married?** a-t-elle été malheureuse quand il s'est marié?; **I don't ~ going with you** je veux bien vous accompagner; **I don't ~ the cold** le froid ne me gêne pas; **would you ~ doing that?** cela vous ennuierait de faire cela?, (*abruptly*) je vous prie de faire cela; **do you ~ the noise?** le bruit vous gêne-t-il?; **I don't ~ what people say** je me moque du qu'en-dira-t-on; **I wouldn't ~ a cup of coffee** je prendrais bien une tasse de café. **(c)** (*take charge of*) *children, animals, shop* garder.
mind out* *vi* faire attention. **~ out!** attention! ♦ **mind-bending*** *adj* renversant. ♦ **mind-blowing*** *adj* hallucinant. ♦ **mind-boggling*** *adj* ahurissant. ♦ **minded** *adj* disposé (*to do* à faire). ♦ **minder** *n* (*of child etc*) gardienne *f*. ♦ **mindful** *adj*: **~ful of** attentif à. ♦ **mindless** *adj* stupide, idiot. ♦ **mindreader** *n*: **he's a ~reader!** il lit dans la pensée des gens!

mine¹ [maɪn] *poss pron* le mien, la mienne, les mien(ne)s. **this pencil is ~** ce crayon est le mien *or* à moi; **a friend of ~** un de mes amis.

mine² [maɪn] **1** *n* **(a)** (*Min*) mine *f*. **coal ~** mine de charbon; **to go down the ~s** travailler à la mine; (*fig*) **a ~ of information** une véritable mine de renseignements. **(b)** (*Mil, Naut etc*) mine *f*. **to lay a ~** poser une mine. **2** *vt* **(a)** (*Min*) *coal, ore* extraire. **(b)** (*Mil etc*) *sea* miner. **3** *vi* exploiter un gisement. to **~ for coal** exploiter une mine (de charbon). **4** *adj*: **~ detector** détecteur *m* de mines; **~ disposal** déminage *m*. ♦ **minefield** *n* champ *m* de mines. ♦ **minelayer** *n* mouilleur *m* de mines. ♦ **minelaying** *n* mouillage *m* de mines. ♦ **miner** *n* mineur *m*. ♦ **mineshaft** *n* puits *m* de mine. ♦ **minesweeper** *n* dragueur *m* de mines. ♦ **mine-sweeping** *n* dragage *m* de mines. ♦ **mining 1** *n* **(a)** (*Min*) exploitation *f* minière; **(b)** (*Mil, Naut*) mouillage *m* de mines; **2** *adj area, village, industry* minier; *engineer* des mines; *family* de mineurs.

mineral ['mɪnərəl] **1** *n* minéral *m*. (*soft drinks*) **~s** boissons *fpl* gazeuses. **2** *adj* minéral. **~ water** (*natural*) eau *f* minérale; (*soft drink*) boisson *f* gazeuse. ♦ **mineralogist** *n* minéralogiste *mf*. ♦ **mineralogy** *n* minéralogie *f*.

mingle ['mɪŋgl] **1** *vt* mêler (*with* à). **2** *vi* (*gen*) se mêler (*with* à); (*consort*) frayer (*with* avec).

mingy* ['mɪndʒɪ] *adj person* radin*; *share* misérable.

mini ['mɪnɪ] **1** *n* (*fashion*) mini *m*; (*~skirt*) mini(-jupe) *f*; (*car*) mini *f* ®. **2** *pref* mini-. **he's a kind of ~-dictator** c'est une sorte de mini-dictateur. ♦ **minibus** *n* minibus *m*. ♦ **minicab** *n* minitaxi *m*. ♦ **minimarket** *or* ♦ **minimart** *n* minilibre-service *m*.

miniature ['mɪnɪtʃəʳ] **1** *n* miniature *f*. **in ~** en miniature. **2** *adj* (*gen*) (en) miniature; (*tiny*) minuscule; *camera* de petit format; *poodle* nain; *railway* miniature; *submarine* de poche. **~ bottle** mini-bouteille *f*; **~ model** maquette *f*. ♦ **miniaturize** *vt* miniaturiser.

minimum ['mɪnɪməm] **1** *n* minimum *m*. **to reduce to a ~** réduire au minimum; **to keep sth to a ~** limiter qch autant que possible. **2** *adj* minimum (*f inv or* -ima). **~ wage** salaire *m* minimum garanti, ≃ SMIC* *m*. ♦ **minimal** *adj* minimal. ♦ **minimize** *vt* minimiser.

minister ['mɪnɪstəʳ] **1** *n* (*gen*) ministre *m*; (*Rel*) pasteur *m*. **M~ of State** ≃ secrétaire *m* d'État; **M~ of Health** ministre de la Santé publique. **2** *vi*: **to ~ to** *needs* pourvoir à; *person* donner ses soins à. ♦ **ministerial** *adj decision, crisis* ministériel; *benches* des ministres. ♦ **ministrations** *npl* soins *mpl*. ♦ **ministry** *n* **(a)** (*Pol etc*) ministère *m*; **Ministry of Health** ministère de la Santé publique; **(b)** (*Rel*) **the ministry** le (saint) ministère; **to go into the ministry** devenir pasteur.

mink [mɪŋk] **1** *n* vison *m*. **2** *adj* de vison.

minnow ['mɪnəʊ] *n* vairon *m*; (*any small fish*) fretin *m*; (*fig: person*) menu fretin *m*.

minor ['maɪnəʳ] **1** *adj* (*gen, Jur, Mus etc*) mineur; *detail, role, expenses, repairs* petit; *importance, interest* secondaire. (*Mus*) **G ~** sol mineur; (*Mus*) **~ key** ton *m* mineur; **in the ~ key** en mineur; **~ offence** ≃ contravention *f* de simple police; (*Med*) **~ operation** opération bénigne; (*Cards*) **~ suit** (couleur *f*) mineure *f*. **2** *n* **(a)** (*Jur*) mineur(e) *m(f)*. **(b)** (*US Univ*) matière *f* secondaire. ♦ **minority** [maɪ'nɒrɪtɪ] **1** *n* minorité *f*; **in the ~ity** en minorité; **2** *adj* (*gen*) minoritaire; *report* soumis par un groupe minoritaire.

Minorca [mɪ'nɔːkə] *n* Minorque *f*. **in ~** à Minorque.

minstrel ['mɪnstrəl] *n* ménestrel *m*.

mint¹ [mɪnt] **1** *n* (hôtel *m* de la) Monnaie *f*; (*fig: big sum*) des sommes *fpl* folles. **to make a ~ of money** faire des affaires d'or. **2** *adj*: **in ~ condition** à l'état de neuf. **3** *vt coins* battre; *gold* monnayer (*into* pour obtenir); (*fig*) *word* inventer. (*fig*) **he ~s money** il fait des affaires d'or.

mint² [mɪnt] **1** *n* (*plant*) menthe *f*; (*sweet*) bonbon *m* à la menthe. **2** *adj* à la menthe. **~ sauce** menthe *f* au vinaigre.

minus ['maɪnəs] **1** *prep* (*Math etc*) moins; (*: *without*) sans. **2** *adj*: **~ quantity** (*Math*) quantité *f* négative; (*: *fig*) quantité négligeable; **~ sign** moins *m*.

minute¹ ['mɪnɪt] **1** *n* **(a)** (*of time*) minute *f*. **it is 20 ~s past 2** il est 2 heures 20 (minutes); **at 4 o'clock to the ~** à 4 heures pile; **we got the train without a ~ to spare** une minute de plus et nous manquions le train; **I'll do it in a ~** je le ferai dans une minute; **the ~ he comes** dès qu'il arrivera; **do it this ~!** fais-le à la minute!; **he went out this ~** il vient tout juste de sortir; **any ~ now** d'une minute à l'autre; **I shan't be a ~** j'en ai pour deux secondes; **it won't take five ~s** ce sera fait en un rien de temps; **wait a ~** attendez une minute *or* un instant; (*indignantly*) minute!; **up to the ~** *equipment* dernier modèle *inv*; *fashion* dernier cri *inv*; *news* de dernière heure. **(b)** (*Geog, Math*) minute *f*. **(c)** (*memorandum*) note *f*. *[meeting]* **~s** procès-verbal *m*; **to take the ~s** rédiger le procès-verbal. **2** *adj* **(a) ~ hand** grande aiguille *f*; **~ steak** entrecôte *f* minute. **(b) ~ book** registre *m* des délibérations. **3** *vt fact, detail* prendre note de.

minute² [maɪ'njuːt] *adj* (*gen*) minuscule; *change, differences* minime, infime; *examination, description* minutieux. **in ~ detail** dans les moindres détails. ♦ **minutely** *adv examine etc* minutieusement; *change* très peu; **~ly resembling ...** ayant très vaguement l'apparence de ... . ♦ **minutiae** *npl* menus détails *mpl*.

miracle ['mɪrəkl] **1** *n* miracle *m* (*also fig*). **by a** *or* **some ~** par miracle; **it is a ~ that** c'est miracle que + *subj*; **it will be a ~ if** ce sera un miracle si. **2** *adj*: **~ cure** *or* **drug** remède-miracle *m*; **~ play** miracle *m* (*Theat*). ♦ **miraculous** *adj* miraculeux. ♦ **miraculously** *adv* miraculeusement.

mirage ['mɪrɑːʒ] *n* mirage *m*.

mirror ['mɪrəʳ] **1** *n* (*gen*) miroir *m*, glace *f*; (*Aut*) rétroviseur *m*. **hand ~** glace à main; **pocket ~** miroir de poche. **2** *adj* **~ image** image *f* invertie. **3** *vt* refléter. **to be ~ed in** se refléter dans.

mirth [mɜːθ] *n* hilarité *f*, rires *mpl*.

misadventure [ˌmɪsəd'ventʃəʳ] *n* mésaventure *f*, (*less serious*) contretemps *m*. (*Jur*) **death by ~** mort *f* accidentelle.

misanthropy [mɪ'zænθrəpɪ] *n* misanthropie *f*. ♦ **misanthropic** *adj* ***person*** misanthrope; ***mood*** misanthropique. ♦ **misanthropist** *n* misanthrope *mf*.

misapply ['mɪsə'plaɪ] *vt* (*gen*) mal employer; ***funds*** détourner.

misapprehension ['mɪsˌæprɪ'henʃən] *n* malentendu *m*, méprise *f*. **he's (labouring) under a ~** il se trompe.

misappropriate ['mɪsə'prəʊprɪeɪt] *vt* détourner. ♦ **misappropriation** *n* détournement *m*.

misbehave ['mɪsbɪ'heɪv] *vi* (*gen*) se conduire mal; *[child]* ne pas être sage. ♦ **misbehaviour,** (*US*) **misbehavior** *n* mauvaise conduite *f*.

miscalculate ['mɪs'kælkjʊleɪt] **1** *vt* mal calculer. **2** *vi* (*fig*) se tromper. ♦ **miscalculation** *n* erreur *f* de calcul.

miscarry [ˌmɪs'kærɪ] *vi* **(a)** *[plan]* échouer, avorter. **(b)** (*Med*) faire une fausse couche. ♦ **miscarriage** *n* **(a)** *[plan]* échec *m*; **miscarriage of justice** erreur *f* judiciaire; **(b)** (*Med*) fausse couche.

miscast ['mɪs'kɑːst] *adj*: **he was ~** on n'aurait jamais dû lui donner ce rôle.

miscellaneous [ˌmɪsɪ'leɪnɪəs] *adj* divers. **~ expenses** frais *mpl* divers. ♦ **miscellany** [mɪ'selənɪ] *n [objects etc]* collection *f*; (*Literat*) recueil *m*; (*Rad, TV*) sélection *f*.

mischance [ˌmɪs'tʃɑːns] *n*: **by (a) ~** par malheur.

mischief ['mɪstʃɪf] *n* **(a)** (*roguishness*) espièglerie *f*; (*naughtiness*) sottises *fpl*; (*maliciousness*) méchanceté *f*. **he's up to (some) ~** *[child]* il prépare une sottise; *[adult]* (*in fun*) il prépare une farce quelconque; (*from malice*) il médite un mauvais coup; **to get into ~** faire des sottises; **to keep sb out of ~** empêcher qn de faire des sottises; **full of ~** espiègle; **bubbling over with ~** pétillant de malice; **to make ~** créer des ennuis (*for sb* à qn); **to make ~ between** semer la discorde entre; **to do o.s. a ~** se faire mal. **(b)** (*: *child*) polisson(ne) *m(f)*. ♦ **mischief-maker** *n* semeur *m*, -euse *f* de discorde; (*esp gossip*) mauvaise langue *f*. ♦ **mischievous** *adj* (*playful, naughty*) espiègle; (*harmful*) malveillant. ♦ **mischievously** *adv* par espièglerie; avec malveillance. ♦ **mischievousness** *n* (*roguishness*) espièglerie *f*; (*naughtiness*) polissonnerie *f*; (*maliciousness*) méchanceté *f*.

misconception ['mɪskən'sepʃən] *n* (*wrong idea/ opinion*) idée/opinion *f* fausse; (*misunderstanding*) malentendu *m*.

misconduct [ˌmɪs'kɒndʌkt] *n* inconduite *f*; (*sexual*) adultère *m*.

misconstrue ['mɪskən'struː] *vt* mal interpréter. ♦ **misconstruction** *n* fausse interprétation *f*.

miscount ['mɪs'kaʊnt] **1** *n* (*gen*) mécompte *m*; (*during election*) erreur *f* dans le compte. **2** *vti* mal compter.

misdeal ['mɪs'diːl] (*vb*: *pret, ptp* **-dealt** [-delt]) (*Cards*) **1** *n* maldonne *f*. **2** *vi* faire maldonne.

misdeed ['mɪs'diːd] *n* méfait *m*.

misdemeanour, (*US*) **-nor** [ˌmɪsdɪ'miːnəʳ] *n* incartade *f*; (*Jur*) infraction *f*.

misdirect ['mɪsdɪ'rekt] *vt* ***letter etc*** mal adresser; ***person*** mal renseigner; ***operation*** mener mal; (*Jur*) ***jury*** mal instruire.

miser ['maɪzəʳ] *n* avare *mf*. ♦ **miserliness** *n* avarice *f*. ♦ **miserly** *adj* avare.

miserable ['mɪzərəbl] *adj* **(a)** (*unhappy*) malheureux, triste; (*deplorable*) ***sight, failure*** pitoyable, lamentable. **to feel ~** avoir le cafard*; (*physically*) être mal fichu*; **to make sb ~** (*depress*) déprimer qn; (*hurt*) peiner qn; **don't look so ~!** ne fais pas cette tête d'enterrement! **(b)** (*filthy, wretched*) misérable, minable. **(c)** (*: *unpleasant*) ***weather etc*** maussade, (*stronger*) sale* (*before n*). **(d)** (*contemptible*) ***meal, gift*** piteux; ***amount, offer*** dérisoire; ***salary*** de misère. **a ~ 50 francs** la misérable somme de 50 F. ♦ **miserably** *adv* ***smile, answer*** pitoyablement; ***fail*** lamentablement; ***live, pay*** misérablement.

misery ['mɪzərɪ] *n* (*unhappiness*) tristesse *f*; (*suffering*) souffrances *fpl*; (*wretchedness*) misère *f*. **a life of ~** une vie de misère; **to make sb's life a ~** rendre qn (constamment) malheureux; **to put an animal out of its ~** achever un animal; **put him out of his ~* and tell him** abrégez son supplice et dites-le-lui; **what a ~ you are!** ce que tu peux être grincheux!

misfire ['mɪs'faɪəʳ] *vi [gun, plan]* faire long feu; *[joke]* foirer*; *[car engine]* avoir des ratés.

misfit ['mɪsfɪt] *n* (*person*) inadapté(e) *m(f)*.

misfortune [mɪs'fɔːtʃən] *n* (*single event*) malheur *m*; (*bad luck*) malchance *f*. **it is his ~ that he is deaf, he has the ~ to be deaf** pour son malheur il est sourd; **that's YOUR ~!** tant pis pour toi!

misgiving [mɪs'gɪvɪŋ] *n* appréhension *f*. **not without ~(s)** non sans appréhension; **to have ~s about** avoir des doutes *mpl* quant à.

misgovern ['mɪs'gʌvən] *vti* mal gouverner.

misguided ['mɪs'gaɪdɪd] *adj* ***person*** abusé; ***attempt*** malencontreux; ***decision, action*** peu judicieux. ♦ **misguidedly** *adv* malencontreusement; peu judicieusement.

mishandle ['mɪs'hændl] *vt* ***object*** manipuler sans précaution; ***person*** s'y prendre mal avec; ***problem*** traiter mal. **he ~d the whole situation** il a été tout à fait maladroit.

mishap ['mɪshæp] *n* mésaventure *f*. **without ~** sans encombre.

mishear ['mɪs'hɪəʳ] *pret, ptp* **-heard** [-hɜːd] *vt* mal entendre.

mishmash* ['mɪʃmæʃ] *n* méli-mélo* *m*.

misinform ['mɪsɪn'fɔːm] *vt* mal renseigner.

misinterpret ['mɪsɪn'tɜːprɪt] *vt* mal interpréter. ♦ **misinterpretation** *n* interprétation *f* erronée (*of* de); (*in translation*) contresens *m*; **open to ~ation** qui prête à contresens.

misjudge ['mɪs'dʒʌdʒ] *vt* ***amount, time*** mal évaluer; (*underestimate*) sous-estimer; ***person*** se méprendre sur le compte de.

mislay [ˌmɪs'leɪ] *pret, ptp* **mislaid** *vt* égarer.

mislead [ˌmɪs'liːd] *pret, ptp* **misled** *vt* tromper. ♦ **misleading** *adj* trompeur.

mismanage ['mɪs'mænɪdʒ] *vt* mal administrer. ♦ **mismanagement** *n* mauvaise administration *f*.

misname ['mɪs'neɪm] *vt* mal nommer.

misnomer ['mɪs'nəʊməʳ] *n* nom *m* impropre.

misogynist [mɪ'sɒdʒɪnɪst] *n* misogyne *mf*.

misplace ['mɪs'pleɪs] *vt* ***word, trust*** mal placer; (*lose*) égarer.

misprint ['mɪsprɪnt] *n* faute *f* d'impression, coquille *f*.

mispronounce ['mɪsprə'naʊns] *vt* prononcer de travers. ♦ **mispronunciation** *n* faute(s) *f(pl)* de prononciation.

misquote ['mɪs'kwəʊt] *vt* citer inexactement. **he was ~d as having said ...** on lui a incorrectement fait dire que ... . ♦ **misquotation** *n* citation *f* inexacte.

misread ['mɪs'riːd] *pret, ptp* **misread** ['mɪs'red] *vt* mal lire; (*misinterpret*) mal interpréter.

misrepresent ['mɪsˌreprɪ'zent] *vt* ***facts*** dénaturer; ***person*** donner une impression incorrecte de.

miss[1] [mɪs] **1** *n* (*shot etc*) coup *m* manqué *or* raté. (*lit, fig*) **that was a near ~** il s'en est fallu de peu *or* d'un cheveu; (*fig*) **to have a near ~** l'échapper belle; **to give sth a ~*** (*job etc*) ne pas faire qch; (*concert etc*) ne pas aller à qch; **I'll give the wine a ~** je me passerai de vin; **give it a ~!*** arrête!

2 *vt* **(a)** (*gen*) *train, target, deadline etc* manquer, rater; *thing looked out for, solution* ne pas trouver; *remark* (*not hear*) ne pas entendre, (*not understand*) ne pas comprendre; (*omit*) *meal, page, day* sauter; *class* manquer, (*deliberately*) sécher*. **it just ~ed me** ça m'a manqué de justesse; **the plane just ~ed the tower** l'avion a failli toucher la tour; (*iro*) **you haven't ~ed much!** vous n'avez pas manqué grand-chose!; (*fig*) **to ~ the boat*** *or* **the bus*** manquer le coche*; **to ~ one's footing** glisser; **she doesn't ~ a trick*** rien ne lui échappe; **to ~ one's way** perdre son chemin; **you can't ~ our house** vous trouverez tout de suite notre maison; **don't ~ the Louvre** ne manquez pas d'aller au Louvre; **we shall ~ Bourges** nous ne verrons pas Bourges; **you're ~ing the point** vous n'y êtes pas. **(b)** (*avoid*) *accident, bad weather* échapper à. **he narrowly ~ed being killed** il a manqué se faire tuer. **(c)** (*long for*) *person* regretter l'absence de. **I do ~ Paris/him** Paris/il me manque beaucoup; **we ~ you very much** tu nous manques beaucoup, nous regrettons beaucoup ton absence; **he won't be ~ed** personne ne le regrettera. **(d)** (*notice loss of*) *money, valuables* remarquer l'absence *or* la disparition de. **I suddenly ~ed my wallet** tout d'un coup je me suis aperçu que je n'avais plus mon portefeuille; **I shan't ~ it** ça ne me fera pas défaut.

3 *vi* **(a)** *[shot, person]* manquer, rater. **you can't ~!** vous ne pouvez pas ne pas réussir!; **he never ~es** il ne manque jamais son coup. **(b) to be ~ing** avoir disparu; **there is one plate ~ing** il manque une assiette; **one of our aircraft is ~ing** un de nos avions n'est pas rentré.

miss out *vt sep* (*accidentally*) sauter, oublier; (*on purpose*) *course at meal* ne pas prendre; *name on list, person* omettre; *word, line of verse, page* sauter; *lecture, museum* ne pas aller à.

miss out on* *vt fus opportunity, bargain* laisser passer, louper*. **he ~ed out on the deal** il n'a pas obtenu tout ce qu'il aurait pu de l'affaire.

♦ **missing** *adj person* absent, disparu; (*Mil*) disparu; *object* (*lost*) perdu, (*left out*) manquant; *word* qui manque; (*Police etc*) **~ing person** personne *f* absente; **the ~ing students** les étudiants dont on est sans nouvelles; (*fig*) **the ~ing link** le chaînon manquant; (*Mil*) **reported ~ing** porté disparu.

miss² [mɪs] *n* mademoiselle *f*. **M~ Smith** Mademoiselle Smith, Mlle Smith; (*in letter*) **Dear M~ Smith** Chère Mademoiselle; **yes M~ Smith** oui mademoiselle; **M~ France 1982** Miss France 1982; **the modern ~** la jeune fille moderne.

missal ['mɪsəl] *n* missel *m*.

misshapen ['mɪs'ʃeɪpən] *adj* difforme.

missile ['mɪsaɪl] **1** *n* (*gen*) projectile *m*; (*Mil*) missile *m*. **2** *adj*: **~ base** base *f* de missiles; **~ launcher** lance-missiles *m inv*.

mission ['mɪʃən] *n* (*all senses*) mission *f*. **trade ~** mission de commerce; **on a ~ to sb** en mission auprès de qn; **his ~ in life is to help others** il s'est donné pour mission d'aider autrui. ♦ **missionary** **1** *n* missionnaire *mf*; **2** *adj* de missionnaire(s).

misspell ['mɪs'spel] *pret, ptp* **misspelt** *vt* mal orthographier. ♦ **misspelling** *n* faute *f* d'orthographe.

mist [mɪst] **1** *n* brume *f*; (*on glass*) buée *f*; *[perfume]* nuage *m*; *[ignorance, tears]* voile *m*. **lost in the ~s of time** perdu dans la nuit des temps. **2** *vi* (**~ over, ~ up**) *[scene, landscape]* se couvrir de brume; *[mirror, eyes]* s'embuer. ♦ **misty** *adj weather* brumeux; *mirror, eyes* embué; *outline, recollection* flou.

mistake [mɪs'teɪk] (*vb: pret* **mistook**, *ptp* **mistaken**) **1** *n* erreur *f*, faute *f*; (*misunderstanding*) méprise *f*. **to make a ~ in a dictation/problem** faire une faute dans une dictée/une erreur dans un problème; **I made a ~ about the book/about him** je me suis trompé sur le livre/sur son compte; **I made a ~ about** *or* **over the road to take/about** *or* **over the dates** je me suis trompé de route/de dates; **make no ~ about it** ne vous y trompez pas; **you're making a big ~** tu fais une grave erreur; **to make the ~ of doing** avoir le tort de faire; **by ~** par erreur, (*carelessly*) par mégarde; **there must be some ~** il doit y avoir erreur; **there must be no ~ about it** qu'on ne s'y trompe pas; **he's wrong and no ~** décidément il a tort; **my ~!** c'est de ma faute! **2** *vt meaning* mal comprendre; *intentions* se méprendre sur; *time, road* se tromper de; *sb's voice* ne pas reconnaître. **to ~ A for B** prendre A pour B. ♦ **mistaken** *adj idea, opinion, conclusion* erroné; *generosity* mal placé; **in the ~n belief that ...** croyant à tort que ...; *[person]* **to be ~n** se tromper (*about* sur); **if I'm not ~n** si je ne me trompe. ♦ **mistakenly** *adv* par erreur; (*carelessly*) par mégarde.

mistime ['mɪs'taɪm] *vt* (*do etc at unsuitable time*) faire *etc* à contretemps.

mistletoe ['mɪsltəʊ] *n* gui *m*.

mistranslate ['mɪstrænz'leɪt] *vt* mal traduire. ♦ **mistranslation** *n* contresens *m*.

mistress ['mɪstrɪs] *n* (*gen*) maîtresse *f*; (*teacher*) professeur *m*. **English ~** professeur d'anglais.

mistrust ['mɪs'trʌst] **1** *n* méfiance *f* (*of* à l'égard de). **2** *vt person, motives* se méfier de; *one's own abilities* douter de. ♦ **mistrustful** *adj* méfiant. ♦ **mistrustfully** *adv* avec méfiance.

misunderstand ['mɪsʌndə'stænd] *pret, ptp* **-stood** *vt* mal comprendre.

♦ **misunderstanding** *n* méprise *f*; (*disagreement*) malentendu *m*. ♦ **misunderstood** *adj person* incompris.

misuse ['mɪs'ju:z] **1** *vt power, authority* abuser de; *word, tool* employer incorrectement; *money, resources, energies, one's time* mal employer; *funds* détourner. **2** ['mɪs'ju:s] *n* abus *m*; emploi *m* incorrect; mauvais emploi; détournement *m*.

mite [maɪt] *n* **(a)** (*small amount*) *[good sense etc]* grain *m*; *[truth]* parcelle *f*. **a ~ of consolation** une toute petite consolation; **the widow's ~** le denier de la veuve. **(b)** (*small child*) petit(e) *m(f)*. **poor little ~** le pauvre petit. **(c)** (*Zool*) mite *f*. **cheese ~** mite de fromage.

mitigate ['mɪtɪgeɪt] *vt* atténuer. **mitigating circumstances** circonstances *fpl* atténuantes. ♦ **mitigation** *n* atténuation *f*.

mitre, (*US*) **miter** ['maɪtəʳ] *n* (*Rel*) mitre *f*; (*Carpentry*) onglet *m*.

mitt [mɪt] *n* (*also* **mitten**) (*cut-off fingers*) mitaine *f*; (*no separate fingers*) moufle *f*; (*Baseball*) gant *m*.

mix [mɪks] **1** *n* mélange *f*. **cake ~** préparation *f* pour gâteau. **2** *vt liquids, ingredients, colours* mélanger (*with* avec); *small objects* mêler, mélanger (*with* à); *metals* allier; *cement, mortar* malaxer; *cake, sauce, cocktails* préparer; *salad* retourner. **to ~ to a smooth paste** battre pour obtenir une pâte homogène; **to ~ business with pleasure** combiner les affaires et le plaisir; **to ~ one's metaphors** faire des métaphores incohérentes. **3** *vi* se mélanger; se mêler; s'allier. **he ~es with all kinds of people** il fréquente toutes sortes de gens; **he doesn't ~ well** il est peu sociable; **they just don't ~** *[patterns]* ils ne vont pas ensemble; *[people]* ils n'ont rien en commun.

mix in *vt sep eggs etc* incorporer (*with* à).

mix together *vt sep* mélanger.

mix up *vt sep* **(a)** (*prepare*) *drink, medicine* mélanger, préparer. **(b)** (*in disorder*) *documents, garments* mêler, mélanger. **(c)** (*confuse*) *two objects, two people* confondre (*with* avec). **(d) to be/get ~ed up in an affair** être/se trouver mêlé à une affaire; **don't get ~ed up in it!** restez à l'écart!; **he has got ~ed up with a lot of criminals** il s'est mis à fréquenter des malfaiteurs. **(e)**

(*muddle*) *person* embrouiller. **to be ~ed up** *[person]* être déboussolé*; *[account, facts]* être embrouillé; **I am all ~ed up about it** je ne sais plus où j'en suis.
♦ **mixed** *adj marriage, school, economy* mixte; *biscuits, nuts* assortis; *weather* variable; *metaphor* incohérent; *motives* complexe; *feelings* contradictoires; *reception* mitigé; (*fig*) **it's a ~ed bag*** il y a un peu de tout; **it's a ~ed blessing** c'est une bonne chose qui a son mauvais côté; **man/woman of ~ed blood** un/une sang-mêlé; **in ~ed company** en présence d'hommes et de femmes; (*Tennis*) **~ed doubles** double *m* mixte; **~ed farming** polyculture *f*. ♦ **mixed-up** *adj person* déboussolé*; *account* embrouillé. ♦ **mixer** *n* **(a)** (*Culin*) mixeur *m*; *[mortar etc]* malaxeur *m*; *[industrial liquids]* agitateur *m*; **cement ~er** bétonnière *f*; **(b) he's a good ~er** il est très sociable *or* liant. ♦ **mixing 1** *n* (*V* **mix 2**) mélange *m*; alliage *m*; malaxage *m*; préparation *f*; **2** *adj*: **~ing bowl** jatte *f*. ♦ **mixture** *n* mélange *m*; (*Med*) préparation *f*, mixture *f*; (*fig*) **it's just the ~ture as before** il n'y a rien de nouveau. ♦ **mix-up** *n* confusion *f* (*over* en ce qui concerne).
moan [məʊn] **1** *n* (*gen*) gémissement *m*; (*: *complaint*) plainte *f*. **2** *vi* (*gen*) gémir; (*: *complain*) se plaindre, rouspéter*. **3** *vt* dire en gémissant.
moat [məʊt] *n* fossés *mpl*.
mob [mɒb] **1** *n [people]* foule *f*, masse *f*; (*disorderly*) cohue *f*; (*rioting*) émeutiers *mpl*; (*pej*) populace *f*; *[criminals, bandits etc]* gang *m*; (*: *group*) bande *f*. **2** *adj*: **~ rule** la loi de la populace. **3** *vt person* assaillir; *place* assiéger.
mobile ['məʊbaɪl] **1** *adj* mobile. (*fig*) **I'm not ~ this week*** je ne suis pas motorisé* cette semaine; **~ canteen** (cuisine) roulante *f*; **~ home** grande caravane *f* (*utilisée comme domicile*); (*Rad, TV*) **~ studio** car *m* de reportage.
2 *n* (*Art*) mobile *m*.
♦ **mobility** *n* mobilité *f*. ♦ **mobilization** *n* mobilisation *f*. ♦ **mobilize** *vti* mobiliser.
mock [mɒk] **1** *vt* (*ridicule*) ridiculiser; (*scoff at*) se moquer de. **2** *vi* se moquer (*at* de). **3** *adj leather etc* imitation *inv* (*before n*), faux (*before n*); *anger* feint. **a ~ battle/trial** un simulacre de bataille/de procès; **~ exam** examen blanc; **~ turtle soup** consommé *m* à la tête de veau.
mock up *vt sep* faire la maquette de.
♦ **mocker** *n* moqueur *m*, -euse *f*. ♦ **mockery** *n* (*gen*) moquerie *f*; (*of justice etc*) parodie *f*; **to make a ~ery of** tourner en dérision. ♦ **mocking 1** *n* moquerie *f*; **2** *adj* moqueur; (*malicious*) narquois. ♦ **mockingbird** *n* moqueur *m* (*oiseau*). ♦ **mockingly** *adv* d'un ton *or* d'un air moqueur. ♦ **mock-up** *n* maquette *f*.
mod* [mɒd] (*abbr of* **modern**) **1** *adj*: **~ cons** *V* **modern 1**. **2** *n*: **~s and rockers** ≈ blousons *mpl* noirs.
mode [məʊd] *n* (*gen*) mode *m*; (*Fashion*) mode *f*. ♦ **modal** *adj* modal.
model ['mɒdl] **1** *n* (*gen, also fig*) modèle *m*; (*small-scale*) modèle réduit; (*Archit, Tech, Town Planning etc*) maquette *f*; (*artist's ~*) modèle; (*fashion ~*) mannequin *m*. **to take sb/sth as one's ~** prendre modèle sur qn/qch; (*Comm*) **a 1978 ~** un modèle 1978; (*Aut*) **sports ~** modèle sport; **factory ~** modèle de fabrique; **male ~** mannequin masculin. **2** *adj* (*gen*) *prison, school, behaviour* modèle; (*small-scale*) *plane, car* modèle réduit *inv*; *railway, village* en miniature. **3** *vt* (*gen*) modeler (*in* en; *on* sur); *garment* présenter. **to ~ o.s. on sb** prendre modèle sur qn. **4** *vi* (*Art etc*) poser (*for* pour); (*Fashion*) être mannequin (*for sb* chez qn).
♦ **modelling,** (*US*) **modeling 1** *n* (*Sculp etc*) modelage *m*; **2** *adj*: **~(l)ing clay** pâte *f* à modeler.
moderate ['mɒdərɪt] **1** *adj* (*gen*) modéré; *climate* tempéré; *language, terms* mesuré; *result* passable. **2** *n* (*esp Pol*) modéré(e) *m(f)*. **3** ['mɒdəreɪt] *vt* modérer. **4** *vi* se modérer. ♦ **moderately** *adv act* avec modération; *successful* modérément; *pleased* plus ou moins; **~ly priced** d'un prix raisonnable. ♦ **moderation** *n* modération *f*; **in moderation** *eat, drink* modérément; **it's all right in moderation** ça ne fait pas de mal à petites doses.
modern ['mɒdən] **1** *adj* moderne. **all ~ conveniences** (*abbr* **mod cons**) tout le confort (moderne); **~ languages** langues *fpl* vivantes. **2** *n* (*person*) moderne *mf*. ♦ **modernity** *n* modernité *f*. ♦ **modernization** *n* modernisation *f*. ♦ **modernize** *vt* moderniser.
modest ['mɒdɪst] *adj* (*all senses*) modeste. **to be ~ about** ne pas se faire gloire de. ♦ **modestly** *adv* modestement. ♦ **modesty** *n* modestie *f*; **with all due ~y** en toute modestie.
modicum ['mɒdɪkəm] *n*: **a ~ of** un minimum de.
modify ['mɒdɪfaɪ] *vt* (*change*) modifier (*also Gram*); (*make less strong*) *demands* modérer. ♦ **modification** *n* modification *f* (*to, in* à). ♦ **modifier** *n* modificateur *m*; (*Gram*) modificatif *m*.
modulate ['mɒdjʊleɪt] *vt* moduler. ♦ **modulation** *n* modulation *f*.
module ['mɒdju:l] *n* module *m*.
mogul ['məʊgəl] *n* grand manitou *m*.
mohair ['məʊhɛəʳ] **1** *n* mohair *m*. **2** *adj* en *or* de mohair.
Mohammed [məʊ'hæmed] *n* Mahomet *m*. ♦ **Mohammedan 1** *adj* mahométan; **2** *n* Mahométan(e) *m(f)*.
moist [mɔɪst] *adj hand, atmosphere* moite; *climate, wind, surface, eyes* humide; *cake* moelleux. ♦ **moisten** *vt* mouiller légèrement; **to ~en one's lips** s'humecter les lèvres. ♦ **moistness** *n* moiteur *f*; humidité *f*. ♦ **moisture** *n* (*gen*) humidité *f*; (*on glass etc*) buée *f*. ♦ **moisturize** *vt air, atmosphere* humidifier; *skin* hydrater. ♦ **moisturizer** *n* (*for skin*) lait *m* hydratant.
molar ['məʊləʳ] *adj, n* molaire (*f*).
molasses [məʊ'læsɪz] *n* mélasse *f*.
mold [məʊld] *etc* (*US*) = **mould** *etc*.
mole¹ [məʊl] *n* taupe *f* (*also fig: spy*). ♦ **molehill** *n* taupinière *f*. ♦ **moleskin** *n* (peau *f* de) taupe *f*; (*Tex*) velours *m* de coton.
mole² [məʊl] *n* (*on skin*) grain *m* de beauté.
molecule ['mɒlɪkju:l] *n* molécule *f*.
molest [məʊ'lest] *vt* (*trouble*) importuner; (*harm*) molester; (*Jur: sexually*) attenter à la pudeur de.
mollify ['mɒlɪfaɪ] *vt* apaiser, calmer.
mollusc, (*US*) **mollusk** ['mɒləsk] *n* mollusque *m*.
mollycoddle ['mɒlɪkɒdl] *vt* chouchouter*.
molten ['məʊltən] *adj* en fusion.
mom* [mɒm] *n* (*US*) maman *f*.
moment ['məʊmənt] *n* **(a)** moment *m*, instant *m*. **man of the ~** homme *m* du moment; **the ~ of truth** la minute de vérité; **just a ~!, one ~!, half a ~!*** un instant!; (*objecting to sth*) minute!; **I shan't be a ~** j'en ai pour un instant; **a ~ ago** il y a un instant; **the ~ he arrives** dès qu'il arrivera; **I've just this ~ heard of it** je viens de l'apprendre à l'instant (même); **it won't take a ~** c'est l'affaire d'un instant; **at the (present) ~, at this ~ in time** en ce moment; **at any ~** d'un moment *or* instant à l'autre; **at the right/last ~** au bon/dernier moment; **for a ~** un instant; **not for a ~!** jamais de la vie!; **from the ~ I saw him** dès l'instant où je l'ai vu; **I'll come in a ~** j'arrive dans un instant; **it was all over in a ~** tout s'est passé en un instant; **I have my** (*or* **he has his** *etc*) **~s*** il m'arrive (*or* il lui arrive *etc*) de faire des étincelles*. **(b)** (*importance*) importance *f*. ♦ **momentarily** *adv* momentanément. ♦ **momentary** *adj* momentané. ♦ **momentous** *adj* très important. ♦ **momentum** *n* (*Phys etc*) moment *m*; (*fig*) élan *m*, vitesse *f* (acquise); **to gather ~um** *[vehicle]* prendre de la

vitesse; *[protests, campaign etc]* gagner du terrain; *(lit, fig)* **to lose ~um** être en perte de vitesse.
Monaco ['mɒnəkəʊ] *n* Monaco *m.*
monarch ['mɒnək] *n* monarque *m.* ♦ **monarchism** *n* monarchisme *m.* ♦ **monarchist** *adj, n* monarchiste *(mf).* ♦ **monarchy** *n* monarchie *f.*
monastery ['mɒnəstərɪ] *n* monastère *m.* ♦ **monastic** *adj* monastique. ♦ **monasticism** *n* monachisme *m.*
Monday ['mʌndɪ] *n* lundi *m*; *for phrases* V **Saturday.**
monetary ['mʌnɪtərɪ] *adj* monétaire. ♦ **monetarism** *n* politique *f* monétaire.
money ['mʌnɪ] **1** *n* argent *m.* **French ~** argent français; **paper ~** papier-monnaie *m*; **~ for jam*** *or* **for old rope*** de l'argent vite gagné; **to make ~** *[person]* gagner de l'argent; *[business etc]* rapporter; **how did he make his ~?** comment est-ce qu'il a fait fortune?; **he's earning good ~** il gagne bien sa vie; **I paid good ~ for it** ça m'a coûté de l'argent; **he's earning big ~** il gagne gros; **that's big ~** c'est une grosse somme; **when do I get my ~?** quand est-ce que j'aurai mon argent?; **to get one's ~'s worth** en avoir pour son argent; **to get one's ~ back** être remboursé; **to put ~ into sth** placer son argent dans qch; **is there ~ in it?** est-ce qu'il y a qch à gagner?; **it's a bargain for the ~** à ce prix-là, c'est une occasion; *(fig)* **for my ~** à mon avis; **he's made of ~*, he has pots of ~*** il roule sur l'or*; **he's got ~ to burn** il a de l'argent à ne savoir qu'en faire; **we're in the ~!*** nous roulons sur l'or*; **~ doesn't grow on trees** l'argent ne se trouve pas sous le pas d'un cheval. **2** *adj difficulties, questions* d'argent, financier. **~ order** mandat *m.* ♦ **moneybox** *n* tirelire *f.* ♦ **moneyed** *adj* riche. ♦ **moneygrubbing 1** *n* rapacité *f*; **2** *adj* rapace. ♦ **moneylender** *n* prêteur *m* sur gages. ♦ **moneylending** *n* prêt *m* à intérêt. ♦ **moneymaker** *n* affaire *f* lucrative. ♦ **moneymaking 1** *n* acquisition *f* d'argent; **2** *adj* qui rapporte.
mongol ['mɒŋgəl] *n (Med)* mongolien(ne) *m(f).*
mongoose ['mɒŋgu:s] *n* mangouste *f.*
mongrel ['mʌŋgrəl] *n* (chien *m*) bâtard *m.*
monitor ['mɒnɪtə^r] **1** *n (Rad: person)* rédacteur *m*, -trice *f* d'un service d'écoute; *(Med, Tech, TV: device)* moniteur *m*; *(Scol)* ≈ chef *m* de classe. **2** *vt (Rad) broadcast* être à l'écoute de; *machine, system* contrôler (les performances de); *progress* contrôler; *discussion, group* assister à (à titre de conseiller).
monk [mʌŋk] *n* moine *m*, religieux *m.* ♦ **monkish** *adj* de moine.
monkey ['mʌŋkɪ] **1** *n* singe *m.* **female ~** guenon *f*; *(child)* **little ~** petit(e) polisson(ne) *m(f).* **2** *adj*: **~ business*** *or* **tricks*** *(dishonest)* qch de louche; *(mischievous)* singeries *fpl*; **no ~ business now!*** pas de blagues!*; **~ nut** cacahuète *f*; *(tree)* **~ puzzle** araucaria *m*; **~ wrench** clef *f* anglaise *or* à molette.
monkey about*, monkey around* *vi (waste time)* perdre son temps; *(play the fool)* faire l'imbécile. **to ~ about with sth** tripoter qch.
mono ['mɒnəʊ] **1** *adj (abbr of* **monophonic***)* mono* *inv.* **2** *n*: **in ~** en monophonie. **3** *pref* mono... .
monochrome ['mɒnəkrəʊm] *n* camaïeu *m.*
monocle ['mɒnəkl] *n* monocle *m.*
monogamy [mɒ'nɒgəmɪ] *n* monogamie *f.* ♦ **monogamous** *adj* monogame.
monogram ['mɒnəgræm] *n* monogramme *m.*
monograph ['mɒnəgræf] *n* monographie *f.*
monolith ['mɒnəʊlɪθ] *n* monolithe *m.*
monologue ['mɒnəlɒg] *n* monologue *m.*
monomania [ˌmɒnəʊ'meɪnɪə] *n* monomanie *f.* ♦ **monomaniac** *n* monomane *mf.*
monoplane ['mɒnəʊpleɪn] *n* monoplan *m.*
monopoly [mə'nɒpəlɪ] *n* monopole *m (of, in* de). ♦ **monopolize** *vt* monopoliser.
monorail ['mɒnəʊreɪl] *n* monorail *m.*
monosyllable ['mɒnəˌsɪləbl] *n* monosyllabe *m.* ♦ **monosyllabic** ['mɒnəʊsɪ'læbɪk] *adj word* monosyllabe; *reply* monosyllabique.
monotone ['mɒnətəʊn] *n*: **in a ~** sur un ton monocorde. ♦ **monotonous** [mə'nɒtənəs] *adj* monotone. ♦ **monotony** *n* monotonie *f.*
monsoon [mɒn'su:n] *n* mousson *f.*
monster ['mɒnstə^r] *n, adj* monstre *(m).* ♦ **monstrosity** *n* monstruosité *f.* ♦ **monstrous** *adj (huge)* colossal; *(dreadful)* monstrueux. ♦ **monstrously** *adv* monstrueusement.
month [mʌnθ] *n* mois *m.* **in the ~ of May** au mois de mai, en mai; **paid by the ~** payé au mois; **every ~** *happen* tous les mois; *pay* mensuellement; **which day of the ~ is it?** le combien sommes-nous?; **he'll never do it in a ~ of Sundays*** il le fera la semaine des quatre jeudis*. ♦ **monthly 1** *adj (gen)* mensuel; *ticket* valable pour un mois; **~ly instalment** *or* **payment** mensualité *f*; **2** *n (Press)* revue *f* mensuelle. **3** *adv pay* mensuellement; *happen* tous les mois.
monument ['mɒnjʊmənt] *n* monument *m (to* à). ♦ **monumental** *adj* monumental; **~al mason** marbrier *m.*
moo [mu:] **1** *n* meuglement *m.* **2** *vi* meugler.
mooch‡ [mu:tʃ] *vi*: **to ~ about** *or* **around** traînasser; **to ~ in** *etc* entrer *etc* en traînant.
mood [mu:d] **1** *n (gen)* humeur *f*; *(Gram, Mus)* mode *m.* **in a good/bad ~** de bonne/mauvaise humeur; **in an ugly ~** *(angry)* d'une humeur massacrante; *(threatening)* menaçant; **I'm in the ~ for dancing** j'ai envie de danser; **I'm in no ~ to listen to him** je ne suis pas d'humeur à l'écouter; **when he's in the ~** quand ça lui chante*; **I'm not in the ~** ça ne me dit rien; **he's in one of his ~s** il est encore mal luné*; **she has ~s** elle a des sautes *fpl* d'humeur; **the ~ of the meeting** l'état *m* d'esprit de l'assemblée. **2** *adj*: **~ music** musique *f* d'ambiance.
♦ **moodily** *adv (bad-temperedly)* d'un air *etc* maussade; *(gloomily)* d'un air morose. ♦ **moodiness** *n (V* **moody***)* humeur *f* changeante *or* maussade. ♦ **moody** *adj (variable)* d'humeur changeante; *(sulky)* maussade.
moon [mu:n] **1** *n* lune *f.* **full/new ~** pleine/nouvelle lune; **there was no ~** c'était une nuit sans lune; **there was a ~** il y avait clair de lune; **by the light of the ~** à la clarté de la lune; **the man in the ~** l'homme (que l'on voit) dans la lune; *(fig)* **to ask** *or* **cry for the ~** demander la lune; **to be over the ~*** être ravi *(about* de). **2** *adj*: **~ landing** alunissage *m*; **~ shot** tir *m* lunaire.
moon about, moon around *vi* musarder en rêvassant.
♦ **moonbeam** *n* rayon *m* de lune. ♦ **moonlight 1** *n* clair *m* de lune; **by ~light** au clair de (la) lune; **2** *adj walk* au clair de lune; *night* de lune; *(fig)* **to do a ~light flit** déménager à la cloche de bois; **3** *vi* (*: *work)* faire du travail noir. ♦ **moonlighting*** *n* travail *m* noir. ♦ **moonlit** *adj* éclairé par la lune; **~lit night** nuit *f* de lune. ♦ **moonrise** *n* lever *m* de (la) lune. ♦ **moonshine*** *n (nonsense)* balivernes *fpl.* ♦ **moonstone** *n* pierre *f* de lune. ♦ **moonstruck** *adj* dans la lune *(fig).*
moor[1] [mʊə^r] *n* lande *f.* ♦ **moorhen** *n* poule *f* d'eau. ♦ **moorland** *n* lande *f.*
moor[2] [mʊə^r] **1** *vt ship* amarrer. **2** *vi* mouiller. ♦ **mooring** *n (place)* mouillage *m*; **at her ~ings** sur ses amarres *fpl.*
moose [mu:s] *n (Zool)* élan *m*; *(Canada)* orignal *m.*
moot [mu:t] **1** *adj*: **it's a ~ point** c'est discutable. **2** *vt*: **it has been ~ed that** on a suggéré que.
mop [mɒp] **1** *n (for floor)* balai *m* laveur; *(for dishes)* lavette *f* (à vaisselle). **~ of hair** tignasse *f*; **~ of curls** toison *f* bouclée. **2** *vt floor, surface* essuyer. **to ~ one's brow** s'éponger le front.

mop up *vt sep liquid* éponger; *surface* essuyer; (*Mil*) *remnants* éliminer.
♦ **mopping-up operations** *npl* (*Mil*) nettoyage *m*.
mope [məʊp] *vi* se morfondre (*about* en pensant à). **to ~ about** *or* **around** passer son temps à se morfondre.
moped ['məʊped] *n* cyclomoteur *m*.
moral ['mɒrəl] **1** *adj* moral. **to have a ~ obligation to do** être dans l'obligation morale de faire; **~ support** soutien *m* moral; **~ philosophy** la morale, l'éthique *f*; **to raise ~ standards** relever les mœurs.
2 *n* **(a)** *[story]* morale *f*. **to point the ~** faire ressortir la morale. **(b)** *[person, act, attitude]* **~s** moralité *f*.
♦ **morale** [mɒ'rɑːl] *n* moral *m*; **to raise sb's ~e** remonter le moral à qn. ♦ **moralist** *n* moraliste *mf*. ♦ **morality** *n* moralité *f*. ♦ **moralize** *vi* moraliser (*about* sur). ♦ **moralizing 1** *adj* moralisateur; **2** *n* leçons *fpl* de morale. ♦ **morally** *adv act* moralement; **~ly wrong** immoral.
morass [mə'ræs] *n* marécage *m*. (*fig*) **a ~ of problems/paperwork** des problèmes/des papiers à n'en plus finir.
morbid ['mɔːbɪd] *adj* (*gen*) morbide; *fear* maladif.
♦ **morbidly** *adv imagine* d'une façon morbide; *obsessed, curious* morbidement.
more [mɔːʳ] *comp of* **many, much 1** *adj, pron* (*greater in number etc*) plus (de), davantage (de); (*additional*) encore (de); (*other*) d'autres. **~ money/books than** plus d'argent/de livres que; **he's got ~ than you** il en a plus que toi; **~ people than we expected** plus de gens que prévu *or* que nous ne l'escomptions; **many came but ~ stayed away** beaucoup de gens sont venus mais davantage *or* un plus grand nombre se sont abstenus; **many ~, a lot ~** beaucoup plus (de); **a few ~ books** encore quelques livres, quelques livres de plus; **a little ~** un peu plus (de); **some ~ meat** encore de la viande, un peu plus de viande; **there's no ~ meat** il n'y a plus de viande; **is there (any) ~ wine?** y a-t-il encore du vin?; **has she any ~ children?** a-t-elle d'autres enfants?; **no ~ shouting!** arrêtez de crier!; **I've got no ~, I haven't any ~** je n'en ai plus, il ne m'en reste plus; **he can't afford ~ than a small house** il ne peut se payer qu'une petite maison; **have you heard any ~ about him?** avez-vous d'autres nouvelles de lui?; **one pound is ~ than 50p** une livre est plus que 50 pence; **~ than a kilo** plus d'un kilo; **~ than enough** plus que suffisant; **I've got ~ like these** j'en ai d'autres comme ça; (*fig*) **you couldn't ask for ~** on ne peut guère en demander plus; **the ~ the merrier** plus on est de fous, plus on rit; **and what's ~ ...** et qui plus est ...; **nothing ~** rien de plus; **sth ~** qch d'autre *or* de plus.
2 *adv* (*gen*) plus; *exercise, sleep* plus (*than* que), davantage. **~ difficult** plus difficile; **~ easily** plus facilement; **~ and ~** de plus en plus; **he's no ~ a duke than I am** il n'est pas plus duc que moi; **~ or less** plus ou moins; **neither ~ nor less** ni plus ni moins (*than* que); **it will ~ than cover the cost** cela couvrira largement les frais; **no ~ can** (*or* **do** *etc*) **I** ni moi non plus; **the ~ I think of it the ~ ashamed I feel** plus j'y pense, plus j'ai honte; **the ~ fool you to go!** tu es d'autant plus idiot d'y aller!; **(all) the ~ so as ...** d'autant plus que ...; **no ~, not any ~** ne ... plus; **I won't do it any ~** je ne le ferai plus; **once ~** une fois de plus, encore une fois.
moreover [mɔː'rəʊvəʳ] *adv* (*further*) de plus, en outre; (*besides*) d'ailleurs, du reste.
morgue [mɔːg] *n* morgue *f*.
moribund ['mɒrɪbʌnd] *adj* moribond.
morning ['mɔːnɪŋ] **1** *n* (*date, part of day*) matin *m*; (*expressing duration*) matinée *f*. **good ~** (*hallo*) bonjour; (*goodbye*) au revoir; **in the ~** le matin, dans la matinée; (*tomorrow*) demain matin; **I work in the ~(s)** je travaille le matin; **a ~'s work** une matinée de travail; **I have a ~ off every week** j'ai une matinée de libre par semaine; **all (the) ~** toute la matinée; **on the ~ of January 23rd** le 23 janvier au matin; **what a beautiful ~!** quelle belle matinée!; **7 o'clock in the ~** 7 heures du matin; **this ~** ce matin; **yesterday ~** hier matin; **one summer ~** par un matin d'été. **2** *adj walk, swim* matinal, du matin; *paper* du matin. **~ dress** habit *m*; **~ prayer** *or* **service** office *m* du matin; **~ sickness** nausées *fpl* matinales.
Morocco [mə'rɒkəʊ] *n* Maroc *m*.
moron ['mɔːrɒn] *n* (*gen*) idiot(e) *m(f)*, crétin(e) *m(f)*; (*Med*†) faible *mf* d'esprit. ♦ **moronic** [mə'rɒnɪk] *adj* crétin.
morose [mə'rəʊs] *adj* morose. ♦ **morosely** *adv* d'un air *etc* morose.
morphia ['mɔːfɪə], **morphine** ['mɔːfiːn] *n* morphine *f*. **~ addict** morphinomane *mf*.
morphology [mɔː'fɒlədʒɪ] *n* morphologie *f*.
Morse [mɔːs] **1** *n* (**~ code**) morse *m*. **2** *adj alphabet* morse; *signals* en morse.
morsel ['mɔːsl] *n* (petit) morceau *m*; *[food]* bouchée *f*.
mortal ['mɔːtl] **1** *adj* (*gen*) mortel; *combat* à mort. **2** *n* mortel(le) *m(f)*. ♦ **mortality** *n* mortalité *f*.
♦ **mortally** *adv* mortellement.
mortar ['mɔːtəʳ] *n* mortier *m*.
mortgage ['mɔːgɪdʒ] **1** *n* (*in house buying*) emprunt-logement *m*; (*second loan*) hypothèque *f*. **to take out a ~** obtenir un emprunt-logement (*on, for* pour), prendre une hypothèque; **to pay off a ~** rembourser un emprunt-logement, purger une hypothèque. **2** *vt* hypothéquer (*also fig*).
mortice, mortise ['mɔːtɪs] *n* mortaise *f*. **~ lock** serrure *f* encastrée.
mortician [mɔː'tɪʃən] *n* entrepreneur *m* de pompes funèbres.
mortify ['mɔːtɪfaɪ] *vt* mortifier. ♦ **mortification** *n* mortification *f* (*also Rel*), humiliation *f*.
♦ **mortifying** *adj* mortifiant.
mortuary ['mɔːtjʊərɪ] *n* morgue *f*.
mosaic [məʊ'zeɪɪk] *n, adj* mosaïque (*f*).
Moslem ['mɒzlem] = **Muslim.**
mosque [mɒsk] *n* mosquée *f*.
mosquito [mɒs'kiːtəʊ] *n* moustique *m*. **~ net** moustiquaire *f*.
moss [mɒs] *n* mousse *f* (*Bot*). ♦ **mossy** *adj* moussu.
most [məʊst] *superl of* **many, much 1** *adj, pron* **(a)** (*gen*) le plus (de), la plus grande quantité (de), le plus grand nombre (de). **(the) ~ money/records** le plus d'argent/de disques; **who has got (the) ~?** qui en a le plus?; **at (the) ~** au maximum, tout au plus; **to make the ~ of** *one's time* bien employer; *respite, opportunity, sunshine, sb's absence* profiter au maximum de; *talents, money* tirer le meilleur parti de; *resources* utiliser au mieux; **make the ~ of it!** profitez-en bien! **(b)** (*largest part*) la plus grande partie (de); (*greatest number*) la majorité (de), la plupart (de). **~ (of the) people/books** *etc* la plupart *or* la majorité des gens/des livres *etc*; **~ of the money** la plus grande partie de l'argent, presque tout l'argent; **~ of it** presque tout; **~ of them** la plupart d'entre eux; **~ of the day** la plus grande partie de la journée; **~ of the time** la plupart du temps; **for the ~ part** pour la plupart, en général; **in ~ cases** dans la plupart des cas.
2 *adv* **(a)** *work etc* le plus. **the ~ intelligent** le plus intelligent (*of, in* de); **~ easily** le plus facilement. **(b)** (*very*) bien, très. **~ likely** très probablement.
♦ **mostly** *adv* (*chiefly*) surtout; (*almost all*) pour la plupart; (*most often*) le plus souvent, la plupart du temps.
motel [məʊ'tel] *n* motel *m*.
moth [mɒθ] *n* papillon *m* de nuit; (*in clothes*) mite

f. ♦ **mothball** *n* boule *f* de naphtaline. ♦ **moth-eaten** *adj* mangé aux mites. ♦ **mothproof 1** *adj* traité à l'antimite; **2** *vt* traiter à l'antimite.

mother [ˈmʌðəʳ] **1** *n* mère *f.* **~'s help** aide *f* familiale; **M~'s Day** la fête des Mères; **M~ Nature** Dame Nature *f*; **M~ Superior** Mère supérieure. **2** *vt* (*fig*) être une vraie mère pour. **3** *adj*: **~ country** mère patrie *f*; **~ love** amour maternel; **~ tongue** langue *f* maternelle. ♦ **mothercraft** *n* puériculture *f.* ♦ **motherhood** *n* maternité *f.* ♦ **mother-in-law** *n* belle-mère *f.* ♦ **motherland** *n* patrie *f.* ♦ **motherly** *adj* maternel. ♦ **mother-of-pearl** *n* nacre *f* (de perle). ♦ **mother-to-be** *n* future maman *f.*

motion [ˈməʊʃən] **1** *n* **(a)** (*gen*) mouvement *m*, marche *f.* **to set in ~** *machine, vehicle* mettre en marche; *process etc* mettre en branle; (*fig*) **to go through the ~s of doing sth** (*mechanically*) faire qch machinalement; (*insincerely*) faire semblant de faire qch. **(b)** (*at meeting etc*) motion *f*; (*Parl*) proposition *f.* **(c)** (*bowel* ~) selles *fpl.* **2** *adj*: **~ picture** film *m*; **~-picture industry** (industrie *f* du) cinéma *m*; **~ sickness** mal *m* de la route (*or* de mer *etc*). **3** *vti*: to **~ (to) sb to do** faire signe à qn de faire. ♦ **motionless** *adj* immobile.

motive [ˈməʊtɪv] *n* (*gen*) motif *m*; (*Jur*) mobile *m* (*for, of* de). **from the best ~s** avec les meilleures intentions, avec les motifs les plus louables; **his ~ for saying that** la raison pour laquelle il a dit cela. ♦ **motivate** *vt act, decision* motiver; *person* pousser (*to do* à faire). ♦ **motivation** *n* motivation *f.*

motley [ˈmɒtlɪ] *adj* (*mixed*) hétéroclite; (*many-coloured*) bariolé.

motocross [ˈməʊtəˌkrɒs] *n* motocross *m.*

motor [ˈməʊtəʳ] **1** *n* (*engine*) moteur *m*; (*car*) voiture *f*, auto(mobile) *f.* **2** *adj* **(a)** *muscle* moteur. **(b)** (*Aut*) *industry* de l'automobile; *accident* de voiture, d'auto. **~ mechanic** mécanicien *m* garagiste; **~ scooter** scooter *m*; **~ mower** tondeuse *f* (à gazon) à moteur; **the M~ Show** le Salon de l'Automobile; **~ vehicle** véhicule *m* automobile. **3** *vi*: **to go ~ing** faire de l'auto. ♦ **motorbike*** *n* moto* *f.* ♦ **motorboat** *n* canot *m* automobile. ♦ **motorcade** *n* (*US*) cortège *m* d'automobiles. ♦ **motorcar** *n* auto(mobile) *f*, voiture *f.* ♦ **motorcycle** *n* motocyclette *f.* ♦ **motorcycling** *n* motocyclisme *m.* ♦ **motorcyclist** *n* motocycliste *mf.* ♦ **motoring** **1** *n* conduite *f* automobile; **2** *adj accident* de voiture; *holiday* en voiture; **the ~ing public** les automobilistes *mpl.* ♦ **motorist** *n* automobiliste *mf.* ♦ **motorization** *n* motorisation *f.* ♦ **motorize** *vt* motoriser. ♦ **motorman** *n* (*US*) conducteur *m* (*d'un train etc électrique*). ♦ **motor-racing** *n* course *f* automobile.

mottled [ˈmɒtld] *adj* tacheté; *complexion* brouillé.

motto [ˈmɒtəʊ] *n* devise *f.*

mould¹ [məʊld] **1** *n* (*Art, Culin, Tech etc*) moule *m.* **2** *vt clay* mouler; *figure* modeler (*in, out of* en); (*fig*) *character, opinion* former. ♦ **moulding** *n* (*Archit etc*) moulure *f.*

mould² [məʊld] *n* (*fungus*) moisissure *f.* ♦ **moulder** *vi [cheese]* moisir; *[building]* tomber en poussière. ♦ **mouldy** *adj* moisi; (**fig: unpleasant*) minable*; **to go ~y** moisir; **to smell ~y** sentir le moisi.

moult, (*US*) **molt** [məʊlt] *vi [snake, bird]* muer; *[dog, cat]* perdre ses poils.

mound [maʊnd] *n* **(a)** *[earth]* tertre *m*; (*Archeol*) tertre artificiel; (*burial* ~) tumulus *m.* **(b)** (*pile*) tas *m.*

mount¹ [maʊnt] *n* (*liter*) mont *m*, montagne *f.* **M~ Everest** le mont Everest.

mount² [maʊnt] **1** *n* **(a)** (*horse*) monture *f.* **(b)** (*support*) *[machine]* support *m*; *[lens, specimen]* monture *f*; *[transparency]* cadre *m* (en carton *etc*). **2** *vt* **(a)** (*gen*) monter sur; (*climb*) *hill, stairs* monter. **(b)** *machine, picture, jewel* monter (*on, in* sur). **(c)** *play, demonstration, plot* monter. (*Mil*) **to ~ guard** monter la garde (*on* sur; *over* auprès de). **3** *vi [prices etc]* monter. **it all ~s up** tout cela finit par chiffrer. ♦ **mounted** *adj* monté, à cheval.

mountain [ˈmaʊntɪn] **1** *n* montagne *f.* **to go to/live in the ~s** aller à/habiter la montagne; **to make a ~ out of a molehill** se faire une montagne d'un rien; (*Econ*) **butter ~** montagne de beurre; **a ~ of work** un travail fou. **2** *adj tribe, people* montagnard; *animal, plant* de(s) montagne(s); *air* de la montagne; *path, scenery, shoes, chalet* de montagne. **~ cat** *or* **lion** puma *m*; **~ range** chaîne *f* de montagnes. ♦ **mountaineer 1** *n* alpiniste *mf*; **2** *vi* faire de l'alpinisme. ♦ **mountaineering** *n* alpinisme *m.* ♦ **mountainous** *adj country* montagneux; (*fig*) gigantesque. ♦ **mountainside** *n*: **to go up/down the ~side** monter/descendre le flanc de la montagne.

mourn [mɔːn] **1** *vi* pleurer. **to ~ for sb** pleurer (la mort de) qn. **2** *vt* pleurer. ♦ **mourner** *n*: **the ~ers** le cortège funèbre. ♦ **mournful** *adj person* mélancolique, triste; *thing* lugubre. ♦ **mournfully** *adv* mélancoliquement; lugubrement. ♦ **mournfulness** *n* tristesse *f*; aspect *m* lugubre. ♦ **mourning** *n* deuil *m*; (*clothes*) vêtements *mpl* de deuil; **in ~ing** en deuil (*for sb* de qn.).

mouse [maʊs] *n, pl* **mice** souris *f.* ♦ **mousehole** *n* trou *m* de souris. ♦ **mousetrap** *n* souricière *f.* ♦ **mousy** *adj person* timide, effacé; *hair* châtain clair *inv* (sans éclat).

mousse [muːs] *n* mousse *f* (*Culin*).

moustache, (*US*) **mustache** [məsˈtɑːʃ] *n* moustache(s) *f(pl).* **man with a ~** homme à moustache.

mouth [maʊθ] **1** *n* (*gen*) bouche *f*; *[dog, cat, lion etc]* gueule *f*; *[river]* embouchure *f*; *[bag]* ouverture *f*; *[hole, cave, harbour etc]* entrée *f*; *[volcano, gun]* bouche *f.* **with one's ~ wide open** bouche bée; **he kept his ~ shut about it** il n'en a parlé à personne; **shut your ~!‡** ferme-la!‡; **you've got a big ~!‡** tu ne pouvais pas la fermer!‡; **it makes my ~ water** cela me fait venir l'eau à la bouche. **2** [maʊð] *vt* prononcer tout bas; (*silently*) faire semblant de prononcer. ♦ **mouthful** *n [food]* bouchée *f*; *[drink]* gorgée *f.* ♦ **mouth organ** *n* harmonica *m.* ♦ **mouthpiece** *n [musical instrument]* bec *m*; *[telephone]* microphone *m*; (*spokesman*) porte-parole *m inv.* ♦ **mouth-to-mouth (resuscitation)** *n* bouche à bouche *m inv.* ♦ **mouthwash** *n* eau *f* dentifrice; (*for gargling*) gargarisme *m.* ♦ **mouth-watering** *adj* appétissant.

move [muːv] **1** *n* **(a)** mouvement *m.* **to be on the ~** être en marche; **to be always on the ~** *[gipsies etc]* se déplacer continuellement; *[military personnel etc]* être toujours en déplacement; *[child, animal]* ne jamais rester en place; (*: *be busy*) ne jamais arrêter; **to make a ~** (*leave*) partir; (*act*) agir; **he made a ~ towards the door** il a esquissé un mouvement vers la porte; **get a ~ on!*** remue-toi!* **(b)** (*change of house*) déménagement *m*; (*change of job*) changement *m* d'emploi. **it's time he had a ~** il a besoin de changer d'horizon. **(c)** (*Chess, Draughts etc: turn*) tour *m*; (*fig*) manœuvre *f.* **knight's ~** marche *f* du cavalier; **a silly ~** (*in game*) un coup stupide; (*fig*) une manœuvre stupide; **it's your ~** c'est à vous de jouer; (*fig*) **he knows every ~ in the game** il connaît toutes les astuces; (*fig*) **one false ~ and ...** un faux pas et ...; **his first ~ after the election** son premier acte après son élection; **what's the next ~?** et maintenant qu'est-ce qu'on fait?; **to make the first ~** faire les premiers pas; **there was a ~ to defeat the proposal** il y a eu une tentative pour faire échec à la proposition.

2 *vt* **(a)** (*change position of*) *object* changer de place, déplacer; *limbs* remuer; *troops, animals* transporter; *chessman* jouer; *employee* (*to another town*) muter (*to* à); (*to another job*) affecter (*to* à). **~ your chair nearer the fire** approchez votre chaise du feu; **they ~d the crowd off the grass** ils ont fait partir la foule de sur la pelouse; **to ~ house** déménager; **to ~ one's job** changer d'emploi; **his firm want to ~ him** son entreprise veut l'envoyer ailleurs; **to ~ heaven and earth to do sth** remuer ciel et terre pour faire qch; **he didn't ~ a muscle** (*flinch*) il n'a pas bronché; **the wind ~s the leaves** le vent agite les feuilles. **(b)** (*fig*) inciter (*sb to do* qn à faire). **I am ~d to ask** je suis incité à demander; **if the spirit ~s me** si le cœur m'en dit. **(c) this did not ~ him** ceci n'a pas réussi à l'ébranler *or* (*emotionally*) l'émouvoir; **she's easily ~d** elle s'émeut facilement; **to ~ sb to tears** émouvoir qn jusqu'aux larmes; **to ~ to anger** mettre en colère; **to ~ to pity** attendrir. **(d)** *resolution etc* proposer (*that* que +*subj*).

3 *vi* **(a)** (*stir*) bouger; (*go*) aller, se déplacer; *[clouds]* passer. *[vehicle]* **to be moving** être en marche; **don't ~!** ne bougez pas!; **he ~d slowly towards the door** il s'est dirigé lentement vers la porte; **let's ~ into the garden** passons dans le jardin; **she ~s well** elle a une démarche aisée; **they ~d across the lawn** ils ont traversé la pelouse; **keep moving** (*to keep warm etc*) ne restez pas sans bouger; (*pass along etc*) circulez; **he ~d into another class** il est passé dans une autre classe; **to ~ freely** *[piece of machinery]* jouer librement; *[people, cars]* circuler aisément; *[traffic]* être fluide; **to keep the traffic moving** assurer la circulation ininterrompue des véhicules; **you can't ~ for books** on ne peut plus se retourner tellement il y a de livres; (*depart*) **it's time we were moving** il est temps que nous partions (*subj*); **things are moving at last!** enfin ça avance!; **he got things moving** avec lui ça a bien démarré. **(b)** (*~ house*) déménager. **to ~ to the country** aller habiter la campagne. **(c)** (*act*) agir. **the government won't ~ until ...** le gouvernement ne fera rien tant que ...; **to ~ first** prendre l'initiative. **(d)** (*in games*) *[player]* jouer; *[chesspiece]* marcher. **it's you to ~** c'est votre tour de jouer.

move about, move around 1 *vi* (*fidget*) remuer; (*walk about*) se déplacer; (*travel*) voyager. **2** *vt sep* déplacer.

move along 1 *vi* (*gen*) avancer; (*on bench etc*) se pousser. **2** *vt sep* faire avancer.

move away 1 *vi* (*gen*) s'éloigner (*from* de); (*move house*) déménager. **2** *vt sep* éloigner (*from* de).

move back 1 *vi* (*gen*) reculer; (*to original position*) retourner, revenir. **2** *vt sep crowd* faire reculer; *troops* replier; *object* reculer; (*to original position*) *person* faire revenir *or* retourner; *object* remettre.

move down 1 *vi* descendre. **2** *vt sep person* faire descendre; *object* descendre.

move forward 1 *vi* (*gen*) avancer; *[troops]* se porter en avant. **2** *vt sep person, vehicle* faire avancer; *troops* porter en avant; *object* avancer.

move in 1 *vi* **(a)** *[police etc]* avancer (*on* sur), intervenir. **(b)** (*to a house*) emménager; (**fig: try for control*) essayer de se tailler une place. **2** *vt sep person* faire entrer; *furniture etc* rentrer; (*on removal day*) installer.

move off 1 *vi* (*gen*) partir; *[car]* démarrer. **2** *vt sep object* enlever.

move on 1 *vi [person, vehicle]* avancer; (*after stopping*) se remettre en route; (*fig: in story etc*) passer (*to* à). **2** *vt sep crowd* faire circuler; *hands of clock* avancer.

move out 1 *vi* déménager (*of* de). **2** *vt sep person, animal* faire sortir; *troops* retirer; *object* sortir, (*on removal day*) déménager.

move over 1 *vi* se pousser. **2** *vt sep* pousser.

move up 1 *vi* (*gen*) monter; *[employee]* avoir de l'avancement; (*Sport: in league*) avancer. **2** *vt sep person* faire monter; *object* monter; (*promote*) *employee* donner de l'avancement à.

♦ **movable** *adj* mobile. ♦ **movement** *n* (*gen*) mouvement *m*; **~ments** *[suspect]* allées et venues *fpl*. ♦ **movie* 1** *n* film *m* (*de cinéma*); **to go to the movies** aller au cinéma *or* au ciné*; **2** *adj industry* du cinéma; **movie camera** caméra *f*. ♦ **moviegoer** *n* amateur *m* de cinéma. ♦ **movie house** *n* (salle *f* de) cinéma *m*. ♦ **movieland** *n* le (monde du) cinéma. ♦ **moving** *adj* **(a)** *vehicle* en marche; *object, crowd* en mouvement; *pavement, staircase* roulant; *power* moteur; *machine-part* mobile; **the moving spirit in the whole affair** l'âme *f* de toute l'affaire; **(b)** (*touching*) *sight* émouvant. ♦ **movingly** *adv* d'une manière émouvante.

mow [məʊ] *pret* **-ed**, *ptp* **-ed** *or* **-n** *vt corn* faucher; *lawn* tondre. **to ~ sb down** faucher qn. ♦ **mower** *n* (*Agr*) faucheuse *f*; (*lawn ~*) tondeuse *f* (à gazon).

Mr ['mɪstəʳ] *n* monsieur *m*. **~ Smith** Monsieur Smith, M. Smith; **yes ~ Smith** oui monsieur; **~ Chairman** monsieur le président.

Mrs ['mɪsɪz] *n* madame *f*. **~ Smith** Madame Smith, Mme Smith; **yes, ~ Smith** oui, madame.

Ms [mɪz, məz] *n titre évitant la distinction entre madame et mademoiselle.*

much [mʌtʃ] *comp* **more**, *superl* **most 1** *adj, pron* **(a)** beaucoup (de). **~ money** beaucoup d'argent; **have you got ~?** est-ce que vous en avez beaucoup?; **does it cost ~?** est-ce que ça coûte cher?; **~ of the town** une bonne partie de la ville; **he hadn't ~ to say** il n'avait pas grand-chose à dire; **we don't see ~ of each other** nous ne nous voyons pas souvent; **it isn't up to ~*** ça ne vaut pas grand-chose; **he's not ~ to look at** il ne paie pas de mine; **he is not ~ of a writer** il n'est pas extraordinaire comme écrivain; **it wasn't ~ of an evening** ce n'était pas une très bonne soirée; **I don't think ~ of that** à mon avis ça ne vaut pas grand-chose; **there wasn't ~ in it** (*in choice*) c'était kif-kif*; (*in race etc*) il a gagné de justesse; **to make ~ of sb/sth** faire grand cas de qn/qch; **I couldn't make ~ of what he was saying** je n'ai pas bien compris ce qu'il disait; **they're ~ of a muchness** c'est blanc bonnet et bonnet blanc; (*fig*) **it's a bit ~!*** c'est un peu fort! **(b)** (*phrases*) **as ~ as** autant que; **as ~ time as** autant de temps que; **as ~ again** encore autant; **twice as ~** deux fois autant *or* plus (de); **it's as ~ as he can do to stand up** c'est tout juste s'il peut se lever; **you could pay as ~ as 20 francs** vous pourriez payer jusqu'à 20 F; **as ~ as to say** comme pour dire; **how ~?** combien (de)?; **however ~ you protest, he ...** vous avez beau protester, il ...; **so ~** tant (de); **so ~ that** tellement *or* tant que ...; **without so ~ as a word** sans même dire un mot; **so ~ for that!** (*resignedly*) tant pis!; (*and now for the next*) et d'une!*; **so ~ for his promises** voilà ce que valaient ses promesses; **this** *or* **that ~ bread** ça de pain; **I know this ~** je sais tout au moins ceci; **this ~ is true** il y a ceci de vrai; **too ~** trop (de); **I've eaten too ~** j'ai trop mangé; **that's too ~, that's a bit ~** c'est trop; (*fig*) c'est trop fort; **this work is too ~ for me** ce travail est trop fatigant pour moi.

2 *adv* beaucoup. **thank you very ~** merci beaucoup, merci bien; **it doesn't ~ matter** cela n'a pas beaucoup d'importance; **~ bigger** beaucoup plus grand; **~ the cleverest** de beaucoup *or* de loin le plus intelligent; **as ~ as** autant que; **as ~ as ever** toujours autant; **I don't like it as ~ as all that** je ne l'aime pas tant que ça; **not so ~ a question of money as of staff** pas tant un problème d'argent que de personnel; **so ~ that** tellement *or* tant que; **so ~ so that** à tel point que; **too ~** trop; **I don't know him, ~ less his father** lui, je ne le connais pas, et son père encore moins; **(very** *or* **pretty)** ~ **the same** presque le même (*as* que); ~ **as I would like to go** bien que je désire (*subj*) beaucoup y aller; ~ **to my amazement** à ma grande stupéfaction.

mucilage ['mju:sɪlɪdʒ] *n* mucilage *m.*

muck [mʌk] *n* (*manure*) fumier *m*; (*mud*) boue *f*; (*dirt*) saletés *fpl*; (*fig: scandal*) cochonneries *fpl.* **dog** ~ crotte *f* de chien.

muck about*, muck around* 1 *vi* (*aimlessly*) traîner, perdre son temps; (*play the fool*) faire l'imbécile. **to** ~ **about with sth** tripoter qch. 2 *vt sep person* créer des complications à.

muck out *vt sep stable* nettoyer.

muck up‡ *vt sep* (*ruin*) *plans, life* gâcher; *car, machine* bousiller*; (*dirty*) *room, clothes* salir.

♦ **muckiness** *n* saleté *f.* ♦ **muckraking** *n* déterrement *m* de scandales. ♦ **muck-up**‡ *n* gâchis *m.* ♦ **mucky** *adj* (*muddy*) boueux; (*filthy*) sale.

mucus ['mju:kəs] *n* mucus *m.*

mud [mʌd] 1 *n* (*gen*) boue *f*; (*in river, sea*) vase *f.* **stuck in the** ~ embourbé; (*fig*) **to throw** ~ **at sb** couvrir qn de boue; **my name is** ~* **here** je suis très mal vu ici. 2 *adj* (*Aut*) ~ **flap** pare-boue *m inv*; ~ **flat** laisse *f* de vase; ~ **hut** hutte *f* de terre; ~ **pie** pâté *m* (de terre). ♦ **mudbank** *n* banc *m* de vase. ♦ **muddy** *adj road, water* boueux; *clothes, hands* couvert de boue; *liquid* trouble; *complexion* terreux. ♦ **mudguard** *n* garde-boue *m inv.* ♦ **mudpack** *n* masque *m* de beauté.

muddle ['mʌdl] 1 *n* (*disorder*) désordre *m*, pagaille *f*; (*perplexity, mix-up*) confusion *f.* **to be in a** ~ *[room, books]* être en désordre; *[person]* ne plus s'y retrouver (*over sth* dans qch); *[ideas]* être embrouillé *or* confus; *[plans, arrangements]* être confus; **to get into a** ~ (*confused*) s'embrouiller (*over* dans); **there's been a** ~ **over the seats** il y a eu confusion en ce qui concerne les places. 2 *vt* (~ **up**) confondre (*A with B* A avec B); *person, story, details* embrouiller. **to get** ~**d (up)** s'embrouiller; **to be** ~**d (up)** être embrouillé.

muddle along, muddle on *vi* continuer tant bien que mal.

muddle through *vi* s'en sortir tant bien que mal.

♦ **muddle-headed** *adj person* brouillon; *plan* confus. ♦ **muddler** *n* esprit *m* brouillon (*personne*). ♦ **muddle-up** *n* confusion *f.*

muff [mʌf] 1 *n* manchon *m.* 2 *vt*: **to** ~ **it*** rater son coup.

muffle ['mʌfl] *vt* **(a)** *sound* assourdir. **(b)** (~ **up**: *wrap up*) emmitoufler. ♦ **muffled** *adj sound, voice* sourd. ♦ **muffler** *n* (*scarf*) cache-nez *m inv*; (*US Aut*) silencieux *m.*

mufti ['mʌftɪ] *n*: **in** ~ en civil.

mug [mʌg] 1 *n* **(a)** chope *f*; (*of metal*) gobelet *m.* **(b)** (‡: *fool*) nigaud(e) *m(f)*, andouille‡ *f.* **what a** ~! quelle andouille‡!; **it's a** ~**'s game*** on se fait toujours avoir*. 2 *vt* (*assault*) agresser.

mug up‡ *vt sep* bûcher*, étudier.

♦ **mugger** *n* agresseur *m.* ♦ **mugging** *n* agression *f.*

muggy ['mʌgɪ] *adj room* qui sent le renfermé; *climate* mou. **it's** ~ il fait lourd.

mulatto [mju:'lætəʊ] *n* mulâtre(sse) *m(f).*

mulberry ['mʌlbərɪ] *n* mûre *f*; (*tree*) mûrier *m.*

mule [mju:l] *n* mulet *m*; (*female*) mule *f.* **stubborn as a** ~ têtu comme une mule. ♦ **mulish** *adj* têtu.

mull [mʌl] *vt wine* chauffer et épicer. ~**ed wine** vin *m* chaud.

mull over *vt sep* ruminer (*fig*).

mullet ['mʌlɪt] *n*: **grey** ~ mulet *m*; **red** ~ rouget *m.*

mulligatawny [ˌmʌlɪgə'tɔ:nɪ] *n* potage *m* au curry.

multi... ['mʌltɪ] *pref* multi... . ♦ **multicoloured** *adj* multicolore. ♦ **multimillionaire** *n* ≃ multimilliardaire *mf.* ♦ **multinational** 1 *adj* multinational; 2 *n* multinationale *f.* ♦ **multipurpose** *adj* multi-usages *inv.* ♦ **multiracial** *adj* multiracial. ♦ **multistorey(ed)** *adj* à étages.

multiple ['mʌltɪpl] 1 *n* multiple *m.* 2 *adj* multiple. ~ **sclerosis** sclérose *f* en plaques; ~ **store** grand magasin *m* à succursales multiples. ♦ **multiple-choice** *adj* à choix multiples. ♦ **multiplication** *n* multiplication *f.* ♦ **multiply** 1 *vt* multiplier (*by* par); 2 *vi* se multiplier.

multitude ['mʌltɪtju:d] *n* multitude *f.*

mum[1]* [mʌm] *n* (*mother*) maman *f.*

mum[2] [mʌm] *adj*: **to keep** ~ **(about sth)** ne pas souffler mot (de qch); ~**'s the word!** motus!

mumble ['mʌmbl] *vti* marmotter.

mumbo jumbo [ˌmʌmbəʊ'dʒʌmbəʊ] *n* charabia* *m.*

mummy[1] ['mʌmɪ] *n* (*embalmed*) momie *f.* ♦ **mummify** *vt* momifier.

mummy[2]* ['mʌmɪ] *n* (*mother*) maman *f.* ~**'s boy** fils *m* à sa mère.

mumps [mʌmps] *nsg* oreillons *mpl.*

munch [mʌntʃ] *vti* mastiquer.

mundane [ˌmʌn'deɪn] *adj* (*humdrum*) banal; (*worldly*) de ce monde.

municipal [mju:'nɪsɪpəl] *adj* municipal. ♦ **municipality** *n* municipalité *f.*

munificence [mju:'nɪfɪsns] *n* munificence *f.* ♦ **munificent** *adj* munificent.

munitions [mju:'nɪʃənz] 1 *npl* munitions *fpl.* 2 *adj*: ~ **dump** entrepôt *m* de munitions.

mural ['mjʊərəl] 1 *adj* mural. 2 *n* peinture *f* murale.

murder ['mɜ:dəʳ] 1 *n* meurtre *m*; (*premeditated*) assassinat *m.* (*fig*) **he was shouting blue** ~* il criait comme un putois; **they get away with** ~* ils peuvent faire n'importe quoi impunément; **it's** ~* c'est infernal; **the roads were** ~* les routes étaient un cauchemar. 2 *adj*: ~ **case** (*Jur*) procès *m* en homicide; (*Police*) affaire *f* d'homicide; ~ **trial** ≃ procès capital; **the** ~ **weapon** l'arme *f* du meurtre. 3 *vt person* assassiner; (*: *fig*) *song* massacrer. **the** ~**ed man** la victime. ♦ **murderer** *n* meurtrier *m*, assassin *m.* ♦ **murderess** *n* meurtrière *f.* ♦ **murderous** *adj* meurtrier.

murky ['mɜ:kɪ] *adj* (*gen*) obscur; *darkness* épais; *water, sb's past* trouble.

murmur ['mɜ:məʳ] 1 *n* murmure *m*; *[bees, traffic, voices]* bourdonnement *m.* **without a** ~ sans murmure; (*Med*) **a heart** ~ un souffle au cœur. 2 *vti* murmurer; bourdonner.

muscle ['mʌsl] *n* muscle *m.*

muscle in* *vi* intervenir. **to** ~ **in on** essayer de s'imposer dans.

♦ **muscular** *adj person, arm* musclé; *tissue, disease* musculaire; **muscular dystrophy** dystrophie *f* musculaire.

muse [mju:z] 1 *vi* songer (*on, about, over* à). 2 *n* muse *f.* ♦ **musing** 1 *adj* songeur; 2 *n* songerie *f.*

museum [mju:'zɪəm] *n* musée *m.*

mushroom ['mʌʃrʊm] 1 *n* champignon *m* (comestible). 2 *adj soup, omelette* aux champignons; *flavour* de champignons; (*colour*) beige rosé *inv*; (*fig*) *town* champignon *inv*; *growth* soudain. ~ **cloud** champignon *m* atomique. 3 *vi* **(a)** (*grow*) pousser comme un champignon. **(b) to go** ~**ing** aller aux champignons.

mushy ['mʌʃɪ] *adj food* en bouillie; *fruit* blet. ~ **peas** purée *f* de pois.

music ['mju:zɪk] 1 *n* musique *f.* **to set to** ~ mettre en musique; (*fig*) **it was** ~ **to his ears** c'était doux à son oreille. 2 *adj teacher, lesson* de musique; *critic* musical. ~ **case** porte-musique *m inv*; ~ **centre** chaîne *f* compacte stéréo; ~ **festival** festival *m*; ~ **hall** music-hall *m*; ~ **lover** mélomane *mf.* ♦ **musical** 1 *adj* (*gen*) musical; *person, family* musicien; ~**al box** boîte *f* à musique; ~**al instrument** instrument *m* de musique; 2 *n* (*Cine, Theat*) comédie *f* musicale. ♦ **musically** *adv* musicalement. ♦ **musician** *n* musicien(ne) *m(f).* ♦ **musicianship** *n* sens *m* de la musique.

♦ **musicologist** *n* musicologue *mf*. ♦ **musicology** *n* musicologie *f*.
musk [mʌsk] *n* musc *m*. ♦ **muskrat** *n* rat *m* musqué.
musket ['mʌskɪt] *n* mousquet *m*.
Muslim ['mʊslɪm] *adj, n* musulman(e) *m(f)*.
muslin ['mʌzlɪn] *n* mousseline *f* (*Tex*).
musquash ['mʌskwɒʃ] *n* rat *m* musqué.
mussel ['mʌsl] *n* moule *f*.
must [mʌst] **1** *modal aux vb* **(a)** (*obligation*) **you ~ leave** vous devez partir, il faut que vous partiez (*subj*); (*on notice*) **'the windows ~ not be opened'** 'défense d'ouvrir les fenêtres'; **you ~n't touch it** il ne faut pas *or* tu ne dois pas y toucher; **sit down if you ~** asseyez-vous si c'est indispensable; **I ~ say** franchement; (*iro*) ça alors!* **(b)** (*certainty*) **he ~ be wrong** il doit se tromper, il se trompe certainement; **is he mad? - he ~ be!** est-ce qu'il est fou? - sûrement!; **I ~ have made a mistake** j'ai dû me tromper.
2 *n*: **this book is a ~*** c'est un livre qu'il faut absolument avoir *or* lire; **a car is a ~*** une voiture est absolument indispensable.
mustache ['mʌstæʃ] (*US*) = **moustache.**
mustard ['mʌstəd] *n* (*Bot, Culin*) moutarde *f*. **~ pot** moutardier *m*.
muster ['mʌstəʳ] **1** *n* (*gathering*) assemblée *f*; (*Mil, Naut:* **~ roll**) rassemblement *m*; (*roll-call*) appel *m*. (*fig*) **to pass ~** être acceptable. **2** *vt number, sum, helpers* réunir; (**~ up**) *strength, energy* rassembler. **he ~ed (up) the courage to say so** il a pris son courage à deux mains pour le dire; **I couldn't ~ (up) enough energy to protest** je n'ai pas eu l'énergie de protester. **3** *vi [people]* se réunir, se rassembler.
musty ['mʌstɪ] *adj taste, smell* de moisi; *room* qui sent le moisi; *ideas* vieux jeu *inv*. **to grow ~** moisir; **to smell ~** avoir une odeur de moisi. ♦ **mustiness** *n* moisi *m*.
mutate [mju:'teɪt] *vi* subir une mutation. ♦ **mutant** *adj, n* mutant (*m*). ♦ **mutation** *n* mutation *f*.
mute [mju:t] **1** *adj* muet. **2** *n* (*Med*) muet(te) *m(f)*; (*Mus*) sourdine *f*. ♦ **muted** *adj voice, sound* assourdi; *colour* sourd; (*Mus*) en sourdine; *criticism, protest* voilé.
mutilate ['mju:tɪleɪt] *vt* mutiler. ♦ **mutilation** *n* mutilation *f*.
mutiny ['mju:tɪnɪ] **1** *n* mutinerie *f*; (*fig*) révolte *f*. **2** *vi* se mutiner; se révolter. ♦ **mutineer** *n* mutiné *m*, mutin *m*. ♦ **mutinous** *adj* mutiné; (*fig*) *attitude, look* rebelle.
mutter ['mʌtəʳ] **1** *n* marmonnement *m*; (*grumbling*) grommellement *m*. **2** *vt* marmonner. **3** *vi* marmonner; (*grumble*) grommeler; *[thunder]* gronder.
mutton ['mʌtn] *n* mouton *m* (*Culin*). **leg of ~** gigot *m*.
mutual ['mju:tjʊəl] *adj affection, help* mutuel; (*common*) *friend, cousin* commun. **the feeling is ~** c'est réciproque. ♦ **mutually** *adv* mutuellement.
Muzak ['mju:zæk] *n* ® musique *f* enregistrée.
muzzle ['mʌzl] **1** *n [dog, fox etc]* museau *m*; *[gun]* bouche *f*; (*anti-biting device: also fig*) muselière *f*. **2** *vt* museler (*also fig*).
muzzy ['mʌzɪ] *adj ideas* confus; *outline* flou. **this cold makes me feel ~** ce rhume m'abrutit.
my [maɪ] *poss adj* mon, ma, mes. **~ book** mon livre; **~ table** ma table; **~ friend** mon ami(e); **~ clothes** mes vêtements; **I've broken ~ leg** je me suis cassé la jambe. ♦ **myself** *pers pron* (*reflexive: direct and indirect*) me; (*emphatic*) moi-même; (*after prep*) moi; **I've hurt ~self** je me suis blessé; **all by ~self** tout seul; **I'm not ~self** je ne suis pas dans mon état normal.
myopic [maɪ'ɒpɪk] *adj* myope.
myrtle ['mɜ:tl] *n* myrte *m*.
mystery ['mɪstərɪ] **1** *n* mystère *m*; (*book:* **~ story**) roman *m* à suspense. **there's no ~ about it** ça n'a rien de mystérieux; **it's a ~ to me how ...** je n'arrive pas à comprendre comment ...; **to make a great ~ of sth** faire grand mystère de qch. **2** *adj ship, man* mystérieux. ♦ **mysterious** *adj* mystérieux. ♦ **mysteriously** *adv* mystérieusement. ♦ **mystification** *n* (*act*) mystification *f*; (*feeling*) perplexité *f*. ♦ **mystify** *vt* mystifier; (*accidentally*) rendre perplexe.
mystic ['mɪstɪk] *adj, n* mystique (*mf*). ♦ **mystical** *adj* mystique. ♦ **mysticism** *n* mysticisme *m*. ♦ **mystique** *n* mystique *f*.
myth [mɪθ] *n* mythe *m*. ♦ **mythical** *adj* mythique. ♦ **mythological** *adj* mythologique. ♦ **mythology** *n* mythologie *f*.
myxomatosis [ˌmɪksəʊmə'təʊsɪs] *n* myxomatose *f*.

N

N, n [en] *n* (*letter*) N, n *m.* **to the nth power** *or* **degree** à la puissance n; **for the nth time*** pour la énième fois.
nab* [næb] *vt wrongdoer* pincer*, attraper; *sb to speak to* coincer*.
nadir ['neɪdɪəʳ] *n* (*Astron*) nadir *m*; (*fig*) point *m* le plus bas.
nag[1] [næg] *n* canasson* *m*, mauvais cheval *m*.
nag[2] [næg] **1** *vti* (~ **at**) être toujours après*; *[doubt etc]* harceler; *[conscience]* travailler. **to ~ sb to do/into doing** harceler qn pour qu'il fasse/jusqu'à ce qu'il fasse. **2** *n*: **he's a dreadful ~*** (*scolding*) il n'arrête pas de faire des remarques; (*pestering*) il n'arrête pas de nous (*or* le *etc*) harceler. ♦ **nagging 1** *adj person* qui n'arrête pas de faire des remarques; *pain, doubt* tenace; **2** *n* remarques *fpl* continuelles, criailleries *fpl*.
nail [neɪl] **1** *n* (*Anat*) ongle *m*; (*Tech*) clou *m*. (*fig*) **to pay on the ~** payer rubis sur l'ongle. **2** *adj*: **~ polish** *or* **varnish** vernis *m* à ongles; **~ polish remover** dissolvant *m*; **~ scissors** ciseaux *mpl* à ongles. **3** *vt* clouer; (*fig*) *wrongdoer* pincer*, attraper; *lie* démasquer; *rumour* démentir. **to ~ the lid on a crate** clouer le couvercle d'une caisse; (*fig*) **to be ~ed to the spot** rester cloué sur place; **~ed shoes** chaussures cloutées.
nail down *vt sep lid* clouer; (*fig*) *hesitating person* obtenir une décision de.
nail up *vt sep picture etc* fixer par des clous; *door, window* condamner (*en clouant*); *box, crate* clouer.
♦ **nailbiting** *n* habitude *f* de se ronger les ongles. ♦ **nailbrush** *n* brosse *f* à ongles. ♦ **nailfile** *n* lime *f* à ongles.
naïve [naɪ'iːv] *adj* naïf. ♦ **naïvely** *adv* naïvement. ♦ **naïveté** *or* ♦ **naïvety** *n* naïveté *f*.
naked ['neɪkɪd] *adj person* (tout) nu; *flame, sword* nu; *facts* brut; *truth* tout nu. **to the ~ eye** à l'œil nu. ♦ **nakedness** *n* nudité *f*.
namby-pamby* ['næmbɪ'pæmbɪ] **1** *n* gnangnan* *mf*. **2** *adj* gnangnan* *inv*.
name [neɪm] **1** *n* nom *m*; (*reputation*) réputation *f*. **what's your ~?** comment vous appelez-vous?; **my ~ is Robert** je m'appelle Robert; **to take sb's ~ and address** prendre les nom et adresse de qn; (*Ftbl etc*) **to have one's ~ taken** recevoir un avertissement; **by the ~ of Smith** du nom de Smith; **by** *or* **under another ~** sous un autre nom; **to go by** *or* **under the ~ of** se faire appeler; **I know him only by ~** je ne le connais que de nom; **he knows them all by ~** il les connaît tous par leur nom; **in ~ only** (*adv*) *reign, exist* de nom seulement; (*adj*) *marriage etc* nominal; **to refer to sb by ~** désigner qn par son nom; **naming** *or* **mentioning no ~s** pour ne nommer personne; **to put one's ~ down for** *job* poser sa candidature à; *competition, class* s'inscrire à; *car, ticket etc* faire une demande pour avoir; **to call sb ~s** traiter qn de tous les noms; **in God's ~** au nom de Dieu; **in the king's ~** de par le roi; **I haven't a penny to my ~*** je n'ai pas le sou; **one of the big ~s in show business** un des grands noms du monde du spectacle; **he has a ~ for honesty** il a la réputation d'être honnête; **to protect one's (good) ~** protéger sa réputation; **to get a bad ~** se faire une mauvaise réputation; **it made his ~** cela l'a rendu célèbre; **to make one's ~** se faire un nom (*as* en tant que).

2 *vt* **(a)** *child, puppy* appeler; *ship* baptiser; *star, new product* donner un nom à. **a person ~d Smith** un(e) nommé(e) Smith; **to ~ a child after sb** donner à un enfant le nom de qn. **(b)** (*give ~ of; designate*) nommer; (*fix*) *date, price* fixer. **he was ~d as chairman/as the thief/as a witness** il a été nommé président/désigné comme étant le voleur/cité comme témoin; **my collaborators are ~d in the preface** mes collaborateurs sont mentionnés dans l'avant-propos; (*wedding*) **to ~ the day** fixer la date du mariage; **you ~ it, they have it*** tout ce que vous pouvez imaginer, ils l'ont!
♦ **name day** *n* fête *f* (*d'une personne*). ♦ **name-dropping** *n*: **there was a lot of ~-dropping* in his speech** son discours était truffé de noms de gens en vue. ♦ **nameless** *adj person* (*unknown*) sans nom; (*anonymous*) anonyme; *fear* indéfinissable; *vice* innommable; **a certain person who shall be ~less** une certaine personne que je ne nommerai pas. ♦ **namely** *adv* à savoir, c'est-à-dire. ♦ **name part** *n* (*Theat*) rôle *m* titulaire. ♦ **nameplate** *n* (*on door etc*) plaque *f*; (*on goods*) plaque du fabricant. ♦ **namesake** *n* homonyme *m* (*personne*).
nanny ['nænɪ] *n* nurse *f*. ♦ **nanny-goat** *n* chèvre *f*.
nap [næp] **1** *n* (*sleep*) petit somme *m*. **afternoon ~** sieste *f*; **to have** *or* **take a ~** faire un petit somme (*or* la sieste).

2 *vi* sommeiller. (*fig*) **to catch sb ~ping** prendre qn au dépourvu (*unawares*) *or* en défaut (*in error etc*).
napalm ['neɪpɑːm] **1** *n* napalm *m*. **2** *adj bomb, bombing* au napalm.
nape [neɪp] *n* nuque *f*.
napkin ['næpkɪn] *n* **(a)** (*table ~*) serviette *f* (de table). **~ ring** rond *m* de serviette. **(b)** (*Brit: also* **nappy**) couche *f* (*de bébé*).
narcissus [nɑː'sɪsəs] *n, pl* **-issi** narcisse *m*. ♦ **narcissistic** *adj* narcissique.
narcotic [nɑː'kɒtɪk] *adj, n* narcotique (*m*).
narrate [nə'reɪt] *vt* raconter. ♦ **narration** *n* narration *f*. ♦ **narrative 1** *n* récit *m*; **2** *adj* narratif. ♦ **narrator** *n* narrateur *m*, -trice *f*.
narrow ['nærəʊ] **1** *adj* (*gen*) étroit; *garment* étriqué; *outlook, mind* étroit, borné; *person* aux vues étroites; *meaning* restreint; *scrutiny* serré; *means, resources, income, existence* limité; *majority* faible; *advantage* petit; *victory* remporté de justesse. **to have a ~ escape** s'en tirer de justesse, l'échapper belle. **2** *vi [road, valley]* se rétrécir; *[majority]* s'amenuiser. **his eyes ~ed** il a plissé les yeux; **to ~ down to** *[search, choice]* se limiter à; *[problem, question]* se ramener à. **3** *vt* (**~ down**) *road* rétrécir; *meaning* préciser; *choice* restreindre. (*fig*) **to ~ the field (down)** restreindre le champ; **with ~ed eyes** en plissant les yeux (*de méfiance etc*).
♦ **narrowly** *adv* **(a)** (*by a small margin*) *miss etc* de justesse; **he ~ly escaped being killed** il a bien failli être tué; **(b)** (*strictly*) *interpret rules etc* strictement; **(c)** (*closely*) *examine* de près, minutieusement. ♦ **narrow-minded** *adj person* aux vues étroites; *ideas, outlook* étroit. ♦ **narrow-mindedness** *n* étroitesse *f* d'esprit. ♦ **narrowness** *n* étroitesse *f*.

nasal ['neɪzəl] *adj* (*Anat, Ling*) nasal; *accent* nasillard. **to speak in a ~ voice** parler du nez. ♦ **nasalize** *vt* nasaliser.

nasturtium [nəs'tɜːʃəm] *n* capucine *f*.

nasty ['nɑːstɪ] *adj person, temper* désagréable (*to* envers, avec), (*stronger*) mauvais; *moment, experience* désagréable, (*stronger*) pénible; *taste, smell, trick* mauvais; *cold, weather, accident, job* sale (*before n*); *remark* méchant; *wound, bend in road* dangereux; (*obscene*) *book, film* obscène. **to taste/smell ~** avoir un mauvais goût/une mauvaise odeur; **a ~ piece of work*** (*action*) un sale coup*; (*person*) un sale type*, une sale bonne femme; **he had a ~ time of it** (*short spell*) il a passé un mauvais quart d'heure; (*longer period*) il a passé de mauvais moments; (*fig*) **what a ~ mess!** quel gâchis épouvantable!; **to have a ~ mind** avoir l'esprit mal tourné; **to have a ~ look in one's eye** avoir l'œil mauvais; **events took a ~ turn** la situation a très mal tourné. ♦ **nastily** *adv* (*unpleasantly*) désagréablement; (*spitefully*) méchamment. ♦ **nastiness** *n* caractère *m* désagréable; méchanceté *f*.

nation ['neɪʃən] *n* (*gen*) nation *f*. **people of all ~s** des gens de toutes les nationalités. ♦ **national 1** *adj* national; **~al anthem** hymne *m* national; **~al debt** dette *f* publique; **~al dress** costume *m* national; (*Brit*) **N~al Health Service, N~al Insurance** ≃ Sécurité *f* sociale; **~al holiday** fête *f* nationale; (*Mil*) **~al service** service *m* militaire; (*Brit*) **N~al Trust** ≃ Caisse *f* Nationale des Monuments Historiques et des Sites; **on a ~al scale** à l'échelon national; **~al strike of miners** grève *f* des mineurs touchant l'ensemble du pays; (*Press*) **the ~al and local papers** la grande presse et la presse locale; **2** *n* (*person*) ressortissant(e) *m(f)*. ♦ **nationalism** *n* nationalisme *m*. ♦ **nationalist** *adj, n* nationaliste (*mf*). ♦ **nationality** *n* nationalité *f*. ♦ **nationalization** *n* nationalisation *f*. ♦ **nationalize** *vt* nationaliser. ♦ **nationally** *adv consider, matter* du point de vue national; *broadcast* dans le pays tout entier; *be known, be felt, apply* dans tout le pays. ♦ **nation-wide** *adj strike, protest* touchant l'ensemble du pays; **there was a ~-wide search for them** on les recherchait à travers tout le pays.

native ['neɪtɪv] **1** *adj* **(a)** *country, town* natal; *language* maternel. **~ land** pays *m* natal, patrie *f*. **(b)** (*innate*) *ability* inné. **(c)** (*indigenous*) *plant, animal* indigène; *product, resources* naturel, du pays. **~ to** originaire de; **French ~ speaker** personne *f* dont la langue maternelle est le français. **(d)** (*of the ~s*) *customs, costume, matters, rights* du pays; *labour, quarter* indigène.

2 *n* autochtone *mf*; (*esp of colony*) indigène *mf*. **a ~ of France** un(e) Français(e) de naissance; **she speaks French like a ~** elle parle français comme si c'était sa langue maternelle; *[person, animal, plant]* **to be a ~ of** être originaire de. ♦ **nativity** *n* nativité *f*; **nativity play** mystère *m* de la Nativité.

natter* ['nætəʳ] **1** *vi* bavarder. **2** *n* causette* *f*.

natty* ['nætɪ] *adj* (*neat*) chic *inv*; (*handy*) astucieux.

natural ['nætʃrəl] **1** *adj* (*gen*) naturel. **it is ~ for you to think** *or* **that you should think** il est naturel *or* normal que vous pensiez (*subj*); **~ childbirth** accouchement *m* sans douleur; (*Jur*) **death from ~ causes** mort *f* naturelle; **to die a ~ death** mourir de sa belle mort; **~ philosophy** physique *f*; (*Mus*) **B ~** si *m* bécarre; **he's a ~ painter** c'est un peintre né. **2** *n* **(a)** (*Mus: sign*) bécarre *m*. **(b) he's a ~!*** il est comme un poisson dans l'eau!
♦ **naturalism** *n* naturalisme *m*. ♦ **naturalist** *adj, n* naturaliste (*mf*). ♦ **naturalization** *n* naturalisation *f*. ♦ **naturalize** *vt*: **to be ~ized** se faire naturaliser. ♦ **naturally** *adv* **(a)** (*of course; as is normal*) naturellement; **~ly not!** bien sûr que non!; **(b)** (*by nature*) de nature; **~ly lazy** paresseux de nature; **her hair is ~ly curly** elle frise naturellement; **it comes ~ly to him to do this** il fait cela tout naturellement; **(c)** (*unaffectedly*) *behave* avec naturel, sans affectation.

nature ['neɪtʃəʳ] **1** *n* **(a)** nature *f*. **the laws of ~** les lois *fpl* de la nature; **to paint from ~** peindre d'après nature; **against ~** contre nature. **(b)** (*character etc*) nature *f*, naturel *m*. **by ~** de nature; **good ~** bon caractère; **he has a nice ~** il a un naturel *or* un caractère facile; **it is not in his ~ to lie** il n'est pas dans sa nature de mentir; **jealous-~d** jaloux de nature, d'un naturel jaloux. **(c)** (*essential quality; type*) nature *f*. **it is in the ~ of things** c'est dans la nature des choses; **in the ~ of this case it is clear that** vu la nature de ce cas il est clair que; **things of this ~** les choses de cette nature *or* de ce genre; **sth in the ~ of an apology** une sorte d'excuse. **2** *adj*: **~ conservancy** protection *f* de la nature; **~ cure** naturisme *m* (*Med*); **~ lover** amoureux *m*, -euse *f* de la nature; **~ reserve** réserve naturelle; **~ study** histoire naturelle; (*Scol*) sciences naturelles; **~ trail** circuit forestier éducatif. ♦ **naturism** *n* naturisme *m*, nudisme *m*. ♦ **naturist** *n* naturiste *mf*, nudiste *mf*.

naught [nɔːt] *n* **(a)** (*Math*) zéro *m*. **~s and crosses** ≃ (jeu *m* du) morpion *m*. **(b)** († *or liter: nothing*) rien *m*.

naughty ['nɔːtɪ] *adj child etc* vilain, pas sage; *joke, story* grivois. **~ word** vilain mot. ♦ **naughtily** *adv say* avec malice; **to behave naughtily** être vilain. ♦ **naughtiness** *n* mauvaise conduite *f*; **a piece of naughtiness** une désobéissance.

nausea ['nɔːsɪə] *n* nausée *f*; (*fig*) écœurement *m*. ♦ **nauseate** *vt* (*Med, fig*) écœurer. ♦ **nauseating** *adj* écœurant. ♦ **nauseatingly** *adv* d'une façon écœurante.

nautical ['nɔːtɪkəl] *adj* nautique.

naval ['neɪvəl] *adj battle, strength, base, college* naval; *affairs, matters* de la marine; *officer* de marine; *hospital, barracks, stores* maritime. **~ architect** ingénieur *m* des constructions navales; **~ aviation** aéronavale *f*; **~ forces** marine *f* de guerre; **one of the ~ powers** l'une des puissances maritimes.

nave [neɪv] *n [church]* nef *f*.

navel ['neɪvəl] *n* nombril *m*. **~ orange** orange *f* navel.

navigate ['nævɪgeɪt] **1** *vi* naviguer. **2** *vt ship* diriger; *seas* naviguer sur. ♦ **navigable** *adj river* navigable. ♦ **navigation** *n* navigation *f*. ♦ **navigator** *n* navigateur *m*.

navvy ['nævɪ] *n* (*Brit*) terrassier *m*.

navy ['neɪvɪ] **1** *n* marine *f* (de guerre). (*Brit*) **Royal N~** marine nationale; **merchant ~** marine marchande; (*US*) **Department of the N~** ministère *m* de la Marine. **2** *adj* (**~-blue**) bleu marine *inv*.

Nazi ['nɑːtsɪ] **1** *n* Nazi(e) *m(f)*. **2** *adj* nazi. ♦ **Nazism** *n* nazisme *m*.

near [nɪəʳ] **1** *adv* **(a)** près (*to* de). **~ at hand** *object* tout près; *event* tout proche; *place* dans le voisinage; **to draw** *or* **come ~** s'approcher (*to* de); *[Christmas, exams]* approcher; **to come ~er** s'approcher davantage; **to come ~ to doing** faillir faire; **to bring sth ~er** rapprocher qch; **~ to where** près de l'endroit où; **~ to tears** au bord des larmes. **(b)** (*nearly*) presque. **nowhere ~ full** loin d'être plein; **as ~ as I can judge** autant que je puisse juger; **that's ~ enough*** ça pourra aller; **60 people, ~ enough*** 60 personnes, à peu près; **as ~ as dammit*** ou c'est tout comme*.

2 *prep* près de. **~ here/there** près d'ici/de là; **he was standing ~ the table** il se tenait près de *or* auprès de la table; **don't come ~ me** ne vous approchez pas de moi; **~ the end of the book** vers la fin du livre; **her birthday is ~ mine** son anniversaire est proche du mien; **he won't go ~* anything illegal** il ne se risquera jamais à faire quoi que ce soit d'illégal; **~ tears** au bord des larmes; **~ death** sur le point de mourir; **the sun was ~ setting** le soleil était près de se coucher; **he was very ~ refusing** il était sur le point de refuser; **the same thing or ~ it** la même chose ou presque *or* ou à peu près; **it's as ~ snowing as makes no difference** il neige ou peu s'en faut; **nobody comes anywhere ~ him at swimming** personne ne lui arrive à la cheville en natation; (*fig*) **that's ~er it** voilà qui est mieux.

3 *adj* **(a)** (*close: gen*) proche. **these glasses make things look ~er** ces lunettes rapprochent les objets; **the N~ East** le Proche-Orient; (*Math*) **to the ~est decimal place** à la plus proche décimale près; **to the ~est pound** à une livre près; **the ~est way** la route la plus directe; **in the ~ future** dans un proche avenir. **(b)** *relative, relationship* proche; *friend, friendship* intime; *guess* près de la vérité; *resemblance* assez exact; *portrait* ressemblant; *race, contest, result* serré. **my ~est and dearest*** mes proches *mpl*; **the ~est equivalent** ce qui s'en rapproche le plus; (*fig*) **that was a ~ thing*** il s'en est fallu de peu; **that's the ~est thing to a compliment** c'est presque un compliment.

4 *vt place* approcher de; *event, date* être près de. **to be ~ing one's goal** toucher au but; **my book is ~ing completion** mon livre est presque achevé.

♦ **nearby 1** *adv* près, tout près; **2** *adj* proche, avoisinant. ♦ **nearly** *adv* (*gen*) presque; **he ~ly laughed** il a failli rire; **she was ~ly crying** elle était sur le point de pleurer; **not ~ly** loin de; **she is not ~ly so old as you** elle est loin d'être aussi âgée que vous; **that's not ~ly enough** c'est loin d'être suffisant. ♦ **nearness** *n* proximité *f*. ♦ **nearside** *n* (*Aut*) (*in Britain*) côté *m* gauche; (*in France, US etc*) côté droit. ♦ **near-sighted** *adj* myope. ♦ **near-sightedness** *n* myopie *f*.

neat [ni:t] *adj* **(a)** (*gen*) net (*f* nette), soigné; *room, handwriting* net; *work* soigné; *desk* bien rangé; *ankles, legs* fin; *phrase, style, solution* élégant; *plan* habile. **~ as a new pin** propre comme un sou neuf; **he is a ~ worker** il est soigneux dans son travail; **she has a ~ figure** elle est bien faite; **a ~ little car** une jolie petite voiture; **to make a ~ job of sth** bien faire qch. **(b)** (*undiluted*) *spirits* pur, sec. **I'll take it ~** je le prendrai sec.

♦ **neaten** *vt dress* ajuster; *desk* ranger. ♦ **neatly** *adv* **(a)** (*tidily*) *fold, wrap, dress* avec soin; *write* proprement; **(b)** (*skilfully*) *avoid, manage* habilement; **~ly put** joliment dit. ♦ **neatness** *n* (*tidiness*) netteté *f*; (*skilfulness*) habileté *f*, adresse *f*.

nebula ['nebjʊlə] *n, pl* **-ae** nébuleuse *f*. ♦ **nebulous** *adj* (*Astron*) nébuleux; (*fig*) nébuleux, vague, flou.

necessary ['nesɪsərɪ] **1** *adj* (*gen*) nécessaire (*to, for* à); *result* inévitable. **it is ~ to do** il faut faire, il est nécessaire de faire; **it is ~ for him to be there** il faut qu'il soit là, il est nécessaire qu'il soit là; **it is ~ that ...** il faut que ... + *subj*, il est nécessaire que ... + *subj*; **if ~** s'il le faut; **to do what is ~** faire le nécessaire (*for* pour); **to make it ~ for sb to do** mettre qn dans la nécessité de faire; **more than is ~** plus qu'il n'en faut; **to do no more than is ~** ne faire que le nécessaire; **all the ~ qualifications** toutes les qualités requises (*for* pour). **2** *n*: **to do the ~*** faire le nécessaire.

♦ **necessarily** *adv* (*gen*) nécessairement, forcément; *lead to, result in* inévitablement. ♦ **necessitate** *vt* nécessiter. ♦ **necessity** *n* (*gen*) nécessité *f* (*of doing, to do* de faire); **from** *or* **out of necessity** par nécessité; **of necessity** nécessairement; **case of absolute necessity** cas *m* de force majeure; **there is no necessity for you to do that** vous n'avez pas besoin de faire cela; **in case of necessity** en cas de besoin; **is there any necessity?** est-ce nécessaire?; **the bare necessities of life** les choses *fpl* nécessaires à la vie; **it's a necessity** c'est une chose indispensable.

neck [nek] **1** *n* **(a)** cou *m*; *[horse, garment]* encolure *f*; *[bottle, vase]* col *m*. **to have a sore ~** avoir mal au cou; **to fling one's arms round sb's ~** se jeter au cou de qn; **to be ~ and ~** être à égalité; **to be up to one's ~ in work** avoir du travail par-dessus la tête; **up to one's ~ in a crime** totalement impliqué dans un crime; **he got it in the ~*** il en a pris pour son grade*; **to stick one's ~ out*** se mouiller‡, prendre des risques; **I don't want him round my ~*** je ne veux pas l'avoir sur le dos; **it's ~ or nothing*** il faut jouer le tout pour le tout; **in your ~ of the woods*** dans vos parages; **~ of mutton** collet *m* de mouton; (*Culin*) **best end of ~** côtelettes *fpl* premières; *[dress]* **high ~** col *m* montant; **square ~** encolure *f* carrée; **dress with a low ~, low-~ed dress** robe décolletée; **shirt with a 38 cm ~** chemise qui fait 38 cm d'encolure. **(b)** (*Brit*‡: *impertinence*) culot* *m*. **2** *vi* (*) se peloter*. **to ~ with sb*** peloter* qn.

♦ **necking*** *n* pelotage* *m*. ♦ **necklace** *n* collier *m*; (*long*) sautoir *m*; **pearl ~lace** collier de perles. ♦ **neckline** *n* encolure *f*. ♦ **necktie** *n* cravate *f*.

nectar ['nektəʳ] *n* nectar *m*.

nectarine ['nektərɪn] *n* brugnon *m*.

need [ni:d] **1** *n* besoin *m*. **if ~ be** si besoin est, s'il le faut; **there's no ~ to hurry** on n'a pas besoin de se presser; **no ~ to tell him** pas besoin de lui dire; **there's no ~ for you to come** vous n'êtes pas obligé de venir; **there is much ~ of food** il y a un grand besoin de vivres; **to have ~ of, to be in ~ of** avoir besoin de; **to be badly** *or* **greatly in ~ of** avoir grand besoin de; **to be in ~** être dans le besoin; **in times of ~** aux heures *fpl* difficiles; **to supply sb's ~s** subvenir aux besoins de qn; **his ~s are few** il a peu de besoins; **the greatest ~s of industry** ce dont l'industrie a le plus besoin.

2 *pret, ptp* **needed** *vt* (*gen*) avoir besoin de. **I ~ money** j'ai besoin d'argent, il me faut de l'argent; **I ~ it** j'en ai besoin, il me le faut; **all that you ~** tout ce qu'il vous faut; **it's just what I ~ed** c'est tout à fait ce qu'il me fallait; **a visa is ~ed** il faut un visa; **a much-~ed holiday** des vacances dont on a (*or* j'ai *etc*) grand besoin; **it** *or* **he doesn't ~ me to tell him** il n'a pas besoin que je le lui dise; **she ~s watching** *or* **to be watched** elle a besoin d'être surveillée; **he ~s to have everything explained to him** il faut tout lui expliquer; **you only ~ed to ask** tu n'avais qu'à demander; **this book ~s careful reading** ce livre doit être lu attentivement; **the situation ~s detailed consideration** la situation doit être considérée *or* exige qu'on la considère (*subj*) dans le détail.

3 *modal auxiliary vb* (*ne s'emploie qu'à la forme interrogative, négative et avec 'hardly', 'scarcely' etc*) **~ he go?** a-t-il besoin *or* est-il obligé d'y aller?, faut-il qu'il y aille?, est-ce qu'il doit vraiment y aller?; **you ~n't wait** vous n'avez pas besoin *or* vous n'êtes pas obligé d'attendre; **you ~n't bother/have bothered to write** ce n'est/n'était pas la peine d'écrire; **~ we go into all this now?** faut-il discuter de tout cela maintenant?; **I ~ hardly say that ...** je n'ai guère besoin de dire que ...; **no one ~ go** *or* **~s to go hungry** personne n'est condamné à avoir faim; **~ that be true?** est-ce nécessairement vrai?; **it ~ not follow that ...** il ne s'ensuit pas nécessairement que ... + *subj*.

♦ **needful 1** *adj* nécessaire; **2** *n*: **to do the ~ful*** faire ce qu'il faut. ♦ **neediness** *n* dénuement *m*, nécessité *f*. ♦ **needless** *adj* inutile; **~less to say it began to rain** inutile de dire que la pluie s'est mise à tomber. ♦ **needlessly** *adv* inutilement. ♦ **needs** *adv* (*ne s'emploie qu'avec 'must'*) **I must ~s leave** il me faut absolument partir; **if ~s must** s'il le faut absolument. ♦ **needy** *adj* nécessiteux; **in ~y circumstances** dans le besoin.

needle ['ni:dl] **1** *n* (*gen*) aiguille *f*; *[record-player]* saphir *m*. **knitting ~** aiguille à tricoter; (*fig*) **to look for a ~ in a haystack** chercher une aiguille dans une botte de foin. **2** *vt* (*) (*annoy*) agacer; (*sting*) piquer au vif; (*nag*) harceler. **she was ~d* into replying** touchée au vif elle a répondu. ♦ **needle-case** *n* porte-aiguilles *m inv*. ♦ **needlecord** *n* velours *m* mille-raies. ♦ **needlepoint** *n* tapisserie *f* à l'aiguille. ♦ **needlework** *n* (*gen*) travaux *mpl* d'aiguille; (*Scol: subject*) couture *f*; (*work*) ouvrage *m*.

ne'er [nɛəʳ] *adv* (*liter*) = **never**. ♦ **ne'er-do-well** *n* propre *mf* à rien.

negative ['negətɪv] **1** *adj* négatif. **2** *n* **(a)** (*answer*) réponse *f* négative. **in the ~** (*adj*) *be* négatif; (*adv*) *answer* négativement. **(b)** (*Gram*) négation *f*. **put into the ~** mettez à la forme négative. **(c)** (*Phot, Elec*) négatif *m*. ♦ **negation** *n* négation *f*. ♦ **negatively** *adv* négativement.

neglect [nɪ'glekt] **1** *vt* (*gen*) négliger (*to do* de faire); *animal, invalid* ne pas s'occuper de, négliger; *one's wife, one's friends* délaisser, négliger; *garden, house, car, machinery* ne pas s'occuper de; *rule, law, advice* ne tenir aucun compte de; *business, work, hobby* se désintéresser de, négliger; *opportunity* laisser échapper, négliger; *promise, duty, obligation* manquer à.

2 *n* (*gen*) manque *m* de soins (*of sb* envers qn); *[duty, obligation]* manquement *m* (*of* à); *[work]* manque d'intérêt (*of* pour). **~ of one's appearance** manque de soins apportés à son apparence; **his ~ of his car** *etc* le fait qu'il ne s'occupe pas de sa voiture *etc*; **in a state of ~** mal tenu; **it happened through ~** c'est dû à la négligence.

♦ **neglected** *adj appearance* négligé, peu soigné; *person* abandonné, délaissé; *house, garden* mal tenu. ♦ **neglectful** *adj* négligent; **to be ~ful of sb/sth** négliger qn/qch. ♦ **neglectfully** *adv* avec négligence.

negligence ['neglɪdʒəns] *n* négligence *f*. ♦ **negligent** *adj* négligent. ♦ **negligently** *adv* **(a)** (*offhandedly*) négligemment; **(b)** (*carelessly*) *omit* par négligence; *behave* avec négligence. ♦ **negligible** *adj* négligeable.

negotiate [nɪ'gəʊʃɪeɪt] **1** *vt* **(a)** *sale, loan, bill* négocier. **(b)** *obstacle, hill* franchir; *river* (*sail on*) naviguer, (*cross*) franchir; *bend in road* prendre; *difficulty* surmonter. **2** *vi* négocier (*with sb for sth* avec qn pour obtenir qch). ♦ **negotiable** *adj* **(a)** (*Fin*) négociable; **(b)** *obstacle* franchissable; *river* navigable; *road* praticable. ♦ **negotiation** *n* négociation *f*. ♦ **negotiator** *n* négociateur *m*, -trice *f*.

Negro ['ni:grəʊ] **1** *adj* noir. **2** *n* Noir *m*. ♦ **Negress** *n* Noire *f*. ♦ **negroid** *adj* négroïde.

neigh [neɪ] **1** *vi* hennir. **2** *n* hennissement *m*.

neighbour, (*US*) **-bor** ['neɪbəʳ] *n* voisin(e) *m(f)*; (*Bible etc*) prochain(e) *m(f)*. ♦ **neighbo(u)rhood** **1** *n* (*gen*) voisinage *m*; **all the children of the ~hood** tous les enfants du voisinage *or* du quartier; **it's not a nice ~hood** ce n'est pas un quartier bien; **in the ~hood of the church** aux alentours *or* dans le voisinage de l'église; **in the ~hood of the crime** dans les parages *mpl* du crime; **in the ~hood of £100** dans les 100 livres; **2** *adj chemist etc* du *or* de quartier. ♦ **neighbo(u)ring** *adj* avoisinant, voisin. ♦ **neighbo(u)rly** *adj person* bon voisin, obligeant; *feelings, action* de bon voisin; *relations* de bon voisinage.

neither ['naɪðəʳ] **1** *adv* ni. **~ ... nor** ni ... ni (+ ne *before vb*); **~ you nor I know** ni vous ni moi ne le savons; **he can ~ read nor write** il ne sait ni lire ni écrire; (*fig*) **that's ~ here nor there** cela n'a rien à voir. **2** *conj*: **if you don't go, ~ shall I** si tu n'y vas pas, je n'irai pas non plus; **~ am I** (*or* **do I** *etc*) moi non plus, ni moi. **3** *adj*: **~ story is true** ni l'une ni l'autre des deux histoires n'est vraie; **in ~ case** ni dans un cas ni dans l'autre. **4** *pron* ni l'un(e) ni l'autre (+ ne *before vb*). **~ of them knows** ni l'un ni l'autre ne le sait, ils ne le savent ni l'un ni l'autre.

neo... ['ni:əʊ] *pref* néo-. **~classical** néo-classique; **~fascist** (*adj, n*) néo-fasciste (*mf*); **~nazi** (*adj, n*) néo-nazi(e) *m(f)*.

neolithic [ˌni:əʊ'lɪθɪk] *adj* néolithique.

neologism [nɪ'ɒlədʒɪzəm] *n* néologisme *m*.

neon ['ni:ɒn] **1** *n* (gaz *m*) néon *m*. **2** *adj* au néon. **~ sign** enseigne *f* au néon.

nephew ['nevju:, 'nefju:] *n* neveu *m*.

nephritis [ne'fraɪtɪs] *n* néphrite *f*.

nerve [nɜ:v] **1** *n* **(a)** nerf *m*; (*Bot*) nervure *f*. **her ~s are bad** elle est très nerveuse; (*before performance*) **to have an attack of ~s** avoir le trac*; **it's only ~s** c'est de la nervosité; **to be a bundle of ~s** être un paquet de nerfs; **he was in a state of ~s, his ~s were on edge** il était sur les nerfs; **he gets on my ~s** il me tape sur les nerfs*; **to have ~s of steel** avoir les nerfs solides; **war of ~s** guerre *f* des nerfs.

(b) (*courage*) courage *m*; (*calm*) sang-froid *m*; (*self-confidence*) assurance *f*, confiance *f* en soi(-même); (*: *cheek*) culot* *m*. **to keep/lose one's ~** conserver/perdre son sang-froid; **he lost his ~, his ~ failed him** il n'a jamais retrouvé sa confiance en lui-même; **I haven't the ~ to do that** je n'ai pas le courage *or* (*cheek*) le culot* de faire ça; **you've got a ~!*** tu as du culot!*

2 *vt*: **to ~ sb to do** donner à qn le courage de faire; **to ~ o.s. to do** s'armer de courage pour faire.

3 *adj cell* nerveux; *gas* neuroplégique. **~ centre** (*Anat*) centre *m* nerveux; (*fig*) centre d'opérations; **~ specialist** neurologue *mf*.

♦ **nerve-racking** *adj* exaspérant. ♦ **nerviness*** *n* (*Brit*) nervosité *f*; (*US*) culot* *m*. ♦ **nervy*** *adj* **(a)** (*Brit: tense*) énervé; **(b)** (*US: cheeky*) qui a du culot*.

nervous ['nɜ:vəs] *adj* (*Anat, Med*) nerveux; (*tense*) nerveux; (*apprehensive*) inquiet; (*self-conscious*) intimidé. **to have a ~ breakdown** faire une dépression nerveuse; **~ energy** vitalité *f*; **~ exhaustion** fatigue *f* nerveuse, (*serious*) surmenage *m* mental; **in a ~ state** très agité; **to feel ~** se sentir mal à l'aise; (*before performance etc*) avoir le trac*; **he makes me ~** (*fearful*) il m'intimide; (*tense*) il m'énerve; (*unsure of myself*) il me fait perdre mes moyens; **I'm rather ~ about diving** j'ai un peu peur de plonger; **he's a ~ wreck*** il est à bout de nerfs. ♦ **nervously** *adv* (*tensely*) nerveusement; (*apprehensively*) avec inquiétude. ♦ **nervousness** *n* nervosité *f*; (*apprehension*) inquiétude *f*; (*before performance*) trac* *m*.

nest [nest] **1** *n* nid *m*. **2** *vi* faire son nid. **3** *adj* (*fig*) **~ egg** pécule *m*.

nestle ['nesl] *vi [person]* se blottir (*up to, against* contre); *[house etc]* se nicher. **to ~ down in bed** se pelotonner dans son lit; **a house nestling among the trees** une maison nichée parmi les arbres.

nestling ['nestlɪŋ, 'neslɪŋ] *n* oisillon *m*.

net[1] [net] **1** *n* **(a)** (*gen*) filet *m*. **hair ~** résille *f*. **(b)** (*Tex*) voile *m*. **2** *vt fish, game* prendre au filet. **3** *adj*: **~ curtains** voilage *m*. ♦ **netball** *n* netball *m*. ♦ **netting** *n* (*nets*) filets *mpl*; (*mesh*) mailles *fpl*; (*Tex*) voile *m* (*pour rideaux*); (*wire ~ting*) treillis *m* (métallique). ♦ **network** *n* (*gen, Elec, TV etc*) réseau *m*; (*fig*) *[streets, veins]* lacis *m*; *[spies, salesmen]* réseau.

net[2], **nett** [net] *adj price, weight* net. **the price is £15 ~** le prix est de 15 livres net.

Netherlands ['neðələndz] *npl* Pays-Bas *mpl*.

nettle ['netl] **1** *n* ortie *f*. (*fig*) **to grasp the ~** prendre le taureau par les cornes. **2** *vt* agacer. **he was ~d into replying** agacé, il a répondu. **3** *adj*: **~**

sting piqûre *f* d'ortie. ♦ **nettlerash** *n* urticaire *f.*
neuralgia [njʊə'rældʒə] *n* névralgie *f.*
neuritis [njʊə'raɪtɪs] *n* névrite *f.*
neuro... ['njʊərəʊ] *pref* neuro..., névro... . ♦ **neurosurgeon** *n* neurochirurgien(ne) *m(f).* ♦ **neurosurgery** *n* neurochirurgie *f.*
neurology [njʊə'rɒlədʒɪ] *n* neurologie *f.* ♦ **neurological** *adj* neurologique. ♦ **neurologist** *n* neurologue *mf.*
neurosis [njʊə'rəʊsɪs] *n, pl* **-oses** névrose *f.* ♦ **neurotic 1** *adj person* névrosé; *disease* névrotique; (*fig*) **she's getting quite neurotic about it** elle en fait une véritable maladie, ça devient une obsession chez elle; **2** *n* névrosé(e) *m(f).*
neuter ['nju:tə^r] **1** *adj* neutre. **2** *n* (*Gram*) neutre *m.* **in the ~** au neutre. **3** *vt cat etc* châtrer.
neutral ['nju:trəl] **1** *adj* neutre. **2** *n* (*Aut*) point *m* mort. **in ~** au point mort. ♦ **neutralist** *adj, n* neutraliste (*mf*). ♦ **neutrality** *n* neutralité *f.* ♦ **neutralize** *vt* neutraliser.
neutron ['nju:trɒn] *n* neutron *m.* **~ bomb** bombe *f* à neutrons.
never ['nevə^r] *adv* ne ... jamais. **I ~ eat it** je n'en mange jamais; **I have ~ seen him** je ne l'ai jamais vu: **~ before had there been such a disaster** jamais on n'avait connu tel desastre; **~ again!** plus jamais!; **I have ~ yet been able to** je n'ai encore jamais pu; **that will ~ do!** c'est inadmissible!; **he ~ said a word** il n'a pas dit le moindre mot; **you've ~ left it behind!** ne me dites pas que vous l'avez oublié!; **~!** ça n'est pas vrai!; **well I ~ (did)!*** ça par exemple!; **~ mind** ça ne fait rien. ♦ **never-ending** *adj* sans fin. ♦ **never-never 1** *n*: **to buy on the ~-~*** acheter à crédit; **2** *adj*: **~-~ land** pays *m* de cocagne. ♦ **nevertheless** *adv* néanmoins, (et) pourtant, quand même. ♦ **never-to-be-forgotten** *adj* inoubliable, qu'on n'oubliera jamais.
new [nju:] *adj* nouveau (*usually before n: before vowel* nouvel, *f* nouvelle); (*brand-new*) neuf (*f* neuve); (*different*) nouveau, autre; *bread, milk, cheese* frais; *wine* nouveau. **I've got a ~ car** (*different*) j'ai une nouvelle *or* une autre voiture; (*brand-new*) j'ai une voiture neuve; **he has written a ~ book** il a écrit un nouveau livre; **~ potatoes** pommes de terre nouvelles; **the ~ moon** la nouvelle lune; **N~ Testament** Nouveau Testament; **the N~ World** le Nouveau Monde; **dressed in ~ clothes** habillé de neuf; **as good as ~** comme neuf, à l'état de neuf; **this idea is not ~** ce n'est pas une idée nouvelle *or* neuve; **the ~ nations** les pays neufs; **a ~ town** une ville nouvelle; **this sort of work is ~ to me** ce genre de travail est qch de nouveau pour moi; **I'm ~ to this kind of work** je n'ai jamais fait ce genre de travail; **he's ~ to the trade** il est nouveau dans le métier; **he's quite ~ to the town** il est tout nouvellement arrivé dans la ville; **~ recruit** nouvelle recrue *f,* bleu* *m;* **the ~ students** *or* **pupils** les nouveaux *mpl,* les nouvelles *fpl;* **the ~ diplomacy** la diplomatie moderne; **the ~ rich** les nouveaux riches *mpl;* **bring me a ~ glass** apportez-moi un autre verre; **that's a ~ one on me!*** on en apprend tous les jours!; **what's ~?*** quoi de neuf? ♦ **newborn** *adj* nouveau-né(e) *m(f).* ♦ **newcomer** *n* nouveau venu *m,* nouvelle venue *f.* ♦ **newfangled** *adj* nouveau genre *inv.* ♦ **new-laid** *adj egg* tout frais. ♦ **new-look** *adj* new-look *inv.* ♦ **newly** *adv* nouvellement, récemment; **~ly made** neuf. ♦ **newly-weds** *npl* jeunes mariés *mpl.* ♦ **newness** *n [fashion, ideas etc]* nouveauté *f; [clothes etc]* état *m* de neuf. ♦ **New Year 1** *n* nouvel an *m,* nouvelle année *f;* **to bring in** *or* **see in the N~ Year** faire le réveillon (de la Saint-Sylvestre *or* du jour de l'an); **Happy N~ Year!** bonne année!; **to wish sb a happy N~ Year** souhaiter une *or* la bonne année à qn; **N~ Year's Day** jour *m or* premier *m* de l'an; **N~ Year's Eve** la Saint-Sylvestre. **2** *adj resolution* de nouvel an. ♦ **New Zealand 1** *n* Nouvelle-Zélande *f;* **2** *adj* néo-zélandais. ♦ **New Zealander** *n* Néo-Zélandais(e) *m(f).*
news [nju:z] **1** *n* **(a)** nouvelles *fpl.* **a piece** *or* **an item of ~** (*gen*) une nouvelle; (*Press*) une information; **have you heard the ~?** vous connaissez la nouvelle?; **have you heard the ~ about Paul?** vous savez ce qui est arrivé à Paul?; **have you any ~ of him?** avez-vous de ses nouvelles?; **what's your ~?** quoi de neuf?; **is there any ~?** y a-t-il du nouveau?; **I've got ~ for you!** j'ai du nouveau à vous annoncer!; **this is ~ to me!** première nouvelle!*; **good ~** bonnes nouvelles; **when the ~ broke** quand on a su la nouvelle; **to make ~** faire parler de soi; (*fig*) **he's in the ~ again** le voilà qui refait parler de lui. **(b)** (*Press, Rad, TV*) informations *fpl;* (*Cine, TV*) actualités *fpl.* **financial/sporting** *etc* **~** chronique *f* financière/sportive *etc.*

2 *adj*: **~ agency** agence *f* de presse; **~ bulletin** (*Rad*) bulletin *m* d'informations; (*TV*) actualités *fpl* télévisées; **~ editor** rédacteur *m;* **~ flash** flash *m* d'information; **~ headlines** titres *mpl* de l'actualité; **~ photographer** reporter *m* photographe; **~ pictures** reportage *m* photographique; **~ sheet** feuille *f* d'informations; **~ stand** kiosque *m* (à journaux); **~ theatre** cinéma *m* d'actualités; **to have ~ value** présenter un intérêt pour le public.

♦ **newsagent** (*Brit*) *or* ♦ **newsdealer** (*US*) *n* marchand(e) *m(f)* de journaux. ♦ **newsboy** *n* vendeur *m* de journaux. ♦ **newscast** *n* (*Rad*) (bulletin *m* d')informations *fpl;* (*TV*) actualités *fpl* (télévisées). ♦ **newscaster** *n* présentateur *m,* -trice *f.* ♦ **newsletter** *n* bulletin *m* (*de société, de compagnie etc*). ♦ **newsman** *n* journaliste *m.* ♦ **newspaper** *n* journal *m;* **~paper office** bureaux *mpl* de la rédaction. ♦ **newspaperman** *n* journaliste *m.* ♦ **newsprint** *n* papier *m* journal. ♦ **newsreader** *n* présentateur *m,* -trice *f.* ♦ **newsreel** *n* actualités *fpl* filmées. ♦ **newsroom** *n* (*Press*) salle *f* de rédaction; (*Rad, TV*) studio *m.* ♦ **newsworthy** *adj* qui présente un intérêt pour le public. ♦ **newsy*** *adj* plein de nouvelles.
newt [nju:t] *n* triton *m.*
next [nekst] **1** *adj* (*immediately adjoining*) *house, room, street* d'à côté, voisin; (*immediately following*) *bus-stop, turning* (*in future*) prochain, (*in past*) suivant; *page, case* suivant. **get off at the ~ stop** descendez au prochain arrêt; **he got off at the ~ stop** il est descendu à l'arrêt suivant; **~ week** la semaine prochaine; **the ~ week** la semaine suivante *or* d'après; **this time ~ week** d'ici huit jours; **the ~ day** le lendemain, le jour suivant; **I will finish this in the ~ 5 days** je finirai ceci dans les 5 jours qui viennent; **the ~ morning** le lendemain matin; **(the) ~ time I see him** la prochaine fois que je le verrai; **the ~ time I saw him** la première fois que je l'ai revu; **the ~ moment** l'instant d'après; **from one moment to the ~** d'un moment à l'autre; **the year after ~** dans deux ans; **who's ~?** à qui le tour?; **you're ~** c'est votre tour, c'est à vous; **I was ~ to speak** ce fut ensuite à mon tour de parler; **the very ~ person I see** la première personne que je verrai; **the ~ thing to do** (*firstly*) la première chose à faire; (*next after this*) ce qu'il faut faire ensuite; **the ~ size** la taille au-dessus.

2 *adv* ensuite, après. **~ we had lunch** ensuite *or* après nous avons déjeuné; **what shall we do ~?** qu'allons-nous faire maintenant?; **when ~ you come to see us** la prochaine fois que vous viendrez nous voir; **when I ~ saw him** quand je l'ai revu (la fois suivante); **what ~?** et puis quoi encore?; **the ~ best thing would be** à défaut le mieux serait; **who's the ~ tallest?** qui est le plus grand après?; **~ to** (*beside*) auprès de, à côté de;

(*almost*) presque; **wool ~ to the skin** de la laine à même la peau; **the ~ to last** l'avant-dernier; **~ to nothing** presque rien; **I got it for ~ to nothing** je l'ai payé trois fois rien.

3 *prep* (*Brit: beside*) à côté de, auprès de.

4 *n* prochain(e) *m(f)*. **the ~ to speak is Paul** c'est Paul qui parle ensuite; **to be continued in our ~** suite au prochain numéro.

♦ **next door 1** *n* la maison d'à côté; **from ~ door** d'à côté; **2** *adv*: **~ door to us** à côté de chez nous; **the boy ~ door** le garçon d'à côté; **3** *adj*: **~-door house** maison *f* d'à côté; **~-door neighbour** voisin(e) *m(f)* d'à côté.

nib [nɪb] *n [pen]* (bec *m* de) plume *f*.

nibble [ˈnɪbl] *vti* grignoter; *[sheep, goats etc]* brouter; *[fish]* toucher. (*fig*) **to ~ (at) an offer** se montrer tenté par une offre.

nice [naɪs] *adj* **(a)** (*gen: pleasant*) agréable; *person* gentil, sympathique; *meal, smell, taste* bon, agréable; (*pretty*) joli. **how ~ you look!** vous êtes vraiment bien!; **be ~ to him** soyez gentil *or* aimable avec lui; **they had a ~ time** ils se sont bien amusés; **how ~ of you to ...** comme c'est gentil *or* aimable à vous de ...; **it's ~ here** on est bien ici; (*fig: iro*) **you're in a ~ mess** vous voilà dans de beaux draps; (*iro*) **that's a ~ way to talk!** c'est du joli ce que vous dites là!; **~ and warm** bien chaud; **~ and easy** très facile; **he gets ~ long holidays** ce qui est bien c'est qu'il a de longues vacances. **(b)** (*respectable, refined*) convenable, comme il faut. **they are not very ~ people** ce ne sont pas des gens très convenables *or* très comme il faut *or* très bien; **that's not very ~** ce n'est pas très convenable, ce n'est pas beau*. **(c)** (*hard to please*) *person* difficile (*about* pour); (*subtle*) *distinction* délicat, subtil. ♦ **nice-looking** *adj* joli, beau. ♦ **nicely** *adv* (*kindly*) gentiment; (*pleasantly*) agréablement; (*prettily*) joliment; (*well*) bien; (*carefully*) minutieusement; (*exactly*) exactement; **that will do ~ly** cela fera très bien l'affaire. ♦ **niceness** *n [person]* gentillesse *f*; *[place, thing]* caractère *m* agréable. ♦ **nicety** *n [judgment]* précision *f*; **to a ~ty** à la perfection; **~ties** finesses *fpl*.

niche [niːʃ] *n* (*Archit*) niche *f*. (*fig*) **to find one's ~** trouver sa voie.

nick [nɪk] **1** *n* **(a)** (*in blade, dish*) ébréchure *f*; (*on skin, in wood*) entaille *f*. (*fig*) **in the ~ of time** juste à temps. **(b)** (‡: *prison*) taule‡ *f*. **in the ~** en taule‡. **(c) in good ~‡** en bonne condition. **2** *vt* **(a)** ébrécher; entailler. **(b)** (‡: *arrest*) pincer*, arrêter. **to get ~ed‡** se faire pincer*. **(c)** (‡: *steal*) piquer‡, voler. **(d)** (*US*) **how much did they ~ you for that suit?‡** tu t'es fait avoir* de combien pour ce costume?

nickel [ˈnɪkl] *n* (*metal*) nickel *m*; (*Can, US: coin*) pièce *f* de cinq cents. ♦ **nickel-plated** *adj* nickelé.

nickname [ˈnɪkneɪm] **1** *n* surnom *m*; (*humorous; malicious*) sobriquet *m*. **2** *vt*: **to ~ sb sth** surnommer qn qch; donner à qn le sobriquet de qch.

nicotine [ˈnɪkətiːn] **1** *n* nicotine *f*. **2** *adj*: **~ poisoning** nicotinisme *m*. ♦ **nicotine-stained** *adj* jauni de nicotine.

niece [niːs] *n* nièce *f*.

nifty‡ [ˈnɪftɪ] *adj car, jacket* très chic *inv*; *tool, gadget* astucieux; *blow, action* habile. **that was a ~ piece of work** ça a été vite fait.

niggardly [ˈnɪgədlɪ] *adj person* pingre; *amount, portion* mesquin.

niggle [ˈnɪgl] **1** *vi* se montrer tatillon. **2** *vt* (*gen*) agacer; *[conscience]* travailler. ♦ **niggling 1** *adj person* tatillon; *details* insignifiant; *doubt, pain* persistant; **2** *n* chicanerie *f*.

night [naɪt] **1** *n* nuit *f*. **at ~, in the ~** la nuit; **by ~, in the ~** de nuit; **last ~** la nuit dernière, cette nuit; (*evening*) hier soir; **tomorrow ~** demain soir; **the ~ before** la veille au soir; **the ~ before last** avant-hier soir; **in the ~, during the ~** pendant la nuit; **Monday ~** lundi soir, la nuit de lundi à mardi; **6 o'clock at ~** 6 heures du soir; **to spend the ~** passer la nuit; **to have a good/bad ~** bien/mal dormir; **~ and day** nuit et jour; **to sit up all ~ talking** passer la nuit entière à bavarder; **to have a ~ out** sortir le soir; **the maid's ~ out** le soir de sortie de la bonne; **let's make a ~ of it** il est trop tôt pour aller se coucher; **he's working ~s** il est de nuit; **I've had too many late ~s** je me suis couché tard trop souvent; **a ~'s sleep** une bonne nuit de sommeil; **a ~'s lodging** un toit pour la nuit; **~ is falling** le soir tombe; (*Theat*) **the last 3 ~s of** les 3 dernières représentations de; **Mozart ~** soirée *f* Mozart. **2** *adj clothes, work, flight, nurse* de nuit. (*fig*) **~ owl** couche-tard *mf*; **~ porter** gardien *m* de nuit; **~ school** cours *mpl* du soir; **~ storage heater/heating** radiateur *m*/chauffage *m* par accumulation; **~ watchman** veilleur *m or* gardien *m* de nuit. ♦ **nightcap** *n* bonnet *m* de nuit; (*drink*) **would you like a ~cap?** voulez-vous boire qch avant de vous coucher? ♦ **nightclub** *n* boîte *f* de nuit. ♦ **nightdress** *or* ♦ **nightgown** *or* ♦ **nightie*** *n* chemise *f* de nuit (*de femme*). ♦ **nightfall** *n*: **at ~fall** à la nuit tombante. ♦ **nightingale** *n* rossignol *m*. ♦ **nightlife** *n* vie *f* nocturne. ♦ **nightlight** *n* (*child's*) veilleuse *f*. ♦ **nightly 1** *adj* de tous les soirs, de toutes les nuits; **2** *adv* tous les soirs, chaque nuit; **twice ~ly** deux fois par soir *or* nuit. ♦ **nightmare** *n* cauchemar *m*. ♦ **nightmarish** *adj* de cauchemar. ♦ **nightshade** *n*: **deadly ~shade** belladone *f*. ♦ **nightshift** *n* (*workers*) équipe *f* de nuit; (*work*) poste *m* de nuit; **on ~shift** de nuit. ♦ **nightshirt** *n* chemise *f* de nuit (*d'homme*). ♦ **night-time** *n* nuit *f*; **at ~-time** la nuit; **in the ~-time** pendant la nuit. ♦ **nightwear** *n* vêtements *mpl* de nuit.

nil [nɪl] *n* rien *m*; (*in form-filling*) néant *m*; (*Sport*) zéro *m*.

nimble [ˈnɪmbl] *adj person, fingers* agile; *old person* alerte; *mind* vif, prompt. ♦ **nimble-fingered/-footed** *adj* aux doigts/pieds agiles. ♦ **nimbleness** *n* agilité *f*; vivacité *f*. ♦ **nimble-witted** *adj* à l'esprit vif. ♦ **nimbly** *adv* agilement.

nincompoop* [nɪŋkəmpuːp] *n* idiot(e) *m(f)*, gourde* *f*.

nine [naɪn] **1** *adj* neuf *inv*. **~ times out of ten** neuf fois sur dix; (*fig*) **he's got ~ lives** il a l'âme chevillée au corps; **a ~ days' wonder** la merveille d'un jour; **a ~-hole golf course** un parcours de neuf trous. **2** *n* neuf *m inv*. **dressed up to the ~s** sur son trente et un; *for other phrases V* **six**. ♦ **ninepins** *npl* (jeu *m* de) quilles *fpl*; **to go down like ~pins** tomber comme des mouches. ♦ **nineteen 1** *adj* dix-neuf *inv*; **2** *n* dix-neuf *m inv*; **to talk ~teen to the dozen*** être un vrai moulin à paroles. ♦ **nineteenth** *adj, n* dix-neuvième (*mf*); (*fraction*) dix-neuvième *m*. ♦ **ninetieth** *adj, n* quatre-vingt-dixième (*mf*); (*fraction*) quatre-vingt-dixième *m*. ♦ **ninety** *adj, n* quatre-vingt-dix (*m*) *inv*; **to be in one's ~ties** avoir plus de quatre-vingt-dix ans. ♦ **ninth** *adj, n* neuvième (*mf*); (*fraction*) neuvième *m*.

nip[1] [nɪp] **1** *n* (*pinch*) pinçon *m*; (*bite*) morsure *f*. **there's a ~ in the air** l'air est piquant. **2** *vt* (*pinch*) pincer; (*bite*) donner un (petit) coup de dent à; *[cold] face etc* piquer; *plants* brûler. (*fig*) **to ~ in the bud** écraser dans l'œuf. **3** *vi*: **to ~* up/out** *etc* monter/sortir *etc* en courant; **he ~ped into the café** il a fait un saut au café; **I've just ~ped in for a minute** je ne fais qu'entrer et sortir. ♦ **nippy*** *adj* **(a)** (*spry*) alerte, preste; **be ~py about it!** fais vite!; **(b)** *wind* piquant, coupant; **it's ~py** l'air est piquant; **(c)** *flavour* fort, piquant.

nip[2] [nɪp] *n* (*drink*) goutte *f*, petit verre *m*.

nipple [ˈnɪpl] *n* (*Anat*) bout *m* de sein; *[baby's bottle]* tétine *f*.

nit [nɪt] *n* **(a)** *[louse]* lente *f*. **(b)** (‡: *fool*) crétin(e)* *m(f)*. ♦ **nit-pick*** *vi* couper les cheveux en quatre.

♦ **nitty-gritty*** *n*: **to get down to the ~ty-gritty** en venir aux choses sérieuses. ♦ **nitwit*** *n* nigaud(e)* *m(f)*.
nitrogen ['naɪtrədʒən] *n* azote *m*. ♦ **nitric** *adj* nitrique, azotique. ♦ **nitroglycerin(e)** *n* nitroglycérine *f*. ♦ **nitrous** *adj* nitreux, azoteux.
no [nəʊ] **1** *particle, n* non (*m inv*). **I won't take ~ for an answer** il n'est pas question de me dire non.
2 *adj* (*not any*) pas de, aucun, nul (*f* nulle) (*all used with 'ne'*). **she had ~ coat** elle n'avait pas de manteau; **I have ~ idea** je n'ai aucune idée; **I have ~ more money** je n'ai plus d'argent; **~ two men would agree** il n'y a pas deux hommes qui seraient d'accord; **~ other man** nul autre, personne d'autre; **~ sensible man** aucun homme de bon sens; **it's of ~ interest** c'est sans intérêt; **~ go!*** pas moyen!; **~ two are alike** il n'y en a pas deux qui se ressemblent; **he's ~ friend of mine** il n'est pas de mes amis; **he's ~ genius** il n'a rien d'un génie; **this is ~ place for children** ce n'est pas un endroit pour les enfants; **it's ~ small matter** ce n'est pas une petite affaire; **there's ~ such thing** cela n'existe pas; **~ smoking** défense de fumer; **~ parking** stationnement *m* interdit; **~ surrender!** on ne se rend pas!; **there's ~ saying what he'll do** il est impossible de dire ce qu'il fera; **there's ~ pleasing him** quoi qu'on fasse il n'est jamais satisfait.
3 *adv*: **I can go ~ farther** je ne peux pas aller plus loin; **I can bear it ~ longer** *or* **~ more** je ne peux plus le supporter; **~ less than 4** pas moins de 4; **she came herself, ~ less!** elle est venue en personne, voyez-vous ça! (*iro*).
♦ **nobody** *V below*. ♦ **no-claim(s) bonus** *n* bonification *f* pour non-sinistre. ♦ **no-go area** *n* zone *f* interdite (*à la police et à l'armée*). ♦ **no-good*** *adj, n* propre (*mf*) à rien. ♦ **nohow*** *adv* en aucune façon. ♦ **no-man's-land** *n* no man's land *m*. ♦ **no one** = **nobody 1**. ♦ **nothing** *V below*. ♦ **noway(s)** *or* ♦ **nowise** *adv* en aucune façon. ♦ **nowhere** *adv* nulle part (+ ne *before vb*); **he went ~where** il n'est allé nulle part; **~where in Europe** nulle part en Europe; **it's ~where you know** ce n'est pas un endroit que tu connais; **~where else** nulle part ailleurs; **~where to be found** introuvable; **she is ~where to be seen** on ne la voit nulle part; **they appeared from ~where** ils sont apparus comme par miracle; (*fig*) **that will get you ~where** ça ne te servira à rien; **we're getting ~where*** ça ne nous mène strictement à rien; **~where near** (*gen*) loin de; **she is ~where near as clever as he is** elle est loin d'être aussi intelligente que lui; **you're ~where near it!** tu n'y es pas du tout!
nobble* ['nɒbl] *vt* (*Brit*) **(a)** (*bribe*) *person* acheter, soudoyer. **(b)** (*Racing*) *horse, dog* droguer (*pour l'empêcher de gagner*). **(c)** (*catch*) *wrongdoer* pincer*, arrêter; *sb to speak to* coincer.
noble ['nəʊbl] **1** *adj* (*gen*) noble; (*: *unselfish*) magnanime. **2** *n* noble *m*. ♦ **nobility** *n* noblesse *f*. ♦ **nobleman** noble *m*. ♦ **nobly** *adv* (*aristocratically*) noblement; (*magnificently*) *proportioned* majestueusement; (*: *selflessly*) généreusement.
nobody ['nəʊbədɪ] **1** *pron* personne, nul (+ ne *before vb*). **I saw ~** je n'ai vu personne; **~ knows** personne *or* nul ne le sait; **who saw him? – ~** qui l'a vu? – personne. **2** *n*: **he's a ~** c'est un rien du tout; **when he was ~** alors qu'il était encore inconnu.
nocturnal [nɒk'tɜːnl] *adj* nocturne.
nod [nɒd] **1** *n* signe *m* de la tête. **to give sb a ~** faire un signe de (la) tête à qn; (*answering yes*) faire signe que oui à qn.
2 *vi* **(a)** (*also* **~ one's head**) faire un signe de la tête; (*as sign of assent*) faire signe que oui, faire un signe de tête affirmatif. **to ~ to sb** faire un signe de tête à qn; (*in greeting*) saluer qn d'un signe de tête; **he ~ded to me to go** de la tête il m'a fait signe de m'en aller; **we have a ~ding acquaintance** nous nous connaissons vaguement. **(b)** (*doze*) somnoler. **(c)** [*flowers etc*] se balancer.
nod off *vi* s'endormir.
node [nəʊd] *n* nœud *m*.
noise [nɔɪz] *n* (*sound*) bruit *m*; (*din*) bruit, tapage *m*; (*Rad, TV*) parasites *mpl*; (*Telec*) friture *f*. **I heard a small ~** j'ai entendu un petit bruit; **~s in the ears** bourdonnements *mpl* d'oreilles; **a hammering ~** un martèlement; **the ~ of the traffic** le bruit *or* le vacarme de la circulation; **I hate ~** j'ai horreur du bruit; (*lit, fig*) **to make a ~** faire du bruit *or* du tapage; (*fig*) **she made ~s* about wanting to go home** elle a marmonné qu'elle voulait rentrer; (*person*) **a big ~*** une huile*. ♦ **noiseless** *adj* silencieux. ♦ **noiselessly** *adv* sans bruit, silencieusement. ♦ **noisily** *adv* bruyamment. ♦ **noisy** *adj* (*gen*) bruyant; (*boisterous*) bruyant, tapageur; **to be noisy** faire du bruit *or* du tapage.
nomad ['nəʊmæd] *n* nomade *mf*. ♦ **nomadic** *adj* nomade.
nom de plume ['nɒmdə'pluːm] *n* (*Literat*) pseudonyme *m*.
nominal ['nɒmɪnl] *adj* (*gen*) nominal; *rule* de nom seulement; *rent* insignifiant. ♦ **nominally** *adv* nominalement.
nominate ['nɒmɪneɪt] *vt* (*appoint*) nommer (*sb to a post* qn à un poste), désigner; (*propose*) proposer, présenter (*sb for sth* qn comme candidat à qch). ♦ **nomination** *n* nomination *f* (*to* à), proposition *f* de candidat. ♦ **nominative** *adj, n* (*Gram*) nominatif (*m*). ♦ **nominee** *n* personne *f* nommée, candidat(e) *m(f)* agréé(e).
non- [nɒn] *pref* non-. ♦ **non-aggression** *n* non-agression *f*. ♦ **non-alcoholic** *adj* non alcoolisé, sans alcool. ♦ **non-aligned** *adj* non-aligné. ♦ **non-arrival** *n* non-arrivée *f*. ♦ **non-believer** *n* incroyant(e) *m(f)*. ♦ **non-Catholic** *adj, n* non-catholique (*mf*). ♦ **non-combatant** *adj, n* non-combattant (*m*). ♦ **non-combustible** *adj* non-combustible. ♦ **non-commissioned officer** *n* sous-officier *m*. ♦ **nonconformist** *adj, n* non-conformiste (*mf*). ♦ **non-contributory** *adj* sans cotisations. ♦ **non-cooperation** *n* refus *m* de coopération. ♦ **non-essentials** *npl* accessoires *mpl*. ♦ **non-event** *n*: **the meeting was a ~-event*** la réunion n'a jamais démarré. ♦ **non-existence** *n* non-existence *f*. ♦ **non-existent** *adj* inexistant. ♦ **non-fiction** *n* littérature *f* non-romanesque. ♦ **non-greasy** *adj* qui ne graisse pas. ♦ **non-inflammable** *adj* ininflammable. ♦ **non-interference** *n* non-intervention *f*. ♦ **non-intervention** *n* non-intervention *f*. ♦ **non-iron** *adj* qui ne nécessite aucun repassage. ♦ **non-member** *n* personne *f* étrangère (au club *etc*); **open to ~-members** ouvert au public. ♦ **non-party** *adj vote, decision* indépendant (de tout parti politique). ♦ **non-payment** *n* non-paiement *m*. ♦ **non-poisonous** *adj snake* non venimeux; *plant* non-vénéneux; *mixture* non toxique. ♦ **non-professional** *adj, n* amateur (*mf*). ♦ **non-profitmaking** *or* ♦ **non-profit** (*US*) *adj* sans but lucratif. ♦ **non-resident 1** *adj person* non résidant; **2** *n* non-résident(e) *m(f)*; (*in hotel*) client(e) *m(f)* de passage. ♦ **non-returnable** *adj* non consigné. ♦ **non-run** *adj* indémaillable. ♦ **non sequitur** *n*: **it's a ~ sequitur** c'est illogique. ♦ **non-shrink** *adj* irrétrécissable. ♦ **non-skid** *adj* antidérapant. ♦ **non-smoker** *n* non-fumeur *m*, personne *f* qui ne fume pas. ♦ **non-starter** *n* (*fig*) **to be a ~-starter*** ne rien valoir. ♦ **non-stick** *adj saucepan* qui n'attache pas, Téfal *inv* ®. ♦ **non-stop 1** *adj* (*gen*) sans arrêt; *train, flight* direct; **2** *adv talk* sans arrêt; (*Aviat*) sans escale. ♦ **non-taxable** *adj* non-imposable. ♦ **non-union**

adj ***workers, labour*** non syndiqué. ♦ **non-violence** *n* non-violence *f*. ♦ **non-violent** *adj* non-violent. ♦ **non-white 1** *n* personne *f* de couleur; **2** *adj* de couleur.

nonchalant [ˈnɒnʃələnt] *adj* nonchalant. ♦ **nonchalance** *n* nonchalance *f*. ♦ **nonchalantly** *adv* nonchalamment.

noncommittal [ˈnɒnkəˈmɪtl] *adj person* réservé; *statement* qui n'engage à rien; *answer* diplomatique.

nondescript [ˈnɒndɪskrɪpt] *adj colour* indéfinissable; *person* quelconque.

none [nʌn] **1** *pron* **(a)** (*thing*) aucun(e) *m(f)* (+ ne *before vb*); (*form-filling*) néant *m*. **~ of the books** aucun livre, aucun des livres; **~ of this** rien de ceci; **~ of that!** pas de ça!; **he would have ~ of it** il ne voulait rien savoir; **~ at all** rien, pas du tout, (*not a single one*) pas un(e) seul(e); **~ of this money** pas un centime de cet argent; **~ of this milk** pas une goutte de ce lait; **there's ~ left** il n'en reste plus. **(b)** (*person*) personne, aucun(e) *m(f)* (+ *ne*). **~ of them** aucun d'entre eux; **~ but you can do it** vous seul êtes capable de le faire; **I know, ~ better, that ...** je sais mieux que personne que ...; **their guest was ~ other than ...** leur invité n'était autre que ... .

2 *adv*: **he's ~ the worse for it** il ne s'en porte pas plus mal; **I'm ~ the worse for having eaten it** je ne me ressens pas de l'avoir mangé; **I like him ~ the worse for it** je ne l'en aime pas moins pour cela; **he was ~ the wiser** il n'était pas plus avancé; **it's ~ too warm** il ne fait pas tellement chaud; **and ~ too soon either!** et ce n'est pas trop tôt!

♦ **nonetheless** = **nevertheless**.

nonentity [nɒˈnentɪtɪ] *n* personne *f* insignifiante, nullité *f*.

nonplus [ˈnɒnˈplʌs] *vt* déconcerter, dérouter.

nonsense [ˈnɒnsəns] **1** *n* absurdités *fpl*, sottises *fpl*, idioties *fpl*. **to talk ~** dire *or* débiter des absurdités; **that's a piece of ~!** c'est une absurdité *or* sottise *or* idiotie!; **~!** ne dis pas de sottises *or* d'idioties!; **it is ~ to say** il est absurde *or* idiot de dire; **he will stand no ~** il ne se laissera pas faire (*from* par; *about* en ce qui concerne); **no ~!** pas d'histoires!*; **there's no ~ about him** c'est un homme très carré; **to make (a) ~ of sth** rendre qch complètement ridicule. **2** *adj*: **~ verse** vers *mpl* amphigouriques.

♦ **nonsensical** *adj* absurde.

noodles [ˈnuːdlz] *npl* nouilles *fpl*.

nook [nʊk] *n* coin *m*. **~s and crannies** coins et recoins.

noon [nuːn] *n* midi *m*. **at ~** à midi.

noose [nuːs] *n* nœud *m* coulant; (*as trap*) collet *m*; *[cowboy]* lasso *m*; *[hangman]* corde *f*. (*fig*) **to put one's head in the ~** se jeter dans la gueule du loup.

nor [nɔːʳ] *conj* **(a)** (*following 'neither'*) ni. **neither you ~ I can do it** ni vous ni moi (nous) ne pouvons le faire; **she neither eats ~ drinks** elle ne mange ni ne boit. **(b)** (= *and not*) **I don't know, ~ do I care** je ne sais pas et d'ailleurs je m'en moque; **~ do I** (*or* **can I** *etc*) ni moi non plus.

norm [nɔːm] *n* norme *f*. ♦ **normal 1** *adj* normal; **it was quite ~al for him to object** il était tout à fait normal *or* naturel qu'il fasse des objections; **it's quite a ~al thing for children to fight** c'est une chose très normale que les enfants se battent (*subj*); **2** *n* normale *f*; **below ~al** au-dessous de la normale. ♦ **normalcy** *or* ♦ **normality** *n* normalité *f*. ♦ **normalize** *vt* normaliser, régulariser. ♦ **normally** *adv* normalement.

Norman [ˈnɔːmən] **1** *adj* normand; (*Archit*) roman. **2** *n* Normand(e) *m(f)*. ♦ **Normandy** *n* Normandie *f*.

Norse [nɔːs] *n* (*Ling*) norrois *m*.

north [nɔːθ] **1** *n* nord *m*. **(to the) ~ of** au nord de; *[wind]* **to veer to the ~, to go into the ~** tourner au nord; **the wind is in the ~** le vent est au nord; **to live in the ~** habiter dans le nord; **in the ~ of** dans le nord de; (*US Hist*) **the N~** les États *mpl* du nord.

2 *adj* (*gen*) nord *inv*; *coast, door* nord, septentrional; *wind* du nord. **in the N~ Atlantic** dans l'Atlantique *m* Nord; **N~ Africa** Afrique *f* du Nord; **N~ African** (*adj*) nord-africain; (*n*) Nord-Africain(e) *m(f)*; **N~ America** Amérique *f* du Nord; **N~ American** (*adj*) nord-américain; (*n*) Nord-Américain(e) *m(f)*; **N~ Sea** mer *f* du Nord; **N~ Sea oil** pétrole *m* de la mer du Nord; **~ Star** étoile *f* polaire.

3 *adv* au nord, vers le nord. **the town lies ~ of the border** la ville est située au nord de la frontière; **we drove ~ for 100 km** nous avons roulé pendant 100 km en direction du nord; **to sail due ~** aller droit vers le nord, avoir le cap au nord (*Naut*).

♦ **northbound** *adj traffic* en direction du nord; *carriageway* nord *inv*. ♦ **north-country** *adj* du Nord (de l'Angleterre). ♦ **north-east 1** *adj, n* nord-est (*m*) *inv*; **2** *adv* vers le nord-est. ♦ **north-eastern** *adj* nord-est *inv*. ♦ **northerly** *adj wind* du nord; *situation, aspect* au nord; **in a ~erly direction** vers le nord. ♦ **northern** *adj region* nord *inv*, du nord; *wall, side* exposé au nord; *coast* nord, septentrional; **in ~ern Spain** dans le nord de l'Espagne; **~ern lights** aurore *f* boréale. ♦ **northerner** *n* homme *m* *or* femme *f* du Nord; (*US Hist*) Nordiste *mf*. ♦ **northernmost** *adj* le plus au nord. ♦ **north-north-east 1** *adj, n* nord-nord-est (*m*) *inv*; **2** *adv* vers le nord-nord-est. ♦ **northward 1** *adj* au nord; **2** *adv* (*also* **~wards**) vers le nord. ♦ **north-west 1** *adj, n* nord-ouest (*m*) *inv*; **2** *adv* vers le nord-ouest. ♦ **north-western** *adj* nord-ouest *inv*.

Norway [ˈnɔːweɪ] *n* Norvège *f*. ♦ **Norwegian 1** *adj* norvégien; **2** *n* Norvégien(ne) *m(f)*; (*Ling*) norvégien *m*.

nose [nəʊz] **1** *n* nez *m*. **his ~ was bleeding** il saignait du nez; **to speak through one's ~** parler du nez; **red-~d** au nez rouge; (*fig*) **right under his ~** juste sous son nez; **his ~ is out of joint** il est dépité; **to lead sb by the ~** mener qn par le bout du nez; **to look down one's ~ at sb/sth** faire le nez à qn/devant qch; **to turn up one's ~** faire le dégoûté (*at* devant); **to keep one's ~ to the grindstone** travailler sans répit; **to poke *or* stick one's ~ into sth** mettre son nez dans qch; **to have a (good) ~ for ...** avoir du flair pour ...; **a line of cars ~ to tail** une file de voitures pare-choc contre pare-choc. **2** *adj*: **~ drops** gouttes *fpl* pour le nez.

nose about, nose around *vi* fouiller, fureter.

nose out *vt sep [dog]* flairer; (*fig*) *secret* découvrir; *person* dénicher.

♦ **nosebag** *n* musette *f* mangeoire. ♦ **nosebleed** *n* saignement *m* de nez; **to have a ~bleed** saigner du nez. ♦ **nose-dive** (*Aviat*) **1** *n* piqué *m*; **2** *vi* descendre en piqué. ♦ **nosegay** *n* petit bouquet *m*. ♦ **nos(e)y*** *adj* curieux; **don't be so ~y** mêlez-vous de ce qui vous regarde!; **N~y Parker** fouinard(e)* *m(f)*.

nostalgia [nɒsˈtældʒɪə] *n* nostalgie *f*. ♦ **nostalgic** *adj* nostalgique.

nostril [ˈnɒstrəl] *n* narine *f*; *[horse]* naseau *m*.

not [nɒt] *adv* ne ... pas. **he is ~ here** il n'est pas ici; **he hasn't come** il n'est pas venu; **he won't stay** il ne restera pas; **he told me ~ to come** il m'a dit de ne pas venir; **~ to mention ...** pour ne pas parler de ...; **I hope ~** j'espère que non; **whether he comes or ~** qu'il vienne ou non; **~ at all** pas du tout, (*after thanks*) il n'y a pas de quoi; **~ in the least** pas du tout, nullement; **~ that I know of** pas que je sache; **why ~?** pourquoi pas?; **~ a few ...** bien des ...; **~ without reason** et pour cause; **~ I!** moi pas!, pas moi!; **~ one book** pas un livre; **~ yet** pas encore; **~ guilty** non coupable.

notable [ˈnəʊtəbl] **1** *adj* (*gen*) notable. **it is ~ that**

... il est remarquable que ... + *subj.* **2** *n* notable *m.*
♦ **notably** *adv* (*in particular*) notamment; (*outstandingly*) notablement.

notary [ˈnəʊtərɪ] *n* (~ **public**) notaire *m.*

notation [nəʊˈteɪʃən] *n* notation *f.*

notch [nɒtʃ] **1** *n* (*in wood, stick*) encoche *f*; (*in belt*) cran *m*; (*in wheel, saw, board*) dent *f*; (*in blade*) ébréchure *f*; (*Sewing*) cran. **2** *vt stick etc* encocher; *blade* ébrécher; *seam* cranter.

notch up *vt sep score etc* marquer.

note [nəʊt] **1** *n* **(a)** (*gen, Diplomacy, Liter etc*) note *f.* **to take** *or* **make a ~ of sth** prendre note de qch; (*fig*) **I must make a ~ to buy some more** il faut que je me souvienne d'en racheter; **to take** *or* **make ~s** prendre des notes; **lecture ~s** notes de cours. **(b)** (*informal letter*) mot *m.* (*to secretary*) **take a ~ to Mr ...** je vais vous dicter un mot pour M. ...; **just a quick ~ to tell you ...** un petit mot à la hâte pour vous dire ... . **(c)** (*Mus*) note *f*; *[piano]* touche *f*; *[bird]* note. **to play** (*or* **sing**) **a false ~** faire une fausse note; (*fig*) **his speech struck the right/wrong ~** son discours était bien dans la note/n'était pas dans la note; **with a ~ of anxiety in his voice** avec une note d'anxiété dans la voix; **a ~ of desperation** un accent de désespoir; **a ~ of warning** un avertissement discret. **(d)** (*Comm, Banking*) billet *m.* **bank ~** billet de banque; **one-pound ~** billet d'une livre. **(e)** (*of person*) **of ~** éminent, de marque; **nothing of ~** rien d'important. **(f)** (*notice*) **to take ~ of** prendre note de; **worthy of ~** digne d'attention.

2 *vt* (*take ~ of*) noter (*that* que), prendre note de; (*notice*) remarquer, constater; (~ **down**) noter, inscrire.

♦ **notebook** *n* carnet *m*; (*Scol*) cahier *m*; *[stenographer]* bloc-notes *m.* ♦ **note-case** *n* porte-feuille *m.* ♦ **noted** *adj* (bien) connu (*for* pour), célèbre. ♦ **notepad** *n* bloc-notes *m.* ♦ **notepaper** *n* papier *m* à lettres. ♦ **noteworthy** *adj* notable.

nothing [ˈnʌθɪŋ] **1** *n* rien *m* (+ ne *before vb*); (*numeral*) zéro *m.* **I saw ~** je n'ai rien vu; **~ happened** il ne s'est rien passé; **to eat ~** ne rien manger; **~ to eat** rien à manger; **there is ~ that pleases him** il n'y a rien qui lui plaise; **~ new** rien de nouveau; **~ on earth** rien au monde; **you look like ~ on earth*** tu as l'air de je ne sais quoi; **as if ~ had happened** comme si de rien n'était; **fit for ~** propre à rien; **to say ~ of ...** sans parler de ...; **I can do ~ about it** je n'y peux rien; **he is ~ if not polite** il est avant tout poli; **for ~** (*in vain*) en vain; (*without payment*) gratuitement; (*for no reason*) sans raison; (*hum*) **I'm not Scottish for ~*** je ne suis pas écossais pour rien; **it's ~** ce n'est rien; **that is ~ to you** (*easy for you*) pour vous ce n'est rien; (*not your business*) cela ne vous regarde pas; **she means ~ to him** elle n'est rien pour lui; **it's ~ to me whether he comes or not** il m'est indifférent qu'il vienne ou non; **she is ~ to** *or* **~ compared with her sister** elle ne vaut pas sa sœur; **I can make ~ of it** je n'y comprends rien; **to have ~ on** (*be naked*) être nu; **I have ~ on for this evening** je n'ai rien de prévu ce soir; **there's ~ in it** (*not interesting*) c'est sans intérêt; (*not true*) ce n'est absolument pas vrai; (*almost the same*) c'est du pareil au même*; **there's ~ in it for us** nous n'avons rien à y gagner; **there's ~ to it*** c'est facile comme tout*; **there's ~ like exercise for keeping one fit** il n'y a rien de tel que l'exercice pour garder la forme; **to come to ~** ne rien donner; **~ much** pas grand-chose; **~ but** rien que; **he does ~ but eat** il ne fait que manger; **I get ~ but complaints** je n'entends que des plaintes; **there's ~ for it but to go** il ne nous reste qu'à partir; **~ less than** rien moins que; **~ more** rien de plus; **~ else** (*no other thing*) rien d'autre; (*nothing further*) rien de plus; **there's ~ else for it** c'est inévitable; **that has ~ to do with us** nous n'avons rien à voir là-dedans; **I've got ~ to do with it** je n'y suis pour rien; **have ~ to do with it!** ne vous en mêlez pas!; **that has ~ to do with it** cela n'a rien à voir; **there is ~ to laugh at** il n'y a pas de quoi rire; **I have ~ against him** je n'ai rien contre lui; **there was ~ doing* at the club** il ne se passait rien d'intéressant au club; **~ doing!*** rien à faire!; **it's a mere ~ compared with** ça n'est rien en comparaison de; **he's just a ~** c'est une nullité.

2 *adv* nullement, pas du tout. **it was ~ like as big as** c'était loin d'être aussi grand que.

♦ **nothingness** *n* néant *m.*

notice [ˈnəʊtɪs] **1** *n* **(a)** (*warning*) avis *m*, notification *f*; (*period*) délai *m.* **advance** *or* **previous ~** préavis *m*; **a week's ~** une semaine de préavis; **to give ~ to** (*to tenant*) donner congé à; (*to landlord etc*) donner un préavis de départ à; **to give sb ~** (*Admin etc: inform*) aviser qn (*to do* de faire; *that* que); (*sack*) (*employee*) licencier qn, (*servant etc*) congédier qn; **to give ~** *[professional or office worker]* donner sa démission; *[servant]* donner ses huit jours; **to give ~ of sth** annoncer qch; **to give sb ~ of sth** prévenir qn de qch; **give me a week's ~ if you want to do ...** prévenez-moi une semaine à l'avance si vous voulez faire ...; **until further ~** jusqu'à nouvel ordre; **at very short ~** *leave* dans les plus brefs délais; *inform* très peu de temps à l'avance; **at a moment's ~** sur-le-champ; **at 3 days' ~** dans un délai de 3 jours.

(b) (*announcement*) avis *m*, annonce *f*; (*poster*) affiche *f*; (*sign*) pancarte *f.* **public ~** avis au public; **to put a ~ in the paper** mettre une annonce *or* un entrefilet dans le journal; (*Press*) **death** *etc* **~** annonce de décès *etc.*

(c) (*review: play*) compte rendu *m*, critique *f.*

(d) **to take ~ of sb/sth** tenir compte de qn/qch, faire attention à qn/qch; **to take no ~ of sb/sth** ne tenir aucun compte de qn/qch, ne pas faire attention à qn/qch; **take no ~!** ne faites pas attention!; **it has attracted a lot of ~** cela a suscité un grand intérêt; **it escaped his ~ that ...** il n'a pas remarqué que ...; **to avoid ~** passer inaperçu; **it came to his ~ that ...** il s'est aperçu que ...; **it has been brought to my ~ that ...** il a été porté à ma connaissance que ...; **beneath my ~** indigne de mon attention.

2 *vt* (*perceive*) remarquer, s'apercevoir de; (*heed*) faire attention à. **I ~d a tear in his coat** j'ai remarqué un accroc dans son manteau; **when he ~d me** quand il s'est aperçu que j'étais là; **I'm afraid I didn't ~** malheureusement je n'ai pas remarqué; **I ~ you have a new dress** je vois que vous avez une nouvelle robe.

3 *adj*: **~ board** panneau *m* d'affichage.

♦ **noticeable** *adj* (*perceptible*) perceptible; (*obvious*) évident, net; **it isn't really ~able** ça ne se voit pas vraiment. ♦ **noticeably** *adv* perceptiblement; nettement.

notify [ˈnəʊtɪfaɪ] *vt*: **to ~ sth to sb** signaler *or* notifier qch à qn; **to ~ sb of sth** aviser qn de qch.
♦ **notification** *n* annonce *f*, notification *f*; (*announcement*) annonce; (*to authorities*) déclaration *f.*

notion [ˈnəʊʃən] *n* **(a)** idée *f.* **he somehow got hold of the ~ that she ...** il s'est mis en tête l'idée qu'elle ...; **according to his ~** selon sa façon de penser; **if that's your ~ of fun ...** si c'est ça que tu appelles t'amuser ...; **I've got some ~ of physics** j'ai quelques notions de physique; **to have no ~ of time** ne pas avoir la notion du temps; **I haven't the least** *or* **slightest** *or* **foggiest* ~** je n'en ai pas la moindre idée; **I have a ~ that** j'ai dans l'idée que; **I had no ~ that** j'ignorais absolument que; **can you give me a rough ~ of how many?** pouvez-vous m'indiquer en gros combien? **(b)** (*US: ribbons etc*) **~s** mercerie *f* (*articles*).

notorious [nəʊˈtɔːrɪəs] *adj event, act* d'une triste notoriété; *crime* notoire, célèbre; *person, case*

tristement célèbre; *liar, thief, criminal* notoire; *place* mal famé. ~ **for his dishonesty** d'une malhonnêteté notoire; **it is** ~ **that ...** il est de notoriété publique que ... . ♦ **notoriety** *n* notoriété *f*. ♦ **notoriously** *adv* notoirement.
notwithstanding [ˌnɒtwɪθˈstændɪŋ] **1** *prep* malgré, en dépit de. **2** *adv* néanmoins, malgré tout. **3** *conj*: ~ **that** quoique + *subj*, bien que + *subj*.
nought [nɔːt] *n* = **naught.**
noun [naʊn] *n* nom *m*, substantif *m*.
nourish [ˈnʌrɪʃ] *vt* nourrir (*with* de). ♦ **nourishing** *adj* nourrissant. ♦ **nourishment** *n* nourriture *f*, aliments *mpl*; **to take** ~**ment** s'alimenter.
novel [ˈnɒvəl] **1** *n* (*Literat*) roman *m*. **2** *adj* nouveau (*after n*), original. ♦ **novelette** *n* nouvelle *f*; (*love story*) roman *m* à l'eau de rose. ♦ **novelist** *n* romancier *m*, -ière *f*. ♦ **novelty** *n* nouveauté *f*; (*idea, thing*) innovation *f*; (*Comm*) article *m* de nouveauté.
November [nəʊˈvembəʳ] *n* novembre *m*; *for phrases V* **September.**
novice [ˈnɒvɪs] *n* novice *mf* (*at* en).
now [naʊ] **1** *adv* **(a)** (*gen*) maintenant; (*these days*) actuellement, en ce moment; (*at that time*) alors. **right** ~ en ce moment, à l'instant même; ~ **is the time to do it** c'est le moment de le faire; ~ **is the best time to go** c'est maintenant le meilleur moment pour y aller; **I saw him come in just** ~ je l'ai vu arriver a l'instant; **they won't be long** ~ ils ne vont plus tarder; **here and** ~ sur-le-champ; ~ **and again, (every)** ~ **and then** de temps en temps, par moments; **it's** ~ **or never!** c'est le moment ou jamais!
(b) (*with prep*) **you should have done that before** ~ vous auriez dû l'avoir déjà fait; **long before** ~ il y a longtemps déjà; **between** ~ **and next Tuesday** d'ici (à) mardi prochain; **they should have arrived by** ~ ils devraient être déjà arrivés; **haven't you finished by** ~? vous n'avez toujours pas fini?; **that will do for** ~ ça ira pour le moment; **from** ~ **on(wards)** à partir de maintenant; **in 3 weeks from** ~ d'ici (à) 3 semaines; **from** ~ **until then** d'ici là; **until** ~, **up to** ~ jusqu'à présent; ~ **here,** ~ **there** tantôt par ici, tantôt par là; ~ **(then)!** bon!, alors!, (*remonstrating*) allons!; **well,** ~! eh bien!; ~, **they had been looking for him** or, ils l'avaient cherché.
2 *conj*: ~ **(that)** maintenant que, à présent que.
♦ **nowadays** *adv* aujourd'hui, actuellement.
nowt [naʊt] *n* (*Brit dial*) = **nothing.**
noxious [ˈnɒkʃəs] *adj* nocif.
nozzle [ˈnɒzl] *n* *[hose, flamethrower]* ajutage *m*; *[syringe]* canule *f*; *[bellows]* bec *m*; *[vacuum cleaner]* suceur *m*; (*for icing*) douille *f*.
nuclear [ˈnjuːklɪəʳ] *adj* (*gen*) nucléaire. ~ **physicist** physicien(ne) *m(f)* atomiste; ~ **physics** physique *f* nucléaire; ~ **scientist** (savant *m*) atomiste *m*. ♦ **nuclear-powered** *adj* nucléaire.
nucleus [ˈnjuːklɪəs] *n, pl* **-ei** (*Astron, Phys*) noyau *m*; (*Bio*) nucléus *m*; (*fig*) éléments *mpl* de base.
nude [njuːd] **1** *adj* nu. **2** *n* (*Art*) nu *m*. **in the** ~ nu. ♦ **nudism** *n* nudisme *m*. ♦ **nudist** *adj, n* nudiste (*mf*); **nudist camp** camp *m* de nudistes. ♦ **nudity** *n* nudité *f*.
nudge [nʌdʒ] **1** *vt* pousser du coude. **2** *n* coup *m* de coude.
nugget [ˈnʌgɪt] *n* pépite *f*.
nuisance [ˈnjuːsns] *n* (*thing, event*) ennui *m*, embêtement* *m*; (*person*) peste *f*, fléau *m*. **it's a** ~ c'est ennuyeux *or* embêtant* (*that* que + *subj*; *doing* de devoir faire); **it/he is a** ~ ça/il m'embête*; **what a** ~! quelle barbe!*; **you're being a** ~ tu nous embêtes*; **to make a** ~ **of o.s.** embêter le monde*; **a public** ~* une calamité publique*.
null [nʌl] *adj* (*Jur*) ~ **and void** nul et non avenu. ♦ **nullify** *vt* infirmer, invalider. ♦ **nullity** *n* nullité *f*.
numb [nʌm] *adj* engourdi (*with* par); (*fig*) paralysé (*with fright etc* par la peur *etc*). ♦ **numbness** *n* engourdissement *m*.
number [ˈnʌmbəʳ] **1** *n* **(a)** (*Math*) nombre *m*, chiffre *m*; (*gen, Gram etc*) nombre. **even/odd** ~ nombre pair/impair; **in round** ~**s** en chiffres ronds. **(b)** (*quantity, amount*) nombre *m*, quantité *f*. **a** ~ **of people** un certain nombre de gens, plusieurs personnes; **a large** ~ **of** *people, mistakes, cases* un grand nombre de; *things* une grande quantité de; **on a** ~ **of occasions** à plusieurs occasions; **a fair** ~ un assez grand nombre; **in equal** ~**s** en nombre égal; ~**s being equal** à nombre égal; **10 in** ~ au nombre de 10; **in small/large** ~**s** en petit/grand nombre; **times without** ~ à maintes reprises; **any** ~ **can play** le nombre de joueurs est illimité; **the power of** ~**s** le pouvoir du nombre; **by force of** ~**s, by sheer** ~**s** par la force du nombre; **one of their** ~ un d'entre eux. **(c)** *[house, page etc]* numéro *m*. (*Telec*) **wrong** ~ faux numéro; **at** ~ **4** au (numéro) 4; **reference** ~ numéro de référence; (*Aut, Mil*) **registration** ~ numéro d'immatriculation; (*fig*) **I've got his** ~**!*** je le connais, lui!; **his** ~**'s up*** il est fichu*; **the** ~ **one player** le meilleur joueur; **he's the** ~ **one there** c'est lui qui dirige tout là-dedans; **he's my** ~ **two*** il est mon second. **(d)** *[goods, clothes, car]* modèle *m*; *[newspaper]* numéro *m*. **the January** ~ le numéro de janvier. **(e)** *[music hall, circus]* numéro *m*; *[pianist, dance band]* morceau *m*; *[singer]* chanson *f*; *[dancer]* danse *f*.
2 *adj*: (*Aut*) ~ **plate** plaque *f* d'immatriculation *or* minéralogique.
3 *vt* **(a)** (*give a number to*) numéroter. **they are not** ~**ed** ils n'ont pas de numéro; (*fig*) **his days were** ~**ed** ses jours étaient comptés. **(b)** (*include, amount to*) compter (*among* parmi).
4 *vi* (~ **off**) se numéroter (*from* en partant de).
♦ **numbering** *n* *[houses etc]* numérotage *m*.
♦ **numberless** *adj* innombrable, sans nombre.
numeral [ˈnjuːmərəl] *n* chiffre *m*, nombre *m*.
numerate [ˈnjuːmərɪt] *adj*: **to be** ~ savoir compter. ♦ **numeracy** *n* notions *fpl* de calcul.
numerical [njuːˈmerɪkəl] *adj* numérique. **in** ~ **order** dans l'ordre numérique. ♦ **numerically** *adv* numériquement.
numerous [ˈnjuːmərəs] *adj* nombreux.
numismatics [ˌnjuːmɪzˈmætɪks] *nsg* numismatique *f*. ♦ **numismatist** *n* numismate *mf*.
nun [nʌn] *n* religieuse *f*, bonne sœur* *f*.
nuptial [ˈnʌpʃəl] *adj* nuptial.
nurse [nɜːs] **1** *n* **(a)** infirmière *f*. **(b)** (*children's* ~) nurse *f*, bonne *f* d'enfants. **2** *vt* (*Med*) soigner; (*suckle*) allaiter; (*cradle in arms*) bercer (dans ses bras); *hope, wrath* nourrir; *horse, car engine* ménager. **she** ~**d him back to health** il a guéri grâce à ses soins; **to** ~ **a constituency** soigner les électeurs. ♦ **nursemaid** *n* bonne *f* d'enfants.
♦ **nursing 1** *adj* **(a)** *mother* qui allaite; **(b)** *[hospital]* **the nursing staff** le personnel soignant *or* infirmier; **nursing auxiliary** aide *f* soignante; **nursing home** clinique *f*; **nursing studies** études *fpl* d'infirmière; **2** *n* (*care of invalids*) soins *mpl*; (*profession of nurse*) profession *f* d'infirmière; **she's going in for nursing** elle va être infirmière.
nursery [ˈnɜːsərɪ] **1** *n* (*room*) nursery *f*, chambre *f* d'enfants; (*institution*) pouponnière *f*; (*Agr*) pépinière *f*. **2** *adj*: ~ **education** enseignement *m* de la maternelle; ~ **rhyme** comptine *f*; ~ **school** (*state-run*) école *f* maternelle; (*private*) jardin *m* d'enfants; (*Ski*) ~ **slopes** pentes *fpl* pour débutants.
♦ **nurseryman** *n* pépiniériste *m*.
nut [nʌt] **1** *n* **(a)** (*Bot*) *terme générique pour fruits à écale* (*no generic term in French*). **a bag of mixed** ~**s** un sachet de noisettes, cacahuètes, amandes *etc* panachées; ~**s and raisins** mendiants *mpl*; (*fig*) **he's a tough** ~ c'est un dur à

cuire*; **a hard ~ to crack** (*problem*) un problème difficile à résoudre; **he can't paint for ~s**‡ il peint comme un pied‡. **(b)** (*Tech*) écrou *m*. **(c)** (‡: *mad person, also* **nutcase**‡) fou *m*, folle *f*, cinglé(e)* *m(f)*. **2** *excl*: ~s!* des clous!‡ **3** *adj chocolate* aux amandes (*or* noisettes *etc*). ♦ **nutcracker(s)** *npl* casse-noix *m inv*, casse-noisettes *m inv*. ♦ **nuthouse**‡ *n* maison *f* de fous. ♦ **nutmeg** *n* (*nut*) (noix *f*) muscade *f*; (*tree*) muscadier *m*. ♦ **nuts**‡ *adj* dingue‡, fou (*about* de); **to go ~s*** perdre la boule‡. ♦ **nutshell** *n* coquille *f* de noix *or* noisette *etc*; (*fig*) **(to put) in a ~shell** (résumer) en un mot. ♦ **nutty** *adj* **(a)** *chocolate etc* aux noisettes (*etc*); *flavour* au goût de noisette *etc*; **(b)** (‡: *mad*) = **nuts.**

nutrient ['nju:triənt] **1** *adj* nutritif. **2** *n* élément *m* nutritif. ♦ **nutrition** *n* nutrition *f*, alimentation *f*. ♦ **nutritional** *adj* alimentaire. ♦ **nutritious** *or* ♦ **nutritive** *adj* nutritif.

nuzzle ['nʌzl] *vi*: **to ~ up/into** fourrer son nez contre/dans.

nylon ['naɪlɒn] **1** *n* nylon *m*. **2** *adj* de *or* en nylon. **~ stockings, ~s** bas *mpl* nylon.

nymph [nɪmf] *n* nymphe *f*.

nymphomania [ˌnɪmfəʊ'meɪnɪə] *n* nymphomanie *f*. ♦ **nymphomaniac** *adj*, *n* nymphomane (*f*).

O

O, o [əʊ] *n* (*letter*) O, o *m*; (*number: Telec etc*) zéro *m*.
oaf [əʊf] *n* (*awkward*) balourd(e)* *m(f)*; (*bad-mannered*) mufle *m*. ♦ **oafish** *adj person* mufle; *behaviour* de mufle.
oak [əʊk] **1** *n* chêne *m*. **2** *adj* (*made of* ~) de *or* en chêne. ~ **apple** galle *f* du chêne. ♦ **oakwood** *n* (*forest*) bois *m* de chênes.
oakum ['əʊkəm] *n* étoupe *f*.
oar [ɔːʳ] *n* aviron *m*, rame *f*. (*fig*) **he always puts his ~ in** il faut toujours qu'il y mette son grain de sel. ♦ **oarlock** *n* tolet *m*. ♦ **oarsman** *n* rameur *m*; (*Naut, also Sport*) nageur *m*.
oasis [əʊ'eɪsɪs] *n, pl* **oases** oasis *f*.
oat [əʊt] **1** *n*: ~**s** avoine *f*. ♦ **oatcake** *n* biscuit *m* d'avoine. ♦ **oatmeal 1** *n* flocons *mpl* d'avoine; **2** *adj* (*colour*) beige.
oath [əʊθ] *n* **(a)** (*Jur etc*) serment *m*. **to take the ~** prêter serment; **to swear an ~** *or* **on one's ~** jurer (*to do* de faire; *that* que); **on** *or* **under ~** sous serment; *witness* assermenté; **to put sb on ~** faire prêter serment à qn; **to put sb on** *or* **under ~ to do sth** faire promettre à qn sous serment de faire qch; **on my ~!** je vous le jure! **(b)** (*bad language*) juron *m*.
obdurate ['ɒbdjʊrɪt] *adj* (*stubborn*) obstiné; (*unyielding*) inflexible; (*unrepentant*) impénitent. ♦ **obduracy** *n* obstination *f*; inflexibilité *f*; impénitence *f*.
obedient [ə'biːdɪənt] *adj* obéissant (*to sb* envers qn; *to sth* à qch). ♦ **obedience** *n* obéissance *f* (*to* à); (*Rel*) obédience *f* (*to* à); **in obedience to sth** conformément à qch. ♦ **obediently** *adv* docilement; *smile* d'un air soumis.
obelisk ['ɒbɪlɪsk] *n* obélisque *m*.
obese [əʊ'biːs] *adj* obèse. ♦ **obesity** *n* obésité *f*.
obey [ə'beɪ] **1** *vt* (*gen*) obéir à; *instructions* se conformer à. **the machine ~s the controls** la machine répond aux commandes. **2** *vi* obéir.
obituary [ə'bɪtjʊərɪ] *n*: ~ **(notice)** nécrologie *f*; ~ **column** nécrologie (*rubrique*).
object ['ɒbdʒɪkt] **1** *n* **(a)** (*gen*) objet *m*. (*pej*) **what an ~ she looks!*** de quoi est-ce qu'elle a l'air!* **(b)** (*Gram*) complément *m* (d'objet). **(c)** (*aim*) but *m*, objectif *m*. **with this ~ in view** *or* **in mind** dans ce but, à cette fin; **with the ~ of doing** dans le but de faire; **what ~ is there in doing that?** à quoi bon faire cela?; **'distance no ~'** 'toutes distances'.
2 *adj*: (*fig*) ~ **lesson** démonstration *f* (*in* de).
3 [əb'dʒekt] *vi* élever une objection (*to* contre), trouver à redire. **I ~!** je proteste! (*to* contre); **if you don't ~** si vous n'y voyez pas d'objection; **he didn't ~ when ...** il n'a élevé aucune objection quand ...; **he ~s to her behaviour/her drinking** il désapprouve sa conduite/qu'elle boive; **do you ~ to my smoking?** est-ce que cela vous gêne si je fume?; **I don't ~ to helping you** je veux bien vous aider; **to ~ to sb** soulever des objections contre qn; **I wouldn't ~ to a bite to eat*** je mangerais bien un morceau.
4 [əb'dʒekt] *vt* objecter (*that* que).
♦ **objection** *n* objection *f*; (*drawback*) inconvénient *m*, obstacle *m*; **to have an ~ion to** = **to object to** (*V* 3 *above*); **to make** *or* **raise an ~ion** soulever *or* élever une objection (*to* contre). ♦ **objectionable** *adj person, behaviour, smell* extrêmement désagréable; *remark, language* choquant. ♦ **objective 1** *adj* **(a)** (*impartial*) objectif (*about* en ce qui concerne); **(b)** (*Gram*) *case* accusatif; *pronoun* complément d'objet; **2** *n* objectif *m*; (*Gram*) accusatif *m*. ♦ **objectively** *adv* objectivement. ♦ **objectivity** *n* objectivité *f*. ♦ **objector** *n*: **the ~ors to ...** ceux qui s'opposent à ...
obligation [ˌɒblɪ'geɪʃən] *n* obligation *f*. **to be/put sb under an ~ to do** être/mettre qn dans l'obligation de faire; **I'm under no ~ to do it** rien ne m'oblige à le faire; **'without ~'** sans engagement'; **to meet/fail to meet one's ~s** satisfaire à/manquer à ses obligations; **to be under an ~ to sb for sth** devoir de la reconnaissance à qn pour qch. ♦ **obligatory** [ɒ'blɪgətərɪ] *adj* obligatoire; (*imposed by custom*) de rigueur; **to make it obligatory for sb to do** imposer à qn l'obligation de faire.
oblige [ə'blaɪdʒ] *vt* **(a)** (*compel*) obliger (*sb to do* qn à faire). **to be ~d to do** être obligé de faire, devoir faire. **(b)** (*do a favour to*) rendre service à, obliger. **anything to ~!*** toujours prêt à rendre service!; **to be ~d to sb for sth** être reconnaissant à qn de qch; **I am much ~d to you** je vous remercie infiniment. ♦ **obliging** *adj* obligeant; **it is very obliging of them** c'est très aimable de leur part. ♦ **obligingly** *adv* obligeamment, aimablement; **the books which you obligingly gave me** les livres que vous avez eu l'obligeance *or* l'amabilité de me donner.
oblique [ə'bliːk] **1** *adj* (*gen*) oblique; *allusion, route, method* indirect. **2** *n* (*Typ*) oblique *f*. ♦ **obliquely** *adv* obliquement; (*fig*) indirectement.
obliterate [ə'blɪtəreɪt] *vt* (*gen*) effacer; *stamp* oblitérer. ♦ **obliteration** *n* effacement *m*; oblitération *f*.
oblivion [ə'blɪvɪən] *n* oubli *m*. ♦ **oblivious** *adj* (*forgetful*) oublieux (*to, of* de); (*unaware*) inconscient (*to, of* de).
oblong ['ɒblɒŋ] **1** *adj* oblong. ~ **dish** plat *m* rectangulaire. **2** *n* rectangle *m*.
obnoxious [əb'nɒkʃəs] *adj person, behaviour* odieux; *smell* infect.
oboe ['əʊbəʊ] *n* hautbois *m*.
obscene [əb'siːn] *adj* obscène. ♦ **obscenely** *adv* d'une manière obscène. ♦ **obscenity** *n* obscénité *f*.
obscure [əb'skjʊəʳ] **1** *adj* (*gen*) obscur; *feeling, memory* vague. **2** *vt* (*darken*) obscurcir; (*hide*) *sun, view* cacher; *argument, idea* embrouiller. **to ~ the issue** embrouiller la question. ♦ **obscurely** *adv* obscurément. ♦ **obscurity** *n* obscurité *f*.
obsequies ['ɒbsɪkwɪz] *npl* obsèques *fpl*.
obsequious [əb'siːkwɪəs] *adj* obséquieux (*to* devant). ♦ **obsequiously** *adv* obséquieusement.
observance [əb'zɜːvəns] *n* **(a)** (*act of observing*) *[rule]* observation *f*; *[rite, custom, Sabbath]* observance *f*. **(b)** (*custom etc*) observance *f*. **religious ~s** observances religieuses. ♦ **observant** *adj* observateur.
observation [ˌɒbzə'veɪʃən] **1** *n* **(a)** (*gen, Med*) observation *f*; (*Police, Mil etc*) surveillance *f*. **to keep under ~** *patient* garder en observation; *suspect, place* surveiller; **powers of ~** facultés *fpl* d'observation. **(b)** (*remark*) observation *f*,

remarque *f.* **2** *adj balloon, post* d'observation. (*US Rail*) ~ **car** voiture *f* panoramique; ~ **tower** mirador *m.* ♦ **observatory** *n* observatoire *m.*

observe [əb'zɜːv] *vt* **(a)** (*obey, note, study*) observer; *anniversary* célébrer. **(b)** (*remark*) faire remarquer, faire observer (*that* que). ♦ **observer** *n* observateur *m,* -trice *f.*

obsess [əb'ses] *vt* obséder, hanter. ♦ **obsession** *n* (*gen*) obsession *f* (*with* de); (*of sth unpleasant*) hantise *f* (*with* de); **sport is an ~ion with him** le sport c'est son idée fixe, le sport tient de l'obsession chez lui; **his ~ion with her** la manière dont elle l'obsède; **his ~ion with death** son obsession *or* sa hantise de la mort. ♦ **obsessive** *adj* obsessionnel. ♦ **obsessively** *adv* d'une manière obsédante; (*Psych*) obsessionnellement.

obsolete ['ɒbsəliːt] *adj attitude, idea, process* dépassé, démodé; *passport, ticket* périmé; *goods, machine* vieux; *law* caduc; *word* obsolète, vieilli; (*Bio*) atrophié. **to become** ~ tomber en désuétude. ♦ **obsolescence** *n [goods, words]* vieillissement *m*; *[machinery]* obsolescence *f*; **planned** *or* **built-in obsolescence** obsolescence calculée. ♦ **obsolescent** *adj machinery* obsolescent; *word* vieilli; *goods* vieux.

obstacle ['ɒbstəkl] **1** *n* obstacle *m.* **to be an ~ to, to put an ~ in the way of** faire obstacle à. **2** *adj race* d'obstacles.

obstetrics [ɒb'stetrɪks] *nsg* obstétrique *f.* ♦ **obstetric(al)** *adj techniques etc* obstétrical; *clinic* obstétrique. ♦ **obstetrician** *n* médecin *m* accoucheur.

obstinate ['ɒbstɪnɪt] *adj* (*gen*) obstiné (*in doing* à faire; *about* sur); *pain, illness* persistant; *fever* rebelle. **as ~ as a mule** têtu comme une mule. ♦ **obstinacy** *n* obstination *f* (*in doing* à faire). ♦ **obstinately** *adv* obstinément; **he tried ~ly to do it** il s'est obstiné à le faire.

obstreperous [əb'strepərəs] *adj* (*noisy*) tapageur; (*unruly*) chahuteur; (*rebellious*) rouspéteur*. ♦ **obstreperously** *adv* tapageusement; en rouspétant*.

obstruct [əb'strʌkt] *vt* (*block*) *road* encombrer (*with* de), boucher (*with* avec); *pipe, view* boucher (*with* avec, *by* par); *artery* obstruer; *traffic* bloquer; (*hinder*) entraver; (*Sport*) faire obstruction à. ♦ **obstruction** *n* (*sth which obstructs*) obstacle *m*; (*to pipe*) bouchon *m*; (*to artery*) caillot *m*; (*in road etc*) **to cause an ~ion** (*gen*) encombrer la voie publique; (*Aut*) bloquer la circulation. ♦ **obstructionist** *adj* obstructionniste. ♦ **obstructive** *adj* obstructionniste; **you're being ~ive** vous ne pensez qu'à mettre des bâtons dans les roues.

obtain [əb'teɪn] *vt* (*gen*) obtenir; *goods* se procurer; (*for sb else*) procurer (*for sb* à qn). (*Comm*) **it may be ~ed from ...** on peut se le procurer chez .... ♦ **obtainable** *adj*: **where is that ~able?** où peut-on se le procurer?

obtrude [əb'truːd] **1** *vt* imposer (*on* à). **2** *vi* s'imposer. ♦ **obtrusion** *n* intrusion *f.* ♦ **obtrusive** *adj person* importun; *opinions* ostentatoire; *smell* pénétrant; *building etc* trop en évidence. ♦ **obtrusively** *adv* importunément.

obtuse [əb'tjuːs] *adj* obtus. ♦ **obtuseness** *n* stupidité *f.*

obverse ['ɒbvɜːs] *n [coin]* face *f*; *[statement]* contrepartie *f.*

obviate ['ɒbvɪeɪt] *vt* obvier à.

obvious ['ɒbvɪəs] *adj* évident, manifeste. **it's ~ that** il est évident *or* manifeste que, il est de toute évidence que; **the ~ thing to do is to leave** la chose à faire c'est évidemment de partir; **that's the ~ one** c'est bien évidemment celui-là; ~ **statement** truisme *m*; **we must not be too ~ about it** il va falloir ne pas trop montrer notre jeu. ♦ **obviously** *adv* évidemment, manifestement; **he was ~ly not drunk** il était évident qu'il n'était pas ivre; **he was not ~ly drunk** il n'était pas visiblement ivre; **~ly!** bien sûr!, évidemment!

occasion [ə'keɪʒən] **1** *n* **(a)** occasion *f,* circonstance *f.* **on the ~ of** à l'occasion de; **on the first ~ that ...** la première fois que ...; **on that ~** à cette occasion, cette fois-là; **on several ~s** à plusieurs occasions; **on rare ~s** en de rares occasions; **on great ~s** dans les grandes occasions; **on ~** à l'occasion; **should the ~ arise** le cas échéant; **this would be a good ~ to try it out** c'est l'occasion tout indiquée pour l'essayer; **to rise to the ~** se montrer à la hauteur de la situation; **there was no ~ for it** ce n'était pas nécessaire; **you had no ~ to say that** vous n'aviez aucune raison de dire cela; **I had ~ to say** j'ai eu l'occasion de dire. **(b)** (*event*) événement *m.* **a big ~** un grand événement; **it was quite an ~** cela n'a pas été un petit événement.

2 *vt* occasionner, causer.

♦ **occasional** *adj event* qui a lieu de temps en temps; *visits* espacés; *rain, showers* intermittent; **we have an ~al visitor** il nous arrive d'avoir qn de temps en temps; **they had passed an ~al car** ils avaient croisé quelques rares voitures; **~al table** guéridon *m.* ♦ **occasionally** *adv* de temps en temps, quelquefois; **very ~ally** très peu souvent.

occident ['ɒksɪdənt] *n* (*liter*) occident *m.* ♦ **occidental** *adj* occidental.

occult [ɒ'kʌlt] **1** *adj* occulte. **2** *n* surnaturel *m.*

occupant ['ɒkjʊpənt] *n* (*gen*) occupant(e) *m(f)*; (*tenant*) locataire *mf*; *[job, post]* titulaire *mf.*

occupation [ˌɒkjʊ'peɪʃən] **1** *n* **(a)** (*gen, Mil*) occupation *f.* **house ready for ~** maison prête à être habitée; **in ~** installé; **army of ~** armée *f* d'occupation; **under military ~** sous occupation militaire. **(b)** (*trade*) métier *m*; (*profession*) profession *f*; (*work*) emploi *m,* travail *m*; (*activity, pastime*) occupation *f.* **he is a plumber by ~** il est plombier de son métier. **2** *adj troops* d'occupation. ♦ **occupational** *adj disease* du travail; *hazard* du métier; **~al therapist** ergothérapeute *mf*; **~al therapy** ergothérapie *f.*

occupy ['ɒkjʊpaɪ] *vt* occuper. **occupied in** *or* **with doing** occupé à faire; **to ~ o.s.** *or* **one's time** s'occuper (*with or by doing* à faire); **to keep one's mind occupied** s'occuper l'esprit. ♦ **occupier** *n* (*gen*) occupant(e) *m(f)*; (*tenant*) locataire *mf.*

occur [ə'kɜːʳ] *vi* **(a)** *[event]* avoir lieu, arriver; *[word, error, plant, disease]* se rencontrer, se trouver; *[difficulty, opportunity]* se présenter; *[change]* s'opérer. **don't let it ~ again!** que cela ne se reproduise plus!; **if a vacancy ~s** en cas de poste vacant; **should the case ~** le cas échéant. **(b) it ~s to me that ...** il me vient à l'esprit que ...; **it didn't ~ to him to refuse** il n'a pas eu l'idée de refuser; **an idea ~red to me** une idée m'est venue; **it ~red to me that we could ...** j'ai pensé *or* je me suis dit que nous pourrions .... ♦ **occurrence** *n* événement *m*; **an everyday ~rence** un fait journalier; **this is a common ~rence** ceci arrive souvent.

ocean ['əʊʃən] **1** *n* océan *m.* **~s of*** énormément de. **2** *adj climate, region* océanique; *cruise* sur l'océan. ~ **bed** fond *m* sous-marin. ♦ **ocean-going** *adj* de haute mer. ♦ **oceanic** [ˌəʊʃɪ'ænɪk] *adj* océanique. ♦ **oceanography** *n* océanographie *f.*

ocelot ['əʊsɪlɒt] *n* ocelot *m.*

ochre, (*US*) **ocher** ['əʊkəʳ] *n* ocre *f.*

o'clock [ə'klɒk] *adv*: **it is one ~** il est une heure; **what ~ is it?** quelle heure est-il?; **at 5 ~** à 5 heures; **at twelve ~** (*midday*) à midi; (*midnight*) à minuit.

octagon ['ɒktəgən] *n* octogone *m.* ♦ **octagonal** *adj* octogonal.

octane ['ɒkteɪn] *n* octane *m.* **high-~ petrol** carburant *m* à indice d'octane élevé.

octave ['ɒktɪv] *n* (*Mus, Rel*) octave *f*; (*Poetry*) huitain *m.*

octavo [ɒk'teɪvəʊ] *n* in-octavo *m*.
octet [ɒk'tet] *n* octuor *m*.
October [ɒk'təʊbəʳ] *n* octobre *m*; *for phrases V* **September.**
octogenarian [ˌɒktəʊdʒɪ'nɛərɪən] *adj, n* octogénaire (*mf*).
octopus ['ɒktəpəs] *n* pieuvre *f*.
oculist ['ɒkjʊlɪst] *n* oculiste *mf*.
odd [ɒd] *adj* **(a)** (*strange*) bizarre, étrange, curieux. **how ~ that ...** comme c'est curieux que + *subj*; **what an ~ thing for him to do!** c'est curieux *or* bizarre qu'il ait fait cela!; **he says some very ~ things** il dit de drôles de choses. **(b)** (*Math*) *number* impair. **(c)** (*extra, left over*) qui reste(nt); (*from pair*) *shoe, sock* dépariè; (*from set*) dépareillé. **£5 and some ~ pennies** 5 livres et quelques pennies; **a few ~ hats** deux ou trois chapeaux; **to be the ~ one over** être en surnombre; **the ~ man out, the ~ one out** l'exception *f*; **60-~** 60 et quelques. **(d)** (*occasional*) **in ~ moments he ...** à ses moments perdus il ...; **at ~ times** de temps en temps; **any ~ piece of wood** un morceau de bois quelconque; **~ jobs** menus travaux *mpl*; **to do ~ jobs about the house** (*gen*) faire de menus travaux domestiques; (*do-it-yourself*) bricoler dans la maison; **I've got one or two ~ jobs for you to do** j'ai deux ou trois choses à te faire faire; **he has written the ~ article** il a écrit un ou deux articles; **I get the ~ letter from him** de temps en temps je reçois une lettre de lui. ♦ **oddball‡** *adj, n* excentrique (*mf*). ♦ **oddity** *n* **(a)** (*also* **oddness**) étrangeté *f*, bizarrerie *f*; **(b)** (*person/thing etc*) personne *f*/chose *f etc* étrange *or* bizarre. ♦ **odd-job man** *n* homme *m* à tout faire. ♦ **oddly** *adv* bizarrement, curieusement; **~ly enough she was at home** chose curieuse elle était chez elle; **she was ~ly attractive** elle avait un charme insolite. ♦ **oddment** *n* (*Comm*) fin *f* de série; *[cloth]* coupon *m*.
odds [ɒdz] **1** *npl* **(a)** (*Betting*) cote *f* (*of 5 to 1* de 5 contre 1). **short/long ~** faible/forte cote; (*fig*) **the ~ are against his coming/that he will come** il y a peu de chances/de fortes chances qu'il vienne; **to fight against heavy ~** lutter contre des forces supérieures; **he succeeded against all the ~** il a réussi alors que tout était contre lui; **by all the ~** d'après ce que l'on sait; **it makes no ~** cela n'a pas d'importance, ça m'est égal; **what's the ~?*** qu'est-ce que ça peut bien faire? **(b) to be at ~** être en désaccord (*with sb over sth* avec qn sur qch). **(c) ~ and ends** (*gen*) des petites choses qui restent; *[cloth]* bouts *mpl*; *[food]* restes *mpl*.
ode [əʊd] *n* ode *f* (*to* à, *on* sur).
odious ['əʊdɪəs] *adj* odieux. ♦ **odium** *n* réprobation *f* générale.
odour, (*US*) **odor** ['əʊdəʳ] *n* odeur *f*. (*fig*) **to be in good/bad ~ with sb** être bien/mal vu de qn. ♦ **odo(u)rless** *adj* inodore.
odyssey ['ɒdɪsɪ] *n* odyssée *f*.
oecology [ɪ'kɒlədʒɪ] *etc* = **ecology** *etc*.
oestrogen ['iːstrəʊdʒən] *n* œstrogène *m*.
of [ɒv, əv] *prep* **(a)** (*gen*) de. **the wife ~ the doctor** la femme du médecin; **a friend ~ ours** un de nos amis; **that funny nose ~ hers** son drôle de nez; **there were 6 ~ us** nous étions 6; **he asked the six ~ us to lunch** il nous a invités tous les six à déjeuner; **~ the ten only one was ...** sur les dix un seul était ...; **he is not one ~ us** il n'est pas des nôtres; **the 2nd ~ June** le 2 juin; **today ~ all days** ce jour entre tous; (*US*) **a quarter ~ 6** 6 heures moins le quart; **girl ~ 10** petite fille de 10 ans; **question ~ no importance** question sans importance; **town ~ narrow streets** ville aux rues étroites; **that idiot ~ a doctor** cet imbécile de docteur; **it was horrid ~ him to say so** c'était méchant de sa part (que) de dire cela. **(b)** (*concerning*) de. **what do you think ~ him?** que pensez-vous de lui?; **what ~ it?** et alors? **(c)** (*origin, cause*) de. **~ noble birth** de naissance noble; **to die ~ hunger** mourir de faim; **dress (made) ~ wool** robe en *or* de laine.
off [ɒf] **1** *adv* **(a)** (*distance*) **5 km ~** à 5 km; **my holiday is a week ~** je serai en vacances dans une semaine; (*Theat*) **voices ~** voix *fpl* dans les coulisses. **(b)** (*departure*) **to be ~** partir, s'en aller; **~ you go!** va-t'en!, sauve-toi!*; (*Sport*) **they're ~!** et les voilà partis!; **where are you ~ to?** où allez-vous?; **we're ~ to France today** nous partons pour la France aujourd'hui; **he's ~ fishing** (*going*) il va à la pêche; (*gone*) il est à la pêche. **(c)** (*absence*) **he's ~ on Tuesdays** il n'est pas là le mardi; **she's ~ at 4 o'clock** elle est libre à 4 heures; **to take a day ~** prendre un jour de congé; **I've got this afternoon ~** j'ai congé cet après-midi; **to be ~ sick** être absent pour cause de maladie; **he's been ~ for 3 weeks** cela fait 3 semaines qu'il est absent. **(d)** (*removal*) **he had his coat ~** il avait enlevé son manteau; **with his hat ~** sans chapeau; **~ with those socks!** enlève tes chaussettes!; **the lid was ~** on avait enlevé le couvercle; **the handle is ~** la poignée s'est détachée; **there are 2 buttons ~** il manque 2 boutons; **I'll give you 5% ~** je vais vous faire une remise de 5%. **(e)** (*not functioning*) **to be ~** *[brakes]* être desserré; *[machine, television, light]* être éteint; *[engine, gas at main, electricity, water]* être coupé; *[tap, gas-tap]* être fermé. **(f) the play is ~** (*cancelled*) la pièce est annulée; (*no longer running*) la pièce a quitté l'affiche; **their engagement is ~** ils ont rompu leurs fiançailles; (*in restaurant*) **the cutlets are ~** il n'y a plus de côtelettes. **(g)** (*stale etc*) **to be ~** *[meat]* être mauvais *or* avancé; *[milk]* être tourné; *[butter]* être rance; (*fig*) **that's a bit ~!*** c'est un peu exagéré!* **(h)** (*phrases*) **~ and on, on and ~** de temps à autre; **right ~*, straight ~*** tout de suite.

2 *prep* **(a)** (*gen*) de. **he fell/jumped ~ the wall** il est tombé/a sauté du mur; **he took the book ~ the table** il a pris le livre sur la table; **there are buttons ~ my coat** il manque des boutons à mon manteau; **the lid was ~ the tin** on avait ôté le couvercle de la boîte; **they eat ~ chipped plates** ils mangent dans des assiettes ébréchées; **they dined ~ a chicken** ils ont dîné d'un poulet; **a slice ~ the cake** une tranche du gâteau; **sth ~ the price** une remise (sur le prix). **(b)** (*distant from*) éloigné de. (*Naut*) **~ Portland Bill** au large de Portland Bill; **a yard ~ me** à un mètre de moi; **height ~ the ground** hauteur *f* à partir du sol; **street (leading) ~ the square** rue qui part de la place; **house ~ the main road** maison à l'écart de la grand-route; **I'm ~** *or* **I've gone ~ sausages*** je n'aime plus les saucisses.

3 *adj*: **he was having an ~ day*** il n'était pas en forme ce jour-là.

♦ **offbeat** *adj* (*fig*) excentrique, original. ♦ **off-centre** *adj* décentré; *construction* en porte-à-faux. ♦ **off-chance** *n*: **on the ~-chance** à tout hasard; **on the ~-chance of seeing her** *or* **that I could see her** au cas où je pourrais la voir. ♦ **off-colour** *adj person* mal fichu*. ♦ **offhand** **1** *adj* (*also* **offhanded**) (*casual*) désinvolte, sans-gêne *inv*; (*curt*) brusque; **2** *adv*: **I can't just say ~hand** je ne peux pas vous le dire à l'improviste *or* comme ça*. ♦ **offhandedly** *adv* avec désinvolture, avec sans-gêne; avec brusquerie. ♦ **offhandedness** *n* désinvolture *f*, sans-gêne *m*; brusquerie *f*. ♦ **offing** *n*: **in the ~ing** en perspective. ♦ **off-key** *adj, adv* (*Mus*) faux. ♦ **off-licence** *n* (*Brit*) magasin *m* de vins et de spiritueux. ♦ **off-limits** *adj* (*US Mil*) interdit (au personnel militaire). ♦ **off-load** *vt goods, passengers* débarquer; *task* passer (*onto sb* à qn). ♦ **off-peak** *adj hours* creux; *traffic* aux heures creuses; *tariff* réduit; *ticket* bénéficiant du tarif réduit; *heating* par accumulation. ♦ **off-putting*** *adj task* rebutant; *food* peu ragoûtant; *person, manner, welcome* peu engageant. ♦ **off-season** *n* morte saison *f.* ♦ **offset** (*vb: pret, ptp* **offset**) **1** *n* (*Typ*) ~**set printing** offset *m*; **2** *vt* compenser. ♦ **offshoot** *n* (*Bot*) rejeton *m*; *[organization]* ramification *f*; *[discussion, action etc]* conséquence *f.* ♦ **offshore** *adj breeze* de terre; *island* proche du littoral; *waters, fishing* côtier. ♦ **offside** **1** *n* (*Aut*) (*in Britain*) côté *m* droit; (*in France, US etc*) côté gauche; **2** *adj* de droite; de gauche; (*Sport*) hors jeu. ♦ **offspring** *n* (*pl inv*) progéniture *f.* ♦ **offstage** *adj, adv* dans les coulisses. ♦ **off-white** *adj* blanc cassé *inv.*

offal ['ɒfəl] *n* abats *mpl.*

offence, (*US*) **offense** [ə'fens] *n* **(a)** (*Jur*) délit *m* (*against* contre); (*Rel etc*) offense *f.* (*Jur etc*) **it is an ~ to do that** il est contraire à la loi de faire cela; **capital ~** crime *m* capital. **(b) to give ~ to sb** offenser qn; **to take ~** se vexer, s'offenser (*at* de).

offend [ə'fend] **1** *vt person* blesser, offenser; *ears, eyes, reason* choquer. **to be ~ed (at)** se vexer (de), s'offenser (de). **2** *vi*: **to ~ against** *law, rule* enfreindre; *good taste, common sense* être une insulte à. ♦ **offender** *n* (*lawbreaker*) délinquant(e) *m(f)*; (*against traffic regulations etc*) contrevenant(e) *m(f)*; (*Jur*) **first ~er** délinquant(e) primaire. ♦ **offending** *adj word, object* incriminé. ♦ **offensive** **1** *adj* **(a)** (*shocking*) offensant, choquant; (*disgusting*) repoussant; (*insulting*) injurieux; **to be offensive to sb** insulter qn; **(b)** *tactics, weapon* offensif; **2** *n* (*Mil*) offensive *f*; **to be on the offensive** avoir pris l'offensive. ♦ **offensively** *adv behave* d'une manière offensante *or* choquante; *say* d'une manière injurieuse.

offer ['ɒfəʳ] **1** *n* (*gen*) offre *f* (*of* de; *for* pour; *to do* de faire). **~ of marriage** demande *f* en mariage; **to make sb an ~ for sth** faire une offre à qn pour qch; (*in advertisement*) **£5 or nearest ~** 5 livres ou au plus offrant; (*Comm*) **on ~** en promotion. **2** *vt job, gift, prayers, apology, opportunity* offrir (*to* à); *help, object, money* proposer (*to* à); *remark, opinion* émettre. **to ~ to do** offrir *or* proposer de faire. ♦ **offering** *n* offrande *f.* ♦ **offertory** *n* (*part of service*) offertoire *m*; (*collection*) quête *f.*

office ['ɒfɪs] **1** *n* **(a)** (*place*) bureau *m*; *[lawyer]* étude *f*; *[doctor]* cabinet *m.* **our London ~** notre bureau *or* notre section *f* de Londres; *[house etc]* **'usual ~s'** 'cuisine, sanitaires'. **(b)** (*function*) fonction *f*; (*duty*) fonctions, devoir *m.* **to be in ~, to hold ~** *[mayor, chairman]* être en fonctions; *[minister]* avoir un portefeuille; *[political party]* être au pouvoir; **public ~** fonctions officielles; **through his good ~s** par ses bons offices *mpl*; **through the ~s of** par l'entremise de. **(c)** (*Rel*) office *m.* **2** *adj staff, furniture, work* de bureau. *[club, society]* **~ bearer** membre *m* du comité directeur; **~ block** immeuble *m* de bureaux; **~ boy** garçon *m* de bureau; **~ hours** heures *fpl* de bureau. ♦ **office-worker** *n* employé(e) *m(f)* de bureau.

officer ['ɒfɪsəʳ] *n* **(a)** (*Aviat, Mil, Naut*) officier *m.* **~s' mess** mess *m.* **(b)** *[local government]* fonctionnaire *m*; *[organization, club]* membre *m* du comité directeur. **police ~** agent *m* (de police).

official [ə'fɪʃəl] **1** *adj* (*gen*) officiel; *language, style* administratif; *uniform* réglementaire. **2** *n* (*gen, Sport etc*) officiel *m*; *[civil service, local government]* fonctionnaire *mf*; *[railways, post office etc]* employé(e) *m(f).* ♦ **officialdom** *n* bureaucratie *f.* ♦ **officialese** *n* jargon *m* administratif. ♦ **officially** *adv* officiellement. ♦ **officiate** *vi* (*Rel*) officier; (*gen*) **to officiate as** remplir les fonctions de.

officious [ə'fɪʃəs] *adj* trop empressé. ♦ **officiously** *adv* avec un empressement excessif. ♦ **officiousness** *n* excès *m* d'empressement.

often ['ɒfən] *adv* souvent, fréquemment. **as ~ as not, more ~ than not** le plus souvent; **every so ~** (*in time*) de temps en temps; (*in spacing, distance etc*) çà et là; **once too ~** une fois de trop; **it cannot be said too ~ that ...** on ne répétera jamais assez que ...; **how ~ have you seen her?** combien de fois l'avez-vous vue?; **how ~ do the boats leave?** les bateaux partent tous les combien?

ogle ['əʊgl] *vt* lorgner*.

ogre ['əʊgəʳ] *n* ogre *m.*

oh [əʊ] *excl* oh!; (*cry of pain*) aïe!

oil [ɔɪl] **1** *n* **(a)** (*Geol, Comm, Ind etc*) pétrole *m.* (*fig*) **to pour ~ on troubled waters** ramener le calme. **(b)** (*Art, Aut, Culin etc*) huile *f.* **fried in ~** frit à l'huile; **~ and vinegar (dressing)** vinaigrette *f*; **painted in ~s** peint à l'huile.

2 *vt* graisser, lubrifier. (*fig*) **to ~ the wheels** mettre de l'huile dans les rouages.

3 *adj industry, shares* pétrolier; *magnate etc* du pétrole; *lamp, stove* à pétrole; (*Aut*) *level, pressure* d'huile; (*Aut*) **~ filter** filtre *m* à huile; **~ gauge** jauge *f* de niveau d'huile; (*Art*) **~ paint** couleur *f* à l'huile; **~ painting** peinture *f* à l'huile; **she's no ~ painting*** ce n'est vraiment pas une beauté; **~ pollution** pollution *f* aux hydrocarbures; **~ rig** (*land*) derrick *m*; (*sea*) plate-forme *f* pétrolière; **~ slick** nappe *f* de pétrole, (*on beach*) marée *f* noire; **~ storage tank** (*for central heating*) cuve *f* à mazout; **~ tanker** (*ship*) pétrolier *m*; (*truck*) camion-citerne *m* (à pétrole); **~ well** puits *m* de pétrole.

♦ **oil-burning** *adj lamp* à pétrole; *stove* (*paraffin*) à pétrole, (*fuel oil*) à mazout. ♦ **oilcan** *n* (*for lubricating*) burette *f* à huile; (*for storage*) bidon *m* à huile. ♦ **oilcloth** *n* toile *f* cirée. ♦ **oilfield** *n* gisement *m* or champ *m* pétrolifère. ♦ **oil-fired** *adj boiler* à mazout; *central heating* au mazout. ♦ **oiliness** *n* (*V* **oily** *below*) aspect *m* huileux *or* graisseux *or* (*Culin*) gras; onction *f.* ♦ **oilskins** *npl* ciré *m.* ♦ **oily** *adj liquid, consistency* huileux; *stain* d'huile; *rag, clothes, hands* graisseux; *cooking, food* gras; (*fig pej*) *manners, tone* onctueux.

ointment ['ɔɪntmənt] *n* onguent *m*, pommade *f.*

O.K.* ['əʊ'keɪ] (*vb: pret, ptp* **O.K.'d**) **1** *excl* d'accord!, O.K.! (*don't fuss*) **~, ~!** ça va, ça va! **2** *adj* (*good*) très bien; (*not bad*) pas mal. **is it ~ with you if I come too?** ça ne vous ennuie pas que je vous accompagne? (*subj*); **I'm coming too, ~?** je viens aussi, d'accord?; **I'm ~** ça va; **the car is ~** la voiture est (*undamaged*) intacte *or* (*repaired etc*) en bon état; **everything's ~** tout va bien. **3** *vt* approuver.

okapi [əʊ'kɑːpɪ] *n* okapi *m.*

old [əʊld] **1** *adj* **(a)** (*gen*) vieux (*before vowel etc* vieil, *f* vieille). **an ~ man** un vieil homme, un vieillard; (*pej*) **he's a real ~ woman** il a des manies de petite vieille; **~ people, ~ folk** personnes *fpl* âgées, vieux *mpl*; **~ people's home, ~ folks' home** hospice *m* de vieillards, (*private*) maison *f* de retraite; **~ for his years** mûr pour son âge; **to grow *or* get ~(er)** vieillir, se faire vieux; **in his ~ age** sur ses vieux jours; **the ~ country** la mère patrie; **Old English** vieil anglais; **~ maid** vieille fille *f*; (*Art*) **~ master** (*artist*) grand peintre *m*; (*painting*) tableau *m* de maître; **the Old World** l'ancien monde *m*; **an ~ chair** une vieille chaise, (*valuable*) une chaise ancienne; **~ wine** vin *m* vieux; **that's an ~ one!** ce n'est pas nouveau!; **as ~ as the hills** vieux comme les chemins; **the ~ part of Nice** le vieux Nice; **~ friends** de vieux amis; **any ~ how/where*** *etc* n'importe comment/où *etc*; **any ~ thing*** n'importe quoi; **we had a great ~ time*** on s'est vraiment bien amusé; (*fig*) **it's the same ~ story*** c'est toujours la même histoire; **~ Paul here*** ce bon vieux Paul; **a good ~**

dog un brave chien; **you ~ scoundrel!** sacré vieux!*; **I say, ~ man** *or* **~ fellow** dites donc mon vieux*.

(b) how ~ are you? quel âge avez-vous?; **he is 10 years ~** il a 10 ans; **at 10 years ~** à (l'âge de) 10 ans; **a 6-year-~ boy** un garçon de 6 ans; **~ enough to dress himself** assez grand pour s'habiller tout seul; **~ enough to vote** en âge de voter; **you're ~ enough to know better!** à ton âge tu devrais avoir plus de bon sens!; **too ~ for that sort of work** trop âgé pour ce genre de travail; (*to child*) **when you're ~er** quand tu seras plus grand; **if I were ~er** si j'étais plus âgé; **if I were 10 years ~er** si j'avais 10 ans de plus; **~er than you** plus âgé que toi; **he's 6 years ~er than you** il a 6 ans de plus que toi; **~er brother** frère aîné; **the ~er generation** la génération antérieure.

(c) (*former*) *school, mayor, home* ancien (*before n*). **~ boy** ancien élève; **in the ~ days** dans le temps, autrefois; **the good ~ days** le bon vieux temps; **this is the ~ way of doing it** on s'y prenait comme cela autrefois; **~ soldier** vétéran *m*.

2 *n* **(a) the ~** les vieux *mpl*, les vieillards *mpl*, les vieilles gens *mpl*.

(b) (in days) of ~ autrefois, jadis; **the men of ~** les hommes de jadis; **I know him of ~** je le connais depuis longtemps.

♦ **old-age** *adj*: **~-age pension** pension *f* vieillesse (*de la Sécurité sociale*); **~-age pensioner** retraité(e) *m(f)*. ♦ **olden** *adj*: **in ~en times** *or* **days** jadis. ♦ **old-established** *adj* ancien (*after n*). ♦ **old-fashioned** *adj* (*old*) d'autrefois; (*out-of-date*) démodé; *person, attitude* vieux jeu *inv*; (*fig*) **to give sb/sth an ~-fashioned look*** regarder qn/qch de travers. ♦ **old-style** *adj* à l'ancienne (mode). ♦ **old-time** *adj* du temps jadis; *dancing* d'autrefois. ♦ **old-timer*** *n* vieillard *m*, ancien *m*. ♦ **old wives' tale** *n* conte *m* de bonne femme. ♦ **old-womanish** *adj* qui a des manies de petite vieille. ♦ **old-world** *adj place* très vieux et pittoresque; *charm, style* d'autrefois.

oleaginous [ˌəʊlɪˈædʒɪnəs] *adj* oléagineux.

oleander [ˌəʊlɪˈændəʳ] *n* laurier-rose *m*.

oligarchy [ˈɒlɪgɑːkɪ] *n* oligarchie *f*.

olive [ˈɒlɪv] **1** *n* olive *f*; (**~** *tree*) olivier *m*. (*fig*) **to hold out the ~ branch** se présenter le rameau d'olivier à la main. **2** *adj* **(a)** *skin* olivâtre. **~ oil** huile *f* d'olive. **(b)** (*also* **olive-green**) vert olive *inv*.

Olympic [əʊˈlɪmpɪk] *adj* olympique. **~ Games, ~s** Jeux *mpl* olympiques.

ombudsman [ˈɒmbʊdzmən] *n* médiateur *m* (*Admin*).

omelet(te) [ˈɒmlɪt] *n* omelette *f*.

omen [ˈəʊmən] *n* présage *m*, augure *m*. **it is a good ~ that ...** il est de bon augure que ... + *subj*. ♦ **ominous** *adj event* de mauvais augure; *look, cloud, voice* menaçant; *sound, sign* alarmant. ♦ **ominously** *adv* d'une façon menaçante *or* alarmante; **he was ominously silent** son silence ne présageait rien de bon.

omit [əʊˈmɪt] *vt* (*accidentally*) omettre (*to do* de faire); (*deliberately*) omettre, négliger (*to do* de faire).

♦ **omission** *n* omission *f*.

omni... [ˈɒmnɪ] *pref* omni ... .

omnibus [ˈɒmnɪbəs] *n* (†: *bus*) omnibus† *m*; (*book*) recueil *m*.

omnipotent [ɒmˈnɪpətənt] *adj* omnipotent. ♦ **omnipotence** *n* omnipotence *f*.

omnivorous [ɒmˈnɪvərəs] *adj* omnivore; *reader* insatiable.

on [ɒn] **1** *prep* **(a)** (*position, direction*) sur, à. **~ the table** sur la table; **with a coat ~ his arm** un manteau sur le bras; **with a ring ~ her finger** une bague au doigt; **the ring ~ her finger** la bague qu'elle avait au doigt; **I have no money ~ me** je n'ai pas d'argent sur moi; **he turned his back ~ us** il nous a tourné le dos; **~ the right** à droite; **~ the blackboard/ceiling** au tableau/plafond; **he hung his hat ~ the nail** il a suspendu son chapeau au clou; **house ~ the main road** maison sur la grand-route. **(b)** (*fig*) **~ the/his violin** au/sur son violon; **with Louis Armstrong ~ the trumpet** avec Louis Armstrong à la trompette; **he swore it ~ the Bible** il l'a juré sur la Bible; **an attack ~ the government** une attaque contre le gouvernement; **it works ~ oil** cela marche au mazout; **~ the radio** à la radio; **~ the BBC** (*TV*) sur la B.B.C.; (*Rad*) à la B.B.C.; (*Rad*) **~ France-Inter** sur France-Inter; **I'm ~ £6,000 a year** je gagne 6 000 livres par an; **a student ~ a grant** un boursier; **he's ~ a course** il suit un cours; **to be ~ the team/committee** faire partie de l'équipe/du comité; **to be ~ pills** prendre des pilules; **to be ~ drugs** se droguer; **he's ~ heroin** il se drogue à l'héroïne; **I'm back ~ cigarettes** je me suis remis à fumer; **we're ~ irregular verbs** nous en sommes aux verbes irréguliers; **let's have a drink ~ it** on va boire un coup* pour fêter ça; **prices are up ~ last year's** les prix sont en hausse par rapport à ceux de l'année dernière; **this round's ~ me** c'est ma tournée; **have it ~ me** je vous le paie; **~ the train/plane** *etc* dans le train/l'avion *etc*.

(c) (*time*) **~ Sunday** dimanche; **~ Sundays** le dimanche; **~ December 1st** le 1er décembre; **~ the evening of December 3rd** le 3 décembre au soir; **~ or about the 20th** vers le 20; **~ and after the 20th** à partir du 20; **~ Easter Day** le jour de Pâques; **it's just ~ 5 o'clock** il va être 5 heures; **~ my arrival** à mon arrivée; **~ my refusal to go away** lorsque j'ai refusé de partir; **~ hearing this** en entendant cela.

(d) (*about, concerning*) sur, de. **he lectures ~ Dante** il fait un cours sur Dante; **a book ~ grammar** un livre de grammaire; **an essay ~ ...** une dissertation sur ...; **he spoke ~ oil** il a parlé du pétrole; **have you heard him ~ V.A.T.?** vous l'avez entendu parler de la T.V.A.?; **Jones ~ Marx** ce que Jones a écrit sur Marx; **I'm ~ a new project** je travaille à un nouveau projet; **away ~ an errand** parti faire une course; **while we're ~ the subject** pendant que nous y sommes.

2 *adv* **(a)** (*covering*) **he had his coat ~** il avait mis son manteau; **~ with your pyjamas!** allez, mets ton pyjama!; **she had nothing ~** elle était toute nue; **what had he got ~?** qu'est-ce qu'il portait?; **the lid is ~** le couvercle est mis.

(b) (*forward*) **from that time ~** à partir de ce moment-là; **it's getting ~ for 2 o'clock** il n'est pas loin de 2 heures; **well ~ in May** bien avant dans le mois de mai; **it was well ~ into May** mai était déjà bien avancé.

(c) (*continuation*) **go ~ with your work** continuez votre travail; **and so ~** et ainsi de suite; **they talked ~ and ~** ils ont parlé sans discontinuer *or* sans arrêt.

(d) (*functioning etc*) **to be ~** *[machine, engine]* être en marche; *[light]* être allumé; *[TV, radio]* être allumé, marcher; *[tap]* être ouvert; *[brake]* être serré; *[meeting, programme etc]* être en cours; **while the meeting was ~** pendant la réunion; **the show is ~ already** le spectacle a déjà commencé; **the play is still ~** la pièce est encore à l'affiche; **what's ~ at the cinema?** qu'est-ce qu'on donne au cinéma?; (*Rad, TV*) **what's ~?** qu'y a-t-il à la radio/à la télé?; (*Rad, TV*) **X is ~ tonight** il y a X ce soir; **you're ~ now!** c'est à vous maintenant!

(e) (*phrases*) **we are going out, are you ~?*** nous sortons, vous venez?; **you're ~!*** tope là!; **it's not ~*** (*refusing*) pas question!; (*not done*) cela ne se fait pas; **he is always ~ at me*** il est toujours après moi*; **to get ~ to sb** se mettre en rapport avec qn (*about sth* à propos de qch); **I'm ~ to something** je

suis sur une piste intéressante; **the police are ~ to him** la police est sur sa piste; **she's ~ to the fact that ...** elle sait que ... .
♦ **oncoming** *adj car* venant en sens inverse. ♦ **onlooker** *n* spectateur *m*, -trice *f*. ♦ **onrush** *n* *[people]* ruée *f*; *[water]* torrent *m*. ♦ **onset** *n* (*start*) début *m*; (*approach*) approche *f*. ♦ **onshore** *adj wind* de mer. ♦ **onslaught** *n* attaque *f*. ♦ **onto** *prep* = **on to.** ♦ **onward 1** *adv* (*also* **onwards**) en avant; **from this time ~ward(s)** désormais; **from today ~ward(s)** à partir d'aujourd'hui; **2** *adj* en avant.

once [wʌns] **1** *adv* **(a)** (*on one occasion*) une fois. **~ only** une seule fois; **~ before** une fois déjà; **~ when I was young** un jour quand j'étais jeune; **~ again, ~ more** encore une fois; **~ and for all** une fois pour toutes; **~ a week** une fois par semaine; **~ in a while, ~ in a way** de temps en temps; **more than ~** plus d'une fois; **~ or twice** une fois ou deux; **for ~** pour une fois; **just this ~** juste pour cette fois-ci; **not ~, never ~** pas une seule fois; **if ~ you ...** si jamais vous ...; **~ a journalist always a journalist** qui a été journaliste le reste toute sa vie. **(b)** (*formerly*) jadis, autrefois. **~ upon a time there was** il y avait une fois, il était une fois; **~ powerful** jadis *or* autrefois puissant. **(c) at ~** (*immediately*) tout de suite; (*simultaneously*) à la fois; **all at ~** (*suddenly*) tout à coup, soudain.

2 *conj* une fois que. **~ she'd seen him she ...** une fois qu'elle l'eut vu *or* après l'avoir vu* elle ... .
♦ **once-over*** *n*: **to give sth the ~-over** vérifier qch très rapidement.

one [wʌn] **1** *adj* **(a)** un(e). **~ hundred and twenty** cent vingt; **twenty-~ apples** vingt et une pommes; **that's ~ way of doing it** c'est une façon de le faire; **she is ~ (year old)** elle a un an; **it's ~ o'clock** il est une heure; **for ~ thing ...** d'abord ...; **with ~ voice** d'une seule voix; **~ day** un jour; **~ Sunday morning** un dimanche matin; **~ hot summer afternoon** par un chaud après-midi d'été. **(b)** (*sole*) un(e) seul(e). **there is ~ man who** il y a un seul homme qui + *subj*; **the ~ man who** le seul qui + *subj*; **~ and only** seul et unique. **(c)** (*same*) (le) même. **in the ~ car** dans la même voiture; **~ and the same person** une seule et même personne; **~ and the same thing** exactement la même chose.

2 *n* un(e) *m(f)*. **twenty-~** vingt et un(e); **~ hundred and ~** cent un(e); **there are three ~s in her phone number** il y a trois uns dans son numéro de téléphone; **~ of them** (*people*) l'un d'eux, l'une d'elles; (*things*) (l')un, (l')une; **chapter ~** chapitre un; **I for ~ don't believe it** pour ma part je ne le crois pas; **who doesn't agree? – I for ~!** qui n'est pas d'accord? – moi pour commencer!; **~ by ~** un à un; **in ~s and twos** *arrive* par petits groupes; *get, send* quelques-uns à la fois; **~ after the other** l'un après l'autre; **~ and all** tous sans exception; **it's all ~** c'est tout un; **it's all ~ to me** cela m'est égal; **to be ~ up*** avoir l'avantage (*on sb* sur qn); **to go ~ better than sb** faire mieux que qn.

3 *pron* **(a)** (*indefinite*) un(e) *m(f)*. **would you like ~?** en voulez-vous un?; **have you got ~?** en avez-vous un?; **the question is ~ of money** c'est une question d'argent; **~ of my best friends** un de mes meilleurs amis; **he's ~ of us** il est des nôtres; **you can't have ~ without the other** on ne peut avoir l'un sans l'autre. **(b)** (*specific*) **this ~** celui-ci, celle-ci; **that ~** celui-là, celle-là; **the ~ who** *or* **that** *or* **which** celui qui, celle qui; **the ~ on the floor** celui *or* celle qui est par terre; **he's the ~ with brown hair** c'est celui qui a les cheveux bruns; **which ~?** lequel?, laquelle?; **I want the red ~** je veux le rouge; **you've taken the wrong ~** vous n'avez pas pris le bon; **that's a difficult ~!** ça c'est difficile!; **the little ~s** les petits; **my dearest ~** mon chéri, ma chérie; **he's a clever ~** c'est un malin; **for ~ who claims to know the language, he** ... pour quelqu'un qui prétend connaître la langue, il ...; **he's not ~ to do that sort of thing** il n'est pas de ceux qui font cela; **he's a great ~* for chess** c'est un mordu* des échecs. **(c) ~ another** = **each other**; *V* **each 2b. (d)** (*impersonal*) (*subject*) on; (*object*) vous. **~ must remember** on doit *or* il faut se souvenir; **it tires ~ too much** cela vous fatigue trop; **~ likes to see ~'s friends happy** on aime que ses amis soient heureux.
♦ **one-armed** *adj* manchot; **~-armed bandit*** machine *f* à sous (*jeu*). ♦ **one-eyed** *adj* borgne. ♦ **one-horse town*** *n* bled* *m*, trou* *m*. ♦ **one-legged** *adj* unijambiste. ♦ **one-man** *adj job* fait *or* à faire par un seul homme; *business* que fait marcher un seul homme; *exhibition etc* consacré à un seul artiste; *woman etc* qui n'aime qu'un seul homme; (*Mus: person*) **~-man band** homme-orchestre *m*; (*fig*) **it's a ~-man band*** un seul homme fait marcher toute l'affaire; (*variety*) **~-man show** one-man show *m*. ♦ **one-night stand** *n* (*Theat*) représentation *f* unique. ♦ **one-off*** *or* ♦ **one-shot*** (*US*) *adj* rarissime, exceptionnel. ♦ **one-one** *adj* (*US*) univoque. ♦ **one-room(ed)** *adj* d'une pièce. ♦ **oneself** *pron* se, soi-même; (*after prep*) soi(-même); (*emphatic*) soi-même; **to hurt ~self** se blesser; **to dress ~self** s'habiller; **to speak to ~self** se parler à soi-même; **to be sure of ~self** être sûr de soi; **one must do it ~self** il faut le faire soi-même; **(all) by ~self** (tout) seul. ♦ **one-sided** *adj decision* unilatéral; *contest, game* inégal; *judgment, account* partial; *contract* inéquitable. ♦ **one-time** *adj* ancien (*before n*). ♦ **one-to-one** *adj* univoque. ♦ **one-track** *adj*: **to have a ~-track mind*** n'avoir qu'une idée en tête. ♦ **one-upmanship*** *n* (*hum*) art *m* de faire mieux que les autres. ♦ **one-way** *adj street* à sens unique; *traffic* en sens unique; *ticket* simple; *emotion etc* non partagé.

onerous ['ɒnərəs] *adj task* pénible; *responsibility* lourd.

onion ['ʌnjən] **1** *n* oignon *m*. **2** *adj soup* à l'oignon; *skin* d'oignon; *stew* aux oignons. ♦ **onion-shaped** *adj* bulbeux.

only ['əʊnlɪ] **1** *adj* seul. **the ~ book that remains** le seul livre qui reste (*subj*); **~ child** enfant *mf* unique; **you're the ~ one to think of that** vous êtes le seul à y avoir pensé; **it's the ~ one left** c'est le seul qui reste (*subj*); **the ~ thing is that it's too late** seulement il est trop tard; **that's the ~ way to do it** c'est la seule façon de le faire.

2 *adv* seulement, simplement, ne ... (plus) que. **~ Paul can wait** il n'y a que Paul qui puisse attendre; **he can ~ wait** il ne peut qu'attendre; **I can ~ say that ...** tout ce que je peux dire c'est que ...; **it's ~ that I thought ...** simplement, je pensais ...; **I will ~ say that ...** je dirai simplement que ...; **it will ~ take a minute** ça ne prendra qu'une minute; **I'm ~ the secretary** je ne suis que le secrétaire; **a ticket for one person ~** un billet pour une seule personne; **'ladies ~'** 'réservé aux dames'; **I ~ looked at it** je n'ai fait que le regarder; **you've ~ to ask** vous n'avez qu'à demander; **~ to think of it** rien que d'y penser; **it's ~ too true** ce n'est que trop vrai; **not ~ A but also B** non seulement A mais aussi B; **~ yesterday** pas plus tard qu'hier; **he has ~ just arrived** il vient tout juste d'arriver; **I caught the train but ~ just** j'ai eu le train mais de justesse; **if ~** si seulement.

3 *conj* seulement, mais. **I would buy it, ~ it's too dear** je l'achèterais bien, seulement *or* mais il est trop cher.

onomatopoeia [ˌɒnəʊmætəʊ'piːə] *n* onomatopée *f*.

onus ['əʊnəs] *n* (*no pl*) **the ~ is on him** c'est sa responsabilité (*to do* de faire).

onyx ['ɒnɪks] *n* onyx *m*.

ooze [uːz] **1** *n* vase *f*. **2** *vi [water, pus, walls]* suinter; *[resin, gum]* exsuder. **3** *vt*: **his wounds ~d pus** le pus suintait de ses blessures; (*fig pej*)

she was oozing charm le charme lui sortait par tous les pores.

ooze away *vi*: **his strength** *etc* **was oozing away** ses forces *etc* l'abandonnaient.

opal ['əupəl] *n* opale *f*.

opaque [əʊ'peɪk] *adj* opaque.

open ['əupən] **1** *adj* **(a)** (*gen*) ouvert. **wide ~** grand ouvert; **half-~, slightly ~** entrouvert; **to welcome with ~ arms** *person* accueillir à bras ouverts; *news* accueillir avec joie; **our grocer is ~ on Mondays** notre épicier ouvre *or* est ouvert le lundi; (*fig*) **to keep ~ house** tenir table ouverte; (*Brit*) **~ day** journée *f* du public.

(b) (*fig*) *boat, letter, cheque, city* ouvert; *river* (*not obstructed*) ouvert à la navigation, (*not frozen*) non gelé; *road, corridor* dégagé; *pipe* ouvert, non bouché; *car* décapoté; *sewer* à ciel ouvert; *prison* à régime libéral; (*Med*) *bowels* relâché; *pores* dilaté. **road ~ to traffic** route ouverte à la circulation; **the way to Paris lay ~** la route de Paris était libre; **the ~ road** la grand-route; **the ~ air** le plein air; **in the ~ air** (*gen*) en plein air; *sleep* à la belle étoile; **in ~ country** en rase campagne; **patch of ~ ground** (*between trees*) clairière *f*; (*in town*) terrain *m* vague; **the ~ sea** la haute mer, le large; **~ space** espace *m* libre; **~ to the elements/to attack** exposé aux éléments/à l'attaque; **~ sandwich** canapé *m* (froid); **~ to persuasion** ouvert à la persuasion; **I'm ~ to advice** je me laisserais volontiers conseiller; **I'm ~ to correction, but ...** dites-moi si je me trompe, mais ...; **~ to improvement** que l'on peut améliorer; **it is ~ to doubt whether ...** on peut douter que ... + *subj*.

(c) *market, meeting, trial* public; *competition, scholarship* ouvert à tous. **the course is not ~ to schoolchildren** ce cours n'est pas ouvert aux lycéens; **several choices were ~ to them** plusieurs choix s'offraient à eux; **this post is still ~** ce poste est encore vacant; (*Jur*) **in ~ court** en audience publique; (*Sport*) **~ season** saison *f* de la chasse; **the O~ University** = le Centre de Télé-enseignement universitaire.

(d) (*frank, not hidden*) *person, face* ouvert, franc; *enemy* déclaré; *admiration, envy* manifeste; *attempt* non dissimulé; *scandal* public. **in ~ revolt** en rébellion ouverte (*against* contre); **it's an ~ secret that** ce n'est un secret pour personne que.

(e) (*undecided*) *question* non résolu, non tranché. **the race was still wide ~** l'issue de la course était encore indécise; **it's an ~ question whether ...** on ne sait pas si ...; **to leave ~** *matter* laisser en suspens; *date* ne pas préciser; **to have an ~ mind on sth** ne pas avoir formé d'opinion sur qch; (*Jur*) **~ verdict** (*not stating cause of death*) verdict *m* de décès avec causes indéterminées; (*where guilty party unknown*) verdict sans désignation de coupable; **~ ticket** billet *m* open.

2 *n*: **out in the ~** (*out of doors*) dehors, en plein air; *sleep* à la belle étoile; (*in the country*) au grand air; **to come out into the ~** (*lit*) sortir au grand jour; (*fig*) *[secret, plans]* se faire jour; *[person]* parler franchement (*about* de); **to bring out into the ~** divulguer.

3 *vt* (*gen: lit, fig*) ouvrir; *bowels* relâcher; *pores* dilater; *legs* écarter; *hole* percer; *conversation, negotiations* engager. **to ~ wide** ouvrir tout grand; **to ~ slightly** entrouvrir; **to ~ again** rouvrir; (*lit, fig*) **he didn't ~ his mouth** il n'a pas ouvert la bouche; **to ~ Parliament** ouvrir la session parlementaire; (*Mil*) **to ~ fire** ouvrir le feu (*on* sur).

4 *vi* **(a)** (*gen*) s'ouvrir; *[shop, museum, bank etc]* ouvrir. **this door never ~s** cette porte n'ouvre jamais; **the door ~ed** la porte s'est ouverte; **to ~ slightly** s'entrouvrir; **to ~ again** se rouvrir; *[door, room]* **to ~ on to** *or* **into** donner sur.

(b) (*begin*) *[class, debate, meeting, play, book]* s'ouvrir, commencer (*with* par); *[speaker]* commencer (*with* par); (*Bridge*) ouvrir (*with* de). (*Theat*) **the play ~s next week** la première a lieu la semaine prochaine.

open out 1 *vi [flower, person]* s'ouvrir; *[passage, tunnel, street]* s'élargir. **to ~ out on to** déboucher sur. **2** *vt sep* ouvrir.

open up 1 *vi* **(a)** *[flower, shop, career, opportunity]* s'ouvrir (*fig: to sb* à qn; *about sth* de qch). **(b)** (*start shooting*) ouvrir le feu. **2** *vt sep* (*gen*) ouvrir; *jungle* rendre accessible; *blocked road* dégager; *prospects, possibility* découvrir, révéler; *horizons, career* ouvrir.

♦ **open-air** *adj games, activities* de plein air; *swimming pool, market, meeting* en plein air; *theatre* de verdure. ♦ **open-and-shut case** *n* cas *m* incontestable. ♦ **opencast mining** *n* exploitation *f* à ciel ouvert. ♦ **open-ended** *or* ♦ **open-end** (*US*) *adj tube* à deux ouvertures; *discussion, meeting* sans limite de durée; *offer* flexible. ♦ **opener** *n* (*for bottles*) ouvre-bouteilles *m inv*; (*for tins*) ouvre-boîtes *m inv*; (*Theat: act*) lever *m* de rideau. ♦ **open-handed** *adj* généreux. ♦ **open-hearted** *adj* franc, sincère. ♦ **open-heart surgery** *n* chirurgie *f* à cœur ouvert. ♦ **opening 1** *n* **(a)** (*gen*) ouverture *f*; (*in wall*) brèche *f*; (*in trees, forest, clouds*) trouée *f*; (*in roof*) percée *f*; **(b)** (*beginning*) ouverture *f*; **(c)** (*opportunity*) occasion *f* (*to do* de faire); (*trade outlet*) débouché *m* (*for* pour); (*job*) poste *m* vacant; (*work*) travail *m*; **to give one's opponent an ~ing** prêter le flanc à son adversaire; **2** *adj ceremony, speech* d'inauguration; *remark* préliminaire; (*St Ex*) *price* d'ouverture; (*Theat*) **~ing night** première *f*; (*Brit*) **~ing time** l'heure *f* d'ouverture (*des pubs*). ♦ **openly** *adv* (*frankly*) ouvertement; (*publicly*) publiquement. ♦ **open-minded** *adj* à l'esprit ouvert. ♦ **open-mouthed** *adj, adv* bouche bée. ♦ **open-necked** *adj* à col ouvert, échancré. ♦ **openness** *n* (*candour*) franchise *f*. ♦ **open-plan** *adj house, office* sans cloisons.

opera ['ɒpərə] **1** *n* opéra *m*. **2** *adj*: **~ glasses** jumelles *fpl* de théâtre; **~ house** (théâtre *m* de l')opéra *m*; **~ singer** chanteur *m*, -euse *f* d'opéra. ♦ **opera-goer** *or* ♦ **opera-lover** *n* amateur *m* d'opéra. ♦ **operatic** *adj* d'opéra. ♦ **operetta** *n* opérette *f*.

operate ['ɒpəreɪt] **1** *vi* (*gen*) opérer; (*Med*) opérer (*on sb* qn; *for sth* de qch); *[drug, propaganda]* opérer (*on* sur); *[machine, vehicle]* marcher, fonctionner (*by electricity etc* à l'électricité *etc*); *[system, sb's mind]* fonctionner; *[factors]* jouer (*to produce* pour produire). **he was ~d on for appendicitis** il a été opéré de l'appendicite; **to ~ on sb's eyes** opérer qn des yeux.

2 *vt* **(a)** *[person] machine, telephone, brakes etc* faire marcher, faire fonctionner; *[switch]* actionner. **a machine ~d by electricity** une machine qui marche à l'électricité.

(b) *business, factory* diriger; *coalmine, oil well* exploiter; *system, changes* opérer; *swindle* réaliser.

♦ **operable** *adj* opérable. ♦ **operating** *adj* **(a)** (*Comm*) *costs* opérationnel; **(b)** (*Med*) *table* d'opération; **operating theatre** salle *f* d'opération. ♦ **operation** *n* **(a)** (*gen, Med, Mil etc*) opération *f*; **to have an operation** se faire opérer; **a lung operation** une opération au poumon; **to perform an operation on sb** opérer qn; **(b)** (*act of operating*) **to be in operation** *[machine]* être en service; *[business etc]* fonctionner; *[mine etc]* être en exploitation; *[law, system]* être en vigueur; **to come into operation** entrer en service (*or* en vigueur *etc*); **to put into operation** mettre en service *etc*. ♦ **operational** *adj* opérationnel. ♦ **operative 1** *adj law, measure, system* en vigueur; **the operative word** le mot clef; **2** *n*

(*worker*) ouvrier *m*, -ière *f*; (*machine operator*) opérateur *m*, -trice *f*; **the steel operatives** la main-d'œuvre des aciéries. ♦ **operator** *n* (*gen*) opérateur *m*, -trice *f*; *[telephones]* téléphoniste *mf*; **radio operator** radio *m*; **tour operator** organisateur *m*, -trice *f* de voyages.
ophthalmia [ɒf'θælmɪə] *n* ophtalmie *f*. ♦ **ophthalmic** *adj surgeon* ophtalmologique.
opiate ['əʊpɪɪt] *n* opiat *m*.
opinion [ə'pɪnjən] **1** *n* (*point of view*) opinion *f*, avis *m*; *[lawyer, doctor]* avis; (*belief*) opinion. **in my ~** à mon avis, d'après moi; **in the ~ of** d'après, selon; **public ~** l'opinion publique; **it's a matter of ~ whether ...** c'est une affaire d'opinion pour ce qui est de savoir si ...; **I'm of your ~** je suis de votre avis *or* opinion; **to be of the ~ that** être d'avis que, estimer que; **political ~s** opinions politiques; **to have a high/low ~ of** avoir/ne pas avoir bonne opinion de; **what is your ~ of this book?** que pensez-vous de ce livre?; (*Med*) **to take a second ~** prendre l'avis d'un autre médecin. **2** *adj*: **~ poll** sondage *m* d'opinion. ♦ **opinionated** *adj* dogmatique.
opium ['əʊpɪəm] *n* opium *m*. **~ addict** opiomane *mf*.
opossum [ə'pɒsəm] *n* opossum *m*.
opponent [ə'pəʊnənt] *n* (*gen*) adversaire *mf*; (*in discussion, debate*) antagoniste *mf*. **he has always been an ~ of ...** il a toujours été contre ... .
opportune ['ɒpətju:n] *adj* opportun. ♦ **opportunely** *adv* opportunément. ♦ **opportuneness** *n* opportunité *f*. ♦ **opportunism** *n* opportunisme *m*. ♦ **opportunist** *adj, n* opportuniste (*mf*).
opportunity [ˌɒpə'tju:nɪtɪ] *n* occasion *f*. **to have the** *or* **an ~ to do** *or* **of doing** avoir l'occasion de faire; **to take the ~ of doing** *or* **to do** profiter de l'occasion pour faire; **at the earliest ~** à la première occasion; **when the ~ occurs** à l'occasion; **if you get the ~** si vous en avez l'occasion; **equality of ~** égalité *f* de chances; **to make the most of one's opportunities** profiter pleinement de ses chances; **this job offers great opportunities** ce poste offre des perspectives *fpl* d'avenir.
oppose [ə'pəʊz] *vt* (*gen*) s'opposer à; *motion, resolution* (*Pol*) faire opposition à, (*in debate*) parler contre. **he ~s our coming** il s'oppose à ce que nous venions (*subj*). ♦ **opposed** *adj* opposé, hostile (*to* à); **I'm ~d to your doing that** je m'oppose à ce que vous fassiez cela; **as ~d to** par opposition à; **as ~d to that, ...** par contre, ... ♦ **opposing** *adj army* opposé.
opposite ['ɒpəzɪt] **1** *adj house etc* d'en face; *side, end, direction, point of view* opposé. **'see map on ~ page'** 'voir plan ci-contre'; **the ~ sex** l'autre sexe *m*; **his ~ number** son homologue *mf*. **2** *adv* (d')en face. **the house ~** la maison d'en face; **the house is directly ~** la maison est directement en face. **3** *prep* en face de. **~ one another** en vis-à-vis; **they live ~ us** ils habitent en face de chez nous; (*Theat etc*) **to play ~ sb** partager la vedette avec qn. **4** *n* contraire *m*, opposé *m*. **quite the ~!** au contraire!; **he told me just the ~** il m'a dit le contraire.
opposition [ˌɒpə'zɪʃən] **1** *n* opposition *f* (*to* à). **in ~ to** en opposition avec; (*Pol*) **the ~** l'opposition; **the party in ~** le parti de l'opposition; (*Pol*) **to be in ~** être dans l'opposition; **the ~*** (*Sport, Pol*) l'adversaire *m*; (*Comm*) la concurrence; **they put up considerable ~** ils opposèrent une vive résistance. **2** *adj* (*Pol*) de l'opposition.
oppress [ə'pres] *vt* (*Mil, Pol etc*) opprimer; *[anxiety, heat etc]* oppresser. ♦ **oppression** *n* oppression *f*. ♦ **oppressive** *adj* (*Mil, Pol etc*) oppressif; *anxiety, heat* accablant; *weather* lourd. ♦ **oppressively** *adv* (*Mil, Pol etc*) tyranniquement; **it was ~ively hot** il faisait une chaleur accablante. ♦ **oppressor** *n* oppresseur *m*.
opprobrium [ə'prəʊbrɪəm] *n* opprobre *m*.
opt [ɒpt] *vi*: **to ~ for sth** opter pour qch (*also Jur*); **to ~ to do** choisir de faire.
opt in* *vi* choisir de participer (*to* à).
opt out* *vi* choisir de ne pas participer (*of* à), se récuser. **to ~ out of doing** choisir de ne pas faire.
optical ['ɒptɪkəl] *adj glass, lens* optique; *instrument, illusion* d'optique. ♦ **optician** *n* opticien(ne) *m(f)*. ♦ **optics** *nsg* optique *f*.
optimism ['ɒptɪmɪzəm] *n* optimisme *m*. ♦ **optimist** *n* optimiste *mf*. ♦ **optimistic** *adj* optimiste. ♦ **optimistically** *adv* avec optimisme.
optimum ['ɒptɪməm] *adj* optimum.
option ['ɒpʃən] *n* option *f* (*on* sur); (*Scol*) matière *f* à option. (*Jur*) **6 months with the ~ of a fine** 6 mois avec substitution d'amende; **I have no ~** je n'ai pas le choix; **he had no ~ but to come** il n'a pas pu faire autrement que de venir; **you have the ~ of remaining here** vous pouvez rester ici si vous voulez; (*fig*) **he kept his ~s open** il n'a pas voulu s'engager. ♦ **optional** *adj* (*gen, Scol etc*) facultatif; (*Comm*) **~al extras** accessoires *mpl* en option.
opulent ['ɒpjʊlənt] *adj* opulent. ♦ **opulence** *n* opulence *f*. ♦ **opulently** *adv* avec opulence.
or [ɔ:ʳ] *conj* ou; (*with neg*) ni. **~ else** ou bien; **do it ~ else!*** fais-le, sinon!*; **without tears ~ sighs** sans larmes ni soupirs; **he could not read ~ write** il ne savait ni lire ni écrire; **an hour ~ so** environ une heure.
oracle ['ɒrəkl] *n* oracle *m*.
oral ['ɔ:rəl] **1** *adj* oral. **2** *n* oral *m*, épreuve *f* orale. ♦ **orally** *adv* oralement; (*Pharm*) par voie orale.
orange ['ɒrɪndʒ] **1** *n* (*fruit*) orange *f*; (*~-tree*) oranger *m*; (*colour*) orange *m*. **2** *adj* (*colour*) orange *inv*; *drink, flavour* d'orange; *liqueur* à l'orange. **~ blossom** fleur(s) *f(pl)* d'oranger; **~ marmalade** confiture *f* d'oranges; **~ stick** bâtonnet m (*pour manucure etc*). ♦ **orangeade** *n* orangeade *f*.
orang-outang [ɔ:ˌræŋu:'tæŋ], **orang-utan** [ɔ:ˌræŋu:'tæn] *n* orang-outang *m*.
oration [ɔ:'reɪʃən] *n* discours *m* solennel. **funeral ~** oraison *f* funèbre. ♦ **orator** ['ɒrətəʳ] *n* orateur *m*, -trice *f*. ♦ **oratorical** *adj* oratoire. ♦ **oratorio** *n* oratorio *m*. ♦ **oratory** *n* (*art*) art *m* oratoire; (*what is said*) éloquence *f*; **piece of oratory** discours *m*.
orbit ['ɔ:bɪt] **1** *n* orbite *f*. **in(to) ~** en orbite (*around* autour de); (*fig*) **that doesn't come within my ~** ceci n'est pas de mon domaine; **the American ~** la sphère d'influence américaine. **2** *vti* orbiter.
orchard ['ɔ:tʃəd] *n* verger *m*. **apple ~** verger de pommiers.
orchestra ['ɔ:kɪstrə] *n* orchestre *m*. ♦ **orchestral** [ɔ:'kestrəl] *adj music* orchestral; *concert* symphonique. ♦ **orchestrate** *vt* orchestrer. ♦ **orchestration** *n* orchestration *f*.
orchid ['ɔ:kɪd] *n* orchidée *f*. **wild ~** orchis *m*.
ordain [ɔ:'deɪn] *vt* **(a)** décréter (*that* que). (*fig*) **it was ~ed that** le destin a voulu que + *subj*. **(b)** (*Rel*) ordonner (*sb priest* qn prêtre).
ordeal [ɔ:'di:l] *n* (terrible) épreuve *f*. **it was a real ~ for him** cela le mettait au supplice.
order ['ɔ:dəʳ] **1** *n* **(a)** (*sequence*) ordre *m*. **word ~** ordre des mots; **what ~ should these cards be in?** dans quel ordre ces cartes devraient-elles être?; **in ~ of merit/appearance** par ordre de mérite/d'entrée en scène; **the cards were out of ~** les cartes n'étaient pas en ordre; **to put in(to) ~** mettre en ordre; **in the ~ of things** dans l'ordre des choses; **the old ~ is changing** l'ancien état de choses change. **(b)** (*good ~*) ordre *m*. **in ~** *room etc* en ordre; *passport, documents* en règle; **to put in ~** mettre en ordre; (*US*) **in short ~** tout de suite; **out of ~, not in working** *or* **running ~** *machine* en panne, détraqué; (*Telec*) *line* en

dérangement; **to be in running** *or* **working** ~ marcher bien. **(c) in ~ to do** pour faire, afin de faire; **in ~ that** afin que + *subj*, pour que + *subj*. **(d)** (*correct procedure*) ordre *m*. (*Parl*) ~, ~! à l'ordre!; **to call sb to ~** rappeler qn à l'ordre; **on a point of ~** sur une question de forme *or* de procédure; **is it in ~ to do that?** est-il permis de faire cela?; **his request is quite in ~** sa demande est tout à fait normale. **(e)** (*peace, control*) ordre *m*. **to keep ~** *[police etc]* maintenir l'ordre; *[teacher]* faire régner la discipline; **to keep sb in ~** tenir qn. **(f)** (*Bio*) ordre *m*; (*social class*) classe *f*. (*fig*) **of a high ~** de premier ordre; **of the ~ of 500** de l'ordre de 500; **Benedictine O~** ordre des bénédictins; **(holy) ~s** ordres *mpl* (majeurs); **to be in/take ~s** être/entrer dans les ordres. **(g)** (*command*) ordre *m*, consigne *f* (*Mil*). **to give sb ~s to do sth** ordonner à qn de faire qch; **I don't take ~s from you!** je ne suis pas à vos ordres!; **on the ~s of** sur l'ordre de; **by ~ of** par ordre de; **to be under ~s to do** avoir reçu l'ordre de faire; (*fig*) **strikes were the ~ of the day** les grèves étaient à l'ordre du jour; (*Jur*) **~ of the Court** injonction *f* de la cour; **deportation ~** arrêté *m* d'expulsion. **(h)** (*Comm*) commande *f*. **made to ~** fait sur commande; **to place an ~ with sb (for sth)** passer une commande (de qch) à qn; **they are on ~** ils sont commandés; (*Comm, fig*) **to ~** sur commande; **~ to view** permis *m* de visiter; **money ~** mandat *m*; (*Banking*) **to the ~ of** à l'ordre de.

2 *adj*: **~ book** carnet *m* de commandes; **~ form** bon *m* de commande.

3 *vt* **(a)** (*command*) ordonner (*sb to do* à qn de faire; *that* que + *subj*). **he was ~ed to be quiet** on lui a ordonné de se taire; **to ~ sb in/up** *etc* ordonner à qn d'entrer/de monter *etc*. **(b)** *goods, meal* commander; *taxi* faire venir. **(c)** (*put in* ~) *one's affairs etc* régler.

4 *vi* (*in restaurant etc*) passer sa commande.

order about, order around *vt sep* commander. ♦ **orderliness** *n* (habitudes *fpl* d')ordre *m*. ♦ **orderly 1** *adj room* en ordre; *mind* méthodique; *life* réglé; *person* qui a de l'ordre; *crowd* discipliné; **in an ~ly way** avec ordre; **2** *n* (*Mil*) planton *m*; (*Med*) garçon *m* de salle; **~ly room** salle *f* de rapport.

ordinal ['ɔːdɪnl] *adj, n* ordinal (*m*).

ordinance ['ɔːdɪnəns] *n* ordonnance *f* (*Admin*).

ordinary ['ɔːdnrɪ] **1** *adj* **(a)** (*usual*) ordinaire (*also pej*), habituel. **in the ~ way** en temps normal; **for all ~ purposes** pour l'usage courant. **(b)** (*average*) *intelligence, reader etc* moyen. **just an ~ fellow** un homme comme les autres. **2** *n*: **out of the ~** qui sort de l'ordinaire. ♦ **ordinarily** *adv* ordinairement.

ordination [ˌɔːdɪ'neɪʃən] *n* ordination *f*.

ordnance ['ɔːdnəns] (*Mil*) **1** *n* artillerie *f*. **2** *adj*: **O~ Corps** Service *m* du matériel; (*Brit*) **O~ Survey map** ≈ carte *f* d'État-Major.

ore [ɔːʳ] *n* minerai *m*. **iron ~** minerai de fer.

oregano [ˌɒrɪ'gɑːnəʊ] *n* origan *m*.

organ ['ɔːgən] **1** *n* (*Anat, also fig, Press etc*) organe *m*; (*Mus*) orgue *m*, orgues *fpl*. **2** *adj*: **~ grinder** joueur *m*, -euse *f* d'orgue de Barbarie; **~ loft** tribune *f* d'orgue. ♦ **organic** *adj* (*gen, Bio etc*) organique; *part* fondamental; *being* organisé; **~ic whole** tout *m* systématique. ♦ **organically** *adv* organiquement; (*basically*) foncièrement. ♦ **organism** *n* organisme *m* (*Bio*). ♦ **organist** *n* organiste *mf*.

organize ['ɔːgənaɪz] *vt* organiser. **to get ~d** s'organiser. ♦ **organization** *n* **(a)** organisation *f*; **charitable organization** œuvre *f* charitable; **(b)** organisation *f*; **his work lacks organization** son travail manque d'organisation. ♦ **organized** *adj* organisé; **~d labour** main-d'œuvre syndiquée. ♦ **organizer** *n* organisateur *m*, -trice *f*. ♦ **organizing** *adj* *committee* chargé de l'organisation; (*bossy*) autoritaire.

orgasm ['ɔːgæzəm] *n* orgasme *m*.

orgy ['ɔːdʒɪ] *n* (*lit, fig*) orgie *f*.

orient ['ɔːrɪənt] *n* orient *m*. ♦ **oriental 1** *adj* oriental; **2** *n*: **O~** Oriental(e) *m(f)*. ♦ **orientate** *vt* orienter. ♦ **orientation** *n* orientation *f*. ♦ **orienteering** *n* (*Sport*) exercice *m* d'orientation sur le terrain.

origami [ˌɒrɪ'gɑːmɪ] *n* (art *m* du) pliage *m*.

origin ['ɒrɪdʒɪn] *n* origine *f*. ♦ **original 1** *adj* **(a)** (*first*) *sin, inhabitant, purpose, meaning* originel; **(b)** (*not copied etc*) *painting, idea, writer* original; (*unconventional*) *character, person* original, excentrique; **2** *n [painting etc]* original *m*; **to read Dante in the ~al** lire Dante dans l'original. ♦ **originality** *n* originalité *f*. ♦ **originally** *adv* **(a)** (*in the beginning*) à l'origine; (*at first*) originellement; **(b)** (*not copying*) originalement. ♦ **originate 1** *vt [person]* être l'auteur de; *[event, effect]* donner naissance à; **2** *vi [person]* être originaire (*from* de); *[stream, custom]* prendre naissance (*in* dans); *[goods]* provenir (*from* de); *[suggestion, idea]* émaner (*from* de). ♦ **originator** *n* auteur *m*.

Orkneys ['ɔːknɪz] *npl* Orcades *fpl*.

orlon ['ɔːlɒn] ® **1** *n* orlon *m* ®. **2** *adj* en orlon.

ornament ['ɔːnəmənt] **1** *n* (*gen*) ornement *m*; (*object*) bibelot *m*. **2** *vt style, dress* orner (*with* de); *room, building, ceiling* ornementer (*with* de). ♦ **ornamental** *adj* (*gen*) ornemental; *garden, lake* d'agrément. ♦ **ornamentation** *n* ornementation *f*.

ornate [ɔː'neɪt] *adj* très orné.

ornithology [ˌɔːnɪ'θɒlədʒɪ] *n* ornithologie *f*. ♦ **ornithological** *adj* ornithologique. ♦ **ornithologist** *n* ornithologue *mf*.

orphan ['ɔːfən] **1** *adj, n* orphelin(e) *m(f)*. **2** *vt*: **to be ~ed** devenir orphelin(e). ♦ **orphanage** *n* orphelinat *m*.

orthodontics [ˌɔːθəʊ'dɒntɪks] *nsg* orthodontie *f*.

orthodox ['ɔːθədɒks] *adj* orthodoxe. ♦ **orthodoxy** *n* orthodoxie *f*.

orthography [ɔː'θɒgrəfɪ] *n* orthographe *f*.

orthopaedic, (*US*) **orthopedic** [ˌɔːθəʊ'piːdɪk] *adj surgery etc* orthopédique. **~ surgeon** chirurgien(ne) *m(f)* orthopédiste. ♦ **orthop(a)edics** *nsg* orthopédie *f*. ♦ **orthop(a)edist** *n* orthopédiste *mf*.

oscillate ['ɒsɪleɪt] **1** *vi* osciller. **2** *vt* faire osciller. ♦ **oscillation** *n* oscillation *f*.

osprey ['ɒspreɪ] *n* orfraie *f*.

ossify ['ɒsɪfaɪ] *vi* s'ossifier. ♦ **ossification** *n* ossification *f*.

ostensible [ɒs'tensəbl] *adj* prétendu, apparent. ♦ **ostensibly** *adv*: **he was ostensibly a student** il était soi-disant étudiant; **he went out, ostensibly to telephone** il est sorti sous prétexte de téléphoner.

ostentatious [ˌɒsten'teɪʃəs] *adj surroundings, person* prétentieux; *dislike, attempt* exagéré, ostentatoire. ♦ **ostentation** *n* ostentation *f*. ♦ **ostentatiously** *adv* avec ostentation.

osteo... ['ɒstɪəʊ] *pref* ostéo... . ♦ **osteoarthritis** *n* ostéoarthrite *f*. ♦ **osteopath** *n* ostéopathe *mf*. ♦ **osteopathy** *n* ostéopathie *f*.

ostracize ['ɒstrəsaɪz] *vt* frapper d'ostracisme. ♦ **ostracism** *n* ostracisme *m*.

ostrich ['ɒstrɪtʃ] *n* autruche *f*.

other ['ʌðəʳ] **1** *adj* autre. **the ~ one** l'autre *mf*; **the ~ 5** les 5 autres; **~ people have done it** d'autres l'ont fait; **~ people's property** la propriété d'autrui; **the ~ day** l'autre jour; **some ~ day** un autre jour; **~ than** autre que; **someone or ~ said** je ne sais qui a dit; **some writer or ~** je ne sais quel écrivain; **some fool or ~** un idiot quelconque.

2 *pron* autre *mf*. **some ~s** d'autres; **several ~s** plusieurs autres; **one after the ~** l'un après l'autre; **some ... ~s ...** les uns ... les autres ...; **one or ~ of them will come** il y en aura bien un qui

viendra; **that man of all ~s** cet homme entre tous; **you and no ~** vous et personne d'autre; **no ~ than** nul autre que.

3 *adv* autrement (*than* que). **I couldn't do ~ than come** je ne pouvais faire autrement que de venir; **no one ~ than** nul autre que.

♦ **otherwise 1** *adv* (*in another way*) autrement; (*in other respects*) autrement, à part cela; **it cannot be ~wise** il ne peut en être autrement; **he was ~wise engaged** il était occupé à autre chose; **except where ~wise stated** sauf indication contraire; **should it be ~wise** dans le cas contraire; **an ~wise excellent essay** une dissertation par ailleurs excellente; **2** *conj* autrement, sinon.

otter ['ɒtəʳ] *n* loutre *f*.

ouch [aʊtʃ] *excl* aïe!

ought[1] [ɔːt] *pret* **ought** *modal aux vb* **I ~ to do it** je devrais le faire, il faudrait que je le fasse; **I ~ to have done it** j'aurais dû le faire; **he thought he ~ to tell you** il a pensé qu'il devait vous le dire; **if they behave as they ~** s'ils se conduisent comme ils le doivent.

ought[2] [ɔːt] *n* = **aught.**

ounce [aʊns] *n* once *f* (= *28,35 grammes*).

our ['aʊəʳ] *poss adj* notre, *pl* nos. ♦ **ours** *poss pron* le nôtre, la nôtre, les nôtres; **this car is ~s** cette voiture est à nous *or* nous appartient *or* est la nôtre; **a friend of ~s** un de nos amis (à nous), un ami à nous*. ♦ **ourselves** *pers pron* (*reflexive: direct and indirect*) nous; (*emphatic*) nous-mêmes; (*after prep*) nous; **we've hurt ~selves** nous nous sommes blessés; **we said to ~selves** nous nous sommes dit, on s'est dit*; **we saw it ~selves** nous l'avons vu nous-mêmes; **we were talking amongst ~selves** nous discutions entre nous; **(all) by ~selves** tout seuls, toutes seules.

oust [aʊst] *vt* évincer (*from* de), supplanter (*sb as* qn comme).

out [aʊt] **1** *adv* **(a)** (*outside; not here etc*) dehors. **he's ~ in the garden** il est dans le jardin; **Paul is ~** Paul est sorti *or* n'est pas là; **he's ~ fishing** il est parti à la pêche; **to be ~ and about again** être de nouveau sur pied; **you should be ~ and about!** ne restez donc pas enfermé!; **to go** *ou* **get ~** sortir; **to lunch ~** déjeuner dehors; **to have a day ~** sortir pour la journée; **it's her evening ~** c'est sa soirée de sortie; **let's have a night ~** si on sortait?; **~ there** là-bas; **~ here** ici; **when he was ~ in Iran** lorsqu'il était en Iran; **the voyage ~** l'aller *m*; **the boat was 10 km ~** le bateau était à 10 km du rivage; **5 days ~ from Liverpool** à 5 jours de Liverpool; (*Sport*) **the ball is ~** le ballon est sorti; (*Tennis*) '**~**!' 'dehors!'; **~ loud** tout haut; **~ with it!** vas-y, parle!

(b) (*fig*) **to be ~** *[person]* (*unconscious*) être sans connaissance; (*out of game etc*) être éliminé; (*on strike*) être en grève; (*out of fashion*) être démodé; (*have appeared etc*) *[roses etc]* être épanoui; *[trees]* être vert, (*in blossom*) être en fleurs; *[stars]* briller; *[moon, sun]* être levé; *[secret, news]* être révélé; *[book]* être publié; *[tide]* être bas; (*extinguished*) *[light, fire, gas]* être éteint; **the socialists are ~** les socialistes ne sont plus au pouvoir; **before the month was ~** avant la fin du mois; (*wrong*) **he was ~ in his calculations, his calculations were ~** il s'est trompé dans ses calculs (*by 20 cm* de 20 cm); **you're not far ~** tu ne te trompes pas de beaucoup; **my watch is 10 minutes ~** ma montre (*fast*) avance *or* (*slow*) retarde de 10 minutes; (*want*) **to be ~ for sth/to do** vouloir à tout prix qch/faire; **they were ~ to get him** ils avaient résolu sa perte; **to be all ~*** être éreinté; **the car was going all ~** *or* **flat ~** la voiture fonçait à toute vitesse; (*unequivocally*) **right ~, straight ~** franchement; **it's the best car ~*** c'est la meilleure voiture qu'il y ait; **~ and away the youngest** de loin le plus jeune.

2 out of *prep* **(a)** (*outside*) en dehors de, hors de. **to go** *or* **come ~ of the room** sortir de la pièce; **let's get ~ of here!** ne restons pas ici!, partons!; **~ of the window** par la fenêtre; **~ of the way!** écartez-vous!; **you're well ~ of it** c'est aussi bien que vous ne soyez pas dans le coup*; **to feel ~ of it** ne pas se sentir dans le coup*. **(b)** (*cause, motive*) par. **~ of curiosity** par curiosité. **(c)** (*origin, source*) de; dans. **one chapter ~ of a novel** un chapitre d'un roman; **a box made ~ of onyx** une boîte en onyx; **he made the table ~ of a crate** il a fait la table avec une caisse; **carved ~ of wood** sculpté dans le bois; **to eat/drink ~ of sth** manger/boire dans qch; **to take sth ~ of a drawer** prendre qch dans un tiroir; **he copied the poem ~ of a book** il a copié le poème dans un livre; **it was like sth ~ of a nightmare** on aurait dit un cauchemar. **(d)** (*from among*) sur. **in 9 cases ~ of 10** dans 9 cas sur 10; **one ~ of 5 smokers** un fumeur sur 5. **(e)** (*without*) sans. **to be ~ of money** être sans argent, ne plus avoir d'argent.

♦ **out-and-out** *adj fool, liar, crook* fieffé; *revolutionary, believer* à tout crin; *defeat, victory* total. ♦ **outback** *n* (*Austr*) intérieur *m* du pays. ♦ **outbid** *pret* **- bid,** *ptp* **-bidden** *vt* enchérir sur. ♦ **outboard** *adj, n* hors-bord (*m*) *inv*. ♦ **outbreak** *n [war, fighting, disease, epidemic etc]* début *m*; *[violence, spots]* éruption *f*; *[emotion, anger, fever]* accès *m*; *[demonstrations]* vague *f*; **at the ~break of war** lorsque la guerre a éclaté. ♦ **outbuildings** *npl* dépendances *fpl*. ♦ **outburst** *n* explosion *f*; (*angry ~*) crise *f* de colère. ♦ **outcast** *n* proscrit(e) *m(f)*; (*socially*) paria *m*. ♦ **outcome** *n* issue *f*, résultat *m*. ♦ **outcrop** *n* (*Geol*) affleurement *m*. ♦ **outcry** *n* protestations *fpl*; **to raise an ~cry about sth** ameuter l'opinion sur qch. ♦ **outdated** *adj* (*gen*) démodé; *word, custom* vieilli. ♦ **outdistance** *vt* distancer. ♦ **outdo** *pret* **outdid,** *ptp* **outdone** *vt* l'emporter sur (*sb in sth* qn en qch); **he was not to be ~done** il refusait de s'avouer vaincu. ♦ **outdoor** *adj activity, games* de plein air; *swimming pool* à ciel ouvert; *clothes* chaud, imperméable; *life* au grand air. ♦ **outdoors 1** *adv stay, play* dehors; *live* au grand air; *sleep* à la belle étoile; **2** *n*: **the great ~doors** le grand air. ♦ **outer** *adj door, wrapping* extérieur; *garments* de dessus; *space* cosmique; **the ~er suburbs** la grande banlieue. ♦ **outermost** *adj* le plus à l'extérieur. ♦ **outfit** *etc V below*. ♦ **outgoing** *adj tenant, president* sortant; *train, boat, plane, mail* en partance; *tide* descendant; (*fig*) *person, personality* ouvert. ♦ **outgoings** *npl* dépenses *fpl*. ♦ **outgrow** *pret* **outgrew,** *ptp* **outgrown** *vt clothes* devenir trop grand pour; *hobby* ne plus s'intéresser à (en grandissant); *habit* perdre en prenant de l'âge. ♦ **outhouse** *n* appentis *m*. ♦ **outing** *n* sortie *f*, excursion *f*. ♦ **outlandish** *adj* exotique; (*pej*) bizarre. ♦ **outlast** *vt* survivre à. ♦ **outlaw 1** *n* hors-la-loi *m inv*; **2** *vt person* mettre hors la loi; *conduct* proscrire. ♦ **outlay** *n* frais *mpl*, dépenses *fpl*. ♦ **outlet 1** *n* (*for water etc*) sortie *f*; (*US Elec*) prise *f* de courant; *[lake]* déversoir *m*; *[river, stream]* embouchure *f*; *[tunnel]* sortie; (*for manufactured goods, talents etc*) débouché *m*; (*for energy, emotions*) exutoire *m* (*for* à); **2** *adj pipe, valve* d'échappement. ♦ **outline** *V below*. ♦ **outlive** *vt* survivre à (*by* de). ♦ **outlook** *n* (*view*) vue *f* (*on, over* sur); (*fig: prospect*) perspective *f* (d'avenir); (*point of view*) attitude *f* (*on* à l'égard de), point *m* de vue (*on* sur); **the ~look for June is wet** on annonce de la pluie pour juin; **the ~look is rather rosy*** les choses s'annoncent assez bien (*for* pour). ♦ **outlying** *adj* (*peripheral*) périphérique; (*remote*) écarté. ♦ **outmoded** = **outdated.** ♦ **outnumber** *vt* surpasser en nombre. ♦ **out-of-date** *adj passport, ticket* périmé; *custom* désuet; *clothes, theory, concept* démodé; *word* vieilli. ♦ **out-of-doors** *adv* = **outdoors 1.**

♦ **out-of-pocket expenses** *npl* débours *mpl*. ♦ **out-of-the-way** *adj place* écarté, perdu; (*unusual*) insolite. ♦ **outpace** *vt* distancer. ♦ **outpatient** *n* malade *mf* en consultation externe; ~**patients department** service *m* (hospitalier) de consultation externe. ♦ **outpost** *n* avant-poste *m*. ♦ **output** *n* (*gen*) production *f*; *[land, machine, factory worker]* rendement *m*; (*Computers*) sortie *f*; (*Elec*) puissance *f* fournie. ♦ **outrage** *V below*. ♦ **outrider** *n* motocycliste *m*, motard* *m* (*d'une escorte*). ♦ **outright 1** *adv kill* sur le coup; *win, own* complètement; *buy* comptant; *reject, refuse, deny* catégoriquement; (*forthrightly*) *say* carrément; **2** *adj win* complet, total; *selfishness* pur; *denial etc* catégorique; *supporter* inconditionnel; *winner* incontesté. ♦ **outrun** *pret* **-ran**, *ptp* **-run** *vt* distancer. ♦ **outset** *n* début *m*. ♦ **outshine** *pret, ptp* **-shone** *vt* éclipser. ♦ **outside** *V below*. ♦ **outsize** *adj* (*gen*) énorme; *clothes* grande taille *inv*; *shop* spécialisé dans les grandes tailles. ♦ **outskirts** *npl [town]* faubourgs *mpl*, banlieue *f*; *[forest]* lisière *f*. ♦ **outspoken** *adj* franc. ♦ **outspokenly** *adv* franchement, carrément. ♦ **outspokenness** *n* franchise *f*. ♦ **outstanding** *adj* **(a)** (*exceptional*) remarquable, exceptionnel; *detail, event* marquant; *feature* dominant; **(b)** (*unfinished etc*) *business* en suspens; *account, debt* impayé; *interest* à échoir; *problem* non résolu; **the work is still ~standing** ce travail reste à faire. ♦ **outstandingly** *adv* remarquablement, exceptionnellement. ♦ **outstay** *vt*: **to ~stay sb** rester plus longtemps que qn; **to ~stay one's welcome** abuser de l'hospitalité de qn. ♦ **outstretched** *adj body, leg* étendu; *arm* tendu; *wings* déployé. ♦ **outstrip** *vt* devancer. ♦ **outward 1** *adv* (*also* ~**wards**) vers l'extérieur; (*Naut*) ~**ward bound** en partance (*for* pour, *from* de); **2** *adj movement* vers l'extérieur; *ship, freight* en partance; *appearance etc* extérieur; ~**ward journey** aller *m*; **with an ~ward show of pleasure** en faisant mine d'être ravi. ♦ **outwardly** *adv* extérieurement, du dehors; (*apparently*) en apparence. ♦ **outweigh** *vt* l'emporter sur. ♦ **outwit** *vt* se montrer plus malin que. ♦ **outworn** *adj clothes* usé; *custom, doctrine, idea* périmé.

outfit ['aʊtfɪt] *n* **(a)** (*clothes and equipment*) équipement *m*; (*tools*) matériel *m*. **a Red Indian ~** une panoplie d'Indien; **puncture repair ~** trousse *f* de réparation (de pneus). **(b)** (*set of clothes*) tenue *f*. **skiing ~** tenue *f* de ski. **(c)** (*: *organization etc*) équipe* *f*. **he's not in our ~** il n'est pas un des nôtres.

♦ **outfitter** *n*: **gents' ~ter** spécialiste *mf* de confection pour hommes; **sports ~ter's** maison *f* d'articles de sport.

outline ['aʊtlaɪn] **1** *n [object]* contour *m*; *[building, tree, face]* profil *m*; (*shorthand*) sténogramme *m*; (*résumé*) esquisse *f*. (*main features*) ~**s** grandes lignes *fpl*; **rough ~ of an article** canevas *m* d'un article; **to give the broad ~s of sth** esquisser qch à grands traits.

2 *vt theory, plan, idea* exposer les grandes lignes de; *book, event* faire un bref compte rendu de; *facts, details* passer brièvement en revue; *situation* donner un aperçu de.

outrage ['aʊtreɪdʒ] **1** *n* (*act*) atrocité *f*; (*during riot etc*) acte *m* de violence; (*emotion*) intense indignation *f*. **it's an ~ against humanity** c'est un crime contre l'humanité; **an ~ against justice** un outrage à la justice; **bomb ~** attentat *m* à la bombe; **it's an ~!** c'est un scandale! **2** *vt* [aʊt'reɪdʒ] *sb's feelings* outrager. **to be ~d by sth** trouver qch monstrueux. ♦ **outrageous** *adj crime, suffering, action* atroce, monstrueux; *remark* outrageant; *sense of humour* scabreux; *price* exorbitant; *hat, fashion* extravagant; **it's ~ous that ...** il est scandaleux que ... + *subj*. ♦ **outrageously** *adv suffer* atrocement; *behave, speak, lie* outrageusement; *dress* de manière grotesque; *expensive* atrocement.

outside [ˌaʊt'saɪd] **1** *adv* (au) dehors, à l'extérieur. **go and play ~** va jouer dehors; **the box was clean ~** la boîte était propre à l'extérieur; **to go ~** sortir.

2 *prep* **(a)** (*lit*) à l'extérieur de, hors de. **~ the house** dehors, à l'extérieur de la maison, hors de la maison; **~ the door** à la porte; **don't go ~ the garden** ne sors pas du jardin; **~ the harbour** au large du port. **(b)** (*fig*) en dehors de. **~ the festival proper** en dehors du vrai festival; **it's ~ the normal range** ceci sort de la gamme normale.

3 *n* extérieur *m* (*also fig*), dehors *m*. **~ in** = **inside out** (*V* **inside**); (*fig*) **judging from the ~** à en juger par les apparences; **he passed the car on the ~** il a doublé la voiture (*Brit*) sur la droite *or* (*US, Europe etc*) sur la gauche; **at the very ~** tout au plus, au maximum.

4 *adj* extérieur (*also fig*); (*maximum*) maximum. (*in plane etc*) **an ~ seat** une place côté couloir; (*Aut*) **the ~ lane** (*Brit*) la voie de droite; (*US, Europe etc*) la voie de gauche; (*Rad, TV*) **~ broadcast** émission *f* réalisée à l'extérieur; **to get an ~ opinion** demander l'avis d'une personne indépendante; (*fig*) **an ~ chance** une très faible chance.

♦ **outside-left/-right** *n* ailier *m* gauche/droit. ♦ **outsider** *n* (*stranger*) étranger *m*, -ère *f*; (*horse or person unlikely to win*) outsider *m*.

oval ['əʊvəl] *adj*, *n* ovale (*m*).

ovary ['əʊvərɪ] *n* ovaire *m*.

ovation [əʊ'veɪʃən] *n* ovation *f*.

oven ['ʌvn] **1** *n* four *m*. (*Culin*) **in the ~** au four; **in a hot/cool ~** à four chaud/doux; **it is like an ~** c'est une fournaise. **2** *adj*: **~ glove** gant *m* isolant. ♦ **ovenproof** *adj* allant au four. ♦ **oven-ready** *adj* prêt à cuire. ♦ **ovenware** *n* plats *mpl* allant au four.

over ['əʊvə^r] **1** *adv* **(a)** (*above*) (par-)dessus. **children of 8 and ~** enfants à partir de 8 ans. **(b)** (*across*) **~ here** ici; **~ there** là-bas; **he has gone ~ to Belgium** il est parti en Belgique; **they're ~ from Canada** ils arrivent du Canada; **he drove us ~ to the other side of town** il nous a conduits de l'autre côté de la ville; (*Telec etc*) **~ to you!** à vous!; **he went ~ to his mother's** il est passé chez sa mère; **let's ask Paul ~** si on invitait Paul à venir nous voir?; **I'll be ~ at 7 o'clock** je passerai à 7 heures; **they were ~ for the day** ils sont venus passer la journée; (*fig*) **he went ~ to the enemy** il est passé à l'ennemi; (*fig*) **I've gone ~ to a new brand of coffee** j'ai changé de marque de café; **~ against the wall** là-bas contre le mur. **(c) all ~** partout; **the world ~** dans le monde entier; **covered all ~ with dust** tout couvert de poussière; **embroidered all ~** tout brodé; **he was trembling all ~** il tremblait de tous ses membres; (*fig*) **that's him all ~!** c'est bien de lui! **(d)** (*down etc*) **he hit her and ~ she went** il l'a frappée et elle a basculé; **he turned the watch ~ and ~** il a retourné la montre dans tous les sens. **(e)** (*again*) encore (une fois). **~ and ~ (again)** à maintes reprises; **5 times ~** 5 fois de suite; **start all ~ again** recommencez au début. **(f)** (*finished*) fini. **the rain is ~** la pluie s'est arrêtée; **the danger was ~** le danger était passé; **it was just ~** cela venait de finir *or* de se terminer; **~ and done with** tout à fait fini. **(g)** (*too*) trop, très. **she's not ~ strong** elle n'est pas trop *or* tellement solide. **(h)** (*remaining*) en plus. **if there is any meat (left) ~** s'il reste de la viande; **there are 3 ~** il en reste 3; **6 metres and a bit ~** un peu plus de 6 mètres.

2 *prep* **(a)** (*on top of*) sur, par-dessus. **he spread the blanket ~ the bed** il a étendu la couverture sur le lit; **I spilled coffee ~ it** j'ai renversé du café dessus; **she put on a cardigan ~ her blouse** elle a mis un gilet par-dessus son corsage. **(b)** (*above*) au-dessus de. **a lamp ~ the table** une lampe au-dessus de la table. **(c)** (*across*) par-dessus; de l'autre côté de. **the house ~ the road** la maison d'en face; **there is a café ~ the road** il y a un café en face; **the bridge ~ the river** le pont qui traverse la rivière; **it's just ~ the river** c'est juste de l'autre côté de la rivière; **tourists from ~ the Atlantic** touristes *mpl* d'outre-Atlantique; **to look ~ the wall/sb's shoulder** regarder par-dessus le mur/l'épaule de qn; **to jump ~ a wall** sauter un mur; **~ the border** au-delà de la frontière. **(d)** (*fig*) (*during*) au cours de, pendant; (*near*) près de. **~ Friday** jusqu'à vendredi soir; **~ a period of** sur une période de; **sitting ~ the fire** assis tout près du feu; **~ a cup of coffee** (tout) en buvant une tasse de café; **~ the phone** au téléphone; **~ the radio** à la radio; **how long will you be ~ it?** combien de temps cela te prendra-t-il?; **what came ~ you?** qu'est-ce qui t'a pris?; **they fell out ~ money** ils se sont brouillés pour une question d'argent; **an increase ~** une augmentation par rapport à; **~ and above what ...** sans compter ce que ...; **but ~ and above that ...** mais en outre *or* par-dessus le marché ... . **(e)** (*everywhere in*) **all ~ France** partout en France; **all ~ the world** dans le monde entier. **(f)** (*more than*) plus de, au-dessus de. **~ 3 hours** plus de 3 heures; **she is ~ sixty** elle a plus de soixante ans; **women ~ 21** les femmes (âgées) de plus de 21 ans; **all numbers ~ 20** tous les chiffres au-dessus de 20.

3 *pref e.g.* **overabundant** surabondant; **overcautious** trop prudent, prudent à l'excès; **overcautiousness** excès *m* de prudence.

♦ **overact** *vi* exagérer son rôle. ♦ **overactive** *adj* trop actif. ♦ **overall 1** *adv survey* en général; *measure, decorate* d'un bout à l'autre; **2** *adj study, survey* d'ensemble; *width, length* total; (*Aut*) **~all measurements** encombrement *m*; **3** *n* blouse *f* (*de travail*); (*Ind etc*) **~s** bleus *mpl* (de travail). ♦ **overanxious** *adj* trop anxieux. ♦ **overawe** *vt* impressionner. ♦ **overbalance 1** *vi* basculer; **2** *vt* faire basculer. ♦ **overbearing** *adj* autoritaire. ♦ **overboard** *adv* par-dessus bord; **man ~board!** un homme à la mer!; (*fig*) **to go ~board for sth** s'emballer* pour qch. ♦ **overburden** *vt* surcharger (*with* de). ♦ **overcast** *adj* couvert. ♦ **overcharge 1** *vt* **(a) to ~charge sb for sth** faire payer qch trop cher à qn; **(b)** (*Elec*) surcharger; **2** *vi* demander un prix excessif. ♦ **overcoat** *n* manteau *m*; *[soldier]* capote *f*; *[sailor]* caban *m*. ♦ **overcome** *pret* **~came**, *ptp* **~come** *vt enemy, opposition* triompher de; *temptation, obstacle* surmonter; *one's rage etc* maîtriser; **we shall ~come!** nous vaincrons!; **to be ~come by** succomber à; **~come with fear** paralysé par la peur; **she was quite ~come** elle était saisie. ♦ **overconfidence** *n* suffisance *f*, présomption *f*. ♦ **overconfident** *adj* suffisant, présomptueux. ♦ **overcook** *vt* faire trop cuire. ♦ **overcrowded** *adj room, bus* bondé; *house, town* surpeuplé; *class* surchargé. ♦ **overcrowding** *n* (*in housing, town*) surpeuplement *m*; (*in classroom*) effectifs *mpl* surchargés; (*in bus etc*) encombrement *m*. ♦ **overdo** *pret* **~did**, *ptp* **~done** *vt* (*exaggerate*) exagérer; (*overcook*) faire trop cuire; **don't ~do the smoking** ne fume pas trop; **to ~do it, to ~do things** (*exaggerate*) exagérer; (*work etc too hard*) s'éreinter, se surmener. ♦ **overdone** *adj* exagéré; (*overcooked*) trop cuit. ♦ **overdose** *n* surdose *f*; **to take an ~dose*** prendre une surdose de sédatifs (*or* barbituriques *etc*). ♦ **overdraft** *n* (*Fin*) découvert *m*; **I've got an ~draft** mon compte est à découvert. ♦ **overdraw** *pret* **~drew**, *ptp* **~drawn** *vt* (*Fin*) mettre à découvert. ♦ **overdrawn** *adj* à découvert. ♦ **overdress 1** *n* robe-chasuble *f*; **2** *vi* s'habiller avec trop de recherche. ♦ **overdrive** *n* (*Aut*) (vitesse *f*) surmultipliée *f*. ♦ **overdue** *adj train, bus* en retard; *reform* qui tarde (à être réalisé); *acknowledgement, apology* tardif; *account* impayé; **the plane is 20 minutes ~due** l'avion a 20 minutes de retard; **that change is long ~due** ce changement se fait attendre depuis longtemps. ♦ **overeat** *pret* **~ate**, *ptp* **~eaten** *vi* trop manger. ♦ **overeating** *n* excès *mpl* de table. ♦ **overestimate** *vt* surestimer. ♦ **overexcited** *adj* surexcité. ♦ **overexert** *vt*: **to ~exert o.s.** se surmener. ♦ **overexertion** *n* surmenage *m*. ♦ **overexpose** *vt* surexposer. ♦ **overfeed** *pret, ptp* **~fed** *vt* suralimenter. ♦ **overfeeding** *n* suralimentation *f*. ♦ **overflow 1** *n* (*outlet*) trop-plein *m*; *[reservoir etc]* déversoir *m*; (*excess people, objects*) excédent *m*; **2** *vt* déborder de; **3** *vi* déborder (*with* de); **to fill/full to ~flowing** remplir/plein à ras bords; **4** *adj pipe* d'écoulement. ♦ **overfly** *pret* **~flew**, *ptp* **~flown** *vt* survoler. ♦ **overgrown** *adj path* envahi par l'herbe; **~grown with** recouvert de. ♦ **overhang** *pret, ptp* **~hung 1** *vt* surplomber; **2** *n* surplomb *m*. ♦ **overhanging** *adj* en surplomb. ♦ **overhaul 1** *n [vehicle, machine]* révision *f*; *[ship]* radoub *m*; **2** *vt* **(a)** (*check*) réviser; radouber; **(b)** (*catch up with*) rattraper. ♦ **overhead 1** *adv* au-dessus; (*in the sky*) dans le ciel; **2** *adj cables, railway* aérien; *lighting* vertical; **3** *n* (*US*) **~head**, (*Brit*) **~heads** frais *mpl* généraux. ♦ **overhear** *pret, ptp* **~heard** *vt* entendre (*souvent par hasard*). ♦ **overheat 1** *vt* surchauffer; **2** *vi [engine]* chauffer. ♦ **overheated** *adj room* surchauffé; *brakes, engine* qui chauffe. ♦ **overjoyed** *adj* ravi, enchanté (*at, by* de; *to do* de faire; *that* que + *subj*). ♦ **overkill** *n* (*Mil*) (capacité *f* de) surextermination *f*. ♦ **overladen** *adj* surchargé. ♦ **overland** *adj, adv* par voie de terre. ♦ **overlap 1** *n* chevauchement *m*; **2** *vi* se chevaucher. ♦ **overlay 1** *vt* recouvrir (*with* de); **2** *n* revêtement *m*. ♦ **overleaf** *adv* au verso. ♦ **overload 1** *n* surcharge *f*; **2** *vt circuit, truck* surcharger (*with* de); *engine* surmener. ♦ **overlook** *vt* **(a)** *[house etc]* donner sur; **our garden is not ~looked** les voisins n'ont pas vue sur notre jardin; **(b)** (*miss*) oublier; **(c)** (*ignore*) fermer les yeux sur. ♦ **overlord** *n* (*gen*) chef *m* suprême; (*Hist*) suzerain *m*. ♦ **overmuch 1** *adv* trop; **2** *adj* trop de. ♦ **overnight 1** *adv* (*during the night*) (pendant) la nuit; (*until next day*) jusqu'à demain *or* au lendemain; (*suddenly*) du jour au lendemain; **2** *adj stay* d'une nuit; *journey* de nuit; (*fig*) *change* soudain; **~night bag** nécessaire *m* de voyage. ♦ **overpass** *n* (*Aut*) pont *m* autoroutier. ♦ **overpay** *pret, ptp* **~paid** *vt* trop payer; **he was ~paid by £5** on lui a payé 5 livres de trop. ♦ **overpayment** *n* surpaye *f*. ♦ **overpopulated** *adj* surpeuplé. ♦ **overpopulation** *n* surpopulation *f* (*in* dans). ♦ **overpower** *vt* (*subdue physically*) maîtriser; (*defeat*) vaincre; (*fig*) accabler. ♦ **overpowering** *adj strength, desire* irrésistible; *smell, heat* suffocant. ♦ **overrate** *vt* surestimer, faire trop grand cas de. ♦ **overrated** *adj* surfait. ♦ **overreach** *vt*: **to ~reach o.s.** vouloir trop entreprendre. ♦ **overreact** *vi* réagir avec excès. ♦ **override** *pret* **~rode**, *ptp* **~ridden** *vt law* fouler aux pieds; *decision* annuler; *objections, order, wishes* passer outre à; *person* passer outre aux opinions de; **this fact ~rides all others** ce fait l'emporte sur tous les autres. ♦ **overriding** *adj importance* primordial; *factor, item* prépondérant. ♦ **overrule** *vt judgment, decision* annuler; *claim, objection* rejeter; **he was ~ruled by the chairman** la décision du président a prévalu contre lui. ♦ **overrun** *pret* **~ran**, *ptp* **~run 1** *vt [rats, weeds]* envahir; *[troops]* occuper; **2** *vi [programme]* dépasser l'heure prévue (*by* de). ♦ **overseas 1** *adv* outre-mer; (*abroad*) à l'étranger; 2 *adj colony, market* d'outre-mer; *trade* extérieur; *visitor* (venu) d'outre-mer, étranger; *aid* aux pays étrangers; **Ministry of O~seas Development** ≈ ministère *m* de la Coopération. ♦ **oversee** *pret* **~saw,** *ptp* **~seen** *vt* surveiller. ♦ **overseer** *n* (*foreman*) contremaître *m*; *[prisoners, slaves]* surveillant *m*. ♦ **overshadow** *vt [clouds]* obscurcir; (*fig*) éclipser. ♦ **overshoot** *pret, ptp* **~shot** *vt* dépasser. ♦ **oversight** *n* omission *m*, oubli *m*; **by** *or* **through an ~sight** par inadvertance. ♦ **oversimplification** *n* simplification *f* excessive. ♦ **oversimplify** *vt* simplifier à l'extrême. ♦ **oversize(d)** *adj* (*gen*) trop grand; *class* surchargé; *family* trop nombreux. ♦ **oversleep** *pret, ptp* **~slept** *vi* dormir trop longtemps. ♦ **overspend** *pret, ptp* **~spent** *vt* dépenser au-dessus *or* au-delà de. ♦ **overspill** *n* excédent *m* de population; **an ~spill town** une ville-satellite. ♦ **overstep** *vt* outrepasser; **to ~step the mark** dépasser la mesure. ♦ **overtake** *pret* **~took,** *ptp* **~taken** *vt* (*catch up*) rattraper; (*pass*) *car* doubler; *competitor* dépasser; *[storm, night]* surprendre; *[fate]* frapper; **~taken by events** dépassé par les événements. ♦ **overtax** *vt* (*Fin*) surimposer; (*fig*) *sb's strength, patience* abuser de; *person* surmener. ♦ **overthrow** *pret* **~threw,** *ptp* **~thrown** 1 *vt enemy, country* vaincre (définitivement); *dictator, government* renverser; 2 *n* défaite *f*; renversement *m*. ♦ **overtime** *n* (*work, pay*) heures *fpl* supplémentaires; **to work ~time** faire des heures supplémentaires; (*fig*) mettre les bouchées doubles (*to do* pour faire). ♦ **overtone** *n [hostility, anger]* accent *m*; **political ~tones** sous-entendus *mpl* politiques. ♦ **overturn** 1 *vt* (*gen*) renverser; *boat* faire chavirer; 2 *vi* se renverser; *[car, plane, railway coach]* se retourner; *[boat]* chavirer. ♦ **overuse** *vt* abuser de. ♦ **overvalue** *vt* surestimer. ♦ **overweight** *adj*: **to be ~weight** *[person]* être trop gros; *[suitcase etc]* être en excès du poids réglementaire; **to be 5 kilos ~weight** peser 5 kilos de trop. ♦ **overwhelm** *vt [flood, avalanche]* engloutir; *[beauty etc]* bouleverser; *enemy, opponent* écraser; *[emotions, misfortunes, shame]* accabler; *[praise, kindness]* rendre confus; **to ~whelm sb with questions** accabler qn de questions; **~whelmed by his kindness** tout confus de sa bonté; **~whelmed** (*happy*) au comble de la joie; (*sad*) accablé (par la douleur); **~whelmed with work/offers** débordé de travail/submergé d'offres. ♦ **overwhelming** *adj victory, majority, defeat* écrasant; *desire, power, pressure* irrésistible; *misfortune, sorrow, heat* accablant; *welcome* extrêmement chaleureux. ♦ **overwhelmingly** *adv win, defeat* d'une manière écrasante; *vote, accept* en masse. ♦ **overwork** 1 *n* surmenage *m*; 2 *vt* surmener; 3 *vi* se surmener. ♦ **overwrought** *adj* excédé.

overt [əʊ'vɜːt] *adj* déclaré, non déguisé. ♦ **overtly** *adv* ouvertement.

ovulate ['ɒvjʊleɪt] *vi* produire des ovules. ♦ **ovulation** *n* ovulation *f*. ♦ **ovum** *n, pl* **ova** ovule *m*.

owe [əʊ] *vt* (*gen*) devoir (*to* à). **to ~ sb a grudge** garder rancune à qn (*for* de); **you ~ it to yourself to make a success of it** vous vous devez de réussir. ♦ **owing 1** *adj* dû; **the amount owing on ...** ce qui reste dû sur ...; **the money still owing to me** la somme qu'on me doit encore; **2 owing to** *prep* par suite de, en raison de.

owl [aʊl] *n* hibou *m*. ♦ **owlish** *adj* de hibou. ♦ **owlishly** *adv* comme un hibou.

own [əʊn] 1 *adj* propre (*before n*). **his (very) ~ car** sa propre voiture, sa voiture à lui; **with my ~ eyes** de mes propres yeux; **it's all my ~ work!** c'est moi qui ai tout fait moi-même!; **he does his ~ cooking** il fait sa cuisine lui-même; **the house has its ~ garage** la maison a son garage particulier; **my ~ one** mon chéri, ma chérie.

2 *pron* **(a) that's my ~** c'est à moi, c'est le mien; **those are his ~** ceux-là sont à lui, ceux-là sont les siens; **my time is my ~** je suis libre de mon temps; **it's all my ~** c'est tout à moi; **a charm all its ~** *or* **of its ~** un charme qui lui est propre; **for reasons of his ~** pour des raisons personnelles; **a copy of your ~** votre propre exemplaire; **a house of your very ~** une maison bien à vous *or* à vous tout seul; **I have money of my ~** j'ai de l'argent à moi. **(b)** (*phrases*) **(all) on one's ~** tout seul; **to see sb on his ~** voir qn seul à seul; (*fig*) **you're on your ~ now!** à toi de jouer!; **he's got nothing to call his ~** il n'a rien à lui; **to come into one's ~** réaliser sa destinée; **to get one's ~ back** prendre sa revanche (*on sb for sth* sur qn de qch).

3 *vt* **(a)** (*possess*) *object, vehicle* posséder; *house, newspaper, company* être le (*or* la) propriétaire de. **who ~s this?** à qui est-ce que cela appartient?; **he looks as if he ~s the place*** on dirait qu'il est chez lui. **(b)** (*acknowledge*) avouer, reconnaître (*that* que).

4 *vi*: **to ~ to** *mistake* reconnaître avoir commis; *debts* reconnaître avoir. **he ~ed to having done it** il a avoué l'avoir fait.

own up *vi* avouer. **to ~ up to (doing) sth** admettre (avoir fait) qch.

♦ **owner** *n* propriétaire *mf*; **who is the ~er of this book?** à qui appartient ce livre?; **all dog ~ers** tous ceux qui ont un chien. ♦ **owner-driver** *n* conducteur *m* propriétaire. ♦ **owner-occupied** *adj* occupé par son propriétaire. ♦ **owner-occupier** *n* occupant *m* propriétaire. ♦ **ownership** *n* possession *f*; (*Comm*) **'under new ~ership'** 'changement de propriétaire'.

ox [ɒks] *n, pl* **oxen** bœuf *m*. ♦ **oxcart** *n* char *m* à bœufs. ♦ **ox-eye daisy** *n* marguerite *f*. ♦ **oxtail soup** *n* soupe *f* à la queue de bœuf.

oxide ['ɒksaɪd] *n* oxyde *m*. ♦ **oxidize** 1 *vt* oxyder; 2 *vi* s'oxyder.

oxyacetylene ['ɒksɪə'setɪliːn] *adj*: **~ burner** chalumeau *m* oxyacétylénique.

oxygen ['ɒksɪdʒən] 1 *n* oxygène *m*. 2 *adj cylinder* d'oxygène; *mask, tent* à oxygène.

oyster ['ɔɪstəʳ] *n* huître *f*. **the world is his ~** le monde est à lui; **~ bed** banc *m* d'huîtres. **~ shell** coquille *f* d'huître.

ozone ['əʊzəʊn] *n* ozone *m*.

P

P, p [piː] *n* **(a)** (*letter*) P, p *m*. **to mind one's Ps and Qs*** se surveiller. **(b) 1 p** un (nouveau) penny; **2 p** deux (nouveaux) pence.
pa* [pɑː] *n* papa *m*.
pace [peɪs] **1** *n* **(a)** (*measure*) pas *m*. **20 ~s away** à 20 pas; (*fig*) **to put sb through his ~s** mettre qn à l'épreuve. **(b)** (*speed*) pas *m*, allure *f*. **at a good ~** d'un bon pas, à vive allure; **at a slow ~** à pas lents, à petite allure; **at a walking ~** au pas; **to set the ~** (*Sport*) donner l'allure; (*fig*) donner le ton; **to keep ~ with** aller à la même allure que, (*fig*) marcher de pair avec. **2** *vi*: **to ~ up and down** faire les cent pas. **3** *vt* **(a)** *room, street* arpenter. **to ~ sth out** mesurer qch au pas. **(b)** (*Sport*) *runner* régler l'allure de. ♦ **pacemaker** *n* (*Med*) stimulateur *m* cardiaque.
pacify ['pæsɪfaɪ] *vt person, fears* apaiser; *country, creditors* pacifier. ♦ **pacific** *adj* pacifique; **the Pacific (Ocean)** le Pacifique, l'océan *m* Pacifique. ♦ **pacification** *n* apaisement *m*; pacification *f*. ♦ **pacifier** *n* (*dummy-teat*) tétine *f*; (*person*) pacificateur *m*, -trice *f*. ♦ **pacifism** *n* pacifisme *m*. ♦ **pacifist** *adj, n* pacifiste (*mf*).
pack [pæk] **1** *n* **(a)** *[goods, cotton]* balle *f*; *[pedlar]* ballot *m*; *[~ animal]* bât *m*; (*Mil*) sac *m* (d'ordonnance); (*Comm*) paquet *m*. (*US*) **~ of cigarettes** paquet de cigarettes. **(b)** (*group*) *[hounds]* meute *f*; *[wolves, thieves]* bande *f*. **~ of lies** tissu *m* de mensonges. **(c)** *[cards]* jeu *m*. **(d)** (*Rugby*) pack *m*. **(e)** (*Med*) **cold/wet ~** enveloppement *m* froid/humide.
2 *vt* **(a)** (*put into box etc*) *objects, goods* emballer. (*Comm*) **~ed in dozens** en paquets de douze; **~ed lunch** repas froid; **~ed in straw** enveloppé dans de la paille. **(b)** (*fill*) *box, suitcase* remplir (*with* de); *room, vehicle, memory* bourrer (*with* de). **to ~ one's case** faire sa valise; **to ~ one's bags** faire ses bagages *or* ses valises, (*fig*) plier bagage. **(c)** (*crush together*) *earth, objects* tasser (*into* dans); *people* entasser (*into* dans). **~ed like sardines** serrés comme des sardines.
3 *vi* **(a)** (*do one's luggage*) faire sa valise *or* ses bagages. **(b)** *[people]* se presser, s'entasser (*into* dans).
pack away *vt sep* ranger.
pack in‡ **1** *vi* (*break down*) *[car, watch etc]* tomber en panne. **2** *vt sep* (*stop*) laisser tomber*.
pack off* *vt sep* envoyer promener*. **to ~ sb off to** expédier* qn à.
pack up **1** *vi* **(a)** (*do one's luggage*) faire sa valise. **(b)** (*) (*give up*) plier bagage; *[watch, machine]* tomber en panne. **2** *vt sep* **(a)** *clothes, belongings* mettre dans une valise; *object, book* emballer. **(b)** (‡: *give up*) *work, school* laisser tomber*.
♦ **package** **1** *n* (*parcel*) paquet *m*, colis *m*; **2** *adj tour, holiday* organisé; **~age deal** marché *m* global; **3** *vt* (*Comm*) emballer. ♦ **packaging** *n* (*materials*) emballage *m*. ♦ **packed** *adj room, vehicle* bondé. ♦ **packer** *n* (*person*) emballeur *m*, -euse *f*; (*device*) emballeuse *f*. ♦ **packet** *n* (*gen*) paquet *m*; *[needles, sweets]* sachet *m*; **to cost a ~et*** coûter les yeux de la tête. ♦ **packhorse** *n* cheval *m* de charge. ♦ **packing** **1** *n* **(a) to do one's ~ing** faire sa valise; **(b)** (*material*) emballage *m*; **2** *adj*: **~ing case** caisse *f* d'emballage.
pact [pækt] *n* pacte *m*, traité *m*.
pad [pæd] **1** *n* **(a)** (*to prevent friction, damage*) coussinet *m*; (*Tech*) tampon *m* (amortisseur); (*Ftbl*) protège-cheville *m inv*; (*Hockey etc*) jambière *f*; (*for inking*) tampon encreur. **(b)** (*writing ~*) bloc *m* (de papier à lettres); (*note ~*) bloc-notes *m*. **(c)** *[rabbit]* patte *f*; *[cat, dog]* coussin *m* charnu. **(d)** (*launching ~*) rampe *f* (de lancement). **(e)** (*: *sanitary towel*) serviette *f* hygiénique. **2** *vi*: **to ~ along/up** *etc* marcher/monter *etc* à pas feutrés. **3** *vt cushion, clothing, shoulders* rembourrer; *furniture, door* capitonner; (**~ out**) *speech* délayer. **~ded cell** cabanon *m*. ♦ **padding** *n* rembourrage *m*; (*in book etc*) délayage *m*.
paddle ['pædl] **1** *n* pagaie *f*. **2** *adj*: **~ steamer** bateau *m* à roues; **paddling pool** bassin *m* pour enfants; (*for garden*) petite piscine *f* (*démontable*). **3** *vt*: **to ~ a canoe** pagayer. **4** *vi* **(a)** (*walk*) barboter. **(b)** (*in canoe*) pagayer. **to ~ up/down the river** remonter/descendre la rivière en pagayant.
paddock ['pædək] *n* enclos *m* (*pour chevaux*); (*Racing*) paddock *m*.
paddy ['pædɪ] *n*: **~ field** rizière *f*.
padlock ['pædlɒk] **1** *n* *[door, chain]* cadenas *m*; *[cycle]* antivol *m*. **2** *vt* cadenasser; mettre un antivol à.
padre ['pɑːdrɪ] *n* (*Mil, Naut etc*) aumônier *m*.
paediatric, (*US*) **pediatric** [ˌpiːdɪ'ætrɪk] *adj department* de pédiatrie; *illness, medicine, surgery* infantile. ♦ **p(a)ediatrician** *n* pédiatre *mf*. ♦ **p(a)ediatrics** *nsg* pédiatrie *f*.
pagan ['peɪgən] *adj, n* (*lit, fig*) païen(ne) *m(f)*.
page¹ [peɪdʒ] *n* page *f*. **on ~ 10** (à la) page 10; **continued on ~ 20** suite page 20.
page² [peɪdʒ] **1** *n* (*also* **~ boy**) (*in hotel*) groom *m*; (*at court*) page *m*. **2** *vt client* faire appeler; *[page boy]* appeler.
pageant ['pædʒənt] *n* spectacle *m* historique. ♦ **pageantry** *n* apparat *m*.
paid [peɪd] (*pret, ptp of* **pay**) *adj gunman etc* à gages. ♦ **paid-up** *adj member* qui a payé sa cotisation.
pail [peɪl] *n* seau *m*.
pain [peɪn] **1** *n* **(a)** (*physical*) douleur *f*; (*mental*) peine *f*, (*stronger*) douleur. **to be in (great) ~** souffrir (beaucoup); **to cause ~ to** (*physically*) faire mal à; (*mentally*) faire de la peine à; **I have a ~ in my shoulder** j'ai mal à l'épaule; **to give sb a ~ in the neck*** enquiquiner qn*; **he's a ~ (in the neck)*** il est casse-pieds*. **(b)** (*trouble*) **~s** peine *f*; **to take ~s to do sth** faire qch très soigneusement; **to take ~s over sth** se donner beaucoup de mal pour qch; **to spare no ~s** ne pas ménager ses efforts (*to do* pour faire). **(c) on ~ of death** sous peine de mort. **2** *vt* faire de la peine à, faire souffrir. ♦ **pained** *adj* peiné. ♦ **painful** *adj wound* douloureux; *sight, task, duty* pénible; **my hand is ~ful** j'ai mal à la main; **it is ~ful to see her** elle fait peine à voir. ♦ **painfully** *adv throb* douloureusement; *walk* péniblement; (*) *thin* terriblement*; **it was ~fully clear that ...** il n'était que trop évident que ... . ♦ **painkiller** *n* calmant *m*. ♦ **painless** *adj operation* indolore; *extraction, childbirth* sans douleur; (*fig*) *experience* bénin;

exam pas trop méchant*. ♦ **painlessly** *adv* sans douleur. ♦ **painstaking** *adj work* soigné; *person* appliqué, soigneux. ♦ **painstakingly** *adv* avec soin.
paint [peɪnt] **1** *n* peinture *f.* **~s** couleurs *fpl*; **box of ~s** boîte *f* de couleurs. **2** *vt* (*gen, Art*) peindre; (*Med*) badigeonner. **to ~ a wall red** peindre un mur en rouge; **to ~ one's nails** se vernir les ongles; (*fig*) **to ~ the town red** faire la bringue*. **3** *vi* peindre. ♦ **paintbox** *n* boîte *f* de couleurs. ♦ **paintbrush** *n* pinceau *m.* ♦ **painter**[1] *n* (*Art*) peintre *m*; **portrait ~er** portraitiste *mf*; **~er and decorator** peintre décorateur. ♦ **painting** *n* **(a)** (*activity*) (*Art*) peinture *f*; *[buildings]* décoration *f*; **(b)** (*picture*) tableau *m*, toile *f.* ♦ **paintpot** *n* pot *m* de peinture. ♦ **paint-remover** *n* décapant *m* (pour peinture). ♦ **paint-spray** *n* pulvérisateur *m* (de peinture). ♦ **paint-stripper** *n* (*chemical*) décapant *m*; (*tool*) racloir *m.* ♦ **paintwork** *n* peintures *fpl.*
painter[2] ['peɪntəʳ] *n* (*Naut*) amarre *f.*
pair [pɛəʳ] *n* paire *f*; (*man and wife*) couple *m.* **a ~ of trousers** un pantalon; **a ~ of scissors** une paire de ciseaux; **in ~s** à *or* par deux; **the happy ~** l'heureux couple.
pair off *vi [people]* s'arranger deux par deux.
pajamas [pə'dʒɑːməz] *npl* (*US*) pyjama *m.*
Pakistan [ˌpɑːkɪs'tɑːn] *n* Pakistan *m.* ♦ **Pakistani** **1** *adj* pakistanais; **2** *n* Pakistanais(e) *m(f).*
pal* [pæl] *n* copain* *m*, copine* *f.*
palace ['pælɪs] *n* palais *m* (*bâtiment*).
palate ['pælɪt] *n* (*Anat, fig*) palais *m.* ♦ **palatable** *adj food* agréable au goût; *fact etc* acceptable.
palatial [pə'leɪʃəl] *adj* grandiose, magnifique.
palaver* [pə'lɑːvəʳ] *n* (*talk*) palabres *fpl*; (*fuss*) histoires* *fpl*, affaire *f.*
pale [peɪl] **1** *adj face, person* (*naturally*) pâle, (*from sickness, fear*) blême; *colour* pâle. **to grow ~** pâlir; **~ blue eyes** yeux *mpl* bleu pâle. **2** *vi [person]* pâlir, devenir blême. **to ~ into insignificance** perdre toute importance (*beside* comparé à). ♦ **paleness** *n* pâleur *f.*
Palestine ['pælɪstaɪn] *n* Palestine *f.* ♦ **Palestinian** **1** *adj* palestinien; **2** *n* Palestinien(ne) *m(f).*
palette ['pælɪt] *n* palette *f.*
paling ['peɪlɪŋ] *n* (*fence*) palissade *f.*
pall[1] [pɔːl] *vi* perdre son charme (*on sb* pour qn). **it never ~s on you** on ne s'en lasse jamais.
pall[2] [pɔːl] *n* drap *m* mortuaire; *[smoke]* voile *m.*
palliate ['pælɪeɪt] *vt* pallier. ♦ **palliative** *adj, n* palliatif (*m*).
pallid ['pælɪd] *adj* blême, blafard. ♦ **pallor** *n* pâleur *f.*
palm[1] [pɑːm] **1** *n [hand]* paume *f.* (*fig*) **to have sb in the ~ of one's hand** faire de qn ce qu'on veut; (*fig*) **to grease sb's ~** graisser la patte* à qn. **2** *vt* escamoter.
palm off *vt sep* refiler* (*on, onto* à).
♦ **palmist** *n* chiromancien(ne) *m(f).* ♦ **palmistry** *n* chiromancie *f.*
palm[2] [pɑːm] **1** *n* (*tree*) palmier *m*; (*branch*) palme *f*; (*Rel*) rameau *m.* **2** *adj*: **P~ Sunday** dimanche *m* des Rameaux.
palpable ['pælpəbl] *adj* palpable; *error* manifeste. ♦ **palpably** *adv* manifestement.
palpitate ['pælpɪteɪt] *vi* palpiter. ♦ **palpitation** *n* palpitation *f.*
paltry ['pɔːltrɪ] *adj* dérisoire.
pamper ['pæmpəʳ] *vt* dorloter, choyer.
pamphlet ['pæmflɪt] *n* brochure *f.*
pan[1] [pæn] **1** *n* **(a)** (*Culin*) casserole *f*, poêlon *m.* **frying ~** poêle *f*; **roasting ~** plat *m* à rôtir. **(b)** *[scales]* plateau *m*; *[lavatory]* cuvette *f.* **2** *adj*: **~ scrubber** tampon *m* à récurer. **3** *vt* (*: *criticize harshly*) *film, book* éreinter.
pan outǃ *vi* tourner, se passer; (*turn out well*) réussir.
pan[2] [pæn] *vti*: **to ~ (the camera)** panoramiquer.
pan... [pæn] *pref* pan.... ♦ **Pan-African** *adj* panafricain. ♦ **Pan-American** *adj* panaméricain. ♦ **Pan-Asian** *adj* panasiatique.
pancake ['pænkeɪk] **1** *n* crêpe *f.* **as flat as a ~** plat comme une galette. **2** *adj*: **P~ Tuesday** Mardi gras.
panchromatic [ˌpænkrəʊ'mætɪk] *adj* panchromatique.
pancreas ['pæŋkrɪəs] *n* pancréas *m.*
panda ['pændə] *n* panda *m.* **~ car** ≈ voiture *f* pie *inv* (*de la police*).
pandemonium [ˌpændɪ'məʊnɪəm] *n* tohu-bohu *m.*
pander ['pændəʳ] *vi*: **to ~ to** *person* se prêter aux exigences de; *whims* se plier à; *tastes* flatter bassement.
pane [peɪn] *n* vitre *f*, carreau *m.*
panel ['pænl] **1** *n* **(a)** *[door, wall]* panneau *m*; *[ceiling]* caisson *m*; *[dress]* pan *m.* **instrument ~** tableau *m* de bord. **(b)** (*Jur, Admin etc*) (*jury*) jury *m*; (*Rad, TV etc*) (*gen*) invités *mpl*; (*for game*) jury *m.* (*Brit*) **to be on a doctor's ~** être inscrit sur le registre d'un médecin conventionné. **2** *adj*: **~ discussion** réunion-débat *f*; (*Rad/TV*) **~ game** jeu *m* radiophonique/télévisé. **3** *vt* lambrisser. **~led door** porte *f* à panneaux; **oak-~led** lambrissé de chêne. ♦ **panelling,** (*US*) **paneling** *n* panneaux *mpl*, lambris *m.* ♦ **panellist,** (*US*) **panelist** *n* (*Rad, TV*) invité(e) *m(f)*; membre *m* d'un jury.
pang [pæŋ] *n* (*gen*) pincement *m* de cœur. **~s** *[death]* affres *fpl*; *[conscience]* remords *mpl*; **he saw her go without a ~** il l'a vue partir sans regret; **to feel the ~s of hunger** ressentir des tiraillements d'estomac.
panic ['pænɪk] **1** *n* panique *f*, affolement *m.* **to throw into a ~** *crowd* semer la panique dans; *person* affoler, paniquer*; **to get into a ~** s'affoler, paniquer*. **2** *adj fear* panique; *decision* de panique. **it was ~ stations**ǃ ça a été la panique générale*. **3** *vi* s'affoler, être pris de panique. **don't ~!*** pas d'affolement! ♦ **panicky** *adj report, newspaper* alarmiste; *decision, action* de panique; *person* paniquard*. ♦ **panic-stricken** *adj* affolé.
pannier ['pænɪəʳ] *n* (*gen*) panier *m*; *[motorcycle etc]* sacoche *f.*
panorama [ˌpænə'rɑːmə] *n* panorama *m.* ♦ **panoramic** *adj* panoramique.
pansy ['pænzɪ] *n* (*Bot*) pensée *f*; (ǃ *pej*) tanteǃ *f.*
pant [pænt] **1** *vi* haleter. **to ~ for breath** chercher à reprendre son souffle; **he ~ed up the hill** il a grimpé la colline en haletant. **2** *vt* dire en haletant.
pantechnicon [pæn'teknɪkən] *n* grand camion *m* de déménagement.
pantheism ['pænθiːɪzəm] *n* panthéisme *m.*
panther ['pænθəʳ] *n* panthère *f.*
pantomime ['pæntəmaɪm] *n* (*Xmas show: Brit*) spectacle *m* de Noël (*tiré d'un conte de fée*); (*mime*) pantomime *f*; (*pej: fuss*) comédie *f* (*fig pej*). **in ~** en mimant.
pantry ['pæntrɪ] *n* garde-manger *m inv.*
pants [pænts] *npl* (*underwear*) slip *m*; (*trousers*) pantalon *m.* **to catch sb with his ~ down**ǃ prendre qn au dépourvu.
papacy ['peɪpəsɪ] *n* papauté *f.* ♦ **papal** *adj* papal; *bull, legate* du Pape.
paper ['peɪpəʳ] **1** *n* **(a)** papier *m.* **a piece of ~** (*odd bit*) un bout de papier; (*sheet*) une feuille de papier; (*document etc*) un papier; **identity ~s** papiers d'identité; **old ~** paperasses *fpl*; **to put sth down on ~** mettre qch par écrit; **it's a good plan on ~** c'est un bon plan sur le papier. **(b)** (*newspaper*) journal *m.* **to write for the ~s** faire du journalisme; **in the ~** dans le journal. **(c)** (*exam questions*) épreuve *f* (écrite); (*written answers*) copie *f.* **(d)** (*scholarly work*) article *m*;

(*at seminar*) exposé *m*; (*at conference*) communication *f*.

2 *adj doll, towel, handkerchief, napkin* en papier, de papier; *plates, cups* en carton; *industry* du papier; *profit etc* théorique. ~ **bag** sac *m* en papier, (*small*) pochette *f*; ~ **chase** rallye-papier *m*; ~ **clip** trombone *m*; ~ **knife** coupe-papier *m inv*; ~ **mill** (usine *f* de) papeterie *f*; ~ **money** papier-monnaie *m*; ~ **shop*** marchand *m* de journaux; ~ **work** paperasserie *f* (*pej*).

3 *vt room* tapisser. (*fig*) **to ~ over the cracks** replâtrer* la situation.

♦ **paperback 1** *n* livre *m* de poche; **2** *adj* de poche. ♦ **paperboy** *n* (*delivering*) livreur *m* de journaux; (*selling*) vendeur *m* de journaux. ♦ **paperweight** *n* presse-papiers *m inv*.

paprika ['pæprɪkə] *n* paprika *m*.

par [pɑːʳ] *n*: **to be on a ~ with** aller de pair avec; **to feel below ~** ne pas se sentir en forme.

parable ['pærəbl] *n* parabole *f*.

parachute ['pærəʃuːt] **1** *n* parachute *m*. **2** *adj jump* en parachute; *regiment* de parachutistes. **~ drop, ~ landing** parachutage *m*. **3** *vi* descendre en parachute. **4** *vt* parachuter. ♦ **parachutist** *n* parachutiste *mf*.

parade [pə'reɪd] **1** *n* (*procession*) défilé *m*; (*ceremony*) parade *f*, revue *f*. **to be on ~** défiler; **~ ground** terrain *m* de manœuvres; **fashion ~** présentation *f* de collections; **mannequin ~** défilé *m* de mannequins. **2** *vt one's wealth* faire étalage de. **3** *vi* défiler. (*fig*) **to ~* about** *or* **around** se balader*.

paradise ['pærədaɪs] *n* paradis *m*. **bird of ~** oiseau *m* de paradis.

paradox ['pærədɒks] *n* paradoxe *m*. ♦ **paradoxical** *adj* paradoxal. ♦ **paradoxically** *adv* paradoxalement.

paraffin ['pærəfɪn] **1** *n* (*Chem*) paraffine *f*; (*fuel*) pétrole *m*. **liquid ~** huile *f* de paraffine. **2** *adj lamp* à pétrole.

paragon ['pærəgən] *n* modèle *m* (de vertu).

paragraph ['pærəgrɑːf] *n* **(a)** paragraphe *m*, alinéa *m*. **'new ~'** 'à la ligne'; **to begin a new ~** aller à la ligne. **(b)** (*newspaper item*) entrefilet *m*.

parallel ['pærəlel] **1** *adj* parallèle (*with, to* à). **to run ~ to** être parallèle à. **2** *n* (*Geog*) parallèle *m*; (*Math*) (ligne *f*) parallèle *f*. (*fig*) **to draw a ~ between** établir un parallèle entre. ♦ **parallelogram** *n* parallélogramme *m*.

paralysis [pə'ræləsɪs] *n* paralysie *f*. ♦ **paralytic** [,pærə'lɪtɪk] *adj* (*Med*) paralytique; (*: *drunk*) ivre mort. ♦ **paralyze** ['pærəlaɪz] *vt* (*Med, fig*) paralyser; **his arm is paralyzed** il est paralysé du bras; **paralyzed with fear** paralysé de peur.

paramilitary [,pærə'mɪlɪtərɪ] *adj* paramilitaire.

paramount ['pærəmaʊnt] *adj chief* souverain; *importance* suprême (*before n*).

paranoia [,pærə'nɔɪə] *n* paranoïa *f*. ♦ **paranoiac** *adj, n* paranoïaque (*mf*). ♦ **paranoid** *adj* paranoïde.

parapet ['pærəpɪt] *n* parapet *m*.

paraphernalia [,pærəfə'neɪlɪə] *npl* attirail *m*.

paraphrase ['pærəfreɪz] **1** *n* paraphrase *f*. **2** *vt* paraphraser.

paraplegia [,pærə'pliːdʒə] *n* paraplégie *f*. ♦ **paraplegic** *adj, n* paraplégique (*mf*).

parasite ['pærəsaɪt] *n* parasite *m*. ♦ **parasitic(al)** *adj* parasite (*on* de).

parasol [,pærə'sɒl] *n* ombrelle *f*; (*over table etc*) parasol *m*.

paratrooper ['pærətruːpəʳ] *n* parachutiste *m* (*Mil*). ♦ **paratroops** *npl* parachutistes *mpl*.

parboil ['pɑːbɔɪl] *vt* faire bouillir à demi.

parcel ['pɑːsl] **1** *n* colis *m*, paquet *m*; *[land]* parcelle *f*; *[shares]* paquet; *[lies, liars etc]* tas* *m*. **2** *adj*: **~ bomb** paquet *m* piégé; **~ office** bureau *m* de messageries; **by ~ post** par colis postal. **3** *vt* (**~ up**) empaqueter.

parcel out *vt sep* distribuer; (*share*) partager; *land* lotir.

parched [pɑːtʃt] *adj crops, land* desséché, brûlé. *[person]* **to be ~** mourir de soif.

parchment ['pɑːtʃmənt] *n* parchemin *m*.

pardon ['pɑːdn] **1** *n* pardon *m*; (*Rel*) indulgence *f*; (*Jur: free ~*) grâce *f*. **general ~** amnistie *f*. **2** *vt* pardonner (*sb for sth* qch à qn; *sb for doing* à qn d'avoir fait); (*Jur*) gracier; amnistier. **3** *excl* (*apologizing*) pardon!; (*not hearing*) comment? ♦ **pardonable** *adj* pardonnable. ♦ **pardonably** *adv* de façon bien pardonnable.

pare [pɛəʳ] *vt fruit* peler; *nails* rogner; (**~ down**) *expenses* réduire.

parent ['pɛərənt] **1** *n* père *m or* mère *f*. **his ~s** ses parents *mpl*. **2** *adj*: **the ~ animals** (*or* **birds** *etc*) les parents *mpl*; (*Comm, Fin*) **~ company** maison *f* mère. ♦ **parentage** *n* naissance *f*, origine *f*; **of unknown ~age** de parents inconnus. ♦ **parental** [pə'rentl] *adj* parental. ♦ **parenthood** *n* paternité *f or* maternité *f*. ♦ **parent-teacher association** *n* association *f* des parents d'élèves et des professeurs.

parenthesis [pə'renθɪsɪs] *n, pl* **-eses** parenthèse *f*. **in ~** entre parenthèses. ♦ **parenthetic(al)** *adj* entre parenthèses. ♦ **parenthetically** *adv* entre parenthèses.

Paris ['pærɪs] *n* Paris. ♦ **Parisian 1** *adj* parisien; **2** *n* Parisien(ne) *m(f)*.

parish ['pærɪʃ] **1** *n* (*Rel*) paroisse *f*; (*civil*) commune *f*. **2** *adj church* paroissial; *hall* paroissial, municipal. ♦ **parishioner** *n* paroissien(ne) *m(f)*.

parity ['pærɪtɪ] *n* parité *f*.

park [pɑːk] **1** *n* (*gen*) parc *m*; (*public*) jardin *m* public, parc. **2** *adj*: **~ keeper** gardien *m* de parc. **3** *vt* garer, parquer. **4** *vi* se garer, stationner (*Admin*). **I've ~ed** *or* **I'm ~ed by the church** je suis garé près de l'église. ♦ **parking 1** *n* stationnement *m*; **'~ing'** 'stationnement autorisé'; **'no ~ing'** 'stationnement interdit'; **~ing is difficult** il est difficile de trouver à se garer; **2** *adj*: **~ing attendant** gardien *m* de parking; **~ing bay** lieu *m* de stationnement (autorisé); **~ing lights** feux *mpl* de position; **~ing lot** parking *m*; **~ing meter** parcmètre *m*; **~ing place** (*marked out*) créneau *m* de stationnement; **I couldn't find a ~ing place** je n'ai pas pu trouver à me garer; **~ing ticket** P.-V.* *m*, procès-verbal *m*. ♦ **parkway** *n* (*US*) avenue *f*.

parka ['pɑːkə] *n* parka *m*.

parliament ['pɑːləmənt] *n* parlement *m*. **to go into P~** se faire élire député; **member of P~** ≃ député *m* (*for* de); *V* **house**. ♦ **parliamentarian** *adj, n* parlementaire (*mf*). ♦ **parliamentary** *adj* (*gen*) parlementaire; *election* législatif; (*Brit*) **P~ary Secretary** ≃ chef *m* de Cabinet (*to* de).

parlour, (*US*) **parlor** ['pɑːləʳ] **1** *n* (petit) salon *m*. **2** *adj*: **~ game** jeu *m* de société.

parmesan [,pɑːmɪ'zæn] *n* parmesan *m*.

parochial [pə'rəʊkɪəl] *adj* (*Rel*) paroissial; (*fig pej*) de clocher.

parody ['pærədɪ] **1** *n* parodie *f*. **2** *vt* parodier.

parole [pə'rəʊl] **1** *n*: **on ~** (*Mil*) sur parole; (*Jur*) en liberté conditionnelle. **2** *vt* mettre en liberté conditionnelle.

paroxysm ['pærəksɪzəm] *n* (*Med*) paroxysme *m*; *[grief, pain]* paroxysme; *[anger]* accès *m*; *[delight]* transport *m*; *[tears, laughter]* crise *f*.

parquet ['pɑːkeɪ] *n* (**~ flooring**) parquet *m*.

parrot ['pærət] *n* perroquet *m*. **~ fashion** (*adv phr*) comme un perroquet.

parry ['pærɪ] *vt blow* parer; *question* éluder.

parsimony ['pɑːsɪmənɪ] *n* parcimonie *f*. ♦ **parsimonious** *adj* parcimonieux. ♦ **parsimoniously** *adv* parcimonieusement.

parsley ['pɑːslɪ] *n* persil *m*. **~ sauce** sauce *f* persillée.

parsnip ['pɑːsnɪp] n panais m.

parson ['pɑːsn] n (C of E etc) pasteur m; (gen) ecclésiastique m. (Culin) ~'s nose croupion m. ♦ **parsonage** n presbytère m.

part [pɑːt] 1 n (a) (section etc: gen) partie f; (Tech) pièce f. spare ~ pièce détachée; in ~(s) en partie; for the most ~ dans l'ensemble; to be ~ (and parcel) of faire partie (intégrante) de; the hundredth ~ le centième; a man of ~s un homme très doué; the funny ~ of it is that ... le plus drôle dans l'histoire c'est que ...; in ~ two of the book dans la deuxième partie du livre; four-~ serial feuilleton m à quatre épisodes; (Culin) three ~s water to one ~ milk trois mesures d'eau pour une mesure de lait; [verb] principal ~s temps mpl principaux; what ~ of speech is it? à quelle catégorie grammaticale est-ce que cela appartient?; the violin ~ la partie de violon; two-~ song chant m à deux voix; in these ~s dans cette région; in this ~ of the world par ici; in foreign ~s à l'étranger. (b) (share: also Theat etc) rôle m. he had a large ~ in the organization of ... il a joué un grand rôle dans l'organisation de ...; she had some ~ in it elle y était pour qch; to take ~ in participer à; I want no ~ in it je ne veux pas m'en mêler. (c) (side) parti m; (behalf) part f. to take sb's ~ prendre parti pour qn; for my ~ pour ma part, quant à moi; on the ~ of de la part de; to take sth in good ~ prendre qch du bon côté.

2 adj: ~ exchange reprise f en compte; to take sth in ~ exchange reprendre qch en compte; ~ owner copropriétaire mf; ~ payment règlement m partiel; ~ song chant m à plusieurs voix.

3 adv en partie. ~ French en partie français.

4 vt (a) crowd ouvrir un passage dans; boxers, fighters séparer. they were ~ed during the war la guerre les a séparés. (b) to ~ one's hair se faire une raie; his hair was ~ed at the side il portait une raie sur le côté. (c) to ~ company with (leave) fausser compagnie à; (disagree with) ne plus être d'accord avec.

5 vi [crowd] s'ouvrir; [boxers etc] se séparer; [friends] se quitter; [rope] se rompre. to ~ from se séparer de; to ~ with money débourser; possessions se défaire de.

♦ **parting** 1 n séparation f; [waters] partage m; [hair] raie f; (lit, fig) the ~ing of the ways la croisée des chemins; 2 adj gift, words d'adieu; (fig) ~ing shot flèche f du Parthe. ♦ **partly** adv en partie. ♦ **part-time** adj, adv à temps partiel; (half-time) à mi-temps. ♦ **part-timer** n employé(e) m(f) à temps partiel.

partake [pɑː'teɪk] pret partook, ptp partaken vi: to ~ of meal prendre.

partial ['pɑːʃəl] adj (a) (in part) partiel. (b) (biased) partial (towards envers), injuste. (*: like) to be ~ to avoir un faible pour. ♦ **partiality** n (bias) partialité f (for pour; towards envers); (liking) penchant m (for pour). ♦ **partially** adv (a) (partly) en partie; (b) (with bias) avec partialité.

participate [pɑː'tɪsɪpeɪt] vi participer (in à). ♦ **participant** n participant(e) m(f) (in à). ♦ **participation** n participation f (in à).

participle ['pɑːtɪsɪpl] n participe m. past/present ~ participe passé/présent.

particle ['pɑːtɪkl] n (gen, Ling, Phys) particule f; [dust, truth, sense] grain m.

particular [pə'tɪkjʊlər] 1 adj (a) (distinct, special) particulier; (personal) personnel. in this ~ case dans ce cas particulier; for no ~ reason sans raison précise; that ~ brand cette marque-là (et non pas une autre); her ~ choice/type of humour son choix/humour personnel; her ~ bed son lit à elle; nothing ~ rien de particulier or de spécial; he took ~ care over it il y a mis un soin particulier; to pay ~ attention to sth faire bien attention à qch; a ~ friend of his un de ses meilleurs amis. (b) (fussy etc) méticuleux, difficile. she is ~ about whom she goes out with elle ne sort pas avec n'importe qui; ~ about his food difficile pour la nourriture; I'm not ~ cela m'est égal.

2 n (a) in ~ en particulier; nothing in ~ rien en or de particulier. (b) (detail) in every ~ en tout point; he is wrong in one ~ il se trompe sur un point; ~s (information) détails mpl, renseignements mpl; (description) description f, [person] signalement m; (name, address) nom m et adresse f; full ~s tous les renseignements; for further ~s apply to ... pour plus amples renseignements s'adresser à ... .

♦ **particularity** n particularité f. ♦ **particularize** vt spécifier, préciser. ♦ **particularly** adv (in ~) en particulier, spécialement; (notably) notamment, particulièrement; (very carefully) méticuleusement.

partisan [ˌpɑːtɪ'zæn] n partisan m.

partition [pɑː'tɪʃən] 1 n (a) cloison f. glass ~ cloison vitrée. (b) (dividing) [country] partition f; [lands] morcellement m.

2 vt country partager; lands morceler; (~ off) room cloisonner.

partitive ['pɑːtɪtɪv] adj, n partitif (m).

partner ['pɑːtnər] n (Comm, Jur, Med etc) associé(e) m(f); (Sport) partenaire mf; (co-driver) coéquipier m, -ière f; (Dancing) cavalier m, -ière f; (in marriage) époux m, épouse f. senior/junior ~ associé principal/adjoint; ~s in crime complices mpl dans le crime. ♦ **partnership** n association f; to be in ~ship être en association (with avec), être associé (with à); to go into ~ship s'associer (with avec); to take sb into ~ship prendre qn comme associé.

partridge ['pɑːtrɪdʒ] n perdrix f; (Culin) perdreau m.

party ['pɑːtɪ] 1 n (a) (Pol etc) parti m. (b) (group) [travellers] groupe m; [workmen] équipe f; (Mil) détachement m. (c) (Jur etc) partie f. third ~ tierce personne f, tiers m; innocent ~ innocent(e) m(f); to be (a) ~ to être mêlé à; (Jur) être complice de. (d) (celebration) réception f. to give a ~ inviter des amis, donner une surprise-partie, (more formally) donner une soirée, recevoir; birthday ~ fête f d'anniversaire; dinner ~ dîner m; evening ~ soirée f; private ~ réunion f intime; tea ~ thé m. 2 adj politics, leader de parti, du parti; disputes de partis. ~ dress robe f habillée; ~ line (Pol) ligne f du parti; (Telec) ligne commune à deux abonnés; (Rad, TV) ~ political broadcast *émission réservée à un parti politique*, ≃ 'tribune f libre'; ~ political question question f qui relève de la ligne du parti; ~ spirit (Pol) esprit m de parti; (*: gaiety) entrain m; ~ wall mur m mitoyen.

pass [pɑːs] 1 n (a) (permit) [journalist, worker etc] laissez-passer m inv; (Rail etc) carte f d'abonnement; (Theat) billet m de faveur; (Naut) lettre f de mer; (safe conduct) sauf-conduit m. (b) (in mountains) col m, défilé m. (c) (in exam) moyenne f. to get a ~ in history avoir la moyenne en histoire. (d) this is a pretty ~! voilà à quoi on en est arrivé!; things have reached such a ~ that ... les choses en sont arrivées à un tel point que ... . (e) (Ftbl etc) passe f. (fig) to make a ~* at a woman faire du plat* à une femme.

2 adj: ~ degree licence f libre.

3 vi (a) (come, go) passer (through par); [procession] défiler; (Aut: overtake) doubler. to ~ down the street descendre la rue; to ~ into oblivion tomber dans l'oubli; to ~ out of sight disparaître; letters ~ed between them ils ont échangé des lettres. (b) (be accepted) [coins] avoir cours; [behaviour] convenir, être acceptable; [project] passer. to ~ under the name of être connu sous le nom de; what ~es for a hat these days ce qui de nos jours passe pour un

chapeau; **he tried to ~ for a doctor** il a essayé de se faire passer pour un docteur; **she would ~ for 20** on lui donnerait 20 ans; **will this do? - oh it'll ~** est-ce que ceci convient? - oh, ça peut aller; **he let it ~** il l'a laissé passer; **he couldn't let it ~** il ne pouvait pas laisser passer ça comme ça; **the estate ~ed to my brother** la propriété est revenue à mon frère. **(c)** *[time, afternoon etc]* passer. **how time ~es!** que le temps passe vite! **(d)** (**~ away**) *[memory, opportunity]* s'effacer, disparaître; *[pain]* passer. **(e)** (*in exam*) être reçu (*in* en). **(f)** (*take place*) se passer, avoir lieu. **all that ~ed between them** tout ce qui s'est passé entre eux; (*liter*) **it came to ~ that** il advint que. **(g)** (*Cards*) passer; (*Ftbl etc*) faire une passe.

4 *vt* **(a)** (*go past*) *building* passer devant; *person* croiser, rencontrer; *barrier, frontier, customs* passer; (*overtake*) (*gen, Sport*) dépasser; (*Aut*) doubler. **when you have ~ed the town hall** quand vous serez passé devant *or* quand vous aurez dépassé la mairie; **to ~ comprehension** dépasser l'entendement; **to ~ belief** être incroyable; **the film ~ed the censors** le film a reçu le visa de la censure. **(b)** *exam* être reçu à, réussir; *candidate* recevoir; (*Parl*) *bill* voter. **the censors have/haven't ~ed the film** le film a été autorisé/interdit par la censure; (*Scol, Univ*) **they didn't ~ him** ils l'ont refusé; **the doctor ~ed him fit for work** le docteur l'a déclaré en état de reprendre le travail; (*Typ*) **to ~ the proofs (for press)** donner le bon à tirer. **(c)** *time* passer. **to ~ the evening reading** passer la soirée à lire. **(d)** (*hand over*) (faire) passer; (*move*) passer; (*Sport*) *ball* passer; *forged money, stolen goods* écouler. **~ me the box** passez-moi la boîte; **the telegram was ~ed round the room** on a fait passer le télégramme dans la salle; **to ~ sth down the line** faire passer qch (de main en main); **to ~ a rope through a ring** passer une corde dans un anneau; **to ~ blood** avoir du sang dans les urines; **to ~ a stone** évacuer un calcul; **to ~ water** uriner. **(e)** (*utter*) *comment* faire; *opinion* émettre. **to ~ remarks about** faire des observations sur; **to ~ judgment** prononcer un jugement (*on* sur); (*Jur*) **to ~ sentence** prononcer une condamnation (*on sb* contre qn).

pass along 1 *vi* passer. **2** *vt sep* faire passer.

pass away *vi* (*die*) mourir, s'éteindre; *[memory etc]* disparaître.

pass back *vt sep* rendre.

pass by 1 *vi* passer (à côté); *[procession]* défiler. **2** *vt sep* négliger, ignorer. **life has ~ed me by** je n'ai pas vraiment vécu.

pass down 1 *vi [inheritance etc]* être transmis (*to* à). **2** *vt sep* transmettre.

pass off 1 *vi* **(a)** *[faintness etc]* passer. **(b)** *[event]* se passer. **everything ~ed off smoothly** tout s'est passé sans accroc. **2** *vt sep* **(a)** faire passer. **to ~ o.s. off as** se faire passer pour. **(b) to ~ sth off on sb** repasser qch à qn.

pass on 1 *vi* **(a)** (*die*) s'éteindre, mourir. **(b)** (*continue one's way*) passer son chemin. **to ~ on to a new subject** passer à un nouveau sujet. **2** *vt sep* (*hand on*) *object* faire passer (*to* à); *old clothes* repasser (*to sb* à qn); *news* faire circuler; *message* transmettre. **you've ~ed your cold on to me** tu m'as passé ton rhume.

pass out 1 *vi* **(a)** (*faint*) s'évanouir; (*from drink*) tomber ivre mort. **(b)** (*US*) **to ~ out of high school** terminer ses études secondaires. **2** *vt sep leaflets etc* distribuer.

pass over *vt sep*: **to ~ over Paul in favour of Robert** préférer Robert à Paul.

pass round *vt sep bottle* faire passer; *sweets, leaflets* distribuer. (*fig*) **to ~ round the hat** faire la quête.

pass through 1 *vi* passer. **2** *vt fus hardships* subir, endurer; *town, country* traverser.

pass up *vt sep* (*lit*) passer; (**: forego*) *opportunity* laisser passer.

◆ **passable** *adj* **(a)** (*tolerable*) passable; **(b)** *road* praticable; *river* franchissable. ◆ **passably** *adv* passablement, assez. ◆ **passage** *n* **(a)** (*passing*) passage *m*; *[bill, law]* adoption *f*; **with the ~age of time** avec le temps; **(b)** (*Naut*) traversée *f*; **(c)** (*way through*) passage *m*; (*corridor*) couloir *m*; **(d)** *[music, text]* passage *m*. ◆ **passageway** *n* passage *m*. ◆ **passbook** *n* livret *m* (bancaire). ◆ **passer-by** *n* passant(e) *m(f)*. ◆ **passing 1** *adj person, car* qui passe; *remark* en passant; *happiness, guest* passager; *desire* fugitif; **2** *n* (*Aut*) dépassement *m*; (*death*) mort *f*; **with the ~ing of time** avec le temps. ◆ **passing-out parade** *n* défilé *m* de promotion. ◆ **passkey** *n* passe-partout *m inv*. ◆ **passmark** *n* moyenne *f*. ◆ **Passover** *n* Pâque *f* des Juifs. ◆ **passport** *n* passeport *m*; (*fig*) **~port to** clef *f* de. ◆ **password** *n* mot *m* de passe.

passé ['pæseɪ] *adj* vieux jeu *inv*.

passenger ['pæsɪndʒə^r] **1** *n* (*in train*) voyageur *m*, -euse *f*; (*in boat, plane, car*) passager *m*, -ère *f*; (*fig pej*) poids *m* mort. **2** *adj coach, train* de voyageurs; (*Aviat*) *list* des passagers. (*Aut*) **~ seat** siège *m* du passager.

passion ['pæʃən] **1** *n* passion *f*; (*anger*) emportement *m*. **to have a ~ for music** avoir la passion de la musique; **to be in a ~** être furieux. **2** *adj* (*Rel*) **P~ play/Sunday** *etc* mystère *m*/dimanche *m etc* de la Passion. ◆ **passionate** *adj* (*gen*) passionné; *speech* véhément. ◆ **passionately** *adv* passionnément; **to be ~ately fond of** adorer. ◆ **passionflower** *n* passiflore *f*.

passive ['pæsɪv] **1** *adj* (*all senses*) passif. **2** *n* passif *m*. **in the ~** au passif. ◆ **passively** *adv* passivement; (*Gram*) au passif. ◆ **passiveness** *or* ◆ **passivity** *n* passivité *f*.

past [pɑːst] **1** *n* passé *m*. **in the ~** autrefois, dans le passé; (*Gram*) au passé; **it's a thing of the ~** cela n'existe plus, c'est fini.

2 *adj* passé. **for some time ~** depuis quelque temps; **in times ~** autrefois; **the ~ week** la semaine dernière *or* passée; **the ~ few days** ces derniers jours; **all that is ~** tout cela c'est du passé; **~ president** ancien président; **to be a ~ master at doing sth** avoir l'art de faire qch; (*Gram*) **in the ~ tense** au passé.

3 *prep* **(a)** (*in time*) plus de. **it is ~ 11 o'clock** il est plus de 11 heures, il est 11 heures passées; (*Brit*) **half ~ 3** 3 heures et demie; **quarter ~ 3** 3 heures et quart; **at 20 ~ 3** à 3 heures 20; (*Brit*) **the train goes at 5 ~*** le train part à 5*; **she is ~ 60** elle a plus de 60 ans, elle a 60 ans passés. **(b)** (*beyond*) plus loin que. **just ~ the post office** un peu plus loin que la poste, juste après la poste. **(c)** (*in front of*) devant. **he goes ~ the house** il passe devant la maison. **(d)** (*beyond limits of*) au delà de. **~ endurance** insupportable; **~ all belief** incroyable; **I'm ~ caring** je ne m'en fais plus; **he is ~ work** il n'est plus en état de travailler; **he's a bit ~ it*** il n'est plus dans la course*; **that cake is ~ its best** ce gâteau n'est plus si bon; **I wouldn't put it ~ her to have done it** cela ne m'étonnerait pas d'elle qu'elle l'ait fait.

4 *adv* auprès, devant. **to go** *or* **walk ~** passer.

pasta ['pæstə] *n* (*Culin*) pâtes *fpl*.

paste [peɪst] **1** *n* **(a)** (*gen, also Culin*) pâte *f*; *[meat etc]* pâté *m*. **almond ~** pâte d'amandes; **liver ~** pâté de foie; **tomato ~** concentré *m* de tomate; **tooth ~** dentifrice *m*. **(b)** (*glue*) colle *f* (de pâte). **2** *adj jewellery* en strass. **3** *vt* coller; *wallpaper* enduire de colle.

paste up *vt sep notice, list* afficher.

◆ **pasteboard** *n* carton *m*. ◆ **pasting‡** *n* (*thrashing*) rossée* *f*; **to give sb a pasting** flanquer une rossée à qn*. ◆ **pasty** ['peɪstɪ] **1** *adj* pâteux; (*pej*) *face, complexion* terreux; **2** ['pæstɪ] *n* (*Culin*) petit pâté *m*.

pastel ['pæstəl] **1** *n* pastel *m*. **2** *adj* pastel *inv*.
pasteurize ['pæstəraɪz] *vt* pasteuriser.
pastille ['pæstɪl] *n* pastille *f*.
pastime ['pɑːstaɪm] *n* passe-temps *m inv*.
pastor ['pɑːstəʳ] *n* pasteur *m*.
pastry ['peɪstrɪ] *n* **(a)** pâte *f*. **(b)** (*cake*) pâtisserie *f*. ♦ **pastrycase** *n* croûte *f*. ♦ **pastrycook** *n* pâtissier *m*, -ière *f*.
pasture ['pɑːstʃəʳ] *n* pâturage *m*.
pat¹ [pæt] **1** *vt* tapoter; *animal* caresser. **2** *n* **(a)** petite tape *f*; (*on animal*) caresse *f*. **to give o.s. a ~ on the back** s'applaudir. **(b) ~ of butter** noix *f* de beurre.
pat² [pæt] **1** *adv*: **to answer ~** avoir une réponse toute prête. **2** *adj answer, explanation* tout prêt.
patch [pætʃ] **1** *n* **(a)** (*for clothes*) pièce *f*; (*for tube, airbed*) rustine *f*; (*over eye*) bandeau *m*. **he isn't a ~ on his brother*** il n'arrive pas à la cheville de son frère. **(b)** (*small area*) *[colour]* tache *f*; *[sky]* morceau *m*; *[land]* parcelle *f*; *[vegetables]* carré *m*; *[ice]* plaque *f*; *[mist]* nappe *f*; *[water]* flaque *f*. (*fig*) **to strike a bad ~** être dans la déveine*; **bad ~es** moments *mpl* difficiles. **2** *vt clothes* rapiécer; *tyre* réparer.
patch up *vt sep clothes* rapiécer; *machine* rafistoler*; (*) *marriage* replâtrer*. **to ~ up a quarrel** se raccommoder.
♦ **patchwork** *n* patchwork *m*. ♦ **patchy** *adj* inégal.
patent ['peɪtənt] **1** *adj* **(a)** (*obvious*) manifeste, patent. **(b)** *invention* breveté. **~ medicine** spécialité *f* pharmaceutique; **~ leather** cuir *m* verni. **2** *n* brevet *m* d'invention. **3** *vt* faire breveter. ♦ **patently** *adv* manifestement.
paternity [pə'tɜːnɪtɪ] *n* paternité *f*. (*Jur*) **~ order** reconnaissance *f* de paternité judiciaire. ♦ **paternal** *adj* paternel. ♦ **paternalist(ic)** *adj* paternaliste. ♦ **paternally** *adv* paternellement.
path [pɑːθ] *n* **(a)** (*gen*) sentier *m*, chemin *m*; (*in garden*) allée *f*; (*fig*) sentier. **(b)** *[river]* cours *m*; *[sun]* route *f*; *[missile, planet]* trajectoire *f*. ♦ **pathway** *n* sentier *m*.
pathetic [pə'θetɪk] *adj* (*gen*) pitoyable (*also fig pej*); *attempt* désespéré. **it was ~ to see it** cela faisait peine à voir. ♦ **pathetically** *adv* pitoyablement; **~ally thin** d'une maigreur pitoyable; **she was ~ally glad** son plaisir vous serrait le cœur.
pathology [pə'θɒlədʒɪ] *n* pathologie *f*. ♦ **pathological** *adj* pathologique. ♦ **pathologist** *n* pathologiste *mf*.
pathos ['peɪθɒs] *n* pathétique *m*.
patience ['peɪʃəns] *n* **(a)** patience *f*. **to have ~** être patient, (*on one occasion*) prendre patience, patienter; **to lose ~** s'impatienter (*with sb* contre qn); **I have no ~ with these people** ces gens m'exaspèrent. **(b)** (*Cards*) réussite *f*. **to play ~** faire des réussites. ♦ **patient 1** *adj* patient; **2** *n* (*Med*) patient(e) *m(f)*; (*in hospital*) malade *mf*. ♦ **patiently** *adv* patiemment.
patriarch ['peɪtrɪɑːk] *n* patriarche *m*.
patriot ['peɪtrɪət] *n* patriote *mf*. ♦ **patriotic** *adj deed, speech* patriotique; *person* patriote. ♦ **patriotically** *adv* patriotiquement. ♦ **patriotism** *n* patriotisme *m*.
patrol [pə'trəʊl] **1** *n* patrouille *f*. **to be on ~** être de patrouille. **2** *adj vehicle* de patrouille. **~ car** voiture *f* de police; **~ leader** chef *m* de patrouille; (*US*) **~ wagon** voiture *f* cellulaire. **3** *vt district* patrouiller dans. **4** *vi* patrouiller. (*fig*) **to ~ up and down** faire les cent pas. ♦ **patrolman** *n* **(a)** (*US*) agent *m* de police; **(b)** (*Aut*) agent *m* de la sécurité routière.
patron ['peɪtrən] *n* **(a)** *[artist]* protecteur *m*, -trice *f*; *[a charity]* patron(ne) *m(f)*. **~ saint** saint(e) patron(ne) *m(f)*. **(b)** *[hotel, shop]* client(e) *m(f)*; *[theatre]* habitué(e) *m(f)*. ♦ **patronage** *n [artist etc]* patronage *m*. ♦ **patronize** *vt* **(a)** (*pej*) traiter avec condescendance; **(b)** *shop* donner sa clientèle à; *cinema* fréquenter. ♦ **patronizingly** *adv* d'un air condescendant.
patter¹ ['pætəʳ] *n* (*talk*) baratin* *m*.
patter² ['pætəʳ] **1** *n [rain etc]* crépitement *m*. **a ~ of footsteps** un petit bruit de pas pressés. **2** *vi [footsteps, person]* trottiner; *[rain, hail]* crépiter (*on* contre).
pattern ['pætən] **1** *n* **(a)** (*design: on wallpaper etc*) dessin(s) *m(pl)*, motif *m*. **(b)** (*Sewing etc: paper ~*) patron *m*; (*fig*) modèle *m*. **it followed the usual ~** cela s'est passé selon la formule habituelle; **behaviour ~s of teenagers** les types *mpl* de comportement chez les adolescents. **(c)** (*sample of material etc*) échantillon *m*. **2** *adj*: **~ book** *[material, wallpaper etc]* album *m* d'échantillons; (*Sewing*) catalogue *m or* album *m* de modes. **3** *vt* modeler (*on* sur). ♦ **patterned** *adj* à motifs.
paunch [pɔːntʃ] *n* panse *f*.
pauper ['pɔːpəʳ] *n* indigent(e) *m(f)*.
pause [pɔːz] **1** *n* (*gen*) pause *f*, arrêt *m*; (*Mus*) repos *m*. **a ~ in the conversation** un petit silence. **2** *vi* (*stop*) faire une pause, s'arrêter un instant; (*hesitate*) hésiter; (*linger*) s'arrêter (*on* sur). **to ~ for breath** s'arrêter pour reprendre haleine.
pave [peɪv] *vt* paver. **~d with gold** pavé d'or; (*fig*) **to ~ the way** préparer le chemin (*for* pour). ♦ **pavement** *n* **(a)** (*Brit*) trottoir *m*; **(b)** (*US*) chaussée *f*. ♦ **paving** *n* (*stones*) pavés *mpl*; (*flagstones*) dalles *fpl*; (*tiles*) carreaux *mpl*. ♦ **paving stone** *n* pavé *m*.
pavilion [pə'vɪlɪən] *n* pavillon *m*.
paw [pɔː] **1** *n* patte *f*. **2** *vt* **(a)** *[animal]* donner un coup de patte à. *[horse]* **to ~ the ground** piaffer. **(b)** (*sexually*) **to ~ sb*** tripoter* qn.
pawn¹ [pɔːn] *n* (*Chess*) pion *m*. (*fig*) **to be sb's ~** se laisser manœuvrer par qn.
pawn² [pɔːn] **1** *vt* mettre en gage. **2** *n*: **in ~** en gage. ♦ **pawnbroker** *n* prêteur *m*, -euse *f* sur gages. ♦ **pawnshop** *n* bureau *m* de prêteur sur gages.
pay [peɪ] (*vb: pret, ptp* **paid**) **1** *n* (*gen*) salaire *m*; *[manual worker]* paie *f or* paye *f*; (*Mil, Naut*) solde *f*, paie. **in the ~ of** à la solde de; **the ~'s not very good** ce n'est pas très bien payé; **holidays with ~** congés *mpl* payés.
2 *adj*: **~ day** jour *m* de paie; **~ desk** caisse *f*; **~ increase** *or* **rise** augmentation *f* de salaire; **~ packet,** (*US*) **~ envelope** enveloppe *f* de paie; (*fig*) paie *f*; **~ phone,** (*US*) **~ station** cabine *f* téléphonique; **~ TV** télé-banque *f*.
3 *vt* **(a)** *money, person* payer (*to do* à faire; *for doing* pour faire); *tradesman, bill, fee* payer, régler; *deposit* verser; *debt* régler; *loan* rembourser; *interest* rapporter; *dividend* distribuer. **to ~ sb £10** payer 10 livres à qn; **he paid them for the book** il leur a payé le livre; **he paid me £2 for the ticket** il m'a payé le billet 2 livres; **he paid £2 for the ticket** il a payé le billet 2 livres; **he paid a lot for his suit** il a payé son costume très cher; **we're not paid for that** on n'est pas payé pour cela; **that's what you're paid for** c'est pour cela qu'on vous paie; **they ~ good wages** ils paient bien; **I get paid on Fridays** je touche ma paie le vendredi; **to ~ money into an account** verser de l'argent à un compte; (*fig*) **to ~ the penalty** subir les conséquences; **to ~ the price of** payer le prix de; **this paid dividends** ceci a porté ses fruits; **it's ~ing its way** ça couvre ses frais; **he likes to ~ his way** il aime payer sa part; **to put paid to** *plans* mettre par terre; *person* régler son compte à; **it will ~ you to be nice to him** vous gagnerez à *or* vous avez intérêt à être aimable avec lui; **it won't ~ him to tell the truth** il ne gagnera rien à dire la vérité. **(b)** *attention, compliments* faire; *homage* rendre; *V* **visit**.
4 *vi* payer. (*lit, fig*) **to ~ for sth** payer qch; (*fig*) **he paid dearly for it** il l'a payé cher (*fig*); **we'll have to ~ through the nose for it*** cela va nous

coûter les yeux de la tête*; **'~ as you earn' system (P.A.Y.E.)** système *m* fiscal de prélèvement à la source; **does it ~?** est-ce que ça paie?, c'est rentable?; **this business doesn't ~** cette affaire n'est pas rentable; **it ~s to advertise** la publicité rapporte; **it doesn't ~ to tell lies** cela ne sert à rien de mentir; **crime doesn't ~** le crime ne paie pas.

pay back *vt sep* **(a)** *stolen money* restituer; *loan, person* rembourser. **to ~ sb back sth** rembourser qch à qn. **(b)** (*get even with*) **to ~ sb back for doing sth** faire payer à qn qch qu'il a fait; **I'll ~ you back for that!** je vous le revaudrai!

pay down *vt sep* (*as deposit*) verser un acompte de.

pay in *vt sep* (*at bank etc*) verser (*to* à).

pay off 1 *vi [trick, scheme]* être payant; *[decision]* être valable; *[patience]* être récompensé. **2** *vt sep* **(a)** *debts* régler; *creditor* rembourser. **to ~ off a grudge** régler un vieux compte. **(b)** (*discharge*) *worker, staff* licencier; *servant* congédier; *crew* débarquer.

pay out *vt sep* **(a)** *rope* laisser filer. **(b)** *money* (*spend*) dépenser; *[cashier etc]* payer. **(c)** = **pay back (b).**

pay up 1 *vi* payer. **2** *vt sep amount* payer; *debts* régler.

♦ **payable** *adj* payable (*in* dans; *over* en); **to make a cheque ~able to sb** faire un chèque à l'ordre de qn. ♦ **payee** *n* bénéficiaire *mf*. ♦ **paying** *adj business, scheme* rentable; **~ing guest** pensionnaire *mf*, hôte *m* payant. ♦ **pay-in slip** *n* (*Banking*) bordereau *m* de versement. ♦ **paymaster** *n* (*Mil*) trésorier *m*. ♦ **payment** *n* (*gen*) paiement *m*; *[deposit, cheque]* versement *m*; *[bill, fee]* règlement *m*; *[debt, loan]* remboursement *m*; (*reward*) récompense *f*; **on ~ment of £50** moyennant la somme de 50 livres; **in ~ment for** *goods* en règlement de; *sum owed* en remboursement de; *work, help* en paiement de; *sb's trouble, efforts* en récompense de; **method of ~ment** mode *m* de règlement; **without ~ment** à titre gracieux; **~ment in full** règlement complet; **~ment by instalments** paiement à tempérament; **in monthly ~ments of £10** payable en versements de 10 livres par mois. ♦ **payoff*** *n* remboursement *m*; (*reward*) récompense *f*; (*outcome*) résultat *m* final; (*climax*) comble *m*. ♦ **payroll** *n* (*list*) registre *m* du personnel; (*money*) paie *f* (de tout le personnel); (*employees*) personnel *m*; **to be on a firm's ~roll** être employé par une société. ♦ **payslip** *n* feuille *f or* bulletin *m* de paie.

pea [pi:] **1** *n* pois *m*. **(green) ~s** (petits) pois; (*fig*) **they are as like as two ~s** ils se ressemblent comme deux gouttes d'eau. **2** *adj*: **~ soup** soupe *f* aux pois. ♦ **peagreen** *adj* vert pomme *inv*. ♦ **peashooter** *n* sarbacane *f*.

peace [pi:s] **1** *n* (*not war*) paix *f*; (*calm*) paix, tranquillité *f*. **at** *or* **in ~** en paix; **at ~ with** en paix avec; **to make ~** faire la paix; (*fig*) **to make one's ~ with** se réconcilier avec; **~ of mind** tranquillité d'esprit; **to disturb sb's ~ of mind** troubler l'esprit de qn; **leave him in ~, give him some ~** laisse-le tranquille, fiche-lui la paix*; **anything for ~ and quiet** n'importe quoi pour avoir la paix; (*Jur*) **to disturb the ~** troubler l'ordre public; **to keep the ~** *[citizen]* ne pas troubler l'ordre public; *[police]* veiller à l'ordre public; (*fig: stop disagreement*) maintenir la paix.

2 *adj*: **~ conference** conférence *f* pour la paix; (*fig*) **~ offering** cadeau *m* de réconciliation; **~ talks** pourparlers *mpl* de paix; **~ treaty** traité *m* de paix.

♦ **peaceable** *adj* (*calm*) paisible; (*~-loving*) pacifique. ♦ **peaceably** *adv* paisiblement; pacifiquement. ♦ **peaceful** *adj reign, period, person* paisible; *life, place, sleep* paisible, tranquille; *meeting* calme; *demonstration* non-violent; *coexistence* pacifique; **the ~ful uses of atomic energy** l'utilisation pacifique de l'énergie nucléaire. ♦ **peacefully** *adv demonstrate, reign* paisiblement; *work, lie, sleep* paisiblement, tranquillement. ♦ **peacefulness** *n* paix *f*, tranquillité *f*. ♦ **peace-keeping** *adj force* de maintien de la paix; *operation, policy* de pacification. ♦ **peace-loving** *adj* pacifique. ♦ **peacemaker** *n* pacificateur *m*, -trice *f*. ♦ **peacetime** *n*: **in ~time** en temps de paix.

peach [pi:tʃ] **1** *n* pêche *f*; (*tree*) pêcher *m*. **2** *adj* (*colour*) pêche *inv*.

peacock ['pi:kɒk] *n* paon *m*. **~ blue** bleu paon *inv*. ♦ **peahen** *n* paonne *f*.

peak [pi:k] **1** *n [mountain]* cime *f*, sommet *m*; (*mountain itself*) pic *m*; *[roof etc]* faîte *m*; *[cap]* visière *f*; (*on graph*) sommet; (*fig*) *[career, power]* apogée *m*. **at its ~** *fame, career, empire* à son apogée; *demand, traffic* à son maximum; *business* à son point culminant; *discontent* à son comble. **2** *adj demand, production* maximum; *hours* d'affluence; *period* de pointe; *traffic* aux heures d'affluence. ♦ **peaky** *adj* fatigué, qui n'a pas l'air très en forme*.

peal [pi:l] **1** *n [thunder]* coup *m*. **~ of bells** carillon *m*; **~ of laughter** éclat *m* de rire. **2** *vi* (**~ out**) *[bells]* carillonner; *[thunder]* gronder; *[organ]* retentir; *[laughter]* éclater. **3** *vt bells* sonner (à toute volée).

peanut ['pi:nʌt] **1** *n* (*nut*) cacahuète *f*; (*plant*) arachide *f*. (*fig*) **it's just ~s**‡ c'est une bagatelle. **2** *adj*: **~ butter** beurre *m* de cacahuètes; **~ oil** huile *f* d'arachide.

pear [pɛəʳ] *n* poire *f*; (*tree*) poirier *m*. ♦ **pear-shaped** *adj* en forme de poire.

pearl [pɜ:l] **1** *n* perle *f*. **mother of ~** nacre *f*; **real/cultured ~s** perles fines/de culture; (*fig*) **~s of wisdom** trésors *mpl* de sagesse; (*fig*) **to cast ~s before swine** jeter des perles aux pourceaux. **2** *adj necklace* de perles; *button* de nacre. **~ barley** orge *m* perlé; **~ diver** pêcheur *m*, -euse *f* de perles. ♦ **pearly** *adj* nacré; (*hum*) **the P~y Gates** les portes *fpl* du Paradis.

peasant ['pezənt] *adj, n* paysan(ne) *m(f)*.

peat [pi:t] *n* tourbe *f*. ♦ **peaty** *adj* tourbeux.

pebble ['pebl] *n* caillou *m*; (*on beach*) galet *m*. (*fig*) **he's not the only ~ on the beach** il n'y a pas que lui. ♦ **pebbledash** *n* crépi *m* moucheté. ♦ **pebbly** *adj road* caillouteux; *beach* de galets.

pecan [pɪ'kæn] *n* pacane *f*; (*tree*) pacanier *m*.

peck [pek] **1** *n* coup *m* de bec; (*hasty kiss*) bise* *f*. **2** *vt object, ground* becqueter; *food* picorer; *person, attacker* donner un coup de bec à; *hole* faire à coups de bec. **3** *vi [bird]* **to ~ at** picorer; *[person]* **to ~ at one's food** manger du bout des dents. ♦ **pecking order** *n* hiérarchie *f*. ♦ **peckish*** *adj*: **to be ~ish** avoir un peu faim.

peculiar [pɪ'kju:lɪəʳ] *adj* **(a)** (*particular*) *importance, qualities* particulier. **its (own) ~ dialect** son dialecte particulier, son propre dialecte; **~ to** particulier à, propre à. **(b)** (*odd*) bizarre, curieux, étrange. ♦ **peculiarity** *n* **(a)** (*distinctive feature*) particularité *f*; **(b)** (*oddity*) bizarrerie *f*. ♦ **peculiarly** *adv* (*specially*) particulièrement; (*oddly*) étrangement.

pecuniary [pɪ'kju:nɪərɪ] *adj* pécuniaire. **~ difficulties** ennuis *mpl* d'argent.

pedagogic(al) [ˌpedə'gɒdʒɪk(əl)] *adj* pédagogique.

pedal ['pedl] **1** *n* pédale *f*. **2** *vi* pédaler. **he ~led through the town** il a traversé la ville (à bicyclette). ♦ **pedalbin** *n* poubelle *f* à pédale. ♦ **pedalboat** *n* pédalo *m*. ♦ **pedalcar** *n* voiture *f* à pédales.

pedant ['pedənt] *n* pédant(e) *m(f)*. ♦ **pedantic** *adj* pédant. ♦ **pedantically** *adv* avec pédantisme. ♦ **pedantry** *n* pédantisme *m*.

peddle ['pedl] *vt goods, gossip* colporter; *drugs* faire le trafic de. ♦ **peddler** *or* ♦ **pedlar** *n* (*door to*

door) colporteur *m*; (*in street*) camelot *m*; *[drugs]* revendeur *m*, -euse *f*.
pederast ['pedəræst] *n* pédéraste *m*. ♦ **pederasty** *n* pédérastie *f*.
pedestal ['pedɪstl] *n* piédestal *m* (*also fig*).
pedestrian [pɪ'destrɪən] **1** *n* piéton *m*. **2** *adj* **(a)** (*fig*) prosaïque, plat. **(b)** ~ **crossing** passage *m* pour piétons, passage clouté; ~ **precinct** zone *f* piétonnière.
pediatric *etc* (*US*) = **paediatric** *etc*.
pedicure ['pedɪkjʊəʳ] *n* soins *mpl* des pieds.
pedigree ['pedɪgri:] **1** *n [animal]* pedigree *m*; *[person]* (*lineage*) ascendance *f*, lignée *f*; (*family tree*) arbre *m* généalogique. **2** *adj animal* de (pure) race.
pedometer [pɪ'dɒmɪtəʳ] *n* podomètre *m*.
pee‡ [pi:] *vi* faire pipi*, pisser‡.
peek [pi:k] *n*, *vi*: **to (take a)** ~ **at** jeter un coup d'œil (furtif) à *or* sur.
peel [pi:l] **1** *n [apple, potato]* épluchure *f*; *[orange]* écorce *f*; (*Culin, also in drink*) zeste *m*. **candied** ~ écorce confite. **2** *vt fruit, potato* éplucher; *stick* écorcer; *shrimps* décortiquer. **to keep one's eyes ~ed‡** ouvrir l'œil* (*for* pour trouver). **3** *vi [paint]* s'écailler; *[skin]* peler.
peel away 1 *vi [skin]* peler; *[paint]* s'écailler; *[wallpaper]* se décoller. **2** *vt sep rind* peler; *film, covering* décoller.
peel back *vt sep film, covering* décoller.
peel off 1 *vi* **(a)** = **peel away 1. (b)** *[plane]* s'écarter de la formation. **2** *vt sep* **(a)** = **peel away 2. (b)** *clothes* enlever.
♦ **peeler** *n* (couteau-)éplucheur *m*. ♦ **peeling 1** *adj wallpaper* qui se décolle; **2** *npl*: **~ings** épluchures *fpl*.
peep [pi:p] **1** *n* (petit) coup *m* d'œil. **to have** *or* **take a** ~ **at sth** jeter un (petit) coup d'œil à *or* sur qch. **2** *vi* jeter un (petit) coup d'œil (*at* à, sur; *into* dans; *over* par-dessus). **he was ~ing at us from ...** il nous regardait furtivement *or* à la dérobée de ... . ♦ **peephole** *n* trou *m* (pour épier). ♦ **Peeping Tom** *n* voyeur *m*.
peer[1] [pɪəʳ] *vi*: **to** ~ **at** regarder.
peer[2] [pɪəʳ] *n* pair *m*. ♦ **peerage** *n* pairie *f*; **to be given a ~age** être anobli. ♦ **peeress** *n* pairesse *f*. ♦ **peerless** *adj* sans pareil.
peevish ['pi:vɪʃ] *adj* maussade; *child* de mauvaise humeur. ♦ **peeved‡** *adj* fâché, en rogne*. ♦ **peevishly** *adv* maussadement; avec (mauvaise) humeur.
peewit ['pi:wɪt] *n* vanneau *m*.
peg [peg] **1** *n* (*wooden*) cheville *f*; (*metal*) fiche *f*; (*for coat, hat*) patère *f*; (*tent* ~) piquet *m*; (*clothes* ~) pince *f* à linge. **I bought this off the** ~ c'est du prêt-à-porter, j'ai acheté ça tout fait; **to take sb down a ~ (or two)** rabattre le caquet à qn; (*fig*) **a ~ to hang a complaint on** un prétexte pour se plaindre. **2** *vt* (*Tech*) cheviller; *prices, wages* stabiliser. **to ~ clothes (out) on the line** étendre du linge sur la corde (à l'aide de pinces).
peg down *vt sep tent* fixer avec des piquets. (*fig*) **to ~ sb down to doing** réussir à décider qn à faire.
peg out‡ *vi* (*die*) claquer‡, mourir.
pejorative [pɪ'dʒɒrɪtɪv] *adj* péjoratif.
pekin(g)ese [ˌpi:kɪ'ni:z] *n* pékinois *m* (*chien*).
pelargonium [ˌpelə'gəʊnɪəm] *n* pélargonium *m*.
pelican ['pelɪkən] *n* pélican *m*.
pellet ['pelɪt] *n [paper, bread]* boulette *f*; (*for gun*) plomb *m*; (*Med*) pilule *f*; *[chemicals]* pastille *f*.
pelmet ['pelmɪt] *n* (*wooden*) lambrequin *m*; (*cloth*) cantonnière *f*.
pelota [pɪ'ləʊtə] *n* pelote *f* basque.
pelt [pelt] **1** *vt* bombarder, cribler (*with* de). **2** *vi* **(a) the rain is** *or* **it's ~ing (down)*** il tombe des cordes*; **~ing rain** pluie *f* battante. **(b)** (*: *run*) **to ~ across** *etc* traverser *etc* à fond de train.
pelvis ['pelvɪs] *n* bassin *m*, pelvis *m*.
pen[1] [pen] **1** *n* plume *f*; (*ball-point*) stylo *m* à bille; (*felt-tip*) feutre *m*; (*fountain* ~) stylo. **to put ~ to paper** écrire; **to put one's ~ through sth** barrer qch. **2** *adj*: ~ **name** pseudonyme *m* (littéraire); ~ **nib** bec *m* de plume. **3** *vt letter* écrire; *article* rédiger. ♦ **pen-and-ink drawing** *n* dessin *m* à la plume. ♦ **penfriend** *n* correspondant(e) *m(f)*. ♦ **penknife** *n* canif *m*.
pen[2] [pen] **1** *n [animals]* parc *m*, enclos *m*; (*play*~) parc (d'enfant). **2** *vt* (~ **in**, ~ **up**) *animals* parquer; *people* enfermer.
penal ['pi:nl] *adj law, clause, code* pénal; *offence* punissable; *colony* pénitentiaire. (*Jur*) ~ **servitude** travaux *mpl* forcés. ♦ **penalize** *vt* **(a)** (*punish; also Sport*) pénaliser (*for* pour); **(b)** (*handicap*) handicaper; **the strike ~izes those who ...** la grève touche les gens qui ... .
penalty ['penəltɪ] **1** *n* (*punishment: gen*) pénalité *f* (*for* pour); (*Sport*) pénalisation *f*; (*Ftbl etc*) penalty *m*. **on ~ of** sous peine de; **the ~ for not doing this is ...** si on ne fait pas cela la pénalité est ...; (*fig*) **to pay the** ~ subir les conséquences; (*in games*) **a 5-point ~ for** une pénalisation de 5 points pour.
2 *adj* (*Ftbl*) ~ **area** surface *f* de réparation; ~ **goal** but *m* sur pénalité; ~ **kick** coup *m* de pied de pénalité.
penance ['penəns] *n* pénitence *f*. **to do ~ for** faire pénitence pour.
pence [pens] *npl of* **penny**.
pencil ['pensl] **1** *n* crayon *m*. **in** ~ au crayon. **2** *adj note, drawing, mark* au crayon. **3** *vt* écrire au crayon, crayonner. ♦ **pencil-case** *n* trousse *f* (d'écolier). ♦ **pencil-sharpener** *n* taille-crayon *m*.
pending ['pendɪŋ] **1** *adj business, question* pendant, en suspens; (*Jur*) *case* pendant, en instance. **2** *prep* (*until*) en attendant.
pendulum ['pendjʊləm] *n* (*gen*) pendule *m*; *[clock]* balancier *m*.
penetrate ['penɪtreɪt] *vti* (*also* ~ **into**) pénétrer (dans); *[bullet, knife]* pénétrer; *[sound]* pénétrer dans; *[person, vehicle] forest* pénétrer dans; *enemy territory* pénétrer en; *business firm, political party* s'infiltrer dans; *plans, mystery* pénétrer. **to ~ through** traverser. ♦ **penetrable** *adj* pénétrable. ♦ **penetrating** *adj* pénétrant. ♦ **penetratingly** *adv* avec pénétration. ♦ **penetration** *n* pénétration *f*.
penguin ['peŋgwɪn] *n* pingouin *m*; (*in Antarctic*) manchot *m*.
penicillin [ˌpenɪ'sɪlɪn] *n* pénicilline *f*.
peninsula [pɪ'nɪnsjʊlə] *n* péninsule *f*.
penis ['pi:nɪs] *n* pénis *m*.
penitent ['penɪtənt] *adj* pénitent. ♦ **penitence** *n* pénitence *f*. ♦ **penitentiary** *n* (*US*) prison *f*. ♦ **penitently** *adv* d'un air contrit.
penny ['penɪ] *n*, *pl* **pence** (*valeur*), **pennies** (*pièces*) penny *m*. **one old/new** ~ un ancien/un nouveau penny; (*fig*) **he is not a ~ the wiser** il n'est pas plus avancé*; **he hasn't a ~ to his name** il n'a pas le sou; **a ~ for your thoughts!** à quoi pensez-vous?; **the ~ has dropped!*** il a (*or* j'ai *etc*) enfin pigé!‡; (*fig*) **he keeps turning up like a bad** ~ pas moyen de se débarrasser de lui; **in for a ~ in for a pound** (au point où on en est) autant faire les choses jusqu'au bout. ♦ **penniless** *adj* sans le sou.
pension ['penʃən] **1** *n* (*state payment*) pension *f*; (*from company etc*) retraite *f*; (*to servant etc*) pension. **old age** ~ pension vieillesse (de la Sécurité sociale); **retirement** ~ (pension de) retraite. **2** *adj*: ~ **fund** fonds *m* vieillesse; ~ **scheme** caisse *f* de retraite.
pension off *vt sep* mettre à la retraite.
♦ **pensionable** *adj post* qui donne droit à une pension; *age* de la retraite. ♦ **pensioner** *n* retraité(e) *m(f)*.
pensive ['pensɪv] *adj* pensif, songeur. ♦ **pensively** *adv* pensivement.

pentagon ['pentəgən] *n* pentagone *m*. ♦ **pentagonal** *adj* pentagonal.
pentathlon [pen'tæθlən] *n* pentathlon *m*.
Pentecost ['pentɪkɒst] *n* la Pentecôte.
penthouse ['penthaʊs] *n* (~ **flat** *or* **apartment**) appartement *m* de grand standing (*construit sur le toit d'un immeuble*).
pent-up ['pent'ʌp] *adj emotions, energy* refoulé; *person* tendu.
penultimate [pɪ'nʌltɪmɪt] *adj, n* pénultième (*mf*).
penury ['penjʊrɪ] *n* indigence *f*. ♦ **penurious** *adj* indigent.
peony (rose) ['pɪənɪ('rəʊz)] *n* pivoine *f*.
people ['pi:pl] **1** *n* **(a)** (*pl: persons*) gens *mpl* (*adj fem if before n*), personnes *fpl*. **old** ~ les personnes âgées, les vieilles gens, les vieux *mpl*; **young** ~ les jeunes gens *mpl*, les jeunes *mpl*; **clever** ~ les gens intelligents; **a lot of** ~ beaucoup de gens *or* de monde; **what a lot of** ~! que de monde!; **several** ~ **said ...** plusieurs personnes ont dit ...; **how many** ~? combien de personnes?; **several English** ~ plusieurs Anglais; **what do you** ~ **think?** qu'est-ce que vous en pensez, vous autres? **(b)** (*pl: in general*) on, les gens. ~ **say ...** on dit ..., les gens disent ...; **don't tell** ~ **that** il ne faut pas dire ça aux gens. **(c)** (*pl: inhabitants*) *[a country]* peuple *m*; *[district, town]* habitants *mpl*. **country** ~ les gens de la campagne, les populations rurales; **town** ~ les habitants des villes, les citadins *mpl*; **the French** ~ les Français, le peuple français. **(d)** (*pl*) (*Pol: citizens*) peuple *m*; (*general public*) public *m*. **government by the** ~ gouvernement *m* par le peuple; **the king and his** ~ le roi et son peuple; **the** ~ **at large** le grand public; **man of the** ~ homme *m* du peuple. **(e)** (*sg: nation etc*) peuple *m*, nation *f*. **(f)** (*pl: family*) famille *f*, parents *mpl*. **I am writing to my** ~* j'écris à ma famille. **2** *vt* peupler (*with* de).
pep* [pep] **1** *n* entrain *m*, dynamisme *m*. **2** *adj*: ~ **pill** excitant *m*; ~ **talk** petit laïus* *m* d'encouragement.
pep up* *vt sep person* ragaillardir; *party, conversation* animer; *drink, plot* corser.
pepper ['pepəʳ] **1** *n* **(a)** (*spice*) poivre *m*. **white/black** ~ poivre blanc/gris. **(b)** (*vegetable*) poivron *m*. **red/green** ~ poivron rouge/vert. **2** *vt* poivrer. ♦ **pepper-and-salt** *adj* poivre et sel *inv*. ♦ **peppercorn** *n* grain *m* de poivre. ♦ **peppermint 1** *n* (*sweet*) pastille *f* de menthe; **2** *adj* à la menthe. ♦ **pepperpot** *n* poivrière *f*. ♦ **peppery** *adj food* poivré; *person* irascible.
peptic ['peptɪk] *adj*: ~ **ulcer** ulcère *m* à l'estomac.
per [pɜ:ʳ] *prep* par. ~ **annum** par an; ~ **capita** par personne; ~ **cent** pour cent; ~ **day** par jour; ~ **head** par tête, par personne; **100 km** ~ **hour** 100 km à l'heure; **she is paid 15 francs** ~ **hour** on la paie 15 F (de) l'heure; **3 francs** ~ **kilo** 3 F le kilo; **4 hours** ~ **person** 4 heures par personne. ♦ **percentage** *n* pourcentage *m*.
perceive [pə'si:v] *vt sound, meaning* percevoir; (*notice*) remarquer (*that* que); *object, person* apercevoir, remarquer. ♦ **perceptible** *adj* perceptible. ♦ **perceptibly** *adv* sensiblement. ♦ **perception** *n* perception *f*. ♦ **perceptive** *adj analysis, person* pénétrant, perspicace.
perch¹ [pɜ:tʃ] *n* (*fish*) perche *f*.
perch² [pɜ:tʃ] **1** *n* perchoir *m*. **2** *vi [bird, person]* se percher. **3** *vt* percher, jucher.
percolate ['pɜ:kəleɪt] **1** *vt coffee* passer. ~**d coffee** café fait dans une cafetière à pression. **2** *vi* passer (*through* par); *[news]* filtrer. ♦ **percolator** *n* cafetière *f* à pression.
percussion [pə'kʌʃən] **1** *n* percussion *f*. **2** *adj* (*Mus*) *instrument* à *or* de percussion.
peregrine ['perɪgrɪn] *adj*: ~ **falcon** faucon *m* pèlerin.
peremptory [pə'remptərɪ] *adj* péremptoire. ♦ **peremptorily** *adv* péremptoirement.
perennial [pə'renɪəl] **1** *adj* (*gen*) perpétuel; *plant* vivace. **2** *n* plante *f* vivace. ♦ **perennially** *adv* perpétuellement.
perfect ['pɜ:fɪkt] **1** *adj* **(a)** (*gen*) parfait. **the** ~ **moment to speak to him about it** le moment idéal pour lui en parler; (*Mus*) ~ **pitch** l'oreille *f* absolue; (*Gram*) ~ **tense** parfait *m*. **(b)** (*emphatic*) *idiot etc* véritable. **he's a** ~ **stranger to me** je ne le connais absolument pas. **2** *n* (*Gram*) parfait *m*. **in the** ~ au parfait. **3** [pə'fekt] *vt work* achever, parfaire; *technique* mettre au point. **to** ~ **one's French** parfaire ses connaissances de français. ♦ **perfection** *n* perfection *f*. ♦ **perfectionist** *adj, n* perfectionniste (*mf*). ♦ **perfectly** *adv* parfaitement.
perfidy ['pɜ:fɪdɪ] *n* perfidie *f*. ♦ **perfidious** *adj* perfide. ♦ **perfidiously** *adv* perfidement.
perforate ['pɜ:fəreɪt] *vt* perforer. ~**d line** pointillé *m*. ♦ **perforation** *n* perforation *f*.
perform [pə'fɔ:m] **1** *vt* **(a)** *task* exécuter, accomplir; *function* remplir; *duty, miracle* accomplir; *rite* célébrer. **to** ~ **an operation** (*gen*) exécuter une opération; (*Med*) pratiquer une opération. **(b)** (*Theat etc*) *play, ballet, opera* donner; *symphony* jouer; *solo, acrobatics* exécuter. **2** *vi* **(a)** *[company etc]* donner une *or* des représentation(s); *[actor]* jouer; *[singer]* chanter; *[dancer]* danser; *[acrobat, trained animal]* exécuter un *or* des numéro(s). **to** ~ **on the violin** jouer du violon; ~**ing seals** *etc* phoques *etc* savants. **(b)** *[machine, vehicle]* marcher, fonctionner.
♦ **performance** *n* **(a)** (*presentation*) *[play, opera, ballet, circus]* représentation *f*; *[film, concert]* séance *f*; (*fig: fuss*) **what a** ~**ance!** quelle affaire!, quelle histoire!*; **(b)** *[actor, musician, dancer etc]* interprétation *f*; *[acrobat]* numéro *m*; *[racehorse, athlete, team etc]* performance *f*; **(c)** *[machine]* fonctionnement *m*; *[vehicle]* performance *f*. ♦ **performer** *n* artiste *mf*.
perfume ['pɜ:fju:m] **1** *n* parfum *m*. **2** [pə'fju:m] *vt* parfumer. ♦ **perfumery** *n* parfumerie *f*.
perfunctory [pə'fʌŋktərɪ] *adj* négligent, pour la forme. ♦ **perfunctorily** *adv bow, greet, perform* négligemment; *answer, agree* sans conviction.
perhaps [pə'hæps, præps] *adv* peut-être. ~ **so/not** peut-être que oui/que non; ~ **he will come** peut-être viendra-t-il, il viendra peut-être, peut-être qu'il viendra.
peril ['perɪl] *n* péril *m*, danger *m*. **in** ~ **of** en danger de; **at your** ~ à vos risques et périls. ♦ **perilous** *adj* périlleux. ♦ **perilously** *adv* périlleusement; **they were** ~**ously near disaster** ils frôlaient la catastrophe.
perimeter [pə'rɪmɪtəʳ] *n* périmètre *m*.
period ['pɪərɪəd] **1** *n* **(a)** (*length of time*) période *f*; (*stage: in career, development etc*) époque *f*, moment *m*. **the classical** ~ la période classique; **furniture of the** ~ meubles de l'époque; **the postwar** ~ (la période de) l'après-guerre *m*; **at that** ~ **in** *or* **of his life** à cette époque *or* à ce moment de sa vie; **the holiday** ~ la période des vacances; (*Met*) **rainy** ~**s** périodes de pluie; **in the** ~ **of a year** en l'espace d'une année; **within a 3-month** ~ dans un délai de 3 mois. **(b)** (*Scol*) cours *m*, leçon *f*. **(c)** (*full stop*) point *m*. **(d)** (*menstruation*) règles *fpl*. **2** *adj costume* de l'époque; *furniture* d'époque. (*fig*) ~ **piece** curiosité *f*. ♦ **periodic** *adj* périodique. ♦ **periodical** *adj, n* périodique (*m*). ♦ **periodically** *adv* périodiquement.
peripatetic [ˌperɪpə'tetɪk] *adj* ambulant; *teacher* qui dessert plusieurs établissements.
periphery [pə'rɪfərɪ] *n* périphérie *f*. ♦ **peripheral** *adj* périphérique.
periscope ['perɪskəʊp] *n* périscope *m*.
perish ['perɪʃ] *vi* (*die*) périr, mourir; *[rubber, foods etc]* se détériorer. ♦ **perishable 1** *adj*

périssable; **2** *n*: ~**ables** denrées *fpl* périssables. ♦ **perished*** *adj* frigorifié*. ♦ **perishing** *adj*: **it's ~ing*** il fait très froid.

peritonitis [ˌperɪtəˈnaɪtɪs] *n* péritonite *f*.

periwinkle [ˈperɪˌwɪŋkl] *n* (*Bot*) pervenche *f*; (*Zool*) bigorneau *m*.

perjure [ˈpɜːdʒəʳ] *vt*: **to ~ o.s.** se parjurer; (*Jur*) faire un faux serment; (*Jur*) ~**d evidence** faux serment. ♦ **perjury** *n* parjure *m*; (*Jur*) faux serment; **to commit perjury** se parjurer; (*Jur*) faire un faux serment.

perk [pɜːk] **1** *vi*: **to ~ up** (*cheer up*) se ragaillardir; (*show interest*) s'animer. **2** *vt* ragaillardir. (*lit, fig*) **to ~ one's ears up** dresser l'oreille. ♦ **perkily** *adv* (*gaily*) d'un air guilleret; (*in lively manner*) avec entrain; (*cheekily*) avec effronterie. ♦ **perky** *adj* guilleret; plein d'entrain; effronté.

perks* [pɜːks] *npl* petits bénéfices *mpl*.

perm [pɜːm] **1** *n* (*abbr of* **permanent wave**) permanente *f*. **2** *vt*: **to ~ sb's hair** faire une permanente à qn; **to have one's hair ~ed** se faire faire une permanente.

permanent [ˈpɜːmənənt] *adj* (*gen*) permanent. **I'm not ~ here** je ne suis pas ici à titre définitif; ~ **address** adresse *f* fixe; (*Brit*) **P~ Undersecretary** ≃ secrétaire *m* général (de ministère); ~ **wave** permanente *f*; (*Rail*) ~ **way** voie *f* ferrée. ♦ **permanence** *n* permanence *f*. ♦ **permanency** *n* (*job*) emploi *m* permanent. ♦ **permanently** *adv* *remain* en permanence, de façon permanente; *appoint* à titre définitif.

permeate [ˈpɜːmɪeɪt] **1** *vt* filtrer à travers; (*fig*) se répandre dans *or* parmi. (*lit, fig*) ~**d with** imprégné de. **2** *vi* s'infiltrer; (*fig*) se répandre.

permission [pəˈmɪʃən] *n* permission *f*; (*official*) autorisation *f*. **to give sb ~ to do** permettre à qn de faire, autoriser qn à faire. ♦ **permissible** *adj* *action* permis (*to do* de faire); *attitude etc* acceptable (*to do* de faire). ♦ **permissive** *adj* *person* (trop) tolérant; *morals, law* laxiste; *society* de tolérance.

permit [ˈpɜːmɪt] **1** *n* (*gen*) autorisation *f* (écrite); (*for specific activity*) permis *m*; (*entrance pass*) laissez-passer *m inv*; (*for goods at Customs*) passavant *m*. **building/fishing/residence ~** permis de construire/de pêche/de séjour. **2** [pəˈmɪt] *vt* permettre (*sb to do* à qn de faire); (*more formally*) autoriser (*sb to do* qn à faire). **he was ~ted to ...** on lui a permis de ..., on l'a autorisé à ...; **to ~ sth to happen** permettre que qch se produise, laisser qch se produire. **3** [pəˈmɪt] *vi*: **to ~ of sth** permettre qch.

pernicious [pəˈnɪʃəs] *adj* nuisible; (*Med*) pernicieux.

pernickety* [pəˈnɪkɪtɪ] *adj* difficile (*about* pour), pointilleux; *job* minutieux.

peroxide [pəˈrɒksaɪd] *n* peroxyde *m*.

perpendicular [ˌpɜːpənˈdɪkjʊləʳ] **1** *adj* (*gen*) perpendiculaire (*to* à); *cliff, slope* à pic. **2** *n* perpendiculaire *f*. ♦ **perpendicularly** *adv* perpendiculairement.

perpetrate [ˈpɜːpɪtreɪt] *vt* (*gen*) faire; *crime* perpétrer. ♦ **perpetrator** *n* auteur *m* (*d'un crime*).

perpetual [pəˈpetjʊəl] *adj* (*gen*) perpétuel. **he's a ~ nuisance** il ne cesse d'enquiquiner* le monde. ♦ **perpetually** *adv* perpétuellement. ♦ **perpetuate** *vt* perpétuer. ♦ **perpetuity** *n*: **in perpetuity** à perpétuité.

perplex [pəˈpleks] *vt* rendre perplexe. **I was ~ed by it** cela m'a rendu perplexe. ♦ **perplexed** *adj* perplexe. ♦ **perplexedly** *adv* d'un air perplexe. ♦ **perplexing** *adj* embarrassant, confus. ♦ **perplexity** *n* embarras *m*, perplexité *f*.

perquisite [ˈpɜːkwɪzɪt] *n* à-côté *m*.

persecute [ˈpɜːsɪkjuːt] *vt* persécuter (*for* pour). ♦ **persecution** *n* persécution *f*; **persecution mania** folie *f* de la persécution. ♦ **persecutor** *n* persécuteur *m*, -trice *f*.

persevere [ˌpɜːsɪˈvɪəʳ] *vi* persévérer (*in sth* dans qch), persister (*in sth* dans qch; *at doing sth* à faire qch). ♦ **perseverance** *n* persévérance *f*, ténacité *f*. ♦ **persevering** *adj* persévérant.

Persia [ˈpɜːʃə] *n* Perse *f*. ♦ **Persian 1** *adj* (*Hist*) perse; (*modern*) persan; *carpet* de Perse; ~**n Gulf** golfe *m* Persique; **2** *n* Persan(e) *m(f)*; (*Hist*) Perse *mf*; (*Ling*) persan *m*.

persist [pəˈsɪst] *vi* persister (*in sth* dans qch; *in doing* à faire). ♦ **persistence** *n* persistance *f*. ♦ **persistent** *adj* (*persevering*) persévérant; (*obstinate*) obstiné; *smell, pain, cough* persistant; *warnings, noise* continuel; (*Jur*) ~**ent offender** multi-récidiviste *mf*. ♦ **persistently** *adv* (*consistently*) constamment; (*obstinately*) obstinément.

person [ˈpɜːsn] *n* personne *f*. **in ~** en personne; **in the ~ of** dans *or* en la personne de; (*Telec*) **a ~ to ~ call** une communication avec préavis; **he had a knife on his ~** il avait un couteau sur lui; (*Gram*) **in the first ~ singular** à la première personne du singulier. ♦ **personable** *adj* qui présente bien. ♦ **personage** *n* personnage *m*.

personal [ˈpɜːsnl] *adj* (*gen, also Gram*) personnel; *liberty, rights etc* individuel; *habits, hygiene* intime; *application* fait en personne; *remark, question* indiscret. ~ **assistant** secrétaire *mf* particulier (-ière); **I have no ~ knowledge of this** personnellement je ne sais rien à ce sujet; **a letter marked '~'** une lettre marquée 'personnel'; **the argument grew ~** la discussion a pris un tour personnel; **don't let's get ~!** abstenons-nous de remarques désobligeantes!; **his ~ appearance** son apparence personnelle; **to make a ~ appearance** apparaître en personne; (*Brit Telec*) ~ **call** (*person-to-person*) communication *f* avec préavis; (*private*) communication privée; (*Press*) ~ **column** annonces *fpl* personnelles; **as a ~ favour to him** pour lui rendre service; ~ **friend** ami(e) *m(f)* intime; **his ~ life** sa vie privée; **to give sth the ~ touch** ajouter une note personnelle à qch.
♦ **personality** *n* (*gen*) personnalité *f*; (*celebrity*) personnalité, personnage *m* connu; **a television ~ity** une vedette de la télévision; **let's keep ~ities out of this** abstenons-nous de remarques désobligeantes. ♦ **personally** *adv* (*in person*) en personne; (*for my part*) personnellement, pour ma part; ~**ly responsible** personnellement responsable; **don't take it ~ly!** ne croyez pas que vous soyez personnellement visé!; **I like him ~ly but not as an employer** je l'aime en tant que personne mais pas en tant que patron.

personify [pɜːˈsɒnɪfaɪ] *vt* personnifier. ♦ **personification** *n* personnification *f*.

personnel [ˌpɜːsəˈnel] **1** *n* personnel *m*. **2** *adj*: ~ **department** service *m* du personnel; ~ **management** direction *f* du personnel; ~ **manager** chef *m* du personnel; ~ **officer** responsable *mf* du personnel.

perspective [pəˈspektɪv] *n* (*gen, Archit, Art, Surv*) perspective *f*. (*fig*) **let's get this into ~** ne perdons pas le sens des proportions.

perspex [ˈpɜːspeks] *n* ® plexiglas *m* ®.

perspicacious [ˌpɜːspɪˈkeɪʃəs] *adj* *person* perspicace; *analysis* pénétrant. ♦ **perspicacity** *n* perspicacité *f*.

perspire [pəsˈpaɪəʳ] *vi* transpirer. ♦ **perspiration** *n* transpiration *f*; **bathed in perspiration** en nage.

persuade [pəˈsweɪd] *vt* persuader (*sb of sth* qn de qch; *sb that* qn que; *sb to do* qn de faire). **they ~d me not to** on m'en a dissuadé. ♦ **persuasion** *n* (*gen*) persuasion *f*; (*Rel*) religion *f*, confession *f*. ♦ **persuasive** *adj* *person* persuasif; *argument* convaincant. ♦ **persuasively** *adv* d'une manière persuasive. ♦ **persuasiveness** *n* pouvoir *m* de persuasion.

pert [pɜːt] *adj* coquin, hardi. ♦ **pertly** *adv* coquinement, hardiment. ♦ **pertness** *n* hardiesse *f*.

pertinacious [ˌpɜːtɪˈneɪʃəs] *adj* entêté. ♦ **pertinaciously** *adv* avec entêtement. ♦ **pertinacity** *n* entêtement *m*.

pertinent [ˈpɜːtɪnənt] *adj* pertinent. ~ **to** qui a rapport à. ♦ **pertinently** *adv* pertinemment.

perturb [pəˈtɜːb] *vt* perturber. **I was ~ed to hear that ...** j'ai appris avec inquiétude que ... . ♦ **perturbation** *n* perturbation *f*. ♦ **perturbing** *adj* troublant, inquiétant.

Peru [pəˈruː] *n* Pérou *m*.

peruse [pəˈruːz] *vt* lire. ♦ **perusal** *n* lecture *f*.

pervade [pɜːˈveɪd] *vt [smell]* se répandre dans; *[influence, ideas]* pénétrer dans; *[gloom]* envahir; *[feeling, atmosphere]* se retrouver partout dans. ♦ **pervasive** *adj smell, ideas* pénétrant; *gloom* envahissant; *influence* qui se fait sentir un peu partout.

perverse [pəˈvɜːs] *adj* (*wicked*) mauvais, pervers; (*contrary*) contrariant; *desire* pervers. ♦ **perversely** *adv* (*wickedly*) par pure méchanceté, avec perversité; (*contrarily*) par esprit de contradiction. ♦ **perversion** *n* (*gen, Med, Psych*) perversion *f*; *[justice, truth]* travestissement *m*. ♦ **perversity** *or* ♦ **perverseness** *n* (*wickedness*) méchanceté *f*, perversité *f*; (*contrariness*) caractère *m* contrariant, esprit *m* de contradiction. ♦ **pervert** **1** *vt* pervertir; **2** [ˈpɜːvɜːt] *n* perverti(e) *m(f)* sexuel(le).

pessary [ˈpesərɪ] *n* pessaire *m*.

pessimism [ˈpesɪmɪzəm] *n* pessimisme *m*. ♦ **pessimist** *n* pessimiste *mf*. ♦ **pessimistic** *adj* pessimiste (*about* au sujet de, sur). ♦ **pessimistically** *adv* avec pessimisme.

pest [pest] **1** *n* (*insect/animal*) insecte *m*/animal *m* nuisible; (*person*) casse-pieds* *mf inv*. **it's a ~ having to go** quelle barbe* d'avoir à y aller. **2** *adj*: ~ **control officer** agent *m* préposé à la lutte antiparasitaire. ♦ **pesticide** *n* pesticide *m*. ♦ **pestilence** *n* peste *f*. ♦ **pestilent** *or* ♦ **pestilential** *adj* (*exasperating*) sacré* (*before n*).

pester [ˈpestəʳ] *vt* harceler (*sb to do* qn pour qu'il fasse; *sb with questions* qn de questions), casser les pieds à*. **she has been ~ing me for an answer** elle n'arrête pas de me réclamer une réponse; **stop ~ing me** fiche-moi la paix* (*about* avec).

pestle [ˈpesl] *n* pilon *m*.

pet [pet] **1** *n* **(a)** (*animal*) animal *m* familier. **he hasn't got any ~s** il n'a pas d'animaux chez lui; **she keeps a goldfish as a ~** en fait d'animal elle a un poisson rouge; **'no ~s allowed'** 'les animaux sont interdits'. **(b)** (*: *favourite*) chouchou(te)* *m(f)*. **be a ~*** sois un chou*; **come here ~*** viens ici mon chou*. **2** *adj* **(a)** *lion, snake* apprivoisé. **he's got a ~ rabbit** il a un lapin; ~ **shop** boutique *f* d'animaux. **(b)** (*fig*) ~ **aversion*** bête *f* noire; ~ **name** petit nom *m* (d'amitié); ~ **subject** marotte *f*, dada* *m*. **3** *vt* (*indulge*) chouchouter*; (*fondle*) câliner. **4** *vi* (*: *sexually*) se peloter*. ♦ **petting*** *n* pelotage* *m*.

petal [ˈpetl] *n* pétale *m*.

peter [ˈpiːtəʳ] *vi*: **to ~ out** *[supplies]* s'épuiser; *[stream, conversation]* tarir; *[plans]* tomber à l'eau; *[book]* tourner court; *[fire]* mourir; *[road]* se perdre.

petite [pəˈtiːt] *adj* menu (*dit d'une femme*).

petition [pəˈtɪʃən] **1** *n* (*list of signatures*) pétition *f* (*for* en faveur de; *against* contre); (*prayer*) prière *f*; (*request, also Jur*) requête *f*. **2** *vt person* adresser une pétition à (*for sth* pour demander qch). **3** *vi* (*Jur*) **to ~ for divorce** faire une demande en divorce.

petrify [ˈpetrɪfaɪ] *vt* pétrifier; (*fig*) pétrifier de peur. ♦ **petrified** *adj* pétrifié; pétrifié de peur.

petrol [ˈpetrəl] (*Brit*) **1** *n* essence *f*. **high-octane ~** supercarburant *m*; **to be heavy on ~** consommer beaucoup; **we've run out of ~** nous sommes en panne d'essence. **2** *adj engine* à essence; *rationing* d'essence. ~ **can** bidon *m* à essence; ~ **cap** bouchon *m* de réservoir (d'essence); ~ **gauge** jauge *f* d'essence; ~ **pump** (*at garage*) pompe *f* d'essence; ~ **station** station-service *f*; ~ **tank** réservoir *m* (d'essence). ♦ **petroleum** *n* pétrole *m*; **~eum jelly** vaseline *f*.

petticoat [ˈpetɪkəʊt] *n* (*skirt*) jupon *m*; (*slip*) combinaison *f*.

petty [ˈpetɪ] *adj farmer, official* petit; (*trivial*) *detail, complaint* insignifiant, sans importance; (*petty-minded*) mesquin. ~ **cash** caisse *f* de dépenses courantes; (*Naut*) ~ **officer** second maître *m*. ♦ **pettifogging** *adj details* insignifiant; *objections* chicanier. ♦ **pettily** *adv* avec mesquinerie. ♦ **pettiness** *n* insignifiance *f*; mesquinerie *f*.

petulant [ˈpetjʊlənt] *adj* irritable. ♦ **petulance** *n* irritabilité *f*. ♦ **petulantly** *adv* avec mauvaise humeur.

pew [pjuː] *n* banc *m* (d'église). **take a ~**‡ assieds-toi.

pewter [ˈpjuːtəʳ] *n* étain *m*.

phantom [ˈfæntəm] *n, adj* fantôme (*m*).

pharmacy [ˈfɑːməsɪ] *n* pharmacie *f*. ♦ **pharmaceutical** *adj* pharmaceutique. ♦ **pharmacist** *n* pharmacien(ne) *m(f)*. ♦ **pharmacology** *n* pharmacologie *f*.

phase [feɪz] **1** *n* (*gen*) phase *f*. **it's just a ~ he's going through** ce n'est qu'une période difficile, ça lui passera. **2** *vt operation* faire progressivement; *execution of plan* procéder par étapes à. **a ~d withdrawal of troops** un retrait progressif des troupes.

phase in *vt sep* introduire progressivement.

phase out *vt sep machinery* retirer progressivement; *jobs* supprimer graduellement.

pheasant [ˈfeznt] *n* faisan *m*.

phenobarbitone [ˈfiːnəʊˈbɑːbɪtəʊn] *n* phénobarbital *m*.

phenomenon [fɪˈnɒmɪnən] *n, pl* **-ena** phénomène *m*. ♦ **phenomenal** *adj* phénoménal. ♦ **phenomenally** *adv* phénoménalement.

philander [fɪˈlændəʳ] *vi* courir après les femmes. ♦ **philanderer** *n* coureur *m* (de jupons).

philanthropy [fɪˈlænθrəpɪ] *n* philanthropie *f*. ♦ **philanthropic** *adj* philanthropique. ♦ **philanthropist** *n* philanthrope *mf*.

philately [fɪˈlætəlɪ] *n* philatélie *f*. ♦ **philatelist** *n* philatéliste *mf*.

philharmonic [ˌfɪlɑːˈmɒnɪk] *adj* philharmonique.

philology [fɪˈlɒlədʒɪ] *n* philologie *f*. ♦ **philological** *adj* philologique. ♦ **philologist** *n* philologue *mf*.

philosophy [fɪˈlɒsəfɪ] *n* philosophie *f*. **his ~ of life** sa philosophie, sa conception de la vie. ♦ **philosopher** *n* philosophe *mf*. ♦ **philosophic(al)** *adj* philosophique; (*fig: resigned*) philosophe, résigné. ♦ **philosophically** *adv* philosophiquement. ♦ **philosophize** *vi* philosopher (*about, on* sur).

phlebitis [flɪˈbaɪtɪs] *n* phlébite *f*.

phlegm [flem] *n* flegme *m*. ♦ **phlegmatic** [flegˈmætɪk] *adj* flegmatique. ♦ **phlegmatically** *adv* flegmatiquement.

phobia [ˈfəʊbɪə] *n* phobie *f*.

phone [fəʊn] *n, vti abbr of* **telephone**. ♦ **phone-in (programme)** *n* programme *m* à ligne ouverte.

phoneme [ˈfəʊniːm] *n* phonème *m*.

phonetic [fəʊˈnetɪk] *adj* phonétique. ♦ **phonetician** *n* phonéticien(ne) *m(f)*. ♦ **phonetics** *nsg* phonétique *f*.

phoney* [ˈfəʊnɪ] **1** *adj name* faux; *jewels* en toc*; *emotion* factice, simulé; *firm, company* bidon* *inv*. **he's ~** c'est un fumiste; **it sounds ~** cela a l'air d'être de la blague*. **2** *n* (*person*) fumiste* *mf*.

phonograph [ˈfəʊnəgrɑːf] *n* électrophone *m*.

phonology [fəʊ'nɒlədʒɪ] *n* phonologie *f*. ♦ **phonological** *adj* phonologique.
phosphate ['fɒsfeɪt] *n* phosphate *m*.
phosphorus ['fɒsfərəs] *n* phosphore *m*. ♦ **phosphorescence** *n* phosphorescence *f*. ♦ **phosphorescent** *adj* phosphorescent.
photo ['fəʊtəʊ] **1** *n* (*abbr of* **photograph**) photo *f*. **2** *pref* photo ... . ♦ **photocopier** *n* photocopieur *m*. ♦ **photocopy 1** *n* photocopie *f*; **2** *vt* photocopier. ♦ **photocopying** *n* photocopie *f*. ♦ **photo finish** *n* photo-finish *f*. ♦ **photogenic** *adj* photogénique. ♦ **photograph 1** *n* photographie *f*; **to take a ~(graph) of sb/sth** prendre une photo de qn/qch, prendre qn/qch en photo; **in** *or* **on this ~(graph)** sur cette photo; **2** *adj*: **~(graph) album** album *m* de photos; **3** *vt* photographier, prendre en photo. ♦ **photographer** [fə'tɒgrəfəʳ] *n* photographe *mf*; **newspaper ~grapher** reporter *m* photographe; **street ~grapher** photostoppeur *m*; **he's a keen ~grapher** il est passionné de photo. ♦ **photographic** *adj* photographique. ♦ **photographically** *adv* photographiquement. ♦ **photography** [fə'tɒgrəfɪ] *n* photographie *f*. ♦ **photostat = photocopy.**
phrase [freɪz] **1** *n* **(a)** (*saying*) expression *f*; (*Gram*) locution *f*. (*Ling*) **verb ~** syntagme *m* verbal. **(b)** (*Mus*) phrase *f*.
2 *vt* **(a)** *thought* exprimer; *letter* rédiger. **(b)** (*Mus*) phraser.
♦ **phrasal verb** *n* verbe *m* à postposition. ♦ **phrasebook** *n* recueil *m* d'expressions. ♦ **phraseology** [ˌfreɪzɪ'ɒlədʒɪ] *n* phraséologie *f*. ♦ **phrasing** *n* (*Mus*) phrasé *m*.
physical ['fɪzɪkəl] *adj* (*gen*) physique; *world, object* matériel. **~ examination** examen médical; **~ exercises, ~ training,** (*Brit*) **~ jerks*** gymnastique *f*; **it's a ~ impossibility for him to do it** il lui est matériellement impossible de le faire. ♦ **physically** *adv* physiquement; **he is ~ly handicapped** c'est un handicapé physique. ♦ **physician** *n* médecin *m*. ♦ **physicist** *n* physicien(ne) *m(f)*. ♦ **physics** *nsg* physique *f*.
physiognomy [ˌfɪzɪ'ɒnəmɪ] *n* physionomie *f*.
physiology [ˌfɪzɪ'ɒlədʒɪ] *n* physiologie *f*. ♦ **physiological** *adj* physiologique. ♦ **physiologist** *n* physiologiste *mf*.
physiotherapy [ˌfɪzɪə'θerəpɪ] *n* kinésithérapie *f*. ♦ **physiotherapist** *n* kinésithérapeute *mf*.
physique [fɪ'ziːk] *n* (*health etc*) constitution *f*; (*appearance*) physique *m*.
piano ['pjɑːnəʊ] **1** *n* piano *m*. **grand ~** piano à queue. **2** *adj lesson, teacher* de piano. **~ duet** morceau *m* pour quatre mains; **~ stool** tabouret *m*; **~ tuner** accordeur *m* (de piano). ♦ **pianist** *n* pianiste *mf*. ♦ **piano accordion** *n* accordéon *m* à clavier. ♦ **pianola** *n* ® piano *m* mécanique.
pick [pɪk] **1** *n* **(a)** (**~*axe***) pioche *f*, pic *m*. **(b)** (*choice*) choix *m*. **to take one's ~** faire son choix; **the ~ of the bunch** le meilleur de tous. **2** *vt* **(a)** (*choose*) choisir; (*Sport*) *sides* former, sélectionner. **to ~ a winner** choisir le gagnant, (*fig*) tirer le bon numéro (*in sb* avec qn); **to ~ one's way through** avancer avec précaution à travers; **to ~ a quarrel** chercher querelle (*with* à); **to ~ a fight** chercher la bagarre* (*with* avec). **(b)** (*gather*) *fruit, flower* cueillir. **(c)** *spot, scab* gratter. **to ~ one's nose** se mettre les doigts dans le nez; **to ~ the bones of a chicken** sucer les os d'un poulet; **to ~ one's teeth** se curer les dents; (*fig*) **to ~ holes in** relever les défauts de; **to ~ sb's brains** faire appel aux lumières de qn; **to ~ a lock** crocheter une serrure; **to ~ pockets** pratiquer le vol à la tire; **I've had my pocket ~ed** on m'a fait les poches. **3** *vi*: **to ~ and choose** prendre son temps pour choisir; **to ~ at one's food** manger du bout des dents; **don't ~ at that spot** ne gratte pas ce bouton.
pick off *vt sep* **(a)** *paint* gratter; *flower, leaf* cueillir. **(b)** (*shoot*) abattre (*après avoir visé soigneusement*).
pick on *vt fus* **(a)** (*: *harass*) harceler, être toujours sur le dos de*. **(b)** (*single out*) choisir, désigner; (*for punishment*) s'en prendre à.
pick out *vt sep* **(a)** (*choose*) choisir. **(b)** (*distinguish*) *object, acquaintance, place etc* distinguer; (*in identification parade*) identifier; (*on photo*) reconnaître. **(c)** *tune on piano* retrouver.
pick over *vt sep fruit, goods* trier, examiner.
pick up 1 *vi* **(a)** (*improve: gen*) s'améliorer; *[prices, wages]* remonter; *[invalid]* se rétablir; *[trade]* reprendre. **(b)** (*: *continue*) continuer, reprendre. **we ~ed up where we'd left off** nous avons repris le travail (*etc*) où nous l'avions laissé. **2** *vt sep* **(a)** (*lift*) *sth dropped* ramasser; *sb fallen* relever; *child, dog* prendre dans ses bras; *telephone* décrocher; (*rescue*) *survivors* recueillir, (*from sea*) repêcher; (*arrest*) arrêter; (*fig*) *points, marks* gagner; *sb's error* relever. **to ~ up speed** prendre de la vitesse; (*fig*) **we ~ed up a rabbit in the headlights** nous avons aperçu un lapin dans la lumière des phares; **the cameras/lights ~ed him up** il est entré dans le champ des caméras/lumières; **to ~ sb up for having made a mistake** reprendre qn pour une faute; (*fig*) **to ~ up the bill*** payer, casquer*. **(b)** (*collect*) *object, goods, passenger* passer prendre. (*fig*) **he ~ed up a girl at the cinema** il a ramassé une fille au cinéma. **(c)** (*acquire*) découvrir; *sale bargain* tomber sur, trouver; *accent, habit* prendre; *information* avoir; (*learn*) apprendre. **you'll soon ~ it up again** vous vous y remettrez vite. **(d)** (*Rad, Telec*) *station, message* capter.
♦ **pickaback** *n*: **to give sb a ~aback** porter qn sur son dos. ♦ **pickaxe** *n* pic *m*, pioche *f*. ♦ **picked** *adj* (*hand-~ed*) *objects* sélectionné; *men* trié sur le volet. ♦ **picker** *n*: **apple-~er** cueilleur *m*, -euse *f* de pommes. ♦ **pickings** *npl* gratte* *f*. ♦ **pick-me-up*** *n* remontant *m*. ♦ **pickpocket** *n* pickpocket *m*. ♦ **pickup** *n* **(a)** *[record-player]* pick-up *m inv*, lecteur *m*; **(b)** (*truck*) pick-up *m inv*; **(c)** (*: *casual lover*) partenaire *mf* de rencontre.
picket ['pɪkɪt] **1** *n* (*gen*) piquet *m*; (*Ind*) piquet de grève; (*Mil*) (*sentry*) sentinelle *f*; (*group*) détachement *m* (de soldats). **2** *adj* (*Ind*) **to be on ~ duty** faire partie d'un piquet de grève; **~ line** cordon *m* de piquet de grève. **3** *vt [strikers]* mettre un piquet de grève aux portes de; *[demonstrators]* former un cordon devant.
pickle ['pɪkl] **1** *n*: **~(s)** pickles *mpl*; (*fig*) **to be in a (pretty) ~*** être dans le pétrin. **2** *vt* conserver dans du vinaigre.
picnic ['pɪknɪk] (*vb: pret, ptp* **picnicked**) **1** *n* pique-nique *m*. (*fig*) **it's no ~*** ça n'est pas une partie de plaisir*; **~ basket** panier *m* à pique-nique. **2** *vi* pique-niquer, faire un pique-nique. ♦ **picnicker** *n* pique-niqueur *m*, -euse *f*.
pictorial [pɪk'tɔːrɪəl] **1** *adj magazine* illustré; *record* en images; *masterpiece* de peinture. **2** *n* illustré *m*. ♦ **pictorially** *adv* au moyen d'images.
picture ['pɪktʃəʳ] **1** *n* **(a)** (*gen*) image *f*; (*illustration*) image, illustration *f*; (*painting*) tableau *m*; (*portrait*) portrait *m*. **I took a ~ of him** j'ai pris une photo de lui; (*TV*) **we have the sound but no ~** nous avons le son mais pas l'image; **to paint a ~** faire un tableau; **to draw a ~** faire un dessin; **to paint/draw a ~ of sth** peindre/dessiner qch; (*fig*) **the garden is a ~ in June** le jardin est ravissant en juin; **he looks the ~ of health** il respire la santé; (*fig*) **the other side of the ~** le revers de la médaille; **his face was a ~!*** si vous aviez vu sa tête!* **(b)** (*Cine*) film *m*. **they made a ~ about it** on en a fait un film; **to go to the ~s** aller au cinéma. **(c)** (*description*) tableau *m*, image *f*; (*mental image*) image. **to give sb a ~ of sth** décrire qch à qn; **he painted a black ~ of ...** il nous a peint un sombre tableau de ...; **I have a clear ~ of him**

(*remembering*) je le revois clairement; (*imagining*) je me le représente très bien; **the general ~** le tableau général de la situation; **do you get the ~?*** tu vois le tableau?*; **to put sb in the ~** mettre qn au courant. **2** *adj*: **~ book** livre *m* d'images; **~ frame** cadre *m*; **~ gallery** (*public*) musée *m* (de peinture); (*private*) galerie *f* (de peinture); **~ postcard** carte *f* postale (illustrée); **~ window** fenêtre *f* panoramique. **3** *vt* se représenter; (*remembering*) revoir. ♦ **picturegoer** *n* amateur *m* de cinéma. ♦ **picturesque** *adj* pittoresque.

pie [paɪ] *n [fruit, fish, meat with gravy etc]* tourte *f*; *[compact filling]* pâté *m* en croûte. **apple ~** tourte aux pommes; **pork ~** pâté de porc en croûte. ♦ **piecrust** *n* croûte *f* de pâté. ♦ **pie dish** *n* terrine *f*. ♦ **pie-eyed*** *adj* parti*, soûl.

piebald ['paɪbɔːld] *adj* pie *inv*.

piece [piːs] *n* (*gen*) morceau *m*; (*smaller*) bout *m*; *[ribbon, string]* bout; (*Comm, Ind, Chess, jigsaw*) pièce *f*; (*Draughts*) pion *m*. **a ~ of land** (*for agriculture*) une parcelle de terre; (*for building*) un lotissement; **a ~ of advice** un conseil; **a ~ of carelessness** de la négligence; **by a ~ of luck** par un coup de chance; **a ~ of music** un morceau de musique; **piano ~** morceau pour piano; **a ~ of poetry** un poème; **a good ~ of work** du bon travail; **a ~ out of 'Ivanhoe'** un passage d''Ivanhoé'; **made in one ~** fait d'une seule pièce; **in one ~** *object* intact; (*) *person* indemne, entier*; **a 5-franc ~** une pièce de 5 F; **a 30-~ tea set** un service à thé de 30 pièces; (*Mus*) **10-~ band** orchestre *m* de 10 exécutants; **3 ~s of luggage** 3 valises *fpl* (*or* sacs *mpl etc*); **~ by ~** pièce à pièce, morceau par morceau; **in ~s** (*broken*) en morceaux; (*not yet assembled*) en pièces détachées; **to come to ~s** (*break*) partir en morceaux; (*dismantle*) se démonter; **to take sth to ~s** démonter qch; **to go to ~s*** (*collapse*) s'effondrer; (*lose one's grip*) lâcher pied (*fig*); **to cut sth to ~s** couper qch en morceaux *or* pièces; **to smash sth to ~s** briser qch en mille morceaux.

piece together *vt sep broken object, facts* rassembler; *jigsaw* assembler; *events* reconstituer.

♦ **piecemeal 1** *adv* petit à petit; **2** *adj* (*gen*) fait (*or* raconté *etc*) petit à petit; *essay, argument* qui manque de rigueur. ♦ **piecework** *n* travail *m* à la pièce. ♦ **pieceworker** *n* ouvrier *m*, -ière *f* payé(e) à la pièce.

pier [pɪəʳ] *n* (*with amusements etc*) jetée *f* (*promenade*); (*landing stage*) embarcadère *m*.

pierce [pɪəs] *vt* (*gen*) percer; *[cold, wind, arrow, bullet]* transpercer. **to have one's ears ~d** se faire percer les oreilles. ♦ **piercing** *adj sound, voice, look* perçant; *cold, wind* glacial.

piety ['paɪətɪ] *n* piété *f*.

pig [pɪg] **1** *n* cochon *m*, porc *m*. (*fig*) **to buy a ~ in a poke** acheter chat en poche; **to make a ~ of o.s.** manger comme un goinfre; **you ~!*** (*mean*) espèce de chameau!*; (*dirty*) espèce de cochon!*; (*greedy*) espèce de goinfre! **2** *adj breeding, industry* porcin. ♦ **piggery** *n* porcherie *f*. ♦ **piggyback** = **pickaback.** ♦ **pigheaded** *adj* entêté. ♦ **pigheadedly** *adv* avec entêtement. ♦ **pigheadedness** *n* entêtement *m*. ♦ **piglet** *n* petit cochon *m*. ♦ **pigman** *n* porcher *m*. ♦ **pigskin 1** *n* peau *f* de porc; **2** *adj* en peau de porc. ♦ **pigsty** *n* porcherie *f*. ♦ **pigtail** *n [hair]* natte *f*.

pigeon ['pɪdʒən] *n* pigeon *m* (*also Culin*). **wood-~** ramier *m*; (*fig*) **that's your ~*** c'est toi que ça regarde, c'est tes oignons*. ♦ **pigeon-fancier** *n* colombophile *mf*. ♦ **pigeonhole 1** *n* casier *m*; **2** *vt* classer (*as* comme). ♦ **pigeon-loft** *n* pigeonnier *m*. ♦ **pigeon-toed** *adj*: **to be ~-toed** avoir les pieds tournés en dedans.

pigment ['pɪgmənt] *n* pigment *m*. ♦ **pigmentation** *n* pigmentation *f*.

pike [paɪk] *n* (*fish*) brochet *m*.

pilchard ['pɪltʃəd] *n* pilchard *m*.

pile[1] [paɪl] *n* (*Constr etc*) pieu *m* de fondation; (*in water*) pilotis *m*; *[bridge]* pile *f*.

pile[2] [paɪl] **1** *n* **(a)** (*heap*) pile *f*, (*less tidy*) tas *m*. **in a ~** en pile, en tas; **atomic ~** pile atomique; (*fig*) **to make one's ~*** faire fortune; **~s of*, a ~ of*** *butter, honey* des masses de*; *cars, flowers* un tas de*. **(b)** (*Med*) **~s** hémorroïdes *fpl*. **2** *vt* (*stack*) empiler; (*heap*) entasser. **~d (high) with books** couvert de piles de livres; **I ~d* the children into the car** j'ai entassé les enfants dans la voiture. **3** *vi* (*) *[people]* s'entasser, s'empiler (*into* dans). **to ~ in*** s'entasser, s'empiler; **to ~ on/off*** *etc* monter/descendre *etc* en se bousculant.

pile on *vt sep*: **to ~ it on*** exagérer, en rajouter; **to ~ on the agony*** dramatiser, faire du mélo*.

pile up 1 *vi [snow etc]* s'amonceler; *[reasons, proof, work, business]* s'accumuler. **2** *vt sep* **(a)** *objects* (*stack*) empiler; (*heap*) entasser; *evidence, reasons* accumuler. **(b)** (*: *crash*) *car* bousiller*.

♦ **pile-up*** *n* (*Aut*) carambolage *m*.

pile[3] [paɪl] *n [cloth, carpet]* poils *mpl*.

pilfer ['pɪlfəʳ] **1** *vt* chaparder*. **2** *vi* se livrer au chapardage*. ♦ **pilferer** *n* chapardeur* *m*, -euse* *f*. ♦ **pilfering** *n* chapardage* *m*.

pilgrim ['pɪlgrɪm] *n* pèlerin *m*. ♦ **pilgrimage** *n* pèlerinage *m*; **to go on a ~age** faire un pèlerinage.

pill [pɪl] *n* pilule *f*. (*fig*) **to sweeten the ~** dorer la pilule (*for sb* à qn); **to be on the ~** prendre la pilule.

pillage ['pɪlɪdʒ] **1** *n* pillage *m*. **2** *vt* piller. **3** *vi* se livrer au pillage.

pillar ['pɪləʳ] *n* (*gen*) pilier *m*; *[fire, smoke]* colonne *f*. **he was pushed around from ~ to post** on se le renvoyait de l'un à l'autre; **~ of salt** statue *f* de sel; **~ of the Church** pilier de l'Église; **he was a ~ of strength** il a vraiment été d'un grand soutien.

♦ **pillar-box** *n* (*Brit*) boîte *f* aux *or* à lettres; **~-box red** rouge sang *inv*.

pillion ['pɪljən] **1** *n* siège *m* arrière (*d'une moto etc*). **~ passenger** passager *m* de derrière. **2** *adv*: **to ride ~** monter derrière.

pillow ['pɪləʊ] *n* oreiller *m*. ♦ **pillowcase** *or* ♦ **pillowslip** *n* taie *f* d'oreiller.

pilot ['paɪlət] **1** *n* pilote *m*. **2** *adj*: **~ scheme** projet *m* d'essai, projet-pilote *m*; **~ film** film-pilote *m*; **~ light** veilleuse *f* (*de cuisinière etc*). **3** *vt* (*Aviat, Naut*) piloter; (*gen: guide*) guider, diriger.

pimento [pɪ'mentəʊ] *n* piment *m*.

pimp [pɪmp] *n* souteneur *m*.

pimple ['pɪmpl] *n* bouton *m* (*Med*). ♦ **pimply** *adj* boutonneux.

pin [pɪn] **1** *n* **(a)** (*gen*) épingle *f*; (*safety ~*) épingle de sûreté *or* de nourrice; (*drawing ~*) punaise *f*. **as neat as a new ~** *room* impeccable; *person* tiré à quatre épingles; **you could have heard a ~ drop** on aurait entendu voler une mouche; **to have ~s and needles** avoir des fourmis (*in* dans); **for two ~s* I'd smack his face** pour un peu je le giflerais. **(b)** *[machine, device, hand-grenade]* goupille *f*; (*Elec*) fiche *f*; (*Med: in limb*) broche *f*; (*Bowling*) quille *f*. (*Elec*) **3-~ plug** prise *f* à 3 fiches. **2** *adj*: **~ money** argent *m* de poche. **3** *vt* (*gen*) épingler (*to* à; *onto* sur); *papers* attacher avec une épingle (*or* une punaise *etc*); (*Tech*) goupiller. **to ~ sb's arms to his sides** lier les bras de qn contre son corps; **to ~ sb against a wall** clouer qn à un mur; **to ~ one's hopes on sth** mettre tous ses espoirs dans qch; **to ~ a crime on sb*** mettre un crime sur le dos de qn.

pin down *vt sep* fixer (avec une épingle *etc*); *[fallen tree] person* coincer; (*Mil*) *troops* bloquer. (*fig*) **to ~ sb down to a promise** obliger qn à tenir sa promesse; **I can't ~ him down** je n'arrive pas à le coincer* (*fig*); **to ~ sb down to doing** décider qn à faire; **there's sth wrong but I can't ~ it down** il y

a qch qui ne va pas mais je n'arrive pas à mettre le doigt dessus.
pin on *vt sep* épingler.
pin up *vt sep notice* afficher; *hem* épingler; *hair* relever avec des épingles.
♦ **pinball** *n* flipper *m*. ♦ **pincushion** *n* pelote *f* à épingles. ♦ **pinpoint** *vt place* localiser avec précision; *problem* mettre le doigt sur. ♦ **pinprick** *n* piqûre *f* d'épingle; (*fig: annoyance*) coup *m* d'épingle. ♦ **pinstripe suit** *n* costume *m* rayé. ♦ **pinup (girl)*** *n* pin-up *f inv*.
pinafore ['pɪnəfɔːʳ] *n* (*apron*) tablier *m*; (*overall*) blouse *f* (*de travail*). ~ **dress** robe-chasuble *f*.
pincers ['pɪnsəz] *npl* tenailles *fpl*.
pinch [pɪntʃ] **1** *n* **(a)** (*action*) pincement *m*; (*mark*) pinçon *m*. **to give sb a** ~ pincer qn; (*fig*) **to feel the** ~ commencer à être serré *or* à être à court; (*fig*) **at a** ~, (*US*) **in a** ~ à la rigueur; **when it comes to the** ~ au moment critique. **(b)** *[salt]* pincée *f*; *[snuff]* prise *f*. (*fig*) **to take sth with a** ~ **of salt** ne pas prendre qch pour argent comptant. **2** *vt* **(a)** (*gen*) pincer; *[shoes]* serrer; *bud* épincer. **(b)** (*: *steal*) piquer*, voler (*from sb* à qn). **(c)** (‡: *arrest*) pincer*, arrêter. **3** *vi [shoe]* serrer. (*fig*) **to** ~ **and scrape** économiser sur tout. ♦ **pinched** *adj* **(a)** (*drawn*) qui a les traits tirés; ~**ed with cold** transi de froid; **(b)** ~**ed for money** à court d'argent; ~**ed for space** à l'étroit.
pine[1] [paɪn] **1** *n* (~ *tree*) pin *m*. **2** *adj*: ~ **kernel** *or* **nut** pigne *f*; ~ **needle** aiguille *f* de pin. ♦ **pinecone** *n* pomme *f* de pin. ♦ **pinewood** *n* (*grove*) pinède *f*; (*material*) (bois *m* de) pin *m*.
pine[2] [paɪn] *vi*: **to** ~ **for** *sth* désirer ardemment; *sb* s'ennuyer de; **to** ~ **away** languir.
pineapple ['paɪn,æpl] *n* ananas *m*.
ping [pɪŋ] **1** *n* bruit *m* métallique; *[bell, clock]* tintement *m*. **2** *vi* faire un bruit métallique; tinter. ♦ **ping-pong** *n* ping-pong *m*.
pinion ['pɪnjən] *n* (*Tech*) pignon *m*.
pink[1] [pɪŋk] **1** *n* **(a)** (*colour*) rose *m*. (*fig*) **to be in the** ~* se porter comme un charme. **(b)** (*Bot*) mignardise *f*. **2** *adj* (*gen*) rose; (*Pol*) gauchisant. **to turn** ~ *[thing]* rosir; *[person]* rougir. ♦ **pinkish** *adj* rosâtre, rosé.
pink[2] [pɪŋk] *vt* (*Sewing*) denteler. ♦ **pinking shears** *npl* ciseaux *mpl* à denteler.
pinkie* ['pɪŋkɪ] *n* petit doigt *m*.
pinnacle ['pɪnəkl] *n* (*Archit*) pinacle *m*; *[mountain]* cime *f*; (*fig*) apogée *m*.
pint [paɪnt] *n* pinte *f*, ≈ demi-litre *m* (*Brit = 0,57 litre; US = 0,47 litre*). **a** ~ **of beer** ≈ un demi (de bière). ♦ **pinta*** *n abbr of* **pint of milk**. ♦ **pint-size(d)** *adj* tout petit.
pioneer [,paɪə'nɪəʳ] **1** *n* pionnier *m*. **2** *vt*: **to** ~ **sth** être l'un des premiers à faire qch. **3** *adj research etc* complètement nouveau.
pious ['paɪəs] *adj* pieux; (*iro*) *hope* légitime. ♦ **piously** *adv* pieusement.
pip [pɪp] **1** *n [fruit]* pépin *m*; *[card, dice]* point *m*; (*Radar*) spot *m*; (*Brit Mil*: on uniform*) ≈ galon *m*. (*Telec: sound*) ~**s** bip-bip *m*; (*fig*) **he gives me the** ~‡ il me hérisse le poil*. **2** *vt*: **to be** ~**ped at the post*** se faire coiffer au poteau.
pipe [paɪp] **1** *n* **(a)** (*tube*) tube *m*; (*for water, gas*) tuyau *m*, conduite *f*. **(b)** (*Mus: instrument*) pipeau *m*; *[organ]* tuyau *m*. **(bag)**~**s** cornemuse *f*. **(c)** pipe *f*. **he smokes a** ~ il fume la pipe; ~ **of peace** calumet *m* de la paix; **put that in your** ~ **and smoke it!*** si ça ne te plaît pas c'est le même prix!* **2** *adj tobacco* à pipe. ~ **cleaner** cure-pipe *m*; (*fig*) ~ **dream** château *m* en Espagne (*fig*). **3** *vt* **(a)** *oil, water* (*by* ~*line*) transporter (*or* amener *etc*) par tuyau *or* conduite *etc*; (*through tube, hose etc*) verser (*into* dans). **to** ~ **icing on a cake** décorer un gâteau de fondant (à la douille); ~**d music** musique *f* de fond enregistrée. **(b)** (*Naut*) **to** ~ **sb aboard** *etc* saluer l'arrivée *etc* de qn (au son du sifflet). **(c)** (*Sewing*) passepoiler (*with* de). **(d)** (*say*) dire d'une voix flûtée.
pipe down‡ *vi* mettre la sourdine*, se taire.
pipe up* *vi* se faire entendre.
♦ **pipeline** *n* (*gen*) pipe-line *m*; *[oil]* oléoduc *m*; *[natural gas]* gazoduc *m*; (*fig*) **it's in the** ~**line** ça va venir, on s'en occupe. ♦ **piper** *n* (*bagpiper*) cornemuseur *m*. ♦ **piping 1** *n* (*pipes*) tuyauterie *f*; (*Sewing*) passepoil *m*; **2** *adj voice* flûté; **3** *adv*: **piping hot** tout bouillant.
pippin ['pɪpɪn] *n* (pomme *f*) reinette *f*.
piquant ['piːkənt] *adj* piquant. ♦ **piquancy** *n* (*flavour*) goût *m* piquant; *[story]* piquant *m*.
pique [piːk] **1** *vt* dépiter. **2** *n* dépit *m*.
pirate ['paɪərɪt] **1** *n* pirate *m*; (*Comm: gen*) contrefacteur *m*; (*in publishing*) démarqueur *m*. **2** *adj ship* de pirates; *radio* pirate. **3** *vt book* publier en édition pirate; *product* contrefaire; *invention, idea* s'approprier. ♦ **piracy** *n* piraterie *f*. ♦ **pirated** *adj* (*Comm*) contrefait; *edition* pirate.
Pisces ['paɪsiːz] *n* (*Astron*) les Poissons *mpl*.
piss‡ [pɪs] *vi* pisser‡.
pistachio [pɪs'tɑːʃɪəʊ] *n* pistache *f*.
pistol ['pɪstl] **1** *n* pistolet *m*. **2** *adj*: **at** ~ **point** sous la menace du pistolet; ~ **shot** coup *m* de pistolet.
piston ['pɪstən] **1** *n* piston *m* (*lit*). **2** *adj engine* à pistons. ~ **ring** segment *m* (de pistons); ~ **rod** tige *f* de piston.
pit[1] [pɪt] **1** *n* **(a)** (*large hole*) trou *m*; (*on moon etc*) cratère *m*; (*coal* ~) mine *f*, puits *m* de mine; (*as game trap, in garage etc*) fosse *f*; (*quarry*) carrière *f*; (*in motor racing*) stand *m*. **chalk** ~ carrière à chaux; **he works in the** ~**s** il travaille à la mine; **in the** ~ **of his stomach/back** au creux de l'estomac/des reins. **(b)** (*Brit Theat*) (fauteuils *mpl* d')orchestre *m*.
2 *adj*: ~ **pony** cheval *m* de mine; ~ **worker** mineur *m* de fond.
3 *vt* **(a)** opposer (*sb against sb* qn à qn). **to** ~ **o.s.** *or* **one's wits against sb** se mesurer avec qn. **(b)** (*mark*) *metal* piqueter; *skin* grêler.
♦ **pithead** *n* (*Min*) carreau *m* de la mine.
pit[2] [pɪt] **1** *n* (*fruit-stone*) noyau *m*. **2** *vt* dénoyauter.
pitapat ['pɪtə'pæt] *adv*: **to go** ~ *[feet]* trottiner; *[heart]* palpiter; *[rain]* crépiter.
pitch[1] [pɪtʃ] **1** *n* **(a)** (*degree*) degré *m*, point *m*; *[voice]* hauteur *f*; (*Mus*) ton *m*, diapason *m*. (*fig*) **at its (highest)** ~ à son comble; **things have reached such a** ~ **that ...** les choses en sont arrivées à un point tel que ... . **(b)** (*Sport*) terrain *m*. **football** *etc* ~ terrain de football *etc*.
2 *vt* **(a)** (*throw*) *ball* lancer; *object* jeter, lancer. **(b)** (*Mus*) *note* donner. **to** ~ **the voice higher/lower** hausser/baisser le ton de la voix; **this song is** ~**ed too low** cette chanson est dans un ton trop bas; **the speech must be** ~**ed at the right level for the audience** le ton du discours doit être adapté au public. **(c)** (*set up*) *tent* dresser; *camp* établir.
3 *vi* (*fall*) tomber; (*be jerked*) être projeté. **the ship** ~**ed (and tossed)** le navire tanguait.
pitch in* *vi* s'attaquer au boulot*.
pitch into* *vt fus* (*attack, abuse*) tomber sur; (*start*) *meal, work* s'attaquer à.
♦ **pitched** *adj*: ~**ed battle** (*Mil*) bataille *f* rangée; (*fig*) véritable bataille. ♦ **pitchfork 1** *n* fourche *f* à foin; **2** *vt*: **to be** ~**forked into doing sth** être forcé de faire qch immédiatement.
pitch[2] [pɪtʃ] *n* (*tar*) poix *f*. ♦ **pitch-black** *adj* **(a)** noir comme poix; **(b)** (*also* **pitch-dark**) **it's** ~**-black** *or* ~**-dark** il fait noir comme dans un four.
♦ **pitchpine** *n* pitchpin *m*.
pitcher ['pɪtʃəʳ] *n* cruche *f*; (*bigger*) broc *m*.
pitfall ['pɪtfɔːl] *n* piège *m*.
pith [pɪθ] *n [bone, plant]* moelle *f*; *[orange]* peau *f* blanche; (*fig: essence*) essence *f*. ♦ **pithy** *adj* (*forceful*) vigoureux; (*terse*) concis; (*pointed*) piquant.

pittance ['pɪtəns] *n* somme *f* dérisoire; (*income*) maigre revenu *m*; (*wage*) salaire *m* de misère.

pity ['pɪtɪ] **1** *n* **(a)** pitié *f*, compassion *f*. **for ~'s sake** de grâce; **to have/take ~ on sb** avoir/prendre pitié de qn; **to feel ~ for sb** avoir pitié de qn. **(b)** (*misfortune*) dommage *m*. **it is a (great) ~** c'est (bien) dommage; **it's a ~ that** il est dommage que +*subj*; **what a ~!** quel dommage!; **(the) more's the ~!** c'est d'autant plus dommage!; **the ~ of it is that ...** le plus malheureux c'est que ... . **2** *vt* plaindre, avoir pitié de. ♦ **piteous** *adj* pitoyable. ♦ **piteously** *adv* pitoyablement. ♦ **pitiable** *adj hovel, situation* pitoyable; *appearance, attempt* piteux. ♦ **pitiful** *adj* pitoyable; (*pej*) *efforts, cowardice* lamentable. ♦ **pitifully** *adv* (*gen*) pitoyablement; *thin etc* à faire pitié; (*pej*) lamentablement. ♦ **pitiless** *adj* impitoyable. ♦ **pitilessly** *adv* impitoyablement. ♦ **pitying** *adj* compatissant. ♦ **pityingly** *adv* avec pitié.

pivot ['pɪvət] **1** *n* (*Mil, Tech, fig*) pivot *m*. **2** *vt* faire pivoter. **3** *vi* (*Tech*) pivoter; *[person]* tourner.

placard ['plækɑːd] **1** *n* affiche *f*, placard *m*. **2** *vt wall* placarder; *announcement* afficher.

placate [plə'keɪt] *vt* calmer, apaiser.

place [pleɪs] **1** *n* **(a)** (*gen*) endroit *m*, (*more formally*) lieu *m*. **to take ~** avoir lieu; **this is the ~** c'est ici, voici l'endroit; (*US*) **no ~*, not any ~*** (ne ...) nulle part; (*US*) **some ~*** quelque part; **this is no ~ for children** cela n'est pas un endroit convenable pour des enfants; **this isn't the ~ to start an argument** nous ne pouvons pas commencer à discuter ici; **from ~ to ~** d'un endroit à l'autre, de lieu en lieu; **he went from ~ to ~ looking for her** il l'a cherchée de ville en ville (*etc*); **all over the ~** partout; **to find/lose one's ~ in a book** trouver/perdre sa page dans un livre; **to keep/lose one's ~ in the queue** garder/perdre sa place dans la queue; **to laugh at the right ~** rire au bon endroit *or* moment; **to go ~s*** (*travel*) voyager; (*make good*) faire son chemin; (*make progress*) obtenir des résultats; **~ of amusement/birth/work** lieu de distractions/de naissance/de travail; **~ of worship** lieu de culte; **the time and ~ of the crime** l'heure et le lieu du crime; **it's a small ~** (*village*) c'est un petit village; (*house*) c'est une petite maison; **the town is such a big ~ now that ...** la ville s'est tellement agrandie *or* étendue que ...; **he needs a bigger ~** il lui faut qch de plus grand; **at Paul's ~*** chez Paul. **(b)** (*in street names etc*) **Washington P~** rue de Washington; **market ~** place *f* du marché. **(c)** (*seat*) place *f*; (*at table*) place, couvert *m*. **(d)** (*position, situation etc*) place *f*; *[star, planet]* position *f*. **in ~ of** à la place de, au lieu de; **to take the ~ of sb/sth** remplacer qn/qch; **out of ~** *object, remark* déplacé; **I feel rather out of ~** je ne me sens pas à ma place; **in his** (*or* **its** *etc*) **~** à sa place; (*fig*) **to put sb in his ~** remettre qn à sa place; **(if I were) in your ~ ...** (si j'étais) à votre place ...; **it's not your ~ to criticize** ce n'est pas à vous de critiquer; **to give ~ to** céder la place à. **(e)** (*job, vacancy*) place *f*, poste *m*; (*in school etc*) place. **I have got a ~ on the sociology course** j'ai été admis à faire sociologie. **(f)** (*in series, rank*) **in the first ~** en premier lieu, premièrement; **in the second ~** en second lieu, deuxièmement; **in the next ~** ensuite; **in the last ~** enfin; **to 5 decimal ~s** jusqu'à la 5e décimale; **he took second ~ in the race** il a été second dans la course; (*Ftbl etc*) **the team was in third ~** l'équipe était placée troisième; **he took second ~ in history/in the history exam** il a été deuxième en histoire/à l'examen d'histoire; **people in high ~s** les gens haut placés.

2 *adj*: **~ card** carte *f* marque-place; **~ mat** set *m* (de table); **~ name** nom *m* de lieu; **~ setting** couvert *m*.

3 *vt* **(a)** (*put: gen*) placer, mettre. **she ~d the matter in the hands of her solicitor** elle a remis l'affaire entre les mains de son avocat. **(b)** (*situate*) placer, situer. **awkwardly ~d** *shop, house* mal situé *or* placé; (*fig*) *person* dans une situation assez délicate; **well ~d to decide** bien placé pour décider. **(c)** (*in exam, race*) placer. **he was ~d first in French/in the race** il s'est placé premier en français/dans la course. **(d)** (*find ~ for*) *object, goods, employee, money* placer; (*Comm*) *order* passer (*with sb* à qn); *bet* placer (*with sb* chez qn); *contract* passer (*with sb* avec qn). **to ~ a book with a publisher** faire accepter un livre par un éditeur. **(e)** (*remember; identify*) *person* se rappeler; *face* reconnaître; *accent* situer.

♦ **placement** *n* (*Fin*) placement *m*; (*during studies*) stage *m*. ♦ **placing** *n [money, funds]* placement *m*; *[ball, players]* position *f*.

placid ['plæsɪd] *adj* placide, calme. ♦ **placidity** *n* placidité *f*. ♦ **placidly** *adv* avec placidité.

plagiarism ['pleɪdʒjərɪzəm] *n* plagiat *m*. ♦ **plagiarist** *n* plagiaire *mf*. ♦ **plagiarize** *vt* plagier.

plague [pleɪg] **1** *n* (*Med*) peste *f*; (*fig*) (*nuisance*) fléau *m*; (*person*) plaie *f*. **to avoid like the ~** fuir comme la peste. **2** *vt* tourmenter, harceler. **to ~ sb with questions** harceler qn de questions.

plaice [pleɪs] *n* plie *f*.

plaid [plæd] *n* tissu *m* écossais.

plain [pleɪn] **1** *adj* **(a)** (*obvious*) clair, évident (*that* que); *path etc* clairement tracé *or* marqué. **it must be ~ to everyone that ...** il est clair pour tout le monde que ...; **as ~ as a pikestaff** *or* **as the nose on your face*** clair comme le jour; **a ~ case of jealousy** un cas manifeste *or* évident de jalousie; **he made his feelings ~** il n'a pas caché ce qu'il ressentait; **to make sth ~ to sb** faire comprendre qch à qn. **(b)** (*unambiguous*) *statement, meaning* clair; *answer* direct, sans ambages; *person* franc. **~ talk** propos *mpl* sans équivoque; **to be a ~ speaker, to like ~ speaking** aimer la franchise; **to use ~ language** appeler les choses par leur nom; **in ~ words, in ~ English** très clairement; **~ dealings** procédés *mpl* honnêtes; **the ~ truth of the matter is (that) ...** à dire vrai ...; **do I make myself ~?** est-ce que je me fais bien comprendre? **(c)** (*utter*) (tout) pur. **it's ~ madness** c'est pure folie, c'est de la folie toute pure. **(d)** (*simple, unadorned*) *dress, food* simple; (*in one colour*) *fabric* uni. (*unlined*) **~ paper** papier uni; **I'm a ~ man** je suis un homme tout simple; **they used to be called ~ Smith** ils s'appelaient Smith tout court; (*Knitting*) **~ stitch** maille *f* à l'endroit; **in ~ clothes** (*not uniform*) en civil; **~ chocolate** chocolat *m* à croquer; **to send under ~ cover** envoyer sous pli discret. **(e)** (*not pretty*) quelconque, ordinaire (*pej*).

2 *adv* **(a)** (*unambiguously*) franchement, carrément. **I can't put it ~er than this** je ne peux pas m'exprimer plus clairement que cela. **(b)** (*in truth*) tout bonnement. **she's just ~ shy** elle est tout bonnement timide.

3 *n* plaine *f*.

♦ **plain-clothes policeman** *n* policier *m* en civil. ♦ **plainly** *adv* (*obviously*) clairement, manifestement; (*unambiguously*) *speak* carrément, sans détours; *remember, see, explain* clairement; (*simply*) *dress* simplement. ♦ **plainness** *n* (*simplicity*) simplicité *f*; (*lack of beauty*) manque *m* de beauté. ♦ **plainsong** *n* plain-chant *m*. ♦ **plain-spoken** *adj* qui a son franc-parler.

plaintiff ['pleɪntɪf] *n* (*Jur*) plaignant(e) *m(f)*.

plaintive ['pleɪntɪv] *adj voice* plaintif. ♦ **plaintively** *adv* plaintivement.

plait [plæt] **1** *n* natte *f*. **2** *vt* natter.

plan [plæn] **1** *n* **(a)** (*drawing, map*) plan *m*. **(b)** (*project*) plan *m*, projet *m*. **~ of campaign** plan de campagne; **five-year ~** plan quinquennal; **development ~** projet de développement; **to**

draw up a ~ dresser un plan; **everything is going according to ~** tout se passe comme prévu; **to make ~s** faire des projets; **to change one's ~s** prendre d'autres dispositions; **the best ~ would be to leave** le mieux serait de partir; **the ~ is to come back here** notre idée est de revenir ici; **have you got any ~s for tonight?** est-ce que vous avez prévu qch pour ce soir?

2 *vt* **(a)** *house, estate, garden etc* dresser les plans de; *programme, holiday, journey, campaign, attack* organiser; *research, industry, economy* planifier; *crime* combiner; *essay* faire le plan de. **well-~ned house** maison bien conçue; **that wasn't ~ned** cela n'était pas prévu; **as ~ned** comme prévu; **to ~ one's family** pratiquer le contrôle des naissances dans son foyer; **~ned parenthood** contrôle des naissances. **(b)** (*have in mind*) *visit, holiday* projeter. **to ~ to do** avoir l'intention de faire.

3 *vi* faire des projets (*for sth* pour qch). (*fig: expect*) **we didn't ~ for so many visitors** nous n'avions pas prévu tant de visiteurs.

♦ **planner** *n* (*Econ*) planificateur *m*, -trice *f*; **town ~ner** urbaniste *mf*. ♦ **planning 1** *n* (*gen*) organisation *f*; (*Econ*) planification *f*; **2** *adj*: **~ning committee** service *m* de planning; **~ning permission** permis *m* de construire.

plane[1] [pleɪn] *n* (*abbr of* **aeroplane, airplane**) avion *m*.

plane[2] [pleɪn] **1** *n* (*tool*) rabot *m*. **2** *vt* raboter.

plane[3] [pleɪn] *n* (*tree*) platane *m*.

plane[4] [pleɪn] *n* (*Art, Math etc*) plan *m*.

plane[5] [pleɪn] *vi* *[bird, glider, boat]* planer; *[car]* faire de l'aquaplanage.

planet ['plænɪt] *n* planète *f*. ♦ **planetarium** *n* planétarium *m*.

plank [plæŋk] *n* planche *f*.

plankton ['plæŋktən] *n* plancton *m*.

plant [plɑːnt] **1** *n* **(a)** (*Bot*) plante *f*. **(b)** (*machinery etc*) matériel *m*, équipement *m*; (*fixed*) installation *f*; (*buildings*) bâtiments *mpl*; (*factory*) usine *f*. **2** *adj*: **the ~ kingdom** le règne végétal; **~ life** flore *f*; **~ pot** pot *m* (de fleurs). **3** *vt* *seeds, flag, object, kiss* planter; *field* planter (*with* en); *colonists etc* établir; *idea* implanter (*in sb's head* dans la tête de qn). (*fig*) **to ~* a revolver on sb** cacher un revolver sur qn (pour le faire incriminer).

plant out *vt sep seedlings* repiquer.

♦ **plantation** *n* plantation *f*. ♦ **planter** *n* planteur *m*.

plaque [plæk] *n* plaque *f*.

plaster ['plɑːstəʳ] **1** *n* **(a)** (*Constr*) plâtre *m*. **(b)** (*Med: for broken bones*) plâtre *m*. **~ of Paris** plâtre de moulage; **he had his leg in ~** il avait la jambe dans le plâtre; **sticking ~** sparadrap *m*; **a (piece of) ~** un pansement adhésif. **2** *adj mould etc* de *or* en plâtre. **~ cast** (*Med*) plâtre *m*; (*Sculp*) moule *m* (en plâtre). **3** *vt* plâtrer; (*fig: cover*) couvrir (*with* de). **to ~ mud on sth** couvrir qch de boue; **~ed with** couvert de. ♦ **plasterboard** *n* carreau *m* de plâtre. ♦ **plastered**‡ *adj* (*drunk*) beurré‡, soûl. ♦ **plasterer** *n* plâtrier *m*.

plastic ['plæstɪk] **1** *n* matière *f* plastique, plastique *m*. **~s** matières plastiques. **2** *adj object* en *or* de (matière) plastique; *art, substance* plastique. **~ explosive** plastic *m*; **~(s) industry** industrie *f* plastique; **~ surgeon** spécialiste *mf* de chirurgie esthétique; **~ surgery** chirurgie *f* esthétique. ♦ **plasticine** *n* ® pâte *f* à modeler.

plate [pleɪt] **1** *n* **(a)** assiette *f*; (*platter*) plat *m*; (*for church collection*) plateau *m* de quête. (*fig*) **he was handed it on a ~** on lui a apporté ça sur un plateau d'argent; (*fig*) **to have a lot on one's ~*** avoir un travail fou. **(b) gold/silver ~** (*objects*) vaisselle *f* d'or/d'argent; (*electroplated metal*) métal doré/argenté. **(c)** (*Phot, Tech, also on door, battery*) plaque *f*; (*Aut: number ~*) plaque d'immatriculation; (*on cooker: hot ~*) plaque chauffante; (*book illustration*) gravure *f*; (*dental ~*) dentier *m*. **2** *vt* (*with metal*) plaquer; (*with gold/silver etc*) dorer/argenter *etc*. ♦ **plateful** *n* assiettée *f*, assiette *f*. ♦ **plate-glass 1** *n* verre *m* à vitre très épais; **2** *adj*: **~-glass window** baie *f* vitrée. ♦ **platelayer** *n* (*Rail*) poseur *m* de rails. ♦ **plate-rack** *n* égouttoir *m*. ♦ **plate-warmer** *n* chauffe-assiettes *m inv*.

plateau ['plætəʊ] *n* plateau *m* (*Geog*).

platform ['plætfɔːm] **1** *n* (*on bus, scales, in scaffolding etc*) plate-forme *f*; (*for band, in hall*) estrade *f*; (*Rail*) quai *m*. **he was on the ~ at the meeting** il était sur l'estrade *or* il était à la tribune lors de la réunion. **2** *adj*: **the ~ party** la tribune; **~ scales** (balance *f* à) bascule *f*; **~ soles** semelles *fpl* compensées; **~ ticket** billet *m* de quai.

platinum ['plætɪnəm] *n* platine *m*. **~ blond(e)** (*adj*) platiné.

platitude ['plætɪtjuːd] *n* platitude *f*.

platonic [plə'tɒnɪk] *adj* platonique.

platoon [plə'tuːn] *n* (*Mil*) section *f*.

platter ['plætəʳ] *n* plat *m*.

plausible ['plɔːzəbl] *adj* *argument* plausible; *person* convaincant. ♦ **plausibility** *n* plausibilité *f*. ♦ **plausibly** *adv* plausiblement.

play [pleɪ] **1** *n* **(a)** (*amusement*) jeu *m*. **the children were at ~** les enfants jouaient *or* s'amusaient; **to say sth in ~** dire qch par jeu; **a ~ on words** un jeu de mots; (*Sport*) **there was some good ~ in the second half** il y a eu du beau jeu à la deuxième mi-temps; **in/out of ~** *ball* en/hors jeu; **~ starts at 11 o'clock** le match commence à 11 heures; (*fig*) **to make a ~ for sth** tout faire pour avoir qch; **to bring *or* call sth into ~** faire entrer qch en jeu; **to make great ~ with sth** faire grand cas de qch. **(b)** (*Tech etc*) jeu *m*. **too much ~ in the clutch** trop de jeu dans l'embrayage; (*fig*) **to give full *or* free ~ to** donner libre cours à. **(c)** (*Theat*) pièce *f* (de théâtre). **to go to (see) a ~** aller au théâtre; **radio ~** pièce radiophonique; **television ~** dramatique *f*.

2 *vt* **(a)** *game, cards* jouer à; *card, chesspiece* jouer; *opponent, opposing team* jouer contre; *match* disputer (*against* avec). **England will be ~ing Smith in the team** l'Angleterre a sélectionné Smith pour l'équipe; **the match will be ~ed on Saturday** le match aura lieu samedi; **to ~ the game, to ~ fair** (*Sport etc*) jouer franc jeu; (*fig*) jouer le jeu; **don't ~ games with me!** ne vous moquez pas de moi!; **to ~ soldiers** jouer aux soldats; **he ~ed the ball into the net** il a mis la balle dans le filet; (*fig*) **to ~ ball*** coopérer (*with sb* avec qn); (*Cards*) **to ~ hearts** jouer cœur; **to ~ one's ace** jouer son as, (*fig*) jouer sa carte maîtresse; (*fig*) **to ~ one's cards well *or* right** bien jouer son jeu; **to ~ a fish** fatiguer un poisson; (*St Ex*) **to ~ the market** jouer à la Bourse; (*fig*) **to ~ the field*** jouer sur plusieurs tableaux; (*fig*) **to ~ it cool*** garder son sang-froid; **to ~ a joke *or* trick on sb** jouer un tour à qn. **(b)** (*Theat etc*) jouer. **let's ~ it for laughs*** jouons-le en farce; (*lit, fig*) **to ~ one's part well** bien jouer; (*fig*) **he was only ~ing a part** il jouait la comédie; (*fig*) **to ~ a part in sth** contribuer à qch; (*fig*) **he ~ed no part in it** il n'y était pour rien; **to ~ the fool** faire l'imbécile. **(c)** (*Mus etc*) *instrument* jouer de; *note, tune, concerto* jouer; *record* passer; *radio* faire marcher. **they were ~ing Beethoven** ils jouaient du Beethoven. **(d)** *hose, searchlight* diriger (*on* sur).

3 *vi* **(a)** (*gen*) jouer; *[lambs etc]* folâtrer; *[light, fountain]* jouer (*on* sur). **to ~ at chess** jouer aux échecs; **to ~ with sth** jouer avec qch, (*fiddle with it*) tripoter qch; **he just ~s at being a soldier** il ne prend pas au sérieux son métier de soldat; **to ~ at soldiers** jouer aux soldats; **to ~ for money/matches** jouer de l'argent/des allumettes; (*lit, fig*) **to ~ for high stakes** jouer gros jeu; (*fig*) **to ~ with**

fire jouer avec le feu; (*fig*) to ~ **for time** essayer de gagner du temps; to ~ **hard to get*** se faire désirer; to ~ **fast and loose with sb** traiter qn à la légère; to ~ **into sb's hands** faire le jeu de qn; **he's just ~ing with you** il vous fait marcher; to ~ **with an idea** caresser une idée. **(b)** (*Mus*) jouer; *[radio]* marcher. to ~ **on the piano** jouer du piano. **(c)** (*Theat etc*) jouer. (*fig*) to ~ **dead** faire le mort.

play about, play around *vi [children etc]* jouer, s'amuser. to ~ **about** *or* **around with sth** (*fiddle with it*) tripoter qch.

play along 1 *vi* (*fig*) to ~ **along with sb** entrer dans le jeu de qn. **2** *vt sep* (*fig*) to ~ **sb along** tenir qn en haleine.

play back *vt sep tape* (ré)écouter, repasser.

play down *vt sep* (*fig*) minimiser.

play off *vt sep* **(a)** (*fig*) to ~ **off A against B** monter A contre B (pour en tirer profit). **(b)** (*Sport*) to ~ **a match off** jouer la belle.

play on *vt fus sb's credulity, good nature* jouer sur. to ~ **on sb's nerves** agacer qn.

play out *vt sep*: **to be ~ed out*** *[person]* être éreinté*; *[argument]* être périmé.

play over, play through *vt sep music* jouer.

play up 1 *vi* **(a)** (*: *give trouble*) *[engine, child]* faire des siennes. **his leg is ~ing up** sa jambe le tracasse. **(b)** (*curry favour with*) to ~ **up to sb** chercher à se faire bien voir de qn. **2** *vt sep*: **his leg is ~ing him up** sa jambe le tracasse; **that boy ~s his father up** ce garçon en fait voir à son père.

♦ **playact** *vi* jouer la comédie (*fig*). ♦ **playacting** *n* comédie *f* (*fig*). ♦ **play-back** *n* réécoute *f*. ♦ **playbill** *n* affiche *f* (de théâtre). ♦ **playboy** *n* playboy *m*. ♦ **player** *n* **(a)** (*Sport*) joueur *m*, -euse *f*; **football ~er** joueur de football; **(b)** (*Theat*) acteur *m*, -trice *f*; **(c)** (*Mus*) musicien(ne) *m(f)*; **flute ~er** joueur *m*, -euse *f* de flûte. ♦ **playful** *adj* espiègle. ♦ **playfully** *adv* avec espièglerie. ♦ **playfulness** *n* espièglerie *f*. ♦ **playgoer** *n* amateur *m* de théâtre. ♦ **playground** *n* cour *f* de récréation. ♦ **playgroup** *or* ♦ **playschool** *n* ≃ garderie *f*. ♦ **playhouse** *n* (*Theat*) théâtre *m*; (*for children*) maison *f* (pliante). ♦ **playing 1** *n*: **some fine ~ing** (*Sport*) du beau jeu; (*Mus*) des passages bien joués; **2** *adj*: **~ing card** carte *f* à jouer; **~ing field** terrain *m* de jeu *or* de sport. ♦ **playmate** *or* ♦ **playfellow** *n* petit(e) camarade *m(f)*. ♦ **play-off** *n* (*Sport*) belle *f*. ♦ **playpen** *n* parc *m* (pour petits enfants). ♦ **play-reading** *n* lecture *f* d'une pièce (de théâtre). ♦ **playroom** *n* salle *f* de jeux (*pour enfants*). ♦ **plaything** *n* (*lit, fig*) jouet *m*. ♦ **playtime** *n* (*Scol*) récréation *f*. ♦ **playwright** *n* auteur *m* dramatique.

plea [pli:] *n* **(a)** (*excuse*) excuse *f*; (*claim*) allégation *f*; (*entreaty*) appel *m* (*for* à). **(b)** (*Jur*) (*statement*) argument *m*; (*defence*) défense *f*. **to put forward a ~ of self-defence** plaider la légitime défense.

plead [pli:d] *pret, ptp* **pleaded** *or* (*: *esp US*) **pled 1** *vi* **(a)** to ~ **with sb to do** supplier *or* implorer qn de faire; to ~ **for sth** (*beg for*) implorer qch; (*make speech in favour of*) plaider pour qch; **he ~ed for help** il a imploré *or* supplié qu'on l'aide (*subj*). **(b)** (*Jur*) plaider (*for* pour, en faveur de; *against* contre). to ~ **guilty/not guilty** plaider coupable/non coupable. **2** *vt* **(a)** (*Jur etc: argue*) plaider. (*Jur*) to ~ **sb's case,** (*fig*) to ~ **sb's cause** plaider la cause de qn. **(b)** (*give as excuse*) *ignorance etc* alléguer, invoquer; (*Jur*) *insanity etc* plaider. ♦ **pleading 1** *n* prières *fpl* (*for sb* en faveur de qn); **2** *adj* suppliant. ♦ **pleadingly** *adv* d'un air suppliant.

pleasant ['pleznt] *adj* (*gen*) agréable; *person* (*attractive*) sympathique, charmant; (*polite*) aimable. **to have a ~ time** passer un bon moment; **it's very ~ here** on est bien ici. ♦ **pleasantly** *adv* (*gen*) agréablement; *behave, smile, answer* aimablement. ♦ **pleasantness** *n [person, manner]* amabilité *f*; *[place, house]* charme *m*. ♦ **pleasantry** *n* (*joke*) plaisanterie *f*; (*polite remarks*) **~ries** propos *mpl* aimables.

please [pli:z] **1** *vi* **(a)** (*also* **if you ~**) s'il vous plaît, s'il te plaît. **yes ~** oui s'il vous plaît; **come in ~** entrez, je vous prie, (*more formally*) veuillez entrer; (*notice*) **~ do not smoke** prière de ne pas fumer; **~ do!** je vous en prie!, mais bien sûr!; **~ don't!** ne faites pas ça s'il vous plaît! **(b)** (*think fit*) **do as you ~!** faites comme vous voulez *or* comme bon vous semble; **as you ~!** comme vous voulez!; **as many as you ~** autant qu'il vous plaira. **(c)** *[gift etc]* plaire, faire plaisir. **our aim is to ~** nous ne cherchons qu'à satisfaire; **anxious to ~** désireux de plaire.

2 *vt* **(a)** (*give pleasure to*) plaire à, faire plaisir à; (*satisfy*) satisfaire, contenter. **I did it just to ~ you** je ne l'ai fait que pour te faire plaisir; **that will ~ him** ça va lui faire plaisir, il va être content; **easy/hard to ~** facile/difficile à satisfaire; **there's no pleasing him** il n'y a jamais moyen de le contenter *or* de le satisfaire. **(b) to ~ o.s.** faire comme on veut; **~ yourself!** comme vous voulez!; **you must ~ yourself whether ...** c'est à vous de décider si ... .

♦ **pleased** *adj* content (*with* de; *to do* de faire; *that* que + *subj*); **as ~d as Punch** heureux comme tout; **~d to meet you!*** enchanté!; **we are ~d to inform you that ...** nous avons le plaisir de vous informer que ... . ♦ **pleasing** *adj personality* sympathique; *sight, news* qui fait plaisir, agréable. ♦ **pleasingly** *adv* agréablement.

pleasure ['pleʒə^r] **1** *n* **(a)** plaisir *m*. **with ~** avec plaisir, volontiers; **it's a ~!** je vous en prie!; **it's a ~ to see you** quel plaisir de vous voir!; **it gave me much ~ to hear that ...** cela m'a fait grand plaisir d'apprendre que ...; **to find/take great ~ in (doing) sth** trouver/prendre beaucoup de plaisir à (faire) qch; **a life of ~** une vie de plaisirs. **(b) at ~** à volonté; **at your ~** à votre gré; (*Comm*) **we await your ~** nous attendons votre décision. **2** *adj*: **~ boat** bateau *m* de plaisance; **~ cruise** croisière *f*. ♦ **pleasurable** *adj* (très) agréable. ♦ **pleasurably** *adv* (très) agréablement.

pleat [pli:t] **1** *n* pli *m*. **2** *vt* plisser.

plebeian [plɪ'bi:ən] *adj, n* plébéien(ne) *m(f)*.

plebiscite ['plebɪsɪt] *n* plébiscite *m*. **to hold a ~** faire un plébiscite.

pledge [pledʒ] **1** *n* **(a)** (*security, token*) gage *m*. **(b)** (*promise*) engagement *m* (*to do* de faire); (*agreement*) pacte *m*. **to be under a ~ of secrecy** avoir promis de garder le secret; (*fig*) **to sign the ~** faire vœu de tempérance. **2** *vt* **(a)** (*pawn*) mettre en gage. **(b)** (*promise*) promettre (*sth* qch; *to do* de faire); (*vow*) faire vœu (*to do* de faire). **to ~ sb to secrecy** faire promettre le secret à qn. **(c)** (*toast*) boire à la santé de.

plenary ['pli:nərɪ] *adj power* absolu; *assembly* plénier. **in ~ session** en séance plénière.

plenipotentiary [ˌplenɪpə'tenʃərɪ] *adj* plénipotentiaire.

plenty ['plentɪ] *n* **(a)** abondance *f*. **in ~** *grow* en abondance; *live* dans l'abondance; **land of ~** pays *m* de cocagne. **(b) ~ of** (*lots of*) beaucoup de; (*enough*) bien assez de; **I've got ~** j'en ai bien assez; **he's got ~ of friends** il a beaucoup d'amis; **10 is ~** 10 suffisent (largement *or* amplement); **that's ~** ça suffit (amplement). ♦ **plenteous** *or* ♦ **plentiful** *adj harvest, food* abondant; *meal, amount* copieux; **eggs are plentiful** il y a une abondance d'œufs.

pleurisy ['plʊərɪsɪ] *n* pleurésie *f*.

pliable ['plaɪəbl] *adj substance* flexible; *person* docile. ♦ **pliability** *n* flexibilité *f*; docilité *f*.

pliers ['plaɪəz] *npl*: **(pair of) ~** pince(s) *f(pl)*, tenailles *fpl*.

plight [plaɪt] *n* triste situation *f*. **the country's**

economic ~ les difficultés *fpl* économiques du pays.

plimsoll ['plɪmsəl] *n* (*Brit*) (chaussure *f* de) tennis *f*.

plinth [plɪnθ] *n* plinthe *f*.

plod [plɒd] *vi*: **to ~ in/out** *etc* entrer/sortir *etc* d'un pas lent *or* lourd; (*fig*) **we must ~ on** il faut persévérer; (*fig*) **he was ~ding through his maths** il faisait méthodiquement son devoir de maths. ♦ **plodder** *n* bûcheur* *m*, -euse* *f*. ♦ **plodding** *adj step* pesant; *worker* bûcheur*.

plonk [plɒŋk] **1** *n* (*: *cheap wine*) vin *m* ordinaire. **2** *adv*: **~ in the middle of** au beau milieu de. **3** *vt* (**~ down**) poser (bruyamment). **to ~ o.s. down** se laisser tomber.

plop [plɒp] **1** *n* plouf *m*. **2** *vi [stone]* faire plouf; *[raindrops]* faire flic flac.

plosive ['pləʊsɪv] (*Ling*) **1** *adj* explosif. **2** *n* consonne *f* explosive.

plot [plɒt] **1** *n* **(a)** (*ground*) terrain *m*, lotissement *m*. **~ of grass** gazon *m*; **building ~** terrain à bâtir; **the vegetable ~** le carré des légumes. **(b)** (*conspiracy*) complot *m* (*against* contre; *to do* pour faire). **(c)** (*Literat, Theat*) intrigue *f*. (*fig*) **the ~ thickens** l'affaire se corse. **2** *vt* **(a)** (**~ out**) *course, route* déterminer; *graph, curve* tracer point par point; *boundary, piece of land* relever. (*Naut*) **to ~ one's position on the map** pointer la carte. **(b)** (*conspire*) *sb's death etc* comploter (*to do* de faire). ♦ **plotter** *n* conspirateur *m*, -trice *f*. ♦ **plotting** *n* complots *mpl*.

plough [plaʊ] **1** *n* charrue *f*. **2** *vt field* labourer; *furrow* creuser. **3** *vi* **(a)** (*Agr*) labourer. **(b)** (*fig*) **to ~ (one's way) through the mud** avancer péniblement dans la boue; **the car ~ed through the fence** la voiture a défoncé la barrière; **to ~ through a book** lire un livre méthodiquement.

plough back *vt sep profits* réinvestir (*into* dans).

plough up *vt sep* (*lit, fig*) labourer.

♦ **ploughing** *n* labour *m*; *[field etc]* labourage *m*; (*fig*) **the ~ing back of profits** le réinvestissement des bénéfices. ♦ **ploughman** *n* laboureur *m*; **~man's (lunch)** ≃ sandwich *m* (*au fromage*).

plover ['plʌvəʳ] *n* pluvier *m*.

plow [plaʊ] (*US*) = **plough.**

ploy* [plɔɪ] *n* stratagème *m* (*to do* pour faire).

pluck [plʌk] **1** *n* (*courage*) courage *m*, cran* *m*. **2** *vt fruit, flower* cueillir; (*Mus*) *strings* pincer; *guitar* pincer les cordes de; (*Culin*) *bird* plumer. **to ~ one's eyebrows** s'épiler les sourcils. **3** *vi*: **to ~ at sb's sleeve** tirer qn doucement par la manche.

pluck off, pluck out *vt sep feathers* arracher; (*gen*) enlever.

pluck up *vt sep*: **he ~ed up (the) courage to tell her** il a pris son courage à deux mains et le lui a dit.

♦ **pluckily** *adv* avec cran*, courageusement. ♦ **plucky** *adj* courageux, qui a du cran*.

plug [plʌg] **1 n (a)** *[bath, basin, barrel]* bonde *f*; (*to stop a leak*) tampon *m*; (*stopper*) bouchon *m*; *[volcano]* culot *m*. (*in lavatory*) **to pull the ~** tirer la chasse d'eau. **(b)** (*Elec*) prise *f* (de courant); *[switchboard]* fiche *f*; (*Aut: sparking ~*) bougie *f*. **(c)** (*: *publicity*) publicité *f* (indirecte). **to give sth/sb a ~*** donner un coup de pouce (publicitaire) à qch/qn. **2** *vt* **(a)** (**~ up**) *hole, jar* boucher; *leak* colmater; *tooth* obturer (*with* avec). **(b)** (*: *publicize*) faire de la publicité pour.

plug away* *vi* travailler méthodiquement (*at sth* pour faire qch). **he was ~ging away at his maths** il bûchait* ses maths.

plug in (*Elec*) **1** *vi* se brancher. **2** *vt sep* brancher.

♦ **plughole** *n* vidange *f*; **it went down the ~hole** c'est tombé dans le trou (du lavabo *etc*).

plum [plʌm] **1** *n* prune *f*; (*tree*) prunier *m*. (*choice thing*) **the** *or* **a ~*** le meilleur. **2** *adj* **(a)** (*~-coloured)* lie de vin *inv*. **(b)** (*: *best*) **the ~ job** le meilleur travail; **a ~ job** un boulot* en or. ♦ **plum pudding** *n* (plum-)pudding *m*.

plumb [plʌm] **1** *n* plomb *m*. **2** *adj* vertical, d'aplomb. **3** *adv* en plein. **~ in the middle of** en plein milieu de. **4** *vt* **(a)** sonder. **to ~ the depths** (*lit*) sonder les profondeurs; (*fig*) toucher le fond du désespoir. **(b) to ~ in a machine** faire le raccordement d'une machine.

♦ **plumber** *n* plombier *m*. ♦ **plumbing** *n* plomberie *f*. ♦ **plumbline** *n* fil *m* à plomb; (*Naut*) sonde *f*.

plume [plu:m] *n* plumet *m*, (*larger*) panache *m* (*also of smoke*).

plummet ['plʌmɪt] *vi [aircraft, bird]* descendre à pic; *[temperature, prices, sales]* baisser brusquement; *[spirits, morale]* tomber à zéro.

plump[1] [plʌmp] **1** *adj person* rondelet; *child, hand, arm* potelé; *cheek, face, cushion* rebondi; *chicken* dodu. **2** *vt* (**~ up**) *pillow* tapoter. ♦ **plumpness** *n [person]* rondeur *f*.

plump[2] [plʌmp] **1** *vt* (**~ down**) flanquer*. **2** *adv* en plein, exactement. **~ in the middle of** en plein milieu de.

plump down *vi* (*also* **~ o.s. down**) s'affaler.

plump for *vt fus* se décider pour.

plunder ['plʌndəʳ] **1** *n* (*act*) pillage *m*; (*loot*) butin *m*. **2** *vt* piller. ♦ **plunderer** *n* pillard *m*. ♦ **plundering 1** *n* pillage *m*; **2** *adj* pillard.

plunge [plʌndʒ] **1** *n* (*gen*) plongeon *m*; (*steep fall*) chute *f*; (*rash investment*) spéculation *f* hasardeuse (*on* sur). (*fig*) **to take the ~** se jeter à l'eau, sauter le pas. **2** *vt* plonger (*into* dans). **3** *vi* **(a)** (*dive: gen*) plonger (*into* dans; *from* de); *[ship]* piquer de l'avant; (*fig*) *[person]* se lancer (*into* dans). **(b)** (*fall: gen*) *[person]* tomber (*from* de). **the plane ~d to the ground/into the sea** l'avion s'est écrasé au sol/abîmé dans la mer. **(c)** (*rush*) **to ~ in/out** *etc* entrer/sortir *etc* précipitamment. ♦ **plunger** *n* (*for blocked pipe*) ventouse *f*.

pluperfect ['plu:'pɜ:fɪkt] *n* plus-que-parfait *m*.

plural ['plʊərəl] **1** *adj form* pluriel, du pluriel; *verb, noun* au pluriel. **2** *n* (*Gram*) pluriel *m*. **in the ~** au pluriel.

plus [plʌs] **1** *prep* plus. **2** *adj* (*Elec, Math*) positif. (*fig*) **a ~ factor** un atout; **10-~ hours** plus de 10 heures. **3** *n* (*Math*) (signe *m*) plus *m*; (*fig: advantage*) atout *m*.

plush [plʌʃ] **1** *n* (*Tex*) peluche *f*. **2** *adj* (*) *hotel etc* somptueux.

Pluto ['plu:təʊ] *n* (*Astron*) Pluton *f*; (*Myth*) Pluton *m*.

plutocracy [ˌplu:'tɒkrəsɪ] *n* ploutocratie *f*. ♦ **plutocrat** *n* ploutocrate *m*.

plutonium [plu:'təʊnɪəm] *n* plutonium *m*.

ply[1] [plaɪ] *n*: **three-~ wool** laine *f* trois fils. ♦ **plywood** *n* contre-plaqué *m*.

ply[2] [plaɪ] **1** *vt needle, tool, oar* manier; *river* naviguer sur. **to ~ one's trade** exercer son métier (*as* de); **to ~ sb with questions** presser qn de questions; **he plied them with drink** il ne cessait de remplir leur verre. **2** *vi*: **to ~ between** faire la navette entre; **to ~ for hire** faire un service de taxi.

pneumatic [nju:'mætɪk] *adj* pneumatique. **~ drill** marteau-piqueur *m*.

pneumonia [nju:'məʊnɪə] *n* (*Med*) pneumonie *f*.

poach[1] [pəʊtʃ] *vt* (*Culin*) pocher. **~ed eggs** œufs *mpl* pochés. ♦ **poacher**[1] *n* pocheuse *f*.

poach[2] [pəʊtʃ] *vti* braconner. **to ~ for salmon** braconner du saumon; (*fig*) **to ~ on sb's preserves** braconner sur les terres de qn. ♦ **poacher**[2] *n* braconnier *m*. ♦ **poaching** *n* braconnage *m*.

pocket ['pɒkɪt] **1** *n* poche *f*. **with his hands in his ~s** les mains dans les poches; **to go through sb's ~s** faire les poches à qn; (*fig*) **to put one's hand in one's ~** débourser; **it put £100 in his ~** cela lui a rapporté 100 livres; **to have sb/sth in one's ~**

avoir qn/qch dans sa poche; **to line one's ~s** se remplir les poches; **to be out of ~** en être de sa poche; **I was £5 in/out of ~** j'avais fait un bénéfice/essuyé une perte de 5 livres; **air ~** trou *m* d'air; **~ of gas/resistance** poche de gaz/de résistance. **2** *adj flask, calculator, edition* de poche. **3** *vt* empocher (*also fig: gain, steal*); (*fig*) *one's pride* mettre dans sa poche. ♦ **pocketbook** *n* (*wallet*) portefeuille *m*; (*notebook*) calepin *m*; (*US: book*) livre *m* de poche; (*US: handbag*) sac *m* à main. ♦ **pocketful** *n* poche *f* pleine. ♦ **pocket-handkerchief 1** *n* mouchoir *m* de poche; **2** *adj* grand comme un mouchoir de poche. ♦ **pocket-knife** *n* canif *m*. ♦ **pocket-money** *n* argent *m* de poche. ♦ **pocket-size(d)** *adj* (*fig*) tout petit.

pock-marked ['pɒkmɑːkt] *adj face* grêlé; *surface* criblé de petits trous.

pod [pɒd] *n [bean, pea etc]* cosse *f*.

podgy* ['pɒdʒɪ] *adj* rondelet.

podiatry [pɒ'diːətrɪ] *n* (*US*) soins *mpl* du pied. ♦ **podiatrist** *n* pédicure *mf*.

poem ['pəʊɪm] *n* poème *m*. ♦ **poet** *n* poète *m*. ♦ **poetess** *n* poétesse *f*. ♦ **poetic** *adj* poétique; **poetic justice** bonne justice *f*. ♦ **poetically** *adv* poétiquement. ♦ **poetry** *n* poésie *f*; **to write poetry** écrire des poèmes. ♦ **poetry-reading** *n* lecture *f* de poèmes.

poignant ['pɔɪnjənt] *adj* poignant. ♦ **poignancy** *n* caractère *m* poignant. ♦ **poignantly** *adv* d'une manière poignante.

point [pɔɪnt] **1** *n* **(a)** *[pencil, knife etc]* pointe *f*; (*Geog*) pointe, cap *m*. **with a sharp ~** très pointu; (*fig*) **not to put too fine a ~ on it** pour dire les choses comme elles sont; **star with 5 ~s** étoile à 5 branches *fpl*; (*Ballet*) **to be on ~s** faire des pointes; **at the ~ of a sword/revolver** à la pointe de l'épée/sous la menace du revolver.

(b) (*dot: gen*) point *m*; (*decimal ~*) virgule *f* (décimale). **3 ~ 6 (3.6)** 3 virgule 6 (3,6); (*Geom*) **~ A** le point A.

(c) (*on scale, in space, in time*) point *m*. **from that ~ onwards** (*in space*) à partir de là; (*in time*) à partir de ce moment-là; **at this** *or* **that ~** (*in space*) à cet endroit-là; (*in time*) à ce moment-là; **at this ~ in time** en ce moment; **~ of the compass** aire *f* de vent; **from all ~s (of the compass)** de tous côtés; **the train stops at Slough, and all ~s west** le train s'arrête à Slough et dans toutes les gares à l'ouest de Slough; **~ of departure/entry** point de départ/d'arrivée; **from that ~ of view** de ce point de vue; **at that ~ in the road** à cet endroit de la route; (*Brit Elec*) **wall** *or* **power ~** prise *f* de courant (*femelle*); **boiling/freezing ~** point d'ébullition/de congélation; **full to bursting ~** plein à craquer; **to be on the ~ of doing** être sur le point de faire; **the ~ of no return** le point de non-retour; (*fig*) **up to a ~** jusqu'à un certain point; **when it comes to the ~** en fin de compte; **when it came to the ~ of paying** quand le moment de payer est arrivé; **severe to the ~ of cruelty** sévère au point d'être cruel.

(d) (*counting unit: Scol, Sport, St Ex, Typ; also on scale*) point *m*; (*on thermometer*) degré *m*. (*Boxing*) **on ~s** aux points; **to go up 2 ~s** augmenter de 2 points.

(e) (*subject, item*) point *m*. **the ~ at issue** la question qui nous (*or* les *etc*) concerne; **~ of interest** point intéressant; **just as a ~ of interest, did you ...?** à titre d'information, est-ce que vous ...?; **12-~ plan** plan *m* en 12 points; **a ~ of detail/law/honour** *etc* un point de détail/de droit/d'honneur *etc*; **on a ~ of principle** sur une question de principe; **in ~ of fact** en fait, à vrai dire; **~ by ~** point par point; **to make a ~** faire une remarque; **to make the ~ that** faire remarquer que; **you've made your ~!** vous avez dit ce que vous aviez à dire!; **I take your ~** je vois où vous voulez en venir; **~ taken!, you have a ~ there!** c'est juste!; **to win one's ~** avoir gain de cause; **he gave me a few ~s on what to do** il m'a donné quelques conseils sur ce que je devais faire.

(f) (*important part, main idea etc*) *[argument etc]* point *m* essentiel; *[joke etc]* astuce *f*; (*meaning, purpose*) intérêt *m*, sens *m*; (*relevance*) pertinence *f*. **there's no ~ in waiting** cela ne sert à rien d'attendre; **what's the ~ of** *or* **in waiting?** à quoi bon attendre?; **I don't see any ~ in doing that** je ne vois aucun intérêt à faire cela; **the ~ is that ...** le fait est que ..., c'est que ...; **the whole ~ was ...** tout l'intérêt était ...; **that's the (whole) ~!** justement!; **that's not the ~** il ne s'agit pas de cela; **beside the ~** à côté de la question; **off the ~** hors de propos; **very much to the ~** très pertinent; **the ~ of this story is that ...** là où je veux en venir avec cette histoire, c'est que ...; **a long story that seemed to have no ~ at all** une longue histoire qui ne rimait à rien; **I missed the ~ of that joke** je n'ai pas compris l'astuce; **you've missed the whole ~!** vous n'avez rien compris!; **to see** *or* **get the ~** comprendre, saisir; **to come to the ~** en venir au fait; **let's get back to the ~** revenons à ce qui nous préoccupe; **to keep** *or* **stick to the ~** rester dans le sujet; **to make a ~ of doing** ne pas manquer de faire.

(g) (*characteristic*) **good ~s** qualités *fpl*; **bad ~s** défauts *mpl*; **his strong ~** son fort; **he has his ~s** il a certaines qualités; **the ~s to look for when buying ...** les détails *mpl* qu'il faut prendre en considération lors de l'achat de ... .

(h) (*Rail*) **~s** aiguilles *fpl*.

2 *adj* (*Police etc*) **to be on ~ duty** diriger la circulation.

3 *vt* **(a)** (*direct*) *telescope, hosepipe etc* pointer, diriger (*on* sur); *gun* braquer (*at* sur). **he ~ed his finger at me** il m'a montré du doigt. **(b)** (*mark, show*) montrer, indiquer. (*fig*) **it ~s the way to ...** cela montre la voie pour ...; (*fig*) **to ~ the moral** souligner la morale. **(c)** (*Constr*) *wall* jointoyer (*with* de).

4 *vi* **(a) to ~ at sth/sb** montrer qch/qn du doigt; (*fig*) **I want to ~ to one or two facts** je veux attirer votre attention sur un ou deux faits; **all the evidence ~s to him** *or* **to his guilt** tous les témoignages l'accusent; **it all ~s to the fact that ...** tout laisse à penser que ...; **everything ~s that way** tout nous amène à cette conclusion. **(b)** *[signpost]* indiquer la direction (*towards* de); *[gun]* être braqué (*at* sur); *[vehicle etc]* être tourné (*towards* vers). *[needle, clock-hand]* **to be ~ing to sth** indiquer qch.

point out *vt sep* **(a)** (*show*) montrer, indiquer (*to sb* à qn). **(b)** (*mention*) faire remarquer (*that* que). **to ~ sth out to sb** signaler qch à qn; **I should ~ out that ...** je dois vous dire que ... .

point up *vt sep* mettre en évidence.

♦ **point-blank 1** *adj shot* à bout portant; *refusal* catégorique; *request* de but en blanc; **at ~-blank range** à bout portant; **2** *adv* à bout portant; catégoriquement; de but en blanc. ♦ **point-by-point** *adj account etc* méthodique. ♦ **pointed** *adj* (*gen*) pointu; *beard* en pointe; *arch* en ogive; *remark* lourd de sens. ♦ **pointedly** *adv reply* d'une manière significative; *say* d'un ton plein de sous-entendus. ♦ **pointer** *n* **(a)** (*stick*) baguette *f*; (*on scale*) (*indicator*) index *m*, (*needle*) aiguille *f*; (*clue, indication*) indice *m* (*to* de); (*piece of advice*) conseil *m* (*on* sur); (*fig*) **this is a ~er to ...** ceci laisse entrevoir ...; **(b)** (*dog*) chien *m* d'arrêt. ♦ **pointing** *n* (*Constr*) jointoiement *m*. ♦ **pointless** *adj attempt, task, suffering* inutile, vain; *existence* dénué de sens; *murder* gratuit; *explanation, joke, story* qui ne rime à rien; **it is ~less to complain** il ne sert à rien de se plaindre. ♦ **pointlessly** *adv try, work, suffer* inutilement; *kill* sans raison. ♦ **pointlessness** *n [task]* inutilité *f*; *[murder]* gratuité *f*.

poise [pɔɪz] **1** *n* (*balance*) équilibre *m*; (*carriage*) maintien *m*; (*self-confidence*) assurance *f*; (*grace*) grâce *f*. **2** *vt* (*balance*) mettre en équilibre; (*hold balanced*) tenir en équilibre. **to be ~d** (*balanced*) être en équilibre; (*held, hanging, hovering*) être suspendu (en l'air); **~d ready to attack** tout prêt à attaquer; (*fig*) **~d on the brink of success** au bord de la réussite.

poison ['pɔɪzn] **1** *n* (*lit, fig*) poison *m*; *[snake]* venin *m*. **to take ~** s'empoisonner; **to die of ~** mourir empoisonné; **they hate each other like ~** ils ne peuvent pas se sentir*. **2** *adj gas* toxique. **~ ivy** sumac *m* vénéneux. **3** *vt* (*gen*) empoisonner. **it's ~ing his system** cela l'intoxique; **to ~ sb's mind** (*corrupt*) corrompre qn; (*instil doubts*) faire douter qn (*against sb* de qn). ♦ **poisoner** *n* empoisonneur *m*, -euse *f* (*lit*). ♦ **poisoning** *n* (*V* **poison 3**) empoisonnement *m*; intoxication *f*; **to die of ~ing** mourir empoisonné; **arsenic ~ing** empoisonnement à l'arsenic. ♦ **poisonous** *adj snake* venimeux; *plant* vénéneux; *gas, fumes, substance* toxique; (*fig*) *rumours, doctrine* pernicieux; (*) *person* ignoble; (*) *coffee etc* infect.

poke [pəʊk] **1** *n* (*push*) poussée *f*; (*jab*) petit coup *m* (*de coude etc*); (*US*: punch*) coup de poing. **I got a ~ in the eye from his umbrella** j'ai reçu son parapluie dans l'œil. **2** *vt* (*with elbow, finger, stick etc*) donner un coup de coude (*or* avec le doigt *or* de canne) à; (*US*: punch*) donner un coup de poing à; (*thrust*) *stick, finger etc* enfoncer (*into* dans; *through* à travers); *rag etc* fourrer (*into* dans); *fire* tisonner. **he ~d me with his umbrella** il m'a donné un petit coup de parapluie; **he ~d his finger in her eye** il lui a mis le doigt dans l'œil; **he ~d me in the ribs** il m'a enfoncé son coude (*or* son doigt *etc*) dans les côtes; **to ~ one's head out of the window** passer la tête par la fenêtre; (*fig*) **to ~ one's nose into sth*** fourrer le nez dans qch. **3** *vi* **(a)** (**~ out**) sortir, dépasser (*from, through* de). **(b) to ~ about** *or* **around in sth** fourrager *or* fouiner (*pej*) dans qch. ♦ **poker**[1] *n* tisonnier *m*. ♦ **pokerwork** *n* pyrogravure *f*.

poker[2] ['pəʊkə^r] *n* (*Cards*) poker *m*. ♦ **poker-faced** *adj* au visage impassible.

poky ['pəʊkɪ] *adj* (*pej*) exigu et sombre.

Poland ['pəʊlənd] *n* Pologne *f*. ♦ **Pole** *n* Polonais(e) *m(f)*. ♦ **Polish 1** *adj* polonais; **2** *n* (*Ling*) polonais *m*.

polar ['pəʊlə^r] *adj* (*Elec, Geog*) polaire. **~ bear** ours *m* blanc. ♦ **polarity** *n* polarité *f*. ♦ **polarization** *n* polarisation *f*. ♦ **polarize** *vt* (*lit, fig*) polariser.

pole[1] [pəʊl] **1** *n* (*gen*) perche *f*; (*telegraph ~; in fences etc*) poteau *m*; (*flag ~; tent ~*) mât *m*; (*curtain ~*) tringle *f*; (*rod; also for vaulting, punting*) perche. (*fig*) **up the ~*** (*mad*) qui déraille*; (*mistaken*) qui se fiche dedans*. **2** *adj*: **~ vault(ing)** saut *m* à la perche. ♦ **poleax(e)** *vt person* terrasser.

pole[2] [pəʊl] **1** *n* (*Elec, Geog*) pôle *m*. **North/South P~** pôle Nord/Sud; **from ~ to ~** d'un pôle à l'autre; (*fig*) **they are ~s apart** ils sont aux antipodes (l'un de l'autre). **2** *adj*: **~ star** étoile *f* polaire.

polemic [pɒ'lemɪk] *n* polémique *f*.

police [pə'liːs] **1** *n* (*organization*) ≃ police *f* (*gen in towns*), gendarmerie *f* (*throughout France*). **the ~** la police, les gendarmes *mpl*; **to join the ~** entrer dans la police; **river/railway ~** police fluviale/des chemins de fer; **the ~ are on his track** la police est sur sa piste. **2** *adj escort, vehicle, protection, inquiry* de la police *or* de la gendarmerie. **~ car** voiture *f* de police *or* de la gendarmerie; (*Brit*) **~ constable** ≃ agent *m* de police, gendarme *m*; **~ dog** chien policier; **the ~ force** la police, les gendarmes *mpl*; **~ inspector** ≃ inspecteur *m* de police; **~ officer** agent *m* (de police), gendarme *m*; **to have a ~ record** avoir un casier judiciaire; **~ state** état *m* policier; **~ station** commissariat *m* de police, gendarmerie *f*; **~ superintendent** commissaire *m* de police. **3** *vt [vigilantes, volunteers etc] district, road, football match etc* faire la police dans (*or* à, sur *etc*); (*Mil*) *frontier, territory* contrôler; (*fig*) *agreements, controls* veiller à l'application de; *prices etc* contrôler. ♦ **policeman** *n* agent *m* (de police), gendarme *m*. ♦ **policewoman** *n* femme-agent *f*.

policy[1] ['pɒlɪsɪ] **1** *n* (*gen*) politique *f*. **the government's policies** la politique du gouvernement; **what is company ~?** quelle est la ligne suivie par la compagnie?; **to follow a ~ of doing sth** faire qch systématiquement; **it's a matter of ~** c'est une question de principe; **it has always been our ~ to do that** nous avons toujours eu pour règle de faire cela; **it would be good/bad ~ to do that** ce serait une bonne/mauvaise politique que de faire cela; **it would not be ~ to refuse** il ne serait pas politique de refuser. **2** *adj decision, matter, statement* de principe; *discussion* de politique générale.

policy[2] ['pɒlɪsɪ] *n* (*Insurance*) police *f* (d'assurance). **to take out a ~** souscrire à une police d'assurance; **~ holder** assuré(e) *m(f)*.

polio ['pəʊlɪəʊ] *n* polio *f*. **~ victim** polio *mf*.

poliomyelitis ['pəʊlɪəʊmaɪə'laɪtɪs] *n* poliomyélite *f*.

polish ['pɒlɪʃ] **1** *n* **(a)** (*for shoes*) cirage *m*; (*for floor, furniture*) cire *f*; (*for nails*) vernis *m* (à ongles). **metal ~** produit *m* d'entretien pour les métaux; **to give sth a ~, to put a ~ on sth** faire briller qch; **my shoes need a ~** mes chaussures ont besoin d'être cirées. **(b)** (*fig*) *[person]* raffinement *m*; *[style, work, performance]* élégance *f*. **2** *vt* (**~ up**) *stones, glass* polir; *shoes, floor, furniture* cirer; *car, pans, metal* astiquer; *one's French etc* perfectionner.

polish off *vt sep food, drink* finir; *work, correspondence* expédier.

♦ **polished** *adj surface, stone, glass* poli; *floor, shoes* ciré; *silver, ornaments* brillant; (*fig*) *person* qui a de l'éducation; *manners* raffiné; *style* poli; *performer* accompli; *performance* impeccable. ♦ **polisher** *n* (*machine*) polissoir *m*; (*for floors*) cireuse *f*.

polite [pə'laɪt] *adj* poli (*to sb* avec qn). **be ~ about his car!** ne dis pas de mal de sa voiture!; **in ~ society** dans la bonne société. ♦ **politely** *adv* poliment. ♦ **politeness** *n* politesse *f*.

politic ['pɒlɪtɪk] *adj* politique, diplomatique. ♦ **political** *adj* politique; **to ask for ~al asylum** demander le droit d'asile politique. ♦ **politically** *adv* politiquement. ♦ **politician** *n* homme *m* politique, femme *f* politique, politicien(ne) *m(f)* (*pej*). ♦ **politics** *nsg* (*gen*) politique *f*; (*Univ: study*) sciences *fpl* politiques; **to talk ~s** parler politique; **to go into ~s** se lancer dans la politique.

poll [pəʊl] **1** *n* **(a)** (*general vote*) vote *m*; (*at election*) scrutin *m*; (*election*) élection *f*. **to take a ~ on sth** procéder à un vote sur qch; **to go to the ~s** aller aux urnes; **a defeat at the ~s** une défaite aux élections; **there was an 84% turnout at the ~s** la participation électorale était de 84%; **he got 20% of the ~** il a obtenu 20% des suffrages exprimés. **(b)** (*survey*) sondage *m*. **opinion ~** sondage d'opinion; **to take a ~** sonder l'opinion (*of* de); **the Gallup ~** le sondage Gallup. **2** *vt votes* obtenir; *people* sonder l'opinion de. ♦ **polling 1** *n* élections *fpl*; **2** *adj day* des élections; **~ing booth** isoloir *m*; **~ing station** bureau *m* de vote.

pollen ['pɒlən] *n* pollen *m*. ♦ **pollinate** *vt* féconder.

pollute [pə'luːt] *vt* polluer; (*fig*) contaminer. ♦ **pollution** *n* pollution *f*; contamination *f*.

polo ['pəʊləʊ] *n* polo *m*. ♦ **polonecked** *adj* à col roulé.

poltergeist ['pɔːltəgaɪst] *n* esprit *m* frappeur.

poly... ['pɒlɪ] *pref* poly.... ♦ **polyandry** *n* polyandrie *f.* ♦ **polyanthus** *n* primevère *f* (*multiflore*). ♦ **polyester** *n* polyester *m.* ♦ **polyethylene** *n* (*US*) polyéthylène *m.* ♦ **polygamy** *n* polygamie *f.* ♦ **polyglot** *adj, n* polyglotte (*mf*). ♦ **polygon** *n* polygone *m.* ♦ **polygonal** *adj* polygonal. ♦ **polymer** *n* polymère *m.* ♦ **polyphonic** *adj* polyphonique. ♦ **polyphony** *n* polyphonie *f.* ♦ **polystyrene** *n* polystyrène *m*; **~styrene cement** colle *f* polystyrène; **~styrene chips** billes *fpl* de polystyrène. ♦ **polysyllabic** *adj* polysyllabe. ♦ **polysyllable** *n* polysyllabe *m.* ♦ **polytechnic** *n* (*Brit*) ≃ IUT *m*, Institut *m* Universitaire de Technologie. ♦ **polythene** *n* (*Brit*) polyéthylène *m*; **~thene bag** sac *m* en plastique. ♦ **polyurethane** *n* polyuréthane *m.*

polyp ['pɒlɪp] *n* polype *m.*

pomegranate ['pɒmə,grænɪt] *n* grenade *f* (*fruit*).

pommyᵻ ['pɒmɪ] (*Australia pej*) **1** *n* Anglais(e) *m(f).* **2** *adj* anglais.

pomp [pɒmp] *n* pompe *f*, faste *m.* **~ and circumstance** grand apparat *m.*

pompous ['pɒmpəs] *adj* (*pej*) pompeux. ♦ **pomposity** *n* manières *fpl* pompeuses. ♦ **pompously** *adv* pompeusement.

poncho ['pɒntʃəʊ] *n* poncho *m.*

pond [pɒnd] *n* étang *m*; (*stagnant*) mare *f*; (*artificial*) bassin *m.*

ponder ['pɒndə^r] **1** *vt* considérer, réfléchir à *or* sur. **2** *vi* réfléchir (*over, on* à, sur).

ponderous ['pɒndərəs] *adj* (*gen*) pesant; *style, joke* lourd. ♦ **ponderously** *adv* pesamment.

pongᵻ [pɒŋ] **1** *n* puanteur *f.* **2** *vi* puer.

pontiff ['pɒntɪf] *n* pontife *m*; (*pope*) souverain pontife *m.* ♦ **pontifical** *adj* pontifical. ♦ **pontificate** *vi* pontifier (*about* au sujet de, sur).

pontoon [pɒn'tu:n] *n* ponton *m*; (*Cards*) vingt-et-un *m.*

pony ['pəʊnɪ] **1** *n* poney *m.* **2** *adj*: **hair in a ~tail** cheveux *mpl* en queue de cheval. ♦ **pony trekking** *n*: **to go ~ trekking** faire une randonnée *f* à cheval.

poodle ['pu:dl] *n* caniche *m.*

poofᵻ [pʊf] *n* (*pej*) tanteᵻ *f*, tapetteᵻ *f.*

pooh-pooh [pu:'pu:] *vt* faire fi de.

pool [pu:l] **1** *n* **(a)** *[water, rain]* flaque *f*; *[blood]* mare *f*; *[light]* rond *m*; (*pond*) étang *m*; (*artificial*) bassin *m*; (*in river*) plan *m* d'eau; (*water hole*) point *m* d'eau; (*swimming ~*) piscine *f.* **(b)** (*money: gen, also Cards*) cagnotte *f*; (*common supply: gen*) fonds *m* commun (*of* de); *[cars]* parc *m*; *[ideas, experience, ability]* réservoir *m*; *[advisers, experts]* équipe *f*; (*Comm, Econ: consortium*) pool *m.* **typing ~** pool de dactylos. **(c) to win sth on the (football) ~s** gagner qch en pariant sur les matchs de football. **(d)** (*US: billiards*) billard *m* américain. **2** *vt money, resources, objects* mettre en commun; *knowledge, efforts* unir. ♦ **poolroom** *n* salle *f* de billard.

poor [pʊə^r] **1** *adj* (*gen*) pauvre; (*inferior*) médiocre; *light, sight* faible; *effort* insuffisant; *memory, health* mauvais; *soil* pauvre; *loser etc* mauvais. **as ~ as a church mouse** pauvre comme Job; **to become ~er** s'appauvrir; (*lacking*) **~ in** pauvre en; **~ things*, they look cold** les pauvres, ils ont l'air d'avoir froid; **you ~ thing!*** mon pauvre!, ma pauvre!; **it's a ~ thing when ...** c'est malheureux que ... +*subj*; **it was a ~ evening** la soirée n'était pas une réussite; **to be ~ at (doing) sth** ne pas être doué pour (faire) qch; **he is a ~ traveller** il supporte mal les voyages. **2** *n*: **the ~** les pauvres *mpl.* ♦ **poorly 1** *adj* souffrant; **2** *adv live, dress* pauvrement; *work, write, explain* médiocrement, mal; *lit, paid* mal. ♦ **poorness** *n* pauvreté *f*; médiocrité *f.*

pop[1] [pɒp] **1** *n* **(a)** *[cork etc]* pan *m.* **~!** pan!; **to go ~** faire pan. **(b)** (**: drink*) boisson *f* gazeuse. **2** *vt* **(a)** *balloon* crever; *cork, press stud* faire sauter. **(b)** (*put: gen*) mettre. **to ~ one's head round the door** passer brusquement la tête par la porte; (*fig*) **to ~ the question** faire sa demande (en mariage). **3** *vi* **(a)** *[balloon]* crever; *[cork, press stud etc]* sauter; *[corn]* éclater; *[ears]* se déboucher. **his eyes were ~ping out of his head** les yeux lui sortaient de la tête. **(b)** (*go*) **to ~ over** (*or* **round** *or* **across** *or* **out**) faire un saut (*to* à *etc*); **he ~ped into a café** il est entré en vitesse dans un café.

pop in *vi* entrer en passant.

pop off *vi* (*leave*) partir; (ᵻ: *die*) claquer*, mourir.

pop up *vi [person]* surgir.

♦ **popcorn** *n* pop-corn *m.* ♦ **popeyed** *adj* aux yeux écarquillés. ♦ **popgun** *n* pistolet *m* à bouchon. ♦ **popper** *n* (*press stud*) pression *f.*

pop[2] [pɒp] (*abbr of* **popular**) **1** *adj song, singer, art* pop *inv.* **2** *n* (musique *f*) pop *m.* **it's top of the ~s** c'est en tête du hit-parade.

pop[3]* [pɒp] *n* (*esp US*) papa *m.*

pope [pəʊp] *n* pape *m.* **P~ Paul** le pape Paul. ♦ **popery** *n* papisme *m.* ♦ **popish** *adj* papiste.

poplar ['pɒplə^r] *n* peuplier *m.*

poplin ['pɒplɪn] *n* popeline *f.*

poppet* ['pɒpɪt] *n*: **yes, ~** oui, mon petit chou; **she's a ~** c'est un amour.

poppy ['pɒpɪ] **1** *n* pavot *m*; (*growing wild*) coquelicot *m.* **2** *adj*: **P~ Day** anniversaire *m* de l'armistice; **~ seed** graine *f* de pavot. ♦ **poppycock*** *n* balivernes *fpl.*

populace ['pɒpjʊlɪs] *n* peuple *m*, foule *f.*

popular ['pɒpjʊlə^r] *adj* **(a)** (*well-liked*) populaire; (*fashionable*) à la mode. **he is ~ with his colleagues** ses collègues l'aiment beaucoup; **he is ~ with the girls** il a du succès auprès des filles; **I'm not very ~ with the boss*** je ne suis pas très bien vu du patron. **(b)** (*for, by the people: gen, Pol*) populaire; *lecture, journal* de vulgarisation. **by ~ request** à la demande générale. ♦ **popularity** *n* popularité *f* (*with* auprès de; *among* parmi). ♦ **popularize** *vt music, fashion, product* rendre populaire; *science, ideas* vulgariser. ♦ **popularizer** *n* vulgarisateur *m*, -trice *f.* ♦ **popularly** *adv* communément.

populate ['pɒpjʊleɪt] *vt* peupler. ♦ **population 1** *n* population *f*; **2** *adj increase, explosion* démographique.

porcelain ['pɔ:səlɪn] *n* porcelaine *f.* **a piece of ~** une porcelaine.

porch [pɔ:tʃ] *n* porche *m.* **sun ~** véranda *f.*

porcupine ['pɔ:kjʊpaɪn] *n* porc-épic *m.*

pore[1] [pɔ:^r] *n* (*Anat*) pore *m.*

pore[2] [pɔ:^r] *vi*: **to ~ over** *book* être absorbé dans; *letter, map* étudier de près; *problem* méditer longuement.

pork [pɔ:k] (*Culin*) **1** *n* porc *m.* **2** *adj chop etc* de porc. **~ butcher** ≃ charcutier *m*; **~ pie** ≃ pâté *m* en croûte.

pornography [pɔ:'nɒgrəfɪ] *n* pornographie *f.* ♦ **porn*** *n* porno* *m or f*; **soft/hard porn** pornographie douce/dure; **porn shop** boutique *f* pornographique. ♦ **pornographic** *adj* pornographique.

porous ['pɔ:rəs] *adj* poreux, perméable.

porpoise ['pɔ:pəs] *n* marsouin *m* (*Zool*).

porridge ['pɒrɪdʒ] *n* porridge *m.* **~ oats** flocons *mpl* d'avoine.

port[1] [pɔ:t] **1** *n* port *m.* **~ of call** (port d')escale *f*; **naval/fishing ~** port militaire/de pêche; **to come into ~** entrer dans le port; **to leave ~** appareiller; (*fig*) **any ~ in a storm** nécessité n'a pas de loi. **2** *adj facilities, authorities* portuaire.

port[2] [pɔ:t] (*Naut: left*) **1** *n* bâbord *m.* **2** *adj* de bâbord.

port[3] [pɔ:t] *n* (*wine*) porto *m.*

portable ['pɔ:təbl] **1** *adj* portatif. **2** *n* modèle *m* portatif.

porter ['pɔ:tə^r] *n* (*for luggage*) porteur *m*; (*US: on train*) employé(e) *m(f)* des wagons-lits; (*door-*

keeper) concierge *mf*; *[public building]* gardien(ne) *m(f)*. ♦ **porterhouse (steak)** *n* ≃ chateaubriand *m*.
portfolio [pɔːtˈfəulɪəu] *n* portefeuille *m* (*Admin*).
porthole [ˈpɔːthəul] *n* hublot *m*.
portion [ˈpɔːʃən] *n* (*gen*) portion *f*; *[train, ticket etc]* partie *f*.
portly [ˈpɔːtlɪ] *adj* corpulent.
portmanteau [pɔːtˈmæntəu] *n* grosse valise *f*. ~ **word** mot-valise *m*.
portrait [ˈpɔːtrɪt] **1** *n* portrait *m*. **2** *adj gallery* de portraits. ~ **painter** portraitiste *mf*. ♦ **portray** [pɔːˈtreɪ] *vt [painter]* peindre, faire le portrait de; *[painting]* représenter; **he portrayed him as ...** *[painter]* il l'a peint sous les traits de ...; *[writer, actor]* il en a fait ... .
Portugal [ˈpɔːtjugəl] *n* Portugal *m*. ♦ **Portuguese 1** *adj* portugais; **2** *n* (*person: pl inv*) Portugais(e) *m(f)*; (*language*) portugais *m*.
pose [pəuz] **1** *n* pose *f*. **to strike a** ~ poser (pour la galerie); **it's only a** ~ c'est de la pose. **2** *vi* (*Art etc*) poser (*for* pour; *as* en); (*fig: attitudinize*) poser. **to** ~ **as a doctor** se faire passer pour un docteur. **3** *vt* **(a)** *artist's model* faire prendre une pose à; *person* faire poser. **(b)** *problem, question* poser; *difficulties* créer. ♦ **poser** *n* question *f* difficile. ♦ **poseur** *n* poseur *m*, -euse *f*.
posh* [pɒʃ] **1** *adj* (*gen*) chic *inv*; *accent* distingué. **2** *adv*: **to talk** ~ parler comme les gens bien.
posh up* *vt sep house* embellir; (*clean up*) briquer; *child* pomponner, bichonner. **to** ~ **o.s. up** se pomponner; **he was all** ~**ed up** il était sur son trente et un, il était bien sapé*.
posit [ˈpɒzɪt] *vt* énoncer, poser en principe.
position [pəˈzɪʃən] **1** *n* (*gen*) position *f*; *[house, shop, town, gun]* emplacement *m*; (*circumstances, also job*) situation *f*. **in(to)** ~ en place, en position; **to change the** ~ **of sth** changer qch de place; **to take up (one's)** ~ prendre position; (*Sport*) **what** ~ **do you play in?** à quelle place jouez-vous?; (*lit, fig*) **to jockey** *or* **manoeuvre for** ~ manœuvrer pour se placer avantageusement; **in a horizontal** ~ en position horizontale; **in an uncomfortable** ~ dans une position incommode; **he finished in 3rd** ~ il est arrivé en 3e position *or* place; **his** ~ **in the government** son poste *or* sa fonction dans le gouvernement; **a** ~ **of trust** un poste de confiance; **to be in a** ~ **to do sth** être en mesure de faire qch; **to be in a good** ~ **to do sth** être bien placé pour faire qch; **put yourself in my** ~ mettez-vous à ma place; **a man in his** ~ un homme dans sa situation; **the economic** ~ la situation économique, la conjoncture; **in an awkward** ~ dans une situation délicate; **you must make your** ~ **clear** vous devez dire franchement quelle est votre position (*on* sur).
2 *vt* **(a)** (*adjust angle of*) *light etc* mettre en position. **(b)** (*put in place: gen*) placer; *army, ship* mettre en position. **to** ~ **o.s.** se mettre, se placer.
positive [ˈpɒzɪtɪv] *adj* **(a)** (*gen*) positif; (*affirmative*) affirmatif; (*constructive*) *help* concret; *attitude, criticism* positif. **(b)** (*definite*) *order* formel; *fact, proof* indéniable; *change, increase, improvement* réel, tangible; *contribution* effectif. **it's a** ~ **miracle*** c'est un vrai miracle; **he's a** ~ **genius*** c'est un véritable génie. **(c)** (*certain*) *person* sûr, certain (*about, on, of* de); *tone* assuré. **I'm quite** ~ j'en suis sûr *or* certain. ♦ **positively** *adv* (*indisputably*) indéniablement; (*categorically*) formellement; (*affirmatively*) affirmativement; (*with certainty*) de façon certaine; (*emphatically*) positivement; (*absolutely*) complètement; **to think** ~**ly** penser de façon constructive.
possess [pəˈzes] *vt* posséder. **like one** ~**ed** comme un possédé; **what can have** ~**ed him to say that?** qu'est-ce qui l'a pris de dire ça? ♦ **possession** *n* possession *f*; **in** ~**ion of** en possession de; **to have in one's** ~**ion** avoir en sa possession; **to get** ~**ion of** acquérir, obtenir, (*improperly*) s'emparer de; **to come into sb's** ~**ion** tomber en la possession de qn; **the information in my** ~**ion** les renseignements dont je dispose; **to take** ~**ion of** prendre possession de, (*improperly*) s'approprier, (*confiscate*) confisquer; (*Jur*) **to be in** ~**ion** occuper les lieux; **a house with vacant** ~**ion** une maison avec jouissance immédiate. ♦ **possessive 1** *adj* possessif (*with sb* à l'égard de qn); **to be** ~**ive about sth** ne pas vouloir partager qch; **an over-**~**ive mother** une mère abusive; **2** *n* (*Gram*) possessif *m*; **in the** ~**ive** au possessif. ♦ **possessively** *adv* d'une façon possessive. ♦ **possessiveness** *n* possessivité *f*. ♦ **possessor** *n* possesseur *m*; **the proud** ~**or of** l'heureux propriétaire de.
possibility [ˌpɒsəˈbɪlɪtɪ] *n* (*gen*) possibilité *f*. **some** ~**/not much** ~ **of success** quelques chances/peu de chances de succès; **there is some/no** ~ **that** il est/n'est pas possible que +*subj*; **it's a distinct** ~ c'est bien possible; **he is a** ~ **for the job** c'est un candidat possible; **the job has real possibilities** c'est un emploi qui offre toutes sortes de possibilités; (*of idea etc*) **it's got possibilities** c'est possible, c'est à voir.
possible [ˈpɒsəbl] **1** *adj* possible. **it is** ~ **that** il se peut que +*subj*, il est possible que +*subj*; **it's** ~ **to do so** il est possible de le faire; **it is** ~ **for him to leave** il lui est possible de partir; **if** ~ si possible; **as far as** ~ dans la mesure du possible; **as much as** ~ autant que possible; **he did as much as** ~ il a fait tout ce qu'il pouvait; **the best** ~ **result** le meilleur résultat possible; **one** ~ **result** un résultat possible *or* éventuel; **what** ~ **interest can you have in it?** qu'est-ce qui peut bien vous intéresser là-dedans?; **a** ~ **candidate** un candidat possible *or* acceptable. **2** *n*: **a list of** ~**s* for the job** une liste de personnes susceptibles d'être retenues pour ce poste; **he's a** ~* **for the match** c'est un joueur possible pour le match. ♦ **possibly** *adv* **(a)** (*with 'can' etc*) **as often as I possibly can** aussi souvent qu'il m'est matériellement possible de le faire; **all he possibly can** *or* **could do** tout son possible (*to help etc* pour aider *etc*); **if I possibly can** si cela m'est possible; **I cannot possibly come** il m'est absolument impossible de venir; **(b)** (*perhaps*) peut-être.
post[1] [pəust] **1** *n* (*gen*) poteau *m*; (*door* ~ *etc*) montant *m*. (*Sport*) **starting/winning** ~ poteau de départ/d'arrivée; **to be beaten at the** ~ être battu sur le poteau. **2** *vt* **(a)** (~ **up**) *notice, list* afficher. **(b)** (*announce*) annoncer. (*Mil etc*) **to** ~ **sth/sb missing** porter qch/qn disparu. ♦ **poster** *n* affiche *f*; (*decorative*) poster *m*; ~**er paint** gouache *f*.
post[2] [pəust] **1** *n* **(a)** (*Mil, gen*) poste *m*. **at one's** ~ à son poste; (*bugle call*) **last** ~ extinction *f* des feux, (*at funerals*) sonnerie *f* aux morts. **(b)** (*trading* ~) comptoir *m*. **(c)** (*job*) poste *m*. **a** ~ **as a manager** un poste de directeur. **2** *vt* **(a)** *sentry, guard* poster. **(b)** (*send*) *person* affecter (*to* à).
post[3] [pəust] **1** *n* poste *f*; (*letters*) courrier *m*. **by** ~ par la poste; **by return of** ~ par retour du courrier; **first-/second-class** ~ ≃ tarif *m* normal/réduit; **to put sth in the** ~ poster qch; **it's in the** ~ c'est déjà posté; **it went first** ~ **this morning** c'est parti ce matin par le premier courrier; **to catch/miss the** ~ avoir/manquer la levée; **take this to the** ~ portez ceci à la poste; **has the** ~ **come yet?** est-ce que le courrier est arrivé?; (*cost*) ~ **and packing** frais *mpl* de port et d'emballage; **Ministry of P**~**s and Telecommunications** ministère *m* des Postes et Télécommunications. **2** *vt* **(a)** (*send*) envoyer par la poste; (*put in mailbox*) mettre à la poste, poster. **to** ~ **sth on** faire suivre qch. **(b)** (*fig*) **to keep sb** ~**ed** tenir qn au courant. ♦ **postage** *n* tarifs *mpl* postaux (*to* pour);

(*in account*) '~**age: £2**' 'frais *mpl* de port: 2 livres'; ~**age due 20p** surtaxe *f* 20 pence. ♦ **postal** *adj district, code, charges* postal; *application* par la poste; *vote* par correspondance; ~**al order** mandat *m* (postal) (*for 10 francs* de 10 F); ~**al worker** employé(e) *m(f)* des postes. ♦ **postbag** *n* sac *m* postal. ♦ **postbox** *n* boîte *f* aux lettres. ♦ **postcard** *n* carte *f* postale. ♦ **poste restante** *n* poste *f* restante. ♦ **post-free** *adv* franco de port. ♦ **posthaste** *adv* le plus vite possible. ♦ **postmark 1** *n* cachet *m* de la poste; **letter with a French** ~**mark** lettre timbrée de France; **2** *vt* tamponner, timbrer; **it is** ~**marked Paris** il y a 'Paris' sur le cachet. ♦ **postmaster** *n* receveur *m* des postes; (*Brit*) **P**~**master General** ministre *m* des Postes et Télécommunications. ♦ **postmistress** *n* receveuse *f* des postes. ♦ **post office 1** *n* (*place*) (bureau *m* de) poste *f*; (*organization*) service *m* des postes; **he works in the** ~ **office** il est employé des postes; **the main** ~ **office** la grande poste; **2** *adj*: **P**~ **Office Box** (*abbr* **P.O. Box**) **24** boîte *f* postale no. 24 (*abbr* B.P. 24); (*US*) **P**~ **Office Department** ministère *m* des Postes et Télécommunications; **P**~ **Office Savings Bank** ≃ Caisse *f* d'Épargne.

post- [pəʊst] *pref* post-. ~**-1950** (*adj*) postérieur à 1950, d'après 1950; (*adv*) après 1950. ♦ **postdate** *vt* postdater. ♦ **postgraduate 1** *adj studies, grant* ≃ de troisième cycle (universitaire); *diploma* décerné après la licence; **2** *n* ≃ étudiant(e) *m(f)* de 3ᵉ cycle. ♦ **post-impressionism** *n* post-impressionnisme *m*. ♦ **post-mortem** *n* autopsie *f* (*on* de). ♦ **postnatal** *adj* post-natal. ♦ **postwar** *adj* de l'après-guerre; **the** ~**war period** l'après-guerre *m*.

posterior [pɒsˈtɪərɪəʳ] *adj* postérieur (*to* à). ♦ **posterity** *n* postérité *f*.

posthumous [ˈpɒstjʊməs] *adj* posthume. ♦ **posthumously** *adv* (*gen*) après sa (*etc*) mort; *award* à titre posthume.

postpone [pəʊstˈpəʊn] *vt* remettre (*for* de, *until* à); renvoyer (à plus tard). ♦ **postponement** *n* renvoi *m* (à plus tard).

postscript [ˈpəʊsskrɪpt] *n* post-scriptum *m inv*.

postulate [ˈpɒstjʊleɪt] *vt* poser comme principe; (*Philos*) postuler.

posture [ˈpɒstʃəʳ] **1** *n* posture *f*. **2** *vi* (*pej*) poser.

posy [ˈpəʊzɪ] *n* petit bouquet *m* (de fleurs).

pot [pɒt] **1** *n* **(a)** (*for flowers, jam etc*) pot *m*; (*piece of pottery*) poterie *f*; (*for cooking*) marmite *f*; (*saucepan*) casserole *f*; (*tea*~) théière *f*; (*coffee* ~) cafetière *f*; (*chamber*~) pot (de chambre). **jam** ~ pot à confiture; ~ **of jam** pot de confiture; ~**s and pans** casseroles; (*fig*) ~**s of*** des tas* de; **to have** ~**s of money*** avoir un argent fou*; **to go to** ~* *[person]* se laisser complètement aller; *[business]* aller à la dérive; *[plans]* aller à vau-l'eau. **(b)** (*: *marijuana*) marie-jeanne* *f*. **2** *adj*: ~ **roast** rôti *m* braisé. **3** *vt* **(a)** *plant, jam* mettre en pot. ~**ted meat** ≃ rillettes *fpl* de viande; ~**ted plant** plante *f* en pot; (*fig*) **a** ~**ted version of** un abrégé de. **(b)** (*: *shoot*) *pheasant etc* descendre*. **(c)** (*) *baby* mettre sur le pot. **4** *vi* **(a)** (*make pottery*) faire de la poterie. **(b)** (*shoot*) to ~ **at sth** tirer qch. ♦ **potbellied** *adj* (*from overeating*) bedonnant*; (*from malnutrition*) au ventre ballonné. ♦ **potbound** *adj plant* (trop) à l'étroit dans son pot. ♦ **potherbs** *npl* herbes *fpl* potagères. ♦ **pothole** *n* (*in road*) fondrière *f*; (*underground*) caverne *f*, (*larger*) gouffre *m*. ♦ **potholer** *n* spéléologue *mf*. ♦ **potholing** *n* spéléologie *f*; **to go** ~**holing** faire de la spéléologie. ♦ **potluck** *n*: **to take** ~**luck** (*for food*) manger à la fortune du pot; (*for other things*) courir le risque. ♦ **pot-scourer** *or* ♦ **pot-scrubber** *n* tampon *m* à récurer. ♦ **potsherd** *n* tesson *m* (de poterie). ♦ **potshot** *n*: **to take a** ~**shot at sth** tirer qch à vue de nez.

potash [ˈpɒtæʃ] *n* potasse *f*.

potassium [pəˈtæsɪəm] *n* potassium *m*.

potato [pəˈteɪtəʊ] *pl* ~**es 1** *n* pomme *f* de terre. **sweet** ~ patate *f* douce. **2** *adj field, salad* de pommes de terre. (*US*) ~ **chips,** (*Brit*) ~ **crisps** pommes *fpl* chips. ♦ **potato-peeler** *n* épluche-légumes *m inv*.

potent [ˈpəʊtənt] *adj* (*gen*) puissant; *drink* fort. ♦ **potency** *n* puissance *f*; *[drink]* forte teneur *f* en alcool.

potential [pəʊˈtenʃəl] **1** *adj* (*gen*) potentiel; *sales, uses* possible, éventuel. **a** ~ **prime minister** un premier ministre en puissance. **2** *n* (*Elec, Math, Mil etc*) potentiel *m*; (*fig: possibilities*) potentialités *fpl*. **to have great** ~ être très prometteur; **he hasn't yet realized his full** ~ il n'a pas encore donné toute sa mesure. ♦ **potentially** *adv* potentiellement.

potpourri [pəʊˈpʊrɪ] *n [flowers]* fleurs *fpl* séchées; (*fig, Mus*) pot-pourri *m*.

potter¹ [ˈpɒtəʳ] *vi* mener sa petite vie tranquille, bricoler*. **to** ~ **(about) round the house** faire des petits travaux dans la maison; **to** ~ **round the shops** faire les magasins sans se presser.

potter² [ˈpɒtəʳ] *n* potier *f*. ~**'s wheel** tour *m* de potier. ♦ **pottery 1** *n* (*craft, place*) poterie *f*; (*objects*) poteries; **a piece of** ~**y** une poterie; **2** *adj jug, dish* de *or* en terre.

potty¹* [ˈpɒtɪ] *n* pot *m* (de bébé). ♦ **potty-trained** *adj* propre.

potty²* [ˈpɒtɪ] *adj person* toqué* (*about* de); *idea* farfelu.

pouch [paʊtʃ] *n* petit sac *m*; (*for money*) bourse *f*; (*for tobacco*) blague *f*; (*US Diplomacy*) valise *f* (diplomatique); (*Anat, Zool*) poche *f*.

pouf(fe) [puːf] *n* **(a)** (*seat*) pouf *m*. **(b)** (‡) = **poof.**

poultice [ˈpəʊltɪs] *n* cataplasme *m*.

poultry [ˈpəʊltrɪ] **1** *n* volaille *f*, volailles. **2** *adj*: ~ **dealer** marchand *m* de volailles; ~ **farm** élevage *m* de volailles; ~ **farmer** éleveur *m*, -euse *f* de volailles; ~ **farming** élevage *m* de volailles. ♦ **poulterer** *n* marchand *m* de volailles.

pounce [paʊns] **1** *n* bond *m*, attaque *f* subite. **2** *vi* bondir, sauter (*on* sur). (*fig*) **to** ~ **on** *object* se précipiter sur; *suggestion* sauter sur.

pound¹ [paʊnd] *n* **(a)** (*weight*) livre *f* (= *453,6 grammes*). **sold by the** ~ vendu à la livre; **80p a** ~ 80 pence la livre. **(b)** (*money*) livre *f*. ~ **sterling** livre sterling (*inv*); ~ **note** billet *m* d'une livre.

pound² [paʊnd] **1** *vt drugs, spices, nuts* piler; *meat* attendrir; *dough* battre; *earth, paving slabs* pilonner; *rocks* concasser; *[guns, bombs]* pilonner; *[sea]* battre sans arrêt contre; *[person] door etc* marteler; *typewriter, piano* taper sur; *person* bourrer de coups. **to** ~ **sth to a pulp** réduire qch en bouillie. **2** *vi* **(a)** *[heart]* battre fort; *[drums]* battre; *[sea, waves]* battre (*on, against* contre). *[person]* **to** ~ **on** *door* marteler; *table* frapper (du poing) sur; *piano etc* taper sur. **(b) to** ~ **in** *etc* entrer *etc* (*heavily*) en martelant le plancher *or* (*at a run*) en courant bruyamment. ♦ **pounding** *n*: **to take a** ~**ing** *[boat]* être battu par les vagues; *[bombed etc city]* être pillonné; *[team]* se faire battre à plate couture.

pound³ [paʊnd] *n* (*for dogs, cars*) fourrière *f*.

pour [pɔːʳ] **1** *vt liquid* verser. **to** ~ **water away** *or* **off** vider de l'eau; **he** ~**ed me a drink** il m'a versé *or* servi à boire; (*fig*) **to** ~ **money into a scheme** investir énormément d'argent dans un projet. **2** *vi* **(a)** *[water, blood etc]* ruisseler (*from* de). **to come** ~**ing in** *[water, sunshine]* entrer à flots; *[letters]* arriver en avalanche; *[people, cars]* arriver en masse; **smoke was** ~**ing from the chimney** des nuages de fumée s'échappaient de la cheminée; (*fig*) **goods are** ~**ing out of the factories** les usines déversent des quantités de marchandises. **(b) it is** ~**ing (with rain)** il pleut à torrents.

pour out *vt sep drinks* verser, servir (*for sb* à qn);

dregs, unwanted liquid vider; (*fig*) *anger, emotion* donner libre cours à; *troubles* épancher; *complaint* déverser; *story* raconter d'un seul jet. ♦ **pouring** *adj sauce etc* liquide; *rain* torrentiel; **a ~ing wet day** une journée de pluie torrentielle.

pout [paʊt] **1** *n* moue *f*. **2** *vi* faire la moue.

poverty ['pɒvətɪ] *n* (*gen*) pauvreté *f*. **to live in ~** vivre dans le besoin; **extreme ~** misère *f*; **~ of resources** manque *m* de ressources. ♦ **poverty-stricken** *adj person, family* dans la misère; *district, conditions* misérable; (*hum: hard up*) fauché*.

powder ['paʊdəʳ] **1** *n* poudre *f*. **2** *adj*: **~ compact** poudrier *m*; **~ puff** houppette *f*; **~ room** toilettes *fpl* (pour dames). **3** *vt* **(a)** *chalk, rocks* pulvériser. **~ed milk** lait *m* en poudre; (*US*) **~ed sugar** sucre *m* glace. **(b)** *face, body* poudrer. **to ~ one's nose** se mettre de la poudre; (**fig: go to lavatory*) ≃ se refaire une beauté. ♦ **powdery** *adj substance, snow* poudreux; *surface* couvert de poudre.

power ['paʊəʳ] **1** *n* **(a)** (*ability,capacity*) pouvoir *m*, capacité *f*; (*faculty*) faculté *f*. **it is not within my ~ to help you** il n'est pas en mon pouvoir de vous aider; **he did everything in his ~ to help us** il a fait tout ce qui était en son pouvoir pour nous aider; **mental ~s** facultés mentales; **the ~ of movement** la faculté de se mouvoir; **he lost the ~ of speech** il a perdu la parole; **~s of persuasion** pouvoir de persuasion; **~s of resistance** capacité de résistance; **~s of imagination** faculté d'imagination.

(b) (*force*) *[person, blow, sun, explosion]* puissance *f*, force *f*; *[engine, telescope etc]* puissance; (*energy*) énergie *f*. **it works by nuclear ~** ça fonctionne à l'énergie nucléaire; (*Elec*) **they cut off the ~** ils ont coupé le courant; (*Elec*) **consumption of ~** consommation *f* d'électricité; **engines at half ~** moteurs à mi-régime; **the ship returned under her own ~** le navire est rentré par ses propres moyens; **sea/air ~** puissance navale/aérienne.

(c) (*authority*) pouvoir *m* (*also Pol*), autorité *f*. **student ~** le pouvoir des étudiants; **that is beyond my ~(s)** ceci ne relève pas de ma compétence; **at the height of his ~** à l'apogée de son pouvoir; **the ~ of veto** le droit de veto; (*Jur*) **the ~ of attorney** la procuration; (*Pol*) **in ~** au pouvoir; **to come to ~** accéder au pouvoir; **to have ~ over sb** avoir autorité sur qn; **to have sb in one's ~** avoir qn en son pouvoir; **to fall into sb's ~** tomber au pouvoir de qn; **they are the real ~** ce sont eux qui détiennent le pouvoir réel; (*fig*) **the ~ behind the throne** celui (*or* celle) qui tire les ficelles; **a ~ in the land** un homme très puissant; **the ~s of darkness/evil** les forces *fpl* des ténèbres/du mal; **the ~s that be** les autorités constituées; **the world ~s** les puissances mondiales; **it did me a ~ of good*** ça m'a fait un bien immense.

(d) (*Math*) puissance *f*. **5 to the ~ of 3** 5 puissance 3.

2 *adj* **(a)** *saw, loom, lathe* mécanique. **(b)** (*Elec*) *cable* électrique; *line* à haute tension. **~ cut** coupure *f* de courant; **~ point** prise *f* de courant; **~ station** centrale *f* (électrique *or* nucléaire). **(c) they are engaged in ~ politics** ils manœuvrent pour s'assurer une place prépondérante; **~ structure** répartition *f* des pouvoirs.

3 *vt* faire fonctionner; (*propel*) propulser. **~ed by nuclear energy, nuclear-~ed** qui fonctionne à l'énergie nucléaire; **~ed by jet engines** propulsé par des moteurs à réaction.

♦ **power-assisted** *adj* assisté. ♦ **powerboat** *n* hors-bord *m inv*. ♦ **power-driven** *adj* à moteur; (*Elec*) électrique. ♦ **powerful** *adj* puissant. ♦ **powerfully** *adv hit, strike* avec force; *affect* fortement; *write etc* puissamment; **to be ~fully built** avoir une carrure puissante. ♦ **powerhouse** *n* (*Elec*) centrale *f* électrique; (*fig*) personne *f etc* très dynamique; **a ~house of new ideas** une mine d'idées nouvelles. ♦ **powerless** *adj* impuissant (*to do* à faire). ♦ **powerlessly** *adv* impuissamment. ♦ **power-sharing** *n* (*Pol*) partage *m* du pouvoir.

practicable ['præktɪkəbl] *adj* praticable. ♦ **practicability** *n [road, path]* praticabilité *f*; *[scheme, suggestion]* possibilité *f* de réalisation.

practical ['præktɪkəl] *adj* (*gen*) pratique. **~ joke** farce *f*; **for all ~ purposes** en réalité; **he's very ~** il a beaucoup de sens pratique. ♦ **practicality** *n [person]* sens *m* pratique; *[scheme, suggestion]* aspect *m* pratique; **~ities** détails *mpl* pratiques. ♦ **practically** *adv* (*in a practical way*) d'une manière pratique; *say, suggest* d'une manière pragmatique; (*in practice*) dans la pratique; (*almost*) pratiquement.

practice ['præktɪs] **1** *n* **(a)** (*habits, usage*) pratique *f*, usage *m*. **to make a ~ of doing** avoir l'habitude de faire; **it's common ~** c'est courant. **(b)** (*exercise, training*) entraînement *m*; (*rehearsal*) répétition *f*. **target ~** exercices *mpl* de tir; **he does 6 hours' piano ~ a day** il fait 6 heures de piano par jour; **out of ~** rouillé (*fig*); **~ makes perfect** c'est en forgeant qu'on devient forgeron. **(c)** (*as opp to theory*) pratique *f*. **in(to) ~** en pratique. **(d)** *[doctor, lawyer]* **to be in ~** exercer; **to go into ~ as a doctor** s'établir docteur; **he has a large ~** il a un cabinet important. **2** *adj flight, run* d'entraînement. **3** *vti* (*US*) = **practise.**

practise ['præktɪs] **1** *vt* **(a)** (*put into practice*) *charity, one's religion* pratiquer; *method* employer. **to ~ medicine/law** exercer la profession de médecin/d'avocat; **to ~ what one preaches** mettre en pratique ce que l'on prêche. **(b)** (*exercise*) s'entraîner, s'exercer (*doing* à faire); *sport* s'entraîner à; *violin etc* s'exercer à; *song, recitation* travailler; (*Mus*) *scales* faire. **I'm practising my German on him** je m'exerce à parler allemand avec lui.

2 *vi* **(a)** (*Mus*) s'exercer; (*Sport*) s'entraîner; *[beginner]* faire des exercices. **he ~s for 2 hours every day** il fait 2 heures d'entraînement (*or* d'exercices) par jour. **(b)** *[doctor, lawyer]* exercer.

♦ **practised,** (*US*) **practiced** *adj teacher, nurse, soldier* expérimenté; *eye, ear* exercé; *movement* expert. ♦ **practising,** (*US*) **practicing** *adj doctor* exerçant; *lawyer* en exercice; *Catholic, Buddhist* pratiquant; *homosexual etc* actif. ♦ **practitioner** *n* (*of an art*) praticien *m*, -ienne *f*; (*Med*) médecin *m*.

pragmatic [præg'mætɪk] *adj* pragmatique.

prairie ['prɛərɪ] *n* plaine *f* (herbeuse). (*US*) **the ~(s)** la Grande Prairie.

praise [preɪz] **1** *n* éloge *m*. **in ~ of** à la louange de; **to speak** (*or* **write** *etc*) **in ~ of sb/sth** faire l'éloge de qn/qch; **I have nothing but ~ for what he has done** je ne peux que le louer de ce qu'il a fait; **a hymn of ~** un cantique; **~ be to God!** Dieu soit loué!; **~ be!*** Dieu merci! **2** *vt* louer (*sb for sth/for doing* qn de qch/d'avoir fait). **to ~ sb to the skies** porter qn aux nues. ♦ **praiseworthy** *adj* digne d'éloges.

pram [præm] *n* (*Brit*) voiture *f* d'enfant.

prance [prɑːns] *vi [horse, dancer etc]* caracoler. **to ~ in/out** *etc* entrer/sortir *etc* (*arrogantly*) en se pavanant *or* (*gaily*) gaiement.

prank [præŋk] *n* (*escapade*) frasque *f*; (*joke*) farce *f*, tour *m*. **a childish ~** une gaminerie; **to play a ~ on sb** jouer un tour à qn.

prattle ['prætl] *vi* babiller; *[several people]* papoter.

prawn [prɔːn] *n* crevette *f* rose, bouquet *m*. **~ cocktail** salade *f* de crevettes.

pray [preɪ] **1** *vi* prier (*for sb* pour qn). **they ~ed to God to help them** ils prièrent Dieu de les secourir; **he ~ed for forgiveness/to die** il pria Dieu de lui pardonner/de le laisser mourir; **we're ~ing for fine weather** nous faisons des prières pour qu'il fasse beau; **he's past ~ing for*** c'est un cas désespéré. **2** *vt* prier (*sb to do* qn de faire; *that* que + *subj*). ♦ **prayer 1** *n* prière *f*; **to say one's ~ers** faire sa prière; (*as service*) **~ers** office *m*; **2** *adj*: **~er book** livre *m* de messe; **the P~er Book** le rituel de l'Église anglicane; **~er mat** tapis *m* de prière; **~er meeting** service *m* religieux non-conformiste.

pre- [pri:] *pref* pré-. **~-1950** (*adj*) antérieur à 1950, d'avant 1950; (*adv*) avant 1950. ♦ **prearrange** *vt* fixer à l'avance. ♦ **precool** *vt* refroidir d'avance. ♦ **pre-establish** *vt* préétablir.

preach [pri:tʃ] **1** *vi* prêcher. **to ~ to sb** prêcher qn; (*fig*) **to ~ to the converted** prêcher un converti. **2** *vt* (*gen*) prêcher; *sermon* faire. ♦ **preacher** *n* prédicateur *m*; (*US: clergyman*) pasteur *m*.

preamble [pri:'æmbl] *n* préambule *m*.

precarious [prɪ'kɛərɪəs] *adj* précaire. ♦ **precariously** *adv* précairement.

precast ['pri:'kɑ:st] *adj*: **~ concrete** béton *m* précoulé.

precaution [prɪ'kɔ:ʃən] *n* précaution *f* (*against* contre). **as a ~** par précaution; **to take ~s** prendre ses précautions; **to take the ~ of doing** prendre la précaution de faire. ♦ **precautionary** *adj measure* de précaution.

precede [prɪ'si:d] *vt* (*in space, time*) précéder; (*in rank*) avoir la préséance sur. ♦ **precedence** ['presɪdəns] *n* (*in rank*) préséance *f*; (*in importance*) priorité *f*; **to take precedence over** *person* avoir la préséance sur; *event, problem, need* avoir la priorité sur. ♦ **precedent** *n* précédent *m*; **to form** *or* **create a precedent** constituer un précédent. ♦ **preceding** *adj* précédent.

precept ['pri:sept] *n* précepte *m*.

precinct ['pri:sɪŋkt] *n* **(a)** (*round cathedral etc*) enceinte *f*. (*neighbourhood*) **~s** alentours *mpl*; (*fig*) **within the ~s of** dans les limites de. **(b)** (*US: Police, Pol*) circonscription *f*.

precious ['preʃəs] **1** *adj* précieux. **~ stone** pierre *f* précieuse; **(my) ~!** mon trésor!; (*iro*) **your ~ son*** ton fils chéri (*iro*). **2** *adv* (*) **~ few, ~ little** très peu.

precipice ['presɪpɪs] *n* à-pic *m inv*. **to fall over a ~** tomber dans un précipice.

precipitate [prɪ'sɪpɪteɪt] **1** *vt* (*gen, Chem*) précipiter; (*Met*) condenser. **2** *adj* hâtif. ♦ **precipitately** *adv* précipitamment.

precipitous [prɪ'sɪpɪtəs] *adj* **(a)** *slope* escarpé, à pic. **(b)** (*hasty*) hâtif. ♦ **precipitously** *adv* à pic.

précis ['preɪsi:] *n* résumé *m*.

precise [prɪ'saɪs] *adj* **(a)** (*gen*) précis; *measurement, meaning, account* exact, précis. **there were 8 to be ~** il y en avait 8 pour être exact *or* précis; **that ~ book** ce livre même; **at that ~ moment** à ce moment précis. **(b)** (*meticulous*) *movement* précis; *person, manner* minutieux; (*pej: over-~*) pointilleux. **in that ~ voice of hers** de sa façon de parler si nette. ♦ **precisely** *adv explain* avec précision; (*exactly*) précisément; **at 10 o'clock ~ly** à 10 heures précises; **what ~ly does he do for a living?** que fait-il au juste pour gagner sa vie? ♦ **precision 1** *n* précision *f*; exactitude *f*; minutie *f*; **2** *adj instrument, bombing* de précision.

preclude [prɪ'klu:d] *vt doubt* écarter; *misunderstanding* prévenir; *possibility* exclure. **to be ~d from doing** être dans l'impossibilité de faire; **that ~s his leaving** cela le met dans l'impossibilité de partir.

precocious [prɪ'kəʊʃəs] *adj* précoce. ♦ **precociously** *adv* précocement. ♦ **precociousness** *or* ♦ **precocity** *n* précocité *f*.

preconceived ['pri:kən'si:vd] *adj* préconçu. ♦ **preconception** *n* préconception *f*.

precondition ['pri:kən'dɪʃən] *n* condition *f* requise.

precook [pri:'kuk] *vt* précuire.

precursor [pri:'kɜ:səʳ] *n* (*person, thing*) précurseur *m*; (*event*) signe *m* avant-coureur.

predate ['pri:'deɪt] *vt* (*put earlier date on*) antidater; (*come before in time*) précéder.

predator ['predətəʳ] *n* prédateur *m*. ♦ **predatory** *adj animal etc* prédateur; *habits* de prédateur; *person* rapace; *armies* pillard; *look* vorace.

predecease ['pri:dɪ'si:s] *vt* prédécéder.

predecessor ['pri:dɪsesəʳ] *n* prédécesseur *m*.

predestine [pri:'destɪn] *vt* prédestiner (*to* à; *to do* à faire). ♦ **predestination** *n* prédestination *f*.

predetermine ['pri:dɪ'tɜ:mɪn] *vt* déterminer d'avance; (*Philos, Rel*) prédéterminer.

predicament [prɪ'dɪkəmənt] *n* situation *f* difficile *or* fâcheuse. **I'm in a real ~** (*puzzled*) je ne sais vraiment pas que faire; (*in a fix*) me voilà dans de beaux draps.

predicative [prɪ'dɪkətɪv] *adj* (*Gram*) attribut *inv*. ♦ **predicatively** *adv* en tant qu'attribut.

predict [prɪ'dɪkt] *vt* prédire. ♦ **predictable** *adj* prévisible. ♦ **predictably** *adv behave etc* d'une manière prévisible; **~ably, he did not appear** comme on pouvait le prévoir, il ne s'est pas montré. ♦ **prediction** *n* prédiction *f*.

predilection [ˌpri:dɪ'lekʃən] *n* prédilection *f* (*for* pour).

predispose ['pri:dɪs'pəʊz] *vt* prédisposer (*to sth* à qch; *to do* à faire). ♦ **predisposition** *n* prédisposition *f*.

predominate [prɪ'dɒmɪneɪt] *vi* prédominer (*over* sur). ♦ **predominance** *n* prédominance *f*. ♦ **predominant** *adj* prédominant. ♦ **predominantly** *adv* surtout.

pre-eminent [pri:'emɪnənt] *adj* prééminent. ♦ **pre-eminence** *n* prééminence *f*. ♦ **pre-eminently** *adv* avant tout.

preen [pri:n] *vt [bird]* lisser. (*fig*) **to ~ o.s.** (*before mirror etc*) se pomponner; (*be proud*) s'enorgueillir (*on* de).

prefabricate [ˌpri:'fæbrɪkeɪt] *vt* préfabriquer. ♦ **prefab*** *n* maison *etc* préfabriquée.

preface ['prefɪs] *n* (*to book*) préface *f*; (*to speech*) introduction *f*.

prefect ['pri:fekt] *n* (*French Admin*) préfet *m*; (*Brit Scol*) *élève des grandes classes chargé(e) de la discipline*. ♦ **prefecture** *n* préfecture *f*.

prefer [prɪ'fɜ:ʳ] *vt* **(a)** préférer, aimer mieux (*doing, to do* faire). **to ~ A to B** préférer A à B, aimer mieux A que B; **I ~ taking the train to going by car** je préfère prendre le train que d'aller en voiture; **I ~ you to leave** je préfère que vous partiez (*subj*); **I much ~** je préfère de beaucoup. **(b)** (*Jur*) *charge* porter; *action* intenter; *complaint* déposer. ♦ **preferable** ['prefərəbl] *adj* préférable (*to sth* à qch). ♦ **preferably** *adv* de préférence. ♦ **preference 1** *n* (*liking*) préférence *f* (*for* pour); (*priority*) priorité *f* (*over* sur); **in ~ence to sth/to doing** plutôt que qch/que de faire; **2** *adj*: **~ence shares** actions *fpl* privilégiées. ♦ **preferential** *adj* préférentiel.

prefix ['pri:fɪks] **1** *n* préfixe *m*. **2** *vt* préfixer.

pregnant ['pregnənt] *adj woman* enceinte; *animal* pleine; (*fig*) *silence* lourd de sens. **3 months ~** enceinte de 3 mois; (*fig*) **~ with** gros de. ♦ **pregnancy** *n [woman]* grossesse *f*.

prehistory ['pri:'hɪstərɪ] *n* préhistoire *f*. ♦ **prehistoric** *adj* préhistorique.

prejudge ['pri:'dʒʌdʒ] *vt question* préjuger de; *person* juger d'avance.

prejudice ['predʒʊdɪs] **1** *n* **(a)** préjugé *m*; (*collective n*) préjugés. **racial ~** préjugés raciaux; **to have a ~ against** avoir un préjugé contre. **(b)** (*Jur*) préjudice *m*. **without ~** sans préjudice (*to* de). **2** *vt* **(a)** *person* prévenir (*against* contre). **(b)** (*also Jur*) *claim, chance* porter préjudice à. ♦ **prejudiced** *adj person* plein de préjugés; *idea* préconçu; **to be ~d against/in favour of** avoir un préjugé contre/en faveur de. ♦ **prejudicial** *adj* préjudiciable (*to* à).

prelate ['prelɪt] *n* prélat *m*.

preliminary [prɪ'lɪmɪnərɪ] *adj, n* préliminaire (*m*).

prelude ['prelju:d] *n* prélude *m* (*to* de).

premarital ['pri:'mærɪtl] *adj* avant le mariage.

premature ['premətʃʊər] *adj* (*gen*) prématuré. **you are a little ~** vous anticipez un peu. ♦ **prematurely** *adv* (*gen*) prématurément; *be born* avant terme.

premeditate [pri:'medɪteɪt] *vt* préméditer. ♦ **premeditation** *n* préméditation *f*.

premenstrual ['pri:'menstrʊəl] *adj*: **~ tension** syndrome *m* prémenstruel.

premier ['premɪər] **1** *adj* premier, primordial. **2** *n* (*Pol*) Premier ministre *m*.

première ['premɪɛər] *n* première *f* (*Theat*).

premise ['premɪs] *n* **(a)** (*hypothesis*) prémisse *f*. **(b)** (*property*) **~s** locaux *mpl*; **business ~s** locaux commerciaux; **on/off the ~s** sur les/hors des lieux; **to see sb off the ~s** escorter qn jusqu'à sa sortie des lieux.

premium ['pri:mɪəm] **1** *n* prime *f*. **to be at a ~** faire prime; **to put a ~ on** *[person]* faire grand cas de; *[situation, event]* donner beaucoup d'importance à.

2 *adj*: **~ bond** bon *m* à lots.

premonition [ˌpri:mə'nɪʃən] *n* pressentiment *m*.

prenatal ['pri:'neɪtl] *adj* prénatal.

preoccupy [pri:'ɒkjʊpaɪ] *vt* préoccuper. ♦ **preoccupation** *n* (*gen*) préoccupation *f*; **his preoccupation with money** son obsession *f* de l'argent.

prep* [prep] (*Scol*) *abbr of* **preparation, preparatory.**

prepack(age) ['pri:'pæk(ɪdʒ)] *vt* (*Comm*) préconditionner.

prepaid ['pri:'peɪd] *adj* payé d'avance; *reply, carriage* payé.

prepare [prɪ'pɛər] **1** *vt* préparer (*sth for sb* qch à qn; *sth for sth* qch pour qch; *sb for a shock/exam/piece of news* qn à un choc/un examen/une nouvelle; *sb for an operation* qn pour une opération). **to ~ the way/ground for sth** préparer la voie/le terrain pour qch.

2 *vi*: **to ~ for** (*make arrangements*) *journey, sb's arrival, event* faire des préparatifs pour; (*~ o.s. for*) *flood, meeting* se préparer pour; *war* se préparer à; *examination* préparer; **to ~ to do sth** se préparer à faire qch.

♦ **preparation** *n* **(a)** préparation *f*; **preparations** préparatifs *mpl* (*for* de); **in preparation** en préparation; **in preparation for** en vue de; **(b)** (*Scol*) devoirs *mpl*. ♦ **preparatory** *adj work* préparatoire; *measure, step* préliminaire; **preparatory school** (*Brit*) école *f* primaire privée; (*US*) lycée *m* privé; **preparatory to sth/to doing** avant qch/de faire. ♦ **prepared** *adj person, army, country* prêt; *statement, answer* préparé à l'avance; (*Culin*) *sauce, soup* tout prêt; **be ~d for bad news** préparez-vous à une mauvaise nouvelle; **I am ~d for anything** (*can cope*) j'ai tout prévu; (*won't be surprised*) je m'attends à tout; **to be ~d to do sth** être prêt à faire qch. ♦ **preparedness** *n* état *m* de préparation.

preponderance [prɪ'pɒndərəns] *n* prépondérance *f*. ♦ **preponderant** *adj* prépondérant. ♦ **preponderantly** *adv* surtout.

preposition [ˌprepə'zɪʃən] *n* préposition *f*.

prepossessing [ˌpri:pə'zesɪŋ] *adj appearance* avenant. **he is very ~** il fait très bonne impression; **a very ~ young man** un jeune homme très bien*.

preposterous [prɪ'pɒstərəs] *adj* ridicule. ♦ **preposterously** *adv* ridiculement.

prerecord ['pri:rɪ'kɔ:d] *vt song, programme* enregistrer à l'avance. **a ~ed broadcast** une émission en différé.

prerequisite ['pri:'rekwɪzɪt] *n* condition *f* préalable.

prerogative [prɪ'rɒgətɪv] *n* prérogative *f*.

Presbyterian [ˌprezbɪ'tɪərɪən] *adj, n* presbytérien(ne) *m(f)*.

preschool ['pri:'sku:l] *adj years* préscolaire; *child* d'âge préscolaire. **~ playgroup** ≃ garderie *f*.

prescribe [prɪs'kraɪb] *vt* (*gen, Med*) prescrire (*sth for sb* qch pour qn). ♦ **prescribed** *adj* (*gen, Jur, Med*) prescrit; **~d books** œuvres *fpl* inscrites au programme. ♦ **prescription 1** *n* (*Med*) ordonnance *f*; **to make out a prescription for sb** faire une ordonnance pour qn; **to make up** *or* (*US*) **fill a prescription** exécuter une ordonnance; **it's on prescription only** on ne peut l'obtenir que sur ordonnance; **2** *adj* (*Brit Med*) **prescription charges** *somme f fixe à payer lors de l'exécution de l'ordonnance*.

present ['preznt] **1** *adj* **(a)** (*there; in existence*) présent. **to be ~ at sth** être présent à qch, assister à qch; **who was ~?** qui était là?; **is there a doctor ~?** y a-t-il un docteur ici? **(b)** (*existing now: also Gram*) *year, circumstances* présent. **her ~ husband** son mari actuel; **at the ~ day** *or* **time** actuellement, à présent; (*Gram*) **~ perfect** passé *m* composé.

2 *n* **(a)** (*~ time*) présent *m*. **up to the ~** jusqu'à présent; **for the ~** pour le moment; **at ~** actuellement, à présent, en ce moment; **as things are at ~** au point où en sont les choses; (*Gram*) **in the ~** au présent. **(b)** (*gift*) cadeau *m*. **she gave me the book as a ~** elle m'a offert le livre; **to make sb a ~ of sth** faire cadeau de qch à qn.

3 [prɪ'zent] *vt* **(a)** (*hand over etc: gen*) présenter (*to* à); *proof, evidence* fournir; (*Jur etc*) *case* exposer. **to ~ sb with sth, to ~ sth to sb** (*give as gift*) offrir qch à qn, faire cadeau de qch à qn; (*hand over*) *prize, medal* remettre qch à qn; **we were ~ed with a fait accompli** nous nous sommes trouvés devant un fait accompli; (*Mil*) **to ~ arms** présenter les armes; **to ~ o.s. at the desk/for an interview** se présenter au bureau/à une entrevue. **(b)** (*offer*) *problem, difficulties, features* présenter; *opportunity* donner. **it ~ed an easy target** cela offrait une cible facile. **(c)** *play, concert* donner; *film,* (*Rad, TV*) *play, programme* donner, passer; (*act as presenter of*) présenter. **(d)** (*introduce*) présenter (*sb to sb* qn à qn). **may I ~ ...?** permettez-moi de vous présenter ... .

♦ **presence** *n* présence *f*; **presence of mind** présence d'esprit; **in the presence of** en présence de; **he certainly made his presence felt*** il n'est vraiment pas passé inaperçu. ♦ **presentable** [prɪ'zentəbl] *adj* présentable. ♦ **presentation** [ˌprezən'teɪʃən] *n* **(a)** (*gen*) présentation *f*; **on ~ation of** *ticket etc* sur présentation de; **(b)** (*gift*) cadeau *m*; (*ceremony*) ≃ vin *m* d'honneur; **who made the ~ation?** qui a remis le cadeau (*or* la médaille *etc*)? ♦ **present-day** *adj* actuel, d'aujourd'hui. ♦ **presenter** [prɪ'zentər] *n* (*Rad, TV*) présentateur *m*, -trice *f*. ♦ **presently** *adv* (*in a little while*) tout à l'heure; (*esp US: now*) à présent.

presentiment [prɪ'zentɪmənt] *n* pressentiment *m*.

preserve [prɪ'zɜ:v] **1** *vt* **(a)** (*keep, maintain*) *building, traditions* conserver; *leather, wood* entretenir; *memory, dignity, sense of humour, reputation, silence* garder; *peace* maintenir. **well-~d** en bon état de conservation, (*hum*) *person* bien conservé (pour son âge). **(b)** (*from harm etc*) préserver (*from* de). **~ me from that!*** le ciel m'en préserve! **(c)** (*Culin*) *fruit etc* conserver, mettre en conserve. **~d** en conserve. **2** *npl*: **~s** (*jam*) confiture *f*; (*bottled fruit/vegetables*) fruits *mpl*/légumes *mpl* en conserve. ♦ **preservation** *n* conservation *f*; (*from harm*) préservation *f*; **to put a preservation order on a**

building classer un édifice. ♦ **preservative** *n* (*Culin*) agent *m* de conservation.

preshrunk ['pri:'ʃrʌŋk] *adj* irrétrécissable.

preside [prɪ'zaɪd] *vi* présider. **to ~ at** *or* **over sth** présider qch.

president ['prezɪdənt] *n* (*Pol etc*) président *m*; (*US Comm*) président-directeur général, P.D.G. *m*.
♦ **presidency** *n* présidence *f*. ♦ **presidential** *adj* présidentiel.

press [pres] **1** *n* (*apparatus, machine: gen*) presse *f*; (*for wine, olives, cheese etc*) pressoir *m*; (*newspapers collectively*) presse. **in the ~** (*being printed*) sous presse; (*in the papers*) dans la presse; **to go to ~** être mis sous presse; **the national ~** la grande presse; **a member of the ~** un(e) journaliste; **to get a good/bad ~** avoir bonne/mauvaise presse.
2 *adj campaign, card, agency etc* de presse. **~ agent** agent *m* de publicité; **~ box,** (*Parl*) **~ gallery** tribune *f* de la presse; **~ conference** conférence *f* de presse; **~ cutting** coupure *f* de presse; **~-cutting agency** argus *m* de la presse; **~ photographer** reporter *m* photographe; **~ release** communiqué *m* de presse; **~ report** reportage *m*.
3 *vt* **(a)** (*push*) *button, switch, trigger* appuyer sur; (*squeeze etc*) *grapes, lemons, flowers, sb's hand* presser. **he ~ed them together** il les a pressés les uns contre les autres; **he ~ed his nose against the window** il a collé son nez à la fenêtre; **he ~ed her to him** il l'a serrée contre lui. **(b)** *clothes etc* repasser, donner un coup de fer à. **(c)** (*fig*) *attack, advantage* pousser; *claim, demand* renouveler; *opponent* presser; *[creditor]* poursuivre. **to ~ sb for an answer** presser qn de répondre; **to ~ a gift on sb** presser qn d'accepter un cadeau; **to ~ sb to do sth** presser qn de faire qch; **to ~ sb into doing sth** forcer qn à faire qch; **we were ~ed into service** nous avons été obligés d'offrir nos services; (*Jur*) **to ~ charges against sb** engager des poursuites contre qn; **I shan't ~ the point** je n'insisterai pas.
4 *vi [person]* appuyer (*on* sur); *[weight, burden]* faire pression (*on* sur); *[debts, troubles]* peser (*on sb* à qn). **time ~es!** le temps presse!; (*fig*) **to ~ for sth/for sth to be done** faire pression pour obtenir qch/pour que qch soit fait; **he ~ed through the crowd** il s'est frayé un chemin dans la foule; **they ~ed round his car** ils se pressaient autour de sa voiture.
press down 1 *vi* appuyer (*on* sur). **2** *vt sep* appuyer sur.
press on *vi* (*in work, journey etc*) continuer. (*fig*) **to ~ on with sth** continuer (à faire) qch.
♦ **press-button** *n* bouton(-pression) *m*. ♦ **pressed** *adj* (*very busy*) débordé (de travail); **to be ~ed for sth** être à court de qch, manquer de qch. ♦ **press-gang** *vt*: **to ~-gang sb into doing sth** forcer la main à qn pour qu'il fasse qch. ♦ **pressing 1** *adj business, problem* urgent; *danger, invitation* pressant; **he was very ~ing** il a beaucoup insisté; **2** *n [clothes]* repassage *m*. ♦ **pressman** *n* journaliste *m*. ♦ **press stud** *n* pression *f*. ♦ **press-up** *n* traction *f*.

pressure ['preʃəʳ] **1** *n* pression *f*. **water ~** pression de l'eau; **a ~ of 2 kg to the square cm** une pression de 2 kg par cm²; **blood ~** pression artérielle; **high-/low-~** (*adj*: *Tech*) à pression haute/basse; (*Tech*) **at full ~** à pression maxima; **because of parental ~** à cause de la pression des parents; **to put ~ on sth/sb** faire pression sur qch/qn (*to do* pour qu'il fasse); **they're putting the ~ on now** ils nous (*etc*) talonnent maintenant; **under ~ from his staff** sous la pression de son personnel; **to use ~ to obtain sth** user de contrainte pour obtenir qch; **the ~ of these events** la tension créée par ces événements; **~ of work prevented him from going** il n'a pas pu y aller parce qu'il avait trop de travail; **he is under a lot of ~** il est sous pression. **2** *adj spacesuit, cabin* pressurisé. **~ group** groupe *m* de pression. **3** *vt*: **to ~* sb to do** faire pression sur qn pour qu'il fasse; **to ~ sb* into doing** forcer qn à faire. ♦ **pressure cooker** *n* cocotte-minute *f* ®. ♦ **pressure gauge** *n* manomètre *m*. ♦ **pressurization** *n* pressurisation *f*. ♦ **pressurize** *vt* **(a)** *cabin, spacesuit* pressuriser; **(b)** (** fig*) = **pressure 3.**

prestige [pres'ti:ʒ] *n* prestige *m*. ♦ **prestigious** *adj* prestigieux.

presume [prɪ'zju:m] **1** *vt* (*suppose*) présumer (*that* que); (*take liberty*) se permettre (*to do* de faire). **2** *vi* prendre des libertés. **to ~ (up)on** abuser de. ♦ **presumably** *adv*: **you are presumably his son** je suppose *or* présume que vous êtes son fils. ♦ **presumption** *n* **(a)** (*supposition*) présomption *f*; **there is a strong presumption that** tout laisse à présumer que; **(b)** (*presumptuousness*) présomption *f*, audace *f*. ♦ **presumptuous** *adj* présomptueux. ♦ **presumptuously** *adv* présomptueusement.

presuppose [ˌpri:sə'pəuz] *vt* présupposer. ♦ **presupposition** *n* présupposition *f*.

pretence, (*US*) **pretense** [prɪ'tens] *n* (*pretext*) prétexte *m*; (*claim*) prétention *f*; (*affectation*) prétention. **under** *or* **on the ~ of (doing) sth** sous prétexte de (faire) qch; **to make a ~ of doing** faire semblant de faire; **it's all (a) ~** tout cela est pure comédie; **his ~ of sympathy** sa feinte sympathie.

pretend [prɪ'tend] **1** *vt* **(a)** (*feign*) faire semblant (*to do* de faire; *that* que); *ignorance, illness* feindre. **let's ~ we're soldiers** jouons aux soldats; (*pej*) **he was ~ing to be a doctor** il se faisait passer pour un docteur. **(b)** (*claim*) prétendre (*that* que; *to do* de faire). **2** *vi* (*feign*) faire semblant. **I was only ~ing!** je plaisantais!; **let's stop ~ing!** assez joué la comédie! **3** *adj* (*) *money, house etc* pour rire*.
♦ **pretended** *adj* prétendu. ♦ **pretender** *n* prétendant(e) *m(f)* (*to the throne* au trône). ♦ **pretension** *n* prétention *f* (*to* à). ♦ **pretentious** *adj* prétentieux. ♦ **pretentiously** *adv* prétentieusement. ♦ **pretentiousness** *n* prétention *f*.

preterite ['pretərɪt] *n* prétérit *m*, passé *m* simple.

pretext ['pri:tekst] *n* prétexte *m* (*to do* pour faire). **under** *or* **on the ~ of (doing) sth** sous prétexte de (faire) qch.

pretty ['prɪtɪ] **1** *adj* (*gen*) joli (*before n*). **as ~ as a picture** *person* joli à croquer; *garden etc* ravissant; **it wasn't a ~ sight** ce n'était pas beau à voir; (*to parrot*) **~ polly!** bonjour Jacquot!; **it will cost a ~ penny** cela coûtera une jolie somme. **2** *adv* assez. **~ well** (*not badly*) pas mal; (*also* **~ nearly**: *almost*) presque, pratiquement; **~ much the same thing** pratiquement la même chose. ♦ **prettily** *adv* joliment. ♦ **pretty-pretty*** *adj* un peu trop joli.

pretzel ['pretsl] *n* bretzel *m*.

prevail [prɪ'veɪl] *vi* **(a)** (*win*) prévaloir (*against* contre; *over* sur). **(b)** (*be in force etc*) *[conditions, attitude, fashion, wind]* prédominer; *[style]* être en vogue. **the situation which now ~s** la situation actuelle. **(c) to ~ (up)on sb to do** persuader qn de faire. ♦ **prevailing** *adj wind* dominant; *belief, attitude* courant; *conditions, situation, customs, fashion* actuel; *style* en vogue.

prevalent ['prevələnt] *adj belief, attitude* courant; *conditions, situation, customs, fashion* actuel; *illness* répandu; *style* en vogue. **it is very ~** cela se voit partout. ♦ **prevalence** *n [illness, belief, attitude]* fréquence *f*; *[conditions, situation, customs]* caractère *m* généralisé; *[style]* vogue *f*.

prevaricate [prɪ'værɪkeɪt] *vi* user de faux-fuyants. ♦ **prevarication** *n* faux-fuyant(s) *m(pl)*.

prevent [prɪ'vent] *vt* (*gen*) empêcher (*sb from*

doing, sb's doing qn de faire); *illness* prévenir; *accident, fire, war* éviter. ♦ **preventable** *adj* évitable. ♦ **preventative** *adj* préventif. ♦ **prevention** *n* prévention *f*; **Society for the P~ion of Cruelty to ...** Société Protectrice des ... . ♦ **preventive** *adj* préventif.

preview ['pri:vju:] *n [film, exhibition]* avant-première *f*. (*fig*) **to give sb a ~ of sth** donner à qn un aperçu de qch.

previous ['pri:vɪəs] **1** *adj* précédent, antérieur. **the ~ letter** la lettre précédente; **a ~ letter** une lettre précédente *or* antérieure; **the ~ evening** la veille au soir; **in a ~ life** dans une vie antérieure; **~ to** antérieur à; **have you made any ~ applications?** avez-vous déjà fait des demandes?; **I have a ~ engagement** je suis déjà pris; (*Comm*) **~ experience** expérience préalable; (*Jur*) **to have no ~ convictions** avoir un casier judiciaire vierge; **he has 3 ~ convictions** il a déjà 3 condamnations. **2** *adv*: **~ to** avant. ♦ **previously** *adv* (*before*) précédemment, auparavant; (*in the past*) dans le temps; (*already*) déjà.

prewar ['pri:'wɔ:ʳ] *adj* d'avant-guerre.

prey [preɪ] **1** *n* (*lit, fig*) proie *f*. **bird of ~** oiseau *m* de proie; (*fig*) **to be a ~ to** être en proie à (*fig*); **to fall a ~ to** être la victime de. **2** *vi*: **to ~ on** *[animal etc]* faire sa proie de; *[person]* s'attaquer à; *[fear, anxiety]* ronger, miner; **sth is ~ing on her mind** il y a qch qui la travaille*.

price [praɪs] **1** *n* (*gen, also fig*) prix *m*; (*estimate*) devis *m*; (*Betting*) cote *f*; (*St Ex*) cours *m*. **to go up in ~** augmenter; **to go down in ~** baisser; **what is the ~ of this book?** combien coûte *or* vaut ce livre?; **to put a ~ on sth** fixer le prix de qch, (*estimate value*) évaluer qch; (*fig*) **he puts a high ~ on** il attache beaucoup de valeur à; (*liter*) **beyond ~** sans prix; **we pay top ~s for gold** nous achetons l'or au prix fort; **high-~d** coûteux, cher; **he got a good ~ for it** il l'a vendu cher; (*fig*) **to pay a high ~ for sth** payer qch chèrement; (*fig*) **it's a small ~ to pay for it** c'est consentir un bien petit sacrifice pour l'avoir; **every man has his ~** tout homme est corruptible à condition d'y mettre le prix; **I wouldn't do it at any ~** je ne le ferais à aucun prix; **peace at any ~** la paix à tout prix; (*fig*) **not at any ~!** pour rien au monde!; (*fig*) **at what a ~!** à quel prix!; **he'll do it for a ~** il le fera si on y met le prix; (*St Ex*) **market ~** cours *m* du marché; **to put a ~ on sb's head** mettre à prix la tête de qn; (*fig*) **what ~* all his promises now?** que valent toutes ses promesses maintenant?

2 *adj control, index, war, reduction, rise* des prix. **~ cut** réduction *f*, rabais *m*; **~ cutting** réductions *fpl* de prix; **~ fixing** (*by government*) contrôle *m* des prix; (*pej: by firms: also* **~ rigging**) alignement *m* des prix; **~ freeze** blocage *m* des prix; **to put a ~ limit on sth** fixer le prix maximum de qch; **~ list** tarif *m*; **~ range** gamme *f* de prix; **within my ~ range** dans mes prix; **~s and incomes policy** politique *f* des prix et des revenus; **~ tag *or* ticket** étiquette *f*.

3 *vt* (*fix ~ of*) fixer le prix de; (*mark ~ on*) marquer le prix de; (*ask ~ of*) demander le prix de; (*fig: estimate value of*) évaluer. **it is ~d at £10** ça coûte 10 livres; **to ~ sth down/up** baisser/augmenter le prix de qch; **to ~ one's goods out of the market** perdre un marché à vouloir demander des prix trop élevés.

♦ **priceless** *adj* (*gen*) inestimable, sans prix; (*: *amusing*) impayable*. ♦ **pricey*** *adj* coûteux, cher.

prick [prɪk] **1** *n* (*act, sensation, mark*) piqûre *f*. (*fig*) **~s of conscience** aiguillons *mpl* de la conscience. **2** *vt* **(a)** (*gen*) piquer; *balloon, blister* crever. **she ~ed her finger** elle s'est piqué le doigt (*with* avec); **to ~ a hole in sth** faire un trou d'épingle (*etc*) dans qch; (*fig*) **his conscience ~ed him** il n'avait pas la conscience tranquille. **(b) to ~ (up) one's ears** *[animal]* dresser les oreilles; *[person]* (*fig*) dresser l'oreille. **3** *vi* (*gen*) piquer. **my eyes are ~ing** les yeux me cuisent.

prick out *vt sep seedlings* repiquer.

pricking ['prɪkɪŋ] *n* picotement *m*, sensation cuisante. (*fig*) **~s of conscience** remords *m(pl)*.

prickle ['prɪkl] **1** *n* **(a)** *[plant]* épine *f*; *[hedgehog etc]* piquant *m*. **(b)** (*sensation*) picotement *m*. **2** *vt* piquer. **3** *vi* picoter. ♦ **prickly** *adj plant* épineux; *animal* armé de piquants; *beard* qui pique; (*fig*) *person* irritable; *subject* épineux. **prickly heat** fièvre *f* miliaire; **prickly pear** figue *f* de Barbarie.

pride [praɪd] **1** *n* **(a)** (*self-respect*) amour-propre *m*; (*satisfaction*) fierté *f*; (*arrogance*) orgueil *m*. **his ~ was hurt** il était blessé dans son amour-propre; **he has too much ~ to ask for help** il est trop fier pour demander de l'aide; **she has no ~** elle n'a pas d'amour-propre; **false ~** vanité *f*; **it is a great source of ~ to her** elle en est très fière; **her ~ in her family** la fierté qu'elle tire de sa famille; **he spoke of them with ~** il a parlé d'eux avec fierté; **to take (a) ~ in** *children, achievements* être très fier de; *house, car etc* prendre grand soin de; **to take (a) ~ in doing** mettre sa fierté à faire; **to have ~ of place** avoir la place d'honneur; **she is her father's ~ and joy** elle est la fierté de son père. **(b)** *[lions]* troupe *f*.

2 *vt*: **to ~ o.s. on (doing) sth** être fier de (faire) qch.

priest [pri:st] *n* (*gen*) prêtre *m*; (*Catholic parish ~*) curé *m*. ♦ **priestess** *n* prêtresse *f*. ♦ **priesthood** *n*: **to enter the ~hood** se faire prêtre. ♦ **priestly** *adj* sacerdotal.

prig [prɪg] *n* pharisien(ne) *m(f)*. **what a ~ she is!** ce qu'elle peut se prendre au sérieux!; **don't be such a ~!** ne fais pas le petit saint! (*or* la petite sainte!). ♦ **priggish** *adj* suffisant. ♦ **priggishness** *n* suffisance *f*.

prim [prɪm] *adj* (*prudish: also* **~ and proper**) collet monté *inv*, guindé; (*demure*) *person, dress* très convenable; *manner, smile, look* guindé; *house, garden* trop coquet. ♦ **primly** *adv* d'une manière guindée; (*demurely*) d'un petit air sage. ♦ **primness** *n [person]* air *m* collet monté; façons *fpl* très convenables.

prima facie ['praɪmə'feɪʃɪ] **1** *adv* à première vue. **2** *adj* légitime (à première vue). **to have a ~ case** (*Jur*) avoir une affaire recevable; (*gen*) avoir raison à première vue.

primal ['praɪməl] *adj* primordial.

primary ['praɪmərɪ] **1** *adj* **(a)** (*gen: first*) primaire. **~ education/school** enseignement *m*/école *f* primaire; **~ (school)teacher** instituteur *m*, -trice *f*. **(b)** (*basic*) principal; *colour* fondamental; *importance* primordial; *meaning of word* primitif. **2** *n* (*US Pol*) primaire *f*. ♦ **primarily** *adv* (*chiefly*) principalement; (*originally*) primitivement.

primate ['praɪmɪt] *n* **(a)** (*Rel*) primat *m*. **(b)** ['praɪmeɪt] (*Zool*) primate *m*.

prime [praɪm] **1** *adj* **(a)** (*chief, principal*) *cause, reason* principal, primordial; *factor, importance* primordial; *advantage* de premier ordre. **P~ Minister** Premier ministre *m*. **(b)** (*excellent*) *meat* de premier choix; *quality* premier (*before n*). **in ~ condition** en parfaite condition; **a ~ example of** un excellent exemple de. **(c)** (*Math*) premier. **2** *n*: **in the ~ of life, in one's ~** dans la fleur de l'âge; *[empire, civilisation etc]* **in its ~** à son apogée; **he is past his ~** il est sur le retour*. **3** *vt gun, pump* amorcer; *surface for painting* apprêter; (*fig: instruct*) *person* mettre au courant. **they ~d him about what he should say** ils lui ont bien fait répéter ce qu'il avait à dire; **she arrived well ~d** elle est arrivée tout à fait préparée. ♦ **primer** *n* (*textbook*) livre *m* élémentaire; (*paint*) apprêt *m*.

primeval [praɪ'miːvəl] *adj* primordial; *forest* vierge.
primitive ['prɪmɪtɪv] *adj, n* primitif (*m*).
primordial [praɪ'mɔːdɪəl] *adj* primordial.
primrose ['prɪmrəʊz] **1** *n* primevère *f* (jaune). **2** *adj* (~ **yellow**) primevère *inv*.
primula ['prɪmjʊlə] *n* primevère *f*.
prince [prɪns] *n* prince *m*. **P~ Charles** le prince Charles; **the P~ of Wales** le prince de Galles; ~ **consort/regent** prince consort/régent. ♦ **princely** *adj* princier. ♦ **princess** *n* princesse *f*.
principal ['prɪnsɪpəl] **1** *adj* (*gen*) principal. **the ~ horn in the orchestra** le premier cor dans l'orchestre; ~ **parts of a verb** temps *mpl* primitifs d'un verbe. **2** *n* **(a)** *[school, institution etc]* directeur *m*, -trice *f*; (*in orchestra*) chef *m* de pupitre; (*Theat*) vedette *f*. **(b)** (*Fin*) ~ **and interest** principal *m or* capital *m* et intérêts.
♦ **principality** *n* principauté *f*. ♦ **principally** *adv* principalement.
principle ['prɪnsəpl] *n* principe *m*. **to go back to first ~s** remonter jusqu'au principe; **in ~** en principe; **on ~, as a matter of ~** par principe; **I make it a ~ never to do that, it's against my ~s to do that** j'ai pour principe de ne jamais faire cela; **that would be totally against my ~s** cela irait à l'encontre de tous mes principes; **a man of ~(s)** un homme qui a des principes; **on the same ~** sur *or* selon le même principe.
print [prɪnt] **1** *n* **(a)** (*mark*) *[foot, tyre etc]* empreinte *f*. **finger~** empreinte digitale; **a thumb ~** l'empreinte d'un pouce; (*Police etc*) **to take sb's ~s** prendre les empreintes de qn. **(b)** (*Typ*) (*actual letters*) caractères *mpl*; (*~ed material*) texte *m* imprimé. **in small/large ~** en petits/gros caractères; **the book is out of ~/in ~** le livre est épuisé/disponible; **he wants to see himself in ~** il veut se faire imprimer. **(c)** (*Art*) gravure *f*; (*Phot*) épreuve *f*; (*Tex*) imprimé *m*; (*~ed dress*) robe *f* imprimée. (*Phot*) **to make a ~ from a negative** tirer une épreuve d'un cliché.
2 *adj dress etc* (en) imprimé.
3 *vt* (*Typ, Tex, fig*) imprimer; (*Phot*) tirer; (*write in block letters*) écrire en caractères d'imprimerie. **~ed in England** imprimé en Angleterre; **it is being ~ed** c'est sous presse; **he has had several books ~ed** il a publié plusieurs livres; (*fig*) **~ed in sb's memory** gravé dans la mémoire.
4 *vi [machine]* imprimer. (*Phot*) **this negative won't ~** ce cliché ne donnera rien.
print out *vt sep* (*Computers*) imprimer.
♦ **printable** *adj* imprimable; (*hum*) **it's just not ~able** on ne peut vraiment pas le répéter. ♦ **printed** *adj* (*gen*) imprimé; *writing paper* à entête; **~ed matter** *or* **papers** imprimés *mpl*; **the ~ed word** la chose imprimée. ♦ **printer** *n* imprimeur *m*; **~er's error** faute *f* d'impression, coquille *f*; **~er's ink** encre *f* d'imprimerie. ♦ **printing 1** *n* impression *f*; (*Phot*) tirage *m*; (*block writing*) écriture *f* en caractères d'imprimerie; **2** *adj*: **~ing press** presse *f* typographique; **~ing works** imprimerie *f* (*atelier*).
prior[1] ['praɪəʳ] **1** *adj* antérieur (*to* à). **without ~ notice** sans préavis; **to have a ~ claim to sth** avoir droit à qch par priorité. **2** *adv*: **~ to** antérieurement à, avant. ♦ **priority** *n* priorité *f*; **to have** *or* **take ~ity over** avoir la priorité sur; **to give first** *or* **top ~ity to sth** donner la priorité absolue à qch; **you must get your ~ities right** vous devez décider de ce qui compte le plus pour vous.
prior[2] ['praɪəʳ] *n* (*Rel*) prieur *m*. ♦ **prioress** *n* prieure *f*. ♦ **priory** *n* prieuré *m*.
prise [praɪz] *vt* (*Brit*) **to ~ open a box** ouvrir une boîte en faisant levier, forcer une boîte; **to ~ the lid off a box** forcer le couvercle d'une boîte.
prism ['prɪzəm] *n* prisme *m*. ♦ **prismatic** *adj* prismatique.
prison ['prɪzn] **1** *n* prison *f*. **in ~** en prison; **to be/put sb in ~** être/mettre qn en prison; **to send sb to ~** condamner qn à la prison; **to send sb to ~ for 5 years** condamner qn à 5 ans de prison; **he was in ~ for 5 years** il a fait 5 ans de prison. **2** *adj food, conditions* dans la *or* les prison(s), pénitentiaire; *system, colony* pénitentiaire. ~ **camp** camp *m* de prisonniers; ~ **officer** gardien(ne) *m(f) or* surveillant(e) *m(f)* de prison. ♦ **prisoner** *n* détenu(e) *m(f)*, prisonnier *m*, -ière *f*; (*Mil, fig*) prisonnier, -ière; **~er of war** prisonnier de guerre; (*Jur*) **~er at the bar** accusé(e) *m(f)*, inculpé(e) *m(f)*; **the enemy took him ~er** il a été fait prisonnier par l'ennemi.
privacy ['prɪvəsɪ] *n* intimité *f*, solitude *f*. **his desire for ~** son désir d'être seul, *[public figure etc]* son désir de préserver sa vie privée; **there is no ~ in these flats** on ne peut avoir aucune vie privée dans ces appartements; **he told me in strictest ~** il me l'a dit dans le plus grand secret; **in the ~ of his own home** dans l'intimité *f* de son foyer.
private ['praɪvɪt] **1** *adj* **(a)** (*not public*) *conversation, meeting, land, road* privé; (*confidential*) *letter* confidentiel, de caractère privé; *agreement* officieux; *funeral* qui a lieu dans l'intimité. '~' (*on door etc*) 'privé'; (*on envelope*) 'personnel'; (*Admin, Jur*) ~ **hearing** audience *f* à huis clos; **I have ~ information that ...** je sais de source privée que ...; **in (his) ~ life** dans sa vie privée; **he's a very ~ person** il aime être seul; (*Theat etc*) ~ **performance** représentation *f* privée; ~ **place** coin *m* retiré; ~ **soldier** (simple) soldat *m*; (*Art etc*) ~ **view** vernissage *m*.
(b) (*for one person*) *house, car, lesson, secretary* particulier; (*personal*) *bank account, advantage, joke, reasons* personnel. **a ~ income, ~ means** une fortune personnelle; **it is my ~ opinion that ...** pour ma part je pense que ...; (*Anat*) ~ **parts** parties *fpl* génitales; ~ **pupil** élève *mf* en leçons particulières; ~ **teacher, ~ tutor** (*for full education*) précepteur *m*, institutrice *f*; (*for one subject*) répétiteur *m*, -trice *f* (*for* en); ~ **tuition** leçons *fpl* particulières.
(c) (*not official or state-controlled etc*) *company, institution, army, school* privé; *doctor, nursing home* privé, non conventionné. (*Econ*) ~ **enterprise** entreprise *f* privée; (*Econ, Ind*) **the ~ sector** le secteur privé; (*esp Brit Med*) **to be a ~ patient** ≃ ne pas être remboursé par la Sécurité sociale; **to be in ~ practice** ≃ être médecin non conventionné; (*esp Brit Med*) ~ **treatment** ≃ traitement *m* non remboursé par la Sécurité sociale; ~ **detective, ~ investigator, ~ eye*** détective *m* privé; **a ~ citizen** un simple citoyen; (*Parl*) ~ **member** simple député *m*.
2 *n* **(a)** (*Mil*) (simple) soldat *m*. **(b) in ~** = **privately a** *and* **b**.
♦ **privately** *adv* **(a)** (*secretly, personally*) dans son for intérieur; **(b)** (*not publicly*) en privé; **(c)** (*unofficially*) *write, apply* à titre personnel.
privation [praɪ'veɪʃən] *n* privation *f*.
privet ['prɪvɪt] *n* troène *m*. ~ **hedge** haie *f* de troènes.
privilege ['prɪvɪlɪdʒ] **1** *n* privilège *m*; (*Parl etc*) prérogative *f*. **to have the ~ of doing** avoir le privilège de faire; **I hate ~** je déteste les privilèges. **2** *vt* (*passive only*) **to be ~d to do** avoir le privilège de faire. ♦ **privileged** *adj* (*gen*) privilégié; *information* confidentiel; **a ~d few** quelques privilégiés; *mpl*; **the ~d few** la minorité privilégiée.
privy ['prɪvɪ] **1** *adj*: **P~ Council/Councillor** conseil *m*/conseiller *m* privé. **2** *n* cabinets *mpl*, W.-C. *mpl*.
prize[1] [praɪz] **1** *n* (*gen*) prix *m*; (*in lottery*) lot *m*. **to win first ~** (*Scol etc*) remporter le premier prix (*in* de); (*in lottery*) gagner le gros lot; **the Nobel P~** le prix Nobel. **2** *adj novel, entry* primé. **a ~ sheep** un mouton primé; **his ~ sheep** son meilleur

mouton; a ~ **example of** un parfait exemple de; a ~ **idiot*** un(e) idiot(e) de premier ordre; ~ **draw** tombola *f*; ~ **fighter** boxeur *m* professionnel; ~ **fighting** boxe *f* professionnelle; ~ **list** palmarès *m*; ~ **money** argent *m* du prix; (*Boxing*) ~ **ring** ring *m*. **3** *vt* faire grand cas de, priser. ~**d possession** bien *m* très précieux. ♦ **prize-giving** *n* (*Scol etc*) distribution *f* des prix. ♦ **prizewinner** *n* (*Scol, gen*) lauréat(e) *m(f)*; (*in lottery*) gagnant(e) *m(f)*. ♦ **prizewinning** *adj essay, novel, entry etc* primé; *ticket* gagnant.

prize² [praɪz] *vt* = **prise.**

pro¹ [prəʊ] **1** *pref* (*in favour of*) pro...; ~**-French** profrançais; **he was** ~**-Hitler** il était partisan d'Hitler. **2** *n*: **the** ~**s and the cons** le pour et le contre.

pro²* [prəʊ] *n* (*abbr of* **professional**) pro *mf*.

probable ['prɒbəbl] *adj* **(a)** (*likely*) *reason, success* probable. **it is** ~ **that** il est probable que + *indic*; **it is hardly** ~ **that** il est peu probable que + *subj*. **(b)** (*credible*) *explanation etc* vraisemblable. ♦ **probability** *n* probabilité *f*; **in all probability** selon toute probabilité. ♦ **probably** *adv* probablement, selon toute probabilité.

probate ['prəʊbɪt] *n* (*Jur*) homologation *f* (d'un testament).

probation [prə'beɪʃən] **1** *n*: **to be on** ~ (*Jur*) ≃ être en sursis avec mise à l'épreuve, *[minors]* être en liberté surveillée; (*gen: in employment etc*) être engagé à l'essai; (*Rel*) être novice; (*Jur*) **to put sb on** ~ mettre qn en sursis avec mise à l'épreuve *etc*. **2** *adj* (*Jur*) ~ **officer** agent *m* de probation; (*for minors*) ≃ délégué(e) *m(f)* à la liberté surveillée. ♦ **probationary** *adj* (*gen*) d'essai. ♦ **probationer** *n* (*gen*) employé(e) *m(f)* engagé(e) à l'essai; (*Rel*) novice *mf*.

probe [prəʊb] **1** *n* (*gen, Med, Space*) sonde *f*; (*investigation*) enquête *f* (*into* sur), investigation *f* (*into* de). **2** *vt hole, crack* explorer, examiner; (*Med*) sonder; (*Space*) explorer; (*also* ~ **into**) *sb's subconscious, past* sonder, explorer; *causes, crime, mystery* chercher à éclaircir. ♦ **probing** *adj question, study* pénétrant; *interrogation* serré; *look* inquisiteur.

probity ['prəʊbɪtɪ] *n* probité *f*.

problem ['prɒbləm] **1** *n* problème *m* (*also Math*). **the housing** ~ le problème du logement; **he is a great** ~ **to his mother** il pose de gros problèmes à sa mère; **we've got** ~**s with the car** nous avons des ennuis *mpl* avec la voiture; **drink** ~**s** des tendances *fpl* à l'alcoolisme; **it's not my** ~ ça ne me concerne pas; **that's no** ~ **to him** ça ne lui pose pas de problème; **that's no** ~! pas de problème!; **what's the** ~? qu'est-ce qui ne va pas?; **I had no** ~ **in getting the money** je n'ai eu aucun mal à obtenir l'argent. **2** *adj child* caractériel; *family* inadapté; *novel, play* à thèse. (*Press*) ~ **page** courrier *m* du cœur. ♦ **problematic(al)** *adj* problématique; **it is** ~**atical whether ...** il n'est pas du tout certain que ... + *subj*.

procedure [prə'siːdʒəʳ] *n* procédure *f*. **the correct** ~ **is to do** la procédure normale, c'est de faire; **what's the** ~?* comment doit-on procéder?, qu'est-ce qu'il faut faire?

proceed [prə'siːd] *vi* (*go*) aller, avancer; (*continue*) continuer. **you must** ~ **cautiously** il faut avancer *or* (*fig: act*) procéder avec prudence; **let us** ~ **to the next item** passons à la question suivante; **I am not sure how to** ~ je ne sais pas très bien comment m'y prendre; **to** ~ **to do sth** se mettre à faire qch; **to** ~ **with sth** continuer *or* poursuivre qch; **it is all** ~**ing according to plan** tout se passe *or* se déroule ainsi que prévu; (*originate*) **to** ~ **from** provenir de; (*Jur*) **to** ~ **against sb** engager des poursuites contre qn. ♦ **proceeding** *n* (*course of action*) façon *f or* manière *f* d'agir. ♦ **proceedings** *npl* (*ceremony*) cérémonie *f*; (*meeting*) séance *f*; (*discussions*) débats *mpl*; (*records: of learned society*) actes *mpl*; (*measures*) mesures *fpl*; (*Jur: legal* ~*ings*) procès *m*; **to take** ~**ings** (*gen*) prendre des mesures (*in order to do* pour faire); (*Jur*) intenter un procès (*against sb* à qn). ♦ **proceeds** ['prəʊsiːdz] *npl* produit *m*, somme *f* recueillie.

process¹ ['prəʊses] **1** *n* **(a)** (*operation*) processus *m*. **the** ~ **of growing up** le processus de la croissance; **a natural/chemical** ~ un processus naturel/chimique; **it's a slow** *or* **long** ~ (*Chem etc*) c'est un processus lent; (*fig*) ça prend du temps; **he supervised the whole** ~ il a supervisé l'opération *f* du début à la fin; **in the** ~ **of cleaning the picture, they ...** pendant qu'ils nettoyaient le tableau ils ...; **to be in** ~ être en cours (*of sth* de qch); **in (the)** ~ **of doing** en train de faire. **(b)** (*specific method*) procédé *m*, méthode *f*. **the Bessemer** ~ le procédé Bessemer; **a** ~ **for doing sth** un procédé *or* une méthode pour faire qch. **(c)** (*Jur*) (*action*) procès *m*; (*summons*) citation *f*.

2 *vt* (*Ind*) *raw materials, food, computer data* traiter; (*Phot*) *film* développer; (*Admin etc*) *an application, papers* s'occuper de. ~**ed cheese** fromage *m* fondu.

♦ **processing** *n* traitement *m*; développement *m*; **food** ~**ing** préparation *f* des aliments; **data** ~**ing** informatique *f*.

process² [prə'ses] *vi* (*go in procession*) défiler; (*Rel*) aller en procession. ♦ **procession** *n [people, cars]* défilé *m*; (*Rel*) procession *f*.

proclaim [prə'kleɪm] *vt* (*gen*) proclamer (*that* que; *sb king etc* qn roi *etc*); *peace, one's love* déclarer; *edict* promulguer; (*fig: show*) révéler. ♦ **proclamation** *n* proclamation *f*.

procrastinate [prəʊ'kræstɪneɪt] *vi* faire traîner les choses. ♦ **procrastination** *n* procrastination *f*.

procreate ['prəʊkrɪeɪt] *vt* procréer. ♦ **procreation** *n* procréation *f*.

procure [prə'kjʊəʳ] **1** *vt* (*for o.s.*) se procurer, obtenir; (*for sb else*) obtenir; (*Jur*) *prostitute etc* procurer. **to** ~ **sth for sb, to** ~ **sb sth** procurer qch à qn, faire obtenir qch à qn. **2** *vi* (*Jur*) faire du proxénétisme. ♦ **procurer** *n* (*Jur*) proxénète *m*. ♦ **procuring** *n [goods, objects]* obtention *f*; (*Jur*) proxénétisme *m*.

prod [prɒd] **1** *n* (*push*) poussée *f*; (*jab*) (petit) coup *m* (*de canne, avec le doigt etc*). **to give sb a** ~ pousser qn doucement (du doigt *or* avec la pointe d'un bâton *etc*); (*fig*) pousser *or* stimuler qn. **2** *vt* pousser doucement (du doigt *or* avec la pointe d'un bâton *etc*). **he** ~**ded the map with his finger** il a planté son doigt sur la carte; **to** ~ **sb into doing sth** pousser qn à faire qch; (*fig*) **he needs** ~**ding** il a besoin d'être stimulé.

prodigal ['prɒdɪgəl] *adj* prodigue.

prodigy ['prɒdɪdʒɪ] *n* prodige *m*, merveille *f*. **child** ~ enfant *mf* prodige.

♦ **prodigious** *adj* prodigieux. ♦ **prodigiously** *adv* prodigieusement.

produce [prə'djuːs] **1** *vt* **(a)** (*make: gen*) produire; *magazine* éditer; *book* (*write*) écrire, (*publish*) publier; (*Fin*) *interest, profit* rapporter; (*give birth to*) donner naissance à. **he has** ~**d a new pop record** il a sorti un nouveau disque pop; **oil-producing countries** pays *mpl* producteurs de pétrole. **(b)** (*bring, show*) *gift, documents, gun* sortir (*from* de), produire; *witness* produire; *proof* fournir. **I can't** ~ **£100!** je ne peux pas trouver 100 livres! **(c)** (*cause: gen*) provoquer, causer; *results, impression* produire, donner; *pleasure, interest* susciter; (*Elec*) *current* engendrer; *spark* faire jaillir. **(d)** (*Theat*) mettre en scène; (*Cine*) produire; (*Rad*) *play* mettre en ondes; (*Rad, TV*) *programme* réaliser; (*TV*) *play, film* mettre en scène.

2 ['prɒdjuːs] *n* produit(s) *m(pl)* (*d'alimentation*).

♦ **producer** *n* (*V* **produce 1a** *and* **1d**) producteur *m*, -trice *f*; metteur *m* en scène; metteur en ondes; réalisateur *m*.

product ['prɒdʌkt] *n* produit *m*; (*fig*) résultat *m*. ♦ **production 1** *n* **(a)** (*Ind*) production *f*; **to put sth into ~ion** entreprendre la production de qch; **to take sth out of ~ion** retirer qch de la production; **the factory is in full ~ion** l'usine tourne à plein rendement; **car ~ion has risen** la production automobile a augmenté; **(b)** (*showing*) présentation *f*; **on ~ion of this ticket** sur présentation de ce billet; **(c)** (*V* **produce 1d**) mise *f* en scène; production *f*; mise *f* en ondes; réalisation *f*; **(d)** (*work produced*) (*Theat*) pièce *f*; (*Cine, Rad, TV*) production *f*; **2** *adj* (*Ind*) **~ion line** chaîne *f* de fabrication; **~ion manager** directeur *m* de la production. ♦ **productive** *adj land, imagination* fertile; *meeting, work* fructueux; *employment, labour* productif; (*Ling*) productif; **I've had a very ~ive day** j'ai bien travaillé aujourd'hui. ♦ **productivity 1** *n* (*Econ, Ind*) productivité *f*; **2** *adj fall, increase* de productivité; **~ivity agreement** accord *m* de productivité; **~ivity bonus** prime *f* à la productivité.

profane [prə'feɪn] **1** *adj* (*secular*) profane; (*pej*) *language etc* impie. **2** *vt* profaner. ♦ **profanity** *n* (*oath*) juron *m*.

profess [prə'fes] *vt* (*gen*) professer. **he ~ed himself satisfied** il s'est déclaré satisfait; **I don't ~ to be an expert** je ne prétends pas être expert en la matière. ♦ **professed** *adj atheist etc* déclaré; (*Rel*) *monk, nun* profès (*f* -esse).

profession [prə'feʃən] *n* (*all senses: gen*) profession *f*. **the ~s** les professions libérales; **by ~** de son (*or* mon *etc*) métier; **the medical ~** (*calling*) la profession de médecin; (*doctors collectively*) les médecins *mpl*; **~ of faith** profession de foi. ♦ **professional 1** *adj* (*gen*) professionnel; *diplomat, soldier* de carrière; *play, piece of work* de haute qualité; **~al people** les membres *mpl* des professions libérales; **to take ~al advice** (*medical/legal*) consulter un médecin/un avocat; (*on practical problem*) consulter un professionnel; (*Sport*) **to turn ~al** passer professionnel; **to have a very ~al attitude to sth** prendre qch très au sérieux; **it is well up to ~al standards** c'est d'un niveau de professionnel; **2** *n* (*all senses*) professionnel(le) *m(f)*. ♦ **professionally** *adv* (*gen*) professionnellement; (*Sport*) *play* en professionnel; **I never met him ~ally** je n'ai jamais eu de rapports de travail avec lui; **~ally qualified** diplômé; **have you ever sung ~ally?** avez-vous jamais été chanteur professionnel?

professor [prə'fesəʳ] *n* (*Univ: Brit, US*) professeur *m* (titulaire d'une chaire); (*US: teacher*) professeur. ♦ **professorial** *adj* professoral.

proffer ['prɒfəʳ] *vt object, hand* tendre; *remark* faire; *thanks, apologies* présenter.

proficient [prə'fɪʃənt] *adj* très compétent (*in* en). ♦ **proficiency** *n* grande compétence *f*.

profile ['prəʊfaɪl] *n* (*gen*) profil *m*; (*fig*) *[person]* portrait *m*; *[situation etc]* esquisse *f*. **in ~** de profil; (*fig*) **to keep a low ~** essayer de ne pas trop se faire remarquer.

profit ['prɒfɪt] **1** *n* (*Comm*) profit *m*, bénéfice *m*; (*fig*) profit. **~ and loss** profits et pertes; **gross/net ~** bénéfice brut/net; **to make a ~** faire un bénéfice (*of* de; *on* sur); **to sell sth at a ~** vendre qch à profit; **to yield a ~** rapporter un bénéfice.

2 *adj*: **~ margin** marge *f* bénéficiaire.

3 *vi*: **to ~ by** *or* **from sth** tirer profit de qch. ♦ **profitability** *n* rentabilité *f*. ♦ **profitable** *adj* (*Comm etc*) rentable; (*fig*) *scheme, agreement* avantageux; *meeting, visit* profitable. ♦ **profitably** *adv sell* à profit; *deal* avec profit; (*fig*) avec profit, avec fruit. ♦ **profiteer** (*pej*) **1** *n* profiteur *m* (*pej*); **2** *vi* faire des bénéfices excessifs. ♦ **profitless** *adj* sans profit. ♦ **profit-making** *adj* à but lucratif; **non-~-making** à but non lucratif. ♦ **profit-sharing** *n* participation *f* aux bénéfices.

profligate ['prɒflɪgɪt] *adj* (*debauched*) débauché; (*extravagant*) extrêmement prodigue. ♦ **profligacy** *n* débauche *f*; extrême prodigalité *f*.

profound [prə'faʊnd] *adj* profond. ♦ **profoundly** *adv* profondément. ♦ **profundity** *n* profondeur *f*.

profuse [prə'fju:s] *adj vegetation, bleeding* abondant; *thanks, praise, apologies* profus. ♦ **profusely** *adv bleed, sweat* abondamment; *thank, praise* avec effusion; **to apologize ~ly** se confondre en excuses. ♦ **profusion** *n* profusion *f*; **in profusion** à profusion.

progeny ['prɒdʒɪnɪ] *n* progéniture *f*. ♦ **progenitor** *n* (*lit*) ancêtre *m*; (*fig*) auteur *m*.

prognosis [prɒg'nəʊsɪs] *n, pl* **-oses** pronostic *m*. ♦ **prognosticate** *vt* pronostiquer. ♦ **prognostication** *n* pronostic *m*.

programme, (*US*) **program** ['prəʊgræm] **1** *n* (*most senses*) programme *m*; (*Rad, TV: broadcast*) émission *f* (*on* sur; *about* au sujet de); (*Rad: station*) poste *m*; (*TV: station*) chaîne *f*; *[course etc]* emploi *m* du temps. (*fig*) **what's the ~ for today?*** qu'est-ce qu'on fait aujourd'hui?; **on the ~** au programme; **on the other ~** (*TV*) sur l'autre chaîne; (*Rad*) sur l'autre poste. **2** *adj* (*Rad, TV*) **~ editor** éditorialiste *mf*; (*Theat*) **~ seller** vendeur *m*, -euse *f* de programmes. **3** *vt* (*gen, Tech, fig*) programmer (*to do* pour faire). **the meeting was ~d to start at 7** le début de la réunion était prévu pour 19 heures. ♦ **programmer** *n* (*computer ~*) programmeur *m*, -euse *f*; (*device*) programmateur *m*. ♦ **programming** *n* programmation *f*.

progress ['prəʊgres] **1** *n* (*gen*) progrès *m(pl)*. **in the name of ~** au nom du progrès; **to make ~** (*gen*) faire des progrès; (*walk etc forward*) avancer; **the patient is making ~** l'état *m* (de santé) du malade s'améliore; **the ~ of events** le cours des événements; **the meeting is in ~** la réunion est en cours.

2 *adj*: **~ report** (*Med*) bulletin *m* de santé; (*Admin etc*) compte rendu *m* des travaux; (*Scol*) bulletin scolaire.

3 *vi* [prə'gres] (*lit,fig*) aller, avancer (*towards* vers); *[student etc]* faire des progrès; *[patient]* aller mieux; *[investigations, studies etc]* progresser. **as the game ~ed** à mesure que la partie se déroulait.

♦ **progression** *n* progression *f*. ♦ **progressive 1** *adj* (*gradually increasing*) *disease, improvement* progressif; (*forward-looking*) *idea, party, person* progressiste; *age* de progrès. **2** *n* (*Pol etc*) progressiste *mf*. ♦ **progressively** *adv* progressivement, petit à petit.

prohibit [prə'hɪbɪt] *vt* (*forbid*) interdire, défendre (*sb from doing* à qn de faire); (*prevent*) empêcher (*sb from doing* qn de faire); (*Admin, Jur etc*) *weapons, drugs, swearing* prohiber. **smoking ~ed** défense de fumer, il est interdit *or* défendu de fumer; **pedestrians are ~ed from using this bridge** il est interdit aux piétons d'utiliser ce pont. ♦ **prohibition** *n* interdiction *f*, défense *f*; prohibition *f* (*also against alcohol*). ♦ **prohibitive** *adj* prohibitif.

project ['prɒdʒekt] **1** *n* **(a)** (*plan, scheme*) projet *m*, plan *m* (*to do, for doing* pour faire); (*undertaking*) opération *f*, entreprise *f*; (*study*) étude *f* (*on* de); (*Scol*) dossier *m* (*on* sur). **(b)** (*US: housing ~*) cité *f*, lotissement *m*. **2** [prə'dʒekt] *vt* (*all senses*) projeter. **3** *vi* faire saillie. **to ~ over** surplomber; **to ~ into** s'avancer dans. ♦ **projecting** *adj construction, part, knob* saillant; *tooth* qui avance. ♦ **projection 1** *n* **(a)** projection *f*; **(b)** (*overhang*) saillie *f*; **2** *adj* (*Cine*) **~ion booth, ~ion room** cabine *f* de projection. ♦ **projectionist** *n* projectionniste *mf*. ♦ **projector** *n* projecteur *m*.

prolapse ['prəʊlæps] *n* descente *f* d'organe.

proletarian [ˌprəʊləˈtɛərɪən] **1** *n* (*abbr* **prole***) prolétaire *mf* (*abbr* prolo*). **2** *adj class, party* prolétarien; *life, mentality* de prolétaire. ♦ **proletariat** *n* prolétariat *m*.
proliferate [prəˈlɪfəreɪt] *vi* proliférer. ♦ **proliferation** *n* prolifération *f*. ♦ **prolific** *adj* prolifique.
prologue [ˈprəʊlɒg] *n* prologue *m* (*Literat: to* de; *fig: to* à).
prolong [prəˈlɒŋ] *vt* prolonger. ♦ **prolongation** *n* (*in space*) prolongement *m*; (*in time*) prolongation *f*.
prom* [prɒm] *n abbr of* **promenade** *and* **promenade concert.**
promenade [ˌprɒmɪˈnɑːd] **1** *n* promenade *f*. **2** *adj* (*Brit*) ~ **concert** *concert donné dans une salle à promenoir;* (*Naut*) ~ **deck** pont *m* promenade. **3** *vi* (*walk*) se promener. **4** *vt* promener. ♦ **promenader*** *n* auditeur *m*, -trice *f* d'un 'promenade concert'.
prominent [ˈprɒmɪnənt] *adj ridge, structure, nose* proéminent; *cheekbones* saillant; *tooth* qui avance; (*striking*) frappant; (*outstanding*) *person* important, très en vue. **to be ~ in** jouer un rôle important dans; **in a ~ position** bien en vue. ♦ **prominence** *n* proéminence *f*; aspect saillant *or* frappant; importance *f*. ♦ **prominently** *adv display, place, set* bien en vue; **his name figured ~ly in the case** on a beaucoup entendu parler de lui dans l'affaire.
promiscuous [prəˈmɪskjʊəs] *adj* (*sexually*) *person* de mœurs faciles; *conduct* léger, libre. ♦ **promiscuity** *or* ♦ **promiscuousness** *n* promiscuité *f* sexuelle. ♦ **promiscuously** *adv* immoralement.
promise [ˈprɒmɪs] **1** *n* promesse *f*. **to make sb a ~** faire une promesse à qn (*to do* de faire); **is it a ~?** c'est promis?; **to keep one's ~** tenir sa promesse; **a young man of ~** un jeune homme qui promet; **it holds out a ~ of peace** cela fait espérer la paix. **2** *vt* promettre (*sth to sb* qch à qn; *sb to do* à qn de faire; *that* que). **I ~!** je vous le promets!; **I can't ~** je ne vous promets rien; (*fig*) **to ~ sb the earth** *or* **the moon** promettre la lune à qn; **to ~ o.s. (to do) sth** se promettre (de faire) qch. **3** *vi* (*fig*) **to ~ well** *[person]* promettre; *[situation, first book, event]* être prometteur; *[crop, business]* s'annoncer bien. ♦ **promising** *adj situation, event* prometteur; *person* qui promet; **the future is promising** l'avenir s'annonce bien; **that's promising** c'est prometteur; (*iro*) ça promet! ♦ **promisingly** *adv* d'une façon prometteuse.
promontory [ˈprɒməntrɪ] *n* promontoire *m*.
promote [prəˈməʊt] *vt* **(a)** *person* promouvoir (*to* au poste de, (*Mil*) au rang de). (*Ftbl etc*) **to be ~d to the first division** monter en première division. **(b)** (*encourage*) *cause, plan, sales, product* promouvoir; *trade* développer; (*Comm*) *firm, campaign* lancer. ♦ **promoter** *n [sport]* organisateur *m*, -trice *f*; *[product]* promoteur *m* de vente; *[business, company]* fondateur *m*, -trice *f*. ♦ **promotion** *n* promotion *f*; **to get promotion** obtenir de l'avancement, être promu.
prompt [prɒmpt] **1** *adj* (*speedy*) *action* rapide, prompt; *delivery, reply, payment, service* rapide; (*punctual*) ponctuel. **to be ~ to do** faire avec promptitude. **2** *adv*: **at 6 o'clock ~** à 6 heures exactement. **3** *vt* **(a)** pousser, inciter (*sb to do* qn à faire). **~ed by a desire to see ...** poussé par un désir de voir ...; **regret ~ed by the sight of ...** regret provoqué par la vue de ... . **(b)** (*Theat*) souffler. ♦ **prompter** *n* (*Theat*) souffleur *m*, -euse *f*. ♦ **prompting** *n*: **at my ~ing** à mon instigation; **without (any) ~ing** de son propre chef. ♦ **promptly** *adv* rapidement, promptement; ponctuellement. ♦ **promptness** *n* promptitude *f*; ponctualité *f*.
prone [prəʊn] *adj* **(a)** (*face down*) étendu face contre terre. **(b)** (*liable*) enclin (*to sth* à qch, *to do* à faire).
prong [prɒŋ] *n [fork]* dent *f*. **three-~ed** *fork* à trois dents; *attack, advance* sur trois fronts.
pronoun [ˈprəʊnaʊn] *n* pronom *m*.
pronounce [prəˈnaʊns] **1** *vt* **(a)** *word etc* prononcer. **how is it ~d?** comment ça se prononce? **(b)** prononcer (*that* que). (*Jur*) **to ~ sentence** prononcer la sentence; **they ~d him unfit to drive** ils l'ont déclaré inapte à la conduite; **to ~ o.s. in favour of** se prononcer *or* se déclarer en faveur de. **2** *vi* se prononcer (*on* sur); (*Jur*) prononcer (*for* en faveur de, *against* contre). ♦ **pronounceable** *adj* prononçable. ♦ **pronounced** *adj* prononcé, marqué. ♦ **pronouncement** *n* déclaration *f*. ♦ **pronunciation** *n* prononciation *f*.
pronto* [ˈprɒntəʊ] *adv* illico*.
proof [pruːf] **1** *n* **(a)** (*gen, Jur, Math etc*) preuve *f*. **~ of identity** pièce(s) *f(pl)* d'identité; **as (a) ~ of, in ~ of** pour preuve de; **I've got ~ that he did it** j'ai la preuve qu'il l'a fait; (*fig*) **to show ~ of** faire preuve de. **(b) to put sth to the ~** mettre qch à l'épreuve. **(c)** (*Typ, Phot*) épreuve *f*. **(d) this whisky is 70° ~** ≃ ce whisky titre 40° d'alcool. **2** *adj*: **~ against** *bullets, time, wear* à l'épreuve de; *temptation, suggestion* insensible à. **3** *vt anorak, tent* imperméabiliser. ♦ **proofread** *vt* corriger les épreuves de. ♦ **proofreader** *n* correcteur *m*, -trice *f* d'épreuves.
prop¹ [prɒp] **1** *n* support *m*; (*for wall; in tunnel etc*) étai *m*; (*for clothes-line*) perche *f*; (*fig*) soutien *m* (*to, for* de). **2** *vt* (**~ up**) (*lean*) *ladder, cycle* appuyer (*against* contre); (*support*) *tunnel, wall* étayer; *clothes-line, lid* caler; (*fig*) *régime* maintenir; *business, company* renflouer; *organization* soutenir; (*Fin*) *the pound* venir au secours de. **to ~ o.s. (up) against** se caler contre.
prop²* [prɒp] *n* (*Theat*) *abbr of* **property 1c.**
propaganda [ˌprɒpəˈgændə] *n* propagande *f*.
propagate [ˈprɒpəgeɪt] **1** *vt* propager. **2** *vi* se propager. ♦ **propagation** *n* propagation *f*.
propel [prəˈpel] *vt vehicle etc* propulser; *person* pousser (*into* dans). **to ~ sth/sb along** faire avancer qch/qn (en le poussant). ♦ **propellant** *n [rocket]* combustible *m*. ♦ **propeller** *n* hélice *f*. ♦ **propelling pencil** *n* porte-mine *m inv*.
propensity [prəˈpensɪtɪ] *n* propension *f* (*to, towards, for* à; *to do, for doing* à faire).
proper [ˈprɒpəʳ] **1** *adj* **(a)** (*appropriate, suitable, correct*) *clothes* indiqué, convenable; *tool, answer* bon, qui convient; *spelling, order* correct; *method, treatment* indiqué, correct. **in the ~ way** comme il faut; (*Admin*) dans les règles; **in the ~ meaning** *or* **sense of the word** au sens propre du mot; **at the ~ time** à la bonne heure, à l'heure dite; (*Admin etc*) **to go through the ~ channels** passer par la filière officielle; **to make a ~ job of sth** bien réussir qch (*also iro*); **to do the ~ thing by sb** bien agir envers qn; (*Gram*) **~ noun** nom *m* propre; **if you think it ~ to do so** si vous jugez bon de faire ainsi; (*Philos, Chem etc*) **~ to** propre à. **(b)** (*seemly*) *person* comme il faut; *book, behaviour* convenable, correct. **it isn't ~ to do that** cela ne se fait pas. **(c)** (*authentic*) véritable. **he's not a ~ electrician** il n'est pas un véritable électricien; **outside Paris ~** en dehors de Paris proprement dit; **he's a ~ fool** c'est un imbécile fini; **I felt a ~ idiot** je me suis senti vraiment idiot; **he's a ~ gentleman** c'est un monsieur très comme il faut; **he made a ~ mess of it** il (en) a fait un beau gâchis.

2 *adv* (‡) *talk* comme il faut; (*very*) vraiment, très.
♦ **properly** *adv* **(a)** (*appropriately, correctly*) *dress* convenablement; *use* correctement, comme il faut; *speak, spell* correctement; **~ly speaking** à proprement parler; **he very ~ly**

refused il a refusé et avec raison; **(b)** (*in seemly way*) *behave, dress* convenablement, comme il faut; *speak* bien; **(c)** (*: *completely*) vraiment.
property ['prɒpətɪ] **1** *n* **(a)** (*possessions*) biens *mpl*, propriété *f*; (*land, building*) propriété; (*estate*) domaine *m*. (*Jur*) **personal** ~ biens personnels; **is this your** ~? cela vous appartient?; **a man of** ~ un homme qui a des biens. **(b)** (*Chem etc*) propriété *f*. **(c)** (*Theat*) accessoire *m*. **2** *adj* **(a)** *owner, tax* foncier; *market* immobilier. ~ **developer** promoteur *m* (de construction). **(b)** (*Theat*) ~ **man/mistress** accessoiriste *m/f*. ♦ **propertied** *adj* possédant.
prophecy ['prɒfɪsɪ] *n* prophétie *f*. ♦ **prophesy** ['prɒfɪsaɪ] **1** *vt* prédire (*that* que). **2** *vi* prophétiser. ♦ **prophet** *n* prophète *m*. ♦ **prophetess** *n* prophétesse *f*. ♦ **prophetic(al)** *adj* prophétique. ♦ **prophetically** *adv* prophétiquement.
propitiate [prə'pɪʃɪeɪt] *vt* se concilier. ♦ **propitiation** *n* propitiation *f*.
propitious [prə'pɪʃəs] *adj* propice. ♦ **propitiously** *adv* d'une manière propice.
proportion [prə'pɔːʃən] **1** *n* **(a)** (*ratio*) proportion *f* (*of sth to sth* de qch par rapport à qch). **the** ~ **of blacks to whites** la proportion *or* le pourcentage des noirs par rapport aux blancs; **in perfect** ~ parfaitement proportionné; **in** ~ **as** à mesure que; **in** ~ **to** en proportion de; **to be in** ~ **to** être proportionné à; **out of** ~ **to** hors de proportion avec, disproportionné par rapport à; **it's out of** ~ *[drawing]* c'est mal proportionné; (*fig*) c'est hors de proportion; (*lit, fig*) **he has no sense of** ~ il n'a pas le sens des proportions. **(b)** (*size*) ~**s** proportions *fpl*. **(c)** (*part*) part *f*, partie *f*. **in equal** ~**s** à parts égales; **a certain** ~ **of the staff** une certaine partie du personnel. **2** *vt* proportionner (*to* à). **well-**~**ed** bien proportionné.
♦ **proportional** *or* ♦ **proportionate** *adj* proportionnel (*to* à). ♦ **proportionally** *adv* proportionnellement.
propose [prə'pəʊz] **1** *vt* **(a)** (*suggest*) proposer (*sth to sb* qch à qn; *doing* de faire; *that* que + *subj*; *sb for sth* qn pour qch). **to** ~ **a toast to sb** porter un toast à la santé de qn; **to** ~ **marriage to sb** demander qn en mariage. **(b)** (*have in mind*) **to** ~ **to do** *or* **doing** se proposer de faire. **2** *vi* (*offer marriage*) faire une demande en mariage (*to sb* à qn).
♦ **proposal** *n* **(a)** (*offer*) proposition *f*; (*of marriage*) demande *f* en mariage; **(b)** (*plan*) projet *m*, plan *m* (*for sth* de *or* pour qch; *to do* pour faire); (*suggestion*) proposition *f* (*to do* de faire). ♦ **proposer** *n* (*Admin, Parl etc*) auteur *m* de la proposition. ♦ **proposition 1** *n* (*gen*) proposition *f*; (*fig*) **that's quite another proposition** ça c'est une tout autre affaire; **the journey alone is quite a proposition** rien que le voyage n'est pas une petite affaire; **to be a tough proposition** être ardu, *[person]* être coriace; **2** *vt* faire des propositions (déshonnêtes) à.
propound [prə'paʊnd] *vt theory, idea* proposer, soumettre; *problem* poser; *programme* exposer.
proprietor [prə'praɪətəʳ] *n* propriétaire *m*. ♦ **proprietary** *adj* (*Comm*) *article* de marque déposée; **proprietary brand** (produit *m* de) marque *f* déposée; **proprietary medicine** spécialité *f* pharmaceutique; **proprietary name** marque *f* déposée. ♦ **proprietress** *n* propriétaire *f*.
propriety [prə'praɪətɪ] *n* **(a)** (*decency*) bienséance *f*, convenance *f*. **to observe the proprieties** respecter les bienséances *or* les convenances. **(b)** (*appropriateness etc*) *[behaviour, step, phrase]* justesse *f*.
propulsion [prə'pʌlʃən] *n* propulsion *f*.
prosaic [prəʊ'zeɪɪk] *adj* prosaïque. ♦ **prosaically** *adv* prosaïquement.
proscribe [prəʊs'kraɪb] *vt* proscrire. ♦ **proscription** *n* proscription *f*.
prose [prəʊz] **1** *n* **(a)** prose *f*. **in** ~ en prose. **(b)** (*Scol etc:* ~ **translation**) thème *m*. **2** *adj*: ~ **writer** prosateur *m*.
prosecute ['prɒsɪkjuːt] *vt* **(a)** (*Jur etc*) poursuivre (en justice) (*for doing sth* pour qch). **(b)** (*further*) *enquiry* poursuivre. ♦ **prosecution** *n* (*Jur*) (*act, proceedings*) poursuites *fpl* judiciaires; **the prosecution** ≈ le ministère public; **witness for the prosecution** témoin *m* à charge. ♦ **prosecutor** *n* **(public prosecutor)** ≈ procureur *m* (de la République).
prosody ['prɒsədɪ] *n* prosodie *f*.
prospect ['prɒspekt] **1** *n* (*gen*) perspective *f* (*of, from* de); (*future*) (perspectives d')avenir *m*; (*hope*) espoir *m* (*of sth* de qch; *of doing* de faire). **this** ~ **cheered him up** cette perspective l'a réjoui; **to have sth in** ~ avoir qch en perspective *or* en vue; **there is little** ~ **of his coming** il y a peu de chances qu'il vienne; **he has little** ~ **of succeeding** il a peu de chances de réussir; **there is no** ~ **of that** rien ne laisse prévoir cela; **there is every** ~ **of success/of succeeding** tout laisse prévoir le succès/qu'on réussira; **the** ~**s for the harvest are good** la récolte s'annonce bien; **what are his** ~**s?** quelles sont ses perspectives d'avenir?; **'good** ~**s of promotion'** 'situation *f* d'avenir'; **it offered the** ~ **of** cela offrait la possibilité de; **he is a good** ~ **for the team** c'est un bon espoir pour l'équipe; **to seem quite a good** ~ sembler prometteur.
2 [prəs'pekt] *vti* prospecter (*for* pour trouver). ♦ **prospecting** *n* (*Min etc*) prospection *f*. ♦ **prospective** *adj son-in-law, home, legislation* futur (*before n*); *journey* en perspective; *customer* possible. ♦ **prospector** *n* prospecteur *m*, -trice *f*; **gold** ~**or** chercheur *m* d'or. ♦ **prospectus** *n* prospectus *m*.
prosper ['prɒspəʳ] *vi* prospérer. ♦ **prosperity** *n* prospérité *f*. ♦ **prosperous** *adj* prospère.
prostate ['prɒsteɪt] *n* (~ **gland**) prostate *f*.
prostitute ['prɒstɪtjuːt] **1** *n* prostituée *f*. **male** ~ prostitué *m*. **2** *vt* prostituer. ♦ **prostitution** *n* prostitution *f*.
prostrate ['prɒstreɪt] **1** *adj* à plat ventre; (*in respect, submission*) prosterné; (*exhausted*) prostré. **2** [prɒs'treɪt] *vt*: **to** ~ **o.s.** se prosterner; **the news** ~**d him** la nouvelle l'a accablé. ♦ **prostration** *n* (*Med*) prostration *f*.
protagonist [prəʊ'tægənɪst] *n* protagoniste *m*.
protect [prə'tekt] *vt* (*gen*) protéger (*from* de; *against* contre); *interests, rights* sauvegarder. ♦ **protection 1** *n* protection *f* (*against* contre); sauvegarde *f*; **under his** ~**ion** sous sa protection; **2** *adj*: **to pay** ~**ion money** verser de l'argent à un racketteur; ~**ion racket** racket *m*. ♦ **protectionism** *n* protectionnisme *m*. ♦ **protectionist** *adj*, *n* protectionniste (*mf*). ♦ **protective** *adj* (*gen*) protecteur; *clothing, covering* de protection. ♦ **protectively** *adv* d'un geste (*or* ton *etc*) protecteur. ♦ **protector** *n* protecteur *m*. ♦ **protectorate** *n* protectorat *m*.
protein ['prəʊtiːn] *n* protéine *f*.
protest ['prəʊtest] **1** *n* protestation *f* (*against* contre; *about* à propos de). **to do sth under** ~ faire qch en protestant. **2** *adj meeting* de protestation. ~ **march** *or* **demonstration** manifestation *f*. **3** [prə'test] *vt* protester (*that* que); *one's innocence, loyalty* protester de. **4** [prə'test] *vi* protester (*against* contre; *about* à propos de; *to sb* auprès de qn). ♦ **Protestant** ['prɒtɪstənt] *adj, n* protestant(e) *m(f)*. ♦ **Protestantism** *n* protestantisme *m*. ♦ **protestation** *n* protestation *f*. ♦ **protester** *n* protestataire *mf*; (*on march, in demonstration*) manifestant(e) *m(f)*.
protocol ['prəʊtəkɒl] *n* protocole *m*.
prototype ['prəʊtəʊtaɪp] *n* prototype *m*.
protract [prə'trækt] *vt* prolonger, faire traîner. ♦ **protracted** *adj* prolongé.

protrude [prəˈtruːd] *vi [stick, gutter, rock, shelf]* dépasser; *[teeth]* avancer; *[eyes]* être globuleux. ♦ **protruding** *adj* qui dépasse; qui avance; globuleux.

protuberant [prəˈtjuːbərənt] *adj* protubérant. ♦ **protuberance** *n* protubérance *f.*

proud [praʊd] *adj* **(a)** *person* fier (*of* de; *that* que + *subj*; *to do* de faire); (*arrogant*) fier, orgueilleux. **that's nothing to be ~ of!** il n'y a pas de quoi être fier!; **as ~ as a peacock** fier comme Artaban, (*pej*) vaniteux comme un paon; **to do o.s. ~*** ne se priver de rien; **to do sb ~*** se mettre en frais pour qn. **(b)** (*splendid*) *ship* majestueux. ♦ **proudly** *adv* fièrement; (*arrogantly*) orgueilleusement; (*splendidly*) majestueusement.

prove [pruːv] **1** *vt* **(a)** (*gen*) prouver (*that* que). **you can't ~ anything against me** vous n'avez aucune preuve contre moi. **(b)** *will* homologuer. **to ~ o.s.** faire ses preuves. **2** *vi*: **he/it ~d to be ...** on s'est rendu compte plus tard qu'il était/que c'était ...; **he ~d (to be) incapable of helping us** il s'est révélé incapable de nous aider; **if it ~s otherwise** s'il en est autrement.

Provence [prɒˈvɑ̃ːns] *n* Provence *f.* ♦ **Provençal** *adj, n* provençal (*m*).

proverb [ˈprɒvɜːb] *n* proverbe *m.* ♦ **proverbial** *adj* proverbial. ♦ **proverbially** *adv* proverbialement.

provide [prəˈvaɪd] **1** *vt* **(a)** (*supply*) fournir (*sb with sth, sth for sb* qch à *or* pour qn); (*equip*) pourvoir (*sb with sth* qn de qch; *sth with sth* qch à qch). **to ~ o.s. with sth** se munir de qch; **the field ~s plenty of space for a car park** le champ offre suffisamment d'espace pour un parc à autos; **~d with** pourvu de. **(b)** *[legislation etc]* stipuler, prévoir (*that* que). **2** *vi* (*financially*) **to ~ for sb** pourvoir aux besoins de qn; (*in the future*) assurer l'avenir de qn; **the Lord will ~** Dieu y pourvoira; (*make arrangements*) **to ~ for sth** prévoir qch. ♦ **provided** *or* ♦ **providing** *conj* pourvu que + *subj*, à condition de + *infin.*

providence [ˈprɒvɪdəns] *n* providence *f.* ♦ **providential** *adj* providentiel. ♦ **providentially** *adv* providentiellement.

province [ˈprɒvɪns] *n* province *f.* **the ~s** (*collectively*) la province; **in the ~s** en province; (*fig*) **that is not (within) my ~** cela n'est pas de mon domaine. ♦ **provincial** *adj, n* provincial(e) *m(f).*

provision [prəˈvɪʒən] **1** *n* **(a)** (*supply*) provision *f.* **to lay in a ~ of** faire provision de; (*food etc*) **~s** provisions *fpl*; **to get in** *or* **lay in ~s** faire des provisions; **the ~ of housing** le logement; **~ of food to the soldiers** approvisionnement *m* des soldats en nourriture; **to make ~ for** *one's family etc* assurer l'avenir de; *journey, siege* prendre des dispositions pour. **(b)** *[legislation etc]* disposition *f*, clause *f.* **~ to the contrary** clause contraire; **there is no ~ for this in the rules** le règlement ne prévoit pas cela.
2 *adj*: **~ merchant** marchand *m* de comestibles.
3 *vt* approvisionner.
♦ **provisional** *adj government, arrangement, licence* provisoire; (*Admin*) *appointment* à titre provisoire; (*Jur*) provisionnel. ♦ **provisionally** *adv agree* provisoirement; *appoint* à titre provisoire. ♦ **proviso** *n* condition *f*; (*Jur*) clause *f* restrictive; **with the proviso that** à condition que + *subj.*

provoke [prəˈvəʊk] *vt* provoquer (*sb to sth* qn à faire qch; *sb to do or into doing* qn à faire). ♦ **provocation** *n* provocation *f*; **under provocation** en réponse à une provocation. ♦ **provocative** *adj* (*gen*) provocant; (*thought-provoking*) *book, title, talk* qui donne à penser. ♦ **provocatively** *adv* d'un air *or* d'un ton provocant. ♦ **provoking** *adj* agaçant.

provost [ˈprɒvəst] *n* (*Brit Univ*) principal *m*; (*US Univ*) ≈ doyen *m*; (*Scot: mayor*) maire *m*; (*Rel*) doyen *m.*

prow [praʊ] *n* proue *f.*

prowess [ˈpraʊɪs] *n* prouesse *f.*

prowl [praʊl] *vi* (**~ about, ~ around**) rôder. ♦ **prowler** *n* rôdeur *m*, -euse *f.*

proximity [prɒkˈsɪmɪtɪ] *n* proximité *f.* **in ~ to** à proximité de.

proxy [ˈprɒksɪ] *n* (*power*) procuration *f*; (*person*) mandataire *mf.* **by ~** par procuration.

prude [pruːd] *n* prude *f*, bégueule *f.* ♦ **prudery** *n* pruderie *f.* ♦ **prudish** *adj* prude.

prudent [ˈpruːdənt] *adj* prudent. ♦ **prudence** *n* prudence *f.* ♦ **prudently** *adv* prudemment.

prune[1] [pruːn] *n* (*fruit*) pruneau *m.*

prune[2] [pruːn] *vt tree* tailler; (**~ down**) *article, essay* faire des coupures dans. ♦ **pruning 1** *n* taille *f*; **2** *adj*: **pruning knife** serpette *f.*

prurient [ˈprʊərɪənt] *adj* lascif. ♦ **prurience** *n* lascivité *f.*

Prussia [ˈprʌʃə] *n* Prusse *f.* ♦ **Prussian 1** *adj* prussien; **2** *n* Prussien(ne) *m(f).*

pry[1] [praɪ] *vi* s'occuper de ce qui ne vous regarde pas. **to ~ into sb's desk** fureter dans le bureau de qn; **to ~ into a secret** chercher à découvrir un secret. ♦ **prying** *adj* fureteur, indiscret.

pry[2] [praɪ] *vt* (*US*) = **prise.**

psalm [sɑːm] *n* psaume *m.* ♦ **psalmist** *n* psalmiste *m.*

pseudo- [ˈsjuːdəʊ] *pref* pseudo-. **~autobiography** pseudo-autobiographie *f*; **~apologetically** sous couleur de s'excuser. ♦ **pseud*** *n* bêcheur* *m*, -euse* *f.* ♦ **pseudo*** *adj* insincère, faux.

pseudonym [ˈsjuːdənɪm] *n* pseudonyme *m.*

psoriasis [sɒˈraɪəsɪs] *n* psoriasis *m.*

psyche [ˈsaɪkɪ] *n* psychisme *m*, psyché *f.*

psychedelic [ˌsaɪkɪˈdelɪk] *adj* psychédélique.

psychiatry [saɪˈkaɪətrɪ] *n* psychiatrie *f.* ♦ **psychiatric** *adj hospital, treatment, medicine* psychiatrique; *disease* mental. ♦ **psychiatrist** *n* psychiatre *mf.*

psychic(al) [ˈsaɪkɪk(əl)] *adj* **(a)** (*supernatural*) *phenomenon, research* métapsychique; (*telepathic*) télépathe. **I'm not ~*** je ne suis pas devin. **(b)** (*Psych*) psychique.

psychoanalysis [ˌsaɪkəʊəˈnælɪsɪs] *n* psychanalyse *f.* ♦ **psychoanalyst** *n* psychanalyste *mf.* ♦ **psychoanalytic(al)** *adj* psychanalytique. ♦ **psychoanalyze** *vt* psychanalyser.

psychology [saɪˈkɒlədʒɪ] *n* psychologie *f.* ♦ **psychological** *adj* psychologique. ♦ **psychologically** *adv* psychologiquement. ♦ **psychologist** *n* psychologue *mf.*

psychopath [ˈsaɪkəʊpæθ] *n* psychopathe *mf.* ♦ **psychopathic** *adj person* psychopathe; *condition* psychopathique.

psychosis [saɪˈkəʊsɪs] *n, pl* **-oses** psychose *f.* ♦ **psychotic** *adj, n* psychotique (*mf*).

psychosomatic [ˈsaɪkəʊsəʊˈmætɪk] *adj* psychosomatique.

psychotherapy [ˈsaɪkəʊˈθerəpɪ] *n* psychothérapie *f.* ♦ **psychotherapist** *n* psychothérapeute *mf.*

ptomaine [ˈtəʊmeɪn] *n* ptomaïne *f.* **~ poisoning** intoxication *f* alimentaire.

pub [pʌb] (*Brit abbr of* **public house**) *n* pub *m*, ≈ bistrot* *m.* **to go on a ~ crawl*** faire la tournée des bistrots *or* des pubs.

puberty [ˈpjuːbətɪ] *n* puberté *f.*

pubis [ˈpjuːbɪs] *n* pubis *m.* ♦ **pubic** *adj*: **pubic hair** poils *mpl* du pubis.

public [ˈpʌblɪk] **1** *adj* (*gen*) public (*f* -ique); (*Econ*: **~ly** *owned*) *company* nationalisé. **to make sth ~** rendre qch public, porter qch à la connaissance du public; (*of copyright*) **in the ~ domain** dans le domaine public; (*Econ, Ind*) **the ~ sector** le secteur public; **his ~ support of the communists** son appui déclaré aux communistes; **2 ~ rooms and 3 bedrooms** 5 pièces dont 3 chambres;

~ **address system** (installation *f* de) sonorisation *f*; **to be in the ~ eye** être très en vue; **he's a ~ figure, he's in ~ life** c'est un homme public; ~ **holiday** fête *f* légale; (*Brit*) ~ **house** pub *m*, ≃ café *m*, bistrot *m*; ~ **lavatory** toilettes *fpl*, W.-C. *mpl*; ~ **library** bibliothèque *f* municipale; (*Pol Econ*) ~ **ownership** étatisation *f*; ~ **relations** relations *fpl* publiques, public-relations* *fpl*; ~ **relations officer** public-relations* *mf*; ~ **school** (*Brit*) collège *m* secondaire privé; (*US*) école *f* publique; ~ **servant** fonctionnaire *mf*; ~ **service** service *m* public; (*US*) ~ **service** corporation service public non étatisé; **he is a good ~ speaker** il parle bien en public; ~ **speaking** art *m* oratoire; ~ **spirit** civisme *m*; ~ **transport** transports *mpl* en commun.

2 *n* public *m*. **in ~** en public; **the reading/sporting ~** les amateurs *mpl* de lecture/de sport; **he couldn't disappoint his ~** il ne pouvait pas décevoir son public.

♦ **publican** *n* patron(ne) *m(f)* de bistrot. ♦ **publicly** *adv* publiquement, en public; (*Econ*) **~ly-owned** nationalisé. ♦ **public-spirited** *adj* qui fait preuve de civisme.

publication [ˌpʌblɪˈkeɪʃən] *n* publication *f*. **this is not for ~** ceci doit rester entre nous.

publicity [pʌbˈlɪsɪtɪ] **1** *n* publicité *f*; (*posters, advertisements etc*) publicité *f*, réclame *f*. **2** *adj agency, agent* de publicité. ♦ **publicize** *vt* **(a)** (*make public*) rendre public, publier; **I don't publicize the fact, but ...** je ne le crie pas sur les toits, mais ...; **(b)** (*advertise*) faire de la publicité pour.

publish [ˈpʌblɪʃ] *vt news, banns, book* publier; *author* éditer. **'just ~ed'** 'vient de paraître'. ♦ **publisher** *n* éditeur *m*, -trice *f*. ♦ **publishing** *n [book etc]* publication *f*; **he's in ~ing** il travaille dans l'édition; **~ing house** maison *f* d'édition.

pucker [ˈpʌkəʳ] **1** *vi* (**~ up**) *[face]* se plisser; (*Sewing*) goder. **2** *vt* (*Sewing*) faire goder.

pudding [ˈpʊdɪŋ] **1** *n* (*dessert*) dessert *m*; (*steamed ~, meat ~*) pudding *m*. (*sausage*) **black/white ~** boudin *m* noir/blanc. **2** *adj*: **~ basin** jatte *f*.

puddle [ˈpʌdl] *n* flaque *f* d'eau.

puerile [ˈpjʊəraɪl] *adj* puéril.

puff [pʌf] **1** *n* **(a)** *[air, wind, smoke]* bouffée *f*; (*from mouth*) souffle *m*; (*sound of engine*) teuf-teuf *m*. **he took a ~ at his cigarette** il a tiré une bouffée de sa cigarette. **(b)** (*powder ~*) houppe *f*, (*small*) houppette *f*. (*cake*) **jam ~** feuilleté *m* à la confiture. **(c)** (*: *Press, Rad, TV advertisement*) réclame *f*. **he gave the record a ~** il a fait de la réclame *or* du boniment pour le disque. **2** *adj*: **~ pastry,** (*US*) **~ paste** pâte *f* feuilletée; **~(ed) sleeves** manches *fpl* bouffantes. **3** *vi* (*blow*) souffler; (*pant*) haleter; *[wind]* souffler. **he was ~ing and panting** il soufflait comme un phoque; **to ~ (away) at one's pipe** tirer des bouffées de sa pipe. **4** *vt* **(a) to ~ (out) smoke** envoyer des bouffées de fumée. **(b)** (*also* **~ out**) *sails, cheeks, chest* gonfler. **his eyes are ~ed up** il a les yeux gonflés *or* bouffis. **(c) to be ~ed (out)*** être à bout de souffle. ♦ **puffball** *n* vesse-de-loup *f*. ♦ **puffiness** *n* gonflement *m*, bouffissure *f*. ♦ **puffy** *adj* gonflé, bouffi.

puffin [ˈpʌfɪn] *n* macareux *m*.

pug [pʌg] *n* carlin *m*. ♦ **pug-nosed** *adj* au nez rond retroussé.

pugilism [ˈpjuːdʒɪlɪzəm] *n* boxe *f*. ♦ **pugilist** *n* pugiliste *m*.

pugnacious [pʌgˈneɪʃəs] *adj* batailleur. ♦ **pugnaciously** *adv* avec pugnacité. ♦ **pugnacity** *n* pugnacité *f*.

puke‡ [pjuːk] *vi* vomir, dégobiller‡.

pukka* [ˈpʌkə] *adj* (*genuine*) véritable; (*excellent*) de premier ordre; (*socially superior*) snob *inv*.

pull [pʊl] **1** *n* **(a)** (*act, effect*) traction *f*; *[moon, magnet, the sea, sb's personality]* attraction *f*; *[current, family ties etc]* force *f*. **to give sth a ~** tirer sur qch; **one more ~!** encore un coup!; **I felt a ~ at my sleeve** j'ai senti qn qui tirait ma manche; **it was a long ~ up the hill** la montée était longue (et raide); (*fig*) **to have some ~ with sb** avoir de l'influence auprès de qn. **(b) he took a ~ at the bottle** il a bu une gorgée à même la bouteille; **he took a ~ at his pipe** il a tiré sur sa pipe. **(c)** (*handle*) poignée *f*; (*cord*) cordon *m*.

2 *vt* **(a)** (*draw*) *cart, caravan, curtains* tirer. **to ~ a door shut** tirer une porte derrière soi; **to ~ a door open** ouvrir une porte en la tirant; **~ your chair closer to the table** approchez votre chaise de la table; **he ~ed the box over to the window** il a traîné la caisse jusqu'à la fenêtre; **he ~ed her towards him** il l'a attirée vers lui. **(b)** (*tug*) *bell, rope* tirer; *trigger* presser; *oars* manier. **to ~ to pieces** *or* **to bits** *toy, box etc* mettre en pièces, démolir; (*fig*) *argument, scheme* démolir; *play, film, person* éreinter; **to ~ sb's hair** tirer les cheveux à qn; (*fig*) **to ~ sb's leg** faire marcher qn*; **he didn't ~ any punches** il n'y est pas allé de main morte; (*fig*) **to ~ strings** se faire pistonner*; **to ~ strings for sb** exercer son influence pour aider qn, pistonner* qn; (*fig*) **to ~ one's weight** faire sa part du travail. **(c)** (*draw out*) *tooth, weeds* arracher; *cork, stopper* enlever; *gun, knife* sortir; *flowers* cueillir; *beer* tirer; (*Culin*) *chicken* vider. **he ~ed a gun on me** il a soudain braqué un revolver sur moi. **(d)** (*strain, tear*) *thread* tirer; *muscle, tendon* se déchirer. **(e)** (*fig: make, do*) *bank raid, burglary* effectuer. **to ~ a fast one on sb*** rouler qn*, avoir qn*.

3 *vi* **(a)** (*tug*) tirer (*at, on* sur). **he ~ed at her sleeve** il l'a tirée par la manche; **the car is ~ing to the left** la voiture tire à gauche. **(b)** (*move*) **the coach ~ed slowly up the hill** le car a gravi lentement la colline; **the train ~ed into/out of the station** le train est entré en gare/est sorti de la gare; **he ~ed clear of the traffic** il a laissé le gros de la circulation derrière lui; **he ~ed away from the kerb** il s'est éloigné du trottoir; **the car isn't ~ing very well** la voiture manque de reprises. **(c)** (*row*) ramer (*for* vers).

pull about, pull around *vt sep* **(a)** *wheeled object etc* tirer derrière soi. **(b)** (*handle roughly*) *watch, ornament etc* tirailler; *person* malmener.

pull along *vt sep wheeled object etc* tirer derrière soi. **to ~ o.s. along** se traîner.

pull apart *vt sep* **(a)** (*pull to pieces*) démonter; (*break*) mettre en pièces. **(b)** (*separate*) séparer.

pull away 1 *vi [vehicle, ship, train]* démarrer. **2** *vt sep object* arracher (*from sb* à qn, des mains de qn). **he ~ed the child away from the fire** il a écarté l'enfant du feu.

pull back 1 *vi* (*withdraw*) se retirer. **2** *vt sep object* retirer (*from* de); *person* tirer en arrière (*from* loin de); (*Mil*) retirer; *curtains* ouvrir; *lever* tirer (sur).

pull down *vt sep* **(a)** *blind* baisser, descendre; *one's skirt, hat* tirer; *one's opponent* mettre à terre; *object from shelf etc* faire tomber (*from* de). **his illness has ~ed him down** la maladie l'a affaibli. **(b)** (*demolish*) *building* démolir, abattre.

pull in 1 *vi* (*Aut etc: arrive*) arriver; *[train]* entrer en gare; (*enter*) entrer; (*stop*) s'arrêter. **2** *vt sep* **(a)** *rope, fishing line* ramener; *person* (*into room, car*) faire entrer, (*into pool etc*) faire piquer une tête dans l'eau à. **(b)** (*restrain*) *horse* retenir. **(c)** (*: *earn*) *[person]* gagner; *[business, shop etc]* rapporter.

pull off *vt sep* **(a)** (*remove*) *handle, gloves, coat* enlever. **(b)** (*fig*) *plan, aim* réaliser; *deal* mener à bien; *attack, hoax* réussir. **he didn't ~ it off** il n'a pas réussi son coup.

pull on *vt sep* mettre.

pull out 1 *vi* **(a)** (*leave*) *[train, car, ship]*

démarrer; (*withdraw: lit, fig*) se retirer (*of* de). (*Aviat*) **to ~ out of a dive** se redresser. **(b)** (*Aut*) déboîter. **he ~ed out to overtake the truck** il a déboîté pour doubler le camion. **2** *vt sep* **(a)** (*extract*) (*gen*) arracher; *splinter, cork* enlever; *gun, knife, cigarette lighter, person* sortir, tirer (*of* de). **(b)** (*withdraw*) *troops, police etc* retirer (*of* de).

pull over 1 *vi* (*Aut*) **to ~ over (to one side)** se ranger sur le côté. **2** *vt sep* **(a)** *box* traîner (*to* jusqu'à); *person* entraîner (*to* vers). **(b)** (*topple*) faire tomber.

pull round 1 *vi [unconscious person]* revenir à soi; *[sick person]* se rétablir. **2** *vt sep chair, person etc* faire pivoter; *unconscious person* ranimer; *sick person* tirer de là.

pull through 1 *vi* (*from illness, difficulties*) s'en tirer. **2** *vt sep rope etc* faire passer; (*fig*) *person* (*from illness, difficulties*) tirer de là.

pull together *vt sep* (*fig*) **to ~ o.s. together** se ressaisir; **~ yourself together!** ressaisis-toi!, ne te laisse pas aller!

pull up 1 *vi* (*stop*) s'arrêter (net). **2** *vt sep* **(a)** *object* remonter; (*haul up*) hisser; *stockings* tirer. **(b)** *weed, tree* arracher. (*fig*) **to ~ up one's roots** se déraciner (*fig*). **(c)** (*halt*) *vehicle, horse* arrêter; (*scold*) réprimander.

♦ **pull-in** *n* (*Brit*) (*lay-by*) parking *m*; (*café*) café *m* au bord de la route. ♦ **pull-out 1** *n* (*magazine section*) supplément *m* détachable; **2** *adj page* détachable; *table leaf* rétractable. ♦ **pullover** *n* pull *m*, pull-over *m*.

pullet ['pʊlɪt] *n* jeune poule *f*.

pulley ['pʊlɪ] *n* poulie *f*.

Pullman ['pʊlmən] *n* (**~ car**) pullman *m*, voiture-salon *f*.

pulp [pʌlp] **1** *n* (*part of fruit*) pulpe *f*; (*for paper*) pâte *f* à papier. **crushed to a ~** complètement écrasé. **2** *adj magazine, book* à sensation. **3** *vt* réduire en pulpe *or* en pâte; *book* mettre au pilon.

pulpit ['pʊlpɪt] *n* chaire *f* (*Rel*).

pulsate [pʌl'seɪt] *vi* (*gen*) émettre des pulsations; *[heart, blood]* battre; *[music]* vibrer. ♦ **pulsating** *adj* rythmique. ♦ **pulsation** *n* pulsation *f*.

pulse[1] [pʌls] *n* (*Med*) pouls *m*; (*Elec, Phys, Rad*) pulsation *f*; *[radar]* impulsion *f*. **to take sb's ~** prendre le pouls de qn.

pulse[2] [pʌls] *n* (*Culin*) légume *m* sec.

pulverize ['pʌlvəraɪz] *vt* pulvériser.

puma ['pju:mə] *n* puma *m*.

pumice ['pʌmɪs] *n* (**~ stone**) pierre *f* ponce.

pummel ['pʌml] *vt* bourrer *or* rouer de coups. ♦ **pummelling** *n* volée *f* de coups.

pump [pʌmp] **1** *n* pompe *f*. **bicycle ~** pompe à bicyclette; **petrol ~** pompe d'essence.

2 *adj*: **~ attendant** pompiste *mf*; **~ house, ~ing station** station *f* de pompage; **~ room** buvette *f* (*de station thermale*).

3 *vt* **(a) to ~ sth out of sth** pomper qch de qch; **to ~ sth into sth** (*foam into walls etc*) injecter *or* (*oil into pipeline etc*) faire passer qch dans qch (au moyen d'une pompe); **to ~ water into sth** pomper de l'eau dans qch; **to ~ air into a tyre** gonfler un pneu (avec une pompe); **the water is ~ed up to the house** l'eau est amenée jusqu'à la maison au moyen d'une pompe; **they ~ed the tank dry** ils ont vidé le réservoir (à la pompe); **the heart ~s the blood** le cœur fait circuler le sang; (*fig*) **to ~ money into sth** injecter de plus en plus d'argent dans qch; (*fig: question*) **to ~ sb for sth** essayer de soutirer qch à qn. **(b)** *handle etc* lever et abaisser vigoureusement.

pump in *vt sep* injecter *or* faire passer (à l'aide d'une pompe).

pump out *vt sep* pomper.

pump up *vt sep tyre* gonfler.

pumpkin ['pʌmpkɪn] *n* citrouille *f*; (*bigger*) potiron *m*. **~ pie** tarte *f* au potiron.

pun [pʌn] *n* calembour *m*, jeu *m* de mots.

Punch [pʌntʃ] *n* Polichinelle *m*. **~ and Judy Show** (théâtre *m* de) guignol *m*.

punch[1] [pʌntʃ] **1** *n* **(a)** (*blow*) coup *m* de poing; *[boxer]* punch *m*; (*fig: drive*) *[publicity, statement]* force *f*; *[person]* punch* *m*. **(b)** (*tool*) (*for tickets*) poinçonneuse *f*; (*for holes in paper*) perforateur *m*; (*for metal*) emporte-pièce *m inv*; (*for nails*) chasse-clou *m*. **2** *vt* **(a)** (*with fist*) *person* donner un coup de poing à; *ball, door* frapper d'un coup de poing. **to ~ sb's nose** donner un coup de poing sur le nez à qn. **(b)** poinçonner; perforer; découper à l'emporte-pièce; enfoncer (au chasse-clou). **to ~ a hole in sth** faire un trou dans qch; (*Ind*) **to ~ one's card** pointer. ♦ **punchball** *or* ♦ **punching bag** (*US*) *n* sac *m* de sable. ♦ **punch(ed) card** *n* carte *f* perforée. ♦ **punch-drunk** *adj* abruti. ♦ **punch-line** *n [joke]* astuce *f*; *[speech]* phrase-clé *f*. ♦ **punch-up*** *n* bagarre* *f*.

punch[2] [pʌntʃ] *n* (*drink*) punch *m*. **~ bowl** bol *m* à punch.

punctilious [pʌŋk'tɪlɪəs] *adj* pointilleux. ♦ **punctiliously** *adv* de façon pointilleuse.

punctual ['pʌŋktjʊəl] *adj person for appointment, train* à l'heure; *employee, payment* ponctuel. ♦ **punctuality** *n* exactitude *f*. ♦ **punctually** *adv arrive* à l'heure; **~ly at 7** à 7 heures précises.

punctuate ['pʌŋktjʊeɪt] *vt* ponctuer (*with* de). ♦ **punctuation** *n* ponctuation *f*; **punctuation mark** signe *m* de ponctuation.

puncture ['pʌŋktʃər] **1** *n* (*in tyre*) crevaison *f*; (*in skin, paper etc*) piqûre *f*. (*Aut etc*) **I've got a ~** j'ai crevé. **2** *adj*: **~ repair kit** trousse *f* de secours pour crevaisons. **3** *vt* crever; piquer. **4** *vi [tyre etc]* crever.

pundit ['pʌndɪt] *n* expert *m*, pontife *m*.

pungent ['pʌndʒənt] *adj smell, taste* âcre; *sauce* piquant; *remark* mordant. ♦ **pungency** *n* âcreté *f*; goût *m* piquant; mordant *m*. ♦ **pungently** *adv remark* d'un ton mordant.

punish ['pʌnɪʃ] *vt* (*gen*) punir (*for sth* de qch; *for doing* pour avoir fait); (*fig*) *opponent, boxer* malmener; *engine* fatiguer; *roast beef* faire honneur à. **he was ~ed by having to clean it up** pour le punir on le lui a fait nettoyer. ♦ **punishable** *adj offence* punissable; **~able by death** passible de la peine de mort. ♦ **punishing 1** *n* punition *f*; **2** *adj* (*fig: exhausting*) exténuant. ♦ **punishment** *n* punition *f*, (*solemn*) châtiment *m*; **as a ~ment** en punition (*for* de); **capital ~ment** peine *f* capitale; **to take one's ~ment** subir sa punition; **to make the ~ment fit the crime** adapter le châtiment au crime; (*fig*) **to take a lot of ~ment** *[boxer, fighter]* encaisser*; *[opposing team]* se faire malmener.

punk [pʌŋk] *n* (*nonsense*) foutaises‡ *fpl*; (*music, person*) punk *m*. **~ rock** le punk rock.

punt[1] [pʌnt] **1** *n* (*boat*) bachot *m* à fond plat. **2** *vt boat* faire avancer à la perche. **3** *vi*: **to go ~ing** faire un tour sur la rivière.

punt[2] [pʌnt] *vi* (*bet*) parier. ♦ **punter** *n* parieur *m*, -ieuse *f*.

puny ['pju:nɪ] *adj person, animal* chétif; *effort* piteux.

pup [pʌp] *n* jeune chien(ne) *m(f)*. (*fig*) **he's an insolent young ~** c'est un petit morveux*. ♦ **puppy 1** *n* = **pup**; **2** *adj*: **~py fat** rondeurs *fpl* d'adolescent(e); **~py love** premier amour *m* (*d'adolescent*).

pupil[1] ['pju:pl] **1** *n* (*Scol etc*) élève *mf*. **2** *adj*: **~ power** pouvoir *m* des lycéens; **~ teacher** professeur *m* stagiaire.

pupil[2] ['pju:pl] *n [eye]* pupille *f*.

puppet ['pʌpɪt] **1** *n* marionnette *f*. **2** *adj theatre, play* de marionnettes; (*fig*) *state, leader* fantoche. **~ show** (spectacle *m* de) marionnettes *fpl*. ♦ **puppeteer** *n* marionnettiste *mf*.

purchase ['pɜ:tʃɪs] **1** *n* **(a)** (*Comm etc*) achat *m*. **(b)** (*grip, hold*) prise *f*. **to get a ~ on** avoir une prise sur. 2 *adj*: ~ **price** prix *m* d'achat; ~ **tax** taxe *f* à l'achat. 3 *vt* acheter (*sth from sb* qch à qn; *sth for sb* qch pour *or* à qn). ♦ **purchaser** *n* acheteur *m*, -euse *f*. ♦ **purchasing power** *n* pouvoir *m* d'achat.

pure [pjʊəʳ] *adj* pur. **as ~ as the driven snow** innocent comme l'enfant qui vient de naître; ~ **in heart** au cœur pur; ~ **science** science pure; **a ~ wool suit** un complet pure laine; ~ **and simple** pur et simple; **it was a ~ accident** c'était un pur accident; **it was ~ chance/madness** c'était un pur hasard/de la pure folie. ♦ **purebred 1** *adj* de race; 2 *n* animal *m* de race; (*horse*) pur-sang *m inv*. ♦ **pure-hearted** *adj* (au cœur) pur. ♦ **purely** *adv* purement; **~ly and simply** purement et simplement. ♦ **pure-minded** *adj* pur d'esprit. ♦ **pureness** *n* pureté *f*.

purgative ['pɜːgətɪv] *adj, n* purgatif (*m*).

purgatory ['pɜːgətərɪ] *n* purgatoire *m*. (*fig*) **it was ~** c'était un vrai purgatoire.

purge [pɜːdʒ] **1** *n* (*gen, Med, Pol*) purge *f*. **2** *vt* **(a)** (*gen, Med, Pol*) purger (*of* de); *traitors* éliminer. **(b)** (*Jur*) *person* disculper (*of* de); *accusation* se disculper de; *offence* purger.

purify ['pjʊərɪfaɪ] *vt* purifier. ♦ **purification** *n* *[water, metal etc]* épuration *f*; *[person]* purification *f*. ♦ **purifier** *n* purificateur *m*.

purist ['pjʊərɪst] *adj, n* puriste (*mf*).

puritan ['pjʊərɪtən] *adj, n* puritain(e) *m(f)*. ♦ **puritanical** *adj* puritain. ♦ **puritanism** *n* puritanisme *m*.

purity ['pjʊərɪtɪ] *n* pureté *f*.

purl [pɜːl] **1** *adj* à l'envers. **2** *vt* tricoter à l'envers.

purloin [pɜː'lɔɪn] *vt* dérober.

purple ['pɜːpl] **1** *adj* violet, pourpre. **to go ~ in the face** devenir cramoisi. (*fig*) ~ **passages** morceaux *mpl* de bravoure. **2** *n* (*colour*) violet *m*, pourpre *m*. (*Rel*) **the ~** la pourpre.

purport ['pɜːpət] **1** *n* signification *f*, portée *f*. **2** [pɜː'pɔːt] *vt*: **to ~ to be** prétendre être.

purpose ['pɜːpəs] *n* (*aim, intention*) but *m*, objet *m*; (*use*) usage *m*, utilité *f*. **a ~ in life** un but *or* un objectif dans la vie; **a film with a ~** un film qui contient un message; **with the ~ of doing** dans le but *or* l'intention de faire; **for this ~** dans ce but; **sense of ~** résolution *f*; **for my ~s** pour ce que je veux faire; **for the ~s of the meeting** pour les besoins de cette réunion; **on ~** exprès, délibérément; **on ~ to annoy me** exprès pour me contrarier; **to no ~** en vain; **to no ~ at all** en pure perte; **to some ~, to good ~** utilement; **to the ~** à propos; **not to the ~** hors de propos. ♦ **purpose-built** *adj* fonctionnalisé. ♦ **purposeful** *adj* (*determined*) résolu; (*intentional*) réfléchi. ♦ **purposefully** *adv* délibérément. ♦ **purposely** *adv* exprès, délibérément.

purr [pɜːʳ] **1** *vi [cat]* ronronner. **2** *n* ronronnement *m*.

purse [pɜːs] **1** *n* (*for coins*) porte-monnaie *m inv*, bourse *f*; (*wallet*) portefeuille *m*; (*US: handbag*) sac *m* à main; (*esp Sport: prize*) prix *m*. (*fig*) **beyond my ~** au-delà de mes moyens. **2** *adj* (*fig*) **to hold/tighten the ~ strings** tenir/serrer les cordons de la bourse. **3** *vt*: **to ~ (up) one's lips** pincer les lèvres. ♦ **purser** *n* (*Naut*) commissaire *m* du bord.

pursue [pə'sjuː] *vt* **(a)** (*chase: gen*) poursuivre; *pleasure, fame* rechercher; *[misfortune etc]* suivre. **(b)** (*carry on*) *studies, career, plan, inquiry* poursuivre; *course of action* suivre. ♦ **pursuer** *n* poursuivant(e) *m(f)*.

pursuit [pə'sjuːt] *n* **(a)** (*chase*) poursuite *f*; (*fig: of pleasure, happiness*) recherche *f*. **to go in ~ of sb/sth** se mettre à la poursuite de qn/qch; **with two policemen in hot ~** avec deux agents à ses (*or* mes *etc*) trousses. **(b)** (*occupation*) occupation *f*; (*work*) travail *m*.

purveyor [pɜː'veɪəʳ] *n* (*Comm etc*) fournisseur *m*, -euse *f* (*of sth* en qch; *to sb* de qn).

pus [pʌs] *n* pus *m*.

push [pʊʃ] **1** *n* **(a)** (*shove*) poussée *f*. **to give sb/sth a ~** pousser qn/qch; (*Brit fig*) **to give sb the ~*** *[employer]* flanquer qn à la porte*; *[boyfriend etc]* laisser tomber qn*. **(b)** (*Mil: advance*) poussée *f*; (*fig*) (*effort*) gros effort *m*; (*campaign*) campagne *f*. **at a ~*** au besoin, à la rigueur; **when it comes to the ~*** au moment critique. **(c)** (*: *drive, energy*) dynamisme *m*, initiative *f*.

2 *vt* **(a)** (*shove, prod*) pousser (*into* dans; *off* de); (*press*) *knob, button* appuyer sur; *stick, finger etc* enfoncer (*into* dans, *between* entre); *rag etc* fourrer (*into* dans). **to ~ sb in/out** *etc* faire entrer/sortir *etc* qn en le poussant; **he ~ed him down the stairs** il l'a poussé et l'a fait tomber dans l'escalier; **they ~ed the car off the road** ils ont poussé la voiture sur le bas-côté; **he ~ed his head through the window** il a passé la tête par la fenêtre; **he ~ed the book into my hand** il m'a fourré* le livre dans la main; **to ~ a door open** ouvrir une porte en poussant; **to ~ one's way through a crowd** se frayer un chemin dans la foule; (*fig*) **it ~ed the matter right out of my mind** cela m'a fait complètement oublier l'affaire; **he's ~ing forty*** il approche de la quarantaine.

(b) (*fig: press, advance*) *advantage* poursuivre; *claim* présenter avec insistance; *one's views* mettre en avant; *product* pousser la vente de; *candidate etc* soutenir. **to ~ home an attack** pousser à fond une attaque; **to ~ the export side** donner priorité aux exportations; **to ~ drugs** revendre de la drogue; **don't ~ your luck*** vas-y doucement!; **he's ~ing his luck*** il y va un peu fort.

(c) (*put pressure on*) pousser; (*force*) forcer, obliger; (*harass*) harceler. **to ~ sb for payment** presser qn à payer; **he ~es himself too hard** il exige trop de lui-même; **don't ~ him too hard** *or* **too far** ne soyez pas trop dur envers lui; **to ~ sb to do** pousser qn à faire; **to ~ sb into doing** forcer qn à faire; **to be ~ed* for time/money/boxes** être à court de temps/d'argent/de boîtes; **I'm really ~ed* today** je suis vraiment bousculé aujourd'hui; **that's ~ing it a bit!*** (*indignantly*) c'est un peu fort!; (*not much room*) c'est un peu juste!

3 *vi* **(a)** pousser. '~' (*on door*) 'poussez'; (*on bell*) 'sonnez'; (*fig*) **he ~es too much** il se met trop en avant; (*fig*) **to ~ for better conditions** faire pression pour obtenir de meilleures conditions. **(b) they ~ed into the room** ils sont entrés dans la pièce en se frayant un passage; **he ~ed past me** il a réussi à passer en me bousculant; **she ~ed through the crowd** elle s'est frayé un chemin dans la foule.

push about, push around *vt sep* **(a)** *cart, toy* pousser de-ci de-là. **(b)** (*: *bully*) marcher sur les pieds à (*fig*).

push aside *vt sep* écarter (brusquement).

push away *vt sep* repousser.

push back *vt sep cover, blankets, lock of hair* rejeter; *curtains* ouvrir; *crowd, enemy* faire reculer; (*fig*) *desire* réprimer.

push down 1 *vi* appuyer (*on* sur). **2** *vt sep switch, lever* abaisser; *knob, button* appuyer sur; *pin, stick* enfoncer; (*knock over*) *fence, barrier, person* renverser. **he ~ed the books down into the box** il a entassé les livres dans la caisse.

push forward 1 *vi* avancer (en poussant). **2** *vt sep person, box etc* pousser en avant. **he ~ed himself forward** il s'est avancé, (*fig*) il s'est mis en avant.

push in 1 *vi* (*into room*) s'introduire de force; (*into discussion etc*) intervenir. **2** *vt sep* **(a)** *stick, pin, finger* enfoncer; *rag* fourrer dedans; *knob, button* appuyer sur; *person* faire entrer (en poussant), (*into water*) pousser dedans. **(b)** (*break*) *door, sides of box* enfoncer.

push off 1 *vi* **(a)** (*Naut*) pousser au large. **(b)** (*: *leave*) filer*, partir. **2** *vt sep* **(a)** *top, lid* enlever en poussant; *vase from shelf etc* faire tomber (*from* de); *person from cliff etc* pousser (*from* de, du haut de). **(b)** (*Naut*) déborder.
push on 1 *vi* (*in journey*) pousser (*to* jusqu'à); (*in work*) continuer. **2** *vt sep* pousser, inciter (*sb to do* qn à faire).
push out *vt sep* **(a)** *person, object* pousser dehors; *boat* pousser au large; *stopper* faire sortir (en poussant); (*fig*) *employee* se débarrasser de. **(b)** *roots, shoots* produire.
push over *vt sep* **(a)** *object* pousser (*to sb* vers qn); (*over cliff etc*) pousser. **(b)** (*topple*) *chair, person* renverser.
push through 1 *vi* se frayer un chemin. **2** *vt sep stick, hand etc* enfoncer; (*fig*) *deal, business* conclure à la hâte; *decision* faire accepter à la hâte; (*Parl*) *bill* réussir à faire voter.
push to *vt sep door* pousser (pour fermer).
push up *vt sep lever, switch, spectacles* relever; (*fig*) (*gen*) augmenter; *sb's temperature, blood pressure, total* faire monter.
◆ **push-bike*** *n* vélo *m*. ◆ **push-button** *adj* presse-bouton *inv*. ◆ **push-chair** *n* poussette *f* (*pour enfant*). ◆ **pusher** *n* **(a)** (*pej*) arriviste *mf*; **(b)** *[drugs]* revendeur *m*, -euse *f*. ◆ **pushful*** *or* ◆ **pushy*** *adj* qui se met trop en avant. ◆ **pushing** *adj person* dynamique, entreprenant; (*pej*) arriviste, qui se met trop en avant. ◆ **pushover*** *n*: **it was a ~over** c'était un jeu d'enfant. ◆ **push-up** *n* traction *f* (*Sport*).
pusillanimous [ˌpju:sɪ'lænɪməs] *adj* pusillanime.
puss* [pʊs], **pussy*** ['pʊsɪ] *n* minet *m*, -ette *f*.
put [pʊt] *pret, ptp* **put 1** *vt* **(a)** (*gen*) mettre; (*place*) placer; (*lay down*) poser; *energy, time* consacrer (*into* à); *money, savings* placer (*into* dans); *advertisement in paper* passer (*in* dans); *signature* apposer (*on, to* à); *mark* faire (*on* sur, à). **he ~ some more coal on the fire** il a remis du charbon sur le feu; **to ~ one's arms round sb** prendre qn dans ses bras; **he ~ his head through the window** il a passé la tête par la fenêtre; **he ~ his hand over his mouth** il s'est mis la main devant la bouche; **he ~ me on the train** il m'a mis *or* accompagné au train; **he ~ me into a non-smoker** il m'a trouvé une place dans un compartiment non-fumeurs; **to ~ sb off a train** *etc* débarquer qn d'un train *etc*; **to ~ sb on to/off a committee** nommer qn à/renvoyer qn d'un comité; **to ~ one's confidence in** placer sa confiance en; **you get out of life what you ~ into it** on ne retire de la vie que ce qu'on y met soi-même; **he has ~ a lot into his marriage** il a fait beaucoup d'efforts pour que son mariage soit une réussite; **he ~ £10 on Black Beauty** il a parié *or* misé 10 livres sur Black Beauty; **I shouldn't ~ him among the greatest poets** je ne le place pas parmi les plus grands poètes.
(b) (*thrust; direct*) *pointed object* enfoncer (*into* dans). **to ~ one's fist through a window** passer le poing à travers une vitre; **I ~ a bullet through his head** je lui ai tiré une balle dans la tête; (*Sport*) **to ~ the shot** *or* **the weight** lancer le poids.
(c) (*cause to be*) **to ~ sb in a good/bad mood** mettre qn de bonne/mauvaise humeur; **to ~ sb on a diet** mettre qn au régime; **to ~ sb to some trouble** déranger qn; **they ~ him to digging the garden** ils lui ont fait bêcher le jardin; **I ~ him to work at once** je l'ai mis au travail aussitôt; **they had to ~ 4 men on to this job** ils ont dû employer 4 hommes à ce travail.
(d) (*with preposition*) **to ~ one across** *or* **over on sb*** faire marcher* qn; **to ~ sb against sb** monter qn contre qn; **to ~ sb off his food** couper l'appétit à qn; **it almost ~ me off opera for good** cela a failli me dégoûter de l'opéra pour toujours; **to ~ sb off doing** ôter à qn l'envie de faire; **to ~ sb off his work** distraire qn de son travail; **to ~ sb through an examination** faire subir un examen à qn; **they really ~ him through it*** ils lui en ont fait voir de dures*.
(e) (*express*) dire, exprimer (*to sb* à qn). **can you ~ it another way?** pouvez-vous vous exprimer autrement?; **to ~ it bluntly** pour parler franc; **as he would ~ it** selon son expression; **as Shakespeare ~s it** comme le dit Shakespeare; **I don't know how to ~ it** je ne sais pas comment le dire; **how shall I ~ it?** comment dire?; **to ~ an expression into French** mettre une expression en français; **how would you ~ it in French?** comment le dirais-tu en français?; **to ~ into verse** mettre en vers.
(f) (*expound*) *case, problem* exposer; *proposal, resolution, arguments* présenter; *question* poser. **I ~ it to you that ...** n'est-il pas vrai que ...?; **it was ~ to me that** on m'a fait clairement comprendre que.
(g) (*estimate*) estimer, évaluer (*at* à). **what would you ~ it at?** à combien l'estimez-vous? *or* l'évaluez-vous?; **I'd ~ her age at 50** je lui donnerais 50 ans.
2 *vi* (*Naut*) **to ~ into port** faire escale, entrer au port; **to ~ into Southampton** entrer au port de Southampton; **to ~ to sea** appareiller, lever l'ancre.
put about 1 *vi* (*Naut*) virer de bord. **2** *vt sep* (*rumour: also* **~ around**) **he ~ it about** *or* **he ~ about the rumour that ...** il a fait courir le bruit que ... .
put across *vt sep* **(a)** (*communicate*) *ideas, intentions* faire comprendre, communiquer (*to sb* à qn); (*Comm*) *new product* faire accepter (*to sb* à qn). **to ~ sth across to sb** faire comprendre qch à qn; **he can't ~ himself across** il n'arrive pas à se mettre en valeur. **(b) to ~ one** *or* **it across on sb*** faire marcher* qn.
put aside *vt sep* **(a)** (*lay down*) *one's book etc* poser; (*save*) mettre de côté. (*Comm*) **I have had it ~ aside for you** je vous l'ai fait mettre de côté. **(b)** (*fig*) *doubts, idea, hope* écarter.
put away *vt sep* **(a)** = **put aside. (b)** *clothes, toys, books* ranger; *car* rentrer. **(c)** (*confine*) (*in prison*) mettre en prison; (*in mental hospital*) (faire) enfermer. **(d)** (*: *consume*) *food* engloutir; *drink* siffler*. **(e)** = **put down 2 h.**
put back 1 *vi* (*Naut*) rentrer (*to* à). **2** *vt sep* **(a)** (*replace*) remettre (à sa place). **(b)** (*retard*) *development, progress* retarder; *project* retarder la réalisation de; *clock* retarder (*by* de); *clock hands* remettre en arrière. **this will ~ us back 10 years** cela nous ramènera où nous en étions il y a 10 ans; (*fig*) **you can't ~ the clock back** ce qui est fait est fait. **(c)** (*postpone*) remettre (*to* à).
put by *vt sep* = **put aside a.**
put down 1 *vi [aircraft]* se poser. **2** *vt sep* **(a)** (*gen*) poser; (*Aut*) *passenger* déposer; *umbrella* fermer; *wine* mettre en cave. (*fig*) **I couldn't ~ that book down** je ne pouvais pas m'arracher à ce livre. **(b)** (*pay*) *deposit, money* verser (*on* pour). **(c)** (*suppress*) *revolt* réprimer; *custom, practice* supprimer. **(d)** (*snub*) rabrouer; (*humiliate*) humilier. **(e)** (*record*) noter, inscrire. **to ~ sth down on paper** mettre qch par écrit; (*Comm*) **~ it down on my account** mettez-le sur mon compte; **I have ~ you down as a teacher/for £10** je vous ai inscrit comme professeur/pour 10 livres. **(f)** (*attribute*) attribuer (*sth to sth* qch à qch). **(g)** (*assess*) **I had ~ him down as a complete fool** je l'avais pris pour *or* je le considérais comme un parfait imbécile; **I'd ~ her down as about forty** je lui donnerais environ quarante ans. **(h)** (*euph: kill*) *dog, cat* faire piquer; *horse* abattre.
put forth *vt sep* (*liter*) *leaves* produire; *arm* tendre; *idea* avancer.

put forward *vt sep* **(a)** (*propose*) *theory, argument* avancer; *opinion* exprimer; *plan, person* proposer (*as* comme; *for* pour). **he ~ himself forward for the job** il a posé sa candidature au poste. **(b)** (*advance*) *meeting, starting time* avancer (*by* de; *to, until* à).
put in 1 *vi* (*Naut*) faire escale (*at* à). **2** *vt sep* **(a)** (*into box, drawer, room etc*) mettre dedans; *seeds* planter. (*packing*) **have you ~ in your shirts?** est-ce que tu as pris tes chemises? **(b)** (*insert*) *word, remark* ajouter; (*include: in letter, publication*) inclure. **have you ~ in why ...?** est-ce que vous avez expliqué pourquoi ...? **(c)** (*enter*) *document, claim* présenter; *application* faire; *one's name* avancer; *protest* élever. (*Jur*) **to ~ in a plea** plaider; **to ~ sb in for an exam** présenter qn à un examen; **to ~ sb in for a job/promotion** proposer qn pour un poste/pour de l'avancement. **(d)** (*esp Pol: elect*), *party, person* élire. **(e)** *time* passer (*on sth* à qch; *on doing* à faire). **we have an hour to ~ in before ...** nous avons une heure à perdre avant ...; **he has ~ in a full day's work** il a fait sa journée, (*fig*) il a bien travaillé; **can you ~ in a few hours at the weekend?** pourrais-tu travailler quelques heures pendant le week-end?; **she ~s in an hour a day at the piano** elle fait une heure de piano par jour.
put in for *vt fus job* poser sa candidature pour *or* à; *promotion, social benefits* faire une demande de.
put off 1 *vi* (*Naut*) démarrer (*from* de). **2** *vt sep* **(a)** (*postpone*) *departure, appointment, decision* repousser, remettre à plus tard; *visitor* renvoyer à plus tard. **to ~ off doing sth** remettre qch (*for* de; *until* jusqu'à); (*fig*) **he ~ her off with vague promises** il l'a dissuadée avec de vagues promesses; **he is not easily ~ off** il ne se laisse pas facilement démonter; **he ~s me off when he laughs like that** cela me déconcerte quand il rit de cette façon; **the colour ~ me off** la couleur m'a plutôt dégoûté. **(b)** *coat, hat etc* enlever; *passenger* déposer. **(c)** (*extinguish etc*) *light, gas* éteindre; *radio, TV, heater* fermer.
put on *vt sep* **(a)** *garment, glasses* mettre. **(b)** (*add, increase*) *pressure, speed* augmenter. **to ~ on weight** grossir, prendre du poids. **(c)** (*assume*) *indignation* affecter, simuler; *air, accent* prendre; (*: *deceive*) *person* faire marcher*. **he's just ~ting it on** il fait seulement semblant; **you're ~ting me on!*** tu me fais marcher!* **(d)** *concert, play, show* organiser; *film* projeter; *extra train, bus etc* mettre en service. (*Telec*) **~ me on to Mr Brown** passez-moi M. Brown. **(e)** *light, gas* allumer; *radio, TV, heater* ouvrir. **~ the kettle on** mets l'eau à chauffer; **I'll just ~ the soup on** je vais juste mettre la soupe à cuire; **to ~ the brakes on** freiner. **(f)** (*advance*) *clock* avancer (*by* de). **(g)** (*wager*) parier. **(h)** (*inform, indicate*) indiquer. **they ~ the police on to him** ils l'ont signalé à la police; **can you ~ me on to a good dentist?** pourriez-vous m'indiquer un bon dentiste?; **Paul ~ us on to you** c'est Paul qui nous envoie; **what ~ you on to it?** qu'est-ce qui vous y a fait penser?
put out 1 *vi*: **to ~ out to sea/from Dieppe** quitter le port/Dieppe. **2** *vt sep* **(a)** (*~ outside*) *chair etc* sortir, mettre dehors; (*get rid of*) *rubbish* sortir; (*expel*) *person, country, organization* expulser (*of* de); *the cat* faire sortir. (*fig*) **to ~ sth out of one's head** ne plus penser à qch. **(b)** (*Naut*) *boat* mettre à la mer. **(c)** (*stretch out, extend*) *arm, leg* étendre; *foot* avancer; *tongue* tirer (*at sb* à qn); *leaves* produire. **to ~ out one's hand** tendre la main, *[car driver, traffic policeman]* tendre le bras; **to ~ one's head out of the window** passer la tête par la fenêtre. **(d)** (*lay out in order*) (*gen*) sortir; *papers, cards* étaler; *chessmen etc* disposer. **(e)** (*extinguish*) *light, flames, cigarette* éteindre; *heater* fermer. **(f)** (*disconcert*) déconcerter (*by, about* par); (*vex*) contrarier, ennuyer (*by, about* par); (*inconvenience*) déranger. **she ~ herself out for us** elle s'est donné beaucoup de mal pour nous. **(g)** (*issue*) *news* annoncer; *report, regulations, book* publier; *rumour* faire courir; *propaganda, statement* faire. **(h)** (*spend*) dépenser (*on* pour). **(i)** (*Comm*) *repairs, small jobs* donner au dehors; (*Ind: subcontract*) donner à des sous-traitants. **(j)** (*exert*) *one's strength, tact* déployer, user de. **(k)** (*dislocate*) *shoulder, back* démettre.
put over *vt sep* = **put across.**
put through *vt sep* **(a)** (*make, complete*) *deal* conclure, mener à bien; *decision* prendre; *proposal* faire accepter. **(b)** (*Telec: connect*) *call* passer. **I'm ~ting you through now** je vous mets en communication, vous êtes en ligne; **~ me through to Mr Smith** passez-moi M. Smith.
put together *vt sep* **(a)** (*lit*) mettre ensemble, placer l'un à côté de l'autre. **he's worth more than the rest of the family ~ together** à lui tout seul il vaut largement le reste de la famille. **(b)** (*assemble*) *table, radio* monter; *jigsaw* assembler; *book, story, account* composer; (*piece together*) *facts, what happened* reconstituer; (*mend*) réparer. **she ~ together an excellent supper** elle a improvisé un délicieux dîner.
put up 1 *vi* **(a)** (*lodge*) descendre (*at* dans); (*for one night*) passer la nuit (*at* à). **(b)** (*offer o.s.*) se porter candidat(e) (*for* à). **2** *vt sep* **(a)** (*raise*) *hand* lever; *flag, sail* hisser; *tent, fence, ladder* dresser; *collar, window* remonter; *umbrella* ouvrir; *notice, picture* mettre (*on* sur); *missile, rocket* lancer; *building, bridge* construire. **~ them up!*** (*in robbery etc*) haut les mains!; (*challenge to fight*) défends-toi! **(b)** (*increase*) (*gen*) augmenter; *temperature, blood pressure, total* faire monter. **(c)** (*offer*) *proposal, idea* présenter, soumettre; *plea, resistance* offrir; (*nominate*) *person* proposer comme candidat (*for* à; *as* comme). **to ~ sth up for sale/auction** mettre qch en vente/aux enchères; **he was ~ up by his local branch** il a été présenté comme candidat par sa section locale; **to ~ sb up for a club** proposer qn comme membre d'un club. **(d)** (*provide*) *money, funds* fournir (*for* pour); *reward* offrir. **how much can you ~ up?** combien pouvez-vous (y) mettre? **(e)** (*prepare*) *picnic, sandwiches, prescription* préparer; (*Comm*) *order* exécuter. **(f)** (*lodge*) loger. **(g)** (*incite*) **to ~ sb up to doing** pousser qn à faire. **(h)** (*inform about*) **to ~ sb up to sth** mettre qn au courant de qch.
put upon *vt fus*: **to ~ upon sb** en imposer à qn; **I won't be ~ upon any more!** je ne vais plus me laisser marcher sur les pieds!
put up with *vt fus* supporter, encaisser*. **he has a lot to ~ up with** il a beaucoup de problèmes.
♦ **put-up job*** *n* coup *m* monté. ♦ **put-you-up** *n* canapé-lit *m*.
putrefy ['pju:trɪfaɪ] **1** *vt* putréfier. **2** *vi* se putréfier. ♦ **putrefaction** *n* putréfaction *f*.
putrid ['pju:trɪd] *adj* putride; (* *fig*) dégoûtant.
putsch [pʊtʃ] *n* putsch *m*, coup *m* d'État.
putt [pʌt] (*Golf*) **1** *n* putt *m*. **2** *vti* putter.
♦ **putting** *n* putting *m*. ♦ **putting green** *n* green *m*.
putty ['pʌtɪ] *n* mastic *m* (*ciment*).
puzzle ['pʌzl] **1** *n* **(a)** (*mystery*) énigme *f*, mystère *m*. **he is a real ~ to me** c'est une énigme vivante pour moi; **it is a ~ to me how ...** je n'arriverai jamais à comprendre comment ... . **(b)** (*game*) casse-tête *m inv*; (*word game*) rébus *m*; (*crossword*) mots *mpl* croisés; (*jigsaw*) puzzle *m*; (*riddle*) devinette *f*. **2** *vt* laisser perplexe. **I am ~d to know why** je n'arrive pas à comprendre pourquoi; **he was ~d about what to say** il ne savait pas quoi dire. **3** *vi*: **to ~ over** *or* **about** *problem, mys-*

tery essayer de résoudre; *sb's actions, intentions* essayer de comprendre; **I'm still puzzling over why ...** j'en suis encore à me demander pourquoi ... .

puzzle out *vt sep problem* résoudre; *mystery* éclaircir; *writing* déchiffrer; *answer, solution* trouver; *sb's actions, attitude* comprendre. **I'm trying to ~ out why** j'essaie de comprendre pourquoi.

♦ **puzzled** *adj* perplexe. ♦ **puzzlement** *n* perplexité *f.* ♦ **puzzler** *n* casse-tête *m inv.* ♦ **puzzling** *adj* incompréhensible.

pygmy ['pɪgmɪ] **1** *n* pygmée *m.* **2** *adj* pygmée (*f inv*).

pyjamas [pɪ'dʒɑːməz] *npl* (*Brit*) pyjama *m.* **in (one's) ~** en pyjama.

pylon ['paɪlən] *n* pylône *m.*

pyramid ['pɪrəmɪd] *n* pyramide *f.*

pyre ['paɪəʳ] *n* bûcher *m* funéraire.

Pyrenees [pɪrə'niːz] *npl* Pyrénées *fpl.*

Pyrex ['paɪreks] *n* ® pyrex *m* ®.

pyro... ['paɪərəʊ] *pref* pyro... . ♦ **pyromaniac** *n* pyromane *mf.* ♦ **pyrotechnic** *adj* pyrotechnique.

python ['paɪθən] *n* python *m.*

Q

Q, q [kjuː] *n* (*letter*) Q, q *m*. **on the q.t.*** en douce*.
quack[1] [kwæk] **1** *n* coin-coin *m*. **2** *vi* faire coin-coin.
quack[2] [kwæk] **1** *n* (*pej*) charlatan *m*; (*: *doctor*) toubib* *m*. **2** *adj* de charlatan.
quad [kwɒd] *n abbr of* **quadruplet** *and* **quadrangle b.**
quadrangle ['kwɒdræŋgl] *n* **(a)** (*Math*) quadrilatère *m*. **(b)** (*courtyard*) cour *f* (*d'un collège etc*).
quadraphonic ['kwɒdrə'fɒnɪk] *adj* quadriphonique. **in ~ sound** en quadriphonie.
quadratic [kwɒ'drætɪk] *adj* du second degré.
quadrilateral [ˌkwɒdrɪ'lætərəl] *adj, n* quadrilatère (*m*).
quadruped ['kwɒdrʊped] *adj, n* quadrupède (*m*).
quadruple ['kwɒdrʊpl] **1** *adj, n* quadruple (*m*). **2** ['kwɒ'druːpl] *vti* quadrupler. ♦ **quadruplet** *n* quadruplé(e) *m(f)*.
quagmire ['kwægmaɪəʳ] *n* bourbier *m*.
quail[1] [kweɪl] *vi* (*flinch*) perdre courage.
quail[2] [kweɪl] *n* (*bird*) caille *f*.
quaint [kweɪnt] *adj* (*odd*) bizarre, original; (*picturesque*) pittoresque; (*old-fashioned etc*) au charme vieillot.
♦ **quaintly** *adv* d'une manière originale *or* pittoresque.
quake [kweɪk] **1** *vi* trembler (*with* de). **2** *n* (*earth-~*) tremblement *m* de terre.
Quaker [kweɪkəʳ] *n* quaker(esse) *m(f)*.
qualification [ˌkwɒlɪfɪ'keɪʃən] *n* **(a)** ~s (*gen*) conditions *fpl* requises; (*degrees etc*) titres *mpl*, diplômes *mpl*; **what are your ~s?** (*skill, degrees, experience etc*) quelle est votre formation?; (*paper ~s*) qu'est-ce que vous avez comme diplômes?; **teaching ~s** les diplômes requis pour enseigner. **(b)** (*limitation*) réserve *f*, restriction *f*. **to accept with/without ~s** accepter avec des/sans réserves.
qualify ['kwɒlɪfaɪ] **1** *vt* **(a)** (*make competent*) qualifier (*to do* pour faire); (*Admin*) donner qualité à (*for* pour; *to do* pour faire). **(b)** (*modify*) *attitude, praise* mitiger; *approval, support* mettre des réserves à; *statement, opinion* nuancer. **(c)** (*Gram*) qualifier. **2** *vi* obtenir son diplôme (*or* son brevet *etc*); (*Sport*) se qualifier (*for* pour). **to ~ as an engineer** obtenir son diplôme d'ingénieur; **to ~ for a job** obtenir les diplômes nécessaires pour un poste; **does he ~?** est-ce qu'il remplit les conditions requises?; (*fig*) **he hardly qualifies as a poet** il ne mérite pas vraiment le nom de poète. ♦ **qualified** *adj* **(a)** (*gen*) qualifié (*for* pour; *to do* pour faire); *engineer, doctor, teacher* diplômé; **he was not qualified for this job** il ne remplissait pas les conditions requises pour ce poste; **to be qualified to do** (*gen*) être qualifié pour faire, avoir les diplômes requis pour faire; (*Admin: officially*) avoir qualité pour faire; **they are not qualified to vote** ils ne sont pas habilités à voter; **(b)** (*modified*) *praise* mitigé; *support, acceptance* conditionnel; *success* modéré. ♦ **qualifying** *adj mark* de passage; *examination* d'entrée; *score* qui permet de se qualifier.
quality ['kwɒlɪtɪ] **1** *n* qualité *f*. **of the best ~** de première qualité; **of good/poor ~** de bonne/de mauvaise qualité. **2** *adj product* de qualité; *newspaper* sérieux.
qualm [kwɑːm] *n* (*scruple*) scrupule *m*; (*misgiving*) inquiétude *f* (*about* sur). **to have ~s about doing** avoir des scrupules à faire.
quandary ['kwɒndərɪ] *n*: **to be in a ~** être dans l'embarras *or* dans un dilemme; **to be in a ~ about what to do** être bien embarrassé de savoir quoi faire.
quantity ['kwɒntɪtɪ] **1** *n* quantité *f*. **in ~** en grande quantité. **2** *adj*: **~ surveying** métrage *m*; **~ surveyor** métreur *m* (vérificateur).
quantum ['kwɒntəm], *pl* **-ta 1** *n* quantum *m*. **2** *adj mechanics, number* quantique. **~ theory** théorie *f* des quanta.
quarantine ['kwɒrəntiːn] **1** *n* quarantaine *f*. **in ~** en quarantaine. **2** *vt* mettre en quarantaine.
quarrel ['kwɒrəl] **1** *n* querelle *f*, dispute *f*; (*breach*) brouille *f*. **to have a ~ with** se disputer *or* se quereller avec; **to pick a ~ with sb** chercher querelle à qn; **I have no ~ with you** je n'ai rien contre vous. **2** *vi* se disputer, se quereller (*with sb* avec qn; *about, over* à propos de); (*break off*) se brouiller (*with sb* avec qn). (*fig*) **I cannot ~ with that** je n'ai rien à redire à cela. ♦ **quarrelling,** (*US*) **quarreling** *n* disputes *fpl*, querelles *fpl*. ♦ **quarrelsome** *adj* querelleur.
quarry[1] ['kwɒrɪ] **1** *n* carrière *f* (*mine*). **2** *vt stone* extraire; *hillside* exploiter. **3** *vi*: **to ~ for marble** exploiter une carrière de marbre. ♦ **quarryman** *n* (ouvrier *m*) carrier *m*. ♦ **quarry-tiled** *adj* carrelé.
quarry[2] ['kwɒrɪ] *n* (*animal, bird etc*) proie *f*; (*Hunting*) gibier *m*; (*person*) personne *f* pourchassée.
quart [kwɔːt] *n* ≃ litre *m* (*Brit = 1,136 litres; US = 0,946 litre*).
quarter ['kwɔːtəʳ] **1** *n* **(a)** (*fourth part*) (*gen*) quart *m*; *[object, apple, beef, moon]* quartier *m*; *[year]* trimestre *m*. **to divide sth into ~s** diviser qch en quatre *or* en quartiers; **a ~ (of a pound) of tea** un quart (de livre) de thé; **a ~ as big as** quatre fois moins grand que; **a ~ of an hour** un quart d'heure; **a ~ to 7,** (*US*) **a ~ of 7** 7 heures moins le quart; **a ~ past 6,** (*US*) **a ~ after 6** 6 heures un *or* et quart; **a ~'s rent** un terme (de loyer). **(b)** (*US, Can: money*) quart *m* de dollar, 25 cents. **(c)** (*direction*) direction *f*, côté *m*; (*compass point*) point *m* cardinal. (*Naut*) **on the port ~** par la hanche de bâbord; **from all ~s** de toutes parts; **you must report that to the proper ~** vous devez signaler cela à qui de droit; **in responsible ~s** dans les milieux autorisés. **(d)** (*part of town*) quartier *m*. **(e)** (*lodgings*) ~s résidence *f*; (*Mil*) quartiers *mpl*, (*temporary*) cantonnement *m*.
2 *vt* **(a)** (*divide into four*) diviser en quatre, diviser en quartiers. **(b)** (*lodge*) *troops* caserner, (*temporarily*) cantonner; (*gen*) loger (*on* chez).
3 *adj* d'un quart. **a ~ share in sth** un quart de qch.
♦ **quarter-deck** *n* (*Naut*) plage *f* arrière. ♦ **quarter-final** *n* quart *m* de finale. ♦ **quarterly 1** *adj* trimestriel; **2** *n* (*periodical*) publication *f* trimestrielle. ♦ **quartermaster** *n* **(a)** (*Mil*) intendant *m* militaire de troisième classe; **(b)** (*Naut*) maître *m* de manœuvre.

quartet(te) [kwɔː'tet] *n* (*gen; also classical music*) quatuor *m*; (*jazz*) quartette *m*.
quarto ['kwɔːtəʊ] *n, adj* in-quarto (*m*) *inv*.
quartz ['kwɔːts] **1** *n* quartz *m*. **2** *adj* de *or* en quartz; *clock* à quartz. ~ **crystal** cristal *m* de quartz.
quash [kwɒʃ] *vt verdict* casser; *rebellion* réprimer; *proposal* rejeter.
quasi- ['kwɑːzɪ] *pref* quasi- (+ *n*), quasi (+*adj*). ~**marriage** quasi-mariage *m*; ~**revolutionary** quasi révolutionnaire.
quaver ['kweɪvəʳ] **1** *n* (*Mus: note*) croche *f*. **2** *vti* (*tremble*) chevroter.
◆ **quavering 1** *adj voice* chevrotant; **2** *n* chevrotement *m*.
quay [kiː] *n* quai *m*. **at the ~side** à quai.
queasy ['kwiːzɪ] *adj*: **to feel ~** avoir mal au cœur, avoir envie de vomir.
◆ **queasiness** *n* nausée *f*.
Quebec [kwɪ'bek] **1** *n* Québec *m*. **2** *adj* québécois.
queen [kwiːn] **1** *n* **(a)** reine *f*; (*Chess, Cards*) dame *f*. **Q~ Elizabeth** la reine Elisabeth; **Q~ Mother** reine mère; **~ bee** reine des abeilles. **(b)** (**:** *pej: homosexual*) pédé**:** *m* (*pej*). **2** *vt* (*) **to ~ it** prendre des airs d'impératrice (*over sb* avec qn).
◆ **queenly** *adj* de reine.
queer [kwɪəʳ] **1** *adj* **(a)** (*odd*) étrange, bizarre, drôle de (*before n*). (*pej*) **a ~ customer** un drôle de type*; **~ in the head*** toqué*; **to be in Q~ Street*** se trouver dans une mauvaise passe. **(b)** (*suspicious*) louche, suspect. **there's sth ~ going on** il se passe qch de louche. **(c)** (*: *unwell*) mal fichu*. **to feel ~** être pris d'un malaise. **(d)** (*: *homosexual*) homosexuel. **he's ~*** c'est un pédé**:**. **2** *n* (*: *homosexual*) (*male*) pédé**:** *m*; (*female*) lesbienne *f*. **3** *vt*: **to ~ sb's pitch** couper l'herbe sous le pied à *or* de qn. ◆ **queerly** *adv* étrangement, bizarrement. ◆ **queerness** *n* étrangeté *f*, bizarrerie *f*.
quell [kwel] *vt* (*gen*) réprimer; *cheeky etc person* faire rentrer sous terre.
quench [kwentʃ] *vt flames* éteindre. **to ~ one's thirst** se désaltérer.
querulous ['kwerʊləs] *adj* ronchonneur*, bougon.
◆ **querulously** *adv* d'un ton bougon.
query ['kwɪərɪ] **1** *n* **(a)** (*question*) question *f*; (*doubt*) doute *m* (*about* sur). **this raises a ~ about the scheme** cela met le projet en question. **(b)** (*question mark*) point *m* d'interrogation. **2** *vt* mettre en question.
quest [kwest] *n* quête *f* (*for* de). **in ~ of** en quête de.
question ['kwestʃən] **1** *n* **(a)** question *f*. **to ask sb a ~, to put a ~ to sb** poser une question à qn. **(b)** (*doubt*) doute *m*. **without ~** sans aucun doute; **there is no ~ about it** il n'y a pas de doute; **to call sth into ~** mettre qch en doute. **(c)** (*matter*) question *f*, affaire *f*. **that's the ~!** c'est là toute la question!; **that's not the ~** là n'est pas la question; **that's another ~** ça, c'est une autre affaire; **the person in ~** la personne en question; **there's some/no ~ of closing the shop** il est/il n'est pas question de fermer le magasin; **there's no ~ of that, that is out of the ~** il n'en est pas question; **the ~ is how many** la question, c'est de savoir combien; **the ~ is to decide ...** il s'agit de décider ...; **it's a ~ of what you want to do** tout dépend de ce que tu veux faire; **it's an open ~** personne ne sait (*whether* si).
2 *adj*: **~ mark** point *m* d'interrogation; (*Parl*) **~ time** heure *f* réservée aux questions orales.
3 *vt* **(a)** *person* interroger, questionner (*on* sur; *about* au sujet de, à propos de). **(b)** *motive, account* mettre en doute *or* en question; *claim* contester. **to ~ whether** douter que +*subj*.
◆ **questionable** *adj* discutable; (*pej*) douteux.
◆ **questioner** *n* personne *f* qui pose des questions.
◆ **questioning 1** *adj* interrogateur, questionneur; **2** *n* interrogation *f*. ◆ **question-master** *n* meneur *m* de jeu, (*Rad, TV*) animateur *m*.
◆ **questionnaire** *n* questionnaire *m*.
queue [kjuː] (*Brit*) **1** *n [people]* queue *f*, file *f* (d'attente); *[cars]* file. **to stand in a ~, to form a ~** faire la queue; **the theatre ~** les personnes qui font (*or* faisaient *etc*) la queue au théâtre; **ticket ~** queue devant les guichets. **2** *vi* (**~ up**) *[people, cars]* faire la queue.
quibble ['kwɪbl] **1** *n* chicane *f*, ergotage *m*. **2** *vi* chicaner (*over* sur).
quick [kwɪk] **1** *adj* **(a)** (*rapid*) *train, route, method* rapide; *recovery, answer* prompt. **be ~!** dépêche-toi!, fais vite!; **try to be ~er** essaie de faire plus vite; (*Mil*) **~ march!** en avant, marche!; **we had a ~ meal** nous avons mangé en vitesse; **to have a ~ one*** prendre un pot* en vitesse; **it's ~er by train** c'est plus rapide *or* ça va plus vite par le train. **(b)** (*lively*) *mind, child* vif, éveillé. **he's too ~ for me** il va trop vite pour moi; **he was ~ to see that ...** il a tout de suite vu que ...; **to be ~ to take offence** être prompt à s'offenser; **to have a ~ temper** s'emporter facilement; **he is ~ at figures** il calcule vite.
2 *n* (*fig*) **to cut sb to the ~** piquer qn au vif; **the ~ and the dead** les vivants *mpl* et les morts *mpl*.
3 *adv* vite. **as ~ as lightning** *or* **as a flash** avec la rapidité de l'éclair.
◆ **quick-acting** *adj* à action rapide. ◆ **quicken 1** *vt* accélérer, hâter; (*fig*) *feelings* stimuler; **to ~en one's pace** accélérer son allure; **2** *vi*: **the pace ~ened** l'allure s'est accélérée. ◆ **quick-freeze,** *pret* **-froze,** *ptp* **-frozen** *vt* surgeler.
◆ **quickie*** *n* chose faite en vitesse; (*drink*) pot* pris en vitesse; (*question*) question *f* éclair *inv*.
◆ **quicklime** *n* chaux *f* vive. ◆ **quickly** *adv* (*fast*) vite, rapidement; (*without delay*) promptement, sans tarder. ◆ **quickness** *n* vitesse *f*, rapidité *f*; promptitude *f*; *[mind]* vivacité *f*. ◆ **quicksands** *npl* sables *mpl* mouvants. ◆ **quickset hedge** *n* haie *f* vive. ◆ **quicksilver** *n* vif-argent *m*, mercure *m*. ◆ **quickstep** *n* fox-trot *m*. ◆ **quick-tempered** *adj* prompt à s'emporter. ◆ **quick-witted** *adj* à l'esprit vif.
quid: [kwɪd] *n* (*pl inv: Brit*) livre *f* (*sterling*).
quiescence [kwaɪ'esns] *n* calme *m*. ◆ **quiescent** *adj* passif, calme.
quiet ['kwaɪət] **1** *adj* **(a)** (*silent, still: gen*) tranquille, calme. **you're very ~** tu ne dis pas grand-chose; **be ~!, keep ~!** taisez-vous!; **isn't it ~!** que c'est calme *or* tranquille!; **it was ~ as the grave** il y avait un silence de mort; **try to be a little ~er** essayez de ne pas faire autant de bruit; **to keep** *or* **stay ~** (*still*) se tenir *or* rester tranquille; (*silent*) garder le silence; **to keep sb ~** (*still*) faire tenir qn tranquille; (*silent*) faire taire qn. **(b)** (*not loud*) *music* doux; *voice, tone* bas; *footstep, sound* léger; *cough, laugh* petit. **keep the radio ~** baisse le volume (de la radio). **(c)** (*subdued*) *person* doux; *dog, horse* docile; *dress, colour* discret. **she's a very ~ girl** elle n'est pas expansive. **(d)** (*peaceful, calm*) calme, paisible, tranquille. **he had a ~ sleep** il a dormi tranquillement; (*Mil etc*) **all ~** rien de nouveau; **a ~ life** une vie tranquille; **this town is too ~** cette ville manque d'animation; **business is ~** les affaires sont calmes; **~ mind** esprit *m* tranquille. **(e)** (*secret*) *envy* caché; *irony, humour* discret; (*private*) *evening, dinner* intime. **they had a ~ wedding** ils se sont mariés dans l'intimité; **I'll have a ~ word with her** je vais lui glisser un mot à l'oreille; **they had a ~ laugh over it** ils en ont ri doucement; **he kept the whole thing ~** il n'en a pas parlé.
2 *n* (*silence*) silence *m*; (*peace*) calme *m*, tranquillité *f*. (*) **on the ~** *do* en cachette, en douce*; *tell* en confidence.
3 *vt* = **quieten 1**.
◆ **quieten 1** *vt* (*gen*) calmer; *conscience*

tranquilliser; **2** *vi* (~**en down**) se calmer; (*after unruly youth*) se ranger. ♦ **quietly** *adv* (*silently*) silencieusement, sans (faire de) bruit; (*not loudly*) *speak, sing* doucement; (*gently*) doucement, calmement; (*without fuss*) simplement; (*secretly*) en cachette, en douce*; *marry* dans la plus stricte intimité. ♦ **quietness** *n* (*silence*) silence *m*; (*stillness, peacefulness*) calme *m*, tranquillité *f*; (*gentleness*) douceur *f*.
quill [kwɪl] *n* (*feather*) penne *f*; (*also* ~**-pen**) plume *f* d'oie; *[porcupine etc]* piquant *m*.
quilt [kwɪlt] **1** *n* édredon *m* (piqué). **continental** ~ couette *f*. **2** *vt eiderdown, cover* ouater et piquer; *dressing gown* molletonner; *furniture* capitonner.
quin [kwɪn] *n abbr of* **quintuplet.**
quince [kwɪns] *n* coing *m*; (*tree*) cognassier *m*.
quinine [kwɪ'ni:n] *n* quinine *f*.
quintessence [kwɪn'tesns] *n* quintessence *f*.
quintet(te) [kwɪn'tet] *n* quintette *m*.
quintuple ['kwɪntjʊpl] **1** *adj, n* quintuple (*m*). **2** ['kwɪn'tju:pl] *vti* quintupler. ♦ **quintuplet** *n* quintuplé(e) *m(f)*.
quip [kwɪp] *n* mot *m* piquant.
quire ['kwaɪəʳ] *n* ≃ main *f* (*de papier*).
quirk [kwɜ:k] *n* bizarrerie *f*. **by a** ~ **of fate** par un caprice du destin. ♦ **quirky** *adj* capricieux.
quit [kwɪt] *pret, ptp* **quit** *or* **quitted** **1** *vt place, activity* quitter; (*esp US: stop*) arrêter (*doing* de faire). **to** ~ **hold** lâcher prise; **to** ~ **hold of sth** lâcher qch; ~ **fooling!** arrête de faire l'idiot! **2** *vi* (*give up: in game etc*) se rendre; (*accept defeat*) abandonner la partie; (*resign*) démissionner. **3** *adj*: ~ **of** débarrassé de.
quite [kwaɪt] *adv* **(a)** (*entirely*) tout à fait, complètement, entièrement. ~ **(so)!** exactement!; **I** ~ **understand** je comprends très bien; **I** ~ **believe it** je le crois volontiers; **I don't** ~ **know** je ne sais pas trop; **that's** ~ **enough!** ça suffit comme ça!; **it wasn't** ~ **what I wanted** ce n'était pas tout à fait *or* exactement ce que je voulais; **that's** ~ **another matter** c'est une tout autre affaire; **he was** ~ **right** il avait bien raison *or* tout à fait raison; ~ **new** tout (à fait) neuf; ~ **alone** tout seul; **she was** ~ **a beauty** c'était une véritable beauté. **(b)** (*to some degree*) assez. ~ **a long time** assez longtemps; ~ **a few people** un assez grand nombre de gens; ~ **good** pas mal du tout; ~ **a good singer** un assez bon chanteur; **I** ~ **like it** j'aime assez ça.
quits [kwɪts] *adj* quitte (*with sb* envers qn). **let's call it** ~ restons-en là.
quiver¹ ['kwɪvəʳ] *vi [person, voice]* frémir, trembler (*with* de); *[eyelids]* battre.
quiver² ['kwɪvəʳ] *n* (*for arrows*) carquois *m*.
quixotic [kwɪk'sɒtɪk] *adj person* chevaleresque; (*visionary*) chimérique; *plan, feeling* donquichottesque. ♦ **quixotically** *adv* sans penser à soi.
quiz [kwɪz] **1** *n* (*Rad/TV*) jeu-concours *m* (radiophonique/télévisé); (*in magazine etc*) série *f* de questions. **2** *vt*: **to** ~ **sb** presser qn de questions (*about* au sujet de).
♦ **quizmaster** *n* meneur *m* de jeu; (*Rad, TV*) animateur *m*. ♦ **quizzical** *adj* narquois. ♦ **quizzically** *adv* d'un air narquois.
quoit [kwɔɪt] *n* palet *m*. **to play** ~**s** jouer au palet.
quorum ['kwɔ:rəm] *n* quorum *m*. **to have a** ~ atteindre le quorum.
quota ['kwəʊtə] *n* (*share*) quote-part *f*; (*permitted amount*) *[imports, immigrants]* quota *m*.
quote [kwəʊt] **1** *vt* **(a)** *author, poem, fact* citer; *reference number etc* rappeler. **don't** ~ **me** ne dites pas que c'est moi qui vous l'ai dit; **he was** ~**d as saying that** ... il aurait dit que ...; ~ ... **unquote** (*in dictation*) ouvrez les guillemets ... fermez les guillemets; (*in report, lecture etc*) je cite ..., fin de citation. **(b)** *price* (*Comm*) indiquer, proposer; (*St Ex*) coter (*at* à). **2** *vi* **(a)** faire des citations. **to** ~ **from** citer. **(b)** (*Comm*) **to** ~ **for** établir un devis pour. **3** *n* **(a)** = **quotation 1. (b) he said,** ~ **'I will never do it'** il a dit, (*in dictation*) ouvrez les guillemets *or* (*in lecture, report etc*) je cite 'je ne le ferai jamais'; ~**s** = **quotation marks.** ♦ **quotable** *adj* digne d'être cité. ♦ **quotation 1** *n* **(a)** citation *f* (*from* de); **(b)** (*Comm: estimate*) devis *m*; **2** *adj*: **in quotation marks** entre guillemets *mpl*.
quotient ['kwəʊʃənt] *n* quotient *m*.

R

R, r [ɑːʳ] *n* (*letter*) R, r *m*. **the three R's** la lecture, l'écriture *f* et l'arithmétique *f*.
rabbi ['ræbaɪ] *n* rabbin *m*.
rabbit ['ræbɪt] **1** *n* lapin *m*. **doe** ~ lapine *f*. **2** *vi*: **to go ~ing** chasser le lapin. **3** *adj*: ~ **hole** terrier *m* (de lapin); ~ **hutch** clapier *m*.
rabble ['ræbl] *n* cohue *f*, foule *f* (confuse). (*pej*) **the** ~ la populace.
rabid ['ræbɪd] *adj* (*fanatical*) fanatique; (*furious*) forcené; *hate* farouche; (*Vet*) enragé.
rabies ['reɪbiːz] **1** *n* rage *f* (*Med*). **2** *adj* (*) *injection* contre la rage.
rac(c)oon [rə'kuːn] *n* raton *m* laveur.
race[1] [reɪs] **1** *n* (*Sport etc*) course *f*. **the 100 metres** ~ la course sur 100 mètres, le 100 mètres; **cycle/horse** ~ course cycliste/de chevaux; ~ **against time** course contre la montre. **2** *vt* **(a)** *person* faire une course avec. **I'll ~ you to school!** à qui arrivera le premier à l'école! **(b)** *horse* faire courir. **the champion ~s Ferraris** le champion court sur Ferrari; (*Aut*) **to ~ the engine** emballer le moteur. **3** *vi* **(a) to ~ against sb** faire la course avec qn; (*fig*) **to ~ against time** courir contre la montre. **(b)** (*rush*) courir à toute allure. **to ~ in/across** *etc* entrer/traverser *etc* à toute allure. **(c)** *[engine]* s'emballer; *[propeller]* s'affoler; *[pulse]* être très rapide. ♦ **racecourse** *n* champ *m* de courses, hippodrome *m*. ♦ **racegoer** *n* turfiste *mf*. ♦ **racehorse** *n* cheval *m* de course. ♦ **racetrack** *n* (*gen*) piste *f*; (*for horses*) champ *m* de courses. ♦ **racing 1** *n* courses *fpl*; **horse/motor racing** courses de chevaux/d'automobiles; **2** *adj* *stables, cycle, car* de course; **racing driver** pilote *m* de course.
race[2] [reɪs] **1** *n* race *f*. **the human** ~ la race *or* l'espèce humaine. **2** *adj* *hatred, prejudice* racial. ~ **relations** rapports *mpl* entre les races; ~ **riot** bagarres *fpl* raciales. ♦ **racial** *adj* racial. ♦ **racialism** *n* racisme *m*. ♦ **racialist** *or* ♦ **racist** *adj, n* raciste (*mf*). ♦ **racism** *n* racisme *m*.
rack[1] [ræk] *n* (*for bottles, documents, files*) casier *m*; (*for fodder, bicycles*) râtelier *m*; (*for luggage*) filet *m*; (*for hats, coats*) porte-manteau *m*; (*in shops*) étagère *f*, rayon *m*. **roof** ~ galerie *f*.
rack[2] [ræk] **1** *n* (*torture*) chevalet *m*. **2** *vt* *[pain]* torturer. (*fig*) **~ed by remorse** tenaillé par le remords; **to ~ one's brains** se creuser la tête.
rack[3] [ræk] *n*: **to go to ~ and ruin** *[building]* tomber en ruine; *[business, economy]* aller à vau-l'eau; *[person, country]* aller à la ruine.
racket[1], **racquet** ['rækɪt] *n* raquette *f*.
racket[2] ['rækɪt] *n* **(a)** (*noise*) *[people]* tapage *m*, raffut* *m*; *[machine]* vacarme *m*. **to make a** ~ faire du raffut* *or* du vacarme. **(b)** (*organized crime*) racket *m*; (*dishonest scheme*) escroquerie *f*. **the drug/stolen car ~*** le trafic de la drogue/des voitures volées; **they're on to quite a ~*** ils ont trouvé une jolie combine*; **it was a dreadful ~*** c'était du vol manifeste!; **he's in on the ~*** il est dans le coup*. ♦ **racketeer** *n* racketteur *m*. ♦ **racketeering** *n* racket *m*.
racy ['reɪsɪ] *adj* *speech, style* plein de verve.
radar ['reɪdɑːʳ] **1** *n* radar *m*. **by** ~ au radar. **2** *adj* *screen, station* radar *inv*. ~ **operator** radariste *mf*; (*Aut Police*) ~ **trap** piège *m* radar.
radiate ['reɪdɪeɪt] **1** *vi* (*gen*) rayonner (*from* de); (*Phys*) irradier. **2** *vt* *heat* émettre, dégager; (*fig*) *happiness* rayonner de; *enthusiasm* respirer. ♦ **radiance** *n* éclat *m*, rayonnement *m*. ♦ **radiant** *adj* (*gen*) rayonnant (*with* de); *colour* éclatant; *heat* radiant; *heater* à foyer rayonnant; *heating* direct. ♦ **radiantly** *adv* *smile* d'un air radieux; **to be radiantly happy** rayonner de joie. ♦ **radiation 1** *n* *[heat etc]* rayonnement *m*; (*radioactivity*) radiation *f*; **2** *adj*: **radiation sickness** mal *m* des rayons; (*Med*) **radiation treatment*** radiothérapie *f*. ♦ **radiator 1** *n* radiateur *m*; **2** *adj* (*Aut*) **radiator cap** bouchon *m* de radiateur; **radiator grill** calandre *f*.
radical ['rædɪkəl] *adj, n* radical (*m*). ♦ **radically** *adv* radicalement.
radio ['reɪdɪəʊ] **1** *n* **(a)** (~ **set**) poste *m* (de radio), radio *f*. **on the** ~ à la radio. **(b)** (*Telec*) radio *f*, radiotélégraphie *f*. **by** ~ par radio. **2** *vt* *person* appeler par radio; *one's position* signaler par radio; *message* envoyer par radio. **3** *vi*: **to ~ for help** appeler au secours par radio. **4** *adj* *beam, silence* radio *inv*; *programme, broadcast* de radio, radiophonique. ~ **announcer** speaker(ine) *m(f)*; ~ **beacon** radiophare *m*; ~ **communication** contact *m* radio *inv*; ~ **link** liaison *f* radio *inv*; ~ **operator** opérateur *m* (radio), radio *m*; ~ **programme** émission *f* (de radio); ~ **station** station *f* de radio; ~ **telescope** radiotélescope *m*; ~ **wave** onde *f* hertzienne. ♦ **radioactive** *adj* radioactif. ♦ **radioactivity** *n* radioactivité *f*. ♦ **radio-controlled** *adj* téléguidé. ♦ **radiogram** *n* (*message*) radiogramme *m*; (*apparatus*) combiné *m*. ♦ **radiographer** *n* radiologue *mf* (*technicien*). ♦ **radiography** *n* radiographie *f*. ♦ **radiologist** *n* radiologue *mf* (*médecin*). ♦ **radiology** *n* radiologie *f*. ♦ **radio-taxi** *n* radio-taxi *m*. ♦ **radiotelephone** *n* radiotéléphone *m*. ♦ **radiotherapy** *n* radiothérapie *f*.
radish ['rædɪʃ] *n* radis *m*.
radium ['reɪdɪəm] *n* radium *m*.
radius ['reɪdɪəs] *n, pl* **radii** rayon *m* (*also Math*). **within a ~ of** dans un rayon de.
raffia ['ræfɪə] *n* raphia *m*.
raffle ['ræfl] **1** *n* tombola *f*. ~ **ticket** billet *m* de tombola. **2** *vt* mettre en tombola.
raft [rɑːft] *n* radeau *m*.
rafter ['rɑːftəʳ] *n* (*Archit*) chevron *m*.
rag[1] [ræg] **1** *n* **(a)** lambeau *m*; (*for wiping etc*) chiffon *m*. **~s** (*for paper-making*) chiffons; (*old clothes*) haillons *mpl*; **in ~s** en lambeaux; **dressed in ~s** vêtu de haillons; **in ~s and tatters** tout en loques; **to feel like a wet ~*** se sentir complètement vidé*. **(b)** (**pej: newspaper*) torchon* *m* (*journal*). **2** *adj* *doll* de chiffon; **the ~ trade*** la confection.
♦ **rag-and-bone-man** *n* chiffonnier *m*. ♦ **ragbag** *n* sac *m* à chiffons; (*fig*) ramassis *m*. ♦ **ragged** ['rægɪd] *adj* *clothes* en lambeaux; *person* en haillons; *cuff* effiloché. ♦ **ragman** *or* ♦ **ragpicker** *n* chiffonnier *m*.
rag[2]* [ræg] **1** *n* (*joke*) farce *f*, blague* *f*. **2** *vt* (*tease*) taquiner; (*trick*) faire une blague* à.
rage [reɪdʒ] **1** *n* rage *f*, fureur *f*. **in a** ~ en rage, en fureur; **to fly into a** ~ se mettre en rage; (*fig*) **to be (all) the** ~ faire fureur. **2** *vi* *[person]* être furieux (*against* contre); *[battle]* faire rage; *[sea]*

être en furie; *[storm, wind]* se déchaîner. ♦ **raging** *adj person* furieux; *thirst* ardent; *pain* atroce; *fever* violent; *sea* en furie; *wind, storm* déchaîné; **in a raging temper** dans une rage folle; **raging toothache** rage *f* de dents.

raid [reɪd] **1** *n* (*Mil*) raid *m*; (*by police*) rafle *f*; (*by bandits*) razzia *f*; (*by thieves*) hold-up *m inv*. **air ~** bombardement *m* aérien; **bank ~** hold-up d'une banque. **2** *vt* faire un raid *or* une rafle dans; razzier; faire un hold-up à; bombarder; (*fig*) *cashbox* puiser dans; *larder, orchard* dévaliser. ♦ **raider** *n* (*bandit*) pillard *m*; (*criminal*) brigand *m*; (*ship*) raider *m*; (*plane*) bombardier *m*; (*Mil*) **the ~ers** le commando.

rail [reɪl] **1** *n* **(a)** (*bar*) *[bridge, boat]* rambarde *f*; *[balcony, terrace]* balustrade *f*; (*banister*) rampe *f*; (*for curtains, spotlights etc*) tringle *f*; (*towel* ~) porte-serviettes *m inv*. (*fence*) **~s** grille *f*. **(b)** (*for train, tram*) rail *m*. **by ~** *travel* en train; *send* par chemin de fer; **to go off the ~s** *[train etc]* dérailler; *[person]* (*err*) s'écarter du droit chemin; (*be confused*) être déboussolé*. **2** *adj strike* des employés de chemin de fer; *traffic* ferroviaire. **~ workers** employés *mpl* du chemin de fer. ♦ **railing** *n* **(a)** (*V* **rail 1a**) rambarde *f*; balustrade *f*; rampe *f*; **(b)** (*part of fence*) barreau *m*; (*fence: also* **~ings**) grille *f*. ♦ **railroad 1** *n* (*US*) = **railway**; **2** *vt* (*fig*) **to ~road sb into doing sth*** forcer qn à faire qch sans qu'il ait le temps de réfléchir.

railway ['reɪlweɪ] **1** *n* (*system*) chemin *m* de fer; (*track*) voie *f* ferrée. **2** *adj bridge, ticket* de chemin de fer. **~ guide** indicateur *m* des chemins de fer; **~ line** ligne *f* de chemin de fer; (*track*) voie ferrée; **~ network** réseau *m* ferroviaire; **~ station** gare *f*; **~ timetable** horaire *m* des chemins de fer. ♦ **railwayman** *n* cheminot *m*.

rain [reɪn] **1** *n* pluie *f*. **it looks like ~** le temps est à la pluie; **in the ~** sous la pluie; **heavy/light ~** pluie battante/fine; **the ~s** la saison des pluies. **2** *vi* pleuvoir (*also fig*). **it is ~ing** il pleut; **it is ~ing heavily, it's ~ing cats and dogs** il pleut à torrents, il tombe des cordes*. ♦ **rainbow** *n* arc-en-ciel *m*. ♦ **raincheck** *n*: **I'll take a ~check*** je m'en souviendrai à l'occasion. ♦ **raincoat** *n* imperméable *m*. ♦ **raindrop** *n* goutte *f* de pluie. ♦ **rainfall** *n* (*shower*) chute *f* de pluie; (*amount*) hauteur *f* des précipitations. ♦ **rainproof 1** *adj* imperméable; **2** *vt* imperméabiliser. ♦ **rainstorm** *n* pluie *f* torrentielle. ♦ **rainwater** *n* eau *f* de pluie. ♦ **rainy** *adj* pluvieux; *season* des pluies; (*fig*) **to put sth away for a ~y day** mettre de l'argent de côté.

raise [reɪz] **1** *vt* **(a)** (*lift: gen*) lever; *object, weight* lever, soulever; *building, level* élever; *sunken ship* renflouer; *dust* soulever; (*fig: to power, in rank*) élever. (*fig*) **he didn't ~ an eyebrow** il n'a pas sourcillé; **to ~ one's hat to sb** donner un coup de chapeau à qn, (*fig*) tirer son chapeau à qn*; **to ~ one's hand to sb** lever la main sur qn; **to ~ sb from the dead** ressusciter qn (d'entre les morts); **to ~ one's voice** élever la voix; **to ~ sb's spirits** remonter le moral de qn; **to ~ sb's hopes** donner à espérer à qn. **(b)** (*increase*) *salary, price* augmenter; *standard* élever; *temperature* faire monter. **(c)** (*erect*) *monument* élever; *building* construire. **(d)** (*produce*) *ghosts* faire apparaître; *question, problems, difficulties* soulever; *objection, protest* élever; *suspicions* faire naître; *blister* provoquer. **to ~ a laugh** faire rire; **to ~ a smile** (*oneself*) ébaucher un sourire; (*in others*) faire sourire; **to ~ Cain*** *or* **hell‡** *or* **the roof*** (*noise*) faire du boucan‡; (*fuss*) faire une scène de tous les diables*. **(e)** (*grow, breed*) *animals, children* élever; *crops* cultiver. **(f)** (*get together*) *army, taxes* lever; *money* se procurer; *funds* réunir. **to ~ a loan** emprunter; **to ~ money on sth** emprunter de l'argent sur qch; **I can't ~ the £500** je n'arrive pas à me procurer les 500 livres. **(g)** (*end*) *siege, embargo* lever. **(h)** (*contact*) **to ~ sb on the radio** entrer en contact avec qn par radio. **2** *n* (*US, also Brit**: *payrise*) augmentation *f* (de salaire).

raise up *vt sep* lever, soulever. **to ~ o.s. up** se soulever.

rake[1] [reɪk] **1** *n* râteau *m*. **2** *vt garden* ratisser; *hay* râteler; *fire* tisonner; (*fig: with gun*) balayer. **3** *vi* (*fig: search*) **to ~ through** fouiller dans.

rake in* *vt sep money* amasser.

rake off *vt sep stones etc* enlever à l'aide d'un râteau.

rake out *vt sep fire* éteindre en faisant tomber la braise.

rake up *vt sep leaves* ramasser avec un râteau; (*fig*) *grievance* rappeler; *the past* revenir sur; *sb's past* fouiller dans.

♦ **rake-off*** *n* profit *m* (*souvent illégal*).

rake[2]† [reɪk] *n* (*person*) roué† *m*, débauché *m*. ♦ **rakish** *adj person* débauché; *appearance* cavalier; **hat at a rakish angle** chapeau campé sur le coin de l'œil.

rally ['rælɪ] **1** *n [troops]* ralliement *m*; *[people]* rassemblement *m*; (*Pol*) rassemblement, meeting *m*; (*Aut*) rallye *m*; (*Tennis*) échange *m*. **peace ~** rassemblement en faveur de la paix. **2** *vt troops, supporters* rallier. **3** *vi [troops, people]* se rallier (*also fig: to* à); *[sick person]* reprendre le dessus. **~ing point** point *m* de ralliement; (*St Ex*) **the market rallied** les cours ont repris.

rally round *vi* (*fig*) venir en aide.

ram [ræm] **1** *n* bélier *m* (*also Astron*). **2** *vt* **(a)** (*push down*) enfoncer; (*pack down*) tasser (*into* dans). **his hat ~med down over his ears** le chapeau enfoncé jusqu'aux oreilles; (*fig*) **to ~ sth down sb's throat** rebattre les oreilles à qn de qch; **to ~ sth into sb's head** enfoncer qch dans le crâne de qn. **(b)** (*crash into*) (*Naut*) heurter de l'avant, (*in battle*) éperonner; (*Aut*) *another vehicle* emboutir; *post, tree* percuter (contre).

ramble ['ræmbl] **1** *n* randonnée *f*. **2** *vi* (*wander about*) se promener au hasard; (*go on hike*) faire une randonnée; (*pej: in speech*: **~ on**) parler pour ne rien dire; *[old person]* radoter. ♦ **rambler** *n* **(a)** (*person*) excursionniste *mf*; **(b)** (*rose*) rosier *m* grimpant. ♦ **rambling** *adj speech, writing* décousu; *person* qui radote; *town* construit au hasard; *house* plein de coins et de recoins; *plant* grimpant.

ramify ['ræmɪfaɪ] **1** *vt* ramifier. **2** *vi* se ramifier. ♦ **ramification** *n* ramification *f*.

ramp [ræmp] *n* (*on road etc*) rampe *f*; (*in garage etc*) pont *m* de graissage. (*Aviat*) **(boarding) ~** passerelle *f*; (*Aut: sign*) '**~**' 'dénivellation'.

rampage [ræm'peɪdʒ] **1** *n*: **to go on the ~** se déchaîner. **2** *vi* (**~ about, ~ around**) se déchaîner.

rampant ['ræmpənt] *adj* (*fig*) **to be ~** sévir.

rampart ['ræmpɑːt] *n* rempart *m*.

ramshackle ['ræm,ʃækl] *adj building* délabré; *table* branlant; *machine* déglingué*.

ran [ræn] *pret of* **run**.

ranch [rɑːntʃ] *n* ranch *m*.

rancid ['rænsɪd] *adj* rance. **to smell ~** sentir le rance.

rancour, (*US*) **-or** ['ræŋkə^r] *n* rancœur *f*. ♦ **rancorous** *adj* plein de rancœur.

random ['rændəm] **1** *n*: **at ~** au hasard, (*stronger*) à l'aveuglette. **2** *adj choice* fait au hasard; *bullet* perdu; *sample* prélevé au hasard.

rang [ræŋ] *pret of* **ring**[2].

range [reɪndʒ] **1** *n* **(a)** (*scope, distance covered*) *[telescope, gun, missile]* portée *f*; *[plane, ship]* rayon *m* d'action. **at a ~ of** à une distance de; **at long ~** à longue portée; (*Mil*) **to find the ~** régler son tir; **out of ~** hors de portée; **within (firing) ~** à portée de tir; **~ of vision** champ *m* visuel. **(b)** (*extent between limits*) *[temperature]* variations *fpl*; *[prices, salaries, values]* échelle *f*; *[musical instrument, voice]* étendue *f*; (*selection*) *[colours, feelings, speeds]* gamme *f*; *[patterns, goods]* choix *m*. **a wide ~ of subjects** un grand choix de sujets. **(c)** (*domain, sphere*) *[activity]* champ *m*, rayon *m*; *[influence]* sphère *f*; *[knowledge]* étendue *f*. **(d)** (*row*) rangée *f*, rang *m*; *[mountains]* chaîne *f*. **(e)** (*US: grazing land*) prairie *f*. **(f)** (*shooting* ~) (*Mil*) champ *m* de tir; (*at fair*) stand *m* (de tir). **(g)** (*cooking stove*) fourneau *m* de cuisine. **2** *vt objects* ranger; *troops* aligner. **3** *vi* **(a)** (*extend*) *[discussion, search]* s'étendre (*from* ... *to* de ... à; *over* sur); *[numbers, opinions]* aller (*from* ... *to* de ... à); *[results, temperatures]* varier (*from* ... *to* entre ... et). (*fig*) **researches ranging over a wide field** recherches qui embrassent un large domaine. **(b)** (*roam*) **to ~ over** parcourir. **(c)** *[guns, missiles, shells]* to ~ **over** avoir une portée de. ♦ **rangefinder** *n* télémètre *m*. ♦ **ranger** *n* *[forest etc]* garde *m* forestier; (*US: mounted patrolman*) gendarme *m* à cheval.

rank[1] [ræŋk] **1** *n* **(a)** (*row*) rang *m*. **taxi ~** station *f* de taxis. **(b)** (*Mil*) rang *m*. **to break ~s** rompre les rangs; **the ~s**, (*Brit*) **other ~s** les sous-officiers *mpl* et hommes *mpl* de troupe; **the ~ and file** (*Mil*) les hommes de troupe; (*fig*) la masse; *[political party]* les membres *mpl* ordinaires; **to rise from the ~s** sortir du rang; **to reduce to the ~s** casser. **(c)** (*social etc position*) rang *m*; (*Mil: grade*) grade *m*. **the ~ of general** le grade de général; **people of all ~s** des gens de toutes conditions; **a person of ~** une personne de haut rang. **2** *vt* classer, ranger (*among* parmi). **3** *vi* compter (*among* parmi). **to ~ above/below sb** être supérieur/inférieur à qn.

rank[2] [ræŋk] *adj* **(a)** *plants* exubérant. **(b)** *smell, drains* fétide; *fats* rance; *person* répugnant. **(c)** *disgrace* absolu; *traitor, insolence* véritable; *injustice, lie* flagrant; *liar* fieffé (*before n*).

rankle ['ræŋkl] *vi*: **to ~ with sb** rester sur le cœur à qn.

ransack ['rænsæk] *vt town* mettre à sac; *room, drawer* fouiller (à fond) (*for* pour trouver).

ransom ['rænsəm] **1** *n* rançon *f*. **to hold sb to ~** mettre qn à rançon; **~ demand** demande *f* de rançon. **2** *vt* racheter.

rant [rænt] *vi* tempêter (*at sb* contre qn).

rap [ræp] **1** *n* (*noise*) petits coups *mpl* secs; (*blow*) tape *f*. **there was a ~ at the door** on a frappé bruyamment à la porte; **to take the ~*** payer les pots cassés. **2** *vt* **(a)** **to ~ sb over the knuckles** donner sur les doigts de qn. **(b)** (**~ out**) *words* dire brusquement; *order, retort* lancer. **3** *vi* frapper (*at* à), donner de petits coups secs (*on* sur). ♦ **rapping** *n* coups *mpl* secs et durs.

rapacious [rə'peɪʃəs] *adj* rapace. ♦ **rapaciously** *adv* avec rapacité. ♦ **rapacity** *n* rapacité *f*.

rape [reɪp] **1** *n* viol *m*. **2** *vt* violer. ♦ **rapist** *n* violeur *m*, auteur *m* d'un viol.

rapid ['ræpɪd] **1** *adj* rapide. **2** *npl* (*Geog*) **~s** rapides *mpl*. ♦ **rapidity** *n* rapidité *f*. ♦ **rapidly** *adv* rapidement.

rapier ['reɪpɪə^r] *n* rapière *f*.

rapt [ræpt] *adj attention* profond; *smile* ravi.

rapture ['ræptʃə^r] *n* ravissement *m*, extase *f*. **to be in ~s over** *object* être ravi de; *person* être en extase devant; **to go into ~s over** s'extasier sur. ♦ **rapturous** *adj smile* de ravissement; *welcome* chaleureux; *applause* frénétique. ♦ **rapturously** *adv* avec ravissement; avec frénésie.

rare [rɛə^r] *adj* (*gen*) rare; *atmosphere* raréfié; *meat* saignant. **it is ~ for her to come** il est rare qu'elle vienne; **to grow ~(r)** *[plants, atmosphere]* se raréfier; *[visits]* devenir plus rares; **we had a ~ old time*** nous nous sommes drôlement* bien amusés; **a very ~ steak** un bifteck bleu. ♦ **rarebit** *n*: **Welsh ~bit** toast *m* au fromage fondu. ♦ **rarefied** ['rɛərɪfaɪd] *adj atmosphere* raréfié; (*fig*) trop raffiné. ♦ **rarely** *adv* rarement. ♦ **rareness** *or* ♦ **rarity** *n* rareté *f*.

rascal ['rɑːskəl] *n* (*scoundrel*) vaurien *m*; (*scamp*) polisson(ne) *m(f)*. ♦ **rascally** *adj person* retors; *trick* vilain (*before n*).

rash[1] [ræʃ] *n* (*Med: gen*) rougeurs *fpl*; (*from food etc*) urticaire *f*; (*in measles etc*) éruption *f*. **to come out in a ~** avoir une éruption *etc*.

rash[2] [ræʃ] *adj person* imprudent; *words* irréfléchi. ♦ **rashly** *adv* imprudemment; sans réfléchir. ♦ **rashness** *n* imprudence *f*.

rasher ['ræʃə^r] *n* (mince) tranche *f* (de lard).

rasp [rɑːsp] **1** *n* (*tool*) râpe *f*; (*noise*) grincement *m*. **2** *vt* **(a)** (*Tech*) râper. **(b)** (*speak*) dire d'une voix grinçante. **3** *vi* grincer. ♦ **rasping** *adj* grinçant.

raspberry ['rɑːzbərɪ] **1** *n* framboise *f*; (*bush*) framboisier *m*. (*fig*) **to blow a ~*** faire un bruit de dérision. **2** *adj ice cream* (à la) framboise *inv*; *jam* de framboise.

rat [ræt] **1** *n* rat *m*. **he's a (dirty) ~*** c'est un salaud‡. **2** *adj*: **~ poison** mort-aux-rats *f*; **~ race** foire *f* d'empoigne. **3** *vi*: **to ~ on sb*** (*desert*) lâcher* qn; (*inform on*) moucharder* qn. ♦ **ratcatcher** *n* chasseur *m* de rats. ♦ **rat-trap** *n* ratière *f*.

ratchet ['rætʃɪt] *n* cliquet *m*. **~ wheel** roue *f* à rochet.

rate [reɪt] **1** *n* **(a)** (*ratio, proportion*) taux *m*, proportion *f*; (*speed*) vitesse *f*, allure *f*. **birth/death ~** (taux de) la natalité/la mortalité; **the failure ~** le pourcentage d'échecs; **~ of consumption** taux de consommation; (*Elec, Water*) **~ of flow** débit *m* moyen; **at the ~ of** (*amount etc*) à raison de; (*speed*) à une vitesse de; (*Med*) **pulse ~** fréquence *f* des pulsations; **at a great ~, at a ~ of knots*** à toute allure; **if you continue at this ~** si vous continuez à ce train-là; **at his ~ of working** au rythme auquel il travaille; (*fig*) **at any ~** en tout cas, de toute façon; **at that ~** dans ce cas. **(b)** (*Comm, Fin*) taux *m*, tarif *m*. **~ of exchange/interest/pay** taux du change/d'intérêt/de rémunération; **postage/advertising ~s** tarifs postaux/de publicité; **insurance ~s** primes *fpl* d'assurance; **reduced ~** tarif réduit. **(c)** (*municipal tax*) **~s** impôts *mpl* locaux; **~s and taxes** impôts et contributions; **a penny on/off the ~s** une augmentation/réduction d'un pour cent des impôts locaux.

2 *vt* **(a)** (*estimate worth of, appraise*) évaluer (*at* à); (*fig: consider*) considérer (*as* comme), compter (*among* parmi). **to ~ sb/sth highly** faire grand cas de qn/qch; **how does he ~ that film?** que pense-t-il de ce film? **(b)** **house ~d at £100 per annum** ≈ maison *f* dont la valeur locative imposable est de 100 livres par an. **(c)** (*deserve*) mériter.

3 *vi* (*be classed*) être classé (*as* comme). ♦ **rateable** *adj*: **~able value** valeur *f* locative imposable. ♦ **ratepayer** *n* contribuable *mf* (*impôts locaux*). ♦ **rating** *n* **(a)** (*assessment*) estimation *f*, évaluation *f*; **(b)** (*Naut*) **the ratings** les matelots et gradés *mpl*.

rather ['rɑːðə^r] *adv* **(a)** (*for preference*) plutôt. **~ than wait, he ...** plutôt que d'attendre, il ...; **I would ~ have the blue dress** je préférerais *or* j'aimerais mieux la robe bleue; **I would much ~ ...** je préférerais de beaucoup ..., j'aimerais mieux ...; **I would ~ do that than wait for him** je préférerais faire ça plutôt que de l'attendre; **I would ~ you came** je préférerais que vous veniez (*subj*); **I'd ~ not** j'aime mieux pas*; **I'd ~ not go** j'aimerais mieux ne pas y aller. **(b)** (*more accurately*) plus exactement, plutôt. **(c)** (*to a considerable degree*) plutôt; (*to some extent*) un peu; (*somewhat*) quelque peu; (*fairly*) assez; (*slightly*) légèrement. **he's ~ clever** il est plutôt intelligent; **it's ~ more difficult than you think** c'est un peu plus difficile que vous ne croyez; **his book is ~ good** son livre n'est pas mauvais du tout; **that costs ~ a lot** cela coûte assez cher; **I ~ think that** je crois bien que; (*excl*) **~!*** et comment!*

ratify ['rætɪfaɪ] *vt* ratifier. ♦ **ratification** *n* ratification *f*.

ratio ['reɪʃɪəʊ] *n* proportion *f*, raison *f*. **in the ~ of 100 to 1** dans la proportion de 100 contre 1; **inverse ~** raison inverse.

ration ['ræʃən] **1** *n* (*allowance: of food, goods etc*) ration *f*. (*food*) **~s** vivres *mpl*. **2** *adj*: **~ book** carte *f* de rationnement. **3** *vt thing, person* rationner. **he was ~ed to 1 kg** sa ration était 1 kg. ♦ **rationing** *n* rationnement *m*.

rational ['ræʃənl] *adj creature* doué de raison; (*Med: lucid*) lucide; *faculty* rationnel; *action, argument, person* raisonnable; *explanation, solution* logique, rationnel. ♦ **rationalization** *n* rationalisation *f*. ♦ **rationalize** **1** *vt* **(a)** *event, conduct etc* justifier (après coup); **(b)** (*organize efficiently*) *industry, production* rationaliser; **2** *vi* chercher une justification (après coup). ♦ **rationally** *adv* raisonnablement, rationnellement.

rattle ['rætl] **1** *n* **(a)** (*sound*) *[vehicle]* bruit *m* (de ferraille); *[chains, bottles, dice, typewriter]* cliquetis *m*; *[hailstones, bullets]* crépitement *m*; *[rattlesnake]* sonnettes *fpl*. **death ~** râle *m*. **(b)** (*object*) *[child]* hochet *m*; *[sports fan]* crécelle *f*. **2** *vi [box, object]* faire du bruit; *[articles in box]* s'entrechoquer; *[vehicle]* faire un bruit de ferraille; *[bullets, hailstones]* crépiter; *[machinery]* cliqueter; *[window]* trembler. *[vehicle]* **to ~ along** rouler dans un bruit de ferraille. **3** *vt* **(a)** *box, dice* agiter; *bottles, cans* faire s'entrechoquer; *keys* faire cliqueter. **(b)** (*: *worry*) troubler. **to get ~d** se mettre dans tous ses états.
rattle off *vt sep poem* débiter à toute allure.
rattle on *vi* parler sans arrêt (*about sth* de qch).
♦ **rattlesnake** *n* serpent *m* à sonnettes.

ratty* ['rætɪ] *adj* en rogne*.

raucous ['rɔːkəs] *adj* rauque. ♦ **raucously** *adv* d'une voix rauque.

ravage ['rævɪdʒ] **1** *n* ravage *m*. **2** *vt* ravager.

rave [reɪv] **1** *vi* (*be delirious*) délirer; (*talk wildly*) divaguer; (*furiously*) tempêter (*at, against* contre); (*enthusiastically*) s'extasier (*about, over* sur). **2** *adj*: **~ review*** critique *f* dithyrambique. ♦ **raving** *adj* délirant; **raving mad** fou furieux (*f* folle furieuse). ♦ **ravings** *npl* délire *m*.

raven ['reɪvn] *n* corbeau *m*. ♦ **raven-haired** *adj* aux cheveux de jais.

ravenous ['rævənəs] *adj animal, appetite* vorace; *person* affamé; *hunger* dévorant. **I'm ~*** j'ai une faim de loup. ♦ **ravenously** *adv* voracement.

ravine [rə'viːn] *n* ravin *m*.

ravioli [ˌrævɪ'əʊlɪ] *n* ravioli *mpl*.

ravish ['rævɪʃ] *vt* ravir. ♦ **ravishing** *adj* ravissant; **~ing beauty** beauté *f* enchanteresse. ♦ **ravishingly** *adv*: **she is ~ingly beautiful** elle est belle à ravir.

raw [rɔː] **1** *adj* **(a)** *food, colour* cru; *cloth, leather* écru; *ore, sugar* brut; *spirit, alcohol* pur. **to give sb a ~ deal*** faire un sale coup à qn*; **to get a ~ deal*** être traité fort mal; **~ material(s)** matières *fpl* premières. **(b)** (*inexperienced*) inexpérimenté; (*uncouth*) mal dégrossi. **~ recruit** bleu* *m*. **(c)** (*sore*) irrité; *skin* écorché; *wound, nerves* à vif. *[cloth etc]* **~ edge** bord *m* coupé. **(d)** *climate, wind* âpre; *air* vif. **2** *n*: **to get sb on the ~** toucher qn au vif; **nature in the ~** la nature telle qu'elle est. ♦ **rawboned** *adj* décharné. ♦ **rawness** *n* **(a)** (*lack of experience*) inexpérience *f*; **(b)** (*on skin*) irritation *f*; **(c)** *[climate]* froid *m* humide; *[wind]* âpreté *f*.

rawlplug ['rɔːlplʌg] *n* cheville *f* (*Menuiserie*).

ray¹ [reɪ] *n* rayon *m*; (*of hope*) lueur *f*.

ray² [reɪ] *n* (*fish*) raie *f*.

rayon ['reɪɒn] *n* (*Tex*) rayonne *f*.

raze [reɪz] *vt* (**~ to the ground**) raser.

razor ['reɪzəʳ] **1** *n* rasoir *m*. **2** *adj*: **~ blade** lame *f* de rasoir. ♦ **razor-sharp** *adj knife etc* tranchant comme un rasoir; (*fig*) *person, mind* très vif; *wit* acéré.

re¹ [reɪ] *n* (*Mus*) ré *m*.

re² [riː] *prep* (*referring to*) au sujet de.

re... [riː] *pref* (*before consonant*) re..., ré...; (*before vowel*) r..., ré... . **to ~do** refaire; **to ~heat** réchauffer; **to ~open** rouvrir; **to ~-elect** réélire.

reach [riːtʃ] **1** *n* **(a)** portée *f*. **within ~** à portée; **out of ~** hors de portée; **within sb's ~** à (la) portée de qn; **within easy ~** *or* **within my ~** à portée de main, sous la main; **not within easy ~** difficilement accessible; **within easy ~ of the sea** à proximité de la mer; **beyond the ~ of the law** à l'abri de la justice; **this subject is beyond his ~** ce sujet le dépasse. **(b)** (*esp Boxing*) allonge *f*. **(c)** *[river]* étendue *f*; *[canal]* bief *m*.
2 *vt* **(a)** (*get as far as*) *place* atteindre, arriver à; *age, goal, limit* atteindre; *agreement, conclusion, page* arriver à. **when we ~ed him** quand nous sommes arrivés auprès de lui; **the letter ~ed him** la lettre lui est parvenue; **the news ~ed us too late** nous avons appris la nouvelle trop tard; **you can ~ me at my hotel** vous pouvez me joindre à mon hôtel. **(b)** (*get and give*) passer. **~ me (over) that book** passez-moi ce livre.
3 *vi* **(a)** *[territory etc]* s'étendre; *[voice, sound]* porter (*to* jusqu'à). **(b)** (*stretch out hand*: **~ across, ~ out, ~ over**) étendre le bras (*for sth* pour prendre qch; *to grasp etc* pour saisir *etc*).

react [riː'ækt] *vi* réagir (*against* contre; *on* sur; *to* à). ♦ **reaction** *n* (*all senses*) réaction *f*. ♦ **reactionary** *adj*, *n* réactionnaire (*mf*). ♦ **reactor** *n* réacteur *m*.

read [riːd] *pret, ptp* **read** [red] **1** *vt* **(a)** (*gen*) lire; *meter* relever; *proofs* corriger. **I brought you sth to ~** je vous ai apporté de la lecture; **to be well-read** être très cultivé; (*fig*) **to ~ sb a lesson*** faire la leçon à qn; **to take sth as read** (*as self-evident*) considérer qch comme allant de soi; (*as agreed*) considérer qch comme convenu; (*Admin*) **to take the minutes as read** passer à l'ordre du jour; **to ~ sb's hand** lire les lignes de la main à qn; (*fig*) **these words can be read in several ways** ces mots peuvent s'interpréter de plusieurs façons; **to ~ between the lines** lire entre les lignes; **to ~ sb's mind** *or* **thoughts** lire la pensée de qn; **I can ~ him like a book** je sais toujours ce qu'il pense; **we mustn't ~ too much into this** nous ne devons pas y attacher trop d'importance; (*Telec*) **do you ~ me?** est-ce que vous me recevez? **(b)** (*Univ: study*) étudier, faire. **to ~ medicine/English** faire des études de médecine/d'anglais. **(c)** *[instruments]* marquer, indiquer. **2** *vi* lire. **he likes ~ing** il aime lire, il aime la lecture; **to ~ to sb** faire la lecture à qn; **I read about it in the paper** je l'ai lu dans le journal; **I've read about him** j'ai lu qch à son sujet. **3** *n*: **she enjoys a good ~*** elle aime bien la lecture, elle aime bouquiner*; **to have a quiet ~*** bouquiner* tranquillement.
read back *vt sep* relire.
read off *vt sep* **(a)** (*without pause*) lire d'un trait; (*at sight*) lire à livre ouvert. **(b)** *instrument readings* relever.
read out *vt sep* lire à haute voix.
read over *vt sep* relire.
read through *vt sep* (*rapidly*) parcourir; (*thoroughly*) lire d'un bout à l'autre.
read up *vt sep*, **read up on** *vt fus* étudier, potasser*.
♦ **readable** *adj handwriting* lisible; *book* facile à lire. ♦ **reader** *n* **(a)** lecteur *m*, -trice *f*; **publisher's ~er** lecteur, -trice dans une maison d'édition; **he's a great ~er** il aime beaucoup lire; **(b)** (*Brit Univ*) ≃ maître *m* de conférences; **(c)** (*read-

ing book) livre *m* de lecture; (*anthology*) recueil *m* de textes. ♦ **readership** *n [newspaper]* nombre *m* de lecteurs. ♦ **reading 1** *n* **(a)** (*gen*) lecture *f*; *[proofs]* correction *f*; **she likes ~ing** elle aime bien lire *or* la lecture; **it makes very interesting ~ing** c'est très intéressant (à lire); **I'd prefer some light ~ing** je préférerais un livre d'une lecture facile; **(b)** (*recital: of play, poems*) (séance *f* de) lecture *f*; **(c)** (*interpretation*) interprétation *f*; **(d)** (*variant*) variante *f*; **(e) to take a ~ing** (*from instrument*) lire un instrument, (*from meter*) relever un compteur; **the ~ing is ...** l'instrument indique ...; **2** *adj book* de lecture; *glasses* pour lire; **to have a ~ing knowledge of Spanish** savoir lire l'espagnol; **~ing lamp** lampe *f* de bureau; **~ing matter** choses *fpl* à lire; **~ing room** salle *f* de lecture.

readdress ['riːə'dres] *vt letter etc* faire suivre.

readjust ['riːə'dʒʌst] **1** *vt* rajuster. **2** *vi* se réadapter (*to* à).

ready ['redɪ] **1** *adj* **(a)** (*gen*) prêt. **'dinner's ~!'** 'à table!'; **everything is ~ for his visit** tout est prêt pour sa visite; **~ for anything** prêt à toute éventualité; **~ to use** *or* **for use** prêt à l'usage; **to be ~ to do** être prêt à faire; **to get ~ to do** se préparer à faire; **to be ~ with an excuse** avoir une excuse toute prête; **to get sth ~** préparer qch; (*Sport*) **~, steady, go!** prêts? 1-2-3 partez!; **I'm ~ for him!** je l'attends de pied ferme!; **get ~ for it!** tenez-vous prêt!, (*before momentous news etc*) tenez-vous bien!; (*Publishing*) **'now ~'** 'vient de paraître'; **~ money** (argent *m*) liquide *m*; **~ reckoner** barème *m*; **he is ~ to help** il est prêt à rendre service; **I am quite ~ to see him** je suis tout à fait disposé à le voir; **he was ~ to cry** il était sur le point de pleurer. **(b)** (*prompt*) *reply, wit* prompt. **to have a ~ tongue** avoir la langue déliée; **to have a ~ sale** se vendre facilement. **2** *n*: **at the ~** (*Mil*) prêt à faire feu; (*fig*) tout prêt. **3** *adv* (*in cpds*) **~-cooked/-furnished** *etc* tout cuit/meublé *etc* (d'avance). ♦ **readily** *adv* (*willingly*) volontiers; (*easily*) facilement. ♦ **readiness** *n* empressement *m* (*to do* à faire); **in readiness for** prêt pour. ♦ **ready-made** *adj curtains* tout fait; *clothes* de confection; *solution, answer* tout prêt. ♦ **ready-mix** *n* préparation *f* instantanée (*pour gâteaux etc*). ♦ **ready-to-serve** *adj* prêt à servir. ♦ **ready-to-wear** *adj* prêt à porter.

real [rɪəl] **1** *adj* véritable, vrai (*both before n*), réel; *reason, jewels* vrai (*before n*), véritable; *flowers, silk* naturel; (*Philos*) réel. **in ~ life, in ~ terms** dans la réalité; **he is the ~ boss** c'est lui le véritable patron; **he has no ~ power** il n'a pas de pouvoir effectif; **when you've tasted the ~ thing, this whisky ...** quand tu as (*or* auras) goûté du vrai whisky, celui-ci ...; **it's the ~ thing*** c'est du vrai de vrai*. **2** *adv* (*: *very*) rudement*. **3** *n*: **for ~*** pour de vrai*. ♦ **real estate** *n* (*US*) immobilier *m*; **~-estate office** agence *f* immobilière. ♦ **realism** *n* réalisme *m*. ♦ **realist** *adj, n* réaliste (*mf*). ♦ **realistic** *adj* réaliste. ♦ **realistically** *adv* avec réalisme, d'une façon réaliste. ♦ **reality** [riː'ælɪtɪ] *n* réalité *f*; **in ~ity** en réalité. ♦ **really** *adv* vraiment.

realize ['rɪəlaɪz] *vt* **(a)** (*become aware of*) se rendre compte de, prendre conscience de; (*understand*) comprendre. **the committee ~s the gravity of the situation** le comité se rend compte de *or* a pris conscience de la gravité de la situation; **he had not fully ~d that she was dead** il n'avait pas vraiment réalisé qu'elle était morte; **I ~d it was raining** je me suis rendu compte qu'il pleuvait, j'ai réalisé* qu'il pleuvait; **I made her ~ that I was right** je lui ai bien fait comprendre que j'avais raison; **I ~ that ...** je me rends compte du fait que ..., je sais bien que ...; **I ~d how/why** j'ai compris comment/pourquoi. **(b)** *hope, plan, assets* réaliser; *price* atteindre; *interest* rapporter. **how much did it ~?** combien est-ce que cela vous a rapporté? ♦ **realization** *n [assets, hope]* réalisation *f*; (*awareness*) prise *f* de conscience, découverte *f* soudaine (*that* que).

realm [relm] *n* royaume *m*; (*fig*) domaine *m*.

realtor ['rɪəltɔːʳ] *n* (*US*) agent *m* immobilier.

ream [riːm] *n* ≈ rame *f* (*de papier*). (*fig*) **~s*** des volumes *mpl*.

reap [riːp] *vt* moissonner, faucher; (*fig*) *profit* récolter, tirer. ♦ **reaper** *n* (*person*) moissonneur *m*, -euse *f*; (*machine*) moissonneuse *f*; **~er and binder** moissonneuse-lieuse *f*.

reappear ['riːə'pɪəʳ] *vi* réapparaître, reparaître. ♦ **reappearance** *n* réapparition *f*.

reappraisal ['riːə'preɪzəl] *n* réévaluation *f*.

rear¹ [rɪəʳ] **1** *n* **(a)** (*back part*) arrière *m*, derrière *m*; (*: *buttocks*) derrière*. **in** *or* **at the ~** à l'arrière; **from the ~** de derrière. **(b)** (*Mil*) arrière-garde *f*; *[squad]* dernier rang *m*; *[column]* queue *f*. **to bring up the ~** fermer la marche. **2** *adj* (*gen*) de derrière; (*Aut*) *door, window etc* arrière *inv*. **~ admiral** contre-amiral *m*. ♦ **rearguard** *n* (*Mil*) arrière-garde *f*; **~guard action** combat *m* d'arrière-garde. ♦ **rearmost** *adj* dernier. ♦ **rear-view mirror** *n* rétroviseur *m*.

rear² [rɪəʳ] **1** *vt* **(a)** *animals, family* élever; *plants* cultiver. **(b)** *a ladder, one's head* dresser. **violence ~s its ugly head** la violence fait son apparition dans toute son horreur. **(c)** *monument* dresser, ériger. **2** *vi* (**~ up**) *[animal]* se cabrer; *[snake]* se dresser.

rearm [ˌriː'ɑːm] *vti* réarmer. ♦ **rearmament** *n* réarmement *m*.

rearrange ['riːə'reɪndʒ] *vt* réarranger. ♦ **rearrangement** *n* nouvel arrangement *m*.

reason ['riːzn] **1** *n* **(a)** (*cause: gen*) raison *f* (*for sth* de qch; *why* pour laquelle). **my ~ for going** la raison pour laquelle je pars; **the ~ why** (le) pourquoi; **I have (good** *or* **every) ~ to believe that ...** j'ai (tout) lieu de croire que ...; **for no ~** sans raison; **for some ~ or another** pour une raison ou pour une autre; **for ~s best known to himself** pour des raisons qu'il est seul à connaître; **all the more ~ for doing** *or* **to do** raison de plus pour faire; **with ~** avec juste raison; **by ~ of** en raison de. **(b)** (*mental faculty, common sense*) raison *f*. **to lose one's ~** perdre la raison; **it stands to ~ that** il va sans dire que; **anything within ~** tout ce qui est raisonnablement possible. **2** *vi* raisonner (*with sb* qn). **3** *vt* conclure, calculer (*that* que). ♦ **reasonable** *adj* (*gen*) raisonnable; *essay, results* acceptable; (*Jur*) *doubt* bien fondé; *chance, amount, hope* certain (*before n*). ♦ **reasonableness** *n* caractère *m* raisonnable. ♦ **reasonably** *adv* raisonnablement; **one can ~ably think that ...** il est raisonnable de penser que ...; **~ably priced** à un prix raisonnable. ♦ **reasoned** *adj* raisonné. ♦ **reasoning** *n* raisonnement *m*.

reassemble [ˌriːə'sembl] **1** *vt tool, machine* remonter. **2** *vi [people]* se rassembler. **school ~s tomorrow** c'est la rentrée demain.

reassure [ˌriːə'ʃʊəʳ] *vt* rassurer. ♦ **reassurance** *n* réconfort *m*. ♦ **reassuring** *adj* rassurant.

reawaken ['riːə'weɪkən] **1** *vt* réveiller de nouveau. **2** *vi* se réveiller de nouveau.

rebate ['riːbeɪt] *n* (*discount*) rabais *m*; (*money back*) remboursement *m*; *[rent]* dégrèvement *m*.

rebel ['rebl] **1** *adj, n* rebelle (*mf*). **2** [rɪ'bel] *vi* se rebeller (*against* contre). ♦ **rebellion** *n* rébellion *f*. ♦ **rebellious** *adj* rebelle; (*fig*) *child* désobéissant. ♦ **rebelliousness** *n* esprit *m* de rébellion.

rebirth ['riː'bɜːθ] *n* renaissance *f*.

rebound [rɪ'baʊnd] **1** *vi* rebondir. **2** ['riːbaʊnd] *n [ball]* rebond *m*; *[bullet]* ricochet *m*.

rebuff [rɪ'bʌf] **1** *n* rebuffade *f*. **2** *vt* repousser.

rebuild [ˌriː'bɪld] *pret, ptp* **rebuilt** *vt* rebâtir.

rebuke [rɪ'bjuːk] **1** *n* reproche *m*. **2** *vt* faire des

reproches à. **to ~ sb for sth/sb for doing** reprocher qch à qn/à qn d'avoir fait.
rebut [rɪ'bʌt] *vt* réfuter. ♦ **rebuttal** *n* réfutation *f*.
recalcitrant [rɪ'kælsɪtrənt] *adj* récalcitrant.
recall [rɪ'kɔːl] **1** *vt* **(a)** (*call back: gen*) rappeler; (*Fin*) *capital* faire rentrer; *Parliament* convoquer en session extraordinaire. **(b)** (*remember*) se rappeler (*doing* avoir fait; *that* que). **2** *n* rappel *m* (*also Mil*). **beyond ~** (*adv*) irrévocablement.
recant [rɪ'kænt] *vi* se rétracter; (*Rel*) abjurer.
recap[1]* ['riːkæp] **1** *n abbr of* **recapitulation. 2** [riː'kæp] *vti abbr of* **recapitulate**: **to ~, ...** en résumé ... .
recap[2] ['riːkæp] (*US*) **1** *n* (*tyre*) pneu *m* rechapé. **2** *vt* rechaper.
recapitulate [ˌriːkə'pɪtjʊleɪt] *vti* récapituler. ♦ **recapitulation** *n* récapitulation *f*.
recapture ['riː'kæptʃəʳ] **1** *vt escapee* reprendre; *atmosphere* retrouver, *[book etc]* recréer. **2** *n [territory]* reprise *f*; *[escapee]* arrestation *f*.
recast ['riː'kɑːst] *vt play* changer la distribution de.
recede [rɪ'siːd] *vi* (*gen*) s'éloigner; *[tide]* descendre; *[chin]* être fuyant. **his hair is receding** son front se dégarnit. ♦ **receding** *adj chin, forehead* fuyant; **receding hairline** front dégarni.
receipt [rɪ'siːt] **1** *n* **(a)** (*for payment*) reçu *m*, quittance *f* (*for* de); (*for parcel, letter*) accusé *m* de réception. **(b)** (*esp Comm*) réception *f*. **to acknowledge ~ of** accuser réception de; **on ~ of** dès réception de; **I am in ~ of ...** j'ai reçu ... . **(c)** (*money taken*) **~s** recettes *fpl*. **2** *adj*: **~ book** livre *m* de quittances. **3** *vt bill* acquitter.
receive [rɪ'siːv] *vt* (*gen*) recevoir; *money, salary* recevoir, toucher; *refusal, setback* essuyer; (*Rad, TV*) *transmissions* capter, recevoir; (*Jur*) *stolen goods* receler. (*Jur*) **to ~ (a sentence of) 2 years' imprisonment** être condamné à 2 ans de prison; (*Comm*) **~d with thanks** pour acquit; **his suggestion was well ~d** sa suggestion a reçu un accueil favorable. ♦ **received** *adj opinion* reçu; (*Ling*) **~d pronunciation** prononciation *f* standard (de l'anglais). ♦ **receiver** *n* **(a)** (*gen*) personne *f* qui reçoit qch; *[letter]* destinataire *mf*; *[goods]* réceptionnaire *mf*; *[stolen property]* receleur *m*, -euse *f*; (*in bankruptcy*) administrateur *m* judiciaire (en matière de faillite); **(b)** *[telephone]* combiné *m*; **to lift the ~r** décrocher; **to replace the ~r** raccrocher. ♦ **receiving** *n [stolen goods]* recel *m*.
recent ['riːsnt] *adj* (*gen*) récent; *development* nouveau; *acquaintance etc* de fraîche date. **in ~ years** ces dernières années. ♦ **recently** *adv* récemment; **as ~ly as** pas plus tard que; **until quite ~ly** jusqu'à ces derniers temps.
receptacle [rɪ'septəkl] *n* récipient *m*.
reception [rɪ'sepʃən] **1** *n* (*all senses*) réception *f*. **to get a favourable ~** être bien accueilli; **to give sb a warm ~** faire un accueil chaleureux à qn. **2** *adj*: **~ centre** centre *m* d'accueil; **~ desk** (bureau *m* de) réception *f*. ♦ **receptionist** *n* réceptionniste *mf*.
receptive [rɪ'septɪv] *adj* réceptif (*to* à). ♦ **receptivity** *n* réceptivité *f*.
recess [rɪ'ses] **1** *n* **(a)** (*cessation of business*) (*Jur, Parl*) vacances *fpl*; (*US Jur: short break*) suspension *f* d'audience; (*Scol, esp US*) récréation *f*. **(b)** (*alcove*) renfoncement *m*; *[bed]* alcôve *f*; *[door, window]* embrasure *f*; *[statue]* niche *f*. **2** *vi* (*US Jur, Parl*) être en vacances. ♦ **recession** *n* (*Econ*) récession *f*.
recessive [rɪ'sesɪv] *adj* rétrograde; (*Genetics*) récessif.
recharge ['riː'tʃɑːdʒ] *vt battery, gun* recharger.
recidivism [rɪ'sɪdɪvɪzəm] *n* récidive *f*. ♦ **recidivist** *adj, n* récidiviste (*mf*).
recipe ['resɪpɪ] *n* (*Culin*) recette *f* (*for* de).
recipient [rɪ'sɪpɪənt] *n [letter]* destinataire *mf*; *[cheque]* bénéficiaire *mf*; *[award]* récipiendaire *m*; (*Jur*) donataire *mf*.
reciprocate [rɪ'sɪprəkeɪt] **1** *vt* (*gen*) donner *or* offrir en retour; *smile* rendre; *kindness* retourner. **2** *vi* en faire autant. ♦ **reciprocal** *adj* réciproque. ♦ **reciprocally** *adv* réciproquement. ♦ **reciprocity** *n* réciprocité *f*.
recite [rɪ'saɪt] **1** *vt poetry* réciter; *facts, details* énumérer. **2** *vi* réciter. ♦ **recital** *n* **(a)** *[poetry, music]* récital *m*; **(b)** (*account*) récit *m*; *[details]* énumération *f*. ♦ **recitation** *n* récitation *f*. ♦ **recitative** *n* récitatif *m*.
reckless ['reklɪs] *adj* (*gen*) imprudent; *person* insouciant, (*stronger*) imprudent; (*Aut*) *driving, driver* imprudent. ♦ **recklessly** *adv* avec insouciance; imprudemment. ♦ **recklessness** *n* insouciance *f*; imprudence *f*.
reckon ['rekən] **1** *vt* (*calculate*) *time, numbers, points* compter; *cost, surface* calculer; (*judge*) considérer (*sb to be* qn comme étant), compter (*among* parmi); (*: *think*) penser, croire; (*estimate*) estimer (*that* que). **about thirty, I ~** une trentaine, à mon avis. **2** *vi* compter, calculer; (*fig*) compter (*on* sur; *with* avec; *without sb* sans qn). **I wasn't ~ing on having to do that** je ne m'attendais pas à devoir faire ça; **a person to be ~ed with** une personne avec laquelle il faut compter; **he ~ed without the fact that ...** il n'avait pas tenu compte du fait que ... . ♦ **reckoning** *n* compte *m*, calcul *m*; **to be out in one's ~ing** s'être trompé dans ses calculs; **on the day of ~ing** le jour où il faudra rendre des comptes; **to the best of my ~ing** pour autant que je puisse en juger.
reclaim [rɪ'kleɪm] *vt land* (*from forest*) défricher; (*from sea*) assécher; (*Ind*) (*by-product*) récupérer; (*demand back*) réclamer (*from sb* à qn).
recline [rɪ'klaɪn] *vi [person]* être étendu *or* allongé. **the seat ~s** le dossier est réglable. ♦ **reclining** *adj seat* à dossier réglable.
recluse [rɪ'kluːs] *n* reclus(e) *m(f)*.
recognition [ˌrekəg'nɪʃən] *n* reconnaissance *f*. **in ~ of** en reconnaissance de; **to gain ~** être reconnu; **to change/change sth beyond all ~** devenir/rendre qch méconnaissable; **to improve out of (all) ~** s'améliorer jusqu'à en être méconnaissable.
recognize ['rekəgnaɪz] *vt* (*all senses*) reconnaître (*by* à; *as* comme étant; *that* que). ♦ **recognizable** *adj* reconnaissable. ♦ **recognized** *adj* reconnu.
recoil [rɪ'kɔɪl] **1** *vi [person]* reculer (*from* devant; *in disgust* de dégoût); *[gun]* reculer; (*fig*) *[actions etc]* retomber (*on* sur). **to ~ from doing** se refuser à faire. **2** *n [gun]* recul *m*; (*fig*) dégoût *m*.
recollect [ˌrekə'lekt] **1** *vt* se rappeler, se souvenir de. **2** *vi* se souvenir. ♦ **recollection** *n* souvenir *m*; **to the best of my ~ion** autant que je m'en souvienne.
recommend [ˌrekə'mend] *vt* **(a)** recommander (*sb/sth for* qn/qch pour; *sb as* qn comme; *sb to do* à qn de faire). **it is/is not to be ~ed** c'est à conseiller/à déconseiller; **she has a lot to ~ her** elle a beaucoup de qualités en sa faveur. **(b)** (*commit*) *child, one's soul* confier (*to* à). ♦ **recommendation** *n* recommandation *f*.
recompense ['rekəmpens] **1** *n* récompense *f*; (*Jur: for damage*) dédommagement *m*. **2** *vt* récompenser (*for* de); (*Jur*) dédommager.
reconcile ['rekənsaɪl] *vt person* réconcilier (*to* avec); *two facts or ideas* concilier. *[people]* **to become ~d** se réconcilier; **to ~ o.s. to sth** se résigner à qch; **what ~d him to it was ...** ce qui le lui a fait accepter, c'était ... . ♦ **reconcilable** *adj* conciliable (*with* avec). ♦ **reconciliation** *n* réconciliation *f*.
recondition ['riːkən'dɪʃən] *vt* (*gen*) remettre à neuf; *engine, machine* réviser.
reconnaissance [rɪ'kɒnɪsəns] **1** *n* (*Aviat, Mil*)

reconnaissance *f*. 2 *adj patrol* de reconnaissance.

reconnoitre, (*US*) **-ter** [ˌrekəˈnɔɪtəʳ] (*Mil*) 1 *vt* reconnaître. 2 *vi* faire une reconnaissance.

reconsider [ˈriːkənˈsɪdəʳ] *vt* reconsidérer. ♦ **reconsideration** *n* remise *f* en cause.

reconstruct [ˈriːkənˈstrʌkt] *vt building* reconstruire; *crime* reconstituer. ♦ **reconstruction** *n* reconstruction *f*; reconstitution *f*.

record [rɪˈkɔːd] 1 *vt* **(a)** (*register*) rapporter (*that* que); *population* recenser; *protest, disapproval* prendre acte de; *event etc* noter, (*describe*) décrire; *[thermometer etc]* enregistrer, marquer. **to ~ the proceedings** tenir le procès-verbal; **to ~ one's vote** voter; **the author ~s that ...** l'auteur rapporte que ... . **(b)** *speech, music* enregistrer (*on tape* sur bande).

2 [ˈrekɔːd] *n* **(a)** (*report*) rapport *m*; (*minutes: of meeting*) procès-verbal *m*, (*of act, decision*) minute *f*; (*Jur*) enregistrement *m*; (*historical report*) document *m*. **~ of attendance** registre *m* des présences; **the society's ~s** les actes *mpl* de la société; **public ~s** archives *fpl*; **to make** *or* **keep a ~ of sth, to put sth on ~** noter *or* consigner qch; (*fig*) **it is on ~ that ...** il est établi que ...; **there is no similar example on ~** aucun exemple semblable n'est attesté; **to go on ~ as saying that ...** déclarer publiquement que ...; **there is no ~ of his having said** il n'est noté *or* consigné nulle part qu'il ait dit; **to set the ~ straight** dissiper toute confusion possible; **strictly off the ~*** à titre purement confidentiel *or* officieux. **(b)** (*case history*) dossier *m*; (*card*) fiche *f*. **police ~** casier *m* judiciaire; **~ of previous convictions** dossier (*d'un prévenu*); (*Police*) **he's got a clean ~, he hasn't got a ~*** il a un casier judiciaire vierge; **France's splendid ~** les succès glorieux de la France; **his past ~** sa conduite passée; (*Scol*) **his attendance ~ is bad** il a été souvent absent; **a good ~ at school** un bon dossier scolaire; **a good safety ~** une bonne tradition de sécurité. **(c)** (*gramophone ~*) disque *m*. **to make** *or* **cut a ~** graver un disque. **(d)** (*Sport, fig*) record *m*. **to beat** *or* **break the ~** battre le record; **to hold the ~** détenir le record; **long-jump ~** record du saut en longueur.

3 *adj* **(a)** *amount, result* record *inv*. (*Sport*) **~ holder** détenteur *m*, -trice *f* du record; **to do sth in ~ time** faire qch en un temps record. **(b)** (*Mus etc*) *programme, album* de disques. **~ changer** changeur *m* de disques automatique; **~ dealer** disquaire *mf*; **~ library** discothèque *f* (*collection*); **~ player** électrophone *m*; **~ token** chèque-disque *m*. **(c) ~ card** fiche *f*.

♦ **record-breaking** *adj* qui bat tous les records. ♦ **recorded** *adj* **(a)** *music* enregistré; (*Rad*) *programme* enregistré à l'avance; **(b)** *fact, occurrence* attesté, noté; (*Brit Post*) **by ~ed delivery** ≃ avec avis de réception. ♦ **recorder** *n* **(a)** (*tape ~er*) magnétophone *m*; **(b)** (*Jur*) ≃ juge *m* suppléant; **(c)** (*Mus*) flûte *f* à bec. ♦ **recording** 1 *n* *[sound, facts]* enregistrement *m*; (*Rad*) **'this programme is a ~ing'** 'ce programme est enregistré'; 2 *adj artist* qui enregistre; *apparatus* enregistreur; *session, studio* d'enregistrement; (*Rad, TV*) **~ing van** car *m* de reportage.

recount [rɪˈkaʊnt] *vt* (*relate*) raconter.

re-count [ˌriːˈkaʊnt] 1 *vt* recompter. 2 [ˈriːkaʊnt] *n [votes]* deuxième dépouillement *m* du scrutin.

recoup [rɪˈkuːp] *vt* récupérer (*ses pertes*).

recourse [rɪˈkɔːs] *n* recours *m* (*to* à).

recover [rɪˈkʌvəʳ] 1 *vt sth lost, appetite, reason, balance* retrouver; *property* reprendre (*from sb* à qn), récupérer; *lost territory* reconquérir; *sth floating* repêcher; *space capsule, wreck*, (*Ind etc*) *materials* récupérer; *debt, expenses, sight, health* recouvrer; *one's breath, strength, consciousness* reprendre; (*Jur*) *damages* obtenir. **to ~ land from the sea** conquérir du terrain sur la mer; (*fig*) **to ~ lost ground** se rattraper; **to ~ o.s.** *or* **one's composure** se ressaisir; **to ~ one's losses** récupérer ses pertes.

2 *vi* (*after accident, illness*) se rétablir (*from* de); (*regain consciousness*) reprendre connaissance; *[the economy, the dollar]* se redresser; *[stock market]* reprendre; *[shares]* remonter. **she is** *or* **has ~ed** elle est rétablie.

♦ **recovery** *n* **(a)** (*V* **recover 1**) récupération *f*; reconquête *f*; recouvrement *m*; obtention *f*; **(b)** (*V* **recover 2**) rétablissement *m*; redressement *m*; reprise *f*; remontée *f*; (*Med*) **on the way to ~y** en voie de guérison; (*Sport*) **to make a ~y** se ressaisir.

re-cover [ˌriːˈkʌvəʳ] *vt chair etc* recouvrir.

recreation [ˌrekrɪˈeɪʃən] 1 *n* récréation *f*. 2 *adj*: **~ ground** terrain *m* de jeux; **~ room** salle *f* de récréation. ♦ **recreational** *adj* de récréation.

recrimination [rɪˌkrɪmɪˈneɪʃən] *n* récrimination *f*.

recruit [rɪˈkruːt] 1 *n* recrue *f*. 2 *vt* recruter. **to ~ sb to help** embaucher* qn pour aider. ♦ **recruiting** *or* ♦ **recruitment** *n* recrutement *m*.

rectangle [ˈrekˌtæŋgl] *n* rectangle *m*. ♦ **rectangular** *adj* rectangulaire.

rectify [ˈrektɪfaɪ] *vt* rectifier; *omission* réparer.

rectitude [ˈrektɪtjuːd] *n* rectitude *f*.

rector [ˈrektəʳ] *n* (*Rel*) pasteur *m* (*anglican*); *[school]* proviseur *m* (de lycée); (*Univ*) président *m* élu. ♦ **rectory** *n* presbytère *m* (*anglican*).

rectum [ˈrektəm] *n* rectum *m*.

recumbent [rɪˈkʌmbənt] *adj* étendu, couché.

recuperate [rɪˈkuːpəreɪt] 1 *vi* (*Med*) se rétablir. 2 *vt object, losses* récupérer. ♦ **recuperation** *n* (*Med*) rétablissement *m*; *[materials etc]* récupération *f*. ♦ **recuperative** *adj powers* de récupération.

recur [rɪˈkɜːʳ] *vi [error, event]* se reproduire, se répéter; *[theme]* se retrouver, réapparaître; *[illness]* réapparaître; *[opportunity, problem]* se représenter. ♦ **recurrence** *n* répétition *f*; réapparition *f*; **a ~rence of the illness** une rechute. ♦ **recurrent** *adj* fréquent, qui revient souvent. ♦ **recurring** *adj* (*Math*) périodique.

recycle [ˌriːˈsaɪkl] *vt* recycler, récupérer.

red [red] 1 *adj* (*gen, also Pol*) rouge; *hair* roux (*f* rousse). **~ as a beetroot** rouge comme une tomate; **~ in the face** tout rouge; (*fig*) rouge de confusion; **to go** *or* **turn ~** rougir; **to see ~** voir rouge; **like a ~ rag to a bull** comme le rouge pour les taureaux; (*fig*) **to roll out the ~ carpet for sb** recevoir qn en grande pompe; **~ light** feu *m* rouge; (*Aut*) **to go through the ~ light** brûler un feu rouge; (*fig*) **to see the ~ light*** se rendre compte du danger; **R~ Cross** Croix-Rouge *f*; **~ deer** cerf *m* commun; **that's a ~ herring** c'est pour brouiller les pistes; **R~ Indian** Peau-Rouge *mf*; (*fig*) **~ tape** paperasserie *f*, bureaucratie *f* tatillonne.

2 *n* (*colour*) rouge *m*; (*Pol: person*) rouge *mf*. (*fig*) **to be in the ~*** *[individual]* être à découvert; *[company]* être en déficit.

♦ **red-blooded** *adj* vigoureux. ♦ **red-brick university** *n* (*Brit*) université *f* de l'ère industrielle. ♦ **redcurrant** *n* groseille *f* (rouge). ♦ **redden** 1 *vt* rendre rouge; 2 *vi [person]* rougir; *[foliage]* roussir. ♦ **reddish** *adj* rougeâtre; *hair* qui tire sur le roux. ♦ **red-eyed** *adj* aux yeux rouges. ♦ **red-faced** *adj* rougeaud; (*fig*) rouge de confusion. ♦ **red-haired** *or* ♦ **red-headed** *adj* roux. ♦ **red-handed** *adj*: **to be caught ~-handed** être pris en flagrant délit. ♦ **redhead** *n* roux *m*, rousse *f*. ♦ **red-hot** *adj* brûlant. ♦ **red-letter day** *n* jour *m* mémorable. ♦ **red-light district** *n* quartier *m* réservé (*prostitution*). ♦ **redness** *n* rougeur *f*; *[hair]* rousseur *f*. ♦ **redskin** *n* Peau-Rouge *mf*. ♦ **redwood** *n* séquoia *m*.

redeem [rɪˈdiːm] *vt* (*buy back*) racheter; (*from*

pawn) dégager; (*Fin*) *debt* amortir; *mortgage* purger; *promise* tenir; *obligation* s'acquitter de; *sinner, failing* racheter; *fault* réparer. **to ~ o.s.** se racheter. ♦ **Redeemer** *n* Rédempteur *m*. ♦ **redeeming** *adj quality* qui rachète les défauts; **only ~ing feature** seul bon côté. ♦ **redemption** *n* (*Rel*) rédemption *f*.

redirect [ˌriːdaɪˈrekt] *vt letter* faire suivre.

redouble [riːˈdʌbl] *vt* redoubler; (*Bridge*) surcontrer.

redoubtable [rɪˈdaʊtəbl] *adj* redoutable.

redound [rɪˈdaʊnd] *vi* retomber (*upon* sur). **to ~ to sb's credit** être tout à l'honneur de qn.

redress [rɪˈdres] **1** *vt* redresser. **2** *n* réparation *f*.

reduce [rɪˈdjuːs] **1** *vt* (*gen*) réduire (*to/by a certain quantity* à une/d'une certaine quantité), diminuer; *drawing, expenses* réduire; *price* baisser; *speed, voltage, tax* diminuer; (*Med*) *swelling* résorber; *temperature* faire descendre; (*Culin*) *sauce* faire réduire. (*Mil*) **to ~ to the ranks** casser; **to ~ sth to pieces/to ashes** réduire qch en morceaux/en cendres; **to ~ sb to silence/despair** réduire qn au silence/au désespoir; **~d to nothing** réduit à zéro; **he's ~d to a skeleton** il n'est plus qu'un squelette ambulant; **to be ~d to doing** être réduit *or* contraint à faire; **to ~ sb to tears** faire pleurer qn. **2** *vi* (*slim*) maigrir. **to be reducing** être au régime. ♦ **reduced** *adj* réduit; **to buy at a ~d price** *ticket* acheter à prix réduit; *goods* acheter au rabais; (*Comm*) **~d goods** soldes *mpl*; **in ~d circumstances** dans la gêne. ♦ **reduction** [rɪˈdʌkʃən] *n* réduction *f*; diminution *f*; baisse *f*; (*Comm*) **to make a reduction on sth** faire un rabais sur qch; **to sell at a reduction** *ticket* vendre à prix réduit; *goods* vendre au rabais; **reduction for cash** escompte *m* au comptant.

redundant [rɪˈdʌndənt] *adj* (*gen*) superflu; (*Literat etc*) redondant; *helper, worker* en surnombre. (*Ind*) **to be made ~, to become ~** être licencié (pour raisons économiques). ♦ **redundancy 1** *n* excès *m*, superfluité *f*; (*Literat*) redondance *f*; (*Ind*) licenciement *m* (pour raisons économiques); **there is a lot of redundancy** il y a beaucoup de licenciements; **2** *adj*: **redundancy payment** indemnité *f* de licenciement.

reed [riːd] **1** *n* (*Bot*) roseau *m*; *[wind instrument]* anche *f*; (*liter: pipe*) pipeau *m*. (*Mus*) **the ~s** les instruments *mpl* à anche. **2** *adj basket etc* de *or* en roseau(x). ♦ **reedy** *adj instrument, sound* aigu (*f* -guë); *voice* flûté.

reef¹ [riːf] *n* **(a)** récif *m*; (*fig*) écueil *m*. **(b)** (*Min*) filon *m*.

reef² [riːf] **1** *n* (*Naut*) ris *m*. **2** *vt* prendre un ris dans. **3** *adj*: **~ knot** nœud *m* plat. ♦ **reefer** *n* **(a)** (*jacket*) caban *m*; **(b)** (꞉) joint꞉ *m* (*de marijuana*).

reek [riːk] *vi*: **to ~ of sth** puer *or* empester qch.

reel [riːl] **1** *n* **(a)** (*gen*) bobine *f*; (*Fishing*) moulinet *m*; (*Cine*) *[film]* bande *f*. **(b)** (*dance*) reel *m* (*danse écossaise*). **2** *vi* chanceler, vaciller; *[drunken man]* tituber. **to ~ back from** s'écarter en chancelant de; (*fig*) **my head is ~ing** la tête me tourne; **I ~ed at the very thought** cette pensée m'a donné le vertige.

reel in *vt sep* ramener.

reel off *vt sep verses, list* débiter.

re-enact [ˈriːɪˈnækt] *vt scene, crime* reconstituer.

re-enter [ˌriːˈentəʳ] **1** *vi* **(a)** rentrer. **(b) to ~ for an exam** se représenter à un examen. **2** *vt* rentrer dans. ♦ **re-entry** *n* rentrée *f*.

re-examine [ˈriːɪgˈzæmɪn] *vt* examiner de nouveau; (*Jur*) *witness* interroger de nouveau.

ref꞉ [ref] *n* (*Sport: abbr of* **referee**) arbitre *m*.

refectory [rɪˈfektərɪ] *n* réfectoire *m*.

refer [rɪˈfɜːʳ] **1** *vt* (*gen*) soumettre (*to* à). **it was ~red to us for (a) decision** on nous a demandé de prendre une décision là-dessus; **I ~red him to the manager** je lui ai dit de s'adresser au gérant; **to ~ sb to the article on ...** renvoyer qn à l'article sur ...; **to ~ a cheque to drawer** refuser d'honorer un chèque.

2 *vi* **(a)** (*allude*) (*directly*) parler (*to* de); (*indirectly*) faire allusion (*to* à). **we shall not ~ to it again** nous n'en reparlerons pas; (*Comm*) **~ring to your letter** comme suite *or* en réponse à votre lettre. **(b)** (*apply*) s'appliquer (*to* à). **does that ~ to me?** est-ce que cela s'applique à moi? **(c)** (*consult*) **to ~ to sb/sth** consulter qch/qn.

♦ **reference** [ˈrefrəns] **1** *n* **(a)** (*allusion*) (*direct*) mention *f* (*to* de), (*indirect*) allusion *f* (*to* à); (*connection*) rapport *m* (*to* avec); **this has no ~ence to ...** cela n'a aucun rapport avec ...; **with ~ence to** en ce qui concerne, (*Comm*) comme suite à; **without ~ence to** sans tenir compte de; **(b)** (*testimonial*) **~ence(s)** références *fpl*; **to give sb a good ~ence** fournir de bonnes références à qn; **to give a ~ence for sb** fournir des renseignements sur qn; **to give sb as a ~ence** donner qn en référence; **(c)** (*in book, on letter*) référence *f*; (*on map*) coordonnées *fpl*; **2** *adj number, point* de référence; **~ence book** ouvrage *m* de référence *or* à consulter; **~ence library** bibliothèque *f* d'ouvrages à consulter.

referee [ˌrefəˈriː] **1** *n* **(a)** (*Sport, fig*) arbitre *m*. **(b) to be ~ for sb** fournir des références à qn; **to give sb as a ~** donner qn en référence. **2** *vt* arbitrer. **3** *vi* être arbitre.

referendum [ˌrefəˈrendəm] *n, pl* **-enda**: **to hold a ~** organiser un référendum.

refill [ˌriːˈfɪl] **1** *vt* (*gen*) remplir à nouveau; *pen, lighter* recharger. **2** [ˈriːfɪl] *n [ballpoint, lipstick]* recharge *f*; *[propelling pencil]* mine *f* de rechange; *[cartridge pen]* cartouche *f*; *[notebook]* feuilles *fpl* de rechange.

refine [rɪˈfaɪn] **1** *vt ore, taste* affiner; *oil, sugar* raffiner; *machine, technique* perfectionner. **2** *vi* s'affiner. **to ~ upon sth** raffiner sur qch. ♦ **refined** *adj* (*gen*) raffiné; *ore* affiné. ♦ **refinement** *n* **(a)** *[person, language]* raffinement *m*; **(b)** (*in machine*) perfectionnement *m* (*in* de). ♦ **refiner** *n* raffineur *m*. ♦ **refinery** *n* raffinerie *f*; **oil ~ry** raffinerie de pétrole.

refit [ˌriːˈfɪt] **1** *vt* (*Naut*) remettre en état. **2** [ˈriːfɪt] *n* remise *f* en état.

reflate [ˌriːˈfleɪt] *vt* (*Econ*) relancer. ♦ **reflation** *n* relance *f*. ♦ **reflationary** *adj* de relance.

reflect [rɪˈflekt] **1** *vt* **(a)** *heat, sound* renvoyer; *light, image* refléter; *[mirror]* réfléchir; (*fig: show*) refléter; *credit, discredit* faire rejaillir (*on* sur). **the moon is ~ed in the lake** la lune se reflète dans le lac; **I saw him ~ed in the mirror** j'ai vu son image dans le miroir *or* réfléchie par le miroir; **this is ~ed in his report** son rapport reflète cela. **(b)** (*think*) se dire, penser (*that* que). **2** *vi* **(a)** (*meditate*) réfléchir, méditer (*on* sur). **(b)** (*discredit*) **to ~ (up)on** *person* faire tort à; *reputation* nuire à; *motives, reasons* discréditer. ♦ **reflection** *n* **(a)** (*act*) réflexion *f*; (*in mirror etc*) reflet *m*; **(b)** (*thought*) réflexion *f* (*on* sur); **on ~ion** réflexion faite; **~ions** pensées *fpl*, réflexions *fpl* (*on, upon* sur); **(c)** (*adverse criticism*) réflexion désobligeante (*on* sur); (*on sb's honour*) atteinte *f* (*on* à); **to be a ~ion on sb/sth** discréditer qn/qch.

♦ **reflector** *n* réflecteur *m*.

reflex [ˈriːfleks] **1** *n* réflexe *m*. **2** *adj* (*gen*) réflexe; (*Math*) *angle* rentrant. **~ camera** (appareil *m*) reflex *m*.

reflexion [rɪˈflekʃən] *n* = **reflection.**

reflexive [rɪˈfleksɪv] **1** *adj* réfléchi. **2** *n* verbe *m* réfléchi.

refloat [ˌriːˈfləʊt] *vt* renflouer.

reform [rɪˈfɔːm] **1** *n* réforme *f*. **2** *adj measures* de réforme. **3** *vt* réformer. **4** *vi [person]* s'amender.

♦ **reformation** *n* réforme *f*. ♦ **reformed** *adj* (*gen*) réformé; *behaviour, person* amendé. ♦ **reformer** *n* réformateur *m*, -trice *f*.

refrain[1] [rɪ'freɪn] *vi* s'abstenir (*from sth* de qch; *from doing* de faire). **I couldn't ~ from laughing** je n'ai pas pu m'empêcher de rire.

refrain[2] [rɪ'freɪn] *n* (*Mus etc*) refrain *m*.

refresh [rɪ'freʃ] *vt [drink, bath]* rafraîchir; *[food, sleep]* redonner des forces à; (*fig*) *memory* rafraîchir. ♦ **refresher** *adj course* de recyclage. ♦ **refreshing** *adj fruit, drink* rafraîchissant; *sleep* réparateur (*f* -trice); *sight, news* réconfortant; *change* agréable; *idea, approach, point of view* nouveau. ♦ **refreshment 1** *n*: **~ments** rafraîchissements *mpl*; **2** *adj*: **~ment bar** buvette *f*; (*Rail*) **~ment room** buffet *m*.

refrigerate [rɪ'frɪdʒəreɪt] *vt* réfrigérer. ♦ **refrigeration** *n* réfrigération *f*. ♦ **refrigerator** *n* réfrigérateur *m*, frigidaire *m* ®.

refuel ['riː'fjʊəl] **1** *vi* se ravitailler en carburant. **2** *vt* ravitailler. ♦ **refuelling** *n* ravitaillement *m* en carburant; (*Aviat*) **~ling stop** escale *f* technique.

refuge ['refjuːdʒ] *n* (*lit, fig*) refuge *m* (*from* contre). **place of ~** asile *m*; (*lit, fig*) **to take ~ in** se réfugier dans. ♦ **refugee 1** *n* réfugié(e) *m(f)*; **2** *adj camp* de réfugiés.

refund [rɪ'fʌnd] **1** *vt cost, postage* rembourser (*to sb* à qn). **to ~ sb's expenses** rembourser qn de ses frais. **2** ['riːfʌnd] *n* remboursement *m*. **to get a ~** se faire rembourser.

refurbish [ˌriː'fɜːbɪʃ] *vt* remettre à neuf.

refuse[1] [rɪ'fjuːz] **1** *vt* refuser (*sb sth* qch à qn; *to do* de faire), se refuser (*to do* à faire); *offer, candidate* refuser; *request, marriage proposal, suitor* rejeter. **they were ~d permission to do** on leur a refusé la permission de faire. **2** *vi* refuser. ♦ **refusal** *n* refus *m* (*to do* de faire); **to give sb first refusal of sth** accorder à qn l'option sur qch.

refuse[2] ['refjuːs] **1** *n* détritus *mpl*, ordures *fpl*; (*industrial or food waste*) déchets *mpl*. **household ~** ordures ménagères; **garden ~** détritus de jardin. **2** *adj*: **~ bin** poubelle *f*, boîte *f* à ordures; **~ collection** ramassage *m* d'ordures; **~ collector** éboueur *m*; **~ disposal** traitement *m* des ordures; **~ disposal service** service *m* de voirie; **~ dump** (*public*) décharge *f* (publique); **~ lorry** voiture *f* d'éboueurs.

refute [rɪ'fjuːt] *vt* réfuter. ♦ **refutation** *n* réfutation *f*.

regain [rɪ'geɪn] *vt* (*gen*) regagner; *health, one's sight* recouvrer; *territory* reconquérir. **to ~ consciousness** reprendre connaissance; **to ~ possession** rentrer en possession (*of* de).

regal ['riːgəl] *adj* royal; (*fig*) majestueux.

regale [rɪ'geɪl] *vt* régaler (*sb with sth* qn de qch).

regard [rɪ'gɑːd] **1** *vt* **(a)** (*consider*) considérer, regarder (*as* comme). **we ~ it as worth doing** à notre avis ça vaut la peine de le faire. **(b)** (*concern*) concerner, regarder. **as ~s ...** pour *or* en ce qui concerne ... . **2** *n* **(a)** (*concern*) **to have** *or* **show little ~ for** faire peu de cas de; **to have** *or* **show no ~ for** ne faire aucun cas de; **without ~ to** *or* **for** sans égard pour; **out of ~ for** par égard pour; **in this ~** à cet égard; **with** *or* **in ~ to** relativement à. **(b)** (*esteem*) estime *f*. **to have a great ~ for sb** avoir beaucoup d'estime pour qn. **(c)** (*in messages*) **give him my ~s** faites-lui mes amitiés; **Paul sends his (kind) ~s** Paul vous fait ses amitiés; (*as letter-ending*) **(kindest) ~s** amicalement. ♦ **regarding** *prep* relativement à. ♦ **regardless 1** *adj*: **~less of** *sb's feelings, fate* indifférent à; *future, danger* insouciant de; *consequences, cost* sans se soucier de; *rank* sans distinction de; **2** *adv*: **he did it ~less*** il l'a fait quand même.

regatta [rɪ'gætə] *n* régates *fpl*.

regenerate [rɪ'dʒenəreɪt] **1** *vt* régénérer. **2** *vi* se régénérer. ♦ **regeneration** *n* régénération *f*.

regent ['riːdʒənt] *n* régent(e) *m(f)*. **prince ~** prince *m* régent. ♦ **regency 1** *n* régence *f*; **2** *adj*: **Regency** Régence *inv*.

reggae ['regeɪ] *n* reggae *m*.

régime [reɪ'ʒiːm] *n* régime *m* (*politique etc*).

regiment ['redʒɪmənt] *n* régiment *m*. ♦ **regimental** *adj* du régiment. ♦ **regimentation** *n* (*pej*) discipline *f* excessive. ♦ **regimented** *adj* soumis à une discipline excessive.

region ['riːdʒən] *n* (*all senses*) région *f*. (*fig*) **in the ~ of** environ, aux alentours de. ♦ **regional** *adj* régional; (*Brit Admin*) **~al development** ≃ aménagement *m* du territoire.

register ['redʒɪstə^r] **1** *n* **(a)** (*gen*) registre *m*; (*of members etc*) liste *f*. **electoral ~** liste électorale; **~ of births, marriages and deaths** registre d'état civil. **(b)** (*Tech*) compteur *m*. **cash ~** caisse *f* (enregistreuse).

2 *vt* **(a)** (*record*) *fact, figure* enregistrer; *birth, death* déclarer; *vehicle* (faire) immatriculer; *trademark* déposer; *one's disappointment etc* exprimer. **~ed as disabled** officiellement reconnu comme handicapé; **to ~ a protest** protester. **(b)** (*take note of*) *fact* enregistrer; (*: *realize*) réaliser* (*that* que), se rendre compte de. **(c)** (*indicate*) *speed, quantity* enregistrer, indiquer. **he ~ed no emotion** il n'a pas paru ému. **(d)** (*Post*) *letter* recommander; (*Rail*) *luggage* faire enregistrer (*to* jusqu'à).

3 *vi* **(a)** (*gen*) s'inscrire; (*in hotel*) signer le registre. **to ~ with a doctor** se faire inscrire comme patient chez un médecin; **to ~ with the police** se déclarer à la police; **to ~ for military service** se faire recenser; **to ~ for a course** s'inscrire à un cours. **(b)** (*: *be understood*) être compris, pénétrer. **it hasn't ~ed (with him)** cela n'a pas encore pénétré, il n'a pas saisi. ♦ **registered** *adj* **(a)** *student, voter* inscrit; *vehicle* immatriculé; *name, trademark* déposé; *nursing home, charity* reconnu par les autorités; (*US*) **~ed nurse** infirmière *f* diplômée d'État; **(b)** *letter* recommandé; *luggage* enregistré; **by ~ed post** par envoi recommandé. ♦ **registrar** *n* (*Admin*) officier *m* de l'état civil; (*Jur: in court*) greffier *m*; (*Univ*) secrétaire *m* (général); (*Med*) interne *mf*. ♦ **registration 1** *n* enregistrement *m*; déclaration *f*; inscription *f*; *[letter]* recommandation *f*; *[luggage]* enregistrement; (*Scol*) **during registration (period)** ≃ pendant l'appel *m*; **2** *adj*: **registration fee** (*Post*) taxe *f* de recommandation; (*Univ*) droits *mpl* d'inscription; (*Aut*) **registration number** numéro *m* d'immatriculation; **car (with) registration number X** voiture immatriculée X; **a T-registration car** *immatriculation indiquant l'année de fabrication d'une voiture*. ♦ **registry office** *n* (*Brit*) bureau *m* de l'état civil; **to get married in a registry office** se marier civilement *or* à la mairie.

regress [rɪ'gres] *vi* régresser (*to* à). ♦ **regression** *n* régression *f*.

regret [rɪ'gret] **1** *vt* regretter (*doing, to do* de faire; *that* que +*subj*). **he is very ill, I ~ to say** il est très malade, hélas; **we ~ to hear that ...** nous sommes désolés d'apprendre que ...; **it is to be ~ted that ...** il est regrettable que ... +*subj*. **2** *n* regret *m* (*for* de). **much to my ~** à mon grand regret; **I have no ~s** je ne regrette rien. ♦ **regretful** *adj person* plein de regrets; *look* de regret. ♦ **regretfully** *adv* (*sadly*) avec regret; (*unwillingly*) à regret. ♦ **regrettable** *adj* regrettable (*that* que +*subj*). ♦ **regrettably** *adv late, poor* fâcheusement; **~tably, he ...** malheureusement, il ... .

regroup [ˌriː'gruːp] *vi* se regrouper.

regular ['regjʊlə^r] **1** *adj* **(a)** (*gen*) *pulse, shape, verb, employment, reminders* régulier. **at ~ intervals** à intervalles réguliers; **a ~ bus service to town** un service régulier d'autobus allant en ville; **he is as ~ as clockwork** il est très ponctuel;

visits as ~ as clockwork visites très régulières. **(b)** (*in order*) *action, procedure* régulier, en règle; (*habitual*) habituel; (*Comm*) *size* standard *inv*; *price* normal; *listener, reader* fidèle; *staff* permanent; (*not conscript*) *soldier, army* de métier, *officer* de carrière; (*not territorial*) d'active. **his ~ time for getting up** l'heure à laquelle il se lève habituellement; **it is quite ~ to do so** il est tout à fait régulier de faire cela; **a ~ idiot** un véritable imbécile; (*US*) **~ guy*** chic type* *m*. **2** *n* (*Mil*) soldat *m* de métier; (*habitual customer etc*) habitué(e) *m(f)*. (*Rad, TV*) **he's one of the ~s on that programme** il participe régulièrement à ce programme. ♦ **regularity** *n* régularité *f*. ♦ **regularize** *vt* régulariser. ♦ **regularly** *adv* régulièrement. ♦ **regulate** *vt* régler (*by* sur). ♦ **regulation 1** *n* règlement *m*; **2** *adj* réglementaire. ♦ **regulator** *n* régulateur *m*.

rehabilitate [ˌriːəˈbɪlɪteɪt] *vt the disabled* (*to everyday life*) rééduquer, (*to work*) réadapter; *refugees* réadapter; *demobilized troops* réintégrer (dans la vie civile); *disgraced person* réhabiliter. ♦ **rehabilitation** *n* rééducation *f*; réadaptation *f*; réintégration *f* (dans la vie civile); réhabilitation *f*; (*Admin*) **rehabilitation centre** centre *m* de rééducation (professionnelle).

rehash [ˌriːˈhæʃ] **1** *vt literary material etc* remanier. **2** [ˈriːhæʃ] *n* réchauffé *m*.

rehearse [rɪˈhɜːs] *vt* (*Theat*) répéter; *what one is going to say* préparer; *facts, grievances* énumérer. ♦ **rehearsal** *n* répétition *f*; **dress rehearsal** (répétition) générale *f*; **this play is in rehearsal** on répète cette pièce.

rehouse [ˌriːˈhaʊz] *vt* reloger.

reign [reɪn] **1** *n* règne *m*. **in the ~ of** sous le règne de; (*fig*) **~ of terror** régime *m* de terreur. **2** *vi* (*lit, fig*) régner. **to ~ supreme** *[champion etc]* être sans rival; *[justice, peace]* régner en souverain(e). ♦ **reigning** *adj* régnant.

reimburse [ˌriːɪmˈbɜːs] *vt* rembourser (*sb for sth* qn de qch). ♦ **reimbursement** *n* remboursement *m*.

rein [reɪn] *n* (*gen*) rêne *f*; *[horse in harness]* guide *f*. (*lit, fig*) **to hold the ~s** tenir les rênes; (*fig*) **to keep a tight ~ on** surveiller étroitement; **to give free ~ to** lâcher la bride à.
rein in *vt sep* serrer la bride à.

reincarnation [ˈriːɪnkɑːˈneɪʃən] *n* réincarnation *f*.

reindeer [ˈreɪndɪəʳ] *n, pl inv* renne *m*.

reinforce [ˌriːɪnˈfɔːs] *vt army, structure, wall* renforcer; *one's demands etc* appuyer. **~d concrete** béton *m* armé. ♦ **reinforcement 1** *n* (*action*) renforcement *m*; (*thing*) armature *f*; (*Mil, fig*) **~ments** renforts *mpl*; **2** *adj troops* de renfort.

reinstate [ˈriːɪnˈsteɪt] *vt* rétablir (*in* dans). ♦ **reinstatement** *n* rétablissement *m*.

reissue [ˌriːˈɪʃjuː] *vt book* rééditer; *film* ressortir.

reiterate [riːˈɪtəreɪt] *vt* réitérer. ♦ **reiteration** *n* réitération *f*.

reject [rɪˈdʒekt] **1** *vt* (*gen*) rejeter; *damaged goods etc [customer, shopkeeper]* refuser, *[producer]* mettre au rebut; *candidate, manuscript* refuser; (*Med*) *[body]* rejeter. **2** [ˈriːdʒekt] *n* (*Comm*) article *m* de rebut. **3** [ˈriːdʒekt] *adj goods* de rebut. **~ shop** magasin *m* de deuxième choix. ♦ **rejection 1** *n* rejet *m*; refus *m*; **2** *adj*: **~ion slip** lettre *f* de refus.

rejoice [rɪˈdʒɔɪs] *vi* se réjouir, être enchanté (*at, over* de). **to ~ in sth** jouir de qch, posséder qch. ♦ **rejoicing** *n* réjouissances *fpl*.

rejoin[1] [ˌriːˈdʒɔɪn] *vt* (*gen*) rejoindre. **to ~ ship** rallier le bord.

rejoin[2] [rɪˈdʒɔɪn] *vi* (*reply*) répliquer. ♦ **rejoinder** *n* réplique *f*.

rejuvenate [rɪˈdʒuːvɪneɪt] *vti* rajeunir.

rekindle [ˌriːˈkɪndl] *vt fire* rallumer; *enthusiasm* raviver.

relapse [rɪˈlæps] **1** *n* rechute *f*. **to have a ~** faire une rechute. **2** *vi* (*gen*) retomber (*into* dans); *[invalid]* rechuter.

relate [rɪˈleɪt] **1** *vt* **(a)** (*recount*) *story* raconter, relater; *details* rapporter. **strange to ~ ...** chose curieuse (à dire) ... . **(b)** (*link*) rattacher (*sth to sth* qch à qch); *two facts etc* établir un rapport entre. **to ~ the cause to the effect** établir un rapport de cause à effet. **2** *vi* se rapporter (*to* à). ♦ **related** *adj* (*in family*) parent (*to* de); (*connected*) *ideas, subjects* liés, connexes; *substances, languages* apparentés; *[person]* **to be closely/distantly ~d** être proche parent/parent éloigné. ♦ **relating to** *prep* relatif à.

relation [rɪˈleɪʃən] *n* **(a)** (*relationship*) rapport *m*, relation *f*. **to bear a ~ to** avoir rapport à; **in ~ to** relativement à; **to have business ~s with** être en rapports *or* relations d'affaires avec; **diplomatic/international ~s** relations diplomatiques/internationales; **sexual ~s** rapports sexuels. **(b)** (*family: person*) parent(e) *m(f)*; (*kinship*) parenté *f*. **to be a ~ of sb's, to be some ~ to sb** avoir des liens de parenté avec qn. ♦ **relationship** *n* **(a)** (*family ties*) liens *mpl* de parenté; **what is your ~ship to him?** quels sont vos liens de parenté avec lui?; **(b)** (*connection: between 2 things*) rapport *m* (*between* entre); (*with sb*) relations *fpl*; (*personal ties*) rapports; **to see a ~ship between** voir un rapport *or* un lien entre; **friendly/business ~ship** relations d'amitié/d'affaires; **to have a ~ship with sb** (*general*) avoir des relations avec qn; (*sexual*) avoir une liaison avec qn; **he has a good ~ship with his clients** il est en bons rapports avec ses clients; **they have a good ~ship** ils s'entendent bien.

relative [ˈrelətɪv] **1** *adj* (*gen*) relatif (*to* à). **the ~ merits of A and B** les mérites respectifs de A et de B. **2** *n* (*person*) parent(e) *m(f)*; (*Gram*) relatif *m*. ♦ **relatively** *adv* relativement; respectivement; (*fairly, rather*) assez. ♦ **relativity** *n* relativité *f*.

relax [rɪˈlæks] **1** *vt* (*gen*) relâcher; *muscles* décontracter; *restrictions* modérer; *person, one's mind* détendre. **2** *vi [sb's hold]* se relâcher; (*rest*) se détendre. (*calm down*) **~!*** du calme! ♦ **relaxation** [ˌriːlækˈseɪʃən] *n* détente *f*. ♦ **relaxed** *adj* (*gen*) relâché; *person, voice* détendu; (*Med*) **~ed throat** gorge *f* irritée *or* enflammée. ♦ **relaxing** *adj climate* reposant, amollissant (*pej*); *atmosphere, activity* qui procure de la détente.

relay [ˈriːleɪ] **1** *n* (*gen*) relais *m*. **in ~s** par relais; **~ race** course *f* de relais. **2** *vt* relayer. **to ~ each other** se relayer.

release [rɪˈliːs] **1** *n* **(a)** (*gen*) libération *f*; (*from Customs*) congé *m*. **on his ~ from prison he ...** dès sa sortie de prison, il ... . **(b)** *[news]* autorisation *f* de publier; *[film, book, record]* sortie *f*. **this film is now on general ~** ce film n'est plus en exclusivité. **(c)** (*record/film etc*) **new ~** nouveau disque/film *etc*; **his latest ~** son dernier disque *etc*. **2** *vt* **(a)** (*set free*) (*gen*) libérer (*from* de); (*Jur*) remettre en liberté; (*from wreckage*) dégager (*from* de); (*from promise, vow*) relever (*from* de). **his employer agreed to ~ him** son patron lui a permis de cesser son travail; (*temporarily*) son patron a accepté de le rendre disponible. **(b)** (*let go*) *object, pigeon* lâcher; *bomb* larguer; *gas* dégager. **to ~ one's hold of** *or* **one's grip on sth** lâcher qch. **(c)** (*issue*) *book, record, film* sortir; *goods* mettre en vente; *news* autoriser la publication de; *statement* publier. **(d)** *clasp, catch* faire jouer; (*Phot*) *shutter* déclencher; *handbrake* desserrer.

relegate [ˈrelɪgeɪt] *vt* reléguer (*to* à; *Sport: to* en). ♦ **relegation** *n* relégation *f*.

relent [rɪˈlent] *vi* se laisser fléchir; (*change one's mind*) changer d'avis. ♦ **relentless** *adj* implacable. ♦ **relentlessly** *adv* implacablement.

relevant ['reləvənt] *adj remark, fact* pertinent (*to* à); *regulation, reference* approprié (*to* à); *information, course* utile. **to be ~ to sth** avoir rapport à qch; **that is not ~** c'est sans rapport.

reliable [rɪ'laɪəbl] *adj person, employee* sérieux, sur qui l'on peut compter; *firm, company* sérieux; *machine* solide; *memory, description* bon, auquel on peut se fier. **a ~ source of information** une source sûre. ♦ **reliability** *n [person, character]* sérieux *m*; *[device, machine]* solidité *f*. ♦ **reliably** *adv work* sérieusement; *informed* de source sûre.

reliant [rɪ'laɪənt] *adj* (*trusting*) confiant (*on* en); (*dependent*) dépendant (*on* de). ♦ **reliance** *n* confiance *f*; dépendance *f*.

relic ['relɪk] *n* relique *f* (*also Rel*). **~s** restes *mpl*; (*fig: of the past*) vestiges *mpl*.

relief [rɪ'li:f] **1** *n* **(a)** (*from pain, anxiety*) soulagement *m* (*from* à). **to my ~** à mon grand soulagement; **that's a ~!** quel soulagement!; **it was a ~ to find it** j'ai été soulagé de le retrouver. **(b)** (*assistance*) secours *m*. **to go to the ~ of** aller au secours de. **(c)** (*Mil*) *[town]* délivrance *f*. **(d)** (*tax* ~) dégrèvement *m*. **(e)** (*Art, Geog*) relief *m*. **to throw sth into ~** mettre qch en relief. **2** *adj* **(a)** *coach, typist* supplémentaire; *fund, work, organization, troops* de secours; *valve* de sûreté. **~ road** route *f* de délestage; **~ supplies** secours *mpl*. **(b)** *map* en relief.

relieve [rɪ'li:v] *vt* **(a)** *person, anxiety, pain* soulager; *fear, boredom* dissiper; *poverty, situation* remédier à. **to be ~d to learn** être soulagé d'apprendre; **to ~ sb of his coat** débarrasser qn de son manteau; **to ~ sb of a duty** décharger qn d'une obligation; (*Mil*) **to ~ sb of a command** relever qn de ses fonctions; **to ~ sb's mind** tranquilliser qn; **he ~d his feelings** il a déchargé sa colère; **to ~ congestion in sth** décongestionner qch; (*go to lavatory*) **to ~ o.s.** faire ses besoins*. **(b)** (*help*) secourir, aider; (*take over from*) relayer; (*Mil*) *guard* relever; *town* délivrer.

religion [rɪ'lɪdʒən] *n* (*gen*) religion *f*. **the Christian ~** la religion chrétienne; **a new ~** un nouveau culte; **it's against my ~** c'est contraire à ma religion (*to do* de faire); **to get ~*** devenir bigot.

religious [rɪ'lɪdʒəs] **1** *adj* (*gen*) religieux (*also fig*); *person* pieux (*also pej*), croyant; *book* de piété; *wars* de religion. **2** *n* religieux *m*, -ieuse *f*. ♦ **religiously** *adv* religieusement.

relinquish [rɪ'lɪŋkwɪʃ] *vt object* lâcher; (*give up: gen*) abandonner; *plan, right* renoncer à (*to sb* en faveur de qn); *habit* renoncer à. **to ~ one's hold on sth** lâcher qch.

reliquary ['relɪkwərɪ] *n* reliquaire *m*.

relish ['relɪʃ] **1** *n* goût *m* (*for* pour). **with great ~** *do sth* avec délectation; *eat* de bon appétit; (*fig*) **it had lost all ~** cela avait perdu tout attrait. **2** *vt food, wine* savourer. **to ~ doing** se délecter à faire; **I don't ~ the thought** l'idée ne me dit rien.

reluctant [rɪ'lʌktənt] *adj person* peu disposé (*to do* à faire), peu enthousiaste; *action* fait *etc* à contrecœur; *consent, praise* accordé à contrecœur. ♦ **reluctance** *n* répugnance *f* (*to do* à faire). ♦ **reluctantly** *adv* à contrecœur, sans enthousiasme.

rely [rɪ'laɪ] *vi*: **to ~ (up)on sb/sth** compter sur qn/qch; **to ~ on sb's doing sth** compter sur le fait que qn fera qch; **I ~ on him for my income** je dépends de lui pour mes revenus; **you can ~ on me not to say anything about it** vous pouvez compter sur moi pour ne pas en parler.

remain [rɪ'meɪn] *vi* rester. **nothing ~s to be said** il ne reste plus rien à dire; **it ~s to be seen whether** ... reste à savoir si ...; **that ~s to be seen** c'est ce que nous verrons; **the fact ~s that** il n'en est pas moins vrai que; **to ~ faithful** demeurer *or* rester fidèle; **to ~ behind** rester; **to ~ silent** garder le silence; **it ~s unsolved** ce n'est toujours pas résolu; (*in letters*) **I ~, yours faithfully** je vous prie d'agréer l'expression de mes sentiments distingués. ♦ **remainder** *n* (*thing or things left over*) reste *m* (*also Math*); (*people*) autres *mfpl*; **~ders** (*Comm*) (*books etc*) invendus *mpl* soldés; (*other articles*) fins *fpl* de série. ♦ **remaining** *adj* qui reste; **I have one ~ing** il n'en reste qu'un; **the ~ing cakes** le reste des gâteaux, les gâteaux qui restent. ♦ **remains** *npl* (*gen*) restes *mpl*; *[fortune, army]* débris *mpl*.

remake ['ri:meɪk] *n* (*Cine*) remake *m*.

remand [rɪ'mɑ:nd] **1** *vt* (*Jur*) renvoyer (*to* à). **to ~ in custody** renvoyer avec détention provisoire. **2** *n*: **on ~** en détention préventive; **~ home** ≃ maison *f* d'arrêt.

remark [rɪ'mɑ:k] **1** *n* remarque *f*, réflexion *f*. **worthy of ~** digne d'attention. **2** *vt* **(a)** (*say*) (faire) remarquer. **(b)** (*notice*) remarquer, observer. **3** *vi* faire des remarques (*on* sur). ♦ **remarkable** *adj* remarquable (*for* par). ♦ **remarkably** *adv* remarquablement.

remarry ['ri:'mærɪ] *vi* se remarier.

remedy ['remədɪ] **1** *n* remède *m* (*for* contre). **2** *vt* remédier à. ♦ **remedial** [rɪ'mi:dɪəl] *adj action* réparateur; *measures* de redressement; (*Med*) *treatment* curatif; *class* de rattrapage; **remedial exercises** gymnastique *f* corrective.

remember [rɪ'membə^r] *vt* (*gen*) se souvenir de, se rappeler; (*commemorate*) *a battle, the fallen* commémorer. **to ~ that** se rappeler que; **I ~ doing it** je me rappelle l'avoir fait; **I ~ed to do it** j'ai pensé à le faire; **that's worth ~ing** c'est bon à savoir; **I can't ~ everything** je ne peux pas penser à tout; **I ~ when ...** je me souviens de l'époque où ...; **I can't ~** je ne sais plus, je ne me souviens pas; **as far as I ~** autant qu'il m'en souvienne; **if I ~ right(ly)** si j'ai bonne mémoire; **don't you ~ me?** (*face to face*) vous ne me reconnaissez pas?; (*phone*) vous ne vous souvenez pas de moi?; **I don't ~ a thing about it** je ne me souviens de rien; **let us ~ that ...** n'oublions pas que ...; **sth to ~ him by** un souvenir de lui; **to ~ o.s.** se reprendre; **to ~ sb in one's prayers** ne pas oublier qn dans ses prières; **~ me to your mother** rappelez-moi au bon souvenir de votre mère. ♦ **remembrance** *n* souvenir *m*; **Remembrance Day** l'Armistice *m*, le 11 novembre; **in remembrance of** en souvenir de.

remind [rɪ'maɪnd] *vt* rappeler (*sb of sth* qch à qn, *sb that* à qn que). **you are ~ed that ...** nous vous rappelons que ...; **to ~ sb to do** faire penser à qn à faire; **she ~ed him of his mother** elle lui rappelait sa mère; **that ~s me!** à propos! ♦ **reminder** *n* (*note etc*) pense-bête *m*; (*Comm: letter*) lettre *f* de rappel; **as a ~er that** pour (vous *etc*) rappeler que; **to be a ~er of sth/sb** rappeler qch/qn.

reminisce [ˌremɪ'nɪs] *vi* raconter ses souvenirs (*about* de). ♦ **reminiscence** *n* réminiscence *f*. ♦ **reminiscent** *adj*: **reminiscent of** qui rappelle, qui fait penser à. ♦ **reminiscently** *adv smile* à ce souvenir; **to talk reminiscently of** évoquer des souvenirs de.

remiss [rɪ'mɪs] *adj* négligent. **he was ~ in not doing it** c'est négligent de sa part de ne pas l'avoir fait.

remission [rɪ'mɪʃən] *n* (*gen, Med, Rel*) rémission *f*; (*Jur*) remise *f* (*for* pour).

remit [rɪ'mɪt] *vt* **(a)** *sins* pardonner; *fee, penalty* remettre. **(b)** (*send*) *money* envoyer. **(c)** (*Jur*) *case* renvoyer. ♦ **remittal** *n* (*Jur*) renvoi *m*. ♦ **remittance** *n* (*sending*) envoi *m* (*de fonds*); (*money sent*) versement *m*; **enclose your ~tance** joignez le paiement.

remnant ['remnənt] **1** *n* (*gen*) reste *m*, restant *m*; *[cloth]* coupon *m*; *[custom, splendour]* vestige *m*; *[food, fortune, army]* débris *mpl*. (*Comm*) **~s** soldes *mpl* (de fins de série). **2** *adj*: **~ sale** soldes *mpl* (de coupons).

remonstrate ['remənstreɪt] *vti* protester (*against* contre; *that* que). **to ~ with sb about sth** faire des remontrances à qn au sujet de qch. ♦ **remonstrance** *n* (*protest*) protestation *f*; (*reproof*) remontrance *f*.

remorse [rɪ'mɔːs] *n* remords *m* (*at* de; *for* pour). **a feeling of ~** un remords; **without ~** sans pitié. ♦ **remorseful** *adj* plein de remords. ♦ **remorsefully** *adv* avec remords. ♦ **remorseless** *adj* dénué de remords; (*fig*) implacable. ♦ **remorselessly** *adv* sans remords; implacablement.

remote [rɪ'məʊt] *adj* **(a)** *place* (*distant*) lointain, éloigné; (*isolated*) isolé; *time* lointain; *ancestor, relative* éloigné; *person* distant. **~ control** télécommande *f*; **in the ~st parts of Africa** au fin fond de l'Afrique; **~ from a main road** loin d'une grande route; **~ from the subject in hand** éloigné de la question. **(b)** (*slight*) *resemblance* vague; *possibility* petit. **not the ~st idea/hope** pas la moindre idée/le moindre espoir; **there is a ~ possibility that** il y a une petite chance que + *subj*. ♦ **remote-controlled** *adj* télécommandé. ♦ **remotely** *adv* (*slightly*) vaguement; **~ly possible** tout juste possible. ♦ **remoteness** *n* (*in space*) éloignement *m*, isolement *m*; (*in time*) éloignement; *[person]* attitude *f* distante.

remould ['riːməʊld] *n* (*tyre*) pneu *m* rechapé.

remove [rɪ'muːv] **1** *vt* (*gen, also Med*) enlever (*from* de); *[removers]* déménager; *stain, graffiti* enlever, faire partir; *word, item on list* rayer; *threat, abuse* supprimer; *objection* réfuter; *difficulty, problem* résoudre; *obstacle, doubt* écarter; *suspicion, fear* dissiper; *official* déplacer. **he was ~d to the cells** on l'a emmené en cellule; **to ~ a child from school** retirer un enfant de l'école; **to ~ sb's name** rayer qn (*from* de); **to ~ one's make-up** se démaquiller; (*fig*) **far ~d from** loin de; **cousin once ~d** cousin(e) *m(f)* au deuxième degré. **2** *vi* déménager (*from* de). **to ~ to London** aller s'installer à Londres. **3** *n* (*fig*) **only a few ~s from** tout proche de; **it's a far ~ from ...** c'est loin d'être ... . ♦ **removable** *adj* (*detachable*) *part, piece* amovible, détachable. ♦ **removal** **1** *n* enlèvement *m*; déménagement *m*; suppression *f*; *[pain]* soulagement *m*; (*Surgery*) ablation *f*; **2** *adj allowance, expenses* de déménagement; **removal man** déménageur *m*; **removal van** camion *m* de déménagement. ♦ **remover** *n* **(a)** (*removal man*) déménageur *m*; **(b)** *[varnish]* dissolvant *m*; *[stains]* détachant *m*; *[paint]* décapant *m*; **make-up ~r** démaquillant *m*.

remunerate [rɪ'mjuːnəreɪt] *vt* rémunérer. ♦ **remuneration** *n* rémunération *f* (*for* de). ♦ **remunerative** *adj* rémunérateur.

renaissance [rɪ'neɪsɑ̃ːns] **1** *n* renaissance *f*. **2** *adj*: **R~** *art, scholar* de la Renaissance; *style, palace* Renaissance *inv*.

renal ['riːnl] *adj* rénal.

render ['rendəʳ] *vt* **(a)** *service, homage* rendre; *assistance* prêter; *account* présenter. **to account ~ed £10** facture de rappel - 10 livres. **(b)** *music* interpréter; *text* traduire (*into* en). **(c)** (*make*) rendre. **it ~ed him helpless** cela l'a rendu infirme. **(d)** (*Culin*) *fat* faire fondre. **(e)** (*Constr*) plâtrer. ♦ **rendering** *n [music]* interprétation *f*; (*translation*) traduction *f* (*into* en).

rendez-vous ['rɒndɪvuː] **1** *n, pl inv* rendez-vous *m*. **2** *vi* se retrouver. **to ~ with sb** rejoindre qn.

renew [rɪ'njuː] *vt* (*gen*) renouveler; *negotiations, discussions, strength* reprendre. **to ~ one's acquaintance with sb** renouer connaissance avec qn. ♦ **renewable** *adj* renouvelable. ♦ **renewal** *n* renouvellement *m*; reprise *f*; *[strength]* regain *m*; **~al of subscription** réabonnement *m*. ♦ **renewed** *adj* accru. **with ~ed vigour** avec une force accrue.

renounce [rɪ'naʊns] *vt* (*gen*) renoncer à; *religion* abjurer; *treaty* dénoncer; *cause* renier.

renovate ['renəʊveɪt] *vt clothes, house* remettre à neuf; *building, painting* restaurer. ♦ **renovation** *n* remise *f* à neuf; restauration *f*.

renown [rɪ'naʊn] *n* renommée *f*. ♦ **renowned** *adj thing* renommé (*for* pour); *person* célèbre (*for* pour).

rent [rent] **1** *n* loyer *m*. (*US*) **for ~** à louer; **quarter's ~** terme *m*. **2** *adj*: **~ collector** receveur *m* de loyers; **~ rebate** dégrèvement *m* de loyer. **3** *vt* **(a)** (*take for ~*) louer, prendre en location. **we don't own it, only ~ it** nous ne sommes pas propriétaires, mais locataires seulement. **(b)** (*also ~ out*) louer, donner en location. ♦ **rental** *n [house, land]* loyer *m*; *[television etc]* (prix *m* de) location *f*; *[telephone]* abonnement *m*. ♦ **rent-free** **1** *adj accommodation* exempt de loyer; **2** *adv live* sans payer de loyer.

renunciation [rɪˌnʌnsɪ'eɪʃən] *n* (*V* **renounce**) renonciation *f* (*of* à); abjuration *f*; dénonciation *f*; reniement *m*.

reopen [ˌriː'əʊpən] **1** *vt* (*gen*) rouvrir; *fight, battle, hostilities* reprendre. **2** *vi* (*gen*) rouvrir; *[wound]* se rouvrir. ♦ **reopening** *n* réouverture *f*.

reorganize ['riː'ɔːgənaɪz] **1** *vt* réorganiser. **2** *vi* se réorganiser. ♦ **reorganization** *n* réorganisation *f*.

rep* [rep] *n abbr of* **repertory company** *and* (*Comm*) **representative**.

repair [rɪ'pɛəʳ] **1** *vt* réparer. **2** *n* (*gen*) réparation *f*; *[roof, road]* réfection *f*. **under ~** en réparation; **damaged beyond ~** irréparable; **closed for ~s** fermé pour cause de travaux; **'road ~s'** 'chantier'; **in good/bad ~** en bon/mauvais état; **to keep in good ~** entretenir. **3** *adj*: **~ kit** *or* **outfit** trousse *f* de réparation; **~ shop** atelier *m* de réparations. ♦ **repairable** *or* ♦ **reparable** ['repərəbl] *adj* réparable. ♦ **repairer** *n* réparateur *m*, -trice *f*; *[shoes]* cordonnier *m*. ♦ **reparation** *n* réparation *f*; **to make reparations for** réparer (*une injure etc*).

repartee [ˌrepɑː'tiː] *n* repartie *f*, réplique *f*.

repatriate [riː'pætrɪeɪt] *vt* rapatrier. ♦ **repatriation** *n* rapatriement *m*.

repay [riː'peɪ] *pret, ptp* **repaid** *vt money* rendre, rembourser; *lender* rembourser; *debt, obligation* s'acquitter de; *sb's kindness* payer de retour; *helper* récompenser (*for* de). ♦ **repayable** *adj* remboursable. ♦ **repayment** *n [money]* remboursement *m*.

repeal [rɪ'piːl] **1** *vt law* abroger; *sentence* annuler. **2** *n* abrogation *f*; annulation *f*.

repeat [rɪ'piːt] **1** *vt* (*gen*) répéter; *demand, promise* réitérer; *efforts* renouveler; (*Mus*) reprendre; (*recite*) *poem etc* réciter (par cœur); (*Scol*) *class* redoubler. (*Comm*) **this offer will never be ~ed** c'est une offre exceptionnelle; **to ~ o.s.** se répéter. **2** *n* répétition *f*; (*Mus, Rad, TV*) reprise *f*. **3** *adj* (*Comm*) *order* renouvelé. (*fig*) **a ~ performance** exactement la même chose. ♦ **repeated** *adj requests, criticism* répété; *efforts* renouvelé. ♦ **repeatedly** *adv* à maintes reprises, très souvent; **I have ~edly told you** je ne cesse de vous répéter; **he had ~edly proclaimed ...** il n'avait pas cessé de proclamer ... .

repel [rɪ'pel] *vt* repousser; (*fig: disgust*) dégoûter. ♦ **repellent** *adj* **(a)** (*disgusting*) repoussant, répugnant; **(b)** **water-~lent** imperméabilisateur.

repent [rɪ'pent] **1** *vi* se repentir (*of* de). **2** *vt* se repentir de. ♦ **repentance** *n* repentir *m*. ♦ **repentant** *adj* repentant.

repercussion [ˌriːpə'kʌʃən] *n* répercussion *f* (*on* sur).

repertory ['repətərɪ] **1** *n* (*Theat, fig: also* **repertoire**) répertoire *m*. **~ (theatre)** théâtre *m* de répertoire; **to act in ~** faire partie d'une troupe de répertoire. **2** *adj*: **~ company** troupe *f* de répertoire.

repetition [ˌrepɪ'tɪʃən] *n* répétition *f*. ♦ **repetitive** [rɪ'petɪtɪv] *adj person* rabâcheur; *writing* plein de redites; *work* monotone.

replace [rɪ'pleɪs] *vt* **(a)** (*put back*) remettre (à sa place), ranger. (Telec) to ~ the receiver raccrocher. (b) (be or provide substitute for) remplacer (by, with par). ◆ **replaceable** adj remplaçable. ◆ **replacement** 1 n (person) remplaçant(e) m(f); (product) produit m de remplacement; 2 adj engine, part de rechange.

replenish [rɪ'plenɪʃ] vt remplir de nouveau (with de). to ~ one's supplies of sth se réapprovisionner en qch. ◆ **replenishment** n remplissage m.

replete [rɪ'pli:t] adj rempli (with de); (well-fed) rassasié. ◆ **repletion** n satiété f.

replica ['replɪkə] n (gen) réplique f; [document, book] fac-similé m.

reply [rɪ'plaɪ] 1 n réponse f; (quick) réplique f. in ~ en réponse (to à). 2 vti répondre; (quickly) répliquer. 3 adj (Post) ~ coupon coupon-réponse m. ◆ **reply-paid** adj avec réponse payée.

report [rɪ'pɔ:t] 1 n (a) (gen) rapport m; [speech, debate, meeting] compte rendu m; (Scol) bulletin m scolaire; (Press, Rad, TV) reportage m; (at regular intervals: on weather, sales etc) bulletin; (rumour) rumeur f. Government ~ rapport d'enquête parlementaire (on sur); (Comm) annual/chairman's ~ rapport annuel/présidentiel; to make a progress ~ on dresser un état périodique de; to make or do a ~ on faire un rapport sur, (Press, Rad, TV) faire un reportage sur; (rumour) there is a ~ that ... on dit que ...; I have heard a ~ that ... j'ai entendu dire que .... (b) (explosion) détonation f; [gun] coup m de fusil etc.
2 vt (a) (state) annoncer (that que); facts, figures annoncer, rapporter; (give account of) rendre compte de; [newspaper, TV programme] signaler; speech faire le compte rendu de. to ~ one's findings présenter ses conclusions; to ~ progress faire un exposé de l'état de la situation; he is ~ed as having said il aurait dit; a prisoner is ~ed to have escaped un détenu se serait évadé; (Gram) ~ed speech style or discours indirect; our correspondent ~s from Rome that ... notre correspondant à Rome nous apprend que ...; it is ~ed from Paris that ... on annonce à Paris que ... . (b) (notify) accident, crime, one's position signaler (to à); criminal, culprit signaler (sb for sth qn pour qch), dénoncer (to à) (often pej). to ~ sb sick signaler que qn est malade; ~ed missing porté disparu; nothing to ~ rien à signaler.
3 vi (a) se présenter (to sb chez qn). to ~ for duty se présenter au travail; (Mil) to ~ to one's unit rallier son unité; to ~ sick se faire porter malade. (b) (give a ~) faire un rapport (on sur); (Press, Rad, TV) faire un reportage (on sur).
report back vi (a) (return) (Mil etc) rentrer au quartier; (gen) être de retour. (b) (make report) présenter son rapport (to à).
◆ **reporter** n (Press) journaliste mf; (Rad, TV) reporter m.

repose [rɪ'pəuz] 1 n (rest, peace) repos m; (sleep) sommeil m. in ~ au repos. 2 vi se reposer; [dead] reposer. ◆ **repository** n (safe place) dépôt m; (warehouse) entrepôt m; [facts etc] mine f.

reprehend [ˌreprɪ'hend] vt réprimander. ◆ **reprehensible** adj répréhensible. ◆ **reprehensibly** adv de façon répréhensible.

represent [ˌreprɪ'zent] vt (all senses) représenter (as comme, comme étant). many countries were ~ed at the ceremony de nombreux pays s'étaient fait représenter à la cérémonie; I ~ Mrs Wolff je viens de la part de Mme Wolff. ◆ **representation** n (gen) représentation f; (protest) to make ~ations to faire une démarche auprès de. ◆ **representative** 1 adj représentatif (of de); 2 n représentant(e) m(f); (Comm) représentant (de commerce); (US Pol) R~ député m.

repress [rɪ'pres] vt (gen) réprimer; (Psych) refouler. ◆ **repressed** adj réprimé; refoulé. ◆ **repression** n répression f; refoulement m. ◆ **repressive** adj attitude, government répressif; measures de répression.

reprieve [rɪ'pri:v] 1 n (Jur) commutation f de la peine capitale; (delay: also gen) sursis m. 2 vt (Jur) accorder une commutation de la peine capitale à; (delay) surseoir à l'exécution de. [building etc] to be ~d bénéficier d'un sursis.

reprimand ['reprɪmɑ:nd] 1 n réprimande f. 2 vt réprimander.

reprint [ˌri:'prɪnt] 1 vt réimprimer. it is being ~ed c'est en réimpression. 2 vi être en réimpression. 3 ['ri:prɪnt] n réimpression f.

reprisal [rɪ'praɪzəl] n: ~s représailles fpl; to take ~s user de représailles; as a ~ for en représailles de.

reproach [rɪ'prəutʃ] 1 n reproche m. (fig) to be a ~ to être la honte de; above ~ irréprochable. 2 vt faire des reproches à. to ~ sb for sth/for having done reprocher à qn qch/d'avoir fait; he has nothing to ~ himself with il n'a rien à se reprocher. ◆ **reproachful** adj look, tone, person réprobateur; words de reproche. ◆ **reproachfully** adv avec reproche.

reproduce [ˌri:prə'dju:s] 1 vt reproduire. 2 vi se reproduire. ◆ **reproduction** 1 n (all senses) reproduction f; 2 adj: reproduction furniture imitations fpl de meubles anciens. ◆ **reproductive** adj reproducteur.

re-proof ['ri:'pru:f] vt garment réimperméabiliser.

reproof [rɪ'pru:f] n réprimande f.

reprove [rɪ'pru:v] vt person blâmer (for de). ◆ **reproval** n blâme m. ◆ **reproving** adj réprobateur. ◆ **reprovingly** adv d'un air or ton réprobateur.

reptile ['reptaɪl] adj, n (also fig pej) reptile (m).

republic [rɪ'pʌblɪk] n république f. ◆ **republican** adj, n républicain(e) m(f). ◆ **republicanism** n républicanisme m.

republish ['ri:'pʌblɪʃ] vt book rééditer.

repudiate [rɪ'pju:dɪeɪt] vt friend etc renier; secret agent désavouer; wife, accusation répudier; [government etc] debt, treaty refuser d'honorer. ◆ **repudiation** n reniement m; désaveu m; répudiation f; refus m d'honorer (un traité etc).

repugnant [rɪ'pʌgnənt] adj répugnant. to be ~ to sb répugner à qn; to find it ~ to do répugner à faire. ◆ **repugnance** n répugnance f (to pour).

repulse [rɪ'pʌls] vt repousser. ◆ **repulsion** n répulsion f. ◆ **repulsive** adj répulsif, repoussant. ◆ **repulsiveness** n caractère m repoussant.

reputable ['repjutəbl] adj de bonne réputation.

reputation [ˌrepju'teɪʃən] n réputation f (as a singer etc de chanteur etc). to have a ~ for honesty avoir la réputation d'être honnête.

repute [rɪ'pju:t] 1 n réputation f, renom m. by ~ de réputation; of ~ réputé, en renom. 2 vt: to be ~d to be être réputé être. ◆ **reputedly** adv d'après ce qu'on dit.

request [rɪ'kwest] 1 n demande f, requête f. at sb's ~ à la demande de qn; by popular ~ à la demande générale; on or by ~ sur demande; to make a ~ for sth faire une demande de qch. 2 vt demander (sth from sb qch à qn; sb to do à qn de faire). 'you are ~ed not to smoke' 'vous êtes priés de ne pas fumer'. 3 adj (Rad) programme des auditeurs; bus stop facultatif.

requiem ['rekwɪem] n requiem m. ~ mass messe f de requiem.

require [rɪ'kwaɪəʳ] vt (a) [person] avoir besoin de; [thing, action] demander, nécessiter. all I ~ tout ce qu'il me faut, tout ce dont j'ai besoin; it ~s great care cela demande or nécessite beaucoup de soin; if ~d au besoin; when ~d quand il le faut; what qualifications are ~d? quels sont les diplômes nécessaires or requis? (b) (order) exiger (sb to do de qn qu'il fasse; sth of sb qch de qn). as ~d by law comme la loi l'exige. ◆ **required** adj *conditions, qualifications* requis; *amount* voulu; **in the ~d time** dans les délais prescrits. ♦ **requirement** *n* **(a)** (*need*) exigence *f*; **to meet sb's ~ments** satisfaire aux exigences de qn; **(b)** (*condition*) condition *f* requise; **to fit the ~ments** remplir les conditions.

requisite ['rekwɪzɪt] **1** *n* chose *f* nécessaire (*for* pour). (*Comm*) **office ~s** articles *mpl* de bureau; **toilet ~s** accessoires *mpl* de toilette. **2** *adj* requis, nécessaire.

requisition [ˌrekwɪ'zɪʃən] **1** *n* réquisition *f*. **2** *vt* réquisitionner.

reredos ['rɪədɒs] *n* retable *m*.

reroute ['riː'ruːt] *vt* dérouter (*through* par).

rescind [rɪ'sɪnd] *vt* *judgment* rescinder; *law* abroger; *contract, decision* annuler.

rescue ['reskjuː] **1** *n* (*help*) secours *mpl*; (*saving*) sauvetage *m*; (*freeing*) délivrance *f*. **to go/come to sb's ~** aller/venir au secours de qn; **to the ~** à la rescousse. **2** *vt* (*save*) secourir, sauver; (*free*) délivrer (*from* de). **3** *adj* *operation, attempt* de sauvetage. **~ party** équipe *f* de sauvetage. ♦ **rescued** *npl*: **the ~d** les rescapés *mpl*. ♦ **rescuer** *n* sauveteur *m*; (*from imprisonment*) libérateur *m*, -trice *f*.

research [rɪ'sɜːtʃ] **1** *n* recherche(s) *f(pl)*. **a piece of ~** un travail de recherche; **to do ~** faire de la recherche (*on* sur). **2** *vi* faire des recherches (*into, on* sur). **3** *vt* *article* faire des recherches pour. **4** *adj* *student* qui fait de la recherche; *laboratory* de recherches. **~ establishment** centre *m* de recherches; (*Univ*) **~ fellow** ≃ chercheur *m*, -euse *f* attaché(e) à l'université. ♦ **researcher** *n* chercheur *m*, -euse *f*.

resemble [rɪ'zembl] *vt* ressembler à. ♦ **resemblance** *n* ressemblance *f*; **to bear a strong/faint resemblance to** avoir une grande/vague ressemblance avec.

resent [rɪ'zent] *vt* être contrarié de, (*stronger*) être indigné de. **I ~ that!** je proteste!; **I ~ your tone** votre ton me déplaît; **he ~ed your having seen her** il était très contrarié du fait que tu l'aies vue. ♦ **resentful** *adj* plein de ressentiment (*about* à cause de). ♦ **resentfully** *adv* avec ressentiment. ♦ **resentment** *n* ressentiment *m*.

reservation [ˌrezə'veɪʃən] *n* **(a)** réserve *f*. **without ~** sans réserve; **with ~s** avec certaines réserves; **mental ~** restriction *f* mentale; **to have ~s about** avoir des doutes sur. **(b)** (*booking*) réservation *f*. **to make a ~ at the hotel** réserver une chambre à l'hôtel; **to have a ~** (*seat/room/table*) avoir une place/chambre/table réservée. **(c)** (*area of land*) réserve *f*. *[roadway]* **central ~** bande *f* médiane.

reserve [rɪ'zɜːv] **1** *vt* (*most senses*) réserver. **to ~ one's strength** ménager ses forces, (*Sport*) se réserver; **to ~ judgment** se réserver de prononcer un jugement; **to ~ the right to do** se réserver le droit de faire. **2** *n* (*most senses*) réserve *f*; (*Sport: substitute*) remplaçant(e) *m(f)*. **cash ~** réserve de caisse; **gold ~s** réserves d'or; (*Mil*) **the R~** la réserve; **in ~** en réserve; **without ~** sans réserve; **he treated me with some ~** il s'est tenu sur la réserve avec moi. **3** *adj* *fund* de réserve; *price* minimum. (*Aut*) **~ tank** réservoir *m* de secours; **~ team** deuxième équipe *f*. ♦ **reserved** *adj* (*gen*) réservé; **to be ~d about ...** rester sur la réserve quant à ... . ♦ **reservist** *n* réserviste *m*. ♦ **reservoir** ['rezəvwɑːʳ] *n* réservoir *m*.

resettle [ˌriː'setl] *vt* *refugee* établir; *land* repeupler.

reshuffle [ˌriː'ʃʌfl] **1** *n* (*Pol*) **Cabinet ~** remaniement *m* ministériel. **2** *vt* remanier.

reside [rɪ'zaɪd] *vi* résider (*fig: in, with* dans). ♦ **residence** ['rezɪdəns] *n* (*gen*) résidence *f*; (*hostel*) foyer *m*; **to take up ~nce** s'installer, élire domicile (*Admin*); **in ~nce** *monarch etc* en résidence; *students etc* rentrés; *doctor* résidant; **~nce permit** permis *m* de séjour. ♦ **residency** *n* résidence *f* officielle. ♦ **resident** **1** *n* habitant(e) *m(f)*; (*in foreign country*) résident(e) *m(f)*; (*in street*) riverain(e) *m(f)*; (*in hostel*) pensionnaire *mf*; **2** *adj* (*gen*) résidant; *chaplain, tutor* à demeure; *population* fixe; **they are ~nt in France** ils résident en France. ♦ **residential** *adj* *area* résidentiel; *work* qui demande résidence.

residue ['rezɪdjuː] *n* reste(s) *m(pl)*; (*Chem*) résidu *m*; (*Math*) reste; (*Jur*) reliquat *m*. ♦ **residual** [re'zɪdjuəl] *adj* restant; (*Chem*) résiduel. ♦ **residuary** *adj* restant; (*Chem*) résiduaire; (*Jur*) **residuary legatee** ≃ légataire *mf* universel(le).

resign [rɪ'zaɪn] **1** *vt* *one's post* démissionner de; *the leadership etc* céder (*to* à). **to ~ one's commission** démissionner (*se dit d'un officier*); **to ~ o.s. to (doing) sth** se résigner à (faire) qch. **2** *vi* démissionner (*from* de). ♦ **resignation** [ˌrezɪg'neɪʃən] *n* **(a)** (*from job*) démission *f*; **to tender one's ~ation** donner sa démission; **(b)** (*mental state*) résignation *f*. ♦ **resigned** *adj* résigné; **to become ~ed to (doing) sth** se résigner à (faire) qch. ♦ **resignedly** *adv* avec résignation.

resilient [rɪ'zɪlɪənt] *adj* *substance* élastique; *character* qui réagit. **he's very ~** (*physically*) il a beaucoup de résistance; (*mentally etc*) il a du ressort. ♦ **resilience** *n* résistance *f*; ressort *m*.

resin ['rezɪn] *n* résine *f*. ♦ **resinous** *adj* résineux.

resist [rɪ'zɪst] **1** *vt* (*gen*) résister à; *order* refuser d'obéir à; *change* s'opposer à. **I couldn't ~ (eating) another cake** je n'ai pas pu m'empêcher de manger encore un gâteau; **she can't ~ him** elle ne peut rien lui refuser. **2** *vi* résister. ♦ **resistance** **1** *n* (*gen, Elec, Med, Mil, Phys*) résistance *f*; **he offered no ~ance** il n'a pas résisté (*to* à); (*Med*) **his ~ance was very low** il n'offrait presque plus de résistance (au mal); **2** *adj*: **~ance fighter** résistant(e) *m(f)*; **the ~ance movement** la résistance. ♦ **resistant** *adj* résistant; (*of virus, strain*) **~ant to** rebelle à.

resit ['riː'sɪt] *pret, ptp* **resat** **1** *vt* se représenter à. **2** ['riːsɪt] *n* deuxième session *f* (*d'un examen*).

resolute ['rezəluːt] *adj* résolu. ♦ **resolutely** *adv* résolument.♦ **resoluteness** *n* résolution *f*.

resolution [ˌrezə'luːʃən] *n* (*all senses*) résolution *f*. **to make a ~** prendre une résolution.

resolve [rɪ'zɒlv] **1** *vt* (*gen*) résoudre (*into* en); *problem, difficulty* résoudre. **2** *vi* résoudre, décider (*to do* de faire; *that* que), se décider (*to do* à faire). **it has been ~d that** il a été résolu que. **3** *n* résolution *f*. **to make a ~ to do** prendre la résolution de faire. ♦ **resolved** *adj* résolu (*to do* à faire).

resonant ['rezənənt] *adj* résonant. ♦ **resonance** *n* résonance *f*.

resort [rɪ'zɔːt] **1** *n* **(a)** (*recourse*) recours *m*; (*thing ~ed to*) ressource *f*. **without ~ to violence** sans recourir à la violence; **as a last ~, in the last ~** en dernier ressort; **it was the only ~ left to them** c'était la seule ressource qui leur restait. **(b)** (*place*) lieu *m* de séjour. **holiday ~** lieu de vacances; **seaside/summer ~** station *f* balnéaire/estivale; **winter sports ~** station de sports d'hiver. **2** *vi* avoir recours (*to sth/sb* à qch/qn), en venir (*to doing* à faire).

resound [rɪ'zaʊnd] *vi* retentir (*with* de); (*fig*) avoir un retentissement. ♦ **resounding** *adj* *shout, victory, success* retentissant; *defeat* écrasant.

resource [rɪ'sɔːs] *n* ressource *f*. **as a last ~** en dernière ressource; **mineral ~s** ressources en minerais; **left to his own ~s** livré à ses propres ressources. ♦ **resourceful** *adj* *person* plein de ressources, débrouillard*; *scheme* ingénieux. ♦ **resourcefully** *adv* d'une manière ingénieuse. ♦ **resourcefulness** *n* ressource *f* (*qualité*).

respect [rɪs'pekt] **1** *n* (*gen*) respect *m*. **to have ~ for** respecter; **to treat with ~** traiter avec respect; **out of ~ for** par respect *or* égard pour; **with due ~ I still think ...** sans vouloir vous contredire je crois toujours ...; **with ~ to** pour *or* en ce qui concerne; **in ~ of** quant à; **in some ~s** à certains égards; **to pay one's ~s to sb** présenter ses respects à qn; **give my ~s** to présentez mes respects à. **2** *vt* respecter. ♦ **respectability** *n* respectabilité *f*. ♦ **respectable** *adj* **(a)** (*decent: gen*) respectable; *clothes, behaviour* convenable; **they are very ~able people** ce sont de très braves gens; **that's not ~able** ça ne se fait pas; **(b)** (*quite big*) *size, income* considérable, respectable. ♦ **respectably** *adv dress, behave* convenablement; (*quite well*) passablement; **very ~ably** pas mal du tout*. ♦ **respecter** *n*: **he is no ~er of persons** il ne s'en laisse imposer par personne. ♦ **respectful** *adj* respectueux. ♦ **respectfully** *adv* respectueusement. ♦ **respecting** *prep* concernant, touchant. ♦ **respective** *adj* respectif. ♦ **respectively** *adv* respectivement.

respire [rɪsˈpaɪəʳ] *vti* respirer. ♦ **respiration** [ˌrespɪˈreɪʃən] *n* respiration *f*. ♦ **respirator** *n* (*Med*) respirateur *m*; (*Mil*) masque *m* à gaz. ♦ **respiratory** *adj* respiratoire.

respite [ˈrespaɪt] *n* répit *m*.

resplendent [rɪsˈplendənt] *adj* resplendissant.

respond [rɪsˈpɒnd] *vi* (*gen*) répondre (*to* à; *with* par). *[patient]* **to ~ to treatment** bien réagir au traitement; **the illness ~ed to treatment** le traitement a agi sur la maladie.

response [rɪsˈpɒns] *n* (*gen*) réponse *f*; (*to treatment*) réaction *f*; (*Rel*) répons *m*. **in ~ to** en réponse à.

responsible [rɪsˈpɒnsəbl] *adj* responsable (*for* de; *to sb for sth* de qch devant qn). **to be directly ~ to sb** relever directement de qn; **he is very ~** il a un grand sens des responsabilités; **it's a ~ job** c'est un poste qui comporte des responsabilités. ♦ **responsibility 1** *n* responsabilité *f*; **to put** *or* **place the responsibility for sth on sb** tenir qn pour responsable de qch; **to take responsibility for sth** prendre la responsabilité de qch; **it's not my responsibility to do that** ce n'est pas à moi de faire ça; **on my own responsibility** sous ma responsabilité; **2** *adj*: **responsibility payment** prime *f* de fonction. ♦ **responsibly** *adv* avec sérieux.

responsive [rɪsˈpɒnsɪv] *adj audience, class, pupil* qui réagit bien; *person* qui n'est pas du tout réservé; (*to affection*) très affectueux.

rest [rest] **1** *n* **(a)** (*gen*) repos *m*; (*Mus*) silence *m*; (*Poetry*) césure *f*. **to need ~/a ~** avoir besoin de repos/de se reposer; **to have a ~** se reposer; **to have a good night's ~** passer une bonne nuit; **to be at ~** (*dead*) reposer en paix; **to lay to ~** porter en terre; **to set sb's mind at ~** tranquilliser qn; **to come to ~** *[object]* s'immobiliser; *[bird]* se poser (*on* sur); **it will give him a ~** ça le reposera; **give it a ~!*** laisse tomber!* **(b)** (*support*) support *m*, appui *m*. **arm ~** accoudoir *m*. **(c)** (*remainder*) **the ~** *[substance, money]* le reste, le restant; *[things, people]* les autres *mfpl*; **the ~ of us will wait here** nous (autres), nous attendrons ici; **and all the ~ of it*** et tout ça*.

2 *adj cure, day* de repos. **~ centre** centre *m* d'accueil; **~ home** maison *f* de repos; (*US*) **~ room** toilettes *fpl*.

3 *vi* **(a)** (*repose*) se reposer; *[the dead]* reposer. (*fig*) **he won't ~ till he finds out ...** il n'aura de cesse qu'il ne découvre (*subj*) ...; (*fig: of actor*) **to be ~ing** se trouver sans engagement; **may he ~ in peace** qu'il repose en paix. **(b)** (*remain*) rester, demeurer. **~ assured that** soyez assuré que; **there the matter ~s** l'affaire en est là; **it ~s with him to decide** il lui appartient de décider; **it doesn't ~ with me** cela ne dépend pas de moi. **(c)** (*lean*) *[person]* s'appuyer (*on* sur; *against* contre); *[roof, ladder]* appuyer (*on* sur; *against* contre); *[reputation, case]* reposer (*on* sur); *[eyes, gaze]* se poser (*on* sur). **a heavy responsibility ~s on him** il a de lourdes responsabilités.

4 *vt* **(a)** laisser reposer. **I am quite ~ed** je me sens tout à fait reposé; **God ~ his soul!** que Dieu ait son âme! **(b)** (*lean*) *hand, small object* poser; *ladder, cycle* appuyer (*on* sur, *against* contre). ♦ **restful** *adj* reposant. ♦ **restless** *adj* agité; **to have a ~less night** mal dormir; **to get ~less** s'agiter, s'impatienter. ♦ **restlessly** *adv move* avec agitation; *fidget* nerveusement. ♦ **restlessness** *n* agitation *f*, impatience *f*.

restaurant [ˈrestərɔ̃:ŋ] **1** *n* restaurant *m*. **2** *adj* (*Rail*) **~ car** wagon-restaurant *m*; **~ owner** restaurateur *m*, -trice *f*.

restitution [ˌrestɪˈtju:ʃən] *n* restitution *f*. **to make ~ of sth** restituer qch.

restive [ˈrestɪv] *adj horse* rétif; *person* agité, énervé.

restore [rɪsˈtɔ:ʳ] *vt* **(a)** (*give back: gen*) rendre (*to* à); *rights, order, calm* rétablir; *confidence* redonner (*to sb* à qn; *in* dans). **~d to health** rétabli; **to ~ sb to life** ramener qn à la vie; **to ~ sth to its former condition** remettre qch en état; **to ~ sb's strength** redonner des forces à qn; **to ~ to the throne** replacer sur le trône; **to ~ to power** ramener au pouvoir. **(b)** (*repair*) *building etc* restaurer. ♦ **restoration** *n* rétablissement *m*; restauration *f* (*also Hist*). ♦ **restorative** *adj, n* reconstituant (*m*). ♦ **restorer** *n* (*Art etc*) restaurateur *m*, -trice *f*.

restrain [rɪsˈtreɪn] *vt* (*gen*) retenir (*sb from doing* qn de faire); *sb's activities* limiter; *anger* réprimer; *feelings* dominer; *struggling person* maîtriser. **to ~ o.s.** se retenir; **~ yourself!** maîtrisez-vous! ♦ **restrained** *adj emotions* contenu; *voice, words* mesuré; *person* maître de soi; *style* sobre. ♦ **restraint** *n* **(a)** (*restriction*) contrainte *f*; **wage ~t** contrôle *m* des salaires; **(b)** (*moderation*) *[person, speech]* retenue *f*; *[style]* sobriété *f*; **to show a lack of ~t** manquer de maîtrise de soi.

restrict [rɪsˈtrɪkt] *vt authority, freedom* restreindre; *visits, price rise* limiter (*to* à). ♦ **restricted** *adj* restreint, limité; *document* confidentiel; *point of view, horizon* étroit; (*Aut*) **~ed area** zone *f* à vitesse limitée. ♦ **restriction** *n* (*gen*) restriction *f*, limitation *f*; *[prices etc]* contrôle *m*; **to place ~ions on** apporter des restrictions à; (*Aut*) **speed ~ion** limitation de vitesse. ♦ **restrictive** *adj* restrictif; (*Ind*) **~ive practices** pratiques *fpl* restrictives de production.

result [rɪˈzʌlt] **1** *n* (*gen*) résultat *m*. **as a ~ he ...** en conséquence il ...; **to be the ~ of** être dû à; **as a ~ of my inquiry** par suite de mon enquête; **to get ~s*** *[person]* obtenir *or* *[action]* donner de bons résultats. **2** *vi* résulter (*from* de). **to ~ in** aboutir à, se terminer par. ♦ **resultant** *adj* résultant.

resume [rɪˈzju:m] **1** *vt* **(a)** (*restart: gen*) reprendre; *relations* renouer. **to ~ one's seat** se rasseoir. **(b)** (*sum up*) résumer. **2** *vi* *[classes etc]* reprendre. ♦ **resumption** *n* reprise *f*.

resurrect [ˌrezəˈrekt] *vt* ressusciter; (*fig*) *fashion, ideas* faire revivre; *memories* réveiller. ♦ **resurrection** *n* (*Rel, fig*) résurrection *f*.

resuscitate [rɪˈsʌsɪteɪt] *vt* (*Med*) réanimer. ♦ **resuscitation** *n* réanimation *f*.

retail [ˈri:teɪl] **1** *n* vente *f* au détail. **2** *vt* vendre au détail; (*fig*) *gossip* colporter. **3** *vi* se vendre au détail (*at* à). **4** *adv* au détail. **5** *adj business, price* de détail. ♦ **retailer** *n* détaillant(e) *m(f)*.

retain [rɪˈteɪn] *vt* (*keep*) conserver, garder; *heat* conserver; (*hold*) retenir, maintenir; *lawyer* retenir, engager; (*remember*) garder en mémoire. ♦ **retainer** *n* (*fee*) provision *f*.

retaliate [rɪˈtælɪeɪt] *vi* se venger (*against sb/sth* de qn/qch; *by doing* en faisant), user de représailles (*against sb* envers qn). ♦ **retaliation** *n* vengeance *f*, représailles *fpl*; **in retaliation** par représailles; **in retaliation for** pour venger. ♦ **retaliatory** *adj*: **retaliatory measures** représailles *fpl*.

retarded [rɪ'tɑːdɪd] *adj* (*Med*) retardé, arriéré. **mentally** ~ arriéré.

retch [retʃ] *vi* avoir des haut-le-cœur.

retention [rɪ'tenʃən] *n* conservation *f*, maintien *m*; (*memory*) mémoire *f*; (*Med*) rétention *f*.

retentive [rɪ'tentɪv] *adj memory* fidèle; *person* qui a bonne mémoire.

reticent ['retɪsənt] *adj* réticent, réservé. **to be ~ about** ne pas parler beaucoup de. ♦ **reticence** *n* réticence *f*.

retina ['retɪnə] *n* rétine *f*.

retinue ['retɪnjuː] *n* suite *f*, escorte *f*.

retire [rɪ'taɪəʳ] **1** *vi* **(a)** (*withdraw*) se retirer (*from* de; *to* à); (*Mil*) reculer; (*Sport*) abandonner. **(b)** (*go to bed*) (aller) se coucher; (*give up work*) prendre sa retraite. **to ~ from business** se retirer des affaires. **2** *vt employee* mettre à la retraite. ♦ **retired** *adj* **(a)** (*no longer working*) retraité, à la retraite; **a ~d person** un(e) retraité(e); **(b)** (*secluded*) *life* retiré. ♦ **retirement** *n* (*stopping work*) retraite *f*. ♦ **retiring** *adj* **(a)** (*shy*) réservé; **(b)** (*departing*) *chairman etc* sortant; **(c)** *age* de la retraite.

retort¹ [rɪ'tɔːt] **1** *n* (*reply*) riposte *f*. **2** *vt* riposter.

retort² [rɪ'tɔːt] *n* (*Chem*) cornue *f*.

retrace [rɪ'treɪs] *vt developments etc* (*research into*) reconstituer, (*give account of*) retracer. **to ~ one's steps** revenir sur ses pas.

retract [rɪ'trækt] **1** *vt* (*gen*) rétracter; (*Aviat*) *undercarriage* rentrer. **2** *vi* se rétracter.

retrain ['riː'treɪn] **1** *vt* recycler (*personne*). **2** *vi* se recycler. ♦ **retraining** *n* recyclage *m*.

retread ['riːtred] *n* (*tyre*) pneu *m* rechapé.

retreat [rɪ'triːt] **1** *n* **(a)** (*esp Mil*) retraite *f*, recul *m*. (*Mil*) **to be in ~** battre en retraite; (*fig*) **to beat a hasty ~** partir en vitesse. **(b)** (*place: also Rel*) retraite *f*. **a country ~** une maison tranquille à la campagne. **2** *vi* (*Mil*) battre en retraite; (*withdraw*) se retirer (*from* de); *[flood, glacier]* reculer; *[chin, forehead]* être fuyant.

retrench [rɪ'trentʃ] **1** *vt* réduire. **2** *vi* faire des économies.

retrial ['riː'traɪəl] *n* (*Jur*) nouveau procès *m*.

retribution [ˌretrɪ'bjuːʃən] *n* châtiment *m*.

retrieve [rɪ'triːv] *vt* (*recover*) *object* récupérer (*from* de); *[dog]* rapporter; *money* recouvrer; *information* extraire; *fortune, honour, position* rétablir; (*set to rights*) *error* réparer; *situation* redresser; (*rescue*) sauver (*from* de). ♦ **retrievable** *adj object, material* récupérable; *money* recouvrable; *error, loss* réparable. ♦ **retrieval** *n* récupération *f*; recouvrement *m*; réparation *f*; **beyond** *or* **past retrieval** irréparable. ♦ **retriever** *n* chien *m* d'arrêt.

retrograde ['retrəʊgreɪd] *adj* rétrograde.

retrospect ['retrəʊspekt] *n*: **in ~** rétrospectivement. ♦ **retrospective 1** *adj pay rise* rétroactif; **2** *n* (*Art*) rétrospective *f*. ♦ **retrospectively** *adv* rétroactivement.

return [rɪ'tɜːn] **1** *vi* (*come back*) revenir; (*go back*) retourner; *[symptoms, doubts]* réapparaître. **to ~ home** rentrer; **have they ~ed?** sont-ils revenus *or* rentrés?; **to ~ to** *work, habit* reprendre; *subject, idea* revenir à; **to ~ to school** rentrer (en classe).

2 *vt* **(a)** (*give back*) (*gen*) rendre; *money* rembourser (*to sb* à qn); (*bring back*) rapporter; (*put back*) remettre; (*send back*) renvoyer; *compliment, salute, blow, visit, book* rendre; *sb's love* répondre à. (*on letter*) '**~ to sender**' 'retour à l'envoyeur'; to **~ sb's favour** rendre service à qn en retour. **(b)** (*reply*) répliquer. **(c)** (*declare*) *income, details* déclarer; (*Jur*) *verdict* rendre. (*Jur*) **to ~ a verdict of guilty on sb** déclarer qn coupable; **to ~ a verdict of murder** conclure au meurtre. **(d)** (*Parl*) *candidate* élire.

3 *n* **(a)** (*coming, going, giving back*) retour *m*; (*sending back*) renvoi *m*; *[sth lost etc]* restitution *f*; *[money]* remboursement *m*. **on my ~** dès mon retour; **~ home** retour; **by ~ of post** par retour du courrier; **many happy ~s (of the day)!** bon anniversaire! **(b)** (**~** *ticket*) aller et retour *m*. **(c)** (*recompense*) récompense *f* (*for* de); (*from land, business, mine*) rapport *m* (*on* de). **~s** (*profits*) bénéfice *m*; (*receipts*) recettes *fpl*; **small profits and quick ~s** de bas prix et un gros chiffre d'affaires; **in ~** en revanche; **in ~ for** en échange de. **(d) official ~s** statistiques *fpl* officielles; **the population ~s** le recensement; **the election ~s** les résultats *mpl* de l'élection; **tax ~** déclaration *f* de revenus *or* d'impôts. **(e)** (*Parl*) *[candidate]* élection *f*.

4 *adj*: **~ fare, ~ ticket** aller et retour *m*; **~ flight** vol *m* de retour; *[ticket]* **~ half** coupon *m* de retour; (*Pol*) **~ing officer** scrutateur *m*; **~ journey** retour *m*; **~ match** match *m* retour; (*Tech*) **~ stroke** course *f* retour.

♦ **returnable** *adj* qu'on doit rendre; *bottle etc* consigné.

reunification ['riːˌjuːnɪfɪ'keɪʃən] *n* réunification *f*.

reunion [rɪ'juːnjən] *n* réunion *f*.

reunite ['riːjuː'naɪt] *vt* réunir.

rev* [rev] **1** *n* (*Aut*) tour *m*. **~ counter** compte-tours *m inv*; **4,000 ~s per minute** 4000 tours minute. **2** *vt engine* emballer. **3** *vi* (**~ up**) *[engine]* s'emballer; *[driver]* emballer le moteur.

reveal [rɪ'viːl] *vt* révéler (*that* que); (*uncover*) *hidden object etc* découvrir. ♦ **revealing** *adj* révélateur; *dress* décolleté. ♦ **revelation** [ˌrevə'leɪʃən] *n* révélation *f*; **(the Book of the) Revelation** l'Apocalypse *f*.

reveille [rɪ'vælɪ] *n* (*Mil*) réveil *m*.

revel ['revl] **1** *vi* se délecter (*in sth* de qch; *in doing* à faire). **2** *npl*: **~s** festivités *fpl*. ♦ **reveller** *n*: **the ~lers** les gens *mpl* de la fête. ♦ **revelry** *n* festivités *fpl*.

revenge [rɪ'vendʒ] **1** *n* vengeance *f*; (*Sport etc*) revanche *f*. **to take ~ on sb for sth** se venger de qch sur qn; **to get one's ~** se venger; **in ~ he ...** pour se venger il ... . **2** *vt* venger. **to be ~d** se venger (*on sb* de qn; *on sb for sth* de qch sur qn).

revenue ['revənjuː] *n* revenu *m*.

reverberate [rɪ'vɜːbəreɪt] *vi* se répercuter; (*fig*) se propager. ♦ **reverberation** *n* répercussion *f*.

revere [rɪ'vɪəʳ] *vt* révérer, vénérer. ♦ **reverence** ['revərəns] **1** *n* vénération *f*; **2** *vt* révérer. ♦ **reverend** *adj*: **the R~nd Robert Martin** (*Anglican*) le révérend Robert Martin; (*Roman Catholic*) l'abbé (Robert) Martin; (*Nonconformist*) le pasteur (Robert) Martin; **R~nd Mother** révérende mère *f*. ♦ **reverent** *adj* respectueux. ♦ **reverently** *adv* avec vénération.

reverse [rɪ'vɜːs] **1** *adj* (*gen*) contraire; *direction* contraire, opposé; *movement, image* inverse. **~ side** *V* **2 b** *below*; **in ~ order** en ordre inverse; (*Aut*) **~ gear** marche *f* arrière.

2 *n* **(a)** (*opposite*) **the ~** le contraire, l'opposé; **quite the ~!** bien au contraire!; (*Aut*) **in ~** en marche arrière. **(b)** (**~** *side*) *[coin]* revers *m*; *[sheet of paper]* verso *m*; *[cloth]* envers *m*; *[painting]* dos *m*. **(c)** (*setback*) revers *m*; (*defeat*) défaite *f*.

3 *vt* **(a)** (*turn the other way round*) *object, garment* retourner; *trend, policy, situation* renverser; *2 objects, order, result* inverser. **to ~ one's policy** faire volte-face (*fig*); **to ~ a procedure** procéder par ordre inverse; (*Brit Telec*) **to ~ the charges** téléphoner en P.C.V.; **~d charge call** communication *f* en P.C.V. **(b)** (*move backwards*) *moving belt* renverser la direction de; *typewriter ribbon* changer de sens. **to ~ one's car**

= **to reverse** (*V* 4). **(c)** (*Jur: annul*) *verdict, judgment* réformer.

4 *vi* (*Aut*) faire marche arrière. **to ~ into the garage** rentrer dans le garage en marche arrière; **to ~ into a tree** heurter un arbre en faisant une marche arrière; **to ~ across the road** faire une marche arrière en travers de la route; **reversing lights** feux *mpl* de marche arrière.

♦ **reversal** *n* (*turning upside down*) renversement *m*; (*switching over of 2 objects*) interversion *f*; *[opinion, view etc]* revirement *m*; (*Jur*) réforme *f*. ♦ **reversible** *adj* réversible.

revert [rɪˈvɜːt] *vi* (*gen*) retourner (*to* à); (*to subject*) revenir (*to* à). (*Bio*) **to ~ to type** retourner au type primitif; (*fig*) **he has ~ed to type** le naturel a repris le dessus. ♦ **reversion** *n* retour *m* (*to* à); (*Bio*) réversion *f*.

review [rɪˈvjuː] **1** *n* **(a)** *[situation, development, the past]* revue *f*, examen *m*; (*Mil etc*) revue; *[book, film, play etc]* critique *f*. **to come up for ~** *or* **come under ~** être révisé; **to keep sth under ~** suivre qch de très près; **to give a ~ of sth** passer qch en revue. **(b)** (*magazine*) revue *f*. **2** *adj [book]* **~ copy** exemplaire *m* de service de presse. **3** *vt one's life, the past, troops* passer en revue; *the situation* réexaminer; *book, play, film* faire la critique de.

♦ **reviewer** *n* critique *m*; **book/film ~er** critique littéraire/de cinéma.

revile [rɪˈvaɪl] *vt* insulter.

revise [rɪˈvaɪz] **1** *vt* **(a)** (*change*) *opinion, estimate* réviser, modifier; *proof* corriger; *text* réviser. **~d edition** édition *f* revue et corrigée; (*Brit*) *[Bible]* **R~d Version** traduction (anglaise) de la Bible de 1884. **(b)** (*learn up*) réviser. **2** *vi* réviser (*for* pour). ♦ **revision** *n* révision *f*.

revive [rɪˈvaɪv] **1** *vt person* (*from fainting*) ranimer, (*from exhaustion*) remonter, (*from near death, esp Med*) réanimer; *fashion* remettre en vogue; *conversation, fire* ranimer; *hope, interest* faire renaître; *law* remettre en vigueur; *custom, usage* rétablir; *play* reprendre. **to ~ sb's courage** redonner du courage à qn.

2 *vi [person]* reprendre connaissance; *[hope, feelings]* renaître; *[business, trade]* reprendre.

♦ **revival** *n [custom, ceremony]* reprise *f*; *[faith]* renouveau *m*; **revival meeting** réunion *f* pour le renouveau de la foi.

revoke [rɪˈvəʊk] **1** *vt law* abroger; *order, edict* révoquer; *promise* revenir sur; *decision* annuler; *licence* retirer. **2** *vi* (*Cards*) faire une fausse renonce. ♦ **revocation** *n* abrogation *f*; révocation *f*; annulation *f*; retrait *m*.

revolt [rɪˈvəʊlt] **1** *n* révolte *f*. **to rise** *or* **be in ~** se révolter (*against* contre). **2** *vi* se révolter (*against* contre). **3** *vt* révolter. ♦ **revolting** *adj* révoltant, (*less strong*) dégoûtant; (*: *unpleasant*) *weather, colour* épouvantable.

revolution [ˌrevəˈluːʃən] *n* (*all senses*) révolution *f*. ♦ **revolutionary** *adj, n* révolutionnaire (*mf*). ♦ **revolutionize** *vt* révolutionner.

revolve [rɪˈvɒlv] **1** *vt* (*lit*) faire tourner. (*fig*) **to ~ a problem in one's mind** retourner un problème dans son esprit. **2** *vi* tourner. **to ~ on an axis/around the sun** tourner sur un axe/autour du soleil; (*fig*) **everything ~s around him** tout dépend de lui. ♦ **revolving** *adj light, stage* tournant; *chair, bookcase* pivotant; (*Tech*) rotatif; **revolving door** tambour *m*.

revolver [rɪˈvɒlvəʳ] *n* revolver *m*.

revue [rɪˈvjuː] *n* (*Theat*) revue *f*.

revulsion [rɪˈvʌlʃən] *n* dégoût *m*.

reward [rɪˈwɔːd] **1** *n* récompense *f*. **as a ~ for sth** en récompense de qch; **as a ~ for doing** pour vous (*or* le *etc*) récompenser d'avoir fait. **2** *vt* récompenser (*for* de). **to ~ sb with a smile** remercier qn d'un sourire. ♦ **rewarding** *adj* (*financially*) rémunérateur; (*fig*) *book/film* qui vaut la peine d'être lu/vu; *activity* qui a sa récompense.

rewire [ˈriːˈwaɪəʳ] *vt house* refaire l'installation électrique de.

rhapsody [ˈræpsədɪ] *n* (*Mus*) rhapsodie *f*; (*fig*) dithyrambe *m*. ♦ **rhapsodize** *vi* s'extasier (*over, about* sur).

rheostat [ˈriːəʊstæt] *n* rhéostat *m*.

rhesus [ˈriːsəs] **1** *n* rhésus *m*. **2** *adj factor* rhésus *inv*. **~ monkey** rhésus *m*.

rhetoric [ˈretərɪk] *n* rhétorique *f*. ♦ **rhetorical** *adj style* ampoulé (*pej*); **~al question** question *f* pour la forme. ♦ **rhetorically** *adv declaim* en orateur; *ask* pour la forme.

rheumatism [ˈruːmətɪzəm] *n* rhumatisme *m*. ♦ **rheumatic fever** *n* rhumatisme *m* articulaire aigu. ♦ **rheumatics** *npl* rhumatismes *mpl*. ♦ **rheumatoid arthritis** *n* rhumatisme *m* chronique polyarticulaire.

rhinoceros [raɪˈnɒsərəs] *n* rhinocéros *m*.

rhododendron [ˌrəʊdəˈdendrən] *n* rhododendron *m*.

rhubarb [ˈruːbɑːb] **1** *n* rhubarbe *f*. **2** *adj jam* de rhubarbe; *pie* à la rhubarbe.

rhyme [raɪm] **1** *n* rime *f*; (*poetry*) vers *mpl*; (*poem*) poème *m*. (*fig*) **without ~ or reason** sans rime ni raison. **2** *vt* faire rimer (*with* avec). **3** *vi* rimer (*with* avec).

rhythm [ˈrɪðəm] *n* rythme *m*. (*Med*) **~ method** méthode *f* des températures. ♦ **rhythmic(al)** *adj movement* rythmique; *music* rythmé. ♦ **rhythmically** *adv* de façon rythmée.

rib [rɪb] *n* (*Anat, Culin*) côte *f*; *[leaf, ceiling]* nervure *f*; *[umbrella]* baleine *f*; *[knitting]* côte. **to dig** *or* **poke sb in the ~s** pousser qn du coude.

ribald [ˈrɪbəld] *adj* paillard. ♦ **ribaldry** *n* paillardises *fpl*.

ribbon [ˈrɪbən] **1** *n* ruban *m*. **in ~s** (*tatters*) en lambeaux. **2** *adj*: **~ development** extension *f* urbaine linéaire en bordure de route.

rice [raɪs] **1** *n* riz *m*. **2** *adj*: **~ pudding** riz *m* au lait. ♦ **ricefield** *n* rizière *f*. ♦ **rice-growing** **1** *n* riziculture *f*; **2** *adj* producteur de riz.

rich [rɪtʃ] *adj* (*gen*) riche (*in* en); *profit* gros; *furniture, gift, clothes* somptueux; *voice* ample; *district of town* très chic. **to grow** *or* **get ~(er)** s'enrichir; **to make ~** enrichir; (*iro*) **that's ~!*** ça c'est pas mal!* (*iro*). ♦ **riches** *npl* richesse(s) *f(pl)*. ♦ **richly** *adv* richement; somptueusement; *deserve* largement. ♦ **richness** *n* richesse *f* (*in* en); somptuosité *f*; ampleur *f*; *[colour]* éclat *m*.

rickets [ˈrɪkɪts] *n* rachitisme *m*. **to have ~** être rachitique. ♦ **rickety** *adj* (*Med*) rachitique; *furniture, stairs* branlant.

ricochet [ˈrɪkəʃeɪ] **1** *n* ricochet *m*. **2** *vi* ricocher.

rid [rɪd] *pret, ptp* **rid** *or* **ridded** *vt* (*of pests, disease*) débarrasser (*of* de); (*of bandits etc*) délivrer (*of* de). **to get ~ of, to ~ o.s. of** *fleas, spots, cold* se débarrasser de; *habit, desire, fears* perdre; *debts* liquider; **to be ~ of** être débarrassé de; **the body gets ~ of waste** l'organisme élimine les déchets. ♦ **riddance** *n* débarras *m*; **good ~dance!*** bon débarras!*

ridden [ˈrɪdn] (*ptp of* **ride**) *adj ending*: **fear-~** hanté par la peur; **remorse-~** tourmenté par le remords.

riddle[1] [ˈrɪdl] **1** *n* crible *m*. **2** *vt coal, soil etc* passer au crible; *stove* agiter la grille de; (*fig*) cribler (*with bullets etc* de balles *etc*).

riddle[2] [ˈrɪdl] *n* (*mystery*) énigme *f*. **to ask sb a ~** poser une devinette à qn.

ride [raɪd] (*vb: pret* **rode**, *ptp* **ridden**) **1** *n* **(a)** promenade *f* (*à cheval, à bicyclette etc*), tour *m*; (*distance covered*) trajet *m*. **horse ~, ~ on horseback** (*for pleasure*) promenade *or* tour à cheval; (*long journey*) chevauchée *f*; **he gave the child a ~ on his back** il a promené l'enfant sur son dos; **coach ~** tour *or* excursion *f* en car; **it's a short taxi ~** ce n'est pas loin en taxi (*to* jusqu'à); **he has a**

long (car/bus) ~ to work il a un long trajet (en voiture/en autobus) jusqu'à son travail; **to go for a ~ in a car** faire un tour *or* une promenade en voiture; **to take sb for a ~** (*in car etc*) emmener qn en promenade; (*fig: make fool of*) mener qn en bateau*; (*swindle*) rouler qn*; **I've never had a ~ in a train** je n'ai jamais pris le train; **can I have a ~ on your bike?** est-ce que je peux monter sur ton vélo?; **a ~ on the merry-go-round** un tour sur le manège. **(b)** (*forest path*) allée *f* cavalière.

2 *vi* **(a)** (*~ a horse*) monter à cheval, faire du cheval. **can you ~?** savez-vous monter à cheval?; **he ~s well** il monte bien, il est bon cavalier. **(b)** (*go on horseback/by bicycle/by motorcycle*) aller à cheval/à bicyclette/en moto. **to ~ down/away** *etc* descendre/s'éloigner *etc* à cheval (*or* à bicyclette *etc*); **the witch was riding on a broomstick** la sorcière était à cheval sur un balai; **they were riding on a bus/in a car/in a train** ils étaient en autobus/en voiture/en train; **they rode in a bus to** ... ils sont allés en autobus à ...; (*fig*) **to be riding for a fall** courir à un échec; **to ~ at anchor** être à l'ancre; **to let things ~** laisser courir*.

3 *vt*: **to ~ a horse/donkey/camel** monter à cheval/à dos d'âne/à dos de chameau; **he was riding Malfi** il montait Malfi; **I have never ridden Flash** je n'ai jamais monté Flash; **he rode Cass at Newmarket** il montait Cass à Newmarket; **he rode Buster into town** il a pris Buster pour aller en ville; **Jason will be ridden by J. Bean** Jason sera monté par J. Bean; **he ~s his pony to school** il va à l'école à dos de poney; **he rode his motorbike/cycle to the station** il est allé à la gare en moto/à bicyclette; **I have never ridden a bicycle/a motorbike** je ne suis jamais monté à bicyclette/à moto; **can I ~ your bike?** est-ce que je peux monter sur ton vélo?; **he was riding a bicycle** il était à bicyclette; **he always ~s a bicycle** il va partout à bicyclette; **they had ridden 10 km** ils avaient fait 10 km à cheval (*or* à bicyclette *etc*).

ride out *vt sep* (*fig*) *difficult period* surmonter, survivre à. **to ~ out the storm** (*Naut*) étaler la tempête; (*fig*) surmonter la crise.

ride up *vi* [*skirt etc*] remonter.

♦ **rider** *n* **(a)** [*horse*] cavalier *m*, -ière *f*; [*racehorse*] jockey *m*; [*circus horse*] écuyer *m*, -ère *f*; **a good ~r** un bon cavalier, une bonne cavalière; **(b)** (*addition: to document*) annexe *f*; (*to insurance policy, jury's verdict*) avenant *m*. ♦ **riding 1** *n* (*horse-riding*) équitation *f*; (*horsemanship*) monte *f*; **2** *adj boots, breeches* de cheval; *teacher* d'équitation; **riding crop** *or* **whip** cravache *f*; **riding habit** tenue *f* d'amazone; **riding school** *or* **stables** manège *m*.

ridge [rɪdʒ] **1** *n* [*roof, nose, line of hills*] arête *f*; (*ledge on hillside*) corniche *f*; (*chain of mountains*) chaîne *f*; (*on sand*) ride *f*; (*in ploughed land*) billon *m*; (*on cliff, rockface*) strie *f*. (*Met*) **a ~ of high pressure** une ligne de hautes pressions. **2** *adj*: **~ tent** tente *f* à armature simple.

ridicule ['rɪdɪkju:l] **1** *n* raillerie *f*, ridicule *m*. **to hold sb/sth up to ~** tourner qn/qch en ridicule. **2** *vt* ridiculiser. ♦ **ridiculous** [rɪ'dɪkjʊləs] *adj* ridicule; **to make o.s. (look) ridiculous** se rendre ridicule. ♦ **ridiculously** *adv* ridiculement. ♦ **ridiculousness** *n* ridicule *m* (*état*).

rife [raɪf] *adj* [*disease, corruption*] **to be ~** sévir; **rumour is ~** des bruits courent.

riffraff ['rɪfræf] *n* racaille *f*.

rifle[1] ['raɪfl] *vt town* piller; *sb's pockets* puiser dans; *drawer, till, house* dévaliser.

rifle[2] ['raɪfl] **1** *n* (*gun*) fusil *m* (rayé); (*for hunting*) carabine *f* de chasse. **2** *adj*: **~ range** (*outdoor*) champ *m* de tir; (*indoor*) stand *m* de tir.

rift [rɪft] *n* (*gen*) fissure *f*; (*in clouds*) trouée *f*; (*Pol: in party*) division *f*.

rig [rɪg] **1** *n* (*oil ~*) (*land*) derrick *m*; (*sea*) plateforme *f* pétrolière. **2** *vt election* truquer; *prices* faire monter (*or* baisser) de façon factice. **it was ~ged** c'était un coup monté.

rig out *vt sep* habiller (*with* de; *as* en).

rig up *vt sep boat* gréer; (*with mast*) mâter; (*set up*) *equipment* monter; (*make hastily*) faire avec des moyens de fortune; (*arrange*) arranger. ♦ **rigging** *n* (*Naut*) gréement *m*. ♦ **rigout*** *n* tenue *f* (*vestimentaire*).

right [raɪt] **1** *adj* **(a)** (*just*) juste, équitable; (*morally good*) bien *inv*. **it isn't ~ to lie** ce n'est pas bien de mentir; **to do what is ~** faire ce qui est conforme au devoir *or* à la morale, se conduire bien; **he thought it ~ to warn me** il a cru *or* jugé bon de m'avertir; **it seemed only ~ to do it** il ne semblait que juste de le faire; **it is only ~ that she should go** il n'est que juste qu'elle y aille; **it is only ~ to point out that** ... en toute justice il faut signaler que ...; **would it be ~ to tell him?** ferait-on bien de le lui dire?; **to do the ~ thing by sb** agir honorablement envers qn.

(b) (*correct*) juste, exact. **to be ~** [*person*] avoir raison (*to do* de faire); [*answer*] être juste, être exact; [*clock*] être à l'heure; **that's ~** c'est juste, c'est exact; **the ~ answer/road/table** la bonne réponse/route/table; **the ~ time** l'heure exacte *or* juste; **at the ~ time** au bon moment; **on the ~ road** sur le bon chemin, (*fig*) sur la bonne voie; **to get one's sums ~** réussir ses additions; **to get one's facts ~** être sûr de ce qu'on avance; **let's get it ~ this time!** essayons d'y arriver cette fois-ci!; **to put** *or* **set ~** *error* corriger; *mistaken person* détromper; *sick person* guérir; *situation* redresser; *clock* remettre à l'heure; **to put things ~** arranger les choses; **put me ~ if I'm wrong** dites-moi si je me trompe; **the ~ clothes** les vêtements appropriés; **what's the ~ thing to do?** qu'est-ce qu'il vaut mieux faire?; **to do sth the ~ way** s'y prendre bien; **that is the ~ way of looking at it** c'est bien ainsi qu'il faut l'envisager; **the ~ word** le mot juste; **the ~ man for the job** l'homme qu'il faut; **the ~ size** la taille qu'il faut; **what is ~ for the country** ce qui est dans l'intérêt du pays; **she is on the ~ side of 40** elle n'a pas encore 40 ans; **to get on the ~ side of sb*** s'insinuer dans les bonnes grâces de qn; **the ~ side of the material** l'endroit *m* du tissu; **to know the ~ people** avoir des relations utiles; **more than is ~** plus que de raison; **~!, ~-oh!*, ~ you are!*** d'accord!; **that's ~!** mais oui!, c'est ça!; **he's the ~ sort*** c'est un type bien*; **all ~** *V* **all 3 b.**

(c) (*well*) **I don't feel quite ~** je ne me sens pas très bien; **to be as ~ as rain*** (*after illness*) se porter comme un charme; (*after fall*) être indemne; **the car's not ~*** il y a qch qui cloche* dans la voiture; **he put the engine ~** il a remis le moteur en état; **to be in one's ~ mind** avoir toute sa raison; **not ~ in the head**‡ un peu dingue‡.

(d) (*Math*) droit. **at ~ angles** à angle droit (*to* avec).

(e) (*opposite of left*) droit, de droite. **~ hand** main droite; **I'd give my ~ hand to know** ... je donnerais cher* pour savoir ... .

2 *adv* **(a)** (*straight*) tout droit, directement; (*exactly, completely*) tout, tout à fait. **~ in front of you** (tout) droit devant vous; **~ behind you** juste derrière vous; **go ~ on** continuez tout droit; **~ away, ~ off*** (*immediately*) tout de suite; (*at the first attempt*) du premier coup; **~ now** en ce moment; (*at once*) tout de suite; **~ here** ici même; **~ in the middle** en plein milieu; **~ at the start** dès le tout début; **~ round the house** tout autour de la maison; **rotten ~ through** complètement pourri; **to turn ~ round** se retourner; **~ at the top of the mountain** tout en haut de la montagne; **~ at the back, ~ at the bottom** tout au fond; **push it ~ in** enfoncez-le complètement *or* jusqu'au bout.

(b) (*correctly*) *do, remember* bien; *guess, calculate* juste; *answer* correctement; (*well*) bien. **if I remember** ~ si je me souviens bien; **you did** ~ **to refuse** vous avez eu raison de refuser; **if everything goes** ~ si tout va bien; **if I get you** ~* si je comprends bien; **I'll see you** ~: je veillerai à ce que vous n'y perdiez (*subj*) pas.

(c) (*opposite of left*) à droite. ~ **and left** *look etc* à droite et à gauche; (*fig*) ~, **left and centre*** de tous les côtés.

3 *n* **(a)** ~ **and wrong** le bien et le mal; **to be in the** ~ avoir raison, être dans le vrai; **I want to know the** ~**s and wrongs of it** je veux savoir qui a tort et qui a raison là-dedans; **to put** *or* **set sth to** ~s mettre qch en ordre. **(b)** droit *m*. **to have a** ~ **to sth** avoir droit à qch; **to have a** *or* **the** ~ **to do** avoir le droit de faire; **what** ~ **have you to say that?** de quel droit dites-vous cela?; **within his** ~**s** dans son droit; **by** ~s en toute justice; (*Jur*) **in his own** ~ de son propre chef; **she's a good actress in her own** ~ elle est elle-même une bonne actrice; **women's** ~**s movement** mouvement *m* pour les droits de la femme. **(c)** (*not left*) droite *f*. **on** *or* **to the** ~ à droite (*of* de); **to keep to the** ~ (*gen*) garder la droite; (*Aut*) tenir sa droite; **on my** ~ à ma droite; (*Pol*) **the R**~ la droite.

4 *vt vehicle, wrong etc* redresser; *injustice* réparer. **to** ~ **itself** *[vehicle]* se redresser; *[problem]* s'arranger.

♦ **right-angled** *adj* à angle droit; *triangle* rectangle. ♦ **righteous** *adj person* vertueux; *anger, indignation* justifié. ♦ **righteousness** *n* droiture *f*, vertu *f*. ♦ **rightful** *adj* légitime. ♦ **rightfully** *adv* à juste titre. ♦ **right-hand** *adj side* droit; ~**-hand drive car** voiture *f* avec la conduite à droite; **his** ~**-hand man** son bras droit (*personne*). ♦ **right-handed** *adj person* droitier; *punch, throw* du droit; *screw* fileté à droite. ♦ **rightly** *adv* **(a)** (*correctly*) bien, correctement; **I don't** ~**ly know*** je ne sais pas au juste; **(b)** (*justifiably*) à juste titre; ~**ly or wrongly** à tort ou à raison. ♦ **right-minded** *or* ♦ **right-thinking** *adj* sensé. ♦ **right-of-way** *n* (*across property*) droit *m* de passage; (*Aut: priority*) priorité *f*. ♦ **right-wing** **1** *n* (*Sport: also* ~**-winger**) ailier *m* droit; (*Pol*) droite *f*; **2** *adj* (*Pol*) de droite.

rigid ['rɪdʒɪd] *adj material* rigide; *person* rigide, inflexible; *specifications, interpretation* strict; *system* qui manque de flexibilité. **he's quite** ~ **about it** il est inflexible là-dessus. ♦ **rigidity** *n* rigidité *f*; inflexibilité *f* ♦ **rigidly** *adv stand etc* avec raideur; (*fig*) *behave, treat* inflexiblement; *oppose* absolument.

rigmarole ['rɪgmərəʊl] *n* (*speech*) galimatias *m*; (*complicated procedure*) comédie* *f*, histoire* *f*.

rigour, (*US*) **-or** ['rɪgə^r] *n* rigueur *f*. ♦ **rigor mortis** *n* rigidité *f* cadavérique. ♦ **rigorous** *adj* rigoureux. ♦ **rigorously** *adv* rigoureusement.

rim [rɪm] *n [cup, bowl]* bord *m*; *[wheel]* jante *f*; *[spectacles]* monture *f*. ♦ **rimless** *adj spectacles* à verres non cerclés.

rind [raɪnd] *n* (*on fruit*) peau *f*, (*cut off*) pelure *f*; *[cheese]* croûte *f*; *[bacon]* couenne *f*.

ring¹ [rɪŋ] **1** *n* **(a)** (*gen*) anneau *m*; (*on finger*) anneau, (*with stone*) bague *f*; (*for napkin*) rond *m*; (*for swimmer*) bouée *f* de natation; (*for invalid to sit on*) rond (pour malade). **wedding** ~ alliance *f*. **(b)** (*circle*) (*of people; in tree trunk*) cercle *m*; (*of smoke, in water etc*) rond *m*. **the** ~**s of Saturn** les anneaux *mpl* de Saturne; **to have** ~**s round the eyes** avoir les yeux cernés; **to stand in a** ~ se tenir en cercle; (*fig*) **to run** ~**s round sb*** battre qn à plate couture. **(c)** (*group*) (*gen*) coterie *f*; *[dealers]* cartel *m*; *[spies]* réseau *m*. **(d)** (*enclosure*) (*at circus*) piste *f*; (*at exhibition*) arène *f*; (*Horse-racing*) enceinte *f* des bookmakers; (*Boxing*) ring *m*. **2** *vt* (*surround*) entourer, encercler; (*put* ~ *on*) *item on list etc* entourer d'un cercle; *bird, tree* baguer. **3** *adj*: ~ **binder** classeur *m* à anneaux; ~ **finger** annulaire *m*; ~ **road** route *f* de ceinture, (*motorway-type*) périphérique *m*. ♦ **ringleader** *n* meneur *m*. ♦ **ringlet** *n* frisette *f*; (*long*) anglaise *f*. ♦ **ringmaster** *n* ≃ 'Monsieur Loyal'. ♦ **ringworm** *n* teigne *f*.

ring² [rɪŋ] (*vb: pret* **rang**, *ptp* **rung**) **1** *n* **(a)** *[bell]* sonnerie *f*, (*lighter*) tintement *m*; *[electric bell]* retentissement *m*; *[telephone]* sonnerie. **there was a** ~ **at the door** on a sonné à la porte; **his voice had an angry** ~ il y avait un accent de colère dans sa voix; **that has the** ~ **of truth** ça sonne juste. **(b)** (*: *phone call*) coup *m* de téléphone *or* de fil*. **to give sb a** ~ donner *or* passer un coup de téléphone *or* de fil* à qn.

2 *vi* **(a)** *[bell]* sonner, retentir, (*lightly*) tinter; *[alarm clock, telephone]* sonner. **to** ~ **for sb/sth** sonner qn/pour demander qch; **to** ~ **for the lift** appeler l'ascenseur. **(b)** (*telephone*) téléphoner. **(c)** *[words]* retentir (*through the room* dans la salle; *in his ears* à ses oreilles); *[voice]* vibrer (*with* de); *[coin]* sonner, tinter; (*resound*) résonner, retentir (*with* de); *[ears]* tinter, bourdonner. **to** ~ **false/true** *[coin]* sonner faux/clair; (*fig*) sonner faux/juste.

3 *vt* **(a)** *bell* faire sonner; *coin* faire tinter. **to** ~ **the doorbell** sonner (à la porte); **to** ~ **the bell** sonner, donner un coup de sonnette; (*fig*) **his name** ~**s a bell*** son nom me dit qch; *[bells]* **to** ~ **the changes** carillonner; (*fig*) **to** ~ **the changes on** varier. **(b)** (*Telec:* ~ **up**) téléphoner à, passer un coup de fil* à.

ring back *vi, vt sep* (*Telec*) rappeler.

ring off *vi* (*Telec*) raccrocher.

ring out *vi [bell]* sonner; *[voice]* résonner; *[shot]* retentir.

ring up *vt sep* (*Telec*) = **ring 3 b.**

♦ **ringing** **1** *adj voice, tone* retentissant; (*Telec*) ~**ing tone** tonalité *f*; **2** *n [bell, telephone]* sonnerie *f*, (*lighter*) tintement *m*; *[electric bell]* retentissement *m*; (*in ears*) bourdonnement *m*.

rink [rɪŋk] *n [ice-skating]* patinoire *f*; *[roller-skating]* skating *m*.

rinse [rɪns] **1** *n* rinçage *m*. **to give sth a** ~ rincer qch. **2** *vt clothes etc* rincer. **to** ~ **(the soap off) one's hands** se rincer les mains; (*colour*) **to** ~ **one's hair** se faire un rinçage.

rinse out *vt sep colour, dirt* faire partir à l'eau; *cup* rincer. **to** ~ **out one's mouth** se rincer la bouche.

riot ['raɪət] **1** *n* émeute *f*, bagarre *f*; *[flowers, colours]* profusion *f*. **2** *adj*: ~ **police** forces *fpl* d'intervention (de police); (*fig*) **to read sb the** ~ **act** tancer qn vertement. **3** *vi* manifester avec violence, (*stronger*) faire une émeute. ♦ **rioter** *n* émeutier *m*, -ière *f*. ♦ **riotous** *adj scene* tapageur; (*: *hilarious*) tordant*; ~**ous living** vie *f* de débauche; **a** ~**ous success** un succès fou* *or* monstre*. ♦ **riotously** *adv* tapageusement; ~**ously funny*** vachement rigolo:.

rip [rɪp] **1** *n* déchirure *f*. **2** *vt* déchirer, fendre. **to** ~ **open** ouvrir en hâte. **3** *vi* **(a)** *[cloth]* se déchirer. **(b)** (*Aut*) **let her** ~**!** fonce!*; **he let** ~* **a string of oaths** il a lâché un chapelet de jurons; **he let** ~* **at me** il m'a passé un bon savon*.

rip off *vt sep* **(a)** arracher (*from* de). **(b)** (*: *steal*) voler; (*: *burgle*) cambrioler.

♦ **rip-roaring*** *adj* exubérant; *success* monstre*.

ripe [raɪp] *adj* (*gen*) mûr (*for* pour); *cheese* fait. **to a** ~ **old age** jusqu'à un bel âge. ♦ **ripen** **1** *vt* (faire) mûrir; **2** *vi* mûrir. ♦ **ripeness** *n* maturité *f*.

ripple ['rɪpl] **1** *n* (*movement: on water, corn*) ondulation *f*; (*noise*) *[waves]* clapotis *m*; *[voices]* murmures *mpl*; *[laughter]* cascade *f*. **2** *vi* onduler.

rise [raɪz] (*vb: pret* **rose**, *ptp* **risen**) **1** *n* **(a)** *[theatre curtain, sun]* lever *m*; (*Mus*) hausse *f*; (*increase*) hausse, (*in wages*) augmentation *f*; (*fig*) *[person, party]* ascension *f*; *[town, industry, empire]* essor *m*. *[employee]* **to ask for a** ~

demander une augmentation (de salaire); (*fig*) **his ~ to power** sa montée au pouvoir; (*fig*) **to get a ~ out of sb*** faire marcher qn*. **(b)** (*small hill*) élévation *f*; (*slope*) côte *f*, pente *f*. **(c)** (*origin*) source *f* (*also fig*). (*fig*) **to give ~ to** donner lieu à.

2 *vi* **(a)** (*get up: gen*) se lever; (*after falling*) se relever. **to ~ to one's feet** se mettre debout, se lever; **to ~ from the dead** ressusciter (des morts). **(b)** (*go higher: gen*) monter; *[balloon]* s'élever; *[curtain, sun, wind]* se lever; *[dough]* lever; *[hair]* se dresser; *[barometer]* remonter; *[fish]* mordre; *[hopes, anger]* croître; (*in society, rank*) s'élever; *[cost of living]* augmenter; *[stocks, shares]* être en hausse; (*fig*) *[mountain, tower]* se dresser (*before sb* devant qn). **to ~ to the surface** remonter à la surface; (*fig*) **he rose to the bait** il a mordu à l'hameçon; **he won't ~ to that** il ne réagira pas à ça; **his eyebrows rose** il a levé les sourcils; **the mountain ~s to 3,000 metres** la montagne a une altitude de 3 000 mètres; **to ~ to the occasion** se montrer à la hauteur de la situation; **I can't ~ to £10** je ne peux pas aller jusqu'à 10 livres; **to ~ in price** augmenter (de prix); *temperature, level* **to ~ above sth** dépasser qch; **her spirits rose** son moral a remonté; **to ~ in the world** réussir; **to ~ from nothing** partir de rien; (*Mil*) **to ~ from the ranks** sortir du rang; **he rose to be President/a captain** il s'est élevé jusqu'à devenir Président/jusqu'au grade de capitaine. **(c)** (*adjourn*) *[assembly]* clore la session; *[meeting]* lever la séance. (*Parl*) **the House rose** l'Assemblée a levé la séance. **(d)** (*start*) *[river]* prendre sa source (*in* dans). **(e)** (*rebel:* **~ up**) se soulever (*against* contre).

rise up *vi [person]* se lever; *V also* **rise 2e.**

♦ **risen** ['rɪzn] *adj* (*Rel*) **the ~n Lord** le Christ ressuscité. ♦ **riser** *n*: **to be an early/a late ~r** (aimer) se lever tôt/tard. ♦ **rising 1** *n* (*rebellion*) soulèvement *m*; **2** *adj sun* levant; *prices, temperature* en hausse; *tide* montant; *wind* qui se lève; *tone* qui monte; *anger, fury* croissant; *ground* qui monte en pente; (*fig*) *generation* nouveau; **rising damp** humidité *f* (par capillarité); **rising young doctor** jeune médecin d'avenir; **she's rising six*** elle va sur ses six ans.

risk [rɪsk] **1** *n* risque *m*. **to take** *or* **run ~s** courir des risques; **to run the ~ of doing** courir le risque de faire; **it's not worth the ~** ça ne vaut pas la peine de courir un tel risque; **there is no ~ that he will come** il ne risque pas de venir; **at your own ~** à vos risques et périls; **at the ~ of seeming stupid** au risque de paraître stupide; **at the ~ of his life** au péril de sa vie; **at ~** *child* en danger; *job* menacé; **fire ~** risque d'incendie. **2** *vt life, future, savings* risquer; *battle, defeat, quarrel* s'exposer aux risques de; *accident* risquer d'avoir; (*venture*) *criticism, remark* risquer. **you ~ falling** vous risquez de tomber; **she won't ~ coming** elle ne se risquera pas à venir; **I'll ~ it** je vais risquer le coup*; **to ~ one's neck** risquer sa peau*. ♦ **riskiness** *n* risques *mpl*. ♦ **risky** *adj* risqué.

rissole ['rɪsəʊl] *n* croquette *f*.

rite [raɪt] *n* (*gen*) rite *m*. **last ~s** derniers sacrements *mpl*. ♦ **ritual** ['rɪtjʊəl] *adj, n* rituel (*m*). ♦ **ritually** *adv* rituellement.

rival ['raɪvəl] **1** *n* rival(e) *m(f)*. **2** *adj firm* rival; *attraction, claim* opposé. **3** *vt*: **to ~ sb in sth** rivaliser de qch avec qn. ♦ **rivalry** *n* rivalité *f*.

river ['rɪvəʳ] **1** *n* rivière *f*, (*major*) fleuve *m* (*also fig*). **down ~** en aval; **up ~** en amont; **the R~ Seine** la Seine. **2** *adj police, system, fishing* fluvial; *fish* de rivière. ♦ **riverbank** *n* rive *f*, berge *f*. ♦ **riverbed** *n* lit *m* de rivière *or* de fleuve. ♦ **riverside 1** *n* bord *m* de la rivière *or* du fleuve; **by the ~side** au bord de l'eau; **along the ~side** le long de la rivière *etc*; **2** *adj* au bord de la rivière.

rivet ['rɪvɪt] **1** *n* rivet *m*. **2** *vt* river. **3** *adj*: **~ joint** assemblage *m* par rivets. ♦ **riveter** *n* (*person*) riveur *m*; (*machine*) riveuse *f*. ♦ **rivet(t)ing 1** *n* rivetage *m*; **2** *adj* (*: *fig*) fascinant.

Riviera [ˌrɪvɪ'ɛərə] *n*: **the French ~** la Côte d'Azur; **the Italian ~** la Riviera (italienne).

road [rəʊd] **1** *n* (*gen*) route *f*; (*minor*) chemin *m*; (*in town*) rue *f*; (*fig*) chemin, voie *f*. **trunk ~** grande route, nationale *f*; **country ~** petite route, route de campagne; '**~ up**' 'attention travaux'; **just across the ~** juste en face (*from* de; *from us* de chez nous); **my car is off the ~** ma voiture est (*laid up*) sur cales *or* (*being repaired*) en réparation; **this vehicle shouldn't be on the ~** on ne devrait pas laisser circuler un véhicule dans cet état; **he is a danger on the ~** au volant c'est un danger public; **to take the ~** se mettre en route; *[salesman, theatre company]* **to be on the ~** être en tournée; **we were on the ~ at 6 o'clock** nous étions sur la route à 6 heures; **we were on the ~ to Paris** nous étions en route pour Paris; **the ~ to London** la route de Londres; (*in towns*) **London R~** rue de Londres; (*fig*) **on the ~ to success** sur le chemin du succès; (*fig*) **somewhere along the ~** à un moment donné; **you're in my ~*** vous m'empêchez de passer; **(get) out of the ~!*** dégagez!; **to have one for the ~*** prendre un dernier verre avant de partir.

2 *adj bridge, map, safety, traffic* routier. **~ accident** accident *m* de la route; **~ book** guide *m* routier; **~ haulage** *or* **transport** transports *mpl* routiers; **~ haulier** entrepreneur *m* de transports routiers; *[driver]* **~ sense** sens *m* de la conduite (sur route); (*Theat*) **~ show** spectacle *m* de tournée; **~ sign** panneau *m* indicateur; **international ~ signs** signalisation *f* routière internationale.

♦ **roadblock** *n* barrage *m* routier. ♦ **roadhog** *n* chauffard *m*. ♦ **roadhouse** *n* relais *m*. ♦ **roadmaking** *n* construction *f* de route. ♦ **roadman** *or* ♦ **roadmender** *n* cantonnier *m*. ♦ **roadroller** *n* rouleau *m* compresseur. ♦ **roadside 1** *n* bord *m* de la route; **along** *or* **by the ~side** au bord de la route; **2** *adj* au bord de la route. ♦ **roadsweeper** *n* (*person*) balayeur *m*, -euse *f*; (*vehicle*) balayeuse *f*. ♦ **road-test 1** *n* essais *mpl* sur route; **2** *vt*: **to ~-test a car** faire les essais sur route. ♦ **road-user** *n* usager *m* de la route. ♦ **roadway** *n* chaussée *f*. ♦ **roadworks** *npl* travaux *mpl* (d'entretien des routes). ♦ **roadworthy** *adj* en état de marche.

roam [rəʊm] **1** *vt streets etc* (*gen*) parcourir, *[child, dog]* traîner dans. **2** *vi* errer, rôder; *[thoughts]* vagabonder. ♦ **roaming 1** *adj* errant, vagabond; **2** *n* vagabondage *m*.

roan [rəʊn] *adj, n* (*horse*) rouan (*m*).

roar [rɔːʳ] **1** *vi [person, crowd]* hurler (*with* de); *[lion]* rugir; *[bull, wind, sea]* mugir; *[thunder, gun, waterfall, vehicle]* gronder; (*Aut: rev*) vrombir; *[fire in hearth]* ronfler. **to ~ with laughter** rire à gorge déployée; **to ~ past** *[trucks]* passer bruyamment à toute allure; *[car]* passer en vrombissant. **2** *vt* (**~ out**) *order* vociférer; *song* chanter à tue-tête; *one's disapproval* hurler. **3** *n* hurlement(s) *m(pl)*; rugissement *m*; mugissement *m*; grondement *m*; vrombissement *m*; ronflement *m*. **~s of laughter** de gros éclats *mpl* de rire. ♦ **roaring** *adj* hurlant; rugissant; mugissant; grondant; vrombissant; ronflant; (*in hearth*) **a ~ing fire** une belle flambée; **~ing success** succès *m* fou; **to do a ~ing trade** faire des affaires d'or*.

roast [rəʊst] **1** *n* rôti *m*. **2** *adj* (*gen*) rôti. **~ beef** rôti *m* de bœuf. **3** *vt* (*gen*) rôtir; *coffee beans* torréfier. **4** *vi [meat]* rôtir. **I'm ~ing!*** je crève* de chaleur! ♦ **roasting 1** *n* rôtissage *m*; **2** *adj* **(a)** (*: *hot*) *day* torride; **(b)** *chicken etc* à rôtir.

rob [rɒb] *vt person, shop* dévaliser; *orchard* piller. **to ~ sb of sth** (*purse etc*) voler *or* dérober qch à qn; (*rights etc*) priver qn de qch; **to ~ the till** voler de l'argent dans la caisse; **he's been ~bed of his watch** on lui a volé sa montre; **I've been ~bed!** j'ai été volé! ♦ **robber** *n* voleur *m*. ♦ **robbery** *n* vol *m*; **highway ~bery** (*lit*) vol de grand chemin; (**fig*) vol manifeste.

robe [rəʊb] *n* **(a)** (*garment*) robe *f* (de cérémonie); (*for house wear*) peignoir *m*. **his ~ of office** la robe de sa charge. **(b)** (*US: rug*) couverture *f*.

robin [ˈrɒbɪn] *n* rouge-gorge *m*.

robot [ˈrəʊbɒt] **1** *n* robot *m*. **2** *adj* automatique.

robust [rəʊˈbʌst] *adj person, humour* robuste; *defence* vigoureux; *material, appetite* solide. ♦ **robustness** *n* robustesse *f*; solidité *f*.

rock¹ [rɒk] **1** *vt* **(a)** *child* bercer; *cradle, rocking chair* balancer; *boat* (*gently*) balancer, (*roughly*) ballotter; *[explosion etc]* ébranler. **(b)** (*shake; also fig*: startle*) secouer. (*fig*) **to ~ the boat*** semer le trouble, compromettre la situation. **2** *vi* (*gently*) se balancer; (*violently*) être ébranlé. **to ~ with laughter*** se tordre de rire. **3** *n* (*music*) rock *m*. ♦ **rock-and-roll** *n* rock (and roll) *m*. ♦ **rocker** *n* **(a)** (*chair*) fauteuil *m* à bascule; **(b) off one's ~er*** cinglé*. ♦ **rocking chair** *n* fauteuil *m* à bascule. ♦ **rocking horse** *n* cheval *m* à bascule. ♦ **rocky¹** *adj table, government* branlant; *health, situation, finances* chancelant.

rock² [rɒk] **1** *n* **(a)** (*gen*) roche *f*; (*hard*) roc *m*; (*~ face*) rocher *m*; (*large mass, huge boulder*) rocher, (*smaller*) roche. **a huge ~ blocked their way** un énorme rocher leur bouchait le chemin; **a pile of fallen ~s** des éboulis *mpl* de roches; **the R~ of Gibraltar** le rocher de Gibraltar; (*fig*) **as solid as a ~** solide comme le roc; **the ship went on the ~s** le bateau est allé donner sur les écueils *mpl*; **on the ~s** *drink* avec des glaçons; (*) *person* qui n'a pas le sou; (*) *marriage* en train de craquer*. **(b)** (*sweet*) **stick of ~** ≈ bâton *m* de sucre d'orge. **2** *adj*: **~ crystal** cristal *m* de roche; **~ face** paroi *f* rocheuse; **~ fall** chute *f* de rochers; **~ garden** rocaille *f*; **~ painting** peinture *f* rupestre; **~ plant** plante *f* de rocaille; **~ salmon** roussette *f*; **~ salt** sel *m* gemme.

♦ **rock-bottom** *n* (*fig*) **to have reached ~-bottom*** *[person]* ne pas pouvoir tomber plus bas; (*in spirits*) avoir le moral à zéro*; *[prices]* être tombé au niveau le plus bas. ♦ **rock-bun** *or* ♦ **rock-cake** *n* rocher *m* (*Culin*). ♦ **rock-climber** *n* varappeur *m*, -euse *f*. ♦ **rock-climbing** *n* varappe *f*. ♦ **rockery** *n* rocaille *f*. ♦ **rocky²** *adj hill* rocheux; *path* rocailleux; **the R~y Mountains** les montagnes *fpl* Rocheuses.

rocket [ˈrɒkɪt] **1** *n* fusée *f*. **to fire** *or* **send up a ~** lancer une fusée; (*fig*) **to give sb a ~*** passer un savon* à qn. **2** *vi [prices]* monter en flèche. **3** *adj*: **~ base, ~ range** base *f* de lancement de missiles; **~ launcher** lance-fusées *m inv*. ♦ **rocketry** *n* (*rockets collectively*) fusées *fpl*.

rod [rɒd] *n* (*wooden*) baguette *f*; (*metallic*) tringle *f*; *[machinery]* tige *f*; (*fishing ~*) canne *f* à pêche; (*symbol of authority*) verge *f*. **curtain/stair ~** tringle à rideaux/d'escalier; (*fig*) **to make a ~ for one's own back** se préparer des ennuis; **to rule with a ~ of iron** *country* gouverner d'une main de fer; *family* mener à la baguette.

rode [rəʊd] *pret of* **ride**.

rodent [ˈrəʊdənt] *adj, n* rongeur (*m*).

roe¹ [rəʊ] *n [fish]* **hard ~** œufs *mpl* (de poisson); **soft ~** laitance *f*.

roe²(-deer) [ˈrəʊ(dɪəʳ)] *n* (*species*) chevreuil *m*; (*female deer*) chevreuil *m* femelle. ♦ **roebuck** *n* chevreuil *m* mâle.

rogue [rəʊg] **1** *n* (*scoundrel*) gredin *m*; (*scamp*) coquin(e) *m(f)*. (*Police*) **~s' gallery** photographies *fpl* de repris de justice. **2** *adj elephant* solitaire. ♦ **roguish** *adj* espiègle, coquin. ♦ **roguishly** *adv speak* avec espièglerie; *look* d'un œil coquin.

role [rəʊl] *n* rôle *m*.

roll [rəʊl] **1** *n* **(a)** (*gen*) rouleau *m*; *[banknotes]* liasse *f*; *[flesh, fat]* bourrelet *m*. **(b)** (*bread ~*) petit pain *m*. **(c)** (*movement*) *[ship]* roulis *m*; (*Aviat*) vol *m* en tonneau. **(d)** *[thunder, drums]* roulement *m*; *[organ]* ronflement *m*. **(e)** (*list*) liste *f*, tableau *m*; (*for court, ship's crew etc*) rôle *m*. **we have 60 pupils on our ~** nous avons 60 élèves inscrits; **to call the ~** faire l'appel; **~ of honour** (*Mil*) liste des combattants morts pour la patrie; (*Scol*) tableau d'honneur; (*Jur*) **to strike sb off the ~s** radier qn des listes.

2 *vi* **(a)** *[ball, ship, eyes]* rouler; *[horse, dog]* se rouler. **to ~ over and over** *[object]* rouler sur soi-même, *[person]* se rouler; **it ~ed under the table** ça a roulé sous la table; **to ~ down a slope** (*falling*) dégringoler une pente; (*playing*) rouler le long d'une pente; **tears were ~ing down her cheeks** les larmes roulaient sur ses joues; **the waves were ~ing on to the beach** les vagues déferlaient sur la plage; **the newspapers were ~ing off the presses** les journaux tombaient des rotatives; (*Aut*) **to ~ along** rouler; (*fig*) **to keep the ball** *or* **things ~ing** veiller à ce que tout marche bien; (*fig*) **he's ~ing in money*** il roule sur l'or; **they were ~ing in the aisles*** (*laughing*) ils se tordaient de rire. **(b)** *[thunder, drums, words]* rouler; *[voice]* retentir.

3 *vt ball* faire rouler; *umbrella, cigarette, lawn* rouler; *pastry, dough* étendre au rouleau; *metal* laminer; *road* cylindrer. **to ~ sth in/out** *etc* faire entrer/sortir *etc* qch en le roulant; **to ~ one's eyes** rouler les yeux; **to ~ one's r's** rouler les r; **to ~ string into a ball** enrouler de la ficelle en pelote.

roll about *vi [coins, marbles]* rouler çà et là; *[ship]* rouler; *[person, dog]* se rouler par terre.

roll away *vi [clouds, vehicle]* s'éloigner; *[ball]* rouler au loin.

roll back *vt sep carpet* rouler; *sheet* enlever (en roulant). (*fig*) **to ~ back the years** ramener le temps passé.

roll by *vi [vehicle, years]* passer.

roll in *vi [letters, contributions]* affluer; (*) *[person]* arriver, s'amener*.

roll on *vi [time]* s'écouler. **~ on Tuesday!*** vivement qu'on soit mardi!

roll out *vt sep* **(a)** *sentence, verse* débiter. **(b)** *pastry* étendre au rouleau; *metal* laminer.

roll over **1** *vi [object]* rouler; *[person, animal]* (*once*) se retourner (sur soi-même), (*several times*) se rouler. **2** *vt sep* retourner.

roll up **1** *vi* **(a)** *[animal]* se rouler (*into* en). **(b)** (*: *arrive*) arriver, s'amener*. (*fairground*) **~ up!** approchez! **2** *vt sep cloth, paper, map* rouler; *one's sleeves* retrousser.

♦ **roll-call** *n* appel *m*. ♦ **rolled gold** **1** *n* plaqué *m* or; **2** *adj* plaqué or *inv*. ♦ **roller** *n* **(a)** (*gen*) rouleau *m*; (*Papermaking, Tex*) calandre *f*; (*in metallurgy*) laminoir *m*; *[blind]* enrouleur *m*; (*little wheel*) roulette *f*; **table on ~ers** table *f* à roulettes; **road ~er** rouleau compresseur; **(b)** (*wave*) lame *f* de houle. ♦ **roller-blind** *n* store *m*. ♦ **roller-coaster** *n* montagnes *fpl* russes. ♦ **roller-skate** **1** *n* patin *m* à roulettes; **2** *vi* faire du patin à roulettes. ♦ **roller-skating** *n* patinage *m* à roulettes. ♦ **roller-towel** *n* essuie-mains *m* à rouleau. ♦ **rolling** *adj ship* qui roule; *sea* houleux; *countryside, ground* onduleux; (*fig*) **he's a ~ing stone** il roule sa bosse*; **~ing pin** rouleau *m* (à pâtisserie); (*Rail*) **~ing stock** matériel *m* roulant. ♦ **roll-neck(ed)** *adj* à col roulé. ♦ **roll-top desk** *n* bureau *m* à cylindre.

rollicking [ˈrɒlɪkɪŋ] *adj* joyeux (et bruyant).

Roman [ˈrəʊmən] **1** *adj* romain. **~ Catholic** (*adj, n*) catholique (*mf*); (*Typ*) **r~ letters** caractères *mpl* romains; **~ nose** nez *m* aquilin; **~ numerals** chiffres *mpl* romains. **2** *n* Romain(e) *m(f)*.

romance [rəʊˈmæns] **1** *n* (*tale of chivalry*) roman *m*; (*love story/film*) roman/film *m* à l'eau de rose; (*Mus*) romance *f*; (*love affair*) idylle *f*; (*attrac-*

tion) charme *m.* **it's quite a ~** c'est un vrai roman; (*fig: lies*) **it's pure ~** c'est du roman. **2** *adj* (*Ling*) **R~** roman. **3** *vi* enjoliver (à plaisir). ♦ **romantic 1** *adj* (*gen*) romantique; *adventure, setting* romanesque; **2** *n* romantique *mf.* ♦ **romantically** *adv write, describe* d'une façon romanesque; *sing, woo* en romantique. ♦ **romanticism** *n* romantisme *m.* ♦ **romanticize** *vti* romancer.

Romanesque [ˌrəʊmə'nesk] *adj* roman (*Archit*).

Romania [rəʊ'meɪnɪə] *n* = **Rumania.**

Rome [rəʊm] *n* Rome. **when in ~ do as the Romans do** à Rome il faut vivre comme les Romains; **the Church of ~** l'Église *f* (catholique) romaine.

romp [rɒmp] **1** *n* jeux *mpl* bruyants. **2** *vi [children, puppies]* jouer bruyamment. **the horse ~ed home** le cheval est arrivé dans un fauteuil*; (*fig*) **to ~ through an exam** passer un examen haut la main. ♦ **rompers** *npl* barboteuse *f* (*pour enfant*).

roof [ru:f] **1** *n* (*gen*) toit *m*; *[cave, tunnel]* plafond *m.* **the ~ of the mouth** la voûte du palais; **without a ~ over one's head** sans abri; **red-~ed** à toit rouge; **under her ~** chez elle; **to live under the same ~ as sb** vivre sous le même toit que qn; (*fig*) **to go through the ~*** *[person]* piquer une crise*; *[price, claim]* devenir excessif; (*fig*) **to raise the ~** faire un boucan terrible*. **2** *adj*: **~ garden** jardin *m* sur le toit; **~ light** plafonnier *m*; (*Aut*) **~ rack** galerie *f.* **3** *vt*: **to ~ sth over** recouvrir qch d'un toit. ♦ **rooftop** *n* toit *m.*

rook[1] [rʊk] **1** *n* (*bird*) corneille *f.* **2** *vt* (*: *swindle*) rouler*. ♦ **rookery** *n* colonie *f* de corneilles.

rook[2] [rʊk] *n* (*Chess*) tour *f.*

rookie* ['rʊkɪ] *n* (*esp Mil*) bleu* *m.*

room [rʊm] **1** *n* **(a)** (*in house, building*) pièce *f*; (*large*) salle *f*; (*bed~*) chambre *f*; (*office, study*) bureau *m.* **~s to let** chambres à louer; **~ and board** pension *f*; **his ~s** son appartement *m*; **they live in ~s** ils habitent un meublé; **a 6-~ed house** une maison de 6 pièces. **(b)** (*space*) place *f* (*for* pour). **is there ~?** y a-t-il de la place?; **there's no ~** il n'y a pas de place; **to make ~ for sb/sth** faire une place pour qn/de la place pour qch; **there is ~ for improvement** cela laisse à désirer. **2** *vi* partager une chambre (*with* avec). **3** *adj*: **~ divider** meuble *m* de séparation; **ring for ~ service** appelez le garçon d'étage; **wine at ~ temperature** vin *m* chambré. ♦ **roomful** *n* pleine salle *f.* ♦ **rooming-house** *n* (*US*) meublé *m* (*immeuble*). ♦ **roommate** *n* camarade *mf* de chambre. ♦ **roomy** *adj flat, handbag* spacieux; *garment* ample.

roost [ru:st] **1** *n* juchoir *m.* **to rule the ~** faire la loi. **2** *vi* jucher. (*fig*) **to come home to ~** retomber sur son auteur. ♦ **rooster** *n* coq *m.*

root [ru:t] **1** *n* (*gen, Ling, Math*) racine *f*; (*fig: of trouble etc*) cause *f.* **to pull up by the ~s** déraciner; **to take ~** prendre racine; **she has no ~s** c'est une déracinée; **to put down ~s in a country** s'enraciner dans un pays; (*fig*) **~ and branch** radicalement; **that is at the ~ of ...** c'est à l'origine de ... . **2** *adj*: **~ cause** cause *f* première; **~ crops** racines *fpl* alimentaires; **~ word** mot *m* racine *inv.* **3** *vt* enraciner. (*fig*) **~ed to the spot** cloué sur place. **4** *vi [plant etc]* s'enraciner.

root about, root around *vi* fouiller (*for sth* pour trouver qch).

root for *vt fus* (*: *esp US*) encourager.

root out *vt sep* (*find*) dénicher; (*remove*) extirper.

rope [rəʊp] **1** *n* corde *f*; (*Naut*) cordage *m*; *[bell]* cordon *m.* (*fig*) **to give sb more ~** lâcher la bride à qn; (*fig*) **to know/learn the ~s*** être/se mettre au courant; **to show sb the ~s*** mettre qn au courant; **a ~ of pearls** un collier de perles. **2** *adj*: **~ ladder** échelle *f* de corde; **Indian ~ trick** tour *m* de la corde (*prestidigitation*). **3** *vt case* corder; *climbers* encorder.

rope in* *vt sep helper* enrôler, embringuer*. **to get ~d in for sth** se laisser embringuer* pour faire qch.

rope off *vt sep part of area* réserver par une corde; (*block off*) interdire l'accès de.

♦ **rop(e)y*** *adj* (*bad*) pas fameux*.

rosary ['rəʊzərɪ] *n* chapelet *m.*

rose[1] [rəʊz] *pret of* **rise.**

rose[2] [rəʊz] **1** *n* **(a)** (*flower*) rose *f*; (**~bush, ~ tree**) rosier *m.* **wild ~** églantine *f*; (*fig*) **my life isn't all ~s*** tout n'est pas rose dans ma vie. **(b)** *[watering can]* pomme *f*; (*on ceiling*) rosace *f* (de plafond). **(c)** (*colour*) rose *m.* **2** *adj* (*colour*) rose; *leaf, petal* de rose. **~ garden** roseraie *f*; **~ window** rosace *f.* ♦ **rosé** *n* rosé *m* (*vin*). ♦ **rosebed** *n* massif *m* de rosiers. ♦ **rosebud** *n* bouton *m* de rose. ♦ **rose-coloured** *adj* (*fig*) **to see sth through ~-coloured spectacles** voir qch en rose. ♦ **rose-grower** *n* rosiériste *mf.* ♦ **rose-hip** *n* gratte-cul *m.* ♦ **rosemary** *n* romarin *m.* ♦ **rose-red** *adj* vermeil. ♦ **rosette** *n* rosette *f*; (*Sport: as prize*) cocarde *f.* ♦ **rosewood** *n* bois *m* de rose. ♦ **rosy** *adj* rose; (*fig*) *future, situation* qui se présente bien; **to paint a rosy picture of sth** dépeindre qch en rose.

rostrum ['rɒstrəm] *n* tribune *f.*

rot [rɒt] **1** *n* pourriture *f*; (*Bot, Med*) carie *f*; (**fig: nonsense*) bêtises *fpl.* (*fig*) **but the ~ set in*** mais les problèmes ont commencé; (*fig*) **to stop the ~** redresser la situation; **that's a lot of ~*** ça, c'est de la blague*. **2** *vi* pourrir. **to ~ away** tomber en pourriture. **3** *vt* (faire) pourrir.

rota ['rəʊtə] *n* tableau *m* (de service).

rotate [rəʊ'teɪt] **1** *vt* (*revolve*) faire tourner; (*change round*) *crops* alterner; *[two people] jobs* faire à tour de rôle. **2** *vi* tourner; être alterné. ♦ **rotary** *adj* rotatif. ♦ **rotating** *adj* tournant; alternant. ♦ **rotation** *n* rotation *f*; **in** *or* **by rotation** à tour de rôle. ♦ **rotor** *n* rotor *m.*

rotten ['rɒtn] *adj* **(a)** (*gen*) pourri; *tooth* gâté; (*fig: corrupt*) corrompu. **~ to the core** complètement pourri. **(b)** (*: *bad*) mauvais. **to feel ~** se sentir mal fichu*; **what ~ luck!** quelle poisse!*; **what a ~ trick!** quel sale tour!*

rotund [rəʊ'tʌnd] *adj person* rondelet; *object* rond, arrondi.

rouble, (*US*) **ruble** ['ru:bl] *n* rouble *m.*

rouge [ru:ʒ] *n* rouge *m* (à joues).

rough [rʌf] **1** *adj* **(a)** (*uneven*) *ground* accidenté; *skin, cloth, surface* rugueux; *path, road* rocailleux. **~ hands** *[peasant]* mains *fpl* rugueuses, *[housewife]* mains rêches. **(b)** (*fig*) *sound, voice* rude; *taste* âpre; (*coarse, unrefined*) *person, manners, life* rude; (*harsh etc*) *person, play, game* brutal; *neighbourhood, weather, sea crossing, tongue* mauvais; *waves, sea* gros. **~ handling of sth** manque *m* de soin envers qch; **~ stuff*** brutalité *f*; **these boys are very ~** ces garçons sont très durs; **a ~ customer*** un dur*; **to have a ~ time (of it)** en voir de dures*; **to give sb a ~ time (of it)** malmener qn, (*fig*) en faire voir de toutes les couleurs à qn*; (*fig*) **to make things ~ for sb*** mener la vie dure à qn; **it is ~ on him*** ce n'est pas marrant* pour lui; **to feel ~*** (*ill*) être mal fichu*. **(c)** (*approximate*) *plan* ébauché; *calculation, translation* approximatif. **~ copy, ~ draft, ~ work** brouillon *m*; **~ sketch** ébauche *f*; **~ paper** papier *m* de brouillon; **~ justice** justice *f* sommaire; **~ estimate** approximation *f*; **at a ~ estimate** *or* **guess** approximativement; **in its ~ state** à l'état brut; (*fig*) **he's a ~ diamond** sous ses dehors frustes c'est un brave garçon. **2** *adv live, sleep* à la dure; *play* brutalement. (*fig*) **to cut up ~*** (*angry*) se mettre en rogne*; (*violent*) devenir violent. **3** *n* **(a) to take the ~ with the smooth** prendre les choses comme elles viennent. **(b)** (*: *person*) voyou *m*, dur* *m.* **4** *vt*: **to ~ it*** vivre à la dure.

rough out *vt sep plan etc* ébaucher.

♦ **roughage** *n* aliments *mpl* qui régularisent les fonctions intestinales. ♦ **rough-and-ready** *adj method, equipment* rudimentaire; *work* fait à la hâte; *person* sans façons. ♦ **rough-and-tumble** *n* mêlée *f*, bagarre *f*. ♦ **roughen** *vt* rendre rude *or* rugueux *or* rêche. ♦ **rough-house*** *n* bagarre *f*. ♦ **roughly** *adv* **(a)** (*not gently*) *push, play* brutalement; *answer, order* avec brusquerie; **to treat sth/sb ~ly** malmener qch/qn; **(b)** (*not finely*) *make, sew* grossièrement; **~ly made** grossier; **to sketch sth ~ly** faire un croquis de qch; **(c)** (*approximately*) en gros, à peu près; **~ly speaking** en gros; **she is ~ly 40** elle a à peu près 40 ans. ♦ **roughneck*** *n* voyou *m*, dur *m* à cuire*. ♦ **roughness** *n [hands, surface]* rugosité *f*; *[person]* rudesse *f*, brusquerie *f*, (*stronger*) brutalité *f*; *[sea]* agitation *f*; *[road]* inégalités *fpl*. ♦ **roughshod** *adv*: **to ride ~shod over** *person* passer sur le corps de; *objection* passer outre à. ♦ **rough-spoken** *adj* au langage grossier.

roulette [ruːˈlet] *n* roulette *f* (*jeu*).

Roumania [ruːˈmeɪnɪə] *n* = **Rumania.**

round [raʊnd] **1** *adv*: **right ~, all ~** tout autour; **he went ~ by the bridge** il a fait le détour par le pont; **the long way ~** le chemin le plus long; **it's a long way ~** ça fait un grand détour; **come ~ and see me** venez me voir; **I asked him ~ for a drink** je l'ai invité à passer prendre un verre (chez moi); **I'll be ~ at 8 o'clock** je serai là à 8 heures; **all the year ~** pendant toute l'année; **drinks all ~!*** je paie une tournée!*; (*fig*) **taking things all ~** tout compte fait; **~ about** *V* **2b** *below*.

2 *prep* **(a)** (*of place etc*) autour de. **~ the table/house** *etc* autour de la table/maison *etc*; **sitting ~ the fire** assis au coin du feu; **the villages ~ Lewes** les villages des environs de Lewes; **if you're ~ this way** si tu passes par ici; (*Aut*) **to go ~ a corner** prendre un virage; **to go ~ an obstacle** contourner un obstacle; **to look ~ a house** visiter une maison; **to show sb ~ a town** faire visiter une ville à qn; **they went ~ the cafés looking for ...** ils ont fait le tour des cafés à la recherche de ...; **put a blanket ~ him** enveloppez-le d'une couverture. **(b)** (*approximately: also* **~ about**) environ.

3 *adj* rond. **to have ~ shoulders** avoir le dos rond; (*fig*) **a ~ dozen** une douzaine tout rond; **in ~ figures** en chiffres ronds; **~ robin** pétition *f*; **the ~ trip** le voyage aller et retour.

4 *n* **(a)** (*circle etc*) rond *m*, cercle *m*; (*slice: of bread, meat*) tranche *f*. **(b) to do** *or* **make one's ~(s)** *[watchman, policeman]* faire sa ronde; *[postman, milkman]* faire sa tournée; *[doctor]* faire ses visites; **he has got a paper ~** il distribue des journaux; *[infection, a cold etc]* **to go the ~s** circuler; **the story is going the ~s that ...** le bruit court que ...; (*fig*) **the daily ~** la routine quotidienne; **one long ~ of pleasures** une longue suite de plaisirs. **(c)** *[cards, golf]* partie *f*; (*Boxing*) round *m*; (*Horse-riding*) parcours *m*; *[competition, tournament]* manche *f*; *[election]* tour *m*; *[talks, discussions]* série *f*. **a ~ of drinks** une tournée*; **~ of ammunition** cartouche *f*; **a ~ of applause** une salve d'applaudissements. **(d)** (*Mus*) canon *m*. **(e) in the ~** (*Theat*) en rond; (*fig*) en détail.

5 *vt* **(a)** (*make* **~**) *edges etc* arrondir. **(b)** (*go* **~**) *corner* tourner; *bend* prendre; (*Naut*) *cape* doubler; *obstacle* contourner.

round off *vt sep speech, list, series* terminer; *sentence* parachever; *meeting* mettre fin à.

round up *vt sep* **(a)** (*bring together*) *people, cattle* rassembler; *criminals* effectuer une rafle de. **(b)** *prices etc* arrondir (au chiffre supérieur).

round (up)on *vt fus* attaquer.

♦ **roundabout 1** *adj route* détourné; *means* contourné; **~about phrase** circonlocution *f*; **2** *n* (*Brit: merry-go-~*) manège *m* (*de fête foraine*); (*at road junction*) rond-point *m* (à sens giratoire). ♦ **rounded** *adj* (*gen*) arrondi; *sentences* élégant. ♦ **rounders** *n* (*Brit*) *sorte de baseball*. ♦ **round-eyed** *adj* aux yeux ronds. ♦ **round-faced** *adj* au visage rond. ♦ **roundly** *adv say, tell* carrément. ♦ **round-necked** *adj pullover* ras du cou *inv*. ♦ **roundness** *n* rondeur *f*. ♦ **round-shouldered** *adj* voûté. ♦ **roundsman** *n, pl* **-men** (*Brit*) livreur *m*; **milk ~sman** laitier *m*. ♦ **round-up** *n [cattle, people]* rassemblement *m*; *[criminals, suspects]* rafle *f*.

rouse [raʊz] *vt* (*gen*) éveiller; (*fig*) *admiration, interest* susciter; *indignation* soulever; *suspicions* éveiller. **to ~ sb to action** pousser qn à agir; **to ~ sb (to anger)** mettre qn en colère. ♦ **rousing** *adj speech, sermon* vibrant; *cheers, applause* frénétique; *music* entraînant.

rout[1] [raʊt] **1** *n* (*defeat*) déroute *f*. **2** *vt* mettre en déroute.

rout[2] [raʊt] *vi* (*search:* **~ about**) fouiller.

rout out *vt sep* (*find*) dénicher; (*force out*) déloger; (*from bed*) tirer.

route [ruːt] **1** *n* (*gen, also of train, plane, ship etc*) itinéraire *m*. **shipping/air ~s** routes *fpl* maritimes/aériennes; **we're on a bus ~** nous sommes sur une ligne d'autobus; **a good ~ to London** un bon itinéraire pour aller à Londres; **en ~** en route (*for* pour). **2** *adj* (*Mil*) **~ march** marche *f* d'entraînement. **3** *vt train etc* faire passer (*through* par); *luggage etc* expédier (*through* par).

routine [ruːˈtiːn] **1** *n* **(a)** routine *f*. **daily ~** train-train *m* de la vie quotidienne; **office ~** travail *m* courant du bureau; **as a matter of ~** automatiquement. **(b)** (*Theat*) numéro *m*. **dance ~** numéro de danse. **2** *adj procedure, inquiry* d'usage; *work etc* habituel, (*pej*) de routine. **it was quite ~** ça n'avait rien de spécial.

roving [ˈrəʊvɪŋ] *adj* vagabond. **he has a ~ eye** il aime reluquer* les filles; **~ ambassador** ambassadeur *m* itinérant; **~ reporter** reporter *m* volant.

row[1] [rəʊ] *n [objects, people]* rang *m*; (*behind one another*) file *f*, ligne *f*; *[houses, trees, figures]* rangée *f*; *[cars]* file; (*Knitting*) rang. **in the front ~** au premier rang; **sitting in a ~** assis en rang; **4 failures in a ~** 4 échecs de suite.

row[2] [rəʊ] **1** *vt boat* faire aller à la rame *or* à l'aviron. **to ~ sb across** faire traverser qn en canot. **2** *vi* ramer. **to ~ away/back** s'éloigner/revenir à la rame; **to go ~ing** (*for pleasure*) faire du canotage; (*Sport*) faire de l'aviron. ♦ **rowboat** *or* ♦ **rowing boat** *n* canot *m* (à rames). ♦ **rower** *n* rameur *m*, -euse *f*. ♦ **rowing 1** *n* canotage *m*; (*Sport*) aviron *m*; **2** *adj*: **~ing club** club *m* d'aviron. ♦ **rowlock** [ˈrɒlək] *n* dame *f* de nage.

row[3]* [raʊ] **1** *n* (*noise*) tapage *m*, vacarme *m*; (*quarrel*) querelle *f*, dispute *f*; (*scolding*) réprimande *f*, savon* *m*. **to make a ~** faire du tapage; **to have a ~** se disputer (*with* avec); **to give sb a ~** passer un savon à qn*; **to get (into) a ~** se faire passer un savon*. **2** *vi* se disputer (*with* avec).

rowan [ˈraʊən] *n* sorbier *m*.

rowdy [ˈraʊdɪ] **1** *adj* (*noisy*) chahuteur; (*rough*) bagarreur*. **2** *n* (*) voyou *m*. ♦ **rowdyism** *n* chahut *m*; bagarre* *f*; (*at football match etc*) violence *f*.

royal [ˈrɔɪəl] **1** *adj* (*gen*) royal. **~ blue** bleu roi *inv*; (*Brit*) **R~ Commission** Commission *f* extraparlementaire; **the ~ household** la maison du roi *or* de la reine; (*fig*) **the ~ road to** la voie royale de; **they gave him a ~ welcome** ils l'ont reçu de façon royale. **2** *n*: **the ~s*** la famille royale. ♦ **royalist** *adj, n* royaliste (*mf*). ♦ **royally** *adv* royalement. ♦ **royalty** *n* **(a)** (*persons*) la famille royale; **(b) ~ties** (*from book*) droits *mpl* d'auteur; (*from oil well, patent*) royalties *fpl*.

rub [rʌb] **1** *n*: **to give sth a ~** (*furniture, shoes, silver*) donner un coup de chiffon à qch; (*sore place, one's arms*) frotter qch; (*fig*) **there's the ~!**

c'est là la difficulté! **2** *vt* frotter; (*Art*) *brass, inscription* prendre un frottis de. **to ~ one's nose** se frotter le nez; **to ~ one's hands together** se frotter les mains; **to ~ sth dry** sécher qch en le frottant; **to ~ a hole in sth** faire un trou dans qch à force de frotter; **to ~ sth through a sieve** passer qch au tamis; **to ~ lotion into the skin** faire pénétrer de la lotion dans la peau; (*fig*) **to ~ shoulders with** coudoyer; (*fig*) **to ~ sb's nose in sth** ne jamais laisser oublier qch à qn. **3** *vi [thing]* frotter (*against* contre); *[person, cat]* se frotter (*against* contre).

rub along* *vi [two people]* s'accorder tant bien que mal.

rub away *vt sep* faire disparaître (en frottant), effacer.

rub down *vt sep horse* bouchonner; *person* frictionner (*with* avec); *wall, paintwork* (*clean*) nettoyer (du haut en bas), (*sandpaper*) poncer.

rub in *vt sep liniment* faire pénétrer en frottant; (*fig*) *idea* insister sur; *lesson* faire entrer (*to* à). (*fig*) **don't ~ it in!*** pas besoin de me le rappeler!

rub off 1 *vi*: **the blue will ~ off on to your hands** tu vas avoir les mains toutes bleues; (*fig*) **it might ~ off on to her brother*** elle en passera peut-être à son frère. **2** *vt sep writing* effacer; *dirt* enlever en frottant.

rub out 1 *vi* s'effacer. **2** *vt sep* effacer.

rub up 1 *vi* (*fig*) **to ~ up against all sorts of people** côtoyer toutes sortes de gens. **2** *vt sep vase, table* frotter, astiquer. (*fig*) **to ~ sb up the right/wrong way** savoir/ne pas savoir s'y prendre avec qn.

♦ **rubbing** *n* frottement *m*; (*Art*) frottis *m*.

rubber[1] ['rʌbəʳ] **1** *n* (*material*) caoutchouc *m*; (*eraser*) gomme *f*. (*shoes*) **~s** caoutchoucs. **2** *adj goods, boots etc* de *or* en caoutchouc. **~ band** élastique *m*; **~ plantation** plantation *f* de hévéas; **~ ring** (*for swimming*) bouée *f* de natation; **~ solution** dissolution *f*; **~ stamp** tampon *m*; **~ tree** hévéa *m*. ♦ **rubberized** *adj* caoutchouté. ♦ **rubbery** *adj* caoutchouteux.

rubber[2] ['rʌbəʳ] *n* (*Bridge*) robre *m*.

rubbish ['rʌbɪʃ] **1** *n* (*waste material*) détritus *mpl*; (*household ~*) ordures *fpl*, immondices *fpl*; *[garden]* détritus; *[factory]* déchets *mpl*; *[building site]* décombres *mpl*; (*nonsense*) bêtises *fpl*, absurdités *fpl*. **this shop sells a lot of ~** ce magasin ne vend que de la camelote*; **it's just ~** (*nonsense*) ça ne veut rien dire; **to talk ~** débiter des bêtises *or* des absurdités; **~!*** quelle blague!*; **it is ~ to say that ...** c'est idiot de dire que ... . **2** *adj* (*Brit*) **~ bin** poubelle *f*, boîte *f* à ordures; **~ cart** voiture *f* d'éboueurs; **~ collection** ramassage *m* d'ordures; **~ dump** décharge *f* publique. ♦ **rubbishy** *adj goods, ideas, book* sans valeur; *shoes etc* de mauvaise qualité.

rubble ['rʌbl] *n* (*ruins*) décombres *mpl*; (*in road-building*) blocaille *f*. **it was reduced to a heap of ~** il n'en restait qu'un tas de décombres.

rubicund ['ru:bɪkənd] *adj* rougeaud.

ruby ['ru:bɪ] **1** *n* rubis *m*. **2** *adj* (*colour*) rubis *inv*; (*made of rubies*) *necklace, ring* de rubis.

rucksack ['rʌksæk] *n* sac *m* à dos.

ructions* ['rʌkʃənz] *npl* (*rows*) disputes *fpl*, grabuge* *m*; (*riots*) bagarres *fpl*. **there'll be ~ if ...** il va y avoir du grabuge* si ... .

rudder ['rʌdəʳ] *n* gouvernail *m*.

ruddy ['rʌdɪ] *adj* **(a)** *complexion* coloré; *sky, glow* rougeoyant. **(b)** (**Brit*) fichu*, sacré* (*before n*).

rude [ru:d] *adj* **(a)** (*impolite*) impoli, mal élevé, (*stronger*) insolent; (*coarse*) grossier; (*improper*) indécent. **to be ~ to sb** être grossier envers qn; **it's ~ to stare** c'est très mal élevé de dévisager les gens; **~ word** gros mot *m*. **(b)** *shock* brusque, rude. (*fig*) **to have a ~ awakening** être rappelé brusquement à la réalité. **(c)** (*primitive*) primitif. **(d)** (*vigorous*) *health* robuste. ♦ **rudely** *adv* impoliment; insolemment; grossièrement; brusquement. ♦ **rudeness** *n* impolitesse *f*; insolence *f*; grossièreté *f*; brusquerie *f*.

rudiment ['ru:dɪmənt] *n* rudiment *m*. ♦ **rudimentary** *adj* rudimentaire.

rueful ['ru:fʊl] *adj look, person* attristé; *situation* attristant. ♦ **ruefully** *adv* avec regret.

ruffian ['rʌfɪən] *n* voyou *m*, brute *f*.

ruffle ['rʌfl] *vt hair, feathers* ébouriffer; *surface, water* agiter; *clothes* déranger, froisser; *person* (*upset*) froisser, (*annoy*) contrarier. **to grow ~d** perdre son calme.

rug [rʌg] *n* petit tapis *m*; (*bedside etc*) carpette *f*; (*travelling ~*) couverture *f*; (*in tartan*) plaid *m*.

rugby ['rʌgbɪ] **1** *n* (*abbr* **rugger***) rugby *m*. **2** *adj*: **~ league** le rugby à treize; **~ player** rugbyman *m*.

rugged ['rʌgɪd] *adj country, ground, road* accidenté; *cliff, coast, mountains* aux contours déchiquetés; *bark* rugueux; *features* irrégulier; *character, person* bourru; *resolve* farouche.

ruin ['ru:ɪn] **1** *n* ruine *f*. **to fall into ~** tomber en ruine; **in ~s** en ruine. **2** *vt* (*gen*) ruiner; *clothes* abîmer; *event, enjoyment* gâter. ♦ **ruined** *adj building* en ruine; *person* ruiné. ♦ **ruinous** *adj* ruineux. ♦ **ruinously** *adv*: **~ously expensive** ruineux.

rule [ru:l] **1** *n* **(a)** (*gen*) règle *f*; (*regulation*) règlement *m*. **the ~s of the game** la règle du jeu; **against the ~s** contraire à la règle *or* au règlement; **~s and regulations** statuts *mpl*; (*Ind*) **work(ing) to ~** grève *f* du zèle; **it's a ~ that ...** il est de règle que ... + *subj*; **~ of the road** règle générale de la circulation; **by ~ of thumb** à vue de nez; **golden ~** règle d'or; (*fig: usual*) **it's the ~** c'est normal; **he makes it a ~ to get up early** il a pour règle de se lever tôt; **as a ~** en règle générale, normalement. **(b)** (*authority*) **under British ~** sous l'autorité *f* britannique; (*Pol etc*) **majority ~** le gouvernement par la majorité; **the ~ of law** l'autorité de la loi. **(c)** (*for measuring*) règle *f* (graduée). **folding ~** mètre *m* pliant.

2 *adj*: **~ book** règlement *m*.

3 *vt* **(a)** *country* gouverner; *business firm etc* diriger. **~d by his wife** mené par sa femme. **(b)** *[umpire, judge]* décider, déclarer (*that* que). **(c)** (*draw lines on*) *paper* régler; *line* tirer à la règle.

4 *vi* **(a)** *[monarch]* régner (*over* sur). (*fig*) **the prices ruling in Paris** les cours pratiqués à Paris. **(b)** (*Jur*) statuer (*against* contre; *in favour of* en faveur de; *on* sur).

rule out *vt sep* exclure, écarter. **the age limit ~s him out** il est exclu du fait de la limite d'âge; **murder can't be ~d out** il est impossible d'exclure l'hypothèse d'un meurtre.

♦ **ruler** *n* **(a)** (*sovereign*) souverain(e) *m(f)*; (*political leader*) chef *m* (d'État); **the country's ~rs** les dirigeants *mpl* du pays; **(b)** (*for measuring*) règle *f*. ♦ **ruling 1** *adj principle* souverain; *factor, passion* dominant; *price* actuel; **the ruling class** la classe dirigeante; (*Pol*) **the ruling party** le parti au pouvoir; **2** *n* (*Admin, Jur*) décision *f*; **to get/give a ruling** obtenir/rendre un jugement.

rum [rʌm] *n* rhum *m*.

Rumania [ru:'meɪnɪə] *n* Roumanie *f*.

rumble ['rʌmbl] **1** *vi* (*gen*) gronder; *[stomach, pipes]* gargouiller. *[vehicle]* **to ~ past** passer avec fracas. **2** *n* grondement *m*; gargouillement *m*. ♦ **rumbling** *n* grondement *m*; gargouillement *m*; **tummy rumblings*** borborygmes *mpl*.

ruminate ['ru:mɪneɪt] *vti* ruminer. ♦ **ruminant** *adj, n* ruminant (*m*). ♦ **ruminative** *adj* pensif.

rummage ['rʌmɪdʒ] **1** *vi* (**~ about, ~ around**) fouiller (*among, in* dans; *for* pour trouver). **2** *adj*: **~ sale** vente *f* de charité (*de bric-à-brac*).

rumour, (*US*) rumor ['ru:məʳ] **1** *n* rumeur *f*, bruit *m*. **~ has it that there will be war, there is a ~ of war** le bruit court *or* on dit qu'il va y avoir la guerre. **2** *vt*: **it is ~ed that ...** on dit que ..., le bruit court que ... .

rump [rʌmp] *n [animal]* croupe *f*; (*Culin*) culotte *f* (de bœuf); *[person]* derrière *m*. ◆ **rumpsteak** *n* culotte *f* (de bœuf); (*single steak*) rumsteck *m*.

rumple ['rʌmpl] *vt* (*gen*) chiffonner; *hair* ébouriffer.

rumpus* ['rʌmpəs] **1** *n* chahut *m*. **to make a ~** faire du chahut. **2** *adj*: **~ room** salle *f* de jeux.

run [rʌn] (*vb: pret* **ran**, *ptp* **run**) **1** *n* **(a) to go for a ~** faire un peu de course à pied; **to go for a 2-km ~** faire 2 km de course à pied; **at a ~** au pas de course, en courant; **to break into a ~** se mettre à courir; **to make a ~ for it** prendre la fuite; **to have the ~ of a place** avoir un endroit à son entière disposition; **to be on the ~** être en cavale*; **to be on the ~ from the police** être recherché par la police; **to have the enemy on the ~** avoir mis l'ennemi en fuite; **to keep the enemy on the ~** harceler l'ennemi; **we've given him** (*etc*) **a good ~ for his money** on ne s'est pas avoué vaincu d'avance; (*on retirement, death*) **he's had a good ~** il a bien profité de l'existence. **(b)** (*outing*) tour *m*, excursion *f*. **to go for a ~ in the car** faire un tour *or* une promenade en voiture; **I'll give you a ~ up to town** je vais vous conduire en ville. **(c)** *[bus, tram, boat, plane]* (*distance*) trajet *m*; (*route*) parcours *m*. **it's a 30-minute bus ~** il y a une demi-heure de trajet en autobus; **the boat no longer does that ~** le bateau ne fait plus cette traversée; **the ships on the China ~** les paquebots qui font la Chine. **(d)** (*series*) série *f*, suite *f*; (*Cards*) séquence *f*; (*Roulette*) série *f* (*on* à). (*Theat*) **the London ~** la saison à Londres; (*Theat*) **the play had a long ~** la pièce a tenu longtemps l'affiche; (*gen*) **it's had a long ~** ça a duré longtemps; **in the long ~** finalement; **to have a ~ of luck** être en veine*; **a ~ of bad luck** une période de malchance. **(e)** (*great demand*) ruée *f* (*on* sur). **there has been a ~ on** on s'est rué sur. **(f)** *[tide]* flux *m*; (*fig: trend*) tendance *f*. **the common ~ of mankind** le commun des mortels; **the ordinary ~ of things** le train-train habituel. **(g)** (*track for sledging, skiing etc*) piste *f*; (*animal enclosure*) enclos *m*. **(h)** (*Typ*) **a ~ of 5,000 copies** un tirage de 5 000 exemplaires.

2 *vi* **(a)** courir. **to ~ in/off** *etc* entrer/partir *etc* en courant; **she came ~ning out** elle est sortie en courant; **to ~ for the bus** courir pour attraper l'autobus; **she ran to meet him/to help him** elle a couru à sa rencontre/à son secours; **the car ran into a tree** la voiture a heurté un arbre; (*fig*) **the news ran like wildfire** la nouvelle s'est répandue comme une traînée de poudre; **a ripple of fear ran through the town** la peur a gagné toute la ville; **how does the last sentence ~?** comment la dernière phrase est-elle rédigée?; **so the story ~s** c'est ainsi que l'histoire est racontée; (*Pol etc*) **to ~ for President, to ~ for the Presidency** être candidat à la présidence.

(b) (*flee*) fuir, se sauver. **to ~ for one's life** se sauver à toutes jambes; **~ for it!** sauvez-vous!

(c) (*become etc*) *[river]* **to ~ dry** se tarir; **my pen's ~ dry** je n'ai plus d'encre; *[resources etc]* **to ~ dry** *or* **short** *or* **low** s'épuiser; **to ~ short of sth** se trouver à court de qch; **to ~ riot** *[people, imagination]* être déchaîné; *[vegetation]* pousser follement; **to ~ wild** *[person, children]* être déchaîné; *[animals]* courir en liberté; *[plants, garden]* retourner à l'état sauvage.

(d) (*move*) filer; *[drawer, curtains]* glisser; (*flow*) couler; *[river, tears, tap, eyes, nose]* couler; *[pen]* fuir; *[sore, abscess]* suppurer; (*melt*) fondre; *[cheese]* couler; *[colour, ink]* baver; (*in washing*) déteindre. **the rope ran through his fingers** la corde lui a filé entre les doigts; **rivers ~ into the sea** les fleuves se jettent dans la mer; **the street ~s into the square** la rue débouche dans la place; **to ~ high** *[river]* être haut; *[sea]* être gros; *[feelings]* être exacerbé; *[prices]* être très haut; **to leave a tap ~ning** laisser un robinet ouvert; **to ~ with blood/sweat/moisture** ruisseler de sang/de sueur/d'humidité; (*fig*) **his blood ran cold** son sang s'est glacé dans ses veines.

(e) (*continue*) *[play]* tenir l'affiche, se jouer; *[film]* passer; *[contract]* être valide. (*Rad, TV*) **the programme ran for 50 minutes** le programme a duré 50 minutes; **the expenditure ~s into millions** les dépenses s'élèvent à des millions; **I can't ~ to a new car** je ne peux pas me payer* une nouvelle voiture; **the funds won't ~ to ...** les fonds ne permettent pas d'acheter ... .

(f) (*Naut*) **to ~ before the wind** courir vent arrière; **to ~ ashore** *or* **aground** s'échouer; (*fig*) **to ~ foul of sb** indisposer qn contre soi.

(g) this train ~s between ce train fait le service entre; **the buses ~ once an hour** les autobus passent toutes les heures.

(h) (*function*) *[machine, factory]* marcher; *[wheel]* tourner. **the car is ~ning smoothly** la voiture marche bien; **to leave the engine ~ning** laisser tourner le moteur; **to ~ on diesel/on electricity/off batteries** marcher au gas-oil/à l'électricité/sur piles.

(i) (*pass*) *[road, river etc]* passer (*through* à travers; *past* devant); *[mountain range]* s'étendre. **the road ~s north and south** la route va du nord au sud; **he has a scar ~ning across his chest** il a une cicatrice en travers de la poitrine; (*fig*) **this theme ~s through** ce thème se retrouve dans; **it ~s in the family** c'est de famille.

(j) *[stockings]* filer; *[knitting]* se démailler.

3 *vt* **(a)** courir. **he ~s 3 km every day** il fait 3 km de course à pied tous les jours; **to ~ a race** courir dans une épreuve; **to ~ errands** faire des commissions; **to ~ a blockade** forcer un blocus; (*fig*) **to ~ sb close** serrer qn de près; **you're ~ning things a bit close!*** ça va être juste!; **to ~ its course** suivre son cours; **to ~ a temperature** avoir de la fièvre; **to ~ the car into a tree** heurter un arbre.

(b) to ~ to earth finir par trouver; **to ~ a horse in the Derby** faire courir un cheval dans le Derby; **to ~ sb out of town** chasser qn de la ville; **she is ~ off her feet*** elle ne sait plus où donner de la tête.

(c) (*transport*) *person* conduire; *thing* transporter; (*smuggle*) *guns* passer en contrebande. **he ran her home** il l'a ramenée chez elle (en voiture).

(d) (*operate etc*) *machine* faire marcher. **he ~s a Rolls** il a une Rolls; **this car is very cheap to ~** cette voiture est très économique; **to ~ into the ground** *car* garder jusqu'à ce qu'elle soit bonne pour la ferraille; *business* laisser péricliter.

(e) (*organize etc*) *business, school, mine, hotel* diriger; *course, competition* organiser. **they ~ trains to London every hour** il y a un train pour Londres toutes les heures; **to ~ extra buses** mettre en service des autobus supplémentaires; **to ~ a house** tenir une maison; **I want to ~ my own life** je veux être maître de ma vie; **she ~s everything** c'est elle qui dirige tout; (*fig*) **I'm ~ning this show!*** c'est moi qui commande ici!

(f) (*move*) *hand, fingers, comb* passer (*over* sur; *through* dans). **to ~ one's finger down a list** suivre une liste du doigt; **to ~ one's eye over** jeter un coup d'œil sur; **he ran the vacuum cleaner over the carpet** il a passé rapidement le tapis à l'aspirateur; **she ran her pencil through the word** elle a barré le mot d'un coup de crayon; **to ~ a rope through** faire passer une corde dans; **to ~ water into a bath** faire couler de l'eau dans une baignoire; **I'll ~ you a bath** je vais te faire couler un bain.

(g) (*issue*) *article* publier; *film* présenter.

run about, run around *vi* courir çà et là.

run across 1 *vi* traverser en courant. **2** *vt fus*

(*meet, find*) *person, thing, fact* tomber sur.
run along *vi* courir; (*go away*) s'en aller.
run away 1 *vi* **(a)** partir en courant; (*flee*) *[person]* s'enfuir; *[horse]* s'emballer. **to ~ away from home** s'enfuir (de chez soi); (*fig*) **don't ~ away with the idea that ...** n'allez pas vous mettre dans la tête que ... . **(b)** *[water]* s'écouler. **2** *vt sep water* laisser s'écouler.
run away with *vt fus money etc* épuiser.
run down 1 *vi [watch etc]* s'arrêter; *[battery]* se décharger. **2** *vt sep* **(a)** (*Aut*) (*knock over*) renverser, (*run over*) écraser; *ship* heurter par l'avant; (*in battle*) éperonner. **(b)** (*reduce*) *production* restreindre de plus en plus; *factory* restreindre la production de; *shop* réduire peu à peu l'ampleur de. (*Med*) **to be ~ down** être fatigué. **(c)** (*: *disparage*) dénigrer.
run in *vt sep* **(a)** *car* roder. **'~ning in'** 'en rodage'. **(b)** (*: *arrest*) emmener au poste.
run into *vt fus* (*meet*) *person* rencontrer par hasard, tomber sur; *difficulties, trouble* se heurter à; *danger* se trouver exposé à. **to ~ into debt** s'endetter.
run off 1 *vi* = **run away 1a. 2** *vt sep* (*Typ*) tirer.
run on 1 *vi* **(a)** (**fig: in talking etc*) parler sans arrêt. **it ran on for 4 hours** ça a duré 4 bonnes heures. **(b)** (*Typ*) suivre sans alinéa. **2** *vt sep letters, words* faire suivre sans laisser d'espace.
run out 1 *vi* **(a)** *[rope, chain]* se dérouler; *[liquid]* couler. **(b)** (*end*) *[lease, contract]* expirer; *[supplies]* s'épuiser; *[period of time]* s'écouler. **when the money ~s out** quand il n'y aura plus d'argent. **2** *vt sep rope, chain* laisser filer.
run out of *vt fus money, time* manquer de.
run over 1 *vi* **(a)** (*overflow*) déborder. **(b)** (*go briefly*) passer, faire un saut (*to sb's house* chez qn). **2** *vt fus* (*reread*) revoir; (*recapitulate*) reprendre. **3** *vt sep* (*Aut*) écraser.
run through *vt fus* **(a)** (*use up*) *fortune* gaspiller. **(b)** (*read quickly*) *notes, text* jeter un coup d'œil sur. **(c)** (*rehearse*) *play* répéter; (*recapitulate*) reprendre. **let's ~ through it again** reprenons cela encore une fois.
run up *vt sep* **(a)** *flag* hisser. **(b)** *bill* laisser accumuler. **(c)** (*: *sew quickly*) fabriquer*.
run up against* *vt fus person* tomber sur; *difficulties* se heurter à.
♦ **runabout 1** *n* (*car*) petite voiture *f*; (*boat*) runabout *m*; **2** *adj* (*Rail*) **~about ticket** billet *m* circulaire. ♦ **runaway 1** *n* fugitif *m*, -ive *f*; **2** *adj person* fugitif; *horse* emballé; *car* fou; *wedding, couple* clandestin; *inflation* galopant. ♦ **rundown** *n* **(a)** réduction *f* (*in, of* de); **(b) to give sb a ~down*** on mettre qn au courant de. ♦ **runner** *n* **(a)** (*athlete*) coureur *m*; (*horse*) partant *m*; (*messenger*) messager *m*; **(b)** (*sliding part*) *[sledge]* patin *m*; *[skate]* lame *f*; *[drawer]* coulisseau *m*; *[curtain]* anneau *m*; **(c)** (*table-runner*) chemin *m* de table; (*hall/stair carpet*) chemin de couloir/d'escalier. ♦ **runner-bean** *n* haricot *m* à rames. ♦ **runner-up** *n* second(e) *m(f)*. ♦ **running 1** *n* (*fig*) **to make the ~ning** mener la course; **to be in the ~ning** avoir des chances de réussir; **in the ~ning for the job** sur les rangs pour avoir le poste; **2** *adj tap* qui coule; *sore* qui suppure; **a ~ning stream** un cours d'eau; **~ning water (in every room)** eau courante (dans toutes les chambres); **to keep up a ~ning battle** être en lutte continuelle (*with* avec); **~ning commentary** (*Rad, TV*) commentaire *m* suivi; (*fig*) commentaire détaillé (*on* sur); **4 days ~ning** 4 jours de suite; **~ning board** marchepied *m*; **~ning costs** frais *mpl* d'exploitation; **the ~ning costs of the car are high** la voiture revient cher; (*US Pol*) **~ning mate** candidat *m* à la vice-présidence; **in ~ning order** en état de marche. ♦ **runny** *adj substance* qui coule; *omelette* baveux. ♦ **run-of-the-mill** *adj* banal. ♦ **run-through** *n* essai *m*. ♦ **runup** *n* période *f* préparatoire (*to* à). ♦ **runway** *n* (*Aviat*) piste *f* (d'envol *or* d'atterrissage).
rung[1] [rʌŋ] *ptp of* **ring**[2].
rung[2] [rʌŋ] *n [ladder, chair]* barreau *m*.
rupture [ˈrʌptʃəʳ] **1** *n* rupture *f*; (*Med**: *hernia*) hernie *f*. **2** *vt* rompre. (*Med*) **to ~ o.s.*** se donner une hernie. **3** *vi* se rompre.
rural [ˈrʊərəl] *adj* (*gen*) rural; *scenery* de la campagne.
ruse [ruːz] *n* ruse *f*.
rush[1] [rʌʃ] **1** *n* **(a)** ruée *f* (*for* vers; *on* sur); (*Mil: attack*) assaut *m*. **gold ~** ruée vers l'or; **we have a ~ on in the office** c'est le coup de feu au bureau; **the Christmas ~** la bousculade des fêtes de fin d'année; **we've had a ~ of orders** on nous a submergés de commandes; **a ~ of warm air** une bouffée d'air tiède. **(b)** (*hurry*) **to be in a ~** être extrêmement pressé; **I had a ~ to get here in time** j'ai dû me dépêcher pour arriver à l'heure; **I did it in a ~** je l'ai fait à toute vitesse; **what's all the ~?** pourquoi est-ce que c'est si pressé? **(c)** (*Cine*) projection *f* d'essai.
2 *adj*: **~ hours** heures *fpl* de pointe; **~ job** travail *m* d'urgence, (*botched*) travail bâclé.
3 *vi [person]* se précipiter; *[car]* foncer. **to ~ up/down** *etc* monter/descendre *etc* précipitamment; **to ~ at sth** se jeter *or* se ruer sur qch; (*fig*) **don't ~ at it, take it slowly** ne fais pas ça trop vite, prends ton temps; **the train ~ed into the tunnel** le train est entré à toute vitesse dans le tunnel; **I'm ~ing to finish it** je me dépêche pour en avoir fini; **to ~ through** *book* lire à la hâte; *meal* prendre sur le pouce*; *town* traverser à toute vitesse; *work* expédier; **the blood ~ed to his face** le sang lui est monté au visage.
4 *vt* **(a)** (*do hurriedly*) *job, task* dépêcher; *order* exécuter d'urgence. **to ~ sb to hospital** transporter qn d'urgence à l'hôpital; **they ~ed him out of the room** ils l'ont fait sortir en toute hâte de la pièce; **I don't want to ~ you** je ne voudrais pas vous bousculer; **to be ~ed off one's feet** être débordé; **to ~ sb into a decision** forcer qn à prendre une décision à la hâte. **(b)** (*take by storm*) *town* prendre d'assaut; *fence* franchir sur son élan; *[crowd] police* s'élancer contre.
rush about, rush around *vi* courir çà et là.
rush through *vt sep* (*Comm*) *order* exécuter d'urgence; *goods, supplies* envoyer de toute urgence.
rush up 1 *vi* (*arrive*) accourir. **2** *vt sep help, reinforcements* faire parvenir d'urgence (*to* à).
rush[2] [rʌʃ] *n* (*Bot*) jonc *m*. **~ matting** tapis *m* tressé.
rusk [rʌsk] *n* ≃ biscotte *f*.
russet [ˈrʌsɪt] **1** *n* (*apple*) reinette *f* grise. **2** *adj* feuille-morte *inv*.
Russia [ˈrʌʃə] *n* Russie *f*. ♦ **Russian 1** *adj* russe; **2** *n* russe *m*; (*person*) Russe *mf*.
rust [rʌst] **1** *n* rouille *f*. **2** *vt* rouiller. **3** *vi* se rouiller. ♦ **rust-coloured** *adj* rouille *inv*. ♦ **rustproof** *or* ♦ **rust-resistant** *adj* inoxydable. ♦ **rusty** *adj* (*lit, fig*) rouillé; (*lit*) **to get** *or* **go ~y** se rouiller; (*fig*) **my English is ~y** mon anglais est un peu rouillé.
rustic [ˈrʌstɪk] *adj* rustique.
rustle [ˈrʌsl] **1** *n* bruissement *m*. **2** *vi* bruire. **3** *vt* **(a)** *papers* faire bruire. **(b)** (*steal*) *cattle* voler.
rustle up* *vt sep* (*find*) se débrouiller* pour trouver; (*make*) préparer en vitesse.
♦ **rustler** *n* voleur *m* de bétail. ♦ **rustling** *n* vol *m* de bétail.
rut [rʌt] *n* ornière *f* (*also fig*). *[person]* **to be in** *or* **get into a ~** suivre l'ornière.
ruthless [ˈruːθlɪs] *adj* impitoyable. ♦ **ruthlessly** *adv* impitoyablement. ♦ **ruthlessness** *n* caractère *m* impitoyable.
rye [raɪ] **1** *n* seigle *m*; (*US: whisky*) whisky *m* (américain). **2** *adj*: **~ bread** pain *m* de seigle.

S

S, s [es] *n* (*letter*) S, s *m*.
Sabbath ['sæbəθ] *n* (*Jewish*) sabbat *m*; (†: *Sunday*) dimanche *m*. ♦ **sabbatical** *adj* sabbatique.
sable ['seɪbl] **1** *n* zibeline *f*. **2** *adj fur* de zibeline, de martre; *brush* en poil de martre.
sabotage ['sæbətɑːʒ] **1** *n* sabotage *m*. **an act of ~** un sabotage. **2** *vt* saboter. ♦ **saboteur** *n* saboteur *m*, -euse *f*.
sabre, (*US*) **saber** ['seɪbəʳ] *n* sabre *m*.
saccharin(e) ['sækərɪn,-iːn] *n* saccharine *f*.
sachet ['sæʃeɪ] *n* sachet *m*.
sack¹ [sæk] **1** *n* (*bag*) sac *m*. **coal ~** sac à charbon; **~ of coal** sac de charbon; (*fig*) **to give sb the ~*** renvoyer qn, mettre qn à la porte; **to get the ~*** être renvoyé, être mis à la porte. **2** *adj*: **~ race** course *f* en sac. ♦ **sackcloth** *n* (*Rel*) **~cloth and ashes** le sac et la cendre. ♦ **sackful** *n* plein sac *m*. ♦ **sacking** *n* **(a)** (*cloth*) toile *f* à sac; **(b)** (*: *dismissal*) renvoi *m*.
sack² [sæk] **1** *n* (*plundering: also* **~ing**) sac *m*. **2** *vt* mettre à sac.
sacrament ['sækrəmənt] *n* sacrement *m*. **to receive the ~s** communier.
sacred ['seɪkrɪd] *adj* sacré (*after n*). **the S~ Heart** le Sacré-Cœur; **~ writings** livres *mpl* sacrés; **~ to the memory of** consacré à la mémoire de; **is nothing ~?** vous ne respectez donc rien?; (*fig*) **~ cow*** chose *f* sacro-sainte.
sacrifice ['sækrɪfaɪs] **1** *n* sacrifice *m*. **to make great ~s** faire de grands sacrifices (*for sb* pour qn; *to do* pour faire). **2** *vt* sacrifier (*to* à; *for sb* pour qn; *for sth* pour avoir qch). ♦ **sacrificial** *adj* (*Rel*) sacrificiel; *price* extrêmement bas.
sacrilege ['sækrɪlɪdʒ] *n* sacrilège *m*. ♦ **sacrilegious** *adj* sacrilège.
sacristy ['sækrɪstɪ] *n* sacristie *f*. ♦ **sacristan** *n* sacristain(e) *m(f)*.
sacrosanct ['sækrəʊsæŋkt] *adj* sacro-saint.
sad [sæd] *adj person, smile* triste; *news, duty, condition* triste (*before n*); *loss* douloureux; *mistake* fâcheux. **to make sb ~** attrister qn; **to grow ~** devenir triste; **a ~ business** une triste affaire. ♦ **sadden** *vt* attrister. ♦ **sad-eyed** *adj* aux yeux tristes. ♦ **sadly** *adv* (*unhappily*) tristement; (*regrettably*) fâcheusement; **~ly incompetent** fort incompétent; **~ly lacking in ...** qui manque fort de ... . ♦ **sadness** *n* tristesse *f*.
saddle ['sædl] **1** *n* selle *f*. **in(to) the ~** en selle; (*fig*) **when he was in the ~** quand c'était lui qui tenait les rênes; **~ of lamb** selle d'agneau. **2** *vt* (**~ up**) *horse* seller. (*fig*) **to ~ sb with (doing) sth*** imposer qch à qn, coller qch à qn*; **we're ~d with it** nous voilà avec ça sur les bras. ♦ **saddlebag** *n* sacoche *f*. ♦ **saddler** *n* sellier *m*. ♦ **saddlery** *n* sellerie *f*.
sadism ['seɪdɪzəm] *n* sadisme *m*. ♦ **sadist** *adj, n* sadique (*mf*). ♦ **sadistic** *adj* sadique.
safari [sə'fɑːrɪ] *n* safari *m*. **to go** *or* **be on ~** faire un safari; **~ park** réserve *f*.
safe [seɪf] **1** *adj* **(a)** (*not in danger*) *person* en sécurité, hors de danger. **~ and sound** sain et sauf; **to be ~ from** être à l'abri de; **no girl is ~ with him** les filles courent toujours un risque avec lui; **you'll be quite ~ here** vous êtes en sécurité ici; **his life was not ~** sa vie était en danger; **I don't feel very ~ on this ladder** je ne me sens pas très en sécurité sur cette échelle; *[jewel, secret]* **it's quite ~** ça ne risque rien. **(b)** (*not dangerous*) *toy, animal, action* sans danger; *method, vehicle* sûr; *ice, ladder, bridge* solide; *beach, bathing* qui n'est pas dangereux; (*secure*) *hiding place, harbour, investment* sûr; (*prudent*) *choice, guess, estimate* prudent. **is it ~ to come out?** est-ce qu'on peut sortir sans danger?; **it's not ~ to go alone** il est dangereux d'y aller tout seul; **is that dog ~?** ce chien n'est pas méchant?; **that dog isn't ~ with children** il ne faut pas laisser les enfants s'approcher du chien; **~ journey!** bon voyage!; **I'll keep it ~** *or* **in a ~ place for you** je vais vous le garder en lieu sûr; **in ~ hands** en mains sûres; **it's ~ as houses** (*runs no risk*) cela ne court aucun risque; (*offers no risk*) cela ne présente aucun risque; (*Med*) **the ~ period*** la période sans danger; **the ~st thing to do would be to wait** le plus sûr serait d'attendre; **just to be on the ~ side** pour être plus sûr; **better ~ than sorry!** mieux vaut être trop prudent!; **it's a ~ bet he'll win** il gagnera à coup sûr; (*Pol*) **a ~ seat** un siège assuré; **it is ~ to predict ...** on peut prédire sans risque d'erreur ... .
2 *n* (*for money, valuables*) coffre-fort *m*; (*for food*) garde-manger *m inv*.
♦ **safe-breaker** *n* perceur *m* de coffre-fort. ♦ **safe-conduct** *n* sauf-conduit *m*. ♦ **safe-deposit** *n* (*vault*) dépôt *m* de coffres-forts; (*box*) coffre *m*. ♦ **safeguard** **1** *vt* sauvegarder (*against* contre); **2** *n* sauvegarde *f* (*against* contre). ♦ **safekeeping** *n*: **in ~keeping** en sécurité; **I gave it to him for ~keeping** je le lui ai donné à garder. ♦ **safely** *adv* (*without mishap*) sans accident; *arrive* bien; (*without risk*) sans danger; *say* sans risque d'erreur; (*securely*) en sûreté; *store* en lieu sûr. ♦ **safeness** *n [construction, equipment]* solidité *f*.
safety ['seɪftɪ] **1** *n [person, valuables]* sécurité *f*; *[construction, equipment]* solidité *f*. **in a place of ~** en lieu sûr; **he reached ~ at last** il était enfin en sûreté *or* en sécurité; **to play for ~** ne pas prendre de risques; **there is ~ in numbers** plus on est nombreux moins il y a de danger; **for ~'s sake** pour plus de sûreté, par mesure de sécurité; **~ on the roads** la sécurité sur les routes; **~ first!** la sécurité d'abord!; (*Aut*) soyez prudents!; **~-first campaign** campagne *f* de sécurité. **2** *adj belt, device, margin, measure, regulations, screen* de sécurité; *bolt, lock, razor, blade, chain, match* de sûreté. **~ catch** cran *m* de sécurité; (*Theat*) **~ curtain** rideau *m* de fer; **~ glass** verre *m* Sécurit ®; **~ net** filet *m* (de protection); **~ pin** épingle *f* de sûreté; **~ valve** soupape *f* de sûreté.
saffron ['sæfrən] **1** *n* safran *m*. **2** *adj colour* safran *inv*.
sag [sæg] *vi [roof, chair]* s'affaisser; *[beam, prices]* fléchir; *[breasts, hemline]* pendre; *[rope]* pendre au milieu, être détendu; *[gate]* être affaissé. ♦ **sagging** *adj* affaissé; fléchi; pendant; détendu.
saga ['sɑːgə] *n* saga *f*; (*novel*) roman-fleuve *m*; (*fig*) aventure *f* épique.
sagacious [sə'geɪʃəs] *adj person* sagace; *comment* perspicace. ♦ **sagaciously** *adv* avec sagacité. ♦ **sagacity** *n* sagacité *f*.
sage¹ [seɪdʒ] *n* sauge *f*. **~ and onion stuffing** farce *f* à l'oignon et à la sauge; **~ green** vert cendré *inv*.

sage² [seɪdʒ] *adj, n* (*wise*) sage (*m*). ♦ **sagely** *adv say, act* avec sagesse; *nod* d'un air solennel.
Sagittarius [ˌsædʒɪ'tɛərɪəs] *n* le Sagittaire.
sago ['seɪgəʊ] *n* sagou *m*. ~ **pudding** sagou au lait.
Sahara [sə'hɑːrə] *n* Sahara *m*.
said [sed] *pret, ptp of* **say**.
sail [seɪl] **1** *n [boat]* voile *f*; *[windmill]* aile *f*. **under** ~ à la voile; *[boat]* **to set** ~ prendre la mer; **to set** ~ **for** *[boat]* partir à destination de; *[person]* partir pour; **to go for a** ~ faire un tour en bateau. **2** *vi* **(a)** *[boat]* **to** ~ **into harbour** entrer au port; **the ship** ~**ed into Cadiz** le bateau est arrivé à Cadix; **to** ~ **round the cape** doubler le cap; **the boat** ~**s at 6 o'clock** le bateau part à 6 heures. **(b)** *[person]* **to** ~ **away/back** *etc* partir/revenir *etc* en bateau; **to** ~ **round the world** faire le tour du monde en bateau; **he goes** ~**ing** il fait de la voile; (*fig*) **he was** ~**ing close to the wind** il jouait un jeu dangereux. **(c)** (*fig*) *[swan, clouds etc]* glisser. **the book** ~**ed out of the window** le livre est allé voler par la fenêtre; **she** ~**ed into the room*** elle est entrée dans la pièce toutes voiles dehors. **3** *vt* **(a) to** ~ **the seas** parcourir les mers; **to** ~ **the Atlantic** traverser l'Atlantique (en bateau). **(b)** *boat* piloter.
sail through* **1** *vi* (*succeed*) réussir haut la main. **2** *vt fus exam, driving test* avoir haut la main.
♦ **sailboat** *n* (*US*) voilier *m*. ♦ **sailcloth** *n* toile *f* à voile. ♦ **sailing** *n* (*act*) navigation *f* à voile; (*pastime*) la voile; (*departure*) départ *m*. ♦ **sailing boat** *n* voilier *m*. ♦ **sailing dinghy** *n* dériveur *m*. ♦ **sailing ship** *n* voilier *m*. ♦ **sailmaker** *n* voilier *m* (*personne*). ♦ **sailor** *n* (*gen*) marin *m*; (*before the mast*) matelot *m*; **to be a good/bad** ~**or** avoir/ne pas avoir le pied marin. ♦ **sailplane** *n* planeur *m*.
saint [seɪnt] *n* saint(e) *m(f)*. ~**'s day** fête *f* (de saint); **All S**~**s' Day** la Toussaint; **S**~ **Peter** saint Pierre; **S**~ **Patrick's Day** la Saint-Patrick; **S**~ **Peter's Church** (l'église *f*) Saint-Pierre; **he's no** ~* ce n'est pas un petit saint. ♦ **saint-like** *or* ♦ **saintly** *adj quality* de saint; *smile* plein de bonté; *person* saint (*before n*). ♦ **saintliness** *n* sainteté *f*.
sake [seɪk] *n*: **for sb's** ~ pour (l'amour de) qn; **for God's** ~ pour l'amour de Dieu; **for my** ~ pour moi; **for your own** ~ pour ton bien; **to eat for the** ~ **of eating** manger pour le plaisir de manger; **for old times'** ~ en souvenir du passé; **for argument's** ~ à titre d'exemple; **art for art's** ~ l'art pour l'art; **for the** ~ **of peace** pour avoir la paix.
salad ['sæləd] **1** *n* salade *f*. **tomato** ~ salade de tomates; **ham** ~ jambon accompagné de salade. **2** *adj*: ~ **bowl** saladier *m*; ~ **cream** ≃ mayonnaise *f* (*en bouteille etc*); (*fig*) ~ **days** années *fpl* de jeunesse et d'inexpérience; ~ **dressing** ≃ mayonnaise *f*, (*oil and vinegar*) vinaigrette *f*; ~ **oil** huile *f* de table; ~ **servers** couvert *m* à salade.
salary ['sælərɪ] **1** *n* (*professional etc*) traitement *m*, appointements *mpl*; (*pay in general*) salaire *m*. **2** *adj*: ~ **earner** personne *f* qui touche un traitement; ~ **range/scale** éventail *m*/échelle *f* des traitements. ♦ **salaried** *adj* (*Ind*) **salaried staff** employés *mpl* touchant un traitement (*or* des appointements).
sale [seɪl] **1** *n* **(a)** (*act*) vente *f*. **to put up for** ~ mettre en vente; **(up) for** ~ à vendre; **on** ~ en vente; **sold on a** ~ **or return basis** vendu avec possibilité de rendre; ~**s are up/down** les ventes ont augmenté/baissé; **auction** ~ vente aux enchères; ~ **in aid of the blind** vente de charité en faveur des aveugles. **(b)** (*Comm: also* ~s) soldes *mpl*. **the** ~**s are on** c'est la saison des soldes; **in the** *or* **a** ~ en solde. **2** *adj*: ~ **price** prix *m* de solde; ~**s department** service *m* des ventes; ~**s force** ensemble *m* des représentants; ~**s manager** directeur *m* commercial; ~**s talk*** boniment *m* (*often pej*). ♦ **saleable** *adj* vendable. ♦ **sale-of-work** *n* vente *f* de charité. ♦ **saleroom** *n* salle *f* des ventes. ♦ **salesman** *n* (*in shop*) vendeur *m*; (*representative*) représentant *m* de commerce. ♦ **salesmanship** *n* art *m* de la vente. ♦ **saleswoman** *n* vendeuse *f*.
salient ['seɪlɪənt] *adj, n* saillant (*m*).
saliva [sə'laɪvə] *n* salive *f*.
sallow ['sæləʊ] *adj* jaunâtre. ♦ **sallowness** *n* teint *m* jaunâtre.
sally ['sælɪ] *n* (*wit*) saillie *f*.
sally forth, sally out *vi* sortir gaiement.
salmon ['sæmən] **1** *n* saumon *m*. **2** *adj*: ~ **fishing** pêche *f* au saumon; ~ **pink** saumon *inv*; ~ **steak** darne *f* de saumon; ~ **trout** truite *f* saumonée.
salmonella [ˌsælmə'nelə] *n* salmonellose *f*.
salon ['sælɔ̃ːŋ] *n* salon *m*.
saloon [sə'luːn] *n* **(a)** (*public room*) salle *f*; (*Brit:* ~ **bar**) ≃ salle de café; (*US: bar*) bar *m*, saloon *m*. **(b)** (*Brit: car*) conduite *f* intérieure.
salsify ['sælsɪfɪ] *n* salsifis *m*.
salt [sɔːlt] **1** *n* sel *m*. **there's too much** ~ **in the potatoes** les pommes de terre sont trop salées; (*fig*) **to rub** ~ **in the wound** retourner le couteau dans la plaie; **he's not worth his** ~ il ne vaut pas grand-chose; **to take sth with a pinch of** ~ ne pas prendre qch au pied de la lettre; (*sailor*) **an old** ~ un vieux loup de mer. **2** *adj water, butter, beef, taste* salé; *mine* de sel; *spoon* à sel. ~ **flats** salants *mpl*; ~ **pork** petit salé *m*. **3** *vt meat, one's food* saler.
salt away *vt sep meat* saler; (*fig*) *money* mettre à gauche*.
♦ **saltcellar** *n* salière *f*. ♦ **salt-free** *adj* sans sel. ♦ **saltiness** *n [water]* salinité *f*; *[food]* goût *m* salé. ♦ **saltpetre,** (*US*) **-ter** *n* salpêtre *m*. ♦ **saltwater** *adj fish* de mer. ♦ **salty** *adj taste* salé.
salubrious [sə'luːbrɪəs] *adj* salubre.
salutary ['sæljʊtərɪ] *adj* salutaire.
salute [sə'luːt] **1** *n* (*with hand*) salut *m*; (*with guns*) salve *f*. **to take the** ~ passer les troupes en revue. **2** *vt* (*Mil etc*) saluer; (*fig: acclaim*) saluer (*as* comme). **to** ~ **the flag** saluer le drapeau. **3** *vi* faire un salut.
salvage ['sælvɪdʒ] **1** *n* **(a)** (*saving*) *[ship etc]* sauvetage *m*; (*for re-use*) récupération *f*. **(b)** (*things saved from fire, wreck*) objets *mpl or* biens *mpl* sauvés; (*for re-use*) objets récupérables. **to collect newspapers for** ~ récupérer les vieux journaux. **(c)** (*payment*) prime *f* de sauvetage. **2** *adj operation, vessel* de sauvetage. **3** *vt* sauver (*from* de); (*for re-use*) récupérer.
salvation [sæl'veɪʃən] *n* (*gen, Rel*) salut *m*. ♦ **Salvation Army** *n* Armée *f* du Salut. ♦ **salvationist** *n* salutiste *mf*.
salve [sælv] **1** *n* baume *m*. **2** *vt*: **to** ~ **his conscience** pour être en règle avec sa conscience.
salver ['sælvəʳ] *n* plateau *m* (*de métal*).
salvo ['sælvəʊ] *n* (*Mil*) salve *f*.
Samaritan [sə'mærɪtən] *n*: **the Good** ~ le bon Samaritain; (*organization*) **the** ~**s** ≃ S.O.S. Amitié.
same [seɪm] **1** *adj* même. **the** ~ **book as** le même livre que; **the** ~ **day** le même jour; **the very** ~ **day** le jour même; **that** ~ **day** ce même jour; **in the** ~ **way ...** de même ...; **the** ~ **table as usual** la table habituelle; **it was just the** ~ **as usual** c'était comme d'habitude; **one and the** ~ **person** une seule et même personne; **always the** ~ **old thing** toujours la même chose; **it comes to the** ~ **thing** cela revient au même; **at the** ~ **time** en même temps; **at the very** ~ **time as ...** au moment même où ...; (*fig pej*) **to go the** ~ **way as sb** suivre les traces de qn; (*in health*) **she's much about the** ~ son état est inchangé. **2** *pron*: **the** ~ (*gen*) le même, la même; (*the* ~ *thing*) la même chose; (*Jur: aforementioned*) le susdit, la susdite. **the film is the** ~ **as before** le film est le même

qu'avant; **it's always the ~ in politics** c'est toujours la même chose en politique; **the price is the ~ as last year** c'est le même prix que l'année dernière; **do the ~ as your brother** fais comme ton frère; **he left and I did the ~** il est parti et j'en ai fait autant; **I would do the ~ again** je recommencerais; **I'll do the ~ for you** je te rendrai ça; (*in bar etc*) **the ~ again please** la même chose s'il vous plaît; **I don't feel the ~ about it as I did** maintenant je vois la chose différemment; **I still feel the ~ about you** mes sentiments à ton égard n'ont pas changé; **it's all the ~ to me** cela m'est égal; **all** *or* **just the ~** tout de même, quand même; **it's not the ~ as before** ce n'est plus pareil; **it's the ~ everywhere** c'est partout pareil; **and the ~ to you!** à toi aussi, (*as retort: in quarrel etc*) et je te souhaite la pareille!; **~ here!*** moi aussi! ◆ **sameness** *n* (*monotony*) monotonie *f*.

sample [ˈsɑːmpl] **1** *n* (*gen*) échantillon *m*; (*Med*) *[urine]* échantillon; *[blood, tissue]* prélèvement *m*. **as a ~** à titre d'échantillon. **2** *adj*: **~ bottle** (*or* **cigarette** *or* **selection** *etc*) échantillon *m*; **~ line** (*or* **verse** *etc*) exemple *m*; **a ~ section of** une section représentative de. **3** *vt food, wine* goûter.

sanatorium [ˌsænəˈtɔːrɪəm] *n, pl* **-ia** sanatorium *m*; (*Scol*) infirmerie *f*.

sanctify [ˈsæŋktɪfaɪ] *vt* sanctifier. ◆ **sanctity** *n [person]* sainteté *f*; *[oath, place]* caractère *m* sacré; *[marriage]* inviolabilité *f*.

sanctimonious [ˌsæŋktɪˈməʊnɪəs] *adj* moralisateur. ◆ **sanctimoniously** *adv say* d'un ton moralisateur.

sanction [ˈsæŋkʃən] **1** *n* (*all senses*) sanction *f*. **to impose economic ~s on** prendre des sanctions économiques contre. **2** *vt* (*gen*) sanctionner. **~ed by usage** consacré par l'usage.

sanctuary [ˈsæŋktjʊərɪ] *n* (*holy place*) sanctuaire *m*; (*refuge*) asile *m*; (*for wild life*) réserve *f*. **to seek ~** chercher asile.

sand [sænd] **1** *n* sable *m*. (*beach*) **~s** plage *f*; **miles and miles of golden ~s** des kilomètres de plages de sable doré. **2** *adj*: **~ dune** dune *f* (de sable); **~ flea** puce *f* de mer. **3** *vt* **(a)** *road* sabler. **(b)** (**~ down**) *wood etc* poncer au papier de verre. ◆ **sandbag** *n* sac *m* de sable. ◆ **sandbank** *n* banc *m* de sable. ◆ **sandbox** *n* tas *m* de sable. ◆ **sandcastle** *n* château *m* de sable. ◆ **sandpaper 1** *n* papier *m* de verre; **2** *vt* poncer au papier de verre. ◆ **sandpit** *n* carrière *f* de sable; (*for children*) tas *m* de sable. ◆ **sandshoes** *npl* (*rubber-soled*) tennis *fpl*; (*rope-soled*) espadrilles *fpl*. ◆ **sandstone** *n* grès *m*. ◆ **sandstorm** *n* tempête *f* de sable. ◆ **sandy** *adj soil, path* sablonneux; *water, deposit* sableux; *beach* de sable; (*colour*) sable *inv*; *hair* blond roux *inv*.

sandal [ˈsændl] *n* sandale *f*; (*rope-soled*) espadrille *f*.

sandwich [ˈsænwɪdʒ] **1** *n* sandwich *m*. **cheese ~** sandwich au fromage; **open ~** canapé *m*. **2** *adj*: **~ loaf** pain *m* de mie; (*Ind*) **~ course** ≃ cours *mpl* de formation professionnelle; **~ man** homme-sandwich *m*. **3** *vt* (**~ in**) *person, appointment* intercaler. **~ed between** pris en sandwich entre*.

sane [seɪn] *adj person* sain d'esprit; *judgment* sain. **he isn't quite ~** il n'a pas toute sa raison. ◆ **sanely** *adv* sainement. ◆ **sanity** *n [person]* santé *f* mentale, raison *f*; **sanity prevailed** le bon sens l'a emporté.

sang [sæŋ] *pret of* **sing.**

sanguinary [ˈsæŋgwɪnərɪ] *adj* sanglant.

sanguine [ˈsæŋgwɪn] *adj* **(a)** *person* optimiste. **(b)** *complexion* sanguin.

sanitarium [ˌsænɪˈtɛərɪəm] *n* = **sanatorium.**

sanitary [ˈsænɪtərɪ] *adj* **(a)** (*clean*) hygiénique. **(b)** *system, equipment* sanitaire. **~ engineer** ingénieur *m* sanitaire; **~ inspector** inspecteur *m*, -trice *f* de la Santé publique; **~ towel,** (*US*) **~ napkin** serviette *f* hygiénique. ◆ **sanitation** *n* (*in house*) installations *fpl* sanitaires; (*in town*) système *m* sanitaire.

sank [sæŋk] *pret of* **sink**[1].

Santa Claus [ˌsæntəˈklɔːz] *n* le père Noël.

sap[1] [sæp] *n* (*Bot*) sève *f*.

sap[2] [sæp] *vt strength, confidence* saper.

sapling [ˈsæplɪŋ] *n* jeune arbre *m*.

sapper [ˈsæpəʳ] *n* (*Mil*) sapeur *m*. (*Brit*) **the S~s*** le génie.

sapphire [ˈsæfaɪəʳ] **1** *n* saphir *m*. **2** *adj ring* de saphir(s). **~ blue** saphir *inv*.

sarcasm [ˈsɑːkæzəm] *n* sarcasme *m*. ◆ **sarcastic** *adj* sarcastique; **sarcastic remarks** sarcasmes *mpl*. ◆ **sarcastically** *adv* sarcastiquement.

sardine [sɑːˈdiːn] *n* sardine *f*. **tinned** *or* (*US*) **canned ~s** ≃ sardines à l'huile.

Sardinia [sɑːˈdɪnɪə] *n* Sardaigne *f*.

sardonic [sɑːˈdɒnɪk] *adj* sardonique. ◆ **sardonically** *adv* sardoniquement.

Sark [sɑːk] *n* Sercq *m*.

sartorial [sɑːˈtɔːrɪəl] *adj* vestimentaire.

sash[1] [sæʃ] *n* (*on uniform*) écharpe *f*; (*on dress etc*) large ceinture *f* à nœud.

sash[2] [sæʃ] *adj*: **~ window** fenêtre *f* à guillotine.

sat [sæt] *pret, ptp of* **sit.**

Satan [ˈseɪtn] *n* Satan *m*. ◆ **satanic** *adj* satanique.

satchel [ˈsætʃəl] *n* cartable *m*.

satellite [ˈsætəlaɪt] *adj, n* satellite (*m*).

satiated [ˈseɪʃɪeɪtɪd] *adj* assouvi (*with* de). ◆ **satiation** *n* assouvissement *m*; **to satiation point** (jusqu')à satiété. ◆ **satiety** *n* satiété *f*.

satin [ˈsætɪn] **1** *n* satin *m*. **2** *adj dress* en *or* de satin; *paper, finish* satiné.

satire [ˈsætaɪəʳ] *n* satire *f* (*on* contre). ◆ **satirical** *adj* satirique. ◆ **satirically** *adv* d'une manière satirique. ◆ **satirist** *n* (*writer etc*) écrivain *m etc* satirique; (*cartoonist*) caricaturiste *mf*; (*in cabaret etc*) ≃ chansonnier *m*. ◆ **satirize** *vt* faire la satire de.

satisfaction [ˌsætɪsˈfækʃən] *n* satisfaction *f* (*at* de). **it was a great ~ to us to hear that ...** nous avons appris avec beaucoup de satisfaction que ...; **it has not been proved to my ~** cela n'a pas été prouvé de façon à me convaincre; **has it been done to your ~?** est-ce que vous en êtes satisfait?

satisfactory [ˌsætɪsˈfæktərɪ] *adj* (*gen*) satisfaisant. **to bring sth to a ~ conclusion** mener qch à bien. ◆ **satisfactorily** *adv* d'une manière satisfaisante.

satisfy [ˈsætɪsfaɪ] *vt* **(a)** *person* satisfaire, contenter. **(b)** *hunger, need, condition, creditor* satisfaire; (*Comm*) *demand* satisfaire à. **(c)** (*convince*) convaincre, assurer (*sb that* qn que; *of* de). **to ~ o.s. of sth** s'assurer de qch. ◆ **satisfied** *adj person, voice* satisfait, content; **he was satisfied to remain ...** il a accepté de rester ...; **I am not satisfied with that** cela ne me satisfait pas; **to be satisfied that ...** être convaincu *or* persuadé que ... . ◆ **satisfying** *adj* satisfaisant; *food* substantiel.

saturate [ˈsætʃəreɪt] *vt* saturer (*with* de). ◆ **saturated** *adj* (*soaked*) trempé. ◆ **saturation 1** *n* saturation *f*; **2** *adj*: **saturation bombing** tactique *f* de saturation (par bombardement); **to reach saturation point** arriver à saturation.

Saturday [ˈsætədɪ] *n* samedi *m*. **on ~** samedi; **on ~s** le samedi; **next ~, ~ next** samedi prochain; **last ~** samedi dernier; **every ~** tous les samedis, chaque samedi; **every other ~, every second ~** un samedi sur deux; **it is ~ today** nous sommes aujourd'hui samedi; **on ~ January 23rd** le samedi 23 janvier; **the ~ after next, a week on ~, ~ week** samedi en huit; **a fortnight on ~, ~ fortnight** samedi en quinze; **a week/fortnight past on ~** il y a huit/quinze jours samedi dernier; **the following ~** le samedi suivant; **the ~ before last** l'autre

samedi; ~ **morning** samedi matin; ~ **afternoon** samedi après-midi; ~ **evening** samedi soir; ~ **night** samedi soir, (*overnight*) la nuit de samedi; (*TV*) ~ **evening viewing** émissions *fpl* du samedi soir; (*Comm*) ~ **closing** fermeture *f* le samedi; (*Press*) **the** ~ **edition** l'édition de *or* du samedi.
Saturn ['sætən] *n* (*Myth*) Saturne *m*; (*Astron*) Saturne *f*.
sauce [sɔːs] *n* **(a)** (*Culin*) sauce *f*. **mint** ~ sauce à la menthe. **(b)** (*: *impudence*) toupet* *m*. ♦ **sauceboat** *n* saucière *f*. ♦ **saucepan** *n* casserole *f*. ♦ **saucily** *adv say* avec impertinence; *look* d'un air coquin. ♦ **sauciness** *n* (*cheekiness*) toupet* *m*. ♦ **saucy** *adj* (*cheeky*) impertinent; *look* coquin; *hat* coquet.
saucer ['sɔːsəʳ] *n* soucoupe *f*.
Saudi Arabia ['saʊdɪə'reɪbɪə] *n* Arabie *f* Saoudite.
sauerkraut ['saʊəkraʊt] *n* choucroute *f*.
sauna ['sɔːnə] *n* sauna *m*.
saunter ['sɔːntəʳ] *vi*: **to** ~ **in/out** *etc* entrer/sortir *etc* d'un pas nonchalant.
sausage ['sɒsɪdʒ] **1** *n* saucisse *f*; (*pre-cooked*) saucisson *m*. **2** *adj*: ~ **meat** chair *f* à saucisse; ~ **roll** ≃ friand *m*.
sauté ['səʊteɪ] **1** *vt* faire sauter (*Culin*). **2** *adj* sauté.
savage ['sævɪdʒ] **1** *adj* **(a)** (*fierce*) (*gen*) féroce; *person* brutal. **(b)** (*primitive*) *tribe, customs* sauvage. **2** *n* sauvage *mf*. **3** *vt [dog etc]* attaquer férocement; *[critics etc]* attaquer violemment. ♦ **savagely** *adv* férocement; brutalement. ♦ **savagery** *n* (*cruelty*) férocité *f*; brutalité *f*.
save¹ [seɪv] **1** *vt* **(a)** (*rescue*) sauver (*from* de). **to** ~ **sb from death/drowning** *etc* sauver qn de la mort/de la noyade *etc*; **to** ~ **sb from falling** empêcher qn de tomber; **to** ~ **sb's life** sauver la vie à *or* de qn; **I couldn't do it to** ~ **my life** je ne le ferais pour rien au monde; (*fig*) **to** ~ **one's bacon*** se tirer du pétrin; **to** ~ **one's skin*** *or* **neck*** *or* **hide*** sauver sa peau*; **to** ~ **face** sauver la face; **God** ~ **the Queen!** vive la reine!; (*Sport*) **to** ~ **a goal** sauver un but; **they** ~**d the palace for posterity** on a préservé le palais pour la postérité. **(b)** (*store away*: ~ **up**) *money* mettre de côté; *food, newspapers* garder; (*collect*) *stamps etc* collectionner. **I've** ~**d you a piece of cake** je t'ai gardé un morceau de gâteau; **I** ~**d your letter till the last** j'ai gardé ta lettre pour la bonne bouche. **(c)** (*not spend, not use*) *money, labour, petrol* économiser; *time* gagner. **you have** ~**d me a lot of trouble** vous m'avez évité bien des ennuis; **to** ~ **time let's assume that ...** pour gagner du temps admettons que ... + *subj*; **it will** ~ **you 10 minutes** cela vous fera gagner 10 minutes; **to** ~ **one's strength for** se ménager pour. **2** *vi* **(a)** (~ **up**) faire des économies. **to** ~ **up for sth** mettre de l'argent de côté pour qch. **(b) to** ~ **on sth** économiser sur qch. **3** *n* (*Sport*) arrêt *m* (*du ballon*). ♦ **saving 1** *n [time, money etc]* économie *f*; **to make savings** économiser, faire des économies; **to live on one's savings** vivre de ses économies; (*Econ*) **to encourage saving(s)** encourager l'épargne; **small savings** la petite épargne; **2** *adj*: **generosity is his saving grace** il se rachète par sa générosité. ♦ **savings bank** *n* caisse *f* d'épargne.
save² [seɪv] *prep* (*except*) sauf.
saveloy ['sævəlɔɪ] *n* cervelas *m*.
saviour, (*US*) **savior** ['seɪvjəʳ] *n* sauveur *m*.
savory ['seɪvərɪ] *n* (*herb*) sarriette *f*.
savour, (*US*) **savor** ['seɪvəʳ] **1** *n* saveur *f*. **2** *vt* savourer. **3** *vi*: **to** ~ **of sth** sentir qch. ♦ **savo(u)ry 1** *adj* (*appetizing*) savoureux; (*not sweet*) salé (*par opposition à sucré*); (*fig*) **not very** ~**y** *subject* peu appétissant; *district* peu recommandable; **2** *n* mets *m* non sucré; (*on toast*) canapé *m* chaud.
saw¹ [sɔː] (*vb*: *pret* **sawed**, *ptp* **sawed** *or* **sawn**) **1** *n* scie *f*. **2** *vt* scier. **to** ~ **sth off/up** enlever/débiter qch à la scie. **3** *vi*: **to** ~ **through sth** scier qch. ♦ **sawdust** *n* sciure *f* (de bois). ♦ **saw-edged knife** *n* couteau-scie *m*. ♦ **sawmill** *n* scierie *f*. ♦ **sawn-off shotgun** *n* carabine *f* à canon scié.
saw² [sɔː] *pret of* **see¹**.
saxophone ['sæksəfəʊn] *n* (*abbr* **sax***) saxophone *m*, saxo* *m*. ♦ **saxophonist** *n* saxophoniste *mf*.
say [seɪ] *pret, ptp* **said 1** *vti* **(a)** (*gen*) dire (*sth to sb* qch à qn; *that* que); *lesson, poem* réciter; *[dial, gauge, clock]* marquer. (*Rel*) **to** ~ **mass/a prayer** dire la messe/une prière; (*fig*) **to** ~ **yes/no to an invitation** accepter/refuser une invitation; ~ **after me ...** répétez après moi ...; **to** ~ **sth again** répéter qch; **I shall have more to** ~ **about that** je reviendrai là-dessus plus tard; **let's** ~ **no more about it** n'en parlons plus; **I've got nothing more to** ~ je n'ai rien à ajouter; **all of that can be said in 2 sentences** tout cela tient en 2 phrases; **something was said about it** on en a parlé, il en a été question; **I should like to ask Mr Smith to** ~ **a few words** je voudrais prier M. Smith de prendre la parole; **he said I was to give you this** il m'a dit de vous donner ceci; **to** ~ **one's say** dire ce qu'on a à dire; **it** ~**s in the rules** il est dit dans le règlement; **he is said to have ...** on dit qu'il a ...; **I** ~ **he should take it** je suis d'avis qu'il le prenne; **I should** ~ **she's intelligent** je pense qu'elle est intelligente; **what would you** ~ **is the population of Paris?** quelle est à votre avis *or* d'après vous la population de Paris?; ~ **someone left you a fortune** si vous héritiez d'une fortune.

(b) (*in phrases*) dire. **'10 o'clock' he said to himself** '10 heures' se dit-il; **and so** ~ **all of us** nous sommes tous d'accord là-dessus; **to** ~ **nothing of her sister/of her breaking it** sans parler de sa sœur/du fait qu'elle l'a cassé; **that's** ~**ing a lot*** ce n'est pas peu dire; **that isn't** ~**ing much*** ça ne veut pas dire grand-chose; **that doesn't** ~ **much for him** cela en dit long sur lui (*iro*); **it** ~**s a lot for his courage that he stayed** il a bien prouvé son courage en restant; **she has nothing to** ~ **for herself** (*no explanation*) elle se trouve sans excuse; (*no conversation*) elle n'a pas de conversation; **he always has a lot to** ~ **for himself** il a toujours son mot à dire; **you might as well** ~ **the earth is flat!** autant dire que la terre est plate!; **you can** ~ THAT **again!*** c'est le cas de le dire!; (*emphatic*) **you've said it!*** tu l'as dit!*; **enough said!*** en voilà assez!; **to** ~ **the least** c'est le moins qu'on puisse dire; **it goes without** ~**ing that ...** il va sans dire que ...; **just** ~ **the word and I'll go** vous n'avez qu'un mot à dire pour que je parte; **he hadn't a good word to** ~ **for her** il n'a rien trouvé à dire en sa faveur; **there's sth to be said for it** cela a du bon; **there's sth to be said for waiting** il y a peut-être intérêt à attendre; **it's easier** *or* **sooner said than done!** c'est plus facile à dire qu'à faire!; **when all is said and done** tout compte fait; **what do you** ~ **to a cup of tea?** que diriez-vous d'une tasse de thé?; **there's no** ~**ing what he'll do** il est impossible de dire ce qu'il fera; **so to** ~ pour ainsi dire; **that is to** ~ c'est-à-dire; **I** ~**!*** dites donc!; **you don't** ~**!*** pas possible!; **if there were,** ~**, 500** s'il y avait, disons, 500; **that's not for me to** ~ ce n'est pas à moi de dire ça.

2 *n*: **to have one's** ~ dire son mot, dire ce qu'on a à dire; **to have a** ~**/no** ~ **in the matter** avoir/ne pas avoir voix au chapitre.

♦ **saying** *n* dicton *m*; **as the** ~**ing goes** comme on dit. ♦ **say-so*** *n*: **on your** ~**-so** parce que vous le dites.
scab [skæb] *n* **(a)** croûte *f* (*Med*). **(b)** (‡*pej*: *blackleg*) jaune *m*.
scaffold ['skæfəld] *n* **(a)** (*gallows*) échafaud *m*. **(b)** (*Constr*: *also* ~**ing**) échafaudage *m*.
scald [skɔːld] *vt* ébouillanter; (*sterilize*) stériliser. ♦ **scalding (hot)** *adj* brûlant.
scale¹ [skeɪl] **1** *n* **(a)** (*gen*) échelle *f*; *[numbers]*

série *f.* ~ **of charges** barème *m*; **(drawn) to ~** à l'échelle; **on a ~ of 1 cm to 5 km** à une échelle de 1 cm pour 5 km; **on a large/small ~** sur une grande/petite échelle; **on a national ~** à l'échelle nationale. **(b)** (*Mus*) gamme *f.* **2** *adj*: **~ drawing** dessin *m* à l'échelle; **~ model** modèle *m* réduit. **3** *vt wall, mountain* escalader.

scale down *vt sep* (*gen*) réduire proportionnellement; *drawing* réduire l'échelle de; *production* réduire.

scale[2] [skeɪl] **1** *n [fish, rust etc]* écaille *f*; (*on skin*) squame *f.* **2** *vt teeth, kettle* détartrer.

scales [skeɪlz] *npl*: **(pair** *or* **set of) ~** (*in kitchen, shop*) balance *f*; (*in bathroom*) pèse-personne *m inv*; (*for luggage, heavy goods*) bascule *f.* (*Astron*) **the S~** la Balance; **to turn the ~ at 80 kilos** peser 80 kilos; (*fig*) **to tip the ~** faire pencher la balance (*in sb's favour* du côté de qn; *against sb* contre qn).

scallop ['skɒləp] *n* coquille *f* Saint-Jacques. **~ shell** coquille.

scalp [skælp] **1** *n* cuir *m* chevelu; (*trophy*) scalp *m.* **2** *vt* scalper.

scalpel ['skælpəl] *n* scalpel *m.*

scamp[1]* [skæmp] *n* (*child*) polisson(ne) *m(f).*

scamp[2] [skæmp] *vt one's work etc* bâcler*.

scamper ['skæmpəʳ] *vi [children]* **to ~ in/out** *etc* entrer/sortir *etc* en gambadant; **to ~ about** gambader.

scampi ['skæmpɪ] *npl* langoustines *fpl.*

scan [skæn] **1** *vt* **(a)** (*examine closely*) *horizon, sb's face* scruter; *crowd* fouiller du regard; *newspaper* lire attentivement. **(b)** (*glance at*) *horizon* promener son regard sur; *crowd* parcourir des yeux; *newspaper* parcourir rapidement. **(c)** (*Radar, TV*) balayer; (*Computers*) scruter. **2** *vi* (*Poetry*) se scander. ♦ **scanner** *n* (*Med*) scanner *m.* ♦ **scansion** *n* scansion *f.*

scandal ['skændl] *n* **(a)** (*disgrace*) scandale *m.* **it's a ~** c'est scandaleux; **it's a ~ that ...** c'est un scandale que ... + *subj.* **(b)** (*gossip*) ragots* *mpl.* **there's a lot of ~ going around about him** il y a beaucoup de ragots* qui circulent sur son compte. ♦ **scandalize** *vt* scandaliser; **to be ~ized by** se scandaliser de. ♦ **scandalous** *adj* scandaleux. ♦ **scandalously** *adv* scandaleusement.

Scandinavia [ˌskændɪ'neɪvɪə] *n* Scandinavie *f.* ♦ **Scandinavian 1** *adj* scandinave; **2** *n* Scandinave *mf.*

scant [skænt] *adj*: **with ~ courtesy** avec bien peu de politesse; **to pay ~ attention** faire à peine attention; **~ praise** éloge *m* des plus brefs. ♦ **scantily** *adv* insuffisamment; **~ily clad** vêtu du strict minimum. ♦ **scanty** *adj meal, harvest* peu abondant; *income, swimsuit* minuscule.

scapegoat ['skeɪpgəʊt] *n* bouc *m* émissaire.

scar [skɑːʳ] **1** *n* (*gen*) cicatrice *f*; (*esp on face*) balafre *f.* (*fig*) **it left a deep ~ on his mind** il en est resté profondément marqué (*fig*). **2** *vt* marquer d'une cicatrice; (*on face*) balafrer. **~red by smallpox** grêlé par la petite vérole; **war-~red town** ville *f* qui porte des cicatrices de la guerre.

scarce [skɛəs] *adj food, money* peu abondant; *edition* rare. **corn is getting ~** le blé se fait rare; **such people are ~** de telles gens sont rares; **to make o.s. ~*** se sauver*. ♦ **scarcely** *adv see, touch* à peine; **~ly anybody knows** il y a très peu de gens qui savent; **he ~ly ever goes there** il n'y va presque jamais; **I can ~ly believe it** j'ai du mal à le croire. ♦ **scarceness** *or* ♦ **scarcity** *n* pénurie *f.*

scare [skɛəʳ] **1** *n*: **to give sb a ~** effrayer qn, faire peur à qn; **to raise a ~** semer la panique; **the war ~** les rumeurs *fpl* de guerre. **2** *vt* effrayer, faire peur à. **to ~ sb stiff*** faire une peur bleue à qn; **to be ~d** avoir peur (*of* de); **to be ~d stiff*, to be ~d to death*, to be ~d out of one's wits*** avoir une peur bleue *or* une frousse* terrible (*of* de).

scare away, scare off *vt sep [dog etc]* faire fuir; *[price]* faire peur à.
♦ **scarecrow** *n* épouvantail *m.* ♦ **scared** *adj* effrayé, affolé (*of* par); *V also* **scare 2** *above.* ♦ **scaremonger** *n* alarmiste *mf.* ♦ **scary*** *adj* qui donne la frousse*.

scarf [skɑːf] *n* écharpe *f*; (*square*) foulard *m.*

scarlatina [ˌskɑːlə'tiːnə] *n* scarlatine *f.*

scarlet ['skɑːlɪt] *adj* écarlate. **~ fever** scarlatine *f.*

scarper‡ ['skɑːpəʳ] *vi* (*Brit*) ficher le camp*.

scathing ['skeɪðɪŋ] *adj remark* cinglant. **to be ~ about sth** critiquer qch de façon cinglante. ♦ **scathingly** *adv* d'une manière cinglante; **to look ~ly at sb** foudroyer qn du regard.

scatter ['skætəʳ] **1** *vt* **(a)** *crumbs, papers* éparpiller; *seeds* semer à la volée; *sand, salt, sawdust* répandre; *coins* jeter à la volée; *cushions* jeter çà et là. **(b)** *clouds, crowd* disperser; *enemy* mettre en déroute. **his paintings are ~ed all over the country** ses tableaux sont dispersés aux quatre coins du pays. **2** *vi [clouds, crowd]* se disperser. ♦ **scatterbrain** *n* écervelé(e) *m(f).* ♦ **scatterbrained** *adj* écervelé.

scavenge ['skævɪndʒ] *vi* fouiller (*for* pour trouver). ♦ **scavenger** *n* (*insect/animal*) insecte *m*/animal *m* nécrophage; (*street cleaner*) éboueur *m*; (*person on dump etc*) maraudeur *m*, -euse *f.*

scenario [sɪ'nɑːrɪəʊ] *n* scénario *m.*

scene [siːn] **1** *n* **(a)** (*gen, Theat*) scène *f.* (*Cine, TV*) **outdoor ~** extérieur *m*; **the ~ is set in Paris** la scène se passe à Paris; (*fig*) **the ~ was set for** toutes les conditions étaient réunies pour; **this set the ~ for** ceci a préparé le terrain pour; (*Theat, fig*) **behind the ~s** dans les coulisses; **~s of violence** scènes de violence; **there were angry ~s** des incidents violents ont eu lieu; (*fuss*) **to make a ~** faire toute une scène *or* toute une histoire*. **(b)** (*place*) lieu *m*, endroit *m.* **the ~ of the crime/accident** le lieu du crime/de l'accident; **he needs a change of ~** il a besoin de changer de cadre; **to come on the ~** arriver; **it's not my ~**‡ ça n'est pas mon genre*. **(c)** (*sight*) spectacle *m*; (*view*) vue *f.* **the ~ from the top** la vue *or* le panorama du sommet; **a ~ of utter destruction** un spectacle de destruction totale. **2** *adj* (*Theat*) **~ change** changement *m* de décors; **~ painter** peintre *m* de décors; **~ shifter** machiniste *m.* ♦ **scenery** *n* (*countryside*) paysage *m*; (*Theat*) décors *mpl*; (*fig*) **a change of ~ry** un changement de cadre. ♦ **scenic** *adj* scénique; (*Rail*) **scenic car** voiture *f* panoramique; **scenic railway** (*panoramic*) petit train *m* d'agrément; (*Brit: switchback*) montagnes *fpl* russes; **scenic road** route *f* touristique.

scent [sent] **1** *n* **(a)** (*perfume*) parfum *m.* **(b)** (*animal's track*) fumet *m*; (*fig*) piste *f.* **to lose the ~** perdre la piste; **to put sb off the ~** déjouer qn. **2** *adj*: **~ bottle** flacon *m* à parfum; **~ spray** vaporisateur *m*; (*aerosol*) atomiseur *m.* **3** *vt* **(a)** (*make ~ed*) parfumer (*with* de). **(b)** (*smell*) *game, danger* flairer.

sceptic, (*US*) **skeptic** ['skeptɪk] *adj, n* sceptique (*mf*). ♦ **sceptical** *adj* sceptique (*of, about* sur). ♦ **sceptically** *adv* avec scepticisme. ♦ **scepticism** *n* scepticisme *m.*

sceptre, (*US*) **-ter** ['septəʳ] *n* sceptre *m.*

schedule ['ʃedjuːl, (*US*) 'skedjuːl] *n* **(a)** *[work, duties, visits]* programme *m*; *[trains etc]* horaire *m*; *[events]* calendrier *m.* **to go according to ~** se passer comme prévu; **on** *or* **up to ~** *train* à l'heure; *work* à jour; **to be behind ~** avoir du retard; **to be ahead of ~** (*in work*) avoir de l'avance sur son programme; **to work to a very tight ~** avoir un programme de travail très serré. **(b)** (*list*) *[goods, contents]* liste *f*, inventaire *m*; *[prices]* barème *m*; (*Customs, Tax etc*) tarif *m.* ♦ **scheduled** *adj time, date, activity* prévu; *price* tarifé; *train or bus service* régulier; *stop* indiqué

dans l'horaire; **he is ~d to leave at midday** il doit partir à midi.
scheme [ski:m] **1** *n* **(a)** (*plan*) plan *m*, projet *m* (*of doing* de faire; *to do, for doing* pour faire; *for sth* pour qch). **a ~ of work** un plan de travail; **profit-sharing ~** système *m* de participation (aux bénéfices); **it's not a bad ~*** ça n'est pas une mauvaise idée. **(b)** (*plot*) complot *m* (*to do* pour faire). **2** *vi* comploter (*to do* pour faire). ♦ **schemer** *n* (*small-scale*) intrigant(e) *m(f)*; (*large-scale*) comploteur *m*, -euse *f*. ♦ **scheming** **1** *adj* intrigant; **2** *n* intrigues *fpl*.
schism ['sɪzəm] *n* schisme *m*.
schizophrenia [ˌskɪtsəʊ'fri:nɪə] *n* schizophrénie *f*. ♦ **schizophrenic** *adj, n* schizophrène (*mf*).
scholar ['skɒlə^r] *n* lettré(e) *m(f)*, érudit(e) *m(f)*. **a Dickens ~** un(e) spécialiste de Dickens. ♦ **scholarly** *adj* érudit, savant. ♦ **scholarship** **1** *n* (*knowledge*) érudition *f*; (*award*) bourse *f* (d'études) (*obtenue sur concours*); **2** *adj*: **~ship holder** boursier *m*, -ière *f*. ♦ **scholastic** *adj* scolaire.
school[1] [sku:l] **1** *n* **(a)** (*gen*) école *f*; (*primary ~*) école; (*secondary ~*) collège *m*; (*grammar ~*) lycée *m*; (*lessons*) cours *mpl*, (*in primary ~*) classes *fpl*. **~ of motoring** auto-école *f*; **to** *or* **at** *or* **in ~** à l'école (*or* au collège *etc*); **to leave ~** quitter l'école *etc*; (*Art*) **the Dutch ~** l'école hollandaise; **a ~ of thought** une école de pensée; (*fig*) **of the old ~** de la vieille école. **(b)** (*Univ*) faculté *f*. **he's at law/medical ~** il fait son droit/sa médecine; **S~ of Linguistics** *etc* Institut *m or* Département *m* de Linguistique *etc*.
2 *adj doctor, holidays, life, report etc* scolaire. **~ attendance** scolarisation *f*; **~ attendance officer** fonctionnaire *mf* chargé(e) de faire respecter les règlements de la scolarisation; **~ bus** car *m* de ramassage scolaire; **~ bus service** service *m* de ramassage scolaire; **~ fees** frais *mpl* de scolarité; **during ~ hours, in ~ time** pendant les heures de classe.
3 *vt animal* dresser; *feelings, reactions* contrôler; *voice etc* discipliner. **to ~ o.s. to do** s'astreindre à faire.
♦ **school-age** *adj* d'âge scolaire. ♦ **schoolbag** *n* cartable *m*. ♦ **schoolbook** *n* livre *m* de classe. ♦ **schoolboy** **1** *n* élève *m*, écolier *m*; **2** *adj*: **~boy slang** argot *m* scolaire. ♦ **schoolchild** *n* écolier *m*, -ière *f*, lycéen(ne) *m(f)*, collégien(ne) *m(f)*. ♦ **schooldays** *npl* années *fpl* d'école. ♦ **schoolgirl** *n* élève *f*, écolière *f*. ♦ **schooling** *n* (*gen*) études *fpl*; **compulsory ~ing** scolarité *f* obligatoire. ♦ **school-leaver** *n* jeune *mf* qui a terminé ses études secondaires. ♦ **school-leaving age** *n* âge *m* de fin de scolarité. ♦ **schoolmarm*** *n* (*pej*) institutrice *f*. ♦ **schoolmaster** *n* (*primary*) instituteur *m*; (*secondary*) professeur *m*. ♦ **schoolmate** *n* camarade *mf* de classe. ♦ **schoolmistress** *n* (*primary*) institutrice *f*; (*secondary*) professeur *m*. ♦ **schoolroom** *n* salle *f* de classe. ♦ **schoolteacher** *n* (*primary*) instituteur *m*, -trice *f*; (*secondary*) professeur *m*. ♦ **schoolteaching** *n* enseignement *m*.
school[2] [sku:l] *n [fish]* banc *m*.
schooner ['sku:nə^r] *n* (*Naut*) goélette *f*.
sciatica [saɪ'ætɪkə] *n* sciatique *f*.
science ['saɪəns] **1** *n* science *f*; (*subject for study*) sciences. **it's a real ~** c'est une véritable science; **the S~ Faculty** la faculté des Sciences. **2** *adj equipment, subject* scientifique; *exam, teacher* de sciences. **~ fiction** science-fiction *f*. ♦ **scientific** *adj* (*gen*) scientifique; *instrument* de précision. ♦ **scientifically** *adv* scientifiquement. ♦ **scientist** *n* scientifique *mf*; **one of our leading scientists** l'un de nos grands savants.
Scilly Isles ['sɪlɪaɪlz] *npl* Sorlingues *fpl*.
scintillate ['sɪntɪleɪt] *vi [star, jewel]* scintiller; *[person]* pétiller d'esprit. ♦ **scintillating** *adj* scintillant; *conversation etc* pétillant.
scissors ['sɪzəz] *npl* ciseaux *mpl*.
scoff [skɒf] *vi* se moquer (*at* de). ♦ **scoffer** *n* moqueur *m*, -euse *f*.
scold [skəʊld] *vt* réprimander (*for doing* pour avoir fait); *child* gronder, attraper (*for doing* pour avoir fait). ♦ **scolding** *n* réprimande *f*, gronderie *f*; **to get a ~ing from sb** se faire réprimander *or* gronder par qn.
scone [skɒn] *n* ≈ petit pain *m* au lait.
scoop [sku:p] **1** *n* **(a)** (*for flour, sugar*) pelle *f* (*à main*); (*for water*) écope *f*; (*for ice cream/potatoes*) cuiller *f* à glace/à purée. **(b) to make a ~** (*Comm*) faire un gros bénéfice; (*Press*) faire un scoop. **2** *vt* (*Comm*) *market* s'emparer de; *competitor* devancer; *profit* ramasser; (*Press*) *story* publier en exclusivité.
scoop out *vt sep water* vider; *hole* creuser.
scoop up *vt sep* ramasser.
scooter ['sku:tə^r] *n* scooter *m*; *[child]* trottinette *f*.
scope [skəʊp] *n* (*opportunity: for activity, action etc*) possibilités *fpl*; (*range*) *[law, regulation]* étendue *f*, portée *f*; (*capacity*) *[person]* compétence *f*, capacité(s) *f(pl)*. **a programme of considerable ~** un programme d'une envergure considérable; **to extend the ~ of one's activities** élargir le champ de ses activités; **it is within/beyond his ~** cela entre dans/dépasse ses compétences; **it is within/beyond the ~ of this book** cela entre dans/dépasse les limites *fpl* de ce livre.
scorch [skɔ:tʃ] **1** *n* (**~ mark**) brûlure *f* légère. **2** *vt linen* roussir; *grass [fire etc]* brûler; *[sun]* dessécher. **~ed earth policy** tactique *f* de la terre brûlée. **3** *vi [car]* **to ~ along** rouler à toute vitesse. ♦ **scorcher*** *n* journée *f* torride. ♦ **scorching** *adj heat* torride; *sand* brûlant; *sun* de plomb; *weather* très chaud.
score [skɔ:^r] **1** *n* **(a)** (*Sport*) score *m*; (*Cards*) marque *f*. **to keep (the) ~** (*gen*) compter les points; (*Cards*) tenir la marque; (*Tennis*) tenir le score; (*Ftbl*) **there's no ~ yet** on n'a pas encore marqué (de but); **there was no ~ in the match** ils ont fait match nul; **what's the ~?** (*Sport*) où en est le jeu *or* le match?; (**fig*) où en sommes-nous?; (*fig*) **to know the ~*** en connaître un bout*; (*fig*) **he's got an old ~ to settle with him** il a un compte à régler avec lui. **(b)** (*account*) titre *m*. **on that ~** à ce titre. **(c)** (*mark: on wood etc*) rayure *f*; (*on leather etc*) incision *f*. **(d)** (*Mus*) partition *f*. **piano ~** partition de piano; **the film ~** la musique du film. **(e)** (*twenty*) **a ~** vingt; **a ~ of people** une vingtaine de personnes; (*fig*) **~s of** un grand nombre de, des tas* de.
2 *vt* **(a)** *goal, point* marquer. **to ~ 70% in an exam** avoir 70 sur 100 à un examen; **to ~ a hit** (*Fencing*) toucher; (*Shooting*) viser juste; (*fig*) remporter un grand succès. **(b)** (*cut*) *rock* strier; *wood, metal* rayer; *leather, skin* inciser. **(c)** *music* écrire (*for violin etc* pour violon *etc*); *film etc* composer la musique de.
3 *vi [player]* marquer un *or* des point(s); *[footballer etc]* marquer un but; *[scorer]* marquer les points; (*fig*) avoir l'avantage. (*fig*) **to ~ over** *or* **off sb** marquer un point aux dépens de qn.
score off, score out *vt sep* rayer, barrer.
♦ **scoreboard** *n* tableau *m*. ♦ **scorecard** *n* (*Shooting*) carton *m*; (*Golf*) carte *f* du parcours; (*Cards*) feuille *f* de marque. ♦ **scorer** *n* (*keeping ~*) marqueur *m*; (*goal ~r*) marqueur (de but).
scorn [skɔ:n] **1** *n* mépris *m*. **2** *vt person, action* mépriser; *advice, danger* faire fi de; *suggestion* rejeter. **to ~ to tell a lie** dédaigner de mentir. ♦ **scornful** *adj* méprisant; **to be ~ful about sth** parler de qch avec mépris. ♦ **scornfully** *adv* avec mépris.
Scorpio ['skɔ:pɪəʊ] *n* le Scorpion (*Astron*).
scorpion ['skɔ:pɪən] *n* scorpion *m*.
Scot [skɒt] *n* Écossais(e) *m(f)*.

Scotch [skɒtʃ] **1** *n* **(a)** whisky *m*, scotch *m*. **(b)** (*abusivement pour* **Scottish** *ou* **Scots**) **the** ~ les Écossais *mpl*. **2** *adj* (*abusivement*) écossais. ~ **egg** *œuf dur enrobé de chair à saucisse*; ~ **mist** bruine *f*; ~ **tape** ® scotch *m* ®, ruban adhésif.
scotch [skɒtʃ] *vt rumour* étouffer; *plan, attempt* faire échouer; *revolt, uprising* réprimer; *claim* démentir.
scot-free ['skɒt'fri:] *adj* (*unpunished*) sans être puni; (*not paying*) sans payer; (*unhurt*) indemne.
Scotland ['skɒtlənd] *n* Écosse *f*.
Scots [skɒts] *adj, n* écossais (*m*). ♦ **Scotsman** *n* Écossais *m*. ♦ **Scotswoman** *n* Écossaise *f*.
Scottish ['skɒtɪʃ] *adj* écossais. **the** ~ **Office** le ministère des Affaires écossaises.
scoundrel ['skaʊndrəl] *n* vaurien *m*; (*child*) coquin(e) *m(f)*.
scour ['skaʊə^r] *vt* **(a)** *pan, sink* récurer; *table, floor* frotter; (*with water*) nettoyer à grande eau; *metal* décaper. **(b)** (*search*) parcourir (*for* à la recherche de). ♦ **scourer** *n* (*powder*) poudre *f* à récurer; (*pad*) tampon *m* abrasif.
scourge [skɜ:dʒ] *n* fléau *m*.
scout [skaʊt] **1** *n* **(a)** (*Mil*) éclaireur *m*; (*boy*) scout *m* (*gen Catholic*); éclaireur (*gen non-Catholic*). **(b) to have a** ~ **round*** reconnaître le terrain. **2** *adj camp, movement* scout; *uniform* de scout. **3** *vi* (*Mil*) aller en reconnaissance. (*gen*) **to** ~ **about for** chercher. ♦ **scouting** *n* scoutisme *m*. ♦ **scoutmaster** *n* chef *m* scout.
scowl [skaʊl] **1** *n* mine *f* renfrognée. **he said with a** ~ dit-il en se renfrognant. **2** *vi* se renfrogner, froncer les sourcils. **to** ~ **at** jeter un regard mauvais à.
scrabble ['skræbl] **1** *vi*: **to** ~ **about** *or* **around for sth** chercher qch à tâtons. **2** *n* (*game*) **S**~ ® Scrabble *m* ®.
scraggy ['skrægɪ] *adj person, animal* efflanqué; *neck, limb* décharné.
scram* [skræm] *vi* ficher le camp*.
scramble ['skræmbl] **1** *vi* **(a) to** ~ **up/down/along** grimper/descendre/avancer tant bien que mal (et à toute vitesse); **to** ~ **for** *coins, seats* se bousculer pour (avoir); *jobs etc* faire des pieds et des mains pour (avoir). **(b)** (*Sport*) **to go scrambling** faire du moto-cross. **2** *vt* (*Culin, Telec*) brouiller. ~**d eggs** œufs brouillés. **3** *n* **(a)** (*rush*) ruée *f* (*for* pour). **(b)** (*motorcycle*) (réunion *f* de) moto-cross *m*. ♦ **scrambler** *n* (*Telec*) brouilleur *m*. ♦ **scrambling** *n* (*Sport*) moto-cross *m*.
scrap[1] [skræp] **1** *n* **(a)** (*piece: gen*) (petit) bout *m*; *[writing]* quelques lignes *fpl*; *[conversation]* bribe *f*; *[news]* fragment *m*. ~**s** (*broken pieces*) débris *mpl*; *[food]* restes *mpl*; **not a** ~ **of evidence/use** pas la moindre preuve/utilité; **not a** ~ pas du tout. **(b)** (~ **metal**) ferraille *f*. **to sell for** ~ vendre à la casse; **what is it worth as** ~? qu'est-ce que cela vaudrait à la casse? **2** *adj car* mis à la ferraille. ~ **dealer** *or* **merchant** marchand *m* de ferraille; (*fig*) **to throw sth on the** ~ **heap** mettre qch au rebut; ~ **iron** ferraille *f*; ~ **paper** (*for scribbling on*) papier *m* de brouillon; (*newspapers etc*) vieux papiers; ~ **yard** chantier *m* de ferraille; (*for cars*) cimetière *m* de voitures. **3** *vt* jeter; *car, ship* envoyer à la ferraille; *equipment* mettre au rebut; *project* laisser tomber. ♦ **scrapbook** *n* album *m* (*de coupures de journaux etc*). ♦ **scrappy** *adj conversation, essay* décousu; *education* incomplet; *meal* sur le pouce*.
scrap[2]* [skræp] **1** *n* (*fight*) bagarre *f*. **2** *vi* se bagarrer* (*with* avec).
scrape [skreɪp] **1** *n* **(a)** (*action*) coup *m* de racloir; (*sound*) raclement *m*; (*mark*) éraflure *f*. **(b)** (*: *trouble*) **to get into/out of a** ~ se mettre dans un/se sortir d'un mauvais pas. **2** *vt* (*clean*) racler; *vegetables* gratter; (*scratch*) érafler; (*just touch*) frôler. **to** ~ **one's plate clean** tout manger; **to** ~ **sth off sth** enlever qch de qch en raclant; **to** ~ **a living** vivoter; (*Naut*) **to** ~ **the bottom** talonner; (*fig*) **to** ~ **the bottom of the barrel** en être réduit aux raclures; **to** ~ **(up) an acquaintance with sb** réussir à faire la connaissance de qn. **3** *vi* (*make sound*) racler, gratter; (*rub*) frotter (*against* contre). **to** ~ **along the wall** frôler le mur; **to** ~ **through the doorway** réussir de justesse à passer par la porte; **to** ~ **through an exam** réussir un examen de justesse.
scrape along *vi* (*manage*) se débrouiller; (*live*) vivoter.
scrape away, scrape off *vt sep* enlever en raclant.
scrape through *vi* (*succeed*) réussir de justesse.
scrape together, scrape up *vt sep objects* rassembler; *money* réunir à grand-peine.
♦ **scraper** *n* racloir *m*; (*at doorstep*) grattoir *m*.
scratch [skrætʃ] **1** *n* **(a)** (*mark*) (*on skin*) égratignure *f*; (*on paint*) éraflure *f*; (*on glass, record*) rayure *f*. (*unharmed*) **without a** ~ indemne. **(b)** (*action, noise*) grattement *m*; (*by claw/nail*) coup *m* de griffe/d'ongle. **(c)** (*Sport*) scratch *m*. (*fig*) **to start from** ~ partir de zéro*; **to come up to** ~ se montrer à la hauteur; **to bring/keep sb up to** ~ amener/maintenir qn au niveau voulu. **2** *adj crew, team* de fortune; *race, golfer* scratch *inv*. **3** *vt* **(a)** (*with nail, claw*) griffer; *varnish* érafler; *record, glass* rayer; *one's name* graver. **to** ~ **a hole in sth** creuser un trou en grattant qch; **he** ~**ed his hand on a nail** il s'est éraflé la main sur un clou. **(b)** (*to relieve itch*) gratter. **to** ~ **one's head** se gratter la tête; (*fig*) **you** ~ **my back and I'll** ~ **yours** un petit service en vaut un autre. **(c)** (*cancel*) *meeting, game* annuler; *competitor, horse* scratcher. **4** *vi [person, dog etc]* se gratter; *[hens]* gratter le sol; *[pen]* gratter. **the dog was** ~**ing at the door** le chien grattait à la porte.
scratch out *vt sep* (*from list*) rayer. **to** ~ **sb's eyes out** arracher les yeux à qn.
♦ **scratchy** *adj material* rêche; *pen* qui gratte.
scrawl [skrɔ:l] **1** *n* gribouillage *m*, griffonnage *m*; (*brief letter*) mot *m* griffonné. **2** *vt* gribouiller, griffonner; *letter* griffonner.
scrawny ['skrɔ:nɪ] *adj person, animal* efflanqué; *neck, limb* décharné.
scream [skri:m] **1** *n [pain, fear]* cri *m* perçant, hurlement *m*; *[laughter]* éclat *m*. **to give a** ~ pousser un cri; (*fig*) **it was a** ~* c'était à se tordre (de rire); **he's a** ~* il est impayable*. **2** *vi* (~ **out**) crier (*at sb* après qn; *for help* à l'aide), hurler (*with pain/rage* de douleur/de colère). **to** ~ **with laughter** rire aux éclats. **3** *vt* (~ **out**) *[person]* hurler (*at* à); *[headlines, posters]* annoncer en toutes lettres. ♦ **screamingly*** *adv*: ~**ingly funny** tordant*.
scree [skri:] *n* éboulis *m* (*en montagne*).
screech [skri:tʃ] **1** *n [person, siren]* hurlement *m*; *[brakes]* grincement *m*; *[tyres]* crissement *m*; *[owl]* cri *m* (rauque et perçant). **she gave a** ~ **of laughter** elle est partie d'un rire perçant. **2** *vi* hurler; grincer; crisser; crier. **3** *vt* crier à tue-tête. ♦ **screech-owl** *n* effraie *f*.
screeds* [skri:dz] *npl*: **to write** ~ écrire des volumes.
screen [skri:n] **1** *n* **(a)** (*in room*) paravent *m*; (*for fire*) écran *m* de cheminée; (*fig: of troops, trees*) rideau *m*. **(b)** (*Cine, TV etc*) écran *m*. (*Cine*) **the** ~ l'écran, le cinéma; (*Cine/TV*) **the large/small** ~ le grand/petit écran; **to write for the** ~ écrire des scénarios. **2** *adj actor* de cinéma. ~ **test** essai *m* à l'écran; ~ **writer** scénariste *mf*. **3** *vt* **(a)** (*hide*) masquer (*from sight* aux regards), cacher; (*protect*) protéger (*from* de). **he** ~**ed the book with his hand** il a caché le livre de sa main. **(b)** *film* projeter. **(c)** (*sieve*) *coal* cribler. (*fig*) **to** ~ **sb (for a job)** vérifier le curriculum vitae de qn; (*Med*) **to** ~ **sb for cancer** faire subir à qn un test de dépis-

tage du cancer. ♦ **screening** *n* **(a)** *[film]* projection *f*; **(b)** (*Med*) test *m* de dépistage. ♦ **screenplay** *n* scénario *m*.
screw [skru:] **1** *n* **(a)** vis *f*; (*action*) tour *m* de vis. (*Brit*) **a ~ of sweets** *etc* un cornet de bonbons *etc*; (*fig*) **he's got a ~ loose*** il lui manque une case*; **to put the ~(s) on sb*** forcer la main à qn. **(b)** (*propeller*) hélice *f*. **(c)** (*Brit*‡: *income*) salaire *m*. **(d)** (‡: *prison officer*) garde-chiourme *m*. **2** *vt* **(a)** (**~ down, ~ on**) visser (*on* sur; *to* à). **to ~ sth tight** visser qch à bloc; (*fig*) **he's got his head ~ed on all right*** il a la tête sur les épaules. **(b)** (*extort*) soutirer (*out of* à). **3** *vi* (**~ down, ~ on**) se visser.
screw off **1** *vi* se dévisser. **2** *vt sep* dévisser.
screw round *vt sep* tourner, visser. **to ~ one's head round** se dévisser la tête.
screw together *vt sep two parts* fixer avec une vis; *object* assembler avec des vis.
screw up *vt sep paper* froisser; *handkerchief* rouler; *one's eyes* plisser; (‡: *spoil*) bousiller*. **to ~ up one's face** faire la grimace; (*fig*) **to ~ up one's courage** prendre son courage à deux mains (*to do* pour faire).
♦ **screwball**‡ *adj, n* cinglé(e) *m(f)*. ♦ **screwdriver** *n* tournevis *m*. ♦ **screw-top(ped)** *adj* avec couvercle à pas de vis. ♦ **screwy**‡ *adj* (*mad*) cinglé*.
scribble ['skrɪbl] **1** *vti* gribouiller, griffonner. **2** *n* griffonnage *m*.
scribble down *vt sep notes* griffonner.
♦ **scribbler** *n* (*bad author*) plumitif *m*. ♦ **scribbling** *n* gribouillage *m*. ♦ **scribbling pad** *n* bloc-notes *m*.
scribe [skraɪb] *n* scribe *m*.
scrimmage ['skrɪmɪdʒ] *n* bagarre *f*.
script [skrɪpt] **1** *n* **(a)** (*Cine*) scénario *m*; (*Rad, Theat, TV*) texte *m*; (*in exam*) copie *f*. **(b)** (*handwriting*) script *m*. **2** *vt film* écrire le scénario de. ♦ **scripted** *adj* (*Rad, TV*) *talk* préparé d'avance. ♦ **script-girl** *n* script(-girl) *f*. ♦ **scriptwriter** *n* scénariste *mf*.
Scripture ['skrɪptʃəʳ] *n* Écriture *f* sainte.
scroll [skrəʊl] *n [parchment]* rouleau *m*; (*ancient book*) manuscrit *m*; (*Archit*) volute *f*.
scrounge* [skraʊndʒ] **1** *vt meal, clothes etc* se faire payer (*from, off sb* par qn). **to ~ money from sb** taper qn‡; **he ~d £5 off him** il l'a tapé de 5 livres‡. **2** *vi*: **to ~ on sb** vivre aux crochets de qn. ♦ **scrounger*** *n* parasite *m*; (*for meals*) pique-assiette *mf inv*.
scrub[1] [skrʌb] **1** *n*: **to give sth a good ~** bien nettoyer qch (à la brosse); **give your face a ~!** lave-toi bien la figure! **2** *vt* **(a)** *floor* nettoyer *or* laver à la brosse; *pan* récurer. **to ~ one's hands** se brosser les mains. **(b)** (*: *cancel*) *match etc* annuler.
scrub down *vt sep room* nettoyer à fond. **to ~ o.s. down** faire une toilette en règle.
scrub off *vt sep mark, stain* enlever en frottant.
♦ **scrubber** *n* (*pan-scrubber*) tampon *m* à récurer. ♦ **scrubbing-brush** *n* brosse *f* dure. ♦ **scrubwoman** *n* (*US*) femme *f* de ménage.
scrub[2] [skrʌb] *n* (*brushwood*) broussailles *fpl*.
scruff [skrʌf] *n* **(a) by the ~ of the neck** par la peau du cou. **(b)** (*: *untidy person*) personne *f* débraillée. ♦ **scruffiness** *n [person]* débraillé *m*; *[building, clothes]* miteux *m*. ♦ **scruffy** *adj appearance* négligé; *person* débraillé; *building, clothes* miteux; **he looks ~y** il fait sale.
scrum [skrʌm] *n* (*Rugby*) mêlée *f*; (*: *in crowd*) bousculade *f*. (*Rugby*) **~ half** demi *m* de mêlée.
scrumptious* ['skrʌmpʃəs] *adj* succulent.
scruple ['skru:pl] *n* scrupule *m* (*about* au sujet de). **he had no ~s about doing it** il ne se faisait pas scrupule de le faire. ♦ **scrupulous** *adj* scrupuleux. ♦ **scrupulously** *adv pay, do* scrupuleusement; **scrupulously honest/clean** d'une honnêteté scrupuleuse/d'une propreté irréprochable. ♦ **scrupulousness** *n* scrupules *mpl*.
scrutinize ['skru:tɪnaɪz] *vt* (*gen*) scruter; *votes* pointer. ♦ **scrutiny** *n* (*gen*) regard *m* scrutateur; *[document, conduct]* examen *m* minutieux; *[votes]* pointage *m*.
scuba ['sku:bə] *n* scaphandre *m* autonome.
scuff [skʌf] *vt shoes* érafler; *feet* traîner.
scuffle ['skʌfl] **1** *n* bagarre *f*. **2** *vi* se bagarrer* (*with* avec).
scull [skʌl] *vi*: **to go ~ing** faire de l'aviron.
scullery ['skʌlərɪ] *n* arrière-cuisine *f*.
sculpt [skʌlpt] *vti* sculpter (*out of* dans). ♦ **sculptor** *n* sculpteur *m*. ♦ **sculptress** *n* femme *f* sculpteur. ♦ **sculpture** **1** *n* sculpture *f*; **2** *vti* sculpter.
scum [skʌm] *n* écume *f*. **to remove the ~ (from)** écumer; (*fig*) **the ~ of the earth** le rebut du genre humain.
scurf [skɜ:f] *n* pellicules *fpl* (*du cuir chevelu*).
scurrilous ['skʌrɪləs] *adj* calomnieux.
scurry ['skʌrɪ] *vi*: **to ~ along/away** *etc* avancer/partir *etc* à toute vitesse.
scuttle[1] ['skʌtl] *vi*: **to ~ in/through** *etc* entrer/traverser *etc* précipitamment.
scuttle[2] ['skʌtl] *vt ship* saborder; *plans* faire échouer.
scythe [saɪð] **1** *n* faux *f*. **2** *vt* faucher.
sea [si:] **1** *n* mer *f*. **on the ~** *boat* en mer; *town* au bord de la mer; **by** *or* **beside the ~** au bord de la mer; **over** *or* **beyond the ~(s)** (*adj*) *lands etc* d'outre-mer; (*adv*) *lie etc* outre-mer; **to go to ~** *[boat]* prendre la mer; *[person]* devenir *or* se faire marin; **to put to ~** prendre la mer; **by ~** par mer, en bateau; **look out to ~** regardez au large; **(out) at ~** en mer; (*fig*) **I'm all at ~** je nage* complètement; (*fig*) **the call of the ~** l'appel *m* du large; **what's the ~ like?** (*for sailing*) quel est l'état de la mer?; (*for bathing*) est-ce que l'eau est bonne?; **the ~ was very rough** la mer était très mauvaise; (*fig*) **a ~ of faces** une multitude de visages.
2 *adj air* de la mer, marin; *bird, breeze, fish, water* de mer; *god, scout* marin; *battle, power* naval; *route, transport* maritime. **~ anemone** anémone *f* de mer; **~ bathing** bains *mpl* de mer; **~ bed** fond *m* de la mer; **~ captain** capitaine *m* (de marine marchande); **~ coast** côte *f*; **~ front** front *m* de mer; **to find one's ~ legs** s'habituer à la mer; **~ level** niveau *m* de la mer; **~ loch** bras *m* de mer; **~ wall** digue *f*.
♦ **seaboard** *n* littoral *m*. ♦ **seafarer** *n* marin *m*. ♦ **seafaring** *n* vie *f* de marin. ♦ **seafood** *n* fruits *mpl* de mer. ♦ **sea-green** *adj* vert glauque *inv*. ♦ **seagull** *n* mouette *f*. ♦ **sea-lion** *n* otarie *f*. ♦ **seaman** *n, pl* **-men** marin *m*. ♦ **seamanship** *n* qualités *fpl* de marin. ♦ **seaplane** *n* hydravion *m*. ♦ **seaport** *n* port *m* de mer. ♦ **seascape** *n* (*Art*) marine *f*. ♦ **seashell** *n* coquillage *m*. ♦ **seashore** *n* rivage *m*, plage *f*; **by the ~shore** au bord de la mer; **on the ~shore** sur la plage, sur le rivage. ♦ **seasick** *adj*: **to be ~sick** avoir le mal de mer. ♦ **seasickness** *n* mal *m* de mer. ♦ **seaside** **1** *n* bord *m* de la mer; **at** *or* **beside** *or* **by the ~side** au bord de la mer; **2** *adj holiday, town* au bord de la mer; *hotel* sur le bord de la mer; **~side resort** station *f* balnéaire. ♦ **sea-urchin** *n* oursin *m*. ♦ **seawards** *adv* vers le large. ♦ **seaway** *n* route *f* maritime. ♦ **seaweed** *n* algue(s) *f(pl)*. ♦ **seaworthiness** *n* bon état *m* de navigabilité. ♦ **seaworthy** *adj* en état de naviguer.
seal[1] [si:l] *n* phoque *m*. ♦ **sealer** *n* (*ship*) navire *m* équipé pour la chasse au phoque. ♦ **sealskin** *n* peau *f* de phoque.
seal[2] [si:l] **1** *n* (*gen*) sceau *m*; (*on letter*) cachet *m*; (*on package*) plomb *m*. (*fig*) **to set one's ~ to sth, to give sth the ~ of approval** donner son approbation à qch; (*fig*) **to set the ~ on sth** sceller qch. **2** *vt* **(a)** (*put ~ on*) *document* sceller; (*close*) *envelope*

coller; *jar* fermer hermétiquement; *tin* souder; (*Culin*) *meat* saisir. **~ed orders** instructions *fpl* secrètes; **my lips are ~ed** mes lèvres sont scellées. **(b)** (*decide*) *fate* régler; *bargain* conclure.

seal off *vt sep* (*close up*) *door, room* condamner; (*forbid entry to*) interdire l'accès de; (*with police etc*) *district* mettre un cordon autour de.

seal up *vt sep jar, door* fermer hermétiquement.

♦ **sealing wax** *n* cire *f* à cacheter.

seam [si:m] *n* **(a)** (*in fabric, rubber*) couture *f*; (*in plastic, metal*) joint *m*; (*in welding*) soudure *f*. **to come apart at the ~s** se découdre; (*fig*) **bursting at the ~s*** plein à craquer. **(b)** (*Min*) veine *f*; (*Geol*) couche *f*. ♦ **seamstress** *n* couturière *f*. ♦ **seamy** *adj district* louche; **the ~y side of life** le côté peu reluisant de la vie.

seance ['seɪɑ̃:ns] *n* séance *f* de spiritisme.

search [sɜ:tʃ] **1** *n* **(a)** (*for sth lost*) recherches *fpl*. **in ~ of** à la recherche de; **to make a ~ for sb/sth** entreprendre des recherches pour retrouver qn/qch; **to begin a ~ for** *person* partir à la recherche de; *thing* se mettre à la recherche de. **(b)** *[person, building, drawer, pocket, district]* fouille *f*; (*Admin*) *[luggage etc]* visite *f*. **2** *vt* **(a)** (*hunt through*) *house, woods, district* fouiller (*for sb/sth* à la recherche de qn/qch). **(b)** (*examine*) (*gen*) fouiller (*for* pour essayer de retrouver); (*Admin*) *luggage* visiter. **they ~ed him for a weapon** ils l'ont fouillé pour s'assurer qu'il n'avait pas d'arme. **(c)** (*scan*) *documents, records, photograph* examiner (en détail) (*for* pour trouver); *one's conscience* sonder; *memory* chercher dans. (*fig*) **he ~ed her face for some sign of affection** il a cherché sur son visage un signe d'affection. **3** *vi* chercher. **to ~ after** *or* **for sth** chercher qch; **to ~ through sth** fouiller qch. ♦ **searcher** *n* chercheur *m*, -euse *f* (*for, after* en quête de). ♦ **searching** *adj look* pénétrant; *examination* minutieux. ♦ **searchlight** *n* projecteur *m* (*pour éclairer*). ♦ **search-party** *n* équipe *f* *or* expédition *f* de secours. ♦ **search-warrant** *n* mandat *m* de perquisition.

season ['si:zn] **1** *n* saison *f*. **to be in/out of ~** être/ne pas être de saison; **a word in ~** un mot dit à propos; (*fig*) **in ~ and out of ~** à tout bout de champ; **the Christmas ~** la période de Noël *or* des fêtes; **the busy ~** (*for shops etc*) la période de pointe; (*for hotels etc*) la pleine saison; **the fishing/football** *etc* **~** la saison de la pêche/de football *etc*; **'S~'s greetings'** 'Joyeux Noël et Bonne Année'; **the off-~** la morte-saison; **during the off-~** hors saison; (*Theat*) **he did a ~ at the Old Vic** il a joué à l'Old Vic pendant une saison; **the film is here for a short ~** le film sera projeté quelques semaines; (*Vet*) **in ~** en chaleur. **2** *adj*: **~ ticket** carte *f* d'abonnement; **~ ticket holder** personne *f* qui possède une carte d'abonnement. **3** *vt* **(a)** *wood* faire sécher. **(b)** (*Culin*) assaisonner; (*spice*) épicer, relever. **a highly ~ed dish** un plat relevé. ♦ **seasonable** *adj weather* de saison. ♦ **seasonal** *adj* saisonnier. ♦ **seasoned** *adj wood* séché; (*fig*) *worker, actor etc* expérimenté; *troops* aguerri; **a ~ed campaigner for** un vétéran des campagnes pour. ♦ **seasoning** *n* assaisonnement *m*; **to add ~ing** assaisonner.

seat [si:t] **1** *n* **(a)** (*gen: chair etc*) siège *m*; (*in theatre etc*) fauteuil *m*; (*in bus, train, car etc*) (*individual*) siège, (*for several people*) banquette *f*; (*on cycle*) selle *f*; (*place: on train, in theatre*) place *f*. **to take a ~** s'asseoir; **to take one's ~** prendre place; **there were 4 ~s in the room** il y avait 4 sièges dans la pièce; (*Theat*) **2 ~s for ...** 2 places pour ...; **keep a ~ for me** gardez-moi une place; **there are ~s for 70 people** il y a 70 places assises; **a two-~er car** une (voiture à) deux places. **(b)** (*part of chair*) siège *m*; *[trousers]* fond *m*; (*: *buttocks*) postérieur* *m*. **(c)** (*Parl*) siège *m*. **to keep/lose one's ~** être/ne pas être réélu; **to take one's ~ in the Commons** prendre son siège aux Communes; **a majority of 50 ~s** une majorité de 50 (députés *etc*). **(d)** (*centre*) *[government, learning]* siège *m*; *[commerce]* centre *m*; *[infection]* foyer *m*. **country ~** château *m*. **2** *adj*: **~ belt** ceinture *f* de sécurité. **3** *vt child* (faire) asseoir; (*at table*) *guest* placer. **to ~ o.s., to be ~ed** s'asseoir; **to be ~ed** (*sitting*) être assis; **to remain ~ed** rester assis; (*find room for*) **we cannot ~ them all** nous n'avons pas assez de sièges pour tout le monde; **how many does the hall ~?** combien y a-t-il de places assises dans la salle?; **this table/this car ~s 8** on peut tenir à 8 à cette table/dans cette voiture. ♦ **seating 1** *n* sièges *mpl*; (*as opp to standing room*) places *fpl* assises; **2** *adj*: **~ing capacity** nombre *m* de places assises.

secateurs [ˌsekə'tɜ:z] *npl* sécateur *m*.

secede [sɪ'si:d] *vi* faire sécession (*from* de). ♦ **secession** *n* sécession *f*.

secluded [sɪ'klu:dɪd] *adj house* à l'écart; *garden* isolé; *life, place* retiré. ♦ **seclusion** *n* solitude *f*; **to live in seclusion** vivre retiré du monde.

second[1] ['sekənd] **1** *adj* (*esp one of many*) deuxième; (*gen one of two*) second. **to be ~ in the queue** être le (*or* la) deuxième dans la queue; **to be ~ in command** (*Mil*) commander en second; (*gen*) être deuxième dans la hiérarchie; (*Scol*) **he was ~ in French** il a été deuxième en français; (*fig*) **he's a ~ Beethoven** c'est un autre Beethoven; **give him a ~ chance** donnez-lui encore une chance; **you won't get a ~ chance to do it** vous ne retrouverez pas l'occasion de le faire; **every ~ day** un jour sur deux; (*Aut*) **~ gear** seconde *f*; (*Med*) **to ask for a ~ opinion** demander l'avis d'un autre médecin; **~ cousin** cousin(e) *m(f)* issu(e) de germain; (*Gram*) **~ person** deuxième personne *f*; **in the ~ place** deuxièmement; **Charles the S~** Charles Deux, Charles II; **to play ~ fiddle to sb** jouer un rôle secondaire auprès de qn; **it's ~ nature to him** c'est une seconde nature chez lui; **~ to none** sans pareil; **my ~ self** un(e) autre moi-même; **to have ~ sight** avoir le don de seconde vue; **to have ~ thoughts** changer d'avis (*about* en ce qui concerne); **on ~ thoughts** ... réflexion faite ...; *for other phrases V* **sixth**.

2 *adv* **(a)** (*in race, exam, competition*) en seconde place. **he came ~** (*in race, exam*) il s'est classé deuxième *or* second; (*at meeting etc*) il est arrivé le deuxième; **the ~ largest book** le plus grand livre sauf un. **(b)** = **secondly**. **(c)** (*Rail etc*) **to travel ~** voyager en seconde.

3 *n* **(a)** deuxième *mf*, second(e) *m(f)*. **he came a good ~** il s'est fait battre de justesse; **he came a poor ~** il a été largement battu (en deuxième place); (*Comm*) **~s** articles *mpl* de second choix. **(b)** (*Boxing*) soigneur *m*; (*in duel*) second *m*. **(c)** (*Aut: ~ gear*) seconde *f*. **in ~** en seconde.

4 *vt* **(a)** *motion* appuyer; *speaker* appuyer la motion de. (*fig*) **I'll ~ that** je suis d'accord. **(b)** [sɪ'kɒnd] *employee* détacher (*to* à).

♦ **secondary** *adj* secondaire (*V* **school**). ♦ **second-best 1** *n*: **as a ~-best** faute de mieux; **2** *adv*: **to come off ~-best** perdre. ♦ **second-class** *adj mail* à tarif réduit; (*Rail*) de seconde (classe); (*pej*) *food, goods etc* de qualité inférieure; **~-class citizen** déshérité(e) *m(f)* dans la société. ♦ **secondhand 1** *adj clothes, car* d'occasion; *information* de seconde main; **~hand bookseller/bookshop** libraire *m*/librairie *f* d'occasion; **~hand dealer** marchand(e) *m(f)* d'occasion; **2** *adv buy* d'occasion; *hear sth* de qn d'autre. ♦ **second-in-command** *n* (*Mil*) commandant *m* en second; (*Naut*) second *m*; (*gen*) adjoint *m*. ♦ **secondly** *adv* deuxièmement, (*more formally*) en second lieu. ♦ **secondment** [sɪ'kɒndmənt] *n* détachement *m*; **on ~ment** en détachement (*to* à). ♦ **second-rate** *adj* médiocre, de deuxième ordre.

second[2] ['sekənd] **1** *n* seconde *f* (*also Geog, Math*

etc). **at that very ~** à cet instant précis; **just a ~!, half a ~!*** une (petite) seconde! **2** *adj*: **~(s) hand** trotteuse *f*.
secret ['si:krɪt] **1** *n* secret *m*. **to keep a ~** garder un secret; **to let sb into the ~** mettre qn dans le secret; **to let sb into a ~** révéler un secret à qn; **to be in the ~** être au courant; **there's no ~ about it** cela n'a rien de secret; **to have no ~s from sb** ne pas avoir de secrets pour qn; **he makes no ~ of the fact that** il ne cache pas que; **in ~** en secret. **2** *adj* (*gen*) secret (*f* -ète); (*secluded*) retiré. **to keep sth ~** ne pas révéler qch (*from sb* à qn); **~ agent** agent *m* secret; **~ police** police *f* secrète; **the S~ Service** les services *mpl* secrets; **~ society** société *f* secrète. ♦ **secrecy** *n* secret *m*; **in secrecy** en secret; **there's no secrecy about it** on n'en fait pas un mystère; **an air of secrecy** un air mystérieux. ♦ **secretive** *adj* (*by nature*) secret, dissimulé (*pej*); **to be ~ive about sth** se montrer très réservé à propos de qch. ♦ **secretly** *adv* secrètement, en secret.
secretary ['sekrətrɪ] *n* secrétaire *mf*; (*company* ~) secrétaire général (*d'une société*). **S~ of State** (*Brit*) ministre *m* (*for* de); (*US*) ≈ ministre des Affaires étrangères. ♦ **secretarial** *adj work, college* de secrétariat; **secretarial course** études *fpl* de secrétaire. ♦ **secretariat** *n* secrétariat *m*. ♦ **secretary-general** *n* secrétaire *m* général.
secrete [sɪ'kri:t] *vt* **(a)** (*Anat, Bio, Med*) sécréter. **(b)** (*hide*) cacher. ♦ **secretion** *n* sécrétion *f*.
sect [sekt] *n* secte *f*. ♦ **sectarian** *adj* sectaire.
section ['sekʃən] **1** *n* **(a)** (*gen*) section *f*, partie *f*; *[country]* partie; *[town]* quartier *m*; *[machine, furniture]* élément *m*; (*Mil*) groupe *m* (de combat). (*Press*) **the financial ~** les pages *fpl* financières; (*Admin*) **~ 2 of the by-laws** l'article *m* 2 des arrêtés. **(b)** (*department*) section *f*. **(c)** (*cut*) coupe *f*. **2** *vt* sectionner. **to ~ off** séparer. ♦ **sectional** *adj bookcase etc* à éléments, démontable; *interests* d'un groupe; *drawing* en coupe.
sector ['sektəʳ] *n* secteur *m*.
secular ['sekjʊləʳ] *adj authority* séculier; *school* laïque; *writer, music* profane.
secure [sɪ'kjʊəʳ] **1** *adj* **(a)** (*solid, firm*) *padlock, nail, knot* solide; *rope* bien attaché; *door* bien fermé; *ladder* qui ne bouge pas; *hold* bon. **to make ~** *rope* bien attacher; *door, window* bien fermer; *tile* bien fixer. **(b)** (*in safe place*) en sûreté; *place* sûr; (*certain*) *career, fame* assuré. **~ from** *or* **against** à l'abri de. **(c)** (*unworried*) tranquille, sans inquiétude. **to feel ~ about** ne pas avoir d'inquiétudes au sujet de; **~ in the knowledge that** ayant la certitude que. **2** *vt* **(a)** (*get*) *object* obtenir (*for sb* pour qn); *staff, performer* engager. **(b)** (*fix*) *rope* attacher; *door, window* bien fermer; *tile* fixer; (*tie up*) *person, animal* attacher. **(c)** (*make safe*) préserver (*against, from* de); *career, future* assurer. ♦ **securely** *adv* (*firmly*) solidement, bien; (*safely*) en sécurité.
security [sɪ'kjʊərɪtɪ] **1** *n* **(a)** (*safety*) sécurité *f*. **in ~** en sécurité; (*Admin, Ind*) **job ~** sécurité de l'emploi; (*Jur*) **~ of tenure** bail *m* assuré. **(b)** (*against spying*) sécurité *f*. **~ was very lax** les mesures *fpl* de sécurité étaient très relâchées. **(c)** (*Fin: for loan*) caution *f*, garantie *f*. **loans without ~** crédit *m* à découvert; **to stand ~ for sb** se porter garant pour *or* de qn. **(d)** (*St Ex*) **securities** valeurs *fpl*, titres *mpl*; **government securities** fonds *mpl* d'État. **2** *adj council, forces* de sécurité; *officer, inspector* chargé de la sécurité. **~ guard** garde *m* chargé de la sécurité; (*transporting money*) convoyeur *m* de fonds; **~ leak** fuite *f* (*de secrets etc*); **~ police** services *mpl* de la sûreté; **he is a ~ risk** il n'est pas sûr.
sedate [sɪ'deɪt] **1** *adj* posé, calme. **2** *vt* (*Med*) mettre sous sédation. ♦ **sedately** *adv* posément, calmement. ♦ **sedation** *n* sédation *f*. ♦ **sedative** ['sedətɪv] *adj, n* sédatif (*m*).
sedentary ['sedntrɪ] *adj* sédentaire.
sediment ['sedɪmənt] *n* (*Geol, Med*) sédiment *m*; (*in boiler, liquids*) dépôt *m*.
sedition [sə'dɪʃən] *n* sédition *f*. ♦ **seditious** *adj* séditieux.
seduce [sɪ'dju:s] *vt* séduire. ♦ **seducer** *n* séducteur *m*, -trice *f*. ♦ **seduction** *n* séduction *f*. ♦ **seductive** *adj person, charms* séduisant; *smile, perfume* séducteur; *offer* alléchant. ♦ **seductively** *adv* d'une manière séduisante.
see[1] [si:] *pret* **saw**, *ptp* **seen** *vti* **(a)** (*gen*) voir. **I can ~ him** je le vois; **I saw him read/reading the letter** je l'ai vu lire/qui lisait la lettre; **he was ~n to read the letter** on l'a vu lire la lettre; **there was no one to be ~n** il n'y avait pas âme qui vive; **there was not a house to be ~n** il n'y avait pas une seule maison en vue; **you can ~ for miles** on y voit à des kilomètres; **I'll go and ~** je vais aller voir; **let me ~** (*show me*) montre-moi, fais voir; (*let me think*) voyons (un peu); **~ for yourself** voyez vous-même; **as you can ~** comme vous pouvez le constater; **so I ~** c'est bien ce que je vois; (*in anger*) **~ here!** non, mais dites donc!*; **can I go out? — we'll ~** est-ce que je peux sortir? — on verra; **~ page 10** voir page 10; **to ~ sth with one's own eyes** voir qch de ses propres yeux; **I must be ~ing things*** je dois avoir des visions*; **he couldn't ~ to read** il n'y voyait pas assez clair pour lire; **to ~ in the dark** voir clair la nuit; **can you ~ your way?** est-ce que vous pouvez trouver votre chemin?; (*fig*) **to ~ one's way to doing sth** trouver le moyen de faire qch; **to ~ the world** voyager; **I saw in the paper that** j'ai vu *or* lu dans le journal que; **I ~ nothing wrong in it** je n'y trouve rien à redire; **I don't know what she ~s in him** je ne sais pas ce qu'elle lui trouve (de bien); **~ who's at the door** allez voir qui est à la porte; **to go and ~ sb, to go to ~ sb** aller voir qn; **they ~ a lot of him** ils le voient souvent; **~ you soon!*, I'll be ~ing you!*** à bientôt!, salut!*; **~ you later!*** à tout à l'heure!; **~ you on Sunday** à dimanche; **this hat has ~n better days** ce chapeau a connu des jours meilleurs; **I never thought we'd ~ the day when ...** je n'aurais jamais cru qu'un jour ...; **I couldn't ~ her left alone** je ne pouvais pas supporter qu'on la laisse (*subj*) toute seule; **I've ~n some things in my time* but ...** j'en ai vu des choses dans ma vie* mais ... .
(b) (*understand*) voir, comprendre; *joke* comprendre. **do you ~ what I mean?** vous voyez ce que je veux dire?; **I don't** *or* **can't ~ how ...** je ne vois pas du tout comment ...; **the way I ~ it, as I ~ it** à mon avis; **as far as I can ~** pour autant que je puisse en juger.
(c) (*accompany*) accompagner, conduire. **to ~ sb to the station** accompagner *or* conduire qn à la gare; **to ~ sb home** raccompagner qn jusque chez lui; **to ~ the children to bed** coucher les enfants.
(d) (*ensure*) s'assurer. **~ that he has all he needs** (*make sure*) faites en sorte qu'il ait tout ce dont il a besoin; (*check*) assurez-vous qu'il ne manque de rien; **I'll ~ he gets the letter** je me charge de lui faire parvenir la lettre.
(e) (*imagine*) imaginer, voir. **I can't ~ him as Prime Minister** je ne le vois *or* ne l'imagine pas du tout en Premier ministre; **I can't ~ myself doing that** je me vois mal *or* je m'imagine mal faisant cela; **I can't ~ myself being elected** je ne vois pas très bien comment je pourrais être élu.
see about *vt fus* **(a)** (*deal with*) s'occuper de. **(b)** (*consider*) **to ~ about sth** voir si qch est possible; **we'll ~ about it** on verra.
see in *vt sep*: **to ~ the New Year in** fêter la Nouvelle Année.
see off *vt sep*: **I saw him off at the station** je l'ai accompagné à la gare; **we'll come and ~ you off** on viendra vous dire au revoir à la gare (*etc*).
see out *vt sep person* raccompagner à la porte.

I'll ~ myself out* ne vous dérangez pas, je trouverai le chemin; **he won't ~ the week out** il ne passera pas la semaine.
see over *vt fus* (*visit*) visiter.
see through 1 *vt fus person* ne pas se laisser tromper par; *behaviour, promises* voir clair dans. **I saw through him at once** j'ai tout de suite compris où il voulait en venir. **2** *vt sep project, deal* mener à bonne fin. **£10 should ~ you through** 10 livres devraient vous suffire; **I'll ~ you through** vous pouvez compter sur moi.
see to *vt fus* (*deal with*) s'occuper de; (*mend*) réparer. **please ~ to it that ...** veillez s'il vous plaît à ce que ... + *subj*.
♦ **seeing** *conj*: **~ing (that)** vu que, étant donné que. ♦ **see-through** *adj* transparent.
see[2] [si:] *n [bishop]* siège *m* épiscopal.
seed [si:d] **1** *n* **(a)** (*Agr, Bot etc*) graine *f*; (*in apple, grape etc*) pépin *m*. (*for sowing*) **the ~** les graines *fpl*, la semence; **to go to ~** *[plant etc]* monter en graine; *[person]* se laisser aller. **(b)** (*Tennis*: **~ed player**) tête *f* de série. **2** *adj potato etc* de semence. **~ pearls** semence *f* de perles. **3** *vt* **(a)** *lawn, clouds* ensemencer; *raisin, grape* épépiner. **(b)** (*Tennis*) **he was ~ed third** il était classé troisième tête de série. **4** *vi* monter en graine. ♦ **seedless** *adj grapes etc* sans pépins. ♦ **seedling** *n* semis *m*. ♦ **seed-merchant** *or* ♦ **seedsman** *n* grainetier *m*. ♦ **seedy** *adj* (*shabby*) miteux; (*: *ill*) mal fichu*.
seek [si:k] *pret, ptp* **sought 1** *vt* (*gen*) chercher (*to do* à faire); *solution, person, thing* chercher; *fame, honours* rechercher; *advice, help* demander (*from sb* à qn). **to ~ one's fortune** chercher fortune. **2** *vi*: **to ~ for** *or* **after** rechercher; **sought after** recherché, demandé.
seek out *vt sep person* aller voir.
♦ **seeker** *n* chercheur *m*, -euse *f* (*after* en quête de).
seem [si:m] *vi* sembler, paraître, avoir l'air; (*impersonal vb*) paraître, sembler. **he ~s honest** il semble (être) honnête, il paraît honnête, il a l'air honnête; **she ~s to know you** elle semble vous connaître; **she ~s not to want to leave** on dirait qu'elle ne veut pas partir; **we ~ to have met before** il me semble que nous nous sommes déjà rencontrés; **I ~ to have heard that before** il me semble avoir déjà entendu cela; **I can't ~ to do it** je n'arrive pas à le faire; **I ~ed to be floating** j'avais l'impression de planer; **how did she ~ to you?** comment l'as-tu trouvée?; **how does it ~ to you?** qu'en penses-tu?; **it ~s that the government is going to fall** (*looks as if*) il semble bien que le gouvernement va tomber; (*people say*) il paraît que le gouvernement va tomber; **it ~s she's right** il semble qu'elle a raison; **it doesn't ~ she's right, it ~s she's not right** il ne semble pas qu'elle ait raison; **does it ~ that she is right?** est-ce qu'il semble qu'elle ait raison?; **it ~s to me that ...** il me semble que ...; **does it ~ to you as though ...?** est-ce que tu crois que ...?; **so it ~s** il paraît; **it ~s not** il paraît que non; **he died yesterday, it ~s** il est mort hier, paraît-il; **I did what ~ed best** j'ai fait ce que j'ai jugé bon; **it ~s ages since we last met** il y a des siècles* que nous ne nous sommes vus; **there ~s to be a mistake** il semble y avoir une erreur.
♦ **seeming** *adj* apparent. ♦ **seemingly** *adv* à ce qu'il paraît, apparemment. ♦ **seemly** *adj behaviour* convenable; *dress* correct.
seen [si:n] *ptp of* **see**[1].
seep [si:p] *vi* filtrer (*through* à travers).
seep away *vi* s'écouler peu à peu.
seep in *vi* s'infiltrer peu à peu.
seep out *vi* suinter.
♦ **seepage** *n* déperdition *f*.
seersucker ['sɪəˌsʌkəʳ] *n* crépon *m* de coton.
seesaw ['si:sɔ:] **1** *n* (jeu *m* de) bascule *f*. **2** *adj motion* de bascule. **3** *vi* (*fig*) osciller.
seethe [si:ð] *vi [liquid]* bouillonner; *[crowd]* s'agiter. (*fig*) **to ~ (with anger)** bouillir de colère; **the streets were seething with people** les rues grouillaient de monde.
segment ['segmənt] *n* (*gen*) segment *m*; *[orange etc]* quartier *m*.
segregate ['segrɪgeɪt] *vt* (*gen, also Pol*) séparer (*from* de); *contagious patient etc* isoler (*from* de). ♦ **segregated** *adj* (*Pol*) *school, club* où la ségrégation (raciale) est appliquée. ♦ **segregation** *n* (*Pol*) ségrégation *f*; (*gen*) séparation *f*, isolement *m* (*from* de). ♦ **segregationist** *adj, n* ségrégationniste (*mf*).
seismic ['saɪzmɪk] *adj* sismique. ♦ **seismograph** *n* sismographe *m*. ♦ **seismology** *n* sismologie *f*.
seize [si:z] *vt* (*gen*) saisir; (*Mil, Police*) s'emparer de. **she ~d (hold of) his hand, she ~d him by the hand** elle lui a saisi la main; **to be ~d with rage** avoir un accès de rage; **she was ~d with fear/with this desire** la peur/ce désir l'a saisie; **he was ~d with a bout of coughing** il a eu un accès de toux.
seize up *vi* (*Tech*) se gripper; (*Med*) s'ankyloser.
seize (up)on *vt fus idea, chance* saisir.
♦ **seizure** *n* **(a)** *[goods, gun, property]* saisie *f*; *[city, ship]* capture *f*; *[power, territory]* prise *f*; **(b)** (*Med*) crise *f*, attaque *f*.
seldom ['seldəm] *adv* rarement, peu souvent.
select [sɪ'lekt] **1** *vt team, candidate* sélectionner (*from, among* parmi); *gift, book, colour* choisir (*from, among* parmi). **~ed works** œuvres *fpl* choisies. **2** *adj audience, group* choisi; *club* fermé; *restaurant* chic *inv*, sélect. **a ~ few** quelques privilégiés *mpl*. ♦ **selection 1** *n* sélection *f*, choix *m*; (*Literat, Mus*) **~ions from** morceaux *mpl* choisis de; **2** *adj committee* de sélection.
♦ **selective** *adj* (*gen*) sélectif; *school* à recrutement sélectif; **to be ~ive** savoir faire un choix.
♦ **selectivity** *n* (*gen*) sélectivité *f*; (*Scol*) sélection *f*. ♦ **selector** *n* (*person*) sélectionneur *m*, -euse *f*; (*Tech*) sélecteur *m*.
self [self] **1** *n, pl* **selves**: **the ~** le moi *inv*; **his better ~** le meilleur de lui-même; **her real ~** son vrai moi; **she's her old ~ again** elle est redevenue complètement elle-même.
2 *pref*: **~-adjusting/-cleaning** *etc* à réglage/nettoyage *etc* automatique; **~-adhesive** autoadhésif; **~-criticism** critique *f* de soi; **~-inflicted** que l'on s'inflige à soi-même.
♦ **self-addressed envelope** *n* enveloppe *f* à mon (*or* son *etc*) nom et adresse. ♦ **self-assurance** *n* assurance *f*. ♦ **self-assured** *adj* plein d'assurance. ♦ **self-centred** *adj* égocentrique. ♦ **self-confessed** *adj*: **he is a ~-confessed thief** *etc* il est voleur *etc* de son propre aveu. ♦ **self-confidence** *n* confiance *f* en soi. ♦ **self-confident** *adj* sûr de soi. ♦ **self-conscious** *adj* embarrassé, gêné (*about* de). ♦ **self-consciousness** *n* gêne *f*. ♦ **self-contained** *adj* indépendant. ♦ **self-control** *n* maîtrise *f* de soi. ♦ **self-controlled** *adj* maître (*f* maîtresse) de soi. ♦ **self-defeating** *adj* infructueux. ♦ **self-defence** *n* légitime défense *f*. ♦ **self-denial** *n* abnégation *f*. ♦ **self-determination** *n* autodétermination *f*. ♦ **self-discipline** *n* discipline *f* (personnelle). ♦ **self-drive** *adj* (*Aut*) sans chauffeur. ♦ **self-educated** *adj* autodidacte. ♦ **self-employed** *adj* qui travaille à son compte. ♦ **self-esteem** *n* amour-propre *m*. ♦ **self-evident** *adj* évident. ♦ **self-explanatory** *adj* qui se passe d'explication. ♦ **self-expression** *n* expression *f* libre. ♦ **self-governing** *adj* autonome. ♦ **self-government** *n* autonomie *f*. ♦ **self-help** *n* débrouillardise* *f*. ♦ **self-importance** *n* suffisance *f*. ♦ **self-important** *adj* suffisant, m'as-tu-vu* *inv*. ♦ **self-indulgence** *n* sybaritisme *m*. ♦ **self-indulgent** *adj* qui ne se refuse rien, sybarite. ♦ **self-interest** *n* intérêt *m* (personnel). ♦ **selfish** *adj person, behaviour* égoïste; *motive* intéressé. ♦ **selfishly** *adv* égoïstement.

♦ **selfishness** *n* égoïsme *m*. ♦ **selfless** *adj* désintéressé. ♦ **selflessly** *adv* d'une façon désintéressée. ♦ **selflessness** *n* désintéressement *m*. ♦ **self-made man** *n* self-made man *m*. ♦ **self-pity** *n* apitoiement *m* sur soi-même. ♦ **self-portrait** *n* autoportrait *m*. ♦ **self-possessed** *adj* qui garde son sang-froid. ♦ **self-possession** *n* sang-froid *m*. ♦ **self-preservation** *n* instinct *m* de conservation. ♦ **self-raising flour** *or* (*US*) ♦ **self-rising flour** *n* farine *f* à levure. ♦ **self-reliant** *adj* indépendant. ♦ **self-respect** *n* respect *m* de soi. ♦ **self-respecting** *adj* qui se respecte. ♦ **self-righteous** *adj* satisfait de soi. ♦ **self-righteousness** *n* satisfaction *f* de soi. ♦ **self-sacrifice** *n* abnégation *f*. ♦ **selfsame** *adj* même. ♦ **self-satisfied** *adj* suffisant. ♦ **self-service** *n* libre-service *m inv*. ♦ **self-starter** *n* démarreur *m*. ♦ **self-sufficiency** *n* indépendance *f*; (*economic*) indépendance économique. ♦ **self-sufficient** *adj* indépendant; économiquement indépendant. ♦ **self-supporting** *adj* qui subvient à ses propres besoins. ♦ **self-taught** *adj* autodidacte.

sell [sel] *pret, ptp* **sold 1** *vt* vendre. **to ~ sth for 2 francs** vendre qch 2 F; **he sold it (to) me for 10 francs** il me l'a vendu 10 F; **are stamps sold here?** est-ce qu'on vend des timbres ici?; **I was sold this in Grenoble** on m'a vendu cela à Grenoble; (*fig*) **to ~ the pass** trahir la cause; **to ~ one's life dearly** vendre chèrement sa vie; **to ~ sb down the river** lâcher qn*; **to ~ sb a pup**‡ rouler qn*; **to ~ sb an idea** faire accepter une idée à qn; **he doesn't ~ himself very well** il n'arrive pas à se mettre en valeur; **to be sold on* sb/sth** être emballé* par qn/qch.

2 *vi* se vendre. **these books ~ at** *or* **for 10 francs each** ces livres se vendent 10 F pièce.

sell off *vt sep stock, shares* liquider; *goods* solder.

sell out 1 *vi* (*Comm*) vendre son affaire. (*fig*) **to ~ out to the enemy** passer à l'ennemi. **2** *vt sep* (*Comm*) **this item is sold out** cet article est épuisé; **we are sold out** on n'en a plus; **we are sold out of milk** on n'a plus de lait; (*Theat*) **the house was sold out** toutes les places étaient louées.

sell up (*esp Brit Comm*) **1** *vi* vendre son affaire. **2** *vt sep business* liquider.

♦ **seller** *n* vendeur *m*, -euse *f*; **~er's market** marché *m* vendeur; **onion-~er** marchand(e) *m(f)* d'oignons. ♦ **selling price** *n* prix *m* de vente. ♦ **sellout** *n* **(a)** (*Theat etc*) **it was a ~out** on a joué à guichets fermés; **(b)** (*betrayal*) trahison *f* (*of* de); capitulation *f* (*to* devant).

sellotape ['seləʊteɪp] ® **1** *n* scotch *m* ®, ruban *m* adhésif. **2** *vt* coller avec du ruban adhésif.

seltzer ['seltsəʳ] *n* eau *f* de Seltz.

selvage, selvedge ['selvɪdʒ] *n* lisière *f* (*d'un tissu*).

semantic [sɪ'mæntɪk] *adj* sémantique. ♦ **semantically** *adv* du point de vue de la sémantique. ♦ **semantics** *nsg* sémantique *f*.

semaphore ['seməfɔːʳ] *n* **(a)** signaux *mpl* à bras. **(b)** (*Rail*) sémaphore *m*.

semblance ['sembləns] *n* semblant *m*.

semen ['siːmən] *n* sperme *m*.

semester [sɪ'mestəʳ] *n* semestre *m*.

semi ['semɪ] *pref* semi-, demi-, à demi, à moitié. ♦ **semicircle** *n* demi-cercle *m*. ♦ **semicircular** *adj* en demi-cercle. ♦ **semicolon** *n* point-virgule *m*. ♦ **semiconscious** *adj* à demi conscient. ♦ **semidarkness** *n* pénombre *f*. ♦ **semidetached house** *n* maison *f* jumelée. ♦ **semifinal** *n* demi-finale *f*. ♦ **semifinalist** *n* joueur *m*, -euse *f* de demi-finale. ♦ **semiofficial** *adj* semi-officiel. ♦ **semiprecious** *adj* semi-précieux. ♦ **semi-skilled** *adj worker* spécialisé; *work* d'ouvrier spécialisé.

seminal ['semɪnl] *adj* (*fig*) fécond.

seminar ['semɪnɑːʳ] *n* séminaire *m* (*discussion*); (*Univ*) séance *f* de travaux pratiques. ♦ **seminarist** *n* séminariste *m*. ♦ **seminary** *n* séminaire *m* (*Rel*).

semolina [ˌseməˈliːnə] *n* semoule *f*. **~ pudding** semoule au lait.

senate ['senɪt] *n* (*Pol*) sénat *m*; (*Univ*) conseil *m* de l'université. ♦ **senator** *n* sénateur *m*.

send [send] *pret, ptp* **sent** *vt* **(a)** (*gen*) envoyer (*to sb* à qn); *letter, parcel* envoyer, expédier; *ball, rocket, arrow* lancer. **I'll ~ a car for you** j'enverrai une voiture vous chercher; **to ~ sb for sth** envoyer qn chercher qch; **to ~ sb to do sth** envoyer qn faire qch; **~ him along to see me** envoie-le-moi; **to ~ sb to bed** envoyer qn se coucher; **to ~ sb home** renvoyer qn chez lui, (*from abroad*) rapatrier qn; **to ~ sb to sleep** endormir qn; **he was sent to prison** on l'a envoyé en prison; **the rain sent us indoors** la pluie nous a fait rentrer; (*fig*) **to ~ sb packing*** *or* **about his business*** envoyer promener qn*; (*fig*) **to ~ sb to Coventry** mettre qn en quarantaine; **the explosion sent a cloud of smoke into the air** l'explosion a projeté un nuage de fumée en l'air; **to ~ a shiver down sb's spine** faire passer un frisson dans le dos de qn; **the sight of the dog sent her running to her mother** en voyant le chien elle s'est précipitée vers sa mère; **the blow sent him sprawling** le coup l'a envoyé par terre; **he sent the plate flying** il a envoyé voler l'assiette; **to ~ sb flying** envoyer qn rouler à terre. **(b)** (*cause to become*) rendre. **to ~ sb mad** rendre qn fou. **(c)** (‡) emballer*. **this music ~s me** cette musique m'emballe*.

send away 1 *vi*: **to ~ away for sth** commander qch par correspondance. **2** *vt sep person* envoyer (*to* à); *parcel, letter, goods* envoyer, expédier; (*post*) mettre à la poste; (*dismiss*) renvoyer.

send back *vt sep* renvoyer.

send down *vt sep person* faire descendre, (*expel*) renvoyer; *prices* faire baisser.

send for *vt fus* **(a)** *doctor, police etc* faire venir; *help* envoyer chercher. **(b)** (*order by post*) commander par correspondance.

send in *vt sep person* faire entrer; *troops, request, names, resignation* envoyer; *report* envoyer, soumettre. **to ~ in an application** faire une demande; (*for job*) poser sa candidature.

send off 1 *vi* = **send away 1. 2** *vt sep person* envoyer (*to do* faire); *letter, parcel, goods* envoyer, expédier; (*post*) mettre à la poste; (*Ftbl etc*) *player* renvoyer du terrain.

send on *vt sep letter* faire suivre; *luggage* (*in advance*) expédier à l'avance, (*afterwards*) faire suivre; *object left behind* renvoyer.

send out 1 *vi*: **to ~ out for sth** envoyer chercher qch. **2** *vt sep* **(a)** *person, dog etc* faire sortir. **she sent the children out to play** elle a envoyé les enfants jouer dehors. **(b)** (*post*) *correspondence, leaflets* envoyer (par la poste). **(c)** *scouts, messengers* envoyer. **(d)** (*emit*) *smell, smoke, heat* émettre, répandre; *light* diffuser.

send round *vt sep document, bottle etc* faire circuler; *person* envoyer (*to sb's* chez qn). **I'll ~ it round to you as soon as it's ready** je vous le ferai parvenir dès que cela sera prêt.

send up *vt sep* **(a)** *person, luggage* faire monter; *smoke* répandre; *aeroplane* envoyer; *spacecraft, flare* lancer; *prices* faire monter en flèche. **(b)** (*: *make fun of*) *person* mettre en boîte*; *book* parodier. **(c)** *entry form* envoyer. **(d)** (*blow up*) faire sauter*.

♦ **sender** *n* expéditeur *m*, -trice *f*, envoyeur *m*, -euse *f*. ♦ **send-off*** *n*: **to give sb a ~-off** faire des adieux chaleureux à qn. ♦ **send-up*** *n* parodie *f*.

senile ['siːnaɪl] *adj* sénile. ♦ **senility** *n* sénilité *f*.

senior ['siːnɪəʳ] **1** *adj* **(a)** (*older*) aîné, plus âgé. **he is 3 years ~ to me** il est mon aîné de 3 ans, il est plus âgé que moi de 3 ans; **Smith S~** Smith père; **~ citizen** personne *f* âgée; **the problems of ~ citi-**

zens les problèmes du troisième âge; (*US*) ~ **high school** lycée *m*; (*US: Scol, Univ*) ~ **year** dernière année *f* d'études. **(b)** (*of higher rank*) *employee* de grade supérieur; *officer, executive, position* supérieur. **he is ~ to me in the firm** il est au-dessus de moi dans l'entreprise; **the ~ partner** l'associé *m* principal.

2 *n* **(a)** (*in age*) aîné(e) *m(f)*. **(b)** (*US Univ*) étudiant(e) *m(f)* de dernière année.

♦ **seniority** *n* (*in age*) priorité *f* d'âge; (*in rank*) supériorité *f*; (*in years of service*) ancienneté *f*; **promotion by ~ity** avancement *m* à l'ancienneté.

sensation [sen'seɪʃən] *n* **(a)** (*physical feeling; impression*) sensation *f* (*of doing* de faire). **(b)** (*excitement*) sensation *f*. **to be** *or* **cause a ~** faire sensation. ♦ **sensational** *adj* **(a)** *event, fashion* qui fait sensation; **(b)** *film, novel, newspaper* à sensation; *account, description* dramatique; **(c)** (*: *marvellous*) sensationnel*, formidable*. ♦ **sensationally** *adv report, describe* en recherchant le sensationnel; **~ally successful** qui a connu un succès extraordinaire.

sense [sens] **1** *n* **(a)** (*faculty etc*) sens *m*. **~ of hearing/smell** *etc* ouïe *f*/odorat *m etc*; **to come to one's ~s** (*regain consciousness*) reprendre connaissance (*V also* **1c**); **~ of colour/direction** sens de la couleur/de l'orientation; **~ of duty/humour** sens du devoir/de l'humour; **to lose all ~ of time** perdre toute notion de l'heure; **to have no ~ of shame** ne pas savoir ce que c'est que la honte. **(b)** (*sensation, impression*) (*physical*) sensation *f*; (*mental*) sentiment *m*. **a ~ of warmth** une sensation de chaleur; **a ~ of guilt** un sentiment de culpabilité. **(c)** (*sanity*) **~s** raison *f*; **to take leave of one's ~s** perdre la raison; **to come to one's ~s** (*become reasonable*) revenir à la raison; **to bring sb to his ~s** ramener qn à la raison; **no one in his ~s would do that** il faudrait être fou pour faire ça. **(d)** (*common ~*) bon sens, intelligence *f*. **you should have had more ~ than to do it** vous auriez dû avoir assez de bon sens pour ne pas le faire; **to see ~** entendre raison; **there's no ~ in doing that, what's the ~ of** *or* **in doing that?** à quoi bon faire cela?; *[words, speech]* **to make ~** avoir du sens; **what she did makes ~** ce qu'elle a fait est logique; **to make ~ of sth** arriver à comprendre qch. **(e)** (*meaning*) sens *m*. **in the literal/figurative ~** au sens propre/figuré; **in every ~ of the word** dans toute l'acception du terme; **in a ~** dans un certain sens; **to get the ~ of what sb says** saisir l'essentiel de ce que dit qn.

2 *vt* (*gen*) *sb's presence, interest* sentir (intuitivement) (*that* que); *danger* pressentir.

♦ **senseless** *adj* **(a)** (*stupid*) insensé; **(b)** (*unconscious*) sans connaissance. ♦ **senselessly** *adv* d'une façon insensée. ♦ **senselessness** *n [person]* manque *m* de bon sens; *[action, idea]* absurdité *f*.

sensible ['sensəbl] *adj* **(a)** (*wise etc*) *person* raisonnable, sensé; *act, decision, choice* raisonnable, judicieux; *clothes* pratique. **(b)** (*perceptible*) *change, difference* sensible, appréciable. ♦ **sensibility** *n* sensibilité *f*; **sensibilities** susceptibilité *f*. ♦ **sensibleness** *n* bon sens *m*. ♦ **sensibly** *adv* **(a)** (*reasonably*) raisonnablement; **(b)** (*perceptibly*) sensiblement.

sensitive ['sensɪtɪv] *adj person, tooth, film* sensible (*to* à); (*delicate*) *skin, question* délicat; (*easily offended*) susceptible. **she is ~ about her nose** elle n'aime pas qu'on lui parle (*subj*) de son nez. ♦ **sensitively** *adv* avec sensibilité. ♦ **sensitiveness** *or* ♦ **sensitivity** *n* sensibilité *f*; délicatesse *f*; susceptibilité *f*. ♦ **sensitize** *vt* sensibiliser.

sensual ['sensjʊəl] *adj* sensuel. ♦ **sensuality** *n* sensualité *f*. ♦ **sensually** *adv* sensuellement.

sensuous ['sensjʊəs] *adj* voluptueux. ♦ **sensuously** *adv* voluptueusement. ♦ **sensuousness** *n* volupté *f*.

sent [sent] *pret, ptp of* **send.**

sentence ['sentəns] **1** *n* **(a)** (*Gram*) phrase *f*. **(b)** (*Jur*) (*judgment*) condamnation *f*, sentence *f*; (*punishment*) peine *f*. (*lit, fig*) **to pass ~ on sb** prononcer une condamnation contre qn; **~ of death** condamnation à mort; **under ~ of death** condamné à mort; **he got a 5-year ~** il a été condamné à 5 ans de prison; **a long ~** une longue peine.

2 *vt*: **to ~ sb to death/to 5 years** condamner qn à mort/à 5 ans de prison.

sententious [sen'tenʃəs] *adj* sentencieux. ♦ **sententiously** *adv* sentencieusement.

sentiment ['sentɪmənt] *n* **(a)** (*feeling*) sentiment *m*; (*opinion*) opinion *f*. **(b)** (*sentimentality*) sentimentalité *f*. ♦ **sentimental** *adj* sentimental. ♦ **sentimentalist** *n* sentimental(e) *m(f)*. ♦ **sentimentality** *n* sentimentalité *f*. ♦ **sentimentally** *adv* sentimentalement.

sentinel ['sentɪnl] *n* sentinelle *f*.

sentry ['sentrɪ] **1** *n* sentinelle *f*. **2** *adj*: **~ box** guérite *f*; **on ~ duty** en *or* de faction.

sepal ['sepəl] *n* sépale *m*.

separate ['seprɪt] **1** *adj* (*gen*) séparé; *career, existence, organization* indépendant; *department* spécial; *entrance* particulier; *occasion, day, issue* différent, autre. **they have ~ rooms** ils ont chacun leur propre chambre; **Paul and his wife sleep in ~ beds/rooms** Paul et sa femme font lit/chambre à part; (*in restaurant etc*) **we want ~ bills** nous voudrions des additions séparées; **there will be ~ discussions on this question** cette question sera discutée séparément; **keep the novels ~ from the textbooks** séparez les romans des livres de classe. **2** *n* (*clothes*) **~s** coordonnés *mpl*. **3** ['sepəreɪt] *vt* séparer (*from* de); (*sort out*) séparer, trier; (*divide up*) diviser; *strands* dédoubler; *milk* écrémer. **they are ~d but not divorced** ils sont séparés mais ils n'ont pas divorcé. **4** ['sepəreɪt] *vi [liquids, people]* se séparer (*from* de); *[fighters]* rompre; *[married couple]* se séparer; *[non-married couple]* rompre. ♦ **separable** *adj* séparable. ♦ **separately** *adv* séparément. ♦ **separation** *n* (*all senses*) séparation *f* (*from sth* de qch; *from sb* d'avec qn). ♦ **separatist** *adj, n* séparatiste (*mf*).

sepia ['siːpjə] *n* sépia *f*.

September [sep'tembəʳ] *n* septembre *m*, mois *m* de septembre. **the first of ~** le premier septembre; **(on) the tenth of ~** le dix septembre; **in ~** en septembre; **in the month of ~** au mois de septembre; **each** *or* **every ~** chaque année en septembre; **at the beginning/in the middle/at the end of ~** au début/au milieu/à la fin (du mois) de septembre; **during ~** pendant le mois de septembre; **there are 30 days in ~** il y a 30 jours au mois de septembre; **~ was cold** septembre a été froid, il a fait froid en septembre.

septic ['septɪk] *adj* septique; *wound* infecté. **to go** *or* **become ~** s'infecter; **~ tank** fosse *f* septique. ♦ **septicaemia,** (*US*) **-cemia** *n* septicémie *f*.

sepulchre, (*US*) **-er** ['sepəlkəʳ] *n* sépulcre *m*. ♦ **sepulchral** [sɪ'pʌlkrəl] *adj* sépulcral.

sequel ['siːkwəl] *n [book, film etc]* suite *f*; *[event etc]* suites *fpl*.

sequence ['siːkwəns] *n* **(a)** (*order*) ordre *m*. **in ~** par ordre; (*Gram*) **~ of tenses** concordance *f* des temps. **(b)** (*series*) suite *f* (*of* de); (*Mus, Cards*) séquence *f*. **film ~** séquence; **dance ~** numéro *m* (de danse).

sequin ['siːkwɪn] *n* paillette *f*.

serenade [ˌserə'neɪd] **1** *n* sérénade *f*. **2** *vt* donner une sérénade à.

serene [sə'riːn] *adj person, sky* serein; *sea* calme. ♦ **serenely** *adv smile, say* avec sérénité; **~ly indifferent to** suprêmement indifférent à. ♦ **serenity** [sɪ'renɪtɪ] *n* sérénité *f*.

serge [sɜːdʒ] *n* serge *f*.

sergeant ['sɑ:dʒənt] *n* (*Infantry*) sergent *m*; (*Artillery, Cavalry*) maréchal *m* des logis; (*US Air Force*) caporal-chef *m*; (*Police*) brigadier *m*. ♦ **sergeant-major** *n* (*Infantry*) sergent-major *m*; (*Artillery, Cavalry*) maréchal *m* des logis-chef.

serial ['sɪərɪəl] **1** *n* feuilleton *m*. **television** ~ feuilleton télévisé; **3-part** ~ feuilleton en 3 épisodes. **2** *adj*: ~ **number** *[goods, car engine]* numéro *m* de série; *[soldier]* matricule *m*; *[cheque, banknote]* numéro. ♦ **serialize** *vt* (*Press*) publier en feuilleton; (*Rad, TV*) adapter en feuilleton.

series ['sɪərɪz] *n, pl inv* (*gen*) série *f*; (*Rad, TV*) série (d'émissions); (*set of books*) collection *f*; (*set of stamps*) série.

serious ['sɪərɪəs] *adj* **(a)** (*in earnest*) (*gen*) sérieux; *attitude, voice, smile* plein de sérieux, grave; *tone, look* sérieux, grave. **I'm quite** ~ je parle sérieusement, je ne plaisante pas; **to give** ~ **thought to sth** (*ponder*) bien réfléchir à qch; (*intend*) songer sérieusement à (faire) qch; **to be** ~ **about one's work** être sérieux dans son travail; **the** ~ **student of jazz** qn qui s'intéresse sérieusement au jazz. **(b)** (*causing concern*) *illness, mistake, situation, threat* grave, sérieux; *damage* important; *loss, doubt* grave (*before n*). **the patient's condition is** ~ le patient est dans un état grave. ♦ **seriously** *adv* **(a)** (*in earnest*) sérieusement; **to take sth/sb** ~**ly** prendre qch/qn au sérieux; **(b)** (*dangerously*) *ill* gravement; *wounded* grièvement; *worried* sérieusement. ♦ **seriousness** *n* (*gen*) sérieux *m*; *[report, information]* caractère *m* sérieux; *[situation, illness, mistake, injury]* gravité *f*; *[damage]* importance *f*; **in all** ~**ness** sérieusement.

sermon ['sɜ:mən] *n* sermon *m* (*on* sur).

serpent ['sɜ:pənt] *n* serpent *m*.

serrated [se'reɪtɪd] *adj edge* en dents de scie; *knife* à dents de scie. ♦ **serration** *n* dentelure *f*.

serum ['sɪərəm] *n* sérum *m*.

serve [sɜ:v] **1** *vt* **(a)** (*work for*) *master, employer, God, one's country, a cause* servir. **(b)** (*be used as etc*) **it** ~**s her as a table** ça lui sert de table; **it** ~**s its** (*or* **my** *or* **his** *etc*) **purpose** cela fait l'affaire; **it** ~**s a variety of purposes** cela sert à divers usages; **it** ~**s no useful purpose** cela ne sert à rien; **his knowledge** ~**d him well** ses connaissances lui ont bien servi *or* été très utiles; **it** ~**s him right** c'est bien fait pour lui; **it** ~**s you right for being so stupid** cela t'apprendra à être si stupide. **(c)** *food, meal* servir (*to sb* à qn); (*Tennis*) servir. (*in shop, restaurant*) **to** ~ **sb (with) sth** servir qch à qn; **are you being** ~**d?** est-ce qu'on vous sert?; **the bus** ~**s 6 villages** le car dessert 6 villages; **the power station** ~**s a large district** la centrale alimente une zone étendue. **(d)** (*work out*) **to** ~ **one's time** *[apprentice]* faire son apprentissage (*as* de); (*Mil*) faire son temps de service; (*Prison*) faire son temps de prison; (*in prison*) **to** ~ **time** faire de la prison; **to** ~ **a prison sentence** purger une peine (de prison). **(e)** (*Jur*) *summons* remettre (*on* à); *warrant* délivrer (*on* à). **to** ~ **notice on sb to the effect that** notifier à qn que; **to** ~ **a writ on sb** assigner qn.

2 *vi* **(a)** *[servant, waiter, soldier]* servir (*also Rel, Tennis*). **to** ~ **on a committee** être membre d'un comité; **he has** ~**d for 2 years as chairman** cela fait 2 ans qu'il exerce la fonction de président. **(b)** (*be useful*) servir (*for, as sth* de qch) **it** ~**s to explain** cela sert à expliquer.

3 *n* (*Tennis etc*) service *m*.

serve out *vt sep meal, soup* servir; *rations, provisions* distribuer.

serve up *vt sep* servir, mettre sur la table. ♦ **servant** *n* domestique *mf*; (*maid*) bonne *f*; (*fig*) serviteur *m*. ♦ **server** *n* **(a)** (*Rel*) servant *m*; (*Tennis etc*) serveur *m*, -euse *f*; **(b)** (*tray*) plateau *m*; (*piece of cutlery*) couvert *m* à servir.

service ['sɜ:vɪs] **1** *n* **(a)** (*gen; also Mil etc*) service *m*. (*Mil*) **to see** ~ servir (*as* comme); **on Her Majesty's** ~ au service de Sa Majesté; *[domestic servant]* **in** ~ en service; **at your** ~ à votre service; **to be of** ~ **to sb** être utile à qn, rendre service à qn; **to bring/come into** ~ mettre/entrer en service; (*in shop, hotel etc*) **the** ~ **is very poor** le service est très mauvais; (*on bill*) **15%** ~ **included** service 15% compris. **(b)** (*department; system*) service *m*. **medical/social** *etc* ~**s** services médicaux/sociaux *etc*; **customs** ~ douane *f*; (*Mil*) **the S**~**s** l'armée *f* (*or* la marine *or* l'aviation *f*), les forces *fpl* armées; **the train** ~ **to London** les trains *mpl* pour Londres; **the number 4 bus** ~ la ligne du numéro 4. **(c)** (*help etc rendered*) service *m*. **to do sb a** ~ rendre service à qn. **(d)** (*Rel*) service *m*. **to hold a** ~ célébrer un service. **(e)** (*maintenance work*) révision *f*. **to put one's car in for** ~ donner sa voiture à réviser. **(f)** (*set of crockery*) service *m*. **coffee** ~ service à café. **(g)** (*Tennis etc*) service *m*.

2 *adj [motorway]* ~ **area** aire *f* de services; ~ **charge** service *m*; (*Mil*) ~ **families** familles *fpl* de militaires; (*Brit*) ~ **flat** appartement *m* avec service; ~ **hatch** passe-plat *m*; (*Aut*) ~ **road** voie *f* de service; ~ **station** station-service *f*.

3 *vt car, washing machine etc* réviser. ♦ **serviceable** *adj building, clothes* (*practical*) commode; (*durable*) solide; (*usable, working*) utilisable. ♦ **serviceman** *n* militaire *m*. ♦ **servicing** *n [car etc]* révision *f*.

serviette [ˌsɜ:vɪ'et] *n* (*esp Brit*) serviette *f* (de table). ~ **ring** rond *m* de serviette.

servile ['sɜ:vaɪl] *adj* servile.
♦ **servility** [sɜ:'vɪlɪtɪ] *n* servilité *f*.

servitude ['sɜ:vɪtju:d] *n* servitude *f*.

servo- ['sɜ:vəʊ] *pref* servo... . ~**assisted** servo-commandé.

session ['seʃən] *n* **(a)** (*sitting, meeting*) séance *f*. **to be in** ~ (*gen*) siéger; *[court]* être en séance; **I had a** ~ **with him** (*work*) nous avons travaillé ensemble; (*discussion*) nous avons eu une longue discussion. **(b)** (*Scol, Univ*) (*year*) année *f* universitaire *or* scolaire; (*US: term*) trimestre *m* universitaire.

set [set] (*vb: pret, ptp* **set**) **1** *n* **(a)** (*gen*) jeu *m*, série *f*; (*kit*) trousse *f*; *[keys, golf clubs, knives, spanners]* jeu; *[chairs, rugs, saucepans, numbers, stamps etc]* série; *[books, toy cars, bracelets, magazines]* collection *f*; *[dishes etc]* service *m*; *[tyres]* train *m*. **a** ~ **of rooms** un appartement; ~ **of teeth** dentition *f*; ~ **of false teeth** dentier *m*; **a** ~ **of dining-room furniture** un mobilier de salle à manger; **a whole** ~ **of telephones on his desk** toute une collection de téléphones sur son bureau; **in** ~**s** en jeux complets, en séries complètes; **sewing** ~ trousse de couture; **painting** ~ boîte *f* de peinture; **chess/draughts** ~ jeu d'échecs/de dames (*objet*). **(b)** (*Tennis*) set *m*; (*Math, Philos*) ensemble *m*. **(c)** (*Elec*) appareil *m*; (*Rad, TV*) poste *m*. **(d)** (*group*) bande *f* (*also pej*); (*larger*) monde *m*. **a** ~ **of thieves** une bande de voleurs; **the golfing** ~ le monde du golf. **(e)** (*stage*) (*Cine*) plateau *m*; (*Theat etc*) scène *f*; (*scenery*) décor *m*. **on the** ~ sur le plateau, en scène. **(f)** (*Hairdressing*) mise *f* en plis. **to have a** ~ se faire faire une mise en plis.

2 *adj* **(a)** (*unchanging: gen*) fixe; *smile etc* figé; *purpose, dogma* déterminé; *opinion, idea* arrêté; *lunch* à prix fixe; (*prearranged*) *time, date* fixe, décidé d'avance; (*Scol etc*) *book, subject* au programme; *speech, talk* préparé d'avance; *prayer* liturgique. ~ **in one's ways** qui tient à ses habitudes; ~ **in one's opinions** immuable dans ses convictions; (*Met*) ~ **fair** au beau fixe; ~ **phrase** expression *f* consacrée. **(b)** (*determined*) résolu; (*ready*) prêt. **to be** ~ **on (doing) sth** vouloir à tout prix (faire) qch; **to be dead** ~ **against** s'opposer absolument à; to **be all ~ to do** être prêt pour faire; (*fig*) **the scene is ~ for** tout est prêt pour.

3 *vt* **(a)** (*gen*) mettre; (*place*) placer; (*put down*) poser; *signature etc* apposer; *guard* poster. **house ~ on a hill** maison située sur une colline; **his stories, ~ in Paris** ses histoires, situées à Paris; **we must ~ the advantages against the disadvantages** il faut mettre en balance les avantages et les inconvénients; **to ~ fire to sth** mettre le feu à qch; *V also* **foot, store** *etc.* **(b)** (*arrange, adjust*) *clock, mechanism* régler; *alarm clock* mettre; (*on display*) *specimen, butterfly etc* monter; *type, page* composer; (*Med*) *arm, leg* (*in plaster*) plâtrer; (*with splint*) mettre une attelle à; *fracture* réduire. **he ~ the needle to zero** il a mis l'aiguille à zéro; **to have one's hair ~** se faire faire une mise en plis; *V also* **sail, table** *etc.* **(c)** (*fix, establish*) *date, limit* fixer; *record* établir; *V also* **course, fashion** *etc.* **(d)** (*assign*) *task, subject* donner; *exam, test* choisir les questions de; *texts, books* mettre au programme. **to ~ sb a problem** poser un problème à qn; **I ~ him the job of clearing up** je l'ai chargé de ranger; *V also* **example** *etc.* **(e)** (*cause to do, begin etc*) **to ~ a dog on sb** lancer un chien contre qn; **she ~ my brother against me** elle a monté mon frère contre moi; **to ~ sth going** mettre qch en marche; **to ~ sb thinking** faire réfléchir qn; **to ~ sb to do sth** faire faire qch à qn; **to ~ o.s. to do** entreprendre de faire. **(f)** *gem* monter (*in* sur); *ring* orner (*with* de). **(g)** *jelly, concrete* faire prendre; *dye, colour* fixer.

4 *vi* **(a)** *[sun, moon etc]* se coucher. **(b)** *[broken bone, limb]* se ressouder; *[jelly, jam]* prendre; *[glue, concrete]* durcir; *[character]* se former. **his face ~ in a hostile expression** son visage s'est figé dans une expression hostile. **(c)** (*begin: gen*) se mettre, commencer (*to doing* à faire). **to ~ to work** se mettre au travail.

set about *vt fus* **(a)** (*begin*) *task, essay* se mettre à. **to ~ about doing** se mettre à faire; **I don't know how to ~ about it** je ne sais pas comment m'y prendre. **(b)** (*attack*) attaquer.

set apart *vt sep object etc* mettre à part; (*fig*) *person* distinguer (*from* de).

set aside *vt sep* **(a)** (*keep, save*) mettre de côté. **(b)** (*lay aside*) *book etc* poser. **(c)** (*reject*) *objection* rejeter; *will* annuler; *judgment* casser.

set back *vt sep* **(a)** (*replace*) remettre. **(b) the house was ~ back from the road** la maison était en retrait de la route. **(c)** (*retard*) *progress, clock* retarder (*by* de). **(d)** (*: *cost*) coûter.

set down *vt sep* **(a)** (*put down*) *object, passenger* déposer; *plane* poser. **(b)** (*record*) noter, inscrire. **to ~ sth down in writing** *or* **on paper** mettre qch par écrit. **(c)** (*attribute*) attribuer (*sth to sth* qch à qch).

set in 1 *vi [complications, difficulties]* surgir; *[disease]* se déclarer; *[reaction]* s'amorcer. **the rain has ~ in for the night** il va pleuvoir toute la nuit. **2** *vt sep* (*Sewing*) *sleeve* rapporter.

set off 1 *vi* (*leave*) se mettre en route. **to ~ off on a journey/an expedition** partir en voyage/en expédition. **2** *vt sep* **(a)** *bomb* faire exploser; *firework* faire partir; *mechanism* déclencher. **(b)** (*enhance*) *hair, furnishings etc* mettre en valeur. **(c)** (*balance etc*) **to ~ off profits against losses** balancer les pertes et les profits.

set out 1 *vi* partir (*for* pour; *from* de; *in search of* à la recherche de). **to ~ out to do** (*intend*) chercher à faire; (*attempt*) entreprendre de faire; **the book ~s out to show ...** ce livre a pour objet de montrer ... . **2** *vt sep books, goods* exposer; *chessmen etc on board* disposer; *reasons, ideas* présenter, exposer.

set to *vi* (*start*) se mettre (*to do* à faire); (*start work*) s'y mettre*.

set up 1 *vi* (*Comm etc*) **to ~ up (in business) as a grocer** s'établir épicier. **2** *vt sep* **(a)** (*place in position*) *chairs, stall* installer; *tent, statue* dresser; *type* assembler; *camp* établir. **(b)** (*fig: start*) *school, institution* fonder; *business, company, fund* créer, lancer; *tribunal, government* constituer; *fashion* lancer; *irritation, quarrel* provoquer; *record* établir; *theory* avancer; *inquiry* ouvrir. **to ~ up house** s'installer; **they ~ up house together** ils se sont mis en ménage; (*Comm, also fig*) **to ~ up shop** s'établir; **to ~ sb up in business** lancer qn dans les affaires; **I've ~ it all up for you** je vous ai tout installé *or* préparé; **I've never ~ myself up as a scholar** je n'ai jamais prétendu être savant. **(c)** (*after illness*) remettre sur pied. **(d)** (*equip*) munir (*with* de).

set upon *vt fus* (*attack*) attaquer.

♦ **setback** *n* (*hitch*) contretemps *m*; (*more serious*) revers *m*; (*in health*) rechute *f*. ♦ **setting 1** *n* **(a)** *[jewel]* monture *f*; (*fig: framework, background*) cadre *m*; **(b)** (*Mus: of poem etc*) mise *f* en musique; **~ting for piano** arrangement *m* pour piano; **2** *adj*: **~ting lotion** lotion *f* pour mise en plis. ♦ **setting-up** *n [institution etc]* création *f*. ♦ **set-to*** *n* (*fight*) bagarre *f*; (*quarrel*) prise *f* de bec*. ♦ **setup*** *n* (*situation*) situation *f*; (*business, firm etc*) affaire *f*.

sett [set] *n* (*in roadway etc*) pavé *m*.

settee [se'ti:] *n* canapé *m*. **~ bed** canapé-lit *m*.

setter ['setəʳ] *n* **(a)** (*dog*) setter *m*, chien *m* d'arrêt. **(b)** (*person*) *V* **typesetter** *etc.*

settle[1] ['setl] *n* banc *m* à haut dossier.

settle[2] ['setl] **1** *vt* **(a)** (*place carefully*) placer *or* poser délicatement; (*stop wobbling*) stabiliser; (*adjust*) ajuster; *person* installer. **to ~ o.s., to get ~d** s'installer. **(b)** (*arrange, solve etc*) *question, details, conditions, bill, account* régler; *date* fixer; *difficulty, problem* résoudre; *debt* rembourser; (*decide*) décider. **that ~s it** (*no more problem*) comme ça, le problème est réglé; (*that's made my mind up*) ça me décide; **that's ~d then?** alors, c'est convenu?; **nothing is ~d** rien n'est décidé; (*Jur*) **to ~ a case out of court** régler une affaire à l'amiable. **(c)** (*calm; stabilize*) *nerves* calmer; *doubts* dissiper. **to ~ one's digestion** calmer les douleurs d'estomac; **the weather is ~d** le temps est au beau fixe. **(d)** (*Jur*) **to ~ sth on sb** constituer qch à qn. **(e)** (*colonize*) *land* coloniser.

2 *vi* **(a)** *[bird, insect]* se poser (*on* sur); *[dust etc]* retomber; *[sediment, coffee grounds etc]* se déposer; *[building]* se tasser; *[emotions]* s'apaiser; *[conditions, situation]* s'arranger. *[dust, snow]* **to ~ on sth** couvrir qch; (*fig*) **when the dust has ~d** quand les choses se seront arrangées; **to ~ into** *armchair* s'installer confortablement dans; *new job* se faire à; *routine* adopter; *habit* prendre; **I can't ~ to anything** je suis incapable de me concentrer. **(b)** (*go to live*) s'installer, se fixer; (*as colonist*) s'établir. **(c) to ~ with sb for the cost of the meal** régler le prix du repas à qn; (*Jur*) **to ~ out of court** arriver à un règlement à l'amiable; **he ~d for £200** il a accepté 200 livres; **they ~d on £200** ils se sont mis d'accord sur 200 livres; **to ~ on sth** (*choose it*) fixer son choix sur qch.

settle down *vi [person]* (*in armchair, house etc*) s'installer (*in* dans); (*become calmer*) se calmer; (*after wild youth etc*) se ranger; *[situation]* s'arranger. **to ~ down to work** se mettre au travail; **he has ~d down in his new job** il s'est fait à son nouvel emploi; **to get married and ~ down** se marier et mener une vie stable; **when things have ~d down again** quand les choses seront redevenues normales.

settle in *vi* (*get things straight*) s'installer; (*get used to things*) s'adapter.

settle up *vi* régler (la note). **to ~ up with sb** (*pay*) régler qn; (*fig*) régler son compte à qn*.

♦ **settlement** *n* **(a)** *[question, bill, debt]* règlement *m*; **(b)** (*agreement*) accord *m*; **(c)** (*dowry*) dot *f*; **(d)** (*colony*) colonie *f*; (*village*) village *m*. ♦ **settler** *n* colon *m*.

seven ['sevn] *adj, n* sept (*m*) *inv*; *for phrases V* **six.** ♦ **seventeen** *adj, n* dix-sept (*m*) *inv*. ♦ **seventeenth** *adj, n* dix-septième (*mf*); (*fraction*) dix-septième *m*. ♦ **seventh** *adj, n* septième (*mf*); (*fraction*) septième *m*. ♦ **seventieth** *adj, n* soixante-dixième (*mf*); (*fraction*) soixante-dixième *m*. ♦ **seventy** *adj, n* soixante-dix (*m*) *inv*; **he's in his ~ties** il a plus de soixante-dix ans.

sever ['sevəʳ] *vt rope etc* couper; (*fig*) *relations* rompre; *communications* interrompre. ♦ **severance** *n* séparation *f* (*from* de); (*Ind*) **~ance pay** indemnité *f* de licenciement.

several ['sevrəl] **1** *adj* plusieurs. **~ times** plusieurs fois. **2** *pron* plusieurs *mfpl*. **~ of us** plusieurs d'entre nous. ♦ **severally** *adv* séparément, individuellement.

severe [sɪ'vɪəʳ] *adj* (*gen*) sévère (*with, on, towards* pour, envers); *examination* dur, difficile; *competition* acharné; *climate, winter* rigoureux; *cold, frost* intense; *pain* violent; *wound, defeat, illness* grave. (*Med*) **a ~ cold** un gros rhume. ♦ **severely** *adv* (*gen*) sévèrement; *injure* grièvement; *ill* gravement; **to leave ~ly alone** *object* ne jamais toucher à; *politics, deal* ne pas du tout se mêler de; *person* ignorer complètement. ♦ **severity** [sɪ'verɪtɪ] *n* sévérité *f*; difficulté *f*; rigueur *f*; intensité *f*; violence *f*; gravité *f*.

sew [səʊ] *pret* **sewed,** *ptp* **sewn** *or* **sewed** *vti* coudre. **to ~ a button on sth** coudre un bouton à qch.

sew on *vt sep button etc* coudre; (*~ back on*) recoudre.

sew up *vt sep tear, wound* recoudre; *seam* faire; *sack* fermer par une couture. **to ~ sth up in a sack** coudre qch dans un sac; (*fig*) **it's all ~n up*** c'est dans la poche*.

♦ **sewing 1** *n* couture *f*; **2** *adj*: **~ing basket** boîte *f* à couture; **~ing cotton** fil *m* de coton; **~ing machine** machine *f* à coudre.

sewage ['sjuːɪdʒ] **1** *n* vidanges *fpl*. **2** *adj*: **~ disposal** évacuation *f* des vidanges; **~ works** champ *m* d'épandage. ♦ **sewer** *n* égout *m*.

sex [seks] **1** *n* sexe *m*. **to have ~ with sb** coucher avec qn*. **2** *adj discrimination, education, instinct* sexuel. **~ act** acte *m* sexuel; **~ appeal** sex-appeal *m*; **~ maniac** obsédé(e) *m(f)* sexuel(le); **~ offender** délinquant(e) *m(f)* sexuel(le); **~ shop** sex-shop *m*; **~ urge** pulsion *f* sexuelle. ♦ **sexual** *adj* sexuel; **~ual intercourse** rapports *mpl* sexuels. ♦ **sexuality** *n* sexualité *f*. ♦ **sexually** *adv* sexuellement. ♦ **sexy*** *adj* sexy* *inv*.

sextet [seks'tet] *n* sextuor *m*.

sexton ['sekstən] *n* sacristain *m*.

shabby ['ʃæbɪ] *adj garment* usé; *furniture* minable; *house, district* miteux; *person* pauvrement vêtu, miteux; *behaviour* mesquin. **a ~ trick** un vilain tour. ♦ **shabbily** *adv* pauvrement; mesquinement. ♦ **shabbiness** *n [dress]* aspect *m* usé; *[person]* mise *f* pauvre; *[behaviour]* mesquinerie *f*.

shack [ʃæk] **1** *n* cabane *f*, hutte *f*. **2** *vi*: **to ~ up with sb‡** se coller avec qn‡.

shade [ʃeɪd] **1** *n* **(a)** ombre *f*. **in the ~** à l'ombre; (*Art*) **light and ~** les clairs *mpl* et les ombres; (*fig*) **to put sth in the ~** éclipser qch. **(b)** *[colour]* nuance *f*, ton *m*; *[opinion]* nuance. **several ~s darker** plus sombre de plusieurs tons; **a new ~ of lipstick** un nouveau ton de rouge à lèvres; **~ of meaning** nuance; **not a ~ of difference** pas la moindre différence; **a ~ bigger** un tout petit peu plus grand. **(c)** (*lamp~*) abat-jour *m inv*; (*eye~*) visière *f*; (*US: blind*) store *m*. (*US: sunglasses*) **~s** lunettes *fpl* de soleil. **2** *vt* **(a)** (*from sun*) abriter du soleil; (*from light*) abriter de la lumière; *eyes* abriter; *light, lamp* voiler. **~d place** endroit *m* ombragé. **(b)** (*~ in*) *outline, drawing* hachurer.

shade off 1 *vi [colours]* se fondre (*into* en). **2** *vt sep colours etc* estomper.

♦ **shady** *adj* ombragé; (*dishonest*) louche.

shadow ['ʃædəʊ] **1** *n* ombre *f*. **in the ~** dans l'ombre (*of* de); **to cast a ~ over sth** projeter une ombre sur qch, (*fig*) assombrir qch; **without a ~ of doubt** sans l'ombre d'un doute; **he's only a ~ of his former self** il n'est plus que l'ombre de lui-même; **to have ~s under one's eyes** avoir les yeux cernés; (*on chin*) **five o'clock ~** la barbe du soir. **2** *adj*: **~ boxing** boxe *f* à vide; (*Parl*) **~ cabinet** cabinet *m* fantôme (*de l'opposition*); (*Parl*) **the ~ Foreign Secretary** le porte-parole de l'opposition pour les Affaires étrangères. **3** *vt* (*follow*) filer (*un suspect etc*). ♦ **shadowy** *adj form, plan* vague.

shaft [ʃɑːft] *n* **(a)** (*stem etc*) *[arrow, spear]* hampe *f*; *[tool, golf club]* manche *m*; *[feather]* tuyau *m*; *[column]* fût *m*; (*on cart, carriage, plough etc*) brancard *m*; (*Aut, Tech*) arbre *m*. **(b)** (*liter: arrow*) flèche *f*; *[light]* rayon *m*; *[sarcasm]* trait *m*. **~ of lightning** éclair *m*. **(c)** *[mine]* puits *m*; *[lift, elevator]* cage *f*; (*for ventilation*) cheminée *f*.

shaggy ['ʃægɪ] *adj hair, mane* broussailleux; *animal* à longs poils rudes. (*fig*) **~ dog story** anecdote *f* embrouillée.

shake [ʃeɪk] (*vb: pret* **shook,** *ptp* **shaken**) **1** *n*: **to give sth a ~** secouer qch; **with a ~ of his head** avec un hochement de tête; **he's got the ~s*** il a la tremblote*; **I'll be there in a ~*** j'arrive dans un instant; **it is no great ~s*** ça ne casse rien*; **he's no great ~s* at swimming** il ne casse rien* comme nageur.

2 *vt* **(a)** (*gen*) *object, person* secouer; *dice, bottle* agiter; *house, windows etc* ébranler; (*brandish*) *stick etc* brandir. **to ~ one's head** (*in refusal etc*) faire non de la tête; (*at bad news etc*) secouer la tête; **he shook his finger at me** il m'a fait signe du doigt; **to ~ one's fist at sb** menacer qn du poing; **to ~ hands with sb** serrer la main à qn; **they shook hands** ils se sont serré la main; **they shook hands on it** ils se sont serré la main en signe d'accord; **to ~ o.s.** se secouer; **he shook the sand out of his shoes** il a secoué ses chaussures pour en vider le sable; **he shook himself free** il s'est libéré d'une secousse. **(b)** (*harm*) *confidence, belief, health* ébranler; *opinion* affecter; *reputation* nuire à; (*amaze*) stupéfier; (*disturb*) secouer. **even torture could not ~ him** même la torture ne l'a pas ébranlé; **to feel ~n** être bouleversé *or* très secoué; **this will ~ you!** tu vas en être soufflé!*; **4 days which shook the world** 4 jours qui ébranlèrent le monde.

3 *vi* **(a)** *[person, hand, table]* trembler; *[building, windows, walls]* trembler, être ébranlé; *[leaves, grasses]* trembler, être agité. **to ~ with cold/fear** trembler de froid/de peur; **he was shaking with laughter** il se tordait de rire. **(b)** (*~ hands*) **they shook on the deal** ils ont scellé leur accord d'une poignée de main; **(let's) ~ on it!** topez là!

shake down *vt sep*: **to ~ down apples from a tree** faire tomber des pommes en secouant l'arbre.

shake off *vt sep dust, sand, water* secouer (*from* de); *cold, cough* se débarrasser de; *yoke* se libérer de; *habit* se défaire de, perdre; *pursuer* semer*.

shake out *vt sep flag, sail* déployer; *blanket* bien secouer; *bag* vider en secouant. **she shook some money out of her bag** elle a secoué son sac et en a fait tomber de l'argent.

shake up *vt sep* **(a)** *pillow* secouer; *bottle* agiter. **(b)** (*disturb*) bouleverser, secouer. **(c)** (*rouse, stir*) *person* secouer, stimuler; *firm, organization* réorganiser de fond en comble.

♦ **shake-up** *n* (*fig*) grande réorganisation *f*. ♦ **shakily** *adv* (*gen*) en tremblant; *walk* d'un pas mal assuré; *write* d'une main tremblante; *say, reply* d'une voix tremblante. ♦ **shaky** *adj* (*trembling*) tremblant; (*nervous*) mal assuré; *writing* tremblé; *table, building* branlant; (*fig*) *health, memory, knowledge* assez mauvais; **I feel a bit shaky** je me sens faible.

shale [ʃeɪl] *n* schiste *m* argileux.

shall [ʃæl] *modal aux vb* **(a)** (*1st person future tense and questions*) **I ~ *or* I'll arrive on Monday** j'arriverai lundi, je vais arriver lundi; **~ I open the door?** voulez-vous que j'ouvre (*subj*) la porte?; **I'll buy 3, ~ I?** je vais en acheter 3, n'est-ce pas *or* d'accord*?; **let's go in, ~ we?** entrons, voulez-vous?; **~ we ask him to come with us?** si on lui demandait de venir avec nous? **(b)** (*command etc*) **it ~ be done this way** cela doit être fait de cette façon; **thou shalt not kill** tu ne tueras point.

shallot [ʃə'lɒt] *n* échalote *f*.

shallow ['ʃæləʊ] *adj* *water, dish* peu profond; *breathing, person, conversation* superficiel. ♦ **shallowness** *n* manque *m* de profondeur; esprit *m* superficiel. ♦ **shallows** *npl* hauts-fonds *mpl*.

sham [ʃæm] **1** *n*: **to be a ~** *[person]* être un imposteur; *[jewellery, furniture]* être du toc*; *[election, organization]* être de la frime*. **2** *adj* *jewellery* faux, en toc*; *piety* feint; *title* faux; *illness, fight* simulé. **3** *vt* *sickness, emotion* feindre, simuler. **to ~ ill** faire semblant d'être malade; **he is only ~ming** il fait seulement semblant.

shamble ['ʃæmbl] *vi*: **to ~ in/out** *etc* entrer/sortir *etc* en traînant les pieds. ♦ **shambles** *n, no pl* (*after fire, bombing*) scène *f* de dévastation; (*muddle*) pagaille* *f*; **his room was (in) a ~s** sa chambre était sens dessus dessous; **the match degenerated into a ~s** le match s'est terminé dans la pagaille*.

shame [ʃeɪm] **1** *n* **(a)** (*feeling*) honte *f*. **he hung his head in ~** il a baissé la tête de honte *or* de confusion; **to bring ~ on sb** déshonorer qn; **to put sb/sth to ~** faire honte à qn/qch. **(b) it is a ~** c'est dommage (*that* que + *subj*; *to do* de faire); **what a ~ he isn't here** quel dommage qu'il ne soit pas ici. **2** *vt* (*bring disgrace on*) déshonorer; (*make ashamed*) faire honte à. **to ~ sb into doing sth** obliger qn à faire qch en lui faisant honte; **to be ~d into doing sth** faire qch par amour-propre.

♦ **shamefaced** *adj* (*ashamed*) honteux; (*confused*) confus. ♦ **shamefacedly** *adv* d'un air honteux; avec confusion. ♦ **shamefacedness** *n* air *m* honteux; confusion *f*. ♦ **shameful** *adj* honteux; **it's ~ful to do that** c'est une honte de faire cela. ♦ **shamefully** *adv* *behave* honteusement; *bad, late* scandaleusement, abominablement; **he is ~fully ignorant** il est si ignorant que c'en est une honte. ♦ **shameless** *adj* *person* éhonté; *behaviour* effronté; **he is quite ~less about it** il n'en a pas du tout honte. ♦ **shamelessly** *adv* effrontément, sans honte. ♦ **shamelessness** *n* effronterie *f*. ♦ **shaming** *adj* humiliant.

shammy* ['ʃæmɪ] *n* (**~ leather**) peau *f* de chamois.

shampoo [ʃæm'puː] **1** *n* (*product, process*) shampooing *m*. **~ and set** shampooing et mise *f* en plis. **2** *vt* *hair* faire un shampooing à; *carpet* shampooer. **to have one's hair ~ed and set** se faire faire un shampooing et mise en plis.

shamrock ['ʃæmrɒk] *n* trèfle *m* (*de l'Irlande*).

shandy ['ʃændɪ] *n* (*Brit*) panaché *m* (*bière*).

shan't [ʃɑːnt] = **shall not**.

shanty[1] ['ʃæntɪ] *n* (*hut*) baraque *f*. **~ town** bidonville *m*.

shanty[2] ['ʃæntɪ] *n* (**sea ~**) chanson *f* de marins.

shape [ʃeɪp] **1** *n* forme *f*. **what ~ is the room?** quelle est la forme de la pièce?; **of all ~s and sizes** de toutes les formes et de toutes les tailles; **his nose is a funny ~** son nez a une drôle de forme; **in the ~ of a cross** en forme de croix; **I can't stand racism in any ~ or form** je ne peux pas tolérer le racisme sous quelque forme que ce soit; **to take the ~ of sth** prendre la forme de qch; **the news reached him in the ~ of a telegram** c'est par un télégramme qu'il a appris la nouvelle; **that's the ~ of things to come** cela donne une idée de ce qui nous attend; **to take ~** prendre tournure; **to be in good ~** *[person]* être en forme; *[business etc]* marcher bien; **in poor ~** *person, business* mal en point; **to carve** (*or* **hammer** *etc*) **sth into ~** façonner qch; (*fig*) **to knock** *or* **lick* into ~** *assistant, soldier* dresser*; *team, plan* mettre au point; **to get o.s. into ~** retrouver la forme; **to get one's ideas into ~** préciser ses idées; **a ~ loomed up out of the darkness** une forme imprécise a surgi de l'obscurité.

2 *vt* *clay, stone* façonner (*into* en); (*fig*) *ideas, character* former; (*influence*) *course of events, sb's fate* influencer. **oddly ~d** d'une forme bizarre; **heart-~d** en forme de cœur.

3 *vi* (*fig*) **things are shaping (up) well** tout marche bien; **how is he shaping?** comment s'en sort-il?*; **he is shaping (up) nicely** il fait des progrès.

♦ **shapeless** *adj* informe. ♦ **shapelessness** *n* manque *m* de forme. ♦ **shapeliness** *n* belles proportions *fpl*, beauté *f*. ♦ **shapely** *adj* *object* bien proportionné; *woman, legs* bien fait.

share [ʃɛəʳ] **1** *n* **(a)** part *f* (*of, in* de). **to get a ~ of** *or* **in sth** avoir part à qch; **he has a ~ in the business** il est l'un des associés dans cette affaire; **he has a half-~ in the firm** il possède la moitié de l'entreprise; (*fig*) **he had a ~ in it** il y était pour qch; **to go ~s in sth** partager qch; **to take a ~ in sth** participer à qch; **he isn't doing his ~** il ne fournit pas sa part d'efforts; **more than his fair ~ of misfortune** plus que sa part de malheurs; **he does his full ~ of work** il fournit toute sa part de travail. **(b)** (*Fin etc*) action *f* (*in a company* d'une compagnie). **2** *adj* (*St Ex*) *prices* des actions. **~ index** indice *m* de la Bourse. **3** *vt* **(a)** (*gen*) partager (*with sb* avec qn); (*get one's ~ of*) *profits etc* avoir part à. **they ~d the money between them** ils se sont partagé l'argent; (*Telec*) **~d line** ligne *f* partagée; **they ~ certain characteristics** ils ont certaines caractéristiques en commun; **I ~ your hope that ...** j'espère comme vous que ... . **(b)** (**~ out**) partager, répartir (*among, between* entre). **4** *vi* partager. **~ and ~ alike** à chacun sa part; **to ~ in** (*get one's ~ in*) *profits etc* avoir part à; (*have etc with other people*) *expenses, work, blame, joy* partager. ♦ **sharecropper** *n* (*US*) métayer *m*, -ère *f*. ♦ **sharecropping** *n* (*US*) métayage *m*. ♦ **shareholder** *n* actionnaire *mf*. ♦ **share-out** *n* partage *m*.

shark [ʃɑːk] *n* requin *m*; (*swindler*) escroc *m*. ♦ **sharkskin** *n* (*Tex*) peau *f* d'ange.

sharp [ʃɑːp] **1** *adj* **(a)** *razor, knife* tranchant, bien aiguisé; *point, needle* aigu (*f* -guë), acéré; *teeth* acéré; *pencil, nose, chin* pointu; *features* anguleux; *corner, angle* aigu; *bend in road* brusque. **(b)** (*abrupt*) *descent* raide; *fall in price, change* soudain. **(c)** (*well-defined*) *outline*, (*TV*) *picture* net; *difference* marqué. **(d)** (*Mus*) **C ~** do *m* dièse; **the note was ~** la note était trop haute. **(e)** (*harsh*) *cry, voice* perçant; *wind, cold* pénétrant, âpre; *frost* fort; *pain* vif; *smell, taste* piquant, âpre (*pej*); *words, retort, tone* cinglant; *rebuke* sévère. (*fig*) **to have a ~ tongue** avoir la langue acérée. **(f)** (*brisk etc*) *pace, quarrel* vif. **look ~ about it!** dépêche-toi! **(g)** (*acute*) *eyesight* perçant; *hearing, smell* fin; *intelligence, mind* pénétrant; *person* vif, dégourdi*. (*pej*) **~ practice** procédés *mpl* malhonnêtes.

2 *adv* **(a)** (*Mus*) *sing, play* trop haut. **(b)** (*abruptly*) *stop* brusquement. **take ~ left** tournez tout à fait à gauche. **(c)** (*punctually*) **at 3 o'clock ~** à 3 heures pile.

3 *n* (*Mus*) dièse *m*. ♦ **sharpen** *vt* **(a)** *blade, tool* aiguiser; *pencil* tailler; **(b)** *outline,* (*TV*) *picture* rendre plus net; *difference* rendre plus marqué; *appetite* aiguiser; *desire* exciter; *pain, feeling* aviver; *intelligence* affiner; **to ~en one's wits** se dégourdir. ♦ **sharpener** *n* (*for knives*) aiguisoir *m*; (*for pencils*) taille-crayons *m inv*. ♦ **sharp-faced** *or* ♦ **sharp-featured** *adj* aux traits anguleux. ♦ **sharply** *adv* **(a)** (*abruptly*) *change, rise, stop* brusquement; **(b)** (*harshly*) *criticize* sévèrement; *observe, retort* sèchement; **(c)** (*distinctly*) *show up, stand out, differ* nettement; **(d)** (*alertly*) *say, ask, look* avec intérêt. ♦ **sharpness** *n* **(a)** *[razor, knife]* tranchant *m*; *[pencil etc]* pointe *f* aiguë; **(b)** *[turn, bend]* angle *m* brusque; *[outline etc]* netteté *f*; *[pain]* violence *f*; *[criticism, reproach, rebuke]* sévérité *f*; *[tone, voice]* brusquerie *f*; *[taste, smell]* piquant *m*, âpreté *f* (*pej*); *[wind, cold]* âpreté. ♦ **sharpshooter** *n* tireur *m* d'élite. ♦ **sharp-sighted** *adj* à qui rien n'échappe. ♦ **sharp-tempered** *adj* coléreux. ♦ **sharp-witted** *adj* à l'esprit vif.

shatter ['ʃætəʳ] **1** *vt window, door* fracasser (*against* contre); *glasses, health, self-confidence, career* briser; *faith* détruire; *hopes, chances* ruiner; *sb's nerves* démolir. **2** *vi [glass, windscreen, cup]* voler en éclats; *[box etc]* se fracasser (*against* contre). ♦ **shattered** *adj* (*grief-stricken*) anéanti; (*: *aghast*) bouleversé; (*: *exhausted*) éreinté. ♦ **shattering** *adj* (*fig*) *attack* destructeur; *defeat* écrasant; *news, experience, disappointment* bouleversant; **this was a ~ing blow to our hopes** nos espoirs ont été gravement compromis.

shave [ʃeɪv] **1** *n*: **to have a ~** se raser; (*fig*) **to have a close** *or* **narrow ~** l'échapper belle. **2** *vt person* raser; *wood* raboter; (*fig: graze*) frôler. **3** *vi* se raser.

shave off *vt sep* **(a) to ~ off one's beard** se raser la barbe. **(b)** *piece of wood* enlever au rabot.

♦ **shaver** *n* rasoir *m* électrique. ♦ **shaving** *n* (*wood etc*) copeau *m*. ♦ **shaving brush** *n* blaireau *m*. ♦ **shaving cream** *n* crème *f* à raser. ♦ **shaving soap** *n* savon *m* à barbe. ♦ **shaving stick** *n* bâton *m* de savon à barbe.

shawl [ʃɔːl] *n* châle *m*.

she [ʃiː] *pers pron* **(a)** (*stressed, unstressed*) elle. **~ has come** elle est venue; **here ~ is** la voici; **~ is a doctor** elle est médecin, c'est un médecin; **SHE didn't do it** ce n'est pas elle qui l'a fait; **younger than ~** plus jeune qu'elle. **(b)** (+ *rel pron*) celle. **~ who** celle qui. **(c) it's a ~** (*animal*) c'est une femelle; (*baby*) c'est une fille. ♦ **she-bear** *n* ourse *f*.

sheaf [ʃiːf] *n [corn]* gerbe *f*; *[papers]* liasse *f*.

shear [ʃɪəʳ] *pret* **-ed**, *ptp* **-ed** *or* **shorn** *vt sheep* tondre. (*fig*) **shorn of** dépouillé de.

shear off *vt sep wool* tondre; *projecting part, nail* arracher; *car wing etc* emporter.

shear through *vt fus cloth* trancher; *wood, metal* fendre.

♦ **shearer** *n* (*person*) tondeur *m*, -euse *f*; (*machine*) tondeuse *f*. ♦ **shearing** *n* (*process*) tonte *f*. ♦ **shears** *npl* (*Gardening*) cisaille *f*; (*gen*) grands ciseaux *mpl*.

sheath [ʃiːθ] *n [sword]* fourreau *m*; *[scissors etc]* étui *m*; *[dagger, electric cable, flex]* gaine *f*; (*Bio, Bot*) enveloppe *f*; (*contraceptive*) préservatif *m*. ♦ **sheath-knife** *n* couteau *m* à gaine.

shed[1] [ʃed] *n* (*for tools, cycles etc*) remise *f*; (*smaller*) cabane *f*; (*huge, open-sided: Rail, Agr etc*) hangar *m*; (*for cattle etc*) étable *f*; (*Ind: part of factory*) atelier *m*.

shed[2] [ʃed] *pret, ptp* **shed** *vt* **(a)** (*get rid of*) *leaves, fur, horns, weight* perdre; *[truck] load* déverser; *coat etc* enlever; *unwanted thing, assistant* se débarrasser de. **the snake ~s its skin** le serpent mue. **(b)** *blood, tears* verser. **(c)** (*send out*) *light, warmth, happiness* répandre. **to ~ light on** (*lit*) éclairer; (*fig*) *sb's motives etc* jeter de la lumière sur; *problem* éclaircir; *subject* éclairer.

sheen [ʃiːn] *n* lustre *m*.

sheep [ʃiːp] **1** *n, pl inv* mouton *m* (*animal*); (*ewe*) brebis *f*. (*fig*) **to make ~'s eyes at** faire les yeux doux à; **we must divide the ~ from the goats** il ne faut pas mélanger les torchons et les serviettes* (*fig*). **2** *adj*: **~ farm** ferme *f* d'élevage de moutons; **~ farmer** éleveur *m* de moutons; **~ farming** élevage *m* de moutons. ♦ **sheepdog** *n* chien *m* de berger. ♦ **sheepish** *adj* penaud. ♦ **sheepishly** *adv* d'un air penaud. ♦ **sheepishness** *n* air *m* penaud. ♦ **sheepskin** *n* peau *f* de mouton; **~skin jacket** canadienne *f*.

sheer[1] [ʃɪəʳ] *adj* **(a)** (*utter*) *chance, kindness, madness* pur; *impossibility, necessity* absolu; *waste* véritable (*before n*). **it was ~ mud** ce n'était que de la boue; **by a ~ accident** tout à fait par hasard; **by ~ hard work** uniquement grâce au travail; **~ robbery** du vol manifeste. **(b)** *stockings, material* extra-fin. **(c)** *rock, cliff* à pic. **a ~ drop** *or* **fall** un à-pic.

sheer[2] [ʃɪəʳ] *vi* (*swerve*) **to ~ off** *[ship]* faire une embardée; (*gen*) changer de direction.

sheet [ʃiːt] **1** *n* **(a)** (*on bed*) drap *m*; (*dust ~*) housse *f*; (*tarpaulin*) bâche *f*. **(b)** (*piece etc*) *[plastic, rubber]* morceau *m*; *[paper, notepaper]* feuille *f*; *[iron, steel]* tôle *f*; *[glass, metal, ice etc]* plaque *f*; *[water, snow]* étendue *f*; *[flames]* rideau *m*. *[paper]* **an odd** *or* **a loose ~** une feuille volante; (*Comm*) **order ~** bulletin *m* de commande. **2** *adj*: **~ lightning** éclair *m* en nappes; **~ metal** tôle *f*; **~ music** partitions *fpl*.

sheik(h) [ʃeɪk] *n* cheik *m*.

shelf [ʃelf] **1** *n, pl* **shelves (a)** étagère *f*, rayon *m*; (*in shop*) rayon; (*in oven*) plaque *f*. **a set of shelves** un rayonnage; **on the ~** *woman* laissée pour compte. **(b)** (*edge*) (*in rock*) rebord *m*; (*underwater*) écueil *m*. **2** *adj* (*Comm*) **~ life** durée *f* de conservation avant vente; (*Libraries*) **~ mark** cote *f*.

shell [ʃel] **1** *n* **(a)** *[egg, nut, oyster, snail etc]* coquille *f*; *[tortoise, lobster]* carapace *f*; (*seashell*) coquillage *m*; *[peas]* cosse *f*. (*lit, fig*) **to come out of one's ~** sortir de sa coquille. **(b)** *[building]* carcasse *f*; *[ship]* coque *f*. (*Culin*) **pastry ~** fond *m* de tarte. **(c)** (*Mil*) obus *m*. **2** *adj necklace etc* de *or* en coquillages. **3** *vt* **(a)** *peas* écosser; *nut, crab, shrimp* décortiquer; *lobster* retirer de sa carapace. **(b)** (*Mil*) bombarder (d'obus).

shell out* **1** *vi* casquer‡ (*for* pour), payer. **2** *vt sep* cracher‡, payer.

♦ **shellfish** *n, pl inv* (*lobster, crab*) crustacé *m*; (*mollusc*) coquillage *m*; (*pl: Culin*) fruits *mpl* de mer. ♦ **shelling** *n* (*Mil*) bombardement *m* (*par obus*). ♦ **shellproof** *adj* blindé.

shelter ['ʃeltəʳ] **1** *n* **(a)** abri *m*. **under the ~ of** sous l'abri de; **to take ~, to get under ~** se mettre à l'abri *or* à couvert; **to take ~ from/under** s'abriter de/sous; **to seek ~** chercher un abri (*from* contre). **(b)** (*on mountain*) abri *m*, refuge *m*; (*for sentry*) guérite *f*; (*bus ~*) abribus *m*; (*air-raid ~*) abri. **2** *vt* **(a)** (*protect*) (*from wind, shells etc*) abriter, protéger (*from* de); (*from blame etc*) protéger (*from* de); *criminal etc* protéger, (*hide*) cacher. **~ed from the wind** à l'abri du vent. **(b)** (*give lodging to*) recueillir. **3** *vi* s'abriter (*from* de; *under* sous). ♦ **sheltered** *adj place* abrité; (*fig*) *life* bien protégé; *childhood* sans soucis; *conditions, environment, workshop* protégé.

shelve [ʃelv] **1** *vt* **(a)** (*fig: postpone*) mettre en sommeil. **(b)** (*lit*) *cupboard, wall* garnir de rayons. **2** *vi* (*slope*: **~ down**) descendre en pente douce. ♦ **shelving** *n* rayonnages *mpl*.

shepherd ['ʃepəd] **1** *n* berger *m*; (*Rel*) pasteur *m*.

(*Culin*) **~'s pie** ≃ hachis *m* Parmentier. **2** *vt* (*fig*) **to ~ sb in** faire entrer qn; **to ~ sb out** escorter qn jusqu'à la porte; **he ~ed us round Paris** il nous a servi de guide dans Paris. ♦ **shepherdess** *n* bergère *f*.

sherbet [ˈʃɜːbət] *n* (*Brit: powder*) poudre *f* acidulée; (*US: water ice*) sorbet *m*.

sheriff [ˈʃerɪf] *n* shérif *m*.

sherry [ˈʃerɪ] *n* xérès *m*, sherry *m*.

Shetland [ˈʃetlənd] **1** *n* (*also* **the ~ Isles, the ~s**) les îles *fpl* Shetland. **2** *adj*: **~ pony** poney *m* shetlandais; **~ wool** shetland *m*.

shield [ʃiːld] **1** *n* (*gen*) bouclier *m*; (*not round*) écu *m*; (*on machine, against radiation etc*) écran *m* (de protection). **2** *vt* protéger (*from* de, contre). **to ~ sb with one's body** faire à qn un rempart de son corps.

shift [ʃɪft] **1** *n* **(a)** (*change*) changement *m* (*in* de); (*Ling*) mutation *f*; (*movement: of cargo, load etc*) déplacement *m* (*in* de). **a sudden ~ in policy** un retournement de la politique; **a sudden ~ in the wind** une saute de vent. **(b)** (*period of work*) poste *m*. **to be on day/night ~** être (au poste) de jour/de nuit; **he works ~s** il travaille par roulement; **I work an 8-hour ~** je fais un poste de 8 heures; **they worked in ~s to save him** ils se sont relayés pour le sauver. **(c)** (*expedient*) expédient *m*, truc* *m*. **to make ~** se débrouiller (*with* avec; *without* sans; *to do* pour faire). **(d)** (*US Aut: gear~*) changement *m* de vitesse.

2 *adj [typewriter]* **~ key** touche *f* de majuscule; (*Ind*) **~ work** travail *m* en poste *or* par roulement.

3 *vt object, furniture* déplacer, changer de place; *one's head, arm etc* bouger, remuer; (*Theat*) *scenery* changer; *screw, lid* débloquer; *employee* (*to another town*) muter (*to* à); (*to another job, department*) affecter (*to* à); (*fig*) *blame, responsibility* rejeter (*on to* sur). **to ~ sth in/out/nearer** *etc* rentrer/sortir/approcher *etc* qch; **to ~ position** changer de position; (*US Aut*) **to ~ gears** changer de vitesse.

4 *vi* **(a)** (*go*) aller; (*move house*) déménager; (*change position, stir*) *[person, limb]* bouger; *[wind]* tourner; *[cargo, load]* se déplacer; *[opinions]* changer; (*change one's mind*) changer d'avis. **he ~ed over to the window** il s'est approché de la fenêtre; **~ off the rug** va-t'en du tapis; **to ~ over** *or* **along** *or* **up** se pousser; (*Aut*) **to ~ into second gear** passer la deuxième; **he won't ~** il ne bougera pas; (*fig*) **to ~ from one's position** modifier sa position; **come on, ~!*** allez, remue-toi!* **(b) to ~ for o.s.** se débrouiller* tout seul. ♦ **shiftily** *adv behave* sournoisement; *answer* de façon évasive. ♦ **shiftiness** *n* sournoiserie *f*; caractère *m* évasif. ♦ **shiftless** *adj* manquant de ressource. ♦ **shiftlessness** *n* manque *m* de ressource. ♦ **shifty** *adj person, behaviour* louche, sournois; *answer* évasif; *look* fuyant.

shilly-shally [ˈʃɪlɪˌʃælɪ] *vi* hésiter. **stop ~ing!** décide-toi enfin! ♦ **shilly-shallying** *n* hésitations *fpl*.

shimmer [ˈʃɪməʳ] *vi [satin, jewels]* chatoyer; *[water, heat haze]* miroiter. ♦ **shimmering** *adj* chatoyant; miroitant.

shin [ʃɪn] **1** *n* tibia *m*. **2** *vi*: **to ~ up a tree** grimper à un arbre; **to ~ down a tree** dégringoler lestement d'un arbre; **to ~ over a wall** escalader un mur. ♦ **shinbone** *n* tibia *m*.

shindy* [ˈʃɪndɪ] *n* (*brawl*) bagarre *f*; (*commotion*) boucan* *m*. **to kick up a ~** faire du boucan*.

shine [ʃaɪn] (*vb: pret, ptp* **shone**) **1** *n [sun, metal]* éclat *m*; *[shoes]* brillant *m*. **to give sth a ~** faire briller qch; **to take the ~ off** *brass, shoes* ternir; (**fig*) *success, news* diminuer l'effet de. **2** *vi* briller. **the sun is shining** il y a du soleil, le soleil brille; **the moon is shining** il y a clair de lune; **to ~ on sth** éclairer qch; **the light was shining in my eyes** j'avais la lumière dans les yeux; **the light shone through the curtains** la lumière passait à travers les rideaux; **her face shone with happiness** son visage rayonnait de bonheur; (*fig*) **to ~ at football** briller au football. **3** *vt* **(a) ~ your torch** *or* **~ the light over here** éclairez par ici. **(b)** (*polish: pret, ptp* **shone** *or* **shined**) faire briller. ♦ **shining** *adj furniture etc* reluisant; (*happy*) *face* rayonnant; *eyes, hair* brillant; *example* resplendissant. ♦ **shiny** *adj* (*gen*) brillant; (*pej*) *clothes* lustré.

shingle [ˈʃɪŋgl] *n* (*on beach etc*) galets *mpl*; (*on roof*) bardeaux *mpl*; (*US**: *signboard*) petite enseigne *f*. ♦ **shingly** *adj beach* de galets.

shingles [ˈʃɪŋglz] *nsg* (*Med*) zona *m*.

ship [ʃɪp] **1** *n* (*gen*) bateau *m*; (*large*) navire *m*; (*vessel*) vaisseau *m*, bâtiment *m*. **His** *or* **Her Majesty's S~** (*abbr* **HMS**) **Maria/Falcon** la Maria/le Falcon; **~'s boat** chaloupe *f*; **~'s company** équipage *m*; **~'s papers** papiers *mpl* de bord. **2** *vt* **(a)** (*transport*) transporter; (*send*: **~ off**) expédier. **(b)** (*put or take on board*) *cargo, water* embarquer; *oars* rentrer. ♦ **shipbuilder** *n* constructeur *m* de navires. ♦ **shipbuilding** *n* construction *f* navale. ♦ **shipload** *n* (*lit*) charge *f*; (*fig*) grande quantité *f*. ♦ **shipmate** *n* camarade *m* de bord. ♦ **shipment** *n* cargaison *f*. ♦ **shipowner** *n* armateur *m*. ♦ **shipper** *n* expéditeur *m*. ♦ **shipping 1** *n* (*ships collectively*) navires *mpl*; (*traffic*) navigation *f*; (*Rad*) **attention all ~ping!** avis à la navigation!; **a danger to ~ping** un danger pour la navigation; **canal closed to British ~ping** canal fermé aux navires britanniques; **2** *adj*: **~ping agent** agent *m* maritime; **~ping company, ~ping line** compagnie *f* de navigation; **~ping lane** voie *f* de navigation. ♦ **shipshape** *adj* en ordre. ♦ **ship-to-shore radio** *n* liaison *f* radio avec la côte. ♦ **shipwreck 1** *n* (*event*) naufrage *m*; (*wrecked ship*) épave *f*; **2** *vt*: **to be ~wrecked** faire naufrage; **~wrecked on a desert island** échoué sur une île déserte. ♦ **shipwrecked** *adj* naufragé. ♦ **shipwright** *n* constructeur *m* de navires. ♦ **shipyard** *n* chantier *m* naval.

shire [ˈʃaɪəʳ] *n* (*Brit*) comté *m*. **~ horse** cheval *m* de gros trait.

shirk [ʃɜːk] **1** *vt task, work* ne pas faire; *duty, difficulty, issue* esquiver. **to ~ doing** s'arranger pour ne pas faire. **2** *vi* tirer au flanc*. ♦ **shirker** *n* tire-au-flanc* *m inv*.

shirt [ʃɜːt] *n* (*man's*) chemise *f*; (*woman's*) chemisier *m*. **in (one's) ~ sleeves** en bras *or* manches de chemise; (*Betting*) **to put one's ~ on sth** jouer tout ce qu'on a sur qch. ♦ **shirty*** *adj* (*esp Brit*) en rogne*.

shiver[1] [ˈʃɪvəʳ] **1** *vi* frissonner (*with* de). **2** *n* frisson *m*. **it sent ~s down his spine** cela lui a donné froid dans le dos; **to give sb the ~s** donner le frisson à qn. ♦ **shivery** *adj* (*from cold*) qui a des frissons; (*from fever*) fiévreux; (*from fear/emotion etc*) frissonnant (de peur/d'émotion *etc*).

shiver[2] [ˈʃɪvəʳ] **1** *n [glass]* éclat *m*. **2** *vi* voler en éclats. **3** *vt* fracasser.

shoal [ʃəʊl] *n* banc *m* (*de poissons*).

shock [ʃɒk] **1** *n* (*gen*) choc *m*; *[earthquake, explosion]* secousse *f*; (*Elec*) décharge *f* (électrique). (*Elec*) **to get a ~** recevoir une décharge (électrique) (*from sth* en touchant qch), prendre le jus*; **he got such a ~ when he heard that ...** cela lui a donné un tel choc *or* un tel coup d'apprendre que ...; **the ~ of the election results** les résultats *mpl* stupéfiants de l'élection; **it came as a ~ to me** ça m'a stupéfié; **it comes as a ~ to hear that ...** il est stupéfiant d'apprendre que ...; **you gave me a ~!** vous m'avez fait peur!; **I got such a ~!** j'ai eu une de ces émotions!*; **the ~ killed him** il est mort d'émotion; **pale with ~** pâle de saisissement; (*Med*) **in a state of ~** en état de choc. **2** *adj* **(a)** (*Mil etc*) *tactics, troops* de choc. (*Aut*) **~ absorber** amortisseur *m*; **~ wave** onde *f* de choc.

(b) (*) *result, reaction* stupéfiant. **3** *vt* (*take aback*) secouer, (*stronger*) bouleverser; (*scandalize*) choquer. **easily ~ed** qui se choque facilement. ♦ **shocking** *adj* (*appalling*) *crime, news, sight* atroce; (*scandalizing*) *book, behaviour* choquant; *decision, waste, price* scandaleux; (*very bad*) *weather, results, handwriting* épouvantable. ♦ **shockingly** *adv unfair, expensive* terriblement; (*very badly*) très mal.

shoddy [ˈʃɒdɪ] *adj* de mauvaise qualité. ♦ **shoddily** *adv made* mal. ♦ **shoddiness** *n* mauvaise qualité *f*.

shoe [ʃuː] (*vb: pret, ptp* **shod**) **1** *n* chaussure *f*, soulier *m*; (*horse~*) fer *m* (à cheval); (*brake ~*) sabot *m* (de frein). **to shake** *or* **shiver in one's ~s** avoir une peur bleue; (*fig*) **I wouldn't like to be in his ~s** je n'aimerais pas être à sa place. **2** *adj*: **~ polish** cirage *m*; **~ repair** réparation *f* de chaussures. **3** *vt horse* ferrer. *[person]* **well/badly shod** bien/mal chaussé.
♦ **shoebrush** *n* brosse *f* à chaussures. ♦ **shoehorn** *n* chausse-pied *m*. ♦ **shoelace** *n* lacet *m* de soulier. ♦ **shoemaker** *or* ♦ **shoe-repairer** *n* cordonnier *m*; **~maker's shop** cordonnerie *f*. ♦ **shoeshop** *n* magasin *m* de chaussures. ♦ **shoestring** *n* lacet *m*; (*fig*) **on a ~string** à peu de frais. ♦ **shoetree** *n* embauchoir *m*.

shone [ʃɒn] *pret, ptp of* **shine.**

shoo [ʃuː] *vt* (**~ away, ~ off**) chasser.

shook [ʃʊk] *pret of* **shake.**

shoot [ʃuːt] (*vb: pret, ptp* **shot**) **1** *n* **(a)** *[plant]* pousse *f*. **(b)** (*chute*) glissière *f*, déversoir *m*. **(c)** (*fig*) **the whole ~**‡ tout le tremblement*.
2 *vt* **(a)** (*hit*) atteindre d'un coup de fusil *etc*; (*hunt*) chasser; (*kill*) abattre; (*execute*) fusiller. **shot in the head** (*hit*) atteint *or* (*killed*) tué d'une balle dans la tête; (*fig*) **you'll get shot for that!*** tu vas te faire incendier* pour ça. **(b)** (*fire*) *gun* tirer *or* lâcher un coup de (*at* sur); *arrow, rocket, missile* lancer (*at* sur); *bullet* tirer (*at* sur). **to ~ a goal** marquer un but; **he shot the bolt** (*fastened*) il a mis le verrou; (*opened*) il a tiré le verrou; (*fig*) **he has shot his bolt** il a joué sa dernière carte; (*fig*) **to ~ a line about sth**‡ raconter des histoires à propos de qch; **to ~ dice** jeter les dés. **(c)** (*direct*) *look* lancer (*at* à); *smile* jeter (*at* à); *[searchlight etc] beam of light* braquer (*at* sur). **to ~ questions at sb** bombarder qn de questions. **(d)** (*Cine etc*) *film, scene* tourner; *person, subject* prendre (en photo). **(e)** *rapids* descendre.
3 *vi* **(a)** (*with gun, bow*) tirer (*at* sur). **to go ~ing** chasser; **to ~ to kill** tirer pour abattre; **to ~ on sight** tirer à vue. **(b)** (*rush*) **to ~ in/past** *etc* entrer/passer *etc* à toute vitesse; **the bullet shot past his ears** la balle lui a sifflé aux oreilles; *[flames, water]* **to ~ out** *or* **up** *etc* jaillir; **the pain went ~ing up his arm** la douleur au bras le lancinait. **(c)** (*Ftbl etc*) shooter, tirer. **to ~ at goal** shooter. **(d)** (*Bot*) bourgeonner, pousser.

shoot down *vt sep plane, person* abattre.

shoot up *vi* **(a)** *[flame, water]* jaillir; *[rocket, price etc]* monter en flèche. **(b)** (*grow quickly*) pousser vite.
♦ **shooting 1** *n* **(a)** (*shots*) coups *mpl* de feu; (*continuous*) fusillade *f*; **(b)** (*murder*) meurtre *m* (avec une arme à feu); (*execution*) exécution *f*; **(c)** (*Hunting*) chasse *f*; **2** *adj pain* lancinant; **~ing brake** break *m*; **~ing gallery** stand *m* de tir; **~ing incidents** échanges *mpl* de coups de feu; (*fig*) **the whole ~ing match*** tout le tremblement*; **~ing star** étoile *f* filante; **~ing stick** canne-siège *f*.

shop [ʃɒp] **1** *n* **(a)** magasin *m*, (*small*) boutique *f*. **wine ~** marchand *m* de vins; **at the butcher's ~** à la boucherie, chez le boucher; (*lit, fig*) **to shut up ~** fermer boutique; (*fig*) **you've come to the wrong ~*** tu te trompes d'adresse*; (*fig*) **to talk ~** parler boutique; (*fig*) **all over the ~*** (*everywhere*) partout; (*in confusion*) en pagaille*. **(b)** (*Ind: work~*) atelier *m*.
2 *adj* (*Brit*) **~ assistant** vendeur *m*, -euse *f*; (*Ind*) **~ steward** délégué(e) syndical(e) *m(f)*; **~ window** vitrine *f*.
3 *vi* faire ses courses (*at* chez). **to go ~ping** (*locally etc*) faire les courses; (*on shopping expedition*) faire des courses; **I was ~ping for a coat** je cherchais un manteau.
4 *vt* (‡: *betray*) vendre, donner*.

shop around *vi* comparer les prix. **to ~ around for sth** comparer les prix avant d'acheter qch.
♦ **shop-floor** *n* (*Ind*) **he works on the ~-floor** c'est un ouvrier; **the ~-floor (workers)** les ouvriers. ♦ **shopgirl** *n* (*Brit*) vendeuse *f*. ♦ **shopkeeper** *n* commerçant(e) *m(f)*. ♦ **shoplift** *vi* voler à l'étalage. ♦ **shoplifter** *n* voleur *m*, -euse *f* à l'étalage. ♦ **shoplifting** *n* vol *m* à l'étalage. ♦ **shopper** *n* **(a)** (*person*) personne *f* qui fait ses courses; (*customer*) client(e) *m(f)*; **(b)** (*: *bag*) cabas *m*. ♦ **shopping 1** *n* (*goods*) achats *mpl*; **2** *adj street, district* commerçant; **~ping bag** cabas *m*; **~ping basket** panier *m* (à provisions); **~ping centre** centre *m* commercial. ♦ **shopsoiled** *adj* qui a fait la vitrine.

shore[1] [ʃɔːʳ] **1** *n [sea]* rivage *m*; *[lake]* rive *f*; (*coast*) côte *f*; (*beach*) plage *f*. **on ~** à terre; **to go on ~** débarquer. **2** *adj* (*Naut*) **~ leave** permission *f* à terre.

shore[2] [ʃɔːʳ] *vt*: **to ~ up** étayer, (*fig*) consolider.

shorn [ʃɔːn] *ptp of* **shear.**

short [ʃɔːt] **1** *adj* **(a)** (*gen*) court; *person* petit, de petite taille; *step, walk* petit; *visit, vowel, syllable* bref. **a ~ distance away** à peu de distance; **to take a ~ holiday** prendre quelques jours de vacances; **a ~ time** *or* **while** peu de temps; **time is getting ~** il ne reste plus beaucoup de temps; **the days are getting ~er** les jours raccourcissent; **make the skirt ~er** raccourcis la jupe; **that was ~ and sweet** ça n'a pas traîné; **to take a ~ cut** prendre un raccourci; **a ~ drink** un petit verre d'apéritif (*or* d'alcool); **to win by a ~ head** (*Racing*) gagner d'une courte tête; (*fig*) gagner de justesse; **~ list** liste *f* des candidats sélectionnés; **~ story** nouvelle *f*; **~-story writer** nouvelliste *mf*; **they want a ~er working week** on veut réduire la semaine de travail; **to have a ~ temper** être coléreux; (*Ind*) **to work ~ time** être en chômage partiel; (*fig*) **to make ~ work of** *job etc* ne pas mettre beaucoup de temps à faire; (*) *person* envoyer promener*. **(b)** (*phrases*) **in ~** bref; **'TV' is ~ for 'television'** 'TV' est l'abréviation de 'television'; **he's called Fred for ~** son diminutif est Fred; **to be ~ of sugar** être à court de sucre; **I'm £2 ~** il me manque 2 livres; **not far ~ of £100** pas loin de 100 livres; **it's little ~ of suicide** c'est presque un suicide; **it's nothing ~ of robbery** c'est du vol ni plus ni moins; **~ of asking him yourself** à moins de lui demander vous-même; **everything ~ of (doing) sth** tout sauf (faire) qch; **to go ~ of sth** manquer de qch; **they never went ~** ils n'ont jamais manqué du nécessaire; (*fig*) **to be taken ~*** être pris d'un besoin pressant; **petrol is ~** *or* **in ~ supply** on manque d'essence; **to give ~ weight** *or* **~ measure** ne pas donner le poids juste, (*deliberately*) tricher sur le poids. **(c)** (*curt*) *reply, manner* brusque, sec. **to be rather ~ with sb** se montrer assez sec *or* brusque à l'égard de qn.
2 *vti* (*Elec*) = **short-circuit,** *V below.*
♦ **shortage** *n* (*gen*) manque *m*, pénurie *f*; **there was no ~age of water** on ne manquait pas d'eau; **the food ~age** la disette; **the housing ~age** la crise du logement. ♦ **shortbread** *or* ♦ **shortcake** *n* sablé *m*. ♦ **short-change** *vt* ne pas donner son dû à. ♦ **short-circuit 1** *n* court-circuit *m*; **2** *vt* court-circuiter; **3** *vi* se mettre en court-circuit. ♦ **shortcoming** *n* défaut *m*. ♦ **short(crust) pastry** *n* pâte *f* brisée. ♦ **shorten 1** *vt skirt, rope* rac-

courcir; *holiday, journey* écourter; *life, book, programme* abréger; *distance, time* réduire; **2** *vi [days etc]* raccourcir. ♦ **shortening** *n* (*Culin*) matière *f* grasse. ♦ **shortfall** *n* manque *m*. ♦ **shorthand 1** *n* sténo(graphie) *f*; **in ~hand** en sténo; **2** *adj notes* en sténo; *notebook* de sténo. ♦ **shorthand-typing** *n* sténodactylo *f*. ♦ **shorthand-typist** *n* sténodactylo *mf*. ♦ **shorthand-writer** *n* sténo(graphe) *mf*. ♦ **short-list** *vt* mettre sur la liste des candidats sélectionnés. ♦ **short-lived** *adj* (*fig*) de courte durée. ♦ **shortly** *adv* **(a)** (*soon*) bientôt, dans peu de temps; **~ly before twelve** peu avant midi; **(b)** (*curtly*) sèchement, brusquement. ♦ **shortness** *n* peu *m* de longueur; petite taille *f*; brièveté *f*; *[vowel, syllable]* brévité *f*; (*curtness*) sécheresse *f*. ♦ **short-range** *adj weather forecast* à court terme. ♦ **shorts** *npl*: **(a pair of) ~s** un short. ♦ **short-sighted** *adj person* myope; *policy, measure* qui manque de vision. ♦ **short-sightedness** *n* myopie *f*; manque *m* de vision. ♦ **short-staffed** *adj*: **to be ~-staffed** manquer de personnel. ♦ **short-tempered** *adj* (*in general*) coléreux; (*in a bad temper*) d'humeur irritable. ♦ **short-term** *adj* à court terme. ♦ **short-wave** (*Rad*) **1** *n* ondes *fpl* courtes; **2** *adj radio* à ondes courtes; *transmission* sur ondes courtes.

shot [ʃɒt] **1** *n* **(a)** (*act of firing*) coup *m*; (*sound*) coup de feu (*or* de fusil *etc*); (*bullet*) balle *f*; (*pellets:* **lead ~**) plomb *m*. (*fig*) **a ~ across the bows, a warning ~** un avertissement; **the first ~ killed him** la première balle l'a tué; **he is a good/bad ~** il est bon/mauvais tireur; (*fig*) **big ~*** personnage *m* important, gros bonnet* *m*; **Parthian ~** flèche *f* du Parthe; (*fig*) **that was a ~ in the dark** c'était dit à tout hasard; **like a ~** *leave, go* comme une flèche; *agree* sans hésiter. **(b)** (*Space*) **moon ~** tir *m* lunaire. **(c)** (*Ftbl, Golf, Tennis etc*) coup *m*; (*throw*) lancer *m*. **good ~**! bien joué!; (*Shooting*) bien visé!; **to put the ~** lancer le poids; **~ put** lancer du poids; **a ~ at goal** un tir au but. **(d)** (*attempt*) essai *m*, coup *m*; (*turn to play*) tour *m*. **to have a ~ at (doing) sth** essayer (de faire) qch; **have a ~ at it!** (*try it*) tentez le coup!; (*guess*) dites voir!* **(e)** (*Phot*) photo *f*; (*Cine*) prise *f* de vues. **(f)** (*injection*) piqûre *f* (*against* contre); (*of alcohol*) coup *m*. (*fig*) **a ~ in the arm** un coup de fouet. **2** *pret, ptp of* **shoot. to get ~ of‡** se débarrasser de. **3** *adj*: **~ with yellow** strié de jaune; **~ silk** soie *f* gorge-de-pigeon. ♦ **shotgun 1** *n* fusil *m* de chasse; **2** *adj*: **~gun wedding** mariage *m* forcé.

should [ʃʊd] *modal aux vb* **(a)** (*obligation, advisability*) **I ~ go and see her** je devrais aller la voir, il faudrait que j'aille la voir; **he thought he ~ tell you** il a pensé qu'il ferait bien de vous le dire; **you ~ have been a teacher** vous auriez dû être professeur; **everything is as it ~ be** tout est en ordre; **how ~ I know?** comment voulez-vous que je le sache? **(b)** (*probability*) **he ~ win the race** il devrait gagner la course, il va probablement gagner la course; **he ~ have got there by now** il a dû arriver à l'heure qu'il est; **why ~ he suspect me?** pourquoi me soupçonnerait-il? **(c)** (*conditional tense*) **I ~ go, I'd go** j'irais; **we ~ have come** nous serions venus; **I ~ like to** j'aimerais bien; **who ~ come in but Paul!** et devinez qui est entré? Paul!

shoulder ['ʃəʊldə^r] **1** *n* **(a)** épaule *f*. **to have broad ~s** être large d'épaules; **put it round your ~s** mets-le sur tes épaules; **to weep on sb's ~** pleurer sur l'épaule de qn; **over one ~** à l'épaule; **to look over sb's ~** regarder par-dessus l'épaule de qn, (*fig*) surveiller qn constamment; **~ to ~** coude à coude; (*fig*) **to put one's ~ to the wheel** s'atteler à la tâche. **(b)** *[road]* accotement *m*, bas-côté *m*; *[hill]* contrefort *m*. **hard/soft ~** accotement stabilisé/non stabilisé. **2** *adj*: **~ bag** sac *m* à bandoulière; **~ blade** omoplate *f*; **between the ~ blades** en plein entre les épaules; *[garment]* **~ strap** bretelle *f*. **3** *vt load* charger sur son épaule; *responsibility* endosser; *task* se charger de. (*Mil*) **to ~ arms** porter l'arme; **to ~ sb aside** écarter qn d'un coup d'épaule. ♦ **shoulder-high** *adv*: **to carry sb ~-high** porter qn en triomphe.

shout [ʃaʊt] **1** *n* cri *m* (*of joy etc* de joie *etc*). **there were ~s of applause/protest/laughter** des acclamations/des protestations bruyantes/des éclats de rire ont retenti; **to give sb a ~** appeler qn. **2** *vt* crier. **3** *vi* crier (*to sb to do* à qn de faire; *at sb* après qn; *for help* au secours), pousser des cris (*for joy etc* de joie *etc*). **to ~ with laughter** éclater de rire; **she ~ed for someone to help her** elle a appelé pour qu'on l'aide (*subj*).

shout down *vt sep speaker* huer.

shout out 1 *vi* pousser un cri. **2** *vt sep* crier.

♦ **shouting** *n* cris *mpl*; (*noise of quarrelling*) éclats *mpl* de voix; (*fig*) **it's all over bar the ~ing** c'est dans le sac*.

shove [ʃʌv] **1** *n* poussée *f*. **to give sb/sth a ~** pousser qn/qch. **2** *vt* (*push*) pousser; (*with effort*) pousser avec peine; (*thrust*) *stick, finger etc* enfoncer (*into* dans; *between* entre); *rag* fourrer (*into* dans); (*jostle*) bousculer; (*put*) mettre. **to ~ sth in/out** *etc* faire entrer/sortir *etc* qch en poussant; **to ~ sth into a drawer/one's pocket** fourrer qch dans un tiroir/sa poche. **3** *vi* pousser. **he ~d (his way) past me** il m'a dépassé en me bousculant; **he ~d (his way) through the crowd** il s'est frayé un chemin à travers la foule.

shove off* *vi* (*leave*) ficher le camp*.

shove over* *vi* (*move over*) se pousser.

shovel ['ʃʌvl] **1** *n* pelle *f*; (*mechanical*) pelleteuse *f*. **2** *vt coal, grain* pelleter; (**~ out**) *mud etc* enlever à la pelle; (**~ up**) *sth spilt etc* ramasser avec une pelle; *snow* enlever à la pelle. ♦ **shovelful** *n* pelletée *f*.

show [ʃəʊ] (*vb: pret* **-ed**, *ptp* **-n** *or* **-ed**) **1** *n* **(a)** *[hatred, affection etc]* démonstration *f*; (*semblance*) semblant *m*; (*ostentation*) parade *f*. **some fine pieces on ~** quelques beaux objets exposés; **~ of power** étalage *m* de force; **a ~ of hands** un vote à main levée; **the dahlias make a splendid ~** les dahlias sont splendides à voir; **they make a great ~ of their wealth** ils font parade de leur richesse; **with a ~ of emotion** en affectant l'émotion; **to make a ~ of doing** faire semblant de faire; **just for ~** pour l'effet. **(b)** (*exhibition: Agr, Art, Tech etc*) exposition *f*; (*Comm*) foire *f*; (*Agr: contest*) concours *m*. **the Boat S~** le Salon de la Navigation. **(c)** (*Theat etc*) spectacle *m*; (*variety* **~**) show *m*. **I often go to a ~** je vais souvent au spectacle; **the last ~ starts at 9** (*Theat*) la dernière représentation *or* (*Cine*) la dernière séance commence à 21 heures; **on with the ~!** que la représentation commence (*or* continue)! **(d)** (*phrases*) **good ~!*** bravo!; **to put up a good ~** bien se défendre*; **to make a poor ~** faire piètre figure; **it's a poor ~*** il n'y a pas de quoi être fier; **this is Paul's ~*** c'est Paul qui commande ici; **to run the ~*** faire marcher l'affaire; **to give the ~ away*** vendre la mèche*.

2 *adj house, flat* témoin *f inv*.

3 *vt* **(a)** (*gen*) montrer; *film, slides* passer; (*exhibit*) *goods for sale, picture, dog* exposer; (*express*) *interest, surprise* montrer, manifester; *gratitude, respect* témoigner; (*indicate*) *[clock, dial etc]* indiquer, marquer. **~ it me!** faites voir!, montrez-le-moi!; **what is ~ing at the Odeon?** qu'est-ce qu'on donne à l'Odéon?; **it has been ~n on television** c'est passé à la télévision; (*fig*) **there's nothing to ~ for it** on ne le dirait pas; **he has nothing to ~ for it** ça ne lui a rien donné; **he daren't ~ his face there again** il n'ose plus s'y montrer; (*fig*) **to ~ one's hand** *or* **cards** abattre son jeu; (*fig*) **to ~ sb the door** mettre qn à la porte; (*fig*) **to ~ the flag** faire acte de présence; **to ~ a**

loss/profit indiquer une perte/un bénéfice; **roads are ~n in red** les routes sont marquées en rouge; **to ~ loyalty** se montrer loyal (*to sb* envers qn); **this skirt ~s the dirt** cette jupe est salissante; **it ~ed signs of having been used** il était visible qu'on s'en était servi; **to ~ fight** faire montre de combativité; **that ~s his good taste** cela témoigne de son bon goût; **to ~ one's age** faire son âge; **this ~s great intelligence** cela révèle *or* dénote beaucoup d'intelligence; **he ~ed himself (to be) a coward** il s'est montré *or* révélé lâche; **it all goes to ~ that ...** tout cela montre bien que ...; **it only goes to ~!*** c'est bien ça la vie!; **I ~ed him that it was impossible** je lui ai prouvé que c'était impossible; (*fig*) **I'll ~ him!*** je lui apprendrai! **(b)** (*conduct*) **to ~ sb in/up** *etc* faire entrer/monter *etc* qn; **to ~ sb to his seat** placer qn; **to ~ sb out, to ~ sb to the door** reconduire qn jusqu'à la porte; **to ~ sb over** *or* **round a house** faire visiter une maison à qn.

4 *vi* *[emotion]* être visible; *[stain, scar]* se voir; *[underskirt etc]* dépasser. **it doesn't ~** cela ne se voit pas.

show off 1 *vi* crâner*; (*show one's knowledge*) étaler sa science. **she's always ~ing off** c'est une crâneuse*; **he's ~ing off again** il essaie encore d'en fiche plein la vue*. **2** *vt sep* **(a)** *sb's beauty, complexion etc* mettre en valeur. **(b)** (*pej*) *one's wealth, knowledge* faire étalage de.

show through *vi* se voir au travers.

show up 1 *vi* **(a)** (*stand out*) *[feature]* ressortir; *[mistake]* être visible; *[stain]* se voir. **it ~ed up clearly against the sky** cela se détachait nettement sur le ciel. **(b)** (*: *appear*) arriver, se pointer*. **2** *vt sep* **(a)** *fraud, impostor* démasquer; *flaw, defect* faire ressortir. **(b)** (*embarrass*) faire honte à (en public).

♦ **show business** *or* ♦ **show biz‡** *n* le monde du spectacle, l'industrie *f* du spectacle. ♦ **showcase** *n* vitrine *f*. ♦ **showdown** *n* épreuve *f* de force. ♦ **showgirl** *n* girl *f*. ♦ **showground** *n* champ *m* de foire. ♦ **showing** *n* *[film]* projection *f*; (*cinema session*) séance *f*. ♦ **showing-off** *n* pose *f* (*affectation*). ♦ **showjumping** *n* concours *m* hippique. ♦ **showman** *n* (*in fair etc*) forain *m*. ♦ **showmanship** *n* (*fig*) sens *m* de la mise en scène. ♦ **show-off** *n* m'as-tu-vu(e)* *m(f)* (*pl inv*). ♦ **showpiece** *n* (*of exhibition etc*) trésor *m*; (*new school etc*) modèle *m* du genre. ♦ **showplace** *n* (*tourist attraction*) lieu *m* de grand intérêt touristique. ♦ **showroom** *n* salle *f* d'exposition. ♦ **showy** *adj colour* éclatant, voyant (*pej*).

shower [ˈʃaʊəʳ] **1** *n* **(a)** *[rain]* averse *f*; (*fig*) *[blows]* grêle *f*; *[sparks, stones, arrows]* pluie *f*. **(b)** (~ **bath**) douche *f*. **to have** *or* **take a ~** prendre une douche. **2** *adj*: ~ **cap** bonnet *m* de douche; ~ **unit** bloc-douche *m*. **3** *vt* (*fig*) **to ~ sb with gifts/praise, to ~ gifts/praise on sb** combler qn de cadeaux/de louanges; **to ~ blows on sb** faire pleuvoir des coups sur qn; **to ~ abuse** *or* **insults on sb** accabler qn d'injures. ♦ **showerproof** *adj* imperméable. ♦ **showery** *adj day* pluvieux; **it will be ~y** il y aura des averses.

shrank [ʃræŋk] *pret of* **shrink.**

shrapnel [ˈʃræpnl] *n* éclats *mpl* d'obus.

shred [ʃred] **1** *n [cloth, paper etc]* lambeau *m*; (*fig*) *[truth, commonsense]* grain *m*. **not a ~ of evidence** pas la moindre preuve; **in ~s** en lambeaux; **to tear to ~s** mettre en lambeaux; (*fig*) *argument etc* démolir entièrement. **2** *vt paper etc* mettre en lambeaux; *carrots etc* râper; *cabbage* couper en lanières. ♦ **shredder** *n* (*for documents*) destructeur *m*.

shrew [ʃru:] *n* (*Zool*) musaraigne *f*; (*woman*) mégère *f*.

shrewd [ʃru:d] *adj person, assessment* perspicace; *businessman, lawyer* habile; *reasoning* judicieux; *plan* astucieux. **I have a ~ idea that ...** je soupçonne fortement que ... . ♦ **shrewdly** *adv suspect* avec perspicacité; *reason* judicieusement; *guess* astucieusement. ♦ **shrewdness** *n* perspicacité *f*; habileté *f*; astuce *f*.

shriek [ʃri:k] **1** *n* hurlement *m*. **~s of laughter** grands éclats *mpl* de rire. **2** *vti* hurler (*with* de). **to ~ with laughter** rire à gorge déployée.

shrill [ʃrɪl] *adj voice, cry* perçant; *whistle, laugh* strident. ♦ **shrillness** *n* ton *m* perçant. ♦ **shrilly** *adv* d'un ton perçant.

shrimp [ʃrɪmp] **1** *n* crevette *f*. **2** *adj*: ~ **cocktail** hors-d'œuvre *m* de crevettes. **3** *vi*: **to go ~ing** aller pêcher la crevette.

shrine [ʃraɪn] *n* (*place*) lieu *m* saint; (*tomb*) tombeau *m* de saint; (*reliquary*) châsse *f*.

shrink [ʃrɪŋk] *pret* **shrank**, *ptp* **shrunk 1** *vi* **(a)** *[clothes]* rétrécir; *[area]* se réduire; *[boundaries]* se resserrer; *[piece of meat]* réduire; *[body, person]* se ratatiner; *[wood]* se contracter; *[quantity, amount]* diminuer. **(b)** (~ **away,** ~ **back**) reculer (*from sth* devant qch; *from doing* devant l'idée de faire). **she shrank (away** *or* **back) from him** elle a eu un mouvement de recul; **he did not ~ from saying** il n'a pas craint de dire. **2** *vt wool* faire rétrécir; *metal* contracter. ♦ **shrinkage** *n* rétrécissement *m*; contraction *f*; diminution *f*.

shrivel [ˈʃrɪvl] (~ **up**) **1** *vi [apple, body]* se ratatiner; *[skin]* se rider; *[leaf, steak]* se racornir. **2** *vt* ratatiner; rider; racornir.

shroud [ʃraʊd] **1** *n* **(a)** *[corpse]* linceul *m*. **(b)** (*Naut*) hauban *m*. **2** *vt* (*fig*) **~ed in** *mist, snow* sous un linceul de; *mystery* enveloppé de.

Shrove Tuesday [ˌʃrəʊvˈtju:zdɪ] *n* Mardi *m* gras.

shrub [ʃrʌb] *n* arbrisseau *m*; (*small*) arbuste *m*. ♦ **shrubbery** *n* massif *m* d'arbustes.

shrug [ʃrʌg] **1** *n* haussement *m* d'épaules. **to give a ~ of contempt** hausser les épaules en signe de mépris; **... he said with a ~ ...** dit-il en haussant les épaules. **2** *vti*: **to ~ (one's shoulders)** hausser les épaules.

shrug off *vt sep suggestion, warning* dédaigner; *remark* ne pas relever; *infection, a cold* se débarrasser de.

shrunk [ʃrʌŋk] *ptp of* **shrink.** ♦ **shrunken** *adj person, body* ratatiné.

shudder [ˈʃʌdəʳ] **1** *n [person]* frisson *m*; *[vehicle, ship, engine]* vibration *f*. **to give a ~** *[person]* frissonner, frémir; *[vehicle, ship]* être ébranlé; **it gives me the ~s*** ça me donne des frissons; **he realized with a ~ that ...** il a frissonné *or* frémi, comprenant que ... . **2** *vi [person]* frissonner; *[thing]* vibrer. **I ~ to think what might have happened** je frémis rien qu'à la pensée de ce qui aurait pu se produire; **I ~ to think!** j'en frémis d'avance!

shuffle [ˈʃʌfl] **1** *n* (*fig*) **a cabinet (re)~** un remaniement ministériel. **2** *vt* **(a) to ~ one's feet** traîner les pieds. **(b)** *cards* battre; *dominoes* mêler; *papers* remuer. **3** *vi* **(a)** traîner les pieds. **to ~ in/out** *etc* entrer/sortir *etc* d'un pas traînant. **(b)** (*Cards*) battre (les cartes).

shun [ʃʌn] *vt place, temptation, person, publicity* fuir; *work, obligation* esquiver.

shunt [ʃʌnt] *vt* (*Rail*) (*direct*) aiguiller; (*divert*) détourner; (*move about*) manœuvrer; (*position*) garer. ♦ **shunting 1** *n* manœuvres *fpl* d'aiguillage; **2** *adj*: **~ing yard** voies *fpl* de garage et de triage.

shush [ʃʊʃ] **1** *excl* chut! **2** *vt* (*) faire chut à; (*silence*) faire taire.

shut [ʃʌt] *pret, ptp* **shut 1** *vt* (*gen*) fermer. **to ~ one's finger in a drawer** se pincer le doigt dans un tiroir; **to ~ sb in a room** enfermer qn dans une pièce; **~ your mouth!‡** la ferme!‡ **2** *vi [door, box, lid]* se fermer, fermer; *[museum, theatre, shop]* fermer. **the door ~** la porte s'est (re)fermée; **the door ~s badly** la porte ferme mal.

shut away *vt sep person, animal* enfermer;

valuables mettre sous clef.
shut down 1 *vi [business, theatre]* fermer (définitivement). **2** *vt sep lid* fermer, rabattre; *business, theatre* fermer (définitivement); *machine* arrêter.
shut in *vt sep* enfermer.
shut off *vt sep* **(a)** (*stop*) *electricity, engine, supplies* couper. **(b)** (*isolate*) *person* isoler (*from* de).
shut out *vt sep* **(a) he found himself ~ out** il s'est aperçu qu'il ne pouvait pas entrer; **I ~ the cat out** j'ai mis le chat dehors; **close the door and ~ out the noise** ferme la porte pour qu'on n'entende pas le bruit. **(b)** (*block*) *view* boucher; *memory* chasser de son esprit.
shut up 1 *vi* (*: *be quiet*) se taire. **2** *vt sep* **(a)** *factory, business, theatre, house* fermer. **(b)** *person, animal* enfermer; *valuables* mettre sous clef. **to ~ sb up in prison** mettre qn en prison. **(c)** (*: *silence*) faire taire.
♦ **shutdown** *n* fermeture *f*. ♦ **shut-in** *adj* enfermé.
shutter [ˈʃʌtəʳ] **1** *n* volet *m*; (*Phot*) obturateur *m*. **2** *adj*: **~ speed** vitesse *f* d'obturation. ♦ **shuttered** *adj house* aux volets fermés.
shuttle [ˈʃʌtl] **1** *n [loom, sewing machine]* navette *f*; (*fig: plane etc*) (avion *m etc* qui fait la) navette. **2** *adj* (*Aviat, Rail etc*) **~ service** service *m* de navette. **3** *vi [person, vehicle, boat]* faire la navette (*between* entre). **4** *vt*: **to ~ sb to and fro** envoyer qn à droite et à gauche; **to ~ sb back and forth** faire faire la navette à qn; **the papers were ~d from one department to another** les documents ont été renvoyés d'un service à l'autre. ♦ **shuttlecock** *n* volant *m* (*Badminton*).
shy¹ [ʃaɪ] **1** *adj* (*gen*) timide; (*unsociable*) sauvage. **to make sb feel ~** intimider qn; **don't be ~** ne fais pas le (*or* la) timide; **don't be ~ of saying** n'ayez pas peur de dire, n'hésitez pas à dire. **2** *vi [horse]* se cabrer (*at* devant). ♦ **shyly** *adv* timidement. ♦ **shyness** *n* timidité *f*.
shy² [ʃaɪ] *vt* (*throw*) lancer, jeter.
Siamese [ˌsaɪəˈmiːz] *adj* siamois. **~ twins** (frères) siamois *mpl*, (sœurs) siamoises *fpl*.
sibilant [ˈsɪbɪlənt] **1** *adj* sifflant. **2** *n* sifflante *f*.
sibling [ˈsɪblɪŋ] *n*: **one of his ~s** l'un de ses frères et sœurs; **Paul and Lucy are ~s** Paul et Lucie sont frère et sœur.
Sicily [ˈsɪsɪlɪ] *n* Sicile *f*.
sick [sɪk] **1** *adj* **(a)** (*ill*) *person* malade; *pallor* maladif. **he's a ~ man** c'est un malade; **he's off ~** il n'est pas là, il est malade; **to go ~** se faire porter malade; **to fall** *or* **take ~** tomber malade; (*vomiting*) **to be ~** vomir; **to feel ~** avoir mal au cœur; **a ~ feeling** un malaise; **I get ~ in planes** je suis malade en avion; **~ headache** migraine *f*. **(b)** (*fig*) *mind, imagination, joke* malsain; *humour* noir. **to be ~ at heart** avoir la mort dans l'âme; **to be ~ of sth/sb*** en avoir marre* de qch/qn; **to be ~ and tired of, to be ~ to death of*** en avoir par-dessus la tête de; **to be ~ of the sight of sth/sb*** en avoir marre* de voir qch/qn; **it makes me ~ to think that ...** ça me dégoûte de penser que ...; **~ benefit** assurance *f* maladie; **on ~ leave** en congé *m* de maladie; **on the ~ list** (*Admin*) porté malade; (*: *ill*) malade; **~ pay** indemnité *f* de maladie (*versée par l'employeur*).
2 *npl*: **the ~** les malades *mpl*.
sick up* *vt sep* vomir.
♦ **sickbay** *n* infirmerie *f*. ♦ **sickbed** *n* lit *m* de malade. ♦ **sicken 1** *vt* dégoûter; **2** *vi* tomber malade; **to ~en for sth** couver qch; **to ~en of** se lasser de. ♦ **sickening** *adj sight, smell* écœurant; (*fig*) *cruelty, crime* ignoble; *waste* dégoûtant; (*: *annoying*) *person, behaviour* exaspérant. ♦ **sickeningly** *adv*: **~eningly polite*** d'une politesse écœurante. ♦ **sickliness** *n [person]* état *m* maladif; *[cake]* goût *m* écœurant. ♦ **sickly** *adj person* maladif; *complexion* blafard; *climate* malsain; *plant* étiolé; *smile* faible; *colour, smell, cake* écœurant; **~ly sweet** douceâtre. ♦ **sickness 1** *n* maladie *f*; **there's a lot of ~ness in the village** il y a beaucoup de malades dans le village; (*vomiting*) **bouts of ~ness** vomissements *mpl*; **mountain ~ness** mal *m* des montagnes; **2** *adj*: **~ness benefit** (prestations *fpl* de l')assurance *f* maladie. ♦ **sickroom** *n* chambre *f* de malade.
sickle [ˈsɪkl] *n* faucille *f*.
side [saɪd] **1** *n* **(a)** *[person]* côté *m*; *[animal]* flanc *m*. **he had the phone by his ~** il avait le téléphone à côté de lui; **she was at** *or* **by his ~** elle était à ses côtés; **~ by ~** (*people*) côte à côte; (*things*) à côté l'un de l'autre; **~ of bacon** flèche *f* de lard; **~ of beef/mutton** quartier *m* de bœuf/mouton.
(b) (*as opp to top, bottom etc*) *[box, house, triangle etc]* côté *m*; *[ship, mountain]* flanc *m*; (*inside*) *[cave, ditch, box]* paroi *f*. **by the ~ of the church** à côté de *or* tout près de l'église; **go round the ~ of the house** contournez la maison.
(c) (*outer surface*) (*gen*) côté *m*; *[cube, record, coin]* côté, face *f*; (*fig*) *[matter, problem etc]* aspect *m*. *[garment, cloth]* **the right ~** l'endroit *m*; **the wrong ~** l'envers *m*; **right/wrong ~ out** à l'endroit/l'envers; **right/wrong ~ up** dans le bon/mauvais sens; (*on box etc*) **'this ~ up'** 'haut'; **write on both ~s of the paper** écrivez au recto et au verso; **three-~d** à trois côtés; **many-~d** multilatéral; **I've written 6 ~s** j'ai écrit 6 pages; (*fig*) **the other ~ of the coin** le revers de la médaille; **there are two ~s to every quarrel** dans toute querelle il y a deux points de vue; **he's got a nasty ~* to him** il a un côté très déplaisant.
(d) (*edge*) bord *m*. **by the ~ of** au bord de.
(e) (*lateral part*) *[street, town, face]* côté *m*. **on the other ~ of** de l'autre côté de; (*fig*) **the science ~ of the college** la section sciences du collège; **from all ~s, from every ~** de tous côtés, de toutes parts; **from ~ to ~** d'un côté à l'autre; **he moved to one ~** il s'est écarté; **to take sb on one ~** prendre qn à part; **to put sth to** *or* **on one ~** mettre qch de côté; **on this ~ of London** entre ici et Londres; **he's on the wrong ~ of 50** il a passé la cinquantaine; **he's on the right ~ of 50** il n'a pas encore 50 ans; **he makes a bit of money on the ~*** il se fait un peu d'argent en plus; **a cousin on his mother's ~** un cousin du côté de sa mère; (*fig*) **on the heavy/cold ~*** plutôt lourd/froid.
(f) (*team*) (*gen*) camp *m*, côté *m*; (*Sport*) équipe *f*; (*Pol etc*) parti *m*. **he's on our ~** il est avec nous; **we have time on our ~** nous avons le temps pour nous; **whose ~ are you on?** qui soutenez-vous?; **there are faults on both ~s** les deux côtés ont des torts; **to take ~s** prendre parti (*with sb* pour qn); **to pick** *or* **choose ~s** se former les camps; **he let the ~ down** il ne leur (*etc*) a pas fait honneur.
(g) (*conceit*) **he's got no ~*** ce n'est pas un crâneur*; **to put on ~*** crâner*.
2 *adj entrance, chapel, seat* latéral; (*fig*) *effect, issue* secondaire. **~ dish** plat *m* d'accompagnement; (*Phot*) **~ face** de profil; **~ glance** regard *m* de côté; **~ plate** petite assiette *f*; **~ road** route *f* transversale; **~ street** rue *f* transversale; **~ view** vue *f* de côté.
3 *vi*: **to ~ with sb** prendre parti pour qn.
♦ **sideboard** *n* buffet *m*. ♦ **sideboards** *or* (*US*) ♦ **sideburns** *npl* rouflaquettes* *fpl*. ♦ **sidecar** *n* side-car *m*. ♦ **sidekick*** *n* (*assistant*) sous-fifre* *m*; (*friend*) copain* *m*, copine* *f*. ♦ **sidelight** *n* (*Aut*) lanterne *f*; (*fig*) **it gives us a ~light on ...** cela nous donne un aperçu de .... ♦ **sideline** *n* **(a)** (*Sport, fig*) **on the ~lines** sur la touche; **(b)** activité *f* (*or* travail *m*) secondaire; **he sells wood as a ~line** il a aussi un petit commerce de bois; (*Comm*) **it's just a ~line** ce n'est pas notre spécialité. ♦ **sidelong** *adj* oblique, de côté. ♦ **sidesaddle** *adv* en amazone. ♦ **sideshows** *npl*

attractions *fpl.* ♦ **side-splitting*** *adj* tordant*. ♦ **side-step 1** *vt* éviter; **2** *vi* (*lit*) faire un pas de côté; (*fig*) rester évasif; (*Boxing*) esquiver. ♦ **sidetrack** *vt* (*fig*) faire dévier de son sujet; **to get ~tracked** s'écarter de son sujet. ♦ **sidewalk** *n* (*US*) trottoir *m.* ♦ **sideways 1** *adj* oblique, de côté; **2** *adv look, fit in* de côté; *walk* en crabe; *stand* de profil. ♦ **side-whiskers** *npl* favoris *mpl.* ♦ **siding** *n* (*Rail*) voie *f* de garage.

sidle ['saɪdl] *vi*: **to ~ in/out** *etc* entrer/sortir *etc* (*sideways*) de côté *or* (*furtively*) furtivement; **he ~d up to me** il s'est glissé vers moi.

siege [siːdʒ] *n* siège *m.* **in a state of ~** en état de siège.

sienna [sɪ'enə] *n* terre *f* de Sienne.

siesta [sɪ'estə] *n* sieste *f.* **to have a ~** faire une sieste.

sieve [sɪv] **1** *n* (*for coal, stones*) crible *m*; (*for sugar, flour, soil*) tamis *m*; (*for liquids*) passoire *f.* (*Culin*) **to rub through a ~** passer au tamis; **he's got a memory like a ~*** sa mémoire est une vraie passoire. **2** *vt* passer au crible; tamiser; passer.

sift [sɪft] **1** *vt* **(a)** *flour, sugar, sand* tamiser; *coal, stones, evidence* passer au crible. **to ~ flour on to sth** saupoudrer qch de farine. **(b)** (**~ out**) *facts, truth* dégager. **2** *vi* (*fig*) **to ~ through sth** examiner qch. ♦ **sifter** *n* saupoudreuse *f.*

sigh [saɪ] **1** *n* soupir *m.* **to heave a ~** pousser un soupir. **2** *vt* soupirer. **3** *vi* soupirer; *[wind]* gémir. **to ~ with relief** pousser un soupir de soulagement; **to ~ for sth** soupirer après qch; (*for sth lost: also* **~ over sth**) regretter qch. ♦ **sighing** *n* soupirs *mpl*; *[wind]* gémissements *mpl.*

sight [saɪt] **1** *n* **(a)** (*act of seeing etc*) vue *f.* **to have good/poor ~** avoir une bonne/mauvaise vue; **to lose one's ~** perdre la vue; **to know by ~** connaître de vue; **to shoot on** *or* **at ~** tirer à vue; **at first ~** à première vue; **love at first ~** le coup de foudre; **it was my first ~ of Paris** c'était la première fois que je voyais Paris; **at the ~ of** à la vue de, en voyant; **the train was still in ~** on voyait encore le train; **the end/a solution is in ~** on entrevoit la fin/une solution; **we live within ~ of the sea** de chez nous on voit la mer; **to come into ~** apparaître; **keep the luggage in ~, don't let the luggage out of your ~** ne perdez pas les bagages de vue; **out of ~** hors de vue; **to keep out of ~** (*vi*) ne pas se montrer; (*vt*) cacher; **it is out of ~** on ne le voit pas; **keep out of his ~!** qu'il ne te voie pas!; **to catch ~ of** apercevoir; **to lose ~ of sb/sth** perdre qn/qch de vue; **the ~ of the cathedral/of blood** *etc* la vue de la cathédrale/du sang *etc*; **I can't bear** *or* **stand the ~ of him** je ne peux pas le voir *or* le sentir*; **in the ~ of the law** devant la loi. **(b)** (*spectacle*) spectacle *m* (*also pej*). **it is a ~ to be seen** cela vaut la peine d'être vu; **to see the ~s** faire du tourisme, visiter la ville; **it's one of the ~s of Paris** c'est l'une des choses à voir à Paris; **it's not a pretty ~** ça n'est guère joli à voir; **it was a ~ for sore eyes** (*welcome*) c'était un spectacle à réjouir le cœur; (**pej*) c'était à en pleurer; **I must look a ~!** je dois avoir une de ces allures!* **(c)** (*on gun*) mire *f.* **to take ~** viser; **in one's ~s** dans sa ligne de tir; (*fig*) **to set one's ~s** viser (*on sth* qch). **(d)** (*phrases*) **not by a long ~** loin de là; **a far** *or* **long ~ better** infiniment mieux; **a ~ too clever*** bien trop malin.

2 *vt* apercevoir.

♦ **sighted 1** *adj* qui voit, doué de vision; **to be partially ~ed** avoir un certain degré de vision; **2** *npl*: **the ~ed** les voyants *mpl* (*lit*). ♦ **sighting** *n*: **numerous ~ings have been reported** de nombreuses personnes ont déclaré l'avoir vu. ♦ **sightly** *adj* beau à voir. ♦ **sightread** *vt* déchiffrer (*Mus*). ♦ **sightreading** *n* déchiffrage *m.* ♦ **sightseeing** *n* tourisme *m*; **to do some ~seeing, to go ~seeing** (*gen*) faire du tourisme; (*in town*) visiter la ville. ♦ **sightseer** *n* touriste *mf.*

sign [saɪn] **1** *n* **(a)** signe *m.* **they communicated by ~s** ils se parlaient par signes; **to make a ~ to sb** faire signe à qn (*to do* de faire); **to make the ~ of the Cross** faire le signe de la croix (*over* sur), (*cross o.s.*) se signer; **as a ~ of** en signe de; **it's a good/bad ~** c'est bon/mauvais signe; **a ~ of the times** un signe des temps; **a sure ~** un signe infaillible; **at the slightest ~ of** au moindre signe de; **there is no ~ of his agreeing** rien ne laisse à penser qu'il va accepter; **no ~ of life** aucun signe de vie; **there's no ~ of him anywhere** on n'arrive pas à le retrouver. **(b)** (*notice*) (*gen and for traffic*) panneau *m*; (*on inn, shop*) enseigne *f.* **2** *adj*: **~ language** langage *m* par signes; **in ~ language** par signes. **3** *vt* **(a)** *letter etc* signer. **to ~ one's name** signer; **he ~s himself John Smith** il signe 'John Smith'. **(b)** (*Ftbl etc*) *player* engager. **4** *vi* **(a)** signer. **you have to ~ for the key** vous devez signer pour obtenir la clef; **he ~ed for the parcel** il a signé le reçu de livraison du paquet; (*Ftbl*) **Smith has ~ed for Celtic** Smith a signé un contrat d'engagement avec le Celtic. **(b) to ~ to sb to do sth** faire signe à qn de faire qch.

sign away *vt sep* signer l'abandon de son droit sur.

sign in *vi* (*in factory etc*) pointer (à l'arrivée); (*in hotel*) signer le registre.

sign off *vi* (*in factory etc*) pointer (au départ); (*Rad, TV*) terminer l'émission.

sign on 1 *vi* (*Mil*) s'engager (*as* comme); (*Ind etc*) se faire embaucher (*as* comme); (*on arrival at work*) pointer (à l'arrivée); (*enrol*) s'inscrire. **I've ~ed on for German conversation** je me suis inscrit au cours de conversation allemande. **2** *vt sep employee* embaucher; (*Mil*) engager.

sign over *vt sep* céder par écrit (*to* à).

sign up *vi, vt sep* = **sign on.**

♦ **signpost 1** *n* poteau *m* indicateur; **2** *vt place* indiquer. ♦ **signposting** *n* signalisation *f.*

signal ['sɪgnl] **1** *n* (*gen*) signal *m* (*for* de). **at a prearranged ~** à un signal convenu; (*Naut*) **flag ~s** signaux par pavillons; **traffic ~s** feux *mpl* de circulation; (*Rad*) **station ~** indicatif *m* (de l'émetteur); (*Telec*) **I'm getting the engaged ~** ça sonne occupé; (*TV*) **the ~ is very weak** (*sound*) le son *or* (*picture*) l'image *f* est très faible; (*Mil*) **the S~s** les Transmissions *fpl.* **2** *adj* (*avant n*) *success* remarquable; *importance* capital. (*Rail*) **~ box** poste *m* d'aiguillage. **3** *vt message* communiquer par signaux. **to ~ sb on/through** *etc* faire signe à qn d'avancer/de passer *etc*; (*Aut*) **to ~ a turn** indiquer un changement de direction. **4** *vi* (*gen*) faire des signaux; (*Aut*) indiquer. **to ~ to sb** faire signe à qn (*to do* de faire). ♦ **signally** *adv* (*gen*) singulièrement; *fail* totalement. ♦ **signalman** *n* (*Rail*) aiguilleur *m.*

signature ['sɪgnətʃəʳ] **1** *n* **(a)** signature *f.* **to put one's ~ to sth** apposer sa signature à qch. **(b)** (*Mus: key* **~**) armature *f.* **2** *adj*: **~ tune** indicatif *m* musical. ♦ **signatory** *n* signataire *mf* (*to* de).

signet ['sɪgnɪt] *n* sceau *m.* **~ ring** chevalière *f.*

signify ['sɪgnɪfaɪ] **1** *vt* (*mean*) signifier (*that* que); (*indicate*) indiquer; (*make known*) indiquer, faire comprendre (*that* que); *one's approval* signifier. **2** *vi* avoir de l'importance. ♦ **significance** *n* (*meaning*) signification *f*; *[event, speech]* importance *f*, portée *f*; **that is of no significance** cela importe peu. ♦ **significant** *adj achievement, increase, amount* considérable; *event* important; *look* significatif; **it is significant that ...** il est significatif *or* révélateur que ... + *subj.* ♦ **significantly** *adv smile etc* d'une façon significative; *improve, change* considérablement; **significantly, he refused** fait révélateur, il a refusé. ♦ **signification** *n* signification *f.*

silence ['saɪləns] **1** *n* silence *m.* (*lit, fig*) **there was**

~ on a gardé le silence (*about* en ce qui concernait); **in ~** en silence; (*fig*) **to pass sth over in ~** passer qch sous silence. **2** *vt person, opposition* réduire au silence; *noise* étouffer; *conscience* faire taire. ♦ **silencer** *n* silencieux *m* (*dispositif*). ♦ **silent** *adj* (*gen*) silencieux; *film, reproach* muet; **it was as silent as the grave** il y avait un silence de mort; **to be** *or* **fall** *or* **remain silent** se taire; **silent 'h'** 'h' muet. ♦ **silently** *adv* silencieusement.

silhouette [ˌsɪluːˈet] **1** *n* silhouette *f.* **2** *vt*: **to be ~d against** se découper contre.

silicon [ˈsɪlɪkən] *n* silicium *m.* **~ chip** microplaquette *f,* plaquette *f* de silicium. ♦ **silicone** *n* silicone *f.* ♦ **silicosis** *n* silicose *f.*

silk [sɪlk] **1** *n* soie *f.* **2** *adj blouse etc* de *or* en soie. **~ factory** soierie *f* (*fabrique*); **~ industry** soierie (*industrie*); **~ manufacturer** fabricant *m* en soierie. ♦ **silkscreen printing** *n* sérigraphie *f.* ♦ **silkworm** *n* ver *m* à soie. ♦ **silky** *adj* soyeux; *voice* doucereux.

sill [sɪl] *n* rebord *m*; (*Aut*) bas *m* de marche.

silly [ˈsɪlɪ] *adj* (*stupid*) bête, idiot, stupide; (*ridiculous*) ridicule. **you ~ fool!** espèce d'idiot(e)!; **don't be ~** ne fais pas l'idiot(e); **to do sth ~** faire une bêtise. ♦ **silliness** *n* bêtise *f,* stupidité *f.*

silo [ˈsaɪləʊ] *n* silo *m.*

silt [sɪlt] *n* vase *f.*

silt up **1** *vi* (*with mud*) s'envaser; (*with sand*) s'ensabler. **2** *vt sep* envaser; ensabler.

silver [ˈsɪlvəʳ] **1** *n* (*metal*) argent *m*; (*~ware, cutlery etc*) argenterie *f.* (*money*) **have you got any ~?** est-ce que vous avez de la monnaie?; **£2 in ~** 2 livres en pièces d'argent. **2** *adj cutlery, jewellery etc* d'argent, en argent. **~ birch** bouleau *m* argenté; **~ coin** pièce *f* d'argent; **~ fir** sapin *m*; **~ foil, ~ paper** papier *m* d'argent; **~ gilt** plaqué *m* argent; **~ jubilee** vingt-cinquième anniversaire *m* (*d'un événement*); (*fig*) **to be born with a ~ spoon in one's mouth** naître avec une cuiller d'argent dans la bouche; **~ wedding** noces *fpl* d'argent. ♦ **silver-grey** *adj* argenté. ♦ **silver-haired** *adj* aux cheveux argentés. ♦ **silver-plate** *n* (*objects*) argenterie *f*; (*material*) plaqué *m* argent. ♦ **silver-plated** *adj* argenté. ♦ **silver-plating** *n* argenture *f.* ♦ **silverside** *n* tranche *f* (grasse) (*viande*). ♦ **silversmith** *n* orfèvre *mf.* ♦ **silverware** *n* argenterie *f.* ♦ **silvery** *adj colour, scales* argenté; *sound* argentin.

similar [ˈsɪmɪləʳ] *adj* semblable (*to* à); (*less strongly*) comparable (*to* à). **a ~ house** une maison presque pareille; **~ in size** de dimensions comparables; **the houses are so ~ that ...** les maisons sont si semblables que ...; **and ~ products** et produits similaires; **vehicles ~ to the bicycle** véhicules apparentés à la bicyclette. ♦ **similarity** [ˌsɪmɪˈlærɪtɪ] *n* ressemblance *f* (*to* avec; *between* entre), similarité *f* (*between* entre). ♦ **similarly** *adv* de la même façon; **and ~ly, ...** et de même ... .

simile [ˈsɪmɪlɪ] *n* comparaison *f* (*Literat*).

simmer [ˈsɪməʳ] **1** *vi* [*water*] frémir; [*vegetables, soup*] cuire à feu doux; (*fig*) (*with excitement*) être en ébullition; (*with rage/discontent*) bouillir de rage/de mécontentement; [*revolt, anger*] couver. **2** *vt* laisser frémir; faire cuire à feu doux.

simmer down* *vi* (*fig*) se calmer.

simper [ˈsɪmpəʳ] **1** *n* sourire *m* affecté. **2** *vi* minauder. ♦ **simpering** **1** *n* minauderies *fpl*; **2** *adj* minaudier.

simple [ˈsɪmpl] *adj* (*gen*) simple. **as ~ as ABC** simple comme bonjour; **he's a ~ labourer** c'est un simple ouvrier; **they're ~ people** ce sont des gens simples; **to make ~(r)** simplifier; **in ~ terms** *or* **language** pour parler simplement *or* clairement; **in ~ English** ≈ en bon français; **the ~ fact that ...** le simple fait que ...; **the ~ truth** la vérité pure et simple; **for the ~ reason that ...** pour la seule *or* simple raison que ...; **~ equation** équation *f* du premier degré; (*Fin*) **~ interest** intérêts *mpl* simples; **a ~ Simon** un nigaud; **he's a bit ~** il est un peu simple d'esprit. ♦ **simple-minded** *adj* simple d'esprit. ♦ **simple-mindedness** *n* simplicité *f* d'esprit. ♦ **simpleton** *n* nigaud(e) *m(f).* ♦ **simplicity** *n* simplicité *f.* ♦ **simplification** *n* simplification *f.* ♦ **simplify** *vt* simplifier. ♦ **simplistic** *adj* simpliste. ♦ **simply** *adv talk, live* simplement, avec simplicité; (*only*) (tout) simplement; (*absolutely*) **you simply MUST come!** il faut absolument que vous veniez! (*subj*).

simulate [ˈsɪmjʊleɪt] *vt* simuler. ♦ **simulation** *n* simulation *f.* ♦ **simulator** *n* simulateur *m.*

simultaneous [ˌsɪməlˈteɪnɪəs] *adj* (*gen*) simultané. (*Math*) **~ equations** équations *fpl* équivalentes. ♦ **simultaneity** *n* simultanéité *f.* ♦ **simultaneously** *adv* simultanément; **~ly with** en même temps que.

sin [sɪn] **1** *n* péché *m.* **~s of omission/commission** péchés par omission/par action; **a ~ against God** un manquement à la loi de Dieu; **it's a ~ to do that** (*Rel*) c'est un péché que de faire cela; (**fig*) c'est un crime de faire cela. **2** *vi* pécher (*against* contre). ♦ **sinful** *adj* (*gen*) coupable; *act, waste* scandaleux. ♦ **sinfully** *adv* d'une façon coupable; scandaleusement. ♦ **sinfulness** *n* [*person*] péchés *mpl*; [*deed*] caractère *m* coupable *or* scandaleux. ♦ **sinner** *n* pécheur *m,* -eresse *f.*

since [sɪns] **1** *conj* **(a)** (*in time*) depuis que. **~ I have been here** depuis que je suis ici; **ever ~ I met him** depuis que je l'ai rencontré; **it's a week ~ I saw him** cela fait une semaine que je ne l'ai pas vu. **(b)** (*because*) puisque, comme. **2** *adv* depuis. **he has not been here ~** il n'est pas venu depuis; **he has been my friend ever ~** il est resté mon ami depuis ce moment-là; **not long ~** il y a peu de temps. **3** *prep* depuis. **~ arriving** *or* **his arrival** depuis son arrivée, depuis qu'il est arrivé; **I have been waiting ~ 10 o'clock** j'attends depuis 10 heures; **~ then** depuis; **ever ~ that we ...** depuis que cela s'est produit nous ...; **how long is it ~ the accident?** il s'est passé combien de temps depuis l'accident?

sincere [sɪnˈsɪəʳ] *adj* sincère. **are they ~ in their desire to help us?** est-ce que leur désir de nous aider est vraiment sincère? ♦ **sincerely** *adv* sincèrement; (*letter-ending*) **Yours ~ly** ≈ Je vous prie d'agréer, Monsieur (*or* Madame *etc*), l'expression de mes sentiments les meilleurs; (*less formally*) cordialement à vous, bien à vous. ♦ **sincerity** [sɪnˈserɪtɪ] *n* sincérité *f.*

sine [saɪn] *n* sinus *m* (*Math*).

sinecure [ˈsaɪnɪkjʊəʳ] *n* sinécure *f.*

sinew [ˈsɪnjuː] *n* (*Anat*) tendon *m.* **~s** (*muscles*) muscles *mpl*; (*strength*) force *f.* ♦ **sinewy** *adj* nerveux.

sing [sɪŋ] *pret* **sang**, *ptp* **sung** **1** *vt* chanter. **2** *vi* [*person, bird, kettle*] chanter; [*ears*] bourdonner; [*wind*] siffler. **to ~ like a lark** chanter comme un rossignol; **to ~ soprano** chanter soprano.

sing out* *vi* (*call*) appeler (bien fort).

♦ **singer** *n* chanteur *m,* -euse *f.* ♦ **singing** **1** *n* [*person, bird*] chant *m*; [*kettle, wind*] sifflement *m*; (*in ears*) bourdonnement *m*; **2** *adj lessons, teacher* de chant. ♦ **singsong** *n*: **to have a ~song** chanter en chœur; **to repeat sth in a ~song (voice)** répéter qch sur deux tons.

singe [sɪndʒ] **1** *vt* brûler légèrement; *cloth, clothes* roussir; *poultry* flamber. **2** *n* légère brûlure.

single [ˈsɪŋgl] **1** *adj* **(a)** (*only one*) seul (*before n*). **a ~ rose in the garden** une seule rose dans le jardin; **he gave her a ~ rose** il lui a donné une rose; **if there is a ~ objection** s'il y a une seule *or* la moindre objection; **the ~ survivor** le seul *or* l'unique survivant; (*Rail*) **~ track** voie *f* unique;

every ~ day tous les jours sans exception; **not a ~ person spoke** pas une seule personne n'a parlé; **I didn't see a ~ soul** je n'ai vu personne; **I haven't a ~ moment to lose** je n'ai pas une minute à perdre; **a** *or* **one ~ department should deal with it all** un service unique devrait traiter tout cela. **(b)** (*not double etc*) *knot, flower* simple. **a ~ ticket** un aller simple (*to* pour); **~ fare** prix *m* d'un aller simple; **~ bed** lit *m* d'une personne; **~ room** chambre *f* pour une personne; (*Typ*) **in ~ spacing** à simple interligne. **(c)** (*unmarried*) célibataire. **~ people** célibataires *mpl*.

2 *n* **(a)** (*Tennis*) **~s** simple *m*; **ladies' ~s** simple dames. **(b)** (*Rail etc: ticket*) aller *m* simple. **(c)** (*record*) **a ~** un 45 tours.

single out *vt sep* (*distinguish*) distinguer; (*choose*) choisir.

♦ **single-breasted** *adj* (*Dress*) droit. ♦ **single-decker** *n* autobus *m* sans impériale. ♦ **single-engined** *adj* monomoteur. ♦ **single-handed 1** *adv* tout seul, sans aucune aide; **2** *adj achievement* fait sans aide; *sailing, voyage* en solitaire. ♦ **single-minded** *adj person, attempt* résolu; *determination* tenace; **to be ~-minded about sth** concentrer tous ses efforts sur qch. ♦ **singleness** *n*: **~ness of purpose** ténacité *f*. ♦ **single-party** *adj* (*Pol*) à parti unique. ♦ **single-seater aeroplane** *n* (avion *m*) monoplace *m*. ♦ **singleton** *n* singleton *m*. ♦ **singly** *adv* séparément, un(e) à un(e).

singlet ['sɪŋglɪt] *n* maillot *m* de corps.

singular ['sɪŋgjʊləʳ] **1** *adj* **(a)** (*Gram*) *noun, verb* au singulier; *form, ending* du singulier. **the masculine ~** le masculin singulier. **(b)** (*outstanding, strange*) singulier. **2** *n* (*Gram*) singulier *m*. **in the ~** au singulier. ♦ **singularity** *n* singularité *f*. ♦ **singularly** *adv* singulièrement.

sinister ['sɪnɪstəʳ] *adj* sinistre; (*Heraldry*) sénestre. ♦ **sinisterly** *adv* sinistrement.

sink[1] [sɪŋk] *pret* **sank**, *ptp* **sunk 1** *vi* (*in water*) couler; (*fig: into despair, sleep*) sombrer (*into* dans); *[ground]* s'affaisser; *[sun]* se coucher; *[foundation, building]* se tasser; *[level, river]* baisser; *[prices, sales, temperature]* baisser (beaucoup); *[shares, the dollar]* tomber (*to* à). **to ~ to the bottom** couler au fond; **to ~ like a stone** couler à pic; (*fig*) **it was ~ or swim** il fallait bien s'en sortir* tout seul; **to ~ out of sight** disparaître; **to ~ to one's knees** tomber à genoux; **to ~ to the ground** s'affaisser; **he sank into a chair** il s'est laissé tomber dans un fauteuil; **he sank into the mud** il s'est enfoncé dans la boue; **the water slowly sank into the ground** l'eau a pénétré lentement dans le sol; (*dying*) **he is ~ing fast** il baisse rapidement; **he has sunk in my estimation** il a baissé dans mon estime; **his voice sank** sa voix s'est faite plus basse; **his heart sank at the thought** il a été pris de découragement à cette idée; **it's enough to make your heart ~** c'est à vous démoraliser *or* à vous donner le cafard*.

2 *vt* **(a)** *ship* couler; *object* faire couler au fond; (*fig*) *project, book, person* couler. (*fig*) **they sank their differences** ils ont enterré leurs querelles; **sunk in thought/despair** plongé dans ses pensées/le désespoir; **I'm sunk*** je suis fichu*. **(b)** *mine, well, foundations* creuser; *pipe etc* noyer; *stake* enfoncer (*into* dans). (*Golf*) **to ~ the ball** faire entrer la balle dans le trou; (*fig*) **to ~ a lot of money in a project** placer beaucoup d'argent dans une entreprise.

sink back *vi [object in water]* retomber; *[person in chair etc]* se laisser retomber.

sink down *vi*: **to ~ down into a chair** se laisser tomber dans un fauteuil; **to ~ down on one's knees** tomber à genoux; **to ~ down out of sight** disparaître.

sink in *vi [person, post etc]* s'enfoncer; *[water, ointment etc]* pénétrer; (*fig*) *[explanation]* rentrer; *[remark]* faire son effet. **it hasn't really sunk in yet** il *etc* ne réalise* pas encore; **it took a long time to ~ in** il *etc* a mis longtemps à comprendre.

♦ **sinking 1** *adj*: **to have a ~ing feeling** avoir un serrement de cœur; (*stronger*) avoir la mort dans l'âme; **to have a ~ing feeling that ...** avoir le pénible pressentiment que ...; **2** *n* (*shipwreck*) naufrage *m*.

sink[2] [sɪŋk] **1** *n* évier *m*. **2** *adj*: **~ tidy** coin *m* d'évier (*ustensile ménager*); **~ unit** bloc-évier *m*.

Sino- ['saɪnəʊ] *pref* sino-.

sinuous ['sɪnjʊəs] *adj* sinueux.

sinus ['saɪnəs] *n* sinus *m inv* (*Med*). ♦ **sinusitis** *n* sinusite *f*.

sip [sɪp] **1** *n* petite gorgée *f*. **a ~ of rum** une goutte de rhum. **2** *vt* boire à petites gorgées.

siphon ['saɪfən] **1** *n* siphon *m*. **2** *vt* siphonner.

siphon off *vt sep liquid* siphonner; (*fig*) *people etc* séparer; *profits, funds* canaliser, (*illegally*) détourner.

sir [sɜːʳ] *n* monsieur *m*. **yes, ~** oui, Monsieur; (*to army officer*) oui, mon capitaine (*or* mon lieutenant *etc*); (*to surgeon*) oui, docteur; (*in letter*) **(Dear) S~** Monsieur; **S~ John Smith** sir John Smith.

siren ['saɪərən] *n* sirène *f*.

sirloin ['sɜːlɔɪn] *n* aloyau *m*. **a ~ steak** un bifteck dans l'aloyau.

sisal ['saɪsəl] *n* sisal *m*.

sissy* ['sɪsɪ] *n* (*coward*) poule *f* mouillée. (*effeminate*) **he's a bit of a ~** il est un peu efféminé.

sister ['sɪstəʳ] **1** *n* **(a)** sœur *f*. **(b)** (*Rel*) (bonne) sœur *f*. **yes, ~** oui, ma sœur; **S~ Mary** sœur Marie. **(c)** (*Brit Med*) infirmière *f* en chef. **yes, ~** oui, Madame (*or* Mademoiselle). **2** *adj*: **~ nations/organizations** nations *fpl*/organisations *fpl* sœurs; **~ peoples/countries** peuples *mpl*/pays *mpl* frères; **~ ship** sister-ship *m*. ♦ **sisterhood** *n* fraternité *f*. ♦ **sister-in-law** *n* belle-sœur *f*. ♦ **sisterly** *adj* de sœur, fraternel.

sit [sɪt] *pret, ptp* **sat 1** *vi* **(a) to ~ (down)** s'asseoir; **to be ~ting (down)** être assis; (*to dog*) **~!** assis!; **~ by me** assieds-toi près de moi; **she just ~s at home** elle reste chez elle à ne rien faire; **he was ~ting over his books all evening** il a passé toute la soirée dans ses livres; **to ~ through a play** *etc* assister à une pièce *etc* jusqu'au bout; **don't just ~ there, DO something!** ne reste pas là à ne rien faire!; **to ~ still/straight** se tenir tranquille/droit; **to ~ tight** ne pas bouger; (*fig*) **to be ~ting pretty*** tenir le bon bout*; **to ~ for one's portrait/for an artist** poser pour son portrait/pour un artiste; **to ~ on a committee** être membre d'un comité; **to ~ for an exam** passer un examen, se présenter à un examen; (*Parl*) **he ~s for Moordown** il est (le) député de Moordown. **(b)** *[bird, insect]* se poser, se percher. **to be ~ting** être perché, (*on eggs*) couver; **to ~ on eggs** couver des œufs. **(c)** *[committee, assembly etc]* être en séance, siéger. **the committee is ~ting now** le comité est en séance; **it ~s from November to June** il siège de novembre à juin. **(d)** *[dress, coat etc]* tomber (*on sb* sur qn).

2 *vt* **(a)** (**~ down**) *child, invalid* asseoir, installer; *guest* faire asseoir. **(b)** *exam* passer, se présenter à.

sit about, sit around *vi* rester assis (à ne rien faire), traîner.

sit back *vi* (*in an armchair*) se caler. **to ~ back and do nothing about it** s'abstenir de faire quoi que ce soit.

sit down 1 *vi* s'asseoir; (*at table*) s'attabler. **to be ~ting down** être assis; (*fig*) **to ~ down under an insult** encaisser* une insulte. **2** *vt sep* asseoir.

sit in *vi* **(a) to ~ in on a discussion** assister à une discussion (sans y prendre part). **(b)** *[demonstrators]* **to ~ in in an office** occuper un bureau.

sit on* *vt fus* (*fig*) **(a)** (*keep secret*) *news, facts,*

report garder secret; (*not pass on*) *file, document* garder pour soi. **(b)** *person* (*silence*) faire taire; (*snub*) remettre à sa place.
sit out *vt sep lecture, play* rester jusqu'à la fin de.
sit up 1 *vi* **(a)** (~ *upright*) se redresser. **to be ~ting up** être assis bien droit; **he was ~ting up in bed** il était assis dans son lit; **you can ~ up now** vous pouvez vous asseoir maintenant; (*fig*) **to make sb ~ up** secouer *or* étonner qn; (*fig*) **to ~ up and take notice** se secouer; (*after illness*) reprendre intérêt à la vie. **(b)** (*stay up*) ne pas se coucher. **to ~ up late** se coucher tard; **to ~ up all night** ne pas se coucher de la nuit; **to ~ up with an invalid** veiller un malade. **2** *vt sep doll, child* asseoir.
♦ **sit-down** *adj*: **to have a ~-down lunch** déjeuner à table; **~-down strike** grève *f* sur le tas. ♦ **sit-in** *n* *[demonstrators]* sit-in *m inv*; *[workers]* grève *f* sur le tas; **to hold a ~-in** (*gen*) occuper les lieux; *[workers]* faire une grève sur le tas. ♦ **sitter** *n* (*Art*) modèle *m*; (*baby-~ter*) baby-sitter *mf*. ♦ **sitting 1** *n [committee etc]* séance *f*; (*for portrait*) séance de pose; (*in canteen etc*) service *m*; **2** *adj tenant* en possession des lieux; (*fig*) **~ting duck*** victime *f* facile; (*Parl*) **~ting member** député *m* en exercice; **~ting room** salon *m*.
sitcom* ['sɪtkɒm] *n* (*Rad, TV etc*) comédie *f* de situation.
site [saɪt] **1** *n [town, building]* emplacement *m*; (*Archeol*) site *m*; (*Constr*) chantier *m*; (*camp* ~) camping *m*. **the ~ of the battle** le champ de bataille. **2** *vt* placer, situer.
situate ['sɪtjʊeɪt] *vt* (*locate*) *building, town* placer; (*put into perspective*) *problem, event* situer. **the house is ~d in the country** la maison se trouve *or* est située à la campagne; **we are rather badly ~d as there is no bus** nous sommes assez mal situés car il n'y a pas d'autobus; (*fig*) **he is rather badly ~d** il est en assez mauvaise posture; **I am well ~d to do that** je suis bien placé pour faire cela; **how are you ~d for money?** est-ce que tu as besoin d'argent? ♦ **situation 1** *n* (*all senses*) situation *f*; **in a very difficult situation** dans une situation très difficile; **to save the situation** sauver la situation; **'situations vacant/wanted'** 'offres *fpl*/demandes *fpl* d'emploi'; **2** *adj*: **situation comedy** comédie *f* de situation.
six [sɪks] **1** *adj* six *inv*. **he is ~ (years old)** il a six ans; **he lives in number ~** il habite au (numéro) six. **2** *n* six *m inv*. **there were about ~** il y en avait six environ; **~ of the girls came** six des filles sont venues; **there are ~ of us** nous sommes six; **all ~ of us left** nous sommes partis tous les six; **it is ~ o'clock** il est six heures; **come at ~** venez à six heures; **it struck ~** six heures ont sonné; **they are sold in ~es** cela se vend par (lots *or* paquets de) six; **the children arrived in ~es** les enfants sont arrivés par groupes de six; **he lives at ~ Churchill Street** il habite (au) six rue Churchill; (*fig*) **to be at ~es and sevens** *[books, houses etc]* être sens dessus dessous; *[person]* être tout retourné*; (*fig*) **it's ~ of one and half a dozen of the other** c'est du pareil au même*. ♦ **sixfold 1** *adj* sextuple; **2** *adv* au sextuple. ♦ **six-footer*** *n* ≃ grand *m* d'un mètre quatre-vingts. ♦ **sixish** *adj*: **he is ~ish** il a dans les six ans; **he came at ~ish** il est venu vers six heures. ♦ **six-pack** *n* pack *m* de six. ♦ **six-shooter** *n* pistolet *m* automatique. ♦ **six-sided** *adj* hexagonal. ♦ **sixteen** *adj, n* seize (*m*) *inv*. ♦ **sixteenth** *adj, n* seizième (*mf*); (*fraction*) seizième *m*. ♦ **sixth 1** *adj* sixième; **to be ~th in a competition/in German** être sixième à un concours/en allemand; **she was the ~th to arrive** elle est arrivée la sixième; **Charles the S~th** Charles Six; **the ~th of November, November the ~th** le six novembre; (*fig*) **~th sense** sixième sens *m*; **2** *n* sixième *mf*; (*fraction*) sixième *m*; (*Mus*) sixte *f*; **he wrote on the ~th** il a écrit le six; (*Scol*) **the lower ~th** ≃ la classe de première; **the upper ~th** ≃ la classe terminale; **3** *adv* **(a)** (*in race, exam, competition*) en sixième place; **he came** *or* **was placed ~th** il s'est classé sixième; **(b)** (*sixthly*) sixièmement. ♦ **sixthly** *adv* sixièmement, en sixième lieu. ♦ **sixtieth** *adj, n* soixantième (*mf*); (*fraction*) soixantième *m*. ♦ **sixty** *adj, n* soixante (*m*) *inv*; **about ~ty** une soixantaine, environ soixante; **about ~ty books** une soixantaine de livres; **he is about ~ty** il a une soixantaine d'années; **to be in one's ~ties** avoir la soixantaine, être sexagénaire; (*1960s etc*) **in the ~ties** dans les années soixante; **the temperature was in the ~ties** ≃ il faisait entre quinze et vingt degrés; (*Aut*) **to do ~ty*** ≃ faire du cent (à l'heure). ♦ **sixty-first** *adj, n* soixante et unième (*mf*); (*fraction*) soixante et unième *m*. ♦ **sixty-four** *adj* (*fig*) **that's the ~ty-four (thousand) dollar question*** c'est toute la question. ♦ **sixty-odd*** *adj, n*: **there were ~ty-odd** il y en avait soixante et quelques*. ♦ **sixty-one** *adj, n* soixante et un (*m*) *inv*. ♦ **sixty-second** *adj, n* soixante-deuxième (*mf*). ♦ **sixty-two** *adj, n* soixante-deux (*m*) *inv*. ♦ **six-year-old 1** *adj child, horse* de six ans; *house, car* vieux de six ans; **2** *n* (*child/horse*) enfant *mf*/cheval *m* de six ans.
size[1] [saɪz] **1** *n* (*for plaster etc*) colle *f*. **2** *vt* encoller.
size[2] [saɪz] *n* **(a)** *[person, animal, sb's head, hands]* taille *f*; *[room, building, car, chair, parcel]* dimensions *fpl*; *[egg, fruit, jewel]* grosseur *f*; *[book, photograph, sheet of paper, envelope]* taille, dimensions; (*format*) format *m*; *[sum]* montant *m*; *[estate, country, difficulty]* étendue *f*; *[operation, campaign]* envergure *f*. **medium-~d** de taille (*or* grosseur *etc*) moyenne; *[packet, tube etc]* **the small/large ~** le petit/grand modèle; **the ~ of the town** l'importance *f* de la ville; **building of vast ~** bâtiment de belles dimensions; **it's the ~ of a brick** c'est de la taille d'une brique; **it's the ~ of a walnut** c'est de la grosseur d'une noix; **it's the ~ of a house/an elephant** c'est grand comme une maison/un éléphant; **he's about your ~** il est à peu près de la même taille que vous; (*fig*) **that's about the ~ of it!** c'est à peu près ça!; **he cut the wood to ~** il a coupé le bois à la dimension voulue. **(b)** *[garment]* taille *f*; *[shoes, gloves]* pointure *f*; *[shirt]* encolure *f*. **what ~ are you?, what ~ do you take?** (*in dress etc*) quelle taille faites-vous?; (*in shoes, gloves*) quelle pointure faites-vous?; (*in hats*) quel est votre tour de tête?; **what ~ of collar or shirt?** quelle encolure?; **I take ~ 12** je prends du 12; **hip ~** tour *m* de hanches; **I take ~ 5 shoes** ≃ je fais du 38.
size up *vt sep person* juger; *situation* mesurer; *problem* mesurer l'étendue de.
♦ **siz(e)able** *adj dog, building, estate* assez grand; *egg, fruit, jewel* assez gros; *operation* assez important; *sum, problem* assez considérable.
sizzle ['sɪzl] **1** *vi* grésiller. **2** *n* grésillement *m*.
skate[1] [skeɪt] *n* (*fish*) raie *f*.
skate[2] [skeɪt] **1** *n* patin *m*. (*fig*) **get your ~s on!*** dépêche-toi! **2** *vi* patiner. **to ~ across/down** *etc* traverser/descendre *etc* en patinant; **to go skating** (*ice*) faire du patin *or* du patinage; (*roller*) faire du patin à roulettes; (*fig*) **it went skating across the room** cela a glissé à travers la pièce.
skate over, skate round *vt fus problem, objection* glisser sur.
♦ **skateboard** *n* planche *f* à roulettes. ♦ **skater** *n* (*ice*) patineur *m*, -euse *f*; (*roller*) personne *f* qui fait du skating. ♦ **skating 1** *n* (*ice*) patinage *m*; (*roller*) patinage à roulettes; **2** *adj*: **skating rink** (*ice*) patinoire *f*; (*roller*) skating *m*.
skein [skeɪn] *n [wool etc]* écheveau *m*.
skeleton ['skelɪtn] **1** *n [person, building, ship, model etc]* squelette *m*; *[plan, novel etc]* schéma *m*. **a walking ~** un cadavre ambulant; **staff**

reduced to a ~ personnel réduit au strict minimum; (*fig*) **the** ~ **at the feast** le *or* la trouble-fête *inv*; (*fig*) **the** ~ **in the cupboard** la honte cachée de la famille. **2** *adj army, staff* squelettique (*fig*); *map* schématique. ~ **key** passe(-partout) *m inv*; *[proposals etc]* ~ **outline** résumé *m*. ♦ **skeletal** *adj* squelettique.

skeptic(al) ['skeptɪk(əl)] (*US*) = **sceptic(al).**

sketch [sketʃ] **1** *n* **(a)** (*drawing*) croquis *m*, esquisse *f*; (*fig*) *[ideas, proposals etc]* aperçu *m*, ébauche *f*. **a rough** ~ (*drawing*) une ébauche; (*fig: of one's plans etc*) un aperçu. **(b)** (*Theat*) sketch *m*, saynète *f*. **2** *adj*: ~**(ing) book/pad** carnet *m*/bloc *m* à dessins; ~ **map** carte faite à main levée. **3** *vi* faire des croquis. **4** *vt view, castle, figure* faire un croquis *or* une esquisse de; *map* faire à main levée; (*fig*: ~ **out**) *ideas, novel, plan* ébaucher, esquisser.

sketch in *vt sep detail* ajouter.

♦ **sketchily** *adv answer* incomplètement; *know* superficiellement. ♦ **sketchy** *adj* (*gen*) incomplet; *knowledge* superficiel.

skewer ['skjʊəʳ] **1** *n* (*for roast etc*) broche *f*; (*for kebabs*) brochette *f*. **2** *vt* embrocher.

ski [ski:] **1** *n* ski *m* (*équipement*); (*Aviat*) patin *m*. **2** *adj school, clothes* de ski. ~ **binding** fixation *f*; ~ **boot** chaussure *f* de ski; ~**(ing) instructor** moniteur *m*, -trice *f* de ski; ~ **lift** remonte-pente *m inv*; ~**(ing) pants** *or* **trousers** fuseau *m* (de ski); ~ **resort** station *f* de ski; ~ **run** piste *f* de ski; ~ **stick** bâton *m* de ski; ~ **tow** téléski *m*. **3** *vi* faire du ski, skier. **to go** ~**ing** faire du ski; (*as holiday*) partir aux sports d'hiver; **to** ~ **down a slope** descendre une pente à skis. ♦ **skier** *n* skieur *m*, -euse *f*. ♦ **skiing 1** *n* ski *m* (*sport*); **2** *adj clothes, school* de ski; *holiday* aux sports d'hiver; **to go on a** ~**ing holiday** partir aux sports d'hiver. ♦ **skijump** *n* (*place*) tremplin *m* de ski. ♦ **skijumping** *n* saut *m* à skis.

skid [skɪd] **1** *n* (*Aut*) dérapage *m*. **to get** *or* **go into a** ~ déraper; **to get out of a** ~, **to correct a** ~ redresser un dérapage. **2** *adj* (*US*) ~ **row** quartier *m* de clochards. **3** *vi* déraper. **to** ~ **to a halt** s'arrêter en dérapant; **to** ~ **into a tree** déraper et percuter un arbre; **the toy** ~**ded across the room** le jouet a glissé jusqu'à l'autre bout de la pièce. ♦ **skidlid*** *n* casque *m* (de moto). ♦ **skidmark** *n* trace *f* de dérapage. ♦ **skidpan** *n* piste savonnée.

skiff [skɪf] *n* skiff *m*, yole *f*.

skill [skɪl] *n* **(a)** (*ability*) habileté *f*, adresse *f* (*at* à); (*gen manual*) dextérité *f*; (*talent*) savoir-faire *m*, talent *m* (*at* en matière de). **his** ~ **in persuading them** l'habileté dont il a fait preuve en les persuadant; **lack of** ~ maladresse *f*. **(b)** (*in craft etc*) technique *f*. **it's a** ~ **that has to be acquired** c'est une technique qui s'apprend; **we could make good use of his** ~**s** ses capacités *or* ses compétences nous seraient bien utiles. ♦ **skilful,** (*US*) **skillful** *adj* habile, adroit (*at doing* à faire). ♦ **skil(l)fully** *adv* habilement, adroitement. ♦ **skil(l)fulness** *n* habileté *f*, adresse *f*. ♦ **skilled** *adj* **(a)** *person* habile, adroit (*in, at doing* pour faire; *in, at sth* en qch); *movement, stroke* adroit; ~**ed in diplomacy** qui a beaucoup d'expérience en diplomatie; ~**ed in the art of** versé dans l'art de; **(b)** (*Ind*) *worker, engineer etc* qualifié; *work* de spécialiste; **it's a** ~**ed job** (*gen*) ça demande beaucoup d'adresse; (*Ind*) c'est un travail de spécialiste.

skillet ['skɪlɪt] *n* poêlon *m*.

skim [skɪm] **1** *vt* **(a)** *milk* écrémer; *soup* écumer. **to** ~ **the cream/scum/grease from sth** écrémer/écumer/dégraisser qch; ~**(med) milk** lait *m* écrémé. **(b)** *stone* faire ricocher (*across* sur). *[bird etc]* **to** ~ **the ground/water** raser le sol/l'eau. **2** *vi*: **to** ~ **across the water/along the ground** raser l'eau/le sol; (*fig*) **to** ~ **through a book** parcourir un livre.

skim off *vt sep cream, grease* enlever; (*fig*) *best pupils etc* mettre à part.

skimp [skɪmp] *vti* (*also* ~ **on**) *butter, cloth etc* lésiner sur; *praise, thanks* être chiche de; *piece of work* faire à la va-vite. ♦ **skimpily** *adv serve, provide* avec parcimonie; *live* chichement. ♦ **skimpiness** *n* (*gen*) insuffisance *f*; *[dress etc]* ampleur *f* insuffisante. ♦ **skimpy** *adj* (*gen*) insuffisant; *dress* étriqué.

skin [skɪn] **1** *n* (*gen*) peau *f*; *[boat, aircraft]* revêtement *m*; (*for duplicating*) stencil *m*; (*for wine*) outre *f*. **fair -**~**ned** à la peau claire; **next to the** ~ à même la peau; **wet** *or* **soaked to the** ~ trempé jusqu'aux os; **the snake casts its** ~ le serpent mue; **rabbit** ~ peau de lapin; **potatoes in their** ~**s** pommes de terre *fpl* en robe des champs; **banana** ~ peau de banane; (*fig*) **to be** ~ **and bone** n'avoir que la peau sur les os; **to escape by the** ~ **of one's teeth** l'échapper belle; **we caught the train by the** ~ **of our teeth** nous avons attrapé le train de justesse; (*fig*) **to have a thick/thin** ~ être insensible/susceptible; (*fig*) **to get under sb's** ~* taper sur les nerfs à qn*; (*fig*) **I've got you under my** ~* je t'ai dans la peau‡; (*fig*) **it's no** ~ **off my nose‡** (*does not hurt me*) pour ce que ça me coûte!; (*does not concern me*) ce n'est pas mon problème. **2** *adj disease, colour* de (la) peau. **3** *vt animal* écorcher; *fruit, vegetable* éplucher. (*fig*) **I'll** ~ **him alive!*** je vais l'écorcher tout vif!; **to** ~ **one's knee** s'écorcher le genou. ♦ **skin-deep** *adj* superficiel; **it's only** ~**-deep** ça n'est pas bien sérieux. ♦ **skin diver** *n* plongeur *m*, -euse *f* sous-marin(e). ♦ **skin diving** *n* plongée sous-marine. ♦ **skinflick‡** *n* film *m* porno* *inv*. ♦ **skinflint** *n* radin(e)* *m(f)*. ♦ **skinful‡** *n*: **to have (had) a** ~**ful** être soûl*. ♦ **skinhead** *n* jeune homme *m* aux cheveux tondus ras; (*thug*) jeune voyou *m*. ♦ **skinny** *adj* maigrichon; *sweater* moulant; (*Fashion*) **the** ~**ny look** la mode ultra-mince. ♦ **skintight** *adj* très ajusté.

skip¹ [skɪp] **1** *n* petit bond, petit saut. **2** *vi* sautiller; (*with rope*) sauter à la corde. **to** ~ **in/out** *etc* entrer/sortir *etc* en sautillant; (*fig*) **he** ~**ped off without paying** il a décampé sans payer; **he** ~**ped over that point** il a glissé sur ce point; **to** ~ **from one subject to another** sauter d'un sujet à un autre. **3** *vt* (*omit*) *page, class, meal* sauter. ~ **it!*** laisse tomber!*; **to** ~ **school** sécher les cours. ♦ **skipping** *n* saut *m* à la corde. ♦ **skipping rope,** (*US*) **skip rope** *n* corde *f* à sauter.

skip² [skɪp] *n* (*container*) benne *f*.

skipper ['skɪpəʳ] *n* (*Naut*) capitaine *m*, patron *m*; (*Sport**) capitaine.

skirmish ['skɜ:mɪʃ] *n* escarmouche *f*.

skirt [skɜ:t] **1** *n* jupe *f*. **2** *vti* (~ **round**) *town, obstacle* contourner; *difficulty* esquiver. ♦ **skirting (board)** *n* plinthe *f*.

skit [skɪt] *n* parodie *f* (*on* de); (*Theat*) sketch *m* satirique.

skittle ['skɪtl] *n* quille *f*. ~**s** (jeu *m* de) quilles.

skive* [skaɪv] *vi* tirer au flanc*. **to** ~ **off** se défiler*. ♦ **skiver*** *n* tire-au-flanc* *m inv*.

skivvy* ['skɪvɪ] *n* boniche *f* (*pej*).

skulduggery* [skʌl'dʌgərɪ] *n* maquignonnage *m*.

skulk [skʌlk] *vi* (~ **about**) rôder furtivement. **to** ~ **in/out** *etc* entrer/sortir *etc* furtivement.

skull [skʌl] *n* crâne *m*. ~ **and crossbones** tête *f* de mort, (*flag*) pavillon *m* à tête de mort. ♦ **skullcap** *n* calotte *f*.

skunk [skʌŋk] *n* mouffette *f*; (*fur*) sconse *m*; (**pej: person*) mufle* *m*.

sky [skaɪ] *n* ciel *m*. **in the** ~ dans le ciel; **under the open** ~ à la belle étoile; **the skies of England** le ciel *or* les ciels d'Angleterre; **under warmer skies** sous des cieux plus cléments; **to praise sb to the skies** porter qn aux nues; (*fig*) **the** ~**'s the limit*** tout est possible. ♦ **sky-blue** *adj* bleu ciel *inv*. ♦ **skydiving** *n* parachutisme *m* (en chute libre).

♦ **sky-high 1** *adv throw* très haut (dans le ciel); to **blow ~-high** *bridge* faire sauter; *theory* démolir; **2** *adj prices, temperature* extrêmement haut. ♦ **Skylab** *n* Skylab *m.* ♦ **skylark 1** *n* (*bird*) alouette *f* (des champs); **2** *vi* (**fig*) chahuter. ♦ **skylarking*** *n* chahut *m.* ♦ **skylight** *n* lucarne *f.* ♦ **skyline** *n* ligne *f* d'horizon; *[city]* ligne des toits. ♦ **skyscraper** *n* gratte-ciel *m inv.* ♦ **skyway** *n* (*US Aut*) route *f* surélevée. ♦ **skywriting** *n* publicité *f* tracée par un avion.

slab [slæb] *n [stone, wood]* bloc *m*; (*paving ~*) dalle *f*; (*flat*) plaque *f*; *[meat]* pièce *f*, (*smaller*) pavé *m*; *[cake]* pavé, (*smaller*) grosse tranche *f*; *[chocolate]* plaque, (*smaller*) tablette *f.*

slack [slæk] **1** *adj* **(a)** (*loose*) *rope* lâche; *joint, knot* desserré; *grip* faible. **to be ~** *[screw etc]* avoir du jeu; *[rope etc]* avoir du mou. **(b)** (*inactive*) *demand, market, trade* faible. **~ periods** périodes *fpl* creuses, (*in the day*) heures *fpl* creuses; **the ~ season** la morte-saison. **(c)** (*lacking energy*) mou; (*lax*) négligent; *student, worker* peu consciencieux. **to be ~ about one's work** négliger son travail; **to grow ~** se laisser aller. **2** *n* **(a) to take up the ~ in a rope** tendre un cordage. **(b)** (*coal*) poussier *m.* **3** *vi* (*) ne pas travailler comme il le faudrait.

slack off* *vi* (*stop working etc*) se relâcher; *[trade, demand]* ralentir.

♦ **slacken (off) 1** *vt rope* donner du mou à; *cable* donner du ballant à; *reins* relâcher; *screw* desserrer; *pressure etc* diminuer; **to ~en speed** *or* **one's pace** ralentir; **2** *vi* prendre du mou *or* du ballant; se desserrer; *[gale, speed, effort, pressure]* diminuer; *[activity, trade]* ralentir. ♦ **slacker*** *n* flemmard(e)* *m(f).* ♦ **slackness** *n [rope etc]* manque *m* de tension; (*) *[person]* laisser-aller *m*; *[trade]* ralentissement *m.* ♦ **slacks** *npl* pantalon *m.*

slag [slæg] *n* (*Metal*) scories *fpl*; (*Min*) crasses *fpl.* **~ heap** (*Metal*) crassier *m*; (*Min*) terril *m.*

slain [sleɪn] (*ptp of* **slay**) *npl*: **the ~** les morts *mpl* (tombés au champ d'honneur).

slake [sleɪk] *vt one's thirst* étancher.

slam [slæm] **1** *vt door, lid* (faire) claquer. **to ~ on the brakes** freiner à mort*; **she ~med the books on the table** elle a flanqué* les livres sur la table; **he ~med the ball into the net** d'un coup violent il a envoyé le ballon dans le filet. **2** *vi [door, lid]* claquer. **3** *n* (*Bridge*) chelem *m.*

slander ['slɑːndəʳ] **1** *n* calomnie *f*; (*Jur*) diffamation *f.* **2** *vt* calomnier; (*Jur*) diffamer. ♦ **slanderous** *adj* calomnieux; diffamatoire. ♦ **slanderously** *adv* calomnieusement; de façon diffamatoire.

slang [slæŋ] **1** *n* argot *m.* **in ~** en argot; **army/school ~** argot militaire/d'écolier; **that word is ~** c'est un mot d'argot; **to talk ~** parler argot. **2** *adj word* d'argot. ♦ **slanging match*** *n* échange *m* d'insultes. ♦ **slangy*** *adj* argotique.

slant [slɑːnt] **1** *n* inclinaison *f*; (*fig: point of view*) angle *m* (*on* sur). **to give/get a new ~* on sth** présenter/voir qch sous un angle nouveau. **2** *vi* pencher. **3** *vt line* faire pencher; (*fig*) *account, news* présenter avec parti-pris. ♦ **slant-eyed** *adj* aux yeux bridés. ♦ **slanting** *adj roof, surface* incliné; *handwriting, line* penché; *rain* oblique. ♦ **slantwise** *adv* de biais.

slap [slæp] **1** *n* (*gen*) claque *f.* **a ~ on the bottom** une fessée; (*lit, fig*) **a ~ in the face** une gifle; **a ~ on the back** une grande tape dans le dos. **2** *adv* (*) en plein (*into* dans). **~ in the middle** en plein milieu. **3** *vt* **(a)** (*hit*) *person* donner une tape *or* (*stronger*) claque à (*on the back* dans le dos). **to ~ a child's bottom** donner une fessée à un enfant; **to ~ sb's face** *or* **sb in the face** gifler qn. **(b)** (*put*) flanquer*. **he ~ped a coat of paint on the wall** il a flanqué* un coup de peinture sur le mur; (*fig*) **to ~ sb down*** rembarrer* qn. ♦ **slap-bang*** *adv* en plein (*into* dans). ♦ **slapdash** *adj person* insouciant; *work* fait à la va-vite. ♦ **slapstick (comedy)** *n* grosse farce *f.* ♦ **slap-up*** *adj meal* fameux*.

slash [slæʃ] **1** *n* entaille *f.* **2** *vt* **(a)** entailler, (*several cuts*) taillader; *rope* trancher; *face* balafrer; (*with whip, stick*) cingler. **to ~ sb** taillader qn; **~ed sleeves** manches *fpl* à crevés. **(b)** *prices* casser*; *costs, expenses* réduire radicalement; *speech, text* couper radicalement. **(c)** (*: *condemn*) *book, play* éreinter.

slat [slæt] *n* lame *f*; *[blind]* lamelle *f.*

slate [sleɪt] **1** *n* ardoise *f.* (*fig*) **put it on the ~*** mettez-le sur mon compte. **2** *adj industry* ardoisier; *roof* en ardoise. **~ blue/grey** bleu/gris ardoise *inv*; **~ quarry** ardoisière *f.* **3** *vt* **(a)** *roof* ardoiser. **(b)** (*) *book, play, actor* éreinter; (*scold*) attraper*. ♦ **slate-coloured** *adj* ardoise *inv.*

slaughter ['slɔːtəʳ] **1** *n [animals]* abattage *m*; *[people]* carnage *m.* **the ~ on the roads** les hécatombes *fpl* sur la route. **2** *vt animal* abattre; *person* tuer sauvagement; *people* massacrer. ♦ **slaughterhouse** *n* abattoir *m.*

Slav [slɑːv] **1** *adj* slave. **2** *n* Slave *mf.*

slave [sleɪv] **1** *n* esclave *mf* (*fig: to sth* de qch). **2** *adj* (*fig*) **~ driver** négrier *m*, -ière *f*; (*fig*) **~ labour** travail *m* de forçat; **~ labour camp** camp *m* de travaux forcés; **~ trade** commerce *m* des esclaves. **3** *vi* (**~ away**) travailler comme un nègre. **to ~ away at sth/at doing** s'escrimer sur qch/à faire. ♦ **slavery** *n* esclavage *m.* ♦ **slavey*** *n* boniche* *f.* ♦ **slavish** *adj subjection* d'esclave; *imitation, devotion* servile. ♦ **slavishly** *adv* servilement.

slaver ['slævəʳ] *vi* (*dribble*) baver.

slay [sleɪ] *pret* **slew**, *ptp* **slain** *vt* (*liter*) tuer.

sleazy* ['sliːzɪ] *adj* minable, miteux.

sledge [sledʒ] **1** *n* (*also* **sled**) traîneau *m*; (*child's*) luge *f.* **2** *vi*: **to go sledging** faire de la luge; **to ~ down** descendre en luge *or* en traîneau.

sledgehammer ['sledʒˌhæməʳ] **1** *n* marteau *m* de forgeron. **2** *adj blow* violent, magistral.

sleek [sliːk] *adj hair, fur* lisse et brillant; *cat* au poil soyeux; *person* (trop) soigné, (*in manner*) onctueux. ♦ **sleekly** *adv reply* doucereusement.

sleep [sliːp] (*vb: pret, ptp* **slept**) **1** *n* sommeil *m.* **to be in a deep** *or* **sound ~** dormir profondément; **to talk/walk in one's ~** parler/marcher en dormant; **she sang the child to ~** elle a chanté jusqu'à ce que l'enfant s'endorme; **to have a ~, to get some ~** dormir, (*short while*) faire un somme; **to get** *or* **go to ~** s'endormir; **my leg has gone to ~** j'ai la jambe engourdie; **to put to ~** endormir; (*put down*) *cat* faire piquer; **a 3-hour ~** 3 heures de sommeil; **to have a good night's ~** passer une bonne nuit; **he didn't lose any ~ over it** il n'en a pas perdu le sommeil pour autant. **2** *vi* **(a)** dormir. **to ~ like a log** *or* **a top** dormir comme une souche; **~ tight!** dors bien!; **to ~ deeply** *or* **soundly** dormir profondément; (*without fear*) **to ~ soundly** dormir sur ses deux oreilles; **to ~ lightly** (*regularly*) avoir le sommeil léger; (*on one occasion*) dormir d'un sommeil léger; **I didn't ~ a wink all night** je n'ai pas fermé l'œil de la nuit; **to ~ on a problem/a letter/a decision** attendre le lendemain pour résoudre un problème/répondre à une lettre/prendre une décision; **I'll have to ~ on it** il faut que j'attende demain pour décider; **he slept through the storm** l'orage ne l'a pas réveillé; **he slept through the alarm clock** il n'a pas entendu son réveil. **(b)** (*spend night*) coucher. **he slept at his aunt's** il a couché chez sa tante; (*have sex*) **to ~ with sb** coucher* avec qn. **3** *vt*: **the house ~s 8** on peut coucher 8 personnes dans cette maison.

sleep around* *vi* coucher* avec n'importe qui.

sleep in *vi* (*lie late*) faire la grasse matinée;

(*oversleep*) ne pas se réveiller à temps.

sleep off *vt sep*: **to ~ sth off** dormir pour faire passer qch.

♦ **sleeper** *n* **(a) to be a light/heavy ~er** avoir le sommeil léger/lourd; **(b)** (*Rail*) (*track*) traverse *f*; (*berth*) couchette *f*; (*train*) train-couchettes *m*; **(c)** (*earring*) clou *m*. ♦ **sleepily** *adv* d'un air *or* ton endormi. ♦ **sleepiness** *n [person]* envie *f* de dormir. ♦ **sleeping** *adj person* qui dort, endormi; **~ing bag** sac *m* de couchage; **the S~ing Beauty** la Belle au bois dormant; (*Rail*) **~ing car** wagon-couchettes *m*; **~ing draught** soporifique *m*; (*Comm*) **~ing partner** commanditaire *m*; **~ing pill** *or* **tablet** somnifère *m*; **~ing sickness** maladie *f* du sommeil. ♦ **sleepless** *adj person* qui ne dort pas, éveillé; *hours* sans sommeil; **to have a ~less night** ne pas dormir de la nuit. ♦ **sleeplessly** *adv* sans dormir. ♦ **sleeplessness** *n* insomnie *f*. ♦ **sleepwalk** *vi* marcher en dormant, être somnambule. ♦ **sleepwalker** *n* somnambule *mf*. ♦ **sleepwalking** *n* somnambulisme *m*. ♦ **sleepwear** *n* vêtements *mpl* de nuit. ♦ **sleepy** *adj person* qui a envie de dormir; *voice, look, village* endormi; **to be** *or* **feel ~y** avoir sommeil. ♦ **sleepyhead*** *n* endormi(e) *m(f)*.

sleet [sliːt] **1** *n* neige *f* fondue. **2** *vi*: **it is ~ing** il tombe de la neige fondue.

sleeve [sliːv] *n [garment]* manche *f*; *[record]* pochette *f*; *[cylinder etc]* chemise *f*. **long-~d** à manches longues; (*fig*) **he's always got sth up his ~** il a plus d'un tour dans son sac; **he's got sth up his ~** il a qch en réserve. ♦ **sleeveboard** *n* jeannette *f*.

sleigh [sleɪ] *n* traîneau *m*.

sleight [slaɪt] *n*: **~ of hand** tour *m* de passe-passe.

slender [ˈslendəʳ] *adj person* mince; *stem, hand, neck, waist* fin; (*fig*) *hope, chance, majority* faible; *income, means, knowledge* maigre. *[person]* **tall and ~** élancé; **small and ~** menu. ♦ **slenderness** *n* minceur *f*; finesse *f*.

slept [slept] *pret, ptp of* **sleep**.

sleuth [sluːθ] *n* limier *m*.

slew [sluː] *pret of* **slay**.

slice [slaɪs] **1** *n* **(a)** (*gen*) tranche *f*; *[lemon, cucumber, sausage]* rondelle *f*, tranche. **~ of bread and butter** tartine *f* (beurrée); (*fig*) **a ~ of the profits** une bonne partie des bénéfices; **~ of life** tranche de vie; **~ of luck** coup *m* de chance. **(b)** (*utensil*) truelle *f*.

2 *vt* couper (en tranches *or* en rondelles); *rope etc* couper net; (*Sport*) *ball* couper. **to ~ sth thin** couper qch en tranches *or* rondelles fines; **a ~d loaf** un pain en tranches.

slice off *vt sep meat* couper; *piece of rope etc* couper net.

slice through *vt fus rope* couper net; (*fig*) *the air, the waves* fendre.

slice up *vt sep* couper en tranches *or* en rondelles.

♦ **slicer** *n* coupe-jambon *m inv*.

slick [slɪk] **1** *adj explanation* trop prompt; *excuse, answer* facile; *person* (*glib*) qui a la parole facile; (*cunning*) rusé. **a ~ customer*** une fine mouche. **2** *n* (*oil ~*) nappe *f* de pétrole. **3** *vt*: **to ~ (down) one's hair** (*with comb*) se lisser les cheveux; (*with haircream*) se brillantiner les cheveux. ♦ **slickly** *adv answer* habilement.

slide [slaɪd] (*vb*: *pret, ptp* **slid**) **1** *n* (*action*) glissade *f*; (*land~*) glissement *m* (de terrain); (*fig: in prices etc*) baisse *f* (*in* de); (*in playground, pool etc*) toboggan *m*; *[microscope]* porte-objet *m*; (*Phot*) diapositive *f*; (*Mus: between notes*) coulé *m*; (*hair ~*) barrette *f*. **2** *adj* (*Phot*) **~ box** classeur *m* pour diapositives; **~ projector** projecteur *m* de diapositives; **~ rule** règle *f* à calcul. **3** *vi* (*gen*) glisser; (*move silently*) se glisser. **to ~ down the bannisters** descendre en glissant sur la rampe; to **~ down a slope** descendre une pente en glissant; **he slid into the room** il s'est glissé dans la pièce; **to let things ~** laisser les choses aller à la dérive. **4** *vt box, case, small object* glisser (*into* dans; *across* à travers); *chair, larger object* faire glisser. **to ~ the top back onto a box** remettre le couvercle sur une boîte; **he slid the gun out of the holster** il a sorti le revolver de l'étui. ♦ **sliding** *adj part* qui glisse; *panel, door, seat* coulissant; (*Aut*) *roof* ouvrant; (*Admin etc*) **sliding scale** échelle *f* mobile.

slight [slaɪt] **1** *adj* **(a)** *person* (*slim*) menu; (*frail*) frêle. **(b)** (*small: gen*) petit, léger (*before n*); (*negligible: gen*) faible, insignifiant; *error* petit. **some ~ optimism** un peu d'optimisme; **not the ~est danger** pas le moindre danger; **not in the ~est** pas le moins du monde; **he takes offence at the ~est thing** il se pique pour un rien. **2** *vt* manquer d'égards envers; (*stronger*) offenser. **3** *n* manque *m* d'égards; (*stronger*) affront *m*. ♦ **slighting** *adj* offensant. ♦ **slightingly** *adv* d'une manière offensante. ♦ **slightly** *adv* **(a)** *sick, better* légèrement, un peu; *know etc* un peu; **(b) ~ly built** menu.

slim [slɪm] **1** *adj person, ankle, book* mince; (*fig*) *hope, excuse* faible; *evidence, resources* insuffisant. **2** *vi* maigrir; (*diet*) être au régime (pour maigrir). **3** *vt* faire maigrir. ♦ **slimmer** *n* personne *f* suivant un régime amaigrissant. ♦ **slimming** *adj diet, pills* amaigrissant, pour maigrir; *food* qui ne fait pas grossir; *dress etc* amincissant. ♦ **slimness** *n* minceur *f*.

slime [slaɪm] *n* (*mud*) vase *f*; (*sticky substance*) dépôt *m* visqueux; (*from snail*) bave *f*. ♦ **sliminess** *n* nature *f* vaseuse; viscosité *f*. ♦ **slimy** *adj* (*gen*) visqueux; *walls* suintant; (*muddy*) *stone, hands* couvert de vase; (*fig*) servile.

sling [slɪŋ] (*vb*: *pret, ptp* **slung**) **1** *n* (*catapult*) fronde *f*; (*child's*) lance-pierre *m inv*; (*Med*) écharpe *f*. **in a ~** en écharpe. **2** *vt* **(a)** (*throw*) lancer (*at sb* à *or* contre qn; *at sth* sur qch). **(b)** (*hang*) *hammock* suspendre; *load etc* hisser. **to ~ across one's shoulder** *rifle, satchel* mettre en bandoulière; *load, coat* jeter par derrière l'épaule.

sling out* *vt sep person* flanquer* à la porte; *object* jeter.

slink [slɪŋk] *pret, ptp* **slunk** *vi*: **to ~ away/out** *etc* s'en aller/sortir *etc* furtivement. ♦ **slinkily*** *adv walk* d'une démarche ondulante. ♦ **slinking** *adj* furtif. ♦ **slinky*** *adj woman* aguichant; *body* sinueux; *walk* ondulant; *dress* moulant.

slip [slɪp] **1** *n* **(a)** (*slide*) dérapage *m*; (*trip*) faux pas *m*; (*mistake*) erreur *f*, bévue *f*; (*oversight*) oubli *m*; (*moral*) écart *m*. **~ of the tongue, ~ of the pen** lapsus *m*; **earth ~** éboulement *m* (de terre); **to give sb the ~** fausser compagnie à qn. **(b)** (*pillow~*) taie *f* (d'oreiller); (*underskirt*) combinaison *f*. **(c) in the ~s** (*Naut*) sur cale *f*; (*Theat*) dans les coulisses *fpl*. **(d)** (*paper: in filing system etc*) fiche *f*. **a ~ of paper** (*small sheet*) un bout de papier; (*strip*) une bande de papier; (*fig*) **a mere ~ of a boy/girl** un gamin/une gamine.

2 *vi* **(a)** (*slide*) *[person, food, hand, object]* glisser (*on* sur; *out of* de); (*Aut*) *[clutch]* patiner. (*fig*) **money ~s through her fingers** l'argent lui file entre les doigts; **several errors had ~ped into the report** plusieurs erreurs s'étaient glissées dans le rapport; **to let ~ an opportunity** laisser échapper une occasion; **he let (it) ~ that ...** il a laissé échapper que ...; **he's ~ping*** (*getting old, less efficient*) il baisse; (*making more mistakes*) il ne fait plus assez attention. **(b)** (*move quickly*) **to ~ into/out of** *[person]* se glisser dans/hors de; *[vehicle]* se faufiler dans/hors de; **to ~ away** *[vehicle, boat]* s'éloigner doucement; *[person]* s'esquiver; **to ~ back** *[vehicle, boat]* revenir doucement; *[guest]* revenir discrètement; *[thief, spy]* revenir furtivement; **I'll just ~ through the garden** je vais passer par le jardin; **I must just ~ out for some cigarettes** il faut que je sorte un instant chercher des cigarettes; **she ~ped out to the shops** elle a fait un saut jusqu'aux magasins; **the secret ~ped out** le secret a été révélé par mégarde; **the words ~ped out before he realized it** les mots lui ont échappé avant même qu'il ne s'en rende compte; **the years ~ped past** les années passèrent; **to ~ into/out of a dress** enfiler/enlever (rapidement) une robe; (*fig*) **to ~ into bad habits** prendre insensiblement de mauvaises habitudes.

3 *vt* **(a)** (*slide*) *coin, small object* glisser (*to sb* à qn; *into* dans). **he ~ped the gun out of its holster** il a sorti le revolver de son étui; **the question was ~ped into the exam** l'épreuve a comporté cette question inattendue; (*Med*) **a ~ped disc** une hernie discale. **(b)** (*escape*) échapper à; *anchor, moorings* filer; *[dog] collar* se dégager de; (*Knitting*) *stitch* glisser. **to ~ sb's attention** *or* **notice** échapper à qn (*that* que); **it ~ped my memory** cela m'était complètement sorti de la tête.

slip up* *vi* (*make mistake*) gaffer*, cafouiller*. ♦ **slipcovers** *npl* housses *fpl*. ♦ **slipknot** *n* nœud *m* coulant. ♦ **slip-on** *adj* facile à mettre. ♦ **slippery** *adj* glissant; (*fig pej*) *person* fuyant; **it's ~pery underfoot** le sol est glissant; (*fig pej*) **he's as ~pery as an eel** il glisse comme une anguille. ♦ **slippy*** *adj* glissant. ♦ **slip-road** *n [motorway]* bretelle *f* d'accès. ♦ **slipshod** *adj person, work* négligé; *dress* débraillé; *worker* négligent. ♦ **slipstream** *n* (*Aviat*) sillage *m*. ♦ **slip-up*** *n* gaffe* *f*, bévue *f*; (*in communications*) cafouillage* *m*. ♦ **slipway** *n* (*Naut*) cale *f*.

slipper ['slɪpəʳ] *n* pantoufle *f*, (*warmer*) chausson *m*.

slit [slɪt] (*vb: pret, ptp* **slit**) **1** *n* (*opening*) fente *f*; (*cut*) incision *f*; (*tear*) déchirure *f*. **2** *vt* fendre; inciser; déchirer; *sb's throat* trancher. **to ~ open** *letter* ouvrir; *sack* éventrer. ♦ **slit-eyed** *adj* aux yeux bridés.

slither ['slɪðəʳ] *vi [person, animal]* glisser; *[snake]* onduler. **to ~ about** déraper.

sliver ['slɪvəʳ] *n [glass, wood]* éclat *m*; *[cheese etc]* lamelle *f*.

slob* [slɒb] *n* rustaud(e) *m(f)*.

slobber ['slɒbəʳ] *vi* baver.

sloe [sləʊ] *n* prunelle *f*. **~ gin** eau-de-vie *f* de prunelle.

slog [slɒg] **1** *n* (*work*) long travail *m* pénible, travail de Romain*; (*effort*) gros effort *m*; (*task*) corvée *f*. **2** *vt ball, opponent* donner un grand coup à. **3** *vi* **(a)** (*work etc*) travailler très dur. **he ~ged through the book** il s'est forcé à lire le livre; **to ~ away** travailler comme un nègre*; **to ~ away at sth** trimer* sur qch. **(b)** (*walk*) **to ~ along** avancer avec effort; **he ~ged up the hill** il a gravi la colline avec effort. ♦ **slogger*** *n* (*hard worker*) bosseur‡ *m*, -euse‡ *f*.

slogan ['sləʊgən] *n* slogan *m*.

slop [slɒp] **1** *n*: **~s** (*for invalids*) bouillon *m*; (*dirty water*) eaux *fpl* sales; (*in teacup*) fond *m* de tasse. **2** *vt* répandre (*par mégarde*) (*onto* sur; *into* dans). **3** *vi* (**~ over**) déborder. ♦ **sloppily** *adv* (*carelessly*) sans soin; (*sentimentally*) avec sensiblerie. ♦ **sloppiness** *n* (*carelessness*) manque *m* de soin; (*sentimentality*) sensiblerie *f*. ♦ **sloppy** *adj food* (trop) liquide; *work* peu soigné, bâclé*; *appearance, language* négligé; *garment* trop grand; (*: *sentimental*) débordant de sensiblerie; (*sweater*) **~py joe*** gros pull *m* vague.

slope [sləʊp] **1** *n* pente *f*. **~ up** montée *f*; **~ down** descente *f*; **on the ~s of Mount Etna** sur les flancs *mpl* de l'Etna; **the southern ~s of the Himalayas** le versant sud de l'Himalaya. **2** *vi [ground, roof]* être en pente; *[handwriting]* pencher. **to ~ up** monter; **to ~ down** descendre. **3** *vt* pencher, incliner. ♦ **sloping** *adj ground, roof* en pente; *handwriting* penché; *shoulders* tombant.

slosh* [slɒʃ] **1** *vt water, paint* répandre, flanquer* (*onto, over* sur; *into* dans). **2** *vi*: **to ~ about in water/mud** patauger dans l'eau/la boue. ♦ **sloshed‡** *adj* (*drunk*) bourré‡, soûl*.

slot [slɒt] **1** *n* (*slit: in machine, box etc*) fente *f*; (*groove*) rainure *f*; (*fig: in timetable etc*) heure *f*; (*Rad, TV*) créneau *m*. **2** *adj*: **~ machine** (*selling things*) distributeur *m* (automatique); (*for amusement*) machine *f* à sous; **~ meter** compteur *m* à paiement préalable. **3** *vt object* emboîter (*into* dans); (*fig*) insérer (*into a programme* dans une grille de programmes). **4** *vi* s'emboîter (*into* dans); (*fig*) s'insérer (*into* dans).

sloth [sləʊθ] *n* **(a)** paresse *f*. **(b)** (*animal*) paresseux *m*. ♦ **slothful** *adj* paresseux.

slouch [slaʊtʃ] *vi*: **to ~ in/out** *etc* entrer/sortir *etc* en se traînant; **he was ~ing in a chair** il était affalé dans un fauteuil; **she always ~es** elle ne se tient jamais droite; **stop ~ing!** tiens-toi droit!

slovenly ['slʌvnlɪ] *adj person* débraillé; *work* qui manque de soin. ♦ **slovenliness** *n* débraillé *m*; manque *m* de soin.

slow [sləʊ] **1** *adj* (*gen*) lent; (*fig*) *track, surface* lourd; (*boring*) *party, novel, play* ennuyeux; *person* (*phlegmatic*) flegmatique; (*stupid*) lent; (*Med*) *child* retardé. **~ but sure** lent mais sûr; **a ~ train** un omnibus; **at a ~ speed** à petite vitesse; (*lit, fig*) **it's ~ going** on n'avance pas vite; **it's ~ work** c'est un travail qui avance lentement; **he's a ~ worker** il travaille lentement; **~ to anger** lent à se mettre en colère; (*brain working ~ly*) **~ to understand/notice** *etc*, **~ in understanding/noticing** *etc* lent à comprendre/remarquer *etc*; (*taking one's time*) **~ to act/decide** *etc*, **~ in acting/deciding** *etc* long à agir/décider *etc*; **my watch is (10 minutes) ~** ma montre retarde (de 10 minutes); **in a ~ oven** à four doux; **business is ~** les affaires stagnent; (*Cine etc*) **in ~ motion** au ralenti. **2** *adv* lentement. **to go ~** *[walker, vehicle]* aller lentement; (*be cautious*) y aller doucement; (*be less active*) ralentir ses activités; (*Ind*) faire la grève perlée; *[watch etc]* prendre du retard; **to go ~er** ralentir; **~-acting/-burning** *etc* à action/combustion *etc* lente; **it is ~-acting** *etc* cela agit *etc* lentement. **3** *vt* (**~ down, ~ up**) (*gen*) retarder; *walker* faire ralentir; *vehicle, machine, traffic* ralentir; *horse* ralentir le pas de; *progress, production, negotiations, reaction* ralentir, retarder. **these interruptions have ~ed us down** ces interruptions nous ont retardés. **4** *vi* (**~ down, ~ off, ~ up**) ralentir. ♦ **slowcoach** *or* (*US*) ♦ **slowpoke*** *n* (*dawdler*) lambin(e)* *m(f)*; (*dullard*) esprit lent. ♦ **slowdown** *n* ralentissement *m*. ♦ **slowly** *adv* lentement; (*little by little*) peu à peu; **~ly but surely** lentement mais sûrement; **to go** (*or* **work** *etc*) **more ~ly** ralentir. ♦ **slow-moving** *adj* lent. ♦ **slowness** *n* lenteur *f*. ♦ **slow-witted** *adj* qui a l'esprit lent. ♦ **slow-worm** *n* orvet *m*.

sludge [slʌdʒ] *n* (*mud, sediment*) boue *f*; (*sewage*) vidanges *fpl*.

slug [slʌg] **1** *n* (*Zool*) limace *f*; (*bullet*) balle *f*; (*blow*) coup *m*. **a ~* of whisky** un coup* de whisky sec. **2** *vt* (*: *hit*) frapper comme une brute.

sluggish ['slʌgɪʃ] *adj* (*gen*) lent; (*lazy*) paresseux; *engine* peu nerveux; *market, business* stagnant; *sales* difficile; *liver* paresseux. **to feel ~** se sentir mou. ♦ **sluggishly** *adv* lentement.

sluice [sluːs] **1** *n* écluse *f*; (**~ gate, ~ valve**) vanne *f*; (**~ way**) canal *m* (à vannes). **2** *vt* (**~ down**) laver à grande eau.

slum [slʌm] **1** *n* (*house*) taudis *m*. **the ~s** les quartiers *mpl* pauvres, les bas quartiers. **2** *adj*: **~ area** quartier *m* pauvre; **~ clearance** aménagement *m* des quartiers insalubres; **~ clearance campaign**

lutte *f* contre les taudis. ♦ **slummy** *adj* misérable, sordide.

slumber ['slʌmbəʳ] **1** *n* (*liter: also* ~s) sommeil *m*. **2** *adj* (*Comm*) ~ **wear** lingerie *f* de nuit. **3** *vi* dormir paisiblement.

slump [slʌmp] **1** *n* (*gen*) baisse *f* soudaine (*in* de); (*Econ*) crise *f* économique; (*St Ex*) effondrement *m* des cours; (*in prices*) effondrement (*in* de). **the 1929** ~ la crise de 1929. **2** *vi* **(a)** (*gen*) baisser brutalement; *[prices]* s'effondrer. **(b)** (~ **down**) s'effondrer, s'affaisser (*into* dans; *onto* sur). ~**ed on the floor** effondré par terre; ~**ed over the wheel** affaissé sur le volant.

slung [slʌŋ] *pret, ptp of* **sling**.

slunk [slʌŋk] *pret, ptp of* **slink**.

slur [slɜːʳ] **1** *n* (*stigma*) atteinte *f* (*on* à); (*insult*) affront *m*. **it's no ~ on him to say ...** ce n'est pas le calomnier que de dire ... . **2** *vt* (*join*) *sounds, words* lier à tort; (*Mus*) lier; (*indistinctly*) *word etc* mal articuler. **his speech was ~red** il n'arrivait pas à articuler. **3** *vi* (*fig*) **to ~ over sth** glisser sur qch.

slurp [slɜːp] *vti* boire à grand bruit.

slush [slʌʃ] **1** *n* (*snow*) neige *f* fondante; (*mud*) gadoue *f*; (*sentiment*) sentimentalité *f*. **2** *adj*: ~ **fund** fonds *mpl* servant à des pots-de-vin. ♦ **slushy** *adj* fondant; (*fig*) fadement sentimental.

slut [slʌt] *n* (*dirty*) souillon *f*; (*immoral*) salope‡ *f*. ♦ **sluttish** *adj appearance* de souillon; *behaviour* de salope‡.

sly [slaɪ] **1** *adj* (*wily*) rusé; (*secretive*) dissimulé; (*underhand*) sournois; (*mischievous*) espiègle. **2** *n*: **on the** ~ en cachette, en douce*. ♦ **slyly** *adv* de façon rusée *or* dissimulée; sournoisement; avec espièglerie; (*in secret*) en cachette, en douce*. ♦ **slyness** *n* ruse *f*; dissimulation *f*; sournoiserie *f*; espièglerie *f*.

smack[1] [smæk] *vi*: **to ~ of sth** sentir qch.

smack[2] [smæk] **1** *n* (*slap*) tape *f*, (*stronger*) claque *f*; (*on face*) gifle *f*; (*sound*) bruit *m* sec. **it was a ~ in the eye for them*** (*snub*) c'était une gifle pour eux; (*setback*) c'était un revers pour eux; (*fig*) **to have a ~ at doing sth*** essayer de faire qch. **2** *vt person* donner une tape *or* une claque à. **to ~ sb's face** gifler qn; **to ~ sb's bottom** donner la fessée à qn; **to ~ one's lips** se lécher les babines. **3** *adv* (*) en plein. ~ **in the middle** en plein milieu. ♦ **smacking** *n* fessée *f*; **to give sb a ~ing** donner une *or* la fessée à qn.

smack[3] [smæk] *n* (**fishing** ~) barque *f* de pêche.

small [smɔːl] **1** *adj* **(a)** (*gen*) petit; *audience, population* peu nombreux; *income, sum* modeste; *meal* léger; *waist* mince; (*morally mean*) *person, mind* mesquin, petit. **the ~est details** les moindres détails; **the ~est possible number of books** le moins de livres possible; **a ~ proportion of** un pourcentage limité *or* restreint de; **to grow *or* get ~er** (*gen*) diminuer; *[town, organization]* décroître; **to make ~er** *income, amount* diminuer; *organization* réduire; *garden, object, garment* rapetisser; (*Typ*) **in ~ letters** en minuscules *fpl*; **he is a ~ eater** il ne mange pas beaucoup; ~ **shopkeeper/farmer** petit commerçant/cultivateur; **to feel** ~ se sentir tout honteux; **to make sb feel** ~ humilier qn; ~ **ads** petites annonces *fpl*; (*TV*) **the ~ screen** le petit écran; ~ **talk** papotage *m*; **he's got plenty of ~ talk** il a de la conversation; *V also* **print, way** *etc.* **(b)** (*little or no*) **to have ~ cause *or* reason to do** n'avoir guère de raisons de faire; **a matter of no ~ consequence** une affaire d'une grande importance.

2 *adv*: **to cut up ~** *paper* couper en tout petits morceaux; *meat* hacher menu.

3 *n*: **the ~ of the back** le creux des reins; (*Dress: esp Brit*) ~**s*** dessous *mpl*, sous-vêtements *mpl*.

♦ **small-arms** *npl* (*Mil*) armes *fpl* portatives. ♦ **smallholder** *n* (*Agr*) ≃ petit cultivateur *m*. ♦ **smallholding** *n* ≃ petite ferme *f* (*de moins de deux hectares*). ♦ **small-minded** *adj* mesquin. ♦ **small-mindedness** *n* mesquinerie *f*. ♦ **smallness** *n [person]* petite taille *f*; *[hand, foot, object]* petitesse *f*; *[income, sum, contribution etc]* modicité *f*. ♦ **smallpox** *n* variole *f*. ♦ **small-scale** *adj* peu important; *undertaking* de peu d'importance. ♦ **small-time** *adj* peu important; **a ~-time crook** un escroc à la petite semaine. ♦ **small-town** *adj* (*pej*) provincial.

smarm* [smɑːm] *vi* (*Brit*) **to ~ over sb** flagorner qn. ♦ **smarmy*** *adj* flagorneur.

smart [smɑːt] **1** *adj* **(a)** (*not shabby*) (*gen*) chic *inv*, élégant; *hotel, shop, car, house* élégant; (*fashionable*) à la mode. **she was looking very ~** elle était très élégante *or* très chic; **the ~ set** le grand monde. **(b)** (*clever*) intelligent, dégourdi*; (*shrewd*) malin; (*pej*) retors. **a ~ lad***, (*US*) **a ~ guy*** un malin; **he's trying to be ~** il fait le malin; **he's too ~ for me** il est beaucoup trop futé pour moi. **(c)** (*quick*) *pace* vif, rapide; *action* prompt. **that was ~ work!** tu n'as pas (*or* il n'a pas *etc*) mis longtemps!; **look ~ about it!** remue-toi!* **2** *vi [cut, graze]* brûler; *[iodine etc]* piquer; (*fig: feel offended*) être piqué au vif. **my eyes were ~ing** j'avais les yeux qui me brûlaient *or* piquaient; **to ~ under an insult** ressentir vivement une insulte. ♦ **smart-alec(k)*** *n* bêcheur* *m*. ♦ **smarten (up)** **1** *vt* (*beautify*) *house, town* (bien) arranger; *child* pomponner; (*speed up*) accélérer; **2** *vi [person]* se faire beau. ♦ **smartly** *adv* (*elegantly*) avec beaucoup de chic *or* d'élégance; (*cleverly*) astucieusement; (*quickly*) *move* vivement; *answer* du tac au tac. ♦ **smartness** *n* (*in appearance etc*) chic *m*, élégance *f*; (*cleverness*) intelligence *f*, astuce *f*; (*quickness*) promptitude *f*. ♦ **smarty*** *n* bêcheur* *m*, -euse* *f*.

smash [smæʃ] **1** *n* **(a)** (*sound*) fracas *m*; (*blow*) coup *m* violent; (*Tennis etc*) smash *m*. **(b)** (*also* ~**-up***) accident *m*. **car/rail ~** accident de voiture/de chemin de fer. **(c)** (*Econ, Fin: collapse*) effondrement *m* (financier); (*St Ex*) krach *m*. **2** *adj*: **it was a ~ hit*** cela a eu un succès foudroyant; **the ~ hit* of the year** le succès de l'année. **3** *adv* (*) en plein. ~ **into a wall** en plein dans un mur. **4** *vt* (*break*) casser, briser; (*shatter*) fracasser; (*fig*) *spy ring etc* détruire; *hopes* ruiner; *enemy* écraser; *opponent, sports record* pulvériser. **to ~ sth to pieces *or* to bits** briser qch en mille morceaux; (*Tennis*) **he ~ed the ball into the net** il a envoyé son smash dans le filet. **5** *vi [cup etc]* se briser (en mille morceaux), se fracasser. **the car ~ed into the tree** la voiture s'est écrasée contre l'arbre.

smash down *vt sep door, fence* fracasser.

smash in *vt sep door* enfoncer. **to ~ sb's face in*** casser la figure à qn*.

smash up *vt sep room etc* tout casser dans; *car* accidenter, bousiller*.

♦ **smash-and-grab (raid)** *n* cambriolage *m* (commis en brisant une devanture). ♦ **smasher‡** *n*: **to be a ~er** (*in appearance*) être vachement‡ beau; (*in character etc*) être vachement chouette‡; **it's a ~er** c'est sensationnel*. ♦ **smashing*** *adj* formidable*, terrible*.

smattering ['smætərɪŋ] *n*: **a ~ of** quelques connaissances *fpl* vagues en.

smear [smɪəʳ] **1** *n* trace *f*, (*longer*) traînée *f*; (*dirty mark*) tache *f*; (*on reputation etc*) tache (*on* sur); (*insult*) calomnie *f*; (*Med*) frottis *m*. **2** *adj*: ~ **campaign** campagne *f* de diffamation. **3** *vt* **(a)** *butter etc* étaler (*on* sur). **to ~ cream on one's hands** s'enduire les mains de crème; **he ~ed his face with mud** il s'est barbouillé le visage de boue; **hands ~ed with ink** mains barbouillées d'encre. **(b)** *page of print* maculer; *wet paint* faire une marque sur; *lettering* étaler (accidentellement).

(*fig*) **to ~ sb** porter atteinte à la réputation de qn. **4** *vi [ink, paint]* se salir.

smell [smel] (*vb: pret, ptp* **smelled** *or* **smelt**[1]) **1** *n* (*sense of* ~) odorat *m*; (*odour*) odeur *f*; (*stench*) mauvaise odeur. **he has no sense of** ~ il n'a pas d'odorat; **it has a nice/nasty** ~ cela sent bon/ mauvais; **what a ~ in here!** que ça sent mauvais ici!; **a ~ of burning** une odeur de brûlé.

2 *vt* sentir; (*fig*) *danger* pressentir; (*sniff at*) sentir, renifler; *[animal]* flairer. **he could** ~ *or* **he smelt sth burning** il sentait que qch brûlait; **he smelt the meat to see if it were bad** il a senti *or* reniflé la viande pour voir si elle était encore bonne; **the dog could ~ the bone** le chien a flairé l'os; (*fig*) **to ~ a rat** soupçonner qch.

3 *vi* **(a) to ~ at sth** renifler qch. **(b) it doesn't ~ at all** *[mixture etc]* ça ne sent rien, ça n'a pas d'odeur; *[gas]* c'est inodore; **these socks** ~ ces chaussettes sentent mauvais; **his breath ~s** il a mauvaise haleine; **that ~s like chocolate** ça sent le chocolat; **to ~ of onions** sentir l'oignon; **to ~ good** *or* **sweet** sentir bon; **to ~ bad** sentir mauvais; **it ~s delicious!** ça embaume!; **it ~s dreadful!** ça pue!; (*fig*) **that deal ~s a bit*** cette affaire semble plutôt louche; **that idea ~s!‡** cette idée ne vaut rien!; **he ~s!‡** c'est un sale type!*

smell out *vt sep* **(a)** *[dog etc]* découvrir en flairant; *[person] criminal, treachery* découvrir. **(b) it's ~ing the room out** ça empeste la pièce.

♦ **smelling salts** *npl* sels *mpl*. ♦ **smelly** *adj* qui sent mauvais; **to be ~y** sentir mauvais, (*stronger*) puer.

smelt[2] [smelt] *vt ore* fondre; *metal* extraire par fusion. ♦ **smelting** *n* fonte *f*; extraction *f* par fusion; **~ing works** fonderie *f*.

smile [smaɪl] **1** *n* sourire *m*. **he said with a** ~ dit-il en souriant; **he had a happy ~ on his face** il avait un sourire heureux; **to give sb a** ~ faire un sourire à qn; **she gave a little** ~ elle a eu un petit sourire; **to be all ~s** être tout souriant *or* tout sourire; **take that ~ off your face!** arrête donc de sourire comme ça! **2** *vi* sourire (*at, to sb* à qn; *at sth* de qch). **to keep smiling** garder le sourire. ♦ **smiling** *adj* souriant. ♦ **smilingly** *adv* en souriant.

smirk [smɜːk] **1** *n* petit sourire *m* (*self-satisfied*) satisfait *or* (*knowing*) narquois *or* (*affected*) affecté. **2** *vi* sourire d'un air satisfait *etc*.

smith [smɪθ] *n* (*shoes horses*) maréchal-ferrant *m*; (*forges iron*) forgeron *m*. ♦ **smithy** *n* forge *f*.

smithereens [ˌsmɪðəˈriːnz] *npl*: **to smash sth to** ~ briser qch en mille morceaux; **in** ~ brisé en mille morceaux.

smitten [ˈsmɪtn] *adj*: **to be ~ with** *remorse, desire* être pris de; *terror, deafness* être frappé de; (*) *sb's beauty* être enchanté par; *idea* s'enthousiasmer pour; (*in love*) *person* être toqué* de.

smock [smɒk] *n* (*dress, overall, maternity top*) blouse *f*; (*maternity dress*) robe *f* de grossesse. ♦ **smocking** *n* smocks *mpl*.

smog [smɒg] *n* smog *m*.

smoke [sməʊk] **1** *n* **(a)** fumée *f*. **there's no ~ without fire** il n'y a pas de fumée sans feu; **to go up in** ~ *[house etc]* brûler; *[plans, hopes etc]* partir en fumée. **(b) to have a** ~ fumer une cigarette (*or* une pipe *etc*). **2** *adj*: **~ bomb** bombe *f* fumigène; **~ screen** (*Mil*) rideau *m* de fumée; (*fig*) paravent *m* (*fig*); **~ signal** signal *m* de fumée. **3** *vi* (*all senses*) fumer. **4** *vt* (*all senses*) fumer. **he ~s cigarettes/a pipe** il fume la cigarette/la pipe; **~d salmon** saumon *m* fumé.

smoke out *vt sep insects, snake etc* enfumer.

♦ **smokeless** *adj*: **~less fuel** combustible *m* non polluant; **~less zone** zone *f* où l'usage de combustibles solides est réglementé. ♦ **smoker** *n* **(a)** fumeur *m*, -euse *f*; **~r's cough** toux *f* de fumeur; **heavy ~r** grand fumeur; **(b)** (*Rail*) wagon *m* fumeurs. ♦ **smoking** *n*: **'no smoking'** 'défense de fumer'; **smoking can damage your health** le tabac est nuisible à la santé; **to give up smoking** arrêter de fumer. ♦ **smoky** *adj atmosphere, room* enfumé; *fire* qui fume; *glass* fumé.

smolder [ˈsməʊldəʳ] *vi* (*US*) = **smoulder**.

smooth [smuːð] **1** *adj* **(a)** (*gen*) lisse; *surface* lisse, égal; *road* à la surface égale; (*hairless*) *chin* glabre; *paste, sauce* onctueux; *flavour, wine* moelleux; *voice, sound* doux. **(b)** *movement etc* régulier, sans à-coups; *takeoff* en douceur; *flight* confortable; *sea crossing, trip* par mer calme; *breathing, pulse* régulier; *day, life* calme. **~ running** *[machinery etc]* bon fonctionnement; *[organization]* bonne marche; (*fig*) **the way is now** ~ il n'y a plus d'obstacles maintenant. **(c)** (*suave*) doucereux, mielleux. **he's a ~ operator*** il sait s'y prendre; **a ~ talker** un beau parleur.

2 *vt* **(a)** (**~ down**) *sheets, pillow, hair* lisser; *wood* rendre lisse. (*fig*) **to ~ the way for sb** aplanir le terrain pour qn. **(b) to ~ cream into one's skin** faire pénétrer la crème dans la peau.

smooth out *vt sep dress* défroisser; *wrinkles, creases* faire disparaître; *difficulties* aplanir.

smooth over *vt sep* (*fig*) **to ~ things over** arranger les choses.

♦ **smoothie‡** *n* (*pej*) beau parleur. ♦ **smoothly** *adv* (*easily*) facilement; (*gently*) doucement; *move* sans à-coups; *talk, say* doucereusement; **everything is going ~ly** tout marche comme sur des roulettes; **it went off ~ly** cela s'est bien passé. ♦ **smoothness** *n* qualité *f* or aspect *m* lisse *or* égal(e); moelleux *m*; douceur *f*; *[sea]* calme *m*; rythme *m* régulier; régularité *f*; caractère *or* ton doucereux. ♦ **smooth-running** *adj engine, machinery* qui n'a pas d'à-coups; *business, scheme* qui marche bien. ♦ **smooth-spoken** *or* ♦ **smooth-tongued** *adj* enjôleur.

smother [ˈsmʌðəʳ] **1** *vt* **(a)** (*stifle*) étouffer. **(b)** (*cover*) couvrir (*with, in* de). **2** *vi* mourir étouffé.

smoulder [ˈsməʊldəʳ] *vi* couver.

smudge [smʌdʒ] **1** *n* (légère) tache *f*. **2** *vt face* salir; *print* maculer; *paint* faire une marque sur; *writing* étaler accidentellement. **3** *vi* se salir; se maculer; s'étaler.

smug [smʌg] *adj person* suffisant; *optimism, satisfaction* béat. ♦ **smugly** *adv* avec suffisance. ♦ **smugness** *n [person]* suffisance *f*; *[voice, reply]* ton *m* suffisant.

smuggle [ˈsmʌgl] **1** *vt tobacco, drugs* passer en contrebande. **to ~ in** *etc goods* faire entrer *etc* en contrebande; (*fig*) *letters, person, animal* faire entrer *etc* clandestinement; **to ~ sth past** *or* **through the customs** passer qch en contrebande. **2** *vi* faire de la contrebande. ♦ **smuggler** *n* contrebandier *m*, -ière *f*. ♦ **smuggling** *n [goods]* contrebande *f* (*action*); *[drugs]* trafic *m*.

smut [smʌt] *n* (*dirt*) petite saleté *f*; (*soot*) flocon *m* de suie; (*mark*) tache *f* de suie; (*in conversation etc*) cochonneries* *fpl*. ♦ **smutty** *adj object* noirci; *joke, film* cochon*.

snack [snæk] *n* casse-croûte *m inv*. **to have a** ~ manger un petit quelque chose. ♦ **snack-bar** *n* snack *m*.

snag [snæg] *n* (*drawback*) inconvénient *m*; (*tear: in cloth*) accroc *m*; (*in stocking*) fil *m* tiré. **there's a ~ in it** il y a un inconvénient *or* une difficulté là-dedans; **to hit a** ~ tomber sur un os*; **that's the ~!** voilà la difficulté!; **the ~ is that ...** l'embêtant*, c'est que ... .

snail [sneɪl] *n* escargot *m*. **at a ~'s pace** à un pas de tortue.

snake [sneɪk] *n* serpent *m*. (*fig*) **~ in the grass** traître(sse) *m(f)*. ♦ **snakebite** *n* morsure *f* de serpent. ♦ **snake-charmer** *n* charmeur *m* de serpent. ♦ **snakes-and-ladders** *n* jeu *m* de l'oie. ♦ **snakeskin** *n* peau *f* de serpent.

snap [snæp] **1** *n* **(a)** (*noise*) bruit *m* sec. **with a ~ of his fingers he ...** faisant claquer ses doigts il ...; (*Met*) **a cold** ~ une brève vague de froid. **(b)**

(~*shot*) photo *f* (d'amateur). **(c)** (*Cards*) (jeu *m* de) bataille *f*. **2** *adj vote, strike* subit; *judgment, answer* irréfléchi. **to make a ~ decision** (se) décider tout d'un coup. **3** *vi* **(a)** (*break*) se casser net *or* avec un bruit sec. **(b)** *[whip, elastic]* claquer. **to ~ open** s'ouvrir avec un bruit sec; **to ~ back into place** revenir à sa place avec un claquement. **(c) to ~ at sb** *[dog]* essayer de mordre qn; *[person]* parler à qn d'un ton brusque. **4** *vt* **(a)** (*break*) casser net *or* avec un bruit sec. **(b) to ~ one's fingers** faire claquer ses doigts; (*fig*) **to ~ one's fingers at sb** faire la nique à qn; **to ~ sth open/shut** ouvrir/fermer qch d'un coup sec. **(c) 'shut up!' he ~ped** 'silence!' fit-il avec brusquerie.

snap off *vt sep* casser net. (*fig*) **to ~ sb's head off** rabrouer qn, rembarrer* qn.

snap out 1 *vi*: **to ~ out of*** se sortir de, se tirer de; **~ out of it!*** secoue-toi!* **2** *vt sep question/order* poser/lancer d'un ton brusque.

snap up *vt sep [dog etc]* happer; (*fig*) *bargain* sauter sur.

♦ **snapdragon** *n* gueule-de-loup *f*. ♦ **snap-fastener** *n* (*on clothes*) pression *f*; (*on handbag etc*) fermoir *m*. ♦ **snapshot** *n* photo *f* (d'amateur). ♦ **snappish** *adj* hargneux, cassant. ♦ **snappy*** *adj reply* bien envoyé; *phrase, slogan* qui a du punch*; **look ~py!** grouille-toi!*

snare [snɛəʳ] **1** *n* piège *m*. **2** *vt* prendre au piège.

snarl¹ [snɑ:l] **1** *vi [dog]* gronder en montrant les dents; *[person]* lancer un grondement (*at sb* à qn). **2** *vt*: **'no' he ~ed** 'non' dit-il avec hargne. **3** *n* grondement *m* féroce.

snarl² [snɑ:l] **1** *n* (*in wool etc*) nœud *m*; (*in traffic:* **~-up**) embouteillage *m*. **2** *vt*: **to get ~ed up** *[wool etc]* s'emmêler; *[traffic]* se bloquer.

snatch [snætʃ] **1** *n* **(a)** *[jewellery, wages etc]* vol *m* (à l'arraché); *[child etc]* enlèvement *m*. **there was a wages ~** des voleurs se sont emparés des salaires. **(b)** (*small piece*) fragment *m*. **a ~ of music/poetry** quelques mesures *fpl*/vers *mpl*; **a ~ of conversation** des bribes *fpl* de conversation; **to work in ~es** travailler par à-coups. **2** *vt* (*grab*) *object* saisir, s'emparer (brusquement) de; *few minutes' peace, short holiday* réussir à avoir; *opportunity* sauter sur; *kiss* voler (*from sb* à qn); *sandwich, drink* avaler à la hâte; (*steal*) voler (*from sb* à qn); (*kidnap*) enlever. **to ~ sth from sb** arracher qch à qn; **to ~ some sleep** réussir à dormir un peu; **to ~ a meal** déjeuner (*or* dîner) à la hâte. **3** *vi*: **to ~ at** *object* essayer de saisir; *opportunity* sauter sur.

snatch away *vt sep* enlever d'un geste brusque.

snatch up *vt sep* ramasser vivement.

sneak [sni:k] **1** *n* (*) rapporteur* *m*, -euse* *f*. **2** *adj attack, visit* subreptice. **~ thief** chapardeur* *m*, -euse* *f*. **3** *vi* **(a) to ~ in/out** *etc* entrer/sortir *etc* à la dérobée; **to ~ into the house** se faufiler dans la maison. **(b)** (*) moucharder* (*on sb* qn). **4** *vt*: **to ~ a look at sth** lancer un coup d'œil furtif à qch; **he was ~ing a cigarette** il était en train de fumer en cachette. ♦ **sneaker*** *n* (chaussure *f* de) tennis *f*. ♦ **sneaking** *adj dislike, preference* inavoué, secret; **I had a ~ing feeling that** je ne pouvais m'empêcher de penser que; **to have a ~ing suspicion that** soupçonner secrètement que. ♦ **sneaky*** *adj* sournois.

sneer [snɪəʳ] **1** *vi* ricaner. **to ~ at sb** se moquer de qn d'un air méprisant; **to ~ at sth** tourner qch en ridicule. **2** *n* (*act*) ricanement *m*; (*remark*) sarcasme *m*. ♦ **sneering 1** *adj* ricaneur, sarcastique; **2** *n* ricanements *mpl*, sarcasmes *mpl*. ♦ **sneeringly** *adv* de façon sarcastique.

sneeze [sni:z] **1** *n* éternuement *m*. **2** *vi* éternuer. (*fig*) **it is not to be ~d at** ce n'est pas à dédaigner.

snide [snaɪd] *adj* narquois.

sniff [snɪf] **1** *n* reniflement *m*. **one ~ of that is enough to kill you** il suffit de respirer cela une fois pour en mourir. **2** *vi* renifler; (*disdainfully*) faire la grimace. **to ~ at sth** *[dog, person]* renifler qch; (*fig*) faire la grimace à qch; **it's not to be ~ed at** ce n'est pas à dédaigner. **3** *vt [dog]* renifler, flairer; *[person] food, bottle* renifler, (*suspiciously*) flairer; *air, perfume* humer; *smelling salts, glue etc* respirer; *drug, inhalant etc* aspirer.

♦ **sniffle 1** *n* (*slight cold*) petit rhume *m* (de cerveau); **2** *vi* renifler. ♦ **sniffy*** *adj* **(a)** (*disdainful*) dédaigneux; **to be ~y about sth** faire le (*or* la) dégoûté(e) devant qch; **(b)** (*smelly*) qui a une drôle d'odeur.

snigger ['snɪgəʳ] **1** *n* rire *m* en dessous. **2** *vi* pouffer de rire. **to ~ at** *remark, question* pouffer de rire en entendant; *sb's appearance etc* se moquer de. ♦ **sniggering** *n* rires *mpl* en dessous.

snip [snɪp] **1** *n* (*cut*) petit coup *m*; (*small piece*) petit bout *m*; (*: *bargain*) bonne affaire *f*. **2** *vt* couper.

snipe [snaɪp] **1** *n* (*pl inv: bird*) bécassine *f*. **2** *vi*: **to ~ at sb/sth** (*shoot*) canarder* qn/qch; (*fig: verbally*) critiquer qn/qch par en dessous. ♦ **sniper** *n* tireur embusqué, canardeur* *m*.

snippet ['snɪpɪt] *n [cloth, paper]* petit bout *m*; *[conversation, news]* bribes *fpl*.

snivel ['snɪvl] *vi* pleurnicher. ♦ **sniveller** *n* pleurnicheur *m*, -euse *f*. ♦ **snivelling 1** *adj* pleurnicheur; **2** *n* pleurnicheries *fpl*.

snob [snɒb] *n* snob *mf*. **he's a terrible ~** il est terriblement snob. ♦ **snobbery** *n* snobisme *m*. ♦ **snobbish** *adj* (*gen*) snob *inv*; *lowly placed person* très impressionné par les gens importants (*or* riches *etc*). ♦ **snobbishness** *n* snobisme *m*. ♦ **snobby*** *adj* snob *inv*.

snog‡ [snɒg] *vi* (*Brit*) se peloter*.

snooker ['snu:kəʳ] *n* ≃ jeu *m* de billard.

snoop [snu:p] *vi* se mêler des *or* fourrer son nez* dans les affaires des autres. **he's been ~ing around here again** il est revenu fourrer son nez* par ici; **to ~ on sb** espionner qn. ♦ **snooper** *n* personne *f* qui fourre son nez* partout.

snooze* [snu:z] **1** *n* petit somme *m*. **2** *vi* sommeiller.

snore [snɔ:ʳ] **1** *vi* ronfler (*en dormant*). **2** *n* (*also* **snoring**) ronflement *m*.

snorkel ['snɔ:kl] *n* (*Sport*) tuba *m*.

snort [snɔ:t] **1** *vi [horse etc]* s'ébrouer; *[person]* grogner; (*laughing*) s'étrangler de rire. **2** *n* ébrouement *m*; grognement *m*. ♦ **snorter*** *n* **(a)** **a ~er of a question/problem** une question/un problème vache‡; **a ~er of a game** un match formidable*; **(b)** (*drink*) petit verre *m*.

snot* [snɒt] *n* morve *f*. ♦ **snotty*** *adj nose* qui coule; *face, child* morveux.

snout [snaʊt] *n* museau *m*.

snow [snəʊ] **1** *n* neige *f*; (*on TV screen*) neige; (*Drugs sl*) neige‡, cocaïne *f*. **hard/soft ~** neige dure/molle; (*Met*) **~ report** bulletin *m* d'enneigement. **2** *vi* neiger. **3** *vt*: **to be ~ed in** *or* **up** être bloqué par la neige; (*fig*) **to be ~ed under** être submergé (*with* de). ♦ **snowball 1** *n* boule *f* de neige; **~ball fight** bataille *f* de boules de neige; **2** *vi* se lancer des boules de neige; (*fig*) *[project etc]* faire boule de neige. ♦ **snow-blindness** *n* cécité *f* des neiges. ♦ **snowbound** *adj road, country* complètement enneigé; *village, person* bloqué par la neige. ♦ **snow-capped** *adj* couronné de neige. ♦ **snowcat** *or* (*US*) ♦ **snowmobile** *n* autoneige *f*. ♦ **snow-covered** *adj* enfoui sous la neige. ♦ **snowdrift** *n* congère *f*. ♦ **snowdrop** *n* perce-neige *m inv*. ♦ **snowfall** *n* chute *f* de neige. ♦ **snowflake** *n* flocon *m* de neige. ♦ **snowline** *n* limite *f* des neiges (éternelles). ♦ **snowman** *n* bonhomme *m* de neige; **the abominable ~man** l'abominable homme *m* des neiges. ♦ **snowplough** *or* (*US*) ♦ **snowplow** *n* chasse-neige *m inv*. ♦ **snowshoe** *n* raquette *f*. ♦ **snowslide** *n* avalanche *f.* ♦ **snowstorm** *n* tempête *f* de neige. ♦ **snow-white** *adj* blanc comme neige. ♦ **Snow White** *n* Blanche-Neige *f.* ♦ **snowy** *adj weather, region* neigeux; *hills, roof* enneigé; *day etc* de neige; (*fig*) *linen* neigeux; *hair* de neige; **it was very ~y yesterday** il a beaucoup neigé hier.

snub[1] [snʌb] **1** *n* rebuffade *f.* **2** *vt person* snober; *offer* repousser. **to be ~bed** essuyer une rebuffade.

snub[2] [snʌb] *adj nose* retroussé. ♦ **snub-nosed** *adj* au nez retroussé.

snuff [snʌf] *n* tabac *m* à priser. **pinch of ~** prise *f*; **to take ~** priser. ♦ **snuffbox** *n* tabatière *f.*

snug [snʌg] *adj* (*cosy*) douillet, confortable; (*safe*) *harbour* bien abrité; *hideout* très sûr. **it's nice and ~ here** il fait bon ici; **~ in bed** bien au chaud dans son lit. ♦ **snuggle** *vi* (**~gle down, ~gle up**) se blottir (*into sth* dans qch; *beside sb* contre qn). ♦ **snugly** *adv* douillettement, confortablement; **to fit ~ly** *[garment]* être bien ajusté; *[object in box etc]* rentrer juste bien.

so [səʊ] **1** *adv* **(a)** (*to such an extent*) si, tellement, aussi. **~ tiring** si *or* tellement fatigant; **he was ~ clumsy that he ...** il était si *or* tellement maladroit qu'il ...; **the body was ~ burnt that it ...** le cadavre était brûlé à un point tel qu'il ...; **he ~ loves her that he ...** il l'aime tant *or* tellement qu'il ...; **~ ... as to** + *infin* assez ... pour + *infin*; **he was ~ stupid as to tell her** il a été assez stupide pour le lui dire; **he was not ~ stupid as to say that to her** il n'a pas été bête au point de lui dire cela; **he is not ~ clever as his brother** il n'est pas aussi *or* si intelligent que son frère; **it's not ~ big as all that!** ce n'est pas si grand que ça!

(b) (*~ as to, ~ that*) **~ as to do** pour faire; **~ as not to be late** pour ne pas être en retard; **~ that** (*purpose*) pour + *infin*, pour que + *subj*; (*result*) si bien que + *indic*; **I'm going early ~ that I'll get a ticket** j'y vais tôt pour obtenir un billet; **I brought it ~ that you could read it** je l'ai apporté pour que vous le lisiez; **he refused to move, ~ that the police had to carry him away** il a refusé de bouger, si bien que les agents ont dû l'emporter de force.

(c) (*very*) si, tellement. **I'm ~ tired!** je suis si *or* tellement fatigué!; **~ very tired** vraiment si fatigué; **~ much to do** tellement *or* tant de choses à faire.

(d) (*thus, in this way*) ainsi, comme ceci *or* cela. **you should stand just ~** vous devriez vous tenir ainsi *or* comme ceci; **he likes everything to be just ~** il aime que tout soit fait comme ça et pas autrement*; **as A is to B ~ C is to D** C est à D ce que A est à B; **~ it was that ...** c'est ainsi que ...; (*frm*) **~ be it** soit; **it ~ happened that** il s'est trouvé que.

(e) (*phrases*) **~ saying ...** sur ces mots ...; **~ I believe** c'est ce qu'il me semble; **is that ~?** vraiment?; **that is ~** c'est exact; **if that is ~ ...** s'il en est ainsi ...; **if ~** si oui; **perhaps ~** peut-être bien que oui; **just ~!, quite ~!** exactement!; **I told you ~ yesterday** je vous l'ai dit hier; **I told you ~!** je vous l'avais bien dit!; **he certainly said ~** il l'a bien dit; **do ~** faites-le; **I think ~** je (le) crois, je (le) pense; **I hope ~** je l'espère bien; **... only more ~** ... mais encore plus; **how ~?** comment?; **he said they would be there and ~ they were** il a dit qu'ils seraient là, et en effet ils y étaient; **~ do I!, ~ have I!, ~ am I!** *etc* moi aussi!; **~ he did!** (*or* **~ it is!** *etc*) en effet!; **I didn't say that! — you did so!*** je n'ai pas dit ça! — mais si tu l'as dit!; **20 or ~** à peu près 20, environ 20, une vingtaine; **and ~ on (and ~ forth)** et ainsi de suite; **~ long!*** à bientôt!

2 *conj* donc, par conséquent; alors. **he was late, ~ he missed the train** il est arrivé en retard, donc *or* par conséquent il a manqué le train; **~ there he is!** le voilà donc!; **the roads are busy, ~ be careful** il y a beaucoup de circulation, alors fais bien attention; **~ you're selling it?** alors vous le vendez?; **and ~ you see ...** alors comme vous voyez ...; **~ what?*** et alors?

♦ **so-and-so** *n*: **Mr S~-and-~*** Monsieur un tel; **Mrs S~-and-~*** Madame une telle; **he's an old ~-and-~*** c'est un vieil imbécile; **if you ask me to do ~-and-~** si vous me demandez de faire ci et ça. ♦ **so-called** *adj* soi-disant *inv*, prétendu. ♦ **so-so*** *adj* comme ci comme ça.

soak [səʊk] **1** *vt* **(a)** faire tremper (*in* dans). **to be ~ed through** être trempé; **to be/get ~ed to the skin** être trempé/se faire tremper jusqu'aux os; **bread ~ed in milk** pain *m* imbibé de lait. **(b)** (‡: *take money from*) (*by overcharging*) estamper‡. (*by taxation*) **to ~ the rich** faire casquer* les riches. **2** *vi* tremper (*in* dans). **3** *n* (‡: *drunkard*) soûlard* *m.*

soak in *vi [liquid]* pénétrer. (*fig*) **I told him what I thought and left it to ~ in*** je lui ai donné mon opinion et je l'ai laissé méditer dessus.

soak up *vt sep* (*lit, fig*) absorber.

♦ **soaking (wet)** *adj* trempé.

soap [səʊp] **1** *n* savon *m.* **2** *vt* (**~ down**) savonner. ♦ **soapdish** *n* porte-savon *m.* ♦ **soapflakes** *npl* paillettes *fpl* de savon. ♦ **soap-opera** *n* mélo* *m* à épisodes. ♦ **soap-powder** *n* lessive *f.* ♦ **soapsuds** *npl* (*lather*) mousse *f* de savon; (*~y water*) eau *f* savonneuse. ♦ **soapy** *adj water* savonneux; *taste* de savon; (**fig pej*) *person* doucereux.

soar [sɔːʳ] *vi* (*often* **~ up**) *[bird, aircraft, prices etc]* monter en flèche; *[ball etc]* voler (*over* par-dessus); *[tower]* s'élancer vers le ciel; *[ambitions, hopes]* grandir démesurément; *[spirits, morale]* remonter en flèche. ♦ **soaring** *adj* qui monte en flèche; élancé.

sob [sɒb] **1** *vi* sangloter. **2** *vt* dire en sanglotant. **3** *n* sanglot *m.* **4** *adj*: **~ story*** histoire *f* à (vous) fendre le cœur; **~ stuff*** mélo* *m*, sensiblerie *f.* ♦ **sobbing 1** *n* sanglots *mpl*; **2** *adj* sanglotant.

sober [ˈsəʊbəʳ] **1** *adj* **(a)** (*moderate*) *person* sérieux; *estimate, statement* modéré; *occasion* solennel; *suit, colour* sobre. **the ~ truth** la vérité toute simple; **the ~ fact of the matter** les faits tels qu'ils sont; **in a ~ mood** plein de gravité. **(b)** (*not drunk*) **I'm perfectly ~** je n'ai vraiment pas trop bu; **he's never ~** il est toujours ivre; **he is ~ now** il est désenivré maintenant; **to be as ~ as a judge, to be stone-cold ~** n'être absolument pas ivre. **2** *vt* (**~ up**) **(a)** (*calm*) calmer; (*deflate*) dégriser. **(b)** (*stop being drunk*) désenivrer. **3** *vi* (**~ up**) (*calm down*) se calmer; (*grow sadder*) être dégrisé; (*stop being drunk*) désenivrer. (*fig*) **it had a ~ing effect on him** ça lui a donné à réfléchir.

♦ **soberly** *adv speak, say* avec modération; *behave, act* de façon posée; *furnish, dress* sobrement. ♦ **soberness** *or* ♦ **sobriety** *n* sérieux *m*; modération *f*; sobriété *f.*

soccer [ˈsɒkəʳ] **1** *n* football *m*, foot* *m.* **2** *adj match, pitch, team* de football, de foot*; *season* du football. **~ player** footballeur *m.*

sociable [ˈsəʊʃəbl] *adj person, animal* sociable; *evening, gathering* amical. **I'll have a drink just to be ~** je prendrai un verre rien que pour vous faire plaisir; **I'm not feeling very ~** je n'ai pas envie de voir des gens. ♦ **sociability** *n* sociabilité *f.* ♦ **sociably** *adv invite, say* amicalement.

social [ˈsəʊʃəl] **1** *adj* **(a)** *behaviour, class, problems, customs, reforms* social. **a ~ outcast** un paria; **~ anthropology** anthropologie *f* sociale; **S~ Democracy** social-démocratie *f*; **S~ Democrat** social-démocrate *mf*; (*US*) **~ insurance** sécurité *f* sociale; **~ science** sciences *fpl* humaines; **~ scientist** spécialiste *mf* des sciences humaines; **~ security** (*n*) aide *f* sociale; (*adj*) *benefits etc* de la sécurité sociale; **to be on ~ security*** recevoir l'aide sociale; **the ~ services** les services *mpl* sociaux; **Department of S~**

Services ministère *m* des Affaires sociales; ~ **studies** sciences sociales; ~ **welfare** sécurité sociale; ~ **work** assistance *f* sociale; ~ **worker** assistant(e) *m(f)* de service social, assistant(e) social(e). **(b)** (*in society*) *engagements, life* mondain. ~ **climber** (*still climbing*) arriviste *mf*; (*arrived*) parvenu(e) *m(f)*; (*Press*) ~ **column** carnet *m* mondain; **a gay ~ life** une vie très mondaine; **we've got no ~ life** nous ne sortons jamais; **how's your ~ life?*** est-ce que tu sors beaucoup? **(c)** (*gregarious*) *person* sociable; *evening* agréable. ~ **club** association *f* amicale.
 2 *n* fête *f*.
♦ **socialism** *n* socialisme *m*. ♦ **socialist** *adj, n* socialiste (*mf*). ♦ **socialite** *n* personnalité *f* en vue dans la haute société. ♦ **socialize** 1 *vt* (*Pol, Psych*) socialiser; 2 *vi* (*be with people*) fréquenter des gens; (*make friends*) se faire des amis; (*chat*) bavarder (*with sb* avec qn). ♦ **socially** *adv interact, be valid* socialement; *acceptable* en société; **I know him ~ly** nous nous rencontrons en société.

society [sə'saɪətɪ] **1** *n* **(a)** (*community*) société *f*. **to live in ~** vivre en société; **it is a danger to ~** cela met la société en danger. **(b)** (*high* ~) haute société *f*. **polite ~** la bonne société. **(c)** (*companionship*) compagnie *f*. **in the ~ of** en compagnie de; **I enjoy his ~** je me plais en sa compagnie. **(d)** (*association, group*) société *f*, association *f*; (*Scol, Univ etc*) club *m*, association. **dramatic ~** club théâtral, association théâtrale; **learned ~** société savante. **2** *adj photographer, wedding* mondain.

socio... ['səʊsɪəʊ] *pref* socio... . **~economic** socio-économique.

sociology [ˌsəʊsɪ'ɒlədʒɪ] *n* sociologie *f*. ♦ **sociological** *adj* sociologique. ♦ **sociologist** *n* sociologue *mf*.

sock[1] [sɒk] *n* chaussette *f*, (*shorter*) socquette *f*. (*fig*) **to pull up one's ~s*** se secouer*.

sock[2]**ꜝ** [sɒk] *n*: **to give sb a ~ on the jaw** flanquer un coup sur la gueuleꜝ à qn.

socket ['sɒkɪt] *n* (*gen*) cavité *f* (*où qch s'emboîte*); *[bone]* cavité articulaire; *[eye]* orbite *f*; *[tooth]* alvéole *f*; (*Elec: for light bulb*) douille *f*; (*Elec: also* **wall** ~) prise *f* de courant (*femelle*).

soda ['səʊdə] **1** *n* **(a)** (*Chem*) soude *f*; (*washing* ~) cristaux *mpl* de soude. **(b)** (~ **water**) eau *f* de Seltz. **whisky and ~** whisky *m* soda. **(c)** (*US:* ~ **pop**) soda *m*. **2** *adj*: ~ **fountain** buvette *f*; ~ **siphon** siphon *m* (d'eau gazeuse).

sodden ['sɒdn] *adj ground* détrempé; *clothes* trempé.

sodium ['səʊdɪəm] **1** *n* sodium *m*. **2** *adj*: ~ **bicarbonate** bicarbonate *m* de soude; ~ **light** lampe *f* à vapeur de sodium.

sofa ['səʊfə] *n* sofa *m*, canapé *m*.

soft [sɒft] **1** *adj* **(a)** (*not hard etc*) *mattress, pillow* doux (*f* douce), (*unpleasantly so*) mou (*f* molle); *mud, snow, ground, collar, cheese* mou; *substance* malléable; *wood, stone, pencil* tendre; *butter, leather, brush* souple; *fabric, hand, skin* doux; *hair* soyeux; *toy* de peluche; (*pej: flabby*) *person, muscle* avachi. ~ **fruit** ≃ fruits *mpl* rouges; (*Comm*) ~ **furnishings** tissus *mpl* d'ameublement (*rideaux etc*); (*Comm*) ~ **goods** textiles *mpl*; (*Anat*) ~ **palate** voile *m* du palais; **to grow** *or* **become ~(er)** = **soften 2**; **to make ~(er)** = **soften 1**; **this sort of life makes you ~** ce genre de vie vous ramollit; ~ **currency** devise *f* faible; ~ **drinks** boissons *fpl* non alcoolisées; ~ **drugs** drogues *fpl* douces; (*fig*) ~ **soap*** flagornerie *f*; **to be a ~ touch*** se faire avoir (facilement); (*Aut*) ~ **verges** accotements *mpl* non stabilisés; ~ **water** eau *f* qui n'est pas calcaire. **(b)** (*not rough*) *tap, pressure* doux, léger; *breeze, rain, weather* doux; (*Aviat*) *landing* en douceur. **(c)** (*not harsh*) *look, smile* doux, gentil; *answer* aimable, gentil; *heart* tendre; *life, job, option* facile; *person* indulgent (*with or on sb* envers qn). **he has a ~ time of it*** il se la coule douce*; **to have a ~ spot for** avoir un faible pour; ~ **sell** promotion *f* de vente discrète. **(d)** (*not loud*) *sound, laugh* doux, léger; *tone, music, voice* doux; *steps* feutré. **in a ~ voice** d'une voix douce; **the radio is too ~** la radio ne joue pas assez fort; **the music is too ~** la musique n'est pas assez forte; ~ **pedal** pédale *f* douce. **(e)** *light, colour,* (*Ling*) *consonant* doux. (*Phot*) ~ **focus** flou *m* artistique. **(f)** (*: *stupid*) stupide. **(g)** (*: *no stamina*) **he's ~** il n'a pas de nerf.
 2 *adv* doucement.
♦ **soft-boiled egg** *n* œuf *m* à la coque. ♦ **soften (up)** **1** *vt* **(a)** (*gen*) adoucir; *butter, clay, ground* ramollir; *collar, leather* assouplir; *outline* estomper; *resistance* amoindrir; (*fig*) **to ~en the blow** amortir le choc; **(b)** *person* attendrir; (*: *by cajoling*) *customer etc* baratinerꜝ; (*: *by bullying*) intimider; **2** *vi* s'adoucir; se ramollir; s'assouplir; s'estomper; **his heart ~ened** il s'est attendri; **his eyes ~ened** son regard s'est adouci. ♦ **softener** *n* (*water softener*) adoucisseur *m*; (*fabric softener*) adoucissant *m*. ♦ **soft-hearted** *adj* au cœur tendre. ♦ **softie*** *n* (*tender-hearted*) tendre *mf*; (*no stamina*) mauviette *f*; (*coward*) poule *f* mouillée. ♦ **softly** *adv* (*quietly*) *say, sing* doucement; *walk* à pas feutrés; (*gently*) *tap* légèrement; (*tenderly*) *smile, look* tendrement, gentiment. ♦ **softness** *n* (*gen*) douceur *f*; *[bed, mattress, pillow]* douceur, mollesse *f* (*pej*); *[snow, ground, butter]* mollesse; *[substance]* malléabilité *f*; *[leather, brush, collar]* souplesse *f*; *[person, muscle]* avachissement *m*; *[outline, photograph]* flou *m*; *[words, glance]* douceur, gentillesse *f*; *[answer]* amabilité *f*, gentillesse; (*indulgence*) manque *m* de sévérité (*towards* envers). ♦ **soft-spoken** *adj* à la voix douce. ♦ **software** *n* (*Computers*) software *m*, logiciel *m*. ♦ **softwood** *n* bois *m* tendre.

soggy ['sɒgɪ] *adj ground* détrempé; *clothes* trempé; *bread* mal cuit; *heat, pudding* lourd.

soh [səʊ] *n* (*Mus*) sol *m*.

soil [sɔɪl] **1** *n* sol *m*, terre *f*. **rich/chalky ~** sol *or* terre riche/calcaire; **cover it over with ~** recouvre-le de terre; **on French ~** sur le sol français. **2** *vt* (*dirty*) salir. **~ed linen** linge *m* sale. **3** *vi* *[material, garment]* se salir.

solar ['səʊlə^r] *adj* (*gen*) solaire; *heating* à l'énergie solaire. ~ **plexus** plexus *m* solaire.

sold [səʊld] *pret, ptp of* **sell**.

solder ['səʊldə^r] **1** *n* soudure *f*. **2** *vt* souder. **~ing iron** fer *m* à souder.

soldier ['səʊldʒə^r] **1** *n* soldat *m*, militaire *m*. **girl ~** femme *f* soldat; **to play at ~s** (*pej*) jouer à la guerre; *[children]* jouer aux soldats; **old ~** vétéran *m*. **2** *vi* servir dans l'armée. (*fig*) **to ~ on** persévérer (malgré tout). ♦ **soldierly** *adj* typiquement militaire.

sole[1] [səʊl] *n, pl inv* (*fish*) sole *f*.

sole[2] [səʊl] **1** *n [shoe]* semelle *f*; *[foot]* plante *f*. **2** *vt* ressemeler.

sole[3] [səʊl] *adj* **(a)** (*only*) seul, unique. **the ~ reason** la seule *or* l'unique raison. **(b)** (*exclusive*) *right* exclusif. (*Comm*) ~ **agent** concessionnaire *mf* (*for* de). ♦ **solely** *adv* (*only*) seulement, uniquement; (*entirely*) entièrement.

solecism ['sɒləsɪzəm] *n* (*Ling*) solécisme *m*; (*social offence*) faute *f* de goût.

solemn ['sɒləm] *adj* (*gen*) solennel; *duty* sacré; *warning* plein de gravité. ♦ **solemnity** [sə'lemnɪtɪ] *n* solennité *f*; caractère *m* sacré; gravité *f*. ♦ **solemnization** *n [marriage]* célébration *f*. ♦ **solemnize** *vt* célébrer. ♦ **solemnly** *adv promise, utter* solennellement; *say, smile* gravement, d'un air solennel.

sol-fa ['sɒl'fɑː] *n* solfège *m*.

solicit [sə'lɪsɪt] **1** *vt* solliciter (*from* de). **2** *vi*

[prostitute] racoler. ♦ **soliciting** *n* racolage *m*.
solicitor [sə'lɪsɪtəʳ] *n* (*Brit*) ≃ avocat *m*; (*US*) ≃ juriste *m* conseil.
solicitous [sə'lɪsɪtəs] *adj* (*anxious*) préoccupé (*for, about* de); (*eager*) désireux (*of* de; *to do* de faire). ♦ **solicitude** *n* sollicitude *f*.
solid ['sɒlɪd] **1** *adj* (*gen*) *substance, structure, reasons, character* solide; *ball, block, tyre* plein; *crowd* dense; *row, line* continu; *vote* unanime. **frozen** ~ complètement gelé; **to become** ~ se solidifier; ~ **geometry** géométrie *f* dans l'espace; **cut out of** ~ **rock** taillé à même la pierre; **in** ~ **gold/oak** en or/chêne massif; ~ **fuel** combustible *m* solide; **a** ~ **stretch of yellow** une étendue de jaune uni; **he was 6 ft 2 of** ~ **muscle** c'était un homme de 2 mètres de haut et tout en muscles; **on** ~ **ground** sur la terre ferme, (*in discussion etc*) en terrain sûr; ~ **common sense** solide bon sens *m*; **a good** ~ **worker** un travailleur sérieux; **he's a good** ~ **bloke*** c'est qn sur qui on peut compter; **the square was** ~ **with cars*** la place était complètement embouteillée; **Moordown is** ~ **for Labour** Moordown vote massivement pour les travaillistes; **a** ~ **hour** une heure entière; **2** ~ **days** 2 jours d'affilée; **a** ~ **day's work** une journée entière de travail.
2 *n* (*gen*) solide *m*. (*food*) ~**s** aliments *mpl* solides.
♦ **solidarity** *n* solidarité *f*. ♦ **solidification** *n* solidification *f*. ♦ **solidify 1** *vt* solidifier; **2** *vi* se solidifier. ♦ **solidity** *n* solidité *f*. ♦ **solidly** *adv build etc* solidement; *vote* massivement; **they are** ~**ly behind him** ils le soutiennent à l'unanimité. ♦ **solid-state** *adj* (*Phys*) des solides; (*Electronics*) transistorisé.
soliloquy [sə'lɪləkwɪ] *n* soliloque *m*.
solitary ['sɒlɪtərɪ] *adj* **(a)** (*alone: gen*) solitaire; *hour* de solitude; (*lonely*) seul. (*Jur*) **in** ~ **confinement** au régime cellulaire; **to take a** ~ **walk** se promener tout seul. **(b)** (*only one*) seul, unique (*before n*). **a** ~ **example** un seul *or* unique exemple; **not a** ~ **one** pas un seul. ♦ **solitude** *n* solitude *f*.
solo ['səʊləʊ] **1** *n* (*Mus*) solo *m*. **piano** ~ solo de piano. **2** *adv play, sing* en solo; *fly* en solitaire. **3** *adj violin etc* solo *inv*; *flight etc* en solitaire. ♦ **soloist** *n* soliste *mf*.
solstice ['sɒlstɪs] *n* solstice *m*.
soluble ['sɒljʊbl] *adj* (*all senses*) soluble. ♦ **solubility** *n* solubilité *f*.
solution [sə'lu:ʃən] *n* (*all senses*) solution *f* (*to* de).
solve [sɒlv] *vt equation, problem* résoudre; *crossword puzzle* réussir; *mystery* éclaircir; *riddle* trouver la solution de.
solvent ['sɒlvənt] **1** *adj* (*Fin*) solvable; (*Chem*) dissolvant. **2** *n* (*Chem*) solvant *m*. ♦ **solvency** *n* solvabilité *f*.
sombre, (*US*) **somber** ['sɒmbəʳ] *adj* sombre.
some [sʌm] **1** *adj* **(a)** (*a certain amount or number of*) ~ **tea/ice/water/cakes** du thé/de la glace/de l'eau/des gâteaux; **there are** ~ **children outside** il y a des enfants *or* quelques enfants dehors; ~ **old shoes** de vieilles chaussures; ~ **dirty shoes** des chaussures sales; **will you have** ~ **more meat?** voulez-vous encore de la viande?
(b) (*unspecified*) ~ **woman was asking for her** il y avait une dame qui la demandait; **in** ~ **book or other** quelque part dans un livre; **at** ~ **place in Africa** quelque part en Afrique; ~ **day** un de ces jours, un jour ou l'autre; ~ **day next week** dans le courant de la semaine prochaine; ~ **other day** un autre jour; ~ **other time!** pas maintenant!; ~ **time last week** un jour la semaine dernière; ~ **more talented person** quelqu'un de plus doué; **there must be** ~ **solution** il doit bien y avoir une solution quelconque.
(c) (*contrasted with others*) ~ **children like school** certains enfants aiment l'école, il y a des enfants qui aiment l'école; ~ **people say that ...** il y a des gens qui disent que ...; **in** ~ **ways, he's right** dans un (certain) sens, il a raison; **in** ~ **way or (an)other** d'une façon ou d'une autre.
(d) (*a considerable amount of*) **it took** ~ **courage to refuse** il a fallu un certain courage *or* pas mal de* courage pour refuser; **at** ~ **length** assez longuement; ~ **distance away** à quelque distance; **I haven't seen him for** ~ **years** cela fait quelques années que je ne l'ai pas vu; *V* **time**.
(e) (*emphatic: a little*) **we still have** SOME **money left** il nous reste quand même un peu d'argent; **that's** SOME **consolation** c'est quand même une petite consolation.
(f) (*intensive*) **that's** ~ **fish!*** quel poisson!; **that was** ~ **film!*** c'était un film formidable; (*iro*) **you're** ~ **help!*** tu parles* d'une aide!
2 *pron* **(a)** (*a certain number*) quelques-un(e)s *m(f)pl*, certain(e)s *m(f)pl*. ~ **went this way and others went that** il y en a qui sont partis par ici et d'autres par là; ~ **(of them) have been sold** certains (d'entre eux) ont été vendus, on en a vendu un certain nombre; **I've still got** ~ **of them** j'en ai encore quelques-uns; ~ **of my friends** certains *or* quelques-uns de mes amis; **I've got** ~ j'en ai quelques-uns. **(b)** (*a certain amount*) **I've got** ~ j'en ai; **have** ~! prenez-en!; **have** ~ **more** reprenez-en; **if you find** ~ si vous en trouvez; **have** ~ **of this cake** prenez un peu de ce gâteau; ~ **(of it) has been eaten** on en a mangé (un morceau); ~ **of this work** une partie de ce travail; ~ **of what you said** certaines choses que vous avez dites.
3 *adv* (*about*) quelque, environ. ~ **twenty houses** quelque vingt maisons, une vingtaine de maisons.
somebody ['sʌmbədɪ] *pron* quelqu'un. **there is** ~ **at the door** il y a quelqu'un à la porte; **there is** ~ **knocking at the door** on frappe à la porte; ~ **else** quelqu'un d'autre; ~ **strong** quelqu'un de fort; ~ **French** un Français, quelqu'un de français; ~ **or other** quelqu'un, je ne sais qui; **Mr S~-or-other** Monsieur Machin*; **she thinks she's** ~ elle se prend pour quelqu'un (d'important).
somehow ['sʌmhaʊ] *adv* **(a)** (*in some way*) **it must be done** ~ **(or other)** il faut que ce soit fait d'une façon ou d'une autre; **he managed it** ~ il y est arrivé tant bien que mal; **we'll manage** ~ on se débrouillera*; **we saved him** ~ **or other** nous l'avons sauvé je ne sais comment. **(b)** (*for some reason*) ~ **he's never succeeded** pour une raison ou pour une autre il n'a jamais réussi; **it seems odd** ~ je ne sais pas pourquoi, mais ça semble bizarre.
someone ['sʌmwʌn] *pron* = **somebody**.
someplace ['sʌmpleɪs] *adv* (*US*) = **somewhere**.
somersault ['sʌməsɔ:lt] **1** *n* (*on ground; also accidental*) culbute *f*; (*by child*) galipette *f*; (*in air*) saut *m* périlleux; (*by car*) tonneau *m*. **2** *vi* (*also* **turn a** ~) faire la culbute *or* un saut périlleux *or* un tonneau.
something ['sʌmθɪŋ] **1** *pron* quelque chose. ~ **moved** il y a quelque chose qui a bougé; ~ **has happened** quelque chose est arrivé; ~ **unusual** quelque chose d'inhabituel; **there must be** ~ **wrong** il doit y avoir quelque chose qui ne va pas; **did you say** ~? pardon?, comment?; **I want** ~ **to read** je veux quelque chose à lire; **would you like** ~ **to drink?** voulez-vous boire quelque chose?; **give him** ~ **to drink** donnez-lui quelque chose à boire; ~ **to live for** une raison de vivre; **I have** ~ **else to do** j'ai quelque chose d'autre à faire; ~ **or other** quelque chose; ~ **of the kind** quelque chose dans ce genre-là; **there's** ~ **about her I don't like** il y a chez elle quelque chose que je n'aime pas; **there's** ~ **in what you say** il y a du vrai dans ce que vous dites; **here's** ~ **for your trouble** voici pour votre peine; **give him** ~ **for himself** donnez-lui un petit quelque chose; **you've got** ~ **there!*** c'est

vrai ce que tu dis là!; **that really is ~!*** c'est pas rien!*; **that certain ~* which makes all the difference** ce petit je ne sais quoi qui fait toute la différence; **he's called Paul ~** il s'appelle Paul quelque chose; **the 4-~ train** le train de 4 heures et quelques; **I hope to see ~ of you** j'espère vous voir un peu; **it is really ~* to find good coffee** ça n'est pas rien* de trouver du bon café; **that's ~!*** ça n'est pas rien!*; **that's always ~** c'est toujours ça; **or ~** ou quelque chose dans ce genre-là; **he is ~ of a miser** il est plutôt avare; **he is ~ of a pianist** il est assez bon pianiste.

2 *adv*: **~ like 200** quelque chose comme 200; **~ over £5,000** plus de 5 000 livres; **~ under £10** un peu moins de 10 livres; **~ like his father** un peu comme son père; **that's ~ like a claret!** ça au moins, c'est du bordeaux!; **that's ~ like it!*** ça au moins, c'est bien!; **it was ~ dreadful*** c'était vraiment épouvantable.

sometime ['sʌmtaɪm] 1 *adv*: **~ last month** le mois dernier, au cours du mois dernier; **it was ~ last winter** c'était pendant l'hiver dernier (je ne sais plus exactement quand); **I'll do it ~** je le ferai un de ces jours; **~ soon** bientôt; **~ before January** d'ici janvier; **~ next year** (dans le courant de) l'année prochaine; **~ after my birthday** après mon anniversaire; **~ or (an)other it will have to be done** il faudra bien le faire tôt ou tard. 2 *adj* (*former*) ancien (*before n*).

sometimes ['sʌmtaɪmz] *adv* **(a)** quelquefois, parfois, de temps en temps. **(b) ~ happy, ~ sad** tantôt gai, tantôt triste.

somewhat ['sʌmwɒt] *adv* quelque peu, assez.

somewhere ['sʌmwɛəʳ] *adv* **(a)** (*in space*) quelque part. **~ else** autre part, ailleurs; **he's ~ about** il est quelque part par ici; **~ near Paris** quelque part pas bien loin de Paris; **~ or other** je ne sais où, quelque part; **~ or other in France** quelque part en France. **(b)** (*approximately*) environ. **~ about 10 o'clock** vers 10 heures, à 10 heures environ; **~ about £12** environ 12 livres, dans les 12 livres.

somnambulism [sɒm'næmbjʊlɪzəm] *n* somnambulisme *m*. ♦ **somnambulist** *n* somnambule *mf*.

somnolence ['sɒmnələns] *n* somnolence *f*. ♦ **somnolent** *adj* somnolent.

son [sʌn] *n* fils *m*. **come here, ~*** viens ici, mon gars*. ♦ **son-in-law** *n* gendre *m*, beau-fils *m*.

sonar ['səʊnɑːʳ] *n* sonar *m*.

sonata [sə'nɑːtə] *n* sonate *f*.

song [sɒŋ] *n* (*gen*) chanson *f*; (*more formal*) chant *m*; *[birds]* chant. **to burst into ~** se mettre à chanter; **give us a ~** chante-nous qch; **~ without words** romance *f* sans paroles; (*fig*) **it was going for a ~** c'était à vendre pour une bouchée de pain; **to make a ~ and dance*** faire toute une histoire* (*about* à propos de). ♦ **songbird** *n* oiseau *m* chanteur. ♦ **songbook** *n* recueil *m* de chansons. ♦ **song hit** *n* chanson *f* à succès, tube* *m*. ♦ **songwriter** *n* compositeur *m*, -trice *f* de chansons.

sonic ['sɒnɪk] *adj* (*gen*) sonique. **~ depth-finder** sonde *f* à ultra-sons.

sonnet ['sɒnɪt] *n* sonnet *m*.

sonorous ['sɒnərəs] *adj* sonore. ♦ **sonority** *n* sonorité *f*. ♦ **sonorously** *adv* d'un ton sonore.

soon [suːn] *adv* **(a)** (*before long*) bientôt; vite. **we shall ~ be in Paris** nous serons bientôt à Paris; **you would ~ get lost** vous seriez vite perdu; **he ~ changed his mind** il a vite changé d'avis; **see you ~!** à bientôt!; **very ~** très vite, très bientôt; **quite ~** dans assez peu de temps, assez vite; **~ afterwards** peu après; **all too ~ it was over** ce ne fut que trop vite fini. **(b)** (*early*) tôt. **why have you come so ~?** pourquoi êtes-vous venu si tôt?; **much ~er than this** bien plus tôt que cela, bien avant; **how ~ can you get here?** dans combien de temps au plus tôt peux-tu être ici?; **how ~ will it be ready?** dans combien de temps est-ce que ce sera prêt? **(c)** (*in phrases*) **as ~ as possible** dès que possible, aussitôt que possible. **I'll do it as ~ as I can** je le ferai aussitôt que je le pourrai *or* aussitôt que possible; **let me know as ~ as you've finished** prévenez-moi dès que *or* aussitôt que vous aurez fini; **as ~ as 7 o'clock** dès 7 heures; **the ~er we get started the ~er we'll be done** plus tôt nous commencerons plus tôt nous aurons fini; **the ~er the better** le plus tôt sera le mieux; **~er or later** tôt ou tard; **no ~er had he finished than ...** à peine avait-il fini que ... . **(d)** (*expressing preference*) **I'd as ~ do that** j'aimerais autant faire ça; **I'd ~er you didn't tell him** je préférerais que vous ne le lui disiez (*subj*) pas; **I would ~er stay here than go** je préférerais *or* j'aimerais mieux rester ici plutôt que d'y aller; **I'd ~er not, I'd as ~ not** je n'y tiens pas; **I'd ~er die!** plutôt mourir!; **~er you than me!*** je n'aimerais pas être à ta place.

soot [sʊt] *n* suie *f*. ♦ **sooty** *adj surface, hands* noir de suie.

soothe [suːð] *vt person, nerves, pain* calmer; *anger, anxieties* apaiser. ♦ **soothing** *adj medicine, ointment* lénitif; *tone, voice, words* apaisant; *sb's presence* rassurant; *hot bath* relaxant. ♦ **soothingly** *adv* d'une manière apaisante; *say* d'un ton apaisant.

sop [sɒp] *n* **(a)** (*Culin*) **~s** aliments *mpl* semi-liquides; (*fig*) **as a ~ to his pride** pour flatter son amour-propre; **he said that as a ~ to the unions** il a dit cela pour amadouer les syndicats. **(b)** (*: *sissy*) poule *f* mouillée.

sop up *vt sep [sponge, rag]* absorber; *[person]* éponger (*with* avec).

♦ **sopping (wet)** *adj* trempé. ♦ **soppy*** *adj* sentimental; (*sissy*) mollasson.

sophisticated [sə'fɪstɪkeɪtɪd] *adj person, mind, tastes* raffiné; *clothes, room* d'une élégance raffinée; *film, book, discussion* subtil; *song* plein de recherche; *machine, method* sophistiqué, hautement perfectionné. **he's not very ~** il est très simple. ♦ **sophistication** *n* raffinement *m*; élégance *f*; subtilité *f*; recherche *f*; sophistication *f*.

sophomore ['sɒfəmɔːʳ] *n* (*US*) étudiant(e) *m(f)* de seconde année.

soporific [ˌsɒpə'rɪfɪk] *adj* soporifique.

soprano [sə'prɑːnəʊ] 1 *n* soprano *mf*. 2 *adj voice* de soprano.

sorbet ['sɔːbɪt] *n* sorbet *m*.

sorcery ['sɔːsərɪ] *n* sorcellerie *f*. ♦ **sorcerer** *n* sorcier *m*.

sordid ['sɔːdɪd] *adj* (*gen*) sordide; *agreement, deal, film, book* ignoble.

sore [sɔːʳ] 1 *adj* **(a)** (*painful*) douloureux; (*inflamed*) irrité, enflammé. **that's ~!** ça me fait mal!; **where is it ~?** où est-ce que vous avez mal?; **I'm ~ all over** j'ai mal partout; **I have a ~ finger** j'ai mal au doigt; (*fig*) **a ~ point** un point délicat. **(b)** (*: *offended*) en rogne* (*about* à cause de; *with sb* contre qn). **he was feeling very ~ about it** il en était vraiment ulcéré; **to get ~** râler*, être en rogne*. 2 *n* (*Med*) plaie *f*. (*fig*) **to open up an old ~** rouvrir une ancienne blessure. ♦ **sorely** *adv wounded* grièvement; *missed, regretted* amèrement; *tempted* fortement; **it is ~ly needed** on en a grandement besoin. ♦ **soreness** *n* (*painfulness*) endolorissement *m*; (*irritation*) irritation *f*; (*: *anger*) colère *f*, rogne* *f*.

sorrel ['sɒrəl] *n* (*Bot*) oseille *f*; (*horse*) alezan *m* clair.

sorrow ['sɒrəʊ] 1 *n* peine *f*, chagrin *m*, tristesse *f*; (*stronger*) douleur *f*. **his ~ at the loss of his son** la douleur qu'il a éprouvée à la mort de son fils; **this was a great ~ to me** j'en ai eu beaucoup de peine *or* de chagrin; **more in ~ than in anger** avec plus de peine que de colère. 2 *vi*: **to ~ over sth** pleurer qch. ♦ **sorrowful** *adj person* triste, (*stronger*) affligé. ♦ **sorrowfully** *adv* tristement. ♦ **sorrowing** *adj* affligé.

sorry ['sɒrɪ] *adj* **(a)** (*regretful*) désolé. **I was ~ to hear of your accident** j'étais désolé d'apprendre que vous avez eu un accident; **I am ~ I cannot come/she cannot come** je regrette *or* je suis désolé de ne pas pouvoir venir/qu'elle ne puisse pas venir; **I am ~ to tell you that ...** je regrette de vous dire que ...; **he didn't pass, I'm ~ to say** il a échoué, malheureusement; **I am ~ I am late** excusez-moi d'être en retard; **say you're ~** demande pardon; **~!, ~ about that!*** pardon!, excusez-moi!; **I'm very** *or* **terribly ~** je suis vraiment désolé *or* navré; **I'm ~, but you're wrong** je regrette, mais vous avez tort; **~ about that vase** excusez-moi pour ce vase; **you'll be ~ for this** vous le regretterez. **(b)** (*pitying*) **to be** *or* **feel ~ for sb** plaindre qn, être désolé pour qn; **I feel so ~ for her** elle me fait pitié; **to be** *or* **feel ~ for o.s.** s'apitoyer sur son propre sort; **he looked very ~ for himself** il faisait piteuse mine. **(c)** (*woeful*) *condition, tale* triste, lamentable; *excuse* piètre (*before n*), lamentable; *sight* désolant, affligeant. **in a ~ state** en piteux état.

sort [sɔːt] **1** *n* (*gen*) genre *m*, espèce *f*, sorte *f*; (*make*) *[car, machine, coffee etc]* marque *f*. **this ~ of thing** ce genre de chose; **what ~ do you want?** vous en voulez de quelle sorte?; **what ~ of man is he?** quel genre d'homme est-ce?; **what ~ of dog is he?** qu'est-ce que c'est comme chien?; **he is not the ~ of man to refuse** ce n'est pas le genre d'homme à refuser; **he's the ~ that will cheat** il est du genre à tricher; **he's not that ~ of person** ce n'est pas son genre; **that's the ~ of person I am** c'est comme ça que je suis; **what ~ of an answer do you call that?** vous appelez ça une réponse?; **and all that ~ of thing** et tout ça*; **you know the ~ of thing I mean** vous voyez ce que je veux dire; **that ~ of behaviour** ce genre de conduite; **they're not our ~*** ce ne sont pas des gens comme nous; **it's my ~* of film** c'est le genre de film que j'aime; **sth of the ~** qch de ce genre(-là); **nothing of the ~!** pas le moins du monde!; (*pej*) **beef of a ~** qch qui peut passer pour du bœuf; **a painter of ~s** un peintre si l'on peut dire; **after a ~, in some ~** en quelque sorte; **to be out of ~s** ne pas être dans son assiette; (*fig*) **a good ~*** un brave type*, une brave fille; **there was a ~ of box** il y avait une sorte *or* une espèce de boîte, il y avait qch qui ressemblait à une boîte; **I was ~ of* frightened that ...** j'avais un peu peur que ... + ne + *subj*; **it's ~ of* blue** c'est plutôt bleu.

2 *vt* (**~ out**) (*classify*) *documents, stamps* classer; (*select those to keep*) *documents, clothes*, (*Post*) *letters etc* trier (*according to* selon); (*separate*) séparer (*from* de).

sort out *vt sep* **(a)** = **sort 2. (b)** (*tidy*) *papers, clothes* ranger; *ideas* mettre de l'ordre dans; (*solve*) *problem* régler; *difficulties* venir à bout de; (*fix, arrange*) arranger. **can you ~ this out?** est-ce que vous pourriez régler *or* arranger ça?; **we've got it all ~ed out now** nous avons réglé *or* résolu la question; **things will ~ themselves out** les choses vont s'arranger d'elles-mêmes; **I couldn't ~ out what had happened** je n'ai pas pu comprendre ce qui s'était passé; **did you ~ out with him when you had to be there?** est-ce que tu as décidé *or* fixé avec lui l'heure à laquelle tu dois y être?; **to ~ sb out*** (*by threatening etc*) régler son compte à qn*; (*get him out of difficulty etc*) tirer qn d'affaire.

♦ **sorter** *n* (*person*) trieur *m*, -euse *f*; (*machine*) trieur *m*. ♦ **sorting-office** *n* bureau *m* de tri.

sortie ['sɔːtɪ] *n* (*Aviat, Mil*) sortie *f*.

soufflé ['suːfleɪ] *n* soufflé *m*. **cheese ~** soufflé au fromage; **~ dish** moule *m* à soufflé.

sought [sɔːt] *pret, ptp of* **seek**.

soul [səʊl] **1** *n* **(a)** âme *f*. **with all one's ~** de toute son âme; **All S~s' Day** le jour des Morts; **he cannot call his ~ his own** il est complètement dominé; **the ~ of discretion** la discrétion même. **(b)** (*person*) âme *f*, personne *f*. **the ship sank with all ~s** le bateau a péri corps et biens; **I didn't see a (single** *or* **living) ~** je n'ai pas vu âme qui vive; **you poor ~!** mon (*or* ma) pauvre!; **he's a good ~** c'est une excellente personne. **2** *adj*: **~ mate** âme *f* sœur; **~ music** soul music *f*. ♦ **soul-destroying** *adj* (*boring*) abrutissant; (*depressing*) démoralisant. ♦ **soulful** *adj expression, music* attendrissant; *eyes, glance* expressif. ♦ **soulfully** *adv* de façon attendrissante; d'un air expressif. ♦ **soulless** *adj person* sans cœur; *task* abrutissant. ♦ **soul-searching** *n*: **after a lot of ~-searching he ...** après avoir bien fait son examen de conscience il ... .

sound[1] [saʊnd] **1** *n* (*gen*) son *m*; *[sea, breaking glass, car brakes etc]* bruit *m*. **the speed of ~** la vitesse du son; **within ~ of** à portée du son de; **to the ~ of the national anthem** au son de l'hymne national; **there was not a ~ to be heard** on n'entendait pas le moindre bruit; **without a ~** sans bruit; **we heard the ~ of voices** nous avons entendu un bruit de voix; **the Glenn Miller ~** la musique de Glenn Miller; (*fig*) **I don't like the ~ of it** (*it doesn't attract me*) ça ne me dit rien; (*it's worrying*) ça m'inquiète.

2 *adj film, recording* sonore. **~ archives** phonothèque *f*; **~ barrier** mur *m* du son; (*Rad etc*) **~ effects** bruitage *m*; (*Cine, Rad etc*) **~ engineer** ingénieur *m* du son; (*Cine*) **~ track** bande *f* sonore; **~ wave** onde *f* sonore.

3 *vi* **(a)** *[bell, trumpet, voice]* sonner, retentir; *[car horn, siren, signal, order]* retentir. **footsteps/a gun ~ed a long way off** on entendit un bruit de pas/un coup de canon dans le lointain; **it ~s better if you read it slowly** ça sonne mieux si vous le lisez lentement. **(b) that ~s like a flute** on dirait le son de la flûte; **it ~s empty** on dirait que c'est vide; **a language which ~ed like Dutch** une langue qui semblait être du hollandais; **he ~s like an Australian** à l'entendre parler on dirait un Australien; **it ~ed as if sb were coming in** on aurait dit que qn entrait; **that ~s like Paul arriving** ça doit être Paul qui arrive; **she ~s tired** elle semble fatiguée; **you ~ like your mother** tu me rappelles ta mère. **(c)** (*seem*) **how does it ~ to you?** qu'en penses-tu?; **it ~s like a good idea** ça a l'air d'être une bonne idée, ça semble être une bonne idée; **it doesn't ~ too good** ce n'est pas très prometteur; **it ~s as if she'll come** il semble qu'elle viendra; **it ~s as if she isn't coming** il semble qu'elle ne vienne pas.

4 *vt* **(a)** *bell, alarm*, (*Mil*) *retreat* sonner; *trumpet, bugle* sonner de. (*Aut*) **to ~ one's horn** klaxonner; (*fig*) **to ~ a note of warning** lancer un avertissement. **(b)** (*Ling*) *a letter* prononcer. **(c)** (*Med*) **to ~ sb's chest** ausculter qn.

sound off‡ *vi* (*proclaim one's opinions*) faire de grands discours (*about* sur); (*boast*) se vanter (*about* de); (*grumble*) râler* (*about* à propos de).

♦ **soundless** *adj* silencieux. ♦ **soundlessly** *adv* sans bruit, en silence. ♦ **soundproof 1** *vt* insonoriser; **2** *adj* insonorisé. ♦ **soundproofing** *n* insonorisation *f*.

sound[2] [saʊnd] **1** *adj* (*gen*) sain; *heart, bank, organization* solide; *structure, bridge* en bon état; *alliance, investment* sûr, sans danger; *sleep* profond; (*sensible*) *reasoning, judgment* juste; *doctrine, argument, case, training* solide; *decision, opinion, policy, behaviour* sensé, valable; *claim* valable; *statesman, player, worker etc* compétent. **of ~ mind** sain d'esprit; **to be ~ in wind and limb** avoir bon pied bon œil; **as ~ as a bell** en parfait état; **he is a ~ socialist** c'est un bon socialiste; **he is ~ enough on theory** il connaît très bien la théorie; **he is a ~ chap** il est très sérieux; **~ sense** bon sens *m*; **that was a ~ move** c'était une action judicieuse *or* sensée; **a ~ thrashing** une bonne correction; **he is a ~ sleeper** il dort bien. **2** *adv*: **to be ~ asleep** être profondément endormi. ♦ **soundly** *adv sleep* profondément; *advise, reason, argue* de façon sensée, avec justesse; *organize, manage, invest* bien; (*Sport*) *play* de façon compétente; **he was ~ly beaten** (*defeated*) il a été battu à plates coutures; (*thrashed*) il a reçu une bonne correction. ♦ **soundness** *n [body, mind]* santé *f*; *[business, argument]* solidité *f*; (*solvency*) solvabilité *f*; *[judgment]* justesse *f*.

sound³ [saʊnd] *vt* (*gen, Med, Naut etc*) sonder; (*fig*: **~ out**) *person* sonder (*on, about* sur). ♦ **sounding** *n* (*Naut etc*) sondage *m*. ♦ **sounding line** *n* ligne *f* de sonde.

soup [suːp] **1** *n* soupe *f*; (*thinner or sieved*) potage *m*; (*very smooth*) velouté *m*. (*fig*) **to be in the ~*** être dans le pétrin*. **2** *adj*: **~ cube** potage *m* en cube; (*stock cube*) cube *m* de bouillon; **~ plate/spoon** assiette *f*/cuiller *f* à soupe; **~ tureen** soupière *f*. ♦ **souped-up*** *adj* au moteur gonflé*. ♦ **soupy** *adj liquid, fog* épais.

sour ['saʊəʳ] **1** *adj* (*gen*) aigre; *fruit, juice* acide; *milk* tourné; (*fig*) *person, voice, remark* acerbe, aigre; *face* revêche. **whisky ~** cocktail *m* de whisky au citron; **~(ed) cream** ≈ crème *f* aigre; **to turn ~** *[milk]* tourner; *[relationship]* tourner au vinaigre; *[plans]* mal tourner; **in a ~ mood** d'humeur revêche; (*fig*) **it was clearly ~ grapes on his part** il l'a manifestement fait (*or* dit *etc*) par dépit. **2** *vt* aigrir. ♦ **sour-faced** *adj* à la mine revêche. ♦ **sourly** *adv* avec aigreur. ♦ **sourness** *n* aigreur *f*; acidité *f*; humeur *f or* ton *m* revêche.

source [sɔːs] *n* (*gen*) source *f*. (*Med*) **a ~ of infection** un foyer d'infection; **what is the ~ of this information?** quelle est la provenance de cette nouvelle?; **I have it from a reliable ~ that ...** je tiens de source sûre que ... .

souse [saʊs] *vt* (*immerse*) tremper (*in* dans); (*soak*) faire tremper (*in* dans); (*Culin*) mariner. **to ~ sth with water** inonder qch d'eau.

south [saʊθ] **1** *n* sud *m*. **to the ~ of** au sud de; **in the ~ of Scotland** dans le sud de l'Écosse; **the wind is in the ~/from the ~** le vent est au sud/vient du sud; **the S~ of France** le Sud de la France, le Midi.

2 *adj* (*gen*) sud *inv*; *coast, door* sud, méridional; *wind* du sud. **the ~ Atlantic** l'Atlantique *m* Sud; **S~ Africa** Afrique *f* du Sud; **S~ African** (*adj*) sud-africain; (*n*) Sud-Africain(e) *m(f)*; **S~ America** Amérique *f* du Sud; **S~ American** (*adj*) sud-américain; (*n*) Sud-Américain(e) *m(f)*; **S~ Sea Islands** Océanie *f*; **the S~ Seas** les Mers *fpl* du Sud.

3 *adv* au sud, vers le sud. **~ of the border** au sud de la frontière; **to go ~** aller en direction du sud *or* du midi; **to sail due ~** aller droit vers le sud, (*Naut*) avoir le cap au sud.

♦ **southbound** *adj traffic* en direction du sud; *carriageway* sud *inv*. ♦ **south-east 1** *adj, n* sud-est (*m*) *inv*; **S~-East Asia** le Sud-Est asiatique; **2** *adv* vers le sud-est. ♦ **south-eastern** *adj* sud-est *inv*. ♦ **southerly** ['sʌðəlɪ] *adj wind* du sud; *situation, aspect* au sud, au midi; **in a ~erly direction** vers le sud *or* le midi. ♦ **southern** ['sʌðən] *adj region* sud *inv*, du sud; *wall, side* exposé au sud; *coast* sud, méridional; **S~ern Africa** Afrique *f* australe; **~ern France** le Sud de la France, le Midi; **in ~ern Spain** dans le Sud de l'Espagne. ♦ **southerner** ['sʌðənəʳ] *n* homme *m or* femme *f* du Sud; (*in France*) Méridional(e) *m(f)*. ♦ **southernmost** ['sʌðənməʊst] *adj* le plus au sud. ♦ **south-south-east 1** *adj, n* sud-sud-est (*m*) *inv*; **2** *adv* vers le sud-sud-est. ♦ **southward 1** *adj* au sud; **2** *adv* (*also* **~wards**) vers le sud. ♦ **south-west 1** *adj, n* sud-ouest (*m*) *inv*; **2** *adv* vers le sud-ouest. ♦ **south-western** *adj* sud-ouest *inv*.

souvenir [ˌsuːvə'nɪəʳ] *n* souvenir *m* (*objet*).

sovereign ['sɒvrɪn] **1** *n* souverain(e) *m(f)*. **2** *adj power, state, remedy* souverain (*after n*); *rights* de souveraineté; (*fig*) *contempt* souverain (*before n*). ♦ **sovereignty** *n* souveraineté *f*.

soviet ['səʊvɪət] **1** *n* soviet *m*. **2** *adj* soviétique. **S~ Russia** Russie *f* soviétique; **the S~ Union** l'Union *f* soviétique.

sow¹ [saʊ] *n* (*pig*) truie *f*.

sow² [səʊ] *pret* **sowed**, *ptp* **sown** *or* **sowed** *vt seed, grass*, (*fig*) *doubt* semer; *field* ensemencer (*with* en). ♦ **sower** *n* (*person*) semeur *m*, -euse *f*; (*machine*) semoir *m*. ♦ **sowing** *n* semailles *fpl*.

soy [sɔɪ] *or* **soya** ['sɔɪə] *n* (**~ bean**) graine *f* de soja. **~ flour** farine *f* de soja.

spa [spɑː] *n* station *f* thermale.

space [speɪs] **1** *n* **(a)** (*gen, Phys etc*) espace *m*. **the rocket vanished into ~** la fusée a disparu dans l'espace; **to stare into ~** regarder dans le vide. **(b)** (*room*) espace *m*, place *f*. **to clear a ~ for sth** faire de la place pour qch; **to take up a lot of ~** *[car, books, piece of furniture]* prendre beaucoup de place; *[building]* occuper un grand espace; **there isn't enough ~ for it** il n'y a pas assez de place pour ça; **to buy ~ in a newspaper** acheter de l'espace dans un journal. **(c)** (*gap between objects, words etc*) espace *m*; (*Mus*) interligne *m*. **leave a ~ for the name** laissez de la place *or* un espace pour le nom; **in the ~ provided** dans la partie réservée à cet effet; **in an enclosed ~** dans un espace clos; **I'm looking for a ~ to park the car** je cherche une place pour me garer. **(d)** (*interval*) **after a ~ of 10 minutes** après un intervalle de 10 minutes; **for the ~ of a month** pendant une période d'un mois; **a ~ of 5 years** une période de 5 ans; **in the ~ of 3 generations/one hour** en l'espace de 3 générations/d'une heure; **a short ~ of time** un court laps de temps; **for a ~** pendant un certain temps.

2 *adj research, age, capsule, laboratory* spatial. *[typewriter]* **~ bar** barre *f* d'espacement; **~ fiction** science-fiction *f*; **~ flight** (*act of flying in space*) voyages *mpl* spatiaux; (*journey*) voyage spatial *or* dans l'espace; **~ heater** radiateur *m*; **~ station** station *f* spatiale.

3 *vt* (**~ out**) (*gen*) espacer; *payments* échelonner (*over* sur).

♦ **space-age** *adj* de l'ère spatiale. ♦ **spacecraft** *or* ♦ **spaceship** *n* engin spatial. ♦ **spaceman** *n* astronaute *m*, cosmonaute *m*. ♦ **space-saving** *adj* qui gagne de la place. ♦ **spacesuit** *n* scaphandre *m* de cosmonaute. ♦ **spacing** *n* espacement *m* (*also Typ*); échelonnement *m*; (*Typ*) **in single/double spacing** avec un interligne simple/double. ♦ **spacious** *adj room, car* spacieux, grand; *garden* grand; *garment* ample. ♦ **spaciousness** *n* grandes dimensions *fpl*.

spade [speɪd] *n* **(a)** bêche *f*, pelle *f*; (*child's*) pelle. (*fig*) **to call a ~ a ~** appeler un chat un chat, ne pas avoir peur des mots. **(b)** (*Cards*) pique *m*. **to play ~s** jouer pique; **one ~** un pique; **he played a ~** il a joué pique; **the six of ~s** le six de pique. ♦ **spadeful** *n* pelletée *f*. ♦ **spadework** *n* (*fig*) gros *m* du travail.

spaghetti [spə'getɪ] **1** *n* spaghetti *mpl*. **2** *adj* (*Aut*) **~ junction** échangeur *m* à niveaux multiples.

Spain [speɪn] *n* Espagne *f*.

span [spæn] **1** *n [hands, arms]* envergure *f*; *[bridge]* travée *f*; *[arch, roof]* portée *f*; *[plane, bird]* (**wing~**) envergure. **the average ~ of life** la durée moyenne de vie; **for a brief ~ of time** pendant un court espace de temps. **2** *vt [bridge etc]* enjamber, franchir. (*fig*) **it ~s almost two thousand years** cela embrasse presque deux mille ans.

Spaniard ['spænjəd] *n* Espagnol(e) *m(f)*.

spaniel ['spænjəl] *n* épagneul *m*.

Spanish ['spænɪʃ] **1** *adj* (*gen*) espagnol; *king, embassy, onion* d'Espagne; *teacher* d'espagnol; (*Culin*) *omelette, rice* à l'espagnole. **~ America**

les pays *mpl* d'Amérique du Sud de langue espagnole. 2 *n* espagnol *m*. (*people*) **the ~** les Espagnols *mpl*.

spank [spæŋk] *vt* donner une fessée à. ♦ **spanking** *n* fessée *f*.

spanner ['spænəʳ] *n* clef *f* (à écrous). (*fig*) **to put a ~ in the works** mettre des bâtons dans les roues.

spar¹ [spɑːʳ] *n* (*Naut*) espar *m*.

spar² [spɑːʳ] *vi* (*Boxing*) s'entraîner (*with* avec); (*argue*) se disputer (*with* avec). ♦ **sparring partner** *n* sparring-partner *m*.

spare [spɛəʳ] **1** *adj* (*reserve*) de réserve, de rechange; (*surplus*) en trop, dont on n'a pas besoin. **take a ~ pen** prends un stylo de réserve *or* de rechange; **there are 2 going ~** il y en a 2 en trop *or* dont on n'a pas besoin; **2 ~ seats for the film** 2 places disponibles pour le film; **~ bed/room** lit *m*/chambre *f* d'ami; **~ cash** (*small amount*) argent *m* en trop; (*larger*) argent disponible; **I have very little ~ time** j'ai très peu de temps libre; **in my ~ time** pendant mes moments de loisir; **~-time activities** loisirs *mpl*; (*Tech*) **~ part** pièce *f* de rechange *or* détachée; (*Aut*) **~ tyre** pneu *m* de rechange; **~ wheel** roue *f* de secours.

2 *vt* **(a)** (*do without*) se passer de. **can you ~ it?** pouvez-vous vous en passer?, vous n'en avez pas besoin?; **can you ~ £10?** est-ce que tu as 10 livres en trop?; **can you ~ me £5?** est-ce que tu peux me passer 5 livres?; **I've only a few minutes to ~** je ne dispose que de quelques minutes; **I can ~ you 5 minutes** je peux vous accorder 5 minutes; **I can't ~ the time to do it** je n'ai pas le temps de le faire; **he had time to ~** il avait du temps devant lui; **to ~ a thought for** penser à; **I've got none to ~** j'en ai juste ce qu'il me faut; **I've enough and to ~** j'en ai plus qu'il ne m'en faut; **with 2 minutes to ~** avec 2 minutes d'avance; **we did it with £5 to ~** nous l'avons fait et il nous reste encore 5 livres. **(b)** (*show mercy to*) *person, life, tree etc* épargner. **if I'm ~d*** si Dieu me prête vie; **to ~ sb's feelings** ménager les sentiments de qn; **he doesn't ~ himself** il ne se ménage pas. **(c)** *suffering, embarrassment* épargner (*to sb* à qn). **you could have ~d yourself the trouble, you could have ~d your pains** vous vous êtes donné du mal pour rien, vous auriez pu vous épargner tout ce mal; **I'll ~ you the details** je vous fais grâce des détails. **(d)** (*refrain from using etc*) *one's strength, efforts* ménager. **he ~d no expense to do it** il a dépensé sans compter pour le faire; **'no expense ~d'** 'sans considération de frais'.

♦ **sparerib** *n* travers *m* de porc. ♦ **sparing** *adj amount, use* modéré; **sparing of praise** avare de compliments. ♦ **sparingly** *adv eat, live* frugalement; *spend, drink, praise, use* avec modération.

spark [spɑːk] **1** *n* (*gen*) étincelle *f* (*also Elec*); *[common sense, interest]* lueur *f*. (*fig*) **to make the ~s fly** mettre le feu aux poudres. **2** *vi* jeter des étincelles. **3** *vt* (**~ off**) *rebellion, complaints, quarrel* déclencher; *interest, enthusiasm* susciter (*in sb* chez qn). ♦ **spark(ing) plug** *n* (*Aut*) bougie *f*.

sparkle ['spɑːkl] **1** *vi* (*gen*) étinceler; *[surface of water, lake, diamond etc]* scintiller; *[wine]* pétiller; *[person]* briller; *[conversation, play, eyes]* pétiller (*with* de), être étincelant. **2** *n* étincellement *m*; scintillement *m*; (*fig*) éclat *m*. ♦ **sparkling** *adj* étincelant (*with* de); scintillant; pétillant (*with* de); brillant.

sparrow ['spærəʊ] *n* moineau *m*. ♦ **sparrowhawk** *n* épervier *m*.

sparse [spɑːs] *adj* clairsemé. ♦ **sparsely** *adv wooded, furnished, populated* peu.

spartan ['spɑːtən] *adj* spartiate.

spasm ['spæzəm] *n* spasme *m*; *[coughing, activity etc]* accès *m* (*of* de). ♦ **spasmodic** *adj work, attempt* intermittent. ♦ **spasmodically** *adv work, try* par à-coups.

spastic ['spæstɪk] **1** *adj movement, colon, paralysis* spasmodique; *child etc* handicapé moteur. **2** *n* (*Med*) handicapé(e) *m(f)* moteur.

spat [spæt] *pret, ptp of* **spit¹**.

spate [speɪt] *n* (*fig*) *[letters, orders etc]* avalanche *f*; *[words, abuse]* torrent *m*. *[river]* **in ~** en crue; **to have a ~ of work** être débordé de travail.

spatial ['speɪʃəl] *adj* spatial.

spatter ['spætəʳ] *vt*: **to ~ mud on sth, to ~ sth with mud** (*accidentally*) éclabousser *or* (*deliberately*) asperger qch de boue.

spatula ['spætjʊlə] *n* spatule *f*.

spawn [spɔːn] **1** *n [fish, frog]* frai *m*, œufs *mpl*; *[mushroom]* blanc *m*. **2** *vt* (*fig pej*) engendrer. **3** *vi [fish]* frayer.

spay [speɪ] *vt* châtrer.

speak [spiːk] *pret* **spoke**, *ptp* **spoken 1** *vi* parler (*to* à; *of, about, on* de; *with* avec). **to ~ in a whisper** chuchoter; **to ~ to o.s.** parler tout seul; **I don't know him to ~ to** je ne le connais pas assez bien pour lui parler; **I'll never ~ to him again** je ne lui adresserai plus jamais la parole; **you have only to ~** tu n'as qu'un mot à dire; **so to ~** pour ainsi dire; **biologically ~ing** biologiquement parlant; **~ing personally** personnellement; **~ing as a member of the society I ...** en tant que membre de la société je ...; (*Telec*) **who's ~ing?** qui est à l'appareil?, (*passing on call*) c'est de la part de qui?; **this is Paul ~ing** c'est Paul à l'appareil; **~ing!** lui- *or* elle-même!; (*Parl*) **to ~ in the House** faire un discours à l'Assemblée; **to ~ in a debate** *[proposer, seconder]* prendre la parole au cours d'un débat; (*from floor of house*) participer à un débat; **~ for yourself!*** parle pour toi!*; **let him ~ for himself** laisse-le dire lui-même ce qu'il a à dire; **it ~s for itself** c'est évident; **the facts ~ for themselves** les faits parlent d'eux-mêmes; **that is already spoken for** c'est déjà retenu; **he is very well spoken of** on dit beaucoup de bien de lui; **~ing of holidays** à propos de vacances; **he has no money to ~ of** il n'a pour ainsi dire pas d'argent; **it's nothing to ~ of** ce n'est pas grand-chose. **2** *vt language* parler; *a poem, one's lines, the truth* dire. **'English spoken'** 'ici on parle anglais'; **French is spoken everywhere** le français se parle partout; **to ~ one's mind** dire ce que l'on pense; **I didn't ~ a word** je n'ai rien dit.

speak out, speak up *vi* (*fig*) **he's not afraid to ~ out** il n'a pas peur de dire ce qu'il pense; **to ~ out for sb** parler en faveur de qn; **to ~ out against sth** s'élever contre qch.

♦ **speaker** *n* **(a)** (*gen*) celui (*or* celle) qui parle; (*in dialogue*) interlocuteur *m*, -trice *f*; (*in public*) orateur *m*; (*lecturer*) conférencier *m*, -ière *f*; **he's a good/poor ~er** il parle bien/mal; **the previous ~er** la personne qui a parlé la dernière; (*Brit Parl*) **the S~er** le Président de la Chambre des Communes; **(b) French ~er** personne *f* qui parle français, (*as native or official language*) francophone *mf*; **he is not a Welsh ~er** il ne parle pas gallois; **(c)** (*loudspeaker*) haut-parleur *m*. ♦ **speaking 1** *adj doll etc* parlant; **German-~ing** parlant allemand; **to be on ~ing terms with sb** adresser la parole à qn; **~ing tube** tuyau *m* acoustique; **2** *n* (*skill*) art *m* de parler.

spear [spɪəʳ] *n* lance *f*. ♦ **spearhead 1** *n* (*fig, Mil*) fer *m* de lance. **2** *vt attack etc* être le fer de lance de. ♦ **spearmint** *n* menthe *f* verte; (*chewing gum*) chewing-gum *m* à la menthe.

spec* [spek] *n*: **on ~** à tout hasard.

special ['speʃəl] **1** *adj* **(a)** (*specific: gen*) *notebook, box, room* spécial, réservé à cet usage. **are you thinking of any ~ date?** est-ce que tu penses à une date particulière?; **I've no ~ person in mind** je ne pense à personne en particulier. **(b)** (*exceptional*) *attention, pleasure, effort* tout particulier; *favour, price, study, skill, care* spécial; *occasion, situation, case, circumstances* exceptionnel; (*Pol etc*) *powers, legislation* extraordinaire. **take ~ care of it** fais-y particulièrement attention; (*Comm*) **~ offer** réclame *f*; **her ~ friend** l'amie qui lui est particulièrement chère; **you're extra ~!*** tu es quelqu'un à part!; **this is a ~ day for me** c'est une journée importante pour moi; **to ask for ~ treatment** demander à être considéré comme un cas à part; **a ~ feature of the village** une caractéristique du village; (*Press*) **~ feature** article *m* spécial; **my ~ chair** mon fauteuil préféré; (*Univ etc*) **~ subject** option *f*; **nothing ~** rien de spécial *or* de particulier; (*when thanked*) **it's nothing ~** c'est bien normal; **what's so ~ about her?** qu'est-ce qu'elle a d'extraordinaire?; **~ agent** (*Comm etc*) concessionnaire *mf*; (*spy*) agent *m* secret; (*Brit*) **~ constable** auxiliaire *m* de police; (*Press, Rad, TV*) **~ correspondent** envoyé(e) *m(f)* spécial(e); (*Post*) **by ~ delivery** en exprès; (*Jur*) **~ licence** dispense *f*; **by ~ messenger** par messager spécial.

2 *n* (*train*) train *m* supplémentaire; (*newspaper*) édition *f* spéciale. **the chef's ~** la spécialité du chef.

♦ **specialist 1** *n* (*gen, also Med*) spécialiste *mf* (*in* de); (*Med*) **an eye/a heart ~ist** un(e) ophtalmologiste/cardiologue; **2** *adj knowledge, dictionary* spécial. ♦ **speciality** [ˌspeʃɪˈælɪtɪ] *n* spécialité *f*; **to make a ~ity of sth** se spécialiser dans qch. ♦ **specialization** *n* spécialisation *f* (*in* dans). ♦ **specialize** *vi* se spécialiser (*in* dans). ♦ **specialized** *adj* spécial. ♦ **specially** *adv* (*specifically*) spécialement; (*particularly*) particulièrement, surtout; (*on purpose*) tout spécialement, exprès.

species [ˈspiːʃiːz] *n, pl inv* espèce *f*.

specify [ˈspesɪfaɪ] *vt* spécifier, préciser. **unless otherwise specified** sauf indication contraire. ♦ **specific** [spəˈsɪfɪk] *adj statement, instruction* précis, explicite; *purpose, meaning, case* précis, particulier; *example* précis; (*Bio, Phys etc*) spécifique; **he was very specific on that point** il s'est montré très explicite sur ce point; (*Phys*) **specific gravity** densité *f*. ♦ **specifically** [spəˈsɪfɪkəlɪ] *adv* (*explicitly*) *warn, state etc* explicitement, de façon précise; (*especially*) *design, intend* particulièrement; **I told you quite specifically** je vous l'avais bien précisé *or* spécifié. ♦ **specification** *n* (*gen*) spécification *f*; (*item in contract etc*) stipulation *f*.

specimen [ˈspesɪmɪn] **1** *n [rock, species, style]* spécimen *m*; *[blood, tissue]* prélèvement *m*; *[urine]* échantillon *m*; (*fig: example*) exemple *m* (*of* de). (*fig: person*) **an odd ~*** un drôle de type*, une drôle de bonne femme*. **2** *adj*: **~ copy** spécimen *m*; **~ page** page *f* spécimen; **~ signature** spécimen *m* de signature.

specious [ˈspiːʃəs] *adj* spécieux.

speck [spek] *n [dust, soot, truth etc]* grain *m*; *[dirt, ink]* petite tache *f*. **I've got a ~ in my eye** j'ai une poussière dans l'œil; **a ~ on the horizon** un point noir à l'horizon. ♦ **speckled** *adj* tacheté.

spectacle [ˈspektəkl] **1** *n* spectacle *m*. **2** *adj*: **~ case** étui *m* à lunettes. ♦ **spectacles** *npl* (*abbr* **specs***) lunettes *fpl*. ♦ **spectacular** [spekˈtækjʊləʳ] **1** *adj* (*gen*) spectaculaire; *success* fou; **2** *n* (*Cine, Theat*) superproduction *f*.

spectator [spekˈteɪtəʳ] **1** *n* spectateur *m*, -trice *f*. **2** *adj sport* qui attire un très grand nombre de spectateurs.

spectre, (*US*) **-ter** [ˈspektəʳ] *n* spectre *m*, fantôme *m*.

spectrum [ˈspektrəm] **1** *n, pl* **-tra** (*Phys*) spectre *m*; (*fig*) gamme *f* (*fig*). **2** *adj colours* spectral.

speculate [ˈspekjʊleɪt] *vi* (*wonder*) s'interroger (*about, on* sur; *whether* pour savoir si); (*Philos, Fin*) spéculer. ♦ **speculation** *n* (*guessing*) conjectures *fpl* (*about* sur); (*Fin, Philos etc*) spéculation *f*. ♦ **speculative** *adj* spéculatif. ♦ **speculator** *n* spéculateur *m*, -trice *f*.

sped [sped] *pret, ptp of* **speed.**

speech [spiːtʃ] **1** *n* **(a)** (*faculty*) parole *f*; (*enunciation*) élocution *f*; (*manner of speaking*) façon *f* de parler, langage *m*; (*as opp to writing*) parole; (*language: of district or group*) parler *m*; (*Gram*) discours *m*. **to lose the power of ~** perdre l'usage de la parole; **better in ~ than in writing** mieux oralement que par écrit; **free ~, freedom of ~** liberté *f* d'expression; (*Gram*) **direct/indirect ~** discours direct/indirect. **(b)** (*formal talk*) discours *m* (*on* sur). **2** *adj*: **~ day** distribution *f* des prix; **~ impediment** défaut *m* d'élocution; (*Anat*) **~ organ** organe *m* de la parole; **~ therapist** orthophoniste *mf*; **~ therapy** orthophonie *f*; **~ training** leçons *fpl* d'élocution. ♦ **speechless** *adj* muet (*with* de); **it left him ~less** il en est resté sans voix. ♦ **speechmaking** *n* (*slightly pej*) beaux discours *mpl*.

speed [spiːd] (*vb: pret, ptp* **sped** *or* **speeded**) **1** *n* **(a)** (*rate of movement*) vitesse *f*; (*rapidity*) rapidité *f*; (*promptness*) promptitude *f*. **shorthand/typing ~s** nombre *m* de mots-minute en sténo/en dactylo; (*Aut*) **what ~ were you doing?** quelle vitesse faisiez-vous?; **at a ~ of 80 km/h** à une vitesse de 80 km/h; **at a great ~** à toute vitesse; **at top ~** *go, run* à toute vitesse; *do sth* très vite; **with such ~** si vite; **to pick up** *or* **get up** *or* **gather ~** prendre de la vitesse. **(b)** (*Tech: gear*) vitesse *f*. **a 3-~ gear** une boîte à 3 vitesses. **(c)** (*Phot*) *[film]* rapidité *f*; (*width of aperture*) degré *m* d'obturation; (*length of exposure*) durée *f* d'exposition.

2 *adj*: **~ cop** ≃ motard *m*; (*Brit*) **there's no ~ limit** il n'y a pas de limitation *f* de vitesse; **the ~ limit is 80 km/h** la vitesse maximale permise est 80 km/h; **~ merchant*** mordu(e)* *m(f)* de la vitesse; (*Aut*) **~ restriction** limitation *f* de vitesse; (*Aut*) **~ trap** piège *m* de police pour contrôle de vitesse.

3 *vi* **(a)** *pret, ptp* **sped**: **to ~ along/across** *etc* aller/traverser *etc* à toute vitesse. **(b)** *pret, ptp* **speeded** (*Aut: go too fast*) conduire trop vite.

speed up *pret, ptp* **speeded up 1** *vi* (*gen*) aller plus vite; *[walker/worker/train etc]* marcher/travailler/rouler *etc* plus vite; (*Aut*) accélérer; *[engine, machine etc]* tourner plus vite; *[production]* s'accélérer. **2** *vt sep* (*gen*) accélérer; *machine* faire tourner plus vite; *person* faire aller (*or* faire travailler) plus vite. **to ~ things up** activer les choses.

♦ **speedboat** *n* vedette *f* (*Naut*). ♦ **speedily** *adv* (*quickly*) *move, work* vite; (*promptly*) *reply, return* promptement; (*soon*) bientôt. ♦ **speeding** *n* (*Aut*) excès *m* de vitesse. ♦ **speedometer** *n* indicateur *m* de vitesse. ♦ **speed-up** *n* accélération *f*; (*Ind*) **~-up of production** amélioration *f* de rendement. ♦ **speedway racing** *n* courses *fpl* de moto. ♦ **speedy** *adj* rapide.

speleology [ˌspiːlɪˈɒlədʒɪ] *n* spéléologie *f*. ♦ **speleologist** *n* spéléologue *mf*.

spell[1] [spel] *n* charme *m*; (*words*) formule *f* magique. **an evil ~** un maléfice; **to put** *or* **cast a ~ on sb** jeter un sort à qn, (*fig*) ensorceler qn; (*fig*) **under the ~ of** ensorcelé par; **to break the ~** rompre le charme. ♦ **spellbinding** *adj* ensorcelant. ♦ **spellbound** *adj* (*fig*) envoûté; (*fig*) **to hold sb ~bound** tenir qn sous le charme.

spell[2] [spel] *n* **(a)** (*turn*) tour *m*. **~ of duty** tour de service. **(b)** (*brief period*) période *f*. (*Met*) **cold/sunny ~s** périodes de froid/ensoleillées; **after a ~** après un certain temps; **for a short ~** pendant un petit moment.

spell[3] [spel] *pret, ptp* **spelt** *or* **spelled 1** *vt* (*in writing*) écrire; (*aloud*) épeler. **how do you ~ it?** comment est-ce que cela s'écrit?; **d-o-g ~s 'dog'** d-o-g forment le mot 'dog'; (*fig*) **that would ~ ruin for him** cela signifierait la ruine pour lui. **2** *vi*: **to**

learn to ~ apprendre l'orthographe; **he can't ~** il fait des fautes d'orthographe.
spell out *vt sep (fig) consequences, alternatives* expliquer bien clairement (*for sb* à qn). **do I have to ~ it out for you?** faut-il que je mette les points sur les i?
◆ **spelling 1** *n* orthographe *f*; **2** *adj*: **~ing mistake** faute *f* d'orthographe.
spend [spend] *pret, ptp* **spent** *vt* **(a)** *money* dépenser (*on sth bought: on* en; *on person, car etc bought for: on* pour; *on doing* pour faire). **without ~ing a penny** sans dépenser un sou; (*Brit fig*) **to ~ a penny*** aller au petit coin*. **(b)** (*pass*) *holiday, time, one's life* passer (*on sth* sur qch; *in doing* à faire); (*devote*) *labour, care* consacrer (*on sth* à qch; *doing, in doing* à faire). **I spent 2 hours on that letter** j'ai passé 2 heures sur cette lettre.
◆ **spender** *n*: **to be a big ~er** dépenser beaucoup.
◆ **spending 1** *n* dépenses *fpl*; **government ~ing** dépenses publiques; **2** *adj*: **~ing money** argent *m* de poche; **~ing power** pouvoir *m* d'achat.
◆ **spendthrift** *n, adj* dépensier *m*, -ière *f*. ◆ **spent** *adj match, cartridge etc* utilisé; *supplies* épuisé.
sperm [spɜːm] *n* sperme *m*. **~ whale** cachalot *m*.
sphere [sfɪəʳ] *n* (*gen*) sphère *f*. **~ of influence** sphère d'influence; **the ~ of poetry** le domaine de la poésie; **in the social ~** dans le domaine social; **in many ~s** dans de nombreux domaines; **within a limited ~** dans un cadre restreint; **that is outside my ~** cela n'entre pas dans mes compétences. ◆ **spherical** ['sferɪkəl] *adj* sphérique.
sphinx [sfɪŋks] *n* sphinx *m*.
spice [spaɪs] **1** *n* (*Culin*) épice *f*. **mixed ~(s)** épices mélangées; (*fig*) **a story with a bit of ~ to it** une histoire qui a du piquant; **the ~ of adventure** le piment de l'aventure. **2** *vt* (*Culin*) épicer (*with* de); (*fig*) relever (*with* de). ◆ **spicy** *adj food* épicé, relevé; (*fig*) piquant.
spick-and-span ['spɪkən'spæn] *adj* propre comme un sou neuf.
spider ['spaɪdəʳ] *n* araignée *f*. **~'s web** toile *f* d'araignée. ◆ **spidery** *adj writing* tremblé.
spiel* [spiːl] *n* baratin* *m* (*about* sur).
spike [spaɪk] **1** *n* (*gen*) pointe *f*; (*for letters, bills etc*) pique-notes *m inv*; (*Bot*) épi *m*. (*shoes*) **~s*** chaussures *fpl* à pointes. **2** *vt* (*fig*) **to ~ sb's guns** mettre des bâtons dans les roues à qn. ◆ **spiky** *adj branch, wall* hérissé de pointes.
spill [spɪl] *pret, ptp* **spilt** *or* **spilled 1** *vt* renverser. **to ~ blood** verser le sang; (*fig*) **to ~ the beans*** vendre la mèche*; (*Naut*) **to ~ (wind from) a sail** étouffer une voile. **2** *vi [liquid, salt etc]* se répandre.
spill out 1 *vi* se répandre; *[people etc]* sortir avec précipitation. **they ~ed out into the streets** ils se sont précipités dans la rue. **2** *vt sep contents etc* répandre; (*fig*) *story, details* révéler.
spill over *vi* déborder (*into* dans).
spin [spɪn] (*vb: pret, ptp* **spun**) **1** *n* (*turn*) tournoiement *m*; (*Aviat*) vrille *f*. **to give a wheel a ~** faire tourner une roue; (*on washing machine*) **long/short ~** essorage *m* complet/léger; (*Sport*) **to put a ~ on a ball** donner de l'effet à une balle; (*Aviat*) **to go into a ~** tomber en vrille; (*fig*) *[person]* **to get into a ~*** paniquer*; **everything was in a ~*** c'était la pagaille* complète; (*fig: try out*) **to give sth a ~*** essayer qch; (*ride*) **to go for a ~*** faire un petit tour en voiture (*or* en vélo *etc*). **2** *vt* **(a)** *wool, glass etc* filer (*into* en, pour en faire); *thread etc* fabriquer; *[spider etc]* tisser. (*fig*) **to ~ a yarn** (*make up*) inventer *or* (*tell*) débiter une longue histoire (*about sth* sur qch). **(b)** *wheel etc* (**~ round**) faire tourner; *top* lancer; *clothes* essorer; (*Sport*) *ball* donner de l'effet à. **to ~ a coin** jouer à pile ou face. **3** *vi* **(a)** *[spinner etc]* filer; *[spider]* tisser sa toile. **(b)** (*often* **~ round**: *gen*) tourner; *[person]* se retourner vivement; *[car wheel]* patiner; *[ball]* tournoyer. **to ~ round and round** tournoyer; **to send sth/sb ~ning** envoyer rouler qch/qn; (*fig*) **my head is ~ning** j'ai la tête qui tourne; (*fig*) **the room was ~ning** la chambre tournait. **(c)** (*Fishing*) **to ~ for trout** pêcher la truite à la cuiller.
spin out *vt sep story, visit, money* faire durer.
◆ **spindrift** *n* embruns *mpl*. ◆ **spin-dry** *vt* essorer (à la machine). ◆ **spin-dryer** *n* essoreuse *f*. ◆ **spinner** *n* (*person*) fileur *m*, -euse *f*; (*Fishing*) cuiller *f*; (*spin-dryer*) essoreuse *f*; (*Baseball, Cricket*) **he sent down a ~ner*** il a donné de l'effet à la balle. ◆ **spinning 1** *n* (*by hand*) filage *m*; (*by machine*) filature *f*; (*Fishing*) pêche *f* à la cuiller; **2** *adj*: **~ning mill** filature *f*; **~ning top** toupie *f*; **~ning wheel** rouet *m*. ◆ **spin-off** *n* (*gen*) avantage *m* inattendu; (*Ind, Tech etc*) application *f* secondaire.
spinach ['spɪnɪdʒ] *n* (*Culin*) épinards *mpl*.
spindle ['spɪndl] *n* (*Spinning*) fuseau *m*, (*on machine*) broche *f*; (*Tech*) *[pump]* axe *m*; *[lathe]* arbre *m*; *[valve]* tige *f*. ◆ **spindly** *adj legs, person* grêle; *plant* étiolé.
spine [spaɪn] *n* (*Anat*) colonne *f* vertébrale; *[fish]* épine *f*; *[hedgehog]* piquant *m*; (*Bot*) épine; *[book]* dos *m*; *[hill etc]* crête *f*. ◆ **spinal** *adj nerve, muscle* spinal; *column, disc* vertébral; *injury* à la colonne vertébrale; **spinal anaesthetic** péridurale *f*; **spinal cord** moelle *f* épinière. ◆ **spine-chilling** *adj* à vous glacer le sang. ◆ **spineless** *adj* (*fig*) mou, sans caractère. ◆ **spiny** *adj* épineux.
spinney ['spɪnɪ] *n* bosquet *m*.
spinster ['spɪnstəʳ] *n* célibataire *f* (*also Admin*), vieille fille *f* (*pej*).
spiral ['spaɪərəl] **1** *adj movement, decoration, spring* en spirale; *nebula, galaxy* spiral; (*Aviat*) en vrille. **~ staircase** escalier *m* en colimaçon. **2** *n* spirale *f*. **in a ~** en spirale; **the wage-price ~** la montée inexorable des salaires et des prix; **the inflationary ~** la spirale inflationniste. **3** *vi [smoke]* monter en spirale; *[prices]* monter en flèche; *[prices and wages]* former une spirale; *[plane]* **to ~ down** descendre en vrille; *[rocket etc]* **to ~ up** monter en spirale.
spire ['spaɪəʳ] *n* (*Archit*) flèche *f*.
spirit ['spɪrɪt] **1** *n* **(a)** (*soul*) esprit *m*. **he was there in ~** il était présent en esprit; **one of the greatest ~s of his day** un des plus grands esprits de son temps; **the leading ~ in the party** l'âme *f* du parti. **(b)** (*supernatural being, ghost etc*) esprit *m*. **evil ~** esprit malin. **(c)** (*attitude etc*) esprit *m*. **in a ~ of forgiveness** dans un esprit de pardon; **he's got the right ~** il a la disposition *or* l'attitude qu'il faut; **you must take it in the ~ in which it was meant** prenez-le dans l'esprit où c'était voulu; **to take sth in the right/wrong ~** prendre qch en bonne/mauvaise part; **you must enter into the ~ of the thing** il faut y participer de bon cœur; **the ~, not the letter of the law** l'esprit et non la lettre de la loi; **that's the ~!** voilà comment il faut réagir!; **community ~** civisme *m*. **(d) in good ~s** de bonne humeur; **in poor *or* low ~s** qui n'a pas le moral; **to keep one's ~s up** garder le moral; **my ~s rose** j'ai repris courage; **to raise sb's ~s** remonter le moral à qn. **(e)** (*courage*) courage *m*, cran* *m*; (*energy*) énergie *f*; (*vitality*) entrain *m*. **(f)** (*Chem*) alcool *m*. (*drink*) **~s** spiritueux *mpl*, alcool; **raw ~s** alcool pur.
2 *adj* **(a)** *lamp etc* à alcool. **(b)** (*Spiritualism*) *help, world* des esprits.
spirit away, spirit off *vt sep person* faire disparaître comme par enchantement; *object, document etc* subtiliser.
◆ **spirited** *adj person, horse, reply, speech* fougueux; *conversation* animé; *music* plein d'allant; *undertaking, defence* courageux; (*Mus*) **he gave a ~ed performance** il a joué avec fougue *or* avec brio. ◆ **spirit-level** *n* niveau *m* à bulle.

♦ **spiritual 1** *adj* spirituel (*par opp à matériel*); **2** *n* chant *m* religieux; (*also* **Negro ~ual**) negro-spiritual *m*. ♦ **spiritualism** *n* (*Rel*) spiritisme *m*. ♦ **spiritualist** *adj, n* spirite (*mf*). ♦ **spirituality** *n* spiritualité *f*. ♦ **spiritually** *adv* spirituellement.

spit[1] [spɪt] (*vb: pret, ptp* **spat**) **1** *n* (*spittle*) crachat *m*; (*saliva*) salive *f*; (*Bot*) crachat de coucou. **~ and polish** astiquage *m*; (*fig*) **he's the dead ~* of his uncle** c'est le portrait craché* de son oncle. **2** *vt* cracher. **3** *vi* cracher (*at sb* sur qn); *[fire, fat]* crépiter. **it was ~ting with rain** il tombait quelques gouttes de pluie.

spit out *vt sep* cracher. (*fig: say it*) **~ it out!*** allons, dis-le!

♦ **spitfire** *n*: **to be a ~fire** s'emporter pour un rien. ♦ **spitting 1** *n*: **'~ting prohibited'** 'défense de cracher'; **2** *adj*: **to be the ~ting image of sb*** être le portrait craché* de qn. ♦ **spittle** *n* (*ejected*) crachat *m*; (*dribbled*) salive *f*; *[animal]* bave *f*. ♦ **spittoon** *n* crachoir *m*.

spit[2] [spɪt] *n* (*Culin*) broche *f*; (*Geog*) langue *f* de terre. ♦ **spitroast** *vt* faire rôtir à la broche.

spite [spaɪt] **1** *n* **(a)** (*ill-feeling*) rancune *f*, dépit *m*. **out of pure ~** par pure rancune *or* malveillance; **to have a ~ against sb*** avoir une dent contre qn. **(b) in ~ of** malgré, en dépit de; **in ~ of the fact that** bien que +*subj*; **in ~ of everyone** envers et contre tous. **2** *vt* vexer. ♦ **spiteful** *adj person, remark, comment* malveillant; *tongue* venimeux. ♦ **spitefully** *adv* par dépit.

splash [splæʃ] **1** *n* (*sound*) plouf *m*; (*series of sounds*) clapotement *m*; (*mark*) éclaboussure *f*; (*fig*) *[colour]* tache *f*; *[publicity]* étalage *m*. (*fig*) **to make a ~*** faire sensation. **2** *vt* éclabousser (*sth over sb/sth* qch sur qn/qch; *sb/sth with sth* qn/qch de qch). **to ~ milk on the floor** renverser du lait par terre; **he ~ed paint on the floor** il a fait des éclaboussures de peinture par terre; **to ~ cold water on one's face** s'asperger la figure d'eau froide; **the news was ~ed across the front page** la nouvelle a fait cinq colonnes à la une. **3** *vi* **(a)** *[liquid, mud etc]* faire des éclaboussures. **to ~ over sth** éclabousser qch. **(b)** *[person, animal]* barboter, patauger (*in* dans). **to ~ across a stream** traverser un ruisseau en pataugeant; *[stone]* **to ~ into the water** tomber dans l'eau avec un gros plouf.

splash down *vi [spacecraft]* amerrir.

splash out* *vi* (*in spending*) faire une folie (*achat*).

splash up *vi* gicler (*on sb* sur qn).

♦ **splashboard** *n* (*Aut etc*) garde-boue *m inv*. ♦ **splashdown** *n* (*Space*) amerrissage *m*.

spleen [spli:n] *n* (*Anat*) rate *f*; (*bad temper*) mauvaise humeur *f*.

splendid ['splendɪd] *adj* (*imposing etc*) *ceremony, beauty* splendide; (*excellent*) *holiday, idea, teacher etc* excellent, formidable*. **that's ~!** c'est formidable!* ♦ **splendidly** *adv* splendidement; de façon excellente, formidablement*; **it all went ~ly** tout a très bien marché. ♦ **splendour,** (*US*) **splendor** *n* splendeur *f*.

splice [splaɪs] *vt rope, film* épisser.

splint [splɪnt] *n* (*Med*) éclisse *f*. **to put in ~s** éclisser; **leg in ~s** jambe éclissée.

splinter ['splɪntəʳ] **1** *n [glass, wood]* éclat *m*; *[bone]* esquille *f*; (*in finger etc*) écharde *f*. **2** *adj*: **~ group** groupe *m* dissident. **3** *vt wood* fendre en éclats; *glass, bone* briser en éclats; (*fig*) *party etc* fragmenter. **4** *vi* se fendre *or* se briser en éclats; se fragmenter.

split [splɪt] (*vb: pret, ptp* **split**) **1** *n* **(a)** (*in garment, fabric*) fente *f*, (*tear*) déchirure *f*; (*in wood, earth's surface*) crevasse *f*; (*fig: quarrel*) rupture *f*; (*Pol*) scission *f*. **there was a 3-way ~ in the committee** le comité s'est trouvé divisé en 3 clans; **to do the ~s** faire le grand écart. **(b)** (*cake etc*) **jam ~** brioche *f* fourrée à la confiture; **banana ~** banana split *m*.

2 *adj* (*Gram*) **~ infinitive** *infinitif où un adverbe est intercalé entre 'to' et le verbe*; **~ peas** pois *mpl* cassés; **~ personality** double personnalité *f*; **a ~ second** une fraction de seconde; **in a ~ second** en un rien de temps; **~-second timing** *[military operation etc]* précision *f* à la seconde près; *[actor, comedian]* sens *m* du moment.

3 *vt* **(a)** (*gen*) fendre; *slate* cliver; (*tear*) déchirer; (*fig*) *party etc* diviser. **to ~ the atom** fissionner l'atome; **to ~ sth open** ouvrir qch en le fendant; **he ~ his head open** il s'est fendu le crâne; **to ~ sth in two** (*cut*) couper *or* (*break*) briser qch en deux; (*fig*) **to ~ hairs** couper les cheveux en quatre; (*fig*) **to ~ one's sides (laughing)** se tordre de rire; **it ~ the party down the middle** cela a divisé le parti en deux. **(b)** (*divide*) partager (*between* entre); (*share*) se partager. **let's ~ a bottle of wine** si on prenait une bouteille de vin à deux (*or* trois *etc*)?; **to ~ the difference** partager la différence; **they ~ the work** ils se sont partagé le travail.

4 *vi* **(a)** (*gen*) se fendre; (*tear*) se déchirer; (*fig*) *[party etc]* se diviser. **to ~ open** se fendre; (*fig*) **my head is ~ting** j'ai atrocement mal à la tête. **(b)** (*divide*) *[group]* se diviser, se séparer. **(c) to ~ on sb*** dénoncer qn.

split off 1 *vi [piece of wood]* se détacher (*from* de); *[group]* se séparer (*from* de). **2** *vt sep piece* enlever (*from* de); *group* séparer (*from* de).

split up 1 *vi [ship]* se briser; *[boulder etc]* se fendre; *[meeting, crowd]* se disperser; *[party, movement]* se diviser; *[married couple]* se séparer; *[friends, engaged couple]* rompre. **2** *vt sep wood, stones* fendre (*into* en); *money, work* partager; *compound, party, organization* diviser (*into* en); *meeting* mettre fin à; *crowd* disperser; *friends* séparer. **we must ~ the work up amongst us** nous devons nous partager le travail.

♦ **split-cane** *adj* en osier. ♦ **split-level** *adj cooker* à plaques de cuisson et four indépendants; *house* à deux niveaux. ♦ **split-off** *n* séparation *f* (*from* de). ♦ **split-site** *adj* sur plusieurs emplacements. ♦ **splitting 1** *n* (*V* **split 3a** *above*) fendage *m*; clivage *m*; déchirement *m*; division *f*; *[atom]* fission *f*; **2** *adj*: **I have a ~ting headache** j'ai atrocement mal à la tête. ♦ **split-up** *n [engaged couple, friends]* rupture *f*; *[married couple]* séparation *f*; *[political party]* scission *f*.

splodge [splɒdʒ], **splotch** [splɒtʃ] *n [ink, colour, dirt etc]* tache *f*; *[cream]* monceau *m*.

splutter ['splʌtəʳ] **1** *vi [person]* (*spit*) crachoter; (*stutter*) bafouiller*; *[fire, fat]* crépiter; *[engine]* bafouiller*. **2** *vt* (**~ out**) bafouiller*. **3** *n* crachotement *m*; bafouillage* *m*; crépitement *m*.

spoil [spɔɪl] *pret, ptp* **spoiled** *or* **spoilt 1** *vt* **(a)** (*damage*) *paint, dress etc* abîmer; *ballot paper* rendre nul. **to ~ one's eyes** s'abîmer la vue. **(b)** (*detract from*) *view, style, effect, food* gâter; *holiday, occasion, pleasure, one's life* gâcher; *garden etc* enlaidir; *sb's peace of mind* empoisonner. **to ~ sb's fun** gâcher l'amusement de qn; **to ~ one's appetite** se couper l'appétit; **if you tell me the ending you'll ~ the film for me** si vous me racontez la fin vous me gâcherez tout l'intérêt du film. **(c)** (*pamper*) *child etc* gâter. **2** *vi* **(a)** *[food]* s'abîmer; (*in warehouse etc*) s'avarier. **(b) to be ~ing for a fight** brûler de se battre. **3** *n* (*gen pl*) **~(s)** (*booty*) butin *m*. ♦ **spoilt** *adj ballot paper* nul; *child* gâté.

spoke[1] [spəʊk] *n* rayon *m*. (*fig*) **to put a ~ in sb's wheel** mettre des bâtons dans les roues à qn.

spoke[2], **spoken** ['spəʊk(ən)] *pret, ptp of* **speak**.

♦ **spokesman** *n* porte-parole *m inv* (*of, for* de).

sponge [spʌndʒ] **1** *n* **(a)** éponge *f*. (*fig*) **to throw in the ~*** s'avouer vaincu. **(b)** (**~ cake**) gâteau *m* de Savoie. **2** *adj*: **~ bag** sac *m* de toilette. **3** *vt* éponger. **4** *vi* (*: *cadge*) **to ~ on sb** vivre aux crochets de qn.

sponge down *vt sep person, walls* laver à l'éponge; *horse* éponger.

♦ **sponger*** *n* (*pej*) parasite *m*. ♦ **spongy** *adj* spongieux.

sponsor ['spɒnsəʳ] **1** *n* (*gen: of appeal etc*) personne *f* qui accorde son patronage; (*for loan etc*) répondant(e) *m(f)*; (*for baptism, club membership*) parrain *m*, marraine *f*; (*Rad, TV, Advertising*) personne (*or* organisme *m*) qui assure le patronage; (*for fund-raising event*) donateur *m*, -trice *f*. **2** *vt appeal, proposal, announcement, programme* patronner; (*Fin*) *borrower* se porter caution pour; (*Rel*) être le parrain (*or* la marraine) de; *club member* parrainer; *fund-raising walker etc* s'engager à rémunérer (en fonction de sa performance). ♦ **sponsorship** *n* patronage *m*; cautionnement *m*; parrainage *m*; (*Rad, TV*) commande *f* publicitaire.

spontaneous [spɒn'teɪnɪəs] *adj* (*gen*) spontané. **~ combustion** combustion *f* vive. ♦ **spontaneity** *n* spontanéité *f*. ♦ **spontaneously** *adv* spontanément.

spook* [spu:k] *n* revenant *m*. ♦ **spooky*** *adj* qui donne le frisson.

spool [spu:l] *n* (*gen*) bobine *f*; *[fishing reel]* tambour *m*; *[sewing machine]* canette *f*; *[wire]* rouleau *m*.

spoon [spu:n] **1** *n* cuiller *f or* cuillère *f*. **2** *vt*: **to ~ sth into a plate** verser qch dans une assiette avec une cuiller. ♦ **spoonfeed** *vt* nourrir à la cuiller; (*fig*) mâcher le travail à. ♦ **spoonful** *n* cuillerée *f*.

spoonerism ['spu:nərɪzəm] *n* contrepèterie *f*.

spoor [spʊəʳ] *n* foulées *fpl*, trace *f*, piste *f*.

sporadic [spə'rædɪk] *adj* sporadique. **~ fighting** échauffourées *fpl*. ♦ **sporadically** *adv* sporadiquement.

sport [spɔ:t] **1** *n* **(a)** sport *m*. **he is good at ~** il est très sportif; **outdoor/indoor ~s** sports de plein air/d'intérieur. **(b)** (*amusement*) divertissement *m*. **to have good ~** (*Hunting/Fishing*) faire bonne chasse/bonne pêche; (*gen*) bien se divertir. **(c)** (*: *person*) chic type* *m*, chic fille* *f*. **be a ~!** sois chic!* **2** *vt* arborer. ♦ **sporting** *adj* sportif, chic* *inv*; **there's a ~ing chance that** il est possible que +*subj*. ♦ **sportingly** *adv* (*fig*) très sportivement. ♦ **sports 1** *npl* (*meeting*) réunion *f* sportive; **2** *adj* (*gen*) de sport; *clothes* sport *inv*; **~s car** voiture *f* de sport; **~s ground** terrain *m* de sport; **~s jacket** veston *m* sport *inv*. ♦ **sportsman** *n* sportif *m*; (*fig*) **he's a real ~sman** il est très sportif. ♦ **sportsmanlike** *adj* sportif, chic* *inv*. ♦ **sportsmanship** *n* esprit *m* sportif. ♦ **sportswear** *n* vêtements *mpl* de sport. ♦ **sportswoman** *n* sportive *f*. ♦ **sporty*** *adj* sportif.

spot [spɒt] **1** *n* **(a)** (*gen*) tache *f* (*on* sur); (*polka dot*) pois *m*; (*on dice, domino*) point *m*; (*pimple*) bouton *m*. **a ~ of dirt** une tache; **a dress with red ~s** une robe à pois rouges; **a ~ of rain** quelques gouttes *fpl* de pluie; **to have ~s before the eyes** voir des mouches volantes devant les yeux; **to come out in ~s** avoir une éruption de boutons. **(b)** (*small amount*) **a ~ of** un peu de; *whisky, coffee etc* une goutte de; *truth, common sense* un grain de; **a ~ of sleep** un petit somme; **he did a ~ of work** il a travaillé un peu; **there's been a ~ of trouble** il y a eu un petit incident; **how about a ~ of lunch?*** et si on mangeait un morceau? **(c)** (*place*) endroit *m*. **a good ~ for a picnic** un bon endroit *or* coin pour un pique-nique; **a tender ~ on the arm** un point sensible au bras; **the police were on the ~ in 2 minutes** la police est arrivée sur les lieux en 2 minutes; **it's easy if you're on the ~** c'est facile si vous êtes sur place; **the man on the ~** la personne qui est sur place; (*Press etc*) l'envoyé spécial; **an on-the-~ report** un reportage sur place; **he decided on the ~** il s'est décidé sur le champ *or* tout de suite; (*fig*) **to be in a (bad or tight) ~*** être dans le pétrin. **(d)** (*: *Rad, Theat, TV: in show*) numéro *m*; (*Rad, TV: advertisement*) spot *m*. **(e)** = **spotlight**.

2 *adj*: **~ cash** argent *m* comptant; **~ remover** détachant *m*.

3 *vt* **(a)** (*speckle*) tacher (*with* de). **(b)** (*notice*) *person, vehicle* apercevoir, repérer*; *mistake* relever; (*recognize*) *bargain, winner, sb's ability* découvrir.

♦ **spotless** *adj* (*lit*: **~lessly clean**) reluisant de propreté; (*fig*) sans tache. ♦ **spotlight** *n* (*Theat: beam*) rayon *m* de projecteur; (*Theat: lamp*) projecteur *m*, spot *m*; (*Aut*) phare *m* auxiliaire; (*Theat*) **in the ~light** sous le feu des projecteurs; (*fig*) **the ~light was on him** il était en vedette. ♦ **spotted** *adj animal* tacheté; *fabric* à pois. ♦ **spotter** *n* **(a)** (*as hobby*) **train ~ter** passionné(e) *m(f)* de trains; **(b)** (*Mil etc*) (*for enemy aircraft*) guetteur *m*; (*during firing*) observateur *m*. ♦ **spotty** *adj face* boutonneux.

spouse [spaʊz] *n* époux *m*, épouse *f*; (*Jur*) conjoint(e) *m(f)*.

spout [spaʊt] **1** *n* (*gen*) bec *m*; (*for tap*) brise-jet *m inv*; *[gutter, pump etc]* dégorgeoir *m*; *[fountain]* jet *m*. (*Brit fig*) **to be up the ~‡** être fichu*. **2** *vt liquid* faire jaillir; *smoke, lava* vomir; (**fig*) *poem etc* débiter.

sprain [spreɪn] **1** *n* entorse *f*, (*less serious*) foulure *f*. **2** *vt muscle etc* fouler. **to ~ one's ankle** se donner une entorse à la cheville, (*less serious*) se fouler la cheville.

sprang [spræŋ] *pret of* **spring**.

sprawl [sprɔ:l] **1** *vi* (*fall*) tomber, s'étaler*; (*lie*) être affalé; *[plant]* ramper (*over* sur); *[handwriting, town]* s'étaler (*over* dans). **2** *n*: **an ugly ~ of buildings down the valley** d'affreux bâtiments qui s'étalent dans la vallée; **London's suburban ~** l'étalement *m* de la banlieue londonienne. ♦ **sprawling** *adj person* affalé; *handwriting* étalé; *city* tentaculaire.

spray¹ [spreɪ] **1** *n* **(a)** (*gen*) nuage *m* de gouttelettes *fpl*; (*from sea*) embruns *mpl*; (*from hose pipe*) pluie *f*; (*from atomizer*) spray *m*; (*from aerosol*) pulvérisation *f*; (*from fountain*) jet *m*. **(b)** (*container*) (*aerosol*) bombe *f*, aérosol *m*; (*for scent etc*) atomiseur *m*, (*refillable*) vaporisateur *m*; (*larger: for garden etc*) pulvérisateur *m*. **insecticide ~** (*aerosol*) bombe (d')insecticide; (*contents*) insecticide *m* (*en bombe*). **(c)** (**~ attachment, ~ nozzle**) pomme *f*. **2** *adj deodorant, insecticide* (présenté) en bombe *etc*. **~ can** bombe *f etc* (*V* **1b**); **~ gun** pistolet *m* (*à peinture etc*); **~ paint** peinture *f* en bombe. **3** *vt* **(a)** *roses, garden, crops* faire des pulvérisations sur; *room* faire des pulvérisations dans; *hair* vaporiser (*with* de). **they ~ed the oil slick with detergent** ils ont répandu du détergent sur la nappe de pétrole; (*fig*) **to ~ sth/sb with bullets** arroser qch/qn de balles. **(b)** *water, insecticide, paint* pulvériser (*on* sur); *scent* vaporiser. **they ~ed foam on the flames** ils ont projeté de la neige carbonique sur les flammes. ♦ **sprayer** *n* **(a)** = **spray¹ 1b**; **(b)** (*aircraft*: **crop-~er**) avion-pulvérisateur *m*. ♦ **spraying machine** *n* (*Agr*) pulvérisateur *m*.

spray² [spreɪ] *n [flowers]* gerbe *f*; *[greenery]* branche *f*; (*brooch*) aigrette *f*.

spread [spred] (*vb: pret, ptp* **spread**) **1** *n* **(a)** *[fire, disease, infection]* propagation *f*; *[nuclear weapons]* prolifération *f*; *[idea, knowledge]* diffusion *f*; *[education]* progrès *m*. **(b)** (*extent*) *[wings]* envergure *f*; *[arch]* ouverture *f*; *[bridge]* travée *f*; *[marks, prices, ages etc]* échelle *f*. **he's got a middle-age ~** il a pris de l'embonpoint avec l'âge. **(c)** (*cover*) (*for table*) dessus *m* de table; (*bed~*) dessus-de-lit *m inv*. **(d)** (*Culin*) pâte *f* (à tartiner). **cheese ~** fromage *m* à tartiner; **anchovy ~** ≃

pâte d'anchois. **(e)** (**fig: meal*) festin *m.* **(f)** (*Press, Typ*) (*two pages*) double page *f*; (*across columns*) deux (*or* trois *etc*) colonnes *fpl.*

2 *vt* **(a)** (~ **out**) (*gen*) étendre (*on sth* sur qch); *wings, sails* déployer; *fingers, toes, arms, legs* écarter. (*fig*) **to ~ one's wings** élargir ses horizons. **(b)** *bread etc* tartiner (*with* de); *butter, glue* étaler (*on* sur). **(c)** (*distribute*) *sand etc* répandre (*on, over* sur); *fertilizer* épandre (*over, on* sur); (~ **out**) *objects, cards, goods* étaler (*on* sur); *soldiers etc* disposer (*along* le long de). **policemen ~ out all over the hillside** des agents de police dispersés sur toute la colline. **(d)** *disease, infection* propager; *germs* disséminer; *wealth* distribuer; *rumours* faire courir; *news, knowledge, panic, indignation* répandre; (*in time:* ~ **out**) *payment, studies etc* échelonner (*over* sur). **our resources are ~ very thinly** nous n'avons plus aucune marge dans l'emploi de nos ressources.

3 *vi* (*gen*) se répandre; *[river, stain]* s'étaler; *[flood, weeds, fire, disease, pain]* s'étendre. **to ~ into** *or* **over sth** (*gen*) se répandre dans *or* sur qch; *[fire, pain, disease]* atteindre qch; *[weeds, panic]* envahir qch; **the desert ~s (out) over 500 square miles** le désert s'étend sur 500 milles carrés.

spread out 1 *vi [people, animals]* se disperser; *[valley]* s'élargir. **2** *vt sep*: **the valley lay ~ out before him** la vallée s'étendait à ses pieds; **he was ~ out on the floor** il était étendu de tout son long par terre.

♦ **spread-eagled** *adj* étendu bras et jambes écartés.

spree [spri:] *n* fête *f.* **to go on** *or* **have a ~** faire la fête; **to go on a spending ~** faire des folies (*achats*).

sprig [sprɪg] *n* rameau *m*, brin *m.*

sprightly ['spraɪtlɪ] *adj* alerte, actif.

spring [sprɪŋ] (*vb: pret* **sprang**, *ptp* **sprung**) **1** *n* **(a)** (*leap*) bond *m*, saut *m.* **in** *or* **with** *or* **at one ~** d'un bond, d'un saut. **(b)** (*for mattress, watch etc; also Tech*) ressort *m.* (*Aut*) **the ~s** la suspension. **(c)** (*resilience*) *[mattress]* élasticité *f.* **(d)** *[water]* source *f.* **hot ~** source chaude. **(e)** (*season*) printemps *m.* **in (the) ~** au printemps; **~ is in the air** il fait un temps de printemps.

2 *adj* **(a)** *weather, day, flowers* printanier, de printemps. (*Brit*) **~ onion** ciboule *f.* **(b)** *mattress* à ressorts. (*file*) **~ binder** classeur *m* à ressort.

3 *vi* **(a)** (*leap*) bondir, sauter (*at* sur). **to ~ in/across** *etc* entrer/traverser *etc* d'un bond; (*fig*) **to ~ to sb's help** bondir à l'aide de qn; **to ~ to the rescue** se précipiter pour porter secours; **he sprang into action** il est passé à l'action; **to ~ into existence/into view** apparaître du jour au lendemain/soudain; **to ~ to mind** venir à l'esprit; **the door sprang open** la porte s'est brusquement ouverte; **hope ~s eternal** l'espoir fait vivre. **(b)** (*originate*) provenir, découler (*from* de).

4 *vt trap, lock* faire jouer. (*fig*) **to ~ a surprise on sb** surprendre qn; **to ~ a question/a piece of news on sb** poser une question/annoncer une nouvelle à qn de but en blanc; **he sprang it on me** il m'a pris de court *or* au dépourvu.

spring up *vi [person]* se lever d'un bond; *[flowers, buildings]* surgir de terre; *[corn]* lever brusquement; *[wind, storm]* se lever brusquement; *[rumour, doubt, fear, friendship, alliance]* naître; *[problem, obstacle]* surgir.

♦ **springboard** *n* tremplin *m.* ♦ **spring-clean** *vt* nettoyer de fond en comble. ♦ **spring-cleaning** *n* grand nettoyage *m.* ♦ **spring-like** *adj* printanier. ♦ **springtime** *n* printemps *m.* ♦ **springy** *adj* (*gen*) souple; *rubber, mattress* élastique; *carpet* moelleux; *plank* flexible.

sprinkle ['sprɪŋkl] *vt* (*with water*) asperger (*with* de); (*with sugar*) saupoudrer (*with* de). **to ~ sand on** *or* **over sth** répandre une légère couche de sable sur qch; **to ~ sand/grit on the roadway** sabler/cendrer la route. ♦ **sprinkler** *n* (*for lawn etc*) arroseur *m*; (*for sugar etc*) saupoudreuse *f*; (*for fire-fighting*) diffuseur *m* (d'extincteur automatique d'incendie). ♦ **sprinkling** *n [water]* quelques gouttes *fpl*; *[sand]* légère couche *f*; (*fig*) **there was a sprinkling of young people** il y avait quelques jeunes çà et là.

sprint [sprɪnt] **1** *n* (*Sport*) sprint *m.* **2** *vi* (*Sport*) sprinter; (*gen*) foncer (*for the bus* pour attraper l'autobus). **to ~ down the street** descendre la rue à toutes jambes. ♦ **sprinter** *n* (*Sport*) sprinteur *m*, -euse *f.*

sprout [spraʊt] **1** *n* (*from bulbs, seeds*) germe *m.* **(Brussels) ~s** choux *mpl* de Bruxelles. **2** *vi [bulbs, onions etc]* germer; (*grow quickly*) *[plants]* bien pousser; *[child]* pousser vite*; (*appear*) surgir. **3** *vt leaves* produire; (*) *moustache* se laisser pousser. *[potatoes, bulbs]* **to ~ shoots** germer.

spruce[1] [spru:s] *n* (*tree*) épicéa *m.*

spruce[2] [spru:s] *adj* pimpant, net.

spruce up *vt sep child* faire beau; *house* bien astiquer. **all ~d up** *person* tiré à quatre épingles.

sprung [sprʌŋ] (*ptp of* **spring**) *adj seat, mattress* à ressorts. (*Aut*) **well-~** bien suspendu.

spry [spraɪ] *adj* alerte, vif.

spud* [spʌd] *n* patate* *f*, pomme *f* de terre.

spun [spʌn] *pret, ptp of* **spin.**

spur [spɜ:ʳ] **1** *n* éperon *m*; (*fig*) aiguillon *m.* (*fig*) **to win one's ~s** faire ses preuves; **on the ~ of the moment** sous l'impulsion du moment. **2** *adj*: **~ road** route *f* d'accès. **3** *vt* (~ **on**) *horse* éperonner; *[ambition etc]* éperonner, aiguillonner. **to ~ sb (on) to do sth** pousser qn à faire qch.

spurious ['spjʊərɪəs] *adj* (*gen*) faux; *claim* fallacieux; *interest, affection* simulé.

spurn [spɜ:n] *vt* repousser (avec mépris).

spurt [spɜ:t] **1** *n [water, flame]* jaillissement *m*; *[anger, enthusiasm, energy]* sursaut *m.* **to put on a ~** (*Sport*) sprinter; (*in running for bus etc*) foncer; (*fig: in work etc*) donner un coup de collier. **2** *vi* (~ **out,** ~ **up**) jaillir (*from* de).

spy [spaɪ] **1** *n* (*gen*) espion(ne) *m(f).* **police ~** indicateur *m*, -trice *f* de police. **2** *adj film, story etc* d'espionnage. **3** *vi* (*gen*) espionner; (*Ind, Pol*) faire de l'espionnage (*for a country* au service d'un pays). **to ~ on sb/sth** espionner qn/épier qch. **4** *vt* (*catch sight of*) apercevoir.

spy out *vt sep*: **to ~ out the land** reconnaître le terrain.

♦ **spyglass** *n* lunette *f* d'approche. ♦ **spyhole** *n* petit trou *m.* ♦ **spying** *n* espionnage *m.*

squabble ['skwɒbl] **1** *n* chamaillerie* *f.* **2** *vi* se chamailler* (*over sth* à propos de qch). ♦ **squabbling** *n* chamailleries* *fpl.*

squad [skwɒd] **1** *n [policemen, workmen, prisoners]* escouade *f*; *[soldiers]* groupe *m*; (*US Sport*) équipe *f.* (*Ftbl*) **the England ~** le contingent anglais. **2** *adj* (*Police*) **~ car** voiture *f* de police.

squadron ['skwɒdrən] *n* (*Mil*) escadron *m*; (*Aviat, Naut*) escadrille *f.*

squalid ['skwɒlɪd] *adj* (*gen*) sordide; *motive* vil. ♦ **squalor** *n* conditions *fpl* sordides.

squall [skwɔ:l] **1** *n* (*Met*) rafale *f or* bourrasque *f* de pluie; (*at sea*) grain *m.* **2** *vi [baby]* hurler, brailler. ♦ **squalling** *adj* criard, braillard*.

squander ['skwɒndəʳ] *vt time, money, talents* gaspiller; *inheritance* dilapider; *opportunity* perdre.

square [skwɛəʳ] **1** *n* **(a)** (*gen*) carré *m*; *[chessboard, crossword, graph paper]* case *f*; (*in pattern, on fabric*) carreau *m*; (*head~*) carré, foulard *m.* **to fold into a ~** plier en carré; (*fig*) **now we're back to ~ one*** nous repartons à zéro*; **~ dance** quadrille *m.* **(b)** (*in town*) place *f*; (*with gardens*) square *m*; (*US: block of houses*) pâté *m* de maisons; (*Mil:* **barrack ~**) cour *f* (de caserne). **the town ~** la grand-place. **(c)** (*Math*) carré *m.* **4**

is the ~ of 2 4 est le carré de 2. **(d)** (*pej*) **he's a real ~*** il est vraiment vieux jeu.

2 *adj* **(a)** (*in shape*) carre. **to cut sth ~** couper qch au carré; (*Typ*) **~ bracket** crochet *m*; (*fig*) **he is a ~ peg in a round hole** il n'est pas à son affaire; (*fig*) **a ~ meal** un repas convenable. **(b)** (*even, balanced*) *books, accounts, figures* en ordre. **to get one's accounts ~** mettre ses comptes en ordre; **to get ~ with sb** (*financially*) régler ses comptes avec qn; (*get even with*) régler son compte à qn; (*fig*) **to be all ~** être quitte; (*Sport*) être à égalité. **(c)** (*honest*) *dealings* honnête, régulier*. **he is absolutely ~** il est l'honnêteté même; **to get** *or* **have a ~ deal** être traité équitablement; **to give sb a ~ deal** agir honnêtement avec qn. **(d)** (*Math etc*) *number* carré. **6 ~ metres** 6 mètres carrés; **6 metres ~** de 6 mètres sur 6; **~ root** racine *f* carrée. **(e)** (**pej: conventional*) vieux jeu *inv*, rétro* *inv*.

3 *adv*: **~ in the middle** en plein milieu; **to look sb ~ in the face** regarder qn bien en face.

4 *vt* **(a)** (*make ~*) *figure, shape* rendre carré; *stone, timber* équarrir; *shoulders* redresser. **(b)** (*settle etc*) *books, accounts* mettre en ordre; *debts, creditors* régler; (*reconcile*) faire cadrer (*A with B* A avec B). **I can't ~ that with what he told me** ça ne cadre pas avec ce qu'il m'a dit; **he managed to ~ it with his conscience/the boss** il s'est arrangé avec sa conscience/le patron; **I can ~* him** je m'occupe de lui. **(c)** (*Math*) *number* élever au carré. **four ~d is sixteen** quatre au carré fait seize.

5 *vi* cadrer, s'accorder (*with* avec).

square off *vt sep paper* quadriller; *wood, edges* équarrir.

square up *vi* **(a)** *[boxers, fighters]* se mettre en garde (*to sb* devant qn). **(b)** (*pay debts*) régler ses comptes (*with sb* avec qn).

♦ **square-bashing** *n* (*Brit Mil sl*) exercice *m*. ♦ **square-built** *adj* trapu. ♦ **square-cut** *adj* coupé à angle droit. ♦ **square-faced** *adj* au visage carré. ♦ **squarely** *adv* **(a)** (*completely*) carrément; **we must face this ~ly** nous devons carrément y faire face; **~ly in the middle** en plein milieu; **(b)** (*honestly*) *treat etc* honnêtement.

squash [skwɒʃ] **1** *n* **(a)** (*crowd, crush*) cohue *f*. **(b) lemon/orange ~** citronnade *f*/orangeade *f* (concentrée). **(c)** (*Sport*: **~ rackets**) squash *m*. **~ court** terrain *m* de squash.

2 *vt* (*gen*) écraser; (*fig*) *argument* réfuter; (*snub*) *person* remettre à sa place. **to ~ flat** *fruit, beetle* écraser; *hat, box* aplatir.

3 *vi* **(a)** *[people]* **they ~ed into the elevator** ils se sont entassés dans l'ascenseur; **they ~ed out of the gate** ils sont sortis en se bousculant près du portail. **(b)** *[fruit, parcel etc]* s'écraser.

squash in **1** *vi [people]* s'entasser. **2** *vt sep* (*into box, suitcase etc*) réussir à faire rentrer.

squash together **1** *vi [people]* se serrer (les uns contre les autres). **2** *vt sep objects* serrer.

squash up **1** *vi [people]* se serrer. **2** *vt sep object* écraser; *paper* chiffonner en boule.

♦ **squashy** *adj fruit* mou.

squat [skwɒt] **1** *adj person* ramassé; *building* lourd; *object* petit et épais. **2** *vi* **(a)** (**~ down**) *[person]* s'accroupir; *[animal]* se tapir. **to be ~ting (down)** *[person]* être accroupi; *[animal]* être tapi. **(b)** *[squatters]* faire du squattage*. **to ~ in a house** squatteriser* une maison. ♦ **squatter** *n* squatter *m*.

squawk [skwɔ:k] **1** *vi [hen, parrot]* pousser un gloussement; *[baby]* brailler; *[person]* pousser un cri rauque; (*: *complain*) râler*. **2** *n* gloussement *m*; braillement *m*; cri *m* rauque.

squeak [skwi:k] **1** *vi [hinge, wheel, pen, chalk]* grincer; *[shoe]* craquer; *[mouse, doll]* vagir; *[person]* glapir. **2** *vt*: **'no' she ~ed** 'non' glapit-elle. **3** *n* grincement *m*; craquement *m*; vagissement *m*; glapissement *m*. **to give a ~ of surprise** pousser un petit cri de surprise; **not a ~*!** pas un murmure, hein!; **I don't want another ~ out of you** je ne veux plus t'entendre. ♦ **squeaky** *adj hinge, wheel* grinçant; *shoes* qui craquent.

squeal [skwi:l] **1** *vi* **(a)** *[animal, person]* pousser un cri aigu; *[brakes]* hurler; *[tyres]* crisser. **(b)** (*‡: inform*) vendre la mèche*. **to ~ on sb** dénoncer qn, donner* qn. **2** *vt*: **'help' he ~ed** 'au secours' cria-t-il d'une voix perçante. **3** *n* cri *m* aigu; hurlement *m*; crissement *m*. **to give a ~ of pain** pousser un cri de douleur; **with a ~ of laughter** avec un rire aigu.

squeamish ['skwi:mɪʃ] *adj* (*easily nauseated; fastidious*) facilement dégoûté; (*queasy*) qui a mal au cœur; (*easily shocked*) qui s'effarouche facilement. **I'm too ~ to do that** je n'ose pas faire cela. ♦ **squeamishness** *n* (*queasiness*) nausée *f*; (*prudishness*) pruderie *f*.

squeeze [skwi:z] **1** *n* (*act, pressure*) pression *f*, compression *f*; (*in crowd*) cohue *f*. **a ~ of lemon** quelques gouttes *fpl* de citron; **a ~ of toothpaste** un peu de dentifrice; **it was a tight ~ to get through** il y avait à peine la place de passer; (*fig*) **to put the ~ on sb‡** harceler qn; (*Econ*) **credit ~** restrictions *fpl* de crédit. **2** *vt* **(a)** (*press*) (*gen*) presser; *doll, teddy bear* appuyer sur; *sb's hand, arm* serrer. **she ~d it into the case** elle a réussi à le faire rentrer dans la valise; (*fig*) **he ~d his victim dry*** il a saigné sa victime à blanc. **(b)** (*extract*: **~ out**) *water, toothpaste* exprimer (*from, out of* de); *names, information, money* soutirer, arracher (*out of* à). **3** *vi* se glisser (*under* sous; *into* dans). **he ~d past me** il s'est glissé devant moi en me poussant un peu; **they all ~d into the car** ils se sont entassés dans la voiture; **he ~d through the crowd** il a réussi à se faufiler à travers la foule; **the car ~d into the empty space** il y avait juste assez de place pour la voiture.

squeeze in **1** *vi [person]* trouver une petite place; *[car etc]* rentrer tout juste. **can I ~ in?** est-ce qu'il y a une petite place pour moi? **2** *vt sep object into box,* (**fig*) *item on programme etc* réussir à faire rentrer.

♦ **squeezer** *n* presse-fruits *m inv*; **lemon ~r** presse-citron *m inv*.

squelch [skweltʃ] *vi*: **to ~ in/out** *etc* entrer/sortir *etc* en pataugeant.

squib [skwɪb] *n* pétard *m*.

squid [skwɪd] *n* calmar *m*.

squiggle ['skwɪgl] **1** *n* gribouillis *m*. **2** *vi* gribouiller.

squint [skwɪnt] **1** *n* (*Med*) strabisme *m*; (*quick glance*) coup *m* d'œil. (*Med*) **to have a ~** loucher. **2** *vi* (*Med*) loucher. **to ~ at sth** (*obliquely*) regarder qch du coin de l'œil; (*quickly*) jeter un coup d'œil à qch.

squire ['skwaɪəʳ] *n* ≈ châtelain *m*; (*Hist*) écuyer *m*.

squirm [skwɜ:m] *vi [worm etc]* se tortiller; *[person]* (*from embarrassment*) ne pas savoir où se mettre; (*from distaste*) avoir un haut-le-corps.

squirrel ['skwɪrəl] **1** *n* écureuil *m*. **2** *adj coat etc* en petit-gris.

squirt [skwɜ:t] **1** *vt water* faire jaillir (*at, on, onto* sur; *into* dans); *oil* injecter; *detergent* verser une giclée de; (*from aerosol*) *insecticide etc* pulvériser (*on* sur). (*scent etc*) **to ~ sb with sth** asperger qn de qch. **2** *vi [liquid]* jaillir (*from* de). **the water ~ed into my eye** j'ai reçu une giclée d'eau dans l'œil. **3** *n [water]* jet *m*; *[detergent]* giclée *f*; *[scent]* quelques gouttes *fpl*.

stab [stæb] **1** *n* (*with dagger/knife etc*) coup *m* (de poignard/de couteau *etc*). (*fig*) **a ~ in the back** un coup déloyal; **a ~ of pain** un élancement; **a ~ of remorse/grief** un remords/une douleur lancinant(e); (*fig*) **to have a ~ at (doing) sth*** s'essayer à (faire) qch. **2** *adj*: ~ **wound** coup *m* de poignard (*or* couteau *etc*). **3** *vt* (*with dagger*) poignarder; (*with knife*) donner un coup de couteau à. **to ~ sb to death** tuer qn d'un coup de couteau *etc*; **he was ~bed through the heart** il a reçu un coup de couteau *etc* dans le cœur; (*lit, fig*) **to ~ sb in the back** poignarder qn dans le dos. ♦ **stabbing 1** *n* agression *f* (à coups de couteau *etc*); **2** *adj pain* lancinant.

stable[1] ['steɪbl] *adj* (*gen*) stable; *prices* stable, (*St Ex*) ferme; *relationship, marriage* solide; *person* équilibré. ♦ **stability** *n* stabilité *f*; fermeté *f*; solidité *f*; équilibre *m*. ♦ **stabilize** *vt* stabiliser. ♦ **stabilizer** *n* (*Aut, Naut*) stabilisateur *m*; (*Aviat*) empennage *m*.

stable[2] ['steɪbl] **1** *n* (*gen*) écurie *f*. **racing** ~ écurie de courses; **riding ~s** manège *m*. **2** *vt horse* mettre à l'écurie. ♦ **stableboy** *or* ♦ **stablelad** *n* lad *m*.

stack [stæk] **1** *n* **(a)** (*gen*) tas *m*; (*hay*~) meule *f*. **~s* of** un tas*de; **to have ~s* of money** rouler sur l'or; **we've got ~s* of time** on a tout le temps. **(b)** (*chimney*) cheminée *f*. **2** *vt* (~ **up**) *objects* empiler; *aircraft* faire attendre (sur niveaux différents); (*fig pej*) *jury, committee* sélectionner avec partialité (*in favour of* pour favoriser; *against* pour défavoriser).

stadium ['steɪdɪəm] *n* stade *m* (*sportif*).

staff [stɑːf] **1** *n* **(a)** (*work force: gen*) personnel *m*; (*Scol, Univ*) professeurs *mpl*; (*servants*) domestiques *mpl*; (*Mil*) état-major *m*. **a large ~** un personnel nombreux; **to be on the ~** faire partie du personnel; **he joined our ~ in 1974** il est entré chez nous en 1974. **(b)** (*liter: pole*) bâton *m*; (*flag*~) mât *m*. **2** *adj* (*Mil*) ~ **college** école *f* supérieure de guerre; (*Scol, Univ*) ~ **meeting** conseil *m* des professeurs. **3** *vt school etc* pourvoir en personnel. **it is ~ed mainly by immigrants** le personnel se compose surtout d'immigrants; **well-~ed** pourvu d'un personnel nombreux. ♦ **staffroom** *n* (*Scol etc*) salle *f* des professeurs.

stag [stæg] **1** *n* cerf *m*. **2** *adj*: ~ **party*** réunion *f* entre hommes. ♦ **stag beetle** *n* cerf-volant *m* (*Zool*).

stage [steɪdʒ] **1** *n* **(a)** (*platform: in theatre*) scène *f*; (*in hall*) estrade *f*. (*profession etc*) **the ~** le théâtre; **on ~** sur scène; **to come on ~** entrer en scène; **to go on the ~** monter sur la scène, (*fig: as career*) monter sur les planches; **to write for the ~** écrire des pièces de théâtre; (*fig*) **to hold the ~** occuper le devant de la scène. **(b)** (*point, part*) *[journey]* étape *f*; *[road, pipeline]* section *f*; *[rocket]* étage *m*; *[operation, process, disease]* stade *m*; *[career]* échelon *m*. *[bus]* **fare ~** section; **in ~s** *travel* par étapes; *study* par degrés; **in** *or* **by easy ~s** par petites étapes, par degrés; **in the early ~s** au début; **at an early ~ in** vers le début de; **at this ~ in the negotiations** à ce stade des négociations; **it has reached the ~ of being translated** c'en est au stade de la traduction; **we have reached a ~ where ...** nous en sommes arrivés à un stade où ...; **he's going through a difficult ~** il passe par une période difficile. **2** *adj*: ~ **designer** décorateur *m*, -trice *f* de théâtre; ~ **director** metteur *m* en scène; ~ **door** entrée *f* des artistes; ~ **fright** trac* *m*; ~ **manager** régisseur *m*; ~ **name** nom *m* de théâtre; (*fig*) **in a ~ whisper** en aparté. **3** *vt* (*Theat*) monter, mettre en scène; (*fig*) *accident etc* (*organize*) organiser; (*feign*) monter. **to ~ a demonstration** (*organize*) organiser une manifestation; (*carry out*) manifester; **to ~ a strike** (*organize*) organiser une grève; (*go on strike*) faire la grève; **that was ~d** c'était un coup monté. ♦ **stagecraft** *n* technique *f* de la scène. ♦ **stagehand** *n* machiniste *m*. ♦ **stage-manage** *vt play, production* être régisseur pour; (*fig*) *event, confrontation* organiser, monter. ♦ **stage-struck** *adj*: **to be ~-struck** brûler d'envie de faire du théâtre.

stagger ['stægəʳ] **1** *vi* chanceler, tituber. **to ~ along/in** *etc* avancer/entrer *etc* en chancelant *or* titubant. **2** *vt* **(a)** (*amaze*) renverser, stupéfier; (*upset*) bouleverser. **(b)** (*space out*) *objects* espacer; *visits, payments* échelonner; *working hours, holidays* étaler. ♦ **staggering** *adj* renversant, bouleversant; (*lit, fig*) **~ing blow** coup *m* de massue.

stagnant ['stægnənt] *adj* stagnant. ♦ **stagnate** *vi [water]* être stagnant; (*fig*) stagner. ♦ **stagnation** *n* stagnation *f*.

staid [steɪd] *adj* (trop) sérieux, (trop) posé. ♦ **staidness** *n* caractère *m* trop sérieux *or* posé.

stain [steɪn] **1** *n* **(a)** (*mark*) tache *f* (*on* sur). **grease ~** tache de graisse; **without a ~ on his character** sans une tache à sa réputation. **(b)** (*colouring*) colorant *m*. **wood ~** couleur *f* pour bois. **2** *adj*: ~ **remover** détachant *m*. **3** *vt* **(a)** tacher (*with* de). **(b)** (*colour*) *wood* teinter; *glass* colorer. **~ed glass** (*substance*) verre *m* coloré; (*windows collectively*) vitraux *mpl*; **~ed-glass window** vitrail *m*. ♦ **stainless steel** *n* acier *m* inoxydable, inox *m*.

stair [stɛəʳ] **1** *n* (*step*) marche *f*; (*also* ~**s**) escalier *m*. **on the ~s** dans l'escalier; **below ~s** à l'office. **2** *adj carpet* d'escalier. ~ **rod** tringle *f* d'escalier. ♦ **staircase** *or* ♦ **stairway** *n* escalier *m*.

stake [steɪk] **1** *n* **(a)** (*gen*) pieu *m*, poteau *m*; (*for plant*) tuteur *m*. (*Hist*) **to be burnt at the ~** mourir sur le bûcher. **(b)** (*Betting*) enjeu *m*; (*share*) intérêt *m*. (*horse-race*) **~s** course *f* de chevaux; (*lit, fig*) **to play for high ~s** jouer gros jeu; **to be at ~** être en jeu; **there is a lot at ~** l'enjeu est considérable; **he has got a lot at ~** il joue gros jeu, il a gros à perdre; **to have a ~ in sth** avoir des intérêts dans qch, (*on large scale*) avoir de gros investissements dans qch. **2** *vt* **(a)** (~ **out**) *area* marquer avec des piquets. **to ~ one's claim to** établir son droit à. **(b)** (~ **up**) *plant* mettre un tuteur à. **(c)** (*bet*) jouer (*on* sur). **I'd ~ my life on it** j'en mettrais ma tête à couper.

stalactite ['stæləktaɪt] *n* stalactite *f*.

stalagmite ['stæləgmaɪt] *n* stalagmite *f*.

stale [steɪl] *adj meat, eggs etc* qui n'est plus frais; *bread* rassis, (*stronger*) dur; *air* confiné; *news* déjà vieux; *joke* rebattu; *athlete* surentraîné. **the room smells ~** cette pièce sent le renfermé; **I'm getting ~** je perds mon enthousiasme. ♦ **stalemate** *n* (*Chess*) pat *m*; (*fig*) impasse *f*; **to have reached ~mate** être dans l'impasse; **to break the ~mate** sortir de l'impasse. ♦ **staleness** *n* (*gen*) manque *m* de fraîcheur.

stalk[1] [stɔːk] *n [plant]* tige *f*; *[fruit]* queue *f*; *[cabbage]* trognon *m*.

stalk[2] [stɔːk] **1** *vt game, prey* traquer; *suspect* filer. **2** *vi*: **to ~ in/off** *etc* entrer/partir *etc* avec raideur; **he ~ed in angrily** il est entré d'un air furieux.

stall [stɔːl] **1** *n* (*in market, at fair*) éventaire *m*; (*in exhibition*) stand *m*; (*in stable, cowshed*) stalle *f*. (*Theat*) **the ~s** l'orchestre *m*; **newspaper/flower ~** kiosque *m* à journaux/de fleuriste; **station book~** librairie *f* de gare; **coffee ~** buvette *f*. **2** *vi [car, engine]* caler; *[aircraft]* être en perte de vitesse. (*fig*) **to ~ for time** essayer de gagner du temps. **3** *vt* (*Aut*) caler; (*Aviat*) causer une perte de vitesse à. (*fig*) **I managed to ~ him** j'ai réussi à le tenir à distance. ♦ **stallholder** *n* marchand(e) *m(f)* (*en plein air*).

stallion ['stæljən] *n* étalon *m* (*cheval*).

stalwart ['stɔːlwət] *adj* (*in build*) vigoureux; (*in spirit*) résolu. **to be a ~ supporter of sb/sth** soutenir qn/qch de façon inconditionnelle.

stamen ['steɪmen] *n* (*Bot*) étamine *f*.

stamina ['stæmɪnə] *n* résistance *f*, endurance *f*. **he's got ~** il est résistant.

stammer ['stæmə^r] **1** *n* bégaiement *m.* **2** *vti* bégayer. ♦ **stammerer** *n* bègue *mf.* ♦ **stammering** *n* bégaiement *m.* ♦ **stammeringly** *adv* en bégayant.

stamp [stæmp] **1** *n* **(a)** timbre *m.* **postage ~** timbre-poste *m*; **savings ~** timbre-épargne *m*; **trading ~** timbre-prime *m*; **National Insurance ~** cotisation *f* à la Sécurité sociale. **(b)** (*rubber ~*) timbre *m.* **date ~** timbre dateur. **(c)** (*mark*) **look at the date ~** regardez la date sur le cachet; (*fig*) **the ~ of genius/truth** le sceau du génie/de la vérité. **2** *adj*: **~ album** album *m* de timbres-poste; **~ collecting** philatélie *f*; **~ collection** collection *f* de timbres(-poste); **~ collector** philatéliste *mf*; **~ dealer** marchand(e) *m(f)* de timbres(-poste); **~ duty** droit *m* de timbre; **~ machine** distributeur *m* automatique de timbres(-poste). **3** *vt* **(a) to ~ one's foot** taper du pied; **to ~ one's feet** (*in rage*) trépigner; (*in dance*) frapper du pied; (*to keep warm*) battre la semelle. **(b)** (*stick a ~ on*) *letter, insurance card* timbrer. **~ed addressed envelope** enveloppe timbrée pour la réponse. **(c)** (*mark with ~*) timbrer; *passport, document* viser; *visa, date* apposer (*on* sur); *metal* poinçonner. **4** *vi* taper du pied; *[horse]* piaffer. **to ~ on sth** piétiner qch; (*angrily*) **to ~ in/out** *etc* entrer/sortir *etc* en tapant du pied.

stamp out *vt sep fire* éteindre en piétinant; *rebellion* enrayer; *custom, tendency* détruire.

stampede [stæm'pi:d] **1** *n [animals, people]* débandade *f*, sauve-qui-peut *m inv*; (*fig: rush*) ruée *f* (*for sth* pour obtenir qch; *for the door* vers la porte). **2** *vi* s'enfuir à la débandade (*from* de), fuir à la débandade (*towards* vers); (*fig: rush*) se ruer (*for sth* pour obtenir qch; *for the door* vers la porte). **3** *vt animals, people* jeter la panique parmi. (*fig*) **we mustn't let ourselves be ~d** il faut que nous prenions le temps de réfléchir.

stance [stæns] *n* position *f.*

stand [stænd] (*vb: pret, ptp* **stood**) **1** *n* **(a)** (*position: lit, fig*) position *f*; (*resistance: Mil, fig*) résistance *f*, opposition *f*. (*lit, fig*) **to take (up) one's ~** prendre position (*against* contre); **he took (up) his ~ beside me** (*lit*) il s'est placé à côté de moi; (*fig*) il m'a soutenu; (*fig*) **to make a ~** résister (*against* à), prendre position (*against* contre). **(b)** (*taxi ~*) station *f* (de taxis). **(c)** (*for plant, bust etc*) guéridon *m*; (*for displaying goods*) étalage *m*; (*at exhibition, trade fair*) stand *m*; (*at fair*) baraque *f*; (*market stall*) éventaire *m*; (*US: witness ~*) barre *f*; (*in sports stadium, along procession route etc*) tribune *f*. **lamp ~** support *m or* pied *m* de lampe; **hat ~** porte-chapeaux *m inv*; **coat ~** portemanteau *m*; **music ~** pupitre *m* à musique; **newspaper ~** kiosque *m* à journaux; **band ~** kiosque (à musique).

2 *vt* **(a)** (*place*: **~ up**) *object* mettre, poser (*on* sur; *against* contre). **to ~ sth on its end** faire tenir qch debout. **(b)** (*tolerate, withstand*) supporter. **I can't ~ it any longer** (*pain etc*) je ne peux plus le supporter; (*boredom etc*) j'en ai assez, j'en ai par-dessus la tête*; **I can't ~ (the sight of) her** je ne peux pas la supporter *or* la voir*; **she can't ~ being laughed at** elle ne supporte pas qu'on se moque (*subj*) d'elle; **I can't ~ gin/Giraudoux** je déteste le gin/Giraudoux; **to ~ the strain** *[rope, beam etc]* supporter la tension; *[person]* tenir le coup; **it won't ~ close examination** cela ne résiste pas à un examen serré; **the town stood constant bombardment** la ville a résisté à un bombardement continuel. **(c)** (*pay for*) payer, offrir. **to ~ sb a drink** payer *or* offrir à boire à qn; **to ~ the cost of sth** payer le coût de qch. **(d)** (*phrases*) **to ~ a chance** avoir une bonne chance (*of doing* de faire); **to ~ no chance** ne pas avoir la moindre chance (*of doing* de faire); **to ~ one's ground** tenir bon; **to ~ trial** passer en jugement (*for* pour).

3 *vi* **(a)** (*be ~ing*: **~ up**) être debout; (*stay ~ing*) rester debout. **too weak to ~** trop faible pour se tenir debout; **to ~ erect** (*stay upright*) rester debout; (*straighten up*) se redresser; **~ up straight!** tiens-toi droit!; (*fig*) **to ~ on one's own feet** se débrouiller tout seul; **he ~s over 6 feet** il fait plus de 1 mètre 80; **the house is still ~ing** la maison existe toujours; **not much still ~s of the walls** il ne reste plus grand-chose des murs; **they didn't leave a stone ~ing** ils n'ont rien laissé debout.

(b) (*rise*: **~ up**) se lever, se mettre debout.

(c) (**~** *still*) rester (debout), être (debout). **we stood talking for an hour** nous sommes restés là à parler pendant une heure; **he stood in the doorway** il se tenait dans l'embrasure de la porte; **don't ~ there, do something!** ne reste pas là à ne rien faire!; (*fig*) **he left the others ~ing** il dépassait les autres d'une tête; **the man ~ing over there** cet homme là-bas; **~ over there till ...** mets-toi là-bas jusqu'à ce que ...; **they stood in a circle** ils se tenaient en cercle; **to ~ in line** faire la queue; **~ still!** ne bougez pas!; (*fig*) **time seemed to ~ still** le temps semblait s'être arrêté; (*lit, fig*) **to ~ fast** *or* **firm** tenir bon; (*lit*) **to ~ in sb's way** barrer le passage à qn; (*fig*) **I won't ~ in your way** je ne vous ferai pas obstacle; **nothing ~s in our way** la voie est libre; **his age ~s in his way** son âge constitue un sérieux handicap; **that was all that stood between him and ...** c'était tout ce qui le séparait de ...; **to ~ clear** s'écarter; **you're ~ing on my foot** tu me marches sur le pied; (*Aut*) **to ~ on the brakes** freiner à mort; (*fig*) **to ~ on ceremony** faire des manières; **to ~ on one's dignity** garder ses distances; **it ~s to reason that ...** il va sans dire que ...; **where do you ~ on this question?** quelle est votre position sur cette question?; **I like to know where I ~** j'aime savoir où j'en suis.

(d) (*be situated*) se trouver. **the village ~s in the valley** le village se trouve dans la vallée; *[statue, argument etc]* **to ~ on** reposer sur.

(e) (*be*) être. **to ~ accused/convicted of** être accusé/déclaré coupable de; (*Parl*) **to ~ (as a candidate** *or* **for election)** être candidat (*for* à); **he stood for the council** il était candidat au poste de conseiller; (*have reached*) **to ~ at** *[thermometer, clock]* indiquer; *[offer, price, bid]* être à; *[score]* être de; **accept the offer as it ~s** acceptez l'offre telle quelle; (*Sport etc*) **the record stood at ...** le record est resté à ...; **as things ~** les choses étant ce qu'elles sont; **how do things ~?** où en sont les choses?

(f) (*remain undisturbed*) *[liquid, dough etc]* reposer; *[tea, coffee]* infuser; *[offer]* demeurer valable. **let the matter ~ as it is** laissez les choses comme elles sont; **they let the regulation ~** ils n'ont rien changé au règlement; *[project, results]* **to ~ or fall by sth** reposer sur qch.

(g) (*be likely*) **to ~ to lose** risquer de perdre; **to ~ to win** avoir des chances de gagner; **he ~s to make a fortune** il pourrait bien faire fortune.

(h) (*Naut*) **to ~ out to sea** (*move*) mettre le cap sur le large; (*stay*) être *or* rester au large.

stand about, stand around *vi* rester là, traîner (*pej*). **to keep sb ~ing about** faire faire le pied de grue à qn.

stand aside *vi* s'écarter, se pousser. (*fig*) **to ~ aside in favour of sb** laisser la voie libre à qn.

stand back *vi* (*move back*) reculer, s'écarter. **the farm ~s back from the motorway** la ferme est à l'écart de l'autoroute.

stand by 1 *vi* **(a)** (*be onlooker*) rester là (à ne rien faire). **(b)** *[troops]* être en état d'alerte; *[person, ship, vehicle]* (*be ready*) se tenir prêt; (*be at hand*) attendre sur place. **~ by for takeoff** paré pour le décollage; **~ by to drop anchor** paré à mouiller l'ancre; **~ by for further news** tenez-vous prêt à recevoir d'autres nouvelles. **2** *vt fus promise* tenir; *sb else's decision* accepter; *one's*

own decision s'en tenir à; *friend* ne pas abandonner; *colleague etc* soutenir.
stand down *vi [troops]* être déconsigné (en fin d'alerte); (*fig: withdraw*) *[candidate]* se désister.
stand for *vt fus* **(a)** (*represent*) *[initials, political party]* représenter. **(b)** (*tolerate*) supporter, tolérer.
stand in *vi*: **to ~ in for sb** remplacer qn.
stand out *vi* (*project*) *[ledge, buttress]* avancer (*from* sur); *[vein etc]* ressortir (*on* sur); (*be conspicuous*) ressortir, se détacher (*against* sur). (*fig*) **he ~s out above all the rest** il surpasse tout le monde; (*fig*) **that ~s out a mile!*** cela saute aux yeux!; **to ~ out for sth** revendiquer qch; **to ~ out against** *attack* résister à; *demand* s'opposer fermement à.
stand over 1 *vi [items for discussion]* rester en suspens. **2** *vt fus person* surveiller, être sur le dos de.
stand to *vi* (*Mil*) se mettre en état d'alerte.
stand up 1 *vi* (*rise*) se lever, se mettre debout; (*be ~ing*) être debout; (*fig*) *[argument, case]* être valable. (*fig*) **to ~ up for sb/sth** défendre qn/qch; **to ~ up to** *opponent* affronter; (*in argument*) tenir tête à; *rough treatment, cold etc* résister à; *V also* **stand 3a, 3b. 2** *vt sep box etc* mettre debout. (*fig*) **she stood me up*** elle m'a fait faux bond; *V also* **stand 2a.**
♦ **stand-by 1** *n*: **it's a useful ~-by** ça peut toujours être utile; **to be on ~-by** *[troops]* être sur pied d'intervention; *[plane]* se tenir prêt à décoller; *[doctor]* être de garde; **2** *adj car, battery etc* de réserve; *generator* de secours; (*Aviat*) *ticket, passenger* sans garantie. ♦ **stand-in** *n* remplaçant(e) *m(f)*; (*Cine*) doublure *f*. ♦ **stand-offish** *adj* (*pej*) distant, froid. ♦ **stand-offishly** *adv* avec froideur. ♦ **standpoint** *n* point *m* de vue. ♦ **standstill** *n* arrêt *m*; **to come to a ~still** s'arrêter; **to bring to a ~still** arrêter; **to be at a ~still** *[person, car]* être immobile; *[production]* être paralysé; *[discussion]* être au point mort; *[trade]* être dans le marasme complet. ♦ **stand-to** *n* (*Mil*) alerte *f*. ♦ **stand-up** *adj collar* droit; *meal etc* (pris) debout; *fight, quarrel* en règle.
standard ['stændəd] **1** *n* **(a)** (*flag*) étendard *m*; (*Naut*) pavillon *m*. **(b)** (*norm*) norme *f*; (*criterion*) critère *m*; (*for weights and measures*) étalon *m*; (*intellectual etc*) niveau *m* (voulu). **monetary ~** titre *m* de monnaie; **the gold ~** l'étalon or; (*fig*) **to be** *or* **come up to ~** *[person]* être à la hauteur; *[thing]* être de la qualité voulue; **you are applying a double ~** vous appliquez deux mesures; **his ~s are high** il cherche l'excellence; (*morally, artistically*) **he has set us a high ~** il a établi un modèle difficile à surpasser; **first-year university ~** du niveau de première année d'université; **high/low ~ of living** niveau de vie élevé/bas; **to have high moral ~s** avoir un sens moral très développé; **I couldn't accept their ~s** je ne pouvais pas accepter leur échelle de valeurs. **(c)** (*street light*) pylône *m* d'éclairage; (*base: for lamp, street light*) pied *m*. **2** *adj size, height, procedure* ordinaire, normal; *metre, weight etc* étalon *inv*; (*Comm: regular*) *design, model, size* standard *inv*; (*Statistics*) *deviation etc* type; *reference book* classique, de base; *pronunciation, usage* correct. **it is now ~ practice to do so** c'est maintenant courant de faire ainsi; **a ~ model car** une voiture de série; **~ time** l'heure légale. ♦ **standard-bearer** *n* porte-étendard *m inv*. ♦ **standardization** *n* standardisation *f*; normalisation *f*. ♦ **standardize** *vt* (*gen*) standardiser; *product, terminology* normaliser. ♦ **standard-lamp** *n* lampadaire *m*.
standing ['stændɪŋ] **1** *adj* **(a)** *passenger* debout *inv*; *crop* sur pied. (*in bus etc*) **~ room** places *fpl* debout; **~ stone** pierre *f* levée. **(b)** (*permanent*) *army, committee, invitation* permanent; *rule* fixe; *grievance, reproach* constant. **~ expenses** frais *mpl* généraux; **a ~ joke** un sujet de plaisanterie continuel; **~ order** (*Banking*) virement *m* automatique; (*Comm*) commande *f* permanente (*for* pour); (*Mil, Parl*) **~ orders** règlement *m*. **2** *n* **(a)** (*importance etc*) *[person, newspaper]* importance *f*; *[restaurant, business]* réputation *f*, standing *m*. **social ~** position *f* sociale, standing; **professional ~** rang *m or* standing professionnel; **firms of that ~** des compagnies aussi réputées; **he has no ~ in this matter** il n'a aucune autorité dans cette affaire. **(b)** (*duration*) **of 10 years' ~** *friendship* qui dure depuis 10 ans; *agreement, contract* qui existe depuis 10 ans; *doctor, teacher* qui a 10 ans de métier; **of long ~** de longue date.
stank [stæŋk] *pret of* **stink.**
stanza ['stænzə] *n [poem]* strophe *f*; *[song]* couplet *m*.
staple[1] ['steɪpl] *adj crop, industry* principal; *products, foods* de base. **~ diet** nourriture *f* de base.
staple[2] ['steɪpl] **1** *n* (*for papers*) agrafe *f*; (*Tech*) crampon *m*. **2** *vt* (**~ together**) agrafer (*on to* à); cramponner. ♦ **stapler** *n* agrafeuse *f*.
star [stɑːʳ] **1** *n* **(a)** étoile *f*; (*Typ etc*) astérisque *m*. **the S~s and Stripes** la Bannière étoilée; **3-~ hotel** hôtel *m* 3 étoiles; **4-~ petrol** super* *m*; (*US*) **four-~ general** général *m* à quatre étoiles; **born under a lucky ~** né sous une bonne étoile; **you can thank your (lucky) ~s* that ...** tu peux remercier le ciel de ce que ...; (*fig*) **to see ~s*** voir trente-six chandelles; (*horoscope*) **the ~s** l'horoscope *m*; **it was written in his ~s that ...** il était écrit que ... . **(b)** (*Cine, Sport etc*) vedette *f*; (*actress only*) star *f*. **2** *adj* (*Theat etc*) **~ part** premier rôle; **a ~(ring) role** l'un des principaux rôles; (*Theat, fig*) **the ~ turn** la vedette. **3** *vt*: **the film ~s John Wayne** John Wayne est la vedette du film; **~ring Greta Garbo as ...** avec Greta Garbo dans le rôle de ... . **4** *vi* être la vedette (*in a film* d'un film); (*fig*) briller. **he ~red as Hamlet** c'est lui qui a joué le rôle de Hamlet. ♦ **stardom** *n* (*Cine, Sport etc*) célébrité *f*. ♦ **starfish** *n* étoile *f* de mer. ♦ **stargaze** *vi*: **to be ~gazing** être dans la lune. ♦ **starlet** *n* (*Cine*) starlette *f*. ♦ **starlight** *n*: **by ~light** à la lumière des étoiles. ♦ **starlit** *adj* étoilé. ♦ **starry** *adj sky, night* étoilé. ♦ **starry-eyed** *adj* (*idealistic*) idéaliste; (*innocent*) innocent; (*from wonder*) éberlué; (*from love*) éperdument amoureux. ♦ **star-studded** *adj sky* parsemé d'étoiles; (*fig*) *cast etc* à vedettes.
starboard ['stɑːbəd] (*Naut*) **1** *n* tribord *m*. **2** *adj* de tribord.
starch [stɑːtʃ] **1** *n* (*gen*) amidon *m*. (*food*) **~es** féculents *mpl*. **2** *vt collar* amidonner, empeser. ♦ **starch-reduced** *adj bread* de régime. ♦ **starchy** *adj*: **~y food** féculents *mpl*.
stare [stɛəʳ] **1** *n* regard *m* (fixe). **curious/vacant ~** long regard curieux/vague. **2** *vi*: **to ~ at sb/sth** regarder qn/qch fixement, fixer qn/qch du regard; **to ~ at sb/sth in surprise** regarder qn/qch avec surprise; **what are you staring at?** qu'est-ce que tu regardes comme ça?; **to ~ into space** avoir le regard perdu dans le vague. **3** *vt*: **to ~ sb in the face** fixer qn du regard, dévisager qn; (*fig*) **they're staring you in the face!** ils sont là devant ton nez; **that ~s you in the face** cela crève les yeux.
stare out *vt sep* faire baisser les yeux à.
stark [stɑːk] **1** *adj countryside* morne; *décor* austère. (*fig*) **the ~ truth** la vérité telle qu'elle est. **2** *adv*: **~ raving** *or* **staring mad*** complètement fou *or* dingue*; **~ naked** complètement nu.
starling ['stɑːlɪŋ] *n* étourneau *m* (*oiseau*).
start [stɑːt] **1** *n* **(a)** (*beginning: gen*) commencement *m*, début *m*; *[negotiations]* ouverture *f*; *[race etc]* départ *m*; (**~ing line**) point *m* de départ. **the ~ of the academic year** la rentrée universitaire et scolaire; **that was the ~ of all the**

trouble c'est là que tous les ennuis ont commencé; **from the ~** dès le début, dès le commencement; **for a ~** d'abord; **from ~ to finish** du début jusqu'à la fin; **to get off to a good ~** bien commencer, prendre un bon départ; **to get a good ~ in life** bien débuter dans la vie; **a good ~ to his career** un bon début pour sa carrière; **to make a ~** commencer; **to make an early ~** commencer de bonne heure, (*in journey*) partir de bonne heure; **to make a fresh ~** recommencer. **(b)** (*advantage*) (*Sport*) avance *f*; (*fig*) avantage *m* (*over* sur). **to give sb 10 metres' ~** *or* **a 10-metre ~** donner 10 mètres d'avance à qn; (*fig*) **that gave him a ~ over the others** cela lui a donné un avantage sur les autres. **(c)** (*sudden movement*) *[person]* sursaut *m*; *[animal]* tressaillement *m*. **to wake with a ~** se réveiller en sursaut; **to give a ~** sursauter; **to give sb a ~** faire sursauter qn; **you gave me such a ~!** ce que vous m'avez fait peur!

2 *vt* **(a)** (*begin*) (*gen*) commencer (*to do, doing* à faire, de faire); *work* commencer, se mettre à; *task* entreprendre; *bottle, cheese etc* entamer. **to ~ a journey** partir en voyage; **to ~ life as** débuter dans la vie comme; **to ~ again** *or* **afresh** recommencer (*to do* à faire). **(b)** (**~ off, ~ up**) *discussion* commencer, ouvrir; *conversation* engager; *quarrel, rumour* faire naître; *reform, series of events* déclencher; *fashion, policy* lancer; *phenomenon, institution* donner naissance à; *war* causer. **to ~ a fire** (*in grate etc*) faire du feu; (*accidentally*) provoquer un incendie; **she has ~ed a baby*** elle est enceinte. **(c)** (*also* **~ up, get ~ed**) *engine, vehicle* mettre en marche, démarrer; *clock* mettre en marche; (**~ off**) *race* donner le signal du départ. **to ~ sb (off** *or* **out) on a career** lancer qn dans une carrière; **if you ~ him (off) on that subject ...** si tu le lances sur ce sujet ...; **that ~ed him remembering** alors il s'est mis à se souvenir; (*fig*) **now you've ~ed sth!** quelle histoire!; **to get ~ed on (doing) sth** commencer (à faire) qch; **let's get ~ed** allons-y; **to get sb ~ed on (doing) sth** faire commencer qch à qn; **once I get ~ed I work very quickly** une fois lancé, je travaille très vite.

3 *vi* **(a)** (*also* **~ off, ~ up**: *gen*) commencer (*with* par; *by doing* par faire); *[road]* partir (*at* de). **to ~ on** *book, study* commencer; *new bottle* entamer; **we must ~ at once** il faut commencer *or* nous y mettre immédiatement; **it's ~ing (off) rather well/badly** cela s'annonce plutôt bien/mal; **to ~ in business** se lancer dans les affaires; **before October ~s** avant le début d'octobre; **to ~ again** *or* **afresh** recommencer; **~ing from Monday** à partir de lundi; **to ~ with, there were only 3** d'abord, ils n'étaient que 3; **~ on a new page** prenez une nouvelle page; **he ~ed (out) to say that ...** son intention était de dire que ... . **(b)** (*leave*: **~ off, ~ out**) partir (*from* de; *for* pour; *on a journey* en voyage). **he ~ed (off** *or* **out) down the street** il a commencé à descendre la rue; (*fig*) **to ~ (off) as a clerk** débuter comme employé; **to ~ (off** *or* **out) as a Marxist** commencer par être marxiste. **(c)** (**~ up**) *[car, machine]* démarrer; *[clock]* se mettre à marcher. **(d)** (*jump nervously*) *[person]* sursauter; *[animal]* tressaillir.

♦ **starter** *n* **(a)** (*Sport*) (*official*) starter *m*; (*horse, runner*) partant *m*; (*Scol etc*) **the child was a late ~er** cet enfant a mis du temps à se développer; (*fig*) **it's a non-~er*** ça ne vaut rien; **(b)** (*Aut*) démarreur *m*; (*on machine etc*) bouton *m* de démarrage; **(c) for ~ers*** (*Culin*) comme hors-d'œuvre *m inv*; (*for a start*) pour commencer. ♦ **starting** *adj*: **~ing point** point *m* de départ; **~ing price** (*St Ex*) prix *m* initial; (*Racing*) cote *f* de départ.

startle ['stɑːtl] *vt* *[sound, sb's arrival]* faire sursauter *or* tressaillir; *[news, telegram]* alarmer. **to ~ sb out of his wits** donner un choc à qn; **you ~d me!** vous m'avez fait peur! ♦ **startled** *adj animal* effarouché; *person, voice* très surpris. ♦ **startling** *adj* (*surprising*) surprenant; (*alarming*) alarmant.

starve [stɑːv] **1** *vt* **(a)** (*deliberately*) affamer. **to ~ sb to death** laisser qn mourir de faim; **she ~d herself to feed him** elle s'est privée de nourriture pour lui donner à manger; **to ~ sb into submission** soumettre qn par la faim. **(b)** (*deprive*) priver (*sb of sth* qn de qch). **2** *vi* manquer de nourriture, être affamé. **to ~ (to death)** mourir de faim. ♦ **starvation 1** *n* inanition *f*; **2** *adj rations, wages* de famine. ♦ **starving** *adj* affamé; (*fig*) **I'm starving*** je meurs de faim.

stash* [stæʃ] *vt* (**~ away**) (*hide*) cacher; (*store away*) mettre de côté. **£500 ~ed away** 500 livres (*stored away*) en réserve *or* (*safe*) en lieu sûr.

state [steɪt] **1** *n* **(a)** état *m*. **~ of alert/war** état d'alerte/de guerre; **in your ~ of health/mind** dans votre état de santé/d'esprit; **in an odd ~ of mind** d'une humeur étrange; **you're in no ~ to reply** vous n'êtes pas en état de répondre; **to lie in ~** être exposé solennellement; **to live in ~** mener grand train; (*fig*) **what's the ~ of play?** où en est-on?; **in a good/bad ~ of repair** bien/mal entretenu; **to be in a good/bad ~** *[chair, car, house]* être en bon/mauvais état; *[person, marriage]* aller bien/mal; **the ~ the car was in** l'état de la voiture; **he's not in a fit ~ to drive** il est hors d'état de conduire; **what a ~ you're in!** vous êtes dans un bel état!; **he got into a terrible ~ about it*** ça l'a mis dans tous ses états; **don't get into such a ~!*** ne vous affolez pas! **(b)** (*Pol*) **the S~** l'État *m*; (*US*) **the S~s** les États-Unis *mpl*; **affairs of ~** affaires *fpl* de l'État.

2 *adj business, secret* d'État; *security, control* de l'État; *medicine* étatisé; (*US: often* **S~**) *law, prison* d'État. **~ apartments** appartements *mpl* officiels; **~ banquet** banquet *m* de gala; (*US*) **S~ Department** Département *m* d'État, ≃ ministère *m* des Affaires étrangères; (*Brit*) **~ education** enseignement *m* public; (*US*) **the S~ line** la frontière entre les états; (*US*) **S~'s attorney** procureur *m*; (*Brit*) **~ school** école publique; (*US*) **~ trooper** ≃ CRS *m*; **to make a ~ visit to a country** se rendre en visite officielle dans un pays.

3 *vt* déclarer (*that* que); *one's views, the facts, problem* exposer; *time, place* fixer, spécifier; *conditions, theory, restrictions* formuler. **it is ~d in the records that ...** il est écrit dans les archives que ...; **as ~d above** ainsi qu'il est dit plus haut; **~ your name and address** déclinez vos nom, prénoms et adresse; **cheques must ~ the sum clearly** les chèques doivent indiquer la somme clairement; **to ~ one's case** présenter ses arguments.

♦ **state-controlled** *adj* étatisé. ♦ **stated** *adj date, sum* fixé; *interval* fixe; *limit* prescrit; **on ~d days** à jours fixes; **at the time ~d** à l'heure dite. ♦ **state-enrolled nurse** *n* (*Brit*) infirmier *m*, -ière *f* auxiliaire, aide-soignante *mf*. ♦ **stateless** *adj* apatride; **~less person** apatride *mf*. ♦ **stateliness** *n* majesté *f*. ♦ **stately** *adj* majestueux; (*Brit*) **~ly home** château *m* (*de l'aristocratie*). ♦ **statement** *n* **(a)** *[views]* exposition *f*; *[conditions]* formulation *f*; (*written, verbal*) déclaration *f*; (*Jur*) déposition *f*; **official ~ment** communiqué *m* officiel; **to make a ~ment** faire une déclaration; **(b)** (*Comm: bill*) facture *f*; **bank ~ment** relevé *m* de compte. ♦ **state-owned** *adj* étatisé. ♦ **state-registered nurse** *n* (*Brit*) infirmier *m*, -ière *f* diplômé(e) d'État. ♦ **stateroom** *n [palace]* grande salle *f* de réception; *[ship, train]* cabine *f* de luxe. ♦ **statesman** *n* homme *m* d'État; (*fig*) **he is a real ~sman** il est extrêmement diplomate. ♦ **statesmanlike** *adj* diplomatique. ♦ **statesmanship** *n* habileté *f* politique. ♦ **state-subsidized** *adj* subventionné par l'État. ♦ **state-wide** *adj, adv* d'un bout à l'autre de l'État.

static ['stætɪk] **1** *adj* statique. **2** *n* **(a)** ~s statique *f*. **(b)** (*Elec, Rad etc*) parasites *mpl*.

station ['steɪʃən] **1** *n* **(a)** (*place*) poste *m*, station *f*; (*Mil*) poste. **fire** ~ caserne *f* de pompiers; **lifeboat** ~ centre *m* de secours en mer; **police** ~ commissariat *m* (de police), gendarmerie *f*; **radio** ~ station de radio; **one's** ~ **in life** sa situation sociale; (*Rel*) **the S~s of the Cross** le Chemin de Croix. **(b)** (*Rail*) gare *f*; *[underground]* station *f*. **bus** *or* **coach** ~ gare routière; **the train came into the** ~ le train est entré en gare, (*in underground*) la rame est entrée dans la station. **2** *adj* (*Rail*) *staff, bookstall etc* de (la) gare. (*US Rad*) ~ **break** page *f* de publicité; (*Rail*) ~ **master** chef *m* de gare; (*Aut*) ~ **wag(g)on** break *m*. **3** *vt* (*gen*) placer; *look-out, troops* poster. **to** ~ **o.s.** se placer; **to be** ~**ed at** *[troops]* être en garnison à; *[sailors]* être en station à. ♦ **stationary** *adj* stationnaire. ♦ **stationer** *n* papetier *m*, -ière *f*; ~**er's (shop)** papeterie *f* (*magasin*). ♦ **stationery 1** *n* papeterie *f* (*articles*); (*writing paper*) papier *m* à lettres; **2** *adj* (*Brit*) **the S~ery Office** ≃ l'Imprimerie nationale.

statistics [stə'tɪstɪks] *npl* statistique *f*; (*measurements*) statistiques; (*hum: woman's*) mensurations *fpl*. **a set of** ~ une statistique. ♦ **statistical** *adj error* de statistiques; *probability, table* statistique; *expert* en statistiques. ♦ **statistically** *adv* statistiquement. ♦ **statistician** [,stætɪs'tɪʃən] *n* statisticien(ne) *m(f)*.

statue ['stætju:] *n* statue *f*. ♦ **statuesque** *adj* sculptural. ♦ **statuette** *n* statuette *f*.

stature ['stætʃəʳ] *n* stature *f*, taille *f*; (*fig*) envergure *f*. (*fig*) **his** ~ **increased when ...** il a pris de l'envergure quand ...; **moral/intellectual** ~ envergure sur le plan moral/intellectuel.

status ['steɪtəs] **1** *n* **(a)** (*economic etc position*) situation *f*, position *f*; (*Admin, Jur*) statut *m*. **social** ~ standing *m*; **civil** ~ état *m* civil; **what is his official** ~? quelle est sa position officielle?; **economic** ~ situation économique; **the** ~ **of the black population** la condition sociale *or* (*Admin*) le statut de la population noire; **his** ~ **as an assistant director** son standing de directeur-adjoint. **(b)** (*prestige*) *[person, job]* prestige *m*. **2** *adj*: ~ **symbol** signe *m* extérieur de richesse. ♦ **status quo** *n* statu quo *m*.

statute ['stætju:t] **1** *n* (*Jur etc*) loi *f*. **by** ~ selon la loi. **2** *adj*: ~ **book** code *m*. ♦ **statutory** *adj duty, right, control* statutaire; *holiday* légal; *offence, rape* défini par un article de loi.

staunch[1] [stɔ:ntʃ] *vt flow* arrêter; *blood* étancher.

staunch[2] [stɔ:ntʃ] *adj support* loyal; *friend, ally* à toute épreuve. ♦ **staunchly** *adv* loyalement.

stave [steɪv] (*vb: pret, ptp* **stove** *or* **staved**) *n* *[barrel etc]* douve *f*; (*Mus*) portée *f*; (*Poetry*) stance *f*, strophe *f*.

stave in *vt sep* enfoncer.

stave off *vt sep danger, threat* écarter; *disaster, defeat* éviter; *hunger* tromper; *attack* parer.

stay [steɪ] **1** *n* **(a)** séjour *m*. **he is in Rome for a short** ~ il est à Rome pour une courte visite *or* un bref séjour; **a** ~ **in hospital** un séjour à l'hôpital. **(b)** (*Jur*) ~ **of execution** sursis *m* à l'exécution (d'un jugement).

2 *vt* **(a)** (*check*) arrêter; *disease, epidemic* enrayer; (*delay*) retarder; (*Jur*) *judgment* surseoir à; *proceedings* suspendre; *decision* remettre. **(b) to** ~ **the course** (*Sport*) aller jusqu'au bout; (*fig*) tenir bon.

3 *vi* (*remain*) rester. ~ **there!** restez là!; **to** ~ **still, to** ~ **put*** ne pas bouger; **to** ~ **to dinner** rester dîner; (*Rad*) ~ **tuned!** restez à l'écoute!; ~ **with it*** tenez bon; **it is here to** ~ c'est bien établi; **he's here to** ~ il est là pour de bon; **if the weather** ~**s fine** si le temps se maintient au beau; **has she come to** ~? est-ce qu'elle est venue avec l'intention de rester?; **she came to** ~ **for a few weeks** elle est venue passer quelques semaines; **I'm** ~**ing with my aunt** je loge chez ma tante; **to** ~ **in a hotel** descendre à l'hôtel; **he was** ~**ing in Paris** il séjournait à Paris.

stay away *vi*: **he** ~**ed away for 3 years** il n'est pas rentré avant 3 ans; **he** ~**ed away from the meeting/from school** il n'est pas allé à la réunion/à l'école.

stay behind *vi* rester (en arrière *or* à la fin).

stay down *vi* rester en bas; (*bending*) rester baissé; (*lying down*) rester couché; (*under water*) rester sous l'eau.

stay in *vi* (*at home*) rester à la maison, ne pas sortir; (*Scol*) être en retenue; *[screw etc]* tenir.

stay out *vi* (*away from home*) ne pas rentrer; (*outside*) rester dehors; (*on strike*) rester en grève. **get out and** ~ **out!** sortez et ne revenez pas!; **to** ~ **out late** rentrer tard; **to** ~ **out all night** ne pas rentrer de la nuit; (*fig*) **to** ~ **out of** *argument etc* ne pas se mêler de; *prison* éviter; **to** ~ **out of trouble** se tenir tranquille.

stay over *vi* s'arrêter (un *or* plusieurs jour(s)), faire une halte. **can you** ~ **over till Thursday?** est-ce que vous pouvez rester jusqu'à jeudi?

stay up *vi [person]* rester debout, ne pas se coucher; *[trousers, fence etc]* tenir. **to** ~ **up late** se coucher tard.

♦ **stay-at-home** *n, adj* casanier (*m*), -ière (*f*). ♦ **stayer** *n* (*horse*) cheval *m or* (*runner*) coureur *m* qui a du fond; (*fig*) **he's a** ~**er** il n'abandonne pas facilement. ♦ **staying power** *n* endurance *f*.

stead [sted] *n*: **in my/his** *etc* ~ à ma/sa *etc* place; **to stand sb in good** ~ être très utile à qn.

steadfast ['stedfəst] *adj* (*unshakeable*) ferme; (*constant*) constant. ♦ **steadfastly** *adv* fermement. ♦ **steadfastness** *n* fermeté *f*.

steady ['stedɪ] **1** *adj* **(a)** (*firm*) *table, pole, boat* stable; *hand* sûr; *gaze* franc; *nerves* solide; *person* sérieux, (*not nervous*) calme. **he isn't very** ~ **on his feet** il n'est pas très solide sur ses jambes; **he plays a very** ~ **game** il a un jeu très régulier; ~ **on!*** doucement! **(b)** (*regular: gen*) *temperature, demand, speed* constant; *improvement, progress* régulier; *job, prices, sales, market* stable. **to keep prices** ~ stabiliser les prix; **we were doing a** ~ **60 km/h** nous roulions à une vitesse constante de 60 km/h; **her** ~ **boyfriend** son petit ami. **2** *adv*: **to go** ~ **with sb*** sortir avec qn; **they're going** ~ ils sortent ensemble. **3** *vt wobbling object* assujettir; *chair, table* (*with hand*) maintenir, (*wedge*) caler; *nervous person, horse* calmer. **to** ~ **o.s.** reprendre son aplomb; **to** ~ **one's nerves** se calmer; **to have a** ~**ing effect on sb** (*make less nervous*) calmer qn; (*make less wild*) assagir qn. ♦ **steadily** *adv* **(a)** *walk* d'un pas ferme; *hold, grasp* d'une main ferme; *gaze, look* longuement; *stay, reply, insist* avec fermeté; **(b)** *improve, decrease, rise* régulièrement; *rain, work, continue* sans arrêt. ♦ **steadiness** *n* **(a)** (*V* **steady 1a**) stabilité *f*; sûreté *f*; sérieux *m*; calme *m*; **(b)** (*V* **steady 1b**) constance *f*; régularité *f*; stabilité *f*.

steak [steɪk] **1** *n [beef]* bifteck *m*, steak *m*; *[other meat, fish]* tranche *f*. **frying** ~ bifteck; **stewing** ~ bœuf *m* à braiser; ~ **and kidney pie** tourte *f* à la viande de bœuf et aux rognons. **2** *adj*: ~ **knife** couteau *m* à steak. ♦ **steakhouse** *n* ≃ grill-room *m*.

steal [sti:l] *pret* **stole**, *ptp* **stolen** **1** *vt* (*gen*) voler (*from sb* à qn). **he stole money from the drawer** *etc* il a volé de l'argent dans le tiroir *etc*; **to** ~ **the credit for sth** s'attribuer tout le mérite de qch; **to** ~ **a glance at** jeter un coup d'œil furtif à; **to** ~ **a march on sb*** prendre qn de vitesse; (*fig*) **he stole the show** on n'a eu d'yeux que pour lui. **2** *vi*: **to** ~ **up/out** *etc* monter/sortir *etc* à pas de loup; **he stole into the room** il s'est glissé dans la pièce. ♦ **stealing** *n* vol *m*.

stealth [stelθ] *n*: **by ~** furtivement. ♦ **stealthily** *adv* furtivement. ♦ **stealthy** *adj* furtif.

steam [sti:m] **1** *n* vapeur *f*. **it works by ~** ça marche à la vapeur; (*Naut*) **full ~ ahead!** en avant toute!; (*fig*) **it's going full ~ ahead** ça va de l'avant à plein régime; **to get up ~** *[train, ship]* chauffer; *[worker, project]* démarrer vraiment*; (*fig*) **to run out of ~** *[speaker, worker]* s'essouffler (*fig*); *[programme, project]* tourner court; **under one's own ~** par ses propres moyens; **to let off ~*** (*energy*) se défouler*; (*anger*) épancher sa bile. **2** *adj boiler, iron, engine* à vapeur. **3** *vt* (*Culin*) cuire à la vapeur. **~ed pudding** pudding *m* cuit à la vapeur; **to ~ open an envelope** décacheter une enveloppe à la vapeur. **4** *vi* **(a)** *[liquid, wet clothes]* fumer. **(b) to ~ along/away** *etc [ship, train]* avancer/partir *etc*; (**fig*) *[person, car]* avancer/partir *etc* à toute vapeur*; **the ship ~ed up the river** le vapeur remontait la rivière.

steam up 1 *vi [glass]* se couvrir de buée. **2** *vt sep* embuer. (*fig*) **to get ~ed up*** se mettre dans tous ses états (*about* à propos de).

♦ **steamboat** *n* vapeur *m*. ♦ **steam-driven** *adj* à vapeur. ♦ **steamer** *n* **(a)** (*boat*) vapeur *m*; (*liner*) paquebot *m*; **(b)** (*Culin*) ≃ couscoussier *m*. ♦ **steamroller 1** *n* rouleau *m* compresseur; **2** *adj tactics* dictatorial. ♦ **steamship** *n* paquebot *m*. ♦ **steamy** *adj atmosphere, heat* humide; *room, window* embué.

steel [sti:l] **1** *n* acier *m*. (*fig*) **to be made of ~** avoir une volonté de fer; **nerves of ~** nerfs *mpl* d'acier. **2** *adj knife, tool* d'acier; *engraving* sur acier; *industry* sidérurgique; (*St Ex*) *shares, prices* de l'acier. **~ band** steel band *m*; **~ guitar** guitare *f* aux cordes d'acier; **~ helmet** casque *m*; **~ wool** paille *f* de fer. **3** *vt* (*fig*) **to ~ o.s. to do** s'armer de courage pour faire; **to ~ o.s. against** se cuirasser contre. ♦ **steel-plated** *adj* revêtu d'acier. ♦ **steelworker** *n* sidérurgiste *m*. ♦ **steelworks** *n* aciérie *f*. ♦ **steely** *adj substance* dur comme l'acier; *colour* acier *inv*; (*fig*) *person, eyes, expression* dur; *refusal, attitude* inflexible; **~y blue/grey** bleu/gris acier *inv*.

steep[1] [sti:p] *adj slope, stairs, climb* raide; *cliff* à pic; *hill, path, road* escarpé; (**fig*) *price* (trop) élevé. (*fig*) **it's rather ~ if ...** c'est un peu fort* que ... + *subj*. ♦ **steeply** *adv*: **to rise** *or* **climb ~ly** *[road etc]* monter en pente raide; *[prices etc]* monter en flèche. ♦ **steepness** *n [road etc]* pente *f* (raide); *[slope]* abrupt *m*.

steep[2] [sti:p] **1** *vt* (*in water, dye etc*) tremper (*in* dans); *washing* faire tremper; (*Culin*) macérer (*in* dans). (*fig*) **~ed in** *ignorance, vice* croupissant dans; *prejudice* imbu de; *history, the classics* imprégné de. **2** *vi [clothes etc]* tremper; (*Culin*) macérer.

steeple ['sti:pl] *n* clocher *m*, flèche *f*. ♦ **steeple-chase** *n* steeple-chase *m* (*course*). ♦ **steeple-chasing** *n* steeple-chase *m* (*sport*). ♦ **steeplejack** *n* réparateur *m* de hautes cheminées *etc*.

steer[1] [stɪə^r] *n* (*ox*) bœuf *m*; (*esp US: castrated*) bouvillon *m*.

steer[2] [stɪə^r] **1** *vt* **(a)** (*handle controls of*) *ship* gouverner; *boat* barrer. **(b)** (*move*) *ship, boat, conversation* diriger (*towards* vers); *car* conduire; (*fig*) *person* guider. **2** *vi* (*Naut*) tenir le gouvernail (*or* la barre); (*Aut*) conduire. **to ~ by the stars** se guider sur les étoiles; **to ~ for sth** faire route vers qch; (*fig*) **to ~ clear of** éviter. ♦ **steering 1** *n* (*Aut, Naut*) conduite *f*; **2** *adj* **(a)** (*Aut*) **~ing arm/column** bras *m*/colonne *f* de direction; **~ing gear** (*Aut*) boîte *f* de direction; (*Aviat*) direction *f*; (*Aut*) **~ing lock** antivol *m* de direction; **~ing wheel** volant *m*; **(b)** *committee* d'organisation.

stem[1] [stem] *vt* (*stop*) *flow* contenir; *river* endiguer; *disease, attack* juguler. (*fig*) **to ~ the course of events** endiguer la marche des événements; (*fig*) **to ~ the tide** *or* **flow of** endiguer.

stem[2] [stem] **1** *n* **(a)** *[flower, plant]* tige *f*; *[fruit, leaf]* queue *f*; *[glass]* pied *m*; *[word]* radical *m*. **(b)** (*Naut*) **from ~ to stern** de bout en bout. **2** *vi*: **to ~ from** provenir de.

stench [stentʃ] *n* puanteur *f*.

stencil ['stensl] **1** *n* (*gen*) pochoir *m*; (*of paper*) poncif *m*; (*in typing etc*) stencil *m*; (*decoration*) décoration *f* au pochoir. (*Typing*) **to cut a ~** préparer un stencil.

2 *vt lettering* marquer au pochoir; *document* polycopier.

stenographer [ste'nɒgrəfə^r] *n* sténographe *mf*. ♦ **stenography** *n* sténographie *f*.

step [step] **1** *n* **(a)** (*gen*) pas *m*. **to take a ~ back/forward** faire un pas en arrière/en avant; **with slow ~s** à pas lents; (*lit, fig*) **at every ~** à chaque pas; **~ by ~** pas à pas, (*fig*) petit à petit; **he didn't move a ~** il n'a pas bougé d'un pas; **a waltz ~** un pas de valse; (*fig*) **it is a great ~ for them to take** c'est pour eux un grand pas à faire; **a ~ in the right direction** un pas dans la bonne voie; **a ~ up in his career** une promotion pour lui; **to take ~s** prendre des dispositions *or* des mesures (*to do* pour faire); **what's the next ~?** qu'est-ce qu'il faut faire maintenant?; **the first ~ is to decide ...** la première chose à faire est de décider ...; **to keep (in) ~** (*in marching*) marcher au pas; (*in dance*) danser en mesure; (*lit, fig*) **to keep ~ with sb** ne pas se laisser distancer par qn; **to fall into ~** se mettre au pas; **to get out of ~** rompre le pas. **(b)** (*stair*) marche *f*; (*door~*) seuil *m*; (*on bus etc*) marchepied *m*. **(flight of) ~s** (*indoors*) escalier *m*; (*outdoors*) perron *m*; **(pair of) ~s** escabeau *m*; **mind the ~** attention à la marche.

2 *vi* faire un (*or* des) pas, aller. **~ this way** venez par ici; **to ~ off sth** descendre de qch; **to ~ aside/back** *etc* s'écarter/reculer *etc*; **he ~ped into the car** il est monté dans la voiture; **to ~ on sth** marcher sur qch; **to ~ on the brakes** donner un coup de frein; (*Aut*) **to ~ on the gas*** appuyer sur le champignon*; (*fig*) **~ on it!*** dépêche-toi!; (*fig*) **to ~ out of line** s'écarter du droit chemin (*iro*).

step down *vi* descendre (*from* de); (*fig*) se désister (*in favour of sb* en faveur de qn).

step forward *vi* faire un pas en avant; (*fig*) se faire connaître.

step in *vi* entrer; (*fig*) intervenir.

step up *vt sep production, sales* augmenter; *campaign, efforts* intensifier; *attempts* multiplier; (*Elec*) *current* augmenter.

♦ **stepbrother** *n* demi-frère *m*. ♦ **step-by-step** *adj instructions* point par point. ♦ **stepchild** *n* beau-fils *m*, belle-fille *f* (*remariage*). ♦ **stepdaughter** *n* belle-fille *f*. ♦ **stepfather** *n* beau-père *m*. ♦ **stepladder** *n* escabeau *m*. ♦ **stepmother** *n* belle-mère *f*. ♦ **stepping-stone** *n* (*lit*) pierre *f* de gué; (*fig*) tremplin *m* (*to* pour obtenir à). ♦ **stepsister** *n* demi-sœur *f*. ♦ **stepson** *n* beau-fils *m*.

stereo ['stɪərɪəʊ] **1** *n* (*system*) stéréo *f*; (*record player/radio etc*) chaîne *f*/radio *f etc* stéréo *inv*. **in ~** en stéréo. **2** *adj record player, tape etc* stéréo *inv*; *broadcast, recording* en stéréo. ♦ **stereophonic** *adj* stéréophonique. ♦ **stereoscope** *n* stéréoscope *m*. ♦ **stereoscopic** *adj* stéréoscopique. ♦ **stereotype 1** *n* (*Psych etc*) stéréotype *m*; **2** *vt* stéréotyper.

sterile ['steraɪl] *adj* stérile. ♦ **sterility** *n* stérilité *f*. ♦ **sterilization** *n* stérilisation *f*. ♦ **sterilize** *vt* stériliser.

sterling ['stɜ:lɪŋ] **1** *n* (*Econ*) livre *f* sterling *inv*. **2** *adj gold, silver* fin; (*Econ*) *pound, area* sterling *inv*; (*fig*) *qualities, worth* à toute épreuve; *person* de confiance.

stern[1] [stɜ:n] *n* (*Naut*) arrière *m*, poupe *f*.

stern[2] [stɜ:n] *adj* (*gen*) sévère; *discipline* strict. **he was made of ~er stuff** il était d'une autre

trempe. ♦ **sternly** *adv* sévèrement. ♦ **sternness** *n* sévérité *f.*
steroid ['stɪərɔɪd] *n* stéroïde *m.*
stet [stet] *impers vb* (*Typ*) à maintenir.
stethoscope ['steθəskəʊp] *n* stéthoscope *m.*
stevedore ['stiːvɪdɔːʳ] *n* docker *m.*
stew [stjuː] **1** *n [meat]* ragoût *m*; *[rabbit, hare]* civet *m.* (*fig*) **in a ~*** dans tous ses états. **2** *vt meat* cuire en ragoût; *rabbit, hare* cuire en civet; *fruit* faire cuire. **3** *vi [food]* cuire; *[tea]* devenir trop infusé. (*fig*) **to let sb ~ in his own juice** laisser qn mijoter dans son jus. ♦ **stewed** *adj meat* en ragoût; *fruit* en compote; (*pej*) *tea* trop infusé; (**: drunk*) soûl*. ♦ **stewpan** *or* ♦ **stewpot** *n* cocotte *f.*
steward ['stjuːəd] *n* (*on estate, in club etc*) intendant *m*; (*on ship, plane*) steward *m*; (*at meeting*) membre *m* du service d'ordre; (*at dance*) organisateur *m.* **shop ~** délégué(e) *m(f)* syndical(e). ♦ **stewardess** *n* hôtesse *f.* ♦ **stewardship** *n* (*duties*) intendance *f*, économat *m.*
stick [stɪk] (*vb: pret, ptp* **stuck**) **1** *n* (*gen*) bâton *m*; (*twig*) brindille *f*; (*walking ~*) canne *f*; (*support for plants*) tuteur *m*; (*Mil, Mus*) baguette *f*; (*Hockey, Lacrosse*) crosse *f*; (*Ice Hockey*) stick *m*; (*piece: of chalk etc: gen*) bâton; *[chewing gum]* tablette *f*; *[celery]* branche *f*; *[rhubarb]* tige *f*; *[bombs]* chapelet *m.* (*for fire*) **~s** du petit bois; **a few ~s of furniture** quelques pauvres meubles *mpl*; (*pej: backwoods*) **in the ~s*** dans l'arrière-pays, en pleine cambrousse*; (*fig*) **to wield the big ~** manier la trique (*fig*), (*Pol*) faire de l'autoritarisme; **the policy of the big ~** la politique du bâton; (*fig*) **to give sb ~** engueuler* qn; (*fig*) **to get hold of the wrong end of the ~** mal comprendre; **he is a dull old ~*** il est rasoir*.
2 *vt* **(a)** (*thrust: gen*) enfoncer, planter (*into* dans); *pin, needle* piquer, enfoncer (*into* dans). **to ~ a pin through sth** transpercer qch avec une épingle; **I stuck the needle into my finger** je me suis piqué le doigt avec l'aiguille. **(b)** (*put: gen*) mettre (*on* sur; *under* sous; *into* dans); (*put down*) mettre, poser (*on* sur); (*into drawer, pocket, hole*) mettre, fourrer (*into* dans). **he stuck his head through the window** il a passé la tête par la fenêtre. **(c)** (*glue*) coller (*on sth* sur qch; *on the wall* au mur; *with* avec). **(d)** (*tolerate*) *thing* supporter; *person* souffrir, sentir*. **(e) to be stuck** (*gen*) être coincé (*between* entre); (*in mud, sand*) être enlisé; (*broken down*) *[vehicle, machine, lift]* être en panne; **stuck fast** bien coincé; **it got stuck in my throat** ça s'est mis en travers de ma gorge; (*fig*) **he was stuck here all summer/for the night** il a été obligé de rester ici tout l'été/de passer la nuit ici; **I'm stuck at home all day** je suis cloué à la maison toute la journée; **I was stuck* with him all evening** je l'ai eu sur le dos toute la soirée; **to be stuck for an answer** ne pas savoir que répondre; (*in puzzle, essay etc*) **I'm stuck*** je sèche*; **I'll help you if you're stuck*** je t'aiderai si tu as un problème; **I was stuck* with organizing it all** on m'a collé* le boulot de tout organiser.
3 *vi* **(a)** *[needle, spear etc]* se planter, s'enfoncer (*into* dans). **a knife ~ing into it** un couteau planté là-dedans; **the nail was ~ing through the plank** le clou dépassait de la planche. **(b)** *[glue, paste]* tenir (*to* à); *[stamp, label]* être collé (*to* à); (*Culin*) *[sauce etc]* attacher (*to* à); (*fig*) *[habit, name etc]* rester (*to sb* à qn). **it stuck to the table** c'est resté collé à la table. **(c)** (*stay*) rester. **to ~ close to sb** rester aux côtés de qn; (*fig*) **to ~ by sb** rester fidèle à qn, ne pas abandonner qn; (*fig*) **to ~ to sb like a limpet** se cramponner à qn; **to ~ to** *promise* tenir; *principles* rester fidèle à; *one's post* rester à; *the facts* s'en tenir à; *the subject* ne pas s'éloigner de; **to ~ at a job** rester dans un emploi; **~ at it!** persévère!; **to ~ to one's guns*** ne pas en démordre; **he stuck to his story** il a maintenu ce qu'il avait dit; **decide what you're going to say then ~ to it** décidez ce que vous allez dire et tenez-vous-y; **to ~ with sb*** (*stay beside*) rester avec qn; (*stay loyal*) rester fidèle à qn. **(d)** (*get jammed*) (*gen*) être coincé; (*in mud, sand*) être enlisé; (*break down*) *[vehicle, machine, lift]* être en panne. **to ~ fast** être bien coincé; **it stuck in my throat** ça s'est mis en travers de ma gorge; (*fig*) je ne suis pas arrivé à digérer* ça; (*balk*) **he will ~ at nothing to get what he wants** il ne recule devant rien pour obtenir ce qu'il veut; **he wouldn't ~ at murder** il irait jusqu'au meurtre.
stick around* *vi* (*stay near*) rester dans les parages; (*hang about*) traîner (à attendre).
stick down *vt sep envelope etc* coller.
stick in 1 *vi* (*) persévérer. **2** *vt sep* (*put in*) (*gen*) enfoncer, planter; *needle, pin* piquer, enfoncer; *photo in album etc* coller. (*fig*) **he stuck in a few quotations** il a collé* quelques citations par-ci par-là; (*fig*) **to get stuck in*** s'y mettre sérieusement.
stick on *vt sep label, stamp* coller.
stick out 1 *vi* **(a)** (*protrude*) (*gen*) sortir (*from* de); *[teeth]* avancer; *[rod etc]* dépasser; *[balcony etc]* faire saillie. **his ears ~ out** il a les oreilles décollées; (*fig*) **it ~s out a mile*** ça crève les yeux (*that* que). **(b)** (*persevere etc*) **to ~ out for more money** tenir bon dans ses revendications pour une augmentation de salaire. **2** *vt sep* **(a)** *one's arm, head* sortir (*of* de); *one's chest* bomber. **to ~ one's tongue out** tirer la langue. **(b)** (**: endure*) supporter. **to ~ it out** tenir le coup.
stick together 1 *vi [labels, pages, objects]* rester collés ensemble; (*stay together*) *[people]* rester ensemble; (*fig*) se serrer les coudes. **2** *vt sep* coller (ensemble).
stick up 1 *vi* **(a) to ~ up out of the water** sortir de l'eau. **(b) to ~ up for sb/sth*** défendre qn/qch. **2** *vt sep* **(a)** *notice etc* afficher. **(b)** *one's hand* lever la main. **~ 'em up!*** haut les mains! **(c)** (*rob*) *person, bank* dévaliser.
♦ **sticker** *n* **(a)** (*label*) auto-collant *m*; **(b)** (*fig*) **he's a ~er*** il n'abandonne pas facilement. ♦ **stickiness** *n* (*V* **sticky**) caractère poisseux *or* collant *or* gluant; moiteur *f.* ♦ **sticking-plaster** *n* sparadrap *m.* ♦ **stick insect** *n* phasme *m.* ♦ **stick-in-the-mud*** *adj, n* encroûté(e)* *m(f).* ♦ **stick-on** *adj* adhésif. ♦ **stick-up*** *n* hold-up *m.* ♦ **sticky** *adj* **(a)** *paste* poisseux, collant; *label* adhésif; *paint, toffee, road, surface, pitch* gluant; *hands* (*sweaty*) moite, (*with jam etc*) poisseux; *climate* chaud et humide; **~y tape** scotch *m* ®, ruban *m* adhésif; **(b)** (**fig*) *problem, situation* délicat; *person* peu accommodant; (*fig*) **to be on a ~y wicket** être dans une situation délicate; **to come to a ~y end** mal finir; **to have a ~y time*** passer un mauvais quart d'heure; **he's very ~y about lending his car*** il répugne à prêter sa voiture.
stickleback ['stɪklbæk] *n* épinoche *f.*
stickler ['stɪkləʳ] *n*: **to be a ~ for** être pointilleux sur le chapitre de, insister sur.
stiff [stɪf] *adj* **(a)** (*gen*) raide, rigide; *arm, joint* ankylosé; *door, lock, brush* dur; *dough, paste* ferme; (*starched*) *shirt etc* empesé. **as ~ as a poker** *or* **a ramrod** raide comme un piquet; **you'll feel ~ tomorrow** vous aurez des courbatures demain; **he's getting ~ as he grows older** il se raidit avec l'âge; **to have a ~ back** avoir mal au dos; **to have a ~ neck** avoir le torticolis; **~ with cold** engourdi par le froid; (*fig*) **to keep a ~ upper lip** rester impassible. **(b)** (*fig*) *smile, reception, person* froid, distant; *resistance* opiniâtre; *exam, course, task* difficile; *climb* raide; *wind, breeze* fort; *price, bill* (trop) élevé. **that's a bit ~!*** c'est un peu fort!*; **I could do with a ~ drink** je boirais bien qch de fort; **a ~ whisky** un grand verre de whisky. ♦ **stiffen (up) 1** *vt* (*gen*) raidir; *joint* ankyloser; (*fig*) *morale, resistance etc* affermir;

2 *vi* (*gen*) devenir raide *or* rigide; *[limb, joint]* s'ankyloser; *[door, lock]* devenir dur; *[resistance]* devenir opiniâtre; *[morale]* s'affermir; **he ~ened when ...** il s'est raidi quand ... . ♦ **stiffly** *adv move, bend* avec raideur; *stand to attention* sans bouger un muscle; (*fig*) *smile, greet, say* froidement. ♦ **stiffness** *n* **(a)** raideur *f*, rigidité *f*; ankylose *f*; dureté *f*; fermeté *f*; **(b)** froideur *f*; difficulté *f*.

stifle ['staɪfl] **1** *vt person, fire, sobs* étouffer; *anger, smile, desire* réprimer. **to ~ a yawn** réprimer une envie de bâiller. **2** *vi* étouffer. ♦ **stifling** *adj fumes* suffocant; *heat* étouffant; **it's stifling*** on étouffe.

stigma ['stɪgmə] *n, pl* (*gen*) **-s**, (*Bot, Rel*) **-mata** stigmate *m* (*on* sur). ♦ **stigmatize** *vt* stigmatiser.

stile [staɪl] *n* échalier *m*; (*turn~*) tourniquet *m*.

stiletto [stɪ'letəʊ] *n* stylet *m*. **~ heel** talon *m* aiguille.

still[1] [stɪl] **1** *adv* **(a)** (*up to now*) encore, toujours. **he is ~ in bed** il est encore *or* toujours au lit; **he ~ hasn't arrived** il n'est pas encore arrivé, il n'est toujours pas arrivé; **you ~ don't believe me** vous ne me croyez toujours pas. **(b)** (+ *comparative: even*) encore. **~ better, better ~** encore mieux. **(c)** (*nonetheless*) quand même, tout de même. **you'll ~ come?** vous viendrez quand même *or* tout de même?; **he's ~ your brother** il n'en est pas moins votre frère. **2** *conj* (*nevertheless*) néanmoins, quand même.

still[2] [stɪl] **1** *adj* (*motionless*) immobile; (*peaceful*) calme, tranquille; (*quiet*) silencieux; (*not fizzy*) *lemonade* non gazeux. **keep ~!** reste tranquille!, ne bouge pas!; (*Art*) **~ life** nature *f* morte. **2** *adv sit, stand, hold* sans bouger. **3** *n* **(a)** **in the ~ of the night** dans le silence de la nuit. **(b)** (*Cine*) photo *f*. ♦ **stillbirth** *n* enfant *m(f)* mort-né(e). ♦ **stillborn** *adj* mort-né. ♦ **stillness** *n* calme *m*, tranquillité *f*; silence *m*.

still[3] [stɪl] *n* (*object*) alambic *m*; (*place*) distillerie *f*.

stilts [stɪlts] *npl* échasses *fpl*. ♦ **stilted** *adj* guindé, qui manque de naturel.

stimulate ['stɪmjʊleɪt] *vt* (*Physiol, gen*) stimuler. **to ~ sb to do** inciter qn à faire. ♦ **stimulant** *adj, n* stimulant (*m*). ♦ **stimulating** *adj* stimulant. ♦ **stimulation** *n* stimulation *f*. ♦ **stimulus** *n, pl* **-li** (*Physiol*) stimulus *m*; (*fig*) stimulant *m*; **it gave trade a new stimulus** cela a donné une nouvelle impulsion au commerce; **under the stimulus of** stimulé par.

sting [stɪŋ] (*vb: pret, ptp* **stung**) **1** *n [insect]* dard *m*; (*pain, mark*) *[insect, nettle etc]* piqûre *f*; *[iodine etc]* brûlure *f*; *[attack, criticism, remark]* mordant *m*. (*fig*) **a ~ in the tail** une mauvaise surprise à la fin. **2** *vt [insect, nettle]* piquer; *[iodine]* brûler; *[rain, hail, whip]* cingler; *[remark, criticism]* piquer au vif. **stung by remorse** bourrelé de remords; **to ~ sb into action** pousser qn à agir; (*fig: robbed*) **I've been stung!*** je me suis fait avoir!* **3** *vi* **(a)** piquer; brûler; *[blow, whip]* provoquer une sensation cuisante; *[remark, criticism]* être cuisant. **(b)** *[eyes]* piquer; *[cut, skin]* brûler. **the fumes made his eyes ~** les fumées picotaient ses yeux. ♦ **stinging** *adj cut, remark* cuisant; **~ing nettle** ortie *f* brûlante.

stingy ['stɪndʒɪ] *adj person* avare, ladre; *portion* misérable. **to be ~ with** *food* lésiner sur; *praise* être chiche de. ♦ **stingily** *adv spend* avec avarice; *serve* en lésinant. ♦ **stinginess** *n* avarice *f*.

stink [stɪŋk] (*vb: pret* **stank**, *ptp* **stunk**) **1** *n* **(a)** puanteur *f*. **what a ~!** ce que ça pue! **(b)** (*fig: trouble*) **to make *or* kick up a ~‡** faire toute une scène (*about* à propos de). **2** *vi* puer (*also fig*), empester (*of sth* qch); (‡: *fig*) *[idea, coffee etc]* être infect; *[person]* être dégueulasse‡. (*lit, fig*) **it ~s to high heaven*** cela sent à plein nez. **3** *vt* (**~ out**) *room etc* empester. ♦ **stinker‡** *n* (*person*) salaud‡ *m*, salope‡ *f*; (*question, essay etc*) vacherie‡ *f*; (*meeting/task etc*) sale* réunion *f*/corvée *f etc*; (*angry letter*) lettre *f* d'engueulade‡. ♦ **stinking 1** *adj substance* puant; (‡*fig*) infect; **to have a ~ing‡ cold** avoir un rhume épouvantable; **2** *adv*: **~ing rich‡** bourré de fric‡.

stint [stɪnt] **1** *n*: **to do one's ~** (*daily work*) faire son travail (quotidien); (*do one's share*) faire sa part de travail; **he does a ~ in the gym every day** il passe un certain temps chaque jour au gymnase; **I've done my ~ at the wheel** j'ai pris mon tour au volant. **2** *vt* (*also* **~ on**) *food* lésiner sur; *compliments* être chiche de. **to ~ sb of sth** mesurer qch à qn; **to ~ o.s.** se priver (*of* de).

stipend ['staɪpend] *n* (*Rel*) traitement *m*.

stipulate ['stɪpjʊleɪt] *vt* (*gen*) stipuler (*that* que); *quantity* prescrire. ♦ **stipulation** *n* stipulation *f*; **on the stipulation that ...** à la condition expresse que ... (+*future or subj*).

stir [stɜːʳ] **1** *n*: **to give sth a ~** remuer qch; (*fig*) **there was a great ~ about ...** il y a eu beaucoup d'agitation à propos de ...; **to cause a ~** faire sensation. **2** *vt* **(a)** *tea, soup* remuer; *mixture* tourner; *fire* tisonner. **to ~ sth into sth** ajouter qch à qch (en tournant). **(b)** (*move etc*) *papers, leaves* agiter; *curiosity, passions, imagination* exciter; *emotions* éveiller; *person* émouvoir. (*fig*) **to ~ o.s.*** se secouer; **to ~ sb to do sth** inciter qn à faire qch; **to ~ sb's blood** réveiller l'enthousiasme de qn. **3** *vi [person]* bouger (*from* de); *[leaves, curtains etc]* remuer. **nobody is ~ring yet** personne n'est encore levé.

stir up *vt sep* (*fig*) (*gen*) exciter; *memories* réveiller; *revolt, hatred* susciter; *mob* ameuter; *trouble* provoquer; *person* secouer (*fig*). **to ~ sb up to (do) sth** pousser qn à (faire) qch.

♦ **stirring** *adj speech, music* enthousiasmant; *years* passionnant.

stirrup ['stɪrəp] *n* étrier *m*.

stitch [stɪtʃ] **1** *n* (*Sewing*) point *m*; (*Knitting*) maille *f*; (*Surgery*) point de suture; (*pain in side*) point de côté. **she put a few ~es in the tear** elle a fait un point à la déchirure; **to put ~es in a wound** suturer une plaie; (*Med*) **to get one's ~es out** se faire retirer ses fils de suture; (*fig*) **he hadn't a ~ (of clothing) on*** il était tout nu *or* à poil‡; (*fig*) **to be in ~es*** se tenir les côtes (de rire); **it had us in ~es*** on se tordait de rire. **2** *vt* (*by hand*) coudre; (*on machine*) piquer; (*Med*) suturer. **3** *vi* coudre.

stitch down *vt sep* rabattre.

stitch on *vt sep button* coudre; *button that's come off* recoudre.

stitch up *vt sep* coudre; (*mend*) recoudre; (*Med*) suturer.

stoat [stəʊt] *n* hermine *f* (*d'été*).

stock [stɒk] **1** *n* **(a)** *[goods]* réserve *f*, (*Comm*) stock *m*; *[money]* réserve; *[learning]* fonds *m*. (*Comm*) **in ~** en stock; **out of ~** épuisé; **to lay in a ~ of** s'approvisionner en; **to take ~** (*Comm*) faire l'inventaire; (*fig*) faire le point; (*fig*) **to take ~ of** *situation, prospects etc* faire le point de; *person* évaluer les mérites de. **(b)** (*Agr: animals and equipment*) cheptel *m* (vif et mort). **live~** bétail *m*; (*Rail*) **rolling ~** matériel *m* roulant. **(c)** (*Cards*) talon *m*. **(d)** (*Culin*) bouillon *m*. **(e)** (*Fin*) valeurs *fpl*, titres *mpl*; (*government* **~s**) fonds *mpl* d'État; (*company shares*) actions *fpl*. **~s and shares** valeurs (mobilières), titres. **(f)** (*flower*) giroflée *f*. **(g)** **to be on the ~s** *[ship]* être sur cale; (*fig*) *[piece of work, scheme]* être en chantier; (*Hist*) **the ~s** le pilori. **(h)** (*lineage*) souche *f*, lignée *f*.

2 *adj* (*Comm*) *goods, size* courant; (*stereotyped*) *argument, excuse* classique. (*Aut, Sport*) **~ car** stock-car *m*; (*Culin*) **~ cube** bouillon-cube *m*; **~ market** Bourse *f*, marché *m* financier; (*fig*) **~ phrase** expression *f* toute faite.

3 *vt* **(a)** (*supply*) *shop, larder* approvisionner

(*with* en); *library/farm* monter en livres/en bétail; *river, lake* peupler (*with* de). **well-~ed** *shop etc* bien approvisionné; *library, farm, garden* bien fourni. **(b)** (*Comm: hold in* ~) avoir, vendre.

stock up 1 *vi* s'approvisionner (*with, on* en; *for* pour). **2** *vt sep shop, cupboard* garnir; *library* accroître le stock de livres de; *river, lake* empoissonner.

♦ **stockbreeder** *n* éleveur *m*, -euse *f*. ♦ **stockbroker** *n* agent *m* de change. ♦ **stock exchange** *n* Bourse *f* (des valeurs); **on the ~ exchange** à la Bourse. ♦ **stockholder** *n* actionnaire *mf*. ♦ **stock-in-trade** *n* (*goods*) marchandises *fpl* en stock; (*tools, materials etc: also fig*) outils *mpl* du métier. ♦ **stockist** *n* stockiste *mf*. ♦ **stockpile** *vt* stocker. ♦ **stockpiling** *n* stockage *m*. ♦ **stockpot** *n* (*Culin*) marmite *f* de bouillon. ♦ **stockroom** *n* réserve *f*, magasin *m*. ♦ **stock-still** *adv*: **to stand ~-still** rester planté comme une borne, (*in fear, amazement*) rester cloué sur place. ♦ **stocktaking 1** *n* inventaire *m*; **2** *vi*: **to be ~taking** (*Comm*) faire l'inventaire; (*fig*) faire le point. ♦ **stocky** *adj* trapu, râblé.

stockade [stɒ'keɪd] *n* palanque *f*, palissade *f*.

stocking ['stɒkɪŋ] **1** *n* bas *m*. **2** *adj*: **in one's ~ feet** sans chaussures; (*Knitting*) **~ stitch** point *m* de jersey. ♦ **stockinet(te)** *n* jersey *m*.

stodge* [stɒdʒ] *n* (*food*) aliment *m* bourratif. ♦ **stodgy** *adj food* bourratif; (*heavy*) *cake* lourd; *book* indigeste; (*: *dull*) *person* sans imagination.

stoic(al) ['stəʊɪk(əl)] *adj* stoïque. ♦ **stoically** *adv* stoïquement. ♦ **stoicism** *n* stoïcisme *m*.

stoke [stəʊk] *vt* (~ **up**) *fire* garnir; *furnace* alimenter; *engine, boiler* chauffer. ♦ **stoker** *n* chauffeur *m* (*Naut etc*).

stole[1] [stəʊl] *n* étole *f*.

stole[2] [stəʊl], **stolen** ['stəʊlən] *pret, ptp of* **steal.**

stolid ['stɒlɪd] *adj* impassible. ♦ **stolidly** *adv* avec impassibilité.

stomach ['stʌmək] **1** *n* (*gen*) ventre *m*; (*Anat*) estomac *m*. **lying on his ~** couché sur le ventre; **to have a pain in one's ~** avoir mal au ventre. **2** *adj ulcer* à l'estomac. **~ ache** mal *m* de *or* au ventre; **~ pump** pompe *f* stomacale; **~ trouble** ennuis *mpl* gastriques. **3** *vt* (*fig*) tolérer, digérer*.

stone [stəʊn] **1** *n* **(a)** (*gen*) pierre *f*; (*pebble*) caillou *m*; (*on beach etc*) galet *m*; (*gravestone*) pierre tombale; (*in fruit*) noyau *m*; (*Med*) calcul *m*. **(made) of ~** de pierre; (*fig*) **within a ~'s throw of** à deux pas de; (*fig*) **to leave no ~ unturned** remuer ciel et terre (*to do* pour faire); **to turn to ~** (*vt*) pétrifier; (*vi*) se pétrifier. **(b)** (*Brit: weight: pl gen inv*) = *6,348 kg*. **2** *adj building* de *or* en pierre. **S~ Age** l'âge *m* de la pierre. **3** *vt* **(a)** *person, object* lancer *or* jeter des pierres sur. **to ~ sb to death** lapider qn. **(b)** *date, olive* dénoyauter. ♦ **stone-blind** *adj* complètement aveugle. ♦ **stone-cold** *adj* complètement froid; **~-cold sober*** pas du tout ivre. ♦ **stoned*** *adj* (*drunk*) soûl*; (*Drugs*) défoncé*. ♦ **stone-deaf** *adj* sourd comme un pot*. ♦ **stonemason** *n* tailleur *m* de pierre(s). ♦ **stonewall** *vi* (*fig*) donner des réponses évasives. ♦ **stoneware** *n* poterie *f* de grès. ♦ **stonework** *n* maçonnerie *f*. ♦ **stonily** *adv* avec froideur. ♦ **stony** *adj road, soil* pierreux; *beach* de galets; (*fig*) *person, heart* de pierre, dur; *look, welcome* froid. ♦ **stony-broke*** *adj* fauché comme les blés*. ♦ **stony-faced** *adj* au visage impassible.

stood [stʊd] *pret, ptp of* **stand.**

stooge [stu:dʒ] *n* (*Theat*) comparse *mf*; (*gen pej*) laquais *m*.

stool [stu:l] *n* **(a)** tabouret *m*; (*folding*) pliant *m*. (*fig*) **to fall between two ~s** se retrouver le bec dans l'eau*. **(b)** (*Med*) selle *f*. ♦ **stool-pigeon*** *n* indicateur *m*, -trice *f* (*de police*).

stoop [stu:p] **1** *n*: **to have a ~** avoir le dos voûté. **2** *vi* (*have a* ~) avoir le dos voûté; (~ **down**) se courber; (*fig*) s'abaisser (*to sth* jusqu'à qch; *to do, to doing* jusqu'à faire). (*fig*) **he would ~ to anything** il est prêt à toutes les bassesses. ♦ **stooping** *adj* voûté, courbé.

stop [stɒp] **1** *n* **(a)** (*halt*) arrêt *m*; (*short stay*) halte *f*. **a ~ for coffee** une pause-café; **6 hours without a ~** 6 heures *fpl* d'affilée; **a 5-minute ~** 5 minutes d'arrêt; **to be at a ~** *[traffic, vehicle]* être à l'arrêt; *[work, production]* avoir cessé; **to come to a ~** *[traffic etc]* s'arrêter; *[work etc]* cesser; **to bring to a ~** *traffic etc* arrêter; *work etc* faire cesser; **to make a ~** *[bus, train]* s'arrêter; *[plane, ship]* faire escale; **to put a ~ to sth** mettre fin *or* un terme à qch. **(b)** (*place*) *[bus, train]* arrêt *m*; *[plane, ship]* escale *f*. **(c)** *[flute, trumpet etc]* clef *f*; *[organ]* jeu *m*. (*fig*) **to pull out all the ~s** faire un suprême effort (*to do* pour faire). **(d)** (*Punctuation*) point *m*; (*in telegrams*) stop *m*.

2 *adj button, lever, signal* d'arrêt. (*Aut*) **~ sign** stop *m* (*panneau*).

3 *vt* **(a)** (~ **up**) *hole, pipe, leak, jar* boucher; *tooth* plomber. **to ~ one's ears** se boucher les oreilles; **to ~ a gap** boucher un trou, (*fig*) combler une lacune. **(b)** (*halt, block: gen*) arrêter; *noise* étouffer; *activity, progress* interrompre, (*suspend*) suspendre; (*Boxing*) *fight* suspendre; *allowance, leave* supprimer; *part of wages* retenir (*out of* sur); *gas, electricity, water supply* couper; *subscription* résilier; *cheque* faire opposition à; *light* empêcher de passer; *pain, worry, enjoyment* mettre fin à. **to ~ sb short** *or* **in his tracks** (*lit*) arrêter qn net; (*fig*) couper qn dans son élan; (*silence*) couper la parole à qn; **he ~ped a bullet*** il a reçu une balle; **rain ~ped play** la pluie a interrompu la partie; *[bank]* **to ~ payment** suspendre ses paiements; **he ~ped the milk for a week** il a fait interrompre la livraison du lait pendant une semaine. **(c)** (*cease*) arrêter, cesser (*doing* de faire). **~ it!** ça suffit!; **~ that noise!** assez de bruit!; **to ~ work** arrêter *or* cesser de travailler. **(d)** (*prevent*) empêcher (*sb's doing, sb from doing* qn de faire; *sth happening, sth from happening* que qch n'arrive (*subj*)). **there's nothing to ~ you** rien ne vous en empêche.

4 *vi* **(a)** (*halt: gen*) s'arrêter; (*end: gen*) cesser, se terminer; *[allowance, privileges]* être supprimé; *[play, programme, concert]* finir, se terminer. **~ thief!** au voleur!; **you can ~ now** vous pouvez (vous) arrêter maintenant; **he ~ped (dead) in his tracks** il s'est arrêté net *or* pile*; **I'd ~ short of murder** je n'irais pas jusqu'au meurtre; **he never knows where to ~** il ne sait pas s'arrêter; **he will ~ at nothing** il ne recule devant rien (*to do* pour faire). **(b)** (*) (*remain*) rester; (*live temporarily*) loger (*with sb* chez qn).

stop by* *vi* s'arrêter en passant.

stop off, stop over *vi* s'arrêter, faire une halte.

stop up *vt sep hole, pipe, jar* boucher. **my nose is ~ped up** j'ai le nez bouché.

♦ **stopcock** *n* robinet *m* d'arrêt. ♦ **stopgap 1** *n* bouche-trou *m*; **2** *adj measure* intérimaire. ♦ **stoplight** *n* (*traffic light*) feu *m* rouge; (*brake light*) stop *m*. ♦ **stop-off** *n* arrêt *m*. ♦ **stopover** *n* halte *f*. ♦ **stoppage** *n* (*gen*) arrêt *m*; (*interruption*) interruption *f*; (*strike*) grève *f*; *[leave, wages, payment]* suspension *f*; (*amount deducted*) retenue *f*. ♦ **stopper** *n* bouchon *m*; **to put the ~per in/take the ~per out of sth** boucher/déboucher qch; (*fig*) **to put a ~per on sth*** mettre un terme à qch; *V* **conversation. 2** *vt* boucher. ♦ **stopping 1** *n* (*gen*) arrêt *m*; (*in tooth*) plombage *m*; **2** *adj* (*Aut*) **we were looking for a ~ping place** nous cherchions un coin où nous arrêter; **~ping train** omnibus *m*. ♦ **stop-press** *n* nouvelles *fpl* de dernière heure. ♦ **stopwatch** *n* chronomètre *m*.

storage ['stɔ:rɪdʒ] **1** *n* *[goods, fuel, food]* entreposage *m*; *[heat, electricity]* accumulation *f*; *[documents]* conservation *f*; (*Computers*) mise *f* en réserve. **to put in(to) ~** entreposer. **2** *adj capacity, problems* d'entreposage; *charges* de magasinage. **~ battery** accumulateur *m*; **~ heater** radiateur *m* électrique par accumulation; **~ space** espace *m* de rangement; *[oil etc]* **~ tank** réservoir *m* d'emmagasinage; **~ unit** meuble *m* de rangement.

store [stɔːʳ] **1** *n* **(a)** (*supply*) provision *f*, réserve *f*; *[learning, information]* fonds *m*. **~s** provisions *fpl*; **to lay in ~s** s'approvisionner, faire des provisions; **to get in** *or* **lay in a ~ of sth** faire provision de qch; (*fig*) **to set great ~/little ~ by sth** faire grand cas/peu de cas de qch. **(b)** (*depot, warehouse*) entrepôt *m*; (*furniture* **~**) garde-meuble *m*; *[ammunition etc]* dépôt *m*; (*in office, factory etc: also* **~s**) réserve *f*, (*larger*) service *m* des approvisionnements. **to put in(to) ~** *goods etc* entreposer; *furniture* mettre au garde-meuble; **to keep sth in ~** garder qch en réserve; (*fig*) **to have sth in ~ for sb** réserver qch à qn. **(c)** (*shop*) magasin *m*; (*large*) grand magasin; (*small*) boutique *f*. **book ~** librairie *f*.

2 *vt* **(a)** (*keep, collect:* **~ up**) *food, fuel, goods* mettre en réserve; *documents* conserver; *electricity, heat* accumuler, emmagasiner; (*fig: in one's mind*) *facts etc* enregistrer dans sa mémoire. **(b)** (*place in* **~**: **~ away**) *food, fuel, goods* entreposer; *one's furniture* mettre au garde-meuble; *crops* engranger; (*Computers*) mettre en réserve; *information* (*in filing system etc*) classer; (*in mind*) enregistrer. **I've got them ~d (away)** je les ai mis de côté.

3 *vi [food]* **to ~ well** bien se conserver. ♦ **storehouse** *n* entrepôt *m*; (*fig: of information etc*) mine *f*. ♦ **storekeeper** *n* magasinier *m*; (*shopkeeper*) commerçant(e) *m(f)*. ♦ **storeroom** *n* réserve *f*.

storey ['stɔːrɪ] *n* étage *m*. **on the 3rd** *or* (*US*) **4th ~** au 3e (étage); **4-~(ed) building** bâtiment de 4 étages.

stork [stɔːk] *n* cigogne *f*.

storm [stɔːm] **1** *n* tempête *f*; (*thunder*~) orage *m*; (*fig*) *[arrows, missiles]* grêle *f*; *[abuse]* torrent *m*; *[cheers, protests, applause]* tempête. (*fig*) **a ~ in a teacup** une tempête dans un verre d'eau; (*fig*) **it caused quite a ~** cela a provoqué une véritable tempête; **to take by ~** (*Mil*) prendre d'assaut; (*fig*) *audience etc* conquérir. **2** *adj signal, warning* de tempête; *window, door* double. (*US*) **~ cellar** abri *m* tempête; (*fig*) **~ centre** centre *m* de l'agitation; **~ cloud** nuage *m* orageux; (*fig*) nuage noir; (*Mil*) **~ troops** troupes *fpl* d'assaut. **3** *vt* (*Mil, also fig*) prendre d'assaut. **4** *vi [wind, rain]* faire rage; (*fig*) *[person]* fulminer (*with rage* de colère; *at sb* contre qn). **to ~ in/out** *etc* entrer/sortir *etc* comme un ouragan. ♦ **stormy** *adj weather, sky* orageux; *sea* démonté; (*fig*) *meeting* houleux; *person* violent.

story[1] ['stɔːrɪ] *n* **(a)** (*gen*) histoire *f*; *[play, film]* action *f*. **short ~** nouvelle *f*; **do you know the ~ about ...?** connaissez-vous l'histoire de ...?; **it's a long ~** c'est toute une histoire; **that's not the whole ~** mais ce n'est pas tout; **according to your ~** d'après ce que vous dites, d'après votre version des faits; **or so the ~ goes** ou du moins c'est ce qu'on raconte; **quite another ~** une tout autre histoire; **it's the same old ~** c'est toujours la même histoire; (*fig*) **it tells its own ~** cela en dit long; **to tell stories*** (*fibs*) raconter des histoires. **(b)** (*Press: article*) article *m*. **he was sent to cover the ~ of the refugees** on l'a envoyé faire un reportage sur les réfugiés; **they daren't print that ~** ils n'osent pas publier cette nouvelle. ♦ **storybook** *n* livre *m* de contes *or* d'histoires. ♦ **storyteller** *n* conteur *m*, -euse *f*; (*: *fibber*) menteur *m*, -euse *f*.

story[2] ['stɔːrɪ] *n* (*US*) = **storey**.

stout [staʊt] **1** *adj* **(a)** (*fat*) gros, corpulent. **to grow ~** prendre de l'embonpoint. **(b)** (*strong*) (*gen*) solide; *horse* vigoureux; *resistance, soldier* vaillant. **with ~ hearts** vaillamment; **a ~ fellow*** un brave type*. **2** *n* (*beer*) bière *f* brune (*forte*). ♦ **stout-hearted** *adj* vaillant. ♦ **stoutly** *adv defend* vaillamment; *deny* catégoriquement; *maintain* dur comme fer. ♦ **stoutness** *n* (*fatness*) embonpoint *m*.

stove [stəʊv] *n* **(a)** (*heater*) poêle *m*. **(b)** (*cooker*) (*solid fuel*) fourneau *m*; (*gas, electricity*) cuisinière *f*; (*small*) réchaud *m*. **(c)** (*Ind, Tech*) four *m*.

stow [stəʊ] *vt* (*put away*) ranger; (*hide*) cacher. **stow away 1** *vi* s'embarquer clandestinement. **2** *vt sep* (*put away*) ranger; (*hide*) cacher. ♦ **stowaway** *n* passager *m*, -ère *f* clandestin(e).

straddle ['strædl] *vt* être à cheval sur.

straggle ['strægl] *vi*: **to ~ in/out** *etc* entrer/sortir *etc* par petits groupes détachés. ♦ **straggler** *n* (*person*) traînard(e) *m(f)*. ♦ **straggling** *or* ♦ **straggly** *adj plant, village* tout en longueur; *hair* en désordre; *objects in row* disséminés; *line* irrégulier.

straight [streɪt] **1** *adj* **(a)** (*not curved, not askew: gen*) *line, edge, picture* droit; *route* direct; *hair* raide; *posture, back* bien droit; (*Geom*) *angle* plat; (*in order*) *room, books* en ordre. **to put** *or* **set ~** *picture* remettre d'aplomb; *hat, tie* ajuster; *house, books, accounts* mettre de l'ordre dans; **the picture isn't ~** le tableau est de travers; (*fig*) **to keep a ~ face** garder son sérieux; (*Theat*) **a ~ man** un faire-valoir; **let's get this ~** entendons-nous bien sur ce point; **to put** *or* **set sb ~ about sth** éclairer qn sur qch; **to keep sb ~ about sth** empêcher qn de se tromper sur qch; (*don't owe anything*) **now we're ~** maintenant on est quitte. **(b)** (*frank*) franc; (*honest*) honnête; *dealing* régulier; *denial, refusal* catégorique. **~ speaking, ~ talking** franc-parler *m*; **to play a ~ game** agir loyalement; **he's ~** il est très honnête; (*: *not homosexual*) c'est un hétéro*; (*: *not criminal*) il est régulier. **(c)** (*plain etc*) *whisky etc* sans eau; (*Theat*) *part, actor* sérieux. **a ~ play** une pièce de théâtre proprement dite; (*Pol*) **a ~ fight** une campagne électorale à deux candidats.

2 *n* **(a)** *[racecourse etc]* **the ~** la ligne droite; (*fig*) **we're in the ~** ça va aller comme sur des roulettes. **(b) to cut sth on the ~** couper qch droit fil; (*fig*) **to keep to the ~ and narrow** rester dans le droit chemin.

3 *adv* **(a)** (*in a* **~** *line*) *walk, grow, stand* droit; *sit* correctement. **he came ~ at me** il est venu tout droit vers moi; **to shoot ~** tirer juste; **I can't see ~*** j'y vois trouble; **~ up in the air** droit en l'air; **~ above/across** juste au-dessus/en face; **~ ahead** *go* tout droit; *look* droit devant soi; **to look sb ~ in the face/the eye** regarder qn bien en face/droit dans les yeux; *[criminal]* **to go ~** rester dans le droit chemin. **(b)** (*directly*) tout droit, directement; (*immediately*) tout de suite, aussitôt. **~ away, ~ off** tout de suite, sur-le-champ; **~ out, ~ off** (*without hesitation*) sans hésiter; (*without beating about the bush*) sans mâcher ses mots; (*fig*) **~ from the horse's mouth** de source sûre; **I'm telling you ~** je vous le dis tout net.

♦ **straightedge** *n* (*tool*) limande *f* (*Menuiserie*).

♦ **straighten 1** *vt* (**~en out**) *wire, nail* redresser; *road* refaire en éliminant les tournants; *hair* défriser; (**~en up**) *tie, hat* ajuster; *picture* remettre d'aplomb; *room* mettre de l'ordre dans; *papers* ranger; **to ~en one's shoulders** se redresser; **2** *vi* (**~en up**) *[person]* se redresser.

♦ **straighten out** *vt sep situation* débrouiller; *problem* résoudre; *ideas* mettre de l'ordre dans; **to ~en things out*** arranger les choses; **to ~en sb out*** remettre qn dans la bonne voie. ♦ **straight-faced** *adv* en gardant son sérieux.

♦ **straightforward** *adj* (*frank*) franc; (*uncomplicated*) simple. ♦ **straightforwardly** *adv answer* franchement; *behave* honnêtement; (*without a hitch*) sans anicroche. ♦ **straightforwardness** *n* franchise *f*; simplicité *f*.

strain[1] [streɪn] **1** *n* **(a)** (*Tech: on rope etc*) tension *f* (*on* de); (*on beam*) pression *f* (*on* sur); (*on person*) (*physical*) effort *m* (physique); (*mental*) tension nerveuse; (*overwork*) surmenage *m*; (*tiredness*) fatigue *f*. **under the ~** sous la tension *or* la pression; **to take the ~ off sth** diminuer la tension de qch *or* la pression sur qch; (*fig*) **to put a great ~ on** *friendship* mettre à rude épreuve; *the economy, savings, budget* grever; *person* épuiser nerveusement; **the ~(s) of city life** la tension de la vie urbaine; **listening for 3 hours is a ~** écouter pendant 3 heures demande un grand effort; **the ~ of climbing the stairs** l'effort requis pour monter l'escalier; **he has been under a great deal of ~** ses nerfs ont été mis à rude épreuve. **(b)** (*Med: sprain*) entorse *f*, foulure *f*. **(c)** (*Mus*) **to the ~s of** aux accents *mpl* de.

2 *vt* **(a)** *rope, beam* tendre excessivement; (*Med*) *muscle* froisser; *arm, ankle* fouler; (*fig*) *friendship, marriage, sb's patience* mettre à rude épreuve; *resources, savings, budget, the economy* grever; *meaning* forcer. **to ~ one's back** se donner un tour de reins; **to ~ one's heart** se fatiguer le cœur; **to ~ one's shoulder** se froisser un muscle dans l'épaule; **to ~ one's voice** forcer sa voix; **to ~ one's eyes** s'abîmer les yeux; **to ~ one's ears to hear sth** tendre l'oreille pour entendre qch; **to ~ every nerve to do** fournir un effort intense pour faire; **to ~ o.s.** (*physically*) faire un faux mouvement; (*mentally*) se surmener; (*iro*) **don't ~ yourself!** surtout ne te fatigue pas! **(b)** (*filter*) *liquid, soup* passer; *vegetables* égoutter.

3 *vi*: **to ~ to do** (*physically*) peiner pour faire; (*mentally*) s'efforcer de faire; **to ~ at sth** (*pushing/pulling*) pousser/tirer qch de toutes ses forces.

strain off *vt sep liquid* vider.

♦ **strained** *adj* **(a)** *arm, ankle* foulé; *muscle* froissé; *eyes* fatigué; *voice, smile, cough* forcé; *look* contraint; *person, relations, atmosphere, nerves* tendu; *style* affecté; **he has a ~ed shoulder/back** il s'est froissé un muscle dans l'épaule/le dos; **(b)** *baby food* en purée. ♦ **strainer** *n* (*Culin*) passoire *f*.

strain[2] [streɪn] *n* (*breed, lineage*) race *f*; *[virus]* souche *f*. **a ~ of madness** des tendances *fpl* à la folie; (*fig*) **a lot more in the same ~** encore beaucoup du même genre; **he continued in this ~** il a continué dans ce sens.

strait [streɪt] *n* (*Geog: also* **~s**: *gen*) détroit *m*. **the S~s of Dover** le Pas de Calais; (*fig*) **in dire ~s** dans une situation difficile. ♦ **straitened** *adj*: **in ~ened circumstances** dans la gêne. ♦ **strait-jacket** *n* camisole *f* de force. ♦ **strait-laced** *adj* collet monté *inv*.

strand [strænd] *n [thread, wire]* brin *m*; *[pearls]* rang *m*; (*in narrative etc*) fil *m*. **a ~ of hair** une mèche.

stranded ['strændɪd] *adj ship* échoué; (*fig*) *person* en rade*. **to leave sb ~** laisser qn en rade*.

strange [streɪndʒ] *adj* **(a)** (*unfamiliar*) *language, country* inconnu; *work, activity* inaccoutumé. **you'll feel rather ~** vous vous sentirez un peu dépaysé; **several ~ people** plusieurs personnes que je ne connaissais pas, plusieurs inconnus; **I never sleep well in a ~ bed** je ne dors jamais bien dans un lit autre que le mien. **(b)** (*odd, unusual*) étrange, bizarre. **it is ~ that** il est étrange *or* bizarre que +*subj*; **~ as it may seem** aussi étrange que cela puisse paraître. ♦ **strangely** *adv* étrangement, curieusement; **~ly enough, ...** chose curieuse, ... ♦ **strangeness** *n* étrangeté *f*, bizarrerie *f*. ♦ **stranger** *n* (*unknown*) inconnu(e) *m(f)*; (*from another place*) étranger *m*, -ère *f*; **he's a ~r to me** il m'est inconnu; **I'm a ~r here** je ne suis pas d'ici; **I am a ~r to Paris** je ne connais pas Paris; **a ~r to politics** un novice en matière de politique.

strangle ['stræŋgl] *vt* étrangler (*also fig*). ♦ **stranglehold** *n*: **to have a ~hold on** tenir à la gorge. ♦ **strangler** *n* étrangleur *m*, -euse *f*. ♦ **strangulation** *n* strangulation *f*.

strap [stræp] **1** *n* (*of leather, cloth*) courroie *f*, sangle *f*; (*on shoe*) lanière *f*; (*ankle ~*) bride *f*; (*on garment*) bretelle *f*; (*on shoulder bag*) bandoulière *f*; (*watch ~*) bracelet *m*; (*in bus, tube*) poignée *f* de cuir; (*Tech*) lien *m*. **2** *vt* (*tie*: **~ down, ~ in, ~ on, ~ up**) attacher (*sth to sth* qch à qch). ♦ **straphanger** *n* voyageur *m*, -euse *f* debout *inv* (*dans le métro etc*). ♦ **strapless** *adj dress, bra* sans bretelles. ♦ **strapping** *adj* costaud* *f inv*.

strategy ['strætɪdʒɪ] *n* stratégie *f*. ♦ **stratagem** *n* stratagème *m*. ♦ **strategic(al)** *adj* stratégique. ♦ **strategist** *n* stratège *m*.

stratosphere ['strætəʊsfɪər] *n* stratosphère *f*.

stratum ['strɑːtəm] *n, pl* **-ta** (*Geol, fig*) couche *f*.

straw [strɔː] **1** *n* (*all senses*) paille *f*. **to drink sth through a ~** boire qch avec une paille; (*fig*) **to clutch at a ~** se raccrocher désespérément à un semblant d'espoir; (*fig*) **a ~ in the wind** une indication des choses à venir; (*fig*) **the last ~** *or* **the ~ that breaks the camel's back** la goutte d'eau qui fait déborder le vase. **2** *adj* (*made of ~*) de paille. **~ hat** chapeau *m* de paille; (*fig*) **~ vote** sondage *m* d'opinion. ♦ **strawberry 1** *n* (*fruit*) fraise *f*; (*plant*) fraisier *m*; **wild ~berry** fraise des bois; **2** *adj jam* de fraises; *ice cream* à la fraise; *tart* aux fraises; (*Anat*) **~berry mark** fraise *f*, envie *f*. ♦ **straw-coloured** *adj* paille *inv*.

stray [streɪ] **1** *adj dog, child, bullet* perdu; *sheep, cow* égaré; *taxi, shot etc* isolé. **a few ~ cars** quelques rares voitures; **a ~ motorist** un des rares automobilistes. **2** *n* (*child/dog*) enfant *mf*/chien *m* perdu(e). **3** *vi [person, animal]* s'égarer; *[thoughts]* vagabonder. **to ~ from** s'écarter de; **to ~ into enemy territory** s'égarer et se retrouver en territoire ennemi.

streak [striːk] **1** *n* (*line, band*) raie *f*; *[ore, mineral]* veine *f*; *[light, blood, paint]* filet *m*. **his hair had ~s of grey in it** ses cheveux commençaient à grisonner; (*deliberate*) **blond ~s** mèches blondes; **like a ~ of lightning** comme un éclair; **a ~ of jealousy** des tendances *fpl* à la jalousie; **a ~ of luck** une période de chance. **2** *vt* zébrer, strier (*with* de). **~ed with** *[sky]* strié de; *[mirror]* zébré de; *[clothes]* maculé de; **hair ~ed with grey** cheveux qui commencent à grisonner. **3** *vi* **(a) to ~ in/past** *etc* entrer/passer *etc* comme un éclair. **(b)** (*: *naked*) courir tout nu en public. ♦ **streaker*** *n* streaker *m*, -euse *f*. ♦ **streaky** *adj colour* marbré; *window, mirror, sky* zébré; *bacon* pas trop maigre.

stream [striːm] **1** *n* **(a)** (*brook*) ruisseau *m*. (*current*) **against the ~** contre le courant. **(b)** (*flow*) *[water, blood, light, excuses, cars etc]* flot *m*; *[cold air]* courant *m*. *[oil]* **to be/come on ~** être/être mis en service; **~s of people** des flots de gens; (*Brit Scol*) **divided into 5 ~s** répartis en 5 classes de niveau; (*Brit Scol*) **the B ~** le groupe B. **2** *vi [liquid, walls]* ruisseler (*with* de). **his eyes were ~ing** il pleurait à chaudes larmes; *[cold air, sunlight]* **to ~ into** entrer à flots dans; *[people, cars etc]* **to ~ in/past** *etc* entrer/passer *etc* à flots. **3** *vt* (*Scol*) *pupils* répartir par niveau. **to ~ French** répartir les élèves par niveau en français. ♦ **streamer** *n* serpentin *m*. ♦ **streaming 1** *n* (*Scol*) répartition *f* des élèves par niveau; **2** *adj*: **a ~ing cold** un gros rhume. ♦ **streamline** *vt* (*Aut, Aviat*) donner un profil aérodynamique à; (*fig*) rationaliser. ♦ **streamlined** *adj* (*Aviat*) fuselé; (*Aut*) aérodynamique; (*fig*) rationalisé.

street [striːt] **1** *n* rue *f*. **in the ~** dans la rue; (*fig*)

the man in the ~ l'homme de la rue; **she is on the ~s** elle fait le trottoir*; (*fig*) **that is right up my ~*** c'est tout à fait dans mes cordes; **he is not in the same ~ as you*** il ne vous vient pas à la cheville; **to be ~s ahead of sb*** dépasser qn de loin; (*fig*) **~s better*** beaucoup mieux. **2** *adj*: **~ directory** *or* **guide** répertoire *m* des rues; **~ door** porte *f* sur la rue; **~ fighting** combats *mpl* de rue; **~ lamp** réverbère *m*; **at ~ level** au rez-de-chaussée; **~ lighting** éclairage *m* des rues; **~ map** plan *m* des rues; **~ market** marché *m* à ciel ouvert; **~ musician** musicien *m* des rues; **~ sweeper** (*person*) balayeur *m*; (*machine*) balayeuse *f*; **~ urchin** gamin *m* des rues. ♦ **streetcar** *n* (*US*) tramway *m*.

strength [streŋθ] *n* **(a)** (*gen*) force *f*; *[building, wood, shoes, claim, case]* solidité *f*; *[current]* intensité *f*; *[drink]* teneur *f* en alcool; *[solution]* titre *m*. **he hadn't the ~ to lift it** il n'avait pas la force de le soulever; **his ~ failed him** ses forces l'ont abandonné; **to get one's ~ back** reprendre des forces; **~ of character** force de caractère; **~ of purpose** résolution *f*; **~ of will** volonté *f*; (*Fin*) **the ~ of the pound** la solidité de la livre; (*fig*) **on the ~ of** en vertu de. **(b)** (*Mil, Naut*) effectif *m*. **fighting ~** effectif mobilisable; **they are below** *or* **under ~** leur effectif n'est pas au complet; (*fig*) **they were there in ~** ils étaient là en grand nombre; (*gen*) **to be on the ~** faire partie du personnel. ♦ **strengthen 1** *vt* (*gen*) renforcer; *person, muscle* fortifier; *eyesight* améliorer; (*Fin*) *the pound* consolider; **2** *vi [muscle, limb]* se fortifier; *[wind, influence, characteristic]* augmenter. ♦ **strengthening** *n* renforcement *m*; amélioration *f*; consolidation *f*.

strenuous ['strenjʊəs] *adj exercise, work* ardu; *game, march, day* fatigant; *life, holiday* très actif; *effort, resistance* acharné; *protest* vigoureux, énergique. (*Med*) **he must not do anything too ~** il ne doit pas se fatiguer. ♦ **strenuously** *adv work, protest* énergiquement; *exercise, pull* vigoureusement; *resist, try* avec acharnement.

stress [stres] **1** *n* **(a)** (*load: on bridge, beam etc*) charge *f* (*of* de); (*on metal*) travail *m*; (*pressure: psychological, moral etc*) pression *f*; (*mental, nervous*) tension *f* nerveuse, stress *m*. **in times of ~** à des moments de grande tension; **the ~es and strains of modern life** les agressions *fpl* de la vie moderne; **to be under ~** être sous tension. **(b)** (*emphasis*) insistance *f*; (*Ling, Mus, Poetry*) accent *m*. **2** *adj* (*Ling*) **~ mark** accent *m*. **3** *vt* (*gen*) insister sur; (*Ling, Mus, Poetry*) accentuer. ♦ **stressful** *adj* difficile, stressant.

stretch [stretʃ] **1** *n* **(a) there's a lot of ~ in this material** ce tissu prête bien; **by a ~ of the imagination** en faisant un effort d'imagination; **there's a straight ~ (of road)** la route est toute droite; **a magnificent ~ of country** une campagne magnifique; **in that ~ of the river** dans cette partie de la rivière; (*distance*) **for a long ~** sur des kilomètres; **not by a long ~!** loin de là! **(b)** (*time*) période *f*. **a long ~ of time** longtemps; **for hours at a ~** pendant des heures d'affilée; (*Prison*) **he's done a 10-year ~‡** il a fait 10 ans de prison. **2** *adj fabric, garment* extensible; (*elasticated*) élastique. **3** *vt* **(a)** *rope, spring* tendre; *elastic* étirer; *shoe, glove, hat* élargir; *muscle* distendre; (*fig*) *law, rules* tourner; *meaning, truth* forcer; *one's principles* adapter; *one's authority* outrepasser. (*fig*) **to ~ a point** faire une concession. **(b)** (*often* **~ out**) *neck* tendre; *arm, leg* tendre, (*extend*) allonger; *wing* déployer; *net, rope* tendre (*between* entre; *above* au-dessus de); *rug, linen* étendre; (*fig*) *athlete, student* pousser. (*fig: go for walk*) **I'm just going to ~ my legs** je vais me dégourdir les jambes; **to be fully ~ed** *[rope etc]* être complètement tendu; *[engine, factory]* tourner à plein; *[person]* donner son plein; **the work he is doing does not ~ him enough** le travail qu'il fait n'exige pas assez de lui. **4** *vi* **(a)** *[person, animal]* s'étirer. **he ~ed across and touched her cheek** il a tendu la main et touché sa joue. **(b)** (*lengthen*) s'allonger; (*widen*) *[shoes]* s'élargir; *[elastic]* s'étirer; *[fabric, jersey]* prêter. **(c)** *[forest, procession, influence]* s'étendre (*over* sur); (*in time*) *[meeting etc]* se prolonger (*into* jusqu'à). **the rope won't ~ to that post** la corde ne va pas jusqu'à ce poteau; **how far will it ~?** jusqu'où ça va?; (*fig*) **my money won't ~* to a new car** mon budget ne me permet pas d'acheter une nouvelle voiture.

stretch out 1 *vi* s'étendre. **2** *vt sep* (*reach*) *arm, hand, foot* tendre; (*extend*) *leg etc* allonger, étendre; *wing* déployer; *net, rope* tendre; *rug, linen* étendre; (*lengthen*) *meeting, discussion* prolonger; *story, explanation* allonger.

♦ **stretcher 1** *n* (*Med*) brancard *m*, civière *f*; **2** *adj*: **~er case** malade *mf* *or* blessé(e) *m(f)* qui ne peut pas marcher. ♦ **stretcher-bearer** *n* brancardier *m*. ♦ **stretchy** *adj* extensible.

strew [stru:] *pret* **strewed**, *ptp* **strewed** *or* **strewn** *vt straw, sand* répandre (*on, over* sur); *flowers, objects, wreckage* éparpiller (*over* sur); *ground, room* joncher (*with* de).

stricken ['strɪkən] *adj* (*wounded*) grièvement blessé; (*grief-~*) affligé; (*damaged*) *city* dévasté; *ship* très endommagé. **~ with remorse/fear** pris de remords/peur.

strict [strɪkt] *adj* **(a)** (*severe: gen*) *person, principle, views* strict, sévère (*with sb* avec qn); *ban, rule* strict; *order* formel; *etiquette* rigide. **(b)** (*precise*) *meaning* strict (*after n*); *translation, time limit* précis; (*absolute*) *accuracy, secrecy, truth* strict (*before n*). **in the ~ sense of the word** au sens strict du mot. ♦ **strictly** *adv* (*gen*) strictement; **~ly between ourselves** strictement entre nous; **~ly speaking** à strictement parler; **~ly prohibited** formellement interdit. ♦ **strictness** *n [person etc]* sévérité *f*. ♦ **stricture** *n* critique *f* (*on* de).

stride [straɪd] (*vb: pret* **strode**, *ptp* **stridden**) **1** *n* grand pas *m*; *[runner]* foulée *f*. **with giant ~s** à pas de géant; **in a few ~s** en quelques enjambées; (*fig*) **to make great ~s** faire de grands progrès (*in French* en français; *in one's studies* dans ses études; *in doing* pour ce qui est de faire); **to get into one's ~** prendre le rythme; **to take in one's ~** *changes etc* accepter avec équanimité; *exam/interrogation etc* passer/subir *etc* sans le moindre effort. **2** *vi*: **to ~ along/away** *etc* avancer/s'éloigner *etc* à grands pas; **he was striding up and down the room** il arpentait la pièce.

strident ['straɪdənt] *adj* strident.

strife [straɪf] *n* conflits *mpl*, dissensions *fpl*. **internal ~** dissensions intestines; **industrial ~** conflits sociaux.

strike [straɪk] (*vb: pret, ptp* **struck**) **1** *n* **(a)** (*Ind*) grève *f* (*of, by* de). **electricity/rail ~** grève des employés de l'électricité/du chemin de fer; **to be on ~** être en grève (*for* pour obtenir; *against* pour protester contre); **to go on ~, to come out on ~** se mettre en grève; **to call a ~** lancer un ordre de grève. **(b)** (*Aviat, Mil*) raid *m* (aérien). **(c)** (*Fishing*) touche *f*; (*Baseball, Bowling*) strike *m*; (*of oil etc*) découverte *f*. (*Miner etc*) **to make a ~** découvrir un gisement; (*fig*) **a lucky ~** un coup de chance.

2 *adj* **(a)** (*Ind*) *committee, fund* de grève; *leader* des grévistes; *pay* de gréviste. **(b)** (*Aviat, Mil*) **~ force** détachement *m* d'avions.

3 *vt* **(a)** (*hit*) *person, ball* frapper; *nail, table* frapper sur; (*knock against*) heurter; (*Mus*) *string* toucher; *[snake]* mordre. **to ~ sth with one's fist** frapper du poing sur qch; (*fig*) **to ~ a man when he is down** frapper un homme à terre; **to ~ the first blow** donner le premier coup; (*fig*) to ~ **a blow for freedom** rompre une lance pour la liberté; to ~ **sth from sb's hand** faire tomber qch de la main de qn; to ~ **fear into sb** remplir qn d'effroi; to ~ **terror into sb** terroriser qn; **he struck his head against the table** sa tête a heurté la table, il s'est cogné la tête contre la table; **the stone struck him on the head** la pierre l'a frappé à la tête; **he was struck by a bullet** il a reçu une balle; **to be struck by lightning** être frappé par la foudre; to ~ **sb dumb** rendre qn muet; (*fig*) **I was struck by his intelligence** j'ai été frappé par son intelligence; **I wasn't very struck* with him** il ne m'a pas fait très bonne impression; **the funny side of it struck me** le côté drôle de la chose m'a frappé; **that ~s me as a good idea** cela me semble une bonne idée; **an idea struck him** il a eu une idée; **it ~s me that ...** j'ai l'impression que ...; **how did the film ~ you?** qu'avez-vous pensé du film? **(b)** (*find, discover*) *gold* trouver; (*fig*) *hotel, road* tomber sur; (*fig*) *difficulty, obstacle* rencontrer. **to ~ oil** (*Miner*) trouver du pétrole; (*fig*) trouver le filon*; (*fig*) **to ~ it rich** faire fortune. **(c)** (*make, produce etc*) *coin, medal* frapper; *sparks, fire* faire jaillir (*from* de); *match* gratter. **to ~ a light** allumer une allumette (*or* un briquet *etc*); **to ~ an average** établir une moyenne; **to ~ a balance** trouver le juste milieu; **to ~ a bargain** conclure un marché; **to ~ an attitude** poser; **to ~ an attitude of surprise** faire l'étonné(e). **(d)** *chord, note* sonner; *[clock]* sonner (*3 o'clock* 3 heures). (*fig*) **that ~s a chord** cela me dit qch; (*fig*) **to ~ a false note** sonner faux; **it has just struck six** six heures viennent juste de sonner. **(e)** (*take down*) *tent* plier; *camp* lever; *flag* baisser. **(f)** (*delete: from list, record*) *name* rayer (*from* de); (*from professional register*) radier (*from* de).

4 *vi* **(a)** (*hit*) frapper; (*Mil*) attaquer; *[snake]* mordre; *[tiger]* sauter sur sa proie; *[disease etc]* frapper; *[panic]* s'emparer des esprits. (*lit, fig*) **to ~ home** faire mouche; **to ~ at** *person* porter un coup à; (*fig*) *root of sth* porter atteinte à; *evil etc* attaquer; **his foot struck against a rock** son pied a heurté un rocher. **(b)** *[clock]* sonner. **(c)** (*Ind: go on* ~) faire grève (*for* pour obtenir; *against* pour protester contre). **(d)** (*turn, go*) aller, prendre. **~ left** prenez à gauche; **to ~ uphill** se mettre à grimper la côte; **he struck (out** *or* **off) across the fields** il s'en est allé à travers champs.

strike back *vi* (*Mil*) user de représailles (*at sb* à l'égard de qn); (*gen*) se venger (*at sb* de qn).

strike down *vt sep* terrasser.

strike off *vt sep* **(a)** *sb's head* trancher; *branch* couper. **(b)** (*from list*) rayer; *doctor etc* radier.

strike out 1 *vi* (*hit out*) se débattre. **he struck out at his attackers** il a lancé des coups dans la direction de ses attaquants; (*in business*) **to ~ out on one's own** se mettre à son propre compte. **2** *vt sep* (*delete*) *word, question* rayer.

strike up 1 *vi [band etc]* commencer à jouer; *[music]* commencer. **2** *vt sep [band]* se mettre à jouer; *[singers]* se mettre à chanter. **~ up the band!** faites jouer l'orchestre!; **to ~ up an acquaintance/a friendship** lier connaissance/amitié (*with sb* avec qn).

♦ **strikebound** *adj* immobilisé par une grève. ♦ **strikebreaker** *n* briseur *m* de grève. ♦ **strikebreaking** *n*: **he was accused of ~breaking** on l'a accusé d'être un briseur de grève. ♦ **striker** *n* (*Ind*) gréviste *mf*; (*Ftbl*) buteur *m*. ♦ **striking** *adj* **(a)** *change, sight* frappant, saisissant; **(b)** (*Mil*) *power* de frappe; (*Mil, fig*) **within striking distance of** à portée de; **(c)** (*Ind*) *workers* en grève. ♦ **strikingly** *adv change, improve* d'une manière frappante; *beautiful etc* remarquablement.

string [strɪŋ] (*vb: pret, ptp* **strung**) **1** *n* **(a)** (*gen*) ficelle *f*; *[violin, bow, racket etc]* corde *f*; *[apron, bonnet]* cordon *m*. **a piece of ~** un bout de ficelle; (*fig*) **there are no ~s attached** cela ne vous *etc* engage à rien; **to have more than one ~ to one's bow** avoir plus d'une corde à son arc; **his first/second ~** sa première/deuxième ressource; (*Mus*) **the ~s** les (instruments *mpl* à) cordes. **(b)** *[beads, pearls]* rang *m*; *[onions, garlic, lies, excuses]* chapelet *m*; *[people, vehicles]* file *f*; *[racehorses]* écurie *f*. **2** *adj* **(a)** *instrument, orchestra, quartet* à cordes; *serenade, piece* pour cordes. **(b) ~ bag** filet *m* à provisions; **~ bean** haricot *m* vert; **~ vest** tricot *m* de corps à grosses mailles. **3** *vt racket* corder; *violin etc* monter; *bow* garnir d'une corde; *beads, pearls* enfiler; *rope* tendre (*across* en travers de; *between* entre); *lights, decorations* suspendre, attacher (*on* sur; *between* entre); *beans* enlever les fils de.

string along* 1 *vi* suivre. **to ~ along with sb** accompagner qn. **2** *vt sep* (*pej*) faire marcher (*fig*).

string out 1 *vi [people, things]* s'échelonner (*along a road* le long d'une route). **2** *vt sep lanterns, washing etc* suspendre; *guards, posts* échelonner.

string up *vt sep lantern, onions* suspendre; (*: *lynch*) pendre. (*fig*) **to be strung up** être très tendu (*about* à la pensée de).

♦ **stringed** *adj* (*Mus*) à cordes. ♦ **stringpulling** *n* (*fig*) piston* *m* (*fig*). ♦ **stringy** *adj celery, meat* filandreux; *cooked cheese* filant; *plant* tout en longueur.

stringent ['strɪndʒənt] *adj* (*gen*) rigoureux; *reasons, arguments* irrésistible; *necessity* impérieux. ♦ **stringency** *n* rigueur *f*; **economic stringency** austérité *f*.

strip [strɪp] **1** *n* **(a)** (*piece: gen*) bande *f*; *[water, sea]* bras *m*. **a ~ of garden** un petit jardin tout en longueur; **comic ~, ~ cartoon** bande dessinée; (*fig*) **to tear a ~ off sb**‡ bien sonner les cloches à qn*. **(b)** (*Aviat: landing* ~) piste *f* d'atterrissage. **(c)** (*Sport: clothes*) tenue *f*. **2** *adj*: **~ lighting** éclairage *m* au néon; **~ poker** strip-poker *m*; **~ show** strip-tease *m*. **3** *vt person* déshabiller; (*often* **~ down**) *room, house* vider; *car, engine, gun* démonter complètement; *screw, gears* arracher le filet de; *branches, bushes* dépouiller; *bed* défaire complètement; (*remove*) *wallpaper, decorations etc* enlever (*from sth* de qch; *from sb* à qn); *paint, furniture* décaper; (*deprive*) *person, object* dépouiller (*of* de). **~ped pine furniture** meubles *mpl* anciens en pin; **to ~ the walls** enlever le papier peint; **to ~ a room of all its pictures** enlever tous les tableaux dans une pièce; (*Fin*) **to ~ a company of its assets** cannibaliser* une compagnie. **4** *vi* (*undress*) se déshabiller; *[striptease artist]* faire du strip-tease. **to ~ naked** se mettre nu; **to ~ to the waist** se déshabiller jusqu'à la ceinture; **~ped to the waist** nu jusqu'à la ceinture.

strip off 1 *vi* se déshabiller complètement. **2** *vt sep* (*gen*) enlever (*from sth* de qch); *leaves* faire tomber (*from* de); *berries* prendre (*from* de).

♦ **stripper** *n* **(a)** (*paint-stripper*) décapant *m*; **(b)** (*: *striptease*) strip-teaseuse *f*. ♦ **striptease** *n* strip-tease *m*.

stripe [straɪp] *n* **(a)** rayure *f*, raie *f*. (*pattern*) **~s** rayures; **yellow with a white ~** jaune rayé de blanc. **(b)** (*Mil*) galon *m*. ♦ **striped** *adj* rayé (*with* de).

stripling ['strɪplɪŋ] *n* tout jeune homme.

strive [straɪv] *pret* **strove**, *ptp* **striven** *vi* s'efforcer (*to do* de faire; *for sth* d'obtenir qch).

strode [strəʊd] *pret of* **stride**.

stroke [strəʊk] **1** *n* **(a)** (*movement; blow: gen*) coup *m*; (*Swimming: style*) nage *f*. (*lit, fig*) **at a ~, at one ~** d'un seul coup; **with a ~ of his axe** d'un coup de hache; **to put sb off his ~** (*Sport*) faire perdre son rythme à qn; (*fig*) faire perdre tous ses moyens à qn; **he hasn't done a ~ (of work)** il n'a rien fait du tout; **~ of diplomacy** chef-d'œuvre *m* de diplomatie; ~ **of genius** trait *m* de génie; ~ **of luck** coup de chance; **master** ~ coup de maître. **(b)** (*mark*) *[pen, pencil]* trait *m*; *[brush]* touche *f*; (*Typ: oblique*) barre *f*. **with a** ~ **of the pen** d'un trait de plume. **(c)** *[bell, clock]* coup *m*. **on the** ~ **of 10** sur le coup de 10 heures; **in the** ~ **of time** juste à temps. **(d)** (*Med*) **to have a** ~ avoir une attaque. **(e)** (*Tech: of piston*) course *f*. **a two-/four-**~ **engine** un moteur à deux/quatre temps. **(f)** (*Rowing: person*) chef *m* de nage. **2** *vt* caresser.

stroll [strəʊl] **1** *n* petite promenade *f*. **to take a** ~, **to go for a** ~ aller faire un tour. **2** *vi*: **to** ~ **in/away** *etc* entrer/s'éloigner *etc* nonchalamment. ♦ **stroller** *n* (*person*) flâneur *m*, -euse *f*; (*US: push-chair*) poussette *f*.

strong [strɒŋ] **1** *adj* (*gen*) fort; (*solid, robust*) *wall, table, shoes, bolt, reasons, evidence stomach, heart, nerves* solide; *eyesight* très bon; *candidate, contender* sérieux; *magnet* puissant; (*Elec*) *current* intense; *characteristic* marqué; *emotion, desire, interest* vif; (*St Ex*) *market* ferme; (*Econ*) *the pound, dollar* solide; *letter, protest, measures* énergique; (*Mus*) *beat* fort; *solution* concentré. **to be as** ~ **as a horse** *or* **an ox** (*powerful*) être fort comme un bœuf; (*healthy*) avoir une santé de fer; (*in circus etc*) ~ **man** hercule *m*; **do you feel** ~? est-ce que vous avez des forces?; (*in health*) **when you are** ~ **again** quand vous aurez repris des forces; **she has never been very** ~ elle a toujours eu une petite santé; (*in courage etc*) **you must be** ~ soyez courageux; (*mentally etc*) **he's a very** ~ **person** c'est un homme qui a du ressort; **an army 500** ~ une armée de 500 hommes; **they were 100** ~ ils étaient au nombre de 100; **in a** ~ **position** bien placé (*to do* pour faire); **his** ~ **suit** (*Cards*) sa couleur forte; (*fig: also* **his** ~ **point**) son fort; **to be** ~ **in maths** être fort en maths; **in** ~ **terms** en termes non équivoques; **there are** ~ **indications that ...** tout semble indiquer que ...; **a** ~ **effect** beaucoup d'effet; (*fig: too much*) **that's a bit** ~!* ça c'est un peu fort!*; **I had a** ~ **sense of ...** je ressentais vivement ...; **I've a** ~ **feeling that ...** j'ai bien l'impression que ...; **he's got** ~ **feelings on this matter** cette affaire lui tient à cœur; **it is my** ~ **opinion that** je suis fermement convaincu que; **a** ~ **socialist** un socialiste fervent; ~ **supporters of** d'ardents partisans de; **I am a** ~ **believer in** je crois fermement à; ~ **verb** verbe *m* irrégulier; ~ **drink** alcool *m*; **it has a** ~ **smell** ça sent fort.

2 *adv*: **to be going** ~ *[person]* être toujours solide; *[car etc]* marcher toujours bien; *[firm, business]* être florissant; *[relationship]* aller bien.

♦ **strong-arm** *adj* brutal. ♦ **strongbox** *n* coffre-fort *m*. ♦ **stronghold** *n* (*Mil*) forteresse *f*; (*fig*) bastion *m*. ♦ **strongly** *adv fight, attack, protest* énergiquement; *attract, influence, desire* vivement; *accentuate, remind, indicate* fortement; *believe* fermement; *feel, sense* profondément; *constructed, made* solidement; ~**ly-worded letter** lettre *f* bien sentie; **it smells very** ~**ly** cela sent très fort; **it smells** ~**ly of onions** cela a une forte odeur d'oignons. ♦ **strong-minded** *adj* qui sait ce qu'il veut. ♦ **strong-mindedly** *adv* avec ténacité. ♦ **strongroom** *n* chambre *f* forte. ♦ **strong-willed** *adj*: to be ~**-willed** avoir de la volonté.

strove [strəʊv] *pret of* **strive.**

struck [strʌk] *pret, ptp of* **strike.**

structure ['strʌktʃəʳ] **1** *n* **(a)** (*gen, Chem etc*) structure *f*; **social/administrative** ~ structure sociale/administrative. **(b)** (*Constr: of building etc*) ossature *f*; (*the building, bridge etc itself*) édifice *m*. **2** *vt* structurer. ♦ **structural** *adj* **(a)** (*gen, Chem etc*) structural; **(b)** (*Constr*) *fault etc* de construction; *alterations* des parties portantes; **structural engineering** ponts et chaussées *mpl*. ♦ **structurally** *adv* (*gen, Chem etc*) du point de vue de la structure; (*Constr*) du point de vue de la construction.

struggle ['strʌgl] **1** *n* (*lit, fig*) lutte *f* (*for* pour; *against* contre; *with* avec; *to do* pour faire). **to put up a** ~ résister; **he lost his glasses in the** ~ il a perdu ses lunettes dans la bagarre; **without a** ~ *surrender etc* sans résistance; (*without difficulty*) sans beaucoup de difficulté; **the** ~ **to find somewhere to live** les difficultés qu'on a à trouver un logement; **I had a** ~ **to persuade him** j'ai eu beaucoup de mal à le persuader; **it was a** ~ cela a demandé beaucoup d'efforts.

2 *vi* **(a)** (*fight*) se battre, lutter (*against sth* contre qch; *with sb* avec qn); (*resist*) résister (*against sth* à qch); (*thrash around*) se débattre; (*fig: try hard*) se démener (*to do* pour faire). **they were struggling for power** ils se disputaient le pouvoir; (*fig*) **he was struggling to make ends meet** il avait beaucoup de mal à joindre les deux bouts. **(b) to** ~ **in/out** *etc* entrer/sortir *etc* avec peine; **to** ~ **through the crowd** se frayer péniblement un chemin à travers la foule; **he** ~**d to his feet** (*from armchair etc*) il s'est levé non sans peine; (*during fight etc*) il s'est relevé péniblement; **he** ~**d into a jersey** il a enfilé non sans peine un pullover.

struggle through *vi* (*fig*) s'en sortir.

♦ **struggling** *adj artist etc* qui vit péniblement.

strum [strʌm] *vti* (~ **on**) *piano* tapoter de; *guitar etc* racler.

strung [strʌŋ] *pret, ptp of* **string.**

strut[1] [strʌt] *vi*: **to** ~ **about** *or* **around** se pavaner; **to** ~ **in/along** *etc* entrer/avancer *etc* d'un air important.

strut[2] [strʌt] *n* (*support*) étai *m*, support *m*.

strychnine ['strɪkni:n] *n* strychnine *f*.

stub [stʌb] **1** *n [tree, plant]* souche *f*; *[pencil]* bout *m*; *[cigarette, cigar]* mégot* *m*; *[cheque, ticket]* talon *m*. **2** *vt* **(a) to** ~ **one's toe** se cogner le doigt de pied (*against* contre). **(b)** (~ **out**) *cigar, cigarette* écraser. ♦ **stubby** *adj person* trapu; *finger* boudiné; *pencil* gros et court.

stubble ['stʌbl] *n* (*Agr*) chaume *m*; (*on chin*) barbe *f* de plusieurs jours.

stubborn ['stʌbən] *adj* (*gen*) opiniâtre; *person* têtu, obstiné; *animal* rétif; *fever, disease* rebelle. ♦ **stubbornly** *adv* obstinément. ♦ **stubbornness** *n* opiniâtreté *f*; entêtement *m*; obstination *f*.

stucco ['stʌkəʊ] *n* stuc *m*.

stuck [stʌk] *pret, ptp of* **stick.** ♦ **stuck-up*** *adj* prétentieux.

stud[1] [stʌd] **1** *n* (*gen, also on roadway*) clou *m* (à grosse tête); (*on football boots*) crampon *m*. **collar** ~ bouton *m* de col. **2** *vt* clouter. (*fig*) ~**ded with** parsemé de.

stud[2] [stʌd] **1** *n* (*racing* ~) écurie *f* (de courses); (~ *farm*) haras *m*. **to be at** ~ étalonner. **2** *adj*: ~ **book** stud-book *m*; ~ **horse** étalon *m*; ~ **mare** poulinière *f*.

student ['stju:dənt] **1** *n* (*gen*) étudiant(e) *m(f)*; (*at school*) élève *mf*. **medical** ~ étudiant(e) en médecine; **he is a** ~ **of bird life** il étudie la vie des oiseaux; **he is a keen** ~ il est très studieux. **2** *adj life, power, unrest* étudiant; *residence, restaurant* universitaire; *attitudes, opinions* des étudiants. **the** ~ **community** les étudiants *mpl*; ~ **teacher** élève *mf* professeur. ♦ **studentship** *n* bourse *f* d'études.

studio ['stju:dɪəʊ] **1** *n* studio *m* (*de TV, d'artiste etc*). **2** *adj*: ~ **couch** divan *m*; (*Phot*) ~ **portrait** portrait *m* photographique.

studious ['stju:dɪəs] *adj person* studieux; *piece of work* soigné; *effort* assidu; *politeness* étudié; *avoidance* délibéré. ♦ **studiously** *adv* studieusement; soigneusement; délibérément; ~**ly polite**

d'une politesse étudiée. ♦ **studiousness** *n* application *f* (à l'étude).

study ['stʌdɪ] **1** *n* **(a)** étude *f* (*of* sur). (*fig*) **his face was a ~** il fallait voir son visage. **(b)** (*room*) bureau *m* (*particulier*). **2** *adj visit, hour* d'étude; *group* de travail. **3** *vt* (*gen*) étudier; *sb's face, reactions, stars* observer. **4** *vi* étudier. **to ~ hard** travailler dur; **to ~ under sb** (*Univ*) travailler sous la direction de qn; *[painter, composer]* être l'élève de qn; **to ~ for an exam** préparer un examen; **he is ~ing to be a doctor/teacher** il fait des études de médecine/pour devenir professeur.
♦ **studied** *adj calm, politeness* étudié; *insult, avoidance* délibéré; (*pej*) *style* affecté.

stuff [stʌf] **1** *n* **(a)** (*substance*) **what's this ~ in this jar?** qu'est-ce que c'est que ça dans ce pot?; **it's good ~** c'est bien *or* bon; **there's some good ~ in it** il y a de bonnes choses là-dedans; **it's poor ~** ça ne vaut pas grand-chose; **it's dangerous ~** c'est dangereux; **I can't listen to his ~ at all** je ne peux pas souffrir sa musique (*or* sa poésie *etc*); (*pej*) **all that ~ about how he ...** tous ces grands discours comme quoi il ...; **that's the ~!*** bravo, c'est ça!; **~ and nonsense!*** balivernes!; **he is the ~ that heroes are made of** il a l'étoffe d'un héros; **he knows his ~*** il s'y connaît; **do your ~!*** vas-y!, c'est à toi!; **he did his ~ very well*** il s'en est bien sorti; **put your ~ away** range tes affaires; **he brought back a lot of ~** il a rapporté des tas de choses. **(b)** (*cloth*) étoffe *f*.
2 *vt* (*fill*) *cushion etc* rembourrer (*with* avec); (*Taxidermy*) *animal* empailler; *box, pockets* bourrer (*with* de); (*Culin*) farcir (*with* avec); *hole* boucher (*with* avec); (*cram*) *objects* fourrer (*in, into* dans). **to ~ one's fingers into one's ears** fourrer ses doigts dans ses oreilles; **he ~ed some money into my hand** il m'a fourré de l'argent dans la main; (*fig*) **he is a ~ed shirt*** il est pompeux; **~ed toy** jouet *m* de peluche; **to ~ o.s. with food** se gaver de nourriture.
3 *vi* (‡: *guzzle*) se gaver.
♦ **stuffed-up** *adj*: **my nose is ~ed-up** j'ai le nez bouché. ♦ **stuffily** *adv say etc* d'un ton désapprobateur. ♦ **stuffiness** *n* (*in room*) manque *m* d'air; *[person]* esprit *m* vieux jeu. ♦ **stuffing** *n* (*gen*) rembourrage *m*; (*Culin*) farce *f*; (*fig*) **he's got no ~ing** c'est une chiffe molle; **to knock the ~ing out of sb** *[boxer, blow]* dégonfler qn; *[illness, news]* mettre qn à plat. ♦ **stuffy** *adj* **(a)** *room* mal aéré; **it's ~y in here** on manque d'air ici; **it smells ~y** ça sent le renfermé; **(b)** *person* vieux jeu *inv*.

stumble ['stʌmbl] *vi* trébucher (*over* sur, contre); *[horse]* broncher. **to ~ in/along** *etc* entrer/avancer *etc* en trébuchant; (*fig*) **to ~ across** *or* **on sth** tomber sur qch; **he ~d through the first verse** il a récité la première strophe d'une voix hésitante. ♦ **stumbling block** *n* pierre *f* d'achoppement.

stump [stʌmp] **1** *n [tree]* souche *f*; *[limb, tail]* moignon *m*; *[tooth]* chicot *m*; *[cigar, pencil, chalk etc]* bout *m*; (*Cricket*) piquet *m*. **2** *vt* **(a)** (*: *puzzle*) faire sécher*. **to be ~ed by sth** être incapable de répondre à qch, sécher* sur qch. **(b)** (*Cricket*) mettre hors jeu. **3** *vi*: **to ~ in/along** *etc* entrer/avancer *etc* (*heavily*) à pas lourds *or* (*limping*) clopin-clopant*.

stump up* (*Brit*) **1** *vi* casquer‡, payer. **2** *vt sep* cracher*, y aller de.
♦ **stumpy** *adj person* ramassé; *object* épais et court.

stun [stʌn] *vt* étourdir; (*fig: amaze*) stupéfier. ♦ **stunned** *adj* stupéfait (*by* de). ♦ **stunning** *adj* étourdissant; stupéfiant; (*: *lovely*) *girl, dress, car* sensationnel*.

stung [stʌŋ] *pret, ptp of* **sting**.

stunk [stʌŋk] *ptp of* **stink**.

stunt^{1} [stʌnt] *n* (*feat*) tour *m* de force; (*Aviat*) acrobatie *f*; (*trick*) truc* *m*, coup *m* monté; (*publicity ~*) truc* publicitaire. ♦ **stuntman** *n* (*Cine etc*) cascadeur *m*.

stunt^{2} [stʌnt] *vt growth* retarder; *person, plant* retarder la croissance de. ♦ **stunted** *adj* rabougri.

stupefy ['stju:pɪfaɪ] *vt [blow]* étourdir; *[drink, drugs]* abrutir; (*fig: astound*) stupéfier. ♦ **stupefaction** *n* stupéfaction *f*. ♦ **stupefying** *adj* (*fig*) stupéfiant.

stupendous [stju(:)'pendəs] *adj ceremony, beauty* prodigieux; (*) *film, holiday* fantastique.
♦ **stupendously** *adv* formidablement*.

stupid ['stju:pɪd] *adj* stupide, idiot; (*from sleep, drink etc*) abruti. **I've done a ~ thing** j'ai fait une bêtise; **you ~ idiot!*** espèce d'idiot(e)!; **he drank himself ~** il s'est abruti d'alcool. ♦ **stupidity** *or* ♦ **stupidness** *n* stupidité *f*, bêtise *f*. ♦ **stupidly** *adv look, smile* stupidement; **I ~ly told him your name** j'ai été assez bête pour lui dire votre nom.

stupor ['stju:pə^{r}] *n* stupeur *f*.

sturdy ['stɜ:dɪ] *adj person, chair* robuste; (*fig*) *resistance, refusal* énergique. ♦ **sturdily** *adv* robustement; énergiquement. ♦ **sturdiness** *n* robustesse *f*.

sturgeon ['stɜ:dʒən] *n* esturgeon *m*.

stutter ['stʌtə^{r}] **1** *n* bégaiement *m*. **2** *vti* bégayer.
♦ **stutterer** *n* bègue *mf*. ♦ **stuttering** *n* bégaiement *m*.

sty [staɪ] *n [pigs]* porcherie *f*.

sty(e) [staɪ] *n* (*Med*) orgelet *m*.

style [staɪl] **1** *n* **(a)** (*gen*) style *m*; (*sort, type*) genre *m*. **in the Renaissance ~** de style Renaissance; **~ of life** *or* **living** style de vie; **he won in fine ~** il l'a emporté haut la main; **just the ~ of book I like** justement le genre de livre que j'aime; (*fig*) **it's not my ~*** ce n'est pas mon genre; **that's the ~!*** bravo! **(b)** (*Dress etc*) modèle *m*; (*Hairdressing*) coiffure *f*. **in the latest ~** (*adv*) à la dernière mode; (*adj*) du dernier cri; **sth in that ~** qch dans ce genre *or* dans ce goût-là. **(c)** (*distinction*) *[person]* allure *f*, chic *m*; *[building, car, film, book]* style *m*, cachet *m*. **to live in ~** vivre sur un grand pied; **he does things in ~** il fait bien les choses; **they got married in ~** ils se sont mariés en grande pompe; **he certainly travels in ~** quand il voyage il fait bien les choses. **2** *vt* **(a)** (*call, designate*) appeler. **(b) to ~ sb's hair** créer une nouvelle coiffure pour qn. ♦ **styling** *n* (*Hairdressing*) coupe *f*. ♦ **stylish** *adj person* qui a du chic; *garment, hotel, district* chic *inv*; *film, book, car* qui a une certaine élégance. ♦ **stylishly** *adv live, dress* élégamment; *travel* dans les règles de l'art. ♦ **stylishness** *n* élégance *f*, chic *m*.
♦ **stylist** *n* (*Literat*) styliste *mf*; (*Hairdressing*) coiffeur *m*, -euse *f*. ♦ **stylistic 1** *adj* (*Literat etc*) stylistique; **2** *n*: **stylistics** stylistique *f*. ♦ **stylize** *vt* styliser.

stylus ['staɪləs] *n* (*tool*) style *m*; *[record player]* pointe *f* de lecture.

suave [swɑ:v] *adj* doucereux. ♦ **suavely** *adv* doucereusement. ♦ **suavity** *n* manières *fpl* doucereuses.

sub... [sʌb] **1** *pref* sub..., sous-. **2** (*) *abbr of* **subaltern, submarine, subscription, substitute.**
♦ **subcommittee** *n* sous-comité *m*; (*in local government*) sous-commission *f*; **the Housing S~committee** la sous-commission du logement.
♦ **subcontinent** *n* sous-continent *m*. ♦ **subcontract 1** *n* sous-traité *m*; **2** *vt* sous-traiter.
♦ **subcontractor** *n* sous-traitant *m*. ♦ **subdivide 1** *vt* subdiviser (*into* en); **2** *vi* se subdiviser.
♦ **subdivision** *n* subdivision *f*. ♦ **sub-edit** *vt* préparer pour l'impression. ♦ **sub-editor** *n* secrétaire *mf* de rédaction. ♦ **subhead(ing)** *n* sous-titre *m*. ♦ **subhuman** *adj* moins qu'humain.
♦ **sublet** (*pret, ptp* **~let**) **1** *n* sous-location *f*; **2** *vti* sous-louer. ♦ **sub-librarian** *n* bibliothécaire *mf* adjoint(e). ♦ **sub-lieutenant** *n* (*Naut*) enseigne *m*

de vaisseau. ♦ **submachine gun** *n* mitraillette *f*. ♦ **subnormal** *adj temperature* au-dessous de la normale; *person* arriéré. ♦ **sub-post office** *n* petit bureau *m* de poste (*de quartier etc*). ♦ **subsoil** *n* (*Agr*) sous-sol *m*. ♦ **subsonic** *adj* subsonique. ♦ **substandard** *adj* (*gen*) inférieur; *goods* de qualité inférieure; *housing* inférieur aux normes exigées. ♦ **substratum** *n, pl* ~**strata** substrat *m*. ♦ **subtenant** *n* sous-locataire *mf*. ♦ **subtitle 1** *n* sous-titre *m*; **2** *vt* sous-titrer. ♦ **subtitling** *n* sous-titrage *m*. ♦ **subtotal** *n* total *m* partiel. ♦ **sub-zero** *adj* au-dessous de zéro.

subaltern ['sʌbltən] *n* (*Brit Mil*) lieutenant *m*.

subconscious ['sʌb'kɒnʃəs] *adj, n* inconscient (*m*). ♦ **subconsciously** *adv* inconsciemment.

subdue [səb'dju:] *vt people, country* soumettre; *feelings* maîtriser. ♦ **subdued** *adj emotion* contenu; *reaction, response* faible; *voice, tone* bas; *conversation, discussion* à voix basse; *light* voilé; **she was very** ~**d** elle avait perdu son entrain.

subject ['sʌbdʒɪkt] **1** *n* (*gen: most senses*) sujet *m* (*of, for* de); (*Scol etc*) matière *f*; (*citizen*) sujet(te) *m(f)*. **he is a French** ~ (*in France*) c'est un sujet français, il est de nationalité française; (*elsewhere*) c'est un ressortissant français; **to get off the** ~ sortir du sujet; **let's get back to the** ~ revenons à nos moutons; **on the** ~ **of** au sujet de; **while we're on the** ~ **of ...** à propos de ...; (*Scol, Univ*) **his best** ~ sa matière forte.

2 *adj* **(a)** *people, tribes, state* soumis. ~ **to** (*liable to*) *disease etc* sujet à; *flooding, subsidence etc* exposé à; *the law, taxation* soumis à; (*conditional upon*) sous réserve de; **our prices are** ~ **to alteration** nos prix sont donnés sous réserve de modifications; ~ **to doing that** à condition de faire cela. **(b)** ~ **heading** rubrique *f*; ~ **index** (*in book*) index *m* des matières; (*in library*) fichier *m* par matières; ~ **matter** (*theme*) sujet *m*; (*content*) contenu *m*.

3 [səb'dʒekt] *vt*: **to** ~ **sb to sth** soumettre qn à qch; **to** ~ **sth to heat** exposer qch à la chaleur; **he was** ~**ed to much criticism** il a été très critiqué. ♦ **subjection** *n* sujétion *f*, soumission *f*. ♦ **subjective** *adj* subjectif. ♦ **subjectively** *adv* subjectivement.

subjugate ['sʌbdʒʊgeɪt] *vt* subjuguer.

subjunctive [səb'dʒʌŋktɪv] *adj, n* subjonctif *(m)*. **in the** ~ au subjonctif.

sublime [sə'blaɪm] *adj* (*gen*) sublime; *contempt, indifference* suprême (*before n*); (*: *excellent*) *dinner, person* divin, fantastique. ♦ **sublimate** *vt* sublimer. ♦ **sublimation** *n* sublimation *f*. ♦ **sublimely** *adv* **(a)** ~**ly beautiful** d'une beauté sublime; **(b)** *contemptuous etc* suprêmement; ~**ly unaware of** dans une ignorance absolue de. ♦ **subliminal** *adj* subliminal. ♦ **subliminally** *adv* au-dessous du niveau de la conscience.

submarine [ˌsʌbmə'ri:n] *adj, n* sous-marin (*m*).

submerge [səb'mɜ:dʒ] **1** *vt* submerger. **to** ~ **sth in sth** immerger qch dans qch. **2** *vi [submarine]* s'immerger.

submit [səb'mɪt] **1** *vt* soumettre (*to* à). **to** ~ **that** suggérer que. **2** *vi* (*Mil, also fig*) se soumettre (*to* à). ♦ **submission** *n* (*all senses*) soumission (*to* à); **starved/beaten into submission** réduit par la faim/les coups. ♦ **submissive** *adj* soumis, docile. ♦ **submissively** *adv* avec soumission, docilement. ♦ **submissiveness** *n* soumission *f*, docilité *f*.

subordinate [sə'bɔ:dnɪt] **1** *adj* (*gen*) subalterne; (*Gram*) subordonné. **2** *n* subordonné(e) *m(f)*. **3** [sə'bɔ:dɪneɪt] *vt* subordonner (*to* à). ♦ **subordination** *n* subordination *f*.

subpoena [səb'pi:nə] (*Jur*) **1** *n* citation *f*, assignation *f*. **2** *vt* citer *or* assigner (à comparaître).

subscribe [səb'skraɪb] **1** *vt money* donner (*to* à). **2** *vi* verser une somme d'argent. **to** ~ **to** *new publication, fund* souscrire à; *newspaper* être abonné à; *idea, project* être partisan de. ♦ **subscriber** *n* souscripteur *m*, -trice *f* (*to* de); abonné(e) *m(f)* (*to* de) (*also Telec*); partisan *m* (*to* de); ~**r trunk dialling** automatique *m*. ♦ **subscription** *n* souscription *f*; abonnement *m*; (*to club*) cotisation *f*; **to pay one's subscription** payer sa cotisation *or* son abonnement; (*Press*) **to take out a subscription to** s'abonner à.

subsequent ['sʌbsɪkwənt] *adj* ultérieur, suivant. **a** ~ **visit** une visite ultérieure; **his** ~ **visit** sa visite suivante; ~ **to** à la suite de.

subservient [səb'sɜ:vɪənt] *adj* obséquieux. ♦ **subservience** *n* obséquiosité *f*.

subside [səb'saɪd] *vi [land, building]* s'affaisser; *[flood, river]* baisser; *[wind, emotion]* tomber; *[threat]* s'éloigner; *[person]* (*fall*) s'affaisser (*into* dans; *on to* sur); (*: *be quiet*) se taire. ♦ **subsidence** *n [land etc]* affaissement *m* (*de terrain*).

subsidiary [səb'sɪdɪərɪ] **1** *adj* subsidiaire. **2** *n* (~ *company*) filiale *f*.

subsidize ['sʌbsɪdaɪz] *vt* subventionner. ♦ **subsidy** *n* subvention *f*; **government** *or* **state subsidy** subvention de l'État.

subsist [səb'sɪst] *vi* subsister. **to** ~ **on sth** vivre de qch. ♦ **subsistence 1** *n* existence *f*, subsistance *f*; (*allowance*) frais *mpl* de subsistance; **2** *adj wage* tout juste suffisant pour vivre; **to live at** ~**ence level** avoir tout juste de quoi vivre.

substance ['sʌbstəns] *n* (*gen*) substance *f*. **the** ~ **of his speech** la substance *or* l'essentiel de son discours; **a man of** ~ un homme riche; **to lack** ~ *[film, book]* manquer d'étoffe; *[argument]* être plutôt mince; *[accusation, claim]* être sans grand fondement. ♦ **substantial** *adj* **(a)** (*large*) (*gen*) important, considérable; *meal* substantiel; *firm* solide; *landowner, businessman* riche; *house etc* grand; **(b)** (*real*) substantiel, réel. ♦ **substantially** *adv* **(a)** (*considerably*) *improve etc* considérablement; **substantially bigger** beaucoup plus grand; **substantially different** très différent; **(b)** (*to a large extent*) en grande partie; **(c)** *built, constructed* solidement. ♦ **substantiate** *vt* justifier.

substantive ['sʌbstəntɪv] *n, adj* (*Gram*) substantif (*m*).

substitute ['sʌbstɪtju:t] **1** *n* (*person*) remplaçant(e) *m(f)* (*for* de); (*thing*) produit *m* de remplacement, succédané *m* (*gen pej*) (*for* de). (*Comm*) **'beware of** ~**s'** 'se méfier des contrefaçons'; **there is no** ~ **for wool** rien ne peut remplacer la laine. **2** *adj player etc* remplaçant. ~ **coffee** succédané *m* de café. **3** *vt* substituer (*A for B* A à B), remplacer (*A for B* B par A). **4** *vi*: **to** ~ **for sb** remplacer qn. ♦ **substitution** *n* substitution *f*, remplacement *m*.

subterfuge ['sʌbtəfju:dʒ] *n* subterfuge *m*.

subterranean [ˌsʌbtə'reɪnɪən] *adj* souterrain.

subtle ['sʌtl] *adj* (*gen*) subtil; *person* subtil, qui a beaucoup de finesse; *mind, intelligence* subtil, pénétrant. ♦ **subtleness** *or* ♦ **subtlety** *n* subtilité *f*; finesse *f*. ♦ **subtly** *adv* subtilement.

subtract [səb'trækt] *vt* soustraire (*from* de). ♦ **subtraction** *n* soustraction *f*.

suburb ['sʌbɜ:b] *n* faubourg *m*. **the** ~**s** la banlieue; **in the** ~**s** en banlieue; **the outer** ~**s** la grande banlieue. ♦ **suburban** *adj* (*gen*) de banlieue, suburbain; (*pej*) *person, accent* banlieusard*. ♦ **suburbanite** *n* banlieusard(e) *m(f)*. ♦ **suburbia** *n* la banlieue.

subvention [səb'venʃən] *n* subvention *f*.

subvert [səb'vɜ:t] *vt the law, tradition* bouleverser; (*corrupt*) *person* corrompre. ♦ **subversion** *n* subversion *f*. ♦ **subversive** *adj* subversif.

subway ['sʌbweɪ] *n* (*underpass*) passage *m* souterrain; (*railway: esp US*) métro *m*.

succeed [sək'si:d] **1** *vi* **(a)** (*be successful: gen*) réussir (*in sth* dans qch; *in doing* à faire). **he ~s in all he does** il réussit tout ce qu'il entreprend; **to ~ in business/as a politician** réussir en affaires/en tant qu'homme politique. **(b)** (*follow*) succéder (*to sth* à qch). **2** *vt* succéder à. **he was ~ed by his son** son fils lui a succédé. ♦ **succeeding** *adj* (*in past*) suivant; (*in future*) à venir, futur; **each ~ing year brought ...** chaque année qui passait apportait ...; **each ~ing year will bring ...** chacune des années à venir apportera ...; **on 3 ~ing Saturdays** 3 samedis consécutifs *or* de suite.

success [sək'ses] **1** *n [plan, venture, attempt, person]* succès *m*, réussite *f* (*in an exam* à un examen; *in maths* en maths; *in one's aim* dans son but; *in business* en affaires; *in one's career* dans sa carrière). **his ~ in doing sth** le fait qu'il ait réussi à faire qch; **his ~ in his attempts** la réussite qui a couronné ses efforts; **without ~** sans succès, en vain; **to make a ~ of** *project, enterprise* mener à bien; *job, meal* réussir; **he was a ~ at last** il avait enfin réussi; **he was a great ~ at the dinner/as Hamlet/as a writer** il a eu beaucoup de succès au dîner/dans le rôle de Hamlet/en tant qu'écrivain; **it was a ~** (*gen*) c'était une réussite; *[play, book, attempt]* ça a été couronné de succès; *[hotel etc]* on en a été très content. **2** *adj*: **~ story** (histoire *f* d'une) réussite *f*. ♦ **successful** *adj plan, venture, application, deal* couronné de succès; *writer, painter, book* à succès; *candidate* (*in exam*) reçu, (*in election*) élu; *marriage, outcome* heureux; *career, businessman* prospère; *[performer, play etc]* **to be ~ful** avoir un succès fou; **to be ~ful in doing** réussir à faire. ♦ **successfully** *adv* avec succès.

succession [sək'seʃən] *n* (*gen*) succession *f*. **in ~** successivement; **4 times in ~** 4 fois de suite; **in close ~** coup sur coup; **in ~ to his father** à la suite de son père. ♦ **successive** *adj generations, discoveries* successif; *days, months* consécutif; **on 4 successive days** pendant 4 jours consécutifs *or* de suite; **each successive failure** chaque nouvel échec. ♦ **successively** *adv* successivement. ♦ **successor** *n* successeur *m* (*to, of* de); (*to throne*) héritier *m*, -ière *f* (*to* de).

succinct [sək'sɪŋkt] *adj* succinct. ♦ **succinctly** *adv* succinctement.

succulent ['sʌkjʊlənt] **1** *adj* succulent. **2** *n* (*Bot*) **~s** plantes *fpl* grasses. ♦ **succulence** *n* succulence *f*.

succumb [sə'kʌm] *vi* succomber (*to* à).

such [sʌtʃ] **1** *adj* tel, pareil. **~ a book** un tel livre, un livre pareil; **~ books** de tels livres, des livres pareils; **we had ~ a case last year** nous avons eu un cas semblable l'année dernière; **in ~ cases** en pareil cas; **did you ever hear of ~ a thing?** avez-vous jamais entendu une chose pareille?; **there's no ~ thing!** ça n'existe pas!; **there are no ~ things as unicorns** les licornes n'existent pas; **there is no ~ thing in France** il n'y a rien de tel en France; **I said no ~ thing!** je n'ai jamais dit cela!; **or some ~ thing** ou une chose de ce genre; **no ~ book exists** un tel livre n'existe pas; **~ was my reply** telle a été ma réponse; **~ is life!** c'est la vie!; **it was SUCH weather!** il a fait un de ces temps!; **I had ~ a fright!** j'ai eu une de ces peurs!; **a friend ~ as Paul, ~ a friend as Paul** un ami tel que *or* comme Paul; **~ writers as Molière** des écrivains tels que Molière; **he's not ~ a fool as you think** il n'est pas aussi bête que vous croyez; **I'm not ~ a fool as to believe that!** je ne suis pas assez bête pour croire ça!; **have you ~ a thing as a penknife?** auriez-vous un canif par hasard?; **~ as?** quel genre de choses?; **~ books as I have** les quelques livres que je possède; **you can take my car, ~ as it is** vous pouvez prendre ma voiture pour ce qu'elle vaut; (*so much*) **~ a noise** tellement de bruit.

2 *adv* **(a)** (*so very*) si, tellement. **~ good coffee** un si bon café; **~ big boxes** de si grandes boîtes, des boîtes si grandes; **it was SUCH a long time ago!** il y a si *or* tellement longtemps de ça!; **~ an expensive car that ...** une voiture si *or* tellement chère que ... . **(b)** (*in comparisons*) aussi. **I haven't had ~ good coffee for years** ça fait des années que je n'ai pas bu un aussi bon café; **~ lovely children as his** des enfants aussi gentils que les siens.

3 *pron*: **~ as wish to go** ceux qui veulent partir; **~ as I have** ceux que j'ai; **teachers as ~ are ...** les professeurs en tant que tels sont ...; **the work as ~ is boring but ...** le travail en soi est ennuyeux mais ...; **there are no houses as ~** il n'y a pas de maisons à proprement parler; **he was not recognized as ~** il n'était pas considéré comme tel; **teachers and doctors and ~(like)*** les professeurs, les docteurs et autres gens de la sorte.

♦ **such-and-such** **1** *n*: **Mr S~-and-~*** Monsieur Untel; **2** *adj*: **in ~-and-~ a street** dans telle rue. ♦ **suchlike*** *adj* de la sorte; *V also* **such 3**.

suck [sʌk] **1** *vt* (*gen*) sucer; (*through straw*) *drink* aspirer (*through* avec); *[baby]* téter; *[pump, machine]* aspirer (*from* de). **to ~ one's thumb** sucer son pouce; **to ~ dry** *orange etc* sucer tout le jus de; (*fig*) *person* (*of money*) sucer jusqu'au dernier sou; (*of energy*) sucer jusqu'à la moelle. **2** *vi [baby]* téter. **to ~ at sth** sucer qch.

suck down *vt sep [sea, mud]* engloutir.

suck in *vt sep [sea, mud]* engloutir; *[pump, machine]* aspirer.

suck out *vt sep [person]* sucer (*of, from* de); *[machine]* refouler à l'extérieur (*of, from* de).

suck up **1** *vi* (*:*) **to ~ up to sb** lécher les bottes* de qn. **2** *vt sep* aspirer.

♦ **sucker** *n* **(a)** (*on machine, octopus etc*) ventouse *f*; (*plunger*) piston *m*; (*Bot*) surgeon *m*; **(b)** (*:* *person*) poire* *f*, imbécile *mf*; **to be a ~er for sth*** ne pas pouvoir résister à qch. ♦ **suckle** **1** *vt* allaiter; **2** *vi* téter. ♦ **suction** **1** *n* succion *f*; **2** *adj device* de succion; *pump* aspirant.

sudden ['sʌdn] *adj* (*gen*) soudain, brusque; *death, inspiration* subit; *bend in road, marriage, appointment* imprévu. **all of a ~** soudain, tout à coup; **it's all so ~!** c'est arrivé tellement vite! ♦ **suddenly** *adv* (*gen*) brusquement, tout à coup, soudain; *die* subitement. ♦ **suddenness** *n* soudaineté *f*; caractère *m* imprévu.

suds [sʌdz] *npl* (**soap~**) (*lather*) mousse *f* de savon; (*soapy water*) eau *f* savonneuse.

sue [su:] **1** *vt* (*gen*) poursuivre en justice (*for sth* pour obtenir qch; *over, about* au sujet de). **to ~ sb for damages** poursuivre qn en dommages-intérêts; **to ~ sb for libel** intenter un procès en diffamation à qn; **to ~ sb for divorce** entamer une procédure de divorce contre qn. **2** *vi* intenter un procès. **to ~ for divorce** entamer une procédure de divorce.

suede [sweɪd] **1** *n* daim *m* (*cuir*). **2** *adj* (*gen*) de daim; *gloves* de suède.

suet ['sʊɪt] *n* graisse *f* de rognon.

suffer ['sʌfər] **1** *vt* **(a)** (*undergo*) (*gen*) subir; *martyrdom, hardship* souffrir; *punishment, change, pain* éprouver; *hunger, headaches* souffrir de. **he ~ed a lot of pain** il a beaucoup souffert. **(b)** (*bear*) *pain* endurer, tolérer; (*allow*) *opposition, sb's rudeness, refusal etc* tolérer. **he doesn't ~ fools gladly** il n'a aucune patience pour les imbéciles.

2 *vi* (*gen*) souffrir. **he ~ed for it** il en a souffert les conséquences; **you'll ~ for this** vous le paierez (*fig*); **to ~ from** *rheumatism, heart trouble, the cold, hunger* souffrir de; *deafness* être atteint de; *a cold, influenza, frostbite, pimples, bad memory* avoir; **he ~s from a limp/stammer** il boite/bégaie; **he was ~ing from shock** il était commotionné; **to ~ from the effects of** *fall, illness* se ressentir de; *alcohol, drug* subir le contrecoup de; **she ~s from lack of friends** son problème, c'est qu'elle n'a pas d'amis; **the house**

is ~ing from neglect la maison se ressent du manque d'entretien; **your health will ~** votre santé en souffrira; **the regiment ~ed badly** le régiment a essuyé de grosses pertes.
♦ **sufferance** *n*: **on ~ance** par tolérance.
♦ **sufferer** *n* (*from illness*) malade *mf*; **diabetes ~ers** diabétiques *mfpl*. ♦ **suffering 1** *n* souffrances *fpl*; **2** *adj* qui souffre.

suffice [sə'faɪs] **1** *vi* suffire. **~ it to say** qu'il suffise de dire. **2** *vt* suffire à.

sufficient [sə'fɪʃənt] *adj* (*enough*) *money, food, people* assez de, suffisamment de; (*big enough*) *number, quantity* suffisant. **to be ~** être suffisant *or* assez (*for* pour), suffire (*for* à); **I've got ~** j'en ai assez *or* suffisamment; **~ to eat** assez à manger; **he earns ~ to live on** il gagne de quoi vivre; **that's quite ~** cela suffit. ♦ **sufficiency** *n* quantité *f* suffisante. ♦ **sufficiently** *adv* suffisamment, assez; **~ly clever to do** suffisamment *or* assez intelligent pour faire; **~ly large** *amount, number* suffisant.

suffix ['sʌfɪks] *n* suffixe *m*.

suffocate ['sʌfəkeɪt] *vti* suffoquer (*with* de).
♦ **suffocating** *adj* suffocant; (*fig*) étouffant; **it's suffocating in here** on étouffe ici. ♦ **suffocation** *n* suffocation *f*; (*Med*) asphyxie *f*; **to die from suffocation** mourir asphyxié.

suffrage ['sʌfrɪdʒ] *n* suffrage *m*. **universal ~** suffrage universel. ♦ **suffragette** *n* suffragette *f*.

sugar ['ʃʊgəʳ] **1** *n* sucre *m*. **2** *vt* sucrer. (*fig*) **to ~ the pill** dorer la pilule. **3** *adj*: **~(ed) almond** dragée *f*; **~ basin** *or* **bowl** sucrier *m*; **~ beet** betterave *f* à sucre; **~ cane** canne *f* à sucre; (*fig*) **~ daddy*** vieux protecteur *m*; **~ lump** morceau *m* de sucre; **~ maple** érable *m* à sucre; **~ plantation** plantation *f* de canne à sucre; **~ refinery** raffinerie *f* de sucre; **~ tongs** pince *f* à sucre.
♦ **sugar-free** *or* ♦ **sugarless** *adj* sans sucre.
♦ **sugary** *adj food, drink, taste* sucré; (*fig pej*) *person, voice* mielleux.

suggest [sə'dʒest] *vt* suggérer (*sth to sb* qch à qn; *that* que). **I ~ that we go there** je suggère qu'on y aille; **he ~ed that they should go there** il leur a suggéré d'y aller; **what are you trying to ~?** que voulez-vous dire par là?; **the facts ~ that he did it** les faits semblent indiquer qu'il l'a fait.
♦ **suggestible** *adj* influençable. ♦ **suggestion** *n* (*gen*) suggestion *f*; (*insinuation*) allusion *f*; **have you any ~ions?** avez-vous qch à suggérer?; **there is no ~ion of** il ne saurait être question de; (*trace*) **a ~ion of** un soupçon de. ♦ **suggestive** *adj* suggestif (*also pej*).

suicide ['sʊɪsaɪd] **1** *n* suicide *m*. **it was political ~** cela représentait un véritable suicide politique. **2** *adj*: **~ attempt, ~ bid** tentative *f* de suicide.
♦ **suicidal** *adj* suicidaire; (*fig*) **that would be suicidal!** ce serait un véritable suicide!

suit [su:t] **1** *n* **(a)** (*man's*) costume *m*, complet *m*; (*woman's*) tailleur *m*, ensemble *m*; (*driver's, astronaut's etc*) combinaison *f*. **~ of clothes** tenue *f*; **~ of armour** armure *f* complète. **(b)** (*Jur*) procès *m*. **to bring a ~** intenter un procès (*against sb* à qn). **(c)** (*Cards*) couleur *f*. **long** *or* **strong ~** couleur longue, (*fig*) fort *m*.
2 *vt* (*gen*) convenir à; *[garment, colour, hairstyle]* aller à. **it doesn't ~ me to leave now** cela ne me convient pas *or* ne m'arrange pas de partir maintenant; **it ~ed him perfectly, it just ~ed his book*** cela lui convenait *or* l'arrangeait parfaitement; **~ yourself!*** c'est comme vous voudrez!; **~s me!*** ça me va!; **the part ~ed him perfectly** le rôle lui allait comme un gant *or* était fait pour lui; **to be ~ed to sth** être fait pour qch; **they are well ~ed** ils sont faits l'un pour l'autre; **to ~ the action to the word** joindre le geste à la parole.
♦ **suitability** *n* fait *m* de convenir *etc* (*V 2 above*); *[action, reply, example, choice]* à-propos *m*; **his ~ability for the post** son aptitude *f* au poste.
♦ **suitable** *adj* (*gen*) approprié (*to* à); *climate, food* qui convient; *colour, size* qui va; *place, time* propice; *clothes* approprié, (*socially*) convenable; **the most ~able man for the job** l'homme le plus apte à faire ce travail; **I can't find anything ~able** je ne trouve rien qui me convienne; (*clothes*) je ne trouve rien qui m'aille; **the 25th is the most ~able for me** c'est le 25 qui m'arrange le mieux; **he is not at all a ~able person** ce n'est pas du tout l'homme qu'il faut; **the film isn't ~able for children** ce n'est pas un film pour les enfants.
♦ **suitably** *adv reply* à propos; *explain* de manière adéquate; *thank, apologize* comme il convient (*or* convenait *etc*); *behave* convenablement; **~ably impressed** favorablement impressionné. ♦ **suitcase** *n* valise *f*. ♦ **suiting** *n* (*Tex*) tissu *m* pour complet. ♦ **suitor** *n* soupirant *m*.

suite [swi:t] *n* (*gen*) suite *f*; (*furniture*) mobilier *m*.

sulk [sʌlk] **1** *npl*: **to be in the ~s, to have the ~s** bouder, faire la tête. **2** *vi* bouder. ♦ **sulkily** *adv* en boudant. ♦ **sulkiness** *n* (*state*) bouderie *f*; (*temperament*) caractère *m* boudeur. ♦ **sulky** *adj* boudeur; **to be** *or* **look ~y** faire la tête.

sullen ['sʌlən] *adj* (*gen*) maussade; *comment, silence* renfrogné. ♦ **sullenly** *adv say etc* d'un ton maussade; *promise, agree* de mauvaise grâce.
♦ **sullenness** *n* humeur *f or* aspect *m* maussade.

sulphur, (*US*) **sulfur** ['sʌlfəʳ] *n* soufre *m*.
♦ **sulphate** *n* sulfate *m*. ♦ **sulphide** *n* sulfure *m*.
♦ **sulphonamide** *n* sulfamide *m*. ♦ **sulphuric** *adj* sulfurique. ♦ **sulphurous** *adj* sulfureux.

sultan ['sʌltən] *n* sultan *m*.

sultana [sʌl'tɑ:nə] *n* raisin *m* sec (de Smyrne).

sultry ['sʌltrɪ] *adj heat, atmosphere* étouffant; *weather, air* lourd; (*fig*) *voice, look, smile* sensuel; *person* passionné.

sum [sʌm] **1** *n* (*amount, total*) somme *f* (*of* de). (*Scol: arithmetic*) **~s** le calcul; **~ of money** somme d'argent. **2** *adj*: **~ total** (*amount*) somme *f* totale; (*money*) montant *m* global; (*fig: result*) résultat *m*.
sum up 1 *vi* (*gen*) résumer (*also Jur*). **to ~ up, let me say that ...** en résumé, je voudrais dire que ... . **2** *vt sep* **(a)** (*summarize*) résumer; *facts, arguments* récapituler. **(b)** (*assess*) *person* jauger; *situation* apprécier d'un coup d'œil.
♦ **summarily** *adv* sommairement. ♦ **summarize** *vt* (*gen*) résumer; *facts, arguments* récapituler.
♦ **summary 1** *n* résumé *m*; **a ~mary of the news** les nouvelles *fpl* en bref; **2** *adj* (*all senses*) sommaire. ♦ **summing-up** *n* résumé *m* (*also Jur*).

summer ['sʌməʳ] **1** *n* été *m*. **in ~** en été; **in the ~ of 1977** au cours de l'été 1977. **2** *adj weather, day, activities* d'été, estival. **~ camp** colonie *f* de vacances; **~ holidays** grandes vacances *fpl*; **~ lightning** éclair *m* de chaleur; **~ school** cours *mpl* de vacances; (*by clock*) **~ time** heure *f* d'été; **~ visitor** estivant(e) *m(f)*. ♦ **summerhouse** *n* pavillon *m* (dans un jardin). ♦ **summertime** *n* (*season*) été *m*. ♦ **summery** *adj* d'été.

summit ['sʌmɪt] **1** *n* (*gen, also Pol*) sommet *m*; (*fig*) *[power, honours, glory]* apogée *m*; *[ambition]* summum *m*. **2** *adj* (*Pol*) *meeting* au sommet.

summon ['sʌmən] *vt* (*gen*) appeler, faire venir; (*to meeting*) convoquer (*to* à); (*Jur*) citer, assigner (*as* comme); *help, reinforcements* requérir. **to ~ sb to do** sommer qn de faire; (*Jur*) **to ~ sb to appear** citer *or* assigner qn; **to ~ sb in** appeler qn.
summon up *vt sep one's energy, strength, courage* rassembler (*to do* pour faire); *interest, enthusiasm* faire appel à.
♦ **summons 1** *n* sommation *f* (*also Mil*); (*Jur*) assignation *f*; (*Jur*) **to take out a ~s against sb** faire assigner qn; **2** *vt* (*Jur*) citer, assigner (*à comparaître*).

sump [sʌmp] *n* (*Tech*) puisard *m*; (*Aut*) carter *m*. **~ oil** huile *f* de carter.
sumptuous ['sʌmptjʊəs] *adj* somptueux. ♦ **sumptuously** *adv* somptueusement. ♦ **sumptuousness** *n* somptuosité *f*.
sun [sʌn] **1** *n* soleil *m*. **the ~ is shining** il fait du soleil, le soleil brille; **in the ~** au soleil; **right in the ~** en plein soleil; **a place in the ~** (*lit*) un endroit ensoleillé; (*fig*) une place au soleil; **the ~ is in my eyes** j'ai le soleil dans les yeux; **everything under the ~** tout ce qu'il est possible d'imaginer; **nothing under the ~** rien au monde; **there's no prettier place under the ~** il n'est pas de plus joli coin au monde; **no reason under the ~** pas la moindre raison; **there is nothing new under the ~** il n'y a rien de nouveau sous le soleil.
2 *vt*: **to ~ o.s.** *[lizard, cat]* se chauffer au soleil; *[person]* prendre un bain de soleil.
3 *adj oil, lotion* solaire. **~ umbrella** parasol *m*. ♦ **sunbathe** *vi* prendre un bain *or* des bains de soleil. ♦ **sunbather** *n* personne *f* qui prend un bain de soleil. ♦ **sunbathing** *n* bains *mpl* de soleil. ♦ **sunbeam** *n* rayon *m* de soleil. ♦ **sunbed** *n* fauteuil *m* bain de soleil. ♦ **sunblind** *n* store *m*. ♦ **sunburn** *n* (*tan*) bronzage *m*; (*painful*) coup *m* de soleil. ♦ **sunburned** *or* ♦ **sunburnt** *adj* (*tanned*) bronzé; (*painfully*) brûlé par le soleil; **to get ~burnt** bronzer; prendre un coup de soleil. ♦ **sundial** *n* cadran *m* solaire. ♦ **sundown** *n* coucher *m* du soleil. ♦ **sun-drenched** *adj* inondé de soleil. ♦ **sun-dried** *adj* séché au soleil. ♦ **sunflower** **1** *n* tournesol *m*; **2** *adj oil, seeds* de tournesol. ♦ **sunglasses** *npl* lunettes *fpl* de soleil. ♦ **sun-lamp** *n* lampe *f* à rayons ultraviolets. ♦ **sunlight** *n* (lumière *f* du) soleil *m*; **in the ~light** au soleil, à la lumière du soleil. ♦ **sunlit** *adj* ensoleillé. ♦ **sunlounger** *n* fauteuil *m* bain de soleil. ♦ **sunny** *adj* ensoleillé; (*fig*) *smile, person* épanoui; **it is ~ny** il fait du soleil; (*Met*) **~ny intervals** éclaircies *fpl*; (*Met*) **the outlook is ~ny** on prévoit du soleil; (*fig*) **he always sees the ~ny side of things** il voit tout du bon côté. ♦ **sunrise** *n* lever *m* du soleil. ♦ **sun-roof** *n* toit *m* ouvrant. ♦ **sunset** *n* coucher *m* du soleil. ♦ **sunshade** *n* (*lady's parasol*) ombrelle *f*; (*for eyes*) visière *f*; (*for table, on pram*) parasol *m*; (*in car*) pare-soleil *m inv*. ♦ **sunshine** **1** *n* (lumière *f* du) soleil *m*; **in the ~shine** au soleil; (*Met*) **5 hours of ~shine** 5 heures *fpl* d'ensoleillement; (*iro*) **he's a real ray of ~shine** il est gracieux comme une porte de prison; **2** *adj* (*Aut*) **~shine roof** toit *m* ouvrant. ♦ **sunspecs*** *npl* lunettes *fpl* de soleil. ♦ **sunspot** *n* tache *f* solaire. ♦ **sunstroke** *n* insolation *f*. ♦ **sunsuit** *n* costume *m* bain de soleil. ♦ **suntan** **1** *n* bronzage *m*; **to get a ~tan** bronzer; **2** *adj*: **~tan lotion/oil** lotion *f*/huile *f* solaire. ♦ **suntanned** *adj* bronzé. ♦ **suntrap** *n* coin *m* très ensoleillé. ♦ **sunup*** *n* lever *m* du soleil.
sundae ['sʌndeɪ] *n* dessert *m* à la glace et aux fruits.
Sunday ['sʌndɪ] **1** *n* dimanche *m*; *for phrases V* **Saturday**. **2** *adj clothes, paper* du dimanche; *walk, rest, peace* dominical. **in one's ~ best** en habits du dimanche; **~ school** ≈ catéchisme *m*.
sundry ['sʌndrɪ] **1** *adj* divers, différent. **all and ~** tout le monde. **2** *npl*: **sundries** articles *mpl* divers.
sung [sʌŋ] *ptp of* **sing**.
sunk [sʌŋk] *ptp of* **sink**[1]. ♦ **sunken** *adj ship, rock* submergé; *eyes, cheeks* creux; *garden* en contrebas; *bath* encastré (*au ras du sol*).
super* ['su:pəʳ] *adj* formidable*, sensationnel*.
super... ['su:pəʳ] *pref* super..., sur..., hyper... . **~-salesman** super-vendeur *m*; (*Pol*) **~power** superpuissance *f*; **~fine** surfin; **~-sensitive** hypersensible. ♦ **superabundant** *adj* surabondant. ♦ **supercharged** *adj* surcomprimé. ♦ **supercharger** *n* compresseur *m*. ♦ **superego** *n* sur-moi *m*. ♦ **superhuman** *adj* surhumain. ♦ **superman** *n, pl* **~men** surhomme *m*. ♦ **supermarket** *n* supermarché *m*. ♦ **supernatural** *adj, n* surnaturel (*m*). ♦ **supersonic** *adj* supersonique. ♦ **supersonically** *adv* en supersonique. ♦ **superstructure** *n* superstructure *f*. ♦ **supertanker** *n* pétrolier *m* géant.
superannuate [ˌsu:pə'rænjʊeɪt] *vt* mettre à la retraite. (*fig*) **~d** suranné. ♦ **superannuation** *n* (*pension*) pension *f* de retraite; (*contribution*) cotisations *fpl* pour la pension.
superb [su:'pɜ:b] *adj* superbe. ♦ **superbly** *adv* superbement; **he is ~ly fit** il est dans une forme éblouissante.
supercilious [ˌsu:pə'sɪlɪəs] *adj* hautain. ♦ **superciliously** *adv* d'un air *or* d'un ton hautain. ♦ **superciliousness** *n* hauteur *f*.
superficial [ˌsu:pə'fɪʃəl] *adj* superficiel. ♦ **superficiality** *n* caractère superficiel, manque *m* de profondeur. ♦ **superficially** *adv* superficiellement.
superfluous [sʊ'pɜ:flʊəs] *adj* (*gen*) superflu. **it is ~ to say that ...** inutile de dire que ...; **he felt rather ~*** il se sentait de trop. ♦ **superfluity** *n* surabondance *f* (*of* de). ♦ **superfluously** *adv* d'une manière superflue.
superimpose [ˌsu:pərɪm'pəʊz] *vt* superposer (*on* à). (*Cine, Phot*) **~d** en surimpression.
superintend [ˌsu:pərɪn'tend] *vt work, shop, department* diriger; *exam* surveiller; *production* contrôler; *vote-counting* présider à. ♦ **superintendence** *n* direction *f*; surveillance *f*; contrôle *m*. ♦ **superintendent** *n [institution, orphanage]* directeur *m*, -trice *f*; *[department]* chef *m*; (*Police*) ≈ commissaire *m* (de police).
superior [sʊ'pɪərɪəʳ] **1** *adj* supérieur (*to* à); *product, goods* de qualité supérieure; (*pej: smug*) *person* suffisant; *air, smile* de supériorité, suffisant. **he felt rather ~** il a éprouvé un certain sentiment de supériorité. **2** *n* supérieur(e) *m(f)*. ♦ **superiority** **1** *n* supériorité *f* (*to, over* par rapport à); **2** *adj*: **~ity complex** complexe *m* de supériorité.
superlative [sʊ'pɜ:lətɪv] **1** *adj quality, achievement* sans pareil; *happiness, indifference* suprême; (*Gram*) superlatif. **2** *n* (*Gram*) superlatif *m*. **in the ~** au superlatif. ♦ **superlatively** *adv* extrêmement.
supernumerary [ˌsu:pə'nju:mərərɪ] *adj, n* surnuméraire (*mf*).
supersede [ˌsu:pə'si:d] *vt belief, object, order* remplacer; *person* supplanter. **~d method** méthode périmée.
superstition [ˌsu:pə'stɪʃən] *n* superstition *f*. ♦ **superstitious** *adj* superstitieux. ♦ **superstitiously** *adv* superstitieusement.
supervise ['su:pəvaɪz] *vt* (*gen*) surveiller; (*Univ*) *research* diriger. ♦ **supervision** *n* surveillance *f*. ♦ **supervisor** *n* (*gen*) surveillant(e) *m(f)*; (*Comm*) chef *m* de rayon; (*Univ: for studies*) directeur *m*, -trice *f* de thèse. ♦ **supervisory** *adj duty* de surveillance.
supine ['su:paɪn] *adj* étendu sur le dos.
supper ['sʌpəʳ] *n* (*main meal*) dîner *m*; (*after theatre etc*) souper *m*; (*snack*) collation *f*. **to have ~** dîner (*or* souper); (*Rel*) **the Last S~** la Cène. ♦ **suppertime** *n* l'heure *f* du dîner; **at ~time** au dîner.
supplant [sə'plɑ:nt] *vt* supplanter.
supple ['sʌpl] *adj* souple. **to become ~(r)** s'assouplir. ♦ **suppleness** *n* souplesse *f*. ♦ **supply**[1] ['sʌplɪ] *adv* avec souplesse.
supplement ['sʌplɪmənt] **1** *n* supplément *m* (*to* à). **2** [ˌsʌplɪ'ment] *vt income* augmenter (*by doing* en faisant); *book, information* ajouter à, compléter. ♦ **supplementary** *adj* supplémentaire; (*Admin*) **~ary benefit** allocation *f* supplémentaire.
supplication [ˌsʌplɪ'keɪʃən] *n* supplication *f*.
supply[2] [sə'plaɪ] **1** *n* **(a)** (*amount, stock*) provision

f, réserve *f*, stock *m* (*also Comm*). **to get** *or* **lay in a ~ of** faire des provisions de; **to get in a fresh ~ of sth** se réapprovisionner en qch; **supplies** (*gen*) provisions, réserves; (*food*) vivres *mpl*; (*Mil*) approvisionnements *mpl*; **electrical supplies** matériel *m* électrique; **office supplies** fournitures *fpl* de bureau. **(b)** alimentation *f*. **the ~ of fuel to the engine** l'alimentation du moteur en combustible; **the electricity/gas ~** l'alimentation en électricité/gaz; (*Econ*) **~ and demand** l'offre et la demande.

2 *adj train, truck, ship* ravitailleur; *pharmacist etc* intérimaire. **~ teacher** remplaçant(e) *m(f)*.

3 *vt* **(a)** (*gen*) fournir (*sth to sb* qch à qn; *sb with goods* qn en marchandises; *sb with help/information* de l'aide/des renseignements à qn); (*Comm*) fournir, approvisionner (*with* en, de). **to ~ electricity/gas/water to the town** alimenter la ville en électricité/gaz/eau; **they kept us supplied with milk** grâce à eux nous n'avons jamais manqué de lait; **a battery is not supplied with the torch** une pile n'est pas livrée avec la torche. **(b)** (*make good*) *need, deficiency* suppléer à; *sb's needs* subvenir à; *loss* compenser.

♦ **supplier** *n* fournisseur *m*.

support [sə'pɔːt] **1** *n* **(a)** appui *m*, soutien *m*. **he leaned on me for ~** il s'est appuyé sur moi, (*fig*) il a cherché mon appui; **to give ~ to sb/sth** soutenir qn/qch; (*fig*) **the proposal got no ~** personne n'a parlé en faveur de la proposition; **in ~ of the motion** en faveur de la motion; **in ~ of his theory/claim** à l'appui de sa théorie/revendication; **to give** *or* **lend one's ~ to** prêter son appui à; **that lends ~ to it** ceci le corrobore; **they stopped work in ~** ils ont cessé le travail par solidarité; **he has no visible means of ~** il n'a pas de moyens d'existence connus. **(b)** (*object*) (*gen*) appui *m*; (*Constr, Tech*) support *m*, soutien *m*; (*fig: moral, financial etc*) soutien; (*US Econ: subsidy*) subvention *f*. **the sole ~ of his family** le seul soutien de sa famille; **he has been a great ~ to me** il a été pour moi un soutien précieux.

2 *adj* (*Mil etc*) *troops, vessel* de soutien.

3 *vt* **(a)** (*hold up*) *[pillar, beam]* soutenir, supporter; *[bridge]* porter; *[person]* soutenir. **the elements necessary to ~ life** les éléments nécessaires à l'entretien de la vie. **(b)** (*uphold*) (*gen*) être en faveur de, être partisan de; *candidate, action, protest* soutenir; *team* être supporter de. **the socialists will ~ it** les socialistes seront *or* voteront pour; **I cannot ~ what you are doing** je ne peux pas approuver ce que vous faites; **a subsidy to ~ the price of beef** une subvention pour maintenir le prix du bœuf; (*Ftbl*) **he ~s Celtic** c'est un supporter du Celtic. **(c)** (*financially*) subvenir aux besoins de. **he has a wife and 3 children to ~** il doit subvenir aux besoins de sa femme et de ses 3 enfants; **to ~ o.s.** subvenir à ses propres besoins; **the school is ~ed by money from ...** l'école reçoit une aide financière de ... . **(d)** (*endure*) supporter, tolérer.

♦ **supportable** *adj* supportable, tolérable. ♦ **supporter** *n [party]* partisan *m*; *[cause, opinion]* adepte *mf*, partisan; (*Sport*) supporter *m*. ♦ **supporting** *adj wall* de soutènement; *film* qui passe en premier; (*Theat*) *role* secondaire; *actor* qui a un rôle secondaire; **~ing cast** partenaires *mpl*.

suppose [sə'pəʊz] *vt* **(a)** (*imagine*) supposer (*that* que + *subj*); (*assume*) supposer (*that* que + *indic*). **~ he doesn't come?** et s'il ne vient pas?; **you'll come, I ~?** vous viendrez, je suppose?; (*as suggestion*) **~** *or* **supposing we go for a walk?** et si nous allions nous promener?; **even supposing that** à supposer même que + *subj*; **always supposing that** en supposant que + *subj*. **(b)** (*believe*) supposer, penser, imaginer (*that* que). **what do you ~ he wants?** à votre avis, que peut-il bien vouloir?; **he is generally ~d to be rich** on dit qu'il est riche; **I don't ~ he'll agree** je suppose qu'il ne sera pas d'accord, je ne pense pas qu'il soit d'accord; **I ~ so** probablement; **I ~ not** je ne (le) pense pas, probablement pas. **(c)** (*ought*) **to be ~d to do sth** être censé faire qch, devoir faire qch; **he isn't ~d to know** il n'est pas censé le savoir; **you're not ~d to do that** il ne vous est pas permis de faire cela. ♦ **supposed** *adj* (*presumed*) présumé, supposé; (*so-called*) prétendu. ♦ **supposedly** *adv* soi-disant, à ce que l'on suppose (*or* supposait *etc*). ♦ **supposition** *n* supposition *f*; **on the supposition that ...** à supposer que ... + *subj*.

suppository [sə'pɒzɪtərɪ] *n* suppositoire *m*.

suppress [sə'pres] *vt* (*gen*) supprimer; *revolt, one's feelings* réprimer; *yawn, scandal* étouffer; *facts, truth* dissimuler; *publication* interdire; (*Psych*) refouler; (*Elec, Rad etc*) éliminer; (*: *silence*) *heckler etc* faire taire. **to ~ a cough/sneeze** *etc* se retenir de tousser/d'éternuer *etc*. ♦ **suppression** *n* suppression *f*; répression *f*; étouffement *m*; dissimulation *f*; interdiction *f*; refoulement *m*; élimination *f*. ♦ **suppressor** *n* dispositif *m* antiparasite.

suppurate ['sʌpjʊəreɪt] *vi* suppurer. ♦ **suppuration** *n* suppuration *f*.

supra... ['suːprə] *pref* supra... . **~national** supranational.

supreme [sʊ'priːm] *adj* (*all senses*) suprême. **to make the ~ sacrifice** faire le sacrifice de sa vie. ♦ **supremacy** *n* suprématie *f* (*over* sur). ♦ **supremo*** *n* grand patron* *m*.

surcharge ['sɜːtʃɑːdʒ] **1** *n* (*gen*) surcharge *f*; (*tax*) surtaxe *f*. **2** [sɜː'tʃɑːdʒ] *vt* surcharger; surtaxer.

sure [ʃʊəʳ] **1** *adj* (*gen*) sûr (*of* de). **it is ~ that she will come, she is ~ to come** il est sûr *or* certain qu'elle viendra; **it is not ~ that she will come, she is not ~ to come** il n'est pas sûr *or* certain qu'elle vienne; **it's ~ to rain** il va pleuvoir à coup sûr; **be ~ to tell me** ne manquez pas de me le dire; **you're ~ of a good meal** un bon repas vous est assuré; **he's ~ of success** *or* **of succeeding** *or* **to succeed** il est sûr *or* certain de réussir; **to be ~ of sb** être sûr de qn; **to make ~ of sth** s'assurer de qch; **get a ticket and make ~** prenez un billet pour plus de sûreté; **I've made ~ of having enough coffee** j'ai veillé à ce qu'il y ait assez de café; **~ thing!*** oui, bien sûr!; (*excl*) **well, to be ~!*** bien ça alors!; **he'll leave for ~** il partira sans aucun doute; **I'll find out for ~** je me renseignerai pour savoir exactement ce qu'il en est; **do you know for ~?** êtes-vous absolument certain?; **I'll do it for ~** je le ferai sans faute; **I'm ~ I've seen him** je suis sûr de l'avoir vu; **I'm ~ he'll help us** je suis sûr qu'il nous aidera; **I'm not ~** je ne suis pas sûr (*that* que + *subj*); **I'm not ~ how/why** *etc* je ne sais pas très bien comment/pourquoi *etc*; **I'm not ~ (if) he can** je ne suis pas sûr qu'il puisse; **I'm ~ I didn't mean to** je ne l'ai vraiment pas fait exprès; **~ of o.s.** sûr de soi.

2 *adv*: **and ~ enough he did arrive** et effectivement *or* en effet il est arrivé; **~ enough!** assurément!; **as ~ as my name's Smith** aussi sûr que je m'appelle Smith; **as ~ as fate, as ~ as anything, as ~ as eggs is eggs*** aussi sûr que deux et deux font quatre; (*: *esp US*) **he can ~ play the piano** il sait drôlement* bien jouer du piano.

♦ **sure-fire*** *adj* certain, infaillible. ♦ **surefooted** *adj* au pied sûr. ♦ **surely** *adv* **(a)** (*expressing confidence: assuredly*) sûrement, certainement; (*expressing incredulity*) tout de même; **~ly he didn't say that!** il n'a pas pu dire ça, tout de même!; **there is ~ly some mistake** il doit sûrement *or* certainement y avoir quelque erreur; **that's ~ly not true** ça ne peut pas être vrai; **~ly not!** pas possible!; (*US: with pleasure*) **~ly!** bien volontiers!; **(b) slowly but ~ly** lentement mais sûrement. ♦ **sureness** *n* (*certainty*) certitude *f*; *[judgment, method, footing]* sûreté *f*; *[aim, shot]* justesse *f*. ♦ **surety** *n* (*Jur*) caution *f*; **to stand ~ty for sb** se porter caution pour qn.

surf [sɜːf] **1** *n* (*waves*) vague *f* déferlante; (*foam*) écume *f*. **2** *vi*: **to go ~ing** surfer. ♦ **surfboard 1** *n* planche *f* de surf; **2** *vi* surfer. ♦ **surfboarder** *or* ♦ **surfrider** *n* surfeur *m*, -euse *f*. ♦ **surfboarding** *or* ♦ **surfriding** *n* surf *m*. ♦ **surf-boat** *n* surf-boat *m*. ♦ **surfing** *n* surf *m*.

surface [ˈsɜːfɪs] **1** *n* (*gen*) surface *f*; (*side: of solid*) côté *m*, face *f*. *[sea, lake etc]* **under the ~** sous l'eau; **he rose to the ~** il est remonté à la surface; **on the ~** (*Naut*) en surface; (*Min: also* **at the ~**) à la surface; (*fig*) à première vue; **on the ~ of the table** sur la surface de la table; **his faults are all on the ~** il a des défauts, mais il a bon fond; **the road ~** la chaussée. **2** *adj tension* superficiel (*also fig*); (*Naut*) *vessel etc* de surface; (*Min*) *work* à la surface. **by ~ mail** par voie de terre. **3** *vt road* revêtir (*with* de). **4** *vi [diver, whale]* remonter à la surface; *[submarine]* faire surface; (**fig*) (*after absence*) réapparaître; (*after hard work*) faire surface. ♦ **surface-to-air** *adj* (*Mil*) sol-air *inv*.

surfeit [ˈsɜːfɪt] *n* excès *m* (*of* de). **to have a ~ of** avoir une indigestion de (*fig*).

surge [sɜːdʒ] **1** *n [rage, enthusiasm]* vague *f*. **the ~ of the sea** la houle; **he felt a ~ of anger** il a senti la colère monter en lui. **2** *vi* **(a)** *[waves]* s'enfler; *[anger]* monter (*within sb* en qn). **the sea ~d against the rocks** la houle battait les rochers; (*Elec*) **the power ~d suddenly** il y a eu une brusque surtension de courant; **the blood ~d to his cheeks** le sang lui est monté au visage. **(b)** *[crowd, vehicles etc]* déferler. **to ~ in/out** *etc* entrer/sortir *etc* à flots; **they ~d round the car** ils se pressaient autour de la voiture; **they ~d forward** ils se sont lancés en avant. ♦ **surging** *adj sea* houleux; *crowd* déferlant.

surgeon [ˈsɜːdʒən] *n* chirurgien *m*. ♦ **surgery 1** *n* (*gen*) chirurgie *f*; (*consulting room*) cabinet *m* (de consultation); (*interview*) consultation *f*; **come to the surgery** venez à la consultation; **when is his surgery?** à quelle heure sont ses consultations?; **during his surgery** pendant ses heures de consultation; **2** *adj*: **surgery hours** heures *fpl* de consultation. ♦ **surgical** *adj* chirurgical; **surgical cotton** coton *m* hydrophile; **surgical dressing** pansement *m*; **surgical spirit** alcool *m* à 90 (degrés).

surly [ˈsɜːlɪ] *adj* revêche, maussade. ♦ **surliness** *n* caractère *m or* air *m* revêche.

surmise [ˈsɜːmaɪz] **1** *n* conjecture *f*. **2** [sɜːˈmaɪz] *vt* conjecturer (*from sth* d'après qch; *that* que).

surmount [sɜːˈmaʊnt] *vt* surmonter.

surname [ˈsɜːneɪm] *n* nom *m* de famille.

surpass [sɜːˈpɑːs] *vt person* surpasser (*in* en); *hopes* dépasser.

surplice [ˈsɜːplɪs] *n* surplis *m*.

surplus [ˈsɜːpləs] **1** *n* (*gen*) surplus *m*; (*Fin*) boni *m*, excédent *m*. **2** *adj* (*gen*) en surplus; (*Fin*) de boni, excédentaire. **it is ~ to requirements** cela excède nos besoins; *[book, document etc]* **~ copies** exemplaires *mpl* de passe; **~ stock** surplus *mpl*; **~ wheat** surplus *or* excédent *m* de blé; **his ~ energy** son surcroît d'énergie; **~ store** magasin *m* de surplus.

surprise [səˈpraɪz] **1** *n* (*gen*) surprise *f*, étonnement *m*; (*event etc*) surprise. **much to my ~** à ma grande surprise, à mon grand étonnement; **to take by ~** *person* prendre au dépourvu; (*Mil*) *fort, town* prendre par surprise; **a look of ~** un regard surpris; **to give sb a ~** faire une surprise à qn; **nasty ~** mauvaise surprise; **it came as a ~ to me to learn that ...** j'ai eu la surprise d'apprendre que ... .

2 *adj* (*gen*) inattendu; *attack* par surprise.

3 *vt* **(a)** (*astonish*) surprendre, étonner. **he was ~d to hear that ...** il a été surpris *or* étonné d'apprendre que ...; **I shouldn't be ~d if it snowed** cela ne m'étonnerait pas qu'il neige (*subj*); **don't be ~d if he refuses** ne soyez pas étonné *or* surpris s'il refuse; **I'm ~d at his ignorance** son ignorance me surprend; **I'm ~d at you!** cela me surprend de votre part!; **I'm ~d he agreed** j'ai été étonné *or* surpris qu'il accepte (*subj*); (*iro*) **go on, ~ me!** allez, étonne-moi!; **he ~d me into agreeing to do it** j'ai été tellement surpris que j'ai accepté de le faire. **(b)** (*catch unawares*) surprendre.

♦ **surprised** *adj* surpris, étonné. ♦ **surprising** *adj* surprenant, étonnant; **it is surprising that** il est surprenant *or* étonnant que + *subj*. ♦ **surprisingly** *adv big, sad etc* étonnamment; **you look surprisingly cheerful for sb who ...** vous m'avez l'air de bien bonne humeur pour qn qui ...; **surprisingly enough, ...** chose étonnante, ...; **not surprisingly he didn't come** comme on pouvait s'y attendre, il n'est pas venu.

surrealism [səˈrɪəlɪzəm] *n* surréalisme *m*. ♦ **surrealist** *adj, n* surréaliste (*mf*). ♦ **surrealistic** *adj* surréaliste.

surrender [səˈrendəʳ] **1** *vi* se rendre (*to* à). **to ~ to the police** se livrer à la police. **2** *vt* (*Mil*) *town, hill* livrer (*to* à); *firearms* rendre (*to* à); *stolen property, documents* remettre (*to* à); *lease* céder; *one's rights, claims, liberty* renoncer à; *hopes* abandonner. **3** *n* (*Mil etc*) reddition *f* (*to* à). **no ~!** on ne se rend pas!

surreptitious [ˌsʌrəpˈtɪʃəs] *adj entry, removal* subreptice; *movement, gesture* furtif. ♦ **surreptitiously** *adv* subrepticement; furtivement.

surround [səˈraʊnd] **1** *vt* entourer; (*totally*) encercler. **~ed by** entouré de; (*Police etc*) **you are ~ed** vous êtes encerclé. **2** *n* bordure *f*. ♦ **surrounding 1** *adj* environnant; **the ~ing countryside** les environs *mpl*; **2** *npl*: **~ings** *[town]* environs *mpl*; (*setting*) cadre *m*; **in their natural ~ings** dans leur cadre naturel.

surtax [ˈsɜːtæks] *n* tranche *f* supérieure de l'impôt sur le revenu.

surveillance [sɜːˈveɪləns] *n* surveillance *f*. **to keep sb under ~** garder qn à vue.

survey [ˈsɜːveɪ] **1** *n* **(a)** (*comprehensive view*) *[prospects, development etc]* vue *f* d'ensemble (*of* de). **he gave a general ~ of the situation** il a fait un tour d'horizon de la situation. **(b)** (*study*) enquête *f* (*of* sur). **to carry out a ~ of** enquêter sur; **~ of public opinion** sondage *m* d'opinion. **(c)** (*Surveying: of land, coast etc*) levé *m*; (*in house-buying*) visite *f* d'expert; (*report*) expertise *f*. **2** *adj*: **~ ship** bateau *m* hydrographique. **3** [sɜːˈveɪ] *vt* **(a)** (*look at*) (*gen*) regarder; *view, crowd* embrasser du regard; *prospects, trends* passer en revue. **(b)** (*study*) *ground etc* inspecter; *needs, prospects* enquêter sur. **(c)** *site, land* faire le levé de; *house, building* inspecter; *country, coast* faire le levé topographique de; *seas* faire le levé hydrographique de.

♦ **surveying** *n* arpentage *m*. ♦ **surveyor** *n [property, buildings etc]* expert *m*; *[land, site]* arpenteur *m* géomètre; *[country, coastline]* topographe *mf*; *[seas]* hydrographe *mf*.

survive [səˈvaɪv] **1** *vi* (*gen*) survivre. **only three volumes ~** il ne reste *or* il ne subsiste plus que trois tomes; (*iro*) **you'll ~!** vous n'en mourrez pas! **2** *vt* (*gen*) survivre à; *injury, disease* réchapper de. ♦ **survival 1** *n* (*gen*) survie *f*; **the survival of the fittest** la persistance du plus apte; **it's the survival of an old law** c'est la survivance d'une vieille loi; **2** *adj*: **survival course/kit** cours *m*/kit *m* de survie. ♦ **survivor** *n* survivant(e) *m(f)*.

sus [sʌs] *adj*: **~ law** garde *f* à vue préventive.

susceptible [səˈseptəbl] *adj* (*sensitive*) sensible; (*touchy*) susceptible. **to be ~ to** (*gen*) être sensible à; *suggestion, sb's influence* être ouvert à; (*Med*) *disease* être prédisposé à; *treatment* répondre à; ~ **of** susceptible de. ♦ **susceptibility** *n* vive sensibilité *f*; susceptibilité *f*; (*Med*) prédisposition *f* (*to* à).

suspect ['sʌspekt] **1** *n* suspect(e) *m(f)*. **2** *adj evidence, act* suspect. **3** [səs'pekt] *vt* (*gen*) soupçonner (*that* que; *of a crime* d'un crime; *of doing* de faire *or* d'avoir fait); *ambush, swindle* flairer, soupçonner; (*have doubts about*) *sb's motives etc* suspecter, douter de. **I ~ed as much** je m'en doutais; **he'll come, I ~** il viendra, j'imagine.

suspend [səs'pend] *vt* **(a)** (*hang*) suspendre (*from* à). **(b)** (*stop: gen*) suspendre; *licence, permission* retirer provisoirement; *bus service* interrompre provisoirement; *employee* suspendre (*from* de); *student, pupil* renvoyer temporairement. (*Jur*) **he received a ~ed sentence of 6 months** il a été condamné à 6 mois de prison avec sursis; (*fig*) **to be in a state of ~ed animation** ne donner aucun signe de vie. ♦ **suspender 1** *n*: **~ers** (*Brit*) (*for stockings*) jarretelles *fpl*; (*for socks*) fixe-chaussettes *mpl*; (*US*) bretelles *fpl*; **2** *adj* (*Brit*) **~er belt** porte-jarretelles *m inv*. ♦ **suspense** *n* incertitude *f*; (*in book, film etc*) suspense *m*; **we waited in great suspense** nous avons attendu haletants; **to keep sb in suspense** tenir qn en suspens; **to put sb out of his suspense** mettre fin à l'incertitude de qn; **novel of suspense** roman *m* à suspense; **the suspense is killing me!*** ce suspense me tue! (*also iro*). ♦ **suspension 1** *n* suspension *f* (*also Aut*); retrait *m* provisoire; interruption *f* provisoire; **2** *adj bridge* suspendu.

suspicion [səs'pɪʃən] *n* soupçon *m*. **laden with ~** chargé de soupçons; **above ~** au-dessus de tout soupçon; **under ~** considéré comme suspect; **he was regarded with ~** on s'est montré soupçonneux à son égard; (*Jur*) **to arrest on ~** arrêter sur des présomptions; **on ~ of murder** sur présomption de meurtre; **I had a ~ that ...** je soupçonnais que ...; **I had no ~ that ...** je ne me doutais pas du tout que ...; **I had (my) ~s about that** j'avais mes doutes là-dessus. ♦ **suspicious** *adj* **(a)** (*feeling ~*) soupçonneux, méfiant; **to be suspicious about sb/sth** avoir des soupçons à l'égard de qn/quant à qch; **to be suspicious of** se méfier de; **(b)** (*causing ~*: **suspicious-looking**) *person, vehicle* suspect; *move, action* louche. ♦ **suspiciously** *adv examine, glance, ask etc* avec méfiance; *behave, run away etc* d'une manière suspecte *or* louche; **it looks suspiciously like measles** ça m'a tout l'air d'être la rougeole; **it sounds suspiciously as though ...** ça m'a tout l'air de signifier que ...; **he arrived suspiciously early** il me paraît suspect qu'il soit arrivé si tôt. ♦ **suspiciousness** *n* caractère *m* soupçonneux *or* suspect.

suss* [sʌs] *vt* (*Brit*) **to ~ out** découvrir.

sustain [səs'teɪn] *vt* **(a)** *weight, beam etc* supporter; *body* donner des forces à; *life* maintenir; (*Mus*) *note* tenir; *effort, role, theory* soutenir; *pretence* poursuivre. (*Jur*) **objection ~ed** ≃ objection accordée. **(b)** (*suffer*) *attack, damage* subir; *loss* éprouver; *injury* recevoir. ♦ **sustained** *adj effort, applause* prolongé. ♦ **sustaining** *adj food* nourrissant. ♦ **sustenance** *n* (*food*) nourriture *f*; (*means of livelihood*) moyens *mpl* de subsistance; **there's not much sustenance in it** cela n'est pas très nourrissant.

swab [swɒb] **1** *n* (*mop, cloth*) serpillière *f*; (*Med: cotton wool etc*) tampon *m*; (*Med: specimen*) prélèvement *m* (*of* dans). **2** *vt* (**~ down**) *floor etc* nettoyer, essuyer; (**~ out**) *wound* tamponner.

swagger ['swægəʳ] **1** *n*: **to walk with a ~** marcher d'un air fanfaron. **2** *vi*: **to ~ about/in** *etc* se promener/entrer *etc* d'un air fanfaron. ♦ **swaggering 1** *adj gait* assuré; *person, look, gesture* fanfaron; **2** *n* air *m* fanfaron.

swallow¹ ['swɒləʊ] **1** *n* (*bird*) hirondelle *f*. **2** *adj*: **~ dive** saut *m* de l'ange. ♦ **swallowtail butterfly** *n* machaon *m*.

swallow² ['swɒləʊ] **1** *n* (*act*) avalement *m*; (*amount*) gorgée *f*. **at one ~** d'un seul coup. **2** *vi* avaler. (*emotionally*) **he ~ed hard** sa gorge s'est serrée. **3** *vt food, story, insult* avaler; *anger, pride* ravaler. (*fig*) **to ~ the bait** se laisser prendre à l'appât; **that's hard to ~** c'est dur à avaler; **they ~ed it whole** ils ont tout avalé.

swallow up *vt sep* (*fig*) engloutir. **he was ~ed up in the crowd** il a disparu dans la foule.

swam [swæm] *pret of* **swim**.

swamp [swɒmp] **1** *n* marais *m*, marécage *m*. **2** *adj*: **~ fever** paludisme *m*. **3** *vt* (*flood*) inonder; *boat* emplir d'eau; (*fig*) submerger (*with* de). (*fig*) **~ed with requests/letters** submergé de requêtes/lettres; **~ed* with work** débordé de travail; (*Ftbl etc*) **towards the end of the game they ~ed us** vers la fin de la partie ils ont fait le jeu. ♦ **swampland** *n* marécages *mpl*. ♦ **swampy** *adj* marécageux.

swan [swɒn] **1** *n* cygne *m*. **2** *adj* (*US*) **~ dive** saut *m* de l'ange; (*fig*) **~ song** chant *m* du cygne. **3** *vi* (*) **he ~ned off to London** il est parti à Londres sans s'en faire*; **he's ~ning around in Paris** il se balade dans Paris sans s'en faire*. ♦ **swansdown** *n* duvet *m* de cygne.

swank* [swæŋk] **1** *n* **(a)** esbroufe* *f*. **out of ~** pour faire de l'esbroufe*. **(b)** (*person*) esbroufeur* *m*, -euse* *f*. **2** *vi* chercher à en mettre plein la vue*. **to ~ about sth** se vanter de qch. ♦ **swanky*** *adj* qui en met plein la vue*.

swap* [swɒp] **1** *n* troc *m*, échange *m*. **it's a fair ~** ça se vaut; (*stamps etc*) **~s** doubles *mpl*. **2** *vt* échanger (*A for B* A contre B; *with sb* avec qn). **let's ~ places** changeons de place (l'un avec l'autre); **I'll ~ you!** tu veux échanger avec moi? **3** *vi* échanger.

swarm¹ [swɔːm] **1** *n [bees, flying insects]* essaim *m*; *[ants, crawling insects]* grouillement *m*; *[people]* nuée *f*. (*fig*) **in ~s** en masse. **2** *vi [bees]* essaimer. *[crawling insects]* **to ~ about** grouiller; *[people]* **to ~ in/out** *etc* entrer/sortir *etc* en masse; *[ground, town]* **to ~ with** grouiller de.

swarm² [swɔːm] *vt* (**~ up**) *tree* grimper à toute vitesse à.

swarthy ['swɔːðɪ] *adj* basané. ♦ **swarthiness** *n* teint *m* basané.

swastika ['swɒstɪkə] *n* swastika *m*; (*Nazi*) croix *f* gammée.

swat [swɒt] **1** *vt* écraser. **2** *n* (**fly ~**, *also* **~ter**) tapette *f*.

swathe [sweɪð] *vt* emmailloter (*in bandages* de bandages), envelopper (*in blankets* dans des couvertures).

sway [sweɪ] **1** *n* **(a)** (*motion*) (*gen*) oscillation *f*; *[boat]* balancement *m*. **(b)** (*liter*) emprise *f* (*over* sur). **under his ~** sous son emprise. **2** *vi* (*gen*) osciller, se balancer; *[tower block, bridge]* osciller; *[train]* tanguer; *[person]* tanguer, osciller; (*fig: vacillate*) balancer (*between* entre). **3** *vt* **(a)** *hanging object* balancer, faire osciller; *hips* rouler; *[wind, waves]* balancer. **(b)** (*influence*) influencer.

swear [swɛəʳ] *pret* **swore**, *ptp* **sworn 1** *vt* jurer (*on sth* sur qch; *that* que; *to do* de faire). **to ~ an oath** (*solemnly*) prêter serment; (*curse*) lâcher un juron; **I could have sworn he touched it** j'aurais juré qu'il l'avait touché; **to ~ sb to secrecy** faire jurer le secret à qn. **2** *vi* **(a)** jurer. **to ~ to the truth of sth** jurer que qch est vrai; **I wouldn't ~ to it** je n'en jurerais pas; (*fig*) **he ~s by vitamin C tablets** il ne jure que par les vitamines C. **(b)** (*curse*) jurer (*at* contre, après). **to ~ like a trooper** jurer comme un charretier.

swear in *vt sep jury etc* faire prêter serment à. ♦ **swearword** *n* juron *m*, gros mot.

sweat [swet] **1** *n* sueur *f*. **by the ~ of his brow** à la sueur de son front; **to be dripping with ~** ruisseler de sueur; (*fig*) **to be in a cold ~*** avoir des sueurs froides; **it was an awful ~*** on en a eu du mal!; **no ~!**‡ pas de problème! **2** *vi* *[person, animal, cheese]* suer (*with, from* de); *[walls]* suinter. **to ~ like a bull** suer comme un bœuf; **he was ~ing profusely/over his essay*** il suait à grosses gouttes/sur sa dissertation. **3** *vt* **(a)** (*fig*) *workers* exploiter. **~ed labour** main-d'œuvre *f* exploitée. **(b) to ~ blood*** (*work hard*) suer sang et eau (*over sth* sur qch); (*be anxious*) avoir des sueurs froides.

sweat out* *vt sep* (*fig*) **you'll have to ~ it out** il faudra t'armer de patience; **they left him to ~ it out** ils n'ont rien fait pour l'aider.

♦ **sweatband** *n* (*Sport*) bandeau *m*. ♦ **sweater** *n* pullover *m*, pull* *m*. ♦ **sweating** *n* transpiration *f*; (*Med*) sudation *f*; *[wall]* suintement *m*. ♦ **sweatshirt** *n* sweat-shirt *m*. ♦ **sweat-shop** *n* atelier *m* où les ouvriers sont exploités. ♦ **sweaty** *adj body* en sueur; *feet* qui suent; *hand* moite; *smell* de sueur; *sock* mouillé de sueur.

swede [swi:d] *n* rutabaga *m*.

Sweden ['swi:dn] *n* Suède *f*. ♦ **Swede** *n* Suédois(e) *m(f)*. ♦ **Swedish 1** *adj* suédois; **2** *n* suédois *m*; **the Swedish** les Suédois *mpl*.

sweep [swi:p] (*vb: pret, ptp* **swept**) **1** *n* **(a)** (**chimney ~**) ramoneur *m*. **(b)** (*movement*) *[arm]* grand geste *m*; *[sword, net]* grand coup *m*; *[scythe]* mouvement *m* circulaire; *[lighthouse etc beam]* trajectoire *f*; (*fig*) *[progress, events]* marche *f*. **with one ~** d'un seul coup; **with a ~ of his arm** d'un geste large; **the police made a ~ of the district** la police a ratissé le quartier; **a wide ~ of meadowland** une vaste étendue de prairie.

2 *vt room, street, snow etc* balayer; *chimney* ramoner; *channel, mines* draguer. (*Naut*) **to ~ sth clean of mines** déminer qch; **to ~ the horizon** (*with binoculars*) parcourir l'horizon; *[lighthouse beam]* balayer l'horizon; **his glance swept the room** il a parcouru la pièce du regard; **a wave of indignation swept the city** une vague d'indignation a déferlé sur la ville; **he swept the rubbish off the pavement** il a enlevé les ordures du trottoir d'un coup de balai; (*fig*) **to ~ sth under the carpet** tirer le rideau sur qch; **to ~ sth on to the floor** faire tomber qch par terre d'un geste large; (*fig*) **to ~ everything before one, to ~ the board** remporter un succès complet; **they swept the board at the election** ils ont remporté l'élection haut la main; **the crowd swept him into the square** la foule l'a emporté sur la place; **the wave swept him overboard** la vague l'a jeté par-dessus bord; **the current swept the boat downstream** le courant a emporté le bateau; **the water swept him off his feet** le courant lui a fait perdre pied; (*fig*) **to be swept off one's feet** être enthousiasmé (*by* par); (*fig*) **he swept her off her feet** elle a eu le coup de foudre pour lui.

3 *vi*: **to ~ in/out/along** *etc* entrer/sortir/avancer *etc* (*swiftly*) rapidement *or* (*impressively*) majestueusement *or* (*angrily*) avec furie; **the car swept round the corner** la voiture a pris le virage comme un bolide; **the rain swept across the plain** la pluie a balayé la plaine; **panic swept through the city** la panique s'est emparée de la ville; **the Alps ~ down to the coast** les Alpes descendent majestueusement vers la côte.

sweep along *vt sep [crowd, flood]* emporter.

sweep aside *vt sep object, person, suggestion* repousser; *difficulty, obstacle* écarter.

sweep away *vt sep dust, snow, rubbish* balayer; *[crowd, current, gale]* entraîner.

sweep out *vt sep* balayer.

sweep up 1 *vi* balayer. **2** *vt sep leaves, dust etc* balayer; (*pick up*) *books etc* ramasser d'un geste brusque.

♦ **sweeper** *n* (*person*) balayeur *m*; (*machine*) balayeuse *f*; (*carpet ~er*) balai *m* mécanique; (*vacuum cleaner*) aspirateur *m*. ♦ **sweeping** *adj movement, gesture* large; *bow, curtsy* profond; *glance* circulaire; *change, reorganization* radical; *reduction* considérable; *price cut* imbattable; **~ing statement** *or* **generalization** généralisation *f* hâtive; **that's pretty ~ing!** c'est beaucoup dire! ♦ **sweepstake** *n* sweepstake *m*.

sweet [swi:t] **1** *adj* **(a)** (*not sour*) *apple, cider, wine* doux (*f* douce); *tea, biscuit, taste* sucré. **to have a ~ tooth** être friand de sucreries; **I love ~ things** j'aime les sucreries *fpl*; (*Culin*) **~ and sour** aigre-doux; **a sickly ~ smell** une odeur fétide. **(b)** (*pleasant etc*) *air, breath* frais; *water* pur; *soil* sain; *scent* agréable; *sound, voice* mélodieux; *running of engine* sans à-coups; *person* gentil, charmant; *revenge, success, character, smile* doux; *child, dog, house, dress* mignon. (*fig*) **the ~ smell of success** la douceur exquise du succès; **it was ~ to his ear** c'était doux à son oreille; (*pej*) **~ words** *or* **talk** flagorneries *fpl*; **~ corn** maïs doux; **~ herbs** fines herbes *fpl*; **~ potato** patate *f* douce; **he carried on in his own ~ way** il a continué comme il l'entendait; **to be ~ on sb*** avoir le béguin* pour qn; **~ Fanny Adams**‡ rien de rien*; **a ~ old lady** une adorable vieille dame; **~ little baby** mignon petit bébé *m*.

2 *adv*: **to smell ~** sentir bon; **to taste ~** avoir un goût sucré.

3 *n* (*toffee etc*) bonbon *m*; (*dessert*) dessert *m*. ♦ **sweetbread** *n* ris *m* de veau *or* d'agneau. ♦ **sweeten** *vt food etc* sucrer; *air* purifier; (*fig*) *person, temper, task* adoucir; (*: *bribe*) graisser la patte à*. ♦ **sweetener** *n* (*Culin*) saccharine *f*, sucrette *f*; (**fig: bribe*) pot-de-vin *m*. ♦ **sweetening** *n* (*substance*) édulcorant *m*. ♦ **sweetheart** *n* petit(e) ami(e) *m(f)*; **yes ~heart** oui mon ange. ♦ **sweetie*** *n* (*toffee etc*) bonbon *m*; **she's a ~ie** c'est un ange; **yes ~ie** oui mon ange. ♦ **sweetly** *adv sing, play* mélodieusement; *smile, answer* gentiment; *[engine] run* sans à-coups. ♦ **sweet-natured** *or* ♦ **sweet-tempered** *adj* d'un naturel doux. ♦ **sweetness** *n* (*gen*) douceur *f*; (*to taste*) goût sucré; (*in smell*) odeur *f* suave. ♦ **sweetpea** *n* pois *m* de senteur. ♦ **sweet-scented** *or* ♦ **sweet-smelling** *adj* parfumé, odorant. ♦ **sweetshop** *n* confiserie *f*. ♦ **sweet-william** *n* œillet *m* de poète.

swell [swel] (*vb: pret* **swelled**, *ptp* **swollen** *or* **swelled**) **1** *n [sea]* houle *f*; (*Mus*) crescendo *m inv*. **2** *adj* (*: *esp US: excellent*) sensationnel*, formidable*. **3** *vi* (**~ up**) *[tyre, airbed, sails]* se gonfler; *[part of body]* enfler; *[wood]* gonfler; *[river]* grossir; *[sound, music, voice]* s'enfler; *[numbers, membership]* augmenter. **4** *vt sail* gonfler; *sound* enfler; *river, population* grossir; *number* augmenter. **swollen with pride** gonflé d'orgueil. ♦ **swellheaded*** *adj* bêcheur. ♦ **swelling** *n* (*Med*) enflure *f*; (*lump*) grosseur *f*; (*on tyre etc*) hernie *f*.

swelter ['sweltəʳ] *vi* étouffer de chaleur. ♦ **sweltering** *adj* oppressant; **it's ~ing in here** on étouffe de chaleur ici.

swept [swept] *pret, ptp of* **sweep**.

swerve [swɜ:v] **1** *vi [boxer, fighter]* faire un écart; *[ball]* dévier; *[vehicle, ship]* faire une embardée; *[driver]* donner un coup de volant; (*fig*) dévier (*from* de). **2** *n* écart *m*; embardée *f*.

swift [swɪft] **1** *adj* (*gen*) prompt (*to do* à faire), rapide; *vehicle, journey* rapide; *movement* vif. **2** *n* (*Orn*) martinet *m*. ♦ **swiftly** *adv* rapidement, vite. ♦ **swiftness** *n* promptitude *f*; rapidité *f*.

swig* [swɪg] **1** *n* lampée* *f*, (*larger*) coup *m*. **to take a ~ at a bottle** boire un coup à même la bouteille. **2** *vt* lamper*.

swill [swɪl] **1** *n* (*for pigs etc*) pâtée *f*; (*garbage*) eaux *fpl* grasses. **2** *vt* **(a)** (**~ out**) *floor* laver à grande eau; *glass* rincer. **(b)** (*: *drink*) boire à grands traits.

swim [swɪm] (*vb: pret* **swam**, *ptp* **swum**) **1** *n*: **to go for a ~, to have a ~ = to go ~ming** (*V* **2**); **after a 2-km ~** après avoir fait 2 km à la nage; **I had a lovely ~** ça m'a fait du bien de nager comme ça; (*fig*) **to be in the ~** être dans le mouvement.

2 *vi* (*gen*) nager; (*as sport*) faire de la natation. **to go ~ming** (*in sea etc*) aller nager, aller se baigner; (*in ~ming baths*) aller à la piscine; **to ~ away/back** *etc [person]* s'éloigner/revenir *etc* à la nage; *[fish]* s'éloigner/revenir *etc*; **he swam under the boat** il est passé sous le bateau; (*fig*) **to ~ with the tide** suivre le courant; (*fig*) **the meat was ~ming in gravy** la viande baignait dans la sauce; **eyes ~ming with tears** yeux baignés de larmes; **the bathroom was ~ming*** la salle de bains était inondée; **the room swam before his eyes** la pièce semblait tourner autour de lui; **his head was ~ming** la tête lui tournait.

3 *vt* traverser à la nage. **it was first swum in 1900** la première traversée à la nage a eu lieu en 1900; **to ~ 10 km** faire 10 km à la nage; **I can't ~ a stroke** je suis incapable de faire une brasse. ♦ **swimmer** *n* nageur *m*, -euse *f*. ♦ **swimming 1** *n* nage *f*, (*as sport*) natation *f*; **2** *adj*: **~ming bath(s)** *or* **pool** piscine *f*; **~ming cap** bonnet *m* de bain; **~ming costume** *or* **suit** maillot *m* (de bain) une pièce; **~ming gala** fête *f* de natation; **~ming trunks** caleçon *m* de bain. ♦ **swimmingly** *adv*: **to go ~mingly** aller à merveille. ♦ **swimsuit** *n* maillot *m* (de bain).

swindle ['swɪndl] **1** *n* escroquerie *f*. **it's a ~** c'est du vol. **2** *vt* escroquer, rouler*. **to ~ sb out of sth, to ~ sth out of sb** escroquer qch à qn. ♦ **swindler** *n* escroc *m*.

swine [swaɪn] *n, pl inv* pourceau *m*; (*‡fig: person*) salaud‡ *m*.

swing [swɪŋ] (*vb: pret, ptp* **swung**) **1** *n* **(a)** (*movement*) balancement *m*; *[pendulum, needle, pointer]* oscillations *fpl*; (*distance*) arc *m*; (*Boxing, Golf*) swing *m*. **to take a ~ at sb** décocher un coup de poing à qn; (*fig*) **the ~ of the pendulum** le mouvement du pendule; (*Pol*) **a ~ of 5% to the left** un revirement de 5% en faveur de la gauche; **to walk with a ~ (in one's step)** marcher d'un pas rythmé; **music that goes with a ~** musique *f* entraînante; (*fig*) **to go with a ~** *[evening, party]* marcher du tonnerre*; *[business, shop]* très bien marcher; **to be in full ~** battre son plein; **to get into the ~ of things** se mettre dans le bain. **(b)** (*play equipment*) balançoire *f*. **to have a ~** se balancer; (*fig*) **what you gain on the ~s you lose on the roundabouts** ce qu'on gagne d'un côté on perd de l'autre. **(c)** (**~ music**) swing *m*.

2 *adj* **(a)** (*Mus*) *band* de swing. **(b)** *bridge* tournant; *door* battant.

3 *vi* (*gen*) se balancer; *[pendulum]* osciller; (*pivot:* **~ round**) tourner, pivoter; *[person]* se retourner. **~ing by his hands** suspendu par les mains; **to ~ to and fro** se balancer; **it swung round through the air** cela a décrit une courbe dans l'air; **he swung across on the rope** agrippé à la corde il s'est élancé et est passé de l'autre côté; **the door swung open/shut** la porte s'est ouverte/refermée; **he swung round on his heels** il a virevolté; **to ~ along/away** *etc* avancer/s'éloigner *etc* d'un pas rythmé; (*fig*) **to ~ into action** passer à l'action; **music that really ~s** musique *f* au rythme entraînant; **the river ~s north** la rivière décrit une courbe vers le nord; (*fig Pol*) **to ~ to the right** virer à droite; (*be hanged*) **he'll ~ for it*** on lui mettra la corde au cou pour cela.

4 *vt* **(a)** (*gen*) balancer; *child on swing* pousser; (*brandish*) brandir. **he swung the case (up) on to his shoulders** il a balancé la valise sur ses épaules; **he swung himself over the wall** il a sauté par-dessus le mur; **to ~ o.s. up into the saddle** sauter en selle; **to ~ one's hips** rouler *or* balancer les hanches. **(b)** (**~ round**) *propeller* lancer; *starting handle* tourner. **to ~ a door open/shut** ouvrir/fermer une porte. **(c)** (*influence*) *election, decision* influencer. **to ~ a deal*** emporter une affaire. **(d)** (*Mus*) *the classics etc* jouer de manière rythmée.

swing round 1 *vi [person]* se retourner; *[crane etc]* pivoter; *[vehicle]* virer, (*after collision*) faire un tête-à-queue; (*fig*) *[voters]* virer de bord; *[opinions etc]* connaître un revirement. **2** *vt sep object on rope etc* faire tourner.

♦ **swinging** *adj step* rythmé; *music, rhythm* entraînant; (**fig*) (*lively*) dynamique; (*fashionable etc*) dans le vent*; *party* du tonnerre*. ♦ **swing-wing** *adj* (*Aviat*) à géométrie variable.

swingeing ['swɪndʒɪŋ] *adj blow, attack* violent; *defeat, majority* écrasant; *damages, taxation, price* énorme.

swipe [swaɪp] **1** *n* (*) (*at ball etc*) grand coup *m*; (*slap*) gifle *f*. **2** *vt* **(a)** (*: *hit*) *ball* frapper à toute volée; *person* gifler à toute volée. **(b)** (‡: *steal*) piquer*, voler (*sth from sb* qch à qn).

swirl [swɜːl] **1** *n* (*gen*) tourbillon *m*; *[cream etc]* volute *f*. **2** *vi* tourbillonner.

swish [swɪʃ] **1** *vi [cane, whip]* siffler, cingler l'air; *[water, long grass, skirts]* bruire. **2** *vt whip, cane* faire siffler. **3** *n* sifflement *m*; bruissement *m*. **4** *adj* (‡: *smart: also* **swishy***) rupin‡.

Swiss [swɪs] **1** *adj* suisse. **~ French/German** suisse romand/allemand; (*Culin*) **~ roll** gâteau *m* roulé. **2** *n, pl inv* Suisse(sse) *m(f)*.

switch [swɪtʃ] **1** *n* **(a)** (*Elec*) interrupteur *m*, commutateur *m*; (*Aut*: **ignition ~**) contact *m*. (*Elec*) **the ~ was on/off** c'était allumé/éteint. **(b)** (*Rail: points*) aiguille *f*. **(c)** *[opinion, allegiance]* revirement *m*; *[funds]* transfert *m* (*from* de; *to* en faveur de). (*Bridge*) **the ~ to hearts** le passage à cœur.

2 *vt* **(a)** (*transfer*) *one's support, allegiance, attention* reporter (*from* de; *to* sur). **to ~ the conversation to another subject** changer de sujet de conversation. **(b)** (*exchange*) échanger (*A for B* A contre B; *sth with sb* qch avec qn); (**~ over, ~ round**) *two objects, letters in word* intervertir; (*rearrange:* **~ round**) *books, objects* changer de place. **to ~ plans** changer de projet. **(c)** (*Rail*) aiguiller (*to another track* sur une autre voie). **(d)** (*Elec etc*) **to ~ the heater to 'low'** mettre le radiateur sur 'doux'; **to ~ the radio/TV to another programme** changer de station/de chaîne.

3 *vi* (**~ over**) **he ~ed (over) to Conservative** il a voté conservateur cette fois; **we ~ed (over) to gas** (nous avons changé et) nous avons maintenant fait installer le gaz; **many have ~ed (over) to teaching** beaucoup se sont recyclés dans l'enseignement.

switch back 1 *vi* (*gen*) revenir (*to* à). (*Rad, TV*) **to ~ back to the other programme** remettre l'autre émission. **2** *vt sep*: **to ~ the heater back to 'low'** remettre le radiateur sur 'doux'; (*Elec*) **to ~ back on** rallumer.

switch off 1 *vi* **(a)** (*Elec*) éteindre; (*Rad, TV*) éteindre le poste; (*fig: lose interest*) décrocher*. **(b)** *[heater, oven etc]* s'éteindre. **2** *vt sep* éteindre. (*Rad, TV*) **he ~ed the programme off** il a fermé le poste; (*Aut*) **to ~ off the engine** arrêter le moteur.

switch on 1 *vi* **(a)** (*Elec*) allumer; (*Rad, TV*) allumer le poste. **(b)** *[heater, oven etc]* s'allumer. **2** *vt sep* (*gen*) allumer; *water supply* ouvrir; *engine, machine* mettre en marche; (‡*fig: excite*) exciter. **to ~ on the light** allumer; (*fig*) **to be ~ed on‡** (*up-to-date*) être dans le vent*; (*by drugs*) planer*; (*sexually*) être tout excité (*by* par).

switch over *vi* (*TV/Rad*) changer de chaîne/de station. (*Rad, TV*) **to ~ over to sth** mettre qch. ♦ **switchback 1** *n* montagnes *fpl* russes (*also fig*); **2** *adj* (*up and down*) tout en montées et descentes. ♦ **switchblade (knife)** *n* (*US*) couteau *m* à cran

d'arrêt. ♦ **switchboard** **1** *n* (*Elec*) tableau *m* de distribution; (*Telec*) standard *m*; **2** *adj* (*Telec*) **~board operator** standardiste *mf*. ♦ **switchover** *n* passage *m* (*from* de; *to* à).
Switzerland ['swɪtsələnd] *n* Suisse *f*. **French-/German-/Italian-speaking ~** la Suisse romande/allemande/italienne.
swivel ['swɪvl] **1** *n* pivot *m*. **2** *adj seat etc* pivotant. **3** *vt* (**~ round**) faire pivoter. **4** *vi* (**~ round**) pivoter.
swollen ['swəʊlən] (*ptp of* **swell**) *adj arm, face* enflé; *eyes, stomach* gonflé (*with* de); *river, lake* en crue; *population* accru. **to have ~ glands** avoir une inflammation des ganglions. ♦ **swollen-headed*** *adj* bêcheur.
swoon [swu:n] *vi* se pâmer; (*fig*) se pâmer d'admiration (*over sb/sth* devant qn/qch).
swoop [swu:p] **1** *n* (*attack*) attaque *f* en piqué (*on* sur); *[police etc]* descente *f* (*on* dans). **at one fell ~** d'un seul coup. **2** *vi* (**~ down**) *[bird]* fondre; *[aircraft]* descendre en piqué; *[police etc]* faire une descente.
swop [swɒp] = **swap**.
sword [sɔ:d] **1** *n* épée *f*. **to wear a ~** porter l'épée. **2** *adj wound* d'épée. **~ arm** bras *m* droit; **~ dance** danse *f* du sabre. ♦ **swordfish** *n* espadon *m*. ♦ **swordsman** *n*: **to be a good ~sman** être une fine lame. ♦ **swordsmanship** *n* habileté *f* dans le maniement de l'épée. ♦ **swordstick** *n* canne *f* à épée. ♦ **sword-swallower** *n* avaleur *m* de sabres.
swore [swɔ:ʳ] *pret of* **swear**.
sworn [swɔ:n] (*ptp of* **swear**) *adj evidence, statement* donné sous serment; *enemy* juré; *ally, friend* à la vie et à la mort.
swot* [swɒt] **1** *n* bûcheur* *m*, -euse* *f*. **2** *vti* bûcher*. **to ~ for an exam** bachoter; **to ~ up (on) sth** potasser* qch. ♦ **swotting*** *n* bachotage *m*.
swum [swʌm] *ptp of* **swim**.
swung [swʌŋ] (*pret, ptp of* **swing**) *adj* (*Typ*) **~ dash** tilde *m*.
sycamore ['sɪkəmɔ:ʳ] *n* sycomore *m*.
sycophant ['sɪkəfənt] *n* flagorneur *m*, -euse *f*.
syllable ['sɪləbl] *n* syllabe *f*. ♦ **syllabic** *adj* syllabique.
syllabus ['sɪləbəs] *n* (*Scol, Univ*) programme *m*. **on the ~** au programme.
syllogism ['sɪlədʒɪzəm] *n* syllogisme *m*.
sylph [sɪlf] *n* sylphe *m*. ♦ **sylphlike** *adj woman* gracile; *figure* de sylphide.
symbiosis [ˌsɪmbɪ'əʊsɪs] *n* (*also fig*) symbiose *f*.
symbol ['sɪmbəl] *n* symbole *m*. ♦ **symbolic(al)** *adj* symbolique. ♦ **symbolically** *adv* symboliquement. ♦ **symbolism** *n* symbolisme *m*. ♦ **symbolist** *adj, n* symboliste (*mf*). ♦ **symbolization** *n* symbolisation *f*. ♦ **symbolize** *vt* symboliser.
symmetry ['sɪmɪtrɪ] *n* symétrie *f*. ♦ **symmetric(al)** *adj* symétrique. ♦ **symmetrically** *adv* symétriquement.
sympathy ['sɪmpəθɪ] *n* **(a)** (*pity*) compassion *f*. **please accept my deepest ~** veuillez agréer mes condoléances; **to feel ~ for** éprouver de la compassion pour; **to show one's ~ for sb** témoigner sa sympathie à qn. **(b)** (*fellow feeling*) solidarité *f* (*for* avec). **I have no ~ with lazy people** je n'ai aucune indulgence pour les paresseux; **he is in ~ with the workers** il est du côté des ouvriers; **I am in ~ with your proposals** je suis en accord avec vos propositions; **to strike in ~ with sb** faire grève en solidarité avec qn. ♦ **sympathetic** *adj* (*showing pity*) compatissant (*to, towards* envers); (*kind*) bien disposé (*to* envers), compréhensif; **you will find him very sympathetic** vous le trouverez bien disposé à votre égard. ♦ **sympathetically** *adv* (*showing pity*) avec compassion; (*kindly*) avec bienveillance. ♦ **sympathize** *vi*: **her cousin called to sympathize** sa cousine est venue témoigner sa sympathie; **I sympathize with you in your grief** je m'associe à votre douleur; **I sympathize with you** (*pity*) je vous plains; (*understand*) je comprends votre point de vue. ♦ **sympathizer** *n* (*in adversity*) personne *f* qui compatit; (*fig: esp Pol*) sympathisant(e) *m(f)* (*with* de).
symphony ['sɪmfənɪ] **1** *n* symphonie *f*. **2** *adj concert, orchestra* symphonique. ♦ **symphonic** *adj* symphonique.
symposium [sɪm'pəʊzɪəm] *n, pl* **-ia** symposium *m*.
symptom ['sɪmptəm] *n* symptôme *m*. ♦ **symptomatic** *adj* symptomatique (*of* de).
synagogue ['sɪnəgɒg] *n* synagogue *f*.
synchronize ['sɪŋkrənaɪz] **1** *vt* synchroniser. **2** *vi* *[events]* se passer en même temps (*with* que). ♦ **synchronization** *n* synchronisation *f*.
syncopate ['sɪŋkəpeɪt] *vt* syncoper. ♦ **syncopation** *n* syncope *f* (*Mus*).
syndicate ['sɪndɪkɪt] **1** *n* (*Comm etc*) syndicat *m*, coopérative *f*. **2** ['sɪndɪkeɪt] *vt* **(a)** (*US Press*) *article etc* vendre *or* publier par l'intermédiaire d'un syndicat de distribution. **(b)** *workers* syndiquer. ♦ **syndicalism** *n* syndicalisme *m*. ♦ **syndicalist** *n* syndicaliste *mf*.
syndrome ['sɪndrəʊm] *n* (*also fig*) syndrome *m*.
synod ['sɪnəd] *n* synode *m*.
synonym ['sɪnənɪm] *n* synonyme *m*. ♦ **synonymous** *adj* synonyme (*with* de). ♦ **synonymy** *n* synonymie *f*.
synopsis [sɪ'nɒpsɪs] *n, pl* **-ses** résumé *m*.
syntax ['sɪntæks] *n* syntaxe *f*. ♦ **syntactic(al)** *adj* syntaxique.
synthesis ['sɪnθəsɪs] *n, pl* **-ses** synthèse *f*. ♦ **synthesize** *vt* (*combine*) synthétiser; (*produce*) produire synthétiquement. ♦ **synthetic** **1** *adj* synthétique; **2** *n* produit *m* synthétique; (*Tex*) **synthetics** fibres *fpl* synthétiques.
syphilis ['sɪfɪlɪs] *n* syphilis *f*. ♦ **syphilitic** *adj, n* syphilitique (*mf*).
syphon ['saɪfən] = **siphon**.
Syria ['sɪrɪə] *n* Syrie *f*.
syringe [sɪ'rɪndʒ] **1** *n* seringue *f*. **2** *vt* seringuer.
syrup ['sɪrəp] *n* sirop *m*; (*Culin*: **golden ~**) mélasse *f* raffinée. ♦ **syrupy** *adj* sirupeux.
system ['sɪstəm] *n* (*gen*) système *m*; (*Physiol*) organisme *m*. **railway ~** réseau *m* de chemin de fer; **digestive ~** appareil *m* digestif; **a shock to his ~** une secousse pour son organisme; (*fig*) **to get sth out of one's ~** se purger de qch; (*Pol*) **down with the ~!** à bas le système!; (*order*) **to lack ~** manquer de méthode. ♦ **systematic** *adj* systématique. ♦ **systematically** *adv* systématiquement. ♦ **systematization** *n* systématisation *f*. ♦ **systematize** *vt* systématiser. ♦ **systems analyst** *n* analyste-programmeur *mf*.

T

T, t [tiː] *n* (*letter*) T, t *m*. (*fig*) **that's it to a T*** c'est exactement ça; **it fits him to a T*** ça lui va comme un gant. ♦ **T-junction** *n* intersection *f* en T. ♦ **T-shirt** *n* T-shirt *m*. ♦ **T-square** *n* équerre *f* en T.
ta* [tɑː] *excl* merci!
tab [tæb] *n* (*part of garment*) patte *f*; (*loop on garment etc*) attache *f*; (*label*) étiquette *f*; (*on shoelace*) ferret *m*; (*marker: on file etc*) onglet *m*; (*US*: café check*) addition *f*. **to keep ~s on*** *person* avoir à l'œil*; *thing* avoir l'œil sur*; (*lit, fig*) **to pick up the ~*** payer l'addition.
tabby ['tæbɪ] *n* (**~ cat**) chat(te) *m(f)* tigré(e).
tabernacle ['tæbənækl] *n* tabernacle *m*.
table ['teɪbl] **1** *n* **(a)** table *f*. **ironing/garden ~** table à repasser/de jardin; **at ~** à table; **to sit down to ~** se mettre à table; **to lay** *or* **set the ~** mettre la table *or* le couvert; (*fig: drunk*) **he was nearly under the ~** un peu plus et il roulait sous la table*. **(b)** *[facts, statistics]* table *f* (*also Math*); *[prices, names]* liste *f*; (*Sport:* **league ~**) classement *m*. **~ of contents** table des matières; (*Math*) **the two-times ~** la table de deux.
2 *vt bill, motion etc* (*Brit: submit*) présenter; (*US: postpone*) ajourner.
3 *adj wine, knife, lamp* de table. **he has good ~ manners** il sait se tenir à table; **~ napkin** serviette *f* (de table); **~ salt** sel *m* fin.
♦ **tablecloth** *n* nappe *f*. ♦ **table-cover** *n* tapis *m* de table. ♦ **table d'hôte 1** *adj* à prix fixe; **2** *n* repas *m* à prix fixe. ♦ **tableland** *n* (*Geog*) (haut) plateau *m*. ♦ **tablemat** *n* (*of linen*) napperon *m*; (*heat-resistant*) dessous-de-plat *m inv*. ♦ **table-runner** *n* chemin *m* de table. ♦ **tablespoon** *n* cuiller *f* de service; (*measurement*: **~spoonful**) cuillerée *f* à soupe (*US Culin = 29,5 ml*). ♦ **table-tennis 1** *n* ping-pong *m*; **2** *adj* de ping-pong; **~-tennis player** joueur *m*, -euse *f* de ping-pong. ♦ **tabletop** *n* dessus *m* de table. ♦ **table-turning** *n* spiritisme *m* par les tables tournantes. ♦ **tableware** *n* vaisselle *f*.
tableau ['tæbləʊ] *n, pl* **-x** (*Theat*) tableau *m* vivant; (*fig*) tableau.
tablet ['tæblɪt] *n* (*stone: inscribed*) plaque *f* commémorative; (*of wax, slate etc*) tablette *f*; (*Pharm*) comprimé *m*; (*for sucking*) pastille *f*; *[chocolate]* tablette. **~ of soap** savonnette *f*.
tabloid ['tæblɔɪd] *n* (*newspaper*) tabloïd *m*.
taboo, tabu [tə'buː] *adj, n* tabou (*m*).
tabular ['tæbjʊlə^r] *adj* tabulaire. ♦ **tabulate** *vt* (*gen*) mettre sous forme de table; *results etc* classifier; (*Typing*) mettre en colonnes. ♦ **tabulator** *n* *[typewriter]* tabulateur *m*.
tachograph ['tækəgrɑːf] *n* tachygraphe *m*.
tacit ['tæsɪt] *adj* tacite. ♦ **tacitly** *adv* tacitement.
taciturn ['tæsɪtɜːn] *adj* taciturne. ♦ **taciturnity** *n* taciturnité *f*.
tack [tæk] **1** *n* **(a)** (*for wood, lino, carpets etc*) broquette *f*; (*for upholstery*) semence *f*; (*US:* **thumb~**) punaise *f*. **(b)** (*Sewing*) point *m* de bâti. **(c)** (*Naut*) bord *m*. **to make a ~** tirer un bord; **on a starboard ~** tribord amures; (*fig*) **on the wrong ~** sur la mauvaise voie; (*fig*) **to try another ~** essayer une autre tactique. **(d)** (*for horse*) sellerie *f* (*articles*). **2** *vt* (*Sewing*) bâtir. **3** *vi* (*make a ~*) tirer un bord. **to ~ along** avancer en tirant des bords.
tack on *vt sep wood, lino* clouer; (*Sewing*) bâtir; (*fig*) ajouter après coup (*to* à).
♦ **tacking** *n* (**~ing stitches**) points *mpl* de bâti.
♦ **tackroom** *n* sellerie *f* (*endroit*).
tackle ['tækl] **1** *n* **(a)** (*esp Naut: ropes, pulleys*) appareil *m* de levage; (*gen: gear*) équipement *m*. **fishing ~** matériel *m* de pêche. **(b)** (*Ftbl etc*) plaquage *m*. **2** *vt* (*Ftbl etc*) plaquer; *thief, intruder* saisir (à bras le corps); *task, problem* s'attaquer à; *question, subject* aborder; (*) *meal, food* attaquer*. **I'll ~ him about it** je vais lui en parler; **I ~d him about what he had done** je l'ai questionné sur ce qu'il avait fait.
tacky ['tækɪ] *adj glue* qui commence à prendre; *paint* pas tout à fait sec; *surface* poisseux.
tact [tækt] *n* tact *m*. ♦ **tactful** *adj person, answer* plein de tact; *hint, inquiry, reference* discret (*f* -ète); **to be ~ful with sb** agir envers qn avec tact; **you could have been a bit more ~ful** tu aurais pu avoir un peu plus de tact. ♦ **tactfully** *adv* avec tact. ♦ **tactless** *adj person, answer* qui manque de tact; *hint* grossier; *inquiry, reference* indiscret.
♦ **tactlessly** *adv* sans tact.
tactic ['tæktɪk] *n* tactique *f*. **~s** la tactique.
♦ **tactical** *adj* (*gen*) tactique; *error etc* de tactique. ♦ **tactically** *adv* du point de vue tactique.
♦ **tactician** *n* tacticien *m*.
tadpole ['tædpəʊl] *n* têtard *m*.
taffeta ['tæfɪtə] *n* taffetas *m*.
tag [tæg] **1** *n* **(a)** *[shoelace, cord etc]* ferret *m*; (*on garment etc: loop*) attache *f*; (*label*) étiquette *f*; (*marker: on file etc*) onglet *m*. **(b)** (*quotation*) citation *f*; (*cliché*) cliché *m*; (*catchword*) slogan *m*. **question ~** queue *f* de phrase interrogative. **(c)** (*game*) (jeu *m* du) chat *m*. **2** *vt* **(a)** (*label*) étiqueter. **(b)** (*: *follow*) suivre; *[detective]* filer.
tag along *vi* suivre le mouvement*. **to ~ along behind sb** traîner derrière qn; **to ~ along with sb** venir (*or* aller) avec qn.
tail [teɪl] **1** *n* (*gen*) queue *f*; *[shirt]* pan *m*; *[coin]* pile *f*. (*Dress*) **~s*** queue de pie; **heads or ~s** pile ou face; **long-~ed** à la queue longue; (*fig*) **with his ~ between his legs** la queue entre les jambes; **he was right on my ~** il me suivait de très près; (*fig: have followed*) **to put a ~ on sb*** faire filer qn. **2** *adj*: **~ coat** habit *m*; **~ end** (*gen*) bout *m*; *[procession etc]* queue *f*; *[storm, debate]* toutes dernières minutes *fpl*; (*Aut, Rail etc*) **~ lamp** *or* **light** feu *m* arrière *inv*. **3** *vt* (*) *suspect etc* suivre, filer.
tail away, tail off *vi [sounds]* se taire peu à peu; *[interest, numbers]* diminuer petit à petit.
♦ **tailback** *n* (*Aut*) bouchon *m*. ♦ **tailboard** *or* ♦ **tailgate** *n* (*Aut*) hayon *m*. ♦ **tailspin** *n* (*Aviat*) vrille *f*. ♦ **tailwind** *n* vent *m* arrière *inv*.
tailor ['teɪlə^r] **1** *n* tailleur *m*. **~'s chalk** craie *f* de tailleur; **~'s dummy** mannequin *m*. **2** *vt garment* façonner; (*fig*) *speech, book* adapter (*to, to suit* à; *for* pour). **a ~ed skirt** une jupe ajustée. ♦ **tailor-made** *adj garment* fait sur mesure; (*fig*) *building* fonctionnalisé (*for* pour); *lesson* préparé spécialement (*for* pour); **the job was ~-made for him** le poste était fait pour lui.
taint [teɪnt] *vt* (*gen*) polluer; *meat, food* gâter; (*fig*) *reputation* porter tache à. ♦ **tainted** *adj* pollué; gâté; entaché; *action* impur; *money* mal acquis.

take [teɪk] (*vb: pret* **took,** *ptp* **taken**) **1** *n* (*Cine, Phot*) prise *f* de vues; (*Sound recording*) enregistrement *m.*

2 *vt* **(a)** (*gen*) prendre (*from sth* dans qch; *from sb* à qn); *prize, degree* avoir, obtenir; *a bet* accepter. **to ~ sb's hand** prendre la main de qn; **to ~ sb by the throat** saisir qn à la gorge; **to ~ sth from one's pocket** prendre qch dans *or* tirer qch de sa poche; **I took these statistics from ...** j'ai tiré ces statistiques de ...; (*Math*) **~ 6 from 9** 9 moins 6; **he took 10 francs off the price** il a rabattu 10 F sur le prix; **he must be ~n alive** il faut le prendre *or* le capturer vivant; (*Cards*) **to ~ a trick** faire une levée; **my ace took his king** j'ai pris son roi avec mon as; **the grocer ~s about £500 per day** l'épicier se fait à peu près 500 livres de recette par jour; **you'll have to ~ your** *or* **a chance** il va falloir que tu prennes le risque; **to ~ sth upon o.s.** prendre qch sur soi; **to ~ it upon o.s. to do** prendre sur soi de faire; (*Med*) **to ~ cold** prendre froid; **to be ~n ill** tomber malade; **to ~ fright** prendre peur; **he took no food for 4 days** il n'a rien mangé *or* pris pendant 4 jours; **how much alcohol has he ~n?** combien d'alcool a-t-il bu?; **I can't ~ alcohol** je ne supporte pas l'alcool; **to ~ one's seat** s'asseoir; **is this seat ~n?** cette place est-elle prise *or* occupée?; **to ~ the train** prendre le train; **~ the first on the left** prenez la première à gauche; **the bus ~s 60 passengers** l'autobus a une capacité de 60 places; **the hall will ~ 200 people** la salle contient jusqu'à 200 personnes; **he won't ~ less than £50 for it** il en demande au moins 50 livres; **~ it from me!** croyez-moi!; **~ it or leave it** c'est à prendre ou à laisser; **I can ~ it or leave it*** j'aime ça mais sans plus; **how did he ~ the news?** comment a-t-il réagi en apprenant la nouvelle?; **she took his death quite well/very badly** elle s'est montrée très calme/a été très affectée en apprenant sa mort; **you must ~ us as you find us** vous devez nous prendre comme nous sommes; **to ~ things as they come/are** prendre les choses comme elles viennent/sont; (*handing over task etc*) **will you ~ it from here?** pouvez-vous prendre la suite?

(b) (*require*) prendre, demander; (*Gram*) être suivi de. **the journey ~s 5 days** le voyage prend *or* demande 5 jours; **it took me 2 hours to do it, I took 2 hours to do it** j'ai mis 2 heures à le faire; **~ your time!** prenez votre temps!, **that ~s courage** cela demande du courage; **it ~s a brave man to do that** il faut être courageux pour faire cela; **it ~s some doing*** cela n'est pas facile (à faire); **it ~s some believing*** c'est à peine croyable; **it took 3 policemen to hold him down** il a fallu 3 gendarmes pour le tenir; **he has got what it ~s to do the job** il est à la hauteur.

(c) (*carry*) *child, object* porter, apporter, emporter; *one's gloves, umbrella* prendre; (*lead*) emmener, conduire; (*accompany*) accompagner. **he took her some flowers** il lui a apporté des fleurs; **~ his suitcase upstairs** montez sa valise; **he took her to the cinema** il l'a emmenée au cinéma; **they took him over the factory** ils lui ont fait visiter l'usine; **to ~ sb to hospital** transporter qn à l'hôpital; **he took me home in his car** il m'a ramené dans sa voiture; **this road/bus will ~ you to ...** cette route/cet autobus vous mènera à ...; (*fig*) **what took you to Lille?** qu'est-ce qui vous a fait aller à Lille?

(d) (*negotiate*) *bend* prendre; *hill* grimper; *fence* sauter; *exam, test* se présenter à; (*study*) *subject* prendre, faire.

(e) (*tolerate*) accepter. **he won't ~ no for an answer** il n'acceptera pas un refus; **I can't ~ it any more** je n'en peux plus; **we can ~ it!** on ne se laissera pas abattre!

(f) (*assume*) supposer, imaginer. **I ~ it that ...** je suppose *or* j'imagine que ...; **how old do you ~ him to be?** quel âge lui donnez-vous?; **what do you ~ me for?** pour qui me prenez-vous?; **I took him to be foreign** je le croyais étranger, je l'ai pris pour un étranger; **now ~ Ireland** prenons par exemple l'Irlande; **taking one thing with another** ... tout bien considéré ... .

3 *vi [fire, vaccination, plant etc]* prendre.

take after *vt fus* ressembler à, tenir de.

take along *vt sep person* emmener; *camera etc* prendre.

take apart *vt sep machine, toy* démonter; (**fig: criticize harshly*) démolir*.

take aside *vt sep* prendre à part.

take away 1 *vi*: **it ~s away from its value** cela diminue sa valeur. **2** *vt sep* **(a)** (*carry, lead away*) *object* emporter; *person* emmener. **(b)** (*remove*) *object* prendre, enlever (*from sb* à qn; *from sth* de qch); *sb's child, wife* enlever (*from sb* à qn). **she took her children away from the school** elle a retiré ses enfants de l'école. **(c)** (*Math*) soustraire, ôter (*from* de).

take back *vt sep* **(a)** *gift, promise, one's wife etc* reprendre. **(b)** (*return*) *book, goods* rapporter (*to* à); (*accompany*) *person* raccompagner (*to* à). (*fig*) **it ~s me back to my childhood** cela me rappelle mon enfance; **that ~s me back!** ça me rappelle de vieux souvenirs!

take down *vt sep* **(a)** *vase from shelf etc* descendre (*from, off* de); *trousers* baisser; *picture, poster* enlever. **(b)** (*dismantle*) *scaffolding* démonter; *building* démolir. **(c)** (*write etc*) *notes, letter, address* prendre.

take in *vt sep* **(a)** *chairs, harvest* rentrer; *person* faire entrer; *lodgers* prendre; *friend* recevoir; *orphan, stray dog* recueillir; *newspaper etc* prendre; *sewing, washing* prendre à domicile. **(b)** *skirt, dress, waistband* reprendre; *knitting* diminuer. **(c)** (*include, cover*) couvrir, inclure. **we cannot ~ in all the cases** nous ne pouvons pas couvrir *or* inclure tous les cas; (*fig*) **we took in Venice on the way home** nous avons visité Venise sur le chemin du retour. **(d)** (*grasp, understand*) saisir, comprendre. **the children were taking it all in** les enfants étaient tout oreilles; **he hadn't fully ~n in that she was dead** il n'avait pas vraiment réalisé* qu'elle était morte; **he took in the situation at a glance** il a apprécié la situation en un clin d'œil. **(e)** (*: *cheat, deceive*) avoir*, rouler*. **he's easily ~n in** il se fait facilement avoir*; **to be ~n in by appearances/a disguise** se laisser prendre aux apparences/à un déguisement.

take off 1 *vi [person]* partir (*for* pour); *[aircraft]* décoller, (*head for*) s'envoler (*for* pour); *[high jumper etc]* s'élancer. **2** *vt sep* **(a)** (*remove*) *garment, price tag, lid* enlever; *telephone receiver* décrocher; *item on menu, train* supprimer. (*Med*) **they had to ~ his leg off** on a dû l'amputer d'une jambe; (*Comm*) **he took £5 off** il a fait un rabais de 5 livres. **(b)** (*lead etc away*) *person* emmener; *object* emporter. **he took her off to lunch** il l'a emmenée déjeuner; **to ~ sb off to jail** emmener qn en prison; **he was ~n off to hospital** on l'a transporté à l'hôpital; **to ~ o.s. off** s'en aller. **(c)** (*imitate*) imiter.

take on 1 *vi* **(a)** *[song, fashion etc]* prendre, marcher*. **(b)** (*: *be upset*) s'en faire*. **2** *vt sep* **(a)** *work, responsibility, bet* accepter; *challenger* (*for game/fight*) accepter de jouer/de se battre contre. **I'll ~ you on** (*Betting*) je parie avec vous; (*Sport*) je joue contre vous; **he has ~n on more than he bargained for** il n'avait pas compté prendre une si lourde responsabilité. **(b)** *employee* prendre; *cargo, passenger* embarquer; *form, qualities* revêtir.

take out *vt sep* **(a)** (*lead, carry outside*) *prisoner* faire sortir; *chair, dog, children etc* sortir. **he took her out to lunch/the theatre** il l'a emmenée déjeuner/au théâtre; **he has often ~n her out** il l'a souvent sortie. **(b)** (*from pocket, drawer*) prendre (*from, of* dans); (*remove*) sortir, enlever (*from, of* de); *tooth* arracher; *appendix, tonsils* enlever; *stain* ôter, enlever (*from* de). (*fig*) **that will ~ you out of yourself** cela vous changera les idées; (*fig*) **that ~s it out of you*** ces choses-là fatiguent beaucoup; **to ~ it out on sb** s'en prendre à qn. **(c)** *insurance, patent* prendre; *licence* se procurer.

take over 1 *vi [dictator, political party etc]* prendre le pouvoir. **to ~ over from sb** prendre la relève de qn; **let him ~ over** cédez-lui la place. **2** *vt sep* **(a)** (*assume responsibility for*) *business, goods etc* reprendre; *new car* prendre livraison de; *sb's debts* prendre à sa charge. **to ~ a job over from sb** remplacer qn à un poste. **(b)** (*Fin*) *another company* absorber. (*fig*) **the tourists have ~n over Venice** les touristes ont envahi Venise.

take to *vt fus* **(a)** (*conceive liking for*) *person* se prendre d'amitié pour, sympathiser avec; *game, action, study* prendre goût à. **I didn't ~ to the idea** l'idée ne m'a rien dit. **(b)** (*start, adopt*) *habit* prendre; *hobby* se mettre à. **to ~ to drink/drugs** se mettre à boire/à se droguer; **she took to saying ...** elle s'est mise à dire ... . **(c) to ~ to one's bed** s'aliter; **to ~ to the woods** *[walker]* passer par les bois; *[hunted man]* s'enfuir à travers bois; **to ~ to the boats** abandonner le navire.

take up 1 *vi*: **to ~ up with sb** se lier avec qn. **2** *vt sep* **(a)** (*lead, carry upstairs, uphill etc*) *person* faire monter; *object* monter. **(b)** (*lift*) *object from ground etc* ramasser; *carpet* enlever; *roadway, pavement* dépaver; *hem, skirt* raccourcir; *passenger* prendre; (*fig: after interruption*) *one's work, conversation, book etc* reprendre. **(c)** (*occupy*) *space, attention* occuper; *time* prendre. **he's very ~n up** il est très pris; **he's quite ~n up with her/with his plan** il ne pense plus qu'à elle/qu'à son projet. **(d)** (*absorb*) *liquids* absorber. **(e)** (*raise question of*) *subject* aborder. **I'll ~ that up with him** je lui en parlerai. **(f)** (*start doing etc*) *hobby, sport etc* se mettre à; *career* embrasser; *method* adopter; *challenge* relever; *shares* souscrire à; *person* adopter. (*fig*) **I'll ~ you up on your promise** je me souviendrai de votre promesse. **(g)** (*understand*) comprendre. **you've ~n me up wrongly** vous m'avez mal compris.

♦ **takeaway 1** *n* café *m* qui fait des plats à emporter; **2** *adj food, meal* à emporter. ♦ **take-home pay** *n* salaire *m* net. ♦ **taken** *adj seat* pris, occupé; (*fig*) **to be very ~n with sb/sth** être très impressionné par qn/qch; **I'm not very ~n with him** il ne m'a pas fait une grosse impression; **I'm quite ~n with** *or* **by that idea** cette idée me plaît énormément. ♦ **takeoff** *n* **(a)** (*Aviat*) décollage *m*; (*fig*) démarrage *m*; **(b)** (*imitation*) pastiche *m*. ♦ **takeover 1** *n* (*Fin etc*) absorption *f*; **2** *adj*: **~over bid** offre *f* publique d'achat. ♦ **taker** *n*: **drug-~rs** les drogués *mpl*; **at £5 he found no ~rs** il n'a pas trouvé de preneurs pour 5 livres. ♦ **taking 1** *adj person, manners* engageant, attirant; **2** *n* (*Mil: capture*) prise *f*. ♦ **takings** *npl* (*Comm*) recette *f*.

talc [tælk], **talcum (powder)** ['tælkəm(ˌpaʊdəʳ)] *n* talc *m*.

tale [teɪl] *n* (*gen*) histoire *f*; (*story*) conte *m*; (*legend*) légende *f*; (*account*) récit *m*. **'T~s of King Arthur'** 'La Légende du Roi Arthur'; **he told us the ~ of his adventures** il nous a fait le récit de ses aventures; **I've been hearing ~s about you** on m'a raconté des choses sur vous; **to tell ~s** rapporter, cafarder*; (*fig*) **to tell ~s out of school** raconter ce qu'on devait taire. ♦ **talebearer** *n* rapporteur *m*, -euse *f*. ♦ **talebearing** *or* ♦ **taletelling** *n* rapportage *m*.

talent ['tælənt] **1** *n* talent *m*. **to have a ~ for drawing** être doué pour le dessin; **he is looking for ~ amongst the schoolboy players** il cherche de futurs grands joueurs parmi les lycéens. **2** *adj*: **~ scout** *or* **spotter** (*Theat/Sport*) dénicheur *m*, -euse *f* de vedettes/de futurs grands joueurs. ♦ **talented** *adj person* doué; *book, painting etc* plein de talent.

talisman ['tælɪzmən] *n* talisman *m*.

talk [tɔːk] **1** *n* **(a)** conversation *f*, discussion *f*; (*more formal*) entretien *m*; (*chat*) causerie *f*. **we've had several ~s about this** nous en avons parlé *or* discuté plusieurs fois; **I must have a ~ with him** il faut que je lui parle. **(b)** (*informal lecture*) exposé *m* (*on* sur); (*less academic*) causerie *f* (*on* sur). **to give a ~** faire un exposé, donner une causerie; **he will give us a ~ on ...** il va nous parler de ...; **to give a ~ on the radio** parler à la radio. **(c)** propos *mpl*; (*gossip*) bavardages *mpl*; (*pej*) racontars *mpl*. **the ~ was all about the wedding** les propos tournaient autour du mariage; **there is some ~ of his returning** (*being discussed*) il est question qu'il revienne; (*being rumoured*) on dit qu'il va peut-être revenir; **it's common ~ that ...** on dit partout que ...; **it's just ~** ce ne sont que des racontars; **there has been a lot of ~ about her** il a beaucoup été question d'elle, on a raconté beaucoup d'histoires sur elle (*pej*); **I've heard a lot of ~ about the factory** j'ai beaucoup entendu parler de l'usine; **all that ~ about what he was going to do!** tous ces beaux discours sur ce qu'il allait faire!; (*pej*) **he's all ~** c'est un hâbleur; **she's the ~ of the town** on ne parle que d'elle.

2 *adj* (*Rad/TV*) **~ show** entretien *m* (radiodiffusé/télévisé).

3 *vi* **(a)** (*speak*) parler (*to sb* à qn; *with sb* avec qn; *about, of sth* de qch); (*chatter*) bavarder (*with* avec); (*converse*) discuter (*to, with* avec); (*more formally*) s'entretenir (*to, with* avec). **to ~ to o.s.** se parler tout seul; **the Foreign Ministers ~ed about ...** les ministres des Affaires étrangères se sont entretenus de ...; **try to keep him ~ing** essaie de le faire parler aussi longtemps que possible; **to get o.s. ~ed about** faire parler de soi; **now you're ~ing!*** voilà qui devient intéressant!; **it's all right for him to ~** il peut parler; **look who's ~ing!*** tu peux toujours parler, toi!*; **he ~s too much** il parle trop, (*indiscreet*) il ne sait pas se taire; **don't ~ to me like that!** ne me parle pas sur ce ton!; **he knows what he's ~ing about when he's on the subject of cars** il s'y connaît quand il parle de voitures; **he doesn't know what he's ~ing about** il ne sait pas ce qu'il dit; **he was ~ing of going to Greece** il parlait d'aller en Grèce; **I'm not ~ing to him any more** je ne lui adresse plus la parole; **~ing of films, have you seen ...?** à propos de films, avez-vous vu ...?; **~ about a stroke of luck!*** tu parles d'une aubaine!*; **who were you ~ing to?** à qui parlais-tu?; **I saw them ~ing (to each other)** je les ai vus en conversation l'un avec l'autre.

4 *vt a language, slang* parler. **to ~ business/politics** parler affaires/politique; **to ~ sb into doing sth** persuader qn de faire qch (*à force de paroles*); **to ~ sb out of doing** dissuader qn de faire (en lui parlant).

talk down 1 *vi*: **to ~ down to sb** parler à qn comme à un enfant. **2** *vt sep* (*Aviat*) *pilot, aircraft* aider à atterrir par radio-contrôle.

talk over *vt sep* discuter de. **I must ~ it over with my wife** je dois en parler à ma femme. ♦ **talkative** *adj* bavard, volubile. ♦ **talkativeness** *n* volubilité *f*. ♦ **talker** *n* causeur *m*, -euse *f*; (*pej*) bavard(e) *m(f)*. ♦ **talkie*** *n* (*Cine*) film *m* parlant; **the ~ies** le cinéma parlant. ♦ **talking 1** *n* bavardage *m*; **he did all the ~ing** il a fait tous les frais de la conversation; **'no ~ing'** 'silence s'il vous plaît'; **2** *adj doll, parrot, film* parlant; **~ing book** livre *m* enregistré; **~ing point** sujet *m* de conversation. ♦ **talking-to*** *n*: **to give sb a good ~ing-to** passer un bon savon à qn*.

tall [tɔːl] *adj person* grand, de haute taille; *building etc* haut, élevé. **how ~ is that mast?** quelle est la hauteur de ce mât?; **how ~ are you?** combien mesurez-vous?; **he is 6 feet ~** ≃ il mesure 1 mètre 80; (*fig*) **a ~ story** une histoire à dormir debout; **that's a ~ order!** c'est demander un peu trop! ♦ **tallboy** *n* commode *f*. ♦ **tallness** *n* grande taille *f*; hauteur *f*.

tally ['tælɪ] **1** *n* compte *m*. **to keep a ~ of** (*count*) tenir le compte de; (*mark off on list*) pointer. **2** *vi* correspondre (*with* à).

talon ['tælən] *n [bird]* serre *f*; *[tiger etc]* griffe *f*.

tamarisk ['tæmərɪsk] *n* tamaris *m*.

tambourine [ˌtæmbə'riːn] *n* tambourin *m*.

tame [teɪm] **1** *adj bird, animal* apprivoisé; (*fig*) *story, match* insipide. **to become** *or* **grow ~(r)** s'apprivoiser; (*hum*) **our ~ American** notre Américain de service. **2** *vt bird, wild animal* apprivoiser; *esp lion, tiger* dompter; (*fig*) *passion* maîtriser; *person* mater. ♦ **tamely** *adv agree* docilement. ♦ **tamer** *n* dresseur *m*, -euse *f*; **lion-~r** dompteur *m*, -euse *f* (de lions).

tamper ['tæmpəʳ] *vi*: **to ~ with** (*gen*) toucher à (*sans permission*); *lock* essayer de crocheter; *document, text,* (*Jur*) *evidence* falsifier.

tampon ['tæmpən] *n* (*Med*) tampon *m*.

tan [tæn] **1** *n* (**sun~**) bronzage *m*. **she's got a lovely ~** elle est bien bronzée. **2** *adj* brun roux *inv*. **3** *vt* **(a)** *hides* tanner. (*fig*) **to ~ sb's hide*** rosser qn*. **(b)** *[sun] sunbather* bronzer; *sailor, farmer etc* basaner. **to get ~ned** = **to tan** (*V* 4). **4** *vi* bronzer. ♦ **tanned** *adj* (**sun~ned**) bronzé; basané. ♦ **tanner** *n* tanneur *m*. ♦ **tannery** *n* tannerie *f* (*établissement*). ♦ **tanning** *n [hides]* tannage *m*; (*‡fig: beating*) tannée‡ *f*; (*suntanning*) bronzage *m*.

tang [tæŋ] *n* (*taste*) saveur *f* forte et piquante; (*smell*) odeur forte et piquante.

tangent ['tændʒənt] *n* (*Math*) tangente *f*. (*fig*) **to fly off at a ~** partir dans une digression.

tangerine [ˌtændʒə'riːn] **1** *n* mandarine *f*. **2** *adj* (*colour*) mandarine *inv*.

tangible ['tændʒəbl] *adj* (*gen*) tangible; *assets* matériel, réel. ♦ **tangibly** *adv* tangiblement.

tangle ['tæŋgl] **1** *n [wool, rope, bushes]* enchevêtrement *m*; (*fig: muddle*) confusion *f*. **to get into a ~** (*gen*) s'enchevêtrer; *[hair]* s'emmêler; (*fig*) *[accounts etc]* s'embrouiller; *[traffic]* se bloquer; *[person]* s'embrouiller; **the whole affair was a hopeless ~** toute cette histoire était affreusement embrouillée. **2** *vt* (**~ up**: *lit, fig*) enchevêtrer, embrouiller. **~d** *string, rope, wool* embrouillé, enchevêtré; *hair* emmêlé, enchevêtré; **to get ~d (up)** = **to get into a tangle** (*V* 1). **3** *vi* (**fig*) **to ~ with sb** se colleter avec qn*.

tank [tæŋk] *n* **(a)** (*container*) (*for storage: for gas, petrol etc*) réservoir *m*; (*esp for rainwater*) citerne *f*; (*for transporting*) réservoir, cuve *f*; (*esp oil*) tank *m*; (*for fermenting, processing etc*) cuve (*also Phot*); (*for fish*) aquarium *m*. **fuel ~** réservoir à carburant. **(b)** (*Mil*) char *m* (de combat), tank *m*.

tank up* *vi* (*Aut*) faire le plein.

♦ **tanker** *n* (*truck*) camion-citerne *m*; (*ship*) pétrolier *m*; (*aircraft*) avion-ravitailleur *m*; (*Rail*) wagon-citerne *m*. ♦ **tankful** *n*: **a ~ful of petrol** un réservoir (plein) d'essence; **a ~ful of water** une citerne (pleine) d'eau.

tankard ['tæŋkəd] *n* chope *f* (à bière).

tannoy ['tænɔɪ] *n* ®: **over the ~** par les haut-parleurs.

tantalize ['tæntəlaɪz] *vt* tourmenter (*par de faux espoirs*). ♦ **tantalizing** *adj* (*gen*) terriblement tentant; *smell* terriblement appétissant; *slowness etc* désespérant. ♦ **tantalizingly** *adv* d'une façon cruellement tentante; **tantalizingly slowly** avec une lenteur désespérante.

tantamount ['tæntəmaʊnt] *adj*: **~ to** équivalent à.

tantrum ['tæntrəm] *n* (**temper ~**) crise *f* de colère. **to have** *or* **throw a ~** piquer une colère.

tap[1] [tæp] **1** *n* (*Brit*) robinet *m*. **beer on ~** bière *f* en fût; (*fig*) **funds/resources on ~** fonds *mpl*/ressources *fpl* disponibles. **2** *adj*: (*Brit*) **~ water** eau *f* du robinet. **3** *vt cask, barrel* mettre en perce; *pine* gemmer; *other tree* inciser; (*Elec*) *current* capter; *wire* brancher; *telephone* mettre sur écoute; (*fig*) *resources, supplies* exploiter. **my phone is being ~ped** mon téléphone est sur écoute; **they ~ped her for a loan*** ils lui ont demandé un prêt; **to ~ sb for information** soutirer des renseignements à qn. ♦ **taproom** *n* salle *f* de bistrot. ♦ **taproot** *n* (*Bot*) racine *f* pivotante.

tap[2] [tæp] **1** *n* petit coup *m*. **there was a ~ at the door** on a frappé doucement à la porte. **2** *vi* frapper doucement. **3** *vt* (*knock*) frapper doucement; (*pat*) tapoter. **he ~ped me on the shoulder** il m'a tapé sur l'épaule; **to ~ out a message in Morse** transmettre un message en morse. ♦ **tap-dance 1** *n* claquettes *fpl*; **2** *vi* faire des claquettes. ♦ **tap-dancer** *n* danseur *m*, -euse *f* de claquettes.

tape [teɪp] **1** *n* (*gen*) ruban *m*, bande *f*; (*Sewing: decoration*) ruban, ganse *f*; (*Sewing: for binding*) extra-fort *m*; (*for parcels*) bolduc *m*; (*sticky ~*) scotch *m* ®; (*Med*) sparadrap *m*; (*for recording*) bande magnétique; (*Sport*) fil *m* d'arrivée; (*at opening ceremonies*) ruban. **the message was coming through on the ~** le message nous parvenait sur bande (perforée). **2** *adj*: **~ deck** platine *f* de magnétophone; (*Brit*) **~ machine** téléscripteur *m*; **~ measure** mètre *m* à ruban. **3** *vt* **(a)** (**~ up**) *parcel etc* attacher avec du ruban *or* du bolduc, (*with sticky ~*) coller avec du scotch; (**~ up, ~ together**) *broken vase etc* recoller avec du scotch *etc*. (*Brit fig*) **I've got him/it all ~d*** je sais parfaitement ce qu'il vaut/de quoi il retourne*; **they had the game/situation ~d*** ils avaient le jeu/la situation bien en main. **(b)** (*record*) *song, message, video material* enregistrer. ♦ **tape-record** *vt* enregistrer. ♦ **tape-recorder** *n* magnétophone *m*. ♦ **tape-recording** *n* enregistrement *m* (au magnétophone). ♦ **tapeworm** *n* ténia *m*, ver *m* solitaire.

taper ['teɪpəʳ] **1** *n* (*for lighting*) bougie *f* fine; (*Rel: narrow candle*) cierge *m*. **2** *vt table leg, trouser leg* fuseler; *hair* effiler; *structure, shape* terminer en pointe.

taper off *vi [sound, storm]* aller en diminuant; *[speech, conversation]* s'effilocher.

♦ **tapered** *or* ♦ **tapering** *adj column, fingers* fuselé; *structure etc* en pointe.

tapestry ['tæpɪstrɪ] *n* tapisserie *f*.

tapioca [ˌtæpɪ'əʊkə] *n* tapioca *m*.

tar [tɑːʳ] **1** *n* goudron *m*. **2** *vt* goudronner. ♦ **tarring** *n* goudronnage *m*. ♦ **tarry** *adj substance* goudronneux; (*tarstained*) plein de goudron.

tarantula [tə'ræntjʊlə] *n* tarentule *f*.

tardy ['tɑːdɪ] *adj* tardif.

target ['tɑːgɪt] **1** *n* (*gen; also fig: of criticism etc*) cible *f*; (*Mil: in attack; fig: objective*) objectif *m*. **to be on ~** *[missile etc]* suivre la trajectoire prévue; *[remark, criticism]* mettre en plein dans le mille; (*in timing etc*) ne pas avoir de retard; **dead on ~!** pile!; **to set o.s. a ~ of £100** se fixer comme objectif de réunir 100 livres. **2** *adj date, amount etc* fixé, prévu. **~ practice** exercices *mpl* de tir.

tariff ['tærɪf] *n* (*tax*) tarif *m* douanier; (*price list*) tarif.

tarmac ['tɑːmæk] ® **1** *n* (*substance*) macadam *m* goudronné; (*runway*) piste *f*; (*airport apron*) aire *f* d'envol. **2** *vt* goudronner.

tarnish ['tɑːnɪʃ] **1** *vt* (*gen*) ternir; *[mirror]* désargenter. **2** *vi* se ternir; se désargenter.

tarot ['tærəʊ] *n* tarot *m*. ~ **card** tarot.
tarpaulin [tɑː'pɔːlɪn] *n* (*material*) toile *f* goudronnée; (*sheet*) bâche *f* (goudronnée).
tarragon ['tærəgən] *n* estragon *m*.
tart[1] [tɑːt] *adj* (*gen*) âpre; *answer etc* acerbe. ♦ **tartly** *adv* d'une manière acerbe. ♦ **tartness** *n* aigreur *f*.
tart[2] [tɑːt] *n* **(a)** (*Culin*) tarte *f*; (*small*) tartelette *f*. **apple** ~ tarte(lette) aux pommes. **(b)** (‡: *prostitute*) poule‡ *f*, putain‡ *f*.
tart up‡ *vt sep* retaper*.
tartan ['tɑːtən] **1** *n* tartan *m*. **2** *adj garment* écossais. ~ **rug** plaid *m*.
tartar[1] ['tɑːtəʳ] *n* (*Chem etc*) tartre *m*. ♦ **tartaric** *adj* tartrique.
tartar[2] ['tɑːtəʳ] **1** *n* homme *m* intraitable; (*woman*) mégère *f*. **2** *adj* (*Culin*) tartare.
task [tɑːsk] **1** *n* tâche *f*. **a hard** ~ une lourde tâche; **to take sb to** ~ prendre qn à partie (*for, about* pour). **2** *vt brain, patience* mettre à l'épreuve. **it didn't** ~ **him too much** cela ne lui a pas demandé trop d'effort. **3** *adj* (*Mil, Police*) ~ **force** détachement *m* spécial. ♦ **taskmaster** *n*: **a hard** ~**master** un véritable tyran.
tassel ['tæsəl] *n* gland *m* (*de tapisserie*).
taste [teɪst] **1** *n* goût *m*. **it has no** ~ cela n'a aucun goût; **it left a bad** ~ cela m'a laissé un goût déplaisant, (*fig*) j'en ai gardé une amertume; (*fig*) **to have (good)** ~ avoir du goût; **he has no** ~ il a très mauvais goût; **in good/bad** ~ de bon/mauvais goût; **would you like a** ~ ? voulez-vous y goûter?; **I gave him a** ~ **of the wine** je lui ai fait goûter le vin; (*fig*) **it gave him a** ~ **of the work** cela lui a donné un aperçu du travail; **a** ~ **of happiness** une idée du bonheur; (*small amount*) **a** ~ **of** un tout petit peu de; **to be to sb's** ~ plaire à qn; **to have a** ~ **for** avoir du goût *or* un penchant pour; **to acquire a** ~ **for** prendre goût à; (*Culin*) **sweeten to** ~ sucrer à volonté; **there's no accounting for** ~ des goûts et des couleurs on ne discute pas; **each to his own** ~, ~**s differ** chacun son goût; **one's** ~**(s) in music** ses goûts musicaux; **he has expensive** ~**s in cars** il a le goût des voitures de luxe.

2 *vt* **(a)** (*perceive flavour of*) sentir (le goût de). **I can't** ~ **the garlic** je ne sens pas l'ail; **you won't** ~ **it** tu n'en sentiras pas le goût. **(b)** (*sample*) *food, drink, power, freedom* goûter à; (*esp for first time*) goûter de; (*to test quality*) *food, drink* goûter; *wine* (*at table*) goûter, (*at wine-tasting etc*) déguster. ~ **this!** goûtez à ça!; **I have never** ~**d snails** je n'ai jamais mangé d'escargots; **he had not** ~**d food for a week** il n'avait rien mangé depuis une semaine.

3 *vi*: **it doesn't** ~ **at all** cela n'a aucun goût; **to** ~ **bitter** avoir un goût amer; **to** ~ **good/bad** avoir bon/mauvais goût; **to** ~ **of** *or* **like sth** avoir un goût de qch; **it** ~**s all right to me** d'après moi cela a un goût normal.

♦ **tasteful** *adj* de bon goût. ♦ **tastefully** *adv* avec goût. ♦ **tastefulness** *n* bon goût *m*. ♦ **tasteless** *adj food* fade; *medicine* qui n'a aucun goût; *remark, decoration* de mauvais goût. ♦ **tastelessly** *adv* sans goût. ♦ **tastelessness** *n* fadeur *f*; mauvais goût *m*. ♦ **taster** *n* dégustateur *m*, -trice *f*. ♦ **tastiness** *n* saveur *f* agréable. ♦ **tasty** *adj food* savoureux; *titbit* succulent.
ta-ta* ['tæ'tɑː] *excl* (*Brit*) salut!*
tatters ['tætəz] *npl* lambeaux *mpl*. ♦ **tattered** *adj object* en lambeaux; *person* déguenillé.
tattle ['tætl] **1** *vi* cancaner. **2** *n* cancans *mpl*. ♦ **tattler** *n* commère *f* (*pej*).
tattoo[1] [tə'tuː] **1** *vt* tatouer. **2** *n* tatouage *m*.
tattoo[2] [tə'tuː] *n* (*Mil: show*) parade *f* militaire.
tatty* ['tætɪ] *adj* (*gen*) défraîchi; *paint* écaillé; *poster, book* écorné.
taught [tɔːt] *pret, ptp of* **teach**.
taunt [tɔːnt] **1** *n* raillerie *f*. **2** *vt* railler. **to** ~ **sb with cowardice** taxer qn de lâcheté. ♦ **taunting 1** *adj* railleur; **2** *n* railleries *fpl*.
Taurus ['tɔːrəs] *n* (*Astron*) le Taureau.
taut [tɔːt] *adj* (*lit, fig*) tendu.
tautology [tɔː'tɒlədʒɪ] *n* tautologie *f*. ♦ **tautological** *adj* tautologique.
tavern† ['tævən] *n* taverne† *f*.
tawdry ['tɔːdrɪ] *adj goods* de camelote*, médiocre; *clothes* tapageur; (*fig*) *motive etc* indigne. ♦ **tawdriness** *n* qualité *f* médiocre.
tawny ['tɔːnɪ] *adj* fauve (*couleur*).
tax [tæks] **1** *n* (*on goods, services*) taxe *f*, impôt *m* (*on* sur); (*income* ~) impôts. **before/after** ~ avant/après l'impôt; **half of it goes in** ~ on en perd la moitié en impôts; **how much** ~ **do you pay?** combien d'impôts payez-vous?; **I paid £1,000 in** ~ j'ai payé 1 000 livres d'impôts *or* de contributions; **free of** ~ exempt d'impôt; **to put a** ~ **on sth** taxer *or* imposer qch; **petrol** ~ taxe sur l'essence. **2** *adj authorities, system etc* fiscal. ~ **evasion** fraude *f* fiscale; ~ **form** feuille *f* d'impôts; **for** ~ **purposes** pour des raisons fiscales. **3** *vt* **(a)** *goods etc* taxer, imposer; *income, profits, person* imposer; (*fig*) *patience etc* mettre à l'épreuve. **(b)** taxer (*sb with sth* qn de qch). **to** ~ **sb with doing** accuser qn de faire (*or* d'avoir fait). ♦ **taxable** *adj* imposable. ♦ **taxation 1** *n* (*act*) taxation *f*; (*taxes*) impôts *mpl*; **2** *adj authority, system* fiscal. ♦ **tax-collector** *n* percepteur *m*. ♦ **tax-deductible** *adj* sujet à dégrèvements (d'impôts). ♦ **tax-free** *adj* exempt d'impôts. ♦ **taxing** *adj* éprouvant. ♦ **taxman*** *n*: **the** ~**man** le percepteur. ♦ **taxpayer** *n* contribuable *mf*.
taxi ['tæksɪ] **1** *n* taxi *m*. **by** ~ en taxi. **2** *adj charges etc* de taxi. **3** *vi* **(a)** *[aircraft]* **to** ~ **along the runway** rouler lentement le long de la piste. **(b)** (*go by* ~) aller en taxi. ♦ **taxicab** *n* taxi *m*. ♦ **taxi-driver** *n* chauffeur *m* de taxi. ♦ **taximeter** *n* taximètre *m*. ♦ **taxi-rank** *n* station *f* de taxis.
taxidermy ['tæksɪdɜːmɪ] *n* empaillage *m*, taxidermie *f*. ♦ **taxidermist** *n* empailleur *m*, -euse *f*.
tea [tiː] *n* **(a)** thé *m*. **she made a pot of** ~ elle a fait du thé; **mint** *etc* ~ tisane *f* de menthe *etc*; **beef** ~ bouillon *m* de viande; (*fig*) **not for all the** ~ **in China** pour rien au monde. **(b)** (*meal*) thé *m*; (*for children*) ≃ goûter *m*. **to have** ~ prendre le thé; *[children]* goûter. ♦ **tea-bag** *n* sachet *m* de thé. ♦ **tea-break** *n* pause-thé *f*; **to have a** ~**-break** faire la pause-thé. ♦ **tea-caddy** *n* boîte *f* à thé. ♦ **teacake** *n* petit pain *m* brioché. ♦ **tea-chest** *n* caisse *f* (à thé). ♦ **teacloth** *n* (*for dishes*) torchon *m*; (*for table*) nappe *f*; (*for trolley, tray*) napperon *m*. ♦ **tea-cosy** *n* couvre-théière *m*. ♦ **teacup** *n* tasse *f* à thé. ♦ **tea-leaf** *n* feuille *f* de thé; **to read the** ~**-leaves** ≃ lire dans le marc du café. ♦ **tea party** *n* thé *m* (*réception*). ♦ **tea-plate** *n* petite assiette. ♦ **teapot** *n* théière *f*. ♦ **tearoom** *n* salon *m* de thé. ♦ **tea-service** *or* ♦ **tea-set** *n* service *m* à thé. ♦ **teashop** *n* pâtisserie-salon de thé *f*. ♦ **teaspoon** *n* petite cuiller *f*. ♦ **teaspoonful** *n* cuillerée *f* à café. ♦ **tea-things** *npl* service *m* à thé; (*dirty dishes*) vaisselle *f* après le thé. ♦ **teatime** *n* l'heure *f* du thé. ♦ **tea-towel** *n* torchon *m* (à vaisselle).
teach [tiːtʃ] *pret, ptp* **taught 1** *vt* (*gen*) apprendre (*sb sth, sth to sb* qch à qn); (*Scol, Univ etc*) enseigner (*sb sth, sth to sb* qch à qn). **to** ~ **sb (how) to do** apprendre à qn à faire; **I'll** ~ **you what to do** je t'apprendrai ce qu'il faut faire; **he** ~**es French** il enseigne le français; (*US*) **to** ~ **school** être professeur (*or* instituteur *etc*); **to** ~ **o.s. (to do) sth** apprendre (à faire) qch tout seul; (*fig*) **that will** ~ **him a lesson!** ça lui apprendra!; **that will** ~ **you to mind your own business!** ça t'apprendra à te mêler de tes affaires!

2 *vi* (*gen*) enseigner. **he wanted to** ~ il voulait enseigner; **he had been** ~**ing all morning** il avait fait cours toute la matinée.

♦ **teachable** *adj subject* enseignable. ♦ **teacher** *n* (*gen*) professeur *m*; (*primary school*) instituteur *m*, -trice *f*; **she is a maths ~er** elle est professeur de maths; **the ~ers accepted the government's offer** les enseignants *mpl* ont accepté l'offre du gouvernement; **~er's handbook** livre *m* du maître; **~er(s') training college** ≈ école *f* normale; **~er training** formation *f* pédagogique; **to get one's ~er training certificate** (*primary*) ≈ sortir de l'école normale; (*secondary*) ≈ avoir son C.A.P.E.S. *etc*. ♦ **teach-in** *n* séance *f* d'études. ♦ **teaching 1** *n* (*gen*) enseignement *m* (*on, about* sur); **to go into ~ing** entrer dans l'enseignement; **2** *adj staff* enseignant; *material* pédagogique; *machine* à enseigner; **~ing hospital** centre *m* hospitalo-universitaire; **the ~ing profession** (*teachers collectively*) les enseignants *mpl*.

teak [tiːk] *n* teck *m*.

team [tiːm] **1** *n* (*gen*) équipe *f*; *[horses, oxen]* attelage *m*. **football/research ~** équipe de football/de chercheurs. **2** *adj*: **~ games/spirit** jeux *mpl*/esprit *m* d'équipe; **~ teaching** enseignement *m* coordonné pour groupes. **3** *vt* (**~ up**) *person* mettre en collaboration (*with* avec); *thing* associer (*with* avec).

team up *vi [people]* faire équipe (*with* avec; *to do* pour faire).

♦ **team-mate** *n* coéquipier *m*, -ière *f*. ♦ **team-member** *n* équipier *m*, -ière *f*. ♦ **teamster** *n* (*US*) camionneur *m*. ♦ **teamwork** *n* collaboration *f* (d'équipe).

tear[1] [tɛəʳ] (*vb: pret* **tore**, *ptp* **torn**) **1** *n* déchirure *f*, accroc *m*. **to make a ~ in sth** déchirer qch; **it has a ~ in it** c'est déchiré. **2** *vt* **(a)** (*gen*) déchirer. **to ~ a hole in** faire une déchirure *or* un accroc à; **to ~ to pieces** *or* **to bits*** *paper* déchirer en menus morceaux; *garment* mettre en lambeaux; *prey* mettre en pièces; (*fig*) *play etc* éreinter; *argument* démolir; **to ~ open** *envelope* déchirer; *letter* déchirer l'enveloppe de; *parcel* ouvrir en déchirant l'emballage de; **to ~ one's hair** s'arracher les cheveux; (*Med*) **to ~ a muscle** se déchirer un muscle; (*fig*) **that's torn it!*** voilà qui flanque tout par terre!*; (*fig*) **torn by war/remorse** *etc* déchiré par la guerre/le remords *etc*; **to be torn between ...** balancer entre ... . **(b)** (*snatch*) arracher (*from sb* à qn; *out of, off, from sth* de qch). **3** *vi* **(a)** *[cloth etc]* se déchirer. **(b)** (*rush*) **to ~ out/down** *etc* sortir/descendre *etc* à toute allure.

tear away *vt sep* (*lit, fig*) arracher (*from sb* à qn; *from sth* de qch). (*fig*) **I couldn't ~ myself away** je n'arrivais pas à m'en arracher.

tear down *vt sep poster, flag* arracher (*from* de); *building* démolir.

tear off *vt sep wrapping* arracher (*from* de); *sth perforated* détacher (*from* de).

tear out *vt sep* arracher (*from* de); *cheque, ticket* détacher (*from* de).

tear up *vt sep* **(a)** *paper*, (*fig*) *contract* déchirer; *offer* reprendre. **(b)** *stake, shrub* arracher.

♦ **tearing 1** *n* déchirement *m*; **2** *adj*: **in a ~ing hurry*** terriblement pressé.

tear[2] [tɪəʳ] *n* larme *f*. **in ~s** en larmes; **there were ~s in her eyes** elle avait les larmes aux yeux; **near** *or* **close to ~s** au bord des larmes; **to burst into ~s** fondre en larmes; **it brought ~s to his eyes** cela lui a fait venir les larmes aux yeux. ♦ **teardrop** *n* larme *f*. ♦ **tearful** *adj* (*gen*) larmoyant; **she was very ~ful** elle a beaucoup pleuré. ♦ **tearfully** *adv* les larmes aux yeux. ♦ **teargas** *n* gaz *m* lacrymogène. ♦ **tear-stained** *adj* barbouillé de larmes.

tease [tiːz] **1** *vt* (*playfully*) taquiner; (*cruelly*) tourmenter. **2** *n* (*person*) taquin(e) *m(f)*. ♦ **teasel** *n* (*Bot*) cardère *f*. ♦ **teaser** *n* problème *m* (difficile). ♦ **teasing 1** *n* taquineries *fpl*; **2** *adj* taquin.

teat [tiːt] *n [animal, bottle etc]* tétine *f*; *[woman]* bout *m* de sein.

technical ['teknɪkəl] *adj* (*gen*) technique. **~ college** collège *m* technique; **~ hitch** incident *m* technique; (*Jur*) **~ offence** contravention *f*. ♦ **technicality** *n* (*detail/difficulty/fault*) détail *m*/difficulté *f*/ennui *m* technique; **the ~ities** les détails techniques. ♦ **technically** *adv* techniquement; (*fig*) **~ly we shouldn't be here** en principe on ne devrait pas être là. ♦ **technician** *n* technicien(ne) *m(f)*. ♦ **technique** [tek'niːk] *n* technique *f*.

technology [tek'nɒlədʒɪ] *n* technologie *f*. **Ministry of T~** ministère *m* des Affaires technologiques. ♦ **technological** *adj* technologique. ♦ **technologist** *n* technologue *mf*.

teddy ['tedɪ] *n* (**~ bear**) nounours *m* (*baby talk*), ours *m* en peluche.

tedious ['tiːdɪəs] *adj* ennuyeux, assommant*. ♦ **tediously** *adv* d'une façon ennuyeuse. ♦ **tediousness** *or* ♦ **tedium** *n* ennui *m*.

tee [tiː] (*Golf*) *n* tee *m*.

teem [tiːm] *vi* **(a)** *[crowds, river, street]* grouiller (*with* de). **(b) it was ~ing (with rain), the rain was ~ing down** il pleuvait à verse. ♦ **teeming** *adj* **(a)** *crowd* grouillant; *street* grouillant de monde; *river* grouillant de poissons; **(b)** *rain* battant.

teenage ['tiːneɪdʒ] *adj* adolescent (*de 13 à 19 ans*); *behaviour* d'adolescent, de jeune; *fashions* pour jeunes. ♦ **teenager** *n* jeune *mf*, adolescent(e) *m(f)*. ♦ **teens** *npl* jeunesse *f*, adolescence *f*; **still in his teens** encore adolescent; **he is in his early teens** il a un peu plus de treize ans.

teeny* ['tiːnɪ] *adj* tout petit.

tee-shirt ['tiːʃɜːt] *n* T-shirt *m*.

teeter ['tiːtəʳ] *vi [person]* chanceler; *[pile]* vaciller. **to ~ on the edge of** être prêt à tomber dans.

teeth [tiːθ] *npl of* **tooth**. ♦ **teethe** [tiːð] *vi* faire ses dents. ♦ **teething 1** *n* poussée *f* des dents; **2** *adj*: **~ing ring** anneau *m* (*de bébé qui fait ses dents*); (*fig*) **~ing troubles** difficultés *fpl* initiales.

teetotal ['tiː'təʊtl] *adj* qui ne boit jamais d'alcool. ♦ **teetotaller**, (*US*) **teetotaler** *n* personne *f* qui ne boit jamais d'alcool.

tele... ['telɪ] *pref* télé... . ♦ **telecommunications** *npl* télécommunications *fpl*.

telegram ['telɪgræm] *n* télégramme *m*; (*Diplomacy, Press*) dépêche *f*.

telegraph ['telɪgrɑːf] **1** *n* télégraphe *m*. **~ pole** poteau *m* télégraphique. **2** *vti* télégraphier. ♦ **telegraphic** *adj* télégraphique. ♦ **telegraphist** [tɪ'legrəfɪst] *n* télégraphiste *mf*. ♦ **telegraphy** [tɪ'legrəfɪ] *n* télégraphie *f*.

telepathy [tɪ'lepəθɪ] *n* télépathie *f*. ♦ **telepathic** [ˌtelɪ'pæθɪk] *adj* télépathique; (*iro*) **I'm not telepathic!*** je ne suis pas devin!

telephone ['telɪfəʊn] **1** *n* téléphone *m*. **on the ~** au téléphone. **2** *vt person* téléphoner à; *message* téléphoner (*to* à). **3** *vi* téléphoner. **4** *adj*: **~ book** *or* **directory** annuaire *m*; **~ booth** *or* **box** *or* **kiosk** cabine *f* téléphonique; **~ call** coup *m* de téléphone*, appel *m* téléphonique; **~ exchange** central *m* téléphonique; **~ line** ligne *f* téléphonique; **~ message** message *m* téléphonique; **~ number** numéro *m* de téléphone; **~ operator** standardiste *mf*, téléphoniste *mf*; **~ subscriber** abonné(e) *m(f)* au téléphone. ♦ **telephonic** [ˌtelɪ'fɒnɪk] *adj* téléphonique. ♦ **telephonist** [tɪ'lefənɪst] *n* téléphoniste *mf*.

telephoto ['telɪ'fəʊtəʊ] *adj*: **~ lens** téléobjectif *m*.

teleprint ['telɪˌprɪnt] *vt* transmettre par téléscripteur. ♦ **teleprinter** *n* téléscripteur *m*.

telescope ['telɪskəʊp] **1** *n* (*reflecting, also Astron*) télescope *m*; (*refracting*) lunette *f* d'approche. **2** *vi [railway carriages etc]* se télescoper; *[umbrella]* se plier. ♦ **telescopic** [ˌtelɪs'kɒpɪk] *adj* télescopique; *umbrella* pliant; **telescopic lens** téléobjectif *m*.

teletype ['telɪtaɪp] ® (*US*) = **teleprint, teleprinter.**
televiewer ['telɪˌvjuːəʳ] *n* téléspectateur *m*, -trice *f*. ♦ **televiewing** *n* (*watching TV*) la télévision; **this evening's televiewing contains ...** le programme de la télévision pour ce soir comprend ... .
television ['telɪˌvɪʒən] **1** *n* télévision *f*; (~ **set**) télévision, téléviseur *m*. **on** ~ à la télévision, à la télé*; **colour** ~ télévision (en) couleur. **2** *adj actor, camera, studio* de télévision; *play, report, serial* télévisé. ~ **programme** émission *f* de télévision. ♦ **televise** *vt* téléviser.
telex ['teleks] **1** *n* télex *m*. **2** *vt* envoyer par télex.
tell [tel] *pret, ptp* **told 1** *vt* **(a)** (*gen*) dire (*sb sth* qch à qn; *sb to do* à qn de faire; *that* que); *story, adventure* raconter (*to* à); *a lie, the truth* dire; *secret, sb's age* révéler (*to* à); *the future* prédire. **I told him where/why** je lui ai dit où/pourquoi; **I told him the way to London** je lui ai expliqué comment aller à Londres; **to** ~ **sb sth again** répéter *or* redire qch à qn; **he's mad, I can** ~ **you!** il est fou, c'est moi qui te le dis!*; **don't** ~ **me you've lost it!** tu ne vas pas me dire que tu l'as perdu!; **I told you so!** je te l'avais bien dit!; **... or so I've been told** ... ou du moins c'est ce qu'on m'a dit; **do as you're told** fais ce qu'on te dit; **I** ~ **you what*, let's go ...** tiens, si on allait ...*; **you're** ~**ing me!*** à qui le dis-tu!; ~ **me another!*** à d'autres!*; **to** ~ **sb's fortune** dire la bonne aventure à qn; **to** ~ **fortunes** dire la bonne aventure; **can you** ~ **the time?** sais-tu lire l'heure?; **can you** ~ **me the time?** peux-tu me dire l'heure qu'il est?; **that** ~**s me all I need to know** maintenant je sais tout ce qu'il me faut savoir; **that** ~**s us a lot about ...** cela nous en dit long sur ...; **she was** ~**ing him about it** elle lui en parlait; **I told him about what had happened** je lui ai dit ce qui était arrivé.

(b) (*distinguish*) distinguer (*sth from sth* qch de qch); (*know*) savoir. **I can't** ~ **them apart** je ne peux pas les distinguer l'un de l'autre; **how can I** ~ **what he will do?** comment puis-je savoir ce qu'il va faire?; **there's no** ~**ing what ...** impossible de dire ce que ...; **no one can** ~ **what ...** personne ne peut savoir ce que ...; **you can** ~ **he's clever** on voit bien qu'il est intelligent; **I can't** ~ **the difference** je ne vois pas la différence (*between* entre); **you can't** ~ **much from his letter** sa lettre n'en dit pas très long.

(c) 30 all told 30 en tout.

2 *vi* **(a)** parler (*of, about* de). **more than words can** ~ plus qu'on ne peut dire; **I won't** ~**!** je ne le répéterai à personne!; **to** ~ **on sb*** rapporter *or* cafarder* sur qn. **(b)** (*know*) savoir. **how can I** ~? comment le saurais-je?; **I can't** ~ je n'en sais rien; **who can** ~? qui sait?; **you never can** ~ on ne sait jamais; **you can't** ~ **from his letter** on ne peut pas savoir d'après sa lettre. **(c)** (*have effect*) se faire sentir (*on sb/sth* sur qn/qch). **his age told against him** il était handicapé par son âge.
tell off* *vt sep* gronder, attraper* (*sb for sth* qn pour qch; *for doing* pour avoir fait). **to be told off*** se faire attraper*.

♦ **teller** *n* (*Banking*) caissier *m*, -ière *f*; *[votes]* scrutateur *m*, -trice *f*. ♦ **telling** *adj figures, point* révélateur; *argument, style* efficace; *blow* bien assené. ♦ **telling-off*** *n* attrapade* *f*; **to get/give a good** ~**ing-off*** recevoir/passer un bon savon* (*from* de; *to* à). ♦ **telltale 1** *n* rapporteur *m*, -euse *f*, cafard* *m*; **2** *adj mark etc* révélateur.
telly* ['telɪ] *n* (*abbr of* **television**) télé* *f*. **on the** ~ à la télé.
temerity [tɪ'merɪtɪ] *n* audace *f*, témérité *f*.
temp* [temp] *n* (*abbr of* **temporary**) intérimaire *mf*.
temper ['tempəʳ] **1** *n* (*nature, disposition*) tempérament *m*, caractère *m*; (*mood*) humeur *f*; (*fit of bad* ~) (accès *m* de) colère *f*. **to have an even** ~, **to be even-**~**ed** être d'un caractère *or* tempérament égal; **to have a hot** *or* **quick** ~ être soupe au lait; **to have a nasty** ~ avoir un sale caractère; **in a foul** ~ d'une humeur massacrante; **in a good/bad** ~ de bonne/mauvaise humeur; **to keep one's** ~ garder son calme; **to lose one's** ~ se mettre en colère; **to be in a** ~ être en colère (*with sb* contre qn; *over, about sth* à propos de qch); **to put sb into a** ~ mettre qn en colère; **in a fit of** ~ **he ...** dans un accès de colère il ...; **he flew into a** ~ il a explosé. **2** *vt* (*fig*) *effects etc* tempérer (*with* par). ♦ **temperament** *n* (*nature*) tempérament *m*; (*moodiness*) humeur *f*. ♦ **temperamental** *adj* **(a)** (*capricious*) capricieux; **(b)** (*innate*) inné.
temperance ['tempərəns] **1** *n* modération *f*; (*in drinking*) tempérance *f*. **2** *adj movement* antialcoolique; *hotel* où l'on ne sert pas de boissons alcoolisées. ♦ **temperate** *adj* tempéré.
temperature ['temprɪtʃəʳ] *n* température *f*. **at a high** ~ à une forte température; **to have** *or* **run a** ~ avoir de la température *or* de la fièvre; **to take sb's** ~ prendre la température de qn.
tempest ['tempɪst] *n* tempête *f*. ♦ **tempestuous** *adj* (*fig*) *meeting, relationship* orageux; *person* passionné.
template ['templɪt] *n* patron *m*, modèle *m*.
temple[1] ['templ] *n* (*Rel*) temple *m*.
temple[2] ['templ] *n* (*Anat*) tempe *f*.
tempo ['tempəʊ] *n, pl* **-pi** tempo *m*.
temporal ['tempərəl] *adj* temporel.
temporary ['tempərərɪ] *adj job, worker* temporaire; *secretary* intérimaire; *teacher* suppléant; *ticket, licence* valide à titre temporaire; *building, decision, method, powers* provisoire; *relief, improvement* passager. ♦ **temporarily** *adv agree, appoint etc* provisoirement, temporairement; *lame, disappointed etc* pendant un certain temps. ♦ **temporize** *vi* chercher à gagner du temps.
tempt [tempt] *vt* tenter. **to** ~ **sb to do** donner à qn l'envie *or* la tentation de faire; **try and** ~ **her to eat** tâchez de la persuader de manger; **I am very** ~**ed to accept** je suis très tenté d'accepter; **I'm very** ~**ed** c'est très tentant; **to** ~ **Providence** *or* **fate** tenter la Providence. ♦ **temptation** *n* tentation *f*; **there is no** ~**ation to do so** on n'est nullement tenté de le faire. ♦ **tempter** *n* tentateur *m*. ♦ **tempting** *adj* tentant; *food* appétissant. ♦ **temptingly** *adv* d'une manière tentante. ♦ **temptress** *n* tentatrice *f*.
ten [ten] *adj, n* dix (*m*) *inv*. **there were about** ~ il y en avait une dizaine; **about** ~ **books** une dizaine de livres; ~**s of thousands of ...** des milliers de ...; **to count in** ~**s** compter par dizaines; (*fig*) ~ **to one he won't come** je parie qu'il ne viendra pas; (*fig*) **they're** ~ **a penny** il y en a tant qu'on en veut; *for other phrases V* **six**. ♦ **ten-cent store** *n* (*US*) bazar *m*. ♦ **tenth** *adj, n* dixième (*mf*); (*fraction*) dixième *m*; **nine-**~**ths of** les neuf dixièmes de; (*fig*) la majeure partie de.
tenable ['tenəbl] *adj* défendable.
tenacious [tɪ'neɪʃəs] *adj* tenace. ♦ **tenaciously** *adv* avec ténacité. ♦ **tenacity** *n* ténacité *f*.
tenant ['tenənt] *n* locataire *mf*. ♦ **tenancy** *n* location *f*.
tench [tentʃ] *n* tanche *f*.
tend[1] [tend] *vt sheep, shop* garder; *invalid* soigner; *machine* surveiller.
tend[2] [tend] *vi* avoir tendance (*to do* à faire). **to** ~ **towards** incliner à *or* vers; **I** ~ **to think that ...** j'incline *or* j'ai tendance à penser que ...; **that** ~**s to be the case with ...** c'est en général le cas avec ...; **grey** ~**ing to blue** gris tirant sur le bleu. ♦ **tendency** *n* tendance *f*; **to have a** ~**ency to do** avoir tendance à faire; **the** ~**ency towards socialism** les tendances socialistes.
tender[1] ['tendəʳ] *n* (*boat*) vedette *f* (*de liaison*).
tender[2] ['tendəʳ] **1** *vt* (*proffer*) *object, money,*

apologies offrir; *resignation* donner. **2** *vi* (*Comm*) faire une soumission (*for sth* pour qch). **3** *n* **(a)** (*Comm*) soumission *f* (*for sth* pour qch). **to invite ~s for sth, to put sth out to ~** mettre qch en adjudication. **(b)** (*Fin*) **that is no longer legal ~** cela n'a plus cours.

tender³ ['tendəʳ] *adj* (*gen*) tendre; *flower* délicat, fragile; *spot, bruise* sensible; *conscience, subject* délicat. ♦ **tender-hearted** *adj* sensible. ♦ **tenderloin** *n* filet *m*. ♦ **tenderly** *adv* tendrement. ♦ **tenderness** *n* tendresse *f* (*towards* envers); *[meat etc]* tendreté *f*; délicatesse *f*; fragilité *f*; sensibilité *f*.

tendon ['tendən] *n* tendon *m*.

tendril ['tendrɪl] *n* (*Bot*) vrille *f*.

tenement ['tenɪmənt] *n* (**~ house**) immeuble *m*.

tenet ['tenət] *n* principe *m*.

tennis ['tenɪs] **1** *n* tennis *m*. **a game of ~** une partie de tennis. **2** *adj player, racket, club, shoe* de tennis. **~ ball** balle *f* de tennis; **~ court** (court *m* de) tennis *m*; (*Med*) **~ elbow** synovite *f* du coude.

tenor ['tenəʳ] **1** *n* **(a)** *[speech etc]* sens *m*, substance *f*; *[life, events]* cours *m*. **(b)** (*Mus*) ténor *m*. **2** *adj* (*Mus*) *voice, part* de ténor; *aria* pour ténor; *recorder, saxophone etc* ténor *inv*.

tense¹ [tens] *n* (*Gram*) temps *m*. **in the present ~** au temps présent.

tense² [tens] **1** *adj muscles, person, voice* tendu; *period* de tension; *smile* crispé. **they were ~ with fear** ils étaient crispés de peur; **things were getting ~** l'atmosphère devenait tendue. **2** *vt muscles* tendre. ♦ **tensely** *adv say* d'une voix tendue; *wait* dans l'anxiété. ♦ **tenseness** *or* ♦ **tension** *n* tension *f*.

tent [tent] **1** *n* tente *f*. **2** *adj*: **~ peg/pole** piquet *m*/montant *m* de tente. **3** *vi* camper.

tentacle ['tentəkl] *n* tentacule *m*.

tentative ['tentətɪv] *adj suggestion, gesture, smile* timide; *offer, voice* hésitant; *scheme* expérimental; *conclusion, solution, plan* provisoire. **everything is very ~** rien n'est encore décidé. ♦ **tentatively** *adv* timidement; avec hésitation; expérimentalement; provisoirement.

tenterhooks ['tentəhʊks] *npl*: **on ~** sur des charbons ardents.

tenuous ['tenjʊəs] *adj* ténu.

tenure ['tenjʊəʳ] *n* bail *m*.

tepid ['tepɪd] *adj* (*lit, fig*) tiède. ♦ **tepidly** *adv* (*fig*) sans enthousiasme.

term [tɜ:m] **1** *n* **(a)** (*limit*) terme *m*; (*period*) période *f*. **in the long ~** à long terme; **in the short ~** dans l'immédiat; **long-/short-~** *loan* à long/court terme; *view* à longue/brève échéance; **his ~ of office** la période où il exerçait ses fonctions; **~ of imprisonment** peine *f* de prison.

(b) (*Scol, Univ*) trimestre *m*; (*Jur*) session *f*. **the autumn/spring/summer ~** le premier/deuxième/troisième trimestre.

(c) (*Math, Philos*) terme *m*. **A expressed in ~s of B** A exprimé en fonction de B; (*fig*) **in ~s of production** sur le plan de la production.

(d) (*conditions*) **~s** (*gen*) conditions *fpl*; *[contract etc]* termes *mpl*; (*Comm etc*) prix *mpl*, tarif *m*; **you can name your own ~s** vous êtes libre de stipuler vos conditions; **not on any ~s** à aucune condition; **on his own ~s** sans concessions de sa part; **to come to ~s with** *person* arriver à un accord avec; *problem, situation* accepter; (*Jur*) **~s and conditions** modalités *fpl*; **~s of surrender/of payment** conditions de la reddition/de paiement; **it is not within our ~s of reference** cela n'entre pas dans les termes de notre mandat; **credit ~s** conditions de crédit; (*Comm*) **we offer it on easy ~s** nous offrons des facilités *fpl* de paiement; **our ~s for full board** notre tarif pension complète; **'inclusive ~s: £20'** '20 livres tout compris'.

(e) (*relationship*) **to be on good/bad ~s with sb** être en bons/mauvais termes *or* rapports avec qn; **they're on fairly friendly ~s** ils ont des rapports assez amicaux.

(f) (*expression*) terme *m*, expression *f*. **technical/colloquial ~** terme technique/familier; **in plain *or* simple ~s** en termes clairs.

2 *adj exams etc* trimestriel.

3 *vt* appeler, nommer.

♦ **termtime** *n*: **in ~time** pendant le trimestre.

terminal ['tɜ:mɪnl] **1** *adj stage* terminal; *illness* dans sa phase terminale; *patient* en phase terminale. **2** *n* **(a)** (*Rail, Coach*) terminus *m inv*. **air ~** aérogare *f*; **container ~** terminus de containers; **oil ~** terminal *m* de conduites pétrolières. **(b)** (*Elec*) borne *f*. ♦ **terminate 1** *vt* (*gen*) terminer; *contract* résilier; **2** *vi* se terminer (*in* en, par). ♦ **termination** *n* fin *f*; *[contract]* résiliation *f*; (*Med*) **termination of pregnancy** interruption *f* de grossesse. ♦ **terminus** *n, pl* **-ni** terminus *m inv*.

terminology [,tɜ:mɪ'nɒlədʒɪ] *n* terminologie *f*. ♦ **terminological** *adj* de terminologie.

termite ['tɜ:maɪt] *n* termite *m*.

tern [tɜ:n] *n* hirondelle *f* de mer.

terrace ['terəs] **1** *n* (*gen*) terrasse *f*; (*houses*) rangée *f* de maisons (*attenantes les unes aux autres*). (*Sport*) **the ~s** les gradins *mpl*. **2** *vt hillside* arranger en terrasses. ♦ **terraced** *adj garden, hillside* en terrasses; *house* attenant aux maisons voisines.

terracotta ['terə'kɒtə] *n* terre *f* cuite.

terrain [te'reɪn] *n* terrain *m* (*sol*).

terrestrial [tɪ'restrɪəl] *adj* terrestre.

terrible ['terəbl] *adj* (*gen*) terrible, effroyable; *heat, pain* atroce, terrible; (*less strong*) *holiday, disappointment, report* épouvantable. ♦ **terribly** *adv* (*very*) terriblement; (*very badly*) *play, sing* affreusement mal.

terrier ['terɪəʳ] *n* terrier *m*.

terrific [tə'rɪfɪk] *adj* **(a)** (*terrifying*) terrifiant, épouvantable. **(b)** (*: *extreme etc*) *amount, height* énorme, fantastique; *speed* fou; *noise* épouvantable; *hill, climb* terriblement raide; *heat, cold, anxiety* terrible; *pleasure* formidable*, terrible*. **(c)** (*: *excellent*) *result, news* formidable*. ♦ **terrifically*** *adv* **(a)** (*extremely*) terriblement; (*pej*) épouvantablement. **(b)** (*very well*) *sing, play* formidablement bien*.

terrify ['terɪfaɪ] *vt* terrifier. **to be terrified of** avoir une terreur folle de. ♦ **terrifying** *adj* terrifiant, épouvantable. ♦ **terrifyingly** *adv loud, near* épouvantablement; *bellow etc* de façon terrifiante.

territory ['terɪtərɪ] *n* territoire *m*. ♦ **territorial 1** *adj* territorial; **2** *n* (*Mil*) **Territorial** territorial *m*; **the Territorials** l'armée territoriale.

terror ['terəʳ] *n* terreur *f*. **to go in ~ of** avoir très peur de; **he went in ~ of his life** il craignait fort pour sa vie; **I have a ~ of flying** j'ai la terreur de monter en avion; **he's a ~ on the roads*** c'est un danger public sur les routes; **that child is a ~*** cet enfant est une vraie terreur*. ♦ **terrorism** *n* terrorisme *m*. ♦ **terrorist** *adj, n* terroriste (*mf*). ♦ **terrorize** *vt* terroriser. ♦ **terror-stricken** *adj* épouvanté.

terry ['terɪ] *n* (**~ towelling**) tissu *m* éponge.

terse [tɜ:s] *adj* laconique. ♦ **tersely** *adv* laconiquement. ♦ **terseness** *n* laconisme *m*.

tertiary ['tɜ:ʃərɪ] *adj* (*gen*) tertiaire. **~ education** enseignement *m* du troisième cycle.

terylene ['terəli:n] *n* ® tergal *m* ®.

test [test] **1** *n* (*of product*) essai *m*; (*of strength etc*) épreuve *f*; (*Med: of blood, urine*) analyse *f*; (*Med: of organ*) examen *m*; (*Pharm, Chem*) analyse; (*Physiol, Psych etc*) test *m*; (*Scol*) interrogation *f* écrite (*or* orale); (*criterion*) critère *m*. (*Pharm etc*) **to do a ~ for sugar** faire une recherche de sucre; **they did a ~ for diphtheria**

ils ont fait une analyse pour voir s'il s'agissait de la diphthérie; **they did ~s on the water** ils ont analysé l'eau; **driving ~** (examen du) permis *m* de conduire; **hearing ~** examen de l'ouïe; **it wasn't a fair ~ of her abilities** cela n'a pas permis d'évaluer correctement ses aptitudes; **to put to the ~** mettre à l'essai *or* à l'épreuve; **to stand the ~** *[person]* se montrer à la hauteur*; *[machine, vehicle]* résister aux épreuves; **to stand the ~ of time** résister au passage du temps.

2 *adj pilot, flight, shot etc* d'essai; *district, experiment, year* test *inv.* **~ ban treaty** traité *m* d'interdiction d'essais nucléaires; *[oil]* **~ bore** sondage *m* de prospection; (*TV*) **~ card** *or* (*US*) **pattern** mire *f*; (*Jur*) **~ case** affaire-test *f* (*destinée à faire jurisprudence*); **the strike is a ~ case** c'est une grève-test; (*Cricket, Rugby*) **~ match** ≃ match international; **~ tube** éprouvette *f*; **~-tube baby** bébé-éprouvette *m.*

3 *vt object, product, machine* essayer, mettre à l'essai; (*Comm*) *goods* vérifier; (*Chem*) *metal, water* analyser; (*Pharm*) *blood* faire des analyses de; *new drug etc* expérimenter; (*Psych*) *person, animal* tester; (*gen*) *person, intelligence, nerves* mettre à l'épreuve; *sight, hearing* examiner; *sb's reactions* mesurer. **they ~ed the material for resistance to ...** ils ont soumis le matériau à des essais destinés à vérifier sa résistance à ...; **these conditions ~ a car's tyres/strength** ces conditions mettent à l'épreuve les pneus/la résistance d'une voiture; **they ~ed him for hearing difficulties** ils lui ont fait passer un examen de l'ouïe; **they ~ed the children in geography** ils ont fait subir aux enfants une interrogation de contrôle en géographie; **they ~ed him for the job** ils lui ont fait passer des tests d'aptitude pour le poste.

4 *vi*: **to ~ for sugar** faire une recherche de sucre; **to ~ for a gas leak** faire des essais pour découvrir une fuite de gaz; (*Telec etc*) **'~ing, ~ing'** ≃ 'un, deux, trois'.

♦ **test-drive** (*Aut*) **1** *n* essai *m* de route; **2** *vt* faire faire un essai de route à. ♦ **testing** *adj*: **~ing ground** terrain *m* d'essai; (*fig*) **a ~ing time** une période éprouvante (*for sb* pour qn).

testament ['testəmənt] *n* testament *m.* **the Old/New T~** l'Ancien/le Nouveau Testament.

testicle ['testɪkl] *n* testicule *m.*

testify ['testɪfaɪ] **1** *vt* témoigner (*that* que). **2** *vi* porter témoignage. **to ~ against/in favour of sb** déposer contre/en faveur de qn; **to ~ to sth** (*Jur*) attester qch; (*gen*) témoigner de qch. ♦ **testimonial** *n* (*reference*) recommandation *f*; (*gift*) témoignage *m* d'estime (*offert à qn par ses collègues etc*). ♦ **testimony** *n* (*Jur*) témoignage *m*, déposition *f*; (*statement*) déclaration *f.*

testy ['testɪ] *adj* grincheux. ♦ **testily** *adv* d'un ton *or* d'un air irrité.

tetanus ['tetənəs] *n* tétanos *m.*

tetchy ['tetʃɪ] *adj* irritable.

tête-à-tête ['teɪtɑː'teɪt] *n* tête à tête *m inv.*

tether ['teðəʳ] **1** *n* longe *f.* (*fig*) **at the end of one's ~** à bout de forces *or* de nerfs. **2** *vt* attacher (*to* à).

text [tekst] *n* texte *m.* ♦ **textbook** *n* manuel *m*, cours *m.* ♦ **textual** *adj error* de texte.

textile ['tekstaɪl] *adj, n* textile (*m*).

texture ['tekstʃəʳ] *n* (*gen*) texture *f*; *[cloth]* contexture *f*; *[skin, wood etc]* grain *m.*

thalidomide [θə'lɪdəʊmaɪd] *n* ® thalidomide *f* ®. **~ baby** victime *f* de la thalidomide.

Thames [temz] *n* Tamise *f.* (*fig*) **he'll never set the ~ on fire** il n'a pas inventé la poudre.

than [ðæn, *weak form* ðən] *conj* **(a)** que. **more ~** plus que; **taller ~** plus grand que; **I'd do anything rather ~ admit it** je ferais tout plutôt que d'avouer cela; **no sooner did he arrive ~ ...** il était à peine arrivé que ...; **it was a better play ~ we expected** la pièce était meilleure que nous ne l'avions prévu. **(b)** (*with numerals*) de. **more/less ~ 20** plus/moins de 20; **less ~ half** moins de la moitié; **more ~ once** plus d'une fois.

thank [θæŋk] **1** *vt* remercier, dire merci à (*sb for sth* qn de qch; *for doing* de faire, d'avoir fait). **~ you** merci (*for sth* pour qch; *for doing* d'avoir fait); **~ you very much** merci bien (*also iro*), merci beaucoup; **no ~ you** (non) merci; **~ goodness*, ~ heaven(s)*, ~ God*** Dieu merci; (*fig*) **you've got him to ~ for that** c'est à lui que tu dois cela; **he's only got himself to ~** il ne peut s'en prendre qu'à lui-même. **2** *npl*: **~s** remerciements *mpl*; (*excl*) **~s!*** merci!; **many ~s** merci mille fois; **with my best ~s** avec mes remerciements les plus sincères; **give him my ~s** remerciez-le de ma part; **to give ~s to God** rendre grâces à Dieu; **~s to you** grâce à toi. ♦ **thankful** *adj* reconnaissant (*for* de); **let us be ~ful that** estimons-nous heureux que + *subj*; **I was ~ful that** j'ai été bien content que + *subj.* ♦ **thankfully** *adv* (*gratefully*) avec reconnaissance; (*with relief*) avec soulagement. ♦ **thankless** *adj* ingrat. ♦ **thanksgiving** *n* action *f* de grâces; (*Can, US*) **T~sgiving Day** fête *f* nationale.

that [ðæt, *weak form* ðət] **1** *dem adj, pl* **those (a)** (*unstressed*) ce (*before vowel or mute 'h'* cet), cette *f*, ces *mfpl.* **~ book** ce livre; **~ man** cet homme; **~ car** cette voiture; **those books** ces livres; **those cars** ces voitures; **I love ~ house of yours!** votre maison, je l'adore!; **~ awful car of theirs** leur fichue* voiture; **what about ~ £5?** et ces 5 livres? **(b)** (*stressed; or as opposed to* **this, these**) ce ...-là, cet ...-là, cette ...-là, ces ...-là. **I mean THAT book** c'est de ce livre-là que je parle; **I like ~ photo better than this one** je préfère cette photo-là à celle-ci; **~ hill over there** cette colline là-bas.

2 *dem pron, pl* **those (a)** cela, ça; ce. **what's ~?** qu'est-ce que c'est que ça?; **who's ~?** qui est-ce?; **is ~ you, Paul?** c'est toi, Paul?; **~'s what they've been told** c'est *or* voilà ce qu'on leur a dit; **those are my children** ce sont mes enfants, (*pointing out*) voilà mes enfants; **do you like ~?** vous aimez ça *or* cela?; **~'s fine!** c'est parfait!; **~'s enough!** ça suffit!; **she's not as stupid as (all) ~** elle n'est pas si bête que ça; **you're not going and ~'s ~!** tu n'y vas pas, un point c'est tout!; **well, ~'s ~!** eh bien voilà!; **~ was ~** les choses se sont arrêtées là; **if it comes to ~ ...** en fait ...; **before ~** avant cela; **with** *or* **at ~ she ...** là-dessus *or* sur ce, elle ...; **there were 6 at ~!** en plus il y en avait 6!; **~ is (to say) ...** c'est-à-dire ...; **like ~** comme ça; **friendship and all ~*** l'amitié et tout ça. **(b)** (**~** *one*) celui-là *m*, celle-là *f*, ceux-là *mpl*, celles-là *fpl.* **I prefer this to ~** je préfère celui-ci à celui-là (*or* celle-ci à celle-là); **those over there** ceux-là (*or* celles-là) là-bas. **(c)** (*before rel pron*) celui *m*, celle *f*, ceux *mpl*, celles *fpl.* **those who** ceux qui.

3 *adv* (*so*) si, aussi. **it's ~ high** c'est haut comme ça; **it's not ~ cold!** il ne fait pas si froid que ça!; **he was ~ ill!*** il était vraiment malade.

4 *rel pron* **(a)** (*nominative*) qui; (*accusative*) que; (*with prep*) lequel *m*, laquelle *f*, lesquels *mpl*, lesquelles *fpl.* **the man ~ came to see you** l'homme qui est venu vous voir; **the letter ~ I sent** la lettre que j'ai envoyée; **fool ~ I am!** imbécile que je suis!; **the men ~ I was speaking to** les hommes auxquels je parlais; **the girl ~ I told you about** la jeune fille dont je vous ai parlé. **(b)** (*in expressions of time*) où. **the evening/summer** *etc* **~ ...** le soir/l'été *etc* où ... .

5 *conj* que. **he said ~ he had seen her** il a dit qu'il l'avait vue, il a dit l'avoir vue; **so big ~ ...** si grand que ...; **not ~ I want to do it** non pas que je veuille le faire; **so ~, in order ~** pour que + *subj*, afin que + *subj.*

thatch [θætʃ] **1** *n* chaume *m.* **2** *vi* faire un toit de chaume. ♦ **thatched** *adj roof* de chaume; **~ed cottage** chaumière *f.*

thaw [θɔː] **1** *n* (*Met*) dégel *m*; (*fig: Pol etc*) détente *f*. **2** *vt* (~ **out**) (*gen; also fig*) dégeler; *ice, snow* faire fondre. **3** *vi* (~ **out**) (*gen, Met; also fig*) dégeler; *[ice, snow]* fondre.

the [ðiː, *weak form* ðə] **1** *def art* **(a)** le, la, (*before vowel or mute 'h'*) l', les. **of** ~, **from** ~ du, de la, de l', des; **to** ~, **at** ~ au, à la, à l', aux. **(b)** (*with sg n denoting whole class*) ~ **aeroplane is an invention of our century** l'avion est une invention de notre siècle. **(c)** (*distributive use*) **50p** ~ **pound** 50 pence la livre; **2 dollars to** ~ **pound** 2 dollars la livre; **paid by** ~ **hour** payé à l'heure; **30 miles to** ~ **gallon** ≈ 9 litres au 100 (km). **(d)** (*with names etc*) **Charles** ~ **First/Second/Third** Charles premier/deux/trois; ~ **Browns** les Brown. **(e)** (*stressed*) **THE Professor Smith** le célèbre professeur Smith; **it's THE restaurant in this part of town** c'est le meilleur restaurant du quartier; **it's THE book just now** c'est le livre à lire en ce moment. **(f)** (*with demonstrative force*) ~ **summer we went to France** l'été où nous sommes allés en France; ~ **shop over there** le magasin là-bas; **he hasn't** ~ **sense to refuse** il n'a pas assez de bon sens pour refuser; **how's** ~ **leg?*** et cette jambe?* **2** *adv*: ~ **more he works** ~ **more he earns** plus il travaille plus il gagne d'argent; ~ **sooner** ~ **better** le plus tôt sera le mieux; **all** ~ **more difficult** d'autant plus difficile.

theatre, (*US*) **-er** ['θɪətəʳ] **1** *n* **(a)** théâtre *m*. **to go to the** ~ aller au théâtre; **it makes good** ~ c'est du bon théâtre. **(b)** (*large room*) salle *f* de conférences. **lecture** ~ amphithéâtre *m*; **operating** ~ salle *f* d'opération. **(c)** (*Mil etc*) théâtre *m*. ~ **of war** théâtre des hostilités. **2** *adj visit* au théâtre; *management* du théâtre. ~ **company** troupe *f* de théâtre. ◆ **theatregoer** *n* habitué(e) *m(f)* du théâtre. ◆ **theatreland** *n*: **London's** ~**land** le Londres des théâtres. ◆ **theatrical 1** *adj* théâtral (*also fig pej*); **2** *npl*: **amateur theatricals** théâtre *m* d'amateurs; (*fig pej*) **all those theatricals** toute cette comédie. ◆ **theatrically** *adv* théâtralement.

thee [ðiː] *pron* (†, *liter*) te; (*before vowel*) t'; (*stressed; after prep*) toi.

theft [θeft] *n* vol *m*.

their [ðɛəʳ] *poss adj* leur (*f inv*). ◆ **theirs** *poss pron* le leur, la leur, les leurs; **this car is** ~**s** cette voiture est à eux (*or* à elles); **a friend of** ~**s** un de leurs amis (à eux *or* à elles); (*pej*) **that car of** ~**s** leur fichue* voiture.

them [ðem, *weak form* ðəm] *pers pron pl* **(a)** (*direct*) (*unstressed*) les; (*stressed*) eux *mpl*, elles *fpl*. **I have seen** ~ je les ai vu(e)s; **I don't know THEM** eux (*or* elles), je ne les connais pas; **if I were** ~ si j'étais à leur place; **it's** ~! ce sont eux!, les voilà! **(b)** (*indirect*) leur. **I gave** ~ **the book** je leur ai donné le livre; **I'm speaking to** ~ je leur parle. **(c)** (*after prep etc*) eux *mpl*, elles *fpl*. **I'm thinking of** ~ je pense à eux; **as for** ~ quant à eux; **younger than** ~ plus jeune qu'eux; **both of** ~ tous (*or* toutes) les deux; **several of** ~ plusieurs d'entre eux; **give me a few of** ~ donnez-m'en quelques-un(e)s; **I don't like either of** ~ je ne les aime ni l'un(e) ni l'autre; **none of** ~ **would do it** aucun d'entre eux (*or* aucune d'entre elles) n'a voulu le faire; **it was very good of** ~ c'était très gentil de leur part. ◆ **themselves** *pers pron pl* (*reflexive*) se; (*emphatic*) eux-mêmes *mpl*, elles-mêmes *fpl*; (*after prep*) eux, elles; **they've hurt** ~**selves** ils se sont blessés, elles se sont blessées; **they said to** ~**selves** ils (*or* elles) se sont dit; **they saw it** ~**selves** ils l'ont vu eux-mêmes; **they were talking amongst** ~**selves** ils discutaient entre eux; **all by** ~**selves** tout seuls, toutes seules.

theme [θiːm] **1** *n* thème *m*, sujet *m*; (*Mus*) thème, motif *m*. **2** *adj*: ~ **song** chanson principale (*d'un film etc*); (*signature tune*) indicatif *m*; (*fig*) refrain *m* habituel.

then [ðen] **1** *adv* **(a)** (*at that time*) alors, à cette époque-là, à ce moment-là. **we had 2 dogs** ~ nous avions alors 2 chiens, nous avions 2 chiens à cette époque-là; **I'll see him** ~ je le verrai à ce moment-là; **(every) now and** ~ de temps en temps; ~ **and there** sur-le-champ; **from** ~ **on** dès lors, dès cette époque-là *or* ce moment-là; **before** ~ avant cela, avant ce moment-là; **between now and** ~ d'ici là; **until** ~ jusque-là, jusqu'alors. **(b)** (*afterwards*) ensuite, puis, alors. **first to London,** ~ **to Paris** d'abord à Londres, puis *or* et ensuite à Paris; **and** ~ **what?** et puis après? **(c)** (*in that case*) alors, donc. ~ **it must be in the sitting room** alors ça doit être au salon; **someone had warned you** ~? on vous avait donc prévenu?; **now** ~ ... alors ... . **(d)** (*and also*) et puis, d'ailleurs. ~ **there's my aunt** et puis il y a ma tante; **... and** ~ **it's none of my business** ... et d'ailleurs cela ne me regarde pas; **and** ~ **again ...** remarquez ... . **2** *adj*: **the** ~ **Prime Minister** le premier ministre de l'époque.

thence [ðens] *adv* (†, *liter*) de là.

theodolite [θɪ'ɒdəlaɪt] *n* théodolite *m*.

theology [θɪ'ɒlədʒɪ] *n* théologie *f*. ◆ **theologian** *n* théologien(ne) *m(f)*. ◆ **theological** *adj* théologique; **theological college** séminaire *m*.

theorem ['θɪərəm] *n* théorème *m*.

theory ['θɪərɪ] *n* théorie *f*. **in** ~ en théorie. ◆ **theoretic(al)** *adj* théorique. ◆ **theoretically** *adv* théoriquement. ◆ **theoretician** *or* ◆ **theorist** *n* théoricien(ne) *m(f)*. ◆ **theorize** *vi [scientist etc]* élaborer des théories (*about* sur); (*fig*) se lancer dans de grandes théories (*about* sur).

therapy ['θerəpɪ] *n* thérapie *f*. ◆ **therapeutic(al)** *adj* thérapeutique. ◆ **therapeutics** *nsg* thérapeutique *f*. ◆ **therapist** *n* thérapeute *mf*.

there [ðɛəʳ] **1** *adv* **(a)** (*place*) y, là. **we shall be** ~ nous y serons, nous serons là; **put it** ~ posez-le là; **we left** ~ nous en sommes partis, nous sommes partis de là; **on** ~ là-dessus; **in** ~ là-dedans; **back** *or* **down** *or* **over** ~ là-bas; **about** *or* **around** ~ par là-bas; **here and** ~ çà et là, par-ci par-là; **from** ~ de là; **they went** ~ **and back** ils ont fait l'aller et retour; ~ **and then** sur-le-champ; **he's all** ~* c'est un malin; **he's not all** ~* il est un peu demeuré. **(b)** ~ **is,** ~ **are** il y a; **once upon a time** ~ **was ...** il était une fois ...; ~ **will be dancing** on dansera; ~ **are 3 apples left** il reste 3 pommes; ~ **comes a time when** ... il vient un moment où ...; ~**'s no denying it** c'est indéniable. **(c)** (*pointing out etc*) ~**'s my brother!** voilà mon frère!; ~ **are the others!** voilà les autres!; ~ **he is!** le voilà!; **that man** ~ cet homme-là; **hey you** ~! hé toi, là-bas!; **hurry up** ~! dépêchez-vous, là-bas!; ~**'s my mother calling me** voilà ma mère qui m'appelle; **I disagree with you** ~ là je ne suis pas d'accord avec vous; **you press this switch and** ~ **you are!** tu appuies sur ce bouton et ça y est!; ~ **you are, I told you that would happen** voilà *or* tiens, je t'avais dit que ça allait arriver; ~ **you go again***, ... ça y est, tu recommences à ... . **2** *excl*: ~, **what did I tell you?** alors, qu'est-ce que je t'avais dit?; ~, ~! allons, allons!; **but** ~, **what's the use?** mais enfin, à quoi bon?

◆ **thereabouts** *adv* (*place*) par là, près de là; **£5 or** ~**abouts** environ 5 livres. ◆ **thereafter** *adv* par la suite. ◆ **thereby** *adv* de cette façon; ~**by hangs a tale!** c'est toute une histoire! ◆ **therefore** *adv* donc, par conséquent. ◆ **thereupon** *adv* (*then*) sur ce; (*on that subject*) à ce sujet.

therm [θɜːm] *n* = 1,055 × 10^8 joules; (*formerly*) thermie *f*. ◆ **thermal** *adj* thermal; (*Elec, Phys*) thermique; ~**al baths** thermes *mpl*.

thermo... ['θɜːməʊ] *pref* therm(o)... . ◆ **thermodynamic** *adj* thermodynamique. ◆ **thermonuclear** *adj* thermonucléaire.

thermometer [θə'mɒmɪtəʳ] *n* thermomètre *m*.

Thermos ['θɜːməs] *n* ®: ~ **(flask)** (bouteille *f*) thermos *f*.

thermostat ['θɜːməstæt] *n* thermostat *m*.

thesaurus [θɪ'sɔːrəs] *n [words]* dictionnaire *m* synonymique.
these [ðiːz] *pl of* **this.**
thesis ['θiːsɪs] *n, pl* **-ses** thèse *f.*
they [ðeɪ] *pers pron pl* **(a)** ils *mpl,* elles *fpl;* (*stressed*) eux *mpl,* elles *fpl.* **~ have gone** ils sont partis, elles sont parties; **there ~ are!** les voilà!; **~ are teachers** ce sont des professeurs; THEY **know nothing about it** eux, ils n'en savent rien. **(b)** (*people in general*) on. **~ say that ...** on dit que ... .
thick [θɪk] **1** *adj* (*gen*) épais (*f* -aisse); *book, lips, nose, wool* épais, gros (*f* grosse); *print* gras (*f* grasse); *honey, vegetation* épais, touffu; (*stupid*) bête, borné. **to grow ~(er)** (s')épaissir; **to make ~(er)** épaissir; **wall 50 cm ~** mur de 50 cm d'épaisseur; (*fig*) **to give sb a ~ ear*** frotter les oreilles à qn*; (*fig*) **that's a bit ~!*** ça, c'est un peu fort!*; **the air is very ~ in here** on manque d'air ici; **furniture ~ with dust** meubles couverts de poussière; **road ~ with cars** rue encombrée de voitures; **town ~ with tourists** ville envahie de touristes; (*fig*) **they are as ~ as thieves** ils s'entendent comme larrons en foire; **Paul and he are very ~*** lui et Paul sont comme les deux doigts de la main.
2 *adv spread, lie etc* en couche épaisse; *cut* en tranches épaisses. **the snow fell ~** la neige tombait dru; (*fig*) **he lays it on a bit ~*** il exagère un peu.
3 *n*: **in the ~ of** *crowd* au plus fort de; *fight* en plein cœur de; **they were in the ~ of it** ils étaient en plein dedans; **through ~ and thin** à travers toutes les épreuves.
♦ **thicken 1** *vt sauce* épaissir; **2** *vi* (*gen; also fig*) s'épaissir; *[crowd]* grossir. ♦ **thickheaded*** *adj* bête, borné. ♦ **thick-knit** *adj* en grosse laine. ♦ **thick-lipped** *adj* aux lèvres charnues. ♦ **thickly** *adv spread* en une couche épaisse; *cut* en tranches épaisses; *speak, say* (*from head cold, fear*) d'une voix voilée; (*from drink*) d'une voix pâteuse; *wooded, populated* très; **~ly spread (*or* covered *etc*) with** couvert d'une épaisse couche de; **the snow fell ~ly** la neige tombait dru. ♦ **thickness** *n* **(a)** (*gen*) épaisseur *f; [lips etc]* grosseur *f; [fog, forest]* densité *f; [hair]* abondance *f;* **(b)** (*layer*) épaisseur *f.* ♦ **thickset** *adj* (*and small*) râblé; (*and tall*) bien bâti. ♦ **thickskinned** *adj orange* à la peau épaisse; (*fig*) *person* peu sensible.
thicket ['θɪkɪt] *n* fourré *m,* hallier *m.*
thief [θiːf] *n, pl* **thieves** voleur *m,* -euse *f.* **set a ~ to catch a ~** à voleur voleur et demi; **stop ~!** au voleur! ♦ **thieve** *vti* voler. ♦ **thieving 1** *adj* voleur; **2** *n* vol *m.*
thigh [θaɪ] *n* cuisse *f.* **~ boots** cuissardes *fpl.* ♦ **thighbone** *n* fémur *m.*
thimble ['θɪmbl] *n* dé *m* (à coudre).
thin [θɪn] **1** *adj* **(a)** (*gen*) mince; *glass* fin; *paper, waist, nose* mince, fin; *leg, person* mince, maigre (*slightly pej*); *string* petit. *[person]* **to get ~(ner)** maigrir; **as ~ as a rake** maigre comme un clou. **(b)** *soup, gravy, oil* peu épais (*f* -aisse); *cream, honey, mud* liquide; *hair, eyebrows, hedge* clairsemé; *fog, smoke* léger; *crowd* épars; *voice* grêle; *blood* anémié. **he's rather ~ on top*** il perd ses cheveux; **the air is ~** l'air est raréfié; (*fig*) **to vanish into ~ air** se volatiliser. **(c)** *profits* maigre; *excuse, story* peu convaincant; *disguise* facilement percé à jour. **to have a ~ time of it*** passer par une période plutôt pénible. **2** *adv spread* en une couche mince; *cut* en tranches minces. **3** *vt* (**~ down**) *paint, sauce* délayer; (**~ out**) *trees, hair* éclaircir. **4** *vi* (**~ out**) *[fog, crowd]* se disperser. **his hair is ~ning** il perd ses cheveux. ♦ **thin-lipped** *adj* aux lèvres minces, (*with rage etc*) les lèvres pincées. ♦ **thinly** *adv cut* en tranches minces; *spread* en couche mince; *wooded etc* peu; *clad* insuffisamment; **~ly disguised as** à peine déguisé en. ♦ **thinness** *n* minceur *f;* maigreur *f.* ♦ **thin-skinned** *adj orange etc* à la peau mince; (*fig*) *person* susceptible.
thine [ðaɪn] (†, *liter*) **1** *poss pron* le tien, la tienne, les tiens, les tiennes. **2** *poss adj* ton, ta, tes.
thing [θɪŋ] *n* **(a)** (*gen*) chose *f.* **~ of beauty** bel objet, belle chose; **such ~s as** des choses comme; **the ~ he loves most is ...** ce qu'il aime le plus au monde c'est ...; **what's that ~?** qu'est-ce que c'est que cette chose-là *or* ce machin-là* *or* ce truc-là?*; **what sort of ~ is that to say?** ça n'est pas une chose à dire; **the good ~s in life** les plaisirs *mpl* de la vie; **he thinks the right ~s** il pense comme il faut; **the ~ is this** voilà de quoi il s'agit; **as ~s are** dans l'état actuel des choses; **the next ~ to do is ...** ce qu'il y a à faire maintenant c'est ...; **the best ~ would be to refuse** le mieux serait de refuser; **the last ~ on the agenda** le dernier point à l'ordre du jour; **you worry about ~s too much** tu te fais trop de soucis; **I must think ~s over** il faut que j'y réfléchisse; **how are ~s with you?** et vous, comment ça va?; **to expect great ~s of** attendre beaucoup de; **they were talking of one ~ and another** ils parlaient de choses et d'autres; **taking one ~ with another** somme toute; **the ~ is to know ...** la question est de savoir ...; **the ~ is, she'd already seen him** ce qu'il y a, c'est qu'elle l'avait déjà vu; **it's a strange ~, but ...** c'est drôle, mais ...; **for one ~, it doesn't make sense** d'abord, ça n'a pas de sens; **and for another ~ ...** et en plus ...; **it's the usual ~** c'est le coup* classique; **it's just one of those ~s** ce sont des choses qui arrivent; **it's just one ~ after another** les embêtements se succèdent; **I hadn't done a ~ about it** je n'avais strictement rien fait.
(b) (*belongings etc*) **~s** affaires *fpl;* **to take off one's ~s** se débarrasser de son manteau *etc;* **do take your ~s off!** débarrassez-vous!; **your swimming ~s** tes affaires de bain; **the first-aid ~s** la trousse de secours.
(c) he's doing his own ~* il fait ce qui lui plaît; **she has got a ~ about spiders*** elle a horreur des araignées; **he has got a ~ about blondes*** il est obsédé par les blondes; **he made a great ~ of it** il en a fait tout un plat*; **Mr T~* rang up** Monsieur Machin* a téléphoné; **poor little ~!** pauvre petit(e)!; **poor ~, he's very ill** le pauvre, il est très malade; **she's a spiteful ~** c'est une rosse*; **that's just the ~ for me** voilà justement ce qu'il me faut; **yoga is the ~ nowadays** le yoga c'est le truc* à la mode aujourd'hui; **it's quite the ~** ça se fait beaucoup; **the latest ~ in hats** un chapeau dernier cri.
♦ **thingumabob*** *or* ♦ **thingumajig*** *or* ♦ **thingummy*** *n* machin* *m,* truc* *m.*
think [θɪŋk] (*vb: pret, ptp* **thought**) **1** *vi* **(a)** (*gen*) penser (*of, about* à; *of, about doing* à faire); (*more carefully*) réfléchir (*of, about* à). **you can't ~ of everything** on ne peut pas penser à tout; **I've too many things to ~ of** j'ai trop de choses en tête; **he ~s about nothing but money** il ne pense qu'à l'argent; **what else is there to ~ about?** c'est ce qu'il y a de plus important; **~ carefully** réfléchissez bien; **~ twice before speaking** réfléchissez-y à deux fois avant de parler; **~ again!** (*reflect on it*) repensez-y!; (*have another guess*) ce n'est pas ça, recommencez!; **to ~ ahead** tout prévoir; **let me ~** que je réfléchisse*, laissez-moi réfléchir; **to ~ aloud** penser tout haut; **to ~ big*** avoir de grandes idées; (*iro*) **I don't ~!*** ça m'étonnerait!; **I'll ~ about it** j'y penserai, je vais y réfléchir; **it's not worth ~ing about** ça ne vaut pas la peine d'y penser; **there's so much to ~ about** il y a tant de choses à prendre en considération; **what are you ~ing about?** à quoi pensez-vous?; **what were you ~ing about!** où avais-tu la tête?; **I wouldn't ~ of**

such a thing! ça ne me viendrait jamais à l'idée!; **would** YOU ~ **of letting him go alone?** vous le laisseriez partir seul?; **I didn't** ~ **to ask** *or* **of asking** je n'ai pas eu l'idée de demander.

(b) (*remember, consider*) penser (*of, about* à). **he** ~**s of nobody but himself** il ne pense qu'à lui; **he's got his children to** ~ **of** *or* **about** il faut qu'il pense à ses enfants; **I can't** ~ **of her name** je n'arrive pas à me rappeler son nom; **I couldn't** ~ **of the right word** le mot juste ne me venait pas.

(c) (*imagine*) **to** ~ **of** imaginer; ~ **of what might have happened** imagine ce qui aurait pu arriver; **just** ~! imagine un peu!

(d) (*devise etc*) **to** ~ **of** (*gen*) avoir l'idée de (*doing* faire); *plan* inventer; *solution* trouver; **what will he** ~ **of next?** qu'est-ce qu'il va encore inventer?

(e) (*have as opinion*) penser (*of* de). **to** ~ **well** *or* **highly** *or* **a lot of sb/sth** avoir une haute opinion de qn/qch; **very well thought of** très respecté; **I don't** ~ **much of that** cela ne me semble pas très bon; **to** ~ **better of doing sth** décider à la réflexion de ne pas faire qch; **he thought better of it** il a changé d'avis; ~ **nothing of it!** n'y attachez aucune importance!; **he thought nothing of walking there** il trouvait tout naturel d'y aller à pied; **to my way of** ~**ing** à mon avis.

2 *vt* **(a)** (*believe*) penser, croire (*that* que). **I** ~ **so/not** je pense *or* crois que oui/non; **I rather** ~ **so** j'ai plutôt l'impression que oui; **I thought as much!, I thought so!** je m'en doutais!; **she's pretty, don't you** ~? elle est jolie, tu ne trouves pas?; **I don't know what to** ~ je ne sais pas qu'en penser; **I** ~ **that** je pense *or* crois que + *indic*; **I don't** ~ **that** je ne pense *or* crois pas que + *subj*; **do you** ~ **that** croyez-vous que + *subj*; **what do you** ~? qu'est-ce que tu en penses?; (*iro*) **what do** YOU ~? qu'est-ce que tu crois, toi?; **what do you** ~ **of him?** comment le trouves-tu?; **who do you** ~ **you are?** pour qui te prends-tu?; **you must** ~ **me very rude** vous devez me trouver très impoli; **he** ~**s he is intelligent** il se croit intelligent; **they are thought to be rich** ils passent pour être riches; **I didn't** ~ **to see you here** je ne m'attendais pas à vous voir ici.

(b) (*imagine*) imaginer. ~ **what we could do** imagine ce que nous pourrions faire; **I can't** ~ **what he means** je ne vois vraiment pas ce qu'il veut dire; **who would have thought it!** qui l'aurait dit!; **to** ~ **that she's only 10!** quand on pense qu'elle n'a que 10 ans!; **to** ~ **evil thoughts** avoir de mauvaises pensées.

(c) (*reflect*) penser à. ~ **what you're doing** pense à ce que tu fais; **we must** ~ **how to do it** il faut nous demander comment le faire; **I was** ~**ing (to myself) how ill he looked** je me disais qu'il avait l'air bien malade; **I didn't** ~ **to let him know** il ne m'est pas venu à l'idée de le mettre au courant; **did you** ~ **to bring it?** est-ce que tu as pensé à l'apporter?

3 *n*: **to have a** ~* **about sth** penser à qch; **to have a good long** ~* **about sth** bien réfléchir à qch; **he's got another** ~ **coming*** il se fait des illusions.

4 *adj*: ~ **tank** groupe *m* d'experts.

think back *vi* essayer de se souvenir (*to* de).

think out *vt sep problem, proposition* étudier; *plan, answer* préparer.

think over *vt sep offer, suggestion* bien réfléchir à. **I'll have to** ~ **it over** il va falloir que j'y réfléchisse.

think up *vt sep plan, improvement* avoir l'idée de; *idea* avoir; *answer* trouver; *excuse* inventer. **what will he** ~ **up next?** qu'est-ce qu'il va encore bien pouvoir inventer?

♦ **thinkable** *adj*: **it's not** ~**able that** il n'est pas pensable que + *subj*. ♦ **thinker** *n* penseur *m*, -euse *f*. ♦ **thinking 1** *adj creature* rationnel; **to any** ~**ing person** pour toute personne qui réfléchit; **to put on one's** ~**ing cap** réfléchir; **2** *n* (*act*) pensée *f*, réflexion *f*; (*thoughts*) opinions *fpl* (*on, about* sur); **I'll have to do some** ~**ing about it** il va falloir que j'y réfléchisse.

third [θɜːd] **1** *adj* troisième. ~ **person**, (*Jur*) ~ **party** tiers *m*; ~ **party insurance** assurance *f* au tiers; ~ **time lucky!** la troisième fois sera la bonne; **the** ~ **finger** le majeur; **the T**~ **World** le Tiers-Monde. **2** *n* troisième *mf*; (*fraction*) tiers *m*; (*Mus*) tierce *f*; (*Aut:* ~ *gear*) troisième vitesse *f*. **in** ~ en troisième; *for phrases V* **sixth. 3** *adv* **(a)** (*in race, exam*) **to come** *or* **be placed** ~ se classer troisième. **(b)** (*thirdly*) troisièmement.

♦ **third-class 1** *adj* (*gen, Rail etc*) de troisième classe; *hotel* de troisième catégorie; (*fig pej*) *meal, goods* de qualité très inférieure; (*Univ*) ~**-class degree** ≃ licence *f* sans mention; **2** *adv* (*Rail*) *travel* en troisième. ♦ **thirdly** *adv* troisièmement. ♦ **third-rate** *adj* de qualité très inférieure.

thirst [θɜːst] **1** *n* soif *f* (*for* de). **2** *vi* (*liter*) avoir soif (*for* de). (*fig*) ~**ing for** assoiffé de. ♦ **thirsty** *adj* qui a soif, (*stronger*) assoiffé; (*fig*) *land* desséché; **to be** ~**y** avoir soif (*for* de); **it makes you** ~**y, it's** ~**y work** ça donne soif.

thirteen [θɜːˈtiːn] *adj, n* treize (*m*) *inv*; *for phrases V* **six**. ♦ **thirteenth** *adj, n* treizième (*mf*); (*fraction*) treizième *m*.

thirty [ˈθɜːtɪ] *adj, n* trente (*m*) *inv*. **about** ~ une trentaine; **about** ~ **books** une trentaine de livres; *for other phrases V* **sixty**. ♦ **thirtieth** *adj, n* trentième (*mf*); (*fraction*) trentième *m*.

this [ðɪs] **1** *dem adj, pl* **these (a)** ce (*before vowel and mute 'h'* cet), cette *f*, ces *mfpl*. ~ **book** ce livre; ~ **man** cet homme; ~ **woman** cette femme; **these books** ces livres; **these women** ces femmes; ~ **week** cette semaine; ~ **time last week** la semaine dernière à pareille heure; ~ **time next year** l'année prochaine à la même époque; ~ **coming week** la semaine prochaine. **(b)** (*stressed; or as opposed to* **that, those**) ce ...-ci, cet ...-ci, cette ...-ci, ces ...-ci. **I like** ~ **photo better than that one** je préfère cette photo-ci à celle-là; ~ **chair over here** cette chaise-ci.

2 *dem pron, pl* **these (a)** ceci, ce. **what is** ~? qu'est-ce que c'est?; **who's** ~? qui est-ce?; ~ **is my son** (*in introduction*) je vous présente mon fils; (*in photo etc*) c'est mon fils; ~ **is the boy I told you about** c'est *or* voici le garçon dont je t'ai parlé; (*on phone*) ~ **is Joe Brown** Joe Brown à l'appareil; ~ **is Tuesday/May** nous sommes mardi/en mai; ~ **is what he showed me** voici ce qu'il m'a montré; ~ **is where we live** c'est ici que nous habitons; **it was like** ~ ... voici comment les choses se sont passées ...; **do it like** ~ faites-le comme ceci; **after** ~ après ceci; **before** ~ **I'd never noticed him** je ne l'avais jamais remarqué auparavant; **it ought to have been done before** ~ cela devrait être déjà fait; **we were talking of** ~ **and that** nous parlions de choses et d'autres; **so it has come to** ~! nous en sommes donc là!; **at** ~ sur ce; **with** ~ **he left us** sur ces mots il nous a quittés; **what's all** ~ **I hear about your new job?** qu'est-ce que j'apprends, vous avez un nouvel emploi? **(b)** (~ *one*) celui-ci *m*, celle-ci *f*, ceux-ci *mpl*, celles-ci *fpl*. **I prefer that to** ~ je préfère celui-là à celui-ci (*or* celle-là à celle-ci).

3 *adv*: ~ **long** aussi long que ça; ~ **far** jusqu'ici.

thistle [ˈθɪsl] *n* chardon *m*. ♦ **thistledown** *n* duvet *m* de chardon.

thither [ˈðɪðəʳ] *adv* (†, *liter*) là, y.

tho' [ðəʊ] *abbr of* **though.**

thong [θɒŋ] *n* lanière *f* (*de cuir*).

thorax [ˈθɔːræks] *n* thorax *m*.

thorn [θɔːn] *n* épine *f*; (*haw*~) aubépine *f*. (*fig*) **a** ~ **in sb's flesh** une épine dans le pied de qn.
♦ **thorny** *adj* (*lit, fig*) épineux.

thorough [ˈθʌrə] *adj work, worker* consciencieux;

search, research minutieux; *knowledge, examination* approfondi; (*fig*) *hooligan, idiot* véritable (*before n*); *scoundrel, rogue* fieffé. **to give sth a ~ clean** nettoyer qch à fond. ♦ **thoroughbred 1** *adj horse* pur-sang *inv*; *other animal* de race; **2** *n* pur-sang *m inv*; bête *f* de race. ♦ **thoroughfare** *n* (*street*) rue *f*; (*public highway*) voie *f* publique; **'no ~fare'** 'passage interdit'. ♦ **thoroughgoing** *adj examination, revision* complet; *hooligan* véritable (*before n*); *rogue, scoundrel* fieffé. ♦ **thoroughly** *adv* (*gen*) à fond; *understand* parfaitement; *agree* tout à fait; (*very*) *clean, nasty* tout à fait, tout ce qu'il y a de*; **to search ~ly** *house* fouiller de fond en comble; *drawer* fouiller à fond. ♦ **thoroughness** *n [worker etc]* minutie *f*.

those [ðəuz] *pl of* **that.**

thou [ðau] *pers pron* (†, *liter*) tu; (*stressed*) toi.

though [ðəu] **1** *conj* **(a)** (*despite the fact that*) bien que +*subj*, quoique +*subj*. **~ it's raining** bien qu'il pleuve, malgré la pluie. **(b)** (*even if*) **strange ~ it may seem** si *or* pour étrange que cela puisse paraître; **even ~ I shan't be there I'll think of you** je ne serai pas là, mais je n'en penserai pas moins à toi. **(c)** (*gen*) **as ~** comme si; **it looks as ~** il semble que + *subj*. **2** *adv* pourtant, cependant. **it's not easy ~** ce n'est pourtant pas facile.

thought [θɔːt] (*pret, ptp of* **think**) *n* **(a)** (*gen*) pensée *f*; (*daydreaming*) rêverie *f*. **lost** *or* **deep in ~** plongé dans ses pensées *or* dans une rêverie; **after much ~** après mûre réflexion; **without ~** sans réfléchir; **without ~ for** *or* **of himself** sans considérer son propre intérêt; **to take ~ for, to give a ~ to** penser à; **to give ~ to** bien réfléchir à; **don't give it another ~** n'y pensez plus. **(b)** (*idea*) pensée *f*, idée *f*. **it's a happy ~** voilà une idée qui fait plaisir; **what a ~!*** imagine un peu!; **what a horrifying ~!*** quel cauchemar!; **what a lovely ~!*** comme ça serait bien!; **what a brilliant ~!*** quelle idée de génie!; **that's a ~!*** tiens, mais c'est une idée!; **the mere ~ of it** rien que d'y penser; **my ~s were elsewhere** j'avais l'esprit ailleurs; **the T~s of Chairman Mao** les pensées du Président Mao; **scientific ~ on the subject** les opinions *fpl* des scientifiques sur la question; **I had ~s of going to Paris** j'avais vaguement l'intention d'aller à Paris; **he gave up all ~ of marrying her** il a renoncé à toute idée de l'épouser; **it's the ~ that counts** c'est l'intention *f* qui compte; (*fig*) **it is a ~ too large** c'est un tout petit peu trop grand. ♦ **thoughtful** *adj* **(a)** (*pensive*) pensif; (*serious*) *person, book, remark* sérieux; **(b)** (*considerate*) *person* prévenant; *act, remark, invitation* gentil; **how ~ful of you!** comme c'est gentil à vous! ♦ **thoughtfully** *adv* pensivement; avec prévenance; **he ~fully offered ...** il a eu la prévenance d'offrir .... ♦ **thoughtfulness** *n* air *m* pensif; prévenance *f*. ♦ **thoughtless** *adj behaviour, words* irréfléchi; *person* étourdi; **he's very ~less** il se soucie fort peu des autres. ♦ **thoughtlessly** *adv* (*carelessly*) étourdiment; (*inconsiderately*) avec insouciance. ♦ **thoughtlessness** *n* (*carelessness*) étourderie *f*; (*lack of consideration*) manque *m* de prévenance. ♦ **thought-provoking** *adj* qui pousse à la réflexion. ♦ **thought-read** *vi* lire dans la pensée de qn. ♦ **thought-reader** *n* liseur *m*, -euse *f* de pensées.

thousand ['θauzənd] *adj, n* mille (*m*) *inv*. **a ~, one ~** mille; **five ~** cinq mille; **a ~ thanks!** mille fois merci!; **about a ~** un millier; **about a ~ men** un millier d'hommes; **~s of** des milliers de; **they came in their ~s** ils sont venus par milliers. ♦ **thousandth** *adj, n* millième (*mf*); (*fraction*) millième *m*.

thrash [θræʃ] *vt* (*beat*) rouer de coups; (*as punishment*) donner une bonne correction à; (*: *Sport etc*) battre à plates coutures.

thrash about *vi* se débattre.

thrash out *vt sep problem, difficulty* (*discuss*) débattre de; (*solve*) démêler; *plan* mettre au point avec difficulté.

♦ **thrashing** *n* correction *f*; **to give sb a good ~ing = to ~ sb.**

thread [θred] **1** *n* **(a)** fil *m*. (*fig*) **to hang by a ~** ne tenir qu'à un fil; (*fig*) **to lose the ~ (of what one is saying)** perdre le fil de son discours; (*fig*) **to pick up the ~ again** retrouver le fil. **(b)** *[screw]* pas *m*, filetage *m*. **2** *vt needle, beads* enfiler; *wire, cotton* faire passer (*through* à travers); *film* monter (*on to* sur). **to ~ one's way through** se faufiler à travers. ♦ **threadbare** *adj rug, clothes* usé, râpé; *room* défraîchi; (*fig*) *excuse* rebattu.

threat [θret] *n* menace *f* (*to sb/sth* pour qn/qch). **to make a ~ against sb** proférer une menace à l'égard de qn; **under the ~ of** menacé de. ♦ **threaten** *vti* menacer (*sb with sth* qn de qch; *to do* de faire); **to ~en** *violence etc* proférer des menaces de; **~ened with** menacé de. ♦ **threatening** *adj* (*gen*) menaçant; *letter* de menaces; (*fig*) **to find sb ~ening** se sentir menacé par qn. ♦ **threateningly** *adv* d'un ton *or* d'une manière menaçant(e).

three [θriː] *adj, n* trois (*m*) *inv*. (*Pol*) **the Big T~** les trois Grands; (*Sport*) **the best of ~** deux jeux et la belle; *for other phrases V* **six.** ♦ **three-cornered** *adj* triangulaire. ♦ **three-dimensional** *adj object* à trois dimensions; *film* en relief. ♦ **three-legged** *adj table* à trois pieds; *race* de pieds liés. ♦ **three-piece suite** *n* salon *m* comprenant canapé et deux fauteuils. ♦ **three-ply** *adj wool* trois fils *inv*. ♦ **three-quarter** *n* (*Rugby*) trois-quarts *m inv*. ♦ **three-quarters** *npl* (*fraction*) trois quarts *mpl*. ♦ **threesome** *n* (*people*) groupe *m* de trois; **in a ~some** à trois. ♦ **three-way** *adj division* en trois; *discussion* à trois. ♦ **three-wheeler** *n* (*car*) voiture *f* à trois roues; (*tricycle*) tricycle *m*.

thresh [θreʃ] *vt* (*Agr*) battre. ♦ **thresher** *n* (*machine*) batteuse *f*. ♦ **threshing** *n* battage *m*.

threshold ['θreʃhəuld] *n* (*lit, fig*) seuil *m*. **to cross the ~** franchir le seuil; (*fig*) **on the ~ of** au seuil de.

threw [θruː] *pret of* **throw.**

thrice [θraɪs] *adv* trois fois.

thrift [θrɪft] *n* économie *f*. ♦ **thriftless** *adj* imprévoyant. ♦ **thrifty** *adj* économe.

thrill [θrɪl] **1** *n* (*gen*) frisson *m*. **what a ~!** quelle émotion!; **it gave me a big ~** ça m'a vraiment fait qch!*; **to get a ~ out of doing sth** se procurer des sensations fortes en faisant qch; **film packed with ~s** film *m* à sensations. **2** *vt* (*gen*) *person, crowd* électriser. **his glance ~ed her** son regard l'a enivrée; **I was ~ed!** j'étais aux anges!; **I was ~ed to meet him** ça m'a vraiment fait qch* de le rencontrer. **3** *vi* frissonner (de joie). ♦ **thriller** *n* (*novel/film*) roman *m*/film *m* à suspense. ♦ **thrilling** *adj play, journey* palpitant; *news* saisissant.

thrive [θraɪv] *pret* **throve, thrived,** *ptp* **thriven, thrived** *vi [person, animal]* être florissant de santé; *[plant]* pousser bien; *[industry, businessman]* prospérer. **children ~ on milk** le lait est excellent pour les enfants; **he ~s on hard work** le travail lui réussit. ♦ **thriving** *adj person etc* florissant de santé; *plant* robuste; *industry etc* prospère.

throat [θrəut] *n* gorge *f*. **to take sb by the ~** prendre qn à la gorge; **I have a sore ~** j'ai mal à la gorge, j'ai une angine; **he had a bone stuck in his ~** il avait une arête dans le gosier; (*fig*) **that sticks in my ~** je n'arrive pas à accepter ça; (*fig*) **to thrust** *or* **shove* sth down sb's ~** rebattre les oreilles de qn avec qch. ♦ **throaty** *adj* guttural.

throb [θrɒb] **1** *vi [heart]* palpiter, battre fort; *[voice, engine]* vibrer; *[drums]* battre (en rythme); *[pain]* lanciner. **town ~bing with life** ville vibrante d'animation; **my head is ~bing** j'ai des élancements dans la tête. **2** *n [heart]* battement *m*; *[engine]* vibration *f*; *[music]* rythme *m* (fort); *[pain]* élancement *m*.

throes [θrəʊz] *npl*: **in the ~ of death** à l'agonie; **in the ~ of** *war, disease, crisis etc* en proie à; *quarrel, debate* au cœur de; **in the ~ of writing a book** aux prises avec la rédaction d'un livre.

thrombosis [θrɒm'bəʊsɪs] *n* thrombose *f*.

throne [θrəʊn] *n* trône *m*. **to come to the ~** monter sur le trône; **on the ~** sur le trône.

throng [θrɒŋ] **1** *n* foule *f*. **2** *vi* se presser (*round* autour de; *to see* pour voir). **3** *vt streets* se presser dans. **~ed with people** plein de monde.

throttle ['θrɒtl] **1** *n* (*Aut, Tech*) papillon *m* des gaz. **to open the ~** mettre les gaz; **to close the ~** réduire l'arrivée des gaz. **2** *vt* (*strangle*) étrangler.

throttle back, throttle down *vt sep engine* mettre au ralenti.

through [θru:] **1** *adv* **(a)** (*gen*) **the nail went right ~** le clou est passé à travers; **just go ~** passez donc; **to let sb ~** laisser passer qn; **to get a train ~ to London** attraper un train direct pour Londres; (*in exam*) **did you get ~?** as-tu été reçu?; **all night ~** toute la nuit; **I knew all ~ that ...** je savais depuis le début que ...; **wet ~** trempé; **wet ~ and ~** complètement trempé; **he's a liar ~ and ~** il ment comme il respire; **he's a Scot ~ and ~** il est écossais jusqu'au bout des ongles; **read it right ~** lis-le jusqu'au bout; **I read it ~ quickly** je l'ai lu rapidement; (*Telec*) **to put sb ~ to sb** passer qn à qn; **I'll put you ~ to her** je vous la passe; **you're ~ now** vous avez votre correspondant; **you're ~ to him** il est en ligne. **(b)** (*finished*) **I'm ~*** ça y est, j'ai fini; **I'm not ~ with you yet*** je n'en ai pas encore fini avec vous; **are you ~ with that book?*** tu n'as plus besoin de ce livre?; **he told me we were ~*** il m'a dit que c'était fini entre nous.

2 *prep* **(a)** (*place*) à travers. **a stream flows ~ the garden** un ruisseau traverse le jardin *or* coule à travers le jardin; **to go ~** *forest, garden, building* traverser; *hedge* passer au travers de; (*Aut*) *red light* griller; (*fig*) *sb's pockets, luggage* fouiller; **to hammer a nail ~ a plank** enfoncer un clou à travers une planche; **he was shot ~ the head** on lui a tiré une balle dans la tête; **to look ~ a window/telescope** regarder par une fenêtre/dans un télescope; **he has really been ~ it*** il en a vu de dures*; **to get ~ an exam** réussir à un examen; **I'm half-way ~ the book** j'en suis à la moitié du livre; **to speak ~ one's nose** parler du nez.

(b) (*time*) pendant, durant. **all** *or* **right ~ his life** pendant *or* durant toute sa vie; **he won't live ~ the night** il ne passera pas la nuit; (*US*) **Monday ~ Friday** de lundi à vendredi; **~ the week** pendant la semaine.

(c) (*by, from*) par; (*thanks to*) grâce à; (*because of*) à cause de. **~ the post** par la poste; **it was all ~ him that ...** c'est à cause de lui que ...; **I heard it ~ my sister** je l'ai appris par ma sœur; **~ his own efforts** par ses propres efforts; **absent ~ illness** absent pour cause de maladie; **~ fear** par peur; **~ not knowing the way he ...** parce qu'il ne connaissait pas le chemin il ... .

3 *adj train, ticket* direct. **'no ~ way'** 'impasse'.

◆ **throughout 1** *prep* **(a)** (*place*) partout dans; **~out the world** partout dans le monde; **(b)** (*time*) pendant; **~out his life** pendant toute sa vie; **2** *adv* (*everywhere*) partout; (*the whole time*) tout le temps. ◆ **throughway** *n* (*US*) autoroute *f* à péage.

throve [θrəʊv] *pret of* **thrive**.

throw [θrəʊ] (*vb: pret* **threw**, *ptp* **thrown**) **1** *n [ball, javelin etc]* **a good ~** un bon jet; **with one ~ of the ball he ...** d'un seul coup il ...; (*in table games*) **you lose a ~** vous perdez un tour.

2 *vt* **(a)** (*gen*) jeter (*to, at* à; *over* sur; *into* dans; *into jail* en prison); *object, stone* lancer, jeter (*to, at* à); *ball, javelin etc* lancer; *dice* jeter; *[fighter etc] opponent* envoyer au sol; *[explosion, car crash etc]* projeter; *pottery* tourner; (*fig*) *responsibility etc* rejeter (*on* sur); (*) *party* organiser (*for sb* en l'honneur de qn); (*: *fig: disconcert*) déconcerter, décontenancer. (*dice*) **to ~ a six** avoir un six; **the horse threw him** le cheval l'a désarçonné; **he was ~n clear of the car** il a été projeté hors de la voiture; **to ~ o.s. to the ground/into sb's arms** se jeter à terre/dans les bras de qn; **to ~ o.s. on sb's mercy** s'en remettre à la merci de qn; (*fig*) **to ~ o.s. into a job** se mettre au travail avec enthousiasme; **to ~ open** *door, window* ouvrir tout grand; (*fig*) *house, gardens* ouvrir au public; *race, competition etc* ouvrir à tout le monde; **to ~ a switch** allumer *or* éteindre brusquement; **to ~ a question at sb** poser une question à qn à brûle-pourpoint; **to ~ sth/sb into confusion** jeter la confusion dans qch/dans l'esprit de qn; **to ~ sb off the trail** dépister qn; (*fig: disconcert*) **I was quite ~n* when ...** je n'en revenais pas quand ... .

(b) (*direct*) *light, shadow, glance* jeter; *slides* projeter; *kiss* envoyer (*to* à); *punch* lancer (*at* à).

throw about, throw around *vt sep litter, confetti* éparpiller. **to be ~n about** être ballotté; (*fig*) **to ~ one's weight about** faire l'important.

throw away *vt sep rubbish etc* jeter; (*fig*) *one's life, talents* gâcher; *money, sb's affection, chance* perdre; *line, remark* (*say casually*) laisser tomber; (*lose effect of*) perdre tout l'effet de. **to ~ o.s. away** gaspiller ses dons.

throw back *vt sep* **(a)** (*return*) *ball etc* renvoyer (*to* à); *fish* rejeter; (*fig*) *image* renvoyer. **(b)** *head, hair* rejeter en arrière; *shoulders* redresser. (*fig*) **to be ~n back upon sth** être obligé de se rabattre sur qch.

throw down *vt sep object* jeter; *weapons* déposer; *challenge* lancer. **to ~ o.s. down** se jeter à terre.

throw in *vt sep object into box etc* jeter; (*Ftbl*) *ball* remettre en jeu; (*fig*) *one's cards* jeter sur la table; (*fig*) *remark, question* interposer; *reference* mentionner en passant. (*fig*) **to ~ in one's hand** *or* **the towel** abandonner la partie; (*as extra*) **with £5 ~n in** avec 5 livres en plus; (*included*) **with meals ~n in** repas compris.

throw off *vt sep* (*get rid of*) (*gen*) se débarrasser de; *disguise* jeter; *pursuers, dogs* perdre, semer*.

throw on *vt sep coal, sticks* ajouter; *clothes* enfiler à la hâte.

throw out *vt sep* **(a)** (*lit*) jeter dehors; *rubbish etc* jeter; *person* expulser; *suggestion,* (*Parl*) *bill* repousser. (*fig*) **to ~ out one's chest** bomber la poitrine. **(b)** (*offer*) *suggestion, idea* laisser tomber; *challenge* lancer. **(c)** (*make wrong*) *calculation, prediction* fausser.

throw over *vt sep* abandonner, laisser tomber* (*for sth else* pour autre chose; *for sb else* pour qn d'autre).

throw together *vt sep* **(a)** (*pack*) *belongings etc* rassembler; (*make hastily*) *object* faire à la six-quatre-deux*; (*) *essay* torcher. **(b)** (*fig: by chance*) *people* réunir (par hasard). **they were ~n together** le hasard les avait réunis.

throw up 1 *vi* (*vomit*) vomir. **2** *vt sep* **(a)** (*into air*) *ball etc* lancer en l'air; *arms* lever. (*fig*) **it threw up several good ideas** quelques bonnes idées en sont sorties. **(b)** (*vomit*) vomir. **(c)** (*: *abandon etc*) *job, studies* abandonner; *opportunity* laisser passer.

◆ **throwaway** *adj packaging* à jeter; *remark* qui n'a l'air de rien. ◆ **throwback** *n* (*fig*) **it's a ~back to** ça remonte à. ◆ **thrower** *n* lanceur *m*, -euse *f*. ◆ **throw-in** *n* (*Ftbl*) remise *f* en jeu.

thru [θru:] (*US*) = **through**.

thrush[1] [θrʌʃ] *n* (*bird*) grive *f*.

thrush[2] [θrʌʃ] *n* (*Med*) muguet *m*.

thrust [θrʌst] (*vb: pret, ptp* **thrust**) **1** *n* **(a)** (*push*) poussée *f* (*also Mil*); (*stab: with knife, stick etc*) coup *m*; (*fig: remark*) pointe *f* (*at sb* contre qn). **(b)** *[propeller, jet engine etc]* poussée *f*; (**fig: energy*) dynamisme *m*. **2** *vt* (*push: gen*) pousser brusquement; *finger, stick, dagger* enfoncer (*into* dans; *between* entre); *sth into drawer, pocket, hole* fourrer* (*into* dans); (*fig*) *job, responsibility* imposer (*upon sb* à qn). **he ~ it into my hand** il me l'a fourré* dans la main; **he ~ it at me** il me l'a brusquement mis sous le nez; **to ~ one's hands into one's pockets** enfoncer les mains dans ses poches; **he ~ his head through the window** il a mis la tête par la fenêtre; (*fig*) **some have greatness ~ upon them** certains ont de la grandeur sans la rechercher; **to ~ o.s. upon sb** imposer sa présence à qn; **to ~ one's way in/out** *etc* entrer/sortir *etc* en se frayant un passage; **to ~ aside** *object, person* écarter brusquement; *suggestion* rejeter violemment.

thud [θʌd] **1** *n* bruit *m* sourd. **2** *vi* faire un bruit sourd (*on, against* en heurtant); *[guns]* gronder sourdement; (*fall*) tomber avec un bruit sourd.

thug [θʌg] *n* voyou *m*.

thumb [θʌm] **1** *n* pouce *m*. (*fig*) **to be under sb's ~** être sous la coupe de qn; **she's got him under her ~** elle le mène par le bout du nez; (*fig*) **to be all ~s** être très maladroit; **he gave me the ~s up sign*** (*all well*) il m'a fait signe que tout allait bien; (*for luck*) il m'a fait signe pour me souhaiter bonne chance. **2** *adj nail, print* du pouce. **~ index** répertoire *m* à onglets. **3** *vt book, magazine* feuilleter. **well ~ed** tout écorné (par l'usage); **to ~ one's nose** faire un pied de nez (*at sb* à qn); **he ~ed a lift to Paris** il est allé à Paris en stop*; **I managed to ~ a lift** je suis arrivé à arrêter une voiture.

thumb through *vt fus book* feuilleter; *card index* consulter rapidement.

♦ **thumbnail** *adj*: **~nail sketch** croquis *m* sur le vif. ♦ **thumbscrew** *n* (*Tech*) vis *f* à papillon. ♦ **thumbtack** *n* (*US*) punaise *f*.

thump [θʌmp] **1** *n* (*blow: with fist/stick etc*) grand coup *m* de poing/de canne *etc*; (*sound*) bruit *m* lourd et sourd. **to fall with a ~** tomber lourdement. **2** *vt person* assener un *or* des coup(s) à; *table* taper sur; *door* cogner à. **3** *vi* cogner, taper (*on* sur; *at* à); *[heart]* battre fort, (*with fear*) battre la chamade. ♦ **thumping*** *adj* (**~ing great**) monumental*.

thunder ['θʌndər] **1** *n* tonnerre *m*; *[applause]* tonnerre; *[hooves, vehicles, trains]* fracas *m*. **there's ~ in the air** il y a de l'orage dans l'air. **2** *vi* (*Met*) tonner; *[guns]* tonner; *[hooves]* retentir. **the train ~ed past** le train est passé dans un grondement de tonnerre. **3** *vt* (**~ out**) *threat, order* proférer d'une voix tonitruante. ♦ **thunderbolt** *n* coup *m* de foudre; (*fig*) coup de tonnerre. ♦ **thunderclap** *n* coup *m* de tonnerre. ♦ **thundercloud** *n* nuage orageux; (*fig*) nuage noir. ♦ **thundering** *adj* **(a)** *rage* fou; *temper* massacrant; **(b)** (*: **~ing great**) monumental*; *success* monstre. ♦ **thunderous** *adj welcome, shouts, noise* étourdissant; *applause* frénétique. ♦ **thunderstorm** *n* orage *m*. ♦ **thunderstruck** *adj* abasourdi. ♦ **thundery** *adj* orageux.

Thursday ['θɜ:zdɪ] *n* jeudi *m*; *for phrases V* **Saturday**.

thus [ðʌs] *adv* ainsi. **~ far** (*up to here*) jusqu'ici; (*up to there*) jusque-là.

thwart [θwɔ:t] *vt plan* contrecarrer; *person* contrecarrer les projets de. **to be ~ed** essuyer un échec.

thy [ðaɪ] *poss adj* (†, *liter*) ton, ta, tes.

thyme [taɪm] *n* thym *m*.

thyroid ['θaɪrɔɪd] *adj, n* (**~ gland**) thyroïde (*f*).

ti [ti:] *n* (*Mus*) si *m*.

tiara [tɪ'ɑ:rə] *n* diadème *m*.

tibia ['tɪbɪə] *n* tibia *m*.

tic [tɪk] *n* tic *m* (nerveux).

tichy‡ ['tɪtʃɪ] *adj* (**~ little**) minuscule.

tick[1] [tɪk] **1** *n* **(a)** *[clock]* tic-tac *m*; (**fig*) instant *m*. **just a ~!*, half a ~!*** un instant!; **in a ~*, in a couple of ~s*** en un rien de temps; **I shan't be a ~*** j'en ai pour une seconde. **(b)** (*mark*) coche *f*. **to put a ~ against sth** cocher qch. **2** *vt name, item* cocher; (*mark right*) *answer etc* marquer juste. **3** *vi [clock, bomb etc]* faire tic-tac. (*fig*) **I don't understand what makes him ~*** il est un mystère pour moi.

tick off *vt sep* **(a)** *name, item* cocher. **(b)** (*: *reprimand*) passer un savon à*.

tick over *vi [engine]* tourner au ralenti; *[taximeter]* tourner; *[business etc]* aller doucettement.

♦ **ticker‡** *n* (*heart*) cœur *m*, palpitant‡ *m*. ♦ **ticker-tape** *n* (*US: at parades etc*) ≈ serpentin *m*; **to get a ~er-tape welcome** être accueilli par une pluie de serpentins. ♦ **ticking[1]** *n [clock]* tic-tac *m*. ♦ **ticking-off*** *n* attrapade* *f*; **to give sb a ~ing-off** passer un savon à qn*; **to get a ~ing-off** se faire attraper. ♦ **tick-tack-toe** *n* (*US*) ≈ jeu *m* de morpion. ♦ **tick-tock** *n [clock]* tic-tac *m*.

tick[2] [tɪk] *n* (*Zool*) tique *f*.

tick[3] [tɪk] *n*: **on ~*** à crédit.

ticket ['tɪkɪt] **1** *n* **(a)** (*gen*) billet *m*; (*for bus, tube, cloakroom*) ticket *m*; (*Comm: label*) étiquette *f*; (*from cash register*) ticket, reçu *m*; (*for left-luggage*) bulletin *m*; (*for library*) carte *f*. **coach ~** billet de car; (*fig*) **that's the ~!*** voilà ce qu'il nous faut!; (*US Pol*) **he is running on the Democratic ~** il se présente sur la liste des démocrates. **(b)** (*Aut: for fine*) P.-V. *m*, papillon *m*. **a ~ on the windscreen** un papillon sur le pare-brise; **to give sb/get a ~ for parking** mettre à qn/attraper un P.-V. pour stationnement illégal. **2** *adj*: (*Theat*) **~ agency** agence *f* de spectacles; **~ collector** contrôleur *m*; **~ holder** personne *f* munie d'un billet; **~ office** guichet *m*. **3** *vt goods* étiqueter.

ticking[2] ['tɪkɪŋ] *n* (*Tex*) toile *f* (à matelas).

tickle ['tɪkl] **1** *vt person, sb's vanity, palate etc* chatouiller; (*: *delight*) faire plaisir à; (*: *amuse*) faire rire. **to be ~d to death‡** *or* **~d pink‡** (*pleased*) être heureux comme tout; (*amused*) rire aux larmes. **2** *vi* chatouiller. **3** *n* chatouillement *m*. ♦ **tickler*** *n* (*problem*) colle* *f*; (*situation*) situation *f* délicate. ♦ **tickling 1** *n* chatouillement *m*; **2** *adj sensation* de chatouillement; *cough* d'irritation. ♦ **ticklish** *or* ♦ **tickly*** *adj* **(a)** *sensation* de chatouillement; *blanket* qui chatouille; *cough* d'irritation; *person* chatouilleux; **(b)** (*touchy*) *person* chatouilleux; (*difficult*) *situation* délicat.

tiddler* ['tɪdlər] *n* (*stickleback*) épinoche *f*; (*tiny fish*) petit poisson *m*; (*child*) petit(e) mioche* *m(f)*.

tiddly* ['tɪdlɪ] *adj* pompette*, ivre. ♦ **tiddlywinks** *n* jeu *m* de puce.

tide [taɪd] **1** *n* marée *f*; (*fig: of events*) cours *m*. **at high/low ~** à marée haute/basse; **the ~ turns at ...** la marée commence à monter (*or* à descendre) à ...; (*fig*) **the ~ has turned** la chance a tourné; (*fig*) **to go with the ~** suivre le courant; **to go against the ~** aller à contre-courant. **2** *vt*: **to ~ sb over (a difficulty)** dépanner* qn (*till* en attendant); **that should ~ me over until ...** avec ça je devrais m'en sortir jusqu'à ... . ♦ **tidal** *adj river* qui a des marées; **tidal wave** raz-de-marée *m inv*; (*of enthusiasm etc*) immense vague *f*. ♦ **tidemark** *n* laisse *f* de haute mer; (*on neck, bath*) ligne *f* de crasse. ♦ **tideway** *n* (*channel*) chenal *m* de marée; (*current*) flux *m*.

tidy ['taɪdɪ] **1** *adj* **(a)** *room, drawer, objects* bien rangé; *dress, hair, schoolwork* net; *habits* d'ordre; *person* (*in appearance*) soigné; (*in character*) ordonné. **to make ~** *or* **tidier** = **to ~** (*V* 3); **to have a ~ mind** avoir l'esprit méthodique. **(b)** (*) *amount, income* rondelet; *speed* bon. **it**

cost him a ~ bit ça lui a coûté une jolie somme; **a ~ bit of his salary** une bonne partie de son salaire. 2 *n* (*in car, cupboard etc*) vide-poches *m inv*. **sink ~** coin *m* d'évier (*ustensile*). 3 *vti* (**~ away, ~ out, ~ up**) ranger. **to ~ o.s. (up)** s'arranger; **to ~ (up) one's hair** arranger sa coiffure. ♦ **tidily** *adv arrange, fold* soigneusement; *write* proprement; *dress* avec soin. ♦ **tidiness** *n [room, drawer, books]* belle ordonnance *f*; *[handwriting, schoolwork]* propreté *f*; *[person]* sens *m* de l'ordre. ♦ **tidy-out*** *or* ♦ **tidy-up*** *n*: **to have a ~-out** *or* **~-up** faire du rangement; **to give sth a (good) ~-out** *or* **~-up** ranger qch à fond.

tie [taɪ] **1** *n* **(a)** (*neck~*) cravate *f*; (*on garment, curtain*) attache *f*; (*on shoe*) lacet *m*; (*Mus*) liaison *f*. (*on invitation*) **black ~** smoking *m*; **white ~** habit *m*; **family ~s** (*links*) liens *mpl* de famille; (*responsibilities*) attaches *fpl* familiales; **children are a great ~** avec les enfants on n'est pas libre. **(b)** (*Sport*) (*draw*) égalité *f* (de points); (*drawn match*) match *m* nul; (*drawn race/competition*) course *f*/concours *m* dont les vainqueurs sont ex æquo. **the match ended in a ~** les deux équipes ont fait match nul; **the election ended in a ~** les candidats ont terminé à égalité de voix; **to play off a ~** rejouer un match nul; **there was a ~ for second place** il y avait deux ex æquo en seconde position; **cup ~** match de coupe.

2 *vt* (*fasten*) attacher (*to* à); (*knot*) nouer (*to* à); *ribbon* faire un nœud à; *shoes* lacer; (*link: also Mus*) lier (*to* à); (*restrict*) restreindre. (*fig*) **his hands are ~d** il a les mains liées; **to be ~d hand and foot** avoir pieds et poings liés; **to ~ a bow in sth** faire un nœud avec qch; **to ~ a knot in sth** faire un nœud à qch; **to get ~d in knots** *[rope etc]* faire des nœuds; (*fig*) *[person]* s'embrouiller; **house ~d to the job** maison liée au travail; **I'm ~d to the house** je suis retenu à la maison; **are we ~d to this plan?** sommes-nous obligés de nous en tenir à ce projet?; **we are very ~d in the evenings** nous sommes rarement libres le soir.

3 *vi* (*draw*) (*Sport etc*) faire match nul; (*in competition*) être ex æquo; (*in election*) obtenir le même nombre de voix. **they ~d for first place** ils ont été premiers ex æquo.

tie back *vt sep curtains* attacher sur les côtés; *hair* retenir (en arrière).

tie down *vt sep* attacher. (*fig*) **to be ~d down** ne pas avoir assez de temps libre; **to ~ sb down to a promise/a price/a time** obliger qn à tenir sa promesse/à fixer un prix/à venir à une certaine heure; **to ~ o.s. down to doing sth** se trouver contraint de faire qch.

tie in 1 *vi* (*be linked*) être lié (*with* à); (*be consistent*) correspondre (*with* à). **2** *vt sep meeting, visit, work* combiner (*with* avec).

tie on *vt sep* attacher.

tie together *vt sep* attacher (ensemble).

tie up 1 *vi* (*Naut*) accoster. **2** *vt sep parcel* ficeler; *prisoner, boat, horse* attacher (*to* à); (*fig*) *money* immobiliser; (*conclude*) *deal etc* conclure; *details* régler. **it's all ~d up** tout est réglé; (*fig*) **to be ~d up** (*linked*) être lié (*with* avec); (*busy*) être très pris; (*muddled*) être embrouillé; (*obstructed*) *[traffic]* être bloqué; *[production, sales]* être arrêté; *[project]* être suspendu.

♦ **tie-breaker** *n* (*Tennis*) tie-break *m*; (*in quiz*) question *f* subsidiaire. ♦ **tie-in** *n* (*link*) lien *m*, rapport *m* (*with* avec). ♦ **tie-on** *adj label* à œillet. ♦ **tiepin** *n* épingle *f* de cravate. ♦ **tie-up** *n* (*connection*) lien *m* (*with* avec; *between* entre).

tier [tɪəʳ] *n* (*in stadium etc*) gradin *m*; (*of cake*) étage *m*. **in ~s** (*gen*) par étages; *seating* en gradins; **to rise in ~s** s'étager; **three-~ed cake** ≃ pièce montée *f* à trois étages.

tiff [tɪf] *n* prise *f* de bec*.

tiger ['taɪgəʳ] **1** *n* tigre *m*. **2** *adj*: **~ lily** lis *m* tigré; **~ moth** écaille *f* (*papillon*). ♦ **tigress** *n* tigresse *f*.

tight [taɪt] **1** *adj* **(a)** (*not loose*) *rope* raide, tendu; *garment* ajusté; (*too ~*) trop étroit; *belt, shoes* qui serre; *tap, lid, drawer* dur; *bend in road* raide; *knot, weave, knitting* serré; *restrictions, control* sévère, strict; *programme, schedule* très chargé. **my shoes are too ~** mes chaussures me serrent; **it's a ~ fit** c'est juste; **to keep a ~ hold on sth** bien tenir qch, (*fig*) avoir qch en main; **it will be ~ but we'll make it in time** ce sera juste, mais nous y arriverons; (*fig*) **in a ~ corner** dans une situation difficile. **(b)** *credit* serré; *business* difficile; *budget* juste; *transaction* qui laisse peu de marge. **money is very ~** (*Econ*) l'argent est rare; (*at home*) les finances sont très justes; **to be ~** (*miserly*) être avare *or* radin*. **(c)** (*: *drunk*) rond*, ivre. **to get ~** se cuiter*.

2 *adv grasp* bien, solidement; *close* bien, hermétiquement; *squeeze* très fort. **screw the nut up ~** serrez l'écrou à bloc; **don't fasten** *or* **tie it too ~** ne le serrez pas trop (fort); *V* **hold, sit, sleep** *etc*.

♦ **tighten 1** *vt* (**~en up**) *rope* tendre; *garment* ajuster; *screw, wheel, grasp* resserrer; *legislation, restrictions* renforcer; (*lit, fig*) **to ~en one's belt** se serrer la ceinture; **2** *vi* (**~en up**) se tendre; se resserrer; être renforcé; (*fig*) **to ~en up on sth** devenir plus strict en matière de qch. ♦ **tight-fisted** *adj* avare, radin*. ♦ **tight-fitting** *adj garment* ajusté; *lid, stopper* qui ferme bien. ♦ **tight-knit** *adj* (*fig*) *family* uni; *programme, schedule* très chargé. ♦ **tightly** *adv* = **tight 2**. ♦ **tightness** *n [garment]* étroitesse *f*; *[screw, lid]* dureté *f*; *[restrictions, control]* sévérité *f*; **he felt a ~ness in his chest** il avait la poitrine oppressée. ♦ **tightrope 1** *n* corde *f* raide; **2** *adj*: **~rope walker** funambule *mf*. ♦ **tights** *npl* collant *m*.

tile [taɪl] **1** *n* (*on roof*) tuile *f*; (*on floor, wall*) carreau *m*. (*fig*) **to be out on the ~s*** faire la noce*. **2** *vt* couvrir de tuiles; carreler. ♦ **tiled** *adj roof* en tuiles; *floor, room etc* carrelé.

till[1] [tɪl] = **until**.

till[2] [tɪl] *n* caisse *f*. (*fig*) **caught with one's hand in the ~** pris sur le fait.

till[3] [tɪl] *vt* (*Agr*) labourer.

tiller ['tɪləʳ] *n* (*Naut*) barre *f* (*du gouvernail*).

tilt [tɪlt] **1** *n* **(a)** (*slope*) inclinaison *f*. **(b) (at) full ~** à toute vitesse. **2** *vt object, one's head* pencher, incliner; *hat* rabattre (*over* sur). **to ~ one's chair back** se balancer sur sa chaise. **3** *vi* (**~ over**) pencher, être incliné.

timber ['tɪmbəʳ] **1** *n* (*wood*) bois *m* de construction; (*trees collectively*) arbres *mpl*. **2** *adj fence etc* en bois. ♦ **timbered** *adj house* en bois; *land* boisé. ♦ **timber-merchant** *n* négociant *m* en bois. ♦ **timberyard** *n* chantier *m* de bois.

time [taɪm] **1** *n* **(a)** (*gen*) temps *m*. **~ and space** le temps et l'espace; **~ flies** le temps passe vite; **only ~ will tell** ≃ qui vivra verra; **~ will show if ...** le temps dira si ...; **with ~, in (the course of) ~, as ~ goes by** avec le temps; **it takes ~** ça prend du temps; **from ~ out of mind** de toute éternité; **I've no ~ for that sort of thing** (*lit*) je n'ai pas le temps de faire ce genre de chose; (*fig*) ce genre de chose m'agace; **I've enough ~** *or* **I have the ~ to go there** j'ai le temps d'y aller; **we've got plenty of ~, we've all the ~ in the world** nous avons tout notre temps; **you've got plenty of ~ to wait for me** vous avez bien le temps de m'attendre; **I can't find ~ to do** *or* **for (doing) that** je n'arrive pas à trouver le temps de faire ça; **to make up for lost ~** rattraper le temps perdu; **in no ~ at all, in less than no ~** en un rien de temps; **he had ~ on his hands** *or* **~ to spare** il avait du temps devant lui; **I spent a lot of ~ preparing this, it took me a lot of ~ to prepare this** il m'a fallu pas mal de temps pour le préparer; **to spend one's ~ doing** passer son temps à faire; **for part** *or* **some of the ~** pendant une partie du temps; **some of the ~ he looks cheerful**

quelquefois *or* par moments il a l'air gai; **most of the ~** la plupart du temps; **all the ~** (*the whole ~*) tout le temps; (*from the start*) dès le début; **take your ~ (over it)** prenez votre temps (pour le faire); (*fig*) **it took me all my ~ to finish it** j'ai eu du mal à le finir; **your ~ is up** (*in exam, visit etc*) c'est l'heure; **free ~, ~ off** temps libre; **in his own good ~** quand bon lui semblera; **in good ~** à temps; **in good ~ for** en avance pour; **all in good ~!** chaque chose en son temps!; **a race against ~** une course contre la montre; **he was working against ~** il travaillait d'arrache-pied (*to finish* pour terminer); **for the ~ being** pour le moment.

(b) (*period, length of ~*) **for a ~** pendant un certain temps; **a long ~** longtemps; **he hasn't been seen for a long ~** on ne l'a pas vu depuis longtemps; **it's a long ~ since ...** il y a bien longtemps que ...; **what a (long) ~ you've been!** il vous en a fallu du temps!; **it took a very long ~ for that to happen** il a fallu attendre longtemps pour que cela arrive (*subj*); **for a long ~ (to come *or* past)** longtemps; **a short ~** peu de temps; **for a short ~** (pendant) un moment; **in a short ~ they were all gone** quelques moments plus tard ils avaient tous disparu; **I waited for some ~** j'ai attendu assez longtemps; **some considerable ~** un temps considérable; **some little ~** un certain temps; **some ~ ago** il y a quelque temps *or* un certain temps; **it won't be ready for some ~** ce ne sera pas prêt avant un certain temps; **in half the ~** deux fois plus vite; **in 2 weeks' ~** dans 2 semaines; **what ~ did he do it in?** il a mis combien de temps?; **cooking ~** temps de cuisson; *[prisoner]* **to do ~*** faire de la prison; **we made good ~** nous avons bien marché; **to be on *or* to work full ~** travailler à plein temps; **to be on ~ and a half** faire des heures supplémentaires payées à 150%; **it is paid at double ~** c'est payé double; **in the firm's ~** pendant les heures de service; **in one's own ~** après les heures de service.

(c) (*era: often pl*) époque *f*. **the ~s we live in** l'époque où nous vivons; **in medieval ~s** à l'époque médiévale; **in Gladstone's ~** du temps de Gladstone; **in ~s past, in former ~s** dans le temps, jadis; **in my ~ it was different** de mon temps c'était différent; **I've seen some queer things in my ~** j'ai vu des choses étranges dans ma vie; **before my ~** (*before I was born*) avant que je ne sois né; (*before I came here*) avant que je ne vienne ici; **in ~(s) of peace** en temps de paix; **peace in our ~** la paix de notre vivant; (*fig*) **he is ahead of his ~, he was born before his ~** il est en avance sur son époque; **to keep up with the ~s** être de son époque; **to be behind the ~s** être vieux jeu *inv*; **at the best of ~s** déjà quand tout va bien; **~s are hard** les temps sont durs; **to have a rough *or* bad *or* tough* ~ (of it)** en voir de dures*; **to give sb a bad ~** en faire voir de dures* à qn; **what great ~s we've had!** c'était le bon temps!; **to have a good ~ (of it)** bien s'amuser; **to have the ~ of one's life** s'amuser comme un fou; **a tense ~** une période très tendue (*for* pour).

(d) (*by clock*) heure *f*. **what is the ~?, what ~ is it?** quelle heure est-il?; **what ~ do you make it?** quelle heure avez-vous?; **have you got the right ~?** est-ce que vous avez l'heure exacte?; **the ~ is 10.30** il est 10.30; **what ~ is he arriving at?** à quelle heure est-ce qu'il arrive?; **he looked at the ~** il a regardé l'heure; **it keeps good ~** c'est toujours à l'heure; **there's a ~ and a place for everything** il y a un temps pour tout; (*fig*) **to pass the ~ of day** échanger quelques mots (*with sb* avec qn); **at this ~ of (the) night** à cette heure de la nuit; **at any ~ of the day or night** à n'importe quelle heure du jour ou de la nuit; **open at all ~s** ouvert à toute heure; (*US*) **midnight, by Eastern ~** minuit, heure de la côte est; **ahead of/behind ~** en avance/retard; **just in ~** juste à temps (*for sth* pour qch; *to do* pour faire); **on ~** à l'heure; **it's ~ for tea, it's tea ~** c'est l'heure du thé; **it's ~ to go** c'est l'heure de partir, il est temps de partir; **it's ~ I was going, it's ~ for me to go** il est temps que je m'en aille; **it's about ~ he was here** il serait temps qu'il arrive (*subj*); **it's (high) ~ that** il est grand temps que + *subj*; **and about ~ too!** et ce n'est pas trop tôt!

(e) (*point of ~*) moment *m*. **at the *or* that ~** à ce moment-là; **at this ~** en ce moment; **at the present ~** en ce moment, actuellement; **at one ~** à un moment donné; **sometimes ... at other ~s ...** quelquefois ... d'autres fois ...; **at all ~s** à tous moments; **I have at no ~ said that** je n'ai jamais dit cela; **at ~s** par moments; **there are ~s when** il y a des moments où; **at his ~ of life** à son âge; **at an inconvenient ~** à un moment inopportun; **he may come (at) any ~** il peut arriver d'un moment à l'autre; **come (at) any ~** venez n'importe quand; **at this ~ of year** à cette époque de l'année; **two things at the same ~** deux choses à la fois; **at the same ~ as** en même temps que; **but at the same ~, you must admit ...** cependant, il faut avouer ...; **by the ~ I had finished** le temps que je termine (*subj*); **by this *or* that ~ they had drunk it all** à ce moment-là ils avaient déjà tout bu; **you must be cold by this ~** vous devez avoir froid maintenant; **by this ~ next year** dans un an; **this ~ tomorrow** demain à cette heure-ci; **this ~ last year** l'année dernière à cette époque-ci; **this ~ last week** il y a exactement huit jours; **in between ~s** entre temps; **from ~ to ~** de temps en temps; **from that ~ *or* this ~ on** (+ *past*) à partir de ce moment; (+ *future*) désormais; **until such ~ as** jusqu'à ce que + *subj*; **this is no ~ for quarrelling** ce n'est pas le moment de se disputer; **to choose one's ~** choisir son moment; **now's the ~ to do it** c'est maintenant qu'il faut le faire; **to die before one's ~** mourir avant l'âge; **his ~ has come** son heure a sonné; **when the ~ comes** quand le moment viendra; **the ~ has come to do ...** il est temps de faire ...; **the ~ has come for us to leave** il est temps que nous partions (*subj*); **it's ~ to get up** c'est l'heure de nous *etc* lever.

(f) (*occasion*) fois *f*. **this ~** cette fois; **(the) next ~ you come** la prochaine fois que vous viendrez; **every *or* each ~** chaque fois; **several ~s** plusieurs fois; **at other ~s** d'autres fois; **at odd ~s** parfois; **many a ~, many ~s** bien des fois; **~ after ~, ~ and (~) again** maintes et maintes fois; **hundreds of ~s*** cent fois; **(the) last ~** la dernière fois; **the previous ~, the ~ before** la dernière fois; **some other ~** une autre fois; **some ~ or other** un jour ou l'autre; **I remember the ~ when** je me rappelle le jour où; **2 at a ~** 2 par 2, (*stairs, steps*) 2 à 2; **for weeks at a ~** pendant des semaines entières; **10 francs a ~** 10 F chaque fois.

(g) (*multiplying*) fois *f*. **2 ~s 3 is 6** 2 fois 3 (font) 6; **10 ~s as big** 10 fois plus grand (*as* que).

(h) (*Mus etc*) mesure *f*. **in ~** en mesure (*to, with* avec); **three-four ~** mesure à trois temps; **to keep ~** rester en mesure.

2 *adj* (a) *bomb, fuse* à retardement; (*US*) *loan etc* à terme. **(b)** (*Phot*) **~ exposure** pose *f*; **to set a ~ limit** fixer une limite de temps *or* un délai (*on, for* pour); **without a ~ limit** sans limitation de temps; (*Ind etc*) **~ sheet** feuille *f* de présence; (*Rad*) **~ signal** signal *m* horaire; **~ switch** (*on apparatus*) minuteur *m*; (*for lighting*) minuterie *f*; **~ zone** fuseau *m* horaire.

3 *vt* (a) (*choose ~ of*) *invasion, visit* fixer (*for* à); *remark, interruption* choisir le moment de. **it was ~d to begin at ...** le commencement était fixé *or* prévu pour ...; **you ~d that perfectly** vous ne pouviez pas mieux choisir votre moment. **(b)** (*count ~ of*) *race, worker etc* chronométrer (*over* sur); *programme, piece of work* minuter; *egg* minuter la cuisson de. **~ how long it takes you**

notez le temps qu'il vous faut pour le faire. ♦ **time (and motion) study** *n* (*Ind etc*) étude *f* des cadences. ♦ **timeclock** *n* (*Ind*) (*machine*) enregistreur *m* de temps; (*place*) pointage *m*. ♦ **time-consuming** *adj* qui prend du temps. ♦ **time-honoured** *adj* consacré (par l'usage). ♦ **timekeeper** *n* (*person: at race etc*) chronométreur *m*; **to be a good ~keeper** être toujours à l'heure. ♦ **time-lag** *n* décalage *m*. ♦ **timeless** *adj* éternel. ♦ **timeliness** *n* à-propos *m*. ♦ **timely** *adj* à propos. ♦ **timeout** *n* (*US*) arrêt *m*. ♦ **timepiece** *n* (*gen*) mécanisme *m* d'horlogerie; (*watch*) montre *f*; (*clock*) horloge *f*. ♦ **timer** *n* (*Culin etc*) compte-minutes *m inv*; (*with sand*) sablier *m*; (*on machine etc*) minuteur *m*; (*Aut*) distributeur *m* d'allumage. ♦ **time-saver** *n*: **it is a great ~-saver** ça fait gagner beaucoup de temps. ♦ **time-saving** **1** *adj* qui fait gagner du temps; **2** *n* gain *m* de temps. ♦ **timeserver** *n* (*pej*) opportuniste *mf*. ♦ **timetable** *n* (*Rail etc*) horaire *m*; (*Scol*) emploi *m* du temps. ♦ **timing** **1** *n* (*Aut*) réglage *m* de l'allumage; (*Ind, Sport*) chronométrage *m*; *[musician etc]* sens *m* du rythme; *[actor]* minutage *m*; (*in formation flying etc*) synchronisation *f*; **the timing of this demonstration** (*date/hour*) la date/l'heure *f* de cette manifestation; (*programme of various stages*) le minutage de cette manifestation; **2** *adj*: **timing mechanism** *[bomb etc]* mouvement *m* d'horlogerie; *[electrical apparatus]* minuteur *m*.

timid ['tɪmɪd] *adj* (*shy*) timide; (*unadventurous*) timoré, craintif. ♦ **timidity** *n* timidité *f*; caractère timoré. ♦ **timidly** *adv* timidement; craintivement.

timorous ['tɪmərəs] *adj* timoré, craintif.

timpani ['tɪmpənɪ] *npl* timbales *fpl*.

tin [tɪn] **1** *n* **(a)** étain *m*; (*~plate*) fer-blanc *m*. **(b)** (*can*) boîte *f* (en fer-blanc); (*mould*) moule *m*; (*dish*) plat *m*. **~ of salmon** boîte de saumon; **cake ~** (*for storing*) boîte à gâteaux; (*for baking*) moule à gâteau; **roasting ~** plat à rôtir. **2** *vt food etc* mettre en conserve. **3** *adj* (*made of ~*) en étain (*or* fer-blanc); *mine* d'étain; *soldier* de plomb. **~ can** boîte *f* (en fer-blanc); **~ hat** casque *m*; **~ whistle** flûteau *m*. ♦ **tinfoil** *n* papier *m* d'aluminium. ♦ **tinned** *adj fruit, salmon* en boîte, en conserve; **~ned food** conserves *fpl*. ♦ **tinny** *adj sound, taste* métallique; (**pej*) *car, machine* de camelote. ♦ **tin-opener** *n* ouvre-boîtes *m*. ♦ **tinplate** *n* fer-blanc *m*. ♦ **tinpot*** *adj* qui ne vaut pas grand-chose. ♦ **tintack** *n* semence *f* (*de tapissier*).

tinder ['tɪndər] *n*: **as dry as ~** sec comme de l'amadou.

tinge [tɪndʒ] **1** *n* teinte *f*. **2** *vt* teinter (*with* de).

tingle ['tɪŋgl] **1** *vi* picoter; (*with excitement*) frissonner. **her face was tingling** le visage lui picotait; **her cheeks were tingling with cold** le froid lui piquait les joues. **2** *n* picotement *m*; frisson *m*. (*sound*) **to have a ~ in one's ears** avoir les oreilles qui tintent. ♦ **tingling** **1** *n* = **tingle 2**; **2** *adj sensation* de picotement.

tinker ['tɪŋkər] **1** *n* (*gen: often pej*) romanichel(le) *m(f)*; (*mending etc*) rétameur *m* ambulant. **2** *vi* (**~ about**) bricoler (*with sth* qch).

tinkle ['tɪŋkl] **1** *vi* tinter. **2** *vt* faire tinter. **3** *n* tintement *m*. (*Telec*) **to give sb a ~*** passer un coup de fil à qn*. ♦ **tinkling** *n* tintement *m*.

tinsel ['tɪnsəl] *n* guirlandes *fpl* de Noël (argentées); (*fig pej*) clinquant *m*.

tint [tɪnt] **1** *n* teinte *f*. **2** *vt* teinter (*with* de). **to ~ one's hair** se faire un shampooing colorant.

tiny ['taɪnɪ] *adj* tout petit, minuscule.

tip¹ [tɪp] *n* (*gen*) bout *m*; (*pointed*) pointe *f*; (*metalled: of cane etc*) embout *m*; *[billiard cue]* procédé *m*. (*fig*) **it's on the ~ of my tongue** je l'ai sur le bout de la langue; (*fig*) **the ~ of the iceberg** la partie émergée de l'iceberg. ♦ **tipped** *adj cigarettes* filtre *inv*; **steel-~ped** qui a un embout de fer. ♦ **tiptoe** **1** *n*: **on ~toe** sur la pointe des pieds; **2** *vi*: **to ~toe in/out** *etc* entrer/sortir *etc* sur la pointe des pieds. ♦ **tiptop*** *adj* excellent.

tip² [tɪp] **1** *n* **(a)** (*gratuity*) pourboire *m*. **the ~ is included** le service est compris. **(b)** (*hint*) suggestion *f*; (*advice*) conseil *m*; (*information; also Racing*) tuyau* *m*. **take my ~** suivez mon conseil.

2 *vt* **(a)** donner un pourboire à. **to ~ sb 5 francs** donner 5 F de pourboire à qn. **(b)** *winner* pronostiquer; *horse* pronostiquer la victoire de (*for the race* dans la course). (*fig*) **he was ~ped for the job** on avait pronostiqué qu'il serait nommé.

tip off *vt sep* (*gen*) donner un tuyau* à (*about sth* sur qch); *police* prévenir.

♦ **tip-off** *n* tuyau* *m*; **to give sb a ~-off** prévenir qn. ♦ **tipster** *n* pronostiqueur *m*.

tip³ [tɪp] **1** *n* (*for rubbish*) décharge *f*. **2** *vt* (**~ over**) incliner; (*overturn*) renverser; (**~ out**) *liquid* verser; *load, rubbish, books etc* déverser (*into* dans; *out of* de). **to ~ sth back** incliner qch en arrière; **to ~ sb into/out of sth** faire tomber qn dans/de qch. **3** *vi* pencher. **to ~ back(wards)** *[chair]* se rabattre en arrière; *[person]* se pencher en arrière.

tip up **1** *vi [table etc]* (*tilt*) pencher; (*overturn*) basculer; *[box, jug]* se renverser; *[seat]* se rabattre; *[truck]* basculer. **2** *vt sep* incliner.

♦ **tipper** *n* (*truck*) camion *m* à benne (basculante). ♦ **tipping** *n*: **'no ~ping'** 'défense de déposer des ordures'.

tipple ['tɪpl] **1** *vi* picoler*. **2** *n*: **gin is his ~** ce qu'il préfère boire c'est du gin. ♦ **tippler** *n* picoleur* *m*, -euse* *f*.

tipsy ['tɪpsɪ] *adj* éméché, parti*. **to get ~** devenir gai.

tirade [taɪ'reɪd] *n* diatribe *f*.

tire¹ ['taɪər] *n* (*US*) = **tyre**.

tire² ['taɪər] **1** *vt* fatiguer; (*weary*) fatiguer, lasser. **2** *vi* se fatiguer; se lasser. **he ~s easily** il se fatigue vite; **he never ~s of saying ...** il ne se lasse jamais de dire ... .

tire out *vt sep* épuiser, crever*.

♦ **tired** *adj person* fatigué; (*weary*) las; *movement, voice* las; (*fig*) *cliché etc* rebattu; **to be ~d of sth/sb** en avoir assez de qch/qn; **to be ~d of doing** en avoir assez de faire; **to get ~d of** commencer à en avoir assez de; **you make me ~d!*** tu me fatigues! ♦ **tiredness** *n* fatigue *f*; lassitude *f*. ♦ **tireless** *adj* infatigable; inlassable. ♦ **tirelessly** *adv* infatigablement; inlassablement. ♦ **tiresome** *adj* ennuyeux. ♦ **tiring** *adj* fatigant.

tissue ['tɪʃu:] **1** *n* (*Anat, Tex*) tissu *m*; (*paper handkerchief*) mouchoir *m* en papier, kleenex *m* ®. (*fig*) **~ of lies** tissu de mensonges. **2** *adj*: **~ paper** papier *m* de soie.

tit¹ [tɪt] *n* (*bird*: **~mouse**) mésange *f*.

tit² [tɪt] *n*: **~ for tat** un prêté pour un rendu.

tit³‡ [tɪt] *n* (*breast*) sein *m*, nichon‡ *m*.

titanic [taɪ'tænɪk] *adj* titanesque.

titbit ['tɪtbɪt] *n [food]* friandise *f*; *[news]* détail *m* croustillant.

titillate ['tɪtɪleɪt] *vt* titiller.

titivate ['tɪtɪveɪt] **1** *vi* se pomponner. **2** *vt* pomponner.

title ['taɪtl] **1** *n* (*gen*) titre *m*; (*Jur*) titres *mpl* (*to* à). (*Cine, TV*) **(credit) ~s** générique *m*. **2** *adj*: **~ deed** titre *m* de propriété; (*Sport*) **~ holder** détenteur *m*, -trice *f* du titre; **~ page** page *f* de titre; (*Theat*) **~ role** = rôle principal. ♦ **titled** *adj person* titré.

titter ['tɪtər] **1** *vi* rire sottement (*at* de). **2** *n* petit rire *m* sot.

tittle-tattle ['tɪtl,tætl] *n* cancans *mpl*.

tizzy* ['tɪzɪ] *n*: **to be in/get into a ~** être/se mettre dans tous ses états.

to [tu:, *weak form* tə] **1** *prep* **(a)** (*gen*) à; (*direction*) à, vers, en, chez. **to give sth ~ sb** donner qch à qn; **he went ~ the door** il est allé à la porte; **he**

was walking ~ the door il marchait vers la porte; **to go ~ school/town** aller à l'école/en ville; **to go ~ France/Canada/the U.S.A.** aller en France/au Canada/aux États-Unis; **to go ~ London/Le Havre** aller à Londres/au Havre; **boats ~ and from Cherbourg** les bateaux à destination ou en provenance de Cherbourg; **to go ~ the doctor('s)** aller chez le docteur; **~ the left** à gauche; **the road ~ London** la route de Londres; **to count ~ 20** compter jusqu'à 20; **it comes ~ £20** ça fait 20 livres (en tout); **it is 90 km ~ Paris** nous sommes à 90 km de Paris; **8 years ago ~ the day** il y a 8 ans jour pour jour; **from morning ~ night** du matin au soir; **from town ~ town** de ville en ville; **50 ~ 60 people** de 50 à 60 personnes; **back ~ back** dos à dos; **bumper ~ bumper** pare-chocs contre pare-chocs; **what's it ~ you?** qu'est-ce que ça peut vous faire?; **be nice ~ her** sois gentil avec elle; **it's a great help ~ him** cela lui est très utile; **known ~ the Ancients** connu des anciens; **assistant ~ the manager** adjoint(e) *m(f)* du directeur; **ambassador ~ France/~ the king** ambassadeur en France/auprès du roi; **he has been a good friend ~ us** il a été pour nous un ami fidèle.

(b) (*in time phrases*) **20 (minutes) ~ 2** 2 heures moins 20; **at (a) quarter ~ 4** à 4 heures moins le quart; **it was 10 ~** il était moins 10.

(c) (*in proportions etc*) **A is ~ B as C is ~ D** A est à B ce que C est à D; **to bet 10 ~ 1** parier 10 contre 1; **by a majority of 10 ~ 7** avec une majorité de 10 contre 7; **they won by 4 goals ~ 2** ils ont gagné 4 (buts) à 2; **one person ~ a room** une personne par chambre; **200 people ~ the square km** 200 personnes au km carré; **how many miles ~ the gallon?** ≃ combien de litres au cent?; **that's nothing ~ what is to come** ce n'est rien à côté de ce qui va venir.

(d) (*phrases*) **here's ~ you!** à la vôtre!; **~ absent friends!** à la santé des absents!; **what would you say ~ a beer?** que diriez-vous d'une bière?; **that's all there is ~ it** (*it's easy*) ça n'est pas plus difficile que ça; (*no ulterior motive etc*) c'est aussi simple que ça; (*Comm*) '**~ repairing cooker: 100 francs**' 'remise en état d'une cuisinière: 100 F'; **~ the best of my recollection** pour autant que je m'en souvienne; **~ my delight** à ma grande joie; (*Math*) **3 ~ the 4th** 3 à la puissance 4.

2 *particle* (*forming infin: shown in French by vb ending*) **~ be** être; **~ eat** manger; **I'll try ~** j'essaierai; **I forgot ~** j'ai oublié.

3 *adv*: **to push the door ~** fermer la porte; **the door is ~** la porte est fermée; **to go ~ and fro** *[person]* aller et venir; (*stride up and down*) faire les cent pas; *[machine part etc]* avoir un mouvement de va-et-vient; *[train, bus etc]* faire la navette (*between* entre).

♦ **to-do*** *n*: **to make a ~-do** faire toute une histoire* (*about* à propos de). ♦ **to-ing and fro-ing** *n* allées et venues *fpl*.

toad [təʊd] *n* crapaud *m*. ♦ **toad-in-the-hole** *n* (*Culin*) *saucisses cuites dans de la pâte à crêpes*. ♦ **toadstool** *n* champignon *m*; (*poisonous*) champignon vénéneux. ♦ **toady 1** *n* flagorneur *m*, -euse *f*; **2** *vi* flagorner; **to ~y to sb** flatter qn bassement. ♦ **toadying** *n* flagornerie *f*.

toast [təʊst] **1** *n* **(a)** pain *m* grillé, toast *m*. **you've burnt the ~** tu as laissé brûler le pain *or* les toasts; **a piece *or* slice of ~** une tartine grillée, un toast; **sardines on ~** sardines *fpl* sur canapé. **(b)** toast *m*. **to drink a ~ to sb** porter un toast à qn (*in champagne* au champagne); **the ~ of the town** la vedette de la ville. **2** *vt* **(a)** *bread etc* faire griller. **(b)** (*drink ~ to*) porter un toast à; *event, victory* arroser (*in champagne* au champagne). ♦ **toaster** *n* grille-pain *m inv* (*électrique*). ♦ **toast-rack** *n* porte-toast *m inv*.

tobacco [təˈbækəʊ] **1** *n* tabac *m*. **2** *adj plantation, company* de tabac; *pouch* à tabac; *industry* du tabac. ♦ **tobacconist** *n* marchand(e) *m(f)* de tabac; **~nist's (shop)** (bureau *m* de) tabac *m*.

toboggan [təˈbɒgən] **1** *n* toboggan *m*; (*child's*) luge *f*. **2** *vi*: **to go ~ing** faire de la luge.

today [təˈdeɪ] *adv, n* aujourd'hui. **all ~** toute la journée aujourd'hui; **a week (past) ~** il y a huit jours aujourd'hui; **~ week, a week (from) ~** aujourd'hui en huit; **what day is (it) ~?** quel jour est-on *or* est-ce aujourd'hui?; **what date is (it) ~?** quelle est la date aujourd'hui?; **~ is Friday/the 4th** aujourd'hui c'est vendredi/le 4; **~ is wet** il pleut aujourd'hui; **~ was a bad day** aujourd'hui ça s'est mal passé; **~'s paper** le journal d'aujourd'hui; (*fig*) **here ~ and gone tomorrow** ça va, ça vient; **the writers of ~** les écrivains d'aujourd'hui.

toddle [ˈtɒdl] *vi [child]* **to ~ in/out** *etc* entrer/sortir *etc* à pas hésitants; *[adult]* **to ~ along*** se balader*. ♦ **toddler** *n* tout(e) petit(e) *m(f)* (qui commence à marcher), bambin* *m*.

toddy [ˈtɒdɪ] *n* ≃ grog *m*.

toe [təʊ] **1** *n* orteil *m*, doigt *m* de pied; *[sock, shoe]* bout *m*. **big/little ~** gros/petit orteil; **three-~d** à trois orteils; (*lit, fig*) **to tread on sb's ~s** marcher sur les pieds de qn; (*fig*) **to keep sb on his ~s** forcer qn à rester alerte. **2** *vt* (*fig*) **to ~ the line** *or* (*US*) **mark** obéir. ♦ **toecap** *n* bout *m* renforcé (*de soulier*). ♦ **toeclip** *n [cyclist]* cale-pied *m inv*. ♦ **toenail** *n* ongle *m* du pied.

toffee [ˈtɒfɪ] *n* caramel *m* (*au beurre*). **~ apple** pomme *f* caramélisée; (*fig*) **he can't do it for ~*** il n'est pas fichu* de le faire.

together [təˈgeðəʳ] *adv* **(a)** (*gen*) ensemble. **I've seen them ~** je les ai vus ensemble; (*fig*) **we're in this ~** (*in same situation*) nous sommes logés à la même enseigne; (*must act ~*) il faut que nous fassions front commun; (*pej*) **they were both in it ~** ils avaient partie liée tous les deux; **tie the ropes ~** nouez les cordes; **all ~ now!** (*shouting, singing*) tous en chœur maintenant!; (*pulling*) (oh!) hisse!; **~ with** avec; **if you look at the reports ~** si vous considérez les rapports conjointement; **for weeks ~** pendant des semaines entières; **for 5 weeks ~** pendant 5 semaines de suite.

(b) (*simultaneously*) en même temps; (*Mus etc*) à l'unisson.

♦ **togetherness** *n* camaraderie *f*.

toggle [ˈtɒgl] *n* (*Dress*) bouton *m* de duffel-coat.

toil [tɔɪl] **1** *n* labeur *m*. **2** *vi* (**~ away**) peiner (*at, over* sur; *to do* pour faire). **to ~ along/up** *etc* avancer/monter *etc* péniblement.

toilet [ˈtɔɪlɪt] **1** *n* **(a)** (*dressing etc*) toilette *f*. **(b)** (*lavatory*) toilettes *fpl*, waters* *mpl*. **to go to the ~** aller aux toilettes *or* aux waters*; **to put sth down the ~** jeter qch dans la cuvette des cabinets. **2** *adj soap, water* de toilette. **~ bag** sac *m* de toilette; **~ case** trousse *f* de toilette; **~ paper** papier *m* hygiénique; **~ roll** rouleau *m* de papier hygiénique. ♦ **toiletries** *npl* articles *mpl* de toilette.

token [ˈtəʊkən] **1** *n* (*symbol*) témoignage *m*, marque *f*; (*metal disc: for telephone etc*) jeton *m*; (*voucher*) bon *m*. **gift ~** bon-cadeau *m*; **book ~** chèque-livre *m*; **record ~** chèque-disque *m*; **milk ~** bon de lait; **as a ~ of, in ~ of** en témoignage de; (*fig*) **by the same ~** de même. **2** *adj payment, strike* symbolique. **a ~ resistance** un semblant de résistance pour la forme.

told [təʊld] *pret, ptp of* **tell**.

tolerate [ˈtɒləreɪt] *vt* (*gen, Med, Tech*) tolérer; *heat, pain* supporter. ♦ **tolerable** *adj* (*bearable*) tolérable; (*fairly good*) passable. ♦ **tolerably** *adv work etc* passablement; *certain, competent* à peu près. ♦ **tolerance** *n* tolérance *f*. ♦ **tolerant** *adj* tolérant (*of sth* de qch, (*Med*) à qch; *of sb* à l'égard de qn). ♦ **tolerantly** *adv* d'une manière tolérante. ♦ **toleration** *n* tolérance *f*.

toll[1] [təʊl] **1** *n* (*gen, also Aut*) péage *m.* (*fig*) **to take a heavy ~ of** *soldiers etc* faire beaucoup de victimes parmi; *sb's strength* ébranler sérieusement; *savings* manger une grande partie de; **the accident ~ on the roads** le nombre des victimes de la route; **the ~ of dead** le nombre des morts. **2** *adj bridge, road* à péage.

toll[2] [təʊl] **1** *vi [bell]* sonner. **2** *vt bell* sonner; *sb's death* sonner le glas pour.

Tom [tɒm] *n* (*fig*) **any ~, Dick or Harry** n'importe qui. ♦ **tom(cat)** *n* matou *m.*

tomato [tə'mɑːtəʊ, (*US*) tə'meɪtəʊ] **1** *n, pl* **-es** tomate *f.* **2** *adj*: **~ juice** jus *m* de tomates; **~ ketchup** ketchup *m*; **~ sauce** sauce *f* tomate.

tomb [tuːm] *n* tombeau *m,* tombe *f.* ♦ **tombstone** *n* pierre *f* tombale.

tomboy ['tɒmbɔɪ] *n* garçon *m* manqué.

tome [təʊm] *n* tome *m,* gros volume *m.*

tomfool ['tɒm'fuːl] *adj* absurde, idiot. ♦ **tomfoolery** *n* âneries *fpl.*

tommy gun ['tɒmɪgʌn] *n* mitraillette *f.*

tomorrow [tə'mɒrəʊ] *adv, n* demain. **all ~** toute la journée demain; **a week (past) ~** il y aura huit jours demain; **~ week, a week from ~** demain en huit; **he'll have been here a week ~** cela fera huit jours demain qu'il est là; **see you ~!** à demain!; **the day after ~** après-demain; **what day will ~ be** *or* **will it be ~?** quel jour sera-t-on demain?; **what date will it be ~?** quelle sera la date demain?; **~ will be Saturday/the 5th** demain ce sera samedi/le 5; **~ will be dry** il ne pleuvra pas demain; **~ never comes** demain n'arrive jamais; **~ is another day!** ça ira peut-être mieux demain!; (*fig*) **the writers of ~** les écrivains de demain; **~ morning/evening** demain matin/soir.

tomtom ['tɒmtɒm] *n* tam-tam *m.*

ton [tʌn] *n* **(a)** (*weight*) tonne *f* (*Brit = 1016,06 kg; Can, US etc = 907,20 kg*). **metric ~** tonne (= *1000 kg*); **a 7-~ truck, a 7-~ner** un camion de 7 tonnes; (*fig*) **~s of*** des tas de*. **(b)** (*Naut*) (*register ~*) tonneau *m*; (*displacement ~*) tonne *f.* **a 60,000-~ steamer** un paquebot de 60 000 tonnes. ♦ **tonnage** *n* tonnage *m.*

tone [təʊn] **1** *n* **(a)** (*sound: gen*) ton *m*; *[musical instrument]* sonorité *f*; (*Telec: also of radio, record player etc*) tonalité *f.* **in low ~s** à voix basse; **in angry ~s** sur le ton de la colère; **don't speak to me in that ~ of voice!** ne me parlez sur ce ton!; (*fig*) **the ~ of his letter** le ton de sa lettre; **the whole ~ of the school** la tenue générale de l'école; (*Fin*) **the ~ of the market** la tenue du marché; **to raise/lower the ~ of sth** rehausser/rabaisser le ton de qch. **(b)** (*colour*) ton *m.* **two-~ car** voiture *f* de deux tons. **(c)** *[muscles etc]* tonus *m.* **2** *adj*: **~ control** bouton *m* de tonalité. **3** *vi* (**~ in**) s'harmoniser (*with* avec).

tone down *vt sep colour* adoucir; *sound, radio etc* baisser; (*fig*) *criticism, effect* atténuer.

tone up *vt sep* (*Med*) tonifier.

♦ **tonal** *adj* tonal. ♦ **tone-deaf** *adj*: **to be ~-deaf** ne pas avoir d'oreille. ♦ **tonelessly** *adv speak* d'une voix blanche.

tongs [tɒŋz] *npl* (**pair of ~**) pinces *fpl*; (*for coal*) pincettes *fpl*; (*for sugar*) pince *f* à sucre; (*curling* ~) fer *m* (à friser).

tongue [tʌŋ] *n* **(a)** (*gen*) langue *f*; *[shoe]* languette *f*; *[bell]* battant *m.* **to put out one's ~** tirer la langue (*at sb* à qn); **his ~ was hanging out** il tirait la langue; (*fig*) **he's lost his ~** il a perdu sa langue; **~ in cheek** ironiquement; **keep a civil ~ in your head!** tâchez d'être plus poli!; **I can't get my ~ round it** je n'arrive pas à le prononcer correctement. **(b)** (*language*) langue *f.* ♦ **tongue-tied** *adj* muet (*fig*). ♦ **tongue-twister** *n* phrase *f* très difficile à prononcer.

tonic ['tɒnɪk] **1** *adj* (*gen*) tonique. (*Mus*) **~ solfa** solfège *m.* **2** *n* **(a)** (*Med; fig*) tonique *m.* (*lit, fig*) **you need a ~** il vous faut un bon tonique; (*fig*) **it was a real ~** cela m'a vraiment remonté le moral. **(b) ~ (water)** ≈ Schweppes *m* ®; **gin and ~** gin-tonic *m.* **(c)** (*Mus*) tonique *f.*

tonight [tə'naɪt] *adv, n* (*before bed*) ce soir; (*during sleep*) cette nuit.

tonsil ['tɒnsl] *n* amygdale *f.* **to have one's ~s out** être opéré des amygdales. ♦ **tonsillectomy** *n* amygdalectomie *f.* ♦ **tonsillitis** *n* amygdalite *f*; **to have ~litis** avoir une angine *or* (*more formally*) une amygdalite.

too [tuː] *adv* **(a)** (*excessively*) trop. **it's ~ hard for me** c'est trop difficile pour moi; **it's ~ hard for me to explain** c'est trop difficile pour que je puisse vous l'expliquer; **~ heavy to carry** trop lourd à porter; **it's ~ heavy for me to carry** c'est trop lourd à porter pour moi; **he's ~ mean to pay for it** il est trop pingre pour le payer; **that's ~ kind of you!** vous êtes vraiment trop aimable!; **I'm not ~ sure about that** je n'en suis pas très certain. **(b)** (*also*) aussi; (*moreover*) en plus, en outre. **I went ~** moi aussi j'y suis allé; **they asked for a discount ~!** et en plus ils ont demandé un rabais!; **and then, ~, there's ...** et puis, il y a aussi ....

took [tʊk] *pret of* **take.**

tool [tuːl] *n* (*gen, Tech*) outil *m*; (*fig*) instrument *m* (*of* de). **set of ~s** panoplie *f* d'outils; **garden ~s** outils *or* ustensiles *mpl* de jardinage; **the ~s of my trade** les outils de mon métier. ♦ **toolbag** *or* ♦ **toolcase** *or* ♦ **toolkit** *n* trousse *f* à outils. ♦ **toolbox** *or* ♦ **toolcase** *or* ♦ **toolchest** *n* boîte *f* à outils. ♦ **tooled** *adj silver* ciselé; *leather* repoussé; *book-cover* en cuir repoussé. ♦ **toolhouse** *or* ♦ **toolshed** *n* cabane *f* à outils. ♦ **toolmaker** *n* outilleur *m.*

toot [tuːt] *vti* klaxonner.

tooth [tuːθ] *n, pl* **teeth** dent *f.* **front ~** dent de devant; **back ~** molaire *f*; **(set of) false teeth** dentier *m*; **to have a ~ out** se faire arracher une dent; (*fig*) **he's a bit long in the ~** il n'est plus tout jeune; (*fig*) **in the teeth of** *wind* contre; *opposition* en dépit de; **~ and nail** avec acharnement; (*fig*) **to get one's teeth into sth** se mettre à fond à qch; **there's nothing you can get your teeth into** ce n'est pas très substantiel; **the legislation has no teeth** la législation est impuissante; (*fig*) **to throw sth in sb's teeth** jeter qch à la tête de qn; **to be sick to the (back) teeth of sth**‡ en avoir ras le bol* de qch. ♦ **toothache** *n* mal *m* de dents; **to have ~ache** avoir mal aux dents. ♦ **toothbrush** *n* brosse *f* à dents. ♦ **toothcomb** *n* peigne *m* fin; (*fig*) **to go through sth with a (fine) ~comb** passer qch au peigne fin. ♦ **toothless** *adj* édenté. ♦ **toothpaste** *n* pâte *f* dentifrice. ♦ **toothpick** *n* cure-dent *m.* ♦ **tooth-powder** *n* poudre *f* dentifrice. ♦ **toothy** *adj*: **to be ~y** avoir des dents de cheval.

top[1] [tɒp] **1** *n* **(a)** *[ladder, page, wall, pile, street etc]* haut *m*; *[mountain, tree, hill, head]* sommet *m*; *[box, container]* dessus *m*; *[plant, vegetable]* fane *f*; *[list, table, classification, queue]* tête *f*; *[profession etc]* faîte *m*; (*surface*) surface *f*; (*roof: of car etc*) toit *m.* **at the ~ of** en haut de, au sommet de, en tête de, au faîte de; **at/near the ~ of the pile** en haut de/vers le haut de la pile; (*Scol*) **to be at the ~ of the class** être premier de la classe; **~ of the milk** crème *f* du lait; **it's ~ of the pops** c'est en tête du hit-parade; **the men at the ~** ceux qui sont au pouvoir; **the ~ of the table** (*solid piece*) le plateau de la table; (*surface*) le dessus de la table; **to sit at the ~ of the table** être assis à la place d'honneur; (*Mil*) **to go over the ~** monter à l'assaut; **on (the) ~ of** sur; **the one on (the) ~** celui qui est en dessus; (*fig*) **to come out on ~** avoir le dessus; (*in career etc*) **he'll get to the ~** il réussira; (*fig*) **he's on ~ of things*** il s'en sort très bien; **things are getting on ~ of her*** elle est dépassée; **on ~ of the one he's got already** en plus de celui qu'il a déjà; **on ~ of all that he ...** et puis par-dessus le marché il ... ; **from ~ to toe** de la tête aux pieds; **from ~ to bottom** *search etc* de fond en comble; (*whole*) *system etc* tout entier; **he's saying that off the ~ of his head*** il dit ça comme ça (mais il n'en est pas certain); **in ~ (gear)** en quatrième; **he's the ~s*** il est champion*; (*on bus*) **seats on ~** places *fpl* à l'étage supérieur; **let's go up on ~** on va en haut. **(b)** (*lid etc*) *[box]* couvercle *m*; *[bottle]* (*screw-on*) bouchon *m*; (*snap-on*) capsule *f*; *[pen]* capuchon *m*. **(c)** (*Dress: blouse etc*) haut *m*; *[pyjamas]* veste *f*.

2 *adj* (*highest*) *shelf, drawer* du haut; (*Mus*) *note* le plus haut; *storey, step* dernier; (*in rank etc*) premier; (*best*) *score, mark etc* (le) meilleur. *[paint]* **the ~ coat** la dernière couche; **the ~ right-hand corner** le coin en haut à droite; **~ price** (*highest*) prix *m* maximum; (*best*) le meilleur prix; **at ~ speed** à toute vitesse; (*Scol*) **~ in maths** premier en maths; (*fig*) **~ marks** vingt sur vingt (*for* pour); **in the ~ class** (*secondary school*) ≈ en terminale; (*primary*) ≈ au cours moyen 2; (**~** *stream*) dans le premier groupe; (*Mus*) **the ~ 20** les 20 premiers du hit-parade; **one of the ~ pianists** un des plus grands pianistes; **a ~ job** un poste prestigieux; **~ people** l'élite *f*; (*fig*) **he's ~ dog* around here** c'est lui qui commande ici.

3 *vt* **(a)** *radish, carrot etc* couper les fanes de. **to ~ and tail fruit** ≈ préparer des fruits. **(b) ~ped by a dome** surmonté d'un dôme. **(c)** (*exceed*) *previous figures etc* dépasser. (*fig*) **and to ~ it all ...** et pour couronner le tout ... . **(d)** *list, queue* être en tête de. (*Theat*) **to ~ the bill** être en tête d'affiche.

top off *vt sep* (*finish*) terminer (*with* par).

top up *vt sep* (*Aut*) *battery* remettre de l'eau dans. **to ~ up a car with oil** remettre de l'huile dans une voiture; **can I ~ up your glass?** je vous en remets?

♦ **topcoat** *n* pardessus *m*. ♦ **topflight*** *adj* de premier ordre. ♦ **top hat** *n* (chapeau *m*) haut-de-forme *m*. ♦ **top-heavy** *adj structure etc* trop lourd du haut; (*fig*) *organization* mal équilibré. ♦ **topless** *adj costume* sans haut; *girl* aux seins nus; **~less swimsuit** monokini* *m*. ♦ **top-level** *adj meeting, discussion* au sommet; *decision* pris au sommet. ♦ **topmost** *adj* le plus haut. ♦ **topping** *n* (*Culin*) **with chocolate ~ping** nappé d'une crème au chocolat. ♦ **top-ranking** *adj* (très) haut placé. ♦ **top-secret** *adj* ultra-secret. ♦ **top-security wing** *n [prison]* quartier *m* sous surveillance spéciale. ♦ **topside** *n* (*Culin*) gîte *m* (à la noix). ♦ **topsoil** *n* couche *f* arable.

top[2] [tɒp] *n* (*toy*) toupie *f*.

topaz ['təʊpæz] *n* topaze *f*.

topic ['tɒpɪk] *n [essay, speech]* sujet *m*; (*for discussion*) sujet de discussion. ♦ **topical** *adj* d'actualité. ♦ **topicality** *n* actualité *f*.

topography [tə'pɒgrəfɪ] *n* topographie *f*.

topple ['tɒpl] **1** *vi* (*wobble*) basculer; (**~ over, ~ down**) tomber. **2** *vt* faire tomber.

topsy-turvy ['tɒpsɪ'tɜ:vɪ] *adj, adv* sens dessus dessous.

torch [tɔ:tʃ] *n* lampe *f* de poche, torche *f* électrique; (*flaming*) flambeau *m*. ♦ **torchlight procession** *n* retraite *f* aux flambeaux.

tore [tɔ:ʳ], **torn** [tɔ:n] *pret, ptp of* **tear**[1].

torment ['tɔ:ment] **1** *n* supplice *m*. **to be in ~** être au supplice; **to suffer ~s** souffrir le martyre. **2** [tɔ:'ment] *vt* (*gen*) tourmenter. **~ed by** torturé par. ♦ **tormentor** *n* persécuteur *m*, -trice *f*.

tornado [tɔ:'neɪdəʊ] *n, pl* **-es** tornade *f*.

torpedo [tɔ:'pi:dəʊ] **1** *n, pl* **-es** torpille *f*. **2** *adj*: **~ boat** torpilleur *m*. **3** *vt* torpiller (*also fig*).

torpid ['tɔ:pɪd] *adj* engourdi. ♦ **torpor** *n* torpeur *f*.

torrent ['tɒrənt] *n* torrent *m* (*also fig*). **the rain was coming down in ~s** il pleuvait à torrents. ♦ **torrential** *adj* torrentiel.

torrid ['tɒrɪd] *adj* torride; (*fig*) ardent.

torso ['tɔ:səʊ] *n* (*Anat*) torse *m*; (*Sculp*) buste *m*.

tortoise ['tɔ:təs] *n* tortue *f*. ♦ **tortoiseshell** *n* écaille *f* (de tortue).

tortuous ['tɔ:tjʊəs] *adj* tortueux.

torture ['tɔ:tʃəʳ] **1** *n* torture *f*, supplice *m*. (*fig*) **it was sheer ~!** c'était un vrai supplice! **2** *vt person* torturer; *language* écorcher; *tune* massacrer.

toss [tɒs] **1** *n* (*throw*) lancement *m*; (*by bull*) coup *m* de cornes. (*from horse*) **to take a ~** faire une chute; **with a ~ of his head** d'un mouvement brusque de la tête; **by the ~ of a coin** à pile ou face; **to win/lose the ~** gagner/perdre à pile ou face; (*Sport: before match*) gagner/perdre le tirage au sort. **2** *vt ball etc* lancer (*to* à); *pancake* faire sauter; *head, mane* rejeter en arrière; *[bull]* projeter en l'air; *[horse]* désarçonner. **to ~ sb in a blanket** faire sauter qn dans une couverture; **to ~ a coin** jouer à pile ou face (*to decide* pour décider); (*Sport: before match*) tirer au sort; **I'll ~ you for it** on le joue à pile ou face; **boat ~ed by the waves** bateau ballotté par les vagues. **3** *vi* **(a)** (**~ about, ~ around**) *[person]* s'agiter; *[trees]* se balancer; *[boat]* tanguer. **to ~ and turn** se tourner et se retourner. **(b)** (**~ up**) jouer à pile ou face (*to decide* pour décider); (*Sport: before match*) tirer au sort. **let's ~ for it** on le joue à pile ou face; **I'll ~ you for the drinks** on joue à pile ou face et le perdant paie à boire.

toss off *vt sep drink* avaler d'un coup; *letter etc* écrire au pied levé.

♦ **toss-up** *n [coin]* coup *m* de pile ou face; (*fig*) **it was a ~-up between the theatre and the cinema** le théâtre ou le cinéma, ça nous était égal.

tot[1] [tɒt] *n* **(a)** (*child*) **(tiny) ~** tout(e) petit(e) enfant *m(f)*. **(b) a ~ of whisky** un petit verre de whisky; **just a ~** juste une goutte.

tot[2] [tɒt] **1** *vt* (**~ up**) faire le total de. **2** *vi*: **to ~ up** faire le total.

total ['təʊtl] **1** *adj* (*gen*) total; *sum* total, global; *ignorance, disagreement* complet. **the ~ losses/sales** le total des pertes/ventes; **it was a ~ loss** on a tout perdu; (*memory*) **~ recall** remémoration *f* totale. **2** *n* **(a)** total *m*. **grand ~** somme *f* globale. **(b) in ~** au total. **3** *vt* **(a)** (*add*: **~ up**) *figures* faire le total de. **(b)** (*amount to*) s'élever à. ♦ **totalitarian** *adj, n* totalitaire (*mf*). ♦ **totalitarianism** *n* totalitarisme *m*. ♦ **totality** *n* totalité *f*. ♦ **totalizator** *or* ♦ **totalizer** *n* (*abbr* **tote**[1]*: *Betting*) pari *m* mutuel. ♦ **totally** *adv* totalement.

tote[2]* [təʊt] *vt* (*gen*) trimballer*; *gun* porter.

totem ['təʊtəm] *n* totem *m*. **~ pole** mât *m* totémique.

totter ['tɒtəʳ] *vi [person]* chanceler; *[object]* vaciller; *[government etc]* chanceler. **to ~ in/out** *etc* entrer/sortir *etc* d'un pas chancelant.

touch [tʌtʃ] **1** *n* **(a)** (*sense of* **~**) toucher *m*; (*act of* **~ing**) contact *m*; (*light brushing*) frôlement *m*; *[pianist, typist]* toucher; *[artist]* touche *f*. **soft to the ~** doux au toucher; **the slightest ~** le moindre contact; **at the ~ of her hand** au contact de sa main; **with the ~ of a finger** à la simple pression d'un doigt; **to put the final** *or* **finishing ~(es) to sth** mettre la dernière touche à qch; **the personal ~** (*gen*) la chaleur humaine; (*in business, décor etc*) la note personnelle; **you've got the right ~ with him** vous savez vous y prendre avec lui; (*fig: borrowing*) **he's a soft** *or* **an easy ~*** il est toujours prêt à se laisser taper*.

(b) (*small amount*) **a ~ of** (*gen*) un tout petit peu de; *colour, gaiety* une touche de; *sadness, humour* une pointe de; *paint* une petite couche de; **a ~ of the sun** un petit coup de soleil; **to have a ~ of flu** être un peu grippé; **to have a ~ of rheumatism** faire un peu de rhumatisme.

(c) (*contact*) **to be in/get in/keep in ~ with sb** être/se mettre/rester en contact *or* en rapport avec qn; **I'll be in ~** je t'écrirai (*or* je te téléphonerai); **keep in ~** ne nous (*or* m')oubliez pas!; **to be out of ~ with, to have lost ~ with**

person ne plus être en contact *or* en rapport avec; *developments etc* ne plus être au courant de; **he's out of ~** il n'est plus dans le coup*; **you can get in ~ with me at this number** vous pouvez me contacter à ce numéro; **I'll put you in ~ with him** je vous mettrai en rapport avec lui.

(d) (*Ftbl, Rugby*) touche *f*. **the ball went into ~** le ballon est sorti en touche; **it is in ~** il y a touche.

2 *vt* **(a)** (*gen*) toucher (*with* de); (*brush lightly*) frôler. **he ~ed her arm** il lui a touché le bras; **the ship ~ed the bottom** le bateau a touché; **to ~ the ground** toucher terre. **(b)** (*tamper with*) toucher à. **don't ~ that!** n'y touchez pas!; **I didn't ~ him!** je ne lui ai rien fait; **~ nothing** ne touchez à rien. **(c)** (*fig*) toucher à; *topic, problem* effleurer; (*concern, move*) toucher. **their land ~es ours** leur terre touche à la nôtre; **Switzerland ~es Italy** la Suisse et l'Italie se touchent; **the fire didn't ~ the paintings** l'incendie a épargné les tableaux; **they can't ~ you if ...** ils ne peuvent rien contre vous si ...; **he won't ~ anything illegal** si c'est illégal il n'y touchera pas; **he didn't ~ his meal** il n'a pas touché à son repas; **I never ~ onions** je ne mange jamais d'oignons; **her cooking can't ~ yours** sa cuisine est loin de valoir la tienne; **there's no pianist to ~ him** personne ne peut l'égaler comme pianiste; **it ~es us all closely** cela nous touche *or* nous concerne tous de très près; **we were very ~ed by your letter** nous avons été très touchés de votre lettre; **to ~ sb for a loan*** taper* qn; **I ~ed him for £10*** je l'ai tapé* de 10 livres.

3 *vi* **(a)** *[hands, ends, lands etc]* se toucher. (*fig*) **to ~ (up)on a subject** effleurer un sujet. **(b)** (*meddle*) **don't ~!** n'y touchez pas!; **'do not ~'** 'défense de toucher'.

touch down *vi* **(a)** (*on land*) atterrir; (*on sea*) amerrir; (*on moon*) alunir. **(b)** (*Rugby etc*) marquer un essai.

touch off *vt sep fuse, firework* faire partir; *mine etc* faire exploser; *explosion, crisis, riot, reaction, argument* déclencher.

touch up *vt sep* retoucher.

♦ **touch-and-go** *adj*: **it's ~-and-go with the sick man** le malade est entre la vie et la mort; **it was ~-and-go whether she did it** elle a failli ne pas le faire; **it was ~-and-go until the last minute** c'est resté incertain jusqu'au bout. ♦ **touch-down** *n* (*on land*) atterrissage *m*; (*on sea*) amerrissage *m*; (*on moon*) alunissage *m*. ♦ **touched** *adj* (*moved*) touché (*by* de); (*: *mad*) toqué*. ♦ **touchiness** *n* susceptibilité *f*. ♦ **touching 1** *adj* touchant; **2** *prep* concernant. ♦ **touchingly** *adv* d'une manière touchante. ♦ **touchline** *n* (*Ftbl etc*) ligne *f* de touche. ♦ **touch-type** *vi* taper au toucher. ♦ **touchy** *adj person* susceptible (*about* sur la question de); *business, situation* délicat; **he's very ~y** il se vexe *or* s'offense pour un rien.

tough [tʌf] **1** *adj* **(a)** *substance, fabric etc* solide, résistant; (*pej*) *meat* dur; (*fig*) *resistance, struggle* acharné; *task, journey* fatigant, pénible; *obstacle, sport* rude; *problem* épineux; *regulations* sévère; *conditions* dur. **it's ~ work** c'est un travail dur *or* pénible. **(b)** (*of person*) (*physically hard*) *mountaineer, athlete etc* robuste, résistant; (*mentally strong*) solide, endurant; (*hard: in character*) *negotiator etc* dur, impitoyable; (*rough*) *criminal, gangster* dur, brutal. **he is a ~ man to deal with** il ne fait pas souvent de concessions; **a ~ guy** un dur*; (*pej*) **they're a ~ lot** ce sont des durs à cuire*; **to get ~ with sb*** se montrer dur envers qn. **(c)** (*unfortunate*) **that's ~*** c'est vache* (*on sb* pour qn); **that's ~ luck on him*** (*pity*) il n'a pas de veine; (*he'll have to put up with it*) tant pis pour lui; **to have a ~ time of it*** en voir de dures*. **2** *n* (*) dur* *m*. ♦ **toughen** *vt substance* renforcer; *person* endurcir; *conditions* rendre plus sévère. ♦ **toughly** *adv fight* avec acharnement; *answer* durement. ♦ **toughness** *n* **(a)** solidité *f*, résistance *f*; dureté *f*; acharnement *m*; caractère *m* fatigant *or* pénible (*or* rude *or* épineux); sévérité *f*; **(b)** résistance *f*; endurance *f*; dureté *f*.

tour [tʊəʳ] **1** *n* (*journey*) voyage *m*; (*by team, actors, musicians etc*) tournée *f*; (*of town, factory, museum etc*) visite *f*, tour *m*; (*day ~*) excursion *f*; (*package ~*) voyage organisé. **to go on a ~ of** *region, country* faire un voyage dans (*or* en *etc*); (*guided ~*) faire un voyage organisé dans (*or* en *etc*); *museums, castles* visiter; **to go on a ~ round the world** faire le tour du monde; **to go on a walking/cycling ~** faire une randonnée à pied/en bicyclette; (*Sport, Theat etc*) **to go on/be on ~** faire une/être en tournée; **~ of inspection** tournée d'inspection; (*Mil etc*) **~ of duty** ronde *f*. **2** *adj*: **~ operator** tour-opérateur *m*, organisateur *m* de voyages. **3** *vt [tourist, visitor]* visiter; *[team, actors, play]* être en tournée en (*or* dans *etc*). **4** *vi*: **to go ~ing** faire du tourisme. ♦ **touring 1** *n* tourisme *m*; **2** *adj team, theatre company* en tournée. ♦ **tourism** *n* tourisme *m*. ♦ **tourist 1** *n* touriste *mf*; **2** *adj class, ticket* touriste *inv*; *attraction, guidebook, season* touristique; *industry* du tourisme; **~ist agency** agence *f* de tourisme; **~ist bureau** *or* **office** syndicat *m* d'initiative; **the ~ist trade** le tourisme; **3** *adv travel* en classe touriste. ♦ **touristy*** *adj* (*pej*) trop touristique.

tournament ['tʊənəmənt] *n* tournoi *m*.

tourniquet ['tʊənɪkeɪ] *n* (*Med*) garrot *m*.

tousled ['taʊzld] *adj hair, person* ébouriffé; *clothes* chiffonné; *bedclothes* en désordre.

tout [taʊt] **1** *n* (*seller*) vendeur ambulant; (*for custom*) racoleur *m*; (*for hotels*) rabatteur *m*; (*Racing*) pronostiqueur *m*. **ticket ~** revendeur *m* de billets (*au marché noir*). **2** *vt wares* vendre (avec insistance); *tickets* revendre. **3** *vi*: **to ~ for custom** racoler les clients.

tow[1] [təʊ] **1** *n*: **on ~** en remorque; **to give sb a ~** remorquer qn; (*Aut*) **to give sb a ~ to start him** faire démarrer qn en remorque; (*fig*) **he had a couple of girls in ~*** il remorquait deux filles. **2** *vt boat, vehicle* remorquer (*to, into* jusqu'à); *caravan, trailer* tirer; *barge* haler. *[police]* **to ~ a car away** emmener une voiture en fourrière. ♦ **towboat** *n* remorqueur *m*. ♦ **towline** *or* ♦ **towrope** *n* câble *m* de remorque. ♦ **towpath** *n* chemin *m* de halage. ♦ **towing-truck** *or* (*US*) ♦ **tow-truck** *n* dépanneuse *f*.

tow[2] [təʊ] *n* (*Tex*) filasse *f*. ♦ **tow-headed** *adj* aux cheveux filasse.

toward(s) [tə'wɔ:d(z)] *prep* (*gen*) vers; (*of attitude*) envers, à l'égard de. **he came ~ me** il est venu vers moi; **we are moving ~ a solution/war** *etc* nous nous acheminons vers une solution/la guerre *etc*; **to save ~ sth** faire des économies pour acheter qch; **~ 10 o'clock/the end of the century** vers 10 heures/la fin du siècle; **my feelings ~ him** mes sentiments à son égard *or* envers lui.

towel ['taʊəl] **1** *n* serviette *f* (de toilette); (*dish ~, tea ~*) torchon *m*; (*for hands*) essuie-mains *m inv*; (*for glasses*) essuie-verres *m inv*; (*sanitary ~*) serviette hygiénique. **2** *adj*: **~ rail** porte-serviettes *m inv*. **3** *vt*: **to ~ o.s. (dry)** se sécher avec une serviette. ♦ **towelling** *n* (*Tex*) tissu *m* éponge.

tower ['taʊəʳ] **1** *n* (*gen*) tour *f*; *[church]* clocher *m*. (*fig*) **a ~ of strength** un grand soutien (*to sb* pour qn). **2** *adj*: **~ block** tour *f* (d'habitation). **3** *vi [building etc]* s'élever très haut. (*lit, fig*) **to ~ over sth/sb** dominer qch/qn. ♦ **towering** *adj building* très haut, imposant; *figure* imposant; (*fig*) **in a ~ing rage** dans une colère noire.

town [taʊn] **1** *n* ville *f*. **in (a) ~, into ~** en ville; **in the ~** dans la ville; **in a little ~** dans une petite ville; **he's out of ~** il est en déplacement, il n'est pas là; **a country ~** une ville de province; (*fig*) **to**

have a night on *or* **to go out on the ~*** faire la bombe*; (*fig*) **he really went to ~ on that essay*** il a mis le paquet* quand il a écrit cette dissertation. **2** *adj centre* de la ville; *house* en ville; *life* urbain. **~ clerk** ≃ secrétaire *m* de mairie; **~ council** conseil *m* municipal; **~ hall** ≃ mairie *f*, hôtel *m* de ville. ♦ **town-and-country planning** *n* ≃ aménagement *m* du territoire. ♦ **town-dweller** *n* citadin(e) *m(f)*. ♦ **town-planner** *n* urbaniste *mf*. ♦ **town-planning** *n* urbanisme *m*. ♦ **township** *n* bourgade *f*. ♦ **townspeople** *npl* citadins *mpl*.

toxic [ˈtɒksɪk] *adj* toxique. ♦ **tox(a)emia** *n* toxémie *f*. ♦ **toxin** *n* toxine *f*.

toy [tɔɪ] **1** *n* jouet *m*. **2** *adj train, car, soldier* petit; *house, railway* miniature; *trumpet* d'enfant; (*fig*) *dog* d'appartement. **3** *vi*: **to ~ with** *object, sb's affections* jouer avec; *idea* caresser; **to ~ with one's food** manger du bout des dents. ♦ **toybox** *n* coffre *m* à jouets. ♦ **toyshop** *n* magasin *m* de jouets.

trace[1] [treɪs] **1** *n* trace *f* (*of* de). **to vanish** *etc* **without ~** disparaître *etc* sans laisser de traces; **there is no ~ of it** il n'en reste plus trace; **we have lost all ~ of them** nous avons complètement perdu leur trace; **without a ~ of ill-feeling** sans la moindre rancune. **2** *vt* **(a)** (*draw*) tracer; (*with tracing paper etc*) décalquer. **(b)** (*locate*) *person, object* retrouver. **to ~ sb** suivre la trace de qn (*as far as* jusqu'à), retrouver la trace de qn (*to* à); **they ~d the weapon (back) to here** ils ont établi que l'arme provenait d'ici; **to ~ back one's family to** faire remonter sa famille à. ♦ **tracer** *n* (*instrument*) traçoir *m*; (*Biochemistry*) traceur *m*; (*bullet*) balle *f* traçante. ♦ **tracery** *n* (*on window*) réseau *m* (*de fenêtre ajourée*); *[frost etc]* dentelles *fpl*. ♦ **tracing** *n* (*process*) calquage *m*; (*result*) calque *m*. ♦ **tracing-paper** *n* papier-calque *m inv*.

trace[2] [treɪs] *n [harness]* trait *m*.

track [træk] **1** *n* **(a)** (*mark, trail*) trace *f*; *[animal, person]* trace, piste *f*; (*route: on radar screen; also of bullet, comet, rocket etc*) trajectoire *f*. **to destroy everything in its ~** tout détruire sur son passage; **to follow in sb's ~s** suivre la trace de qn, (*fig*) marcher sur les traces de qn; **to be on sb's ~** être sur la piste de qn; (*fig*) **to be on the right ~** être sur la bonne voie; **to be on the wrong ~** faire fausse route; **to put** *or* **throw sb off the ~** désorienter qn; **to keep ~ of** *spacecraft, events, developments* suivre; *person* suivre la trace de; (*fig: keep in touch with*) rester en contact avec; **to lose ~ of** *spacecraft etc* perdre; (*fig*) *developments etc* ne plus être au courant de; *person* perdre la trace de; (*fig*) perdre tout contact avec; **I've lost ~ of what he is saying** j'ai perdu le fil de ce qu'il dit; (*fig*) **to make ~s*** filer (*for* à). **(b)** (*path*) chemin *m*, piste *f*; (*Sport*) piste. **sheep ~** piste à moutons; **mule ~** chemin muletier; **race ~** piste; **motor-racing ~** autodrome *m*; **dog-racing ~** cynodrome *m*. **(c)** (*Rail*) voie *f*, rails *mpl*. **to leave the ~(s)** dérailler; **to cross the ~** traverser la voie. **(d)** *[tape]* piste *f*; *[record]* plage *f*. **4-~ tape** bande *f* à 4 pistes. **(e)** *[tractor]* chenille *f*. **(f)** (*US Scol*) **divided into 5 ~s** répartis en 5 classes de niveau; **the B ~** le groupe B.

2 *adj* (*Sport*) *racing, event, athletics* sur piste. (*also fig*) **to have a good ~ record** avoir eu de bons résultats.

3 *vt animal, person, vehicle* suivre la trace de; *game, prey, wanted man* traquer; *rocket, comet* suivre la trajectoire de.

track down *vt sep animal, wanted man* traquer et capturer; *sth or sb wanted* (finir par) retrouver.

♦ **tracked** *adj vehicle* à chenille. ♦ **tracker 1** *n* (*Hunting*) traqueur *m*; (*gen*) poursuivant(e) *m(f)*; **2** *adj*: **~er dog** chien *m* policier. ♦ **tracking** *adj* (*Space*) **~ing station** station *f* d'observation. ♦ **tracksuit** *n* survêtement *m*.

tract[1] [trækt] *n* **(a)** *[land, water]* étendue *f*; (*US: housing estate*) résidence *f*. **(b)** (*Anat*) **digestive ~** appareil *m* digestif.

tract[2] [trækt] *n* (*pamphlet*) tract *m*.

tractable [ˈtræktəbl] *adj person* accommodant; *animal* docile; *material* malléable; *problem* résoluble.

traction [ˈtrækʃən] **1** *n* traction *f*. **2** *adj*: **~ engine** locomobile *f*.

tractor [ˈtræktəʳ] *n* tracteur *m*.

trade [treɪd] **1** *n* **(a)** (*Econ etc*) commerce *m*. **overseas ~** commerce extérieur; **the wool ~** le commerce de la laine; **he's in the wool ~** il est négociant en laine; **to do a lot of ~ with** faire beaucoup de commerce *or* d'affaires avec; **to do a brisk** *or* **roaring ~** vendre beaucoup (*in* de); (*Brit*) **Board of T~**, (*US*) **Department of T~** ministère *m* du Commerce. **(b)** (*job*) métier *m*. **he is a butcher by ~** il est boucher de son métier; **to learn a ~** apprendre un métier; (*lit, fig*) **he's in the ~** il est du métier; **known in the ~ as ...** que les gens du métier appellent ... .

2 *adj association, fair, journal, route, school* commercial; *barriers* douanier; *price* de gros. **~ deficit** balance *f* commerciale déficitaire; **the T~ Descriptions Act** la loi de protection du consommateur; **~ discount** remise *f* au détaillant; **~ figures** *or* **returns** résultats *mpl* financiers; **~ name** marque *f* déposée; (*lit, fig*) **~ secret** secret *m* de fabrication; **~ wind** alizé *m*.

3 *vi* faire le commerce (*in* de; *with* avec). (*fig*) **to ~ on sb's kindness** abuser de la gentillesse de qn.

4 *vt* (*exchange*) échanger (*sth for sth* qch contre qch; *sth with sb* qch avec qn).

trade in *vt sep car, television etc* faire reprendre. **I've ~d it in for a new one** je l'ai fait reprendre quand j'en ai acheté un nouveau.

♦ **trade-in 1** *n* (*Comm*) reprise *f*; **he took it as a ~-in** il me l'a repris; **2** *adj price, value* à la reprise. ♦ **trademark** *n* marque *f* de fabrique; **registered ~mark** marque déposée. ♦ **trade-off** *n* (*US*) échange *m*. ♦ **trader** *n* commerçant(e) *m(f)*; (*bigger*) négociant(e) *m(f)* (*in* en); (*street ~*) vendeur *m*, -euse *f* de rue. ♦ **tradesman** *n* commerçant *m*. ♦ **trade(s) union** *n* syndicat *m*. ♦ **trade(s) unionism** *n* syndicalisme *m*. ♦ **trade(s) unionist** *n* syndicaliste *mf*. ♦ **trading 1** *n* commerce *m*; **2** *adj nation* commerçant; *port, centre* de commerce; (*Brit*) **trading estate** zone *f* industrielle; **trading stamp** timbre-prime *m*.

tradition [trəˈdɪʃən] *n* tradition *f*. **according to ~** selon la tradition; (*fig*) **it's in the best ~** c'est dans la plus pure tradition (*of* de). ♦ **traditional** *adj* traditionnel (*to do* de faire). ♦ **traditionally** *adv* traditionnellement.

traffic [ˈtræfɪk] (*vb: pret, ptp* **trafficked**) **1** *n* **(a)** (*Aut*) circulation *f*; (*Aviat, Naut, Rail, Telec*) trafic *m*. **road ~** circulation routière; **rail ~** trafic ferroviaire; (*Aut*) **holiday ~** circulation des grands départs (*or* des grandes rentrées); **the ~ is heavy** (*Aut*) il y a beaucoup de circulation; (*Aviat etc*) le trafic est intense; (*Aut*) **closed to heavy ~** interdit aux poids lourds; (*Aut*) **build-up** *or* **backlog of ~** bouchon *m*; **~ coming into Paris** la circulation dans le sens province-Paris; **~ in and out of the airport** le trafic à destination et en provenance de l'aéroport. **(b)** (*trade*) commerce *m* (*in* de); (*pej*) trafic *m* (*in* de). **the drug ~** le trafic de la drogue. **2** *vi* faire le commerce *or* le trafic (*pej*) (*in* de). **3** *adj* (*Aut*) *regulations, policeman* de la circulation; *police* de la route; *offence* au code de la route; *sign* de signalisation. (*Aviat*) **~ controller** aiguilleur *m* du ciel; **~ island** refuge *m*; **~ jam** embouteillage *m*; **~ light** *or* **signal** feu *m* (de signalisation); **the ~ lights were at green** le feu était au vert; **~ warden** contractuel(le) *m(f)*. ♦ **trafficker** *n* trafiquant(e) *m(f)* (*in* en).

tragedy ['trædʒɪdɪ] *n* (*gen, Theat*) tragédie *f*. **the ~ of it is that ..., it is a ~ that ...** il est tragique que ... + *subj*. ♦ **tragic** *adj* tragique; **tragic actor** tragédien *m*. ♦ **tragically** *adv* tragiquement.

trail [treɪl] **1** *n* **(a)** (*of blood, smoke; from plane, comet etc*) traînée *f*; (*tracks: gen*) trace *f*; (*Hunting*) piste *f*, trace. **a long ~ of refugees** une longue colonne de réfugiés; **to leave a ~ of destruction** tout détruire sur son passage; (*lit, fig*) **on the ~ of** sur la piste de. **(b)** (*path*) sentier *m*, chemin *m*. **2** *vt* **(a)** (*follow*) suivre la piste de. **(b)** (*tow*) *object on rope etc* traîner; (*Aut*) *caravan etc* tirer. **they ~ed dirt all over the carpet** ils ont couvert le tapis de traces sales; **to ~ one's fingers through the water** laisser traîner ses doigts dans l'eau. **3** *vi* **(a)** *[object]* traîner (*in* dans; *from* de); *[plant]* ramper. (*Sport*) **to ~ by 13 points** être en retard de 13 points. **(b) to ~ along/in** *etc* (*in straggling line*) passer/entrer *etc* à la queue leu leu; (*wearily*) passer/entrer *etc* en traînant les pieds.

trail away, trail off *vi [sound]* s'estomper.

♦ **trailblazer** *n* pionnier *m*, -ière *f*. ♦ **trailer 1** *n* **(a)** (*Aut*) remorque *f*; (*caravan*) caravane *f*; **(b)** (*Cine, TV*) film *m* publicitaire (*for a film* pour un film); **2** *adj* (*US*) **~er park** camp *m* de caravaning. ♦ **trailing** *adj hair, blanket etc* traînant; *plant* rampant.

train [treɪn] **1** *n* **(a)** (*Rail*) train *m*; (*in underground*) rame *f*. **fast ~** rapide *m*; **slow ~** omnibus *m*; **to go by ~** prendre le train; **to go to London by ~** aller à Londres en train *or* par le train; **on** *or* **in the ~** dans le train; **to transport by ~** transporter par voie ferroviaire. **(b)** (*line: of vehicles, camels etc*) file *f*; (*entourage*) suite *f*. (*fig*) **it brought famine in its ~** cela a amené la famine dans son sillage. **(c)** (*series: of events etc*) suite *f*; *[gunpowder]* traînée *f*. **in an unbroken ~** en succession ininterrompue; **his ~ of thought** le fil de ses pensées. **(d)** *[robe etc]* traîne *f*.

2 *adj*: **~ ferry** ferry-boat *m*; **the ~ service to London** les trains pour Londres; **~ set** train *m* électrique (*jouet*).

3 *vt* **(a)** (*instruct etc*) *teacher, craftsman, employee, soldier etc* former; (*Sport*) entraîner; *animal* dresser (*to do* à faire); *voice* travailler; *ear, mind, memory* exercer. (*house~*) **to ~ a puppy/child** apprendre à un chiot/à un enfant à être propre; **to ~ sb to do** apprendre à qn à faire, (*professionally*) former qn à faire; **to ~ o.s. to do** s'entraîner à faire; **to ~ sb in a craft** préparer qn à un métier; **he was ~ed in weaving** *or* **as a weaver** il a reçu une formation de tisserand; **where were you ~ed?** où avez-vous reçu votre formation? **(b)** (*direct etc*) *gun, telescope etc* braquer (*on* sur); *plant* faire grimper (*along* le long de).

4 *vi* recevoir une (*or* sa) formation; (*Sport*) s'entraîner (*for* pour). **to ~ as** *or* **to be a teacher** *etc* recevoir une formation de professeur *etc*.

♦ **trained** *adj person* (*gen*) compétent (*for* pour); (*professionally*) qualifié (*for* pour); *engineer, nurse* diplômé; *teacher* habilité à enseigner; *animal* dressé; *eye, ear* exercé; **she has a ~ed voice** elle a pris des leçons de chant; **he is not ~ed** il n'a reçu aucune formation professionnelle; **well-~ed** *child* bien élevé; *animal*, (*iro*) *husband etc* bien dressé. ♦ **trainee** *adj, n* stagiaire (*mf*); **management ~ee** stagiaire de direction; **~ee typist** dactylo *f* stagiaire. ♦ **trainer** *n* **(a)** (*Sport*) entraîneur *m*; (*in circus*) dresseur *m*, -euse *f*; **(b)** (*shoe*) chaussure *f* de sport. ♦ **training 1** *n* (*for job*) formation *f*; (*Sport*) entraînement *m*; *[animal]* dressage *m*; (*Sport*) **to be in ~ing** (*preparing o.s.*) être en cours d'entraînement; (*on form*) être en forme; **she has had secretarial ~ing** elle a suivi des cours de secrétariat; **2** *adj scheme, centre* (*for job*) de formation; (*Sport*) d'entraînement; **~ing college** (*gen*) école *f* professionnelle; (*for teachers*) ≃ école normale; **~ing course** cours *mpl* professionnels; **~ing plane/ship** avion-/navire-école *m*. ♦ **trainspotter** *n* passionné(e) *m(f)* de trains. ♦ **trainspotting** *n*: **to go ~-spotting** observer les trains.

traipse* [treɪps] *vi*: **to ~ in/out** *etc* entrer/sortir *etc* d'un pas traînant; **to ~ around** se balader*.

trait [treɪt] *n* trait *m* (*de caractère*).

traitor ['treɪtəʳ] *n* traître *m*. **to be a ~ to sth** trahir qch; **to turn ~** passer à l'ennemi. ♦ **traitress** *n* traîtresse *f*.

trajectory [trə'dʒektərɪ] *n* trajectoire *f*.

tram(car) ['træm(kɑːʳ)] *n* tram(way) *m*.

tramp [træmp] **1** *n* **(a)** *[footsteps]* martèlement *m* (de pas). **(b)** (*hike*) randonnée *f* (à pied). **(c)** (*vagabond*) vagabond(e) *m(f)*, clochard(e) *m(f)*. (*pej*) **she's a ~*** elle est coureuse*. **(d) ~ (steamer)** tramp *m*. **2** *vi*: **to ~ along** (*hike*) poursuivre son chemin à pied; (*walk heavily*) marcher d'un pas lourd; *[soldiers etc]* marteler le pavé. **3** *vt*: **to ~ the streets** battre le pavé; **I ~ed the town looking for ...** j'ai parcouru la ville à pied pour trouver ... .

trample ['træmpl] *vti* (*lit, fig*) **to ~ on sth/sb, to ~ sth/sb underfoot** piétiner qch/qn, fouler qch/qn aux pieds; **to ~ on sb's feelings** bafouer les sentiments de qn; **to ~ sth into the ground** enfoncer qch dans le sol.

trampoline ['træmpəlɪn] *n* trampolino *m*.

trance [trɑːns] *n* transe *f*. **to go** *or* **fall into a ~** entrer en transe.

tranquil ['træŋkwɪl] *adj* tranquille. ♦ **tranquillity,** (*US*) **tranquility** *n* tranquillité *f*. ♦ **tranquil(l)ize** *vt* (*Med*) mettre sous tranquillisants. ♦ **tranquil(l)izer** *n* tranquillisant *m*.

trans... [trænz] *pref* trans... . ♦ **transatlantic** *adj* transatlantique.

transact [træn'zækt] *vt* traiter, régler. ♦ **transaction** *n* (*Econ, Fin, St Ex*) transaction *f*; (*in bank, shop*) opération *f*; **cash ~ion** opération au comptant.

transcend [træn'send] *vt* (*gen*) transcender; (*excel over*) surpasser. ♦ **transcendent** *adj* transcendant. ♦ **transcendental** *adj* transcendantal; **~ental meditation** méditation *f* transcendantale.

transcribe [træn'skraɪb] *vt* transcrire. ♦ **transcript** *or* ♦ **transcription** *n* transcription *f*.

transect [træn'sekt] *vt* sectionner (transversalement).

transept ['trænsept] *n* transept *m*.

transfer [træns'fɜːʳ] **1** *vt* (*gen*) transférer (*to* à); *power* faire passer (*from* de; *to* à); *design, drawing, one's affections* reporter (*to* sur). (*Telec*) **to ~ the charges** téléphoner en P.C.V.; **~red charge call** communication *f* en P.C.V. **2** *vi* (*gen*) être transféré (*to* à; *from* de). (*Univ etc*) **he's ~red from Science to Geography** il ne fait plus de science, il s'est réorienté en géographie. **3** ['trænsfɜːʳ] *n* **(a)** (*gen*) transfert *m* (*to* à; *from* de); (*Pol: of power*) passation *f*. **by bank ~** par virement *m* bancaire. **(b)** (*design etc*) (*rub-on type*) décalcomanie *f*; (*stick-on*) auto-collant *m*. ♦ **transferable** *adj* transmissible; **not ~able** personnel.

transfigure [træns'fɪgəʳ] *vt* transfigurer. ♦ **transfiguration** *n* transfiguration *f*.

transfix [træns'fɪks] *vt* (*lit*) transpercer. (*fig*) **~ed** cloué sur place (*with* de).

transform [træns'fɔːm] *vt* transformer (*into* en). **to be ~ed into** se transformer en. ♦ **transformation** *n* transformation *f*. ♦ **transformational** *adj* transformationnel. ♦ **transformer** *n* (*Elec*) transformateur *m*.

transfuse [træns'fjuːz] *vt* transfuser. ♦ **transfusion** *n* (*Med, fig*) transfusion *f*; **to give sb a**

transfusion faire une transfusion à qn.

transgress [træns'gres] *vi* pécher. ♦ **transgressor** *n* pécheur *m*, -eresse *f*.

transient ['trænzıənt] *adj* transitoire, éphémère.

transistor [træn'zıstəʳ] *n* (*Elec, Rad*) transistor *m*. ♦ **transistorize** *vt* transistoriser.

transit ['trænzıt] **1** *n*: **in ~** en transit *m*. **2** *adj goods, passengers* en transit; *documents, visa*, (*Aviat*) *lounge* de transit; (*Mil etc*) *camp* volant. ♦ **transition** *n* transition *f* (*from* de; *to* à). ♦ **transitional** *adj period, government* de transition; *measures* transitoire.

transitive ['trænzıtıv] *adj* transitif.

transitory ['trænzıtərı] *adj* transitoire, éphémère.

translate [trænz'leıt] **1** *vt* traduire (*from* de; *into* en). **the word is ~d as ...** le mot se traduit par ...; (*fig*) **to ~ ideas into actions** passer des idées aux actes. **2** *vi [person]* traduire. **it won't ~** c'est intraduisible. ♦ **translatable** *adj* traduisible. ♦ **translation** *n* traduction *f* (*from* de; *into* en); (*Scol etc*) version *f*. ♦ **translator** *n* traducteur *m*, -trice *f*.

transliterate [trænz'lıtəreıt] *vt* translittérer.

translucence [trænz'lu:sns] *n* translucidité *f*. ♦ **translucent** *adj* translucide.

transmit [trænz'mıt] **1** *vt* (*gen, Aut, Med etc*) transmettre; (*Rad, Telec, TV*) émettre. **2** *vi* (*Rad etc*) émettre. ♦ **transmissible** *adj* transmissible. ♦ **transmission 1** *n* transmission *f*; **2** *adj* (*Aut*) **transmission shaft** arbre *m* de transmission. ♦ **transmitter** *n* (*Telec*) transmetteur *m*; (*microphone*) capsule *f* microphonique; (*Rad, TV*) émetteur *m*. ♦ **transmitting** *adj* (*Telec*) *set, station* émetteur.

transmute [trænz'mju:t] *vt* transmuer (*into* en).

transom ['trænsəm] *n* traverse *f*.

transparent [træns'pɛərənt] *adj* transparent. ♦ **transparency** *n* transparence *f*; (*Phot*) diapositive *f*.

transpire [træns'paıəʳ] *vi* **(a)** (*happen*) se passer. **it ~d that ...** on a appris par la suite que ... . **(b)** (*Bot, Physiol*) transpirer.

transplant [træns'plɑ:nt] **1** *vt* (*gen*) transplanter; (*Med*) greffer; *seedlings etc* repiquer. **2** ['trænsplɑ:nt] *n* (*Med*) transplantation *f*. **he's had a heart ~** on lui a fait une greffe du cœur *or* une transplantation cardiaque.

transport ['trænspɔ:t] **1** *n* **(a)** transport *m*. **road/rail ~** transport par route/par chemin de fer; **Ministry of T~** ministère *m* des Transports; **have you got any ~?*** tu as une voiture? **(b)** *[delight etc]* transport *m*; *[fury etc]* accès *m*. **2** *adj costs, ship etc* de transport; *system* des transports. **~ café** ≃ restaurant *m* de routiers. **3** [træns'pɔ:t] *vt* (*lit, fig*) transporter. ♦ **transportation** *n* transport *m*; *[criminals]* transportation *f*. ♦ **transporter** *n* (*gen*) transporteur *m*; (*car transporter*) (*Aut*) camion *m or* (*Rail*) wagon *m* pour transport d'automobiles.

transpose [træns'pəuz] *vt* transposer. ♦ **transposition** *n* transposition *f*.

transship [træns'ʃıp] *vt* transborder. ♦ **transshipment** *n* transbordement *m*.

transubstantiation ['trænsəbˌstænʃı'eıʃən] *n* transsubstantiation *f*.

transverse ['trænzvɜ:s] *adj* transversal. ♦ **transversely** *adv* transversalement.

transvestite [trænz'vestaıt] *n* travesti(e) *m(f)* (*Psych*).

trap [træp] **1** *n* **(a)** (*gen*) piège *m*; (*gin-~*) collet *m*; (*covered hole*) trappe *f*; (*mouse~*) souricière *f*. (*lit, fig*) **to set** *or* **lay a ~** tendre un piège (*for sb* à qn); **to catch in a ~** prendre au piège; **caught like a rat in a ~** fait comme un rat. **(b) ~(door)** trappe *f*; **keep your ~ shut‡** ferme ta gueule‡. **2** *vt* **(a)** (*snare*) *animal, person* prendre au piège. **(b)** (*catch, cut off*) *miner, climber, vehicle, ship* bloquer; *gas, liquid* retenir; *object, one's finger* coincer (*in sth* dans qch). ♦ **trapper** *n* trappeur *m*. ♦ **trapshooting** *n* ball-trap *m*.

trapeze [trə'pi:z] **1** *n* trapèze *m*. **2** *adj*: **~ artist** trapéziste *mf*.

trappings ['træpıŋz] *npl [kingship etc]* cérémonial *m*; *[success]* signes *mpl* extérieurs.

Trappist ['træpıst] **1** *n* trappiste *m*. **2** *adj* de la Trappe.

trash [træʃ] **1** *n* (*refuse*) ordures *fpl*; (*cheap goods*) camelote* *f*; (*nonsense*) bêtises *fpl*, blagues* *fpl*. **this is ~** ça ne vaut rien, (*message, letter etc*) c'est de la blague*; *[people]* **they're just ~‡** ce sont des moins que rien. **2** *adj*: **~ can** poubelle *f*, boîte *f* à ordures. ♦ **trashy** *adj* (*gen*) qui ne vaut rien; *goods* de camelote*.

trauma ['trɔ:mə] *n* (*Med, Psych*) trauma *m*; (*fig*) traumatisme *m*. ♦ **traumatic** *adj* (*Med*) traumatique; (*Psych, fig*) traumatisant.

travel ['trævl] **1** *vi* **(a)** (*journey*) voyager; (*Comm*) être représentant (*for* de; *in* en). **they have ~led a long way** ils sont venus de loin, (*fig*) ils ont fait beaucoup de chemin; **he is ~ling in Spain** il est en voyage en Espagne; **as he was ~ling across France** pendant qu'il voyageait à travers la France; **to ~ through a region** parcourir une région; **to ~ round the world** faire le tour du monde; **to ~ light** voyager avec peu de bagages; *[food, wine]* **it ~s well** ça supporte bien le voyage. **(b)** (*move, go*) aller; *[machine part etc]* se déplacer. **you were ~ling too fast** vous alliez trop vite; **to ~ at 80 km/h** faire du 80 km/h; **light ~s at a speed of ...** la vitesse de la lumière est de ...; **news ~s fast** les nouvelles circulent vite. **2** *vt country, district, distance* parcourir. **much-~led road** route très fréquentée. **3** *n* les voyages *mpl*. **his ~s** ses voyages; **he's off on his ~s again** il repart en voyage; **on your ~s** au cours de vos voyages, (*fig hum*) au cours de vos allées et venues. **4** *adj allowance, expenses* de déplacement; *story, film* de voyages; *organization* de tourisme. **~ agency** agence *f* de voyages; **~ agent** agent *m* de voyages; **~ brochure** dépliant *m* touristique. ♦ **travelator** *n* tapis roulant. ♦ **traveller**, (*US*) **traveler** *n* voyageur *m*, -euse *f*; (*Comm*) représentant *m* (de commerce) (*in* en); **~ler's cheque**, (*US*) **~er's check** chèque *m* de voyage. ♦ **travel(l)ing 1** *n* voyages *mpl*; **2** *adj* **(a)** *circus, troupe* ambulant; *crane* mobile; (*Comm*) **~(l)ing salesman** représentant *m* de commerce; **(b)** *bag, rug, clock, scholarship* de voyage; *expenses, allowance* de déplacement. ♦ **travelogue** *n* (*talk/film/book*) compte rendu *m*/film *m*/récit *m* de voyages. ♦ **travel-sick** *adj* (*in car/plane/boat*) **to be ~-sick** avoir le mal de la route/de l'air/de mer. ♦ **travel-sickness 1** *n* mal *m* de la route *etc*; **2** *adj pills* contre le mal de la route *etc*.

traverse ['trævəs] *vt* traverser.

travesty ['trævıstı] *n* (*Art, Literat etc*) pastiche *m*; (*pej*) *[freedom, justice]* simulacre *m*.

trawl [trɔ:l] **1** *n* (*net*) chalut *m*. **2** *vi*: **to ~ (for sth)** pêcher (qch) au chalut. ♦ **trawler** *n* chalutier *m*. ♦ **trawling** *n* pêche *f* au chalut.

tray [treı] *n* (*for carrying*) plateau *m*; (*for storing*) (*box*) boîte *f*; (*basket*) corbeille *f*; (*drawer*) tiroir *m*. ♦ **traycloth** *n* napperon *m*.

treacherous ['tretʃərəs] *adj person, action, answer* (*gen; also fig*) traître (*f* traîtresse). **road conditions are ~** il faut se méfier de l'état des routes. ♦ **treacherously** *adv* traîtreusement; *say* perfidement. ♦ **treachery** *n* traîtrise *f*.

treacle ['tri:kl] *n* mélasse *f*.

tread [tred] (*vb: pret* **trod**, *ptp* **trodden**) **1** *n* **(a)** (*footsteps*) pas *mpl*; (*sound*) bruit *m* de pas. **(b)** *[tyre]* chape *f*; *[stair]* giron *m*. **2** *vi* marcher. **to ~ on sth** (*accidentally*) marcher sur qch; (*deliberately*) écraser qch; **to ~ carefully** *or* **warily** avancer avec précaution. **3** *vt path, road* parcourir. **to ~ sth underfoot** fouler qch aux pieds; **to**

~ **grapes** fouler du raisin; **to ~ water** nager en chien. ♦ **treadle 1** *n* pédale *f* (*de tour etc*); **2** *adj machine* à pédale. ♦ **treadmill** *n* (*fig*) routine *f* mortellement ennuyeuse.
treason ['tri:zn] *n* trahison *f*. ♦ **treasonable** *adj* qui constitue une trahison.
treasure ['treʒəʳ] **1** *n* trésor *m*. (*fig*) **she's a real ~** elle est adorable, (*of servant etc*) c'est une perle. **2** *adj*: **~ house** trésor *m* (*lieu*); **~ hunt** chasse *f* au trésor. **3** *vt* (*value*) attacher une grande valeur à; (*keep*: **~ up**) *money, valuables* garder précieusement; *memory, thought* chérir. ♦ **treasurer** *n* trésorier *m*, -ière *f*. ♦ **treasure-trove** *n* trésor *m* (*dont le propriétaire est inconnu*). ♦ **treasury 1** *n* trésorerie *f*; (*Brit*) **the Treasury,** (*US*) **the Department of the Treasury** ≈ le ministère des Finances; **2** *adj*: **treasury bill** ≈ bon *m* du Trésor.
treat [tri:t] **1** *vt* **(a)** traiter (*sb like a child* qn comme un enfant; (*Chem etc*) *sth with sth* qch à qch; (*Med*) *sb for sth* qn pour qch). **to ~ sb well** bien traiter qn, bien se conduire envers qn; **to ~ sb badly** mal se conduire envers qn, traiter qn fort mal; **to ~ sb with respect** montrer du respect envers qn; **to ~ sth with care** faire attention à qch; **it ~s the problems of ...** cela traite les problèmes de ... ; **he ~ed the whole thing as a joke** il a pris tout cela à la plaisanterie; (*Med*) **to ~ sb/sth with penicillin** soigner qn/qch à la pénicilline. **(b) to ~ sb to sth** offrir *or* payer* qch à qn; **to ~ o.s. to sth** se payer* qch.
2 *vi*: **to ~ with sb** traiter avec qn (*for sth* pour qch); *[article etc]* **to ~ of** traiter de.
3 *n* (*pleasure*) plaisir *m*; (*outing*) sortie *f*; (*present*) cadeau *m*. **a ~ in store** un plaisir à venir; **it was a great ~ (for us) to see them** ça nous a vraiment fait plaisir de les voir; **it is a ~ for her to go out to a meal** c'est tout un événement* pour elle de dîner en ville; **to give sb a ~** faire plaisir à qn; **to stand ~** inviter; **this is my ~** c'est moi qui paie*.
♦ **treatise** *n* traité *m* (*on* de). ♦ **treatment** *n* (*gen*) traitement *m*; **his ~ment of his parents/this subject** la façon dont il traite ses parents/ce sujet; **he got good ~ment** (*gen*) on l'a bien traité; (*Med*) il a été bien traité *or* soigné; **to give sb preferential ~ment** accorder à qn un régime de faveur; **medical ~ment** soins *mpl* médicaux, traitement; (*Med*) **to have ~ment for sth** suivre un traitement pour qch. ♦ **treaty** *n* (*Pol*) traité *m* (*with* avec; *between* entre); **to make a ~y** signer un traité.
treble ['trebl] **1** *adj* **(a)** (*triple*) triple. **(b)** (*Mus*) *voice* de soprano (*voix d'enfant*). **the ~ clef** la clef de sol. **2** *adv* (*thrice*) trois fois plus que. **3** *vti* tripler.
tree [tri:] *n* arbre *m*. **cherry ~** cerisier *m*; (*fig*) **to be at the top of the ~** être arrivé au haut de l'échelle. ♦ **tree-covered** *adj* boisé. ♦ **tree-house** *n* cabane *f* construite dans un arbre. ♦ **tree-lined** *adj* bordé d'arbres. ♦ **treetop** *n* cime *f* d'un arbre. ♦ **tree-trunk** *n* tronc *m* d'arbre.
trefoil ['trefɔɪl] *n* (*Bot*) trèfle *m*.
trek [trek] **1** *vi* voyager à la dure. (*fig*) **I had to ~* over to the library** il a fallu que je me traîne jusqu'à la bibliothèque. **2** *n* voyage *m* difficile. **it was quite a ~* to the hotel** il y avait un bon bout de chemin à faire jusqu'à l'hôtel.
trellis ['trelɪs] *n* treillis *m*, (*tougher*) treillage *m*.
tremble ['trembl] **1** *vi* (*gen*) trembler (*with, from* de); (*from fear, passion*) frémir, trembler; *[engine, ship]* vibrer. **2** *n* tremblement *m*. **to be all of a ~*** trembler de la tête aux pieds. ♦ **trembling 1** *adj* tremblant; frémissant; **2** *n* tremblement *m*.
tremendous [trəˈmendəs] *adj* (*huge*) *difference, number, pleasure* énorme; (*dreadful*) *storm, blow* terrible; *victory* foudroyant; *speed, success* fou; (*: *excellent*) formidable*. **we had a ~ time*** on s'est drôlement bien amusé*. ♦ **tremendously** *adv* extrêmement, terriblement.
tremor ['treməʳ] *n* tremblement *m*.
tremulous ['tremjʊləs] *adj* (*timid*) timide; (*trembling*) tremblant. ♦ **tremulously** *adv* timidement; en tremblant.
trench [trentʃ] *n* tranchée *f* (*also Mil*), (*wider*) fossé *m*. ♦ **trenchcoat** *n* trench-coat *m*.
trenchant ['trentʃənt] *adj* incisif, mordant.
trend [trend] *n* (*tendency*) tendance *f* (*towards* à); *[river, road]* direction *f*; *[events]* cours *m*; (*fashion: in clothes etc*) mode *f*. **there is a ~ towards doing/away from doing** on a tendance à faire/à ne plus faire; **~s in popular music** les tendances de la musique populaire. ♦ **trendsetter** *n* personne *f* qui donne le ton. ♦ **trendy*** *adj clothes* dernier cri *inv*; *opinions, person* dans le vent*.
trepidation [ˌtrepɪˈdeɪʃən] *n* vive inquiétude *f*.
trespass ['trespəs] *vi* s'introduire sans permission (*on sb's land* dans la propriété de qn). **'no ~ing'** 'entrée interdite'; **you're ~ing** vous êtes dans une propriété privée. ♦ **trespasser** *n* intrus(e) *m(f)*; **'~ers will be prosecuted'** 'défense d'entrer sous peine de poursuites'.
trestle ['tresl] *adj*: **~ table** table *f* à tréteaux.
trial ['traɪəl] **1** *n* **(a)** (*Jur: proceedings*) procès *m*; (*gen*) jugement *m*. **at** *or* **during the ~** au cours du procès; **~ by jury** jugement par jury; **to be** *or* **go on ~** passer en jugement; **on ~ for theft** jugé pour vol; **he was on ~ for his life** il encourait la peine de mort; **to bring sb to ~** faire passer qn en jugement. **(b)** (*test*) *[machine, vehicle, drug etc]* essai *m*. **~s** (*Ftbl etc*) match *m* de sélection; (*Athletics etc*) épreuve *f* de sélection; *[sheepdogs, horses]* concours *m*; **~ of strength** épreuve *f* de force; **by ~ and error** par tâtonnements; **to be/take on ~** être/prendre à l'essai; **to give sb a ~** mettre qn à l'essai. **(c)** (*hardship*) épreuve *f*. **it was a great ~** cela a été une véritable épreuve (*for* pour); **the ~s of old age** les afflictions *fpl* de la vieillesse; **~s and tribulations** tribulations *fpl*; **he is a ~ to his mother** il donne beaucoup de souci à sa mère. **2** *adj flight, period etc* d'essai; *offer, marriage* à l'essai. **~ run** essai *m*, (*fig*) période *f* d'essai.
triangle ['traɪæŋgl] *n* triangle *m*. ♦ **triangular** *adj* triangulaire.
tribe [traɪb] *n* tribu *f*. ♦ **tribal** *adj* (*gen*) tribal; *warfare* entre tribus. ♦ **tribesman** *n* membre *m* de la tribu.
tribunal [traɪˈbju:nl] *n* (*gen, Jur*) tribunal *m*. **~ of inquiry** commission *f* d'enquête.
tribute ['trɪbju:t] *n* tribut *m*. **to pay ~ to** payer tribut à, rendre hommage à; **that is a ~ to his generosity** cela témoigne de sa générosité. ♦ **tributary** *n* (*river*) affluent *m*.
trice [traɪs] *n*: **in a ~** en un clin d'œil.
trick [trɪk] **1** *n* **(a)** (*ruse*) ruse *f*, truc* *m*; (*joke, hoax*) tour *m*, blague* *f*; *[conjurer, dog etc]* tour; (*special skill*) truc* (*for doing* pour faire). **it's a ~ to make you believe ...** c'est une ruse *or* un truc* pour vous faire croire ...; **to play a ~ on sb** jouer un tour à qn; **a dirty** *or* **low** *or* **shabby** *or* **nasty ~** un sale tour; **a ~ of the trade** une ficelle du métier; **a ~ of the light** une illusion d'optique; **he's up to his old ~s again*** il fait de nouveau des siennes*; (*fig*) **he knows a ~ or two*** c'est un petit malin; **to do the ~*** faire l'affaire; **I'll soon get the ~ of it** je vais bientôt prendre le pli. **(b)** (*habit*) manie *f* (*of doing* de faire); (*mannerism*) tic *m*. **he has a ~ of scratching his ear** il a le tic de se gratter l'oreille; **he has a ~ of arriving just when ...** il a le don d'arriver au moment où ... . **(c)** (*Cards*) levée *f*. **to take a ~** faire une levée; (*fig*) **he never misses a ~** rien ne lui échappe. **2** *adj photograph* truqué. **~ question** question-piège *f*. **3** *vt* (*deceive*) attraper, avoir*; (*swindle*) escroquer. **I've been ~ed!** on m'a eu!*; **to ~ sb into doing** amener qn à faire par la ruse; **to ~ sb out of sth** obtenir qch de qn par la ruse. ♦ **trickery** *n*

ruse *f.* ♦ **trickster** *n* filou *m.* ♦ **tricky** *adj problem, situation, task* difficile, délicat; (*pej*) *person* rusé; **he's a ~y man to deal with** (*scheming*) avec lui il faut se méfier; (*touchy*) il n'est pas commode.

trickle ['trɪkl] **1** *n [water, blood etc]* filet *m.* (*fig*) **a ~ of people** quelques rares personnes; **there was a steady ~ of letters** les lettres arrivaient en petit nombre mais régulièrement. **2** *adj* (*Elec*) **~ charger** chargeur *m* à régime lent. **3** *vi* (*drop slowly*) couler goutte à goutte; (*flow slowly*) couler en un filet. **tears ~d down her cheeks** les larmes coulaient *or* dégoulinaient le long de ses joues; **to ~ in** *[water]* couler goutte à goutte; *[people]* entrer les uns après les autres; *[money, letters]* arriver peu à peu; **the ball ~d into the net** le ballon a roulé doucement dans le filet.

tricolo(u)r ['trɪkələʳ] *n* drapeau *m* tricolore.

tricycle ['traɪsɪkl] *n* tricycle *m.*

trier ['traɪəʳ] *n*: **to be a ~** être persévérant.

trifle ['traɪfl] **1** *n* **(a)** (*object, sum of money*) bagatelle *f.* **it's only a ~** ce n'est rien; **he worries over ~s** il se fait du mauvais sang pour un rien; **a ~ difficult** un peu difficile. **(b)** (*Culin*) ≈ diplomate *m.* **2** *vi*: **to ~ with** traiter à la légère. ♦ **trifling** *adj* insignifiant.

trigger ['trɪgəʳ] **1** *n [gun]* détente *f*, gâchette *f*; *[tool]* déclic *m.* **to press *or* pull the ~** appuyer sur la détente. **2** *vt* (**~ off**) *explosion, revolt* déclencher; *reaction, protest* provoquer. ♦ **trigger-happy*** *adj person* qui a la gâchette facile; (*fig*) *nation etc* prêt à déclencher la guerre pour un rien.

trigonometry [ˌtrɪgəˈnɒmɪtrɪ] *n* trigonométrie *f.*

trill [trɪl] **1** *n* (*Mus*) trille *m*; (*Ling*) consonne roulée. **2** *vi* triller. **3** *vt* (*gen*) triller; (*Ling*) *one's rs* rouler.

trilogy ['trɪlədʒɪ] *n* trilogie *f.*

trim [trɪm] **1** *adj person, clothes* net, soigné; *boat, garden, house* coquet, net. **~ figure** taille *f* svelte. **2** *n* **(a) in (good) ~** *garden, house etc* en bon état; *person, athlete* en forme; *[athlete etc]* **to get into ~** se remettre en forme; (*Naut*) **the ~ of the sails** l'orientation *f* des voiles. **(b)** (*cut*) **to give sth a ~** = **to trim sth** (*V* **3a**); (*at hairdresser's*) **to have a ~** se faire rafraîchir les cheveux. **(c)** (*decoration: Archit*) moulures *fpl*; (*Aut: outside*) finitions *fpl* extérieures; (*on garment*) garniture *f.* **car with blue interior ~** voiture à intérieur bleu. **3** *vt* **(a)** (*cut*) *hair* rafraîchir; *wick, lamp* tailler; *beard, hedge, roses* tailler légèrement; *edges* couper; *wood, paper* couper les bords de, rogner. **to ~ one's nails** se rogner les ongles. **(b)** (*decorate*) *garment* garnir, orner (*with* de); *Christmas tree, shop window* décorer (*with* de). ♦ **trimming** *n* (*on garment*) garniture *f*; (*edging*) bordure *f*; **~mings** (*cuttings*) chutes *fpl*; **it costs £100 without the ~mings** cela coûte 100 livres sans les accessoires *mpl*; (*Culin*) **and all the ~mings** avec la garniture habituelle.

trimaran ['traɪməræn] *n* trimaran *m.*

trinity ['trɪnɪtɪ] *n* trinité *f.* **T~ (Sunday)** la fête de la Trinité.

trinket ['trɪŋkɪt] *n* (*knick-knack*) bibelot *m*; *[jewellery]* colifichet *m.*

trio ['trɪəʊ] *n* trio *m.*

trip [trɪp] **1** *n* **(a)** voyage *m*; (*excursion*) excursion *f.* **away on a ~** en voyage; **to take a ~** (*go on journey*) partir en voyage; (*go*) aller (*to* à); **cheap ~s to Spain** des voyages à prix réduit en Espagne; **he does 3 ~s to Scotland a week** il va en Écosse 3 fois par semaine; **I don't want another ~ to the shops** je ne veux pas retourner dans les magasins. **(b)** (*Drugs sl*) **to be on a ~** faire un trip; **a bad ~** un trip qui tourne mal. **2** *vi* **(a)** (**~ over, ~ up**) trébucher (*on, over* contre, sur), faire un faux pas; (*make mistake:* **~ up**) gaffer*. **(b) to ~ along/in** *etc* marcher/entrer *etc* d'un pas sautillant. **3** *vt* (**~ up**) faire trébucher; (*deliberately*) faire un croche-pied à; (*in questioning etc*) prendre en défaut. ♦ **tripper** *n* touriste *mf*; (*day ~*) excursionniste *mf.* ♦ **tripwire** *n* fil *m* de détente.

tripe [traɪp] *n* (*Culin*) tripes *fpl*; (*: *nonsense*) bêtises *fpl*, foutaises: *fpl.*

triphthong ['trɪfθɒŋ] *n* triphtongue *f.*

triple ['trɪpl] **1** *adj, n* triple (*m*). **2** *adv* trois fois plus que. **3** *vti* tripler. ♦ **triplets** *npl* triplé(e)s *m(f)pl.* ♦ **triplicate** *n*: **in triplicate** en trois exemplaires.

tripod ['traɪpɒd] *n* trépied *m.*

triptych ['trɪptɪk] *n* triptyque *m.*

trite [traɪt] *adj* banal. ♦ **tritely** *adv* banalement.

triumph ['traɪʌmf] **1** *n* (*victory*) triomphe *m* (*for* pour; *of* de; *over* sur); (*sense of ~*) sentiment *m* de triomphe. **in ~** en triomphe. **2** *vi* triompher (*over* de). ♦ **triumphal** *adj* triomphal. ♦ **triumphant** *adj* (*gen*) triomphant; *homecoming* triomphal. ♦ **triumphantly** *adv* triomphalement.

trivia ['trɪvɪə] *npl* futilités *fpl.* ♦ **trivial** *adj amount, reason* insignifiant; *remark, mistake, matter* sans importance; *film, book* banal. ♦ **triviality** *n* caractère *m* insignifiant; manque *m* d'importance; banalité *f*; **~lities** futilités *fpl.*

trod [trɒd], **trodden** ['trɒdn] *pret, ptp of* **tread.**

trolley ['trɒlɪ] **1** *n* (*in station, supermarket*) chariot *m*; (*two-wheeled*) diable *m*; (*tea ~*) table roulante, (*in office*) chariot à boissons. **2** *adj*: **~ bus** trolleybus *m.*

trombone [trɒm'bəʊn] *n* trombone *m* (*Mus*).

troop [tru:p] **1** *n* (*gen*) groupe *m*, troupe *f*; *[scouts]* troupe. (*Mil*) **~s** troupes. **2** *adj movements etc* de troupes; *train* militaire. **~ carrier** (*Aut*) transport *m* de troupes; (*Naut*: *also* **~ship**) transport (*navire*); (*Aviat*) avion *m* de transport militaire. **3** *vi*: **to ~ in/past** *etc* entrer/passer *etc* en groupe. ♦ **trooper** *n* (*Mil*) soldat *m* de cavalerie; (*US: state trooper*) ≈ C.R.S. *m.* ♦ **trooping** *n*: **~ing the colour** le salut au drapeau.

trophy ['trəʊfɪ] *n* trophée *m.*

tropic ['trɒpɪk] *n* tropique *m.* **T~ of Cancer/Capricorn** tropique du cancer/du capricorne; **in the ~s** sous les tropiques. ♦ **tropical** *adj* tropical.

trot [trɒt] **1** *n* (*pace*) trot *m.* **at a ~** au trot; (*fig*) **5 days on the ~*** 5 jours de suite; **to keep sb on the ~*** ne pas accorder une minute de tranquillité à qn. **2** *vi* trotter, courir. *[person]* **to ~ in/past** *etc* entrer/passer *etc* au trot; **she ~ted round to the grocer's** elle a fait un saut chez l'épicier.

trot out *vt sep excuses, reasons* débiter; *names, facts etc* réciter d'affilée.

♦ **trotter** *n* (*Culin*) **pig's ~ters** pieds *mpl* de porc.

trouble ['trʌbl] **1** *n* **(a)** (*difficulties*) ennuis *mpl.* **to be in ~** avoir des ennuis (*with sb* avec qn; *for doing* pour avoir fait), être en difficulté; **to get into ~** s'attirer des ennuis (*for sth* pour qch; *for doing* pour avoir fait); **to get into ~ with sb** s'attirer la colère de qn; **to get sb into ~** causer des ennuis à qn; **to get out of ~** se tirer d'affaire; **to make ~** causer des ennuis (*for sb* à qn); **it's asking for ~** c'est se chercher des ennuis; **there's ~ brewing** il y a de l'orage dans l'air.

(b) (*bother, effort*) mal *m.* **it's no ~** cela ne me dérange pas (*to do* de faire); **it's not worth the ~** ça ne vaut pas la peine; **nothing is too much ~ for her** elle se dépense sans compter; **I had all that ~ for nothing** je me suis donné tout ce mal pour rien; **he went to enormous ~** il s'est donné un mal fou (*to help* pour aider); **to go to the ~ of doing, to take the ~ to do** se donner le mal de faire; **he took a lot of ~ over it** il s'est donné beaucoup de mal pour cela; **to put sb to a lot of ~** donner beaucoup de mal à qn.

(c) (*problem, nuisance*) ennui *m*, problème *m*; (*worry*) souci *m*, ennui; (*Pol etc*) troubles *mpl.* **what's the ~?** qu'est-ce qu'il y a?; **that's the ~!** c'est ça l'ennui!; **the ~ is that** ... l'ennui *or* le problème, c'est que ...; **the carburettor is giving us ~** nous avons des problèmes de carburateur; **he is trying to locate the ~** il essaie de localiser le problème; **there is ~ between them** ils s'entendent mal; **to cause ~ between** causer des désaccords entre; **I'm having ~ with him** il me donne des soucis, il me cause des ennuis; **he is a ~ to his parents** il est un souci pour ses parents; **to have ~ in doing** avoir du mal à faire; **your ~s are over** vous voilà au bout de vos peines; (*Med*) **I have back ~** mon dos me fait souffrir; **kidney ~** ennuis rénaux; (*Aut*) **engine ~** ennuis de moteur; **there is a lot of ~ in Africa** la situation est très tendue en Afrique; **labour ~s** troubles sociaux; **there's ~ at the factory** ça chauffe* à l'usine.

2 *adj*: **~ spot** point *m* chaud *or* névralgique.

3 *vt* (*worry*) inquiéter; (*upset*) troubler; (*bother*) déranger; (*inconvenience*) gêner. **his eyes ~ him** ses yeux le font souffrir; **the heat ~d us** la chaleur nous a gênés; **nothing ~s him** rien ne le trouble; **I am sorry to ~ you** je suis désolé de vous déranger; **does it ~ you if ...** est-ce que cela vous dérange si ... + *indic or* que ... + *subj*; **don't ~ yourself!** ne vous dérangez pas!; **to ~ o.s. to do** se donner la peine de faire; **may I ~ you for a light?** puis-je vous demander du feu?; **I shan't ~ you with the details** je vous ferai grâce des détails.

4 *vi* se déranger. **please don't ~** ne vous dérangez pas; **to ~ to do** se donner la peine de faire.

♦ **troubled** *adj* (*gen*) inquiet; *life, sleep* agité; *water* trouble; **to be ~d about sth** s'inquiéter de qch; **in ~d times** à une époque agitée. ♦ **trouble-free** *adj* (*gen*) sans ennuis *or* problèmes; *car* qui ne tombe jamais en panne. ♦ **troublemaker** *n* provocateur *m*, -trice *f*. ♦ **troubleshooter** *n* (*Tech*) expert *m* (appelé en cas de crise); (*Ind, Pol*) conciliateur *m*. ♦ **troublesome** *adj person* pénible; *request, cough* gênant; *task* ennuyeux; **his back is ~some** son dos le fait souffrir.

trough [trɒf] *n* **(a)** (*dip*) creux *m*; (*fig*) point *m* bas. (*Met*) **~ of low pressure** zone *f* dépressionnaire. **(b)** (*drinking ~*) abreuvoir *m*; (*feeding ~*) auge *f*.

trounce [traʊns] *vt* battre à plates coutures.

troupe [tru:p] *n* troupe *f* (*Theat*).

trousers ['traʊzəz] *npl*: **(pair of) ~** pantalon *m*; **long ~** pantalon long; **short ~** culottes *fpl* courtes; (*fig*) **she wears the ~*** c'est elle qui porte la culotte *or* qui commande. ♦ **trouser-suit** *n* tailleur-pantalon *m*.

trousseau ['tru:səʊ] *n* trousseau *m* (*de mariée*).

trout [traʊt] **1** *n, pl inv* truite *f*. **2** *adj stream* à truites; *fishing* à la truite.

trowel ['traʊəl] *n* (*Constr*) truelle *f*; (*gardening*) déplantoir *m*. (*fig*) **to lay it on with a ~*** y aller un peu fort.

truant ['trʊənt] *n* élève *mf* absent(e) sans autorisation. **to play ~** (*Scol etc*) manquer les cours; (*fig: from office etc*) faire l'école buissonnière. ♦ **truancy** *n* absence *f* non autorisée (*de l'école etc*); **truancy is increasing** le nombre d'élèves qui s'absentent sans autorisation augmente.

truce [tru:s] *n* trêve *f*. **to call a ~** faire trêve (*to* à).

truck[1] [trʌk] *n* **(a)** (*fig*) **to have no ~ with** refuser d'avoir affaire à. **(b)** (*US: vegetables*) produits *mpl* maraîchers. **~ farmer** maraîcher *m*.

truck[2] [trʌk] **1** *n* (*lorry*) camion *m*; (*Rail*) truck *m*; (*luggage handcart*) chariot *m* à bagages, (*two-wheeled*) diable *m*. **2** *vt* (*esp US*) camionner. ♦ **truckdriver** *or* ♦ **trucker** *n* camionneur *m*. ♦ **trucking** *n* camionnage *m*. ♦ **truckload** *n* plein camion.

truculent ['trʌkjʊlənt] *adj* brutal, agressif. ♦ **truculence** *n* brutalité *f*. ♦ **truculently** *adv* brutalement, agressivement.

trudge [trʌdʒ] *vi*: **to ~ in/along** *etc* entrer/marcher *etc* péniblement; **to ~ round the town** se traîner dans la ville.

true [tru:] **1** *adj* **(a)** (*accurate: gen*) vrai; *description, account* exact, véridique; *copy* conforme; *statistics, measure* exact. **it's all ~** tout est vrai; **too ~!*** ah oui alors!; **can it be ~ that** est-il possible que + *subj*; **it is ~ that** il est vrai que + *indic*; **is it ~ that** est-il vrai que + *indic or subj*; **it's not ~ that** il n'est pas vrai que + *indic or subj*; **if it is ~ that** s'il est vrai que + *indic*; **to come ~** se réaliser; **the same holds ~ for** il en est de même pour. **(b)** (*genuine*) *repentance, friendship* vrai (*before n*), véritable; *friend, scholar etc* vrai, véritable (*both before n*). **what is the ~ situation?** quelle est la situation réelle?; **it is not a ~ reptile** ce n'est pas vraiment un reptile. **(c)** (*faithful*) fidèle (*to sb/sth* à qn/qch). **~ to life/to type** conforme à la réalité/au type. **(d)** *wall, upright* d'aplomb; *beam* droit; *machine part* juste; *wheel* dans l'axe; (*Mus*) *voice etc* juste. **2** *n*: **out of ~** *upright, wall* pas d'aplomb; *beam* tordu; *wheel* voilé. **3** *adv aim, sing* juste. ♦ **true-blue*** *adj* loyal. ♦ **truism** *n* truisme *m*. ♦ **truly** *adv* (*genuinely*) *love, believe* vraiment; (*faithfully*) *reflect, show* fidèlement; (*truthfully*) *answer, tell* franchement; (*without doubt*) *great, terrible* vraiment, véritablement; **well and truly** bel et bien; (*letter ending*) **yours truly** je vous prie d'agréer l'expression de mes sentiments respectueux.

truffle ['trʌfl] *n* truffe *f*.

trump [trʌmp] **1** *n* atout *m*. **spades are ~(s)** c'est atout pique; **what's ~(s)?** quel est l'atout?; **no ~(s)** sans atout; (*fig*) **he was holding all the ~s** il avait tous les atouts dans son jeu; (*fig*) **to turn up ~s*** faire des merveilles. **2** *adj* (*lit, fig*) **~ card** atout *m*. **3** *vt* (*Cards*) prendre avec l'atout. (*fig*) **to ~ sb's ace** faire encore mieux que qn.

trump up *vt sep charge etc* inventer de toutes pièces.

trumpet ['trʌmpɪt] **1** *n* (*Mus*) trompette *f*. **2** *vi* *[elephant]* barrir. ♦ **trumpeter** *n* (*Mil*) trompette *m*. ♦ **trumpet-player** *n* (*Mus*) trompettiste *mf*.

truncheon ['trʌntʃən] *n* matraque *f*; (*directing traffic*) bâton *m* (*d'agent de police*).

trundle ['trʌndl] **1** *vt* (*push etc*) pousser *etc* bruyamment. **2** *vi*: **to ~ along/down** rouler/descendre bruyamment.

trunk [trʌŋk] **1** *n* (*Anat, Bot*) tronc *m*; *[elephant]* trompe *f*; (*luggage*) malle *f*; (*US Aut*) coffre *m*. **~s** (*swimming*) slip *m* de bain; (*underwear*) slip (d'homme). **2** *adj* (*Telec*) **~ call** communication *f* interurbaine; (*Rail*) **~ line** grande ligne *f*; **~ road** route *f* nationale.

truss [trʌs] **1** *n [hay etc]* botte *f*; *[flowers, fruit]* grappe *f*; (*Constr*) ferme *f*; (*Med*) bandage *m* herniaire. **2** *vt chicken* trousser; (**~ up**) *prisoner* ligoter.

trust [trʌst] **1** *n* **(a)** confiance *f* (*in* en). **breach of ~** abus *m* de confiance; **to have ~ in** avoir confiance en; **to put one's ~ in** faire confiance à; **you'll have to take it on ~** il vous faudra me (*or* le *etc*) croire sur parole. **(b)** (*Jur*) **to leave money in ~** faire administrer un legs par fidéicommis (*for* à l'intention de). **(c)** (*Fin*) trust *m*.

2 *adj fund, account* en fidéicommis.

3 *vt* **(a)** *person, object* avoir confiance en; *method, promise* se fier à. **he is not to be ~ed** on ne peut pas lui faire confiance; **to ~ sb with sth** confier qch à qn; **to ~ sb to do sth** compter sur qn pour faire qch; **he is too young to be ~ed on the roads** il est trop petit pour qu'on le laisse aller dans la rue tout seul; **I can't ~ him out of my sight** je n'ose pas le quitter des yeux; (*iro*) **~ you!*** pour ça on peut te faire confiance! **(b)** (*entrust*) confier (*sth to sb* qch à qn). **(c)** (*hope*) espérer (*that* que).

4 *vi*: **to ~ in sb** se fier à qn; **to ~ to luck** s'en remettre à la chance.

♦ **trusted** *adj person* en qui l'on a toute confiance; *method* éprouvé. ♦ **trustee** *n* (*Jur*) fidéicommissaire *m*; *[institution, school]* administrateur *m*, -trice *f*; **the ~ees** le conseil d'administration. ♦ **trustful** *or* ♦ **trusting** *adj* confiant. ♦ **trustfully** *or* ♦ **trustingly** *adv* avec confiance. ♦ **trustworthiness** *n [person]* loyauté *f*; *[statement]* véracité *f*. ♦ **trustworthy** *adj person* digne de confiance; *report, account* exact. ♦ **trusty** *adj* (*hum*) fidèle.

truth [tru:θ] *n* vérité *f*. **to tell the ~** dire la vérité; **to tell (you) the ~, ~ to tell** à vrai dire; **there's some/no ~ in what he says** il y a du vrai/il n'y a pas un mot de vrai dans ce qu'il dit; **~ will out** la vérité finira toujours par se savoir; **the ~, the whole ~ and nothing but the ~** la vérité, toute la vérité et rien que la vérité; **the plain unvarnished ~** la vérité toute nue; **in ~** en vérité. ♦ **truthful** *adj person* qui dit la vérité; *statement* véridique. ♦ **truthfully** *adv answer* sans mentir; **I don't mind, ~fully** sincèrement, ça m'est égal. ♦ **truthfulness** *n* véracité *f*.

try [traı] **1** *n* **(a)** (*attempt*) essai *m*, tentative *f*. **to have a ~** essayer (*at doing* de faire); **to give sth a ~** essayer qch; **it was a good ~** il a (*or* tu as *etc*) vraiment essayé; **it's worth a ~** cela vaut le coup d'essayer; **at the first ~** du premier coup; **after 3 tries** après avoir essayé 3 fois. **(b)** (*Rugby*) essai *m*. **to score a ~** marquer un essai.

2 *vt* **(a)** (*attempt*) essayer, tâcher (*to do* de faire). **~ to eat it, ~ and eat it** essaie *or* tâche de le manger; **I'll ~ anything once** je suis toujours prêt à faire un essai; (*warning*) **just you ~ it!** essaie un peu pour voir!*; **he tried 3 questions** il a essayé de répondre à 3 questions; **to ~ one's best** *or* **one's hardest** faire de son mieux (*to do* pour faire); **to ~ one's hand at sth/at doing** s'essayer à qch/à faire; **it's ~ing to rain*** il a l'air de vouloir pleuvoir*. **(b)** (*sample*) *food, method, car etc* essayer. **won't you ~ me for the job?** vous ne voulez pas me faire faire un essai?; **~ pushing that button** essayez de presser ce bouton; (*also *fig*) **~ this for size** essaie ça pour voir. **(c)** (*test etc*) *person, sb's patience, strength* mettre à l'épreuve; *eyes* fatiguer; *vehicle, plane, machine* tester. **to ~ one's strength against sb** se mesurer à qn; **to ~ one's luck** tenter sa chance; **well-tried** qui a fait ses preuves; **sorely tried** durement éprouvé. **(d)** (*Jur*) *person, case* juger (*for* pour).

3 *vi* essayer (*for sth* d'obtenir qch). **~ again!** essaie encore une fois!

try on *vt sep* **(a)** *garment, shoe* essayer. **(b)** (*fig*) **to ~ it on** essayer de voir jusqu'où on peut aller (*with sb* avec qn); **don't ~ anything on!** ne fais pas le malin!

try out *vt sep thing, method* essayer; *employee etc* mettre à l'essai. **~ it out on the cat first** essaie d'abord de voir quelle est la réaction du chat.

♦ **trying** *adj person, experience* pénible; *work* ennuyeux; **to have a ~ing time** passer des moments difficiles. ♦ **try-on*** *n*: **it's a ~-on** c'est du bluff. ♦ **tryout** *n* essai *m*.

tsar [zɑ:ʳ] *n* tsar *m*. ♦ **tsarina** *n* tsarine *f*.

tsetse fly ['tsetsıflaı] *n* mouche *f* tsé-tsé *inv*.

tub [tʌb] *n* (*gen*) cuve *f*; (*for washing clothes*) baquet *m*; (*for flowers*) bac *m*; (*for cream etc*) petit pot *m*; (*bath~*) tub *m*, (*in bathroom*) baignoire *f*. ♦ **tubby*** *adj* replet.

tuba ['tju:bə] *n* tuba *m*.

tube [tju:b] **1** *n* (*gen*) tube *m*; *[tyre]* chambre *f* à air. (*Brit: underground*) **the ~** le métro; **to go by ~** prendre le métro; (*US: TV*) **the ~*** la télé*. **2** *adj*: **~ station** station *f* de métro. ♦ **tubeless** *adj tyre* sans chambre à air. ♦ **tubing** *n* tubes *mpl*; **rubber tubing** tube *m or* tuyau *m* en caoutchouc. ♦ **tubular** *adj* tubulaire.

tuber ['tju:bəʳ] *n* (*Bot*) tubercule *m*. ♦ **tubercle** *n* (*Med*) tubercule *m*. ♦ **tubercular** *adj* tuberculeux. ♦ **tuberculin** *n* tuberculine *f*. ♦ **tuberculin-tested** *adj milk* ≃ certifié. ♦ **tuberculosis** (*abbr* **TB***) *n* tuberculose *f*; **he's got TB*** il est tuberculeux.

tuck [tʌk] **1** *n* (*Sewing etc*) rempli *m*. **to take a ~ in** faire un rempli dans. **2** *vt*: **to ~ sth under one's arm** mettre qch sous son bras; **~ it away out of sight** cache-le; **~ed away among the trees** caché parmi les arbres; **to ~ one's shirt into one's trousers** rentrer sa chemise dans son pantalon; **he was sitting with his feet ~ed under him** il avait les pieds repliés sous lui. **3** *vi*: **to ~ into a meal*** attaquer* un repas.

tuck in 1 *vi* (*: *eat*) bien boulotter*. **~ in!** allez-y! **2** *vt sep shirt, flap* rentrer; *sheets, child* border.

tuck up *vt sep skirt, sleeves* remonter; *legs* replier; (*in bed*) border.

♦ **tuckbox** *n* (*Scol*) boîte *f* à provisions. ♦ **tuck-in*** *n*: **they had a good ~-in** ils ont vraiment bien boulotté*. ♦ **tuck-shop** *n* (*Scol*) boutique *f* à provisions.

Tuesday ['tju:zdı] *n* mardi *m*; *for phrases V* **Saturday.**

tuft [tʌft] *n* touffe *f*. ♦ **tufted** *adj bird* huppé.

tug [tʌg] **1** *n* **(a)** (*pull*) petite saccade *f*. **to give sth a ~** tirer sur qch; **I felt a ~ at my sleeve/on the rope** j'ai senti qu'on me tirait par la manche/qu'on tirait sur la corde. **(b)** (*~boat*) remorqueur *m*. **2** *vt rope, sleeve etc* tirer sur; (*drag*) tirer, traîner; (*Naut*) remorquer. **3** *vi* tirer fort (*at, on* sur). ♦ **tug-of-war** *n* (*Sport*) lutte *f* à la corde; (*fig*) lutte acharnée.

tuition [tjʊ'ıʃən] *n* cours *mpl*. **private ~** cours particuliers (*in* de); **~ fee** frais *mpl* d'inscription.

tulip ['tju:lıp] *n* tulipe *f*.

tulle [tju:l] *n* tulle *m*.

tumble ['tʌmbl] **1** *n* **(a)** (*fall*) chute *f*; *[acrobat etc]* culbute *f*. **to have** *or* **take a ~** faire une chute. **(b)** (*confused heap*) amas *m*. **in a ~** en désordre. **2** *vi* **(a)** (*fall*) tomber; (*trip*) trébucher (*over* sur); *[acrobat etc]* faire des culbutes. **to ~ head over heels** faire la culbute; **to ~ downstairs** dégringoler dans l'escalier. **(b)** (*rush*) **he ~d into bed** il s'est jeté au lit; **he ~d out of bed** il a bondi hors du lit; **they ~d out of the car** ils ont déboulé* de la voiture. **(c)** (*realize*) **to ~ to sth*** réaliser* qch. **3** *vt pile* renverser.

tumble about, tumble around *vi [puppies, children]* gambader; *[acrobat]* cabrioler.

tumble down *vi [building etc]* **to be tumbling down** tomber en ruine.

♦ **tumbledown** *adj* délabré. ♦ **tumbledryer** *n* séchoir *m* à linge (à air chaud). ♦ **tumbler** *n* (*glass*) verre *m* (droit); (*of plastic, metal*) gobelet *m*; (*tumbledryer*) séchoir *m* à linge (à air chaud).

tummy* ['tʌmı] *n* ventre *m*. ♦ **tummy-ache** *n* mal *m* de ventre.

tumour, (*US*) **tumor** ['tju:məʳ] *n* tumeur *f*.

tumult ['tju:mʌlt] *n* tumulte *m*. **in a ~** dans le tumulte; (*emotionally*) en émoi. ♦ **tumultuous** *adj* tumultueux. ♦ **tumultuously** *adv* tumultueusement.

tumulus ['tju:mjʊləs] *n, pl* **-li** tumulus *m*.

tuna ['tju:nə] *n* (**~ fish**) thon *m*.

tundra ['tʌndrə] *n* toundra *f*.

tune [tju:n] **1** *n* **(a)** air *m*. **he gave us a ~** il nous a joué un air; **to the ~ of** *sing* sur l'air de; *march, process* aux accents de; (*fig*) **repairs etc to the ~ of £30** réparations *etc* s'élevant à la coquette somme de 30 livres; (*fig*) **to change one's ~** changer de ton; (*fig*) **to call the ~** commander. **(b) to be in ~/out of ~** *[instrument]* être accordé/désaccordé; *[singer]* chanter juste/faux; **to sing/play in ~** chanter/jouer juste; **to sing/play out of ~** chanter/jouer faux; (*fig*) **in ~ with** en accord avec. **2** *vt* (*Mus*) accorder; (*Rad, TV*) régler (*to* sur); (*Aut*) régler. (*Rad*) **to be ~d (in) to** ... être à l'écoute de ....

tune in (*Rad, TV*) **1** *vi* se mettre à l'écoute (*to* de). **2** *vt sep* régler (*to* sur).

tune up *vi [orchestra]* accorder ses instruments. ♦ **tuneful** *adj* (*gen*) mélodieux; *singer* à la voix mélodieuse. ♦ **tunefully** *adv* mélodieusement. ♦ **tuneless** *adj* peu mélodieux. ♦ **tunelessly** *adv sing* faux. ♦ **tuner 1** *n* **(a) piano-~r** accordeur *m* de pianos; **(b)** (*Rad: knob*) bouton *m* de réglage; **2** *adj*: **~r amplifier** radio-ampli *m*. ♦ **tuning** *n* (*Mus*) accord *m*; (*Aut, Rad, TV*) réglage *m*. ♦ **tuning-fork** *n* diapason *m*. ♦ **tuning-knob** *n* (*Rad etc*) bouton *m* de réglage.

tungsten ['tʌŋstən] *n* tungstène *m*.

tunic ['tju:nɪk] *n* tunique *f*.

Tunisia [tju:'nɪzɪə] *n* Tunisie *f*.

tunnel ['tʌnl] **1** *n* (*gen*) tunnel *m*; (*Min*) galerie *f*. **to make a ~ = to tunnel** (*V* 2). **2** *vi* percer un tunnel (*into* dans; *under* sous). **to ~ in/out** *etc* entrer/sortir *etc* en creusant un tunnel.

tunny ['tʌnɪ] *n* thon *m*.

turban ['tɜ:bən] *n* turban *m*.

turbid ['tɜ:bɪd] *adj* turbide.

turbine ['tɜ:baɪn] *n* turbine *f*.

turbo... ['tɜ:bəʊ] *pref* turbo... . ♦ **turbojet** *n* (*engine*) turboréacteur *m*; (*aircraft*) avion *m* à turboréacteur. ♦ **turboprop** *n* turbopropulseur *m*.

turbot ['tɜ:bət] *n* turbot *m*.

turbulent ['tɜ:bjʊlənt] *adj* turbulent. ♦ **turbulence** *n* turbulence *f*.

tureen [tə'ri:n] *n* soupière *f*.

turf [tɜ:f] **1** *n* (*grass*) gazon *m*; (*one piece*) motte *f* de gazon; (*peat*) tourbe *f*. (*Sport*) **the T~** le turf. **2** *adj*: **~ accountant** bookmaker *m*. **3** *vt* **(a)** (**~ over**) *land* gazonner. **(b)** (*) (*throw*) balancer*, jeter; (*put*) flanquer*. **to ~ sb out** flanquer* qn à la porte.

Turkey ['tɜ:kɪ] *n* Turquie *f*. ♦ **Turkish 1** *adj* turc (*f* turque); **Turkish bath** bain *m* turc; **Turkish delight** loukoum *m*; **2** *n* (*Ling*) turc *m*.

turkey ['tɜ:kɪ] *n* dindon *m*, dinde *f*; (*Culin*) dinde. ♦ **turkey-cock** *n* dindon *m*.

turmeric ['tɜ:mərɪk] *n* safran *m* des Indes.

turmoil ['tɜ:mɔɪl] *n* agitation *f*; (*emotional*) émoi *m*. **everything was in a ~** c'était le bouleversement le plus complet.

turn [tɜ:n] **1** *n* **(a)** *[wheel, handle etc]* tour *m*. **to give sth a ~** tourner qch (une fois); (*Culin*) **done to a ~** à point.

(b) (*bend: in road etc*) tournant *m*. **'no left ~'** 'défense de tourner à gauche'; **take the next left ~** prenez la prochaine route à gauche; (*walk*) **to take a ~ in the park** aller faire un tour dans le parc; **at the ~ of the year/century** en fin d'année/de siècle; (*fig*) **at every ~** à tout instant; **things took a new ~** les choses ont pris une nouvelle tournure; **to take a ~ for the worse** s'aggraver; **to take a ~ for the better** s'améliorer; **a scientific ~ of mind** une tournure d'esprit scientifique; **~ of phrase** tournure *f*.

(c) (*Med*) crise *f*. **he had one of his ~s** il a eu une nouvelle crise; **she has giddy ~s** elle a des vertiges; **it gave me quite a ~*** ça m'a fait un coup*.

(d) (*action etc*) **to do sb a good ~** rendre un service à qn; **to do sb a bad ~** jouer un mauvais tour à qn; **his good ~ for the day** sa bonne action pour la journée; **one good ~ deserves another** un prêté pour un rendu; **it has served its ~** ça a fait son temps.

(e) (*Theat etc*) numéro *m*. **to do a ~** faire un numéro.

(f) (*in game, queue etc*) tour *m*. **it's your ~** c'est à vous (*to play* de jouer); **whose ~ is it?** c'est à qui le tour?; **wait your ~** attendez votre tour; **they answered in ~, they answered ~ and ~ about** ils ont répondu à tour de rôle; **and he, in ~, said** ... et lui, à son tour, a dit ...; **hot and cold by ~s** tour à tour chaud et froid; **to take ~s at doing sth, to take it in ~(s) to do sth** faire qch à tour de rôle; **take it in ~s!** chacun son tour!; **to take ~s at the wheel** se relayer au volant; **to take a ~ at the wheel** faire un bout de conduite*; (*fig*) **to speak out of ~** commettre une indiscrétion.

2 *vt* **(a)** (*gen*) *handle, key, wheel etc* tourner; (*mechanically etc*) faire tourner. **~ the key in the lock** ferme la porte à clef.

(b) *page* tourner; *mattress, steak, record* retourner. **to ~ one's ankle** se tordre la cheville; **it ~s my stomach** cela me soulève le cœur.

(c) (*direct*) *car, object, thoughts* tourner, diriger (*towards* vers); *gun, telescope etc* braquer (*on* sur); *eyes* tourner (*to* vers); *steps* diriger (*to* vers); *conversation* détourner (*to* sur). **to ~ a picture to the wall** tourner un tableau face au mur; **they ~ed hoses on them** ils les ont aspergés avec des lances d'incendie; **he ~ed his back on us** il nous a tourné le dos, (*fig*) il s'est mis à nous battre froid; **he ~ed his back on the past** il a tourné la page; **as soon as his back is ~ed** dès qu'il a le dos tourné; **without ~ing a hair** sans sourciller; (*fig*) **to ~ the other cheek** tendre l'autre joue; **he ~ed his hand to writing** il s'est mis à écrire; **he can ~ his hand to anything** il sait tout faire; (*fig*) **to ~ the tables** renverser les rôles (*on sb* aux dépens de qn); **they ~ed him against his father** ils l'ont monté contre son père.

(d) (*deflect*) *blow* détourner. **to ~ sb from doing** dissuader qn de faire.

(e) (*shape*) *wood, metal* tourner. **well-~ed phrase** expression *f* bien tournée.

(f) (*go past*) **to ~ the corner** tourner le coin de la rue, (*fig*) passer le moment critique; **he has ~ed 40** il a 40 ans passés; **it's ~ed 3 o'clock** il est 3 heures passées.

(g) (*change*) transformer (*sth into sth* qch en qch), changer (*sb into sth* qn en qch); (*translate*) traduire (*into* en); *milk* faire tourner. (*fig*) **it ~ed him into an old man** cela a fait de lui un vieillard; **actor ~ed writer** acteur devenu écrivain; **to ~ a book into a play/film** adapter un livre pour la scène/l'écran; **to ~ sth black** noircir qch; **to ~ a boat adrift** faire partir un bateau à la dérive.

3 *vi* **(a)** *[handle, wheel, key]* tourner; *[person]* (**~ round, ~ over**) se tourner (*to, towards* vers), (*~ right round*) se retourner; *[person, vehicle]* (*change course*: **~ off**) tourner (*into* dans; *towards* vers), (*reverse direction*: **~ round**) faire demi-tour; *[ship]* virer; *[road, river]* faire un coude; *[wind, milk]* tourner; *[tide]* changer de direction; *[weather]* changer; *[leaves]* jaunir. **he ~ed to look at me** il s'est retourné pour me regarder; **~ to face me** tourne-toi vers moi; (*Mil*) **right ~!** à droite, droite!; **to ~ (to the) left** tourner à gauche; **they ~ed and came back** ils ont fait demi-tour et ils sont revenus; (*Aut*) **there's nowhere to ~** il n'y a pas d'endroit où faire demi-tour; **the car ~ed into a side street** la voiture a tourné dans une rue transversale; **it ~s on its axis** cela tourne autour de son axe; (*fig*) **my head is ~ing** j'ai la tête qui tourne; **it all ~s on whether ...** tout dépend si ...; **to ~ tail (and run)** prendre ses jambes à son cou; **he would ~ in his grave if he knew ...** il se retournerait dans sa tombe s'il savait ...; **our luck has ~ed** la chance a tourné pour nous; **the conversation ~ed on ...** la conversation en est venue à ...; **to ~ on sb** attaquer qn; **to ~ against sb** se retourner contre qn; (*fig*) **he didn't know which way to ~** il ne savait plus où donner de la tête; **he ~ed to me for advice** il s'est tourné vers moi pour me demander conseil; **he ~ed to politics** il s'est tourné vers la politique; **he ~ed to drink** il s'est mis à boire.

(b) (*change*) **to ~ into sth** se changer en qch; (*fig*) **he ~ed into an old man overnight** il est

devenu vieux en l'espace d'une nuit; **his admiration ~ed to scorn** son admiration s'est changée en mépris; **to ~ black** noircir; **to ~ angry** se mettre en colère; **to ~ communist/professional** devenir communiste/professionnel.
turn aside 1 *vi* se détourner (*from* de). **2** *vt sep* détourner.
turn away 1 *vi* se détourner (*from* de). **2** *vt sep* **(a)** *object* détourner. **(b)** (*reject*) *person* (*gen*) renvoyer; *beggar* chasser; *offer, business, customers* refuser.
turn back 1 *vi* (*in journey etc*) faire demi-tour; (*to page*) revenir (*to* à). **2** *vt sep* **(a)** *bedclothes, collar* rabattre. **(b)** (*send back*) *person, vehicle* faire faire demi-tour à. **(c)** *clock, hands of clock* reculer (*to* jusqu'à). (*fig*) **to ~ the clock back 50 years** revenir en arrière de 50 ans.
turn down *vt sep* **(a)** *bedclothes, collar* rabattre. **to ~ down the corner of the page** corner la page. **(b)** (*reduce*) *gas, heat, music* baisser. **(c)** (*refuse*) *offer, suitor* rejeter; *candidate, volunteer* refuser.
turn in 1 *vi* **(a)** *[car, person]* tourner (*to* dans). **(b)** (*: *go to bed*) aller se coucher. **2** *vt sep* (*: *hand over*) *object* rendre (*to* à); *wanted man* livrer (à la police); *stolen goods* apporter à la police.
turn off 1 *vi* **(a)** *[person, vehicle]* tourner. **(b)** *[automatic heater etc]* s'éteindre. **2** *vt sep water, electricity, gas, radio, tap* fermer; *light* éteindre; (*at main*) *all services* couper; *engine* arrêter. (*fig*) **it ~ed me off‡** ça m'a totalement rebuté.
turn on 1 *vi [automatic heater etc]* s'allumer. **2** *vt sep tap* ouvrir; *water* faire couler; *gas, electricity, light, radio, heater* allumer; (*at main*) *all services* brancher; *engine, machine* mettre en marche. (*fig*) **that really ~s me on‡** ça me fait vraiment qch*.
turn out 1 *vi* **(a)** (*go out*) sortir; *[troops etc]* aller au rassemblement. **they ~ed out to see her** ils sont venus la voir. **(b)** (*prove to be*) s'avérer; *[person]* se révéler. **it ~ed out that...** il s'est avéré que...; **it ~ed out to be true** cela s'est avéré juste; **he ~ed out to be a good student** il s'est révélé bon étudiant; **as it ~ed out** en l'occurrence; **everything will ~ out all right** tout finira bien. **2** *vt sep* **(a)** *light, gas* éteindre. **(b)** (*empty out*) *pockets, contents* vider (*of* de); *room, cupboard* nettoyer à fond; *cake etc* démouler (*on to* sur; *of* de); (*expel*) *person* mettre à la porte; *tenant* expulser; *employee* renvoyer. **(c)** *troops, police* envoyer. **(d)** (*produce*) *goods* produire; (*fig*) *teachers, salesmen etc* former. (*fig*) **well ~ed out** élégant.
turn over 1 *vi* **(a)** *[person, car etc]* se retourner; *[car engine]* tourner au ralenti. **to ~ over and over** faire des tours sur soi-même; **my stomach ~ed over** (*nausea*) j'ai eu l'estomac retourné; (*fright etc*) mon sang n'a fait qu'un tour. **(b)** (*in reading*) tourner la page. (*in letter etc*) **please ~ over** (*abbr* **PTO**) tournez s'il vous plaît (*abbr* T.S.V.P.). **2** *vt sep* **(a)** *page* tourner; *mattress, patient, card* retourner. (*fig*) **to ~ over an idea in one's mind** retourner une idée dans sa tête. **(b)** (*hand over*) *object* rendre (*to* à); *person* livrer (*to* à).
turn round 1 *vi [person]* se retourner; (*change direction*) *[person, vehicle]* faire demi-tour; (*rotate*) *[object]* tourner. **to ~ round and round** tournoyer sur soi-même. **2** *vt sep* (*gen*) tourner; *vehicle, ship etc* faire faire demi-tour à.
turn up 1 *vi* **(a)** (*arrive*) arriver; (*be found*) être retrouvé; *[playing card]* sortir. **sth will ~ up** on va bien trouver qch. **(b)** (*point upwards*) remonter. **his nose ~s up** il a le nez retroussé. **2** *vt sep* **(a)** *collar, sleeve* remonter. **~ed-up nose** nez *m* retroussé; (*fig: stop*) **~ it up!‡** la ferme!‡ **(b)** *buried object* déterrer; (*find*) *lost object etc* dénicher. **(c)** *heat, gas, television etc* mettre plus fort; (*Rad, TV*) *volume* augmenter.

♦ **turncoat** *n* renégat(e) *m(f)*. ♦ **turning 1** *n* (*side road*) route *f* (*or* rue *f*) latérale; (*fork*) embranchement *m*; (*bend*) coude *m*; **the second ~ing on the left** la deuxième à gauche; **2** *adj* (*fig*) **~ing point** moment *m* décisif (*in* de). ♦ **turnoff** *n* (*in road*) embranchement *m*. ♦ **turnout** *n* **(a)** (*attendance*) **there was a good/bad ~out** beaucoup de gens/peu de gens sont venus; **(b)** (*clean*) **to have a good ~out of a room** *etc* nettoyer une pièce à fond. ♦ **turnover** *n* **(a)** (*Comm etc*) *[stock, goods]* roulement *m*; (*total business*) chiffre *m* d'affaires; **he sold them cheaply hoping for a quick ~over** il les a vendus bon marché pour les écouler rapidement; **a high ~over of staff** de fréquents changements de personnel; **(b)** (*Culin*) **apple** *etc* **~over** chausson *m* aux pommes *etc*. ♦ **turnpike** *n* (*US*) autoroute *f* à péage. ♦ **turnstile** *n* tourniquet *m* (*barrière*). ♦ **turntable** *n [record player]* platine *f*; (*for trains, cars etc*) plaque *f* tournante. ♦ **turn-up** *n [trousers]* revers *m*.
turnip ['tɜːnɪp] *n* navet *m*.
turpentine ['tɜːpəntaɪn] *n* (*abbr* **turps***) térébenthine *f*. **~ substitute** white-spirit *m*.
turquoise ['tɜːkwɔɪz] **1** *n* (*stone*) turquoise *f*; (*colour*) turquoise *m*. **2** *adj ring* de turquoise; (*colour*) turquoise *inv*.
turret ['tʌrɪt] *n* tourelle *f*.
turtle ['tɜːtl] *n* tortue *f* marine. **~ soup** consommé *m* à la tortue; (*fig*) **to turn ~** chavirer. ♦ **turtledove** *n* tourterelle *f*. ♦ **turtlenecked** *adj* à col montant.
tusk [tʌsk] *n* défense *f* (*d'éléphant etc*).
tussle ['tʌsl] **1** *n* (*struggle*) lutte *f* (*for* pour). **to have a ~ with sb** se bagarrer* avec qn. **2** *vi* se battre (*with sb* avec qn; *for sth* pour qch). **to ~ over sth** se disputer qch.
tussock ['tʌsək] *n* touffe *f* d'herbe.
tutor ['tjuːtər] **1** *n* (*private teacher*) précepteur *m*, -trice *f* (*in* de); (*Brit Univ*) ≃ directeur *m*, -trice *f* d'études; (*US Univ*) ≃ assistant(e) *m(f)* (*en faculté*). **2** *vt*: **to ~ sb in Latin** donner des cours particuliers de latin à qn. ♦ **tutorial** *n* (*Univ*) travaux *mpl* pratiques (*in* de).
tuxedo [tʌk'siːdəʊ] *n* (*US*) smoking *m*.
TV* [ˌtiː'viː] *n* (*abbr of* **television**) télé* *f*.
twaddle ['twɒdl] *n* balivernes *fpl*, fadaises *fpl*.
twang [twæŋ] **1** *n [wire etc]* son *m* (de corde pincée); (*in voice*) nasillement *m*. **to speak with a ~** parler du nez. **2** *vt guitar etc* pincer les cordes de. **3** *vi [wire]* vibrer.
tweak [twiːk] *vt ear, nose* tordre; *rope, hair* tirer.
twee* [twiː] *adj* (*pej*) **it's rather ~** ça fait un peu maniéré.
tweed [twiːd] *n* tweed *m*. (*suit*) **~s** costume *m* de tweed.
tweet [twiːt] **1** *n* (*also* **~-~**) gazouillis *m*. **2** *vi* gazouiller.
tweezers ['twiːzəz] *npl* pince *f* à épiler.
twelve [twelv] *adj, n* douze (*m*) *inv*; *for phrases V* **six.** ♦ **twelfth** *adj, n* douzième (*mf*); (*fraction*) douzième *m*; **Twelfth Night** la fête des Rois.
twenty ['twentɪ] *adj, n* vingt (*m*). **about ~** une vingtaine; **about ~ books** une vingtaine de livres; *for phrases V* **sixty.** ♦ **twentieth** *adj, n* vingtième (*mf*); (*fraction*) vingtième *m*.
twerp‡ [twɜːp] *n* andouille‡ *f*, idiot(e) *m(f)*.
twice [twaɪs] *adv* deux fois. **~ as long as** deux fois plus long que; **she is ~ your age** elle a deux fois votre âge; **~ a week** deux fois par semaine.
twiddle ['twɪdl] *vti* (*also* **~ with**: *gen*) tripoter. (*fig*) **to ~ one's thumbs** se tourner les pouces.
twig¹ [twɪg] *n* brindille *f*.
twig²* [twɪg] *vti* (*understand*) piger*, saisir.
twilight ['twaɪlaɪt] *n* (*evening*) crépuscule *m* (*also fig*); (*morning*) aube *f* naissante. **at ~** au crépuscule, à l'aube naissante; (*half light*) **in the ~** dans la pénombre.

twill [twɪl] *n* (*Tex*) sergé *m*.

twin [twɪn] **1** *n* jumeau *m*, -elle *f*. **2** *adj son, brother* jumeau; *daughter, sister* jumelle; *town* jumelé. ~ **beds** lits *mpl* jumeaux. **3** *vt town etc* jumeler (*with* avec). ♦ **twin-engined** *adj* bimoteur. ♦ **twinning** *n* jumelage *m*.

twine [twaɪn] **1** *n* ficelle *f*. **2** *vt* enrouler (*round* autour de). **3** *vi* s'enrouler.

twinge [twɪndʒ] *n*: ~ **(of pain)** élancement *m*; **to feel a** ~ **of sadness** *or* **regret** avoir un pincement au cœur; **a** ~ **of conscience** *or* **remorse** un petit remords.

twinkle ['twɪŋkl] **1** *vi [star, lights]* scintiller; *[eyes]* pétiller. **2** *n* scintillement *m*; pétillement *m*. **... he said with a** ~ **in his eye** ... dit-il avec un pétillement dans les yeux. ♦ **twinkling 1** *adj* scintillant; pétillant; **2** *n*: **in the twinkling of an eye** en un clin d'œil.

twirl [twɜːl] **1** *n [body]* tournoiement *m*; (*in writing*) fioriture *f*. **2** *vi* (~ **round**) *[dancer etc]* tournoyer. **3** *vt* (~ **round**) *cane, lasso* faire tournoyer; *handle* faire pivoter; *moustache* tortiller.

twirp* [twɜːp] *n* = **twerp***.

twist [twɪst] **1** *n* **(a)** (*Med*) foulure *f*. **to give sth a** ~ (*handle*) faire tourner qch; (*wire*) tordre qch; **with a quick** ~ **of the wrist** d'un rapide tour de poignet. **(b)** (*in wire etc*) tortillon *m*; *[events]* tournure *f*. **a** ~ **of** *yarn* une torsade de; *tobacco* un rouleau de; *paper* un tortillon de; *lemon* un zeste de; **road full of** ~**s and turns** route qui fait des zigzags; (*fig*) **to give a new** ~ **to sth** donner un tour nouveau à qch; (*fig*) **to go round the** ~* devenir dingue*. **2** *vt* (*gen*) tordre; (~ **together**) *strands etc* entortiller (*into sth* pour en faire qch); (*coil*) enrouler (*round* autour de); (*turn*) *knob, handle, top* tourner; (*fig*) *meaning, facts, truth* déformer. *[rope etc]* **to get** ~**ed** s'entortiller; **to** ~ **one's ankle** se fouler la cheville; **to** ~ **one's neck** attraper le torticolis; **to** ~ **sb's arm** tordre le bras à qn, (*fig*) forcer la main à qn. **3** *vi [rope etc]* s'enrouler (*round* autour de). *[road, motorcycle etc]* **to** ~ **and turn** zigzaguer.

twist off *vt sep branch* enlever en tordant; *bottle-top* enlever en dévissant.

twist round *vi [person]* se retourner.

♦ **twisted** *adj* (*gen*) tordu; *rope, cord* entortillé; *wrist, ankle* foulé; *socks* tirebouchonnant; (*fig*) *logic* faux; *mind* tordu. ♦ **twister*** *n* escroc *m*. ♦ **twisting 1** *n* (*gen*) torsion *f*; *[meaning]* déformation *f*; **2** *adj path* sinueux.

twit[1] [twɪt] *vt* (*tease*) taquiner (*about* à propos de).

twit[2]* [twɪt] *n* idiot(e) *m(f)*, crétin(e) *m(f)*.

twitch [twɪtʃ] **1** *n* (*nervous*) tic *m* (*in sth* à qch); (*pull on rope etc*) saccade *f*. **to give sth a** ~ tirer d'un coup sec sur qch. **2** *vi [person, animal, hands]* avoir un mouvement convulsif, (*permanent condition*) avoir un tic; *[face, muscle]* se convulser; *[nose, tail, ears]* remuer. **3** *vt rope etc* tirer d'un coup sec. **it** ~**ed its ears** ses oreilles ont remué.

twitter ['twɪtəʳ] **1** *vi [bird]* gazouiller; *[person]* parler avec agitation (*about* de). **2** *n [birds]* gazouillis *m*. (*fig*) **to be in a** ~* être tout sens dessus dessous* (*about* à cause de).

two [tuː] *adj, n* deux (*m*) *inv*. **to cut in** ~ couper en deux; ~ **by** ~ *take, do* deux par deux; *climb steps* deux à deux; **in** ~**s** par deux; **in** ~**s and threes** *sell* deux ou trois à la fois; *arrive* par petits groupes; **they're** ~ **of a kind** ils se ressemblent; (*fig*) **to put** ~ **and** ~ **together** faire le rapport; ~**'s company** on est mieux à deux; *V* **one**, *and for other phrases V* **six**. ♦ **two-edged** *adj* (*lit, fig*) à double tranchant. ♦ **two-faced** *adj* (*fig*) hypocrite. ♦ **twofold 1** *adj* double; **2** *adv* au double. ♦ **two-legged** *adj* bipède. ♦ **two-party** *adj* (*Pol*) bipartite. ♦ **two-piece suit** *n* (*man's*) costume *m* deux-pièces; (*woman's*) tailleur *m*. ♦ **two-ply** *adj wool* à deux fils. ♦ **two-seater** *n* (*car*) voiture *f or* (*plane*) avion *m* (*plane*) à deux places. ♦ **twosome** *n*: **in a** ~**some** à deux. ♦ **two-stroke** *n* (*engine*) deux-temps *m inv*; (*mixture/fuel*) mélange *m*/carburant *m* pour deux-temps. ♦ **two-time*** *vt* doubler*, tromper. ♦ **two-way** *adj switch* à deux départs; *street* à double sens; *traffic* dans les deux sens; **a** ~**-way radio** un émetteur-récepteur. ♦ **two-wheeler** *n* deux-roues *m inv*.

tycoon [taɪ'kuːn] *n* gros homme *m* d'affaires. **oil** ~ magnat *m* du pétrole.

type [taɪp] **1** *n* **(a)** (*gen, Bio, Soc etc*) type *m*; (*sort*) genre *m*, espèce *f*, sorte *f*; (*make: of machine, coffee etc*) marque *f*; *[aircraft, car]* modèle *m*. **true to** ~ conforme au type; **gruyère-**~ **cheese** fromage genre gruyère*; **what** ~ **do you want?** vous en (*or* le *etc*) voulez de quelle sorte?; **what** ~ **of man is he?** quel genre d'homme est-ce?; **you know the** ~ **of thing I mean** vous voyez ce que je veux dire; **he's not my** ~* il n'est pas mon genre*; **it's my** ~ **of film** c'est le genre de film que j'aime; (*person*) **an odd** ~* un drôle de numéro*. **(b)** (*Typ*) (*one letter*) caractère *m*; (*letters collectively: print*) caractères, type *m*. **to set** ~ composer; **in large/small** ~ en gros/petits caractères; **in italic** ~ en italiques.

2 *vt* **(a)** *blood sample etc* classifier. (*Theat etc*) **he is** ~**d as ...** on ne lui donne plus que les rôles de ... . **(b)** (~ **out**) *letter etc* taper (à la machine); (~ **out,** ~ **up**) *notes* taper.

3 *vi* taper à la machine.

♦ **type-cast** *adj* (*Theat etc*) **to be** ~**-cast** se voir toujours attribuer les mêmes rôles. ♦ **typeface** *n* œil *m* de caractère. ♦ **typescript** *n* manuscrit *m* dactylographié. ♦ **typeset** *vt* composer. ♦ **typesetter** *n* compositeur *m*, -trice *f*. ♦ **typesetting** *n* composition *f*. ♦ **typewriter** *n* machine *f* à écrire. ♦ **typewriting** *n* dactylographie *f*. ♦ **typewritten** *adj* tapé à la machine, dactylographié. ♦ **typing 1** *n* (*skill*) dactylo *f*; **pages of typing** pages *fpl* dactylographiées; **2** *adj lesson, teacher* de dactylo; *paper* machine *inv*; **typing error** faute *f* de frappe; **typing pool** dactylo* *f*. ♦ **typist** *n* dactylo *mf*. ♦ **typography** *n* typographie *f*. ♦ **typology** *n* typologie *f*.

typhoid ['taɪfɔɪd] *n* typhoïde *f*.

typhoon [taɪ'fuːn] *n* typhon *m*.

typhus ['taɪfəs] *n* typhus *m*.

typical ['tɪpɪkəl] *adj* (*gen*) typique, caractéristique (*of* de); *case, example* typique, type *inv*. **a** ~ **day in spring** un jour de printemps comme il y en a tant; **the** ~ **Frenchman** le Français type *or* typique; **with** ~ **modesty he said ...** avec sa modestie habituelle il a dit ...; **that's** ~ **of him!** c'est bien lui!; (*iro*) ~**!** ça ne m'étonne pas! ♦ **typically** *adv* typiquement; **he was** ~**ly rude** il s'est conduit avec sa grossièreté habituelle. ♦ **typify** *vt [thing]* être caractéristique de; *[person]* avoir le type même de.

tyrant ['taɪərənt] *n* tyran *m*. ♦ **tyrannic(al)** *adj* tyrannique. ♦ **tyrannize** *vi*: **to tyrannize over sb** tyranniser qn. ♦ **tyranny** *n* tyrannie *f*.

tyre ['taɪəʳ] **1** *n* pneu *m*. **2** *adj*: ~ **gauge** manomètre *m* (pour pneus); ~ **lever** démonte-pneu *m*; ~ **pressure** pression *f* de gonflage.

tyro ['taɪərəʊ] *n* novice *mf*.

tzar [zɑːʳ] *n* = **tsar**.

U

U, u [juː] **1** *n* *(letter)* U, u *m*. **2** *adj* (*: *upper-class*) U distingué; **non-U** vulgaire. ♦ **U-bend** *n* coude *m* (*angle*). ♦ **U-turn** *n* (*Aut*) demi-tour *m*; (*fig, Pol*) volte-face *f inv*.
ubiquitous [juːˈbɪkwɪtəs] *adj* doué d'ubiquité. ♦ **ubiquity** *n* ubiquité *f*.
udder [ˈʌdəʳ] *n* pis *m*, mamelle *f*.
ugh [ɜːh] *excl* pouah!
ugly [ˈʌglɪ] *adj* (*gen*) laid; *custom, vice etc* répugnant; *situation* moche*; *war* brutal; *expression, look* menaçant; *wound, rumour, word* vilain (*before n*). **it is an ~ sight** ce n'est pas beau à voir; **~ customer*** sale individu *m*; (*fig*) **~ duckling** vilain petit canard *m*. ♦ **ugliness** *n* laideur *f*.
ulcer [ˈʌlsəʳ] *n* ulcère *m*. ♦ **ulcerated** *or* ♦ **ulcerous** *adj* ulcéreux.
Ulster [ˈʌlstəʳ] *n* Ulster *m*.
ulterior [ʌlˈtɪərɪəʳ] *adj* ultérieur. **~ motive** motif *m* secret.
ultimate [ˈʌltɪmɪt] *adj* (*gen*) ultime; *destination, outcome* final; *authority* suprême; *principle, cause* fondamental. (*Mil*) **the ~ deterrent** l'ultime moyen de dissuasion; (*fig*) **the ~ (in) luxury** le summum du luxe; **the ~ (in) selfishness** le comble de l'égoïsme. ♦ **ultimately** *adv* (*at last*) finalement; (*eventually*) par la suite; (*in the last analysis*) en dernière analyse. ♦ **ultimatum** *n, pl* **-ta** ultimatum *m*; **to issue an ultimatum** adresser un ultimatum (*to* à). ♦ **ultimo** *adv* (*Comm*) du mois dernier.
ultra... [ˈʌltrə] *pref* ultra..., hyper... . ♦ **ultrafashionable** *adj* du tout dernier cri. ♦ **ultrahigh** *adj*: **~high frequency** très haute fréquence *f*. ♦ **ultramarine** *adj, n* bleu outremer (*m*) *inv*. ♦ **ultramodern** *adj* ultramoderne. ♦ **ultrasensitive** *adj* hypersensible. ♦ **ultrashort** *adj* ultra-court. ♦ **ultrasonic** *adj* ultrasonique. ♦ **ultraviolet** *adj* ultra-violet.
umber [ˈʌmbəʳ] *adj, n* terre (*f*) d'ombre.
umbilical [ˌʌmbɪˈlaɪkəl] *adj* ombilical. **~ cord** cordon *m* ombilical.
umbrage [ˈʌmbrɪdʒ] *n*: **to take ~** prendre ombrage (*at* de).
umbrella [ʌmˈbrelə] **1** *n* parapluie *m*. **beach ~** parasol *m*; (*Mil*) **air ~** écran *m* de protection aérienne; (*fig*) **under the ~ of** sous les auspices *mpl* de. **2** *adj*: **~ pine** pin *m* parasol; **~ stand** porte-parapluies *m inv*.
umlaut [ˈʊmlaʊt] *n* tréma *m*.
umpire [ˈʌmpaɪəʳ] (*Sport*) **1** *n* arbitre *m*. **2** *vt* arbitrer. **3** *vi* être l'arbitre.
umpteen* [ˈʌmptiːn] *adj* je ne sais combien de. ♦ **umpteenth*** *adj* énième.
unabashed [ˈʌnəˈbæʃt] *adj* nullement décontenancé.
unabated [ˈʌnəˈbeɪtɪd] *adj* non diminué.
unable [ˈʌnˈeɪbl] *adj*: **to be ~ to do** (*have no means, power, opportunity*) être incapable de faire, ne pas pouvoir faire; (*not know how to*) ne pas savoir faire.
unabridged [ˈʌnəˈbrɪdʒd] *adj edition* intégral.
unacceptable [ˈʌnəkˈseptəbl] *adj suggestion* inacceptable; *amount, extent* inadmissible.
unaccompanied [ˈʌnəˈkʌmpənɪd] *adj child, luggage* non accompagné; *singing* sans accompagnement; *instrument* seul.
unaccountable [ˈʌnəˈkaʊntəbl] *adj* inexplicable. ♦ **unaccountably** *adv* inexplicablement. ♦ **unaccounted** *adj*: **they are still unaccounted for** ils n'ont toujours pas été retrouvés.
unaccustomed [ˈʌnəˈkʌstəmd] *adj slowness etc* inhabituel, inaccoutumé. **to be ~ to sth/to doing** ne pas avoir l'habitude de qch/de faire.
unacquainted [ˈʌnəˈkweɪntɪd] *adj*: **to be ~ with** ignorer.
unadorned [ˈʌnəˈdɔːnd] *adj* tout simple; (*fig*) *facts* tout nu.
unadulterated [ˈʌnəˈdʌltəreɪtɪd] *adj* (*gen*) pur; *wine* non frelaté; (*fig*) *bliss, nonsense* pur et simple.
unaffected [ˈʌnəˈfektɪd] *adj* **(a)** (*sincere*) *person* naturel, simple; *behaviour* non affecté; *style* sans recherche, simple. **(b)** non affecté (*by* par); (*emotionally*) non touché (*by* par). ♦ **unaffectedly** *adv* sans affectation.
unafraid [ˈʌnəˈfreɪd] *adj* qui n'a pas peur (*of* de).
unaided [ˈʌnˈeɪdɪd] *adj* sans aide, tout seul. **his own ~ efforts** ses propres efforts.
unalloyed [ˈʌnəˈlɔɪd] *adj* (*fig*) sans mélange.
unalterable [ʌnˈɒltərəbl] *adj rule* invariable; *fact* certain; *friendship* inaltérable. ♦ **unaltered** *adj* inchangé.
unambiguous [ˈʌnæmˈbɪgjʊəs] *adj* non ambigu. ♦ **unambiguously** *adv* sans ambiguïté.
unambitious [ˈʌnæmˈbɪʃəs] *adj person* peu ambitieux; *plan* modeste.
un-American [ˈʌnəˈmerɪkən] *adj* antiaméricain.
unanimous [juːˈnænɪməs] *adj group, decision* unanime (*in sth* pour qch; *in doing* à faire); *vote* à l'unanimité. ♦ **unanimity** *n* unanimité *f*. ♦ **unanimously** *adv* à l'unanimité.
unannounced [ˈʌnəˈnaʊnst] *adj* sans se faire annoncer.
unanswerable [ʌnˈɑːnsərəbl] *adj question* à laquelle il est impossible de répondre; *argument* irréfutable. ♦ **unanswered** *adj letter, question* sans réponse; *criticism* non réfuté.
unappetizing [ˈʌnˈæpɪtaɪzɪŋ] *adj* peu appétissant.
unappreciated [ˈʌnəˈpriːʃɪeɪtɪd] *adj person* méconnu; *offer, help* non apprécié. ♦ **unappreciative** *adj* indifférent (*of* à).
unapproachable [ˈʌnəˈprəʊtʃəbl] *adj* d'un abord difficile.
unarmed [ˈʌnˈɑːmd] *adj person* non armé; *combat* sans armes.
unashamed [ˈʌnəˈʃeɪmd] *adj pleasure, greed* effronté. **he was quite ~ about it** il n'en avait absolument pas honte.
unasked [ˈʌnˈɑːskt] *adj do* spontanément; *arrive* sans y avoir été invité.
unassisted [ˈʌnəˈsɪstɪd] *adj* sans aide.
unassuming [ˈʌnəˈsjuːmɪŋ] *adj* modeste.
unattached [ˈʌnəˈtætʃt] *adj part etc* non attaché; (*fig*) *person, group* indépendant; (*not married etc*) sans attaches.
unattainable [ˈʌnəˈteɪnəbl] *adj* inaccessible.
unattended [ˈʌnəˈtendɪd] *adj* (*not looked after*) *luggage* abandonné; *shop, person* laissé sans surveillance.
unattractive [ˈʌnəˈtræktɪv] *adj thing* peu attrayant; *person* déplaisant.
unauthorized [ˈʌnˈɔːθəraɪzd] *adj* non autorisé.

unavailable ['ʌnə'veɪləbl] *adj* (*Comm*) *article* épuisé; *person* qui n'est pas disponible.
unavailing ['ʌnə'veɪlɪŋ] *adj effort* vain, inutile.
unavoidable [ˌʌnə'vɔɪdəbl] *adj* inévitable (*that* que +*subj*). ◆ **unavoidably** *adv slow, large* inévitablement; *prevented, delayed* malencontreusement.
unaware ['ʌnə'wɛəʳ] *adj*: **to be ~ of sth/that ...** ignorer qch/que ... . ◆ **unawares** *adv do sth* inconsciemment; **to catch** *or* **take sb ~s** prendre qn au dépourvu.
unbalanced ['ʌn'bælənst] *adj* déséquilibré.
unbandage ['ʌn'bændɪdʒ] *vt* débander.
unbearable [ʌn'bɛərəbl] *adj* insupportable. ◆ **unbearably** *adv* insupportablement.
unbeatable ['ʌn'biːtəbl] *adj* imbattable. ◆ **unbeaten** *adj army, player* invaincu; *record, price* non battu.
unbecoming ['ʌnbɪ'kʌmɪŋ] *adj garment* peu seyant; *behaviour* malséant.
unbeknown(st) ['ʌnbɪ'nəʊn(st)] *adv*: **~ to** à l'insu de.
unbelievable [ˌʌnbɪ'liːvəbl] *adj* incroyable (*that* que +*subj*). ◆ **unbelievably** *adv* incroyablement. ◆ **unbeliever** *n* incrédule *mf*. ◆ **unbelieving** *adj* incrédule. ◆ **unbelievingly** *adv* d'un air incrédule.
unbend ['ʌn'bend] *pret, ptp* **unbent 1** *vt pipe etc* redresser. **2** *vi* (*fig*) *[person]* se détendre. ◆ **unbending** *adj* (*fig*) inflexible.
unbias(s)ed ['ʌn'baɪəst] *adj* impartial.
unbidden ['ʌn'bɪdn] *adj* sans y avoir été invité.
unbleached ['ʌn'bliːtʃt] *adj linen* écru.
unblemished [ʌn'blemɪʃt] *adj* sans tache.
unblock ['ʌn'blɒk] *vt pipe* déboucher; *road, harbour* dégager.
unblushing [ʌn'blʌʃɪŋ] *adj* effronté. ◆ **unblushingly** *adv* sans rougir.
unbolt ['ʌn'bəʊlt] *vt door* déverrouiller.
unborn ['ʌn'bɔːn] *adj child* qui n'est pas encore né; *generation* à venir, futur.
unbounded [ʌn'baʊndɪd] *adj* sans borne.
unbreakable ['ʌn'breɪkəbl] *adj* incassable.
unbridled [ʌn'braɪdld] *adj* (*fig*) débridé.
unbroken ['ʌn'brəʊkən] *adj* (*gen*) intact; *line* continu, (*Genealogy*) direct; (*fig*) *promise* tenu; *series, silence, sleep* ininterrompu; *record* non battu; *horse* indompté. **his spirit remained ~** il ne s'est pas découragé.
unburden [ʌn'bɜːdn] *vt*: **to ~ o.s.** s'épancher (*to sb* avec qn).
unbusinesslike [ʌn'bɪznɪslaɪk] *adj trader* qui n'a pas le sens des affaires; *transaction* irrégulier; (*fig*) *person* qui manque d'organisation; *report* peu méthodique.
unbutton ['ʌn'bʌtn] *vt* déboutonner.
uncalled-for [ʌn'kɔːldfɔːʳ] *adj criticism* injustifié; *remark* déplacé. **that was quite ~** vous n'aviez nullement besoin de faire (*or* dire) ça.
uncanny [ʌn'kænɪ] *adj sound, atmosphere* étrange, inquiétant; *resemblance, knack* troublant. ◆ **uncannily** *adv silent, cold* sinistrement; *alike* étrangement.
uncared-for ['ʌn'kɛədfɔːʳ] *adj garden, building, child* laissé à l'abandon; *appearance* négligé.
unceasing [ʌn'siːsɪŋ] *adj* incessant. ◆ **unceasingly** *adv* sans cesse.
unceremonious ['ʌnˌserɪ'məʊnɪəs] *adj* brusque. ◆ **unceremoniously** *adv* sans cérémonie.
uncertain [ʌn'sɜːtn] *adj* (*gen*) incertain (*of, about* de); *temper* inégal. **it is ~ whether** on ne sait pas exactement si; **he is ~ whether** il ne sait pas au juste si; **in no ~ terms** en des termes on ne peut plus clairs. ◆ **uncertainly** *adv* d'une manière hésitante. ◆ **uncertainty** *n* incertitude *f*; (*doubts*) doutes *mpl*.
uncertificated ['ʌnsə'tɪfɪkeɪtɪd] *adj* non diplômé.
unchallengeable ['ʌn'tʃælɪndʒəbl] *adj* incontestable. ◆ **unchallenged** *adj leader, rights* incontesté; *statement, figures* non contesté; (*Jur*) *witness* non récusé; **to let sth go unchallenged** laisser passer qch sans protester.
unchangeable [ʌn'tʃeɪndʒəbl] *adj* invariable. ◆ **unchanged** *adj* inchangé. ◆ **unchanging** *adj* invariable.
uncharitable [ʌn'tʃærɪtəbl] *adj* peu charitable.
uncharted ['ʌn'tʃɑːtɪd] *adj* inexploré.
unchecked ['ʌn'tʃekt] *adj* **(a)** (*unrestrained*) *anger* non maîtrisé. **to advance ~** avancer sans rencontrer d'opposition; **to continue ~** continuer sans la moindre opposition. **(b)** (*not verified*) *figures, statement* non vérifié; *typescript* non relu.
unchristian ['ʌn'krɪstjən] *adj* peu chrétien.
uncivilized ['ʌn'sɪvɪlaɪzd] *adj* (*gen*) barbare; *amount, time etc* impossible*.
unclaimed ['ʌn'kleɪmd] *adj* non réclamé.
uncle ['ʌŋkl] *n* oncle *m*. **yes, ~** oui, mon oncle.
unclean ['ʌn'kliːn] *adj* malpropre; (*fig*) impur.
unclear [ˌʌn'klɪəʳ] *adj* qui n'est pas clair. **it is ~ whether ...** il n'est pas clair si ... .
unclouded ['ʌn'klaʊdɪd] *adj* (*lit, fig*) sans nuages.
uncoil ['ʌn'kɔɪl] **1** *vt* dérouler. **2** *vi* se dérouler.
uncollected ['ʌnkə'lektɪd] *adj tax* non perçu; *bus fare* non encaissé; *luggage, lost property* non réclamé; *refuse* non ramassé.
uncoloured ['ʌn'kʌləd] *adj* non coloré; (*fig*) *description* objectif. (*fig*) **~ by** non déformé par.
uncombed ['ʌn'kəʊmd] *adj* non peigné.
uncomfortable [ʌn'kʌmfətəbl] *adj thing* inconfortable; *afternoon* désagréable. *[person]* **to be** *or* **feel ~** ne pas être à l'aise, (*uneasy*) être mal à l'aise (*about sth* au sujet de qch); **this chair is very ~** ce fauteuil n'est pas du tout confortable; **I had an ~ feeling that** je ne pouvais pas m'empêcher de penser que; **to make things ~ for sb** créer des ennuis à qn; **to have an ~ time** passer un moment pénible. ◆ **uncomfortably** *adv hot* désagréablement; *seated, dressed* inconfortablement; (*uneasily*) *think* avec une certaine inquiétude; *say* avec gêne; *near, similar etc* un peu trop.
uncommitted ['ʌnkə'mɪtɪd] *adj* (*gen*) non engagé; *attitude, country* neutraliste.
uncommon [ʌn'kɒmən] *adj* (*unusual*) rare, peu commun; (*outstanding*) rare, extraordinaire. **it is not ~ that** il n'est pas rare que +*subj*. ◆ **uncommonly** *adv* (*extremely*) extraordinairement; **not ~ly** assez souvent.
uncommunicative ['ʌnkə'mjuːnɪkətɪv] *adj* peu communicatif.
uncomplaining ['ʌnkəm'pleɪnɪŋ] *adj* patient, résigné. ◆ **uncomplainingly** *adv* sans se plaindre.
uncomplicated [ʌn'kɒmplɪkeɪtɪd] *adj* peu compliqué, simple.
uncomplimentary ['ʌnˌkɒmplɪ'mentərɪ] *adj* peu flatteur.
uncompromising [ʌn'kɒmprəmaɪzɪŋ] *adj person* intransigeant; *honesty* absolu.
unconcealed ['ʌnkən'siːld] *adj* non dissimulé.
unconcern ['ʌnkən'sɜːn] *n* sang-froid *m*; (*lack of interest*) indifférence *f*. ◆ **unconcerned** *adj* (*unworried*) imperturbable (*by* devant); (*unaffected*) indifférent (*by* à). ◆ **unconcernedly** *adv* sans s'inquiéter; avec indifférence.
unconditional ['ʌnkən'dɪʃənl] *adj* (*gen*) inconditionnel; *surrender* sans condition. ◆ **unconditionally** *adv* inconditionnellement; sans condition.
unconfirmed ['ʌnkən'fɜːmd] *adj* non confirmé.
uncongenial ['ʌnkən'dʒiːnɪəl] *adj person* peu sympathique; *work, place* peu agréable.
unconnected ['ʌnkə'nektɪd] *adj events, facts* sans rapport; *languages* sans connexion; *ideas* décousu; (*Elec*) débranché.
unconscious [ʌn'kɒnʃəs] **1** *adj* **(a)** (*Med*) sans

connaissance. **to be ~ for 3 hours** rester sans connaissance pendant 3 heures; **to become ~** perdre connaissance; **knocked ~** assommé. **(b)** (*unaware*) *person, humour, desire* inconscient (*of* de). **2** *n* (*Psych*) inconscient *m*. ♦ **unconsciously** *adv* inconsciemment, sans s'en rendre compte.

unconstitutional [ˈʌnˌkɒnstɪˈtjuːʃənl] *adj* anticonstitutionnel.

uncontested [ˈʌnkənˈtestɪd] *adj* incontesté; (*Parl*) *seat* non disputé.

uncontrollable [ˈʌnkənˈtrəʊləbl] *adj child, animal* indiscipliné; *desire, emotion* irrésistible; *epidemic, inflation* qui ne peut être enrayé. **to have an ~ temper** ne pas savoir se contrôler. ♦ **uncontrollably** *adv skid etc* sans pouvoir se reprendre; *feel* irrésistiblement; **to laugh uncontrollably** avoir le fou rire. ♦ **uncontrolled** *adj emotion* non contenu; *price rises* effréné; *inflation* incontrôlé.

unconventional [ˈʌnkənˈvenʃənl] *adj* peu conventionnel.

unconvinced [ˈʌnkənˈvɪnst] *adj*: **to be** *or* **remain ~** ne pas être convaincu (*of* de). ♦ **unconvincing** *adj* peu convaincant. ♦ **unconvincingly** *adv* d'une manière peu convaincante.

uncooked [ˈʌnˈkʊkt] *adj* cru.

uncooperative [ˈʌnkəʊˈɒpərətɪv] *adj* peu coopératif.

uncork [ˈʌnˈkɔːk] *vt* déboucher.

uncountable [ˈʌnˈkaʊntəbl] *adj* incalculable; (*Ling*) non comptable.

uncouple [ˈʌnˈkʌpl] *vt train* découpler; *trailer* détacher.

uncouth [ʌnˈkuːθ] *adj* fruste.

uncover [ʌnˈkʌvəʳ] *vt* découvrir.

uncritical [ˈʌnˈkrɪtɪkəl] *adj* qui manque d'esprit critique (*of* à l'égard de); *attitude, report* non critique.

uncrossed [ˈʌnˈkrɒst] *adj cheque* non barré.

uncrushable [ˈʌnˈkrʌʃəbl] *adj* infroissable.

unction [ˈʌŋkʃən] *n*: **extreme ~** extrême-onction *f*.

uncultivated [ˈʌnˈkʌltɪveɪtɪd] *adj* inculte.

uncurl [ˈʌnˈkɜːl] *vt* (*gen*) dérouler; *legs* déplier.

uncut [ˈʌnˈkʌt] *adj* (*gen*) non coupé; *diamond* brut; *gem, stone* non taillé; *edition etc* intégral.

undamaged [ʌnˈdæmɪdʒd] *adj goods* non endommagé; *reputation* intact.

undated [ˈʌnˈdeɪtɪd] *adj* non daté.

undaunted [ˈʌnˈdɔːntɪd] *adj* non intimidé (*by* par). **to carry on ~** continuer sans se laisser intimider.

undecided [ˈʌndɪˈsaɪdɪd] *adj* indécis. **that is still ~** cela n'a pas encore été décidé; **I am ~ whether ...** je n'ai pas décidé si ... .

undefeated [ˈʌndɪˈfiːtɪd] *adj* invaincu.

undefined [ˌʌndɪˈfaɪnd] *adj word* non défini; *sensation etc* vague.

undelivered [ˈʌndɪˈlɪvəd] *adj* non distribué. **if ~ return to sender** ≃ en cas d'absence prière de retourner à l'expéditeur.

undemonstrative [ˈʌndɪˈmɒnstrətɪv] *adj* peu démonstratif.

undeniable [ˌʌndɪˈnaɪəbl] *adj* incontestable. ♦ **undeniably** *adv* incontestablement.

under [ˈʌndəʳ] **1** *adv* **(a)** (*below*) au-dessous, en dessous. **to stay ~** (**~** *water*) rester sous l'eau; (**~** *anaesthetic*) rester sous l'effet de l'anesthésie; (*Comm etc*) **as ~** comme ci-dessous. **(b)** (*less*) au-dessous. **children of 15 and ~** les enfants de 15 ans et au-dessous.

2 *prep* **(a)** (*beneath*) sous. **~ the table** sous la table; **from ~ the bed** de dessous le lit; **it's ~ there** c'est là-dessous; **he went and sat ~ it** il est allé s'asseoir dessous; **to stay ~ water** rester sous l'eau; **~ the microscope** au microscope. **(b)** (*less than*) moins de; (*in series, rank, scale etc*) au-dessous de. **to be ~ age** être mineur; **children ~ 15** enfants de moins de *or* enfants au-dessous de 15 ans; **~ £10** moins de 10 livres; **any number ~ 10** un chiffre au-dessous de 10. **(c)** (*fig*) sous. **~ the Tudors** sous les Tudors; **~ the circumstances** dans les circonstances; **~ an assumed name** sous un faux nom; **you'll find him ~ 'plumbers' in the book** vous le trouverez sous 'plombiers' dans l'annuaire; (*Mil etc*) **to serve ~ sb** servir sous les ordres de qn; **to study ~ sb** *[undergraduate]* suivre les cours de qn; *[postgraduate]* travailler sous la direction de qn; *[painter etc]* être l'élève de qn. **(d)** (*according to*) selon, conformément à. **~ this law** selon *or* conformément à cette loi.

3 (*in compounds*) (*insufficiently*) sous-; (*junior*) aide-, sous-. **~capitalized** sous-financé; **~populated** sous-peuplé; **~cooked** pas assez cuit; **~gardener** aide-jardinier *m*; (*in age*) **the ~-10's** les moins *mpl* de 10 ans.

♦ **underachieve** *vi* ne pas donner toute sa mesure. ♦ **underarm** *adv* par en-dessous. ♦ **underbelly** *n* (*fig*) point *m* vulnérable. ♦ **undercarriage** *n* train *m* d'atterrissage. ♦ **undercharge** *vt* ne pas faire payer assez à. ♦ **underclothes** *npl or* ♦ **underclothing** *n* sous-vêtements *mpl*. ♦ **undercoat** *n [paint]* couche *f* de fond. ♦ **undercover** *adj* secret. ♦ **undercurrent** *n* courant *m* (sous-marin); (*fig*) courant sous-jacent. ♦ **undercut** *pret, ptp* **-cut** *vt* (*Comm*) vendre moins cher que. ♦ **underdeveloped** *adj* (*Anat, Phot*) insuffisamment développé; (*Econ*) sous-développé. ♦ **underdog** *n* (*fig*) **the ~dog** (*in fight*) celui qui perd; (*socially*) l'opprimé *m*. ♦ **underdone** *adj* (*Culin*) saignant; (*pej*) pas assez cuit. ♦ **underemployed** *adj* sous-employé. ♦ **underestimate** *vt* sous-estimer. ♦ **underexpose** *vt* (*Phot*) sous-exposer. ♦ **underexposure** *n* sous-exposition *f*. ♦ **underfeed** *pret, ptp* **-fed** *vt* sous-alimenter. ♦ **underfelt** *n* thibaude *f*. ♦ **under-floor heating** *n* chauffage *m* par le sol. ♦ **underfoot** *adv* sous les pieds; **it is wet ~foot** le sol est humide; **to trample sth ~foot** fouler qch aux pieds. ♦ **undergarment** *n* sous-vêtement *m*. ♦ **undergo** *pret* **-went**, *ptp* **-gone** *vt* (*gen*) subir; *medical treatment* suivre. ♦ **undergraduate** **1** *n* étudiant(e) *m(f)*; **2** *adj circles* étudiant; *opinion* des étudiants; *attitude* d'étudiant. ♦ **underground** **1** *adj* (*gen*) souterrain; (*fig*) *organization* secret; *press* clandestin; (*Art, Cine*) underground *inv*; **2** *adv* sous (la) terre; **to go ~ground** *[wanted man]* entrer dans la clandestinité; *[guerilla]* prendre le maquis; **3** *n*: **the ~ground** (*railway*) le métro; (*Mil, Pol etc*) la résistance; (*Art etc*) le mouvement underground; **by ~ground** en métro. ♦ **undergrowth** *n* sous-bois *m inv*. ♦ **underhand** **1** *adv* (*Sport*) par en-dessous; **2** *adj* (*also* **~handed**) sournois, en sous-main. ♦ **underlay** *n* thibaude *f*. ♦ **underlie** *pret* **-lay**, *ptp* **-lain** *vt* être à la base de. ♦ **underline** *vt* (*lit, fig*) souligner. ♦ **underling** *n* (*pej*) subalterne *m*. ♦ **underlining** *n* soulignement *m*. ♦ **underlying** *adj rock, cause* sous-jacent; *principle* fondamental. ♦ **undermentioned** *adj* (cité) ci-dessous. ♦ **undermine** *vt* (*gen*) saper; *health* miner; *effect* amoindrir. ♦ **underneath** **1** *prep* sous, au-dessous de; **2** *adv* (en) dessous; **3** *adj* d'en dessous; **4** *n* dessous *m*. ♦ **undernourish** *vt* sous-alimenter. ♦ **undernourishment** *n* sous-alimentation *f*. ♦ **underpaid** *adj* sous-payé. ♦ **underpants** *npl* slip *m* (*pour homme*). ♦ **underpass** *n* (*for cars*) passage *m* inférieur (*de l'autoroute*); (*for pedestrians*) passage souterrain. ♦ **underpay** *vt* sous-payer. ♦ **underpin** *vt* (*lit, fig*) étayer. ♦ **underpriced** *adj* dont le prix est trop bas. ♦ **underprivileged** *adj* (*gen*) défavorisé; (*Econ*) économiquement faible; **the ~privileged** les économiquement faibles *mpl*. ♦ **underrate** *vt* sous-estimer. ♦ **underseal** *vt* traiter contre la rouille. ♦ **undersecretary** *n* sous-secrétaire *m*. ♦ **undersexed** *adj* de faible libido. ♦ **undershirt** *n* tricot *m* de corps. ♦ **underside** *n* dessous *m*. ♦ **undersigned** *adj, n* soussigné(e) *m(f)*; **I the ~signed ...** je soussigné(e) ... . ♦ **undersized** *adj* trop petit. ♦ **underskirt** *n* jupon *m*. ♦ **understaffed** *adj* à court de personnel. ♦ **understand** *V below*. ♦ **understate** *vt* minimiser. ♦ **understatement** *n* affirmation *f* en dessous de la vérité; (*Ling*) litote *f*; **that's an ~statement** c'est peu dire. ♦ **understudy 1** *n* doublure *f*; **2** *vt* doubler. ♦ **undertake** *pret* **-took,** *ptp* **-taken** *vt task* entreprendre; *duty* se charger de; *responsibility* assumer; *obligation* contracter; **to ~take to do** s'engager à faire. ♦ **undertaker** *n* entrepreneur *m* des pompes funèbres; **the ~taker's** les pompes funèbres *fpl*. ♦ **undertaking** *n* **(a)** (*operation*) entreprise *f*; **it is quite an ~taking** c'est toute une entreprise; **(b)** (*promise*) engagement *m*; **to give an ~taking** promettre (*that* que; *to do* de faire). ♦ **undertone** *n*: **in an ~tone** à mi-voix. ♦ **undervalue** *vt* (*fig*) sous-estimer. ♦ **undervalued** *adj* (*lit*) qui vaut plus que son prix. ♦ **undervest** *n* tricot *m* de corps. ♦ **underwater** *adj* sous-marin. ♦ **underwear** *n* sous-vêtements *mpl*. ♦ **underworld 1** *n* (*hell*) enfers *mpl*; (*criminals*) milieu *m*, pègre *f*; **2** *adj organization* du milieu; *connections etc* avec le milieu. ♦ **underwrite** *vt* (*gen*) garantir; (*Insurance, St Ex*) souscrire. ♦ **underwriter** *n* souscripteur *m*.

understand [ˌʌndəˈstænd] *pret, ptp* **-stood 1** *vt* (*gen*) comprendre (*that* que; *why etc* pourquoi *etc*). **to make o.s. understood** se faire comprendre; **I can't ~ a word of it** je n'y comprends rien; **I understood we were to be paid** j'ai cru comprendre que nous devions être payés; **I ~ you are leaving** si je comprends bien vous partez; **she is understood to have left** on croit qu'elle est partie; **to let it be understood that** donner à entendre que; **to be understood** *[price, date]* ne pas être spécifié; *[word]* être sous-entendu; **it's understood that** il est entendu que; **that's quite understood** c'est entendu. **2** *vi* comprendre. **now I ~!** je comprends *or* j'y suis maintenant!; **he was, I ~ ...** il était, si j'ai bien compris ... . ♦ **understandable** *adj* compréhensible; **it is ~able that** on comprend que +*subj*; **that's ~able** ça se comprend. ♦ **understandably** *adv*: **he's ~ably angry** il est en colère et ça se comprend, naturellement il est en colère. ♦ **understanding 1** *adj person* compréhensif (*about* à propos de); *smile, look* bienveillant; **2** *n* **(a)** compréhension *f* (*of* de); **to have a good ~ing of sth** bien comprendre qch; **the age of ~ing** l'âge *m* de discernement; **(b)** (*agreement*) accord *m*; (*arrangement*) arrangement *m*; **to come to an ~ing with sb** s'entendre *or* s'arranger avec qn; **on the ~ing that** à condition que +*subj*; **this will encourage ~ing between ...** ceci favorisera l'entente *f* entre ... . ♦ **understandingly** *adv* avec bienveillance.

undeserved [ˈʌndɪˈzɜːvd] *adj* immérité. ♦ **undeservedly** [ˈʌndɪˈzɜːvɪdlɪ] *adv* indûment.

undesirable [ˈʌndɪˈzaɪərəbl] **1** *adj* peu souhaitable (*that* que +*subj*), (*stronger*) indésirable. **2** *n* indésirable *mf*.

undetected [ˈʌndɪˈtektɪd] *adj*: **to go ~** passer inaperçu.

undeveloped [ˈʌndɪˈveləpt] *adj* (*gen*) qui ne s'est pas développé; *film* non développé; *land, resources* non exploité.

undies* [ˈʌndɪz] *npl* dessous *mpl*, lingerie *f*.

undignified [ʌnˈdɪgnɪfaɪd] *adj* qui manque de dignité.

undiluted [ˈʌndaɪˈluːtɪd] *adj concentrate* non dilué; *pleasure* sans mélange; *nonsense* pur.

undiplomatic [ˈʌnˌdɪpləˈmætɪk] *adj person* peu diplomate; *action, answer* peu diplomatique.

undipped [ˈʌnˈdɪpt] *adj* (*Aut*) **his headlights were ~** il était en phares.

undischarged [ˈʌndɪsˈtʃɑːdʒd] *adj bankrupt* non réhabilité; *debt* non acquitté.

undisciplined [ʌnˈdɪsɪplɪnd] *adj* indiscipliné.

undiscovered [ˈʌndɪsˈkʌvəd] *adj* (*unknown*) inconnu. **it remained ~ for 700 years** cela n'a été découvert que 700 ans après.

undiscriminating [ˈʌndɪsˈkrɪmɪneɪtɪŋ] *adj* qui manque de discernement.

undisguised [ˈʌndɪsˈgaɪzd] *adj* non déguisé.

undisputed [ˈʌndɪsˈpjuːtɪd] *adj* incontesté.

undistinguished [ˈʌndɪsˈtɪŋgwɪʃt] *adj* médiocre, quelconque.

undisturbed [ˈʌndɪsˈtɜːbd] *adj* **(a)** *papers, clues* non dérangé; *sleep* paisible. **to work ~** travailler sans être dérangé. **(b)** (*unworried*) non inquiet, calme. **he was ~ by the news** la nouvelle ne l'a pas inquiété.

undivided [ˈʌndɪˈvaɪdɪd] *adj* entier. **your ~ attention** toute votre attention.

undo [ˈʌnˈduː] *pret* **-did,** *ptp* **-done** *vt* (*gen: unfasten etc*) défaire; *good effect* annuler; *mischief, wrong* réparer. ♦ **undoing** *n* perte *f*; **that was his ~ing** c'est ce qui l'a perdu. ♦ **undone** *adj* (*unfastened etc*) défait; **to come undone** se défaire; **to leave sth undone** ne pas faire qch.

undoubted [ʌnˈdaʊtɪd] *adj* indubitable. ♦ **undoubtedly** *adv* indubitablement, sans aucun doute.

undreamed-of [ʌnˈdriːmdɒv] *adj* insoupçonné.

undress [ˈʌnˈdres] **1** *vt* déshabiller. **2** *vi* se déshabiller.

undrinkable [ˈʌnˈdrɪŋkəbl] *adj* (*unpalatable*) imbuvable; (*poisonous*) non potable.

undue [ˈʌnˈdjuː] *adj* excessif. ♦ **unduly** *adv* trop, excessivement.

undulate [ˈʌndjʊleɪt] *vi* onduler. ♦ **undulating** *adj* (*gen*) onduleux; *countryside* vallonné.

undying [ʌnˈdaɪɪŋ] *adj* (*fig*) éternel.

unearned [ˈʌnˈɜːnd] *adj reward* immérité. **~ income** rentes *fpl*.

unearth [ˈʌnˈɜːθ] *vt* (*lit, fig*) déterrer.

unearthly [ʌnˈɜːθlɪ] *adj* surnaturel, sinistre; (**fig*) *noise etc* impossible*. **~ hour*** heure indue.

uneasy [ʌnˈiːzɪ] *adj peace, truce* difficile; *silence* gêné; *sleep, night* agité; *conscience* non tranquille; *person* (*ill-at-ease*) gêné; (*worried*) inquiet. ♦ **uneasily** *adv* (*ill-at-ease*) avec gêne; (*worriedly*) avec inquiétude; *sleep* d'un sommeil agité. ♦ **uneasiness** *n* inquiétude *f*.

uneatable [ˈʌnˈiːtəbl] *adj* immangeable. ♦ **uneaten** *adj* non mangé.

uneconomic(al) [ˈʌnˌiːkəˈnɒmɪk(əl)] *adj machine, car* peu économique; *work, method* peu rentable.

uneducated [ˈʌnˈedjʊkeɪtɪd] *adj person* sans éducation; *speech* populaire (*pej*).

unemotional [ˈʌnɪˈməʊʃənl] *adj* impassible. ♦ **unemotionally** *adv* avec impassibilité.

unemployed [ˈʌnɪmˈplɔɪd] **1** *adj* sans travail, en chômage. **2** *npl* **the ~** les chômeurs *mpl*. ♦ **unemployable** *adj* incapable de travailler. ♦ **unemployment 1** *n* chômage *m*; **2** *adj*: **unemployment benefit** allocation *f* de chômage.

unending [ʌnˈendɪŋ] *adj* interminable.

unendurable [ˈʌnɪnˈdjʊərəbl] *adj* insupportable.

unenterprising [ˈʌnˈentəpraɪzɪŋ] *adj person* qui manque d'initiative; *act* qui manque de hardiesse.

unenthusiastic [ˈʌnɪnˌθuːzɪˈæstɪk] *adj* peu enthousiaste. ♦ **unenthusiastically** *adv* sans enthousiasme.

unenviable [ˈʌnˈenvɪəbl] *adj* peu enviable.

unequal [ˈʌnˈiːkwəl] *adj* (*gen*) inégal. **to be ~ to a task** ne pas être à la hauteur d'une tâche. ♦ **unequalled** *adj* inégalé. ♦ **unequally** *adv* inégalement.

unequivocal [ˈʌnɪˈkwɪvəkəl] *adj* sans équivoque. ♦ **unequivocally** *adv* sans équivoque.

unerring [ˈʌnˈɜːrɪŋ] *adj judgment, accuracy* infaillible; *aim, skill, blow* sûr.
unethical [ˈʌnˈeθɪkəl] *adj* immoral.
uneven [ˈʌnˈiːvən] *adj* inégal. ♦ **unevenly** *adv* inégalement. ♦ **unevenness** *n* inégalité *f*.
uneventful [ˈʌnɪˈventfʊl] *adj* peu mouvementé.
unexceptionable [ˌʌnɪkˈsepʃnəbl] *adj* irréprochable. ♦ **unexceptional** *adj* qui n'a rien d'exceptionnel.
unexciting [ˈʌnɪkˈsaɪtɪŋ] *adj* peu intéressant.
unexpected [ˈʌnɪksˈpektɪd] *adj* inattendu. **it was all very ~** on ne s'y attendait pas du tout. ♦ **unexpectedly** *adv* (*gen*) subitement; *arrive* inopinément.
unexplained [ˈʌnɪksˈpleɪnd] *adj* inexpliqué.
unexposed [ˈʌnɪksˈpəʊzd] *adj film* vierge.
unexpurgated [ˈʌnˈekspɜːgeɪtɪd] *adj* non expurgé.
unfailing [ʌnˈfeɪlɪŋ] *adj supply, zeal* inépuisable; *optimism* inébranlable; *remedy* infaillible. ♦ **unfailingly** *adv* infailliblement.
unfair [ˈʌnˈfɛəʳ] *adj person, decision, deal* injuste (*to sb* envers qn; *that* que +*subj*); *competition, play, tactics* déloyal. ♦ **unfairly** *adv decide* injustement; *play* déloyalement. ♦ **unfairness** *n* injustice *f*; déloyauté *f*.
unfaithful [ˈʌnˈfeɪθfʊl] *adj* infidèle (*to* à).
unfamiliar [ˈʌnfəˈmɪljəʳ] *adj* peu familier, inconnu. **to be ~ with sth** mal connaître qch.
unfashionable [ˈʌnˈfæʃnəbl] *adj dress, subject* démodé; *district, shop* peu chic *inv*. **it is ~ to say** ça ne se fait plus de dire.
unfasten [ˈʌnˈfɑːsn] *vt* (*gen*) défaire; *door* déverrouiller.
unfavourable, (*US*) **unfavorable** [ˈʌnˈfeɪvərəbl] *adj* (*gen*) défavorable; *moment* peu propice. ♦ **unfavo(u)rably** *adv* défavorablement.
unfeeling [ʌnˈfiːlɪŋ] *adj* insensible. ♦ **unfeelingly** *adv* sans pitié.
unfeminine [ʌnˈfemɪnɪn] *adj* peu féminin.
unfinished [ˈʌnˈfɪnɪʃt] *adj* (*gen*) inachevé. **3 ~ letters** 3 lettres à finir; **some ~ business** une affaire à régler; **it looks rather ~** c'est mal fini.
unfit [ˈʌnˈfɪt] *adj* (*incompetent*) inapte (*for* à; *to do* à faire); (*unworthy*) indigne (*to do* de faire). *[footballer etc]* **he's ~** il n'est pas en état de jouer; **he is ~ to be a teacher** il ne devrait pas enseigner; **he was ~ to drive/for work** il n'était pas en état de conduire/de reprendre le travail; **~ for military service** inapte au service militaire; **~ for habitation** inhabitable; **~ for consumption/publication** impropre à la consommation/publication; **road ~ for lorries** route *f* impraticable aux camions.
unflattering [ˈʌnˈflætərɪŋ] *adj* peu flatteur.
unfold [ʌnˈfəʊld] **1** *vt* (*gen*) déplier; *wings* déployer; *arms* décroiser; (*fig*) *plans* exposer; *secret* dévoiler. **2** *vi [view, plot]* se dérouler.
unforeseeable [ˈʌnfɔːˈsiːəbl] *adj* imprévisible. ♦ **unforeseen** *adj* imprévu.
unforgettable [ˈʌnfəˈgetəbl] *adj* inoubliable. ♦ **unforgotten** *adj* inoublié.
unforgivable [ˈʌnfəˈgɪvəbl] *adj* impardonnable. ♦ **unforgivably** *adv* impardonnablement. ♦ **unforgiving** *adj* implacable.
unformed [ˈʌnˈfɔːmd] *adj* informe.
unforthcoming [ˈʌnfɔːθˈkʌmɪŋ] *adj* réticent.
unfortunate [ʌnˈfɔːtʃnɪt] **1** *adj* (*gen*) malheureux (*that* que + *subj*); *circumstances* triste; *event* fâcheux. **how ~!** quel dommage!; **he has been ~** il n'a pas eu de chance. **2** *n* malheureux *m*, -euse *f*. ♦ **unfortunately** *adv* malheureusement.
unfounded [ˈʌnˈfaʊndɪd] *adj* sans fondement.
unframed [ˈʌnˈfreɪmd] *adj picture* sans cadre.
unfreeze [ˈʌnˈfriːz] *pret* **-froze,** *ptp* **-frozen** *vt* dégeler; (*Econ, Fin*) débloquer.
unfriendly [ˈʌnˈfrendlɪ] *adj person, reception* froid; *attitude, behaviour, remark* inamical. **to be ~ towards sb** manifester de la froideur à qn. ♦ **unfriendliness** *n* froideur *f* (*towards* envers).
unfulfilled [ˈʌnfʊlˈfɪld] *adj promise* non tenu; *ambition, prophecy* non réalisé; *desire* insatisfait; *condition* non rempli. *[person]* **to feel ~** se sentir frustré.
unfurl [ʌnˈfɜːl] *vt* déployer.
unfurnished [ˈʌnˈfɜːnɪʃt] *adj* non meublé.
ungainly [ʌnˈgeɪnlɪ] *adj* gauche, disgracieux.
un-get-at-able* [ˈʌngetˈætəbl] *adj* inaccessible.
ungodly [ʌnˈgɒdlɪ] *adj* impie. (*fig*) **~ hour*** heure *f* indue.
ungovernable [ʌnˈgʌvənəbl] *adj country* ingouvernable; *passion* irrépressible.
ungracious [ˈʌnˈgreɪʃəs] *adj* peu gracieux. ♦ **ungraciously** *adv* avec mauvaise grâce.
ungrammatical [ˈʌngrəˈmætɪkəl] *adj* incorrect, non grammatical. ♦ **ungrammatically** *adv* incorrectement.
ungrateful [ʌnˈgreɪtfʊl] *adj* ingrat (*towards* envers). ♦ **ungratefully** *adv* avec ingratitude.
ungrudging [ˈʌnˈgrʌdʒɪŋ] *adj help* donné sans compter; *praise* très sincère. ♦ **ungrudgingly** *adv give* généreusement; *help* de bon cœur.
unguarded [ˈʌnˈgɑːdɪd] *adj* (*Mil etc*) sans surveillance; (*fig*) *remark* irréfléchi. **in an ~ moment** dans un moment d'inattention.
unhappy [ʌnˈhæpɪ] *adj person* (*sad*) malheureux, triste; (*ill-pleased*) mécontent; (*worried*) inquiet; (*unfortunate*) malchanceux; *childhood, remark, coincidence* malheureux; *situation* regrettable; *circumstances* triste. **I feel ~ about it** cela m'inquiète. ♦ **unhappily** *adv* (*miserably*) d'un air malheureux; (*unfortunately*) malheureusement. ♦ **unhappiness** *n* tristesse *f*.
unharmed [ˈʌnˈhɑːmd] *adj person* indemne; *thing* intact.
unhealthy [ʌnˈhelθɪ] *adj person* maladif; *place, habit, curiosity* malsain.
unheard-of [ˈʌnˈhɜːdɒv] *adj* inouï.
unheeded [ˈʌnˈhiːdɪd] *adj* (*ignored*) négligé; (*unnoticed*) inaperçu. **it went ~** on n'y a pas prêté attention.
unhelpful [ˈʌnˈhelpfʊl] *adj person* peu obligeant; *thing* qui n'aide guère. **I found that very ~** ça ne m'a pas aidé du tout.
unhesitating [ʌnˈhezɪteɪtɪŋ] *adj reply, reaction* immédiat; *person* qui n'hésite pas. ♦ **unhesitatingly** *adv* sans hésitation.
unhindered [ˈʌnˈhɪndəd] *adj* sans encombre.
unholy [ʌnˈhəʊlɪ] *adj* impie; (**fig*) impossible*. **~ hour*** heure indue.
unhook [ˈʌnˈhʊk] *vt* décrocher (*from* de).
unhoped-for [ʌnˈhəʊptfɔːʳ] *adj* inespéré.
unhurried [ˈʌnˈhʌrɪd] *adj movement* lent; *reflection* mûr (*before n*); *journey/meal etc* fait/pris *etc* sans se presser. ♦ **unhurriedly** *adv* sans se presser.
unhurt [ˈʌnˈhɜːt] *adj* indemne, sain et sauf.
unhygienic [ˈʌnhaɪˈdʒiːnɪk] *adj* non hygiénique.
unicorn [ˈjuːnɪkɔːn] *n* licorne *f*.
unidentified [ˈʌnaɪˈdentɪfaɪd] *adj* (*gen*) non identifié. **~ flying object** (*abbr* **UFO**) objet *m* volant non identifié (*abbr* O.V.N.I. *m*).
uniform [ˈjuːnɪfɔːm] **1** *n* uniforme *m*. **in ~** en uniforme; **in full ~** en grand uniforme; **out of ~** en civil. **2** *adj length* uniforme; *colour* uni; *temperature* constant. ♦ **uniformed** *adj policeman etc* en uniforme; *organization* qui porte un uniforme. ♦ **uniformity** *n* uniformité *f*. ♦ **uniformly** *adv* uniformément.
unify [ˈjuːnɪfaɪ] *vt* unifier. ♦ **unification** *n* unification *f*.
unilateral [ˈjuːnɪˈlætərəl] *adj* unilatéral. ♦ **unilaterally** *adv* unilatéralement.
unimaginable [ˌʌnɪˈmædʒɪnəbl] *adj* inimaginable. ♦ **unimaginative** *adj* qui manque d'imagination. ♦ **unimaginatively** *adv* sans imagination.

unimpaired ['ʌnɪm'pɛəd] *adj* (*gen*) aussi bon qu'auparavant; *quality* non diminué.
unimportant ['ʌnɪm'pɔːtənt] *adj* sans importance.
unimpressed ['ʌnɪm'prest] *adj* (*gen*) peu impressionné (*by* par); (*unconvinced*) peu convaincu (*by* par). **I was** ~ ça ne m'a pas impressionné.
uninhabitable ['ʌnɪn'hæbɪtəbl] *adj* inhabitable. ♦ **uninhabited** *adj* inhabité.
uninhibited ['ʌnɪn'hɪbɪtɪd] *adj person* sans inhibitions; *emotion* non refréné; *dance* sans retenue.
uninitiated ['ʌnɪ'nɪʃɪeɪtɪd] *npl* (*fig*) **the** ~ les noninitiés *mpl*.
uninjured ['ʌn'ɪndʒəd] *adj* indemne, sain et sauf.
uninspired ['ʌnɪn'spaɪəd] *adj* qui manque d'inspiration. ♦ **uninspiring** *adj* qui n'est guère inspirant.
unintelligent ['ʌnɪn'telɪdʒənt] *adj* inintelligent.
unintelligible ['ʌnɪn'telɪdʒɪbl] *adj* inintelligible. ♦ **unintelligibly** *adv* inintelligiblement.
unintentional ['ʌnɪn'tenʃənl] *adj* involontaire. **it was quite** ~ ce n'était pas fait exprès. ♦ **unintentionally** *adv* involontairement, sans le faire exprès.
uninterested [ʌn'ɪntrɪstɪd] *adj* indifférent (*in* à). ♦ **uninteresting** *adj book, activity* inintéressant; *person* ennuyeux; *offer* non intéressant.
uninterrupted ['ʌn,ɪntə'rʌptɪd] *adj* ininterrompu. ♦ **uninterruptedly** *adv* sans interruption.
uninvited ['ʌnɪn'vaɪtɪd] *adj*: **to arrive** ~ arriver sans invitation; **to do sth** ~ faire qch sans y avoir été invité.
union ['juːnjən] **1** *n* (*gen*) union *f*; (*trade* ~) syndicat *m*. (*US*) **the U~** les États-Unis *mpl*; **U~ of Soviet Socialist Republics** (*abbr* **USSR**) Union des républiques socialistes soviétiques (*abbr* U.R.S.S. *f*). **2** *adj* **(a)** (*Ind*) *card, leader, movement* syndical; *headquarters* du syndicat. ~ **member** membre *m* du syndicat; (*US*) ~ **shop** atelier *m* d'ouvriers syndiqués. **(b) U~ Jack** *drapeau du Royaume-Uni*. ♦ **unionism** *n* (*trade unionism*) syndicalisme *m*. ♦ **unionist** *n* **(a)** (*trade unionist*) syndicaliste *mf*; **the militant** ~**ists** les militants *mpl* syndicaux; **(b)** (*Pol: Ir etc*) unioniste *mf*. ♦ **unionize** *vt* (*Ind*) syndiquer.
unique [juː'niːk] *adj* unique. ♦ **uniquely** *adv* exceptionnellement. ♦ **uniqueness** *n* caractère *m* unique.
unisex ['juːnɪseks] *adj* unisexe.
unison ['juːnɪzn] *n*: **in** ~ (*Mus*) à l'unisson *m*; (*gen*) en chœur.
unit ['juːnɪt] **1** *n* **(a)** (*gen, Elec, Math, Mil etc*) unité *f*. **administrative/linguistic/monetary** ~ unité administrative/linguistique/monétaire; ~ **of length** unité de longueur. **(b)** (*section*) groupe *m*; *[furniture]* élément *m*. **compressor** ~ groupe compresseur; **kitchen** ~ élément de cuisine; **sink** ~ bloc-évier *m*; **research** ~ (*building*) bloc *m* de recherches; (*personnel*) groupe de recherches. **2** *adj* **(a)** *price* unitaire. ~ **trust** société *f* d'investissement. **(b)** ~ **furniture** mobilier *m* par éléments.
unite [juː'naɪt] **1** *vt* (*join*) *countries etc* unir (*A with B* A à B); (*unify*) *one country etc* unifier. **2** *vi* (*join together*) s'unir (*with sth* à qch; *with sb* à *or* avec qn; *against* contre; *in doing, to do* pour faire); *[companies]* fusionner; (*become united*) *[party]* s'unifier. ♦ **united** *adj* (*gen*) uni; (*unified*) unifié; *front* uni; *efforts* conjugué; **U~d Kingdom** Royaume-Uni *m*; **U~d Nations Organization** (*abbr* **UN** *or* **UNO**) Organisation *f* des Nations unies (*abbr* O.N.U. *f*); **U~d States of America** (*abbr* **US** *or* **USA**) États-Unis *mpl*. ♦ **unity** ['juːnɪtɪ] *n* unité *f*; (*fig*) **in unity** en harmonie *f* (*with* avec).
universe ['juːnɪvɜːs] *n* univers *m*. ♦ **universal** *adj* universel; **she's a universal favourite** tout le monde l'aime; **to make sth universal** universaliser qch; **universal joint** joint *m* de cardan. ♦ **universally** *adv* universellement.
university [,juːnɪ'vɜːsɪtɪ] **1** *n* université *f*. **to be at/go to** ~ être/aller à l'université; **to study at** ~ faire des études universitaires. **2** *adj degree, town, library* universitaire; *professor, student* d'université. **he has a** ~ **education** il a fait des études universitaires.
unjust ['ʌn'dʒʌst] *adj* injuste (*to* envers). ♦ **unjustly** *adv* injustement.
unjustifiable [ʌn'dʒʌstɪfaɪəbl] *adj* injustifiable. ♦ **unjustifiably** *adv* sans justification. ♦ **unjustified** *adj* injustifié.
unkempt ['ʌn'kempt] *adj* (*gen*) débraillé; *hair* mal peigné.
unkind [ʌn'kaɪnd] *adj person, behaviour* peu aimable, pas gentil (*to sb* avec qn); (*stronger*) méchant (*to sb* avec qn); *fate* cruel. ♦ **unkindly** *adv* (*gen*) méchamment; **don't take it** ~**ly if ...** ne soyez pas offensé si ... . ♦ **unkindness** *n* manque *m* de gentillesse; méchanceté *f*; **an** ~**ness** une méchanceté.
unknown ['ʌn'nəʊn] **1** *adj* inconnu. **it was** ~ **to him** cela lui était inconnu, il l'ignorait; ~ **to him, the plane had crashed** l'avion s'était écrasé, ce qu'il ignorait; **she did it quite** ~ **to him** elle l'a fait à son insu; **substance** ~ **to science** substance inconnue de la science; (*Math, fig*) ~ **quantity** inconnue *f*; **the U~ Soldier** *or* **Warrior** le Soldat inconnu. **2** *n* **(a)** (*gen*) **the** ~ l'inconnu *m*; (*Math, fig*) **many** ~**s** de nombreuses inconnues *fpl*. **(b)** (*person*) inconnu(e) *m(f)*. ♦ **unknowable** *adj* inconnaissable. ♦ **unknowing** *adj* inconscient. ♦ **unknowingly** *adv* inconsciemment.
unladen ['ʌn'leɪdn] *adj weight* à vide.
unladylike ['ʌn'leɪdɪlaɪk] *adj girl* mal élevée. **it's** ~ **to yawn** une jeune fille bien élevée ne bâille pas.
unlawful ['ʌn'lɔːfʊl] *adj* illégal, illicite. ♦ **unlawfully** *adv* illégalement.
unleavened ['ʌn'levnd] *adj* azyme (*Rel*).
unless [ən'les] *conj* à moins que ... (ne) + *subj*, à moins de + *infin*. **take it,** ~ **you can find another** prenez-le, à moins que vous (n')en trouviez un autre *or* à moins d'en trouver un autre; ~ **I am mistaken** si je ne me trompe; ~ **I hear to the contrary** sauf contrordre; ~ **otherwise stated** sauf indication contraire.
unlicensed ['ʌn'laɪsənst] *adj activity* illicite; *vehicle* sans vignette; *hotel etc* non patenté pour la vente des spiritueux.
unlike ['ʌn'laɪk] **1** *adj* dissemblable, différent. **they are quite** ~ ils ne se ressemblent pas du tout. **2** *prep* à la différence de. ~ **his brother, he ...** à la différence de son frère, il ...; **it's quite** ~ **him to do that** ça ne lui ressemble pas de faire cela; **how** ~ **him!** on ne s'attendait pas à ça de sa part; **it is quite** ~ **mine** ça n'est pas du tout comme le mien.
unlikeable ['ʌn'laɪkəbl] *adj person* peu sympathique; *thing* peu agréable.
unlikely [ʌn'laɪklɪ] *adj happening, outcome* peu probable; *explanation* peu plausible. **it is** ~ **that she will come, she is** ~ **to come** il est peu probable qu'elle vienne, il y a peu de chances pour qu'elle vienne; **she is** ~ **to succeed** elle a peu de chances de réussir; **that is** ~ **to happen** cela ne risque guère d'arriver; **in the** ~ **event of his accepting** dans le cas fort improbable où il accepterait. ♦ **unlikelihood** *n* improbabilité *f*.
unlimited [ʌn'lɪmɪtɪd] *adj* illimité.
unlined ['ʌn'laɪnd] *adj garment* sans doublure; *face* sans rides; *paper* non réglé.
unlit ['ʌn'lɪt] *adj lamp* non allumé; *road* non éclairé; *vehicle* sans feux.
unload ['ʌn'ləʊd] **1** *vt* (*gen*) décharger; (*get rid of*) se débarrasser de; *shares* se défaire de. **to** ~ **sth onto sb** se décharger de qch sur qn. **2** *vi* être déchargé. ♦ **unloaded** *adj gun* qui n'est pas

chargé. ♦ **unloading** *n* déchargement *m*.

unlock ['ʌn'lɒk] *vt* ouvrir. **it is ~ed** ce n'est pas fermé à clef.

unlooked-for [ʌn'lʊktfɔːʳ] *adj* inattendu.

unlovable ['ʌn'lʌvəbl] *adj* peu attachant.

unlucky [ʌn'lʌkɪ] *adj person* malchanceux; *coincidence, event* malencontreux; *choice, decision* malheureux; *day* de malchance; *omen* néfaste; *colour, number* qui porte malheur. **he's ~** il n'a pas de chance; **he tried to get a seat but he was ~** il a essayé d'avoir une place mais il n'y est pas arrivé; **he was ~ enough to meet her** il a eu la malchance de la rencontrer; **it is ~ to do that** ça porte malheur de faire ça. ♦ **unluckily** *adv* malheureusement (*for sb* pour qn). ♦ **unluckiness** *n* manque *m* de chance.

unmade ['ʌn'meɪd] *adj bed* défait.

unmanageable [ʌn'mænɪdʒəbl] *adj vehicle, parcel, size* peu maniable; *animal* indocile; *person* impossible; *hair* rebelle.

unmanned ['ʌn'mænd] *adj spacecraft* inhabité. **it was left ~** il n'y avait personne là.

unmarked ['ʌn'mɑːkt] *adj* (*unscratched etc*) sans marque; (*unnamed*) non marqué; (*uncorrected*) *essay* non corrigé; *police car* banalisé.

unmarried ['ʌn'mærɪd] *adj* célibataire, qui n'est pas marié. **~ mother** mère *f* célibataire.

unmask ['ʌn'mɑːsk] *vt* (*lit, fig*) démasquer.

unmentionable [ʌn'menʃnəbl] *adj* dont il ne faut pas parler.

unmerciful [ʌn'mɜːsɪfʊl] *adj* impitoyable (*towards* pour). ♦ **unmercifully** *adv* impitoyablement.

unmistakable ['ʌnmɪs'teɪkəbl] *adj evidence, sympathy* indubitable; *voice, walk* qu'on ne peut pas ne pas reconnaître. **it is quite ~** on ne peut pas se tromper. ♦ **unmistakably** *adv* manifestement, sans aucun doute.

unmitigated [ʌn'mɪtɪgeɪtɪd] *adj terror, admiration* absolu; *folly* pur; *disaster* total; *scoundrel, liar* fieffé (*before n*).

unmixed ['ʌn'mɪkst] *adj* pur, sans mélange.

unmounted ['ʌn'maʊntɪd] *adj gem, picture* non monté.

unmoved ['ʌn'muːvd] *adj* indifférent (*by* à). **he was ~** ça ne l'a pas ému, ça l'a laissé indifférent.

unmusical ['ʌn'mjuːzɪkəl] *adj sound* peu mélodieux; *person* peu musicien.

unnamed ['ʌn'neɪmd] *adj person* anonyme; *thing* innommé, (*unlabelled*) non marqué.

unnatural [ʌn'nætʃrəl] *adj* anormal; *habit, vice, love* contre nature; (*affected*) qui manque de naturel. **it is ~ for her to do that** il n'est pas normal *or* naturel qu'elle fasse cela. ♦ **unnaturally** *adv* anormalement; (*affectedly*) d'une manière affectée; **not ~ly** naturellement.

unnecessary [ʌn'nesɪsərɪ] *adj* (*useless*) inutile (*to do* de faire); (*superfluous*) superflu. **it is ~ for you to come** il n'est pas nécessaire *or* il est inutile que vous veniez (*subj*). ♦ **unnecessarily** *adv do, say* inutilement; *strict* sans nécessité.

unnerve ['ʌn'nɜːv] *vt* déconcerter. ♦ **unnerving** *adj* déconcertant.

unnoticed ['ʌn'nəʊtɪst] *adj* inaperçu. **to go ~** passer inaperçu.

unnumbered ['ʌn'nʌmbəd] *adj* (*lit*) sans numéro.

unobjectionable ['ʌnəb'dʒekʃnəbl] *adj thing* acceptable; *person* à qui l'on ne peut rien reprocher.

unobserved *adj*: **to escape ~** s'échapper sans être vu; **to go ~** passer inaperçu.

unobstructed ['ʌnəb'strʌktɪd] *adj pipe* non bouché; *road* dégagé. **the driver has an ~ view** le conducteur a une excellente visibilité.

unobtainable ['ʌnəb'teɪnəbl] *adj* impossible à obtenir.

unobtrusive ['ʌnəb'truːsɪv] *adj* discret. ♦ **unobtrusively** *adv* discrètement.

unoccupied ['ʌn'ɒkjʊpaɪd] *adj person* inoccupé, qui n'a rien à faire; *house* inoccupé; *seat*, (*Mil*) *zone* libre; *post* vacant.

unofficial ['ʌnə'fɪʃəl] *adj report etc* officieux; *visit* privé. **in an ~ capacity** à titre privé; (*Ind*) **~ strike** grève *f* sauvage. ♦ **unofficially** *adv* officieusement.

unopened ['ʌn'əʊpənd] *adj* qui n'a pas été ouvert. **to remain ~** rester fermé.

unopposed ['ʌnə'pəʊzd] *adj* sans opposition.

unorganized ['ʌn'ɔːgənaɪzd] *adj* inorganisé; (*badly organized*) mal organisé; *person* qui ne sait pas s'organiser.

unoriginal ['ʌnə'rɪdʒɪnəl] *adj* qui manque d'originalité.

unorthodox ['ʌn'ɔːθədɒks] *adj* peu orthodoxe.

unostentatious ['ʌnˌɒstən'teɪʃəs] *adj* sans ostentation, simple. ♦ **unostentatiously** *adv* sans ostentation.

unpack ['ʌn'pæk] **1** *vt suitcase* défaire; *belongings* déballer. **2** *vi* déballer ses affaires. ♦ **unpacking** *n* déballage *m*; **to do one's ~ing** déballer ses affaires.

unpaid ['ʌn'peɪd] *adj bill* impayé; *debt* non acquitté; *work, helper* non rétribué; *leave* non payé. **to work ~** travailler gratuitement.

unpalatable [ʌn'pælɪtəbl] *adj food* qui n'a pas bon goût; *fact, truth* désagréable.

unparalleled [ʌn'pærəleld] *adj* sans égal.

unpardonable [ʌn'pɑːdnəbl] *adj* impardonnable.

unpatriotic ['ʌnˌpætrɪ'ɒtɪk] *adj person* peu patriote; *thing* antipatriotique.

unperturbed ['ʌnpə'tɜːbd] *adj* non déconcerté. **~ by that, he ...** sans se laisser déconcerter par cela, il ... .

unpick ['ʌn'pɪk] *vt seam* défaire.

unpin ['ʌn'pɪn] *vt* détacher (*from* de).

unplaced ['ʌn'pleɪst] *adj horse* non placé; *athlete* non classé.

unplanned ['ʌn'plænd] *adj occurrence* imprévu; *baby* non prévu.

unpleasant [ʌn'pleznt] *adj* (*gen*) désagréable; *person, remark* désagréable (*to sb* avec qn), déplaisant; *house, town* déplaisant. **he had an ~ time** il a passé de mauvais moments. ♦ **unpleasantly** *adv reply* désagréablement; *behave, smile* de façon déplaisante; **~ly close** un peu trop près. ♦ **unpleasantness** *n* caractère *m* désagréable *or* déplaisant; (*quarrelling*) **a lot of ~ness** beaucoup de frictions *fpl*.

unplug ['ʌn'plʌg] *vt* (*Elec*) débrancher.

unpolished ['ʌn'pɒlɪʃt] *adj furniture, floor, shoes* non ciré; *diamond* non poli; (*fig*) *person* fruste; *manners* peu raffiné; *style* qui manque de poli.

unpolluted ['ʌnpə'luːtɪd] *adj* non pollué.

unpopular ['ʌn'pɒpjʊləʳ] *adj* (*gen*) impopulaire. **to be ~ with sb** *[person]* être impopulaire auprès de qn; *[decision etc]* être impopulaire chez qn; **to make o.s. ~** se rendre impopulaire. ♦ **unpopularity** *n* impopularité *f*.

unpractical ['ʌn'præktɪkəl] *adj thing* peu pratique; *person* qui manque de sens pratique.

unprecedented [ʌn'presɪdəntɪd] *adj* sans précédent.

unpredictable ['ʌnprɪ'dɪktəbl] *adj* (*gen*) imprévisible; *weather* incertain. **he is quite ~** on ne sait jamais ce qu'il va faire.

unprejudiced [ʌn'predʒʊdɪst] *adj* impartial.

unprepared ['ʌnprɪ'pɛəd] *adj speech etc* improvisé. **I was ~ for the exam** je n'avais pas suffisamment préparé l'examen; (*fig*) **he was quite ~ for it** cela l'a pris au dépourvu; **he began it quite ~** il l'a commencé sans y être préparé.

unprepossessing ['ʌnˌpriːpə'zesɪŋ] *adj* qui fait mauvaise impression.

unpretentious ['ʌnprɪ'tenʃəs] *adj* sans prétention.

unprincipled [ʌn'prɪnsɪpld] *adj* sans scrupules.

unprintable ['ʌn'prɪntəbl] *adj* (*lit*) impubliable; (*fig*) que l'on n'oserait pas répéter.
unproductive ['ʌnprə'dʌktɪv] *adj* improductif.
unprofessional ['ʌnprə'feʃənl] *adj* contraire au code professionnel.
unprofitable [ˌʌn'prɒfɪtəbl] *adj* peu rentable; *job* peu lucratif. ♦ **unprofitably** *adv* sans profit.
unpromising [ˌʌn'prɒmɪsɪŋ] *adj* peu prometteur.
unpronounceable [ˌʌnprə'naʊnsəbl] *adj* imprononçable.
unprotected [ˌʌnprə'tektɪd] *adj person, town* sans défense; (*exposed to elements*) découvert.
unprovided-for [ˌʌnprə'vaɪdɪdfɔːʳ] *adj person* sans ressources.
unprovoked [ˌʌnprə'vəʊkt] *adj* sans provocation.
unpublished [ˌʌn'pʌblɪʃt] *adj* inédit. ♦ **unpublishable** *adj* impubliable.
unpunctual ['ʌn'pʌŋktjʊəl] *adj* peu ponctuel.
unpunished ['ʌn'pʌnɪʃt] *adj* impuni. **to go ~** rester impuni.
unqualified ['ʌn'kwɒlɪfaɪd] *adj* **(a)** (*gen*) non qualifié (*to do* pour faire); (*in professions*) non diplômé. **no ~ person will be considered** les candidats n'ayant pas les diplômes requis ne seront pas considérés. **(b)** *statement, promise, approval etc* inconditionnel; *praise* sans réserve; *success* fou; (*) *idiot* fini; *rogue, liar* fieffé (*before n*).
unquestionable [ʌn'kwestʃənəbl] *adj fact* incontestable; *honesty* certain. ♦ **unquestionably** *adv* incontestablement. ♦ **unquestioned** *adj* incontesté. ♦ **unquestioning** *adj acceptance* inconditionnel; *belief, obedience* aveugle.
unravel [ʌn'rævəl] **1** *vt material* effilocher; *knitting* défaire; *threads* démêler; (*fig*) *mystery* débrouiller; *plot* dénouer. **2** *vi* s'effilocher.
unreadable ['ʌn'riːdəbl] *adj* illisible.
unready ['ʌn'redɪ] *adj* mal préparé (*for sth* pour qch). ♦ **unreadiness** *n* impréparation *f*.
unreal ['ʌn'rɪəl] *adj* irréel. ♦ **unrealistic** *adj* peu réaliste. ♦ **unreality** *n* irréalité *f*.
unreasonable [ʌn'riːznəbl] *adj* (*gen*) qui n'est pas raisonnable, déraisonnable; *demand, length* excessif; *price* exagéré. **~ hour** heure *f* indue; **it is ~ to do** on ne peut pas raisonnablement faire. ♦ **unreasonableness** *n [person]* attitude *f* déraisonnable. ♦ **unreasonably** *adv* déraisonnablement; excessivement; exagérément. ♦ **unreasoning** *adj* irraisonné.
unrecognizable ['ʌn'rekəgnaɪzəbl] *adj* méconnaissable, qui n'est pas reconnaissable. ♦ **unrecognized** *adj talent etc* méconnu; (*Pol*) *régime etc* non reconnu; **to do sth unrecognized** faire qch sans être reconnu.
unrecorded ['ʌnrɪ'kɔːdɪd] *adj event etc* non mentionné.
unrefined ['ʌnrɪ'faɪnd] *adj substance* non raffiné; *person* fruste.
unreformed ['ʌnrɪ'fɔːmd] *adj person* non amendé.
unrehearsed ['ʌnrɪ'hɜːst] *adj speech etc* improvisé; *incident* inattendu.
unrelated ['ʌnrɪ'leɪtɪd] *adj*: **to be ~ to** *[facts, events]* n'avoir aucun rapport avec; *[person]* n'avoir aucun lien de parenté avec.
unrelenting ['ʌnrɪ'lentɪŋ] *adj person* implacable; *persecution* acharné.
unreliable ['ʌnrɪ'laɪəbl] *adj person* sur qui on ne peut pas compter; *firm* qui n'est pas sérieux; *car, machine* peu fiable; *map* peu fidèle; *news* sujet à caution; *source of information* douteux. **my watch is ~** je ne peux pas me fier à ma montre. ♦ **unreliability** *n [person etc]* manque *m* de sérieux; *[machine]* manque de fiabilité.
unrelieved ['ʌnrɪ'liːvd] *adj pain, gloom* constant; *boredom* mortel; *grey, black etc* uniforme.
unremarkable ['ʌnrɪ'mɑːkəbl] *adj* médiocre.
unremitting ['ʌnrɪ'mɪtɪŋ] *adj kindness* inlassable; *hatred* opiniâtre.
unremunerative ['ʌnrɪ'mjuːnərətɪv] *adj* peu rémunérateur, mal payé.
unrepeatable ['ʌnrɪ'piːtəbl] *adj offer, bargain* exceptionnel; *comment* que l'on n'ose pas répéter.
unrepentant ['ʌnrɪ'pentənt] *adj* impénitent.
unrepresentative ['ʌnˌreprɪ'zentətɪv] *adj* peu représentatif (*of* de).
unrequited ['ʌnrɪ'kwaɪtɪd] *adj* non partagé.
unreserved ['ʌnrɪ'zɜːvd] *adj seat* non réservé; *admiration* sans réserve. ♦ **unreservedly** *adv* sans réserve.
unresponsive ['ʌnrɪs'pɒnsɪv] *adj* qui ne réagit pas. **~ to** insensible à.
unrest [ʌn'rest] *n* agitation *f*, troubles *mpl*.
unrestricted ['ʌnrɪ'strɪktɪd] *adj time, power* illimité; *access* libre.
unrewarded ['ʌnrɪ'wɔːdɪd] *adj [efforts etc]* **to go ~** rester sans récompense. ♦ **unrewarding** *adj* ingrat; (*financially*) peu rémunérateur.
unripe ['ʌn'raɪp] *adj* vert, qui n'est pas mûr.
unrivalled, (*US*) **-aled** [ʌn'raɪvəld] *adj* sans égal.
unroll ['ʌn'rəʊl] **1** *vt* dérouler. **2** *vi* se dérouler.
unromantic ['ʌnrə'mæntɪk] *adj* peu romantique.
unruffled ['ʌn'rʌfld] *adj hair, water* lisse; *person* calme.
unruled ['ʌn'ruːld] *adj paper* uni, non réglé.
unruly [ʌn'ruːlɪ] *adj* indiscipliné.
unsaddle ['ʌn'sædl] *vt* desseller.
unsafe ['ʌn'seɪf] *adj* **(a)** (*dangerous*) *machine, bridge, toy* dangereux; *journey* périlleux; *method* peu sûr. **~ to eat** *or* **drink** (*gen*) impropre à la consommation; *water* non potable. **(b)** (*in danger*) en danger. **to feel ~** ne pas se sentir en sécurité.
unsaid ['ʌn'sed] *adj*: **to leave sth ~** passer qch sous silence.
unsaleable ['ʌn'seɪləbl] *adj* invendable.
unsatisfactory ['ʌnˌsætɪs'fæktərɪ] *adj* peu satisfaisant, qui laisse à désirer. ♦ **unsatisfied** *adj person, desire* insatisfait (*with* de); *need, demand, appetite* non satisfait; (*unconvinced*) non convaincu. ♦ **unsatisfying** *adj result* peu satisfaisant; *work* ingrat; *food* peu nourrissant.
unsaturated ['ʌn'sætʃəreɪtɪd] *adj* (*Chem*) non saturé.
unsavoury, (*US*) **-ory** ['ʌn'seɪvərɪ] *adj food* mauvais au goût; (*fig*) *person, district* peu recommandable; *reputation* équivoque; *subject* plutôt répugnant. **an ~ business** une sale affaire.
unscathed ['ʌn'skeɪðd] *adj* indemne.
unscientific ['ʌnˌsaɪən'tɪfɪk] *adj* peu scientifique.
unscratched ['ʌn'skrætʃt] *adj surface* intact; *person* indemne.
unscrew ['ʌn'skruː] **1** *vt* dévisser. **2** *vi* se dévisser.
unscripted ['ʌn'skrɪptɪd] *adj* (*Rad, TV*) improvisé.
unscrupulous [ʌn'skruːpjʊləs] *adj person* dénué de scrupules; *act* malhonnête. ♦ **unscrupulously** *adv* sans scrupules. ♦ **unscrupulousness** *n* manque *m* de scrupules; malhonnêteté *f*.
unseasonable [ʌn'siːznəbl] *adj fruit etc* hors de saison; *weather* qui n'est pas de saison. ♦ **unseasonably** *adv*: **unseasonably warm** chaud pour la saison.
unseasoned ['ʌn'siːznd] *adj timber* vert; *food* non assaisonné.
unseat ['ʌn'siːt] *vt rider* désarçonner.
unseemly [ʌn'siːmlɪ] *adj* inconvenant.
unseen ['ʌn'siːn] *adj* inaperçu. **to escape ~** s'échapper sans être vu; **~ translation** version *f* (*sans préparation*).
unselfconscious ['ʌnˌself'kɒnʃəs] *adj* naturel. ♦ **unselfconsciously** *adv* sans la moindre gêne.
unselfish ['ʌn'selfɪʃ] *adj person* généreux; *act* désintéressé. ♦ **unselfishly** *adv* sans penser à soi. ♦ **unselfishness** *n* générosité *f*.

unserviceable ['ʌn'sɜːvɪsəbl] *adj* inutilisable.
unsettle ['ʌn'setl] *vt* perturber. ♦ **unsettled** *adj person* perturbé; *weather, future* incertain; **he feels ~d** il n'est pas bien dans sa peau. ♦ **unsettling** *adj news* inquiétant; *effect* perturbateur.
unshakeable ['ʌn'ʃeɪkəbl] *adj* inébranlable. ♦ **unshaken** *adj resolve* inébranlable; *person* non déconcerté.
unshaven ['ʌn'ʃeɪvn] *adj* non rasé.
unshrinkable ['ʌn'ʃrɪŋkəbl] *adj* irrétrécissable.
unsightly [ʌn'saɪtlɪ] *adj* disgracieux, laid.
unsinkable ['ʌn'sɪŋkəbl] *adj* insubmersible.
unskilful, (*US*) **unskillful** ['ʌn'skɪlfʊl] *adj* (*clumsy*) maladroit; (*inexpert*) malhabile. ♦ **unskil(l)fully** *adv* avec maladresse; malhabilement. ♦ **unskilled** *adj* (*gen*) inexpérimenté; (*Ind*) *work* de manœuvre; **unskilled worker** manœuvre *m*.
unsociable [ʌn'səʊʃəbl] *adj* insociable. **I'm feeling ~** je n'ai guère envie de voir des gens.
unsocial [ʌn'səʊʃəl] *adj* (*Ind*) **~ hours** heures *fpl* de travail peu pratiques.
unsold ['ʌn'səʊld] *adj* invendu.
unsolved ['ʌn'sɒlvd] *adj mystery* non résolu; *crossword* non terminé.
unsophisticated ['ʌnsə'fɪstɪkeɪtɪd] *adj person* simple, naturel; *thing* simple.
unsound ['ʌn'saʊnd] *adj timber* pourri; *structure, floor, bridge* en mauvais état; *organization, business* peu solide; *investment* peu sûr; *judgment, argument* peu valable; *policy, decision, advice* peu judicieux; *statesman, player* incompétent. (*Jur*) **of ~ mind** qui ne jouit pas de toutes ses facultés mentales.
unsparing [ʌn'spɛərɪŋ] *adj* prodigue (*of* de). ♦ **unsparingly** *adv give* généreusement; *work* inlassablement.
unspeakable [ʌn'spiːkəbl] *adj* indescriptible. ♦ **unspeakably** *adv* (*bad etc*) affreusement.
unspoiled ['ʌn'spɔɪld] *adj countryside, beauty* qui n'est pas défiguré; *style* naturel; *person* qui reste simple.
unspoken ['ʌn'spəʊkən] *adj thought* inexprimé; *approval* tacite.
unsporting ['ʌn'spɔːtɪŋ] *adj* déloyal. **that's very ~ of you** ce n'est pas très chic de votre part.
unstable ['ʌn'steɪbl] *adj* instable.
unstamped ['ʌn'stæmpt] *adj letter* non affranchi.
unsteady ['ʌn'stedɪ] *adj ladder, structure* instable, branlant; *hand* tremblant; *voice* mal assuré; *step* chancelant; *rhythm* irrégulier. **to be ~ on one's feet** ne pas très bien tenir sur ses jambes; (*from drink*) tituber. ♦ **unsteadily** *adv walk* d'un pas chancelant; *say* d'une voix mal assurée.
unstick ['ʌn'stɪk] *pret, ptp* **-stuck** *vt* décoller. **to come unstuck** *[stamp etc]* se décoller; (*) *[plan]* tomber à l'eau*; *[person]* tomber sur un bec*.
unstinting [ʌn'stɪntɪŋ] *adj praise* sans réserve; *generosity* sans bornes; *efforts* illimité.
unstressed ['ʌn'strest] *adj* inaccentué.
unsubstantiated ['ʌnsəb'stænʃɪeɪtɪd] *adj accusation* non prouvé; *rumour* non confirmé.
unsuccessful ['ʌnsək'sesfʊl] *adj negotiation, attempt, visit* infructueux, qui est un échec; *candidate, marriage, outcome* malheureux; *application* non retenu; *writer, painter, book* qui n'a pas de succès; *firm* qui ne prospère pas. **to be ~** (*gen*) ne pas réussir (*in doing* à faire); (*Scol etc*) échouer (*in an exam* à un examen; *in maths* en maths); **I tried but I was ~** j'ai essayé mais sans succès; **after 3 ~ attempts** après avoir échoué 3 fois. ♦ **unsuccessfully** *adv* en vain, sans succès.
unsuitable ['ʌn'suːtəbl] *adj* (*gen*) qui ne convient pas; *moment* inopportun; *colour, size* qui ne va pas; *action, example, device* peu approprié. **to be ~ for sth** (*gen*) ne pas convenir à qch; *[film, book]* ne pas être conseillé pour qch; **he is ~ for the post** ce n'est pas l'homme qu'il faut pour le poste. ♦ **unsuited** *adj person* inapte (*to* à); *thing* impropre (*to* à); **they are quite unsuited** ils ne sont pas compatibles.
unsupported ['ʌnsə'pɔːtɪd] *adj structure, hypothesis* non soutenu; *statement* non confirmé; *mother, family* sans soutien financier.
unsure ['ʌn'ʃʊə^r] *adj* incertain (*of, about* de). **to be ~ of o.s.** manquer d'assurance.
unsuspected ['ʌnsəs'pektɪd] *adj* insoupçonné. ♦ **unsuspecting** *adj* qui ne se doute de rien.
unsweetened ['ʌn'swiːtnd] *adj* sans sucre.
unswerving [ʌn'swɜːvɪŋ] *adj* (*fig*) inébranlable.
unsympathetic ['ʌnˌsɪmpə'θetɪk] *adj* indifférent (*to* à). ♦ **unsympathetically** *adv* avec indifférence.
unsystematic ['ʌnˌsɪstɪ'mætɪk] *adj* peu systématique. ♦ **unsystematically** *adv* sans système.
untangle ['ʌn'tæŋgl] *vt wool etc* démêler.
untapped ['ʌn'tæpt] *adj resources* inexploité.
untaxed ['ʌn'tækst] *adj goods* exempt de taxes; *income* non imposable.
unteachable ['ʌn'tiːtʃəbl] *adj person* à qui on ne peut rien apprendre.
untenable ['ʌn'tenəbl] *adj position* intenable.
untested ['ʌn'testɪd] *adj person, theory, method* qui n'a pas été mis à l'épreuve; *product, invention* qui n'a pas été essayé; *new drug* non encore expérimenté.
unthinkable [ʌn'θɪŋkəbl] *adj* impensable (*that* que *+subj*). ♦ **unthinking** *adj* irréfléchi. ♦ **unthinkingly** *adv* sans réfléchir.
untidy [ʌn'taɪdɪ] *adj appearance* négligé; *clothes* débraillé; *hair* mal peigné; *person* désordonné; *writing, work* brouillon; *room, desk* en désordre. ♦ **untidily** *adv work, live* sans ordre; *write, dress* sans soin. ♦ **untidiness** *n* (*in appearance*) débraillé *m*; (*in habits*) manque *m* d'ordre; *[room]* désordre *m*.
untie ['ʌn'taɪ] *vt knot, string, parcel* défaire; *prisoner, hands, bonds* détacher.
until [ən'tɪl] **1** *prep* jusqu'à. **~ such time as** (*in future*) jusqu'à ce que *+subj*; (*in past*) avant que +ne *+subj*; **from morning ~ night** du matin jusqu'au soir; **~ now** jusqu'ici; **~ then** jusque-là; **it won't be ready ~ tomorrow** ce ne sera pas prêt avant demain; **he didn't leave ~ the following day** il n'est parti que le lendemain; **I had heard nothing of it ~ 5 minutes ago** j'en ai seulement entendu parler il y a 5 minutes. **2** *conj* (*in future*) jusqu'à ce que *+subj*; (*in past*) avant que +ne *+subj*. **wait ~ I come** attendez que je vienne; **~ they built the new road** avant qu'ils ne fassent la nouvelle route; **~ they build the new road** en attendant qu'ils fassent la nouvelle route; **he won't come ~ you invite him** il ne viendra pas avant que vous ne l'invitiez *or* avant d'être invité; **do nothing ~ you get my letter/~ I come** ne faites rien avant d'avoir reçu ma lettre/avant que je n'arrive (*subj*).
untimely [ʌn'taɪmlɪ] *adj spring, death* prématuré; *moment, arrival, remark* inopportun. **to come to an ~ end** *[person]* mourir prématurément; *[project]* être enterré prématurément.
untiring [ʌn'taɪərɪŋ] *adj* infatigable. ♦ **untiringly** *adv* infatigablement.
untold ['ʌn'təʊld] *adj amount, wealth* incalculable; *agony, delight* indescriptible.
untouchable [ʌn'tʌtʃəbl] *adj, n* intouchable (*mf*). ♦ **untouched** *adj* **(a)** (*Comm*) **untouched by hand** sans manipulation directe; **he left his meal untouched** il n'a pas touché à son repas; **(b)** (*safe*) *person* indemne; *thing* intact; (*unaffected*) insensible (*by* à).
untoward [ˌʌntə'wɔːd] *adj* fâcheux.
untrained ['ʌn'treɪnd] *adj worker* qui n'a pas reçu de formation professionnelle; *animal* non dressé; *ear* inexercé.

untranslatable [ˈʌntrænzˈleɪtəbl] *adj* intraduisible.
untried [ˈʌnˈtraɪd] *adj product, invention* qui n'a pas été essayé; *person, method* qui n'a pas été mis à l'épreuve.
untroubled [ˈʌnˈtrʌbld] *adj* calme.
untrue [ˈʌnˈtru:] *adj* (*gen*) faux (*f* fausse); *lover etc* infidèle (*to* à). **it is ~ that** il est faux *or* il n'est pas vrai que *+subj*. ♦ **untruth** *n* contre-vérité *f*. ♦ **untruthful** *adj statement* mensonger; *person* menteur. ♦ **untruthfully** *adv* mensongèrement.
untrustworthy [ˌʌnˈtrʌstˌwɜ:ðɪ] *adj person* indigne de confiance; *source of information* douteux.
untwist [ˈʌnˈtwɪst] *vt wire* détordre.
unusable [ˈʌnˈju:zəbl] *adj* inutilisable. ♦ **unused** *adj* **(a)** [ˈʌnˈju:zd] (*new*) neuf; (*not in use*) inutilisé; **(b)** [ˈʌnˈju:st] **to be unused to (doing) sth** ne pas avoir l'habitude de (faire) qch.
unusual [ʌnˈju:ʒʊəl] *adj shape, name* étrange, insolite; *talents, size* exceptionnel. **it is ~ for him to be early** il est rare qu'il arrive (*subj*) de bonne heure; **that's ~ for him!** ce n'est pas dans ses habitudes!; **that's ~!** ça n'arrive pas souvent! ♦ **unusually** *adv* (*unaccustomedly*) *happy, warm* exceptionnellement, anormalement; (*exceedingly*) *tall, gifted* exceptionnellement, extraordinairement; **~ly early** plus tôt que d'habitude.
unutterable [ʌnˈʌtərəbl] *adj joy, boredom* indescriptible; (*) *idiot, fool* fini.
unvarnished [ˈʌnˈvɑ:nɪʃt] *adj wood* non verni; *account, truth* pur et simple.
unvarying [ʌnˈvɛərɪŋ] *adj* invariable, constant.
unveil [ʌnˈveɪl] *vt* dévoiler. ♦ **unveiling** *n* (*ceremony*) inauguration *f*.
unventilated [ˈʌnˈventɪleɪtɪd] *adj* sans ventilation.
unvoiced [ˈʌnˈvɔɪst] *adj opinion* inexprimé; *consonant* sourd.
unwanted [ˈʌnˈwɒntɪd] *adj clothing etc* superflu, dont on n'a pas besoin; *child* non désiré; *effect* non recherché.
unwarranted [ʌnˈwɒrəntɪd] *adj* injustifié.
unwary [ʌnˈwɛərɪ] *adj* imprudent.
unwearying [ʌnˈwɪərɪɪŋ] *adj* inlassable.
unwelcome [ʌnˈwelkəm] *adj visitor, gift* importun; *news, delay, change* fâcheux. **they made us feel ~** ils nous ont mal accueillis.
unwell [ˈʌnˈwel] *adj* souffrant. **to feel ~** ne pas se sentir très bien.
unwholesome [ˈʌnˈhəʊlsəm] *adj* malsain.
unwieldy [ʌnˈwi:ldɪ] *adj* difficile à manier.
unwilling [ˈʌnˈwɪlɪŋ] *adj*: **to be ~ to do** (*reluctant*) être peu disposé à faire; (*refuse*) ne pas vouloir faire. ♦ **unwillingly** *adv* à contrecœur.
unwind [ˈʌnˈwaɪnd] *pret, ptp* **-wound 1** *vt* dérouler. **2** *vi* se dérouler; (*: *relax*) se détendre.
unwise [ˈʌnˈwaɪz] *adj person* malavisé; *move, decision* imprudent. ♦ **unwisely** *adv* imprudemment.
unwitting [ʌnˈwɪtɪŋ] *adj* involontaire. ♦ **unwittingly** *adv* involontairement.
unwonted [ʌnˈwəʊntɪd] *adj* inaccoutumé.
unworkable [ˈʌnˈwɜ:kəbl] *adj scheme etc* impraticable.
unworldly [ˈʌnˈwɜ:ldlɪ] *adj* détaché de ce monde.
unworthy [ʌnˈwɜ:ðɪ] *adj* indigne (*of* de; *to do* de faire).
unwrap [ˈʌnˈræp] *vt* défaire, ouvrir.
unwritten [ˈʌnˈrɪtn] *adj agreement* verbal. **it is an ~ law that ...** il est tacitement admis que ... .
unyielding [ʌnˈji:ldɪŋ] *adj person* inflexible.
unzip [ˈʌnˈzɪp] *vt* ouvrir la fermeture éclair ® de.
up [ʌp] **1** *adv* **(a)** (*gen*) en haut, en l'air; *throw etc* en l'air. **hold it ~ higher** tiens-le plus haut; **~ there** là-haut; **~ in the air** en l'air; **~ in the sky/mountains** dans le ciel/les montagnes; **~ on the hill** sur la colline; **~ on top of** sur; **~ at the top of** en haut de; **~ above** au-dessus; **~ above sth** au-dessus de qch; **he lives 5 floors ~** il habite au 5e étage; **all the way ~** jusqu'en haut; **I met him on my way ~** je l'ai rencontré en montant; **farther ~** (*on wall etc*) plus haut; (*along bench etc*) plus loin; **close ~ to** tout près de; **with his head ~ (high)** la tête haute; **the blinds were ~** les stores étaient levés; **~ against the wall** appuyé contre le mur; **~ on end** debout; **'this side ~'** 'haut'; **you've been ~ and down all evening** tu n'as pas arrêté toute la soirée; *[invalid]* **he's been rather ~ and down** il a eu des hauts et des bas; **to jump ~ and down** sauter; **to walk ~ and down** faire les cent pas.
(b) (*out of bed*) **to be ~** être levé, être debout *inv*; **get ~!** debout!, levez-vous!; **I was ~ late last night** je me suis couché tard hier soir; **he was ~ all night** il ne s'est pas couché de la nuit; **~ and about, ~ and doing*** à l'ouvrage; **to be ~ and about again** ne plus être alité.
(c) (*fig*) **when the sun was ~** quand le soleil était levé; **the tide is ~** la marée est haute; **the river is ~** la rivière a monté; **the road is ~** la route est en travaux; (*Parl*) **the House is ~** la Chambre ne siège pas; **~ with Joe Bloggs!** vive Joe Bloggs!; **~ with** *or* **~ among the leaders** dans les premiers; **he's well ~ in Latin** (*place in class*) il a une bonne place en latin; (*knows a lot*) il est fort en latin; **I'm ~ with him in maths** nous sommes au même niveau en maths; **I'm not very well ~ on what's been going on** je ne suis pas vraiment au fait de ce qui s'est passé; **~ in London** à Londres; **~ in Scotland** en Écosse; **he's ~ from Birmingham** il arrive de Birmingham; **to come ~ to town** venir en ville; **~ north** dans le nord; **I'll play you 100 ~** je vous fais une partie en 100; **Chelsea were 3 goals ~** Chelsea menait par 3 buts; **we were 20 points ~ on them** nous avions 20 points d'avance sur eux; **to be one ~ on sb*** faire mieux que qn; **what's ~?*** (*what's happening*) qu'est-ce qu'il y a?; (*what's wrong*) qu'est-ce qui ne va pas?; **what's ~ with him?*** qu'est-ce qu'il a?; **there's sth ~*** (*happening*) il se passe qch; (*wrong*) il y a qch qui ne va pas (*with sb* chez qn).
(d) (*higher etc*) **to be ~** *[prices, salaries, goods]* avoir augmenté (*by* de); *[temperature, level]* avoir monté (*by* de); *[standard]* être plus élevé; **it is ~ on last year** cela a augmenté par rapport à l'an dernier.
(e) (*upwards*) **from £2 ~** à partir de 2 livres.
(f) (*installed, built etc*) **to be ~** *[curtains, shutters]* être posé; *[pictures]* être accroché; *[building]* être construit; *[tent]* être planté; *[flag]* être hissé; *[notice]* être affiché.
(g) (*finished*) **his leave is ~** sa permission est terminée; **it is ~ on the 20th** ça se termine le 20; **when 3 days were ~** au bout de 3 jours; **time's ~!** c'est l'heure!; **it's all ~ with him*** il est fichu*.
(h) to be ~ against *difficulties* se heurter à; *competitors, competition* avoir affaire à; **you don't know what you're ~ against!** tu n'as pas idée des difficultés qui t'attendent!; **he's ~ against a very powerful man** il a contre lui un homme très puissant; **we're really ~ against it** nous allons avoir du mal à nous en sortir.
(i) (*as far as*) **~ to** jusqu'à; **~ to now** jusqu'à maintenant, jusqu'ici; **~ to here** jusqu'ici; **~ to there** jusque-là; **what page are you ~ to?** à quelle page en êtes-vous?; **~ to and including chapter 5** jusqu'au chapitre 5 inclus.
(j) (*depending on*) **it's ~ to you to decide** c'est à vous de décider; **it's ~ to you (whether you go or not)** c'est à vous de décider (si vous y allez ou non); **it's ~ to us to help him** c'est à nous de l'aider.
(k) (*busy doing etc*) **what is he ~ to?** qu'est-ce qu'il peut bien faire?; **he's ~ to sth** il manigance qch; **what have you been ~ to recently?** qu'est-ce que vous devenez ces temps-ci?; **what have you**

been ~ to? qu'est-ce que tu as manigancé?; **he's ~ to no good** il prépare une bêtise, *[adult]* il prépare un mauvais coup.

(l) (*equal to*) **to be ~ to a task** être à la hauteur d'une tâche; **is he ~ to advanced work?** est-il capable de faire des études supérieures?; **it isn't ~ to his usual standard** d'habitude il fait mieux que ça; **are you feeling ~ to going?** est-ce que tu te sens assez d'attaque* pour y aller?; **I just don't feel ~ to it** je ne m'en sens pas le courage; **he really isn't ~ to going back to work** il n'est vraiment pas en état de reprendre le travail; **it's not ~ to much** ça ne vaut pas grand-chose.

2 *prep*: **to be ~ a tree/~ a ladder** être dans un arbre/sur une échelle; **to go ~** *stairs, street* monter; *river* remonter; **he pointed ~ the hill** il a indiqué du doigt le haut de la colline; **the house is ~ that road** la maison est dans cette rue; **they live just ~ the road** ils habitent un peu plus haut dans la rue; **~ and down the country** un peu partout dans le pays; **he went ~ and down the country** il parcourait le pays; **I've been ~ and down the stairs all evening** je n'ai pas arrêté de monter et descendre les escaliers de toute la soirée; **further ~ the page** plus haut sur la même page; **halfway ~ the hill** à mi-côte.

3 *n*: **~s and downs** (*in road*) accidents *mpl*; (*in career, health*) hauts *mpl* et bas *mpl*; **he is on the ~ and ~*** tout va de mieux en mieux pour lui.

4 *adj* (*Brit*) *train* qui va à Londres.

5 *vi*: **I ~ped and told him** sans plus attendre je lui ai dit.

♦ **up-and-coming** *adj* plein d'avenir. ♦ **up-and-down** *adj movement* de va-et-vient; (*fig*) *career, business* qui a des hauts et des bas. ♦ **upbringing** *n* éducation *f*. ♦ **upcountry** *adv go* vers l'intérieur (*d'un pays*); *be* à l'intérieur. ♦ **update** *vt* mettre à jour. ♦ **upend** *vt box etc* mettre debout; (*fig*) *system etc* renverser. ♦ **upgrade** *vt employee* promouvoir; *job, post* revaloriser. ♦ **upheaval** *n* (*Geol*) soulèvement *m*; (*fig*) bouleversement *m*; (*esp Pol*) perturbations *fpl*; (*esp in home, family*) remue-ménage *m*; **it caused a lot of ~heaval** cela a tout perturbé. ♦ **uphill 1** *adv*: **to go ~hill** monter; **2** *adj road* qui monte; (*fig*) *task* pénible; **it's ~hill all the way** ça monte tout le long; (*fig*) c'est une lutte continuelle. ♦ **uphold** *pret, ptp* **-held** *vt institution, person* soutenir; *law* faire respecter; (*Jur*) *verdict* confirmer. ♦ **upholder** *n* défenseur *m*. ♦ **upholster** *vt* garnir (*in* de); (*pad etc*) rembourrer. ♦ **upholsterer** *n* tapissier *m*. ♦ **upholstery** *n* garniture *f*. ♦ **upkeep** *n* entretien *m*. ♦ **uplands** *npl* hautes terres *fpl*. ♦ **uplifted** *adj* grandi, exalté. ♦ **upon** *prep* = **on 1**. ♦ **upper 1** *adj* (*gen*) supérieur; *part, floor* supérieur, du dessus; (*in place names*) haut; **the ~per classes** les couches *fpl* supérieures de la société; **the ~per middle class** la haute bourgeoisie; (*fig*) **the ~per crust** le gratin*; **the ~per income bracket** la tranche des revenus élevés; **the ~per school** les grandes classes; **2** *n [shoe]* empeigne *f*. ♦ **upper-class** *adj* aristocratique. ♦ **uppermost** *adj* (*highest*) le plus haut, le plus élevé; (*on top*) en dessus; **it was ~permost in my mind** j'y pensais avant tout autre chose. ♦ **uppish*** *adj* prétentieux. ♦ **upright 1** *adj, adv* droit; **2** *n* **(a)** *[door, window]* montant *m*; *[goal-post]* montant de but; **(b)** (*piano*) piano *m* droit. ♦ **uprising** *n* soulèvement *m*, insurrection *f* (*against* contre). ♦ **uproar** *n* (*shouts*) tumulte *m*; (*protesting*) tempête *f* de protestations; **the hall was in (an) ~roar** le tumulte régnait dans la salle. ♦ **uproarious** *adj meeting, evening, discussion* tordant*, désopilant; *joke, mistake* hilarant; *laughter* éclatant; **~roarious success** grand succès comique. ♦ **uproariously** *adv laugh* aux éclats; *greet etc* avec de grands éclats de rire; **~roariously funny** désopilant. ♦ **uproot** *vt* déraciner. ♦ **upset** *etc V below*. ♦ **upshot** *n* résultat *m*. ♦ **upside down 1** *adv hold etc* à l'envers; **to turn ~side down** *object* retourner; (*fig*) *cupboard etc* mettre sens dessus dessous; (*) *plans* flanquer à l'eau*; **2** *adj* (*gen*) à l'envers; (*upturned*) retourné; (*in disorder*) sens dessus dessous. ♦ **upstairs 1** *adv* en haut (*d'un escalier*); **he's ~stairs** il est en haut; **to go ~stairs** monter; **to take ~stairs** *person* faire monter; *luggage etc* monter; **the people ~stairs** les gens du dessus; **the room ~stairs** la pièce d'en haut; **2** *n* étage *m* (*du dessus*); **3** *adj*: **an ~stairs room** une chambre à l'étage. ♦ **upstanding** *adj* (*well-built*) bien bâti; (*honest*) droit; **a fine ~standing young man** un jeune homme très bien. ♦ **upstart** *n* parvenu(e) *m(f)*. ♦ **upstream** *adv be* en amont (*from* de); *sail* vers l'amont; *swim* contre le courant. ♦ **upsurge** *n [feeling]* vague *f*; *[interest]* regain *m*. ♦ **upswept** *adj* (*Aut, Aviat*) profilé. ♦ **uptake** *n*: **to be quick/slow on the ~take** avoir l'esprit vif/lent. ♦ **uptight*** *adj* crispé; **to get ~tight** se crisper (*about* à propos de). ♦ **up-to-date** *adj report, information* très récent; *building, person, ideas* moderne. ♦ **up-to-the-minute** *adj* de dernière heure. ♦ **upturned** *adj nose* retroussé. ♦ **upward 1** *adj movement* ascendant; *pull, thrust* vers le haut; *trend* à la hausse; *glance* levé; **2** *adv* (*also* **~wards**) vers le haut; (*fig*) **from 10 francs ~wards** à partir de 10 F; **from childhood ~wards** dès sa jeunesse; **~wards of 300** 300 et plus.

upset [ʌp'set] *pret, ptp* **-set 1** *vt container, contents* renverser; *boat* faire chavirer; (*fig*) *plan, timetable, system, stomach* déranger; *calculation* fausser; *person* (*offend*) vexer; (*grieve*) faire de la peine à; (*annoy*) contrarier; (*make ill*) rendre malade. **don't ~ yourself** ne vous en faites pas*. **2** *adj stomach, digestion* dérangé; *person* (*offended*) vexé; (*grieved*) peiné, triste; (*annoyed*) fâché, contrarié; (*ill*) souffrant. **to get ~** se vexer, devenir triste, se fâcher; **what are you so ~ about?** qu'est-ce qui ne va pas? **3** ['ʌpset] *n* (*upheaval*) désordre *m*; (*in plans etc*) bouleversement *m* (*in* de); (*emotional*) chagrin *m*. **to have a stomach ~** avoir l'estomac dérangé. ♦ **upsetting** *adj* (*offending*) vexant; (*saddening*) triste, (*stronger*) affligeant; (*annoying*) contrariant.

uranium [jʊə'reɪnɪəm] *n* uranium *m*.

Uranus [jʊə'reɪnəs] *n* (*Astron*) Uranus *f*.

urban ['ɜːbən] *adj* urbain. ♦ **urbanization** *n* urbanisation *f*.

urbane [ɜː'beɪn] *adj* urbain, courtois. ♦ **urbanity** *n* urbanité *f*.

urchin ['ɜːtʃɪn] *n* polisson(ne) *m(f)*.

urge [ɜːdʒ] **1** *n* forte envie *f* (*to do* de faire). **to have the ~ to do** éprouver une forte envie de faire. **2** *vt person* pousser (*to do* à faire), conseiller vivement (*sb to do* à qn de faire); *caution, measure* préconiser, conseiller vivement; (*emphasize*) insister sur. **he needed no urging** il ne s'est pas fait prier; **to ~ that** recommander vivement que +*subj*; **'now!' he ~d** 'tout de suite!' insista-t-il; **to ~ sb in** *etc* presser qn d'entrer *etc*.

urge on *vt sep horse* presser; *person, troops* faire avancer; (*fig*) *worker* presser; *work* activer; (*Sport*) *team* encourager. **to ~ sb on to (do) sth** inciter qn à (faire) qch.

urgent ['ɜːdʒənt] *adj need, case, attention* urgent; *tone* insistant; *entreaty, request* pressant. ♦ **urgency** *n [case etc]* urgence *f*; *[tone, entreaty]* insistance *f*; **a matter of urgency** une affaire urgente. ♦ **urgently** *adv need* d'urgence; *plead* instamment.

urine ['jʊərɪn] *n* urine *f*. ♦ **urinal** *n* urinoir *m*. ♦ **urinary** *adj* urinaire. ♦ **urinate** *vi* uriner.

urn [ɜːn] *n* (*gen*) urne *f*. **tea ~** fontaine *f* à thé.

us [ʌs] *pers pron* nous. **he hit ~** il nous a frappés; **give it to ~** donnez-le-nous; **in front of ~** devant nous; **let ~** *or* **let's go!** allons-y!; **younger than ~** plus jeune que nous; **both of ~** nous deux, tous les deux; **he is one of ~** il est des nôtres; **~ English** nous autres Anglais; (*me*) **give ~ it!‡** donne-le-moi!

use [ju:s] **1** *n* **(a)** (*gen*) usage *m*, emploi *m*; (*way of using*) emploi, utilisation *f*. **the ~ of steel** l'emploi de l'acier; **to learn the ~ of** apprendre à se servir de; **directions for ~** mode *m* d'emploi; **'for the ~ of teachers only'** *book, equipment* 'à l'usage des professeurs seulement'; *room* 'réservé aux professeurs'; **for one's own ~** à son usage personnel; **for ~ in emergency** à utiliser en cas d'urgence; **fit for ~** en état de servir; **ready for ~** prêt à l'emploi; **to improve with ~** s'améliorer à l'usage; **in ~** *machine, word* en usage; **no longer in ~** *machine* hors d'usage; *word* qui ne s'emploie plus; (*notice*) **'out of ~'** 'en dérangement'; **in general ~** d'usage courant; **it is in daily ~** on s'en sert tous les jours; **it's gone out of ~** on ne l'emploie plus; **to make ~ of** se servir de, utiliser; **to make good ~ of, to put to good ~** *time, money* faire un bon emploi de; *opportunity, facilities* tirer parti de; **a new ~ for** un nouvel emploi de, une nouvelle utilisation de; **I'll find a ~ for it** je trouverai un moyen de m'en servir; **I've no further ~ for it** je n'en ai plus besoin; (*fig*) **I've no ~ for that sort of thing!*** je n'ai rien à en faire!

(b) (*usefulness*) **to be of ~** servir, être utile (*for, to* à); **to be (of) no ~** ne servir à rien; **he gave me the ~ of his car** il m'a permis de me servir de sa voiture; **to have lost the ~ of one's arm** avoir perdu l'usage de son bras; **what's the ~ of doing ...?** à quoi bon faire ...?; **is this (of) any ~ to you?** est-ce que cela peut vous être utile?; **he's no ~** il est nul (*as* comme); **it's no ~ protesting** il ne sert à rien de protester; **it's no ~** rien à faire, ça ne sert à rien.

2 [ju:z] *vt* **(a)** (*gen*) se servir de, utiliser, employer (*to do, for doing* pour faire); *a language* utiliser, se servir de; *money* utiliser (*to do* pour faire); *car* prendre, se servir de; *force, discretion* user de; *opportunity* profiter de; *method, means* employer; *sb's name* faire usage de. **are you using this?** vous servez-vous de ceci?; **he ~d it as a hammer** il s'en est servi comme marteau; **I ~ that as a table** ça me sert de table; **'to be ~d regularly'** 'à utiliser régulièrement'; **no longer ~d** *machine, room* qui ne sert plus; *word* qui ne s'emploie plus; **~ your head** *or* **brains!** réfléchis un peu!; **~ your eyes!** ouvre l'œil!; **I could ~ a drink!*** je prendrais bien un verre!; **it could ~ a bit of paint*** une couche de peinture ne ferait pas de mal. **(b)** *petrol etc* user, consommer; (**~ up**) (*finish*) finir; *left-overs* utiliser. **have you ~d all the sellotape?** avez-vous fini le scotch? **(c)** (*treat*) *person* traiter, agir envers. **he was badly ~d** on a mal agi envers lui.

3 *aux vb* (*translated by imperfect tense*) **I ~d to see him every day** je le voyais *or* j'avais l'habitude de le voir tous les jours.

use up *vt sep supplies, strength* épuiser; *food, paper* finir; *scraps* utiliser; *money* dépenser. **it is all ~d up** c'est épuisé, il n'en reste plus.

♦ **usable** *adj* utilisable. ♦ **usage** *n* **(a)** (*custom; also Ling*) usage *m*; **(b)** (*treatment*) *[object]* manipulation *f*; *[person]* traitement *m*; **it's had some rough usage** on s'en est mal servi. ♦ **used** [ju:zd] *adj* **(a)** *stamp* oblitéré; *car* d'occasion; **(b)** [ju:st] (*accustomed*) **to be ~d to (doing) sth** être habitué à *or* avoir l'habitude de (faire) qch; **to get ~d to** s'habituer à; **you'll get ~d to it** vous vous y ferez. ♦ **useful** *adj* (*gen*) utile; *discussion, time* utile, profitable; (*fig*) *player etc* compétent; **it is ~ful for him to be able to ...** il est très utile qu'il puisse ...; **to make o.s. ~ful** se rendre utile; **to come in ~ful** être utile; **to be ~ful** to rendre service à; **he's a ~ful man to know** c'est un homme utile à connaître; **it's a ~ful thing to know** c'est bon à savoir; **he's ~ful with a gun** il sait bien manier un fusil. ♦ **usefully** *adv* utilement. ♦ **usefulness** *n* utilité *f*. ♦ **useless** *adj* (*no good*) qui ne vaut rien; (*unusable*) inutilisable; *remedy* inefficace; *person* incompétent; *volunteer* incapable; **shouting is ~less** il est inutile de crier, il ne sert à rien de crier; **he's ~less** il est nul (*as* comme). ♦ **uselessly** *adv* inutilement. ♦ **user** *n [machine, dictionary etc]* utilisateur *m*, -trice *f*; *[public service, telephone, road, train]* usager *m*; **oil ~rs** consommateurs *mpl* de mazout; **car ~rs** automobilistes *mpl*.

usher ['ʌʃəʳ] **1** *n* (*in law courts etc*) huissier *m* (*audiencier*); (*in theatre, church*) placeur *m*. **2** *vt*: **to ~ sb through/along** *etc* faire traverser/avancer *etc* qn; **to ~ sb to the door** reconduire qn à la porte; **to ~ in** *person* faire entrer; (*fig*) *period* inaugurer. ♦ **usherette** *n* ouvreuse *f*.

usual ['ju:ʒʊəl] **1** *adj* (*gen*) habituel; *word* usuel; *remarks, conditions* d'usage. **the ~ practice** ce qui se fait d'habitude; **his ~ practice** son habitude *f*; **as is ~ with such machines it ...** comme toutes les machines de ce genre elle ...; **as is ~ on these occasions** comme le veut la coutume en ces occasions; **he'll soon be his ~ self again** il retrouvera bientôt sa santé (*or* sa gaieté *etc*); **as ~** comme d'habitude, comme à l'ordinaire; **more than ~** plus que d'habitude *or* d'ordinaire; **it's not ~ for him to be late** il est rare qu'il soit en retard. **2** *n* (*drink*) **the ~!*** comme d'habitude! ♦ **usually** *adv* d'habitude, d'ordinaire; **more than ~ly careful** encore plus prudent que d'habitude.

usurp [ju:'zɜ:p] *vt* usurper. ♦ **usurper** *n* usurpateur *m*, -trice *f*.

usury ['ju:ʒʊrɪ] *n* usure *f* (*prêt*).

utensil [ju:'tensl] *n* ustensile *m*.

uterus ['ju:tərəs] *n* utérus *m*.

utility [ju:'tɪlɪtɪ] **1** *n* (*use*) utilité *f*; (*public ~*) service *m* public. **2** *adj* (*gen*) utilitaire. **~ room** *pièce réservée au repassage etc*. ♦ **utilitarian** *adj* utilitaire. ♦ **utilizable** *adj* utilisable. ♦ **utilization** *n* utilisation *f*. ♦ **utilize** *vt* utiliser.

utmost ['ʌtməʊst] **1** *adj* **(a)** (*greatest*) *simplicity, care etc* le plus grand; *skill* suprême; *danger* extrême. **with the ~ speed** à toute vitesse; **it is of the ~ importance that ...** il est extrêmement important que ... + *subj*; **a matter of the ~ importance** une affaire de la plus haute importance. **(b)** (*furthest*) *place, part* le plus éloigné, extrême. **2** *n*: **to do one's ~** faire tout son possible (*to do* pour faire); **to the ~ of one's ability** à la limite de ses capacités; **to the ~** au plus haut degré; **at the ~** tout au plus.

Utopia [ju:'təʊpɪə] *n* utopie *f*. ♦ **Utopian** *adj* utopique.

utter[1] ['ʌtəʳ] *adj sincerity, disaster* complet, total; *madness* pur; *idiot, fool* fini; *rogue, liar* fieffé (*before n*). **it was ~ nonsense!** c'était complètement absurde; **he's an ~ stranger** il m'est complètement inconnu. ♦ **utterly** *adv* complètement, tout à fait. ♦ **uttermost** = **utmost**.

utter[2] ['ʌtəʳ] *vt word* prononcer; *cry* pousser; *threat, insult* proférer; *libel* publier; *counterfeit money* émettre. **he didn't ~ a word** il n'a pas soufflé mot.

V

V, v [viː] *n* (*letter*) V, v *m*. ♦ **V-neck** *n* décolleté *m* en V *or* en pointe.

vacant [ˈveɪkənt] *adj job* vacant, à remplir; *room, house, seat* libre; *hours* de loisir; *mind* vide; *stare* vague; *person* (*stupid*) stupide; (*dreamy*) sans expression. ♦ **vacancy** *n* (*room*) chambre *f* à louer; (*job*) poste *m* vacant; **vacancy for a typist** poste de dactylo à suppléer, (*notice*) 'on cherche dactylo'; **'no vacancies'** (*of jobs*) 'pas d'embauche'; (*in hotel*) 'complet'. ♦ **vacantly** *adv*: **to gaze ~ly into space** avoir le regard perdu dans le vide. ♦ **vacate** *vt room, seat, job, house* quitter; **to vacate the premises** vider les lieux.

vacation [vəˈkeɪʃən] **1** *n* vacances *fpl*. **on ~** en vacances; **to take a ~** prendre des vacances; (*Scol etc*) **long ~** grandes vacances. **2** *adj*: **~ course** cours *mpl* de vacances.

vaccinate [ˈvæksɪneɪt] *vt* vacciner (*against* contre). **to get ~d** se faire vacciner; **have you been ~d against ...?** est-ce que vous êtes vacciné contre ...? ♦ **vaccination** *n* vaccination *f*. ♦ **vaccine** *n* vaccin *m*; **polio vaccine** vaccin contre la polio.

vacillate [ˈvæsɪleɪt] *vi* hésiter (***between*** entre).

vacuum [ˈvækjʊm] **1** *n* vide *m*; (*Phys*) vacuum *m*. **2** *adj brake, pump* à vide. **~ cleaner** aspirateur *m*; **~ flask** *or* (*US*) **bottle** bouteille *f* thermos ®. **3** *vt carpet* passer à l'aspirateur. ♦ **vacuity** *n* vacuité *f*. ♦ **vacuous** *adj eyes, stare* vide; *remark* bête. ♦ **vacuum-packed** *adj* emballé sous vide.

vagabond [ˈvægəbɒnd] *n* vagabond(e) *m(f)*.

vagary [ˈveɪgərɪ] *n* caprice *m*.

vagina [vəˈdʒaɪnə] *n* vagin *m*. ♦ **vaginal** *adj* vaginal; **~l discharge** pertes *fpl* blanches.

vagrant [ˈveɪgrənt] *n, adj* vagabond(e) *m(f)*. ♦ **vagrancy** *n* vagabondage *m*.

vague [veɪg] *adj* (*not clear: gen*) vague, imprécis; *outline, photograph, memory* flou; *feeling, expression, idea* vague, confus; (*absent-minded*) *person* distrait. **I haven't the ~st idea** je n'en ai pas la moindre idée; **I had a ~ idea that** je pensais vaguement que; **he was ~ about it** (*didn't say exactly*) il ne l'a pas bien précisé; (*didn't know exactly*) il n'en était pas sûr; **to look ~, to have a ~ look in one's eyes** avoir l'air vague. ♦ **vaguely** *adv* vaguement. ♦ **vagueness** *n [person]* distraction *f*, étourderie *f*.

vain [veɪn] *adj* **(a)** (*useless, empty*) *attempt, hope* vain (*before n*); *promise* vide; *words* creux. **in ~** en vain, vainement; **she tried in ~ to open the door** elle a essayé en vain d'ouvrir la porte; **I looked for him in ~, he had left** j'ai eu beau le chercher, il était parti. **(b)** (*conceited*) vaniteux. ♦ **vainly** *adv* **(a)** (*to no effect*) en vain, vainement; **(b)** (*conceitedly*) vaniteusement.

valentine [ˈvæləntaɪn] *n* (**~ card**) carte *f* de la Saint-Valentin (*gage d'amour*).

valet [ˈvæleɪ] *n* valet *m* de chambre.

valiant [ˈvæljənt] *adj* (*gen*) courageux, vaillant. **to make a ~ effort to do** essayer vaillamment de faire. ♦ **valiantly** *adv* vaillamment.

valid [ˈvælɪd] *adj claim, contract, document, ticket* valable, valide (*for* pour); *excuse, argument* valable. ♦ **validate** *vt document etc* valider; *argument* prouver la justesse de. ♦ **validity** *n [document etc]* validité *f*; *[argument]* justesse *f*.

valise [vəˈliːz] *n* sac *m* de voyage.

valley [ˈvælɪ] *n* vallée *f*; (*small*) vallon *m*. **the Seine/Rhône** *etc* **~** la vallée de la Seine/du Rhône *etc*; **the Loire V~** le Val de Loire.

valour, (*US*) **valor** [ˈvæləʳ] *n* bravoure *f*. ♦ **valorous** *adj* valeureux.

value [ˈvæljuː] **1** *n* valeur *f*. **to gain (in) ~** prendre de la valeur; **to lose (in) ~** se déprécier; (*Tax etc*) **increase/decrease in ~** plus-/moins-value *f*; **he paid the ~ of the cup he broke** il a remboursé la tasse qu'il a cassée; **of no ~** sans valeur; **it has been of no ~ to her** ça ne lui a servi à rien; **to be of great ~** valoir cher; **to get good ~ for money** en avoir pour son argent; **it's the best ~** c'est le plus avantageux; **to put too high/too low a ~ on sth** surestimer/sous-estimer qch; **to the ~ of £100** d'une valeur de 100 livres; **at his (*or* its *etc*) proper ~** à sa juste valeur; (*moral standards*) **~s** valeurs. **2** *adj*: **~ added tax (*abbr* V.A.T.)** taxe *f* sur la valeur ajoutée (*abbr* T.V.A.); (*fig*) **~ judgment** jugement *m* de valeur. **3** *vt* **(a)** *house, painting* évaluer (*at* à); (*Comm, Jur*) expertiser (*at* à). **(b)** *friendship* apprécier; *comforts, independence* tenir à. ♦ **valuable 1** *adj object* de valeur; *advice, time* précieux; **2** *npl*: **valuables** objets *mpl* de valeur. ♦ **valuation** *n* (*Comm, Jur*) expertise *f*; (*value decided upon*) appréciation *f*; **to have a valuation made of sth** faire expertiser qch; **the valuation is too high** l'appréciation est trop élevée; (*fig*) **to take sb at his own valuation** prendre qn pour celui qu'il croit être. ♦ **valued** *adj friend* précieux; *colleague* estimé. ♦ **valueless** *adj* sans valeur.

valve [vælv] *n* (*Anat*) valvule *f*; (*Bot, Zool*) valve *f*; (*Tech*) *[machine]* soupape *f*; *[tyre etc]* valve; (*Electronics, Rad*) lampe *f*; *[musical instrument]* piston *m*.

vampire [ˈvæmpaɪəʳ] *n* vampire *m*. **~ bat** vampire (*chauve-souris*).

van[1] [væn] *n* **(a)** (*Aut: large*) camion *m*, fourgon *m*; (*smaller*) camionnette *f*. **(b)** (*Rail*) fourgon *m*. **(c)** (*: *abbr of* **caravan**) caravane *f*. ♦ **van-boy** *or* ♦ **van-man** *n* livreur *m*.

van[2] [væn] *n abbr of* **vanguard.**

vandal [ˈvændəl] *n* vandale *mf*. ♦ **vandalism** *n* vandalisme *m*. ♦ **vandalize** *vt* saccager.

vane [veɪn] *n* (**weather ~**) girouette *f*.

vanguard [ˈvængɑːd] *n* avant-garde *f*. **in the ~** (*Mil etc*) en tête (*of* de); (*fig*) à l'avant-garde (*of* de).

vanilla [vəˈnɪlə] **1** *n* vanille *f*. **2** *adj cream, ice* à la vanille.

vanish [ˈvænɪʃ] *vi* disparaître. **to ~ into thin air** se volatiliser. ♦ **vanishing** *adj*: **~ing cream** crème *f* de jour; **~ing point** point *m* de fuite; **~ing trick** tour *m* de passe-passe.

vanity [ˈvænɪtɪ] **1** *n* vanité *f*. **2** *adj*: **~ case** sac *m* de toilette.

vanquish [ˈvæŋkwɪʃ] *vt* vaincre.

vantage [ˈvɑːntɪdʒ] **1** *n* avantage *m*. **2** *adj*: **~ point,** (*Mil*) **~ ground** position *f* avantageuse.

vapid [ˈvæpɪd] *adj* sans intérêt.

vapour, (*US*) **vapor** [ˈveɪpəʳ] **1** *n* vapeur *f*; (*on glass*) buée *f*. **2** *adj* (*Aviat*) **~ trail** traînée *f* de condensation. ♦ **vaporize 1** *vt* vaporiser; **2** *vi* se vaporiser. ♦ **vaporizer** *n* (*Med*) inhalateur *m*.

varicose ['værɪkəʊs] *adj*: ~ **vein** varice *f*.
varnish ['vɑːnɪʃ] **1** *n* vernis *m*. **nail** ~ vernis à ongles. **2** *vt* vernir. ♦ **varnishing** *n* (*Art*) vernissage *m*.
vary ['vɛərɪ] **1** *vi* (*gen*) varier (*with* selon). **to ~ from sth** différer de qch. **2** *vt* (*gen*) varier; *temperature, results* faire varier. ♦ **variability** *n* variabilité *f*. ♦ **variable** *adj, n* variable (*f*). ♦ **variance** *n [people]* **to be at variance** être en désaccord (*with sb* avec qn; *about, over sth* à propos de qch); *[facts, statements]* ne pas s'accorder (*with* avec). ♦ **variant** *n* variante *f*. ♦ **variation** *n* variation *f*. ♦ **varied** *adj* varié. ♦ **variegated** *adj* bigarré; (*Bot*) panaché. ♦ **variety** [və'raɪətɪ] **1** *n* **(a)** (*gen*) variété *f*; **for a variety of reasons** pour diverses raisons; **a large variety of** un grand choix de; **(b)** (*Theat*) variétés *fpl*; **2** *adj* (*Theat*) *artiste* de variétés; **variety show** (*Theat, TV*) spectacle *m* de variétés; (*Rad, TV*) émission *f* de variétés. ♦ **various** ['vɛərɪəs] *adj* (*different*) divers (*before n*), différent; (*several*) divers (*before n*), plusieurs; **at various times** (*different*) en diverses occasions; (*several*) à plusieurs reprises; **various people** plusieurs *or* diverses personnes. ♦ **variously** *adv* diversement. ♦ **varying** *adj* qui varie, variable; **with ~ing degrees of success** avec plus ou moins de succès.
vase [vɑːz] *n* vase *m*. **flower** ~ vase à fleurs.
vasectomy [væ'sektəmɪ] *n* vasectomie *f*.
vaseline ['væsɪliːn] *n* vaseline *f*.
vast [vɑːst] *adj* (*gen*) vaste (*usually before n*); *success* énorme. **a ~ amount of** énormément de; **to a ~ extent** dans une très large mesure; **at ~ expense** à grands frais; ~ **sums** des sommes folles. ♦ **vastly** *adv grateful, amused* infiniment; *rich* extrêmement; **to be ~ly mistaken** se tromper du tout au tout; **~ly improved** infiniment meilleur. ♦ **vastness** *n* immensité *f*.
vat [væt] *n* cuve *f*, bac *m*.
Vatican ['vætɪkən] *n* Vatican *m*. **the ~ Council** le Concile du Vatican.
vaudeville ['vəʊdəvɪl] *n* spectacle *m* de music-hall.
vault[1] [vɔːlt] *n* **(a)** (*cellar*) cave *f*; (*tomb*) caveau *m*; (*in bank*) salle *f* des coffres. **(b)** (*Archit*) voûte *f*. ♦ **vaulting** *n* (*Archit*) voûtes *fpl*.
vault[2] [vɔːlt] *vti*: **to ~ (over) sth** sauter qch (d'un bond).
vaunt [vɔːnt] *vt*: **much ~ed** dont on (*or* il *etc*) a tant parlé.
veal [viːl] *n* veau *m* (*Culin*). ~ **cutlet** escalope *f* de veau.
veer [vɪəʳ] *vi* (~ **round**) *[wind]* tourner (*to* vers, à); *[ship, car, road]* virer. (*fig: change one's mind*) **to ~ round** changer d'opinion; **to ~ off the subject** s'éloigner du sujet.
vegetable ['vedʒɪtəbl] **1** *n* **(a)** légume *m*. **early ~s** primeurs *fpl*. **(b)** (*generic term: plant*) végétal *m*. **2** *adj oil, matter* végétal; *soup* de légumes. ~ **dish** légumier *m*; ~ **garden** potager *m*; ~ **kingdom** règne *m* végétal; ~ **knife** couteau *m* à éplucher; ~ **salad** macédoine *f* de légumes. ♦ **vegetarian** [ˌvedʒɪ'tɛərɪən] *adj, n* végétarien(ne) *m(f)*. ♦ **vegetarianism** *n* végétarisme *m*. ♦ **vegetate** *vi* végéter. ♦ **vegetation** *n* végétation *f*.
vehement ['viːɪmənt] *adj* (*gen*) véhément; *attack* violent. ♦ **vehemence** *n [feelings, speech]* véhémence *f*; *[actions]* fougue *f*. ♦ **vehemently** *adv speak etc* avec véhémence; *attack* avec violence.
vehicle ['viːɪkl] *n* véhicule *m*. ♦ **vehicular traffic** [vɪ'hɪkjʊlə'træfɪk] *n* circulation *f*.
veil [veɪl] **1** *n* (*gen*) voile *m*; (*on hat*) voilette *f*; (*fig*) voile. (*Rel*) **to take the ~** prendre le voile; (*fig*) **to draw a ~ over** mettre un voile sur. **2** *vt* voiler. ♦ **veiled** *adj* (*lit, fig*) voilé.
vein [veɪn] *n* (*gen*) veine *f*; (*in leaf*) nervure *f*. (*fig*) **a ~ of truth/cruelty** un fond de vérité/de cruauté; **in melancholy ~** d'humeur mélancolique; **in the same ~** dans le même esprit. ♦ **veined** *adj hand, stone* veiné; *leaf* nervuré.
veld(t) [velt] *n* veld(t) *m*.
vellum ['veləm] *n* vélin *m*.
velocity [vɪ'lɒsɪtɪ] *n* vélocité *f*, vitesse *f*.
velour(s) [və'lʊəʳ] *n* velours *m* épais.
velvet ['velvɪt] **1** *n* velours *m*. (*fig*) **to be on ~*** jouer sur du velours*. **2** *adj dress* de velours. ♦ **velveteen** *n* velvet *m*. ♦ **velvety** *adj* velouté.
venal ['viːnl] *adj* vénal. ♦ **venality** *n* vénalité *f*.
vendetta [ven'detə] *n* vendetta *f*.
vending ['vendɪŋ] *n* vente *f*. ~ **machine** distributeur *m* automatique. ♦ **vendor** *n* vendeur *m*, -euse *f*.
veneer [və'nɪəʳ] **1** *n* placage *m*; (*fig*) apparence *f*. **2** *vt* plaquer.
venerate ['venəreɪt] *vt* vénérer. ♦ **venerable** *adj* vénérable. ♦ **veneration** *n* vénération *f*.
venereal [vɪ'nɪərɪəl] *adj*: ~ **disease** (*abbr* **V.D.**) maladie *f* vénérienne.
Venetian [vɪ'niːʃən] *adj* vénitien. ~ **glass** cristal *m* de Venise; ~ **blind** store *m* vénitien.
vengeance ['vendʒəns] *n* vengeance *f*. **to take ~ on** se venger de *or* sur; (*fig*) **with a ~** pour de bon*.
venial ['viːnɪəl] *adj* véniel.
venison ['venɪsən] *n* venaison *f*.
venom ['venəm] *n* venin *m*. ♦ **venomous** *adj* (*lit, fig*) venimeux; *tongue* de vipère. ♦ **venomously** *adv* d'une manière venimeuse.
vent [vent] **1** *n* (*hole*) orifice *m*; (*pipe*) conduit *m*; *[chimney]* tuyau *m*. (*fig*) **to give ~ to** donner libre cours à. **2** *vt* (*fig*) *anger etc* décharger (*on* sur).
ventilate ['ventɪleɪt] *vt room, tunnel* ventiler; (*fig*) *question* livrer à la discussion; *grievance* étaler au grand jour. ♦ **ventilation** *n* ventilation *f*; **ventilation shaft** conduit *m* d'aération. ♦ **ventilator** *n* ventilateur *m*; (*Aut*) déflecteur *m*.
ventricle ['ventrɪkl] *n* ventricule *m*.
ventriloquist [ven'trɪləkwɪst] *n* ventriloque *mf*. ♦ **ventriloquism** *n* ventriloquie *f*.
venture ['ventʃəʳ] **1** *n* entreprise *f* (hasardeuse). **at a ~** au hasard; **~ into business** incursion *f* dans les affaires; **business ~s** tentatives *fpl* commerciales; **a new ~ in publishing** qch de nouveau en matière d'édition. **2** *vt life, fortune, reputation* risquer; *explanation, opinion* hasarder. **to ~ a guess** hasarder une réponse; **he did not ~ to speak** il n'a pas osé parler. **3** *vi* se risquer (*on doing* à faire). **to ~ in/through** *etc* se risquer à entrer/traverser *etc*; **to ~ out of doors** se risquer à sortir; **to ~ into town** s'aventurer dans la ville; **when we ~d on this** quand nous avons entrepris cela.
venue ['venjuː] *n* lieu *m* (de rendez-vous).
Venus ['viːnəs] *n* (*Astron, Myth*) Vénus *f*.
veracious [və'reɪʃəs] *adj* véridique. ♦ **veracity** [və'ræsɪtɪ] *n* véracité *f*.
veranda(h) [və'rændə] *n* véranda *f*.
verb [vɜːb] *n* verbe *m*. ♦ **verbal** *adj* (*gen*) verbal; *memory* auditif. ♦ **verbalize** *vt* exprimer. ♦ **verbally** *adv* verbalement. ♦ **verbatim** *adj, adv* mot pour mot.
verbena [vɜː'biːnə] *n* verveine *f*.
verbiage ['vɜːbɪɪdʒ] *n* verbiage *m*. ♦ **verbose** *adj* verbeux. ♦ **verbosely** *adv* avec verbosité. ♦ **verbosity** *n* verbosité *f*.
verdict ['vɜːdɪkt] *n* (*Jur, also gen*) verdict *m*. ~ **of guilty/not guilty** verdict de culpabilité/de non-culpabilité; (*gen*) **to give one's ~ on** se prononcer sur.
verge [vɜːdʒ] **1** *n [road]* accotement *m*; *[forest]* orée *f*. **to be on the ~ of** *ruin, death* être à deux doigts de; *a discovery* être à la veille de; *tears* être au bord de; **on the ~ of doing** sur le point de faire. **2** *vi* incliner, tendre (*towards* vers). **to ~ on sth** *[ideas, actions]* approcher de qch; *[person]* frôler qch.

verger ['vɜːdʒəʳ] *n* bedeau *m*.
verify ['verɪfaɪ] *vt* (*gen*) vérifier; *documents* contrôler. ♦ **verifiable** *adj* vérifiable. ♦ **verification** *n* vérification *f*.
veritable ['verɪtəbl] *adj* véritable, vrai (*both before n*).
vermicelli [ˌvɜːmɪ'selɪ] *n* vermicelle *m*.
vermilion [və'mɪljən] *adj, n* vermillon (*m*) *inv*.
vermin ['vɜːmɪn] *collective n* (*animals*) animaux *mpl* nuisibles; (*insects, also people*) vermine *f*. ♦ **verminous** *adj* couvert de vermine.
vermouth ['vɜːməθ] *n* vermouth *m*.
vernacular [və'nækjʊləʳ] *n* langue *f* vernaculaire.
veronica [və'rɒnɪkə] *n* véronique *f*.
verruca [və'ruːkə] *n* verrue *f* (*plantaire*).
versatile ['vɜːsətaɪl] *adj* *person* aux talents variés; *mind* souple; *genius* universel. ♦ **versatility** *n [person]* variété *f* de talents.
verse [vɜːs] *n* **(a)** (*poetry*) poésie *f*, vers *mpl*. **in ~** en vers. **(b)** (*stanza*) *[poem]* strophe *f*; *[song]* couplet *m*; *[Bible]* verset *m*. ♦ **versed** *adj* (**well-~d**) versé (*in* dans). ♦ **versification** *n* versification *f*. ♦ **versify** *vi* faire des vers.
version ['vɜːʃən] *n* (*most senses*) version *f*; *[car]* modèle *m*.
versus ['vɜːsəs] *prep* (*Jur, Sport, gen*) contre.
vertebra ['vɜːtɪbrə] *n, pl* **-ae** vertèbre *f*. ♦ **vertebrate** *adj, n* vertébré (*m*).
vertex ['vɜːteks] *n, pl* **-tices** (*gen, Math*) sommet *m*; (*Anat*) vertex *m*.
vertical ['vɜːtɪkəl] **1** *adj* (*gen*) vertical; *cliff* à pic. **2** *n* verticale *f*. ♦ **vertically** *adv* verticalement.
vertigo ['vɜːtɪgəʊ] *n* vertige *m*. **to suffer from ~** avoir des vertiges.
verve [vɜːv] *n* verve *f*, brio *m*.
very ['verɪ] **1** *adv* **(a)** (*extremely*) très, bien. **~ amusing** très *or* fort amusant; **I am ~ cold** j'ai très froid; **~ well** très bien; **~ little** très peu (de); **~ much** beaucoup, bien; **~ much bigger** beaucoup *or* bien plus grand; **he doesn't work ~ much** il ne travaille pas beaucoup; **~ high frequency** (*Rad*) ondes *fpl* ultra-courtes; (*Electronics*) très haute fréquence. **(b)** (*absolutely*) tout, de loin. **~ best quality** toute première qualité; **~ last/first** tout dernier/premier; **the ~ cleverest** de loin le plus intelligent; **at the ~ latest** au plus tard; **at the ~ most/least** tout au plus/moins; **in the ~ best of health** en excellente santé; **the ~ best of friends** les meilleurs amis du monde; **it's my ~ own** c'est à moi tout seul; **the ~ next shop** le magasin tout de suite après; **the ~ same day** le jour même; **the ~ same hat** exactement le même chapeau; **the ~ next day** le lendemain même.
2 *adj* **(a)** (*precise*) même. **that ~ day** ce jour même; **his ~ words** ses propos mêmes; **the ~ thing!** (*of object*) voilà justement ce qu'il me faut; (*of idea etc*) c'est idéal; **the ~ man I need** tout à fait l'homme qu'il me faut. **(b)** (*extreme*) tout. **at the ~ end** *[year]* tout à la fin; *[road]* tout au bout; **to the ~ end** jusqu'au bout; **in the ~ depths of** au plus profond de. **(c)** (*mere*) seul. **the ~ word** le mot seul, rien que le mot; **the ~ thought of it** rien que d'y penser; **the ~ idea!** quelle idée alors!
vespers ['vespəz] *npl* vêpres *fpl*.
vessel ['vesl] *n* (*all senses*) vaisseau *m*.
vest[1] [vest] **1** *n* **(a)** (*Brit*) *[man]* tricot *m* de corps; *[woman]* chemise *f* américaine. **(b)** (*US*) gilet *m*. **2** *adj*: **~ pocket** poche *f* de gilet.
vest[2] [vest] *vt*: **to ~ sb with sth, to ~ sth in sb** investir qn de qch; **the authority ~ed in me** l'autorité dont je suis investi; (*Fin*) **~ed interests** droits *mpl* acquis; (*fig*) **he has a ~ed interest in it** il est directement intéressé là-dedans.
vestibule ['vestɪbjuːl] *n* vestibule *m*.
vestige ['vestɪdʒ] *n* (*gen*) vestige *m*. (*fig*) **not a ~ of truth/common sense** pas une trace de vérité/de bon sens.
vestment ['vestmənt] *n* vêtement *m* sacerdotal.
vestry ['vestrɪ] *n* sacristie *f*.
vet [vet] **1** *n* (*abbr of* **veterinary surgeon**) vétérinaire *mf*. **2** *vt* *text* revoir; *application* examiner minutieusement. **it was ~ted by him** c'est lui qui l'a approuvé; **to ~ sb for a job** se renseigner de façon approfondie au sujet de qn avant de lui offrir un poste.
vetch [vetʃ] *n* vesce *f*.
veteran ['vetərən] **1** *n* vétéran *m*. **war ~** ancien combattant *m*. **2** *adj* *traveller, writer* chevronné. **she is a ~ campaigner for ...** elle fait campagne depuis toujours pour ...; **a ~ teacher/golfer** un vétéran de l'enseignement/du golf; **~ car** voiture *f* d'époque (*avant 1916*).
veterinary ['vetərɪnərɪ] *adj* vétérinaire. **~ surgeon** vétérinaire *mf*.
veto ['viːtəʊ] **1** *n, pl* **-es** veto *m*. **to have a/use one's ~** avoir un/exercer son droit de veto. **2** *vt* (*also* **put a ~ on**) opposer son veto à.
vex [veks] *vt* contrarier, fâcher. ♦ **vexation** *n* ennui *m*. ♦ **vexatious** *or* ♦ **vexing** *adj* contrariant. ♦ **vexed** *adj* fâché (*with sb* contre qn); *question* controversé; **to get ~ed** se fâcher.
via ['vaɪə] *prep* par, via.
viable ['vaɪəbl] *adj* viable. ♦ **viability** *n* viabilité *f*.
viaduct ['vaɪədʌkt] *n* viaduc *m*.
vibesᵗ [vaɪbz] *npl* (*abbr of* **vibrations**) **the ~ are wrong** ça ne gaze pas*.
vibrate [vaɪ'breɪt] *vi* vibrer (*with* de). ♦ **vibrant** *adj* vibrant. ♦ **vibration** *n* vibration *f*.
viburnum [vaɪ'bɜːnəm] *n* viorne *f*.
vicar ['vɪkəʳ] *n* (*C of E*) pasteur *m*; (*RC*) vicaire *m*. ♦ **vicarage** *n* presbytère *m* (*anglican*).
vicarious [vɪ'kɛərɪəs] *adj* *suffering etc* à la place d'un autre. **to get ~ pleasure from** retirer indirectement du plaisir de. ♦ **vicariously** *adv* indirectement.
vice[1] [vaɪs] **1** *n* vice *m*, (*less strong*) défaut *m*. *[animal]* **he has no ~s** il n'est pas vicieux. **2** *adj* (*Police*) **~ squad** brigade *f* des mœurs.
vice[2] [vaɪs] *n* (*tool*) étau *m*.
vice[3] ['vaɪsɪ] *prep* à la place de.
vice- [vaɪs] *pref* vice-. **~admiral** vice-amiral *m*; **~chairman** vice-président(e) *m(f)*; **~chancellor** (*Univ*) recteur *m*; (*Jur*) vice-chancelier *m*; **~president** vice-président(e) *m(f)*. ♦ **viceroy** *n* vice-roi *m*.
vice versa ['vaɪsɪ'vɜːsə] *adv* vice versa.
vicinity [vɪ'sɪnɪtɪ] *n* (*nearby area*) environs *mpl*, alentours *mpl*; (*closeness*) proximité *f*. **in the ~** dans les environs; **in the ~ of** aux alentours de.
vicious ['vɪʃəs] *adj* *remark, look* méchant; *kick, attack* brutal; *tongue* de vipère; *habit, animal, circle* vicieux. ♦ **viciously** *adv* méchamment; brutalement. ♦ **viciousness** *n* méchanceté *f*; brutalité *f*.
vicissitude [vɪ'sɪsɪtjuːd] *n* vicissitude *f*.
victim ['vɪktɪm] *n* victime *f*. **to be the ~ of** être victime de; **to fall (a) ~ to** devenir la victime de; (*fig: to sb's charms etc*) succomber à. ♦ **victimization** *n* représailles *fpl* (*subies par un ou plusieurs des responsables*); **he alleged ~ization** il a prétendu être victime de représailles. ♦ **victimize** *vt* prendre pour victime; (*after strike etc*) exercer des représailles sur; **to be ~ized** être victime de représailles.
Victorian [vɪk'tɔːrɪən] **1** *n* Victorien(ne) *m(f)*. **2** *adj* victorien. ♦ **Victoriana** *n* antiquités *fpl* victoriennes.
victory ['vɪktərɪ] *n* victoire *f*. **to win a ~ over** remporter une victoire sur. ♦ **victor** *n* vainqueur *m*. ♦ **victorious** [vɪk'tɔːrɪəs] *adj* (*gen*) victorieux; *shout* de victoire; **to be victorious** sortir victorieux (*in* de). ♦ **victoriously** *adv* victorieusement.
victuals ['vɪtlz] *npl* victuailles *fpl*.
video ['vɪdɪəʊ] **1** *adj* *system etc* vidéo *inv*. **~ cas-**

sette vidéocassette *f*; ~ **(cassette) recorder** magnétoscope *m*; ~ **recording** enregistrement *m* sur magnétoscope; ~ **frequency** vidéofréquence *f*. **2** *n* (*: *US*) télévision *f*, télé* *f*. ♦ **videophone** *n* vidéophone *m*. ♦ **videotape 1** *n* (bande *f* de) magnétoscope *m*; **2** *vt* enregistrer sur magnétoscope.

vie [vaɪ] *vi* rivaliser (*with sb in doing* avec qn pour faire), lutter (*with sb for sth* avec qn pour (avoir) qch; *with sb for doing* avec qn pour faire).

view [vjuː] **1** *n* **(a)** (*gen*) vue *f*. **in full ~ of** en plein devant; **to come into ~** apparaître; **to come into ~ of** arriver en vue de; **the house is within ~ of the sea** de la maison on voit la mer; **hidden from ~** caché; (*lit, fig*) **to keep sth in ~** ne pas perdre qch de vue; *[exhibit]* **on ~** exposé; **the house is on ~** on peut visiter la maison; **back/front ~ of the house** la maison vue de derrière/de devant; **you'll get a better ~ from here** vous verrez mieux d'ici; **there is a splendid ~** la vue est splendide; **a ~ over ...** une vue sur ...; **50 ~s of Paris** 50 vues de Paris; **a room with a ~** une chambre avec une belle vue. **(b)** (*opinion*) avis *m*, opinion *f*. **in my ~** à mon avis; **to hold ~s on** avoir des opinions sur; **to take the ~ that** penser que; **to take a dim*** *or* **a poor ~ of sth** apprécier médiocrement qch; **to fall in with sb's ~s** tomber d'accord avec qn; **point of ~** point *m* de vue. **(c)** (*survey*) vue *f*, aperçu *m*. **a general** *or* **an overall ~ of a problem** une vue d'ensemble d'un problème; **to take the long ~** prévoir les choses de loin; **in ~ of** étant donné, vu; **in ~ of the fact that** étant donné que, vu que. **(d)** (*intention*) but *m*. **to have in ~** envisager (*sth* qch; *doing* de faire); **with this in ~** dans ce but; **with a ~ to doing** dans l'intention de faire.
2 *vt* **(a)** *house etc* visiter. **(b)** (*consider*) *problem, prospect* envisager.
3 *vi* (*TV*) regarder la télévision.
♦ **viewer** *n* **(a)** (*TV*) téléspectateur *m*, -trice *f*; **(b)** (*for slides*) visionneuse *f*. ♦ **viewfinder** *n* viseur *m*. ♦ **viewpoint** *n* point *m* de vue.

vigil ['vɪdʒɪl] *n* (*gen*) veille *f*; (*by sickbed etc*) veillée *f*; (*Rel*) vigile *f*. ♦ **vigilance** *n* vigilance *f*. ♦ **vigilant** *adj* vigilant. ♦ **vigilante** *n* membre *m* d'un groupe d'autodéfense. ♦ **vigilantly** *adv* avec vigilance.

vigour, (*US*) **vigor** ['vɪgəʳ] *n* vigueur *f*. ♦ **vigorous** *adj* vigoureux. ♦ **vigorously** *adv* vigoureusement.

vile [vaɪl] *adj* (*base, evil*) vil, ignoble; (*extremely bad*) exécrable. **in a ~ temper** d'une humeur massacrante. ♦ **vilely** *adv* vilement. ♦ **vileness** *n* vilenie *f*. ♦ **vilification** [ˌvɪlɪfɪ'keɪʃən] *n* calomnie *f*. ♦ **vilify** *vt* calomnier.

villa ['vɪlə] *n* (*in town*) pavillon *m* (*de banlieue*); (*in country*) maison *f* de campagne; (*by sea*) villa *f*.

village ['vɪlɪdʒ] **1** *n* village *m*, bourgade *f*, patelin* *m*. **2** *adj school etc, idiot* du village. ~ **green** pré *m* communal; **the ~ inn** l'auberge *f* du village; **a ~ inn** une auberge de campagne. ♦ **villager** *n* villageois(e) *m(f)*.

villain ['vɪlən] *n* scélérat *m*; (*in drama, novel*) traître(sse) *m(f)*; (*: *rascal*) coquin(e) *m(f)*; (*Police etc sl: criminal*) bandit *m*. ♦ **villainous** *adj* (*gen*) *deed etc* infâme; (*: *bad*) *coffee, weather* abominable. ♦ **villainy** *n* infamie *f*.

vim* [vɪm] *n* entrain *m*.

vindicate ['vɪndɪkeɪt] *vt* (*gen*) justifier; *rights* faire valoir. ♦ **vindication** *n* justification *f*; **in vindication of** pour justifier.

vindictive [vɪn'dɪktɪv] *adj* vindicatif. ♦ **vindictively** *adv* vindicativement.

vine [vaɪn] *n* vigne *f*. ♦ **vine-grower** *n* viticulteur *m*, vigneron *m*. ♦ **vine-growing** *adj district* viticole. ♦ **vineyard** ['vɪnjəd] *n* vignoble *m*.

vinegar ['vɪnɪgəʳ] *n* vinaigre *m*.

vintage ['vɪntɪdʒ] **1** *n* (*harvesting; season*) vendanges *fpl*; (*year*) année *f*. **what ~ is it?** c'est de quelle année?; **the 1972 ~** le vin de 1972. **2** *adj wine* de grand cru. **a ~ year** une bonne année (*for* pour); ~ **car** voiture *f* d'époque (*1917–1930*).

vinyl ['vaɪnɪl] **1** *n* vinyle *m*. **2** *adj* de vinyle.

viola[1] [vɪ'əʊlə] *n* (*Mus*) alto *m*. ~ **player** altiste *mf*.

viola[2] ['vaɪəʊlə] *n* (*Bot*) pensée *f*.

violate ['vaɪəleɪt] *vt* violer. ♦ **violation** *n* violation *f*; **it's a violation of his privacy** c'est s'ingérer dans sa vie privée.

violence ['vaɪələns] *n* violence *f*. **to use ~ against** employer la violence contre; **there was an outbreak of ~** de violents incidents *mpl* ont éclaté; **racial ~** violents incidents raciaux; **crime of ~** voie *f* de fait; (*Jur*) **robbery with ~** vol *m* avec coups et blessures; (*fig*) **to do ~ to** faire violence à. ♦ **violent** *adj* (*gen*) violent; *halt, braking* brutal; *colour* criard; **to die a violent death** mourir de mort violente; **to have a violent temper** avoir un tempérament violent; **to be in a violent temper** être dans une rage folle; **by violent means** par la violence; **a violent dislike** une vive aversion (*for* envers). ♦ **violently** *adv struggle, react* violemment; (*severely*) *ill, angry* terriblement; **to behave violently** se montrer violent; **to fall violently in love with** tomber follement amoureux de.

violet ['vaɪəlɪt] **1** *n* (*Bot*) violette *f*; (*colour*) violet *m*. **2** *adj* violet.

violin [ˌvaɪə'lɪn] **1** *n* violon *m*. **2** *adj sonata* pour violon. ♦ **violinist** *n* violoniste *mf*.

viper ['vaɪpəʳ] *n* vipère *f*.

virgin ['vɜːdʒɪn] **1** *n* vierge *f*; garçon *m* vierge. **she/he is a ~** elle/il est vierge; **the Blessed V~** la Sainte Vierge. **2** *adj* (*fig*) *forest* vierge; *snow* frais. ♦ **virginity** *n* virginité *f*.

Virginia creeper [və'dʒɪnjə'kriːpəʳ] *n* vigne *f* vierge.

Virgo ['vɜːgəʊ] *n* (*Astron*) la Vierge.

virile ['vɪraɪl] *adj* viril. ♦ **virility** *n* virilité *f*.

virtual ['vɜːtjʊəl] *adj*: **he is the ~ leader** en fait c'est lui le chef; **it was a ~ failure** ce fut pratiquement un échec. ♦ **virtually** *adv* (*when it comes to the bit*) en fait; (*to all intents and purposes*) pratiquement; **he is ~ly the leader** en fait c'est lui le chef; **it ~ly failed** ça a pratiquement échoué; **~ly certain** pratiquement certain.

virtue ['vɜːtjuː] *n* vertu *f*. **to make a ~ of necessity** faire de nécessité vertu; **by ~ of** en vertu de; **to have the ~ of being** *[thing]* avoir l'avantage d'être; *[person]* avoir le mérite d'être; **there is no ~ in doing that** il n'y a aucun mérite à faire cela. ♦ **virtuous** *adj* vertueux. ♦ **virtuously** *adv* vertueusement.

virtuoso [ˌvɜːtjʊ'əʊzəʊ] **1** *n* virtuose *mf*. **violin ~** virtuose du violon. **2** *adj performance* de virtuose. ♦ **virtuosity** *n* virtuosité *f*.

virulence ['vɪrʊləns] *n* virulence *f*. ♦ **virulent** *adj* virulent.

virus ['vaɪərəs] *n* virus *m*. **rabies ~** virus de la rage; ~ **disease** maladie *f* virale.

visa ['viːzə] *n* visa *m* (*de passeport*).

vis-à-vis ['viːzəviː] *prep* vis-à-vis de.

viscera ['vɪsərə] *npl* viscères *mpl*.

viscount ['vaɪkaʊnt] *n* vicomte *m*.

viscous ['vɪskəs] *adj* visqueux.

vise [vaɪs] *n* (*US*) = **vice**[2].

visible ['vɪzəbl] *adj* **(a)** visible. ~ **to the naked eye** visible à l'œil nu; **to become ~** apparaître. **(b)** (*obvious*) manifeste. **with ~ impatience** avec une impatience manifeste. ♦ **visibility** *n* visibilité *f*. ♦ **visibly** *adv* visiblement; (*obviously*) manifestement.

vision ['vɪʒən] *n* (*gen*) vision *f*; (*eyesight*) vue *f*. **a man of ~** un homme qui voit loin; **his ~ of the future** la façon dont il voit l'avenir; **to see ~s** avoir des visions; **to have ~s of wealth** avoir des visions de richesses; **she had ~s of being**

drowned elle s'est vue noyée. ◆ **visionary** *adj, n* visionnaire (*mf*).
visit ['vɪzɪt] **1** *n* (*call, tour*) visite *f*; (*stay*) séjour *m*. **to pay a ~ to** *person* rendre visite à; *place* aller à; **to be on a ~ to** *person* être en visite chez; *place* faire un séjour à; **on a private/an official ~** en visite privée/officielle; (*fig*) **to pay a ~*** aller au petit coin*. **2** *vt* **(a)** (*go and see*) *person* aller voir; (*more formally*) rendre visite à; *town, museum, zoo, theatre* aller à. **(b)** (*stay with or in*) *person* faire un séjour chez; *town, country* faire un séjour à (*or* en). **(c)** (*inspect*) *place* inspecter; *troops* passer en revue. ◆ **visitation** *n [official]* visite *f* d'inspection; *[bishop]* visite pastorale. ◆ **visiting** *adj professor etc* associé; **~ing card** carte *f* de visite; **~ing hours** *or* **time** heures *fpl* de visite; (*Sport*) **the ~ing team** les visiteurs *mpl*; **I'm not on ~ing terms with him** nous ne nous rendons pas visite. ◆ **visitor** *n* (*guest*) invité(e) *m(f)*; (*in hotel*) client(e) *m(f)*; (*tourist; also at exhibition etc*) visiteur *m*, -euse *f*; **~ors' book** livre *m* d'or, (*in hotel*) registre *m*; **~ors to Paris** les visiteurs de passage à Paris; **~ors to the exhibition** les personnes *fpl* visitant l'exposition.
visor ['vaɪzəʳ] *n* visière *f*.
vista ['vɪstə] *n* (*view*) panorama *m*; (*fig*) perspective *f*.
visual ['vɪzjʊəl] *adj* visuel. **to teach with ~ aids** enseigner par des méthodes visuelles. ◆ **visualize** *vt* (*imagine*) se représenter (*sth* qch; *sb doing* qn faisant); (*foresee*) envisager. ◆ **visually** *adv* visuellement.
vital ['vaɪtl] *adj* **(a)** (*gen*) vital; *importance* capital; *error* fatal. **~ statistics** *[population]* statistiques *fpl* démographiques; (*: *woman's*) mensurations *fpl*; **~ to sb/sth** indispensable à qn/pour qch; **it is ~ that ...** il est indispensable *or* vital que ... + *subj*. **(b)** (*lively*) plein d'entrain. ◆ **vitality** *n* vitalité *f*. ◆ **vitally** *adv necessary* absolument; *urgent* extrêmement; **it is ~ly important** c'est d'une importance capitale; **it is ~ly important that** il est absolument indispensable que + *subj*.
vitamin ['vɪtəmɪn] **1** *n* vitamine *f*. **~ A/B** *etc* vitamine A/B *etc*; **with added ~s** vitaminé. **2** *adj content* en vitamines; *tablets* de vitamines. **~ deficiency** carence *f* en vitamines.
vitiate ['vɪʃɪeɪt] *vt* vicier.
vitreous ['vɪtrɪəs] *adj* (*gen*) vitreux; *enamel* vitrifié. ◆ **vitrify** *vt* vitrifier.
vitriol ['vɪtrɪəl] *n* (*Chem, fig*) vitriol *m*. ◆ **vitriolic** *adj* (*fig*) venimeux.
vituperation [vɪˌtju:pəˈreɪʃən] *n* vitupérations *fpl*.
viva ['vaɪvə] *n* oral *m*. ◆ **viva voce** [~'vəʊsɪ] *adv* de vive voix.
vivacious [vɪ'veɪʃəs] *adj* vif, enjoué. ◆ **vivaciously** *adv* avec vivacité. ◆ **vivacity** [vɪ'væsɪtɪ] *n* vivacité *f*.
vivid ['vɪvɪd] *adj colour* vif, éclatant; *tie etc* voyant; *imagination* vif; *recollection* très net; *description* vivant. ◆ **vividly** *adv describe* d'une manière vivante; *imagine* de façon précise; *remember* très nettement. ◆ **vividness** *n [colour, light]* éclat *m*; *[style]* vigueur *f*.
vivisection [ˌvɪvɪ'sekʃən] *n* vivisection *f*.
vixen ['vɪksn] *n* renarde *f*; (*woman*) mégère *f*.
viz [vɪz] *adv* c'est-à-dire.
vizier [vɪ'zɪəʳ] *n* vizir *m*.
vocabulary [vəʊ'kæbjʊlərɪ] *n* (*gen*) vocabulaire *m*; (*in textbook*) lexique *m*.
vocal ['vəʊkəl] *adj* **(a)** (*gen*) vocal. **~ cords** cordes *fpl* vocales. **(b)** (*voicing opinion*) *group, person* qui se fait entendre. ◆ **vocalic** *adj* vocalique. ◆ **vocalist** *n* chanteur *m*, -euse *f* (*dans un groupe*). ◆ **vocalize** *vt* (*Ling*) vocaliser; *opinions etc* exprimer. ◆ **vocally** *adv* vocalement.
vocation [vəʊ'keɪʃən] *n* (*Rel etc*) vocation *f*. **to have a ~ for teaching** avoir la vocation de l'enseignement. ◆ **vocational** *adj training etc* professionnel; **~al guidance** orientation *f* professionnelle.
vocative ['vɒkətɪv] *adj, n* vocatif (*m*).
vociferate [vəʊ'sɪfəreɪt] *vi* vociférer, brailler*. ◆ **vociferous** *adj* bruyant. ◆ **vociferously** *adv* en vociférant.
vodka ['vɒdkə] *n* vodka *f*.
vogue [vəʊg] *n* vogue *f*. **to be the ~** *or* **in ~** être en vogue; **to have a great ~** être très en vogue.
voice [vɔɪs] **1** *n* (*gen, Gram etc*) voix *f*. **to lose one's ~** avoir une extinction de voix; **in good ~** en voix; **in a soft ~** d'une voix douce; **soft-~d** à voix douce; **at the top of his ~** à tue-tête; (*fig*) **to have a ~ in the matter** avoir voix au chapitre; **with one ~** à l'unanimité. **2** *vt feelings etc* exprimer; (*Ling*) *consonant* voiser. ◆ **voiceless** *adj* sans voix; *consonant* sourd.
void [vɔɪd] **1** *n* vide *m*. **to fill the ~** combler le vide. **2** *adj* (*gen*) vide; (*Jur*) nul. **~ of** dépourvu de.
volatile ['vɒlətaɪl] *adj* (*Chem*) volatil; (*fig*) *situation* explosif; *person* versatile.
volcano [vɒl'keɪnəʊ] *n* volcan *m*. ◆ **volcanic** [vɒl'kænɪk] *adj* volcanique.
vole [vəʊl] *n* (*Zool*) campagnol *m*.
volition [vɒ'lɪʃən] *n*: **of one's own ~** de son propre gré.
volley ['vɒlɪ] **1** *n* **(a)** (*Mil*) volée *f*; *[stones]* grêle *f*; *[insults]* bordée *f*; *[applause]* salve *f*. **(b)** (*Sport*) volée *f*. **2** *vt ball* reprendre de volée. ◆ **volleyball** *n* volley(-ball) *m*.
volt [vəʊlt] *n* volt *m*. ◆ **voltage** *n* voltage *m*, tension *f*; **high/low ~age** haute/basse tension.
volte-face ['vɒlt'fɑ:s] *n* volte-face *f inv*.
voluble ['vɒljʊbl] *adj* volubile. ◆ **volubility** *n* volubilité *f*. ◆ **volubly** *adv* avec volubilité.
volume ['vɒlju:m] *n* **(a)** (*book*) volume *m*. **in 6 ~s** en 6 volumes; **~ one** tome *m* premier; **~ two/three** *etc* tome deux/trois *etc*. **(b)** (*size; sound*) volume *m*; *[tank]* capacité *f*. **~ of water/production** volume d'eau/de la production; (*Rad, TV*) **to turn the ~ up/down** augmenter/diminuer le volume; **~s of smoke** nuages *mpl* de fumée; **~s of tears** flots *mpl* de larmes; **to write ~s** écrire des volumes; **it speaks ~s for ...** cela en dit long sur ... . ◆ **voluminous** *adj* volumineux.
volunteer [ˌvɒlən'tɪəʳ] **1** *n* (*Mil, gen*) volontaire *mf*. **2** *adj army, group* de volontaires; *helper* bénévole. **3** *vt help etc* offrir de son plein gré; *information, suggestion, facts* fournir spontanément. **'seven' he ~ed** 'sept' dit-il spontanément. **4** *vi* s'offrir, se proposer (*for sth* pour qch; *to do* pour faire); (*Mil*) s'engager comme volontaire (*for* dans). ◆ **voluntarily** *adv* (*willingly*) volontairement; (*without payment*) bénévolement. ◆ **voluntary** *adj confession, contribution* volontaire; (*unpaid*) *help, work, worker* bénévole.
voluptuous [və'lʌptjʊəs] *adj* voluptueux. ◆ **voluptuously** *adv* voluptueusement. ◆ **voluptuousness** *n* volupté *f*.
vomit ['vɒmɪt] **1** *vti* vomir. **2** *n* vomi *m*. ◆ **vomiting** *n* vomissements *mpl*.
voracious [və'reɪʃəs] *adj* (*gen*) vorace; *reader* avide. ◆ **voraciously** *adv eat* avec voracité. ◆ **voracity** [vɒ'ræsɪtɪ] *n* voracité *f*.
vortex ['vɔ:teks] *n* vortex *m*; (*fig*) tourbillon *m*.
votary ['vəʊtərɪ] *n* fervent(e) *m(f)* (*of* de).
vote [vəʊt] **1** *n* (*gen*) vote *m*; (*~ cast*) vote, voix *f* (*for* pour; *against* contre). **to give the ~ to sb** accorder le droit de vote à qn; **~s for women!** droit de vote pour les femmes!; **to put sth to the ~** mettre qch au vote; **to take a ~** procéder au vote (*on* sur); **~ of censure** *or* **no confidence** motion *f* de censure; **to pass a ~ of censure** voter la censure; **to pass a ~ of confidence in** passer un vote de confiance à l'égard de; **~ of thanks** discours *m* de remerciement; **to win ~s** gagner des voix; **to count the ~s** compter les voix *or* les votes, (*Pol*) dépouiller le scrutin; **the Labour ~** les voix

travaillistes. **2** *vt* **(a)** (~ **through**) *bill, sum of money etc* voter. **the committee ~d to request a subsidy** le comité a voté une demande d'une subvention. **(b)** (*elect*: ~ **in**) élire. **he was ~d chairman** il a été élu président; (*fig*) **they ~d her the best cook** ils l'ont proclamée la meilleure cuisinière; **I ~* we go** je propose qu'on y aille. **3** *vi* voter (*for sb/sth* pour qn/qch; *against* contre). ~ **for Robert!** votez Robert!; **to ~ Socialist** voter socialiste; **to ~ on sth** mettre qch au vote. ♦ **voter** *n* électeur *m*, -trice *f*. ♦ **voting 1** *n* (*process of voting*) scrutin *m*; (*result*) vote *m*; **2** *adj*: **voting booth** isoloir *m*; **voting paper** bulletin *m* de vote.

votive ['vəʊtɪv] *adj* votif.

vouch [vaʊtʃ] *vi*: **to ~ for** (*gen*) répondre de; *truth of sth* garantir. ♦ **voucher** *n* (*gen*) bon *m*; (*receipt*) reçu *m*.

vow [vaʊ] **1** *n* vœu *m*. **to take** *or* **make a ~** faire (le) vœu (*to do* de faire); (*Rel*) **to take one's ~s** prononcer ses vœux. **2** *vt* jurer (*to do* de faire; *that* que); *obedience etc* vouer.

vowel ['vaʊəl] **1** *n* voyelle *f*. **2** *adj* vocalique.

voyage ['vɔɪɪdʒ] **1** *n* voyage *m* par mer, traversée *f*. **to go on a ~** partir en voyage (par mer); **the ~ out/home** le voyage d'aller/de retour; ~ **of discovery** voyage d'exploration. **2** *vi* voyager (par mer). ♦ **voyager** *n* voyageur *m*, -euse *f*.

vulcanize ['vʌlkənaɪz] *vt* vulcaniser. ♦ **vulcanite** *n* ébonite *f*. ♦ **vulcanization** *n* vulcanisation *f*.

vulgar ['vʌlgəʳ] *adj* (*gen*) vulgaire; (*pej*) vulgaire, grossier. ~ **Latin** latin *m* vulgaire; ~ **word** gros mot *m*; ~ **fraction** fraction *f* ordinaire. ♦ **vulgarity** *n* vulgarité *f*. ♦ **vulgarly** *adv* (*all senses*) vulgairement. ♦ **Vulgate** *n* Vulgate *f*.

vulnerable ['vʌlnərəbl] *adj* vulnérable. **his ~ spot** son point faible. ♦ **vulnerability** *n* vulnérabilité *f*.

vulture ['vʌltʃəʳ] *n* vautour *m*.

W

W, w ['dʌbljuː] *n* (*letter*) W, w *m*.

wad [wɒd] **1** *n [cloth, paper, cotton wool]* tampon *m*; *[putty, chewing gum]* boulette *f*; *[straw]* bouchon *m*; *[tobacco]* carotte *f*, (*chewing*) chique *f*; *[documents, banknotes]* liasse *f*. **2** *vt garment* ouater; *quilt* rembourrer. ♦ **wadding** *n* (*gen*) bourre *f*; (*for lining*) rembourrage *m*; (*for garments*) ouate *f*.

waddle ['wɒdl] *vi* se dandiner. **to ~ in/out** *etc* entrer/sortir *etc* en se dandinant.

wade [weɪd] **1** *vi* (*for fun*) barboter. **to ~ through** *water, mud* patauger dans; *long grass* avancer avec difficulté dans; (**fig*) *book, work etc* venir péniblement à bout de; **to ~ ashore** regagner la rive à pied; (*fig*) **to ~ into sb*** (*attack*) tomber sur qn; (*scold*) engueuler‡ qn; **to ~ into a meal*** attaquer* un repas. **2** *vt stream* traverser à gué. ♦ **wader** *n* (*boot*) botte *f* de pêcheur; (*bird*) échassier *m*.

wafer ['weɪfəʳ] *n* (*Culin*) gaufrette *f*; (*Rel*) hostie *f*. ♦ **wafer-thin** *adj* mince comme une pelure d'oignon.

waffle[1] ['wɒfl] *n* (*Culin*) gaufre *f*. **~ iron** gaufrier *m*.

waffle[2]* ['wɒfl] **1** *n* (*words*) verbiage *m*. **2** *vi* parler interminablement (*about* de), parler pour ne rien dire.

wag [wæg] **1** *vt* (*gen*) agiter, remuer (*sth at sb/sth* qch dans la direction de qn/qch). **the dog ~ged its tail at me** le chien a remué la queue en me voyant. **2** *vi [tail]* remuer. (*fig*) **his tongue never stops ~ging** il a la langue bien pendue; **it set tongues ~ging** cela a fait jaser. **3** *n*: **with a ~ of its tail** en remuant la queue. ♦ **wagtail** *n* hochequeue *m*.

wage [weɪdʒ] **1** *n* (*also* **~s**) salaire *m*, paye *f*; *[servant]* gages *mpl*. **hourly/weekly ~** salaire horaire/hebdomadaire; **2 days' ~s** 2 jours de salaire *or* de paye; **his ~s are £75 per week** il touche 75 livres par semaine; **he gets a good ~** il est bien payé. **2** *adj rise* de salaire; *scale, freeze* des salaires. **~ demand** *or* **claim** demande *f* de révision de salaire; **~ earner** salarié(e) *m(f)*; **the family ~ earner** le soutien de la famille; **~ packet** paye *f*; **~s clerk** ≃ aide-comptable *mf*; **~s slip** fiche *f* de paye. **3** *vt*: **to ~ war** faire la guerre (*against* à, contre); **to ~ a campaign** mener une campagne (*for* pour).

wager ['weɪdʒəʳ] **1** *vt* parier (*sth on* qch sur; *that* que). **2** *n* pari *m*.

waggle ['wægl] **1** *vt pencil, tail etc* agiter; *loose screw etc* faire jouer; *hips* tortiller de. **2** *vi [tail]* frétiller; *[tooth]* branler.

waggon, (*esp US*) **wagon** ['wægən] *n* (*horse-drawn*) chariot *m*; (*truck*) camion *m*; (*Rail*) wagon *m* (de marchandises); (*tea trolley*) table *f* roulante, (*larger: for tea urn*) chariot. (*fig*) **to go on the ~*** ne plus boire (d'alcool). ♦ **wag(g)oner** *n* roulier *m*. ♦ **wag(g)onload** *n* (*Agr*) charretée *f*; (*Rail*) wagon *m*.

waif [weɪf] *n* enfant *mf* misérable. **~s and strays** enfants *mpl* abandonnés.

wail [weɪl] **1** *vi* (*gen*) gémir; (*cry*) pleurer; (*whine*) pleurnicher; *[baby]* vagir; *[siren]* hurler. **2** *n* gémissement *m*; pleurs *mpl*; pleurnichements *mpl*; vagissement *m*; hurlement *m*. ♦ **wailing 1** *n* gémissements *mpl*; vagissements *mpl*; hurlements *mpl*; **2** *adj child* gémissant; *sound* plaintif.

wainscot(t)ing ['weɪnskətɪŋ] *n* lambrissage *m* (*en bois*).

waist [weɪst] **1** *n* (*gen*) taille *f*, ceinture *f*. **to put one's arm round sb's ~** prendre qn par la taille; **stripped to the ~** torse nu; **he was up to the ~ in water** l'eau lui arrivait à la ceinture; **high-/low-~ed dress** robe *f* à taille haute/basse. **2** *adj*: **~ measurement** *or* **size** tour *m* de taille. ♦ **waistband** *n* ceinture *f* (*de jupe etc*). ♦ **waistcoat** *n* gilet *m*. ♦ **waistline** *n* taille *f*; **to watch one's ~line** faire attention à sa ligne.

wait [weɪt] **1** *n* **(a)** (*gen*) attente *f*. **a 3-hour ~** 3 heures d'attente; (*between trains*) 3 heures de battement *m*; **to lie in ~** être à l'affût; **to lie in ~ for sb** *[huntsman, lion, reporter]* guetter qn; *[bandits, guerrillas]* dresser un guet-apens à qn. **(b)** (*Brit*) **the ~s** les chanteurs *mpl* de Noël.

2 *vi* **(a)** attendre (*for sb/sth* qn/qch; *for sb to do, until sb does* que qn fasse). **~ a moment!** un instant!; **~ till you're old enough** attends d'être assez grand; **just you ~!** tu vas voir ce que tu vas voir!; **just ~ till your father finds out!** attends un peu que ton père apprenne ça!; **~ and see!** attends voir!; **we'll just have to ~ and see** il va falloir attendre; **to keep sb ~ing** faire attendre qn; **they'll do it while you ~** on va le faire pendant que vous attendez; **'repairs while you ~'** 'réparations à la minute'; **he didn't ~ to be told twice** il ne se l'est pas fait dire deux fois; **that was worth ~ing for** cela valait la peine d'attendre; **I can't ~ to see him again** je meurs d'envie de le revoir; **they can't ~ to reverse this policy** ils brûlent de révoquer cette politique; **parcel ~ing to be collected** colis *m* en souffrance. **(b) to ~ at table** servir à table.

3 *vt* **(a)** attendre. **we'll ~ lunch for you** nous vous attendrons pour nous mettre à table. **(b)** (*US*) **to ~ table** servir à table.

wait about, wait around *vi* attendre (*for sb/sth* qn/qch); (*loiter*) traîner.

wait behind *vi* rester (*for sb* pour attendre qn).

wait on *vt fus [servant]* servir. **she ~s on him hand and foot** elle est aux petits soins pour lui.

wait up *vi* ne pas se coucher (*till 2 o'clock* avant 2 heures; *for sb* avant que qn ne revienne). **don't ~ up for me** couchez-vous sans m'attendre; **you can ~ up to see the programme** tu peux voir le programme avant de te coucher.

wait upon *vt fus [ambassador etc]* présenter ses respects à.

♦ **waiter** *n* garçon *m* (de café); **~er!** garçon!, monsieur! ♦ **waiting 1** *n* attente *f*; (*Aut*) **'no ~ing'** 'stationnement strictement interdit'; **2** *adj crowd etc* qui attend; (*fig*) **to play a ~ing game** (*gen*) attendre son heure; (*in negotiations etc*) mener une politique d'attente; **~ing list** liste *f* d'attente; **~ing room** salon *m* d'attente, (*in station etc*) salle *f* d'attente. ♦ **waitress** *n* serveuse *f*.

waive [weɪv] *vt claim* renoncer à; *condition* abandonner. ♦ **waiver** *n* renonciation *f* (*of* à).

wake[1] [weɪk] *n [ship]* sillage *m*. (*fig*) **in the ~ of** à la suite de; **to bring sth in its ~** amener qch dans son sillage; **to follow in sb's ~** marcher sur les traces de qn.

wake[2] [weɪk] *pret* **woke, waked,** *ptp* **waked, woken**

1 *vi* (~ **up**) se réveiller (*from* de); (*fig: start to work etc*) se secouer. ~ **up!** réveille-toi!; **she woke (up) to find them gone** à son réveil elle s'est aperçue qu'ils étaient partis; (*fig*) **to ~ (up) to sth** prendre conscience de qch. **2** *vt* (~ **up**) *person* réveiller (*from* de); (*fig*) *memories, desires* éveiller. **a noise that would ~ the dead** un bruit à réveiller les morts; (*fig*) **he needs sth to ~ him up** il a besoin d'être secoué. **3** *n* **(a)** (*over corpse*) veillée *f* mortuaire. **(b)** (*N Engl*) **W~s (Week)** *semaine de congé annuel.* ♦ **wakeful** *adj* (*awake*) éveillé; (*alert*) vigilant; *hours etc* sans sommeil. ♦ **waken** *vti* = **wake**². ♦ **wakey-wakey**‡ *excl* réveillez-vous! ♦ **waking 1** *adj* (*not sleeping*) éveillé; **in one's waking hours** pendant les heures de veille; **all his waking hours** chaque heure de sa journée; **2** *n*: **between waking and sleeping** entre la veille et le sommeil.

Wales [weɪlz] *n* pays *m* de Galles. **North/South ~** le Nord/le Sud du pays de Galles; **Secretary of State for ~** ministre *m* chargé du pays de Galles.

walk [wɔːk] **1** *n* **(a)** promenade *f*; (*~ing race*) épreuve *f* de marche. **to go for a ~** se promener, faire une promenade, (*shorter*) faire un tour, (*hike*) faire une randonnée; **a long ~** une grande promenade; **to take sb for a ~** emmener qn se promener; **to take the dog for a ~** promener le chien; **it is 10 minutes' ~ from here** c'est à 10 minutes à pied d'ici; **it's only a short ~ to the shops** il n'y a pas loin à marcher jusqu'aux magasins. **(b)** (*gait*) démarche *f*. **I knew him by his ~** je l'ai reconnu à sa démarche. **(c) to slow down to a ~** ralentir pour aller au pas; **at a ~** sans courir. **(d)** (*avenue*) avenue *f*; (*path: in garden*) allée *f*; (*in country*) chemin *m*. (*fig*) **from all ~s of life** de toutes conditions sociales.

2 *vi* (*gen*) marcher (*on* sur); (*not run*) aller au pas; (*not ride or drive*) aller à pied; (*go for a ~*) se promener; *[ghost]* apparaître. **to ~ back/down** *etc* rentrer/descendre *etc* (à pied *or* sans courir); (*fig*) **you must ~ before you can run** on apprend petit à petit; **he ~s in his sleep** il est somnambule; **he's ~ing in his sleep** il marche en dormant; **to ~ up and down** marcher de long en large; (*fig*) **my pen seems to have ~ed*** mon stylo a fichu le camp*; **to ~ all the way to London** faire tout le chemin à pied jusqu'à Londres; **to ~ home** rentrer à pied; **to ~ into** *trap, ambush* tomber dans; (*bump into*) *table, person* se cogner à.

3 *vt* **(a)** *distance* faire à pied. **you can ~ it in a couple of minutes** à pied cela vous prendra deux minutes; (*fig: easy*) **he ~ed it*** cela a été un jeu d'enfant pour lui. **(b)** *town, road* parcourir. **to ~ the streets** se promener dans les rues; (*from poverty*) errer dans les rues; *[prostitute]* faire le trottoir; **to ~ the plank** subir le supplice de la planche. **(c)** (*cause to ~*) *invalid, prisoner* faire se promener; *dog* promener; *horse* conduire à pied; *cycle* pousser. **I ~ed him round Paris** je l'ai promené dans Paris; **to ~ sb in** *etc* faire entrer *etc* qn; **I'll ~ you home/to the station** je vais vous raccompagner/vous accompagner à la gare; **they ~ed him off his feet** ils l'ont tellement fait marcher qu'il ne tenait plus debout.

walk about, walk around *vi* aller et venir.

walk across *vi* (*over bridge etc*) traverser. **to ~ across to sb** s'approcher de qn.

walk away *vi* s'éloigner (*from* de), partir. (*fig: unharmed*) **to ~ away from an accident** sortir indemne d'un accident; **to ~ away with sth** (*steal*) emporter qch en partant; (*win easily*) gagner qch haut la main.

walk in *vi* entrer. **who should ~ in but Paul!** et voilà que Paul est entré à ce moment-là!; **he just ~ed in and gave me the sack** il est entré sans crier gare et m'a annoncé qu'il me mettait à la porte.

walk off 1 *vi* = **walk away. 2** *vt sep excess weight* perdre en marchant. **to ~ off a headache** faire une promenade pour se débarrasser d'un mal de tête.

walk on *vi* (*Theat*) être figurant(e).

walk out *vi* (*go out*) sortir; (*go away*) partir; (*as protest*) partir en signe de protestation; (*strike*) se mettre en grève. **they ~ed out of the discussion** ils ont quitté la séance de discussion (en signe de protestation); **to ~ out on sb*** laisser tomber qn*.

walk up *vi* (*approach*) s'approcher (*to sb* de qn). (*at fair etc*) ~ **up,** ~ **up!** approchez, approchez!

♦ **walkabout*** *n [celebrity]* bain *m* de foule; **to go on a ~about** prendre un bain de foule. ♦ **walker** *n* **(a)** (*esp Sport*) marcheur *m*, -euse *f*; (*for pleasure*) promeneur *m*, -euse *f*; **he's a good ~er** il est bon marcheur; **he's a fast ~er** il marche vite; **(b)** (*support: for convalescents etc*) déambulateur *m*; (*for babies*) trotte-bébé *m*. ♦ **walkie-talkie** *n* talkie-walkie *m*. ♦ **walk-in** *adj cupboard* de plain-pied. ♦ **walking 1** *n* marche *f* à pied, promenade *f*; **2** *adj shoes* de marche; *miracle* ambulant; (*Mil*) **the ~ing wounded** les blessés *mpl* capables de marcher; **a ~ing encyclopedia** une encyclopédie vivante; **it is within ~ing distance** on peut facilement y aller à pied (*of* de); **we had a ~ing holiday** comme vacances nous avons fait un voyage à pied; **~ing race** épreuve *f* de marche; **~ing stick** canne *f*; **to be on a ~ing tour** faire une longue randonnée à pied. ♦ **walk(ing)-on part** *n* (*Theat*) rôle *m* de figurant(e). ♦ **walkout** *n* (*strike*) grève *f* surprise; (*from meeting etc*) départ *m* en signe de protestation; **to stage a ~out** faire une grève surprise, partir en signe de protestation. ♦ **walkover** *n* (*Racing*) walk-over *m*; (*fig*) (*game etc*) victoire *f* facile; (*exam etc*) jeu *m* d'enfant. ♦ **walk-up** *n* (*US*) (*house*) immeuble *m* sans ascenseur; (*apartment*) appartement *m* dans un immeuble sans ascenseur. ♦ **walkway** *n* passage *m* pour piétons.

wall [wɔːl] **1** *n* (*gen*) mur *m*; (*as defence*) rempart *m*, muraille *f*; (*interior; also of tunnel, stomach etc*) paroi *f*; *[tyre]* flanc *m*; (*fig: of smoke etc*) muraille. **within the (city) ~s** dans les murs; **the Great W~ of China** la grande muraille de Chine; **the Berlin W~** le mur de Berlin; **they left only the bare ~s standing** ils n'en ont laissé que les murs; (*Econ*) **tariff ~** barrière *f* douanière; **~s have ears** les murs ont des oreilles; *[prisoner]* **to go over the ~** s'évader; (*fig*) **to go to the ~** *[person]* perdre la partie; (*go bankrupt*) faire faillite; *[plan, activity]* être sacrifié; **it's the weakest to the ~** les plus faibles doivent céder le pas; (*fig*) **he had his back to the ~, he was up against the ~** il était acculé; (*fig*) **to bang one's head against a brick ~** se taper la tête contre les murs; (*fig*) **to come up against a blank ~** se heurter à un mur; **to drive sb up the ~*** rendre qn dingue* *or* fou. **2** *adj cupboard, clock, map, socket* mural. **~ chart** planche *f* murale (*gravure*); **~ lamp** *or* **light** applique *f* (*lampe*). **3** *vt* (~ **in**) *garden* entourer d'un mur; *city* fortifier. **to ~ sb/sth up** murer qn/qch. ♦ **walled** *adj garden* clos; *city* fortifié. ♦ **wall-eyed** *adj* qui louche. ♦ **wallflower** *n* giroflée *f*; (*fig*) **to be a ~flower** faire tapisserie. ♦ **wallpaper 1** *n* papier *m* peint; **2** *vt* tapisser (de papier peint). ♦ **wall-to-wall carpeting** *n* moquette *f*.

wallaby ['wɒləbɪ] *n* wallaby *m*.

wallet ['wɒlɪt] *n* portefeuille *m*.

Walloon [wɒ'luːn] **1** *adj* wallon. **2** *n* Wallon(ne) *m(f)*; (*Ling*) wallon *m*.

wallop* ['wɒləp] **1** *n* (grand) coup *m*; (*sound*) fracas *m*. **it hit the floor with a ~** vlan! c'est tombé par terre. **2** *vt person* rosser*; *object* taper sur.

♦ **walloping**‡ **1** *adj* (*big etc*) sacré* (*before n*), formidable*; **2** *n* (*beating*) rossée* *f*.

wallow ['wɒləʊ] *vi* (*gen: also in vice etc*) se vautrer (*in* dans); (*in self-pity etc*) se complaire (*in* à); *[ship]* être ballotté.

walnut ['wɔːlnʌt] **1** *n* noix *f*; (*tree, wood*) noyer *m*. **2** *adj table etc* en noyer; *cake* aux noix; *oil* de noix.

walrus ['wɔːlrəs] *n* morse *m* (*Zool*). (*hum*) ~ **moustache** moustache *f* à la gauloise.

waltz [wɔːlts] **1** *n* valse *f*. **2** *vi* valser. (*fig*) **to ~ in/out** *etc* entrer/sortir *etc* (*gaily*) d'un pas joyeux *or* (*brazenly*) avec désinvolture.

wan [wɒn] *adj* (*gen*) pâle; *person, look* triste. ♦ **wanly** *adv smile, say* tristement.

wand [wɒnd] *n* baguette *f* (magique); *[usher etc]* verge *f*, bâton *m*.

wander ['wɒndəʳ] **1** *n*: **to go for a ~ around the town/the shops** aller faire un tour en ville/dans les magasins. **2** *vi* (**~ about, ~ around**) (*gen*) errer; (*idly*) flâner; *[river, road]* serpenter; (*stray*) s'écarter (*from* de), s'égarer. **to ~ in/away** *etc* entrer/partir *etc* sans se presser; **they ~ed round the shop** ils ont flâné dans le magasin; **he ~ed off the path** il s'est écarté du chemin, il s'est égaré; **his thoughts ~ed back to ...** ses pensées se sont distraitement reportées à ...; **my mind was ~ing** j'étais distrait; (*pej*) **his mind is ~ing** il divague. **3** *vt streets, hills* errer dans. **to ~ the world** courir le monde. ♦ **wanderer** *n* vagabond(e) *m(f)*; (*on seeing sb*) **the ~er's returned!** tiens, un revenant! ♦ **wandering 1** *adj way of life, person* errant, vagabond; *river, road* qui serpente; *tribe* nomade; *minstrel* ambulant; *glance* distrait; *thoughts* vagabond; **the W~ing Jew** le Juif errant; **2** *npl*: **~ings** vagabondages *mpl*. ♦ **wanderlust** *n* envie *f* de voir le monde.

wane [weɪn] *vi, n* (*also* **be on the ~**) *[moon]* décroître; *[reputation, interest]* diminuer; *[beauty, strength]* décliner. ♦ **waning** *adj* décroissant; diminuant; déclinant.

wangle* ['wæŋgl] **1** *n* combine *f*. **2** *vt* (*get*) se débrouiller pour obtenir (*sth from sb* qch de qn; *sth for sb* qch pour qn); (*without paying*) carotter* (*sth for sb* qch pour qn; *sth from sb* qch à qn). **I'll ~ it somehow** je me débrouillerai pour arranger ça. ♦ **wangler*** *n* débrouillard(e)* *m(f)*. ♦ **wangling*** *n* système D* *m*.

want [wɒnt] **1** *vt* **(a)** (*gen*) vouloir (*to do* faire); (*wish, desire*) avoir envie de, désirer (*to do* faire). **what do you ~?** que voulez-vous?, que désirez-vous?; **what do you ~ with** *or* **of him?** qu'est-ce que vous lui voulez?; **what does he ~ for that picture?** combien veut-il pour ce tableau?; **I don't ~ to!** je n'en ai pas envie!, (*more definite*) je ne veux pas!; **all I ~ is ...** tout ce que je veux, c'est ...; **I ~ your opinion on this** je voudrais votre avis là-dessus; **I ~ you to tell me ...** je veux que tu me dises ...; **I ~ it done** je veux qu'on le fasse; **I was ~ing to leave** j'avais envie de partir; **to ~ out*** vouloir sortir, (*fig: from project etc*) vouloir laisser tomber*; **you're not ~ed here** on n'a pas besoin de vous ici; **I know when I'm not ~ed!*** je me rends compte que je suis de trop; (*fig*) **you've got him where you ~ him** vous le tenez à votre merci; (*iro*) **you don't ~ much** il n'en faut pas beaucoup pour vous faire plaisir; **he ~s you in his office** il veut vous voir dans son bureau; **you're ~ed on the phone** on vous demande au téléphone; **to be ~ed by the police** être recherché par la police (*for sth* pour qch); **the ~ed man** l'homme que la police recherche; **'good cook ~ed'** 'on demande une bonne cuisinière'; (*Press*) **'articles ~ed'** 'articles demandés'; (*sexually*) **to ~ sb** désirer qn. **(b)** (*need*) *[person]* avoir besoin de; *[task etc] care, skill* exiger; (*: *ought*) devoir (*to do* faire). **we have all we ~** nous avons tout ce qu'il nous faut; **you ~ a hammer if ...** tu as besoin d'un marteau si ...; **the car ~s cleaning** la voiture a besoin d'être lavée; **you ~ to see his boat!*** tu devrais voir son bateau!; (*lack*) **it ~ed only his agreement** il ne manquait que son accord.

2 *vi* (*lack*) **to ~ for sth** manquer de qch, avoir besoin de qch.

3 *n* **(a)** (*lack*) manque *m*. **for ~ of** faute de; **for ~ of anything better** faute de mieux; **for ~ of anything better to do** faute d'avoir quelque chose de mieux à faire; **for ~ of sth to do** par désœuvrement; **it wasn't for ~ of trying that he ...** ce n'était pas faute d'avoir essayé qu'il ...; **there was no ~ of enthusiasm** ce n'était pas l'enthousiasme qui manquait. **(b)** (*poverty*) besoin *m*, misère *f*. **to live in ~** être dans le besoin. **(c)** (*requirement*) **his ~s are few** il a peu de besoins *mpl*; **it meets a long-felt ~** cela comble enfin cette lacune. ♦ **want ad*** *n* (*Press*) demande *f* (*for* de). ♦ **wanting 1** *adj*: **to be ~ing** manquer; **~ing in** qui manque de; **to be tried and found ~ing** *[person]* être jugé insuffisant; *[thing]* ne pas être suffisamment bien; (*pej*) **he is a bit ~ing*** il est simplet; **2** *prep* (*without*) sans; (*minus*) moins.

wanton ['wɒntən] *adj cruelty, destruction* gratuit, injustifié; *woman* dévergondé. ♦ **wantonly** *adv destroy etc* de façon injustifiée.

war [wɔːʳ] **1** *n* guerre *f*. **to be at ~** être en guerre (*with* avec); *[country]* **to go to ~** entrer en guerre (*against* contre; *over* à propos de); *[soldier]* **to go off to ~** partir pour la guerre; (*also fig*) **to make ~ on** faire la guerre à; **the Great W~** la guerre de 14–18; **the period between the ~s** (*1918–39*) l'entre-deux-guerres *m inv*; (*Brit*) **the W~ Office**, (*US*) **the W~ Department** le ministère de la Guerre; **to carry the ~ into the enemy's camp** prendre l'offensive; (*fig*) **it was ~ to the knife** *or* **the death** c'était une lutte à couteaux tirés (*between* entre); (*fig*) **~ of words** guerre de paroles; (*fig*) **you've been in the ~s again*** tu t'es encore fait estropier. **2** *adj* (*gen*) *crime, widow, wound, zone* de guerre. (*fig*) **~ clouds** nuages *mpl* avant-coureurs de la guerre; **~ cry** cri *m* de guerre; **~ dance** danse *f* guerrière; **on a ~ footing** sur le pied de guerre; **~ games** (*Mil: for training*) kriegspiel *m*; (*practice manoeuvres*) manœuvres *fpl* militaires; (*board games*) jeux *mpl* de stratégie militaire; **~ memorial** monument *m* aux morts. **3** *vi* faire la guerre (*against* à). ♦ **war-disabled** *npl* invalides *mfpl* de guerre. ♦ **warfare** *n* guerre *f* (*activité*); **class ~fare** lutte *f* des classes. ♦ **warhead** *n* ogive *f*. ♦ **warhorse** *n* (*fig*) **an old ~horse** (*Mil*) un vieux militaire; (*Pol etc*) un vétéran. ♦ **warlike** *adj* guerrier. ♦ **warmonger** *n* belliciste *mf*. ♦ **warmongering 1** *adj* belliciste; **2** *n* propagande *f* belliciste. ♦ **warpath** *n* (*fig*) **to be on the ~path*** chercher la bagarre*. ♦ **warring** *adj nations* en guerre; (*fig*) *interests* contradictoires; *ideologies* en conflit. ♦ **warship** *n* navire *m* de guerre. ♦ **wartime 1** *n* temps *m* de guerre; **in ~time** en temps de guerre; **2** *adj* de guerre. ♦ **war-weary** *adj* las de la guerre.

warble ['wɔːbl] *vi [bird]* gazouiller; *[person]* roucouler. ♦ **warbler** *n* oiseau *m* chanteur. ♦ **warbling** *n* gazouillis *m*.

ward [wɔːd] **1** *n* **(a)** *[hospital]* salle *f*. **(b)** (*Local Government*) section *f* électorale. **(c)** (*Jur*) pupille *mf*. **~ of court** pupille sous tutelle judiciaire. **2** *vt*: **to ~ sth off** éviter qch. ♦ **warden** *n [city, castle]* gouverneur *m*; *[park, game reserve]* gardien *m*, -ienne *f*; *[institution, student hostel etc]* directeur *m*, -trice *f*; *[youth hostel]* père *m or* mère *f* aubergiste; (*traffic warden*) contractuel(le) *m(f)*. ♦ **warder** *n* gardien *m* (de prison). ♦ **wardress** *n* gardienne *f* (de prison). ♦ **wardroom** *n* (*Naut*) carré *m*.

wardrobe ['wɔːdrəʊb] *n* (*cupboard*) armoire *f*; (*clothes*) garde-robe *f*; (*Theat*) costumes *mpl*. (*Theat*) **~ mistress** costumière *f*.

warehouse ['wɛəhaʊs] *n* entrepôt *m*, magasin *m*. ♦ **warehouseman** *n* magasinier *m*.

wares [wɛəz] *npl* marchandises *fpl*.

warm [wɔːm] **1** *adj* **(a)** (*gen*) (assez) chaud; *iron, oven* moyen. **I am ~** j'ai (assez) chaud; **this room is quite ~** il fait (assez) chaud dans cette pièce; **as ~ as toast** chaud comme une caille; **it's ~, the weather is ~** il fait chaud; **it's nice and ~ in here** il fait bon ici; **in ~ weather** par temps chaud; (*Met*) **~ front** front *m* chaud; **the water is just ~** l'eau est juste chaude; **this coffee's only ~** ce café est tiède; **to get sth ~** chauffer qch; **to get** *or* **grow ~** *[person]* se réchauffer; *[water, object]* chauffer; (*in guessing etc games*) **you're getting ~(er)!** tu chauffes!; **to keep sth ~** tenir qch au chaud; **it keeps me ~** ça me tient chaud; **keep him ~** ne le laissez pas prendre froid; **keep (yourself) ~** ne prenez pas froid; **it's ~ work** c'est du travail qui donne chaud. **(b)** (*fig*) *colour, discussion* chaud; *voice, feelings, welcome, congratulations* chaleureux; *apologies, thanks* vif; *supporter* ardent. **she is a very ~ person** elle est très chaleureuse de nature; (*in letter*) **with ~est wishes** avec tous mes vœux les plus amicaux.

2 *n*: **to give sth a ~*** chauffer qch; **to have a ~* by the fire** se chauffer près du feu; **come and sit in the ~*** venez vous asseoir au chaud.

3 *vt* (**~ up**) *person, room* réchauffer; *water, food, coat* chauffer, réchauffer. **to ~ one's hands** se (ré)chauffer les mains; (*fig*) **it ~ed my heart** ça m'a réchauffé le cœur.

4 *vi* **(a)** (**~ up**) *[person etc]* se réchauffer; *[water etc]* chauffer. **(b)** (*fig*) **to ~ to sth** s'enthousiasmer peu à peu pour qch; **to ~ to sb** se prendre de sympathie pour qn.

warm up 1 *vi* **(a)** = **warm 4a. (b)** *[engine, car]* se réchauffer; *[athlete, dancer]* s'échauffer; *[discussion, audience]* devenir animé; *[party]* commencer à être plein d'entrain; *[game]* devenir excitant. **things are ~ing up** ça commence à chauffer*. **2** *vt sep person, room* réchauffer; *water, food, coat* chauffer; *engine, car* faire chauffer; *discussion* animer; (*Theat etc*) *audience* mettre en train.

♦ **warm-blooded** *adj* à sang chaud. ♦ **warm-hearted** *adj* chaleureux. ♦ **warming-up exercises** *npl* exercices *mpl* d'échauffement. ♦ **warmly** *adv clothe, wrap up* chaudement; (*fig*) *welcome, applaud* chaleureusement; *thank, recommend* vivement; **tucked up ~ly in bed** bordé bien au chaud dans son lit. ♦ **warmth** *n* chaleur *f*. ♦ **warm-up*** *n* (*Sport*) période *f* d'échauffement; (*Theat, TV etc*) mise *f* en train.

warn [wɔːn] *vt* (*gen*) prévenir, avertir (*of* de, *that* que); *authorities, police* alerter. **you have been ~ed!** vous êtes averti!; **to ~ sb against doing** *or* **not to do** conseiller à qn de ne pas faire; **to ~ sb off** *or* **against sth** mettre qn en garde contre qch. ♦ **warning 1** *n* (*gen; also informal note*) avertissement *m*; (*formal letter*) avis *m*; (*signal*) alerte *f*; **without ~ing** *fall, happen* inopinément; *arrive, leave* à l'improviste, sans prévenir; **thank you for the ~ing** merci de m'avoir prévenu; **a note of ~ing in his voice** une mise en garde dans le ton qu'il a pris; **I gave you due ~ing** je vous avais bien prévenu (*that* que); (*Met*) **gale ~ing** avis de grand vent; **2** *adj glance, cry* d'avertissement; *sign* avertisseur; **~ing device** dispositif *m* d'alarme; **~ing light** voyant *m* avertisseur; **~ing shot** (*gen, Mil*) coup *m* tiré en guise d'avertissement; (*Naut*) coup de semonce; (*fig*) avertissement *m*; ... **he said in a ~ing tone** ... dit-il pour mettre en garde.

warp [wɔːp] **1** *n* **(a)** (*Tex*) chaîne *f*; (*fig: essence*) fibre *f*. **(b)** (*distortion: in wood etc*) voilure *f*. **2** *vt object* voiler; (*fig*) *judgment* fausser; *character* corrompre. **3** *vi* se voiler. ♦ **warped** *adj mind* tordu; *sense of humour* morbide; *account* tendancieux.

warrant ['wɒrənt] **1** *n* (*for travel, payment*) bon *m*; (*guarantee*) garantie *f*; (*Mil*) brevet *m*; (*Jur, Police*) mandat *m*. (*Jur*) **there is a ~ out for his arrest** on a émis un mandat d'arrêt contre lui; (*gen*) **he has no ~ for saying so** il ne s'appuie sur rien pour justifier cela. **2** *adj*: **~ officer** adjudant *m* (*auxiliaire de l'officier*). **3** *vt* **(a)** (*justify*) justifier. **the facts do not ~ it** les faits ne le justifient pas. **(b)** (*guarantee*) garantir. **I'll ~ (you) he won't do it again!** je vous assure qu'il ne recommencera pas! ♦ **warranted** *adj goods* garanti; *remark* justifié. ♦ **warranty** *n* autorisation *f*; (*Comm, Jur*) garantie *f*.

warren ['wɒrən] *n [rabbits]* garenne *f*; (*overcrowded house*) taupinière *f* (*fig*). **a ~ of little streets** un dédale de petites rues.

warrior ['wɒrɪə^r] *n* guerrier *m*, -ière *f*.

Warsaw ['wɔːsɔː] *n* Varsovie. **~ Pact** pacte *m* de Varsovie.

wart [wɔːt] *n* verrue *f*. (*fig*) **~s and all** sans aucun embellissement. ♦ **wart-hog** *n* phacochère *m*.

wary ['wɛərɪ] *adj* (*gen*) prudent; *manner* précautionneux. **to be ~ about sb/sth** se méfier de qn/qch; **to be ~ of doing** hésiter beaucoup à faire; **to keep a ~ eye on sb/sth** surveiller qn/qch de près. ♦ **warily** *adv* (*gen*) avec prudence; *say* avec précaution. ♦ **wariness** *n* prudence *f*.

wash [wɒʃ] **1** *n* **(a) to give sth a ~** laver qch; **to have a ~** se laver; **to have a quick ~** se débarbouiller; **it needs a ~** cela a besoin d'être lavé; **to send sth to the ~** envoyer qch au blanchissage; **put your jeans in the ~** mets tes jeans au sale; **your shirt is in the ~** ta chemise est à la lessive; **the colours ran in the ~** cela a déteint à la lessive; (*fig*) **it will all come out in the ~*** (*be known*) on finira bien par savoir ce qu'il en est; (*be all right*) ça finira par se tasser*. **(b)** = **washing 1b. (c)** *[ship]* sillage *m*; (*sound: of waves etc*) clapotis *m*. **(d)** (*with paint*) **to give sth a blue ~** badigeonner qch en bleu.

2 *vt* **(a)** (*gen*) laver. **to ~ o.s.** *[person]* se laver, faire sa toilette; *[cat]* faire sa toilette; (*fig*) **to ~ one's hands of** *sth* se laver les mains de; *sb* se désintéresser de; **he ~ed the dirt off his hands** il s'est lavé les mains (pour en enlever la saleté); **to ~ the dishes/clothes** faire la vaisselle/la lessive; (*fig*) **to ~ one's dirty linen in public** laver son linge sale en public; **to ~ sth clean** bien nettoyer qch; (*fig*) **~ed clean of sin** lavé de tout péché. **(b)** *[river etc]* (*carry away*) emporter; (*to shore*) rejeter; (*flow over*) *coast etc* baigner. **~ed out to sea** entraîné vers le large.

3 *vi* **(a)** (*have a ~*) se laver (*in hot water* à l'eau chaude), faire sa toilette; (*do the washing*) faire la lessive. **this fabric won't ~** ce tissu n'est pas lavable; (*fig*) **that just won't ~*** ça ne prend pas (*with* avec). **(b)** *[waves etc]* **to ~ over sth** balayer qch.

wash away *vt sep* **(a)** *stain* faire partir au lavage; *mud etc* enlever à l'eau; *[rain]* faire partir; (*fig*) *sins* laver. **(b)** *[river etc] boat* emporter; *river bank* éroder; *footprints* effacer.

wash down *vt sep* **(a)** *deck, car* laver à grande eau; *wall* lessiver. **(b)** *pill* faire descendre (*with* avec); *food* arroser (*with* de).

wash off 1 *vi* (*with soap*) partir au lavage; (*with water*) partir à l'eau; (*from walls*) partir au lessivage. **it won't ~ off** ça ne s'en va pas. **2** *vt sep* faire partir au lavage *or* à l'eau; (*from wall*) faire partir en lessivant.

wash out 1 *vi* = **wash off 1. 2** *vt sep* **(a)** = **wash off 2. (b)** (*clean*) *bottle, pan* laver. (*fig*) **the match was ~ed out** le match n'a pas eu lieu à cause de la pluie; **that has ~ed out any chance of ...** ça a anéanti toute possibilité de ...; (*tired etc*) **to be/look ~ed out*** être/avoir l'air complètement lessivé*.

wash through *vt sep* laver rapidement.

wash up 1 *vi* **(a)** (*Brit: dishes*) faire la vaisselle.

(b) (*US: have a* ~) se débarbouiller. **2** *vt sep* **(a)**(*Brit*) *plates, cups* laver. **(b)** *[sea, tide]* rejeter (sur le rivage). **(c)** (*fig*) **to be all ~ed up*** *[scheme]* être fichu*; *[marriage, relationship]* être en ruines.
♦ **washable** *adj* lavable. ♦ **wash-and-wear** *adj shirt* qui ne nécessite aucun repassage; (*on label*) 'ne pas repasser'. ♦ **washbasin** *or* ♦ **washbowl** *or* ♦ **wash-hand basin** *n* lavabo *m*. ♦ **washcloth** *n* gant *m* de toilette. ♦ **washday** *n* jour *m* de lessive. ♦ **washer** *n* **(a)** (*in tap etc*) rondelle *f*; **(b)** (~*ing machine*) machine *f* à laver; (*for windscreen*) lave-glace *m inv*. ♦ **wash-house** *n* lavoir *m*. ♦ **washing 1** *n* **(a)** (*act*) *[car]* lavage *m*; *[clothes]* lessive *f*; *[walls]* lessivage *m*; **(b)** (*clothes themselves*) linge *m*, lessive *f*; **to do the ~ing** faire la lessive; **2** *adj*: **~ing day** jour *m* de lessive; **~ing line** corde *f* à linge; **~ing machine** machine *f* à laver; **~ing powder** lessive *f* (en poudre); **~ing soda** cristaux *mpl* de soude. ♦ **washing-up 1** *n* (*Brit*) vaisselle *f* (*à laver etc*); **to do the ~ing-up** faire la vaisselle; **2** *adj*: **~ing-up bowl** bassine *f*; **~ing-up liquid** lave-vaisselle *m inv* (*produit*); **~ing-up water** eau *f* de vaisselle. ♦ **wash-leather** *n* peau *f* de chamois. ♦ **wash-out*** *n* (*event, play*) fiasco *m*; (*person*) nullité *f*. ♦ **washroom** *n* toilettes *fpl*. ♦ **washstand** *n* lavabo *m*. ♦ **washtub** *n* (*bath*) tub *m*; (*for clothes*) bassine *f*.

wasp [wɒsp] *n* guêpe *f*. **~'s nest** guêpier *m*.
♦ **waspish** *adj* hargneux. ♦ **waspishly** *adv* avec hargne.

waste [weɪst] **1** *n* **(a)** (*gen*) gaspillage *m*; *[time]* perte *f*. **to go** *or* **run to ~** (*gen*) être gaspillé; *[land]* être à l'abandon; **the ~ in the kitchens** le gaspillage *or* le gâchis dans les cuisines; **it's a ~ of money to do that** on gaspille de l'argent en faisant cela; **that machine was a ~ of money** cela ne valait vraiment pas la peine d'acheter cette machine; **a ~ of effort** un effort inutile; **it's a ~ of time doing that** on perd son temps à faire *or* en faisant cela; **it's a ~ of time and energy** c'est peine perdue; **it's a ~ of breath** c'est dépenser sa salive pour rien. **(b)** (~ *material*) déchets *mpl*; (*household* ~) ordures *fpl*; (*water*) eaux *fpl* sales. **nuclear ~** déchets nucléaires. **(c)** (*expanse: of snow etc*) désert *m* (immense); (*in town*) terrain *m* vague.

2 *adj material* de rebut; *energy, heat* perdu; *food* inutilisé; *water* sale; *ground, district* à l'abandon. **~ products** (*Ind*) déchets *mpl* de fabrication; (*Physiol*) déchets de l'organisme; **to lay ~** dévaster.

3 *vt* (*gen*) gaspiller (*on sth* pour qch; *on doing* pour faire); *time, an evening* perdre; *opportunity* laisser passer. **nothing is ~d** il n'y a aucun gaspillage; **to ~ one's breath** dépenser sa salive pour rien; **the sarcasm was ~d on him** il n'a pas compris le sarcasme; **caviar is ~d on him** ça ne vaut pas la peine de lui donner du caviar.

4 *vi [food, goods, resources]* se perdre, être gaspillé. **you mustn't let it ~** il ne faut pas le laisser perdre; **~ not want not** l'économie protège du besoin.

waste away *vi* dépérir.
♦ **wastage** *n* (*gen*) gaspillage *m*; *[time]* perte *f*; (*amount lost from container*) pertes; (*rejects*) déchets *mpl*; (*as part of industrial process etc*) déperdition *f*; (*Comm: through pilfering etc*) coulage *m*; **there is a huge wastage of** on gaspille énormément de. ♦ **wastebasket** *n* corbeille *f* (à papier). ♦ **wastebin** *n* (*basket*) corbeille *f* (à papier); (*in kitchen*) poubelle *f*. ♦ **wasted** *adj* **(a)** *limb* (*from disease, starvation*) décharné; (*withered*) atrophié. **(b)** *food, resources* gaspillé; *effort* inutile, vain; *life* gâché; *time* perdu. ♦ **waste-disposal unit** *n* broyeur *m* d'ordures. ♦ **wasteful** *adj person* gaspilleur; *process* peu rentable; *expenditure* inutile. ♦ **wastefully** *adv spend, throw away* bêtement; **to use sth ~fully** ne pas utiliser qch au mieux. ♦ **wastefulness** *n [person]* manque *m* d'économie; *[process]* manque de rentabilité. ♦ **wasteland** *n* terres *fpl* à l'abandon; (*in town*) terrain *m* vague. ♦ **wastepaper** *n* vieux papiers *mpl*; **~paper basket** corbeille *f* (à papier). ♦ **waste-pipe** *n* (tuyau *m* de) vidange *f*. ♦ **wasting** *adj disease* qui ronge. ♦ **wastrel** *n* (*good-for-nothing*) propre *mf* à rien; (*spendthrift*) dépensier *m*, -ière *f*.

watch [wɒtʃ] **1** *n* **(a)** montre *f*. **by my ~** à ma montre. **(b) to keep ~** faire le guet; **to keep (a) close ~ on** *or* **over sth/sb** surveiller qch/qn de près; **to be on the ~ for** *person, enemy, animal, vehicle* guetter; *danger* être sur ses gardes à cause de; *bargains* être à l'affût de. **(c)** (*Naut*) quart *m*. **to be on ~** être de quart; **officer of the ~** officier *m* de quart.

2 *vt* **(a)** (*gen*) regarder (*sb doing sth* qn faire qch), observer; (*keep an eye on*) *suspect, house, dish cooking, luggage, child, shop* surveiller; *expression, birds etc* observer; *notice board, small ads etc* consulter régulièrement; *political situation, developments* suivre de près. **~ what I do** regarde-moi faire; **he ~ed his chance and slipped out** il a guetté le moment propice et s'est esquivé; **have you ever ~ed an operation?** avez-vous déjà assisté à une opération?; **we are being ~ed** on nous surveille; **~ tomorrow's paper** ne manquez pas de lire le journal de demain. **(b)** (*be careful of*) *money, expenses, dangerous thing* faire attention à. **~ that knife!** fais attention avec ce couteau!; **~ your head!** attention *or* gare à votre tête!; **~ it!*** attention!; **~ your step!, ~ how you go!** (fais) attention!; **to ~ one's step** se surveiller; **I must ~ the time** il faut que je surveille l'heure; **he does tend to ~ the clock** il a tendance à surveiller la pendule; **to ~ sb's interests** veiller aux intérêts de qn; **~ your language** surveille ton langage; **~ you don't burn yourself** attention, ne vous brûlez pas!; **~ that he does his homework** veillez à ce qu'il fasse ses devoirs.

3 *vi* (*gen*) regarder; (*pay attention*) faire attention. **to ~ by sb's bedside** veiller au chevet de qn; **to ~ over sb/sth** surveiller qn/qch; **to ~ for sth/sb** guetter qch/qn; **he's ~ing to see what you're going to do** il attend pour voir ce que vous allez faire.

watch out *vi* (*keep a look-out*) guetter (*for sb/sth* qn/qch); (*take care*) faire attention, prendre garde. **~ out!** attention!; **~ out for cars** faites attention *or* prenez garde aux voitures; **to ~ out for thieves** être sur ses gardes contre les voleurs; **~ out for trouble if ...** préparez-vous à des ennuis si ... .
♦ **watchdog** *n* chien *m* de garde; (*fig*) gardien *m*, -ienne *f*. ♦ **watcher** *n* (*observer*) observateur *m*, -trice *f*; (*hidden or hostile*) guetteur *m*; (*spectator*) spectateur *m*, -trice *f*. ♦ **watchful** *adj* vigilant; **to keep a ~ful eye on sth/sb** garder qch/qn à l'œil; **under the ~ful eye of ...** sous l'œil vigilant de ... . ♦ **watchmaker** *n* horloger *m*, -ère *f*. ♦ **watchmaking** *n* horlogerie *f*. ♦ **watchman** *n* gardien *m*. ♦ **watch-night service** *n* messe *f* de minuit de la Saint-Sylvestre. ♦ **watchstrap** *n* bracelet *m* de montre. ♦ **watchtower** *n* tour *f* de guet. ♦ **watchword** *n* (*password*) mot *m* de passe; (*fig: motto*) mot d'ordre.

water ['wɔːtəʳ] **1** *n* eau *f*. **hot and cold ~ in all rooms** eau courante chaude et froide dans toutes les chambres; **drinking ~** eau potable; **I want a drink of ~** je voudrais un verre d'eau; **to turn on the ~** (*at main*) ouvrir l'eau; (*from tap*) ouvrir le robinet; **the road is under ~** la route est inondée; **to swim under ~** nager sous l'eau; (*tide*) **at high/low ~** à marée haute/basse; **to make ~** *[ship]* faire eau; (*urinate: also* **to pass ~**) uriner; **it won't hold ~** *[container]* ça n'est pas étanche;

[plan, excuse] ça ne tient pas debout; (*fig*) **a lot of ~ has passed under the bridge** il est passé beaucoup d'eau sous les ponts; **he spends money like ~** l'argent lui fond entre les mains; (*fig*) **to pour** *or* **throw cold ~ on sth** se montrer peu enthousiaste pour qch; (*fig*) **it's like ~ off a duck's back*** c'est comme si on chantait*; **lavender/rose ~** eau de lavande/de rose; (*at spa*) **to take the ~s** faire une cure thermale; **in French ~s** dans les eaux territoriales françaises; **the ~s of the Rhine** les eaux du Rhin; (*in pregnancy*) **the ~s** les eaux; (*Med*) **~ on the knee** épanchement *m* de synovie; **~ on the brain** hydrocéphalie *f*.

2 *adj level, pressure, pipe, snake, rat* d'eau; *pump, mill, clock, pistol* à eau; *plant, bird* aquatique. **~ bed** matelas *m* d'eau; **~ biscuit** craquelin *m*; *[soldier etc]* **~ bottle** bidon *m*; **~ cannon** grande lance *f* à eau; (*in streets*) **~ cart** arroseuse *f* (municipale); (*Culin*) **~ ice** sorbet *m*; **~ main** conduite *f* principale d'eau; **~ polo** water-polo *m*; **~ power** énergie *f* hydraulique; **~ purifier** (*device*) épurateur *m* d'eau; (*tablet*) cachet *m* pour purifier l'eau; **~ rate** taxe *f* sur l'eau; **~ softener** adoucisseur *m* d'eau; **~ supply** (*for town*) approvisionnement *m* en eau; (*for house etc*) alimentation *f* en eau; (*for traveller*) provision *f* d'eau; **to cut off the ~ supply** couper l'eau; (*Geog*) **~ table** niveau *m* hydrostatique; **~ tank** réservoir *m* d'eau, citerne *f*; **~ tower** château *m* d'eau.

3 *vi [eyes]* pleurer. **his mouth ~ed** il a eu l'eau à la bouche; **it made his mouth ~** cela lui a fait venir l'eau à la bouche.

4 *vt [gardener, river]* arroser; *animal* donner à boire à; *wine etc* couper (d'eau).

water down *vt sep milk, wine* couper (d'eau); (*fig*) *story, version* édulcorer; *effect* atténuer.

♦ **watercolour 1** *n* (*painting*) aquarelle *f*; (*paints*) **~colours** couleurs *fpl* pour aquarelle; **in ~colours** à l'aquarelle; **2** *adj* à l'aquarelle. ♦ **watercourse** *n* cours *m* d'eau. ♦ **watercress** *n* cresson *m* (de fontaine). ♦ **watered** *adj silk* moiré. ♦ **waterfall** *n* chute *f* d'eau. ♦ **waterfowl** *npl* gibier *m* d'eau. ♦ **waterfront** *n* (*at docks etc*) quais *mpl*; (*sea front*) front *m* de mer. ♦ **water-heater** *n* chauffe-eau *m inv*. ♦ **water-hole** *n* mare *f*. ♦ **watering** *n* arrosage *m*. ♦ **watering-can** *n* arrosoir *m*. ♦ **waterlily** *n* nénuphar *m*. ♦ **waterline** *n* (*Naut*) ligne *f* de flottaison. ♦ **waterlogged** *adj wood* imprégné d'eau; *shoes* imbibé d'eau; *land, pitch* détrempé. ♦ **watermark** *n* (*in paper*) filigrane *m*; (*left by tide*) laisse *f* de haute mer. ♦ **water-meadow** *n* prairie *f* souvent inondée. ♦ **watermelon** *n* pastèque *f*. ♦ **waterproof 1** *adj material* imperméable; *watch* étanche; **~proof sheet** (*for bed*) alaise *f*; (*tarpaulin*) bâche *f*; **2** *n* imperméable *m*; **3** *vt* imperméabiliser. ♦ **waterproofing** *n* imperméabilisation *f*. ♦ **water-repellent** *adj, n* hydrofuge (*m*). ♦ **watershed** *n* (*Geog*) ligne *f* de partage des eaux; (*fig*) grand tournant *m*. ♦ **waterside** *n* bord *m* de l'eau; **at** *or* **on** *or* **by the ~side** au bord de l'eau; **along the ~side** le long de la rive. ♦ **water-ski** *vi* faire du ski nautique. ♦ **water-skiing** *n* ski *m* nautique. ♦ **water-soluble** *adj* soluble dans l'eau. ♦ **waterspout** *n* (*on roof etc*) tuyau *m* de descente; (*Met*) trombe *f*. ♦ **watertight** *adj container* étanche; (*fig*) *excuse, plan* inattaquable; (*fig*) **in ~tight compartments** séparé par des cloisons étanches. ♦ **waterway** *n* voie *f* navigable. ♦ **water-wings** *npl* bouée *f*, flotteurs *mpl* de natation. ♦ **waterworks** *n* (*sg: place*) station *f* hydraulique; (*fig: cry*) **to turn on the ~works*** se mettre à pleurer comme une Madeleine*; **to have sth wrong with one's ~works*** avoir des ennuis de vessie. ♦ **watery** *adj substance* aqueux; *eyes* larmoyant; (*pej*) *tea, coffee* trop faible; *soup* trop liquide; *taste* fade; *colour* délavé.

Waterloo [ˌwɔːtəˈluː] *n* Waterloo. (*fig*) **to meet one's ~** faire naufrage (*fig*).

watt [wɒt] *n* (*Elec*) watt *m*. ♦ **wattage** *n* puissance *f* en watts.

wave [weɪv] **1** *n* **(a)** (*at sea, on lake*) vague *f*; (*on beach*) rouleau *m*; (*on river, pond*) vaguelette *f*; (*in hair, on surface*) ondulation *f*; (*fig: of attack, enthusiasm, strikes etc*) vague. (*liter*) **the ~s** les flots *mpl*; **her hair has a natural ~ in it** ses cheveux ondulent naturellement; **to come in ~s** *[people]* arriver par vagues; *[explosions etc]* se produire par vagues; (*Cine etc*) **the new ~** la nouvelle vague. **(b)** (*Phys, Rad, Telec etc*) onde *f*. **long ~** grandes ondes; **medium/short ~** ondes moyennes/courtes. **(c)** (*gesture*) **to give sb a ~** faire un signe de la main à qn; **with a ~ of his hand** d'un signe de la main.

2 *vi* **(a)** *[person]* faire signe de la main; *[flag]* flotter au vent; *[branch, tree]* être agité; *[grass, corn]* onduler. **to ~ to sb** (*in greeting*) saluer qn de la main; (*as signal*) faire signe à qn (*to do* de faire). **(b)** *[hair]* onduler.

3 *vt* **(a)** *flag, handkerchief etc* agiter; (*threateningly*) *stick, sword* brandir. **he ~d the ticket at me furiously** il a agité vivement le ticket sous mon nez; **to ~ goodbye to sb** dire au revoir de la main à qn; **to ~ sb back/on** *etc* faire signe à qn de reculer/d'avancer *etc*. **(b)** *hair* onduler.

wave about, wave around *vt sep object, one's arms* agiter dans tous les sens.

wave aside, wave away *vt sep person, object* écarter d'un geste; *offer, help* refuser d'un geste.

♦ **waveband** *n* bande *f* de fréquences. ♦ **wavelength** *n* longueur *f* d'ondes; (*fig*) **we're not on the same ~length** nous ne sommes pas sur la même longueur d'ondes. ♦ **wavy** *adj hair, surface* ondulé; *line* onduleux. ♦ **wavy-haired** *adj* aux cheveux ondulés.

waver [ˈweɪvəʳ] *vi [flame, courage]* vaciller; *[voice]* trembler; *[person]* (*weaken*) lâcher pied; (*hesitate*) hésiter (*between* entre). ♦ **waverer** *n* indécis(e) *m(f)*. ♦ **wavering 1** *adj* vacillant; tremblant; hésitant; **2** *n* vacillation *f*; tremblement *m*; hésitations *fpl*.

wax¹ [wæks] **1** *n* (*gen*) cire *f*; (*for skis*) fart *m*; (*in ear*) bouchon *m* de cire. **2** *adj candle etc* de *or* en cire. **~ paper** papier *m* paraffiné. **3** *vt floor, furniture, shoes* cirer; *car* lustrer. ♦ **waxen** *adj colour* cireux. ♦ **waxworks** *n* (*pl: figures*) personnages *mpl* en cire; (*sg: wax museum*) musée *m* de cire. ♦ **waxy** *adj substance, complexion, colour* cireux; *potato* qui ne s'émiette pas.

wax² [wæks] *vi [moon]* croître. **to ~ poetic** *etc* devenir d'humeur poétique *etc*; **to ~ eloquent** déployer toute son éloquence (*about, over* à propos de); **to ~ enthusiastic** s'enthousiasmer (*about* pour).

way [weɪ] **1** *n* **(a)** (*road etc*) chemin *m*, voie *f*. **the ~ across the fields** le chemin qui traverse les champs; **they drove a ~ through the hills** ils ont ouvert un passage à travers les collines; **the Appian W~** la voie Appienne; (*Rel*) **the W~ of the Cross** le chemin de la Croix; **private/public ~** voie privée/publique; **across the ~** de l'autre côté de la rue (*from* par rapport à), en face; (*fig*) **the middle ~** le juste milieu.

(b) (*route*) chemin *m* (*to* de, vers). **which is the ~ to ...?** pouvez-vous m'indiquer le chemin de ...?; **he talked/it rained** *etc* **all the ~** il a parlé/il a plu *etc* pendant tout le chemin (*to* jusqu'à); **there are houses all the ~** il y a des maisons tout le long du chemin; (*fig*) **I'm with you all the ~*** je suis entièrement d'accord avec vous; **the ~ to success** le chemin du succès; **the shortest** *or* **quickest ~ to Leeds** le chemin le plus court pour aller à Leeds; **I went the long ~ round** j'ai pris le chemin le plus long; **on the ~ to London we ...** en allant à Londres nous ...; **it's on the ~ to the station** c'est sur le chemin de la gare; **we met him on the ~** nous l'avons rencontré en route; **on the ~ here I saw ...** en venant ici j'ai vu ...; **on your ~ home** en rentrant chez vous; **I must be on my ~** il faut que je parte; **to start on one's ~** se mettre en route; **to go on one's ~** reprendre son chemin; **he went by ~ of Glasgow** il est passé par Glasgow; **they met him by the ~** ils l'ont rencontré en chemin; (*fig*) **by the ~, what did he say?** à propos, qu'est-ce qu'il a dit?; (*fig*) **that is by the ~** tout ceci est secondaire; **the village is quite out of the ~** le village est vraiment à l'écart; (*fig*) **it's nothing out of the ~** cela n'a rien de spécial; **an out-of-the-~ subject** un sujet peu commun; **if it's not out of my ~** si c'est sur mon chemin; (*fig*) **to go out of one's ~ to do sth** se donner du mal pour faire qch; **don't go out of your ~ to do it** ne vous dérangez pas pour le faire; **to lose the** *or* **one's ~** perdre son chemin (*to* en allant à); **to ask the** *or* **one's ~** demander son chemin (*to* pour aller à); **I know the** *or* **my ~ to the station** je sais comment aller à la gare; (*fig*) **she knows her ~ about** elle sait se débrouiller; **they went their separate ~s** (*lit*) ils sont partis chacun de leur côté; (*fig*) chacun a suivi son chemin; (*fig*) **he went his own ~** il a fait à son idée; (*fig*) **he has gone the ~ of ...** il a fait comme ...; **to make one's ~ towards ...** se diriger vers ...; **to make one's ~ through sth** traverser qch; **to make one's ~ back to sth** retourner *or* revenir vers qch; (*fig*) **he had to make his own ~** il a dû faire son chemin tout seul; **the ~ back** le chemin du retour; **the ~ back to the station** le chemin pour retourner à la gare; **the ~ down/up** le chemin pour descendre/monter; **the ~ forward is dangerous** le chemin devient dangereux plus loin; **the ~ in** l'entrée *f*; **I'm looking for a ~ in/out** je cherche un moyen d'entrer/de sortir; **do you know the ~ into/out of ...?** savez-vous par où on entre dans/sort de ...?; *[fashion etc]* **it's on the ~ in/out** c'est la nouvelle mode/passé de mode; **the ~ out** la sortie; **on the** *or* **your ~ out** en sortant; (*fig*) **there is no ~ out of it** *or* **no ~ round it** il n'y a pas moyen de s'en sortir; **the ~ through the forest** le chemin à travers la forêt; **'no ~ through'** 'sans issue'.

(c) (*path*) **to be in sb's ~** barrer le passage à qn; (*fig*) **am I in the** *or* **your ~?** est-ce que je vous gêne?; **it's out of the ~ over there** ça ne gêne pas là-bas; **to get out of the ~** s'écarter; **to get out of sb's ~** laisser passer qn; **to get out of the ~ of the car** s'écarter de la voiture; **get it out of the ~!** poussez-le!, écartez-le!; **as soon as I've got the exam out of the ~** dès que je serai débarrassé de l'examen; **keep matches out of children's ~** ne laissez pas les allumettes à la portée des enfants; **to keep out of sb's ~** éviter qn; **he kept well out of the ~** il a pris soin de rester à l'écart; **to put sth out of the ~** ranger qch; **to want sb/sth out of the ~*** vouloir se débarrasser de qn/qch; **to put difficulties in sb's ~** créer des difficultés à qn; **he put me in the ~ of one or two good bargains** il m'a indiqué quelques bonnes affaires; **to make ~ for sb** s'écarter pour laisser passer qn, (*fig*) laisser la voie libre à qn; **make ~!** écartez-vous!; (*fig*) **this made ~ for a reform of ...** ceci a préparé le terrain pour une réforme de ...; **to push** *or* **thrust** *or* **elbow one's ~ through a crowd** se frayer un chemin à travers une foule; **to hack** *or* **cut one's ~ through sth** s'ouvrir un chemin à la hache *etc* dans qch; **to crawl/limp** *etc* **one's ~ to the door** ramper/boiter *etc* jusqu'à la porte; **he talked his ~ out of it** il s'en est sorti avec de belles paroles; **to give ~** *V* **give 1d.**

(d) (*distance*) distance *f*. **a long ~ off** *or* **away** loin; **a little ~ away** *or* **off** pas très loin; **it's a long ~** c'est loin (*from* de); **it's a long** *or* **good ~ to London** ça fait loin pour aller à Londres*; **it's a long ~ from here to ...** cela fait loin d'ici à ...; **we've a long ~ to go** (*lit*) nous avons encore un grand bout de chemin à faire; (*fig*) nous ne sommes pas au bout de nos peines; **your work has still a long ~ to go** vous avez encore de grands efforts à faire dans votre travail; (*fig*) **it should go a long ~ towards improving it/paying the bill** cela devrait l'améliorer considérablement/cela devrait couvrir une grande partie de la facture; **he makes a little go a long ~** il tire le meilleur parti de ce qu'il a; **a little kindness goes a long ~** un peu de gentillesse facilite bien des choses.

(e) (*direction*) direction *f*, sens *m*. **this ~** par ici; **'this ~ for** *or* **to the cathedral'** 'vers la cathédrale'; **this ~ and that** par-ci par-là, en tous sens; **which ~ did he go?** par où est-il passé?; **which ~ do we go from here?** (*lit*) par où passons-nous maintenant?; (*fig*) quelle voie devons-nous choisir maintenant?; **are you going my ~?** est-ce que vous allez dans la même direction que moi?; (*fig*) **everything's going his ~*** tout lui sourit; **he went that ~** il est parti par là; **she didn't know which ~ to look** elle ne savait pas où regarder; **he looked the other ~** il a détourné les yeux; **he never looks my ~** il ne regarde jamais dans ma direction; **I'll be down** *or* **round your ~** je serai près de chez vous; **if the chance comes your ~** si jamais vous en avez l'occasion; **over Oxford ~** du côté d'Oxford; (*fig*) **he's in a fair ~ to succeed** il est en passe de réussir; **the right ~ round** *or* **out** à l'endroit; **the wrong ~ round** *or* **out** à l'envers, dans le mauvais sens; **the right ~ up** dans le bon sens; **the wrong ~ up** sens dessus dessous; **the other ~ round** dans l'autre sens; **it's the other ~ round** c'est juste le contraire; **a one-~ street** une rue à sens unique; **a three-~ discussion** une discussion à trois participants.

(f) (*manner, method*) façon *f*, moyen *m* (*to do, of doing* de faire). **there are ~s and means** il y a différents moyens (*of doing* de faire); **we haven't the ~s and means to do it** nous n'avons pas les ressources suffisantes pour le faire; (*Admin*) **W~s and Means Committee** Commission *f* des Finances; **the French ~ of life** la manière de vivre des Français; **(in) this ~** comme ceci, de cette façon; **that's the ~ to do it** voilà comment il faut s'y prendre; (*encouraging*) **that's the ~!** voilà, c'est bien!; (*refusing*) **no ~!*** pas question!*; **do it either ~** fais-le de l'une ou l'autre façon; **either ~* I can't help you** de toute façon je ne peux pas vous aider; **do it your own ~** fais-le à ta façon; **to get one's own ~** obtenir ce que l'on désire; **to want one's own ~** ne vouloir en faire qu'à sa tête; **Arsenal had it all their own ~** Arsenal a complètement dominé le match; **I won't let him have things all his own ~** je ne vais pas lui passer tous ses caprices; **to my ~ of thinking** à mon avis; **her ~ of looking at it** son point de vue sur la question; **that's the ~ the money goes** c'est à ça que l'argent passe; **whatever ~ you like to look at it** de quelque façon que vous envisagiez (*subj*) la chose; **it's the ~ things are** c'est la vie; **it's just the ~ I'm made** c'est comme ça que je suis; **leave it all the ~ it is** laisse les choses comme elles sont; **the ~ things are going we shall have nothing left** du train où vont les choses il ne nous restera rien; **that's always the ~** c'est toujours comme ça; **it was this ~ ...** voici comment cela s'est passé ...; **to do sth the right/wrong ~** faire qch bien/mal; **in a general ~** en général; **once in a ~** de temps en temps; **by ~ of being a joke** en guise de plaisanterie.

(g) (*state; degree*) état *m*. **to be in a bad ~** *[person, situation]* aller mal; *[car etc]* être en piteux état; **there are no two ~s about it** c'est absolument clair; **one ~ or (an)other** d'une façon ou d'une autre; (*Racing*) **each ~** gagnant ou placé; **you can't have it both ~s** il faut choisir; (*fig*) **in a small ~** d'une façon limitée; **in his**

own small ~ dans la limite de ses moyens; **he is a bookseller in a big** ~ c'est un gros libraire; **we lost in a really big** ~ nous avons vraiment beaucoup perdu; **in the ordinary** ~ **of things** normalement.

(h) (*custom*) coutume *f*; (*manner*) façon *f* (*of doing* de faire). **the** ~**s of the Spaniards** les coutumes espagnoles; **the** ~**s of God and men** les voies *fpl* de Dieu et de l'homme; **his foreign** ~**s** ses habitudes *fpl* d'étranger; **he is very slow in his** ~**s** il fait tout très lentement; **he is amusing in his (own)** ~ il est amusant à sa façon; **it's not my** ~ ce n'est pas mon genre (*to do* de faire); **she has a** ~ **with her** elle sait persuader; **he has a** ~ **with people/cars** il sait s'y prendre avec les gens/les voitures; **to mend one's** ~**s** s'amender; **to get into/out of the** ~ **of doing** prendre/perdre l'habitude de faire.

(i) (*respect, detail*) égard *m*, point *m*. **in some** ~**s** à certains égards; **in many** ~**s** à bien des égards; **can I help you in any** ~? puis-je vous aider en quoi que ce soit?; **does that in any** ~ **explain it?** est-ce là une explication satisfaisante?; **he's in no** ~ **to blame** ce n'est vraiment pas sa faute; **without in any** ~ **wishing to do so** sans vouloir le moins du monde le faire; **he's right in a** *or* **one** ~ il a raison dans un certain sens; **what is there in the** ~ **of books?** qu'est-ce qu'il y a comme livres?

(j) *[ship]* **to gather/lose** ~ prendre/perdre de la vitesse; **to have** ~ **on** avoir de l'erre; **to be under** ~ *[ship]* faire route; *[meeting, discussion]* être en cours; *[plans]* être en voie de réalisation; **to get under** ~ *[ship]* appareiller; *[person]* se mettre en route; *[vehicle, meeting, discussion]* démarrer; **to get sth under** ~ faire démarrer qch.

2 *adv*: ~ **back** *etc* = **away back** *etc* (*V* **away 1a**); **you're** ~ **out* in your calculations** tu es très loin du compte dans tes calculs.

♦ **wayfarer** *n* voyageur *m*, -euse *f*. ♦ **wayfaring** *n* voyages *mpl*. ♦ **waylay** *pret, ptp* **-laid** *vt* (*attack*) attaquer; (*speak to*) arrêter au passage. ♦ **way-out*** *adj* excentrique. ♦ **wayside 1** *n* bord *m* *or* côté *m* de la route; **along the** ~**side** le long de la route; **by the** ~**side** au bord de la route; (*fig*) **to fall by the** ~**side** abandonner en route; **2** *adj* *café etc* au bord de la route. ♦ **wayward** *adj* rebelle.

W.C. ['dʌblju(:)'si:] *n* W.-C. *mpl*, waters *mpl*.

we [wi:] *pers pron pl* nous. ~ **know** nous savons; (*stressed*) nous, nous savons; ~ **went to the pictures** nous sommes allés *or* on est allé* au cinéma; ~ **French** nous autres Français; **as** ~ **do in Scotland** comme on fait en Écosse; ~ **all make mistakes** tout le monde peut se tromper.

weak [wi:k] *adj* (*gen*) faible; *structure, material* qui manque de solidité; *coffee, tea* léger; (*fig*) *chin* fuyant; (*Med*) *health, lungs, stomach* fragile. ~ **from** *or* **with hunger** affaibli par la faim; **to grow** ~**(er)** = **to weaken 1**; **to have a** ~ **heart** avoir le cœur malade; **to have** ~ **eyes** *or* **eyesight** avoir une mauvaise vue; ~ **in the head*** faible d'esprit, débile*; **he went** ~ **at the knees** il avait les jambes comme du coton; ~ **in maths** faible en maths; ~ **spot** point *m* faible; (*fig*) **the** ~ **link in the chain** le point faible; ~ **verb** verbe *m* faible. ♦ **weaken 1** *vi* (*gen*) faiblir; (*in health*) s'affaiblir; *[influence, power]* baisser; *[prices]* fléchir; **2** *vt* (*gen*) affaiblir; *join, structure, material* enlever de la solidité à; *heart* fatiguer; *coffee, solution, mixture* diluer. ♦ **weakening 1** *n* (*gen*) affaiblissement *m*; *[structure, material]* fléchissement *m*; **2** *adj* (*gen*) affaiblissant; *disease* débilitant. ♦ **weak-kneed** *adj* mou, faible. ♦ **weakling** *n* (*physically*) mauviette *f*; (*morally etc*) faible *mf*. ♦ **weakly 1** *adj* faible, chétif; **2** *adv* faiblement. ♦ **weak-minded** *adj* faible d'esprit. ♦ **weakness** *n* faiblesse *f*; manque *m* de solidité; fragilité *f*; **one of his** ~**nesses** un de ses points faibles; **to have a** ~**ness for** avoir un faible pour. ♦ **weak-willed** *adj* faible.

weal [wi:l] *n* (*on skin*) marque *f* d'un coup de fouet.

wealth [welθ] *n* (*fact of being rich*) richesse *f*; (*money, possessions, resources*) richesses, fortune *f*. **a man of great** ~ un homme richissime; **mineral** ~ richesses minières; (*fig*) **a** ~ **of ideas** une profusion d'idées. ♦ **wealthy** *adj* (très) riche.

wean [wi:n] *vt* *baby* sevrer; (*fig: from bad habits etc*) détourner (*from, off* de). **I've managed to** ~ **him off gin** je l'ai habitué à se passer de gin.

weapon ['wepən] *n* arme *f*.

wear [wɛəʳ] (*vb: pret* **wore**, *ptp* **worn**) **1** *n*: **clothes for everyday** ~ vêtements *mpl* pour tous les jours; **evening/town** ~ tenue *f* de soirée/de ville; (*Comm*) **children's/summer** ~ vêtements pour enfants/d'été; **what is the correct** ~ quelle est la tenue convenable (*for* pour); **this carpet has had some hard** ~ ce tapis a beaucoup servi; **it will stand up to a lot of** ~ cela fera beaucoup d'usage; **there is still some** ~ **left in it** (*garment*) c'est encore mettable; (*carpet, tyre*) cela fera encore de l'usage; **he got 4 years'** ~ **out of it** cela lui a fait 4 ans; **it has had a lot of** ~ **and tear** c'est très usagé; **fair** ~ **and tear** usure *f* normale; **the** ~ **and tear on the engine** l'usure du moteur; **to show signs of** ~, **to look the worse for** ~ commencer à être fatigué.

2 *vt* **(a)** (*gen*) porter; (*fig*) *smile, look* avoir. **he was** ~**ing a hat** il portait un chapeau, il avait (mis) un chapeau; **I never** ~ **a hat** je ne mets *or* porte jamais de chapeau; **what shall I** ~? qu'est-ce que je vais mettre?; **I've nothing to** ~ je n'ai rien à me mettre; **she was** ~**ing blue** elle était en bleu; **she** ~**s her hair long** elle a les cheveux longs; **I never** ~ **scent** je ne me mets jamais de parfum; **she was** ~**ing make-up** elle était maquillée; **she was** ~**ing lipstick** elle s'était mis du rouge à lèvres; **she wore a frown** elle fronçait les sourcils; (*fig: agree to*) **he won't** ~ **that*** il ne marchera pas*.

(b) (*rub etc*) *clothes, stone etc* user; *groove, path* creuser peu à peu; *hole* faire peu à peu (*in sth* dans *or* à qch). **worn thin** *blade* aminci à l'usage; *rug* complètement râpé; (*fig*) **worn with care** usé par les soucis.

3 *vi* **(a)** (*last*) faire de l'usage. **these shoes will** ~ **for years** ces chaussures feront des années; **to** ~ **well** *[garment, carpet]* faire beaucoup d'usage; *[theory, friendship]* résister au temps; **she has worn well*** elle est bien conservée.

(b) (*rub etc thin*) s'user. **worn at the knees** usé aux genoux; **to** ~ **into holes** se trouer; **the rock has worn smooth** la roche a été polie par le temps; **to** ~ **thin** *[cloth]* être râpé; *[patience]* s'épuiser; (*fig*) **that excuse has worn thin!** cette excuse ne prend plus!

wear away 1 *vi [substance]* s'user; *[inscription]* s'effacer. **2** *vt sep* user; effacer.

wear down 1 *vi [heels, pencil etc]* s'user. **2** *vt sep materials* user; *patience, strength, person* épuiser; *courage, resistance* miner.

wear off *vi [colour, inscription]* s'effacer; *[pain, anger, excitement]* passer; *[effects, anaesthetic]* se dissiper. **the novelty has worn off** cela n'a plus l'attrait de la nouveauté.

wear on *vi [day, winter etc]* avancer; *[war, discussions etc]* se poursuivre. **as the years wore on** avec le temps.

wear out 1 *vi* (*gen*) s'user; *[patience etc]* s'épuiser. **2** *vt sep shoes, clothes* user; *strength, patience, person, horse* épuiser. **to** ~ **o.s. out** s'épuiser (*doing* à faire); **to be worn out** être exténué.

♦ **wearable** *adj* *garment* mettable. ♦ **wearer** *n*: **they will delight the** ~**er** ils feront la joie de la personne qui les portera; **uniform** ~**ers** ceux qui portent l'uniforme; **from maker to** ~**er** du fabricant au client. ♦ **wearing** *adj* épuisant.

weary ['wɪərɪ] **1** *adj person, smile, look* las (*f* lasse) (*of sth* de qch; *of doing* de faire); *sigh* de lassitude; *journey* (*tiring*) fatigant; (*irksome*) lassant. **to grow ~ of sth/of doing** se lasser de qch/de faire; **4 ~ hours** 4 heures mortelles. **2** *vi* se lasser (*of sth* de qch; *of doing* de faire). **3** *vt* (*tire*) fatiguer; (*try patience of*) lasser (*with* à force de). ♦ **wearied** *adj* las. ♦ **wearily** *adv say, sigh, look* avec lassitude; *move* péniblement. ♦ **weariness** *n* lassitude *f*; fatigue *f*. ♦ **wearisome** *adj* (*tiring*) épuisant; (*boring*) lassant, ennuyeux.

weasel ['wi:zl] *n* belette *f*.

weather ['weðəʳ] **1** *n* temps *m*. **~ permitting** si le temps le permet; **what's the ~ like?** quel temps fait-il?; **it's fine/bad ~** il fait beau/mauvais; **in hot ~** par temps chaud; **in all ~s** par tous les temps; (*fig*) **to be under the ~*** être mal fichu*. **2** *vt* **(a)** (*survive*) *tempest, crisis* réchapper à. **(b)** *wood etc* faire mûrir. **~ed rocks** rochers *mpl* patinés par la pluie *etc*. **3** *adj knowledge, map, station* météorologique; *conditions, variations* atmosphérique; (*Naut*) *side, sheet* du vent. (*Brit*) **W~ Centre,** (*US*) **W~ Bureau** Office *m* national de la météorologie; **~ chart** carte *f* du temps; (*fig*) **to keep a ~ eye on sth** surveiller qch; **~ forecast** prévisions *fpl* météorologiques, météo* *f*; **~ report** bulletin *m* météorologique, météo*; **~ ship** navire *m* météo *inv*; **the ~ situation** le temps. ♦ **weather-beaten** *adj person* tanné; *building* dégradé par les intempéries. ♦ **weatherboarding** *n* planches *fpl* de recouvrement. ♦ **weathercock** *or* ♦ **weathervane** *n* girouette *f*. ♦ **weatherman*** *n* météorologiste *m*. ♦ **weatherproof** *adj clothing* imperméable; *house* étanche.

weave [wi:v] (*vb: pret* **wove**, *ptp* **woven**) **1** *n* tissage *m*. **2** *vt* (*gen*) tisser; *strands* entrelacer; *basket, garland* tresser; (*fig*) *story* inventer. **3** *vi* **(a)** (**~ along**) *[road, river]* serpenter. **(b) to ~ (one's way) through sth** se faufiler à travers qch; (*fig*) **let's get weaving!*** allons, remuons-nous! ♦ **weaver** *n* tisserand(e) *m(f)*.

web [web] *n* (*fabric; also of lies etc*) tissu *m*; *[spider]* toile *f*. ♦ **webbed** *adj* palmé. ♦ **webbing** *n* (*on chair*) sangles *fpl*. ♦ **webfooted** *adj*: **to be ~footed** avoir les pieds palmés.

wed [wed] **1** *vt* épouser. (*fig*) *[person]* **to be ~ded to sth** tenir infiniment à qch; **cunning ~ded to ambition** la ruse alliée à l'ambition. **2** *vi* se marier. **3** *npl*: **the newly-~s** les jeunes mariés *mpl*. ♦ **wedding 1** *n* (*ceremony*) mariage *m*; **silver/golden ~ding** noces *fpl* d'argent/d'or; **to have a quiet/a church ~ding** se marier dans l'intimité/à l'église; **2** *adj cake, night* de noces; *present, invitation, anniversary* de mariage; *dress* de mariée; *ceremony, march* nuptial; **~ding breakfast** lunch *m* de mariage; **their ~ding day** le jour de leur mariage; **~ding ring** alliance *f*.

wedge [wedʒ] **1** *n* (*under wheel etc*) cale *f*; (*for splitting sth*) coin *m*; (*piece: of cake etc*) part *f*. (*fig*) **it's the thin end of the ~** c'est le commencement de la fin. **2** *vt* (*fix*) *table, wheels* caler; (*push*) enfoncer (*into* dans; *between* entre). **to ~ a door open** maintenir une porte ouverte à l'aide d'une cale; **car ~d between two trucks** voiture coincée entre deux camions; **to ~ sth in** faire rentrer qch; **to be ~d in** être coincé. ♦ **wedge-heeled** *adj* à semelles compensées.

Wednesday ['wenzdeɪ] *n* mercredi *m*; *for phrases V* **Saturday.**

wee [wi:] *adj* (*Scot*) tout petit.

weed [wi:d] **1** *n* mauvaise herbe *f*; (**pej: person*) mauviette *f*. **2** *vt* désherber.

weed out *vt sep* (*fig*) *person* éliminer (*from* de); *old books, clothes* trier et jeter.

♦ **weeding** *n* désherbage *m*; **I've done some ~ing** j'ai un peu désherbé. ♦ **weed-killer** *n* désherbant *m*. ♦ **weedy** *adj* (*fig*) *person* qui a l'air d'une mauviette.

week [wi:k] *n* semaine *f*. **in a ~** dans une semaine, dans huit jours; **what day of the ~ is it?** quel jour de la semaine sommes-nous?; **~ in ~ out,~ after ~** semaine après semaine; **this ~** cette semaine; **next/last ~** la semaine prochaine/dernière; **in the middle of the ~** vers le milieu *or* dans le courant de la semaine; **a ~ today** aujourd'hui en huit; **a ~ past yesterday** il y a eu une semaine hier; **every two ~s** toutes les deux semaines, tous les quinze jours; **two ~s ago** il y a deux semaines, il y a quinze jours; **in 3 ~s' time** dans 3 semaines; **the ~ ending May 6th** la semaine qui se termine le 6 mai; **the working ~** la semaine de travail; **a 36-hour ~** une semaine de 36 heures.

♦ **weekday 1** *n* jour *m* de semaine; **on ~days** en semaine, (*Comm*) les jours ouvrables; **2** *adj activities, timetable* de la semaine. ♦ **weekend 1** *n* week-end *m*, fin *f* de semaine; **at ~ends** pendant les week-ends; **at the ~end** pendant le week-end; **we're going away for the ~end** nous partons en week-end; **a long ~end** un week-end prolongé; **2** *adj visit, programme* de *or* du week-end; **~end case** sac *m* de voyage; **~end cottage** maison *f* de campagne. ♦ **weekly 1** *adj* hebdomadaire; **2** *adv* une fois par semaine; **twice ~ly** deux fois par semaine; **3** *n* (*magazine*) hebdomadaire *m*.

weep [wi:p] *pret, ptp* **wept 1** *vi* pleurer (*for joy* de joie; *for sb* qn; *over sth* sur qch; *to see* de voir); *[wound etc]* suinter. **to ~ bitterly** pleurer à chaudes larmes; **I could have wept!** j'en aurais pleuré! **2** *n*: **to have a good/a little ~** pleurer un bon coup/un peu. ♦ **weeping 1** *n* larmes *fpl*; **2** *adj person* qui pleure; **~ing willow** saule *m* pleureur. ♦ **weepy** *adj voice* larmoyant; **to be ~y** avoir envie de pleurer.

weevil ['wi:vl] *n* charançon *m*.

weewee* ['wi:wi:] **1** *n* pipi* *m*. **2** *vi* faire pipi*.

weft [weft] *n* (*Tex*) trame *f*.

weigh [weɪ] **1** *vt* **(a)** peser. **it ~s 9 kilos** ça pèse 9 kilos; **what do you ~?** combien est-ce que vous pesez?; (*fig*) **it ~s a ton** c'est du plomb; **to ~ one's words** peser ses mots; **to ~ sth in one's hand** soupeser qch; **to ~ (up) A against B** mettre en balance A et B; **to ~ (up) the pros and cons** peser le pour et le contre. **(b) to ~ anchor** lever l'ancre. **2** *vi [object, responsibilities]* peser (*on* sur). **to ~ heavy/light** peser lourd/peu; (*fig*) **it was ~ing on her mind** cela la tracassait, (*stronger*) cela la tourmentait.

weigh down 1 *vi* peser de tout son poids (*on sth* sur qch). **2** *vt sep branch etc* faire plier. **to be ~ed down by** *load, parcels etc* plier sous le poids de; *responsibilities etc* être accablé de.

weigh in *vi [boxer, jockey etc]* se faire peser. **to ~ in at 70 kilos** peser 70 kilos avant le match (*or* la course).

weigh out *vt sep sugar etc* peser.

weigh up *vt sep* (*consider*) examiner; (*compare*) mettre en balance (*A with B, A against B* A et B).

♦ **weighbridge** *n* pont-bascule *m*. ♦ **weigh-in** *n* (*Sport*) pesage *m*. ♦ **weighing-machine** *n* balance *f*. ♦ **weight 1** *n* **(a)** poids *m* (*also fig*); **atomic ~t** poids atomique; **to be sold by ~t** se vendre au poids; **what is your ~t?** combien pesez-vous?; **what a ~t it is!** que c'est lourd!; **they are the same ~t** ils font le même poids; (*fig*) **it is worth its ~t in gold** cela vaut son pesant d'or; **under-/over~t** trop maigre/gros; **to put on/lose ~t** grossir/maigrir; **he put his full ~t on ...** il a pesé de tout son poids sur ...; **feel the ~t of this box!** soupesez-moi cette boîte!; (*fig*) **it's a ~t off my mind** c'est un gros souci de moins; (*fig*) **to give ~t to sth** donner du poids à qch; **to carry ~t** *[argument, factor]* avoir du poids (*with* pour); *[person]* avoir de l'influence; **(b)** (*for scales etc*) poids *m*; **~ts and measures** poids et mesures; **2** *vt* (**~t down**) (*sink*) lester *or* (*hold down*) maintenir avec un poids (*or* une pierre *etc*). ♦ **weighting** *n* (*on salary*) indemnité *f*; **London ~ting** indemnité de résidence pour Londres. ♦ **weightless** *adj* en état d'apesanteur. ♦ **weightlessness** *n* apesanteur *f*. ♦ **weightlifter** *n* haltérophile *m*. ♦ **weightlifting** *n* haltérophilie *f*. ♦ **weighty** *adj load, responsibility* lourd; *argument, matter* de poids; *reason* probant; *consideration, deliberation* mûr; *problem* grave.

weir [wɪəʳ] *n* barrage *m* (*de rivière*).

weird [wɪəd] *adj* (*eerie*) surnaturel, mystérieux; (*odd*) bizarre, étrange. ♦ **weirdly** *adv* mystérieusement; bizarrement, étrangement. ♦ **weirdness** *n* étrangeté *f*. ♦ **weirdo‡** *or* ♦ **weirdy‡** *n* drôle d'oiseau* *m* (*pej*).

welcome ['welkəm] **1** *adj* **(a)** *reminder, interruption* opportun. *[person, thing]* **to be ~** être le (*or* la) bienvenu(e); **~!** soyez le bienvenu *etc*; **~ to our house/to England** bienvenue chez nous/en Angleterre; **to make sb ~** faire bon accueil à qn; **I didn't feel very ~** je me suis senti de trop; **it was ~ news/a ~ sight** nous avons été (*or* il a été *etc*) heureux de l'apprendre/de le voir; **it is a ~ change** c'est un changement agréable; **it was a ~ relief** j'ai été vraiment soulagé. **(b) thank you — you're ~** merci — il n'y a pas de quoi; **you're ~ to try** libre à vous d'essayer; **you're ~ to use my car** n'hésitez pas à prendre ma voiture; **you're ~ to any help I can give you** si je peux vous être utile, ce sera avec plaisir; (*iro*) **you're ~ to it** je vous souhaite bien du plaisir. **2** *n* accueil *m*. **to bid sb ~** souhaiter la bienvenue à qn; **to give sb a warm ~** faire un accueil chaleureux à qn; **I got a fairly cold ~** j'ai été reçu plutôt froidement. **3** *vt* (*greet formally*) accueillir; (*greet warmly*) accueillir chaleureusement; (*bid ~*) souhaiter la bienvenue à; *news, suggestion, change* se réjouir de. **I'd ~ a cup of coffee** je prendrais volontiers une tasse de café. ♦ **welcoming** *adj smile, handshake* accueillant; *speech* d'accueil.

weld [weld] **1** *n* soudure *f*. **2** *vt* souder (*on to* à). ♦ **welder** *n* (*person*) soudeur *m*; (*machine*) soudeuse *f*. ♦ **welding 1** *n* soudure *f*; **2** *adj*: **~ing torch** chalumeau *m*.

welfare ['welfɛəʳ] **1** *n* **(a)** (*gen*) bien *m*; (*comfort*) bien-être *m*. **the nation's ~, the ~ of all** le bien public; **the physical/spiritual ~ of** la santé physique/morale de; **child/animal ~** protection *f* de l'enfance/des animaux; **to look after sb's ~** avoir la responsabilité de qn. **(b) (social) ~** assistance *f* sociale. **2** *adj milk, meals* gratuit. **~ centre** centre *m* d'assistance sociale; (*gen*) **the W~ State** l'État-providence *m*; **thanks to the W~ State** grâce à la Sécurité sociale; **~ work** travail social; **~ worker** ≃ travailleur *m*, -euse *f* social(e).

well¹ [wel] **1** *n* (*for water etc; also between buildings*) puits *m*; *[staircase, lift]* cage *f*. **2** *vi* **(a)** (**~ up**) *[tears, emotion]* monter. **(b)** (**~ out**) *[spring]* sourdre; *[blood]* couler (*from* de).

well² [wel] **1** *adv, comp* **better**, *superl* **best (a)** (*gen*) bien. **very ~** très bien; **he sings as ~ as he plays** il chante aussi bien qu'il joue; **he sings as ~ as she does** il chante aussi bien qu'elle; **~ done!** bravo!; **~ played!** bien joué!; **to do ~** (*succeed: in work etc*) bien réussir; (*manage sth*) bien se débrouiller; **the patient is doing ~** le malade est en bonne voie; **you did ~ to come** vous avez bien fait de venir; **to do as ~ as one can** faire de son mieux; **he did himself ~** il ne s'est privé de rien; **to do ~ by sb** bien agir envers qn; **you're ~ out of it** c'est une chance que tu n'aies plus rien à voir avec cela (*or* lui *etc*); **how ~ I understand!** comme je vous (*or* le *etc*) comprends!; **~ I know it!** je le sais bien!

(b) (*intensifying etc*) bien. **~ over 100** bien plus de 100; **he is ~ past fifty** il a largement dépassé la cinquantaine; **~ and truly** bel et bien; **he could ~ afford to pay for it** il avait largement les moyens de le payer; **you would be ~ advised to leave** vous feriez bien de partir; **you may ~ be surprised to learn** vous serez sans aucun doute surpris d'apprendre; **one might ~ ask why** on pourrait à juste titre demander pourquoi; **you might ~ ask!** belle question!; **he couldn't very ~ refuse** il ne pouvait guère refuser; **you might as ~ say** autant dire que; **you may as ~ tell me** autant me le dire, tu ferais aussi bien de me le dire; **we might (just) as ~ have stayed** autant valait rester, nous aurions aussi bien fait de rester; **as ~ she might** comme il se devait; **~ she might!** c'était la moindre des choses!

(c) as ~ (*also*) aussi; (*on top of it all*) par-dessus le marché; **by night as ~ as by day** aussi bien de jour que de nuit, de jour comme de nuit; **as ~ as his dog he has ...** en plus de son chien il a ... .

2 *excl* (*gen*) eh bien!; (*resignation*) enfin! (*after interruption*) **~, as I was saying ...** donc, comme je disais ...; (*hesitation*) **~ ...** c'est que ...; (*surprise*) **~, ~, ~!** tiens, tiens, tiens!; **~ I never!** ça par exemple!; **very ~ then** bon, d'accord.

3 *adj, comp* **better**, *superl* **best (a)** bien; bon. **all's ~ that ends well** tout est bien qui finit bien; **all's ~** tout va bien; **all is not ~** il y a qch qui ne va pas; **it's all very ~ to say ...** c'est bien joli de dire ...; **if you want to do it, ~ and good** si vous voulez le faire, d'accord; **it would be ~ to leave** on ferait bien de partir; **it is as ~ to remember** on ferait bien de se rappeler; **it would be just as ~ for you to stay** vous feriez tout aussi bien de rester; **it's as ~ for you that ...** heureusement pour vous que ... .

(b) (*healthy*) **how are you? — very ~** comment allez-vous? — très bien; **I hope you're ~** j'espère que vous allez bien; **to feel ~** se sentir bien; **to get ~** se remettre; **get ~ soon!** remets-toi vite!

4 *n*: **to think/speak ~ of** penser/dire du bien de; **I wish you ~!** je vous souhaite de réussir!; **sb who wishes you ~** qn qui vous veut du bien; **to let** *or* **leave ~ alone** s'arrêter là; **leave ~ alone** (*gen*) il faut savoir s'arrêter là; (*Prov*) le mieux est l'ennemi du bien.

5 *pref*: **well-** bien; **~-chosen/-dressed** *etc* bien choisi/habillé *etc*.

♦ **well-behaved** *adj child* sage; *animal* obéissant. ♦ **well-being** *n* bien-être *m*. ♦ **well-bred** *adj* (*good family*) de bonne famille; (*courteous*) bien élevé; *animal* de bonne race. ♦ **well-built** *adj* solide. ♦ **well-educated** *adj* qui a reçu une bonne éducation. ♦ **well-fed** *adj* bien nourri. ♦ **well-heeled*** *adj* nanti. ♦ **well-informed** *adj* bien informé (*about* sur); (*knowledgeable*) *person* instruit; (*Press etc*) **~-informed sources** milieux *mpl* bien informés. ♦ **well-judged** *adj remark* judicieux; *shot* bien visé; *estimate* juste. ♦ **well-kept** *adj house, garden* bien tenu; *hands* soigné; *hair* bien entretenu; *secret* bien gardé. ♦ **well-known** *adj* bien connu, célèbre. ♦ **well-made** *adj* bien fait. ♦ **well-mannered** *adj* bien élevé. ♦ **well-meaning** *adj person* bien intentionné; (*also* **~-meant**) *remark, action* fait avec les meilleures intentions. ♦ **well-nigh** *adv* presque. ♦ **well-off** *adj* **(a)** (*rich*) riche; **(b)** (*fortunate*) **you don't know when you're ~-off** tu ne connais pas ton bonheur; **she's ~-off without him** elle se passe fort bien de lui. ♦ **well-spent** *adj time* bien employé; *money* utilement dépensé. ♦ **well-thought-of** *adj* bien considéré. ♦ **well-thought-out** *adj* bien conçu. ♦ **well-timed** *adj* opportun, à propos. ♦ **well-to-do** *adj* aisé. ♦ **well-wishers** *npl* amis *mpl*; (*unknown*) amis *or* admirateurs *mpl* inconnus. ♦ **well-worn** *adj path* battu; *carpet, clothes* usagé; (*fig*) *expression* rebattu.

wellington ['welɪŋtən] *n* (**~ boot**: *also* **wellie***) botte *f* de caoutchouc.

Welsh [welʃ] **1** *adj* gallois. **~ dresser** vaisselier *m*; (*Pol*) **the ~ Office** le ministère des Affaires galloises. **2** *n* gallois *m.* (*people*) **the ~** les Gallois *mpl.* ♦ **Welshman** *n* Gallois *m.* ♦ **Welshwoman** *n* Galloise *f.*

welsh* [welʃ] *vi*: **to ~ on sb** lever le pied* en emportant l'argent de qn.

welterweight ['weltəweɪt] *n* (*Boxing*) poids *m* welter.

wend [wend] *vt*: **to ~ one's way** aller son chemin (*to, towards* vers).

went [went] *pret of* **go.**

wept [wept] *pret, ptp of* **weep.**

were [wɜːʳ] *pret of* **be.**

werewolf ['wɪəwʊlf] *n, pl* **-wolves** loup-garou *m.*

west [west] **1** *n* ouest *m.* **(to the) ~ of** à l'ouest de; **in the ~ of** dans l'ouest de; **the wind is in the ~** le vent est à l'ouest; **the wind is from the ~** le vent vient de l'ouest; **to live in the ~** habiter dans l'ouest; (*Pol*) **the W~** l'Occident *m,* l'Ouest *m.* **2** *adj side* ouest *inv*; *wind* d'ouest; *coast, door* ouest, occidental. **W~ Africa** Afrique *f* occidentale; **W~ Indies** Antilles *fpl*; **W~ Indian** (*adj*) antillais; (*n*) Antillais(e) *m(f)*; (*London*) **the W~ End** *le quartier élégant de Londres*; **the W~ Country** le sud-ouest (de l'Angleterre). **3** *adv drive, travel etc* en direction de l'ouest, vers l'ouest. **~ of the border** à l'ouest de la frontière; **to go due ~** aller droit vers l'ouest; (*fig*) **to go ~*** *[thing]* être fichu*; *[person]* passer l'arme à gauche*. ♦ **westbound** *adj traffic, vehicles* en direction de l'ouest; *carriageway* ouest *inv.* ♦ **westerly** *adj wind* de l'ouest; *situation, aspect* à l'ouest; **in a ~erly direction** en direction de l'ouest. ♦ **western 1** *adj region* ouest *inv,* de l'ouest; *coast* ouest, occidental; *wall, side* exposé à l'ouest; **in ~ern France** dans la France de l'ouest; **~ern France** l'Ouest *m* de la France; **W~ern Europe** Europe *f* occidentale; (*Pol*) **W~ern countries** pays *mpl* de l'Ouest *or* occidentaux; **2** *n* (*film*) western *m*; (*novel*) roman *m* d'aventures de cowboys. ♦ **westerner** *n* homme *m or* femme *f* de l'Ouest; (*Pol*) Occidental(e) *m(f).* ♦ **westernization** *n* occidentalisation *f.* ♦ **westernize** *vt* occidentaliser; **to become ~ernized** s'occidentaliser.

wet [wet] **1** *adj* (*gen*) (tout) mouillé; (*damp*) humide; (*soaking* ~) trempé; *paint* frais; *ink, watercolours* pas encore sec; *weather* pluvieux; *climate* humide; *day* de pluie; *season* des pluies. **it grows in ~ places** ça pousse dans les endroits humides; **~ to the skin, ~ through** trempé jusqu'aux os; **to get ~** se mouiller; **to get one's feet ~** se mouiller les pieds; (*fig*) **he's still ~ behind the ears*** il manque d'expérience; (*weather*) **it's going to be ~** il va pleuvoir; (*fig*) **a ~ blanket*** un rabat-joie; **he's really ~‡** c'est une vraie lavette*. **2** *n* **(a) the ~** (*rain*) la pluie; (*damp*) l'humidité *f*; **it got left out in the ~** c'est resté dehors sous la pluie. **(b)** (‡*pej: person*) lavette* *f.* **3** *vt* mouiller. **to ~ one's lips** se mouiller les lèvres; **to ~ o.s.** *or* **one's pants** mouiller sa culotte; **to ~ the bed** mouiller le lit. ♦ **wetness** *n* humidité *f.* ♦ **wetsuit** *n* combinaison *f* de plongée.

whack [wæk] **1** *n* **(a)** (*blow*) grand coup *m*; (*sound*) claquement *m.* (*attempt*) **to have a ~ at doing*** essayer de faire; **I'll have a ~ at it*** je vais tenter le coup*. **(b)** (*: *share*) part *f.* **2** *vt thing, person* donner un grand coup à; (*spank*) fesser; (*: *defeat*) donner une raclée* à. ♦ **whacked‡** *adj* (*exhausted*) crevé*. ♦ **whacker‡** *n* (*fish etc*) poisson *m etc* énorme; (*lie*) mensonge *m* énorme. ♦ **whacking 1** *n* (*spanking*) fessée *f*; (*beating: lit, fig*) raclée* *f*; **2** *adj* (*also* **~ing big***) énorme.

whale [weɪl] **1** *n* baleine *f.* (*fig*) **we had a ~ of a time*** on s'est drôlement* bien amusé; **a ~ of a difference*** une sacrée* différence. **2** *adj*: **~ oil** huile *f* de baleine. **3** *vi* pêcher la baleine. ♦ **whalebone** *n* fanon *m* de baleine; (*in corset etc*) baleine *f.* ♦ **whaler** *n* (*man*) pêcheur *m* de baleine; (*ship*) baleinier *m.* ♦ **whaling 1** *n* pêche *f* à la baleine; **2** *adj industry* baleinier.

wharf [wɔːf] *n* quai *m.* ♦ **wharfage** *n* droits *mpl* de quai.

what [wɒt] **1** *adj* **(a)** quel. **~ play did you see?** quelle pièce avez-vous vue?; **~ news?** quelles nouvelles?; **she showed me ~ book it was** elle m'a montré quel livre c'était; **~ a man!** quel homme!; **~ a nuisance!** que c'est ennuyeux!; **~ fools we are!** que nous sommes bêtes!; **~ a huge house!** quelle maison immense!

(b) I gave him ~ money I had je lui ai donné tout l'argent que j'avais; **~ little I said** le peu que j'ai dit.

2 *pron* **(a)** (*in questions: subject*) qu'est-ce qui; (*object*) que, qu'est-ce que; (*after prep*) quoi. **~'s happening?** qu'est-ce qui se passe?; **~ did you do?** qu'est-ce que vous avez fait?, qu'avez-vous fait?; **~ were you talking about?** de quoi parliez-vous?; **~ is that?** qu'est-ce que c'est que ça?; **~'s that book?** qu'est-ce que c'est que ce livre?; **~ is his address?** quelle est son adresse?; **~ is this called?** comment ça s'appelle?; **~'s the French for 'pen'?** comment dit-on 'pen' en français?; **~ can we do?** qu'est-ce que nous pouvons faire?, que pouvons-nous faire?; **~ will it cost?** combien est-ce que ça coûtera?; **it's** WHAT? c'est quoi?

(b) (*that which: subject*) ce qui; (*object*) ce que. **I wonder ~ will happen** je me demande ce qui va arriver; **tell us ~ you're thinking about** dites-nous ce à quoi vous pensez; **he asked me ~ she'd told me** il m'a demandé ce qu'elle m'avait dit; **I don't know ~ that book is** je ne sais pas ce que c'est que ce livre; **he just doesn't know ~'s ~** il est complètement dépassé*; **I'll show them ~'s ~** je vais leur montrer de quoi il retourne; **~ is done is done** ce qui est fait est fait; **say ~ you like** vous pouvez dire ce que vous voulez; **~ I need is ...** ce dont j'ai besoin c'est ...; **I don't know who is doing ~** je ne sais pas qui fait quoi; **I know ~, I'll tell you ~** tu sais quoi; **he's not ~ he was** il n'est plus ce qu'il était; **I've no clothes except ~ I'm wearing** je n'ai d'autres vêtements que ceux que je porte.

(c) ~ about Robert? et Robert?; **~ about writing that letter?** et si vous écriviez cette lettre?; **~ about the money you owe me?** et l'argent que vous me devez?; **~ about it?** (*so ~?*) et alors?; (*~ do you think?*) alors, qu'est-ce que tu en penses?; **~ about a coffee?** si on prenait un café?; **~ for?** pourquoi?; **~ did you do that for?** pourquoi avez-vous fait ça?; **... and ~ have you*, ... and ~ not*** et je ne sais quoi encore; **and ~ is more** et qui plus est; **and ~ is worse** et ce qui est pire; **and, ~ is less common** et, ce qui est plus inhabituel; **~ with X and Y** avec X et Y en plus; **~ with one thing and another** avec ceci et cela, (*after listing things*) avec tout ça.

3 *excl*: **~, no tea!** quoi *or* comment, pas de thé! ♦ **whatever 1** *adj, adv* (*any*) **~ever (the) book you choose** quel que soit le livre que vous choisissiez (*subj*); (*all*) **~ever money you've got** tout ce que tu as comme argent; **nothing ~ever** absolument rien; **2** *pron* **(a)** (*no matter what*) quoi que + *subj*; **~ever happens** quoi qu'il arrive (*subj*); **~ever you (may) find** quoi que vous trouviez; **~ever it may be** quoi que ce soit; **I'll pay ~ever it costs** je paierai ce que ça coûtera; **~ever it costs, get it** achète-le quel qu'en soit le prix; **(b)** (*anything that*) tout ce que; **do ~ever you please** faites ce que vous voulez; **(c)** (*emphatic*) **~ever did you do?*** qu'est-ce que vous êtes allé faire? ♦ **what's-it*** *or* ♦ **what's-his-name*** *or* ♦ **what-d'ye-call-him*** *etc n* machin* *m.* ♦ **whatsoever** = **whatever.**

wheat [wiːt] **1** *n* blé *m,* froment *m.* **2** *adj flour, field* de blé. ♦ **wheatgerm** *n* germes *mpl* de blé. ♦ **wheatmeal** *n* farine *f* brute (*à 80%*).

wheedle ['wiːdl] *vt* cajoler. **to ~ sth out of sb**

obtenir qch de qn par des cajoleries. ♦ **wheedling 1** *adj* enjôleur; **2** *n* cajoleries *fpl*.

wheel [wi:l] **1** *n* (*gen*) roue *f*; (*Naut*) roue de gouvernail; (*Aut: steering* ~) volant *m*; (*spinning* ~) rouet *m*; (*potter's* ~) tour *m*. ~ **of fortune** roue de la fortune; **at the** ~ (*Naut*) au gouvernail; (*Aut*) au volant; **to take the** ~ (*Naut*) prendre le gouvernail; (*Aut*) se mettre au volant; (*fig*) **the ~s of government** les rouages *mpl* du gouvernement; **to oil** *or* **grease the ~s** huiler les rouages; **there are ~s within ~s** il y a toutes sortes de forces en jeu; **the ~ has come full circle** la boucle est bouclée.

2 *vt barrow, pushchair, bed* pousser, rouler; *cycle* pousser; *person* pousser (dans un landau *or* un fauteuil roulant *etc*). (*fig*) ~ **him in!*** amenez-le!

3 *vi* (~ **round**) *[birds]* tournoyer; *[person]* se retourner (brusquement); (*Mil*) effectuer une conversion; *[procession]* tourner. (*Mil*) **right ~!** à droite!; (*fig*) **to be ~ing and dealing*** chercher des combines *fpl*; **there has been a lot of ~ing and dealing* over that** cela a donné lieu à toutes sortes de combines.

♦ **wheelbarrow** *n* brouette *f*. ♦ **wheelbase** *n* empattement *m*. ♦ **wheelchair** *n* fauteuil *m* roulant. ♦ **wheeled** *adj* à roues; **three-~ed** à trois roues. ♦ **-wheeler** *n ending*: **four-~er** voiture *f* à quatre roues. ♦ **wheelwright** *n* charron *m*.

wheeze [wi:z] **1** *n* respiration *f* bruyante. **2** *vi [person]* avoir du mal à respirer.

whelk [welk] *n* buccin *m*.

whelp [welp] **1** *n* petit(e) *m(f)* (*d'un animal*). **2** *vi* mettre bas.

when [wen] **1** *adv* quand. ~ **does the train leave?** quand *or* à quelle heure part le train?; ~ **is your birthday?** c'est quand, votre anniversaire?; ~ **did Columbus ...?** quand *or* en quelle année Christophe Colomb a-t-il ...?; **I don't know ~ we'll see him again** je ne sais pas quand nous le reverrons; **~'s the wedding?** à quand le mariage?; ~ **is the best time** quel est le meilleur moment (*to do* pour faire); **till ~?** jusqu'à quand?; **he's got to go by ~?** il faut qu'il soit parti quand?; (*iro*) **since ~?*** depuis quand?*

2 *conj* **(a)** (*at the time that*) quand, lorsque. ~ **I heard his voice I smiled** quand *or* lorsque j'ai entendu sa voix j'ai souri; ~ **I was a child there was ...** quand *or* lorsque j'étais enfant il y avait ...; **let me know ~ she comes** faites-moi savoir quand elle arrivera; ~ **writing to her, remember to say ...** quand vous lui écrirez n'oubliez pas de dire ...; ~ **you like** quand vous voulez *or* voudrez; **hardly had I got back ~ ...** je venais à peine de rentrer quand ... .

(b) (*on, at etc which*) où; que. **on the day ~** le jour où; **at the time ~** au moment *or* à l'heure où; **in spring, ~ ...** au printemps, au moment où ...; **on Saturday(s), ~ ...** le samedi, quand ...; (*each Saturday that*) **on Saturday(s) ~ ...** les samedis où ...; (*last etc Saturday ~*) **on Saturday, ~ ...** samedi, quand ...; **at 8 o'clock, ~ ...** à 8 heures, heure à laquelle ...; **at the very moment ~** juste au moment où; **one day ~ the sun was shining** un jour où le soleil brillait; **this is a time ~ we must speak** c'est dans un moment comme celui-ci qu'il faut parler; **there are times ~ ...** il y a des moments où ...; (*drinks etc*) **say ~!*** vous me direz ..., vous m'arrêterez ... .

(c) (*the time that*) **he told me about ~ you ...** il m'a raconté le jour où vous ...; **she spoke of ~ they had visited London** elle a parlé de la semaine (*or* du jour *etc*) où ils avaient visité Londres; **now is ~ I need you** c'est maintenant que j'ai besoin de vous; **that's ~ the train leaves** c'est l'heure à laquelle le train part; **that's ~ Napoleon was born** c'est l'année (*or* le jour) où Napoléon est né; **that's ~ you ought to try ...** c'est le moment d'essayer ...; **that was ~ the trouble started** c'est alors que les ennuis ont commencé.

(d) (*after*) quand, une fois que. ~ **you've read the book you'll know why** quand vous aurez lu le livre vous saurez pourquoi; ~ **it is finished the bridge will measure ...** une fois terminé, le pont mesurera ...; ~ **they had left he ...** après leur départ *or* après qu'ils furent partis, il ...; ~ **he'd been to Greece he ...** après être allé en Grèce, il ...; **do it ~ he's finished** faites-le quand il aura fini.

(e) (*whereas*) alors que. **he walked ~ he could have taken the bus** il est allé à pied alors qu'il aurait pu prendre le bus.

♦ **whenever 1** *conj* **(a)** (*at whatever time*) quand; **~ever you wish** quand vous voulez; **leave ~ever you're ready** partez quand vous serez prêt; **(b)** (*every time that*) chaque fois que; **~ever I see her I think of Jenny** chaque fois que je la vois je pense à Jenny; **2** *adv*: **last Monday, or ~ever** lundi dernier, ou je ne sais quand.

whence [wens] *adv, conj* (*liter*) d'où.

where [wɛəʳ] **1** *adv* où. ~ **do you live?** où habitez-vous?; ~ **are you going (to)?** où allez-vous?; **I wonder ~ ...** je me demande où ...; **~'s the theatre?** où est le théâtre?; ~ **do you come from?** d'où êtes-vous?; **near ~?** près d'où?

2 *conj* **(a)** (*gen*) (là) où. **stay ~ you are** restez où vous êtes; **there is a school ~ our house once stood** il y a une école là où se dressait autrefois notre maison; **go ~ you like** allez où vous voulez; **it's not ~ I left it** ce n'est plus là où je l'avais laissé; **it's not ~ I expected to see it** je ne m'attendais pas à le voir là.

(b) (*in etc which*) où. **the house ~ ...** la maison où ...; **in the place ~** à l'endroit où; **England is ~ you'll find ...** c'est en Angleterre que vous trouverez ...; **this is ~ it was found** c'est là qu'on l'a retrouvé.

(c) (*the place that*) là que. **so that's ~ my gloves have got to!** voilà où sont passés mes gants!; (*fig*) **that's ~ things started to go wrong** c'est là que les choses se sont gâtées; **this is ~ you've got to decide** là il faut que tu décides; **I walked past ~ he was standing** j'ai dépassé l'endroit où il se tenait; **from ~ I am** d'où *or* de là où je suis.

(d) (*whereas*) alors que. **he walked ~ he could have taken the bus** il est allé à pied alors qu'il aurait pu prendre le bus.

♦ **whereabouts 1** *adv* où (donc); **2** *npl*: **to know sb's ~abouts** savoir où est qn. ♦ **whereas** *conj* (*on the other hand*) alors que, tandis que; (*Jur: since*) attendu que. ♦ **wherefore** *n V* **why**. ♦ **whereupon** *conj* sur quoi, et sur ce. ♦ **wherever 1** *conj* **(a)** (*no matter where*) où que +*subj*; **~ver I am I'll always remember** où que je sois, je n'oublierai jamais; **(b)** (*anywhere*) (là) où; **sit ~ver you like** asseyez-vous (là) où vous voulez; **Barcombe, ~ver that is** un endroit qui s'appellerait Barcombe; **(c)** (*everywhere*) partout où; **~ver you go, I'll go too** partout où tu iras, j'irai; **~ver you see it, you know that ...** partout où vous le voyez, vous savez que ...; **2** *adv*: **in London or Liverpool or ~ver*** à Londres, Liverpool ou Dieu sait où. ♦ **wherewithal** *n*: **the ~withal** les moyens *mpl* (*to do* de faire).

whet [wet] *vt* (*lit, fig*) aiguiser. ♦ **whetstone** *n* pierre *f* à aiguiser.

whether ['weðəʳ] *conj* **(a)** si. **I don't know ~ it's true or not** je ne sais pas si c'est vrai ou non; **I don't know ~ to go** je ne sais pas si je dois y aller; **it is doubtful ~** il est peu probable que+*subj*; **I doubt ~** je doute que+*subj*; **I'm not sure ~** je ne suis pas sûr que+*subj*. **(b)** que+*subj*. ~ **it rains or snows** qu'il pleuve ou qu'il neige; ~ **you go or not, he ...** que tu y ailles ou non, il ... . **(c)** soit. ~ **before or after** soit avant, soit après.

whew [hwu:] *excl* ouf!

whey [weɪ] *n* petit-lait *m*.
which [wɪtʃ] **1** *adj* **(a)** (*in questions etc*) quel. **~ card?** quelle carte?, laquelle des cartes?; **I don't know ~ books** je ne sais pas quels livres; **~ one?** lequel (*or* laquelle)?; **~ one of you?** lequel (*or* laquelle) d'entre vous?
(b) in ~ case auquel cas; **a week, during ~ time** ... une semaine au cours de laquelle ... .
2 *pron* **(a)** (*in questions etc*) lequel *m*, laquelle *f*. **~ have you taken?** lequel avez-vous pris?; **~ of your sisters?** laquelle de vos sœurs?; **~ of you?** (*two people*) lequel de vous deux?; (*more than two*) lequel d'entre vous?; **~ are the ripest apples?** quelles sont les pommes les plus mûres?
(b) (*the one or ones that: subject*) celui (*or* celle *etc*) qui; (*object*) celui *etc* que. **show me ~ is the cheapest** montrez-moi celui qui est le moins cher; **I know ~ I'd rather have** je sais celui que je préférerais; **I don't know ~ is ~** je ne peux pas les distinguer; **I don't mind ~** ça m'est égal.
(c) (*that: subject*) qui; (*object*) que; (*after prep*) lequel *etc*. **the book ~ is on the table** le livre qui est sur la table; **the apple ~ you ate** la pomme que vous avez mangée; **the box ~ you put it in** la boîte dans laquelle vous l'avez mis; **the book ~ I told you about** le livre dont je vous ai parlé.
(d) (*and that: subject*) ce qui; (*object*) ce que; (*after prep*) quoi. **you're late, ~ reminds me ...** vous êtes en retard, ce qui me fait penser ...; **she said she was 40, ~ I don't believe** elle a dit qu'elle avait 40 ans, ce que je ne crois pas; **after ~ she left** après quoi elle est partie; **of ~ more later** ce dont je reparlerai plus tard; **from ~ we deduce** d'où nous déduisons.
♦ **whichever 1** *adj* **(a)** (*that one which*) **I'll have ~ever apple you don't want** je prendrai la pomme dont vous ne voulez pas; **keep ~ever one you prefer** gardez celui que vous préférez (peu importe lequel); **(b)** (*no matter which*: *subject*) quel que soit ... qui+*subj*; (*object*) quel que soit ... que+*subj*; **~ever book is left** quel que soit le livre qui reste (*subj*); **~ever dress you wear** quelle que soit la robe que tu portes (*subj*); **~ever way you look at it** de quelque manière que vous le considériez (*subj*); **2** *pron* **(a)** (*the one which*: *subject*) celui *m* (*or* celle *f etc*) qui; (*object*) celui *etc* que; **~ever is best for him** celui qui lui convient le mieux; **~ever you like** celui que vous voulez; **choose ~ever is easiest** choisissez le plus facile; **(b)** (*no matter which one: subject*) quel que soit celui qui+*subj*; (*object*) quel que soit celui que+*subj*; **~ever of the two books he chooses** quel que soit le livre qu'il choisisse; **~ever of the apples is left** quelle que soit la pomme qui reste (*subj*).
whiff [wɪf] *n* (*puff: of chloroform, sea air etc*) bouffée *f*; (*smell*) odeur *f*. **one ~ of this is enough to kill you** il suffit de respirer ça une fois pour mourir; **I caught a ~ of gas** j'ai senti l'odeur du gaz.
while [waɪl] **1** *conj* **(a)** (*during the time that*) pendant que. **~ I was out of the room** pendant que j'étais hors de la pièce; **she fell asleep ~ reading** elle s'est endormie en lisant; **~ you're away I'll write some letters** pendant ton absence *or* pendant que tu seras absent j'écrirai quelques lettres; **and ~ you're about it** et pendant que vous y êtes. **(b)** (*as long as*) tant que. **it won't happen ~ I'm here** cela n'arrivera pas tant que je serai là. **(c)** (*although*) bien que+*subj*, quoique+*subj*. **~ there are a few people who like that** bien qu'il *or* quoiqu'il y ait un petit nombre de gens qui aiment cela **(d)** (*whereas*) alors que, tandis que. **she sings quite well, ~ her sister can't sing a note** elle ne chante pas mal alors que *or* tandis que sa sœur ne sait pas chanter du tout.
2 *n*: **a ~** quelque temps; **a short ~, a little ~** un moment; **a long ~, a good ~** (assez) longtemps; **after a ~** au bout de quelque temps; **for a ~ I thought ...** j'ai pensé un moment ..., (*longer*) pendant quelque temps j'ai pensé ...; **once in a ~** une fois de temps en temps; **in between ~s** entretemps; **all the ~** pendant tout ce temps-là.
while away *vt sep* (faire) passer.
♦ **while-you-wait heel repairs** *npl* ≈ talon minute. ♦ **whilst** *conj* = **while 1.**
whim [wɪm] *n* caprice *m*, fantaisie *f*. **he gives in to her every ~** il lui passe tous ses caprices; **as the ~ takes him** comme l'idée lui vient. ♦ **whimsical** *adj person* fantasque; *smile, book* étrange; *idea* saugrenu. ♦ **whimsically** *adv say, suggest* de façon saugrenue; *smile, look* étrangement.
whimper [ˈwɪmpəʳ] **1** *vi [person, baby]* gémir faiblement; (*whine*) pleurnicher; *[dog]* pousser de petits cris plaintifs. **2** *n* gémissement *m*. ♦ **whimpering 1** *n* gémissements *mpl*; **2** *adj voice* larmoyant; (*whining*) pleurnicheur; *person, animal* qui gémit faiblement.
whin [wɪn] *n* (*Bot*) ajonc *m*.
whine [waɪn] **1** *vi [person, dog]* gémir; (*fig: complain*) se lamenter (*about* sur), se plaindre (*about* de); *[siren]* gémir. **2** *vt*: **'no,' he ~d** 'non,' dit-il d'une voix geignarde. **3** *n* gémissement *m* prolongé; (*fig*) plainte *f*; *[bullet, machine]* plainte stridente. ♦ **whining 1** *n [person, child]* gémissements *mpl* continus, pleurnicheries *fpl*; *[dog]* gémissements; (*fig: complaining*) plaintes *fpl* continuelles; **2** *adj voice, child* geignard; *dog* qui gémit.
whinny [ˈwɪnɪ] **1** *vi* hennir. **2** *n* hennissement *m*.
whip [wɪp] **1** *n* **(a)** fouet *m*; (*riding ~*) cravache *f*. **(b)** (*Parl*) (*person*) chef *m* de file (*d'un groupe parlementaire*). (*summons*) **three-line ~** convocation *f* impérative (*pour voter*). **(c)** (*Culin*) **strawberry** *etc* **~** mousse *f* instantanée à la fraise *etc*.
2 *adj* (*fig*) **to have the ~ hand** avoir l'avantage (*over* sur).
3 *vt* **(a)** fouetter; (*Culin*) battre au fouet. **~ped cream** crème *f* fouettée. **(b)** (*seize etc*) **to ~ sth out of sb's hands** enlever brusquement qch des mains de qn; **he ~ped a gun out of his pocket** il a brusquement sorti un revolver de sa poche; **to ~ sth away** *etc* enlever *etc* qch brusquement. **(c)** (*‡: steal*) faucher*, voler. **(d)** *rope* surlier; (*Sewing*) surfiler.
4 *vi*: **to ~ along/away** *etc* filer/partir *etc* à toute allure; **the car ~ped round the corner** la voiture a pris le tournant à toute allure; **to ~ round** *[person]* se retourner vivement; *[object]* pivoter brusquement.
whip up *vt sep cream etc* battre au fouet; (*fig*) *indignation, interest* stimuler; (*: *prepare*) *meal* préparer en vitesse. **can you ~ us up sth to eat?*** est-ce que vous pourriez nous faire à manger* en vitesse?
♦ **whiplash** *n* (*blow from whip*) coup *m* de fouet; (*fig: in car accident*) coup du lapin*. ♦ **whippersnapper** *n* freluquet *m*. ♦ **whipping 1** *n* (*punishment*) correction *f*; **to give sb a ~ping** fouetter qn; **2** *adj*: **~ping cream** crème fraîche (*à fouetter*); (*fig*) **~ping boy** bouc *m* émissaire. ♦ **whip-round*** *n*: **to have a ~-round** faire une collecte (*for* pour).
whippet [ˈwɪpɪt] *n* whippet *m*.
whirl [wɜːl] **1** *vi* **(a)** (**~ round**) *[leaves, dancers, water]* tourbillonner; *[wheel, merry-go-round]* tourner. **the leaves ~ed down** les feuilles tombaient en tourbillonnant. **(b)** (*move rapidly*) **to ~ along/away** *etc* aller/partir *etc* à toute vitesse. **2** *vt* (**~ round**) *leaves etc* faire tourbillonner; *sword, object on rope* faire tournoyer. (*fig*) **they ~ed us round the Louvre** ils nous ont fait visiter le Louvre à toute vitesse; **the train ~ed us along** le train nous emportait à toute allure. **3** *n* tourbillon *m*. (*fig*) **the social ~** la vie mondaine; **her**

thoughts/emotions were in a ~ tout tourbillonnait dans sa tête/son cœur; **my head is in a ~** la tête me tourne; (*fig: try*) **to give sth a ~*** essayer qch. ♦ **whirlpool** tourbillon *m*. ♦ **whirlwind 1** *n* tornade *f*, trombe *f*; **2** *adj* éclair* *inv*.

whirr [wɜːʳ] **1** *vi [bird's wings, insect's wings]* bruire; *[cameras, machinery]* ronronner, (*louder*) vrombir. **to go ~ing off** partir en vrombissant. **2** *n* bruissement *m*; ronronnement *m*; vrombissement *m*.

whisk [wɪsk] **1** *n* (*Culin*) fouet *m*; (*rotary*) batteur *m* à œufs. **with a ~ of his tail** d'un coup de queue; (*Culin*) **to give sth a good ~** bien battre qch. **2** *vt* **(a)** (*Culin*) battre au fouet; *egg whites* battre en neige. **~ the eggs into it** incorporez-y les œufs avec un fouet. **(b) to ~ sth out of sb's hands** enlever brusquement qch des mains de qn; **she ~ed the letter off the table** elle a prestement fait disparaître la lettre de la table; **to ~ sth away/off** *etc* emporter/enlever *etc* qch brusquement; **the lift ~ed us up to the top floor** l'ascenseur nous a emportés jusqu'au dernier étage à toute allure.

whiskers ['wɪskəz] *npl* (*side ~*) favoris *mpl*; (*beard*) barbe *f*; (*moustache*) moustache *f*; *[animal]* moustaches.

whisky, (*US, Ir*) **whiskey** ['wɪskɪ] *n* whisky *m*. **a ~ and soda** un whisky soda.

whisper ['wɪspəʳ] **1** *vi* (*gen*) chuchoter (*to sb* à l'oreille de qn). **you'll have to ~** il faudra que vous parliez bas. **2** *vt* chuchoter, dire à voix basse (*sth to sb* qch à qn; *that* que). **he ~ed a word in my ear** il m'a dit qch à l'oreille; (*fig*) **it is ~ed that ...** le bruit court que .... **3** *n* (*gen*) chuchotement *m*; *[wind etc]* murmure *m*; (*fig: rumour*) bruit *m*. **in a ~** à voix basse. ♦ **whispering 1** *n* chuchotement *m*; (*fig*) **there has been a lot of ~ing about them** toutes sortes de rumeurs ont couru sur leur compte; **2** *adj* (*fig*) **~ing campaign** campagne *f* (diffamatoire) insidieuse; **~ing gallery** galerie *f* à écho.

whist [wɪst] *n* whist *m*. **~ drive** tournoi *m* de whist.

whistle ['wɪsl] **1** *n* **(a)** (*sound: gen*) sifflement *m*; (*made with a ~*) coup *m* de sifflet; *[audience]* (*cheering*) sifflements d'admiration; (*booing*) sifflets *mpl*. **(b)** (*thing blown*) sifflet *m*. **penny ~** flûteau *m*; **he blew his ~** il a donné un coup de sifflet; **the referee blew his ~ for half-time** l'arbitre a sifflé la mi-temps; **it broke off as clean as a ~** ça a cassé net; (*fig*) **he blew the ~ on it*** (*informed on it*) il a vendu la mèche*; (*stopped it*) il y a mis le holà.

2 *vi* (*gen*) siffler; (*casually, light-heartedly*) siffloter. **to ~ at** *or* **for** *or* **to sb/sth** siffler qn/qch; (*fig*) **he's whistling in the dark** il fait (*or* dit) ça pour se rassurer; (*fig*) **he can ~ for it!*** il peut toujours courir!*; **an arrow ~d past his ear** une flèche a sifflé à son oreille; **the cars ~d past** les voitures passaient à toute allure.

3 *vt tune* siffler; (*casually*) siffloter.

whistle up *vt sep dog, taxi* siffler; (**fig*) *helpers, more food etc* dégoter*, trouver.

♦ **whistle-stop** *adj* (*Pol etc*) **he made a ~-stop tour of ...** il a fait à toute allure le tour de ... .

Whit [wɪt] **1** *n* (*also* **~sun**) la Pentecôte. **2** *adj week, holiday etc* de Pentecôte. **~ Sunday/Monday** le dimanche/lundi de Pentecôte.

whit [wɪt] *n*: **not a ~ of truth** pas un brin de vérité; **it wasn't a ~ better** ce n'était pas mieux du tout.

white [waɪt] **1** *adj* **(a)** (*gen*) blanc (*f* blanche). **as ~ as a sheet/a ghost** pâle comme un linge/la mort; **as ~ as snow** blanc comme neige; **~ with fear** blême de peur; **to go** *or* **turn ~** (*with fear, anger*) blêmir; *[hair]* blanchir; **it gets the clothes ~r than ~** ça lave encore plus blanc; **a ~ Christmas** un Noël sous la neige; (*fig*) **it's a ~ elephant** c'est tout à fait superflu; **the ~ flag** le drapeau blanc; **~ frost** gelée *f* blanche; (*fig*) **the ~ hope of** le grand espoir de; (*at sea*) **~ horses,** (*US*) **~ caps** moutons *mpl*; (*US*) **the W~ House** la Maison Blanche; (*fig*) **a ~ lie** un pieux mensonge; (*Acoustics*) **~ noise** son *m* blanc; (*Parl*) **~ paper** livre *m* blanc (*du gouvernement*) (*on* sur); (*Comm*) **~ sale** vente *f* de blanc; (*Culin*) **~ sauce** béchamel *f*; **~ wedding** mariage *m* en blanc. **(b)** (*racially*) *person, skin* blanc; *supremacy* de la race blanche. **a ~ man** un Blanc; **a ~ woman** une Blanche; **the ~ South Africans** les Blancs d'Afrique du Sud.

2 *n* **(a)** (*colour*) blanc *m*; (*whiteness*) blancheur *f*; *[egg, eye]* blanc. **dressed in ~** vêtu de blanc; (*linen etc*) **the ~s** le linge blanc; **his face was a deathly ~** son visage était d'une pâleur mortelle; **to be a dazzling ~** être d'une blancheur éclatante. **(b)** (*person*) Blanc *m*, Blanche *f*.

♦ **whitebait** *n* (*Culin*) petite friture *f*. ♦ **white-collar** *adj*: **a ~-collar job** un emploi dans un bureau; **~-collar worker** employé(e) *m(f)* de bureau, col *m* blanc. ♦ **white-faced** *adj* blême. ♦ **white-haired** *adj person* aux cheveux blancs. ♦ **white-hot** *adj* chauffé à blanc. ♦ **whiten** *vt* blanchir. ♦ **whiteness** *n* blancheur *f*. ♦ **whitening** *n* (*substance*) blanc *m*. ♦ **white spirit** *n* white-spirit *m*. ♦ **whitethorn** *n* aubépine *f*. ♦ **whitewash 1** *n* lait *m* de chaux; (*fig*) **it was a ~wash of his character** ça visait à blanchir sa réputation; **2** *vt wall etc* blanchir à la chaux; (*fig*) *person, sb's reputation, motives* blanchir; *sb's faults* justifier (par des arguments fallacieux); *event, episode* peindre sous des traits anodins. ♦ **whitish** *adj* blanchâtre.

whiting ['waɪtɪŋ] *n* (*fish*) merlan *m*.

whitlow ['wɪtləʊ] *n* panaris *m*.

whittle ['wɪtl] *vt* tailler au couteau (*out of* dans). **to ~ down** *wood* tailler; (*fig*) *costs* amenuiser.

whiz(z) [wɪz] **1** *n* (*sound*) sifflement *m*. **2** *adj*: **~ kid*** petit prodige *m*. **3** *vi*: **to ~** *or* **go ~ing through the air** fendre l'air (en sifflant); **to ~ past** *etc* passer *etc* à toute vitesse.

who [huː] *pron* **(a)** (*in questions: remplace aussi 'whom' dans le langage parlé*) (qui est-ce) qui; (*after prep*) qui. **~'s there?** qui est là?; **~ are you?** qui êtes-vous?; **~ has the book?** (qui est-ce) qui a le livre?; **~ should it be but Robert!** qui vois-je? Robert!; **I don't know ~'s ~ in the office** je ne connais pas très bien les gens au bureau; **'W~'s W~'** ≃ 'Bottin *m* Mondain'; **~(m) did you see?** qui avez-vous vu?; **~'s the book by?** le livre est de qui?; **you-know-~* said ...** qui vous savez a dit ... . **(b)** (*that*) qui. **my aunt ~ lives in London** ma tante qui habite à Londres; **those ~ can swim** ceux qui savent nager. ♦ **whodunit*** *n* roman *m* policier. ♦ **whoever** *pron* **(a)** (*anyone that*) quiconque; **~ever wishes may ...** quiconque le désire peut ...; **~ever finds it can keep it** celui qui le trouvera pourra le garder; **~ever said that was ...** celui qui a dit ça était ...; **ask ~ever you like** demandez à qui vous voulez; **(b)** (*no matter who: subject*) qui que ce soit qui +*subj*; (*object*) qui que ce soit que +*subj*; **~ever you are** qui que vous soyez; **~ever he marries** qui que ce soit qu'il épouse (*subj*); **(c) ~ever told you that?** qui donc vous a dit ça?

whoa [wəʊ] *excl* (**~ there**) ho!, holà!

whole [həʊl] **1** *adj* **(a)** (*entire*) (+ *sing n*) entier, tout; (+ *pl n*) entier. **the ~ book** le livre entier, tout le livre; **a ~ hour** toute une heure, une heure entière; **3 ~ days** 3 jours entiers; **the ~ world** le monde entier; **~ villages** des villages entiers; **the ~ road** toute la route; **~ milk** lait *m* entier; **to swallow sth ~** avaler qch tout entier; **roasted ~** rôti tout entier; **the ~ truth** toute la vérité; **the ~ point of it** tout l'intérêt de la chose; **with my ~ heart** de tout mon cœur; **the ~ lot** le tout; **the ~ lot of you** vous tous; **a ~ lot better*** vraiment beaucoup mieux; **a ~ lot of things** tout un tas de choses; **to go the ~ hog*** aller jusqu'au bout, s'engager à fond. **(b)** (*unbroken*) *glass, seal, egg* intact; *series, set* complet; (*unhurt*) sain et sauf. (*Math*) ~ **number** nombre *m* entier.

2 *n* **(a)** (*all*) **the ~ of the book** tout le livre, le livre entier; **the ~ of the sum** la somme tout entière, la totalité de la somme; **the ~ of the time** tout le temps; **the ~ of France** la France tout entière; **the ~ of Paris was talking about it** dans tout Paris on parlait de ça; **as a ~** dans son ensemble; **on the ~** dans l'ensemble. **(b)** (*complete unit*) tout *m*. **they make a ~** ils font un tout; **estate sold as a ~** propriété vendue en bloc.

♦ **wholehearted** *adj approval, admiration* sans réserve; **to make a ~hearted attempt** essayer de tout cœur. ♦ **wholeheartedly** *adv* de tout cœur. ♦ **wholemeal** *adj flour* brut; *bread* ≃ complet. ♦ **wholesale 1** *n* (vente *f* en) gros *m*; **2** *adj price, firm, trade etc* de gros; (*fig*) *slaughter, destruction, dismissals* en masse; *criticism, acceptance* en bloc; *campaign, movement* généralisé; **there was a ~sale attempt to do it** on a essayé par tous les moyens de le faire; **3** *adv buy, sell* en gros; *get, obtain* au prix de gros; (*fig*) *dismiss, imprison, destroy* en masse; *reject, accept* en bloc. ♦ **wholesaler** *n* grossiste *mf*. ♦ **wholesome** *adj* (*gen*) sain; *air, climate* sain, salubre. ♦ **wholly** *adv* complètement, entièrement.

whom [hu:m] *pron* **(a)** (*souvent remplacé par 'who' dans le langage parlé*) (*in questions*) qui. **~ did you see?** qui avez-vous vu?; **with ~?** avec qui? **(b)** (*that*) que; (*after prep*) qui. **my aunt, ~ I love** ma tante, que j'aime; **those ~ he had seen** ceux qu'il avait vus; **the man to ~** l'homme à qui, l'homme auquel; **the man of ~** l'homme dont.

whoop [hu:p] **1** *n* cri *m* (*de triomphe etc*). **2** *vi* pousser des cris; (*Med*) avoir des quintes de toux coquelucheuse. **3** *vt*: **to ~ it up‡** bien se marrer‡. ♦ **whoopee 1** *excl* youpi!; **2** *n*: **to make ~ee‡** bien se marrer‡. ♦ **whooping cough** *n* coqueluche *f*. ♦ **whoops** *excl* houp-là!

whopper* ['wɒpəʳ] *n* (*car/parcel etc*) voiture *f*/colis *m etc* énorme; (*lie*) mensonge *m* énorme. ♦ **whopping*** *adj* énorme.

whore‡ [hɔ:ʳ] *n* putain‡ *f*.

whose [hu:z] **1** *poss pron* à qui. **~ is this?** à qui est ceci?; **I know ~ it is** je sais à qui c'est; **let's see ~ lasts longest** voyons celui de qui durera le plus longtemps. **2** *poss adj* **(a)** (*in questions: gen*) de qui; (*ownership*) à qui. **~ hat is this?** à qui est ce chapeau?; **~ son are you?** de qui êtes-vous le fils?; **~ fault is it?** à qui la faute? **(b)** dont, de qui. **the man ~ hat I took** l'homme dont j'ai pris le chapeau; **the boy ~ sister I was talking to** le garçon à la sœur duquel *or* à la sœur de qui je parlais; **those ~ passports are here** ceux dont les passeports sont ici.

why [waɪ] **1** *adv, conj* pourquoi. **~ did you do it?** pourquoi l'avez-vous fait?; **I wonder ~** je me demande pourquoi; **he told me ~ he did it** il m'a dit pourquoi il l'a fait *or* la raison pour laquelle il l'a fait; **that's (the reason) ~** voilà pourquoi; **~ not?** pourquoi pas?; **the reasons ~ he did it** les raisons pour lesquelles il l'a fait; **there's no reason ~ you shouldn't try again** il n'y a pas de raison pour que tu n'essayes (*subj*) pas de nouveau; **~ not phone her?** pourquoi ne pas lui téléphoner? **2** *excl* (*surprise*) tiens!; (*remonstrating*) mais voyons donc!; (*explaining*) eh bien! **3** *n*: **the ~(s) and the wherefore(s)** les causes *fpl* et les raisons *fpl*; **the ~ and the how** le pourquoi et le comment.

wick [wɪk] *n* mèche *f*.

wicked ['wɪkɪd] *adj* (*iniquitous*) *person* méchant; *act* mauvais; *system, policy* inique; (*unpleasant*) *blow, wound* vilain (*before n*); *pain* violent; *satire, criticism* méchant; *waste* scandaleux; (*mischievous etc*) *person, smile, remark* malicieux. **that was a ~ thing to do** c'était vraiment méchant!; **he has a ~ temper** il a un caractère épouvantable; (*fig: admiringly*) **a ~* shot/game** *etc* un coup/un jeu *etc* du tonnerre*. ♦ **wickedly** *adv* (*evilly*) *behave* très mal; *destroy, kill* par un raffinement de méchanceté; (*mischievously*) malicieusement; (*: *skilfully*) *play, manage etc* formidablement bien*. ♦ **wickedness** *n* méchanceté *f*; scandale *m*; malice *f*; *[murder]* atrocité *f*.

wicker ['wɪkəʳ] **1** *n* osier *m*. **2** *adj basket etc* d'osier. ♦ **wickerwork** *n* vannerie *f*.

wicket ['wɪkɪt] *n* **(a)** (*door*) portillon *m*. **(b)** (*Cricket*) guichet *m*. ♦ **wicket-keeper** *n* gardien *m* de guichet.

wide [waɪd] **1** *adj* (*gen*) large; *margin, variety* grand; *ocean, desert* immense; (*fig*) *knowledge* vaste, grand; *survey, study* de grande envergure. **how ~ is the room?** quelle est la largeur de la pièce?; **it is 5 metres ~** cela fait 5 mètres de large; (*Cine*) **~ screen** écran *m* panoramique; (*fig*) **~ boy*** filou *m*; **the shot was ~** le coup est passé à côté; **~ of the target** loin de la cible. **2** *adv aim, shoot, fall* loin du but. **the bullet went ~** la balle est passée à côté; **(set) ~ apart** *trees, houses* largement espacés; *eyes, legs* très écartés; **~ awake** bien éveillé; **~ open** grand ouvert. ♦ **wide-eyed** *adj* aux yeux écarquillés (*from fear etc* de peur *etc*). ♦ **widely** *adv scatter, spread* sur une grande étendue; *travel* beaucoup; *differ, different* radicalement; *spaced* largement; *believed, understood etc* généralement; **~ly-held opinions** des opinions *fpl* très répandues; **~ly known for** connu partout pour; **to be ~ly read** *[author, book]* être très lu; *[reader]* avoir beaucoup lu (*in sth* qch). ♦ **widen 1** *vt* (*gen*) élargir; *margin* augmenter; *knowledge* accroître; *survey, study* accroître la portée de; **2** *vi* (**~n out**) s'élargir; s'accroître. ♦ **wide-ranging** *adj report* de grande envergure; *interests* divers, variés. ♦ **widespread** *adj arms* en croix; *wings* déployés; *belief* très répandu.

widow ['wɪdəʊ] **1** *n* veuve *f*. (*fig*) **she's a golf ~** son mari la délaisse pour aller jouer au golf; **~'s peak** pousse *f* de cheveux en V sur le front. **2** *vt*: **to be ~ed** devenir veuf (*f* veuve); **his ~ed mother** sa mère qui est veuve. ♦ **widower** *n* veuf *m*. ♦ **widowhood** *n* veuvage *m*.

width [wɪdθ] *n* (*gen*) largeur *f*; *[garment]* ampleur *f*. **it is 5 metres in ~** cela fait 5 mètres de large; **a ~ of cloth** une largeur d'étoffe. ♦ **widthwise** *adv* en largeur.

wield [wi:ld] *vt tool, weapon etc* manier; (*brandish*) brandir; *power etc* exercer.

wife [waɪf] *n, pl* **wives** (*gen*) femme *f*; (*Admin etc*) épouse *f*. **the farmer's/butcher's** *etc* **~** la fermière/bouchère *etc*; **the ~‡** la patronne‡; (*Admin etc*) **wives who have ...** les femmes mariées qui ont ...; **old wives' tale** conte *m* de bonne femme; (*woman*) **a poor old ~*** une pauvre vieille. ♦ **wifely** *adj duties* conjugal; *feelings* d'une bonne épouse. ♦ **wife-swapping** *n* échange *m* de partenaires (*par deux couples*).

wig [wɪg] *n* perruque *f*; (*hair-piece*) postiche *m*.

wiggle ['wɪgl] **1** *vt pencil, stick, toes* agiter, remuer; *loose screw, tooth* faire jouer. **to ~ one's hips** tortiller des hanches. **2** *vi [sth loose]* branler; *[tail]* remuer. ♦ **wiggly** *adj line* ondulé.

wigwam ['wɪgwæm] *n* wigwam *m*.

wild [waɪld] **1** *adj* **(a)** *animal, plant, tribe, countryside* sauvage; *rabbit* de garenne. **it was growing ~** ça poussait à l'état sauvage; (*fig*) **~ horses wouldn't make me tell** je ne le dirais pour rien au monde; (*fig*) **to sow one's ~ oats** jeter sa gourme; (*US*) **the W~ West** le Far West. **(b)** *wind* furieux; *sea* en furie; *weather* gros; *night* de tempête. **(c)** (*excited etc*) *person, youth, scheme, laughter* fou (*f* folle); *eyes* égaré; *appearance, look* farouche; *imagination, enthusiasm* débordant; *life, evening* mouvementé; (*: *angry*) furieux. **a gang of ~ kids** une bande de casse-cou; **we had some ~ times** nous avons fait bien des folies; **there was a lot of ~ talk about ...** on a agité des tas d'idées folles au sujet de ...; **to make a ~ guess** risquer à tout hasard une hypothèse (*at sth* sur qch); (*excited*) **to go ~** *[dog etc]* devenir comme fou; *[person]* ne plus se tenir (*with joy* de joie); *[audience]* entrer en délire; **~ with indignation** fou d'indignation; (*enthusiastic*) **to be ~ about sb/sth** être dingue* *or* fou de qn/qch; **I'm not ~ about it*** ça ne m'emballe* pas beaucoup; **it's enough to drive you ~!*** c'est à vous rendre dingue*! *or* fou!

2 *n*: **the call of the ~** l'appel *m* de la nature; **into the ~s** dans les régions *fpl* sauvages; **in the ~s of Alaska** au fin fond de l'Alaska.

♦ **wildcat 1** *n* chat *m* sauvage; **2** *adj* (*fig*) *scheme* insensé; *strike* sauvage. ♦ **wilderness** ['wɪldənɪs] *n* (*gen*) région *f* sauvage; (*Bible; also fig: of streets, snow etc*) désert *m*; (*overgrown garden*) jungle *f*. ♦ **wild-eyed** *adj* aux yeux égarés. ♦ **wildfire** *n*: **to spread like ~fire** se répandre comme une traînée de poudre. ♦ **wildfowl** *npl* (*collective*) oiseaux *mpl* sauvages; (*Hunting*) gibier *m* à plume. ♦ **wildlife 1** *n* la nature; (*more formally*) la flore et la faune; **2** *adj*: **~life sanctuary** réserve *f* naturelle. ♦ **wildly** *adv blow, rage* furieusement; *behave* de façon extravagante; *gesticulate, talk* comme un fou; *applaud* frénétiquement; *protest* violemment; *shoot, hit out, guess* au hasard; *rush around* dans tous les sens; (*: *very*) *happy, enthusiastic* follement; **her heart was beating ~ly** son cœur battait à se rompre; **he looked at them ~ly** il leur a jeté un regard fou. ♦ **wildness** *n [countryside, scenery]* aspect *m* sauvage; *[tribe]* sauvagerie *f*; *[wind, sea]* fureur *f*; *[appearance]* désordre *m*; *[imagination]* extravagance *f*; *[enthusiasm]* ferveur *f*; **the ~ness of the weather** le sale temps qu'il fait (*or* faisait *etc*).

wildebeest ['wɪldɪbi:st] *n* gnou *m*.

wiles [waɪlz] *npl* (*tricks*) ruses *fpl*; (*charms*) artifices *mpl*.

wilful, (*US*) **willful** ['wɪlfʊl] *adj person, character* têtu, obstiné; *action* délibéré; *murder* prémédité; *damage* commis avec préméditation. ♦ **wil(l)fully** *adv* (*obstinately*) obstinément; (*deliberately*) délibérément.

will [wɪl] **1** *modal aux vb* **(a)** (*making future tense*) **he ~** *or* **he'll speak** il parlera; (*near future*) il va parler; **you won't lose it** tu ne le perdras pas; **you ~ come to see us, won't you?** vous viendrez nous voir, n'est-ce pas?; **~ he come? — yes he ~** est-ce qu'il viendra? — oui; **no you won't!** non, certainement pas!; **they'll arrive tomorrow — ~ they?** ils arriveront demain — ah bon?; (*in requests*) **~ you please sit down!** voulez-vous vous asseoir, s'il vous plaît!; (*in commands*) **you ~ speak to no one** vous ne parlerez à personne; **~ you be quiet!** veux-tu bien te taire!

(b) (*conjecture*) **that ~ be the postman** ça doit être le facteur; **that ~ have been last year** c'était l'année dernière, sans doute.

(c) (*willingness*) **I ~ help you** je vous aiderai, je veux bien vous aider; **~ you help me? — yes I ~/no I won't** tu veux m'aider? — oui je veux bien/non je ne veux pas; **if you'll help me** si vous voulez bien m'aider; **won't you come with us?** tu ne veux pas venir avec nous?; **~ you have a cup of coffee?** voulez-vous un petit café?; **won't you have a drink?** vous prendrez bien un verre?; **just a moment, ~ you?** un instant, s'il vous plaît; (*in marriage service*) **I ~** oui; **I WILL see him!** on ne m'empêchera pas de le voir!; **I won't have it!** je n'admets pas ça!; **it won't open** ça ne s'ouvre pas; **do what you ~** faites ce que vous voulez.

(d) (*habit, characteristic: usually present tense in French*) **he ~ sit for hours doing nothing** il reste assis pendant des heures à ne rien faire; **the car ~ do 150 km/h** cette voiture fait 150 km/h; **he WILL talk all the time!** il ne peut pas s'empêcher de parler!; **if you WILL tell her everything** si tu insistes pour lui raconter tout; (*ruefully*) **I WILL call him Richard** il faut toujours que je l'appelle (*subj*) Richard; **accidents ~ happen** il y aura toujours des accidents.

2 *pret, ptp* **willed** *vt* **(a)** (*wish, intend*) vouloir (*sth* qch; *that* que + *subj*). **it is as God ~s** c'est la volonté de Dieu; **you must ~ it really hard** il faut le vouloir très fort; **to ~ sb to do** prier intérieurement pour que qn fasse; **to ~ o.s. to do sth** faire un suprême effort pour faire qch.

(b) (*Jur: leave in one's ~*) léguer (*sth to sb* qch à qn).

3 *n* **(a)** volonté *f*. **he has a ~ of his own** il est très volontaire; **an iron ~** une volonté de fer; **the ~ to live** la volonté de survivre; **where there's a ~ there's a way** vouloir, c'est pouvoir; **it is his ~ that** sa volonté est que + *subj*; **to take the ~ for the deed** juger la chose sur l'intention; **Thy ~ be done** que Ta volonté soit faite; **at ~** (*as much as you like*) *borrow etc* à volonté; (*whenever you like*) *join, leave etc* quand vous le voulez *etc*; **to do sth against one's ~** faire qch à contre-cœur; **with the best ~ in the world** avec la meilleure volonté du monde; **to work with a ~** travailler avec détermination.

(b) (*Jur*) testament *m*. **the last ~ and testament of ...** les dernières volontés *fpl* de ...; **in his ~** dans son testament.

♦ **willing 1** *adj* **(a) I'm quite ~ing to do it** je veux bien le faire, je suis prêt à le faire; **he wasn't very ~ing to help** il n'était pas tellement prêt à aider; **they are ~ing and able to go** ils veulent et ils peuvent y aller; **God ~ing** si Dieu le veut; **(b)** *obedience, help* spontané; *helper, worker* de bonne volonté; **he's very ~ing** il est plein de bonne volonté; **~ing hands** des mains *fpl* empressées; (*fig*) **the ~ing horse** la bonne âme (qui se sacrifie toujours); **2** *n*: **to show ~ing** faire preuve de bonne volonté. ♦ **willingly** *adv* (*with pleasure*) volontiers; (*voluntarily*) volontairement, spontanément; (*agreeing*) **~ingly!** volontiers!; **did he do it ~ingly?** l'a-t-il fait de lui-même *or* volontairement? ♦ **willingness** *n*: **I don't doubt his ~ingness** ce n'est pas sa bonne volonté que je mets en doute; **his ~ingness to help me** son empressement *m* à m'aider. ♦ **willpower** *n* volonté *f*, vouloir *m*.

will-o'-the-wisp ['wɪləðə'wɪsp] *n* (*lit, fig*) feu *m* follet.

willow ['wɪləʊ] *n* saule *m*. ♦ **willowherb** *n* épilobe *m*. ♦ **willow-pattern 1** *n* motif *m* chinois (bleu); **2** *adj china* à motif chinois (bleu). ♦ **willowy** *adj person* élancé; *object* mince.

willy-nilly ['wɪlɪ'nɪlɪ] *adv* bon gré mal gré.

wilt [wɪlt] *vi [flower]* se faner; *[plant]* se dessécher; *[person]* commencer à flancher*; *[effort, enthusiasm etc]* diminuer.

wily ['waɪlɪ] *adj* rusé, malin. **a ~ old devil*** *or* **bird*** un vieux renard.

wimple ['wɪmpl] *n* guimpe *f*.

win [wɪn] (*vb: pret, ptp* **won**) **1** *n* (*Sport etc*) victoire *f* (*for* pour). **to have a ~** gagner; **to back a horse for a ~** jouer un cheval gagnant.

2 *vi* **(a)** gagner, l'emporter (*by a length etc* d'une longueur *etc*). **(b) to ~ free** se dégager (*from sth* de qch).

3 *vt* **(a)** (*gen*) gagner; *prize, victory* remporter; *scholarship* obtenir; *fame, fortune* trouver; *sb's attention* captiver; *sb's friendship, esteem, sympathy, admirers* s'attirer; *friends, reputation* se faire (*as* en tant que). **he won it for growing radishes** il l'a eu pour sa culture de radis; **he won £5 from her** il lui a gagné 5 livres; **to ~ the day** (*Mil*) remporter la victoire; (*gen*) l'emporter;

this won him attention/the prize *etc* ceci lui a valu l'attention/le prix *etc*; **to ~ sb's love/respect** se faire aimer/respecter de qn. **(b)** (*reach*) *shore, goal* parvenir à.
win back *vt sep land, trophy* reprendre (*from* à); *gaming loss etc* recouvrer; *sb's support, girlfriend etc* reconquérir.
win out, win through *vi* y parvenir.
win over, win round *vt sep* convaincre. **I won him over to my point of view** je l'ai gagné à ma façon de voir.
♦ **winner** *n* (*in fight, argument*) vainqueur *m*; (*in game, competition*) gagnant(e) *m(f)*; **to be the ~ner** gagner; (*fig*) **it's a ~ner** c'est sensationnel*; **to pick a ~ner** (*Racing*) choisir un gagneur; (*gen*) tirer le bon numéro. ♦ **winning 1** *adj* **(a)** *person, car etc* gagnant; *goal, shot etc* décisif; **(b)** (*captivating*) *person* charmant; *smile, manner* charmeur; **2** *npl* (*Betting etc*) **~nings** gains *mpl*. ♦ **winning-post** *n* poteau *m* d'arrivée.
wince [wɪns] *vi* tressaillir; (*grimace*) grimacer (de douleur *or* dégoût *etc*). **he ~d at the thought** cette pensée l'a fait tressaillir; **without wincing** sans broncher.
winch [wɪntʃ] **1** *n* treuil *m*. **2** *vt*: **to ~ sth up/down** *etc* monter/descendre *etc* qch au treuil.
wind[1] [wɪnd] **1** *n* **(a)** vent *m*. **high ~** grand vent, vent violent; **the ~ was in the east** le vent venait de l'est; **to go/run like the ~** aller/filer comme le vent; (*Naut*) **to run before the ~** avoir vent arrière; (*fig*) **to sail close to the ~** (*gen*) y aller un peu fort; (*almost illegal*) friser l'illégalité; (*blue joke etc*) friser la vulgarité; (*fig*) **to take the ~ out of sb's sails** couper l'herbe sous le pied de qn; (*fig*) **to see how the ~ blows** voir la tournure que prennent les choses; (*fig*) **the ~ of change is blowing** un grand courant d'air frais souffle; (*fig*) **there's sth in the ~** il y a qch dans l'air; (*fig*) **to get ~ of sth** avoir vent de qch; **he threw caution to the ~s** il a fait fi de toute prudence. **(b)** (*breath*) souffle *m*. **he has still plenty of ~** il a encore du souffle; **he had lost his ~** il avait perdu le souffle; **to get one's ~ back** *or* **one's second ~** reprendre son souffle; (*fig pej*) **it's all ~** ce n'est que du vent; (*fig*) **to put the ~ up sb*** flanquer la frousse* à qn; **to get/have the ~ up*** attraper/avoir la frousse* (*about* à propos de). **(c)** (*Med*) vents *mpl*. **to break ~** lâcher un vent, avoir des gaz; **to bring up ~** avoir un renvoi. **(d)** (*Mus*) **the ~(s)** les instruments *mpl* à vent.
2 *adj erosion etc* éolien; *instrument* à vent.
3 *vt*: **to ~ sb** *[blow, boxer]* couper le souffle à qn; *[fall, exertion]* essouffler qn; **I'm only ~ed** j'ai la respiration coupée, c'est tout.
♦ **windbag*** *n* hâbleur *m*, -euse *f*. ♦ **windbreak** *n* (*tree, fence etc*) abat-vent *m inv*; (*for camping etc*) pare-vent *m inv*. ♦ **windcheater** *n* anorak *m* léger. ♦ **windfall** *n* (*fruit*) fruit *m* abattu par le vent; (*fig*) aubaine *f*. ♦ **wind-gauge** *n* anémomètre *m*. ♦ **windmill** *n* moulin *m* à vent. ♦ **windpipe** *n* (*Anat*) trachée *f*. ♦ **windproof** *adj* qui ne laisse pas passer le vent. ♦ **windscreen** *or* (*US*) ♦ **windshield 1** *n* pare-brise *m inv*; **2** *adj*: **~screen washer** lave-glace *m inv*; **~screen wiper** essuie-glace *m inv*. ♦ **windsleeve** *or* ♦ **windsock** *n* manche *f* à air. ♦ **windswept** *adj* battu des vents. ♦ **windward 1** *adj, adv* du côté du vent; **2** *n*: **to ~ward of sth** contre le vent par rapport à qch. ♦ **windy** *adj* **(a)** *place* battu par les vents, exposé au vent; *day, weather* de grand vent; **it's ~y** il y a du vent; **(b)** (*scared*) **to be** *or* **get ~y* about sth** paniquer* à cause de qch.
wind[2] [waɪnd] (*vb: pret, ptp* **wound**) **1** *n*: **to give sth a ~ = to ~ sth** (V 2).
2 *vt* **(a)** (*roll*) enrouler (*on* sur; *round* autour de). **to ~ wool (into a ball)** enrouler de la laine (en pelote); **he wound his way home** il a pris lentement le chemin du retour. **(b)** *clock, watch, toy* remonter; *handle* donner des tours de. (*with winch etc*) **to ~ sth up/down** monter/descendre qch (avec un treuil *etc*).
3 *vi* (*also* **~ its way**) *[river, path, procession]* serpenter (*through* à travers). **to ~ up/down** *[path etc]* monter/descendre en serpentant; *[stairs]* monter/descendre en tournant.
wind down* *vi* (*relax*) se détendre.
wind up 1 *vi [meeting, discussion]* se terminer (*with* par). **they wound up* in Cannes/in jail** ils se sont retrouvés à Cannes/en prison; **he wound up* as a doctor** il a fini par devenir médecin. **2** *vt sep* **(a)** (*end*) *meeting, speech* clore, terminer (*with* par); (*Comm*) *business* liquider; *account* clore. **(b)** *watch etc* remonter. (*fig: tense*) **to be all wound up*** être crispé (*about* à propos de).
♦ **winding** *adj road, river* sinueux, qui serpente; *staircase* tournant.
windlass ['wɪndləs] *n* treuil *m*.
window ['wɪndəʊ] *n* (*gen*) fenêtre *f*; (*in car, train*) vitre *f*; (*~ pane*) vitre, carreau *m*; (*stained-glass ~*) vitrail *m*, (*larger*) verrière *f*; *[shop, café etc]* vitrine *f*; (*in post office, ticket office etc*) guichet *m*; (*in envelope*) fenêtre. **at the ~** à la fenêtre (*or* vitre); **don't lean out of the ~** ne te penche pas par la fenêtre, (*in train, car etc*) ne te penche pas en dehors; **to look** *etc* **out of the ~** regarder *etc* par la fenêtre, (*in train etc*) regarder *etc* dehors; **to break a ~** casser une vitre; **to clean the ~s** nettoyer les carreaux; *[shop]* **in the ~** en vitrine. ♦ **window-box** *n* jardinière *f* (*à plantes*). ♦ **window-cleaner** *n* (*person*) laveur *m*, -euse *f* de carreaux. ♦ **window-dresser** *n* (*Comm*) étalagiste *mf*. ♦ **window-dressing** *n* (*Comm*) composition *f* d'étalage; (*fig pej*) **it's only ~-dressing** ce n'est qu'une façade. ♦ **window-ledge** *n* rebord *m* de fenêtre. ♦ **window-pane** *n* vitre *f*. ♦ **window-seat** *n* (*in room*) banquette *f* (située sous la fenêtre); (*in vehicle: gen*) place *f* côté fenêtre *inv*; (*in train*) coin *m* fenêtre. ♦ **window-shopping 1** *n* lèche-vitrines *m*; **2** *vi*: **to go ~-shopping** faire du lèche-vitrines. ♦ **windowsill** *n* (*inside*) appui *m* de fenêtre; (*outside*) rebord *m* de fenêtre.
wine [waɪn] **1** *n* vin *m*. **2** *vt*: **to ~ and dine sb** emmener qn faire un très bon dîner. **3** *adj bottle, cellar* à vin; (*colour*) lie-de-vin *inv*. **~ list** carte *f* des vins; **~ merchant** marchand(e) *m(f)* de vin, (*larger scale*) négociant(e) *m(f)* en vins; **~ vinegar** vinaigre *m* de vin; **~ waiter** sommelier *m*. ♦ **wineglass** *n* verre *m* à vin. ♦ **wine-grower** *n* viticulteur *m*, -trice *f*, vigneron(ne) *m(f)*. ♦ **winegrowing 1** *n* viticulture *f*; **2** *adj district, industry* viticole. ♦ **wine-tasting** *n* dégustation *f* (de vins).
wing [wɪŋ] **1** *n* (*gen*) aile *f*; *[armchair]* oreillette *f*; (*Sport: player*) ailier *m*. (*fig*) **to take sb under one's ~** prendre qn sous son aile; (*Theat*) **the ~s** les coulisses *fpl*; (*Theat; fig*) **in the ~s** dans les coulisses; (*Pol*) **on the left ~ of the party** sur l'aile gauche du parti. **2** *adj* (*Aut*) **~ mirror** rétroviseur *m* de côté; **~ tip** bout *m* de l'aile. ♦ **winged** *adj* ailé. ♦ **winger** *n* (*Sport*) ailier *m*. ♦ **wingspan** *n* envergure *f*.
wink [wɪŋk] **1** *n* clin *m* d'œil; (*blink*) clignement *m*. **with a ~** en clignant de l'œil; **in a ~, as quick as a ~** en un clin d'œil. **2** *vi* faire un clin d'œil (*to, at* à); (*blink*) cligner des yeux; *[star]* clignoter; ♦ **winking 1** *adj light* clignotant. **2** *n*: **as easy as ~ing** simple comme bonjour.
winkle ['wɪŋkl] **1** *n* bigorneau *m*. **2** *vt* (*) extirper (*sth/sb out of* qch/qn de).
winter ['wɪntəʳ] **1** *n* hiver *m*. **in ~** en hiver; **in the ~ of 1977** pendant l'hiver de 1977. **2** *adj weather, day, activities, clothes* d'hiver. **~ sports** sports *mpl* d'hiver. ♦ **wintertime** *n* hiver *m*. ♦ **wintry** *adj* d'hiver; (*fig*) *smile* glacial.
wipe [waɪp] **1** *n*: **to give sth a ~** donner un coup de

torchon (*or* d'éponge *etc*) à qch. **2** *vt* (*gen*) essuyer (*with* avec); *blackboard* effacer. **to ~ one's feet** s'essuyer les pieds (*on* sur; *with* avec); **to ~ one's nose** se moucher; **to ~ one's bottom** s'essuyer; **to ~ sth dry** essuyer soigneusement qch; (*fig*) **to ~ the floor with sb*** réduire qn en miettes*.
wipe away *vt sep tears* essuyer; *marks* effacer.
wipe off *vt sep* effacer.
wipe out *vt sep* **(a)** *container* bien essuyer; *writing, insult, memory* effacer; *debt* régler. **(b)** (*annihilate*) *town, people, opposing team* anéantir.
wipe up 1 *vi* (*dry dishes*) essuyer la vaisselle. **2** *vt sep* essuyer.
♦ **wiper** *n* (*Aut*) essuie-glace *m inv.*
wire ['waɪəʳ] **1** *n* **(a)** fil *m* de fer; (*Elec*) fil (électrique); (~ *fence*) grillage *m*. **telephone ~s** fils téléphoniques; (*fig*) **we've got our ~s crossed*** nous ne sommes pas sur la même longueur d'ondes. **(b)** (*telegram*) télégramme *m*. **2** *adj object* en fil de fer; *brush* métallique. **~ cutters** cisaille *f*. **3** *vt* **(a)** (*Elec*) *house* faire l'installation électrique de; *circuit* installer. **to ~ sth to sth** (*tie*) rattacher qch à qch (avec du fil de fer); (*Elec*) brancher qch sur qch; **to ~ a room for sound** sonoriser une pièce. **(b)** (*telegraph*) télégraphier (*to* à). **4** *vi* télégraphier. ♦ **wireless 1** *n* T.S.F. *f*; **by ~less** par sans-fil; **on the ~less** à la T.S.F.; **2** *adj station, programme* radiophonique; **~less message** radio *m*, sans-fil *m*; **~less operator** radiotélégraphiste *mf*; **~less set** poste *m* de T.S.F. ♦ **wire-netting** *n* treillis *m* métallique. ♦ **wirepulling*** *n* intrigues *fpl*, piston* *m*. ♦ **wiretapping** *n* mise *f* sur écoute d'une ligne téléphonique. ♦ **wiring** *n* (*Elec*) installation *f* électrique. ♦ **wiry** *adj hair* dru; *animal* nerveux, vigoureux; *person* maigre et nerveux.
wisdom ['wɪzdəm] **1** *n [person]* sagesse *f*; *[action, remark]* prudence *f*. **2** *adj*: **~ tooth** dent *f* de sagesse.
wise[1] [waɪz] *adj person* sage; (*learned*) savant; *look, nod* averti; *action, remark, advice* judicieux; (*prudent*) prudent. **a ~ man** un sage; **the Three W~ Men** les trois Rois mages; **to grow ~r** s'assagir; **how ~ of you!** vous avez (eu) bien raison; **the ~st thing to do is to wait** le plus sage est d'attendre; **I'm none the ~r** ça ne m'avance pas beaucoup; **nobody will be any the ~r if ...** personne n'en saura rien si ...; **~ guy*** gros malin* *m*; **to put sb/be ~ to sth*** mettre qn/être au courant de qch; **to get ~ to sb*** piger* le petit jeu de qn. ♦ **wisecrack*** *n* vanne* *f*, remarque désobligeante. ♦ **wisely** *adv* sagement; judicieusement; prudemment.
wise[2] [waɪz] **1** *n*: **in no ~** en aucune façon; **in this ~** ainsi. **2** *adv ending, e.g.* **health~** du point de vue santé.
wish [wɪʃ] **1** *vt* **(a)** (*desire*) souhaiter, désirer (*sth* qch; *to do* faire; *that* que +*subj*). **what do you ~ him to do?** que voudrais-tu *or* souhaites-tu *or* désires-tu qu'il fasse?; **I ~ I'd gone with you** j'aurais bien voulu vous accompagner, je regrette de ne pas vous avoir accompagné; **I ~ I hadn't said that** je regrette d'avoir dit cela; **I ~ you'd stop talking!** tu ne peux donc pas te taire!; **I ~ I could!** si seulement je pouvais!; **I ~ to heaven*** *or* **to goodness* he hadn't done it** si seulement il n'avait pas fait ça!; **he doesn't ~ her any harm** il ne lui veut aucun mal; (*fig*) **it was ~ed on to me*** je n'ai pas pu faire autrement que de l'accepter. **(b)** (*bid*) souhaiter. **I ~ you well** je vous souhaite de réussir; (*iro*) **I ~ you luck of it!** je te souhaite bien du plaisir!; **he ~ed us good luck** il nous a souhaité bonne chance; **to ~ sb good-bye** dire au revoir à qn; **to ~ sb a happy birthday** souhaiter bon anniversaire à qn.
2 *vi* faire un vœu. **to ~ for sth/for sth to happen** souhaiter qch/que qch se produise; **everything he could ~ for** tout ce qu'il pourrait désirer; **what more could you ~ for?** que pourrais-tu souhaiter de plus?
3 *n* **(a)** désir *m* (*to do* de faire). **he had no ~ to go** il n'avait pas envie d'y aller; **against my ~(es)** contre mon gré. **(b)** souhait *m*, vœu *m*. **to make a ~** faire un vœu; **3 ~es** 3 souhaits; **his ~ came true, he got his ~** son souhait s'est réalisé. **(c) give him my good** *or* **best ~es** (*in conversation*) faites-lui mes amitiés; (*in letter*) transmettez-lui mes meilleures pensées; **he sends his best ~es** (*in conversation*) il vous fait ses amitiés; (*in letter*) il vous envoie ses meilleures pensées; **best ~es for a happy birthday** tous mes meilleurs vœux pour votre anniversaire; (*in letter*) **with best ~es from Paul** bien amicalement, Paul.
♦ **wishbone** *n* bréchet *m*. ♦ **wishful** *adj*: **it's ~ful thinking** c'est prendre ses désirs pour la réalité.
wishy-washy* ['wɪʃɪˌwɒʃɪ] *adj* (*gen*) fadasse*; *colour* délavé.
wisp [wɪsp] *n [straw]* brin *m*; *[hair]* fine mèche *f*; *[smoke]* mince volute *f*. ♦ **wispy** *adj* (trop) fin.
wisteria [wɪs'tɪərɪə] *n* glycine *f*.
wistful ['wɪstfʊl] *adj* nostalgique. ♦ **wistfully** *adv* avec regret.
wit [wɪt] *n* **(a)** (*intelligence*) **~(s)** esprit *m*, intelligence *f*; **quick-~ted** à l'esprit vif; **native ~** bon sens; **you'll need all your ~s about you** il va te falloir toute ta présence d'esprit; **keep your ~s about you!** restez attentif!; **use your ~s!** sers-toi de ton intelligence!; **it was a battle of ~s** ils jouaient au plus fin; **he lives by his ~s** il vit d'expédients; **to collect one's ~s** rassembler ses esprits; **he was at his ~s' end** il ne savait plus que faire; (*fig*) **out of one's ~s** fou (*f* folle). **(b)** (*wittiness*) esprit *m*; (*witty person*) homme *m or* femme *f* d'esprit. **flash of ~** trait *m* d'esprit. ♦ **witticism** *n* mot *m* d'esprit. ♦ **wittily** *adv* avec beaucoup d'esprit. ♦ **witty** *adj* plein d'esprit.
witch [wɪtʃ] *n* sorcière *f*. ♦ **witchcraft** *n* sorcellerie *f*. ♦ **witch-doctor** *n* sorcier *m* (*de tribu*). ♦ **witch-hunt** *n* (*fig*) chasse *f* aux sorcières.
with [wɪð, wɪθ] *prep* **(a)** (*gen*) avec. **I was ~ her** j'étais avec elle; **she was staying ~ friends** elle était chez des amis; **I'll be ~ you in a minute** je suis à vous dans un instant; **I have no money ~ me** je n'ai pas d'argent sur moi; **she had her umbrella ~ her** elle avait pris son parapluie; **that problem is always ~ us** ce problème ne nous lâche pas; **the hat doesn't go ~ the dress** le chapeau ne va pas avec la robe; (*fig*) **I'm ~ you** (*agree ~ you*) je suis d'accord avec vous; (*support you*) je suis avec vous; **he just wasn't ~ us*** (*didn't understand*) il ne voyait* pas du tout; (*wasn't paying attention*) il était tout à fait ailleurs; (*up-to-date*) **to be ~ it*** être dans le vent*.
(b) (*having etc*) à, qui a. **the boy ~ brown eyes** le garçon aux yeux marron; **a coat ~ a fur collar** un manteau à col de fourrure; **a room ~ a view of the sea** une chambre qui a vue sur la mer.
(c) (*manner, means, cause*) avec, de. **~ my whole heart** de tout mon cœur; **~ pleasure** avec plaisir; **~ all speed** à toute vitesse; **~ no trouble at all** sans la moindre difficulté; **... he said ~ a smile** ... dit-il en souriant *or* avec un sourire; **she left ~ tears in her eyes** elle est partie, les larmes aux yeux; **cut it ~ a knife** coupe-le avec un couteau; **take it ~ both hands** prenez-le à deux mains; **trembling ~ fear** tremblant de peur; **white ~ snow** blanc de neige; **in bed ~ flu** retenu au lit par la grippe; **to go down ~ measles** attraper la rougeole; **~ the price of food these days you can't ...** au prix où est la nourriture de nos jours on ne peut pas ... .
(d) (*as regards*) **the trouble ~ Paul is that** ce qu'il y a avec Paul, c'est que; **it's a habit ~ him** c'est une habitude chez lui; **she's good ~ children**

elle sait bien s'occuper des enfants; **what do you want ~ that book?** qu'est-ce que tu veux faire de ce livre?; **pleased ~** satisfait de.

(e) (*indicating time*) avec. **he rose ~ the sun** il se levait avec le jour; **~ the approach of winter** à l'approche de l'hiver; **~ time** avec le temps; **~ these words** *or* **~ that he left us** là-dessus *or* sur ce il nous a quittés.

(f) (*despite*) malgré. **~ all his faults I still like him** malgré tous ses défauts je l'aime bien quand même; **~ all that, he is still better than ...** malgré tout ça il est encore meilleur que ... .

♦ **with-it‡** *adj* dans le vent*.

withdraw [wɪθ'drɔː] *pret* **-drew,** *ptp* **-drawn 1** *vt* (*gen*) retirer (*from* de); *ambassador* rappeler; *opinion, statement* rétracter; *claim* renoncer à; *order* annuler; (*Comm*) *faulty goods etc* retirer de la vente; *banknotes* retirer de la circulation. **2** *vi* (*gen*) se retirer (*from* de); *[person]* (*move away*) se retirer; (*move back*) reculer (*from* de; *a few paces* de quelques pas); (*retract offer etc*) se rétracter; *[candidate]* se désister (*from* de; *in favour of* en faveur de). (*Mil*) **to ~ to a new position** se replier; (*fig*) **to ~ into o.s.** se replier sur soi-même. ♦ **withdrawal 1** *n* (*gen*) retrait *m* (*of* de); (*Mil: retreat*) repli *m* (*to* sur); **2** *adj* (*Med, Psych*) **to have ~al symptoms** être en état de manque. ♦ **withdrawn** *adj person* renfermé.

wither ['wɪðəʳ] **1** *vi* (*gen*) se flétrir; *[hope, love etc]* s'évanouir; *[beauty]* se faner. **2** *vt plant* flétrir. **to ~ sb with a look** foudroyer qn du regard. ♦ **withered** *adj* flétri; (*gen*) *limb* atrophié; *old person* tout desséché. ♦ **withering** *adj tone, look* profondément méprisant; *remark, criticism* cinglant.

withhold [wɪθ'həʊld] *pret, ptp* **-held** *vt money from pay etc* retenir (*from sth* de qch); *payment, decision* remettre; *one's taxes* refuser de payer; *one's consent, help, support* refuser (*from sb* à qn); *truth, news* cacher (*from sb* à qn).

within [wɪð'ɪn] *prep* **(a)** (*inside*) à l'intérieur de. **~ the box/park** à l'intérieur de la boîte/du parc; **a voice ~ him** une voix en lui; **to be ~ the law** être dans les limites de la légalité; **to live ~ one's income** vivre selon ses moyens. **(b)** (*less than*) **~ a kilometre of** à moins d'un kilomètre de; **correct to ~ a centimetre** correct à un centimètre près; **~ a week of her visit** moins d'une semaine après (*or* avant) sa visite; **~ an hour (from now)** d'ici une heure; **he returned ~ the week** il est revenu avant la fin de la semaine.

without [wɪð'aʊt] *prep* sans. **~ a coat** sans manteau; **~ a coat or hat** sans manteau ni chapeau; **~ any money** sans argent; **he is ~ friends** il n'a pas d'amis; **not ~ difficulty** non sans difficulté; **he was quite ~ shame** il n'avait aucune honte; **~ speaking** sans parler; **~ anybody knowing** sans que personne le sache; **to go** *or* **do ~ sth** se passer de qch.

withstand [wɪθ'stænd] *pret, ptp* **-stood** *vt* résister à.

witness ['wɪtnɪs] **1** *n* **(a)** (*person*) témoin *m* (*to or of an incident* d'un incident; *to sb's signature* certifiant la signature de qn; *to a document* attestant l'authenticité d'un document). (*Jur*) **~ for the defence/prosecution** témoin à décharge/à charge; (*Jur*) **to call sb as ~** citer qn comme témoin. **(b)** (*evidence*) témoignage *m*. **in ~ whereof** en témoignage de quoi; **to bear ~ to sth** *[thing, result etc]* témoigner de qch; *[person]* attester qch; **~ the case of** témoin le cas de. **2** *adj*: **~ box** *or* (*US*) **stand** barre *f* des témoins; **in the ~ box** à la barre. **3** *vt* **(a)** (*see*) *event, crime* être témoin de, (*notice*) *change, improvement* remarquer. **(b)** (*esp Jur*) *document* attester l'authenticité de. **to ~ sb's signature** être témoin. **4** *vi* (*Jur*) témoigner (*to sth* de qch; *to having done* avoir fait).

wizard ['wɪzəd] *n* enchanteur *m*, sorcier *m*. (*fig*) **a financial ~** un génie en matière financière; **a ~ with a paintbrush** un champion* du pinceau.

wizened ['wɪznd] *adj* ratatiné.

wobble ['wɒbl] **1** *vi* (*gen*) trembler; *[object about to fall, compass needle, cyclist etc]* osciller; *[acrobat, dancer]* chanceler; *[wheel]* avoir du jeu. **the table was wobbling** la table tremblait; **this table ~s** cette table est branlante. **2** *n* (*Aut*) **wheel ~** shimmy *m*.

♦ **wobbly** *adj hand, voice* tremblant; *jelly* qui tremble; *table, chair* branlant, bancal; *object about to fall* qui oscille dangereusement; *wheel* qui a du jeu; (*feel weak*) **to be wobbly** se sentir faible.

woe [wəʊ] *n* malheur *m*. **~ is me!** pauvre de moi!; **~ betide him who ...** malheur à celui qui ...; **a tale of ~** une litanie de malheurs. ♦ **woebegone** *adj* désolé, abattu. ♦ **woeful** *adj* (*gen*) malheureux; *news, story, sight* affligeant. ♦ **woefully** *adv* (*sadly*) *say, look* très tristement; (*regrettably*) *small etc* regrettablement.

woke(n) ['wəʊk(n)] *pret (ptp) of* **wake²**.

wold [wəʊld] *n* haute plaine *f*, plateau *m*.

wolf [wʊlf] **1** *n, pl* **wolves** loup *m*; (**fig: Don Juan type*) tombeur *m* de femmes. **she-~** louve *f*; (*fig*) **a ~ in sheep's clothing** un loup déguisé en brebis; **that will keep the ~ from the door** cela nous *etc* mettra à l'abri du besoin. **2** *adj* (*fig*) **he gave a ~ whistle** il a sifflé la fille. **3** *vt* (**~ down**) engloutir. ♦ **wolfhound** *n* chien-loup *m*. ♦ **wolfish** *adj* vorace.

woman ['wʊmən] *pl* **women** ['wɪmɪn] **1** *n* femme *f*. **young ~** jeune femme; **come along, young ~!** allez mademoiselle, venez!; (*hum: wife*) **the little ~‡** ma *etc* petite femme*; **~ of the world** femme d'expérience; **Paul and all his women** Paul et toutes les femmes dans sa vie; **I've got a ~ who comes in 3 times a week** j'ai une femme de ménage qui vient 3 fois par semaine; **Women's Liberation Movement, Women's Lib*** mouvement *m* de libération de la femme, M.L.F. *m*; (*Press*) **the women's page** la page des lectrices; **women's team** équipe *f* féminine. **2** *adj*: **a ~ music teacher** un professeur de musique femme; **~ worker** ouvrière *f*; **women doctors** les femmes *fpl* médecins; **he's got a ~ driver** son chauffeur est une femme; **women drivers are ...** les femmes au volant sont ...; **~ friend** amie *f*. ♦ **woman-hater** *n* misogyne *mf*. ♦ **womanhood** *n* féminité *f*; **to reach ~hood** devenir une femme. ♦ **womanizer** *n* coureur *m* de jupons. ♦ **womankind** *n* les femmes *fpl* (*en général*). ♦ **womanlike 1** *adj* féminin; **2** *adv* d'une manière très féminine. ♦ **womanliness** *n* féminité *f*. ♦ **womanly** *adj figure, bearing* féminin; *behaviour* digne d'une femme; *gentleness etc* tout féminin. ♦ **womenfolk** *npl* les femmes *fpl*.

womb [wuːm] *n* utérus *m*; (*fig: of nature etc*) sein *m*.

won [wʌn] *pret, ptp of* **win**.

wonder ['wʌndəʳ] **1** *n* **(a)** émerveillement *m*, étonnement *m*. **(lost) in ~** émerveillé. **(b)** (*sth wonderful*) merveille *f*, miracle *m*. **the ~s of science** les miracles de la science; **the Seven W~s of the World** les Sept Merveilles du monde; **the ~ of it all is that ...** le plus étonnant dans tout cela c'est que ...; **it's a ~ that ...** c'est extraordinaire que ... + *subj*; **it's a ~ to me that ...** je n'en reviens pas que ... + *subj*; **no ~ he ...** ce n'est pas étonnant qu'il ... + *subj or* si il ... + *indic*; **no ~!** cela n'a rien d'étonnant!; **it's small ~ that ...** il n'est guère étonnant que ... + *subj*.

2 *vi* **(a)** (*marvel*) s'étonner, s'émerveiller (*at sth* de qch). **I ~ that ...** cela m'étonne que ... + *subj*; **he'll be back, I shouldn't ~** cela ne m'étonnerait pas qu'il revienne. **(b)** (*reflect*) penser, songer (*about sth* à qch). **it makes you ~** cela donne à penser; **I'm ~ing about going to the pictures** j'ai à moitié envie d'aller au cinéma.

3 *vt* se demander (*where/who etc* où/qui *etc*; *whether, if* si). **I ~ what to do** je ne sais pas quoi faire.

♦ **wonderful** *adj* merveilleux; **~ful to relate, he ...** chose étonnante, il ... . ♦ **wonderfully** *adv hot, quiet etc* merveilleusement; *manage, work etc* à merveille; **he looks ~fully well** il a très bonne mine. ♦ **wondering** *adj* (*astonished*) étonné; (*thoughtful*) songeur. ♦ **wonderland** *n* pays *m* merveilleux. ♦ **wonderment** *n* émerveillement *m*.

wonky* ['wɒŋkɪ] *adj chair, table* bancal; *machine* détraqué; *person* (*not well*) patraque*. **to go ~** *[machine]* se détraquer; *[TV picture etc]* se dérégler; *[handicraft, drawing]* aller de travers.

won't [wəʊnt] = **will not**; *V* **will.**

woo [wu:] *vt woman* faire la cour à, courtiser; (*fig*) *audience, influential person* chercher à plaire à; *fame, success* rechercher.

wood [wʊd] **1** *n* **(a)** bois *m*. **touch ~!**, (*US*) **knock on ~!** touchons du bois!; **aged in the ~** vieilli au tonneau. **(b)** (*forest*) bois *m*. **~s** bois *mpl*; **a pine ~** un bois de pins; (*fig*) **he can't see the ~ for the trees** les arbres lui cachent la forêt; (*fig*) **we're out of the ~** nous sommes tirés d'affaire. **(c)** (*Golf*) bois *m*; (*Bowls*) boule *f*.

2 *adj* **(a)** *floor, object* de bois, en bois. **~ carving** sculpture *f* en bois; **~ engraving** gravure *f* sur bois; **~ pulp** pâte *f* à papier; **~ shavings** copeaux *mpl* (de bois). **(b)** *nymph etc* des bois. **~ anemone** anémone *f* des bois.

♦ **woodbine** *n* chèvrefeuille *m*. ♦ **woodchuck** *n* marmotte *f* d'Amérique. ♦ **woodcock** *n* bécasse *f*. ♦ **woodcraft** *n* connaissance *f* des forêts. ♦ **woodcut** *n* gravure *f* sur bois. ♦ **woodcutter** *n* bûcheron *m*. ♦ **wooded** *adj* boisé; **thickly/sparsely ~ed** très/peu boisé. ♦ **wooden** *adj object* de bois, en bois; *leg* de bois; (*fig*) *movement* raide; *look, acting* sans expression; *personality, response* gauche. ♦ **woodland 1** *n* région *f* boisée; **2** *adj flower etc* des bois. ♦ **woodlouse** *n, pl* **-lice** cloporte *m*. ♦ **woodman** *n* forestier *m*. ♦ **woodpecker** *n* pic *m*. ♦ **woodpigeon** *n* ramier *m*. ♦ **woodpile** *n* tas *m* de bois. ♦ **woodshed** *n* bûcher *m*. ♦ **woodwind** *npl* (*Mus*) bois *mpl*. ♦ **woodwork** *n* (*craft, subject*) menuiserie *f*; (*more elaborate*) ébénisterie *f*; (*parts of house*) charpente *f*. ♦ **woodworm** *n* ver *m* du bois; **it's got ~worm** c'est vermoulu. ♦ **woody** *adj stem etc* ligneux.

woof[1] [wʊf] *n* (*Tex*) trame *f*.

woof[2] [wʊf] *vi [dog]* aboyer. **~, ~!** oua, oua!

wool [wʊl] **1** *n* laine *f*. **a ball of ~** une pelote de laine; **knitting/darning ~** laine à tricoter/repriser; (*fig*) **to pull the ~ over sb's eyes** en faire accroire à qn; **it's pure ~** c'est pure laine. **2** *adj cloth, trade* de laine; *dress* en *or* de laine; *shop* de laines. ♦ **wool-gathering** *n* (*fig*) **to be ~-gathering** être dans les nuages. ♦ **woollen,** (*US*) **woolen 1** *adj cloth* de laine; *garment* en *or* de laine; *industry* lainier; *manufacturer* de lainages; **2** *npl*: **~lens** lainages *mpl*. ♦ **woolly,** (*US*) **wooly 1** *adj* (*gen*) laineux; (*fig*) *clouds* cotonneux; *ideas* confus; *essay, book* verbeux; **2** *n* tricot *m*; (*collectively*) **~lies** lainages *mpl*. ♦ **wool-merchant** *n* négociant *m* en laines.

word [wɜ:d] **1** *n* **(a)** (*gen*) mot *m*; (*spoken*) mot, parole *f*. *[song etc]* **~s** paroles; **the written/spoken ~** ce qui est écrit/dit; **by ~ of mouth** de vive voix; **man of few ~s** homme peu loquace; **~ for ~** *repeat, copy out* mot pour mot, textuellement; *translate* mot à mot; *analyze, go over* mot par mot; **in other ~s** autrement dit; **in a ~** en un mot; **what's the ~ for 'table' in German?** comment dit-on 'table' en allemand?; **in the ~s of Racine** comme dit Racine; **to put sth into ~s** exprimer qch; **~s fail me!** je ne sais plus que dire!; **without a ~** sans dire un mot; **with these ~s, he ...** sur ces mots, il ...; **too stupid for ~s** vraiment trop stupide; **that's not the ~ for it!** c'est trop peu dire!; **that's a better ~ for it** ce serait plus près de la vérité; **those were his very ~s** c'est ce qu'il a dit mot pour mot; **a flood of ~s** un flot de paroles; **in so many ~s** explicitement; **to have the last ~** avoir le dernier mot; (*fig*) **the last ~ in** ce qu'on fait de mieux en matière de; **a ~ of warning** un petit avertissement; **he won't hear a ~ against her** il n'admet absolument pas qu'on la critique (*subj*); **nobody had a good ~ to say about him** personne n'a trouvé la moindre chose à dire en sa faveur; **to put in a (good) ~ for** glisser un mot en faveur de; **I want a ~ with you** j'ai à vous parler; **I'll have a ~ with him about it** je vais lui en parler; **I never said a ~** je n'ai rien dit du tout; **he didn't say a ~ about it** il n'en a absolument pas parlé; **I can't get a ~ out of him** je ne peux rien en tirer; **you took the ~s right out of my mouth** c'est exactement ce que j'allais dire; **you put ~s into my mouth!** vous me faites dire ce que je n'ai pas dit!; (*quarrel*) **to have ~s with sb** se disputer avec qn.

(b) (*fig: no pl*) (*message*) mot *m*; (*news*) nouvelles *fpl* (*of, about* de). **to leave ~** laisser un mot (*with sb for sb* à qn pour qn; *that* que); **~ came from H.Q. that ...** le Q.G. nous *etc* a fait savoir que ...; **there's no ~ from John yet** on est toujours sans nouvelles de Jean; **~ of command** mot d'ordre; **his ~ is law** c'est lui qui fait la loi; **to give the ~ to advance** donner l'ordre d'avancer; (*Rel*) **the W~** le Verbe; **the W~ of God** la parole de Dieu.

(c) (*promise*) parole *f*. **~ of honour** parole d'honneur; **a man of his ~** un homme de parole; **he was as good as his ~** il a tenu parole; **to give one's ~** donner sa parole (*to sb* à qn; *that* que); **to break/go back on/keep one's ~** manquer à/retirer/tenir sa parole; **to take sb at his ~** prendre qn au mot; **his ~ against mine** sa parole contre la mienne; **I've only got her ~ for it** c'est elle qui le dit, je n'ai aucune preuve; **to take sb's ~ for it** croire qn sur parole; **(upon) my ~!*** ma parole!

2 *adj*: **~ game** jeu *m* avec des mots; **~ list** nomenclature *f*; **~ order** ordre *m* des mots.

3 *vt document, protest* formuler.

♦ **word-blind** *adj* dyslexique. ♦ **word-blindness** *n* dyslexie *f*. ♦ **wordbook** *n* lexique *m*. ♦ **word-for-word** *adj analysis* mot par mot; *translation* mot à mot. ♦ **wordiness** *n* verbosité *f*. ♦ **wording** *n [letter, statement]* termes *mpl*; **the ~ing is clumsy** c'est maladroitement exprimé; **the ~ing is important** le choix des termes est important; **change the ~ing slightly** changez quelques mots. ♦ **word-perfect** *adj*: **to be ~-perfect in sth** savoir qch sur le bout du doigt. ♦ **wordplay** *n* jeu *m* de mots. ♦ **word-processing** *n* traitement *m* des textes. ♦ **word-processor** *n* système *m* de traitement des textes. ♦ **wordy** *adj* verbeux.

wore [wɔ:ʳ] *pret of* **wear.**

work [wɜ:k] **1** *n* **(a)** (*gen*) travail *m*. **to be at ~** travailler (*on* sur), être à l'œuvre *or* au travail; (*fig*) **other forces are at ~** d'autres forces sont en jeu; **to start ~, to set to ~** se mettre au travail *or* à l'œuvre; **to set to ~ doing** se mettre à faire; **to set sb to ~ doing** donner pour tâche à qn de faire; **good ~!** bravo!; **a good piece of ~** du bon travail; **she put a lot of ~ into it** elle a passé beaucoup de temps dessus; **there's a lot of ~ to be done on it** il reste beaucoup à faire; **I'm trying to get some ~ done** j'essaie de travailler un peu; **~ has begun on the bridge** les travaux du pont ont commencé; **it's women's ~** c'est un travail de femme; **it's quite easy ~** ce n'est pas difficile à faire; **it's hot ~** ça donne chaud; **to make short ~ of** *sth* faire très rapidement; (*fig*) *sb* envoyer promener*; **it's the**

~ **of a professional** c'est un travail de professionnel.

(b) (*as employment*) travail *m*. **to go to** ~ aller travailler, aller à l'usine (*or* au bureau *etc*); **to look for** ~ chercher du travail *or* un emploi; **he's at** ~ il est au bureau (*or* à l'usine *etc*); **he is in** ~ il a un emploi; **out of** ~ en chômage, sans emploi; **to put** *or* **throw sb out of** ~ réduire qn au chômage; **he's off** ~ il n'est pas allé (*or* venu) travailler, (*longer-term*) il est absent; **a day off** ~ un jour de congé; **I've got time off** ~ j'ai du temps libre; **domestic** ~ travaux *mpl* domestiques; **office** ~ travail de bureau; **I've done a full day's** ~ (*lit*) j'ai fait ma journée; (*fig*) j'ai eu une journée bien remplie; (*fig*) **it's all in the day's** ~ ça n'a rien d'extraordinaire.

(c) *[writer, musician, politician, scholar etc]* œuvre *f*; (*writing*) ouvrage *m* (*on sb/sth* sur qn/qch; *of fiction etc* de fiction *etc*); (*piece of sewing*) ouvrage. **the** ~**s of God** les œuvres de Dieu; **good** ~**s** bonnes œuvres; **his life's** ~ l'œuvre de sa vie; **his** ~ **will be remembered** son œuvre restera dans la mémoire des hommes; ~ **of art** œuvre d'art; **the complete** ~**s of** les œuvres complètes de; **he sells a lot of his** ~ il vend beaucoup de tableaux (*or* de livres *etc*); (*fig*) **he's a nasty piece of** ~* c'est un sale type*.

(d) (*pl*) ~s (*gen, Admin, Mil*) travaux *mpl*; *[clock, machine etc]* mécanisme *m*. **Ministry of W**~**s** ministère *m* des Travaux publics; **building/road** ~**s** travaux de construction/d'entretien de la route; (*fig*) **they gave him the** ~**s**‡ ils lui en ont fait voir de dures*; (*fig*) **the whole** ~**s*** tout le tralala*.

(e) (*pl inv: factory*) ~s usine *f*; **gas**~**s** usine à gaz.

2 *adj* **(a)** ~ **force** main-d'œuvre *f*; ~ **load** part *f* du travail; **his** ~ **load is too heavy** il a trop de travail; ~ **permit** permis *m* de travail; (*US*) ~ **week of 38 hours** semaine *f* de 38 heures.

(b) ~**s committee** *or* **council** comité *m* d'entreprise; ~**s manager** chef *m* d'exploitation.

3 *vi* **(a)** (*gen*) travailler (*at sth* à qch; *on sth* sur qch; *in wood etc* avec le bois *etc*). **to** ~ **hard** travailler dur; **to** ~ **like a horse** *or* **a Trojan** travailler comme un forçat *or* un bœuf; (*Ind*) **to** ~ **to rule** faire la grève du zèle; (*fig*) **I've been** ~**ing on him** j'ai bien essayé de le convaincre; **the police are** ~**ing on the case** la police enquête sur l'affaire; (*gen*) **we're** ~**ing on it** on y travaille; **they are** ~**ing on the principle that ...** ils partent du principe que ...; **there are not many facts to** ~ **on** on manque de faits sur lesquels on puisse se baser; **to** ~ **for/against sth** lutter pour/contre qch; (*fig*) **to** ~ **towards sth** se diriger petit à petit vers qch.

(b) *[machine, car, scheme]* marcher; *[drug, medicine, spell]* agir; *[brain]* fonctionner. **the lift isn't** ~**ing** l'ascenseur ne marche pas *or* est en panne; **it** ~**s on electricity** ça marche à l'électricité; (*fig*) **that** ~**s both ways** c'est à double tranchant.

(c) (*move*) *[mouth]* se contracter. *[person]* **to** ~ **(one's way) along/up** *etc* arriver petit à petit à avancer/à monter *etc*.

4 *vt* **(a)** (*cause to* ~) *person, staff* faire travailler; *mechanism, machine* faire marcher, actionner. **to** ~ **sb too hard** exiger trop de qn; **he** ~**s himself too hard** il se surmène; **can you** ~ **the machine?** sais-tu te servir de la machine?; **it's** ~**ed by electricity** ça marche à l'électricité.

(b) *miracle* faire, accomplir; *change* apporter. **to** ~ **wonders** *[person]* faire des merveilles; *[thing]* faire merveille; **to** ~ **one's passage** payer son passage en travaillant; **to** ~ **one's way through college** travailler pour payer ses études; (*fig*) **he has managed to** ~ **his promotion*** il s'est débrouillé pour obtenir son avancement; **can you** ~ **it* so that ...** pouvez-vous faire en sorte que ... +*subj*; **I'll** ~ **it*** je le ferai; **to** ~ **o.s. into a rage** se mettre dans une colère noire; **he** ~**ed the rope through the hole** il est petit à petit arrivé à faire passer la corde dans le trou; **to** ~ **sth free/loose** arriver à délier/desserrer qch; **he** ~**ed it into his speech** il s'est arrangé pour l'introduire dans son discours; **to** ~ **one's way along** arriver petit à petit à avancer; **the roots have** ~**ed their way into the foundations** les racines ont pénétré dans les fondations; (*fig*) **to** ~ **one's way into a firm** arriver à se faire une place dans une compagnie.

(c) *mine, land* exploiter; *metal, leather, dough* travailler; *object* façonner (*out of* dans); (*sew*) coudre; (*embroider*) *design etc* broder.

work in *vi [arrangement etc]* cadrer (*with sb's plans* avec les projets de qn).

work off *vt sep* **(a)** *debt, obligation* acquitter en travaillant. **(b)** *surplus fat* se débarrasser de; *weight* éliminer; *annoyance* passer (*on sb* sur qn); *energy* dépenser son surplus de.

work out 1 *vi [plan, arrangement]* réussir, marcher; *[problem, sum]* se résoudre exactement. *[total]* **to** ~ **out at** s'élever à; **it** ~**s out at 5 apples per child** ça fait 5 pommes par enfant; **it's all** ~**ing out as planned** tout se déroule comme prévu; **things didn't** ~ **out for her** les choses ont plutôt mal tourné pour elle; **it will** ~ **out right in the end** tout finira par s'arranger; **how did it** ~ **out?** comment ça a marché?* **2** *vt sep calculation, problem* résoudre; *answer, total* trouver; *code* déchiffrer; *scheme, idea* mettre au point. **I'll have to** ~ **it out** (*gen*) il faut que je réfléchisse; (*counting*) il faut que je calcule; **to** ~ **out where/why** *etc* finir par découvrir où/pourquoi *etc*; (*of behaviour etc*) **I can't** ~ **it out** ça me dépasse*.

work round *vi*: **to** ~ **round to a subject** aborder un sujet (avec tact); **what are you** ~**ing round to?** où voulez-vous en venir?

work up 1 *vi*: **to** ~ **up to sth/to doing** préparer le terrain pour qch/pour faire; **what is he** ~**ing up to?** où veut-il bien en venir? **2** *vt sep trade* développer. **he** ~**ed it up from almost nothing into ...** en partant de rien il a réussi à en faire ...; **to** ~ **one's way up** s'élever à la force du poignet (*from* de; *to be* jusqu'à être); **to** ~ **one's way up to the top** gravir un à un tous les échelons de la hiérarchie; **to** ~ **sb up into a fury** déchaîner la fureur de qn; **to** ~ **up an appetite** s'ouvrir l'appétit; **to** ~ **up enthusiasm for** s'enthousiasmer pour; **to get** ~**ed up** se mettre dans tous ses états.

♦ **workable** *adj arrangement etc* possible, réalisable. ♦ **workaday** *adj clothes* de tous les jours; *event* banal. ♦ **workbag** *n* sac *m* à ouvrage. ♦ **workbasket** *n* corbeille *f* à ouvrage. ♦ **workbench** *n* établi *m*. ♦ **workbook** *n* (*exercise book*) cahier *m* d'exercices; (*manual*) manuel *m*. ♦ **workbox** *n* boîte *f* à ouvrage. ♦ **workdesk** *n* bureau *m* de travail. ♦ **worker 1** *n* travailleur *m*, -euse *f*, ouvrier *m*, -ière *f* (*esp Agr, Ind etc*); **he's a good** ~**er** il travaille bien; **the** ~**ers in this industry** ceux qui travaillent dans cette industrie; (*Ind*) **management and** ~**ers** patronat *m* et travailleurs; **office** ~**er** employé(e) *m(f)* de bureau; **2** *adj participation etc* des travailleurs; ~**er priest** prêtre-ouvrier *m*. ♦ **working** *adj clothes, lunch, week etc* de travail; *wife* qui travaille; *model* qui marche; *partner* actif; **the** ~**ing class** la classe ouvrière (*V also* **working-class**); **8-hour** ~**ing day** journée *f* de travail de 8 heures; (*Pol etc*) ~**ing majority** majorité *f* suffisante; **an ordinary** ~**ing man** un simple ouvrier; ~**ing party** (*committee*) commission *f* d'enquête; (*squad: of soldiers etc*) escouade *f*. ♦ **working-class** *adj background, suburb* ouvrier; *person* qui appartient à la classe ouvrière. ♦ **workings** *npl* (*mechanism*) mécanisme *m*; *[government,* *organization]* rouages *mpl*; (*Min*) chantier *m* d'exploitation; **the ~ings of her mind** ce qui se passe dans sa tête. ♦ **workman** *n,pl* **-men** (*gen, Comm, Ind etc*) ouvrier *m*; **he's a good ~man** il travaille bien. ♦ **workmanlike** *adj method, person* professionnel; *tool, product, essay* bien fait; *attempt* honnête. ♦ **workmanship** *n [craftsman]* habileté *f* professionnelle; **a superb piece of ~manship** un travail superbe. ♦ **workmate** *n* camarade *mf* de travail. ♦ **workout** *n* (*Sport*) séance *f* d'entraînement. ♦ **workroom** *n* salle *f* de travail. ♦ **workshop** *n* atelier *m*. ♦ **workshy** *adj* fainéant. ♦ **work-to-rule** *n* grève *f* du zèle.

world [wɜːld] **1** *n* **(a)** (*gen*) monde *m*. **all over the ~** dans le monde entier; **to go round the ~** faire le tour du monde; **to see the ~** voir du pays; **known throughout the ~** connu dans le monde entier; **alone in the ~** seul au monde; **it's a small ~!** le monde est petit!; **the New W~** le Nouveau Monde; **the ancient ~** l'antiquité *f*; **the ~ we live in** le monde où nous vivons; **since the beginning of the ~** depuis que le monde est monde; **~ without end** dans les siècles des siècles; (*Rel*) **in the ~** dans le siècle; **in this ~** ici-bas, en ce monde; **the next ~, the ~ to come** l'au-delà; **he's not long for this ~** il n'en a plus pour longtemps à vivre; **to bring a child into the ~** mettre un enfant au monde; **the ~ of nature** le monde de la nature; **the business ~** le monde *or* le milieu des affaires.

(b) (*phrases*) **he lives in a ~ of his own** il vit dans un monde à lui; **it's out of this ~** c'est extraordinaire; **to be dead to the ~** (*asleep*) dormir profondément; (*drunk*) être ivre mort; **to be on top of the ~*** être aux anges; **to think the ~ of sb** mettre qn sur un piédestal; **it did him a ~ of good** ça lui a fait énormément de bien; **there's a ~ of difference between ...** il y a un monde entre ...; **~s apart** diamétralement opposés; **it's not the end of the ~** ce n'est pas la fin du monde; **it was for all the ~ as if ...** c'était exactement comme si ...; **the ~'s worst cook** la pire cuisinière qui soit; **I'd give the ~ to know ...** je donnerais tout au monde pour savoir ...; **a man of the ~** un homme d'expérience; **to go up in the ~** faire du chemin (*fig*); **he has come down in the ~** il a connu des jours meilleurs; **the ~ and his wife** absolument tout le monde; **it's what he wants most in (all) the ~** c'est ce qu'il veut plus que tout au monde; **nowhere in the (whole wide) ~** nulle part au monde; **not for anything in the ~** pour rien au monde; **where/why in the ~ has he ...?** où/pourquoi donc a-t-il ...?

2 *adj power, scale* mondial; *record, champion, tour* du monde; *language* universel. (*Ftbl*) **the W~ Cup** la Coupe du monde; (*Comm*) **W~ Fair** Exposition *f* Internationale; **W~ Health Organization** (*abbr* **WHO**) Organisation *f* mondiale de la santé (*abbr* O.M.S.); **W~ War One/Two** la Première/Seconde guerre mondiale.

♦ **world-famous** *adj* de renommée mondiale. ♦ **worldly** *adj matters, pleasures* de ce monde; *attitude, person* matérialiste; (*Rel*) temporel; **all his ~ly goods** tout ce qu'il possède. ♦ **worldly-wise** *adj* qui a l'expérience du monde. ♦ **world-wide** *adj* mondial, universel.

worm [wɜːm] **1** *n* (*gen*) ver *m*. **earth~** ver de terre; (*Med*) **to have ~s** avoir des vers; (*fig*) **the ~ has turned** il *etc* en a eu assez de se faire marcher sur les pieds; (*US fig*) **a can of ~s*** un véritable guêpier; **you ~!*** misérable! **2** *vt* **(a) to ~ (one's way) into sth** se glisser dans qch; (*fig: into group, sb's confidence etc*) s'insinuer dans qch. **(b)** (*extract*) **to ~ it** *or* **information out of sb** tirer les vers du nez à qn (*about* à propos de; *why etc* pour savoir pourquoi *etc*). ♦ **worm-eaten** *adj fruit* véreux; *furniture* vermoulu. ♦ **wormwood** *n* armoise *f*.

worn [wɔːn] (*ptp of* **wear**) *adj object* usé; *person* las. ♦ **worn-out** *adj object* complètement usé; *person* épuisé.

worry ['wʌrɪ] **1** *n* souci *m* (*of doing* de faire; *to sb* pour qn). **the least of my worries** le cadet de mes soucis; **it's causing us a lot of ~** cela nous donne beaucoup de souci. **2** *vi* **(a)** se faire du souci, s'inquiéter (*about, over* au sujet de, pour). **don't ~ about me** ne vous inquiétez pas *or* ne vous en faites pas* pour moi. **(b) to ~ at sth = to ~ sth**; *V* **3b. 3** *vt* **(a)** inquiéter, tracasser. **it worries me that** cela m'inquiète que +*subj*; **don't ~ yourself** *or* **your head* about it** ne te fais pas de mauvais sang pour ça; **to ~ o.s. sick** se rendre malade d'inquiétude (*about* au sujet de); **what's ~ing you?** qu'est-ce qui ne va pas? **(b)** *[dog] bone etc* jouer avec; *sheep* harceler. ♦ **worried** *adj* inquiet (*about* au sujet de); **worried to death*** fou d'inquiétude. ♦ **worrier** *n* anxieux *m*, -euse *f*. ♦ **worrisome** *adj* inquiétant. ♦ **worrying** *adj* inquiétant; **to have a ~ing time** passer un mauvais quart d'heure, (*longer*) en voir de dures*.

worse [wɜːs] **1** *adj* (*comp of* **bad** *and* **ill**) pire, plus mauvais (*than* que). **you're ~ than he is!** tu es pire que lui!; **and, what's ~ ...** le pire, c'est que ...; **~ than ever** pire que jamais; **it could have been ~** ç'aurait pu être pire; **things couldn't be ~** ça ne pourrait pas aller plus mal; **~ things have happened** on a vu pire; **to make matters** *or* **things ~** aggraver la situation (*by doing* en faisant); **and, to make matters** *or* **things ~, he ...** et, pour comble de malheur, il ...; **it gets ~ and ~** ça ne fait qu'empirer; **he is getting ~** (*in behaviour, memory*) il ne s'arrange pas; (*in health*) il va de plus en plus mal; **to get ~** (*gen*) se détériorer; *[rheumatism, smell etc]* empirer; **I feel ~** je me sens plus mal; **so much the ~ for him!** tant pis pour lui!; **~ luck!*** hélas!; **none the ~** *V* **none 2**.

2 *adv* (*comp of* **badly** *and* **ill**) *sing, play etc* plus mal (*than* que); (*more*) *rain, hate etc* plus (*than* que). **you might** *or* **could do ~** vous pourriez faire pire (*than to do* que de faire); **he is ~ off than before** (*gen*) il se retrouve dans une situation pire qu'avant; (*less money*) il y a perdu; **I shan't think any the ~ of you** je n'en aurai pas une moins bonne opinion de toi (*for having done* pour avoir fait).

3 *n* pire *m*. **there's ~ to come** on n'a pas vu le pire; **~ followed** ensuite cela a été pire; **a change for the ~** (*gen*) une détérioration très nette de la situation; (*Med*) une aggravation très nette.

♦ **worsen** *vi* (*gen*) se détériorer, empirer; *[health etc]* empirer; *[chances of success]* diminuer.

worship ['wɜːʃɪp] **1** *n* **(a)** (*gen*) culte *m*. (*Rel*) **place of ~** lieu *m* de culte; **hours of ~** heures *fpl* des offices. **(b) His** *or* **Your W~** (*Mayor*) Monsieur le Maire; (*magistrate*) Monsieur le Juge. **2** *vt* (*Rel*) adorer; (*gen*) *person* adorer, vénérer; *money, success etc* avoir le culte de. **he ~ped the ground she trod on** il vénérait jusqu'au sol qu'elle foulait. **3** *vi* (*Rel*) faire ses dévotions. ♦ **worshipper** *n* adorateur *m*, -trice *f*; (*in church*) **~pers** fidèles *mpl*.

worst [wɜːst] **1** *adj* (*superl of* **bad** *and* **ill**) le (*or* la) plus mauvais(e), le (*or* la) pire. **the ~ student in the class** le plus mauvais élève de la classe; **his ~ mistake** son erreur la plus grave; **the ~ thing he ever did** la pire chose qu'il ait jamais faite; **the ~ winter for 20 years** l'hiver le plus rude depuis 20 ans; **at the ~ possible time** au plus mauvais moment; **the ~ possible job for him** l'emploi le plus contre-indiqué pour lui.

2 *adv* (*superl of* **badly** *and* **ill**) le plus mal. **he sings ~ of all** il chante le plus mal de tous; **the ~-dressed man in England** l'homme le plus mal habillé d'Angleterre; **he came off ~** c'est lui qui s'en est le plus mal sorti; **they are the ~ off** ils sont le plus affectés; (*poorest*) ils sont le plus dans la gêne; **my leg hurts ~ of all** c'est ma jambe qui me fait le plus mal.

3 *n* pire *m*. **the ~ that can happen** le pire *or* la pire chose qui puisse arriver; **at (the) ~** au pis aller; **to be at its** *etc* **~** *[crisis, storm, epidemic]* être à son *etc* point culminant; *[situation, conditions, relationships]* n'avoir jamais été aussi mauvais; **at the ~ of the storm** au plus fort de l'orage; **matters were at their ~** les choses ne pouvaient pas aller plus mal; **the ~ is yet to come** on n'a pas encore vu le pire; **the ~ of it is that ...** le pire c'est que ...; **that's the ~ of ...** ça c'est l'inconvénient de ...; **if the ~ comes to the ~** en mettant les choses au pis; **to get the ~ of it** être le perdant; **do your ~!** vous pouvez toujours essayer!; **it brings out the ~ in me** ça réveille en moi les pires instincts.

worsted ['wʊstɪd] *n* worsted *m*.

worth [wɜːθ] **1** *n* **(a)** (*value*) valeur *f* (*in gold etc* en or *etc*). **I know his ~** je sais ce qu'il vaut; **he showed his true ~** il a montré sa vraie valeur. **(b)** (*quantity*) **he bought 20 pence ~ of sweets** il a acheté pour 20 pence de bonbons; **he bought 20 pence ~** il en a acheté pour 20 pence.

2 *adj*: **to be ~ £10** valoir 10 livres; **what** *or* **how much is it ~?** ça vaut combien?; **how much is he ~?** à combien s'élève sa fortune?; (*lit, fig*) **it's ~ a great deal** ça a beaucoup de valeur (*to me* pour moi); **it's more than my life (***or* **job** *etc***) is ~ to do that** je ne peux pas risquer de faire ça; **to be ~ one's weight in gold** valoir son pesant d'or; **it's not ~ the paper it's written on** ça ne vaut pas le papier sur lequel c'est écrit; **this pen is ~ 10 others** ce stylo en vaut 10 autres; (*fig*) **what's it ~ to you?*** vous donneriez combien pour le savoir (*or* l'avoir *etc*)?; **take it for what it's ~** prenez-le pour ce que ça vaut; **it's well ~ the trouble (***or* **effort** *or* **time)** ça vaut la peine; **it's ~ reading/having** *etc* ça vaut la peine d'être lu/d'en avoir un *etc*; **it's well ~ it** ça vaut la peine *or* le coup*; **life isn't ~ living** la vie ne vaut pas la peine d'être vécue; **it's ~ a visit** ça vaut la visite; **it is ~ while to do that** on gagne à faire ça; **it's not ~ (my) while waiting** je perdrais mon temps à attendre; **it wasn't ~ his while to take the job** ça ne valait pas le coup* qu'il accepte (*subj*) l'emploi; **I'll make it ~ your while*** je vous récompenserai de votre peine.

♦ **worthless** *adj* (*gen*) qui ne vaut rien; *effort* vain; *person* qui ne vaut pas cher. ♦ **worthwhile** *adj visit* qui en vaut la peine; *book/film etc* qui mérite d'être lu/vu *etc*; *work, life* utile; *contribution* très valable; *cause* louable. ♦ **worthy** ['wɜːðɪ] *adj* (*gen*) digne (*of* de; *to do* de faire); *citizen etc* digne (*before n*); *aim, effort* louable; **he found a ~y opponent** il a trouvé un adversaire digne de lui; **it is ~y of note that ...** il est bon de remarquer que ...; **nothing ~y of mention** rien de notable.

would [wʊd] *modal aux vb* (*cond of* **will**) **(a)** (*cond tense*) **he ~ do it if you asked him** il le ferait si vous le lui demandiez; **he ~ have done it if you had asked him** il l'aurait fait si vous le lui aviez demandé; **I wondered if you'd come** je me demandais si vous viendriez *or* si vous alliez venir; **you ~ think she had enough to do** on pourrait penser qu'elle a assez à faire. **(b)** (*conjecture*) **it ~ have been about 8 o'clock** il devait être 8 heures à peu près. **(c)** (*willingness*) **I said I ~ do it** je lui ai dit que je le ferais *or* que je voulais bien le faire; **he ~n't help me** il ne voulait pas m'aider, il n'a pas voulu m'aider; **the car ~n't start** la voiture n'a pas démarré; **~ you like some tea?** voulez-vous *or* voudriez-vous du thé?; **~ you like to go?** voulez-vous y aller?, est-ce que vous aimeriez y aller?; **~ you please help me?** pourriez-vous m'aider, s'il vous plaît? **(d)** (*habit, characteristic*) **he ~ always read in bed** il lisait toujours *or* il avait l'habitude de lire au lit; **50 years ago the streets ~ be empty on Sundays** il y a 50 ans, les rues étaient vides le dimanche; **you WOULD (do that)!** c'est bien de toi (de faire ça)!; **it WOULD rain!** il pleut, naturellement! **(e)** (*liter*) **~ to God that ...** plût à Dieu que ... + *subj*; **~ I were younger!** si seulement j'étais plus jeune! ♦ **would-be** *adj*: **a ~-be poet** *etc* une personne qui veut être poète *etc*; (*pej*) un prétendu poète *etc*.

wound¹ [wuːnd] **1** *n* blessure *f*. **chest/bullet ~** blessure à la poitrine/par balle. **2** *vt* (*lit, fig*) blesser (*in the leg etc* à la jambe *etc*). ♦ **wounded 1** *adj* (*lit, fig*) blessé; **a ~ed man** un blessé; **2** *npl*: **the ~ed** les blessés *mpl*. ♦ **wounding** *adj* blessant.

wound² [waʊnd] *pret, ptp of* **wind²**.

wove(n) ['wəʊv(ən)] *pret (ptp) of* **weave**.

wraith [reɪθ] *n* apparition *f*, spectre *m*.

wrangle ['ræŋgl] **1** *n* (*also* **wrangling**) dispute *f*. **2** *vi* se disputer (*about, over* à propos de).

wrap [ræp] **1** *n* (*shawl*) châle *m*; (*housecoat etc*) peignoir *m*; (*rug, blanket*) couverture *f*. (*on parcel etc*) **~s** emballage *m*; (*fig*) **to keep a scheme under ~s*** ne pas dévoiler un projet.

2 *vt* (*cover: gen*) envelopper (*in* dans); (*pack*) *parcel* emballer (*in* dans); (*wind*) *tape etc* enrouler (*round* autour de). (*fig*) **~ped in mist/mystery** enveloppé de brume/de mystère. **wrap up 1** *vi* (*dress warmly*) s'habiller chaudement. **~ up well!** couvrez-vous bien! **2** *vt sep* **(a)** (*gen*) envelopper (*in* dans); *parcel* emballer (*in* dans). (*fig*) **he ~ped it up a bit*, but what he meant was ...** il ne l'a pas dit franchement, mais ce qu'il voulait dire c'est ...; (*fig: engrossed*) **~ped up in one's work** absorbé par son travail; **he is ~ped up in himself** il ne pense qu'à lui-même. **(b)** (*: *conclude*) *deal* conclure. **he had everything ~ped up** il avait tout arrangé.

♦ **wrapover** *adj skirt* portefeuille *inv*. ♦ **wrapped** *adj bread etc* pré-emballé. ♦ **wrapper** *n [chocolate, parcel]* papier *m* (d'emballage); *[newspaper for post]* bande *f*; *[book]* jaquette *f*. ♦ **wrapping 1** *n [parcel, chocolate]* papier *m* (d'emballage); **2** *adj*: **~ping paper** (*brown paper*) papier *m* d'emballage; (*decorated*) papier cadeau.

wrath [rɒθ] *n* (*liter*) courroux *m*.

wreath [riːθ] *n* couronne *f* (*de fleurs*); *[smoke]* volute *f*. **laurel ~** couronne de laurier. ♦ **wreathed** *adj*: **~ed in mist** enveloppé de brume; **face ~ed in smiles** visage rayonnant.

wreck [rek] **1** *n* (*of ship, plans etc*) naufrage *m*; (*~ed ship*) épave *f*; (*~ed plane/car etc*) avion *m*/voiture *f etc* accidenté(e); (*building*) ruines *fpl*. **the car was a ~** la voiture était bonne à mettre à la ferraille; **he looks a ~** il a une mine de déterré. **2** *vt train* faire dérailler; *plane* détruire; *building, furniture* démolir; *mechanism* détraquer; (*fig*) *marriage, friendship, life, career* briser; *plans, health* ruiner; *negotiations* faire échouer; *chances* anéantir. *[ship, sailor]* **to be ~ed** faire naufrage; **the plane was ~ed** il n'est resté que des débris de l'avion; **he ~ed the whole house** il a tout démoli dans la maison. ♦ **wreckage** *n* (*pieces*) débris *mpl*; *[building]* décombres *mpl*; (*~ed ship*) épave *f*. ♦ **wrecked** *adj ship* naufragé; *train, car* accidenté; *plans* anéanti. ♦ **wrecker** *n* (*unlawful*) vandale *m*; (*lawful*) démolisseur *m*; *[cars]* marchand *m* de ferraille.

wren [ren] *n* roitelet *m*.

wrench [rentʃ] **1** *n* **(a) to give sth a ~** tirer de toutes ses forces sur qch; (*fig: emotional*) **it was a ~** cela a été un déchirement. **(b)** (*tool*) clé *f* (à écrous). **2** *vt handle etc* tirer violemment sur. **to ~ sth off** *or* **out** *or* **away** arracher qch (*of, from sth* de qch; *from sb* des mains de qn); **he ~ed himself free** il s'est dégagé avec un mouvement violent; (*Med*) **to ~ one's ankle** se tordre la cheville.

wrestle ['resl] *vi* lutter (*with sb* contre qn); (*Sport*) pratiquer la lutte libre; (*as staged fight*) catcher (*with sb* contre qn). (*fig*) **to ~ with** *conscience, sums, device* se débattre avec; *temptation* lutter contre. ♦ **wrestler** *n* lutteur *m*, -euse *f*; catcheur *m*, -euse *f*. ♦ **wrestling 1** *n* lutte *f*; **all-in wrestling** catch *m*; **2** *adj*: **wrestling match** rencontre *f* de catch *or* de lutte.

wretch [retʃ] *n* misérable *mf*. (*hum*) **you ~!** misérable!; **little ~!** petit polisson! ♦ **wretched** [ˈretʃɪd] *adj* (*very poor*) *person, conditions, house* misérable; (*unhappy*) malheureux; (*depressed*) déprimé; (*ill*) malade; (*too small*) *wage* de misère; *sum, amount* dérisoire; (*pej*) *behaviour, remark* mesquin; *weather, holiday, results* lamentable; (*conscience-stricken etc*) **I feel ~ed about it** je me sens vraiment coupable; **what ~ed luck!** quelle déveine!*; **they played a ~ed game** ils ont très mal joué; **that ~ed dog*** ce maudit chien. ♦ **wretchedly** *adv live* misérablement; *say, weep, apologize* pitoyablement; *treat, behave, pay, perform, play* très mal. ♦ **wretchedness** *n* (*poverty*) misère *f*; (*unhappiness*) extrême tristesse *f*.

wrick [rɪk] **1** *vt*: **to ~ one's ankle** se tordre la cheville; **to ~ one's neck** attraper un torticolis. **2** *n* entorse *f*; torticolis *m*.

wriggle [ˈrɪgl] **1** *vi* (**~ about**) *[worm, snake, eel]* se tortiller; *[fish]* frétiller; *[person]* (*restlessly*) remuer; (*in embarrassment*) se tortiller; (*excitedly*) frétiller. **to ~ along** *[worm etc]* avancer en se tortillant; *[person]* avancer en rampant; **to ~ free** se dégager en se contorsionnant; **to ~ through sth** se glisser dans qch; (*fig*) **to ~ out of sth** esquiver qch; **he'll manage to ~ out of it** il trouvera un moyen de s'esquiver. **2** *vt toes* remuer. ♦ **wriggly** *or* ♦ **wriggling** *adj worm* qui se tortille; *fish* frétillant; *child* remuant.

wring [rɪŋ] *pret, ptp* **wrung** *vt* **(a)** (*twist*) *handkerchief etc* tordre. **to ~ a chicken's neck** tordre le cou à un poulet; **I'll ~ your neck!*** je te tordrai le cou!*; **to ~ one's hands** se tordre les mains de désespoir; **to ~ sb's hand** serrer longuement la main à qn; (*fig*) **a story to ~ one's heart** une histoire à vous fendre le cœur. **(b)** (**~ out**) *wet clothes etc* essorer; *water* exprimer (*from sth* de qch); (*fig*) *confession etc* arracher (*from sb* à qn); *money* soutirer (*from sb* à qn). ♦ **wringer** *n* essoreuse *f*. ♦ **wringing (wet)** *adj garment* trempé; *person* trempé jusqu'aux os.

wrinkle [ˈrɪŋkl] **1** *n* (*on skin, fruit*) ride *f*; (*in stockings, cloth etc*) pli *m*. **2** *vt* (**~ up**) *skin* rider; *forehead* plisser; *nose* froncer; *rug, sheet* faire des plis dans. **3** *vi* se plisser; se froncer; faire des plis. ♦ **wrinkled** *adj skin, apple* ridé; *brow* plissé; *nose* froncé; *sheet, sweater* qui fait des plis.

wrist [rɪst] *n* poignet *m*. ♦ **wristband** *n [shirt etc]* poignet *m*; *[watch etc]* bracelet *m*. ♦ **wrist-watch** *n* montre-bracelet *f*.

writ [rɪt] *n* (*Jur*) acte *m* judiciaire. **to issue a ~ against sb, to serve a ~ on sb** assigner qn en justice (*for libel etc* pour diffamation *etc*); **~ of habeas corpus** ordre *m* (écrit) d'habeas corpus.

write [raɪt] *pret* **wrote**, *ptp* **written 1** *vt* (*gen*) écrire; *cheque, list, bill* faire; *prescription, certificate* rédiger. **how is it written?** comment est-ce que ça s'écrit?; (*fig*) **it was written all over his face** cela se lisait sur son visage; (*fig*) **he had 'policeman' written all over him*** cela sautait aux yeux qu'il était policier.

2 *vi* écrire (*to sb* à qn; *on, about sth* sur qch). **he can read and ~** il sait lire et écrire; **~ on both sides of the paper** écrivez des deux côtés de la feuille; **he had always wanted to ~** il avait toujours voulu écrire *or* être écrivain; **what shall I ~ about?** sur quoi est-ce que je vais écrire?; (*Comm*) **~ for our brochure** demandez notre brochure.

write away *vi* (*Comm etc*) **to ~ away for** *form, details* écrire pour demander; *goods* commander par lettre.

write back *vi* répondre (par lettre).

write down *vt sep* écrire; (*note*) noter; (*put in writing*) mettre par écrit.

write in 1 *vi*: **a lot of people have written in** beaucoup de gens nous ont écrit; **to ~ in for sth** écrire pour demander qch. **2** *vt sep word, item on list etc* ajouter.

write off 1 *vi* = **write away**. **2** *vt sep debt* passer aux profits et pertes; *operation, scheme* mettre un terme à; (*smash up*) *car, machine* détruire, bousiller*. (*fig*) **I've written off the whole thing** j'ai fait une croix dessus*, je le considère comme perdu; (*fig*) **he had been written off as a failure** on avait décidé qu'il ne ferait jamais rien de bon.

write out *vt sep* (*gen*) écrire; *cheque, list, bill* faire; *prescription, bill* rédiger; (*copy*) *essay etc* recopier.

write up *vt sep notes, diary* mettre à jour; (*write report on*) *developments etc* faire un compte rendu de; (*record*) (*Chem etc*) *experiment* rédiger; (*Archeol etc*) *one's findings* consigner. **to ~ sth up in a notebook** consigner qch dans un agenda.

♦ **write-off** *n* (*Comm*) perte *f* sèche; (*fig*) **the car** *etc* **was a ~-off** la voiture *etc* était bonne pour la ferraille. ♦ **writer** *n* (*of letter, book etc*) auteur *m*; (*as profession*) écrivain *m*; **a thriller ~r** un auteur de romans policiers; **he is a ~r** il est écrivain, c'est un écrivain; **to be a good/bad ~r** écrire bien/mal; **~r's cramp** crampe *f* des écrivains. ♦ **write-up** *n* (*Press*) compte rendu *m* (*about* de); (*review*) critique *f*. ♦ **writing** *n* (*handwriting*) écriture *f*; (*sth written*) qch d'écrit; **in his own writing** écrit de sa main; (*fig*) **he saw the writing on the wall** il a vu le signe sur le mur; **to put sth in writing** mettre qch par écrit; **he devoted his life to writing** il a consacré sa vie à son œuvre d'écrivain; **writing is his hobby** écrire est son passe-temps favori; **in this author's writing(s)** dans les écrits *mpl* de cet auteur. ♦ **writing-case** *n* nécessaire *m* de correspondance. ♦ **writing-desk** *n* secrétaire *m* (*bureau*). ♦ **writing-pad** *n* bloc *m* de papier à lettres, bloc-notes *m*. ♦ **writing-paper** *n* papier *m* à lettres. ♦ **writing-table** *n* bureau *m*. ♦ **written** *adj* (*gen*) écrit, par écrit; *evidence* par écrit; **written exam** écrit *m*.

wrong [rɒŋ] **1** *adj* **(a)** (*bad*) mal *inv*; (*unfair*) injuste. **it is ~ to lie, lying is ~** c'est mal de mentir; **it is ~ that she should do that** il est injuste qu'elle fasse cela; **what's ~ with going to the pictures?** quel mal y a-t-il à aller au cinéma?; **there's nothing ~ in that** il n'y a rien à redire à ça; **there's nothing ~ in** *or* **with doing that** il n'y a aucun mal à faire cela.

(b) (*incorrect*) *belief, guess* erroné; *answer, calculation* faux, inexact; (*Mus*) *note* faux. **to be ~** se tromper (*about* sur, à propos de), avoir tort (*to do, in doing* de faire); **you were ~ to hit him** tu as eu tort de le frapper; **my watch is ~** ma montre n'est pas à l'heure; **to get sth ~** se tromper dans qch; **they got it ~ again** ils se sont encore trompés; **he told me the ~ time** (*gen*) il ne m'a pas donné l'heure exacte; (*for appointment etc*) il ne m'a pas donné la bonne heure; **at the ~ time** à un moment inopportun; **the letter has the ~ date on it** ils se sont trompés de date sur la lettre; (*Telec*) **to get a ~ number** se tromper de numéro; **that's the ~ number** ce n'est pas le bon numéro; **he got on the ~ train** il s'est trompé de train, il n'a pas pris le bon train; (*fig*) **you're on the ~ road** vous faites fausse route; **I'm in the ~ job** ce n'est pas le travail qu'il me faut; **he's got the ~ kind of friends** il a de mauvaises fréquentations; **that's the ~ kind of plug** ce n'est pas la prise qu'il faut; **to say the ~ thing** dire ce qu'il ne fallait pas dire;

that's the ~ way to go about it ce n'est pas comme ça qu'il faut s'y prendre; **the bread went down the ~ way** j'ai avalé le pain de travers; **on the ~ side** du mauvais côté; (*fig*) **he got out of bed on the ~ side, he got out of the ~ side of the bed** il s'est levé du pied gauche; **the ~ side of the cloth** le mauvais côté *or* l'envers *m* du tissu; **he's on the ~ side of forty** il a dépassé la quarantaine; (*fig*) **to get on the ~ side of sb** se faire mal voir de qn; **it's in the ~ place** ce n'est pas à sa place.

(c) (*amiss*) **sth's ~** *or* **there's sth ~ (with it** *or* **him** *etc*) il y a qch qui ne va pas; **sth's ~ with my leg** j'ai qch à la jambe; **sth's ~ with my watch** ma montre ne marche pas comme il faut; **what's ~?** qu'est-ce qui ne va pas?; **there's sth ~** il y a qch qui cloche*; **what's ~ with you?** qu'est-ce que vous avez?; **what's ~ with your arm?** qu'est-ce que vous avez au bras?; **what's ~ with the car?** qu'est-ce qu'elle a, la voiture?; **there's nothing ~** tout va bien; **nothing ~, I hope?** tout va bien, j'espère?; **there's nothing ~ with it** (*theory, translation*) c'est tout à fait correct; (*method, plan*) c'est tout à fait valable; (*machine, car*) ça marche très bien; **there's nothing ~ with him** il va très bien.

2 *adv answer, guess* mal, incorrectement. **you've spelt it ~** vous l'avez mal écrit; **you're doing it all ~** tu t'y prends mal; **you did ~ to refuse** vous avez eu tort de refuser; **you've got it ~** vous avez fait une erreur, (*misunderstood*) vous avez mal compris; **don't get me ~*** comprends-moi bien; **to go ~** (*gen*) se tromper; (*on road*) se tromper de route; *[plan]* mal tourner; *[business deal etc]* tomber à l'eau; *[machine, car]* tomber en panne; *[clock, watch etc]* se détraquer; **you can't go ~** c'est très simple; **you won't go far ~ if ...** vous ne pouvez guère vous tromper si ...; **sth went ~** il est arrivé qch; **sth went ~ with the gears** qch s'est détraqué dans l'embrayage; **nothing can go ~ now** tout doit marcher comme sur des roulettes maintenant; **everything went ~** tout est allé de travers.

3 *n* **(a)** (*evil*) mal *m*. **to do ~** mal agir; (*fig*) **he can do no ~ in her eyes** il lui semble parfait. **(b)** (*injustice*) injustice *f*. **he suffered great ~** il a été la victime de graves injustices; **to right a ~** réparer une injustice. **(c) to be/put sb in the ~** être/mettre qn dans son tort.

4 *vt* faire tort à.

♦ **wrongdoer** *n* malfaiteur *m*, -trice *f*. ♦ **wrongdoing** *n* méfaits *mpl*. ♦ **wrongful** *adj arrest* arbitraire; *accusation, dismissal* injustifié. ♦ **wrongfully** *adv* à tort. ♦ **wrong-headed** *adj* buté. ♦ **wrongly** *adv answer, do, count, state* incorrectement; *treat* injustement; *accuse, dismiss* à tort.

wrote [rəʊt] *pret of* **write.**

wrought [rɔːt] *adj iron* forgé; *silver* ouvré. ♦ **wrought-iron** *adj* en fer forgé. ♦ **wrought-up** *adj* très tendu.

wrung [rʌŋ] *pret, ptp of* **wring.**

wry [raɪ] *adj* désabusé. **to make a ~ face** faire la grimace. ♦ **wryly** *adv* avec une ironie désabusée.

XYZ

X, x [eks] *n* (*letter*) X, x *m*; (*Math*) x *m*. **for x years** pendant x années; **X marks the spot** l'endroit est marqué d'une croix. ♦ **X-certificate** *adj film* interdit aux moins de 18 ans. ♦ **X-ray 1** *n* (*ray*) rayon *m* X; (*photo*) radiographie *f*, radio* *f*; **to have an X-ray** se faire radiographier, se faire faire une radio*; **2** *vt* radiographier; **3** *adj examination* radioscopique; **X-ray photo** radio* *f*; **X-ray treatment** radiothérapie *f*.
Xerox ['zɪərɒks] *vt* ® photocopier.
Xmas ['krɪsməs, 'eksməs] *n abbr of* **Christmas.**
xylophone ['zaɪləfəʊn] *n* xylophone *m*.

Y, y [waɪ] *n* (*letter*) Y, y *m*. **Y-fronts** ® slip *m* (d'homme); **Y-shaped** en forme d'Y.
yacht [jɒt] **1** *n* yacht *m*. **2** *vi*: **to go ~ing** faire de la navigation de plaisance. **3** *adj*: **~ club** cercle *m* nautique. ♦ **yachting 1** *n* yachting *m*, navigation *f* de plaisance; **2** *adj cap* de marin; *magazine etc* de la voile. ♦ **yachtsman** *n* plaisancier *m*.
yak[1] [jæk] *n* (*Zool*) yak *m*.
yak[2]* [jæk] *vi* (*also* **yackety-yak**) caqueter.
yam [jæm] *n* igname *f*; (*sweet potato*) patate *f*.
yank [jæŋk] **1** *n* coup sec. **2** *vt* tirer d'un coup sec. **to ~ sth off** *or* **out** arracher qch.
Yank* [jæŋk] **1** *adj* amerloque‡ (*pej*). **2** *n* Amerloque‡ *mf* (*pej*). ♦ **Yankee*** *n* Yankee *mf*.
yap [jæp] **1** *vi* [*dog*] japper; (*) [*person*] jacasser. **2** *n* jappement *m*. ♦ **yapping 1** *adj dog* jappeur; **2** *n* jappements *mpl*.
yard[1] [jɑːd] *n* **(a)** yard *m* (*91,44 cm*), ≈ mètre *m*. **about a ~ long** long d'un mètre; **by the ~** au mètre; (*fig*) **~s of*** des kilomètres de*. **(b)** (*Naut*) vergue *f*. ♦ **yardage** *n* ≈ métrage *m*. ♦ **yardarm** *n* bout *m* de vergue. ♦ **yardstick** *n* (*fig*) mesure *f*.
yard[2] [jɑːd] *n* (*gen*) cour *f*; (*US: garden*) jardin *m*; (*work-site*) chantier *m*; (*for storage*) dépôt *m*. **back ~** cour de derrière; **builder's/shipbuilding ~** chantier de construction/de construction navale; **timber/coal ~** dépôt de bois/de charbon; (*Brit*) **the Y~, Scotland Y~** Scotland Yard *m* (≈ *le Quai des Orfèvres*).
yarn [jɑːn] *n* **(a)** fil *m*; (*Tech: for weaving*) filé *m*. **nylon etc ~** fil de nylon *etc*. **(b)** (*tale*) longue histoire *f*.
yawn [jɔːn] **1** *vi* [*person*] bâiller (*with boredom* d'ennui); [*chasm etc*] s'ouvrir. **2** *vt*: **to ~ one's head off** bâiller à se décrocher la mâchoire; **'no' he ~ed** 'non' dit-il en bâillant. **3** *n* bâillement *m*. **to give a ~** bâiller. ♦ **yawning** *adj chasm* béant.
yeah* [jɛə] *particle* oui, ouais*.
year [jɪə^r] *n* **(a)** an *m*, année *f*. **this ~** cette année; **next ~** l'an prochain, l'année prochaine; **3 times a ~** 3 fois l'an *or* par an; **in the ~ of grace/of Our Lord** en l'an de grâce/de Notre Seigneur; **in the ~ 1969** en 1969; **~ by ~, from ~ to ~** d'année en année; **from one ~ to the other** d'une année à l'autre; **~ in, ~ out** année après année; **all the ~ round** d'un bout de l'année à l'autre; **over the ~s, as the ~s go by** au fil des années; **taking the good ~s with the bad** bon an mal an; **~s and ~s ago** il y a bien des années; **for ~s together** plusieurs années de suite; **to pay by the ~** payer à l'année; **valid one ~** valide un an; **a ~ last January** il y a eu un an au mois de janvier; **they have not met for ~s** ils ne se sont pas vus depuis des années; (*fig*) **I've been waiting for ~s*** ça fait une éternité que j'attends; **15 ~s' imprisonment** 15 ans de prison; **he is 6 ~s old** il a 6 ans; **in his fortieth ~** dans sa quarantième année; **£10 a ~** 10 livres par an; **that new hat takes ~s off her** ce nouveau chapeau la rajeunit. **(b)** (*age*) **young for his ~s** jeune pour son âge; **to get on in ~s** prendre de l'âge; **~s of discretion** l'âge adulte (*fig*). **(c)** (*Scol, Univ*) année *f*. **she was in my ~ at school** elle était de mon année au lycée; **in the second ~** (*Univ*) en deuxième année; (*school*) ≈ en cinquième. **(d)** [*coin, stamp, wine*] année *f*. ♦ **yearbook** *n* annuaire *m* (*d'un organisme etc*). ♦ **yearling** *n* animal *m* d'un an; (*racehorse*) yearling *m*. ♦ **yearly 1** *adj* annuel; **2** *adv* annuellement; **twice ~ly** deux fois par an.
yearn [jɜːn] *vi* languir (*for sb* après qn), aspirer (*for sth* à qch; *to do* à faire). **to ~ for home** avoir la nostalgie de chez soi. ♦ **yearning** *n* désir *m* ardent (*for* de; *to do* de faire).
yeast [jiːst] *n* levure *f*. **dried ~** levure déshydratée.
yell [jel] **1** *n* (*gen*) hurlement *m*, cri *m* (*of* de). **to give a ~** pousser un hurlement *or* un cri; **a ~ of laughter** un grand éclat de rire. **2** *vti* (**~ out**) hurler (*with* de). ♦ **yelling 1** *n* hurlements *mpl*; **2** *adj* hurlant.
yellow ['jeləʊ] **1** *adj object etc* jaune; *hair, curls* blond; (*fig: cowardly*) lâche. **to go** *or* **turn ~** jaunir; (*Med*) **~ fever** fièvre *f* jaune; (*Telec*) **the ~ pages** ≈ l'annuaire *m* des professions. **2** *n* (*colour: also of egg*) jaune *m*. **3** *vti* jaunir. **~ed with age** jauni par le temps. ♦ **yellowhammer** *n* (*bird*) bruant *m* jaune.
yelp [jelp] **1** *n* [*dog*] jappement *m*; [*fox*] glapissement *m*. **2** *vi* japper; glapir. ♦ **yelping 1** *n* jappements *mpl*; glapissements *mpl*; **2** *adj* jappeur; glapissant.
yen* [jen] *n*: **to have a ~ for sth/to do** avoir grande envie de qch/de faire.
yep‡ [jep] *particle* ouais*, oui.
yes [jes] **1** *particle* oui; (*answering neg question or contradicting*) si. **to say ~** dire oui; **~ certainly** mais oui. **2** *n* oui *m inv*. ♦ **yes-man** *n* béni-oui-oui* *m inv* (*pej*); **he's a ~-man** il dit amen à tout.
yesterday ['jestədeɪ] **1** *adv, n* hier (*m*). **all (day) ~** toute la journée d'hier; **a week (from) ~** d'hier en huit; **a week (past) ~, ~ week** il y a eu hier huit jours; **late ~** hier dans la soirée; **~ was the second** c'était hier le deux; **~ was Friday** c'était hier vendredi; **~ was very wet** il a beaucoup plu hier; **~ was a bad day for him** la journée d'hier s'est mal passée pour lui; **the day before ~** avant-hier (*m*); (*fig*) **the great men of ~** tous les grands hommes du passé *or* d'hier; **all our ~s** tout notre passé. **2** *adj*: **~ evening/morning** hier soir/matin.
yet [jet] **1** *adv* **(a)** (*as ~, still*) encore; (*till now*) jusqu'ici; (*till then*) jusqu'alors. **they haven't ~ returned** ils ne sont pas encore *or* ne sont toujours pas revenus; **no one has come ~** jusqu'ici, personne n'est venu; **no one had come ~** jusqu'alors, personne n'était venu; **places we have ~ to see** des endroits qu'il nous reste encore à voir, des endroits que nous n'avons pas encore vus; **~ more difficult** encore plus difficile; **~ once more**

encore une fois, une fois de plus; **and ~ another** et encore un autre; **he may ~ come** il peut encore *or* toujours venir; **I'll do it ~** je finirai bien par le faire. **(b)** (*so far*) **has he arrived ~?** est-il déjà arrivé?; **I wonder if he's come ~** je me demande s'il est arrivé maintenant; **not (just) ~** pas encore; **don't come in (just) ~** n'entrez pas encore; **must you go just ~?** faut-il que vous partiez (*subj*) déjà?; **I needn't go just ~** je n'ai pas besoin de partir tout de suite. **(c) nor ~** ni, et ... non plus; **I do not like him nor ~ his sister** je ne les aime ni lui ni sa sœur, je ne l'aime pas et sa sœur non plus. **2** *conj* pourtant, néanmoins, quand même. **and ~ everyone liked her** et pourtant *or* néanmoins tout le monde l'aimait, mais tout le monde l'aimait quand même; **strange ~ true** étrange mais pourtant vrai.

yew [juː] *n* if *m*.

Yiddish ['jɪdɪʃ] *n* yiddish *m*.

yield [jiːld] **1** *vt* **(a)** (*produce etc: gen*) rendre; *[mine, oil well]* débiter; *[an industry]* produire; *[business, tax, shares] amount, profit* rapporter; *opportunity* fournir; *results* produire. **(b)** (*surrender: gen, Mil*) céder (*to* à). **2** *vi* (*give way: gen, Mil*) céder (*to* devant), se rendre (*to* à); *[ice, door etc]* céder. **they begged him but he would not ~** ils l'ont supplié mais il n'a pas cédé; (*Mil etc*) **they ~ed to us** ils se rendirent à nous; **to ~ to temptation** succomber à la tentation. **3** *n* (*V* **1a**) rendement *m*; débit *m*; production *f*; rapport *m*.

yippee* [jɪ'piː] *excl* hourra!

yob(bo)* ['jɒb(əʊ)] *n* (*pej*) loubard *m* (*pej*).

yod [jɒd] *n* (*Ling*) yod *m*.

yodel ['jəʊdl] *vi* faire des tyroliennes.

yoga ['jəʊgə] *n* yoga *m*. ♦ **yogi** *n* yogi *m*.

yoghourt, yog(h)urt ['jəʊgət] *n* yaourt *m*.

yoke [jəʊk] **1** *n* **(a)** (*lit, fig*) joug *m*. **under the ~ of** sous le joug de. **(b)** *[dress, blouse]* empiècement *m*. **2** *vt* accoupler.

yokel ['jəʊkəl] *n* rustre *m*.

yolk [jəʊk] *n* jaune *m* (d'œuf).

yonder ['jɒndə^r] *adv* (**over ~**) là-bas.

you [juː] *pers pron* **(a)** (*subject*) tu, vous; (*object*) te, vous; (*stressed and after prep*) toi, vous. **~ are very kind** tu es très gentil, vous êtes très gentil(s); **I shall see ~ soon** je te *or* je vous verrai bientôt; **for ~** pour toi *or* vous; **younger than ~** plus jeune que toi *or* vous; **~ and yours** toi et les tiens, vous et les vôtres; **~ French** vous autres Français; **~ and I will go together** toi et moi *or* vous et moi, nous irons ensemble; **~ fool!** espèce d'imbécile!; **~ darling!** tu es un amour!; **it's ~** c'est toi *or* vous; **there's a fine house for ~!** en voilà une belle maison! **(b)** (*one, anyone*) (*nominative*) on; (*accusative, dative*) vous, te. **~ never know your luck** on ne connaît jamais son bonheur; **fresh air does ~ good** l'air frais (vous *or* te) fait du bien.

♦ **your** [jʊə^r] *poss adj* **(a)** ton, ta, tes; votre, vos; **~r book** ton *or* votre livre; **YOUR book** ton livre à toi, votre livre à vous; **~r table** ta *or* votre table; **~r friend** ton ami(e), votre ami(e); **~r clothes** tes *or* vos vêtements; **give me ~r hand** donne-moi la main; **(b)** (*one's*) son, sa, ses; ton *etc*, votre *etc*; **you give him ~r form and he gives you ~r pass** on lui donne son formulaire et il vous remet votre laissez-passer; **it's good for ~r health** c'est bon pour la santé; **~r ordinary Englishman** l'Anglais moyen. ♦ **you're = you are.** ♦ **yours** *poss pron* le tien, la tienne, les tiens, les tiennes; le vôtre, la vôtre, les vôtres; **this book is ~rs** ce livre est à toi *or* à vous, ce livre est le tien *or* le vôtre; **a cousin of ~rs** un de tes *or* de vos cousins; **it's no fault of ~rs** ce n'est pas de votre faute (à vous); (*pej*) **that dog of ~rs** ton *or* votre sacré* *or* fichu* chien; (*in pub etc*) **what's ~rs?** qu'est-ce que tu prends *or* vous prenez? ♦ **yourself** *pers pron, pl* **-selves** (*reflexive*) te, vous; (*after prep*) toi, vous; (*emphatic*) toi-même, vous-même; **have you hurt ~rself?** tu t'es fait mal?, vous vous êtes fait mal?; **you never speak of ~rself** tu ne parles jamais de toi, vous ne parlez jamais de vous; **you told me ~rself** tu me l'as dit toi-même, vous me l'avez dit vous-même; **all by ~rself** tout seul.

young [jʌŋ] **1** *adj* (*gen*) jeune. **~ people** jeunes *mpl*, jeunes gens *mpl*; **~ lady** (*unmarried*) jeune fille *f*; (*married*) jeune femme *f*; **listen to me, ~ man** écoutez-moi, jeune homme; **~ at heart** jeune de cœur; **~ for his age** jeune pour son âge; **to marry ~** se marier jeune; **3 years ~er than you** plus jeune que vous de 3 ans; **my ~er brother** mon frère cadet; **my ~er sister** ma sœur cadette; **the ~er son** le cadet; **I'm not so ~ as I was** je n'ai plus mes vingt ans; **in my ~ days** quand j'étais jeune; **to grow** *or* **get ~er** rajeunir; **if I were ~er** si j'étais plus jeune; **if I were 10 years ~er** si j'avais 10 ans de moins; **you're only ~ once** jeunesse n'a qu'un temps; **~ Mr Brown, Mr Brown the ~er** le jeune M. Brown; (*as opposed to his father*) M. Brown fils; **the ~er generation** la jeune génération; **the ~ idea** ce que pensent les jeunes, (*fig*) la jeune génération; **~ wine** vin *m* vert; **~ nation** nouvelle nation *f*; (*fig*) **~ blood** sang *m* nouveau *or* jeune. **2** *npl* **(a) the ~** les jeunes *mpl*, les jeunes gens *mpl*; **~ and old** les jeunes commes les vieux; **books for the ~** livres pour les jeunes *or* la jeunesse. **(b)** *[animal]* petits *mpl*. ♦ **youngster** *n* jeune *mf*.

youth [juːθ] **1** *n* **(a)** jeunesse *f*. **in my ~** dans ma jeunesse, lorsque j'étais jeune; **in early ~** dans la première jeunesse. **(b)** (*young man*) jeune homme *m*. **~s** jeunes gens *mpl*. **(c)** (*collective: young people*) jeunesse *f*, jeunes *mpl*. **the ~ of a country** la jeunesse d'un pays; **the ~ of today** les jeunes *or* la jeunesse d'aujourd'hui. **2** *adj orchestra etc* de jeunes, de jeunesse. **~ club** foyer *m* *or* centre *m* de jeunes; **~ hostel** *V* **hostel**; **~ leader** animateur *m*, -trice *f* de groupes de jeunes; **~ movement** mouvement *m* de la jeunesse. ♦ **youthful** *adj* (*gen*) jeune; *air, mistake* de jeunesse; *quality, freshness* juvénile. ♦ **youthfulness** *n* jeunesse *f*.

yowl [jaʊl] *vi [person, dog]* hurler; *[cat]* miauler.

yucky*, **yukky*** ['jʌkɪ] *adj* dégoûtant.

Yugoslavia ['juːgəʊ'slɑːvɪə] *n* Yougoslavie *f*.

Yule [juːl] *n* (†) Noël *m*. **~ log** bûche *f* de Noël. ♦ **Yuletide**† *n* époque *f* de Noël.

yummy* ['jʌmɪ] **1** *adj food* délicieux. **2** *excl* miam, miam!*

Z, z [zed, (*US*) ziː] *n* (*letter*) Z, z *m*.

zany ['zeɪnɪ] *adj* dingue*, fou.

zeal [ziːl] *n* zèle *m* (*for* pour). ♦ **zealot** ['zelət] *n* fanatique *mf*. ♦ **zealous** ['zeləs] *adj* (*fervent*) zélé; (*devoted*) dévoué; **~ous for** plein de zèle pour. ♦ **zealously** *adv* avec zèle.

zebra ['ziːbrə] **1** *n* zèbre *m*. **2** *adj* (*Brit*) **~ crossing** passage *m* pour piétons.

zed [zed], (*US*) **zee** [ziː] *n* (la lettre) z *m*.

zenith ['zenɪθ] *n* zénith *m*.

zephyr ['zefə^r] *n* zéphyr *m*.

zero ['zɪərəʊ] **1** *n,pl* **-s** *or* **-es** zéro *m*. **2** *adj tension, voltage* nul; *altitude, growth* zéro *inv*. **~ hour** (*Mil*) l'heure H; (*fig*) le moment décisif. **3** *vi*: **to ~ in on sth** piquer droit sur qch.

zest [zest] *n* **(a)** (*gusto*) entrain *m*; (*fig: spice*) piquant *m*. **with ~** (*gen*) avec entrain; *eat* avec grand appétit; **~ for living** appétit *m* de vivre; **it adds ~ to the episode** cela donne du piquant à l'histoire. **(b)** (*Culin: of orange etc*) zeste *m*. ♦ **zestful** *adj* plein d'entrain.

zigzag ['zɪgzæg] **1** *n* zigzag *m*. **2** *adj path, course, line* en zigzag; *road* en lacets; *pattern, design* à zigzags. **3** *adv* en zigzag. **4** *vi* zigzaguer. **to ~ out/**

through *etc* sortir/traverser *etc* en zigzaguant.
zinc [zɪŋk] **1** *n* zinc *m*. **2** *adj plate, alloy* de zinc; *roof* zingué.
Zionism ['zaɪənɪzəm] *n* sionisme *m*.
zip [zɪp] **1** *n* **(a)** (*also* ~ **fastener, zipper**) fermeture *f* éclair ®. **pocket with a** ~ poche *f* à fermeture éclair, poche zippée*. **(b)** (*: *energy etc*) entrain *m*. **put a bit of** ~ **into it*** activez-vous! **2** *adj* (*US Post*) ~ **code** code *m* postal. **3** *vt* (~ **up**) *dress, bag* fermer avec une fermeture éclair ®. **to** ~ **sth on** attacher qch avec une fermeture éclair; **she** ~**ped open her bag** elle a ouvert la fermeture éclair de son sac. **4** *vi* **(a)** *[garment etc]* **to** ~ **up/on** *etc* se fermer/s'attacher *etc* avec une fermeture éclair ®. **(b)** (*) *[car, person]* **to** ~ **in/past** *etc* entrer/passer *etc* comme une flèche. ♦ **zip-on** *adj* à fermeture éclair ®.
zircon ['zɜːkən] *n* zircon *m*.
zither ['zɪðəʳ] *n* cithare *f*.
zodiac ['zəʊdɪæk] *n* zodiaque *m*.
zombie* ['zɒmbɪ] *n* (*fig pej*) automate *m*.
zone [zəʊn] **1** *n* (*gen*) zone *f*; (*esp Mil*) (*area*) zone; (*subdivision of town*) secteur *m*. **danger** ~ zone dangereuse. **2** *vt* (*divide into* ~*s*) *area* diviser en zones. **district** ~**d for industry** zone réservée à l'implantation industrielle.
♦ **zonal** *adj* zonal. ♦ **zoning** *n* répartition *f* en zones.
zoo [zuː] *n* zoo *m*. ~ **keeper** gardien(ne) *m(f)* de zoo.
zoology [zəʊ'ɒlədʒɪ] *n* zoologie *f*. ♦ **zoological** *adj* zoologique; **zoological gardens** jardin *m* zoologique. ♦ **zoologist** *n* zoologiste *mf*.
zoom [zuːm] **1** *n* vrombissement *m*. **2** *vi* vrombir. **to** ~ **away/through** *etc* démarrer/traverser *etc* en trombe; (*Cine*) **to** ~ **in** faire un zoom (*on* sur).
♦ **zoom lens** *n* (*Phot*) zoom *m*.
zucchini [zuː'kiːnɪ] *n* (*US*) courgette *f*.

VERBES ANGLAIS À PARTICULE

(a) *vi* = verbe intransitif. ex: **blow off** dans 'his hat blew off'.
(b) *vt sep* = verbe transitif séparable. ex: **blow off** dans 'the wind blew off his hat' ou 'the wind blew his hat off'. Le complément d'objet du verbe peut se mettre soit après la particule, soit entre les deux éléments du verbe en les séparant. Cette dernière structure est d'ailleurs obligatoire lorsque le complément d'objet est un pronom: 'the wind blew it off'.
(c) *vt fus* = verbe transitif fusionné. ex: **admit to** dans 'he admitted to the theft'. Le complément d'objet ne peut jamais s'intercaler entre les deux éléments du verbe, même lorsqu'il s'agit d'un pronom: 'he admitted to it'.
(d) pour beaucoup de verbes qui indiquent un mouvement ou une direction, les verbes à particule correspondants n'ont pas été dissociés de l'article principal, car ils peuvent être déduits des illustrations fournies. Ainsi, à partir de **crawl 2** *vi* (*gén*) ramper; ... **to ~ in/out** *etc* entrer/sortir *etc* en rampant ... vous pouvez construire: 'to crawl across' (traverser en rampant), 'to crawl down' (descendre en rampant) etc.

Verbes forts anglais

Le prétérit et le participe passé des verbes forts anglais sont mentionnés directement après le mot souche.

ENGLISH PHRASAL VERBS

(a) *vi* = verb intransitive, e.g. **blow off** in 'his hat blew off'.
(b) *vt sep* = verb transitive separable, e.g. **blow off** in 'the wind blew off his hat'. The object of the verb may either come after the second part of the phrasal verb, as in this example, or between the two parts ('the wind blew it off').
(c) *vt fus* = verb transitive fused, e.g. **admit to** in 'he admitted to the theft', where the object of the phrasal verb never comes between the two parts (always 'he admitted to it', never 'he admitted it to').
(d) Note that for many verbs which involve movement and direction e.g. 'crawl', the related phrasal verbs have not been taken out of the main verb entry, as they may be constructed on the basis of the samples shown. Thus at **crawl 2** *vi* (*gen*) ramper; ... **to ~ in/out** *etc* entrer/sortir *etc* en rampant ... : you can form from that 'to crawl across' (traverser en rampant), 'to crawl down' (descendre en rampant) and so on.

English Strong Verbs

The forms of the English strong verbs are indicated immediately after the headword.

LE VERBE FRANÇAIS

THE FRENCH VERB

	Present	*Imperfect*	*Future*	*Past Historic*	*Past Part.*	*Subjunctive*
(1) **arriver** (regular: see table at the end of the list)						
(2) **finir** (regular: see table)						
(3) **placer**	je place nous plaçons	je plaçais	je placerai	je plaçai	placé	que je place
bouger	je bouge nous bougeons	je bougeais	je bougerai	je bougeai	bougé	que je bouge
(4) **appeler**	j'appelle nous appelons	j'appelais	j'appellerai	j'appelai	appelé	que j'appelle
jeter	je jette nous jetons	je jetais	je jetterai	je jetai	jeté	que je jette
(5) **geler**	je gèle nous gelons	je gelais	je gèlerai	je gelai	gelé	que je gèle
(6) **céder**	je cède nous cédons	je cédais	je céderai	je cédai	cédé	que je cède
(7) **épier**	j'épie nous épions	j'épiais	j'épierai	j'épiai	épié	que j'épie
(8) **noyer**	je noie nous noyons	je noyais	je noierai	je noyai	noyé	que je noie
envoyer			j'enverrai			
payer	je paie *ou* paye		je paierai *ou* payerai			que je paie *ou* paye
(9) **aller** (see table)						
(10) **haïr**	je hais il hait nous haïssons ils haïssent	je haïssais	je haïrai	je haïs	haï	que je haïsse
(11) **courir**	je cours il court nous courons	je courais	je courrai	je courus	couru	que je coure
(12) **cueillir**	je cueille nous cueillons	je cueillais	je cueillerai	je cueillis	cueilli	que je cueille
(13) **assaillir**	j'assaille nous assaillons	j'assaillais	j'assaillirai	j'assaillis	assailli	que j'assaille
(14) **servir**	je sers il sert nous servons	je servais	je servirai	je servis	servi	que je serve
(15) **bouillir**	je bous il bout nous bouillons	je bouillais	je bouillirai	je bouillis	bouilli	que je bouille
(16) **partir**	je pars il part nous partons	je partais	je partirai	je partis	parti	que je parte
(17) **fuir**	je fuis il fuit nous fuyons ils fuient	je fuyais	je fuirai	je fuis	fui	que je fuie
(18) **couvrir**	je couvre nous couvrons	je couvrais	je couvrirai	je couvris	couvert	que je couvre

	Present	Imperfect	Future	Past Historic	Past Part.	Subjunctive
(19) **mourir**	je meurs il meurt nous mourons ils meurent	je mourais	je mourrai	je mourus	mort	que je meure
(20) **vêtir**	je vêts il vêt nous vêtons	je vêtais	je vêtirai	je vêtis	vêtu	que je vête
(21) **acquérir**	j'acquiers il acquiert nous acquérons ils acquièrent	j'acquérais	j'acquerrai	j'acquis	acquis	que j'acquière
(22) **venir**	je viens il vient nous venons ils viennent	je venais	je viendrai	je vins	venu	que je vienne
(23) **pleuvoir**	il pleut	il pleuvait	il pleuvra	il plut	plu	qu'il pleuve
(24) **prévoir**	je prévois il prévoit nous prévoyons ils prévoient	je prévoyais	je prévoirai	je prévis	prévu	que je prévoie
(25) **pourvoir**	je pourvois il pourvoit nous pourvoyons ils pourvoient	je pourvoyais	je pourvoirai	je pourvus	pourvu	que je pourvoie
(26) **asseoir**	j'assois il assoit nous assoyons ils assoient *ou* j'assieds il assied nous asseyons ils asseyent	j'assoyais *ou* j'asseyais	j'assoirai *ou* j'asseyerai *ou* j'assiérai	j'assis	assis	que j'assoie *ou* que j'asseye
(27) **mouvoir**	je meus il meut nous mouvons ils meuvent	je mouvais nous mouvions	je mouvrai	je mus	mû	que je meuve
	N.B. *émouvoir* and *promouvoir* have the past participles *ému* and *promu* respectively.					
(28) **recevoir**	je reçois il reçoit nous recevons ils reçoivent	je recevais nous recevions	je recevrai	je reçus	reçu	que je reçoive
devoir					dû	
(29) **valoir**	je vaux il vaut nous valons	je valais nous valions	je vaudrai	je valus	valu	que je vaille
falloir	il faut	il fallait	il faudra	il fallut	fallu	qu'il faille
(30) **voir**	je vois il voit nous voyons ils voient	je voyais nous voyions	je verrai	je vis	vu	que je voie
(31) **vouloir**	je veux il veut nous voulons ils veulent	je voulais nous voulions	je voudrai	je voulus	voulu	que je veuille
(32) **savoir**	je sais il sait nous savons	je savais nous savions	je saurai	je sus	su	que je sache

	Present	*Imperfect*	*Future*	*Past Historic*	*Past Part.*	*Subjunctive*
(33) **pouvoir**	je peux *ou* puis il peut nous pouvons ils peuvent	je pouvais nous pouvions	je pourrai	je pus	pu	que je puisse
(34) **avoir** (see table)						
(35) **conclure** **inclure**	je conclus il conclut nous concluons	je concluais	je conclurai	je conclus	conclu inclus	que je conclue
(36) **rire**	je ris il rit nous rions ils rient	je riais	je rirai	je ris	ri	que je rie
(37) **dire** **suffire** **médire** *etc*	je dis il dit nous disons vous dites ils disent vous suffisez vous médisez *etc*	je disais	je dirai	je dis	dit	que je dise
(38) **nuire**	je nuis il nuit nous nuisons	je nuisais	je nuirai	je nuisis	nui	que je nuise
(39) **écrire**	j'écris il écrit nous écrivons	j'écrivais	j'écrirai	j'écrivis	écrit	que j'écrive
(40) **suivre**	je suis il suit nous suivons	je suivais	je suivrai	je suivis	suivi	que je suive
(41) **rendre** **rompre** **battre**	je rends il rend nous rendons il rompt je bats il bat nous battons	je rendais je battais	je rendrai je battrai	je rendis je battis	rendu battu	que je rende que je batte
(42) **vaincre**	je vaincs il vainc nous vainquons	je vainquais	je vaincrai	je vainquis	vaincu	que je vainque
(43) **lire**	je lis il lit nous lisons	je lisais	je lirai	je lus	lu	que je lise
(44) **croire**	je crois il croit nous croyons ils croient	je croyais	je croirai	je crus	cru	que je croie
(45) **clore**	je clos il clôt *ou* clot ils closent	je closais	je clorai	not applicable	clos	que je close
(46) **vivre**	je vis il vit nous vivons	je vivais	je vivrai	je vécus	vécu	que je vive
(47) **moudre**	je mouds il moud nous moulons	je moulais	je moudrai	je moulus	moulu	que je moule

	Present	Imperfect	Future	Past Historic	Past Part.	Subjunctive
(48) **coudre**	je couds il coud nous cousons	je cousais	je coudrai	je cousis	cousu	que je couse
(49) **joindre**	je joins il joint nous joignons	je joignais	je joindrai	je joignis	joint	que je joigne
(50) **traire**	je trais il trait nous trayons ils traient	je trayais	je trairai	not applicable	trait	que je traie
(51) **absoudre**	j'absous il absout nous absolvons	j'absolvais	j'absoudrai	j'absolus	absous	que j'absolve
résoudre					résolu	
(52) **craindre**	je crains il craint nous craignons	je craignais	je craindrai	je craignis	craint	que je craigne
peindre	je peins il peint nous peignons	je peignais	je peindrai	je peignis	peint	que je peigne
(53) **boire**	je bois il boit nous buvons ils boivent	je buvais	je boirai	je bus	bu	que je boive
(54) **plaire**	je plais il plaît nous plaisons	je plaisais	je plairai	je plus	plu	que je plaise
taire	il tait					
(55) **croître**	je croîs il croît nous croissons	je croissais	je croîtrai	je crûs	crû	que je croisse
	N.B. *accroître* and *décroître* have the past participles *accru* and *décru* respectively.					
(56) **mettre**	je mets il met nous mettons	je mettais	je mettrai	je mis	mis	que je mette
(57) **connaître**	je connais il connaît nous connaissons	je connaissais	je connaîtrai	je connus	connu	que je connaisse
(58) **prendre**	je prends il prend nous prenons ils prennent	je prenais	je prendrai	je pris	pris	que je prenne
(59) **naître**	je nais il naît nous naissons	je naissais	je naîtrai	je naquis	né	que je naisse

(60) **faire** (see table)

(61) **être** (see table)

1. **arriver** (regular verb)

INDICATIVE

Present
j'arrive
tu arrives
il arrive
nous arrivons
vous arrivez
ils arrivent

Imperfect
j'arrivais
tu arrivais
il arrivait
nous arrivions
vous arriviez
ils arrivaient

Past Historic
j'arrivai
tu arrivas
il arriva
nous arrivâmes
vous arrivâtes
ils arrivèrent

Future
j'arriverai
tu arriveras
il arrivera
nous arriverons
vous arriverez
ils arriveront

Perfect
je suis arrivé
nous sommes arrivés

Pluperfect
j'étais arrivé

Past Anterior
je fus arrivé

Future Perfect
je serai arrivé

Present Participle
arrivant

Past Participle
arrivé

CONDITIONAL

Present
j'arriverais
tu arriverais
il arriverait
nous arriverions
vous arriveriez
ils arriveraient

Past I
je serais arrivé

Past II
je fusse arrivé

IMPERATIVE

Present
arrive
arrivons
arrivez

Past
sois arrivé
soyons arrivés
soyez arrivés

SUBJUNCTIVE

Present
que j'arrive
que tu arrives
qu'il arrive
que nous arrivions
que vous arriviez
qu'ils arrivent

Imperfect
que j'arrivasse
que tu arrivasses
qu'il arrivât
que nous arrivassions
que vous arrivassiez
qu'ils arrivassent

Past
que je sois arrivé

Pluperfect
que je fusse arrivé

2. **finir** (regular verb)

INDICATIVE

Present
je finis
tu finis
il finit
nous finissons
vous finissez
ils finissent

Imperfect
je finissais
tu finissais
il finissait
nous finissions
vous finissiez
ils finissaient

Past Historic
je finis
tu finis
il finit
nous finîmes
vous finîtes
ils finirent

Future
je finirai
tu finiras
il finira
nous finirons
vous finirez
ils finiront

Perfect
j'ai fini
nous avons fini

Pluperfect
j'avais fini

Past Anterior
j'eus fini

Future Perfect
j'aurai fini

Present Participle
finissant

Past Participle
fini

CONDITIONAL

Present
je finirais
tu finirais
il finirait
nous finirions
vous finiriez
ils finiraient

Past I
j'aurais fini

Past II
j'eusse fini

IMPERATIVE

Present
finis
finissons
finissez

Past
aie fini
ayons fini
ayez fini

SUBJUNCTIVE

Present
que je finisse
que tu finisses
qu'il finisse
que nous finissions
que vous finissiez
qu'ils finissent

Imperfect
que je finisse
que tu finisses
qu'il finît
que nous finissions
que vous finissiez
qu'ils finissent

Past
que j'aie fini

Pluperfect
que j'eusse fini

9. aller

INDICATIVE

Present
je vais
tu vas
il va
nous allons
vous allez
ils vont

Imperfect
j'allais
tu allais
il allait
nous allions
vous alliez
ils allaient

Past Historic
j'allai
tu allas
il alla
nous allâmes
vous allâtes
ils allèrent

Future
j'irai
tu iras
il ira
nous irons
vous irez
ils iront

Present Participle
allant

Past Participle
allé

Past Infinitive
être allé

CONDITIONAL

Present
j'irais
tu irais
il irait
nous irions
vous iriez
ils iraient

IMPERATIVE

Present
va
allons
allez

Past
sois allé
soyons allés
soyez allés

SUBJUNCTIVE

Present
que j'aille
que tu ailles
qu'il aille
que nous allions
que vous alliez
qu'ils aillent

Imperfect
que j'allasse
que tu allasses
qu'il allât
que nous allassions
que vous allassiez
qu'ils allassent

34. avoir

INDICATIVE

Present
j'ai
tu as
il a
nous avons
vous avez
ils ont

Imperfect
j'avais
tu avais
il avait
nous avions
vous aviez
ils avaient

Past Historic
j'eus
tu eus
il eut
nous eûmes
vous eûtes
ils eurent

Future
j'aurai
tu auras
il aura
nous aurons
vous aurez
ils auront

Present Participle
ayant

Past Participle
eu

Past Infinitive
avoir eu

CONDITIONAL

Present
j'aurais
tu aurais
il aurait
nous aurions
vous auriez
ils auraient

IMPERATIVE

Present
aie
ayons
ayez

SUBJUNCTIVE

Present
que j'aie
que tu aies
qu'il ait
que nous ayons
que vous ayez
qu'ils aient

Imperfect
que j'eusse
que tu eusses
qu'il eût
que nous eussions
que vous eussiez
qu'ils eussent

60. **faire**

INDICATIVE

Present
je fais
tu fais
il fait
nous faisons
vous faites
ils font

Imperfect
je faisais
tu faisais
il faisait
nous faisions
vous faisiez
ils faisaient

Past Historic
je fis
tu fis
il fit
nous fîmes
vous fîtes
ils firent

Future
je ferai
tu feras
il fera
nous ferons
vous ferez
ils feront

Present Participle
faisant

Past Participle
fait

Past Infinitive
avoir fait

CONDITIONAL

Present
je ferais
tu ferais
il ferait
nous ferions
vous feriez
ils feraient

IMPERATIVE

Present
fais
faisons
faites

Past
aie fait
ayons fait
ayez fait

SUBJUNCTIVE

Present
que je fasse
que tu fasses
qu'il fasse
que nous fassions
que vous fassiez
qu'ils fassent

Imperfect
que je fisse
que tu fisses
qu'il fît
que nous fissions
que vous fissiez
qu'ils fissent

61. **être**

INDICATIVE

Present
je suis
tu es
il est
nous sommes
vous êtes
ils sont

Imperfect
j'étais
tu étais
il était
nous étions
vous étiez
ils étaient

Past Historic
je fus
tu fus
il fut
nous fûmes
vous fûtes
ils furent

Future
je serai
tu seras
il sera
nous serons
vous serez
ils seront

Present Participle
étant

Past Participle
été

Past Infinitive
avoir été

CONDITIONAL

Present
je serais
tu serais
il serait
nous serions
vous seriez
ils seraient

IMPERATIVE

Present
sois
soyons
soyez

SUBJUNCTIVE

Present
que je sois
que tu sois
qu'il soit
que nous soyons
que vous soyez
qu'ils soient

Imperfect
que je fusse
que tu fusses
qu'il fût
que nous fussions
que vous fussiez
qu'ils fussent

ABRÉVIATIONS ET SIGLES

ADN *nm* Acide désoxyribonucléique

AF *nfpl* Allocations familiales

AFP *nf* Agence France-Presse

AG *nf* Assemblée générale

ANPE *nf* Agence nationale pour l'emploi

Benelux [benelyks] *nm* Union douanière de la Belgique, du Luxembourg et des Pays-Bas

BEPC *nm* Brevet d'études du 1er cycle

BP *nf* Boîte postale

BT(S) *nm* Brevet de technicien (supérieur)

C. Celsius, centigrade

CAP *nm* Certificat d'aptitude professionnelle

CAPES [kɑpɛs] *nm* Certificat d'aptitude au professorat de l'enseignement du second degré

CC *nm* Corps consulaire

CCP *nm* Compte chèques postal

CD *nm* Corps diplomatique

CEE *nf* Communauté économique européenne

CES *nm* Collège d'enseignement secondaire

CET *nm* Collège d'enseignement technique

CFDT *nf* Confédération française et démocratique du travail

CFTC *nf* Confédération française des travailleurs chrétiens

CGC *nf* Confédération générale des cadres

CGT *nf* Confédération générale du travail

CIDUNATI [sidynɑti] *nm* Comité d'information et de défense de l'union nationale des artisans et travailleurs indépendants

CNPF *nm* Conseil national du patronat français

CNRS *nm* Centre national de la recherche scientifique

CROUS [kʀus] *nm* Centre régional des œuvres universitaires et scolaires

CRS *nm* membre des Compagnies républicaines de sécurité

DCA *nf* Défense contre avions

DDT *nm* dichloro-diphényl-trichloréthane

DEA *nm* Diplôme d'études approfondies

DEUG [døg] *nm* Diplôme d'études universitaires générales

DOMTOM [dɔmtɔm] *mpl* Départements et territoires d'outre-mer

DST *nf* direction de la surveillance du territoire

DTTAB *nm* vaccin antityphoïdique et antiparatyphoïdique A et B, antidiphtérique et tétanique

EDF *nf* Électricité de France

ENA [enɑ] *nf* École nationale d'administration

ENS ... [əɛnɛs] *nf* École nationale supérieure ...

F Franc(s)

FB Franc belge

FEN [fɛn] *nf* Fédération de l'éducation nationale

FF frères; franc français

FMI *nm* Fonds monétaire international

FNSEA *nf* Fédération nationale des syndicats d'exploitants agricoles

FO *nf* Force ouvrière

FS Franc suisse

G.O. Grandes ondes

Ha Hectare

HEC *nfpl* Hautes études commerciales

HF Haute fréquence

HLM *nf* Habitation à loyer modéré

IFOP [ifɔp] *nm* Institut français d'opinion publique

INSEE [inse] *nm* Institut national de la statistique et des études économiques

IUT *nm* Institut universitaire de technologie

J-C Jésus-Christ

JO *nm* Journal officiel

Me Maître

Mgr Monseigneur

MLF *nm* Mouvement de libération des femmes

O.C. Ondes courtes

OCDE *nf* Organisation de coopération et de développement économique

OLP *nf* Organisation de libération de la Palestine

OMS *nf* Organisation mondiale de la santé

ONU *nf* Organisation des nations unies

OPEP [opɛp] *nf* Organisation des pays exportateurs de pétrole

OS *nm* Ouvrier spécialisé

OTAN [otɑ̃] *nf* Organisation du traité de l'Atlantique Nord

OUA *nf* Organisation de l'unité africaine

OVNI [ɔvni] *nm* Objet volant non-identifié

PC *nm* Parti communiste; poste de commandement

PCC *nm* Pour copie conforme

PCV *nm* (Per-Ce-Voir) communication téléphonique payable par le destinataire

PDG *nm* Président-directeur général

PME *nfpl* Petites et moyennes entreprises

PMI *nfpl* Petites et moyennes industries

PMU *nm* Pari mutuel urbain

PNB *nm* Produit national brut

P.O. Petites ondes

PTT *nfpl* Postes télégraphes téléphones

P.-V. *nm* Procès-verbal

QG *nm* Quartier général

QI *nm* Quotient intellectuel

RATP *nf* Régie autonome des transports parisiens

RDA *nf* République Démocratique Allemande

RER *nm* Réseau express régional

RF *nf* République française

RFA *nf* République Fédérale Allemande

RN *nf* Route nationale

RPR *nm* Rassemblement pour la république

RSVP Répondez s'il vous plaît

SA(RL) Société anonyme (à responsabilité limitée)

SGDG Sans garantie du gouvernement

SMIC [smik] *nm* Salaire minimum interprofessionnel de croissance

SNCF *nf* Société nationale des chemins de fer français

SOFRES [sofʀɛs] *nf* Société française d'enquêtes pour sondage

SPA *nf* Société protectrice des animaux

SVP S'il vous plaît

TEE *nm* Trans-Europe-Express

TNT *nm* Trinitrotoluène

TSVP Tournez s'il vous plaît

TTC Toutes taxes comprises

TVA *nf* Taxe sur la valeur ajoutée

UDF *nf* Union pour la démocratie française

UER *nf* Unité d'enseignement et de recherche

URSS *nf* Union des Républiques Socialistes Soviétiques

USA *nmpl* États-Unis d'Amérique

VDQS Vin délimité de qualité supérieure

ABBREVIATIONS AND ACRONYMS

A	(*Brit Cine*) adults
AA	1 Automobile Association 2 Alcoholics Anonymous 3 (*Brit Cine*) restricted
AC	alternating current
A.D.	Anno Domini, in the year of our Lord
a.m.	ante meridiem, before noon
B.A.	Bachelor of Arts
BBC	British Broadcasting Corporation
B.C.	before Christ
Benelux	Belgium, Netherlands, Luxembourg
BR	British Rail
B.Sc.	Bachelor of Science
C.	1 (*US Fin*) cent; (*Fin: France*) centime 2 century 3 circa, about 4 cubic
CBI	Confederation of British Industries
cf	confer, compare
CIA	(*US*) Central Intelligence Agency
c/o	care of
D.A.	(*US*) District Attorney
D.C.	direct current
dec.	deceased
D.I.Y.	do-it-yourself
do.	ditto
Dr	doctor
EEC	European Economic Community
e.g.	exempli gratia, for example
Esq.	Esquire
ETA	estimated time of arrival
FA	Football Association
FBI	(*US*) Federal Bureau of Investigation
F.R.S.	Fellow of the Royal Society
ft.	foot, feet
G.B.	Great Britain
G.C.E.	General Certificate of Education
GDR	German Democratic Republic
GHQ	General Headquarters
GMT	Greenwich Mean Time
G.P.	general practitioner
GPO	General Post Office
h. & c.	hot and cold (water)
H.F.	high frequency
HGV	heavy goods vehicle
H.M.	His (Her) Majesty
H.P., h.p.	1 (*Comm*) hire purchase 2 (*Tech*) horsepower
H.R.H.	His (Her) Royal Highness
i.e.	id est, that is, namely
IMF	International Monetary Fund
in., ins.	inch(es)
Inc	(*US*) Incorporated
IOU	I owe you
IQ	intelligence quotient
I.R.A.	Irish Republican Army
J.C.	Jesus Christ
J.P.	Justice of the Peace
K.C.	King's Counsel
KGB	*Russian Secret Police*
K.O.	knock-out
LA	(*US*) Los Angeles
lb	libra, pound
L.P.	long-playing (record)
L.s.d.	Librae, solidi, denarii; pounds, shillings and pence
LSD	lysergic acid diethylomide
Ltd	Limited
M.A.	Master of Arts
M.C.	1 Master of Ceremonies 2 (*US*) Member of Congress 3 (*Mil*) Military Cross
M.I.5	Military Intelligence (5)
M.P.	Member of Parliament
m.p.g.	miles per gallon
m.p.h.	miles per hour
NASA	['næsə] (*US*) National Astronautics and Space Administration
NATO	['neɪtəʊ] North Atlantic Treaty Organization
N.B.	nota bene, note well
N.H.S.	National Health Service
no.	number
NSPCC	National Society for the Prevention of Cruelty to Children
O.A.U.	Organization of African Unity
OECD	Organization for European Cooperation and Development
O.H.M.S.	On His (Her) Majesty's Service
OPEC	['əʊpek] Organization of Petroleum Exporting Countries
oz	ounce(s)
p.	page
p.a.	per annum, yearly
P.A.	personal assistant
P.A.Y.E.	pay as you earn
P.C.	police constable
pd	paid
Ph.D.	Doctor of Philosophy
PLO	Palestinian Liberation Organization
p.m.	post meridiem, after noon
P.M.	Prime Minister
p.o.	postal order
P.O.B.	post office box
p.p.	per procurationem, by proxy
PPS	Parliamentary Private Secretary
P.R.	public relations
P.S.	postscript
PTO	please turn over
PVC	polyvinyl chloride
Q.C.	Queen's Counsel
RAC	Royal Automobile Club
RAF	Royal Air Force
R.I.P.	requiescat in pace, rest in peace
RN	1 Royal Navy 2 (*US*) Registered Nurse
r.p.m.	revolutions per minute
RSPCA	Royal Society for the Prevention of Cruelty to Animals
RSVP	répondez s'il vous plaît
S.A.	South Africa
s.a.e.	stamped addressed envelope
S.R.N.	State Registered Nurse
STD	subscriber trunk dialling
stg	sterling
TB	tuberculosis
T.N.T.	trinitrotoluene
TT	1 teetotal, teetotaller 2 (*Agr*) tuberculin-tested
TUC	Trades Union Congress
U	(*Brit Cine*) universal
UFO	['ju:fəʊ] unidentified flying object
UHF	ultra-high frequency
U.K.	United Kingdom
UN	United Nations
UNESCO	[ju:'neskəʊ] United Nations Educational, Scientific and Cultural Organization
UNICEF	['ju:nɪsef] United Nations International Children's Emergency Fund
UNO	United Nations Organization
USA	United States of America
USSR	Union of Soviet Socialist Republics
VAT	[væt] value-added tax
VHF	very high frequency
VIP	very important person
V.P., V. Pres.	Vice-President
VSOP	Very superior old pale
WHO	World Health Organization
X	(*Brit Cine*) adults only
Xmas	Christmas